# 2008 STANDARD POSTAGE STAMP CATALOGUE

**ONE HUNDRED AND SIXTY-FOURTH EDITION IN SIX VOLUMES**

## VOLUME 6
## COUNTRIES OF THE WORLD
## So-Z

| | |
|---|---|
| EDITOR | James E. Kloetzel |
| ASSOCIATE EDITOR | William A. Jones |
| ASSISTANT EDITOR /NEW ISSUES & VALUING | Martin J. Frankevicz |
| ASSISTANT EDITOR | Charles Snee |
| VALUING ANALYST | Steven R. Myers |
| ADMINISTRATIVE ASSISTANT/IMAGE COORDINATOR | Beth L. Brown |
| DESIGN MANAGER | Teresa M. Wenrick |
| ADVERTISING | Phyllis Stegemoller |
| CIRCULATION / PRODUCT PROMOTION MANAGER | Tim Wagner |
| VICE PRESIDENT/EDITORIAL AND PRODUCTION | Steve Collins |
| PRESIDENT | William Fay |

Released September 2007
Includes New Stamp Listings through the September 2007 *Scott Stamp Monthly* Catalogue Update



***Scott Publishing Co.***
911 Vandemark Road, Sidney, OH 45365-0828
A division of AMOS PRESS, INC., publishers of *Scott Stamp Monthly, Linn's Stamp News, Coin World* and *Coin World's Coin Values.*

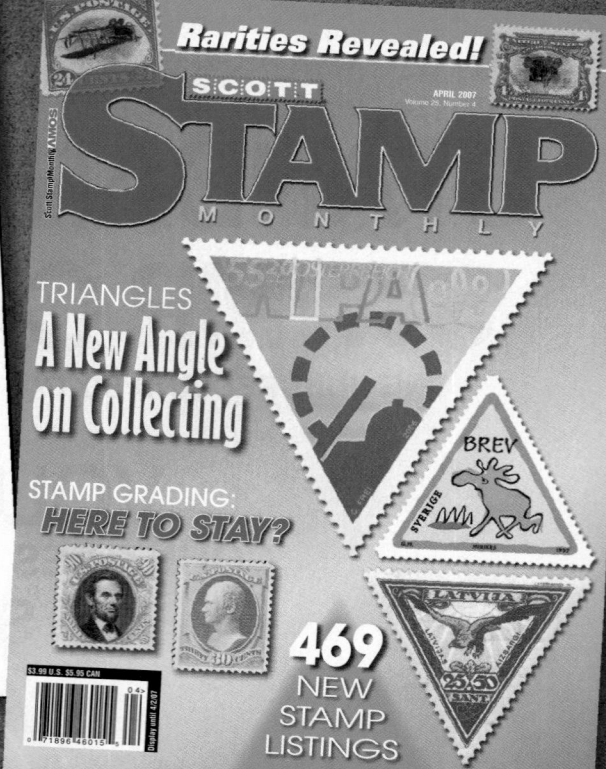

# Table of Contents



**Scott Publishing Mission Statement**

The Scott Publishing Team exists to serve the recreational, educational and commercial hobby needs of stamp collectors and dealers.

We strive to set the industry standard for philatelic information and products by developing and providing goods that help collectors identify, value, organize and present their collections.

Quality customer service is, and will continue to be, our highest priority. We aspire toward achieving total customer satisfaction.

## Copyright Notice



## Trademark Notice



ISBN 0-89487-400-0

Library of Congress Card No. 2-3301

# Scott Publishing Co.

SCOTT 911 VANDEMARK ROAD, SIDNEY, OHIO 45365 937-498-0802

Dear Scott Catalogue User:

In this introductory letter for Volume 6 of the *2008 Scott Standard Postage Stamp Catalogue*, we repeat a question that we have asked in other introductions this year: Is this the first time in several years that you have purchased or consulted a Scott Standard volume? If so, the thousands of value changes plus editorial enhancements contained in the 2008 edition is only the tip of an iceberg.

During the past five years, from the 2003 through the 2007 editions of the Standard catalogues, more than 645,500 value changes have been made in these volumes alone, not counting the tens of thousands of additional changes made in the Scott Specialized Catalogue of United States Stamps and Covers and In the Scott Classic Specialized Catalogue of Stamps and Covers. That is more value changes than the total number of listings in these Standard catalogues and yes, we do keep a count of these things. Most of these value changes are value increases, and many stamps have had their values changed more than once during this time period.

The message here is this: If you have not checked Scott values recently, it is time you did so. Values overall have increased during the last five years, and many values have increased significantly. Staying on top of the current market will allow you to make better buying and selling decisions. And the Scott Standard catalogues reflect that current market.

We continue to receive a great deal of favorable feedback from customers concerning our printing of the catalogues in color. We are constantly adding to and upgrading the images, rescanning when necessary. We are down to the last half of one percent, and the master list of images remaining to be scanned almost seems manageable. Many collectors and dealers have helped, and continue to help, by submitting stamps or scans to replace illustrations that are still in black and white. We thank all of them for their help, for without their generosity this project would have taken much longer than it has to reach completion.

***What's new for Volume 6?***

There are more than 25,500 value changes in this year's Volume 6 of the Standard catalogue, which are many more value changes than have typically been made to this volume in recent years. The value changes in all the volumes this year, which overwhelmingly have been increases so far, have been driven almost totally by market prices and only indirectly, if at all, by currency exchange rates. However, a general statement is in order concerning currency exchange rates. While this volume was being valued, currency exchange rates for both the euro and the British pound versus the United States dollar were continuing to swing significantly in favor of the former currencies. We will have to pay special attention to this trend to see if it sustains itself over time. Economists are telling us that the trend may well sustain itself. Collectors should be aware that if it does, then pressure on the U.S. dollar will become evident in the stamp marketplace as well as other marketplaces. The result will be that desirable foreign stamps will cost more in U.S. dollars and catalogue values may become somewhat understated. If you are in the market for better British and other foreign stamps, it may be prudent to make purchases sooner rather than later.

***What countries have seen the most activity in Volume 6?***

There are many countries in Volume 6 that have large numbers of value changes. Leading the way is Turkey, where a thorough review has resulted in a massive 3,605 new values. Tunisia shows 2,439 value changes, followed by Uruguay (2,148), Venezuela (2,021), Sweden (1,954), Tonga (1,374), Surinam (1,333), Syria (1,246), Somalia (782), Spain (608), Zaire (576), Wallis & Futuna Islands (522) and Thailand (519). Many other countries show significant numbers of value changes.

Value changes in Turkey begin with the earliest issues and continue throughout the listings, with fewer changes noted in the 1950s-1970s period. The first issue is up close to ten percent, but many other value increases are larger. The popular 1914 2pa-200pi Views of Constantinople set, Scott 254-270, jumps to $777.75 unused from $734.20 unused in the 2007 Volume 6.

Values for sets in mint, never hinged condition have been installed from the 1923 issue (Scott 605) up to the breakpoint for the listings of stamps in never-hinged condition only in 1939 (Scott 817). As might be expected, the premiums for Turkey sets in never-hinged condition in this time period are quite large.

In Tunisia, as in Turkey, value changes are seen in profusion throughout the listings. Many changes are significant, such as the increases in the very first set, the 1888 1c-5fr Coat of Arms, Scott 1-8, which jump to $768.50 unused and $508.70 used, from $567 unused and $324.85 used last year. Many lower-value sets also see their values increase by similar percentages.

Most value changes in Sweden tend to be in later issues rather than in the classics, and the sizes of the changes are not as large as those seen in Turkey and Tunisia. The 1970 30o Bird set of 5, Scott 873-877, moves to $4.25 mint, never hinged from $3.50 last year, while the 1991 5k Maps set of 6, Scott 1861-1866, rises to $14.40 mint, never hinged and $9.60 used, from $12 mint, never hinged and $7.50 used. An even larger percentage increase is seen in the 1997 (5k) Classic Cars set, Scott 2248-2253, which climbs to $13.50 both mint, never hinged and used, from $9.60 mint, never hinged and $9 used In the 2007 Volume 6.

Collectors are urged to study the listings from their favorite Volume 6 countries for the voluminous value changes contained in a great many of them. And, as always, collectors should check the Catalogue Number Additions, Deletions & Changes listing for important catalogue editorial changes. In this volume, that listing is on page 1163.

***How do I keep up with all the latest developments in between year editions?***

Subscribe to *Scott Stamp Monthly*. You will find *Scott Stamp Monthly* packed with information. Scott staffers share their research and views each month in a variety of special features (particularly in the "From the Scott Editors" column) and important sidebars. There is also extensive new listing information in the "Scott New Issues Update" section complete with By Topic listings that index new issues according to topical interest.

***Good news on the employment front.***

Beginning with the 2008 Volume 5 catalogue, we welcome a new addition to the Scott Catalogue staff. Chad Snee has joined the Scott editors following a Navy Reserve tour of duty in Afghanistan of almost a year. Collectors and dealers will recognize Snee as the former Senior Editor with Linn's Stamp News. He is a logical thinker who is energetic and knowledgeable – a perfect combination of traits that will serve him well as our new Assistant Catalogue Editor. We are very pleased to have him join the staff, and we know that catalogue users will be pleased also.

***Anything else?***

A hobby is a great gift. Enjoy.

James E. Kloetzel

James E. Kloetzel/Catalogue Editor

# Acknowledgments

Our appreciation and gratitude go to the following individuals who have assisted us in preparing information included in this year's Scott Catalogues. Some helpers prefer anonymity. These individuals have generously shared their stamp knowledge with others through the medium of the Scott Catalogue.

Those who follow provided information that is in addition to the hundreds of dealer price lists and advertisements and scores of auction catalogues and realizations that were used in producing the catalogue values. It is from those noted here that we have been able to obtain information on items not normally seen in published lists and advertisements. Support from these people goes beyond data leading to catalogue values, for they also are key to editorial changes.

A special acknowledgment to Liane and Sergio Sismondo of The Classic Collector for their extraordinary assistance and knowledge sharing that has aided in the preparation of this year's Standard and Classic Specialized Catalogues.

A. R. Allison
Roland Austin
Robert Ausubel (Great Britain Collectors Club)
Dr. H.U. Bantz (S. W. Africa Stamp Study Group)
John Barone (Stamptracks)
Jack Hagop Barsoumian (International Stamp Co.)
William Batty-Smith
George G. Birdsall (Northland Auctions)
John Birkinbine II
John D. Bowman (Carriers and Locals Society)
Roger S. Brody
Keith & Margie Brown
Bernard Bujnak
Alan C. Campbell
Tina & John Carlson (JET Stamps)
Joseph H. Chalhoub
Richard A. Champagne (Richard A. Champagne, Inc.)
Leroy P. Collins III (United Postal Stationery Society)
Frank D. Correl
Andrew Cronin (Canadian Society of Russian Philately)
Francis J. Crown, Jr.
Tony L. Crumbley (Carolina Coin & Stamp, Inc.)
Stephen R. Datz
Tony Davis
Bob Dumaine
Mark Eastzer (Markest Stamp Co.)
Esi Ebrani
Paul G. Eckman
Mehdi Esmaili (Iran Philatelic Study Circle)
Marty Farber
Leon Finik (Loral Stamps)
Henry Fisher
Jeffrey M. Forster
Robert S. Freeman
Ernest E. Fricks (France & Colonies Philatelic Society)
Richard Friedberg
Bob Genisol (Sultan Stamp Center)
Michael A. Goldman (Regency Superior, Ltd.)
Daniel E. Grau
Henry Hahn (Society for Czechoslovak Philately, Inc.)
Joe Hahn (Associated Collectors of El Salvador)
Jerone Hart
John B. Head
Bruce Hecht (Bruce L. Hecht Co.)
Robert R. Hegland
Clifford O. Herrick (Fidelity Trading Co.)
Jack R. Hughes (Fellowship of Samoan Specialists)
Philip J. Hughes (Croatian Philatelic Society)
Wilson Hulme
Doug Iams
Eric Jackson
Michael Jaffe (Michael Jaffe Stamps, Inc)
Peter C. Jeannopoulos
Stephen Joe (International Stamp Service)
Richard Juzwin (Richard Juzwin PTY LTD)
John Kardos
Stanford M. Katz
Lewis Kaufman (The Philatelic Foundation)
Patricia A. Kaufmann
Dr. James W. Kerr
Karlis Kezbers
William V. Kriebel
Elliot Landau
John R. Lewis (The William Henry Stamp Co.)
Ulf Lindahl (Ethiopian Philatelic Society)
William A. Litle
Gary B. Little (Luxembourg Collectors Club)
Pedro Llach (Filatelia Llach S.L.)
George Luzitano
Dennis Lynch
Marilyn R. Mattke
William K. McDaniel
Gary N. McLean
Mark S. Miller (India Study Circle)
Allen Mintz (United Postal Stationery Society)
William E. Mooz
David Mordant
Gary M. Morris (Pacific Midwest Co.)
Peter Mosiondz, Jr.
Bruce M. Moyer (Moyer Stamps & Collectibles)
Richard H. Muller (Richard's Stamps)
James Natale
Albert Olejnik
John E. Pearson (Pittwater Philatelic Service)
John Pedneault
Donald J. Peterson (International Philippine Philatelic Society)
Stanley M. Piller (Stanley M. Piller & Associates)
Todor Drumev Popov
Peter W. W. Powell
Stephen Radin (Albany Stamp Co.)
Ghassan D. Riachi
Eric Roberts
Peter A. Robertson
Michael Rogers (Michael Rogers, Inc.)
Michael Ruggiero
Christopher Rupp
Mehrdad Sadri (Persiphila)
Richard H. Salz
Alex Schauss (Schauss Philatelics)
Jacques C. Schiff, Jr. (Jacques C. Schiff, Jr., Inc.)
Bernard Seckler (Fine Arts Philatelists)
F. Burton Sellers
Guy Shaw
Jeff Siddiqui
Sergio & Liane Sismondo (The Classic Collector)
Merle Spencer (The Stamp Gallery)
Jay Smith
Frank Stanley, III
Richard Stark
Philip & Henry Stevens (postalstationery.com)
Jerry Summers
Steve Unkrich
Philip T. Wall
Daniel C. Warren
Richard A. Washburn
Giana Wayman (Asociacion Filatélica de Costa Rica)
William R. Weiss, Jr. (Weiss Auctions)
Ed Wener (Indigo)
Hans A. Westphal
Ken Whitby
Don White (Dunedin Stamp Centre)
Kirk Wolford (Kirk's Stamp Company)
Robert F. Yacano (K-Line Philippines)
Ralph Yorio
Val Zabijaka
Dr. Michal Zika (Album)

# Addresses, Telephone Numbers, Web Sites, E-Mail Addresses of General & Specialized Philatelic Societies

Collectors can contact the following groups for information about the philately of the areas within the scope of these societies, or inquire about membership in these groups. Aside from the general societies, we limit this list to groups that specialize in particular fields of philately, particular areas covered by the Scott Standard Postage Stamp Catalogue, and topical groups. Many more specialized philatelic society exist than those listed below. These addresses are updated yearly, and they are, to the best of our knowledge, correct and current. Groups should inform the editors of address changes whenever they occur. The editors also want to hear from other such specialized groups not listed.
Unless otherwise noted all website addresses begin with http://

American Philatelic Society
100 Match Factory Place
Bellefonte PA 16823-1367
Ph: (814) 933-3803
www.stamps.org
E-mail: apsinfo@stamps.org

American Stamp Dealers Association
Jim Roselle
3 School St. Suite #205
Glen Cove NY 11542
Ph: (516) 759-7000
www.asdaonline.com
E-mail: asda@erols.com

International Society of Worldwide Stamp Collectors
Terry Myers, MD
9463 Benbrook Blvd. #114
Benbrook TX 76126
www.iswsc.org
E-mail: iswsc@hotmail.com

Royal Philatelic Society
41 Devonshire Place
London, United Kingdom W1G 6JY
www.rpsl.org.uk
E-mail: secretary@rpsl.org.uk

Royal Philatelic Society of Canada
PO Box 929, Station Q
Toronto, ON, Canada M4T 2P1
Ph: (888) 285-4143
www.rpsc.org
E-mail: info@rpsc.org

Young Stamp Collectors of America
Janet Houser
100 Match Factory Place
Bellefonte PA 16823-1367
Ph: (814) 933-3820
www.stamps.org/ysca/intro.htm
E-mail: ysca@stamps.org

### Groups focusing on fields or aspects found in worldwide philately (some may cover U.S. area only)

American Air Mail Society
Stephen Reinhard
PO Box 110
Mineola NY 11501
www.americanairmailsociety.org
E-mail: sreinhard1@optonline.net

American First Day Cover Society
Douglas Kelsey
PO Box 16277
Tucson AZ 85732-6277
Ph: (520) 321-0880
www.afdcs.org
E-mail: afdcs@aol.com

American Revenue Association
Eric Jackson
PO Box 728
Leesport PA 19533-0728
Ph: (610) 926-6200
www.revenuer.org
E-mail: eric@revenuer.com

American Topical Association
Ray E. Cartier
PO Box 57
Arlington TX 76004-0057
Ph: (817) 274-1181
americantopicalassn.org
E-mail: americantopical@msn.com

Errors, Freaks and Oddities Collectors Club
Jim McDevitt
7643 Sequoia Dr., North
Mobile AL 36695-2809
Ph: (251) 607-9253
www.efoers.org
E-mail: cwouscg@aol.com

First Issues Collectors Club
Kurt Streepy
P.O. Box 288
Clear Creek IN 47426-0288
www.firstissues.org
E-mail: orders@firstissues.org

The Joint Stamp Issues Society
Pascal LeBlond
60-600 Rue Cormier
Gatineau, QC, Canada J9H 6B4
jointissues.ovh.org
E-mail: jointissues@yahoo.com

National Duck Stamp Collectors Society
Anthony J. Monico
PO Box 43
Harleysville PA 19438-0043
www.ndscs.org
E-mail: ndscs@hwcn.org

No Value Identified Club
Albert Sauvanet
Le Clos Royal B, Boulevard des Pas Enchantes
St. Sebastien-sur Loire, France 44230
E-mail: alain.vailly@irin.univ nantes.fr

The Perfins Club
Kurt Ottenheimer
462 West Walnut St.
Long Beach NY 11561
Ph: (516) 431-3412
E-mail: oak462@optonline.net

Postage Due Mail Study Group
John Rawlins
13, Longacre
Chelmsford
United Kingdom, CM1 3BJ
E-mail: john.rawlins2@ukonline.co.uk.

Post Mark Collectors Club
David Proulx
7629 Homestead Drive
Baldwinsville NY 13027
E-mail: stampdance@baldcom.net

Postal History Society
Kalman V. Illyefalvi
8207 Daren Court
Pikesville MD 21208-2211
Ph: (410) 653-0665
E-mail: kalphyl@juno.com

Precancel Stamp Society
Arthur Damm
176 Bent Pine Hill
North Wales PA 19454
Ph: (215) 368-6082
E-mail: shirldamm@comcast.net

United Postal Stationery Society
Stuart Leven
1445 Foxworthy Ave. #187
San Jose, CA 95118-1119
www.upss.org
E-mail: poststat@gmail.com

United States Possessions Philatelic Society
Geoffrey Brewster
6453 E. Stallion Rd.
Paradise Valley AZ 85253
Ph: (480) 607-7184

### Groups focusing on U.S. area philately as covered in the Standard Catalogue

Canal Zone Study Group
Richard H. Salz
60 27th Ave.
San Francisco CA 94121-1026

Carriers and Locals Society
John D. Bowman
232 Leaf Lane
Alabaster AL 35007
Ph: (205) 621-8449
www.pennypost.org
E-mail: johndbowman@charter.net

Confederate Stamp Alliance
Patricia A. Kaufmann
10194 N. Old State Road
Lincoln DE 19960
www.csalliance.org
E-mail: trishkauf@comcast.net

Hawaiian Philatelic Society
Kay H. Hoke
PO Box 10115
Honolulu HI 96816-0115
Ph: (808) 521-5721

Plate Number Coil Collectors Club
Ronald E. Maifeld
PO Box 54622
Cincinnati OH 45254-0622
Ph: (513) 213-4208
www.pnc3.org
E-mail: president@pnc3.org

United Nations Philatelists
Blanton Clement, Jr.
P.O. Box 146
Morrisville PA 19067-0146
www.unpi.com
E-mail: bclemjr@yahoo.com

United States Stamp Society
Executive Secretary
PO Box 6634
Katy TX 77491-6631
www.usstamps.org
E-mail: webmaster@usstamps.org

U.S. Cancellation Club
Roger Rhoads
6160 Brownstone Ct.
Mentor OH 44060
www.geocities.com/athens/2088/uscchome.htm
E-mail: rrrhoads@aol.com

U.S. Philatelic Classics Society
Rob Lund
2913 Fulton
Everett WA 98201-3733
www.uspcs.org
E-mail: membershipchairman@uspcs.org

### Groups focusing on philately of foreign countries or regions

Aden & Somaliland Study Group
Gary Brown
PO Box 106
Briar Hill, Victoria, Australia 3088
E-mail: garyjohn951@optushome.com.au

American Society of Polar Philatelists (Antarctic areas)
Alan Warren
PO Box 39
Exton PA 19341-0039
www.polarphilatelists.org
E-mail: alanwar@att.net

Andorran Philatelic Study Circle
D. Hope
17 Hawthorn Dr.
Stalybridge, Cheshire, United Kingdom SK15 1UE
www.chy-an-piran.demon.co.uk/
E-mail: apsc@chy-an-piran.demon.co.uk

Australian States Study Circle of The Royal Sydney Philatelic Club
Ben Palmer
GPO 1751
Sydney, N.S.W., Australia 2001

Austria Philatelic Society
Ralph Schneider
PO Box 23049
Belleville IL 62223
Ph: (618) 277-6152
www.austriaphilatelicsociety.com
E-mail: rschneider39@charter.net

American Belgian Philatelic Society
Walter D. Handlin
1303 Bullens Lane.
Woodlin, PA 19094
groups.hamptonroads.com/ABPS
E-mail: wdhandlin1@comcast.net

Bechuanalands and Botswana Society
Neville Midwood
69 Porlock Lane
Furzton, Milton Keynes, United Kingdom MK4 1JY
www.nevsoft.com
E-mail: bbsoc@nevsoft.com

Bermuda Collectors Society
Thomas J. McMahon
PO Box 1949
Stuart FL 34995
www.bermudacollectorssociety.org

Brazil Philatelic Association
William V. Kriebel
1923 ManningSt.
Philadelphia PA 19103-5728
Ph: (215) 735-3697
E-mail: kriebewv@drexel.edu

British Caribbean Philatelic Study Group
Dr. Reuben A. Ramkissoon
3011 White Oak Lane
Oak Brook IL 60523-2513
Ph: (630) 963-1439
www.bcpsg.com
E-mail: rramkissoon@juno.com

British North America Philatelic Society (Canada & Provinces)
H. P. Jacobi
6-2168 150A St.
Surrey, B.C., Canada V4A 9W4
www.bnaps.org
E-mail: pjacobi@shaw.ca

British West Indies Study Circle
W. Clary Holt
PO Drawer 59
Burlington NC 27216
Ph: (336) 227-7461

Burma Philatelic Study Circle
Michael Whittaker
1, Ecton Leys, Hillside
Rugby, Warwickshire, United Kingdom, CV22 5SL
E-mail: whittaker2004@ntlworld.com

Ceylon Study Group
R. W. P. Frost
42 Lonsdale Road, Cannington
Bridgewater, Somerset, United Kingdom TA5 2JS
E-mail: rodney.frost@tiscali.co.uk

Channel Islands Specialists Society
Miss S. Marshall
3, La Marette, Alderney,
Channel Islands, United Kingdom, GY9 3UQ
E-mail: am012e5360@blueyonder.co.uk

China Stamp Society
Paul H. Gault
PO Box 20711
Columbus OH 43220
www.chinastampsociety.org
E-mail: secretary@chinastampsociety.org

Colombia/Panama Philatelic Study Group (COPAPHIL)
c/o James A. Cross
PO Box 2245
El Cajon CA 92021
www.copaphil.org
E-mail: jimacross@cts.com

Association Filatelic de Costs Rica
Giana Wayman
c/o Interlink 102, PO Box 52-6770
Miami, FL 33152
E-mail: scotland@racsa.co.cr

Society for Costa Rica Collectors
Dr. Hector R. Mena
PO Box 14831
Baton Rouge LA 70808
www.socorico.org
E-mail: hrmena@aol.com

Croatian Philatelic Society (Croatia & other Balkan areas)
Ekrem Spahich
502 Romero, PO Box 696
Fritch TX 79036-0696
Ph: (806) 273-5609
www.croatianstamps.com
E-mail: eckSpahich@cableone.net

Cuban Philatelic Society of America
Ernesto Cuesta
PO Box 34434
Bethesda MD 20827
www.philat.com/cpsa
E-mail: ecuesta@philat.com

Cyprus Study Circle
Jim Wigmore
19 Riversmeet, Appledore
Bideford, N. Devon, United Kingdom EX39 1RE
www.cyprusstudycircle.org/index.htm
E-mail: jameswigmore@aol.com

Society for Czechoslovak Philately
Phil Rhoade
28168 Cedar Trail
Cleveland MN 56017
www.czechoslovakphilately.org
E-mail: philip.rhoade@mnsu.edu

Danish West Indies Study Unit of the Scandinavian Collectors Club
Arnold Sorensen
7666 Edgedale Drive
Newburgh IN 47630
Ph: (812) 853-2653
dwistudygroup.com
E-mail: valbydwi@hotmail.com

East Africa Study Circle
Jonathan Smalley
1 Lincoln Close
Tweeksbury, United Kingdom B91 1AE
easc.org.uk
E-mail: jpasmalley@tiscali.co.uk

Egypt Study Circle
Mike Murphy
109 Chadwick Road
London, United Kingdom SE15 4PY
egyptstudycircle.org.uk
E-mail: egyptstudycircle@hotmail.com

Estonian Philatelic Society
Juri Kirsimagi
29 Clifford Ave.
Pelham NY 10803
Ph: (914) 738-3713

Ethiopian Philatelic Society
Ulf Lindahl
21 Westview Place
Riverside CT 06878
Ph: (203) 866-3540
home.comcast.net/~fbheiser/ethiopia5.htm
E-mail: ulindahl@optonline.net

Falkland Islands Philatelic Study Group
Carl J. Faulkner
Williams Inn, On-the-Green
Williamstown MA 01267-2620
Ph: (413) 458-9371

Faroe Islands Study Circle
Norman Hudson
28 Enfield Road
Ellesmere Port, Cheshire, United Kingdom CH65 8BY
www.faroeislandssc.org.
E-mail: jntropics@hotmail.com

Former French Colonies Specialist Society
BP 628
75367 Paris Cedex 08, France
www.colfra.com
E-mail: clubcolfra@aol.com

France & Colonies Philatelic Society
Edward Grabowski
741 Marcellus Drive
Westfield NJ 07090-2012
www.drunkenboat.net/frandcol/
E-mail: edjjg@alum.mit.edu

Germany Philatelic Society
PO Box 6547
Chesterfield MO 63006
www.gps.nu

German Democratic Republic Study Group of the German Philatelic Society
Ken Lawrence
PO Box 98
Bellefonte PA 16823-0098
Ph: (814) 422-0625
E-mail: apsken@aol.com

Gibraltar Study Circle
David R. Stirrups
34 Glamis Drive
Dundee, United Kingdom DD2 1QP
E-mail: drstirrups@dundee.ac.uk

Great Britain Collectors Club
Timothy Bryan Burgess
3547 Windmill Way
Concord CA 94518
www.gbstamps.com/gbcc
E-mail: Pennyred@earthlink.net

Hellenic Philatelic Society of America (Greece and related areas)
Dr. Nicholas Asimakopulos
541 Cedar Hill Ave.
Wyckoff NJ 07481
Ph: (201) 447-6262
E-mail: nick1821@aol.com

Haiti Philatelic Society
Ubaldo Del Toro
5709 Marble Archway
Alexandria VA 22315
www.haitiphilately.org
E-mail: u007ubi@aol.com

Hong Kong Stamp Society
Dr. An-Min Chung
3300 Darby Rd. Cottage 503
Haverford PA 19041-1064

Society for Hungarian Philately
Robert Morgan
2201 Roscomare Rd.
Los Angeles CA 90077-2222
www.hungarianphilately.org
E-mail: h.alan.hoover@hungarianphilately.org

India Study Circle
John Warren
PO Box 7326
Washington DC 20044
Ph: (202) 564-6876
www.indiastudycircle.org
E-mail: warren.john@epa.gov

Indian Ocean Study Circle
Mrs. S. Hopson
Field Acre, Hoe Benham
Newbury, Berkshire, United Kingdom RG20 8PD
www.iosc.org.uk

Society of Indo-China Philatelists
Ron Bentley
2600 North 24th Street
Arlington VA 22207
www.sicp-online.org
E-mail: ron.bentley@verizon.net

Iran Philatelic Study Circle
Mehdi Esmaili
PO Box 750096
Forest Hills NY 11375
www.iranphilatelic.org
E-mail: m.esmaili@earthlink.net

Eire Philatelic Association (Ireland)
David J. Brennan
PO Box 704
Bernardsville NJ 07924
eirephilatelicassoc.org
E-mail: brennan704@aol.com

Society of Israel Philatelists
Paul S. Aufrichtig
300 East 42nd St.
New York NY 10017

Italy and Colonies Study Circle
Andrew D'Anneo
1085 Dunweal Lane
Calistoga CA 94515
www.icsc.pwp.blueyonder.co.uk
E-mail: audanneo@napanet.net

International Society for Japanese Philately
Kenneth Kamholz
PO Box 1283
Haddonfield NJ 08033
www.isjp.org
E-mail: isjp@isjp.org

Korea Stamp Society
John E. Talmage
PO Box 6889
Oak Ridge TN 37831
www.pennfamily.org/KSS-USA
E-mail: jtalmage@usit.net

Latin American Philatelic Society
Jules K. Beck
30 1/2 Street #209
St. Louis Park MN 55426-3551

Latvian Philatelic Society
Aris Birze
569 Rougemount Dr.
Pickering, ON, Canada L1W 2C1

Liberian Philatelic Society
William Thomas Lockard
PO Box 106
Wellston OH 45692
Ph: (740) 384-2020
E-mail: tlockard@zoomnet.net

Liechtenstudy USA (Liechtenstein)
Paul Tremaine
PO Box 601
Dundee OR 97115
Ph: (503) 538-4500
www.liechtenstudy.org
E-mail: editor@liechtenstudy.org

Lithuania Philatelic Society
John Variakojis
3715 W. 68th St.
Chicago IL 60629
Ph: (773) 585-8649
www.filatelija.lt/lps/and
www.withgusto.org/lps/index.htm
E-mail: variakojis@earthlink.net

Luxembourg Collectors Club
Gary B. Little
7319 Beau Road
Sechelt, BC, Canada VON 3A8
www.luxcentral.com/stamps/LCC
E-mail: lcc@luxcentral.com

Malaya Study Group
David Tett
16 Broadway, Gustard Wood,
Wheathampstead, Herts, United Kingdom AL4 8LN
www.m-s-g/org/uk
E-mail: davidtett@aol.com

Malta Study Circle
Alec Webster
50 Worcester Road
Sutton, Surrey, United Kingdom SM2 6QB
E-mail: alecwebster50@hotmail.com

Mexico-Elmhurst Philatelic Society International
David Pietsch
PO Box 50997
Irvine CA 92619-0997
E-mail: mepsi@msn.com

Society for Moroccan and Tunisian Philately
206, bld. Pereire
75017 Paris, France
members.aol.com/Jhaik5814
E-mail: splm206@aol.com

Natal and Zululand Study Circle
Dr. Guy Dillaway
PO Box 181
Weston MA 02493
www.nzsc.demon.co.uk

Nepal & Tibet Philatelic Study Group
Roger D. Skinner
1020 Covington Road
Los Altos CA 94024-5003
Ph: (650) 968-4163
fuchs-online.com/ntpsc/
E-mail: colinhepper@hotmail.co.uk

American Society of Netherlands Philately
Jan Enthoven
221 Coachlite Ct. S.
Onalaska WI 54650
Ph: (608) 781-8612
www.cs.cornell.edu/Info/People/aswin /NL/neth
E-mail: jenthoven@centurytel.net

New Zealand Society of Great Britain
Keith C. Collins
13 Briton Crescent
Sanderstead, Surrey, United Kingdom CR2 0JN
www.cs.stir.ac.uk/~rgc/nzsgb
E-mail: rgc@cs.stir.ac.uk

Nicaragua Study Group
Erick Rodriguez
11817 S.W. 11th St.
Miami FL 33184-2501
clubs.yahoo.com/clubs/nicaraguastudygroup
E-mail: nsgsec@yahoo.com

Society of Australasian Specialists/ Oceania
Henry Bateman
PO Box 4862
Monroe LA 71211-4862
Ph: (800) 571-0293 members.aol.com/stampsho/saso.html
E-mail: hbateman@jam.rr.com

Orange Free State Study Circle
J. R. Stroud
28 Oxford St.
Burnham-on-sea, Somerset, United Kingdom TA8 1LQ
www.ofssc.org
E-mail: jrstroud@classicfm.net

Pacific Islands Study Circle
John Ray
24 Woodvale Avenue
London, United Kingdom SE25 4AE
www.pisc.org.uk
E-mail: info@pisc.org.uk

Pakistan Philatelic Study Circle
Jeff Siddiqui
PO Box 7002
Lynnwood WA 98046
E-mail: jeffsiddiqui@msn.com

Centro de Filatelistas Independientes de Panama
Vladimir Berrio-Lemm
Apartado 0823-02748
Plaza Concordia Panama, Panama
E-mail: panahistoria@yahoo.es

Papuan Philatelic Society
Steven Zirinsky
PO Box 49, Ansonia Station
New York NY 10023
Ph: (718) 706-0616
E-mail: szirinsky@cs.com

International Philippine Philatelic Society
Robert F. Yacano
PO Box 100
Toast NC 27049
Ph: (336) 783-0768
E-mail: ryacano@tria.d.rr.com

Pitcairn Islands Study Group
Dr. Everett L. Parker
719 Moosehead Lake Rd.
Greenville ME 04441-9727
Ph: (207) 695-3163
www.pisg.org
E-mail: eparker@midmaine.net

Plebiscite-Memel-Saar Study Group of the German Philatelic Society
Clay Wallace
100 Lark Court
Alamo CA 94507
E-mail: clayw1@sbcglobal.net

Polonus Philatelic Society (Poland)
Chris Kulpinski
9350 E. Palm Tree Dr.
Scottsdale AZ 85255
Ph: (480) 585-7114
www.polonus.org
E-mail: ctk@kulpinski.net

International Society for Portuguese Philately
Clyde Homen
1491 Bonnie View Rd.
Hollister CA 95023-5117
www.portugalstamps.com
E-mail: cjh1491@sbcglobal.net

Rhodesian Study Circle
William R. Wallace
PO Box 16381
San Francisco CA 94116
www.rhodesianstudycircle.org.uk
E-mail: bwall8rscr@earthlink.net

Canadian Society of Russian Philately
Andrew Cronin
PO Box 5722, Station A
Toronto, ON, Canada M5W 1P2
Ph: (905) 764-8968
www3.sympatico.ca/postrider/postrider
E-mail: postrider@sympatico.ca

Rossica Society of Russian Philately
Edward J. Laveroni
P.O. Box 320997
Los Gatos CA 95032-0116
www.rossica.org
E-mail: ed.laveroni@rossica.org

Ryukyu Philatelic Specialist Society
Carmine J. DiVincenzo
PO Box 381
Clayton CA 94517-0381

St. Helena, Ascension & Tristan Da Cunha Philatelic Society
Dr. Everett L. Parker
719 Moosehead Lake Rd.
Greenville ME 04441-9727
Ph: (207) 695-3163
ourworld.compuserve.com/homepages/ ST_HELENA_ASCEN_TDC
E-mail: eparker@midmaine.net

St. Pierre & Miquelon Philatelic Society
Jim Taylor
7704 Birch Bay Dr.
Blaine WA 98230
E-mail: jamestaylor@wavehome.com

Associated Collectors of El Salvador
Joseph D. Hahn
1015 Old Boalsburg Rd. Apt G-5
State College PA 16801-6149
www.elsalvadorphilately.org
E-mail: joehahn2@yahoo.com

Fellowship of Samoa Specialists
Jack R. Hughes
PO Box 1260
Boston MA 02117-1260
members.aol.com/tongaJan/foss.html

Sarawak Specialists' Society
Stu Leven
PO Box 24764
San Jose CA 95154-4764
Ph: (408) 978-0193
www.britborneostamps.org.uk
E-mail: stulev@ix.netcom.com

Scandinavian Collectors Club
Donald B. Brent
PO Box 13196
El Cajon CA 92020
www.scc-online.org
E-mail: dbrent47@sprynet.com

Slovakia Stamp Society
Jack Benchik
PO Box 555
Notre Dame IN 46556

Philatelic Society for Greater Southern Africa
Alan Hanks
34 Seaton Drive
Aurora, ON, L4G 2KI, Canada

Spanish Philatelic Society
Robert H. Penn
1108 Walnut Drive
Danielsville PA 18038
Ph: (610) 767-6793

Sudan Study Group
c/o North American Agent
Richard Wilson
53 Middle Patent Road
Bedford NY 10506
www.sudanphilately.co.uk
E-mail: dadu1@verizon.net

American Helvetia Philatelic Society (Switzerland, Liechtenstein)
Richard T. Hall
PO Box 15053
Asheville NC 28813-0053
www.swiss-stamps.org
E-mail: secretary@swiss-stamps.org

Tannu Tuva Collectors Society
Ken Simon
513 Sixth Ave. So.
Lake Worth FL 33460-4507
Ph: (561) 588-5954
www.seflin.org/tuva
E-mail: p003115b@pb.seflin.org

Society for Thai Philately
H. R. Blakeney
PO Box 25644
Oklahoma City OK 73125
E-mail: HRBlakeney@aol.com

Transvaal Study Circle
J. Woolgar
132 Dale Street
Chatham, Kent ME4 6QH, United Kingdom
www.transvaalsc.org

Ottoman and Near East Philatelic Society (Turkey and related areas)
Bob Stuchell
193 Valley Stream Lane
Wayne PA 19087
www.oneps.org
E-mail: rstuchell@msn.com

Ukrainian Philatelic & Numismatic Society
George Slusarczuk
PO Box 303
Southfields NY 10975-0303
www.upns.org
E-mail: Yurko@warwick.net

Vatican Philatelic Society
Sal Quinonez
1 Aldersgate, Apt. 1002
Riverhead NY 11901-1830
Ph: (516) 727-6426
www.vaticanphilately.org

British Virgin Islands Philatelic Society
Giorgio Migliavacca
PO Box 7007
St. Thomas VI 00801-0007
www.islandsun.com/FEATURES/bviphil9198.html
E-mail: issun@candwbvi.net

West Africa Study Circle
Dr. Peter Newroth
Suite 603
5332 Sayward Hill Crescent
Victoria, BC, Canada V8Y 3H8
www.wasc.org.uk/

Western Australia Study Group
Brian Pope
PO Box 423
Claremont, Western Australia, Australia 6910

Yugoslavia Study Group of the Croatian Philatelic Society
Michael Lenard
1514 North 3rd Ave.
Wausau WI 54401
Ph: (715) 675-2833
E-mail: mjlenard@aol.com

## Topical Groups

Americana Unit
Dennis Dengel
17 Peckham Rd.
Poughkeepsie NY 12603-2018
www.americanaunit.org
E-mail: info@americanaunit.org

Astronomy Study Unit
George Young
PO Box 632
Tewksbury MA 01876-0632
Ph: (978) 851-8283
www.fandm.edu/departments/astronomy/miscell/astunit.html
E-mail: george-young@msn.com

Bicycle Stamp Club
Norman Batho
358 Iverson Place
East Windsor NJ 08520
Ph: (609) 448-9547
members.tripod.com/~bicyclestamps
E-mail: normbatho@worldnet.att.net

Biology Unit
Alan Hanks
34 Seaton Dr.
Aurora, ON, Canada L4G 2K1
Ph: (905) 727-6993

Bird Stamp Society
Mrs. Rosie Bradley
31 Park View,
Chepsow, Gwent, United Kingdom NP16 5NA
www.bird-stamps.org/bss
E-mail: bradley666@lycos.co.uk

Canadiana Study Unit
John Peebles
PO Box 3262, Station "A"
London, ON, Canada N6A 4K3
E-mail: john.peebles@sympatico.ca

Captain Cook Study Unit
Brian P. Sandford
173 Minuteman Dr.
Concord MA 01742-1923
www.captaincooksociety.com
E-mail: US@captaincooksociety.com/

Casey Jones Railroad Unit
Norman E. Wright
33 Northumberland Rd.
Rochester NY 14618-2405
Ph: (585) 461-9792
www.uqp.de/cjr/index.htm
E-mail: normaned@rochester.rr.com

Cats on Stamps Study Unit
Mary Ann Brown
3006 Wade Rd.
Durham NC 27705
E-mail: mabrown@nc.rr.com

Chemistry & Physics on Stamps Study Unit
Dr. Roland Hirsch
20458 Water Point Lane
Germantown MD 20874
www.cpossu.org
E-mail: rfhirsch@cpossu.org

Chess on Stamps Study Unit
Anne Kasonic
7625 County Road #153
Interlaken NY 14847
E-mail: akasonic@capital.net

Christmas Philatelic Club
Linda Lawrence
312 Northwood Drive
Lexington KY 40505
Ph: (859) 293-0151
www.hwcn.org/link/cpc
E-mail: stamplinda@aol.com

Christopher Columbus Philatelic Society
Donald R. Ager
PO Box 71
Hillsboro NH 03244-0071
Ph: (603) 464-5379
E-mail: meganddon@tds.net

Collectors of Religion on Stamps
Verna Shackleton
425 North Linwood Avenue #110
Appleton WI 54914
www://my.vbe.com/~cmfourl/coros1.htm
E-mail: corosec@sbcglobal.net

Dogs on Stamps Study Unit
Morris Raskin
202A Newport Rd.
Monroe Township NJ 08831
Ph: (609) 655-7411
www.dossu.org
E-mail: mraskin@cellurian.com

Earth's Physical Features Study Group
Fred Klein
515 Magdalena Ave.
Los Altos CA 94024
epfsu.jeffhayward.com

Ebony Society of Philatelic Events and Reflections (African-American topicals)
Manuel Gilyard
800 Riverside Drive, Ste 4H
New York NY 10032-7412
www.esperstamps.org
E-mail: gilyardmani@aol.com

Embroidery, Stitchery, Textile Unit
Helen N. Cushman
1001 Genter St., Apt. 9H
La Jolla CA 92037
Ph: (619) 459-1194

Europa Study Unit
Donald W. Smith
PO Box 576
Johnstown PA 15907-0576
www.europanews.emperors.net
E-mail: eunity@aol.com or donsmith65@msn.com

Fine & Performing Arts
Deborah L. Washington
6922 So. Jeffery Boulevard #7 - North
Chicago IL 60649
E-mail: brasslady@comcast.net

Fire Service in Philately
Brian R. Engler, Sr.
726 1/2 W. Tilghman St.
Allentown PA 18102-2324
Ph: (610) 433-2782
www.firestamps.com

Gay & Lesbian History on Stamps Club
Joe Petronie
PO Box 190842
Dallas TX 75219-0842
www.glhsc.org
E-mail: glhsc@aol.com

Gems, Minerals & Jewelry Study Unit
George Young
PO Box 632
Tewksbury MA 01876-0632
Ph: (978) 851-8283
www.rockhounds.com/rockshop/gmjsuapp.txt
E-mail: george-young@msn.com

Graphics Philately Association
Mark H Winnegrad
PO Box 380
Bronx NY 10462-0380
www.graphics-stamps.org
E-mail: indybruce1@yahoo.com

Journalists, Authors & Poets on Stamps
Ms. Lee Straayer
P.O. Box 6808
Champaign IL 61826
E-mail: lstraayer@dcbnet.com

Lighthouse Stamp Society
Dalene Thomas
8612 West Warren Lane
Lakewood CO 80227-2352
Ph: (303) 986-6620
www.lighthousestampsociety.org
E-mail: dalene1@champmail.com

Lions International Stamp Club
John Bargus
304-2777 Barry Rd. RR 2
Mill Bay, BC, Canada V0R 2P0
Ph: (250) 743-5782

Mahatma Gandhi On Stamps Study Circle
Pramod Shivagunde
Pratik Clinic, Akluj
Solapur, Maharashtra, India 413101
E-mail: drnanda@bom6.vsnl.net.in

Mask Study Unit
Carolyn Weber
1220 Johnson Drive, Villa 104
Ventura CA 93003-0540
E-mail: cweber@venturalink.net

Masonic Study Unit
Stanley R. Longenecker
930 Wood St.
Mount Joy PA 17552-1926
Ph: (717) 653-1155
E-mail: natsco@usa.net

Mathematical Study Unit
Estelle Buccino
5615 Glenwood Rd.
Bethesda MD 20817-6727
Ph: (301) 718-8898
www.math.ttu.edu/msu/
E-mail: m.strauss@ttu.edu

Medical Subjects Unit
Dr. Frederick C. Skvara
PO Box 6228
Bridgewater NJ 08807
E-mail: fcskvara@verizon.net

Mourning Stamps and Covers Club
John Hotchner
PO Box 1125
Falls Church VA 22041-0125
E-mail: jmhstamp@ix.netcom.com

Napoleonic Age Philatelists
Ken Berry
7513 Clayton Dr.
Oklahoma City OK 73132-5636
Ph: (405) 721-0044
www.nap-stamps.org
E-mail: krb2@earthlink.net

Old World Archeological Study Unit
Caroline Scannel
11 Dawn Drive
Smithtown NY 11787-1761
www.owasu.org
E-mail: editor@owasu.org

Petroleum Philatelic Society International
Linda W. Corwin
5427 Pine Springs Court
Conroe TX 77304
Ph: (936) 441-0216
E-mail: corwin@pdq.net

Philatelic Computing Study Group
Robert de Violini
PO Box 5025
Oxnard CA 93031-5025
www.pcsg.org
E-mail: dviolini@adelphia.net

Philatelic Lepidopterists' Association
Alan Hanks
34 Seaton Dr.
Aurora, ON, Canada L4G 2K1
Ph: (905) 727-6933

Rotary on Stamps Unit
Gerald L. Fitzsimmons
105 Calla Ricardo
Victoria TX 77904
rotaryonstamps.org
E-mail: glfitz@suddenlink.net

Scouts on Stamps Society International
Lawrence Clay
PO Box 6228
Kennewick WA 99336
Ph: (509) 735-3731
www.sossi.org
E-mail: rfrank@sossi.org

Ships on Stamps Unit
Les Smith
302 Conklin Avenue
Penticton, BC, Canada, V2A 2T4
Ph: (250) 493-7486
www.shipsonstamps.org
E-mail: lessmith440@shaw.ca

Space Unit
Carmine Torrisi
PO Box 780241
Maspeth NY 11378
Ph: (718) 386-7882
stargate.1usa.com/stamps/
E-mail: ctorrisi1@nyc.rr.com

Sports Philatelists International
Margaret Jones
5310 Lindenwood Ave.
St. Louis MO 63109-1758
www.sportstamps.org

Stamps on Stamps Collectors Club
Alf Jordan
156 West Elm Street
Yarmouth ME 04096
Ph: (650) 234-1136
www.stampsonstamps.org
E-mail: ajordan1@maine.rr.com

Windmill Study Unit
Walter J. Hollien
PO Box 346
Long Valley NJ 07853-0346
Ph: (862) 812-0030
E-mail: whollien@earthlink.net

Women on Stamps Study Unit
Hugh Gottfried
2232 26th St.
Santa Monica CA 90405-1902
E-mail: hgottfried@adelphia.net

Zeppelin Collectors Club
Cheryl Ganz
PO Box 77196
Washington DC 20013

# Expertizing Services

The following organizations will, for a fee, provide expert opinions about stamps submitted to them. Collectors should contact these organizations to find out about their fees andrequirements before submitting philatelic material to them. The listing of these groups here is not intended as an endorsement by Scott Publishing Co.

## General Expertizing Services

American Philatelic Expertizing Service (a service of the American Philatelic Society)
100 Match Factory Place
Bellefonte PA 16823-1367
Ph: (814) 237-3803
Fax: (814) 237-6128
www.stamps.org
E-mail: ambristo@stamps.org
Areas of Expertise: Worldwide

B. P. A. Expertising, Ltd.
PO Box 137
Leatherhead, Surrey, United Kingdom KT22 0RG
E-mail: sec.bpa@tcom.co.uk
Areas of Expertise: British Commonwealth, Great Britain, Classics of Europe, South America and the Far East

Philatelic Foundation
70 West 40th St., 15th Floor
New York NY 10018
Ph: (212) 221-6555
Fax: (212) 221-6208
www.philatelicfoundation.org
E-mail:philatelicfoundation@verizon.net
Areas of Expertise: U.S. & Worldwide

Professional Stamp Experts
PO Box 6170
Newport Beach CA 92658
Ph: (877) STAMP-88
Fax: (949) 833-7955
www.collectors.com/pse
E-mail: pseinfo@collectors.com
Areas of Expertise: Stamps and covers of U.S., U.S. Possessions, British Commonwealth

Royal Philatelic Society Expert Committee
41 Devonshire Place
London, United Kingdom W1N 1PE
www.rpsl.org.uk/experts.html
E-mail: experts@rpsl.org.uk
Areas of Expertise: All

## Expertizing Services Covering Specific Fields Or Countries

Canadian Society of Russian Philately Expertizing Service
PO Box 5722, Station A
Toronto, ON, Canada M5W 1P2
Fax: (416) 932-0853
Areas of Expertise: Russian areas

China Stamp Society Expertizing Service
1050 West Blue Ridge Blvd
Kansas City MO 64145
Ph: (816) 942-6300
E-mail: hjmesq@aol.com
Areas of Expertise: China

Confederate Stamp Alliance Authentication Service
c/o Patricia A. Kaufmann
10194 N. Old State Road
Lincoln DE 19960-9797
Ph: (302) 422-2656
Fax: (302) 424-1990
www.webuystamps.com/csaauth.htm
E-mail: trishkauf@comcast.net
Areas of Expertise: Confederate stamps and postal history

Croatian Philatelic Society Expertizing Service
PO Box 696
Fritch TX 79036-0696
Ph: (806) 857-0129
E-mail: ou812@arn.net
Areas of Expertise: Croatia and other Balkan areas

Errors, Freaks and Oddities Collectors Club Expertizing Service
138 East Lakemont Dr.
Kingsland GA 31548
Ph: (912) 729-1573
Areas of Expertise: U.S. errors, freaks and oddities

Estonian Philatelic Society Expertizing Service
39 Clafford Lane
Melville NY 11747
Ph: (516) 421-2078
E-mail: esto4@aol.com
Areas of Expertise: Estonia

Hawaiian Philatelic Society Expertizing Service
PO Box 10115
Honolulu HI 96816-0115
Areas of Expertise: Hawaii

Hong Kong Stamp Society Expertizing Service
PO Box 206
Glenside PA 19038
Fax: (215) 576-6850
Areas of Expertise: Hong Kong

International Association of Philatelic Experts
United States Associate members:

Paul Buchsbayew
119 W. 57th St.
New York NY 10019
Ph: (212) 977-7734
Fax: (212) 977-8653
Areas of Expertise: Russia, Soviet Union

William T. Crowe
(see Professional Stamp Experts)
Areas of Expertise: United States

John Lievsay
(see American Philatelic Expertizing Service and Philatelic Foundation)
Areas of Expertise: France

Robert W. Lyman
P.O. Box 348
Irvington on Hudson NY 10533
Ph and Fax: (914) 591-6937
Areas of Expertise: British North America, New Zealand

Robert Odenweller
P.O. Box 401
Bernardsville, NJ 07924-0401
Ph and Fax: (908) 766-5460
Areas of Expertise: New Zealand, Samoa to 1900

Alex Rendon
P.O. Box 323
Massapequa NY 11762
Ph and Fax: (516) 795-0464
Areas of Expertise: Bolivia, Colombia, Colombian States

Sergio Sismondo
10035 Carousel Center Dr.
Syracuse NY 13290-0001
Ph: (315) 422-2331
Fax: (315) 422-2956
Areas of Expertise: British East Africa, Camerouns, Cape of Good Hope, Canada, British North America

International Society for Japanese Philately Expertizing Committee
32 King James Court
Staten Island NY 10308-2910
Ph: (718) 227-5229
Areas of Expertise: Japan and related areas, except WWII Japanese Occupation issues

International Society for Portuguese Philately Expertizing Service
PO Box 43146
Philadelphia PA 19129-3146
Ph: (215) 843-2106
Fax: (215) 843-2106
E-mail: s.s.washburne@worldnet.att.net
Areas of Expertise: Portugal and Colonies

Mexico-Elmhurst Philatelic Society International Expert Committee
PO Box 1133
West Covina CA 91793
Areas of Expertise: Mexico

Ukrainian Philatelic & Numismatic Society Expertizing Service
30552 Dell Lane
Warren MI 48092-1862
Ph: (810) 751-5754
Areas of Expertise: Ukraine, Western Ukraine

V. G. Greene Philatelic Research Foundation
P.O. Box 204, Station Q
Toronto, ON, Canada M4T 2M1
Ph: (416) 921-2073
Fax: (416) 921-1282
E-mail: vggfoundation@on.aibn.com
www.greenefoundation.ca
Areas of Expertise: British North America

# Information on Catalogue Values, Grade and Condition

## Catalogue Value

The Scott Catalogue value is a retail value; that is, an amount you could expect to pay for a stamp in the grade of Very Fine with no faults. Any exceptions to the grade valued will be noted in the text. The general introduction on the following pages and the individual section introductions further explain the type of material that is valued. The value listed for any given stamp is a reference that reflects recent actual dealer selling prices for that item.

Dealer retail price lists, public auction results, published prices in advertising and individual solicitation of retail prices from dealers, collectors and specialty organizations have been used in establishing the values found in this catalogue. Scott Publishing Co. values stamps, but Scott is not a company engaged in the business of buying and selling stamps as a dealer.

Use this catalogue as a guide for buying and selling. The actual price you pay for a stamp may be higher or lower than the catalogue value because of many different factors, including the amount of personal service a dealer offers, or increased or decreased interest in the country or topic represented by a stamp or set. An item may occasionally be offered at a lower price as a "loss leader," or as part of a special sale. You also may obtain an item inexpensively at public auction because of little interest at that time or as part of a large lot.

Stamps that are of a lesser grade than Very Fine, or those with condition problems, generally trade at lower prices than those given in this catalogue. Stamps of exceptional quality in both grade and condition often command higher prices than those listed.

Values for pre-1900 unused issues are for stamps with approximately half or more of their original gum. Stamps with most or all of their original gum may be expected to sell for more, and stamps with less than half of their original gum may be expected to sell for somewhat less than the values listed. On rarer stamps, it may be expected that the original gum will be somewhat more disturbed than it will be on more common issues. Post-1900 unused issues are assumed to have full original gum. From breakpoints in most countries' listings, stamps are valued as never hinged, due to the wide availability of stamps in that condition. These notations are prominently placed in the listings and in the country information preceding the listings. Some countries also feature listings with dual values for hinged and never-hinged stamps.

## Grade

A stamp's grade and condition are crucial to its value. The accompanying illustrations show examples of Very Fine stamps from different time periods, along with examples of stamps in Fine to Very Fine and Extremely Fine grades as points of reference. When a stamp seller offers a stamp in any grade from fine to superb without further qualifying statements, that stamp should not only have the centering grade as defined, but it also should be free of faults or other condition problems.

**FINE** stamps (illustrations not shown) have designs that are quite off center, with the perforations on one or two sides very close to the design but not quite touching it. There is white space between the perforations and the design that is minimal but evident to the unaided eye. Imperforate stamps may have small margins, and earlier issues may show the design just touching one edge of the stamp design. Very early perforated issues normally will have the perforations slightly cutting into the design. Used stamps may have heavier than usual cancellations.

**FINE-VERY FINE** stamps will be somewhat off center on one side, or slightly off center on two sides. Imperforate stamps will have two margins of at least normal size, and the design will not touch any edge. For perforated stamps, the perfs are well clear of the design, but are still noticeably off center. *However, early issues of a country may be printed in such a way that the design naturally is very close to the edges. In these cases, the perforations may cut into the design very slightly.* Used stamps will not have a cancellation that detracts from the design.

**VERY FINE** stamps will be just slightly off center on one or two sides, but the design will be well clear of the edge. The stamp will present a nice, balanced appearance. Imperforate stamps will be well centered within normal-sized margins. *However, early issues of many countries may be printed in such a way that the perforations may touch the design on one or more sides. Where this is the case, a boxed note will be found defining the centering and margins of the stamps being valued.* Used stamps will have light or otherwise neat cancellations. This is the grade used to establish Scott Catalogue values.

**EXTREMELY FINE** stamps are close to being perfectly centered. Imperforate stamps will have even margins that are slightly larger than normal. Even the earliest perforated issues will have perforations clear of the design on all sides.

**Scott Publishing Co. recognizes that there is no formally enforced grading scheme for postage stamps, and that the final price you pay or obtain for a stamp will be determined by individual agreement at the time of transaction.**

## Condition

*Grade* addresses only centering and (for used stamps) cancellation. *Condition* refers to factors other than grade that affect a stamp's desirability.

Factors that can increase the value of a stamp include exceptionally wide margins, particularly fresh color, the presence of selvage, and plate or die varieties. Unusual cancels on used stamps (particularly those of the 19th century) can greatly enhance their value as well.

Factors other than faults that decrease the value of a stamp include loss of original gum, regumming, a hinge remnant or foreign object adhering to the gum, natural inclusions, straight edges, and markings or notations applied by collectors or dealers.

Faults include missing pieces, tears, pin or other holes, surface scuffs, thin spots, creases, toning, short or pulled perforations, clipped perforations, oxidation or other forms of color changelings, soiling, stains, and such man-made changes as reperforations or the chemical removal or lightening of a cancellation.

## Grading Illustrations

On the following two pages are illustrations of various stamps from countries appearing in this volume. These stamps are arranged by country, and they represent early or important issues that are often found in widely different grades in the marketplace. The editors believe the illustrations will prove useful in showing the margin size and centering that will be seen on the various issues.

In addition to the matters of margin size and centering, collectors are reminded that the very fine stamps valued in the Scott catalogues also will possess fresh color and intact perforations, and they will be free from defects.

Examples shown are computer-manipulated images made from single digitized master illustrations.

## Stamp Illustrations Used in the Catalogue

It is important to note that the stamp images used for identification purposes in this catlaogue may not be indicative of the grade of stamp being valued. Refer to the written discussion of grades on this page and to the grading illustrations on the following two pages for grading information.

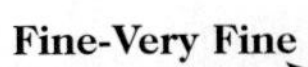
Fine-Very Fine

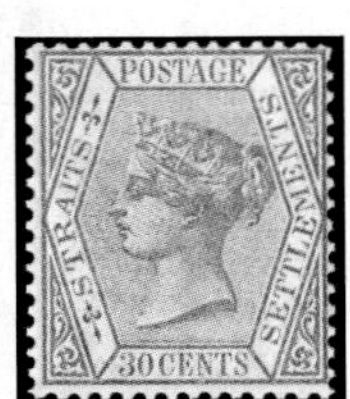

SCOTT CATALOGUES VALUE STAMPS IN THIS GRADE

Very Fine

Extremely Fine

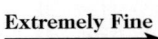

Fine-Very Fine

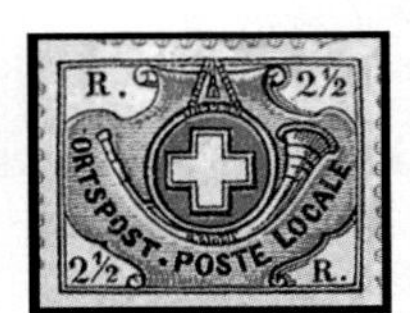

SCOTT CATALOGUES VALUE STAMPS IN THIS GRADE

Very Fine

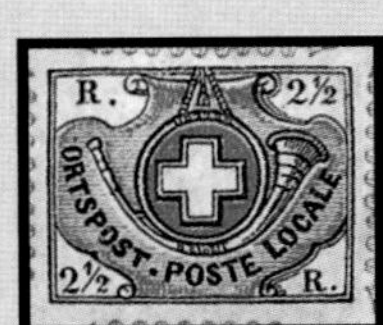

Extremely Fine

Fine-Very Fine →

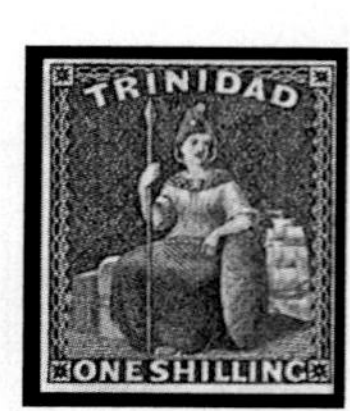


SCOTT CATALOGUES VALUE STAMPS IN THIS GRADE

Very Fine →

Extremely Fine →

Fine-Very Fine →

SCOTT CATALOGUES VALUE STAMPS IN THIS GRADE

Very Fine →

Extremely Fine →

For purposes of helping to determine the gum condition and value of an unused stamp, Scott Publishing Co. presents the following chart which details different gum conditions and indicates how the conditions correlate with the Scott values for unused stamps. Used together, the Illustrated Grading Chart on the previous pages and this Illustrated Gum Chart should allow catalogue users to better understand the grade and gum condition of stamps valued in the Scott catalogues.

| Gum Categories: | MINT N.H. | ORIGINAL GUM (O.G.) | | | | NO GUM |
|---|---|---|---|---|---|---|
| | **Mint Never Hinged** *Free from any disturbance* | **Lightly Hinged** *Faint impression of a removed hinge over a small area* | **Hinge Mark or Remnant** *Prominent hinged spot with part or all of the hinge remaining* | **Large part o.g.** *Approximately half or more of the gum intact* | **Small part o.g.** *Approximately less than half of the gum intact* | **No gum** *Only if issued with gum* |
| Commonly Used Symbol: | ★★ | ★ | ★ | ★ | ★ | (★) |
| Pre-1900 Issues (Pre-1881 for U.S.) | *Very fine pre-1900 stamps in these categories trade at a premium over Scott value* | | | Scott Value for "Unused" | | Scott "No Gum" listings for selected unused classic stamps |
| From 1900 to break-points for listings of never-hinged stamps | Scott "Never Hinged" list-ings for selected unused stamps | Scott Value for "Unused" (Actual value will be affected by the degree of hinging of the full o.g.) | | | | |
| From breakpoints noted for many countries | Scott Value for "Unused" | | | | | |

**Never Hinged (NH; ★★):** A never-hinged stamp will have full original gum that will have no hinge mark or disturbance. The presence of an expertizer's mark does not disqualify a stamp from this designation.

**Original Gum (OG; ★):** Pre-1900 stamps should have approximately half or more of their original gum. On rarer stamps, it may be expected that the original gum will be somewhat more disturbed that it will be on more common issues. Post-1900 stamps should have full original gum. Original gum will show some disturbance caused by a previous hinge(s) which may be present or entirely removed. The actual value of a post-1900 stamp will be affected by the degree of hinging of the full original gum.

**Disturbed Original Gum:** Gum showing noticeable effects of humidity, climate or hinging over more than half of the gum. The significance of gum disturbance in valuing a stamp in any of the Original Gum categories depends on the degree of disturbance, the rarity and normal gum condition of the issue and other variables affecting quality.

**Regummed (RG; (★)):** A regummed stamp is a stamp without gum that has had some type of gum privately applied at a time after it was issued. This normally is done to deceive collectors and/or dealers into thinking that the stamp has original gum and therefore has a higher value. A regummed stamp is considered the same as a stamp with none of its original gum for purposes of grading.

# Understanding the Listings

On the opposite page is an enlarged "typical" listing from this catalogue. Below are detailed explanations of each of the highlighted parts of the listing.

1 **Scott number** — Scott catalogue numbers are used to identify specific items when buying, selling or trading stamps. Each listed postage stamp from every country has a unique Scott catalogue number. Therefore, Germany Scott 99, for example, can only refer to a single stamp. Although the Scott catalogue usually lists stamps in chronological order by date of issue, there are exceptions. When a country has issued a set of stamps over a period of time, those stamps within the set are kept together without regard to date of issue. This follows the normal collecting approach of keeping stamps in their natural sets.

When a country issues a set of stamps over a period of time, a group of consecutive catalogue numbers is reserved for the stamps in that set, as issued. If that group of numbers proves to be too few, capital-letter suffixes, such as "A" or "B," may be added to existing numbers to create enough catalogue numbers to cover all items in the set. A capital-letter suffix indicates a major Scott catalogue number listing. Scott uses a suffix letter only once. Therefore, a catalogue number listing with a capital-letter suffix will not also be found with the same letter (lower case) used as a minor-letter listing. If there is a Scott 16A in a set, for example, there will not also be a Scott 16a. However, a minor-letter "a" listing may be added to a major number containing an "A" suffix (Scott 16Aa, for example).

Suffix letters are cumulative. A minor "b" variety of Scott 16A would be Scott 16Ab, not Scott 16b.

There are times when a reserved block of Scott catalogue numbers is too large for a set, leaving some numbers unused. Such gaps in the numbering sequence also occur when the catalogue editors move an item's listing elsewhere or have removed it entirely from the catalogue. Scott does not attempt to account for every possible number, but rather attempts to assure that each stamp is assigned its own number.

Scott numbers designating regular postage normally are only numerals. Scott numbers for other types of stamps, such as air post, semi-postal, postal tax, postage due, occupation and others have a prefix consisting of one or more capital letters or a combination of numerals and capital letters.

2 **Illustration number** — Illustration or design-type numbers are used to identify each catalogue illustration. For most sets, the lowest face-value stamp is shown. It then serves as an example of the basic design approach for other stamps not illustrated. Where more than one stamp use the same illustration number, but have differences in design, the design paragraph or the description line clearly indicates the design on each stamp not illustrated. Where there are both vertical and horizontal designs in a set, a single illustration may be used, with the exceptions noted in the design paragraph or description line.

When an illustration is followed by a lower-case letter in parentheses, such as "A2(b)," the trailing letter indicates which overprint or surcharge illustration applies.

Illustrations normally are 70 percent of the original size of the stamp. An effort has been made to note all illustrations not illustrated at that percentage. Virtually all souvenir sheet illustrations are reduced even more. Overprints and surcharges are shown at 100 percent of their original size if shown alone, but are 70 percent of original size if shown on stamps. In some cases, the illustration will be placed above the set, between listings or omitted completely. Overprint and surcharge illustrations are not placed in this catalogue for purposes of expertizing stamps.

3 **Paper color** — The color of a stamp's paper is noted in italic type when the paper used is not white.

4 **Listing styles** — There are two principal types of catalogue listings: major and minor.

Major listings are in a larger type style than minor listings. The catalogue number is a numeral that can be found with or without a capital-letter suffix, and with or without a prefix.

Minor listings are in a smaller type style and have a small-letter suffix or (if the listing immediately follows that of the major number) may show only the letter. These listings identify a variety of the major item. Examples include perforation, color, watermark or printing method differences, multiples (some souvenir sheets, booklet panes and se-tenant combinations), and singles of multiples.

Examples of major number listings include 16, 28A, B97, C13A, 10N5, and 10N6A. Examples of minor numbers are 16a and C13Ab.

5 **Basic information about a stamp or set** — Introducing each stamp issue is a small section (usually a line listing) of basic information about a stamp or set. This section normally includes the date of issue, method of printing, perforation, watermark and, sometimes, some additional information of note. *Printing method, perforation and watermark apply to the following sets until a change is noted.* Stamps created by overprinting or surcharging previous issues are assumed to have the same perforation, watermark and printing method as the original. Dates of issue are as precise as Scott is able to confirm and often reflect the dates on first-day covers, rather than the actual date of release.

6 **Denomination** — This normally refers to the face value of the stamp; that is, the cost of the unused stamp at the post office at the time of issue. When a denomination is shown in parentheses, it does not appear on the stamp. This includes the non-denominated stamps of the United States, Brazil and Great Britain, for example.

7 **Color or other description** — This area provides information to solidify identification of a stamp. In many recent cases, a description of the stamp design appears in this space, rather than a listing of colors.

8 **Year of issue** — In stamp sets that have been released in a period that spans more than a year, the number shown in parentheses is the year that stamp first appeared. Stamps without a date appeared during the first year of the issue. Dates are not always given for minor varieties.

9 **Value unused and Value used** — The Scott catalogue values are based on stamps that are in a grade of Very Fine unless stated otherwise. Unused values refer to items that have not seen postal, revenue or any other duty for which they were intended. Pre-1900 unused stamps that were issued with gum must have at least most of their original gum. Later issues are assumed to have full original gum. From breakpoints specified in most countries' listings, stamps are valued as never hinged. Stamps issued without gum are noted. Modern issues with PVA or other synthetic adhesives may appear ungummed. Unused self-adhesive stamps are valued as appearing undisturbed on their original backing paper. Values for used self-adhesive stamps are for examples either on piece or off piece. For a more detailed explanation of these values, please see the "Catalogue Value," "Condition" and "Understanding Valuing Notations" sections elsewhere in this introduction.

In some cases, where used stamps are more valuable than unused stamps, the value is for an example with a contemporaneous cancel, rather than a modern cancel or a smudge or other unclear marking. For those stamps that were released for postal and fiscal purposes, the used value represents a postally used stamp. Stamps with revenue cancels generally sell for less.

Stamps separated from a complete se-tenant multiple usually will be worth less than a pro-rated portion of the se-tenant multiple, and stamps lacking the attached labels that are noted in the listings will be worth less than the values shown.

10 **Changes in basic set information** — Bold type is used to show any changes in the basic data given for a set of stamps. This includes perforation differences from one stamp to the next or a different paper, printing method or watermark.

11 **Total value of a set** — The total value of sets of three or more stamps issued after 1900 are shown. The set line also notes the range of Scott numbers and total number of stamps included in the grouping. The actual value of a set consisting predominantly of stamps having the minimum value of twenty cents may be less than the total value shown. Similary, the actual value or catalogue value of se-tenant pairs or of blocks consisting of stamps having the minimum value of twenty cents may be less than the catalogue values of the component parts.

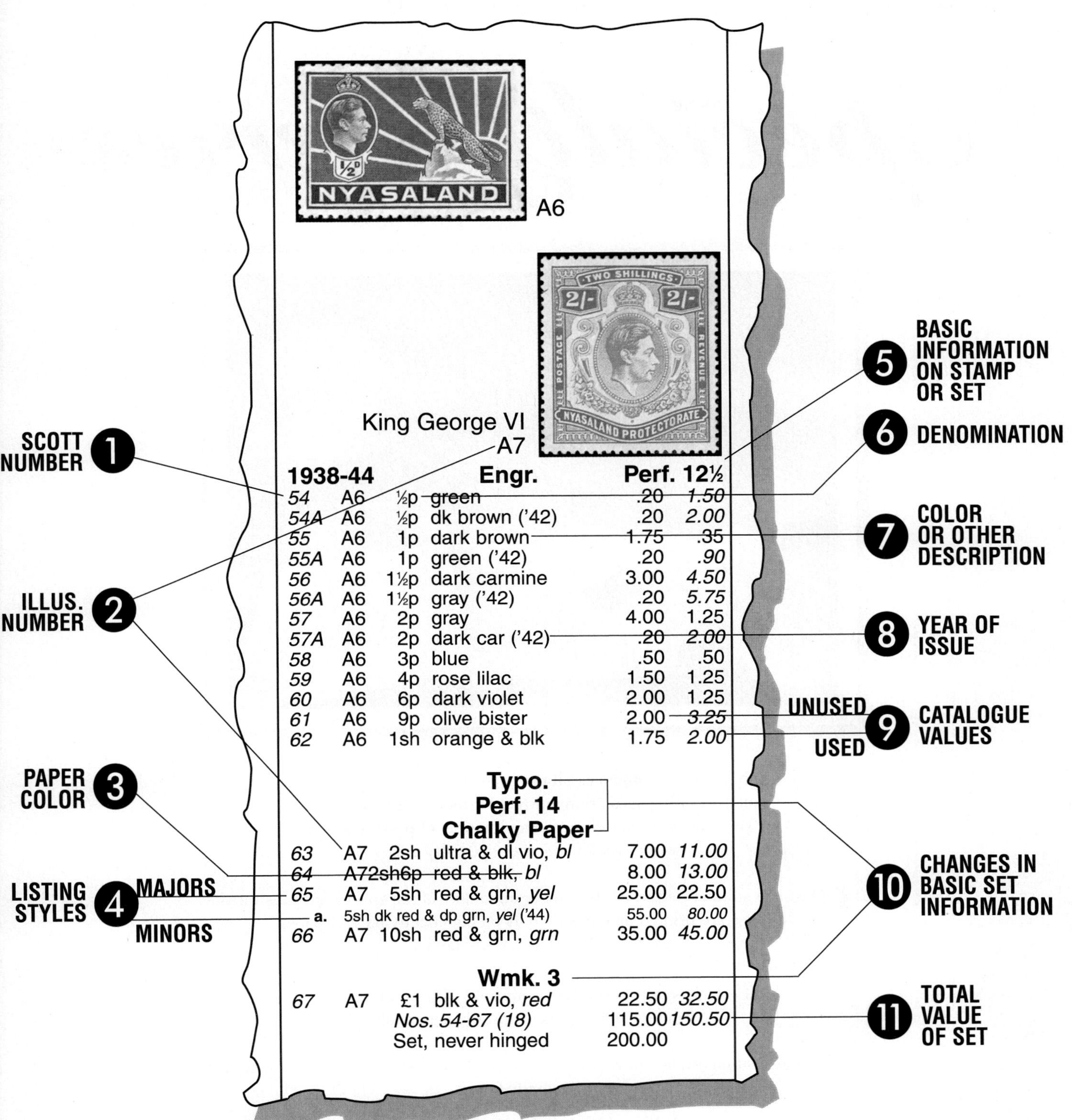


**1938-44 Engr. Perf. 12½**

| | | | | | |
|---|---|---|---|---|---|
| *54* | A6 | ½p | green | .20 | *1.50* |
| *54A* | A6 | ½p | dk brown ('42) | .20 | *2.00* |
| *55* | A6 | 1p | dark brown | 1.75 | .35 |
| *55A* | A6 | 1p | green ('42) | .20 | *.90* |
| *56* | A6 | 1½p | dark carmine | 3.00 | *4.50* |
| *56A* | A6 | 1½p | gray ('42) | .20 | *5.75* |
| *57* | A6 | 2p | gray | 4.00 | 1.25 |
| *57A* | A6 | 2p | dark car ('42) | .20 | *2.00* |
| *58* | A6 | 3p | blue | .50 | .50 |
| *59* | A6 | 4p | rose lilac | 1.50 | 1.25 |
| *60* | A6 | 6p | dark violet | 2.00 | 1.25 |
| *61* | A6 | 9p | olive bister | 2.00 | *3.25* |
| *62* | A6 | 1sh | orange & blk | 1.75 | *2.00* |

**Typo.**
**Perf. 14**
**Chalky Paper**

| | | | | | |
|---|---|---|---|---|---|
| *63* | A7 | 2sh | ultra & dl vio, *bl* | 7.00 | *11.00* |
| *64* | A7 | 2sh6p | red & blk, *bl* | 8.00 | *13.00* |
| *65* | A7 | 5sh | red & grn, *yel* | 25.00 | 22.50 |
| **a.** | | 5sh | dk red & dp grn, *yel* ('44) | 55.00 | *80.00* |
| *66* | A7 | 10sh | red & grn, *grn* | 35.00 | *45.00* |

**Wmk. 3**

| | | | | | |
|---|---|---|---|---|---|
| *67* | A7 | £1 | blk & vio, *red* | 22.50 | *32.50* |
| | | | *Nos. 54-67 (18)* | 115.00 | *150.50* |
| | | | Set, never hinged | 200.00 | |

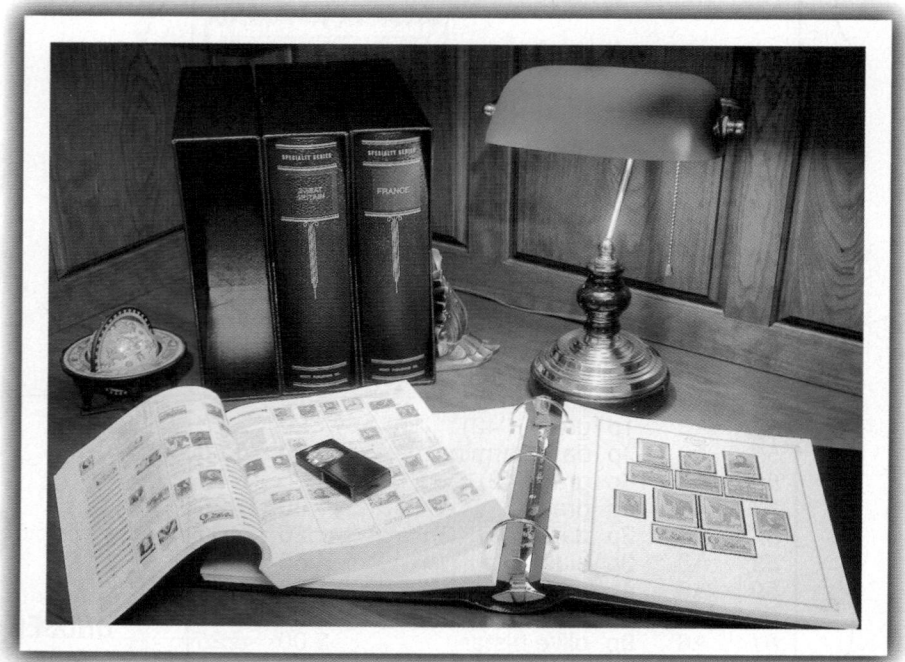

# Catalogue Listing Policy

It is the intent of Scott Publishing Co. to list all postage stamps of the world in the *Scott Standard Postage Stamp Catalogue.* The only strict criteria for listing is that stamps be decreed legal for postage by the issuing country and that the issuing country actually have an operating postal system. Whether the primary intent of issuing a given stamp or set was for sale to postal patrons or to stamp collectors is not part of our listing criteria. Scott's role is to provide basic comprehensive postage stamp information. It is up to each stamp collector to choose which items to include in a collection.

It is Scott's objective to seek reasons why a stamp should be listed, rather than why it should not. Nevertheless, there are certain types of items that will not be listed. These include the following:

1. Unissued items that are not officially distributed or released by the issuing postal authority. If such items are officially issued at a later date by the country, they will be listed. Unissued items consist of those that have been printed and then held from sale for reasons such as change in government, errors found on stamps or something deemed objectionable about a stamp subject or design.

2. Stamps "issued" by non-existent postal entities or fantasy countries, such as Nagaland, Occusi-Ambeno, Staffa, Sedang, Torres Straits and others. Also, stamps "issued" in the names of legitimate, stamp-issuing countries that are not authorized by those countries.

3. Semi-official or unofficial items not required for postage. Examples include items issued by private agencies for their own express services. When such items are required for delivery, or are valid as prepayment of postage, they are listed.

4. Local stamps issued for local use only. Postage stamps issued by governments specifically for "domestic" use, such as Haiti Scott 219-228, or the United States non-denominated stamps, are not considered to be locals, since they are valid for postage throughout the country of origin.

5. Items not valid for postal use. For example, a few countries have issued souvenir sheets that are not valid for postage. This area also includes a number of worldwide charity labels (some denominated) that do not pay postage.

6. Intentional varieties, such as imperforate stamps that look like their perforated counterparts and are usually issued in very small quantities. Also, other egregiously exploitative issues such as stamps sold for far more than face value, stamps purposefully issued in artificially small quantities or only against advance orders, stamps awarded only to a selected audience such as a philatelic bureau's standing order customers, or stamps sold only in conjunction with other products. All of these kinds of items are usually controlled issues and/or are intended for speculation. These items normally will be included in a footnote.

7. Items distributed by the issuing government only to a limited group, club, philatelic exhibition or a single stamp dealer or other private company. These items normally will be included in a footnote.

The fact that a stamp has been used successfully as postage, even on international mail, is not in itself sufficient proof that it was legitimately issued. Numerous examples of so-called stamps from non-existent countries are known to have been used to post letters that have successfully passed through the international mail system.

There are certain items that are subject to interpretation. When a stamp falls outside our specifications, it may be listed along with a cautionary footnote.

A number of factors are considered in our approach to analyzing how a stamp is listed. The following list of factors is presented to share with you, the catalogue user, the complexity of the listing process.

**Additional printings** — "Additional printings" of a previously issued stamp may range from an item that is totally different to cases where it is impossible to differentiate from the original. At least a minor number (a small-letter suffix) is assigned if there is a distinct change in stamp shade, noticeably redrawn design, or a significantly different perforation measurement. A major number (numeral or numeral and capital-letter combination) is assigned if the editors feel the "additional printing" is sufficiently different from the original that it constitutes a different issue.

**Commemoratives** — Where practical, commemoratives with the same theme are placed in a set. For example, the U.S. Civil War Centennial set of 1961-65 and the Constitution Bicentennial series of 1989-90 appear as sets. Countries such as Japan and Korea issue such material on a regular basis, with an announced, or at least predictable, number of stamps known in advance. Occasionally, however, stamp sets that were released over a period of years have been separated. Appropriately placed footnotes will guide you to each set's continuation.

**Definitive sets** — Blocks of numbers generally have been reserved for definitive sets, based on previous experience with any given country. If a few more stamps were issued in a set than originally expected, they often have been inserted into the original set with a capital-letter suffix, such as U.S. Scott 1059A. If it appears that many more stamps than the originally allotted block will be released before the set is completed, a new block of numbers will be reserved, with the original one being closed off. In some cases, such as the U.S. Transportation and Great Americans series, several blocks of numbers exist. Appropriately placed footnotes will guide you to each set's continuation.

**New country** — Membership in the Universal Postal Union is not a consideration for listing status or order of placement within the catalogue. The index will tell you in what volume or page number the listings begin.

**"No release date" items** — The amount of information available for any given stamp issue varies greatly from country to country and even from time to time. Extremely comprehensive information about new stamps is available from some countries well before the stamps are released. By contrast some countries do not provide information about stamps or release dates. Most countries, however, fall between these extremes. A country may provide denominations or subjects of stamps from upcoming issues that are not issued as planned. Sometimes, philatelic agencies, those private firms hired to represent countries, add these later-issued items to sets well after the formal release date. This time period can range from weeks to years. If these items were officially released by the country, they will be added to the appropriate spot in the set. In many cases, the specific release date of a stamp or set of stamps may never be known.

**Overprints** — The color of an overprint is always noted if it is other than black. Where more than one color of ink has been used on overprints of a single set, the color used is noted. Early overprint and surcharge illustrations were altered to prevent their use by forgers.

**Se-tenants —** Connected stamps of differing features (se-tenants) will be listed in the format most commonly collected. This includes pairs, blocks or larger multiples. Se-tenant units are not always symmetrical. An example is Australia Scott 508, which is a block of seven stamps. If the stamps are primarily collected as a unit, the major number may be assigned to the multiple, with minors going to each component stamp. In cases where continuous-design or other unit se-tenants will receive significant postal use, each stamp is given a major Scott number listing. This includes issues from the United States, Canada, Germany and Great Britain, for example.

# Special Notices

## Classification of stamps

The *Scott Standard Postage Stamp Catalogue* lists stamps by country of issue. The next level of organization is a listing by section on the basis of the function of the stamps. The principal sections cover regular postage, semi-postal, air post, special delivery, registration, postage due and other categories. Except for regular postage, catalogue numbers for all sections include a prefix letter (or number-letter combination) denoting the class to which a given stamp belongs. When some countries issue sets containing stamps from more than one category, the catalogue will at times list all of the stamps in one category (such as air post stamps listed as part of a postage set).

The following is a listing of the most commonly used catalogue prefixes.

**Prefix... Category**

C ....... Air Post
M....... Military
P........ Newspaper
N ....... Occupation - Regular Issues
O ....... Official
Q ....... Parcel Post
J......... Postage Due
RA ..... Postal Tax
B........ Semi-Postal
E........ Special Delivery
MR .... War Tax

Other prefixes used by more than one country include the following:

H ....... Acknowledgment of Receipt
I......... Late Fee
CO..... Air Post Official
CQ..... Air Post Parcel Post
RAC... Air Post Postal Tax
CF...... Air Post Registration
CB ..... Air Post Semi-Postal
CBO... Air Post Semi-Postal Official
CE ..... Air Post Special Delivery
EY...... Authorized Delivery
S........ Franchise
G ....... Insured Letter
GY ..... Marine Insurance
MC .... Military Air Post
MQ.... Military Parcel Post
NC..... Occupation - Air Post
NO..... Occupation - Official
NJ ...... Occupation - Postage Due
NRA... Occupation - Postal Tax
NB ..... Occupation - Semi-Postal
NE ..... Occupation - Special Delivery
QY ..... Parcel Post Authorized Delivery
AR ..... Postal-fiscal
RAJ .... Postal Tax Due
RAB ... Postal Tax Semi-Postal
F........ Registration
EB...... Semi-Postal Special Delivery
EO ..... Special Delivery Official
QE ..... Special Handling

## New issue listings

Updates to this catalogue appear each month in the *Scott Stamp Monthly* magazine. Included in this update are additions to the listings of countries found in the *Scott Standard Postage Stamp Catalogue* and the *Specialized Catalogue of United States Stamps*, as well as corrections and updates to current editions of this catalogue.

From time to time there will be changes in the final listings of stamps from the *Scott Stamp Monthly* to the next edition of the catalogue. This occurs as more information about certain stamps or sets becomes available.

The catalogue update section of the *Scott Stamp Monthly* is the most timely presentation of this material available. Annual subscriptions to the *Scott Stamp Monthly* are available from Scott Publishing Co., Box 828, Sidney, OH 45365-0828.

## Number additions, deletions & changes

A listing of catalogue number additions, deletions and changes from the previous edition of the catalogue appears in each volume. See Catalogue Number Additions, Deletions & Changes in the table of contents for the location of this list.

## Understanding valuing notations

The *minimum catalogue value* of an individual stamp or set is 20 cents. This represents a portion of the cost incurred by a dealer when he prepares an individual stamp for resale. As a point of philatelic-economic fact, the lower the value shown for an item in this catalogue, the greater the percentage of that value is attributed to dealer mark up and profit margin. In many cases, such as the 20-cent minimum value, that price does not cover the labor or other costs involved with stocking it as an individual stamp. The sum of minimum values in a set does not properly represent the value of a complete set primarily composed of a number of minimum-value stamps, nor does the sum represent the actual value of a packet made up of minimum-value stamps. Thus a packet of 1,000 different common stamps — each of which has a catalogue value of 20-cents — normally sells for considerably less than 200 dollars!

The *absence of a retail value* for a stamp does not necessarily suggest that a stamp is scarce or rare. A dash in the value column means that the stamp is known in a stated form or variety, but information is either lacking or insufficient for purposes of establishing a usable catalogue value.

Stamp values in *italics* generally refer to items that are difficult to value accurately. For expensive items, such as those priced at $1,000 or higher, a value in italics indicates that the affected item trades very seldom. For inexpensive items, a value in italics represents a warning. One example is a "blocked" issue where the issuing postal administration may have controlled one stamp in a set in an attempt to make the whole set more valuable. Another example is an item that sold at an extreme multiple of face value in the marketplace at the time of its issue.

One type of warning to collectors that appears in the catalogue is illustrated by a stamp that is valued considerably higher in used condition than it is as unused. In this case, collectors are cautioned to be certain the used version has a genuine and contemporaneous cancellation. The type of cancellation on a stamp can be an important factor in determining its sale price. Catalogue values do not apply to fiscal, telegraph or non-contemporaneous postal cancels, unless otherwise noted.

Some countries have released back issues of stamps in canceled-to-order form, sometimes covering as much as a 10-year period. The Scott Catalogue values for used stamps reflect canceled-to-order material when such stamps are found to predominate in the marketplace for the issue involved. Notes frequently appear in the stamp listings to specify which items are valued as canceled-to-order, or if there is a premium for postally used examples.

Many countries sell canceled-to-order stamps at a marked reduction of face value. Countries that sell or have sold canceled-to-order stamps at *full* face value include United Nations, Australia, Netherlands, France and Switzerland. It may be almost impossible to identify such stamps if the gum has been removed, because official government canceling devices are used. Postally used copies of these items on cover, however, are usually worth more than the canceled-to-order stamps with original gum.

## Abbreviations

Scott Publishing Co. uses a consistent set of abbreviations throughout this catalogue to conserve space, while still providing necessary information.

### COLOR ABBREVIATIONS

amb .amber
anil ..aniline
ap ....apple
aqua.aquamarine
az.....azure
bis....bister
bl .....blue
bld ...blood
blk ...black
bril...brilliant
brn...brown
brnshbrownish
brnz .bronze
brt....bright
brnt..burnt
car ...carmine
cer ...cerise
chlky chalky
cham chamois
chnt .chestnut
choc.chocolate
chr ...chrome
cit ....citron
cl .....claret
cob...cobalt
cop...copper
crim .crimson
cr .....cream
dk ....dark
dl .....dull
dp ....deep
db ....drab
emer emerald
gldn .golden
grysh grayish
grn ...green
grnsh greenish
hel ...heliotrope
hn ....henna
ind ...indigo
int....intense
lav....lavender
lem ..lemon
lil .....lilac
lt......light
mag..magenta
man .manila
mar ..maroon
mv ...mauve
multi multicolored
mlky milky
myr ..myrtle
ol .....olive
olvn .olivine
org ...orange
pck...peacock
pnksh pinkish
Prus .Prussian
pur...purple
redsh reddish
res....reseda
ros ...rosine
ryl ....royal
sal ....salmon
saph .sapphire
scar ..scarlet
sep ...sepia
sien ..sienna
sil.....silver
sl......slate
stl.....steel
turq..turquoise
ultra .ultramarine
Ven ..Venetian
ver ...vermilion
vio ...violet
yel....yellow
yelsh yellowish

When no color is given for an overprint or surcharge, black is the color used. Abbreviations for colors used for overprints and surcharges include: "(B)" or "(Blk)," black; "(Bl)," blue; "(R)," red; and "(G)," green.

Additional abbreviations in this catalogue are shown below:

Adm.............Administration
AFL.............American Federation of Labor
Anniv. ..........Anniversary
APS.............American Philatelic Society
Assoc. ..........Association
ASSR...........Autonomous Soviet Socialist Republic
b. ................Born
BEP.............Bureau of Engraving and Printing
Bicent. .........Bicentennial
Bklt. .............Booklet
Brit. .............British
btwn. ...........Between
Bur. ..............Bureau
c. or ca.........Circa
Cat...............Catalogue
Cent.............Centennial, century, centenary
CIO..............Congress of Industrial Organizations
Conf.............Conference
Cong. ...........Congress
Cpl...............Corporal
CTO.............Canceled to order
d. .................Died
Dbl...............Double
EKU .............Earliest known use
Engr. ............Engraved
Exhib. ..........Exhibition
Expo. ...........Exposition
Fed. .............Federation
GB ...............Great Britain
Gen..............General
GPO.............General post office
Horiz............Horizontal
Imperf. .........Imperforate
Impt.............Imprint
Intl...............International
Invtd. ...........Inverted
L ..................Left
Lieut., lt. ......Lieutenant
Litho. ...........Lithographed
LL ................Lower left
LR................Lower right
mm ..............Millimeter
Ms. ..............Manuscript
Natl..............National
No. ..............Number
NY ...............New York
NYC.............New York City
Ovpt. ...........Overprint
Ovptd...........Overprinted
P ..................Plate number
Perf. .............Perforated, perforation
Phil. .............Philatelic
Photo. ..........Photogravure
PO ...............Post office
Pr. ................Pair
P.R. ..............Puerto Rico
Prec. ............Precancel, precanceled
Pres..............President
PTT..............Post, Telephone and Telegraph
Rio ...............Rio de Janeiro
Sgt. ..............Sergeant
Soc...............Society
Souv. ............Souvenir
SSR .............Soviet Socialist Republic, see ASSR
St. ................Saint, street
Surch. ..........Surcharge
Typo.............Typographed
UL ...............Upper left
Unwmkd......Unwatermarked
UPU.............Universal Postal Union
UR ...............Upper Right
US................United States
USPOD ........United States Post Office Department
USSR............Union of Soviet Socialist Republics
Vert. .............Vertical
VP................Vice president
Wmk............Watermark
Wmkd..........Watermarked
WWI............World War I
WWII...........World War II

## Examination

Scott Publishing Co. will not comment upon the genuineness, grade or condition of stamps, because of the time and responsibility involved. Rather, there are several expertizing groups that undertake this work for both collectors and dealers. Neither will Scott Publishing Co. appraise or identify philatelic material. The company cannot take responsibility for unsolicited stamps or covers sent by individuals.

All letters, E-mails, etc. are read attentively, but they are not always answered due to time considerations.

## How to order from your dealer

When ordering stamps from a dealer, it is not necessary to write the full description of a stamp as listed in this catalogue. All you need is the name of the country, the Scott catalogue number and whether the desired item is unused or used. For example, "Japan Scott 422 unused" is sufficient to identify the unused stamp of Japan listed as "422 A206 5y brown."

# Basic Stamp Information

A stamp collector's knowledge of the combined elements that make a given stamp issue unique determines his or her ability to identify stamps. These elements include paper, watermark, method of separation, printing, design and gum. On the following pages each of these important areas is briefly described.

## Paper

Paper is an organic material composed of a compacted weave of cellulose fibers and generally formed into sheets. Paper used to print stamps may be manufactured in sheets, or it may have been part of a large roll (called a web) before being cut to size. The fibers most often used to create paper on which stamps are printed include bark, wood, straw and certain grasses. In many cases, linen or cotton rags have been added for greater strength and durability. Grinding, bleaching, cooking and rinsing these raw fibers reduces them to a slushy pulp, referred to by paper makers as "stuff." Sizing and, sometimes, coloring matter is added to the pulp to make different types of finished paper.

After the stuff is prepared, it is poured onto sieve-like frames that allow the water to run off, while retaining the matted pulp. As fibers fall onto the screen and are held by gravity, they form a natural weave that will later hold the paper together. If the screen has metal bits that are formed into letters or images attached, it leaves slightly thinned areas on the paper. These are called watermarks.

When the stuff is almost dry, it is passed under pressure through smooth or engraved rollers - dandy rolls - or placed between cloth in a press to be flattened and dried.

Stamp paper falls broadly into two types: wove and laid. The nature of the surface of the frame onto which the pulp is first deposited causes the differences in appearance between the two. If the surface is smooth and even, the paper will be of fairly uniform texture throughout. This is known as *wove paper.* Early papermaking machines poured the pulp onto a continuously circulating web of felt, but modern machines feed the pulp onto a cloth-like screen made of closely interwoven fine wires. This paper, when held to a light, will show little dots or points very close together. The proper name for this is "wire wove," but the type is still considered wove. Any U.S. or British stamp printed after 1880 will serve as an example of wire wove paper.

Closely spaced parallel wires, with cross wires at wider intervals, make up the frames used for what is known as *laid paper.* A greater thickness of the pulp will settle between the wires. The paper, when held to a light, will show alternate light and dark lines. The spacing and the thickness of the lines may vary, but on any one sheet of paper they are all alike. See Russia Scott 31-38 for examples of laid paper.

*Batonne*, from the French word meaning "a staff," is a term used if the lines in the paper are spaced quite far apart, like the printed ruling on a writing tablet. Batonne paper may be either wove or laid. If laid, fine laid lines can be seen between the batons.

*Quadrille* is the term used when the lines in the paper form little squares. *Oblong quadrille* is the term used when rectangles, rather than squares, are formed. See Mexico-Guadalajara Scott 35-37 for examples of oblong quadrille paper.

Paper also is classified as thick or thin, hard or soft, and by color if dye is added during manufacture. Such colors may include yellowish, greenish, bluish and reddish.

Brief explanations of other types of paper used for printing stamps, as well as examples, follow.

**Pelure** — Pelure paper is a very thin, hard and often brittle paper that is sometimes bluish or grayish in appearance. See Serbia Scott 169-170.

**Native** — This is a term applied to handmade papers used to produce some of the early stamps of the Indian states. Stamps printed on native paper may be expected to display various natural inclusions that are normal and do not negatively affect value. Japanese paper, originally made of mulberry fibers and rice flour, is part of this group. See Japan Scott 1-18.

**Manila** — This type of paper is often used to make stamped envelopes and wrappers. It is a coarse-textured stock, usually smooth on one side and rough on the other. A variety of colors of manila paper exist, but the most common range is yellowish-brown.

**Silk** — Introduced by the British in 1847 as a safeguard against counterfeiting, silk paper contains bits of colored silk thread scattered throughout. The density of these fibers varies greatly and can include as few as one fiber per stamp or hundreds. U.S. revenue Scott R152 is a good example of an easy-to-identify silk paper stamp.

Silk-thread paper has uninterrupted threads of colored silk arranged so that one or more threads run through the stamp or postal stationery. See Great Britain Scott 5-6 and Switzerland Scott 14-19.

**Granite** — Filled with minute cloth or colored paper fibers of various colors and lengths, granite paper should not be confused with either type of silk paper. Austria Scott 172-175 and a number of Swiss stamps are examples of granite paper.

**Chalky** — A chalk-like substance coats the surface of chalky paper to discourage the cleaning and reuse of canceled stamps, as well as to provide a smoother, more acceptable printing surface. Because the designs of stamps printed on chalky paper are imprinted on what is often a water-soluble coating, any attempt to remove a cancellation will destroy the stamp. *Do not soak these stamps in any fluid.* To remove a stamp printed on chalky paper from an envelope, wet the paper from underneath the stamp until the gum dissolves enough to release the stamp from the paper. See St. Kitts-Nevis Scott 89-90 for examples of stamps printed on this type of chalky paper.

**India** — Another name for this paper, originally introduced from China about 1750, is "China Paper." It is a thin, opaque paper often used for plate and die proofs by many countries.

**Double** — In philately, the term double paper has two distinct meanings. The first is a two-ply paper, usually a combination of a thick and a thin sheet, joined during manufacture. This type was used experimentally as a means to discourage the reuse of stamps.

The design is printed on the thin paper. Any attempt to remove a cancellation would destroy the design. U.S. Scott 158 and other Banknote-era stamps exist on this form of double paper.

The second type of double paper occurs on a rotary press, when the end of one paper roll, or web, is affixed to the next roll to save time feeding the paper through the press. Stamp designs are printed over the joined paper and, if overlooked by inspectors, may get into post office stocks.

**Goldbeater's Skin** — This type of paper was used for the 1866 issue of Prussia, and was a tough, translucent paper. The design was printed in reverse on the back of the stamp, and the gum applied over the printing. It is impossible to remove stamps printed on this type of paper from the paper to which they are affixed without destroying the design.

**Ribbed** — Ribbed paper has an uneven, corrugated surface made by passing the paper through ridged rollers. This type exists on some copies of U.S. Scott 156-165.

Various other substances, or substrates, have been used for stamp manufacture, including wood, aluminum, copper, silver and gold foil, plastic, and silk and cotton fabrics.

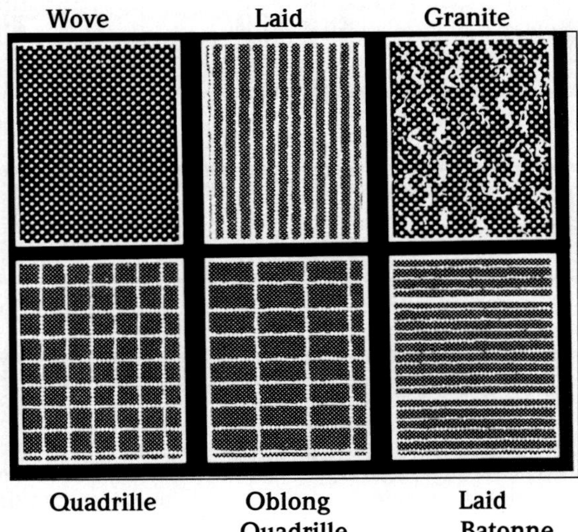


## Watermarks

Watermarks are an integral part of some papers. They are formed in the process of paper manufacture. Watermarks consist of small designs, formed of wire or cut from metal and soldered to the surface of the mold or, sometimes, on the dandy roll. The designs may be in the form of crowns, stars, anchors, letters or other characters or symbols. These pieces of metal - known in the paper-making industry as "bits" - impress a design into the paper. The design sometimes may be seen by holding the stamp to the light. Some are more easily seen with a watermark detector. This important tool is a small black tray into which a stamp is placed face down and dampened with a fast-evaporating watermark detection fluid that brings up the watermark image in the form of dark lines against a lighter background. These dark lines are the thinner areas of the paper known as the watermark. Some watermarks are extremely difficult to locate, due to either a faint impression, watermark location or the color of the stamp. There also are electric watermark detectors that come with plastic filter disks of various colors. The disks neutralize the color of the stamp, permitting the watermark to be seen more easily.

Multiple watermarks of Crown Agents and Burma

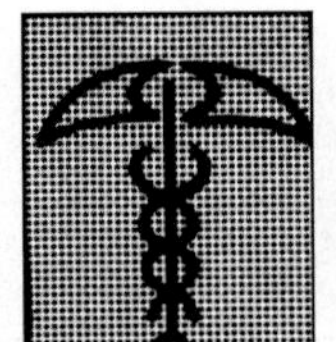

Watermarks of Uruguay, Vatican City and Jamaica

**WARNING: Some inks used in the photogravure process dissolve in watermark fluids (Please see the section on Soluble Printing Inks).** Also, see "chalky paper."

Watermarks may be found normal, reversed, inverted, reversed and inverted, sideways or diagonal, as seen from the back of the stamp. The relationship of watermark to stamp design depends on the position of the printing plates or how paper is fed through the press. On machine-made paper, watermarks normally are read from right to left. The design is repeated closely throughout the sheet in a "multiple-watermark design." In a "sheet watermark," the design appears only once on the sheet, but extends over many stamps. Individual stamps may carry only a small fraction or none of the watermark.

"Marginal watermarks" occur in the margins of sheets or panes of stamps. They occur on the outside border of paper (ostensibly outside the area where stamps are to be printed). A large row of letters may spell the name of the country or the manufacturer of the paper, or a border of lines may appear. Careless press feeding may cause parts of these letters and/or lines to show on stamps of the outer row of a pane.

## Soluble Printing Inks

**WARNING:** Most stamp colors are permanent; that is, they are not seriously affected by short-term exposure to light or water. Many colors, especially of modern inks, fade from excessive exposure to light. There are stamps printed with inks that dissolve easily in water or in fluids used to detect watermarks. Use of these inks was intentional to prevent the removal of cancellations. Water affects all aniline inks, those on so-called safety paper and some photogravure printings - all such inks are known as *fugitive colors. Removal from paper of such stamps requires care and alternatives to traditional soaking.*

## Separation

"Separation" is the general term used to describe methods used to separate stamps. The three standard forms currently in use are perforating, rouletting and die-cutting. These methods are done during the stamp production process, after printing. Sometimes these methods are done on-press or sometimes as a separate step. The earliest issues, such as the 1840 Penny Black of Great Britain (Scott 1), did not have any means provided for separation. It was expected the stamps would be cut apart with scissors or folded and torn. These are examples of imperforate stamps. Many stamps were first issued in imperforate formats and were later issued with perforations. Therefore, care must be observed in buying single imperforate stamps to be certain they were issued imperforate and are not perforated copies that have been altered by having the perforations trimmed away. Stamps issued imperforate usually are valued as singles. However, imperforate varieties of normally perforated stamps should be collected in pairs or larger pieces as indisputable evidence of their imperforate character.

### PERFORATION

The chief style of separation of stamps, and the one that is in almost universal use today, is perforating. By this process, paper between the stamps is cut away in a line of holes, usually round, leaving little bridges of paper between the stamps to hold them together. Some types of perforation, such as hyphen-hole perfs, can be confused with roulettes, but a close visual inspection reveals that paper has been removed. The little perforation bridges, which project from the stamp when it is torn from the pane, are called the teeth of the perforation.

As the size of the perforation is sometimes the only way to differentiate between two otherwise identical stamps, it is necessary to be able to accurately measure and describe them. This is done with a perforation gauge, usually a ruler-like device that has dots or graduated lines to show how many perforations may be counted in the space of two centimeters. Two centimeters is the space universally adopted in which to measure perforations.

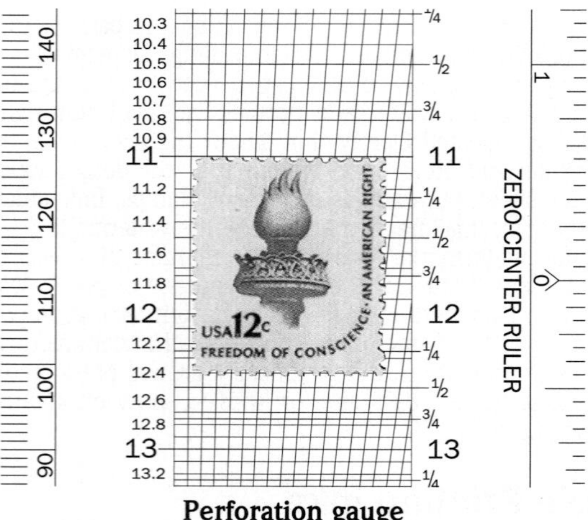


**Perforation gauge**

To measure a stamp, run it along the gauge until the dots on it fit exactly into the perforations of the stamp. If you are using a graduated-line perforation gauge, simply slide the stamp along the surface until the lines on the gauge perfectly project from the center of the bridges or holes. The number to the side of the line of dots or lines that fit the stamp's perforation is the measurement. For example, an "11" means that 11 perforations fit between two centimeters. The description of the stamp therefore is "perf. 11." If the gauge of the perforations on the top and bottom of a stamp differs from that on the sides, the result is what is known as *compound perforations.* In measuring compound perforations, the gauge at top and bottom is always given first, then the sides. Thus, a stamp that measures 11 at top and bottom and 10 1/2 at the sides is "perf. 11 x 10 1/2." See U.S. Scott 632-642 for examples of compound perforations.

Stamps also are known with perforations different on three or all four sides. Descriptions of such items are clockwise, beginning with the top of the stamp.

A perforation with small holes and teeth close together is a "fine perforation." One with large holes and teeth far apart is a "coarse perforation." Holes that are jagged, rather than clean-cut, are "rough perforations." *Blind perforations* are the slight impressions left by the perforating pins if they fail to puncture the paper. Multiples of stamps showing blind perforations may command a slight premium over normally perforated stamps.

The term *syncopated perfs* describes intentional irregularities in the perforations. The earliest form was used by the Netherlands from 1925-33, where holes were omitted to create distinctive patterns. Beginning in 1992, Great Britain has used an oval perforation to help prevent counterfeiting. Several other countries have started using the oval perfs or other syncopated perf patterns.

A new type of perforation, still primarily used for postal stationery, is known as microperfs. Microperfs are tiny perforations (in some cases hundreds of holes per two centimeters) that allows items to be intentionally separated very easily, while not accidentally breaking apart as easily as standard perforations. These are not currently measured or differentiated by size, as are standard perforations.

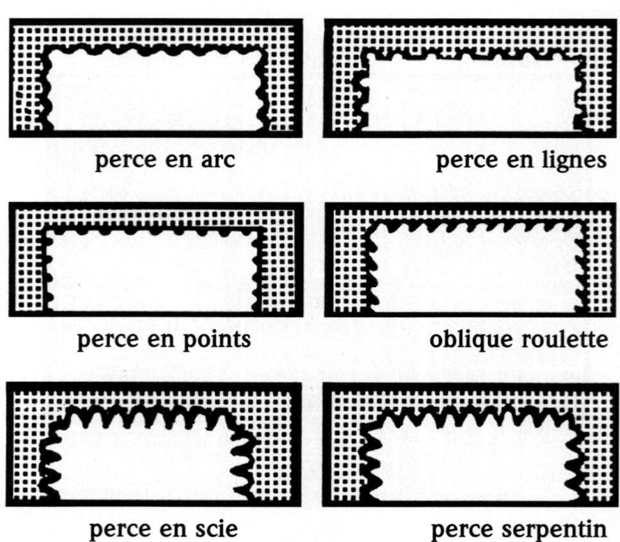

**perce en arc** **perce en lignes**

**perce en points** **oblique roulette**

**perce en scie** **perce serpentin**

### ROULETTING

In rouletting, the stamp paper is cut partly or wholly through, with no paper removed. In perforating, some paper is removed. Rouletting derives its name from the French roulette, a spur-like wheel. As the wheel is rolled over the paper, each point makes a small cut. The number of cuts made in a two-centimeter space determines the gauge of the roulette, just as the number of perforations in two centimeters determines the gauge of the perforation.

The shape and arrangement of the teeth on the wheels varies. Various roulette types generally carry French names:

*Perce en lignes* - rouletted in lines. The paper receives short, straight cuts in lines. This is the most common type of rouletting. See Mexico Scott 500.

*Perce en points* - pin-rouletted or pin-perfed. This differs from a small perforation because no paper is removed, although round, equidistant holes are pricked through the paper. See Mexico Scott 242-256.

*Perce en arc* and *perce en scie* - pierced in an arc or saw-toothed designs, forming half circles or small triangles. See Hanover (German States) Scott 25-29.

*Perce en serpentin* - serpentine roulettes. The cuts form a serpentine or wavy line. See Brunswick (German States) Scott 13-18.

Once again, no paper is removed by these processes, leaving the stamps easily separated, but closely attached.

### DIE-CUTTING

The third major form of stamp separation is die-cutting. This is a method where a die in the pattern of separation is created that later cuts the stamp paper in a stroke motion. Although some standard stamps bear die-cut perforations, this process is primarily used for self-adhesive postage stamps. Die-cutting can appear in straight lines, such as U.S. Scott 2522, shapes, such as U.S. Scott 1551, or imitating the appearance of perforations, such as New Zealand Scott 935A and 935B.

## Printing Processes

### ENGRAVING (Intaglio, Line-engraving, Etching)

**Master die** — The initial operation in the process of line engraving is making the master die. The die is a small, flat block of softened steel upon which the stamp design is recess engraved in reverse.

Master die

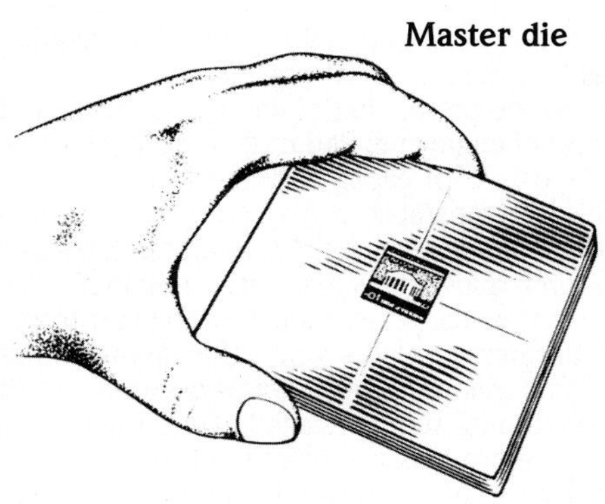

Photographic reduction of the original art is made to the appropriate size. It then serves as a tracing guide for the initial outline of the design. The engraver lightly traces the design on the steel with his graver, then slowly works the design until it is completed. At various points during the engraving process, the engraver hand-inks the die and makes an impression to check his progress. These are known as progressive die proofs. After completion of the engraving, the die is hardened to withstand the stress and pressures of later transfer operations.

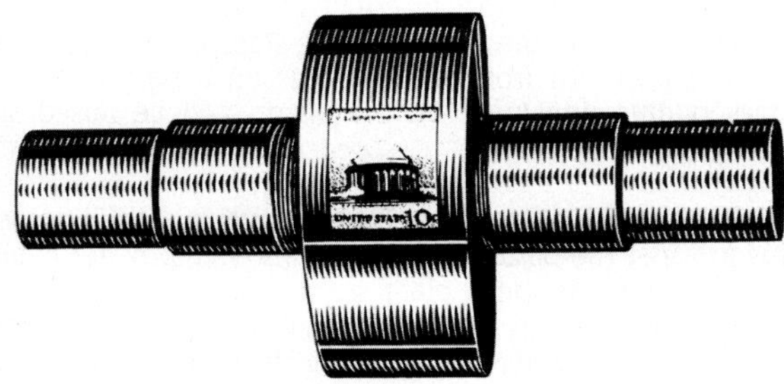

Transfer roll

**Transfer roll** — Next is production of the transfer roll that, as the name implies, is the medium used to transfer the subject from the master die to the printing plate. A blank roll of soft steel, mounted on a mandrel, is placed under the bearers of the transfer press to allow it to roll freely on its axis. The hardened die is placed on the bed of the press and the face of the transfer roll is applied to the die, under pressure. The bed or the roll is then rocked back and forth under increasing pressure, until the soft steel of the roll is forced into every engraved line of the die. The resulting impression on the roll is known as a "relief" or a "relief transfer." The engraved image is now positive in appearance and stands out from the steel. After the required number of reliefs are "rocked in," the soft steel transfer roll is hardened.

Different flaws may occur during the relief process. A defective relief may occur during the rocking in process because of a minute piece of foreign material lodging on the die, or some other cause. Imperfections in the steel of the transfer roll may result in a breaking away of parts of the design. This is known as a relief break, which will show up on finished stamps as small, unprinted areas. If a damaged relief remains in use, it will transfer a repeating defect to the plate. Deliberate alterations of reliefs sometimes occur. "Altered reliefs" designate these changed conditions.

**Plate** — The final step in pre-printing production is the making of the printing plate. A flat piece of soft steel replaces the die on the bed of the transfer press. One of the reliefs on the transfer roll is positioned over this soft steel. Position, or layout, dots determine the correct position on the plate. The dots have been lightly marked on the plate in advance. After the correct position of the relief is determined, the design is rocked in by following the same method used in making the transfer roll. The difference is that this time the image is being transferred from the transfer roll, rather than to it. Once the design is entered on the plate, it appears in reverse and is recessed. There are as many transfers entered on the plate as there are subjects printed on the sheet of stamps. It is during this process that double and shifted transfers occur, as well as re-entries. These are the result of improperly entered images that have not been properly burnished out prior to rocking in a new image.

Modern siderography processes, such as those used by the U.S. Bureau of Engraving and Printing, involve an automated form of rocking designs in on preformed cylindrical printing sleeves. The same process also allows for easier removal and re-entry of worn images right on the sleeve.

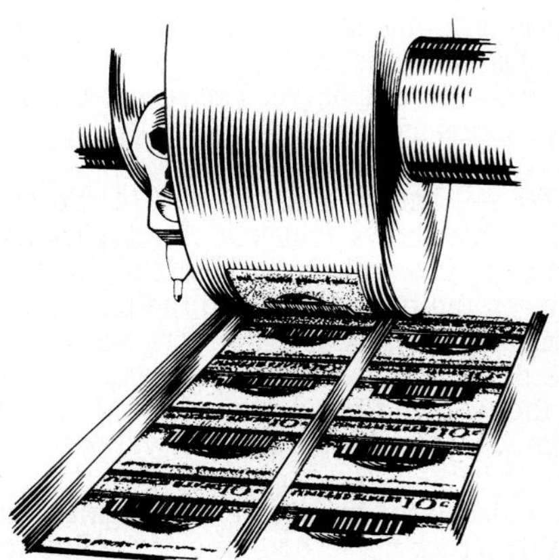

Transferring the design to the plate

Following the entering of the required transfers on the plate, the position dots, layout dots and lines, scratches and other markings generally are burnished out. Added at this time by the siderographer are any required *guide lines, plate numbers* or other *marginal markings.* The plate is then hand-inked and a proof impression is taken. This is known as a plate proof. If the impression is approved, the plate is machined for fitting onto the press, is hardened and sent to the plate vault ready for use.

On press, the plate is inked and the surface is automatically wiped clean, leaving ink only in the recessed lines. Paper is then forced under pressure into the engraved recessed lines, thereby receiving the ink. Thus, the ink lines on engraved stamps are slightly raised, and slight depressions (debossing) occur on the back of the stamp. Prior to the advent of modern high-speed presses and more advanced ink formulations, paper had to be dampened before receiving the ink. This sometimes led to uneven shrinkage by the time the stamps were perforated, resulting in improperly perforated stamps, or misperfs. Newer presses use drier paper, thus both *wet* and *dry printings* exist on some stamps.

**Rotary Press** — Until 1914, only flat plates were used to print engraved stamps. Rotary press printing was introduced in 1914, and slowly spread. Some countries still use flat-plate printing.

After approval of the plate proof, older *rotary press plates* require additional machining. They are curved to fit the press cylinder. "Gripper slots" are cut into the back of each plate to receive the "grippers," which hold the plate securely on the press. The plate is then hardened. Stamps printed from these bent rotary press plates are longer or wider than the same stamps printed from flat-plate presses. The stretching of the plate during the curving process is what causes this distortion.

**Re-entry** — To execute a re-entry on a flat plate, the transfer roll is re-applied to the plate, often at some time after its first use on the press. Worn-out designs can be resharpened by carefully burnishing out the original image and re-entering it from the transfer roll. If the original impression has not been sufficiently removed and the transfer roll is not precisely in line with the remaining impression, the resulting double transfer will make the re-entry obvious. If the registration is true, a re-entry may be difficult or impossible to distinguish. Sometimes a stamp printed from a successful re-entry is identified by having a much sharper and clearer impression than its neighbors. With the advent of rotary presses, post-press re-entries were not possible. After a plate was curved for the rotary press, it was impossible to make a re-entry. This is because the plate had already been bent once (with the design distorted).

However, with the introduction of the previously mentioned modern-style siderography machines, entries are made to the pre-formed cylindrical printing sleeve. Such sleeves are dechromed and softened. This allows individual images to be burnished out and re-entered on the curved sleeve. The sleeve is then rechromed, resulting in longer press life.

**Double Transfer** — This is a description of the condition of a transfer on a plate that shows evidence of a duplication of all, or a portion of the design. It usually is the result of the changing of the registration between the transfer roll and the plate during the rocking in of the original entry. Double transfers also occur when only a portion of the design has been rocked in and improper positioning is noted. If the worker elected not to burnish out the partial or completed design, a strong double transfer will occur for part or all of the design.

It sometimes is necessary to remove the original transfer from a plate and repeat the process a second time. If the finished re-worked image shows traces of the original impression, attributable to incomplete burnishing, the result is a partial double transfer.

With the modern automatic machines mentioned previously, double transfers are all but impossible to create. Those partially doubled images on stamps printed from such sleeves are more than likely re-entries, rather than true double transfers.

**Re-engraved** — Alterations to a stamp design are sometimes necessary after some stamps have been printed. In some cases, either the original die or the actual printing plate may have its "temper" drawn (softened), and the design will be re-cut. The resulting impressions from such a re-engraved die or plate may differ slightly from the original issue, and are known as "re-engraved." If the alteration was made to the master die, all future printings will be consistently different from the original. If alterations were made to the printing plate, each altered stamp on the plate will be slightly different from each other, allowing specialists to reconstruct a complete printing plate.

**Dropped Transfers** — If an impression from the transfer roll has not been properly placed, a dropped transfer may occur. The final stamp image will appear obviously out of line with its neighbors.

**Short Transfer** — Sometimes a transfer roll is not rocked its entire length when entering a transfer onto a plate. As a result, the finished transfer on the plate fails to show the complete design, and the finished stamp will have an incomplete design printed. This is known as a "short transfer." U.S. Scott No. 8 is a good example of a short transfer.

## TYPOGRAPHY (Letterpress, Surface Printing, Flexography, Dry Offset, High Etch)

Although the word "Typography" is obsolete as a term describing a printing method, it was the accepted term throughout the first century of postage stamps. Therefore, appropriate Scott listings in this catalogue refer to typographed stamps. The current term for this form of printing, however, is "letterpress."

As it relates to the production of postage stamps, letterpress printing is the reverse of engraving. Rather than having recessed areas trap the ink and deposit it on paper, only the raised areas of the design are inked. This is comparable to the type of printing seen by inking and using an ordinary rubber stamp. Letterpress includes all printing where the design is above the surface area, whether it is wood, metal or, in some instances, hardened rubber or polymer plastic.

For most letterpress-printed stamps, the engraved master is made in much the same manner as for engraved stamps. In this instance, however, an additional step is needed. The design is transferred to another surface before being transferred to the transfer roll. In this way, the transfer roll has a recessed stamp design, rather than one done in relief. This makes the printing areas on the final plate raised, or relief areas.

For less-detailed stamps of the 19th century, the area on the die not used as a printing surface was cut away, leaving the surface area raised. The original die was then reproduced by stereotyping or electrotyping. The resulting electrotypes were assembled in the required number and format of the desired sheet of stamps. The plate used in printing the stamps was an electroplate of these assembled electrotypes.

Once the final letterpress plates are created, ink is applied to the raised surface and the pressure of the press transfers the ink impression to the paper. In contrast to engraving, the fine lines of letterpress are impressed on the surface of the stamp, leaving a debossed surface. When viewed from the back (as on a typewritten page), the corresponding line work on the stamp will be raised slightly (embossed) above the surface.

## PHOTOGRAVURE (Gravure, Rotogravure, Heliogravure)

In this process, the basic principles of photography are applied to a chemically sensitized metal plate, rather than photographic paper. The design is transferred photographically to the plate through a halftone, or dot-matrix screen, breaking the reproduction into tiny dots. The plate is treated chemically and the dots form depressions, called cells, of varying depths and diameters, depending on the degrees of shade in the design. Then, like engraving, ink is applied to the plate and the surface is wiped clean. This leaves ink in the tiny cells that is lifted out and deposited on the paper when it is pressed against the plate.

Gravure is most often used for multicolored stamps, generally using the three primary colors (red, yellow and blue) and black. By varying the dot matrix pattern and density of these colors, virtually any color can be reproduced. A typical full-color gravure stamp will be created from four printing cylinders (one for each color). The original multicolored image will have been photographically separated into its component colors.

Modern gravure printing may use computer-generated dot-matrix screens, and modern plates may be of various types including metal-coated plastic. The catalogue designation of Photogravure (or "Photo") covers any of these older and more modern gravure methods of printing.

For examples of the first photogravure stamps printed (1914), see Bavaria Scott 94-114.

## LITHOGRAPHY (Offset Lithography, Stone Lithography, Dilitho, Planography, Collotype)

The principle that oil and water do not mix is the basis for lithography. The stamp design is drawn by hand or transferred from engraving to the surface of a lithographic stone or metal plate in a greasy (oily) substance. This oily substance holds the ink, which will later be transferred to the paper. The stone (or plate) is wet with an acid fluid, causing it to repel the printing ink in all areas not covered by the greasy substance.

Transfer paper is used to transfer the design from the original stone or plate. A series of duplicate transfers are grouped and, in turn, transferred to the final printing plate.

**Photolithography** — The application of photographic processes to lithography. This process allows greater flexibility of design, related to use of halftone screens combined with line work. Unlike photogravure or engraving, this process can allow large, solid areas to be printed.

**Offset** — A refinement of the lithographic process. A rubber-covered blanket cylinder takes the impression from the inked lithographic plate. From the "blanket" the impression is *offset* or transferred to the paper. Greater flexibility and speed are the principal reasons offset printing has largely displaced lithography. The term "lithography" covers both processes, and results are almost identical.

### EMBOSSED (Relief) Printing

Embossing, not considered one of the four main printing types, is a method in which the design first is sunk into the metal of the die. Printing is done against a yielding platen, such as leather or linoleum. The platen is forced into the depression of the die, thus forming the design on the paper in relief. This process is often used for metallic inks.

Embossing may be done without color (see Sardinia Scott 4-6); with color printed around the embossed area (see Great Britain Scott 5 and most U.S. envelopes); and with color in exact registration with the embossed subject (see Canada Scott 656-657).

### HOLOGRAMS

For objects to appear as holograms on stamps, a model exactly the same size as it is to appear on the hologram must be created. Rather than using photographic film to capture the image, holography records an image on a photoresist material. In processing, chemicals eat away at certain exposed areas, leaving a pattern of constructive and destructive interference. When the phororesist is developed, the result is a pattern of uneven ridges that acts as a mold. This mold is then coated with metal, and the resulting form is used to press copies in much the same way phonograph records are produced.

A typical reflective hologram used for stamps consists of a reproduction of the uneven patterns on a plastic film that is applied to a reflective background, usually a silver or gold foil. Light is reflected off the background through the film, making the pattern present on the film visible. Because of the uneven pattern of the film, the viewer will perceive the objects in their proper three-dimensional relationships with appropriate brightness.

The first hologram on a stamp was produced by Austria in 1988 (Scott 1441).

### FOIL APPLICATION

A modern tecnique of applying color to stamps involves the application of metallic foil to the stamp paper. A pattern of foil is applied to the stamp paper by use of a stamping die. The foil usually is flat, but it may be textured. Canada Scott 1735 has three different foil applications in pearl, bronze and gold. The gold foil was textured using a chemical-etch copper embossing die. The printing of this stamp also involved two-color offset lithography plus embossing.

### COMBINATION PRINTINGS

Sometimes two or even three printing methods are combined in producing stamps. In these cases, such as Austria Scott 933 or Canada 1735 (described in the preceding paragraph), the multiple-printing technique can be determined by studying the individual characteristics of each printing type. A few stamps, such as Singapore Scott 684-684A, combine as many as three of the four major printing types (lithography, engraving and typography). When this is done it often indicates the incorporation of security devices against counterfeiting.

### INK COLORS

Inks or colored papers used in stamp printing often are of mineral origin, although there are numerous examples of organic-based pigments. As a general rule, organic-based pigments are far more subject to varieties and change than those of mineral-based origin.

The appearance of any given color on a stamp may be affected by many aspects, including printing variations, light, color of paper, aging and chemical alterations.

Numerous printing variations may be observed. Heavier pressure or inking will cause a more intense color, while slight interruptions in the ink feed or lighter impressions will cause a lighter appearance. Stamps printed in the same color by water-based and solvent-based inks can differ significantly in appearance. This affects several stamps in the U.S. Prominent Americans series. Hand-mixed ink formulas (primarily from the 19th century) produced under different conditions (humidity and temperature) account for notable color variations in early printings of the same stamp (see U.S. Scott 248-250, 279B, for example). Different sources of pigment can also result in significant differences in color.

Light exposure and aging are closely related in the way they affect stamp color. Both eventually break down the ink and fade colors, so that a carefully kept stamp may differ significantly in color from an identical copy that has been exposed to light. If stamps are exposed to light either intentionally or accidentally, their colors can be faded or completely changed in some cases.

Papers of different quality and consistency used for the same stamp printing may affect color appearance. Most pelure papers, for example, show a richer color when compared with wove or laid papers. See Russia Scott 181a, for an example of this effect.

The very nature of the printing processes can cause a variety of differences in shades or hues of the same stamp. Some of these shades are scarcer than others, and are of particular interest to the advanced collector.

## Luminescence

All forms of tagged stamps fall under the general category of luminescence. Within this broad category is fluorescence, dealing with forms of tagging visible under longwave ultraviolet light, and phosphorescence, which deals with tagging visible only under shortwave light. Phosphorescence leaves an afterglow and fluorescence does not. These treated stamps show up in a range of different colors when exposed to UV light. The differing wavelengths of the light activates the tagging material, making it glow in various colors that usually serve different mail processing purposes.

Intentional tagging is a post-World War II phenomenon, brought about by the increased literacy rate and rapidly growing mail volume. It was one of several answers to the problem of the need for more automated mail processes. Early tagged stamps served the purpose of triggering machines to separate different types of mail. A natural outgrowth was to also use the signal to trigger machines that faced all envelopes the same way and canceled them.

Tagged stamps come in many different forms. Some tagged stamps have luminescent shapes or images imprinted on them as a form of security device. Others have blocks (United States), stripes, frames (South Africa and Canada), overall coatings (United States), bars (Great Britain and Canada) and many other types. Some types of tagging are even mixed in with the pigmented printing ink (Australia Scott 366, Netherlands Scott 478 and U.S. Scott 1359 and 2443).

The means of applying taggant to stamps differs as much as the intended purposes for the stamps. The most common form of tagging is a coating applied to the surface of the printed stamp. Since the taggant ink is frequently invisible except under UV light, it does not interfere with the appearance of the stamp. Another common application is the use of phosphored papers. In this case the paper itself either has a coating of taggant applied before the stamp is printed, has taggant applied during the papermaking process (incorporating it into the fibers), or has the taggant mixed into the coating of the paper. The latter method, among others, is currently in use in the United States.

Many countries now use tagging in various forms to either expedite mail handling or to serve as a printing security device against counterfeiting. Following the introduction of tagged stamps for public use in 1959 by Great Britain, other countries have steadily joined the parade. Among those are Germany (1961); Canada and Denmark (1962); United States, Australia, France and Switzerland (1963); Belgium and Japan (1966); Sweden and Norway (1967); Italy (1968); and Russia (1969). Since then, many other countries have begun using forms of tagging, including Brazil, China, Czechoslovakia, Hong Kong, Guatemala, Indonesia, Israel, Lithuania, Luxembourg, Netherlands, Penrhyn Islands, Portugal, St. Vincent, Singapore, South Africa, Spain and Sweden to name a few.

In some cases, including United States, Canada, Great Britain and Switzerland, stamps were released both with and without tagging. Many of these were released during each country's experimental period. Tagged and untagged versions are listed for the aforementioned countries and are noted in some other countries' listings. For at least a few stamps, the experimentally tagged version is worth far more than its untagged counterpart, such as the 1963 experimental tagged version of France Scott 1024.

In some cases, luminescent varieties of stamps were inadvertently created. Several Russian stamps, for example, sport highly fluorescent ink that was not intended as a form of tagging. Older stamps, such as early U.S. postage dues, can be positively identified by the use of UV light, since the organic ink used has become slightly fluorescent over time. Other stamps, such as Austria Scott 70a-82a (varnish bars) and Obock Scott 46-64 (printed quadrille lines), have become fluorescent over time.

Various fluorescent substances have been added to paper to make it appear brighter. These optical brightners, as they are known, greatly affect the appearance of the stamp under UV light. The brightest of these is known as Hi-Brite paper. These paper varieties are beyond the scope of the Scott Catalogue.

Shortwave UV light also is used extensively in expertizing, since each form of paper has its own fluorescent characteristics that are impossible to perfectly match. It is therefore a simple matter to detect filled thins, added perforation teeth and other alterations that involve the addition of paper. UV light also is used to examine stamps that have had cancels chemically removed and for other purposes as well.

## Gum

The Illustrated Gum Chart in the first part of this introduction shows and defines various types of gum condition. Because gum condition has an important impact on the value of unused stamps, we recommend studying this chart and the accompanying text carefully.

The gum on the back of a stamp may be shiny, dull, smooth, rough, dark, white, colored or tinted. Most stamp gumming adhesives use gum arabic or dextrine as a base. Certain polymers such as polyvinyl alcohol (PVA) have been used extensively since World War II.

The *Scott Standard Postage Stamp Catalogue* does not list items by types of gum. The *Scott Specialized Catalogue of United States Stamps* does differentiate among some types of gum for certain issues.

Reprints of stamps may have gum differing from the original issues. In addition, some countries have used different gum formulas for different seasons. These adhesives have different properties that may become more apparent over time.

Many stamps have been issued without gum, and the catalogue will note this fact. See, for example, United States Scott 40-47. Sometimes, gum may have been removed to preserve the stamp. Germany Scott B68, for example, has a highly acidic gum that eventually destroys the stamps. This item is valued in the catalogue with gum removed.

## Reprints and Reissues

These are impressions of stamps (usually obsolete) made from the original plates or stones. If they are valid for postage and reproduce obsolete issues (such as U.S. Scott 102-111), the stamps are *reissues.* If they are from current issues, they are designated as *second, third,* etc., *printing.* If designated for a particular purpose, they are called *special printings.*

When special printings are not valid for postage, but are made from original dies and plates by authorized persons, they are *official reprints. Private reprints* are made from the original plates and dies by private hands. An example of a private reprint is that of the 1871-1932 reprints made from the original die of the 1845 New Haven, Conn., postmaster's provisional. *Official reproductions* or imitations are made from new dies and plates by government authorization. Scott will list those reissues that are valid for postage if they differ significantly from the original printing.

The U.S. government made special printings of its first postage stamps in 1875. Produced were official imitations of the first two stamps (listed as Scott 3-4), reprints of the demonetized pre-1861 issues (Scott 40-47) and reissues of the 1861 stamps, the 1869 stamps and the then-current 1875 denominations. Even though the official imitations and the reprints were not valid for postage, Scott lists all of these U.S. special printings.

Most reprints or reissues differ slightly from the original stamp in some characteristic, such as gum, paper, perforation, color or watermark. Sometimes the details are followed so meticulously that only a student of that specific stamp is able to distinguish the reprint or reissue from the original.

## Remainders and Canceled to Order

Some countries sell their stock of old stamps when a new issue replaces them. To avoid postal use, the *remainders* usually are canceled with a punch hole, a heavy line or bar, or a more-or-less regular-looking cancellation. The most famous merchant of remainders was Nicholas F. Seebeck. In the 1880s and 1890s, he arranged printing contracts between the Hamilton Bank Note Co., of which he was a director, and several Central and South American countries. The contracts provided that the plates and all remainders of the yearly issues became the property of Hamilton. Seebeck saw to it that ample stock remained. The "Seebecks," both remainders and reprints, were standard packet fillers for decades.

Some countries also issue stamps *canceled-to-order (CTO),* either in sheets with original gum or stuck onto pieces of paper or envelopes and canceled. Such CTO items generally are worth less than postally used stamps. In cases where the CTO material is far more prevalent in the marketplace than postally used examples, the catalogue value relates to the CTO examples, with postally used examples noted as premium items. Most CTOs can be detected by the presence of gum. However, as the CTO practice goes back at least to 1885, the gum inevitably has been soaked off some stamps so they could pass as postally used. The normally applied postmarks usually differ slightly from standard postmarks, and specialists are able to tell the difference. When applied individually to envelopes by philatelically minded persons, CTO material is known as *favor canceled* and generally sells at large discounts.

## Cinderellas and Facsimiles

*Cinderella* is a catch-all term used by stamp collectors to describe phantoms, fantasies, bogus items, municipal issues, exhibition seals, local revenues, transportation stamps, labels, poster stamps and many other types of items. Some cinderella collectors include in their collections local postage issues, telegraph stamps, essays and proofs, forgeries and counterfeits.

A *fantasy* is an adhesive created for a nonexistent stamp-issuing authority. Fantasy items range from imaginary countries (Occusi-Ambeno, Kingdom of Sedang, Principality of Trinidad or Torres Straits), to non-existent locals (Winans City Post), or nonexistent transportation lines (McRobish & Co.'s Acapulco-San Francisco Line).

On the other hand, if the entity exists and could have issued stamps (but did not) or was known to have issued other stamps, the items are considered *bogus* stamps. These would include the Mormon postage stamps of Utah, S. Allan Taylor's Guatemala and Paraguay inventions, the propaganda issues for the South Moluccas and the adhesives of the Page & Keyes local post of Boston.

*Phantoms* is another term for both fantasy and bogus issues.

*Facsimiles* are copies or imitations made to represent original stamps, but which do not pretend to be originals. A catalogue illustration is such a facsimile. Illustrations from the Moens catalogue of the last century were occasionally colored and passed off as stamps. Since the beginning of stamp collecting, facsimiles have been made for collectors as space fillers or for reference. They often carry the word "facsimile," "falsch" (German), "sanko" or "mozo" (Japanese), or "faux" (French) overprinted on the face or stamped on the back. Unfortunately, over the years a number of these items have had fake cancels applied over the facsimile notation and have been passed off as genuine.

## Forgeries and Counterfeits

Forgeries and counterfeits have been with philately virtually from the beginning of stamp production. Over time, the terminology for the two has been used interchangeably. Although both forgeries and counterfeits are reproductions of stamps, the purposes behind their creation differ considerably.

Among specialists there is an increasing movement to more specifically define such items. Although there is no universally accepted terminology, we feel the following definitions most closely mirror the items and their purposes as they are currently defined.

*Forgeries* (also often referred to as *Counterfeits*) are reproductions of genuine stamps that have been created to defraud collectors. Such spurious items first appeared on the market around 1860, and most old-time collections contain one or more. Many are crude and easily spotted, but some can deceive experts.

An important supplier of these early philatelic forgeries was the Hamburg printer Gebruder Spiro. Many others with reputations in this craft included S. Allan Taylor, George Hussey, James Chute, George Forune, Benjamin & Sarpy, Julius Goldner, E. Oneglia and L.H. Mercier. Among the noted 20th-century forgers were Francois Fournier, Jean Sperati and the prolific Raoul DeThuin.

Forgeries may be complete replications, or they may be genuine stamps altered to resemble a scarcer (and more valuable) type. Most forgeries, particularly those of rare stamps, are worth only a small fraction of the value of a genuine example, but a few types, created by some of the most notable forgers, such as Sperati, can be worth as much or more than the genuine. Fraudulently produced copies are known of most classic rarities and many medium-priced stamps.

In addition to rare stamps, large numbers of common 19th- and early 20th-century stamps were forged to supply stamps to the early packet trade. Many can still be easily found. Few new philatelic forgeries have appeared in recent decades. Successful imitation of well-engraved work is virtually impossible. It has proven far easier to produce a fake by altering a genuine stamp than to duplicate a stamp completely.

*Counterfeit* (also often referred to as *Postal Counterfeit* or *Postal Forgery*) is the term generally applied to reproductions of stamps that have been created to defraud the government of revenue. Such items usually are created at the time a stamp is current and, in some cases, are hard to detect. Because most counterfeits are seized when the perpetrator is captured, postal counterfeits, particularly used on cover, are usually worth much more than a genuine example to specialists. The first postal counterfeit was of Spain's 4-cuarto carmine of 1854 (the real one is Scott 25). Apparently, the counterfeiters were not satisfied with their first version, which is now very scarce, and they soon created an engraved counterfeit, which is common. Postal counterfeits quickly followed in Austria, Naples, Sardinia and the Roman States. They have since been created in many other countries as well, including the United States.

An infamous counterfeit to defraud the government is the 1-shilling Great Britain "Stock Exchange" forgery of 1872, used on telegraph forms at the exchange that year. The stamp escaped detection until a stamp dealer noticed it in 1898.

## Fakes

*Fakes* are genuine stamps altered in some way to make them more desirable. One student of this part of stamp collecting has estimated that by the 1950s more than 30,000 varieties of fakes were known. That number has grown greatly since then. The widespread existence of fakes makes it important for stamp collectors to study their philatelic holdings and use relevant literature. Likewise, collectors should buy from reputable dealers who guarantee their stamps and make full and prompt refunds should a purchased item be declared faked or altered by some mutually agreed-upon authority. Because fakes always have some genuine characteristics, it is not always possible to obtain unanimous agreement among experts regarding specific items. These students may change their opinions as philatelic knowledge increases. More than 80 percent of all fakes on the philatelic market today are regummed, reperforated (or perforated for the first time), or bear forged overprints, surcharges or cancellations.

Stamps can be chemically treated to alter or eliminate colors. For example, a pale rose stamp can be re-colored to resemble a blue shade of high market value. In other cases, treated stamps can be made to resemble missing color varieties. Designs may be changed by painting, or a stroke or a dot added or bleached out to turn an ordinary variety into a seemingly scarcer stamp. Part of a stamp can be bleached and reprinted in a different version, achieving an inverted center or frame. Margins can be added or repairs done so deceptively that the stamps move from the "repaired" into the "fake" category.

Fakers have not left the backs of the stamps untouched either. They may create false watermarks, add fake grills or press out genuine grills. A thin India paper proof may be glued onto a thicker backing to create the appearance an issued stamp, or a proof printed on cardboard may be shaved down and perforated to resemble a stamp. Silk threads are impressed into paper and stamps have been split so that a rare paper variety is added to an otherwise inexpensive stamp. The most common treatment to the back of a stamp, however, is regumming.

Some in the business of faking stamps have openly advertised foolproof application of "original gum" to stamps that lack it, although most publications now ban such ads from their pages. It is believed that very few early stamps have survived without being hinged. The large number of never-hinged examples of such earlier material offered for sale thus suggests the widespread extent of regumming activity. Regumming also may be used to hide repairs or thin spots. Dipping the stamp into watermark fluid, or examining it under long-wave ultraviolet light often will reveal these flaws.

Fakers also tamper with separations. Ingenious ways to add margins are known. Perforated wide-margin stamps may be falsely represented as imperforate when trimmed. Reperforating is commonly done to create scarce coil or perforation varieties, and to eliminate the naturally occurring straight-edge stamps found in sheet margin positions of many earlier issues. Custom has made straight-edged stamps less desirable. Fakers have obliged by perforating straight-edged stamps so that many are now uncommon, if not rare.

Another fertile field for the faker is that of overprints, surcharges and cancellations. The forging of rare surcharges or overprints began in the 1880s or 1890s. These forgeries are sometimes difficult to detect, but experts have identified almost all. Occasionally, overprints or cancellations are removed to create non-overprinted stamps or seemingly unused items. This is most commonly done by removing a manuscript cancel to make a stamp resemble an unused example. "SPECIMEN" overprints may be removed by scraping and repainting to create non-overprinted varieties. Fakers use inexpensive revenues or pen-canceled stamps to generate unused stamps for further faking by adding other markings. The quartz lamp or UV lamp and a high-powered magnifying glass help to easily detect removed cancellations.

The bigger problem, however, is the addition of overprints, surcharges or cancellations - many with such precision that they are very difficult to ascertain. Plating of the stamps or the overprint can be an important method of detection.

Fake postmarks may range from many spurious fancy cancellations to a host of markings applied to transatlantic covers, to adding normally appearing postmarks to definitives of some countries with stamps that are valued far higher used than unused. With the increased popularity of cover collecting, and the widespread interest in postal history, a fertile new field for fakers has come about. Some have tried to create entire covers. Others specialize in adding stamps, tied by fake cancellations, to genuine stampless covers, or replacing less expensive or damaged stamps with more valuable ones. Detailed study of postal rates in effect at the time a cover in question was mailed, including the analysis of each handstamp used during the period, ink analysis and similar techniques, usually will unmask the fraud.

## Restoration and Repairs

Scott Publishing Co. bases its catalogue values on stamps that are free of defects and otherwise meet the standards set forth earlier in this introduction. Most stamp collectors desire to have the finest copy of an item possible. Even within given grading categories there are variances. This leads to a controversial practice that is not defined in any universal manner: stamp *restoration.*

There are broad differences of opinion about what is permissible when it comes to restoration. Carefully applying a soft eraser to a stamp or cover to remove light soiling is one form of restoration, as is washing a stamp in mild soap and water to clean it. These are fairly accepted forms of restoration. More severe forms of restoration include pressing out creases or removing stains caused by tape. To what degree each of these is acceptable is dependent upon the individual situation. Further along the spectrum is the freshening of a stamp's color by removing oxide build-up or the effects of wax paper left next to stamps shipped to the tropics.

At some point in this spectrum the concept of *repair* replaces that of restoration. Repairs include filling thin spots, mending tears by reweaving or adding a missing perforation tooth. Regumming stamps may have been acceptable as a restoration or repair technique many decades ago, but today it is considered a form of fakery.

Restored stamps may or may not sell at a discount, and it is possible that the value of individual restored items may be enhanced over that of their pre-restoration state. Specific situations dictate the resultant value of such an item. Repaired stamps sell at substantial discounts from the value of sound stamps.

# Terminology

**Booklets** — Many countries have issued stamps in small booklets for the convenience of users. This idea continues to become increasingly popular in many countries. Booklets have been issued in many sizes and forms, often with advertising on the covers, the panes of stamps or on the interleaving.

The panes used in booklets may be printed from special plates or made from regular sheets. All panes from booklets issued by the United States and many from those of other countries contain stamps that are straight edged on the sides, but perforated between. Others are distinguished by orientation of watermark or other identifying features. Any stamp-like unit in the pane, either printed or blank, that is not a postage stamp, is considered to be a *label* in the catalogue listings.

Scott lists and values booklet panes. Modern complete booklets also are listed and valued. Individual booklet panes are listed only when they are not fashioned from existing sheet stamps and, therefore, are identifiable from their sheet stamp counterparts.

Panes usually do not have a used value assigned to them because there is little market activity for used booklet panes, even though many exist used and there is some demand for them.

**Cancellations** — The marks or obliterations put on stamps by postal authorities to show that they have performed service and to prevent their reuse are known as cancellations. If the marking is made with a pen, it is considered a "pen cancel." When the location of the post office appears in the marking, it is a "town cancellation." A "postmark" is technically any postal marking, but in practice the term generally is applied to a town cancellation with a date. When calling attention to a cause or celebration, the marking is known as a "slogan cancellation." Many other types and styles of cancellations exist, such as duplex, numerals, targets, fancy and others. See also "precancels," below.

**Coil Stamps** — These are stamps that are issued in rolls for use in dispensers, affixing and vending machines. Those coils of the United States, Canada, Sweden and some other countries are perforated horizontally or vertically only, with the outer edges imperforate. Coil stamps of some countries, such as Great Britain and Germany, are perforated on all four sides and may in some cases be distinguished from their sheet stamp counterparts by watermarks, counting numbers on the reverse or other means.

**Covers** — Entire envelopes, with or without adhesive postage stamps, that have passed through the mail and bear postal or other markings of philatelic interest are known as covers. Before the introduction of envelopes in about 1840, people folded letters and wrote the address on the outside. Some people covered their letters with an extra sheet of paper on the outside for the address, producing the term "cover." Used airletter sheets, stamped envelopes and other items of postal stationery also are considered covers.

**Errors** — Stamps that have some major, consistent, unintentional deviation from the normal are considered errors. Errors include, but are not limited to, missing or wrong colors, wrong paper, wrong watermarks, inverted centers or frames on multicolor printing, inverted or missing surcharges or overprints, double impressions, missing perforations, unintentionally omitted tagging and others. Factually wrong or misspelled information, if it appears on all examples of a stamp, are not considered errors in the true sense of the word. They are errors of design. Inconsistent or randomly appearing items, such as misperfs or color shifts, are classified as freaks.

**Color-Omitted Errors** — This term refers to stamps where a missing color is caused by the complete failure of the printing plate to deliver ink to the stamp paper or any other paper. Generally, this is caused by the printing plate not being engaged on the press or the ink station running dry of ink during printing.

**Color-Missing Errors** — This term refers to stamps where a color or colors were printed somewhere but do not appear on the finished stamp. There are four different classes of color-missing errors, and the catalog indicates with a two-letter code appended to each such listing what caused the color to be missing. These codes are used only for the United States' color-missing error listings.

**FO** = A *foldover* of the stamp sheet during printing may block ink from appearing on a stamp. Instead, the color will appear on the back of the foldover (where it might fall on the back of the selvage or perhaps on the back of the stamp or another stamp). FO also will be used in the case of foldunders, where the paper may fold underneath the other stamp paper and the color will print on the platen.

**EP** = A piece of *extraneous paper* falling across the plate or stamp paper will receive the printed ink. When the extraneous paper is removed, an unprinted portion of stamp paper remains and shows partially or totally missing colors.

**CM** = A misregistration of the printing plates during printing will result in a *color misregistration*, and such a misregistraion may result in a color not appearing on the finished stamp.

**PS** = A *perforation shift* after printing may remove a color from the finished stamp. Normally, this will occur on a row of stamps at the edge of the stamp pane.

**Overprints and Surcharges** — Overprinting involves applying wording or design elements over an already existing stamp. Overprints can be used to alter the place of use (such as "Canal Zone" on U.S. stamps), to adapt them for a special purpose ("Porto" on Denmark's 1913-20 regular issues for use as postage due stamps, Scott J1-J7) or to commemorate a special occasion (United States Scott 647-648).

A *surcharge* is a form of overprint that changes or restates the face value of a stamp or piece of postal stationery.

Surcharges and overprints may be handstamped, typeset or, occasionally, lithographed or engraved. A few hand-written overprints and surcharges are known.

**Personalized Stamps** — In 1999, Australia issued stamps with se-tenant labels that could be personalized with pictures of the customer's choice. Other countries quickly followed suit, with some offering to print the selected picture on the stamp itself within a frame that was used exclusively for personalized issues. As the picture used on these stamps or labels vary, listings for such stamps are for *any* picture within the common frame (or any picture on a se-tenant label), be it a "generic" image or one produced especially for a customer, almost invariably at a premium price.

**Precancels** — Stamps that are canceled before they are placed in the mail are known as precancels. Precanceling usually is done to expedite the handling of large mailings and generally allow the affected mail pieces to skip certain phases of mail handling.

In the United States, precancellations generally identified the point of origin; that is, the city and state. This information appeared across the face of the stamp, usually centered between parallel lines. More recently, bureau precancels retained the parallel lines, but the city and state designations were dropped. Recent coils have a service inscription that is present on the original printing plate. These show the mail service paid for by the stamp. Since these stamps are not intended to receive further cancellations when used as intended, they are considered precancels. Such items often do not have parallel lines as part of the precancellation.

In France, the abbreviation *Affranchts* in a semicircle together with the word *Postes* is the general form of precancel in use. Belgian precancellations usually appear in a box in which the name of the city appears. Netherlands precancels have the name of the city enclosed between concentric circles, sometimes called a "lifesaver." Precancellations of other countries usually follow these patterns, but may be any arrangement of bars, boxes and city names.

Precancels are listed in the Scott catalogues only if the precancel changes the denomination (Belgium Scott 477-478); if the precanceled stamp is different from the non-precanceled version (such as untagged U.S. precancels); or if the stamp exists only precanceled (France Scott 1096-1099, U.S. Scott 2265).

**Proofs and Essays** — Proofs are impressions taken from an approved die, plate or stone in which the design and color are the same as the stamp issued to the public. Trial color proofs are impressions taken from approved dies, plates or stones in colors that vary from the final version. An essay is the impression of a design that differs in some way from the issued stamp. "Progressive die proofs" generally are considered to be essays.

**Provisionals** — These are stamps that are issued on short notice and intended for temporary use pending the arrival of regular issues. They usually are issued to meet such contingencies as changes in government or currency, shortage of necessary postage values or military occupation.

During the 1840s, postmasters in certain American cities issued stamps that were valid only at specific post offices. In 1861, postmasters of the Confederate States also issued stamps with limited validity. Both of these examples are known as "postmaster's provisionals."

**Se-tenant** — This term refers to an unsevered pair, strip or block of stamps that differ in design, denomination or overprint.

Unless the se-tenant item has a continuous design (see U.S. Scott 1451a, 1694a) the stamps do not have to be in the same order as shown in the catalogue (see U.S. Scott 2158a).

**Specimens** — The Universal Postal Union required member nations to send samples of all stamps they released into service to the International Bureau in Switzerland. Member nations of the UPU received these specimens as samples of what stamps were valid for postage. Many are overprinted, handstamped or initial-perforated "Specimen," "Canceled" or "Muestra." Some are marked with bars across the denominations (China-Taiwan), punched holes (Czechoslovakia) or back inscriptions (Mongolia).

Stamps distributed to government officials or for publicity purposes, and stamps submitted by private security printers for official approval, also may receive such defacements.

The previously described defacement markings prevent postal use, and all such items generally are known as "specimens."

**Tete Beche** — This term describes a pair of stamps in which one is upside down in relation to the other. Some of these are the result of intentional sheet arrangements, such as Morocco Scott B10-B11. Others occurred when one or more electrotypes accidentally were placed upside down on the plate, such as Colombia Scott 57a. Separation of the tete-beche stamps, of course, destroys the tete beche variety.

# Currency Conversion

| Country | Dollar | Pound | S Franc | Yen | HK $ | Euro | Cdn $ | Aus $ |
|---|---|---|---|---|---|---|---|---|
| Australia | 1.2174 | 2.4265 | 1.0054 | 0.0101 | 0.1557 | 1.6552 | 1.0992 | — |
| Canada | 1.1075 | 2.2075 | 0.9146 | 0.0092 | 0.1416 | 1.5058 | — | 0.9097 |
| European Union | 0.7355 | 1.4660 | 0.6074 | 0.0061 | 0.0940 | — | 0.6641 | 0.6042 |
| Hong Kong | 7.8204 | 15.588 | 6.4583 | 0.0651 | — | 10.633 | 7.0613 | 6.4239 |
| Japan | 120.14 | 239.45 | 99.211 | — | 15.362 | 163.39 | 108.47 | 98.682 |
| Switzerland | 1.2109 | 2.4136 | — | 0.0101 | 0.1548 | 1.6464 | 1.0934 | 0.9947 |
| United Kingdom | 0.5017 | — | 0.4143 | 0.0042 | 0.0642 | 0.6821 | 0.4530 | 0.4121 |
| United States | — | 1.9932 | 0.8258 | 0.0083 | 0.1279 | 1.3596 | 0.9029 | 0.8214 |

| Country | Currency | U.S. $ Equiv. |
|---|---|---|
| Solomon Islands | dollar | .1400 |
| Somalia | shilling | .0007 |
| South Africa | rand | .1444 |
| S. Georgia & S. Sandwich Isls | British pound | 1.9932 |
| Spain | euro | 1.3596 |
| Sri Lanka | rupee | .0090 |
| Sudan | pound | .0050 |
| Surinam | dollar | .3636 |
| Swaziland | emalangeni | .1434 |
| Sweden | krona | .1482 |
| Switzerland | franc | .8258 |
| Syria | pound | .0192 |
| Tajikistan | somoni | .2908 |
| Tanzania | shilling | .0008 |
| Thailand | baht | .0306 |
| Timor | U.S. dollar | 1.00 |
| Togo | Community of French Africa (CFA) franc | .0021 |
| Tokelau | New Zealand dollar | .7357 |
| Tonga | pa'anga | .5067 |
| Niuafo'ou | pa'anga | .5067 |
| Trinidad & Tobago | dollar | .1590 |
| Tristan da Cunha | British pound | 1.9932 |
| Tunisia | dinar | .7740 |
| Turkey | lira | .7407 |
| Turk. Rep. of Northern Cyprus | lira | .7407 |
| Turkmenistan | manat | .0002 |
| Turks & Caicos Islands | U.S. dollar | 1.00 |
| Tuvalu | Australian dollar | .8214 |
| Uganda | shilling | .0006 |
| Ukraine | hryvnia | .1987 |
| United Arab Emirates | dirham | .2723 |
| Uruguay | peso | .0419 |
| Uzbekistan | sum | .0008 |
| Vanuatu | vatu | .0096 |
| Vatican City | euro | 1.3596 |
| Venezuela | bolivar | .0005 |
| Viet Nam | dong | .00006 |
| Virgin Islands | U.S. dollar | 1.00 |
| Wallis & Futuna Islands | Community of French Pacific (CFP) franc | .0114 |
| Yemen | rial | .0050 |
| Zambia | kwacha | .0002 |
| Zaire (Congo Dem. Rep.) | franc | .0018 |
| Zimbabwe | dollar | .0040 |

*Source: **Wall Street Journal** May 7, 2007. Figures reflect values as of May 4, 2007.*

# COMMON DESIGN TYPES

Pictured in this section are issues where one illustration has been used for a number of countries in the Catalogue. Not included in this section are overprinted stamps or those issues which are illustrated in each country.

## EUROPA

### Europa, 1956

The design symbolizing the cooperation among the six countries comprising the Coal and Steel Community is illustrated in each country.

Belgium 496-497
France 805-806
Germany 748-749
Italy 715-716
Luxembourg 318-320
Netherlands 368-369

### Europa, 1958

"E" and Dove — CD1

European Postal Union at the service of European integration.

**1958, Sept. 13**

Belgium 527-528
France 889-890
Germany 790-791
Italy 750-751
Luxembourg 341-343
Netherlands 375-376
Saar 317-318

### Europa, 1959

6-Link Enless Chain — CD2

**1959, Sept. 19**

Belgium 536-537
France 929-930
Germany 805-806
Italy 791-792
Luxembourg 354-355
Netherlands 379-380

### Europa, 1960

19-Spoke Wheel CD3

First anniverary of the establishment of C.E.P.T. (Conference Europeenne des Administrations des Postes et des Telecommunications.) The spokes symbolize the 19 founding members of the Conference.

**1960, Sept.**

Belgium 553-554
Denmark 379
Finland 376-377
France 970-971
Germany 818-820
Great Britain 377-378
Greece 688
Iceland 327-328
Ireland 175-176
Italy 809-810
Luxembourg 374-375
Netherlands 385-386
Norway 387
Portugal 866-867
Spain 941-942
Sweden 562-563
Switzerland 400-401
Turkey 1493-1494

### Europa, 1961

19 Doves Flying as One — CD4

The 19 doves represent the 19 members of the Conference of European Postal and Telecommunications Administrations C.E.P.T.

**1961-62**

Belgium 572-573
Cyprus 201-203
France 1005-1006
Germany 844-845
Great Britain 383-384
Greece 718-719
Iceland 340-341
Italy 845-846
Luxembourg 382-383
Netherlands 387-388
Spain 1010-1011
Switzerland 410-411
Turkey 1518-1520

### Europa, 1962

Young Tree with 19 Leaves CD5

The 19 leaves represent the 19 original members of C.E.P.T.

**1962-63**

Belgium 582-583
Cyprus 219-221
France 1045-1046
Germany 852-853
Greece 739-740
Iceland 348-349
Ireland 184-185
Italy 860-861
Luxembourg 386-387
Netherlands 394-395
Norway 414-415
Switzerland 416-417
Turkey 1553-1555

### Europa, 1963

Stylized Links, Symbolizing Unity — CD6

**1963, Sept.**

Belgium 598-599
Cyprus 229-231
Finland 419
France 1074-1075
Germany 867-868
Greece 768-769
Iceland 357-358
Ireland 188-189
Italy 880-881
Luxembourg 403-404
Netherlands 416-417
Norway 441-442
Switzerland 429
Turkey 1602-1603

### Europa, 1964

Symbolic Daisy — CD7

5th anniversary of the establishment of C.E.P.T. The 22 petals of the flower symbolize the 22 members of the Conference.

**1964, Sept.**

Austria 738
Belgium 614-615
Cyprus 244-246
France 1109-1110
Germany 897-898
Greece 801-802
Iceland 367-368
Ireland 196-197
Italy 894-895
Luxembourg 411-412
Monaco 590-591
Netherlands 428-429
Norway 458
Portugal 931-933
Spain 1262-1263
Switzerland 438-439
Turkey 1628-1629

### Europa, 1965

Leaves and "Fruit" CD8

**1965**

Belgium 636-637
Cyprus 262-264
Finland 437
France 1131-1132
Germany 934-935
Greece 833-834
Iceland 375-376
Ireland 204-205
Italy 915-916
Luxembourg 432-433
Monaco 616-617
Netherlands 438-439
Norway 475-476
Portugal 958-960
Switzerland 469
Turkey 1665-1666

### Europa, 1966

Symbolic Sailboat — CD9

**1966, Sept.**

Andorra, French 172
Belgium 675-676
Cyprus 275-277
France 1163-1164
Germany 963-964
Greece 862-863
Iceland 384-385
Ireland 216-217
Italy 942-943
Liechtenstein 415
Luxembourg 440-441
Monaco 639-640
Netherlands 441-442
Norway 496-497
Portugal 980-982
Switzerland 477-478
Turkey 1718-1719

### Europa, 1967

Cogwheels CD10

**1967**

Andorra, French 174-175
Belgium 688-689
Cyprus 297-299
France 1178-1179
Germany 969-970
Greece 891-892
Iceland 389-390
Ireland 232-233
Italy 951-952
Liechtenstein 420
Luxembourg 449-450
Monaco 669-670
Netherlands 444-447
Norway 504-505
Portugal 994-996
Spain 1465-1466
Switzerland 482
Turkey B120-B121

### Europa, 1968

Golden Key with C.E.P.T. Emblem CD11

**1968**

Andorra, French 182-183
Belgium 705-706
Cyprus 314-316
France 1209-1210
Germany 983-984
Greece 916-917
Iceland 395-396
Ireland 242-243
Italy 979-980
Liechtenstein 442
Luxembourg 466-467
Monaco 689-691
Netherlands 452-453
Portugal 1019-1021
San Marino 687
Spain 1526
Turkey 1775-1776

### Europa, 1969

"EUROPA" and "CEPT" CD12

Tenth anniversary of C.E.P.T.

**1969**

Andorra, French 188-189
Austria 837
Belgium 718-719
Cyprus 326-328
Denmark 458
Finland 483
France 1245-1246
Germany 996-997
Great Britain 585
Greece 947-948
Iceland 406-407
Ireland 270-271
Italy 1000-1001
Liechtenstein 453
Luxembourg 474-475
Monaco 722-724
Netherlands 475-476
Norway 533-534
Portugal 1038-1040
San Marino 701-702
Spain 1567
Sweden 814-816

Switzerland..............................500-501
Turkey..............................1799-1800
Vatican..............................470-472
Yugoslavia..............................1003-1004

**Europa, 1970**

Interwoven Threads CD13

**1970**

Andorra, French..............................196-197
Belgium..............................741-742
Cyprus..............................340-342
France..............................1271-1272
Germany..............................1018-1019
Greece..............................985, 987
Iceland..............................420-421
Ireland..............................279-281
Italy..............................1013-1014
Liechtenstein..............................470
Luxembourg..............................489-490
Monaco..............................768-770
Netherlands..............................483-484
Portugal..............................1060-1062
San Marino..............................729-730
Spain..............................1607
Switzerland..............................515-516
Turkey..............................1848-1849
Yugoslavia..............................1024-1025

**Europa, 1971**

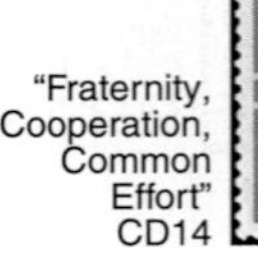

"Fraternity, Cooperation, Common Effort" CD14

**1971**

Andorra, French..............................205-206
Belgium..............................803-804
Cyprus..............................365-367
Finland..............................504
France..............................1304
Germany..............................1064-1065
Greece..............................1029-1030
Iceland..............................429-430
Ireland..............................305-306
Italy..............................1038-1039
Liechtenstein..............................485
Luxembourg..............................500-501
Malta..............................425-427
Monaco..............................797-799
Netherlands..............................488-489
Portugal..............................1094-1096
San Marino..............................749-750
Spain..............................1675-1676
Switzerland..............................531-532
Turkey..............................1876-1877
Yugoslavia..............................1052-1053

**Europa, 1972**

Sparkles, Symbolic of Communications CD15

**1972**

Andorra, French..............................210-211
Andorra, Spanish..............................62
Belgium..............................825-826
Cyprus..............................380-382
Finland..............................512-513
France..............................1341
Germany..............................1089-1090
Greece..............................1049-1050
Iceland..............................439-440
Ireland..............................316-317
Italy..............................1065-1066
Liechtenstein..............................504
Luxembourg..............................512-513
Malta..............................450-453
Monaco..............................831-832
Netherlands..............................494-495
Portugal..............................1141-1143
San Marino..............................771-772
Spain..............................1718
Switzerland..............................544-545
Turkey..............................1907-1908
Yugoslavia..............................1100-1101

**Europa, 1973**

Post Horn and Arrows CD16

**1973**

Andorra, French..............................219-220
Andorra, Spanish..............................76
Belgium..............................839-840
Cyprus..............................396-398
Finland..............................526
France..............................1367
Germany..............................1114-1115
Greece..............................1090-1092
Iceland..............................447-448
Ireland..............................329-330
Italy..............................1108-1109
Liechtenstein..............................528-529
Luxembourg..............................523-524
Malta..............................469-471
Monaco..............................866-867
Netherlands..............................504-505
Norway..............................604-605
Portugal..............................1170-1172
San Marino..............................802-803
Spain..............................1753
Switzerland..............................580-581
Turkey..............................1935-1936
Yugoslavia..............................1138-1139

**Europa, 2000**

CD17

**2000**

Albania..............................2621-2622
Andorra, French..............................522
Andorra, Spanish..............................262
Armenia..............................610-611
Austria..............................1814
Azerbaijan..............................698-699
Belarus..............................350
Belgium..............................1818
Bosnia & Herzegovina (Moslem)....358
Bosnia & Herzegovina (Serb)........111-112
Croatia..............................428-429
Cyprus..............................959
Czech Republic..............................3120
Denmark..............................1189
Estonia..............................394
Faroe Islands..............................376
Finland..............................1129
Aland Islands..............................166
France..............................2771
Georgia..............................228-229
Germany..............................2086-2087
Gibraltar..............................837-840
Great Britain (Guernsey)..........805-809
Great Britain (Jersey)..............935-936
Great Britain (Isle of Man)..............883
Greece..............................1959
Greenland..............................363
Hungary..............................3699-3700
Iceland..............................910
Ireland..............................1230-1231
Italy..............................2349
Latvia..............................504
Liechtenstein..............................1178
Lithuania..............................668
Luxembourg..............................1035
Macedonia..............................187
Malta..............................1011-1012
Moldova..............................355
Monaco..............................2161-2162
Poland..............................3519
Portugal..............................2358
Portugal (Azores)..............................455
Portugal (Madeira)..............................208
Romania..............................4370
Russia..............................6589
San Marino..............................1480
Slovakia..............................355
Slovenia..............................424
Spain..............................3036
Sweden..............................2394
Switzerland..............................1074
Turkey..............................2762
Turkish Rep. of Northern Cyprus....500
Ukraine..............................379
Vatican City..............................1152

The Gibraltar stamps are similar to the stamp illustrated, but none have the design shown above. All other sets listed above include at least one stamp with the design shown, but some include stamps with entirely different designs. Bulgaria Nos. 4131-4132 and Yugoslavia Nos. 2485-2486 are Europa stamps with completely different designs.

**PORTUGAL & COLONIES**
**Vasco da Gama**

Fleet Departing CD20

Fleet Arriving at Calicut — CD21

Embarking at Rastello CD22

Muse of History CD23

San Gabriel, da Gama and Camoens CD24

Archangel Gabriel, the Patron Saint CD25

Flagship San Gabriel — CD26

Vasco da Gama — CD27

Fourth centenary of Vasco da Gama's discovery of the route to India.

**1898**

Azores..............................93-100
Macao..............................67-74
Madeira..............................37-44
Portugal..............................147-154
Port. Africa..............................1-8
Port. Congo..............................75-98
Port. India..............................189-196
St. Thomas & Prince Islands...170-193
Timor..............................45-52

**Pombal**
**POSTAL TAX**
**POSTAL TAX DUES**

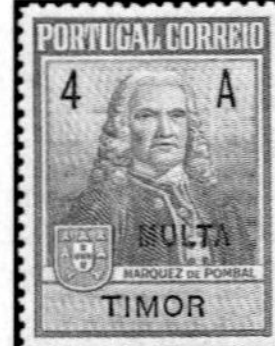


Marquis de Pombal — CD28

Planning Reconstruction of Lisbon, 1755 — CD29

Pombal Monument, Lisbon — CD30

Sebastiao Jose de Carvalho e Mello, Marquis de Pombal (1699-1782), statesman, rebuilt Lisbon after earthquake of 1755. Tax was for the erection of Pombal monument. Obligatory on all mail on certain days throughout the year. Postal Tax Dues are inscribed "Multa."

**1925**

Angola.............. RA1-RA3, RAJ1-RAJ3
Azores............ RA9-RA11, RAJ2-RAJ4
Cape Verde...... RA1-RA3, RAJ1-RAJ3
Macao............ RA1-RA3, RAJ1-RAJ3
Madeira.......... RA1-RA3, RAJ1-RAJ3
Mozambique..... RA1-RA3, RAJ1-RAJ3
Nyassa............ RA1-RA3, RAJ1-RAJ3
Portugal........ RA11-RA13, RAJ2-RAJ4
Port. Guinea..... RA1-RA3, RAJ1-RAJ3
Port. India......... RA1-RA3, RAJ1-RAJ3
St. Thomas & Prince
Islands.............. RA1-RA3, RAJ1-RAJ3
Timor............... RA1-RA3, RAJ1-RAJ3

Vasco da Gama CD34

Mousinho de Albuquerque CD35

Dam CD36

Prince Henry the Navigator CD37

Affonso de Albuquerque CD38

Plane over Globe CD39

**1938-39**

Angola..............................274-291, C1-C9
Cape Verde..............................234-251, C1-C9
Macao..............................289-305, C7-C15
Mozambique..............................270-287, C1-C9
Port. Guinea..............................233-250, C1-C9
Port. India..............................439-453, C1-C8
St. Thomas & Prince
Islands ... 302-319, 323-340, C1-C18
Timor..............................223-239, C1-C9

### Lady of Fatima

Our Lady of the Rosary, Fatima, Portugal — CD40

**1948-49**

| | |
|---|---|
| Angola | 315-318 |
| Cape Verde | 266 |
| Macao | 336 |
| Mozambique | 325-328 |
| Port. Guinea | 271 |
| Port. India | 480 |
| St. Thomas & Prince Islands | 351 |
| Timor | 254 |

A souvenir sheet of 9 stamps was issued in 1951 to mark the extension of the 1950 Holy Year. The sheet contains: Angola No. 316, Cape Verde No. 266, Macao No. 336, Mozambique No. 325, Portuguese Guinea No. 271, Portuguese India Nos. 480, 485, St. Thomas & Prince Islands No. 351, Timor No. 254. The sheet also contains a portrait of Pope Pius XII and is inscribed "Encerramento do Ano Santo, Fatima 1951." It was sold for 11 escudos.

### Holy Year

Church Bells and Dove CD41

Angel Holding Candelabra CD42

Holy Year, 1950.

**1950-51**

| | |
|---|---|
| Angola | 331-332 |
| Cape Verde | 268-269 |
| Macao | 339-340 |
| Mozambique | 330-331 |
| Port. Guinea | 273-274 |
| Port. India | 490-491, 496-503 |
| St. Thomas & Prince Islands | 353-354 |
| Timor | 258-259 |

A souvenir sheet of 8 stamps was issued in 1951 to mark the extension of the Holy Year. The sheet contains: Angola No. 331, Cape Verde No. 269, Macao No. 340, Mozambique No. 331, Portuguese Guinea No. 275, Portuguese India No. 490, St. Thomas & Prince Islands No. 354, Timor No. 258, some with colors changed. The sheet contains doves and is inscribed 'Encerramento do Ano Santo, Fatima 1951.' It was sold for 17 escudos.

### Holy Year Conclusion

Our Lady of Fatima — CD43

Conclusion of Holy Year. Sheets contain alternate vertical rows of stamps and labels bearing quotation from Pope Pius XII, different for each colony.

**1951**

| | |
|---|---|
| Angola | 357 |
| Cape Verde | 270 |
| Macao | 352 |
| Mozambique | 356 |
| Port. Guinea | 275 |
| Port. India | 506 |
| St. Thomas & Prince Islands | 355 |
| Timor | 270 |

### Medical Congress

CD44

First National Congress of Tropical Medicine, Lisbon, 1952. Each stamp has a different design.

**1952**

| | |
|---|---|
| Angola | 358 |
| Cape Verde | 287 |
| Macao | 364 |
| Mozambique | 359 |
| Port. Guinea | 276 |
| Port. India | 516 |
| St. Thomas & Prince Islands | 356 |
| Timor | 271 |

### Postage Due Stamps

CD45

**1952**

| | |
|---|---|
| Angola | J37-J42 |
| Cape Verde | J31-J36 |
| Macao | J53-J58 |
| Mozambique | J51-J56 |
| Port. Guinea | J40-J45 |
| Port. India | J47-J52 |
| St. Thomas & Prince Islands | J52-J57 |
| Timor | J31-J36 |

### Sao Paulo

Father Manuel de Nobrege and View of Sao Paulo — CD46

Founding of Sao Paulo, Brazil, 400th anniv.

**1954**

| | |
|---|---|
| Angola | 385 |
| Cape Verde | 297 |
| Macao | 382 |
| Mozambique | 395 |
| Port. Guinea | 291 |
| Port. India | 530 |
| St. Thomas & Prince Islands | 369 |
| Timor | 279 |

### Tropical Medicine Congress

CD47

Sixth International Congress for Tropical Medicine and Malaria, Lisbon, Sept. 1958. Each stamp shows a different plant.

**1958**

| | |
|---|---|
| Angola | 409 |
| Cape Verde | 303 |
| Macao | 392 |
| Mozambique | 404 |
| Port. Guinea | 295 |
| Port. India | 569 |
| St. Thomas & Prince Islands | 371 |
| Timor | 289 |

### Sports

CD48

Each stamp shows a different sport.

**1962**

| | |
|---|---|
| Angola | 433-438 |
| Cape Verde | 320-325 |
| Macao | 394-399 |
| Mozambique | 424-429 |
| Port. Guinea | 299-304 |
| St. Thomas & Prince Islands | 374-379 |
| Timor | 313-318 |

### Anti-Malaria

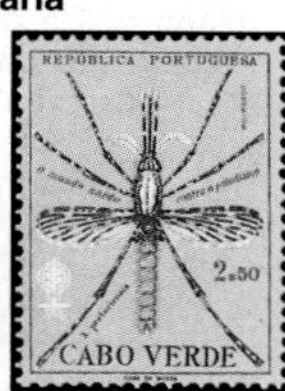


Anopheles Funestus and Malaria Eradication Symbol — CD49

World Health Organization drive to eradicate malaria.

**1962**

| | |
|---|---|
| Angola | 439 |
| Cape Verde | 326 |
| Macao | 400 |
| Mozambique | 430 |
| Port. Guinea | 305 |
| St. Thomas & Prince Islands | 380 |
| Timor | 319 |

### Airline Anniversary

Map of Africa, Super Constellation and Jet Liner — CD50

Tenth anniversary of Transportes Aereos Portugueses (TAP).

**1963**

| | |
|---|---|
| Angola | 490 |
| Cape Verde | 327 |
| Mozambique | 434 |
| Port. Guinea | 318 |
| St. Thomas & Prince Islands | 381 |

### National Overseas Bank

Antonio Teixeira de Sousa — CD51

Centenary of the National Overseas Bank of Portugal.

**1964, May 16**

| | |
|---|---|
| Angola | 509 |
| Cape Verde | 328 |
| Port. Guinea | 319 |
| St. Thomas & Prince Islands | 382 |
| Timor | 320 |

### ITU

ITU Emblem and the Archangel Gabriel — CD52

International Communications Union, Cent.

**1965, May 17**

| | |
|---|---|
| Angola | 511 |
| Cape Verde | 329 |
| Macao | 402 |
| Mozambique | 464 |
| Port. Guinea | 320 |
| St. Thomas & Prince Islands | 383 |
| Timor | 321 |

### National Revolution

CD53

40th anniv. of the National Revolution. Different buildings on each stamp.

**1966, May 28**

| | |
|---|---|
| Angola | 525 |
| Cape Verde | 338 |
| Macao | 403 |
| Mozambique | 465 |
| Port. Guinea | 329 |
| St. Thomas & Prince Islands | 392 |
| Timor | 322 |

### Navy Club

CD54

Centenary of Portugal's Navy Club. Each stamp has a different design.

**1967, Jan. 31**

| | |
|---|---|
| Angola | 527-528 |
| Cape Verde | 339-340 |
| Macao | 412-413 |
| Mozambique | 478-479 |
| Port. Guinea | 330-331 |
| St. Thomas & Prince Islands | 393-394 |
| Timor | 323-324 |

### Admiral Coutinho

CD55

Centenary of the birth of Admiral Carlos Viegas Gago Coutinho (1869-1959), explorer and aviation pioneer. Each stamp has a different design.

**1969, Feb. 17**

| | |
|---|---|
| Angola | 547 |
| Cape Verde | 355 |
| Macao | 417 |
| Mozambique | 484 |
| Port. Guinea | 335 |
| St. Thomas & Prince Islands | 397 |
| Timor | 335 |

### Administration Reform

Luiz Augusto Rebello da Silva — CD56

Centenary of the administration reforms of the overseas territories.

**1969, Sept. 25**

Angola ... 549
Cape Verde ... 357
Macao ... 419
Mozambique ... 491
Port. Guinea ... 337
St. Thomas & Prince Islands ... 399
Timor ... 338

### Marshal Carmona

CD57

Birth centenary of Marshal Antonio Oscar Carmona de Fragoso (1869-1951), President of Portugal. Each stamp has a different design.

**1970, Nov. 15**

Angola ... 563
Cape Verde ... 359
Macao ... 422
Mozambique ... 493
Port. Guinea ... 340
St. Thomas & Prince Islands ... 403
Timor ... 341

### Olympic Games

CD59

20th Olympic Games, Munich, Aug. 26-Sept. 11. Each stamp shows a different sport.

**1972, June 20**

Angola ... 569
Cape Verde ... 361
Macao ... 426
Mozambique ... 504
Port. Guinea ... 342
St. Thomas & Prince Islands ... 408
Timor ... 343

### Lisbon-Rio de Janeiro Flight

CD60

50th anniversary of the Lisbon to Rio de Janeiro flight by Arturo de Sacadura and Coutinho, March 30-June 5, 1922. Each stamp shows a different stage of the flight.

**1972, Sept. 20**

Angola ... 570
Cape Verde ... 362
Macao ... 427
Mozambique ... 505
Port. Guinea ... 343
St. Thomas & Prince Islands ... 409
Timor ... 344

### WMO Centenary

WMO Emblem — CD61

Centenary of international meterological cooperation.

**1973, Dec. 15**

Angola ... 571
Cape Verde ... 363
Macao ... 429
Mozambique ... 509
Port. Guinea ... 344
St. Thomas & Prince Islands ... 410
Timor ... 345

### FRENCH COMMUNITY

**Upper Volta can be found under Burkina Faso in Vol. 1**
**Madagascar can be found under Malagasy in Vol. 3**

### Colonial Exposition

People of French Empire CD70

Women's Heads CD71

France Showing Way to Civilization CD72

"Colonial Commerce" CD73

International Colonial Exposition, Paris.

**1931**

Cameroun ... 213-216
Chad ... 60-63
Dahomey ... 97-100
Fr. Guiana ... 152-155
Fr. Guinea ... 116-119
Fr. India ... 100-103
Fr. Polynesia ... 76-79
Fr. Sudan ... 102-105
Gabon ... 120-123
Guadeloupe ... 138-141
Indo-China ... 140-142
Ivory Coast ... 92-95
Madagascar ... 169-172
Martinique ... 129-132
Mauritania ... 65-68
Middle Congo ... 61-64
New Caledonia ... 176-179
Niger ... 73-76
Reunion ... 122-125
St. Pierre & Miquelon ... 132-135
Senegal ... 138-141
Somali Coast ... 135-138
Togo ... 254-257
Ubangi-Shari ... 82-85
Upper Volta ... 66-69
Wallis & Futuna Isls. ... 85-88

### Paris International Exposition
### Colonial Arts Exposition

"Colonial Resources"
CD74 CD77

Overseas Commerce CD75

Exposition Building and Women CD76

"France and the Empire" CD78

Cultural Treasures of the Colonies CD79

Souvenir sheets contain one imperf. stamp.

**1937**

Cameroun ... 217-222A
Dahomey ... 101-107
Fr. Equatorial Africa ... 27-32, 73
Fr. Guiana ... 162-168
Fr. Guinea ... 120-126
Fr. India ... 104-110
Fr. Polynesia ... 117-123
Fr. Sudan ... 106-112
Guadeloupe ... 148-154
Indo-China ... 193-199
Inini ... 41
Ivory Coast ... 152-158
Kwangchowan ... 132
Madagascar ... 191-197
Martinique ... 179-185
Mauritania ... 69-75
New Caledonia ... 208-214
Niger ... 72-83
Reunion ... 167-173
St. Pierre & Miquelon ... 165-171
Senegal ... 172-178
Somali Coast ... 139-145
Togo ... 258-264
Wallis & Futuna Isls. ... 89

### Curie

Pierre and Marie Curie CD80

40th anniversary of the discovery of radium. The surtax was for the benefit of the Intl. Union for the Control of Cancer.

**1938**

Cameroun ... B1
Cuba ... B1-B2
Dahomey ... B2
France ... B76
Fr. Equatorial Africa ... B1
Fr. Guiana ... B3
Fr. Guinea ... B2
Fr. India ... B6
Fr. Polynesia ... B5
Fr. Sudan ... B1
Guadeloupe ... B3
Indo-China ... B14
Ivory Coast ... B2
Madagascar ... B2
Martinique ... B2
Mauritania ... B3
New Caledonia ... B4
Niger ... B1
Reunion ... B4
St. Pierre & Miquelon ... B3
Senegal ... B3
Somali Coast ... B2
Togo ... B1

### Caillie

Rene Caillie and Map of Northwestern Africa — CD81

Death centenary of Rene Caillie (1799-1838), French explorer. All three denominations exist with colony name omitted.

**1939**

Dahomey ... 108-110
Fr. Guinea ... 161-163
Fr. Sudan ... 113-115
Ivory Coast ... 160-162
Mauritania ... 109-111
Niger ... 84-86
Senegal ... 188-190
Togo ... 265-267

### New York World's Fair

Natives and New York Skyline CD82

**1939**

Cameroun ... 223-224
Dahomey ... 111-112
Fr. Equatorial Africa ... 78-79
Fr. Guiana ... 169-170
Fr. Guinea ... 164-165
Fr. India ... 111-112
Fr. Polynesia ... 124-125
Fr. Sudan ... 116-117
Guadeloupe ... 155-156
Indo-China ... 203-204
Inini ... 42-43
Ivory Coast ... 163-164
Kwangchowan ... 121-122
Madagascar ... 209-210
Martinique ... 186-187
Mauritania ... 112-113
New Caledonia ... 215-216
Niger ... 87-88
Reunion ... 174-175
St. Pierre & Miquelon ... 205-206
Senegal ... 191-192
Somali Coast ... 179-180
Togo ... 268-269
Wallis & Futuna Isls. ... 90-91

### French Revolution

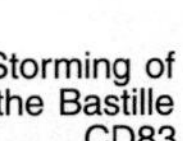


Storming of the Bastille CD83

French Revolution, 150th anniv. The surtax was for the defense of the colonies.

**1939**

Cameroun ... B2-B6
Dahomey ... B3-B7
Fr. Equatorial Africa ... B4-B8, CB1
Fr. Guiana ... B4-B8, CB1
Fr. Guinea ... B3-B7
Fr. India ... B7-B11
Fr. Polynesia ... B6-B10, CB1
Fr. Sudan ... B2-B6
Guadeloupe ... B4-B8
Indo-China ... B15-B19, CB1
Inini ... B1-B5
Ivory Coast ... B3-B7

Kwangchowan B1-B5
Madagascar B3-B7, CB1
Martinique B3-B7
Mauritania B4-B8
New Caledonia B5-B9, CB1
Niger B2-B6
Reunion B5-B9, CB1
St. Pierre & Miquelon B4-B8
Senegal B4-B8, CB1
Somali Coast B3-B7
Togo B2-B6
Wallis & Futuna Isls. B1-B5

Plane over Coastal Area CD85

All five denominations exist with colony name omitted.

**1940**

Dahomey C1-C5
Fr. Guinea C1-C5
Fr. Sudan C1-C5
Ivory Coast C1-C5
Mauritania C1-C5
Niger C1-C5
Senegal C12-C16
Togo C1-C5

### Defense of the Empire

Colonial Infantryman — CD86

**1941**

Cameroun B13B
Dahomey B13
Fr. Equatorial Africa B8B
Fr. Guiana B10
Fr. Guinea B13
Fr. India B13
Fr. Polynesia B12
Fr. Sudan B12
Guadeloupe B10
Indo-China B19B
Inini B7
Ivory Coast B13
Kwangchowan B7
Madagascar B9
Martinique B9
Mauritania B14
New Caledonia B11
Niger B12
Reunion B11
St. Pierre & Miquelon B8B
Senegal B14
Somali Coast B9
Togo B10B
Wallis & Futuna Isls. B7

### Colonial Education Fund

CD86a

**1942**

Cameroun CB3
Dahomey CB4
Fr. Equatorial Africa CB5
Fr. Guiana CB4
Fr. Guinea CB4
Fr. India CB3
Fr. Polynesia CB4
Fr. Sudan CB4
Guadeloupe CB3
Indo-China CB5
Inini CB3
Ivory Coast CB4
Kwangchowan CB4
Malagasy CB5
Martinique CB3
Mauritania CB4
New Caledonia CB4
Niger CB4
Reunion CB4
St. Pierre & Miquelon CB3
Senegal CB5
Somali Coast CB3
Togo CB3
Wallis & Futuna CB3

Cross of Lorraine & Four-motor Plane CD87

**1941-5**

Cameroun C1-C7
Fr. Equatorial Africa C17-C23
Fr. Guiana C9-C10
Fr. India C1-C6
Fr. Polynesia C3-C9
Fr. West Africa C1-C3
Guadeloupe C1-C2
Madagascar C37-C43
Martinique C1-C2
New Caledonia C7-C13
Reunion C18-C24
St. Pierre & Miquelon C1-C7
Somali Coast C1-C7

Transport Plane CD88

Caravan and Plane CD89

**1942**

Dahomey C6-C13
Fr. Guinea C6-C13
Fr. Sudan C6-C13
Ivory Coast C6-C13
Mauritania C6-C13
Niger C6-C13
Senegal C17-C25
Togo C6-C13

### Red Cross

Marianne CD90

The surtax was for the French Red Cross and national relief.

**1944**

Cameroun B28
Fr. Equatorial Africa B38
Fr. Guiana B12
Fr. India B14
Fr. Polynesia B13
Fr. West Africa B1
Guadeloupe B12
Madagascar B15
Martinique B11
New Caledonia B13
Reunion B15
St. Pierre & Miquelon B13
Somali Coast B13
Wallis & Futuna Isls. B9

### Eboue

CD91

Felix Eboue, first French colonial administrator to proclaim resistance to Germany after French surrender in World War II.

**1945**

Cameroun 296-297
Fr. Equatorial Africa 156-157
Fr. Guiana 171-172
Fr. India 210-211
Fr. Polynesia 150-151
Fr. West Africa 15-16
Guadeloupe 187-188
Madagascar 259-260
Martinique 196-197
New Caledonia 274-275
Reunion 238-239
St. Pierre & Miquelon 322-323
Somali Coast 238-239

### Victory

Victory — CD92

European victory of the Allied Nations in World War II.

**1946, May 8**

Cameroun C8
Fr. Equatorial Africa C24
Fr. Guiana C11
Fr. India C7
Fr. Polynesia C10
Fr. West Africa C4
Guadeloupe C3
Indo-China C19
Madagascar C44
Martinique C3
New Caledonia C14
Reunion C25
St. Pierre & Miquelon C8
Somali Coast C8
Wallis & Futuna Isls. C1

### Chad to Rhine

Leclerc's Departure from Chad — CD93

Battle at Cufra Oasis — CD94

Tanks in Action, Mareth — CD95

Normandy Invasion — CD96

Entering Paris — CD97

Liberation of Strasbourg — CD98

"Chad to the Rhine" march, 1942-44, by Gen. Jacques Leclerc's column, later French 2nd Armored Division.

**1946, June 6**

Cameroun C9-C14
Fr. Equatorial Africa C25-C30
Fr. Guiana C12-C17
Fr. India C8-C13
Fr. Polynesia C11-C16
Fr. West Africa C5-C10
Guadeloupe C4-C9
Indo-China C20-C25
Madagascar C45-C50
Martinique C4-C9
New Caledonia C15-C20
Reunion C26-C31
St. Pierre & Miquelon C9-C14
Somali Coast C9-C14
Wallis & Futuna Isls. C2-C7

### UPU

French Colonials, Globe and Plane — CD99

Universal Postal Union, 75th anniv.

**1949, July 4**

Cameroun C29
Fr. Equatorial Africa C34
Fr. India C17
Fr. Polynesia C20
Fr. West Africa C15
Indo-China C26
Madagascar C55
New Caledonia C24
St. Pierre & Miquelon C18
Somali Coast C18
Togo C18
Wallis & Futuna Isls. C10

### Tropical Medicine

Doctor Treating Infant CD100

The surtax was for charitable work.

**1950**

Cameroun ........ B29
Fr. Equatorial Africa ........ B39
Fr. India ........ B15
Fr. Polynesia ........ B14
Fr. West Africa ........ B3
Madagascar ........ B17
New Caledonia ........ B14
St. Pierre & Miquelon ........ B14
Somali Coast ........ B14
Togo ........ B11

### Military Medal

Medal, Early Marine and Colonial Soldier — CD101

Centenary of the creation of the French Military Medal.

**1952**

Cameroun ........ 332
Comoro Isls. ........ 39
Fr. Equatorial Africa ........ 186
Fr. India ........ 233
Fr. Polynesia ........ 179
Fr. West Africa ........ 57
Madagascar ........ 286
New Caledonia ........ 295
St. Pierre & Miquelon ........ 345
Somali Coast ........ 267
Togo ........ 327
Wallis & Futuna Isls. ........ 149

### Liberation

Allied Landing, Victory Sign and Cross of Lorraine — CD102

Liberation of France, 10th anniv.

**1954, June 6**

Cameroun ........ C32
Comoro Isls. ........ C4
Fr. Equatorial Africa ........ C38
Fr. India ........ C18
Fr. Polynesia ........ C22
Fr. West Africa ........ C17
Madagascar ........ C57
New Caledonia ........ C25
St. Pierre & Miquelon ........ C19
Somali Coast ........ C19
Togo ........ C19
Wallis & Futuna Isls. ........ C11

### FIDES

Plowmen CD103

Efforts of FIDES, the Economic and Social Development Fund for Overseas Possessions (Fonds d' Investissement pour le Developpement Economique et Social). Each stamp has a different design.

**1956**

Cameroun ........ 326-329
Comoro Isls. ........ 43
Fr. Polynesia ........ 181
Fr. West Africa ........ 65-72
Madagascar ........ 292-295
New Caledonia ........ 303
Somali Coast ........ 268
Togo ........ 331

### Flower

CD104

Each stamp shows a different flower.

**1958-9**

Cameroun ........ 333
Comoro Isls. ........ 45
Fr. Equatorial Africa ........ 200-201
Fr. Polynesia ........ 192
Fr. So. & Antarctic Terr. ........ 11
Fr. West Africa ........ 79-83
Madagascar ........ 301-302
New Caledonia ........ 304-305
St. Pierre & Miquelon ........ 357
Somali Coast ........ 270
Togo ........ 348-349
Wallis & Futuna Isls. ........ 152

### Human Rights

Sun, Dove and U.N. Emblem CD105

10th anniversary of the signing of the Universal Declaration of Human Rights.

**1958**

Comoro Isls. ........ 44
Fr. Equatorial Africa ........ 202
Fr. Polynesia ........ 191
Fr. West Africa ........ 85
Madagascar ........ 300
New Caledonia ........ 306
St. Pierre & Miquelon ........ 356
Somali Coast ........ 274
Wallis & Futuna Isls. ........ 153

### C.C.T.A.

CD106

Commission for Technical Cooperation in Africa south of the Sahara, 10th anniv.

**1960**

Cameroun ........ 335
Cent. Africa ........ 3
Chad ........ 66
Congo, P.R. ........ 90
Dahomey ........ 138
Gabon ........ 150
Ivory Coast ........ 180
Madagascar ........ 317
Mali ........ 9
Mauritania ........ 117
Niger ........ 104
Upper Volta ........ 89

### Air Afrique, 1961

Modern and Ancient Africa, Map and Planes — CD107

Founding of Air Afrique (African Airlines).

**1961-62**

Cameroun ........ C37
Cent. Africa ........ C5
Chad ........ C7
Congo, P.R. ........ C5
Dahomey ........ C17
Gabon ........ C5
Ivory Coast ........ C18
Mauritania ........ C17
Niger ........ C22
Senegal ........ C31
Upper Volta ........ C4

### Anti-Malaria

CD108

World Health Organization drive to eradicate malaria.

**1962, Apr. 7**

Cameroun ........ B36
Cent. Africa ........ B1
Chad ........ B1
Comoro Isls. ........ B1
Congo, P.R. ........ B3
Dahomey ........ B15
Gabon ........ B4
Ivory Coast ........ B15
Madagascar ........ B19
Mali ........ B1
Mauritania ........ B16
Niger ........ B14
Senegal ........ B16
Somali Coast ........ B15
Upper Volta ........ B1

### Abidjan Games

CD109

Abidjan Games, Ivory Coast, Dec. 24-31, 1961. Each stamp shows a different sport.

**1962**

Chad ........ 83-84
Cent. Africa ........ 19-20
Congo, P.R. ........ 103-104
Gabon ........ 163-164, C6
Niger ........ 109-111
Upper Volta ........ 103-105

### African and Malagasy Union

Flag of Union CD110

First anniversary of the Union.

**1962, Sept. 8**

Cameroun ........ 373
Cent. Africa ........ 21
Chad ........ 85
Congo, P.R. ........ 105
Dahomey ........ 155
Gabon ........ 165
Ivory Coast ........ 198
Madagascar ........ 332
Mauritania ........ 170
Niger ........ 112
Senegal ........ 211
Upper Volta ........ 106

### Telstar

Telstar and Globe Showing Andover and Pleumeur-Bodou — CD111

First television connection of the United States and Europe through the Telstar satellite, July 11-12, 1962.

**1962-63**

Andorra, French ........ 154
Comoro Isls. ........ C7
Fr. Polynesia ........ C29
Fr. So. & Antarctic Terr. ........ C5
New Caledonia ........ C33
Somali Coast ........ C31
St. Pierre & Miquelon ........ C26
Wallis & Futuna Isls. ........ C17

### Freedom From Hunger

World Map and Wheat Emblem CD112

U.N. Food and Agriculture Organization's "Freedom from Hunger" campaign.

**1963, Mar. 21**

Cameroun ........ B37-B38
Cent. Africa ........ B2
Chad ........ B2
Congo, P.R. ........ B4
Dahomey ........ B16
Gabon ........ B5
Ivory Coast ........ B16
Madagascar ........ B21
Mauritania ........ B17
Niger ........ B15
Senegal ........ B17
Upper Volta ........ B2

### Red Cross Centenary

CD113

Centenary of the International Red Cross.

**1963, Sept. 2**

Comoro Isls. ........ 55
Fr. Polynesia ........ 205
New Caledonia ........ 328
St. Pierre & Miquelon ........ 367
Somali Coast ........ 297
Wallis & Futuna Isls. ........ 165

### African Postal Union, 1963

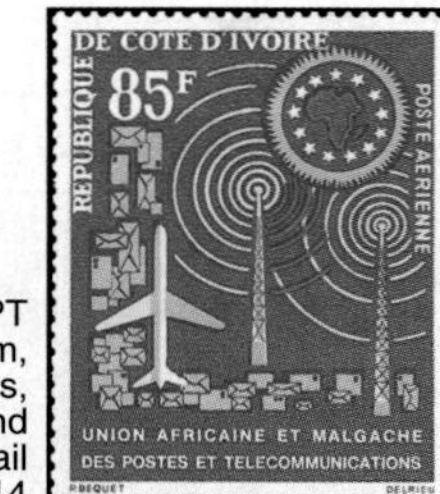


UAMPT Emblem, Radio Masts, Plane and Mail CD114

Establishment of the African and Malagasy Posts and Telecommunications Union.

**1963, Sept. 8**

| | |
|---|---|
| Cameroun | C47 |
| Cent. Africa | C10 |
| Chad | C9 |
| Congo, P.R. | C13 |
| Dahomey | C19 |
| Gabon | C13 |
| Ivory Coast | C25 |
| Madagascar | C75 |
| Mauritania | C22 |
| Niger | C27 |
| Rwanda | 36 |
| Senegal | C32 |
| Upper Volta | C9 |

### Air Afrique, 1963

Symbols of Flight — CD115

First anniversary of Air Afrique and inauguration of DC-8 service.

**1963, Nov. 19**

| | |
|---|---|
| Cameroun | C48 |
| Chad | C10 |
| Congo, P.R. | C14 |
| Gabon | C18 |
| Ivory Coast | C26 |
| Mauritania | C26 |
| Niger | C35 |
| Senegal | C33 |

### Europafrica

Europe and Africa Linked — CD116

Signing of an economic agreement between the European Economic Community and the African and Malagasy Union, Yaounde, Cameroun, July 20, 1963.

**1963-64**

| | |
|---|---|
| Cameroun | 402 |
| Chad | C11 |
| Cent. Africa | C12 |
| Congo, P.R. | C16 |
| Gabon | C19 |
| Ivory Coast | 217 |
| Niger | C43 |
| Upper Volta | C11 |

### Human Rights

Scales of Justice and Globe CD117

15th anniversary of the Universal Declaration of Human Rights.

**1963, Dec. 10**

| | |
|---|---|
| Comoro Isls. | 58 |
| Fr. Polynesia | 206 |
| New Caledonia | 329 |
| St. Pierre & Miquelon | 368 |
| Somali Coast | 300 |
| Wallis & Futuna Isls. | 166 |

### PHILATEC

Stamp Album, Champs Elysees Palace and Horses of Marly CD118

Intl. Philatelic and Postal Techniques Exhibition, Paris, June 5-21, 1964.

**1963-64**

| | |
|---|---|
| Comoro Isls. | 60 |
| France | 1078 |
| Fr. Polynesia | 207 |
| New Caledonia | 341 |
| St. Pierre & Miquelon | 369 |
| Somali Coast | 301 |
| Wallis & Futuna Isls. | 167 |

### Cooperation

CD119

Cooperation between France and the French-speaking countries of Africa and Madagascar.

**1964**

| | |
|---|---|
| Cameroun | 409-410 |
| Cent. Africa | 39 |
| Chad | 103 |
| Congo, P.R. | 121 |
| Dahomey | 193 |
| France | 1111 |
| Gabon | 175 |
| Ivory Coast | 221 |
| Madagascar | 360 |
| Mauritania | 181 |
| Niger | 143 |
| Senegal | 236 |
| Togo | 495 |

### ITU

Telegraph, Syncom Satellite and ITU Emblem CD120

Intl. Telecommunication Union, Cent.

**1965, May 17**

| | |
|---|---|
| Comoro Isls. | C14 |
| Fr. Polynesia | C33 |
| Fr. So. & Antarctic Terr. | C8 |
| New Caledonia | C40 |
| New Hebrides | 124-125 |
| St. Pierre & Miquelon | C29 |
| Somali Coast | C36 |
| Wallis & Futuna Isls. | C20 |

### French Satellite A-1

Diamant Rocket and Launching Installation — CD121

Launching of France's first satellite, Nov. 26, 1965.

**1965-66**

| | |
|---|---|
| Comoro Isls. | C15-C16 |
| France | 1137-1138 |
| Fr. Polynesia | C40-C41 |
| Fr. So. & Antarctic Terr. | C9-C10 |
| New Caledonia | C44-C45 |
| St. Pierre & Miquelon | C30-C31 |
| Somali Coast | C39-C40 |
| Wallis & Futuna Isls. | C22-C23 |

### French Satellite D-1

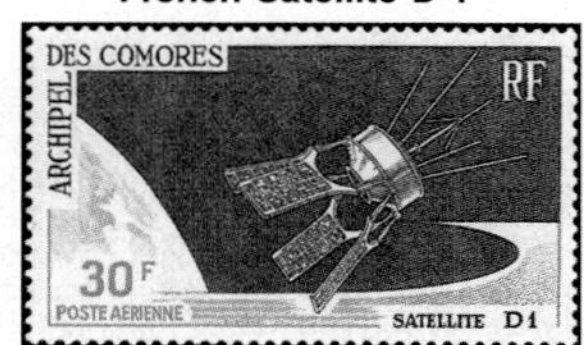


D-1 Satellite in Orbit — CD122

Launching of the D-1 satellite at Hammaguir, Algeria, Feb. 17, 1966.

**1966**

| | |
|---|---|
| Comoro Isls. | C17 |
| France | 1148 |
| Fr. Polynesia | C42 |
| Fr. So. & Antarctic Terr. | C11 |
| New Caledonia | C46 |
| St. Pierre & Miquelon | C32 |
| Somali Coast | C49 |
| Wallis & Futuna Isls. | C24 |

### Air Afrique, 1966

Planes and Air Afrique Emblem — CD123

Introduction of DC-8F planes by Air Afrique.

**1966**

| | |
|---|---|
| Cameroun | C79 |
| Cent. Africa | C35 |
| Chad | C26 |
| Congo, P.R. | C42 |
| Dahomey | C42 |
| Gabon | C47 |
| Ivory Coast | C32 |
| Mauritania | C57 |
| Niger | C63 |
| Senegal | C47 |
| Togo | C54 |
| Upper Volta | C31 |

### African Postal Union, 1967

Telecommunications Symbols and Map of Africa — CD124

Fifth anniversary of the establishment of the African and Malagasy Union of Posts and Telecommunications, UAMPT.

**1967**

| | |
|---|---|
| Cameroun | C90 |
| Cent. Africa | C46 |
| Chad | C37 |
| Congo, P.R. | C57 |
| Dahomey | C61 |
| Gabon | C58 |
| Ivory Coast | C34 |
| Madagascar | C85 |
| Mauritania | C65 |
| Niger | C75 |
| Rwanda | C1-C3 |
| Senegal | C60 |
| Togo | C81 |
| Upper Volta | C50 |

### Monetary Union

Gold Token of the Ashantis, 17-18th Centuries — CD125

West African Monetary Union, 5th anniv.

**1967, Nov. 4**

| | |
|---|---|
| Dahomey | 244 |
| Ivory Coast | 259 |
| Mauritania | 238 |
| Niger | 204 |
| Senegal | 294 |
| Togo | 623 |
| Upper Volta | 181 |

### WHO Anniversary

Sun, Flowers and WHO Emblem CD126

World Health Organization, 20th anniv.

**1968, May 4**

| | |
|---|---|
| Afars & Issas | 317 |
| Comoro Isls. | 73 |
| Fr. Polynesia | 241-242 |
| Fr. So. & Antarctic Terr. | 31 |
| New Caledonia | 367 |
| St. Pierre & Miquelon | 377 |
| Wallis & Futuna Isls. | 169 |

### Human Rights Year

Human Rights Flame — CD127

**1968, Aug. 10**

| | |
|---|---|
| Afars & Issas | 322-323 |

| | |
|---|---|
| Comoro Isls. | 76 |
| Fr. Polynesia | 243-244 |
| Fr. So. & Antarctic Terr. | 32 |
| New Caledonia | 369 |
| St. Pierre & Miquelon | 382 |
| Wallis & Futuna Isls. | 170 |

### 2nd PHILEXAFRIQUE

CD128

Opening of PHILEXAFRIQUE, Abidjan, Feb. 14. Each stamp shows a local scene and stamp.

**1969, Feb. 14**

| | |
|---|---|
| Cameroun | C118 |
| Cent. Africa | C65 |
| Chad | C48 |
| Congo, P.R. | C77 |
| Dahomey | C94 |
| Gabon | C82 |
| Ivory Coast | C38-C40 |
| Madagascar | C92 |
| Mali | C65 |
| Mauritania | C80 |
| Niger | C104 |
| Senegal | C68 |
| Togo | C104 |
| Upper Volta | C62 |

### Concorde

Concorde in Flight CD129

First flight of the prototype Concorde supersonic plane at Toulouse, Mar. 1, 1969.

**1969**

| | |
|---|---|
| Afars & Issas | C56 |
| Comoro Isls. | C29 |
| France | C42 |
| Fr. Polynesia | C50 |
| Fr. So. & Antarctic Terr. | C18 |
| New Caledonia | C63 |
| St. Pierre & Miquelon | C40 |
| Wallis & Futuna Isls. | C30 |

### Development Bank

Bank Emblem — CD130

African Development Bank, fifth anniv.

**1969**

| | |
|---|---|
| Cameroun | 499 |
| Chad | 217 |
| Congo, P.R. | 181-182 |
| Ivory Coast | 281 |
| Mali | 127-128 |
| Mauritania | 267 |
| Niger | 220 |
| Senegal | 317-318 |
| Upper Volta | 201 |

### ILO

ILO Headquarters, Geneva, and Emblem — CD131

Intl. Labor Organization, 50th anniv.

**1969-70**

| | |
|---|---|
| Afars & Issas | 337 |
| Comoro Isls. | 83 |
| Fr. Polynesia | 251-252 |
| Fr. So. & Antarctic Terr. | 35 |
| New Caledonia | 379 |
| St. Pierre & Miquelon | 396 |
| Wallis & Futuna Isls. | 172 |

### ASECNA

Map of Africa, Plane and Airport CD132

10th anniversary of the Agency for the Security of Aerial Navigation in Africa and Madagascar (ASECNA, Agence pour la Securite de la Navigation Aerienne en Afrique et a Madagascar).

**1969-70**

| | |
|---|---|
| Cameroun | 500 |
| Cent. Africa | 119 |
| Chad | 222 |
| Congo, P.R. | 197 |
| Dahomey | 269 |
| Gabon | 260 |
| Ivory Coast | 287 |
| Mali | 130 |
| Niger | 221 |
| Senegal | 321 |
| Upper Volta | 204 |

### U.P.U. Headquarters

CD133

New Universal Postal Union headquarters, Bern, Switzerland.

**1970**

| | |
|---|---|
| Afars & Issas | 342 |
| Algeria | 443 |
| Cameroun | 503-504 |
| Cent. Africa | 125 |
| Chad | 225 |
| Comoro Isls. | 84 |
| Congo, P.R. | 216 |
| Fr. Polynesia | 261-262 |
| Fr. So. & Antarctic Terr. | 36 |
| Gabon | 258 |
| Ivory Coast | 295 |
| Madagascar | 444 |
| Mali | 134-135 |
| Mauritania | 283 |
| New Caledonia | 382 |
| Niger | 231-232 |
| St. Pierre & Miquelon | 397-398 |
| Senegal | 328-329 |
| Tunisia | 535 |
| Wallis & Futuna Isls. | 173 |

### De Gaulle

CD134

First anniversay of the death of Charles de Gaulle, (1890-1970), President of France.

**1971-72**

| | |
|---|---|
| Afars & Issas | 356-357 |
| Comoro Isls. | 104-105 |
| France | 1322-1325 |
| Fr. Polynesia | 270-271 |
| Fr. So. & Antarctic Terr. | 52-53 |
| New Caledonia | 393-394 |
| Reunion | 377, 380 |
| St. Pierre & Miquelon | 417-418 |
| Wallis & Futuna Isls. | 177-178 |

### African Postal Union, 1971

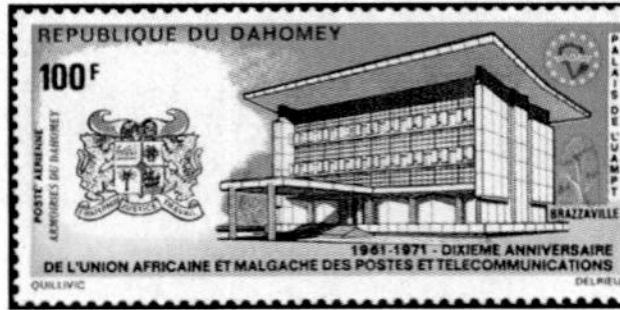


UAMPT Building, Brazzaville, Congo — CD135

10th anniversary of the establishment of the African and Malagasy Posts and Telecommunications Union, UAMPT. Each stamp has a different native design.

**1971, Nov. 13**

| | |
|---|---|
| Cameroun | C177 |
| Cent. Africa | C89 |
| Chad | C94 |
| Congo, P.R. | C136 |
| Dahomey | C146 |
| Gabon | C120 |
| Ivory Coast | C47 |
| Mauritania | C113 |
| Niger | C164 |
| Rwanda | C8 |
| Senegal | C105 |
| Togo | C166 |
| Upper Volta | C97 |

### West African Monetary Union

African Couple, City, Village and Commemorative Coin — CD136

West African Monetary Union, 10th anniv.

**1972, Nov. 2**

| | |
|---|---|
| Dahomey | 300 |
| Ivory Coast | 331 |
| Mauritania | 299 |
| Niger | 258 |
| Senegal | 374 |
| Togo | 825 |
| Upper Volta | 280 |

### African Postal Union, 1973

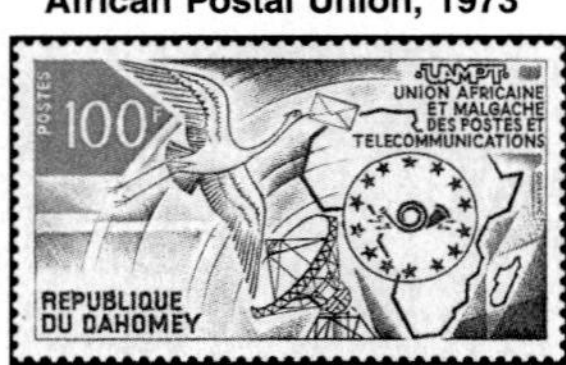


Telecommunications Symbols and Map of Africa — CD137

11th anniversary of the African and Malagasy Posts and Telecommunications Union (UAMPT).

**1973, Sept. 12**

| | |
|---|---|
| Cameroun | 574 |
| Cent. Africa | 194 |
| Chad | 294 |
| Congo, P.R. | 289 |
| Dahomey | 311 |
| Gabon | 320 |
| Ivory Coast | 361 |
| Madagascar | 500 |
| Mauritania | 304 |
| Niger | 287 |
| Rwanda | 540 |
| Senegal | 393 |
| Togo | 849 |
| Upper Volta | 297 |

### Philexafrique II — Essen

CD138

CD139

Designs: Indigenous fauna, local and German stamps. Types CD138-CD139 printed horizontally and vertically se-tenant in sheets of 10 (2x5). Label between horizontal pairs alternately commemoratives Philexafrique II, Libreville, Gabon, June 1978, and 2nd International Stamp Fair, Essen, Germany, Nov. 1-5.

**1978-1979**

| | |
|---|---|
| Benin | C285-C286 |
| Central Africa | C200-C201 |
| Chad | C238-C239 |
| Congo Republic | C245-C246 |
| Djibouti | C121-C122 |
| Gabon | C215-C216 |
| Ivory Coast | C64-C65 |
| Mali | C356-C357 |
| Mauritania | C185-C186 |
| Niger | C291-C292 |
| Rwanda | C12-C13 |
| Senegal | C146-C147 |

## BRITISH COMMONWEALTH OF NATIONS

The listings follow established trade practices when these issues are offered as units by dealers. The Peace issue, for example, includes only one stamp from the Indian state of Hyderabad. The U.P.U. issue includes the Egypt set. Pairs are included for those varieties issues with bilingual designs se-tenant.

### Silver Jubilee

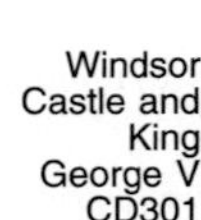

Windsor Castle and King George V CD301

Reign of King George V, 25th anniv.

**1935**

| | |
|---|---|
| Antigua | 77-80 |
| Ascension | 33-36 |
| Bahamas | 92-95 |
| Barbados | 186-189 |
| Basutoland | 11-14 |
| Bechuanaland Protectorate | 117-120 |
| Bermuda | 100-103 |
| British Guiana | 223-226 |
| British Honduras | 108-111 |
| Cayman Islands | 81-84 |
| Ceylon | 260-263 |
| Cyprus | 136-139 |
| Dominica | 90-93 |
| Falkland Islands | 77-80 |
| Fiji | 110-113 |
| Gambia | 125-128 |
| Gibraltar | 100-103 |
| Gilbert & Ellice Islands | 33-36 |

Gold Coast ........ 108-111
Grenada ........ 124-127
Hong Kong ........ 147-150
Jamaica ........ 109-112
Kenya, Uganda, Tanganyika ........ 42-45
Leeward Islands ........ 96-99
Malta ........ 184-187
Mauritius ........ 204-207
Montserrat ........ 85-88
Newfoundland ........ 226-229
Nigeria ........ 34-37
Northern Rhodesia ........ 18-21
Nyasaland Protectorate ........ 47-50
St. Helena ........ 111-114
St. Kitts-Nevis ........ 72-75
St. Lucia ........ 91-94
St. Vincent ........ 134-137
Seychelles ........ 118-121
Sierra Leone ........ 166-169
Solomon Islands ........ 60-63
Somaliland Protectorate ........ 77-80
Straits Settlements ........ 213-216
Swaziland ........ 20-23
Trinidad & Tobago ........ 43-46
Turks & Caicos Islands ........ 71-74
Virgin Islands ........ 69-72

The following have different designs but are included in the omnibus set:

Great Britain ........ 226-229
Offices in Morocco ...... 67-70, 226-229, 422-425, 508-510
Australia ........ 152-154
Canada ........ 211-216
Cook Islands ........ 98-100
India ........ 142-148
Nauru ........ 31-34
New Guinea ........ 46-47
New Zealand ........ 199-201
Niue ........ 67-69
Papua ........ 114-117
Samoa ........ 163-165
South Africa ........ 68-71
Southern Rhodesia ........ 33-36
South-West Africa ........ 121-124

249 stamps

### Coronation

Queen Elizabeth and King George VI CD302

### 1937

Aden ........ 13-15
Antigua ........ 81-83
Ascension ........ 37-39
Bahamas ........ 97-99
Barbados ........ 190-192
Basutoland ........ 15-17
Bechuanaland Protectorate ...... 121-123
Bermuda ........ 115-117
British Guiana ........ 227-229
British Honduras ........ 112-114
Cayman Islands ........ 97-99
Ceylon ........ 275-277
Cyprus ........ 140-142
Dominica ........ 94-96
Falkland Islands ........ 81-83
Fiji ........ 114-116
Gambia ........ 129-131
Gibraltar ........ 104-106
Gilbert & Ellice Islands ........ 37-39
Gold Coast ........ 112-114
Grenada ........ 128-130
Hong Kong ........ 151-153
Jamaica ........ 113-115
Kenya, Uganda, Tanganyika ........ 60-62
Leeward Islands ........ 100-102
Malta ........ 188-190
Mauritius ........ 208-210
Montserrat ........ 89-91
Newfoundland ........ 230-232
Nigeria ........ 50-52
Northern Rhodesia ........ 22-24
Nyasaland Protectorate ........ 51-53
St. Helena ........ 115-117
St. Kitts-Nevis ........ 76-78
St. Lucia ........ 107-109
St. Vincent ........ 138-140
Seychelles ........ 122-124
Sierra Leone ........ 170-172
Solomon Islands ........ 64-66
Somaliland Protectorate ........ 81-83
Straits Settlements ........ 235-237
Swaziland ........ 24-26
Trinidad & Tobago ........ 47-49
Turks & Caicos Islands ........ 75-77
Virgin Islands ........ 73-75

The following have different designs but are included in the omnibus set:

Great Britain ........ 234
Offices in Morocco ........ 82, 439, 514
Canada ........ 237
Cook Islands ........ 109-111
Nauru ........ 35-38
Newfoundland ........ 233-243
New Guinea ........ 48-51
New Zealand ........ 223-225
Niue ........ 70-72
Papua ........ 118-121
South Africa ........ 74-78
Southern Rhodesia ........ 38-41
South-West Africa ........ 125-132

202 stamps

### Peace

King George VI and Parliament Buildings, London CD303

Return to peace at the close of World War II.

### 1945-46

Aden ........ 28-29
Antigua ........ 96-97
Ascension ........ 50-51
Bahamas ........ 130-131
Barbados ........ 207-208
Bermuda ........ 131-132
British Guiana ........ 242-243
British Honduras ........ 127-128
Cayman Islands ........ 112-113
Ceylon ........ 293-294
Cyprus ........ 156-157
Dominica ........ 112-113
Falkland Islands ........ 97-98
Falkland Islands Dep. ........ 1L9-1L10
Fiji ........ 137-138
Gambia ........ 144-145
Gibraltar ........ 119-120
Gilbert & Ellice Islands ........ 52-53
Gold Coast ........ 128-129
Grenada ........ 143-144
Jamaica ........ 136-137
Kenya, Uganda, Tanganyika ........ 90-91
Leeward Islands ........ 116-117
Malta ........ 206-207
Mauritius ........ 223-224
Montserrat ........ 104-105
Nigeria ........ 71-72
Northern Rhodesia ........ 46-47
Nyasaland Protectorate ........ 82-83
Pitcairn Island ........ 9-10
St. Helena ........ 128-129
St. Kitts-Nevis ........ 91-92
St. Lucia ........ 127-128
St. Vincent ........ 152-153
Seychelles ........ 149-150
Sierra Leone ........ 186-187
Solomon Islands ........ 80-81
Somaliland Protectorate ........ 108-109
Trinidad & Tobago ........ 62-63
Turks & Caicos Islands ........ 90-91
Virgin Islands ........ 88-89

The following have different designs but are included in the omnibus set:

Great Britain ........ 264-265
  Offices in Morocco ........ 523-524
Aden
  Kathiri State of Seiyun ........ 12-13
  Qu'aiti State of Shihr and Mukalla ........ 12-13
Australia ........ 200-202
Basutoland ........ 29-31
Bechuanaland Protectorate ...... 137-139
Burma ........ 66-69
Cook Islands ........ 127-130
Hong Kong ........ 174-175
India ........ 195-198
  Hyderabad ........ 51
New Zealand ........ 247-257
Niue ........ 90-93
Pakistan-Bahawalpur ........ O16
Samoa ........ 191-194
South Africa ........ 100-102
Southern Rhodesia ........ 67-70
South-West Africa ........ 153-155
Swaziland ........ 38-40
Zanzibar ........ 222-223

164 stamps

### Silver Wedding

King George VI and Queen Elizabeth

CD304 CD305

### 1948-49

Aden ........ 30-31
  Kathiri State of Seiyun ........ 14-15
  Qu'aiti State of Shihr and Mukalla ........ 14-15
Antigua ........ 98-99
Ascension ........ 52-53
Bahamas ........ 148-149
Barbados ........ 210-211
Basutoland ........ 39-40
Bechuanaland Protectorate ...... 147-148
Bermuda ........ 133-134
British Guiana ........ 244-245
British Honduras ........ 129-130
Cayman Islands ........ 116-117
Cyprus ........ 158-159
Dominica ........ 114-115
Falkland Islands ........ 99-100
Falkland Islands Dep. ........ 1L11-1L12
Fiji ........ 139-140
Gambia ........ 146-147
Gibraltar ........ 121-122
Gilbert & Ellice Islands ........ 54-55
Gold Coast ........ 142-143
Grenada ........ 145-146
Hong Kong ........ 178-179
Jamaica ........ 138-139
Kenya, Uganda, Tanganyika ........ 92-93
Leeward Islands ........ 118-119
Malaya
  Johore ........ 128-129
  Kedah ........ 55-56
  Kelantan ........ 44-45
  Malacca ........ 1-2
  Negri Sembilan ........ 36-37
  Pahang ........ 44-45
  Penang ........ 1-2
  Perak ........ 99-100
  Perlis ........ 1-2
  Selangor ........ 74-75
  Trengganu ........ 47-48
Malta ........ 223-224
Mauritius ........ 229-230
Montserrat ........ 106-107
Nigeria ........ 73-74
North Borneo ........ 238-239
Northern Rhodesia ........ 48-49
Nyasaland Protectorate ........ 85-86
Pitcairn Island ........ 11-12
St. Helena ........ 130-131
St. Kitts-Nevis ........ 93-94
St. Lucia ........ 129-130
St. Vincent ........ 154-155
Sarawak ........ 174-175
Seychelles ........ 151-152
Sierra Leone ........ 188-189
Singapore ........ 21-22
Solomon Islands ........ 82-83
Somaliland Protectorate ........ 110-111
Swaziland ........ 48-49
Trinidad & Tobago ........ 64-65
Turks & Caicos Islands ........ 92-93
Virgin Islands ........ 90-91
Zanzibar ........ 224-225

The following have different designs but are included in the omnibus set:

Great Britain ........ 267-268
  Offices in Morocco ..... 93-94, 525-526
Bahrain ........ 62-63
Kuwait ........ 82-83
Oman ........ 25-26
South Africa ........ 106
South-West Africa ........ 159

138 stamps

### U.P.U.

Mercury and Symbols of Communications — CD306

Plane, Ship and Hemispheres — CD307

Mercury Scattering Letters over Globe CD308

U.P.U. Monument, Bern CD309

Universal Postal Union, 75th anniversary.

### 1949

Aden ........ 32-35
  Kathiri State of Seiyun ........ 16-19
  Qu'aiti State of Shihr and Mukalla ........ 16-19
Antigua ........ 100-103
Ascension ........ 57-60
Bahamas ........ 150-153
Barbados ........ 212-215
Basutoland ........ 41-44
Bechuanaland Protectorate ...... 149-152
Bermuda ........ 138-141
British Guiana ........ 246-249
British Honduras ........ 137-140
Brunei ........ 79-82
Cayman Islands ........ 118-121
Cyprus ........ 160-163
Dominica ........ 116-119
Falkland Islands ........ 103-106
Falkland Islands Dep. ........ 1L14-1L17
Fiji ........ 141-144
Gambia ........ 148-151
Gibraltar ........ 123-126
Gilbert & Ellice Islands ........ 56-59
Gold Coast ........ 144-147
Grenada ........ 147-150
Hong Kong ........ 180-183
Jamaica ........ 142-145
Kenya, Uganda, Tanganyika ........ 94-97
Leeward Islands ........ 126-129
Malaya
  Johore ........ 151-154
  Kedah ........ 57-60
  Kelantan ........ 46-49
  Malacca ........ 18-21
  Negri Sembilan ........ 59-62
  Pahang ........ 46-49
  Penang ........ 23-26
  Perak ........ 101-104
  Perlis ........ 3-6
  Selangor ........ 76-79
  Trengganu ........ 49-52
Malta ........ 225-228
Mauritius ........ 231-234
Montserrat ........ 108-111
New Hebrides, British ........ 62-65
New Hebrides, French ........ 79-82
Nigeria ........ 75-78
North Borneo ........ 240-243
Northern Rhodesia ........ 50-53
Nyasaland Protectorate ........ 87-90
Pitcairn Islands ........ 13-16
St. Helena ........ 132-135
St. Kitts-Nevis ........ 95-98
St. Lucia ........ 131-134
St. Vincent ........ 170-173

Sarawak 176-179
Seychelles 153-156
Sierra Leone 190-193
Singapore 23-26
Solomon Islands 84-87
Somaliland Protectorate 112-115
Southern Rhodesia 71-72
Swaziland 50-53
Tonga 87-90
Trinidad & Tobago 66-69
Turks & Caicos Islands 101-104
Virgin Islands 92-95
Zanzibar 226-229

The following have different designs but are included in the omnibus set:

Great Britain 276-279
  Offices in Morocco 546-549
Australia 223
Bahrain 68-71
Burma 116-121
Ceylon 304-306
Egypt 281-283
India 223-226
Kuwait 89-92
Oman 31-34
Pakistan-Bahawalpur 26-29, O25-O28
South Africa 109-111
South-West Africa 160-162

319 stamps

### University

Arms of University College CD310

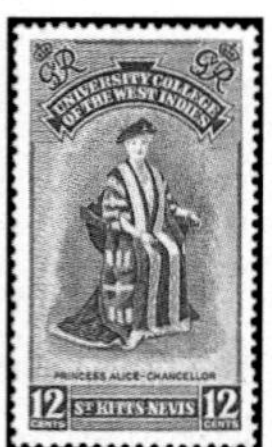
Alice, Princess of Athlone CD311

1948 opening of University College of the West Indies at Jamaica.

**1951**

Antigua 104-105
Barbados 228-229
British Guiana 250-251
British Honduras 141-142
Dominica 120-121
Grenada 164-165
Jamaica 146-147
Leeward Islands 130-131
Montserrat 112-113
St. Kitts-Nevis 105-106
St. Lucia 149-150
St. Vincent 174-175
Trinidad & Tobago 70-71
Virgin Islands 96-97

28 stamps

### Coronation

Queen Elizabeth II — CD312

**1953**

Aden 47
  Kathiri State of Seiyun 28
  Qu'aiti State of Shihr and Mukalla 28
Antigua 106
Ascension 61
Bahamas 157
Barbados 234
Basutoland 45
Bechuanaland Protectorate 153
Bermuda 142
British Guiana 252
British Honduras 143
Cayman Islands 150
Cyprus 167
Dominica 141
Falkland Islands 121
Falkland Islands Dependencies 1L18
Fiji 145
Gambia 152
Gibraltar 131
Gilbert & Ellice Islands 60
Gold Coast 160
Grenada 170
Hong Kong 184
Jamaica 153
Kenya, Uganda, Tanganyika 101
Leeward Islands 132
Malaya
  Johore 155
  Kedah 82
  Kelantan 71
  Malacca 27
  Negri Sembilan 63
  Pahang 71
  Penang 27
  Perak 126
  Perlis 28
  Selangor 101
  Trengganu 74
Malta 241
Mauritius 250
Montserrat 127
New Hebrides, British 77
Nigeria 79
North Borneo 260
Northern Rhodesia 60
Nyasaland Protectorate 96
Pitcairn 19
St. Helena 139
St. Kitts-Nevis 119
St. Lucia 156
St. Vincent 185
Sarawak 196
Seychelles 172
Sierra Leone 194
Singapore 27
Solomon Islands 88
Somaliland Protectorate 127
Swaziland 54
Trinidad & Tobago 84
Tristan da Cunha 13
Turks & Caicos Islands 118
Virgin Islands 114

The following have different designs but are included in the omnibus set:

Great Britain 313-316
  Offices in Morocco 579-582
Australia 259-261
Bahrain 92-95
Canada 330
Ceylon 317
Cook Islands 145-146
Kuwait 113-116
New Zealand 280-284
Niue 104-105
Oman 52-55
Samoa 214-215
South Africa 192
Southern Rhodesia 80
South-West Africa 244-248
Tokelau Islands 4

106 stamps

### Royal Visit 1953

Separate designs for each country for the visit of Queen Elizabeth II and the Duke of Edinburgh.

**1953**

Aden 62
Australia 267-269
Bermuda 163
Ceylon 318
Fiji 146
Gibraltar 146
Jamaica 154
Kenya, Uganda, Tanganyika 102
Malta 242
New Zealand 286-287

13 stamps

### West Indies Federation

Map of the Caribbean CD313

Federation of the West Indies, April 22, 1958.

**1958**

Antigua 122-124
Barbados 248-250
Dominica 161-163
Grenada 184-186
Jamaica 175-177
Montserrat 143-145
St. Kitts-Nevis 136-138
St. Lucia 170-172
St. Vincent 198-200
Trinidad & Tobago 86-88

30 stamps

### Freedom from Hunger

Protein Food CD314

U.N. Food and Agricultural Organization's "Freedom from Hunger" campaign.

**1963**

Aden 65
Antigua 133
Ascension 89
Bahamas 180
Basutoland 83
Bechuanaland Protectorate 194
Bermuda 192
British Guiana 271
British Honduras 179
Brunei 100
Cayman Islands 168
Dominica 181
Falkland Islands 146
Fiji 198
Gambia 172
Gibraltar 161
Gilbert & Ellice Islands 76
Grenada 190
Hong Kong 218
Malta 291
Mauritius 270
Montserrat 150
New Hebrides, British 93
North Borneo 296
Pitcairn 35
St. Helena 173
St. Lucia 179
St. Vincent 201
Sarawak 212
Seychelles 213
Solomon Islands 109
Swaziland 108
Tonga 127
Tristan da Cunha 68
Turks & Caicos Islands 138
Virgin Islands 140
Zanzibar 280

37 stamps

### Red Cross Centenary

Red Cross and Elizabeth II CD315

**1963**

Antigua 134-135
Ascension 90-91
Bahamas 183-184
Basutoland 84-85
Bechuanaland Protectorate 195-196
Bermuda 193-194
British Guiana 272-273
British Honduras 180-181
Cayman Islands 169-170
Dominica 182-183
Falkland Islands 147-148
Fiji 203-204
Gambia 173-174
Gibraltar 162-163
Gilbert & Ellice Islands 77-78
Grenada 191-192
Hong Kong 219-220
Jamaica 203-204
Malta 292-293
Mauritius 271-272
Montserrat 151-152
New Hebrides, British 94-95
Pitcairn Islands 36-37
St. Helena 174-175
St. Kitts-Nevis 143-144
St. Lucia 180-181
St. Vincent 202-203
Seychelles 214-215
Solomon Islands 110-111
South Arabia 1-2
Swaziland 109-110
Tonga 134-135
Tristan da Cunha 69-70
Turks & Caicos Islands 139-140
Virgin Islands 141-142

70 stamps

### Shakespeare

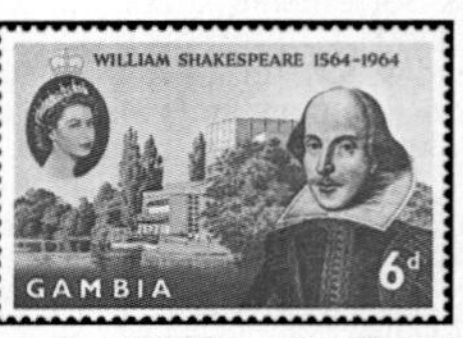

Shakespeare Memorial Theatre, Stratford-on-Avon — CD316

400th anniversary of the birth of William Shakespeare.

**1964**

Antigua 151
Bahamas 201
Bechuanaland Protectorate 197
Cayman Islands 171
Dominica 184
Falkland Islands 149
Gambia 192
Gibraltar 164
Montserrat 153
St. Lucia 196
Turks & Caicos Islands 141
Virgin Islands 143

12 stamps

### ITU

ITU Emblem CD317

Intl. Telecommunication Union, cent.

**1965**

Antigua 153-154
Ascension 92-93
Bahamas 219-220
Barbados 265-266
Basutoland 101-102
Bechuanaland Protectorate 202-203
Bermuda 196-197
British Guiana 293-294
British Honduras 187-188
Brunei 116-117
Cayman Islands 172-173
Dominica 185-186
Falkland Islands 154-155
Fiji 211-212
Gibraltar 167-168
Gilbert & Ellice Islands 87-88
Grenada 205-206
Hong Kong 221-222
Mauritius 291-292
Montserrat 157-158
New Hebrides, British 108-109
Pitcairn Islands 52-53
St. Helena 180-181
St. Kitts-Nevis 163-164
St. Lucia 197-198
St. Vincent 224-225
Seychelles 218-219
Solomon Islands 126-127
Swaziland 115-116
Tristan da Cunha 85-86
Turks & Caicos Islands 142-143
Virgin Islands 159-160

64 stamps

### Intl. Cooperation Year

ICY Emblem CD318

**1965**

Antigua ....155-156
Ascension ....94-95
Bahamas ....222-223
Basutoland ....103-104
Bechuanaland Protectorate ....204-205
Bermuda ....199-200
British Guiana ....295-296
British Honduras ....189-190
Brunei ....118-119
Cayman Islands ....174-175
Dominica ....187-188
Falkland Islands ....156-157
Fiji ....213-214
Gibraltar ....169-170
Gilbert & Ellice Islands ....104-105
Grenada ....207-208
Hong Kong ....223-224
Mauritius ....293-294
Montserrat ....176-177
New Hebrides, British ....110-111
New Hebrides, French ....126-127
Pitcairn Islands ....54-55
St. Helena ....182-183
St. Kitts-Nevis ....165-166
St. Lucia ....199-200
Seychelles ....220-221
Solomon Islands ....143-144
South Arabia ....17-18
Swaziland ....117-118
Tristan da Cunha ....87-88
Turks & Caicos Islands ....144-145
Virgin Islands ....161-162

64 stamps

### Churchill Memorial

Winston Churchill and St. Paul's, London, During Air Attack CD319

**1966**

Antigua ....157-160
Ascension ....96-99
Bahamas ....224-227
Barbados ....281-284
Basutoland ....105-108
Bechuanaland Protectorate ....206-209
Bermuda ....201-204
British Antarctic Territory ....16-19
British Honduras ....191-194
Brunei ....120-123
Cayman Islands ....176-179
Dominica ....189-192
Falkland Islands ....158-161
Fiji ....215-218
Gibraltar ....171-174
Gilbert & Ellice Islands ....106-109
Grenada ....209-212
Hong Kong ....225-228
Mauritius ....295-298
Montserrat ....178-181
New Hebrides, British ....112-115
New Hebrides, French ....128-131
Pitcairn Islands ....56-59
St. Helena ....184-187
St. Kitts-Nevis ....167-170
St. Lucia ....201-204
St. Vincent ....241-244
Seychelles ....222-225
Solomon Islands ....145-148
South Arabia ....19-22
Swaziland ....119-122
Tristan da Cunha ....89-92
Turks & Caicos Islands ....146-149
Virgin Islands ....163-166

136 stamps

### Royal Visit, 1966

Queen Elizabeth II and Prince Philip CD320

Caribbean visit, Feb. 4 - Mar. 6, 1966.

**1966**

Antigua ....161-162
Bahamas ....228-229
Barbados ....285-286
British Guiana ....299-300
Cayman Islands ....180-181
Dominica ....193-194
Grenada ....213-214
Montserrat ....182-183
St. Kitts-Nevis ....171-172
St. Lucia ....205-206
St. Vincent ....245-246
Turks & Caicos Islands ....150-151
Virgin Islands ....167-168

26 stamps

### World Cup Soccer

Soccer Player and Jules Rimet Cup CD321

World Cup Soccer Championship, Wembley, England, July 11-30.

**1966**

Antigua ....163-164
Ascension ....100-101
Bahamas ....245-246
Bermuda ....205-206
Brunei ....124-125
Cayman Islands ....182-183
Dominica ....195-196
Fiji ....219-220
Gibraltar ....175-176
Gilbert & Ellice Islands ....125-126
Grenada ....230-231
New Hebrides, British ....116-117
New Hebrides, French ....132-133
Pitcairn Islands ....60-61
St. Helena ....188-189
St. Kitts-Nevis ....173-174
St. Lucia ....207-208
Seychelles ....226-227
Solomon Islands ....167-168
South Arabia ....23-24
Tristan da Cunha ....93-94

42 stamps

### WHO Headquarters

World Health Organization Headquarters, Geneva — CD322

**1966**

Antigua ....165-166
Ascension ....102-103
Bahamas ....247-248
Brunei ....126-127
Cayman Islands ....184-185
Dominica ....197-198
Fiji ....224-225
Gibraltar ....180-181
Gilbert & Ellice Islands ....127-128
Grenada ....232-233
Hong Kong ....229-230
Montserrat ....184-185
New Hebrides, British ....118-119
New Hebrides, French ....134-135
Pitcairn Islands ....62-63
St. Helena ....190-191
St. Kitts-Nevis ....177-178
St. Lucia ....209-210
St. Vincent ....247-248
Seychelles ....228-229
Solomon Islands ....169-170
South Arabia ....25-26
Tristan da Cunha ....99-100

46 stamps

### UNESCO Anniversary

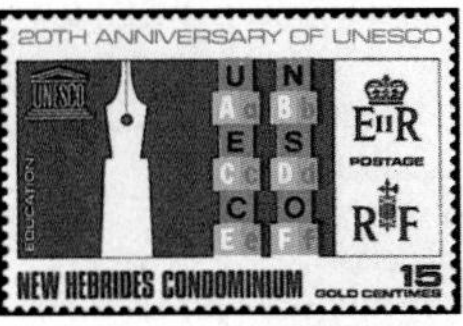


"Education" — CD323

"Science" (Wheat ears & flask enclosing globe). "Culture" (lyre & columns). 20th anniversary of the UNESCO.

**1966-67**

Antigua ....183-185
Ascension ....108-110
Bahamas ....249-251
Barbados ....287-289
Bermuda ....207-209
Brunei ....128-130
Cayman Islands ....186-188
Dominica ....199-201
Gibraltar ....183-185
Gilbert & Ellice Islands ....129-131
Grenada ....234-236
Hong Kong ....231-233
Mauritius ....299-301
Montserrat ....186-188
New Hebrides, British ....120-122
New Hebrides, French ....136-138
Pitcairn Islands ....64-66
St. Helena ....192-194
St. Kitts-Nevis ....179-181
St. Lucia ....211-213
St. Vincent ....249-251
Seychelles ....230-232
Solomon Islands ....171-173
South Arabia ....27-29
Swaziland ....123-125
Tristan da Cunha ....101-103
Turks & Caicos Islands ....155-157
Virgin Islands ....176-178

84 stamps

### Silver Wedding, 1972

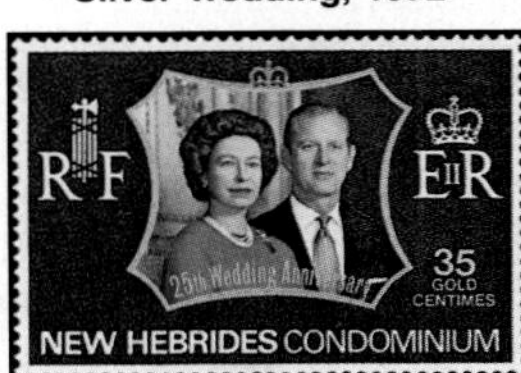


Queen Elizabeth II and Prince Philip — CD324

Designs: borders differ for each country.

**1972**

Anguilla ....161-162
Antigua ....295-296
Ascension ....164-165
Bahamas ....344-345
Bermuda ....296-297
British Antarctic Territory ....43-44
British Honduras ....306-307
British Indian Ocean Territory ....48-49
Brunei ....186-187
Cayman Islands ....304-305
Dominica ....352-353
Falkland Islands ....223-224
Fiji ....328-329
Gibraltar ....292-293
Gilbert & Ellice Islands ....206-207
Grenada ....466-467
Hong Kong ....271-272
Montserrat ....286-287
New Hebrides, British ....169-170
Pitcairn Islands ....127-128
St. Helena ....271-272
St. Kitts-Nevis ....257-258
St. Lucia ....328-329
St.Vincent ....344-345
Seychelles ....309-310
Solomon Islands ....248-249
South Georgia ....35-36
Tristan da Cunha ....178-179
Turks & Caicos Islands ....257-258
Virgin Islands ....241-242

60 stamps

### Princess Anne's Wedding

Princess Anne and Mark Phillips — CD325

Wedding of Princess Anne and Mark Phillips, Nov. 14, 1973.

**1973**

Anguilla ....179-180
Ascension ....177-178
Belize ....325-326
Bermuda ....302-303
British Antarctic Territory ....60-61
Cayman Islands ....320-321
Falkland Islands ....225-226
Gibraltar ....305-306
Gilbert & Ellice Islands ....216-217
Hong Kong ....289-290
Montserrat ....300-301
Pitcairn Island ....135-136
St. Helena ....277-278
St. Kitts-Nevis ....274-275
St. Lucia ....349-350
St. Vincent ....358-359
St. Vincent Grenadines ....1-2
Seychelles ....311-312
Solomon Islands ....259-260
South Georgia ....37-38
Tristan da Cunha ....189-190
Turks & Caicos Islands ....286-287
Virgin Islands ....260-261

44 stamps

### Elizabeth II Coronation Anniv.

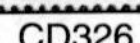

CD326

CD327

CD328

Designs: Royal and local beasts in heraldic form and simulated stonework. Portrait of Elizabeth II by Peter Grugeon. 25th anniversary of coronation of Queen Elizabeth II.

**1978**

Ascension ....229
Barbados ....474
Belize ....397
British Antarctic Territory ....71
Cayman Islands ....404
Christmas Island ....87
Falkland Islands ....275
Fiji ....384
Gambia ....380
Gilbert Islands ....312
Mauritius ....464
New Hebrides, British ....258
St. Helena ....317
St. Kitts-Nevis ....354
Samoa ....472

| | |
|---|---|
| Solomon Islands | 368 |
| South Georgia | 51 |
| Swaziland | 302 |
| Tristan da Cunha | 238 |
| Virgin Islands | 337 |

20 sheets

### Queen Mother Elizabeth's 80th Birthday

CD330

Designs: Photographs of Queen Mother Elizabeth. Falkland Islands issued in sheets of 50; others in sheets of 9.

**1980**

| | |
|---|---|
| Ascension | 261 |
| Bermuda | 401 |
| Cayman Islands | 443 |
| Falkland Islands | 305 |
| Gambia | 412 |
| Gibraltar | 393 |
| Hong Kong | 364 |
| Pitcairn Islands | 193 |
| St. Helena | 341 |
| Samoa | 532 |
| Solomon Islands | 426 |
| Tristan da Cunha | 277 |

12 stamps

### Royal Wedding, 1981

Prince Charles and Lady Diana — CD331

Wedding of Charles, Prince of Wales, and Lady Diana Spencer, St. Paul's Cathedral, London, July 29, 1981.

**1981**

| | |
|---|---|
| Antigua | 623-625 |
| Ascension | 294-296 |
| Barbados | 547-549 |
| Barbuda | 497-499 |
| Bermuda | 412-414 |
| Brunei | 268-270 |
| Cayman Islands | 471-473 |
| Dominica | 701-703 |
| Falkland Islands | 324-326 |
| Falkland Islands Dep. | 1L59-1L61 |
| Fiji | 442-444 |
| Gambia | 426-428 |
| Ghana | 759-761 |
| Grenada | 1051-1053 |
| Grenada Grenadines | 440-443 |
| Hong Kong | 373-375 |
| Jamaica | 500-503 |
| Lesotho | 335-337 |
| Maldive Islands | 906-908 |
| Mauritius | 520-522 |
| Norfolk Island | 280-282 |
| Pitcairn Islands | 206-208 |
| St. Helena | 353-355 |
| St. Lucia | 543-545 |
| Samoa | 558-560 |
| Sierra Leone | 509-517 |
| Solomon Islands | 450-452 |
| Swaziland | 382-384 |
| Tristan da Cunha | 294-296 |
| Turks & Caicos Islands | 486-488 |
| Caicos Island | 8-10 |
| Uganda | 314-316 |
| Vanuatu | 308-310 |
| Virgin Islands | 406-408 |

### Princess Diana

CD332

CD333

Designs: Photographs and portrait of Princess Diana, wedding or honeymoon photographs, royal residences, arms of issuing country. Portrait photograph by Clive Friend. Souvenir sheet margins show family tree, various people related to the princess. 21st birthday of Princess Diana of Wales, July 1.

**1982**

| | |
|---|---|
| Antigua | 663-666 |
| Ascension | 313-316 |
| Bahamas | 510-513 |
| Barbados | 585-588 |
| Barbuda | 544-546 |
| British Antarctic Territory | 92-95 |
| Cayman Islands | 486-489 |
| Dominica | 773-776 |
| Falkland Islands | 348-351 |
| Falkland Islands Dep. | 1L72-1L75 |
| Fiji | 470-473 |
| Gambia | 447-450 |
| Grenada | 1101A-1105 |
| Grenada Grenadines | 485-491 |
| Lesotho | 372-375 |
| Maldive Islands | 952-955 |
| Mauritius | 548-551 |
| Pitcairn Islands | 213-216 |
| St. Helena | 372-375 |
| St. Lucia | 591-594 |
| Sierra Leone | 531-534 |
| Solomon Islands | 471-474 |
| Swaziland | 406-409 |
| Tristan da Cunha | 310-313 |
| Turks and Caicos Islands | 530A-534 |
| Virgin Islands | 430-433 |

### 250th anniv. of first edition of Lloyd's List (shipping news publication) & of Lloyd's marine insurance.

CD335

Designs: First page of early edition of the list; historical ships, modern transportation or harbor scenes.

**1984**

| | |
|---|---|
| Ascension | 351-354 |
| Bahamas | 555-558 |
| Barbados | 627-630 |
| Cayes of Belize | 10-13 |
| Cayman Islands | 522-525 |
| Falkland Islands | 404-407 |
| Fiji | 509-512 |
| Gambia | 519-522 |
| Mauritius | 587-590 |
| Nauru | 280-283 |
| St. Helena | 412-415 |
| Samoa | 624-627 |
| Seychelles | 538-541 |
| Solomon Islands | 521-524 |
| Vanuatu | 368-371 |
| Virgin Islands | 466-469 |

### Queen Mother 85th Birthday

CD336

Designs: Photographs tracing the life of the Queen Mother, Elizabeth. The high value in each set pictures the same photograph taken of the Queen Mother holding the infant Prince Henry.

**1985**

| | |
|---|---|
| Ascension | 372-376 |
| Bahamas | 580-584 |
| Barbados | 660-664 |
| Bermuda | 469-473 |
| Falkland Islands | 420-424 |
| Falkland Islands Dep. | 1L92-1L96 |
| Fiji | 531-535 |
| Hong Kong | 447-450 |
| Jamaica | 599-603 |
| Mauritius | 604-608 |
| Norfolk Island | 364-368 |
| Pitcairn Islands | 253-257 |
| St. Helena | 428-432 |
| Samoa | 649-653 |
| Seychelles | 567-571 |
| Solomon Islands | 543-547 |
| Swaziland | 476-480 |
| Tristan da Cunha | 372-376 |
| Vanuatu | 392-396 |
| Zil Elwannyen Sesel | 101-105 |

### Queen Elizabeth II, 60th Birthday

CD337

**1986, April 21**

| | |
|---|---|
| Ascension | 389-393 |
| Bahamas | 592-596 |
| Barbados | 675-679 |
| Bermuda | 499-503 |
| Cayman Islands | 555-559 |
| Falkland Islands | 441-445 |
| Fiji | 544-548 |
| Hong Kong | 465-469 |
| Jamaica | 620-624 |
| Kiribati | 470-474 |
| Mauritius | 629-633 |
| Papua New Guinea | 640-644 |
| Pitcairn Islands | 270-274 |
| St. Helena | 451-455 |
| Samoa | 670-674 |
| Seychelles | 592-596 |
| Solomon Islands | 562-566 |
| South Georgia | 101-105 |
| Swaziland | 490-494 |
| Tristan da Cunha | 388-392 |
| Vanuatu | 414-418 |
| Zambia | 343-347 |
| Zil Elwannyen Sesel | 114-118 |

### Royal Wedding

Marriage of Prince Andrew and Sarah Ferguson CD338

**1986, July 23**

| | |
|---|---|
| Ascension | 399-400 |
| Bahamas | 602-603 |
| Barbados | 687-688 |
| Cayman Islands | 560-561 |
| Jamaica | 629-630 |
| Pitcairn Islands | 275-276 |
| St. Helena | 460-461 |
| St. Kitts | 181-182 |
| Seychelles | 602-603 |
| Solomon Islands | 567-568 |
| Tristan da Cunha | 397-398 |
| Zambia | 348-349 |
| Zil Elwannyen Sesel | 119-120 |

### Queen Elizabeth II, 60th Birthday

Queen Elizabeth II & Prince Philip, 1947 Wedding Portrait — CD339

Designs: Photographs tracing the life of Queen Elizabeth II.

**1986**

| | |
|---|---|
| Anguilla | 674-677 |
| Antigua | 925-928 |
| Barbuda | 783-786 |
| Dominica | 950-953 |
| Gambia | 611-614 |
| Grenada | 1371-1374 |
| Grenada Grenadines | 749-752 |
| Lesotho | 531-534 |
| Maldive Islands | 1172-1175 |
| Sierra Leone | 760-763 |
| Uganda | 495-498 |

### Royal Wedding, 1986

CD340

Designs: Photographs of Prince Andrew and Sarah Ferguson during courtship, engagement and marriage.

**1986**

| | |
|---|---|
| Antigua | 939-942 |
| Barbuda | 809-812 |
| Dominica | 970-973 |
| Gambia | 635-638 |
| Grenada | 1385-1388 |
| Grenada Grenadines | 758-761 |
| Lesotho | 545-548 |
| Maldive Islands | 1181-1184 |
| Sierra Leone | 769-772 |
| Uganda | 510-513 |

### Lloyds of London, 300th Anniv.

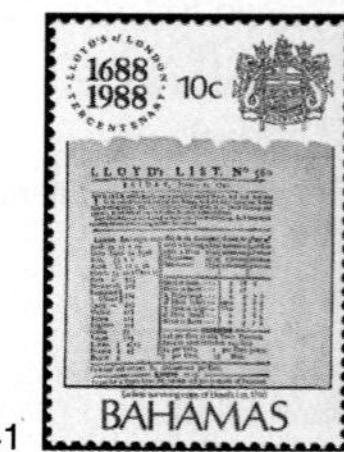


CD341

Designs: 17th century aspects of Lloyds, representations of each country's individual connections with Lloyds and publicized disasters insured by the organization.

**1986**

| | |
|---|---|
| Ascension | 454-457 |
| Bahamas | 655-658 |
| Barbados | 731-734 |
| Bermuda | 541-544 |
| Falkland Islands | 481-484 |
| Liberia | 1101-1104 |
| Malawi | 534-537 |
| Nevis | 571-574 |
| St. Helena | 501-504 |
| St. Lucia | 923-926 |
| Seychelles | 649-652 |
| Solomon Islands | 627-630 |

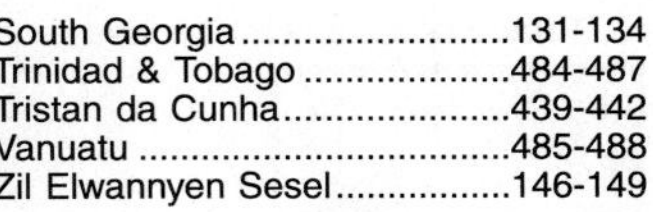

| | |
|---|---|
| South Georgia | 131-134 |
| Trinidad & Tobago | 484-487 |
| Tristan da Cunha | 439-442 |
| Vanuatu | 485-488 |
| Zil Elwannyen Sesel | 146-149 |

### Moon Landing, 20th Anniv.

CD342

Designs: Equipment, crew photographs, spacecraft, official emblems and report profiles created for the Apollo Missions. Two stamps in each set are square in format rather than like the stamp shown; see individual country listings for more information.

**1989**

| | |
|---|---|
| Ascension Is. | 468-472 |
| Bahamas | 674-678 |
| Belize | 916-920 |
| Kiribati | 517-521 |
| Liberia | 1125-1129 |
| Nevis | 586-590 |
| St. Kitts | 248-252 |
| Samoa | 760-764 |
| Seychelles | 676-680 |
| Solomon Islands | 643-647 |
| Vanuatu | 507-511 |
| Zil Elwannyen Sesel | 154-158 |

### Queen Mother, 90th Birthday

CD343 CD344

Designs: Portraits of Queen Elizabeth, the Queen Mother. See individual country listings for more information.

**1990**

| | |
|---|---|
| Ascension Is. | 491-492 |
| Bahamas | 698-699 |
| Barbados | 782-783 |
| British Antarctic Territory | 170-171 |
| British Indian Ocean Territory | 106-107 |
| Cayman Islands | 622-623 |
| Falkland Islands | 524-525 |
| Kenya | 527-528 |
| Kiribati | 555-556 |
| Liberia | 1145-1146 |
| Pitcairn Islands | 336-337 |
| St. Helena | 532-533 |
| St. Lucia | 969-970 |
| Seychelles | 710-711 |
| Solomon Islands | 671-672 |
| South Georgia | 143-144 |
| Swaziland | 565-566 |
| Tristan da Cunha | 480-481 |
| Zil Elwannyen Sesel | 171-172 |

### Queen Elizabeth II, 65th Birthday, and Prince Philip, 70th Birthday

CD345

CD346

Designs: Portraits of Queen Elizabeth II and Prince Philip differ for each country. Printed in sheets of 10 + 5 labels (3 different) between. Stamps alternate, producing 5 different triptychs.

**1991**

| | |
|---|---|
| Ascension Is. | 505-506 |
| Bahamas | 730-731 |
| Belize | 969-970 |
| Bermuda | 617-618 |
| Kiribati | 571-572 |
| Mauritius | 733-734 |
| Pitcairn Islands | 348-349 |
| St. Helena | 554-555 |
| St. Kitts | 318-319 |
| Samoa | 790-791 |
| Seychelles | 723-724 |
| Solomon Islands | 688-689 |
| South Georgia | 149-150 |
| Swaziland | 586-587 |
| Vanuatu | 540-541 |
| Zil Elwannyen Sesel | 177-178 |

### Royal Family Birthday, Anniversary

CD347

Queen Elizabeth II, 65th birthday, Charles and Diana, 10th wedding anniversary: Various photographs of Queen Elizabeth II, Prince Philip, Prince Charles, Princess Diana and their sons William and Henry.

**1991**

| | |
|---|---|
| Antigua | 1446-1455 |
| Barbuda | 1229-1238 |
| Dominica | 1328-1337 |
| Gambia | 1080-1089 |
| Grenada | 2006-2015 |
| Grenada Grenadines | 1331-1340 |
| Guyana | 2440-2451 |
| Lesotho | 871-875 |
| Maldive Islands | 1533-1542 |
| Nevis | 666-675 |
| St. Vincent | 1485-1494 |
| St. Vincent Grenadines | 769-778 |
| Sierra Leone | 1387-1396 |
| Turks & Caicos Islands | 913-922 |
| Uganda | 918-927 |

### Queen Elizabeth II's Accession to the Throne, 40th Anniv.

CD348

CD349

Various photographs of Queen Elizabeth II with local Scenes.

**1992 - CD348**

| | |
|---|---|
| Antigua | 1513-1518 |
| Barbuda | 1306-1309 |
| Dominica | 1414-1419 |
| Gambia | 1172-1177 |
| Grenada | 2047-2052 |
| Grenada Grenadines | 1368-1373 |
| Lesotho | 881-885 |
| Maldive Islands | 1637-1642 |
| Nevis | 702-707 |
| St. Vincent | 1582-1587 |
| St. Vincent Grenadines | 829-834 |
| Sierra Leone | 1482-1487 |
| Turks and Caicos Islands | 978-987 |
| Uganda | 990-995 |
| Virgin Islands | 742-746 |

**1992 - CD349**

| | |
|---|---|
| Ascension Islands | 531-535 |
| Bahamas | 744-748 |
| Bermuda | 623-627 |
| British Indian Ocean Territory | 119-123 |
| Cayman Islands | 648-652 |
| Falkland Islands | 549-553 |
| Gibraltar | 605-609 |
| Hong Kong | 619-623 |
| Kenya | 563-567 |
| Kiribati | 582-586 |
| Pitcairn Islands | 362-366 |
| St. Helena | 570-574 |
| St. Kitts | 332-336 |
| Samoa | 805-809 |
| Seychelles | 734-738 |
| Solomon Islands | 708-712 |
| South Georgia | 157-161 |
| Tristan da Cunha | 508-512 |
| Vanuatu | 555-559 |
| Zambia | 561-565 |
| Zil Elwannyen Sesel | 183-187 |

### Royal Air Force, 75th Anniversary

CD350

**1993**

| | |
|---|---|
| Ascension | 557-561 |
| Bahamas | 771-775 |
| Barbados | 842-846 |
| Belize | 1003-1008 |
| Bermuda | 648-651 |
| British Indian Ocean Territory | 136-140 |
| Falkland Is. | 573-577 |
| Fiji | 687-691 |
| Montserrat | 830-834 |
| St. Kitts | 351-355 |

### Royal Air Force, 80th Anniv.

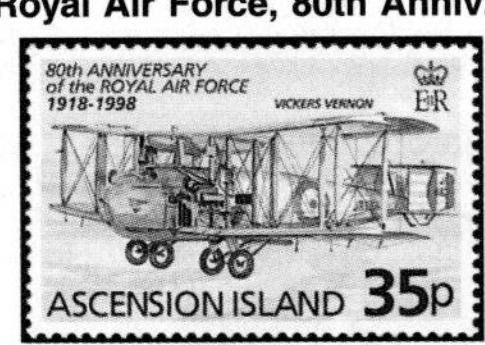

Design CD350 Re-inscribed

**1998**

| | |
|---|---|
| Ascension | 697-701 |
| Bahamas | 907-911 |
| British Indian Ocean Terr | 198-202 |
| Cayman Islands | 754-758 |
| Fiji | 814-818 |
| Gibraltar | 755-759 |
| Samoa | 957-961 |
| Turks & Caicos Islands | 1258-1265 |
| Tuvalu | 763-767 |
| Virgin Islands | 879-883 |

### End of World War II, 50th Anniv.

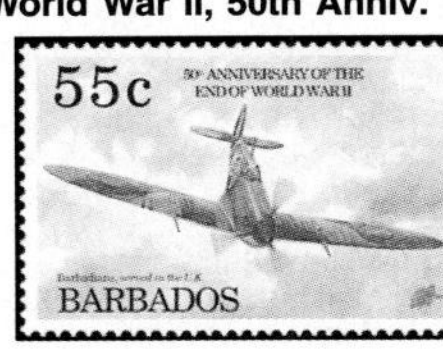

CD351

CD352

**1995**

| | |
|---|---|
| Ascension | 613-617 |
| Bahamas | 824-828 |
| Barbados | 891-895 |
| Belize | 1047-1050 |
| British Indian Ocean Territory | 163-167 |
| Cayman Islands | 704-708 |
| Falkland Islands | 634-638 |
| Fiji | 720-724 |
| Kiribati | 662-668 |
| Liberia | 1175-1179 |
| Mauritius | 803-805 |
| St. Helena | 646-654 |
| St. Kitts | 389-393 |
| St. Lucia | 1018-1022 |
| Samoa | 890-894 |
| Solomon Islands | 799-803 |
| South Georgia & S. Sandwich Is. | 198-200 |
| Tristan da Cunha | 562-566 |

### UN, 50th Anniv.

CD353

**1995**

| | |
|---|---|
| Bahamas | 839-842 |
| Barbados | 901-904 |
| Belize | 1055-1058 |
| Jamaica | 847-851 |
| Liberia | 1187-1190 |
| Mauritius | 813-816 |
| Pitcairn Islands | 436-439 |
| St. Kitts | 398-401 |
| St. Lucia | 1023-1026 |
| Samoa | 900-903 |
| Tristan da Cunha | 568-571 |
| Virgin Islands | 807-810 |

### Queen Elizabeth, 70th Birthday

CD354

**1996**

| | |
|---|---|
| Ascension | 632-635 |
| British Antarctic Territory | 240-243 |
| British Indian Ocean Territory | 176-180 |
| Falkland Islands | 653-657 |
| Pitcairn Islands | 446-449 |
| St. Helena | 672-676 |
| Samoa | 912-916 |
| Tokelau | 223-227 |
| Tristan da Cunha | 576-579 |
| Virgin Islands | 824-828 |

### Diana, Princess of Wales (1961-97)

CD355

**1998**

Ascension ........................................696
Bahamas ..............................901A-902
Barbados ........................................950
Belize ...........................................1091
Bermuda .........................................753
Botswana ...................................659-663
British Antarctic Territory ................258
British Indian Ocean Terr. ...............197
Cayman Islands ....................752A-753
Falkland Islands ..............................694
Fiji ..........................................819-820
Gibraltar ..........................................754
Kiribati ..................................719A-720
Namibia ...........................................909
Niue ................................................706
Norfolk Island ..........................644-645
Papua New Guinea .........................937
Pitcairn Islands ...............................487
St. Helena .......................................711
St. Kitts ................................437A-438
Samoa ..................................955A-956
Seycelles .........................................802
Solomon Islands .......................866-867
South Georgia & S. Sandwich Islands
..........................................................220
Tokelau ................................252B-253
Tonga ...............................................980
Niuafo'ou .......................................201
Tristan da Cunha ............................618
Tuvalu .............................................762
Vanuatu ...........................................719
Virgin Islands ..................................878

### Wedding of Prince Edward and Sophie Rhys-Jones

CD356

**1999**

Ascension ................................729-730
Cayman Islands ........................775-776
Falkland Islands .......................729-730
Pitcairn Islands .........................505-506
St. Helena ................................733-734
Samoa .......................................971-972
Tristan da Cunha .......................636-637
Virgin Islands ............................908-909

### 1st Manned Moon Landing, 30th Anniv.

CD357

**1999**

Ascension ................................731-735
Bahamas ..................................942-946
Barbados ..................................967-971
Bermuda ........................................778
Cayman Islands ........................777-781
Fiji ...........................................853-857
Jamaica ...................................889-893
Kiribati .....................................746-750
Nauru .......................................465-469
St. Kitts ....................................460-464
Samoa .......................................973-977
Solomon Islands .......................875-879
Tuvalu .......................................800-804
Virgin Islands ............................910-914

### Queen Mother's Century

CD358

**1999**

Ascension ................................736-740
Bahamas ..................................951-955
Cayman Islands ........................782-786
Falkland Islands .......................734-738
Fiji ...........................................858-862
Norfolk Island ...........................688-692
St. Helena ................................740-744
Samoa .......................................978-982
Solomon Islands .......................880-884
South Georgia & South
Sandwich Islands .................231-235
Tristan da Cunha .......................638-642
Tuvalu .......................................805-809

### Prince William, 18th Birthday

CD359

**2000**

Ascension ................................755-759
Cayman Islands ........................797-801
Falkland Islands .......................762-766
Fiji ...........................................889-893
South Georgia ...........................257-261
and South Sandwich Islands
Tristan da Cunha .......................664-668
Virgin Islands ............................925-929

### Reign of Queen Elizabeth II, 50th Anniv.

CD360

**2002**

Ascension ................................790-794
Bahamas ..............................1033-1037
Barbados ..............................1019-1023
Belize ...................................1152-1156
Bermuda ...................................822-826
British Antarctic Territory ..........307-311
British Indian Ocean Territory ........239-243
Cayman Islands ........................844-848
Falkland Islands .......................804-808
Gibraltar ...................................896-900
Jamaica ....................................952-956
Nauru .......................................491-495
Norfolk Island ...........................758-762
Papua New Guinea .............1019-1023
Pitcairn Islands ..............................552
St. Helena ................................788-792
St. Lucia ...............................1146-1150
Solomon Islands .......................931-935
South Georgia & So. Sandwich Is. .......
...............................................274-278
Swaziland .................................706-710
Tokelau .....................................302-306
Tonga .........................................1059
Niuafo'ou ........................................239
Tristan da Cunha .......................706-710
Virgin Islands ............................967-971

### Queen Mother Elizabeth (1900-2002)

CD361

**2002**

Ascension ................................799-801
Bahamas ..............................1044-1046
Bermuda ...................................834-836
British Antarctic Territory ..........312-314
British Indian Ocean Territory ........245-247
Cayman Islands ........................857-861
Falkland Islands .......................812-816
Nauru .......................................499-501
Pitcairn Islands .........................561-565
St. Helena ................................808-812
St. Lucia ...............................1155-1159
Seychelles ........................................830
Solomon Islands .......................945-947
South Georgia & So. Sandwich Isls. ....
...............................................281-285
Tokelau .....................................312-314
Tristan da Cunha .......................715-717
Virgin Islands ............................979-983

### Head of Queen Elizabeth II

CD362

**2003**

Ascension ........................................822
Bermuda ...........................................865
British Antarctic Territory ................322
British Indian Ocean Territory .........261
Cayman Islands ...............................878
Falkland Islands ..............................828
St. Helena .......................................820
South Georgia & South Sandwich
Islands .........................................294
Tristan da Cunha ............................731
Virgin Islands ................................1003

### Coronation of Queen Elizabeth II, 50th Anniv.

CD363

**2003**

Ascension ................................823-825
Bahamas ..............................1073-1075
Bermuda ...................................866-868
British Antarctic Territory ..........323-325
British Indian Ocean Territory ........262-264
Cayman Islands ........................879-881
Jamaica ....................................970-972
Kiribati .....................................825-827
Pitcairn Islands .........................577-581
St. Helena ................................821-823
St. Lucia ...............................1171-1173
Tokelau .....................................320-322
Tristan da Cunha .......................732-734
Virgin Islands ..........................1004-1006

### Prince William, 21st Birthday

CD364

**2003**

Ascension ........................................826
British Indian Ocean Territory .........265
Cayman Islands .......................882-884
Falkland Islands ..............................829
South Georgia & South Sandwich
Islands .........................................295
Tokelau ...........................................323
Tristan da Cunha ............................735
Virgin Islands ........................1007-1009

# British Commonwealth of Nations

## Dominions, Colonies, Territories, Offices and Independent Members

Comprising stamps of the British Commonwealth and associated nations.

A strict observance of technicalities would bar some or all of the stamps listed under Burma, Ireland, Kuwait, Nepal, New Republic, Orange Free State, Samoa, South Africa, South-West Africa, Stellaland, Sudan, Swaziland, the two Transvaal Republics and others but these are included for the convenience of collectors.

## 1. Great Britain

Great Britain: Including England, Scotland, Wales and Northern Ireland.

## 2. The Dominions, Present and Past

### AUSTRALIA

The Commonwealth of Australia was proclaimed on January 1, 1901. It consists of six former colonies as follows:

New South Wales
Queensland
South Australia
Victoria
Tasmania
Western Australia

The following islands and territories are, or have been, administered by Australia: Australian Antarctic Territory, Christmas Island, Cocos (Keeling) Islands, Nauru, New Guinea, Norfolk Island, Papua.

### CANADA

The Dominion of Canada was created by the British North America Act in 1867. The following provinces were former separate colonies and issued postage stamps:

British Columbia and Vancouver Island
New Brunswick
Newfoundland
Nova Scotia
Prince Edward Island

### FIJI

The colony of Fiji became an independent nation with dominion status on Oct. 10, 1970.

### GHANA

This state came into existence Mar. 6, 1957, with dominion status. It consists of the former colony of the Gold Coast and the Trusteeship Territory of Togoland. Ghana became a republic July 1, 1960.

### INDIA

The Republic of India was inaugurated on January 26, 1950. It succeeded the Dominion of India which was proclaimed August 15, 1947, when the former Empire of India was divided into Pakistan and the Union of India. The Republic is composed of about 40 predominantly Hindu states of three classes: governor's provinces, chief commissioner's provinces and princely states. India also has various territories, such as the Andaman and Nicobar Islands.

The old Empire of India was a federation of British India and the native states. The more important princely states were autonomous. Of the more than 700 Indian states, these 43 are familiar names to philatelists because of their postage stamps.

### CONVENTION STATES

Chamba
Faridkot
Gwalior
Jhind
Nabha
Patiala

### NATIVE FEUDATORY STATES

Alwar
Bahawalpur
Bamra
Barwani
Bhopal
Bhor
Bijawar
Bundi
Bussahir
Charkhari
Cochin
Dhar
Duttia
Faridkot (1879-85)
Hyderabad
Idar
Indore
Jaipur
Jammu
Jammu and Kashmir
Jasdan
Jhalawar
Jhind (1875-76)
Kashmir
Kishangarh
Las Bela
Morvi
Nandgaon
Nowanuggur
Orchha
Poonch
Rajpeepla
Sirmur
Soruth
Travancore
Wadhwan

### NEW ZEALAND

Became a dominion on September 26, 1907. The following islands and territories are, or have been, administered by New Zealand:

Aitutaki
Cook Islands (Rarotonga)
Niue
Penrhyn
Ross Dependency
Samoa (Western Samoa)
Tokelau Islands

### PAKISTAN

The Republic of Pakistan was proclaimed March 23, 1956. It succeeded the Dominion which was proclaimed August 15, 1947. It is made up of all or part of several Moslem provinces and various districts of the former Empire of India, including Bahawalpur and Las Bela. Pakistan withdrew from the Commonwealth in 1972.

### SOUTH AFRICA

Under the terms of the South African Act (1909) the self-governing colonies of Cape of Good Hope, Natal, Orange River Colony and Transvaal united on May 31, 1910, to form the Union of South Africa. It became an independent republic May 3, 1961.

Under the terms of the Treaty of Versailles, South-West Africa, formerly German South-West Africa, was mandated to the Union of South Africa.

### SRI LANKA (CEYLON)

The Dominion of Ceylon was proclaimed February 4, 1948. The island had been a Crown Colony from 1802 until then. On May 22, 1972, Ceylon became the Republic of Sri Lanka.

## 3. Colonies, Past and Present; ControlledTerritory and Independent Members of the Commonwealth

Aden
Aitutaki
Antigua
Ascension
Bahamas
Bahrain
Bangladesh
Barbados
Barbuda
Basutoland
Batum
Bechuanaland
Bechuanaland Prot.
Belize
Bermuda
Botswana
British Antarctic Territory
British Central Africa
British Columbia and Vancouver Island
British East Africa
British Guiana

British Honduras
British Indian Ocean Territory
British New Guinea
British Solomon Islands
British Somaliland
Brunei
Burma
Bushire
Cameroons
Cape of Good Hope
Cayman Islands
Christmas Island
Cocos (Keeling) Islands
Cook Islands
Crete,
British Administration
Cyprus
Dominica
East Africa & Uganda
Protectorates
Egypt
Falkland Islands
Fiji
Gambia
German East Africa
Gibraltar
Gilbert Islands
Gilbert & Ellice Islands
Gold Coast
Grenada
Griqualand West
Guernsey
Guyana
Heligoland
Hong Kong
Indian Native States
(see India)
Ionian Islands
Jamaica
Jersey

Kenya
Kenya, Uganda & Tanzania
Kuwait
Labuan
Lagos
Leeward Islands
Lesotho
Madagascar
Malawi
Malaya
Federated Malay States
Johore
Kedah
Kelantan
Malacca
Negri Sembilan
Pahang
Penang
Perak
Perlis
Selangor
Singapore
Sungei Ujong
Trengganu
Malaysia
Maldive Islands
Malta
Man, Isle of
Mauritius
Mesopotamia
Montserrat
Muscat
Namibia
Natal
Nauru
Nevis
New Britain
New Brunswick
Newfoundland
New Guinea

New Hebrides
New Republic
New South Wales
Niger Coast Protectorate
Nigeria
Niue
Norfolk Island
North Borneo
Northern Nigeria
Northern Rhodesia
North West Pacific Islands
Nova Scotia
Nyasaland Protectorate
Oman
Orange River Colony
Palestine
Papua New Guinea
Penrhyn Island
Pitcairn Islands
Prince Edward Island
Queensland
Rhodesia
Rhodesia & Nyasaland
Ross Dependency
Sabah
St. Christopher
St. Helena
St. Kitts
St. Kitts-Nevis-Anguilla
St. Lucia
St. Vincent
Samoa
Sarawak
Seychelles
Sierra Leone
Solomon Islands
Somaliland Protectorate
South Arabia
South Australia
South Georgia

Southern Nigeria
Southern Rhodesia
South-West Africa
Stellaland
Straits Settlements
Sudan
Swaziland
Tanganyika
Tanzania
Tasmania
Tobago
Togo
Tokelau Islands
Tonga
Transvaal
Trinidad
Trinidad and Tobago
Tristan da Cunha
Trucial States
Turks and Caicos
Turks Islands
Tuvalu
Uganda
United Arab Emirates
Victoria
Virgin Islands
Western Australia
Zambia
Zanzibar
Zululand

**POST OFFICES IN FOREIGN COUNTRIES**

Africa
East Africa Forces
Middle East Forces
Bangkok
China
Morocco
Turkish Empire

# Colonies, Former Colonies, Offices, Territories Controlled by Parent States

## Belgium

Belgian Congo
Ruanda-Urundi

## Denmark

Danish West Indies
Faroe Islands
Greenland
Iceland

## Finland

Aland Islands

## France

### COLONIES PAST AND PRESENT, CONTROLLED TERRITORIES

Afars & Issas, Territory of
Alaouites
Alexandretta
Algeria
Alsace & Lorraine
Anjouan
Annam & Tonkin
Benin
Cambodia (Khmer)
Cameroun
Castellorizo
Chad
Cilicia
Cochin China
Comoro Islands
Dahomey
Diego Suarez
Djibouti (Somali Coast)
Fezzan
French Congo
French Equatorial Africa
French Guiana
French Guinea
French India
French Morocco
French Polynesia (Oceania)
French Southern &
Antarctic Territories
French Sudan
French West Africa
Gabon
Germany
Ghadames
Grand Comoro
Guadeloupe
Indo-China
Inini
Ivory Coast
Laos
Latakia
Lebanon
Madagascar
Martinique
Mauritania
Mayotte
Memel
Middle Congo
Moheli
New Caledonia
New Hebrides
Niger Territory
Nossi-Be
Obock
Reunion
Rouad, Ile
Ste.-Marie de Madagascar
St. Pierre & Miquelon
Senegal
Senegambia & Niger
Somali Coast
Syria
Tahiti
Togo
Tunisia
Ubangi-Shari
Upper Senegal & Niger
Upper Volta
Viet Nam
Wallis & Futuna Islands

### POST OFFICES IN FOREIGN COUNTRIES

China
Crete
Egypt
Turkish Empire
Zanzibar

## Germany

### EARLY STATES

Baden
Bavaria
Bergedorf
Bremen
Brunswick
Hamburg
Hanover
Lubeck
Mecklenburg-Schwerin
Mecklenburg-Strelitz
Oldenburg
Prussia
Saxony
Schleswig-Holstein
Wurttemberg

### FORMER COLONIES

Cameroun (Kamerun)
Caroline Islands
German East Africa
German New Guinea
German South-West Africa
Kiauchau
Mariana Islands
Marshall Islands
Samoa
Togo

## Italy

### EARLY STATES

Modena
Parma
Romagna
Roman States
Sardinia
Tuscany
Two Sicilies
  Naples
  Neapolitan Provinces
  Sicily

### FORMER COLONIES, CONTROLLED TERRITORIES, OCCUPATION AREAS

Aegean Islands
  Calimno (Calino)
  Caso
  Cos (Coo)
  Karki (Carchi)
  Leros (Lero)
  Lipso
  Nisiros (Nisiro)
  Patmos (Patmo)
  Piscopi
  Rodi (Rhodes)
  Scarpanto
  Simi
  Stampalia
Castellorizo
Corfu
Cyrenaica
Eritrea
Ethiopia (Abyssinia)
Fiume
Ionian Islands
  Cephalonia
  Ithaca
  Paxos
Italian East Africa
Libya
Oltre Giuba
Saseno
Somalia (Italian Somaliland)
Tripolitania

### POST OFFICES IN FOREIGN COUNTRIES

"ESTERO"*
Austria
China
  Peking
  Tientsin
Crete
Tripoli
Turkish Empire
  Constantinople
  Durazzo
  Janina
Jerusalem
Salonika
Scutari
Smyrna
Valona

*Stamps overprinted "ESTERO" were used in various parts of the world.

## Netherlands

Aruba
Netherlands Antilles (Curacao)
Netherlands Indies
Netherlands New Guinea
Surinam (Dutch Guiana)

## Portugal

### COLONIES PAST AND PRESENT, CONTROLLED TERRITORIES

Angola
Angra
Azores
Cape Verde
Funchal
Horta
Inhambane
Kionga
Lourenco Marques
Macao
Madeira
Mozambique
Mozambique Co.
Nyassa
Ponta Delgada
Portuguese Africa
Portuguese Congo
Portuguese Guinea
Portuguese India
Quelimane
St. Thomas & Prince Islands
Tete
Timor
Zambezia

## Russia

### ALLIED TERRITORIES AND REPUBLICS, OCCUPATION AREAS

Armenia
Aunus (Olonets)
Azerbaijan
Batum
Estonia
Far Eastern Republic
Georgia
Karelia
Latvia
Lithuania
North Ingermanland
Ostland
Russian Turkestan
Siberia
South Russia
Tannu Tuva
Transcaucasian Fed. Republics
Ukraine
Wenden (Livonia)
Western Ukraine

## Spain

### COLONIES PAST AND PRESENT, CONTROLLED TERRITORIES

Aguera, La
Cape Juby
Cuba
Elobey, Annobon & Corisco
Fernando Po
Ifni
Mariana Islands
Philippines
Puerto Rico
Rio de Oro
Rio Muni
Spanish Guinea
Spanish Morocco
Spanish Sahara
Spanish West Africa

### POST OFFICES IN FOREIGN COUNTRIES

Morocco
Tangier
Tetuan

# Dies of British Colonial Stamps

DIE A

DIE B

**DIE A:**
**1.** The lines in the groundwork vary in thickness and are not uniformly straight.
**2.** The seventh and eighth lines from the top, in the groundwork, converge where they meet the head.
**3.** There is a small dash in the upper part of the second jewel in the band of the crown.
**4.** The vertical color line in front of the throat stops at the sixth line of shading on the neck.

**DIE B:**
**1.** The lines in the groundwork are all thin and straight.
**2.** All the lines of the background are parallel.
**3.** There is no dash in the upper part of the second jewel in the band of the crown.
**4.** The vertical color line in front of the throat stops at the eighth line of shading on the neck.

DIE I

DIE II

**DIE I:**
**1.** The base of the crown is well below the level of the inner white line around the vignette.
**2.** The labels inscribed "POSTAGE" and "REVENUE" are cut square at the top.
**3.** There is a white "bud" on the outer side of the main stem of the curved ornaments in each lower corner.
**4.** The second (thick) line below the country name has the ends next to the crown cut diagonally.

| DIE Ia. | DIE Ib. |
|---|---|
| 1 as die II. | 1 and 3 as die II. |
| 2 and 3 as die I. | 2 as die I. |

**DIE II:**
**1.** The base of the crown is aligned with the underside of the white line around the vignette.
**2.** The labels curve inward at the top inner corners.
**3.** The "bud" has been removed from the outer curve of the ornaments in each corner.
**4.** The second line below the country name has the ends next to the crown cut vertically.

Wmk. 1
Crown and C C

Wmk. 2
Crown and C A

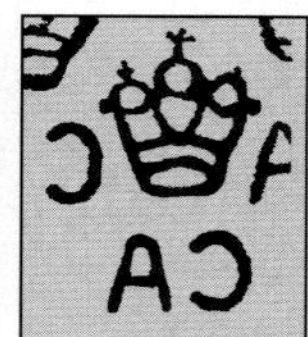
Wmk. 3
Multiple Crown and C A

Wmk. 4
Multiple Crown and Script C A

Wmk. 4a

Wmk. 314
St. Edward's Crown and C A Multiple

Wmk. 373

Wmk. 384

# British Colonial and Crown Agents Watermarks

Watermarks 1 to 4, 314, 373, and 384, common to many British territories, are illustrated here to avoid duplication.

The letters "CC" of Wmk. 1 identify the paper as having been made for the use of the Crown Colonies, while the letters "CA" of the others stand for "Crown Agents." Both Wmks. 1 and 2 were used on stamps printed by De La Rue & Co.

Wmk. 3 was adopted in 1904; Wmk. 4 in 1921; Wmk. 314 in 1957; Wmk. 373 in 1974; and Wmk. 384 in 1985.

In Wmk. 4a, a non-matching crown of the general St. Edwards type (bulging on both sides at top) was substituted for one of the Wmk. 4 crowns which fell off the dandy roll. The non-matching crown occurs in 1950-52 printings in a horizontal row of crowns on certain regular stamps of Johore and Seychelles, and on various postage due stamps of Barbados, Basutoland, British Guiana, Gold Coast, Grenada, Northern Rhodesia, St. Lucia, Swaziland and Trinidad and Tobago. A variation of Wmk. 4a, with the non-matching crown in a horizontal row of crown-CA-crown, occurs on regular stamps of Bahamas, St. Kitts-Nevis and Singapore.

Wmk. 314 was intentionally used sideways, starting in 1966. When a stamp was issued with Wmk. 314 both upright and sideways, the sideways varieties usually are listed also – with minor numbers. In many of the later issues, Wmk. 314 is slightly visible.

Wmk. 373 is usually only faintly visible.

## SOLOMON ISLANDS

'sä-lə-mən 'ī-lənds

British Solomon Islands

LOCATION — West Pacific Ocean, east of Papua
GOVT. — Independent state in British Commonwealth
AREA — 10,954 sq. mi.
POP. — 455,429 (1999 est.)
CAPITAL — Honiara

The Solomons include 10 large islands and four groups of small islands extending over an area of 375,000 square miles.

The British protectorate of British Solomon Islands changed its name to Solomon Islands in 1975 and achieved independence July 7, 1978.

12 Pence = 1 Shilling
20 Shillings = 1 Pound
100 Cents = 1 Dollar (1966)

**Catalogue values for unused stamps in this country are for Never Hinged items, beginning with Scott 80 in the regular postage section and Scott B1 in the semi-postal section.**

War Canoe — A1

**Unwmk.**

**1907, Feb. 14 Litho. *Perf. 11***

1 A1 ½p ultra 10.50 *16.00*
2 A1 1p red 26.00 *30.00*
3 A1 2p dull blue 32.50 *35.00*
*a.* Horiz. pair, imperf. btwn. *12,500.*
4 A1 2½p orange 37.50 *47.50*
*a.* Vert. pair, imperf. btwn. *4,500.*
*b.* Horiz. pair, imperf. btwn. *6,250.* *4,750.*
5 A1 5p yellow green 65.00 *77.50*
6 A1 6p chocolate 60.00 *72.50*
*a.* Vertical pair, imperf. btwn. *4,250.*
7 A1 1sh violet 85.00 *90.00*
*Nos. 1-7 (7)* 316.50 *368.50*

Imperf. between varieties should be accompanied by certificates of authenticity issued by competent authorities. Excellent counterfeits are plentiful.

War Canoe A2

George V A3

**Wmk. Multiple Crown and CA (3)**

**1908-11 Engr. *Perf. 14***

8 A2 ½p green 1.75 1.10
9 A2 1p carmine 1.50 1.10
10 A2 2p gray 1.50 1.10
11 A2 2½p ultra 4.25 2.25
12 A2 4p red, *yel* ('11) 3.75 12.50
13 A2 5p olive green 10.50 8.00
14 A2 6p claret 11.50 7.50
15 A2 1sh black, *green* 9.75 8.00
16 A2 2sh vio, *bl* ('10) 47.50 *65.00*
17 A2 2sh6p red, *bl* ('10) 57.50 *85.00*
18 A2 5sh bl, *yel* ('10) 90.00 *125.00*
*Nos. 8-18 (11)* 239.50 *316.55*

Inscribed "POSTAGE — POSTAGE"

**1913-24 Typo.**

19 A3 ½p green .95 *4.00*
20 A3 1p carmine 1.75 *16.00*
21 A3 3p violet, *yel* 1.00 *4.75*
*a.* 3p violet, *orange buff* 5.00 *27.50*
22 A3 11p dull violet & red 5.75 *13.50*

**Wmk. 4**

23 A3 1½p scarlet ('24) 2.50 .80
*Nos. 19-23 (5)* 11.95 *39.05*

Inscribed "POSTAGE — REVENUE"

**1914-23 Wmk. 3**

28 A3 ½p green .95 *13.50*
*a.* ½p yellow green ('17) 5.25 *21.00*
29 A3 1p carmine 1.75 1.50
*a.* 1p scarlet ('17) 5.50 *7.50*
30 A3 2p gray 3.50 *10.50*
31 A3 2½p ultra 2.25 *5.75*

**Chalky Paper**

32 A3 3p violet, *yel* ('23) 22.50 *97.50*
33 A3 4p blk & red, *yel* 2.25 *3.00*
34 A3 5p dull vio & ol grn 22.50 *35.00*
*a.* 5p brown purple & olive green 22.50 *35.00*
35 A3 6p dull vio & red vio 7.00 *16.00*
36 A3 1sh blk, *green* 5.50 *8.00*
*a.* 1sh blk, *bl grn*, ol back 8.50 *27.50*
37 A3 2sh dull vio & ultra, *bl* 8.00 *11.50*
38 A3 2sh6p blk & red, *bl* 11.00 *22.50*
39 A3 5sh grn & red, *yel* 37.50 *55.00*
*a.* 5sh green & red, *orange buff* 52.50 *80.00*
40 A3 10sh grn & red, *grn* 95.00 *92.50*
41 A3 £1 vio & blk, *red* 275.00 140.00
*Nos. 28-41 (14)* 494.70 *512.25*

Inscribed "POSTAGE - REVENUE"

**1922-31 Wmk. 4**

43 A3 ½p green .40 *4.00*
44 A3 1p carmine ('23) 12.50 12.50
45 A3 1p violet ('27) 1.10 *8.50*
46 A3 2p gray ('23) 4.50 *17.00*
47 A3 3p ultra ('23) .85 *5.25*

**Chalky Paper**

48 A3 4p blk & red, *yel* ('27) 4.00 *26.00*
49 A3 4½p red brn ('31) 3.50 *22.50*
50 A3 5p dull vio & ol grn 3.50 *30.00*
51 A3 6p dull vio & red vio 4.25 *30.00*
52 A3 1sh black, *emer* 3.25 *14.00*
53 A3 2sh dull vio & ultra, *bl* ('27) 9.25 *42.50*
54 A3 2sh6p blk & red, *bl* 8.50 *45.00*
55 A3 5sh grn & red, *yel* 30.00 *62.50*
56 A3 10sh grn & red, *emer* ('25) 110.00 *110.00*
*Nos. 43-56 (14)* 195.60 *429.75*

No. 49 is on ordinary paper.

**Common Design Types**
pictured following the introduction.

**Silver Jubilee Issue**
Common Design Type

**1935, May 6 Engr. *Perf. 13½x14***

60 CD301 1½p car & dk bl 1.25 1.00
61 CD301 3p blue & brown 3.50 *6.50*
62 CD301 6p ol grn & lt bl 10.50 *13.00*
63 CD301 1sh brt vio & ind 8.50 *12.00*
*Nos. 60-63 (4)* 23.75 *32.50*
Set, never hinged 42.50

**Coronation Issue**
Common Design Type

**1937, May 13 *Perf. 11x11½***

64 CD302 1p dark purple .25 *.60*
65 CD302 1½p dark carmine .25 *.50*
66 CD302 3p deep ultra .40 *.40*
*Nos. 64-66 (3)* .90 *1.50*
Set, never hinged 1.25

Spears and Shield — A4

Policeman and Chief — A5

Artificial Island, Malaita — A6

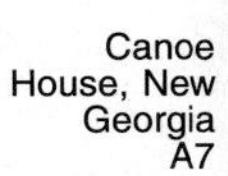
Canoe House, New Georgia A7

Roviana War Canoe — A8

View of Munda Point — A9

Meeting House, Reef Islands A10

Coconut Plantation A11

Breadfruit A12

Tinakula Volcano, Santa Cruz Islands A13

Scrub Fowl — A14

Malaita Canoe — A15

***Perf. 12½, 13½ (A7, A13, A14)***

**1939-51 Wmk. 4**

67 A4 ½p deep grn & ultra .20 *1.10*
68 A5 1p dk pur & choc .20 *1.75*
69 A6 1½p car & sl grn .30 *1.50*
70 A7 2p blk & org brn .35 *1.60*
*a.* 2p black & red brown ('43) .35 *1.75*
Never hinged .70
*b.* Perf. 12 ('51) .20 *1.60*
Never hinged .35
71 A8 2½p ol grn & rose vio 1.00 *2.50*
*a.* Vert. pair, imperf. horiz. *11,500.*
72 A9 3p ultra & blk, perf. 13½ .55 *1.75*
*a.* Perf. 12 ('51) .85 *2.75*
Never hinged 1.75
73 A10 4½p dk brn & yel grn 3.25 *14.00*
74 A11 6p rose lil & dk pur .30 *1.10*
75 A12 1sh blk & grn .70 *1.10*
76 A13 2sh dp org & blk 4.25 *4.50*
*a.* 2sh dp org & vio blk ('43) 4.25 *5.00*
Never hinged 5.50
77 A14 2sh6p dull vio & blk 17.00 6.00
78 A15 5sh red & brt bl green 20.00 13.00
79 A10 10sh red lil & ol ('42) 6.00 *9.50*
*Nos. 67-79 (13)* 54.10 *59.40*
Set, never hinged 100.00

**Catalogue values for unused stamps in this section, from this point to the end of the section, are for Never Hinged items.**

**Peace Issue**
Common Design Type
***Perf. 13½x14***

**1946, Oct. 15 Wmk. 4 Engr.**

80 CD303 1½p carmine .20 .70
81 CD303 3p deep blue .20 .30

**Silver Wedding Issue**
Common Design Types

**1949, Mar. 14 Photo. *Perf. 14x14½***

82 CD304 2p black .40 .40

***Perf. 11½x11***

**Engr.; Name Typo.**

83 CD305 10sh red violet 17.50 13.50

**UPU Issue**
Common Design Types
**Engr.; Name Typo. on 3p and 5p**
***Perf. 13½, 11x11½***

**1949, Oct. 10 Wmk. 4**

84 CD306 2p red brown 1.00 .85
85 CD307 3p indigo 2.40 .85
86 CD308 5p green 1.00 *1.25*
87 CD309 1sh slate 1.00 .85
*Nos. 84-87 (4)* 5.40 3.80

**Coronation Issue**
Common Design Type

**1953, June 2 Engr. *Perf. 13½x13***

88 CD312 2p gray & black .80 .50

Ysabel Canoe A16

Prow of Roviana Canoe — A17

Designs: 1p, Roviana canoe. 1½p, Artificial Island, Malaita. 2p, Canoe house. 3p, Malaita canoe. 5p, 1sh3p, Map. 6p, Trading schooner. 8p, 9p, Henderson Field, Guadalcanal. 1sh, Chart of Solomons and H.M.S. Swallow, recalling Capt. Philip Carteret's voyage of 1767. 2sh, Tinakula Volcano. 2sh6p, Meeting house, Reef Islands. 5sh, Alvaro de Mendana de Neyra and Caravel. 10sh, Constable and Chief. £1, Coat of Arms.

***Perf. 11½x11, 11x11½, 12, 13***

**1956-60 Engr. Wmk. 4**

89 A16 ½p lilac & orange .20 *.50*
90 A16 1p red brn & ol grn .20 .20
91 A16 1½p dk car & sl bl .20 *.90*
92 A16 2p gray grn & choc .20 *.25*
93 A17 2½p gray bl & blk .75 *.75*
94 A16 3p dull red & grn .40 .20
95 A16 5p blue & black .20 *.60*
96 A16 6p bluish grn & blk .35 .20
97 A16 8p black & ultra .40 .20
98 A16 9p black & brt grn 2.50 .70
99 A16 1sh brn org & sl bl .75 *.75*
100 A16 1sh3p blue & black 6.75 1.50
101 A16 2sh car rose & blk 12.50 1.50
102 A17 2sh6p rose lil & emer 9.00 .50
103 A16 5sh red brown 17.50 6.00

| | | | | |
|---|---|---|---|---|
| **104** | A17 | 10sh black brown | 24.00 | 7.00 |
| **105** | A16 | £1 lt blue & blk | 37.50 | *40.00* |
| | | *Nos. 89-105 (17)* | 113.40 | 61.75 |

Issued: £1, 11/5/58; 9p, 1sh3p, 1/28/60; others, 3/1/56.

See Nos. 113-125.

Great Frigate Bird — A18

***Perf. 13x12½***

**1961, Jan. 19 Litho. Wmk. 314**

| | | | | |
|---|---|---|---|---|
| **106** | A18 | 2p blue green & black | .20 | *.25* |
| **107** | A18 | 3p rose red & black | .20 | .20 |
| **108** | A18 | 9p lilac & black | .25 | *.40* |
| | | *Nos. 106-108 (3)* | .65 | .85 |

New constitution, brought into operation Oct. 18, 1960. The watermark is sideways and may be found facing both left and right.

### Freedom from Hunger Issue

Common Design Type

**1963, June 4 Photo. *Perf. 14x14½***

| | | | | |
|---|---|---|---|---|
| **109** | CD314 | 1sh3p ultra | 3.50 | 1.50 |

### Red Cross Centenary Issue

Common Design Type

**1963, Sept. 2 Litho. *Perf. 13***

| | | | | |
|---|---|---|---|---|
| **110** | CD315 | 2p black & red | .40 | .25 |
| **111** | CD315 | 9p ultra & red | 2.00 | 1.75 |

Types of 1956-60

***Perf. 12, 13, 11½x11***

**1963-64 Engr. Wmk. 314**

| | | | | |
|---|---|---|---|---|
| **113** | A16 | 1p red brn & ol grn | .35 | .30 |
| **114** | A16 | 1½p dk car & sl bl | .35 | *.80* |
| **115** | A16 | 2p gray grn & choc | .25 | .25 |
| **117** | A16 | 3p dull red & grn | .70 | .20 |
| **119** | A16 | 6p bluish grn & blk | .90 | .40 |
| **121** | A16 | 9p black & brt grn | 1.00 | .45 |
| **123** | A16 | 1sh3p blue & blk | 1.10 | *1.25* |
| **124** | A16 | 2sh car rose & blk | 2.75 | *5.75* |
| **125** | A17 | 2sh6p rose lil & emer | 17.50 | 14.50 |
| | | *Nos. 113-125 (9)* | 24.90 | 23.90 |

Issued: 3p, 11/16; 6p, 9p, 1sh3p, 7/7/64; 1p, 1½p, 2p, 2sh, 2sh6p, 7/9/64.

### ITU Issue

Common Design Type

***Perf. 11x11½***

**1965, June 28 Litho. Wmk. 314**

| | | | | |
|---|---|---|---|---|
| **126** | CD317 | 2p ver & grnsh blue | .35 | .25 |
| **127** | CD317 | 3p grnsh bl & ol bis | .55 | .40 |

Makira Food Bowl — A19

Designs: 1p, 1sh, 1sh3p, Various orchids. 1½p, Scorpion shell. 2p, Papuan hornbill. 2½p, Ysabel shield. 3p, Rennellese club. 6p, Moorish idol (fish). 9p, Great frigate bird. 2sh, Sanford's sea eagle. 2sh6p, Malaita belt. 5sh, Ornithoptera Victoreae (butterfly). 10sh, White cockatoo. £1, Figurehead, western canoe.

***Perf. 13x12½***

**1965, May 24 Litho. Wmk. 314**

**Design Subject in Black**

| | | | | |
|---|---|---|---|---|
| **128** | A19 | ½p sl blue & lt bl | .20 | *1.25* |
| **129** | A19 | 1p orange & yel | .45 | .30 |
| **130** | A19 | 1½p blue & yel grn | .25 | *1.25* |
| **131** | A19 | 2p vio bl & lt bl | .35 | *1.25* |
| **132** | A19 | 2½p red brn & buff | .20 | *.40* |
| **133** | A19 | 3p grn & lt grn | .20 | .20 |
| **134** | A19 | 6p brt car rose & org | .25 | *.70* |
| **135** | A19 | 9p slate grn & buff | .50 | .20 |
| **136** | A19 | 1sh dp cl & rose | 1.10 | .20 |
| **137** | A19 | 1sh3p ver & buff | 4.75 | 2.10 |
| **138** | A19 | 2sh dp mag & lil | 9.00 | 2.75 |
| **139** | A19 | 2sh6p ol brn & buff | 1.10 | .65 |
| **140** | A19 | 5sh dk vio bl & lil | 13.50 | 4.75 |
| **141** | A19 | 10sh ol grn & yel | 16.50 | 3.75 |
| **142** | A19 | £1 purple & red | 10.00 | 4.75 |
| | | *Nos. 128-142 (15)* | 58.35 | 24.50 |

For surcharges see Nos. 149-166.

### Intl. Cooperation Year Issue

Common Design Type

**1965, Oct. 25 Litho. *Perf. 14½***

| | | | | |
|---|---|---|---|---|
| **143** | CD318 | 1p bl grn & cl | .20 | .20 |
| **144** | CD318 | 2sh6p lt violet & grn | 1.10 | .90 |

### Churchill Memorial Issue

Common Design Type

**1966, Jan. 24 Photo. *Perf. 14***

| | | | | |
|---|---|---|---|---|
| **145** | CD319 | 2p multicolored | .25 | *.30* |
| **146** | CD319 | 9p multicolored | .45 | .30 |
| **147** | CD319 | 1sh3p multicolored | .60 | .30 |
| **148** | CD319 | 2sh6p multicolored | .70 | *.85* |
| | | *Nos. 145-148 (4)* | 2.00 | 1.75 |

Nos. 128-142 Surcharged with New Value and Three Bars in Black or Red

***Perf. 13x12½***

**1966-67 Litho. Wmk. 314**

| | | | | |
|---|---|---|---|---|
| **149** | A19 | 1c on ½p multi | .20 | .20 |
| **150** | A19 | 2c on 1p multi | .20 | .20 |
| **151** | A19 | 3c on 1½p multi | .20 | .20 |
| **152** | A19 | 4c on 2p multi | .20 | .20 |
| **153** | A19 | 5c on 6p multi | .20 | .20 |
| **154** | A19 | 6c on 2½p multi | .20 | .20 |
| **155** | A19 | 7c on 3p multi | .30 | .30 |
| **156** | A19 | 8c on 9p multi | .35 | .35 |
| *b.* | | "8" inverted | 25.00 | 20.00 |
| **157** | A19 | 10c on 1sh | .45 | .45 |
| **158** | A19 | 12c on 1sh3p multi | .80 | .45 |
| **159** | A19 | 13c on 1sh3p multi | 4.00 | .50 |
| **160** | A19 | 14c on 3p multi | .65 | .50 |
| **161** | A19 | 20c on 2sh multi | 4.00 | .85 |
| **162** | A19 | 25c on 2sh6p multi | 3.00 | 1.10 |
| **163** | A19 | 35c on 2p multi | 2.75 | 1.60 |
| **164** | A19 | 50c on 5sh multi (R) | 10.00 | 2.25 |
| **165** | A19 | $1 on 10sh multi | 8.50 | 1.75 |
| **166** | A19 | $2 on £1 multi | 8.75 | 2.75 |
| | | *Nos. 149-166 (18)* | 44.75 | 14.05 |

The 12c, 14c, 35c have watermark sideways.

Issued: 12c, 14c, 35c, 3/1/67; others, 2/14/66.

**1966 Wmk. 314 Sideways**

| | | | | |
|---|---|---|---|---|
| *149a* | A19 | 1c on ½p | .20 | .20 |
| *150a* | A19 | 2c on 1p | .20 | .20 |
| *151a* | A19 | 3c on 1½p | .20 | .20 |
| *152a* | A19 | 4c on 2p | .25 | .25 |
| *153a* | A19 | 5c on 6p | .30 | .30 |
| *154a* | A19 | 6c on 2½p | .35 | .35 |
| *155a* | A19 | 7c on 3p | .40 | .40 |
| *156a* | A19 | 8c on 9p | .45 | .45 |
| *157a* | A19 | 10c on 1sh | .60 | .60 |
| *159a* | A19 | 13c on 1sh3p | .75 | .75 |
| *161a* | A19 | 20c on 2sh | 1.25 | 1.25 |
| *162a* | A19 | 25c on 2sh6p | 1.50 | 1.50 |
| *164a* | A19 | 50c on 5sh (R) | 3.00 | 3.00 |
| *165a* | A19 | $1 on 10sh | 6.00 | 6.00 |
| *166a* | A19 | $2 on £1 | 9.00 | 9.00 |
| | | *Nos. 149a-166a (15)* | 24.45 | 24.45 |

### World Cup Soccer Issue

Common Design Type

**1966, July 1 Litho. *Perf. 14***

| | | | | |
|---|---|---|---|---|
| **167** | CD321 | 8c multicolored | .30 | .30 |
| **168** | CD321 | 35c multicolored | 1.10 | 1.10 |

### WHO Headquarters Issue

Common Design Type

**1966, Sept. 20 Litho. *Perf. 14***

| | | | | |
|---|---|---|---|---|
| **169** | CD322 | 3c multicolored | .20 | .20 |
| **170** | CD322 | 50c multicolored | 1.60 | 1.60 |

### UNESCO Anniversary Issue

Common Design Type

**1966, Dec. 1 Litho. *Perf. 14***

| | | | | |
|---|---|---|---|---|
| **171** | CD323 | 3c "Education" | .40 | .20 |
| **172** | CD323 | 25c "Science" | .95 | .40 |
| **173** | CD323 | $1 "Culture" | 2.40 | 1.90 |
| | | *Nos. 171-173 (3)* | 3.75 | 2.50 |

Henderson Field, Guadalcanal — A20

Design: 35c, US Marines landing, Red Beach, Guadalcanal, 1942.

***Perf. 14x14½***

**1967, Aug. 28 Photo. Wmk. 314**

| | | | | |
|---|---|---|---|---|
| **174** | A20 | 8c multi & silver | .20 | .20 |
| **175** | A20 | 35c multi & gold | .75 | .75 |

Guadalcanal campaign in WW II, 25th anniv.

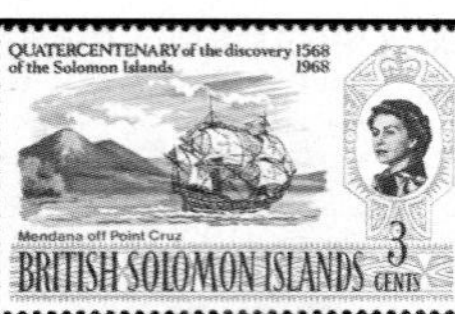


Mendana's Ship Off Puerta de la Cruz (Honiara), Guadalcanal, 1568 — A21

Designs: 8c, Arrival of Missionaries. 35c, Naval battle during World War II. $1, Honor guard raising Union Jack during proclamation of Protectorate.

**1968, Feb. 2 Photo. *Perf. 14½***

| | | | | |
|---|---|---|---|---|
| **176** | A21 | 3c pink & multi | .40 | .20 |
| **177** | A21 | 8c emerald & multi | .40 | .20 |
| **178** | A21 | 35c multicolored | .85 | .20 |
| **179** | A21 | $1 blue & multi | 1.10 | *2.25* |
| | | *Nos. 176-179 (4)* | 2.75 | 2.85 |

400th anniv. of the discovery of the British Solomon Islands by the Spanish navigator Alvaro de Mendana de Neyra.

Vine Fishing A22

Designs: 2c, Kite fishing. 3c, Platform fishing. 4c, Net fishing. 6c, Gold lip shell diving. 8c, Night fishing. 12c, Boat building. 14c, Cocoa harvest. 15c, Road building. 20c, Geological survey by plane. 24c, Hauling timber. 35c, Copra. 45c, Harvesting rice. $1, Honiara Port. $2, Map of the Islands, plane and route of Internal Air Service.

**Wmk. 314**

**1968, May 20 Photo. *Perf. 14½***

| | | | | |
|---|---|---|---|---|
| **180** | A22 | 1c aqua, brn & blk | .20 | .20 |
| **181** | A22 | 2c lt yel grn, brn & blk | .20 | .20 |
| **182** | A22 | 3c brt grn, dk grn & blk | .20 | .20 |
| **183** | A22 | 4c brt rose lil, brn & blk | .20 | .20 |
| **184** | A22 | 6c multicolored | .30 | .20 |
| **185** | A22 | 8c dp ultra, org & blk | .20 | .30 |
| **186** | A22 | 12c bister, red & blk | .85 | .35 |
| **187** | A22 | 14c red org, brn & blk | 4.00 | *2.25* |
| **188** | A22 | 15c multicolored | .90 | .70 |
| **189** | A22 | 20c ultra, red & blk | 4.75 | 3.25 |
| **190** | A22 | 24c scarlet, yel & blk | 2.50 | *3.75* |
| **191** | A22 | 35c multicolored | 2.50 | .45 |
| **192** | A22 | 45c yellow, red & blk | 2.00 | .45 |
| **193** | A22 | $1 vio bl, emer & blk | 3.00 | 1.75 |
| **194** | A22 | $2 multicolored | 7.50 | 4.00 |
| | | *Nos. 180-194 (15)* | 29.30 | 18.25 |

Map of South Pacific and University Degrees — A23

***Perf. 12½x12***

**1969, Feb. 10 Litho. Unwmk.**

| | | | | |
|---|---|---|---|---|
| **195** | A23 | 3c multicolored | .20 | .20 |
| **196** | A23 | 12c multicolored | .25 | .20 |
| **197** | A23 | 35c multicolored | .55 | .50 |
| | | *Nos. 195-197 (3)* | 1.00 | .90 |

Inauguration of the University of the South Pacific in 1969, at the Royal New Zealand Air Force Seaplane Station, Laucala Bay, Fiji.

Field Ball and Games' Emblem — A24

Stained Glass Window with Melanesian Peace Symbol — A25

***Perf. 14½x14***

**1969, Aug. 13 Photo. Wmk. 314**

| | | | | |
|---|---|---|---|---|
| **198** | A24 | 3c shown | .20 | .20 |
| **199** | A24 | 8c Soccer | .20 | .20 |
| **200** | A24 | 14c Running | .35 | .30 |
| **201** | A24 | 45c Rugby | 1.10 | .95 |
| *a.* | | Souvenir sheet of 4, #198-201 | 6.25 | 6.25 |
| | | *Nos. 198-201 (4)* | 1.85 | 1.65 |

3rd S. Pacific Games, Port Moresby, Aug. 13-23.

In No. 201a, shading was added below athlete's foot on 14c, and strengthened on 8c and 45c.

**1969, Nov. 21 Photo. Wmk. 314**

Christmas: 8c, South Sea Islands scene with palms and Star of Bethlehem.

| | | | | |
|---|---|---|---|---|
| **202** | A25 | 8c vio, grnsh bl & blk | .20 | .20 |
| **203** | A25 | 35c black & multi | .60 | .60 |

C. M. Woodford and Stamp of 1907 — A26

Designs: 7c, British Solomon Islands 1906 handstamp and cancellation, and New South Wales No. 99. 18c, British Solomon Islands No. 18 and 1913 Tulagi cancellation. 23c, New General Post Office, Honiara.

**1970, Apr. 15 Litho. *Perf. 13***

| | | | | |
|---|---|---|---|---|
| **204** | A26 | 7c lilac rose & black | .20 | .20 |
| **205** | A26 | 14c lt olive & black | .35 | .35 |
| **206** | A26 | 18c orange, yel & blk | .45 | .45 |
| **207** | A26 | 23c multicolored | .65 | .65 |
| | | *Nos. 204-207 (4)* | 1.65 | 1.65 |

Issued to publicize the opening of the new General Post Office in Honiara.

Map of Solomon Islands A27

18c, British Solomon Islands coat of arms, vert.

***Perf. 14½x14, 14x14½***

**1970, June 15 Litho. Wmk. 314**

| | | | | |
|---|---|---|---|---|
| **208** | A27 | 18c multicolored | .55 | .55 |
| **209** | A27 | 35c multicolored | 1.00 | 1.00 |

Adoption of the new 1970 Constitution.

Red Cross Headquarters, Honiara — A28

35c, Map of British Solomon Islands showing Red Cross stations, wheelchair.

**1970, Aug. 17 *Perf. 14½x14***

| | | | | |
|---|---|---|---|---|
| **210** | A28 | 3c multicolored | .20 | .20 |
| **211** | A28 | 35c multicolored | .95 | .85 |

Centenary of British Red Cross Society.

Carved Angel and Southern Cross — A29

Reredos: Symbols of Trinity and Light at St. Luke's Church, Kia — A30

***Perf. 14x13½, 13½x14***

**1970, Oct. 19 Litho. Wmk. 314**

| | | | | |
|---|---|---|---|---|
| **212** | A29 | 8c violet & bister brn | .25 | .25 |
| **213** | A30 | 45c multicolored | 1.00 | 1.00 |

Christmas 1970.

Count de La Pérouse and "La Boussole" — A31

4c, Astrolabe, Polynesian reed map. 12c, Abel Tasman, sailing ship Heemskerk, 1643. 35c, Te Puki canoe, Santa Cruz.

**1971, Jan. 28** ***Perf. 14½x14***

| | | | | |
|---|---|---|---|---|
| **214** | A31 | 3c multicolored | 1.00 | .50 |
| **215** | A31 | 4c multicolored | 1.00 | .50 |
| **216** | A31 | 12c multicolored | 1.25 | .75 |
| **217** | A31 | 35c multicolored | 1.50 | 1.25 |
| | | *Nos. 214-217 (4)* | 4.75 | 3.00 |

In honor of famous explorers and ships. See Nos. 228-231, 250-253.

Bishop Patteson, J. Atkin and S. Taroniara — A32

Designs: 4c, Last landing of the "Southern Cross" at Nukapu. 14c, Memorial for Bishop Patteson and map of Nukapu, vert. 45c, Ceremonial leaf tag (had been attached to Bishop's body), vert.

***Perf. 14½x14, 14x14½***

**1971, Apr. 5 Litho. Wmk. 314**

| | | | | |
|---|---|---|---|---|
| **218** | A32 | 2c lt green & multi | .25 | .25 |
| **219** | A32 | 4c blue green & multi | .25 | .25 |
| **220** | A32 | 14c brt pink & multi | .25 | .25 |
| **221** | A32 | 45c brown & multi | .50 | .50 |
| | | *Nos. 218-221 (4)* | 1.25 | 1.25 |

Bishop John Coleridge Patteson (1827-71), head of the Melanesian mission.

Boxing, Games Emblem A33

8c, Soccer. 12c, Running. 35c, Spear fishing.

**1971, Aug. 9** ***Perf. 14½x14***

| | | | | |
|---|---|---|---|---|
| **222** | A33 | 3c orange & multi | .30 | .30 |
| **223** | A33 | 8c emerald & multi | .30 | .30 |
| **224** | A33 | 12c yellow & multi | .30 | .30 |
| **225** | A33 | 35c blue & multi | .50 | .50 |
| | | *Nos. 222-225 (4)* | 1.40 | 1.40 |

4th South Pacific Games, Papeete, French Polynesia, Sept. 8-19.

Melanesian Lectern (wood carving) — A34

Christmas: 45c, Stylized birds, painted by school girl Margarita Bara.

**1971, Nov. 15 Litho. Wmk. 314**

| | | | | |
|---|---|---|---|---|
| **226** | A34 | 9c orange & multi | .20 | .20 |
| **227** | A34 | 45c blue & multi | 1.10 | 1.10 |

Explorer Type of 1971

4c, Louis Antoine de Bougainville, La Boudeuse, 1776. 9c, Horizontal planisphere, 1574, ivory backstaff, 1695. 15c, Philip Carteret, H.M.S. Swallow, 1707. 45c, Small canoe of Malaita.

**1972, Feb. 1** ***Perf. 14½***

| | | | | |
|---|---|---|---|---|
| **228** | A31 | 4c brown & multi | .40 | .25 |
| **229** | A31 | 9c green & multi | .60 | .25 |
| **230** | A31 | 15c lt blue & multi | .75 | .50 |
| **231** | A31 | 45c blue & multi | 2.25 | 2.25 |
| | | *Nos. 228-231 (4)* | 4.00 | 3.25 |

Cupha Woodfordi A35

Designs: 1c, 2c, 3c, 4c, $2, Butterflies. 5c, 8c, 9c, 15c, $1. Fishes. 12c, 20c, 25c, 35c, 45c, Orchids. $5, Birds.

**1972-73** ***Perf. 14***

| | | | | |
|---|---|---|---|---|
| **232** | A35 | 1c *shown* | .20 | .20 |
| **233** | A35 | 2c *Ornithoptera priamus* | .30 | .30 |
| **234** | A35 | 3c *Vindula sapor* | .30 | .30 |
| **235** | A35 | 4c *Papilio orssippus* | .30 | .30 |
| **236** | A35 | 5c *Great trevally* | .40 | .40 |
| **237** | A35 | 8c *Little bonito* | .50 | .50 |
| **238** | A35 | 9c *Sapphire demoiselle* | .60 | *.70* |
| **239** | A35 | 12c *Costus speciosus* | 1.50 | .80 |
| **240** | A35 | 15c *Orange anemone* | 1.50 | 1.00 |
| **241** | A35 | 20c *Spathoglottis plicata* | 3.50 | 1.25 |
| **242** | A35 | 25c *Ephemerantha comata* | 3.50 | 1.50 |
| **243** | A35 | 35c *Dendrobium cuthbertsonii* | 3.75 | 2.00 |
| **244** | A35 | 45c *Heliconia salomonica* | 3.00 | 3.00 |
| **245** | A35 | $1 *Blue-finned triggerfish* | 3.75 | *5.00* |
| **246** | A35 | $2 *Ornithoptera allotti* | 11.00 | *17.50* |
| **247** | A35 | $5 *Great frigate bird* | 16.50 | *18.00* |
| | | *Nos. 232-247 (16)* | 50.60 | *52.75* |

Issued: $5, 7/2/73; others, 7/2/72.

For overprints see Nos. 300-311.

**Silver Wedding Issue, 1972**

Common Design Type

Design: Queen Elizabeth II, Prince Philip, scroll and message drum on woven mat.

**1972, Nov. 20 Photo.** ***Perf. 14x14½***

| | | | | |
|---|---|---|---|---|
| **248** | CD324 | 8c car rose & multi | .20 | .20 |
| **249** | CD324 | 45c olive & multi | .50 | .50 |

Explorer Type of 1971

Designs: 4c, Antoine R. J. d'Entrecasteaux and "The Recherche," 1791. 9c, Ship's hourglass, 17th century, and chronometer, 1761. 15c, Lieutenant Shortland and "The Alexander," 1788. 35c, Tomoko (war canoe).

**Wmk. 314**

**1973, Mar. 9 Litho.** ***Perf. 14½***

| | | | | |
|---|---|---|---|---|
| **250** | A31 | 4c blue & multi | .20 | .20 |
| **251** | A31 | 9c blue & multi | .55 | .55 |
| **252** | A31 | 15c blue & multi | 1.00 | 1.00 |
| **253** | A31 | 35c blue & multi | 3.25 | 3.25 |
| | | *Nos. 250-253 (4)* | 5.00 | 5.00 |

Pan Pipes A36

Musical Instruments: 9c, Castanets. 15c, Bamboo flute. 35c, Bauro gongs. 45c, Bamboo band.

**1973, Oct. 1** ***Perf. 13½x14***

| | | | | |
|---|---|---|---|---|
| **254** | A36 | 4c brick red & multi | .20 | .20 |
| **255** | A36 | 9c yellow bis & multi | .25 | .25 |
| **256** | A36 | 15c pink & multi | .40 | .40 |
| **257** | A36 | 35c blue green & multi | .90 | .90 |
| **258** | A36 | 45c multicolored | 1.25 | 1.25 |
| | | *Nos. 254-258 (5)* | 3.00 | 3.00 |

**Princess Anne's Wedding Issue**

Common Design Type

**1973, Nov. 14** ***Perf. 14***

| | | | | |
|---|---|---|---|---|
| **259** | CD325 | 4c slate & multi | .30 | .30 |
| **260** | CD325 | 35c multicolored | .70 | .70 |

Adoration of the Kings, by Jan Brueghel A37

Adoration of the Kings by: 22c, Peter Brueghel, vert. 45c, Botticelli.

**1973, Nov. 26 Litho.** ***Perf. 14***

**Size: 39x25mm, 25x39mm**

| | | | | |
|---|---|---|---|---|
| **261** | A37 | 8c pink & multi | .25 | .25 |
| **262** | A37 | 22c lilac & multi | .50 | .50 |

***Perf. 13½***

**Size: 47x35mm**

| | | | | |
|---|---|---|---|---|
| **263** | A37 | 45c gray & multi | 1.25 | 1.25 |
| | | *Nos. 261-263 (3)* | 2.00 | 2.00 |

Christmas 1973.

Map of Solomon Islands — A38

**1974, Feb. 18 Litho.** ***Perf. 13½***

| | | | | |
|---|---|---|---|---|
| **264** | A38 | 4c blue & multi | .20 | .20 |
| **265** | A38 | 9c citron & multi | .25 | .25 |
| **266** | A38 | 15c violet gray & multi | .45 | .45 |
| **267** | A38 | 35c emerald & multi | 1.50 | 1.50 |
| | | *Nos. 264-267 (4)* | 2.40 | 2.40 |

Visit of British Royal Family.

First Resident Commissioner Landing at Tulagi — A39

Designs: 9c, Marine radar and scanner unit, map of Islands. 15c, Islanders taken to "Blackbirder" ship. 45c, John F. Kennedy's P.T. 109 off Lumbari Island, 1943.

**1974, May 15 Litho.** ***Perf. 14½***

| | | | | |
|---|---|---|---|---|
| **268** | A39 | 4c multicolored | .20 | .20 |
| **269** | A39 | 9c multicolored | .45 | .45 |
| **270** | A39 | 15c multicolored | .60 | .60 |
| **271** | A39 | 45c multicolored | 2.75 | 2.75 |
| | | *Nos. 268-271 (4)* | 4.00 | 4.00 |

Ships and navigators.

Mailman, Map of Islands — A40

9c, Carrier pigeon, horiz. 15c, Angel Gabriel. 45c, Pegasus, horiz. Designs based on origami (folded paper) figures.

**1974, Aug. 29 Wmk. 314** ***Perf. 14***

| | | | | |
|---|---|---|---|---|
| **272** | A40 | 4c brt green & multi | .20 | .20 |
| **273** | A40 | 9c lemon & multi | .30 | .20 |
| **274** | A40 | 15c multicolored | .45 | .35 |
| **275** | A40 | 45c blue & multi | 1.25 | 1.10 |
| | | *Nos. 272-275 (4)* | 2.20 | 1.85 |

Centenary of Universal Postal Union.

Solomon Islands No. 208 A41

**1974, Dec. 16 Litho.** ***Perf. 14½***

| | | | | |
|---|---|---|---|---|
| **276** | A41 | 4c shown | .20 | .20 |
| **277** | A41 | 9c No. 107 | .30 | .30 |
| **278** | A41 | 15c same | .50 | .50 |
| **279** | A41 | 35c like 4c | 1.10 | 1.10 |
| | *a.* | Souvenir sheet of 4, #276-279 | 5.00 | 5.00 |
| | | *Nos. 276-279 (4)* | 2.10 | 2.10 |

New Constitution, inaugurated Oct. 18, 1960.

Golden Whistler A42

Birds: 2c, River kingfisher. 3c, Red-throated fruit dove. 4c, Button quail. $2, Duchess lorikeet.

**1975, Apr. 7 Wmk. 314** ***Perf. 14***

| | | | | |
|---|---|---|---|---|
| **280** | A42 | 1c yellow grn & multi | .45 | .75 |
| **281** | A42 | 2c lt blue & multi | .50 | .90 |
| **282** | A42 | 3c brt pink & multi | .55 | .90 |
| **283** | A42 | 4c orange & multi | .60 | .75 |
| **284** | A42 | $2 dp orange & multi | 13.00 | 12.00 |
| | | *Nos. 280-284 (5)* | 15.10 | 15.30 |

See Nos. 316-320, 323, 330-331. For overprints see Nos. 296-299.

Motor Vessel Walande A43

**1975, May 29** ***Perf. 13½***

| | | | | |
|---|---|---|---|---|
| **285** | A43 | 4c shown | .60 | .20 |
| **286** | A43 | 9c M. V. Melanesian | .80 | .20 |
| **287** | A43 | 15c Ship Marsina, house flag | 1.10 | .25 |
| **288** | A43 | 45c S. S. Himalaya | 2.00 | 1.50 |
| | | *Nos. 285-288 (4)* | 4.50 | 2.15 |

Runner, 800-meters — A44

**1975, Aug. 4 Litho. *Perf. 13½***

| | | | | |
|---|---|---|---|---|
| **289** | A44 | 4c shown | .20 | .20 |
| **290** | A44 | 9c Long jump | .20 | .20 |
| **291** | A44 | 15c Javelin | .35 | .35 |
| **292** | A44 | 45c Soccer | 1.00 | 1.00 |
| *a.* | | Souvenir sheet of 4, #289-292 | 5.00 | 5.00 |
| | | *Nos. 289-292 (4)* | 1.75 | 1.75 |

5th South Pacific Games, Guam, Aug. 1-10.

Nativity and Candles A45

Christmas: 35c, Angels, shepherds and candles. 45c, Three Kings approaching Bethlehem, and candles.

**1975, Oct. 13 Wmk. 373 *Perf. 14***

| | | | | |
|---|---|---|---|---|
| **293** | A45 | 15c multicolored | .35 | .35 |
| **294** | A45 | 35c multicolored | .80 | .80 |
| **295** | A45 | 45c multicolored | 1.10 | 1.10 |
| *a.* | | Souvenir sheet of 3, #293-295 | 5.00 | 5.00 |
| | | *Nos. 293-295 (3)* | 2.25 | 2.25 |

Nos. 236-245, 247, 280-284 Overprinted with Bar Obliterating "British" in Black or Silver

**1975, Nov. 12 Litho. Wmk. 314**

| | | | | |
|---|---|---|---|---|
| **296** | A42 | 1c multicolored | .60 | .50 |
| **297** | A42 | 2c multicolored | 1.10 | .50 |
| **298** | A42 | 3c multicolored | .80 | .50 |
| **299** | A42 | 4c multicolored | 1.10 | .50 |
| **300** | A35 | 5c multicolored | .55 | .50 |
| **301** | A35 | 8c multicolored | .55 | .50 |
| **302** | A35 | 9c multicolored | .55 | .55 |
| **303** | A35 | 12c multicolored | 1.75 | .65 |
| **304** | A35 | 15c multicolored | 1.75 | .70 |
| **305** | A35 | 20c multicolored | 2.25 | .90 |
| **306** | A35 | 25c multicolored | 2.25 | 1.00 |
| **307** | A35 | 35c multicolored | 2.50 | 1.50 |
| **308** | A35 | 45c multicolored | 2.25 | 1.75 |
| **309** | A35 | $1 multicolored | 1.75 | *3.50* |
| **310** | A42 | $2 multicolored | 6.75 | *7.00* |
| **311** | A35 | $5 multicolored (S) | 6.50 | *18.00* |
| | | *Nos. 296-311 (16)* | 33.00 | *38.55* |

Ceremonial Food Bowl — A46

Artifacts: 15c, Barava, chief's money. 35c, Nguzu-nguzu, canoe protector spirit, vert. 45c, Nguzu-nguzu on canoe prow.

**Wmk. 314**

**1976, Jan. 12 Litho. *Perf. 14***

| | | | | |
|---|---|---|---|---|
| **312** | A46 | 4c scarlet & black | .20 | .20 |
| **313** | A46 | 15c lt violet & multi | .25 | .25 |
| **314** | A46 | 35c multicolored | .75 | .75 |
| **315** | A46 | 45c multicolored | .90 | .90 |
| | | *Nos. 312-315 (4)* | 2.10 | 2.10 |

Type of 1975 Inscribed "Solomon Islands" and

Golden Cowries A47

1c, Golden whistler. 2c, River kingfisher. 3c, Red-throated fruit dove. 4c, Button quail. 5c, Willie wagtail. 10c, Glory-of-the-sea cones. 12c, Rainbow lory. 15c, Pearly nautilus. 20c, Venus comb murex. 25c, Commercial trochus. 35c, Melon or baler shell. 45c, Orange spider conch. $1, Pacific triton. $2, Duchess lorikeet. $5, Great frigate bird.

**1976 Wmk. 373 *Perf. 14***

| | | | | |
|---|---|---|---|---|
| **316** | A42 | 1c yel grn & multi | .40 | .35 |
| **317** | A42 | 2c lt blue & multi | .80 | .70 |
| **318** | A42 | 3c pink & multi | .45 | .35 |
| **319** | A42 | 4c orange & multi | .45 | .40 |
| **320** | A42 | 5c red brown & multi | .80 | .70 |
| **321** | A47 | 6c rose & multi | .55 | .50 |
| **322** | A47 | 10c multicolored | .55 | .50 |
| **323** | A42 | 12c yel grn & multi | .90 | .80 |
| **324** | A47 | 15c lilac & multi | .40 | .35 |
| **325** | A47 | 20c ultra & multi | .90 | .75 |
| **326** | A47 | 25c dull grn & multi | .70 | .65 |
| **327** | A47 | 35c bister & multi | .95 | .95 |
| **328** | A47 | 45c fawn & multi | 1.10 | 1.10 |
| **329** | A47 | $1 olive & multi | 2.50 | 2.50 |
| **330** | A42 | $2 multicolored | 5.00 | 5.00 |
| **331** | A42 | $5 multicolored | 9.75 | 9.75 |
| | | *Nos. 316-331 (16)* | 26.20 | 25.35 |

Issue dates: $5, Dec. 6; others Mar. 8.

Coast Watchers, World War II A48

American Bicentennial: 20c, "Amagiri" ramming "P.T.109" and Lt. John F. Kennedy. 35c, Plane on Henderson Airfield. 45c, Map showing landing of US forces on Guadalcanal.

**1976, May 24 *Perf. 14***

| | | | | |
|---|---|---|---|---|
| **333** | A48 | 6c black & multi | .40 | .20 |
| **334** | A48 | 20c black & multi | 1.10 | .55 |
| **335** | A48 | 35c black & multi | 1.50 | .90 |
| **336** | A48 | 45c black & multi | 1.50 | 1.10 |
| *a.* | | Souvenir sheet of 4, #333-336 | 8.00 | 8.00 |
| | | *Nos. 333-336 (4)* | 4.50 | 2.75 |

Alexander Graham Bell — A49

Designs: 20c, Radio-telephone and satellite. 35c, Ericsson's magneto telephone. 45c, Telephone, 1876, and stick telephone.

**1976, July 26 Litho. *Perf. 14½x14***

| | | | | |
|---|---|---|---|---|
| **337** | A49 | 6c lt ultra & multi | .20 | .20 |
| **338** | A49 | 20c multicolored | .45 | .45 |
| **339** | A49 | 35c orange & multi | .70 | .70 |
| **340** | A49 | 45c bister & multi | 1.00 | 1.00 |
| | | *Nos. 337-340 (4)* | 2.35 | 2.35 |

Centenary of first telephone call by Alexander Graham Bell, Mar. 10, 1876.

One-Eleven BAC — A50

Planes: 20c, Solair Britten Norman Islander. 35c, DC-3 Dakota. 45c, De Havilland DH50A.

**1976, Sept. 13 Wmk. 373 *Perf. 14***

| | | | | |
|---|---|---|---|---|
| **341** | A50 | 6c black & multi | .20 | .20 |
| **342** | A50 | 20c black & multi | .65 | .65 |
| **343** | A50 | 35c black & multi | 1.10 | 1.10 |
| **344** | A50 | 45c black & multi | 1.40 | 1.40 |
| | | *Nos. 341-344 (4)* | 3.35 | 3.35 |

1st flight to Solomon Islands, 50th anniv.

Queen Receiving Lei, 1974 Visit — A51

Carved Wooden Figure — A52

35c, Communion plate, cup. 45c, Communion.

**1977, Feb. 7 Litho. *Perf. 14x13½***

| | | | | |
|---|---|---|---|---|
| **345** | A51 | 6c multicolored | .20 | .20 |
| **346** | A51 | 35c multicolored | .50 | .50 |
| **347** | A51 | 45c multicolored | .65 | .65 |
| | | *Nos. 345-347 (3)* | 1.35 | 1.35 |

25th anniv. of the reign of Elizabeth II.

**1977, May 9 *Perf. 14***

Artifacts: 20c, Sea adaro or spirit. 35c, Shark-headed man. 45c, Seated man.

| | | | | |
|---|---|---|---|---|
| **348** | A52 | 6c yellow & multi | .25 | .25 |
| **349** | A52 | 20c blue & multi | .25 | .25 |
| **350** | A52 | 35c rose & multi | .55 | .55 |
| **351** | A52 | 45c multicolored | .70 | .70 |
| | | *Nos. 348-351 (4)* | 1.75 | 1.75 |

Man Spraying House, Anopheles Mosquito — A53

Designs: 20c, Taking blood samples. 35c, Microscope, map of Solomon Islands, Malaria Eradication Program emblem. 45c, Messenger delivering medicine to malaria patient.

**1977, July 27 Litho. Wmk. 373**

| | | | | |
|---|---|---|---|---|
| **352** | A53 | 6c multicolored | .25 | .25 |
| **353** | A53 | 20c multicolored | .40 | .40 |
| **354** | A53 | 35c multicolored | .55 | .55 |
| **355** | A53 | 45c multicolored | .80 | .80 |
| | | *Nos. 352-355 (4)* | 2.00 | 2.00 |

Malaria eradication.

Adoration of the Shepherds — A54

Christmas: 20c, Nativity. 35c, Adoration of the Kings. 45c, Flight into Egypt.

**Wmk. 373**

**1977, Sept. 12 Litho. *Perf. 14***

| | | | | |
|---|---|---|---|---|
| **356** | A54 | 6c multicolored | .25 | .25 |
| **357** | A54 | 20c multicolored | .40 | .40 |
| **358** | A54 | 35c multicolored | .55 | .55 |
| **359** | A54 | 45c multicolored | .80 | .80 |
| | | *Nos. 356-359 (4)* | 2.00 | 2.00 |

Traditional Feather Money — A55

Designs: No. 361, New coins. No. 362, Banknotes. No. 363, Traditional shell money.

**1977, Oct. 24 Litho. *Perf. 14x14½***

| | | | | |
|---|---|---|---|---|
| **360** | | 6c brt green & multi | .20 | .20 |
| **361** | | 6c brt green & multi | .20 | .20 |
| *a.* | A55 | Pair, #360-361 | .30 | .30 |
| **362** | | 45c buff & multi | 1.00 | 1.00 |
| **363** | | 45c buff & multi | 1.00 | 1.00 |
| *a.* | A55 | Pair, #362-363 | 2.00 | 2.00 |
| | | *Nos. 360-363 (4)* | 2.40 | 2.40 |

New coinage.

Shortland Islands Figure — A56

Artifacts: 20c, Ceremonial shield. 35c, Santa Cruz ritual figure. 45c, Decorative combs.

**1978, Jan. 11 *Perf. 14***

| | | | | |
|---|---|---|---|---|
| **364** | A56 | 6c multicolored | .20 | .20 |
| **365** | A56 | 20c multicolored | .45 | .45 |
| **366** | A56 | 35c multicolored | .80 | .80 |
| **367** | A56 | 45c multicolored | 1.00 | 1.00 |
| | | *Nos. 364-367 (4)* | 2.45 | 2.45 |

**Elizabeth II Coronation Anniversary Issue**

Common Design Types

**Souvenir Sheet**

**Unwmk.**

**1978, Apr. 21 Litho. *Perf. 15***

| | | | | |
|---|---|---|---|---|
| **368** | | Sheet of 6 | 3.50 | 3.50 |
| *a.* | | CD326 45c King's dragon | .50 | .50 |
| *b.* | | CD327 45c Elizabeth II | .50 | .50 |
| *c.* | | CD328 45c Sandford eagle | .50 | .50 |

No. 368 contains 2 se-tenant strips of Nos. 368a-368c, separated by horizontal gutter with commemorative and descriptive inscriptions and showing central part of coronation procession with coach.

National Flag — A57

Apostles by Dürer — A58

Independence: 15c, Governor General's flag. 35c, Cenotaph, Honiara, flags of U.S., Great Britain, New Zealand and Australia. 45c, Coat of Arms.

**Wmk. 373**

**1978, July 7 Litho. *Perf. 14***

| | | | | |
|---|---|---|---|---|
| **369** | A57 | 6c multicolored | .20 | .20 |
| **370** | A57 | 15c multicolored | .30 | .30 |
| **371** | A57 | 35c multicolored | .70 | .70 |
| **372** | A57 | 45c multicolored | .95 | .95 |
| | | *Nos. 369-372 (4)* | 2.15 | 2.15 |

**1978, Oct. 4 Litho. *Perf. 14***

| | | | | |
|---|---|---|---|---|
| **373** | A58 | 6c John | .20 | .20 |
| **374** | A58 | 20c Peter | .40 | .40 |
| **375** | A58 | 35c Paul | .70 | .70 |
| **376** | A58 | 45c Mark | .90 | .90 |
| | | *Nos. 373-376 (4)* | 2.20 | 2.20 |

Albrecht Dürer (1471-1528), German painter, 450th death anniversary.

Scouts Making Fire — A59

Designs: 20c, Camping. 35c, Solomon Islands Scouts. 45c, Canoeing.

**1978, Nov. 15 Litho. *Perf. 14***

| | | | | |
|---|---|---|---|---|
| **377** | A59 | 6c multicolored | .20 | .20 |
| **378** | A59 | 20c multicolored | .30 | .30 |
| **379** | A59 | 35c multicolored | .55 | .55 |
| **380** | A59 | 45c multicolored | .70 | .70 |
| | | *Nos. 377-380 (4)* | 1.75 | 1.75 |

50 years of Scouting in Solomon Islands.

Discovery A60

Designs: 18c, Capt. Cook, 1776, painting by Nathaniel Dance. 35c, Sextant. 45c, Capt. Cook after Flaxman / Wedgwood medallion.

**Wmk. 373**

**1979, Jan. 16 Litho. *Perf. 11***

| | | | | |
|---|---|---|---|---|
| **381** | A60 | 8c multicolored | .20 | .20 |
| **382** | A60 | 18c multicolored | .40 | .40 |
| **383** | A60 | 35c multicolored | .80 | .80 |

**Litho.; Embossed**

| | | | | |
|---|---|---|---|---|
| **384** | A60 | 45c multicolored | 1.00 | 1.00 |
| | | *Nos. 381-384 (4)* | 2.40 | 2.40 |

Capt. Cook's voyages.

Fish Net Float A61

Artifacts: 20c, Armband made of shell money, vert. 35c, Ceremonial food bowl. 45c, Forehead ornament, vert.

**1979, Mar. 21 Litho. *Perf. 14***

| | | | | |
|---|---|---|---|---|
| **385** | A61 | 8c multicolored | .30 | .30 |
| **386** | A61 | 20c multicolored | .30 | .30 |
| **387** | A61 | 35c multicolored | .45 | .45 |
| **388** | A61 | 45c multicolored | .60 | .60 |
| | | *Nos. 385-388 (4)* | 1.65 | 1.65 |

6th South Pacific Games A62

**1979, June 4 Litho. Wmk. 373**

| | | | | |
|---|---|---|---|---|
| **389** | A62 | 8c Running | .20 | .20 |
| **390** | A62 | 20c Hurdles | .25 | .25 |
| **391** | A62 | 35c Soccer | .30 | .30 |
| **392** | A62 | 45c Swimming | .50 | .50 |
| | | *Nos. 389-392 (4)* | 1.25 | 1.25 |

Solomon Islands No. 14 — A63

Sea Snake — A64

Designs (Rowland Hill and): 20c, Great Britain No. 27. 35c, Solomon Islands No. 372. 45c, Solomon Islands No. 40.

**1979, Aug. 16 Litho. *Perf. 14***

| | | | | |
|---|---|---|---|---|
| **393** | A63 | 8c multicolored | .20 | .20 |
| **394** | A63 | 20c multicolored | .40 | .40 |
| **395** | A63 | 35c multicolored | .65 | .65 |
| | | *Nos. 393-395 (3)* | 1.25 | 1.25 |

**Souvenir Sheet**

| | | | | |
|---|---|---|---|---|
| **396** | A63 | 45c multicolored | 1.25 | 1.25 |

Sir Rowland Hill (1795-1879), originator of penny postage.

***Perf. 13½x13***

**1979-83 Litho. Wmk. 373**

| | | | | |
|---|---|---|---|---|
| **397** | A64 | 1c Sea snake | .20 | .50 |
| **398** | A64 | 3c Red-banded tree snake | .20 | .75 |
| **399** | A64 | 4c Whip snake | .20 | .75 |
| **400** | A64 | 6c Pacific boa | .20 | .75 |
| **401** | A64 | 8c Skink | .20 | .45 |
| **402** | A64 | 10c Gecko | .20 | .50 |
| **403** | A64 | 12c Monitor | .30 | .50 |
| **404** | A64 | 15c Angelhead | .30 | .75 |
| **405** | A64 | 20c Giant toad | .40 | .35 |
| **406** | A64 | 25c Marsh frog | .45 | .60 |
| **407** | A64 | 30c Horned frog | 1.50 | .60 |
| **408** | A64 | 35c Tree frog | .50 | .60 |
| **408A** | A64 | 40c Burrowing snake | .55 | 1.40 |
| **409** | A64 | 45c Guppy's snake | .65 | .85 |
| **409A** | A64 | 50c Tree gecko | .60 | .85 |
| **410** | A64 | $1 Large skink | 2.00 | 1.25 |
| **411** | A64 | $2 Guppy's frog | 2.50 | 2.50 |
| **412** | A64 | $5 Estuarine crocodile | 6.50 | 6.50 |
| **412A** | A64 | $10 Hawksbill turtle | 11.50 | *13.00* |
| | | *Nos. 397-412A (19)* | 28.95 | 33.45 |

Issued: $10, 9/20/82; 40c, 50c, 1/24/83; others, 9/1979 (undated).

Nos. 403, 406, 410, 412 reissued inscribed "1982." No. 407, "1983."

Madonna and Child, by Morando — A65

IYC Emblem and Madonna and Child: 20c, Bernardino Luini. 35c, Bellini. 50c, Raphael.

**1979, Nov. 15 *Perf. 14½***

| | | | | |
|---|---|---|---|---|
| **413** | A65 | 4c multicolored | .20 | .20 |
| **414** | A65 | 20c multicolored | .25 | .25 |
| **415** | A65 | 35c multicolored | .40 | .40 |
| **416** | A65 | 50c multicolored | .65 | .65 |
| ***a.*** | | Souvenir sheet of 4, #413-416 | 1.75 | 1.75 |
| | | *Nos. 413-416 (4)* | 1.50 | 1.50 |

Christmas 1979, Intl. Year of the Child.

Curacoa and Crest A66

Ships and Crests: 20c, Herald, 1854. 35c, Royalist, 1889. 45c, Beagle, 1878.

**Wmk. 373**

**1980, Jan. 23 Litho. *Perf. 14***

| | | | | |
|---|---|---|---|---|
| **417** | A66 | 8c multicolored | .20 | .20 |
| **418** | A66 | 20c multicolored | .40 | .40 |
| **419** | A66 | 35c multicolored | .65 | .65 |
| **420** | A66 | 45c multicolored | .85 | .85 |
| | | *Nos. 417-420 (4)* | 2.10 | 2.10 |

See Nos. 435-438.

Steel Fishery Training Ship — A67

**1980, Mar. 27 Litho. *Perf. 13½***

| | | | | |
|---|---|---|---|---|
| **421** | A67 | 8c shown | .20 | .20 |
| **422** | A67 | 20c Fishery training ship | .25 | .25 |
| **423** | A67 | 45c Refrigerated carrier | .45 | .40 |
| **424** | A67 | 80c Research ship | .85 | *1.75* |
| | | *Nos. 421-424 (4)* | 1.75 | 2.60 |

"Comliebank," Tulag Cancel — A68

**1980, May 6 Litho. *Perf. 14½***

| | | | | |
|---|---|---|---|---|
| **425** | | Sheet of 4 | 2.00 | 2.00 |
| ***a.*** | A68 | 45c shown | .50 | .50 |
| ***b.*** | A68 | 45c Douglas C-47 | .50 | .50 |
| ***c.*** | A68 | 45c BAC 1-11, Honiara cancel | .50 | .50 |
| ***d.*** | A68 | 45c "Corabank," Auki cancel | .50 | .50 |

London 1980 Intl. Stamp Exhib., May 6-14.

**Queen Mother Elizabeth Birthday Issue**

Common Design Type

**Wmk. 373**

**1980, Aug. 4 Litho. *Perf. 14***

| | | | | |
|---|---|---|---|---|
| **426** | CD330 | 45c multicolored | .50 | .50 |

Angel with Trumpet — A69

Christmas: 20c, Angel with violin. 45c, Angel with trumpet. 80c, Angel with lute.

**Wmk. 373**

**1980, Sept. 2 Litho. *Perf. 14½***

| | | | | |
|---|---|---|---|---|
| **427** | A69 | 8c multicolored | .20 | .20 |
| **428** | A69 | 20c multicolored | .20 | .20 |
| **429** | A69 | 45c multicolored | .40 | .40 |
| **430** | A69 | 80c multicolored | .70 | .70 |
| | | *Nos. 427-430 (4)* | 1.50 | 1.50 |

Parthenos Sylvia — A70

**Wmk. 373**

**1980, Nov. 12 Litho. *Perf. 13½***

| | | | | |
|---|---|---|---|---|
| **431** | A70 | 8c shown | .50 | .40 |
| **432** | A70 | 20c *Delias schoenbergi* | .70 | .60 |
| **433** | A70 | 45c *Jamides cephion* | 1.25 | 1.00 |
| **434** | A70 | 80c *Ornithoptera victoriae* | 1.75 | 1.75 |
| | | *Nos. 431-434 (4)* | 4.20 | 3.75 |

See Nos. 461-464.

Ship & Crest Type of 1980

8c, Mounts Bay, 1959. 20c, Charybdis, 1970. 45c, Hydra, 1972-73. $1, Britannia, 1974.

**1981, Jan. 14**

| | | | | |
|---|---|---|---|---|
| **435** | A66 | 8c multicolored | .20 | .20 |
| **436** | A66 | 20c multicolored | .20 | .20 |
| **437** | A66 | 45c multicolored | .45 | .45 |
| **438** | A66 | $1 multicolored | 1.25 | 1.25 |
| | | *Nos. 435-438 (4)* | 2.10 | 2.10 |

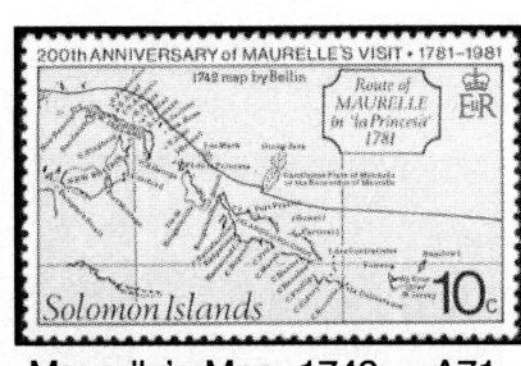
Maurelle's Map, 1742 — A71

**Wmk. 373**

**1981, Mar. 23 Litho. *Perf. 14***

| | | | | |
|---|---|---|---|---|
| **439** | A71 | 8c Francisco Maurelle, vert. | .20 | .20 |
| **440** | A71 | 10c shown | .20 | .20 |
| **441** | A71 | 45c La Princesa | .60 | .60 |
| **442** | A71 | $1 Compass cards, vert. | 1.00 | 1.00 |
| | | *Nos. 439-442 (4)* | 2.00 | 2.00 |

**Souvenir Sheet**

| | | | | |
|---|---|---|---|---|
| **443** | | Sheet of 4 | 1.60 | 1.60 |
| ***a.*** | A71 | 25c any single | .35 | .35 |

Bicent. of arrival of Francisco Antonio Maurelle and of charts of mapmaker Jean Nicholas Buache (1741-1825). No. 443 contains 4 44x28mm stamps, perf. 14½.

Women's Basketball — A72

**Wmk. 373**

**1981, July 7 Litho. *Perf. 12***

| | | | | |
|---|---|---|---|---|
| **444** | A72 | 8c shown | .20 | .20 |
| **445** | A72 | 10c Tennis | .20 | .20 |
| **446** | A72 | 25c Women's running | .35 | .35 |
| **447** | A72 | 30c Soccer | .35 | .35 |
| **448** | A72 | 45c Boxing | .50 | .50 |
| | | *Nos. 444-448 (5)* | 1.60 | 1.60 |

**Souvenir Sheet**

| | | | | |
|---|---|---|---|---|
| **449** | A72 | $1 Emblem | 1.25 | 1.25 |

Mini South Pacific Games, July.

**Royal Wedding Issue**

Common Design Type

**1981, July 22 *Perf. 13½x13***

| | | | | |
|---|---|---|---|---|
| **450** | CD331 | 8c Bouquet | .20 | .20 |
| **451** | CD331 | 45c Charles | .30 | .30 |
| **452** | CD331 | $1 Couple | 1.00 | 1.00 |
| | | *Nos. 450-452 (3)* | 1.50 | 1.50 |

For surcharge see No. B1.

Duke of Edinburgh's Awards, 25th Anniv. — A73

**Wmk. 373**

**1981, Sept. 28 Litho. *Perf. 14***

| | | | | |
|---|---|---|---|---|
| **453** | A73 | 8c Music | .25 | .25 |
| **454** | A73 | 25c Handicrafts | .25 | .25 |
| **455** | A73 | 45c Canoeing | .35 | .35 |
| **456** | A73 | $1 Duke of Edinburgh | .90 | .90 |
| | | *Nos. 453-456 (4)* | 1.75 | 1.75 |

Holy Cross Cathedral, Honiara — A74

Christmas: 8c, 25c, Old churches, diff. 10c, St. Barnabas Anglican Cathedral, Honiara.

**1981, Oct. 12**

| | | | | |
|---|---|---|---|---|
| **457** | A74 | 8c multicolored | .30 | .30 |
| **458** | A74 | 10c multicolored | .30 | .30 |
| **459** | A74 | 25c multicolored | .40 | .40 |
| **460** | A74 | $2 multicolored | 1.50 | 1.50 |
| | | *Nos. 457-460 (4)* | 2.50 | 2.50 |

Butterfly Type of 1980

**Wmk. 373**

**1982, Jan. 5 Litho. *Perf. 13½***

| | | | | |
|---|---|---|---|---|
| **461** | A70 | 10c Doleschallia bisaltide | .40 | .40 |
| **462** | A70 | 25c Papilio bridgei hecataeus | .75 | .70 |

**463** A70 35c Taenaris phorcas .90 .75
**464** A70 $1 Graphium sarpedon 2.40 2.40
*Nos. 461-464 (4)* 4.45 4.25

Sanford's Eagle — A75

**1982, May 15 Litho. *Perf. 14***
**465** A75 12c Pair facing left .60 .60
**466** A75 12c Chick .60 .60
**467** A75 12c Mother feeding chicks .60 .60
**468** A75 12c Pair facing right .60 .60
**469** A75 12c Male flying .60 .60
**470** A75 12c Pair flying .60 .60
*Nos. 465-470 (6)* 3.60 3.60

Se-tenant in sheets of 24. The center horiz. row consists of 4 No. 470 + label. No block of 6 contains all 6 designs.

**Princess Diana Issue**
Common Design Type
***Perf. 14½x14***
**1982, July 1 Litho. Wmk. 373**
**471** CD333 12c Arms .20 .20
**472** CD333 40c Diana .65 .65
**473** CD333 50c Wedding .90 .90
**474** CD333 $1 Portrait 1.75 1.75
*Nos. 471-474 (4)* 3.50 3.50

A76

**1982, Oct. 11 Litho. *Perf. 14***
**475** A76 25c Running .40 .40
**476** A76 25c Boxing .40 .40

**Souvenir Sheet**
**477** Sheet of 3, #475-476, 477a 2.75 2.75
*a.* A76 $1 Britannia facing left 1.75 1.75

12th Commonwealth Games, Brisbane, Australia, Sept. 30-Oct. 9.

**1982, Oct. 11**
**478** A76 12c Royal couple .25 .25
**479** A76 12c Flags .25 .25

**Souvenir Sheet**
**480** Sheet of 3, #478-479, 480a 2.75 2.75
*a.* A76 $1 Britannia facing right 1.75 1.75

Visit of Queen Elizabeth II and Prince Philip.

Scouting Year A78

Designs: Nos. 481, 485, Scout patroller. Nos. 482, 486, Brigade bugler. Nos. 483, 487, Baden-Powell. Nos. 484, 488, William Smith.

**1982, Nov. 30**
**481** A78 12c dark blue & multi .25 .25
**482** A78 12c brown & multi .25 .25
**483** A78 25c dark blue & multi .30 .30
**484** A78 25c brown & multi .30 .30
**485** A78 35c green & multi .30 .30
**486** A78 35c red & multi .30 .30
**487** A78 50c green & multi .50 .50
**488** A78 50c red & multi .50 .50
*Nos. 481-488 (8)* 2.70 2.70

Turtles A79

**1983, Jan. 5 *Perf. 14***
**489** A79 18c Leatherback .50 .50
**490** A79 35c Loggerhead .65 .65
**491** A79 45c Pacific Ridley .90 .90
**492** A79 50c Green .90 .90
*Nos. 489-492 (4)* 2.95 2.95

Commonwealth Day — A80

**1983, Mar. 14**
**493** A80 12c Oliva vidum, conus generalis, murex tribulus .20 .20
**494** A80 35c Romu, kurila, kakadu, money belt .55 .55
**495** A80 45c Shells, bride necklaces .70 .70
**496** A80 50c Trochus niloticus, natural, polished .75 .75
*Nos. 493-496 (4)* 2.20 2.20

Manned Flight Bicentenary — A81

**Wmk. 373**
**1983, June 30 Litho. *Perf. 14***
**497** A81 30c Montgolfliere, 1783 .40 .40
**498** A81 35c Lockheed Hercules .45 .45
**499** A81 40c Wright Brothers' Flyer III, 1905 .50 .50
**500** A81 45c Columbia space shuttle .55 .55
**501** A81 50c Beechcraft Baron-Solair .65 .65
*Nos. 497-501 (5)* 2.55 2.55

Christmas 1983 — A82

**1983, Aug. 25**
**502** A82 12c Weto dance .20 .20
**503** A82 15c Custom wrestling .20 .20
**504** A82 18c Girl dancers .25 .25
**505** A82 20c Devil dancers .30 .30
**506** A82 25c Bamboo band .35 .35
**507** A82 35c Gilbertese dancers .50 .50
**508** A82 40c Pan pipers .60 .60
**509** A82 45c Afufu girl dancers .65 .65
**510** A82 50c Cross, flowers .75 .75
*a.* Souvenir sheet of 9, #502-510 3.75 3.75
*Nos. 502-510 (9)* 3.80 3.80

Stamps in #510a do not have "Christmas 1983."
For overprints see Nos. 519-520.

World Communications Year — A83

**Wmk. 373**
**1983, Dec. 19 Litho. *Perf. 14***
**511** A83 12c Telephone Exchange building .20 .20
**512** A83 18c Ham radio operator .20 .20
**513** A83 25c No. 11 .35 .35
**514** A83 $1 No. 14 1.25 1.25
*a.* Souvenir sheet of 1 1.50 1.50
*Nos. 511-514 (4)* 2.00 2.00

No. 514a is inscribed "1908-1983." See No. 525 for sheet inscribed "1907-1984."

Local Fungi — A84

**1984, Jan. 30 *Perf. 13½***
**515** A84 6c Calvatia gardneri .30 .30
**516** A84 18c Marasmiellus inoderma .50 .50
**517** A84 35c Pycnoporus sanguineus .75 .75
**518** A84 $2 Filoboletus manipularis 3.00 3.00
*Nos. 515-518 (4)* 4.55 4.55

Type of No. 510 overprinted "VISIT OF POPE JOHN PAUL II May 9th, 1984"

**1984, Apr. 16 Wmk. 373**
**519** A82 12c multicolored .20 .20
**520** A82 50c multicolored .70 .70

**Lloyd's List Issue**
Common Design Type
**1984, Apr. 21 Litho. *Perf. 14½x14***
**521** CD335 12c Olivebank, 1892 .65 .20
**522** CD335 15c Tinhow, 1906 .75 .50
**523** CD335 18c Oriana, Point Cruz .80 .60
**524** CD335 $1 Point Cruz view 2.50 2.50
*Nos. 521-524 (4)* 4.70 3.80

WCY Type of 1983
Souvenir Sheet
**Wmk. 373**
**1984, June 18 Litho. *Perf. 14***
**525** A83 $1 multicolored 1.75 1.75

UPU Congress. No. 514a is inscribed "1908-1983," No. 525 inscribed "1907-1984."

Asia-Pacific Broadcasting Union, 20th Anniv. — A86

**1984, July 2 *Perf. 13½***
**526** A86 12c Village drums .20 .20
**527** A86 45c Radio City Guadalcanal .60 .60
**528** A86 60c Broadcasting studio .80 .80
**529** A86 $1 Broadcasting station 1.40 1.40
*Nos. 526-529 (4)* 3.00 3.00

1984 Summer Olympics — A87

***Perf. 13½x14***
**1984, Aug. 4 Litho. Wmk. 373**
**530** A87 12c Flag, vert. .20 .20
**531** A87 25c Lawson Tama Stadium, Honiara .45 .45
**532** A87 50c Honiara Community Center .85 .85
*a.* Booklet pane, 2 ea #531-532 2.75
**533** A87 $1 Olympic Stadium 1.75 1.75
*Nos. 530-533 (4)* 3.25 3.25

**Souvenir Sheet**
**534** A87 95c Bronte Baths 4.50 4.50

Solomon Islds. first olympic participation. No. 534 available in booklet only. Margin shows swimmer A. Wickham (1886-1976).

Little Pied Cormorant (Ausipex '84) A88

**Wmk. 373**
**1984, Sept. 21 Litho. *Perf. 14½***
**535** A88 12c shown .45 .45
**536** A88 18c Australian grey duck .60 .55
**537** A88 35c Nankeen night-heron .80 .60
**538** A88 $1 Dollarbird 1.75 1.75
*a.* Souvenir sheet of 4, #535-538 3.50 3.50
*Nos. 535-538 (4)* 3.60 3.35

EXPO '85, Tsukuba, Japan A89

Designs: 12c, Japanese Memorial Shrine, Mt. Austen, Guadalcanal. 25c, Digital telephone exchange equipment. 45c, Soltai No. 7 fishing vessel. 85c, Coastal village.

**Wmk. 373**
**1985, June 28 Litho. *Perf. 14***
**539** A89 12c multicolored .20 .20
**540** A89 25c multicolored .35 .35
**541** A89 45c multicolored .60 .60
**542** A89 85c multicolored 1.10 1.10
*Nos. 539-542 (4)* 2.25 2.25

**Queen Mother 85th Birthday**
Common Design Type
***Perf. 14½x14***
**1985, June 7 Litho. Wmk. 384**
**543** CD336 12c VE Day, 1945 .20 .20
**544** CD336 25c With Margaret .30 .30
**545** CD336 35c St. Patrick's Day celebration .40 .40
**546** CD336 $1 Holding Prince Henry 1.25 1.25
*Nos. 543-546 (4)* 2.15 2.15

**Souvenir Sheet**
**547** CD336 $1.50 In a gondola, Venice 2.00 2.00

For surcharge see No. B2.

Christmas — A90

**1985, Aug. 30 Wmk. 373 *Perf. 14½***
**548** A90 12c Titiana Village .20 .20
**549** A90 25c Sigana, Santa Isabel .35 .35
**550** A90 35c Artificial Island, Langa Lagoon .45 .45
*Nos. 548-550 (3)* 1.00 1.00

Intl. Youth Year — A91

12c, Girl Guide activities. 15c, Stop Polio Campaign. 25c, Relay runners, views of the islands. 35c, Relay runners, views of Australia. 45c, Saluting natl. flag, badges.

**1985, Sept. 30** ***Perf. 14***

**551** A91 12c multicolored .70 .20
**552** A91 15c multicolored .85 .35
**553** A91 25c multicolored 1.10 .65
**554** A91 35c multicolored 1.25 .75
*a.* Souvenir sheet of 2, #553-554 2.00 2.00
**555** A91 45c multicolored 1.50 1.00
*Nos. 551-555 (5)* 5.40 2.95

Girl Guides 75th anniv., 12c, 45c; IYY, others.

Souvenir Sheet

Audubon Birth Bicent. — A92

Bird illustration by Audubon.

**1985, Nov. 25** **Wmk. 384**

**556** A92 Sheet of 3, 45c, 2 50c 6.50 6.50
*a.* Portrait 1.75 1.75
*b.* Osprey 2.25 2.25

Souvenir Sheet

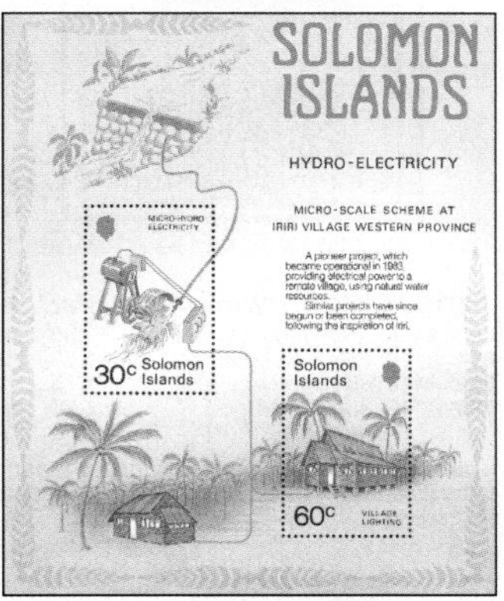
Mini Hydro-Electric Project, Iriri Village — A93

Designs: 30c, Water-driven generator. 60c, Illuminated village house.

**1986, Jan. 24** ***Perf. 14***

**557** A93 Sheet of 2 3.00 3.00
*a.* 30c multicolored 1.00 1.00
*b.* 60c multicolored 1.75 1.75

Halley's Comet A94

Operation Raleigh, 1986: 18c, Construction of Red Cross Center, Gizo. 30c, Exploring rain forest. 60c, Observing Halley's Comet. $1, Ships Sir Walter Raleigh and Zebu.

***Perf. 14½x14***

**1986, Mar. 27** **Wmk. 373**

**558** A94 18c multicolored 1.00 .20
**559** A94 30c multicolored 1.75 .50
**560** A94 60c multicolored 3.00 1.50
**561** A94 $1 multicolored 3.50 2.25
*Nos. 558-561 (4)* 9.25 4.45

**Queen Elizabeth II 60th Birthday**
Common Design Type

Designs: 5c, Visiting Clydebank Town Hall with Prince Philip, 1947. 18c, At Queen Mother's 80th birthday, St. Paul's Cathedral, 1980. 22c, Walking among children of the islands, Pacific tour, 1982. 55c, 50th birthday, Windsor Castle, 1976. $2, Visiting Crown Agents' offices, 1983.

**1986, Apr. 21** **Wmk. 384** ***Perf. 14½***

**562** CD337 5c scarlet, blk & sil .20 .20
**563** CD337 18c ultra & multi .20 .20
**564** CD337 22c green & multi .20 .20
**565** CD337 55c violet & multi .50 .50
**566** CD337 $2 rose vio & multi 1.90 1.90
*Nos. 562-566 (5)* 3.00 3.00

**Royal Wedding Issue, 1986**
Common Design Type

Designs: 55c, Informal portrait. 60c, Andrew aboard royal navy vessel.

**Wmk. 384**

**1986, July 23** **Litho.** ***Perf. 14***

**567** CD338 55c multicolored .50 .50
**568** CD338 60c multicolored .60 .60

Souvenir Sheet

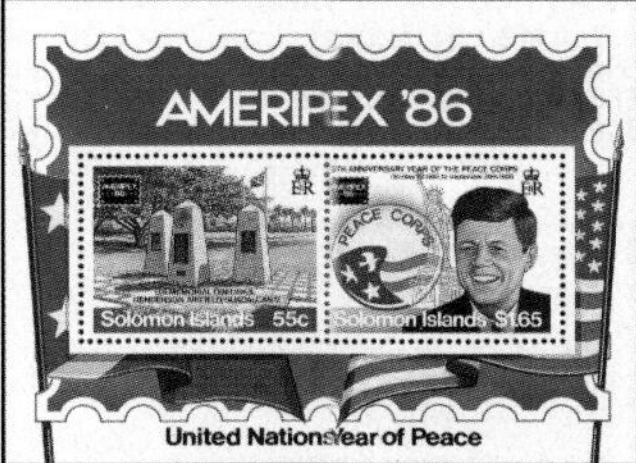
AMERIPEX '86 — A95

55c, U.S. Memorial, Henderson Field, Guadalcanal. $1.65, Peace Corps emblem, Statue of Liberty, Pres. John F. Kennedy.

**1986, May 22** **Litho.** ***Perf. 13½***

**569** A95 Sheet of 2 2.50 2.50
*a.* 55c multicolored .60 .60
*b.* $1.65 multicolored 1.75 1.75

Intl. Peace Year, Peace Corps 25th anniv. For surcharge see No. B3.

1987 America's Cup — A96

Previous winners, challengers, maps and club emblems: No. 570a, America, US, 1851. b, Magic, US, 1870. c, Madeleine, US, 1876. d, Mischief, US, 1881. e, Columbia, US, 1871. f, British Cup course, 1851. g, America II, US, 1987. h, America's Cup. i, Heart of America, US, 1987. j, French Kiss, France, 1987.

No. 571a, Puritan, US, 1885. b, Mayflower, US, 1886. c, Defender, US, 1895. d, Vigilant, US, 1893. e, Volunteer, US, 1887. f, America Cup course, Newport, 1930-1962. g, South Australia, Australia, 1987. h, KA14, Australia, 1987. i, New Zealand II, New Zealand, 1987. j, St. Francis IX, US, 1987.

No. 572a, Columbia, US, 1899. b, Columbia, US, 1901. c, Enterprise, US, 1930. d, Resolute, US, 1920. e, Reliance, US, 1903. f, America Cup course, 1964-1983. g, Kookaburra, Australia, 1987. h, Eagle, US, 1987. i, True North, Canada, 1987. j, Italia, Italy, 1987.

No. 573a, Rainbow, US, 1934. b, Ranger, US, 1937. c, Constellation, US, 1964. d, Weatherly, US, 1962. e, Columbia, US, 1958. f, Western Australia Cup course, 1987. g, Secret Cove, syndicate, 1987. h, Courageous III, US, 1987. i, France, France, 1987. j, Azzurra, Italy, 1987.

No. 574a, Intrepid, US, 1967. b, Intrepid, US, 1970. c, Freedom, US, 1980. d, Courageous, US, 1977. e, Courageous, US, 1974. f, Australia II, Australia, 1983. g, Crusader, Great Britain, 1987. h, Sail America, US, 1987. i, Australia III, Australia, 1987. j, Royal Perth Yacht Club/America's Cup '87 emblem, 1987.

**1986, Aug. 22** **Litho.** ***Perf. 14½***

**570** Strip of 10 + label 5.00 5.00
*a.-d.* A96 18c any single .20 .20
*e.-f.* A96 30c any single .25 .25
*g.-j.* A96 $1 any single .85 .85
**571** Strip of 10 + label 5.00 5.00
*a.-d.* A96 18c any single .20 .20
*e.-f.* A96 30c any single .25 .25
*g.-j.* A96 $1 any single .85 .85
**572** Strip of 10 + label 5.00 5.00
*a.-d.* A96 18c any single .20 .20
*e.-f.* A96 30c any single .25 .25
*g.-j.* A96 $1 any single .85 .85
**573** Strip of 10 + label 5.00 5.00
*a.-d.* A96 18c any single .20 .20
*e.-f.* A96 30c any single .25 .25
*g.-j.* A96 $1 any single .85 .85
**574** Strip of 10 + label 5.00 5.00
*a.-d.* A96 18c any single .20 .20
*e.-f.* A96 30c any single .25 .25
*g.-j.* A96 $1 any single .85 .85
*Nos. 570-574 (5)* 25.00 25.00

Nos. 570-574 printed se-tenant with center labels picturing natl. arms, 1987 America's Cup emblem and trophy in sheets of 50.

Souvenir Sheet

**1987, Feb. 4** **Litho.** ***Perf. 14½***

**575** A96 $5 Stars and Stripes, U.S., victor 5.25 5.25

Coral — A97

***Perf. 14½x14***

**1987, Feb. 11** **Litho.** **Wmk. 384**

**576** A97 18c Dendrophyllia gracilis .50 .20
**577** A97 45c Dendronephthya .95 .50
**578** A97 60c Clavularia 1.25 1.25
**579** A97 $1.50 Melithaea squamata 2.75 2.75
*Nos. 576-579 (4)* 5.45 4.70

Flowering Plants — A98

**1987-88**

**580** A98 1c Cassia fistula .20 .20
**581** A98 5c Allamanda cathartica .20 .20
**582** A98 10c Catharanthus roseus .20 .20
**583** A98 18c Mimosa pudica .40 .20
**584** A98 20c Hibiscus rosa-sinensis .40 .20
**585** A98 22c Clerodendrum thomsonae .45 .25
**586** A98 25c Bauhinia variegata .50 .30
**587** A98 28c Gloriosa rothschildiana .55 .30
**588** A98 30c Heliconia solomonensis .60 .35
**589** A98 40c Episcia hybrid .70 .45
**590** A98 45c Bougainvillea hybrid .75 .50
**591** A98 50c Alpinia purpurata .80 .60
**592** A98 55c Plumeria rubra .90 .60
**593** A98 60c Acacia farnesiana 1.00 .70
**594** A98 $1 Ipomea purpurea 2.50 1.10
**595** A98 $2 Dianella ensifolia 3.50 3.50
**596** A98 $5 Passiflora foetida 5.75 5.75
**596A** A98 $10 Hemigraphis specie ('88) 9.00 9.00
*Nos. 580-596A (18)* 28.40 24.40

Issue dates: $10, Mar. 1; others, May 12.

Mangrove Kingfisher — A99

Orchids — A100

Designs: a, Perched on root. b, Diving. c, Landing in water. d, Emerging with fish.

***Perf. 14x14½***

**1987, July 15** **Wmk. 373**

**597** Strip of 4 13.50 13.50
*a.-d.* A99 60c any single 3.00 3.00

No. 597 has a continuous design.

***Perf. 13½x13***

**1987, Sept. 23** **Wmk. 384**

**598** A100 18c Dendrobium conanthum 1.10 .30
**599** A100 30c Spathoglottis plicata 2.00 .35
**600** A100 55c Dendrobium gouldii 2.25 .75
**601** A100 $1.50 Dendrobium goldfinchii 4.75 4.50
*Nos. 598-601 (4)* 10.10 5.90

Christmas 1987.

Transportation and Communications Decade — A101

Designs: 18c, Telecommunications link. 30c, Express mail service. 60c, Guadalcanal Road Improvement Project. $2, Beechcraft Queen Air, Henderson Airfield control tower.

***Perf. 14x13½***

**1987, Oct. 31** **Litho.** **Unwmk.**

**602** A101 18c multicolored .25 .20
**603** A101 30c multicolored .60 .30
**604** A101 60c multicolored .65 .65
**605** A101 $2 multicolored 2.75 2.75
*Nos. 602-605 (4)* 4.25 3.90

Queen Victoria's Birdwing Butterfly — A102

Designs: No. 606a, Male. No. 606b, Larva. No. 606c, Pupa. No. 606d, Female.

**1987, Nov. 25** **Wmk. 384** ***Perf. 14½***

**606** Strip of 4 16.00 16.00
*a.-d.* A102 45c any single 3.75 3.75

Intl. Fund for Agricultural Development (IFAD), 10th Anniv. — A103

Natl. colors and: No. 607, Student, Natl. Agricultural Training Institute (NATI) farm and emblem (left stamp). No. 608, Students in working in NATI field and emblem (right stamp). No. 609, Flatbed truck transporting produce and emblem (left stamp). No. 610, Canoes, seagulls and emblem (right stamp).

**Wmk. 384**

**1988, Feb. 12 Litho. *Perf. 14½***

| | | | | |
|---|---|---|---|---|
| **607** | | 50c multicolored | .80 | .80 |
| **608** | 120 | 61 multicolored | .80 | .80 |
| *a.* | | A103 Pair, #607-608 | 1.60 | 1.60 |
| **609** | | $1 multicolored | 1.00 | 1.00 |
| **610** | | $1 multicolored | 1.00 | 1.00 |
| *a.* | | A103 Pair, #609-610 | 2.00 | 2.00 |
| | | *Nos. 607-610 (4)* | 3.60 | 3.60 |

EXPO '88, Brisbane, Apr. 30-Oct. 30 — A104

Designs: 22c, Yacht in dry dock. 80c, Canoe. $1.50, Huts.

***Perf. 13½x14***

**1988, Apr. 30 Unwmk.**

| | | | | |
|---|---|---|---|---|
| **611** | A104 | 22c multicolored | .20 | .20 |
| **612** | A104 | 80c multicolored | .80 | .80 |
| **613** | A104 | $1.50 multicolored | 1.50 | 1.50 |
| *a.* | | Souv. sheet of 3, #611-613 | 2.50 | 2.50 |
| *b.* | | As "a," surcharged $3.50 in margin ('90) | 12.00 | 12.00 |
| | | *Nos. 611-613 (3)* | 2.50 | 2.50 |

National Independence, 10th Anniv. — A105

***Perf. 13x13½***

**1988, July 7 Litho. Wmk. 373**

| | | | | |
|---|---|---|---|---|
| **614** | A105 | 22c *Capitana* in Estrella Bay | 1.00 | .20 |
| **615** | A105 | 55c Flag raising, 1893 | 1.75 | .55 |
| **616** | A105 | 80c Supreme Court | 1.50 | 1.25 |
| **617** | A105 | $1 Traditional celebration | 1.75 | 1.75 |
| | | *Nos. 614-617 (4)* | 6.00 | 3.75 |

Australia Bicentennial — A106

Ships: 35c, M.V. *Papuan Chief.* 60c, M.V. *Nimos.* 70c, S.S. *Malaita.* $1.30, S.S. *Makambo.*

**1988, July 30 Wmk. 384 *Perf. 14***

| | | | | |
|---|---|---|---|---|
| **618** | A106 | 35c multicolored | 1.10 | .30 |
| **619** | A106 | 60c multicolored | 1.60 | .45 |
| **620** | A106 | 70c multicolored | 1.60 | .70 |
| **621** | A106 | $1.30 multicolored | 2.00 | 1.60 |
| *a.* | | Souvenir sheet of 4, #618-621 | 3.75 | 3.75 |
| | | *Nos. 618-621 (4)* | 6.30 | 3.05 |

A107

Orchids — A108

**Wmk. 384**

**1988, Aug. 5 Litho. *Perf. 14½***

| | | | | |
|---|---|---|---|---|
| **622** | A107 | 22c Archery | .65 | .20 |
| **623** | A107 | 55c Weight lifting | .90 | .55 |
| **624** | A107 | 70c Running | 1.00 | .70 |
| **625** | A107 | 80c Boxing | 1.25 | .80 |
| | | *Nos. 622-625 (4)* | 3.80 | 2.25 |

**Souvenir Sheet**

**Wmk. 373**

| | | | | |
|---|---|---|---|---|
| **626** | A107 | $2 Olympic Stadium, horiz. | 3.00 | 3.00 |

1988 Summer Olympics, Seoul.

**Lloyds of London, 300th Anniv.**

Common Design Type

Designs: 22c, King George V and Queen Mary at Lloyd's ground-breaking ceremony, 1925. 50c, *Forthbank,* horiz. 65c, Soltel Satellite Ground Station, horiz. $2, *Empress of China.*

**1988, Oct. 31 *Perf. 14***

| | | | | |
|---|---|---|---|---|
| **627** | CD341 | 22c multicolored | .55 | .20 |
| **628** | CD341 | 50c multicolored | 1.40 | .40 |
| **629** | CD341 | 65c multicolored | 1.50 | .60 |
| **630** | CD341 | $2 multicolored | 3.25 | 2.00 |
| | | *Nos. 627-630 (4)* | 6.70 | 3.20 |

***Perf. 13½x13***

**1989, Jan. 20 Litho. Wmk. 373**

| | | | | |
|---|---|---|---|---|
| **631** | A108 | 22c *Bulbophyllum dennisii* | 1.10 | .25 |
| **632** | A108 | 35c *Calanthe langei* | 1.40 | .50 |
| **633** | A108 | 55c *Bulbophyllum blumei* | 1.75 | 1.10 |
| **634** | A108 | $2 *Grammatophyllum speciosum* | 3.50 | 3.50 |
| | | *Nos. 631-634 (4)* | 7.75 | 5.35 |

Intl. Red Cross, 125th Anniv. — A109

***Perf. 14x14½***

**1989, May 16 Wmk. 384**

| | | | | |
|---|---|---|---|---|
| **635** | | 35c Disabled children | .60 | .60 |
| **636** | | 35c Children's Center minibus | .60 | .60 |
| *a.* | | A109 Pair, #635-636 | 1.25 | 1.25 |
| **637** | | $1.50 Patient abed | 1.90 | 1.90 |
| **638** | | $1.50 Physical therapy | 1.90 | 1.90 |
| *a.* | | A109 Pair, #637-638 | 4.00 | 4.00 |
| | | *Nos. 635-638 (4)* | 5.00 | 5.00 |

Sea Slugs A110

**1989, June 30 Wmk. 373 *Perf. 14½***

| | | | | |
|---|---|---|---|---|
| **639** | A110 | 22c *Phyllidia varicosa* | .95 | .25 |
| **640** | A110 | 70c *Chromodoris bullocki* | 2.40 | 1.50 |
| **641** | A110 | 80c *Chromodoris leopardus* | 2.40 | 1.60 |
| **642** | A110 | $1.50 *Phidiana indica* | 3.00 | 3.00 |
| | | *Nos. 639-642 (4)* | 8.75 | 6.35 |

**Moon Landing, 20th Anniv.**

Common Design Type

*Apollo 16*: 22c, Splashdown. 35c, Launch. 70c, Mission emblem. 80c, Ultraviolet color enhancement of Earth. $4, The Moon, as photographed during the *Apollo 11* mission.

**1989, July 20 Wmk. 384 *Perf. 14***

**Size of Nos. 644-645: 29x29mm**

| | | | | |
|---|---|---|---|---|
| **643** | CD342 | 22c multicolored | .60 | .25 |
| **644** | CD342 | 35c multicolored | .95 | .50 |
| **645** | CD342 | 70c multicolored | 1.75 | 1.75 |
| **646** | CD342 | 80c multicolored | 1.90 | 1.90 |
| | | *Nos. 643-646 (4)* | 5.20 | 4.40 |

**Souvenir Sheet**

| | | | | |
|---|---|---|---|---|
| **647** | CD342 | $4 multicolored | 5.00 | 5.00 |

Blowing Soap Bubbles A111

Children's games.

**1989, Nov. 17 Wmk. 384**

| | | | | |
|---|---|---|---|---|
| **648** | A111 | 5c Five stones catch, vert. | .25 | .50 |
| **649** | A111 | 67c shown | 1.75 | 1.75 |
| **650** | A111 | 73c Coconut shell empire | 1.75 | 1.75 |
| **651** | A111 | $1 Seed wind sound, vert. | 2.75 | 2.75 |
| | | *Nos. 648-651 (4)* | 6.50 | 6.75 |

**Souvenir Sheet**

**Wmk. 373**

| | | | | |
|---|---|---|---|---|
| **652** | A111 | $3 Baseball, softball, vert. | 8.25 | 8.25 |

World Stamp Expo '89.

Christmas — A112

**1989, Nov. 30 Wmk. 384**

| | | | | |
|---|---|---|---|---|
| **653** | A112 | 18c Butterfly, fishermen | .60 | .25 |
| **654** | A112 | 25c Nativity | .85 | .30 |
| **655** | A112 | 45c Hospital ward | 1.50 | .45 |
| **656** | A112 | $1.50 Tug of war | 3.25 | 3.25 |
| | | *Nos. 653-656 (4)* | 6.20 | 4.25 |

Personal Ornaments A113

**1990, Feb. 14 Litho. Wmk. 373**

| | | | | |
|---|---|---|---|---|
| **657** | A113 | 5c shown | .30 | .40 |
| **658** | A113 | 12c Necklace | .45 | .30 |
| **659** | A113 | 18c Islander, diff. | .50 | .30 |
| **660** | A113 | $2 Head ornament | 4.75 | 4.75 |
| | | *Nos. 657-660 (4)* | 6.00 | 5.75 |

Cowrie Shells A114

**1990, July 23**

| | | | | |
|---|---|---|---|---|
| **666** | A114 | 4c Spindle cowrie | .35 | .50 |
| **667** | A114 | 20c Map cowrie | .90 | .35 |
| **668** | A114 | 35c Sieve cowrie | 1.25 | .40 |
| **669** | A114 | 50c Egg cowrie | 1.75 | 1.75 |
| **670** | A114 | $1 Prince cowrie | 2.75 | 2.75 |
| | | *Nos. 666-670 (5)* | 7.00 | 5.75 |

**Queen Mother, 90th Birthday**

Common Design Types

25c, Queen Mother, 1987. $5, Inspecting damage to Buckingham Palace, 1940.

**1990, Aug. 4 Wmk. 384 *Perf. 14x15***

| | | | | |
|---|---|---|---|---|
| **671** | CD343 | 25c multicolored | .75 | .25 |

***Perf. 14½***

| | | | | |
|---|---|---|---|---|
| **672** | CD344 | $5 brown & blk | 4.75 | 5.25 |

First Postage Stamp, 150th Anniv. A115

Designs: 35c, Postman, mail van. 45c, Solomon Islands Post Office. 50c, Solomon Islands No. 1. 55c, Young philatelist. 60c, Solomon Islands No. 20, Penny Black.

**1990, Oct. 15 Wmk. 373 *Perf. 14***

| | | | | |
|---|---|---|---|---|
| **673** | A115 | 35c multicolored | 1.10 | .45 |
| **674** | A115 | 45c multicolored | 1.25 | .50 |
| **675** | A115 | 50c multicolored | 1.50 | 1.50 |
| **676** | A115 | 55c multicolored | 1.75 | 1.75 |
| **677** | A115 | 60c multicolored | 1.90 | 1.90 |
| | | *Nos. 673-677 (5)* | 7.50 | 6.10 |

Birds A116

**1990, Dec. 5**

| | | | | |
|---|---|---|---|---|
| **678** | A116 | 10c Purple swamphen | .85 | .75 |
| **679** | A116 | 25c Rufous brown pheasant dove | 1.25 | .50 |
| **680** | A116 | 30c Superb fruit dove | 1.50 | .50 |
| **681** | A116 | 45c Cardinal honey-eater | 1.75 | .70 |
| **682** | A116 | $2 Pigmy parrot | 3.00 | 3.00 |
| | | *Nos. 678-682 (5)* | 8.35 | 5.45 |

Birdpex '90, 20th Intl. Ornithological Congress, New Zealand.

Crop Pests — A117

***Perf. 14x13½***

**1991, Jan. 16 Litho. Wmk. 373**

| | | | | |
|---|---|---|---|---|
| **683** | A117 | 7c Sweet potato weevil | .55 | .40 |
| **684** | A117 | 25c Melon fly | .95 | .30 |
| **685** | A117 | 40c Taro beetle | 1.50 | .50 |
| **686** | A117 | 90c Cocoa weevil borer | 2.00 | 2.00 |
| **687** | A117 | $1.50 Rhinoceros beetle | 2.50 | 2.50 |
| | | *Nos. 683-687 (5)* | 7.50 | 5.70 |

**Elizabeth & Philip, Birthdays**

Common Design Types

**Wmk. 384**

**1991, June 17 Litho. *Perf. 14½***

| | | | | |
|---|---|---|---|---|
| **688** | CD346 | 90c multicolored | 1.40 | 1.40 |
| **689** | CD345 | $2 multicolored | 3.00 | 3.00 |
| *a.* | | Pair, #688-689 + label | 4.50 | 4.50 |

No. 689a exists with two different labels.

Nutritional Foods — A118

**1991, June 24 Wmk. 373 *Perf. 14***

| | | | | |
|---|---|---|---|---|
| **690** | A118 | 5c Coconut water | .30 | .45 |
| **691** | A118 | 75c Feed your child | 1.50 | 1.50 |
| **692** | A118 | 80c Mother's milk | 1.75 | 1.75 |
| **693** | A118 | 90c Local food | 1.90 | 1.90 |
| | | *Nos. 690-693 (4)* | 5.45 | 5.60 |

A 65c value, depicting healthy and unhealthy foods, was prepared but not issued. Value $300.

9th South Pacific Games — A119

**Wmk. 384**

**1991, Aug. 8 Litho. *Perf. 14***

| | | | | |
|---|---|---|---|---|
| **694** | A119 | 25c Volleyball | 1.25 | .30 |
| **695** | A119 | 40c Judo | 1.75 | .60 |
| **696** | A119 | 65c Squash | 2.25 | 2.25 |
| **697** | A119 | 90c Lawn bowling | 2.50 | 2.50 |
| | | *Nos. 694-697 (4)* | 7.75 | 5.65 |

**Souvenir Sheet**

| | | | | |
|---|---|---|---|---|
| **698** | A119 | $2 Games emblem | 6.25 | 6.25 |

Christmas — A120

**Wmk. 373**

**1991, Oct. 28 Litho. *Perf. 14***

**699** A120 10c Food preparation .40 .20
**700** A120 25c Church service .75 .20
**701** A120 65c Feast 1.75 .90
**702** A120 $2 Cricket match 4.50 4.50
*a.* Souvenir sheet of 4, #699-702 7.50 7.50
*Nos. 699-702 (4)* 7.40 5.80

Phila Nippon '91 — A121

Tuna fishing: 5c, Yellowfin tuna. 30c, Boat for pole and line tuna fishing. 80c, Pole and line tuna fishing. $2, Arabushi processing. No. 707a, Food made from tuna, tori nanban. b, Aka miso soup.

**Wmk. 384**

**1991, Nov. 16 Litho. *Perf. 14***

**703** A121 5c multicolored .35 .20
**704** A121 30c multicolored 1.00 .45
**705** A121 80c multicolored 2.50 1.75
**706** A121 $2 multicolored 4.50 4.50
*Nos. 703-706 (4)* 8.35 6.90

**Souvenir Sheet**

**707** A121 80c Sheet of 2, #a.-b. 3.00 3.00

No. 707 contains two 28x45mm stamps.

### Queen Elizabeth II's Accession to the Throne, 40th Anniv.

Common Design Type

**Wmk. 384 (5c, 60c), 373**

**1992, Feb. 6 Litho. *Perf. 14***

**708** CD349 5c multicolored .30 .40
**709** CD349 20c multicolored .60 .20
**710** CD349 40c multicolored .85 .30
**711** CD349 60c multicolored .90 .90
**712** CD349 $5 multicolored 3.75 3.75
*Nos. 708-712 (5)* 6.40 5.55

Alvaro Mendana de Niera (1541-1595), Discoveries in the Solomon Islands — A122

Granada '92: 10c, Thousand Ships Bay. 65c, Route to the Solomon Islands. 80c, Alvaro Mendana de Niera. $1, Graciosa Bay settlement. $5, Sailing ships.

***Perf. 15x14½***

**1992, Apr. 24 Litho. Wmk. 373**

**713** A122 10c multicolored .40 .20
**714** A122 65c multicolored .95 .60
**715** A122 80c multicolored 1.25 1.25
**716** A122 $1 multicolored 2.00 2.00
**717** A122 $5 multicolored 5.00 5.00
*Nos. 713-717 (5)* 9.60 9.05

A123

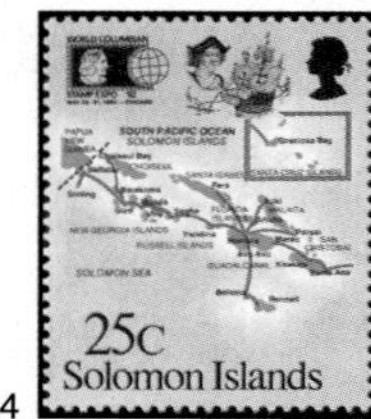

A124

***Perf. 14x13½***

**1992, May 3 Litho. Wmk. 373**

**718** A123 25c Early portrait .60 .35
**719** A123 70c Wearing USMC fatigues 1.25 1.25
**720** A123 90c Wearing uniform, cap 1.25 1.25
*a.* Booklet pane, 2 ea #718, 720 3.75
**721** A123 $2 Statue 1.50 1.50
*a.* Booklet pane, 2 ea #719, 721 5.50
*Nos. 718-721 (4)* 4.60 4.35

**Souvenir Sheet**

**722** A123 $4 In dress uniform 8.25 8.25
*a.* Booklet pane of 1 8.00

Sergeant Major Jacob Vouza (1891-1984). One margin of Nos. 720a, 721a, and 722a is rouletted 8.

**1992, May 22**

World Columbian Stamp Expo '92, Chicago: 25c, Solomon Airlines domestic routes. 80c, Boeing 737-400 airplanes. $1.50, Solomon Airlines international routes. $5, Columbus and Santa Maria.

**723** A124 25c multicolored .90 .20
**724** A124 80c multicolored 1.75 1.25
**725** A124 $1.50 multicolored 2.75 2.75
**726** A124 $5 multicolored 5.75 5.75
*a.* Souvenir sheet of 4, #723-726 12.00 12.00
*b.* As "a," ovptd. with Taipei '93 emblem in sheet margin 6.75 6.75
*Nos. 723-726 (4)* 11.15 9.95

No. 726b issued Aug. 14, 1993.

Miniature Sheets

Battle of Guadalcanal, 50th Anniv. A125

Scenes from battle of Guadalcanal: No. 727a, Japanese landing at Esperance. b, US landings. c, Australian Navy cruiser. d, US Navy post office. e, Royal New Zealand Air Force PBY Catalina.

No. 728a, US Marine Wildcat fighters. b, Henderson Field under construction and attack. c, Heavy cruiser USS Quincy. d, Australian Navy heavy cruiser Canberra. e, US Marines land on Guadalcanal. f, Japanese aircraft carrier Ryujo. g, Japanese Zeke fighters attack US positions. h, Japanese bombers attack American beachhead. i, Japanese destroyers of Tokyo Express. j, Japanese heavy cruiser Chokai.

**Wmk. 384**

**1992, Aug. 7 Litho. *Perf. 14***

**727** A125 30c Sheet of 5, #a.-e. 7.50 7.50
**728** A125 80c Sheet of 10, #a.-j. 15.00 15.00

See No. 889.

Orchids A126

***Perf. 14½x14***

**1992, Dec. 14 Litho. Wmk. 373**

**729** A126 15c Dendrobium hybrid .80 .25
**730** A126 70c Vanda "Amy Laycock" 1.60 1.00
**731** A126 95c Dendrobium mirbelianum 2.00 2.00
**732** A126 $2.50 Dendrobium macrophyllum 2.75 2.75
*Nos. 729-732 (4)* 7.15 6.00

See Nos. 752-755.

Crabs A127

**Wmk. 373**

**1993, Jan. 15 Litho. *Perf. 13***

**733** A127 5c Stalk-eyed ghost .20 .55
**734** A127 10c Red-spotted .20 .55
**735** A127 25c Flat .20 .55
**736** A127 30c Land hermit .20 .20
**737** A127 40c Grapsid .25 .30
**738** A127 45c Red & white painted .25 .30
**739** A127 55c Swift-footed .30 .35
**740** A127 60c Spanner .35 .35
**741** A127 70c Red hermit .45 .45
**742** A127 80c Red-eyed .50 .50
**743** A127 90c Rathbun red .55 .55
**744** A127 $1 Coconut .60 .60
**745** A127 $1.10 Red-spotted white .65 .65
**746** A127 $4 Ghost 2.25 2.75
*a.* Souvenir sheet of 1, perf. 14 2.25 2.25
**747** A127 $10 Mangrove fiddler 6.25 6.25
*Nos. 733-747 (15)* 13.20 14.90

No. 746a for Hong Kong '97. Issued: #733-747, 1/15/93; #746a, 2/3/97.

World War II, 50th Anniv. A128

Designs: 30c, US War Memorial, Skyline Ridge. 80c, Country flags, Guadalcanal. 95c, Major General Alexander A. Vandegrift, map. $4, WWII Scouts, Gizo Islands.

**Wmk. 373**

**1993, Apr. 19 Litho. *Perf. 14***

**748** A128 30c multicolored .50 .30
**749** A128 80c multicolored 1.40 1.25
**750** A128 95c multicolored 1.60 1.60
**751** A128 $4 multicolored 5.00 5.00
*Nos. 748-751 (4)* 8.50 8.15

**Orchid Type of 1992**

***Perf. 14½x14***

**1993 Litho. Wmk. 373**

**752** A126 20c like #729 .40 .25
**753** A126 85c like #730 1.10 1.10
**754** A126 $1.15 like #731 1.40 1.40
**755** A126 $3 like #732 4.00 4.00
*Nos. 752-755 (4)* 6.90 6.75

Nos. 752, 755 are inscribed "World Orchid Conference." Nos. 753-754 are inscribed "Indopex '93 Exhibition."

Issued: #752, 755, 4/24; #753-754, 4/29.

Sinking of PT 109, 50th Anniv. A129

Designs: 30c, PT 109 about to be rammed. 50c, Native, Lt. John F. Kennedy. 95c, Message for help written on coconut, natives in canoe. $1.10, Kennedy, Navy and Marine Corps Medal. $5, PT 109.

**Wmk. 373**

**1993, July 30 Litho. *Perf. 13***

**756** A129 30c multicolored .55 .45
**757** A129 50c multicolored .65 .55
**758** A129 95c multicolored .85 .80
**759** A129 $1.10 multicolored 1.25 1.25
*Nos. 756-759 (4)* 3.30 3.05

**Souvenir Sheet**

***Perf. 13x13½***

**760** A129 $5 multicolored 7.25 7.25

Nicobar Pigeon — A130

**Wmk. 373**

**1993, Sept. 21 Litho. *Perf. 14***

**761** A130 30c shown 1.50 1.00
**762** A130 50c One on ground 2.00 1.25
**763** A130 65c Two on branches 2.50 1.75
**764** A130 70c One on branch 3.50 2.50
**765** A130 $1.10 One on berry branch 1.50 1.50
**766** A130 $3 Two in flight 2.75 2.75
*Nos. 761-766 (6)* 13.75 10.75

World Wildlife Fund.

Dogs A131

**Wmk. 373**

**1994, Feb. 18 Litho. *Perf. 14½***

**767** A131 30c Dachshund .60 .30
**768** A131 80c German shepherd 1.00 1.00
**769** A131 95c Dobermann pinscher 1.25 1.25
**770** A131 $1.10 Australian cattle dog 1.50 1.50
*Nos. 767-770 (4)* 4.35 4.05

**Souvenir Sheet**

**771** A131 $4 Boxer 8.00 8.00

Hong Kong '94.

No. 771 overprinted "19-25 Aug. Jakarta '95 Surcharge $2-00." was available only at the exhibition.

Dolphins A132

**Wmk. 373**

**1994, May 9 Litho. *Perf. 14***

**772** A132 75c Striped 1.00 .85
**773** A132 85c Risso's 1.25 1.00
**774** A132 $1.15 Common 1.50 1.50
**775** A132 $2.50 Spinner 3.00 3.00
**776** A132 $3 Bottlenose 3.50 3.50
*Nos. 772-776 (5)* 10.25 9.85

Miniature Sheet

Butterflies A133

Designs: a, Vindula sapor. b, Papilio aegeus. c, Graphium hicetaon. d, Graphium mendana. e, PHILAKOREA '94 emblem. f, Graphium meeki. g, Danaus schenkii. h, Papilio ptolychus. i, Phaedyma fissizonata.

**Wmk. 373**

**1994, Aug. 16 Litho. *Perf. 13½***

**777** A133 70c Sheet of 9, #a.-i. 6.75 6.75

For overprint see No. 842.

Intl. Year of the Family — A134

Designs: a, Girl writing letter in Brisbane, Australia, family reading letter on Santa Isabel, Solomon Islands. b, Boeing 737-400, Brisbane Intl. Airport, Australia. c, Boeing 737-400, Henderson Airfield, Guadalcanal, DHC 6-Twin Otter. d, Fera Airfield, Buala, Santa Isabel. e, Family.

**1994, Aug. 18** ***Perf. 13***

**778** A134 $1.10 Strip of 5, #a.-e. 5.75 5.75
*f.* Sheet of 1, #778 5.75 5.75

Volcanoes of the Solomon Islands A135

Designs: 30c, Cook Island Volcano erupting under sea, 1967. 70c, Kavachi Volcano erupting from sea, 1977. 80c, Kavachi Volcano forming temporary island, 1978. 90c, Tinakulu Volcano, permanent island.

No. 783: a, Map of Solomon Island volcanoes. b, Diagram illustrating formation of volcanic island archipelago.

**Wmk. 373**

**1994, Oct. 24** **Litho.** ***Perf. 14***

**779** A135 30c multicolored .40 .40
**780** A135 70c multicolored .70 .70
**781** A135 80c multicolored .90 .90
**782** A135 90c multicolored 1.25 1.25
*Nos. 779-782 (4)* 3.25 3.25

**Souvenir Sheet**

**783** A135 $2 Sheet of 2, #a.-b. 4.00 4.00

La Perouse Expedition, 210th Anniv. A136

Designs: 30c, La Perouse, King Louis XVI. 80c, Map of Ile de La Perouse. 95c, L'Astrolabe. $1.10, La Boussole. $3, L'Astrolabe foundering on reef.

**Wmk. 384**

**1994, Dec. 16** **Litho.** ***Perf. 14***

**784** A136 30c multicolored .60 .30
**785** A136 80c multicolored 1.25 1.00
**786** A136 95c multicolored 1.50 1.25
**787** A136 $1.10 multicolored 1.75 1.75
**788** A136 $3 multicolored 3.00 3.00
*Nos. 784-788 (5)* 8.10 7.30

Visit South Pacific Year A137

30c, Tourists watching traditional dance, land hermit crab. 50c, Dendrobium rennellii, milkweed butterfly. 95c, Diver, moorish idol, fish. $1.15, Boats at shore, grapsid crab.

$4, Flower, yellow-bibbed lorry.

***Perf. 15x14½***

**1995, Feb. 17** **Litho.** **Wmk. 373**

**789** A137 30c multicolored .25 .25
**790** A137 50c multicolored .65 .65
**791** A137 95c multicolored .75 .75
**792** A137 $1.15 multicolored .85 .85
*Nos. 789-792 (4)* 2.50 2.50

**Souvenir Sheet**

**793** A137 $4 multicolored 4.25 4.25

FAO, 50th Anniv. A138

**1995, Apr. 5** ***Perf. 12***

**794** A138 70c Banana 1.00 .80
**795** A138 75c Paw paw 1.00 .80
**796** A138 95c Pomelo 1.25 1.25
**797** A138 $2 Star fruit 2.25 2.25
*Nos. 794-797 (4)* 5.50 5.10

**Souvenir Sheet**

**798** A138 $3 Mango 2.75 2.75

**End of World War II, 50th Anniv.**

Common Design Types

Admirals, aircraft carriers: 95c, Vice Adm. Chuichi Nagumo, Akagi. $1, Rear Adm. Frank J. Fletcher, USS Yorktown. $2, Vice Adm. Robert L. Ghormley, USS Wasp. $3, Vice Adm. William F. Halsey, USS Enterprise.

$5, Reverse of War Medal 1939-45.

**1995, May 8** ***Perf. 13½***

**799** CD351 95c multicolored 1.50 1.50
**800** CD351 $1 multicolored 1.50 1.50
**801** CD351 $2 multicolored 2.25 2.25
**802** CD351 $3 multicolored 3.50 3.50
*Nos. 799-802 (4)* 8.75 8.75

**Souvenir Sheet**

***Perf. 14***

**803** CD352 $5 multicolored 4.50 4.50

Orchids — A139

Designs: 45c, Calanthe triplicata. 75c, Dendrobium mohlianum. 85c, Flickingeria comata. $1.15, Dendrobium spectabile.

$4, Coelogyne asperata.

**Wmk. 373**

**1995, Sept. 1** **Litho.** ***Perf. 14***

**804** A139 45c multicolored 1.00 .30
**805** A139 75c multicolored 1.25 1.00
**806** A139 85c multicolored 1.25 1.10
**807** A139 $1.15 multicolored 2.00 2.00
*Nos. 804-807 (4)* 5.50 4.40

**Souvenir Sheet**

**808** A139 $4 multicolored 4.25 4.25

Singapore '95 (#808).

Christmas — A140

Designs: 90c, Start of canoe race. $1.05, Pan pipers, Christmas tree. $1.25, Picnic on beach. $1.45, Local church, nativity.

**1995, Nov. 6** ***Perf. 13x13½***

**810** A140 90c multicolored .85 .75
**811** A140 $1.05 multicolored .90 .80
**812** A140 $1.25 multicolored 1.00 1.00
**813** A140 $1.45 multicolored 1.25 1.25
*Nos. 810-813 (4)* 4.00 3.80

Guglielmo Marconi (1847-1937), Radio, Cent. — A141

Designs: $1.05, Demonstration, Salisbury Plain, 1896. $1.20, Birth of maritime radio, 1900. $1.35, First ground air transmitter, Croydon, 1920. $1.45, Marconi visiting Japan on world tour, 1933-34.

***Perf. 14½x14***

**1996, Feb. 28** **Litho.** **Wmk. 373**

**814** A141 $1.05 multicolored .85 .85
**815** A141 $1.20 multicolored 1.00 1.00
**816** A141 $1.35 multicolored 1.25 1.25
**817** A141 $1.45 multicolored 1.40 1.40
*Nos. 814-817 (4)* 4.50 4.50

Lories A142

**1996, Apr. 10** **Litho.** ***Perf. 14***

**818** A142 75c Palm lorikeet .90 .50
**819** A142 $1.05 Duchess lorikeet 1.00 .70
**820** A142 $1.20 Yellow-bibbed lory 1.25 1.25
**821** A142 $1.35 Cardinal lory 2.00 2.00
**822** A142 $1.45 Meek's lorikeet 2.00 2.00
*Nos. 818-822 (5)* 7.15 6.45

**Souvenir Sheet**

**823** A142 $3 Rainbow lorikeet 3.75 3.75

CAPEX '96 — A143

Island scenes: 40c, Dug-out canoe. 90c, Man, bicycle. $1.20, Mobile Post Office bus. $1.45, "Tulagi Express."

$4, "Tepuke," traditional canoe from Temotu Province.

**Wmk. 384**

**1996, June 8** **Litho.** ***Perf. 13***

**824** A143 40c multicolored .55 .40
**825** A143 90c multicolored 1.00 .80
**826** A143 $1.20 multicolored 1.25 1.25
**827** A143 $1.45 multicolored 2.25 2.25
*Nos. 824-827 (4)* 5.05 4.70

**Souvenir Sheet**

**828** A143 $4 multicolored 3.00 3.00

1996 Summer Olympic Games, Atlanta — A144

Olympic posters: 90c, Tokyo, 1964. $1.20, Los Angeles, 1932. $1.35, Paris, 1924. $2.50, London, 1908.

**Wmk. 384**

**1996, June 30** **Litho.** ***Perf. 14***

**829** A144 90c multicolored .70 .55
**830** A144 $1.20 multicolored .90 .90
**831** A144 $1.35 multicolored 1.00 1.00
**832** A144 $2.50 multicolored 1.50 1.50
*Nos. 829-832 (4)* 4.10 3.95

First Christian Mission, 150th Anniv. — A145

Designs: 40c, Suiesi, Makira Bay, 1846-47. 65c, Original sketches by Rev. L. Verguet, 1846, Surimahe. $1.35, Bishop Epalle's grave, Isabel, 1845. $1.45, Makira Mission, Jean Claude Colin, Marist founder.

**Wmk. 373**

**1996, Sept. 12** **Litho.** ***Perf. 14***

**833** A145 40c multicolored .40 .20
**834** A145 65c multicolored .50 .50
**835** A145 $1.35 multicolored .85 .80
**836** A145 $1.45 multicolored 1.00 1.00
*Nos. 833-836 (4)* 2.75 2.50

**Souvenir Sheet**

Taipei '96 — A146

Illustration reduced.

**1996, Oct. 21**

**837** A146 $1.50 Sandford's eagle 1.25 1.25

UNICEF, 50th Anniv. A147

**Wmk. 373**

**1996, Nov. 21** **Litho.** ***Perf. 14½***

**838** A147 40c Food .35 .25
**839** A147 $1.05 Recreation .75 .75
**840** A147 $1.35 Medicine .95 .95
**841** A147 $2.50 Education 1.50 1.50
*Nos. 838-841 (4)* 3.55 3.45

No. 777 Ovptd. in Red with SINGPEX '97 Emblem

**Wmk. 373**

**1997, Feb. 21** **Litho.** ***Perf. 13½***

**842** A133 70c Sheet of 9, #a.-i. 6.25 6.25

Overprint is centered over entire sheet with each stamp containing portion of SINGPEX '97 emblem.

Overprint exists in black from a limited printing.

Northern Common Cuscus A148

15c, In tree. 60c, Eating berries. $2.50, In tree, climbing right. $3, Two in branches.

**Wmk. 373**

**1997, Apr. 21** **Litho.** ***Perf. 12***

**843** A148 15c multicolored .20 .20
**844** A148 60c multicolored .30 .30
**845** A148 $2.50 multicolored 1.10 1.10
**846** A148 $3 multicolored 1.40 1.40
*Nos. 843-846 (4)* 3.00 3.00

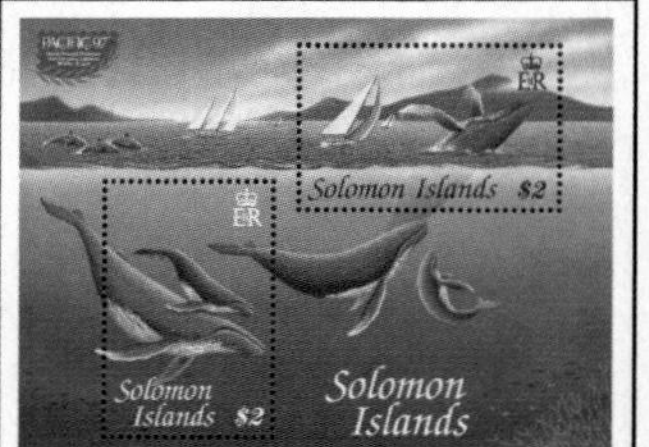


Whales — A149

a, Whale, calf, vert. b, Whale breaching.

**Wmk. 373**

**1997, May 29 Litho. *Perf. 14½***
**847** A149 $2 Sheet of 2, #a.-b. 3.00 3.00

PACIFIC 97.

Queen Elizabeth II & Prince Philip, 50th Wedding Anniv. — A150

#848, Queen with two horses. #849, Prince. #850, Prince on polo pony. #851, Queen. #852, Queen, Prince at Royal Ascot.

**1997, July 10 *Perf. 13***
**848** $3 multicolored 2.75 2.75
**849** $3 multicolored 2.75 2.75
***a.*** A150 Pair, #848-849 6.00 6.00
**850** $3 multicolored 2.75 2.75
**851** $3 multicolored 2.75 2.75
***a.*** A150 Pair, #850-851 6.00 6.00
*Nos. 848-851 (4)* 11.00 11.00

**Souvenir Sheet**

**852** A150 $3 multicolored 2.75 2.75

South Pacific Commission, 50th Anniv. — A151

Chelonia mydas: 50c, Laying eggs. 90c, Young turtles entering water. $1.50, Group swimming under water. $2, Two adults under water.

**Wmk. 384**

**1997, Sept. 29 Litho. *Perf. 14***
**853** A151 50c multicolored .60 .35
**854** A151 90c multicolored .90 .80
**855** A151 $1.50 multicolored 1.25 1.25
**856** A151 $2 multicolored 1.50 1.50
*Nos. 853-856 (4)* 4.25 3.90

Christmas A152

Designs: $1.10, Oni mako. $1.40, Ysabel dancing women with bamboo sticks. $1.50, Pan pipers from Small Malaita. $1.70, Western bamboo band.

No. 861, vert.: a, Pachycephala pectoralis. b, Papilio aegeus, graphium meeki.

**Wmk. 373**

**1997, Nov. 24 Litho. *Perf. 13½***
**857** A152 $1.10 multicolored .60 .60
**858** A152 $1.40 multicolored .80 .80
**859** A152 $1.50 multicolored .85 .85
**860** A152 $1.70 multicolored .95 .95
*Nos. 857-860 (4)* 3.20 3.20

**Souvenir Sheet of 2**

***Perf. 14***

**861** A152 $1.50 #a.-b. 3.50 3.50

China Stamp Exhibition, Bangkok '97 (#861). Issued: #857-860, 11/24; #861, 12/5.

Game Fish — A153

50c, Black marlin. $1.20, Shortbill swordfish. $1.40, Swordfish. $2, Indo-Pacific sailfish.

***Perf. 14½***

**1998, Feb. 27 Litho. Unwmk.**
**862** A153 50c multicolored .75 .40
**863** A153 $1.20 multicolored 1.25 1.00
**864** A153 $1.40 multicolored 1.50 1.50
**865** A153 $2 multicolored 1.75 1.75
***a.*** Souv. sheet of 1, wmk. triangles 2.25 2.25
*Nos. 862-865 (4)* 5.25 4.65

Singpex '98 (#865a). No. 865a issued 7/23 and sold for $3.

**Diana, Princess of Wales (1961-97)**

Common Design Type

$2, Wearing white dress (without hat).

#867: a, Up close. b, Wearing white hat, dress. c, Wearing evening dress, black background. d, Taking flowers from children.

***Perf. 14½x14***

**1998, Mar. 31 Wmk. 373**
**866** CD355 $2 multicolored 1.10 1.10
Complete booklet, 10 #866 11.00

**Sheet of 4**

**867** CD355 $2.50 #a.-d. 5.00 5.00

No. 867 sold for $10 + 50c, with surtax from international sales being donated to the Princess Diana Memorial Fund and surtax from national sales being donated to designated local charity.

Technical Cooperation Between Solomon Islands and Republic of China A154

Designs: 50c, Harvesting watermelons. $1.50, Harvesting rice.

No. 870: a, 80c, Growing cucumbers. b, $1.20, Growing tomatoes.

**Wmk. 373**

**1998, May 29 Litho. *Perf. 13***
**868** A154 50c multicolored .30 .30
**869** A154 $1.50 multicolored .80 .80

**Souvenir Sheet**

**870** A154 Sheet of 2, #a.-b. 1.40 1.40

Melanesian Trade and Culture Show — A155

a, Group raising arms during traditional dance. b, Men with bows and arrow. c, Man smiling in front of water. d, Four men with poles in traditional dance. e, Masked man kneeling down with bow and arrow. f, Man in traditional garb, flowers. g, Group carrying poles. h, Man with spear and shield. i, Man in traditional garb, sun over water.

**1998, July 3 *Perf. 13½***
**871** Sheet of 9 7.50 7.50
***a.-c.*** A155 50c any single .45 .45
***d.-f.*** A155 $1.20 any single .55 .55
***g.-i.*** A155 $1.50 any single .75 .75

Souvenir Sheet

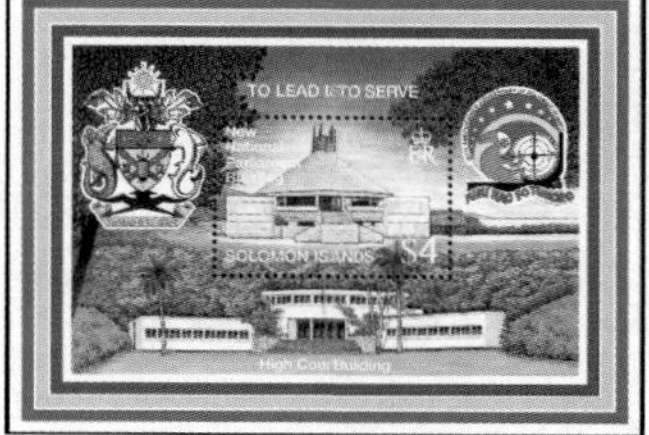

New Natl. Parliament Building — A156

Illustration reduced.

**1998, July 7**
**872** A156 $4 multicolored 2.50 2.50

Independence, 20th anniv.

Souvenir Sheet

Australia '99 World Stamp Expo — A157

Designs: a, HMS Endeavour, 1770. b, Los Reyes being careened at Guadalcanal, 1568.

**1999, Mar. 19 *Perf. 13¼x13¾***
**873** A157 $10 Sheet of 2, #a.-b. 8.50 8.50

PhilexFrance '99, World Philatelic Exhibition. A158

Marine Life: a, Beach. b, Great frigate bird. c, Coconut crab. d, Green turtle. e, Royal Spanish dancer nudibranch. f, Sun moon and stars butterflyfish. g, Striped Sweetlips. h, Saddle-back butterflyfish. i, Cuttlefish. j, Giant clam. k, Lionfish. l, Spiny lobster.

**1999, July 2 *Perf. 13¼***
**874** A158 $1 Sheet of 12, #a.-l. 6.75 6.75

**1st Manned Moon Landing, 30th Anniv.**

Common Design Type

Designs: 50c, Lift-off. $1.50, Lunar module above moon's surface. $2.50, Aldrin beside US flag. $3.40, Splashdown.

$4, Earth as seen from moon.

***Perf. 14x13¾***

**1999, July 20 Litho. Wmk. 384**
**875** CD357 50c multicolored .40 .30
**876** CD357 $1.50 multicolored .90 .90
**877** CD357 $2.50 multicolored 1.75 1.75
**878** CD357 $3.40 multicolored 2.25 2.25
*Nos. 875-878 (4)* 5.30 5.20

**Souvenir Sheet**

***Perf. 14***

**879** CD357 $4 multicolored 3.25 3.25
***a*** Ovptd. in margin in red 3.50 3.50

No. 879 contains one circular stamp 40mm in diameter.

Issued 7/7/2000, overprint on No. 879a reads "WORLD STAMP EXPO - USA VALUE $5.00." Sold for $5.

**Queen Mother's Century**

Common Design Type

Queen Mother: $1, Inspecting bomb damage at Portsmouth, 1941. $1.50, At the Derby, 1983. $2.30, Receiving birthday wishes. $4.90, As colonel-in-chief of Royal Army Medical Corps.

$3, With King George VI, Winston Churchill, V-E Day, 1945.

**1999, Aug. 16 *Perf. 13½***
**880** CD358 $1 multicolored .75 .50
**881** CD358 $1.50 multicolored .85 .85
**882** CD358 $2.30 multicolored 1.25 1.25
**883** CD358 $4.90 multicolored 1.90 1.90
*Nos. 880-883 (4)* 4.75 4.50

**Souvenir Sheet**

**884** CD358 $5 black 3.25 3.25

Ferrari Racing Cars A159

**1999, Sept. 27 Wmk. 373 *Perf. 14***
**885** A159 $1 212E .75 .50
**886** A159 $1.50 250TR .90 .70
**887** A159 $3.30 250LM 1.50 1.50
**888** A159 $4.20 612 Can-Am 2.75 2.75
*Nos. 885-888 (4)* 5.90 5.45

**Guadalcanal Type of 1992**

Designs: a, Flags at half staff. b, Cenotaph, Honiara. c, Solomon Peace Memorial Park. d, US War Memorial, Skyline Ridge. e, Reunion ship Ocean Pearl.

**1999, Aug. 16 Wmk. 384**
**889** A125 30c Strip of 5, #a.-e., + label 2.50 2.50

Melanesian Mission, 150th Anniv. — A160

Christmas: a, $1, Bishop George Augustus Selwyndd. b, $1, Bishop John Coleridge Patteson. c, $3.30, Text. d, $1.50, Stained glass. e, $1.50, Southern Cross.

**1999, Nov. 12 Unwmk.**
**890** A160 Strip of 5, #a.-e. 4.00 4.00

See Norfolk Islands #693.

Millennium A161

Designs: Nos. 891, 893a, $1 Munda lighthouse, war canoe. Nos. 892, 893b, $4, Tulagi lighthouse, security boat.

**2000, Apr. 27 *Perf. 13½x13¼***
**891** A161 $1 multi 1.25 .75
**892** A161 $4 multi 3.75 3.75

**Souvenir Sheet**

**893** A161 Sheet of 2, #a.-b. 6.00 6.00

Nos. 893a, 893b have red violet margins.

Souvenir Sheet

Commonwealth Youth Minister's Meeting — A162

Illustration reduced.

**2000, May 22 Litho.** ***Perf. 13½x13¼***

**894** A162 $6 multi 9.50 9.50

Year of the Dragon A163

Dragon head facing: $1, Front. $3.90, Left.

***Perf. 11¾x11½***

**2000, Nov. 13 Litho. Unwmk.**

**895-896** A163 Set of 2 2.50 2.50

*896a* Souvenir sheet, #895-896 2.50 2.50

East Rennell Island World Heritage Site A164

Map and: 50c, Rennell Island. $3.40, Lake Tegano. $4, Rennell shrikebill. $4.90, Endemic orchid.

***Perf. 11¾x11½***

**2000, Nov. 30 Litho.**

**897-900** A164 Set of 4 7.25 7.25

2000 Summer Olympics and Olymphilex, Sydney — A165

Runners in: $1, 100-meter race. $4.50, 1500-meter race.

**2000, Dec. 11** ***Perf. 14***

**901-902** A165 Set of 2 4.75 4.75

*a.* Souvenir sheet, #901-902 4.25 4.25

Birds A166

Designs: 5c, Yellow-throated white eye. 20c, Purple swamphen. 50c, Blyth's hornbill. 80c, Yellow-faced myna. 90c, Blue-faced parrotfinch. $1, Crested tern. $2, Rainbow lorikeet. $3, Eclectus parrot. $4, Dwarf kingfisher. $10, Beach thick-knee. $20, Brahminy kite. $50, Superb fruit dove.

**2001 Wmk. 373** ***Perf. 14¼x14½***

| | | | | |
|---|---|---|---|---|
| **903** | A166 | 5c multi | .20 | .20 |
| **904** | A166 | 20c multi | .20 | .20 |
| **905** | A166 | 50c multi | .25 | .25 |
| **906** | A166 | 80c multi | .35 | .35 |
| **907** | A166 | 90c multi | .40 | .40 |
| **908** | A166 | $1 multi | .50 | .50 |
| **909** | A166 | $2 multi | .90 | .90 |
| **910** | A166 | $3 multi | 1.25 | 1.25 |
| **911** | A166 | $4 multi | 1.75 | 1.75 |
| **912** | A166 | $10 multi | 3.75 | 3.75 |

**Size: 48x38mm**

***Perf. 13¾x13½***

| | | | | |
|---|---|---|---|---|
| **913** | A166 | $20 multi | 8.25 | 8.25 |
| **913A** | A166 | $50 multi | 22.50 | 22.50 |
| | | *Nos. 903-913 (11)* | 17.80 | 17.80 |

Issued: Nos. 5c-$20, 2/1/01; $50, 6/1/01.

**East Rennell Island Type of 2000 and**

Hong Kong 2001 Stamp Exhibition A167

Snake color: $1.70, Yellow and brown. $2.30, Green and yellow.

**2001, Feb. 1 Litho.** ***Perf. 11¾x11½***

**914-915** A167 Set of 2 3.00 3.00

**Souvenir Sheet**

**916** A164 $5 Like #900 5.00 5.00

UN High Commissioner for Refugees, 50th Anniv. — A168

Designs: 50c, Refugees. $1, Food and medical supplies. $1.90, Shelter. $2.30, Education.

***Perf. 14¼***

**2001, July 28 Litho. Unwmk.**

**917-920** A168 Set of 4 3.75 3.75

Souvenir Sheet

New Year 2001 (Year of the Snake) — A168a

No. 920A: b, Red-banded tree snake. c, Whip snake. d, Pacific boa. e, Guppy's snake.

**920A** A168a $1 Sheet of 4, #b-e 3.25 3.25

Reef Fish A169

Designs: 70c, Amphiprion chrysopterus. 90c, Amphiprion perideraion. $1, Premnas biaculeatus. $1.50, Amphiprion melanopus. $2.10, Amphiprion clarkii. $4.50, Dascyllus trimaculatus.

**Wmk. 373**

**2001, Dec. 27 Litho.** ***Perf. 14***

**921-926** A169 Set of 6 5.75 5.75

*926a* Souvenir sheet, #921-926 5.75 5.75

Worldwide Fund for Nature (WWF) A170

Various depictions of gray cuscus: $1, $1.70, $2.30, $5.

**2002, Jan. 31**

**927-930** A170 Set of 4 5.00 5.00

*a.* Horiz. strip of 4 5.25 5.25

**Reign Of Queen Elizabeth II, 50th Anniv. Issue**

Common Design Type

Designs: Nos. 931, 935a, $1, Princess Elizabeth with baby carriage, 1933. Nos. 932, 935b, $1.90, Wearing sunglasses. Nos. 933, 935c, $2.10, In 1955. Nos. 934, 935d, $2.30, Wearing hat. No. 935e, $10, 1955 portrait by Annigoni (38x50mm).

***Perf. 14¼x14½, 13¾ (#935e)***

**2002, Feb. 6 Litho. Wmk. 373**

**With Gold Frames**

**931-934** CD360 Set of 4 3.75 3.75

**Souvenir Sheet**

**Without Gold Frames**

**935** CD360 Sheet of 5, #a-e 7.50 7.50

Methodist Mission, Cent. A172

Designs: $1, Typical old school building, Western Solomons. $1.70, Mrs. J. F. Goldie and companions. $2.10, Tandanya, first mission schooner. $2.30, Rev. J. F. Goldie and Solomon Islands chiefs.

$5, Rev. Goldie and Sam Aqarao, vert.

**2002, May 23 Unwmk.** ***Perf. 14¼***

**937-940** A172 Set of 4 3.50 3.50

**Souvenir Sheet**

**941** A172 $5 multi 2.75 2.75

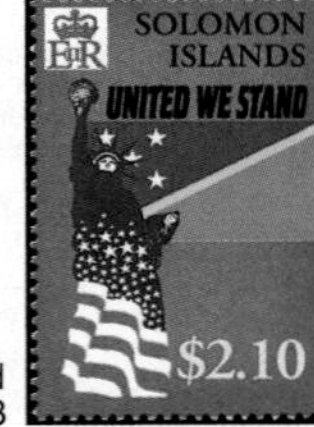


United We Stand — A173

***Perf. 13½x13¼***

**2002, June 17 Unwmk.**

**942** A173 $2.10 multi 2.25 2.25

Souvenir Sheet

New Year 2002 (Year of the Horse) — A173a

No. 942A: b, Horse. c, Horse, horiz.

***Perf. 13½x13¾, 13¾x13½***

**2002, July 7 Litho.**

**942A** A173a $4 Sheet of 2, #a-b 5.25 5.25

No. 942 was printed in sheets of 4.

Cowrie Shells — A174

No. 943: a, $1, Sieve cowrie. b, $1, Kitten cowrie. c, $1, Stolid cowrie, eroded cowrie. d, $1.90, Tapering cowrie. e, $1.90, Tiger cowrie. f, $1.90, Lynx cowrie. g, $2.30, Map cowrie. h, $2.30, Pacific deer cowrie. i, $2.30, Tortoise cowrie.

$10, Golden cowrie.

***Perf. 14¼x14½***

**2002, Aug. 2 Wmk. 373**

**943** A174 Sheet of 9, #a-i 7.00 7.00

**Souvenir Sheet**

**944** A174 $10 multi 5.50 5.50

Phila Korea 2002 World Stamp Exhibition, Seoul.

**Queen Mother Elizabeth (1900-2002)**

Common Design Type

Designs: No. 945, $1, Without hat (sepia photograph). No. 946, $2.30, Wearing blue hat.

No. 947: a, $5, Wearing tiara (black and white photograph). b, $5, Wearing green blue hat.

**Wmk. 373**

**2002, Aug. 5 Litho.** ***Perf. 14¼***

**With Purple Frames**

**945-946** CD361 Set of 2 2.25 2.25

**Souvenir Sheet**

**Without Purple Frames**

***Perf. 14½x14¼***

**947** CD361 Sheet of 2, #a-b 4.75 4.75

Battle of Guadalcanal, 60th Anniv. — A175

US servicemen: $1, No. 952d, Coast Guard signalman First Class Douglas Munro. $1.90, No. 952b, Marine Corps Capt. Joe Foss. $2.10, No. 952c, Marine Corps Platoon Sergeant Mitchell Paige. $2.30, No. 952a, Navy Rear Admiral Norman Scott.

**2002, Aug. 7 Unwmk.** ***Perf. 14***

**948-951** A175 Set of 4 5.00 5.00

**Souvenir Sheet**

**952** A175 $5 Sheet of 4, #a-d 8.50 8.50

Christmas — A176

Paintings: $1, Christmas Night, by Lucas Cranach, the Elder. $2.10, Madonna and Child, by Giovanni Bellini. $2.30, Nativity, by Perugino, horiz. $5, Madonna and Child, by Simone Martini.

**2002, Nov. 25 Litho.** ***Perf. 14***

**953-956** A176 Set of 4 6.00 6.00

New Year 2003 (Year of the Ram) A177

***Perf. 14¼x14½***

**2003, Apr. 15 Litho. Unwmk.**

**957** A177 $3 multi 1.50 1.50

Issued in sheets of 4.

U. S. Medals of Honor — A178

Designs: $1, Air Force Medal of Honor. $1.90 Navy Medal of Honor. $2.10, Army Medal of Honor. $2.30, Medal of Honor ribbon.

**2003, June 6** ***Perf. 14***

**958-961** A178 Set of 4 4.25 4.25

Prince William, 21st Birthday — A179

No. 962: a, In gray suit. b, In red shirt. c, In black suit.
$15, In blue shirt.

**2003, June 21**
**962** A179 $9 Sheet of 3, #a-c 12.00 12.00

**Souvenir Sheet**

**963** A179 $15 multi 5.50 5.50

Solomon Islands — Republic of China Diplomatic Relations, 20th Anniv. A180

Designs: $1.50, Rice farmers. $2.10, Hospital.

**2003, July 8** ***Perf. 14¼***
**964-965** A180 Set of 2 2.25 2.25

Coronation of Queen Elizabeth II, 50th Anniv. — A181

No. 966: a, Wearing tiara. b, Wearing green hat. c, Wearing blue hat.
$15, Wearing tiara, diff.

**2003, June 2 Litho.** ***Perf. 14***
**966** A181 $9 Sheet of 3, #a-c 12.00 12.00

**Souvenir Sheet**

**967** A181 $15 multi 7.50 7.50

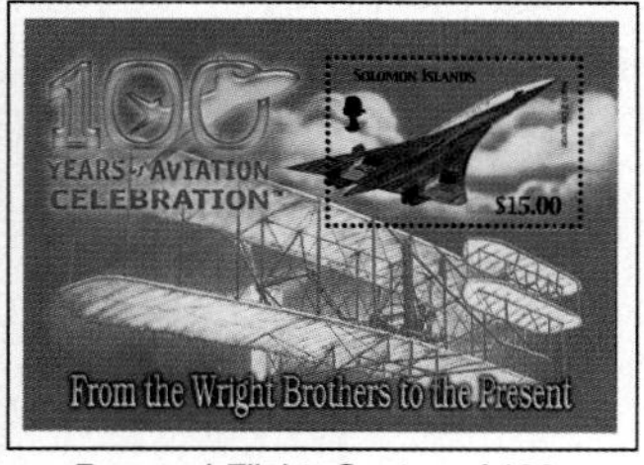

Powered Flight, Cent. — A182

No. 968: a, Boeing 747. b, Boeing 707. c, Lockheed Model 649. d, Boeing Model 247D. e, Fokker F.VII. f, Orville and Wilbur Wright.
$15, Concorde.

**2003, Dec. 17**
**968** A182 $4 Sheet of 6, #a-f 12.00 12.00

**Souvenir Sheet**

**969** A182 $15 multi 5.75 5.75

**Souvenir Sheet**

Visit of Pope John Paul II, 20th Anniv. — A183

No. 970: a, $5, Pope waving. b, $10, Pope with crucifix.

**2004, Aug. 6 Litho.** ***Perf. 14***
**970** A183 Sheet of 2, #a-b 5.50 5.50

2004 Summer Olympics, Athens — A184

Designs: $1.50, Runner at starting blocks. $2, Runner in full stride. $2.20, Runner at finish line. $10, Solomon Islands flag, Olympic rings.

**2004, Aug. 13** ***Perf. 14***
**971-974** A184 Set of 4 5.50 5.50

Orchids A185

No. 975: a, Calanthe triplicata. b, Dendrobium johnsoniae. c, Dendrobium capituliflorum. d, Spathoglottis plicata. e, Dendrobium mirbelianum. f, Dendrobium polysema. g, Paphiopedilum bougainvilleanum. h, Coelogyne asperata. i, Dendrobium macrophyllum. j, Dendrobium spectabile.

**2004, Aug. 28** ***Perf. 13½***

| | | | |
|---|---|---|---|
| **975** | Block of 10 | 11.50 | 11.50 |
| ***a.-e.*** | A185 $2.60 Any single | .75 | .75 |
| ***f.-j.*** | A185 $5 Any single | 1.50 | 1.50 |

Pres. Ronald Reagan (1911-2004) — A186

**2004, Sept. 30 Litho.** ***Perf. 14***
**976** A186 $5 multi 2.00 2.00

Printed in sheets of 4.

Merchant Ships A187

Designs: $1.50, MV Bilikiki. $2.20, MV Spirit of Solomons. $3, SS Oceana. $20, RMS Queen Elizabeth 2.

**2004, Oct. 11** ***Perf. 13¼***
**977-980** A187 Set of 4 7.50 7.50

FIFA (Fédération Internationale de Football Association), Cent. — A188

No. 981, $2.10: a, Player and ball. b, Players.
No. 982, $10: a, Players. b, Player and ball.
Illustration reduced.

**2004, Nov. 1** ***Perf. 14***

**Horiz. Pairs, #a-b**

**981-982** A188 Set of 2 7.00 7.00

Bird Life International — A189

No. 983, $2.10: a, Rufous-tailed waterhen. b, Buff-banded rail. c, Purple swamphen. d, Woodford's rail e, Roviana rail. f, Makira moorhen.
No. 984, $5: a, Solomon Islands hawk-owl (denomination at LR). b, White-throated eared nightjar (denomination at LR). c, Solomon Islands hawk-owl (denomination at LL). d, White-throated eared nightjar (denomination at UR). e, Marbled frogmouth. f, Fearful owl.
No. 985, $7.50: a, Beach kingfisher. b, Collared kingfisher. c, Ultramarine kingfisher. d, Moustached kingfisher. e, Little kingfisher. f, Variable kingfisher.

**2004, Nov. 15** ***Perf. 13¾***

**Sheets of 6, #a-f**

**983-985** A189 Set of 3 25.00 25.00

Christmas — A190

Paintings: 10c, Adoration of the Magi, by Peter Paul Rubens. 50c, Madonna della Tenda, by Raphael, vert. $1.50, Madonna and Child, by Titian, vert. $2.60, Madonna by the Arch, by Albrecht Dürer, vert. $3, Holy Family, by Frans Floris. $10, Madonna and Child, by unknown artist.

**2004, Dec. 8** ***Perf. 14***
**986-991** A190 Set of 6 5.50 5.50

Battle of Trafalgar, Bicent. — A191

No. 992, $1.90: a, Vice-Admiral Horatio Lord Nelson. b, HMS Victory. c, Sir Thomas Masterman Hardy. d, The first engagement. e, Breaking the line. f, The death of Nelson.
No. 993, $2.60: a, Lord Cuthbert Collingwood. b, Napoleon Bonaparte. c, Destruction of the Bucentaure. d, Race and chase, 1805. e, The Nelson Touch — Band of Brothers. f, The Nelson Touch.
No. 994, $5: a, Nelson and Hardy on deck. b, Nelson sends the signal "England expects." c, Attempted siege of HMS Victory. d, Neptune tows Victory to Gibraltar. e, Funeral procession on Thames. f, Nelson's Column.
No. 995, $10: a, Nelson's early years. b, The letters of Nelson. c, Siege of Calvi — Nelson loses the sight of his eye. d, Santa Cruz de Tenerife — Nelson loses his arm. e, The Battle of Cape St. Vincent. f, The Battle of the Nile.

**2005, Jan. 3** ***Perf. 13¼***

**Sheets of 6, #a-f**

**992-995** A191 Set of 4 37.50 37.50

Baha'is in Solomon Islands, 50th Anniv. — A192

Designs: $1.50, Geometric design. $3, Globe, hands, laurel branches. $5, Alvin and Gertrude Blum, horiz.

**2005, Mar. 21 Litho.** ***Perf. 14¼***
**996-998** A192 Set of 3 3.00 3.00

End of World War II, 60th Anniv. — A193

No. 999: a, $2.50, Japanese forces land at Tulagi. b, $2.50, USS Lexington under air attack during Battle of the Coral Sea. c, $2.50, Coastwatcher and Solomon Island scouts. d, $2.50, US forces land at Tulagi and Guadalcanal virtually unopposed. e, $2.50, HMAS Canberra sinking at Iron Bottom Sound. f, $5, Cactus Air Force in action over Henderson Airfield. g, $5, "Tokyo Express" nightly bombardments by Japanese warships. h, $5, P-38 Lightnings shoot down Admiral Yamamoto. i, $5, Lt. John F. Kennedy's PT-109 sank after collision with Japanese warship Amagiri. j, $5, Sgt. Maj. Vouza and medals.
No. 1000, RAN coastwatchers sending enemy intelligence reports by teleradio.

**2005, Apr. 21** ***Perf. 13¾***
**999** A193 Sheet of 10, #a-j 11.00 11.00

**Souvenir Sheet**

**1000** A193 $5 multi 2.00 2.00

Pacific Explorer 2005 World Stamp Expo, Sydney (#1000).

Europa Stamps, 50th Anniv. (in 2006) A194

No. 1001: a, Spain #1262. b, Netherlands #417.
No. 1002: a, Andorra (French) #174. b, Belgium #573.
No. 1003: a, Belgium #496. b, Spain #1567.
No. 1004: a, Austria #657. b, San Marino #701.
No. 1005: a, Netherlands #494. b, Norway #842.
No. 1006: a, Germany #749. b, Italy #750.

**2005, May 16** ***Perf. 13½x13¾***

| | | | |
|---|---|---|---|
| **1001** | Horiz. pair | .55 | .55 |
| ***a.-b.*** | A194 $1 Either single | .25 | .25 |
| ***c.*** | Souvenir sheet, #1001 | .55 | .55 |
| **1002** | Horiz. pair | 1.25 | 1.25 |
| ***a.-b.*** | A194 $2.10 Either single | .60 | .60 |
| ***c.*** | Souvenir sheet, #1002 | 1.25 | 1.25 |
| **1003** | Horiz. pair | 2.00 | 2.00 |
| ***a.-b.*** | A194 $2.50 Either single | .80 | .80 |
| ***c.*** | Souvenir sheet, #1003 | 2.10 | 2.10 |
| **1004** | Horiz. pair | 3.50 | 3.50 |
| ***a.-b.*** | A194 $5 Either single | 1.50 | 1.50 |
| ***c.*** | Souvenir sheet, #1004 | 3.75 | 3.75 |
| **1005** | Horiz. pair | 6.50 | 6.50 |
| ***a.-b.*** | A194 $10 Either single | 3.00 | 3.00 |
| ***c.*** | Souvenir sheet, #1005 | 6.75 | 6.75 |
| **1006** | Horiz. pair | 10.00 | 10.00 |
| ***a.-b.*** | A194 $15 Either single | 4.50 | 4.50 |
| ***c.*** | Souvenir sheet, #1006 | 10.50 | 10.50 |
| | *Nos. 1001-1006 (6)* | 23.80 | 23.80 |

Queen Elizabeth II's Royal Year — A195

No. 1007, $1: a, Order of the Garter. b, Trooping the Color.
No. 1008, $2.10: a, Royal Ascot. b, Garden party.
No. 1009, $2.50: a, Royal visits. b, State visits.
No. 1010, $5: a, State Opening of Parliament. b, Remembrance Day.
No. 1011, $10: a, Investitures. b, Christmas broadcast.
No. 1012, $15: a, Maundy service. b, Chelsea Flower Show.
Illustration reduced.

**2005, June 3** ***Perf. 14½***
**Horiz. Pairs, #a-b**

**1007-1012** A195 Set of 6 22.50 22.50

A196

A197

A198

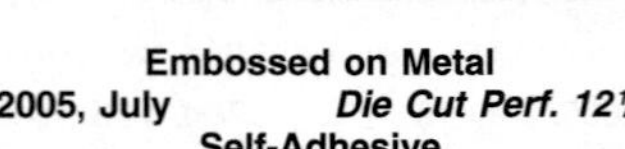
Pope John Paul II (1920-2005) A199

**Embossed on Metal**
**2005, July** ***Die Cut Perf. 12½***
**Self-Adhesive**

| | | | | | |
|---|---|---|---|---|---|
| **1013** | A196 | $1.20 | shown | .60 | .60 |
| **1014** | A196 | $1.20 | Pope, diff. | .60 | .60 |
| **1015** | A197 | $2.60 | shown | 1.25 | 1.25 |
| **1016** | A197 | $2.60 | Pope, diff. | 1.25 | 1.25 |
| **1017** | A198 | $5 | shown | 2.50 | 2.50 |
| **1018** | A198 | $5 | Pope, diff. | 2.50 | 2.50 |
| **1019** | A199 | $10 | shown | 5.50 | 5.50 |
| **1020** | A199 | $10 | Pope, diff. | 5.50 | 5.50 |
| | *Nos. 1013-1020 (8)* | | | 19.70 | 19.70 |

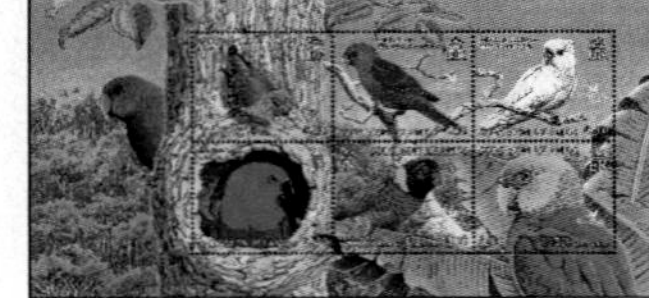
BirdLife International — A200

No. 1021, $2.10: a, Finsch's pygmy parrot. b, Cardinal lory. c, Solomon's cockatoo. d, Eclectus parrot. e, Rainbow lory. f, Song parrot.

No. 1022, $5: a, Red-knobbed imperial pigeon. b, Yellow-bibbed fruit dove. c, Claret-breasted fruit dove. d, Nicobar pigeon. e, Stephan's ground dove. f, Crested cuckoo dove.
No. 1023, $7.50: a, Pied goshawk. b, Imitator sparrowhawk. c, Buff-headed coucal. d, Black-faced pitta. e, Melanesian megapode. f, Blyth's hornbill.

**2005, Sept. 1 Litho.** ***Perf. 14½x14¾***
**Sheets of 6, #a-f**

**1021-1023** A200 Set of 3 25.00 25.00

Rotary International, Cent. — A201

**2005, Sept. 12** ***Perf. 14½***

**1024** A201 $2.50 multi 1.25 1.25

No. 970 Overprinted

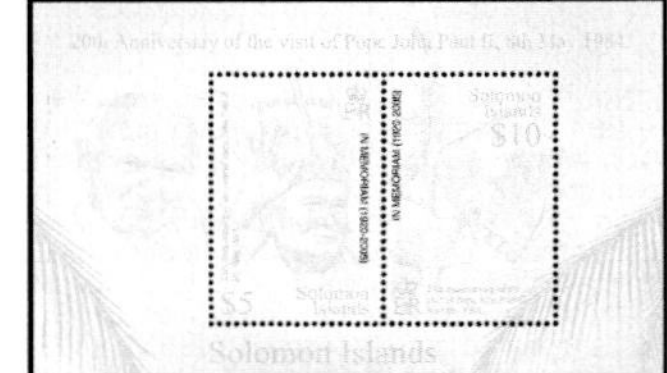

No. 1025: a, $5. b, $10.

**2005, Oct. 3** ***Perf. 14***

**1025** A183 Sheet of 2, #a-b 4.25 4.25

Christmas — A202

Stories by Hans Christian Andersen (1805-75): $1, The Little Fir Tree. $2.10, The Nightingale. $2.50, The Emperor's New Clothes. $5, The Phoenix. $10, The Tinderbox. $15, The Red Shoes.

**2005, Oct. 10**

**1026-1031** A202 Set of 6 11.00 11.00

Battle of Trafalgar, Bicent. — A203

Designs: $5, HMS Victory. $10, Ship in battle, horiz. $20, Admiral Horatio Nelson.

**2005, Oct. 18** ***Perf. 13¼***

**1032-1034** A203 Set of 3 11.00 11.00

Worldwide Fund for Nature (WWF) — A204

Various views of prehensile-tailed skink: $1.50, $2.60, $3, $10.

**2005, Dec. 7** ***Perf. 14½***

**1035-1038** A204 Set of 4 5.25 5.25
*1038a* Sheet, 2 each # 1035-1038 9.50 9.50

Queen Elizabeth II, 80th Birthday A205

Queen Elizabeth II: $2.10, As young girl. $2.50, As woman. $5, Holding camera. $20, Wearing red hat.
No. 1043: a, $10, Like $2.50. b, $15, Like $5.

**2006, Apr. 21 Litho.** ***Perf. 14***
**Stamps With White Frames**

**1039-1042** A205 Set of 4 8.25 8.25

**Souvenir Sheet**
**Stamps Without Frames**

**1043** A205 Sheet of 2, #a-b 7.00 7.00

Anniversaries — A206

No. 1044, $2.20: a, Great Eastern. b, Isambard Kingdom Brunel (1806-59), engineer.
No. 1045, $2.50: a, Charles Darwin. b, Green turtle.
No. 1046, $5: a, Diving bell. b, Edmond Halley (1656-1742), astronomer.
No. 1047, $10: a, Locomotive "Rocket." b, George Stephenson (1781-1848), inventor.

**2006, Apr. 30** ***Perf. 14¾x14½***
**Horiz. Pairs, #a-b**

**1044-1047** A206 Set of 4 11.00 11.00

Darwin's voyage on the Beagle, 175th anniv. (#1045).

Christopher Columbus (1451-1506), Explorer — A207

Designs: $1.90, Niña. $2.20, Pinta. $2.60, Santa Maria. $10, Arms of Columbus.

**2006, May 22** ***Perf. 13¼x13***

**1048-1051** A207 Set of 4 4.75 4.75

Washington 2006 World Philatelic Exhibition.

2006 World Cup Soccer Championships, Germany — A208

Match scenes from: $4, 1954 West Germany finals victory. $5, 1966 England finals victory. $10, 1998 France finals victory. $20, 2006 Solomon Islands vs. Australia playoff.

**2006, June 9** ***Perf. 14***

**1052-1055** A208 Set of 4 11.00 11.00

Victoria Cross, 150th Anniv. A209

Victoria Cross and: $1, Captured Russian gun used to cast the Victoria Cross. $2.20, Midshipman Charles Lucas, first recipient of Victoria Cross. $2.50, Queen Victoria awarding first Victoria Crosses. $5, Corporal Sukanaivalu, Fijian infantryman at Bougainville, 1944. $10, Corporal Rattey, Australian infantryman at Bougainville, 1945. $15, Private Partridge, Australian infantryman at Bougainville, 1945.

**2006, June 26** ***Perf. 14x14½***

**1056-1061** A209 Set of 6 10.00 10.00

Prehistoric Animals — A210

Designs: 5c, Baryonyx. 10c, Diplodocus. $1.50, Pteranodon. $2.15, Argentinosaurus. $2.40, Centrosaurus. $3, Allosaurus. $10, Ankylosaurus. $20, Iguanodon.

**2006, Aug. 14** ***Perf. 13¼x13¾***

**1062-1069** A210 Set of 8 11.00 11.00

Cone Shells — A211

Designs: 5c, Conus marmoreus. 10c, Conus auratinus. 20c, Conus ferrugineus. 50c, Conus consors. 80c, Conus magdalenae. 90c, Conus sulcatus brettinghami. $1, Conus tmetus. $1.50, Conus aureus. $2, Conus corallinus. $3, Conus floccatus. $4, Conus punniculus. $10, Conus pohlianus. $20, Conus proximus. $50, Conus canonicus.

**2006, Oct. 31** ***Perf. 13x12½***

| | | | | | |
|---|---|---|---|---|---|
| **1070** | A211 | 5c | multi | .20 | .20 |
| **1071** | A211 | 10c | multi | .20 | .20 |
| **1072** | A211 | 20c | multi | .20 | .20 |
| **1073** | A211 | 50c | multi | .20 | .20 |
| **1074** | A211 | 80c | multi | .20 | .20 |
| **1075** | A211 | 90c | multi | .25 | .25 |
| **1076** | A211 | $1 | multi | .30 | .30 |
| **1077** | A211 | $1.50 | multi | .40 | .40 |
| **1078** | A211 | $2 | multi | .55 | .55 |
| **1079** | A211 | $3 | multi | .80 | .80 |
| **1080** | A211 | $4 | multi | 1.10 | 1.10 |
| **1081** | A211 | $10 | multi | 2.75 | 2.75 |
| **1082** | A211 | $20 | multi | 5.50 | 5.50 |
| **1083** | A211 | $50 | multi | 13.50 | 13.50 |
| | *Nos. 1070-1083 (14)* | | | 26.15 | 26.15 |

Tales of Beatrix Potter — A212

Designs: $1.50, The Tale of Peter Rabbit. $1.90, The Tale of Squirrel Nutkin. $2.15, The Tailor of Gloucester. $2.40, The Tale of Benjamin Bunny. $2.65, The Tale of Two Bad Mice. $5, The Tale of Mrs. Tiggy-Winkle.

**2006, Dec. 4** ***Perf. 13x13½***

**1084-1089** A212 Set of 6 4.25 4.25
*1089a* Miniature sheet, #1084-1089 4.25 4.25

Wedding of Queen Elizabeth II and Prince Philip, 60th Anniv. — A213

Designs: $2.10, Couple looking straight ahead. $2.50, Couple looking at each other. $5, Wedding ceremony. No. 1093, $20, Elizabeth with flowers.
No. 1094, $20, Wedding party.

**2007, Jan. 31** ***Perf. 13¾***

| | | | | |
|---|---|---|---|---|
| **1090-1093** | A213 | Set of 4 | 8.50 | 8.50 |

**Souvenir Sheet**

***Perf. 14***

| | | | | |
|---|---|---|---|---|
| **1094** | A213 | $20 multi | 5.75 | 5.75 |

No. 1094 contains one 42x56mm stamp.

## SEMI-POSTAL STAMPS

**Catalogue values for unused stamps in this section are for Never Hinged items.**

No. 452 Overprinted in Red: "+ 50c SURCHARGE / CYCLONE RELIEF FUND / 1982"

***Perf. 13½x13***

**1982, May 3 Litho. Wmk. 373**

| | | | | |
|---|---|---|---|---|
| **B1** | CD331 | $1 + 50c multi | 2.25 | 2.25 |

Nos. 546 and 569 Surcharged "Cyclone Relief Fund 1986" and New Value in Scarlet

***Perf. 14½x14***

**1986, Sept. 23 Litho. Wmk. 384**

| | | | | |
|---|---|---|---|---|
| **B2** | CD336 | $1 + 50c multi | 1.75 | 1.75 |

**Souvenir Sheet**

***Perf. 13½***

| | | | | |
|---|---|---|---|---|
| **B3** | | Sheet of 2 | 4.25 | 4.25 |
| *a.* | A95 | 55c + 25c multi | 1.00 | 1.00 |
| *b.* | A95 | $1.65 + 75c multi | 2.75 | 2.75 |

No. 840 Surcharged in Red

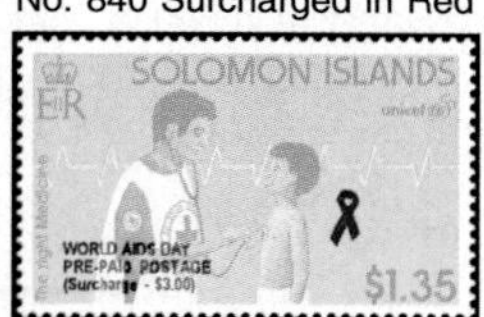


**Wmk. 373**

**2003, Feb. 8 Litho.** ***Perf. 14½***

| | | | | |
|---|---|---|---|---|
| **B4** | A147 | $1.35 +$3 multi | 3.50 | 3.50 |

World AIDS Day.

No. 866 Surcharged in Red

***Perf. 14½x14***

**2003, Mar. 17 Wmk. 373**

| | | | | |
|---|---|---|---|---|
| **B5** | CD355 | $2 +$5 multi | 3.25 | 3.25 |

Surtax for Cyclones Zoe and Beni Relief Fund.

## POSTAGE DUE STAMPS

D1

***Perf. 12***

**1940, Sept. 1 Typo. Wmk. 4**

| | | | | |
|---|---|---|---|---|
| **J1** | D1 | 1p emerald | 4.00 | *7.25* |
| **J2** | D1 | 2p dark red | 4.25 | *7.25* |
| **J3** | D1 | 3p chocolate | 4.25 | *12.00* |
| **J4** | D1 | 4p dark blue | 6.50 | *12.00* |
| **J5** | D1 | 5p deep green | 7.25 | *22.50* |
| **J6** | D1 | 6p brt red vio | 7.25 | *17.50* |
| **J7** | D1 | 1sh dull violet | 9.00 | *27.50* |
| **J8** | D1 | 1sh6p turq green | 16.00 | *50.00* |
| | | *Nos. J1-J8 (8)* | 58.50 | *156.00* |
| | | Set, never hinged | 100.00 | |

# SOMALIA

sō-ˈmä-lē-ə

(Somali Democratic Republic)

(Italian Somaliland)

(Benadir)

LOCATION — Eastern Africa, bordering on the Indian Ocean and the Gulf of Aden
GOVT. — Probably none
AREA — 246,201 sq. mi.
POP. — 7,140,643 (1999 est.)
CAPITAL — Mogadishu

The former Italian colony which included the territory west of the Juba River became known as Oltre Giuba (Trans-Juba), was absorbed into Italian East Africa in 1936. Somalia stamps continued in use in Italian East Africa for several years. It was under British military administration from 1941-49. Italian trusteeship took effect in 1950, with a UN Advisory Council helping the administrator. On July 1, 1960, the former Italian colony merged with Somaliland Protectorate (British) to form the independent Republic of Somalia.

4 Besas = 1 Anna
16 Annas = 1 Rupee
100 Besas = 1 Rupee (1922)
100 Centesimi = 1 Lira (1905, 1925)
100 Centesimi = 1 Somalo (1950)
100 Centesimi = 1 Somali Shilling (1961)

**Catalogue values for unused stamps in this country are for Never Hinged items, beginning with Scott 170 in the regular postage section, Scott B52 in the semi-postal section, Scott C17 in the airpost section, Scott CB11 in the airpost semi-postal section, Scott CE1 in the airpost special delivery section, Scott E8 in the special delivery section, Scott J55 in the postage due section, and Scott Q56 in the parcel post section.**

**Used values in italics are for postally used Italian Somalia stamps. CTO's or stamps with fake cancels sell for about the same as unused, hinged stamps.**

**Watermark**

Wmk. 140 — Crown

**Italian Somaliland**

Elephant — A1

Lion — A2

**Wmk. 140**

**1903, Oct. 12 Typo.** ***Perf. 14***

| | | | | |
|---|---|---|---|---|
| **1** | A1 | 1b brown | 52.50 | 12.00 |
| **2** | A1 | 2b blue green | 1.50 | *7.50* |
| **3** | A2 | 1a claret | 1.50 | *9.00* |
| **4** | A2 | 2a orange brown | 1.75 | *16.00* |
| **5** | A2 | 2½a blue | 1.50 | *16.00* |
| **6** | A2 | 5a orange | 1.75 | *37.50* |
| **7** | A2 | 10a lilac | 1.75 | *37.50* |
| | | *Nos. 1-7 (7)* | 62.25 | *135.50* |

For surcharges see Nos. 8-27, 40-50, 70-77.

Surcharged

**1905, Dec. 29**

| | | | | |
|---|---|---|---|---|
| **8** | A2 | 15c on 5a orange | *3,000.* | 825.00 |
| **9** | A2 | 40c on 10a lilac | 600.00 | 250.00 |

Surcharged

**1906-07**

| | | | | |
|---|---|---|---|---|
| **10** | A1 | 2c on 1b brown | 6.00 | *15.00* |
| **11** | A1 | 5c on 2b blue grn | 6.00 | 10.50 |

Surcharged

| | | | | |
|---|---|---|---|---|
| **12** | A2 | 10c on 1a claret | 6.00 | 10.50 |
| **13** | A2 | 15c on 2a brn org ('06) | 6.00 | 10.50 |
| **14** | A2 | 25c on 2½a blue | 15.00 | 10.50 |
| **15** | A2 | 50c on 5a yellow | 14.00 | 13.00 |

Surcharged

| | | | | |
|---|---|---|---|---|
| **16** | A2 | 1 l on 10a lilac | 21.00 | *32.50* |
| | | *Nos. 10-16 (7)* | 74.00 | *102.50* |

Nos. 15 and 16 with bars over former Surcharge and

**1916, Apr.**

| | | | | |
|---|---|---|---|---|
| **18** | A2 | 5c on 50c on 5a yel | 32.50 | 37.50 |
| **19** | A2 | 20c on 1 l on 10a dl lil | 9.00 | *30.00* |

No. 4 Surcharged

| | | | | |
|---|---|---|---|---|
| **20** | A2 | 20c on 2a org brn | 18.00 | 11.00 |
| | | *Nos. 18-20 (3)* | 59.50 | *78.50* |

Nos. 11-16 Surcharged:

a

b

**1922, Feb. 1**

| | | | | |
|---|---|---|---|---|
| **22** | A1(a) | 3b on 5c on 2b | 10.50 | *19.00* |
| **23** | A2(b) | 6c on 10c on 1a | 18.00 | 15.00 |
| **24** | A2(b) | 9b on 15c on 2a | 18.00 | 19.00 |
| **25** | A2(b) | 15b on 25c on 2½a | 18.00 | 15.00 |
| **26** | A2(b) | 30b on 50c on 5a | 20.00 | *37.50* |
| **27** | A2(b) | 60b on 1 l on 10a | 20.00 | *67.50* |
| | | *Nos. 22-27 (6)* | 104.50 | *173.00* |

**Victory Issue**

Italy Nos. 136-139 Surcharged

**1922, Apr.**

| | | | | |
|---|---|---|---|---|
| **28** | A64 | 3b on 5c olive grn | 1.75 | *6.75* |
| **29** | A64 | 6b on 10c red | 1.75 | *6.75* |
| **30** | A64 | 9b on 15c slate grn | 1.75 | *10.50* |
| **31** | A64 | 15b on 25c ultra | 1.75 | *10.50* |
| | | *Nos. 28-31 (4)* | 7.00 | *34.50* |

Nos. 10-16 Surcharged with Bars and

c

d

**1923, July 1**

| | | | | |
|---|---|---|---|---|
| **40** | A1 | 1b brown | 9.00 | *27.50* |
| **41** | A1(c) | 2b on 2c on 1b | 9.00 | *27.50* |
| **42** | A1(c) | 3b on 2c on 1b | 9.00 | *16.00* |
| **43** | A2(d) | 5b on 50c on 5a | 9.00 | *15.00* |
| **44** | A1(c) | 6b on 5c on 2b | 13.50 | 15.00 |
| **45** | A2(d) | 18b on 10c on 1a | 13.50 | 15.00 |
| **46** | A2(d) | 20b on 15c on 2a | 16.00 | 15.00 |
| **47** | A2(d) | 25b on 15c on 2a | 16.00 | 15.00 |
| **48** | A2(d) | 30b on 25c on 2½a | 18.00 | 15.00 |
| **49** | A2(d) | 60b on 1 l on 10a | 18.00 | *40.00* |
| **50** | A2(d) | 1r on 1 l on 10a | 45.00 | *52.50* |
| | | *Nos. 40-50 (11)* | 176.00 | *253.50* |

No. 40 is No. 10 with bars over the 1907 surcharge.

### Propagation of the Faith Issue

Italy Nos. 143-146 Surcharged

**1923, Oct. 24** **Wmk. 140**

| No. | Type | Description | Unused | Used |
|---|---|---|---|---|
| 51 | A68 | 6b on 20c ol grn & brn org | 7.50 | 37.50 |
| 52 | A68 | 13b on 30c cl & brn org | 7.50 | 37.50 |
| 53 | A68 | 20b on 50c vio & brn org | 4.50 | 45.00 |
| 54 | A68 | 30b on 1 l bl & brn org | 4.50 | 55.00 |
| | | *Nos. 51-54 (4)* | 24.00 | 175.00 |

### Fascisti Issue

Italy Nos. 159-164 Surcharged in Red or Black

**1923, Oct. 29** **Unwmk.** ***Perf. 14***

| No. | Type | Description | Unused | Used |
|---|---|---|---|---|
| 55 | A69 | 3b on 10c dk grn (R) | 9.00 | 13.00 |
| 56 | A69 | 13b on 30c dk vio (R) | 9.00 | 13.00 |
| 57 | A69 | 20b on 50c brn car | 9.00 | 15.00 |
| | | **Wmk. 140** | | |
| 58 | A70 | 30b on 1 l blue | 9.00 | 37.50 |
| 59 | A70 | 1r on 2 l brown | 9.00 | 45.00 |
| 60 | A71 | 3r on 5 l blk & bl (R) | 9.00 | 60.00 |
| | | *Nos. 55-60 (6)* | 54.00 | 183.50 |

### Manzoni Issue

Italy Nos. 165-170 Surcharged in Red

**1924, Apr. 1**

| No. | Type | Description | Unused | Used |
|---|---|---|---|---|
| 61 | A72 | 6b on 10c brn red & blk | 12.00 | 37.50 |
| 62 | A72 | 9b on 15c bl grn & blk | 12.00 | 37.50 |
| 63 | A72 | 13b on 30c blk & sl | 12.00 | 37.50 |
| 64 | A72 | 20b on 50c org brn & blk | 12.00 | 37.50 |

Surcharged

| No. | Type | Description | Unused | Used |
|---|---|---|---|---|
| 65 | A72 | 30b on 1 l bl & blk | 75.00 | 250.00 |
| 66 | A72 | 3r on 5 l vio & blk | 475.00 | 2,000. |
| | | *Nos. 61-66 (6)* | 598.00 | 2,400. |

### Victor Emmanuel Issue

Italy Nos. 175-177 Overprinted

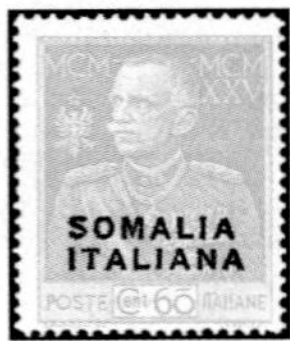

**1925-26** **Unwmk.** ***Perf. 13½, 11***

| No. | Type | Description | Unused | Used |
|---|---|---|---|---|
| 67 | A78 | 60c brown car | 1.50 | 7.50 |
| a. | | Perf. 11 | 90.00 | 150.00 |
| 68 | A78 | 1 l dk bl, perf 11 | 2.25 | 11.00 |
| a. | | Perf. 13½ | 7.50 | 37.50 |
| 69 | A78 | 1.25 l dk blue ('26) | 1.50 | 18.00 |
| a. | | Perf. 11 | 600.00 | 825.00 |
| | | *Nos. 67-69 (3)* | 5.25 | 36.50 |

Stamps of 1907-16 with Bars over Original Values

**1926, Mar. 1** **Wmk. 140** ***Perf. 14***

| No. | Type | Description | Unused | Used |
|---|---|---|---|---|
| 70 | A1 | 2c on 1b brown | 20.00 | 45.00 |
| 71 | A1 | 5c on 2b blue grn | 15.00 | 22.50 |
| 72 | A2 | 10c on 1a rose red | 9.00 | 7.50 |
| 73 | A2 | 15c on 2a org brn | 9.00 | 10.50 |
| 74 | A2 | 20c on 2a org brn | 10.50 | 10.50 |
| 75 | A2 | 25c on 2½a blue | 10.50 | 15.00 |
| 76 | A2 | 50c on 5a yellow | 15.00 | 26.00 |
| 77 | A2 | 1 l on 10a dull lil | 20.00 | 37.50 |
| | | *Nos. 70-77 (8)* | 109.00 | 174.50 |

### Saint Francis of Assisi Issue

Italy Nos. 178-180 Overprinted

**1926, Apr. 12** ***Perf. 14***

| No. | Type | Description | Unused | Used |
|---|---|---|---|---|
| 78 | A79 | 20c gray green | 2.25 | 10.50 |
| 79 | A80 | 40c dark violet | 2.25 | 10.50 |
| 80 | A81 | 60c red brown | 2.25 | 18.00 |

Italy Nos. 182 and Type of 1926 Overprinted in Red

**Unwmk.** ***Perf. 11***

| No. | Type | Description | Unused | Used |
|---|---|---|---|---|
| 81 | A82 | 1.25 l dark blue | 2.25 | 26.00 |
| | | ***Perf. 14*** | | |
| 82 | A83 | 5 l + 2.50 l ol grn | 6.00 | 52.50 |
| | | *Nos. 78-82 (5)* | 15.00 | 117.50 |

Italian Stamps of 1901-26 Overprinted

**1926-30** **Wmk. 140**

| No. | Type | Description | Unused | Used |
|---|---|---|---|---|
| 83 | A43 | 2c orange brown | 3.75 | 6.00 |
| 84 | A48 | 5c green | 3.75 | 6.00 |
| 85 | A48 | 10c claret | 3.00 | .35 |
| 86 | A49 | 20c violet brown | 3.00 | 2.25 |
| 87 | A46 | 25c grn & pale grn | 3.00 | 1.50 |
| 88 | A49 | 30c gray ('30) | 13.50 | 30.00 |
| 89 | A49 | 60c brown orange | 4.50 | 9.00 |
| 90 | A46 | 75c dk red & rose | 97.50 | 30.00 |
| 91 | A46 | 1 l brown & grn | 4.50 | .75 |
| 92 | A46 | 1.25 l blue & ultra | 10.50 | 2.25 |
| 93 | A46 | 2 l dk grn & org | 22.50 | 13.50 |
| 94 | A46 | 2.50 l dk grn & org | 22.50 | 18.00 |
| 95 | A46 | 5 l blue & rose | 60.00 | 37.50 |
| 96 | A51 | 10 l gray grn & red | 60.00 | 60.00 |
| | | *Nos. 83-96 (14)* | 312.00 | 217.10 |

### Volta Issue

Type of Italy, 1927, Overprinted

**1927, Oct. 10**

| No. | Type | Description | Unused | Used |
|---|---|---|---|---|
| 97 | A84 | 20c purple | 4.50 | 30.00 |
| 98 | A84 | 50c deep orange | 7.50 | 18.00 |
| a. | | Double overprint | 160.00 | |
| 99 | A84 | 1.25 l brt blue | 10.50 | 47.50 |
| | | *Nos. 97-99 (3)* | 22.50 | 95.50 |

Italian Stamps of 1927-28 Overprinted in Black or Red

**1928-30**

| No. | Type | Description | Unused | Used |
|---|---|---|---|---|
| 100 | A86 | 7½c lt brown | 18.00 | 52.50 |
| a. | | Double overprint | 400.00 | |
| 101 | A85 | 50c brn & sl (R) | 18.00 | 6.00 |
| 102 | A86 | 50c brt violet ('30) | 37.50 | 52.50 |
| | | ***Perf. 11*** **Unwmk.** | | |
| 103 | A85 | 1.75 l deep brown | 70.00 | 18.00 |
| | | *Nos. 100-103 (4)* | 143.50 | 129.00 |

### Monte Cassino Issue

Types of Monte Cassino Issue of Italy Overprinted in Red or Blue

**1929, Oct. 14** **Wmk. 140** ***Perf. 14***

| No. | Type | Description | Unused | Used |
|---|---|---|---|---|
| 104 | A96 | 20c dk green (R) | 4.50 | 16.00 |
| 105 | A96 | 25c red org (Bl) | 4.50 | 16.00 |
| 106 | A98 | 50c + 10c crim (Bl) | 4.50 | 18.00 |
| 107 | A98 | 75c + 15c ol brn (R) | 4.50 | 18.00 |
| 108 | A96 | 1.25 l + 25c dk vio (R) | 10.50 | 32.50 |
| 109 | A98 | 5 l + 1 l saph (R) | 10.50 | 37.50 |

Overprinted in Red

**Unwmk.**

| No. | Type | Description | Unused | Used |
|---|---|---|---|---|
| 110 | A100 | 10 l + 2 l gray brn | 10.50 | 52.50 |
| | | *Nos. 104-110 (7)* | 49.50 | 190.50 |

### Royal Wedding Issue

Type of Italian Royal Wedding Stamps of 1930 Overprinted

**1930, Mar. 17** **Wmk. 140**

| No. | Type | Description | Unused | Used |
|---|---|---|---|---|
| 111 | A101 | 20c yellow green | 1.50 | 4.50 |
| 112 | A101 | 50c + 10c dp org | 1.10 | 7.50 |
| 113 | A101 | 1.25 l + 25c rose red | 1.10 | 15.00 |
| | | *Nos. 111-113 (3)* | 3.70 | 27.00 |

### Ferrucci Issue

Types of Italian Stamps of 1930 Overprinted in Red or Blue

**1930, July 26**

| No. | Type | Description | Unused | Used |
|---|---|---|---|---|
| 114 | A102 | 20c violet (R) | 3.00 | 3.75 |
| 115 | A103 | 25c dark green (R) | 3.00 | 3.75 |
| 116 | A103 | 50c black (R) | 3.00 | 7.50 |
| 117 | A103 | 1.25 l deep blue (R) | 3.00 | 15.00 |
| 118 | A104 | 5 l + 2 l dp car (bl) | 7.50 | 26.00 |
| | | *Nos. 114-118 (5)* | 19.50 | 56.00 |

### Virgil Issue

Types of Italian Stamps of 1930 Overprinted in Red or Blue

**1930, Dec. 4** **Photo.** **Wmk. 140**

| No. | Type | Description | Unused | Used |
|---|---|---|---|---|
| 119 | A106 | 15c violet blue | 1.10 | 7.50 |
| 120 | A106 | 20c orange brown | 1.10 | 3.00 |
| 121 | A106 | 25c dark green | 1.10 | 3.00 |
| 122 | A106 | 30c lt brown | 1.10 | 3.00 |
| 123 | A106 | 50c dull violet | 1.10 | 3.00 |
| 124 | A106 | 75c rose red | 1.10 | 6.00 |
| 125 | A106 | 1.25 l gray blue | 1.10 | 7.50 |
| | | **Engr.** **Unwmk.** | | |
| 126 | A106 | 5 l + 1.50 l dk vio | 3.25 | 37.50 |
| 127 | A106 | 10 l + 2.50 l ol brn | 3.25 | 55.00 |
| | | *Nos. 119-127 (9)* | 14.20 | 125.50 |

### Saint Anthony of Padua Issue

Types of Italian Stamps of 1931 Overprinted in Blue or Red

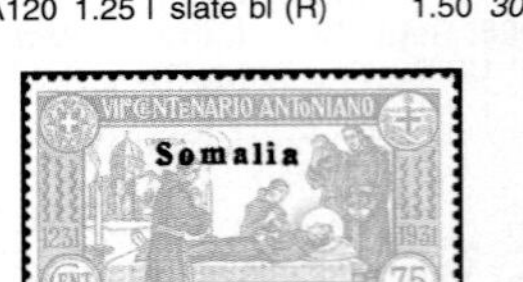

**1931, May 7** **Photo.** **Wmk. 140**

| No. | Type | Description | Unused | Used |
|---|---|---|---|---|
| 129 | A116 | 20c brown (Bl) | 1.50 | 16.00 |
| 130 | A116 | 25c green (R) | 1.50 | 6.00 |
| 131 | A118 | 30c gray brn (Bl) | 1.50 | 6.00 |
| 132 | A118 | 50c dull vio (Bl) | 1.50 | 6.00 |
| 133 | A120 | 1.25 l slate bl (R) | 1.50 | 30.00 |

Overprinted in Red or Black

**Engr.** **Unwmk.**

| No. | Type | Description | Unused | Used |
|---|---|---|---|---|
| 134 | A121 | 75c black (R) | 1.50 | 16.00 |
| 135 | A122 | 5 l + 2.50 l dk brn (Bk) | 6.00 | 62.50 |
| | | *Nos. 129-135 (7)* | 15.00 | 142.50 |

Italy Nos. 218, 221 Overprinted in Red

**1931** **Wmk. 140**

| No. | Type | Description | Unused | Used |
|---|---|---|---|---|
| 136 | A94 | 25c dk green (R) | 11.00 | 18.00 |
| 137 | A95 | 50c purple (R) | 11.00 | 4.00 |

Lighthouse at Cape Guardafui — A3

Tower at Mnara Ciromo — A4

Governor's Palace at Mogadishu — A5

Termite Nest — A6

Ostrich — A7

Hippopotamus — A8

Greater Kudu — A9

Lion — A10

**1932 Wmk. 140 Photo. *Perf. 12***

**138** A3 5c deep brown 6.00 *7.50*
**139** A3 7½c violet 9.00 *18.00*
**140** A3 10c gray black 11.00 .35
**141** A3 15c olive green 4.50 1.10
**142** A4 20c carmine 225.00 .35
**143** A4 25c deep green 4.50 .35
**144** A4 30c dark brown 37.50 1.10
**145** A5 35c dark blue 6.00 *11.00*
**146** A5 50c violet 300.00 .35
**147** A5 75c carmine 6.00 .75
**148** A6 1.25 l dark blue 18.00 .75
**149** A6 1.75 l red orange 11.00 .75
**150** A6 2 l carmine 6.00 .35
**151** A7 2.55 l indigo 30.00 *60.00*
**152** A7 5 l carmine 18.00 7.50
**153** A8 10 l violet 26.00 18.00
**154** A9 20 l dark green 67.50 82.50
**155** A10 25 l dark blue 67.50 *125.00*
*Nos. 138-155 (18)* 853.50 335.70
Set, never hinged 2,075.

**1934-37 *Perf. 14***

*138a* A3 5c deep brown 2.25 .75
*139a* A3 7½c violet 2.25 *22.50*
*140a* A3 10c gray black 2.25 .35
*141a* A3 15c olive green 2.25 *2.10*
*142a* A4 20c carmine 2.25 .20
*143a* A4 25c deep green 2.25 .35
*144a* A4 30c dark brown 3.75 .35
*145a* A5 35c dark blue 7.50 *30.00*
*146a* A5 50c violet 22.50 .35
*147a* A5 75c carmine 37.50 .35
*148a* A6 1.25 l dark blue 60.00 1.10
*149a* A6 1.75 l red orange 150.00 18.00
*150a* A6 2 l carmine 45.00 .75
*151a* A7 2.55 l indigo 175.00 *450.00*
*152a* A7 5 l carmine 15.00 3.00
*153a* A8 10 l violet 150.00 30.00
*154a* A9 20 l dark green *12,000.* *1,350.*
Never hinged 15,000.
*155a* A10 25 l dark blue 675.00 400.00
*Nos. 138a-153a,155a (17)* 1,354. 960.15
Set, never hinged 3,350.

Eleven denominations in the foregoing series exist perf. 12x14 or 14x12.

Types of 1932 Issue Overprinted in Black or Red

**1934, May *Perf. 14***

**156** A3 10c brown (Bk) 9.00 *18.00*
**157** A4 25c green 9.00 *18.00*
**158** A5 50c dull vio (Bk) 7.50 *18.00*
**159** A6 1.25 l blue 7.50 *18.00*
**160** A7 5 l brown black 4.25 *6.50*
**161** A8 10 l car rose (Bk) 9.00
**162** A9 20 l dull blue 9.00
**163** A10 25 l dark green 9.00
*Nos. 156-163 (8)* 64.25 *78.50*
Set, never hinged 160.00

Duke of the Abruzzi (Luigi Amadeo, 1873-1933).

Mother and Child A11

**1934, Oct.**

**164** A11 5c ol grn & brn 3.75 *18.00*
**165** A11 10c yel brn & blk 3.75 *18.00*
**166** A11 20c scarlet & blk 3.75 *15.00*
**167** A11 50c dk violet & brn 3.75 *15.00*
**168** A11 60c org brn & blk 3.75 *22.50*
**169** A11 1.25 l dk blue & grn 3.75 *37.50*
*Nos. 164-169,C1-C6 (12)* 45.00 *250.50*
Set, never hinged 55.00

Second Colonial Arts Exhibition, Naples.

**Catalogue values for unused stamps in this section, from this point to the end of the section, are for Never Hinged items.**

## Somalia

Tower at Mnara Ciromo — A12

Governor's Palace, Mogadishu — A13

Design: 5c, 20c, 60c, Ostrich.

**Wmk. 277**

**1950, Mar. 24 Photo. *Perf. 14***

**170** A12 1c gray black .20 .20
**171** A12 5c carmine rose .20 .20
**172** A13 6c violet .20 .20
**173** A12 8c Prus green .20 .20
**174** A13 10c dark green .20 .20
**175** A12 20c blue green .20 .20
**176** A13 35c red .20 .20
**177** A13 55c brt blue .25 .20
**178** A12 60c purple .30 .20
**179** A12 65c brown .40 .20
**180** A13 1s deep orange .65 .20
*Nos. 170-180,E8-E9 (13)* 10.50 8.45

Council in Session A14

**1951, Oct. 4**

**181** A14 20c dk green & brn 2.25 .25
**182** A14 55c brown & violet 4.00 4.00
*Nos. 181-182,C27A-C27B (4)* 12.75 9.25

Meeting of First Territorial Council.

Fair Emblem, Palm Tree and Minaret — A16

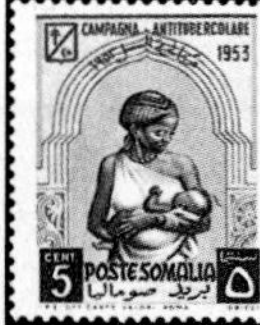

Mother and Child — A17

**1952, Sept. 14 Wmk. 277 *Perf. 14***

**185** A16 25c red & dk brown 1.75 *1.75*
**186** A16 55c blue & dk brown 1.75 *1.75*
*Nos. 185-186,C28 (3)* 5.75 5.75

1st Somali Fair, Mogadishu, Sept. 14-28.

**1953, May 27**

**Center in Dark Brown**

**187** A17 5c rose violet .20 .20
**188** A17 25c rose .20 .20
**189** A17 50c blue .75 .75
*Nos. 187-189,C29 (4)* 2.15 2.15

Anti-tuberculosis campaign.

Laborer at Fair Entrance A18

**1953, Sept. 28 Unwmk. *Perf. 11½***

**190** A18 25c dk green & gray .25 .25
**191** A18 60c blue & gray .50 .50
*Nos. 190-191,C30-C31 (4)* 1.75 1.75

2nd Somali Fair, Mogadishu, 9/28-10/12.

Map and Stamps of 1903 A19

***Perf. 13x13½***

**1953, Dec. 16 Engr. Wmk. 277**

**"Stamps" in Brown and Rose Carmine**

**192** A19 25c deep magenta .30 .30
**193** A19 35c dark green .30 .30
**194** A19 60c orange .30 .30
*Nos. 192-194,C32-C33 (5)* 1.90 1.90

50th anniv. of the 1st Somali postage stamps.

Somalia Brushwood A20

***Perf. 12½x13½***

**1954, June 1 Photo. Unwmk.**

**195** A20 25c dp blue & dk gray .35 .35
**196** A20 60c orange brn & brown .35 .35
*Nos. 195-196,C37-C38 (4)* 1.85 1.80

Convention of Nov. 11, 1953, with the Sovereign Military Order of Malta, providing for the care of lepers.

Somali Flag A21

Adenium Somalense A22

***Perf. 13½x13***

**1954, Oct. 12 Litho. Wmk. 277**

**197** A21 25c blk, grn, bl, red & yel .30 .30

Adoption of a Somali flag. See No. C39.

**1955, Feb. Photo. *Perf. 13***

Flowers: 5c, Haemanthus multiflorus martyn. 10c, Grinum scabrum. 25c, Poinciana elata. 60c, Calatropis procera. 1s, Pancratium. 1.20s, Sesamothamnus bussernus.

**198** A22 1c bl, dp rose & dk ol brn .20 .20
**199** A22 5c bl, rose lil & grn .20 .20
**200** A22 10c lilac & green .20 .20
**201** A22 25c vio brn, yel & grn .30 .30
**202** A22 60c blk, car & grn .20 .20
**203** A22 1s red brn & grn .20 .25
**204** A22 1.20s dk brn, yel & grn .35 .35
*Nos. 198-204,E10-E11 (9)* 3.00 4.20

See #216-220. For overprint see #242.

Weaver at Loom A23

Design: 30c, Cattle fording stream.

***Perf. 13½x14***

**1955, Sept. 24 Wmk. 303**

**205** A23 25c dark brown .30 .30
**206** A23 30c dark green .30 .30
*Nos. 205-206,C46-C47 (4)* 1.40 1.40

3rd Somali Fair, Mogadishu, Sept. 1955.

Casting Ballots — A24

Arms of Somalia — A25

**1956, Apr. 30 *Perf. 14***

**207** A24 5c brown & gray grn .20 .20
**208** A24 10c brown & ol bis .20 .20
**209** A24 25c brown & brn red .20 .20
*Nos. 207-209,C48-C49 (5)* 1.00 1.00

Opening of the territory's first democratically elected Legislative Assembly.

**1957, May 6 Wmk. 303 *Perf. 13½***

**Coat of Arms in Dull Yellow, Blue and Black**

**210** A25 5c lt red brown .20 .20
**211** A25 25c carmine .20 .20
**212** A25 60c bluish violet .20 .20
*Nos. 210-212,C50-C51 (5)* 1.00 1.05

Issued in honor of the new coat of arms.

Dam at Falcheiro A26

10c, Juba River Bridge. 25c, Silos at Margherita.

**1957, Sept. 28 Photo. *Perf. 14***

**213** A26 5c brown & purple .20 .20
**214** A26 10c bister & bl grn .20 .20
**215** A26 25c carmine & blue .20 .20
*Nos. 213-215,C52-C53 (5)* 1.00 1.20

Fourth Somali Fair and Film Festival.

Flower Type of 1955

Flowers: 1c, Adenium Somalense. 10c, Grinum scabrum. 15c, Adansonia digitata. 25c, Poinciana elata. 50c, Gloriosa virescens.

**1956-59 Wmk. 303 Photo. *Perf. 13***

**216** A22 1c bl, dp rose & dk ol brn .20 .20
**217** A22 10c lil, grn & yel ('59) .20 .20
**218** A22 15c red, grn & yel ('58) .30 .30
**219** A22 25c dull lil, grn & yel ('59) .20 .20
**220** A22 50c bl, grn, red & yel ('58) .40 .40
*Nos. 216-220 (5)* 1.30 1.30

Fencer — A27

Soccer Player A28

Designs: 5c, Discus thrower. 6c, Motorcyclist. 8c, Fencer. 10c, Archer. 25c, Boxers.

**1958, Apr. 28 Wmk. 303 *Perf. 14***

**221** A27 2c violet .20 .20
**222** A28 4c green .20 .20
**223** A27 5c vermilion .20 .20
**224** A28 6c gray .20 .20
**225** A27 8c violet blue .20 .20
**226** A28 10c orange .20 .20
**227** A28 25c dark green .20 .20
*Nos. 221-227,C54-C56 (10)* 2.00 2.00

Book and Assembly Palace — A29

White Stork — A30

**1959, June 19**

**228** A29 5c green & ultra .20 .20
**229** A29 25c ocher & ultra .20 .20
*Nos. 228-229,C59-C60 (4)* .80 1.00

Opening of Somalia's Constituent Assembly. See No. C60a.

**1959, Sept. 4 Photo. *Perf. 14***

Birds: 10c, Saddle-billed stork. 15c, Sacred ibis. 25c, Pink-backed pelican.

**230** A30 5c yellow, blk & red .30 .20
**231** A30 10c brown, red & yel .30 .20
**232** A30 15c orange & black .30 .20
**233** A30 25c dk car, blk & org .30 .20
*Nos. 230-233,C61-C62 (6)* 3.20 1.80

Incense Bush — A31

Arms of University Institute — A32

Design: 60c, Girl burning incense.

**1959, Sept. 28 Wmk. 303**

**234** A31 20c orange & black .20 .20
**235** A31 60c blk, org & dk red .20 .25
*Nos. 234-235,C63-C64 (4)* .90 1.20

5th Somali Fair, Mogadishu.

**1960, Jan. 14 Photo. *Perf. 14***

Designs: 50c, Map of Africa and arms, horiz. 80c, Arms of University Institute.

**236** A32 5c brown & salmon .20 .20
**237** A32 50c lt vio bl, brn & blk .20 .20
**238** A32 80c brt red & blk .25 .25
*Nos. 236-238,C65-C66 (5)* 1.25 1.25

Opening of the University Institute of Somalia.

Globe and Uprooted Oak Emblem A33

Palm — A34

Design: 60c, Like 10c but with inscription and emblem rearranged.

**1960, Apr. 7 *Perf. 14***

**239** A33 10c yel brn, grn & blk .20 .20
**240** A33 60c dp bister & blk .20 .20
**241** A34 80c pink, grn & blk .20 .20
*Nos. 239-241,C67 (4)* .85 .85

World Refugee Year, 7/1/59-6/30/60.

**Republic**

No. 217 Overprinted

**Wmk. 303**

**1960, June 26 Photo. *Perf. 13***

**242** A22 10c lilac, grn & yel 11.00 *12.00*
*Nos. 242,C68-C69 (3)* 49.50 50.50

Independence of British Somaliland, which became part of the Republic of Somalia.

Gazelle and Map of Africa — A36

25c, NYC skyline, UN Building and UN flag.

**1960, July 1 *Perf. 14***

**243** A36 5c lilac & brown .30 .30
**244** A36 25c blue .45 .45
*Nos. 243-244,C70-C71 (4)* 2.50 2.00

Somalia independence.

Boy Drawing Giraffe A37

**1960, Nov. 24**

**245** A37 10c shown .20 .20
**246** A37 15c Zebra .20 .20
**247** A37 25c Black rhinoceros .30 .30
*Nos. 245-247,C72 (4)* 2.45 1.70

Olympic Torch, Somalia Flag — A38

Girl Harvesting Papaya — A39

10c, Runners, flag and Olympic rings.

**1960 Wmk. 303 *Perf. 14***

**248** A38 5c green & blue .25 .20
**249** A38 10c yellow & blue .25 .20
*Nos. 248-249,C73-C74 (4)* 1.95 1.60

17th Olympic Games, Rome, 8/25-9/11.

**1961, July 5 Photo.**

Girl harvesting: 10c, Durrah (sorghum). 20c, Cotton. 25c, Sesame. 40c, Sugar cane. 50c, Bananas. 75c, Peanuts, horiz. 80c, Grapefruit, horiz.

**250** A39 5c multicolored .20 .20
**251** A39 10c multicolored .20 .20
**252** A39 20c multicolored .20 .20
**253** A39 25c multicolored .20 .20
**254** A39 40c multicolored .30 .25
**255** A39 50c multicolored .50 .40
**256** A39 75c multicolored .75 .50
**257** A39 80c multicolored 1.25 1.00
*Nos. 250-257 (8)* 3.60 2.95

Shield, Bow and Quiver — A40

Pomacanthus Semicirculatus A41

Design: 45c, Pottery and incense jug.

**1961, Sept. 28**

**258** A40 25c blk, car & ocher .20 .20
**259** A40 45c blk, bl grn & ocher .25 .25
*Nos. 258-259,C82-C83 (4)* 2.20 1.60

6th Somali Fair, Mogadishu.

**1962, Apr. 26 Photo.**

Fish: 15c, Girl embroidering fish on cloth. 40c, Novaculichthys taeniourus.

**260** A41 15c brown, blk & pink .20 .20
**261** A41 25c orange, blk & ultra .20 .20
**262** A41 40c green, blk & rose .80 .60
*Nos. 260-262,C84 (4)* 3.95 2.75

Mosquito Trapped by Sprays A42

Design: 25c, Man with spray gun and malaria eradication emblem, vert.

**1962, Oct. 25 Wmk. 303 *Perf. 14***

**263** A42 10c orange red & grn .20 .20
**264** A42 25c rose lilac, brn & blk .40 .40
*Nos. 263-264,C85-C86 (4)* 2.60 1.80

WHO drive to eradicate malaria.

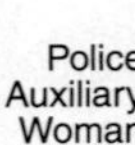

Police Auxiliary Woman A43

10c, Army auxiliary woman. 25c, Radio police car. 75c, First aid army auxiliary, vert.

**1963, May 15 Wmk. 303 *Perf. 14***

**265** A43 5c multicolored .20 .20
**266** A43 10c black & orange .20 .20
**267** A43 25c multicolored .20 .20
**268** A43 75c multicolored .25 .20
*Nos. 265-268,C87-C88 (6)* 1.75 1.20

Women's auxiliary forces.

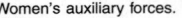

Carved Fork and Spoon and Wheat Emblem A44

**1963, June 25 Photo.**

**269** A44 75c green & red brown .20 .20

FAO "Freedom from Hunger" campaign. See No. C89.

Pres. Aden Abdulla Osman — A45

**1963, Sept. 15 Wmk. 303 *Perf. 14***

**270** A45 25c bl, dk brn, org & lt bl .20 .20
*Nos. 270,C90-C91 (3)* 1.25 .70

3rd anniv. of independence.

Dunes Theater A46

55c, African Merchants' and Artisans' Exhibit.

**1963, Sept. 28 Photo.**

**271** A46 25c blue green .20 .20
**272** A46 55c carmine rose .20 .20
*Nos. 271-272,C92 (3)* 1.25 .80

7th Somali Fair, Mogadishu.

Somali Credit Bank Building A47

**1964, May 16 Wmk. 303 *Perf. 14***

**273** A47 60c indigo, red lil & yel .30 .20
*Nos. 273,C93-C94 (3)* 1.30 .70

10th anniv. of the Somali Credit Bank.

Running — A48

ITU Emblem and Map of Africa — A50

DC-3 A49

**1964, Oct. 10 Wmk. 303 *Perf. 14***

274 A48 10c shown .20 .20
275 A48 25c High jump .20 .20
*Nos. 274-275,C95-C96 (4)* 1.40 .90

18th Olympic Games, Tokyo, Oct. 10-25.

**1964, Nov. 8 Photo. *Perf. 14***

Design: 20c, Passengers leaving DC-3.

276 A49 5c dk blue & lil rose .20 .20
277 A49 20c blue & orange .30 .20
*Nos. 276-277,C97-C98 (4)* 2.35 1.05

Establishment of Somali Air Lines.

**1965, May 17 Wmk. 303 *Perf. 14***

278 A50 25c dp blue & dp org .20 .20
*Nos. 278,C99-C100 (3)* 1.40 .80

ITU centenary.

Tanning Industry A51

25c, Meat industry; cannery, cattle. 35c, Fishing industry; cannery, fishing boats.

**1965, Sept. 28 Photo. *Perf. 14***

279 A51 10c sepia & buff .20 .20
280 A51 25c sepia & pink .20 .20
281 A51 35c sepia & lt blue .20 .20
*Nos. 279-281,C101-C102 (5)* 1.75 1.05

8th Somali Fair, Mogadishu.

Hottentot Fig and Gazelle A52

Designs: 60c, African tulip and giraffes. 1sh, Ninfea and flamingos. 1.30sh, Pervincia and ostriches. 1.80sh, Bignonia and zebras.

**1965, Nov. 1 Wmk. 303 *Perf. 14***
**Flowers in Natural Colors**

282 A52 20c blk & brt bl .20 .20
283 A52 60c blk & dk gray .20 .20
284 A52 1sh blk, sl grn & ol grn .25 .20
285 A52 1.30sh blk & dp grn .50 .20
286 A52 1.80sh blk & brt bl .70 .25
*Nos. 282-286 (5)* 1.85 1.05

Narina's Trogon A53

Birds: 35c, Bateleur eagle, vert. 50c, Vulture. 1.30sh, European roller. 2sh, Vulturine guinea fowl, vert.

**1966, June 1 Photo. Wmk. 303**

287 A53 25c multicolored .20 .20
288 A53 35c brt blue & multi .20 .20
289 A53 50c multicolored .20 .20
290 A53 1.30sh multicolored .30 .20
291 A53 2sh multicolored .50 .25
*Nos. 287-291 (5)* 1.40 1.05

Globe and UN Emblem A54

UN emblem and: 1sh, Map of Africa. 1.50sh, Map of Somalia.

**1966, Oct. 24 Litho. *Perf. 13x12½***

292 A54 35c bl, pur & brt bl .20 .20
293 A54 1sh brn, yel & brick red .20 .20
294 A54 1.50sh grn, blk, bl & yel .25 .25
*Nos. 292-294 (3)* .65 .65

21st anniversary of United Nations.

Woman Sitting on Crocodile A55

Paintings: 1sh, Woman and warrior. 1.50sh, Boy leading camel. 2sh, Women pounding grain.

**Wmk. 303**
**1966, Dec. 1 Photo. *Perf. 14***

295 A55 25c multicolored .20 .20
296 A55 1sh multicolored .20 .20
297 A55 1.50sh multicolored .20 .20
298 A55 2sh multicolored .25 .20
*Nos. 295-298 (4)* .85 .80

Somali art, exhibited in the Garesa Museum, Mogadishu.

UNESCO Emblem A56

**1966, Dec. 20 Wmk. 303 *Perf. 14***

299 A56 35c blk, dk red & gray .20 .20
300 A56 1sh blk, emer & yel .20 .20
301 A56 1.80sh blk, ultra & red .30 .25
*Nos. 299-301 (3)* .70 .65

UNESCO, 20th anniv.

Haggard's Oribi — A57

Dancers — A58

Gazelles: 60c, Long-snouted dik-dik. 1sh, Gerenuk. 1.80sh, Soemmering's gazelle.

**1967, Feb. 20 Photo. *Perf. 14***

302 A57 35c blk, ultra & bis .20 .20
303 A57 60c blk, org & brn .20 .20
304 A57 1sh blk, red & brn .20 .20
305 A57 1.80sh blk, yel grn & brn .30 .25
*Nos. 302-305 (4)* .90 .85

**Unwmk.**
**1967, July 15 Litho. *Perf. 13***

Designs: Various Folk Dances.

306 A58 25c multicolored .20 .20
307 A58 50c multicolored .20 .20
308 A58 1.30sh multicolored .20 .20
309 A58 2sh multicolored .25 .25
*Nos. 306-309 (4)* .85 .85

Boy Scout Giving Scout Sign — A59

Designs: 50c, Boy Scouts with flags. 1sh, Boy Scout cooking and tent. 1.80sh, Jamboree emblem.

**1967, Aug. 15**

310 A59 35c multicolored .20 .20
311 A59 50c multicolored .20 .20
312 A59 1sh multicolored .25 .20
313 A59 1.80sh multicolored .50 .30
*Nos. 310-313 (4)* 1.15 .90

12th Boy Scout World Jamboree, Farragut State Park, Idaho, Aug. 1-9.

Pres. Abdirascid Ali Scermarche and King Faisal — A60

Designs: 1sh, Clasped hands, flags of Somalia and Saudi Arabia.

**Wmk. 303**
**1967, Sept. 21 Photo. *Perf. 14***

314 A60 50c black & lt blue .20 .20
315 A60 1sh multicolored .20 .20
*Nos. 314-315,C103 (3)* .70 .60

Visit of King Faisal of Saudi Arabia.

Gaterin Gaterinus A61

Tropical Fish: 50c, Chaetodon semilarvatus. 1sh, Priacanthus hamrur. 1.80sh, Epinephelus summana.

**1967, Nov. 15 Litho. *Perf. 14***

316 A61 35c dk bl, yel & blk .20 .20
317 A61 50c brt bl, ocher & blk .20 .20
318 A61 1sh emer, org, brn & blk .25 .20
319 A61 1.80sh pur, yel & blk .50 .40
*Nos. 316-319 (4)* 1.15 1.00

Physician Treating Infant A62

Waterbuck A64

Woman and Basket with Lemons A63

WHO, 20th anniv.: 1sh, Physician examining boy and nurse. 1.80sh, Physician and nurse treating patient.

**Wmk. 303**
**1968, Mar. 20 Photo. *Perf. 14***

320 A62 35c blk, scar, bl & brn .20 .20
321 A62 1sh blk, grn & brn .20 .20
322 A62 1.80sh blk, org & brn .30 .25
*Nos. 320-322 (3)* .70 .65

**1968 Litho. *Perf. 11½***

Designs: 10c, Oranges. 25c, Coconuts. 35c, Papayas. 40c, Limes. 50c, Grapefruit. 1sh, Bananas. 1.30sh, Cotton bolls. 1.80sh, Speke's gazelle. 2sh, Lesser kudu. 5sh, Hunter's hartebeest. 10sh, Clark's gazelle (dibatag).

323 A63 5c lt blue & multi .20 .20
324 A63 10c yellow & multi .20 .20
325 A63 25c lt lilac & multi .20 .20
326 A63 35c salmon & multi .20 .20
327 A63 40c buff & multi .20 .20
328 A63 50c multicolored .20 .20
329 A63 1sh lt blue & multi .20 .20
330 A63 1.30sh gray & multi .25 .25
331 A64 1.50sh lt blue & multi .20 .20
332 A64 1.80sh multicolored .30 .25
333 A64 2sh pink & multi .35 .25
334 A64 5sh multicolored 1.00 .80
335 A64 10sh multicolored 2.75 1.25
*Nos. 323-335 (13)* 6.25 4.40

Issued: #323-330, 4/25; #331-335, 5/10.

Javelin — A65

Statuette — A66

**Wmk. 303**
**1968, Oct. 12 Photo. *Perf. 14***

336 A65 35c shown .20 .20
337 A65 50c Running .20 .20
338 A65 80c High jump .20 .20
339 A65 1.50sh Basketball .25 .20
*a.* Souvenir sheet of 4, #336-339 .70 .60
*Nos. 336-339 (4)* .85 .80

19th Olympic Games, Mexico City, Oct. 12-27. No. 339a sold for 3.65sh.

***Perf. 11½x12***
**1968, Dec. 1 Litho. Unwmk.**

Statuettes: 25c, Woman grinding grain. 35c, Woman potter. 2.80sh, Woman mat maker.

340 A66 25c rose lil, blk & brn .20 .20
341 A66 35c brick red, blk & brn .20 .20
342 A66 2.80sh green, blk & brn .50 .35
*Nos. 340-342 (3)* .90 .75

Cornflower and Rhinoceros A67

80c, Sunflower & elephant. 1sh, Oleander & antelopes. 1.80sh, Chrysanthemums & storks.

***Perf. 13x12½***
**1969, Mar. 25 Litho. Unwmk.**

343 A67 40c red & multi .20 .20
344 A67 80c violet & multi .20 .20
345 A67 1sh blue & multi .20 .20
346 A67 1.80sh yellow & multi .30 .25
*Nos. 343-346 (4)* .90 .85

ILO Emblem and Blacksmiths — A68

Designs: 1sh, Oxdrawn plow. 1.80sh, Drawing water from well.

**Wmk. 303**

**1969, May 10 Photo. *Perf. 14***

**347** A68 25c dk red, dp bis & blk .20 .20
**348** A68 1sh car rose, brn & blk .20 .20
**349** A68 1.80sh multicolored .30 .25
*Nos. 347-349 (3)* .70 .65

ILO, 50th anniversary.

Mahatma Gandhi — A69

Designs: 1.50sh, Gandhi, globe and hands releasing dove, horiz. 1.80sh, Gandhi seated.

**Unwmk.**

**1969, Oct. 2 Photo. *Perf. 13***

**Size: 25x35½mm**

**350** A69 35c brown violet .20 .20

***Perf. 14½x14***

**Size: 37½x20mm**

**351** A69 1.50sh bister brn .20 .20

***Perf. 13***

**Size: 25x35½mm**

**352** A69 1.80sh olive gray .25 .25
*Nos. 350-352 (3)* .65 .65

Mohandas K. Gandhi (1869-1948), leader in India's fight for independence.

---

**1970**

US Space Explorations. Set of seven. 60, 80c, 1, 1.50, 1.80, 2, 2.80sh. Souv. sheet, 14sh, issued Feb. 14. Nos. 7001-7008.

---

Nivprale Vevanes A70

Butterflies: 50c, Leschenault. 1.50sh, Papilio (ornytoptera) aeacus. 2sh, Urania riphaeus.

***Perf. 12½x13***

**1970, Mar. 25 Litho. Unwmk.**

**353** A70 25c multicolored .20 .20
**354** A70 50c multicolored .20 .20
**355** A70 1.50sh orange & multi .20 .20
**356** A70 2sh yellow & multi .30 .30
*Nos. 353-356 (4)* .90 .90

**Somali Democratic Republic**

Lenin Addressing Crowd — A71

Designs: 25c, Lenin walking with children. 1.80sh, Lenin in his study, horiz.

***Perf. 12x12½, 12½x12***

**1970, Apr. 22 Litho. Unwmk.**

**357** A71 25c multicolored .20 .20
**358** A71 1sh multicolored .20 .20
**359** A71 1.80sh multicolored .25 .20
*Nos. 357-359 (3)* .65 .60

Lenin (1870-1924), Russian communist leader.

Bird Feeding Young A72

35c, Monument & Battle of Dagahtur. 1sh, Arms of Somalia, UN emblem, vert. 2.80sh, Boy milking camel, & star, vert.

***Perf. 14x13½, 13½x14***

**1970, July 28 Photo. Wmk. 303**

**360** A72 25c blue & multi .20 .20
**361** A72 35c slate & multi .20 .20
**362** A72 1sh violet & multi .20 .20
**363** A72 2.80sh blue & multi .65 .50
*Nos. 360-363 (4)* 1.25 1.10

10th anniversary of independence.

"Agriculture" — A73

40c, Soldier and flag. 1sh, Hand on open book. 1.80sh, Grain, scales of justice and dove.

***Perf. 14x13½***

**1970, Oct. 21 Photo. Wmk. 303**

**364** A73 35c green & multi .20 .20
**365** A73 40c ultra & blk .20 .20
**366** A73 1sh red brown & blk .20 .20
**367** A73 1.80sh multicolored .40 .25
*Nos. 364-367 (4)* 1.00 .85

First anniversary of Oct. 21st Revolution.

Snake Strangling Black Man, Map of South Africa A74

Design: 1.80sh, Concentration camp and symbols of justice holding scales.

***Perf. 14x13½***

**1971, June 20 Photo. Wmk. 303**

**368** A74 1.30sh multicolored .30 .20
**369** A74 1.80sh gray, red & blk .45 .30

Against racial discrimination in South Africa.

Waves A75

Design: 2.80sh, Waves and globe.

**1971, June 30**

**370** A75 25c black & blue .20 .20
**371** A75 2.80sh blk, grn & bl .60 .40

3rd World Telecommunications Day, May 17.

Map of Africa and Telecommunications System — A76

Design: 1.50sh, Map of Africa and telecommunications system, diff.

**1971, July 25**

**372** A76 1sh blk, lt bl & grn .20 .20
**373** A76 1.50sh black & yellow .30 .25

Pan-African Telecommunications system.

White Rhinoceros A77

Wild Animals: 1sh, Cheetahs. 1.30sh, Zebras. 1.80sh, Lion attacking camel.

**1971, Aug. 25**

**374** A77 35c ocher & multi .20 .20
**375** A77 1sh violet & multi .25 .20
**376** A77 1.30sh violet & multi .45 .20
**377** A77 1.80sh multicolored .50 .25
*Nos. 374-377 (4)* 1.40 .85

Headquarters, Mogadishu, Flag, Map of Africa — A78

Design: 1.30sh, Desert Fort.

**1971, Oct. 18**

**378** A78 1.30sh blk & red org .25 .25
**379** A78 1.50sh blk, blue & yel .30 .25

East and Central African Summit Conf.

Revolution Monument A79

1sh, Field workers. 1.35sh, Building workers.

**1971, Oct. 21**

**380** A79 10c black & blue .20 .20
**381** A79 1sh blk, yel brn & grn .20 .20
**382** A79 1.35sh blk, dp brn & yel .35 .20
*Nos. 380-382 (3)* .75 .60

2nd anniversary of 1969 revolution.

Vaccination of Cow — A80

1.80sh, Veterinarian vaccinating cow.

***Perf. 14x13½***

**1971, Nov. 28 Photo. Wmk. 303**

**383** A80 40c blk, red & bl .40 .20
**384** A80 1.80sh lt green & multi .45 .35

Rinderpest campaign.

Postal Union Emblem, Dove and Letter A81

**1972, Jan. 25 Unwmk.**

**385** A81 1.50sh multicolored .50 .45

10th anniv. of APU. See No. C108.

Children and UNICEF Emblem A82

Design: 50c, Mother and child, vert.

**1972, Mar. 30 *Perf. 13x14, 14x13***

**386** A82 50c blk, bis brn & dk brn .20 .20
**387** A82 2.80sh lt blue & multi .70 .50

UNICEF, 25th anniv. (in 1971).

Camel A83

Designs: 10c, Cattle and cargo ship. 20c, Bull. 40c, Sheep. 1.70sh, Goat.

**1972, Apr. 10 *Perf. 14x13***

**388** A83 5c green & multi .20 .20
**389** A83 10c multicolored .20 .20
**390** A83 20c multicolored .20 .20
**391** A83 40c orange red & blk .20 .20
**392** A83 1.70sh dull grn & blk .85 .45
*Nos. 388-392 (5)* 1.65 1.25

Hands Holding Infant A84

1sh, Youth Corps emblem, marchers with flags. 1.50sh, Woman, man, tent, tractor.

**1972, Oct. 21 Photo. *Perf. 14x13½***

**393** A84 70c yellow & multi .20 .20
**394** A84 1sh red & multi .25 .20
**395** A84 1.50sh lt blue & multi .35 .30
*Nos. 393-395 (3)* .80 .70

3rd anniversary of October 21 Revolution.

Folk Dance A85

Folk Dances: 40c, Man and woman, vert. 1sh, Group dance, vert. 2sh, Two men and a woman.

**1973 Photo. *Perf. 14x13½, 13½x14***

**396** A85 5c dull blue & multi .20 .20
**397** A85 40c brown & multi .20 .20
**398** A85 1sh yellow & multi .25 .20
**399** A85 2sh brick red & multi .45 .30
*Nos. 396-399 (4)* 1.10 .90

Hand Writing Somali Script A86

40c, Flame and "FAR SOMALI" inscription, vert. 1sh, Woman and sunburst with Somali script.

***Perf. 13½x14, 14x13½***

**1973, Oct. 21 Photo.**

**400** A86 40c red & multi .20 .20
**401** A86 1sh blue & multi .20 .20
**402** A86 2sh yellow & multi .45 .30
*Nos. 400-402 (3)* .85 .70

Publicity for use of Somali script.

Map of Africa and Emblem — A87

Map of Africa with Target on Somalia — A88

**1974, June 12** ***Perf. 13½x14***
**403** A87 40c multicolored .20 .20
**404** A88 2sh multicolored .50 .30

OAU Meeting, Mogadishu.

Hurdler A89

1sh, Runners. 1.40sh, Netball, vert.

**1974, Aug. 1** ***Perf. 14x13, 13x14***
**405** A89 50c black & orange .20 .20
**406** A89 1sh black & green .25 .20
**407** A89 1.40sh black & olive .35 .25
*Nos. 405-407 (3)* .80 .65

Victory Pioneers — A90

Pioneers Helping Woman — A91

**1974, Aug. 25** **Photo.** ***Perf. 13x14***
**408** A90 40c multicolored .20 .20
**409** A91 2sh multicolored .40 .30

Victory Pioneers, founded Aug. 24, 1972, to defend Socialist Revolution.

Map of Arab Countries A92

Flags of Arab Countries A93

**1974, Sept. 1** ***Perf. 14x13***
**410** A92 1.50sh multicolored .35 .20
**411** A93 1.70sh multicolored .45 .25

Somalia's admission to the Arab League, Feb. 14, 1974.

Tank Tracks in Desert A94

Somalis Reading Books — A95

***Perf. 14x13½, 13½x14***
**1974, Oct. 21** **Litho.**
**412** A94 40c multicolored .20 .20
**413** A95 2sh multicolored .50 .30

5th anniversary of the Oct. 21st Revolution.

Carrier Pigeons A96

Design: 3sh, Postrider.

**1975, Feb. 15** **Litho.** ***Perf. 14x13½***
**414** A96 50c blue & multi .25 .20
**415** A96 3sh multicolored 1.25 .45

UPU centenary (in 1974).

Africa A97

Design: 1.50sh, Carrier pigeons.

**1975, Apr. 10**
**416** A97 1sh multicolored .30 .20
**417** A97 1.50sh multicolored .50 .25

African Postal Union.

Somali Warrior — A98

Designs: Traditional costumes of Somali men (1sh, 10sh) and women (40c, 50c, 5sh).

**1975, Oct. 27** **Photo.** ***Perf. 13½***
**418** A98 10c yellow & multi .20 .20
**419** A98 40c lt blue & multi .20 .20
**420** A98 50c multicolored .20 .20
**421** A98 1sh green & multi .25 .20
**422** A98 5sh claret & multi 1.25 .65
**423** A98 10sh rose & multi 2.50 1.75
*Nos. 418-423 (6)* 4.60 3.20

Monument — A99

IWY Emblem A100

**1975, Dec. 10** **Litho.** ***Perf. 13½x14***
**424** A99 50c blk & red org .20 .20
**425** A100 2.30sh blk, pink & mag .50 .40

International Women's Year.

Abdulla Hassan Monument A101

Abdulla Hassan with Warriors — A102

1.50sh, Abdulla Hassan speaking to his men. 2.30sh, Attacking horsemen, horiz.

***Perf. 14x13½, 13½x14***
**1976, Nov. 30** **Photo.**
**426** A101 50c multicolored .20 .20
**427** A102 60c multicolored .20 .20
**428** A102 1.50sh multicolored .30 .25
**429** A102 2.30sh multicolored .50 .35
*Nos. 426-429 (4)* 1.20 1.00

Sayid Mohammed Abdulla Hassan (1864-1920), poet and military leader.

Cypraea Gracilis A103

Sea Shells: 75c, Charonia bardayi. 1sh, Chlamys townsendi. 2sh, Cymatium ranzanii. 2.75sh, Conus argillaceus. 2.90sh, Strombus oldi.

**1976, Dec. 15** **Photo.** ***Perf. 14x13½***
**430** A103 50c blue & multi .20 .20
**431** A103 75c blue & multi .20 .20
**432** A103 1sh blue & multi .25 .20
**433** A103 2sh blue & multi .50 .30
**434** A103 2.75sh blue & multi .75 .45
**435** A103 2.90sh blue & multi .85 .45
*a.* Souvenir sheet of 6, #430-435 4.00 4.00
*Nos. 430-435 (6)* 2.75 1.80

No. 435a sold for 11sh.

Benin Head and Hunters — A104

Benin Head and: 75c, Handicrafts. 2sh, Dancers. 2.90sh, Musicians.

**1977, Aug. 30** **Photo.** ***Perf. 14x13½***
**436** A104 50c multicolored .20 .20
**437** A104 75c multicolored .20 .20
**438** A104 2sh multicolored .45 .30
**439** A104 2.90sh multicolored .60 .40
*Nos. 436-439 (4)* 1.45 1.10

2nd World Black and African Festival, FESTAC '77, Lagos, Nigeria, Jan. 15-Feb. 12.

Arms of Somalia A105

Designs: 75c, Somali flags, vert. 1.50sh, Pres. Mohammed Siad Barre and globe. 2sh, Arms over rising sun and flags, vert.

***Perf. 13½x14, 14x13½***
**1977, Sept. 30** **Photo.**
**440** A105 75c multicolored .20 .20
**441** A105 1sh multicolored .20 .20
**442** A105 1.50sh multicolored .25 .20
**443** A105 2sh multicolored .45 .40
*Nos. 440-443 (4)* 1.10 1.00

Somali Socialist Revolutionary Party, established July 1, 1976.

Licaon Pictus A106

Protected Animals: 75c, Bush baby. 1sh, Somali ass. 1.50sh, Aardwolf. 2sh, Greater kudu. 3sh, Giraffe.

**1977, Nov. 25** **Photo.** ***Perf. 14x13½***
**444** A106 50c multicolored .20 .20
**445** A106 75c multicolored .20 .20
**446** A106 1sh multicolored .25 .20
**447** A106 1.50sh multicolored .35 .25
**448** A106 2sh multicolored .50 .35
**449** A106 3sh multicolored .70 .60
*a.* Souvenir sheet of 6, #444-449 2.50 2.50
*Nos. 444-449 (6)* 2.20 1.80

Leonardo da Vinci's Flying Machine A107

ICAO Emblem and: 1.50sh, Montgolfier's balloon. 2sh, Wright brothers' plane. 2.90sh, Somali Airlines turbojet.

**1977, Dec. 23** **Photo.** ***Perf. 14x13½***
**450** A107 1sh multicolored .25 .20
**451** A107 1.50sh multicolored .35 .25
**452** A107 2sh multicolored .45 .40
**453** A107 2.90sh multicolored .70 .45
*a.* Souvenir sheet of 4, #450-453 2.25 2.25
*Nos. 450-453 (4)* 1.75 1.30

ICAO, 30th anniv. No. 453a sold for 10sh.

Dome of the Rock — A108

**Lithographed and Engraved**
**1978, Apr. 30** ***Perf. 13x14***
**454** A108 75c multicolored .20 .20
**455** A108 2sh multicolored .45 .35

Palestinian fighters and their families.

Stadium and Soccer Player — A109

Designs: 4.90sh, Stadium and goalkeeper. 5.50sh, Stadium and player.

**1978, Aug. 5 Litho. *Perf. 14x13½***

**456** A109 1.50sh multicolored .35 .20
**457** A109 4.90sh multicolored 1.25 .90
**458** A109 5.50sh multicolored 1.40 1.10
*a.* Souvenir sheet of 3, #456-458 3.75 3.75
*Nos. 456-458 (3)* 3.00 2.20

11th World Cup Soccer Championship, Argentina, June 1-25. No. 458a sold for 14sh.

Acacia Tortilis — A110

Trees: 50c, Ficus sycomorus, vert. 75c, Terminalia catapa, vert. 2.90sh, Baobab.

**1978, Sept. 5 Photo. *Perf. 14***

**459** A110 40c multicolored .20 .20
**460** A110 50c multicolored .20 .20
**461** A110 75c multicolored .20 .20
**462** A110 2.90sh multicolored .40 .40
*Nos. 459-462 (4)* 1.00 1.00

Forest conservation.

Hibiscus — A111

Flowers of Somalia: 1sh, Cassia baccarinii. 1.50sh, Kigelia somalensis. 2.30sh, Dichrostachys glomerata.

**1978, Dec. 15 Photo. *Perf. 13½x14***

**463** A111 50c multicolored .20 .20
**464** A111 1sh multicolored .25 .20
**465** A111 1.50sh multicolored .30 .25
**466** A111 2.30sh multicolored .50 .35
*a.* Souv. sheet, #463-466, perf. 14 2.50 2.50
*Nos. 463-466 (4)* 1.25 1.00

Huri and Siganus Rivulatus A112

Fishery Development: 80c, Sail huri, gaterin gaterinus. 2.30sh, Fishing boats, hypacanthus amia. 2.50sh, Motorized fishing boat, mackerel.

**1979, Sept. 1 Photo. *Perf. 14x13½***

**467** A112 75c multicolored .20 .20
**468** A112 80c multicolored .20 .20
**469** A112 2.30sh multicolored .40 .40
**470** A112 2.50sh multicolored .45 .45
*Nos. 467-470 (4)* 1.25 1.25

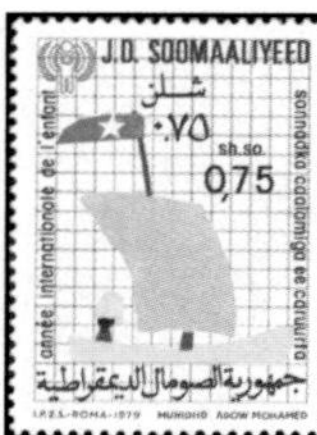

Sailing, IYC Emblem — A113

IYC Emblem, Children's Drawings: 50c, 90c, Schoolboy. 1.50sh, 2.50sh, Houses. 3sh, 4sh, Bird and flower. 1sh, as 75c.

**1979, Sept. 10 Photo. *Perf. 13½x14***

**471** A113 50c multicolored .20 .20
**472** A113 75c multicolored .20 .20
**473** A113 1.50sh multicolored .25 .25
**474** A113 3sh multicolored .50 .50
*Nos. 471-474 (4)* 1.15 1.15

**Souvenir Sheet of 4**

**474A** A113 #b.-e. 1.75 1.75

Intl. Year of the Child. No. 474A contains 90c, 1sh, 2.50sh, 4sh stamps and sold for 10sh.

University Students, Outdoor Classrooms — A114

Flower and: 50c, Housing construction. 75c, Children's recreation. 1sh, Doctor examining child, woman and man carrying grain and fish. 2.40sh, Woman and children carrying produce over dam. 3sh, Dish antenna.

**1979, Nov. 30 Litho. *Perf. 14x13½***

**475** A114 20c multicolored .20 .20
**476** A114 50c multicolored .20 .20
**477** A114 75c multicolored .20 .20
**478** A114 1sh multicolored .25 .20
**479** A114 2.40sh multicolored .60 .25
**480** A114 3sh multicolored .65 .30
*Nos. 475-480 (6)* 2.10 1.35

Oct. 21 revolution, 10th anniversary.

Barbopsis Devecchii A115

Freshwater Fish: 90c, Phreatichthys andruzzii. 1sh, Uegitglanis zammaranoi. 2.50sh, Pardi's catfish.

**1979, Dec. 12**

**481** A115 50c multicolored .25 .20
**482** A115 90c multicolored .30 .20
**483** A115 1sh multicolored .35 .20
**484** A115 2.50sh multicolored 1.00 .30
*a.* Souvenir sheet of 4, #481-484 3.00 3.00
*Nos. 481-484 (4)* 1.90 .90

No. 484a sold for 10sh.

Taleh Fortress, Congress Emblem — A116

**1980, June 1 Photo. *Perf. 14x13½***

**485** A116 2.25sh multicolored .60 .35
**486** A116 3.50sh multicolored .90 .55

1st International Congress of Somalian Studies, Mogadishu, July 6-13.

View of Marka — A117

**1980, July 1 Litho. *Perf. 14***

**487** A117 75c shown .20 .20
**488** A117 1sh Gandershe + label .25 .20
**489** A117 2.30sh Afgooye + label .65 .35
**490** A117 3.50sh Muqdisho + label 1.00 .55
*Nos. 487-490 (4)* 2.10 1.30

See Nos. 502-505, 527-530.

A118

A119

**1980, July 30 Photo. *Perf. 13½x14***

**491** A118 1sh Batis perkeo .30 .20
**492** A118 2.25sh Rynchostruthus socotranus louisae .30 .35
**493** A118 5sh Laniarius ruficeps 1.90 .80
*a.* Souvenir sheet of 3, #491-493 2.75 1.25
*Nos. 491-493 (3)* 2.50 1.35

***Perf. 13½x14, 14x13½***

**1981, Oct. 16 Litho.**

**494** A119 75c Globe, grain .20 .20
**495** A119 3.25sh Emblem, horiz. .75 .50
**496** A119 5.50sh like No. 494 1.50 .90
*Nos. 494-496 (3)* 2.45 1.60

World Food Day.

13th World Telecommunications Day — A120

**1981, Oct. 10 *Perf. 13½x14***

**497** A120 1sh Shepherdess, sheep, dish antenna .30 .20
**498** A120 3sh Emblems 1.10 .50
**499** A120 4.60sh like No. 498 1.10 .55
*Nos. 497-499 (3)* 2.50 1.25

Hegira, 1500th Anniv. — A121

1982 World Cup — A122

**1981, Oct. Photo. *Perf. 13½x14***

**500** A121 1.50sh multicolored .30 .20
**501** A121 3.80sh multicolored .85 .65

View Type of 1980

**1982, May 31 Litho. *Perf. 13½x14***

**502** A117 2.25sh Balcad .65 .35
**503** A117 4sh Jowhar 1.25 .65
**504** A117 5.50sh Golaleey 1.60 .90
**505** A117 8.30sh Muqdisho 2.25 1.25
*Nos. 502-505 (4)* 5.75 3.15

Nos. 502-505 each se-tenant with label showing regional map.

**1982, June 13**

Designs: Various soccer players.

**506** A122 1sh multicolored .35 .20
**507** A122 1.50sh multicolored .55 .25
**508** A122 3.25sh multicolored 1.25 .55
*a.* Souvenir sheet of 3, #506-508 2.25 1.00
*Nos. 506-508 (3)* 2.15 1.00

ITU Plenipotentiaries Conference, Nairobi, Sept. — A123

**1982, Oct. 15 Photo. *Perf. 14x13½***

**509** A123 75c green & multi .20 .20
**510** A123 3.25sh orange & multi .85 .50
**511** A123 5.50sh blue & multi 1.50 .90
*Nos. 509-511 (3)* 2.55 1.60

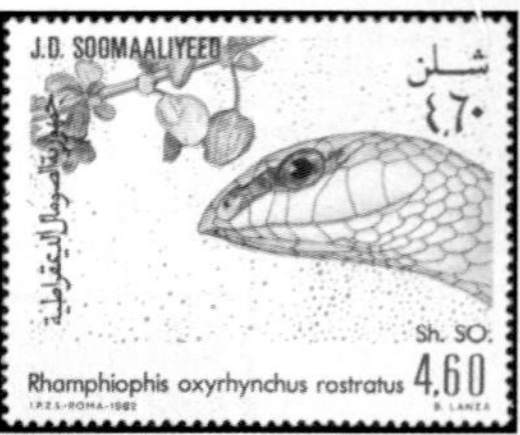

Local Snakes — A124

2.80sh, Bitis arietans. 3.20sh, Psammophis punctulatus. 4.60sh, Rhamphiophis oxyrhynchus. 8.60sh, Sphalerosophis josephscorteccii.

**1982, Dec. 20 Photo. *Perf. 14***

**512** A124 2.80sh multicolored .75 .40
**513** A124 3.20sh multicolored .85 .50
**514** A124 4.60sh multicolored 1.40 .65
*Nos. 512-514 (3)* 3.00 1.55

**Souvenir Sheet**

**515** A124 8.60sh multicolored 4.00 2.25

Somali Woman — A125

A126

**1982, Dec. 30 *Perf. 14x13½***

**516** A125 1sh yel & multi .20 .20
**517** A125 5.20sh lilac & multi .90 .85
**518** A125 5.80sh org & multi .95 .90
**519** A125 6.40sh blue & multi 1.10 1.00

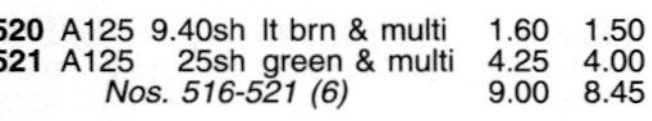

**520** A125 9.40sh lt brn & multi 1.60 1.50
**521** A125 25sh green & multi 4.25 4.00
*Nos. 516-521 (6)* 9.00 8.45

**1983, July 20** ***Perf. 13½x14***
**522** A126 5.20sh multicolored .95 .65
**523** A126 6.40sh multicolored 1.00 .85

World Communications Year.

2nd Intl. Congress of Somali Studies, Hamburg — A127

Various views of Hamburg.

**1983, Aug. 1** ***Perf. 14***
**524** A127 5.20sh multicolored .85 .65
**525** A127 6.40sh multicolored 1.00 .85

Military Uniforms — A128

Designs: a, Air Force. b, Women's Auxiliary Corps. c, Border Police. d, People's Militia. e, Army Infantry. f, Custodial Corps. g, Police. h, Navy.

**1983, Oct. 21** **Litho.** ***Perf. 13½x14***
**526** Strip of 8 2.00
***a.-h.*** A128 3.20sh, any single .25 .20

View Type of 1980

**1983**
**527** A117 2.80sh Barawe .35 .20
**528** A117 3.20sh Bur Hakaba .40 .20
**529** A117 5.50sh Baydhabo .65 .30
**530** A117 8.60sh Dooy Nuunaay 1.10 .50
*Nos. 527-530 (4)* 2.50 1.20

Sea Shells A129

**1984, Feb. 15** **Litho.** ***Perf. 14x13½***
**531** A129 2.80sh Volutocorbis rosavittoriae .25 .20
**532** A129 3.20sh Phalium bituberculosum .25 .20
**533** A129 5.50sh Conus milneedwarsi .40 .30
*Nos. 531-533 (3)* .90 .70

**Souvenir Sheet**

***Perf. 14***

**534** A129 15sh Cypraea broderipi 1.25 .90

Olympics 1984 — A130

Riccione Fair — A131

**1984, Sept.** **Litho.** ***Perf. 13½x14***
**535** A130 1.50sh Runners .20 .20
**536** A130 3sh Discus .25 .20
**537** A130 8sh Pole vaulting .65 .45
***a.*** Souvenir sheet of 3, #535-537 1.25 .90
*Nos. 535-537 (3)* 1.10 .85

No. 537a sold for 15sh.

**1984, Sept.** **Litho.** ***Perf. 13½x14***
**538** A131 5.20sh multicolored .40 .30
**539** A131 6.40sh multicolored .55 .40

Animals A132

**1984, Sept.** **Litho.** ***Perf. 14x13½***
**540** A132 1sh Hystrix cristata .20 .20
**541** A132 1.50sh Ichneumia albicauda .20 .20
**542** A132 2sh Mungos mungo .20 .20
**543** A132 4sh Mellivora capensis .40 .25
***a.*** Souvenir sheet of 4, #540-543 .90 .60
*Nos. 540-543 (4)* 1.00 .85

No. 543a sold for 10sh.

Intl. Civil Aviation Org., 40th Anniv. — A133

**1984, Nov. 20** **Litho.** ***Perf. 14***
**544** A133 3sh multicolored .20 .20
**545** A133 6.40sh multicolored .25 .20

**Souvenir Sheet**

**546** Sheet of 2 .35 .35
***a.*** A133 3sh like No. 544 .20 .20
***b.*** A133 6.40sh like No. 545 .25 .25

No. 546 contains 2 49½x46mm stamps. Sold for 10sh.

Dove — A134

Constellations from the Book of Fixed Stars, by Abd al-Rahman al-Sufi.

**1985, Aug. 10** **Litho.** ***Perf. 13½x14***
**547** A134 4.30sh shown .45 .30
**548** A134 11sh Bull 1.10 .80
**549** A134 12.50sh Rams 1.25 .90
**550** A134 13.80sh Archer 1.50 1.00
*Nos. 547-550 (4)* 4.30 3.00

Architecture — A135

**1985, Sept.** **Litho.** ***Perf. 13½x14***
**551** A135 2sh Ras Kiambone + label .20 .20
**552** A135 6.60sh Hannassa + label .55 .45
**553** A135 10sh Mnarani + label 1.50 1.10
**554** A135 18.60sh as #551, diff. + label 2.75 1.75
*Nos. 551-554 (4)* 5.00 3.50

See Nos. 572-575.

Lady Somalia Seated in Posthorn A136

**1985, Oct.** ***Perf. 14x14½***
**555** A136 2sh multicolored .20 .20
**556** A136 20sh multicolored 2.00 1.50
***a.*** Souvenir sheet of 2, #555-556, perf. 13½ 3.25 3.25

ITALIA '85, Rome. No. 556a sold for 30sh.

Bats A137

**1985, Dec. 25** **Litho.** ***Perf. 14x13½***
**557** A137 2.50sh Triaenops persicus .20 .20
**558** A137 4.50sh Cardioderma cor .20 .20
**559** A137 16sh Tadarida condylura .55 .40
**560** A137 18sh Coleura afra .65 .45
*Nos. 557-560 (4)* 1.60 1.25

**Souvenir Sheet**

**561** Sheet of 4 1.75 1.75
***a.*** A137 2.50sh like #552 .20 .20
***b.*** A137 4.50sh like #553 .20 .20
***c.*** A137 16sh like #554 .70 .70
***d.*** A137 18sh like #555 .80 .80

Nos. 561a-561d printed in continuous design. No. 561 sold for 50sh.

Economic Trade Agreement with Kenya — A138

Design: Presidents Arap Moi and Barre, satellite communications.

**1986, Feb. 15** ***Perf. 14***
**562** A138 9sh multi .30 .25
**563** A138 14.50sh multi .50 .35

EUROFLORA Flower Exhibition, Genoa — A139

3rd Intl. Congress on Somali Studies — A140

**1986, Apr. 25** ***Perf. 13½x14***
**564** A139 10sh Flower arrangement .35 .25
**565** A139 15sh Arrangement, diff. .50 .40
***a.*** Souvenir sheet of 2, #564-565 1.25 1.25

No. 565a sold for 30sh.

**1986, May 26**
**566** A140 11.35sh multi .40 .30
**567** A140 20sh multi .70 .50

1986 World Cup Soccer Championships, Mexico — A141

Various soccer plays.

**1986, June** ***Perf. 14x13½***
**568** A141 3.60sh multi .20 .20
**569** A141 4.80sh multi .20 .20
**570** A141 6.80sh multi .25 .20
**571** A141 22.60sh multi .85 .55
***a.*** Souvenir sheet of 4, #568-571 1.75 1.75
*Nos. 568-571 (4)* 1.50 1.15

No. 571a sold for 50sh.

Architecture Type of 1985

**1986** **Litho.** ***Perf. 13½x14***
**572** A135 10sh Bulaxaar .35 .30
**573** A135 15sh Saylac .50 .40
**574** A135 20sh Saylac, diff. .70 .55
**575** A135 31sh Jasiiradaha Jawaay 1.10 .85
*Nos. 572-575 (4)* 2.65 2.10

Nos. 572-575 each printed se-tenant with decorative label.

Red Crescent — Red Cross Rehabilitation Center, Mogadishu — A143

**1987, May 8** **Litho.** ***Perf. 13½x13***
**576** A143 56sh multi 2.00 1.60

**Souvenir Sheet**

**577** A143 56sh multi, diff. 2.25 2.25

No. 577 sold for 60sh. See Norway No. 908.

A144

A145

**1987, Sept. 27 Litho. *Perf. 13½x14***

**578** A144 20sh Running .90 .70
**579** A144 48sh Javelin 2.00 1.60
*a.* Souvenir sheet of 2, #578-579 3.50 3.50

OLYMPHILEX '87, Rome. No. 579a sold for 75sh.

**1987, Oct. 5 Photo. *Perf. 13½x14½***

**580** A145 53sh multicolored 1.40 1.10
**581** A145 72sh multicolored 1.90 1.40

Intl. Year of Shelter for the Homeless.

GEOSOM '87 — A146

A147

Maps: 10sh, 160,000,000 years ago. 20sh, 60,000,000 years ago. 40sh, 15,000,000 years ago. 50sh, Today.

**1987, Nov. 24 Litho. *Perf. 13½x14***

**582** A146 10sh multi .25 .20
**583** A146 20sh multi, diff. .50 .40
**584** A146 40sh multi, diff. 1.00 .75
**585** A146 50sh multi, diff. 1.25 1.00
*a.* Souv. sheet of 2, #583, 585 5.50 4.00
*Nos. 582-585 (4)* 3.00 2.35

Symposium on the Geology of Somalia, Mogadishu, 11/24-12/1. #585a sold for 130sh.

**1988, Dec. 31 Litho. *Perf. 13½x14***

**586** A147 50sh multicolored .50 .40
**587** A147 168sh multicolored 1.60 1.25

World Health Organization, 40th anniv.

Wildlife A148

***Perf. 13½x14, 14x13½***

**1989, Oct. 20 Litho.**

**588** A148 75sh *Lepus somaliensis* .35 .30
**589** A148 198sh *Syncerus caffer* .90 .70
**590** A148 200sh *Papio hamadryas* .95 .70
**591** A148 216sh *Hippopotamus amphibius* 1.00 .75
*a.* Souvenir sheet of 2, #590-591 3.25 3.25
*Nos. 588-591 (4)* 3.20 2.45

No. 591a contains 2 labels like #588-589. Sold for 700sh.

Somali Revolution, 20th Anniv. A149

Flowers, children's games: 70sh, Kick ball. 100sh, Swinging. 150sh, Teeter-totter. 300sh, Jumping rope, stick and hoop.

**1989, Dec. 12 Litho. *Perf. 14x13½***

**592** A149 70sh multicolored 1.40 1.10
**593** A149 100sh multicolored 2.00 1.60
**594** A149 150sh multicolored 3.00 2.40
**595** A149 300sh multicolored 6.00 4.75
*Nos. 592-595 (4)* 12.40 9.85

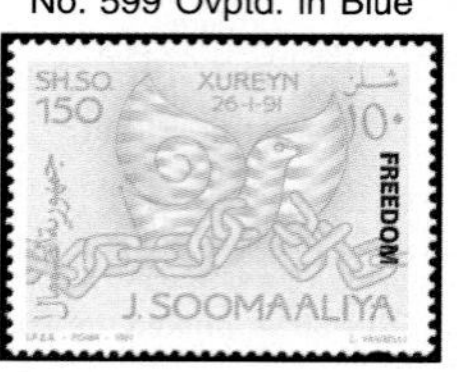

A150 A151

Liberation: Nos. 599-600, Dove breaking chains, horiz.

**1991 Litho. *Perf. 13½x14, 14x13½***

**596** A150 70sh lilac & multi .65 .50
**597** A150 100sh grn bl & multi .90 .70
**598** A150 150sh brt blue & multi 1.40 1.00
**599** A150 150sh yellow & multi 1.40 1.00
**600** A150 300sh yel grn & multi 2.75 2.00
**601** A150 300sh yel grn & multi 2.75 2.00
*Nos. 596-601 (6)* 9.85 7.20

Issued: Nos. 599-600, July 2; others, July 4.

No. 599 Ovptd. in Blue

**1991 Litho. *Perf. 14x13½***

**602** A150 150sh yellow & multi 1.40 1.00

**1991 Litho. *Perf. 14***

Various minarets.

**603** A151 30sh multicolored .30 .30
**604** A151 40sh multicolored .45 .35
**605** A151 50sh multicolored .55 .40
**606** A151 150sh multicolored 1.70 1.25
*Nos. 603-606 (4)* 3.00 2.30

Relief efforts have demonstrated the breakdown of government services in Somalia. It is unclear which faction has control of the Postal Service, if any is operating. The status of Scott Nos. 607-638 will be reviewed once more information is available.

Gazelles A152

**1992 *Perf. 14x13½***

**Inscribed in Black**

**607** A152 500sh Two Speke's 2.50
**608** A152 700sh One Speke's 3.50
**609** A152 800sh One Soemmering's 4.50
**610** A152 1000sh Two Soemmering's 5.50
*Nos. 607-610 (4)* 16.00

World Wildlife Fund.

Without WWF Emblem
**Inscribed in red lilac**

**611** A152 100sh like #607 .55
**612** A152 200sh like #608 1.10
**613** A152 300sh like #609 1.60
**614** A152 400sh like #610 2.25

**Inscribed in black**

**615** A152 1500sh Baboons 8.25
**616** A152 2500sh Hippopotamus 13.00
**617** A152 3000sh Giraffes 16.00
**618** A152 5000sh Leopard 25.00
*Nos. 607-618 (12)* 83.75

Nos. 607-618 are part of an expanding set. Numbers may change.
For overprints see No. 629-632.

Nos. 607-610 Ovptd. "PARTICIPANT / RIO 1992" in Orange

**1992 Litho. *Perf. 14x13½***

**629** A152 500sh on #607 2.75
**630** A152 700sh on #608 3.75
**631** A152 800sh on #609 4.50
**632** A152 1000sh on #610 5.50
*Nos. 629-632 (4)* 16.50

Discovery of America, 500th Anniv. A153

Designs: 100sh, Sighting land from crow's nest. 200sh, Three men pointing from ship. 300sh, Columbus in his cabin. 400sh, Claiming land. 2000sh, Building fort in New World.
No. 638: a, 800sh, like #634. b, 900sh, like #635. c, 1300sh, like #633.

**1992**

**633** A153 100sh multicolored .55
**634** A153 200sh multicolored 1.10
**635** A153 300sh multicolored 1.60
**636** A153 400sh multicolored 2.25
**637** A153 2000sh multicolored 11.00
*Nos. 633-637 (5)* 16.50

**Souvenir Sheet**

**638** A153 Sheet of 3, #a.-c. 16.50

Nos. 638a-638c do not have white border. No. 638 exists imperf.

## SEMI-POSTAL STAMPS

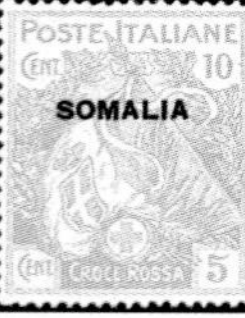

Italy Nos. B1-B4 Overprinted

**1916 Wmk. 140 *Perf. 14***

**B1** SP1 10c + 5c rose 11.00 *30.00*
**B2** SP2 15c + 5c slate 32.50 *40.00*
**B3** SP2 20c + 5c orange 11.00 *37.50*
**B4** SP2 20c on 15c + 5c slate 32.50 *62.50*
*Nos. B1-B4 (4)* 87.00 *170.00*

**Holy Year Issue**

Italy Nos. B20-B25 Surcharged in Black or Red

**1925, June 1 *Perf. 12***

**B5** SP4 6b + 3b on 20c + 10c 3.00 *18.00*
**B6** SP4 13b + 6b on 30c + 15c 3.00 *21.00*
**B7** SP4 15b + 8b on 50c + 25c 3.00 *18.00*
**B8** SP4 18b + 9b on 60c + 30c 3.00 *24.00*
**B9** SP8 30b + 15b on 1 l +50c (R) 3.00 *30.00*
**B10** SP8 1r + 50b on 5 l +2.50 l (R) 3.00 *45.00*
*Nos. B5-B10 (6)* 18.00 *156.00*

**Colonial Institute Issue**

"Peace" Substituting Spade for Sword — SP10

**1926, June 1 Typo. *Perf. 14***

**B11** SP10 5c + 5c brown .90 *7.50*
**B12** SP10 10c + 5c olive grn .90 *7.50*
**B13** SP10 20c + 5c blue grn .90 *7.50*
**B14** SP10 40c + 5c brown red .90 *7.50*
**B15** SP10 60c + 5c orange .90 *7.50*
**B16** SP10 1 l + 5c blue .90 *7.50*
*Nos. B11-B16 (6)* 5.40 *45.00*

The surtax was for the Italian Colonial Institute.

Types of Italian Semi-Postal Stamps of 1926 Overprinted

**1927, Apr. 21 Unwmk. *Perf. 11½***

**B17** SP10 40c + 20c dk brn & blk 2.25 *30.00*
**B18** SP10 60c + 30c brn red & ol brn 2.25 *30.00*
**B19** SP10 1.25 l + 60c dp bl & blk 2.25 *47.50*
**B20** SP10 5 l + 2.50 l dk grn & blk 3.75 *67.50*
*Nos. B17-B20 (4)* 10.50 *175.00*

The surtax was for the charitable work of the Voluntary Militia for Italian National Defense.

Allegory of Fascism and Victory — SP11

**1928, Oct. 15 Wmk. 140 *Perf. 14***

**B21** SP11 20c + 5c blue grn 2.25 *11.00*
**B22** SP11 30c + 5c red 2.25 *11.00*
**B23** SP11 50c + 10c purple 2.25 *11.00*
**B24** SP11 1.25 l + 20c dk blue 3.00 *21.00*
*Nos. B21-B24 (4)* 9.75 *54.00*

46th anniv. of the Societa Africana d'Italia. The surtax aided that society.

Types of Italian Semi-Postal Stamps of 1928 Overprinted

**1929, Mar. 4 Unwmk. Perf. 11**

| | | | | |
|---|---|---|---|---|
| **B25** | SP10 | 30c + 10c red & blk | 3.75 | 18.00 |
| **B26** | SP10 | 50c + 20c vio & blk | 3.75 | 22.00 |
| **B27** | SP10 | 1.25 l + 50c brn & bl | 4.50 | 37.50 |
| **B28** | SP10 | 5 l + 2 l ol grn & blk | 4.50 | 67.50 |
| | | *Nos. B25-B28 (4)* | 16.50 | 145.00 |

The surtax was for the charitable work of the Voluntary Militia for Italian National Defense.

Types of Italian Semi-Postal Stamps of 1926 Overprinted in Black or Red

**1930, Oct. 20 Perf. 14**

| | | | | |
|---|---|---|---|---|
| **B29** | SP10 | 30c + 10c dk grn & bl grn (Bk) | 19.00 | 30.00 |
| **B30** | SP10 | 50c + 10c dk grn & vio (R) | 19.00 | 40.00 |
| **B31** | SP10 | 1.25 l + 30c ol brn & red brn (R) | 19.00 | 52.50 |
| **B32** | SP10 | 5 l + 1.50 l ind & grn (R) | 60.00 | 150.00 |
| | | *Nos. B29-B32 (4)* | 117.00 | 272.50 |

The surtax was for the charitable work of the Voluntary Militia for Italian National Defense.

Irrigation Canal SP14

**1930, Nov. 27 Photo. Wmk. 140**

| | | | | |
|---|---|---|---|---|
| **B33** | SP14 | 50c + 20c olive brn | 3.75 | 18.00 |
| **B34** | SP14 | 1.25 l + 20c dp blue | 3.75 | 18.00 |
| **B35** | SP14 | 1.75 l + 20c green | 3.75 | 20.00 |
| **B36** | SP14 | 2.55 l + 50c purple | 6.00 | 32.50 |
| **B37** | SP14 | 5 l + 1 l dp car | 6.00 | 47.50 |
| | | *Nos. B33-B37 (5)* | 23.25 | 136.00 |

25th anniv. of the Italian Colonial Agricultural Institute. The surtax was for the aid of that institution.

SP15

King Victor Emmanuel III — SP16

**1935, Jan. 1**

| | | | | |
|---|---|---|---|---|
| **B38** | SP15 | 5c + 5c blk brn | 3.00 | 18.00 |
| **B39** | SP15 | 7½c + 7½c vio | 3.00 | 18.00 |
| **B40** | SP15 | 15c + 10c ol blk | 3.00 | 18.00 |
| **B41** | SP15 | 20c + 10c rose red | 3.00 | 18.00 |
| **B42** | SP15 | 25c + 10c dp grn | 3.00 | 18.00 |
| **B43** | SP15 | 30c + 10c brn | 3.00 | 18.00 |
| **B44** | SP15 | 50c + 10c pur | 3.00 | 18.00 |
| **B45** | SP15 | 75c + 15c rose car | 3.00 | 18.00 |
| **B46** | SP15 | 1.25 l + 15c dp bl | 3.00 | 18.00 |
| **B47** | SP15 | 1.75 l + 25c red org | 3.00 | 18.00 |
| **B48** | SP15 | 2.75 l + 25c gray | 18.00 | 75.00 |
| **B49** | SP15 | 5 l + 1 l dp cl | 18.00 | 75.00 |
| **B50** | SP15 | 10 l + 1.80 l red brn | 18.00 | 75.00 |
| **B51** | SP16 | 25 l + 2.75 l brn & red | 150.00 | 300.00 |
| | | *Nos. B38-B51 (14)* | 234.00 | 705.00 |
| | | Set, never hinged | 575.00 | |

Visit of King Victor Emmanuel III.

**Catalogue values for unused stamps in this section, from this point to the end of the section, are for Never Hinged items.**

### Somalia

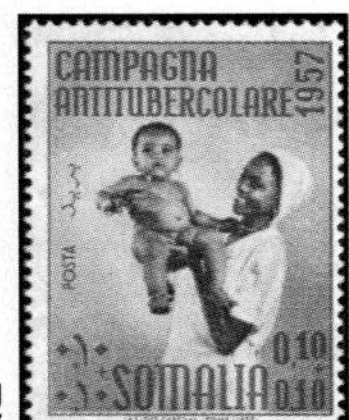

Nurse Holding Infant — SP17

**1957, Nov. 30 Wmk. 303 Perf. 14**

| | | | | |
|---|---|---|---|---|
| **B52** | SP17 | 10c + 10c red & brn | .20 | .20 |
| **B53** | SP17 | 25c + 10c grn & brn | .20 | .20 |
| | | *Nos. B52-B53,CB11-CB12 (4)* | .85 | .95 |

The surtax was for the fight against tuberculosis.

### Republic

Refugees SP18

**1964, Dec. 12 Photo. Perf. 14**

| | | | | |
|---|---|---|---|---|
| **B54** | SP18 | 25c + 10c vio bl & red | .25 | .20 |
| | | *Nos. B54,CB13-CB14 (3)* | 1.55 | .70 |

The surtax was to help refugees.

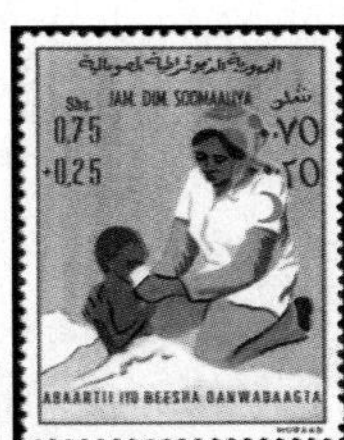
Red Cross Nurse Feeding Child — SP19

Refugees SP20

Famine Relief: 80c+20c, Nomad in parched land, horiz. 2.40sh+10c, Family with fish and produce. 2.90sh+10c, Physician and Aid Society emblem, horiz.

**1976, Dec. 10 Perf. 13x14, 14x13**

| | | | | |
|---|---|---|---|---|
| **B55** | SP19 | 75c + 25c multi | .25 | .25 |
| **B56** | SP19 | 80c + 20c multi | .25 | .25 |
| **B57** | SP19 | 2.40sh + 10c multi | .50 | .50 |
| **B58** | SP19 | 2.90sh + 10c multi | .70 | .70 |
| | | *Nos. B55-B58 (4)* | 1.70 | 1.70 |

**1981, Dec. 15 Photo. Perf. 13½x14**

| | | | | |
|---|---|---|---|---|
| **B59** | SP20 | 2sh + 50c multi | .70 | .40 |
| **B60** | SP20 | 6.80sh + 50c multi | 2.00 | .60 |
| *a.* | | Souvenir sheet of 2, #B59-B60 | 4.00 | 1.60 |

TB Bacillus Centenary — SP31

**1982, Dec. 30 Photo. Perf. 14**

| | | | | |
|---|---|---|---|---|
| **B61** | SP31 | 4.60sh + 60c multi | 2.00 | .85 |
| **B62** | SP31 | 5.80sh + 60c multi | 2.00 | 1.00 |

## AIR POST STAMPS

View of Coast AP1

Cheetahs AP2

**Wmk. 140**

**1934, Oct. Photo. Perf. 14**

| | | | | |
|---|---|---|---|---|
| **C1** | AP1 | 25c sl bl & red org | 3.75 | 18.00 |
| **C2** | AP1 | 50c dk grn & blk | 3.75 | 15.00 |
| **C3** | AP1 | 75c brn & red org | 3.75 | 15.00 |
| *a.* | | Imperf. | | |
| **C4** | AP2 | 80c org brn & blk | 3.75 | 18.00 |
| **C5** | AP2 | 1 l scar & blk | 3.75 | 21.00 |
| **C6** | AP2 | 2 l dk bl & brn | 3.75 | 37.50 |
| | | *Nos. C1-C6 (6)* | 22.50 | 124.50 |
| | | Set, never hinged | 55.00 | |

2nd Colonial Arts Exhibition, Naples.
For overprint see No. CO1.

Banana Tree and Airplane AP3

25c, 1.50 l, Banana tree, plane. 50c, 2 l, Plane over cotton field. 60c, 5 l, Plane over orchard. 75c, 10 l, Plane over field workers. 1 l, 3 l, Small girl watching plane.

**1936 Photo.**

| | | | | |
|---|---|---|---|---|
| **C7** | AP3 | 25c slate green | 1.50 | 6.00 |
| **C8** | AP3 | 50c brown | .75 | .20 |
| **C9** | AP3 | 60c red orange | 2.25 | 9.00 |
| **C10** | AP3 | 75c orange brn | 1.50 | 2.25 |
| **C11** | AP3 | 1 l deep blue | .75 | .20 |
| **C12** | AP3 | 1.50 l purple | 1.50 | .75 |
| **C13** | AP3 | 2 l slate blue | 4.50 | 1.10 |
| **C14** | AP3 | 3 l copper red | 15.00 | 9.00 |
| **C15** | AP3 | 5 l yellow green | 16.00 | 13.50 |
| **C16** | AP3 | 10 l dp rose red | 18.00 | 22.50 |
| | | *Nos. C7-C16 (10)* | 61.75 | 64.50 |
| | | Set, never hinged | 150.00 | |

**Catalogue values for unused stamps in this section, from this point to the end of the section, are for Never Hinged items.**

### Somalia

AP8

**1950-51 Wmk. 277**

| | | | | |
|---|---|---|---|---|
| **C17** | AP8 | 30c yellow brn | .20 | .30 |
| **C18** | AP8 | 45c dk carmine | .20 | .30 |
| **C19** | AP8 | 65c dk blue vio | .20 | .30 |
| **C20** | AP8 | 70c dull blue | .20 | .30 |
| **C21** | AP8 | 90c olive brn | .20 | .30 |
| **C22** | AP8 | 1s lilac rose | .20 | .30 |
| **C23** | AP8 | 1.35s violet | .25 | .70 |
| **C24** | AP8 | 1.50s blue green | .35 | .60 |
| **C25** | AP8 | 3s blue | 2.50 | 2.50 |
| **C26** | AP8 | 5s chocolate | 3.00 | 3.00 |
| **C27** | AP8 | 10s red org ('51) | 3.25 | 2.50 |
| | | *Nos. C17-C27 (11)* | 10.55 | 11.10 |

Scene in Mogadishu AP8a

**1951, Oct. 4**

| | | | | |
|---|---|---|---|---|
| **C27A** | AP8a | 1s vio & Prus bl | 2.50 | 1.25 |
| **C27B** | AP8a | 1.50s ol grn & chnt brn | 4.00 | 3.75 |

First Territorial Council meeting.

Plane, Palm Tree and Minaret — AP9

Mother and Child — AP10

**1952, Sept. 14**

| | | | | |
|---|---|---|---|---|
| **C28** | AP9 | 1.20s ol bis & dp bl | 2.25 | 2.25 |

1st Somali Fair, Mogadishu, Sept. 14-28.

**1953, May 27**

| | | | | |
|---|---|---|---|---|
| **C29** | AP10 | 1.20s dk grn & dk brn | 1.00 | 1.00 |

Somali anti-tuberculosis campaign.

Fair Entrance AP11

**1953, Sept. 28 Unwmk. Perf. 11½**

| | | | | |
|---|---|---|---|---|
| **C30** | AP11 | 1.20s brn car & pink | .50 | .50 |
| **C31** | AP11 | 1.50s yel brn & buff | .50 | .50 |

2nd Somali Fair, Mogadishu, Sept. 28-Oct. 12, 1953.

Plane over Map and Stamps of 1903 AP12

***Perf. 13x13½***

**1953, Dec. 16 Engr. Wmk. 277**

**Early Stamps in Brn and Rose Car**

| | | | | |
|---|---|---|---|---|
| **C32** | AP12 | 60c orange brown | .50 | .50 |
| **C33** | AP12 | 1s greenish black | .50 | .50 |

1st Somali postage stamps, 50th anniv.

"UPU" among Constellations — AP13

*Perf. 11½*

**1953, Dec. 16 Photo. Unwmk.**

**C34** AP13 1.20s red & cream .45 .35
**C35** AP13 1.50s brown & cream .50 .40
**C36** AP13 2s green & lt blue .55 .50
*Nos. C34-C36 (3)* 1.50 1.25

UPU, 75th anniv. (in 1949).

Alexander Island Juba River — AP14

Somali Flag — AP15

**1954, June 1** *Perf. 13½x12½*

**C37** AP14 1.20s dk grn & brn .50 .50
**C38** AP14 2s dk carmine & pur .65 .60

See note after No. 196.

*Perf. 13½x13*

**1954, Oct. 12 Litho. Wmk. 277**

**C39** AP15 1.20s multicolored .30 .30

Adoption of Somali flag.

Haggard's Oribi — AP16

Designs: 45c, Phillip's dik-dik. 50c, Speke's gazelle. 75c, Gerenuk. 1.20s, Soemmering's gazelle. 1.50s, Waterbuck.

**Wmk. 277**

**1955, Apr. 12 Photo.** *Perf. 13½*

**Antelopes in Natural Colors**

**Size: 22x33mm**

**C40** AP16 35c gray grn & blk .35 *.60*
**C41** AP16 45c lilac & blk 1.60 .70
**C42** AP16 50c rose lil & blk .40 *.50*
**C43** AP16 75c red 1.10 .50
**C44** AP16 1.20s dk gray grn 1.10 *1.40*
**C45** AP16 1.50s bright blue 1.60 *2.40*
*Nos. C40-C45 (6)* 6.15 6.10

See Nos. C57-C58.

Caravan at Water Hole AP17

Design: 1.20s, Village well.

*Perf. 13½x14*

**1955, Sept. 24 Wmk. 303**

**C46** AP17 45c brown & orange .35 .35
**C47** AP17 1.20s sapphire & pink .45 .45

3rd Somali Fair, Mogadishu, Sept. 1955.

**Ballot Type of Regular Issue**

**1956, Apr. 30 Photo.** *Perf. 14*

**C48** A24 60c brown & ultra .20 .20
**C49** A24 1.20s brown & org .20 .20

Opening of the territory's first democratically elected Legislative Assembly.

**Arms Type of Regular Issue**

**1957, May 6 Wmk. 303** *Perf. 13½*

**Coat of Arms in Dull Yellow, Blue and Black**

**C50** A25 45c blue .20 .20
**C51** A25 1.20s bluish green .20 .25

Issued in honor of the new coat of arms.

Type of Regular Issue, 1957 and

Oil Well — AP18

Design: 60c, Irrigation canal construction.

**1957, Sept. 28** *Perf. 14*

**C52** A26 60c blue & brown .20 .30
**C53** AP18 1.20s black & ver .20 .30

Fourth Somali Fair and Film Festival.

**Sport Type of Regular Issue**

60c, Runner. 1.20s, Bicyclist. 1.50s, Basketball player.

**1958, Apr. 28 Wmk. 303** *Perf. 14*

**C54** A27 60c brown .20 .20
**C55** A27 1.20s blue .20 .20
**C56** A27 1.50s rose carmine .20 .20
*Nos. C54-C56 (3)* .60 .60

**Animal Type of 1955**

3s, Lesser kudu. 5s, Hunter's hartebeest.

**1958-59 Photo.**

**Size: 20½x36½mm**

**C57** AP16 3s ocher & sepia .60 .85
**C58** AP16 5s gray, blk & yel ('59) .60 .85

See No. CE1.

Police Bugler AP19

**1959, June 19 Photo.**

**C59** AP19 1.20s ocher & ultra .20 .30
**C60** AP19 1.50s olive grn & ultra .20 .30
*a.* Souv. sheet of 4, #228-229, C59-C60 1.25 1.75

Opening of the Constituent Assembly of Somalia.

Marabou AP20

**1959, Sept. 4 Wmk. 303**

**C61** AP20 1.20s shown 1.00 .50
**C62** AP20 2s Great egret 1.00 .50

Incense Shipment, 15th Century B.C. AP21

Design: 2s, Incense burner and view of Mogadishu harbor.

**1959, Sept. 28** *Perf. 14*

**C63** AP21 1.20s red & blk .20 .30
**C64** AP21 2s blue, blk & org .30 .45

5th Somali Fair, Mogadishu.

University Institute and Arms AP22

Design: 1.20s, Front view of Institute.

**1960, Jan. 14**

**C65** AP22 45c grn, blk & org brn .25 .25
**C66** AP22 1.20s blue, ultra & blk .35 .35

Opening of the University Institute of Somalia.

Stork and Uprooted Oak Emblem — AP23

**1960, Apr. 7 Wmk. 303** *Perf. 14*

**C67** AP23 1.50s lt grn, bl & red .25 .25

World Refugee Year, 7/1/59-6/30/60.

**Republic**

**#C42, C44 Overprinted Like #242**

**Wmk. 277**

**1960, June 26 Photo.** *Perf. 13½*

**Antelopes in Natural Colors**

**C68** AP16 50c rose lil & blk 21.00 21.00
**C69** AP16 1.20s dk gray grn 17.50 17.50

See note after No. 242.

Parliament and Italian Flag AP25

1.80s, Somali flag and assembly building.

**1960, July 1 Wmk. 303** *Perf. 14*

**C70** AP25 1s org red, grn & red .50 .25
**C71** AP25 1.80s red org, ultra & blk 1.25 1.00

Somalia's independence.

**Animal Type of Regular Issue**

**1960, Nov. 24**

**C72** A37 3s Leopard 1.75 1.00

**Olympic Games Type**

45c, Runner, flag, Olympic rings. 1.80s, Long distance runner, flag, Olympic rings.

**1960, Nov. 24**

**C73** A38 45c lilac & blue .20 .20
**C74** A38 1.80s org ver & bl 1.25 1.00

17th Olympic Games, Rome, 8/25-9/11.

Amauris Fenestrata and Jet Plane AP26

Various Butterflies.

**1961, Sept. 9**

**C75** AP26 60c blue, brn & yel .40 .20
**C76** AP26 90c yel, blk & grn .50 .25
**C77** AP26 1s multicolored 1.75 .35
**C78** AP26 1.80s org, blk & red .90 .60
**C79** AP26 3s multicolored 1.25 .80
**C80** AP26 5s ver, blk & brt bl 3.50 1.25
**C81** AP26 10s multicolored 7.00 2.75
*Nos. C75-C81 (7)* 15.30 6.20

Wooden Headrest, Comb and Cap AP27

Design: 1.80sh, Camel, metal sculpture.

**1961, Sept. 28 Wmk. 303** *Perf. 14*

**C82** AP27 1sh blk, ultra & ocher .50 .40
**C83** AP27 1.80sh blk, yel & brn 1.25 .75

6th Somali Fair, Mogadishu.

**Fish Type**

Fish: 2.70sh, Lutianus sebae.

**1962, Apr. 26**

**C84** A41 2.70sh ultra, brn & rose brn 2.75 1.75

Mosquitoes and Malaria Eradication Emblem — AP28

Police Auxiliary Women — AP29

**Wmk. 303**

**1962, Oct. 25 Photo.** *Perf. 14*

**C85** AP28 1sh bis brn & blk .75 .30
**C86** AP28 1.80sh lt green & blk 1.25 .90

WHO drive to eradicate malaria.

**1963, May 15 Wmk. 303** *Perf. 14*

Women's Auxiliary Forces: 1.80sh, Army auxiliary women with flag.

**C87** AP29 1sh dk bl, yel & org .30 .20
**C88** AP29 1.80sh multicolored .60 .20

**Freedom from Hunger Type**

Design: 1sh, Sower and wheat.

**1963, June 25**

**C89** A44 1sh dk brn, yel & bl .40 .20

**President Osman Type**

**1963, Sept. 15 Wmk. 303** *Perf. 14*

**C90** A45 1sh multicolored .55 .20
**C91** A45 1.80sh multicolored .50 .30

**Somali Fair Type**

Design: 1.80sh, Government Pavilion.

**1963, Sept. 28 Photo.**

**C92** A46 1.80sh blue .85 .40

Map of Somalia, Animals and Globe AP30

1.80sh, Somali Credit Bank emblem.

**1964, May 16 Wmk. 303** *Perf. 14*

**C93** AP30 1sh multicolored .30 .20
**C94** AP30 1.80sh blk, bl & yel .70 .30

10th anniversary of Somali Credit Bank.

### Olympic Type

**1964, Oct. 10** **Photo.**
**C95** A48 90c Diving .40 .20
**C96** A48 1.80sh Soccer .60 .30
*a.* Souvenir sheet, #274-275, C95-C96 35.00

No. C96a sold for 3.55sh.

Elephants and DC-3
AP31

Design: 1.80sh, Plane over Mogadishu.

**1964, Nov. 8** **Photo.** ***Perf. 14***
**C97** AP31 1sh brown & green .60 .25
**C98** AP31 1.80sh black & blue 1.25 .40

Establishment of Somali Air Lines.

### ITU Type

**1965, May 17** **Wmk. 303** ***Perf. 14***
**C99** A50 1sh dp grn & blk .40 .20
**C100** A50 1.80sh rose lil & brn .80 .40

### Somali Fair Type

Designs: 1.50sh, Sugar industry; harvesting sugar cane and refinery. 2sh, Dairy industry; bottling plant and milk cow.

**1965, Sept. 28** **Photo.** ***Perf. 14***
**C101** A51 1.50sh sepia & pale bl .40 .20
**C102** A51 2sh sepia & rose .75 .25

### Faisal Type

Design: 1.80sh, Ka'aba, Mecca, Pres. Abdirascid Ali Scermarche and King Faisal.

**1967, Sept. 21** **Wmk. 303** ***Perf. 14***
**C103** A60 1.80sh blk, dp rose & org .30 .20

Egret — AP32

Birds: 1sh, Southern carmine bee-eater. 1.30sh, Bruce's green pigeon. 1.80sh, Broad-tailed paradise whydah.

***Perf. 11½***

**1968, Nov. 1** **Unwmk.** **Litho.**
**C104** AP32 35c blue & multi .20 .20
**C105** AP32 1sh green & multi .20 .20
**C106** AP32 1.30sh vio bl & multi .25 .20
**C107** AP32 1.80sh yellow & multi .35 .25
*Nos. C104-C107 (4)* 1.00 .85

### Somali Democratic Republic

Postal Union Type

1.30sh, Postal Union emblem and letter.

***Perf. 14x13½***

**1972, Jan. 25** **Photo.** **Unwmk.**
**C108** A81 1.30sh multicolored .40 .35

## AIR POST SEMI-POSTAL STAMPS

King Victor Emmanuel III
SPAP1

**Wmk. 140**

**1934, Nov. 5** **Photo.** ***Perf. 14***
**CB1** SPAP1 25c + 10c gray grn 6.00 *13.50*
**CB2** SPAP1 50c + 10c brn 6.00 *13.50*
**CB3** SPAP1 75c + 15c rose red 6.00 *13.50*
**CB4** SPAP1 80c + 15c blk brn 6.00 *13.50*
**CB5** SPAP1 1 l + 20c red brn 6.00 *13.50*
**CB6** SPAP1 2 l + 20c brt bl 6.00 *13.50*
**CB7** SPAP1 3 l + 25c pur 21.00 *67.50*
**CB8** SPAP1 5 l + 25c org 21.00 *67.50*
**CB9** SPAP1 10 l + 30c rose vio 21.00 *67.50*
**CB10** SPAP1 25 l + 2 l dp grn 21.00 *67.50*
*Nos. CB1-CB10 (10)* 120.00 *351.00*
Set, never hinged 300.00

65th birthday of King Victor Emmanuel III; non-stop flight from Rome to Mogadishu.
For overprint see No. CBO1.

**Catalogue values for unused stamps in this section, from this point to the end of the section, are for Never Hinged items.**

### Somalia

Type of Semi-Postal Stamps, 1957

**1957, Nov. 30** **Wmk. 303** ***Perf. 14***
**CB11** SP17 55c + 20c dk bl & brn .20 .25
**CB12** SP17 1.20s + 20c vio & brn .25 .30

The surtax was for the fight against tuberculosis.

Type of Semi-Postal Issue, 1964

Designs: 75c+20c, Destroyed Somali village. 1.80sh+50c, Soldier aiding children, and map of Somalia, vert.

**1964, Dec. 12** **Photo.** ***Perf. 14***
**CB13** SP18 75c + 20c blk, org red & brn .40 .20
**CB14** SP18 1.80sh + 50c blk, ol bis & slate .90 .30

## AIR POST SPECIAL DELIVERY STAMP

**Catalogue value for the stamp in this section is for a Never Hinged item.**

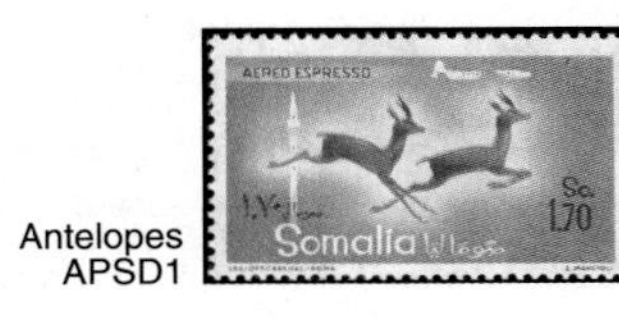

Antelopes
APSD1

**Wmk. 303**

**1958, Oct. 4** **Photo.** ***Perf. 14***
**CE1** APSD1 1.70s org ver & blk .60 .85

## AIR POST OFFICIAL STAMP

No. C1 Overprinted

**Wmk. 140**

**1934, Nov. 11** **Photo.** ***Perf. 14***
**CO1** AP1 25c sl bl & red org *2,500.* *3,350.*
Never hinged 3,750.

Forgeries of this overprint exist.

## AIR POST SEMI-POSTAL OFFICIAL STAMP

Type of Air Post Semi-Postal Stamps, 1934 Overprinted Crown and "SERVIZIO DI STATO" in Black

**1934, Nov. 5** **Wmk. 140** ***Perf. 14***
**CBO1** SPAP1 25 l + 2 l cop red 2,500. *3,750.*
Never hinged 3,000.

## SPECIAL DELIVERY STAMPS

Italy No. E3 Surcharged

**1923, July 16** **Wmk. 140** ***Perf. 14***
**E1** SD1 30b on 60c dl red 24.00 *20.00*

Italy, Type of 1908 Special Delivery Stamp Surcharged

**E2** SD2 60b on 1.20 l bl & red 35.00 *42.50*

"Italia"
SD3

**1924, June** **Engr.** **Unwmk.**
**E3** SD3 30b dk red & brn 9.00 *15.00*
**E4** SD3 60b dk blue & red 15.00 *22.50*

Nos. E3-E4 Surcharged in Black or Red with Bars and

**1926, Oct.**
**E5** SD3 70c on 30b (Bk) 10.00 *16.00*
**E6** SD3 2.50 l on 60b (R) 13.50 *20.00*
*a.* Imperf., pair 375.00

Same Surcharge on No. E3

**1927** ***Perf. 11***
**E7** SD3 1.25 l on 30b 13.50 12.00
*a.* Perf. 14 175.00 *450.00*
*b.* Imperf., pair 750.00

**Catalogue values for unused stamps in this section, from this point to the end of the section, are for Never Hinged items.**

### Somalia

Bananas, Grant's Gazelles
SD4

**Wmk. 277**

**1950, Apr. 24** **Photo.** ***Perf. 14***
**E8** SD4 40c blue green 3.00 2.25
**E9** SD4 80c violet 4.50 4.00

Gardenias
SD5

Design: 1s, Eryrhina melanocantha.

**1955, Feb.** ***Perf. 13***
**E10** SD5 50c lilac & green .50 *1.00*
**E11** SD5 1s bl, rose brn & grn .85 *1.50*

## AUTHORIZED DELIVERY STAMP

Italy No. EY2 Overprinted in Black

**1939** **Wmk. 140** ***Perf. 14***
**EY1** AD2 10c brown 40.00 —

No. EY1 has yellowish gum. A 1941 printing in grayish brown, with white gum, was not issued. Value, 40 cents.

## POSTAGE DUE STAMPS

Postage Due Stamps of Italy Overprinted

**1906-08** **Wmk. 140** ***Perf. 14***
**J1** D3 5c buff & magenta 15.00 *37.50*
**J2** D3 10c buff & magenta 52.50 45.00
**J3** D3 20c org & magenta 37.50 *55.00*
**J4** D3 30c buff & magenta 30.00 *60.00*
**J5** D3 40c buff & magenta 225.00 60.00
**J6** D3 50c buff & magenta 60.00 *75.00*
**J7** D3 60c buff & mag ('08) 52.50 *75.00*
**J8** D3 1 l blue & magenta 1,125. 325.00
**J9** D3 2 l blue & magenta 1,050. 325.00
**J10** D3 5 l blue & magenta 1,050. 325.00
**J11** D3 10 l blue & magenta 185.00 *300.00*
*Nos. J1-J11 (11)* 3,882. *1,682.*

Postage Due Stamps of Italy Overprinted at Top of Stamps

**1909-19**
**J12** D3 5c buff & magenta 7.50 *18.00*
**J13** D3 10c buff & magenta 7.50 *18.00*
**J14** D3 20c buff & magenta 16.00 *37.50*
**J15** D3 30c buff & magenta 37.50 37.50
**J16** D3 40c buff & magenta 37.50 *40.00*
**J17** D3 50c buff & magenta 37.50 *60.00*
**J18** D3 60c buff & mag ('19) 45.00 *52.50*
**J19** D3 1 l blue & magenta 115.00 60.00
**J20** D3 2 l blue & magenta 160.00 160.00
**J21** D3 5 l blue & magenta 175.00 175.00
**J22** D3 10 l blue & magenta 45.00 *60.00*
*Nos. J12-J22 (11)* 683.50 *718.50*

Same with Overprint at Bottom of Stamps

**1920**
*J12a* D3 5c buff & magenta 90.00 125.00
*J13a* D3 10c buff & magenta 90.00 125.00
*J14a* D3 20c buff & magenta 125.00 90.00
*J15a* D3 30c buff & magenta 150.00 90.00
*J16a* D3 40c buff & magenta 150.00 125.00
*J17a* D3 50c buff & magenta 125.00 115.00
*J18a* D3 60c buff & magenta 150.00 115.00

| | | | | |
|---|---|---|---|---|
| *J19a* | D3 | 1 l blue & magenta | 150.00 | 175.00 |
| *J20a* | D3 | 2 l blue & magenta | 150.00 | 175.00 |
| *J21a* | D3 | 5 l blue & magenta | 150.00 | 210.00 |
| | | *Nos. J12a-J21a (10)* | 1,330. | 1,345. |

D4

D5

**1923, July 1**

| | | | | |
|---|---|---|---|---|
| **J23** | D4 | 1b buff & black | 1.50 | *6.00* |
| **J24** | D4 | 2b buff & black | 1.50 | *6.00* |
| *a.* | | Inverted numeral and ovpt. | 450.00 | |
| **J25** | D4 | 3b buff & black | 1.50 | *6.00* |
| **J26** | D4 | 5b buff & black | 3.00 | *6.00* |
| **J27** | D4 | 10b buff & black | 3.00 | *6.00* |
| **J28** | D4 | 20b buff & black | 3.00 | *6.00* |
| **J29** | D4 | 40b buff & black | 3.00 | *6.00* |
| **J30** | D4 | 1r blue & black | 3.75 | *30.00* |
| | | *Nos. J23-J30 (8)* | 20.25 | *72.00* |

Type of Postage Due Stamps of Italy Overprinted

**1926, Mar. 1**

| | | | | |
|---|---|---|---|---|
| **J31** | D3 | 5c buff & black | 19.00 | *26.00* |
| **J32** | D3 | 10c buff & black | 19.00 | 18.00 |
| **J33** | D3 | 20c buff & black | 19.00 | *27.50* |
| **J34** | D3 | 30c buff & black | 19.00 | 18.00 |
| **J35** | D3 | 40c buff & black | 19.00 | 18.00 |
| **J36** | D3 | 50c buff & black | 30.00 | 18.00 |
| **J37** | D3 | 60c buff & black | 30.00 | 18.00 |
| **J38** | D3 | 1 l blue & black | 45.00 | 27.50 |
| **J39** | D3 | 2 l blue & black | 67.50 | 27.50 |
| **J40** | D3 | 5 l blue & black | 75.00 | 40.00 |
| **J41** | D3 | 10 l blue & black | 90.00 | 52.50 |
| | | *Nos. J31-J41 (11)* | 432.50 | 291.00 |

**Numerals and Ovpt. Invtd.**

| | | | |
|---|---|---|---|
| *J32a* | D3 | 10c | 175.00 |
| *J33a* | D3 | 20c | 525.00 |
| *J34a* | D3 | 30c | 175.00 |
| *J35a* | D3 | 40c | 175.00 |
| *J36a* | D3 | 50c | 175.00 |
| *J37a* | D3 | 60c | 175.00 |

Postage Due Stamps of Italy, 1934, Overprinted in Black

**1934, May 12**

| | | | | |
|---|---|---|---|---|
| **J42** | D6 | 5c brown | .75 | *3.75* |
| **J43** | D6 | 10c blue | .75 | *3.75* |
| **J44** | D6 | 20c rose red | 3.00 | 7.50 |
| **J45** | D6 | 25c green | 3.00 | 7.50 |
| **J46** | D6 | 30c red orange | 7.50 | *11.00* |
| **J47** | D6 | 40c black brown | 7.50 | *15.00* |
| **J48** | D6 | 50c violet | 13.50 | 4.50 |
| **J49** | D6 | 60c black | 16.00 | *30.00* |
| **J50** | D7 | 1 l red orange | 21.00 | 13.50 |
| **J51** | D7 | 2 l green | 37.50 | 30.00 |
| **J52** | D7 | 5 l violet | 40.00 | *60.00* |
| **J53** | D7 | 10 l blue | 40.00 | *67.50* |
| **J54** | D7 | 20 l carmine | 45.00 | *82.50* |
| | | *Nos. J42-J54 (13)* | 235.50 | *336.50* |

**Catalogue values for unused stamps in this section, from this point to the end of the section, are for Never Hinged items.**

**Somalia**

**1950 Wmk. 277 Photo. *Perf. 14***

| | | | | |
|---|---|---|---|---|
| **J55** | D5 | 1c dark gray violet | .50 | .50 |
| **J56** | D5 | 2c deep blue | .50 | .50 |
| **J57** | D5 | 5c blue green | .50 | .50 |
| **J58** | D5 | 10c rose lilac | .50 | .50 |
| **J59** | D5 | 40c violet | 2.50 | 2.50 |
| **J60** | D5 | 1s dark brown | 3.50 | 3.50 |
| | | *Nos. J55-J60 (6)* | 8.00 | 8.00 |

## PARCEL POST STAMPS

These stamps were used by affixing them to the way bill so that one half remained on it following the parcel, the other half staying on the receipt given the sender. Most used halves are right halves. Complete stamps were and are obtainable canceled, probably to order. Both unused and used values are for complete stamps.

Parcel Post Stamps of Italy, 1914-17, Overprinted

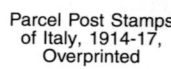

**1917-19 Wmk. 140 *Perf. 13½***

| | | | | |
|---|---|---|---|---|
| **Q1** | PP2 | 5c brown | 4.50 | *37.50* |
| *a.* | | Double overprint | 375.00 | |
| **Q2** | PP2 | 10c blue | 6.00 | *26.00* |
| **Q3** | PP2 | 20c black ('19) | 260.00 | 110.00 |
| **Q4** | PP2 | 25c red | 11.00 | *45.00* |
| *a.* | | Double overprint | — | |
| **Q5** | PP2 | 50c orange | 110.00 | 60.00 |
| **Q6** | PP2 | 1 l lilac | 37.50 | *60.00* |
| **Q7** | PP2 | 2 l green | 52.50 | *60.00* |
| **Q8** | PP2 | 3 l bister | 60.00 | *90.00* |
| **Q9** | PP2 | 4 l slate | 67.50 | *90.00* |
| | | *Nos. Q1-Q9 (9)* | 609.00 | *578.50* |

**Halves Used**

| | |
|---|---|
| Q1, Q4 | .20 |
| Q2 | .20 |
| Q3, Q5 | 2.75 |
| Q6-Q7 | .30 |
| Q8 | .50 |
| Q9 | 1.25 |

Nos. Q5-Q9 were overprinted in 1922 with a slightly different type in which the final "A" of SOMALIA is directly over the final "A" of ITALIANA. They were not regularly issued. Value for set, $400.

Parcel Post Stamps of Italy, 1914-17, Overprinted

**1923**

| | | | | |
|---|---|---|---|---|
| **Q10** | PP2 | 25c red | 22.50 | *25.00* |
| **Q11** | PP2 | 50c orange | 19.00 | *25.00* |
| **Q12** | PP2 | 1 l violet | 27.50 | 25.00 |
| **Q13** | PP2 | 2 l green | 27.50 | 25.00 |
| **Q14** | PP2 | 3 l bister | 47.50 | 25.00 |
| **Q15** | PP2 | 4 l slate | 47.50 | 25.00 |
| | | *Nos. Q10-Q15 (6)* | 191.50 | *150.00* |

**Halves Used**

| | |
|---|---|
| Q10 | 1.10 |
| Q11, Q12 | .30 |
| Q13 | .40 |
| Q14 | .85 |
| Q15 | 1.60 |

Parcel Post Stamps of Italy, 1914-17, Surcharged

**1923**

| | | | | |
|---|---|---|---|---|
| **Q16** | PP2 | 3b on 5c brown | 11.00 | 22.50 |
| **Q17** | PP2 | 5b on 5c brown | 11.00 | 22.50 |
| **Q18** | PP2 | 10b on 10c blue | 11.00 | 18.00 |
| **Q19** | PP2 | 25b on 25c red | 32.50 | 32.50 |
| **Q20** | PP2 | 50b on 50c org | 30.00 | *40.00* |
| **Q21** | PP2 | 1r on 1 l lilac | 37.50 | 47.50 |
| **Q22** | PP2 | 2r on 2 l green | 60.00 | 67.50 |
| **Q23** | PP2 | 3r on 3 l bister | 60.00 | 67.50 |
| **Q24** | PP2 | 4r on 4 l slate | 75.00 | 67.50 |
| | | *Nos. Q16-Q24 (9)* | 328.00 | 385.50 |

**Halves Used**

| | |
|---|---|
| Q16-Q17 | .20 |
| Q18-Q19 | .20 |
| Q20-Q21 | .30 |
| Q22 | .60 |
| Q23 | 1.10 |
| Q24 | 1.60 |

No. Q16 has the numeral "3" at the left also.

Parcel Post Stamps of Italy, 1914-22 Overprinted

**1926-31**

**Red Overprint**

| | | | | |
|---|---|---|---|---|
| **Q25** | PP2 | 5c brown | 22.50 | *45.00* |
| **Q26** | PP2 | 10c blue | 22.50 | *45.00* |
| **Q27** | PP2 | 20c black | 52.50 | 45.00 |
| **Q28** | PP2 | 25c red | 52.50 | 45.00 |
| **Q29** | PP2 | 50c orange | 52.50 | 45.00 |
| **Q30** | PP2 | 1 l violet | 67.50 | 45.00 |
| **Q31** | PP2 | 2 l green | 115.00 | 45.00 |
| **Q32** | PP2 | 3 l yellow | 18.00 | *45.00* |
| **Q33** | PP2 | 4 l slate | 18.00 | *45.00* |
| **Q34** | PP2 | 10 l vio brn ('30) | 37.50 | *60.00* |
| **Q35** | PP2 | 12 l red brn '31) | 37.50 | *60.00* |
| **Q36** | PP2 | 15 l olive ('31) | 37.50 | *95.00* |
| **Q37** | PP2 | 20 l dull vio ('31) | 37.50 | *95.00* |
| | | *Nos. Q25-Q37 (13)* | 571.00 | *715.00* |

**Halves Used**

| | |
|---|---|
| Q25-Q26 | .30 |
| Q27-Q28, Q33 | .70 |
| Q29, Q34 | .90 |
| Q30-Q31 | .50 |
| Q32 | .40 |
| Q35-Q36 | 1.10 |
| Q37 | 1.25 |

Nos. Q25-Q31 come with two types of overprint: I — The first "I" and last "A" of ITALIANA extend slightly at both sides of SOMALIA. II — Only the I" extends. These seven stamps with type I overprint were not regularly issued, and Nos. Q27-Q31 (type I) sell for less than with type II overprint.

**Black Overprint**

| | | | | |
|---|---|---|---|---|
| **Q38** | PP2 | 10 l violet brown | 75.00 | 55.00 |
| **Q39** | PP2 | 12 l red brown | 52.50 | 55.00 |
| **Q40** | PP2 | 15 l olive | 52.50 | 55.00 |
| **Q41** | PP2 | 20 l dull violet | 52.50 | 55.00 |
| | | *Nos. Q38-Q41 (4)* | 232.50 | 220.00 |

**Halves Used**

| | |
|---|---|
| Q38 | .45 |
| Q39-Q41 | .30 |

Same Overprint on Parcel Post Stamps of Italy, 1927-38

**1928-39**

**Black Overprint**

| | | | | |
|---|---|---|---|---|
| **Q42** | PP3 | 25c red ('31) | 40.00 | *30.00* |
| **Q43** | PP3 | 30c ultra | 2.25 | *3.75* |
| **Q43A** | PP3 | 50c orange | *11,250.* | |
| **Q44** | PP3 | 60c red | 2.25 | *6.00* |
| **Q45** | PP3 | 1 l lilac ('31) | 600.00 | *1,300.* |
| **Q46** | PP3 | 2 l green ('31) | 600.00 | *2,000.* |
| **Q47** | PP3 | 3 l bister | 4.50 | *15.00* |
| **Q48** | PP3 | 4 l gray black | 4.50 | *15.00* |
| **Q49** | PP3 | 10 l rose lil ('34) | 400.00 | *425.00* |
| **Q50** | PP3 | 20 l lil brn ('34) | 400.00 | *450.00* |
| | | *Nos. Q42-Q43,Q44-Q50 (9)* | 2,053. | *4,244.* |

**Halves Used**

| | |
|---|---|
| Q42, Q50 | 1.00 |
| Q43, Q44 | .20 |
| Q43A | 40.00 |
| Q45-Q48 | .30 |
| Q49 | 2.00 |

The 25c, 1 l and 2 l come with both types of overprint (see note below No. Q37). Both types were regularly issued. Values are for type I on 25c, type II on 1 l and 2 l.

**Red Overprint**

| | | | | |
|---|---|---|---|---|
| **Q51** | PP3 | 5c brown ('39) | 14.50 | |
| **Q52** | PP3 | 3 l bister ('30) | 30.00 | *55.00* |
| | | Half stamp | | .30 |
| **Q53** | PP3 | 4 l gray black ('30) | 30.00 | *55.00* |
| | | Half stamp | | .30 |
| | | *Nos. Q51-Q53 (3)* | 74.50 | |

Same Overprint in Black on Italy Nos. Q24-Q25

**1940 *Perf. 13***

| | | | | |
|---|---|---|---|---|
| **Q54** | PP3 | 5c brown | 2.25 | *7.50* |
| | | Half stamp | | .20 |
| **Q55** | PP3 | 10c deep blue | 3.00 | *7.50* |
| | | Half stamp | | .20 |

**Catalogue values for unused stamps in this section, from this point to the end of the section, are for Never Hinged items.**

**Somalia**

PP1

**1950 Wmk. 277 Photo. *Perf. 14***

| | | | | |
|---|---|---|---|---|
| **Q56** | PP1 | 1c cerise | .20 | *.50* |
| **Q57** | PP1 | 3c dark gray violet | .20 | *.50* |
| **Q58** | PP1 | 5c rose lilac | .20 | *.50* |
| **Q59** | PP1 | 10c red orange | .20 | *.50* |
| **Q60** | PP1 | 20c dark brown | .20 | *.50* |
| **Q61** | PP1 | 50c blue green | .30 | *.70* |
| **Q62** | PP1 | 1s violet | 1.25 | *3.00* |
| **Q63** | PP1 | 2s brown | 1.60 | *4.00* |
| **Q64** | PP1 | 3s blue | 1.75 | *4.50* |
| | | *Nos. Q56-Q64 (9)* | 5.90 | *14.70* |

**Halves Used**

| | |
|---|---|
| Q56-Q58 | .20 |
| Q59-Q60 | .20 |
| Q61 | .20 |
| Q62 | .20 |
| Q63 | .30 |
| Q64 | .50 |

# SOMALI COAST

sō-'mä-lē 'kōst

(Djibouti)

LOCATION — Eastern Africa, bordering on the Gulf of Aden
GOVT. — French Overseas Territory
AREA — 8,500 sq. mi.
POP. — 86,000 (est. 1963)
CAPITAL — Djibouti (Jibuti)

The port of Obock, which issued postage stamps in 1892-1894, was included in the territory and began to use stamps of Somali Coast in 1902. See Obock in Vol. 4.

On Mar. 19, 1967, the territory changed its name to the French Territory of the Afars and Issas. The Republic of Djibouti was proclaimed June 27, 1977.

100 Centimes = 1 Franc

**Catalogue values for unused stamps in this country are for Never Hinged items, beginning with Scott 224 in the regular postage section, Scott B13 in the semi-postal section, Scott C1 in the airpost section, Scott CB1 in the airpost semi-postal section, and Scott J39 in the postage due section.**

Navigation and Commerce
A1 A2

A3

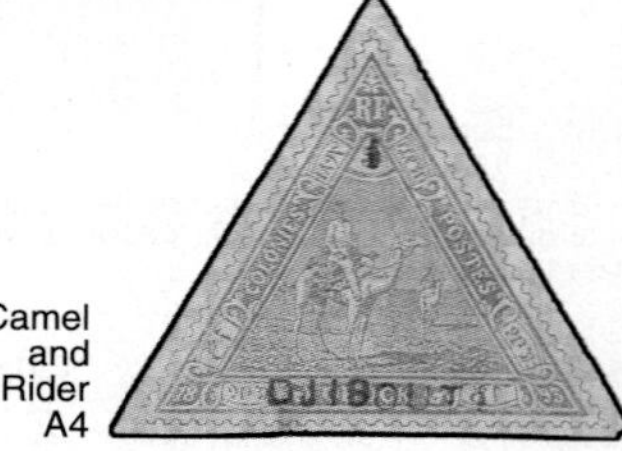
Camel and Rider
A4

Obock Nos. 32-33, 35, 45 with Overprint or Surcharge Handstamped in Black, Blue or Red

**1894 Unwmk. *Perf. 14x13½***

| | | | | |
|---|---|---|---|---|
| **1** | A1 | 5c grn & red, *grnsh* (with bar) | 135.00 | 120.00 |
| *a.* | | Without bar | 1,000. | 700.00 |
| **2** | A2 | 25c on 2c brn & bl, *buff* (Bl & Bk) | 335.00 | 200.00 |
| *a.* | | "25" omitted | 850.00 | 700.00 |
| *b.* | | "DJIBOUTI" omitted | 850.00 | 700.00 |
| *c.* | | "DJIBOUTI" inverted | 975.00 | 900.00 |
| **3** | A3 | 50c on 1c blk & red, *bl* (R & Bl) | 350.00 | 225.00 |
| *a.* | | "5" instead of "50" | 1,350. | 1,000. |
| *b.* | | "0" instead of "50" | 1,350. | 975.00 |
| *c.* | | "DJIBOUTI" omitted | 1,350. | 975.00 |

***Imperf***

| | | | | |
|---|---|---|---|---|
| **4** | A4 | 1fr on 5fr car | 600.00 | 475.00 |
| **5** | A4 | 5fr carmine | 1,650. | 1,200. |

The overprint on No. 1 includes a bar to obliterate "OBOCK."

"DJIBOUTI" is in blue on No. 2, in red on No. 3.

Counterfeits exist of Nos. 4-5.

View of Djibouti, Somali Warriors — A5

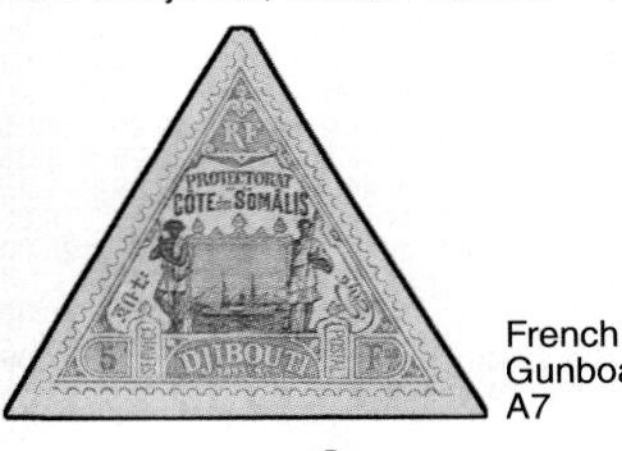

French Gunboat A7

Crossing Desert (Size: 66mm wide, including simulated perfs.) — A8

Designs: 15c, 25c, 30c, 40c, 50c, 75c, Different views of Djibouti. 1fr, 2fr, Djibouti quay.

***Imperf. (Simulated Perforations in Frame Color)***

**1894-1902 Typo.**

**Quadrille Lines Printed on Paper**

6 A5 1c blk & claret 3.25 2.50
7 A5 2c claret & blk 3.25 2.50
8 A5 4c vio brn & bl 12.50 7.50
9 A5 5c bl grn & red 12.50 6.00
10 A5 5c grn & yel grn ('02) 9.00 7.50
11 A5 10c brown & grn 16.50 7.50
a. Half used as 5c on cover ('01) 125.00
12 A5 15c violet & grn 16.50 7.50
13 A5 25c rose & blue 25.00 9.00
14 A5 30c gray brn & rose 16.50 9.00
a. Half used as 15c on cover ('01) 400.00
15 A5 40c org & bl ('00) 49.00 32.50
16 A5 50c blue & rose 25.00 15.00
a. Half used as 25c on cover ('01) 1,450.
17 A5 75c violet & org 42.50 31.50
18 A5 1fr ol grn & blk 20.00 15.00
19 A5 2fr gray brn & rose 87.50 67.50
20 A7 5fr rose & blue 180.00 125.00
21 A8 25fr rose & blue 850.00 *875.00*
22 A8 50fr blue & rose 575.00 575.00
*Nos. 6-20 (15)* 519.00 345.50

High values are found with the overprint "S" (Specimen) erased and, usually, a cancellation added.

For surcharges see Nos. 24-27B.

A9

**1899**

**Black Surcharge**

23 A9 40c on 4c brn & bl *2,950.* 27.50
a. Double surcharge *5,500.* 1,275.

Nos. 17-20 Surcharged

**1902 Blue Surcharge**

24 A5 0.05c on 75c 62.50 36.00
a. Inverted surcharge 525.00 475.00
b. Double surcharge 525.00 475.00
25 A5 0.10c on 1fr 70.00 47.50
a. Inverted surcharge 500.00 375.00
b. Double surcharge 400.00 375.00
26 A5 0.40c on 2fr 575.00 375.00
a. Double surcharge 1,900. 1,725.

**Black Surcharge**

27 A7 0.75c on 5fr 500.00 375.00
a. Inverted surcharge 2,500. 2,000.
c. Double surcharge 2,500. 2,000.

**Obock No. 57 Surcharged in Blue**

27B A7 0.05c on 75c gray lil & org 1,350. 975.00

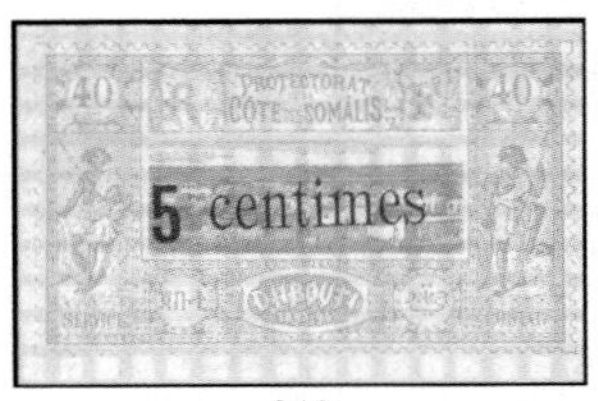


A10

**Nos. 15-16 Surcharged in Black**

28 A10 5c on 40c 7.50 4.50
a. Double surcharge 120.00 100.00
29 A10 10c on 50c 25.00 25.00
a. Inverted surcharge 450.00 450.00
b. Double surcharge 450.00

Surcharged on Stamps of Obock

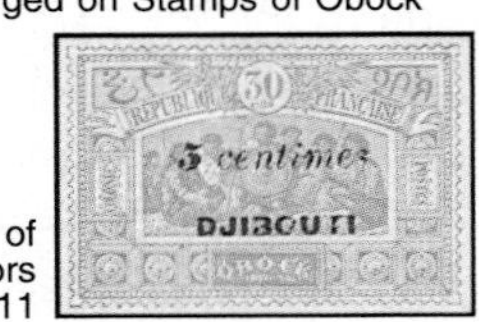

Group of Warriors A11

**Black Surcharge**

30 A11 5c on 30c bis & yel grn 13.50 9.75
a. Inverted surcharge 225.00 225.00
b. Double surcharge 200.00 175.00
c. Triple surcharge

A12

**Red Surcharge**

31 A12 10c on 25c blk & bl 13.50 11.50
a. Inverted surcharge 225.00 225.00
b. Double surcharge 250.00 250.00
c. Triple surcharge 1,500. 1,500.

A13

**Black Surcharge**

32 A13 10c on 10fr org & red vio 32.50 26.50
a. Double surcharge 210.00 200.00
b. Triple surch., one invtd. 1,800. 1,700.

A14

**Black Surcharge**

33 A14 10c on 2fr dl vio & org 60.00 47.50
a. "DJIBOUTI" inverted 250.00 200.00
b. Large "0" in "10" 110.00 82.50
c. Double surcharge 400.00 375.00

**Same Surcharge on Obock No. 53 in Red**

33D A7 10c on 25c blk & bl *30,000.* *20,000.*

A14a

**Black Surcharge on Obock Nos. 63-64**

33E A14a 5c on 25fr brn & bl 57.50 47.50
33F A14a 10c on 50fr red vio & grn 75.00 52.50
g. "01" instead of "10" 190.00 165.00
h. "CENTIMES" inverted 2,500. 2,500.
i. Double surcharge 2,250. 2,250.

Tadjoura Mosque A15

Somalis on Camel A16

Warriors — A17

**1902 Engr. *Perf. 11½***

34 A15 1c brn vio & org .75 .75
35 A15 2c yel brn & yel grn .90 .75
36 A15 4c bl & carmine 2.00 1.50
37 A15 5c bl grn & yel grn 2.00 1.00
38 A15 10c car & red org 5.25 3.25
39 A15 15c brn org & bl 5.25 3.25
40 A16 20c vio & green 11.50 6.00
41 A16 25c blue 17.00 10.50
a. 25c indigo & blue ('03) 20.00 11.00
42 A16 30c red & black 5.00 4.00
43 A16 40c orange & blue 11.50 7.25
44 A16 50c grn & red org 35.00 35.00
45 A16 75c orange & vio 6.50 4.00
46 A17 1fr red org & vio 20.00 12.50
47 A17 2fr yel grn & car 30.00 22.50
a. Without names of designer and engraver at bottom 100.00 100.00
48 A17 5fr orange & blue 18.00 16.00
*Nos. 34-48 (15)* 170.65 128.25

**1903**

49 A15 1c brn vio & blk .75 .65
50 A15 2c yel brn & blk 1.10 .80
51 A15 4c lake & blk 1.50 1.25
a. 4c red & black 1.50 1.25
52 A15 5c bl grn & blk 3.25 2.25
53 A15 10c carmine & blk 6.50 2.50
54 A15 15c org brn & blk 14.50 7.25
55 A16 20c dl vio & blk 20.00 14.50
56 A16 25c ultra & blk 10.00 7.25
58 A16 40c orange & blk 7.25 7.25
59 A16 50c green & blk 18.00 11.00
60 A16 75c buff & blk 9.25 8.50
a. 75c brown orange & black 60.00 60.00
61 A17 1fr orange & blk 15.00 14.50
62 A17 2fr yel grn & blk 8.00 6.25
a. Without names of designer and engraver at bottom 35.00 35.00
63 A17 5fr red org & blk 17.00 14.50
a. 5fr ocher & black 20.00 20.00
*Nos. 49-63 (14)* 132.10 98.45

Imperforates, transposed colors and inverted centers exist in the 1902 and 1903 issues. Most of these were issued from Paris and some are said to have been fraudulently printed.

Tadjoura Mosque A18

Somalis on Camel — A19

Warriors — A20

**1909 Typo. *Perf. 14x13½***

64 A18 1c maroon & brn .65 .60
65 A18 2c vio & ol gray .65 .60
66 A18 4c ol gray & bl .85 .80
67 A18 5c grn & gray grn 1.10 .75
68 A18 10c car & ver 3.25 1.25
69 A18 20c blk & red brn 5.25 4.25
70 A19 25c bl & pale bl 4.00 2.50
71 A19 30c brn & scar 6.00 4.25
72 A19 35c vio & grn 7.25 4.50
73 A19 40c rose & vio 6.50 4.25
74 A19 45c brn & bl grn 6.50 4.25
75 A19 50c maroon & brn 6.50 5.25
76 A19 75c scarlet & grn 14.50 10.00
77 A20 1fr vio & brn 18.00 16.00
78 A20 2fr brn & rose 29.00 22.50
79 A20 5fr vio brn & bl grn 47.50 32.50
*Nos. 64-79 (16)* 157.50 114.25

Drummer A21

Somali Girl A22

Djibouti-Addis Ababa Railroad Bridge — A23

**1915-33 *Perf. 13½x14***

**Chalky Paper**

80 A21 1c brt vio & red brn .20 .20
81 A21 2c ocher & ind .20 .20
82 A21 4c dk brn & red .20 .20
83 A21 5c yel grn & grn .80 .75
84 A21 5c org & dl red ('22) .45 .45
85 A22 10c car & dk red 1.25 .75
86 A22 10c ap grn & grn ('22) .75 .75
87 A22 10c ver & grn ('25) .20 .20
88 A22 15c brn vio & car .65 .35
89 A22 20c org & blk brn .20 .20
90 A22 20c dp grn & bl grn ('25) .20 .20
91 A22 20c dk grn & red ('27) .35 .35
92 A22 25c ultra & dl bl .75 .45
93 A22 25c blk & bl grn ('22) .80 .80
94 A22 30c blk & bl grn 1.60 1.25
95 A22 30c rose & red brn ('22) 1.00 1.00
96 A22 30c vio & ol grn ('25) .20 .20
97 A22 30c grn & dl grn ('27) .35 .35
98 A22 35c lt grn & dl rose .45 .35
99 A22 40c bl & brn vio .60 .45
100 A22 45c red brn & dk bl .65 .55
101 A22 50c car rose & blk 8.00 5.25
102 A22 50c ultra & ind ('24) .90 .90
103 A22 50c dk brn & red vio ('25) .55 .55
104 A22 60c ol grn & red vio ('25) .35 .20
105 A22 65c car rose & ol grn ('25) .55 .35
106 A22 75c dl vio & choc .55 .45
107 A22 75c ind & ultra ('25) .45 .35
108 A22 75c brt vio & ol brn ('27) 1.25 .85
109 A22 85c vio brn & bl grn ('25) .85 .75
110 A22 90c brn red & brt red ('30) 6.25 4.50

**111** A23 1fr bis brn & red 1.25 .75
**112** A23 1.10fr lt brn & ultra ('28) 3.25 3.25
**113** A23 1.25fr dk bl & blk brn ('33) 7.25 6.00
**114** A23 1.50fr lt bl & dk bl ('30) 1.00 .75
**115** A23 1.75fr gray grn & lt red ('33) 6.25 4.00
**116** A23 2fr bl vio & blk 2.25 1.75
**117** A23 3fr red vio ('30) 8.25 5.75
**118** A23 5fr rose red & blk 4.25 2.10
*Nos. 80-118 (39)* 65.30 48.50

No. 99 is on ordinary paper.

For surcharges and overprints see Nos. 119-134, 183-193.

Nos. 83, 92 Surcharged in Green or Blue

**1922**

**119** A21 10c on 5c (G) .45 .45
*a.* Double surcharge 65.00 65.00
**120** A22 50c on 25c (Bl) .45 .45

Type of 1915 Surcharged in Various Colors

**1922**

**121** A22 0,01c on 15c vio & rose (Bk) .20 .20
**122** A22 0,02c on 15c vio & rose (Bl) .35 .35
**123** A22 0,04c on 15c vio & rose (G) .45 .45
**124** A22 0,05c on 15c vio & rose (R) .45 .45
*Nos. 121-124 (4)* 1.45 1.45

Nos. 88, 99 and Type of 1915 Surcharged

**1923-27**

**125** A22 60c on 75c ol grn & vio .35 .35
**126** A22 65c on 15c ('25) 1.40 1.40
**127** A22 85c on 40c ('25) 1.10 1.10
**128** A22 90c on 75c brn red & red ('27) 3.50 3.50
*Nos. 125-128 (4)* 6.35 6.35

No. 118 and Type of 1915-17 Surcharged with New Value and Bars in Black or Red

**1924-27**

**129** A23 25c on 5fr .80 .80
**130** A23 1.25fr on 1fr dk bl & ultra (R) ('26) .75 .75
**131** A23 1.50fr on 1fr lt bl & dk bl ('27) .80 .80
**132** A23 3fr on 5fr ver & red vio ('27) 3.50 3.50
**133** A23 10fr on 5fr brn red & ol brn ('27) 6.00 6.00
**134** A23 20fr on 5fr gray grn & lil rose ('27) 10.00 10.00
*Nos. 129-134 (6)* 21.85 21.85

Common Design Types pictured following the introduction.

### Colonial Exposition Issue

Common Design Types

**Engr., Name of Country Typo. in Black**

**1931** ***Perf. 12½***

**135** CD70 40c deep green 4.00 4.00
**136** CD71 50c violet 4.00 4.00
**137** CD72 90c red orange 4.25 4.25
**138** CD73 1.50fr dull blue 4.25 4.25
*Nos. 135-138 (4)* 16.50 16.50

### Paris International Exposition Issue

Common Design Types

**1937** **Engr.** ***Perf. 13***

**139** CD74 20c deep violet 1.25 1.25
**140** CD75 30c dark green 1.25 1.25
**141** CD76 40c carmine rose 1.25 1.25
**142** CD77 50c dk brn & bl 1.25 1.25
**143** CD78 90c red 1.40 1.40
**144** CD79 1.50fr ultra 1.40 1.40
*Nos. 139-144 (6)* 7.80 7.80

### Colonial Arts Exhibition Issue Souvenir Sheet

Common Design Type

**1937** ***Imperf.***

**145** CD75 3fr dull violet 8.50 *10.00*

Mosque of Djibouti — A24

Somali Warriors — A25

Governor Léonce Lagarde — A26

View of Djibouti — A27

**1938-40** ***Perf. 12x12½, 12½***

**146** A24 2c dull red vio .20 .20
**147** A24 3c slate grn .20 .20
**148** A24 4c dull red brn .20 .20
**149** A24 5c carmine .20 .20
**150** A24 10c blue gray .20 .20
**151** A24 15c slate black .20 .20
**152** A24 20c dark orange .20 .20
**153** A25 25c dark brown .55 .45
**154** A25 30c dark blue .20 .20
**155** A25 35c olive grn .65 .55
**156** A24 40c org brn ('40) .20 .20
**157** A24 45c dull grn ('40) .20 .20
**158** A25 50c red .45 .35
**159** A25 55c dull red vio .65 .55
**160** A25 60c black ('40) .45 .45
**161** A25 65c orange brown .75 .65
**162** A25 70c lt violet ('40) 1.00 1.00
**163** A26 80c gray blk 1.60 1.25
**164** A25 90c rose vio ('39) 1.10 1.10
**165** A26 1fr carmine 2.25 1.50
**166** A26 1fr black ('40) .35 .35
**167** A26 1.25fr magenta ('39) .80 .80
**168** A26 1.40fr pck bl ('40) .85 .85
**169** A26 1.50fr dull green .65 .65
**170** A26 1.60fr brn car ('40) .85 .85
**171** A26 1.75fr ultra .85 .80
**172** A26 2fr dk orange .75 .60
**173** A26 2.25fr ultra ('39) 1.10 1.10
**174** A26 2.50fr org brn ('40) 1.60 1.60
**175** A26 3fr dull violet .75 .60
**176** A27 5fr brn & pale cl 1.60 1.60
**177** A27 10fr ind & pale bl 1.90 1.90
**178** A27 20fr car lake & gray 1.90 1.90
*Nos. 146-178 (33)* 25.40 23.45

For types A24-A26 without "RF," see Nos. 237A-237C.

For overprints and surcharge see Nos. 194-223.

### New York World's Fair Issue

Common Design Type

**1939** **Engr.** ***Perf. 12½x12***

**179** CD82 1.25fr car lake .85 .85
**180** CD82 2.25fr ultra .85 .85

Mosque of Djibouti and Marshal Pétain — A28

**1941, Nov. 10** **Engr.** ***Perf. 12x12½***

**181** A28 1fr yellow brown .55
**182** A28 2.50fr blue .55

For types A24-A26 without "RF," see Nos. 237A-237C. Nos. 181-182 were issued by the Vichy government in France, but were not placed on sale in Somali Coast.

For surcharges, see Nos. B11-B12.

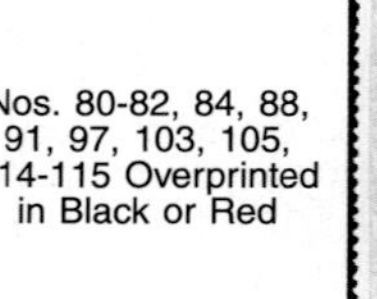

Nos. 80-82, 84, 88, 91, 97, 103, 105, 114-115 Overprinted in Black or Red

***Perf. 13½x14, 14x13½***

**1943** **Unwmk.**

**183** A21 1c .90 .90
**184** A21 2c 1.00 1.00
**185** A21 4c 20.00 20.00
**186** A21 5c 1.25 1.25
**187** A22 15c 5.25 5.25
**188** A22 20c 1.40 1.40
**189** A22 30c 1.40 1.40
**190** A22 50c 1.40 1.40
**191** A22 65c 1.40 1.40
**192** A23 1.50fr (R) 1.40 1.40
**193** A23 1.75fr 8.00 8.00
*Nos. 183-193 (11)* 43.40 43.40

Stamps of 1938-40 Overprinted in Black or Red

On A24

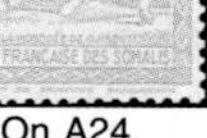


On A25

On A26

On A27

**1943** ***Perf. 12x12½, 12½***

**194** A24 2c dl red vio 1.50 1.50
**195** A24 3c sl grn (R) 1.50 1.50
**196** A24 4c dl red brn 1.50 1.50
**197** A24 5c carmine 1.50 1.50
**198** A24 10c bl gray (R) .65 .65
**199** A24 15c sl blk (R) 1.50 1.50
**200** A24 20c dk org 1.50 1.50
**201** A25 25c dk brn (R) 2.50 2.50
**202** A25 30c dk bl (R) .65 .65
**203** A25 35c olive (R) 3.25 3.25
**204** A24 40c brn org .65 .65
**205** A24 45c dl grn 3.00 3.00
**206** A25 55c dl red vio (R) 1.50 1.50
**207** A25 60c blk (R) .65 .65
**208** A25 70c lt vio (R) .65 .65
*a.* Inverted overprint 190.00 190.00
**209** A26 80c gray blk (R) .85 .85
**210** A25 90c rose vio (R) .65 .65
**211** A26 1.25fr magenta .85 .85
**212** A26 1.40fr pck bl (R) .65 .65
**213** A26 1.50fr dl grn 1.50 1.50
**214** A26 1.60fr brn car .85 .85
**215** A26 1.75fr ultra (R) 7.50 7.50
**216** A26 2fr dk org .90 .90
**217** A26 2.25fr ultra (R) 1.25 1.25
**218** A26 2.50fr chestnut 1.25 1.25
**219** A26 3fr dl vio (R) 1.25 1.25
**220** A27 5fr brn & pale cl 8.00 8.00
**221** A27 10fr ind & pale bl 125.00 125.00
**222** A27 20fr car lake & gray 6.00 6.00

The space between overprint on Nos. 206 and 208 measures 10½mm.

No. 161 Surcharged in Black

**223** A25 50c on 65c org brn .65 .65
*Nos. 194-223 (30)* 179.65 179.65

**Catalogue values for unused stamps in this section, from this point to the end of the section, are for Never Hinged items.**

Locomotive and Palms — A29

**1943** **Unwmk.** **Photo.** ***Perf. 14½x14***

**224** A29 5c royal blue .20 .20
**225** A29 10c pink .20 .20
**226** A29 25c emerald .35 .35
**227** A29 30c gray blk .35 .35
**228** A29 40c violet .35 .35
**229** A29 80c red brn .35 .35
**230** A29 1fr aqua .35 .35
**231** A29 1.50fr scarlet .35 .35
**232** A29 2fr brown .35 .35
**233** A29 2.50fr ultra .55 .55
**234** A29 4fr brt org .80 .80
**235** A29 5fr dp rose lil .80 .80
**236** A29 10fr lt ultra .85 .85
**237** A29 20fr green 1.00 1.00
*Nos. 224-237 (14)* 6.85 6.85

For surcharges see Nos. 240-247.

Types of 1938-40 Without "RF"

**1944, Apr. 3** **Engr.** ***Perf. 12½***

**237A** A24 40c org brn .65
**237B** A25 50c red .85
**237C** A26 1.50fr dull green 1.10
*Nos. 237A-237C (3)* 2.60

Nos. 237A-237C were issued by the Vichy government in France, but were not placed on sale in Somali Coast.

### Eboue Issue

Common Design Type

**1945** **Engr.** ***Perf. 13***

**238** CD91 2fr black .55 .55
**239** CD91 25fr Prus grn 1.10 1.10

Nos. 238 and 239 exist imperforate.

Nos. 224, 226 and 233 Surcharged with New Values and Bars in Carmine or Black

**1945** ***Perf. 14½x14***

**240** A29 50c on 5c (C) .45 .45
**241** A29 60c on 5c (C) .45 .45
**242** A29 70c on 5c (C) .45 .45
*a.* Inverted surcharge 110.00
**243** A29 1.20fr on 5c (C) .55 .55
**244** A29 2.40fr on 25c .65 .55
*a.* Inverted surcharge 110.00

**245** A29 3fr on 25c .65 .65
**246** A29 4.50fr on 25c .65 .65
*a.* Inverted surcharge 110.00
**247** A29 15fr on 2.50fr (C) 1.00 1.00
*Nos. 240-247 (8)* 4.85 4.75

Danakil Tent — A30

Khor-Angar Outpost A31

Obock-Tadjouran Road — A32

Somali Woman A33

Somali Village A34

Djibouti Mosque A35

**1947 Unwmk. Photo. *Perf. 13***

**248** A30 10c vio bl & org .20 .20
**249** A30 30c ol brn & org .20 .20
**250** A30 40c dp plum & org .20 .20
**251** A31 50c bl grn & org .20 .20
**252** A31 60c choc & dp yel .20 .20
**253** A31 80c vio bl & org .20 .20
**254** A32 1fr bl & choc .20 .20
**255** A32 1.20fr bl grn & ol grn 1.00 .65
**256** A32 1.50fr org & vio bl .40 .20
**257** A33 2fr red lil & bl gray .60 .45
**258** A33 3fr dp bl & brn org .90 .65
**259** A33 3.60fr car rose & cop red 1.75 1.25
**260** A33 4fr choc & bl gray 1.25 .85
**261** A34 5fr org & choc .75 .55
**262** A34 6fr gray bl & int bl 1.25 .65
**263** A34 10fr gray bl & red lil 1.50 .75
**264** A35 15fr choc, gray bl & pink 1.50 .85
**265** A35 20fr dk bl, gray bl & org 2.00 1.10
**266** A35 25fr vio brn, lil rose & gray bl 4.00 2.50
*Nos. 248-266 (19)* 18.30 11.85

**Military Medal Issue**
Common Design Type

**1952 Engraved and Typographed**

**267** CD101 15fr blk, grn, yel & dk pur 6.00 6.00

Imperforates
Most stamps of Somali Coast from 1956 onward exist imperforate in issued and trial colors, and also in small presentation sheets in issued colors.

**FIDES Issue**
Common Design Type and

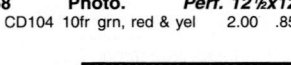

Lighthouse, Ras-Bir — A36

15fr, Loading ship and map, Djibouti.

**1956 Unwmk. Engr. *Perf. 13***

**268** CD103 15fr purple 1.50 1.00
**269** A36 40fr dp ultra & gray 3.00 1.75

**Flower Issue**
Common Design Type

Design: 10fr, Haemanthus, horiz.

**1958 Photo. *Perf. 12½x12***

**270** CD104 10fr grn, red & yel 2.00 .85

Wart Hog — A37

40c, Cheetah. 50c, Gerenuk, vert.

**1958 Engr. *Perf. 13***

**271** A37 30c red brn & sepia .35 .20
**272** A37 40c brn & olive .35 .20
**273** A37 50c brn, grn & gray .45 .20
*Nos. 271-273,C21 (4)* 7.40 4.10

**Human Rights Issue**
Common Design Type

**1958, Dec. 10 Unwmk.**

**274** CD105 20fr brt pur & dk bl 1.50 1.50

Universal Declaration of Human Rights, 10th anniv.

Parrotfish A38

Designs: Various Tropical Fish.

**1959 Engr. *Perf. 13***

**275** A38 1fr brt bl, brn & red org .45 .35
**276** A38 2fr blk, lt bl, yel & grn .45 .35
**277** A38 3fr vio & blk brn .45 .35
**278** A38 4fr brt grnsh bl, org & lt brn .65 .55
**279** A38 5fr brt grnsh bl & blk 1.00 .75
**280** A38 20fr brt bl, dl red brn & rose 2.00 1.50
**281** A38 25fr red, grn & ultra 3.25 2.00
**282** A38 60fr bl & dk grn 7.50 4.00
*Nos. 275-282 (8)* 15.75 9.85

No. 276 is vertical.

Flamingo — A39

Birds: 15fr, Bee-eater, horiz. 30fr, Sacred ibis, horiz. 75fr, Pink-backed pelican.

**1960 Unwmk. *Perf. 13***

**283** A39 10fr bluish grn, bis & cl 2.00 .90
**284** A39 15fr rose lil, grn & yel 2.75 1.00
**285** A39 30fr bl, blk, org & brn 6.25 3.00
**286** A39 75fr grn, sl grn & yel 9.00 5.50
*Nos. 283-286 (4)* 20.00 10.40

Dragon Tree — A40

Klipspringer A41

Meleagrina Margaritifera A42

Designs: 4fr, Cony. 6fr, Large flatfish. 25fr, Fennecs. 40fr, Griffon vulture.

**1962, Mar. 24 Engr. *Perf. 13***

**287** A40 2fr grn, yel, org & brn 1.50 1.00
**288** A40 4fr ocher & choc 1.50 1.10
**289** A40 6fr brn, mar, grn & yel 3.25 2.00
**290** A40 25fr red brn, ocher & grn 6.50 4.00
**291** A40 40fr dk bl, brn & gray 9.25 5.50
**292** A41 50fr bis, bl & lil 9.00 6.50
*Nos. 287-292 (6)* 31.00 20.10

**1962, Nov. 24 Photo.**

Sea Shells: 10fr, Tridacna squamosa, horiz. 25fr, Strombus tricornis, horiz. 30fr, Trochus dentatus.

**Shells in Natural Colors**

**293** A42 8fr red & blk 1.50 1.00
**294** A42 10fr car rose & blk 1.50 1.25
**295** A42 25fr dp bl & brn 3.50 1.50
**296** A42 30fr rose lil & brn 3.50 1.75
*Nos. 293-296 (4)* 10.00 5.50

See Nos. C28-C29.

**Red Cross Centenary Issue**
Common Design Type

**1963, Sept. 2 Engr. *Perf. 13***

**297** CD113 50fr org brn, gray & car 5.00 5.00

Astraea Coral — A43

Design: 6fr, Organ-pipe coral.

**1963, Nov. 30 Photo. *Perf. 13x13½***

**298** A43 5fr multi 2.00 1.10
**299** A43 6fr multi 2.00 1.10

See Nos. C26-C27, C30.

**Human Rights Issue**
Common Design Type

**1963, Dec. 20 Engr. *Perf. 13***

**300** CD117 70fr dk brn & ultra 6.50 6.50

**Philatec Issue**
Common Design Type

**1964, Apr. 7 Unwmk. *Perf. 13***

**301** CD118 80fr dp lil rose, grn & brn 6.00 6.00

Houri (Somali Sailboats) A44

Design: 25fr, Sambouk (Somali sailboats).

**1964, June 9 Engr.**

**302** A44 15fr multi 1.25 .85
**303** A44 25fr multi 2.00 1.25

View of Dadwayya and Map of Somali Coast A45

Design: 20fr, View of Tadjourah and map of Somali Coast.

**1965, Oct. 20 Engr. *Perf. 13***

**304** A45 6fr ultra, sl grn & red brn .90 .55
**305** A45 20fr ultra, org brn & brt grn 1.10 .75

Senna — A46

**1966 Engr. *Perf. 13***

**306** A46 5fr shown 1.00 .65
**307** A46 8fr Poinciana 1.00 .65
**308** A46 25fr Aloe 1.25 1.00
*Nos. 306-308,C41 (4)* 7.25 4.80

Desert Monitor A47

**1967, May 8 Engr. *Perf. 13***

**309** A47 20fr red brn, ocher & sepia 4.00 3.25

Stamps of Somali Coast were replaced in 1967 by those of the French Territory of the Afars and Issas.

## SEMI-POSTAL STAMPS

Somali Girl — SP1

**1915 Unwmk. *Perf. 13½x14***
**Chalky Paper**

**B1** SP1 10c + 5c car & dk red 6.50 6.50

**Curie Issue**
Common Design Type

**1938 Engr. *Perf. 13***

**B2** CD80 1.75fr + 50c brt ultra 6.00 6.00

**French Revolution Issue**
Common Design Type

**Photo., Name and Value Typo. in Black**

**1939**

**B3** CD83 45c + 25c green 7.00 7.00
**B4** CD83 70c + 30c brown 7.00 7.00
**B5** CD83 90c + 35c red org 7.00 7.00
**B6** CD83 1.25fr + 1fr rose pink 7.00 7.00
**B7** CD83 2.25fr + 2fr blue 7.00 7.00
*Nos. B3-B7 (5)* 35.00 35.00

Common Design Type and

Somali Guard SP2

Local Police — SP3

**1941 Photo. *Perf. 13½***

**B8** SP2 1fr + 1fr red 1.00
**B9** CD86 1.50fr + 3fr maroon 1.00
**B10** SP3 2.50fr + 1fr blue 1.00
*Nos. B8-B10 (3)* 3.00

Nos. B8-B10 were issued by the Vichy government in France, but were not placed on sale in Somali Coast.

Nos. 181-182
Surcharged in Black or Red

**1944 Engr. *Perf. 12x12½***

**B11** 50c + 1.50fr on 2.50fr deep blue (R) .55
**B12** + 2.50fr on 1fr yellow brown .55

Colonial Development Fund.

Nos. B11-B12 were issued by the Vichy government in France, but were not placed on sale in Somali Coast.

**Catalogue values for unused stamps in this section, from this point to the end of the section, are for Never Hinged items.**

**Red Cross Issue**
Common Design Type
Inscribed "Djibouti"

**1944 *Perf. 14½x14***

**B13** CD90 5fr + 20fr emerald 1.25 1.25

The surtax was for the French Red Cross and national relief.

**Tropical Medicine Issue**
Common Design Type

**1950 Engr. *Perf. 13***

**B14** CD100 10fr + 2fr red brn & red 5.00 5.00

The surtax was for charitable work.

**Anti-Malaria Issue**
Common Design Type

**1962, Apr. 7 Unwmk. *Perf. 13***

**B15** CD108 25fr + 5fr aqua 6.00 6.00

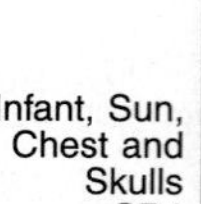

Infant, Sun, Chest and Skulls SP4

**1965, Dec. 10 Engr. *Perf. 13***

**B16** SP4 25fr + 5fr ocher, sl & brt grn 2.00 2.00

Campaign against tuberculosis.

## AIR POST STAMPS

**Catalogue values for unused stamps in this section are for Never Hinged items.**

Common Design Type
Inscribed "Djibouti"

**1941 Unwmk. Photo. *Perf. 14½x14***

**C1** CD87 1fr dk orange .65 .65
**C2** CD87 1.50fr brt red .65 .65
**C3** CD87 5fr brown red .85 .85
**C4** CD87 10fr black .90 .90
**C5** CD87 25fr ultra 1.60 1.60
**C6** CD87 50fr dark green 1.50 1.50
**C7** CD87 100fr plum 2.25 2.25
*Nos. C1-C7 (7)* 8.40 8.40

Obock & Djibouti

**1943, June 21 Engr. *Perf. 13***

**C7A** 1.50fr red brown .55
**C7B** 4fr ultramarine .55

50th Ann. of transfer of capital from Obock to Djibouti.

Nos. C7A-C7B were issued by the Vichy government in France, but were not placed on sale in Somali Coast.

**Victory Issue**
Common Design Type

**1946 *Perf. 12½***

**C8** CD92 8fr deep blue 1.00 1.00

**Chad to Rhine Issue**
Common Design Types

**1946**

**C9** CD93 5fr gray black 1.25 1.25
**C10** CD94 10fr dp orange 1.25 1.25
**C11** CD95 15fr violet brn 1.25 1.25
**C12** CD96 20fr brt violet 1.25 1.25
**C13** CD97 25fr blue green 2.50 2.50
**C14** CD98 50fr lt ultra 2.50 2.50
*Nos. C9-C14 (6)* 10.00 10.00

Somali Gazing Skyward — AP1

Frontier Post, Loyada — AP2

Governor's Mansion, Djibouti — AP3

***Perf. 12½x13, 13x12½***

**1947 Photo. Unwmk.**

**C15** AP1 50fr gray bl & choc 3.50 1.00
**C16** AP2 100fr multicolored 4.50 2.25
**C17** AP3 200fr multicolored 6.50 3.25
*Nos. C15-C17 (3)* 14.50 6.50

**UPU Issue**
Common Design Type

**1949 Engr. *Perf. 13***

**C18** CD99 30fr bl, dp bl, brn red & grn 7.25 7.25

**Liberation Issue**
Common Design Type

**1954, June 6**

**C19** CD102 15fr indigo & purple 6.50 6.50

Somali Woman and Map of Djibouti — AP4

**1956, Feb. 20 Unwmk.**

**C20** AP4 500fr dk vio & rose vio 40.00 40.00

Mountain Reedbucks — AP5

**1958, July 7 Engr. *Perf. 13***

**C21** AP5 100fr ultra, lt grn & dk red brn 6.25 3.50

Albert Bernard, Flag and Troops — AP6

**1960, Jan. 18**

**C22** AP6 55fr ultra, sepia & car 2.00 1.25

25th death anniv. of Administrator Albert Bernard at Moraito.

Great Bustard — AP7

**1960, Oct. 24 Unwmk. *Perf. 13***

**C23** AP7 200fr brn, org & slate 18.00 12.50

Salt Dealers' Caravan at Assal Lake — AP8

**1962, Jan. 6 Engr. *Perf. 13***

**C24** AP8 500fr dk bl, red brn, pink & blk 20.00 12.50

Obock — AP9

**1962, Mar. 11 Unwmk. *Perf. 13***

**C25** AP9 100fr blue & org brn 4.00 2.50

Centenary of the founding of Obock.

Rostellaria Magna — AP10

40fr, Millepore coral. 55fr, Brain coral. 100fr, Lambis bryonia (seashell). 200fr, Branch coral.

**1962-63 Photo. *Perf. 13½x12½***

**C26** AP10 40fr multi ('63) 2.50 1.00
**C27** AP10 55fr multi ('63) 4.00 2.50
**C28** AP10 60fr multi 5.50 2.00
**C29** AP10 100fr multi 8.00 4.00
**C30** AP10 200fr multi ('63) 10.00 6.00
*Nos. C26-C30 (5)* 30.00 15.50

**Telstar Issue**
Common Design Type

**1963, Feb. 9 Engr. *Perf. 13***

**C31** CD111 20fr dp claret & dk grn .75 .75

Zaroug (Somali Sailboats) — AP11

Designs: 50fr, Sambouk (boat) building. 300fr, Zeima sailboat.

**1964-65 Engr. *Perf. 13***

**C32** AP11 50fr blue, ocher & choc 3.00 1.60
**C33** AP11 85fr dk Prus grn, dk brn & mag 4.25 2.00
**C34** AP11 300fr ultra, lt brn & bl grn ('65) 12.50 6.25
*Nos. C32-C34 (3)* 19.75 9.85

Discus Thrower — AP12

**1964, Oct. 10 Engr.**

**C35** AP12 90fr rose lil, red brn & blk 8.50 6.50

18th Olympic Games, Tokyo, Oct. 10-25.

**ITU Issue**
Common Design Type

**1965, May 17**

**C36** CD120 95fr lil rose, brt bl & lt brn 13.00 8.00

Camels in Ghoubet Kharab and Map of Somali Coast — AP13

**1965** **Engr.** ***Perf. 13***
**C37** AP13 45fr Abbe Lake 2.75 1.25
**C38** AP13 65fr shown 3.25 1.25

Issue dates: 45fr, Oct. 20; 65fr, July 16.

### French Satellite A-1 Issue
Common Design Type

Designs: 25fr, Diamant rocket and launching installations. 30fr, A-1 satellite.

**1966, Jan. 28** **Engr.** ***Perf. 13***
**C39** CD121 25fr redsh brn, ol brn & dl red 2.50 2.50
**C40** CD121 30fr ol brn, dl red & redsh brn 2.50 2.50
*a.* Strip of 2, #C39-C40 + label 9.00 9.00

Each sheet contains 16 triptychs (2x8).

Stapelia — AP14

**1966** **Engr.** ***Perf. 13***
**C41** AP14 55fr sl grn, dl mag & emer 4.00 2.50

Feather Starfish and Coral — AP15

Fish: 25fr, Regal angelfish. 40fr, Pomocanthops filamentosus. 50fr, Amphiprion ephippium. 70fr, Squirrelfish. 80fr, Surgeonfish. 100fr, Pterois lunulatus.

**1966** **Photo.** ***Perf. 13***
**C42** AP15 8fr multicolored 1.60 1.60
**C43** AP15 25fr multicolored 3.25 3.25
**C44** AP15 40fr multicolored 4.50 4.50
**C45** AP15 50fr multicolored 6.25 6.25
**C46** AP15 70fr multicolored 9.25 9.25
**C47** AP15 80fr multicolored 12.00 12.00
**C48** AP15 100fr multicolored 16.00 16.00
*Nos. C42-C48 (7)* 52.85 52.85

### French Satellite D-1 Issue
Common Design Type

**1966, June 10** **Engr.** ***Perf. 13***
**C49** CD122 48fr dk brn, brt bl & grn 3.25 2.00

---

## AIR POST SEMI-POSTAL STAMPS

**Catalogue values for unused stamps in this section are for Never Hinged items.**

SPAP1

**Unwmk.**
**1942, June 22** **Engr.** ***Perf. 13***
**CB1** SPAP1 1.50fr+ 3.50fr green 1.00
**CB2** SPAP1 2fr + 6fr brown 1.00

Native children's welfare fund.
Nos. CB1-CB2 were issued by the Vichy government in France, but were not placed on sale in Somali Coast

### Colonial Education Fund
Common Design Type

**1942, June 22**
**CB3** CD86a 1.20fr + 1.80fr blue & red 1.50

No. CB3 was issued by the Vichy government in France, but was not placed on sale in Somali Coast.

Pharaoh Sacrificing before Horus and Hathor — SPAP2

**Unwmk.**
**1964, Aug. 28** **Engr.** ***Perf. 13***
**CB4** SPAP2 25fr + 5fr multi 6.50 6.25

UNESCO world campaign to save historic monuments in Nubia.

---

## POSTAGE DUE STAMPS

D1

**1915** **Unwmk.** **Typo.** ***Perf. 14x13½***
**Chalky Paper**
**J1** D1 5c deep ultra .20 .20
**J2** D1 10c brown red .35 .35
**J3** D1 15c black .55 .55
**J4** D1 20c purple 1.10 1.10
**J5** D1 30c orange 1.10 1.10
**J6** D1 50c maroon 2.25 2.25
**J7** D1 60c green 3.25 3.25
**J8** D1 1fr dark blue 3.50 3.50
*Nos. J1-J8 (8)* 12.30 12.30

See Nos. J11-J20.

Type of 1915 Issue Surcharged

**1927**
**J9** D1 2fr on 1fr light red 6.00 6.00
**J10** D1 3fr on 1fr lilac rose 6.00 6.00

Type of 1915

**1938** **Engr.** ***Perf. 12½x13***
**J11** D1 5c light ultra .20 .20
**J12** D1 10c dark carmine .20 .20
**J13** D1 15c brown black .20 .20
**J14** D1 20c violet .20 .20
**J15** D1 30c orange yellow .85 .85
**J16** D1 50c brown .55 .55
**J17** D1 60c emerald .85 .85
**J18** D1 1fr indigo 1.75 1.75
**J19** D1 2fr red .80 .80
**J20** D1 3fr dark brown 1.10 1.10
*Nos. J11-J20 (10)* 6.70 6.70
Set, never hinged 12.00

Inscribed "Inst de Grav" below design.

Postage Due Stamps of 1915 Overprinted in Red or Black

**1943** **Unwmk.** ***Perf. 14x13½***
**J21** D1 5c ultra (R) .90 .90
**J22** D1 10c brown red .90 .90
**J23** D1 15c black (R) .90 .90
**J24** D1 20c purple .90 .90
**J25** D1 30c orange .90 .90
**J26** D1 50c maroon .90 .90
**J27** D1 60c green .90 .90
**J28** D1 1fr dark blue (R) 5.75 5.75
*Nos. J21-J28 (8)* 12.05 12.05
Set, never hinged 18.00

Postage Due Stamps of 1938 Overprinted in Red or Black

**1943** ***Perf. 12½x13***
**J29** D1 5c lt ultra (R) .90 .90
**J30** D1 10c dark car .90 .90
**J31** D1 15c brn blk (R) .90 .90
**J32** D1 20c violet .90 .90
**J33** D1 30c org yel .90 .90
**J34** D1 50c brown .90 .90
**J35** D1 60c emerald .90 .90
**J36** D1 1fr indigo (R) .90 .90
**J37** D1 2fr red 6.25 6.25
**J38** D1 3fr dk brn (R) 7.25 7.25
*Nos. J29-J38 (10)* 20.70 20.70
Set, never hinged 40.00

For type D1 without "RF," see Nos. J38A-J38E.

Type D1 Without "RF"
**Engraved, Values Typo**
**1944, Apr. 3**
**J38A** D1 30c org yel & lilac .20
**J38B** D1 50c yel brn & blk brn .20
**J38C** D1 60c grn & dk grn .45
**J38D** D1 2fr red & rose .45
**J38E** D1 3fr sepia & blk .85
*Nos. J38A-J38E (5)* 2.15

Nos. J38A-J38E were issued by the Vichy government in France, but were not placed on sale in Somali Coast.

**Catalogue values for unused stamps in this section, from this point to the end of the section, are for Never Hinged items.**

D2

**1947** **Photo.** ***Perf. 13½x13***
**J39** D2 10c purple .20 .20
**J40** D2 30c brown .20 .20
**J41** D2 50c green .35 .35
**J42** D2 1fr deep orange .35 .35
**J43** D2 2fr lilac rose .55 .55
**J44** D2 3fr dk org brn .55 .55
**J45** D2 4fr blue .75 .75
**J46** D2 5fr orange red .75 .75
**J47** D2 10fr olive green .75 .75
**J48** D2 20fr blue violet 1.40 1.40
*Nos. J39-J48 (10)* 5.85 5.85

---

# SOMALILAND PROTECTORATE

sō-ˈmä-lē-ˌland

prə-ˈtek-t(ə-)rət

LOCATION — Eastern Africa, bordering on the Gulf of Aden
GOVT. — British Protectorate
AREA — 68,000 sq. mi.
POP. — 640,000 (estimated)
CAPITAL — Hargeisa

Formerly administered by the Indian Government, the territory was taken over by the British Foreign Office in 1898 and transferred to the Colonial Office in 1905.
Somaliland Protectorate became part of independent Somalia in 1960.

16 Annas = 1 Rupee
100 Cents = 1 Shilling (1951)

**Catalogue values for unused stamps in this country are for Never Hinged items, beginning with Scott 108.**

Stamps of India, 1882-1900, Overprinted at Top of Stamp

**1903** **Wmk. 39** ***Perf. 14***
**1** A17 ½a light green 3.00 *4.50*
**2** A19 1a carmine rose 3.00 *4.00*
**3** A21 2a violet 2.50 1.60
*a.* Double overprint *725.00*
**4** A28 2½a ultra 2.25 *1.90*
**5** A22 3a brown orange 3.50 3.50
**6** A23 4a olive green 4.00 3.00
**7** A25 8a red violet 4.25 *5.50*
**8** A26 12a brown, *red* 3.50 *8.00*
*a.* Inverted overprint *1,200.*
**9** A29 1r car rose & grn 7.50 *11.00*
**10** A30 2r yel brn & car rose 30.00 *52.50*
**11** A30 3r green & brown 25.00 *62.50*
**12** A30 5r violet & blue 42.50 *72.50*
**Wmk. Elephant's Head (38)**
**13** A14 6a bister 5.50 *5.25*
*Nos. 1-13 (13)* 136.50 *235.75*

Nos. 1-5 exist without the 2nd "I" of "BRITISH."

Same, but Overprinted at Bottom of Stamp

**1903** **Wmk. 39**
**14** A28 2½a ultra 3.50 *7.25*
**15** A26 12a violet, *red* 8.00 *14.00*
**16** A29 1r car rose & grn 4.00 *17.50*
**17** A30 2r yel brn & car rose 90.00 *140.00*
**18** A30 3r green & brn 90.00 *150.00*
*a.* Inverted overprint 675.00
**19** A30 5r violet & blue 85.00 *110.00*
**Wmk. 38**
**20** A14 6a bister 6.75 *6.25*
*Nos. 14-20 (7)* 287.25 *445.00*

Stamps of India, 1902-03, Ovptd.

**1903** **Wmk. 39**
**21** A33 ½a light green 2.50 .60
**22** A34 1a car rose 1.40 .35
**23** A35 2a violet 1.90 *2.75*
**24** A37 3a brown orange 2.75 *2.75*
**25** A38 4a olive green 1.60 *4.50*
**26** A40 8a red violet 1.90 *2.50*
*Nos. 21-26 (6)* 12.05 *13.45*

The above overprints vary in length, also in the relative positions of the letters. Nos. 21-23 exist without the second "I" of "British."

A1

King Edward VII — A2

**1904 Wmk. 2 Typo.**

| No. | Type | Description | Unused | Used |
|---|---|---|---|---|
| 27 | A1 | ½a dl grn & grn | 2.10 | *4.50* |
| 28 | A1 | 1a carmine & blk | 13.00 | 3.50 |
| 29 | A1 | 2a red vio & dull vio | 2.25 | *2.40* |
| 30 | A1 | 2½a ultramarine | 4.50 | *4.00* |
| 31 | A1 | 3a gray grn & vio brn | 2.40 | *2.75* |
| 32 | A1 | 4a black & gray grn | 2.50 | *5.00* |
| 33 | A1 | 6a vio & gray grn | 5.75 | *18.00* |
| 34 | A1 | 8a pale blue & blk | 4.50 | *5.75* |
| 35 | A1 | 12a ocher & blk | 7.50 | *11.50* |
| | | **Wmk. Crown and C C (1)** | | |
| 36 | A2 | 1r gray grn | 14.00 | *47.50* |
| 37 | A2 | 2r red vio & dull vio | 47.50 | *85.00* |
| 38 | A2 | 3r blk & gray grn | 47.50 | *95.00* |
| 39 | A2 | 5r carmine & blk | 47.50 | *95.00* |
| | | *Nos. 27-39 (13)* | 201.00 | *379.90* |

**1905 Wmk. 3**

| No. | Type | Description | Unused | Used |
|---|---|---|---|---|
| 40 | A1 | ½a dl grn & grn | 2.00 | *8.00* |
| 41 | A1 | 1a carmine & blk | 13.00 | 1.75 |
| 42 | A1 | 2a red vio & dull vio | 8.25 | *10.00* |
| 43 | A1 | 2½a ultramarine | 4.50 | *11.00* |
| 44 | A1 | 3a gray grn & vio brn | 2.50 | *16.00* |
| 45 | A1 | 4a black & gray grn | 5.00 | *16.00* |
| 46 | A1 | 6a violet & gray grn | 6.00 | *27.50* |
| 47 | A1 | 8a pale blue & blk | 6.75 | *10.00* |
| 48 | A1 | 12a ocher & black | 7.25 | *11.00* |
| | | *Nos. 40-48 (9)* | 55.25 | *111.25* |

Nos. 41, 42, 44-48 are on both ordinary and chalky paper.

**1909**

| No. | Type | Description | Unused | Used |
|---|---|---|---|---|
| 49 | A1 | ½a bluish green | 26.00 | *30.00* |
| 50 | A1 | 1a carmine | 3.00 | 2.25 |

For overprints see Nos. O11-O16.

King George V
A3 A4

The ½, 1 and 2½a of type A3 are on ordinary paper, the other values of types A3 and A4 are on chalky paper.

**1912-19**

| No. | Type | Description | Unused | Used |
|---|---|---|---|---|
| 51 | A3 | ½a green | .70 | 9.25 |
| 52 | A3 | 1a carmine | 2.75 | .60 |
| 53 | A3 | 2a red vio & dull vio | 3.75 | *16.00* |
| 54 | A3 | 2½a ultramarine | 1.10 | *9.75* |
| 55 | A3 | 3a gray grn & vio brn | 2.50 | *7.50* |
| 56 | A3 | 4a blk & grn ('13) | 2.75 | *11.50* |
| 57 | A3 | 6a violet & green | 2.75 | *5.75* |
| 58 | A3 | 8a lt blue & blk | 4.00 | *17.50* |
| 59 | A3 | 12a ocher & blk | 3.75 | *24.00* |
| 60 | A4 | 1r dull grn & grn | 12.00 | *18.00* |
| 61 | A4 | 2r red vio & dull vio ('19) | 20.00 | *75.00* |
| 62 | A4 | 3r blk & gray grn ('19) | 67.50 | *125.00* |
| 63 | A4 | 5r car & blk ('19) | 65.00 | *175.00* |
| | | *Nos. 51-63 (13)* | 188.55 | *494.85* |

**1921 Wmk. 4**

| No. | Type | Description | Unused | Used |
|---|---|---|---|---|
| 64 | A3 | ½a blue green | 3.00 | *11.50* |
| 65 | A3 | 1a scarlet | 3.75 | .80 |
| 66 | A3 | 2a vio & dull vio | 4.50 | 1.10 |
| 67 | A3 | 2½a ultramarine | 1.10 | *5.25* |
| 68 | A3 | 3a gray grn & vio brown | 2.75 | *8.50* |
| 69 | A3 | 4a black & grn | 2.75 | *8.50* |
| 70 | A3 | 6a violet & grn | 1.60 | *15.00* |
| 71 | A3 | 8a lt blue & blk | 2.25 | *6.25* |
| 72 | A3 | 12a ocher & blk | 9.00 | *17.50* |
| 73 | A4 | 1r dull grn & grn | 8.50 | *55.00* |
| 74 | A4 | 2r vio & dull vio | 25.00 | *55.00* |
| 75 | A4 | 3r blk & gray grn | 37.50 | *110.00* |
| 76 | A4 | 5r scarlet & blk | 72.50 | *190.00* |
| | | *Nos. 64-76 (13)* | 174.20 | *484.40* |

**Common Design Types**

pictured following the introduction.

**Silver Jubilee Issue**

Common Design Type

**1935, May 6 Engr. *Perf. 11x12***

| No. | Type | Description | Unused | Used |
|---|---|---|---|---|
| 77 | CD301 | 1a car & dk blue | 2.50 | *3.75* |
| 78 | CD301 | 2a black & ultra | 3.00 | *3.75* |
| 79 | CD301 | 3a ultra & brown | 2.50 | *13.50* |
| 80 | CD301 | 1r brown vio & ind | 7.50 | *13.50* |
| | | *Nos. 77-80 (4)* | 15.50 | *34.50* |
| | | Set, never hinged | 25.00 | |

**Coronation Issue**

Common Design Type

**1937, May 13 *Perf. 13½x14***

| No. | Type | Description | Unused | Used |
|---|---|---|---|---|
| 81 | CD302 | 1a carmine | .20 | *.25* |
| 82 | CD302 | 2a black | .35 | *1.75* |
| 83 | CD302 | 3a bright ultra | .40 | *.90* |
| | | *Nos. 81-83 (3)* | .95 | *2.90* |
| | | Set, never hinged | 2.25 | |

Blackhead Sheep — A5

Greater Kudu — A6

Map of Somaliland Protectorate A7

**1938, May 10 Wmk. 4 *Perf. 12½***

| No. | Type | Description | Unused | Used |
|---|---|---|---|---|
| 84 | A5 | ½a green | .30 | *5.50* |
| 85 | A5 | 1a carmine | .30 | *1.60* |
| 86 | A5 | 2a deep claret | 1.50 | *1.90* |
| 87 | A5 | 3a ultra | 5.75 | *11.00* |
| 88 | A6 | 4a dark brown | 3.50 | *8.75* |
| 89 | A6 | 6a purple | 5.00 | *13.00* |
| 90 | A6 | 8a gray black | 1.25 | *13.50* |
| 91 | A6 | 12a orange | 5.00 | *16.00* |
| 92 | A7 | 1r green | 6.00 | *55.00* |
| 93 | A7 | 2r rose violet | 11.00 | *55.00* |
| 94 | A7 | 3r ultramarine | 13.00 | *32.50* |
| 95 | A7 | 5r black | 14.00 | *32.50* |
| *a.* | | Horiz. pair, imperf. btwn. | *11,000.* | |
| | | *Nos. 84-95 (12)* | 66.60 | *246.25* |
| | | Set, never hinged | 125.00 | |

A8

A9

A10

**1942, Apr. 22**

| No. | Type | Description | Unused | Used |
|---|---|---|---|---|
| 96 | A8 | ½a green | .20 | *.50* |
| 97 | A8 | 1a carmine | .20 | .20 |
| 98 | A8 | 2a deep claret | .40 | .25 |
| 99 | A8 | 3a ultramarine | 1.25 | .25 |
| 100 | A9 | 4a dark brown | 1.75 | .25 |
| 101 | A9 | 6a purple | 1.75 | .25 |
| 102 | A9 | 8a gray | 2.00 | *.25* |
| 103 | A9 | 12a orange | 2.00 | *.50* |
| 104 | A10 | 1r green | 1.25 | *.90* |
| 105 | A10 | 2r rose violet | 1.25 | *5.25* |
| 106 | A10 | 3r ultra | 2.25 | *9.00* |
| 107 | A10 | 5r black | 5.25 | *8.25* |
| | | *Nos. 96-107 (12)* | 19.55 | *25.85* |
| | | Set, never hinged | 37.50 | |

For surcharges see Nos. 116-126.

**Catalogue values for unused stamps in this section, from this point to the end of the section, are for Never Hinged items.**

**Peace Issue**

Common Design Type

***Perf. 13½x14***

**1946, Oct. 15 Engr. Wmk. 4**

| No. | Type | Description | Unused | Used |
|---|---|---|---|---|
| 108 | CD303 | 1a carmine | .20 | .20 |
| *a.* | | Perf. 13½ | 15.00 | *62.50* |
| 109 | CD303 | 3a deep blue | .20 | .20 |

**Silver Wedding Issue**

Common Design Types

**1949, Jan. 28 Photo. *Perf. 14x14½***

| No. | Type | Description | Unused | Used |
|---|---|---|---|---|
| 110 | CD304 | 1a scarlet | .25 | .20 |

**Engraved; Name Typographed**

***Perf. 11½x11***

| No. | Type | Description | Unused | Used |
|---|---|---|---|---|
| 111 | CD305 | 5r gray black | 6.50 | *9.25* |

**UPU Issue**

Common Design Types

Surcharged in Black or Carmine with New Values in Annas

**Engr.; Name Typo. on 3a, 6a**

**1949, Oct. 10 *Perf. 13½, 11x11½***

| No. | Type | Description | Unused | Used |
|---|---|---|---|---|
| 112 | CD306 | 1a on 10c rose car | .25 | .20 |
| 113 | CD307 | 3a on 30c ind (C) | 1.40 | .85 |
| 114 | CD308 | 6a on 50c rose vio | .50 | *1.10* |
| 115 | CD309 | 12a on 1sh red org | .50 | .60 |
| | | *Nos. 112-115 (4)* | 2.65 | 2.75 |

Nos. 96 and 98 to 107 Surcharged with New Value in Black or Carmine

**1951, Apr. 2 Wmk. 4 *Perf. 12½***

| No. | Type | Description | Unused | Used |
|---|---|---|---|---|
| 116 | A8 | 5c on ½a green | .40 | *1.25* |
| 117 | A8 | 10c on 2a deep claret | .40 | *.50* |
| 118 | A8 | 15c on 3a ultramarine | 1.40 | 1.40 |
| 119 | A9 | 20c on 4a dark brown | 2.10 | .25 |
| 120 | A9 | 30c on 6a purple | 2.25 | .60 |
| 121 | A9 | 50c on 8a gray | 2.50 | .25 |
| 122 | A9 | 70c on 12a red | 4.75 | *4.50* |
| 123 | A10 | 1sh on 1r green | 2.25 | .65 |
| 124 | A10 | 2sh on 2r rose violet | 6.00 | *15.00* |
| 125 | A10 | 2sh on 3r ultra | 7.50 | 6.50 |
| 126 | A10 | 5sh on 5r black (C) | 11.00 | 8.50 |
| | | *Nos. 116-126 (11)* | 40.55 | 39.40 |

**Coronation Issue**

Common Design Type

**1953, June 2 Engr. *Perf. 13½x13***

| No. | Type | Description | Unused | Used |
|---|---|---|---|---|
| 127 | CD312 | 15c dark green & blk | .35 | .20 |

Camel Carrying Somali House A11

Askari Militiaman A12

Designs: 35c, 2sh, Rock Pigeon. 50c, 5sh, Martial eagle. 1sh, Blackhead sheep. 1sh30c, Tomb of Sheik Isaaq, Mait. 10sh, Taleh Fort.

**1953-58 Engr. *Perf. 12½***

| No. | Type | Description | Unused | Used |
|---|---|---|---|---|
| 128 | A11 | 5c gray | .20 | *.50* |
| 129 | A12 | 10c red orange | 2.50 | .60 |
| 130 | A11 | 15c blue green | .70 | *.60* |
| 131 | A11 | 20c rose red | .70 | .40 |
| 132 | A12 | 30c lt chocolate | 2.50 | .40 |
| 133 | A11 | 35c blue | 5.75 | 2.00 |
| 134 | A11 | 50c lil rose & brn | 5.75 | .55 |
| 135 | A11 | 1sh grnsh blue | .70 | .30 |
| 136 | A11 | 1sh30c dark gray & ultra ('58) | 12.50 | 3.50 |
| 137 | A11 | 2sh violet & brn | 30.00 | 6.00 |
| 138 | A11 | 5sh emer & brn | 32.50 | 6.50 |
| 139 | A11 | 10sh rose lilac & brn | 20.00 | 15.00 |
| | | *Nos. 128-139 (12)* | 113.80 | 36.35 |

Nos. 131 and 135 Overprinted: "Opening of the Legislative Council 1957"

**1957, May 21**

| No. | Type | Description | Unused | Used |
|---|---|---|---|---|
| 140 | A11 | 20c rose red | .20 | .20 |
| 141 | A11 | 1sh greenish blue | .35 | .30 |

Nos. 131 and 136 Overprinted: "Legislative Council Unofficial Majority, 1960"

**1960, Apr. 5**

| No. | Type | Description | Unused | Used |
|---|---|---|---|---|
| 142 | A11 | 20c rose red | .20 | .20 |
| 143 | A11 | 1sh30c dk gray & ultra | .90 | .30 |

Changes in the Legislative Council.

Three stamps of Somalia were overprinted "Somaliland Independence 26 June 1960" and issued in Hargeisa on that day. Somaliland Protectorate became part of Somalia on July 1, 1960. These three stamps are listed in Vol. 5 as Somalia Nos. 242, C68-C69.

Stamps of Somaliland Protectorate were replaced by those of Somalia in 1960.

## OFFICIAL STAMPS

Official Stamps of India, 1883-1900, Overprinted

**1903, June 1 Wmk. 39 *Perf. 14***

| No. | Type | Description | Unused | Used |
|---|---|---|---|---|
| O1 | A17 | ½a light green | 7.50 | *55.00* |
| O2 | A19 | 1a carmine rose | 17.50 | *9.25* |
| O3 | A21 | 2a violet | 9.25 | *55.00* |
| O4 | A25 | 8a red violet | 11.50 | *425.00* |
| O5 | A29 | 1r car rose & grn | 11.50 | *625.00* |
| | | *Nos. O1-O5 (5)* | 57.25 | *1,169.* |

India Nos. 61-63, 68, 49 Overprinted

**1903**

| No. | Type | Description | Unused | Used |
|---|---|---|---|---|
| O6 | A33 | ½a green | .50 | |
| O7 | A34 | 1a carmine rose | .50 | |
| O8 | A35 | 2a violet | .80 | |
| O9 | A40 | 8a red violet | 5.00 | |
| O10 | A29 | 1r car rose & grn | 20.00 | |
| | | *Nos. O6-O10 (5)* | 26.80 | |

Nos. O6-O10 were not regularly issued.

Regular Issue of 1904 Overprinted

**1904 Wmk. Crown and C A (2)**

| No. | Type | Description | Unused | Used |
|---|---|---|---|---|
| O11 | A1 | ½a gray green | 4.75 | *55.00* |
| O12 | A1 | 1a carmine & blk | 3.75 | *8.00* |
| O13 | A1 | 2a red vio & dull vio | 200.00 | *70.00* |
| O14 | A1 | 8a pale blue & blk | 70.00 | *150.00* |
| | | *Nos. O11-O14 (4)* | 278.50 | *283.00* |

**Wmk. Crown and C C (1)**

| No. | Type | Description | Unused | Used |
|---|---|---|---|---|
| O15 | A2 | 1r gray green | 190.00 | *675.00* |

Same Overprint on No. 42

**1905 Wmk. 3**

| No. | Type | Description | Unused | Used |
|---|---|---|---|---|
| O16 | A1 | 2a red vio & dull vio | 90.00 | *900.00* |

The period after "M" may be found missing on Nos. O11-O14 and O16.

## SOUTH AFRICA

sauth ˈa-fri-kə

LOCATION — Southern Africa
GOVT. — Republic
AREA — 472,730 sq. mi.
POP. — 43,426,386 (1999 est.)
CAPITAL — Pretoria (administrative); Cape Town (legislative); Bloemfontein (Judicial)

The union was formed on May 31, 1910, comprising the former British colonies of Cape of Good Hope, Natal, Transvaal and the Orange Free State, which became provinces. The union became a republic in 1961.

For previous listings, see individual headings.

12 Pence = 1 Shilling
20 Shillings = 1 Pound
100 Cents = 1 Rand (1961)

**Catalogue values for unused stamps in this country are for Never Hinged items, beginning with Scott 74 in the regular postage section, Scott B1 in the semi-postal section, Scott J30 in the postage due section, and Scott O21 in the officials section.**

### Watermarks

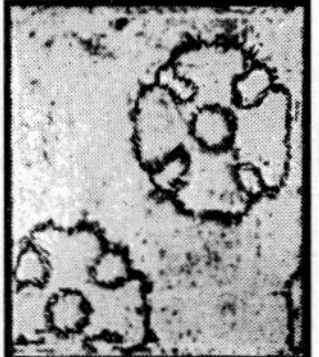

Wmk. 47 — Multiple Rosette

Wmk. 177 — Springbok's Head

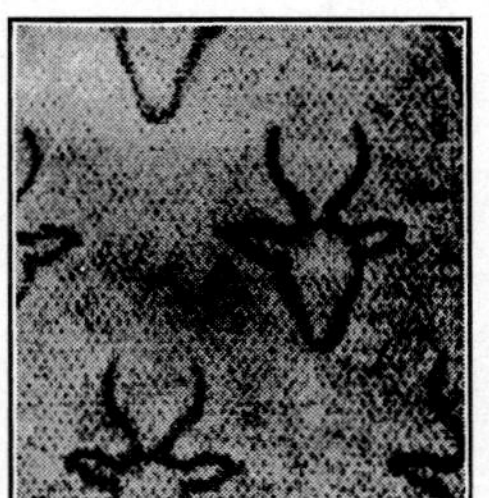

Wmk. 201 — Multiple Springbok's Head

Wmk. 330 — Coat of Arms, Multiple

Wmk. 348 — RSA in Triangle, Multiple

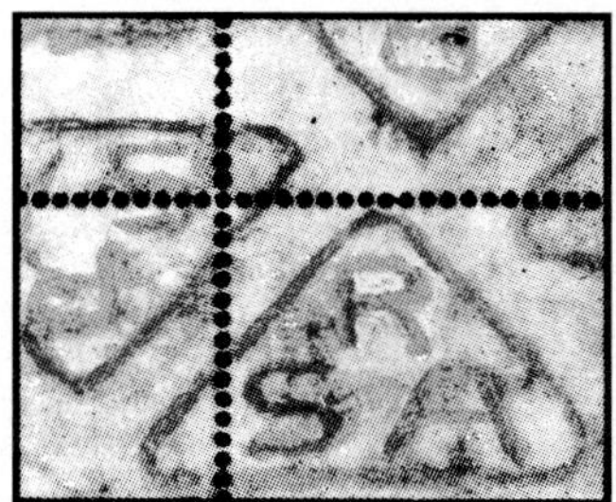


Wmk. 359 — RSA in Triangle, Tete Beche

George V
A1 A2

| **1910** | **Engr.** | **Wmk. 47** | ***Perf. 14*** | |
|---|---|---|---|---|
| 1 | A1 2½p blue | | 3.00 | 1.75 |

Union Parliament opening, Nov. 4, 1910.

Type A2 stamps have very small margins at top and bottom. Values are for copies with perfs close to, or touching the frame.

| **1913-24** | | **Typo.** | | **Wmk. 177** |
|---|---|---|---|---|
| 2 | A2 | ½p green | 1.50 | .20 |
| *a.* | | Double impression | *15,000.* | |
| 3 | A2 | 1p scarlet | 1.50 | .20 |
| 4 | A2 | 1½p org brn ('20) | .75 | .20 |
| *a.* | | Tête bêche pair | 4.50 | *15.00* |
| 5 | A2 | 2p dull violet | 2.25 | .20 |
| 6 | A2 | 2½p ultra | 5.50 | 1.60 |
| 7 | A2 | 3p brn org & blk | 13.00 | .55 |
| 8 | A2 | 3p ultra ('22) | 4.75 | 1.60 |
| 9 | A2 | 4p ol grn & org | 11.00 | .55 |
| 10 | A2 | 6p violet & blk | 9.50 | .70 |
| 11 | A2 | 1sh orange | 20.00 | .70 |
| 12 | A2 | 1sh3p violet ('20) | 17.50 | 11.00 |
| 13 | A2 | 2sh6p green & cl | 70.00 | 5.50 |
| 14 | A2 | 5sh blue & claret | 140.00 | 9.00 |
| 15 | A2 | 10sh ol grn & blue | 225.00 | 14.50 |
| 16 | A2 | £1 red & dp grn ('16) | 850.00 | 450.00 |
| *a.* | | £1 lt red & gray green ('24) | 1,100. | *1,600.* |
| | | *Nos. 2-16 (15)* | 1,372. | 496.50 |

The ½p, 1p and 1½p have the words "Revenue" and "Inkomst" on the stamps. On other stamps of this type these words are replaced by short vertical lines.

All values exist in many shades. No. 4a exists with and without gutter between.

Unwatermarked copies of the 1p are the result of misplaced watermarks.

All values except the 2sh6p and £1 exist with watermark inverted.

For overprint see No. O1.

### Coil Stamps

***Perf. 14 Horizontally***

| | | | | |
|---|---|---|---|---|
| 17 | A2 | ½p green | 9.25 | 1.90 |
| 18 | A2 | 1p scarlet ('14) | 11.50 | 6.25 |
| 19 | A2 | 1½p org brown ('20) | 17.00 | 27.50 |
| 20 | A2 | 2p dull violet ('21) | 18.00 | 9.00 |
| | | *Nos. 17-20 (4)* | 55.75 | 44.65 |

"Hope" — A3

Design: No. 22, inscribed SUIDAFRIKA.

| **1926** | **Engr.** | **Wmk. 201** | ***Imperf.*** | |
|---|---|---|---|---|
| 21 | A3 4p blue gray | | 2.00 | 1.40 |
| 22 | A3 4p blue gray | | 2.00 | 1.40 |

Nos. 21 and 22 were privately rouletted and perforated, but such varieties were not officially made.

No. 21 (English inscription) was printed in a separate sheet from No. 22 (Afrikaans inscription).

### English-Afrikaans Se-Tenant

Stamps with English inscriptions and with Afrikaans inscriptions were printed alternately in the same sheets, starting with No. 23. Major-number listings and values are for horizontal pairs (vertical pairs sell for about one-third less) of such stamps consisting of one English and one Afrikaans-inscribed stamp, unless otherwise described.

Values are for pairs with no fold marks between stamps and no perf separations.

Beware of pairs that have been rejoined.

Springbok
A5

Jan van Riebeek's Ship, Drommedaris — A6

Orange Tree — A7

| **1926** | **Typo.** | ***Perf. 14½x14*** | | |
|---|---|---|---|---|
| 23 | A5 | ½p dk grn & blk, pair | 3.00 | *3.50* |
| *a.* | | Single, English | .25 | .20 |
| *b.* | | Single, Afrikaans | .25 | .20 |
| *c.* | | Tete beche pair | 1,500. | |
| *d.* | | Center omitted | 1,400. | |
| *e.* | | Booklet pane of 6 | 190.00 | |
| *f.* | | As "e," perf. 14 | 300.00 | |
| 24 | A6 | 1p car & blk, pair | 3.00 | *3.00* |
| *a.* | | Single, English | .25 | .20 |
| *b.* | | Single, Afrikaans | .25 | .20 |
| *c.* | | Imperf., pair | 1,350. | |
| *d.* | | Tete beche pair | 1,750. | |
| *e.* | | Center omitted | 275.00 | |
| *f.* | | Booklet pane of 6 | 160.00 | |
| *g.* | | As "f," perf. 14 | 250.00 | |
| 25 | A7 | 6p org & grn, pair | 42.50 | *47.50* |
| *a.* | | Single, English | 3.00 | 2.25 |
| *b.* | | Single, Afrikaans | 3.00 | 2.25 |
| | | *Nos. 23-25 (3)* | 48.50 | *54.00* |

Nos. 23c and 24d are from uncut sheets printed for the perf. 14 booklet panes of 1928, Nos. 23f and 24g.

See Nos. 33-35, 42, 45-50, 59-61, 98-99. For overprints see Nos. O2-O4, O6-O9, O12-O15, O18, O21-O25, O30-O32, O42-O45, O48.

Government Buildings, Pretoria — A8

"Groote Schuur," Rhodes's Home — A9

Native Kraal — A10

Gnu — A11

Trekking — A12

Ox Wagon — A13

Cape Town and Table Mountain — A14

***Perf. 14, 14x13½***

| **1927-28** | | **Engr.** | | **Wmk. 201** |
|---|---|---|---|---|
| 26 | A8 | 2p vio brn & gray, pair | 13.50 | *26.00* |
| *a.* | | Single, English | 2.10 | 1.40 |
| *b.* | | Single, Afrikaans | 2.10 | 1.40 |
| 27 | A9 | 3p red & blk, pair | 24.00 | *37.50* |
| *a.* | | Single, English | 2.10 | 1.40 |
| *b.* | | Single, Afrikaans | 2.10 | 1.40 |
| *c.* | | Perf. 14x13½, pair | 67.50 | *82.50* |
| *d.* | | As "c," single, English | 3.25 | 2.75 |
| *e.* | | As "c," single, Afrikaans | 3.25 | 2.75 |
| 28 | A10 | 4p brown, pair ('28) | 32.50 | *67.50* |
| *a.* | | Single, English | 3.25 | 1.90 |
| *b.* | | Single, Afrikaans | 3.25 | 1.90 |
| 29 | A11 | 1sh dp bl & bis brn, pair | 47.50 | *87.50* |
| *a.* | | Single, English | 6.75 | 2.75 |
| *b.* | | Single, Afrikaans | 6.75 | 2.75 |
| 30 | A12 | 2sh6p brn & bl grn, pair | 140.00 | *400.00* |
| *a.* | | Single, English | 20.00 | 24.00 |
| *b.* | | Single, Afrikaans | 20.00 | 24.00 |
| *c.* | | Perf. 14x13½, pair | 475.00 | 675.00 |
| *d.* | | As "c," single, English | 32.50 | 37.50 |
| *e.* | | As "c," single, Afrikaans | 32.50 | 37.50 |
| 31 | A13 | 5sh dp grn & blk, pair | 275.00 | *650.00* |
| *a.* | | Single, English | 30.00 | 40.00 |
| *b.* | | Single, Afrikaans | 30.00 | 40.00 |
| *c.* | | Perf. 14x13½, pair | 525.00 | 750.00 |
| *d.* | | As "c," single, English | 47.50 | 52.50 |
| *e.* | | As "c," single, Afrikaans | 47.50 | 52.50 |
| 32 | A14 | 10sh ol brn & bl, pair | 200.00 | 200.00 |
| *a.* | | Single, English | 20.00 | 16.00 |
| *b.* | | Single, Afrikaans | 20.00 | 16.00 |
| *c.* | | Perf. 14x13½, pair | 275.00 | 375.00 |
| *d.* | | As "c," single, English | 24.00 | 20.00 |
| *e.* | | As "c," single, Afrikaans | 24.00 | 20.00 |
| | | *Nos. 26-32 (7)* | 732.50 | *1,468.* |

See Nos. 36-41, 43-44, 53-54, 58, 62-66. For overprints see Nos. O5, O10-O111, O16-O17, O19-O20, O28, O33-O35, O39, O41, O49-O53.

### Types of 1926-28 Redrawn "SUIDAFRIKA" (No Hyphen) on Afrikaans Stamps

The photogravure, unhyphenated stamps of 1930-45 are distinguished from the 1926-28 typographed or engraved stamps (also unhyphenated) by the following characteristics:

½p, 1p, 6p. Leg of "R" in AFRICA or AFRIKA ends in a straight line in the photogravure set; in a curved line in the typographed. No. 35 differs from No. 34, having 2mm space between POSSEEL—INKOMSTE instead of 1mm.

2p. A memorial statue has been added just above and leftward of the "2" in value tablet on Nos. 36-37 (photogravure).

3p. Top frame on No. 38 consists of 3 heavy lines. On No. 27 it has 3 heavy and 2 very thin lines.

4p. On Nos. 40-41 the background in upper corners is solid. On No. 28 it consists of horizontal and vertical lines. No. 41 has pretzel-shaped scroll endings at bottom. On No. 40 these scroll endings enclose a solid mass of color.

1sh. No. 43 has no fine shading lines projecting from the curved top of the left inner frame, as No. 29 has. On No. 43 the shading of the last "A" of the country name partly covers the flower below it.

2sh6p. On No. 44 the shading below the country name is solid or shows signs of wear. On No. 30 it is composed of fine lines.

The engraved pictorials are much more finely executed and show details more clearly than the photogravure.

***Perf. 15x14 (½p, 1p, 6p), 14***

**1930-45 Photo. Wmk. 201**

33 A5 ½p bl grn & blk, pair 3.50 3.50
- *a.* Single, English .20 .20
- *b.* Single, Afrikaans .20 .20
- *c.* Tete-beche pair 1,250.
- *d.* As "c," gutter between 1,750.
- *e.* Booklet pane of 6 40.00 40.00
- *f.* Vert. pair, monolingual 5.00 5.00

34 A6 1p car & blk, pair 4.00 3.50
- *a.* Single, English .20 .20
- *b.* Single, Afrikaans .20 .20
- *c.* Center omitted 2,500.
- *d.* Frame omitted 2,500.
- *e.* Tete-beche pair 1,800.
- *f.* As "e," gutter between 1,500.
- *g.* Booklet pane of 6 16.00 16.00

35 A6 1p rose & blk, pair ('32) 35.00 4.50
- *a.* Single, English 1.00 .20
- *b.* Single, Afrikaans 1.00 .20
- *c.* Center omitted 750.00

36 A8 2p vio & gray, pair ('31) 24.00 16.00
- *a.* Single, English 1.10 .40
- *b.* Single, Afrikaans 1.10 .40
- *c.* Frame omitted 1,000.
- *d.* Tete-beche pair 6,500.
- *e.* Booklet pane of 4 200.00 200.00

37 A8 2p vio & ind, pair ('38) 250.00 100.00
- *a.* Single, English 12.50 7.25
- *b.* Single, Afrikaans 12.50 7.25

38 A9 3p red & blk, pair ('31) 72.50 *95.00*
- *a.* Single, English 6.75 6.75
- *b.* Single, Afrikaans 6.75 6.75

39 A9 3p ultra & bl, pair ('33) 22.50 10.00
- *a.* Single, English 1.10 .80
- *b.* Single, Afrikaans 1.10 .80
- *c.* Center omitted 1,000.

40 A10 4p redsh brn, pair ('32) 250.00 210.00
- *a.* Single, English 25.00 11.00
- *b.* Single, Afrikaans 25.00 11.00

41 A10 4p brn, pair ('36) 6.50 5.00
- *a.* Single, English 1.10 .45
- *b.* Single, Afrikaans 1.10 .45

42 A7 6p org & grn, pair ('31) 29.00 6.50
- *a.* Single, English 1.10 .45
- *b.* Single, Afrikaans 1.10 .45

43 A11 1sh dl bl & yel brn, pair 140.00 57.50
- *a.* Single, English 7.25 1.10
- *b.* Single, Afrikaans 7.25 1.10
- *c.* 1sh dp bl & brn, pair ('32) 72.50 32.50
- *d.* As "c," single, English 5.25 .40
- *e.* As "c," single, Afrikaans 5.25 .40

44 A12 2sh 6p brn & bl, pair ('45) 29.00 19.00
- *a.* Single, English 1.75 .70
- *b.* Single, Afrikaans 1.75 .70
- *c.* 2sh6p brn & sl grn ('36), pair 85.00 50.00
- *d.* As "c," single, English 10.00 4.00
- *e.* As "c," single, Afrikaans 10.00 4.00
- *f.* 2sh6p choc & dp grn ('37), pair 75.00 40.00
- *g.* As "f," single, English 9.00 4.00
- *h.* As "f," single, Afrikaans 9.00 4.00
- *i.* 2sh6p red brn & grn, pair ('32) 210.00 200.00
- *j.* As "i," single, English 17.00 6.50
- *k.* As "i," single, Afrikaans 17.00 6.50

*Nos. 33-44 (12)* 866.00 530.50

No. 34 unwatermarked, or watermarked multiple clover leaf, is a proof.

Types of 1926-28 with "SUID-AFRIKA" Hyphenated on Afrikaans Stamps, and

Gold Mine — A15

Government Buildings, Pretoria — A16

Groote Schuur — A17

Groot Constantia — A18

½p. No. 45 shading in leaves and ornaments strengthened; 40 lines in center background. Size: 18½x22½mm.

No. 46 has 28 heavy horizontal shading lines in center background and similar thicker lines in frame. Top and bottom green bars are scored by a white horizontal line. Size: 18½x22½mm.

No. 47 is smaller, 18x22mm.

1p. No. 48, size 18½x22½mm.

No. 49, size 18x22mm.

No. 50. Size: 17½x21½mm.

2p. On Nos. 53-54, S's in SOUTH and POSTAGE are narrower than on Nos. 36-37.

6p. Die I, "SUID-AFRIKA" 16½mm. Shading in leaves framing oval very faint and broken. Size: 18½x22½mm.

Die II, "SUID-AFRIKA" 17mm. Leaves strongly shaded. Heavy lines of shading in background of tree. Size: 18½x22½mm.

Die III, "question mark" scrolls below top panel are cleanly defined without intrusion of background shading. Size: 18x22mm.

Nos. 45-67 were printed in many shades. Some denominations in some printings were partly or wholly screened. Except for No. 47, the screened stamps were issued after 1947.

5sh. No. 65. Type I, letters "U" and "A" in SOUTH AFRICA have projections. Size: 27x21½mm.

No. 66. Type II, letters "U" and "A" redrawn to eliminate projections. Size: 26½x21½mm.

***Perf. 15x14 (½p, 1p, 6p), 14***

**1933-54 Photo. Wmk. 201**

45 A5 ½p grn & gray, pair ('36) 4.00 .80
- *a.* Single, English .25 .20
- *b.* Single, Afrikaans .25 .20
- *c.* Bklt. pane of 6, marginal ads 25.00 25.00
- *d.* Perf. 13½x14 (coil), pair 30.00 *47.50*
- *e.* As "d," single, English 1.75 1.25
- *f.* As "d," single, Afrikaans 1.75 1.25

46 A5 ½p grn & gray, redrawn, pair ('37) 4.00 .40
- *a.* Single, English .20 .20
- *b.* Single, Afrikaans .20 .20
- *c.* Booklet pane of 6 37.50 30.00
- *d.* Booklet pane of 2 8.00 1.00
- *e.* As "c," 4 blank margins 35.00 35.00
- *f.* Perf. 14½x14 (coil), pair 12.50 7.25
- *g.* As "f," single, English 2.25 .80
- *h.* As "f," single, Afrikaans 2.25 .80

47 A5 ½p grn & gray, pair ('47) 1.25 .40
- *a.* Single, English .20 .20
- *b.* Single, Afrikaans .20 .20
- *c.* Bklt. pane of 6, marginal ads 4.00 3.50
- *d.* As "c," no horiz. margins 5.00 3.00

48 A6 1p car & gray, pair ('34) 1.10 .65
- *a.* Single, English .20 .20
- *b.* Single, Afrikaans .20 .20
- *c.* Booklet pane of 6 37.50 37.50
- *d.* Booklet pane of 2 3.00 1.25
- *e.* Perf. 13½x14 (coil), pair 30.00 52.50
- *f.* As "e," single, English 1.40 1.00
- *g.* As "e," single, Afrikaans 1.40 1.00
- *h.* Center omitted, pair 325.00
- *j.* Bklt. pane of 6, marginal ads 27.50 27.50
- *k.* As "j," 4 blank margins 30.00 30.00
- *m.* Perf. 14½x14 (coil), pair 11.00 11.00
- *n.* As "m," single, English 1.40 1.40
- *p.* As "m," single, Afrikaans 1.40 1.40

49 A6 1p rose car & gray blk, pair ('40) 1.50 .30
- *a.* Single, English .20 .20
- *b.* Single, Afrikaans .20 .20
- *c.* Unwmkd., pair 325.00 325.00
- *d.* Booklet pane of 6 3.75 2.75
- *e.* Perf. 14½x14 (coil), pair 4.00 6.00
- *f.* As "e," single, English 1.40 .90
- *g.* As "e," single, Afrikaans 1.40 .90
- *h.* As "d," marginal ads 5.00 4.25

50 A6 1p car & blk, pair ('51) .75 .20
- *a.* Single, English .20 .20
- *b.* Single, Afrikaans .20 .20

51 A15 1½p dk grn & gold, 27x21½mm, pair ('36) 2.00 1.40
- *a.* Single, English .25 .20
- *b.* Single, Afrikaans .25 .20
- *c.* Booklet pane of 4 9.00 8.00
- *d.* Center omitted, pair 1,000.

52 A15 1½p sl grn & och, 22x18mm, pair ('41) 1.25 .25
- *a.* Single, English .20 .20
- *b.* Single, Afrikaans .20 .20
- *c.* Center omitted, pair 900.00
- *d.* Booklet pane of 6 5.75 4.50

53 A8 2p bl vio & dl bl, pair ('38) 40.00 32.50
- *a.* Single, English 3.00 1.25
- *b.* Single, Afrikaans 3.00 1.25

54 A8 2p dl vio & gray, pair ('41) 24.00 *45.00*
- *a.* Single, English .90 .50
- *b.* Single, Afrikaans .90 .50

55 A16 2p pur & sl bl, 27x21½mm, pair ('45) 1.50 *4.00*
- *a.* Single, English .20 .20
- *b.* Single, Afrikaans .20 .20

56 A16 2p same, 21½ x 17¼mm, pair ('50) 1.00 *4.50*
- *a.* Single, English .20 .20
- *b.* Single, Afrikaans .20 .20
- *c.* Booklet pane of 6 ('51) 3.75 2.75

57 A17 3p ultra, pair ('40) 5.00 1.75
- *a.* Single, English .20 .20
- *b.* Single, Afrikaans .20 .20
- *c.* 3p bl, pair ('49) 2.00 *4.00*
- *d.* As "c," single, English .20 .20
- *e.* As "c," single, Afrikaans .20 .20

58 A10 4p choc brn, pair ('52) 1.25 *5.50*
- *a.* Single, English .20 .20
- *b.* Single, Afrikaans .20 .20

59 A7 6p org & bl grn, I, pair ('37) 50.00 22.50
- *a.* Single, English 3.75 1.10
- *b.* Single, Afrikaans 3.75 1.10

60 A7 6p org & grn, II, pair ('38) 22.50 3.00
- *a.* Single, English 1.50 .25
- *b.* Single, Afrikaans 1.50 .25

61 A7 6p red org & bl grn, III ('50), pair 1.75 1.00
- *a.* Single, English .20 .20
- *b.* Single, Afrikaans .20 .20
- *c.* 6p org & grn, III, pair ('46) 13.50 1.90
- *d.* As "c," single, English 1.00 .20
- *e.* As "c," single, Afrikaans 1.00 .20

62 A11 1sh chlky bl & lt brn ('50), pair 9.00 6.00
- *a.* As "f," single, English .55 .20
- *b.* As "f," single, Afrikaans .55 .20
- *c.* 1sh lt bl & ol brn, pair ('39) 35.00 7.50
- *d.* As "c," single, English 1.00 .20
- *e.* As "c," single, Afrikaans 1.00 .20
- *f.* 1sh vio bl & brnsh blk, pair 16.00 10.00
- *g.* Single, English .50 .30
- *h.* Single, Afrikaans .50 .30

63 A12 2sh6p brn & brt grn, pair ('49) 7.50 *24.00*
- *a.* Single, English 1.25 .75
- *b.* Single, Afrikaans 1.25 .75

64 A13 5sh grn & blk, I, pair 55.00 55.00
- *a.* Single, English 2.50 2.00
- *b.* Single, Afrikaans 2.50 2.00

65 A13 5sh bl grn & blk, I, pair ('49) 42.50 *62.50*
- *a.* Single, English 4.00 3.50
- *b.* Single, Afrikaans 4.00 3.50

66 A13 5sh grn & blk, II, pair ('54) 55.00 *75.00*
- *a.* Single, English 4.00 3.50
- *b.* Single, Afrikaans 4.00 3.50

67 A18 10sh ol blk & bl, pair ('39) 50.00 17.50
- *a.* Single, English 3.00 1.00
- *b.* Single, Afrikaans 3.00 1.00

*Nos. 45-67 (23)* 381.85 364.15

See Nos. 98-99. For overprints see Nos. O26-O27, O29, O36-O38, O40, O46-O47, O54.

George V and Springboks — A19

**1935, May 1 Wmk. 201 *Perf. 15x14***

68 A19 ½p Prus grn & blk, pair 3.00 *8.50*
- *a.* Single, English top .25 .25
- *b.* Single, Afrikaans top .25 .25

69 A19 1p car rose & blk, pair 3.00 *8.00*
- *a.* Single, English top .25 .25
- *b.* Single, Afrikaans top .25 .25

70 A19 3p bl & dk bl, pair 14.00 *45.00*
- *a.* Single, English top 1.40 2.75
- *b.* Single, Afrikaans top 1.40 2.75

71 A19 6p org & grn, pair 30.00 *72.50*
- *a.* Single, English top 2.10 *3.00*
- *b.* Single, Afrikaans top 2.10 *3.00*

*Nos. 68-71 (4)* 50.00 *134.00*

Set, never hinged 100.00

25th anniv. of the reign of George V.

English and Afrikaans inscriptions are transposed on alternate stamps. On the ½p, 3p and 6p with "SOUTH AFRICA" at top, "SILWER JUBILEUM" is at left of medallion, but on 1p with English at top, it is at the right.

## Johannesburg International Philatelic Exhibition Issue

Souvenir Sheets

A20

A21

Black Overprint, "JIPEX 1936"

**1936, Nov. 2 *Perf. 15x14***

72 A20 Sheet of 6 (½p) 5.00 9.50

73 A21 Sheet of 6 (1p) 4.00 6.50

Set, never hinged 19.00

Sheets made by overprinting booklet panes Nos. 45c and 48j. Sheets exist with and without horizontal perforations through right margin. Sheet size: 81x72½mm.

**Catalogue values for unused stamps in this section, from this point to the end of the section, are for Never Hinged items.**

George VI — A22

"KRONING SUID-AFRIKA" on alternate stamps.

**1937, May 12 *Perf. 14***

74 A22 ½p grn & ol blk, pair .55 .40
- *a.* Single, English .20 .20
- *b.* Single, Afrikaans .20 .20

75 A22 1p car & ol blk, pair .85 .40
- *a.* Single, English .20 .20
- *b.* Single, Afrikaans .20 .20

76 A22 1½p Prus grn & org, pair .85 .70
- *a.* Single, English .20 .20
- *b.* Single, Afrikaans .20 .20

77 A22 3p bl & ultra, pair 1.75 *2.00*
- *a.* Single, English .20 .20
- *b.* Single, Afrikaans .20 .20

78 A22 1sh Prus bl & org brn, pair 5.00 3.50
- *a.* Single, English .50 .25
- *b.* Single, Afrikaans .50 .25

*Nos. 74-78 (5)* 9.00 7.00

Coronation of George VI and Queen Elizabeth.

Wagon Wheel A23

Voortrekker Family
A24

Alternate stamps inscribed "SOUTH AFRICA," "SUID-AFRIKA."

**1938, Dec. 14** ***Perf. 15x14***

**79** A23 1p rose & slate, pair 7.00 5.50
*a.* Single, English .30 .30
*b.* Single, Afrikaans .30 .30
**80** A24 1½p red brn & Prus bl, pair 8.00 6.50
*a.* Single, English .30 .35
*b.* Single, Afrikaans .30 .35

Issued to commemorate the Voortrekkers.

Infantry
A25

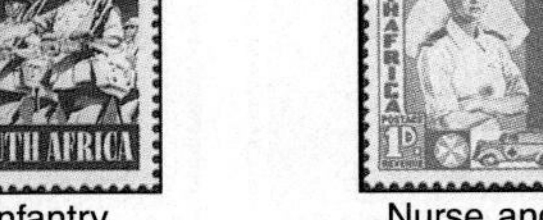

Nurse and Ambulance
A26

Airman and Spitfires (Flight Lt. Robert Kershaw)
A27

Sailor
A28

Women's Services
A29

Artillery — A30

Welder — A31

Tank Corps
A32

Signal Corps — A33

Bilingual inscriptions on 2p and 1sh.

***Perf. 14 (2p, 4p, 6p), 15x14***

**1941-43** **Photo.** **Wmk. 201**

**81** A25 ½p dp bl grn, pair .90 .40
*a.* Single, English .20 .20
*b.* Single, Afrikaans .20 .20
**82** A26 1p brt rose, pair 1.75 .70
*a.* Single, English .20 .20
*b.* Single, Afrikaans .20 .20
**83** A27 1½p Prus grn, pair ('42) 1.10 .40
*a.* Single, English .20 .20
*b.* Single, Afrikaans .20 .20
**84** A28 2p dk violet .50 .20
**85** A29 3p dp blue, pair 14.00 11.50
*a.* Single, English .50 .50
*b.* Single, Afrikaans .50 .50
**86** A30 4p org brn, pair 12.25 8.75
*a.* Single, English .75 .20
*b.* Single, Afrikaans .75 .20
*c.* 4p red brown, pair 32.50 32.50
*d.* As "c," single, English 1.50 1.00
*e.* As "c," single, Afrikaans 1.50 1.00
**87** A31 6p brt red org, pair 11.75 6.75
*a.* Single, English .50 .20
*b.* Single, Afrikaans .50 .20
**88** A32 1sh dark brown 2.25 .50
**89** A33 1sh3p dk ol brn, pair ('43) 10.00 6.00
*a.* Single, English .50 .30
*b.* Single, Afrikaans .50 .30
*c.* 1sh3p dark brown, pair 6.00 6.50
*d.* As "c," single, English .50 .30
*e.* As "c," single, Afrikaans .50 .30
*Nos. 81-89 (9)* 54.50 35.20

Infantry-Nurse
A34 A35

Airman-Sailor
A36 A37

Women's Services — A38

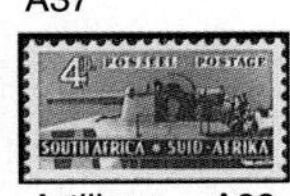

Artillery — A39

Welder — A40

Tank Corps — A41

Bilingual inscriptions on 4p and 1sh.

***Pairs: Perf. 14, Roul. 6½ btwn. Strips of 3: Perf. 15x14, Roul. 6½ btwn.***

**1942-43** **Photo.** **Wmk. 201**

**90** A34 ½p Horiz. strip of 3 .70 .55
*a.* Single, English .20 .20
*b.* Single, Afrikaans .20 .20
*c.* As #90, imperf. between 350.00
**91** A35 1p Horiz. strip of 3 ('43) .90 .60
*a.* Single, English .20 .20
*b.* Single, Afrikaans .20 .20
*c.* As #91, imperf. between 350.00
**92** A36 1½p Horiz. pair .70 .60
*a.* Single, English .20 .20
*b.* Single, Afrikaans .20 .20
*c.* As #92, roul. 13 4.50 4.50
*d.* As #92, imperf. btwn. 350.00 375.00
**93** A37 2p Horiz. pair ('43) .70 .50
*a.* Single, English .20 .20
*b.* Single, Afrikaans .20 .20
*c.* As #93, imperf. btwn. 350.00
**94** A38 3p Vert strip of 3 5.50 *8.50*
*a.* Single, English .20 .20
*b.* Single, Afrikaans .20 .20
**95** A39 4p Vert. strip of 3 16.00 9.00
*a.* Single .20 .20
**96** A40 6p Horiz. pair 3.00 2.75
*a.* Single, English .20 .20
*b.* Single, Afrikaans .20 .20
**97** A41 1sh Vert. pair 12.50 3.50
*a.* Single .20 .20
*Nos. 90-97 (8)* 40.00 26.00

Because of the rouletting these are collected as pairs or strips of three, even on the bilingual stamps.

Types of 1926, Redrawn
"SUID-AFRIKA" Hyphenated
Coil Stamps

**1943** **Photo.** ***Perf. 15x14***

**98** A5 ½p myrtle grn, vert. pair 1.25 *3.00*
*a.* Single, English .20 .20
*b.* Single, Afrikaans .20 .20
**99** A6 1p rose pink, vert. pair 2.00 *3.00*
*a.* Single, English .20 .20
*b.* Single, Afrikaans .20 .20

"Victory" — A42

"Peace" — A43

Design: 3p, Profiles of couple ("Hope").

**1945, Dec. 3** **Photo.** ***Perf. 14***

**100** A42 1p rose pink & choc, pair .25 .25
*a.* Single, English .20 .20
*b.* Single, Afrikaans .20 .20
**101** A43 2p vio & sl bl, pair .25 .25
*a.* Single, English .20 .20
*b.* Single, Afrikaans .20 .20
**102** A43 3p ultra & dp ultra, pair .35 .35
*a.* Single, English .20 .20
*b.* Single, Afrikaans .20 .20
*Nos. 100-102 (3)* .85 .85

World War II victory of the Allies.

George VI — A44

King George VI and Queen Elizabeth
A45

Princesses Margaret Rose and Elizabeth
A46

***Perf. 15x14***

**1947, Feb. 17** **Wmk. 201**

**103** A44 1p cer & gray, pair .25 .25
*a.* Single, English .20 .20
*b.* Single, Afrikaans .20 .20
**104** A45 2p purple, pair .25 .25
*a.* Single, English .20 .20
*b.* Single, Afrikaans .20 .20
**105** A46 3p dk blue, pair .35 .35
*a.* Single, English .20 .20
*b.* Single, Afrikaans .20 .20
*Nos. 103-105 (3)* .85 .85

Visit of the British Royal Family, Mar.-Apr., 1947.

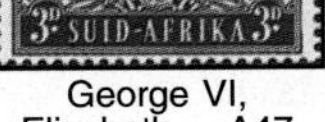

George VI, Elizabeth — A47

Gold Mine — A48

**1948, Apr. 26** **Photo.** ***Perf. 14***

**106** A47 3p dp chlky bl & sil, pair .50 .50
*a.* Single, English .20 .20
*b.* Single, Afrikaans .20 .20

25th anniv. of the marriage of George VI and Queen Elizabeth.

***Vertical Pairs Perf. 14 all around, Rouletted 6½ between***

**1948, Apr.**

**107** A48 1½p sl & och, vert. pair 1.25 *2.00*
*a.* Single, English .20 .20
*b.* Single, Afrikaans .20 .20

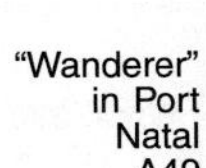

"Wanderer" in Port Natal
A49

**1949, May 2** **Photo.** ***Perf. 15x14***

**108** A49 1½p red brown, pair .45 .45
*a.* Single, English .20 .20
*b.* Single, Afrikaans .20 .20

Mercury and Globe — A50

**1949, Oct. 1** ***Perf. 14x15***

**109** A50 ½p dk green, pair .50 .50
*a.* Single, English .20 .20
*b.* Single, Afrikaans .20 .20
**110** A50 1½p dk red, pair .75 .75
*a.* Single, English .20 .20
*b.* Single, Afrikaans .20 .20
**111** A50 3p ultra, pair 1.25 1.25
*a.* Single, English .20 .20
*b.* Single, Afrikaans .20 .20
*Nos. 109-111 (3)* 2.50 2.50

75th anniv. of the UPU.

Except for Nos. 216, 310-313, 518a, 669a this is the end of bi-lingual multiples in the postage section.

Voortrekkers en Route to Natal — A51

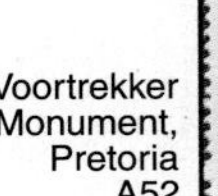

Voortrekker Monument, Pretoria
A52

Voortrekkers Looking Toward Natal, and Open Bible — A53

**1949, Dec. 1** ***Perf. 15x14***

**112** A51 1p magenta .20 .20
**113** A52 1½p dull green .20 .20
**114** A53 3p dark blue .20 .20
*Nos. 112-114 (3)* .60 .60

Inauguration of the Voortrekker Monument at Pretoria.

Riebeeck's Seal and Dutch East India Company Monogram
A54

Maria de la Quellerie — A55

2p, van Riebeeck's Ships. 4½p, Jan van Riebeeck. 1sh, Landing of van Riebeeck.

***Perf. 15x14, 14x15***

**1952, Mar. 14** **Wmk. 201**

**115** A54 ½p dk brn & red vio .20 .20
**116** A55 1p dark green .20 .20
**117** A54 2p dark purple .20 .20
**118** A55 4½p dark blue .20 .20
**119** A54 1sh brown .55 .50
*Nos. 115-119 (5)* 1.35 1.30

300th anniv. of the landing of Jan van Riebeeck at the Cape of Good Hope.

Nos. 116-117 Overprinted "SATISE" (1p) and "SADIPU" (2p)

**1952, Mar. 26**

**120** A55 1p dark green .30 .55
**121** A54 2p dark purple .35 .70

South African Tercentenary Intl. Stamp Exhib., Cape Town, Mar. 26-Apr. 5, 1952.

**Coronation Issue**

Queen Elizabeth II — A97

**1953, June 3** ***Perf. 14x15***

**192** A97 2p violet blue .20 .20

Cape Triangle of 1853 A98

**1953, Sept. 1** ***Perf. 15x14***

**193** A98 1p red & dk brown .20 .20
**194** A98 4p blue & indigo .25 .20

Cent. of the introduction of postage stamps in South Africa.

Merino Ram and Sheep — A99

**1953, Oct. 1** ***Perf. 14***

**195** A99 4½p shown .35 .20
**196** A99 1sh3p Springbok 1.25 .20
**197** A99 1sh6p Aloes 1.00 .30
*Nos. 195-197 (3)* 2.60 .70

Arms of Orange Free State, Pen and Scroll A100

**1954, Feb. 23** ***Perf. 15x14***

**198** A100 2p red org & dk brown .20 .20
**199** A100 4½p gray & rose violet .25 .25

Orange Free State centenary.

Wart Hog A101

White Rhinoceros A102

Lion — A103

**1954, Oct. 14** ***Perf. 15x14***

**200** A101 ½p shown .20 .20
**201** A101 1p Gnu .20 .20
**202** A101 1½p Leopard .20 .20
**203** A101 2p Zebra .20 .20

***Perf. 14***

**204** A102 3p shown .20 .20
**205** A102 4p Elephant .40 .20
**206** A102 4½p Hippopotamus .50 .70
**207** A103 6p shown .45 .20
**208** A102 1sh Kudu 2.75 .20
**209** A103 1sh3p Springbok 1.75 .30
**210** A102 1sh6p Gemsbok 1.60 .45
**211** A102 2sh6p Nyala 3.75 .25
**212** A102 5sh Giraffe 9.25 1.50
**213** A102 10sh Sable antelope 14.00 3.25
*Nos. 200-213 (14)* 35.45 8.05

See Nos. 221-228, 241-244, 247, 250-253.

Paul Kruger — A104

Portrait: 6p, Martinus Wessels Pretorius.

***Perf. 14x15***

**1955, Oct. 21 Photo. Wmk. 201**

**214** A104 3p slate green .25 .20
**215** A104 6p brown violet .50 .25

Centenary of Pretoria.

Andries Pretorius, Church of the Vow and Flag of Natalia — A105

German Wagon and House — A106

**1955, Dec. 1** ***Perf. 14***

Inscribed alternately in English and Afrikaans.

**216** A105 2p ultra & cer, pair .60 3.00
*a.* Single, English .20 .20
*b.* Single, Afrikaans .20 .20

Union Covenant Celebrations, Pietermaritzburg, Dec. 13-18, 1955.

**1958, July 1** ***Perf. 14***

**218** A106 2p pale lilac & brown .20 .20

Cent. of the arrival of German settlers.

Seal of Academy A107

***Perf. 15x14***

**1959, May 1 Photo. Wmk. 201**

**219** A107 3p brt blue & dk blue .20 .20
*a.* Dark blue omitted 1,800.

50th anniv. of the South African Academy of Science and Art, Pretoria.

Globe Showing Antarctica and South Africa — A108

***Perf. 14x15***

**1959, Nov. 16 Wmk. 330**

**220** A108 3p blue grn, brn & org .20 .20

South African Natl. Antarctic Expedition.

Animal Types of 1954

**1959-60 Wmk. 330** ***Perf. 15x14***

**221** A101 ½p Wart hog ('60) .30 *1.75*
**222** A101 1p Gnu .20 .20
*a.* Redrawn .35 .20

***Perf. 14***

**223** A102 3p White rhino .35 .20
**224** A102 4p Elephant 1.00 .25
**225** A103 6p Lion 1.90 .25
**226** A102 1sh Kudu 2.75 .25
**227** A102 2sh6p Nyala 8.50 6.00
**228** A102 5sh Giraffe ('60) 18.00 26.00
*Nos. 221-228 (8)* 33.00 34.90

On No. 222a, the numeral "1" is centered above "S." On No. 222, "1" is slightly to right of "S."

Prime Ministers Botha, Smuts, Hertzog, Malan, Strydom and Verwoerd A109

Flag and Notes from National Anthem — A110

Pushing Wheel Uphill A111

6p, Arms of the Union and of four provinces. 1sh6p, Official Union festival emblem.

***Perf. 14x15, 15x14***

**1960 Photo. Wmk. 330**

**235** A109 3p chocolate .20 .20
**236** A110 4p lt blue & red org .25 .20
**237** A110 6p yel grn, red & brn .35 .20
**238** A111 1sh yel, dk bl & blk .70 .20
**239** A111 1sh6p lt blue & blk 2.50 1.75
*Nos. 235-239 (5)* 4.00 2.55

50th anniv. of the founding of the Union. See Nos. 245-246, 248-249.

Map, Old and New Locomotives — A112

**1960, May 2** ***Perf. 15x14***

**240** A112 1sh3p dark blue 3.25 1.25

Centenary of railways in South Africa.

Types of 1954 and 1960.

Designs: ½c, Wart hog. 1c, Gnu. 1½c, Leopard. 2c, Zebra. 2½c, Prime Ministers. 3½c, Flag and music notes. 5c, Lion. 7½c, Arms of Union and four provinces. 10c, Pushing wheel uphill. 12½c, Springbok. 20c, Gemsbok. 50c, Giraffe. 1r, Sable antelope.

***Perf. 15x14, 14x15, 14 (A102, A103)***

**1961, Feb. 14 Photo. Wmk. 330**

**241** A101 ½c dk bluish grn .20 .20
**242** A101 1c rose brown .20 .20
**243** A101 1½c sepia .20 .20
**244** A101 2c purple .20 .20
**245** A109 2½c chocolate .25 .20
**246** A110 3½c lt bl & red org .40 .25
**247** A103 5c org & dk brn .50 .20
**248** A110 7½c yel grn, red & brn .60 .25
**249** A111 10c yel, dk bl & blk .70 .20
**250** A103 12½c dull grn & dk brn 1.10 .60
**251** A102 20c pink & dk brn 1.90 1.25
**252** A102 50c org yel & blk brn 7.75 *8.25*
**253** A102 1r blue & black 18.00 16.00
*Nos. 241-253 (13)* 32.00 28.00

**Republic**

Natal Pigmy Kingfisher A112a

Coral Tree Flower A112b

Pouring Gold A113

Groot Constantia A114

Designs: 1½c, Afrikander bull. 3c, Crimson-breasted shrike. 5c, Baobab tree. 7½c, Corn. 10c, Castle entrance, Cape Town. 12½c, Protea flower. 20c, Secretary bird. 50c, Cape Town, harbor. 1r, Bird of Paradise flower.

Two types of 2½c:
Type I — Lines of building faint.
Type II — Lines of building very strong; strong line between bottom of building and top of name panel.

***Perf. 14x15, 15x14***

**1961, May 31 Photo. Wmk. 330**

**254** A112a ½c blue, mag & brn .20 .20
*a.* Perf. 14x13½ ('63) .20 .20
**255** A112b 1c gray & red .20 .20
**256** A112a 1½c brown carmine .20 .20

***Perf. 14***

**257** A113 2c ultra & orange .20 .20
**258** A114 2½c violet & grn (I) .30 .20
*a.* Type II .40 .20
**259** A113 3c pink, dk bl & red .30 .20
**260** A114 5c grnsh bl & yel .35 .20
**261** A114 7½c emerald & brn .50 .20
*a.* Brown omitted
**262** A114 10c emer & dk brn .75 .20
**263** A114 12½c dk grn, red & yel 1.50 .20
*a.* Yellow omitted 600.00
**264** A114 20c sal, sl bl & pink 4.00 .30
**265** A113 50c ultra & blk 30.00 2.10
**266** A113 1r blue, org & grn 22.50 2.10
*Nos. 254-266 (13)* 61.00 6.50

**1961-63 Unwmk.** ***Perf. 15x14***

**269** A112b 1c gray & red .25 .20

***Perf. 14***

**270** A113 2c ultra & org ('63) 7.25 .35
**271** A114 2½c violet & grn (II) .30 .20
**272** A113 3c pink, dk bl & red .60 .20
**273** A114 5c grnsh blue & yel .75 .20
**274** A114 7½c emer & brn ('62) 1.10 .35
**275** A114 10c green & dk brn 1.25 .50
**276** A114 20c sal, sl bl & pink ('63) 17.50 4.75
**277** A113 50c ultra & blk ('62) 26.00 5.25
*Nos. 269-277 (9)* 55.00 12.00

See Nos. 289-298, 317-322, 324, 326-338, 340-342, 376-377, 379-382, 383-385 and designs A135-A136.

Boeing 707 and Bleriot Monoplane A115

Folk Dancers A116

*Perf. 14x15*

**1961, Dec. 1 Photo. Wmk. 330**

| | | | | |
|---|---|---|---|---|
| **280** | A115 | 3c blue & red | .50 | .20 |

50th anniv. of South Africa's 1st air mail.

**1962, Mar. 1**

| | | | | |
|---|---|---|---|---|
| **281** | A116 | 2½c lt brn, choc & red org | .30 | .20 |

50th anniv. of folk dancing in South Africa.

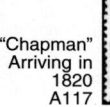

"Chapman" Arriving in 1820 A117

*Perf. 15x14*

**1962, Aug. 20 Photo. Wmk. 330**

| | | | | |
|---|---|---|---|---|
| **282** | A117 | 2½c dp plum & bl grn | .30 | .20 |
| **283** | A117 | 12½c choc & blue | 2.75 | 1.50 |

Unveiling of the precinct stone of the British Settlers Monument at Grahamstown.

Red Disa Orchid, Castle Rock, Kirstenbosch Botanic Gardens — A118

**1963, Mar. 14** ***Perf. 14***

| | | | | |
|---|---|---|---|---|
| **284** | A118 | 2½c multicolored | .35 | .20 |

50th anniv. of the Kirstenbosch Botanic Gardens, Cape Town.

Centenary Emblem and Nurse — A119

12½c, Centenary emblem and globe, horiz.

**1963, Aug. 30 Wmk. 348** ***Perf. 14***

| | | | | |
|---|---|---|---|---|
| **285** | A119 | 2½c rose claret, blk & red | .35 | .20 |

*Perf. 15x14*

| | | | | |
|---|---|---|---|---|
| **286** | A119 | 12½c dk bl gray & red | 3.50 | 1.60 |
| *a.* | | Red Cross omitted | *1,450.* | |

Centenary of the International Red Cross.

Assembly Seat, Bunga Building, Umtata A120

*Perf. 14½x14*

**1963, Dec. 11 Wmk. 348**

| | | | | |
|---|---|---|---|---|
| **287** | A120 | 2½c dk brn & lt grn | .30 | .20 |
| *a.* | | Light green omitted | *1,600.* | |

Transkei Legislative Assembly, 1st meeting.

Types of 1961

*Perf. 15x14, 14x15*

**1963-67 Photo. Wmk. 348**

**Colors as Before**

| | | | | |
|---|---|---|---|---|
| **289** | A112b | 1c | .20 | .20 |
| **290** | A112a | 1½c ('67) | 2.25 | .85 |
| | | ***Perf. 14*** | | |
| **291** | A113 | 2c ('64) | .20 | .20 |
| **292** | A114 | 2½c (II) ('64) | .50 | .20 |
| **293** | A114 | 5c ('66) | 2.25 | .20 |
| **294** | A114 | 7½c ('66) | 11.50 | 2.25 |
| **295** | A114 | 10c ('64) | 1.10 | .20 |
| **296** | A114 | 20c ('64) | 4.50 | .40 |
| **297** | A113 | 50c ('66) | 37.50 | 6.50 |
| **298** | A113 | 1r ('64) | 70.00 | 32.50 |
| | | *Nos. 289-298 (10)* | 130.00 | 43.50 |

Rugby Board Emblem, Springbok and Ball — A121

John Calvin — A122

Design: 12½c, Rugby player diving over goal line, horiz.

*Perf. 14x15, 15x14*

**1964, May 8 Photo. Wmk. 348**

| | | | | |
|---|---|---|---|---|
| **301** | A121 | 2½c dk green & brn | .25 | .20 |
| **302** | A121 | 12½c yellow grn & blk | 3.75 | 2.50 |

South African Rugby Board, 75th anniv.

**1964, July 10** ***Perf. 14***

| | | | | |
|---|---|---|---|---|
| **303** | A122 | 2½c choc, brt car & vio | .35 | .20 |

John Calvin (1509-64), French theologian and leader of the Reformation.

Nurse's Lamp — A123

Design: 12½c, Nurse holding lamp, horiz.

*Perf. 14x15, 15x14*

**1964, Oct. 12 Photo. Wmk. 348**

| | | | | |
|---|---|---|---|---|
| **304** | A123 | 2½c gold & ultra | .25 | .20 |
| **305** | A123 | 12½c ultra & gold | 2.75 | 2.75 |
| *a.* | | Gold omitted | *1,200.* | |

South African Nursing Assoc., 50th anniv.

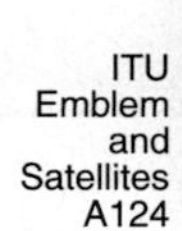

ITU Emblem and Satellites A124

Design: 12½c, ITU emblem, old and new communication equipment.

**1965, May 17** ***Perf. 15x14***

| | | | | |
|---|---|---|---|---|
| **306** | A124 | 2½c brt blue & org | .30 | .20 |
| **307** | A124 | 12½c green & claret | 3.00 | 2.50 |

Cent. of the ITU.

Pulpit, Groote Kerk, Cape Town — A125

Design: 12½c, Emblem of Dutch Reformed Church of South Africa, horiz.

*Perf. 14x15, 15x14*

**1965, Oct. 21 Photo. Wmk. 348**

| | | | | |
|---|---|---|---|---|
| **308** | A125 | 2½c dp brown & yel | .25 | .20 |
| **309** | A125 | 12½c lt ultra, ocher & blk | 3.00 | 2.75 |

Tercentenary of the Dutch Reformed Church in South Africa.

Diamond — A126

**1966, May 31** ***Perf. 14***

2½c, Flying bird, symbol of freedom & the future, horiz. 3c, Corn. 7½c, Table Mountain, horiz. Inscribed alternately in English & Afrikaans.

| | | | | |
|---|---|---|---|---|
| **310** | A126 | 1c blk, yel, dk & lt grn, pair | .50 | .50 |
| *a.* | | Single, English | .20 | .20 |
| *b.* | | Single, Afrikaans | .20 | .20 |
| **311** | A126 | 2½c dk bl, ultra & yel grn, pair | 1.25 | 1.25 |
| *a.* | | Single, English | .20 | .20 |
| *b.* | | Single, Afrikaans | .20 | .20 |
| | | ***Perf. 14x15, 15x14*** | | |
| **312** | A126 | 3c red brn, red & yel, pair | 2.50 | 2.50 |
| *a.* | | Single, English | .20 | .20 |
| *b.* | | Single, Afrikaans | .20 | .20 |
| **313** | A126 | 7½c ultra, vio bl, och & blk, pair | 7.00 | 7.00 |
| *a.* | | Single, English | .50 | .40 |
| *b.* | | Single, Afrikaans | .50 | .40 |
| | | *Nos. 310-313 (4)* | 11.25 | 11.25 |

5th anniversary of the Republic.

Nos. 310-313 with watermark 359 are reprints made for U.P.U. presentation booklets.

Hendrik F. Verwoerd and Union Buildings, Pretoria A127

Designs: 3c, Verwoerd's portrait, vert. 12½c, Verwoerd and map of South Africa.

*Perf. 15x14, 14x15*

**1966, Dec. 6 Photo. Wmk. 348**

| | | | | |
|---|---|---|---|---|
| **314** | A127 | 2½c grnsh blue & blk | .20 | .20 |
| **315** | A127 | 3c yellow grn & blk | .20 | .20 |
| **316** | A127 | 12½c dull blue & blk | 1.40 | 1.25 |
| | | *Nos. 314-316 (3)* | 1.80 | 1.65 |

Dr. Verwoerd (1901-1966), Prime Minister.

Types of 1961 Redrawn and

Industry — A128

(Inscriptions in larger, bolder type)

½c, 1½c and 1r

On the 1r, the "N" of "VAN" is over the final "A" of "AFRIKA." On Nos. 266 and 298, the "N" is over "KA."

1c, 7½c and 12½c

2½c, 5c, 10c and 20c

2c, 3c and 50c (similar)

*Perf. 14x15, 15x14*

**1964-68 Photo. Wmk. 348**

**Colors as Before**

| | | | | |
|---|---|---|---|---|
| **317** | A112a | ½c | .20 | .20 |
| *a.* | | Imperf., pair | 400.00 | |
| **318** | A112b | 1c | .30 | .20 |
| | | ***Perf. 14*** | | |
| **319** | A113 | 2c ('68) | .30 | .20 |
| **320** | A114 | 2½c | .35 | .20 |
| **321** | A113 | 3c | .60 | .20 |
| **322** | A113 | 12½c | 2.25 | .20 |
| **323** | A128 | 15c ('67) | 5.00 | .20 |
| **324** | A113 | 1r | 16.00 | 2.50 |
| | | *Nos. 317-324 (8)* | 25.00 | 3.90 |

See No. 339.

Redrawn Types of 1964-68

4c, Groot Constantia (like 2½c). 6c, Corn (like 7½c). 9c, Protea flower (like 12½c).

**1967-71 Photo. Wmk. 359**

| | | | | |
|---|---|---|---|---|
| **326** | A112a | ½c | .20 | .20 |
| **327** | A112b | 1c | .20 | .20 |
| **328** | A112a | 1½c | .20 | .20 |
| **329** | A113 | 2c ('68) | 1.90 | .20 |
| **330** | A114 | 2½c | .20 | .20 |
| **331** | A113 | 3c | .20 | .20 |
| **332** | A114 | 4c ('71) | .40 | .20 |
| **333** | A114 | 5c ('68) | .20 | .20 |
| **334** | A114 | 6c ('71) | 1.00 | .20 |
| **335** | A114 | 7½c | 1.75 | .20 |
| **336** | A114 | 9c ('71) | 1.25 | .20 |
| **337** | A114 | 10c ('68) | 3.75 | .25 |
| **338** | A114 | 12½c ('70) | 3.00 | .55 |
| **339** | A128 | 15c ('69) | 6.00 | .40 |
| **340** | A114 | 20c ('68) | 7.25 | .55 |
| **341** | A113 | 50c ('68) | 8.00 | .90 |
| **342** | A113 | 1r ('68) | 10.50 | 1.90 |
| | | *Nos. 326-342 (17)* | 46.00 | 6.75 |

Luminescence

Starting in 1969, South Africa began to add phosphorescent "frames" to its definitive stamps.

In 1971, stamps began to appear with the phosphorescent element throughout the paper.

Phosphorescent commemoratives include Nos. 357, 359 et cetera.

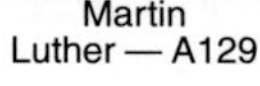

Martin Luther — A129

Door of Wittenberg Church — A130

*Perf. 14x15*

**1967, Oct. 31 Litho. Wmk. 348**

| | | | | |
|---|---|---|---|---|
| **343** | A129 | 2½c pink & black | .20 | .20 |
| | | **Wmk. 359** | | |
| **344** | A130 | 12½c black & orange | 2.25 | 2.00 |

450th anniversary of the Reformation.

Pres. J. J. Fouché — A133

James B. M. Hertzog Statue — A134

Design: 12½c, Full-face portrait.

***Perf. 14x15***

**1968, Apr. 10 Photo. Wmk. 348**

**345** A133 2½c lt rose brn & dk brn .30 .20
**346** A133 12½c grysh bl & vio bl 2.50 2.25

**Wmk. 359**

**347** A133 12½c grysh bl & vio bl 2.75 2.25
*Nos. 345-347 (3)* 5.55 4.70

Pres. Jacobus Johannes Fouché, inauguration.

***Perf. 13½x14, 14x13½***

**1968, Sept. 21 Photo. Wmk. 359**

Designs: 2½c, Hertzog in 1902, with hat, horiz. 3c, Hertzog in 1924, horiz.

**348** A134 2½c dk brn, lem & blk .20 .20

**Wmk. 348**

**349** A134 3c multicolored .30 .20
**350** A134 12½c org brn, org & blk 2.00 1.75
*Nos. 348-350 (3)* 2.50 2.15

Unveiling of a monument in Bloemfontein honoring James Barry Munnik Hertzog (1866-1942), Boer general, prime minister of South Africa (1924-39).

Natal Pigmy Kingfisher A135

Kaffir Boom Flower A136

**1969 Wmk. 359 Photo. *Perf. 14***

**351** A135 ½c blue & multi .20 .20
*a.* Perf. 14x14½ (coil) 1.50 .20
**352** A136 1c grysh brown & multi .20 .20

See Nos. 374-375.

Springbok, Torch and Rings — A137

**1969, Mar. 15 *Perf. 14x13½***

**353** A137 2½c olive, ind & red .20 .20
**354** A137 12½c bister, ind & red 1.60 1.40

South African Natl. Games, Bloemfontein, Mar. 15-Apr. 19.

Groote Schuur Hospital and Dr. Barnard A138

Hands Holding Heart A139

***Perf. 13½x14***

**1969, July 7 Photo. Wmk. 348**

**355** A138 2½c dp rose, pink & plum .20 .20

***Perf. 15x14***

**Wmk. 359**

**356** A139 12½c dp bl & dp car 2.25 1.75

1st heart transplant operation (by Dr. Christiaan Barnard) and opening of the 47th South African Medical Cong., Pretoria.

Stagecoach of 1869 — A140

Transvaal No. 1 — A141

Water Drop and Flower — A142

***Perf. 13½x14, 14x13½***

**1969, Oct. 6 Photo. Wmk. 359**

**357** A140 2½c ocher, Prus bl & yel .35 .20
**358** A141 12½c sal, grn & gold 3.00 2.25

Centenary of South African postage stamps.

**1970, Feb. 14 *Perf. 14***

Design: 3c, Waves, horiz.

**359** A142 2½c brn, brt bl & grn .20 .20
**360** A142 3c pale gray, bl & ind .35 .20

Issued to publicize the Water 70 campaign of the Department of Water Affairs.

Sower — A143

"BIBLIA" A144

**1970, Aug. 24 Photo. *Perf. 14***

**361** A143 2½c multicolored .25 .20

**Photo; Gold Impressed**

**362** A144 12½c ultra, blk & gold 2.60 2.25

150th anniv. of the South African Bible Soc.

Strijdom Tower, Johannes G. Strijdom — A145

Map of Antarctica A146

***Perf. 14x13½, 13½x14***

**1971, May 22 Photo. Wmk. 359**

**363** A145 5c blue, yel & blk .40 .20
**364** A146 12½c grnsh bl, vio bl & red 4.00 4.00

**Wmk. 330**

**365** A145 5c blue, yel & blk 2.00 .90
*Nos. 363-365 (3)* 6.40 5.10

Intl. Stamp Exhib. (INTERSTEX), Cape Town, May 22-31. No. 364 also for the 10th anniv. of the Antarctic Treaty pledging peaceful uses of and scientific cooperation in Antarctica.

Landing of British Settlers, 1820, by Thomas Baines A147

Martinus Steyn, Paul Kruger, Unification Monument — A148

**1971, May 31 Wmk. 359**

**366** A147 2c magenta & rose red .20 .20
**367** A148 4c blue green & blk .30 .20

10th anniv. of the Republic of South Africa.

Hendrik Verwoerd Dam A149

**1972, Mar. 4 Photo. *Perf. 14***

**Size: 37x22mm**

**368** A149 4c shown .25 .20
**369** A149 5c Aerial view of dam .45 .20

**Size: 57x22mm**

**370** A149 10c Dam, reservoir and Verwoerd 1.50 .90
*Nos. 368-370 (3)* 2.20 1.30

Inauguration of the Hendrik F. Verwoerd Dam of the Orange River Project.

Ram's Head and Wool Mark — A150

Lamb and Wool Mark — A151

**1972, May 15 Wmk. 359 *Perf. 14***

**371** A150 4c blue & multi .20 .20
**372** A151 15c dull bl & dk bl 1.75 .40

South African wool industry. Issued in sheets of 100 with advertisements in margin. See Nos. 378-378A, 382A.

Cats — A152

Pylon — A153

**1972, Sept. 19 Wmk. 359**

**373** A152 5c multicolored 1.00 .25

Centenary of the SPCA.

Redrawn Types of 1964-69 and Types of 1972

***Perf. 14x15 (½c), 14 (1c, #382A), 12½***

**1972-74 Photo. Unwmk.**

| | | | | |
|---|---|---|---|---|
| **374** | A135 | ½c blue & multi | 7.50 | 8.25 |
| **375** | A136 | 1c grysh brn & red | .20 | .20 |
| **376** | A113 | 2c brt blue & org | .50 | .20 |
| **377** | A113 | 3c rose red & bluish black | .55 | .65 |
| **378** | A150 | 4c blue & multi | .85 | .20 |
| **378A** | A150 | 4c brown & multi | .40 | .20 |
| **379** | A114 | 5c grnsh bl & yel | 1.00 | .25 |
| **380** | A114 | 6c emerald & brn | 2.50 | 4.00 |
| **381** | A114 | 9c dk grn, red & yel | 2.25 | .75 |
| **382** | A114 | 10c emer & dk brn | 2.50 | .45 |
| **382A** | A151 | 15c dull bl & dk bl | 2.75 | 3.75 |
| **383** | A114 | 20c sal, sl bl & pink | 2.75 | .60 |
| **384** | A113 | 50c ultra & black | 7.25 | 1.75 |
| **385** | A113 | 1r bl, org & grn | 19.00 | 3.75 |
| | | *Nos. 374-385 (14)* | 50.00 | 25.00 |

Issued: 2c, 1972; 6c, 15c, 1974: others, 1973.

**1973, Feb. 1 Photo. *Perf. 12x12½***

Designs: 4c, Electrical usage, pylon, power plant, horiz. 15c, Smokestacks.

**Size: 37½x20mm**

**386** A153 4c blue & multi .25 .20

**Size: 20x27mm**

***Perf. 12½***

**387** A153 5c blue & black .35 .20
**388** A153 15c ocher & multi 3.75 1.50
*Nos. 386-388 (3)* 4.35 1.90

Electricity Supply Commission, 50th anniv.

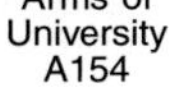

Arms of University A154

Old University, Cape Town A156

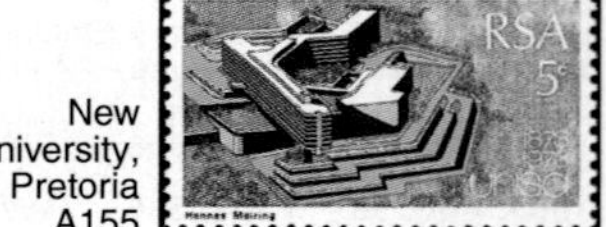


New University, Pretoria A155

**1973, Apr. 2 Unwmk. *Perf. 12½***

**389** A154 4c blue & multi .25 .20

***Perf. 12x12½***

**Wmk. 359**

**390** A155 5c gold & multi .35 .20

**Unwmk. *Perf. 12½***

**391** A156 15c gold & blk 3.25 1.65

Cent. of the Univ. of South Africa (UNISA).

Woltemade, Sailor and Horse — A157

Designs: 5c, Sinking ship in storm. 15c, "De Jonge Thomas" sinking.

**1973, June 2 Photo. *Perf. 12x12½***

392 A157 4c brown red, ol & blk .25 .20
393 A157 5c olive, blk & citron .45 .20
394 A157 15c brown, blk & ocher 5.50 4.50
*Nos. 392-394 (3)* 6.20 4.90

Bicentenary of Wolraad Woltemade's heroism in saving 14 people from the ship "De Jonge Thomas" in Table Bay.

C. J. Langenhoven and Anthem — A158

4c, 5c, vert., Portrait and signature.

**1973, Aug. 1 *Perf. 12½***

**Size: 27x20mm**

395 A158 4c orange, blk & ultra .50 .20

***Perf. 12½x12, 12x12½***

**Size: 21x38mm, 37x21mm**

396 A158 5c orange, blk & ultra .60 .20
397 A158 15c orange, blk & ultra 3.00 1.00
*Nos. 395-397 (3)* 4.10 1.40

Cornelis Jacob Langenhoven (1873-1932), lawyer, writer, who worked for recognition of Afrikaans language.

World Map and Communications Network — A159

***Perf. 12½***

**1973, Oct. 1 Photo. Unwmk.**

398 A159 15c ultra & multi 1.75 1.65
a. Wmk. 359 2.50 2.25

International Telecommunications Day.

Restored Houses, Tulbagh — A160

Design: 5c, Church Street, Tulbagh.

**1974, Mar. 14 Unwmk. *Perf. 12½***

**Size: 27x21mm**

400 A160 4c Prus green & multi .25 .20

**Size: 57x20mm**

401 A160 5c ocher & multi .45 .20

Restoration of historic Church Street in Tulbagh after 1969 earthquake.

Burgerspond A161

Prime Minister D. F. Malan A162

**1974, Apr. 7 Photo. *Perf. 12½x12***

402 A161 9c multicolored .80 .55

Centenary of the first official coin struck in South Africa, 1874. The £1 gold coin shows portrait of Pres. Thomas Francois Burger.

**1974, May 22 Photo. Unwmk.**

403 A162 4c lt ultra & dk blue .30 .20

Centenary of the birth of Daniel F. Malan (1874-1959), prime minister of South Africa.

Congress Emblem A163

**1974, June 13 *Perf. 12x12½***

404 A163 15c silver & dk blue 1.25 .50

15th World Sugar Cong., Durban, 6/13-30.

"50" A164

**1974, July 13 Photo. Unwmk.**

405 A164 4c red & black .35 .20

50th anniversary of radio in South Africa.

Cultural Center, Grahamstown — A165

**1974, July 13 *Perf. 12x12½***

406 A165 5c red & black .35 .20

Natl. Monument to British settlers of 1820.

Natal No. 78, Transvaal No. 145, Cape of Good Hope No. 28 and Orange River Colony No. 4 — A166

**1974, Oct. 9 Photo. *Perf. 12½***

407 A166 15c multicolored 1.25 .90

Centenary of Universal Postal Union.

Wild Iris — A167

Cape Gannet — A168

Galjoen — A169

Bokmakierie (Shrike) — A170

Designs: 2c, Heather. 3c, Geranium. 4c, Calla lily. 7c, Zebrafish. 9c, Angelfish. 10c, Moorish idol. 14c, Roman fish. 15c, Greater double-collared sunbird. 20c, Yellow-billed hornbill. 25c, Barberton daisy. 50c, Blue cranes. 1r, Bateleur eagles.

**Photo. and Engr.**

**1974, Nov. 11 Unwmk. *Perf. 12½***

408 A167 1c pink & multi .20 .20
409 A167 2c yellow & multi .20 .20
410 A167 3c multicolored .20 .20
411 A167 4c multicolored .20 .20
412 A168 5c dull blue & multi .20 .20
413 A169 6c multicolored .25 .20
414 A169 7c lilac & multi .30 .20
415 A169 9c buff & multi .35 .20
416 A169 10c lt blue & multi .40 .20
417 A169 14c salmon & multi .60 .20
418 A168 15c gray & multi .60 .20
419 A168 20c yellow & multi .80 .30
420 A167 25c dk brown & multi 1.10 .35

***Perf. 12x12½***

421 A170 30c gray & multi 4.50 .75
422 A170 50c citron & multi 4.00 1.00
423 A170 1r multicolored 7.50 2.00
*Nos. 408-423 (16)* 21.40 6.60

The coils that follow are two colors while the above sheet stamps are multicolored.

**1974 Photo. *Perf. 12½***

**Coil Stamps**

430 A167 1c pink & violet .45 .30
431 A167 2c yellow & grn .65 .25
432 A168 5c dull blue & blk 1.40 .70
433 A169 10c lt blue & indigo 9.50 5.75
*Nos. 430-433 (4)* 12.00 7.00

**See note on color that follows No. 423.**

**1975-76 *Perf. 14***

**Same Designs**

*430a* A167 1c .55 .25
*431a* A167 2c ('76) .45 .25
*433a* A169 10c ('76) 5.00 5.50
*Nos. 430a-433a (3)* 6.00 6.00

No. 430a has black control number on back of every fifth stamp.

Voortrekker Monument and Encampment — A171

**1974, Dec. 6 Unwmk. *Perf. 12½***

438 A171 4c multicolored .35 .20

Voortrekker Monument, 25th anniversary.

Sasolburg Refinery A172

***Perf. 12x12½, 12½***

**1975, Feb. 26 Litho.**

439 A172 15c red & multi 1.25 .90

25th anniversary of South Africa Coal, Oil and Gas Corp., Ltd. (SASOL).

Pres. Nicolaes Diederichs A173

Jan C. Smuts A174

**Litho. and Engr.**

**1975, Apr. 19 *Perf. 12½x12***

440 A173 4c brown & gold .20 .20

**Litho.**

441 A173 15c ultra & gold .85 .85

Installation of Dr. Nicolaes Diederichs as third State President.

**Litho. and Engraved**

**1975, May 24**

442 A174 4c black .30 .20

Smuts (1870-1950), lawyer, gen., statesman.

Dutch East Indiaman, by Baines A175

Designs: Paintings by John Thomas Baines.

**1975, June 18 Photo. *Perf. 12x12½***

443 A175 5c gold & multi .20 .20
444 A175 9c gold & multi .30 .25
445 A175 15c gold & multi .55 .45
446 A175 30c gold & multi 1.00 1.00
a. Souvenir sheet of 4 3.50 3.50
*Nos. 443-446 (4)* 2.05 1.90

John Thomas Baines (1820-75), painter. #446a contains 4 litho. stamps similar to #443-446.

Gideon Malherbe House, Paarl — A176

**Photo. and Engr.**

**1975, Aug. 14 *Perf. 12½***

447 A176 4c multicolored .30 .20

Society of Real Afrikanders (Genootskap of Regte Afrikaaners), cent.

Automatic Letter Sorting — A177

**1975, Sept. 11 Photo. *Perf. 12½x12***

448 A177 4c brt blue & multi .30 .20

Postal automation.

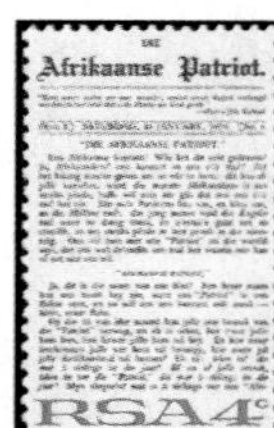


Title Page, First Afrikaans Paper — A178

Afrikaans Monument, Paarl — A179

**1975, Oct. 10 Litho. *Perf. 12½x12***

449 A178 4c black & orange .20 .20
450 A179 5c multicolored .25 .20

Inauguration of Afrikaans Language Monument.

Table Mountain — A180

**1975, Nov. 13 Litho. *Perf. 12½***

451 A180 15c shown 2.25 1.50
452 A180 15c Johannesburg 2.25 1.50
453 A180 15c Cape vineyards 2.25 1.50
454 A180 15c Lions, Kruger Natl. Park 2.25 1.50
a. Block of 4, #451-454 9.00 9.00

Tourist publicity.

Satellites, Radar and Africa on Globe — A181

**1975, Dec. 3 Litho. *Perf. 12½***
**455** A181 15c dk vio blue & multi .60 .50

Satellite communications.

Lawn Bowler — A182

#457, Cricket batsman. #458, Polo player. #459, Golfer (Gary Player).

**1976 Photo. *Perf. 12½x12***
**456** A182 15c green & blk .60 .35
**457** A182 15c yellow grn & blk .60 .35
**458** A182 15c olive & blk .60 .35
**459** A182 15c brt green & blk .60 .35
*a.* Miniature sheet of 4, #456-459 3.75 2.75
*Nos. 456-459 (4)* 2.40 1.40

3rd World Bowling Championships, Zoo Lake Club, Johannesburg, Feb. 1976 (No. 456); cent. of cricket in South Africa (No. 457); intl. polo (No. 458); Gary Player, South African golf champion (No. 459).

Issue dates: #456, Feb. 18. #457, Mar. 12. #458, Aug. 16. #459, 459a, Dec. 2.

No. 456 Overprinted in Gold

**1976, Apr. 6 Photo. *Perf. 12½x12***
**460** A182 15c green & black .45 .45

Victory of South Africa in 3rd World Bowling championships.

Picnic under Baobab Tree A183

Paintings by Erich Mayer: 10c, Wagons at Foot of Blauberg, Transvaal. 15c, Hartbeesspoort Dam, near Pretorial. 20c, Street in Doornfontein.

**1976, Apr. 20 Photo. *Perf. 12x12½***
**461** A183 4c ocher & multi .25 .20
**462** A183 10c dk green & multi .50 .45
**463** A183 15c multicolored .70 .60
**464** A183 20c multicolored 1.10 1.00
*a.* Souvenir sheet of 4, #461-464 3.50 3.50
*Nos. 461-464 (4)* 2.55 2.25

Erich Mayer (1876-1960), painter. Artist's signature in horizontal gutter between 2 se-tenant pairs.

Wildlife Protection A184

**1976, June 5 Litho. *Perf. 12x12½***
**465** A184 3c Cheetah .25 .20
**466** A184 10c Black rhinoceros .55 .35
**467** A184 15c Blesbok 1.10 .70
**468** A184 20c Zebra 1.40 .95
*Nos. 465-468 (4)* 3.30 2.20

All values exist on yellow toned paper. Value, twice that of stamps on white paper.

Emily Hobhouse, by Johan Hoekstra — A185

**1976, June 8 Photo. *Perf. 12½x12***
**469** A185 4c multicolored .25 .20

Emily Hobhouse (1860-1926), the "Angel of Mercy" during Anglo-Boer War.

S.S. Dunrobin Castle, 1876 A186

**1976, Oct. 5 Litho. *Perf. 12x12½***
**470** A186 10c multicolored .75 .30

Ocean Mail Service contract, centenary.

Family with Globe — A187

**1976, Nov. 6 Photo. *Perf. 12½x12***
**471** A187 4c salmon & dull red .25 .20

Family planning.

Wine Glasses A188

Jacob Daniel du Toit A189

**1977, Feb. 14 Litho. *Perf. 12½x12***
**472** A188 15c multicolored .50 .25
*a.* Word "Die" omitted from left inscription 12.00 10.00

Quality of the Vintage Symposium, Cape Town, Feb. 14-21.

**1977, Feb. 21 Photo.**
**473** A189 4c multicolored .25 .20

Dr. Jacob Daniel du Toit (Totius; 1877-1953), theologian, educator, poet.

Transvaal Supreme Court A190

**1977, May 18 Photo. *Perf. 12x12½***
**474** A190 4c red brown .25 .20

Transvaal Supreme Court, centenary.

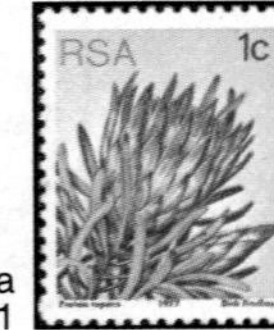

Sugarbush (Protea Repens) — A191

**Photo. (1-5, 8, 10, 15, 20c); Litho. (others)**

**1977, May 27 *Perf. 12½***
**475** A191 1c shown .20 .20
**476** A191 2c P. punctata .20 .20
**477** A191 3c P. neriifolia .20 .20
**478** A191 4c P. longifolia .20 .20
**479** A191 5c P. cynaroides .20 .20
**480** A191 6c P. canaliculata .20 .20
**481** A191 7c P. lorea .20 .20
**482** A191 8c P. mundii .20 .20
**483** A191 9c P. roupelliae .20 .20
**484** A191 10c P. aristata .25 .20
**485** A191 15c P. eximia .25 .20
**486** A191 20c P. magnifica .25 .20
**487** A191 25c P. grandiceps .30 .20
**488** A191 30c P. amplexicaulis .45 .20
**489** A191 50c Leucospermum cordifolium .60 .30
**490** A191 1r Paranomus reflexus 1.10 .65
**491** A191 2r Orothamnus zeyheri 2.50 1.25
*Nos. 475-491 (17)* 7.50 5.00

***Perf. 14***
*477a* A191 3c Litho. .20 .20
*479a* A191 5c .20 .20
*480a* A191 6c .20 .20
*481a* A191 7c .20 .20
*482a* A191 8c .20 .20
*483a* A191 9c .20 .20
*484a* A191 10c .25 .20
*486a* A191 20c Litho. .75 .30
*487a* A191 25c .60 .20
*488a* A191 30c .70 .25
*489a* A191 50c 1.25 .40
*490a* A191 1r 2.50 .80
*491a* A191 2r 4.75 1.50
*Nos. 477a-491a (13)* 12.00 4.85

***Perf. 14 Vertically***
**Photo. Coil Stamps**
**492** A191 1c Silver tree .20 .20
**493** A191 2c Bottle brush .20 .20
**494** A191 5c Blushing bride .20 .20
**495** A191 10c Leucadendrom sessile .20 .20
*Nos. 492-495 (4)* .80 .80

Some printings have control number on back of every fifth stamp.

Gymnastics — A192

**1977, Aug. 15 Litho. *Perf. 12½x12***
**496** A192 15c multicolored .40 .30

8th Intl. Cong. of Physical Education and Sports for Girls and Women, Cape Town, Aug. 14-20.

World Map and "M" A193

**1977, Sept. 15 Litho. *Perf. 12x12½***
**497** A193 15c multicolored .40 .30

Introduction of international metric system.

Nuclear Power Plant and Uranium Atom A194

**1977, Oct. 8**
**498** A194 15c multicolored .40 .30

Uranium development.

Flag of South Africa A195

**1977, Nov. 11**
**499** A195 5c multicolored .20 .20

50th anniversary of national flag.

Walvis Bay, 1878 — A196

**1978, Mar. 10 Litho. *Perf. 12½***
**500** A196 15c multicolored .55 .40

Centenary of Walvis Bay annexation.

Dr. Andrew Murray — A197

**1978, May 9 *Perf. 12½x12***
**501** A197 4c multicolored .20 .20

Dr. Andrew Murray, pioneer theologian, 150th birth anniversary.

Railroad Rail and ISCOR Emblem — A198

**1978, June 5 Litho. *Perf. 12***
**502** A198 15c multicolored .45 .40

50th anniversary of ISCOR (Iron and Steel Industrial Corporation).

Saldanha Bay — A199

Design: No. 504, Richard's Bay.

**1978, July 21 Litho. *Perf. 12½***
**503** A199 15c multicolored .55 .55
**504** A199 15c multicolored .55 .55
*a.* Pair, #503-504 1.10 1.10

Opening of new harbors on east and west coasts of South Africa.

Landscape by Volschenk — A200

Designs: Landscapes by J. E. A. Volschenk.

**1978, Aug. 21**
**505** A200 10c multicolored .35 .35
**506** A200 15c multicolored .50 .50
**507** A200 20c multicolored .70 .70

**508** A200 25c multicolored .90 .90
*a.* Souvenir sheet of 4, #505-508 3.00 3.00
*Nos. 505-508 (4)* 2.45 2.45

Jan Ernst Abraham Volschenk (1853-1936), first South African professional artist.

B. J. Vorster — A201

**1978, Oct. 10 Litho. *Perf. 12½x12***
**509** A201 4c maroon & gold .20 .20
*a.* Perf. 14½x14 .75 .30

***Perf. 14½x14***
**510** A201 15c violet & gold .40 .30

Inauguration of Balthazar John Vorster as president of South Africa.

Golden Gate Highlands National Park — A202

Designs: 15c, Blyde River Canyon, Transvaal. 20c, Amphitheater, Natal National Park. 25c, Cango Caves, Cape Province.

**1978, Nov. 13 *Perf. 12½***
**511** A202 10c multicolored .30 .30
**512** A202 15c multicolored .40 .40
**513** A202 20c multicolored .60 .60
**514** A202 25c multicolored .95 .95
*Nos. 511-514 (4)* 2.25 2.25

Tourist publicity.

Tellurometer and Dr. I. R. Wadley — A203

**1979, Feb. 12 Litho. *Perf. 12½***
**515** A203 15c multicolored .30 .25

15th anniversary of the invention of the tellurometer (to measure radio distances).

South Africa No. C5 A204

**1979, Mar. 30 Litho. *Perf. 14½x14***
**516** A204 15c multicolored .35 .30

First stamp printed by South African Government Printer, 50th anniversary.

"Save Fuel" A205

Fuel Economy: No. 518, Language inscriptions reversed.

**1979, Apr. 2 Photo. *Perf. 12x12½***
**517** A205 4c red & black .20 .20
**518** A205 4c red & black .20 .20
*a.* Pair, #517-518 .25 .25

Battle of Isandlwana, by Melton Prior — A206

15c, Battle of Ulundi, by Louis Creswicke. 20c, Battle of Rorke's Drift, by Lt. Col. Crealock.

**1979, May 25 Litho. *Perf. 14x13½***
**519** A206 4c red & black .20 .20
**520** A206 15c red & black .40 .35
**521** A206 20c red & black .50 .40
*a.* Souv. sheet, #519-521 + label 3.00 3.00
*Nos. 519-521 (3)* 1.10 .95

Centenary of Zulu War.

"Health Care and Service" — A207

**1979, June 19 Litho. *Perf. 12½x12***
**522** A207 4c multicolored .20 .20
*a.* Perf. 14½x14 .25 .25

Health Year.

Boy and Girl Watching Candle — A208

**1979, Sept. 13 Litho. *Perf. 14½x14***
**523** A208 4c multicolored .20 .20

South African Christmas Stamp Fund, 50th anniversary.

Cape Town University, 150th Anniversary — A209

**1979, Oct. 1 Litho. *Perf. 14x14½***
**524** A209 4c multicolored .20 .20
*a.* Perf. 12x12½ .25 .25

Southern Sun Rose — A210

Designs: Roses.

**1979, Oct. 4 Litho. *Perf. 14½x14***
**525** A210 4c multicolored .20 .20
**526** A210 15c multicolored .35 .30
**527** A210 20c multicolored .45 .40
**528** A210 25c multicolored .65 .55
*a.* Souvenir sheet of 4, #525-528 2.25 2.25
*Nos. 525-528 (4)* 1.65 1.45

Rosafari 1979, 4th World Rose Convention, Pretoria, October.

Stellenbosch University — A211

**1979, Nov. 8**
**529** A211 4c shown .20 .20
**530** A211 15c Rhenish Church .30 .25

Stellenbosch (oldest town in South Africa), 300th anniversary.

A212

A213

**1979, Dec. 18 Photo. *Perf. 12½x12***
**531** A212 4c multicolored .20 .20

Federation of Afrikaans Cultural Societies, 50th anniv.

**1980, May 6 Litho. *Perf. 14½x14***

Paintings by Pieter Wenning (1873-1921): 5c, Still Life with Sweet Peas. 25c, House in the Suburbs, Cape Town.

**532** A213 5c multicolored .20 .20

**Size: 45x37mm**

**533** A213 25c multicolored .50 .35
*a.* Souvenir sheet of 2, #532-533 1.75 1.00

Great Star of Africa Diamond — A214

**1980, May 12 Litho. *Perf. 14x14½***
**534** A214 15c shown .45 .35
**535** A214 20c Cullinan II diamond .55 .50

World Diamond Congress.

A215

A216

**1980, Sept. 3 Litho. *Perf. 14½x14***
**536** A215 5c multicolored .20 .20

Christian Louis Leipoldt (1880-1947), writer and physician.

**1980, Oct. 9 Litho.**
**537** A216 5c multicolored .20 .20

University of Pretoria, 50th anniv.

Marine With Ships, by Willem van de Velde — A217

Paintings: 10c, Firetail and Trainer, by George Stubbs. 15c, Lavinia, by Thomas Gainsborough, vert. 20c, Landscape, by Pieter Post.

**1980, Nov. 3 *Perf. 14½x14***
**538** A217 5c multicolored .20 .20
**539** A217 10c multicolored .20 .20
**540** A217 15c multicolored .30 .25
**541** A217 20c multicolored .35 .30
*a.* Souvenir sheet of 4, #538-541 1.50 1.25
*Nos. 538-541 (4)* 1.05 .95

Natl. Gallery, 50th anniv.

P.J. Joubert, Paul Kruger, M.W. Pretorius (First Leaders of Triumvirate Government) — A218

Design: 10c, Monument, flag of South African Republic, 1880, vert.

**1980, Dec. 15 *Perf. 14x14½ 14½x14***
**542** A218 5c multicolored .20 .20
**543** A218 10c multicolored .20 .20

Paardekraal Monument (built on site of founding of triumverate government) centennial.

British Troops in Battle of Amajuba — A219

**1981, Feb. 27 Litho. *Perf. 14x14½***
**544** A219 5c Boer snipers, vert. .20 .20
**545** A219 15c shown .35 .30

Battle of Amajuba centenary (led to independence of Orange Free State).

Scene from Verdi's Aida A220

**1981, May 23 Litho. *Perf. 14½x14***
**546** A220 20c Raka ballet scene .35 .30
**547** A220 25c shown .45 .35
*a.* Souvenir sheet of 2, #546-547 1.00 .80

Opening of State Theater, Pretoria.

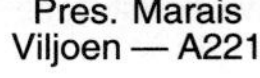

Pres. Marais Viljoen — A221

Deaf Girl Learning to Speak — A222

**1981, May 30** *Perf. 14x14½*
**Size: 57x21mm**
**548** A221 5c Former presidents .20 .20
**549** A221 15c shown .30 .25

**1981, June 12** *Perf. 14½x14*
**550** A222 5c shown .20 .20
**551** A222 15c Man reading braille .30 .25

Institute for the Deaf and Blind, Worcester, centenary.

Natl. Cancer Assn. 50th Anniv. — A223

**1981, July 10**
**552** A223 5c multicolored .20 .20

Calanthe Natalensis A224

Voortrekker Movement, 50th Anniv. A225

**1981, Sept. 11** **Litho.**
**553** A224 5c shown .20 .20
**554** A224 15c Eulophia speciosa .30 .25
**555** A224 20c Disperis fanniniae .40 .30
**556** A224 25c Disa uniflora .50 .40
*a.* Souvenir sheet of 4, #553-556 2.50 2.25
*Nos. 553-556 (4)* 1.40 1.15

10th World Orchid Conf., Durban, 9/11-17.

**1981, Sept. 30** *Perf. 14x14½*
**557** A225 5c multicolored .20 .20

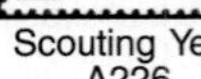
Scouting Year A226

TB Bacillus Centenary A227

**1982, Feb. 22** **Litho.** *Perf. 14½x14*
**558** A226 15c Baden-Powell .30 .25

**1982, Mar. 24** **Litho.**
**559** A227 20c multicolored .30 .25

Return of Simonstown Naval Base, 25th Anniv. — A228

**1982, Apr. 2** *Perf. 14½x14*
**560** A228 8c Submarine .20 .20
**561** A228 15c Strike craft .25 .20
**562** A228 20c Mine sweeper .35 .30
**563** A228 25c Harbor patrol boats .45 .35
*a.* Souvenir sheet of 4, #560-563 2.25 1.90
*Nos. 560-563 (4)* 1.25 1.05

Old Provost, Grahamstown A229

Design: 2c, Tuynhuys, Kaapstad (Cape Town). 3c, Appelhof, Bloemfontein. 4c, Raadsaal, Pretoria. 5c, Die Kasteel, Kaapstad. 6c, Goewermentsgebou, Bloemfontein. 7c, Drostdy, Graaf-Reinet. 8c, Leeuwenhof, Cape Town. 9c, Libertas, Pretoria. 10c, City Hall, Pietermaritzburg. 11c, City Hall, Kimberley. 12c, City Hall, Port Elizabeth. 14c, Johannesburg City Hall. 15c, Hotel Milner, Matjesfontein. 16c, Durban City Hall. 20c, Post Office, Durban. 25c, Melrose House, Pretoria. 30c, Old Legislative Assembly Building, Pietermaritzburg. 50c, Raadsaal, Bloemfontein. 1r, Houses of Parliament, Cape Town. 2r, Uniegebou, Pretoria.

Coils have different designs.

**1982-87** **Litho.** *Perf. 14x14½*
**564** A229 1c brown ('84) .20 .20
**565** A229 2c apple green .20 .20
**566** A229 2c green .75 .20
**567** A229 2c slate grn ('85) .20 .20
**568** A229 3c purple ('85) 1.25 .20
**569** A229 4c olive grn ('85) .20 .20
**570** A229 5c carmine .20 .20
**571** A229 6c brt green .20 .20
**572** A229 7c gray green .20 .20
**573** A229 8c blue .20 .20
**574** A229 8c intense bl ('83) .20 .20
**575** A229 9c brt rose lilac .20 .20
**576** A229 10c lt red brown .20 .20
**577** A229 10c violet brn ('83) .30 .20
**578** A229 11c cerise ('84) .25 .20
**579** A229 12c dp ultra ('85) .35 .20
**580** A229 14c rose brn ('86) .50 .20
**581** A229 16c red ('87) .60 .20
**582** A229 20c vermilion .25 .20
**583** A229 20c black ('85) .60 .20
**584** A229 25c bister .25 .20

**Size: 45x27mm**
*Perf. 14½x14*
**586** A229 30c brown ('86) 1.50 .20
**587** A229 50c Prus blue ('86) 2.25 .20
**588** A229 1r violet blue ('86) 2.50 .20
**589** A229 2r cerise ('85) 5.00 .20
*Nos. 564-589 (25)* 18.55 5.00

For surcharge see No. B12.

**Engr.**
**590** A229 1c dark brown .20 .20
**591** A229 2c slate grn ('83) .20 .20
**592** A229 3c violet .20 .20
**593** A229 4c olive green .20 .20
**594** A229 5c dark lake ('83) .20 .20
**595** A229 6c green blk ('84) .20 .35
**596** A229 15c blue .20 .20
**597** A229 20c black ('83) .50 .20
**598** A229 30c violet brown .45 .25
**599** A229 50c Prus blue .70 .25
**600** A229 1r violet blue 1.50 .20
**601** A229 2r rose carmine 3.00 .30
*Nos. 590-601 (12)* 7.55 2.75

In some cases there are slight design differences from litho. stamp.

*Perf. 14 Horiz.*
**Photo.** **Coil Stamps**
**602** A229 1c Residence, Swellendam .20 .20
**603** A229 2c City Hall, East London .25 .20
**604** A229 5c Rissik St. PO, Johannesburg .30 .20
**605** A229 10c Morgenster, Somerset West .40 .20
*Nos. 602-605 (4)* 1.15 .80

Bradysaurus A230

Prehistoric Animals (Karoo Fossils).

**1982, Dec. 1** **Litho.** *Perf. 14x14½*
**606** A230 8c shown .30 .20
**607** A230 15c Lystrosaurus .60 .20
**608** A230 20c Euparkeria .80 .25
**609** A230 25c Thrinaxodon 1.00 .35
*a.* Souvenir sheet of 4, #606-609 3.00 3.00
*Nos. 606-609 (4)* 2.70 1.00

Weather Station, Gough Island A231

**1983, Jan. 19** **Litho.**
**610** A231 8c shown .20 .20
**611** A231 20c Marion Isld. station .30 .25
**612** A231 25c Reading instruments .40 .30
**613** A231 40c Weather balloon, Antarctica .65 .50
*Nos. 610-613 (4)* 1.55 1.25

Steam Locomotives — A232

**1983, Apr. 27** **Litho.**
**614** A232 10c Class 82, 1952 .25 .20
**615** A232 20c Class 16E, 1935 .45 .35
**616** A232 25c Class 6H, 1901 .55 .45
**617** A232 40c Class 15F, 1939 .95 .70
*Nos. 614-617 (4)* 2.20 1.70

Soccer — A233

***Perf. 14½x14 (10c, 25c), 14x14½ (20c, 40c)***

**1983, July 20** **Litho.**
**618** A233 10c Rugby, vert. .20 .20
**619** A233 20c shown .35 .25
**620** A233 25c Sailing, vert. .45 .30
**621** A233 40c Equestrian .65 .50
*Nos. 618-621 (4)* 1.65 1.25

Plettenberg Bay — A234

**1983, Oct. 12** **Litho.** *Perf. 14½x14*
**622** A234 10c shown .20 .20
**623** A234 20c Durban Beach .30 .20
**624** A234 25c West Coast beach .40 .25
**625** A234 40c Clifton beach scene .65 .45
*a.* Souvenir sheet of 4, #622-625 1.75 1.25
*Nos. 622-625 (4)* 1.55 1.10

English Writers of South Africa — A235

Designs: 10c, Thomas Pringle (1789-1834). 20c, Pauline Smith (1882-1959). 25c, Olive Schreiner (1855-1920). 40c, Percy FitzPatrick (1862-1931).

**1984, Feb. 24** **Litho.** *Perf. 14½x14*
**626** A235 10c multicolored .20 .20
**627** A235 20c multicolored .25 .20
**628** A235 25c multicolored .35 .25
**629** A235 40c multicolored .60 .35
*Nos. 626-629 (4)* 1.40 1.00

Manganese — A236

**1984, June 8** **Litho.** *Perf. 14x14½*
**630** A236 11c shown .25 .20
**631** A236 20c Chromium .45 .25
**632** A236 25c Vanadium .60 .30
**633** A236 30c Titanium .70 .35
*Nos. 630-633 (4)* 2.00 1.10

Bloukrans River Bridge A237

**1984, Aug. 24**
**634** A237 11c shown .20 .20
**635** A237 25c Durban 4-level Bridge Interchange .45 .25
**636** A237 30c Mfolozi Railroad Bridge .55 .30
**637** A237 45c Gouritz River Bridge .80 .45
*Nos. 634-637 (4)* 2.00 1.20

New Constitution A238

Military Medals A239

**1984, Sept. 3** **Litho.** *Perf. 14x14½*
**638** A238 11c Preamble (English) .30 .20
**639** A238 11c Preamble (Afrikaans) .30 .20
*a.* Pair, #638-639 .60 .35
**640** A238 25c Symbolic pillars, anthem .65 .35
**641** A238 30c Arms .75 .40
*Nos. 638-641 (4)* 2.00 1.15

**1984, Nov. 9** *Perf. 14½x14*
**642** A239 11c Pro Patria .20 .20
**643** A239 25c De Wet .40 .25
**644** A239 30c John Chard Decoration .50 .30
**645** A239 45c Honoris Crux .70 .45
*a.* Miniature sheet of 4, #642-645 2.00 1.25
*Nos. 642-645 (4)* 1.80 1.20

Pres. Pieter Willem Botha (b. 1916) — A240

**1984, Nov. 2** **Litho.** *Perf. 14x14½*
**646** A240 11c multicolored .20 .20
**647** A240 25c multicolored .40 .25

Frans David Oerder, Painter (1867-1944) A241

**1985, Feb. 22** **Litho.** *Perf. 14½x14*
**648** A241 11c Reflections .20 .20
**649** A241 25c Ladies in a Garden .40 .25
**650** A241 30c Still-Life with Lobster .50 .30

651 A241 50c Still-Life with Marigolds .80 .45
a. Souvenir sheet of 4, #648-651 2.00 2.00
*Nos. 648-651 (4)* 1.90 1.20

Cape Parliament Cent. A242

**1985, May 15** **Litho.**
652 A242 12c Parliament .20 .20
653 A242 25c Speaker's chair .35 .25
654 A242 30c The National Convention, by Edward Roworth .40 .30
655 A242 50c South African arms .70 .40
*Nos. 652-655 (4)* 1.65 1.15

Indigenous Flowers A243

Cape Silver A244

**1985, Aug. 23** **Litho.** ***Perf. 14½x14***
656 A243 12c Freesia .20 .20
657 A243 25c Nerine .65 .45
658 A243 30c Ixia .75 .50
659 A243 50c Gladiolus 1.40 .90
*Nos. 656-659 (4)* 3.00 2.05

**1985, Nov. 5** ***Perf. 14½x14, 14x14½***
660 A244 12c Sugar bowl, horiz. .20 .20
661 A244 25c Tea pot, horiz. .40 .20
662 A244 30c Goblet .45 .25
663 A244 50c Coffee pot .75 .40
*Nos. 660-663 (4)* 1.80 1.05

Blood Transfusion Services A245

**1986, Feb. 20** ***Perf. 14½x14***
664 A245 12c Blood donation .20 .20
665 A245 20c Transfusion .35 .20
666 A245 25c Surgery .45 .20
667 A245 30c Emergency aid .55 .25
*Nos. 664-667 (4)* 1.55 .85

Republic of South Africa, 25th Anniv. A246

**1986, May 30** **Litho.** ***Perf. 14x14½***
668 A246 14c Text in Afrikaans .25 .20
669 A246 14c Text in English .25 .20
a. Pair, #668-669 .50 .50

Cultural Heritage — A247

Restoration projects: 14c, Drostdyhof, Free Street, Graaff-Reinet, 19th cent. 20c, Pilgrim's Rest, Eastern Transvaal, 1873. 25c, J.T. Strapp and Son importers, c. 1893, Bethlehem. 30c, Palmdene, c. 1897, Pietermaritzburg.

**1986, Aug. 14** ***Perf. 14½x14***
670 A247 14c multicolored .25 .20
671 A247 20c multicolored .35 .25
672 A247 25c multicolored .40 .30
673 A247 30c multicolored .50 .35
*Nos. 670-673 (4)* 1.50 1.10

Johannesburg, Cent. — A248

Discovery of Gold in Roodepoort, Cent. — A249

**1986, Sept. 25** ***Perf. 14x14½***
674 A248 14c Johannesburg, 1886 .25 .20
675 A249 20c Gold mine .35 .25
676 A248 25c Johannesburg, 1986 .40 .30
677 A249 30c Gold .50 .35
a. Souvenir sheet of 1 2.50 2.50
*Nos. 674-677 (4)* 1.50 1.10

No. 677a for Johannesburg stamp exhibition. Sold for 50c.

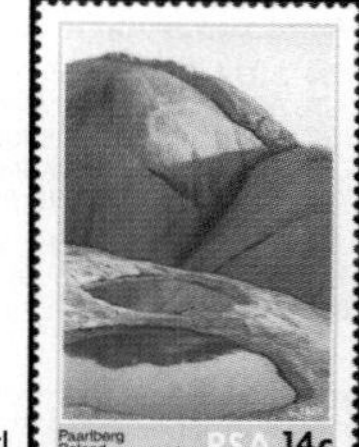

Pearl Mountain — A250

Beetles — A251

**1986, Nov. 20** **Litho.** ***Perf. 14x14½***
678 A250 14c shown .25 .25
679 A250 20c The Column, Drakensburg .35 .35
680 A250 25c Maltese Cross, Cedarberg .45 .45
681 A250 30c Bourke's Luck Potholes .55 .55
*Nos. 678-681 (4)* 1.60 1.60

**1987, Mar. 6** **Litho.** ***Perf. 14x14½***
690 A251 14c *Chaetodera regalis* .25 .25
691 A251 20c *Trichostetha fascicularis* .40 .40
692 A251 25c *Julodis viridipes* .50 .50
693 A251 30c *Ceroplesis militaris* .60 .60
*Nos. 690-693 (4)* 1.75 1.75

Petroglyphs A252

**1987, June 4** ***Perf. 14½x14***
694 A252 16c Eland, Sebaaieni Cave .30 .30
695 A252 20c Leaping lion, Clocolan .40 .40
696 A252 25c Black wildebeest, uMhlwazini Valley .50 .50
697 A252 30c San dance, Floukraal .60 .60
*Nos. 694-697 (4)* 1.80 1.80

Paarl, 300th Anniv. A253

**1987, Sept. 3**
698 A253 16c Oude Pastorie .30 .30
699 A253 20c Winegrowing .40 .40
700 A253 25c Wagon-building .50 .50
701 A253 30c KWV Cathedral Cellar .60 .60
*Nos. 698-701 (4)* 1.80 1.80

A souvenir sheet of one, No. 701, has decorative margin picturing emblem of the natl. philatelic exhibition at Paarl, Sept. 16-19. Sold for 50c.

Map, "The Bible" in 76 Languages — A254

Religious Paintings by Rembrandt A255

Designs: 30c, *Belshazzar's Feast.* 50c, *St. Matthew and the Angel,* vert.

***Perf. 14x14½, 14½x14 (30c)***
**1987, Nov. 19**
702 A254 16c shown .30 .30
703 A255 30c shown .60 .60
704 A255 50c multicolored 1.00 1.00
*Nos. 702-704 (3)* 1.90 1.90

Bible Society of South Africa.

A 40c stamp was prepared and sent to post offices, but was not issued. Some were sold contrary to the withdrawal order, and used examples are known.

For surcharge see No. B13.

Discovery of the Cape of Good Hope by Bartolomeu Dias — A256

Designs: 16c, Dias, astrolabe, Cape of Good Hope. 30c, Kwaaihoek Memorial. 40c, Caravels, 1488. 50c, Martellus Map, c. 1489.

**1988, Feb. 3** ***Perf. 14½x14***
706 A256 16c multicolored .30 .30
707 A256 30c multicolored .55 .55
708 A256 40c multicolored .75 .75
709 A256 50c multicolored .95 .95
*Nos. 706-709 (4)* 2.55 2.55

A souvenir sheet of one, No. 709, has decorative margin picturing emblem of the natl. philatelic exhibition held at Pietermaritzburg, Nov. 22-27. Sold for 70c.

For surcharge see No. B14 .

French Huguenot Settlement of the Cape, 300th Anniv. — A257

**1988, Apr. 13** ***Perf. 14x14½***
710 A257 16c Memorial, Franschhoek .35 .35
711 A257 30c Map of France .60 .60
712 A257 40c French-Dutch Bible, 1672 .80 .80
713 A257 50c St. Bartholomew's Day Massacre, 1572 1.00 1.00
*Nos. 710-713 (4)* 2.75 2.75

For surcharges see Nos. B15-B18 .

Lighthouses A258

**1988, June 9** ***Perf. 14½x14***
714 A258 16c Pelican Point, 1932 .30 .30
715 A258 30c Groenpunt, 1824 .55 .55
716 A258 40c Agulhas, 1849 .75 .75
717 A258 50c Umhlanga Rocks, 1954 .95 .95
a. Souvenir sheet of 4, #714-717 3.50 3.50
*Nos. 714-717 (4)* 2.55 2.55

**"Standardised Mail"**
**"STANDARD POSTAGE"**
**Stamps inscribed thus were sold for the amount shown in ( ) on date of issue.**

Succulents A259

**1988-93** **Litho.** ***Perf. 14x14½***
735 A259 1c *Huernia zebrina* .20 .20
736 A259 2c *Euphorbia symmetrica* .20 .20
737 A259 5c *Lithops dorotheae* .20 .20
738 A259 7c *Gibbaeum newbrownii* .20 .20
739 A259 10c *Didymaotus lapidiformis* .20 .20
740 A259 16c *Vanheerdea divergens* .20 .20
741 A259 18c *Faucaria tigrina* .20 .20
742 A259 20c *Conophytum mundum* .20 .20
743 A259 21c *Gasteria armstrongii* .20 .20
744 A259 25c *Cheiridopsis pecularis* .20 .20
745 A259 30c *Tavaresia barklyi* .20 .20
a. Strip, 2 ea 1c, 2c, 5c, 7c, 30c 6.00
746 A259 35c *Dinteranthus wilmotianus* .25 .20
747 A259 40c *Frithia pulchra* .30 .20
748 A259 (45c) *Stapelia grandiflora* .30 .20
749 A259 50c *Lapidaria margaretae* .35 .35
750 A259 90c *Dioscorea elephantipes* .65 .40
751 A259 1r *Trichocaulon cactiforme* .70 .55
752 A259 2r *Crassula columnaris* 1.40 .75
753 A259 5r *Anacampseros albissima* 5.25 2.00
*Nos. 735-753 (19)* 11.40 6.85

**Coil Stamps**
**Photo.**
***Perf. 14 Horiz.***
754 A259 1c *Adromischus marianiae* 1.00 1.00
755 A259 2c *Titanopsis calcarea* .25 .25
756 A259 5c *Dactylopsis digitata* .25 .25
757 A259 10c *Pleiospilos bolusii* .50 .50
*Nos. 754-757 (4)* 2.00 2.00

Issued: 18c, 4/1/89; 5r, 3/1/90; 21c, 4/2/90; #748, 4/1/93; others, 9/1/88.

Map and Settlers — A260

*Exodus,* Tapestry by W.H. Coetzer Studio — A261

*Crossing the Drakensburg,* Tapestry by Coetzer Studio (illustration reduced) — A262

Church of the Vow, Pietermaritzburg — A263

***Perf. 14x14½, 14½x14 (50c)***

**1988, Nov. 21** **Litho.**

| | | | | |
|---|---|---|---|---|
| **758** | A260 | 16c multicolored | .40 | .25 |
| **759** | A261 | 30c multicolored | .70 | .45 |
| **760** | A262 | 40c multicolored | .95 | .60 |
| **761** | A263 | 50c multicolored | 1.10 | .75 |
| | | *Nos. 758-761 (4)* | 3.15 | 2.05 |

The Great Trek, 150th anniv.

Discovery of a Living Specimen of the Coelacanth, 50th Anniv. A264

Designs: 16c, *Latimeria chalumnae.* 30c, J. L. B. Smith, Margaret Courtenay-Latimer. 40c, Smith Institute of Ichthyology, Grahamstown. 50c, Fish, GEO two-man research submarine.

**1989, Feb. 9** ***Perf. 14½x14***

| | | | | |
|---|---|---|---|---|
| **762** | A264 | 16c multicolored | .30 | .30 |
| **763** | A264 | 30c multicolored | .55 | .55 |
| **764** | A264 | 40c multicolored | .75 | .75 |
| **765** | A264 | 50c multicolored | .95 | .95 |
| ***a.*** | | Souvenir sheet of 1 | 4.50 | 4.50 |
| ***b.*** | | Souvenir sheet of 2 | .55 | .55 |
| | | *Nos. 762-765 (4)* | 2.55 | 2.55 |

No. 765a has decorative margin picturing emblem of the natl. philatelic exhibition WANDERERS 101, held Sept. 6-9. Sold for 1.50r.

No. 765b was issued 6/97, sold for 1r and is inscribed for Old Mutual Environmental Education Center in sheet margin.

Soil Conservation Campaign of the Natl. Grazing Strategy — A265

**1989, May 3** ***Perf. 14x14½***

| | | | | |
|---|---|---|---|---|
| **766** | A265 | 18c Desertification | .35 | .35 |
| **767** | A265 | 30c Eroded gullies | .55 | .55 |
| **768** | A265 | 40c Barrage | .75 | .75 |
| **769** | A265 | 50c Verdant plain | .95 | .95 |
| | | *Nos. 766-769 (4)* | 2.60 | 2.60 |

Natl. Rugby Board, Cent. A266

Springboks, foreign team emblems, match scenes.

**1989, June 22**

| | | | | |
|---|---|---|---|---|
| **770** | A266 | 18c France, 1980 | .30 | .25 |
| **771** | A266 | 30c Australia, 1963 | .55 | .45 |
| **772** | A266 | 40c New Zealand, 1937 | .75 | .60 |
| **773** | A266 | 50c British Isles, 1896 | .90 | .75 |
| | | *Nos. 770-773 (4)* | 2.50 | 2.05 |

Paintings by Jacob Hendrik Pierneef (1886-1957) A267

**1989, Aug. 3** ***Perf. 14½x14***

| | | | | |
|---|---|---|---|---|
| **774** | A267 | 18c *Composition in Blue,* 1928 | .30 | .20 |
| **775** | A267 | 30c *Zanzibar,* 1926 | .55 | .25 |
| **776** | A267 | 40c *The Bushveld,* 1949 | .75 | .30 |
| **777** | A267 | 50c *Cape Homestead,* 1942 | .90 | .40 |
| ***a.*** | | Souvenir sheet of 4, #774-777 | 2.75 | 2.75 |
| | | *Nos. 774-777 (4)* | 2.50 | 1.15 |

Election of Pres. Frederik Willem de Klerk, Aug. 15 — A268

**1989, Sept. 20** ***Perf. 14x14½***

| | | | | |
|---|---|---|---|---|
| **778** | A268 | 18c shown | .35 | .20 |
| **779** | A268 | 45c Portrait, diff. | .90 | .50 |

Fossil Fuels, Nuclear and Thermal Power A269

18c, SOEKOR gas project, Mossel Bay. 30c, SASOL coal conversion plant. 40c, Koeberg nuclear power plant. 50c, ESKOM thermal power station.

**1989, Oct. 19**

| | | | | |
|---|---|---|---|---|
| **780** | A269 | 18c multicolored | .25 | .20 |
| **781** | A269 | 30c multicolored | .45 | .30 |
| **782** | A269 | 40c multicolored | .55 | .35 |
| **783** | A269 | 50c multicolored | .75 | .45 |
| | | *Nos. 780-783 (4)* | 2.00 | 1.30 |

Cooperation in Southern Africa — A270

Maps and: 18c, Cahora Bassa hydroelectric power project. 30c, Railway network. 40c, Lesotho Highlands water project. 50c, Veterinary care.

**1990, Feb. 15** ***Perf. 14½x14***

**Size of 18c, 40c: 68x26mm**

| | | | | |
|---|---|---|---|---|
| **784** | A270 | 18c multicolored | .30 | .25 |
| **785** | A270 | 30c multicolored | .55 | .40 |
| **786** | A270 | 40c multicolored | .70 | .50 |
| **787** | A270 | 50c multicolored | .90 | .65 |
| ***a.*** | | Miniature sheet of 4, #784-787 | 2.50 | 2.50 |
| | | *Nos. 784-787 (4)* | 2.45 | 1.80 |

Stamp Day — A271

Birds — A272

Stamps on stamps: a, Great Britain #1. b, Cape of Good Hope #2. c, Natal #4. d, Orange River Colony #10. e, Transvaal #3.

**1990, May 12** **Litho.**

| | | | | |
|---|---|---|---|---|
| **788** | | Strip of 5 | 1.90 | 1.90 |
| ***a.-e.*** | | A271 21c any single | .35 | .35 |

Penny Black, 150th anniv.

**1990, Aug. 2** **Litho.** ***Perf. 14x14½***

Designs: 21c, *Tauraco corythaix.* 35c, *Cossypha natalensis.* 40c, *Mirafra africana.* 50c, *Telophorus zeylonus.*

| | | | | |
|---|---|---|---|---|
| **789** | A272 | 21c multicolored | .40 | .25 |
| **790** | A272 | 35c multicolored | .65 | .45 |
| **791** | A272 | 40c multicolored | .75 | .50 |
| **792** | A272 | 50c multicolored | .95 | .60 |
| | | *Nos. 789-792 (4)* | 2.75 | 1.80 |

A souvenir sheet of 1 #792 was sold by the Philatelic Foundation of South Africa. Value $3.50.

Karoo Landscape, Near Britstown A273

Tourism: #794, Camps Bay, Cape Peninsula. #795, Giraffes, Kruger Natl. Park. #796, Boschendal homestead, Drakenstein.

**1990, Nov. 1** **Litho.** ***Perf. 14½x14***

| | | | | |
|---|---|---|---|---|
| **793** | A273 | 50c multicolored | .60 | .60 |
| **794** | A273 | 50c multicolored | .60 | .60 |
| **795** | A273 | 50c multicolored | .60 | .60 |
| **796** | A273 | 50c multicolored | .60 | .60 |
| ***a.*** | | Block of 4, #793-796 | 2.50 | 2.50 |

A274

A275

National Decorations: No. 797, Woltemade Cross for Bravery. No. 798, Order of the Southern Cross. No. 799, Order of the Star of South Africa. No. 800, Order for Meritorious Service. No. 801, Order of Good Hope.

**1990, Dec. 6**

| | | | | |
|---|---|---|---|---|
| **797** | A274 | 21c multicolored | .30 | .25 |
| **798** | A274 | 21c multicolored | .30 | .25 |
| **799** | A274 | 21c multicolored | .30 | .25 |
| **800** | A274 | 21c multicolored | .30 | .25 |
| **801** | A274 | 21c multicolored | .30 | .25 |
| ***a.*** | | Souv. sheet of 5, #797-801 | 1.50 | 1.50 |
| ***b.*** | | Strip of 5, #797-801 | 1.50 | 1.50 |

**1991, Feb. 21** **Litho.**

Animal Breeding: a, Boer horse. b, Bonsmara cattle. c, Dorper sheep. d, Ridgeback dog. e, Putterie racing pigeon.

| | | | | |
|---|---|---|---|---|
| **802** | A275 | 21c Strip of 5, #a.-e. | 1.90 | 1.25 |

Achievements — A276

Designs: 25c, First heart transplant, vert. 40c, Matimba power plant. 50c, Dolos breakwater blocks. 60c, Western Deep Levels Gold Mine, world's deepest mine, vert.

***Perf. 14½x14 (25c, 60c), 14x14½ (40c, 50c, #806a)***

**1991, May 30** **Litho.**

| | | | | |
|---|---|---|---|---|
| **803** | A276 | 25c multicolored | .30 | .20 |
| **804** | A276 | 40c multicolored | .50 | .25 |
| **805** | A276 | 50c multicolored | .60 | .30 |
| **806** | A276 | 60c multicolored | .45 | .35 |
| ***a.*** | | Souvenir sheet of 1 | 2.00 | 2.00 |
| | | *Nos. 803-806 (4)* | 1.85 | 1.10 |

30th anniv. of Republic of South Africa.

1st Registration of Nurses & Midwives, Cent. — A277

**1991, Aug. 15** **Litho.** ***Perf. 14x14½***

| | | | | |
|---|---|---|---|---|
| **807** | A277 | 60c multicolored | .75 | .75 |

Creation of South African Post Office Ltd. — A278

**1991, Oct. 1** **Litho.**

| | | | | |
|---|---|---|---|---|
| **808** | | 27c Post office | .30 | .20 |
| **809** | | 27c Telkom SA Ltd. | .30 | .20 |
| ***a.*** | A278 | Pair, #808-809 | .60 | .60 |

South African Scientists A279

Designs: 27c, Sir Arnold Theiler (1867-1936), veterinarian. 45c, Sir Basil Schonland (1896-1972), physicist. 65c, Dr. Robert Broom (1866-1951), paleontologist. 85c, Dr. Alexander L. du Toit (1878-1948), geologist.

**1991, Oct. 9** ***Perf. 14½x14***

| | | | | |
|---|---|---|---|---|
| **810** | A279 | 27c multicolored | .30 | .20 |
| **811** | A279 | 45c multicolored | .50 | .30 |
| **812** | A279 | 65c multicolored | .75 | .40 |
| **813** | A279 | 85c multicolored | .95 | .50 |
| | | *Nos. 810-813 (4)* | 2.50 | 1.40 |

Antarctic Treaty, 30th Anniv. A280

**1991, Dec. 5 Litho.**

814 A280 27c SA Agulhas, penguins .35 .20
815 A280 65c Meteorological chart .90 .40

Conservation — A281

**1992, Feb. 6 Litho. *Perf. 14x14½***

816 A281 27c Prevent erosion .25 .20
817 A281 65c Water pollution .65 .40
818 A281 85c Air pollution .85 .50
*Nos. 816-818 (3)* 1.75 1.10

A souvenir sheet of 1 #817 was sold by Intersapa.

A282

A283

Designs depicting history of postal stones: No. 819, Sailing ships at Table Bay. No. 820, Sailors going ashore at Aguada de Saldanha. No. 821, Sailors discovering postal stone near Versse River. No. 822, Finding letters under postal stones. No. 823, Reading news from other mariners.

**1992, May 9 Litho. *Perf. 14x14½***

819 A282 35c multicolored .35 .30
820 A282 35c multicolored .35 .30
821 A282 35c multicolored .35 .30
822 A282 35c multicolored .35 .30
823 A282 35c multicolored .35 .30
*a.* Strip of 5, #819-823 1.90 1.90

Stamp Day.

***Perf. 14½x14, 14x14½***

**1992, July 9 Litho.**

Antique Cape Furniture: No. 824, Queen Anne settee, c. 1750-70. No. 825, Stinkwood settee, c. 1800. No. 826, Canopy bed, c. 1800, vert. No. 827, Rocking cradle, 19th cent. No. 828, Waterbutt, c. 1800, vert. No. 829, Flemish style cabinet, c. 1700, vert. No. 830, Armoire, c. 1780-1790, vert. No. 831, Church chair, late 17th cent, vert. No. 832, Tub chair, c. 1770-1790, vert. No. 833, Bible desk, c. 1770, vert.

824 A283 35c multicolored .35 .30
825 A283 35c multicolored .35 .30
826 A283 35c multicolored .35 .30
827 A283 35c multicolored .35 .30
828 A283 35c multicolored .35 .30
829 A283 35c multicolored .35 .30
830 A283 35c multicolored .35 .30
831 A283 35c multicolored .35 .30
832 A283 35c multicolored .35 .30
833 A283 35c multicolored .35 .30
*a.* Miniature sheet of 10, #824-833 3.50

Sports A284

**1992, July 24 *Perf. 14x14½***

834 A284 35c Formula 1 Grand Prix .35 .30
835 A284 35c Soccer .35 .30
836 A284 55c Paris-le Cap Rally .55 .45
837 A284 70c Track .65 .55
838 A284 90c Rugby .85 .75
839 A284 1.05r Cricket 1.00 .85
*a.* Souvenir sheet of 6, #834-839 3.75 3.75
*Nos. 834-839 (6)* 3.75 3.20

A285

A286

**1992, Oct. 8 Litho. *Perf. 14½x14***

840 A285 35c Women's Monument .30 .30
841 A285 70c Sekupu Player .70 .55
842 A285 90c The Hunter .90 .75
843 A285 1.05r Postman Lehman 1.10 .85
*a.* Souvenir sheet of 4, #840-843 3.00 3.00
*Nos. 840-843 (4)* 3.00 2.45

Sculptures by Anton van Wouw (1862-1945). No. 843a sold for 3.30r.

**1993, Jan. 28 Litho.**

South African Harbors.

844 A286 35c Walvis Bay .30 .25
845 A286 55c East London .50 .35
846 A286 70c Port Elizabeth .65 .45
847 A286 90c Cape Town .80 .60
848 A286 1.05r Durban 1.00 .70
*a.* Souv. sheet, #844-848 + label 3.25 3.25
*Nos. 844-848 (5)* 3.25 2.35

No. 848a sold for 3.90r.

A287

A288

Aircraft: a, Bristol Boxkite, 1907. b, Voisin, 1909. c, Bleriot XI, 1911. d, Paterson No. 2 biplane, 1913. e, Henri Farman F.27, 1915. f, BE2e, 1918. g, Vickers Vimy Silver Queen, 1920. h, SE-5a, 1921. i, Avro 504K, 1921. j, Armstrong-Whitworth Atalanta, 1930. k, DH66 Hercules, 1931. l, Westland Wapiti, 1931. m, Junkers F.13, 1932. n, Handley Page HP-42, 1933. o, Junkers Ju52/3m, 1934. p, Junkers Ju86, 1936. q, Hawker Hartbees, 1936. r, Short Empire flying boat Canopus, 1937. s, Miles Master II and Airspeed AS-10 Oxford, 1940. t, Harvard Mk IIa, 1942. u, Short Sunderland, 1945. v, Avro York, 1946. w, Douglas DC-7B, 1955. x, Sikorsky S-55C, 1956. y, Boeing 707-344, 1959.

**1993, May 7 Litho. *Perf. 14x14½***
**Miniature Sheet of 25**

849 A287 45c #a.-y. 10.00

A souvenir sheet containing #849a, 849y was sold by the Philatelic Foundation of South Africa.

**1993-95 Litho. *Perf. 14x14½,***

Endangered Fauna: 1c, Heleophryne rosei. 2c, Bradypodion taeniabronchum. 5c, Cordylus giganteus. 10c, Psammobates geometricus. 20c, Atelerix frontalis. 40c, Bunolagus monticularis. #856, Diceros bicornis. #856A, "Black Rhinocerous." 50c, Cercopithecus mitis. 55c, Proteles cristatus. 60c, Lycaon pictus. 70c, Hippotragus equinus. 75c, Poecilogale albinucha. 80c, Otis kori. 85c, Serinus citrinipectus. 90c, Spheniscus demersus. 1r, Grus carunculatus. 2r, Hirundo atrocaerulea. 5r, Polemaetus bellicosus. 10r, Terathopius ecaudatus.

**Inscriptions in Latin**

850 A288 1c multicolored .20 .20
851 A288 2c multicolored .20 .20
852 A288 5c multicolored .20 .20
853 A288 10c multicolored .20 .20
854 A288 20c multicolored .20 .20
*a.* Strip, 1c, 2 ea 2c, 20c .50
*b.* Strip, 20c, 2 ea 5c, 10c .50
*c.* Strip, 20c, 2 each 5c, 10c, perf. 14½ vert. .50
855 A288 40c multicolored .25 .20
856 A288 (45c) multicolored .30 .20
857 A288 50c multicolored .30 .20
*a.* Strip, #850, 852, 857, 2 #851, Perf. 14½ Vert. 1.00
858 A288 55c multicolored .30 .20
859 A288 60c multicolored .35 .20
860 A288 70c multicolored .40 .20
861 A288 75c multicolored .45 .20
862 A288 80c multicolored .50 .20
862A A288 85c multicolored .50 .30
863 A288 90c multicolored .55 .20
*a.* Booklet pane of 10 — —
Complete booklet, #863a —
864 A288 1r multicolored .60 .20
865 A288 2r multicolored 1.25 .20
866 A288 5r multicolored 3.00 .50
867 A288 10r multicolored 6.00 1.50
*Nos. 850-867 (19)* 15.75 5.50

#857a exists with tab showing Reader's Digest emblem in either red or black; also in different order with emblem in blue.

Issued: #854b, 8/24/94; #854c, 10/94; #857a, 9/1/95; 85c, 10/2/95; #863a, 1995; others, 9/3/93.

See designs A336 and A343 (no frames).

**Wildlife Type with English Inscriptions**

Designs: 1c, Table Mountain ghost frog. 2c, Smith's dwarf chameleon. 10c, Geometric tortoise. 20c, Southern African hedgehog. 40c, Riverine rabbit. (45c), Black rhinoceros. 50c, Samango monkey. 60c, Cape hunting dog. 70c, Roan antelope. 90c, Jackass penguin. 1r, Wattled crane. 2r, Blue swallow. 5r, Martial eagle. 20r, Fish Eagle.

***Perf. 14x14¼, 14 Vert. on 1 or 2 sides (1c, 2c, 10c, 55c), 13x14½ (#867F)***

**1996-98 Litho.**

867A A288 1c multicolored .20 .20
867B A288 2c multicolored .20 .20
867C A288 10c multicolored .20 .20
867D A288 20c multicolored .20 .20
867E A288 40c multicolored .20 .20
867F A288 (45c) multicolored .40 .25
*n.* Booklet pane of 10 3.00
Complete booklet, #867Fn 3.00
*o.* Souvenir sheet of 1 .55 .55
867G A288 50c multicolored .20 .20
867H A288 55c multicolored .50 .50
*p.* Strip of 5, 1c, 10c, 55c, 2 2c 1.00
867I A288 70c multicolored .25 .20
867J A288 90c multicolored .35 .20
867K A288 1r multicolored .35 .20
867L A288 2r multicolored .75 .20
867M A288 5r multicolored 1.75 .85

***Perf. 14x14¼ Syncopated***

867Q A288 20c multicolored .20 .20
867R A288 (45c) multicolored .50 .40
867S A288 50c multicolored .40 .25
867T A288 60c multicolored .25 .20
867U A288 1r multicolored 2.75 .25

**Size: 34x25mm**

***Perf. 14¾ Syncopated***

867V A288 20r multicolored 7.00 3.50

No. 867Fn is inscribed in sheet margin for ExpoScience Internationale '97, and sold for 1r.

No. 867Hp has tab showing Reader's Digest emblem and release date in either green or orange.

Issued: #867Hp, 8/1; #867F, 7/7/97.

First Postal Services in South Africa, 190th Anniv. A289

Designs: 45c, Dragoons, Cape Town-False Bay Route. 65c, Ox train, Cape Town-Stellenbosch. 85c, Khoi-Khoin runners. 1.05r, Post riders, Cape Town-eastern districts.

**1993, Oct. 8 *Perf. 14x14½***

868 A289 45c multicolored .30 .30
869 A289 65c multicolored .45 .40
870 A289 85c multicolored .55 .50
871 A289 1.05r multicolored .70 .65
*Nos. 868-871 (4)* 2.00 1.85

Tourism A290

a, Namaqualand. b, North Beach, Durban. c, Lion. d, Apple Express. e, Oryx gazella.

**1993, Nov. 12 Litho. *Perf. 14½x14***

872 A290 85c Strip of 5, #a.-e. 3.25 3.25

Export Fruits A291

**1994, Jan. 28 Litho. *Perf. 14½x14***

873 A291 85c Grapes .60 .50
874 A291 90c Apples .65 .55
875 A291 1.05r Plums .75 .60
876 A291 1.25r Oranges .95 .75
877 A291 1.40r Avocados 1.10 .85
*Nos. 873-877 (5)* 4.05 3.25

A souvenir sheet of 1 #873 was sold for 3r by the Philatelic Foundation of South Africa.

Peace and Goodwill — A292

Childrens' drawings: 45c, Smiling faces, by Nicole Davies. 70c, Dove flying toward olive tree, by Robynne Lawrie. 95c, Three girls, dove, scattered cartridge cases, by Batami Nothmann. 1.15r, Faces surrounding "peace," by Karen Uys.

**1994, Apr. 8 Litho. *Perf. 14½x14***

878 A292 45c multicolored .30 .25
879 A292 70c multicolored .45 .40
880 A292 95c multicolored .60 .55
881 A292 1.15r multicolored .70 .65
*a.* Souvenir sheet of 1 .55 .55
*Nos. 878-881 (4)* 2.05 1.85

No. 881a was issued 8/97, sold for 1.15r and is inscribed "Chernobyl's Children, a decade later 1986-1996" in margin.

Inauguration of Pres. Nelson Mandela — A293

***Perf. 14x14½, 14½x14***

**1994, May 10 Litho.**

882 A293 45c shown .30 .25
883 A293 70c Anthems, horiz. .50 .40
884 A293 95c Flag, horiz. .70 .55
885 A293 1.15r Union Bldgs., horiz. .85 .65
*Nos. 882-885 (4)* 2.35 1.85

Tugboats — A294

**1994, May 13** ***Perf. 14½x14***

**886** A294 45c TS McEwen .30 .25
**887** A294 70c Sir William Hoy .45 .40
**888** A294 95c Sir Charles Elliott .60 .55
**889** A294 1.15r Eland .75 .65
**890** A294 1.35r Pioneer .85 .75
*a.* Souvenir sheet of 5, #886-890 3.25 3.25
*Nos. 886-890 (5)* 2.95 2.60

Our Family — A295

Children's paintings: a, Mother Hands Out Work (C1.5). b, My Friends and I at Play (C2.5). c, Family Life (C3.5). d, Sunday in Church (C4.5). e, I Visit My Brother in the Hospital (C5.5).

**1994, July 10 Litho.** ***Perf. 14x14½***

**891** A295 45c Strip of 5, #a.-e. 1.50 1.50

Stamp Day — A296

**1994, Sept. 30 Litho.** ***Perf. 14***

**892** A296 50c Bulk mail .30 .30
**893** A296 70c Proof of delivery .40 .40
**894** A296 95c Registered mail .55 .55
**895** A296 1.15r Express delivery .65 .65
*Nos. 892-895 (4)* 1.90 1.90

Heather — A297

Designs: a, Erica tenuifolia. b, Erica urna-viridis. c, Erica decora. d, Erica aristata. e, Erica dichrus.

**1994, Nov. 18 Litho.** ***Perf. 14***

**896** A297 95c Strip of 5, #a.-e. 3.25 3.25

Tourism — A298

#897, Phacochoerus aethiopicus, Eastern Transvaal Province. #898, Lost City, Sun City, North West Province. #899, Ceratotherium simum, KwaZulu/Natal Province. #900, Waterfront, Cape Town, Western Cape Province. #901, Adansonia digitata, Northern Transvaal Province. #902, Highland Route, Free State. #903, Augrabies Falls, Northern Cape Province. #904, Addo Elephant Natl. Park, Eastern Cape Province. #905, Union Buildings, Pretoria, Gauteng.
Illustration reduced.

**1995-97 Litho.** ***Perf. 14***

**897** A298 50c multicolored .30 .30
**898** A298 50c multicolored .30 .30
**899** A298 (60c) multicolored .35 .35
**900** A298 (60c) multicolored .35 .35
**901** A298 (60c) multicolored .35 .35
*a.* #901 + label, perf. 14 on one side .55 .55
*b.* Souvenir sheet of 1 .55 .55
**902** A298 (60c) multicolored .35 .35
**903** A298 (60c) multicolored .35 .35
**904** A298 (60c) multicolored .35 .35
**905** A298 (60c) multicolored .35 .35
*a.* Strip of 5, #901-905 1.75 1.75
*Nos. 897-905 (9)* 3.05 3.05

#901a sold for 70c; #901b for 1.10r on date of issue.
Issued: #897, 1/18; #898, 2/15; #899, 4/28; #900, 5/12; #901-905, 6/30; #901a, 2/97; #901b 8/97.

South African Airforce, 75th Anniv. — A299

DeHavilland DH-9 biplane, Cheetah D fighter.

**1995, Feb. 1 Litho.** ***Perf. 14***

**906** A299 50c multicolored .30 .30

First Trans-Africa Flight, 75th Anniv. — A300

Vickers Vimy bomber Silver Queen, map of route.

**1995, Feb. 1**

**907** A300 95c multicolored .55 .55

South Africa, 1995 Rugby World Cup Champions A301

Designs: No. 908, Shown. No. 909, Player running with ball, vert. No. 910, Player holding trophy, vert. No. 911, Like #908, World Champions. No. 912, Scrum, two players.

**1995 Litho.** ***Perf. 14***

**908** A301 (60c) multicolored .30 .30
*a.* Perf. 14 horiz. .30 .30
**909** A301 (60c) multicolored .30 .30
*a.* Souvenir sheet of 1 .50 .50
*b.* Perf. 14 vert. .30 .30
*c.* Booklet pane, 5 each #908a, 909b 3.00
Complete booklet, #909c 3.00
*d.* Booklet pane, 10 #909b 3.00
Complete booklet, #909d 3.00
**910** A301 (60c) multicolored .30 .30
**911** A301 (60c) multicolored .30 .30

**Size: 68x26mm**

**912** A301 1.15r multicolored .55 .55
*Nos. 908-912 (5)* 1.75 1.75

Issued: #910-911, 6/28; others 5/25.

CSIR (Council for Scientific and Industrial Research), 50th Anniv. A302

**1995, June 15**

**913** A302 (60c) Purifying water .35 .35

Marine Science in South Africa, Cent. A303

**1995, Aug. 25 Litho.** ***Perf. 14***

**914** A303 (60c) Dr. JDF Gilchrist .35 .35

**Souvenir Sheet**

Singapore '95 — A304

Illustration reduced.

**1995, Sept. 1**

**915** A304 (60c) multicolored .35 .35

Masakhane Campaign A305

**1995** ***Perf. 14x14¼***

**916** A305 (60c) multicolored .35 .35
*a.* Booklet pane of 10 3.50
Complete booklet, No. 916a 3.50

**Booklet Stamp**
**Size: 29x20mm**

**916B** A305 (60c) multicolored
*c.* Booklet pane of 10
Complete booklet, #916c

Issued: #916, 9/16; #916B, 12/1.

Visit of Pope John Paul II — A306

Mahatma Gandhi — A307

**1995, Sept. 16** ***Perf. 14***

**917** A306 (60c) multicolored .35 .35

**1995, Oct. 2**

Designs: (60c), 1906 Photograph. 1.40r, Ghandhi in later years.

**918** A307 (60c) blue .35 .35
*a.* Souvenir sheet of 1 .50 .50
**919** A307 1.40r brown .80 .80
*a.* Souvenir sheet of 1 .80 .80

No. 918a is inscribed in sheet margin for 50th anniv. of Congress Alliance for Democratic South Africa. Issued July 1997.
Design on stamp in No. 919a extends to perforations.
See India Nos. 1534-1535.

World Post Day — A308

**1995**

**920** A308 (60c) multicolored .35 .35

**Size: 65x60mm**
***Imperf***

**921** A308 5r multicolored 3.00 3.00

Stampex '95.
Issued: (60c), 10/9; 5r, 10/19.

UN, 50th Anniv. A309

**1995, Oct. 24 Litho.** ***Perf. 14***

**922** A309 (60c) multicolored .35 .35

**Souvenir Sheet**

UNESCO, 50th Anniv. — A310

Illustration reduced.

**1995, Oct. 24**

**923** A310 (60c) multicolored .35 .35

Shells — A311

A312

**1995, Nov. 24**

**924** A311 (60c) Afrivoluta priglei .35 .35
**925** A311 (60c) Lyria africana .35 .35
**926** A311 (60c) Marginella mosaica .35 .35
**927** A311 (60c) Conus pictus .35 .35
**928** A311 (60c) Gypreaea fultoni .35 .35
*a.* Strip of 5, #924-928 1.75 1.75

**1996, Jan. 8 Litho.** ***Perf. 14***

1996 African Cup of Nations Soccer Championships: Nos. 929-933, Various soccer plays, map of Africa. No. 934, Player in traditional uniform.

**Color of "RSA"**

**929** A312 (60c) blue .35 .35
**930** A312 (60c) yellow .35 .35
**931** A312 (60c) red .35 .35
**932** A312 (60c) gray .35 .35
**933** A312 (60c) green .35 .35
*a.* Strip of 5, Nos. 929-933 1.75 1.75

**Souvenir Sheet**

**934** A312 (1.15r) multicolored .65 .65

South African Victory in African Nations Soccer Championship A312a

**1996, Feb. 8 Litho.** ***Perf. 14½x14***

**934A** A312a (60c) multicolored .30 .30

City of Bloemfontein, 150th Anniv. — A313

**1996, Mar. 28 Litho. *Perf. 14***
**935** A313 (60c) multicolored .30 .30

Souvenir Sheet

New Year 1996 (Year of the Rat) — A313a

Illustration reduced.

**1996, May 18 Litho. *Perf. 14***
**940D** A313a 60c multicolored .25 .25

CHINA '96.

Man in a Donkey Cart, by Gerard Sekoto (1913-93) — A314

Paintings: #942, 2r, Song of the Pick. #943, 2r, Yellow Houses, Sophiatown, 1940, vert.

**1996, June 1 Litho. *Perf. 14***
**941** A314 1r multicolored .55 .55
**942** A314 2r multicolored 1.10 1.10

**Souvenir Sheet**

**943** A314 2r multicolored 1.10 1.10

Youth Day — A315

**1996, June 8**
**944** A315 (60c) multicolored .30 .30

Comrades Marathon, 75th Anniv. — A316

**1996, June 8 Litho. *Perf. 14***
**945** A316 (60c) multicolored .30 .30

Souvenir Sheet

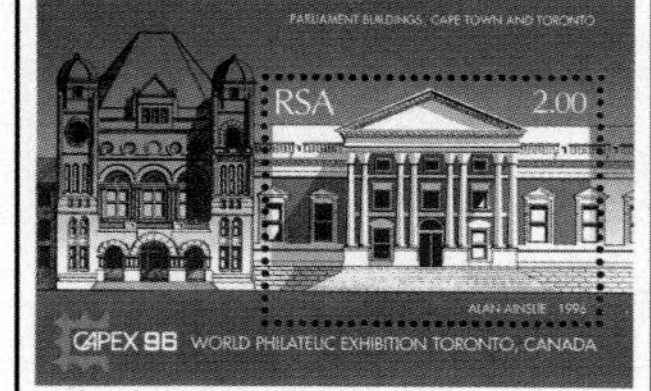

Parliament Building, Toronto — A316a

Illustration reduced.

**1996, June 8 Litho. *Perf. 14***
**945A** A316a 2r multicolored .85 .85

CAPEX '96.

A317

A318

1996 Summer Olympic Games, Atlanta: No. 946: a, Cycling. b, Swimming. c, Boxing. d, Running. e, Pole vault.
1.40r, South African Olympic emblem.

**1996, July 5 Litho. *Perf. 14½x14***
**946** A317 (70c) Strip of 5, #a.-e. 1.75 1.75

***Perf. 14***

**947** A317 1.40r multicolored .65 .65

No. 946 was issued in sheets of 10 stamps.

**1996, Aug. 1 Litho. *Perf. 14***

Background color: a, Vermilion & multi. b, Deep blue & multi. c, Deep yellow & multi. d, Bright blue & multi. e, Red & multi.

**948** Strip of 5 1.75 1.75
*a.-e.* A318 (70c) any single .35 .35

New Democratic Constitution.

South African Merchant Marine, 50th Anniv. — A319

Paintings of ships, by Peter Bilas: No. 949: a, Sea Pioneer. b, SA Winterberg.
No. 950: a, Langloof. b, SA Vaal.
2r, Constantia.

**1996, Aug. 5 Litho. *Perf. 14***
**949** Pair .70 .70
*a.-b.* A319 (70c) any single .35 .35
**950** Pair 1.40 1.40
*a.-b.* A319 1.40r any single .70 .70

**Souvenir Sheet**

**950C** A319 2r multicolored 1.00 1.00

No. 950C contains one 72x30mm stamp.

A320

A321

**1996, Aug. 9 Litho. *Perf. 14***
**951** A320 70c multicolored .35 .35

Natl. Women's Day.

**1996, Oct. 9**
**952** A321 70c multicolored .35 .35

World Post Day.

Christmas — A322

**1996, Oct. 9**
**953** A322 70c multicolored .35 .35

No. 953 exists in a privately produced souvenir, sold at 2r for charitable purposes.

Souvenir Sheet

Bloemfontein, 150th Natl. Stamp Show — A323

Illustration reduced.

**1996, Oct. 9 Litho. *Perf. 14½x14***
**954** A323 2r multicolored 1.00 1.00

South African Nobel Laureates, Death Cent. of Alfred Nobel — A324

a, Max Theiler, medicine, 1951. b, Albert Luthuli, peace, 1960. c, Alfred Nobel (1833-96). d, Allan Cormack, medicine, 1979. e, Aaron Klug, chemistry, 1982. f, Desmond Tutu, peace, 1984. g, Nadine Gordimer, literature, 1991. h, Symbol for Nobel Prizes 1901-96. i, Nelson R. Mandela, peace, 1993. j, F.W. de Klerk, peace, 1993.

**1996, Nov. 4**
**955** A324 (70c) Sheet of 10, #a.-j. 3.50 3.50
*k.* Souvenir sheet, #955c .40 .40

First Motor Car in South Africa, Cent. A325

**1997, Jan. 4 Litho. *Perf. 14***
**956** A325 (70c) multicolored .35 .35

Souvenir Sheet

Hong Kong '97 — A326

***Perf. 14 Syncopated***

**1997, Feb. 12 Litho.**
**957** A326 3r multicolored 1.60 1.60

Natl. Water Week and Water Day — A328

Save water for: No. 959, Farming. No. 960, Gardening. No. 961, Health. No. 962, Housing. No. 963, For all.

***Perf. 14 Syncopated on 2 or 3 Sides***

**1997, Mar. 22 Litho.**

**Booklet Stamps**

**959** A328 (70c) multicolored .50 .50
**960** A328 (70c) multicolored .50 .50
**961** A328 (70c) multicolored .50 .50
**962** A328 (70c) multicolored .50 .50
**963** A328 (70c) multicolored .50 .50
*a.* Booklet pane, 2 each #959-963 5.00
Complete booklet 5.00

***Perf. 14x14¼ on 2 or 3 Sides***

**1997, Mar. Litho.**

**Booklet Stamps**

**963B** A328 (70c) Like #959 .50 .50
**963C** A328 (70c) Like #960 .50 .50
**963D** A328 (70c) Like #961 .50 .50
**963E** A328 (70c) Like #962 .50 .50
**963F** A328 (70c) Like #963 .50 .50
*g.* Bklt. pane, 2 ea #963B-963F 5.00
Complete booklet, #963Fg 5.00

South African Navy, 75th Anniv. — A329

Warships: No. 964, Strike craft SAS Kobie Coetsee. No. 965, Survey ship SAS Protea. No. 966, Mine counter-measures ship SAS Umkomaas. No. 967, Submarine Emily Hobhouse, anti-submarine frigate SAS President Pretorius.

**1997, Apr. 1 *Perf. 14 Syncopated***
**964** A329 (70c) multicolored .35 .35
**965** A329 (70c) multicolored .35 .35
**966** A329 (70c) multicolored .35 .35
**967** A329 (70c) multicolored .35 .35
*a.* Block of 4, #964-967 1.40 1.40

First Democratic Elections, 5th Anniv. — A330

People voting, signs saying: No. 968, "Election Day, 27, April, 1994." No. 969, "Polling Station." No. 970, "Register Here." No. 971, "Vote Here." No. 972, "Ballot Box."

***Perf. 14 Syncopated***

**1997, Apr. 26** **Litho.**

**968** A330 (70c) black & red .50 .50
**969** A330 (70c) black & red .50 .50
**970** A330 (70c) black & red .50 .50
**971** A330 (70c) black & red .50 .50
**972** A330 (70c) black & red .50 .50
*b.* Strip of 5, #968-972 2.50 2.50

Souvenir Sheet

New Year 1997 (Year of the Ox) — A330a

Illustration reduced.

**1997, May 2** **Litho.** ***Perf. 14***

**972A** A330a 4.50r multicolored 2.25 2.25

SAPDA '97.

A331

A332

Cultural Artifacts.

**1997, May 18** ***Perf. 14***

**973** A331 (70c) Zulu baskets .35 .35
**974** A331 (70c) S. Sotho figure .35 .35
**975** A331 (70c) S. Ndebele figure .35 .35
**976** A331 (70c) Venda door .35 .35
**977** A331 (70c) Tsonga medicine gourd .35 .35
**978** A331 (70c) Wooden pot, N. cape .35 .35
**979** A331 (70c) Khoi walking stick .35 .35
**980** A331 (70c) Tswana knife handle .35 .35
**981** A331 (70c) Xhosa pipe .35 .35
**982** A331 (70c) Swazi vessel .35 .35
*a.* Sheet of 10, #973-982 3.50 3.50

**1997, Dec.** ***Perf. 14x15***

*973a* Zulu baskets .50 .50
*974a* S. Sotho figure .50 .50
*975a* S. Ndebele figure .50 .50
*976a* Venda door .50 .50
*977a* Tsonga medicine gourd .50 .50
*978a* Wooden pot, N. cape .50 .50
*979a* Khoi walking stick .50 .50
*980a* Tswana knife handle .50 .50
*981a* Xhosa pipe .50 .50
*982b* Swazi vessel .50 .50
*982c* Bklt. pane, #973a-981a, 982b 5.00
Complete booklet, 2 #982c 10.00

**1997, June 5** ***Perf. 14***

Birds.

**983** A332 (70c) White-breasted cormorant .35 .35
**984** A332 (70c) Hammerkop .35 .35
**985** A332 (70c) Pied kingfisher .35 .35
**986** A332 (70c) Purple heron .35 .35
**987** A332 (70c) Black-headed heron .35 .35
**988** A332 (70c) Darter .35 .35
**989** A332 (70c) Green-backed heron .35 .35
**990** A332 (70c) White-faced duck .35 .35
*a.* Souvenir sheet of 1 .55 .55
**991** A332 (70c) Saddle-billed stork .35 .35
**992** A332 (70c) Water dikkop .35 .35
*a.* Sheet of 10, #983-992 3.50 3.50
*b.* Booklet pane of 10, #983-992, perf. 14x14¾ — —
Complete booklet, 2 #992b —

Birds look bluer and browner on some stamps from No. 992b. No. 992a has Ilsapex 98 emblem in margin, which is not found on No. 992b.

No. 990a, issued 7/11/97, is inscribed in sheet margin for JUNASS '97, and sold for 2r.

Grocott's, Muirhead & Gowie Buildings, Grahamstown — A333

Illustration reduced.

**1997, May 29** **Litho.** ***Perf. 14***

**993** A333 5r multicolored 3.00 3.00

PACIFIC 97.

Indigenous Cattle A335

***Perf. 14½ Syncopated***

**1997, Aug. 10**

**999** A335 (70c) Nguni .50 .50
**1000** A335 (70c) Bonsmara .50 .50
**1001** A335 (70c) Afrikander .50 .50
**1002** A335 (70c) Drakensberger .50 .50
*a.* Block of 4, #999-1002 2.00 2.00

Antarctic Wildlife A336

**1997, Aug. 27** **Litho.** ***Perf. 14***

**1003** A336 (70c) Leopard seal .40 .40
**1004** A336 1.20r Antarctic skua .65 .65
**1005** A336 1.70r King penguin .90 .90
*Nos. 1003-1005 (3)* 1.95 1.95

Enoch Sontonga (1873-1905), Author of Africa's Natl. Anthem — A337

***Perf. 14 Syncopated***

**1997, Sept. 24** **Litho.**

**1006** A337 (70c) shown .50 .50
**1007** A337 (70c) "Nkosi Sikelel iAfrika" .50 .50
*a.* Pair, #1006-1007 1.00 1.00

Heritage Day.

Souvenir Sheet

Cape Town '97 Natl. Stamp Show — A338

**1997, Oct. 8** ***Perf. 14***

**1008** A338 4.50r multicolored 2.25 2.25

Souvenir Sheet

World Post Day — A339

**1997, Oct. 9** ***Perf. 14 Syncopated***

**1009** A339 (70c) multicolored .70 .70

No. 1009 sold for 1r on day of issue.

SANTA (South African Natl. Tuberculosis Assoc., 50th Anniv. — A340

Designs featuring former Christmas seals: No. 1010, Bethlehem. No. 1011, Candles on each side of Cross of Lorraine. No. 1012, Candles, angels, Cross. No. 1013, Cross, angel kneeling. No. 1014, Santa carrying Cross. No. 1015, Madonna and Child, Cross. No. 1016, Christmas trees. No. 1017, Magi. No. 1018, Bell, stained glass window. No. 1019, Native African kneeling, flag.

**1997, Nov. 3** ***Perf. 14 Syncopated***

**1010** A340 (70c) multicolored .50 .50
**1011** A340 (70c) multicolored .50 .50
**1012** A340 (70c) multicolored .50 .50
**1013** A340 (70c) multicolored .50 .50
**1014** A340 (70c) multicolored .50 .50
**1015** A340 (70c) multicolored .50 .50
**1016** A340 (70c) multicolored .50 .50
**1017** A340 (70c) multicolored .50 .50
**1018** A340 (70c) multicolored .50 .50
**1019** A340 (70c) multicolored .50 .50
*a.* Sheet of 10, #1010-1019 5.00 5.00

Souvenir Sheet

New Year 1998 (Year of the Tiger) — A341

Illustration reduced.

**1998, Jan. 28** **Litho.** ***Perf. 14x14½***

**1020** A341 5r multicolored 2.50 2.50

Natl. Sea Rescue Institute A342

**1998, Feb. 11** ***Perf. 14 Syncopated***

**1021** A342 (70c) multicolored .50 .50

Fauna (no frame) — A343

5c, Giant girdle-tailed lizard. 10c, Geometric tortoise. 20c, Southern African hedgehog. 30c, Spotted hyena. 40c, Riverine rabbit. 50c, Samango monkey. 60c, Cape hunting dog. 70c, Roan antelope. 80c, Kori bustard. 90c, Jackass penguin. 1r, Wattled crane. #1032, Impala. #1033, Waterbuck. #1034, Blue wildebeest. #1035, Eland. #1036, Kudu. #1037, Black rhinoceros. #1038, White rhinoceros. #1039, Buffalo. #1040, Lion. #1041, Leopard. #1042, African elephant. #1044, Giraffe. 1.50r, Tawny eagle, vert. 2r, Blue swallow. 2.30r, Cape vulture, vert. 5r, Martial eagle. 10r, Bataleur. 20r, Fish eagle.

***Perf. 14x14¼, 14x14¼, 14¼x14 Syncopated (#1043), 14x14¼ Syncopated on 2 or 3 Sides (#1036B-1036F, 1042B-1042F)***

**1998-2000** **Litho.**

**1021A** A343 5c multi .20 .20
**1022** A343 10c multi .20 .20
**1023** A343 20c multi .20 .20
**1024** A343 30c multi .20 .20
**1025** A343 40c multi .20 .20
**1026** A343 50c multi .20 .20
**1027** A343 60c multi .20 .20
**1028** A343 70c multi .20 .20
**1029** A343 80c multi .30 .30
**1030** A343 90c multi .30 .30
**1031** A343 1r multi .30 .30
**1032** A343 (1.10r) multi, vert. .55 .55
**1033** A343 (1.10r) multi, vert. .55 .55
**1034** A343 (1.10r) multi, vert. .55 .55
**1035** A343 (1.10r) multi, vert. .55 .55
**1036** A343 (1.10r) multi, vert. .55 .55
*a.* Strip of 5, #1032-1036 2.75 2.75
*h.* Booklet pane, 2 each #1032-1036, "Standard" 5mm long 5.50
Booklet, #1036h 5.50
**1036B** A343 (1.10r) Like #1034 .35 .35
**1036C** A343 (1.10r) Like #1035 .35 .35
**1036D** A343 (1.10r) Like #1036 .35 .35
**1036E** A343 (1.10r) Like #1032 .35 .35
**1036F** A343 (1.10r) Like #1033 .35 .35
*g.* Booklet pane, 2 each #1036B-1036F 3.50
Booklet, #1036Fg 3.50
**1037** A343 (1.10r) multi .35 .35
*a.* Booklet pane of 10 3.50
Complete bklt., #1037a 3.50
**1038** A343 (1.30r) multi .45 .45
**1039** A343 (1.30r) multi .45 .45
**1040** A343 (1.30r) multi .45 .45
**1041** A343 (1.30r) multi .45 .45
**1042** A343 (1.30r) multi .45 .45
*a.* Booklet pane, 2 ea #1038-1042 4.50
Complete bklt., #1042a 4.50
**1042B** A343 (1.30r) Like #1038 .45 .45
**1042C** A343 (1.30r) Like #1039 .45 .45
**1042D** A343 (1.30r) Like #1040 .45 .45
**1042E** A343 (1.30r) Like #1041 .45 .45
**1042F** A343 (1.30r) Like #1042 .45 .45
*g.* Booklet pane, 2 each #1042B-1042F 4.50
Complete bklt., #1042Fg 4.50
**1043** A343 2r multi .65 .65
**1043A** A343 2r multi .65 .65
**1044** A343 3r multi 1.00 1.00
**1045** A343 5r multi 1.75 1.75

**Size: 20x38mm**

***Perf. 14¼x13¾***

**1045A** A343 1.50r multi .50 .50
**1045B** A343 2.30r multi .75 .75

**Size: 35x25mm**

***Perf. 14¼x14***

**1046** A343 10r multi 3.25 3.25
*a.* Perf. 14¾ 3.25 3.25

***Perf. 14¾ Syncopated***

**1047** A343 20r multi 6.25 6.25
*Nos. 1021A-1047 (40)* 26.65 26.65

**Self-adhesive**

**Litho.**

***Die Cut Perf. 13x12¾***

**1048** A343 (1.10r) like #1033 .55 .55
**1049** A343 (1.10r) like #1032 .55 .55
**1050** A343 (1.10r) like #1036 .55 .55
**1051** A343 (1.10r) like #1035 .55 .55
**1052** A343 (1.10r) like #1034 .55 .55
*a.* Strip of 5, #1048-1052 2.75
*h.* Booklet, 2 each #1048-1052 5.50

**Booklet Stamps**

**Self-Adhesive**

***Serpentine Die Cut 11x11¼***

**1052B** A343 (1.30r) Like #1035 .40 .40
**1052C** A343 (1.30r) Like #1036 .40 .40
**1052D** A343 (1.30r) Like #1032 .40 .40
**1052E** A343 (1.30r) Like #1034 .40 .40

**1052F** A343 (1.30r) Like #1033 .40 .40
*g.* Booklet pane, 2 each #1052B-1052F 4.00

Nos. 1038-1042F are inscribed "Airmail Postcard."
"Standard" on Nos. 1032-1036, 1036a is 5½mm long.
Nos. 1042B-1042F are booklet stamps. No. 1052Fg is a complete booklet. Nos. 1036B-1036F were issued in a booklet.
Issued: #1037, 1/98; 10c, 40c, 50c, 70c, 90c, 1r, 1/16/98; #1038-1042, 4/98; #1036B-1036F, 5/18/98; 3r, 6/24/98; 20c, 6/25/98; #1032-1036, 1048-1052, 5/18/98; 10r, 20r, 9/21/98; #1046a, 10/28/98; #1043A, 1/9/99; #1052B-1052F, 12/99; 1.50r, 2.30r, 6/5/00; 5c, 7/4/00.

Souvenir Sheet

Leopard — A344

Illustration reduced.

**1998, May 1** ***Perf. 14***
**1053** A344 5r multicolored 2.50 2.50

SAPDA '98 Stamp Show, Johannesburg.

A345

A346

**1998, June 8**
**1054** A345 (1.10r) multicolored .55 .55

1998 World Cup Soccer Championships, France. No. 1054 was issued in sheets of 10.

**1998, June 28** ***Perf. 14x14½***

Early South African History: #1055, Early stone age hand axe. #1056, Musuku. #1057, San rock engravings. #1058, Early iron age pots. #1059, Khoekhoe pot. #1060, Florisbad skull. #1061, San rock art. #1062, Mapungubwe gold. #1063, Lydenburg head. #1064, Taung child.

**1055** A346 (1.10r) multicolored .40 .40
**1056** A346 (1.10r) multicolored .40 .40
**1057** A346 (1.10r) multicolored .40 .40
**1058** A346 (1.10r) multicolored .40 .40
**1059** A346 (1.10r) multicolored .40 .40
**1060** A346 (1.10r) multicolored .40 .40
**1061** A346 (1.10r) multicolored .40 .40
**1062** A346 (1.10r) multicolored .40 .40
**1063** A346 (1.10r) multicolored .40 .40
**1064** A346 (1.10r) multicolored .40 .40
*a.* Sheet of 10, #1055-1064 4.00 4.00
Booklet, 2 #1064a 8.00

Raptors — A347

Designs: No. 1065, Pale chanting goshawk. No. 1066, Jackal buzzard. No. 1067, Lanner falcon. No. 1068, Bearded vulture. No. 1069, Black harrier. No. 1070, Cape vulture. No. 1071, Bateleur. No. 1072, Spotted eagle owl. No. 1073, White-headed vulture. No. 1074, African fish eagle.

**1998, Aug. 16** ***Perf. 14x15***
**1065** A347 (1.10r) multicolored .40 .40
**1066** A347 (1.10r) multicolored .40 .40
**1067** A347 (1.10r) multicolored .40 .40
**1068** A347 (1.10r) multicolored .40 .40
**1069** A347 (1.10r) multicolored .40 .40
**1070** A347 (1.10r) multicolored .40 .40
**1071** A347 (1.10r) multicolored .40 .40
**1072** A347 (1.10r) multicolored .40 .40
**1073** A347 (1.10r) multicolored .40 .40
**1074** A347 (1.10r) multicolored .40 .40
*a.* Sheet of 10, #1065-1074 4.00 4.00
*b.* Booklet pane, #1065-1074 4.00
Complete booklet, 2 #1074b + 2 prepaid postcards 9.75

Vert. and horiz. perforations extend to top, bottom and right edges of sheet on No. 1074a, but do not on No. 1074b.

Natl. Arbor Week A348

Trees: No. 1075, Baobab. No. 1076, Umbrella thorn. No. 1077, Shepherd's tree. No. 1078, Karee.

**1998, Sept. 4** **Litho.** ***Perf. 13¾x14***
**1075** A348 (1.10r) multi .40 .40
**1076** A348 (1.10r) multi .40 .40
**1077** A348 (1.10r) multi .40 .40
**1078** A348 (1.10r) multi .40 .40
*a.* Block of 4, #1075-1078 1.60 1.60

Christmas — A349

**1998, Oct. 9** **Litho.** ***Perf. 14x15***
**1079** A349 (1.10r) Angel .40 .40
**1080** A349 (1.10r) Bell .40 .40
**1081** A349 (1.10r) Package .40 .40
**1082** A349 (1.10r) Christmas tree .40 .40
**1083** A349 (1.10r) Star .40 .40
*a.* Strip of 5, #1079-1083 2.00 2.00

Souvenir Sheet

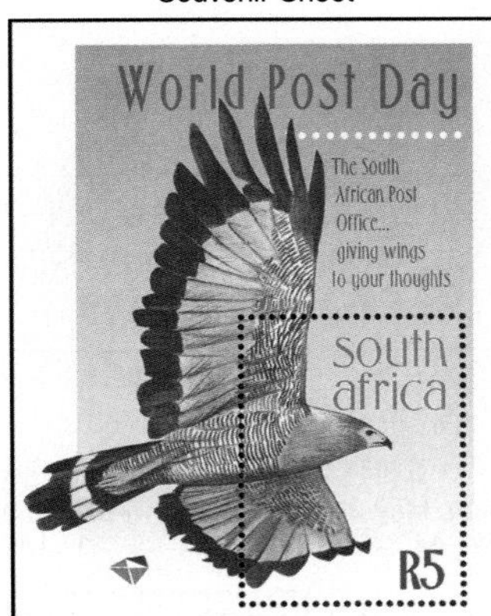

World Post Day — A351

Illustration reduced.

**1998, Oct. 9** **Litho.** ***Perf. 14x14½***
**1089** A351 5r multicolored 1.75 1.75

Souvenir Sheet

ILSAPEX 1998, Midrand, South Africa — A352

Designs of unissued stamps created for 1927 definitive series in colors of: a, Red and green. b, Green and black.

**1998, Oct. 20** **Litho.** ***Perf. 14½x14¼***
**1090** A352 5r Sheet of 2, #a.-b. 3.50 3.50

Souvenir Sheet

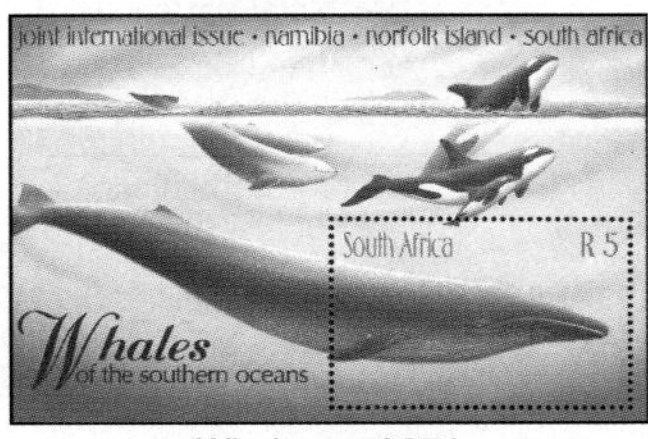

Whales — A354

Illustration reduced.

**1998, Oct. 23** **Litho.** ***Perf. 13½x14***
**1095** A354 5r multicolored 3.00 3.00

See Namibia #919, Norfolk Island #665.

Souvenir Sheet

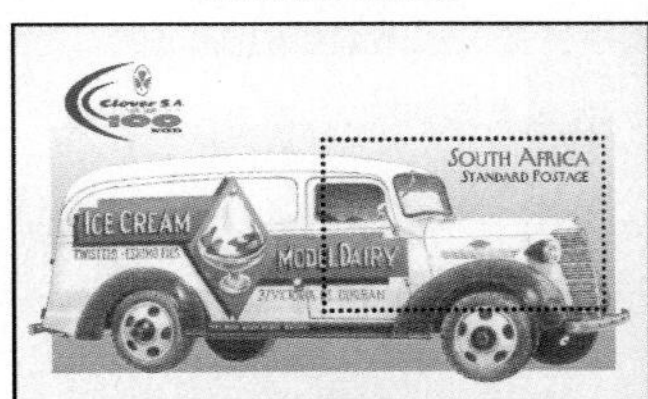

Clover SA Limited, 100th Anniv. — A354a

Illustration reduced.

**1998, Nov. 15** **Litho.** ***Perf. 14¼x14***
**1095A** A354a (1.10r) multicolored .40 .40

Universal Declaration of Human Rights, 50th Anniv. — A355

**1998, Dec. 9** ***Perf. 14¼***
**1096** A355 (1.10r) multicolored .40 .40

UPU, 125th Anniv. A356

Designs: No. 1097, Dennis Royal Mail vehicle, 1913. No. 1098, Ford V8 Mail van, 1935. No. 1099, Mobile post office, 1937. No. 1100, Trojan post office van, 1927.

**1999, Feb. 15** **Litho.** ***Perf. 13¾x14***
**1097** A356 (1.10r) multi .35 .35
**1098** A356 (1.10r) multi .35 .35
**1099** A356 (1.10r) multi .35 .35
**1100** A356 (1.10r) multi .35 .35
*a.* Block of 4, #1097-1100 1.40 1.40

New Year 1999 (Year of the Rabbit) — A357

Illustration reduced.

**1999, Feb. 16** **Litho.** ***Perf. 14x13½***
**1101** A357 5r multicolored 1.75 1.75

Ships of the Southern Oceans — A358

**1999, Mar. 19** **Litho.** ***Perf. 13¾x14***
**1102** A358 (1.10r) Endeavour .35 .35
**1103** A358 (1.10r) HMS Beagle .35 .35
**1104** A358 (1.10r) Discovery .35 .35
**1105** A358 (1.10r) Heemskerck .35 .35
*a.* Block of 4, #1102-1105 1.40 1.40

**Souvenir Sheet**

***Perf. 13¾***

**1106** A358 5r Lawhill, vert. 1.60 1.60

Australia 99 World Stamp Expo (No. 1106).

AIDS Awareness — A359

***Perf. 14¼x14 on 3 sides***

**1999, Apr. 1**
**1107** A359 (1.20r) purple & multi .40 .40
**1108** A359 (1.20r) green & multi .40 .40
*a.* Booklet pane, 5 each #1107-1108 4.00
Complete booklet, #1108a 4.00

Souvenir Sheets

IBRA '99, Nuremberg, Germany — A360

Illustration reduced.

**1999, Apr. 27** ***Perf. 14¼x14***
**1109** A360 5r multi 1.60 1.60

SAPDA '99, Johannesburg — A361

Illustration reduced.

**1999, Apr. 30** *Perf. 13¾*
**1110** A361 5r multi 1.60 1.60

A362

A363

**1999, May 1** *Perf. 14x14¾*
**1111** A362 (1.20r) Nurse .40 .40
**1112** A362 (1.20r) Washerwoman .40 .40
**1113** A362 (1.20r) Lumberjack .40 .40
**1114** A362 (1.20r) Tree planter .40 .40
**1115** A362 (1.20r) Cook .40 .40
**1116** A362 (1.20r) Fisherman .40 .40
**1117** A362 (1.20r) Construction worker .40 .40
**1118** A362 (1.20r) Miner .40 .40
**1119** A362 (1.20r) Mailman .40 .40
**1120** A362 (1.20r) Jackhammerer .40 .40
*a.* Sheet of 10, #1111-1120 4.00 4.00

Labor Day.

**1999, June 16** *Perf. 14x14¼*
**1121** A363 (1.20r) multi .40 .40

Inauguration of Pres. Thabo Mbeki.

Souvenir Sheet

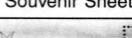

Order of St. John, 900th Anniv. — A364

Illustration reduced.

**1999, June 23** *Perf. 14x14¾*
**1122** A364 2r multi .65 .65

Standard Bank Arts Festival, 25th Anniv. — A365

**1999, June 29** *Perf. 14x14¼*
**1123** A365 (1.20r) shown .40 .40
**1124** A365 (1.20r) Film .40 .40
**1125** A365 (1.20r) Music .40 .40
**1126** A365 (1.20r) Mask, diff. .40 .40
**1127** A365 (1.20r) Painter .40 .40
*a.* Strip of 5, #1123-1127 2.00 2.00

Traditional Wall Art — A366

**1999, Aug. 8** *Perf. 13¼x13¾*
**1128** A366 (1.20r) North Ndebele .40 .40
**1129** A366 (1.20r) South Ndebele .40 .40
**1130** A366 (1.20r) Swazi .40 .40
**1131** A366 (1.20r) Venda .40 .40
**1132** A366 (1.20r) South Sotho .40 .40
**1133** A366 (1.20r) Xhosa .40 .40
**1134** A366 (1.20r) North Sotho .40 .40
**1135** A366 (1.20r) Tsonga .40 .40
**1136** A366 (1.20r) Zulu .40 .40
**1137** A366 (1.20r) Tswana .40 .40
*a.* Sheet of 10, #1128-1137 4.00 4.00

Souvenir Sheet

China 1999 World Philatelic Exhibition — A367

**1999, Aug. 21** *Perf. 14x13¼*
**1138** A367 5r multi 1.60 1.60

Souvenir Sheet

JOPEX '99 — A368

**1999, Sept. 8 Litho.** *Perf. 14¼x14½*
**1139** A368 5r Strelitzia flower 1.60 1.60

Migratory Animals — A369

**1999, Oct. 4 Litho.** *Perf. 14x14¾*
**1140** A369 (1.20r) Barn swallow .40 .40
**1141** A369 (1.20r) Great white shark .40 .40
**1142** A369 (1.20r) Lesser kestrel .40 .40
**1143** A369 (1.20r) Common dolphin .40 .40
**1144** A369 (1.20r) European bee-eater .40 .40
**1145** A369 (1.20r) Loggerhead turtle .40 .40
**1146** A369 (1.20r) Curlew sandpiper .40 .40
**1147** A369 (1.20r) Wandering albatross .40 .40
**1148** A369 (1.20r) Springbok .40 .40
**1149** A369 (1.20r) Lesser flamingo .40 .40
*a.* Sheet of 10, #1140-1149 4.00 4.00
Complete booklet, 2 #1149a (stitched in) + 2 postal cards 9.50

Complete booklet sold for 29r.

Boer War, Cent. A370

**1999, Oct. 11 Litho.** *Perf. 13¾*
**1150** A370 (1.20r) Boer men, woman .40 .40
**1151** A370 (1.20r) Soldiers, ship .40 .40
*a.* Pair, #1150-1151 .80 .80
*b.* Booklet pane, #1150-1151, perf. 13¼x13¾ ('02) .95 —

Issued: No. 1151b, 5/31/02. See note after No. 1282.

Millennium — A371

**2000, Jan. 1 Litho.** *Perf. 13¼x13¾*
**1152** A371 (1.20r) multi .40 .40

Start of National Lottery A372

**2000, Mar. 2 Litho.** *Perf. 13¼x13¾*
**1153** A372 (1.20r) multi .40 .40

Family Day — A373

**2000, Apr. 5 Litho.** *Perf. 13¼*
**1154** A373 (1.30r) multi .40 .40

Souvenir Sheet

The Stamp Show 2000, London — A374

Illustration reduced.

**2000, May 20 Litho.** *Perf. 13¼*
**1155** A374 4.60r multi 1.40 1.40

Frogs and Toads — A375

No. 1156: a, Banded stream frog. b, Yellow-striped reed frog. c, Natal leaf-folding frog. d, Paradise toad. e, Table Mountain ghost frog. f, Banded rubber frog. g, Dwarf grass frog. h, Long-toed tree frog. i, Namaqua rain frog. j, Bubbling kassina.
4.60r, Forest tree frog.

*Perf. 13¼x13¾*
**2000, June 23** **Litho.**
**1156** Sheet of 10 4.00 4.00
*a.-j.* A375 1.30r Any single .40 .40

Souvenir Sheet
*Perf. 13¼*
**1157** A375 4.60r multi 1.40 1.40

Junass 2000, Boksburg (No. 1157). No. 1157 contains one 48x30mm stamp.

Medicinal Plants — A376

No. 1158: a, Stalked bulbine. b, Wild dagga. c, Wild garlic. d, Pig's ear. e, Wild ginger.
No. 1159: a, Red paintbrush. b, Cancer bush. c, Yellow star flower. d, Bitter aloe. e, Sour fig.

**2000, Aug. 1** *Perf. 13¾x13¼*
**1158** Horiz. strip of 5 2.00 2.00
*a.-e.* A376 1.30r Any single .40 .40
**1159** Horiz. strip of 5 3.75 3.75
*a.-e.* A376 2.30r Any single .70 .70

2000 Summer Olympics, Sydney — A377

Olympic rings and: 1.30r, Flagbearer. 1.50r, Elena Meyer of South Africa and Derartu Tulu of Ethiopia. 2.20r, Joshua Thugwane. 2.30r, South African flag. 6.30r, Penny Heyns.

**2000, Sept. 1** *Perf. 13¼x13¾*
**1160-1164** A377 Set of 5 4.25 4.25

Intl. Year for the Culture of Peace A378

**2000, Sept. 19 Litho.** *Perf. 13¼*
**1165** A378 1.30r multi .40 .40

World Heritage Sites — A379

Designs: No. 1166, 1.30r, Robben Island. No. 1167, 1.30r, Greater St. Lucia Wetland Park. No. 1168, 1.30r, Sterkfontein Fossil Hominid Complex.

**2000, Sept. 22** *Perf. 13¼x13¾*
**1166-1168** A379 Set of 3 1.25 1.25

World Post Day — A380

**2000 Litho. *Perf. 13¼x13***

**1169** A380 1.30r multi .40 .40
*a.* Perf. 13¾x13 + label .45 .45

Issued: No. 1169, 10/9; No. 1169a, 11/8. No. 1169a was issued in sheets of 20 stamps + 20 different labels depicting characters on the MTN Gladiators 3 television show that sold for 35r.

Souvenir Sheet

Year of the Dragon — A381

**2000, Oct. 9 Litho. *Perf. 13½x13***

**1170** A381 4.60r multi 1.40 1.40

Writers of the Boer War Era — A382

Medals and: 1.30r, Sol Plaatje, Johanna Brandt. 4.40r, Sir Arthur Conan Doyle, Sir Winston Churchill.

**2000, Oct. 25 Litho. *Perf. 13¼x13¾***

**1171-1172** A382 Set of 2 1.75 1.75
*a.* Booklet pane, #1171-1172 2.25 —

Issued: No. 1172a, 5/31/02. See note after No. 1282.

A383

Fish, Flowers, Butterflies and Birds — A384

Designs: 5c, Palette surgeonfish. 10c, Blue-banded surgeonfish. 20c, Royal angelfish. 30c, Emperor angelfish. 40c, Blackbar triggerfish. 50c, Coral rockcod. 60c, Powder-blue surgeonfish. 70c, Threadfin butterflyfish. 80c, Longhorn cowfish. 90c, Longnose butterflyfish. 1r, Coral beauty. Nos. 1184, 1200, 1205, 1210, 1215, 1219A, 1220, 1225, Botterblom, vert. Nos. 1185, 1201, 1206, 1211, 1216, 1219B, 1221, 1226, Blue marguerite, vert. Nos. 1186, 1202, 1207, 1212, 1217, 1219C, 1222, 1227, Karoo violet, vert. Nos. 1187, 1203, 1208, 1213, 1218, 1219D, 1223, 1228, Tree pelargonium, vert. Nos. 1188, 1204, 1209, 1214, 1219, 1219E, 1224, 1229, Black-eyed susy, vert. 1.40r, Gold-banded forester. 1.50r, Brenton blue. 1.60r, Yellow pansy butterfly. No. 1191, Silver-barred charaxes. No. 1231, Large-spotted acraea butterfly. 2r, Lilac-breasted roller, vert. 2.10r, Koppie charaxes butterfly. 2.30r, Citrus swallowtail. 2.50r, Common grass-yellow butterfly. 3r, Woodland kingfisher, vert. 5r, White-fronted bee-eater, vert. 6.30r, Green-banded swallowtail. 7r, Southern milkweed butterfly. 10r, African green pigeon, vert. 12.60r, False dotted-border. 14r, Lilac tip butterfly. 20r, Purple-crested lourie, vert.

Non-English country name inscriptions at top: Nos. 1200, 1204, 1207, 1217, 1219A, 1219E, 1220, 1224, 1227, Afrika Borwa. Nos. 1201, 1208, 1218, 1219B, 1221, 1228, Ningizimu Afrika. Nos. 1202, 1219C, 1222, Suid-Afrika. Nos. 1203, 1219D, 1223, Afrika Tshipembe. Nos. 1205, 1215, 1225, Afrika Dzonga. Nos. 1206, 1216, 1226, Afrika Sewula. Nos. 1209, 1219, 1229, Mzantsi Afrika.

***Perf. 14½x14¾, 14¾x14½***

**2000, Nov. 15 Litho.**

**1173** A383 5c multi .20 .20
*a.* Perf. 13 .20 .20
**1174** A383 10c multi .20 .20
*a.* Perf. 13 .20 .20
**1175** A383 20c multi .20 .20
*a.* Perf. 13 .20 .20
**1176** A383 30c multi .20 .20
*a.* Perf. 13 .20 .20
**1177** A383 40c multi .20 .20
*a.* Perf. 13 .20 .20
**1178** A383 50c multi .20 .20
*a.* Perf. 13 .20 .20
**1179** A383 60c multi .20 .20
*a.* Perf. 13 .20 .20
**1180** A383 70c multi .20 .20
*a.* Perf. 13 .20 .20
**1181** A383 80c multi .25 .25
*a.* Perf. 13 .25 .25
**1182** A383 90c multi .30 .30
*a.* Perf. 13 .25 .25
**1183** A383 1r multi .30 .30
*a.* Perf. 13 .30 .30
**1184** A383 1.30r multi .40 .40
**1185** A383 1.30r multi .40 .40
**1186** A383 1.30r multi .40 .40
**1187** A383 1.30r multi .40 .40
**1188** A383 1.30r multi .40 .40
*a.* Horiz. strip of 5, #1184-1188 2.00 2.00
**1189** A383 1.40r multi .45 .45
**1190** A383 1.50r multi .50 .50
**1191** A383 1.90r multi .60 .60
**1192** A383 2r multi .65 .65
*a.* Perf. 13 .65 .65
**1193** A383 2.30r multi .70 .70
**1194** A383 3r multi .95 .95
*a.* Perf. 13 .95 .95
**1195** A383 5r multi 1.60 1.60
*a.* Perf. 13 1.60 1.60
**1196** A383 6.30r multi 2.00 2.00
**1197** A383 10r multi 3.00 3.00
*a.* Perf. 13 ('01) 3.00 3.00
**1198** A383 12.60r multi 4.00 4.00
*a.* Perf. 13 ('01) 4.50 4.50
**1199** A383 20r multi 6.25 6.25
*a.* Perf. 13 5.00 5.00

Issued: Nos. 1197a, 1199a, 10/1/01. No. 1179a, 10/1/01. Nos. 1178a, 1192a, 1194a, 1195a, 2002. No. 1173a, 4/2/03; No. 1174a, 5/22/03; Nos. 1175a, 1181a, 9/22/03; Nos. 1176a, 1182a, 1199a, 2/27/03; Nos. 1177a, 1180a, 1183a, 9/23/03.

**Types of 2000**

***Die Cut Perf. 13x12½ on 2 or 3 Sides***

**2000, Nov. 15 Litho.**

**Booklet Stamps**

**Self-Adhesive**

**1200** A384 1.30r multi .40 .40
**1201** A384 1.30r multi .40 .40
**1202** A384 1.30r multi .40 .40
**1203** A384 1.30r multi .40 .40
**1204** A384 1.30r multi .40 .40
**1205** A384 1.30r multi .40 .40
**1206** A384 1.30r multi .40 .40
**1207** A384 1.30r multi .40 .40
**1208** A384 1.30r multi .40 .40
**1209** A384 1.30r multi .40 .40
*a.* Booklet, #1200-1209 4.00

**2001, May 16 Litho. *Perf. 13***

**1210** A383 1.40r multi .45 .45
**1211** A383 1.40r multi .45 .45
**1212** A383 1.40r multi .45 .45
**1213** A383 1.40r multi .45 .45
**1214** A383 1.40r multi .45 .45
*a.* Horiz. strip of 5, #1210-1214 2.25 2.25

**Coil Stamps**

**Self-Adhesive**

***Serpentine Die Cut 13½***

**1215** A384 (1.40r) multi .45 .45
**1216** A384 (1.40r) multi .45 .45
**1217** A384 (1.40r) multi .45 .45
**1218** A384 (1.40r) multi .45 .45
**1219** A384 (1.40r) multi .45 .45
**1219A** A384 (1.40r) multi .45 .45
**1219B** A384 (1.40r) multi .45 .45
**1219C** A384 (1.40r) multi .45 .45
**1219D** A384 (1.40r) multi .45 .45
**1219E** A384 (1.40r) multi .45 .45
*f.* Strip of 10, #1215-1219E 4.50

**Booklet Stamps**

***Die Cut Perf. 13x12½ on 2 or 3 Sides***

**1220** A384 (1.40r) multi .45 .45
**1221** A384 (1.40r) multi .45 .45
**1222** A384 (1.40r) multi .45 .45
**1223** A384 (1.40r) multi .45 .45
**1224** A384 (1.40r) multi .45 .45
**1225** A384 (1.40r) multi .45 .45
**1226** A384 (1.40r) multi .45 .45
**1227** A384 (1.40r) multi .45 .45
**1228** A384 (1.40r) multi .45 .45
**1229** A384 (1.40r) multi .45 .45
*a.* Booklet, #1220-1229 4.50
*Nos. 1173-1229 (62)* 40.40 40.40

**Type of 2000**

**2001, June 16 Litho. *Perf. 13***

**1230** A383 1.60r multi .50 .50
**1231** A383 1.90r multi .60 .60
**1232** A383 2.10r multi .65 .65
**1233** A383 2.50r multi .80 .80
**1234** A383 7r multi 2.25 2.25
**1235** A383 14r multi 4.50 4.50
*Nos. 1230-1235 (6)* 9.30 9.30

Myths and Legends — A385

Designs: 1.30r, The Rain Bull. 1.50r, The Treasure of the Grosvenor. 2.20r, Seven Magic Birds. 2.30r, The Hole in the Wall. 6.30r, Van Hunks and the Devil.

**2001, Jan. 24 Litho. *Perf. 13¾***

**1236-1240** A385 Set of 5 4.25 4.25

Souvenir Sheet

Hong Kong 2001 Stamp Exhibition — A386

**2001, Feb. 1 *Perf. 14½x14***

**1241** A386 4.60r Tree snake 1.40 1.40

Sports Stars A387

Designs: No. 1242, 1.40r, Ernie Els, golfer. No. 1243, 1.40r, Terence Parkin, swimmer. No. 1244, 1.40r, Hezekiel Sepeng, runner. No. 1245, 1.40r, Rosina Magola, netball player. No. 1246, 1.40r, Francois Pienaar, rugby player. No. 1247, 1.40r, Zanele Situ, javelin thrower. No. 1248, 1.40r, Hestrie Cloete, high jumper. No. 1249, 1.40r, Lucas Radebe, soccer player. No. 1250, 1.40r, Vuyani Bungu, boxer. No. 1251, 1.40r, Jonty Rhodes, cricket player.

**2001, Feb. 28 *Perf. 13¾x14***

**1242-1251** A387 Set of 10 4.50 4.50
*1251a* Sheet of 15 #1251 +15 labels, perf. 14½x14 6.50

Labels on No. 1251a depict players from the 2000-01 South African World Cup Cricket team.

Kgalagadi Transfrontier Park — A388

Designs: 1.40r, Gemsboks, flags of South Africa and Botswana. 2.50r, Cheetahs. 2.90r, Sociable weaver birds. 3.60r, Meerkats.

**2001, May 12 Litho. *Perf. 13x13¼***

**1252-1255** A388 Set of 4 3.25 3.25
*1254a* Souvenir sheet, #1253-1254 1.75 1.75

See Botswana Nos. 714-717.

Campaign Against Child Abuse — A389

**2001, May 16 *Perf. 13¾***

**1256** A389 1.40r multi .45 .45

Soweto Uprising, 25th Anniv. — A390

**2001, June 16 Litho. *Perf. 13¾***

**1257** A390 1.40r multi .45 .45

Bats — A391

No. 1258: a, Cape horseshoe bat. b, Welwitsch's hairy bat. c, Schreiber's long-fingered bat. d, Wahlberg's epauletted fruit bat. e, Short-eared trident bat. f, Common slit-faced bat. g, Egyptian fruit bat. h, Egyptian free-tailed bat, vert. i, De Winton's long-eared bat. j, Large-eared free-tailed bat.

***Serpentine Die Cut 11¼***

**2001, June 22**

**Self-Adhesive**

**1258** A391 Sheet of 10, #a-j 4.50 4.50
*a.-j.* 1.40r Any single .45 .45

Boer War, Cent. — A392

Designs: 1.40r, Rev. J. D. Kestell. 3r, Capt. Thomas Crean.

**2001, Aug. 1 *Perf. 13¼***

**1259-1260** A392 Set of 2 1.40 1.40
*a.* Booklet pane, #1259-1260, perf. 13¼x13¾ 1.75 —

Issued: No. 1260a, 5/31/02. See note after No. 1282.

World Conference Against Racism, Durban — A393

No. 1262: a, Kgotlelelo le pharologantsho. b, Kubeketelelana kanye nekwehlukana. c, Verdraagsaamheid en diversiteit. d, U kondelelana na u fhambana. e, Kutlwisiso ka mefutafuta. f, Ku va ni mbilu yo leha ni kuhambana-hambana. g, Ibekezelelwano nehlukahlukano. h, Kgothlelelo le pharologano. i, Ukubekezelelana nokungafani. j, Ukunyamezelana nokungafani.

**2001, Aug. 1** ***Perf. 13¾x13½***

**1261** A393 2.10r shown .65 .65
**1262** Sheet of 10 4.50 4.50
*a.-j.* A393 1.40r Any single .45 .45

See Brazil No. 2809.

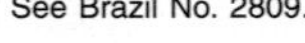

Musical Instruments — A394

Designs: 1.40r, Concertina. 1.90r, Trumpet. 2.50r, Electric guitar. 3r, African drum. 7r, Cello.

**Litho. with Foil Application**

**2001, Aug. 23** ***Perf. 13¼x14***

**1263-1267** A394 Set of 5 5.00 5.00

Christmas A395

Designs: 2r, Tree. 3r, Angel.

**2001, Oct. 1** **Litho.** ***Perf. 13¼***

**1268-1269** A395 Set of 2 1.60 1.60

Frame — A396

**2001, Oct. 1** ***Serpentine Die Cut***

**Self-Adhesive**

**1270** A396 (1.40r) multi .45 .45
*a.* Double-sided pane of 10 + 40 labels 4.50

Volvo Round-the-World Yacht Race — A397

Designs: 1.40r, Yacht. 6r, Yacht, horiz.

**2001, Oct. 23** ***Perf. 13***

**1271** A397 1.40r multi .45 .45

**Souvenir Sheet**

***Perf. 14x13¼***

**1272** A397 6r multi 1.90 1.90

No. 1272 contains one 40x30mm stamp.

2003 ICC Cricket World Cup, South Africa — A398

**2001, Nov. 1** ***Perf. 14x13¾***

**1273** A398 (1.40r) multi .45 .45

**Souvenir Sheet**

New Year 2002 (Year of the Horse) — A399

**2001, Nov. 2** ***Perf. 14x13¼***

**1274** A399 6r multi 1.90 1.90

Marine Life — A400

No. 1275: a, Hammerhead shark. b, Loggerhead turtle, vert. c, Clown triggerfish, vert. d, Cape fur seal, vert. e, Bottlenosed dolphins. f, Crowned seahorse, vert. g, Blue-spotted ribbontail ray, vert. h, Moorish idol. i, Common octopus. j, Coral rock cod.

***Serpentine Die Cut 12¾***

**2001, Nov. 2**

**Self-Adhesive**

**1275** A400 Sheet of 10 4.50 4.50
*a.-j.* (1.40r) Any single .45 .45

Johannesburg World Summit on Sustainable Development — A401

Designs: Nos. 1276a, 1281c, Prosperity, vert. Nos. 1276b, 1281a, People, vert. Nos. 1276c, 1281b, Planet, vert. (1.50r), Water, sanitation and energy for all. No. 1278, Buildings, globe. No. 1279, Clean environment for health. (3.30r), Food security for all.

Sizes: Nos. 1276a-1276c, 22x32mm, Nos. 1281a-1281c, 21x26mm.

***Perf. 13¾x13¼, 13¼x13 (#1277, 1279, 1280), 13¼x13¾ (#1278)***

**2002** **Litho.**

**1276** A401 (1.40r) Strip of 3, #a-c 1.40 1.40
**1277** A401 (1.50r) multi .50 .50
**1278** A401 (3r) multi .95 .95
**1279** A401 (3r) multi .95 .95
**1280** A401 (3.30r) multi 1.00 1.00

**Booklet Stamps**

**Self-Adhesive**

***Serpentine Die Cut on 2 or 3 Sides***

**1281** A401 (1.40r) Strip of 3, #a-c 1.40 1.40
*d.* Booklet pane, 4 #1281a, 3 #1281b-1281c 4.50 4.50
*Nos. 1276-1281 (6)* 6.20 6.20

Issued: Nos. 1276, 1278, 1281, 4/17. Nos. 1277, 1279, 1280, 8/25. No. 1279 is airmail.

**Souvenir Sheet**

End of Boer War, Cent. — A402

No. 1282: a, 1.50r, Army officer. b, 3.30r, Government official.

**2002, May 31** ***Perf. 13¼x13¾***

**1282** A402 Sheet of 2, #a-b 1.50 1.50
*c.* Booklet pane, #1282 1.90 —
Complete booklet, #1151b, 1172a, 1260a, 1282c + 2 postal cards 10.50

No. 1282c has rouletting between margin of No. 1282 and the booklet pane margin. Complete booklet sold for 45r.

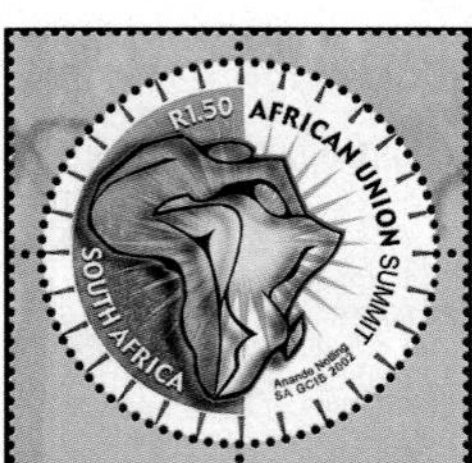

African Union Summit A403

**2002, June 25** ***Perf. 13½***

**1283** A403 1.50r multi .50 .50

Values are for stamps with surrounding selvage.

**Type of 2000**

Designs: 1.80r, Emperor moth. 2.20r, Peach moth. 2.80r, Snouted tiger moth. 9r, False tiger moth. 16r, Moon moth.

**2002, Sept. 20** **Litho.** ***Perf. 13***

**1284** A383 1.80r multi .55 .55
**1285** A383 2.20r multi .70 .70
**1286** A383 2.80r multi .85 .85
**1287** A383 9r multi 2.75 2.75
**1288** A383 16r multi 5.00 5.00
*Nos. 1284-1288 (5)* 9.85 9.85

A404 A405

A406 A407

ICC Cricket World Cup
A408 A409

**2002** ***Perf. 12½x12¾***

**1289** A404 (1.50r) multi .50 .50
**1290** A405 (1.50r) multi .50 .50
**1291** A407 (1.50r) multi .50 .50
**1292** A409 (1.50r) multi .50 .50
**1293** A406 (1.50r) multi .50 .50
**1294** A408 (1.50r) multi .50 .50
*Nos. 1289-1294 (6)* 3.00 3.00

Issued: Nos. 1289, 1290, 9/23; 1292, 1294, 11/1; Nos. 1291, 1293, 12/21.

**Souvenir Sheet**

Steve Biko (1946-77), Anti-apartheid Leader — A410

**2002, Oct. 9** ***Perf. 14¾x14½***

**1295** A410 4.75r multi 1.50 1.50

See note under No. 1321.

**Souvenir Sheet**

World Post Day — A411

**2002, Oct. 9** ***Perf. 13¼x13½***

**1296** A411 4.75r multi 1.50 1.50

Christmas — A412

Stained glass patterns: 1.50r, 3r.

**2002, Oct. 23** ***Perf. 14x14¾***

**1297-1298** A412 Set of 2 1.40 1.40

Souvenir Sheets

Sawfish — A413

Designs: No. 1299, 7r, Pristis pectinata. No. 1300, 7r, Pristis microdon.

**2002, Oct. 23** ***Perf. 13¾***
**1299-1300** A413 Set of 2 4.50 4.50

JUNASS Philatelic Exhibition (#1299); Algoapex Philatelic Exhibition (#1300).

Souvenir Sheet

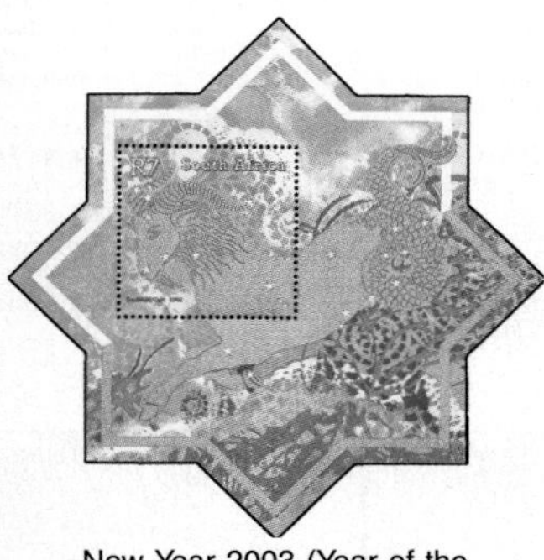

New Year 2003 (Year of the Ram) — A414

**2002, Nov. 1** ***Perf. 14½***
**1301** A414 7r multi 2.25 2.25

AIDS Prevention — A415

No. 1302 — AIDS prevention ribbon and: a, Man with sunglasses, male symbol. b, Woman with open mouth. c, Woman with sunglasses, female symbol. d, Hand holding candle, "Stop." e, Woman, candle. f, Hand holding candle, "Be safe." g, Candle, hand pointing at ribbon. h, Open hand. i, Face in droplet. j, Open hand, pills.

***Serpentine Die Cut 11¾***
**2002, Nov. 29**
**Self-Adhesive**

**1302** Booklet of 10 4.75 4.75
***a.-j.*** A415 (1.50r) Any single .45 .45

Souvenir Sheet

Solar Eclipse of Dec. 4, 2002 — A416

**2002, Dec. 4** ***Perf. 14½***
**1303** A416 4.75r multi 1.50 1.50

ICC Cricket World Cup — A417

No. 1304: a, Huts with windmill blades. b, Horseman. c, Cricket players with bats. d, Bus with people on roof. e, Mother and child. f, Double-decker bus.

**2003, Feb. 28** ***Perf. 14¼x13¾***
**1304** A417 (1.50r) Sheet of 6, #a-f 2.75 2.75

Souvenir Sheet

Tembisile (Chris) Hani (1942-93), African National Congress Leader — A418

**2003, Apr. 27** **Litho.** ***Perf. 14¾***
**1305** A418 (1.65r) multi .45 .45

See note after No. 1321.

Life in Informal Settlements — A419

No. 1306: a, Women carrying water jugs on head. b, Man with guitar. c, Man with rake. d, Woman using sewing machine. e, Two children. f, Drink vendor. g, Shoemakers. h, Woman with green cap. i, Young woman with cap and tire. j, Woman with child.

**2003, May 16** ***Perf. 14x13¾***
**1306** A419 (1.65r) Sheet of 10, #a-j 4.50 4.50

Souvenir Sheet

Africa Day — A420

**2003, May 25** ***Perf. 14¾***
**1307** A420 11.70r multi 3.00 3.00

Souvenir Sheet

Oliver Reginald Tambo (1917-93), African National Congress President — A421

**2003, May 29**
**1308** A421 (1.65r) multi .45 .45

See note after No. 1321.

Ballroom Dancing — A422

Designs: 1.65r, Salsa. 2.20r, Rumba. 2.80r, Waltz. 3.30r, Foxtrot. 3.80r, Tango.

**2003, July 23** ***Perf. 13¼x13¾***
**1309-1313** A422 Set of 5 3.75 3.75

Dogs — A423

No. 1314: a, Africanis. b, Rhodesian Ridgeback. c, Boerboel. d, Basenji.

**2003, Aug. 1** ***Perf. 14½***
**1314** A423 (1.65r) Sheet of 4, #a-d 1.90 1.90

**Type of 2000**

Designs: No. 1315, Botterblom, vert. No. 1316, Blue marguerite, vert. No. 1317, Karoo violet, vert. No. 1318, Tree pelargonium, vert. No. 1319, Black-eyed susy, vert.

**2003, Sept. 15** **Litho.** ***Perf. 13***
**1315** A383 (1.65r) multi .45 .45
**1316** A383 (1.65r) multi .45 .45
**1317** A383 (1.65r) multi .45 .45
**1318** A383 (1.65r) multi .45 .45
**1319** A383 (1.65r) multi .45 .45
***a.*** Horiz. strip of 5, #1315-1319 2.25 2.25

Souvenir Sheet

Walter Max Ulyate Sisulu (1912-2003), African National Congress Deputy President — A424

**2003, Sept. 24** ***Perf. 14¾***
**1320** A424 11.70r multi 3.50 3.50

See note after No. 1321.

Souvenir Sheet

Robert Mangaliso Sobukwe (1924-1978), Pan Africanist Congress President — A425

**2003, Sept. 24** ***Perf. 14¾***
**1321** A425 11.70r multi 3.50 3.50

Nos. 1295, 1305, 1308, 1320 and 1321 were sold in, but unattached to, a commemorative booklet that sold for 60r.

Stamp of Fortune Television Show — A426

**2003, Sept. 29** ***Perf. 14¼x14***
**1322** A426 (1.65r) multi .50 .50

Engineering and Postal Communication — A427

No. 1323: a, Shongweni Dam (60x23mm). b, Kimberley Microwave Tower (30x47mm). c, Northern Cape Legislature Building (30x23mm). d, Durban Westville highway interchange (30x47mm). e, Postal truck on Community Bridge, Limpopo (30x23mm). f, Nelson Mandela Bridge, Johannesburg (60x23mm).

**2003, Oct. 9** ***Perf. 14x14¼***
**1323** A427 (3.30r) Sheet of 6, #a-f 5.75 5.75
***g.*** Like No. 1323, with PIARC World Road Congress inscription in margin 5.75 5.75

Souvenir Sheet

South Africa - India Diplomatic Relations, 10th Anniv. — A428

**2003, Oct. 16** ***Perf. 14¾***
**1324** A428 3.35r multi .95 .95

Bid for Hosting 2010 World Cup Soccer Championships — A429

Emblem, soccer fan with painted face and: No. 1325, (3.80r), Map of Africa. No. 1326, (4.25r), Soccer players.

**2003, Oct. 23**
**1325-1326** A429 Set of 2 2.40 2.40

No. 1325 is airmail.

Cape of Good Hope Triangle Stamps, 150th Anniv.
A430

**2003, Oct. 23 Litho.** ***Perf. 12½x12¾***
**1327** A430 (1.65r) blue .50 .50

Printed in sheets of 4.

A431

Christmas — A432

No. 1328: a, Joseph, Mary on donkey. b, Angels. c, Magi. d, Madonna and Child. e, Dove.

**2003, Nov. 3 Litho.** ***Perf. 14x14¼***
**1328** Horiz. strip of 5 2.40 2.40
***a.-e.*** A431 (1.65r) Any single .45 .45

***Perf. 14¾***

**1329** A432 3.80r shown 1.10 1.10

Elephants — A433

No. 1330: a, African elephants. b, Asian elephant.
Illustration reduced.

**2003, Dec. 9** ***Perf. 14¼x14***
**1330** A433 3.35r Horiz. pair, #a-b 2.10 2.10

South Africa — Thailand diplomatic relations, 10th anniv. See Thailand No. 2105.

Powered Flight, Cent. — A434

No. 1331: a, Paterson Biplane. b, "Silver Queen" Vickers Vimy. c, Wapiti. d, De Havilland DH-9. e, Junkers Ju52/53. f, Sikorsky S-55 helicopter. g, Boeing 707. h, Rooivalk helicopter. i, SUNSAT Microsatellite. j, Mark Shuttleworth, first African in space, and Space Station.

**2003, Dec. 17** ***Perf. 14¼x14***
**1331** A434 (1.65r) Sheet of 10, #a-j 5.00 5.00

Souvenir Sheet

New Year 2004 (Year of the Monkey) — A435

**2004, Jan. 22** ***Perf. 13¾***
**1332** A435 11.70r multi 3.25 3.25

Road Safety — A436

No. 1333 — Inscriptions: a, Be visible. b, Don't drink and drive. c, Maintain your vehicle. d, Slow down. e, Don't drive when tired.

***Perf. 13¼x13¾***

**2004, Mar. 24 Litho.**
**1333** Vert. strip of 5 2.75 2.75
***a.-e.*** A436 (1.70r) Any single .55 .55

End of Apartheid, 10th Anniv. — A437

No. 1334: a, Dove, map of Africa. b, People voting. c, Women and child. d, Sports fans holding flag and trophies. e, Woman with handicrafts.

**2004, Apr. 27 Litho.** ***Perf. 13¼***
**1334** Vert. strip of 5 2.50 2.50
***a.-e.*** A437 (1.70r) Any single .50 .50

Miniature Sheet

Legacy of Slaves — A438

No. 1335: a, Slave bell, Vergelegen, and slave lodge, Cape Town. b, Hidayat al-Islam, first book in Arabic-Afrikaans. c, Chair and cupboard. d, Traditional foods. e, Indian workers in sugar cane fields. f, Chinese mine workers.

**2005, May 1**
**1335** A438 (1.70r) Sheet of 6, #a-f 3.00 3.00

Souvenir Sheet

FIFA (Fédération Internationale de Football Association), Cent. — A439

**2004, Apr. 30 Litho.** ***Perf. 14¾***
**1336** A439 4.35r multi 1.25 1.25

Spiders — A440

No. 1337: a, Hedgehog spider. b, Golden orb-web spider, vert. c, Lynx spider, vert. d, Black button spider, vert. e, Ladybird spider. f, Flower crab spider. g, Rain spider, vert. h, Horn baboon spider. i, Trap door spider. j, Spotted crab spider.

***Serpentine Die Cut 9½x9, 9x9½***

**2004, July 30**

**Self-Adhesive**

**1337** A440 Sheet of 10, #a-j 5.50 5.50
***a.-j.*** (1.70r) Any single .55 .55

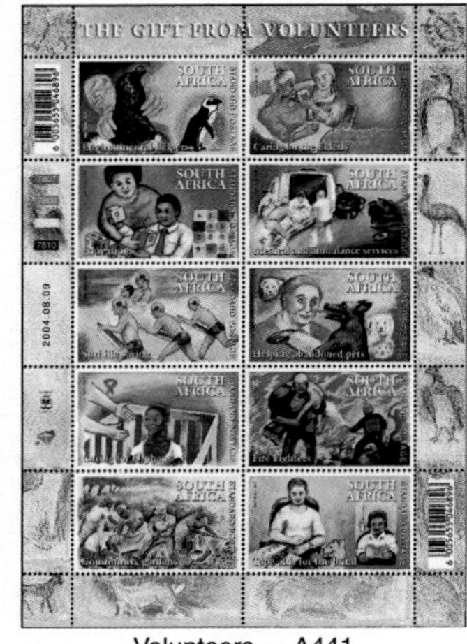
Volunteers — A441

No. 1338: a, Environmental helpers. b, Caring for the elderly. c, Education. d, Medical and ambulance services. e, Surf life saving. f, Helping abandoned pets. g, Caring for orphans. h, Fire fighters. i, Community gardens. j, Tape aids for the blind.

**2004, Aug. 9** ***Perf. 13½x13¾***
**1338** A441 (1.70r) Sheet of 10, #a-j 5.25 5.25

Sports — A442

No. 1339: a, Archery. b, Track. c, Equestrian. d, Cycling. e, Rhythmic gymnastics. f, Canoeing. g, Soccer. h, Swimming. i, Boxing. j, Tennis.

**2004, Aug. 13** ***Perf. 13¾x13½***
**1339** A442 (1.70r) Sheet of 10, #a-j 5.25 5.25

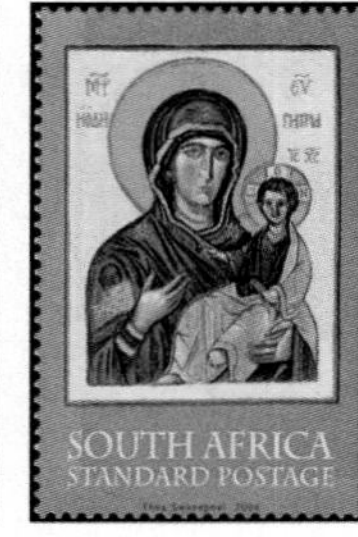
Christmas
A443

Icons: (1.70r), Madonna and Child. (4r), Jesus Christ, Pantocrator.

**2004, Oct. 1**
**1340-1341** A443 Set of 2 1.75 1.75

No. 1341 is inscribed "International Airmail Letter."

Birds — A444

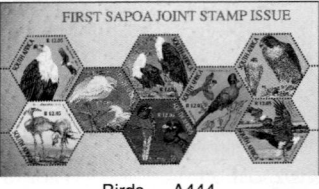

No. 1342: a, African fish eagles, national bird of Namibia. b, African fish eagles, national bird of Zimbabwe. c, Peregrine falcons, national bird of Angola. d, Cattle egrets, national bird of Botswana. e, Purple-crested louries, national bird of Swaziland. f, Blue cranes, national bird of South Africa. g, Bar-tailed trogons. h, African fish eagles, national bird of Zambia.

**2004, Oct. 9** ***Perf. 14***
**1342** A444 12.05r Sheet of 8, #a-h 30.00 30.00

See Angola No. , Botswana Nos. 792-793, Malawi No., Namibia No. 1052, Swaziland Nos. 727-735, Zambia No. 1033, and Zimbabwe No. 975.

Souvenir Sheet

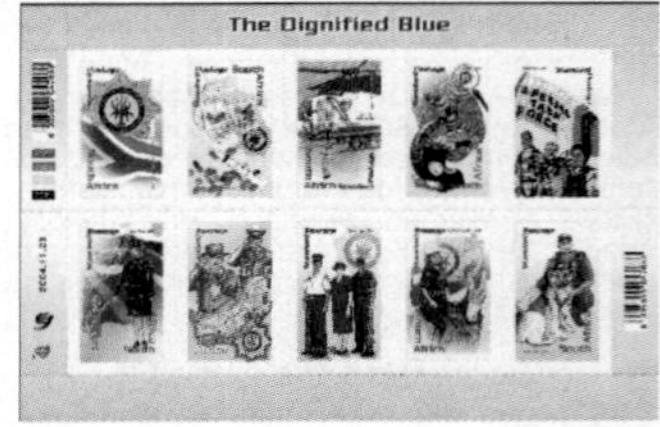
Regular Air Mail Service in South Africa, 75th Anniv. — A445

**Litho. with Hologram**

**2004, Oct. 9** ***Perf. 13¾***
**1343** A445 12.05r multi 3.75 3.75

South African Police Service, 10th Anniv. — A446

No. 1344: a, South African Police Service badge, South African flag. b, Fighting drugs. c, Police air wing. d, Fingerprint and forensic science. e, Special task force. f, Protecting women and children. g, Sector policing. h, The Dignified Blue. i, SAPS mounted unit. j, Dog unit.

***Serpentine Die Cut 13½x13***

**2004, Nov. 23 Litho.**

**Self-Adhesive**

**1344** A446 Sheet of 10 6.00 6.00
***a.-j.*** (1.70r) Any single .60 .60

South African Large Telescope
A447

No. 1345: a, Exterior of building. b, Cut-away view of building. c, Building aperture, top of telescope, Southern Cross constellation. d, Telescope. e, Building aperture, entire telescope.

**2004, Dec. 1** ***Perf. 13¾x13½***

**1345** Horiz. strip of 5 7.00 7.00
***a.-e.*** A447 4r Any single 1.40 1.40

Souvenir Sheet

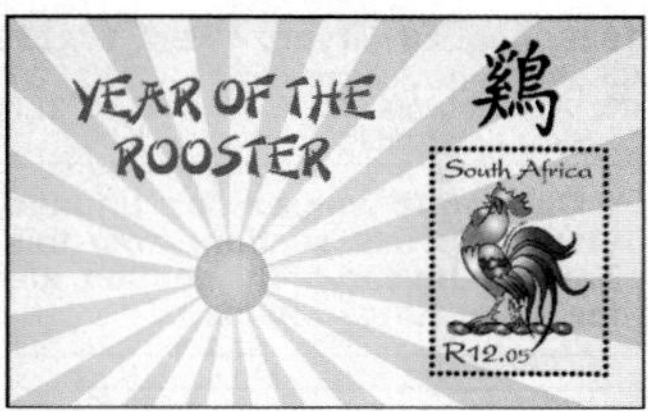


New Year 2005 (Year of the Rooster) — A448

**2005, Feb. 9** ***Perf. 14¾x14½***

**1346** A448 12.05r multi 4.00 4.00

Souvenir Sheet

Freedom Charter, 50th Anniv. — A449

No. 1347: a, "Freedom Charter" in mirror image. b, "Freedom Charter" and "50."

***Perf. 14¼x14¾***

**2005, June 24** **Litho.**

**1347** A449 (1.77r) Sheet of 2, #a-b 1.10 1.10

Miniature Sheet

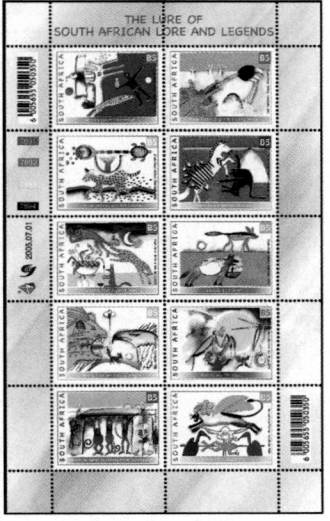

Legends — A450

No. 1348: a, Honeyguide's Revenge. b, How Ostrich Got His Long Neck. c, How Serval Got His Spots. d, How Zebra Got His Stripes. e, Jackal, the Tiger Eater. f, Jackal and Wolf. g, King Lion and King Eagle. h, Mantis and the Moon. i, Words as Sweet as Honey from Sankhambi. j, When Lion Could Fly.

**2005, July 1**

**1348** A450 B5 Sheet of 10, #a-j 11.00 11.00

Nos. 1348a-11348j each sold for 3.75r on day of issue.

Miniature Sheet

Small Mammals — A451

No. 1349: a, Lesser bushbaby (24x60mm). b, Riverine rabbit (24x30mm). c, African wildcat (48x30mm). d, Yellow mongoose (24x60mm). e, Steenbok (48x30mm). f, Cape fox (24x30mm).

**2005, July 15** ***Perf. 14***

**1349** A451 (1.77r) Sheet of 6, #a-f 3.50 3.50

Energy Sources — A452

**2005, Sept. 26** ***Perf. 14x14¼***

**1350** A452 (1.77r) Wave .55 .55
**1351** A452 (3.65r) Wind 1.10 1.10
**1352** A452 (4.25r) Sun 1.40 1.40
*Nos. 1350-1352 (3)* 3.05 3.05

Inscription on No. 1350, Standard Postage; No. 1351, International Airmail Postcard; No. 1352, International Airmail Letter.

Christmas A453

Wire and bead sculptures: (1.77r), Candle, Christmas tree, heart. (4.25r), Angel and dove.

**2005, Oct. 3**

**1353** A453 (1.77r) multi .55 .55
**1354** A453 (4.25r) multi 1.40 1.40

Inscription on No. 1353, Standard Postage; No. 1354, International Airmail Letter.

Prevention of Blindness — A454

**Litho. & Embossed**

**2005, Oct. 13** ***Perf. 14¼x14***

**1355** A454 (1.77r) org brn & gray .55 .55

Souvenir Sheet

New Year 2006 (Year of the Dog) — A455

No. 1356: a, Seeing-eye dog. b, Drug-sniffing dog and luggage. c, Bird-chasing dog at airport.

**2006, Jan. 26** ***Perf. 13¼x13***

**1356** A455 B5 Sheet of 3, #a-c 3.75 3.75

Nos. 1356a-1356c each sold for 3.75r on day of issue.

Rock Art — A456

No. 1357: a, Detail of Linton Panel, Iziko South African Museum. b, Reedbuck, South African Museum of Rock Art (inscription at LR). c, San ritual specialist, South African Museum of Rock Art (inscription at LL). d, Rhinoceros, Wildebeest Kuil rock art site. e, Eland, Game Pass rock art site.

**2006, Feb. 15**

**1357** Horiz. strip of 5 3.00 3.00
***a.-e.*** A456 (1.77r) Any single .60 .60

Miniature Sheet

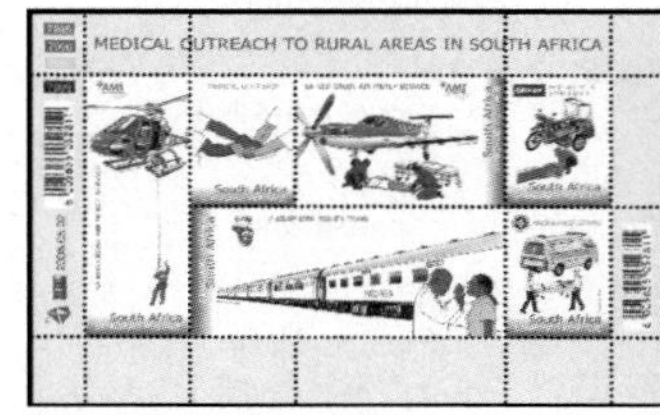


Rural Medical Outreach — A457

No. 1358: a, Helicopter and rescuer (24x60mm). b, Doctors clasping hands (24x30mm). c, Airplane, paramedics tending to man on stretcher, horiz. (48x30mm). d, Motorcycle ambulance, paramedic assisting man (24x30mm). e, Phelophepa Health Train, doctor examining woman, horiz. (72x30mm). f, Ambulance, attendants moving patient on gurney (24x30mm).

**2006, May 2** **Litho.** ***Perf. 13¼***

**1358** A457 (1.85r) Sheet of 6, #a-f 3.75 3.75

Chief Bhambatha Zondi, Leader of 1906 Rebellion — A458

Illustration reduced.

**2006, June 9** ***Perf. 14x13½***

**1359** A458 (1.85r) multi .55 .55

Red Cross War Memorial Children's Hospital, 50th Anniv. — A459

Designs: (1.85r), Nurse and ill child. (4.40r), Hospital building, horiz.

***Perf. 13¾x13½, 13½x13¾***

**2006, June 18**

**1360-1361** A459 Set of 2 1.75 1.75

Inscription on No. 1360 reads "Standard Postage;" on No. 1361, "International Letter."

Souvenir Sheet

Women's Anti-Apartheid March to the Union Building, Pretoria, 50th Anniv. — A460

**2006, Aug. 9** ***Perf. 14¾x14***

**1362** A460 B5 multi 1.10 1.10

No. 1362 sold for 3.75r on day of issue.

Miniature Sheet

Clivia Flowers — A461

No. 1363: a, Clivia nobilis. b, Clivia miniata. c, Clivia gardenii. d, Clivia caulescens. e, Clivia mirabilis. f, Clivia robusta.

**2006, Sept. 6** ***Perf. 13x13¼***

**1363** A461 (1.85r) Sheet of 6, #a-f 3.00 3.00

Animal, Text and Tracks A462

Animal, Herd and Tracks A463

No. 1364: a, Buffalo. b, Elephant. c, Blue wildebeest. d, Hippopotamus. e, Black rhinoceros. f, Giraffe. g, Spotted hyena. h, Leopard. i, Warthog. j, Zebra.

**Litho. & Embossed**

**2006, Sept. 15** ***Perf. 13¾x13¼***

**1364** Sheet of 10 5.00 5.00
***a.-e.*** A462 (1.85r) Any single .50 .50
***f.-j.*** A463 (1.85r) Any single .50 .50

Christmas — A464

No. 1365: a, Antelope. b, Warthog. c, Zebra. d, Hippopotamus. e, Lion, as Santa, in sleigh. (4.40r), Lion as Santa.

**2006, Oct. 2** **Litho.** ***Perf. 13½x13***

**1365** Horiz. strip of 5 2.40 2.40
***a.-e.*** A464 (1.85r) Any single .45 .45
**1366** A464 (4.40r) multi 1.25 1.25

Inscriptions on Nos. 1365a-1365e read "Standard Postage;" on No. 1366, "International Airmail Letter."

World Post Day — A465

No. 1367 — Boy and slogan: a, "Start an Adventure." b, "Be Cool." c, "Learn More." d, "Have Fun." e, "Travel the World."

**2006, Oct. 9** ***Perf. 13x13¼***

| | | | |
|---|---|---|---|
| **1367** | Horiz. strip of 5 | 2.50 | 2.50 |
| *a.-e.* | A465 (1.85r) Any single | .50 | .50 |

## SEMI-POSTAL STAMPS

**Catalogue values for unused stamps in this section are for Never Hinged items.**

English-Afrikaans Se-Tenant

Stamps with English inscriptions and with Afrikaans inscriptions of Nos. B1-B11 were printed alternately in the same sheets. Major-number listings and values are for pairs consisting of one English and one Afrikaans-inscribed stamp.

Church of the Vow — SP1

Cradock's Pass — SP2

Voortrekker — SP3

Voortrekker Woman — SP4

**1933-36 Photo. Wmk. 201** ***Perf. 14***

| | | | |
|---|---|---|---|
| **B1** | SP1 ½p + ½p grn & blk, pair ('36) | 11.00 | 4.75 |
| *a.* | Single, English | .55 | .55 |
| *b.* | Single, Afrikaans | .55 | .55 |
| **B2** | SP2 1p + ½p rose & blk, pair | 7.25 | 3.75 |
| *a.* | Single, English | .45 | .35 |
| *b.* | Single, Afrikaans | .45 | .35 |
| **B3** | SP3 2p + 1p dull vio & gray, pair | 12.00 | 6.00 |
| *a.* | Single, English | .55 | .55 |
| *b.* | Single, Afrikaans | .55 | .55 |
| **B4** | SP4 3p + 1½p dp blue & gray, pair | 18.00 | 9.50 |
| *a.* | Single, English | 1.50 | 1.10 |
| *b.* | Single, Afrikaans | 1.50 | 1.10 |
| | *Nos. B1-B4 (4)* | 48.25 | 24.00 |

Issued to commemorate the Voortrekkers. Surtax went to the National Memorial Fund for a national Voortrekker monument.

Voortrekker Plowing — SP5

Crossing the Drakensberg — SP6

Signing Dingaan-Retief Treaty — SP7

Proposed Monument — SP8

**1938, Dec. 14** ***Perf. 14***

| | | | |
|---|---|---|---|
| **B5** | SP5 ½p + ½p dl grn & ind, pair | 5.50 | 5.25 |
| *a.* | Single, English | .55 | .45 |
| *b.* | Single, Afrikaans | .55 | .45 |
| **B6** | SP6 1p + 1p rose & sl, pair | 7.25 | 6.00 |
| *a.* | Single, English | .65 | .55 |
| *b.* | Single, Afrikaans | .65 | .55 |
| | ***Perf. 15x14*** | | |
| **B7** | SP7 1½p + 1½p Prus grn & choc, pair | 17.50 | 10.50 |
| *a.* | Single, English | 1.10 | 1.10 |
| *b.* | Single, Afrikaans | 1.10 | 1.10 |
| **B8** | SP8 3p + 3p chlky bl, pair | 20.00 | 12.50 |
| *a.* | Single, English | 1.40 | 1.60 |
| *b.* | Single, Afrikaans | 1.40 | 1.60 |
| | *Nos. B5-B8 (4)* | 50.25 | 34.25 |

Voortrekker centenary. Surtax went to the Natl. Memorial Fund for a Voortrekker monument.

"The Old Vicarage," Huguenot Museum — SP9

Rising Sun and Cross — SP10

Huguenot Dwelling, Drakenstein Mountain Valley — SP11

**1939, July 17 Photo.** ***Perf. 14***

| | | | |
|---|---|---|---|
| **B9** | SP9 ½p + ½p Prus grn & gray brn, pair | 6.50 | 4.75 |
| *a.* | Single, English | .50 | .50 |
| *b.* | Single, Afrikaans | .50 | .50 |
| **B10** | SP10 1p + 1p rose car & Prus grn, pair | 6.25 | 6.00 |
| *a.* | Single, English | .60 | .60 |
| *b.* | Single, Afrikaans | .60 | .60 |
| | ***Perf. 15x14*** | | |
| **B11** | SP11 1½p + 1½p, pair | 16.00 | 9.00 |
| *a.* | Single, English | .95 | .95 |
| *b.* | Single, Afrikaans | .95 | .95 |
| | *Nos. B9-B11 (3)* | 28.75 | 19.75 |

250th anniv. of the landing of the Huguenots in South Africa. Surtax went to a fund to build a Huguenot memorial at Paarl.

No. 581 Surcharged in English or Afrikaans

a

b

c

d

**1987, Nov. 16 Litho.** ***Perf. 14x14½***

| | | | |
|---|---|---|---|
| **B12** | Pair | 1.00 | 1.00 |
| *a.* | A229(a) 16c +10c red | .50 | .50 |
| *b.* | A229(b) 16c +10c red | .50 | .50 |

Surcharge for flood relief.

No. 702 Surcharged in English or Afrikaans

**1987, Dec. 1**

| | | | |
|---|---|---|---|
| **B13** | Pair | 1.00 | 1.00 |
| *a.* | A254(a) 16c +10c multicolored | .50 | .50 |
| *b.* | A254(b) 16c +10c multicolored | .50 | .50 |

"+10c" is overprinted below text on Nos. B13a-B13b. Surcharge for flood relief.

No. 706 Surcharged in English or Afrikaans

**1988, Mar. 1** ***Perf. 14½x14***

| | | | |
|---|---|---|---|
| **B14** | Pair | 1.00 | 1.00 |
| *a.* | A256(a) 16c +10c multicolored | .50 | .50 |
| *b.* | A256(b) 16c +10c multicolored | .50 | .50 |

Surcharge for flood relief.

Nos. 710-713 Surcharged in English or Afrikaans

**1988, Apr. 13** ***Perf. 14x14½***

| | | | |
|---|---|---|---|
| **B15** | Pair | .85 | .85 |
| *a.* | A257(c) 16c +10c multicolored | .40 | .40 |
| *b.* | A257(d) 16c +10c multicolored | .40 | .40 |
| **B16** | Pair | 1.60 | 1.60 |
| *a.* | A257(c) 30c +10c multicolored | .80 | .80 |
| *b.* | A257(d) 30c +10c multicolored | .80 | .80 |
| **B17** | Pair | 2.25 | 2.25 |
| *a.* | A257(c) 40c +10c multicolored | 1.10 | 1.10 |
| *b.* | A257(d) 40c +10c multicolored | 1.10 | 1.10 |
| **B18** | Pair | 2.75 | 2.75 |
| *a.* | A257(c) 50c +10c multicolored | 1.25 | 1.25 |
| *b.* | A257(d) 50c +10c multicolored | 1.25 | 1.25 |
| | *Nos. B12-B18 (7)* | 10.45 | 10.45 |

Surcharge for flood relief.

On Nos. B16a, B16b, the "+ 10" is in upper left corner.

## AIR POST STAMPS

Mail Plane — AP1

Biplane in Flight — AP2

Unwmk.

**1925, Feb. 26 Litho.** ***Perf. 12***

| | | | |
|---|---|---|---|
| **C1** | AP1 1p red | 3.00 | 4.75 |
| **C2** | AP1 3p ultramarine | 10.00 | *13.00* |
| **C3** | AP1 6p violet | 17.50 | *24.00* |
| **C4** | AP1 9p gray green | 29.00 | *32.50* |
| | *Nos. C1-C4 (4)* | 59.50 | *74.25* |
| | Set, never hinged | 150.00 | |

Forgeries exist.

**1929, Aug. 16 Typo.** ***Perf. 14x13½***

| | | | |
|---|---|---|---|
| **C5** | AP2 4p blue green | 8.50 | 2.75 |
| **C6** | AP2 1sh orange | 27.50 | 21.00 |
| | Set, never hinged | 75.00 | |

**Catalogue values for unused stamps in this section, from this point to the end of the section, are for Never Hinged items.**

**"AIRMAIL POSTCARD"**
**"AIRMAIL POSTCARD RATE"**

Stamps inscribed thus were sold for the amount shown in ( ) on date of issue.

See Nos. 1038-1042F for stamps included with postage sets.

**Endangered Fauna Type of 1993**

**1996, May 8 Litho.** ***Perf. 14x14½***

| | | | |
|---|---|---|---|
| **C6A** | A288 (1r) White rhinoceros | .50 | .50 |
| **C6B** | A288 (1r) Buffalo | .50 | .50 |
| **C6C** | A288 (1r) Lion | .50 | .50 |
| *f.* | Souvenir sheet of 1 + label | .55 | .55 |
| **C6D** | A288 (1r) Leopard | .50 | .50 |
| **C6E** | A288 (1r) African elephant | .50 | .50 |
| *g.* | Strip of 5, #936-940 | 2.50 | |
| *h.* | Sheet of 10, 2 each #936-940 | 5.00 | |
| *i.* | Booklet pane of 5, #936-940 + 5 labels | 3.00 | |
| | Complete booklet, #940c | 3.00 | |

No. C6Cf is inscribed in sheet margin for Coach House, and sold for 1r.

Issued: #C6Cf, 2/97; #C6Ei, 7/27/97.

Inauguaration of Blue Train — AP3

Designs: No. C7, Double-headed Class 6E 1, electric locomotives, Cape Town to Beaufort West. No. C8, Double-headed Class 6E 1 electric lovomotives, Hex River Valley. No. C9, 1960's Steam powered locomotives between Three Sisters and Huchinson. No. C10, Diesel locomotives, Modder River Bridge near Kimberly. No. C11, Diesel locomotives, Northern Transvaal.

**1997, Aug. 1** ***Perf. 14 Syncopated***

| | | | |
|---|---|---|---|
| **C7** | AP3 (1r) multicolored | .60 | .60 |
| *a.* | Souv. sheet of 1, perf. 14 | .60 | .60 |
| **C8** | AP3 (1r) multicolored | .60 | .60 |
| **C9** | AP3 (1r) multicolored | .60 | .60 |
| *a.* | Souvenir sheet of 1, perf. 14 | .60 | .60 |
| **C10** | AP3 (1r) multicolored | .60 | .60 |
| **C11** | AP3 (1r) multicolored | .60 | .60 |
| *a.* | Strip of 5, #C7-C11 | 3.00 | 3.00 |

No. C7a is inscribed in sheet margin for The Cape Stamp Show and Harmers of London stamp auctioneers.

No. C9a was issued 11/97, sold for 1.30r and is inscribed for Eastgate Universal Stamps & Coins in sheet margin.

**1998, Nov. Litho.** ***Perf. 14¾x14***
**Booklet Stamps**

| | | | |
|---|---|---|---|
| **C12** | AP3 (1r) Like #C7 | .60 | .60 |
| **C13** | AP3 (1r) Like #C8 | .60 | .60 |
| **C14** | AP3 (1r) Like #C9 | .60 | .60 |
| **C15** | AP3 (1r) Like #C10 | .60 | .60 |
| **C16** | AP3 (1r) Like #C11 | .60 | .60 |
| *a.* | Bklt. pane, 2 ea #C12-C16 | 6.00 | |
| | Complete booklet, #C16a | 6.00 | |
| | *Nos. C12-C16 (5)* | 3.00 | 3.00 |

Tourism AP4

Western Cape of South Africa: No. C7, Sandstone Cliffs. No. C8, Robben Island. No. C9, Pinehurst Homestead. No. C10, Waterfront, Capetown. No. C11, Boschendal Wine Estate.

**1998, Sept. 28 Litho. *Perf. 14½x14***

**Booklet Stamps**

| | | | |
|---|---|---|---|
| **C17** | AP4 (1.30r) multicolored | .50 | .50 |
| **C18** | AP4 (1.30r) multicolored | .50 | .50 |
| **C19** | AP4 (1.30r) multicolored | .50 | .50 |
| **C20** | AP4 (1.30r) multicolored | .50 | .50 |
| **C21** | AP4 (1.30r) multicolored | .50 | .50 |
| *a.* | Bklt. pane, 2 ea #C17-C21 + label | 5.00 | |
| | Complete booklet, #C21a | 5.00 | |
| | *Nos. C17-C21 (5)* | 2.50 | 2.50 |

***Perf. 14¾x14 on 3 sides***

**1998, Sept. 28 Litho.**

KwaZulu-Natal: No. C22, Drakensberge. No. C23, Zulu women and huts. No. C24, Rhinoceros and pelicans. No. C25, Rickshaw driver. No. C26, Indian dancers.

| | | | |
|---|---|---|---|
| **C22** | AP4 (1.30r) multicolored | .50 | .50 |
| **C23** | AP4 (1.30r) multicolored | .50 | .50 |
| **C24** | AP4 (1.30r) multicolored | .50 | .50 |
| **C25** | AP4 (1.30r) multicolored | .50 | .50 |
| **C26** | AP4 (1.30r) multicolored | .50 | .50 |
| *a.* | Booklet pane, 2 ea #C22-C26 | 5.00 | |
| | Complete booklet, #C26a | 5.00 | |

Worldwide Fund for Nature AP5

**1998, Oct. 23 Litho. *Perf. 14¾x14***

| | | | |
|---|---|---|---|
| **C27** | AP5 (1.30r) Cuvier's beaked whale | .90 | .90 |
| **C28** | AP5 (1.30r) Minke whale | .90 | .90 |
| **C29** | AP5 (1.30r) Bryde's whale | .90 | .90 |
| **C30** | AP5 (1.30r) Pygmy right whale | .90 | .90 |
| *a.* | Block of 4, #C27-C30 | 3.60 | 3.60 |
| *b.* | Booklet pane, 3 each #C27-C28, 2 each #C29-C30 | 9.00 | |
| | Complete booklet | 9.00 | |
| | Complete booklet, 2 #C30b + 2 postal cards | 25.00 | |

No. C30b exists with and without perfs running through side and bottom pane margins.

**Tourism Type of 1998**

Mpumalanga and Northern Province: No. C31, Blyde River Canyon. No. C32, Lone Creek Falls. No. C33, Ndebele women. No. C34, Pilgrim's Rest historical town. No. C35, Elephants, Thulamela, Kruger National Park.

**1999, Aug. Litho. *Perf. 14¾x14***

| | | | |
|---|---|---|---|
| **C31** | AP4 (1.30r) multi | .40 | .40 |
| **C32** | AP4 (1.30r) multi | .40 | .40 |
| **C33** | AP4 (1.30r) multi | .40 | .40 |
| **C34** | AP4 (1.30r) multi | .40 | .40 |
| **C35** | AP4 (1.30r) multi | .40 | .40 |
| *a.* | Booklet pane, 2 each #C31-C35 | 4.00 | |
| | Complete booklet, #C35a | 4.00 | |

Big Game Animals — AP6

Designs: Nos. C36, C45, Elephant. Nos. C37, C44, Lion. Nos. C38, C43, Rhinoceros. Nos. C39, C42, Leopard. Nos. C40, C41, Buffalo.

***Perf. 14¾x14½ on 3 or 4 Sides***

**2001, Apr. 25 Litho.**

**Booklet Stamps**

| | | | |
|---|---|---|---|
| **C36** | AP6 (1.90r) multi | .60 | .60 |
| **C37** | AP6 (1.90r) multi | .60 | .60 |
| **C38** | AP6 (1.90r) multi | .60 | .60 |
| **C39** | AP6 (1.90r) multi | .60 | .60 |
| **C40** | AP6 (1.90r) multi | .60 | .60 |
| *a.* | Booklet pane, 2 each #C36-C40 | 6.00 | |
| | Booklet, 2 #C40a + 2 postal cards | 12.00 | |

**Self-Adhesive**

**Size: 30x24mm**

***Serpentine Die Cut 12x11½ on 2 or 3 Sides***

| | | | |
|---|---|---|---|
| **C41** | AP6 (1.90r) multi | .60 | .60 |
| **C42** | AP6 (1.90r) multi | .60 | .60 |
| **C43** | AP6 (1.90r) multi | .60 | .60 |
| **C44** | AP6 (1.90r) multi | .60 | .60 |
| **C45** | AP6 (1.90r) multi | .60 | .60 |
| *a.* | Booklet, 2 each #C41-C45 | 6.00 | |

Tourism — AP7

Designs: No. C46, (2.10r), Cango Caves. No. C47, (2.10r), Table Mountain. No. C48, (2.10r), West Coast. No. C49, (2.10r), Snow-covered mountains near Elliot. No. C50, (2.10r), Augrabies Waterfall. No. C51, (2.10r), Stellenbosch vineyard country. No. C52, (2.10r), Flowers, Namaqualand. No. C53, (2.10r), Tsitsikamma Forest. No. C54, (2.10r), Cape Mountain zebras. No. C55, (2.10r), Richtersveld Desert.

**2001, Sept. 6 Litho. *Perf. 13¼x13¾***

| | | | | |
|---|---|---|---|---|
| **C46-C55** | AP7 | Set of 10 | 6.50 | 6.50 |

Pres. Nelson Mandela — AP8

Various photographs. Color of country name and size of stamps: a, Lilac, 31x48mm. b, Red and lilac, 50x38mm. c, Orange, 31x48mm. d, Orange, 31x31mm. e, Orange, 38x50mm. f, White, 38x50mm. g, White, 50x38mm. h, White, 31x48mm. i, Lilac, 38x50mm. j, Red, 31x31mm.

**2001, Nov. 26 *Perf. 14¾x14, 13¾***

| | | | |
|---|---|---|---|
| **C56** | Booklet | 8.50 | |
| *a.-j.* | AP8 (2.10r) Any booklet pane | .85 | .85 |

No. C56 sold for 45r and included two postal cards.

Shaka (1785-1828), Zulu King — AP9

**2003, Sept. 24 Litho. *Perf. 13x13¼***

| | | | |
|---|---|---|---|
| **C57** | AP9 (3.30r) multi | .95 | .95 |

Miniature Sheet

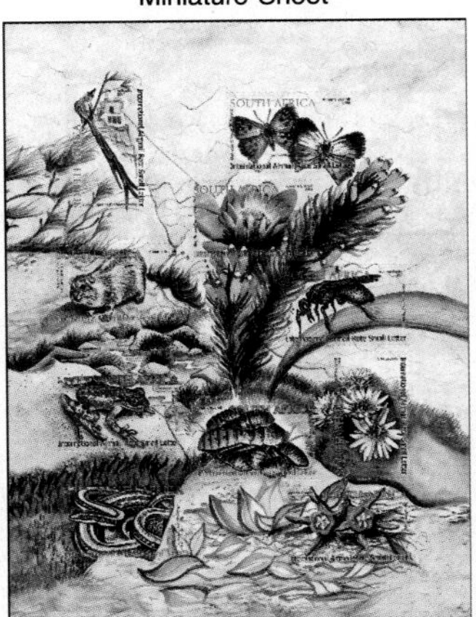


Flora and Fauna of Table Mountain — AP10

No. C58: a, Cape sugarbird, vert. b, Dark opal butterflies. c, King protea. d, Cape rock hyrax. e, Cuckoo wasp. f, Table Mountain ghost frog. g, Table Mountain cockroaches. h, Staavia dodii, vert. i, Spotted skaapsteker. j, Duvalia immaculata.

***Serpentine Die Cut 9x9½, 9½x9***

**2004, Sept. 1 Litho.**

**Self-Adhesive**

| | | | | |
|---|---|---|---|---|
| **C58** | AP10 | Sheet of 10 | 16.00 | 16.00 |
| *a.-j.* | (10r) Any single | | 1.60 | 1.60 |

World Post Day — AP11

**2004, Sept. 23 *Perf. 14***

| | | | |
|---|---|---|---|
| **C59** | AP11 (3.45r) multi | 1.10 | 1.10 |

Rotary International, Cent. — AP12

No. C60: a, Doctor listening to boy's heartbeat, infant receiving oral vaccination. b, Child at computer, welder.

**2005, Feb. 23 *Perf. 14¼x14***

| | | | |
|---|---|---|---|
| **C60** | Horiz. pair | 2.75 | 2.75 |
| *a.-b.* | AP12 (4r) Either single | 1.25 | 1.25 |

Miniature Sheet

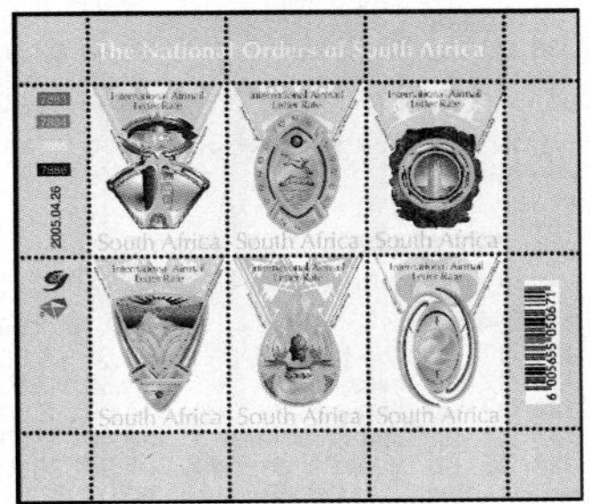


National Orders — AP13

No. C61: a, Order of Mapungubwe. b, Order of Merit for Bravery. c, Order of the Baobab. d, Order of Luthuli. e, Order of Ikhamanga. f, Order of the Companions of O. R. Tambo.

**Litho. & Embossed with Foil Application**

**2005, Nov. 26 *Perf. 14¾x14¼***

| | | | |
|---|---|---|---|
| **C61** | AP13 (4.25r) Sheet of 6, #a-f | 8.50 | 8.50 |

Miniature Sheet

Art — AP14

No. C62: a, Boland Winter, by Eric Laubscher. b, Table Mountain, by Maggie Laubser. c, Fishermen Drawing Nets, by Walter Battis. d, Oh, South Africa, You've Turned My World Completely Upside Down, by Lalitha Jawahirlal. e, Untitled, by Lucky Sibiya. f, Untitled, by Sophie Masiza. g, Azibuye Emasisweni, by Trevor Makhoba. h, Kontantwinkel Riebeck-Wes, by John Kramer. i, Houses in the Hills, by Gladys Mgudlandlu. j, Sequence City, by Usha Seejarim.

**2005, May 6 Litho. *Perf. 14¼x14¾***

| | | | |
|---|---|---|---|
| **C62** | AP14 (3.65r) Sheet of 10, #a-j | 12.50 | 12.50 |

Intl. Year of Physics — AP15

**2005, July 7 *Perf. 14½***

| | | | |
|---|---|---|---|
| **C63** | AP15 (3.65r) multi | 1.10 | 1.10 |

Miniature Sheet

"Hello" in Various Languages and Flag — AP16

No. C64: a, Hallo! b, Hi! c, Sawubona. d, Ndi Masiari! e, Lotjha!. f, Avuxeni. g, Dumela. h, Molo!

**2005, Oct. 9**

| | | | |
|---|---|---|---|
| **C64** | AP16 (3.65r) Sheet of 8, #a-h | 9.00 | 9.00 |

**Big Game Animals Type of 2001**

***Serpentine Die Cut 12¼x12¾ on 2 or 3 Sides***

**2005, Oct. 10**

**Self-Adhesive**

**Booklet Stamps**

**Size: 30x24mm**

| | | | |
|---|---|---|---|
| **C65** | AP6 (3.65r) Buffalo | 1.10 | 1.10 |
| **C66** | AP6 (3.65r) Leopard | 1.10 | 1.10 |
| **C67** | AP6 (3.65r) Rhinoceros | 1.10 | 1.10 |
| **C68** | AP6 (3.65r) Lion | 1.10 | 1.10 |
| **C69** | AP6 (3.65r) Elephant | 1.10 | 1.10 |
| *a.* | Booklet, 2 each # C65-C69 | 11.00 | |

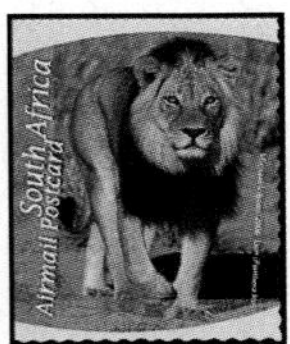


Big Game Animals — AP17

***Serpentine Die Cut 12½x13½***

**2006, Feb. 24**

**Self-Adhesive**

**Booklet Stamps**

| | | | |
|---|---|---|---|
| **C70** | AP17 (3.65r) Lion | 1.25 | 1.25 |
| **C71** | AP17 (3.65r) Buffalo | 1.25 | 1.25 |
| **C72** | AP17 (3.65r) Elephant | 1.25 | 1.25 |
| **C73** | AP17 (3.65r) Rhinoceros | 1.25 | 1.25 |
| **C74** | AP17 (3.65r) Leopard | 1.25 | 1.25 |
| *a.* | Booklet, 2 each #C70-C74 | 12.50 | |

Cyclists — AP18

**2006, Mar. 6 *Perf. 13¼x13¾***

| | | | |
|---|---|---|---|
| **C75** | AP18 (4.25r) multi | 1.40 | 1.40 |

Souvenir Sheet

2010 World Cup Soccer Championships, South Africa — AP19

**2006, July 7 Litho.** ***Perf. 14¾x14½***
**C76** AP19 (4.40r) multi 1.25 1.25

Miniature Sheet

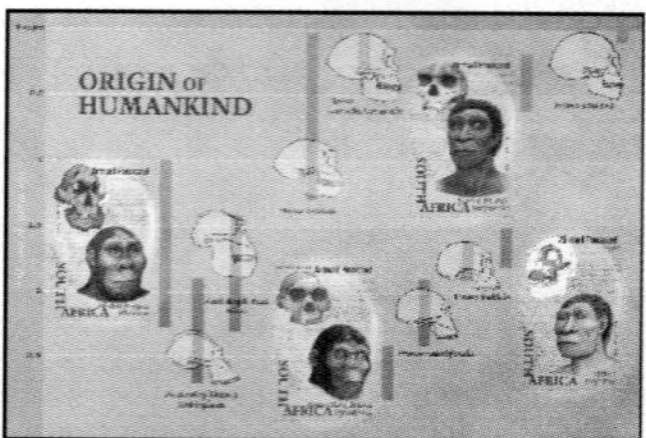


Origins of Humans — AP20

No. C77: a, Paranthropus robustus. b, Australopithecus africanus. c, Homo heidelbergensis. d, Homo ergaster.

***Serpentine Die Cut 11½x11¾***
**2006, Nov. 10**
**Self-Adhesive**
**C77** AP20 (3.80r) Sheet of 4, #a-d 4.25 4.25

## POSTAGE DUE STAMPS

D1

D2

**Wmk. Springbok's Head (177)**
**1914-15 Typo.** ***Perf. 14***
**J1** D1 ½p green & blk .90 3.50
**J2** D1 1p red & blk .90 .20
**J3** D1 2p vio & blk ('14) 4.50 .65
**J4** D1 3p ultra & blk .70 .65
**J5** D1 5p brown & blk 1.75 *15.00*
**J6** D1 6p gray & blk 8.75 *15.00*
**J7** D1 1sh black & red 62.50 *125.00*
*Nos. J1-J7 (7)* 80.00 *160.00*

**1922 Unwmk. Litho.** ***Rouletted 7-8***
**J8** D1 ½p blue grn & blk 1.00 *7.75*
**J9** D1 1p dull red & blk 1.10 .75
**J10** D1 1½p yellow brn & blk 1.25 1.50
*Nos. J8-J10 (3)* 3.35 *10.00*

**1922-26** ***Perf. 14***
**J11** D1 ½p blue grn & blk .20 .20
**J12** D1 1p rose & blk ('23) .35 .20
**J13** D1 1½p yel brn & blk ('24) 1.00 .80
**J14** D1 2p vio & blk ('23) .85 .40
*a.* Imperf. pair 250.00
**J15** D1 3p blue & blk ('26) 5.00 5.00
**J16** D1 6p gray & blue ('23) 10.00 5.00
*Nos. J11-J16 (6)* 17.40 11.60

**1927-28** **Typo.**
**J17** D2 ½p blue green & blk .40 .50
**J18** D2 1p rose & black .40 .40
**J19** D2 2p violet & black .70 .60
**J20** D2 3p ultra & black 6.50 6.50
**J21** D2 6p gray & black 12.00 10.00
*Nos. J17-J21 (5)* 20.00 18.00

Type of 1927-28 Redrawn
***Perf. 15x14***
**1932-40 Photo. Wmk. 201**
**J22** D2 ½p blue grn & blk ('34) 1.00 1.25
**J23** D2 1p rose car & blk ('34) .95 .95
**J24** D2 2p blk violet & blk 4.00 .30
*a.* 2p dark purple & black ('40) 11.00 .20
**J25** D2 3p dp blue & blk 18.00 12.00
**J26** D2 3p ultra & dk bl ('35) 3.50 .40
**J27** D2 3p blue & dk bl ('40) 21.00 2.00
**J28** D2 6p brn org & grn ('33) 18.00 6.00
**J29** D2 6p red org & grn ('38) 8.50 2.00
*Nos. J22-J29 (8)* 74.95 24.90

The ½p No. J22 photogravure has larger but thinner numeral and the "d" is taller and thinner than on No. J17.

The 1p No. J23 photogravure has numeral with parallel sides. The "d" is taller and thicker than on No. J18.

On Nos. J25 and J27 the numeral is followed by a large "d" with thick lines and a large round period below it.

Nos. J22, J24 and J25 have frame in photogravure, value typographed.

**Catalogue values for unused stamps in this section, from this point to the end of the section, are for Never Hinged items.**

See "English-Afrikaans Se-tenant" note preceding No. 23.

D3

***Horiz. strips of Three, Perf. 15x14 All Around, Rouletted 6½ Between***
**1943-44 Photo. Wmk. 201**
**J30** D3 ½p Prus green ('44) 8.50 *22.50*
*a.* Single .20 .20
**J31** D3 1p brt carmine 9.50 5.25
*a.* Single .20 .20
**J32** D3 2p dark purple 9.00 9.00
*a.* Single .20 .20
**J33** D3 3p dark blue 55.00 62.50
*a.* Single .20 .20
*Nos. J30-J33 (4)* 82.00 99.25

Catalogued as strips of 3 because of the perforations.

Type of 1932-38, Redrawn
Thick Numerals, Capital "D"
**1948-49** ***Perf. 15x14***
**J34** D2 ½p blue green & blk 9.00 6.00
**J35** D2 1p deep rose & blk 10.50 2.50
**J36** D2 2p dk pur & blk ('49) 14.00 2.50
**J37** D2 3p ultra & dk blue 12.00 9.00
**J38** D2 6p dp org & grn ('49) 37.50 7.00
*Nos. J34-J38 (5)* 83.00 27.00

Redrawn Type of 1948-49
Hyphen between Suid-Afrika
**1950-58** ***Perf. 15x14***
**J40** D2 1p car rose & blk 1.10 .40
**J41** D2 2p dk pur & blk ('51) .75 .25
**J42** D2 3p ultra & dk blue 5.75 2.25
**J43** D2 4p emer & dk grn ('58) 13.00 10.00
**J44** D2 6p dp org & grn ('52) 10.50 10.50
**J45** D2 1sh brn red & dk brn ('58) 16.00 13.00
*Nos. J40-J45 (6)* 47.10 36.40

D4

D5

***Perf. 15x14***
**1961, Feb. 14 Photo. Wmk. 330**
**J46** D4 1c cerise & blk .20 2.50
**J47** D4 2c purple & blk .20 2.50
**J48** D4 4c brt & dk green 1.100 *6.00*
**J49** D4 5c chalky bl & slate 2.00 *6.50*
**J50** D4 6c vermilion & dk grn 8.00 *7.00*
**J51** D4 10c maroon & dk brn 8.50 *10.00*
*Nos. J46-J51 (6)* 20.90 *34.50*

**Republic**
**1961-69** ***Perf. 15x14***
**Afrikaans Inscription on Top and Left Side**
**J52** D5 1c cerise & blk .40 .40
**J53** D5 4c brt & dk green 3.50 2.50
**J54** D5 6c vermilion & dk grn 7.00 6.00

**English Inscription on Top and Left Side**
**J55** D5 1c cerise & blk ('62) .25 3.00
**J56** D5 2c purple & blk .35 .35
**J57** D5 4c brt & dk grn ('69) 10.00 14.00
**J58** D5 5c chlky bl & dk bl 2.00 2.50
**J59** D5 5c chlky bl & blk ('62) 2.25 9.00
**J60** D5 10c maroon & dk brn 4.00 2.50
*Nos. J52-J60 (9)* 29.75 40.25

**1967-70 Photo. Wmk. 359**
**Afrikaans Inscription on Top and Left Side**
**J61** D5 1c carmine rose & blk .20 .20
**J62** D5 2c brt purple & blk .20 .20
*a.* Perf. 14 ('71) 18.00 18.00
**J63** D5 4c lt grn & blk ('71) 20.00 18.00
*a.* 4c bright & dark green ('70) *75.00 75.00*
**J64** D5 5c dk blue & blk .60 .60
**J65** D5 6c orange & dk grn 3.00 *7.00*
**J66** D5 10c dk rose brown & blk 2.50 1.50

**English Inscription on Top and Left Side**
**J67** D5 1c car rose & blk .20 .20
**J68** D5 2c brt purple & blk .30 .30
*a.* Perf. 14 ('71) 18.00 18.00
**J69** D5 4c lt green & blk ('71) 20.00 18.00
*a.* 4c bright & dark green ('70) *25.00 25.00*
*b.* As "a," perf. 14 ('71) *42.50* 42.50
**J70** D5 5c dk blue & blk .60 .60
**J71** D5 6c orange & dk grn 3.00 *7.00*
**J72** D5 10c dk rose brown & blk 2.50 1.50
*Nos. J61-J72 (12)* 53.10 *55.10*

D6

**1972, Mar. 22** ***Perf. 14x13½***
**J73** D6 1c brt yellow green .40 *1.25*
**J74** D6 2c orange .60 *2.25*
**J75** D6 4c dull purple 1.50 *2.25*
**J76** D6 6c yellow 1.50 *4.00*
**J77** D6 8c bright blue 2.50 *4.00*
**J78** D6 10c rose red 4.50 *6.25*
*Nos. J73-J78 (6)* 11.00 *20.00*

On the 2c, 6c and 10c "TO PAY" in first row at left.

## OFFICIAL STAMPS

Type A2 stamps have very small margins at top and bottom. Values are for copies with perfs close to, or touching the frame.

Regular Issues Overprinted in Black

Periods in Overprint
On No. 5
**1926 Wmk. 177** ***Perf. 14***
**O1** A2 2p dull violet 18.00 2.00

See "English-Afrikaans Se-tenant" note preceding No. 23.

On Nos. 23-25
***Perf. 14½x14***
**Wmk. 201**
**O2** A5 ½p dk grn & blk, pair 6.00 *12.00*
*a.* Single, English .75 1.25
*b.* Single, Afrikaans .75 1.25
**O3** A6 1p car & blk, pair 4.00 *7.00*
*a.* Single, English .25 .50
*b.* Single, Afrikaans .25 .50
**O4** A7 6p org & grn, pair 550.00 75.00
*a.* Single, English 25.00 9.00
*b.* Single, Afrikaans 25.00 9.00

Nos. 26 and 25 Overprinted (Reading Up)

b

No Periods in Overprint
**1928-29** ***Perf. 14, 14½x14***
**Space between words 19mm**
**O5** A8 2p vio brn & gray, pair ('29) 3.50 *10.00*
*a.* Single, English .50 *1.50*
*b.* Single, Afrikaans .50 *1.50*
*c.* Space 17½mm, pair 4.00 *12.50*
*d.* As "c," single, English .50 *2.00*
*e.* As "c," single, Afrikaans .50 *2.00*

**Space between words 11½mm**
**O6** A7 6p org & grn, pair 18.00 *25.00*
*a.* Single, English 2.00 *2.75*
*b.* Single, Afrikaans 2.00 *2.75*

#23-25 Ovptd. type "b" Reading Down
Space between words 13½-14mm
**1929** ***Perf. 14½x14***
**O7** A5 ½p grn & blk, pair 2.00 *2.75*
*a.* Single, English .25 .30
*b.* Single, Afrikaans .25 .30
*c.* Period after "OFFISIEEL" on English stamp 3.25 3.25
*d.* Pair, "c" + normal ½p 30.00 30.00
*e.* Period after "OFFISIEEL." on Afrikaans stamp 3.25 3.25
*f.* Pair, "e" + normal ½p 35.00 35.00
**O8** A6 1p car & blk, pair 2.50 *3.50*
*a.* Single, English .30 .40
*b.* Single, Afrikaans .30 .40
**O9** A7 6p org & grn, pair 7.75 *26.00*
*a.* Single, English 1.25 *3.00*
*b.* Single, Afrikaans 1.25 *3.00*
*c.* Period after "OFFISIEEL." on English stamp 8.00 *10.00*
*d.* Pair, "c" + normal 6p 60.00 *100.00*
*e.* Period after "OFFISIEEL." on Afrikaans stamp 9.00 *12.00*
*f.* Pair, "e" + normal 6p 70.00 *110.00*
*Nos. O7-O9 (3)* 12.25 *32.25*

#29-30 Ovptd. type "b" Reading Down
Space between words 17½-19mm
**1931 Engr.** ***Perf. 14, 14x13½***
**O10** A11 1sh dp bl & bis brn, pair 30.00 *85.00*
*a.* Single, English 3.00 *9.00*
*b.* Single, Afrikaans 3.00 *9.00*
*c.* Period after "OFFICIAL." on Afrikaans stamp 50.00 50.00
*d.* Pair, "c" + normal 1sh 100.00 *225.00*
**O11** A12 2sh6p brn & bl grn, pair 60.00 *150.00*
*a.* Single, English 7.50 *17.50*
*b.* Single, Afrikaans 7.50 *17.50*
*c.* Period after "OFFICIAL." on Afrikaans stamp 72.50 72.50
*d.* Pair, "c" + normal 2sh6p 275.00 *475.00*

Regular Issues of 1930-45 Overprinted type "b" Reading Down
("SUIDAFRIKA" on Afrikaans stamps)
***Perf. 15x14 (½p, 1p, 6p), 14***
**1930-47 Photo. Wmk. 201**
**Space between words 9½-12mm**
**(Various spacings occur in same setting)**
**O12** A5 ½p bl grn & blk (#33), pair ('31) 2.00 *3.50*
*a.* Single, English .20 *.40*
*b.* Single, Afrikaans .20 *.40*
*c.* Period after "OFFISIEEL." on English stamp 3.50 *4.00*
*d.* Pair, "c" + normal ½p 25.00 *42.50*
*e.* Period after "OFFISIEEL." on Afrikaans stamp 3.25 *3.50*
*f.* Pair, "e" + normal ½p 25.00 *40.00*

**Space between words 12½-13½mm**
**O13** A5 ½p bl grn & blk, pair (#33) 3.00 4.00
*a.* Single, English .25 .50
*b.* Single, Afrikaans .25 .50
**O14** A6 1p car & blk, pair (#34) 3.50 3.50
*a.* Single, English .40 .50
*b.* Single, Afrikaans .40 .50
*c.* Period after "OFFISIEEL." on English stamp 3.75 *4.00*
*d.* Pair, "c" + normal 1p 25.00 *32.50*
*e.* Period after "OFFISIEEL." on Afrikaans stamp 3.00 *3.50*
*f.* Pair, "e" + normal 1p 25.00 *32.50*
**O15** A6 1p rose & blk, pair (#35) ('33) 7.50 9.00
*a.* Single, English .75 1.00
*b.* Single, Afrikaans .75 1.00
*c.* Double ovpt., pair 275.00 *300.00*
*d.* As "c," English 45.00
*e.* As "c," Afrikaans 45.00

**Space between words 20½-22mm**
**O16** A8 2p vio & gray, pair (#36) ('31) 4.50 *10.00*
*a.* Single, English .60 *1.25*
*b.* Single, Afrikaans .60 *1.25*
**O17** A8 2p vio & ind, pair (#37) 75.00 *85.00*
*a.* Single, English 6.00 *9.00*
*b.* Single, Afrikaans 6.00 *9.00*

**Space between words 12½-13½mm**
**O18** A7 6p org & grn, pair (#42) 7.00 8.50
*a.* Single, English .75 .90
*b.* Single, Afrikaans .75 .90
*c.* Period after "OFFISIEEL." on English stamp 6.50 6.50
*d.* Pair, "c" + normal 6p 50.00 *60.00*

*e.* Period after "OFFISIEEL." on Afrikaans stamp 5.50 5.50
*f.* Pair, "e" + normal 6p 40.00 *50.00*

**Space between words 21mm**

**O19** A11 1sh dp bl & brn, pair (#43c) ('32) 42.50 *75.00*
*a.* Single, English 4.00 *7.50*
*b.* Single, Afrikaans 4.00 *7.50*
*c.* 1sh dk bl & yel brn (#43), 19mm, pair 42.50 *75.00*
*d.* As "c," single, English 3.00 *7.50*
*e.* As "c," single, Afrikaans 3.00 *7.50*
*f.* As "c," spaced 21mm, pair 42.50 *65.00*
*g.* As "f," single, English 6.00 *7.50*
*h.* As "f," single, Afrikaans 6.00 *7.50*

**Space between words 17½-18½mm**

**O20** A12 2sh6p brn & sl grn (#44c) ('37), pair 65.00 *100.00*
*a.* Single, English 10.00 *12.50*
*b.* Single, Afrikaans 10.00 *12.50*
*c.* Spaced 21mm, pair 45.00 *70.00*
*d.* As "c," single, English 4.50 *8.00*
*e.* As "c," single, Afrikaans 4.50 *8.00*
*f.* 2sh6p red brn & grn, pair (#44i) ('33) 50.00 *90.00*
*g.* As "f," single, English 5.00 *8.50*
*h.* As "f," single, Afrikaans 5.00 *8.50*
*j.* 2sh6p brn & bl, 19-20mm (#44) ('47), pair 30.00 60.00
*k.* As "j," single, English 3.00 *5.00*
*m.* As "j," single, Afrikaans 3.00 *5.00*
*Nos. O12-O20 (9)* 210.00 *298.50*

**Catalogue values for unused stamps in this section, from this point to the end of the section, are for Never Hinged items.**

Regular Issue of 1933-54 Overprinted type "b" Reading Down ("SUID-AFRIKA" Hyphenated)

**1935-50 Photo. *Perf. 15x14, 14***

**Space between words given with each listing**

**O21** A5 ½p grn & gray (#45), 12½-13mm, pair ('36) 3.25 *15.00*
*a.* Single, English .25 *1.25*
*b.* Single, Afrikaans .25 *1.25*
**O22** A5 ½p grn & gray, (#46), 11½-13mm, pair ('38) 12.00 *12.50*
*a.* Single, English .50 *1.00*
*b.* Single, Afrikaans .50 *1.00*
**O23** A5 ½p grn & gray (#47), 11½mm, pair ('48) 1.25 *5.00*
*a.* Single, English .20 *.70*
*b.* Single, Afrikaans .20 *.70*
**O24** A6 1p car & gray (#48), 11-13mm, pair 1.00 1.00
*a.* Single, English .20 .20
*b.* Single, Afrikaans .20 .20
**O25** A6 1p rose car & gray blk (#49), 11½-12mm, pair ('41) 1.00 .50
*a.* Single, English .20 .20
*b.* Single, Afrikaans .20 .20
**O26** A15 1½p dk grn & gold (#51), 19-21mm, pair ('37) 30.00 22.50
*a.* Single, English 2.25 1.75
*b.* Single, Afrikaans 2.25 1.75
**O27** A15 1½p sl grn & och (#52), 16mm, pair ('44) 3.00 *8.00*
*a.* Single, English .30 *.45*
*b.* Single, Afrikaans .30 *.45*
*c.* Ovpt. spaced 14-14½mm, pair 3.00 *5.00*
*d.* As "c," single, English .25 *.80*
*e.* As "c," single, Afrikaans .25 *.80*
**O28** A8 2p bl vio & dl bl (#53), 20-21mm, pair ('39) 80.00 30.00
*a.* Single, English 7.50 2.50
*b.* Single, Afrikaans 7.50 2.50
**O29** A16 2p pur & sl (#55), 19-21mm, pair ('48) 4.50 *16.00*
*a.* Single, English .25 *1.50*
*b.* Single, Afrikaans .25 *1.50*
**O30** A7 6p org & bl grn, I (#59), 12-13mm, pair ('38) 80.00 *40.00*
*a.* Single, English 6.50 3.75
*b.* Single, Afrikaans 6.50 3.75
**O31** A7 6p org & grn, II (#60), 12-13mm, pair ('39) 12.00 10.00
*a.* Single, English 1.25 1.25
*b.* Single, Afrikaans 1.25 1.25
**O32** A7 6p org & grn III (#61), 11½-12mm, pair ('47) 5.50 *8.00*
*a.* Single, English .50 *.90*
*b.* Single, Afrikaans .50 *.90*
**O33** A11 1sh lt bl & ol brn (#62c), 19-21mm, pair ('40) 65.00 27.50
*a.* Single, English 4.50 2.00
*b.* Single, Afrikaans 4.50 2.00

*c.* "OFFICIAL" on both sides 500.00
*d.* "OFFISIEEL" on both sides 500.00
*e.* 1sh chlky bl & lt brn (#62) ('50), pair 10.00 *25.00*
*f.* As "e," single, English .90 *2.50*
*g.* As "e," single, Afrikaans .90 *2.50*
*h.* 1sh vio bl & brnsh blk (#62f), 18-19mm, pair 65.00 27.50
*j.* As "h," single, English 4.50 2.00
*k.* As "h," single, Afrikaans 4.50 2.00
**O34** A13 5sh grn & blk (#64) 19-20mm, pair 55.00 *110.00*
*a.* Single, English 3.50 *12.50*
*b.* Single, Afrikaans 3.50 *12.50*
**O35** A13 5sh bl grn & blk (#65), 20mm, pair 40.00 *110.00*
*a.* Single, English 3.50 *12.50*
*b.* Single, Afrikaans 3.50 *12.50*
**O36** A18 10sh ol blk & bl (#67), 19½-20mm, pair ('48) 85.00 *175.00*
*a.* Single, English 7.50 *22.50*
*b.* Single, Afrikaans 7.50 *22.50*
*Nos. O21-O36 (16)* 478.50 *591.00*

Nos. 52 and 56 Overprinted type "b" Reading Up

Space between words 16mm

**1949-50 Size: 22x18mm *Perf. 14***

**O37** A15 1½p sl grn & ocher, pair 35.00 *40.00*
*a.* Single, English 2.25 *3.50*
*b.* Single, Afrikaans 2.25 *3.50*

**Size: 21½x17½mm**

**O38** A16 2p pur & sl bl, pair ('50) *1,500.* *1,750.*
*a.* Single, English 125. *175.*
*b.* Single, Afrikaans 125. *175.*

Nos. 64, 67 Overprinted

c 

Space between words 18-19mm

**1940 *Perf. 14***

**O39** A13 5sh grn & blk, pair 85.00 *100.00*
*a.* Single, English 3.00 *10.00*
*b.* Single, Afrikaans 3.00 *10.00*
**O40** A18 10sh ol brn & bl, pair *375.00* *350.00*
*a.* Single, English 25.00 *35.00*
*b.* Single, Afrikaans 25.00 *35.00*

No. 54 Overprinted type "c" Reading Up

Space between words 19mm

**1945 *Perf. 14***

**O41** A8 2p dl vio & gray, pair 8.00 *22.50*
*a.* Single, English .50 *2.25*
*b.* Single, Afrikaans .50 *2.25*

No. 47 Overprinted **OFFICIAL OFFISIEEL**

**1947 *Perf. 15x14***

**O42** A5 ½p grn & gray, pair *22.50* 20.00
*a.* Single, English 1.00 *2.00*
*b.* Single, Afrikaans 1.00 *2.00*

Stamps of 1937-54 Overprinted

**1950-54 *Perf. 15x14, 14***

**Space between words 10mm**

**O43** A5 ½p grn & gray, pair (#47) .90 1.50
*a.* Single, English .20 .20
*b.* Single, Afrikaans .20 .20
**O44** A6 1p rose car & gray blk, pair (#49) 1.00 *2.00*
*a.* Single, English .20 .20
*b.* Single, Afrikaans .20 .20
**O45** A6 1p car & blk, pair (#50) 1.00 *1.50*
*a.* Single, English .20 .20

*b.* Single, Afrikaans .20 .20

**Space between words 14½mm**

**O46** A15 1½p sl grn & ocher, pair (#52) 1.50 *3.00*
*a.* Single, English .20 *.35*
*b.* Single, Afrikaans .20 *.35*
**O47** A16 2p pur & sl bl, pair (#56) 1.00 *2.00*
*a.* Single, English .20 *.20*
*b.* Single, Afrikaans .20 *.20*
*c.* Ovpt. reading up, pair

**Space between words 10mm**

**O48** A7 6p red org & bl grn, III, pair (#61c) 2.00 *3.00*
*a.* Single, English .35 *.35*
*b.* Single, Afrikaans .35 *.35*

**Space between words 19mm**

**O49** A11 1sh chlky bl & lt brn, pair (#62) 6.75 *15.00*
*a.* Single, English .50 *1.75*
*b.* Single, Afrikaans .50 *1.75*
*c.* 1sh vio bl & brnsh blk (#62f), pair 140.00 *150.00*
*d.* As "c," single, English 12.50 *17.50*
*e.* As "c," single, Afrikaans 12.50 *17.50*
**O50** A12 2sh6p brn & brt grn, pair (#63) 10.00 *32.50*
*a.* Single, English 1.00 *3.25*
*b.* Single, Afrikaans 1.00 *3.25*
**O51** A13 5sh grn & blk, pair (#64) 175.00 *90.00*
*a.* Single, English 2.00 *9.00*
*b.* Single, Afrikaans 2.00 *9.00*
**O52** A13 5sh bl grn & blk, I, pair (#65) 65.00 *75.00*
*a.* Single, English 3.00 *6.50*
*b.* Single, Afrikaans 3.00 *6.50*
**O53** A13 5sh grn & blk, II, pair (#66) 80.00 *80.00*
*a.* Single, English 4.00 *9.00*
*b.* Single, Afrikaans 4.00 *9.00*
**O54** A18 10sh ol blk & bl, pair (#67) 80.00 *200.00*
*a.* Single, English 5.00 *21.00*
*b.* Single, Afrikaans 5.00 *21.00*
*Nos. O43-O54 (12)* 424.15 *505.50*

## BOPHUTHATSWANA

ˌbō-ˌₚpü-tät-ˈswä-nə

LOCATION — Noncontiguous enclaves, Republic of South Africa
GOVT. — Self-governing tribal homeland
AREA — 27,340 sq. mi.
POP. — 1,660,000 (1985)
CAPITAL — Mmabatho

**Catalogue values for all unused stamps in this country are for Never Hinged items.**

Independence from South Africa — A1

***Perf. 12½***

**1977, Dec. 6 Litho. Unwmk.**

**1** A1 4c Hands, dove released .75 .75
**2** A1 10c Leopard (state emblem) 1.50 1.10
**3** A1 15c Coat of arms 3.00 2.25
**4** A1 20c Flag 4.00 3.00
*Nos. 1-4 (4)* 9.25 7.10

An imperf. souvenir sheet exists containing Nos. 1-4 printed in one color (blue). Not valid for postage.

Tribal Totems — A2

Designs: 1c, African buffalo (Malete, Hwaduba). 2c, Bush pig (Kolobeng). 3c, Chacma baboon (Hurutshe, Thlaro). 4c, Leopard (state emblem). 5c, Crocodile (Kwena-Fokeng). 6c, Savanna monkey (Kgatla). 7c, Lion (Taung). 8c, Spotted hyena (Phiring). 9c, Cape porcupine (Rokologadi). 10c, Aardvark (Tlokwa). 15c, Fish (Tlhaping). 20c, Hunting dog (Tlhalerwa). 25c, Common duiker (Mfatlha). 30c, African elephant (Tlhako, Tloung). 50c, Python (Nogeng). 1r, Hippopotamus (Kubung). 2r, Greater kudu (Rolong).

**1977, Dec. 6**

**5** A2 1c multicolored .20 .20
**6** A2 2c multicolored .20 .20
**7** A2 3c multicolored .20 .20
**8** A2 4c multicolored 5.00 2.40
**9** A2 5c on 4c multi 1.40 .80
**10** A2 6c multicolored .25 .25
**11** A2 7c multicolored 1.25 1.25
**12** A2 8c multicolored .35 .25
**13** A2 9c multicolored .45 .25
**14** A2 10c multicolored .35 .25
**15** A2 15c multicolored .45 .25
**16** A2 20c multicolored .45 .35
**17** A2 25c multicolored .50 .35
**18** A2 30c multicolored .60 .35
**19** A2 50c multicolored .85 .50
**20** A2 1r multicolored 1.75 1.40
**21** A2 2r multicolored 3.25 3.25
*Nos. 5-21 (17)* 17.50 12.50

No. 9 was printed as a 4c stamp. Grass was printed over the 4c at upper right and 5c printed at upper left. Copies exist without the surcharge. No. 9A does not have the 4c.

***Perf. 14***

*5a* A2 1c .20 .20
*6a* A2 2c .20 .20
*7a* A2 3c .20 .20
*8a* A2 4c .20 .20
**9A** A2 5c multicolored .20 .20
*11a* A2 7c .20 .20
*12a* A2 8c .25 .25
*14a* A2 10c .25 .25
*Nos. 5a-14a (8)* 1.70 1.70

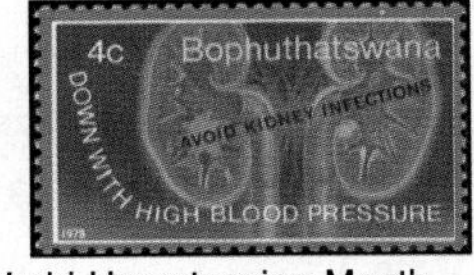


World Hypertension Month — A3

**1978, Apr. 7 *Perf. 12x12½***

**22** A3 4c Avoid kidney infections .60 .60
**23** A3 10c Lower salt intake 1.00 1.00
**24** A3 15c Overeating is dangerous 1.40 1.40
*Nos. 22-24 (3)* 3.00 3.00

Road Safety A4

**1978, July 12**

**25** A4 4c Don't drink and drive .75 .45
**26** A4 10c Keep children off roads 1.10 .65
**27** A4 15c Pedestrians observe crossing signals 1.40 .80
**28** A4 20c Observe stop signs 2.25 1.10
*Nos. 25-28 (4)* 5.50 3.00

Cutting and Polishing Semi-precious Stones — A5

**1978, Oct. 3**

**29** A5 4c Cutting slabs of travertine .40 .20
**30** A5 10c Polishing travertine .75 .55
**31** A5 15c Sorting stones 1.25 .75
**32** A5 20c Factory at Taung 1.60 1.00
*Nos. 29-32 (4)* 4.00 2.50

1st Airplane Flight, 75th Anniv. — A6

Illustration reduced.

**1978, Dec. 1** ***Perf. 12½***

33 A6 10c Wright Flyer 1.00 1.00
34 A6 15c Orville and Wilbur Wright 1.50 1.50

Pres. Lucas M. Mangope — A7

**1978, Dec. 6**

35 A7 4c Profile .20 .20
36 A7 15c Portrait .45 .45

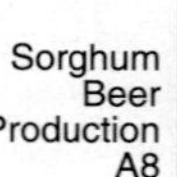

Sorghum Beer Production A8

**1979, Feb. 28** ***Perf. 14x14½***

37 A8 4c Drying germinated wheat .30 .30
38 A8 15c Cooking ground grain .80 .80
39 A8 20c Straining the liquid 1.00 1.00
40 A8 25c Drinking beer 1.40 1.40
*Nos. 37-40 (4)* 3.50 3.50

Tate-Knoetze Boxing Match — A9

**1979, June 2**

41 A9 15c John Tate .90 .90
42 A9 15c Kallie Knoetze .90 .90
*a.* Pair, #41-42 2.00 2.00

Intl. Children's Year — A10

Illustrations by local youths: 4c, Boy dazzled by sun, from a folk tale, by Hendrick Sebapo. 15c, Africans and animal silhouettes, by Daisy Morapedi. 20c, Man in profile and landscape, by Peter Tladi. 25c, Old man, boy and mule, by Sebapo.

**1979, June 7** ***Perf. 14½x14***

43 A10 4c multicolored .20 .20
44 A10 15c multicolored .35 .35
45 A10 20c multicolored .50 .50
46 A10 25c multicolored .70 .70
*Nos. 43-46 (4)* 1.75 1.75

Platinum Industry A11

Designs: 4c, Pouring molten metal. 15c, Platinum in industrial use. 20c, Telecommunications satellite in orbit. 25c, Jewelry.

**1979, Aug. 15** ***Perf. 14x14½***

47 A11 4c multicolored .20 .20
48 A11 15c multicolored .25 .25
49 A11 20c multicolored .35 .35
50 A11 25c multicolored .45 .45
*Nos. 47-50 (4)* 1.25 1.25

Agriculture A12

**1979, Oct. 25**

51 A12 5c Cattle .20 .20
52 A12 15c Picking cotton .25 .25
53 A12 20c Researcher in corn field .35 .35
54 A12 25c Fish in net .45 .45
*Nos. 51-54 (4)* 1.25 1.25

Stop Smoking Campaign A13

Edible Wild Fruit A14

**1980, Mar. 5** ***Perf. 14½x14***

55 A13 5c multicolored .00 .25

**1980, June 4**

56 A14 5c *Landolphia capensis* .20 .20
57 A14 10c *Vangueria infausta* .25 .25
58 A14 15c *Bequaertiodendron magalismontanum* .40 .40
59 A14 20c *Sclerocarya caffra* .50 .50
*Nos. 56-59 (4)* 1.35 1.35

Birds — A15

**1980, Sept. 10**

60 A15 5c Pied babbler .20 .20
61 A15 10c Carmine bee-eater .45 .45
62 A15 15c Shaft-tailed whydah .70 .70
63 A15 20c Meyer's parrot .90 .90
*Nos. 60-63 (4)* 2.25 2.25

Sun City Tourist Attractions A16

**1980, Dec. 5** ***Perf. 14x14½***

64 A16 5c Hotel, casino, country club .20 .20
65 A16 10c Golfer at Gary Player Country Club .40 .40
66 A16 15c Casino interior .60 .60
67 A16 20c Night club dancers .80 .80
*Nos. 64-67 (4)* 2.00 2.00

Intl. Year for the Disabled — A17

**1981, Jan. 30** ***Perf. 14½x14***

68 A17 5c shown .20 .20
69 A17 15c Blind boy .25 .25
70 A17 20c Archer in wheelchair .35 .35
71 A17 25c X-ray (tuberculosis) .45 .45
*Nos. 68-71 (4)* 1.25 1.25

Easter A18

Bible quotes and: 5c, Lamb, sunset. 15c, Bread. 20c, Man holding lamb. 25c, Wheat field.

**1981, Apr. 1** ***Perf. 14x14½***

72 A18 5c multicolored .20 .20
73 A18 15c multicolored .30 .30
74 A18 20c multicolored .45 .45
75 A18 25c multicolored .55 .55
*Nos. 72-75 (4)* 1.50 1.50

Telephones A19

Grasses A20

5c, Siemens & Halske wall telephone, 1885. 15c, Ericsson table model, 1895. 20c, Hasler table model, 1900. 25c, Mix & Genest wall model, 1904.

**1981, July 31** ***Perf. 14½x14***

76 A19 5c multicolored .20 .20
77 A19 15c multicolored .30 .30
78 A19 20c multicolored .35 .35
79 A19 25c multicolored .45 .45
*Nos. 76-79 (4)* 1.30 1.30

**1981, Nov. 25**

80 A20 5c *Themeda triandra* .20 .20
81 A20 15c *Rhynchelytrum repens* .30 .30
82 A20 20c *Eragrostis capensis* .35 .35
83 A20 25c *Monocymbium ceresiiforme* .45 .45
*Nos. 80-83 (4)* 1.30 1.30

Boy Scouts, 75th Anniv. — A21

Easter — A22

**1982, Jan. 29**

84 A21 5c Scout, 1982 .20 .20
85 A21 15c Mafeking Siege stamps .35 .35
86 A21 20c Scout cadet, 1907 .45 .45
87 A21 25c Lord Baden-Powell .55 .55
*Nos. 84-87 (4)* 1.55 1.55

**1982, Apr. 1**

88 A22 15c John 12:1 .20 .20
89 A22 20c Matthew 21:1-2 .20 .20
90 A22 25c Mark 11:5-6 .50 .50
91 A22 30c Matthew 21:7 .60 .60
*Nos. 88-91 (4)* 1.50 1.50

Table Telephones — A23

**1982, Sept. 3**

92 A23 8c Ericsson, 1878 .20 .20
93 A23 15c Ericsson, 1885 .30 .30
94 A23 20c Ericsson, 1893 .35 .35
95 A23 25c Siemens & Halske, 1898 .45 .45
*Nos. 92-95 (4)* 1.30 1.30

Independence, 5th Anniv. — A24

8c, Old parliament building. 15c, New government offices. 20c, University, Mmabatho. 25c, Civic Center, Mmabatho.

**1982, Dec. 6** ***Perf. 14x14½***

96 A24 8c multicolored .20 .20
97 A24 15c multicolored .30 .30
98 A24 20c multicolored .35 .35
99 A24 25c multicolored .45 .45
*Nos. 96-99 (4)* 1.30 1.30

Pilanesberg Nature Reserve — A25

**1983, Jan. 5**

100 A25 8c *Ceratotherium simum* .25 .25
101 A25 20c *Equus burchelli* .60 .60
102 A25 25c *Hippotragus niger* .75 .75
103 A25 40c *Alcelaphus caama* 1.10 1.10
*Nos. 100-103 (4)* 2.70 2.70

Easter A26

**1983, Mar. 30** ***Perf. 14½x14***

104 A26 8c Matthew 21:7 .20 .20
105 A26 20c Mark 11:7 .35 .35
106 A26 25c Matthew 21:8 .40 .40
107 A26 40c Mark 11:9 .65 .65
*Nos. 104-107 (4)* 1.60 1.60

Telephones A27

Birds of the Veld A28

10c, ATM table model, c. 1920. 20c, A/S Elektrisk wall model, c. 1900. 25c, Ericsson wall model, c. 1900. 40c, Ericsson wall model, c. 1900, diff.

**1983, June 22**

108 A27 10c multicolored .20 .20
109 A27 20c multicolored .35 .35
110 A27 25c multicolored .45 .45
111 A27 40c multicolored .70 .70
*Nos. 108-111 (4)* 1.70 1.70

**1983, Sept. 14**

112 A28 10c Kori bustard .25 .25
113 A28 20c Black korhaan .55 .55
114 A28 25c Red-crested korhaan .70 .70
115 A28 40c Stanley bustard 1.25 1.25
*Nos. 112-115 (4)* 2.75 2.75

Grasses — A29

**1984, Jan. 20**

116 A29 10c *Panicum maximum* .20 .20
117 A29 20c *Hyparrhenia dregeana* .30 .30
118 A29 25c *Cenchrus ciliaris* .35 .35
119 A29 40c *Urochloa brachyura* .55 .55
*Nos. 116-119 (4)* 1.40 1.40

Easter
A30

**1984, Mar. 23** ***Perf. 14½x14***

**120** A30 10c Mark 11:11 .20 .20
**121** A30 20c Mark 11:15 .30 .30
**122** A30 25c Matthew 21:19 .40 .40
**123** A30 40c Matthew 21:19, diff. .65 .65
*Nos. 120-123 (4)* 1.55 1.55

See Nos. 165-168, 173-176.

Mining Industry
A31

**1984, Apr. 2** ***Perf. 14½x14***

**124** A31 11c multicolored .35 .35

Telephones — A32

11c, Shuchhardt table model, c. 1905. 20c, Siemens wall model, c. 1925. 25c, Ericsson table model, c. 1900. 30c, Oki table model, c. 1930.

**1984, July 20**

**125** A32 11c multicolored .20 .20
**126** A32 20c multicolored .30 .30
**127** A32 25c multicolored .40 .40
**128** A32 30c multicolored .45 .45
*Nos. 125-128 (4)* 1.35 1.35

Lizards
A33

Designs: 11c, Yellow-throated plated lizard. 25c, Transvaal girdled lizard. 30c, Ocellated sand lizard. 45c, Bibron's thick-toed gecko.

**1984, Sept. 25** ***Perf. 14x14½***

**129** A33 11c multicolored .20 .20
**130** A33 25c multicolored .40 .40
**131** A33 30c multicolored .50 .50
**132** A33 45c multicolored .75 .75
*Nos. 129-132 (4)* 1.85 1.85

Child Health
Care — A34

Mafeking,
Cent. — A35

**1985, Jan. 25**

**133** A34 11c Stop Polio .20 .20
**134** A34 25c Stop Measles .40 .40
**135** A34 30c Stop Diphtheria .50 .50
**136** A34 50c Stop Whooping Cough .80 .80
*Nos. 133-136 (4)* 1.90 1.90

**1985, Mar. 11**

Portraits: 11c, Montshiwa (1814-1896), chief of the Barolong booRatshidi. 25c, Sir Charles Warren (1840-1927), army commander who established the Crown Colony and laid out the town of Mafeking.

**137** A35 11c multicolored .20 .20
**138** A35 25c multicolored .35 .35

Industries
A36

Designs: 1c, Textile mill, Bophuthatswana. 2c, Sewing cloth sacks, Selosesha. 3c, Ceramic tile production line. 4c, Processing sheepskin. 5c, Manufacture of crossbows. 6c, Automobile parts. 7c, Hosiery factory, Babelegi. 8c, Specialized bicycle factory. 9c, Lawn mower assembly line. 10c, Dress factory, Thaba Nchu. 12c, Automobile upholstery factory. 14c, Milling industry, Mafeking. 15c, Manufacturing of plastic bags. 16c, Brickworks, Mmabatho. 18c, Manufacturing of cutlery. 20c, Men's clothing factory. 25c, Chromium plating baby carriage parts. 30c, Spray-painting metal beds. 50c, Milk processing plant. 1r, Printing works. 2r, Industrial complex, Babelegi.

**1985-89** ***Perf. 14½x14***

**139** A36 1c multicolored .20 .20
**140** A36 2c multicolored .20 .20
**141** A36 3c multicolored .20 .20
**142** A36 4c multicolored .20 .20
**143** A36 5c multicolored .20 .20
**144** A36 6c multicolored .20 .20
**145** A36 7c multicolored .20 .20
**146** A36 8c multicolored .20 .20
**147** A36 9c multicolored .20 .20
**148** A36 10c multicolored .20 .20
**149** A36 12c multicolored .25 .25
**150** A36 14c multicolored .30 .30
**151** A36 15c multicolored .35 .35
**152** A36 16c multicolored .35 .35
**153** A36 18c multicolored .40 .40
**154** A36 20c multicolored .45 .45
**155** A36 25c multicolored .60 .60
**156** A36 30c multicolored .70 .70
**157** A36 50c multicolored 1.10 1.10
**158** A36 1r multicolored 2.25 2.25
**159** A36 2r multicolored 4.75 4.75
*Nos. 139-159 (21)* 13.50 13.50

Issued: 1c-10c, 15c, 20c, 25c, 30c-2r, 10/25/85; 12c, 4/1/85; 14c, 4/1/86; 16c, 4/1/87; 18c, 7/3/89.

Easter Type of 1984

**1985, Apr. 2**

**165** A30 12c Matthew 21:14 .20 .20
**166** A30 25c Matthew 21:14, diff. .35 .35
**167** A30 30c Matthew 21:15 .40 .40
**168** A30 50c Matthew 21:15-16 .70 .70
*Nos. 165-168 (4)* 1.65 1.65

Tree Conservation
A37

**1985, July 4** ***Perf. 14x14½***

**169** A37 12c *Fourea saligna* .20 .20
**170** A37 25c *Boscia albitrunca* .45 .45
**171** A37 30c *Erythrina lysistemon* .55 .55
**172** A37 50c *Bequaertiodendron magalismontanum* .90 .90
*Nos. 169-172 (4)* 2.10 2.10

Easter Type of 1984

**1986, Mar. 6** ***Perf. 14½x14***

**173** A30 12c John 12:2 .20 .20
**174** A30 20c John 12:3 .35 .35
**175** A30 25c John 12:3, diff. .45 .45
**176** A30 30c Matthew 26:7 .55 .55
*Nos. 173-176 (4)* 1.55 1.55

Paintings of Thaba Nchu in the Africana Museum, Johannesburg — A38

14c, *Wesleyan Mission Station and Residence of Moroka, Chief of the Barolong, 1834,* by Charles Davidson Bell. 20c, *James Archbell's Congregation, 1834,* by Bell. 25c, *Mission Station at Thaba Nchu, 1850,* by Thomas Baines (1822-75).

**1986, May 15** ***Perf. 14x14½***

**177** A38 14c multicolored .20 .20
**178** A38 20c multicolored .25 .25
**179** A38 25c multicolored .35 .35
*Nos. 177-179 (3)* .80 .80

Incorporation of Thaba Nchu and Bophuthatswana, Oct. 1, 1983.

A souvenir sheet of one No. 179 has decorative margin continuing the painting and picturing the emblem of the philatelic exhibition held at Johannesburg, Oct. 6-11. Sold for 50c.

Temisano Development Projects
A39

**1986, Aug. 6** ***Perf. 14½x14***

**180** A39 14c Agricultural production .20 .20
**181** A39 20c Community development .35 .35
**182** A39 25c Vocational training .40 .40
**183** A39 30c Secondary industries .50 .50
*Nos. 180-183 (4)* 1.45 1.45

BOP Airways, 5th Anniv.
A40

**1986, Oct. 16** ***Perf. 14x14½***

**184** A40 14c Airline personnel, aircraft .30 .30
**185** A40 20c Passengers .45 .45
**186** A40 25c Mmabatho Intl. Airport .60 .60
**187** A40 30c Cessna Citation .65 .65
*Nos. 184-187 (4)* 2.00 2.00

Sports — A41

Wildflowers — A42

**1987, Jan. 22**

**188** A41 14c Netball .30 .30
**189** A41 20c Tennis .45 .45
**190** A41 25c Soccer .55 .55
**191** A41 30c Running .70 .70
*Nos. 188-191 (4)* 2.00 2.00

**1987, Apr. 23**

**192** A42 16c *Berkheya zeyheri* .40 .40
**193** A42 20c *Plumbago auriculata* .50 .50
**194** A42 25c *Pterodiscus speciosus* .65 .65
**195** A42 30c *Gazania krebsiana* .75 .75
*Nos. 192-195 (4)* 2.30 2.30

A souvenir sheet of one No. 194 has decorative black and white inscribed margin picturing the emblem of the natl. philatelic exhibition held at Paarl, Sept. 16-19. Sold for 70c.

Education — A43

Designs: 16c, E.M. Mokgoko Farmer Training Center, Ramatlabama. 20c, Main lecture block, University of Bophuthatswana, Mmabatho. 25c, Manpower Center. 30c, Hotel training school, Odi.

**1987, Aug. 6** ***Perf. 14½x14***

**196** A43 16c multicolored .35 .35
**197** A43 20c multicolored .45 .45
**198** A43 25c multicolored .60 .60
**199** A43 30c multicolored .75 .75
*Nos. 196-199 (4)* 2.15 2.15

Independence, 10th Anniv. — A44

Communications.

**1987, Dec. 4**

**200** A44 16c Postal service .25 .25
**201** A44 30c Telephone .45 .45
**202** A44 40c Radio .65 .65
**203** A44 50c Television .80 .80
*Nos. 200-203 (4)* 2.15 2.15

Easter
A45

**1988, Mar. 31**

**204** A45 16c John 12:12-14 .25 .25
**205** A45 30c Mark 14:10-11 .50 .50
**206** A45 40c John 13:5 .70 .70
**207** A45 50c John 13:26 .85 .85
*Nos. 204-207 (4)* 2.30 2.30

Natl. Parks Board Activities — A46

**1988, June 23** ***Perf. 14½x14***

**208** A46 16c Environmental education .40 .40
**209** A46 30c Conservation .80 .80
**210** A46 40c Catering 1.10 1.10
**211** A46 50c Tourism 1.40 1.40
*Nos. 208-211 (4)* 3.70 3.70

A souvenir sheet of one No. 211 has black and white decorative margin picturing the emblem of the natl. philatelic exhibition held at Pietermaritzburg, Nov. 22-27. Sold for 70c.

Crops
A47

**1988, Sept. 15** ***Perf. 14½x14***

**212** A47 16c Sunflowers .35 .35
**213** A47 30c Peanuts .70 .70
**214** A47 40c Cotton 1.00 1.00
**215** A47 50c Cabbages 1.25 1.25
*Nos. 212-215 (4)* 3.30 3.30

Dams — A48

**1988, Nov. 17**

**216** A48 16c Ngotwane .35 .35
**217** A48 30c Groothoek .65 .65
**218** A48 40c Sehujwane 1.00 1.00
**219** A48 50c Molatedi 1.10 1.10
*Nos. 216-219 (4)* 3.10 3.10

Easter A49

**1989, Mar. 9**

**220** A49 16c Mark 26:26 .35 .35
**221** A49 30c Matthew 26:39 .65 .65
**222** A49 40c Mark 14:45 1.00 1.00
**223** A49 50c John 18:10 1.25 1.25
*Nos. 220-223 (4)* 3.25 3.25

Children's Art — A50

Designs: 18c, "Rooster," by Thembi Atong. 30c, "Thatched Hut in Rural Setting," by Muhammad Mahri. 40c, "Modern World," by Tshepo Mashokwe. 50c, "Cityscape," by Miles Brown.

**1989, May 11**

**224** A50 18c multicolored .45 .45
**225** A50 30c multicolored .70 .70
**226** A50 40c multicolored .95 .95
**227** A50 50c multicolored 1.25 1.25
*Nos. 224-227 (4)* 3.35 3.35

Birds of Prey — A51

**1989, Sept. 1** ***Perf. 14x14½***

**228** A51 18c *Elanus caeruleus* .60 .60
**229** A51 30c *Melierax canorus* 1.00 1.00
**230** A51 40c *Falco naumanni* 1.25 1.25
**231** A51 50c *Circaetus gallicus* 1.65 1.65
*a.* Souvenir sheet of 1 4.00 4.00
*Nos. 228-231 (4)* 4.50 4.50

No. 231a has multicolored decorative margin picturing emblem of the WANDERERS 101 natl. philatelic exhibition held Sept. 6-9. Sold for 1.50r.

Traditional Thatched Dwellings A52

**1989, Nov. 28** ***Perf. 14½x14***

**232** A52 18c shown .40 .40
**233** A52 30c multi, diff. .75 .75
**234** A52 40c multi, diff. .90 .90
**235** A52 50c multi, diff. 1.10 1.10
*Nos. 232-235 (4)* 3.15 3.15

Community Services A53

**1990, Jan. 11**

**236** A53 18c Playground .40 .40
**237** A53 30c Immunization clinic .65 .65
**238** A53 40c Library .95 .95
**239** A53 50c Hospital 1.25 1.25
*Nos. 236-239 (4)* 3.25 3.25

Wildlife (Small Mammals) A54

**1990, Apr. 11 Litho.** ***Perf. 14½x14***

**240** A54 21c *Dendromus mystacalis* .55 .55
**241** A54 30c *Ictonyx striatus* .80 .80
**242** A54 40c *Elephantulus myurus* 1.00 1.00
**243** A54 50c *Procavia capensis* 1.25 1.25
*a.* Souvenir sheet of 1 3.50 3.50
*Nos. 240-243 (4)* 3.60 3.60

No. 243a has multicolored inscribed margin; text publicizes the natl. philatelic exhibition. Sold for 1.50r.

Sandgrouses — A55

**1990, July 12 Litho.** ***Perf. 14x14½***

**244** A55 21c *Pterocles burchelli* .60 .60
**245** A55 35c *Pterocles bicinctus* 1.10 1.10
**246** A55 40c *Pterocles namaqua* 1.25 1.25
**247** A55 50c *Pterocles gutturalis* 1.50 1.50
*Nos. 244-247 (4)* 4.45 4.45

Bus Manufacturing — A56

a, Chassis welding. b, Mounting the engine. c, Body construction. d, Spray painting. e, Completed models and bare chassis.

**1990, Aug. 3** ***Perf. 14½x14***

**248** Strip of 5 3.00 3.00
*a.-e.* A56 21c any single .60 .60

Traditional Activities — A57

**1990, Oct. 4** ***Perf. 14x14½***

**249** A57 21c Basketry .45 .45
**250** A57 35c Tanning .75 .75
**251** A57 40c Beer making .85 .85
**252** A57 50c Pottery making 1.10 1.10
*Nos. 249-252 (4)* 3.15 3.15

Bophuthatswana Air Force, 10th Anniv. — A58

Helicopters: a, Alouette III. b, BK117. Airplanes: c, Pilatus Trainer PC-7. d, Pilatus Porter PC-6. e, Casa 212.

**1990, Dec. 12** ***Perf. 14½x14***

**253** Strip of 5 6.00 6.00
*a.-e.* A58 21c any single 1.00 1.00

Edible Wild Fruit — A59

**1991, Jan. 24 Litho.** ***Perf. 14x14½***

**254** A59 21c Annona senegalensis .45 .45
**255** A59 35c Strychnos pungens .75 .75
**256** A59 40c Ficus sycomorus .95 .95
**257** A59 50c Dovyalis caffra 1.10 1.10
*Nos. 254-257 (4)* 3.25 3.25

Easter A60

**1991, Mar. 21 Litho.** ***Perf. 14½x14***

**258** A60 21c Mark 14:46 .55 .55
**259** A60 35c Mark 14:53 .85 .85
**260** A60 40c Mark 14:65 1.10 1.10
**261** A60 50c Mark 14:67 1.25 1.25
*Nos. 258-261 (4)* 3.75 3.75

Locomotives A61

**1991, July 4** **Litho.**

**Size: 72x25mm (25c, 50c)**

**262** A61 25c Class 6A .60 .60
**263** A61 40c Class 7A 1.00 1.00
**264** A61 50c Class 6Z 1.25 1.25
**265** A61 60c Class 8 1.65 1.65
*Nos. 262-265 (4)* 4.50 4.50

A souvenir sheet of 1 #265 was sold by the Philatelic Foundation of South Africa.

See Nos. 291-294.

Maps of Africa — A62

**1991, Sept. 12 Litho.** ***Perf. 14x14½***

**266** A62 25c Caneiro chart, 1502 .50 .50
**267** A62 40c Cantino chart, 1502 .85 .85
**268** A62 50c Contarini map, 1506 1.10 1.10
**269** A62 60c Waldseemuller map, 1507 1.40 1.40
*Nos. 266-269 (4)* 3.85 3.85

Maps of Africa A63

**1992, Jan. 9 Litho.** ***Perf. 14½x14***

**270** A63 27c Fracanzano, 1508 .45 .45
**271** A63 45c Waldseemuller, 1513 .80 .80
**272** A63 65c Waldseemuller, 1516 1.10 1.10
**273** A63 85c Laurent Fries, 1522 1.40 1.40
*Nos. 270-273 (4)* 3.75 3.75

Easter A64

**1992, Apr. 1** **Litho.**

**274** A64 27c Mark 15:1 .45 .45
**275** A64 45c Mark 15:15 .80 .80
**276** A64 65c Mark 15:17-18 1.10 1.10
**277** A64 85c Mark 15:19 1.40 1.40
*Nos. 274-277 (4)* 3.75 3.75

Acacia Trees — A65

**1992, Sept. 17** **Litho.**

**278** A65 35c Karroo .45 .45
**279** A65 70c Erioloba .90 .90
**280** A65 90c Tortilis 1.10 1.10
**281** A65 1.05r Mellifera 1.25 1.25
*Nos. 278-281 (4)* 3.70 3.70

A souvenir sheet of 1 #279 exists. Sold for 2.50r.

Lost City Hotel Complex, Sun City — A66

a, View from lake. b, Palace. c, Porte cochere. d, Lobby of Palace. e, Tusk bar.

**1992, Nov. 19 Litho.** ***Perf. 14x14½***

**282** Strip of 5 3.25 3.25
*a.-e.* A66 35c any single .65 .65

Chickens A67

**1993, Feb. 12 Litho.** ***Perf. 14½x14***

**283** A67 35c Light Sussex .45 .45
**284** A67 70c Rhode Island red .90 .90
**285** A67 90c Brown leghorn 1.25 1.25
**286** A67 1.05r White leghorn 1.40 1.40
*Nos. 283-286 (4)* 4.00 4.00

A souvenir shet of 1 #284 exists. Sold for 3r.

Easter A68

**1993, Mar. 5**

| | | | | | |
|---|---|---|---|---|---|
| **287** | A68 | 35c | Luke 23:25 | .40 | .40 |
| **288** | A68 | 70c | John 19:17 | .80 | .80 |
| **289** | A68 | 90c | Mark 15:21 | 1.10 | 1.10 |
| **290** | A68 | 1.05r | Mark 15:23 | 1.25 | 1.25 |
| | | | *Nos. 287-290 (4)* | 3.55 | 3.55 |

Trains Type of 1991

Designs: 45c, Mafeking locomotive shed, c. 1933, RR classes 10, 8, & 12. 65c, Locomotive No. 5. 85c, 1934 Royal visit, White Train, SAR Class 16B. 1.05r, SAR class 19D.

**1993, June 18 Litho.**

**Size: 72x25mm (45c, 85c)**

| | | | | | |
|---|---|---|---|---|---|
| **291** | A61 | 45c | multicolored | .50 | .50 |
| **292** | A61 | 65c | multicolored | .75 | .75 |
| **293** | A61 | 85c | multicolored | .95 | .95 |
| **294** | A61 | 1.05r | multicolored | 1.25 | 1.25 |
| *a.* | | | Souvenir sheet of 4, #291-294 | 3.75 | 3.75 |
| | | | *Nos. 291-294 (4)* | 3.45 | 3.45 |

Maps of Africa A69

Name of cartographer, year published: 45c, Sebastian Munster, 1540. 65c, Jacopo Gastaldi, 1564. 85c, Gerardus Mercator the Younger, 1595. 1.05r, Abraham Ortelius, 1570.

**1993, Aug. 20 Litho.**

| | | | | | |
|---|---|---|---|---|---|
| **295** | A69 | 45c | multicolored | .50 | .50 |
| **296** | A69 | 65c | multicolored | .75 | .75 |
| **297** | A69 | 85c | multicolored | .95 | .95 |
| **298** | A69 | 1.05r | multicolored | 1.25 | 1.25 |
| | | | *Nos. 295-298 (4)* | 3.45 | 3.45 |

Easter A70

**1994, Mar. 25 Litho. *Perf. 14½x14***

| | | | | | |
|---|---|---|---|---|---|
| **299** | A70 | 35c | Luke 22:33 | .35 | .35 |
| **300** | A70 | 65c | Luke 23:35-36 | .70 | .70 |
| **301** | A70 | 85c | Luke 23:36 | .90 | .90 |
| **302** | A70 | 1.05r | Luke 23:38 | 1.00 | 1.00 |
| | | | *Nos. 299-302 (4)* | 2.95 | 2.95 |

Bophuthatswana ceased to exist 4/27/94.

## CISKEI

'sis-,kī

LOCATION — Enclave, Republic of South Africa
GOVT. — Self-governing tribal homeland
AREA — 5,592 sq. mi.
POP. — 1,000,000
CAPITAL — Bisho

**Catalogue values for all unused stamps in this country are for Never Hinged Items.**

Independence from South Africa — A1

***Perf. 14x14½***

**1981, Dec. 4 Litho. Unwmk.**

| | | | | | |
|---|---|---|---|---|---|
| **1** | A1 | 5c | Pres. Sebe | .20 | .20 |
| **2** | A1 | 15c | Coat of arms | .25 | .25 |
| **3** | A1 | 20c | Flag | .30 | .30 |
| **4** | A1 | 25c | Mace | .35 | .35 |
| | | | *Nos. 1-4 (4)* | 1.10 | 1.10 |

An imperf. souvenir sheet exists containing Nos. 1-4 printed in one color (black). Not valid for postage.

Birds
A2 A3

**1981-90 *Perf. 14½x14***

| | | | | | |
|---|---|---|---|---|---|
| **5** | A2 | 1c | *Tauraco corythaix* | .20 | .20 |
| **6** | A2 | 2c | *Motacilla capensis* | .20 | .20 |
| **7** | A2 | 3c | *Centropus superciliosus* | .20 | .20 |
| **8** | A2 | 4c | *Nectarinia famosa* | .20 | .20 |
| **9** | A2 | 5c | *Anthropoides paradisea* | .20 | .20 |
| **10** | A2 | 6c | *Onychognathus morio* | .20 | .20 |
| **11** | A2 | 7c | *Ceryle maxima* | .20 | .20 |
| **12** | A2 | 8c | *Bostrychia hagedash* | .25 | .20 |
| **13** | A2 | 9c | *Cuculus clamosus* | .25 | .20 |
| **14** | A2 | 10c | *Lybius torquatus* | .25 | .20 |
| **15** | A2 | 11c | *Oriolus larvatus* | .55 | .20 |
| **16** | A2 | 12c | *Alcedo cristata* | .55 | .20 |
| **17** | A2 | 14c | *Upupa epops* | .65 | .20 |
| **18** | A2 | 15c | *Haliaeetus vocifer* | .25 | .20 |
| **19** | A2 | 16c | *Batis capensis* | .65 | .20 |
| **20** | A3 | 18c | *Euplectes progne* | 1.00 | .20 |
| **21** | A2 | 20c | *Macronyx capensis* | .35 | .25 |
| **22** | A2 | 21c | *Aplopelia larvata* | 3.25 | .20 |
| **23** | A2 | 25c | *Burhinus capensis* | .40 | .25 |
| **24** | A2 | 30c | *Treron calva* | .55 | .35 |
| **25** | A2 | 50c | *Poicephalus robustus* | .90 | .60 |
| **26** | A2 | 1r | *Apaloderma narina* | 1.50 | 1.10 |
| **27** | A2 | 2r | *Bubo capensis* | 3.25 | 2.25 |
| | | | *Nos. 5-27 (23)* | 16.00 | 8.20 |

Issued: 11c, 4/4/82; 12c, 4/1/85; 14c, 4/1/86; 16c, 4/1/87; 18c, 7/3/89; 21c, 7/3/90; others, 12/4/81.

Nursing A4

**1982, Apr. 30 *Perf. 14½x14, 14x14½***

| | | | | | |
|---|---|---|---|---|---|
| **34** | A4 | 8c | Cecilia Makiwane, vert. | .20 | .20 |
| **35** | A4 | 15c | Surgery, vert. | .25 | .25 |
| **36** | A4 | 20c | Nurses pledge to serve | .35 | .35 |
| **37** | A4 | 25c | Hospital care | .45 | .45 |
| | | | *Nos. 34-37 (4)* | 1.25 | 1.25 |

Pineapple Industry A5

**1982, Aug. 20 *Perf. 14x14½***

| | | | | | |
|---|---|---|---|---|---|
| **38** | A5 | 8c | Spraying | .20 | .20 |
| **39** | A5 | 15c | Harvesting | .20 | .20 |
| **40** | A5 | 20c | Transporting fruit to cannery | .20 | .20 |
| **41** | A5 | 30c | Packing | .30 | .30 |
| | | | *Nos. 38-41 (4)* | .90 | .90 |

Small Mammals A6

**1982, Oct. 29**

| | | | | | |
|---|---|---|---|---|---|
| **42** | A6 | 8c | *Lepus capensis* | .20 | .20 |
| **43** | A6 | 15c | *Vulpes chama* | .30 | .30 |
| **44** | A6 | 20c | *Xerus inaurus* | .35 | .35 |
| **45** | A6 | 25c | *Felis caracal* | .40 | .40 |
| | | | *Nos. 42-45 (4)* | 1.25 | 1.25 |

Trees — A7

**1983, Feb. 2 *Perf. 14½x14***

| | | | | | |
|---|---|---|---|---|---|
| **46** | A7 | 8c | *Cussonia spicata* | .20 | .20 |
| **47** | A7 | 20c | *Curtisia dentata* | .30 | .30 |
| **48** | A7 | 25c | *Calodendrum capense* | .35 | .35 |
| **49** | A7 | 40c | *Podocarpus falcatus* | .60 | .60 |
| | | | *Nos. 46-49 (4)* | 1.45 | 1.45 |

**1984, Jan. 6**

| | | | | | |
|---|---|---|---|---|---|
| **50** | A7 | 10c | *Rhus chirindensis* | .20 | .20 |
| **51** | A7 | 20c | *Phoenix reclinata* | .30 | .30 |
| **52** | A7 | 25c | *Ptaeroxylon obliquum* | .35 | .35 |
| **53** | A7 | 40c | *Apodytes dimidiata* | .60 | .60 |
| | | | *Nos. 50-53 (4)* | 1.45 | 1.45 |

Sharks — A8

**1983, Apr. 13 *Perf. 14x14½***

| | | | | | |
|---|---|---|---|---|---|
| **54** | A8 | 8c | Dusky | .20 | .20 |
| **55** | A8 | 20c | Ragged-tooth | .40 | .40 |

**Size: 57x21mm**

| | | | | | |
|---|---|---|---|---|---|
| **56** | A8 | 25c | Tiger | .50 | .50 |
| **57** | A8 | 30c | Scalloped hammerhead | .60 | .60 |
| **58** | A8 | 40c | Great white | .80 | .80 |
| | | | *Nos. 54-58 (5)* | 2.50 | 2.50 |

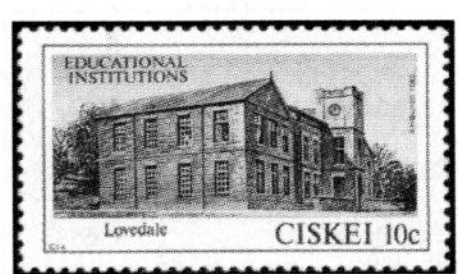


Educational Institutions — A9

**1983, July 6**

| | | | | | |
|---|---|---|---|---|---|
| **59** | A9 | 10c | Lovedale | .20 | .20 |
| **60** | A9 | 20c | Fort Hare | .20 | .20 |
| **61** | A9 | 25c | Healdtown | .25 | .25 |
| **62** | A9 | 40c | Lennox Sebe | .35 | .35 |
| | | | *Nos. 59-62 (4)* | 1.00 | 1.00 |

Military Uniforms — A10

6th Foot, 1st Warwickshire Regiment, 1821-27 (No. 63): a, White drill uniform (D1.5). b, Light Company privates (D2.5). c, Grenadier Company sergeants (D3.5). d, Light Co. Officers (D4.5). e, Officer and field officer (D5.5).

Cape Mounted Rifles, 1827-35 (No. 64): a, Trooper and sergeant, 1830 (D1.5). b, Trooper and sergeant in full dress, 1835 (D2.5). c, Officers, 1830 (D3.5). d, Officers in full dress, 1827-34 (D4.5). e, Officers in full dress, 1834 (D5.5).

**1983, Sept. 28 *Perf. 14½x14***

| | | | | |
|---|---|---|---|---|
| **63** | | Strip of 5 | 1.50 | 1.50 |
| *a.-e.* | A10 | 20c any single | .25 | .25 |

**1984, Oct. 26**

| | | | | |
|---|---|---|---|---|
| **64** | | Strip of 5 | 2.00 | 1.75 |
| *a.-e.* | A10 | 25c any single | .40 | .30 |

Sheets of 10 containing two strips of five.

Coastal Angling A11

Bait.

**1984, Apr. 12 *Perf. 14x14½***

| | | | | | |
|---|---|---|---|---|---|
| **65** | A11 | 11c | Sand prawn | .20 | .20 |
| **66** | A11 | 20c | Coral worm | .20 | .20 |
| **67** | A11 | 25c | Bloodworm | .25 | .25 |
| **68** | A11 | 30c | Red-bait | .35 | .35 |
| | | | *Nos. 65-68 (4)* | 1.00 | 1.00 |

**1985, Mar. 7**

Game fish.

| | | | | | |
|---|---|---|---|---|---|
| **69** | A11 | 11c | *Lithognathus lithognathus* | .20 | .20 |
| **70** | A11 | 25c | *Pachymetopon grande* | .55 | .40 |
| **71** | A11 | 30c | *Argyrosomus hololepidotus* | .65 | .45 |
| **72** | A11 | 50c | *Pomadasys commersonni* | 1.00 | .70 |
| | | | *Nos. 69-72 (4)* | 2.40 | 1.75 |

Migratory Birds and Maps — A12

**1984, Aug. 17 *Perf. 14½x14***

| | | | | | |
|---|---|---|---|---|---|
| **73** | A12 | 11c | Banded sand martin | .25 | .25 |
| **74** | A12 | 25c | House martin | .80 | .80 |
| **75** | A12 | 30c | Greater striped swallow | .90 | .90 |
| **76** | A12 | 45c | European swallow | 1.25 | 1.25 |
| | | | *Nos. 73-76 (4)* | 3.20 | 3.20 |

Brownies A13

**1985, May 3**

| | | | | | |
|---|---|---|---|---|---|
| **77** | A13 | 12c | shown | .20 | .20 |
| **78** | A13 | 25c | Rangers planting saplings | .35 | .35 |
| **79** | A13 | 30c | Guide color guard | .40 | .40 |
| **80** | A13 | 50c | Camping | .70 | .70 |
| | | | *Nos. 77-80 (4)* | 1.65 | 1.65 |

Intl. Year of the Child, 75th anniv. of the Girl Guide movement.

Small Businesses A14

**1985, Aug. 8 *Perf. 14x14½***

| | | | | | |
|---|---|---|---|---|---|
| **81** | A14 | 12c | Furniture | .20 | .20 |
| **82** | A14 | 25c | Dress making | .30 | .30 |
| **83** | A14 | 30c | Welding | .40 | .40 |
| **84** | A14 | 50c | Basketry | .65 | .65 |
| | | | *Nos. 81-84 (4)* | 1.55 | 1.55 |

Troop Ships — A15

**1985, Nov. 15 *Perf. 14½x14***

| | | | | | |
|---|---|---|---|---|---|
| **85** | A15 | 12c | *Antelope* | .25 | .25 |
| **86** | A15 | 25c | *Pilot* | .55 | .55 |
| **87** | A15 | 30c | *Salisbury* | .60 | .60 |
| **88** | A15 | 50c | *Olive Branch* | 1.10 | 1.10 |
| | | | *Nos. 85-88 (4)* | 2.50 | 2.50 |

Miniature Sheet

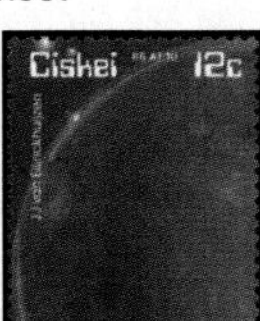


Halley's Comet — A16

Comet streaking through the solar system: a, A1.10. b, A2.10. c, A3.10. d, A4.10. e, A5.10. f, A6.10. g, A7.10. h, A8.10. i, A9.10. j, A10.10.
Illustration reduced.

**1986, Mar. 20**

**89** A16 Sheet of 10 *22.50 22.50*
*a.-j.* 12c any single *2.25 2.25*

Military Uniforms — A17

98th Foot Regiment: 14c, Fifer in winter. 20c, Private in summer. 25c, Grenadier Company sergeant in summer. 30c, Sergeant-major in winter.

**1986, June 12**

**90** A17 14c multicolored .25 .25
**91** A17 20c multicolored .35 .35
**92** A17 25c multicolored .45 .45
**93** A17 30c multicolored .50 .50
*a.* Souvenir sheet of 1 3.50 3.50
*Nos. 90-93 (4)* 1.55 1.55

No. 93a for the natl. philatelic exhibition held at Johannesberg, Oct. 6-11. Sold for 50c.

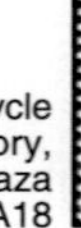

Bicycle Factory, Dimbaza A18

**1986, Sept. 18**

**94** A18 14c Welding frames .25 .25
**95** A18 20c Painting .35 .35
**96** A18 25c Spoke installation .40 .40
**97** A18 30c Assembly .50 .50
*Nos. 94-97 (4)* 1.50 1.50

Independence, 5th Anniv. — A19

14c, Pres. Sebe. 20c, Natl. shrine, Ntaba kaNdoda. 25c, Legislative Assembly, Bisho. 30c, Automatic telephone exchange, Bisho.

**1986, Dec. 4** ***Perf. 14x14½***

**98** A19 14c multicolored .25 .25
**99** A19 20c multicolored .35 .35
**100** A19 25c multicolored .40 .40
**101** A19 30c multicolored .50 .50
*Nos. 98-101 (4)* 1.50 1.50

Edible Mushrooms A20

**1987, Mar. 19**

**102** A20 14c *Boletus edulis* .30 .30
**103** A20 20c *Macrolepiota zeyheri* .45 .45
*a.* Souvenir sheet of 1 3.50 3.50
**104** A20 25c *Termitomyces* .55 .55
**105** A20 30c *Russula capensis* .65 .65
*Nos. 102-105 (4)* 1.95 1.95

No. 103a has fawn and black decorative margin picturing emblem of the natl. philatelic exhibition held at Paarl, Sept. 16-19. Sold for 50c.

Nkone Cattle A21

**1987, June 18** ***Perf. 14½x14***

**106** A21 16c Cow and calf .25 .25
**107** A21 20c Cow .35 .35
**108** A21 25c Bull .40 .40
**109** A21 30c Herd .50 .50
*Nos. 106-109 (4)* 1.50 1.50

Toys — A22

***Perf. 14x14½, 14½x14***

**1987, Sept. 17**

**110** A22 16c Windmill, vert. .25 .25
**111** A22 20c Rag doll, vert. .35 .35
**112** A22 25c Clay horse .40 .40
**113** A22 30c Wire vehicle .50 .50
*Nos. 110-113 (4)* 1.50 1.50

Folklore A23

Legend of Sikulume: 16c, Seven birds. 20c, Sikulume escapes cannibals. 25c, Fights sea monster. 30c, Elopes and is pursued by bride's father.

**1987, Nov. 6** ***Perf. 14½x14***

**114** A23 16c multicolored .25 .25
**115** A23 20c multicolored .35 .35
**116** A23 25c multicolored .40 .40
**117** A23 30c multicolored .50 .50
*Nos. 114-117 (4)* 1.50 1.50

See Nos. 122, 139-142, 147-150.

Endangered and Protected Plant Species — A24

**1988, Mar. 17** ***Perf. 14x14½***

**118** A24 16c *Clivia nobilis* .30 .30
**119** A24 30c *Dierama pulcherrimum* .60 .60
**120** A24 40c *Moraea reticulata* .75 .75
**121** A24 50c *Crinum campanulatum* .95 .95
*a.* Souvenir sheet of 1 3.50 3.50
*Nos. 118-121 (4)* 2.60 2.60

No. 121a margin pictures the emblem of the natl. philatelic exhibition held at Pietermaritzburg, Nov. 22-27. Sold for 1r.

### Folklore Type of 1987
### Miniature Sheet

Legend of Mbulukazi: a, Two wives (B1.10). b, Two doves appear to Numbakatali (B2.10). c, Birth of Mbulukazi and brother (B3.10). d, Mbulukazi and brother at river (B4.10). e, Chief's son announces marriage (B5.10). f, Chief's son presents wives Mbulukazi and Mahlunguluza with huts (B6.10). g, Mahlunguluza drowns Mbulukazi (B7.10). h, Ox tears down Mahlunguluza's hut (B8.10). i, Mbulukazi revived (B9.10). j, Chief's son embraces Mbulukazi, banishes Mahlunguluza (B10.10).

**1988, Aug. 26**
**Size of Nos. 122a-122j: 36x20mm**

**122** Sheet of 10 3.75 3.75
*a.-j.* A23 16c any single .35 .35

Citrus Farming A25

**1988, Sept. 29**

**123** A25 16c Nursery .30 .30
**124** A25 30c Grafting .60 .60
**125** A25 40c Picking fruit .70 .70
**126** A25 50c Grading .95 .95
*Nos. 123-126 (4)* 2.55 2.55

Poisonous Mushrooms A26

**1988, Dec. 1**

**127** A26 16c *Amanita phalloides* .40 .40
**128** A26 30c *Chlorophyllum molybdites* .80 .80
**129** A26 40c *Amanita muscaria* 1.00 1.00
**130** A26 50c *Amanita pantherina* 1.25 1.25
*Nos. 127-130 (4)* 3.45 3.45

Dams — A27

**1989, Mar. 2** ***Perf. 14½x14***

**131** A27 16c Kat River .35 .35
**132** A27 30c Cata .70 .70
**133** A27 40c Binfield Park .90 .90
**134** A27 50c Sandile 1.00 1.00
*Nos. 131-134 (4)* 2.95 2.95

Trout Hatcheries A28

Artificial fertilization: 18c, Obtaining eggs from trout. 30c, Fertilized ova, alevins. 40c, Rainbow trout at 5 weeks. 40c, Adult male rainbow trout.

**1989, June 8**

**135** A28 18c multicolored .50 .50
**136** A28 30c multicolored .75 .75
**137** A28 40c multicolored 1.10 1.10
**138** A28 50c multicolored 1.25 1.25
*a.* Souvenir sheet of 1 4.00 4.00
*Nos. 135-138 (4)* 3.60 3.60

No. 138a margin pictures emblem of the natl. philatelic exhibition WANDERERS 101, held Sept. 6-9. Sold for 1.50r.

### Folklore Type of 1987

Legend of the Little Jackal and the Lion: 18c, Lion and Jackal hunt large eland. 30c, Jackal and offspring climbing to lair. 40c, Lion roaring, jackal under rock. 50c, Lion falling.

**1989, Sept. 21**

**139** A23 18c multicolored .40 .40
**140** A23 30c multicolored .70 .70
**141** A23 40c multicolored .95 .95
**142** A23 50c multicolored 1.25 1.25
*Nos. 139-142 (4)* 3.30 3.30

Early Transportation A29

**1989, Dec. 7** ***Perf. 14x14½***

**143** A29 18c Cape cart .40 .40
**144** A29 30c Jubilee Spider .70 .70
**145** A29 40c Transport wagon .95 .95
**146** A29 50c Voortrekker wagon 1.25 1.25
*Nos. 143-146 (4)* 3.30 3.30

### Folklore Type of 1987

The Legend of Five Heads: 18c, Mpunzikazi presenting offering to Makanda Mahlanu, the 5-headed snake chief. 30c, Snake chief kills Mpunzikazi. 40c, Mpunzanyan presents offering to snake chief. 50c, Snake chief transformed into a man and marries Mpunzanyan.

**1990, Mar. 15** ***Perf. 14½x14***

**147** A23 18c multicolored .40 .40
**148** A23 30c multicolored .70 .70
**149** A23 40c multicolored .95 .95
**150** A23 50c multicolored 1.25 1.25
*Nos. 147-150 (4)* 3.30 3.30

Handmade Carpets — A30

**1990, June 14 Litho.** ***Perf. 14x14½***

**151** A30 21c Hand weaving .50 .50
**152** A30 35c Spinning .80 .80
**153** A30 40c Dyeing yarn .95 .95
**154** A30 50c Hand weaving, diff. 1.10 1.10
*a.* Souvenir sheet of 1 3.50 3.50
*Nos. 151-154 (4)* 3.35 3.35

No. 154a for the 150th anniv. of the Penny Black. Sold for 1.50r.

Plows — A31

**1990, Sept. 6 Litho.** ***Perf. 14½x14***

**155** A31 21c Wooden beam, c. 1855 .35 .35
**156** A31 35c Triple disc, c. 1895 .60 .60
**157** A31 40c Reversible disc, c. 1895 .70 .70
**158** A31 50c "Het Volk", c. 1910 .85 .85
*Nos. 155-158 (4)* 2.50 2.50

Prickly Pear — A32

**1990, Nov. 29** **Litho.**

**159** A32 21c Vendor .55 .55
**160** A32 35c Prickly pear bush .90 .90
**161** A32 40c shown 1.00 1.00
**162** A32 50c Flowering prickly pear 1.25 1.25
*Nos. 159-162 (4)* 3.70 3.70

Owls — A33

**1991, Feb. 2 Litho.** ***Perf. 14x14½***

**163** A33 21c Marsh owl .55 .55
**164** A33 35c Scops owl .90 .90
**165** A33 40c Barn owl 1.10 1.10
**166** A33 50c Wood owl 1.25 1.25
*a.* Miniature sheet of 1 3.75 3.75
*Nos. 163-166 (4)* 3.80 3.80

First Letter From South Africa — A34

Designs: a, Map showing location of Sao Bras (Mossel Bay), 1500. b, Storm-damaged ship off Cabo Tormentoso, 1500. c, Pedro d'Ataide lands at Sao Bras, 1501. d, D'Ataide leaves letter in boot, 1501. e, Joao da Nova finds letter, 1501.

**1991, May 11** **Litho.**

**167** A34 25c Strip of 5, #a.-e. 3.75 3.75

Inscriptions on #167a & 167b are reversed.

Solar System A35

**1991, Aug. 1** **Litho.** ***Perf. 14½x14***

**168** A35 1c Comet nucleus .20 .20
**169** A35 2c Trojan asteroids .20 .20
**170** A35 5c Meteoroid .20 .20
**171** A35 7c Pluto .20 .20
**172** A35 10c Neptune .20 .20
**173** A35 20c Uranus .20 .20
**174** A35 25c Saturn .25 .25
**175** A35 30c Jupiter .30 .30
**176** A35 35c Asteroid belt .35 .35
**177** A35 40c Mars .45 .45
**178** A35 50c Earth's moon .55 .55
**179** A35 60c Earth .65 .65
**180** A35 1r Venus 1.10 1.10
**181** A35 2r Mercury 2.40 2.40
**182** A35 5r Sun 5.50 5.50
*a.* Min. sheet of 15, #168-182 16.00 16.00
*Nos. 168-182 (15)* 12.75 12.75

Frontier Forts A36

Designs: 27c, Xhosa warrior, Fort Armstrong. 45c, Sir George Grey, Keiskamma Hoek Post. 65c, Chief Sandile, Fort Hare. 85c, Cavalryman, Cavalry Barracks, Peddie.

**1991, Nov. 7** **Litho.** ***Perf. 14x14½***

**183** A36 27c multicolored .35 .35
**184** A36 45c multicolored .65 .65
**185** A36 65c multicolored .85 .85
**186** A36 85c multicolored 1.25 1.25
*Nos. 183-186 (4)* 3.10 3.10

Cloud Formations — A37

**1992, Mar. 19** **Litho.**

**187** A37 27c Cumulonimbus .35 .35
**188** A37 45c Altocumulus .65 .65
**189** A37 65c Cirrus .85 .85
**190** A37 85c Cumulus 1.25 1.25
*Nos. 187-190 (4)* 3.10 3.10

Satellites A38

**1992, June 4** **Litho.** ***Perf. 14½x14***

**191** A38 35c Intelsat VI .40 .40
**192** A38 70c GPS Navstar .80 .80
**193** A38 90c Meteosat 1.00 1.00
**194** A38 1.05r Landsat VI 1.10 1.10
*Nos. 191-194 (4)* 3.30 3.30

A souvenir sheet of one No. 192 exists. Sold for 2.50r.

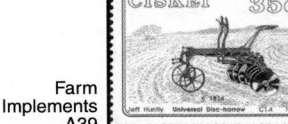

Farm Implements A39

35c, John Deere universal disc-harrow, c. 1914. 70c, John Deere clod crusher & pulverizer, c. 1914. 90c, Self-dump hay rake, c. 1910. 1.05r, McCormick hay tedder, c. 1900.

**1992, Aug. 20** **Litho.**

**195** A39 35c multicolored .40 .40
**196** A39 70c multicolored .80 .80
**197** A39 90c multicolored 1.00 1.00
**198** A39 1.05r multicolored 1.10 1.10
*Nos. 195-198 (4)* 3.30 3.30

Hotels A40

Designs: 35c, Mpekweni Sun Marine Resort. 70c, Katberg Protea Hotel. 90c, Fish River Sun Hotel. 1.05r, Amatola Sun Hotel.

**1992, Nov. 5** **Litho.**

**199** A40 35c multicolored .40 .40
**200** A40 70c multicolored .80 .80
**201** A40 90c multicolored 1.00 1.00
**202** A40 1.05r multicolored 1.10 1.10
*Nos. 199-202 (4)* 3.30 3.30

Famous Explorers A41

Map of voyage, sailing ship, and explorer: 45c, San Gabriel, 1497-98, Vasco da Gama. 65c, Endeavour, 1768-71, James Cook. 85c, Victoria, 1519, Ferdinand Magellan. 90c, Golden Hinde, 1577-80, Sir Francis Drake. 1.05r, Heemskerck, 1642, Abel Tasman.

**1993, May 19** **Litho.**

**203** A41 45c multicolored .35 .35
**204** A41 65c multicolored .60 .60
**205** A41 85c multicolored .70 .70
**206** A41 90c multicolored .75 .75
**207** A41 1.05r multicolored .85 .85
*Nos. 203-207 (5)* 3.25 3.25

Small Cage Birds — A42

Designs: 45c, Serinus canarius domesticus. 65c, Melopsittacus undulatus. 85c, Agapornis roseicollis. 90c, Nymphicus hollandicus. 1.05r, Chloebia gouldiae.

**1993, July 16** **Litho.**

**208** A42 45c multicolored .35 .35
**209** A42 65c multicolored .60 .60
**210** A42 85c multicolored .70 .70
**211** A42 90c multicolored .75 .75
**212** A42 1.05r multicolored .85 .85
*Nos. 208-212 (5)* 3.25 3.25

A souvenir sheet of one No. 209 has inscription for National Philatelic Exhibition. Sold for 3r.

Churches A43

45c, Goshen Mission Church. 65c, Kamastone Mission Church. 85c, Richie Thompson Memorial Church. 1.05r, Bryce Ross Memorial Church.

**1993, Sept. 17** **Litho.**

**213** A43 45c black, buff & red .50 .50
**214** A43 65c black, blue & red .70 .70
**215** A43 85c black, tan & red .95 .95
**216** A43 1.05r blk, lt yel & red 1.25 1.25
*Nos. 213-216 (4)* 3.40 3.40

Invader Plants — A44

**1993, Nov. 5** **Litho.** ***Perf. 14x14½***

**217** A44 45c Opuntia aurantiaca .50 .50
**218** A44 65c Datura stramonium .70 .70
**219** A44 85c Sesbania punicea .95 .95
**220** A44 1.05r Nicotiana glauca 1.25 1.25
*a.* Souvenir sheet, #217-220 3.25 3.25
*Nos. 217-220 (4)* 3.40 3.40

Shipwrecks A45

**1994, Feb. 18** **Litho.** ***Perf. 14½x14***

**221** A45 45c SS Losna, 1921 .45 .45
**222** A45 65c Catherine, 1846 .65 .65
**223** A45 85c Bennebroek, 1713 .80 .80
**224** A45 1.05r Sao Joao Bapista, 1622 1.10 1.10
*Nos. 221-224 (4)* 3.00 3.00

Roses A46

**1994, Apr. 15** **Litho.** ***Perf. 14½x14***

**225** A46 45c Herman Steyn .45 .45
**226** A46 70c Esther Geldenhuys .65 .65
**227** A46 95c Margaret Wasserfall .80 .80
**228** A46 1.15r Prof. Fred Ziady 1.10 1.10
*a.* Souvenir sheet of 4, #225-228 3.00 3.00
*Nos. 225-228 (4)* 3.00 3.00

Ciskei ceased to exist April 27, 1994.

## TRANSKEI

ˌtranˌtˌs-ˈkī

LOCATION — Enclave, East Cape Province, Republic of South Africa
GOVT. — Self-governing tribal homeland
AREA — 16,910 sq. mi.
POP. — 2,876,122 (1985)
CAPITAL — Umtata

**Catalogue values for all unused stamps in this country are for Never Hinged items.**

Independence from South Africa — A1

***Perf. 12½***

**1976, Oct. 26** **Litho.** **Unwmk.**

**1** A1 4c Paramount Chief K.D. Matanzima .50 .50
**2** A1 10c Mace, flag 1.10 1.10
**3** A1 15c Matanzima, diff. 1.90 1.90
**4** A1 20c Coat of arms 2.50 2.50
*Nos. 1-4 (4)* 6.00 6.00

An imperf. souvenir sheet exists containing Nos. 1-4 printed in one color (black). Not valid for postage.

Lubisi Dam — A2

**1976, Oct. 26** ***Perf. 12x12½***

**5** A2 1c shown .20 .20
**6** A2 2c Soil cultivation .20 .20
**7** A2 3c Threshing sorghum .20 .20
**8** A2 4c Transkei matron 3.00 .30
**9** A2 5c Grinding corn 3.00 .30
**10** A2 6c Cutting *Phormium tenax* .25 .20
**11** A2 7c Shepherd boy .25 .20
**12** A2 8c Felling timber .25 .20
**13** A2 9c Agricultural school .30 .25
**14** A2 10c Picking tea .30 .20
**15** A2 15c Wood gathering .35 .25
**16** A2 20c Weaving industry .35 .20
**17** A2 25c Improving cattle breeds .45 .25
**18** A2 30c Sledge transportation .75 .60
**19** A2 50c Map, coat of arms .65 .60
**20** A2 1r Administrative Building, Umtata 1.25 1.25
**21** A2 2r The Bunga, flag 2.25 2.10
*Nos. 5-21 (17)* 14.00 7.50

***Perf. 14***

*5a* A2 1c .20 .20
*6a* A2 2c .20 .20
*7a* A2 3c .20 .20
*8a* A2 4c .20 .20
*9a* A2 5c .20 .20
*10a* A2 6c .20 .20
*12a* A2 8c .20 .20
*13a* A2 9c .20 .20
*14a* A2 10c .30 .30
*15a* A2 15c .40 .40
*16a* A2 20c .55 .55
*17a* A2 25c .70 .70
*18a* A2 30c .90 .90
*19a* A2 50c 1.40 1.40
*Nos. 5a-19a (14)* 5.85 5.85

Transkei Airways Inaugural Flight, Umtata-Johannesburg — A3

**1977, Feb. 11**

**22** A3 4c Aircraft .75 .75
**23** A3 15c Aircraft, terminal 3.00 3.00

*Artemesia affra* — A4

Medicinal plants.

**1977, May 16** ***Perf. 12½x12***

**24** A4 4c shown .50 .50
**25** A4 10c *Bulbine natalensis* 2.00 2.00
**26** A4 15c *Melianthus major* 3.00 3.00
**27** A4 20c *Cotyledon orbiculata* 4.25 4.25
*Nos. 24-27 (4)* 9.75 9.75

**1978, Sept. 25**

Edible fruit.

**28** A4 4c *Carissa bispinosa* .20 .20
**29** A4 10c *Dovyalis caffra* .45 .45
**30** A4 15c *Harpephyllum caffrum* .65 .65
**31** A4 20c *Syzygium cordatum* .90 .90
*Nos. 28-31 (4)* 2.20 2.20

**1981, Apr. 15**

Medicinal plants.

**32** A4 5c *Leonotis leonurus* .20 .20
**33** A4 15c *Euphorbia bupleurifolia* .30 .30
**34** A4 20c *Pelargonium reniforme* .40 .40
**35** A4 25c *Hibiscus trionum* .50 .50
*Nos. 32-35 (4)* 1.40 1.40

Transkei Radio, 1st Anniv. A5

**1977, Oct. 26** ***Perf. 12x12½***
**36** A5 4c Disc jockey .50 .50
**37** A5 15c Announcer 1.25 1.25

"Help the Blind" — A6

**1977, Nov. 18** ***Perf. 12½x12***
**38** A6 4c Basket weaver .20 .20
**39** A6 15c Reading Braille .80 .80
**40** A6 20c Spinning wool 1.00 1.00
*Nos. 38-40 (3)* 2.00 2.00

**1978, Nov. 30**

"Care for Cripples."

**41** A6 4c Leg brace on boy .20 .20
**42** A6 10c Man in wheelchair .55 .55
**43** A6 15c Nurse examining boy .75 .75
*Nos. 41-43 (3)* 1.50 1.50

Men's Pipes A7

**1978, Mar. 1** ***Perf. 12x12½***
**44** A7 4c shown .50 .50
**45** A7 10c multi, diff. .75 .75
**46** A7 15c multi, diff. 1.25 1.25
**47** A7 20c Woman's and witch doctor's pipes 1.50 1.50
*Nos. 44-47 (4)* 4.00 4.00

Weaving Industry A8

**1978, June 9**
**48** A8 4c Angora goat .35 .35
**49** A8 10c Spinning mohair .80 .80
**50** A8 15c Dyeing mohair 1.25 1.25
**51** A8 20c Weaving mohair rug 1.60 1.60
*Nos. 48-51 (4)* 4.00 4.00

Initiation Ceremony of Xhosa Men — A9

**1979, Jan. 30** ***Perf. 12½***
**52** A9 4c Chi Cha youth .20 .20
**53** A9 10c Youths in seclusion .55 .55
**54** A9 15c Umtshilo dance .65 .65
**55** A9 20c Leaving the Sutu .85 .85
*Nos. 52-55 (4)* 2.25 2.25

Chief Matanzima A10

Water Resources A11

**1979, Feb. 20** ***Perf. 14½x14***
**56** A10 4c brn car & gold .20 .20
**57** A10 15c olive grn & gold .40 .40

Inauguration of Matanzima, second state president.

**1979, Mar. 13** ***Perf. 14½x14, 14x14½***
**58** A11 4c Windmill .20 .20
**59** A11 10c Woman filling water jar .40 .40
**60** A11 15c Irrigation, Indwe River, horiz. .60 .60
**61** A11 20c Ncora dam, horiz. .75 .75
*Nos. 58-61 (4)* 1.95 1.95

Waterfalls A12

Child Healh Care A13

**1979, Sept. 4**
**62** A12 4c Magwa Falls .20 .20
**63** A12 10c Bawa Falls .30 .30
**64** A12 15c Waterfall Bluff, horiz. .45 .45
**65** A12 20c Tsitsa Falls, horiz. .60 .60
*Nos. 62-65 (4)* 1.55 1.55

**1979, Dec. 3** ***Perf. 14½x14***
**66** A13 5c Pre-natal nourishment .20 .20
**67** A13 15c Primary feeding .45 .45
**68** A13 20c Immunization .65 .65
*Nos. 66-68 (3)* 1.30 1.30

Fishing Flies — A14

a, Durham ranger. b, Colonel Bates. c, Black gnat. d, Zug bug. e, March brown.

**1980, Jan. 15** ***Perf. 14x14½***
**69** Strip of 5 2.50 2.50
***a.-e.*** A14 5c any single .50 .50

**1981, Jan. 15**

Designs: a, Kent's lightning. b, Wickham's fancy. c, Jock Scott. d, Green highlander. e, Tan nymph.

**70** Strip of 5 1.50 1.50
***a.-e.*** A14 10c any single .30 .30

**1982, Jan. 6**

a, Royal coachman. b, Light spruce. c, Montana nymph. d, Butcher. e, Blue charm.

**71** Strip of 5 1.50 1.50
***a.-e.*** A14 10c any single .30 .30

**1983, Mar. 2**

Designs: a, Alexandra. b, Kent's marbled sedge. c, White marabou. d, Mayfly nymph. e, Silver Wilkinson.

**72** Strip of 5 2.00 2.00
***a.-e.*** A14 20c any single .40 .40

**1984, Feb. 10**

Designs: a, Silver gray. b, Ginger quill. c, Hardy's favorite. d, March brown nymph. e, Kent's spectrum Mohawk.

**73** Strip of 5 2.50 2.50
***a.-e.*** A14 20c any single .50 .50

Rotary Intl., 75th Anniv. — A15

Cycads — A16

**1980, Feb. 22** ***Perf. 14½x14***
**74** A15 15c blk, ultra & gold .40 .40

**1980, Apr. 30**
**75** A16 5c *Encephalartos altensteinii* .20 .20
**76** A16 10c *Encephalartos princeps* .25 .25
**77** A16 15c *Encephalartos vilosus* .35 .35
**78** A16 20c *Encephalartos friderici-guilielmi* .50 .50
*Nos. 75-78 (4)* 1.30 1.30

Birds — A17

**1980, July 30**
**79** A17 5c *Cuculus solitarius* .25 .25
**80** A17 10c *Batis capensis* .55 .55
**81** A17 15c *Balearica pavonina* .85 .85
**82** A17 20c *Ploceus ocularius* 1.10 1.10
*Nos. 79-82 (4)* 2.75 2.75

Tourism — A18

**1980, Oct. 26**
**83** A18 5c Hole in the Wall .20 .20
**84** A18 10c Port St. Johns .30 .30
**85** A18 15c The Citadel .40 .40
**86** A18 20c The Archway .50 .50
*Nos. 83-86 (4)* 1.40 1.40

Xhosa Women's Headdresses — A19

**1981, Aug. 28**
**87** A19 5c Eyamakhwenkwe .20 .20
**88** A19 15c Eyabafana .30 .30
**89** A19 20c Umfazana .35 .35
**90** A19 25c Ixhegokazi .45 .45
***a.*** Souvenir sheet of 4, #87-90 1.90 1.90
*Nos. 87-90 (4)* 1.30 1.30

Independence, 5th Anniv. — A20

**1981, Oct. 26** ***Perf. 14x14½***
**91** A20 5c State House .20 .20
**92** A20 15c University .40 .40

Boy Scout Movement, 75th Anniv. A21

Great Medical Pioneers A22

**1982, May 14** ***Perf. 14½x14***
**93** A21 8c Salute .20 .20
**94** A21 10c Planting tree .20 .20
**95** A21 20c Rafting .40 .40
**96** A21 25c Nature hike with dog .50 .50
*Nos. 93-96 (4)* 1.30 1.30

**1982, Oct. 5**
**97** A22 15c Hippocrates .35 .35
**98** A22 20c Anton van Leeuwenhoek .45 .45
**99** A22 25c William Harvey .55 .55
**100** A22 30c Joseph Lister .65 .65
*Nos. 97-100 (4)* 2.00 2.00

**1983, Aug. 17**
**101** A22 10c Edward Jenner .30 .30
**102** A22 20c Gregor Mendel .65 .65
**103** A22 25c Louis Pasteur .80 .80
**104** A22 40c Florence Nightingale 1.25 1.25
*Nos. 101-104 (4)* 3.00 3.00

**1984, Oct. 12**
**105** A22 11c Nicholas of Cusa .40 .40
**106** A22 25c William Morton .90 .90
**107** A22 30c Wilhelm Roentgen 1.10 1.10
**108** A22 45c Karl Landsteiner 1.65 1.65
*Nos. 105-108 (4)* 4.05 4.05

**1985, Sept. 20**
**109** A22 12c Andreas Vesalius .45 .45
**110** A22 25c Marcello Malpighi 1.10 1.10
**111** A22 30c Francois Magendie 1.40 1.40
**112** A22 50c William Stewart Halsted 2.00 2.00
*Nos. 109-112 (4)* 4.95 4.95
*Nos. 97-112 (16)* 14.00 14.00

Umtata, Cent. A23

Architecture: 8c, City Hall. 15c, The Bunga. 20c, Botha Sigcau Building. 25c, Palace of Justice, Matanzima Building.

**1982, Nov. 10** ***Perf. 14x14½***
**113** A23 8c multicolored .20 .20
**114** A23 15c multicolored .20 .20
**115** A23 20c multicolored .30 .30
**116** A23 25c multicolored .40 .40
*Nos. 113-116 (4)* 1.10 1.10

Wildcoast Holiday Resort, Mzamba A24

**1983, May 25**
**117** A24 10c Hotel complex .20 .20
**118** A24 20c Beach scene .35 .35
**119** A24 25c Casino .45 .45
**120** A24 40c Carousel .65 .65
*Nos. 117-120 (4)* 1.65 1.65

Post Offices A25

**1983, Nov. 9** *Perf. 14½x14*

121 A25 10c Lady Frere .20 .20
122 A25 20c Idutywa .30 .30
123 A25 25c Lusikisiki .40 .40
124 A25 40c Cala .60 .60
*Nos. 121-124 (4)* 1.50 1.50

**1984, May 11**

125 A25 11c Umzimkulu .20 .20
126 A25 20c Mount Fletcher .30 .30
127 A25 25c Qumbu .40 .40
128 A25 30c Umtata .60 .60
*Nos. 125-128 (4)* 1.50 1.50

Xhosa Lifestyle A26

**1984-90**

129 A26 1c Amagqira .20 .20
130 A26 2c Horsemen .20 .20
131 A26 3c Mat maker .20 .20
132 A26 4c Xhosa dancers .20 .20
133 A26 5c Man, donkeys .20 .20
134 A26 6c Musicians .20 .20
135 A26 7c Fingo brides .20 .20
136 A26 8c Tasting beer .20 .20
137 A26 9c Thinning corn .20 .20
138 A26 10c Dance demonstration .20 .20
139 A26 11c Carrying water from the river .20 .20
140 A26 12c Meal preparation .25 .25
141 A26 14c Weeding .25 .25
142 A26 15c Stick fighting .30 .30
143 A26 16c Morning pasture .30 .30
144 A26 20c Abakhwetha dancers .40 .40
145 A26 21c Building initiation hut .40 .40
146 A26 25c Tribesmen singing .45 .45
147 A26 30c Matrons .50 .50
148 A26 50c Pipe maker .95 .95
149 A26 1r Intonjane women 1.90 1.90
150 A26 2r Abakhwetha 4.00 4.00
*Nos. 129-150 (22)* 11.90 11.90

Issued: 11c, 4/2/84; 12c, 4/1/85; 14c, 4/1/86; 16c, 4/1/87; 21c, 7/3/90; others, 7/6/84.

Soil Conservation A27

Designs: 11c, Erosion from over-grazing. 25c, Wall construction to collect sediment. 30c, Regeneration of vegetation. 50c, Cattle grazing on verdant plain.

**1985, Feb. 7**

155 A27 11c shown .20 .20
156 A27 25c multicolored .45 .45
157 A27 30c multicolored .50 .50
158 A27 50c multicolored .85 .85
*Nos. 155-158 (4)* 2.00 2.00

Bridges A28

**1985, Apr. 18**

159 A28 12c Tsitsa .20 .20
160 A28 25c White Kei .45 .45
161 A28 30c Mitchell .50 .50
162 A28 50c Umzimvubu .85 .85
*Nos. 159-162 (4)* 2.00 2.00

Match Industry — A29

**1985, July 25** *Perf. 14½x14*

163 A29 12c Peeling logs .20 .20
164 A29 25c Splint chopping .45 .45
165 A29 30c VPO machine .50 .50
166 A29 50c Filling boxes .85 .85
*Nos. 163-166 (4)* 2.00 2.00

Port St. Johns A30

Designs: 12c, Early street scene. 20c, Coaster *Umzimvubu* at the Old Jetty. 25c, Unloading corn from wagons at the Jetty. 30c, View of the town, 1890's.

**1986, Feb. 6**

167 A30 12c multicolored .20 .20
168 A30 20c multicolored .35 .35
169 A30 25c multicolored .45 .45
170 A30 30c multicolored .55 .55
a. Souvenir sheet of 4, #167-170 2.50 2.50
*Nos. 167-170 (4)* 1.55 1.55

Aloes — A31

**1986, May 1**

171 A31 14c *Aloe ferox* .20 .20
172 A31 20c *Aloe arborescens* .30 .30
173 A31 25c *Aloe maculata* .40 .40
174 A31 30c *Aloe ecklonis* .50 .50
a. Souvenir sheet of 1 4.00 4.00
*Nos. 171-174 (4)* 1.40 1.40

No. 174a margin pictures emblem of the natl. philatelic exhibition held at Johannesburg, Oct. 6-11. Sold for 50c.

Hydroelectric Power Stations A32

14c, First Falls, Umtata River. 20c, Second Falls, Umtata River. 25c, Ncora, Qumanco River. 30c, Collywobbles, Mbashe River.

**1986, July 24**

175 A32 14c shown .25 .25
176 A32 20c multicolored .35 .35
177 A32 25c multicolored .40 .40
178 A32 30c multicolored .50 .50
*Nos. 175-178 (4)* 1.50 1.50

Independence, 10th Anniv. — A33

Designs: 14c, Prime Minister G. M. Matanzima. 20c, Technical College, Umtata. 25c, University of Transkei, Umtata. 30c, Palace of Justice, Umtata.

**1986, Oct. 26**

179 A33 14c multicolored .20 .20
180 A33 20c multicolored .30 .30
181 A33 25c multicolored .35 .35
182 A33 30c multicolored .40 .40
*Nos. 179-182 (4)* 1.25 1.25

Transkei Airways, 10th Anniv. — A34

**1987, Feb. 5**

183 A34 14c shown .30 .30
184 A34 20c Aircraft tail .45 .45
185 A34 25c Nose, propellers .55 .55
186 A34 30c Plane, control tower .65 .65
*Nos. 183-186 (4)* 1.95 1.95

Beadwork — A35

Spiders — A36

**1987, May 22** *Perf. 14x14½*

187 A35 16c Pondo girl .30 .30
188 A35 20c Bomvana woman .40 .40
189 A35 25c Xessibe woman .50 .50
a. Souvenir sheet of 1 3.50 3.50
190 A35 30c Xhosa man .65 .65
*Nos. 187-190 (4)* 1.85 1.85

No. 189a has blue and black decorative margin picturing the emblem of the natl. philatelic exhibition held at Paarl, Sept. 16-19. Sold for 50c.

**1987, Aug. 24**

191 A36 16c *Latrodectus indistinctus* .60 .60
192 A36 20c *Nephila pilipes fenestrata* .75 .75
193 A36 25c *Lycosidae* .95 .95
194 A36 30c *Argiope nigrovittata* 1.10 1.10
*Nos. 191-194 (4)* 3.40 3.40

Domestic Animals A37

**1987, Oct. 22**

195 A37 16c Black pigs .40 .40
196 A37 30c Goats .75 .75
197 A37 40c Merino sheep .95 .95
198 A37 50c Cattle 1.25 1.25
*Nos. 195-198 (4)* 3.35 3.35

Seaweed — A38

**1988, Feb. 18**

199 A38 16c *Plocamium corallorhiza* .40 .40
200 A38 30c *Gelidium amanzil* .70 .70
201 A38 40c *Ecklonia biruncinata* 1.00 1.00
202 A38 50c *Halimeda cuneata* 1.25 1.25
*Nos. 199-202 (4)* 3.35 3.35

Blanket Factory, Butterworth A39

**1988, May 5** *Perf. 14½x14*

203 A39 16c Spinning machines .40 .40
204 A39 30c Warping machine .70 .70
205 A39 40c Weaving machine 1.00 1.00
206 A39 50c Raising the nap 1.25 1.25
*Nos. 203-206 (4)* 3.35 3.35

Wreck of the *Grosvenor*, 1782 — A40

Designs: 16c, Ship, map. 30c, *The Wreck of the Grosvenor,* by R. Smirke. 40c, Dirk hilt, compass and coins salvaged. 50c, *African Hospitality,* by G. Morland.

**1988, Aug. 4**

207 A40 16c multicolored .40 .40
208 A40 30c multicolored .75 .75
209 A40 40c multicolored 1.00 1.00
210 A40 50c multicolored 1.25 1.25
a. Souvenir sheet of 1 4.00 4.00
*Nos. 207-210 (4)* 3.40 3.40

No. 210a margin pictures emblem of the natl. philatelic exhibition at Pietermaritzburg, Nov. 22-27. Sold for 1r.

Endangered Species A41

**1988, Oct. 20**

211 A41 16c *Felis nigripes* .50 .50
212 A41 30c *Philantomba monticola* .95 .95
213 A41 40c *Ourebia ourebi* 1.25 1.25
214 A41 50c *Lycaon pictus* 1.50 1.50
*Nos. 211-214 (4)* 4.20 4.20

Locomotive, Trains and Bridges — A42

Designs: 16c, Class 14 CRB locomotive. 30c, CRB pulling train over Toleni-Halt Bridge. 40c, Train on the Great Kei River Bridge, vert. 50c, Train in the Kei Valley.

**1989, Jan. 19** *Perf. 14x14½, 14½x14*

215 A42 16c multi .45 .45
216 A42 30c multi .85 .85
217 A42 40c multi 1.25 1.25
218 A42 50c multi, vert. 1.40 1.40
*Nos. 215-218 (4)* 3.95 3.95

A souvenir sheet of one No. 218 has margin picturing the emblem of the natl. philatelic exhibition WANDERERS 101, held Sept. 6-9. Sold for 1.50r.

Basketry A43

**1989, Apr. 20** *Perf. 14½x14*

219 A43 18c shown .45 .45
220 A43 30c multi, diff. .75 .75
221 A43 40c multi, diff. .95 .95
222 A43 50c multi, diff. 1.25 1.25
*Nos. 219-222 (4)* 3.40 3.40

Mackerel
A44

**1989, July 20**

| | | | | | |
|---|---|---|---|---|---|
| **223** | A44 | 18c | shown | .50 | .50 |
| **224** | A44 | 30c | Squid | .80 | .80 |
| **225** | A44 | 40c | Brown mussel | 1.00 | 1.00 |
| **226** | A44 | 50c | Rock lobster | 1.40 | 1.40 |
| | | | *Nos. 223-226 (4)* | 3.70 | 3.70 |

Trees
A45

**1989, Oct. 5** ***Perf. 14x14½***

| | | | | | |
|---|---|---|---|---|---|
| **227** | A45 | 18c | Broom cluster fig | .45 | .45 |
| **228** | A45 | 30c | Natal fig | .75 | .75 |
| **229** | A45 | 40c | Broad-leaved coral | .95 | .95 |
| **230** | A45 | 50c | Cabbage tree | 1.25 | 1.25 |
| | | | *Nos. 227-230 (4)* | 3.40 | 3.40 |

Fossils
A46

**1990, Jan. 18**

| | | | | | |
|---|---|---|---|---|---|
| **231** | A46 | 18c | *Ginkgo koningensis* | .60 | .60 |
| **232** | A46 | 30c | *Pseudoctenis spatulata* | 1.10 | 1.10 |
| **233** | A46 | 40c | *Rissikia media* | 1.40 | 1.40 |
| **234** | A46 | 50c | *Taeniopteris anavolans* | 1.90 | 1.90 |
| | | | *Nos. 231-234 (4)* | 5.00 | 5.00 |

Great Medical
Pioneers — A47

Diviners — A48

**1990, Mar. 29** ***Perf. 14x14½***

| | | | | | |
|---|---|---|---|---|---|
| **235** | A47 | 18c | Aretaeus | .60 | .60 |
| **236** | A47 | 30c | Claude Bernard | 1.00 | 1.00 |
| **237** | A47 | 40c | Oscar Minkowski | 1.40 | 1.40 |
| **238** | A47 | 50c | Frederick Banting | 1.75 | 1.75 |
| | | | *Nos. 235-238 (4)* | 4.75 | 4.75 |

**1990, June 28 Litho.** ***Perf. 14x14½***

| | | | | | |
|---|---|---|---|---|---|
| **239** | A48 | 21c | Dancing to the Drum | .65 | .65 |
| **240** | A48 | 35c | Lecturing Imichetywa | 1.10 | 1.10 |
| **241** | A48 | 40c | Initiation ceremony | 1.25 | 1.25 |
| **242** | A48 | 50c | Induction ceremony | 1.50 | 1.50 |
| *a.* | | | Souvenir sheet of 1 | 4.00 | 4.00 |
| | | | *Nos. 239-242 (4)* | 4.50 | 4.50 |

No. 242a for the 150th anniv. of the Penny Black. Sold for 1.50r.

Flowers — A49

Parasitic
Plants — A50

**1990, Sept. 20 Litho.** ***Perf. 14x14½***

| | | | | | |
|---|---|---|---|---|---|
| **243** | A49 | 21c | Cyrtanthus obliquus | .55 | .55 |
| **244** | A49 | 35c | Disa crassicornis | .95 | .95 |
| **245** | A49 | 40c | Sandersonia aurantiaca | 1.10 | 1.10 |
| **246** | A49 | 50c | Podranea ricasoliana | 1.25 | 1.25 |
| | | | *Nos. 243-246 (4)* | 3.85 | 3.85 |

**1991, Jan. 10** **Litho.**

| | | | | | |
|---|---|---|---|---|---|
| **247** | A50 | 21c | Harveya pulchra | .60 | .60 |
| **248** | A50 | 35c | Harveya speciosa | .95 | .95 |
| **249** | A50 | 40c | Alectra sessiliflora | 1.10 | 1.10 |
| **250** | A50 | 50c | Hydnora africana | 1.40 | 1.40 |
| | | | *Nos. 247-250 (4)* | 4.05 | 4.05 |

Dolphins
A51

**1991, Apr. 4 Litho.** ***Perf. 14½x14***

| | | | | | |
|---|---|---|---|---|---|
| **251** | A51 | 25c | Delphinus delphis | .65 | .65 |
| **252** | A51 | 40c | Tursiops truncatus | 1.00 | 1.00 |
| **253** | A51 | 50c | Sousa plumbea | 1.25 | 1.25 |
| **254** | A51 | 60c | Grampus griseus | 1.50 | 1.50 |
| | | | *Nos. 251-254 (4)* | 4.40 | 4.40 |

Birds — A52

Medical
Pioneers — A53

**1991, June 20** **Litho.**

| | | | | | |
|---|---|---|---|---|---|
| **255** | A52 | 25c | Balearica regulorum | .70 | .70 |
| **256** | A52 | 40c | Gyps coprotheres | 1.10 | 1.10 |
| **257** | A52 | 50c | Grus carunculata | 1.40 | 1.40 |
| **258** | A52 | 60c | Neophron percnopterus | 1.60 | 1.60 |
| *a.* | | | Souvenir sheet of 1 | 4.00 | 4.00 |
| | | | *Nos. 255-258 (4)* | 4.80 | 4.80 |

**1991, Sept. 26 Litho.** ***Perf. 14x14½***

Developers of vaccines: 25c, Emil von Behring (1854-1917) and Shibasaburo Kitasato (1852-1931), diphtheria. 40c, Leon Albert Calmette (1863-1933) and Camille Guerin (1872-1961), tuberculosis. 50c, Jonas Salk (b. 1914), polio. 60c, John Franklin Enders (1897-1985), measles.

| | | | | | |
|---|---|---|---|---|---|
| **259** | A53 | 25c | multicolored | .55 | .55 |
| **260** | A53 | 40c | multicolored | .95 | .95 |
| **261** | A53 | 50c | multicolored | 1.10 | 1.10 |
| **262** | A53 | 60c | multicolored | 1.50 | 1.50 |
| | | | *Nos. 259-262 (4)* | 4.10 | 4.10 |

Orchids — A54

**1992, Feb. 20** **Litho.**

| | | | | | |
|---|---|---|---|---|---|
| **263** | A54 | 27c | Eulophia speciosa | .40 | .40 |
| **264** | A54 | 45c | Satyrium sphaerocarpum | .65 | .65 |
| **265** | A54 | 65c | Disa scullyi | 1.00 | 1.00 |
| **266** | A54 | 85c | Disa tysonii | 1.25 | 1.25 |
| | | | *Nos. 263-266 (4)* | 3.30 | 3.30 |

Medical
Pioneers
A55

27c, Thomas Huckle Weller (b. 1915), developer of rubella vaccine. 45c, Ignaz Philipp Semmelweis (1818-65), diagnosed septicaemia. 65c, Sir James Young Simpson (1811-70), 1st to use chloroform in obstetrics. 85c, Rene Theophile Hyacinthe Laennec (1781-1826), inventor of stethoscope.

**1992, Apr. 1 Litho.** ***Perf. 14½x14***

| | | | | | |
|---|---|---|---|---|---|
| **267** | A55 | 27c | multicolored | .45 | .45 |
| **268** | A55 | 45c | multicolored | .80 | .80 |
| **269** | A55 | 65c | multicolored | 1.10 | 1.10 |
| **270** | A55 | 85c | multicolored | 1.40 | 1.40 |
| | | | *Nos. 267-270 (4)* | 3.75 | 3.75 |

Waterfowl — A56

**1992, July 16 Litho.** ***Perf. 14x14½***

| | | | | | |
|---|---|---|---|---|---|
| **271** | A56 | 35c | Anas erythrorhyncha | .45 | .45 |
| **272** | A56 | 35c | Anas hottentota | .45 | .45 |
| *a.* | | | Pair, #271-272 | .90 | .90 |
| **273** | A56 | 70c | Oxyura punctata | .95 | .95 |
| **274** | A56 | 70c | Thalassornis leuconotus | .95 | .95 |
| *a.* | | | Pair, #273-274 | 1.90 | 1.90 |
| **275** | A56 | 90c | Anas sparsa | 1.25 | 1.25 |
| **276** | A56 | 90c | Alopochen aegyptiacus | 1.25 | 1.25 |
| *a.* | | | Pair, #275-276 | 2.50 | 2.50 |
| **277** | A56 | 1.05r | Anas smithi | 1.25 | 1.25 |
| **278** | A56 | 1.05r | Anas capensis | 1.25 | 1.25 |
| *a.* | | | Pair, #277-278 | 2.75 | 2.75 |
| | | | *Nos. 271-278 (8)* | 7.80 | 7.80 |

A souvenir sheet of 1 #273 was sold by the Philatelic Foundation of South Africa.

Fossils
A57

Designs: 35c, Pseudomelania sutherlandi. 70c, Gaudryceras denseplicatum. 90c, Neithea quinquecostata. 1.05r, Pugilina (Mayeria) acuticarinatus.

**1992, Sept. 17 Litho.** ***Perf. 14½x14***

| | | | | | |
|---|---|---|---|---|---|
| **279** | A57 | 35c | multicolored | .45 | .45 |
| **280** | A57 | 70c | multicolored | .90 | .90 |
| **281** | A57 | 90c | multicolored | 1.25 | 1.25 |
| **282** | A57 | 1.05r | multicolored | 1.40 | 1.40 |
| | | | *Nos. 279-282 (4)* | 4.00 | 4.00 |

Dogs — A58

**1993, Feb. 12** **Litho.**

| | | | | | |
|---|---|---|---|---|---|
| **283** | A58 | 35c | Papillon | .45 | .45 |
| **284** | A58 | 70c | Pekingese | .90 | .90 |
| **285** | A58 | 90c | Chihuahua | 1.25 | 1.25 |
| **286** | A58 | 1.05r | Dachshund | 1.40 | 1.40 |
| | | | *Nos. 283-286 (4)* | 4.00 | 4.00 |

A souvenir sheet of one No. 284 exists. Soild for 3r.

Prehistoric
Animals
A59

**1993, June 18** **Litho.**

| | | | | | |
|---|---|---|---|---|---|
| **287** | A59 | 45c | Fabrosaurus | .60 | .60 |
| **288** | A59 | 65c | Diictodon | .85 | .85 |
| **289** | A59 | 85c | Chasmatosaurus | 1.10 | 1.10 |
| **290** | A59 | 1.05r | Rubidgea | 1.40 | 1.40 |
| | | | *Nos. 287-290 (4)* | 3.95 | 3.95 |

Medical
Pioneers
A60

Designs: 45c, Sir Alexander Fleming (1881-1955), discovered penicillin and Lord Howard Walter Florey (1898-1968), purified penicillin for general use. 65c, Alexis Carrel (1873-1944), developed Carrel-Dakin fluid and method to suture blood vessels. 85c, James Lind (1716-1794), recommended citrus fruit to combat scurvy. 1.05r, Santiago Ramon y Cajal (1852-1934), established neuron as basic unit of nervous structure.

**1993, Aug. 20** **Litho.**

| | | | | | |
|---|---|---|---|---|---|
| **291** | A60 | 45c | multicolored | .60 | .60 |
| **292** | A60 | 65c | multicolored | .80 | .80 |
| **293** | A60 | 85c | multicolored | 1.00 | 1.00 |
| **294** | A60 | 1.05r | multicolored | 1.25 | 1.25 |
| | | | *Nos. 291-294 (4)* | 3.65 | 3.65 |

Doves — A61

Designs: 45c, Streptopelia senegalensis. 65c, Turtur tympanistria. 85c, Turtur chalcospilos. 1.05r, Oena capensis.

**1993, Oct. 15 Litho.** ***Perf. 14x14½***

| | | | | | |
|---|---|---|---|---|---|
| **295** | A61 | 45c | multicolored | .60 | .60 |
| **296** | A61 | 65c | multicolored | .85 | .85 |
| **297** | A61 | 85c | multicolored | 1.10 | 1.10 |
| **298** | A61 | 1.05r | multicolored | 1.25 | 1.25 |
| *a.* | | | Souvenir sheet of 4, #295-298 | 4.00 | 4.00 |
| | | | *Nos. 295-298 (4)* | 3.80 | 3.80 |

No. 298a sold for 3.50r.

Modern
Shipwrecks
A62

**1994, Mar. 18 Litho.** ***Perf. 14½x14***

| | | | | | |
|---|---|---|---|---|---|
| **299** | A62 | 45c | Clan Lindsay, 1898 | .55 | .55 |
| **300** | A62 | 65c | Horizon, 1967 | .80 | .80 |
| **301** | A62 | 85c | Oceanos, 1991 | 1.10 | 1.10 |
| **302** | A62 | 1.05r | Forresbank, 1958 | 1.25 | 1.25 |
| | | | *Nos. 299-302 (4)* | 3.70 | 3.70 |

A souvenir sheet of 1 #301 exists. Sold for 3r.

Transkei ceased to exist April 27, 1994.

## VENDA

ˈven-də

LOCATION — Enclave, Republic of South Africa

GOVT. — Self-governing tribal homeland
AREA — 4,040 sq. mi.
POP. — 343,480 (1980)
CAPITAL — Thohoyandou

**Catalogue values for all unused stamps in this country are for Never Hinged items.**

Independence from South Africa — A1

Designs: 4c, Mace, flag. 15c, Administrative buildings. 20c, P.R. Mphephu, paramount chief and president. 25c, Coat of arms.

***Perf. 14½x14***

**1979, Sept. 13 Litho. Unwmk.**

**1** A1 4c multicolored .35 .35
**2** A1 15c multicolored .90 .90
**3** A1 20c multicolored 1.25 1.25
**4** A1 25c multicolored 1.75 1.75
*Nos. 1-4 (4)* 4.25 4.25

Flowers — A2

Wood Carvings — A3

**1979-85** ***Perf. 12½, 14 (11c, 12c)***

**5** A2 1c *Tecomaria capensis* .20 .20
**6** A2 2c *Catophractes alexandri* .20 .20
**7** A2 3c *Tricliceras longipedunculatum* .20 .20
**8** A2 4c *Dissotis princeps* .20 .20
**9** A2 5c *Gerbera jamesonii* 1.75 .55
**10** A2 6c *Hibiscus mastersianus* .20 .20
**11** A2 7c *Nymphaea caerulaea* .20 .20
**12** A2 8c *Crinum lugardiae* .30 .20
**13** A2 9c *Xerophyta retinervis* .20 .20
**14** A2 10c *Hypoxis angustifolia* .25 .20
**15** A2 11c *Combretum microphyllum* .25 .20
**16** A2 12c *Clivia caulescens* .35 .20
**17** A2 15c *Pycnostachys urticifolia* .20 .20
**18** A2 20c *Zantedeschia jucunda* .20 .20
**19** A2 25c *Leonotis mollis* 2.10 .80
**20** A2 30c *Littonia modesta* .35 .25
**21** A2 50c *Protea caffra* .55 .25
**22** A2 1r *Adenium multiflorum* .80 .45
**23** A2 2r *Strelitzia caudata* 1.75 1.10
*Nos. 5-23 (19)* 10.25 6.00

Issue dates: 11c, Apr. 2, 1984; 12c, Apr. 1, 1985; others, Sept. 13, 1979.

***Perf. 14***

*5a* A2 1c .20 .20
*6a* A2 2c .20 .20
*7a* A2 3c .20 .20
*9a* A2 5c .20 .20
*12a* A2 8c .20 .20
*14a* A2 10c .25 .20
*19a* A2 25c .70 .40
*21a* A2 50c 1.50 .80
*Nos. 5a-21a (8)* 3.45 2.40

**1980, Feb. 13** ***Perf. 14½x14, 14x14½***

Designs: 5c, Man with cup. 10c, Woman with corn, bowl and spoon. 15c, King Nebuchadnezzar, horiz. 20c, Python killing woman, horiz.

**24** A3 5c multicolored .20 .20
**25** A3 10c multicolored .35 .35
**26** A3 15c multicolored .50 .50
**27** A3 20c multicolored .70 .70
*Nos. 24-27 (4)* 1.75 1.75

Tea Cultivation A4

**1980, May 14** ***Perf. 14x14½***

**28** A4 5c Plants in nursery .20 .20
**29** A4 10c Harvest .20 .20
**30** A4 15c Withering .40 .40
**31** A4 20c Cut, twist, curl unit .60 .60
*Nos. 28-31 (4)* 1.40 1.40

Banana Industry A5

**1980, Aug. 13**

**32** A5 5c Plants .20 .20
**33** A5 10c Cutting "hands" .20 .20
**34** A5 15c Sorting .40 .40
**35** A5 20c Packing .60 .60
*Nos. 32-35 (4)* 1.40 1.40

Butterflies A6

Sunbirds A7

**1980, Nov. 13** ***Perf. 14½x14***

**36** A6 5c *Precis tugela* .20 .20
**37** A6 10c *Charaxes bohemani* .25 .25
**38** A6 15c *Catacroptera cloanthe* .45 .45
**39** A6 20c *Papilio dardanus* .60 .60
*Nos. 36-39 (4)* 1.50 1.50

**1981, Feb. 16**

**40** A7 5c *Anthreptes collaris* .20 .20
**41** A7 15c *Nectarinia mariquensis* .45 .45
**42** A7 20c *Nectarinia talatala* .60 .60
**43** A7 25c *Nectarinia senegalensis* .75 .75
*Nos. 40-43 (4)* 2.00 2.00

Nwanedi Dam — A8

**1981, May 6**

**44** A8 5c shown .20 .20
**45** A8 15c Mahovhohovho Falls .20 .20
**46** A8 20c Phiphidi Falls .25 .25
**47** A8 25c Lake Fundudzi .35 .35
*Nos. 44-47 (4)* 1.00 1.00

Orchids — A9

Musical Instruments — A10

**1981, Sept. 11**

**48** A9 5c *Cynorkis kassnerana* .20 .20
**49** A9 15c *Eulophia fridericii* .20 .20
**50** A9 20c *Bonatea densiflora* .25 .25
**51** A9 25c *Mystacidium brayboniae* .35 .35
*a.* Souvenir sheet of 4, #48-51 1.50 1.50
*Nos. 48-51 (4)* 1.00 1.00

**1981, Nov. 13** ***Perf. 14x14½***

**52** A10 5c Mbila .20 .20
**53** A10 15c Phalaphala .20 .20
**54** A10 20c Tshizambi .25 .25
**55** A10 25c Ngoma .35 .35
*Nos. 52-55 (4)* 1.00 1.00

Sisal Cultivation A11

**1982, Feb. 26**

**56** A11 5c Harvesting .20 .20
**57** A11 10c Drying .20 .20
**58** A11 20c Grading .25 .25
**59** A11 25c Baling .35 .35
*Nos. 56-59 (4)* 1.00 1.00

History of Writing — A12

Designs: 8c, Bison, petroglyph, Atlamira, Spain. 15c, Animal, petroglyph, eastern California. 20c, Pictographic script on a Sumerian tablet. 25c, Bushman burial stone, Humansdorp, South Africa.

**1982, June 15** ***Perf. 14½x14***

**60** A12 8c multicolored .20 .20
**61** A12 15c multicolored .25 .25
**62** A12 20c multicolored .35 .35
**63** A12 25c multicolored .45 .45
*Nos. 60-63 (4)* 1.25 1.25

**1983, May 11 Size: 21x37mm**

10c, Indus Valley script, 3000 B.C. 20c, Sumerian cuneiform, 2000 B.C. 25c, Egyptian hieroglyphics, 1300 B.C. 40c, Chinese handscroll, A.D. 1100.

**64** A12 10c multicolored .20 .20
**65** A12 20c multicolored .30 .30
**66** A12 25c multicolored .35 .35
**67** A12 40c multicolored .40 .40
*Nos. 64-67 (4)* 1.25 1.25

**1984, Feb. 17** ***Perf. 14x14½***
**Size: 37½x20½mm**

Designs: 10c, Evolution of the cuneiform sign. 20c, Evolution of the Chinese character. 25c, Development of Cretan hieroglyphics. 40c, Development of Egyptian hieroglyphics.

**68** A12 10c multicolored .20 .20
**69** A12 20c multicolored .45 .45
**70** A12 25c multicolored .50 .50
**71** A12 40c multicolored .85 .85
*Nos. 68-71 (4)* 2.00 2.00

**1985, Mar. 21** ***Perf. 14½x14***
**Size: 34x24½mm**

Designs: 11c, Southern Arabic characters. 25c, Phoenician characters. 30c, Aramaic characters. 50c, Canaanite characters.

**72** A12 11c multicolored .20 .20
**73** A12 25c multicolored .50 .50
**74** A12 30c multicolored .60 .60
**75** A12 50c multicolored 1.00 1.00
*Nos. 72-75 (4)* 2.30 2.30

**1986, Apr. 10** ***Perf. 14x14½***
**Size: 24½x34mm**

**76** A12 14c Etruscan .30 .30
**77** A12 20c Greek .45 .45
**78** A12 25c Roman .55 .55
**79** A12 30c Cyrillic .65 .65
*Nos. 76-79 (4)* 1.95 1.95

**1988, Apr. 28** ***Perf. 14½x14***
**Size: 34x26mm**

**80** A12 16c Chinese .40 .40
**81** A12 30c Hindi .65 .65
**82** A12 40c Russian .90 .90
**83** A12 50c Arabic 1.10 1.10
*Nos. 80-83 (4)* 3.05 3.05
*Nos. 60-83 (24)* 11.80 11.80

See Nos. 209-212.

Trees A13

**1982, Sept. 17**

**84** A13 8c *Euphorbia ingens* .20 .20
**85** A13 15c *Pterocarpus angolensis* .25 .25
**86** A13 20c *Ficus ingens* .35 .35
**87** A13 25c *Adansonia digitata* .45 .45
*Nos. 84-87 (4)* 1.25 1.25

**1983, Aug. 3**

**88** A13 10c *Gardenia spatulifolia* .20 .20
**89** A13 20c *Hyphaene natalensis* .35 .35
**90** A13 25c *Albizia adianthifolia* .40 .40
**91** A13 40c *Sesamothamnus lugardii* .70 .70
*Nos. 88-91 (4)* 1.65 1.65

**1984, June 21**

**92** A13 11c *Afzelia quanzensis* .20 .20
**93** A13 20c *Peltophorum africanum* .35 .35
**94** A13 25c *Gyrocarpus americanus* .45 .45
**95** A13 30c *Acacia sieberana* .55 .55
*Nos. 92-95 (4)* 1.55 1.55
*Nos. 84-95 (12)* 4.45 4.45

Frogs — A14

**1982, Nov. 26** ***Perf. 14x14½***

**96** A14 8c *Rana angolensis* .20 .20
**97** A14 15c *Chiromantis xerampelina* .35 .35
**98** A14 20c *Leptopelis* .45 .45
**99** A14 25c *Ptychadena anchietae* .60 .60
*Nos. 96-99 (4)* 1.60 1.60

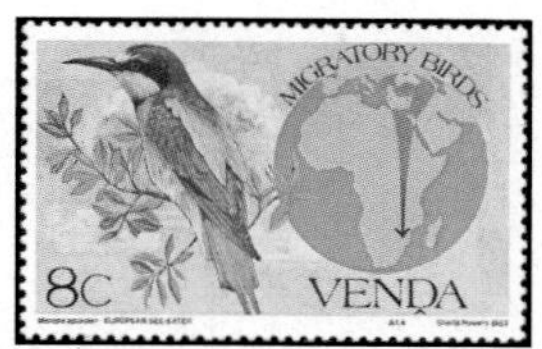

Migratory Birds and Maps — A15

**1983, Feb. 16** ***Perf. 14½x14***

**100** A15 8c European bee-eater .25 .25
**101** A15 20c Steppe eagle .60 .60
**102** A15 25c Plum-colored starling .75 .75
**103** A15 40c White-bellied stork 1.25 1.25
*Nos. 100-103 (4)* 2.85 2.85

Subtropical Fruit A16

**1983, Oct. 26** ***Perf. 14x14½***

**104** A16 10c Avocado .20 .20
**105** A16 20c Mango .25 .25
**106** A16 25c Papaya .30 .30
**107** A16 40c Litchi .55 .55
*Nos. 104-107 (4)* 1.30 1.30

Migratory Birds — A17

**1984, Apr. 26** *Perf. 14½x14*

**108** A17 11c White stork .30 .30
**109** A17 20c Paradise flycatcher .60 .60
**110** A17 25c Yellow-billed kite .75 .75
**111** A17 30c Wood sandpiper .90 .90
*Nos. 108-111 (4)* 2.55 2.55

Independence, 5th Anniv. — A18

**1984, Sept. 13** *Perf. 14½x14*

**112** A18 11c Dzata Ruins .20 .20
**113** A18 25c Traditional hut .40 .40
**114** A18 30c Low-income housing .45 .45
**115** A18 45c Modern home .70 .70
*Nos. 112-115 (4)* 1.75 1.75

Songbirds A19

Food of the Veld A20

**1985, Jan. 10**

**116** A19 11c Heuglin's robin .30 .30
**117** A19 25c Black-collared barbet .65 .65
**118** A19 30c Black-headed oriole .80 .80
**119** A19 50c Kurrichane thrush 1.25 1.25
*Nos. 116-119 (4)* 3.00 3.00

**1985, June 21** *Perf. 14x14½*

**120** A20 12c *Mimusops zeyheri* .25 .25
**121** A20 25c *Ziziphus mucronata* .55 .55
**122** A20 30c *Citrullus lanatus* .60 .60
**123** A20 50c *Berchemia discolor* 1.10 1.10
*Nos. 120-123 (4)* 2.50 2.50

See Nos. 173-176.

Ferns — A21

**1985, Sept. 5** *Perf. 14½x14*

**124** A21 12c *Pellaea dura* .25 .25
**125** A21 25c *Actiniopteris radiata* .55 .55
**126** A21 30c *Adiantum hispidulum* .60 .60
**127** A21 50c *Polypodium polypodioides* 1.10 1.10
*Nos. 124-127 (4)* 2.50 2.50

Reptiles A22

**1986-90** *Perf. 14x14½*

**128** A22 1c *Psammophylax tritaeniatus* .20 .20
**129** A22 2c *Pseudaspis cana* .20 .20
**130** A22 3c *Nucras taeniolata ornata* .20 .20
**131** A22 4c *Bitis arietans* .20 .20
**132** A22 5c *Mabuya capensis* .20 .20
**133** A22 6c *Naja haje annulifera* .20 .20
**134** A22 7c *Mabuya quinquetaeniata margaritifer* .20 .20
**135** A22 8c *Philothamnus semivariegatus* .20 .20
**136** A22 9c *Gerrhosaurus flavigularis* .20 .20
**137** A22 10c *Prosymna sundevallii lineata* .20 .20
**138** A22 14c *Platysaurus intermedius* .30 .30
**139** A22 15c *Lacerta rupicola* .30 .30
**140** A22 16c *Varanus niloticus* .35 .35
**141** A22 18c *Dendroaspis polylepis* .40 .40
**142** A22 20c *Afroedura transvaalica* .45 .45
**143** A22 21c *Chamaeleo dilepsis* .45 .45
**144** A22 25c *Elapsoidea sundevallii longicauda* .55 .55
**145** A22 30c *Pachydactylus tigrinus* .65 .65
**146** A22 50c *Mehelya capensis* 1.10 1.10
**147** A22 1r *Cordylus warreni depressus* 2.25 2.25
**148** A22 2r *Python sebae natalensis* 4.50 4.50
*Nos. 128-148 (21)* 13.30 13.30

Issued: 14c, 4/1/86; 16c, 4/1/87; 18c, 7/3/89; 21c, 8/3/90; others, 1/16/86.

Forestry A23

Designs: 14c, Planting pine seedlings. 20c, Felling and extracting saw timber. 25c, Unloading timber at sawmill. 30c, Construction workers using pre-cut lumber.

**1986, June 26** *Perf. 14x14½*

**153** A23 14c multicolored .20 .20
**154** A23 20c multicolored .35 .35
**155** A23 25c multicolored .40 .40
**156** A23 30c multicolored .50 .50
*Nos. 153-156 (4)* 1.45 1.45

FIVA World Classic Car Rally — A24

**1986, Sept. 4** *Perf. 14½x14*

**157** A24 14c 1910 Maxwell .45 .45
**158** A24 20c 1929 Bentley 4½ l .65 .65
**159** A24 25c 1933 Plymouth Coupe .85 .85
**160** A24 30c 1958 Mercedes Cabriolet 1.00 1.00
*a.* Souvenir sheet of 1 5.00 5.00
*Nos. 157-160 (4)* 2.95 2.95

No. 160a for the natl. philatelic exhibition held at Johannesburg, Oct. 6-11. Sold for 50c.

Waterfowl A25

Wood Carvings A26

**1987, Jan. 8** *Perf. 14x14½, 14½x14*

**161** A25 14c *Sarkidiornis melanotos* .65 .65
**162** A25 20c *Dendrocygna viduata* .90 .90
**163** A25 25c *Plectropterus gambensis* 1.10 1.10
*a.* Souvenir sheet of 1 6.50 6.50
**164** A25 30c *Alopochen aegyptiacus* 1.40 1.40
*Nos. 161-164 (4)* 4.05 4.05

Nos. 163-164 are horiz. No. 163a margin pictures emblem of the natl. philatelic exhibition held at Paarl, Sept. 16-19. Sold for 50c.

**1987, Apr. 9** *Perf. 14½x14*

**165** A26 16c *Iron Master* .35 .35
**166** A26 20c *Distant Drums* .40 .40
**167** A26 25c *Sunrise* .55 .55
**168** A26 30c *Obedience* .70 .70
*Nos. 165-168 (4)* 2.00 2.00

Freshwater Fish — A27

**1987, July 2** *Perf. 14x14½*

**169** A27 16c *Hydrocynus vittatus* .70 .70
**170** A27 20c *Opsardium zambezense* .90 .90
**171** A27 25c *Oreochromis mossambicus* 1.00 1.00
**172** A27 30c *Clarias gariepinus* 1.25 1.25
*Nos. 169-172 (4)* 3.85 3.85

### Food of the Veld Type

**1987, Oct. 2**

**173** A20 16c *Grewia occidentalis* .35 .35
**174** A20 30c *Phoenix reclinata* .70 .70
**175** A20 40c *Halleria lucida* 1.00 1.00
**176** A20 50c *Cucumis africanus* 1.25 1.25
*Nos. 173-176 (4)* 3.30 3.30

Coffee Industry A28

**1988, Jan. 21** *Perf. 14½x14*

**177** A28 16c Harvesting .40 .40
**178** A28 30c Weighing .75 .75
**179** A28 40c Sun drying 1.00 1.00
**180** A28 50c Roasting 1.25 1.25
*Nos. 177-180 (4)* 3.40 3.40

Nurse's Training College, Shayandima A29

**1988, Aug. 18**

**181** A29 16c shown .40 .40
**182** A29 30c Microscopy .70 .70
**183** A29 40c Anatomy lecture 1.00 1.00
**184** A29 50c Clinical training 1.25 1.25
*Nos. 181-184 (4)* 3.35 3.35

Watercolors by Kenneth Thabo A30

**1988, Oct. 6**

**185** A30 16c Fetching Water .40 .40
**186** A30 30c Grinding Maize .70 .70
**187** A30 40c Offering Food 1.00 1.00
**188** A30 50c Kindling the Fire 1.25 1.25
*a.* Souvenir sheet of 1 4.00 4.00
*Nos. 185-188 (4)* 3.35 3.35

No. 188a for the natl. philatelic exhibition held at Pietermaritzburg, Nov. 22-27. Sold for 1.50r.

See Nos. 193-196.

Traditional Kitchenware A31

**1989, Jan. 5**

**189** A31 16c Ndongwana .35 .35
**190** A31 30c Ndilo .65 .65
**191** A31 40c Mufaro .90 .90
**192** A31 50c Muthatha 1.10 1.10
*Nos. 189-192 (4)* 3.00 3.00

### Art Type of 1988

Traditional dances: watercolors by Kenneth Thabo.

**1989, Apr. 5**

**193** A30 18c Domba .35 .35
**194** A30 30c Tshinzerere .65 .65
**195** A30 40c Malende .90 .90
**196** A30 50c Malombo 1.10 1.10
*Nos. 193-196 (4)* 3.00 3.00

Endangered Bird Species — A32

**1989, June 27**

**197** A32 18c *Bucorvus leadbeateri* .60 .60
**198** A32 30c *Torgos tracheliotus* 1.00 1.00
**199** A32 40c *Terathopius ecaudatus* 1.25 1.25
**200** A32 50c *Polemaetus bellicosus* 1.65 1.65
*a.* Souvenir sheet of 1 4.00 4.00
*Nos. 197-200 (4)* 4.50 4.50

No. 200a for the natl. philatelic exhibition WANDERERS 101, held Sept. 6-9. Sold for 1.50r.

Independence, 10th Anniv. — A33

**1989, Sept. 13**

**201** A33 18c Pres. Ravele .35 .35
**202** A33 30c Presidential office .65 .65
**203** A33 40c Presidential residence .80 .80
**204** A33 50c Thohoyandou Stadium 1.00 1.00
*Nos. 201-204 (4)* 2.80 2.80

Wildlife Conservation, Nwanedi Natl. Park — A34

**1990, Mar. 1**

**205** A34 18c *Panthera leo* .50 .50
**206** A34 30c *Equus burchelli* .90 .90
**207** A34 40c *Acinonyx jubatus* 1.10 1.10
**208** A34 50c *Ceratotherium simum* 1.40 1.40
*a.* Souvenir sheet of 1 3.75 3.75
*Nos. 205-208 (4)* 3.90 3.90

No. 208a for the natl. philatelic exhibition. Sold for 1.50r.

### History of Writing Type

Designs: 21c, Calligraphy. 30c, Musical notation, Beethoven's *Moonlight Sonata.* 40c, Computer characters. 50c, Black-and-white television picture transmitted across interstellar distances by the Arecibo radio telescope.

**1990, May 23** **Litho.** *Perf. 14½x14*

**209** A12 21c multicolored .55 .55
**210** A12 30c multicolored .75 .75
**211** A12 40c multicolored 1.00 1.00
**212** A12 50c multicolored 1.40 1.40
*Nos. 209-212 (4)* 3.70 3.70

Aloe Plants — A35

Butterflies — A36

**1990, Aug. 23 Litho. *Perf. 14½x14***

| | | | | |
|---|---|---|---|---|
| **213** | A35 21c | Aloe globuligemma | .55 | .55 |
| **214** | A35 35c | Aloe aculeata | .90 | .90 |
| **215** | A35 40c | Aloe lutescens | 1.10 | 1.10 |
| **216** | A35 50c | Aloe angelica | 1.25 | 1.25 |
| | | *Nos. 213-216 (4)* | 3.80 | 3.80 |

**1990, Nov. 15 *Perf. 14x14½***

| | | | | |
|---|---|---|---|---|
| **217** | A36 21c | Pseudacraea boisduvalii | .70 | .70 |
| **218** | A36 35c | Papilio nireus | 1.25 | 1.25 |
| **219** | A36 40c | Charaxes jasius | 1.40 | 1.40 |
| **220** | A36 50c | Aeropetes tulbaghia | 1.65 | 1.65 |
| | | *Nos. 217-220 (4)* | 5.00 | 5.00 |

Birds A37

A38

**1991, Mar. 7 Litho. *Perf. 14½x14***

| | | | | |
|---|---|---|---|---|
| **221** | A37 21c | Batis capensis | .65 | .65 |
| **222** | A37 35c | Cossypha natalensis | 1.00 | 1.00 |
| **223** | A37 40c | Anthreptes collaris | 1.25 | 1.25 |
| **224** | A37 50c | Phyllastrephus flavostriatus | 1.50 | 1.50 |
| | | *Nos. 221-224 (4)* | 4.40 | 4.40 |

**1991, June 6 Litho. *Perf. 14½x14***

Chinese inventions.

| | | | | |
|---|---|---|---|---|
| **225** | A38 25c | Paper made from pulp | .65 | .65 |
| **226** | A38 40c | Magnetic compass | 1.00 | 1.00 |
| **227** | A38 50c | Abacus | 1.25 | 1.25 |
| **228** | A38 60c | Gunpowder | 1.50 | 1.50 |
| *a.* | | Souvenir sheet of 1 | 4.00 | 4.00 |
| | | *Nos. 225-228 (4)* | 4.40 | 4.40 |

Hotels A39

**1991, Aug. 29 Litho.**

| | | | | |
|---|---|---|---|---|
| **229** | A39 25c | Venda Sun | .50 | .50 |
| **230** | A39 40c | Mphephu Resort | .85 | .85 |
| **231** | A39 50c | Sagole Spa | 1.00 | 1.00 |
| **232** | A39 60c | Luphephe-Nwanedi Resort | 1.40 | 1.40 |
| | | *Nos. 229-232 (4)* | 3.75 | 3.75 |

Trees A40

**1991, Nov. 21 Litho.**

| | | | | |
|---|---|---|---|---|
| **233** | A40 27c | Acacia xanthophloea | .45 | .45 |
| **234** | A40 45c | Faurea saligna | .80 | .80 |
| **235** | A40 65c | Strelitzia caudata | 1.10 | 1.10 |
| **236** | A40 85c | Kigelia africana | 1.40 | 1.40 |
| | | *Nos. 233-236 (4)* | 3.75 | 3.75 |

Clothing Factory A41

**1992, Mar. 5 Litho.**

| | | | | |
|---|---|---|---|---|
| **237** | A41 27c | Setting the web | .35 | .35 |
| **238** | A41 45c | Knitting a pattern | .80 | .80 |
| **239** | A41 65c | Using sewing machine | 1.10 | 1.10 |
| **240** | A41 85c | Testing for flaws | 1.40 | 1.40 |
| | | *Nos. 237-240 (4)* | 3.65 | 3.65 |

Bees A42

**1992, May 21 Litho.**

| | | | | |
|---|---|---|---|---|
| **241** | A42 35c | Honey bee | .50 | .50 |
| **242** | A42 70c | Carder bee | 1.00 | 1.00 |
| **243** | A42 90c | Leafcutter bee | 1.10 | 1.10 |
| **244** | A42 1.05r | Carpenter bee | 1.40 | 1.40 |
| | | *Nos. 241-244 (4)* | 4.00 | 4.00 |

A souvenir sheet of 1 #242 was sold by the Philatelic Foundation of South Africa.

Inventions A43

Designs: 35c, Plow, Egypt 1259 B.C. 70c, Wheel, Mesopotamia, 3200 B.C. 90c, Brickmaking, Egypt, 3000 B.C. 1.05r, Sailing ship, Egypt, 1600 B.C.

**1992, Aug. 13**

| | | | | |
|---|---|---|---|---|
| **245** | A43 35c | multicolored | .50 | .50 |
| **246** | A43 70c | multicolored | 1.00 | 1.00 |
| **247** | A43 90c | multicolored | 1.10 | 1.10 |
| **248** | A43 1.05r | multicolored | 1.40 | 1.40 |
| | | *Nos. 245-248 (4)* | 4.00 | 4.00 |

Crocodile Farming A44

**1992, Oct. 15 Litho.**

| | | | | |
|---|---|---|---|---|
| **249** | A44 35c | Emerging from water | .50 | .50 |
| **250** | A44 70c | Egg laying | 1.00 | 1.00 |
| **251** | A44 90c | Hatchlings | 1.10 | 1.10 |
| **252** | A44 1.05r | Maternal care | 1.40 | 1.40 |
| | | *Nos. 249-252 (4)* | 4.00 | 4.00 |

Domestic Cats — A45

**1993, Mar. 19 Litho.**

| | | | | |
|---|---|---|---|---|
| **253** | A45 45c | Burmese | .50 | .50 |
| **254** | A45 65c | Tabby | 1.00 | 1.00 |
| **255** | A45 85c | Siamese | 1.10 | 1.10 |
| **256** | A45 1.05r | Persian | 1.40 | 1.40 |
| | | *Nos. 253-256 (4)* | 4.00 | 4.00 |

A souvenir sheet of one No. 254 has inscription for National Philatelic Exhibition. Sold for 3r.

Herons A46

Designs: 45c, Butorides striatus. 65c, Nycticorax nycticorax. 85c, Ardea purpurea. 1.05r, Ardea melanocephala.

**1993, July 16 Litho. *Perf. 14½x14***

| | | | | |
|---|---|---|---|---|
| **257** | A46 45c | multicolored | .60 | .60 |
| **258** | A46 65c | multicolored | .90 | .90 |
| **259** | A46 85c | multicolored | 1.10 | 1.10 |
| **260** | A46 1.05r | multicolored | 1.40 | 1.40 |
| *a.* | | Souvenir sheet of 4, #257-260 | 4.00 | 4.00 |
| | | *Nos. 257-260 (4)* | 4.00 | 4.00 |

Shoe Factory — A47

**1993, Sept. 17 Litho. *Perf. 14x14½***

| | | | | |
|---|---|---|---|---|
| **261** | A47 45c | Punching out sole lining | .60 | .60 |
| **262** | A47 65c | Shaping heel | .90 | .90 |
| **263** | A47 85c | Joining upper to inner sole | 1.10 | 1.10 |
| **264** | A47 1.05r | Forming sole | 1.40 | 1.40 |
| | | *Nos. 261-264 (4)* | 4.00 | 4.00 |

Inventions A48

**1993, Nov. 5 Litho. *Perf. 14x14½***

| | | | | |
|---|---|---|---|---|
| **265** | A48 45c | Axe | .60 | .60 |
| **266** | A48 65c | Armor | .90 | .90 |
| **267** | A48 85c | Arch | 1.10 | 1.10 |
| **268** | A48 1.05r | Aqueduct | 1.40 | 1.40 |
| | | *Nos. 265-268 (4)* | 4.00 | 4.00 |

Dogs A49

**1994, Jan. 14 Litho. *Perf. 14½x14***

| | | | | |
|---|---|---|---|---|
| **269** | A49 45c | Cocker spaniel | .60 | .60 |
| **270** | A49 65c | Maltese | .90 | .90 |
| **271** | A49 85c | Scottish terrier | 1.10 | 1.10 |
| **272** | A49 1.05r | Miniature schnauzer | 1.40 | 1.40 |
| | | *Nos. 269-272 (4)* | 4.00 | 4.00 |

A souvenir sheet of 1 #271 was sold for 3r by the Philatelic Foundation of Southern Africa and sold for 1.50r.

Monkeys A50

Designs: 45c, Cercopithecus aethiops. 65c, Galago moholi. 85c, Cercopithecus mitis. 1.05r, Otolemur crassicaudatus.

**1994, Mar. 4 Litho. *Perf. 14½x14***

| | | | | |
|---|---|---|---|---|
| **273** | A50 45c | multicolored | .55 | .55 |
| **274** | A50 65c | multicolored | .85 | .85 |
| **275** | A50 85c | multicolored | 1.10 | 1.10 |
| **276** | A50 1.05r | multicolored | 1.40 | 1.40 |
| *a.* | | Souvenir sheet of 4, #273-276 | 4.00 | 4.00 |
| | | *Nos. 273-276 (4)* | 3.90 | 3.90 |

Starlings A51

45c, Lamprotornis nitens. 70c, Cinnyricinclus leucogaster. 95c, Onychognathus morio. 1.15r, Creatophora cinerea.

**1994, Apr. 29 Litho. *Perf. 14½x14***

| | | | | |
|---|---|---|---|---|
| **277** | A51 45c | multicolored | .55 | .55 |
| **278** | A51 70c | multicolored | .85 | .85 |
| **279** | A51 95c | multicolored | 1.10 | 1.10 |
| **280** | A51 1.15r | multicolored | 1.40 | 1.40 |
| | | *Nos. 277-280 (4)* | 3.90 | 3.90 |

Venda ceased to exist April 27, 1994.

The Venda postal service continued to operate until 1996.

## SOUTH ARABIA

sauth ə-'rā-bē-ə

LOCATION — Southern Arabia
GOVT. — Federation; British dependency
AREA — 61,890 sq. mi.
POP. — 771,000 (est. 1966)
CAPITAL — Al Ittihad

The Federation of South Arabia was established in 1959 and consists of 14 states including Aden colony and part of Aden protectorate. When the Federation became independent, Nov. 30, 1967, it became the People's Republic of Southern Yemen. See People's Democratic Republic of Yemen, Vol. 6.

100 Cents = 1 Shilling
1000 Fils = 1 Dinar (1965)

**Catalogue values for all unused stamps in this country are for Never Hinged items.**

Common Design Types pictured following the introduction.

**Red Cross Centenary Issue**
Common Design Type
**Wmk. 314**

**1963, Nov. 25 Litho. *Perf. 13***
1 CD315 15c black & red .45 .30
2 CD315 1sh25c ultra & red .95 .80

Arms of Federation of South Arabia — A1

Flag of Federation — A2

***Perf. 14½x14***
**1965, Apr. 1 Photo. Unwmk.**
3 A1 5f blue .20 .20
4 A1 10f light violet blue .20 .20
5 A1 15f blue green .20 .20
6 A1 20f green .20 .20
7 A1 25f orange brown .20 .20
8 A1 30f lemon .20 .20
9 A1 35f red brown .20 .20
10 A1 50f rose red .20 .20
11 A1 65f light yellow green .30 .20
12 A1 75f rose carmine .35 .20

***Perf. 14½***
**Flag in Black, Yellow, Green and Blue**
13 A2 100f reddish brown .40 .20
14 A2 250f dark blue 5.50 .60
15 A2 500f dark red 10.00 .75
16 A2 1d violet 16.50 7.50
*Nos. 3-16 (14)* 34.65 11.05

**Intl. Cooperation Year Issue**
Common Design Type with Coat of Arms Replacing Queen's Portrait
**Wmk. 314**

**1965, Oct. 24 Litho. *Perf. 14½***
17 CD318 5f blue grn & claret .25 .20
18 CD318 65f lt violet & green .85 .20

**Churchill Memorial Issue**
Common Design Type with Coat of Arms Replacing Queen's Portrait
**Unwmk.**

**1966, Jan. 24 Photo. *Perf. 14***
**Design in Black, Gold and Carmine Rose**
19 CD319 5f bright blue .20 .20
20 CD319 10f green .45 .20
21 CD319 65f brown 1.10 .50
22 CD319 125f violet 1.60 1.00
*Nos. 19-22 (4)* 3.35 1.90

**World Cup Soccer Issue**
Common Design Type with Coat of Arms Replacing Queen's Portrait

**1966, July 1 Litho. *Perf. 14***
23 CD321 10f multicolored .60 .20
24 CD321 50f multicolored 1.40 .30

**WHO Headquarters Issue**
Common Design Type with Coat of Arms Replacing Queen's Portrait

**1966, Sept. 20 Litho. Unwmk.**
25 CD322 10f multicolored .50 .20
26 CD322 75f multicolored 1.25 .40

**UNESCO Anniversary Issue**
Common Design Type with Coat of Arms Replacing Queen's Portrait

**1966, Dec. 15 Litho. *Perf. 14***
27 CD323 10f "Education" .40 .25
28 CD323 65f "Science" 1.60 1.25
29 CD323 125f "Culture" 3.75 5.00
*Nos. 27-29 (3)* 5.75 6.50

## SOUTHERN NIGERIA

'sə-thərn nī-'jir-ē-ə

LOCATION — In western Africa bordering on the Gulf of Guinea
GOVT. — British Crown Colony and Protectorate
AREA — 90,896 sq. mi.
POP. — 8,590,545
CAPITAL — Lagos

The Protectorate of Southern Nigeria, formed in 1900, absorbed in that year the Niger Coast Protectorate. In 1906 it united with Lagos and became the Colony and Protectorate of Southern Nigeria. An amalgamation was effected in 1914 between Northern and Southern Nigeria to form the Colony and Protectorate of Nigeria. See Nigeria, Northern Nigeria, Niger Coast Protectorate and Lagos.

12 Pence = 1 Shilling
20 Shillings = 1 Pound

Victoria
A1

Edward VII
A2

**Wmk. Crown and C A (2)**
**1901, Mar. Typo. *Perf. 14***
1 A1 ½p yel grn & blk 2.00 2.50
 a. ½p yel grn & sepia ('02) 2.50 3.00
2 A1 1p car rose & blk 1.60 1.75
 a. 1p carmine rose & sepia ('02) 2.50 2.00
3 A1 2p org brn & blk 3.75 4.25
4 A1 4p ol grn & blk 3.25 18.00
5 A1 6p red vio & blk 3.25 7.50
6 A1 1sh blk & gray grn 9.25 30.00
7 A1 2sh6p brn & blk 52.50 92.50
8 A1 5sh yellow & blk 55.00 110.00
9 A1 10sh vio & blk, *yel* 100.00 200.00
*Nos. 1-9 (9)* 230.60 466.50

**1903-04**
10 A2 ½p yel grn & blk 1.10 .35
11 A2 1p car rose & blk 1.50 .80
12 A2 2p org brn & blk 7.50 1.75
13 A2 2½p ultra & blk ('04) 2.25 .85
14 A2 4p ol grn & blk 3.25 6.25
15 A2 6p red vio & blk 4.50 9.25
16 A2 1sh blk & gray grn 35.00 22.50
17 A2 2sh6p brown & blk 30.00 70.00
18 A2 5sh yellow & blk 70.00 160.00
19 A2 10sh vio & blk, *yel* 35.00 100.00
20 A2 £1 pur & gray grn 375.00 750.00
*Nos. 10-20 (11)* 565.10 1,121.

**1904-07 Wmk. 3**
**Chalky Paper**
21 A2 ½p yel grn & blk .60 .20
22 A2 1p carmine & blk 14.00 .25
23 A2 2p org brn & blk 3.00 .50
24 A2 2½p ultra & blk 1.10 1.10
24A A2 3p vio & org brn ('07) 11.00 1.50
25 A2 4p ol grn & blk ('05) 16.00 29.00
26 A2 6p red vio & blk 13.50 4.00
27 A2 1sh blk & gray grn 3.75 4.00
28 A2 2sh6p brn & blk ('05) 27.50 20.00
29 A2 5sh yellow & blk 47.50 85.00
30 A2 10sh vio & blk, *yel* ('08) 110.00 200.00
31 A2 £1 pur & gray grn ('05) 225.00 250.00
*Nos. 21-31 (12)* 472.95 595.55

#23 and 24 are on ordinary paper, #24A and 25 on chalky, and the other values on both papers.

**1907-10**
**Ordinary Paper**
32 A2 ½p green ('08) 2.00 .25
33 A2 1p carmine 4.00 .70
34 A2 2p gray 3.00 .80
35 A2 2½p ultra 2.25 4.25

**Chalky Paper**
36 A2 3p violet, *yel* 2.25 .35
37 A2 4p scar & blk, *yel* 2.50 .90
38 A2 6p red vio & dl vio 29.00 3.75
39 A2 1sh black, *green* 8.00 .50
40 A2 2sh6p car & blk, *bl* 5.75 1.10
41 A2 5sh scar & grn, *yel* 45.00 55.00
42 A2 10sh red & grn, *grn* 75.00 110.00
43 A2 £1 blk & vio, *red* 210.00 250.00
*Nos. 32-43 (12)* 388.75 427.60

**1910 Ordinary Paper Redrawn**
44 A2 1p carmine .85 .20

In the redrawn stamp the "1" of "1d" is not as thick as in No. 33 but the "d" is taller and broader.

King George V — A3

**1912**
45 A3 ½p green 2.50 .20
46 A3 1p carmine 2.25 .20
47 A3 2p gray .85 .95
48 A3 2½p ultra 3.25 3.25
49 A3 3p violet, *yel* 1.10 .35
50 A3 4p scar & blk, *yel* 1.50 2.40
51 A3 6p red vio & dl vio 1.50 1.50
52 A3 1sh black, *green* 3.25 .85
53 A3 2sh6p red & blk, *bl* 9.25 35.00
54 A3 5sh red & grn, *yel* 22.50 87.50
55 A3 10sh red & grn, *grn* 52.50 100.00
56 A3 £1 blk & vio, *red* 190.00 250.00
*Nos. 45-56 (12)* 290.45 482.20

Stamps of Southern Nigeria were replaced in 1914 by those of Nigeria.

## SOUTHERN RHODESIA

'sə-thərn rō-'dē-zh,ē-,ə

LOCATION — Southeastern Africa between Northern Rhodesia and Mozambique
GOVT. — British Colony
AREA — 150,333 sq. mi.
POP. — 4,010,000 (est. 1963)
CAPITAL — Salisbury

Prior to 1923 this territory was administered by the British South Africa Company. The colony was created in that year by the British Government at the request of the inhabitants. In 1953, Southern Rhodesia joined Northern Rhodesia and Nyasaland to form the Federation of Rhodesia and Nyasaland. When the Federation dissolved at the end of 1963, Southern Rhodesia again became an internally self-governing colony. See Rhodesia and Northern Rhodesia.

12 Pence = 1 Shilling
20 Shillings = 1 Pound

**Catalogue values for unused stamps in this country are for Never Hinged items, beginning with Scott 56 in the regular postage section and Scott J1 in the postage due section.**

King George V — A1

**1924-30 Unwmk. Engr. *Perf. 14***
1 A1 ½p dark green 2.50 .20
 a. Vert. pair, imperf. btwn. 950.00 1,050.
 b. Horiz. pair, imperf. btwn. 950.00 1,050.
 c. Horiz. pair, imperf. vert. 1,100.
2 A1 1p scarlet 2.00 .20
 a. Horiz. pair, imperf. btwn. 850.00 950.00
 b. Perf. 12½ (coil) ('30) 3.25 92.50
 c. Vert. pair, imperf. btwn. 1,500.
 d. Vert. pair, imperf. horiz. 950.00
3 A1 1½p bister brown 2.50 .90
 a. Horiz. pair, imperf. btwn. 10,000.
 b. Vert. pair, imperf. btwn. 6,250.
4 A1 2p vio blk & blk 3.50 .80
 a. Horiz. pair, imperf. btwn. 12,500.
5 A1 3p deep blue 2.75 3.50
6 A1 4p org red & blk 3.00 3.25
7 A1 6p lilac & blk 2.25 4.75
 a. Horiz. pair, imperf. btwn. 40,000.
8 A1 8p gray grn & vio 12.50 50.00
9 A1 10p rose red & bl 13.50 57.50
10 A1 1sh turq bl & blk 5.75 7.50
11 A1 1sh6p yellow & blk 22.50 37.50
12 A1 2sh brown & blk 20.00 20.00
13 A1 2sh6p blk brn & bl 35.00 70.00
14 A1 5sh bl grn & bl 70.00 175.00
*Nos. 1-14 (14)* 197.75 431.10

Values for imperf between pairs are for stamps from the same pane. Stamps separated by wide margins are cross-gutter pairs and sell for much lower prices.

George V
A2

Victoria Falls
A3

**1931-37 *Perf. 11½, 14 (1p)***
16 A2 ½p dp green ('33) .75 .20
 a. Bklt. pane of 6 ('32) 150.00
 b. Perf. 12 .95 1.10
 c. Perf. 14 ('35) 1.90 .35
17 A2 1p scarlet ('35) .60 .20
 a. Bklt. pane of 6 ('32) 150.00
 b. Perf. 11½ ('33) 2.00 .20
 c. Perf. 12 1.10 .80
18 A2 1½p dp brown ('32) 3.00 .90
 a. Bklt. pane of 6 ('32) 600.00
 b. Perf. 12 ('33) 62.50 47.50

**Typo. *Perf. 14½x14***
19 A3 2p blk brn & blk 4.75 1.75
20 A3 3p dark blue 11.50 12.50

***Perf. 12, 11½ (2sh6p)***
**Engr.**
21 A2 4p org red & blk 1.50 1.75
 a. Perf. 14 ('37) 37.50 55.00
 b. Perf. 11½ ('35) 20.00 5.75
22 A2 6p rose lilac & blk 2.50 3.50
 a. Perf. 14 ('36) 8.00 1.00
 b. Perf. 11½ ('33) 17.50 1.75
23 A2 8p green & violet 2.00 3.75
 a. Perf. 11½ ('34) 20.00 37.50
24 A2 9p gray grn & ver ('34) 7.00 10.50
25 A2 10p car & ultra 8.00 2.75
 a. Perf. 11½ ('33) 7.00 15.00
26 A2 1sh turq bl & blk 2.25 3.00
 a. Perf. 11½ ('36) 125.00 70.00
 b. Perf. 14 ('37) 225.00 160.00
27 A2 1sh6p ocher & blk 11.50 17.50
 a. Perf. 11½ ('36) 57.50 125.00
28 A2 2sh dk brn & blk 24.00 7.50
 a. Perf. 11½ ('33) 42.50 35.00
29 A2 2sh6p ol brn & ultra ('33) 32.50 35.00
 a. Perf. 12 37.50 40.00
30 A2 5sh bl grn & ultra 55.00 55.00
*Nos. 16-30 (15)* 166.85 155.80

Victoria Falls — A4

**1932, May** ***Perf. 12½***

**31** A4 2p dark brn & grn 4.75 1.10
**32** A4 3p dark blue 4.75 2.10
*a.* Vert. pair, imperf. horiz. *9,000.* *11,000.*
*b.* Vert. pair, imperf. btwn. *21,500.*
Set, never hinged 18.00

See Nos. 37-37A.

**Silver Jubilee Issue**

Victoria Falls and George V A5

**1935, May 6** ***Perf. 11x12***

**33** A5 1p car rose & olive 2.75 1.50
**34** A5 2p blk brn & lt grn 4.25 4.00
**35** A5 3p blue & violet 5.50 *9.50*
**36** A5 6p dp violet & blk 7.50 *12.50*
*Nos. 33-36 (4)* 20.00 *27.50*
Set, never hinged 37.50

25th anniv. of the reign of George V.

"Postage and Revenue" A6

**1935-41** ***Perf. 14***

**37** A6 2p dk brn & grn ('41) 1.10 .25
*b.* Perf. 12½ 1.75 10.00
Never hinged 3.00
**37A** A6 3p deep blue ('38) 1.75 .25
Set, never hinged 6.50

Queen Elizabeth, George VI — A7

**1937, May 12** ***Perf. 12½***

**38** A7 1p carmine & gray grn .60 .70
**39** A7 2p brown & green .65 *1.75*
**40** A7 3p lt blue & violet 3.00 *8.00*
**41** A7 6p red violet & blk 1.75 *3.75*
*Nos. 38-41 (4)* 6.00 14.20
Set, never hinged 11.50

Coronation of George VI & Elizabeth.

King George VI — A8

**1937, Nov. 25** ***Perf. 14***

**42** A8 ½p yellow green .35 .20
**43** A8 1p red .35 .20
**44** A8 1½p red brown .65 .35
**45** A8 4p orange red .85 .20
**46** A8 6p dark gray .85 .60
**47** A8 8p blue green 1.25 2.25
**48** A8 9p blue 1.25 .80
**49** A8 10p violet 1.60 *3.00*
**50** A8 1sh green & blk 1.25 .20
**51** A8 1sh6p ocher & blk 7.25 2.50
**52** A8 2sh brown & blk 10.50 .70
**53** A8 2sh6p violet & blue 7.25 5.50
**54** A8 5sh green & blue 16.00 2.75
*Nos. 42-54 (13)* 49.40 19.25
Set, never hinged 75.00

**Catalogue values for unused stamps in this section, from this point to the end of the section, are for Never Hinged items.**

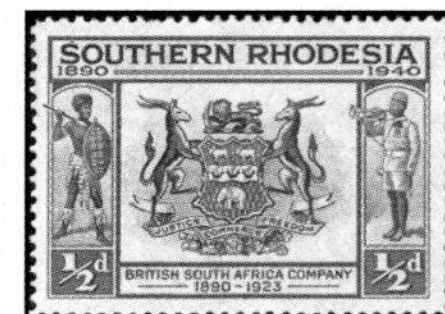

Seal of British South Africa Co. — A9

Fort Salisbury, 1890 — A10

Cecil John Rhodes — A11

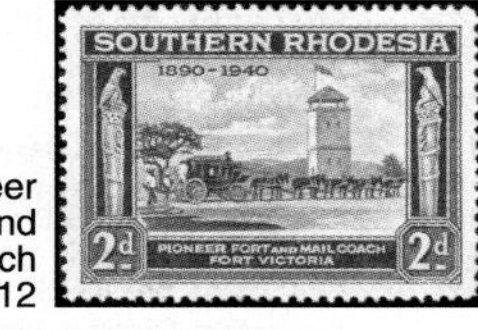

Pioneer Fort and Mail Coach A12

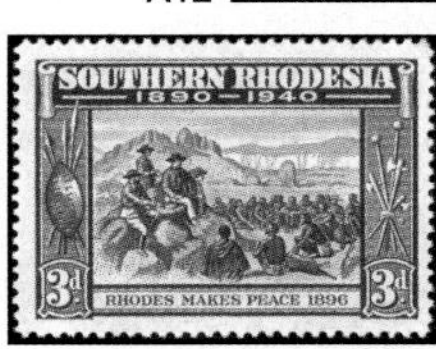

Rhodes Makes Peace, 1896 — A13

Victoria Falls Bridge — A14

Sir Charles Coghlan — A15

Queen Victoria, George VI, Lobengula's Kraal and Government House A16

**Unwmk.**

**1940, June 3** **Engr.** ***Perf. 14***

**56** A9 ½p dp grn & dull vio .20 .40
**57** A10 1p red & vio blue .20 .20
**58** A11 1½p cop brn & blk .20 .50
**59** A12 2p pur & brt grn .50 .40
**60** A13 3p dk blue & blk .80 1.00
**61** A14 4p brn & bl grn 1.00 *1.50*
**62** A15 6p sepia & dull grn 1.00 1.40
**63** A16 1sh dk bl & brt grn 1.10 1.40
*Nos. 56-63 (8)* 5.00 6.80

50th anniv. of the founding of Southern Rhodesia by Cecil John Rhodes.

Pioneer — A17

**1943, Nov. 1** **Photo.** **Wmk. 201**

**64** A17 2p Prus grn & choc .20 .35

50th anniv. of Matabeleland under British control.

Princess Elizabeth and Princess Margaret Rose A18

King George VI and Queen Elizabeth A19

**Unwmk.**

**1947, Apr. 1** **Engr.** ***Perf. 14***

**65** A18 ½p dk green & blk .30 .60
**66** A19 1p carmine & blk .30 .60

Visit of the British Royal Family, Apr., 1947.

**Victory Issue**

Queen Elizabeth A20

George VI A21

Princess Elizabeth A22

Princess Margaret Rose A23

**1947, May 8**

**67** A20 1p deep carmine .20 .20
**68** A21 2p slate black .20 .20
**69** A22 3p deep blue .60 *.50*
**70** A23 6p red orange .40 *.75*
*Nos. 67-70 (4)* 1.40 1.65

Victory of the Allied Nations in WW II.

Common Design Types pictured following the introduction.

**UPU Issue**

Common Design Types

**Engr.; Name Typo.**

**1949, Oct. 10** **Wmk. 4** ***Perf. 11x11½***

**71** CD307 2p slate black .70 .50
**72** CD308 3p slate blue 1.25 *1.75*

75th anniv. of the UPU.

Queen Victoria and King George VI A24

**Unwmk.**

**1950, Sept. 12** **Engr.** ***Perf. 14***

**73** A24 2p choc & blue grn .55 *1.10*

60th anniversary of Rhodesia.

Hospital, Doctor and Natives A25

Designs: 1p, African Scene. 2p, Native Houses, Modern City and Cecil Rhodes. 4½p, Dam and Natives. 1sh, Transportation.

**1953, Apr. 15**

**74** A25 ½p dk brown & blue .20 *.40*
**75** A25 1p blue grn & fawn .20 .20
**76** A25 2p vio & dk bl grn .35 .20
**77** A25 4½p dk bl & bl grn 1.50 *2.25*
**78** A25 1sh chestnut & blk 2.00 .70
*Nos. 74-78 (5)* 4.25 3.75

#77 is inscribed Matabeleland Diamond Jubilee.

Type of Nyasaland Prot., 1953

**1953, May 30** ***Perf. 14x13½***

**79** A17 6p purple .35 .35

Nos. 74-79 were issued to commemorate the Central African Cecil Rhodes Centenary Exhibition.

**Coronation Issue**

Elizabeth II — A26

**1953, June 1** ***Perf. 12x12½***

**80** A26 2sh6p cerise 5.25 *6.00*

Sable Antelope A27

Rhodes' Grave A28

Flame Lily — A29

Designs: 1p, Tobacco planter. 3p, Farm Worker. 4½p, Victoria Falls. 6p, Baobab tree. 9p, Lion. 1sh, Zimbabwe ruins. 2sh, Birchenough Bridge. 2sh6p, Kariba Gorge. 5sh, Basket maker. 10sh, Balancing rocks. £1, Arms.

***Perf. 14x13½, 13½x14***

**1953, Aug. 31**

**Portrait in Various Positions**

**81** A27 ½p rose lake & dk ol grn .20 .25
**82** A27 1p choc & grn .20 .20
**83** A28 2p rose vio & org brn .20 .20

**Size: 28x22½mm**

**84** A29 3p car & sep .45 .50
**85** A29 4p gray, brn, car & grn 2.25 .20

**86** A29 4½p ultra & blk 1.50 1.75
**87** A28 6p aqua & olive 2.00 .20
**88** A29 9p org brn & dp bl 3.00 1.50
**89** A29 1sh grnsh bl & rose vio .95 .20
**90** A29 2sh red & rose vio 8.25 2.50
**91** A29 2sh6p org brn & ol grn 6.00 3.00
**92** A28 5s dk grn & org brn 13.00 7.00

**Size: 37x27mm**

**93** A29 10sh ol grn & red brn 18.00 32.50
**94** A29 £1 dk gray & car 29.00 32.50
*Nos. 81-94 (14)* 85.00 82.50

Ansellia Orchid — A30

**1964, Feb. 19 Photo. *Perf. 14½***

**Size: 23x19mm**

**95** A30 ½p Corn .20 *1.00*
**96** A30 1p Cape buffalo .20 .20
*a.* Purple omitted 1,900.
**97** A30 2p Tobacco .20 .20
**98** A30 3p Kudu .20 .20
**99** A30 4p Oranges .20 .20

***Perf. 13½x13***

**Size: 27x23mm**

**100** A30 6p Flame lily .20 .20
**101** A30 9p shown .80 .80
**102** A30 1sh Emeralds .75 .20
*a.* Green omitted 2,100.
**103** A30 1sh3p Aloe 1.00 .20
**104** A30 2sh Lake Kyle 1.50 1.00
**105** A30 2sh6p Tiger fish 1.75 .80
*a.* Red omitted 2,600.
*b.* Ultra omitted 5,750.

***Perf. 14½x14***

**Size: 32x27mm**

**106** A30 5sh Cattle 4.00 2.50
**107** A30 10sh Guinea fowl 13.00 6.00
**108** A30 £1 Arms 21.00 14.00
*Nos. 95-108 (14)* 45.00 27.50

#95-108 with overprint "Independence 11th November 1965" are listed as Rhodesia #208-221.

Stamps of Southern Rhodesia were replaced in 1965 by those of Rhodesia (formerly Southern Rhodesia).

### POSTAGE DUE STAMPS

**Catalogue values for unused stamps in this section are for Never Hinged items.**

Great Britain Postage Due Stamps of 1938-51 Overprinted in Black

**1951 Wmk. 251 *Perf. 14x14½***

**J1** D1 ½p emerald 3.00 *10.00*
**J2** D1 1p violet blue 2.75 *2.75*
**J3** D1 2p black brown 3.00 *1.60*
**J4** D1 3p violet 3.25 *1.25*
**J5** D1 4p brt blue 2.00 *2.25*
*a.* 4p slate green 150.00 *300.00*
**J6** D1 1sh blue 3.25 *2.00*
*Nos. J1-J6 (6)* 17.25 *19.85*

## SOUTH GEORGIA

'sauth 'jor-jə

LOCATION — Island in South Atlantic Ocean, 1,100 mi. east of Tierra del Fuego
GOVT. — Dependency of Falkland Islands
AREA — 1,450 sq. mi.
POP. — Military and biological staff only.
CAPITAL — Grytviken Harbor (military garrison)

South Georgia remained a dependency of the Falkland Islands in 1962 when three other dependencies became Antarctic Territory, a separate colony. In 1985 South Georgia and the South Sandwich Islands became a separate colony. See Falkland Islands Dependencies Nos. 3L1-3L8.

12 Pence = 1 Shilling
20 Shillings = 1 Pound
100 Pence = 1 Pound (1971)

**Catalogue values for all unused stamps in this country are for Never Hinged items.**

Reindeer A1

Sperm Whale — A2

Designs: 1p, South Sandwich Islands map. 2½p, Penguins. 3p, Fur seals. 4p, Finback whale and ship. 5½p, Elephant seals. 6p, Sooty albatross. 9p, Whaling ship. 1sh, Leopard seal. 2sh, Shackleton's cross. 2sh6p, Wandering albatross. 5sh, Elephant and fur seals. 10sh, Plankton and krill (shrimp). No. 15, Blue whale. No. 16, King penguins.

**Wmk. 314 Upright**

**1963-69 Engr. *Perf. 15***

**1** A1 ½p dull red .55 *.90*
*a.* Perf. 14x15 ('67) 1.25 *1.50*
*b.* Watermark sideways ('70) 1.50 *3.75*
**2** A2 1p violet blue 1.00 *.90*
**3** A2 2p blue green 1.40 .90
**4** A1 2½p black 5.75 2.25
**5** A2 3p olive 3.00 .35
**6** A1 4p green 5.50 .75
**7** A1 5½p dull violet 2.75 .40
**8** A2 6p orange .80 .45
**9** A1 9p blue 6.25 1.75
**10** A1 1sh lilac .90 .30
**11** A1 2sh cit & lt blue 26.00 6.00
**12** A1 2sh6p blue 25.00 4.00
**13** A1 5sh ocher 23.00 4.00
**14** A2 10sh rose claret 40.00 10.00
**15** A1 £1 ultra 100.00 62.50
**16** A2 £1 slate green 12.00 *17.50*
*Nos. 1-16 (16)* 253.90 112.95
Set, hinged 135.00

Issued: No. 16, 12/1/69; others 7/10/63.

Stamps and Type of 1963 Surcharged with New Value (Decimal Currency) and 3 Bars

**Wmk. 314 Upright; Sideways on ½p**

**1971-72 *Perf. 15***

**17** A1 ½p on ½p dull red 1.25 .75
*a.* Wmk. upright ('73) 3.00 2.75
**18** A2 1p on 1p vio blue 1.60 .90
*a.* Wmk. sideways ('76) 2.75 3.25
**19** A1 1½p on 5½p dull vio 1.00 .70
**20** A2 2p on 2p blue grn .90 .50
**21** A1 2½p on 2½p black 2.50 .70
**22** A2 3p on 3p olive 1.25 .75
**23** A1 4p on 4p green 1.25 .90
**24** A2 5p on 6p orange 2.25 1.25
**25** A1 6p on 9p blue 1.75 .55
**26** A1 7½p on 1sh lilac 2.50 2.00
**27** A1 10p on 2sh cit & lt bl 22.50 7.50
**28** A1 15p on 2sh6p blue 20.00 9.00
**29** A1 25p on 5sh ocher 15.00 7.50
**30** A2 50p on 10sh rose claret, glazed paper ('72) 25.00 *20.00*
*a.* Wmk. sideways ('76) 30.00 *30.00*
*c.* Ordinary paper 47.50 25.00
*Nos. 17-30 (14)* 98.75 53.00

Two types of surcharge are found on ½p, 1p, 1½p and 50p.
Issued: Nos. 17-29, 30b, 2/15/71. No. 30, 12/1/72. No. 30a, 3/9/76.

**Wmk. 373 Sideways; Upright on 3p, 50p; Inverted on 1p, 5p**

**1977**

*17b* A1 ½p on ½p dull red 1.75 1.60
*18b* A2 1p on 1p vio blue 1.00 .90
*19b* A1 1½p on 5½p dl vio 1.00 1.00
*21b* A1 2½p on 2½p black 13.00 3.25
*22b* A2 3p on 3p olive 7.75 3.25
*23b* A1 4p on 4p green 20.00 14.00
*24b* A2 5p on 6p orange 4.00 2.75
*26b* A1 7½p on 1sh lilac 1.90 *8.25*
*27b* A1 10p on 2sh cit & lt bl 1.90 *8.25*
*28b* A1 15p on 2sh6p blue 2.75 *8.25*
*29b* A1 25p on 5sh ocher 2.00 *8.25*
*30b* A2 50p on 10sh lil rose ('79) 2.00 *8.25*
*Nos. 17b-30b (12)* 59.05 *68.00*

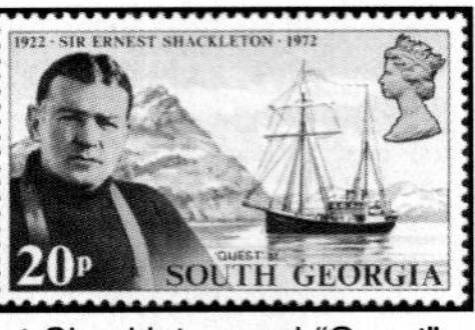

Ernest Shackleton and "Quest" — A3

1½p, "Endurance" in ice of Weddell Sea. 5p, Launching of sailboat "James Caird." 10p, Route of "James Caird" to South Georgia.

**1972, Jan. 5 Litho. *Perf. 13½***

**31** A3 1½p vio bl, blk & yel 1.20 *1.75*
**32** A3 5p bl grn, blk & yel 1.40 *2.25*
**33** A3 10p lt blue & blk 2.00 *2.50*
**34** A3 20p multicolored 2.25 *3.00*
*Nos. 31-34 (4)* 6.85 9.50

Sir Ernest Shackleton (1874-1922), explorer of Antarctica.

Common Design Types pictured following the introduction.

### Silver Wedding Issue, 1972

Common Design Type

Design: Queen Elizabeth II, Prince Philip, elephant seal and king penguins.

**1972, Nov. 20 Photo. *Perf. 14x14½***

**35** CD324 5p slate grn & multi .50 .50
**36** CD324 10p violet & multi 1.00 1.00

### Princess Anne's Wedding Issue

Common Design Type

**1973, Dec. 1 Litho. *Perf. 14***

**37** CD325 5p citron & multi .20 .20
**38** CD325 15p slate & multi .60 .60

Churchill, Parliament and Big Ben — A4

Design: 25p, Churchill and battleship.

**1974, Dec. 14 Litho. *Perf. 14½***

**39** A4 15p vio blue & multi 1.25 1.25
**40** A4 25p orange & multi 2.00 2.00
*a.* Souvenir sheet of 2, #39-40 7.25 7.25

Sir Winston Churchill (1874-1965).

Capt. James Cook — A5

Cook's "Possession" — A6

Design: 16p, Possession Bay.

**1975, Apr. 26 Wmk. 314**

**41** A5 2p multicolored 2.50 1.00
**42** A6 8p multicolored 3.75 1.75
**43** A6 16p multicolored 4.00 2.50
*Nos. 41-43 (3)* 10.25 5.25

Bicentenary of Capt. Cook's discovery of South Georgia.

"Discovery" and Biological Laboratory — A7

Designs: 8p, "William Scoresby" and Nansen-Pettersson water sampling bottles. 11p, "Discovery II" and plankton net. 25p, Biological station and krill (shrimp).

**Wmk. 373**

**1976, Dec. 21 Litho. *Perf. 14***

**44** A7 2p multicolored 1.00 .35
**45** A7 8p multicolored 1.50 1.25
**46** A7 11p multicolored 1.75 1.40
**47** A7 25p multicolored 3.75 2.50
*Nos. 44-47 (4)* 8.00 5.50

25th anniversary of the biological investigations of the "Discovery."

Queen with Regalia and Westminster Abbey — A8

6p, Prince Philip visiting Shackleton Memorial, 1957. 33p, Queen in procession after coronation.

**1977, Feb. 7 *Perf. 13½x14***

**48** A8 6p multicolored .30 .25
**49** A8 11p multicolored .55 .40
**50** A8 33p multicolored 1.25 1.25
*Nos. 48-50 (3)* 2.10 1.90

25th anniv. of the reign of Elizabeth II.

### Elizabeth II Coronation Anniversary Issue

Common Design Types

**Souvenir Sheet**

**Unwmk.**

**1978, June 2 Litho. *Perf. 15***

**51** Sheet of 6 4.50 *4.50*
*a.* CD326 25p Panther of Henry VI 1.00 .90
*b.* CD327 25p Elizabeth II 1.00 .90
*c.* CD328 25p Fur seal 1.00 .90

No. 51 contains 2 se-tenant strips of Nos. 51a-51c, separated by horizontal gutter with commemorative and descriptive inscriptions and showing central part of coronation procession with coach.

Resolution A9

Cook's voyages: 6p, Map of South Georgia and South Sandwich Islands with Cook's route. 11p, King penguin, drawing by Forster. 25p, Cook after Flaxman/Wedgwood medallion.

**1979, Feb. 14 Litho. *Perf. 11***

**52** A9 3p multicolored 1.75 1.00
**53** A9 6p multicolored 1.75 .85
**54** A9 11p multicolored 2.25 1.90

**Lithographed; Embossed**

**55** A9 25p multicolored 2.50 2.25
*Nos. 52-55 (4)* 8.25 6.00

Capt. Cook's voyages.

## SOUTH GEORGIA and SOUTH SANDWICH ISLANDS

### Queen Elizabeth II 60th Birthday

Common Design Type

Designs: 10p, With King George and Queen Mary at christening of Prince Charles, 1948. 24p, Engagement of Prince Charles and Lady Diana, Buckingham Palace Music Room, 1981. 29p, Order of the British Empire, service at St. Paul's Cathedral, London, 1974. 45p, Banquet for Canadian Prime Minister Trudeau during the 1976 Olympics. 58p, Visiting Crown Agents' offices, 1983.

**1986, Apr. 21 Wmk. 384 *Perf. 14½***

**101** CD337 10p multicolored .25 .25
**102** CD337 24p multicolored .60 .60
**103** CD337 29p multicolored .75 .75
**104** CD337 45p multicolored 1.10 1.10
**105** CD337 58p multicolored 1.50 1.50
*Nos. 101-105 (5)* 4.20 4.20

Wedding of Prince Andrew and Sarah Ferguson — A12

**1986, Nov. 10 Litho. *Perf. 14½***

**106** A12 17p Couple at Ascot .80 *1.10*
**107** A12 22p Wedding .90 *1.40*
**108** A12 29p Andrew, helicopter 1.60 1.60
*Nos. 106-108 (3)* 3.30 4.10

Birds A13

**1987, Apr. 24 Litho. Wmk. 384**

**109** A13 1p Dominican gull 1.25 *1.75*
**110** A13 2p Blue-eyed cormorant 1.60 *2.00*
**111** A13 3p Wattled sheathbill 2.00 2.00
**112** A13 4p Brown skua 1.75 1.75
**113** A13 5p Cape pigeon 1.75 1.75
**114** A13 6p South Georgia diving petrel 1.75 1.75
**115** A13 7p South Georgia pipit 2.00 2.00
**116** A13 8p South Georgia pintail 2.00 2.00
**117** A13 9p Fairy prion 2.00 2.00
**118** A13 10p Chinstrap penguin 2.25 2.25
**119** A13 20p Macaroni penguin 2.40 *2.75*
**120** A13 25p Light-mantled sooty albatross 2.50 *2.75*
**121** A13 50p Southern giant petrel 3.25 3.25
**122** A13 £1 Wandering albatross 3.75 *5.00*
**123** A13 £3 King penguin 9.75 *11.00*
*Nos. 109-123 (15)* 40.00 44.00

3, 4, 7, 8, 20, 25, 50p and £3 vert.

Intl. Geophysical Year, 30th Anniv. — A14

**1987, Dec. 5 Litho. *Perf. 14½***

**124** A14 24p shown .90 .80
**125** A14 29p Grytviken Whaling Station 1.00 .90
**126** A14 58p Glaciologist 1.75 1.75
*Nos. 124-126 (3)* 3.65 3.45

Sea Shells A15

**1988, Feb. 26 Wmk. 384 *Perf. 14½***

**127** A15 10p Gaimardia trapesina .75 .60
**128** A15 24p Margarella tropidophoroides 1.40 1.40
**129** A15 29p Trophon scotianus 1.60 1.60
**130** A15 58p Chlanidota densesculpta 3.25 3.25
*Nos. 127-130 (4)* 7.00 6.85

### Lloyds of London, 300th Anniv.

Common Design Type

10p, Queen Mother at the official opening of the Lloyds Building, Lime Street, 1957. 24p, Lindblad Explorer, horiz. 29p, Leith Harbor whaling station, horiz. 58p, Whale oil tanker Horatio on fire.

**1988, Sept. 17 *Perf. 14***

**131** CD341 10p multicolored .70 .40
**132** CD341 24p multicolored 1.10 .90
**133** CD341 29p multicolored 1.10 1.10
**134** CD341 58p multicolored 2.50 2.50
*Nos. 131-134 (4)* 5.40 4.90

Glacier Formations — A16

**1989, July 31**

**135** A16 10p Glacier headwall .65 .50
**136** A16 24p Accumulation area 1.00 1.00
**137** A16 29p Ablation area 1.25 1.25
**138** A16 58p Calving front 2.50 2.50
*Nos. 135-138 (4)* 5.40 5.25

Combined Services Expedition, 1964-65 A17

**1989, Nov. 28 *Perf. 14x14½***

**139** A17 10p "Last ordeal" of the trek .60 .50
**140** A17 24p Survey of Royal Bay 1.25 1.10
**141** A17 29p HMS *Protector* 1.50 1.25
**142** A17 58p 1st Ascent of Mt. Paget 2.50 2.40
*Nos. 139-142 (4)* 5.85 5.25

### Queen Mother, 90th Birthday

Common Design Types

Designs: 26p, Queen Mother. £1, King, Queen & Air Raid Wardens, 1940.

***Perf. 14x15***

**1990, Sept. 15 Wmk. 384**

**143** CD343 26p multicolored 1.25 1.25

***Perf. 14½***

**144** CD344 £1 blue & black 4.50 4.50

Shipwrecks A18

**Wmk. 384**

**1990, Dec. 22 Litho. *Perf. 14***

**145** A18 12p Brutus .60 .50
**146** A18 26p Bayard 1.25 1.00
**147** A18 31p Karrakatta 1.50 1.25
**148** A18 62p Louise 2.75 2.25
*Nos. 145-148 (4)* 6.10 5.00

### Elizabeth & Philip, Birthdays

Common Design Types

**1991, July 2 *Perf. 14½***

**149** CD345 31p multicolored 1.50 1.50
**150** CD346 31p multicolored 1.50 1.50
*a.* Pair, #149-150 + label 6.00 6.00

No. 150a exists with two different labels.

Elephant Seals A19

**1991, Nov. 2 Wmk. 373 *Perf. 14***

**151** A19 12p Two bulls .80 .80
**152** A19 26p One bull 1.60 1.60
**153** A19 29p Using sand as sunscreen 1.60 1.60
**154** A19 31p Bull, close up 1.60 1.60
**155** A19 34p Harem on beach 2.00 2.00
**156** A19 62p Cow and pup 3.25 3.25
*Nos. 151-156 (6)* 10.85 10.85

### Queen Elizabeth II's Accession to the Throne, 40th Anniv.

Common Design Type

**1992, Feb. 6**

**157** CD349 7p multicolored .45 .25
**158** CD349 14p multicolored .70 .55
**159** CD349 29p multicolored 1.10 1.00
**160** CD349 34p multicolored 1.25 1.25
**161** CD349 68p multicolored 2.50 2.50
*Nos. 157-161 (5)* 6.00 5.55

South Georgia Teal A20

**1992, Mar. 22 Wmk. 384**

**162** A20 2p Adult, young .70 .30
**163** A20 6p Adult, nest of eggs .95 .55
**164** A20 12p Four swimming 1.40 1.25
**165** A20 20p Adult, two chicks 2.00 2.00
*Nos. 162-165 (4)* 5.05 4.10

World Wildlife Fund.

South Georgia Whaling Museum A21

Designs: 15p, Abandoned factory, Grytviken. 31p, Whaler's lighter, bones. 36p, King Edward Cove. 72p, Museum Building.

**Wmk. 373**

**1993, June 29 Litho. *Perf. 13½***

**166-169** A21 Set of 4 8.00 8.00

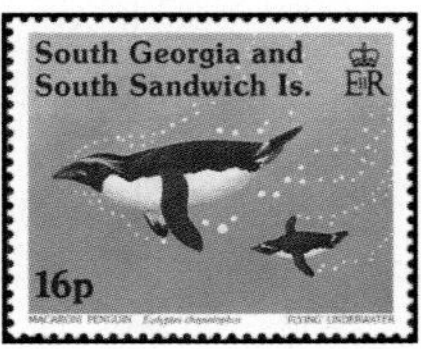


Macaroni Penguins A22

16p, Swimming underwater. 34p, Part of rookery. 39p, Two juveniles. 78p, Two adults.

***Perf. 14x14½***

**1993, Dec. 10 Litho. Wmk. 373**

**170-173** A22 Set of 4 8.00 8.00

Ovptd. with Hong Kong '94 Emblem

**1994, Feb. 18**

**174-177** A22 Set of 4 9.00 9.00

Whales and Dolphins A23

Designs: 1p, Hourglass dolphin. 2p, Southern right whale dolphin. 5p, Long-finned pilot whale. 8p, Southern bottlenose whale. 9p, Killer whale. 10p, Minke whale. 20p, Sei whale. 25p, Humpback whale. 50p, Southern right whale. £1, Sperm whale. £3, Fin whale. £5, Blue whale.

**Wmk. 373**

**1994, Jan. 24 Litho. *Perf. 14***

**178** A23 1p multicolored 1.00 1.00
**179** A23 2p multicolored 1.50 1.50
**180** A23 5p multicolored 2.00 1.75
**181** A23 8p multicolored 2.25 1.75
**182** A23 9p multicolored 2.25 1.75
**183** A23 10p multicolored 2.25 1.75
**184** A23 20p multicolored 3.25 2.75
**185** A23 25p multicolored 3.25 2.75
**186** A23 50p multicolored 4.25 3.00
**187** A23 £1 multicolored 5.50 4.25
**188** A23 £3 multicolored 11.00 11.00
**189** A23 £5 multicolored 18.00 18.00
*Nos. 178-189 (12)* 56.50 51.25

Native Wildlife A24

**Wmk. 384**

**1994, Sept. 28 Litho. *Perf. 14***

**190** A24 17p Bull elephant seals .90 .90
**191** A24 35p Fur seal, vert. 1.75 1.75
**192** A24 40p Gray-headed albatrosses 2.00 2.00
**193** A24 65p King penguins, vert. 3.00 3.00
*Nos. 190-193 (4)* 7.65 7.65

Capt. C. A. Larsen's First Voyage to South Georgia A25

**1994, Dec. 1**

**194** A25 17p Map of Jason Harbor .65 .65
**195** A25 35p Castor, 1886 1.75 1.75
**196** A25 40p Hertha, 1884 2.00 2.00
**197** A25 65p Jason, 1881 3.25 3.25
*Nos. 194-197 (4)* 7.65 7.65

### End of World War II, 50th Anniv.

Common Design Types

#198, HMS Queen of Bermuda moored at Leith Harbor. #199, 4-inch gun, Hansen Point, four men of Norwegian Defense Force.
£1, Reverse of War Medal 1939-45.

**Wmk. 384**

**1995, May 8 Litho. *Perf. 14***

**198** CD351 50p multicolored 3.00 3.00
**199** CD351 50p multicolored 3.00 3.00
*a.* Pair, #198-199 7.50 7.50

**Souvenir Sheet**

**Wmk. 373**

**200** CD352 £1 multicolored 6.75 6.75

No. 199a is a continuous design.

Yachts — A26

**Wmk. 373**

**1995, Nov. 16 Litho. *Perf. 14½***

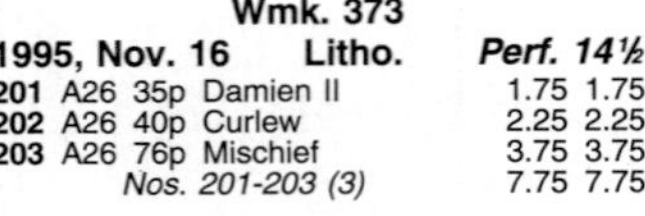

**201** A26 35p Damien II 1.75 1.75
**202** A26 40p Curlew 2.25 2.25
**203** A26 76p Mischief 3.75 3.75
*Nos. 201-203 (3)* 7.75 7.75

Sir Ernest Shackleton's King Haakon Bay-Stromness Trek, 80th Anniv. — A27

Designs: 15p, Shackleton, Ridge 2493 Point of No Return. 20p, Frank Worsley, King Haakon Bay from Shackleton Gap. 30p, Map of Shackleton's route. 65p, Tom Crean, Manager's Villa, Stromness Whaling Station.

**Wmk. 384**

**1996, May 20 Litho. *Perf. 14***

**204** A27 15p multicolored .80 .80
**205** A27 20p multicolored 1.25 1.25
**206** A27 30p multicolored 1.75 1.75
**207** A27 65p multicolored 3.50 3.50
*Nos. 204-207 (4)* 7.30 7.30

Chinstrap Penguins — A28

***Perf. 14½x14***

**1996, Nov. 8 Litho. Wmk. 373**

**208** A28 17p Swimming .90 .90
**209** A28 35p Male, female 1.50 1.50
**210** A28 40p Feeding chicks 1.75 1.75
**211** A28 76p Feeding on krill 3.50 3.50
*a.* Souvenir sheet of 1, perf. 14x14½ 5.00 5.00
*Nos. 208-211 (4)* 7.65 7.65

Return of Hong Kong to China (#211a).

Queen Elizabeth and Prince Philip, 50th Wedding Anniv. — A29

#212, Queen. #213, Prince driving team of horses. #214, Queen looking at horses. #215, Prince. #216, Princess Anne on horseback, Queen. #217, Prince, child on horseback.
£1.50, Queen, Prince in open carriage, horiz.

***Perf. 14½x14***

**1997, July 10 Litho. Wmk. 384**

**212** 15p multicolored 1.00 1.00
**213** 15p multicolored 1.00 1.00
*a.* A29 Pair, #212-213 2.25 2.25
**214** 17p multicolored 1.25 1.25
**215** 17p multicolored 1.25 1.25
*a.* A29 Pair, #214-215 2.75 2.75
**216** 40p multicolored 2.50 2.50
**217** 40p multicolored 5.50 5.50
*a.* A29 Pair, #216-217 8.25 8.25
*Nos. 212-217 (6)* 12.50 12.50

**Souvenir Sheet**

**218** A29 £1.50 multicolored 8.50 8.50

Flora and Fauna A30

a, Reindeer. b, Antarctic tern. c, Gray-headed albatross. d, King penguin. e, Prickly burr. f, Fur seal.

***Perf. 14½x14***

**1998, Mar. 16 Litho. Wmk. 373**

**219** A30 35p Sheet of 6, #a.-f. 9.50 9.50

**Diana, Princess of Wales (1961-97)**

Common Design Type

Designs: a, Looking left. b, In white evening dress. c, In red dress. d, In white.

**1998, Mar. 31**

**220** CD355 35p Sheet of 4, #a.-d. 5.25 5.25

No. 220 sold for £1.40 + 20p, with surtax and 50% of the profits from the issue being donated to the Princess Diana Memorial Fund.

Tourism A31

Designs: 30p, MS Explorer. 35p, Wandering albatross. 40p, Elephant seal. 65p, Post Office, King Edward Point.

**Wmk. 373**

**1998, Sept. 28 Litho. *Perf. 14½***

**221** A31 30p multicolored 2.00 1.50
**222** A31 35p multicolored 2.25 1.75
**223** A31 40p multicolored 2.50 1.90
**224** A31 65p multicolored 3.75 3.25
*Nos. 221-224 (4)* 10.50 8.40

Island Views A32

Designs: 9p, Grytviken and Sugartop Mountain. 17p, Old sealing ships, Grytviken. 35p, King Edward Point. 40p, Arrival at South Georgia. 65p, Church, Grytviken.

**Wmk. 384**

**1999, Jan. 4 Litho. *Perf. 14***

**225** A32 9p multicolored 1.25 1.00
**226** A32 17p multicolored 1.75 1.25
**227** A32 35p multicolored 2.75 2.00
**228** A32 40p multicolored 3.00 2.50
**229** A32 65p multicolored 3.50 3.50
*Nos. 225-229 (5)* 12.25 10.25

**Souvenir Sheet**

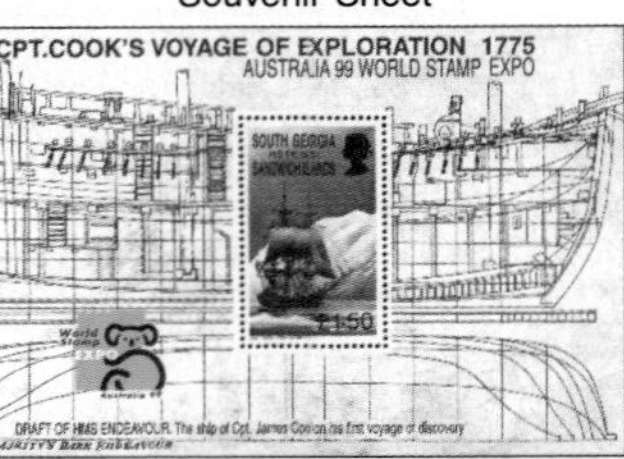


Capt. James Cook's Ship HMS Resolution, 1773 — A33

Illustration reduced.

**1999, Mar. 5 *Perf. 13½***

**230** A33 £1.50 multicolored 12.50 12.50

Australia '99, World Stamp Expo.

**Queen Mother's Century**

Common Design Type

Queen Mother: 25p, At air raid shelter, 1940. 30p, With Prince Edward, Lady Sarah Armstrong-Jones, Viscount Linley, 70th birthday. 35p, With Prince William, 94th birthday. 40p, As colonel-in-chief of Royal Anglian Regiment.
£1, Funeral procession for Queen Victoria, portrait of Victoria.

**Wmk. 384**

**1999, Aug. 18 Litho. *Perf. 13½***

**231** CD358 25p multicolored 2.00 2.00
**232** CD358 30p black 2.75 2.75
**233** CD358 35p multicolored 3.25 3.25
**234** CD358 40p multicolored 3.50 3.50
*Nos. 231-234 (4)* 11.50 11.50

**Souvenir Sheet**

**235** CD358 £1 black 12.50 12.50

Birds — A34

Designs: 1p, Chinstrap penguin, vert. 2p, White chinned petrel. 5p, Gray backed storm petrel, vert. 10p, South Georgia pipit, vert. 11p, Gray headed albatross. 30p, Blue petrel, vert. 35p, Black browed albatross. 40p, South Georgia diving petrel. 50p, Macaroni penguin, vert. £1, Light mantled sooty albatross. £3, South Georgia pintail. £5, King penguin, vert.

**Wmk. 384**

**1999, Nov. 15 Litho. *Perf. 14***

**236** A34 1p multicolored .75 .90
**237** A34 2p multicolored .85 .90
**238** A34 5p multicolored .95 .95
**239** A34 10p multicolored 1.00 1.00
**240** A34 11p multicolored 1.25 1.25
**241** A34 30p multicolored 2.25 2.25
**242** A34 35p multicolored 2.50 2.50
**243** A34 40p multicolored 2.50 2.50
**244** A34 50p multicolored 2.75 2.50
**245** A34 £1 multicolored 4.75 4.75
**246** A34 £3 multicolored 11.00 11.00
**247** A34 £5 multicolored 16.00 16.00
*Nos. 236-247 (12)* 46.55 46.50

Millennium — A35

***Perf. 14½x14¼***

**1999, Dec. 18 Litho. Wmk. 384**

**248** A35 11p Sunrise 1.50 1.25
**249** A35 11p Church 1.50 1.25
**250** A35 11p Albatrosses 1.50 1.25
**251** A35 35p Penguins 2.50 2.50
**252** A35 35p Reindeer 2.50 2.50
**253** A35 35p Sunset 2.50 2.50
*Nos. 248-253 (6)* 12.00 11.25

Sir Ernest Shackleton (1874-1922), Polar Explorer — A36

Designs: 35p, Voyage across Scotia Sea, 1916. 40p, Shackleton, Thomas Crean and Frank Worsley crossing South Georgia. 65p, Shackleton's grave.

**2000, Feb. 20 Wmk. 373 *Perf. 14***

**254** A36 35p multi 2.50 2.50
**255** A36 40p multi 2.75 2.75
**256** A36 65p multi 3.75 3.75
*Nos. 254-256 (3)* 9.00 9.00

See British Antarctic Territory Nos. 285-287, Falkland Islands Nos. 758-760.

**Prince William, 18th Birthday**

Common Design Type

William: 25p, In suit, carrying bag, vert. 30p, With ski equipment, vert. 35p, Wearing suit and wearing sweater. 40p, In suit, waving. 50p, In beret, saluting.

***Perf. 13¾x14¼, 14¼x13¾***

**2000, June 21 Litho. Wmk. 373**

**Stamps With White Border**

**257** CD359 25p multi 2.00 1.75
**258** CD359 30p multi 2.25 2.00
**259** CD359 35p multi 2.50 2.25
**260** CD359 40p multi 3.00 2.75
*Nos. 257-260 (4)* 9.75 8.75

**Souvenir Sheet**

**Stamps Without White Border**

***Perf. 14¼***

**261** Sheet of 5 11.00 11.00
*a.* CD359 25p multi 1.50 1.50
*b.* CD359 30p multi 1.75 1.75
*c.* CD359 35p multi 2.00 2.00
*d.* CD359 40p multi 2.25 2.25
*e.* CD359 50p multi 2.50 2.50

King Penguins — A37

#262, 37p, Penguins at sea. #263, 37p, Adult & creche. #264, 43p, Advertisement walk & courtship. #265, 43p, Nesting.

***Perf. 14¾x14***

**2000, Oct. 16 Litho. Wmk. 373**

**262-265** A37 Set of 4 10.00 10.00

Royal Fleet Auxiliary Vessels A38

Designs: No. 266, 37p, RFA Sir Percivale. No. 267, 37p, RFA Tidespring. No. 268, 43p, RFA Diligence. No. 269, 43p, RFA Gold Rover.

**Wmk. 373**

**2001, May 28 Litho. *Perf. 14***

**266-269** A38 Set of 4 11.00 11.00

Marine Life — A39

Designs: 33p, Icefish. No. 271, 37p, Spiny back crab. No. 272, 37p, Krill, vert. 43p, Toothfish, vert.

**Wmk. 373**

**2001, Oct. 22 Litho. *Perf. 13¾***

**270-273** A39 Set of 4 11.00 11.00

**Reign Of Queen Elizabeth II, 50th Anniv. Issue**

Common Design Type

Designs: Nos. 274, 278a, 20p, With dog, 1952. Nos. 275, 278b, 37p, With Prince Philip, 1997. Nos. 276, 278c, 43p, Examining royal stamp collection, 1946. Nos. 277, 278d, 50p, Wearing blue hat, 1999. No. 278e, 50p, 1955 portrait by Annigoni (38x50mm).

***Perf. 14¼x14½, 13¾ (#278e)***

**2002, Feb. 6 Litho. Wmk. 373**

**With Gold Frames**

**274-277** CD360 Set of 4 9.00 9.00

**Souvenir Sheet**

**Without Gold Frames**

**278** CD360 Sheet of 5, #a-e 11.00 11.00

World Record Animals — A40

No. 279: a, 10p, Fin whale. b, 10p, Blue whale. c, 20p, Sperm whale. d, 37p, Leopard seal with mouth open. e, 37p, Leopard seal on ice. f, 43p, Elephant seal.
£1.50, Elephant seal, diff.

**2002, Mar. 2 Litho. *Perf. 13¾***
**279** A40 Sheet of 6, #a-f 11.00 11.00

**Souvenir Sheet**

**280** A40 £1.50 multi 8.50 8.50

**Queen Mother Elizabeth (1900-2002)**
Common Design Type

Designs: 22p, Wearing hat (black and white photograph). 40p, Wearing tiara. Nos. 283, 285a, 45p, Holding dog (black and white photograph). Nos. 284, 285b, 95p, Wearing white stole.

***Perf. 14¼, 13¾x14¼ (#283-284)***
**2002, Aug. 5 Litho. Wmk. 373**
**With Purple Frames**

**281-284** CD361 Set of 4 8.75 8.75

**Souvenir Sheet**
**Without Purple Frames**
***Perf. 14½x14¼***

**285** CD361 Sheet of 2, #a-b 6.75 6.75

Antarctic Fur Seals — A41

Designs: No. 286, 40p, Seal in water. No. 287, 40p, Two seals on ice. No. 288, 45p, Six seals. No. 289, 45p, One seal.

**Wmk. 373**
**2002, Oct. 25 Litho. *Perf. 13¾***
**286-289** A41 Set of 4 10.00 10.00

Worldwide Fund for Nature (WWF) — A42

Gray-headed albatross: 40p, Adults at nesting ground. No. 291, 45p, Adult and chick (WWF emblem at LL). No. 292, 45p, Two adults (WWF emblem at UL). 70p, Bird's head.

**Wmk. 373**
**2003, Jan. 6 Litho. *Perf. 14***
**290-293** A42 Set of 4 8.00 8.00
*293a* Strip of 4 8.75 8.75

**Head of Queen Elizabeth II**
Common Design Type
**Wmk. 373**
**2003, June 2 Litho. *Perf. 13¾***
**294** CD362 £2 multi 7.75 7.75

**Prince William, 21st Birthday**
Common Design Type

No. 295: a, Color photograph at right. b, Color photograph at left.

**Wmk. 373**
**2003, June 21 Litho. *Perf. 14¼***
**295** Horiz. pair 5.50 5.50
***a.-b.*** CD364 70p Either single 2.50 2.50

History of South Georgia — A43

No. 296: a, HMS Sappho visits Grytviken, 1906. b, Norwegian reindeer introduced, 1911. c, Largest blue whale landed, 1912. d, Shackleton's island crossing, 1916. e, Shackleton Memorial Cross, 1922. f, Discovery investigations, 1925. g, First powered flight over South Georgia, 1938. h, Operation Tabarin, 1943. i, Duke of Edinburgh visits, 1957. j, Bird Island Research Station, 1958. k, Mt. Paget climbed, 1964. l, Liberation of the island, 1982. m, Royal charter and crest, 1985. n, Museum inaugurated, 1992. o, Applied fishery research, 2001. p, Grytviken remedial work, 2003.

**Wmk. 373**
**2004, Feb. 6 Litho. *Perf. 13¼***
**296** A43 40p Sheet of 16, #a-p 26.00 26.00

Royal Navy Ships A44

Designs: 10p, HMS Ajax. 25p, HMS Amazon. 45p, HMS Dartmouth. 50p, HMS Penelope. 70p, HMS St. Austell Bay. £1, HMS Plymouth.

**Wmk. 373**
**2004, Apr. 26 Litho. *Perf. 14***
**297-302** A44 Set of 6 12.00 12.00

Merchant Ships A45

Designs: No. 303, 42p, RMS Queen Elizabeth 2. No. 304, 42p, MS Endeavour. 50p, MS Lindblad Explorer. 75p, SS Canberra.

***Perf. 13¼x13½***
**2004, Nov. 10 Litho.**
**303-306** A45 Set of 4 9.00 9.00

Animal Juveniles — A46

Designs: 1p, Skua. 2p, Reindeer. 3p, Antarctic prion, horiz. 5p, Humpback whale, horiz. 10p, Gentoo penguins. 25p, Antarctic fur seal. 50p, South Georgia pintail, horiz. 75p, Light-mantled sooty albatross. £1, Weddell seal, horiz. £2, King penguin, horiz. £3, Southern right whale, horiz. £5, Wandering albatross.
(42p), Elephant seal, horiz.

***Perf. 13½x13¼, 13¼x13½***
**2004, Nov. 15 Wmk. 373**

| | | | | |
|---|---|---|---|---|
| **307** | A46 | 1p multi | .20 | .20 |
| **308** | A46 | 2p multi | .20 | .20 |
| **309** | A46 | 3p multi | .20 | .20 |
| **310** | A46 | 5p multi | .20 | .20 |
| **311** | A46 | 10p multi | .40 | .40 |
| **312** | A46 | 25p multi | .95 | .95 |
| **313** | A46 | 50p multi | 1.90 | 1.90 |
| **314** | A46 | 75p multi | 3.00 | 3.00 |
| **315** | A46 | £1 multi | 4.00 | 4.00 |
| **316** | A46 | £2 multi | 7.75 | 7.75 |
| **317** | A46 | £3 multi | 11.50 | 11.50 |
| **318** | A46 | £5 multi | 19.50 | 19.50 |
| | | *Nos. 307-318 (12)* | 49.80 | 49.80 |

**Booklet Stamp**
**Self-Adhesive**
**Unwmk.**
***Serpentine Die Cut 12½***

**319** A46 (42p) multi 1.60 1.60
***a.*** Booklet pane of 4 6.50
Complete booklet, 2 #319a 13.00

No. 319 is inscribed "Airmail Postcard."

Grytviken, Cent. — A47

Designs: 24p, Capt. Carl Anton Larsen, founder of Grytviken. 42p, Grytviken from Mount Hodges. 50p, Whale catcher Fortuna. £1, Ski jumper.

**2004, Dec. 10 Wmk. 373 *Perf. 13¾***
**320-323** A47 Set of 4 8.50 8.50

Duncan Carse (1913-2004), Survey Expedition Leader — A48

Designs: No. 324, 50p, Carse. No. 325, 50p, Map of South Georgia, surveyors. 75p, Carse as radio broadcaster. £1, AMOW, Carse's hut, Undine South.

**Wmk. 373**
**2005, Sept. 26 Litho. *Perf. 13¾***
**324-327** A48 Set of 4 9.75 9.75

A49

A50

A51

A52

A53

Penguins A54

**2005, Nov. 1 *Perf. 14***

| | | | | |
|---|---|---|---|---|
| **328** | A49 | 45p multi | 1.60 | 1.60 |
| **329** | A50 | 45p multi | 1.60 | 1.60 |
| **330** | A51 | 45p multi | 1.60 | 1.60 |
| **331** | A52 | 45p multi | 1.60 | 1.60 |
| **332** | A53 | 45p multi | 1.60 | 1.60 |
| **333** | A54 | 45p multi | 1.60 | 1.60 |
| | | *Nos. 328-333 (6)* | 9.60 | 9.60 |

Queen Elizabeth II, 80th Birthday A55

Queen: No. 334, 50p, As child, with dog. Nos. 335, 338a, 50p, As young woman. Nos. 336, 338b, 75p, As older woman. £1, Wearing hat.

**2006, Apr. 21 Litho. *Perf. 14***
**With White Frames**

**334-337** A55 Set of 4 10.50 10.50

**Souvenir Sheet**
**Without White Frames**

**338** A55 Sheet of 2, #a-b 4.75 4.75

BirdLife International A56

Birds: 24p, Black-browed albatross. 45p, Southern giant petrel. 50p, White-chinned petrel. 75p, Wandering albatross.
No. 343: a, Black-browed albatross, diff. b, White-chinned petrel, diff.

**Wmk. 373**
**2006, Oct. 18 Litho. *Perf. 13¾***
**339-342** A56 Set of 4 7.50 7.50

**Souvenir Sheet**

**343** A56 £1 Sheet of 2, #a-b 7.75 7.75

Communications — A57

Designs: 25p, Mail drop from Royal Air Force Hercules plane. 50p, Radio/wireless room. 60p, MV Sigma. £1.05, SS Fleurus.

***Perf. 14¼x14***
**2006, Nov. 30 Litho. Wmk. 373**
**344-347** A57 Set of 4 9.50 9.50

Mapping — A58

No. 348, 50p: a, Map of Neumayer Glacier, 1958. b, Map of Neumayer Glacier, 2003.

No. 349, 60p: a, Kern DKM1 theodolite and map. b, Landsat 7 satellite.
Illustration reduced.

**2007, Jan. 5** **Perf. 13¾**
**Horiz. Pairs, #a-b**

**348-349** A58 Set of 2 8.50 8.50

## SEMI-POSTAL STAMPS

Liberation of South Georgia, 10th Anniv. — SP1

Designs: 14p+6p, King Edward Point, Winter 1982. 29p+11p, Queen Elizabeth 2 in Cumberland Bay. 34p+16p, Royal Marines on South Sandwich Islands. 68p+32p, HMS Endurance and Wasp Helicopter.

**Wmk. 384**
**1992, June 20** **Litho.** **Perf. 14**

**B1** SP1 14p +6p multicolored 1.25 1.25
**B2** SP1 29p +11p multicolored 1.75 1.75
**B3** SP1 34p +16p multicolored 2.00 2.00
**B4** SP1 68p +32p multicolored 4.25 4.25
*a.* Souvenir sheet of 4, #B1-B4 10.00 10.00
*Nos. B1-B4 (4)* 9.25 9.25

Surtax for Soldiers', Sailors' and Airmen's Families Association.

# SOUTH KASAI

This part of a Congo province declared itself an autonomous state and in 1961 issued several series of stamps, some of which were overprints on Congo (ex-Belgian) stamps. Established nations did not recognize South Kasai as an independent state.

# SOUTH MOLUCCAS

(Republik Maluku Selatan)

It appears that stamps of the so-called republic of South Moluccas were privately issued and had no postal use. Accordingly, they are not recognized as postage stamps.

# SOUTH RUSSIA

sauth 'rəsh-ə

LOCATION — An area in southern Russia bordering on the Caspian and Black Seas.

A provisional government set up and maintained by General Denikin in opposition to the Bolshevik forces in Russia following the downfall of the Empire. The stamps were used in the field postal service established for carrying on communication between the various armies united in the revolt. These armies included the Don Cossacks, the Kuban Cossacks, and also the neighboring southern Russian people in favor of the counter-revolution against the Bolsheviks.

100 Kopecks = 1 Ruble

Values for used stamps are for CTO copies. Postally used specimens sell for considerably more.

**Watermark**

Wmk. 171 — Diamonds

**Don Government (Novocherkassk) Rostov Issue**

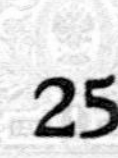

Russian Stamps of 1909-17 Surcharged

**1918** **Unwmk.** **Perf. 14x14½**

**1** A14 25k on 1k dl org yel 2.00 1.90
*a.* Inverted surcharge 30.00 40.00
**2** A14 25k on 2k dl grn .50 .60
*a.* Inverted surcharge 30.00 30.00
**3** A14 25k on 3k car .75 .75
*a.* Double surcharge 35.00 60.00
**4** A15 25k on 4k car 2.50 3.50
*a.* Inverted surcharge 25.00 35.00
**5** A14 50k on 7k blue 5.00 6.50

***Imperf***

**6** A14 25k on 1k orange .60 1.25
*a.* Inverted surcharge 30.00 40.00
**7** A14 25k on 2k gray grn 7.50 12.50
**8** A14 25k on 3k red 4.50 3.00
*Nos. 1-8 (8)* 23.35 30.00

Counterfeits exist of Nos. 1-8.

Ermak, Cossack Leader — A1

Inscription on Back

**1919** **Perf. 11½**

**10** A1 20k green 40.00 85.00

This stamp was available for both postage and currency.

Novocherkassk Issue

**25 1P. 1P.**

Russian stamps with these surcharges are bogus.

**Kuban Government Ekaterinodar Issues**

Russian Stamps of 1909-17 Surcharged:

d

e

f

g

h

i

**1918-20** **Unwmk.** **Perf. 14x14½**

**20** A14(d) 25k on 1k dl org yel .40 .65
*a.* Inverted surcharge 30.00 27.50
*b.* Dbl. surch., one inverted 30.00 25.00
**21** A14(d) 50k on 2k dl grn 6.00 6.00
*a.* Inverted surcharge 30.00 27.50
*b.* Double surcharge 25.00 20.00
*c.* Dbl. surcharge inverted 25.00 20.00
**22** A14(e) 70k on 5k dk cl 2.40 6.00
**23** A14(f) 1r on 3k car 2.40 4.75
*a.* Inverted surcharge 25.00 20.00
*b.* Double surcharge 25.00 15.00
*c.* Pair, one without surch. 25.00 15.00
**24** A14(g) 1r on 3k car .60 1.00
*a.* Inverted surcharge 25.00 20.00
*b.* Double surcharge 25.00 20.00
*c.* Pair, one without surcharge 25.00 20.00
**25** A15(h) 3r on 4k rose 12.00 18.00
*b.* Inverted surcharge 40.00 50.00
*c.* Double surcharge 40.00 60.00
*d.* Dbl. surcharge inverted 40.00 60.00
**26** A15(i) 10r on 4k rose 4.00 5.00
*a.* 10r on 4k carmine 8.00 13.00
*b.* Inverted surcharge 40.00 55.00
**27** A11(i) 10r on 15k red brn & dp bl 1.25 1.60
*a.* Surchd. on face & back 25.00 15.00
*b.* Dbl. surch., one inverted 40.00 60.00
**28** A14(i) 25r on 3k car 2.25 2.00
*a.* Inverted surcharge 15.00 20.00
**29** A14(i) 25r on 7k bl 30.00 27.50
*a.* Inverted surcharge 55.00 60.00
**30** A11(i) 25r on 14k bl & car 60.00 65.00
*a.* Inverted surcharge 80.00 80.00
**31** A11(i) 25r on 25k dl grn & dk vio 30.00 60.00
*a.* Inverted surcharge 65.00 70.00
*Nos. 20-31 (12)* 151.30 197.50

***Imperf***

**35** A14(d) 25d on 1k org 1.25 2.00
**36** A14(d) 50k on 2k gray grn .30 .35
*a.* Inverted surcharge 30.00 25.00
*b.* Double surcharge 30.00 25.00
*c.* Pair, one without surch. 30.00 30.00
**37** A14(e) 70k on 5k claret 2.40 3.25
**38** A14(f) 1r on 3k red 1.25 2.00
*a.* Inverted surcharge 30.00 20.00
*b.* Double surcharge 20.00 15.00
*c.* Pair, one without surch. 20.00 15.00
**39** A14(g) 1r on 3k red .50 .65
*a.* Double surcharge 15.00 20.00
*b.* Pair, one without surch. 15.00 20.00
*c.* As "a," inverted 30.00 45.00
**40** A11(i) 10r on 15k red brn & dp bl 4.75 6.00
**41** A14(i) 25r on 3k red 6.00 9.50
*a.* Inverted surcharge 42.50
*Nos. 35-41 (7)* 16.45 23.75

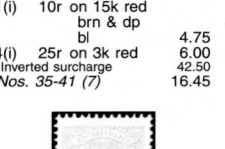

Russian Stamps of 1909-17 Surcharged

**1919** **Perf. 14, 14½x15**

**45** A14 70k on 1k dl org yel 1.25 1.00

***Imperf***

**46** A14 70k on 1k orange 1.25 2.40
*a.* Inverted surcharge 20.00 20.00
*b.* Double surch., one inverted 30.00 25.00

The 1k postal savings stamp with this surcharge inverted is a proof.
Counterfeits exist of Nos. 20-46.

Postal Savings Stamps Surcharged for Postal Use

A2

**1919** **Wmk. 171** **Perf. 14½x15**

**47** A2 10r on 1k red, *buff* 18.00 24.00
*a.* Inverted surcharge 75.00
**48** A2 10r on 5k grn, *buff* 40.00 45.00
*a.* Double surcharge 250.00
**49** A2 10r on 10k brn, *buff* 120.00 150.00
*Nos. 47-49 (3)* 178.00 219.00

Counterfeits exist of Nos. 47-49.

**Crimea**

Russian Stamp of 1917 Surcharged **35 коп.**

**1919** **Unwmk.** **Imperf**

**51** A14 35k on 1k orange .30 1.0
*a.* Comma, instead of period in surcharge 1.00

A3

Paper with Buff Network
Inscription on Back

**1919** **Imperf**

**52** A3 50k brown 40.00 75.00

Available for both postage and currency.

Russia Nos. 77, 82, 123, 73, 119 Surcharged

Nos. 53-57

Nos. 58-59

**1920** **Perf. 14x14½**

**53** A14 5r on 5k dk claret 1.25 2.40
*a.* Inverted surcharge 40.00
*b.* Double surcharge 45.00
**54** A8 5r on 20k dl bl & dk car 1.25 2.40
*a.* Inverted surcharge 30.00
*b.* Double surcharge 40.00
*c.* "5" omitted 30.00

***Imperf***

**55** A14 5r on 5k claret 1.25 2.40
*a.* Double surcharge 25.00

**Same Surcharge on Stamp of Denikin Issue, No. 64**

**57** A5 5r on 35k lt bl 12.00 14.00
*a.* Double surcharge 80.00
*Nos. 53-57 (4)* 15.75 21.20

**1920** **Perf. 14x14½**

**58** A14 100r on 1k dl org yel 3.75
*a.* "10" in place of "100" 55.00
*b.* Inverted surcharge 35.00
*c.* Double surcharge 55.00

***Imperf***

**59** A14 100r on 1k orange 2.75

Nos. 53-57 were issued at Sevastopol during the occupation by General Wrangel's army. Nos. 58-59 were prepared but not used.

**Denikin Issue**

A5

St. George — A6

**1919** **Unwmk.** **Imperf.**

**61** A5 5k orange .20 .25
**62** A5 10k green .20 .25
**63** A5 15k red .20 .35
**64** A5 35k light blue .20 .25
**65** A5 70k dark blue .20 .35
*a.* Tête bêche pair 65.00
**66** A6 1r brown & red .50 .50
**67** A6 2r gray vio & yellow .70 .75
**68** A6 3r dl rose & green .50 .75
**69** A6 5r slate & violet .80 1.10
**70** A6 7r gray grn & rose 1.50 2.75
**71** A6 10r red & gray 1.25 2.00
*Nos. 61-71 (11)* 6.25 9.30

***Perf. 11½***

*68a* A6 3r dull rose & green 1.25 1.25
*69a* A6 5r slate & violet 2.00 2.00
*71a* A6 10r red & gray 1.40 1.60
*Nos. 68a-71a (3)* 4.65 4.85

Nos. 61-71 were issued at Ekaterinodar and used in all parts of South Russia that were occupied by the People's Volunteer Army under Gen. Anton Ivanovich Denikin. The inscription on the stamps reads "United Russia."

Stamps of type A6 with rosettes instead of numerals in the small circles at the sides may be essays. Perforated copies of Nos. 61-67 and 70 are of private origin.

For surcharges see Russia, Offices in Turkish Empire Nos. 303-319.

# SOUTH WEST AFRICA

sauth 'west 'a-fri-kə

## (Namibia)

LOCATION — Southwestern Africa between Angola, Botswana and South Africa, bordering on the Atlantic Ocean
GOVT. — Administered by the Republic of South Africa under a mandate of the League of Nations
AREA — 318,261 sq. mi.
POP. — 1,039,800 (1982)
CAPITAL — Windhoek

Formerly a German possession, South West Africa was occupied by South African forces in 1915 and by the Treaty of Versailles was mandated to the Union of South Africa. On March 20, 1990 it became Namibia.

12 Pence = 1 Shilling
20 Shillings = 1 Pound
100 Cents = 1 Rand (1961)

**Catalogue values for unused stamps in this country are for Never Hinged items, beginning with Scott 125 in the regular postage section, Scott B1 in the semi-postal section, Scott J86 in the postage due section, and Scott O13 in the officials section.**

### Watermarks

Watermarks 177, 201, 330, 348 and 359 can be found at the beginning of South Africa.

Stamps of South Africa, Nos. 2-3, 5 and 9-16, Overprinted in English or Afrikaans alternately throughout the sheets.

**Major-number listings and values of Nos. 1-40 and 85-93 are for pairs with both overprints.**

Setting I

"South West" 14½mm wide
"Zuid-West" 13mm wide
Overprint Spaced 14mm

**1923, Jan. 2 Wmk. 177 *Perf. 14***

**1** A2 ½p green, pair 3.00 *10.50*
  *a.* Single, Dutch 1.10 *1.10*
**2** A2 1p red, pair 3.75 *10.50*
  *a.* Single, Dutch 1.10 *1.10*
  *b.* Inverted overprint, pair 550.00
  *c.* As "b," single, English 125.00
  *d.* As "b," single, Dutch 125.00
  *e.* "Af.rica" 175.00 210.00
  *f.* Double overprint, pair 1,000.
  *g.* As "f," single, English 500.00
  *h.* As "f," single, Dutch 500.00
**3** A2 2p dull vio, pair 4.75 *14.00*
  *a.* Single, Dutch 1.75 *1.75*
  *b.* Inverted overprint, pair 625.00 700.00
  *c.* As "b," single, English 110.00
  *d.* As "b," single, Dutch 110.00
**4** A2 3p ultra, pair 8.50 *19.00*
  *a.* Single, Dutch 3.25 *3.25*
**5** A2 4p ol grn & org, pair 15.00 *52.50*
  *a.* Single, Dutch 4.50 *4.50*
**6** A2 6p vio & blk, pair 9.25 *50.00*
  *a.* Single, Dutch 4.75 *4.75*
**7** A2 1sh orange, pair 27.50 *55.00*
  *a.* Single, Dutch 5.75 *5.25*
**8** A2 1sh3p violet, pair 35.00 *62.50*
  *a.* Single, Dutch 6.50 *6.50*
  *b.* Inverted overprint, pair 375.00
  *c.* As "b," single, English 45.00
  *d.* As "b," single, Dutch 45.00
**9** A2 2sh6p grn & cl, pair 70.00 *150.00*
  *a.* Single, Dutch 22.50 *22.50*
**10** A2 5sh blue & cl, pair 175.00 *375.00*
  *a.* Single, Dutch 57.50 *57.50*
**11** A2 10sh ol grn & bl, pair 1,500. *2,900.*
  *a.* Single, Dutch 475.00 *500.00*
**12** A2 £1 red & dp grn, pair 800.00 *2,000.*
  *a.* Single, Dutch 300.00 *300.00*
  *Nos. 1-12 (12)* 2,651. *5,699.*

Most values exist with "t" of "West" partly or totally missing. Vertical displacement in overprinting accounts for the copies with only one line of overprint.

**For English from setting I "a," see note after No. 27.**

Setting II

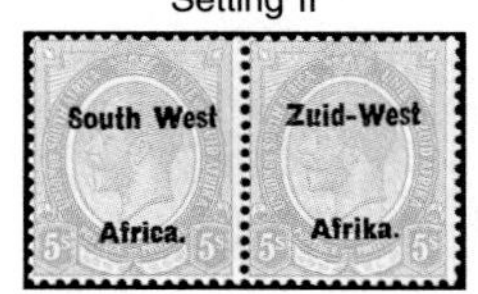


Words Same Width as Setting I
Overprint Spaced 9½-10mm

**1923, Apr.**

**13** A2 5sh blue & cl, pair 160.00 *300.00*
  *a.* Single, English 52.50 *52.50*
  *b.* Single, Dutch 52.50 *52.50*
  *c.* As #13, without period after "Afrika" 1,200. 1,300.
**14** A2 10sh ol grn & bl, pair 575.00 *1,000.*
  *a.* Single, English 160.00 *160.00*
  *b.* Single, Dutch 160.00 *160.00*
  *c.* As #14, without period after "Afrika" 2,600. *3,250.*
**15** A2 £1 red & green, pair 1,150. *1,700.*
  *a.* Single, English 225.00 *225.00*
  *b.* Single, Dutch 225.00 *225.00*
  *c.* As #15, without period after "Afrika" 6,000. 5,750.

Setting III

English as in Setting I
"Zuidwest" 11mm wide, No Hyphen
Overprint Spaced 14mm

**1923-24**

**16** A2 ½p grn, pair ('24) 7.00 *40.00*
  *a.* Single, English .30 *4.25*
  *b.* Single, Dutch .30 *4.25*
**17** A2 1p red, pair 6.25 *10.50*
  *a.* Single, English .30 *1.60*
  *b.* Single, Dutch .30 *1.60*
**18** A2 2p dull vio, pair 6.25 *10.50*
  *a.* Single, English .30 *1.50*
  *b.* Single, Dutch .30 *1.50*
  *c.* Dbl. ovpt., pair 1,200.
  *d.* As "c," single, English 90.00
  *e.* As "c," single, Dutch 90.00
**19** A2 3p ultra, pair 5.75 *11.50*
  *a.* Single, English .50 *1.50*
  *b.* Single, Dutch .50 *1.50*
**20** A2 4p ol grn & org, pair 7.00 *24.00*
  *a.* Single, English .50 *3.25*
  *b.* Single, Dutch .50 *3.25*
**21** A2 6p vio & blk, pair 16.00 *52.50*
  *a.* Single, English 1.00 *5.75*
  *b.* Single, Dutch 1.00 *5.75*
**22** A2 1sh orange, pair 16.00 *52.50*
  *a.* Single, English 1.00 *5.75*
  *b.* Single, Dutch 1.00 *5.75*
**23** A2 1sh3p violet, pair 32.50 *52.50*
  *a.* Single, English 1.75 *6.25*
  *b.* Single, Dutch 1.75 *6.25*
**24** A2 2sh6p grn & cl, pair 52.50 *92.50*
  *a.* Single, English 4.00 *11.50*
  *b.* Single, Dutch 4.00 *11.50*
**25** A2 5sh blue & cl, pair 70.00 *150.00*
  *a.* Single, English 7.50 *21.00*
  *b.* Single, Dutch 7.50 *21.00*
**26** A2 10sh ol grn & bl, pair 190.00 *300.00*
  *a.* Single, English 30.00 *47.50*
  *b.* Single, Dutch 30.00 *47.50*
**27** A2 £1 red & green, pair 350.00 *450.00*
  *a.* Single, English 40.00 *70.00*
  *b.* Single, Dutch 40.00 *70.00*
  *Nos. 16-27 (12)* 759.25 *1,246.*

The English overprint of Setting III is the same as that of Setting I.

Setting IV

**South West** **Zuidwest**

**Africa.** **Afrika.**
g h

"South West" 16mm wide
"Zuidwest" 12mm wide
Overprint Spaced 14mm

**1924, July**

**28** A2 2sh6p grn & cl, pair 92.50 *175.00*
  *a.* Single, English 13.00 *32.50*
  *b.* Single, Dutch 13.00 *32.50*

Setting VI

"South West" 16, 16½mm wide
"Zuidwest" 12½mm wide
Overprint Spaced 9½mm

**1924, Dec.**

**29** A2 ½p green, pair 8.00 *45.00*
  *a.* Single, English .35 *5.75*
  *b.* Single, Dutch .35 *5.75*
**30** A2 1p red, pair 3.75 *11.50*
  *a.* Single, English .25 *1.60*
  *b.* Single, Dutch .25 *1.60*
**31** A2 2p dull vio, pair 5.75 *25.00*
  *a.* Single, English .30 *2.00*
  *b.* Single, Dutch .30 *2.00*
**32** A2 3p ultra, pair 5.25 *32.50*
  *a.* Single, English .45 *3.25*
  *b.* Single, Dutch .45 *3.25*
**33** A2 4p ol grn & org, pair 7.50 *52.50*
  *a.* Single, English .50 *4.50*
  *b.* Single, Dutch .50 *4.50*
**34** A2 6p vio & blk, pair 10.50 *55.00*
  *a.* Single, English .75 *5.75*
  *b.* Single, Dutch .75 *5.75*
**35** A2 1sh orange, pair 12.50 *55.00*
  *a.* Single, English .75 *5.75*
  *b.* Single, Dutch .75 *5.75*
**36** A2 1sh3p violet, pair 17.50 *55.00*
  *a.* Single, English .75 *5.75*
  *b.* Single, Dutch .75 *5.75*
**37** A2 2sh6p grn & cl, pair 32.50 *80.00*
  *a.* Single, English 3.00 *11.50*
  *b.* Single, Dutch 3.00 *11.50*
**38** A2 5sh blue & cl, pair 47.50 *110.00*
  *a.* Single, English 6.00 *16.00*
  *b.* Single, Dutch 6.00 *16.00*
**39** A2 10sh ol grn & bl, pair 75.00 *150.00*
  *a.* Single, English 10.00 *22.50*
  *b.* Single, Dutch 10.00 *22.50*
**40** A2 £1 red & grn, pair 250.00 *475.00*
  *a.* Single, English 40.00 *75.00*
  *b.* Single, Dutch 40.00 *75.00*
  *Nos. 29-40 (12)* 475.75 *1,146.*

Setting VII
South Africa Nos. 21-22 Overprinted:

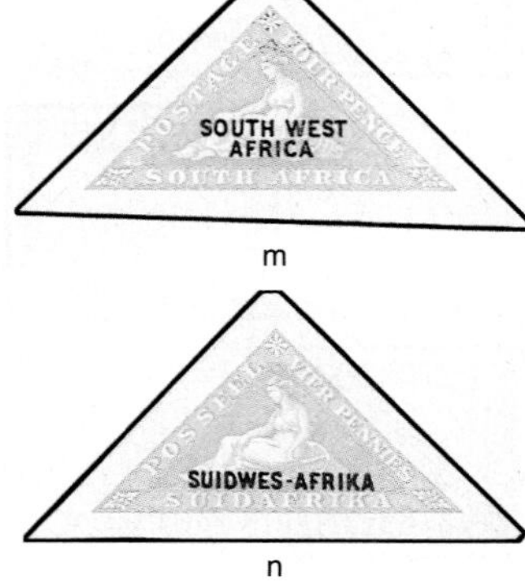

m
n

o

**1926-27 Wmk. 201 *Imperf.***

**81** A3 (m) 4p blue gray .85 *3.50*
**82** A3 (n) 4p blue gray .85 *3.50*
**83** A3 (o) 4p blue gray ('27) 7.00 *22.50*
  *Nos. 81-83 (3)* 8.70 *29.50*

Nos. 81-83 were not officially perforated, but firms and individuals applied various forms of perforation and rouletting for their own convenience. Perf. 11 examples of Nos. 81-82 were made by John Meinert, Ltd., Windhoek, same values.

Setting VIII
South Africa Nos. 23-25 Overprinted Alternately with type "p" on English-inscribed Stamps and type "q" on Afrikaans-inscribed Stamps

"South West" 16½mm wide
"Suidwes" 11mm wide
Overprint Spaced 11½mm

**1926 Typo. *Perf. 14½x14***

**85** A5 ½p dk grn & blk, pair 1.90 *7.50*
  *a.* Single, English .35 *1.00*
  *b.* Single, Afrikaans .35 *1.00*
  *c.* Afrikaans ovpt. on English stamp .35 *1.00*
  *d.* English ovpt. on Afrikaans stamp .35 *1.00*
  *e.* Pair, "c" + "d" 1.75 *6.00*
  *f.* As "e," without period after "Africa" 175.00
**86** A6 1p car & blk, pair 2.25 *3.00*
  *a.* Single, English .35 *.60*
  *b.* Single, Afrikaans .35 *.60*
  *c.* Afrikaans ovpt. on English stamp .35 *.60*
  *d.* English ovpt. on Afrikaans stamp .35 *.60*
  *e.* Pair, "c" + "d" 1.75 *5.00*
  *f.* As "e," without period after "Africa" 325.00
**87** A7 6p org & grn, pair 27.50 *35.00*
  *a.* Single, English 2.50 *5.00*
  *b.* Single, Afrikaans 2.50 *5.00*
  *c.* Afrikaans ovpt. on English stamp 2.00 *3.50*
  *d.* English ovpt. on Afrikaans stamp 2.00 *3.50*
  *e.* Pair, "c" + "d" 12.50 *27.50*
  *f.* As "e," without period after "Africa" 200.00
  *Nos. 85-87 (3)* 31.65 *45.50*

For overprints see Nos. O1-O3.

Setting IX
South Africa Nos. 26-27, 29-32 Overprinted in Blue with types "p" and "q" Spaced 16mm

**1927 Engr. *Perf. 14***

**88** A8 2p vio brn & gray, pair 5.50 *17.50*
  *a.* Single, English .25 *2.00*
  *b.* Single, Afrikaans .25 *2.00*
**89** A9 3p red & blk, pair 5.50 *32.50*
  *a.* Single, English .50 *3.00*
  *b.* Single, Afrikaans .50 *3.00*
**90** A11 1sh dp bl & bis brn, pair 17.50 *37.50*
  *a.* Single, English 1.25 *4.50*
  *b.* Single, Afrikaans 1.25 *4.50*
**91** A12 2sh6p brn & bl grn, pair 40.00 *97.50*
  *a.* Single, English 5.50 *15.00*
  *b.* Single, Afrikaans 5.50 *15.00*
**92** A13 5sh dp grn & blk, pair 85.00 *200.00*
  *a.* Single, English 10.00 *22.50*
  *b.* Single, Afrikaans 10.00 *22.50*
**93** A14 10sh ol brn & bl, pair 75.00 *160.00*
  *a.* Single, English 9.00 *22.50*
  *b.* Single, Afrikaans 9.00 *22.50*
  *Nos. 88-93 (6)* 228.50 *545.00*

South Africa Nos. 12 and 16a Overprinted at Foot

**1927 Typo. Wmk. 177**

**94** A2 1sh3p violet 1.40 *7.50*
a. Without period after "A" 110.00
**95** A2 £1 lt red & gray grn 110.00 190.00
a. Without period after "A" 1,750. *2,600.*

South Africa Nos. 23-25 Overprinted type "r" at Foot

**1927 Wmk. 201 *Perf. 14½x14***

**96** A5 ½p green & blk, pair 2.25 *7.50*
a. Single, English .20 *.90*
b. Single, Afrikaans .20 *.90*
c. As #96, without period after "A" on one stamp 47.50 85.00
**97** A6 1p car & blk, pair 1.50 *3.75*
a. Single, English .20 *.65*
b. Single, Afrikaans .20 *.65*
c. As #97, without period after "A" on one stamp 47.50 85.00
d. Ovpt. at top, pair ('30) 2.00 *16.00*
e. As "d," single, English .35 *1.90*
f. As "d," single, Afrikaans .35 *1.90*
**98** A7 6p org & grn, pair 13.00 *26.00*
a. Single, English 1.25 *3.25*
b. Single, Afrikaans 1.25 *3.25*
c. As #98, without period after "A" on one stamp 125.00
*Nos. 96-98 (3)* 16.75 *37.25*

For overprints see Nos. O5-O7.

South Africa Nos. 26-32 Overprinted type "r" at Top

**1927-28 Engr. *Perf. 14***

**99** A8 2p vio brn & gray, pair 10.50 *27.50*
a. Single, English 1.00 *1.75*
b. Single, Afrikaans 1.00 *1.75*
c. As #99, without period after "A" on one stamp 85.00 125.00
d. Double ovpt., one inverted 800.00 1,050.
**100** A9 3p red & blk, pair 7.00 *26.00*
a. Single, English .50 *3.75*
b. Single, Afrikaans .50 *3.75*
c. As #100, without period after "A" on one stamp 92.50 150.00
**101** A10 4p brn, pair ('28) 17.50 *45.00*
a. Single, English 1.25 *8.00*
b. Single, Afrikaans 1.25 *8.00*
c. As #101, without period after "A" on one stamp 97.50 *150.00*
**102** A11 1sh dp bl & bis brn, pair 22.50 *55.00*
a. Single, English 1.50 *5.75*
b. Single, Afrikaans 1.50 *5.75*
c. As #102, without period after "A" on one stamp 1,500.
**103** A12 2sh6p brn & bl grn, pair 47.50 *97.50*
a. Single, English 6.00 *14.00*
b. Single, Afrikaans 6.00 *14.00*
c. As #103, without period after "A" on one stamp 190.00 *325.00*
**104** A13 5sh dp grn & blk, pair 70.00 *140.00*
a. Single, English 8.00 *21.00*
b. Single, Afrikaans 8.00 *21.00*
c. As #104, without period after "A" on one stamp 275.00 425.00
**105** A14 10sh ol brn & bl, pair 110.00 225.00
a. Single, English 20.00 *32.50*
b. Single, Afrikaans 20.00 *32.50*
c. As #105, without period after "A" on one stamp 375.00 625.00
*Nos. 99-105 (7)* 285.00 *616.00*

For overprint see No. O8.

South Africa Nos. 33-34 Overprinted type "r" at Foot

**1930 Photo. *Perf. 15x14***

**106** A5 ½p bl grn & blk, pair 9.25 *32.50*
a. Single, English .50 *3.25*
b. Single, Afrikaans .50 *3.25*
**107** A6 1p car rose & blk, pair 7.50 *30.00*
a. Single, English .50 *3.25*
b. Single, Afrikaans .50 *3.25*

Kori Bustard — A15

Cape Cross — A16

Mail Transport — A17

Bogenfels — A18

Windhoek — A19

Waterberg — A20

Lüderitz Bay — A21

Bush Scene — A22

Elands — A23

Zebras and Brindled Gnus — A24

Herero Houses — A25

Welwitschia Plant — A26

Okuwahakan Falls — A27

***Perf. 14x13½***

**1931-37 Wmk. 201 Engr.**

**108** A15 ½p grn & blk, pair 2.75 3.00
a. Single, English .20 .20
b. Single, Afrikaans .20 .20
**109** A16 1p red & ind, pair 2.75 3.00
a. Single, English .20 .20
b. Single, Afrikaans .20 .20
**110** A17 1½p vio brn, pair ('37) 25.00 3.50
a. Single, English .20 .30
b. Single, Afrikaans .20 .30
**111** A18 2p dk brn & dk bl, pair .80 *4.25*
a. Single, English .20 .20
b. Single, Afrikaans .20 .20
**112** A19 3p dp bl & gray blk, pair .80 *4.75*
a. Single, English .20 .20
b. Single, Afrikaans .20 .20
**113** A20 4p brn vio & grn, pair 2.10 *8.00*
a. Single, English .20 .25
b. Single, Afrikaans .20 .25
**114** A21 6p ol brn & bl, pair 1.75 *10.50*
a. Single, English .20 .25
b. Single, Afrikaans .20 .25
**115** A22 1sh bl & vio brn, pair 1.75 *11.00*
a. Single, English .20 .30
b. Single, Afrikaans .20 .30
**116** A23 1sh3p ocher & pur, pair 8.75 12.50
a. Single, English .45 .60
b. Single, Afrikaans .45 .60
**117** A24 2sh6p dk gray & rose, pair 22.50 27.50
a. Single, English 1.25 2.00
b. Single, Afrikaans 1.25 2.00
**118** A25 5sh vio brn & ol grn, pair 19.00 *45.00*
a. Single, English 1.25 *3.25*
b. Single, Afrikaans 1.25 *3.25*
**119** A26 10sh grn & brn, pair 52.50 *57.50*
a. Single, English 4.50 *7.00*
b. Single, Afrikaans 4.50 *7.00*
**120** A27 20sh bl grn & mar, pair 85.00 95.00
a. Single, English 12.50 12.50
b. Single, Afrikaans 12.50 12.50
*Nos. 108-120 (13)* 225.45 *285.50*

For overprints see Nos. O13-O27.

George V — A28

**1935, May 6 *Perf. 14x13½***

**121** A28 1p carmine & blk 1.25 .30
**122** A28 2p dk brown & blk 1.25 .30
**123** A28 3p blue & blk 10.00 *21.00*
**124** A28 6p violet & blk 4.50 *11.50*
*Nos. 121-124 (4)* 17.00 *33.10*
Set, never hinged 30.00

25th anniv. of the reign of George V.

**Catalogue values for unused stamps in this section, from this point to the end of the section, are for Never Hinged items.**

**Coronation Issue**

Inscribed alternately in English and Afrikaans

George VI — A29

**1937, May 12 Engr. *Perf. 13½x14***

**125** A29 ½p emer & blk, pair .45 .25
a. Single, English .20 .20
b. Single, Afrikaans .20 .20
**126** A29 1p car & blk, pair .45 .25
a. Single, English .20 .20
b. Single, Afrikaans .20 .20
**127** A29 1½p org & blk, pair .45 .25
a. Single, English .20 .20
b. Single, Afrikaans .20 .20
**128** A29 2p dk brn & blk, pair .45 .30
a. Single, English .20 .20
b. Single, Afrikaans .20 .20
**129** A29 3p brt bl & blk, pair .55 .30
a. Single, English .20 .20
b. Single, Afrikaans .20 .20
**130** A29 4p dk vio & blk, pair .55 .35
a. Single, English .20 .20
b. Single, Afrikaans .20 .20
**131** A29 6p yel & blk, pair .55 *2.75*
a. Single, English .20 .30
b. Single, Afrikaans .20 .30
**132** A29 1sh gray & blk, pair 2.00 *3.25*
a. Single, English .20 .75
b. Single, Afrikaans .20 .75
*Nos. 125-132 (8)* 5.45 7.70

George VI & Queen Elizabeth coronation.

**Voortrekker Issue**

South Africa Nos. 79-80 Overprinted type "r"

**1938, Dec. 14 Photo. *Perf. 15x14***

**133** A23 1p rose & sl, pair 13.00 11.50
a. Single, English 1.00 *1.25*
b. Single, Afrikaans 1.00 *1.25*
**134** A24 1½p red brn & Prus bl, pair 16.00 13.50
a. Single, English 1.50 1.50
b. Single, Afrikaans 1.50 1.50

Issued to commemorate the Voortrekkers.

South Africa Nos. 81-89 Overprinted

136ovpt

***Perf. 14 (2p, 4p, 6p); 15x14***

**1941-43 Wmk. 201**

**135** A25 ½p dp blue grn, pair 1.75 2.10
a. Single, English .20 .20
b. Single, Afrikaans .20 .20
**136** A26 1p brt rose, pair 2.00 2.25
a. Single, English .20 .20
b. Single, Afrikaans .20 .20
**137** A27 1½p Prus grn, pair ('42) 3.00 3.25
a. Single, English .20 .20
b. Single, Afrikaans .20 .20
**138** A28 2p dk violet .60 .50
**139** A29 3p dp blue, pair 15.00 10.00
a. Single, English .75 *1.00*
b. Single, Afrikaans .75 *1.00*
**140** A30 4p brown, pair 6.00 8.25
a. Single, English .30 *.75*
b. Single, Afrikaans .30 *.75*
**141** A31 6p brt red org, pair 3.50 4.00
a. Single, English .30 *1.00*
b. Single, Afrikaans .30 *1.00*
**142** A32 1sh dk brown 1.25 1.00
**143** A33 1sh3p dk ol brn, pair ('43) 15.00 16.00
a. Single, English 1.00 1.25
b. Single, Afrikaans 1.00 1.25
*Nos. 135-143 (9)* 48.10 47.35

South Africa Nos. 90-97 Overprinted

t

u

***Pairs or Strips of 3 Perf. 14 or 15x14 all around, Rouletted 6½ or 13 btwn.***

**1942-45 Wmk. 201**

**144** A34(t) ½p dp grn, horiz. strip of 3 .75 .60
a. Single, English .20 .20
b. Single, Afrikaans .20 .20
c. ½p dp bl grn, horiz. strip of 3 1.50 2.25
d. As "c," single, English .20 .20
e. As "c," single, Afrikaans .20 .20
**145** A35(t) 1p brt car, horiz. strip of 3 .75 .60
a. Single, English .20 .20
b. Single, Afrikaans .20 .20
c. 1p rose car, horiz. strip of 3 1.25 *2.00*
d. As "c," single, English .20 .20
e. As "c," single, Afrikaans .20 .20
**146** A36(u) 1½p cop brn, horiz. pair .75 .60
a. Single, English .20 .20
b. Single, Afrikaans .20 .20
**147** A37(t) 2p dk vio, horiz. pair .75 .75
a. Single, English .20 .20
b. Single, Afrikaans .20 .20
**148** A38(t) 3p dp bl, vert. strip of 3 4.00 *4.25*
a. Single, English .20 *.40*
b. Single, Afrikaans .20 *.40*
**149** A39(t) 4p sl grn, vert. strip of 3 5.00 *6.25*
a. Single .20 *.30*
b. As "c," single 50.00
c. Invtd. ovpt., strip of 3 500.00 300.00
**150** A40(t) 6p brt red org, horiz. pair 2.75 1.60
a. Single, English .20 *.30*
b. Single, Afrikaans .20 *.30*

*c.* Inverted overprint, pair 425.00
*d.* As "c," single, English 50.00 50.00
*e.* As "c," single, Afrikaans 50.00 50.00
**151** A41(u) 1sh dk brn, vert. pair 12.00 11.00
*a.* Single .75 1.50
*b.* As "c," single 70.00
*c.* Inverted overprint, pair 450.00 325.00
**152** A41(t) 1sh dk brn, vert. pair 2.25 1.60
*a.* Single .20 *.30*
*b.* As "c," single 45.00 40.00
*c.* Invtd. ovpt., vert. pair 375.00 275.00
*Nos. 144-152 (9)* 29.00 27.25

Issue years: #144-145, 147-151, 1943; #152, 1944; #144c, 145c, 149c, 1945.

### Peace Issue

South Africa Nos. 100-102 Overprinted Type "w"

**1945, Dec. 3 Wmk. 201 *Perf. 14***
**153** A42 1p rose pink & choc, pair .40 .40
*a.* Single, English .20 .20
*b.* Single, Afrikaans .20 .20
*c.* Inverted overprint, pair 300.00 300.00
*d.* As "c," single, English 37.50
*e.* As "c," single, Afrikaans 37.50
**154** A43 2p vio & sl bl, pair .40 .40
*a.* Single, English .20 .20
*b.* Single, Afrikaans .20 .20
**155** A43 3p ultra & dp ultra, pair 1.25 1.25
*a.* Single, English .20 .20
*b.* Single, Afrikaans .20 .20
*Nos. 153-155 (3)* 2.05 2.05

WW II victory of the Allies.

### Royal Visit Issue

South Africa Nos. 103-105 Overprinted

**1947, Feb. 17 *Perf. 15x14***
**156** A44 1p cerise & gray, pair .30 .20
*a.* Single, English .20 .20
*b.* Single, Afrikaans .20 .20
**157** A45 2p purple, pair .30 .25
*a.* Single, English .20 .20
*b.* Single, Afrikaans .20 .20
**158** A46 3p dk blue, pair .35 .30
*a.* Single, English .20 .20
*b.* Single, Afrikaans .20 .20
*Nos. 156-158 (3)* .95 .75

Visit of the British Royal Family, Mar.-Apr., 1947.

South Africa No. 106 Overprinted

**1948, Apr. 26 *Perf. 14***
**159** A47 3p dp chalky bl & sil, pair 1.25 .30
*a.* Single, English .20 .20
*b.* Single, Afrikaans .20 .20

25th anniv. of the marriage of George VI and Queen Elizabeth.

### UPU Issue

South Africa Nos. 109-111 Overprinted type "w" 13mm wide

**1949, Oct. 1 *Perf. 14x15***
**160** A50 ½p dk green, pair 1.10 *1.50*
*a.* Single, English .20 *.25*
*b.* Single, Afrikaans .20 *.25*
**161** A50 1½p dk red, pair 1.10 *1.50*
*a.* Single, English .20 .20
*b.* Single, Afrikaans .20 .20
**162** A50 3p ultra, pair 1.75 2.00
*a.* Single, English .20 *.25*
*b.* Single, Afrikaans .20 *.25*
*Nos. 160-162 (3)* 3.95 5.00

75th anniv. of the UPU.

---

Except for Nos. 312-313, 423-428, this ends the bi-lingual multiples in the postage section.

---

### Voortrekker Monument Issue

South Africa Nos. 112-114 Overprinted

**1949, Dec. 1 *Perf. 15x14***
**163** A51 1p magenta .20 .20
**164** A52 1½p dull green .20 .20
**165** A53 3p dark blue .30 .30
*Nos. 163-165 (3)* .70 .70

Inauguration of the Voortrekker Monument at Pretoria.

South Africa Nos. 115-119 Overprinted

w

x

**1952, Mar. 14 *Perf. 15x14, 14x15***
**166** A54(w) ½p dk brown & red vio .40 .40
**167** A55(x) 1p dark green .40 .40
**168** A54(w) 2p dark purple .85 .40
**169** A55(x) 4½p dark blue 1.00 1.00
**170** A54(w) 1sh brown 2.00 2.00
*Nos. 166-170 (5)* 4.65 4.20

300th anniv. of the landing of Jan van Riebeeck at the Cape of Good Hope.

### Coronation Issue

Queen Elizabeth II and Flowers — A54

Various flowers.

**1953, June 2 Photo. *Perf. 14***
**244** A54 1p carmine rose .55 .30
**245** A54 2p dark green .55 .30
**246** A54 4p deep magenta 1.10 .65
**247** A54 6p deep blue 1.10 1.00
**248** A54 1sh chestnut brown 1.60 1.25
*Nos. 244-248 (5)* 4.90 3.50

Rock Painting of Two Bucks — A55

Rhinoceros Hunt — A56

Designs: 2p, "White Lady" (rock painting). 4½p, Elephant and giraffe (rock painting). 4½p, Karakul lamb. 6p, Owambo blowing Kudu horn. 1sh, Ukuanjama woman. 1sh3p, Herero woman. 1sh6p, Ukuanjama girl. 2sh6p, Lioness. 5sh, Cape Oryx. 10sh, Elephant.

**1954, Nov. 15 Wmk. 201 *Perf. 14***
**249** A55 1p rose brown .55 .20
**250** A55 2p dk brown .55 .20
**251** A56 3p brown vio 1.25 .20
**252** A56 4p olive gray 1.50 .20
**253** A55 4½p blue vio 1.10 .20
**254** A55 6p gray green 1.50 .40
**255** A55 1sh magenta 2.10 .50
**256** A55 1sh3p rose pink 4.00 1.00
**257** A55 1sh6p dull purple 4.50 1.10
**258** A55 2sh6p yel brown 8.50 2.50
**259** A55 5sh blue 19.00 6.00
**260** A55 10sh dk green 32.50 12.50
*Nos. 249-260 (12)* 77.05 25.00

**1960 Wmk. 330 *Perf. 14***
**261** A55 1p rose brown 1.50 .60
**262** A55 2p dark brown 1.75 .80
**263** A56 3p brown vio 2.40 1.50
**264** A56 4p olive gray 5.50 6.25
**265** A55 1sh6p dull purple 24.00 21.00
*Nos. 261-265 (5)* 35.15 30.15

General Post Office, Windhoek — A57

Fishing Industry — A58

Designs: 1c, Finger Rock, Asab. 1½c, Monument, Mounted Soldier. 2c, Quivertree (aloe dichotoma Masson). 2½c, Administrator's residence. 3c, Swakopmund Lighthouse and flamingoes. 5c, Flamingo. 7½c, Christchurch. 10c, Diamonds. 12½c, Fort Namutoni. 15c, Hardap Dam. 20c, Topaz. 50c, Tourmaline. 1r, Heliodor.

**1961-63 Wmk. 330 Photo. *Perf. 14***
**266** A57 ½c blue & brown .70 .35
**267** A58 1c pale lil & brn .35 .30
**268** A58 1½c sal & dk pur .35 .30
**269** A58 2c yel & green 1.00 1.00
**270** A57 2½c lt bl & red brn .75 .35
**271** A58 3c dp rose & vio bl 5.00 1.25
**272** A58 3½c blue grn & ind 1.00 .40
**273** A58 5c bluish gray & red 7.25 2.10
**274** A58 7½c yellow & brn .90 .90
**275** A58 10c brt blue & yel 1.60 .55
**276** A57 12½c yellow & ind 2.75 2.75
**277** A57 15c dp brn & blue 16.00 5.75
**278** A58 20c sal, brn & blk 5.50 2.10
**279** A58 50c org yel & Prus grn 9.75 5.50
**280** A58 1r brt blue, mar & yel 14.50 11.00
*Nos. 266-280 (15)* 67.40 34.60

Issued: 3c, 10/1/62; 15c, 3/16/63; others, 2/14/61.

**1962-73 Unwmk.**
**281** A57 ½c blue & brn .60 *1.25*
**282** A58 1½c sal & dk pur ('63) 6.25 .25
**283** A58 2c yellow & grn 5.00 3.00
**284** A57 2½c lt bl & red brn ('64) 6.50 3.00
**285** A58 3c dp rose & vio bl ('73) 1.00 1.00
**286** A58 3½c bl grn & ind ('66) 15.00 4.50
**287** A58 5c bluish gray & red 7.25 3.00
*Nos. 281-287 (7)* 41.60 16.00

See Nos. 304-308, 314-328.

Hardap Dam and Development A59

Centenary Emblem and S.W.A. Map A60

**1963, Mar. 16 Wmk. 330**
**294** A59 3c sepia green .90 .90

Opening of Hardap Dam near Mariental.

**1963, Aug. 30 Unwmk. *Perf. 14***

Design: 15c, Emblem and globe.

**295** A60 7½c blue, blk & red 5.75 3.50
**296** A60 15c brn org, blk & red 12.00 7.00

Centenary of the International Red Cross.

Assembly Hall — A61

John Calvin — A62

**1964, May 14 Photo. Wmk. 330**
**297** A61 3c salmon pink & vio bl .90 .75

Issued to commemorate the opening of the new hall of the Legislative Assembly.

**1964, Oct. 1 Unwmk. *Perf. 14***
**298** A62 2½c magenta & gold .85 .55
**299** A62 15c green & gold 4.50 3.50

John Calvin (1509-64), French theologian and leader of the Reformation.

Mail Runner, 1890 — A63

Kurt von François — A64

**Wmk. 348**

**1965, Oct. 18 Photo. *Perf. 14***
**300** A63 3c red & deep brown .55 .30
**301** A64 15c green & deep brn 2.75 1.75

75th anniversary of Windhoek.

Dr. H. H. Vedder, Missionary, Educator and Senator, 90th Birthday — A65

**1966, July 4 *Perf. 14***
**302** A65 3c black & salmon .40 .30
**303** A65 15c black & light blue 2.50 2.25

Types of 1961-62

**1966-67 Wmk. 348 Photo. *Perf. 14***
**Chalky Paper**
**304** A57 ½c lt blue & brn *11.00 3.00*
**304A** A58 1c pale lil & brn .35 .20
**305** A58 2c brt yel & dp grn .35 .20
**306** A57 2½c gray blue & red brn .50 .20
**307** A58 3½c pale grn & vio bl 4.25 2.00
**308** A58 7½c brt yel & brn 4.00 .80
*Nos. 304-308 (6)* *20.45 6.40*

The watermark on Nos. 304, 305-308 is very faint, and these stamps can be distinguished by the shades and by the thick chalky paper. The watermark on No. 304A is clear.

Issued: 2c, 2½c, 1966; others, 1967.

Camelthorn Tree — A66

Verwoerd A67

Swart A68

Design: 3c, Waves breaking against rock.

***Perf. 14, 14x15 (15c)***

**1967, Jan. 6 Litho. Wmk. 348**

**309** A66 2½c green & black .30 .20
**310** A67 3c brt blue & brown .40 .20
**311** A67 15c rose lilac & black 2.75 2.50
*Nos. 309-311 (3)* 3.45 2.90

Dr. Hendrik F. Verwoerd (1901-1966), Prime Minister of South Africa.

***Perf. 14x15***

**1968, Jan. 2 Photo. Wmk. 359**

15c, President and Mrs. C. R. Swart.

**312** Strip of 3 4.50 4.50
*a.* A68 3c Single, English .55 .30
*b.* A68 3c Single, Afrikaans .55 .30
*c.* A68 3c Single, German .55 .30
**313** Strip of 3 11.50 11.50
*a.* A68 15c Single, English 3.00 2.50
*b.* A68 15c Single, Afrikaans 3.00 2.50
*c.* A68 15c Single, German 3.00 2.50

Charles Robberts Swart, 1st president of South Africa, (1961-67).

Types of 1961-62

Designs: 4c, like 2½c. 6c, Christchurch. 9c, Fort Namutoni.

**1968-72 Wmk. 359 Photo. *Perf. 14***

**314** A57 ½c blue & brown 1.00 .25
**315** A57 ½c blue & brn, redrawn ('70) 2.50 1.00
**316** A58 1c pale lilac & brn ('70) 1.00 .25
**317** A58 1½c salmon & dk pur 1.25 .35
**318** A58 1½c sal & dk pur, redrawn ('71) 14.00 6.50
**319** A58 2c yel & grn, redrawn ('70) 1.40 .35
**320** A57 2½c lt bl & red brn ('70) 1.25 .25
**321** A58 3c dp rose & vio bl ('70) 6.00 .30
**322** A57 4c lt bl & red brn ('71) 2.00 .85
**323** A58 5c bluish gray & red 4.25 .45
**324** A58 6c yel & brn ('71) 8.75 3.50
**325** A57 9c yel & ind ('71) 9.00 4.50
**326** A58 10c brt bl & yel ('70) 20.00 1.65
**327** A57 15c dp brn & bl ('72) 24.50 3.50
**328** A58 20c org, brn & blk 19.00 2.00
*Nos. 314-328 (15)* 115.90 25.70

Nos. 315, 318-319 are without inscription "Posgeld Incomste Postage Revenue" and the numerals have been enlarged. The ½c (#315), 2c and 10c were also issued as coils.

Water Type of South Africa, 1970

2½c, Water drop and flower. 3c, Waves, horiz.

**1970, Feb. 14 *Perf. 14***

**329** A142 2½c brown, brt bl & grn .90 .65
**330** A142 3c pale gray, bl & indigo 1.10 .80

Water '70 campaign of the South African Department of Water Affairs.

Bible Society Types of South Africa

Designs: 2½c, Sower, stained glass window. 12½c, "BIBLIA" and open book.

**1970, Aug. 24 Photo. *Perf. 14***

**331** A143 2½c multicolored 1.10 .55

**Photo.; Gold Impressed**

**332** A144 12½c ultra, blk & gold 11.00 8.00

South African Bible Soc., 150th anniv.

Stamp Exhibition Types of South Africa

***Perf. 14x13½, 13½x14***

**1971, May 31 Photo. Wmk. 359**

**333** A145 5c blue, yel & blk 4.00 3.25
**334** A146 12½c grnsh bl, vio bl & red 47.50 27.50

Intl. Stamp Exhib. (INTERSTEX), Cape Town, May 22-31. No. 334 also for the 10th anniv. of the Antarctic Treaty pledging peaceful uses of and scientific cooperation in Antarctica.

Republic Anniversary Types of South Africa

**1971, May 31 *Perf. 14***

**335** A147 2c mag, rose red & buff 2.25 1.40
**336** A148 4c blue green & black 4.00 1.90

10th anniv. of the Republic of South Africa.

Cat Type of South Africa

**1972, Sept. 19 *Perf. 14***

**337** A152 5c multicolored 4.00 3.25

Cent. of the SPCA.

Landscape, by Adolph Jentsch — A69

Designs: Various landscapes by Adolph Jentsch (1888-1977). 10c, 15c, vert.

**1973, Apr. 28 Litho. *Perf. 11½x12½***

**338** A69 2c multicolored .85 .85
**339** A69 4c multicolored 1.40 1.40
**340** A69 5c multicolored 1.75 1.75
**341** A69 10c multicolored 3.75 3.75
**342** A69 15c multicolored 5.50 5.50
*Nos. 338-342 (5)* 13.25 13.25

Sarcocaulon Rigidum A70

Pachypodium Namaqua-num A71

Designs: 1c-50c, Various succulent plants. 1r, Welwitschia. 30c, 1r, horiz.

**1973, Sept. 1 Litho. *Perf. 12½***

**Plants in Natural Colors**

**343** A70 1c light blue .25 .25
**344** A70 2c yellow .25 .25
**345** A70 3c salmon pink .25 .25
**346** A70 4c gray .30 .25
**347** A70 5c blue .60 .25
**348** A70 6c greenish gray .55 .25
**349** A70 7c bright yellow .50 .25
**350** A70 9c dull yellow 1.25 .25
**351** A70 10c blue green .60 .25
**352** A70 14c yellow green 1.50 .50
**353** A70 15c light brown 1.50 .50
**354** A70 20c light olive 3.00 .70
**355** A70 25c orange 1.00 .75

***Perf. 12x12½, 12½x12***

**356** A71 30c dull yellow 1.50 1.00
**357** A71 50c light green 2.00 1.60
**358** A71 1r blue green 3.00 3.00
*Nos. 343-358 (16)* 18.05 10.30

**1979 Same Designs *Perf. 14***

*344a* A70 2c .35 .35
*345a* A70 3c .35 .35
*347a* A70 5c .50 .50
*351a* A70 10c .50 .50
*356a* A70 30c .75 .75
*357a* A70 50c .90 .90
*Nos. 344a-357a (6)* 3.35 3.35

**Coil Stamps**

**1973, Sept. 1 Photo. *Perf. 14***

**359** A70 1c brt pink & black .85 .60
**360** A70 2c yellow & black .65 .55
**361** A70 5c red & black 1.75 .65

**1978 *Perf. 14 Vertically***

**361A** A70 1c brt pink & black 5.00 4.00
**362** A70 2c yellow & black 1.25 .45
**362A** A70 5c red & black 1.25 .65
*Nos. 359-362A (6)* 10.75 6.90

For overprints, see Nos. 423-428.

**NOTE: coil stamps, Nos. 359-362A, are printed in two colors, sheet stamps are multicolored.**

Chat-shrike — A72

Designs: Rare birds.

***Perf. 12½x11½***

**1974, Feb. 13 Litho.**

**363** A72 4c shown 3.50 3.00
**364** A72 5c Rosy-faced lovebirds 5.25 3.50
**365** A72 10c Damara rockjumper 12.00 11.00
**366** A72 15c Ruppell's parrot 21.00 17.00
*Nos. 363-366 (4)* 41.75 34.50

Rock Carvings, Twyfelfontein A73

Mining A74

**1974, Apr. 10 Litho. *Perf. 12½***

**367** A73 4c Giraffe & horse 1.60 .90
**368** A73 5c Elephant 2.10 1.25

***Perf. 12x12½***

**Size: 37x21½mm**

**369** A73 15c Deer, horiz. 10.00 5.50
*Nos. 367-369 (3)* 13.70 7.65

**1974, Sept. 30 *Perf. 12½x11½***

**370** A74 10c Diamonds 4.75 2.00
**371** A74 15c Diamond open pit mining 6.75 3.00

Map Showing Route, Covered Wagons A75

***Perf. 11½x12***

**1974, Nov. 13 Unwmk.**

**372** A75 4c yellow & multi 1.25 .85

Centenary of "Thirstland Trek" from Transvaal through Kalahari Desert to Angola.

Peregrine Falcon — A76

Designs: Protected Birds of Prey.

**1975, Mar. 19 *Perf. 12½x11½***

**373** A76 4c shown 2.50 1.75
**374** A76 5c Black eagle 3.25 2.00
**375** A76 10c Martial eagle 7.25 4.50
**376** A76 15c Egyptian vulture 9.75 6.50
*Nos. 373-376 (4)* 22.75 14.75

Kolmanskop, Ghost Diamond Mining Town — A77

Designs: 9c, German steam traction engine, 1896. 15c, Old Fort, Windhoek and statue of Colonial German trooper on horseback.

**1975, July 23 Litho. *Perf. 12x12½***

**377** A77 5c violet & multi .35 .30
**378** A77 9c ocher & multi .75 .75
**379** A77 15c yellow & multi 1.25 1.25
*Nos. 377-379 (3)* 2.35 2.30

Historic monuments.

Paintings by Otto Schröder (1913-75) A78

**1975, Oct. 15 Litho. *Perf. 12x12½***

**380** A78 15c Luderitz 1.25 1.25
**381** A78 15c Swakopmund 1.25 1.25
**382** A78 15c Unloading freighters 1.25 1.25
**383** A78 15c Ships at anchor, Walvis Bay 1.25 1.25
*a.* Souvenir sheet of 4, #380-383 6.00 6.00
*b.* Block of 4, #380-383 5.00 5.00

No. 383a has a horizontal gutter with black inscription on silver panel.

Elephants A79

Pre-historic Rock Paintings: 10c, Rhinoceros. 15c, Antelope and hunter. 20c, Hunter with bow and arrow.

**1976, Mar. 12 Litho. *Perf. 12x12½***

**384** A79 4c red brown & multi .25 .20
**385** A79 10c red brown & multi .60 .60
**386** A79 15c red brown & multi .90 .90
**387** A79 20c red brown & multi 1.50 1.50
*a.* Souvenir sheet of 4, #384-387 3.75 3.75
*Nos. 384-387 (4)* 3.25 3.20

Schloss Duwisib A80

Castles Built by German Settlers: 10c, Schwerinsburg. 20c, Heynitzburg.

**1976, May 14 Litho. *Perf. 12x12½***

**388** A80 10c multicolored .60 .60
**389** A80 15c multicolored .90 .90
**390** A80 20c multicolored 1.25 1.25
*Nos. 388-390 (3)* 2.75 2.75

Nature Protection A81

**1976, July 16 Litho. *Perf. 11½x12½***

**391** A81 4c Daman .45 .25
**392** A81 10c Dik-diks 1.10 .65
**393** A81 15c Tree squirrel 1.75 1.10
*Nos. 391-393 (3)* 3.30 2.00

Augustineum Training Institute, Windhoek — A82

20c, Katutura State Hospital, Windhoek.

**1976, Sept. 17 Litho. *Perf. 12x12½***

**394** A82 15c ocher & black .60 .60
**395** A82 20c citron & black .80 .80

Owambo Canal System A83

20c, Ruacana Dam and hydroelectric station.

**1976, Nov. 19 Litho. *Perf. 12x12½***

| | | | | |
|---|---|---|---|---|
| **396** | A83 | 15c multicolored | .60 | .60 |
| **397** | A83 | 20c multicolored | .80 | .80 |

Water and electricity supply.

Sinking Ship off Namib Shore — A84

Designs: Namib Desert, various views.

**1977, Mar. 29 Litho. *Perf. 12½***

| | | | | |
|---|---|---|---|---|
| **398** | A84 | 4c multicolored | .20 | .20 |
| **399** | A84 | 10c multicolored | .50 | .45 |
| **400** | A84 | 15c multicolored | .75 | .65 |
| **401** | A84 | 20c multicolored | 1.10 | .95 |
| | | *Nos. 398-401 (4)* | 2.55 | 2.25 |

Owambo Kraal A85

Designs: 10c, Giant grain baskets. 15c, Women pounding corn. 20c, Body painting.

**1977, July 15 Litho. *Perf. 12x12½***

| | | | | |
|---|---|---|---|---|
| **402** | A85 | 4c multicolored | .20 | .20 |
| **403** | A85 | 10c multicolored | .40 | .40 |
| **404** | A85 | 15c multicolored | .55 | .55 |
| **405** | A85 | 20c multicolored | .85 | .85 |
| | | *Nos. 402-405 (4)* | 2.00 | 2.00 |

Traditions of the Wambo people.

J. G. Strijdom Airport, Windhoek — A86

**1977, Aug. 22 *Perf. 12½***

| | | | | |
|---|---|---|---|---|
| **406** | A86 | 20c multicolored | .50 | .50 |

Drostdy, Lüderitz, 1910 A87

Historic Houses: 10c, Woermannhaus, Swakopmund, 1895. 15c, Neu-Heusis, Windhoek. 20c, Schmelenhaus, Bethanie, 1814.

**1977, Nov. 4 Litho. *Perf. 12x12½***

| | | | | |
|---|---|---|---|---|
| **407** | A87 | 5c multicolored | .20 | .20 |
| **408** | A87 | 10c multicolored | .40 | .40 |
| **409** | A87 | 15c multicolored | .60 | .60 |
| **410** | A87 | 20c multicolored | .80 | .80 |
| *a.* | | Souvenir sheet of 4, #407-410 | 2.40 | 2.40 |
| | | *Nos. 407-410 (4)* | 2.00 | 2.00 |

Side-winding Adder — A88

Small Animals of the Namib Desert: 10c, Golden sand mole. 15c, Palmato gecko. 20c, Namaqua chameleon.

**1978, Feb. 6 Litho. *Perf. 12½***

| | | | | |
|---|---|---|---|---|
| **411** | A88 | 4c multicolored | .20 | .20 |
| **412** | A88 | 10c multicolored | .45 | .45 |
| **413** | A88 | 15c multicolored | .65 | .65 |
| **414** | A88 | 20c multicolored | .90 | .90 |
| | | *Nos. 411-414 (4)* | 2.20 | 2.20 |

Bushman Hunter Disguised as Ostrich A89

Bushmen: 10c, Woman carrying ostrich eggs on back. 15c, Making fire. 20c, Family sitting in front of hut.

**1978, Apr. 14 Litho. *Perf. 12x12½***

| | | | | |
|---|---|---|---|---|
| **415** | A89 | 4c brown, buff & blk | .20 | .20 |
| **416** | A89 | 10c brown, buff & blk | .35 | .35 |
| **417** | A89 | 15c brown, buff & blk | .55 | .55 |
| **418** | A89 | 20c brown, buff & blk | .70 | .70 |
| | | *Nos. 415-418 (4)* | 1.80 | 1.80 |

Lutheran Church, Windhoek — A90

Designs: 10c, Lutheran Church, Swakopmund. 15c, Rhenish Mission Church, Otjimbingwe. 20c, Rhenish Mission Church, Keetmanshoop.

**1978, June 16 Litho. *Perf. 12½***

| | | | | |
|---|---|---|---|---|
| **419** | A90 | 4c ol bister & blk | .20 | .20 |
| **420** | A90 | 10c bister & blk | .35 | .35 |
| **421** | A90 | 15c pale red brn & blk | .55 | .55 |
| **422** | A90 | 20c blue gray & blk | .70 | .70 |
| *a.* | | Souvenir sheet of 4, #419-422 | 1.90 | 1.90 |
| | | *Nos. 419-422 (4)* | 1.80 | 1.80 |

Type of 1973 Inscribed in English, German or Afrikaans:

a, UNIVERSAL / SUFFRAGE
b, ALLGEMEINES / WAHLRECHT
c, ALGEMENE / STEMREG

**1978, Nov. 1 Litho. *Perf. 12½***

| | | | |
|---|---|---|---|
| **423** | Strip of 3 | .25 | .25 |
| *a.-c.* | A70 4c any single | .20 | .20 |
| **424** | Strip of 3 | .30 | .30 |
| *a.-c.* | A70 5c any single | .20 | .20 |
| **425** | Strip of 3 | .60 | .60 |
| *a.-c.* | A70 10c any single | .20 | .20 |
| **426** | Strip of 3 | .95 | .95 |
| *a.-c.* | A70 15c any single | .30 | .30 |
| **427** | Strip of 3 | 1.25 | 1.25 |
| *a.-c.* | A70 20c any single | .40 | .40 |
| **428** | Strip of 3 | 1.60 | 1.60 |
| *a.-c.* | A70 25c any single | .55 | .55 |
| | *Nos. 423-428 (6)* | 4.95 | 4.95 |

General suffrage. Printed se-tenant with inscriptions alternating horizontally and vertically in sheets of 30 (3x10).

Greater Flamingoes A91

Water Birds: 15c, White-breasted cormorants. 20c, Chestnut-banded plovers. 25c, White pelicans.

**1979, Apr. 5 Litho. *Perf. 14x14½***

| | | | | |
|---|---|---|---|---|
| **429** | A91 | 4c multicolored | .20 | .20 |
| **430** | A91 | 15c multicolored | .45 | .45 |
| **431** | A91 | 20c multicolored | .60 | .60 |
| **432** | A91 | 25c multicolored | .75 | .75 |
| | | *Nos. 429-432 (4)* | 2.00 | 2.00 |

Silver Topaz A92

**1979, Nov. 26 Litho. *Perf. 14x14½***

| | | | | |
|---|---|---|---|---|
| **433** | A92 | 4c shown | .35 | .35 |
| **434** | A92 | 15c Aquamarine | .55 | .55 |
| **435** | A92 | 20c Malachite | .85 | .85 |
| **436** | A92 | 25c Amethyst | 1.00 | 1.00 |
| | | *Nos. 433-436 (4)* | 2.75 | 2.75 |

Killer Whale — A93

**1980, Mar. 25 Litho. *Perf. 14x14½***

| | | | | |
|---|---|---|---|---|
| **437** | A93 | 4c shown | .35 | .30 |
| | | **Size: 37½x21mm** | | |
| **438** | A93 | 5c Humpback whale | .40 | .30 |
| **439** | A93 | 10c Southern right whale | .80 | .60 |
| | | **Size: 57½x21mm** | | |
| **440** | A93 | 15c Sperm whale, giant squid | 1.40 | .90 |
| **441** | A93 | 20c Fin whale | 1.90 | 1.25 |
| | | **Size: 87½x21mm** | | |
| **442** | A93 | 25c Blue whale, diver | 2.00 | 1.50 |
| *a.* | | Souvenir sheet of 6, #437-442 | 7.50 | 7.50 |
| | | *Nos. 437-442 (6)* | 6.85 | 4.85 |

Impala A94

**1980, June 25 Litho. *Perf. 14½x14***

| | | | | |
|---|---|---|---|---|
| **443** | A94 | 5c shown | .20 | .20 |
| **444** | A94 | 10c Tsessebe | .30 | .30 |
| **445** | A94 | 15c Roan antelope | .45 | .45 |
| **446** | A94 | 20c Sable antelope | .60 | .60 |
| | | *Nos. 443-446 (4)* | 1.55 | 1.55 |

Cape Hunting Dog — A95

**1980-85 Litho. *Perf. 14½x14***

| | | | | |
|---|---|---|---|---|
| **447** | A95 | 1c Black backed jackal | .25 | .25 |
| **448** | A95 | 2c shown | .25 | .25 |
| **449** | A95 | 3c Hyena | .25 | .25 |
| **450** | A95 | 4c Dorcas antelope | .25 | .25 |
| **451** | A95 | 5c Oryx | .25 | .25 |
| **452** | A95 | 6c Greater kudu | .25 | .25 |
| | | ***Perf. 14x1414½*** | | |
| **453** | A95 | 7c Zebra, horiz. | .25 | .25 |
| **454** | A95 | 8c Porcupine, horiz. | .25 | .25 |
| **455** | A95 | 9c Honey badger, horiz. | .25 | .25 |
| **456** | A95 | 10c Cheetah, horiz. | .25 | .25 |
| **456A** | A95 | 11c Blue wildebeest ('84) | .90 | .35 |
| **456B** | A95 | 12c Syncerus caffer, horiz. ('85) | .55 | .30 |
| *c.* | | Booklet pane of 10 | 4.50 | |
| **457** | A95 | 15c Hippopotamus, horiz. | .30 | .30 |
| **458** | A95 | 20c Taurotragus oryx, horiz. | .45 | .45 |
| **459** | A95 | 25c Rhinoceros, horiz. | .55 | .55 |
| **460** | A95 | 30c Lion, horiz. | .65 | .65 |
| | | ***Perf. 14½x14*** | | |
| **461** | A95 | 50c Giraffe | 1.25 | 1.25 |
| **462** | A95 | 1r Leopard | 2.10 | 2.10 |
| **463** | A95 | 2r Elephant | 4.25 | 4.25 |
| | | *Nos. 447-463 (19)* | 13.50 | 12.70 |

Coil Stamps

**1980, Oct. 1 Litho. *Perf. 14 Vert.***

| | | | | |
|---|---|---|---|---|
| **464** | A95 | 1c Suricate suricate | .45 | .45 |
| **465** | A95 | 2c Guenon | .45 | .45 |
| **466** | A95 | 5c South African chacma | .45 | .45 |
| | | *Nos. 464-466 (3)* | 1.35 | 1.35 |

See Nos. 556-557.

Von Bach Dam, Swakop River — A96

**1980, Nov. 25 Litho. *Perf. 14x14½***

| | | | | |
|---|---|---|---|---|
| **467** | A96 | 5c shown | .20 | .20 |
| **468** | A96 | 10c Swakoppoort Dam | .20 | .20 |
| **469** | A96 | 15c Naute Dam | .25 | .25 |
| **470** | A96 | 20c Hardap Dam | .35 | .35 |
| | | *Nos. 467-470 (4)* | 1.00 | 1.00 |

Water conservation in the desert.

Fish River Canyon — A97

Designs: Views of Fish River Canyon.

**1981, Mar. 20 Litho. *Perf. 14½x14***

| | | | | |
|---|---|---|---|---|
| **471** | A97 | 5c multicolored | .20 | .20 |
| **472** | A97 | 15c multicolored | .20 | .20 |
| **473** | A97 | 20c multicolored | .25 | .25 |
| **474** | A97 | 25c multicolored | .35 | .35 |
| | | *Nos. 471-474 (4)* | 1.00 | 1.00 |

Aloe Erinacea — A98

**1981, Aug. 14**

| | | | | |
|---|---|---|---|---|
| **475** | A98 | 5c shown | .20 | .20 |
| **476** | A98 | 15c Aloe viridiflora | .20 | .20 |
| **477** | A98 | 20c Aloe pearsonii | .30 | .30 |
| **478** | A98 | 25c Aloe littoralis | .35 | .35 |
| | | *Nos. 475-478 (4)* | 1.05 | 1.05 |

Paul Weiss-Haus Building, 1909, Luderitz — A99

Designs: Historic buildings in Luderitz.

**1981, Oct. 16**

| | | | | |
|---|---|---|---|---|
| **479** | A99 | 5c shown | .20 | .20 |
| **480** | A99 | 15c Deutsche Afrika Bank, 1906 | .25 | .25 |
| **481** | A99 | 20c Schroederhaus, 1911 | .35 | .35 |
| **482** | A99 | 25c Imperial P.O., 1908 | .45 | .45 |
| *a.* | | Souvenir sheet of 4, #479-482 | 1.40 | 1.40 |
| | | *Nos. 479-482 (4)* | 1.25 | 1.25 |

Salt Making A100

**1981, Dec. 4 Litho. *Perf. 14x14½***

**483** A100 5c Salt pan .20 .20
**484** A100 15c Dumping and washing .20 .20
**485** A100 20c Stockpiling .25 .25
**486** A100 25c Loading .35 .35
*Nos. 483-486 (4)* 1.00 1.00

Kalahari Starred Tortoise A101

**1982, Mar. 12**

**487** A101 5c shown .20 .20
**488** A101 15c Leopard tortoise .25 .25
**489** A101 20c Angulated tortoise .40 .40
**490** A101 25c Speckled padloper .50 .50
*Nos. 487-490 (4)* 1.35 1.35

Discoverers of South-West Africa — A102

**1982, May 28 Litho. *Perf. 14½x14***

**491** A102 15c Archbishop Olaus Magnus, sea monster .25 .25
**492** A102 20c Bartolomeu Dias, ships, map .45 .35
**493** A102 25c Caravel .70 .45
**494** A102 30c Dias erecting cross, Angra das Voltas .75 .55
*Nos. 491-494 (4)* 2.15 1.60

The Needle, Upper Brandberg A103

Designs: Mountain peaks.

**1982, Aug. 3 Litho. *Perf. 14x14½***

**495** A103 6c Brandberg .20 .20
**496** A103 15c Omatako twin peaks .20 .20
**497** A103 20c shown .25 .25
**498** A103 25c Spitzkuppe, Karakul sheep .35 .35
*Nos. 495-498 (4)* 1.00 1.00

Traditional Headdress, Herero Tribe — A104

**1982, Oct. 15 Litho. *Perf. 14x14½***

**499** A104 6c shown .20 .20
**500** A104 15c Himba .25 .25
**501** A104 20c Ngandjera .35 .35
**502** A104 25c Kwanyama .45 .45
*Nos. 499-502 (4)* 1.25 1.25

See Nos. 524-527.

Fort Vogelsang A105

Bethany Chief Joseph Fredericks — A106

***Perf. 14x14½ (6c, 25c), 14½x14 (20c, 30-40c)***

**1983, Mar. 16**

**503** A105 6c shown .20 .20
**504** A106 20c shown .30 .30
**505** A105 25c Angra Pequena Bay .40 .40
**506** A106 30c Explorer Heinrich Vogelsang .45 .45
**507** A106 40c Adolf Luderitz (1834-1886) .65 .65
*Nos. 503-507 (5)* 2.00 2.00

City of Luderitz centenary (1982).

Diamond Field, 1908 A107

Ernest Oppenheimer (1880-1957), Diamond Industry Leader — A108

***Perf. 14x14½ (10-20c), 14½x14 (25-40c)***

**1983, June 8 Litho.**

**508** A107 10c shown .20 .20
**509** A107 20c Field, diff. .40 .40
**510** A108 25c shown .50 .50
**511** A108 40c August Stauch, prospector .80 .80
*Nos. 508-511 (4)* 1.90 1.90

75th anniv. of discovery of diamonds at Luderitz.

Zebras Drinking, by J.J. van Ellinckhuijzen (b. 1940) — A109

Paintings: 20c, Rossing Mountain, by Herman H.-J. Henckert (b. 1906). 25c, Stampeding Buffalo, by Fritz Krampe (1913-1966). 40c, Erongo Mountains, by Johann Blatt (1905-1973).

**1983, Sept. 1 *Perf. 14x14½***

**512** A109 10c multicolored .20 .20
**513** A109 20c multicolored .35 .35
**514** A109 25c multicolored .45 .45
**515** A109 40c multicolored .70 .70
*Nos. 512-515 (4)* 1.70 1.70

Lobster Industry A110

**1983, Nov. 23 *Perf. 13½x14***

**516** A110 10c Lobsters .20 .20
**517** A110 20c Dinghies .35 .35
**518** A110 25c Raising trap .45 .45
**519** A110 40c Packaging .70 .70
*Nos. 516-519 (4)* 1.70 1.70

Historic Buildings, Swakopmund — A111

**1984, Mar. 8 Litho. *Perf. 14x13½***

**520** A111 10c Hohenzollern House .20 .20
**521** A111 20c Railway Station .40 .40
**522** A111 25c Imperial District Bureau .50 .50
**523** A111 30c Ritterburg .60 .60
*Nos. 520-523 (4)* 1.70 1.70

Headdress Type of 1982

**1984, May 25 Litho.**

**524** A104 11c Kwambi .20 .20
**525** A104 20c Bushman .40 .40
**526** A104 25c Kwaluudhi .50 .50
**527** A104 30c Mbukushu .60 .60
*Nos. 524-527 (4)* 1.70 1.70

German Colonization Centenary — A112

**1984, Aug. 7 Litho. *Perf. 13½x14***

**528** A112 11c Map, flag .25 .25
**529** A112 25c Flag raising .60 .60
**530** A112 30c Land marker .70 .70
**531** A112 45c Corvettes Elisabeth & Leipzig 1.40 1.40
*Nos. 528-531 (4)* 2.95 2.95

Spring Flowers — A113

**1984, Nov. 22 Litho. *Perf. 14½x14***

**532** A113 11c Sweet thorn .20 .20
**533** A113 25c Camel thorn .50 .50
**534** A113 30c Hook thorn .60 .60
**535** A113 45c Candle-pod acacia .90 .90
*Nos. 532-535 (4)* 2.20 2.20

Ostrich A114

**1985, Mar. 15**

**536** A114 11c Head of bird .25 .25
**537** A114 25c Female nesting .70 .70
**538** A114 30c Chick, eggs .80 .80
**539** A114 50c Male mating dance 1.40 1.40
*Nos. 536-539 (4)* 3.15 3.15

Historic Buildings, 1900-1912, Windhoek — A115

**1985, June 6**

**540** A115 12c Erkrath, Gathemann Buildings, Kaiser Street .20 .20
**541** A115 25c Gymnasium .35 .35
**542** A115 30c Supreme Court .45 .45
**543** A115 50c Railway Station .80 .80
*Nos. 540-543 (4)* 1.80 1.80

600mm Narrow-gauge Locomotives — A116

**1985, Aug. 2**

**544** A116 12c Zwilling Schmalspur, 1898 .35 .35
**545** A116 25c Feldspur Side-Tank .70 .70
**546** A116 30c 0-6-2 Side-Tank, 1904 .80 .80
**547** A116 50c Henschel hd Smalspoor, 1912 1.50 1.50
*Nos. 544-547 (4)* 3.35 3.35

Swakopmund-Tsumeb Railway line, 79th anniv.

Endemic Musical Instruments A117

**1985, Oct. 17**

**548** A117 12c Lidumu-dumu .20 .20
**549** A117 25c Ngoma .30 .30
**550** A117 30c Okambulum bumbwa .35 .35
**551** A117 50c Gwashi .60 .60
*Nos. 548-551 (4)* 1.45 1.45

Diogo Cao, Portuguese Explorer, 1486 Visit to SWA A118

**1986, Jan. 24 *Perf. 14½x14***

**552** A118 12c Erecting padroes on shore .30 .30
**553** A118 20c Cao coat of arms .55 .55
**554** A118 25c Caravel .70 .70
**555** A118 30c Portrait .90 .90
*Nos. 552-555 (4)* 2.45 2.45

Wildlife Type of 1980

**1986-87 Litho. *Perf. 14x14½***

**556** A95 14c Caracal, horiz. 4.00 4.00
**557** A95 16c Warthog, horiz. 2.50 2.50

Issue dates: 14c, Apr. 1; 16c, Apr. 1, 1987.

Rock Formations A119

Designs: 14c, Granite bornhardt, Erongo. 20c, Vingerklip, Outjo. 25c, Aeolian sandstone, Kuiseb River. 30c, Columnar dolerite, Twyfelfontein.

**1986, Apr. 24 *Perf. 14½x14***

**566** A119 14c multicolored .35 .35
**567** A119 20c multicolored .55 .55
**568** A119 25c multicolored .70 .70
**569** A119 30c multicolored 1.00 1.00
*Nos. 566-569 (4)* 2.60 2.60

Karakul Wool (Swakara) Industry — A120

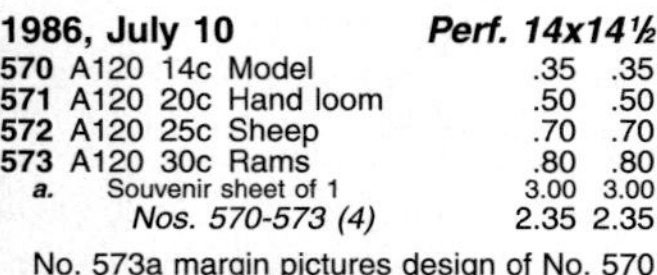

**1986, July 10** ***Perf. 14x14½***

**570** A120 14c Model .35 .35
**571** A120 20c Hand loom .50 .50
**572** A120 25c Sheep .70 .70
**573** A120 30c Rams .80 .80
*a.* Souvenir sheet of 1 3.00 3.00
*Nos. 570-573 (4)* 2.35 2.35

No. 573a margin pictures design of No. 570 and Johannesburg stamp exhib. emblem. Sold for 50c to benefit stamp exhib.

Caprivi Strip — A121

**1986, Nov. 6** **Litho.** ***Perf. 14½x14***

**574** A121 14c Lake Liambezi .35 .35
**575** A121 20c Stock and crop farming .55 .55
**576** A121 25c Settlement .70 .70
**577** A121 30c Map .90 .90
*Nos. 574-577 (4)* 2.50 2.50

Paintings by Thomas Baines (1820-1875) A122

Designs: 14c, *Rhenish Mission Church at Gababis,* 1863. 20c, *Outspan in October,* 1861. 25c, *Outspan Under Oomahaama Tree,* 1862. 30c, *Swa-Kop River S.W. Africa,* 1861.

**1987, Feb. 19** **Litho.** ***Perf. 14½x14***

**578** A122 14c multicolored .50 .50
**579** A122 20c multicolored .75 .75
**580** A122 25c multicolored .90 .90
*a.* Souvenir sheet of 1 2.75 2.75
**581** A122 30c multicolored 1.10 1.10
*Nos. 578-581 (4)* 3.25 3.25

No. 580a for the natl. philatelic exhibition at Paarl, Sept. 16-19. Sold for 50c.

Insects A123

**1987, May 7**

**582** A123 16c *Garreta nitens* .75 .75
**583** A123 20c *Alcimus stenurus* .90 .90
**584** A123 25c *Anthophora caerulea* 1.10 1.10
**585** A123 30c *Hemiempusa capensis* 1.25 1.25
*Nos. 582-585 (4)* 4.00 4.00

Resorts — A124

**1987, July 23**

**586** A124 16c Okaukuejo, Etosha Natl. Park .40 .40
**587** A124 20c Daan Viljoen Game Park .55 .55
**588** A124 25c Ai-Ais Hot Springs .65 .65
**589** A124 30c Hardap, Mariental .75 .75
*Nos. 586-589 (4)* 2.35 2.35

Shipwrecks A125

**1987, Oct. 15**

**590** A125 16c *Hope,* 1804 .50 .50
**591** A125 30c *Tilly,* 1885 1.10 1.10
**592** A125 40c *Eduard Bohlen,* 1909 1.40 1.40
**593** A125 50c *Dunedin Star,* 1942 1.75 1.75
*Nos. 590-593 (4)* 4.75 4.75

Discovery of the Cape of Good Hope by Bartolomeu Dias, 500th Anniv. — A126

**1988, Jan. 7** ***Perf. 14x14½***

**594** A126 16c shown .45 .45
**595** A126 30c Caravel .75 .75
**596** A126 40c The Cantino Map, 1502 1.10 1.10
**597** A126 50c King John II 1.40 1.40
*Nos. 594-597 (4)* 3.70 3.70

Historic Sites A127

**1988, Mar. 3** ***Perf. 14½x14***

**598** A127 16c Sossusvlei Clay Pans .40 .40
**599** A127 30c Sesriem Canyon .65 .65
**600** A127 40c Hoaruseb clay castles .90 .90
**601** A127 50c Hoba meteorite 1.50 1.50
*Nos. 598-601 (4)* 3.45 3.45

Postal Service, Cent. A128

**1988, July 7** ***Perf. 14x14½***

**602** A128 16c Otyimbingue P.O., 1888 .35 .35
**603** A128 30c Windhoek P.O., 1904 .70 .70
**604** A128 40c Mail runner, 1888 1.00 1.00
**605** A128 50c Camel post, 1904 1.25 1.25
*a.* Souvenir sheet of 1 3.75 3.75
*Nos. 602-605 (4)* 3.30 3.30

No. 605a for the natl. philatelic exhibition held at Windhoek, July 7-9. Sold for 1r.

Birds — A129

**1988, Nov. 3**

**606** A129 16c *Namibornis hereo* 1.00 1.00
**607** A129 30c *Ammomanes grayi* 1.50 1.50
**608** A129 40c *Eupodotis rueppelii* 1.75 1.75
**609** A129 50c *Tockus monteiri* 1.90 1.90
*Nos. 606-609 (4)* 6.15 6.15

Missionaries and Mission Stations — A130

16c, Carl Hahn (1818-95) & Gross-Barmen Mission. 30c, Johann Kronlein (1826-92) & Berseba Mission. 40c, Franz Kleinschmidt (1812-64) & Rehoboth Mission. 50c, Johann Schmelen (1777-1848) & Bethanien Mission.

**1989, Feb. 16**

**610** A130 16c multicolored .45 .45
**611** A130 30c multicolored .75 .75
**612** A130 40c multicolored 1.00 1.00
**613** A130 50c multicolored 1.40 1.40
*Nos. 610-613 (4)* 3.60 3.60

Aviation Industry, 75th Anniv. A131

Maps and aircraft.

**1989, May 18** ***Perf. 14½x14***

**614** A131 18c Beechcraft 1900 .75 .75
**615** A131 30c Ryan Navion, 1948 1.10 1.10
**616** A131 40c Junkers F13, 1930 1.40 1.40
**617** A131 50c Pfalz Otto biplane, 1914 2.00 2.00
*a.* Souvenir sheet of 1 4.50 4.50
*Nos. 614-617 (4)* 5.25 5.25

No. 617a has decorative bright blue and black inscribed margin picturing emblem of natl. philatelic exhibition WANDERERS 101, held Sept. 6-9. Sold for 1.50r.

Namib Desert Sand Dunes — A132

**1989, Aug. 14** ***Perf. 14x14½***
**Size of 30c, 50c: 31x21½mm**

**618** A132 18c Barchan dunes .30 .30
**619** A132 30c Star dunes .55 .55
**620** A132 40c Transverse dunes .75 .75
**621** A132 50c Crescent dunes .90 .90
*Nos. 618-621 (4)* 2.50 2.50

Suffrage, UN Resolution 435 — A133

**1989, Aug. 24**

**622** A133 18c dull org & gray vio .30 .30
**623** A133 35c green & blue .60 .60
**624** A133 45c yellow & purple .85 .85
**625** A133 60c golden brn & gray grn 1.25 1.25
*Nos. 622-625 (4)* 3.00 3.00

Minerals — A134

Mines A135

**1989-90** ***Perf. 14½x14***

**626** A134 1c Gypsum .20 .20
**627** A134 2c Fluorite .20 .20
**628** A134 5c Mimetite .20 .20
**629** A134 7c Cuprite .20 .20
**630** A134 10c Azurite .20 .20
**631** A134 18c Boltwoodite .30 .30
**631A** A134 18c see footnote *14.00* *8.00*
**632** A134 20c Dioptase .30 .30
**633** A135 25c Alluvial diamond field, Oranjemund .35 .35
**634** A135 30c Lead, copper & zinc mine, Tsumeb .40 .40
**635** A135 35c Zinc mine, Rosh Pinah .50 .50
**636** A134 40c Diamonds .55 .55
**637** A134 45c Wulfenite .65 .65
**638** A135 50c Tin mine, Uis .70 .70
**639** A135 1r Uranium mine, Rossing 1.50 1.50
**640** A134 2r Gold 3.00 3.00
*Nos. 626-640 (16)* *23.25* 17.25

#631 has formula, K(H3O)(UO2)(SiO4); #631A K2(UO2)2(SiO3)2(OH)2.5HO2O.

Issued: #631A, 10/25/90; others, 11/16/89.

This set remained in use until Namibia issued a definitive set Jan. 2, 1991.

Flora — A136

**1990, Feb. 1** ***Perf. 14½x14***

**641** A136 18c *Adenium boehmianum* .45 .45
**642** A136 35c *Adansonia digitata* .85 .85
**643** A136 45c *Kigelia africana* 1.10 1.10
**644** A136 60c *Harpagophytum procumbens* 1.40 1.40
*a.* Souvenir sheet of 1 2.50 2.50
*Nos. 641-644 (4)* 3.80 3.80

No. 644a margin publicizes the natl. phil. exhib. Sold for 1.50r.

---

## SEMI-POSTAL STAMPS

**Catalogue values for unused stamps in this section are for Never Hinged items.**

### Voortrekker Monument Issue

South Africa Nos. B1-B4 Overprinted

**1935-36** **Wmk. 201** ***Perf. 14***

**B1** SP1 ½p + ½p grn & blk, pair 3.00 *6.25*
*a.* Single, English .25 *.85*
*b.* Single, Afrikaans .25 *.85*
**B2** SP2 1p + ½p rose & blk, pair 4.00 3.75
*a.* Single, English .30 .45
*b.* Single, Afrikaans .30 .45
**B3** SP3 2p + 1p dl vio & gray, pair 13.00 7.00
*a.* Single, English .75 .90
*b.* Single, Afrikaans .75 .90
**B4** SP4 3p + 1½p dp bl & gray, pair 25.00 37.50
*a.* Single, English 1.50 *4.50*
*b.* Single, Afrikaans 1.50 *4.50*
*Nos. B1-B4 (4)* 45.00 54.50

### Voortrekker Centenary Issue

South Africa Nos. B5-B8 Overprinted

**1938, Dec. 14** ***Perf. 14***

**B5** SP5 ½p + ½p dl grn & indigo, pair 9.00 8.75
*a.* Single, English .75 1.25
*b.* Single, Afrikaans .75 1.25

***Perf. 15x14***

**B6** SP6 1p + 1p rose & sl, pair 20.00 13.00
*a.* Single, English .50 *1.00*
*b.* Single, Afrikaans .50 *1.00*
**B7** SP7 1½p + 1½p Prus grn & choc, pair 26.00 18.00
*a.* Single, English 1.25 2.50
*b.* Single, Afrikaans 1.25 2.50
**B8** SP8 3p + 3p chlky bl, pair 50.00 37.50
*a.* Single, English 2.75 5.00
*b.* Single, Afrikaans 2.75 5.00
*Nos. B5-B8 (4)* 105.00 77.25

Same Overprint on South Africa Nos. B9-B11

**1939, July 17** *Perf. 14*

**B9** SP9 ½p + ½p Prus grn & gray brn, pair 8.50 6.75
- *a.* Single, English .85 .85
- *b.* Single, Afrikaans .85 .85

**B10** SP10 1p + 1p rose car & Prus grn, pair 16.00 12.50
- *a.* Single, English 1.00 1.00
- *b.* Single, Afrikaans 1.00 1.00

*Perf. 15x14*

**B11** SP11 1½p + 1½p rose vio, dk vio & Prus grn, pair 28.00 20.00
- *a.* Single, English 1.25 1.25
- *b.* Single, Afrikaans 1.25 1.25

*Nos. B9-B11 (3)* 52.50 39.25

250th anniv. of the landing of the Huguenots in South Africa. Surtax went to a fund to build a Huguenot memorial at Paarl.

## AIR POST STAMPS

South Africa Nos. C5-C6 Overprinted

**1930** **Unwmk.** *Perf. 14x13½*

**C1** AP2 4p blue green 8.00 32.50
- *a.* Without period after "A" 80.00 150.00

**C2** AP2 1sh orange 12.50 57.50
- *a.* Without period after "A" 475.00 625.00

Overprinted

**C3** AP2 4p blue green 1.50 7.00
- *a.* Double overprint 200.00
- *b.* Inverted overprint 200.00
- *c.* Small "I" in "AIR" 6.00

**C4** AP2 1sh orange 4.25 17.50
- *a.* Double overprint 575.00

Monoplane over Windhoek — AP3

Biplane over Windhoek — AP4

**Wmk. 201**

**1931, Mar. 5** **Engr.** *Perf. 14*

**C5** AP3 3p blue & dk brn, pair 30.00 35.00
- *a.* Single, English 2.00 3.00
- *b.* Single, Afrikaans 2.00 3.00

**C6** AP4 10p brn vio & blk, pair 45.00 75.00
- *a.* Single, English 3.00 6.00
- *b.* Single, Afrikaans 3.00 6.00

## POSTAGE DUE STAMPS

Postage Due Stamps of South Africa and Transvaal Overprinted like Regular Issues.

Setting I

On South Africa Nos. J11, J14

**1923** **Unwmk.** *Perf. 14*

**J1** D1 ½p blue grn & blk, pair 5.00 15.00
- *a.* Single, English .35 4.00
- *b.* Single, Dutch .35 4.00
- *c.* As #J1, without period after "Afrika" 100.00
- *d.* Inverted ovpt., pair 325.00

**J2** D1 2p vio & blk, pair 3.00 20.00
- *a.* Single, English .20 4.00
- *b.* Single, Dutch .20 4.00
- *c.* As #J2, without period after "Afrika" 70.00 70.00

**On South Africa Nos. J9-J10**

*Rouletted 7-8*

**J3** D1 1p dull red & blk, pair 7.00 12.00
- *a.* Single, English .20 3.00
- *b.* Single, Dutch .20 3.00
- *c.* As #J3, without period after "Afrika" 70.00 70.00
- *d.* Pair, imperf. between 825.00

**J4** D1 1½p yel brn & blk, pair 1.00 8.00
- *a.* Single, English .20 1.75
- *b.* Single, Dutch .20 1.75
- *c.* As #J4, without period after "Afrika" 42.50 42.50

**On South Africa Nos. J3-J4, J6**

*Perf. 14*

**Wmk. 177**

**J5** D1 2p vio & blk, pair 17.00 27.50
- *a.* Single, English 1.75 7.50
- *b.* Single, Dutch 1.75 7.50
- *c.* As #J5, without period after "Afrika" 150.00

**J6** D1 3p ultra & blk, pair 9.00 27.50
- *a.* Single, English .85 7.50
- *b.* Single, Dutch .85 7.50

**J7** D1 6p gray & blk, pair 24.00 40.00
- *a.* Single, English 2.50 12.50
- *b.* Single, Dutch 2.50 12.50

*Nos. J5-J7 (3)* 50.00 95.00

**On Transvaal Nos. J5-J6**

**Wmk. Multiple Crown and C A (3)**

**J8** D1 5p vio & blk, pair 4.00 27.50
- *a.* Single, English .50 7.50
- *b.* Single, Dutch .50 7.50
- *c.* As #J8, without period after "Afrika" 85.00 85.00

**J9** D1 6p red brn & blk, pair 17.00 27.50
- *a.* Single, Dutch 1.75 7.50
- *b.* As #J9, without period after "Afrika" 140.00

For No. J9 single in English see No. J17a and note after No. 27.

The "t" of "West" may be found partly or entirely missing on Nos. J1, J3-J6, J8-J9.

**Setting II**

**On South Africa No. J9**

*Rouletted*

**Unwmk.**

**J10** D1 1p dull red & blk, pair 8,000.
- *a.* Single, English 800.00 —
- *b.* Single, Dutch 800.00 —

**On South Africa Nos. J3-J4**

*Perf. 14*

**Wmk. 177**

**J11** D1 2p vio & blk, pair 14.00 25.00
- *a.* Single, English 1.25 7.00
- *b.* Single, Dutch 1.25 7.00
- *c.* As #J11, without period after "Afrika" 110.00 125.00

**J12** D1 3p ultra & blk, pair 7.00 20.00
- *a.* Single, English .75 5.00
- *b.* Single, Dutch .75 5.00
- *c.* As #J12, without period after "Afrika" 70.00 80.00

**On Transvaal No. J5**

**Wmk. Multiple Crown and C A (3)**

**J13** D1 5p vio & blk, pair 75.00 140.00
- *a.* Single, English 15.00
- *b.* Single, Dutch 15.00

**Setting III**

**On South Africa Nos. J11, J12, J9**

**Unwmk.**

**J14** D1 ½p blue grn & blk, pair 7.00 17.50
- *a.* Single, Dutch .75 4.50

**J15** D1 1p rose & blk, pair 8.00 20.00
- *a.* Single, English .75 4.50
- *b.* Single, Dutch .75 4.50

*Rouletted 7*

**J16** D1 1p dull red & blk, pair 2.00 20.00
- *a.* Single, Dutch .20 4.00

For Nos. J14 and J16 singles in English see Nos. J1a and J3a and note after No. 27.

**On Transvaal No. J6**

*Perf. 14*

**Wmk. 3**

**J17** D1 6p red brown & blk, pair 17.00 60.00
- *a.* Single, English 1.75 17.50
- *b.* Single, Dutch 1.75 17.50

See note below No. 27.

Setting IV

On South Africa Nos. J11-J12, J16

**1924** **Unwmk.**

**J18** D1 ½p blue grn & blk, pair 3.50 20.00
- *a.* Single, English .45 5.00
- *b.* Single, Dutch .45 5.00

**J19** D1 1p rose & blk, pair 5.00 20.00
- *a.* Single, English .60 5.00
- *b.* Single, Dutch .60 5.00

**J20** D1 6p gray & blk, pair 2.25 27.50
- *a.* Single, English .30 8.00
- *b.* Single, Dutch .30 8.00

**On Transvaal No. J5**

**Wmk. Multiple Crown and C A (3)**

**J21** D1 5p violet & blk, pair 400.00 1,000.
- *a.* Single, English 100.00
- *b.* Single, Dutch 100.00

Setting V

i

j

"South West" 16mm wide
"Zuidwest" 12mm wide
Overprint Spaced 12mm

On South Africa Nos. J4, J11, J13

**1924** **Unwmk.**

**J22** D1 ½p green & blk, pair 2.00 22.50
- *a.* Single, English .25 6.50
- *b.* Single, Dutch .25 6.50

**J23** D1 1½p yel brown & blk 4.00 22.50
- *a.* Single, English .50 6.50
- *b.* Single, Dutch .50 6.50

**Wmk. Springbok's Head (177)**

**J24** D1 3p ultra & black, pair 12.50 37.50
- *a.* Single, English 1.40 10.00
- *b.* Single, Dutch 1.40 10.00

On Transvaal No. J5

**Wmk. Multiple Crown and C A (3)**

**J25** D1 5p violet & blk, pair 3.00 25.00
- *a.* Single, English .40 7.50
- *b.* Single, Dutch .40 7.50

Setting VI

On South Africa Nos. J4, J11-J16

**1924, Dec.** **Unwmk.**

**J26** D1 ½p blue grn & blk, pair 5.00 25.00
- *a.* Single, English .60 6.00
- *b.* Single, Dutch .60 6.00

**J27** D1 1p rose & blk, pair 1.50 7.50
- *a.* Single, English .20 1.75
- *b.* Single, Dutch .20 1.75
- *c.* As #J27, without period after "Africa" 87.50

**J28** D1 1½p yel brown & blk, pair 2.50 22.50
- *a.* Single, English .30 5.50
- *b.* Single, Dutch .30 5.50
- *c.* As #J28, without period after "Africa" 75.00

**J29** D1 2p vio & blk, pair 2.50 12.50
- *a.* Single, English .30 3.00
- *b.* Single, Dutch .30 3.00
- *c.* As #J29, without period after "Africa" 55.00

**J30** D1 3p bl & blk, pair 3.00 15.00
- *a.* Single, English .75 3.50
- *b.* Single, Dutch .75 3.50
- *c.* As #J30, without period after "Africa" 70.00

**J31** D1 6p gray & blk, pair 8.00 45.00
- *a.* Single, English 1.00 12.50
- *b.* Single, Dutch 1.00 12.50
- *c.* As #J31, without period after "Africa" 100.00

*Nos. J26-J31 (6)* 22.50 127.50

**Wmk. Springbok's Head (177)**

**J32** D1 3p ultra & black, pair 6.00 35.00
- *a.* Single, English .75 9.00
- *b.* Single, Dutch .75 9.00

On Transvaal No. J5

**Wmk. 3**

**J33** D1 5p violet & blk, pair 2.00 12.50
- *a.* Single, English .25 3.00
- *b.* Single, Dutch .25 3.00
- *c.* As #J33, without period after "Africa" 55.00 75.00

Setting VIII

On South Africa Nos. J18, J13-J16

**1927** **Unwmk.**

**J34** D2 1p rose & blk, pair .90 9.00
- *a.* Single, English .20 2.00
- *b.* Single, Afrikaans .20 2.00
- *c.* As #J34, without period after "Africa" 10.50 17.50

**J35** D1 1½p yel brown & blk, pair .90 10.00
- *a.* Single, English .20 2.50
- *b.* Single, Afrikaans .20 2.50
- *c.* As #J35, without period after "Africa" 50.00 60.00

**J36** D1 2p vio & blk, pair 2.50 12.50
- *a.* Single, English .30 3.25
- *b.* Single, Afrikaans .30 3.25
- *c.* As #J36, without period after "Africa" 50.00 60.00

**J37** D1 3p bl & blk, pair 10.00 40.00
- *a.* Single, English 1.25 10.00
- *b.* Single, Afrikaans 1.25 10.00
- *c.* As #J37, without period after "Africa" 70.00 70.00

**J38** D1 6p gray & blk, pair 7.50 27.50
- *a.* Single, English 1.00 8.00
- *b.* Single, Afrikaans 1.00 8.00
- *c.* As #J38, without period after "Africa" 100.00 115.00

*Nos. J34-J38 (5)* 21.80 99.00

On Transvaal No. J5

**Wmk. Multiple Crown and C A (3)**

**J39** D1 5p violet & blk, pair 16.00 75.00
- *a.* Single, English 1.75 20.00
- *b.* Single, Afrikaans 1.75 20.00

South Africa Nos. J15-J16 Overprinted

**1928** **Unwmk.**

**J79** D1 3p blue & black 1.65 12.00
- *a.* Without period after "A" 30.00 35.00

**J80** D1 6p gray & black 7.50 22.50
- *a.* Without period after "A" 125.00

**Same Overprint on South Africa Nos. J17-J21**

**J81** D2 ½p blue grn & blk .40 6.00

**J82** D2 1p rose & black .50 3.00
- *a.* Without period after "A" 40.00 45.00

**J83** D2 2p violet & black .65 3.75
- *a.* Without period after "A" 60.00

**J84** D2 3p ultra & black 1.50 17.50

**J85** D2 6p gray & black 1.75 15.00
- *a.* Without period after "A" 40.00 55.00

*Nos. J81-J85 (5)* 4.80 45.25

**Catalogue values for unused stamps in this section, from this point to the end of the section, are for Never Hinged items.**

D3

D4

**Wmk. 201**

**1931, Feb. 23** **Litho.** *Perf. 12*

**Size: 19x22mm**

**J86** D3 ½p yel green & blk .85 8.50

**J87** D3 1p rose & black .85 1.65

**J88** D3 2p violet & black .85 3.25

**J89** D3 3p blue & black 3.25 18.00

**J90** D3 6p gray & black 13.00 27.50

*Nos. J86-J90 (5)* 18.80 58.90

**Photo. (Frame) & Typo. (Center)**

**1959** *Perf. 14½x14*

**Size: 17x21mm**

**J91** D3 1p rose & black 2.00 13.00

**J92** D3 2p violet & black 2.00 13.00

**J93** D3 3p blue & black 2.00 14.50

*Nos. J91-J93 (3)* 6.00 40.50

**1960** **Wmk. 330**

**Size: 17x21mm**

**J94** D3 1p rose & black 3.50 4.00

**J95** D3 3p blue & black 3.50 5.50

**1961, Feb.** **Photo.** *Perf. 14½x14*

**J96** D4 1c green & black 1.00 4.25

**J97** D4 2c red & black 1.00 4.25

**J98** D4 4c lilac & black 1.00 4.25

**J99** D4 5c blue & black 1.60 5.25

**J100** D4 6c emerald & black 2.00 7.50

**J101** D4 10c yellow & black 4.00 9.50

*Nos. J96-J101 (6)* 10.60 35.00

Type of South Africa, 1972

**1972** **Wmk. 359** *Perf. 14x13½*

**J102** D6 1c bright green 1.00 3.75

**J103** D6 8c violet blue 3.75 7.25

## OFFICIAL STAMPS

Nos. 85-87 (Setting VIII) Overprinted at top with type "c" on English-inscribed Stamps and type "d" on Afrikaans-inscribed Stamps

c d

Without Periods after Words

**1927 Wmk. 201** ***Perf. 14½x14***

**O1** A5 ½p dk green & blk, pair 75.00 *175.00*
*a.* Single, English 9.00 *25.00*
*b.* Single, Afrikaans 9.00 *25.00*
**O2** A6 1p car & blk, pair 75.00 *175.00*
*a.* Single, English 9.00 *25.00*
*b.* Single, Afrikaans 9.00 *25.00*
**O3** A7 6p org & grn, pair 90.00 *175.00*
*a.* Single, English 9.50 *25.00*
*b.* Single, Afrikaans 9.50 *25.00*

**South Africa No. 5 Overprinted As Nos. 85-87 plus "c" and "d"**

***Perf. 14***

**Wmk. 177**

**O4** A2 2p dull violet 190.00 *275.00*
*a.* Single, English 22.50 *40.00*
*b.* Single, Afrikaans 22.50 *40.00*

Nos. 96-98 Overprinted like Nos. J79-J85 at foot, Overprinted Types "c" and "d" at Top

**1929 Wmk. 201** ***Perf. 14½x14***

**O5** A5 ½p green & blk, pair .85 *10.00*
*a.* Single, English .20 *2.50*
*b.* Single, Afrikaans .20 *2.50*
**O6** A6 1p car & blk, pair 1.00 *11.00*
*a.* Single, English .20 *2.50*
*b.* Single, Afrikaans .20 *2.50*
**O7** A7 6p org & grn, pair 3.75 *15.00*
*a.* Single, English .75 *3.50*
*b.* Single, Afrikaans .75 *3.50*
*Nos. O5-O7 (3)* 5.60 *36.00*

No. 99 Overprinted like Nos. J79-J85 at foot,
Overprinted at top

**OFFICIAL. OFFISIEEL.**

With Periods after Words

***Perf. 14***

**O8** A8 2p vio brn & gray, pair 2.50 *17.00*
*a.* Single, English .30 *3.75*
*b.* Single, Afrikaans .30 *3.75*
*c.* Without period after "OFFI-CIAL" 5.00 *30.00*
*d.* Pair, "c" + normal 2p 15.00 *80.00*
*e.* Without period after "OF-FISIEEL" 5.00 *30.00*
*f.* Pair, "e" + normal 2p 15.00 *80.00*
*g.* Pair, "c" + "e" 15.00 *80.00*

In each sheet of 120 stamps there were 12 No. O8c and 10 No. O8e.

South Africa Nos. 23-25 Overprinted

Without Periods after Words

**1929 Wmk. 201** ***Perf. 14½x14***

**O9** A5 ½p green & blk, pair .60 *11.00*
*a.* Single, English .20 *2.50*
*b.* Single, Afrikaans .20 *2.50*
**O10** A6 1p car & blk, pair .70 *11.00*
*a.* Single, English .20 *2.50*
*b.* Single, Afrikaans .20 *2.50*
**O11** A7 6p org & grn, pair 2.50 *25.00*
*a.* Single, English .30 *6.00*
*b.* Single, Afrikaans .30 *6.00*
*Nos. O9-O11 (3)* 3.80 *47.00*

South Africa No. 26 Overprinted

With Periods after Words

***Perf. 14***

**O12** A8 2p vio brn & gray, pair 1.00 *15.00*
*a.* Single, English .20 *3.50*
*b.* Single, Afrikaans .20 *3.50*
*c.* Without period after "OFFI-CIAL" 3.50 *35.00*
*d.* Pair, "c" + normal 2p 12.50 *70.00*
*e.* Without period after "OF-FISIEEL" 3.50 *35.00*
*f.* Pair, "e" + normal 2p 12.50 *70.00*
*g.* Pair, "c" + "e" 17.50 *80.00*

**Catalogue values for unused stamps in this section, from this point to the end of the section, are for Never Hinged items.**

Nos. 108-109, 111 and 114 Overprinted in Red

**OFFICIAL OFFISIEEL**

**1931**

**O13** A15 ½p green & blk, pair 8.50 *15.00*
*a.* Single, English 1.00 *3.50*
*b.* Single, Afrikaans 1.00 *3.50*
**O14** A16 1p red & indigo, pair .65 *15.00*
*a.* Single, English .20 *3.50*
*b.* Single, Afrikaans .20 *3.50*
**O15** A18 2p dk brn & dk bl, pair 1.00 *9.00*
*a.* Single, English .20 *2.00*
*b.* Single, Afrikaans .20 *2.00*
**O16** A21 6p ol brn & bl, pair 2.00 *13.00*
*a.* Single, English .25 *3.00*
*b.* Single, Afrikaans .25 *3.00*
*Nos. O13-O16 (4)* 12.15 *52.00*

No. 110 Overprinted in Red

**1938, July 1 Wmk. 201**

**O17** A17 1½p violet brn, pair 25.00 *35.00*
*a.* Single, English 2.75 *6.00*
*b.* Single, Afrikaans 2.75 *6.00*

Nos. 108-111, 114 Ovptd. in Red

**1945-50 Wmk. 201** ***Perf. 14x13½***

**O18** A15 ½p grn & blk, pair 8.00 *21.00*
*a.* Single, English 1.00 *4.25*
*b.* Single, Afrikaans 1.00 *4.25*
**O19** A16 1p red & ind, pair ('50) 2.00 *12.50*
*a.* Single, English .25 *3.00*
*b.* Single, Afrikaans .25 *3.00*
**O20** A17 1½p vio brn, pair 30.00 27.50
*a.* Single, English 5.00 5.00
*b.* Single, Afrikaans 5.00 5.00
**O21** A18 2p dk brn & dk bl, pair ('47) 425.00 *600.00*
*a.* Single, English 75.00 *100.00*
*b.* Single, Afrikaans 75.00 *100.00*
**O22** A21 6p ol brn & bl, pair 7.00 *27.50*
*a.* Single, English .80 *5.00*
*b.* Single, Afrikaans .80 *5.00*
*Nos. O18-O20,O22 (4)* 47.00 *88.50*

Nos. 108-111, 114 Ovptd. in Red

**1951-52**

**O23** A15 ½p grn & blk, pair ('52) 11.00 *15.00*
*a.* Single, English 1.25 *4.00*
*b.* Single, Afrikaans 1.25 *4.00*
**O24** A16 1p red & ind, pair 2.25 *9.00*
*a.* Single, English .30 *1.75*
*b.* Single, Afrikaans .30 *1.75*
*c.* Ovpt. transposed, pair 50.00 *82.50*
*d.* As "c," single, English ovpt. 10.00
*e.* As "c," single, Afrikaans ovpt. 10.00
**O25** A17 1½p violet brn, pair 22.50 22.50
*a.* Single, English 3.00 5.00
*b.* Single, Afrikaans 3.00 5.00
*c.* Ovpt. transposed, pair 60.00 75.00
*d.* As "c," single, English ovpt. 7.50
*e.* As "c," single, Afrikaans ovpt. 7.50
**O26** A18 2p dk brn & dk bl, pair 1.50 *13.00*
*a.* Single, English .20 *3.50*
*b.* Single, Afrikaans .20 *3.50*
*c.* Ovpt. transposed, pair 32.50 *90.00*
*d.* As "c," single, English ovpt. 4.50
*e.* As "c," single, Afrikaans ovpt. 4.50
**O27** A21 6p ol brn & blue, pair 2.75 *30.00*
*a.* Single, English .35 *7.00*
*b.* Single, Afrikaans .35 *7.00*
*c.* Ovpt. transposed, pair 20.00 *110.00*
*d.* As "c," single, English ovpt. 4.00
*e.* As "c," single, Afrikaans ovpt. 4.00
*Nos. O23-O27 (5)* 40.00 *89.50*

"Overprint transposed" means English inscription on Afrikaans stamp, or vice versa.

Use of official stamps ceased in Jan. 1955.

# SPAIN

ˈspān

LOCATION — Southwestern Europe, Iberian Peninsula
GOVT. — Monarchy
AREA — 194,884 sq. mi.
POP. — 39,167,744 (1999 est.)
CAPITAL — Madrid

Spain was a monarchy until about 1931, when a republic was established. After the Civil War (1936-39), the Spanish State of Gen. Francisco Franco was recognized. The monarchy was restored in 1975.

32 Maravedis = 8 Cuartos = 1 Real
1000 Milesimas = 100 Centimos = 1 Escudo (1866)
100 Milesimas = 1 Real
4 Reales = 1 Peseta
100 Centimos = 1 Peseta (1872)
100 Cents = 1 Euro (2002)

**Catalogue values for unused stamps in this country are for Never Hinged items, beginning with Scott 909 in the regular postage section, Scott B139 in the semi-postal section, Scott C159 in the airpost section, and Scott E21 in the special delivery section.**

## Watermarks

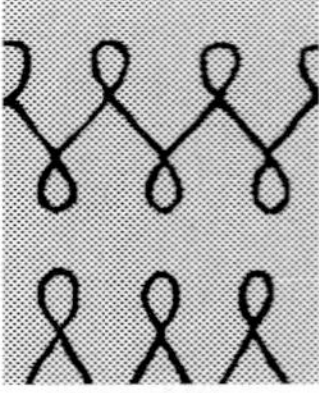
Wmk. 104 — Loops

Wmk. 105 — Crossed Lines

Wmk. 116 — Crosses and Circles

Wmk. 178 — Castle

Stamps punched with a small round hole have done telegraph service. In this condition most of them sell for 20 cents to $20.

Stamps of 1854 to 1882 canceled with three parallel horizontal bars or two thin lines are remainders. Most of these are valued through No. 101.

For additional shades see the *Scott Classic Catalogue*.

## Kingdom

Queen Isabella II
A1 A2

6 CUARTOS:
Type I — "T" and "O" of CUARTOS separated.
Type II — "T" and "O" joined.

**Unwmk.**

**1850, Jan. 1 — Litho. — *Imperf.***

| No. | Type | Description | Unused | Used |
|---|---|---|---|---|
| 1 | A1 | 6c blk, thin paper (II) | 675.00 | 15.00 |
| a. | | Thick paper (II) | 675.00 | 25.00 |
| b. | | Thick paper (I) | 800.00 | 20.00 |
| c. | | Thin paper (I) | 800.00 | 25.00 |
| 2 | A2 | 12c lilac | 2,300. | 260.00 |
| a. | | Thin paper | *3,200.* | 275.00 |
| 3 | A2 | 5r red | 2,300. | 250.00 |
| 4 | A2 | 6r blue | 3,000. | 725.00 |
| 5 | A2 | 10r green | 4,100. | 2,100. |

Stamps of types A2, A3, A4, A6, A7a and A8 are inscribed "FRANCO" on the cuarto values and "CERTIFICADO," "CERTIFO" or "CERT DO" on the reales values.

A3 A4

**1851, Jan. 1 — Typo.**

**Thin Paper**

| No. | Type | Description | Unused | Used |
|---|---|---|---|---|
| 6 | A3 | 6c black | 250.00 | 2.50 |
| a. | | Thick paper | 475.00 | 10.00 |
| 7 | A3 | 12c lilac | 4,250. | 140.00 |
| 8 | A3 | 2r red | *17,500.* | *9,500.* |
| 9 | A3 | 5r rose | 2,100. | 225.00 |
| a. | | 5r red brown (error) | *13,000.* | — |
| 10 | A3 | 6r blue | 3,600. | 900.00 |
| a. | | Cliche of 2r in plate of 6r | *125,000.* | *100,000.* |
| 11 | A3 | 10r green | 2,600. | 375.00 |

**1852, Jan. 1**

**Thick Paper**

| No. | Type | Description | Unused | Used |
|---|---|---|---|---|
| 12 | A4 | 6c rose | 350.00 | 2.25 |
| a. | | Thin paper | 400.00 | 3.50 |
| 13 | A4 | 12c lilac | 1,800. | 120.00 |
| 14 | A4 | 2r pale red | *15,000.* | *4,500.* |
| 15 | A4 | 5r yellowish green | 1,900. | 85.00 |
| 16 | A4 | 6r grnsh blue | *3,100.* | 375.00 |

Arms of Madrid — A5

Isabella II — A6

**1853, Jan. 1**

**Thin Paper**

| No. | Type | Description | Unused | Used |
|---|---|---|---|---|
| 17 | A5 | 1c bronze | 2,400. | 450.00 |
| 18 | A5 | 3c bronze | *12,500.* | *6,250.* |
| 19 | A6 | 6c carmine rose | 400.00 | 1.75 |
| a. | | Thick paper | 525.00 | 11.00 |
| b. | | Thick bluish paper | 775.00 | 16.00 |
| 20 | A6 | 12c red violet | 1,950. | 100.00 |
| 21 | A6 | 2r vermilion | *10,500.* | *2,750.* |
| 22 | A6 | 5r lt green | 2,200. | 85.00 |
| 23 | A6 | 6r deep blue | 3,000. | 325.00 |

Nos. 17-18 were issued for use on Madrid city mail only. *They were reprinted on this white paper in duller colors.*

A7

A7a

Coat of Arms of Spain — A8

**1854**

**Thin White Paper**

| No. | Type | Description | Unused | Used |
|---|---|---|---|---|
| 24 | A7 | 2c green | 2,650. | 400.00 |
| c. | | Thick paper | 1,750. | 425.00 |
| 25 | A7a | 4c carmine | 375.00 | 1.75 |
| a. | | Thick paper | 400.00 | 10.00 |
| 26 | A8 | 6c carmine | 275.00 | 1.40 |
| 27 | A7a | 1r indigo | 3,300. | 250.00 |
| | | Bar cancellation | | 12.00 |
| 28 | A8 | 2r scarlet | 1,400. | 90.00 |
| | | Bar cancellation | | 3.50 |
| c. | | Thick paper | — | 125.00 |
| 29 | A8 | 5r green | 1,325. | 90.00 |
| | | Bar cancellation | | 8.50 |
| 30 | A8 | 6r blue | 2,200. | 260.00 |
| | | Bar cancellation | | 12.50 |

See boxed note on bar cancellation before #1.

**Thick Bluish Paper**

| No. | Type | Description | Unused | Used |
|---|---|---|---|---|
| 31 | A7 | 2c green | *11,000.* | *1,700.* |
| b. | | Thin paper | *5,000.* | *1,300.* |
| 32 | A7a | 4c carmine | 350.00 | 4.75 |
| c. | | Thin paper | 250.00 | 8.50 |
| 32A | A8 | 6c carmine | 525.00 | 11.00 |
| d. | | Thin paper | — | 55.00 |
| 33 | A7a | 1r pale blue | | *6,500.* |
| | | Bar cancellation | | 100.00 |
| a. | | Thin paper | — | *6,000.* |
| 34 | A8 | 2r dull red | *4,500.* | 450.00 |
| a. | | Thin paper | *4,500.* | 450.00 |

The 2c with watermark 104 is a proof.

Isabella II — A9

**1855, Apr. 1 — Wmk. 104**

**Blue Paper**

| No. | Type | Description | Unused | Used |
|---|---|---|---|---|
| 36 | A9 | 2c green | *2,250.* | 100.00 |
| a. | | 2c yellow green | *2,350.* | 125.00 |
| | | Bar cancellation, #36 or 36a | | 6.00 |
| 37 | A9 | 4c brown red | 225.00 | .65 |
| a. | | 4c carmine | 240.00 | 1.40 |
| b. | | 4c lake | 240.00 | .90 |
| | | Bar cancellation, #37, 37a or 37b | | 1.50 |
| 38 | A9 | 1r green blue | 975.00 | 14.00 |
| a. | | 1r blue | 1,000. | 14.50 |
| | | Bar cancellation, #38 or 38a | | 3.00 |
| b. | | Cliché of 2r in plate of 1r | *13,000.* | *2,000.* |
| | | Bar cancellation | | 500.00 |
| 39 | A9 | 2r reddish violet | 725.00 | 12.50 |
| a. | | 2r deep violet | 750.00 | 13.00 |
| | | Bar cancellation | | 2.25 |

**1856, Jan. 1 — Wmk. 105**

**Rough Yellowish Paper**

| No. | Type | Description | Unused | Used |
|---|---|---|---|---|
| 40 | A9 | 2c green | *2,750.* | 200.00 |
| | | Bar cancellation | | 8.50 |
| 41 | A9 | 4c rose | 7.25 | 1.75 |
| | | Bar cancellation | | 1.50 |
| 42 | A9 | 1r grnsh blue | *2,900.* | 160.00 |
| a. | | 1r dull blue | *3,400.* | 180.00 |
| | | Bar cancellation, #42 or 42a | | 5.00 |
| 43 | A9 | 2r brown violet | 425.00 | 20.00 |
| a. | | 2r dark reddish violet | 450.00 | 30.00 |
| | | Bar cancellation, #43 or 43a | | 5.00 |

**1856, Apr. 11 — Unwmk.**

**White Smooth Paper**

| No. | Type | Description | Unused | Used |
|---|---|---|---|---|
| 44 | A9 | 2c blue green | 450.00 | 35.00 |
| a. | | 2c yellow green | 475.00 | 37.50 |
| | | Bar cancellation, #44 or 44a | | 5.00 |
| 45 | A9 | 4c rose | 3.75 | .30 |
| a. | | 4c carmine | 25.00 | 17.50 |
| 46 | A9 | 1r blue | 17.50 | 19.00 |
| a. | | 1r pale greenish blue | 19.00 | 20.00 |
| | | Bar cancellation, #46 or 46a | | 2.25 |
| 47 | A9 | 2r brown lilac | 57.50 | 21.00 |
| a. | | 2r dull lilac | 65.00 | 22.50 |
| | | Bar cancellation, #47 or 47a | | 4.75 |

Three types of No. 45.

**1859**

| No. | Type | Description | Unused | Used |
|---|---|---|---|---|
| 48 | A9 | 12c dark orange | 137.50 | |
| | | Bar cancellation | | 30.00 |

No. 48 was never put in use. *Reprints exist.*

A10

A11

**1860-61**

**Tinted Paper**

| No. | Type | Description | Unused | Used |
|---|---|---|---|---|
| 49 | A10 | 2c green, *grn* | 275.00 | 17.50 |
| | | Bar cancellation | | 2.00 |
| 50 | A10 | 4c orange, *grn* | 30.00 | .65 |
| 51 | A10 | 12c car, *buff* | 290.00 | 11.00 |
| | | Bar cancellation | | 2.25 |
| 52 | A10 | 19c brn, *buff* ('61) | 2,400. | 1,100. |
| 53 | A10 | 1r blue, *grn* | 260.00 | 11.00 |
| | | Bar cancellation | | 2.25 |
| 54 | A10 | 2r lilac, *lil* | 325.00 | 9.00 |
| | | Bar cancellation | | 2.00 |

**1862, July 16**

| No. | Type | Description | Unused | Used |
|---|---|---|---|---|
| 55 | A11 | 2c dp bl, *yel* | 27.50 | 9.00 |
| 56 | A11 | 4c dk brn, *redsh buff* | 1.90 | .50 |
| a. | | 4c brown, *white* | 17.50 | 5.00 |
| 57 | A11 | 12c blue, *pnksh* | 37.50 | 7.50 |
| | | Bar cancellation | | 2.25 |
| 58 | A11 | 19c car, *lil* | 160.00 | 200.00 |
| a. | | 19c carmine, *white* | 225.00 | 210.00 |
| 59 | A11 | 1r brown, *yel* | 50.00 | 17.50 |
| | | Bar cancellation | | 2.50 |
| 60 | A11 | 2r green, *pnksh* | 29.00 | 11.00 |
| | | Bar cancellation | | 2.25 |
| | | *Nos. 55-60 (6)* | 305.90 | 245.50 |

A12

A13

**1864, Jan. 1**

| No. | Type | Description | Unused | Used |
|---|---|---|---|---|
| 61 | A12 | 2c dk bl, *lil* | 37.50 | 16.00 |
| 62 | A12 | 4c rose, *redsh buff* | 2.00 | .60 |
| a. | | 4c carmine, *reddish buff* | 12.50 | 4.00 |
| 63 | A12 | 12c green, *pnksh* | 37.50 | 9.50 |
| 64 | A12 | 19c violet, *pnksh* | 160.00 | 160.00 |
| 65 | A12 | 1r brown, *grn* | 145.00 | 57.50 |
| | | Bar cancellation | | 3.00 |
| 66 | A12 | 2r bl, *pnksh* | 37.50 | 9.50 |
| | | Bar cancellation | | 2.50 |
| | | *Nos. 61-66 (6)* | 419.50 | 253.10 |

**1865, Jan. 1 Litho. *Imperf.***

**67** A13 2c rose 250.00 25.00
**68** A13 4c blue *2,400.*
**69** A13 12c blue & rose 325.00 17.50
Bar cancellation 4.50
*a.* Frame inverted *13,500.* 900.00
**70** A13 19c brown & rose 1,200. 600.00
Bar cancellation 60.00
**71** A13 1r yellow grn 350.00 45.00
Bar cancellation 17.50
**72** A13 2r red lilac 350.00 25.00
Bar cancellation 16.00
**73** A13 2r rose 375.00 55.00
Bar cancellation 8.50
*a.* 2r salmon 350.00 57.50
Bar cancellation 12.50

No. 68 is without gum and was never put into use.

A majority of the perforated stamps from 1865 to about 1950 are rather poorly centered. The very fine examples that are valued will be fairly well centered. Poorly centered stamps sell for less. Stamps of some issues are almost always badly centered, and our values will be for examples with fine centering. Such issues will be noted.

**1865, Jan. 1 *Perf. 14***

**74** A13 2c rose red 450.00 90.00
Bar cancellation 8.50
**75** A13 4c blue 32.50 .65
**76** A13 12c blue & rose 450.00 47.50
Bar cancellation 7.00
*a.* Frame inverted *16,500.* *1,650.*
As "a," bar cancel 50.00
**77** A13 19c brown & rose *3,250.* *1,750.*
**78** A13 1r yellow grn 1,300. 400.00
Bar cancellation 17.50
**79** A13 2r violet 1,000. 175.00
Bar cancellation 16.00
**80** A13 2r rose 1,100. 250.00
*a.* 2r salmon 1,100. 250.00
*b.* 2r dull orange 1,100. 250.00
Bar cancellation 22.50

Values for Nos. 74-80 are for stamps with perforations touching the frame on at least one side.

A14

A14a

**1866, Jan. 1**

**81** A14 2c rose 170.00 22.50
Bar cancellation 3.50
**82** A14 4c blue 32.50 .65
Bar cancellation 3.50
**83** A14 12c orange 185.00 9.50
*a.* 12c orange yellow 275.00 19.00
**84** A14 19c brown 850.00 325.00
Bar cancellation 25.00
*Nos. 81-84 (4)* 1,237. 357.65

**1866**

**85** A14 10c green 225.00 19.00
Bar cancellation 3.00
**86** A14 20c lilac 150.00 15.00
Bar cancellation 3.00
**87** A14a 20c dull lilac 850.00 57.50
Bar cancellation 2.25
*Nos. 85-87 (3)* 1,225. 91.50

For the Type A14a 20c in green, see Cuba No. 25.

A15

A15a

A15b

A15c

**1867-68**

**88** A15 2c yellow brown 375.00 37.50
**89** A15a 4c blue 27.50 1.00
**90** A15b 12c orange yellow 190.00 7.75
*a.* 12c dark orange 250.00 12.00
*b.* 12c red orange ('68) 850.00 37.50
**91** A15c 19c rose 1,100. 425.00
Bar cancellation 22.50

See Nos. 100-102. For overprints see Nos. 114a-115a, 124-128, 124a-128a, 124c-124c, 124e-126e.

A15d

A15e

**92** A15d 10c blue green 250.00 20.00
Bar cancellation 2.50
**93** A15e 20c lilac 130.00 8.75
Bar cancellation 2.50

For overprints see Nos. 116-117, 116a-117a, 116c-117c, 117d, 117e, 117f.

A16

A17

A18

A19

**94** A16 5m green 42.50 17.00
Bar cancellation 2.50
**95** A17 10m brown 42.50 17.00
*a.* Tête bêche pair *16,500.*
**96** A18 25m blue & rose 225.00 20.00
*a.* Frame inverted *16,000.*
Bar cancellation 5.00
**97** A18 50m bister brown 20.00 .75
*Nos. 94-97 (4)* 330.00 54.75

See No. 98. For overprints see Nos. 118-122, 118a-122a, 120c-122c, 122d, 120e, 122e, 119f, 122f.

**1868-69**

**98** A18 25m blue 250.00 15.00
Bar cancellation 3.50
**99** A19 50m violet 25.00 .60
**100** A15b 100m brown 525.00 65.00
Bar cancellation 2.50
**101** A15c 200m green 190.00 14.00
Bar cancellation 2.50
**102** A15c 19c brown 2,250. 500.00

For overprints see Nos. 123, 123a, 123c, 123e.

**Provisional Government**

Excellent counterfeits exist of the provisional and provincial overprints.

**For Madrid**

Regular Issues Handstamped in Black

**1868-69**

**116** A15d 10c green 22.50 14.50
**117** A15e 20c lilac 19.00 11.00
**118** A16 5m green 14.50 5.00
**119** A17 10m brown 11.00 5.00
**120** A18 25m blue & rose 32.50 13.00
**121** A18 25m blue 32.50 11.00
**122** A18 50m bister brown 6.50 4.50
**123** A19 50m violet 6.50 4.50
**124** A15b 100m brown 65.00 26.00
**125** A15c 200m green 22.50 8.25
**126** A15b 12c orange 45.00 15.00
**127** A15c 19c rose 300.00 125.00
**128** A15c 19c brown 650.00 150.00
*Nos. 116-128 (13)* 1,227. 392.75

Nos. 116-128 exist with handstamp in blue, a few in red. These sell for more.

**For Andalusian Provinces**

Regular Issues Handstamped Vertically in Blue

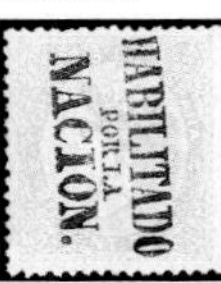


*114a* A15 2c brown 65.00 32.50
*115a* A15a 4c blue 30.00 22.50
*116a* A15d 10c green 32.50 13.00
*117a* A15e 20c lilac 25.00 14.00
*118a* A16 5m green 17.00 7.25
*119a* A17 10m brown 11.50 5.00
*120a* A18 25m blue & rose 37.50 13.00
*b.* Frame inverted *22,000.*
*121a* A18 25m blue 37.50 14.00
*122a* A18 50m bister brown 8.25 5.00
*123a* A19 50m violet 8.25 5.00
*124a* A15b 100m brown 82.50 30.00
*125a* A15c 200m green 27.50 11.00
*126a* A15b 12c orange yel 30.00 12.00
*127a* A15c 19c rose 375.00 190.00
*128a* A15c 19c brown 700.00 250.00
*Nos. 114a-128a (15)* 1,487. 624.25

**For Valladolid Province**

Regular Issues Handstamped in Black

**(Two types of overprint)**

*116c* A15d 10c green 35.00 15.00
*117c* A15e 20c lilac 32.50 16.00
*120c* A18 25m blue & rose 50.00 13.00
*121c* A18 25m blue 50.00 19.00
*122c* A18 50m bister brown 13.00 8.25
*123c* A19 50m violet 13.00 6.50
*124c* A15b 100m brown 100.00 32.50
*125c* A15c 200m green 32.50 13.00
*126c* A15b 12c orange 35.00 11.50
*127c* A15c 19c rose *325.00* *160.00*
*128c* A15c 19c brown *850.00* *210.00*
*Nos. 116c-126c (9)* 361.00 134.75

**For Asturias Province**

Regular Issues Handstamped in Black

***Habilitado por la Junta Revolucionaria***

*117d* A15e 20c lilac 160.00 110.00
*122d* A18 50m bister brown 175.00 110.00

**For Teruel Province**

Regular Issues Handstamped in Black

*117e* A15e 20c lilac 65.00 50.00
*120e* A18 25m blue & rose 82.50 50.00
*122e* A18 50m bister brown 60.00 30.00
*123e* A19 50m violet 60.00 30.00
*124e* A15b 100m brown 140.00 65.00
*125e* A15c 200m green 100.00 40.00
*126e* A15b 12c orange 82.50 55.00
*Nos. 117e-126e (7)* 590.00 320.00

**For Salamanca Province**

Regular Issues Handstamped in Blue

*117f* A15e 20c lilac 65.00 50.00
*119f* A17 10m brown 60.00 37.50
*122f* A18 50m bister brown 65.00 45.00
*Nos. 117f-122f (3)* 190.00 132.50

**Duke de la Torre Regency**

"España" — A20

**1870, Jan. 1 Typo.**

**159** A20 1m brn lil, *buff* 6.50 6.50
Bar cancellation 2.00
*b.* 1m brown lilac, *pinkish buff* 7.00 7.75
**161** A20 2m blk, *pinkish* 7.75 8.00
*a.* 2m black, *buff* 8.75 9.00

**163** A20 4m bister brn 15.00 13.50
**164** A20 10m rose 17.00 6.00
*a.* 10m carmine 21.00 7.50
**165** A20 25m lilac 52.50 6.50
Bar cancellation 2.00
*a.* 25m gray lilac 55.00 6.50
*b.* 25m aniline violet 85.00 8.25
**166** A20 50m ultra 10.00 .35
*a.* 50m dull blue 125.00 5.00
**167** A20 100m red brown 29.00 5.25
Bar cancellation 2.00
*a.* 100m claret 30.00 6.25
*b.* 100m orange brown 30.00 5.50
**168** A20 200m pale brn 27.50 5.25
Bar cancellation 2.00
**169** A20 400m green 250.00 22.50
Bar cancellation 3.00
**170** A20 1e600m dull lilac 1,350. 850.00
Bar cancellation 22.50
**171** A20 2e blue 1,100. 525.00
Bar cancellation 27.50
**172** A20 12c red brown 225.00 6.50
**173** A20 19c yel grn 300.00 160.00

The 12c carmine rose and 12c blue on pink paper were never put into use. Value, $1,350.

**Kingdom**

A21

A22

King Amadeo

A23 A24

**1872, Oct. 1 *Imperf.***

**174** A21 ¼c ultra 2.25 2.25
*a.* Complete 1c (block of 4 ¼c) 100.00 82.50
*b.* As "a," one cliche inverted 1,800. *1,750.*

See No. 221A.

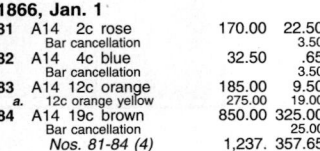

**1872-73** *Perf. 14*

**176** A22 2c gray lilac 17.50 7.75
*a.* 2c violet 27.50 17.00
*b.* Imperf. 70.00
**177** A22 5c green 125.00 60.00
*a.* Imperf. 160.00
**178** A23 5c rose ('73) 20.00 5.50
**179** A23 6c blue 120.00 37.50
**180** A23 10c brown lilac 350.00 225.00
**181** A23 10c ultra ('73) 7.50 .50
**182** A23 12c gray lilac 17.50 2.10
Bar cancellation 2.00
**183** A23 20c gray vio ('73) 140.00 82.50
Bar cancellation 5.00
**184** A23 25c brown 70.00 11.50
Bar cancellation 2.00
**185** A23 40c pale red brn 62.50 10.00
Bar cancellation 2.00
**186** A23 50c deep green 100.00 10.50
Bar cancellation 2.00
**187** A24 1p lilac 100.00 52.50
Bar cancellation 3.25
**188** A24 4p red brown 625.00 600.00
Bar cancellation 7.50
**189** A24 10p deep green 2,200. 2,300.
Bar cancellation 250.00

### First Republic

Mural Crown A25

"España" A26

**1873, July 1** *Imperf.*

**190** A25 ¼c green 1.00 1.00
*a.* Complete 1c (block of 4 ¼c) 37.50 19.00
As "a," bar cancellation 2.50
*d.* As "a," ultra (error) 190.00 160.00

**1873, July 1** *Perf. 14*

**191** A26 2c orange 13.00 6.00
**192** A26 5c claret 29.00 6.00
Bar cancellation 2.00
**193** A26 10c green 6.50 .35
Bar cancellation 2.00
*a.* Tête bêche pair 32,500.
**194** A26 20c black 80.00 22.50
Bar cancellation 3.75
**195** A26 25c deep brown 30.00 6.00
Bar cancellation 2.00
**196** A26 40c brown vio 32.50 6.00
Bar cancellation 2.00
**197** A26 50c ultra 16.50 6.75
Bar cancellation 2.00
**198** A26 1p lilac 52.50 30.00
Bar cancellation 2.00
**199** A26 4p red brown 575.00 475.00
Bar cancellation 12.50
**200** A26 10p violet brn 1,750. 1,750.
Bar cancellation 13.50

Only one example of No. 193a is known, and it is in a block of six stamps.

"Justice" A27

Coat of Arms A28

**1874, July 1**

**201** A27 2c yellow 17.50 8.00
Bar cancellation 2.00
**202** A27 5c violet 32.50 9.50
Bar cancellation 2.00
*a.* 5c red violet 30.00 9.50
**203** A27 10c ultra 9.75 .35
*a.* Imperf. 12.00
**204** A27 20c dark green 140.00 42.50
Bar cancellation 3.75
**205** A27 25c red brown 30.00 6.50
Bar cancellation 2.00
*a.* 25c lilac (error) 300.00 —
Bar cancellation 27.50
*b.* Imperf. 55.00
**206** A27 40c violet 300.00 7.50
Bar cancellation 2.00
*a.* 40c brown (error) 225.00 —
*b.* Imperf. 175.00
**207** A27 50c yellow 95.00 7.75
Bar cancellation 2.00
*a.* Imperf. 110.00
**208** A27 1p yellow green 75.00 32.50
Bar cancellation 2.00
*a.* 1p emerald 85.00 45.00
*b.* Imperf. 160.00
**209** A27 4p rose 625.00 390.00
Bar cancellation 7.50
*a.* 4p carmine 725.00 575.00
**210** A27 10p black 2,750. 1,800.
Bar cancellation 10.00

**1874, Oct. 1**

**211** A28 10c red brown 22.50 .65
Bar cancellation 1.50
*a.* 10c brown 37.50 3.25
*b.* Imperf. 75.00

### Kingdom

Nos. 212-221 are almost always badly centered and are often irregularly perforated. Values are for stamps with complete perforations and fine centering. Sound stamps with average centering are worth about 50% of these values. Stamps with very fine centering sell for more.

King Alfonso XII — A29

**1875, Aug. 1**

**Blue Framed Numbers on Back, 1-100 on Each Sheet**

**212** A29 2c orange brown 22.50 11.00
*a.* 2c chocolate brown 30.00 15.00
*b.* Imperf. 45.00 45.00
**213** A29 5c lilac 77.50 13.00
*a.* Imperf. 87.50 87.50
**214** A29 10c blue 9.25 .40
Bar cancellation 1.90
*a.* Imperf. 22.50 22.50
**215** A29 20c brown orange 275.00 125.00
**216** A29 25c rose 65.00 8.00
Bar cancellation 1.90
**217** A29 40c deep brown 125.00 37.50
Bar cancellation 4.50
*a.* Imperf. 140.00 140.00
**218** A29 50c gray lilac 175.00 42.50
Bar cancellation 5.25
**219** A29 1p black 190.00 80.00
Bar cancellation 3.00
**220** A29 4p dark green 475.00 525.00
**221** A29 10p ultra 1,500. 1,750.

**1876, June 1** *Imperf.*

**221A** A21 ¼c green .25 .20
*b.* Complete 1c (block 4 ¼c) 1.10 .30
*c.* As "b," two ¼c sideways, one invtd. 110.00 110.00
*d.* As "b," both upper ¼c invtd. 140.00 140.00
*e.* As "b," upper left ¼c invtd. 1,000. 500.00
*f.* As "b," both lower ¼c invtd. 140.00 140.00

No. 221Ac has one stamp upright, one inverted, one facing right and one facing left.

Nos. 222-230 are almost always badly centered. Values are for stamps with fine centering, fresh color and, in the case of mint stamps, full original gum. Sound stamps with average centering are worth about 50% of these values. Stamps with very fine centering sell for more.

King Alfonso XII
A30 A31

ONE PESETA:
Type I — Thin figures of value and "PESETA" in thick letters.
Type II — Thick figures of value and "PESETA" in thin letters.

**Wmk. 178**

**1876, June 1** **Engr.** *Perf. 14*

**222** A30 5c yellow brown 14.00 3.75
**223** A30 10c blue 3.75 .45
**224** A30 20c bronze green 17.50 13.00
**225** A30 25c brown 7.75 5.50
**226** A30 40c black brown 75.00 100.00
**227** A30 50c green 15.00 6.75
**228** A30 1p dp blue, I 20.00 9.00
*a.* 1p ultra, II 27.50 13.00
**229** A30 4p brown violet 47.50 55.00
**230** A30 10p vermilion 125.00 125.00
*Nos. 222-230 (9)* 325.50 318.45

***Imperf***

| | | | |
|---|---|---|---|
| *222a* | A30 | 5c | 11.00 |
| *223a* | A30 | 10c | 5.50 |
| *225a* | A30 | 25c | 12.00 |
| *227a* | A30 | 50c | 17.00 |
| *228b* | A30 | 1p | 25.00 |
| *229a* | A30 | 4p | 87.50 |
| *230a* | A30 | 10p | 190.00 |

Two plates each were used for the 5c, 10c, 25c, 50c, 1p and 10p. The 1p plates are most easily distinguished.

The 20c value also exists imperf. Value $500.

**Unwmk.**

**1878, July 1** **Typo.** *Perf. 14*

**232** A31 2c mauve 32.50 11.00
*a.* Imperf. 60.00
**233** A31 5c orange 40.00 14.00
**234** A31 10c brown 7.75 .50
Bar cancellation 3.00
**235** A31 20c black 160.00 125.00
*a.* Imperf. 275.00
**236** A31 25c olive bister 22.50 2.75
Bar cancellation 6.25
**237** A31 40c red brown 150.00 140.00
**238** A31 50c blue green 87.50 11.00
Bar cancellation 2.00
**239** A31 1p gray 72.50 21.00
Bar cancellation 2.00
**240** A31 4p violet 190.00 125.00
**241** A31 10p blue 375.00 350.00
*a.* Imperf. 450.00
*Nos. 232-241 (10)* 1,137. 800.25

A32 A33

**1879, May 1**

**242** A32 2c black 8.25 4.50
Bar cancellation 3.00
**243** A32 5c gray green 14.00 1.10
Bar cancellation 3.00
**244** A32 10c rose 13.50 .45
Bar cancellation 2.00
**245** A32 20c red brown 110.00 15.00
Bar cancellation 2.00
**246** A32 25c bluish gray 14.00 .45
Bar cancellation 2.00
**247** A32 40c brown 26.00 5.50
Bar cancellation 2.00
**248** A32 50c dull buff 100.00 5.00
Bar cancellation 2.00
*a.* 50c yellow 170.00 7.00
**249** A32 1p brt rose 125.00 2.25
Bar cancellation 2.00
**250** A32 4p lilac gray 575.00 32.50
Bar cancellation 3.00
**251** A32 10p olive bister 1,650. 175.00
Bar cancellation 6.25

**1882, Jan. 1**

**252** A33 15c salmon 7.75 .20
Bar cancellation 2.00
*a.* 15c reddish orange 27.50 .45
**253** A33 30c red lilac 310.00 5.25
Bar cancellation 2.00
**254** A33 75c gray lilac 210.00 4.75
Bar cancellation 2.00
*a.* Imperf. 300.00

Nos. 255-270 are usually poorly centered and often exhibit defective perforations. Values are for fine to very fine examples, well centered but not very fine, fresh and without perforation faults. Average copies sell for about half these values.

King Alfonso XIII
A34 A35

**1889-99**

**255** A34 2c blue green 6.00 .45
**256** A34 2c black ('99) 35.00 7.25
**257** A34 5c blue 11.00 .20
**258** A34 5c blue grn ('99) 125.00 1.40
**259** A34 10c yellow brown 13.00 .20
**260** A34 10c red ('99) 225.00 4.50
**261** A34 15c violet brown 4.75 .20
**262** A34 20c yellow green 45.00 4.75
**263** A34 25c blue 17.50 .20
**264** A34 30c olive gray 72.50 5.25
**265** A34 40c brown 72.50 3.00
**266** A34 50c rose 70.00 2.10
**267** A34 75c orange 210.00 4.25
**268** A34 1p dark violet 55.00 .45
*a.* 1p carmine rose (error) 350.00
**269** A34 4p carmine rose 650.00 47.50
**270** A34 10p orange red 1,050. 110.00

The 15c yellow, type A34 is an official stamp listed as No. O9.

Several values exist imperf.

Nos. 272-286 are almost always badly centered. Values are for stamps with fine centering, fresh color and, if unused, full original gum. Sound stamps with average centering sell for about half these values. Very fine copies sell for more.

Control Number on Back

**1900-05** **Engr.** **Unwmk.**

**272** A35 2c bister brown 3.25 .20
**273** A35 5c dark green 5.75 .20
**274** A35 10c rose red 8.75 .20
**275** A35 15c blue black 14.00 .20
**276** A35 15c dull lilac ('02) 10.50 .20
**277** A35 15c purple ('05) 5.75 .20
**278** A35 20c grnsh black 32.50 2.75
**279** A35 25c blue 5.25 .40
**280** A35 30c deep green 37.50 .35
**281** A35 40c olive bister 125.00 5.00
**282** A35 40c rose ('05) 300.00 4.50
**283** A35 50c slate blue 32.50 .55
**284** A35 1p lake 30.00 .80
**285** A35 4p dk violet 250.00 22.50
**286** A35 10p brown orange 225.00 72.50
*Nos. 272-286 (15)* 1,085. 110.55
Set, never hinged 1,650.

There are numerous shades and unissued colors for this issue.

***Imperf***

| | | | |
|---|---|---|---|
| *272a* | A35 | 2c | 57.50 |
| *273a* | A35 | 5c | 25.00 |
| *274a* | A35 | 10c | 25.00 |
| *275a* | A35 | 15c | 110.00 |
| *276a* | A35 | 15c | 22.50 |
| *277a* | A35 | 15c | 17.00 |
| *278a* | A35 | 20c | 90.00 |
| *279a* | A35 | 25c | 17.00 |
| *280b* | A35 | 30c | 110.00 |
| *282a* | A35 | 40c | 300.00 |
| *283a* | A35 | 50c | 125.00 |
| *284a* | A35 | 1p | 57.50 |
| *285a* | A35 | 4p | 200.00 |
| *286a* | A35 | 10p | 190.00 |

The 15c in red brown (value $700), 30c blue ($900), 1p olive ($800), 1p blue green ($750) and 1p dark violet ($750) were prepared but not issued.

Nos. 287-296 are almost always badly centered. Values are for stamps with fine centering, fresh color and, if unused, full original gum. Sound stamps with average centering sell for about half these values. Very fine copies sell for more.

Don Quixote Starts Forth A36

10c, Don Quixote attacks windmill. 15c, Meets country girls. 25c, Sancho Panza tossed in blanket. 30c, Don Quixote knighted. 40c, Tilting at sheep. 50c, On Wooden horse. 1p, Adventure with lions. 4p, In bullock cart, 10p, The Enchanted Lady.

Control Number on Back

**1905, May 1** **Typo.**

**287** A36 5c dark green 1.25 1.10
*a.* Imperf. 55.00
**288** A36 10c orange red 2.50 1.75
**289** A36 15c violet 2.50 1.75
*a.* Imperf. 82.50
**290** A36 25c dark blue 6.50 3.25
**291** A36 30c dk blue green 47.50 9.25
**292** A36 40c bright rose 75.00 30.00
**293** A36 50c slate 19.00 6.25
**294** A36 1p rose red 250.00 80.00
**295** A36 4p dk violet 120.00 80.00
**296** A36 10p brown orange 175.00 125.00
*Nos. 287-296 (10)* 699.25 338.35
Set, never hinged 1,350.

300th anniversary of the publication of Cervantes' "Don Quixote."

Counterfeits exist of Nos. 287-296.

For surcharges see Nos. 586-588, C91.

Six stamps picturing King Alfonso XIII and Queen Victoria Eugenia were put on sale Oct. 1, 1907, at the Madrid Industrial Exhibition. They were not valid for postage. Value, unused $40, mint never hinged $60.

The original labels were engraved and perf 11½. Examples printed by other methods or with other perfs are reprints. Value $2.

Alfonso XIII — A46

A47

Blue Control Number on Back

*Perf. 13x12½, 13, 13½x13, 14*

**1909-22** **Engr.**

**297** A46 2c dark brown .55 .55
*a.* No control number .55 .20
Never hinged 1.00
**298** A46 5c green 1.25 .20
**299** A46 10c carmine 2.10 .20
**300** A46 15c violet 9.50 .20
**301** A46 20c olive green 50.00 .90
**302** A46 25c deep blue 4.75 .20
**303** A46 30c blue green 8.50 .20
**304** A46 40c rose 15.50 .65
**305** A46 50c blue ('22) 11.50 .40
*a.* 50c slate blue 12.50 .40
Never hinged 18.50
**306** A46 1p lake 30.00 .40
**307** A46 4p deep violet 80.00 12.00
**309** A46 10p orange 100.00 26.00
*Nos. 297-309 (12)* 313.65 41.90
Set, never hinged 725.00

Nos. 297-309 exist imperforate. Value, unused $500.

The 5c exists in carmine; the 10c in yellow orange (value $400); the 15c in blue (value $400); the 4p in lake (value $1,000). The 5c and 15c are unissued trial colors, privately perforated and back-numbered. The 4p lake is known only with perfin "B.H.A." (Banco Hispano-Americano). 100 copies of the 4p exist, most poorly centered.

See Nos. 310, 315-317. For overprints see Nos. C1-C5, C58-C61.

Counterfeits exist.

Control Number on Back in Red or Orange

**1917**

**310** A46 15c yellow ocher 3.50 .35
Never hinged 6.00
*a.* Control number in blue 14.50 1.10

Control Number on Back in Blue

**1918**

**313** A46 40c light red 82.50 5.75
Never hinged 150.00

**1920** **Typo.** ***Imperf.***

**314** A47 1c blue green .20 .20

***Perf. 13x12½***

**Litho.**

**315** A46 2c bister 5.00 .20
**316** A46 20c violet 42.50 .20
*Nos. 314-316 (3)* 47.70 .60
Set, never hinged 145.00

Nos. 314-315 have no control number on back.

For overprints and surcharge see Nos. 358, 449, 457, 468, 10L1, 11LB1.

**1921** **Engr.**

**317** A46 20c violet 30.00 .20
Never hinged 52.50

Madrid Post Office — A48

**1920, Oct. 1** **Typo.** ***Perf. 13½***

**Center and Portrait in Black**

**318** A48 1c blue green .20 .25
**319** A48 2c olive bister .20 .25

**Control Number on Back**

**320** A48 5c green .85 .90
**321** A48 10c red .85 .90
**322** A48 15c yellow 1.40 1.10
**323** A48 20c violet 1.60 1.50
**324** A48 25c gray blue 2.25 2.50
**325** A48 30c dark green 6.25 4.75
**326** A48 40c rose 25.00 6.50
**327** A48 50c brt blue 27.50 17.50
**328** A48 1p brown red 27.50 14.50
**329** A48 4p brown violet 85.00 60.00
**330** A48 10p orange 175.00 125.00
*Nos. 318-330 (13)* 353.60 235.65
Set, never hinged 1,050.

Universal Postal Union Congress, Madrid, Oct. 10-Nov. 30.

Nos. 318, 320, 322-326, 330 exist perf 14. See *Scott Classic Specialized Catalogue* for listings.

Nos. 318-330 exist imperforate. Value, $2,500. stamps.

King Alfonso XIII
A49 A49a

FIFTEEN CENTIMOS:
Die I — Narrow "5."
Die II — Wide "5."

TWENTY FIVE CENTIMOS:
Die I — "25" is 2¾mm high. Vertical stroke of "5" is 1mm long.
Die II — "25" is 3mm high. Vertical stroke of "5" is 1½mm long.

***Perf. 11 to 14, Compound***

**1922-26** **Engr.** **Unwmk.**

**331** A49 2c olive green .75 .20
*a.* 2c deep orange (error) 87.50 *210.00*
Never hinged *110.00*

**Control Number on Back**

**332** A49 5c red violet 3.50 .20
**333** A49 5c claret 1.50 .20
**334** A49 10c carmine 1.50 1.00
**335** A49 10c yellow green 1.40 .20
*a.* 10c blue green ('23) 2.25 .20
Never hinged 5.50
**336** A49 15c slate bl (I) 6.50 .20
*a.* 15c black green (II) 27.50 2.25
Never hinged 47.50
**337** A49 20c violet 3.25 .20
**338** A49 25c carmine (I) 3.25 .20
*a.* 25c rose red (II) 5.50 1.00
Never hinged 11.00
*b.* 25c lilac rose (error) 100.00 160.00
Never hinged *175.00*
**339** A49 30c black brn ('26) 12.00 .20
**340** A49 40c deep blue 3.75 .20
**341** A49 50c orange 16.00 .20
*a.* 50c orange red 77.50 1.90
Never hinged 110.00
**342** A49a 1p blue black 15.00 .20
**343** A49a 4p lake 70.00 3.50
**344** A49a 10p brown 30.00 12.00
*Nos. 331-344 (14)* 168.40 18.70
Set, never hinged 390.00

Nos. 331, 334, 336-344 exist imperf.

The 5c exists in vermilion (value $110); the 25c in dark blue (value $200). The 50c exists in red brown, the 4p in brown and 10p in lake; value, each $90. These five were not regularly issued.

For overprints see Nos. 359-370, 467.

"Santa Maria" and View of Seville A50

Herald of Barcelona — A51

Exposition Buildings — A52

King Alfonso XIII and View of Barcelona A53

**1929, Feb. 15** ***Perf. 11***

**345** A50 1c grnsh blue 2.25 2.25
**346** A51 2c pale yel grn .25 .25
**347** A52 5c rose lake .45 .45

**Control Number on Back**

**348** A53 10c green .45 .45
**349** A50 15c Prus blue .75 .75
**350** A51 20c purple .50 .50
**351** A50 25c brt rose .50 .50
**352** A52 30c black brn 3.75 4.25
**353** A53 40c dark blue 7.00 7.25
**354** A51 50c deep orange 3.75 4.25
**355** A52 1p blue black 10.50 11.00
**356** A53 4p deep rose 22.50 22.50
**357** A53 10p brown 60.00 62.50
*Nos. 345-357,E2 (14)* 130.15 136.90
Set, never hinged 250.00

***Perf. 14***

*345a* A50 1c greenish blue .70 .70
*348a* A53 10c green 20.00 37.50
*349a* A50 15c Prus blue 22.50 22.50
*350a* A51 20c purple 26.00 37.50
*351a* A50 25c bright rose 32.50 37.50
*352a* A52 30c black brown 32.50 37.50
*353a* A53 40c dark blue 70.00 90.00
*354a* A51 50c deep orange 32.50 37.50
*355a* A52 1p blue black 32.50 37.50
*356a* A53 4p deep rose 25.00 25.00
*357a* A53 10p brown 110.00 140.00
*Nos. 345a-357a,E2a (12)* 433.20 535.70
Set, never hinged 700.00

Seville and Barcelona Exhibitions.

Nos. 345-357 exist imperf. Value, $75 each. See note after No. 432.

Nos. 314, 331, 333, 335-344 Overprinted in Red or Blue

**1929, June 10** ***Imperf.***

**358** A47 1c blue green .50 .80

***Perf. 13½x12½***

**359** A49 2c olive green .50 .90
**360** A49 5c claret (Bl) .50 .90
**361** A49 10c yellow green .50 .90
**362** A49 15c slate blue .50 .90
**363** A49 20c violet .50 .90
**364** A49 25c carmine (Bl) .50 .90
**365** A49 30c black brown 2.10 3.50
**366** A49 40c deep blue 2.10 3.50
**367** A49 50c orange (Bl) 2.10 3.50
**368** A49a 1p blue black 10.00 17.50
**369** A49a 4p lake (Bl) 10.00 19.00
**370** A49a 10p brown (Bl) 35.00 65.00
*Nos. 358-370,E4 (14)* 76.80 143.20
Set, never hinged 150.00

55th assembly of League of Nations at Madrid June 10-16. The stamps were available for postal use only on those days.

Nos. 359-370 values are for off-center copies. Well-centered stamps sell for about 4 times these values.

Exposition Building — A54

**1930** **Litho.** ***Perf. 11***

**371** A54 5c dk blue & salmon 5.50 5.00
**372** A54 5c dk violet & blue 5.50 5.00
Set, never hinged 19.00

Barcelona Philatelic Congress and Exhibition. "C. F. y E. F." are the initials of "Congreso Filatelico y Exposicion Filatelica." For each admission ticket, costing 2.75 pesetas, the holder was allowed to buy one of each of these stamps.

A55

Locomotives A56

**1930, May 10** ***Perf. 14***

**373** A55 1c light blue .50 .60
**374** A55 2c apple green .50 .60

**Control Number on Back**

**375** A55 5c lake .50 .60
**376** A55 10c yellow green .50 .60
**377** A55 15c bluish gray .50 .60
**378** A55 20c purple .50 .60
**379** A55 25c brt rose .50 .60
**380** A55 30c olive gray 1.60 1.40
**381** A55 40c dark blue 1.60 1.50
**382** A55 50c dk orange 3.50 4.50
**383** A56 1p dark gray 4.25 5.00
**384** A56 4p deep rose 77.50 60.00
**385** A56 10p bister brn 300.00 300.00
*Nos. 373-385,C12-C17,E6 (20)* 526.20 510.85
Set, never hinged 1,100.

11th Intl. Railway Congress, Madrid, 1930.

These stamps were on sale May 10-21, 1930, exclusively at the Palace of the Senate in Madrid and at the Barcelona and Seville expositions.

Francisco de Goya at Age 80
("1746 1828") ("1828 1928")
A57 A59

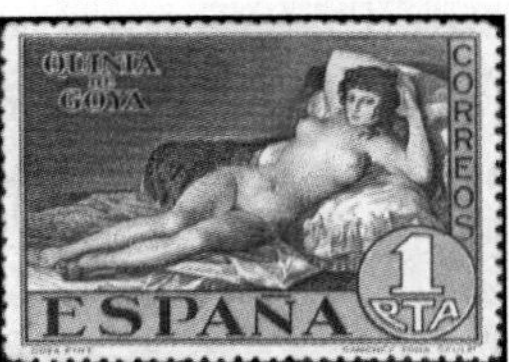


"La Maja Desnuda" — A58

**1930, June 15** **Litho.** ***Perf. 12½***

**Inscribed "Correos Espana"**

**386** A57 1c yellow .20 .20
**387** A57 2c bister brn .20 .20
**388** A57 5c lilac rose .20 .20
**389** A57 10c green .20 .20

**Engr.**

**390** A57 15c lt blue .20 .20
**391** A57 20c brown violet .20 .20
**392** A57 25c red .20 .20
**393** A57 30c brown 4.25 4.25
**394** A57 40c dark blue 4.25 4.25
**395** A57 50c vermilion 4.25 4.25
**396** A57 1p black 5.25 5.25
**397** A58 1p dark violet .75 .65
**398** A58 4p slate gray .55 .50
**399** A58 10p red brown 10.50 8.00

**Inscribed "1828 Goya 1928"**

**Litho.**

**400** A59 2c olive green .20 .20
**401** A59 5c gray violet .20 .20

**Engr.**

**402** A59 25c rose carmine .25 .25
*Nos. 386-402,C18-C30,CE1,E7 (32)* 46.60 44.05
Set, never hinged 60.00

To commemorate the death of Francisco de Goya y Lucientes, painter and engraver.

Nos. 386-399 were issued in connection with the Spanish-American Exposition at Seville.

Nos. 386-402 exist imperf. Value, set $300. See note after No. 432.

King Alfonso XIII — A61

Two types of the 40c:

Type I

Type II

**1930** *Perf. 11½, 12x11½*

| | | | | | |
|---|---|---|---|---|---|
| **406** | A61 | 2c | red brown | .20 | .20 |

**Control Number on Back**

| | | | | | |
|---|---|---|---|---|---|
| **407** | A61 | 5c | black brown | .65 | .20 |
| **408** | A61 | 10c | green | 3.00 | .20 |
| **409** | A61 | 15c | slate green | 10.00 | .20 |
| **410** | A61 | 20c | dark violet | 5.50 | .65 |
| **411** | A61 | 25c | carmine | .65 | .20 |
| **412** | A61 | 30c | brown lake | 14.00 | 1.60 |
| **413** | A61 | 40c | dk blue (I) | 19.00 | 1.00 |
| *a.* | | | Type II | 25.00 | 1.00 |
| | | | Never hinged | 45.00 | |
| **414** | A61 | 50c | orange | 17.50 | 1.75 |
| | | | *Nos. 406-414 (9)* | 70.50 | 6.00 |
| | | | Set, never hinged | 190.00 | |

#406-414 exist imperf. Value for set, $350.

For overprints see #450-455, 458-466, 469-487.

**1930, Sept. 29** **Litho.** *Perf. 12½*

| | | | | | |
|---|---|---|---|---|---|
| **418** | A63 | 1c | olive gray | .20 | .20 |
| **419** | A64 | 2c | olive green | .20 | .20 |
| **420** | A63 | 2c | olive green | .20 | .20 |
| **421** | A64 | 5c | red brown | .20 | .20 |
| **422** | A63 | 5c | red brown | .20 | .20 |
| **423** | A64 | 10c | blue green | .85 | .70 |
| **424** | A63 | 15c | ultra | .85 | .90 |
| **425** | A64 | 20c | violet | 1.25 | 1.10 |

**Engr.**

| | | | | | |
|---|---|---|---|---|---|
| **426** | A65 | 25c | dark red | 1.25 | 1.10 |
| **427** | A66 | 30c | bis brn, bl & blk brn | 6.00 | 5.25 |
| **428** | A65 | 40c | ultra | 5.50 | 5.75 |
| **429** | A66 | 50c | dk vio, bl & vio brn | 7.75 | 5.75 |
| **430** | A65 | 1p | black | 7.75 | 5.75 |
| **431** | A67 | 4p | blk & dk blue | 8.75 | 6.50 |
| **432** | A67 | 10p | red brn & dk brn | 35.00 | 32.50 |
| | | | *Nos. 418-432,E8 (16)* | 77.70 | 68.05 |
| | | | Set, never hinged | 140.00 | |

Christopher Columbus tribute.

Nos. 418 to 432 were privately produced. Their promoters presented a certain quantity of these labels to the Spanish Postal Authorities, who placed them on sale and allowed them to be used for three days, retaining the money obtained from the sale.

This note will also apply to Nos. 345-357, 386-402, 433-448, 557-571, B1-B105, C18-C57, C73-C87, CB1-CB5, CE1, E2, E7-E9, E15 and EB1.

Many so-called "errors" of color and perforation are known.

Nos. 418-432 exist imperf. Value, set $450.

See Nos. 2671, B194.

Bow of "Santa Maria" — A63

Stern of "Santa Maria" — A64

"Santa Maria," "Niña," "Pinta" — A65

Columbus Leaving Palos — A66

Columbus Arriving in America — A67

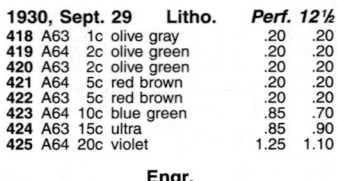

Arms of Spain, Bolivia, Paraguay — A68

Pavilion and Map of Central America — A69

Exhibition Pavilion of Ecuador — A70

Colombia Pavilion — A71

Dominican Republic Pavilion A72

Uruguay Pavilion A73

Argentina Pavilion A74

Chile Pavilion A75

Brazil Pavilion A76

Mexico Pavilion A77

Cuba Pavilion A78

Peru Pavilion A79

U.S. Pavilion A80

Exhibition Pavilion of Portugal — A81

King Alfonso XIII and Queen Victoria — A82

**Unwmk.**

**1930, Oct. 10** **Photo.** *Perf. 14*

| | | | | | |
|---|---|---|---|---|---|
| **433** | A68 | 1c | blue green | .20 | .20 |
| **434** | A69 | 2c | bister brown | .20 | .20 |
| **435** | A70 | 5c | olive brown | .20 | .20 |
| **436** | A71 | 10c | dark green | .30 | .30 |
| **437** | A72 | 15c | indigo | .30 | .30 |
| **438** | A73 | 20c | violet | .30 | .30 |
| **439** | A74 | 25c | car rose | .30 | .30 |
| **440** | A75 | 25c | car rose | .30 | .30 |
| **441** | A76 | 30c | rose lilac | 1.50 | 1.50 |
| **442** | A77 | 40c | slate blue | .90 | .90 |
| **443** | A78 | 40c | slate blue | .90 | .90 |
| **444** | A79 | 50c | brown org | 1.50 | 1.50 |
| **445** | A80 | 1p | ultra | 2.25 | 2.25 |
| **446** | A81 | 4p | brown violet | 30.00 | 27.50 |
| **447** | A82 | 10p | brown | 2.10 | 2.10 |

*Perf. 11, 14*

**Engr.**

| | | | | | |
|---|---|---|---|---|---|
| **448** | A82 | 10p | orange brown | 42.50 | 42.50 |
| | | | *Nos. 433-448,C50-C57,E9 (25)* | 104.30 | 96.00 |
| | | | Set, never hinged | 265.00 | |

Spanish-American Union Exhibition, Seville.

The note after No. 432 will also apply to Nos. 433-448. All values exist imperforate. Value, set: hinged $250; never hinged $325.

*Reprints of Nos. 433-448 have blurred colors, yellowish paper and an inferior, almost invisible gum. They sell for about $1 per set.*

## Revolutionary Issues
## Madrid Issue

Regular Issues of 1920-30 Overprinted in Black, Green or Red

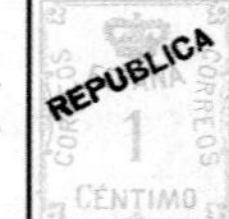


On No. 314

**1931** *Imperf.*

| | | | | | |
|---|---|---|---|---|---|
| **449** | A47 | 1c | blue green | .20 | .20 |

On Nos. 406-411

*Perf. 11½*

| | | | | | |
|---|---|---|---|---|---|
| **450** | A61 | 2c | red brown (G) | .30 | .25 |
| **451** | A61 | 5c | black brn (R) | .40 | .40 |
| **452** | A61 | 10c | green | .70 | .70 |
| **453** | A61 | 15c | slate grn (R) | 1.40 | 1.50 |
| **454** | A61 | 20c | dk violet (R) | 1.40 | 1.50 |
| **455** | A61 | 25c | carmine (G) | 1.90 | 2.25 |
| | | | *Nos. 449-455,E10 (8)* | 10.80 | 11.30 |
| | | | Set, never hinged | 22.50 | |

The status of Nos. 449-455, E10 has been questioned.

## First Barcelona Issue

Regular Issues of 1920-30 Overprinted in Black or Red

On No. 314

**1931** *Imperf.*

| | | | | | |
|---|---|---|---|---|---|
| **457** | A47 | 1c | blue green | .20 | .20 |

**On Nos. 406-414**

*Perf. 11½*

| | | | | | |
|---|---|---|---|---|---|
| **458** | A61 | 2c | red brown | .20 | .20 |
| **459** | A61 | 5c | black brown | .20 | .20 |
| **460** | A61 | 10c | green | .55 | .55 |
| **461** | A61 | 15c | slate grn (R) | .60 | .60 |
| **462** | A61 | 20c | dk violet (R) | .60 | .60 |
| **463** | A61 | 25c | carmine | .60 | .60 |
| **464** | A61 | 30c | brown lake | 4.50 | 4.50 |
| **465** | A61 | 40c | dk blue (R) | 1.25 | 1.25 |
| **466** | A61 | 50c | orange | 1.25 | 1.25 |

**On Stamp of 1922-26**

| | | | | | |
|---|---|---|---|---|---|
| **467** | A49a | 1p | blue blk (R) | 7.50 | 6.25 |
| | | | *Nos. 457-467,E11 (12)* | 22.45 | 21.20 |
| | | | Set, never hinged | 45.00 | |

Nos. 457-467 are known both with and without accent over "U."

The status of Nos. 457-467, E11 has been questioned.

### Second Barcelona Issue

Regular Issues of 1920-30 Overprinted in Black or Red

On No. 314
*Imperf*

**468** A47 1c blue green .20 .20

On Nos. 406-414
*Perf. 11½*

**469** A61 2c red brown .20 .20
**470** A61 5c black brown (R) .20 .20
**471** A61 10c green .20 .20
**472** A61 15c slate grn (R) 1.40 1.25
**473** A61 20c dark violet (R) .40 .45
**474** A61 25c carmine .40 .45
**475** A61 30c brown lake 5.75 5.75
**476** A61 40c dark blue (R) 1.25 1.25
**477** A61 50c orange 4.50 3.50
*Nos. 468-477 (10)* 14.50 13.45
Set, never hinged 27.50

The status of Nos. 469-477, C58-C61 has been questioned.

### General Issue of the Republic

Nos. 406-414, 342 Overprinted in Blue or Red

**1931, May 27**

**478** A61 2c red brown .20 .20
**479** A61 5c black brn (R) .20 .20
**480** A61 10c green (R) .25 .20
**481** A61 15c slate grn (R) 2.75 .20
**482** A61 20c dk violet (R) 1.25 .75
**483** A61 25c carmine .40 .20
**484** A61 30c brown lake 3.50 .75
**485** A61 40c dk blue (R) 3.50 .45
**486** A61 50c orange 6.00 .45
**487** A49a 1p blue blk (R) 45.00 .75
*Nos. 478-487,E12 (11)* 68.55 5.15
Set, never hinged 150.00

The setting contained 18 repetitions of "Republica Espanola" for each vertical row of 10 stamps. According to its sheet position, a stamp received different parts of the overprinted words.

Overprint position varieties include: reading down on 25c, 30c, 40c and 50c; double on 1p; double, both reading down, on 25c, 40c and 50c.

---

"Republica Espanola"
Stamps of various Spanish colonies overprinted "Republica Espanola" are listed with the colonies.

---

Fountain of Lions, The Alhambra, Granada
A84

Interior of Mosque, Córdoba — A85

Alcántara Bridge and Alcazar, Toledo
A86

Francisco García y Santos
A87

Puerta del Sol, Madrid, on April 14, 1931 as Republic Was Proclaimed
A88

*Perf. 12½*

**1931, Oct. 10** **Unwmk.** **Engr.**

**491** A84 5c violet brown .20 .25
**492** A85 10c blue green .30 .30
**493** A86 15c dark violet .30 .30
**494** A85 25c deep red .30 .30
**495** A87 30c olive green .30 .30
**496** A84 40c indigo .90 .90
**497** A85 50c orange red .90 .90
**498** A86 1p black 1.75 1.75
**499** A88 4p red violet 8.50 8.50
**500** A88 10p red brown 27.50 *30.00*
*Nos. 491-500,C62-C67,CO1-CO6,O20-O29 (32)* 93.20 97.15
Set, never hinged 125.00

3rd Pan-American Postal Union Cong., Madrid.

Nos. 491-500 exist imperforate. Value, set: hinged $150; never hinged $250.

Symbolical of Montserrat Cut With a Saw — A89

Abbott Oliva and Monastery Workman — A90

"Black Virgin"
A91 A92

Montserrat Monastery — A93

**1931, Dec. 9** *Perf. 11, 14*

**501** A89 1c myrtle green 1.10 1.40
*a.* Perf. 14 19.00 19.00
Never hinged 37.50
**502** A89 2c red brown .65 1.00
*a.* Perf. 14 14.00 15.00
Never hinged 27.50

#### Control Number on Back

**503** A89 5c black brown .75 1.25
*a.* Perf. 14 14.00 15.00
Never hinged 27.50
**504** A89 10c yellow green .85 1.25
*a.* Perf. 14 14.00 17.00
Never hinged 27.50
**505** A90 15c myrtle green 1.10 1.60
*a.* Perf. 14 19.00 22.50
Never hinged 37.50
**506** A91 20c dark violet 2.25 2.25
*a.* Perf. 11 100.00 140.00
Never hinged *190.00*
**507** A92 25c lake 3.25 3.25
*a.* Perf. 14 5.75 6.50
Never hinged 11.50
**508** A91 30c deep red 35.00 32.50
*a.* Perf. 14 37.50 37.50
Never hinged 77.50
**509** A93 40c dull blue 20.00 17.50
*a.* Perf. 11 140.00 160.00
Never hinged *275.00*
**510** A90 50c dark orange 45.00 42.50
*a.* Perf. 14 62.50 72.50
Never hinged *125.00*
**511** A92 1p gray black 45.00 42.50
*a.* Perf. 11 80.00 100.00
Never hinged *160.00*
**512** A93 4p lilac rose 450.00 450.00
*a.* Perf. 14 475.00 825.00
Never hinged *875.00*
**513** A92 10p deep brown 350.00 300.00
*a.* Perf. 14 725.00 875.00
Never hinged *1,400.*
*Nos. 501-511,C68-C72,E13 (17)* 244.20 236.25
Set, never hinged 375.00
*Nos. 501-513,C68-C72,E13 (19)* 1,044. 986.25
Set, never hinged 2,100.

Commemorative of the building of the old Monastery at Montserrat, started in 1031, and of the image of the Black Virgin (said to have been carved by St. Luke) which was crowned by Pope Leo XIII in 1881.

Nos. 501-513 exist imperforate. Value, set $4,000.

For surcharges see Nos. 589, C92-C96.

Francisco Pi y Margall — A95

Joaquín Costa — A96

Nicolás Salmerón
A97

Pablo Iglesias
A99

Emilio Castelar — A100

**1931-32** *Perf. 11½*

#### Control Number on Back

**516** A95 5c brnsh black 3.00 .30
**517** A96 10c yellow green 7.25 .30
**518** A97 15c slate green 4.75 .20
**520** A99 25c lake 22.50 .70
*b.* Imperf. 175.00
Never hinged 225.00
**521** A99 30c carmine rose 7.25 .20
*c.* Imperf. 82.50
Never hinged 125.00
**522** A100 40c dark blue 42.50 4.50
**523** A97 50c orange 52.50 7.75
*Nos. 516-523 (7)* 139.75 13.95
Set, never hinged 400.00

#### Without Control Number

*516a* A95 5c brownish blk ('32) 4.50 .20
*517a* A96 10c yel grn ('32) 4.00 .20
*518a* A97 15c slate green ('32) .60 .20
*520a* A99 25c lake 32.50 .20
*521a* A99 30c carmine rose 1.90 .20
*522a* A100 40c dark blue ('32) .20 .20
*523a* A97 50c orange ('32) 26.00 .50
*Nos. 516a-523a (7)* 69.70 1.70
Set, never hinged 150.00

#### Without Control Number, Imperf.

*516b* A95 5c 6.50
*517b* A96 10c 11.00
*518b* A97 15c 6.25
*520c* A99 25c *110.00*
*521b* A99 30c 5.50
*522b* A100 40c 14.00
*523b* A97 50c 125.00
*Nos. 516b-523b (7)* 278.25
Set, never hinged 550.00

See Nos. 532, 538, 550, 579, 579a.

For overprints and surcharges see Nos. 7LC12-7LC13, 7LC15-7LC16, 7LC18, 7LE4, 8LB6, 8LB9-8LB10, 9LC17-9LC18, 10L7, 10L10-10L12, 10L16-10L18, 10L22-10L23, 11L7, 11L10-11L12, 11LB8, 12L4, 12L8, 12L11-12L12, 13L8, 14L6, 14L10-14L12, 14L18, 14L22-14L24.

Blasco Ibáñez
A103

Manuel Ruiz-Zorrilla
A104

#### Without Control Number

**1931-34** *Perf. 11½*

**526** A103 2c red brown ('32) .20 .20
**528** A103 5c chocolate ('34) .20 .20
**532** A95 20c dark violet .25 .20
**534** A104 25c lake ('34) .45 .20
**538** A100 60c apple green ('32) .20 .20
*Nos. 526-538 (5)* 1.30 1.00
Set, never hinged 2.50

*Imperf*

*526a* A103 2c 14.00
*528a* A103 5c 2.75
*532a* A95 20c 6.25
*534a* A104 25c 5.25
*538a* A100 60c 6.25
*Nos. 526a-538a (5)* 34.50
Set, never hinged 70.00

For overprints and surcharges see Nos. 8LB3, 8LB7, 9LC3, 9LC8-9LC9, 9LC14, 10L6, 10L13, 11L4, 11L8, 11LB5, 11LB9, 12L5, 12L9, 13L5, 13L7, 14L3, 14L7, 14L15, 14L19.

Cliff Houses, Cuenca — A105

Alcázar of Segovia — A106

Gate of the Sun at Toledo — A107

**1932-38** *Perf. 10*

**539** A105 1p gray black ('38) .20 .20
**540** A106 4p magenta ('38) .30 .40
**541** A107 10p deep brn ('38) .65 .70
*Nos. 539-541 (3)* 1.15 1.30
Set, never hinged 2.75

*Imperf*

*539a* A105 1p 5.25 2.75
*540a* A106 4p 9.00 6.50
*541a* A107 10p 6.50 6.00
*Nos. 539a-541a (3)* 20.75 15.25
Set, never hinged 45.00

*Perf. 11½*

*539b* A105 1p .20 .20
*540b* A106 4p .70 .85
*541b* A107 10p 1.90 3.00
*Nos. 539b-541b (3)* 2.80 4.05
Set, never hinged 5.00

For overprints and surcharge see Nos. 9LC19, 10L19, 13L9, 14L25, 14L27-14L28.

Numeral
A108

Santiago Ramón y Cajal
A109

**1933 Unwmk. Typo. *Imperf.***

**542** A108 1c blue green .20 .20

***Perf. 11½***

**543** A108 2c buff .20 .20
*a.* Perf. 13½x13 .65 .20
Never hinged 1.40
Set, never hinged .65

See Nos. 592-597. For surcharges and overprints see Nos. 590-590A, 634A-634D, 8LB1-8LB2, 9LC1-9LC2, 9LC4-9LC7, 9LC11-9LC12, 9LC20, 9LC26, 10L2-10L4, 11L1-11L2, 11LB2-11LB3, 12L1-12L2, 13L1-13L3, 14L1, 14L13.

**1934 Engr. *Perf. 11½x11***

**545** A109 30c black brown 6.00 1.10
Never hinged 15.00
*a.* Perf. 14 22.50 30.00
Never hinged 42.50
*b.* Imperf. 32.50
Never hinged 55.00

Type of 1931 and

Mariana Pineda
A110

Concepción Arenal
A111

Gumersindo de Azcarate
A112

Gaspar Melchor de Jovellanos
A113

**1935-36**

**546** A110 10c light green .20 .20
*b.* 10c blue green ('36) .20 .20
**547** A111 15c dark green .20 .20
*b.* 15c yellow green ('36) .20 .20
**548** A112 30c carmine rose 7.25 .20
**549** A113 30c rose red .20 .20
**550** A97 50c dark blue 1.00 .30
*Nos. 546-550 (5)* 8.85 1.10
Set, never hinged 20.00

***Imperf***

*546a* A110 10c 1.60
*547a* A111 15c 5.25
*548a* A112 30c 26.00
*549a* A113 30c 1.90
*550a* A97 50c *225.00*
*Nos. 546a-550a (5)* 259.75
Set, never hinged 500.00

Shades exist.

For overprints and surcharges see Nos. 7LE3, 8LB4-8LB5, 8LB8, 10L8-10L9, 10L14, 10L20-10L21, 11L5-11L6, 11L9, 11LB6-11LB7, 11LB10, 12L6-12L7, 12L10, 13L6, 14L4-14L5, 14L8, 14L16-14L17, 14L20.

Lope's Bookplate
A116

Lope de Vega
A117

Alcántara and Alcázar, Toledo
A118

**1935, Oct. 12 *Perf. 11½x11, 11x11½***

**552** A116 15c myrtle green 5.75 .30
**553** A117 30c rose red 2.50 .30
**554** A117 50c dark blue 11.00 3.00
**555** A118 1p blue black 21.00 2.00
*Nos. 552-555 (4)* 40.25 5.60
Set, never hinged 95.00

***Imperf***

*552a* A116 15c 400.00
*553a* A117 30c 11.00
*554a* A117 50c 65.00
*555a* A118 1p 60.00
*Nos. 552a-555a (4)* 536.00
Set, never hinged 850.00

***Perf. 14***

*553b* A117 30c 6.50 14.50
*554b* A117 50c 29.00 45.00
*555b* A118 1p 32.50 50.00
*Nos. 553b-555b (3)* 68.00 109.50
Set, never hinged 150.00

Lope Felix de Vega Carpio (1562-1635), Spanish dramatist and poet.
For surcharge see No. 11LB11.

Map of Amazon by Bartolomeo Oliva, 16th Century
A119

**1935, Oct. 12 *Perf. 11½***

**556** A119 30c rose red 1.90 .95
Never hinged 3.75
*a.* Perf. 14 22.50
Never hinged 45.00
*b.* Imperf. 32.50
Never hinged 60.00

Proposed Iglesias Amazon Expedition.

Miguel Moya — A120

Torcuato Luca de Tena — A121

José Francos Rodríguez
A122

Alejandro Lerroux
A123

Nazareth School and Rotary Press — A124

**1936, Feb. 14 Photo. *Perf. 12½***

**Size: 22x26mm**

**557** A120 1c crimson .20 .20
**558** A121 2c orange brown .20 .20
**559** A122 5c black brown .20 .20
**560** A123 10c emerald .20 .20

**Size: 24x28½mm**

**561** A120 15c blue green .20 .20
**562** A121 20c violet .20 .20
**563** A122 25c red violet .20 .20
**564** A123 30c crimson .20 .20

**Size: 25½x30½mm**

**565** A120 40c orange .50 .35
**566** A121 50c ultra .20 .20
**567** A122 60c olive green .50 .35
**568** A123 1p gray black .50 .35
**569** A124 2p lt blue 6.50 3.00
**570** A124 4p lilac rose 6.50 6.00
**571** A124 10p red brown 17.00 14.00
*Nos. 557-571,E15 (16)* 33.55 26.15
Set, never hinged 55.00
*Nos. 557-571,C73-C87,E15 (31)* 61.25 45.00
Set, never hinged 110.00

Madrid Press Association, 40th anniversary.
Nos. 557-571 exist imperf. Values about 7 times those of perf. stamps.
See note after No. 432. See Nos. C73-C87.

Arms of Madrid — A125

**1936, Apr. 2 Engr. *Imperf.***

**572** A125 10c brown black 42.50 42.50
**573** A125 15c dark green 42.50 42.50
Set, never hinged 120.00

1st National Philatelic Exhibition which opened in Madrid, Apr. 2, 1936.
For overprints see Nos. C88-C89.

"Republica Espanola"
A126

Gregorio Fernández
A127

**1936 Litho. *Perf. 11½, 13½x13***

**574** A126 2c orange brown .20 .20
Never hinged .30

For surcharges & overprints see #591, 9LC24, 10L5, 11L3, 11LB4, 12L3, 13L4, 14L2, 14L14.

**1936, Mar. 10 Engr. *Perf. 11½***

**576** A127 30c carmine 1.10 .85
Never hinged 2.00
*a.* Perf. 14 9.00 8.25
Never hinged 17.50
*b.* Imperf. 15.00
Never hinged 22.50

Tercentenary of the death of Gregorio Fernandez, sculptor.
For overprints see Nos. 7LC20-7LC21.

Type of 1931 and

Pablo Iglesias
A128 A129

Velázquez
A130

Fermín Salvoechea
A131

**1936-38 *Perf. 11, 11½, 11½x11***

**577** A128 30c rose red .20 .20
**578** A129 30c car rose 1.10 .50
**579** A100 40c car rose ('37) 1.10 .50
**580** A129 45c carmine ('37) .20 .20
**581** A130 50c dark blue .20 .20
**582** A131 60c indigo ('37) .75 .90
**583** A131 60c dp orange ('38) 6.00 5.00
*Nos. 577-583 (7)* 9.55 7.50
Set, never hinged 26.00

***Perf. 14***

*577a* A128 30c rose red 6.50
*578a* A129 30c carmine rose 6.75
*579a* A100 40c carmine rose 6.50
*580a* A129 45c carmine 6.00
*582a* A131 60c indigo 6.00
*583a* A131 60c deep orange 9.50
*Nos. 577a-583a (6)* 41.25
Set, never hinged 90.00

Nos. 577-583 exist imperf. Value, set $70. Set, never hinged, $150.
For overprints see Nos. C90, 7LC17, 7LC22-7LC23, 10L15, 14L21.

Statue of Liberty, Spanish and US Flags — A132

**1938, June 1 Photo. *Perf. 11½***

**585** A132 1p multicolored 15.00 16.00
Never hinged 26.00
*a.* Imperf., pair 75.00 50.00
Never hinged 100.00
*b.* Horiz. pair, imperf. vert. 57.50 75.00
Never hinged 85.00
*c.* Souvenir sheet of 1 25.00 30.00
Never hinged 40.00
*d.* As "c," imperf. 275.00 225.00
Never hinged 475.00

150th anniv. of the U.S. Constitution.
For surcharge see No. C97.

No. 289 Surcharged in Black

**1938 *Perf. 14***

**586** A36 45c on 15c violet 14.00 14.00
Never hinged 17.50

7th anniversary of the Republic.
Values are for examples with perforations nearly touching the design on one or two sides.

No. 289 Surcharged in Black:

a

b

**1938, May 1**

**587** A36 45c on 15c violet 3.00 3.00
**588** A36 1p on 15c violet 5.25 5.25
Set, never hinged 12.00

Issued to commemorate Labor Day.
Values are for examples with perforations nearly touching the design on one or two sides.

No. 507 Surcharged in Black

**1938, Nov. 10** *Perf. 11½*

**589** A92 2.50p on 25c lake .20 .20
Never hinged .20
*b.* Perf. 14 3.50 6.00
Never hinged 6.00

Types of 1933-36 Surcharged in Blue or Red

**1938** *Perf. 10, 11, 13½x13, 13x14*

**590** A108 45c on 1c grn (R) .40 .25
*b.* Imperf. 6.00 5.00
Never hinged 10.00
**590A** A108 45c on 2c buff (Bl) 17.00 14.00
**591** A126 45c on 2c org brn (Bl) .20 .20
*Nos. 590-591 (3)* 17.60 14.45
Set, never hinged 29.00

Many overprint varieties exist.

Numeral Type of 1933

**1938-39** **Litho.** *Perf. 11½, 13*

**White or Gray Paper**

**592** A108 5c gray brown .20 .20
**593** A108 10c yellow green .20 .20
**594** A108 15c slate green .20 .20
**595** A108 20c vio, gray paper .20 .20
**596** A108 25c red violet .20 .20
**597** A108 30c scarlet .20 .20
*Nos. 592-597 (6)* 1.20 1.20
Set, never hinged 1.40

"Republic" — A133

**1938** *Perf. 11½*

**598** A133 40c rose red .20 .20
**599** A133 45c car rose .20 .20
*a.* Printed on both sides 11.00 11.00
Never hinged 27.50
**600** A133 50c ultra .20 .20
**601** A133 60c dp ultra .50 .30
*Nos. 598-601 (4)* 1.10 .90
Set, never hinged 1.10

Nos. 598-601 exist imperf. Value for set $22.50.

Machine Gunners A134

Infantry — A135

*Perf. 11½x11, 11x11½, Imperf.*

**1938, Sept. 1** **Photo.**

**602** A134 25c dark green 9.25 9.25
**603** A135 45c red brown 9.25 9.25
Set, never hinged 50.00

43rd Division of the Republican Army. Sold only at the Philatelic Agency and for foreign exchange.

Blast Furnace A136

Steel Mill and Sculpture, "Defenders of Numantia" A137

**1938, Aug. 9** *Perf. 16*

**604** A136 45c black .20 .20
**605** A137 1.25p dark blue .20 .20
Set, never hinged .30

Issued in honor of the workers of Sagunto.

Submarine — A137a

Designs: 1p, 15p, U-Boat D1. 2p, 6p, U-Boat A1. 4p, 10p, U-Boat B2.

**1938, Aug. 11** *Perf. 16*

**605A** A137a 1p blue 5.50 5.50
**605B** A137a 2p red brown 10.00 10.00
**605C** A137a 4p red orange 12.00 12.00
**605D** A137a 6p deep blue 27.50 27.50
**605E** A137a 10p magenta 45.00 45.00
**605F** A137a 15p dp gray green 500.00 500.00
*Nos. 605A-605F (6)* 600.00 600.00
Set, never hinged 725.00

**Souvenir Sheet**

*Perf. 10½*

**605G** A137a Sheet of 3 550.00 550.00
Never hinged 700.00
*a.* 4p carmine & gray black 125.00 125.00
*b.* 6p dull blue & gray black 125.00 125.00
*c.* 15p green & gray black 125.00 125.00

Nos. 605A-605G were issued for use on a proposed submarine mail service between Barcelona and Mahon, Minorca. One voyage was made on this mail route, carrying 300 agency-prepared covers. The stamps were also valid for ordinary mail.

Nos. 605A-605G were sold only at the Philatelic Agency in Barcelona, for double their face value.

Nos. 605A-605G exist imperf. Value: set of 6 stamps, $775 unused, $1,000 never hinged; souvenir sheet, $2,250 unused, $2,900 never hinged.

Riflemen A138

Machine Gunners A139

Bomb Throwing — A140

**1938, Nov. 25** **Engr.** *Perf. 10*

**606** A138 5c sepia 3.50 3.50
**607** A138 10c dp violet 3.50 3.50
**608** A138 25c blue green 3.50 3.50
**609** A139 45c rose red 3.50 3.50
**610** A139 60c dark blue 6.25 6.25
**611** A139 1.20p black 125.00 125.00
**612** A140 2p orange 37.50 37.50
**613** A140 5p dark brown 220.00 220.00
**614** A140 10p dk blue grn 40.00 40.00
*Nos. 606-614 (9)* 442.75 442.75
Set, never hinged 725.00

Honoring the Militia. Sold only at the Philatelic Agency and for foreign exchange. Exist imperf. Value, set $1,200. Set, never hinged, $1,800.

**Spanish State**

Arms of Spain — A141

**1936** **Litho.** *Imperf.*

**Thin Transparent Paper**

**615** A141 30c blue 190.00
**616** A141 30c pale green 190.00

*Perf. 11*

**Thick Wove Paper**

**617** A141 30c dark blue 550.00 110.00
Set, never hinged 1,200.

Issued in Granada during siege. After the city was liberated, these stamps were used throughout the province of Granada.

Well-centered copies of No. 617 are worth twice as much as the values above.

Many forgeries exist.

A143

Cathedral of Burgos — A145

University of Salamanca A146

Cathedral del Pilar, Zaragoza — A147

"La Giralda," Seville — A148

Xavier Castle, Navarre — A149

Court of Lions, Alhambra at Granada A150

Mosque, Córdoba A151

Alcántara Bridge and Alcázar, Toledo — A152

Soldier Carrying Flag — A153

Troops Landing at Algeciras A154

Two types of 30c:

Type I — Imprint 12mm long; "3" does not touch frame.

Type II — Imprint 8mm long; "3" touches frame.

**1936** **Unwmk.** **Litho.** *Imperf.*

**623** A143 1c green 6.00 4.50

*Perf. 11½*

**624** A143 2c orange brown .60 .45
**625** A145 5c gray brown .60 .55
**626** A146 10c green .60 .45
**627** A147 15c dull green .60 .45
**628** A148 25c rose lake .85 .45
**629** A149 30c carmine (I) .60 .45
*a.* Type II .70 .55
Never hinged 1.40
**630** A150 50c deep blue 14.00 8.75
**631** A151 60c yellow green .95 .70
**632** A152 1p black 5.25 3.75
**633** A153 4p rose vio, red & yel 52.50 29.00
**634** A154 10p light brown 52.50 29.00
*Nos. 623-634 (12)* 135.05 78.50
Set, never hinged 240.00

Nos. 624-634 exist imperf. Value, set $275.

Nos. 625-631, 633-634 were privately overprinted "VIA AEREA" and plane, supposedly for use in Ifni.

For surcharges see Nos. 9LC21, 9LC23.

Nos. 542-543 Surcharged "Habilitado 0'05 ptas." in Two Lines

**1936** *Imperf., Perf. 11½*

**634A** A108 5c on 1c bl grn 2.25 3.00
**634B** A108 5c on 2c buff 2.25 3.00
**634C** A108 10c on 1c bl grn 2.25 3.00
**634D** A108 15c on 2c buff 2.25 3.00
*Nos. 634A-634D (4)* 9.00 12.00
Set, never hinged 15.00

Issued in the Balearic Islands to meet a shortage of these values. Nos. 634A and 634C are imperf., Nos. 634B and 634D are perf. 11½.

St. James of Compostela — A155

St. James Cathedral A156

Pórtico de la Gloria A157

Two types of 30c:

I — No dots in "1937."

II — Dot before and after "1937."

**1937** *Perf. 11½, 11x11½*

**635** A155 15c violet brown .95 1.25
**636** A156 30c rose red (I) 5.00 .55
*a.* Type II 17.50 14.00
Never hinged 35.00

**637** A157 1p blue & org 14.50 3.25
*a.* Center inverted 275.00 250.00
Never hinged 425.00
*Nos. 635-637 (3)* 20.45 5.05
Set, never hinged 50.00

Holy Year of Compostela. Nos. 635-637 exist imperf. Value for set $150.

"Estado Espanol"
A159 A160

"El Cid" — A161

Isabella I — A162

Two types of 5c, 30c and 10p:
5 Centimos: Type I Imprint 9½mm long. Type II Imprint 14mm long.
30 Centimos: Type I Imprint, "Hija De B. Fournier Burgos." Type II Imprint, "Fournier Burgos".
10 Pesetas: Type I "10" 2½mm high. Type II "10" 3mm high.

With Imprint

**1936-40** ***Imperf.***
**638** A159 1c green .20 .20

***Perf. 11***
**640** A160 2c brown .20 .20

***Perf. 11, 11½, 11½x11, 11½x10½***
**641** A161 5c brown (I) .45 .20
**642** A161 5c brown (II) .20 .20
**643** A161 10c green .20 .20

***Perf. 11, 11x11½***
**644** A162 15c gray black .20 .20
**645** A162 20c dark violet .40 .20
**646** A162 25c brown lake .20 .20
**647** A162 30c rose (I) .50 .20
**648** A162 30c rose (II) 17.50 2.10
**649** A162 40c orange 1.60 .20
**650** A162 50c dark blue 1.60 .20
**651** A162 60c yellow .30 .20
**652** A162 1p blue 16.50 .50
**653** A162 4p magenta 21.00 5.25
**654** A161 10p dk bl (I) ('37) 75.00 40.00
**655** A161 10p dp bl (II) ('40) 32.50 15.00
*Nos. 638-655 (17)* 168.55 65.25
Set, never hinged 375.00

No. 638 was privately perforated. See Nos. 662-667. For overprint and surcharges see Nos. E18, 9LC10, 9LC13, 9LC15-9LC16, 9LC22, 9LC25, 9LC27-9LC30, 9LC34-9LC53.

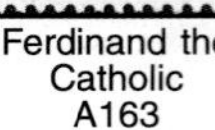

Ferdinand the Catholic
A163

Emblem of the Falange
A164

**1938** ***Perf. 10½, 11½x11***

**Imprint: "Lit Fournier Vitoria"**
**656** A163 15c deep green 1.25 .20
**657** A163 30c deep red 3.75 .20

**Imprint: "Fournier Vitoria"**

***Perf. 10***
**658** A163 15c deep green 1.25 .20
**659** A163 20c purple 8.25 1.25
**660** A163 25c brown car .60 .20
**661** A163 30c deep red 3.75 .20
*Nos. 656-661 (6)* 18.85 2.25
Set, never hinged 65.00

Nos. 656-661 exist imperf.; value for set, $150 hinged, $225 never hinged. Part-perf. varieties exist.
For overprints see Nos. C98-C99.

Without Imprint

**1938-50** ***Perf. 11, 13½x13¼***

Two types of the 15 Centimos:
Type I — Medieval style numerals with diagonal line through "5."
Type II — Modern numerals. Narrower "5" without diagonal line.

**662** A159 1c green, imperf. .20 .20
**663** A160 2c brn (18½x22mm; '40) .20 .20
*a.* 2c bis brn (17½x21mm; '48) .20 .20
Never hinged .20
**664** A161 5c gray brn ('39) .20 .20
*a.* Perf 13½x13¼ ('49) .20 .20
**665** A161 10c dk carmine .25 .20
*a.* 10c rose .35 .20
Never hinged .75
*b.* Perf 13½x13¼ ('49) .20 .20
**666** A161 15c dk green (I) .90 .20
**666A** A161 15c dk green (II) .60 .20
*b.* Perf 13½x13¼ ('50) .65 .20
Never hinged 1.25
**667** A162 70c dk blue ('39) .75 .20
*Nos. 662-667 (7)* 3.10 1.40
Set, never hinged 4.25

**1938, July 17** ***Perf. 10***
**668** A164 15c bl grn & lt grn 4.25 3.75
**669** A164 25c rose red & rose 4.25 3.75
**670** A164 30c bl & lt bl 2.25 2.50
**671** A164 1p brown & yellow 90.00 80.00
*Nos. 668-671 (4)* 100.75 90.00
Set, never hinged 190.00

Second anniversary of the Civil War.
Nos. 678-681 exist imperforate, Value, set $725 hinged, $950 never hinged .

Isabella I
A165

Gen. Francisco Franco
A166

**1938-39** **Litho.** ***Perf. 10***
**672** A165 20c brt violet ('39) .50 .20
**673** A165 25c brown carmine 5.25 .60
**674** A165 30c rose red .20 .20
**675** A165 40c dull violet .25 .20
**676** A165 50c indigo ('39) 22.50 2.50
**677** A165 1p deep blue 7.50 .90
*Nos. 672-677 (6)* 36.20 4.60
Set, never hinged 87.50

Nos. 672-677 exist imperforate. Value set, $225 hinged, $300 never hinged.

Imprint: "Sanchez Toda"

**1939-40** ***Perf. 10***
**678** A166 20c brt violet .30 .20
**679** A166 25c rose lake .30 .20
**680** A166 30c rose carmine .25 .20
**681** A166 40c slate green .20 .20
**682** A166 45c vermilion ('40) 1.75 1.60
**683** A166 50c indigo .25 .20
**684** A166 60c orange 2.75 2.50
**685** A166 70c blue .35 .20
**686** A166 1p black 11.00 .20
**687** A166 2p dark brown 16.50 1.10
**688** A166 4p dark violet 87.50 16.00
**689** A166 10p light brown 45.00 40.00
*Nos. 678-689 (12)* 166.15 62.60
Set, never hinged 290.00

#686-689 have value & "Pta." on 1 line while #702-705 have value & "Pta." on 2 lines.
Nos. 678-689 exist imperforate. Value set, $525 hinged, $650 never hinged.

Without Imprint

***Perf. 9½x10¼***

**1939-47** **Litho.** **Unwmk.**
**690** A166 5c dull brn vio .40 .20
**691** A166 10c brown orange 1.75 .60
**692** A166 15c lt green .45 .20
**693** A166 20c brt violet ('40) .40 .20
**694** A166 25c dp claret ('40) .40 .20
**695** A166 30c blue ('40) .40 .20
**697** A166 40c Prus grn ('40) .40 .20
*a.* 40c greenish black .55 .20
Never hinged .65
**698** A166 45c ultra ('41) .45 .20
**699** A166 50c indigo ('40) .40 .20
*a.* Perf. 11½ ('47) 30.00 3.00
Never hinged 50.00
**700** A166 60c dull org ('40) .55 .20
**701** A166 70c blue ('40) .65 .20
**702** A166 1p gray blk ('40) 6.25 .20
**703** A166 2p dull brn ('41) 7.75 .20
**704** A166 4p dull rose ('40) 29.00 .20
**705** A166 10p lt brown ('40) 140.00 2.50
*Nos. 690-705 (15)* 189.25 5.70
Set, never hinged 330.00

***Perf. 13x13¼***

**1949-53** **Litho.** **Unwmk.**
*693a* A166 20c brt violet .20 .20
*694a* A166 25c dp claret .20 .20
*695a* A166 30c blue .20 .20
**696** A166 35c aqua ('51) .20 .20
*697b* A166 40c Prus grn ('50) .20 .20
*698a* A166 45c ultra ('52) .20 .20
*699b* A166 50c indigo .20 .20
*700a* A166 60c dull org .20 .20
*701a* A166 70c blue ('53) 16.00 .20
*702a* A166 1p gray blk ('51) 8.25 .20
*703a* A166 2p dull brn ('50) 3.00 .20
*704a* A166 4p dull rose 5.00 .20
*705a* A166 10p lt brown ('53) 1.10 .30
*Nos. 693a-705a (13)* 34.95 2.70
Set, never hinged 80.00

The 40c exists in three types, with variations in the value tablet: I. "CTS" does not touch bottom line. II. Light background in tablet. "CTS" touches bottom line. III. As type I, but with well defined lines of white and color around rectangle.
The 60c exists in two types: I. Top and left side of value tablet touch rest of design. II. Tablet separated from rest of design by white lines.
Five values exist with perf. 10: 5c, 10c, 45c, 4p and 10p.
The imperforate 10c dull claret, type A166, without imprint, is a postal tax stamp, RA14.

**1944** **Redrawn**
**706** A166 1p gray 50.00 .65
Never hinged 110.00

"PTS" instead of "PTA" as No. 702.
Nos. 690-704 and 706 exist imperforate. Value, set $925.

The value reads "PTAS" instead of "PTS"

**1944** **Unwmk.** ***Perf. 9½x10½, 13***
**709** A166 10p brown 14.00 .30
Never hinged 20.00

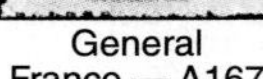

General Franco — A167

St. John of the Cross — A168

**1942-48** **Engr.** ***Perf. 12½x13***
**712** A167 40c chestnut .40 .20
**713** A167 75c dk bl, perf. 9½x10½ ('46) 3.50 .40
**714** A167 90c dk green ('48) .30 .20
*a.* Perf. 9½x10½ ('47) 1.40 .20
**715** A167 1.35p purple ('48) .90 .20
*a.* Perf. 9½x10½ ('46) 2.00 .40
*Nos. 712-715 (4)* 5.10 1.00
Set, never hinged 8.00

**1942** **Litho.** ***Perf. 9½x10½***
**721** A168 20c violet .50 .20
**722** A168 40c salmon 1.10 .60
**723** A168 75c ultra 1.40 1.75
*Nos. 721-723 (3)* 3.00 2.55
Set, never hinged 4.25

St. John of the Cross (1542-1591).
Nos. 721-723 exist imperforate. Value, $65 hinged, $80 never hinged.

**Holy Year Issues**

Statue in St. James Cathedral
A169

St. James of Compostela
A170

Incense Burner — A171

Carvings in St. James Cathedral
A172 A174

St. James — A173

St. James' Casket — A175

East Portal of Cathedral
A176

St. James Cathedral
A177

***Perf. 9½x10½***

**1943, Oct.** **Litho.** **Unwmk.**
**724** A169 20c deep blue .20 .20
**725** A170 40c dk red brown .45 .20
**726** A171 75c deep blue 1.90 1.90

Nos. 725 and 727 exist imperforate. Value, $550.

**1943-44** ***Perf. 9½x10½, 10½x9½***
**727** A172 20c rose red ('44) .20 .20
**728** A173 40c dull green .45 .20
**729** A174 75c dk blue ('44) 2.50 2.00

**1944**
**730** A175 20c red violet .20 .20
**731** A176 40c dull brown .65 .20
**732** A177 75c bright blue 27.50 29.00
*Nos. 724-732 (9)* 34.05 34.10
Set, never hinged 72.50

**Millenium of Castile Issues**

Arms of Soria — A178

Arms of Castile — A179

Arms of Avila
A180

Fortress
A181

Arms of Segovia
A182

Arms of Fernan González
A183

Arms of Burgos A185

Arms of Santander A186

**1944 Litho.** ***Perf. 9½x10½***

| | | | |
|---|---|---|---|
| **733** A178 20c violet | .20 | .20 |
| **734** A179 40c dull brown | 2.50 | .45 |
| **735** A180 75c blue | 2.50 | *2.75* |

**1944**

| | | |
|---|---|---|
| **736** A181 20c rose violet | .20 | .20 |
| **737** A182 40c dull brown | 2.50 | .45 |
| **738** A183 75c dull blue | 2.40 | *2.50* |

**1944**

| | | |
|---|---|---|
| **739** A180 20c red violet | .20 | .20 |
| **740** A185 40c dull brown | 1.90 | .45 |
| **741** A186 75c blue | 2.75 | *3.00* |
| *Nos. 733-741 (9)* | 15.15 | 10.20 |
| Set, never hinged | 24.00 | |

Nos. 733, 738 and 741 exist imperforate. Value, $650. Value never hinged, $900.
No. 739 exists imperforate on grayish paper.

Francisco Gomez de Quevedo y Villegas (1580-1645), Writer — A187

**1945, Sept. 8 Engr.** ***Perf. 10***

| | | |
|---|---|---|
| **742** A187 40c dark brown | .65 | .55 |
| Never hinged | 1.10 | |

Exists imperf. Value $80.

Type of Semi-Postal Stamp, 1940, Without Imprint at Lower Left and Right

**1946, Jan. 1 Litho.** ***Perf. 11***

| | | |
|---|---|---|
| **743** SP20 50c (40c + 10c) sl grn & rose vio | 1.40 | .25 |
| Never hinged | 2.40 | |

No. 743 was used as an ordinary postage stamp of 50c denomination.
Exists imperf. Value $80.

Elio Antonio de Nebrija — A188

University of Salamanca and Signature of Francisco de Vitoria — A189

**1946, Oct. 12 Engr.** ***Perf. 9½x10***

| | | |
|---|---|---|
| **744** A188 50c deep plum | .40 | .30 |
| **745** A189 75c deep blue | .50 | .45 |
| *Nos. 744-745,C121 (3)* | 2.80 | 3.25 |
| Set, never hinged | 4.75 | |

Stamp Day and the Day of the Race, Oct. 12, 1946.
Nos. 744-745 and C121 exist imperforate. Value set, $160 inged, $240 never hinged.

Francisco de Goya A190

Benito Jeronimo Feijoo y Montenegro A191

**1946, Oct 26**

| | | |
|---|---|---|
| **746** A190 25c deep plum | .20 | .20 |
| **747** A190 50c green | .20 | .20 |
| **748** A190 75c dark blue | .60 | .75 |
| *Nos. 746-748 (3)* | | 1.15 |
| Set, never hinged | 1.00 | |

Francisco de Goya, birth bicentenary.
Nos. 746-748 exist imperforate. Value set, $25 hinged, $32.50 never hinged.

**1947, June 1 Unwmk.**

| | | |
|---|---|---|
| **749** A191 50c deep green | .45 | .35 |
| Never hinged | .65 | |

No. 749 exists imperforate. Value, $35.

Don Quixote Reading A192

"Don Quixote" by Zuloaga A193

**1947, Oct. 9 Engr.** ***Perf. 9½x10½***

| | | |
|---|---|---|
| **750** A192 50c sepia | .20 | .25 |
| **751** A193 75c dark blue | .35 | .45 |
| *Nos. 750-751,C122 (3)* | 4.55 | 4.70 |
| Set, never hinged | 6.65 | |

Stamp Day and the 400th anniv. of the birth of Miguel de Cervantes Saavedra.
Nos. 750-751 and C122 exist imperforate. Value set, $550 hinged, $650 never hinged.

General Franco
A194 A195

**1948 Litho.** ***Perf. 12½x13***

| | | |
|---|---|---|
| **752** A194 15c green | .20 | .20 |
| **753** A195 50c violet | .80 | .20 |
| Set, never hinged | 1.25 | |

Nos. 752 and 753 exist imperforate. Value set, $400 hinged, $550 never hinged.
See Nos. 760-768, 780, 801-803. For surcharges see Nos. B137-B138.

Hernando Cortez — A196

Mateo Aleman — A197

**1948, June 15 Engr.** ***Perf. 12½x13***

| | | |
|---|---|---|
| **754** A196 35c black | .20 | .20 |

***Perf. 9½x10½***

| | | |
|---|---|---|
| **755** A197 70c dk violet brn | 1.40 | 2.00 |
| *a.* Perf. 12½x13 | 25.00 | 25.00 |
| Set, never hinged | 2.25 | |

No. 754 exists imperforate. Value set, $100 hinged, $125 never hinged.

Ferdinand III (The Saint) — A198

Grandson of Adm. Ramon de Bonifaz — A199

**1948, Sept. 20 Litho.** ***Perf. 12½x13***

| | | |
|---|---|---|
| **756** A198 25c rose violet | .20 | .20 |
| **757** A199 30c scarlet | .20 | .20 |
| Set, never hinged | .50 | |

700th anniversary of the Spanish navy and of the capture of Seville by Ferdinand the Saint.

José de Salamanca y Mayol — A200

Train Crossing Pancorbo Viaduct — A201

***Perf. 12½x13, 13x12½***

**1948, Oct. 9 Unwmk.**

| | | |
|---|---|---|
| **758** A200 50c brown | .50 | .20 |
| **759** A201 5p deep green | 1.40 | .20 |
| *Nos. 758-759,C125 (3)* | 3.40 | 1.90 |
| Set, never hinged | 5.50 | |

Centenary of Spanish railroads.

Franco Types of 1948

**1948-49 Litho.** ***Perf. 12½x13***

| | | |
|---|---|---|
| **760** A194 5c brown | .20 | .20 |
| **761** A195 25c vermilion | .20 | .20 |
| **762** A195 35c blue green | .20 | .20 |
| **763** A195 40c red brown | .55 | .20 |
| **764** A195 45c car rose ('49) | .30 | .20 |
| **765** A194 50c bister | .80 | .20 |
| **766** A195 70c purple ('49) | 1.50 | .25 |
| **767** A195 75c dk vio blue | 1.25 | .25 |
| **768** A195 1p rose pink | 4.00 | .20 |
| *Nos. 760-768 (9)* | 9.00 | 1.90 |
| Set, never hinged | 13.00 | |

Imperforates exist of Nos. 761 ($100), 762 ($300), 764 ($300) and 768 ($500)

Symbols of UPU A202

**1949, Oct. 9**

| | | |
|---|---|---|
| **769** A202 50c red brown | .35 | .20 |
| **770** A202 75c violet blue | .35 | .55 |
| *Nos. 769-770,C126 (3)* | .90 | 1.20 |
| Set, never hinged | 1.90 | |

75th anniv. of the UPU.

St. John of God — A203

Pedro Calderon de la Barca — A204

**1950, Mar. 8 Engr. Unwmk.**

| | | |
|---|---|---|
| **771** A203 1p dark violet | 6.25 | 4.00 |
| Never hinged | 11.50 | |

400th anniversary of the death of St. John of God, humanitarian.

**1950-53 Photo.** ***Perf. 12½***

Designs: 10c Lope de Vega. 15c, Tirso de Molina. 20c, Juan Ruiz de Alarcon, dramatist. 50c, St. Antonio Maria Claret y Clara.

| | | |
|---|---|---|
| **772** A204 5c brown ('51) | .20 | .20 |
| **773** A204 10c dp rose brn ('51) | .20 | .20 |
| **773A** A204 15c dk sl grn ('53) | .20 | .20 |
| **774** A204 20c violet | .20 | .20 |

***Perf. 12½x13***

**Engr.**

| | | |
|---|---|---|
| **775** A204 50c dk blue ('51) | 2.50 | 1.50 |
| *Nos. 772-775 (5)* | 3.30 | 2.30 |
| Set, never hinged | 4.35 | |

No. 774 exists imperforate. Value, $250.

Stamp of 1850 — A205

Queen Isabella I — A206

**1950, Oct. 12 Engr.** ***Imperf.***

| | | |
|---|---|---|
| **776** A205 50c purple | 4.75 | 6.50 |
| **777** A205 75c ultra | 4.75 | 6.50 |
| **778** A205 10p dk slate grn | 85.00 | 87.50 |
| **779** A205 15p red | 85.00 | 87.50 |
| *Nos. 776-779,C127-C130 (8)* | 348.50 | 376.00 |
| Set, never hinged | 575.00 | |

Centenary of Spain's stamps.

Franco Type of 1948

**1950 Litho.** ***Perf. 12½x13***

| | | |
|---|---|---|
| **780** A195 45c red | .60 | .20 |
| Never hinged | .90 | |

**1951, Apr. 22 Photo.** ***Perf. 12½***

| | | |
|---|---|---|
| **781** A206 50c brown | .50 | .35 |
| **782** A206 75c blue | .60 | .35 |
| **783** A206 90c rose brown | .35 | .25 |
| **784** A206 1.50p orange | 8.00 | 7.50 |
| **785** A206 2.80p olive grn | 20.00 | 20.00 |
| *Nos. 781-785 (5)* | 29.45 | 28.45 |
| Set, never hinged | 52.50 | |

500th anniversary of the birth of Queen Isabella I. See Nos. C132-C136.

Ferdinand, the Catholic A210

Maria Michaela Dermaisiéres A211

**1952, May 10 Photo.** ***Perf. 13***

| | | |
|---|---|---|
| **787** A210 50c green | .45 | .30 |
| **788** A210 75c indigo | 2.75 | 1.40 |
| **789** A210 90c rose brown | .40 | .35 |
| **790** A210 1.50p orange | 7.75 | 8.00 |
| **791** A210 2.80p brown | 15.00 | 16.00 |
| *Nos. 787-791 (5)* | 26.35 | 26.05 |
| Set, never hinged | 50.00 | |

500th anniversary of the birth of Ferdinand the Catholic of Spain. See Nos. C139-C143.

**1952, May 26** ***Perf. 12½x13***

| | | |
|---|---|---|
| **792** A211 90c claret | .20 | .20 |
| Never hinged | .20 | |

35th International Eucharistic Congress, Barcelona, 1952. See No. C137.

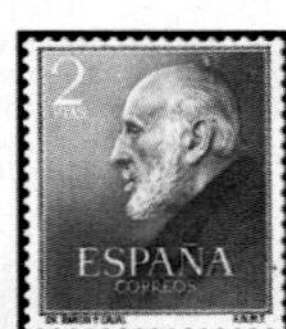
Dr. Santiago Ramon y Cajal — A212

Portrait: 4.50p, Dr. Jaime Ferran y Clua.

**1952, July 8 Photo.**

| | | |
|---|---|---|
| **793** A212 2p bright blue | 13.50 | .50 |
| **794** A212 4.50p red brown | .50 | .80 |
| Set, never hinged | 22.50 | |

Centenary of the births of Dr. Santiago Ramon y Cajal and Dr. Jaime Ferran y Clua.

University Seal — A213

Luis de Leon — A214

Cathedral of Salamanca A215

**1953, Oct. 12** ***Perf. 12½x13, 13x12½***

**795** A213 50c deep magenta .45 .30
**796** A214 90c dark olive gray 1.65 2.00
**797** A215 2p brown 11.00 3.25
*Nos. 795-797 (3)* 13.10 5.55
Set, never hinged 17.00

Stamp Day, 10/12/53, and 700th anniv. of the founding of the University of Salamanca.

The Magdalene — A216

**1954, Jan. 10** ***Perf. 12½x13***

**798** A216 1.25p deep magenta .20 .20
Never hinged .20

José de Ribera, painter, 300th death anniv.

St. James of Compostela A217

St. James Cathedral A218

**1954, Mar. 1**

**799** A217 50c dark brown .20 .20
**800** A218 3p blue 27.50 3.00
Set, never hinged 47.50

Holy year of Compostela, 1954.

Franco Types of 1948

**1954** **Litho.** ***Perf. 12½x13***

**801** A194 5c olive gray .20 .20
**802** A195 30c deep green .20 .20
**803** A194 80c dull car rose 1.65 .20
*Nos. 801-803 (3)* 2.05 .60
Set, never hinged 5.00

Virgin by Alonso Cano — A219

Marcelino Menendez y Pelayo — A220

Virgins: 15c, Begoña. 25c, Of the Abandoned. 30c, Black. 50c, Of the Pillar. 60c, Covadonga. 80c, Kings'. 1p, Almudena. 2p, Africa. 3p, Guadalupe.

**1954, July 18** **Photo.** ***Perf. 12½x13***

**804** A219 10c dk car rose .20 .20
**805** A219 15c olive green .20 .20
**806** A219 25c purple .20 .20
**807** A219 30c brown .25 .20
**808** A219 50c brown olive .55 .20
**809** A219 60c gray .25 .20
**810** A219 80c grnsh gray 2.50 .20
**811** A219 1p lilac gray 2.50 .20

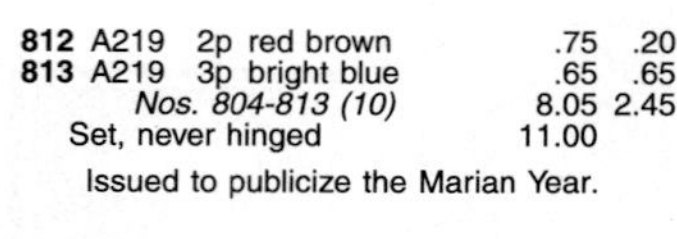
**812** A219 2p red brown .75 .20
**813** A219 3p bright blue .65 .65
*Nos. 804-813 (10)* 8.05 2.45
Set, never hinged 11.00

Issued to publicize the Marian Year.

**1954, Oct. 12**

**814** A220 80c dk gray grn 5.75 .40
Never hinged 10.00

Stamp Day, October 12, 1954.

Gen. Franco — A221

Imprint: "F.N.M.T."

**1954-56** ***Perf. 12½x13***

**815** A221 10c dk car lake .20 .20
**816** A221 15c bister .20 .20
**817** A221 20c dk ol grn ('55) .20 .20
**818** A221 25c blue violet .20 .20
**819** A221 30c brown .20 .20
**820** A221 40c rose vio ('55) .20 .20
**821** A221 50c dk brn olive .20 .20
**822** A221 60c dk vio brown .20 .20
**823** A221 70c dk green .20 .20
**824** A221 80c dk blue grn .20 .20
**825** A221 1p dp orange .20 .20
**826** A221 1.40p lil rose ('56) .20 .20
**827** A221 1.50p lt bl grn ('56) .20 .20
**828** A221 1.80p emerald ('56) .20 .20
**829** A221 2p red 13.00 1.25
**830** A221 2p red lilac ('56) .20 .20
**831** A221 3p Prus blue .20 .20
**832** A221 5p dk red brn .20 .20
**833** A221 6p dk gray ('55) .20 .20
**834** A221 8p brt vio ('56) .20 .20
**835** A221 10p yel grn ('55) .25 .20
*Nos. 815-835 (21)* 17.05 5.25
Set, never hinged 20.00

Coils: The 1.50p, No. 830, the 3p and the 6p were issued in coils in brighter tones (the 3p in 1974, others in 1973). Every fifth stamp has a black control number on the back.

See Nos. 937-938, 1852-1855.

St. Ignatius of Loyola — A222

St. Ignatius and Loyola Palace A223

***Perf. 13x12½, 12½x13***

**1955, Oct. 12** **Photo.** **Unwmk.**

**836** A222 25c dull purple .20 .20
**837** A223 60c bister .40 .30
**838** A222 80c Prus green 1.65 .25
*Nos. 836-838 (3)* 2.25 .75
Set, never hinged 4.25

4th cent. of the death of St. Ignatius of Loyola, founder of the Jesuit Order, and Day of the Stamp.

Symbols of Telegraph and Radio Communication A224

St. Vincent Ferrer A225

**1955, Dec. 8** ***Perf. 13x12½***

**839** A224 15c dk olive bis .30 .20
**840** A224 80c Prus green 4.50 .25
**841** A224 3p bright blue 8.50 1.25
*Nos. 839-841 (3)* 13.30 1.70
Set, never hinged 27.50

Spanish telegraph system centenary.

**1955, Dec. 20** ***Perf. 13***

**842** A225 15c olive bister .40 .25
Never hinged .85

Canonization of St. Vincent Ferrer, 5th cent.

"Holy Family" by El Greco — A226

Marching Soldiers and Dove — A227

**1955, Dec. 24** ***Perf. 13x12½***

**843** A226 80c dark green 3.75 .95
Never hinged 6.00

**1956, July 17** **Unwmk.**

**844** A227 15c olive bis & brn .20 .20
**845** A227 50c lt ol grn & ol .50 .30
**846** A227 80c mag & grnsh blk 4.25 .25
**847** A227 3p ultra & dp blue 4.25 1.40
*Nos. 844-847 (4)* 9.20 2.15
Set, never hinged 19.00

20th anniversary of Civil War.

Ciudad de Toledo A228

**1956, Aug. 3** ***Perf. 12½x13***

**848** A228 3p blue 3.50 2.00
Never hinged 5.75

Issued to publicize the voyage of the S. S. Ciudad de Toledo to Central and South America carrying the First Floating (Industrial) Exposition.

Black Virgin of Montserrat A229

Archangel Gabriel by Fra Angelico A230

Design: 60c, Monastery of Montserrat, mountains and crucifix.

**1956, Sept. 11** ***Perf. 13x12½***

**849** A229 15c bister .20 .20
**850** A229 60c violet black .20 .20
**851** A229 80c blue green .35 .45
*Nos. 849-851 (3)* .75 .85
Set, never hinged .85

75th anniv. of the coronation of the Black Virgin of Montserrat.

**1956, Oct. 12** **Engr.**

**852** A230 80c dull green .90 .45
Never hinged 1.25

Stamp Day, Oct. 12.

Statistical Chart A231

**1956, Nov. 3** ***Perf. 12½x13***

**853** A231 15c dk olive bis .35 .35
**854** A231 80c green 3.50 .90
**855** A231 1p red orange 3.50 .90
*Nos. 853-855 (3)* 7.35 2.15
Set, never hinged 10.00

Centenary of Spanish Statistics.

Hermitage and Monument A232

**1956, Dec. 4**

**856** A232 80c dull blue grn 2.00 .25
Never hinged 5.50

20th anniversary of the nomination of Gen. Franco as chief of state and commander in chief of the army.

Hungarian Children A233

St. Marguerite Alacoque's Vision of Jesus A234

**1956, Dec. 17** ***Perf. 13x12½***

**857** A233 10c brown lake .20 .20
**858** A233 15c dk bister .20 .20
**859** A233 50c olive gray .30 .20
**860** A233 80c dk blue grn 2.25 .20
**861** A233 1p red orange 2.50 .20
**862** A233 3p brt blue 6.50 2.50
*Nos. 857-862 (6)* 11.95 3.50
Set, never hinged 20.00

Issued in sympathy to the children of Hungary.

**1957, Oct. 12** **Photo.** **Unwmk.**

**863** A234 15c dk olive bis .20 .20
**864** A234 60c violet blk .25 .20
**865** A234 80c dk blue grn .35 .20
*Nos. 863-865 (3)* .80 .60
Set, never hinged 1.00

Centenary of the feast of the Sacred Heart of Jesus and for Stamp Day 1957.

Gonzalo de Cordoba — A235

**1958, Feb. 28** **Engr.** ***Perf. 13x12½***

**866** A235 1.80p yellow green .25 .20
Never hinged .35

Issued in honor of El Gran Capitan, 15th century military leader.

"The Parasol," by Goya — A236

"Wife of the Bookseller of Carretas Street" — A237

Goya Paintings: 50c, Duke of Fernan-Nunez. 60c, The Crockery Seller. 70c, Isabel Cobos de Porcel. 80c, Goya by Vicente Lopez. 1p, "El Pelele" (Carnival Doll). 1.80p, Goya's grandson Marianito. 2p, The Vintage. 3p, The Drinker.

**1958, Mar. 24 Photo. *Perf. 13***
**Gold Frame**

| | | | | | |
|---|---|---|---|---|---|
| **867** | A236 | 15c | bister | .20 | .20 |
| **868** | A237 | 40c | plum | .20 | .20 |
| **869** | A237 | 50c | olive gray | .20 | .20 |
| **870** | A237 | 60c | violet gray | .20 | .20 |
| **871** | A237 | 70c | dp yellow grn | .20 | .20 |
| **872** | A237 | 80c | dk slate grn | .20 | .20 |
| **873** | A237 | 1p | orange red | .20 | .20 |
| **874** | A237 | 1.80p | brt green | .20 | .20 |
| **875** | A237 | 2p | red lilac | .40 | .45 |
| **876** | A236 | 3p | brt blue | .65 | .85 |
| | | | *Nos. 867-876 (10)* | 2.65 | 2.90 |
| | | | Set, never hinged | 2.40 | |

Issued to honor Francisco Jose de Goya and for the "Day of the Stamp," Mar. 24.

See Nos. 1111-1114. For other art types see A240a, A246a, A257, A272, A285a, A300, A310, A324, A340-A341, A360, A371 and footnote following No. 1606.

Exhibition Emblem and Globe — A238

**1958, June 7 *Perf. 13x12½***

| | | | | | |
|---|---|---|---|---|---|
| **877** | A238 | 80c | car, dk brn & gray | .45 | .20 |
| *a.* | | | Souvenir sheet, imperf. | 20.00 | 20.00 |
| **878** | A238 | 3p | car, vio blk & bl | 1.75 | .90 |
| *a.* | | | Souvenir sheet, imperf. | 20.00 | 20.00 |
| | | | Set, never hinged | 2.75 | |
| | | | #877a-878a never hinged | 55.00 | |

No. 877a sold for 2p, No. 878a for 5p.
Universal and Intl. Exposition at Brussels.

Charles V — A239

Various Portraits of Charles V: 50c, 1.80p, with helmet. 70c, 2p, facing left. 80c, 3p, with beret.

**1958, July 30 Photo. *Perf. 13***

| | | | | | |
|---|---|---|---|---|---|
| **879** | A239 | 15c | buff & brown | .20 | .20 |
| **880** | A239 | 50c | lt grn & ol brn | .20 | .20 |
| **881** | A239 | 70c | gray, grn & blk | .20 | .20 |
| **882** | A239 | 80c | pale brn & Prus grn | .20 | .20 |
| **883** | A239 | 1p | bis & brick red | .20 | .20 |
| **884** | A239 | 1.80p | pale grn & brt grn | .20 | .20 |
| **885** | A239 | 2p | gray & lilac | .30 | .30 |
| **886** | A239 | 3p | pale brn & brt bl | .85 | .65 |
| | | | *Nos. 879-886 (8)* | 2.35 | 2.15 |
| | | | Set, never hinged | 3.25 | |

400th anniv. of the death of Charles V (Carlos I of Spain.)

Escorial and Streamlined Train — A240

Designs: 60c, 2p, Railroad bridge at Despeñaperros, vert. 80c, 3p, Train and Castle de La Mota.

**1958, Sept. 29 *Perf. 12½x13***

| | | | | | |
|---|---|---|---|---|---|
| **887** | A240 | 15c | dk olive bis | .20 | .20 |
| **888** | A240 | 60c | dk purple | .20 | .20 |
| **889** | A240 | 80c | dk blue grn | .20 | .20 |
| **890** | A240 | 1p | red orange | .20 | .20 |
| **891** | A240 | 2p | red lilac | .20 | .20 |
| **892** | A240 | 3p | blue | .70 | .40 |
| | | | *Nos. 887-892 (6)* | 1.70 | 1.40 |
| | | | Set, never hinged | 3.00 | |

Intl. Railroad Cong., Madrid, Sept. 28-Oct. 7.

Velazquez Self-portrait A240a

Velazquez Paintings: 15c, The Drinkers, horiz. 40c, The Spinners. 50c, Surrender of Breda. 60c, The Little Princesses. 70c, Prince Balthazar. 1p, The Coronation of Our Lady. 1.80p, Aesop. 2p, Vulcan's Forge. 3p, Menippus.

**1959, Mar. 24 Photo. *Perf. 13***
**Gold Frame**

| | | | | | |
|---|---|---|---|---|---|
| **893** | A240a | 15c | dk brown | .20 | .20 |
| **894** | A240a | 40c | rose violet | .20 | .20 |
| **895** | A240a | 50c | olive | .20 | .20 |
| **896** | A240a | 60c | black brown | .20 | .20 |
| **897** | A240a | 70c | dp yellow grn | .20 | .20 |
| **898** | A240a | 80c | dk slate grn | .20 | .20 |
| **899** | A240a | 1p | orange red | .20 | .20 |
| **900** | A240a | 1.80p | emerald | .20 | .20 |
| **901** | A240a | 2p | red lilac | .20 | .20 |
| **902** | A240a | 3p | brt blue | .35 | .45 |
| | | | *Nos. 893-902 (10)* | 2.15 | 2.25 |
| | | | Set, never hinged | 2.00 | |

Issued to honor Diego de Silva Velazquez (1599-1660) and for Stamp Day, Mar. 24.

For other art types see A236-A237, A246a, A257, A272, A285a, A300, A310, A324, A340-A341, A360, A371 and footnote following No. 1606.

Civil War Memorial — A241

**1959, Apr 1. Litho. Unwmk.**

| | | | | | |
|---|---|---|---|---|---|
| **903** | A241 | 80c | yel grn & dk sl grn | .20 | .20 |
| | | | Never hinged | .30 | |

Inauguration of the war memorial at the monastery of the Holy Cross in the Valley of the Fallen.

Louis XIV and Philip IV — A242

**1959, Oct. 24 Photo. *Perf. 13x12½***

| | | | | | |
|---|---|---|---|---|---|
| **904** | A242 | 1p | gold & rose brn | .20 | .20 |
| | | | Never hinged | .30 | |

300th anniv. of the signing of the Treaty of the Pyrenees. Design shows the French-Spanish meeting at Isle des Faisans in 1659, as pictured in the Lebrun Tapestry, Versailles.

Monastery of Guadalupe A243

80c, Monastery, different view. 1p, Portals.

**1959, Nov. 16 Engr. *Perf. 12½x13***

| | | | | | |
|---|---|---|---|---|---|
| **905** | A243 | 15c | lt red brown | .20 | .20 |
| **906** | A243 | 80c | slate | .20 | .20 |
| **907** | A243 | 1p | rose red | .20 | .20 |
| | | | *Nos. 905-907 (3)* | .60 | .60 |
| | | | Set, never hinged | .60 | |

Entrance of the Franciscan Brothers into Guadalupe monastery, 50th anniv.

Holy Family, by Goya — A244

**1959, Dec. 10 Photo. *Perf. 13x12½***

| | | | | | |
|---|---|---|---|---|---|
| **908** | A244 | 1p | orange brown | .20 | .20 |
| | | | Never hinged | .40 | |

**Catalogue values for unused stamps in this section, from this point to the end of the section, are for Never Hinged items.**

Lidian Bull A245

Bullfighter, 19th Century — A246

Designs: 20c, Rounding up bulls. 25c, Running with the bulls, Pamplona. 30c, Bull entering arena. 50c, Bullfighting with cape. 70c, Bullfighting with banderillas. 80c, 1p, 1.40p, 1.50p, Fighting with muleta, various poses. 1.80p, Mounted bullfighter placing banderillas.

***Perf. 12½x13, 13x12½***

**1960, Feb. 29 Engr. Unwmk.**

| | | | | | |
|---|---|---|---|---|---|
| **909** | A245 | 15c | sepia & bis | .20 | .20 |
| **910** | A245 | 20c | vio & bl vio | .20 | .20 |
| **911** | A246 | 25c | gray | .20 | .20 |
| **912** | A246 | 30c | sepia & bister | .20 | .20 |
| **913** | A246 | 50c | dull vio & sep | .20 | .20 |
| **914** | A246 | 70c | sepia & sl grn | .20 | .20 |
| **915** | A246 | 80c | blue grn & grn | .20 | .20 |
| **916** | A246 | 1p | red & brn | .20 | .20 |
| **917** | A246 | 1.40p | brown & lake | .20 | .20 |
| **918** | A246 | 1.50p | grnsh bl & grn | .20 | .20 |
| **919** | A245 | 1.80p | grn & dk grn | .20 | .20 |
| **920** | A246 | 5p | brn & brn car | .55 | .45 |
| | | | *Nos. 909-920,C159-C162 (16)* | 3.90 | 3.65 |

Murillo Self-portrait A246a

Christ of Lepanto A247

Murillo Paintings: 25c, The Good Shepherd. 40c, Rebecca and Eliezer. 50c, Virgin of the Rosary. 70c, Immaculate Conception. 80c, Children with Shell. 1.50p, Holy Family with Bird, horiz. 2.50p, Children Playing Dice. 3p, Children Eating. 5p, Children counting Money.

**1960, Mar. 24 Photo. *Perf. 13***
**Gold Frame**

| | | | | | |
|---|---|---|---|---|---|
| **921** | A246a | 25c | dull violet | .20 | .20 |
| **922** | A246a | 40c | plum | .20 | .20 |
| **923** | A246a | 50c | olive gray | .20 | .20 |
| **924** | A246a | 70c | dp yel grn | .20 | .20 |
| **925** | A246a | 80c | deep green | .20 | .20 |
| **926** | A246a | 1p | violet brown | .20 | .20 |
| **927** | A246a | 1.50p | blue green | .20 | .20 |
| **928** | A246a | 2.50p | rose car | .20 | .20 |
| **929** | A246a | 3p | brt blue | 1.25 | .60 |
| **930** | A246a | 5p | deep red brn | .35 | .25 |
| | | | *Nos. 921-930 (10)* | 3.20 | 2.45 |

Issued to honor Bartolome Esteban Murillo (1617-1682) and for Stamp Day, Mar. 24.

For other art types see A236-A237, A240a, A257, A272, A285a, A300, A310, A324, A340-A341, A360, A371 and footnote following No. 1606.

**1960, Mar. 27 *Perf. 13x12½***

80c, 2.50p, 10p, Holy Family Church, Barcelona.

| | | | | | |
|---|---|---|---|---|---|
| **931** | A247 | 70c | brn car & grn | 1.60 | 1.25 |
| **932** | A247 | 80c | blk & ol grn | 1.60 | 1.25 |
| **933** | A247 | 1p | cl & brt red | 1.60 | 1.25 |
| **934** | A247 | 2.50p | brt vio & gray vio | 1.60 | 1.25 |
| **935** | A247 | 5p | sepia & bister | 1.60 | 1.25 |
| **936** | A247 | 10p | sepia & bister | 1.60 | 1.25 |
| | | | *Nos. 931-936,C163-C166 (10)* | 28.60 | 20.50 |

First International Congress of Philately, Barcelona, March 26-Apr. 5. Nos. 931-936 could be bought at the exhibition upon presentation of 5p entrance ticket.

Franco Type of 1954-56
Imprint: "F.N.M.T.-B"

**1960, Mar. 31 Photo. *Perf. 13***

| | | | | | |
|---|---|---|---|---|---|
| **937** | A221 | 1p | deep orange | 1.40 | .60 |
| **938** | A221 | 5p | dark red brown | 1.40 | .60 |

Printed and issued at the International Congress of Philately in Barcelona.

St. Juan de Ribera — A248

St. Vincent de Paul — A249

**1960, Aug. 16 Photo. *Perf. 13***

| | | | | | |
|---|---|---|---|---|---|
| **939** | A248 | 1p | orange red | .20 | .20 |
| **940** | A248 | 2.50p | lilac rose | .20 | .20 |

Canonization of St. Juan de Ribera.

Common Design Types pictured following the introduction.

**Europa Issue, 1960**
Common Design Type

**1960, Sept. 19 *Perf. 12½x13***
**Size: 38½x21½mm**

| | | | | | |
|---|---|---|---|---|---|
| **941** | CD3 | 1p | sl grn & ol bis | *.75* | .20 |
| **942** | CD3 | 5p | choc & salmon | *.75* | .50 |

**1960, Sept. 27 Unwmk. *Perf. 13***

| | | | | | |
|---|---|---|---|---|---|
| **943** | A249 | 25c | violet | .20 | .20 |
| **944** | A249 | 1p | orange red | .40 | .20 |

3rd centenary of the death of St. Vincent de Paul.

Pedro Menendez de Aviles — A250

Runner — A251

70c, 2.50p, Hernando de Soto. 80c, 3p, Ponce de Leon. 1p, 5p, Alvar Nunez Cabeza de Vaca.

**1960, Oct. 12** ***Perf. 13x12½***

**945** A250 25c vio bl, *bl* .20 .20
**946** A250 70c slate grn, *pink* .20 .20
**947** A250 80c dk grn, *pale brn* .20 .20
**948** A250 1p org brn, *yel* .20 .20
**949** A250 2p dk car rose, *pink* .30 .20
**950** A250 2.50p lil rose, *buff* .60 .20
**951** A250 3p dk blue, *grnsh* 2.75 .50
**952** A250 5p dk brown, *cit* 2.25 .85
*Nos. 945-952 (8)* 6.70 2.55

Florida's discovery & colonization, 4th cent.

***Perf. 13x12½, 12½x13***

**1960, Oct. 31** **Photo.**

Sports: 40c, 2p, Bicycling, horiz. 70c, 2.50p, Soccer, horiz. 80c, 3p, Athlete with rings. 1p, 5p, Hockey on roller skates, horiz.

**953** A251 25c dk vio, brn & blk .20 .20
**954** A251 40c purple, org & blk .20 .20
**955** A251 70c brt green & red .30 .20
**956** A251 80c dp grn, car & blk .25 .20
**957** A251 1p red org, brt grn & blk .55 .20
**958** A251 1.50p Prus grn, brn & blk .40 .20
**959** A251 2p red lil, emer & blk 1.10 .20
**960** A251 2.50p lil rose & green .40 .20
**961** A251 3p ultra, red & blk .75 .20
**962** A251 5p red brn, bl & blk .75 .35
*Nos. 953-962,C167-C170 (14)* 7.70 3.65

Isaac Albeniz — A252

**1960, Nov. 7** ***Perf. 13***

**963** A252 25c dark gray .20 .20
**964** A252 1p orange red .20 .20

Isaac Albeniz, composer, birth centenary.

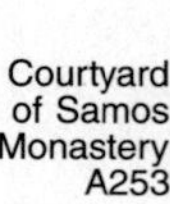

Courtyard of Samos Monastery A253

1p, Fountain, vert. 5p, Facade, vert.

***Perf. 12½x13, 13x12½***

**1960, Nov. 21** **Engr.**

**965** A253 80c bl grn & Prus grn .20 .20
**966** A253 1p org brn & car rose 1.10 .20
**967** A253 5p sepia & ocher 1.10 .45
*Nos. 965-967 (3)* 2.40 .85

Issued in honor of the reconstructed Benedictine monastery at Samos, Lugo.

Adoration, by Velazquez — A254

**1960, Dec. 1** **Photo.** ***Perf. 13x12½***

**968** A254 1p orange red .30 .20

Flight into Egypt by Francisco Bayeu A255

**1961, Jan. 23** ***Perf. 12½x13***

**969** A255 1p copper red .25 .20
**970** A255 5p dull red brown .45 .30

World Refugee Year.

Leandro F. de Moratin, by Goya — A256

St. Peter by El Greco — A257

**1961, Feb. 13** ***Perf. 13***

**971** A256 1p henna brown .20 .20
**972** A256 1.50p dk blue green .20 .20

Leandro Fernandez de Moratin (1760-1828), poet and dramatist, 200th birth anniv.

**1961, Mar. 24** ***Perf. 13***

El Greco Paintings: 40c, Virgin Mary. 70c, Head of Christ. 80c, Knight with Hand on Chest. 1p, Self-portrait. 1.50p, Baptism of Christ. 2.50p, Holy Trinity. 3p, Burial of Count Orgaz. 5p, Christ Stripped of His Garments. 10p, St. Mauritius and the Theban Legion.

**Gold Frame**

**973** A257 25c violet black .20 .20
**974** A257 40c lilac .20 .20
**975** A257 70c green .25 .20
**976** A257 80c Prus green .25 .20
**977** A257 1p chocolate 2.25 .20
**978** A257 1.50p grnsh blue .25 .20
**979** A257 2.50p dk car rose .45 .20
**980** A257 3p bright blue 1.10 .45
**981** A257 5p black brown 3.25 1.40
**982** A257 10p purple .55 .30
*Nos. 973-982 (10)* 8.75 3.55

El Greco and Stamp Day, March 24.

For other art types see A236-A237, A240a, A246a, A272, A285a, A300, A310, A324, A340-A341, A360, A371 and footnote following No. 1606.

Diego Velazquez — A258

Canceled Stamp — A259

Velazquez Paintings: 1p, Duke de Olivares. 2.50p, Infanta Margarita. 10p, Detail from The Spinners, horiz.

**Unwmk.**

**1961, Apr. 17** **Engr.** ***Perf. 13***

**983** A258 80c dk blue & sl grn 1.90 .75
a. Souvenir sheet 7.75 *8.25*
**984** A258 1p brn red & choc 5.50 .75
a. Souvenir sheet 7.75 *8.25*
**985** A258 2.50p vio bl & bl 1.40 1.00
a. Souvenir sheet 7.75 *8.25*
**986** A258 10p grn & yel grn 6.25 2.50
a. Souvenir sheet 7.75 *8.25*
*Nos. 983-986 (4)* 15.05 5.00

300th anniversary (in 1960) of the death of Velazquez, painter.

Each souvenir sheet contains one imperf. stamp. The colors of the stamps have been changed: 80c, red brown & slate; 1p, blue & violet; 2.50p, green & blue; 10p, slate blue & greenish blue. The sheets were sold at a premium.

**1961, May 6** **Photo.** ***Perf. 13x12½***

**987** A259 25c gray & red .20 .20
**988** A259 1p orange & blk 1.10 .20
**989** A259 10p olive grn & brn 1.10 .60
*Nos. 987-989 (3)* 2.40 1.00

Issued for International Stamp Day.

Juan Vazquez de Mella — A260

Flag, Angel and Peace Doves — A261

**1961, June 8** **Unwmk.** ***Perf. 13***

**990** A260 1p henna brown .45 .20
**991** A260 2.30p red lilac .20 .20

Birth centenary of Juan Vazquez de Mella y Fanjul, politician and writer.

**1961, July 10**

Designs: 80c, Ships and Strait of Gibraltar. 1p, Alcazar and horseman. 1.50p, Ruins and triumphal arch. 2p, Horseman over Ebro. 2.30p, Victory parade. 2.50p, Ship building. 3p, Steel industry. 5p, Map of Spanish irrigation dams and statue, horiz. 6p, Dama de Elche statue and power station. 8p, Mining development. 10p, General Franco.

**992** A261 70c multicolored .20 .20
**993** A261 80c multicolored .20 .20
**994** A261 1p multicolored .20 .20
**995** A261 1.50p gold, pink & brn .20 .20
**996** A261 2p gold, gray & bl .20 .20
**997** A261 2.30p multicolored .20 .20
**998** A261 2.50p multicolored .20 .20
**999** A261 3p gold, red & dk gray .35 .25
**1000** A261 5p bl grn, ol gray & pink 2.25 1.10
**1001** A261 6p multicolored 1.10 .75
**1002** A261 8p gold, ol & sep .70 .55
**1003** A261 10p gold, gray & grn .70 .55
*Nos. 992-1003 (12)* 6.50 4.60

25th anniversary of national uprising.

Christ, San Clemente, Tahull A262

Luis de Argote y Gongora A263

Designs: 25c, Bas-relief, Compostela Cathedral. 1p, Cloister of Silos. 2p, Virgin of Irache.

**1961, July 24** **Unwmk.** ***Perf. 13***

**Gold Frame**

**1004** A262 25c blue violet .40 .20
**1005** A262 1p orange brown .55 .20
**1006** A262 2p deep plum .75 .20
**1007** A262 3p grnsh bl, sal & blk .95 .40
*Nos. 1004-1007 (4)* 2.65 1.00

Seventh Exposition of the Council of Europe dedicated to Romanesque art, Barcelona-Santiago de Compostela, July 10-Oct. 10.

**1961, Aug. 10** **Photo.** ***Perf. 13***

**1008** A263 25c violet black .20 .20
**1009** A263 1p henna brown .50 .20

400th anniversary of the birth of Luis de Argote y Gongora, poet.

**Europa Issue, 1961**

Common Design Type

**1961, Sept. 18** ***Perf. 12½x13***

**Size: 37½x21½mm**

**1010** CD4 1p brt vermilion .20 .20
**1011** CD4 5p brown *.45 .30*

Cathedral at Burgos A264

Sebastian de Belalcazar A265

**1961, Oct. 1** ***Perf. 13***

**1012** A264 1p gold & olive green .20 .20

25th anniversary of the nomination of Gen. Francisco Franco as Head of State.

**Builders of the New World**

Portraits: 70c, 2.50p, Blas de Lezo. 80c, 3p, Rodrigo de Bastidas. 1p, 5p, Nuflo de Chaves.

**1961, Oct. 12** **Photo.** ***Perf. 13x12½***

**1013** A265 25c indigo, *grn* .20 .20
**1014** A265 70c grn, *cream* .20 .20
**1015** A265 80c sl grn, *pnksh* .20 .20
**1016** A265 1p dk blue, *sal* .60 .20
**1017** A265 2p dk car, *bluish* 3.75 .20
**1018** A265 2.50p lil, *pale lil* .90 .45
**1019** A265 3p blue, *grysh* 1.90 .80
**1020** A265 5p brown, *yel* 2.00 .90
*Nos. 1013-1020 (8)* 9.75 3.15

Issued to honor the discoverers and conquerors of Colombia and Bolivia.

See Nos. 1131-1138, 1187-1194, 1271-1278, 1316-1323, 1377-1384, 1489-1496, 1548, 1550, 1587-1588, 1632-1633.

Patio of the Kings, Escorial — A266

Views of Escorial: 80c, Patio. 1p, Garden of the Monks and Escorial, horiz. 2.50p, Staircase. 5p, General view of Escorial, horiz. 6p, Main altar.

***Perf. 13x12½, 12½x13***

**1961, Oct. 31** **Engr.** **Unwmk.**

**1021** A266 70c bl grn & ol grn .20 .20
**1022** A266 80c Prus grn & ind .20 .20
**1023** A266 1p ocher & dk red .55 .20
**1024** A266 2.50p cl & dull vio .55 .20
**1025** A266 5p bister & dk brn 1.60 .70
**1026** A266 6p sl bl & dull pur 2.25 1.50
*Nos. 1021-1026 (6)* 5.35 3.00

Alfonso XII Monument, Retiro Park — A267

Church of St. Mary, Naranco — A268

Designs: 1p, King Philip II. 2p, Town hall, horiz. 2.50p, Cibeles fountain, horiz. 3p, Alcala gate, horiz. 5p, Cervantes memorial, Plaza de Espagna.

**Photogravure (25c, 2p, 5p)**
**Engraved (1p, 2.50p, 3p)**

**1961, Nov. 13** **Unwmk.** ***Perf. 13***

**1027** A267 25c gray & dull pur .20 .20
**1028** A267 1p bis brn & gray .30 .20
**1029** A267 2p claret & gray .30 .20
**1030** A267 2.50p black & lilac .25 .20
**1031** A267 3p slate & ind .60 .35

1032 A267 5p Prus grn & beige 1.10 .55
*Nos. 1027-1032 (6)* 2.75 1.70

400th anniv. of Madrid as capital of Spain.

**1961, Nov. 27**

Designs: 1p, King Fruela I, founder of Oviedo. 2p, Cross of the Angels. 2.50p, King Alfonso II. 3p, King Alfonso III. 5p, Apostles from Oviedo Cathedral (sculpture).

**1033** A268 25c pur & gray grn .20 .20
**1034** A268 1p bis brn & brn .30 .20
**1035** A268 2p dk brn & pale pur .65 .20
**1036** A268 2.50p claret & ind .30 .20
**1037** A268 3p slate & indigo .65 .45
**1038** A268 5p ol & ol grn 1.25 .55
*Nos. 1033-1038 (6)* 3.35 1.80

1200th anniversary of the founding of Oviedo, capital of Asturia.

Nativity Sculptured by José Gines — A269

"La Cierva" Autogiro — A270

**1961, Dec. 1 Photo. *Perf. 13x12½***
**1039** A269 1p dull purple .30 .20

**1961, Dec. 11 Unwmk. *Perf. 13***

2p, Hydroplane "Plus Ultra.," horiz. 3p, "Jesus del Gran Poder," plane of Madrid-Manila flight, horiz. 5p, Bustard hunt by plane. 10p, Madonna of Loretto, patron saint of Spanish airmen.

**1040** A270 1p indigo & blue .20 .20
**1041** A270 2p grn, dl pur & blk .20 .20
**1042** A270 3p blk & ol grn 1.10 .35
**1043** A270 5p dl pur, gray bl & blk 2.25 .90
**1044** A270 10p blk, lt bl & ol gray 1.10 .60
*Nos. 1040-1044 (5)* 4.85 2.25

50th anniversary of Spanish aviation.

### Provincial Arms Issue

Alava — A271

Arms of Spain — A271a

**1962 Photo. *Perf. 13***
**1045** A271 5p Alava .20 .20
**1046** A271 5p Albacete .20 .20
**1047** A271 5p Alicante .25 .20
**1048** A271 5p Almeria .25 .20
**1049** A271 5p Avila .25 .20
**1050** A271 5p Badajoz .20 .20
**1051** A271 5p Baleares .20 .20
**1052** A271 5p Barcelona .20 .20
**1053** A271 5p Burgos .65 .40
**1054** A271 5p Caceres .35 .25
**1055** A271 5p Cadiz .45 .35
**1056** A271 5p Castellon de la Plana 3.50 1.50
*Nos. 1045-1056 (12)* 6.70 4.10

**1963**
**1057** A271 5p Ciudad Real .45 .35
**1058** A271 5p Cordoba 3.50 1.25
**1059** A271 5p Coruña .55 .35
**1060** A271 5p Cuenca .55 .35
**1061** A271 5p Fernando Po .80 .75
**1062** A271 5p Gerona .20 .20
**1063** A271 5p Gran Canaria .20 .20
**1064** A271 5p Granada .25 .25
**1065** A271 5p Guadalajara .55 .35
**1066** A271 5p Guipuzcoa .20 .20
**1067** A271 5p Huelva .20 .20
**1068** A271 5p Huesca .20 .20
*Nos. 1057-1068 (12)* 7.65 4.65

**1964**
**1069** A271 5p Ifni .20 .20
**1070** A271 5p Jaen .20 .20
**1071** A271 5p Leon .20 .20
**1072** A271 5p Lerida .20 .20
**1073** A271 5p Logrono .20 .20
**1074** A271 5p Lugo .20 .20
**1075** A271 5p Madrid .20 .20
**1076** A271 5p Malaga .20 .20
**1077** A271 5p Murcia .20 .20
**1078** A271 5p Navarra .20 .20
**1079** A271 5p Orense .20 .20
**1080** A271 5p Oviedo .20 .20
*Nos. 1069-1080 (12)* 2.40 2.40

**1965**
**1081** A271 5p Palencia .20 .20
**1082** A271 5p Pontevedra .20 .20
**1083** A271 5p Rio Muni .20 .20
**1084** A271 5p Sahara .20 .20
**1085** A271 5p Salamanca .20 .20
**1086** A271 5p Santander .20 .20
**1087** A271 5p Segovia .20 .20
**1088** A271 5p Seville .20 .20
**1089** A271 5p Soria .20 .20
**1090** A271 5p Tarragona .20 .20
**1091** A271 5p Tenerife .20 .20
**1092** A271 5p Teruel .20 .20
*Nos. 1081-1092 (12)* 2.40 2.40

**1966**
**1093** A271 5p Toledo .20 .20
**1094** A271 5p Valencia .20 .20
**1094A** A271 5p Valladolid .20 .20
**1094B** A271 5p Vizcaya .20 .20
**1094C** A271 5p Zamora .20 .20
**1094D** A271 5p Zaragoza .20 .20
**1094E** A271 5p Ceuta .20 .20
**1094F** A271 5p Melilla .20 .20
**1094G** A271a 10p black .20 .20
*Nos. 1093-1094G (9)* 1.80 1.80
*Nos. 1045-1094G (57)* 20.95 15.35

Zurbaran Self-portrait A272

Zurbaran Paintings: 25c, Martyr, horiz. 40c, Burial of St. Catherine. 70c, St. Casilda. 80c, Jesus crowning St. Joseph. 1.50p, St. Jerome. 2.50p, Virgin of Grace. 3p, The Apotheosis of St. Thomas Aquinas. 5p, The Virgin as a child. 10p, The Immaculate Virgin.

**Unwmk.**
**1962, Mar. 24 Photo. *Perf. 13***
**Gold Frame**
**1095** A272 25c olive gray .40 .20
**1096** A272 40c purple .40 .20
**1097** A272 70c green .50 .20
**1098** A272 80c Prus green .40 .20
**1099** A272 1p chocolate 7.50 .20
**1100** A272 1.50p brt blue grn .90 .20
**1101** A272 2.50p dk car rose .90 .20
**1102** A272 3p bright blue 1.00 .35
**1103** A272 5p deep brown 2.50 .75
**1104** A272 10p olive green 2.50 .75
*Nos. 1095-1104 (10)* 17.00 3.25

Issued to honor Francisco de Zurbaran (1598-1664) and for Stamp Day, March 24.

For other art types see A236-A237, A240a, A246a, A257, A285a, A300, A310, A324, A340-A341, A360, A371 and footnote following No. 1606.

San Jose Convent, Avila A272a

St. Theresa (by Velázquez?) A273

Design: 1p, St. Theresa by Bernini.

**1962, Apr. 10 *Perf. 13***
**1105** A272a 25c bluish blk .20 .20
**1106** A272a 1p brown .20 .20

***Perf. 13x12½***
**1107** A273 3p bright blue 1.25 .40
*Nos. 1105-1107 (3)* 1.65 .80

4th centenary of St. Theresa's reform of the Carmelite order.

Mercury — A274

**1962, May 7**
**1108** A274 25c vio, rose & mag .20 .20
**1109** A274 1p brn, org & lt brn .20 .20
**1110** A274 10p dp grn, ol grn & brt grn 1.75 .80
*Nos. 1108-1110 (3)* 2.15 1.20

International Stamp Day, May 7.

Painting Type of 1958

Rubens Paintings: 25c, Ferdinand of Austria. 1p, Self-portrait. 3p, Philip II. 10p, Duke of Lerma on horseback.

**1962, May 28 *Perf. 13***
**Gold Frame**
**Size: 25x30mm**
**1111** A237 25c violet black .65 .30
**1112** A237 1p chocolate 5.75 .30
**1113** A237 3p blue 5.25 2.00

***Perf. 13x12½***
**Size: 26x38mm**
**1114** A237 10p slate green 4.00 2.75
*Nos. 1111-1114 (4)* 15.65 5.35

St. Benedict A275

El Cid, Statue by Cristobal A276

Berruguete Sculptures: 80c, Apostle. 1p, St. Peter. 2p, St. Christopher carrying Christ Child. 3p, Ecce Homo (Christ). 10p, St. Sebastian.

**1962, July 9 *Perf. 13x12½***
**1115** A275 25c lt blue & plum .20 .20
**1116** A275 80c sal & ol gray .30 .20
**1117** A275 1p gray & red .40 .20
**1118** A275 2p gray & magenta 3.25 .20
**1119** A275 3p brn pink & dk bl 1.25 .85
**1120** A275 10p rose & brown 1.25 .50
*Nos. 1115-1120 (6)* 6.65 2.15

Alonso Berruguete (1486-1561), architect, sculptor and painter.

***Perf. 13x12½, 12½x13***
**1962, July 30 Engr.**

2p, Equestrian statue by Anna Huntington. 3p, El Cid's treasure chest, horiz. 10p, Oath-taking ceremony at Santa Gadea, horiz.

**1121** A276 1p lt green & gray .25 .20
**1122** A276 2p brown & choc 1.40 .20
**1123** A276 3p blue & sl grn 4.25 1.10
**1124** A276 10p lt grn & sl grn 2.75 .60
*Nos. 1121-1124 (4)* 8.65 2.10

El Cid Campeador (Rodrigo Diaz de Vivar, 1040-99), Spain's national hero.

### Europa Issue, 1962

Bee and Honeycomb — A277

**1962, Sept. 13 Photo. *Perf. 12½x13***
**1125** A277 1p deep rose .20 .20
**1126** A277 5p dull green 1.00 .40

Discus Thrower A278

UPAE Emblem A279

80c, Runner. 1p, Hurdler. 3p, Sprinter at start.

**1962, Oct. 7 *Perf. 13x12½***
**1127** A278 25c pale pink & vio blk .20 .20
**1128** A278 80c pale yel & dk grn .25 .20
**1129** A278 1p pale rose & brn .20 .20
**1130** A278 3p pale bl & dk bl .25 .30
*Nos. 1127-1130 (4)* .90 .90

Second Spanish-American Games, Madrid, Oct. 7-12.

### Builders of the New World

Portrait Type of 1961

Portraits: 25c, 2p, Alonso de Mendoza. 70c, 2.50p, Jiménez de Quesada. 80c, 3p, Juan de Garay. 1p, 5p, Pedro de la Gasca.

**1962, Oct. 12 Unwmk.**
**1131** A265 25c rose lil, *gray* .20 .20
**1132** A265 70c grn, *pale pink* 1.00 .20
**1133** A265 80c dk grn, *pale yel* .70 .20
**1134** A265 1p red brn, *gray* 1.40 .20
**1135** A265 2p car, *lt bl* 3.25 .20
**1136** A265 2.50p dk vio, *pnksh* .70 .25
**1137** A265 3p dp bl, *pale pink* 7.00 1.25
**1138** A265 5p brn, *pale yel* 3.50 1.50
*Nos. 1131-1138 (8)* 17.75 4.00

**1962, Oct. 20 Engr. *Perf. 13***
**1139** A279 1p sepia & green .20 .20

50th anniv. of the founding of the Postal Union of the Americas and Spain, UPAE.

The Annunciation, by Murillo — A280

Holy Family by Pedro de Mena — A281

Mysteries of the Rosary: 70c, The Visitation, Correa. 80c, Nativity, Murillo. 1p, The Presentation, Pedro de Campaña. 1.50p, The Finding in the Temple, (unknown painter). 2p, The Agony in the Garden, Gianquinto. 2.50p, The Scourging at the Pillar, Alonso Cano. 3p, The Crowning with Thorns, Tiepolo. 5p, Carrying of the Cross, El Greco. 8p, The Crucifixion, Murillo. 10p, The Resurrection, Murillo.

**1962, Oct. 26**
**1140** A280 25c lilac & brown .20 .20
**1141** A280 70c grn & dk bl grn .20 .20
**1142** A280 80c ol & dk bl grn .20 .20
**1143** A280 1p green & gray 4.00 .70
**1144** A280 1.50p green & dk bl .20 .20
**1145** A280 2p brown & violet 1.10 .50
**1146** A280 2.50p dk brn & rose claret .40 .20
**1147** A280 3p lilac & gray .40 .20
**1148** A280 5p brn & dk car .60 .35
**1149** A280 8p vio brn & blk .60 .25
**1150** A280 10p grn & yel grn .95 .25
*Nos. 1140-1150,C171-C174 (15)* 11.45 4.40

**1962, Dec. 6 Photo. *Perf. 13x12½***
**1151** A281 1p olive gray .35 .20

Malaria Eradication Emblem A282

**1962, Dec. 21** ***Perf. 12½x13***

**1152** A282 1p blk, yel grn & yel .20 .20

WHO drive to eradicate malaria.

Pope John XXIII and St. Peter's, Rome A283

**1962, Dec. 29** **Engr.**

**1153** A283 1p dp plum & blk .25 .20

Vatican II, the 21st Ecumenical Council of the Roman Catholic Church. See No. 1199.

St. Paul, by El Greco A284

Courtyard, Poblet Monastery A285

**1963, Jan. 25** ***Perf. 13***

**1154** A284 1p brn, blk & olive .30 .20

St. Paul's visit to Spain, 1,900th anniv.

***Perf. 12½x13, 13x12½***

**1963, Feb. 25** **Unwmk.**

Designs: 1p, Royal sepulcher. 3p, View of monastery, horiz. 5p, Gothic arch.

**1155** A285 25c choc & slate grn .20 .20
**1156** A285 1p org ver & rose car .35 .20
**1157** A285 3p vio bl & dk bl 1.10 .20
**1158** A285 5p brown & ocher 2.40 .90
*Nos. 1155-1158 (4)* 4.05 1.50

Issued in honor of the Cistercian monastery of Santa Maria de Poblet.

José de Ribera, Self-portrait A285a

Coach A286

Ribera Paintings: 25c, Archimedes. 40c, Jacob's Flock. 70c, Triumph of Bacchus. 80c, St. Christopher. 1.50p, St. Andrew. 2.50p, St. John the Baptist. 3p, St. Onofre. 5p, St. Peter. 10p, The Immaculate Virgin.

**Unwmk.**

**1963, Mar. 24** **Photo.** ***Perf. 13***

**Gold Frame**

**1159** A285a 25c violet .35 .20
**1160** A285a 40c red lilac .40 .20
**1161** A285a 70c green 1.00 .20
**1162** A285a 80c dark green 1.00 .20
**1163** A285a 1p brown 1.00 .20
**1164** A285a 1.50p blue green 1.00 .20
**1165** A285a 2.50p car rose 2.75 .20
**1166** A285a 3p dark blue 3.00 .50
**1167** A285a 5p olive 10.50 2.25
**1168** A285a 10p dull red brn 4.00 1.40
*Nos. 1159-1168 (10)* 25.00 5.55

Issued to honor José de Ribera (1588-1652) and for Stamp Day, Mar. 24.

For other art types see A236-A237, A240a, A246a, A257, A272, A300, A310, A324, A340-A341, A360, A371 and footnote following No. 1606.

**1963, May 3** ***Perf. 13x12½***

**1169** A286 1p multicolored .20 .20

First Intl. Postal Conference, Paris, 1863.

Globe A287

**1963, May 8** ***Perf. 12½x13***

**1170** A287 25c multicolored .20 .20
**1171** A287 1p multicolored .20 .20
**1172** A287 10p multicolored 1.10 .65
*Nos. 1170-1172 (3)* 1.50 1.05

Issued for International Stamp Day, 1963.

"Give us this Day our Daily Bread..." A288

**1963, June 1** **Unwmk.**

**1173** A288 1p multicolored .20 .20

FAO "Freedom from Hunger" campaign.

"Pillars of Hercules" and Globes — A289

Seal of Council of San Sebastian A290

Designs: 80c, Fleet of Columbus. 1p, Columbus and compass rose.

**1963, June 4** ***Perf. 13***

**1174** A289 25c multicolored .20 .20
**1175** A289 80c brn, lt grn & gold .20 .20
**1176** A289 1p sl grn, sepia & gold .25 .20
*Nos. 1174-1176 (3)* .65 .60

Cong. of Institutions of Spanish Culture, June 5-15.

**1963, June 27** **Photo.**

80c, Burning of city, 1813. 1p, View, 1836.

**1177** A290 25c vio, grn & blk .20 .20
**1178** A290 80c dk brn, gray & red .20 .20
**1179** A290 1p dk grn, grn & ol .30 .20
*Nos. 1177-1179 (3)* .70 .60

Rebuilding of San Sebastian, 150th anniv.

**Europa Issue, 1963**

Our Lady of Europe — A291

**1963, Sept. 16** **Engr.** ***Perf. 13x12½***

**1180** A291 1p bis brn & choc .20 .20
**1181** A291 5p bluish grn & blk *.55* *.40*

Arms of Order of Mercy — A292

King James I — A293

Designs: 1p, Our Lady of Mercy. 1.50p, St. Pedro Nolasco. 3p, St. Raimundo de Penafort.

**1963, Sept. 24** **Photo.** ***Perf. 13***

**1182** A292 25c blk, car rose & gold .20 .20

**Engr.**

**1183** A293 80c sepia & green .20 .20
**1184** A293 1p gray vio & brn vio .20 .20
**1185** A293 1.50p dull bl & blk .20 .20
**1186** A293 3p gray & black .20 .20
*Nos. 1182-1186 (5)* 1.00 1.00

Coronation of Our Lady of Mercy, 75th anniv.

**Builders of the New World**

Portrait Type of 1961

25c, 2p, Father Junipero Serra. 70c, 2.50p, Vasco Nuñez de Balboa. 80c, 3p, José de Galvez. 1p, 5p, Diego Garcia de Paredes.

**1963, Oct. 12** ***Perf. 13x12½***

**1187** A265 25c vio bl, *bl* .20 .20
**1188** A265 70c grn, *pale rose* .20 .20
**1189** A265 80c dk grn, *yel* .50 .20
**1190** A265 1p dk bl, *pale rose* .60 .20
**1191** A265 2p magenta, *lt bl* 1.75 .20
**1192** A265 2.50p vio blk, *dl rose* 1.10 .20
**1193** A265 3p brt bl, *pink* 2.40 1.00
**1194** A265 5p brown, *yel* 3.00 2.25
*Nos. 1187-1194 (8)* 9.75 4.45

The Good Samaritan — A294

**1963, Oct. 28** **Unwmk.**

**1195** A294 1p gold, pur & brt car .20 .20

Centenary of International Red Cross.

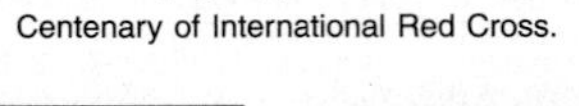

Holy Family by Alonso Berruguete (1486-1561) A295

Father Raymond Lully A296

**1963, Dec. 2** **Photo.** ***Perf. 13x12½***

**1196** A295 1p dark green .20 .20

Christmas 1963. See No. 1279.

**1963, Dec. 5** **Engr.**

Portrait: 1.50p, Cardinal Luis Antonio de Belluga (1662-1743).

**1197** A296 1p dk violet & blk .20 .20
**1198** A296 1.50p sepia & dull vio .20 .20
*Nos. 1197-1198,C175-C176 (4)* 3.40 1.35

Papal Type of 1962

Design: 1p, Pope Paul VI and St. Peter's, Rome.

**1963, Dec. 30** ***Perf. 12½x13***

**1199** A283 1p dk green & blk .20 .20

Second session of Vatican II, the 21st Ecumenical Council of the Roman Catholic Church.

Alcazar, Segovia A297

Dragon Caves, Majorca — A298

Tourism: 40c, Potes, Santander. 50c, Leon Cathedral. No. 1202, Crypt of San Isidro at Leon. No. 1203, Costa Brava. 80c, Christ of the Lanterns, Cordova. No. 1206, Court of Lions, Alhambra, Granada. No. 1208, Interior of La Mezquita, Cordova. 1.50p, View of Gerona.

**1964** **Engr.** ***Perf. 13***

**1200** A297 40c sepia & blue .20 .20
**1201** A298 50c gray & sepia .20 .20
**1202** A297 70c ind & dk bl grn .20 .20
**1203** A298 70c violet & brown .20 .20
**1204** A298 80c dp ultra & blk .20 .20
**1205** A297 1p vio bl & pur .20 .20
**1206** A297 1p rose red & dl pur .20 .20
**1207** A298 1p dk green & blk .20 .20
**1208** A298 1p brn vio & rose .20 .20
**1209** A297 1.50p gray grn, brn & blk .20 .20
*Nos. 1200-1209 (10)* 2.00 2.00

See Nos. 1280-1289.

Santa Maria de Huerta Monastery A299

Joaquin Sorolla, Self-portrait A300

Designs: 1p, Great Hall. 5p, View of monastery with apse, horiz.

**1964, Feb. 24** ***Perf. 13x12½, 12½x13***

**1212** A299 1p gray grn & grn .20 .20
**1213** A299 2p grnsh blue & sepia .25 .20
**1214** A299 5p dark blue 1.50 .75
*Nos. 1212-1214 (3)* 1.95 1.15

Santa Maria Monastery, Huerta, 8th cent.

**1964, Mar. 24** **Photo.** ***Perf. 13***

Sorolla Paintings: 25c, The Jug (woman and child). 40c, Oxen and Driver, horiz. 70c, Man and Woman from La Mancha. 80c, Fisher Woman of Valencia. 1p, Self-portrait. 1.50p, Round up, horiz. 2.50p, Fishermen, horiz. 3p, Children at the Beach, horiz. 5p, Unloading the Boat. 10p, Man and Woman on Horseback, Valencia.

**Gold Frame**

**1215** A300 25c violet .20 .20
**1216** A300 40c purple .20 .20
**1217** A300 70c dp yellow grn .20 .20
**1218** A300 80c bluish grn .20 .20
**1219** A300 1p brown .20 .20
**1220** A300 1.50p Prus blue .20 .20
**1221** A300 2.50p dk car rose .20 .20
**1222** A300 3p violet blue .45 .45

**1223** A300 5p chocolate 1.40 1.00
**1224** A300 10p deep green .65 .35
*Nos. 1215-1224 (10)* 3.90 3.20

Issued to honor Joaquin Sorolla y Bastida (1863-1923) and for Stamp Day, March 24.
For other art types see A236-A237, A240a, A246a, A257, A272, A285a, A310, A324, A340-A341, A360, A371 and footnote following No. 1606.

"Peace" A301

"Sport" — A302

Designs: 40c, Radio and television. 50c, New apartments. 70c, Agriculture. 80c, Reforestation. 1p, Economic development. 1.50p, Modern architecture. 2p, Transportation. 2.50p, Hydroelectric development. 3p, Electrification. 5p, Scientific achievements. 6p, Buildings, tourism. 10p, Generalissimo Franco.

**1964, Apr. 1**
**1225** A301 25c blk, emer & gold .20 .20
**1226** A302 30c blk, bl & sal pink .20 .20
**1227** A301 40c gold & blk .20 .20
**1228** A302 50c multicolored .20 .20
**1229** A301 70c multicolored .20 .20
**1230** A301 80c multicolored .20 .20
**1231** A302 1p multicolored .25 .20
**1232** A302 1.50p multicolored .20 .20
**1233** A301 2p multicolored .20 .20
**1234** A302 2.50p multicolored .20 .20
**1235** A301 3p gold, blk & red .90 .90
**1236** A302 5p gold, grn & red .30 .30
**1237** A301 6p multicolored .45 .45
**1238** A302 10p multicolored .55 .55
*Nos. 1225-1238 (14)* 4.25 4.20

Issued to commemorate 25 years of peace.

Bullfight and Unisphere A303

Stamp of 1850 and Modern Stamps A304

Designs: 1p, Spanish pavilion, horiz. 2.50p, La Mota castle, Medina de Campo. 5p, Spanish dancer. 50p, Jai alai.

***Perf. 12½x13, 13x12½***
**1964, Apr. 23** **Engr.**
**1239** A303 1p bl grn & yel grn .20 .20
**1240** A303 1.50p carmine & brn .20 .20
**1241** A303 2.50p dk bl & sl grn .20 .20
**1242** A303 5p car & dk car rose .30 .30
**1243** A303 50p vio bl & dk bl .85 .40
*Nos. 1239-1243 (5)* 1.75 1.30

New York World's Fair, 1964-65.

**1964, May 6** ***Perf. 13x12½***
**1244** A304 25c dk car rose & dl pur .20 .20
**1245** A304 1p yel grn & dk bl .20 .20
**1246** A304 10p orange & rose red .40 .35
*Nos. 1244-1246 (3)* .80 .75

Issued for International Stamp Day, 1964.

Virgin of Hope — A305

Santa Maria — A306

**1964, May 31** **Photo.** ***Perf. 13x12½***
**1247** A305 1p dark green .20 .20

Canonical coronation of the Virgin of Hope (La Macarena) in St. Gil's Church, Seville, May 31.

**1964, July 16** ***Perf. 13***

Designs (ships): 15c, 13th cent. ship of King Alfonso X, from medieval manuscript, vert. 25c, Carrack, from 15th cent. engraving, vert. 50c, Galley. 70c, Galleon. 80c, Xebec. 1p, Warship, Santisima Trinidad, vert. 1.50p, 18th cent. corvette, Atrevida, vert. 2p, Steamer, Isabel II. 2.50p, Frigate, Numancia, Spain's 1st armored ship. 3p, Destroyer. 5p, Submarine of Isaac Peral. 6p, Cruiser, Baleares. 10p, Training ship, Juan Sebastian Elcano.

**1248** A306 15c dp rose & vio blk .20 .20
**1249** A306 25c org yel & gray grn .20 .20
**1250** A306 40c ultra & dk bl .20 .20
**1251** A306 50c slate grn & dk bl .20 .20
**1252** A306 70c vio & dk bl .20 .20
**1253** A306 80c dl bl grn & ultra .20 .20
**1254** A306 1p org & vio brn .20 .20
**1255** A306 1.50p car & sepia .20 .20
**1256** A306 2p blk & slate grn .75 .20
**1257** A306 2.50p rose car & dl vio .20 .20
**1258** A306 3p sepia & indigo .20 .20
**1259** A306 5p dk bl, lt grn & vio .90 .90
**1260** A306 6p lt green & vio .80 .80
**1261** A306 10p org yel & rose red .35 .20
*Nos. 1248-1261 (14)* 4.80 4.10

Issued to honor the Spanish Navy.

**Europa Issue, 1964**
Common Design Type
**1964, Sept. 14** **Photo.** ***Perf. 12½x13***
**Size: 21½x39mm**
**1262** CD7 1p bis, red & grn *.30* .20
**1263** CD7 5p brt bl, mag & grn *1.00* .55

Madonna of Alcazar — A307

Shot Put — A308

**1964, Oct. 9** **Photo.** ***Perf. 13***
**1264** A307 25c bister & brn .20 .20
**1265** A307 1p gray & indigo .20 .20

Reconquest of Jerez de la Frontera, 700th anniv.

**1964, Oct. 10**
**Gold Olympic Rings**
**1266** A308 25c shown .20 .20
**1267** A308 80c Broad jump .20 .20
**1268** A308 1p Slalom .20 .20
**1269** A308 3p Judo .20 .20
**1270** A308 5p Discus .20 .20
*Nos. 1266-1270 (5)* 1.00 1.00

1964 Olympic Games.

**Builders of the New World**
Portrait Type of 1961

25c, 2p, Diego de Almagro. 70c, 2.50p, Francisco de Toledo. 80c, 3p, Archbishop Toribio de Mogrovejo. 1p, 5p, Francisco Pizarro.

**1964, Oct. 12** ***Perf. 13x12½***
**1271** A265 25c pale grn & vio .20 .20
**1272** A265 70c pink & ol gray .20 .20
**1273** A265 80c buff & Prus grn .30 .20
**1274** A265 1p buff & gray vio .30 .20
**1275** A265 2p pale bl & ol gray .30 .20
**1276** A265 2.50p pale grn & cl .25 .20
**1277** A265 3p gray & dk bl 3.00 1.00
**1278** A265 5p yellow & brown 1.75 1.25
*Nos. 1271-1278 (8)* 6.30 3.45

**Christmas Type of 1963**

Nativity by Francisco de Zurbaran (1598-1664).

**1964, Dec. 4** **Photo.**
**1279** A295 1p olive black .20 .20

**Tourism Types of 1964**

Designs: 25c, Columbus monument, Barcelona. 30s, Facade of Santa Maria, Burgos. 50c, Santa Maria la Blanca (medieval synagogue), Toledo. 70c, Bridge, Zamora. 80c, La Giralda (tower) and Cathedral of Seville. 1p, Boat and nets in Cudillero harbor. No. 1286, Cathedral of Burgos, interior. No. 1287, View of Mogrovejo, Santander. 3p, Bridge, Cambados, Pontevedra. 6p, Silk merchants' hall (Lonja), Valencia, interior.

**1965** **Engr.** ***Perf. 13***
**1280** A298 25c dk blue & blk .20 .20
**1281** A298 30c dull grn & sep .20 .20
**1282** A298 50c cl & rose car .20 .20
**1283** A297 70c vio bl & ind .20 .20
**1284** A298 80c rose cl & dk pur .20 .20
**1285** A298 1p dp cl, car & blk .20 .20
**1286** A298 2.50p brn vio & bis .20 .20
**1287** A297 2.50p dull bl & gray .20 .20
**1288** A298 3p rose car & dk brn .20 .20
**1289** A298 6p slate & black .20 .20
*Nos. 1280-1289 (10)* 2.00 2.00

Alfonso X, the Wise (1232-84) A309

Julio Romero de Torres, Self-portrait A310

25c, Juan Donoso-Cortes (1809-53). 2.50p, Gaspar M. Jovellanos (1744-1810). 5p, St. Dominic de Guzman (1170-1221).

**1965, Feb. 25** **Engr.** ***Perf. 13x12½***
**1292** A309 25c slate bl & blk .20 .20
**1293** A309 70c blue & indigo .20 .20
**1294** A309 2.50p slate grn & sep .20 .20
**1295** A309 5p dull grn & sl grn .25 .25
*Nos. 1292-1295 (4)* .85 .85

**1965, Mar. 24** **Photo.** ***Perf. 13***

De Torres Paintings: 25c, Girl with Jar. 40c, "The Song" (girl with guitar). 70c, Madonna of the Lanterns. 80c, Girl with guitar. 1.50p, "The Poem of Cordova" (pensive woman). 2.50p, Martha and Mary. 3p, "The Poem of Cordova" (two women holding statue of angel). 5p, Girl with the Charcoal. 10p, Back of woman's head.

**Gold Frame**
**1296** A310 25c dull purple .20 .20
**1297** A310 40c purple .20 .20
**1298** A310 70c olive green .20 .20
**1299** A310 80c slate green .20 .20
**1300** A310 1p dk red brn .20 .20
**1301** A310 1.50p blue green .20 .20
**1302** A310 2.50p lilac rose .20 .20
**1303** A310 3p dark blue .35 .25
**1304** A310 5p brown .35 .25
**1305** A310 10p slate green .50 .30
*Nos. 1296-1305 (10)* 2.60 2.20

Issued to honor Julio Romero de Torres (1880-1930) and for Stamp Day, March 24.
For other art types see A236-A237, A240a, A246a, A257, A272, A285a, A300, A324, A340-A341, A360, A371 and footnote following No. 1606.

Bull and Symbolic Stamps — A311

**1965, May 6** ***Perf. 13x12½***
**1306** A311 25c multicolored .20 .20
**1307** A311 1p orange & multi .20 .20
**1308** A311 10p multicolored .50 .30
*Nos. 1306-1308 (3)* .90 .70

Issued for International Stamp Day, 1965.

ITU Emblem, Old and New Communication Equipment — A312

**1965, May 17** ***Perf. 12½x13***
**1309** A312 1p salmon, blk & red .20 .20

International Telecommunication Union, cent.

Pilgrim — A313

Explorer, Royal Flag of Spain and Ships — A314

Design: 2p, Pilgrim (profile).

**1965, July 25** **Photo.** ***Perf. 13***
**1310** A313 1p multicolored .20 .20
**1311** A313 2p multicolored .20 .20

Issued to commemorate the Holy Year of St. James of Compostela, patron saint of Spain.

**1965, Aug. 28** ***Perf. 13x12½***
**1312** A314 3p red, blk & yel .20 .20

400th anniv. of the settlement of Florida, and the 1st permanent European settlement in the continental US, St. Augustine, Fla. See US No. 1271.

St. Benedict — A315

Sports Palace, Madrid — A316

**Europa Issue, 1965**
**1965, Sept. 27** **Engr.** ***Perf. 13x12½***
**1313** A315 1p yel grn & sl grn .20 .20
**1314** A315 5p lilac & violet *.40* .25

**1965, Oct. 9 Photo. *Perf. 13***

| | | | | | |
|---|---|---|---|---|---|
| **1315** | A316 | 1p | gray, gold & dk brn | .20 | .20 |

Issued to commemorate the meeting of the International Olympic Committee in Madrid.

**Builders of the New World**

Portrait Type of 1961

25c, 2p, Don Fadrique de Toledo. 70c, 2.50p, Father José de Anchieta. 80c, 3p, Francisco de Orellana. 1p, 5p, St. Luis Beltran.

**1965, Oct. 12 Photo. *Perf. 13x12½***

| | | | | | |
|---|---|---|---|---|---|
| **1316** | A265 | 25c | pale grn & dp pur | .20 | .20 |
| **1317** | A265 | 70c | pink & brown | .20 | .20 |
| **1318** | A265 | 80c | cream & Prus grn | .20 | .20 |
| **1319** | A265 | 1p | buff & dk vio | .20 | .20 |
| **1320** | A265 | 2p | lt bl & dk ol grn | .20 | .20 |
| **1321** | A265 | 2.50p | lt blue & pur | .20 | .20 |
| **1322** | A265 | 3p | gray & dk bl | 1.00 | .35 |
| **1323** | A265 | 5p | yellow & brn | 1.00 | .30 |
| | | | *Nos. 1316-1323 (8)* | 3.20 | 1.85 |

Chamber of Charles V, Yuste Monastery A317

Stamp of 1865 (No. 78) A318

Yuste Monastery: 1p, Courtyard, horiz. 5p, View of monastery, horiz.

***Perf. 12½x13, 13x12½***

**1965, Nov. 15 Engr.**

| | | | | | |
|---|---|---|---|---|---|
| **1324** | A317 | 1p | bl gray & blk | .20 | .20 |
| **1325** | A317 | 2p | red brn & brn blk | .20 | .20 |
| **1326** | A317 | 5p | grayish bl & grn | .25 | .25 |
| | | | *Nos. 1324-1326 (3)* | .65 | .65 |

Monastery of Yuste, Estremadura.

**1965, Nov. 22 *Perf. 13x12½***

Designs: 1p, Stamp of 1865 (No. 77). 5p, Stamp of 1865 (No. 80).

| | | | | | |
|---|---|---|---|---|---|
| **1327** | A318 | 80c | blk & yel grn | .20 | .20 |
| **1328** | A318 | 1p | plum, brn & rose | .20 | .20 |
| **1329** | A318 | 5p | sepia & org brn | .20 | .20 |
| | | | *Nos. 1327-1329 (3)* | .60 | .60 |

Cent. of the 1st Spanish perforated postage stamps.

Nativity A319

**1965, Dec. 1 Photo. *Perf. 12½x13***

| | | | | | |
|---|---|---|---|---|---|
| **1330** | A319 | 1p | bright green | .20 | .20 |

Virgin of Peace, Antipolo A320

Globe and Four Beasts of Apocalypse A321

Design: 3p, Father Andres de Urdaneta.

**1965, Dec. 3 *Perf. 13x12½***

| | | | | | |
|---|---|---|---|---|---|
| **1331** | A320 | 1p | pale sal & ol brn | .20 | .20 |
| **1332** | A320 | 3p | gray & dp blue | .20 | .20 |

Christianization of the Philippines, 400th anniv.

**1965, Dec. 29 Photo. *Perf. 13x12½***

| | | | | | |
|---|---|---|---|---|---|
| **1333** | A321 | 1p | grnsh bl, yel & brn | .20 | .20 |

Vatican II, the 21st Ecumenical Council of the Roman Catholic Church, 10/11/62-12/8/65.

Adm. Alvaro de Bazan (1526-88) A322

Exhibition Emblem; Type Block "P" A323

2p, Daza de Valdes, scientist, 17th cent.

**1966, Feb. 26 Engr. *Perf. 13x12½***

| | | | | | |
|---|---|---|---|---|---|
| **1334** | A322 | 25c | dull blue & gray | .20 | .20 |
| **1335** | A322 | 2p | magenta & violet | .20 | .20 |

See Nos. C177-C178.

**1966, Mar. 4 Photo. *Perf. 13***

| | | | | | |
|---|---|---|---|---|---|
| **1336** | A323 | 1p | red, grn & vio bl | .20 | .20 |

Graphic Arts and Advertising Packaging Exhibition "Graphispack," Barcelona, 3/4-13.

José Maria Sert, Self-portrait A324

Santa Maria Church, Guernica — A325

Sert Paintings: 25c, The Magic Ball. 40c, Evocation of Toledo, horiz. 70c, Christ on the Cross. 80c, Parachutists. 1.50p, "Audacity." 2.50p, "Justice." 3p, Jacob Wrestling with the Angel. 5p, "The Five Continents." 10p, Sts. Peter and Paul.

**1966, Mar. 24**

**Gold Frame**

| | | | | | |
|---|---|---|---|---|---|
| **1337** | A324 | 25c | dk purple | .20 | .20 |
| **1338** | A324 | 40c | dp magenta | .20 | .20 |
| **1339** | A324 | 70c | green | .20 | .20 |
| **1340** | A324 | 80c | dk ol grn | .20 | .20 |
| **1341** | A324 | 1p | claret brn | .20 | .20 |
| **1342** | A324 | 1.50p | dull blue | .20 | .20 |
| **1343** | A324 | 2.50p | dk red | .20 | .20 |
| **1344** | A324 | 3p | deep blue | .20 | .20 |
| **1345** | A324 | 5p | sepia | .20 | .20 |
| **1346** | A324 | 10p | grnsh blk | .20 | .20 |
| | | | *Nos. 1337-1346 (10)* | 2.00 | 2.00 |

Issued to honor José Maria Sert (1876-1945) and for Stamp Day, Mar. 24.

For other art types see A236-A237, A240a, A246a, A257, A272, A285a, A300, A310, A340-A341, A360, A371 and footnote following No. 1606.

**1966, Apr. 28 Photo. *Perf. 13***

Designs: 1p, Arms of Guernica and Luno. 3p, Tree of Guernica.

| | | | | | |
|---|---|---|---|---|---|
| **1347** | A325 | 80c | bl, sepia & grn | .20 | .20 |
| **1348** | A325 | 1p | yel grn & multi | .20 | .20 |
| **1349** | A325 | 3p | bl, grn & vio brn | .20 | .20 |
| | | | *Nos. 1347-1349 (3)* | .60 | .60 |

Founding of Guernica and Luno, 6th cent.

Cover with Stamp of 1850 (#1) A326

Designs (covers): 1p, 5r (#3). 10p, 10r (#5).

**1966, May 6 *Perf. 12½x13***

| | | | | | |
|---|---|---|---|---|---|
| **1350** | A326 | 25c | rose vio, blk & red | .20 | .20 |
| **1351** | A326 | 1p | red brn, org & blk | .20 | .20 |
| **1352** | A326 | 10p | ol grn, grn & org | .25 | .20 |
| | | | *Nos. 1350-1352 (3)* | .65 | .60 |

Issued for International Stamp Day, 1966.

Bohi Valley — A327

Torla, Huesca A328

Tourism: 40c, Portal of Sigena Monastery, Huesca. 50c, Santo Domingo Church, Soria. 80c, Torre del Oro, Seville. 1p, Palm and view, Pico de Teyde, Santa Cruz de Tenerife. 1.50p, Monastery of Guadalupe, Caceres. 2p, Alcala de Henares University. 3p, Seo Cathedral, Lerida. 10p, Courtyard of St. Gregorio, Valladolid.

**1966 Engr. *Perf. 13***

| | | | | | |
|---|---|---|---|---|---|
| **1353** | A327 | 10c | gray grn & bl grn | .20 | .20 |
| **1354** | A328 | 15c | gray grn & brn | .20 | .20 |
| **1355** | A327 | 40c | bis brn & brn | .20 | .20 |
| **1356** | A327 | 50c | car rose & dp cl | .20 | .20 |
| **1357** | A327 | 80c | lilac & rose vio | .20 | .20 |
| **1358** | A327 | 1p | vio bl & bl grn | .20 | .20 |
| **1359** | A328 | 1.50p | dk bl & blk | .20 | .20 |
| **1360** | A328 | 2p | sl bl & sepia | .20 | .20 |
| **1361** | A328 | 3p | ultra & blk | .20 | .20 |
| **1362** | A327 | 10p | brt bl & grnsh bl | .20 | .20 |
| | | | *Nos. 1353-1362 (10)* | 2.00 | 2.00 |

Tree and Globe A329

**1966, June 6 Photo. *Perf. 12½x13***

| | | | | | |
|---|---|---|---|---|---|
| **1363** | A329 | 1p | brn & dk grn | .20 | .20 |

6th Intl. Forestry Cong., Madrid, June 6-18.

Navy Emblem — A330

**1966, July 1 Photo. *Perf. 13***

| | | | | | |
|---|---|---|---|---|---|
| **1364** | A330 | 1p | gray & dk bl | .20 | .20 |

Naval Week, Barcelona, July 1-8.

Guadamur Castle — A331

Castles: 25c, Alcazar, Segovia. 40c, La Mota. 50c, Olite. 70c, Monteagudo. 80c, Butron, vert. 1p, Manzanares. 3p, Almansa, vert.

**1966, Aug. 13 Engr. *Perf. 13***

| | | | | | |
|---|---|---|---|---|---|
| **1365** | A331 | 10c | grysh bl & sep | .20 | .20 |
| **1366** | A331 | 25c | violet & purple | .20 | .20 |
| **1367** | A331 | 40c | grnsh bl & bl grn | .20 | .20 |
| **1368** | A331 | 50c | grnsh bl & ultra | .20 | .20 |
| **1369** | A331 | 70c | vio bl & ind | .20 | .20 |
| **1370** | A331 | 80c | vio & sl grn | .20 | .20 |
| **1371** | A331 | 1p | ol bis & gray | .20 | .20 |
| **1372** | A331 | 3p | rose & red lil | .20 | .20 |
| | | | *Nos. 1365-1372 (8)* | 1.60 | 1.60 |

Don Quixote, Dulcinea and Aldonza Lorenzo — A332

**1966, Sept. 5 Photo. *Perf. 13***

| | | | | | |
|---|---|---|---|---|---|
| **1373** | A332 | 1.50p | sal, lt grn & blk | .20 | .20 |

4th World Congress of Psychiatry, Madrid.

**Europa Issue, 1966**

The Rape of Europa A333

**1966, Sept. 28 Photo. *Perf. 12½x13***

| | | | | | |
|---|---|---|---|---|---|
| **1374** | A333 | 1p | multicolored | .20 | .20 |
| **1375** | A333 | 5p | multicolored | .25 | .20 |

Don Quixote and Sancho Panza on Clavileno A334

Title Page of "Dotrina Christiana" A335

**1966, Oct. 9 *Perf. 13x12½***

| | | | | | |
|---|---|---|---|---|---|
| **1376** | A334 | 1.50p | sl bl, red brn & dk brn | .20 | .20 |

17th Cong. of the Intl. Astronautical Federation.

**Builders of the New World**

Types of 1961 and A335

30c, Antonio de Mendoza. 1p, José A. Manso de Velasco. 1.20p, Coins of Lima, 1699. 1.50p, Manuel de Castro y Padilla. 3p, Portal of Oruro Convent, Bolivia. 3.50p, Manuel de Amat. 6p, Inca courier, El Chasqui.

**1966, Oct. 12**

| | | | | | |
|---|---|---|---|---|---|
| **1377** | A265 | 30c | pale pink & brn | .20 | .20 |
| **1378** | A335 | 50c | pale bis & brn | .20 | .20 |
| **1379** | A265 | 1p | gray & vio | .20 | .20 |
| **1380** | A335 | 1.20p | gray & slate | .20 | .20 |
| **1381** | A265 | 1.50p | pale grn & dp grn | .20 | .20 |
| **1382** | A335 | 3p | pale gray & dp bl | .20 | .20 |
| **1383** | A265 | 3.50p | pale lil & pur | .25 | .25 |
| **1384** | A265 | 6p | buff & sepia | .20 | .20 |
| | | | *Nos. 1377-1384 (8)* | 1.65 | 1.65 |

Ramon del Valle Inclan — A336

Portraits: 3p, Carlos Arniches. 6p, Jacinto Benavente y Martinez.

**1966, Nov. 7 Photo. *Perf. 13***

| | | | | | |
|---|---|---|---|---|---|
| 1385 | A336 | 1.50p | blk & green | .20 | .20 |
| 1386 | A336 | 3p | blk & gray vio | .20 | .20 |
| 1387 | A336 | 6p | blk & slate | .20 | .20 |
| | | | *Nos. 1385-1387 (3)* | .60 | .60 |

Issued to honor Spanish writers.
See design A355.

Carthusian Monastery, Jerez A337

St. Mary Carthusian Monastery: 1p, Portal, vert. 5p, Entrance gate.

***Perf. 13x12½, 12½x13***

**1966, Nov. 24 Engr.**

| | | | | | |
|---|---|---|---|---|---|
| 1388 | A337 | 1p | grnsh bl & sl bl | .20 | .20 |
| 1389 | A337 | 2p | green & yel grn | .20 | .20 |
| 1390 | A337 | 5p | lilac & claret | .20 | .20 |
| | | | *Nos. 1388-1390 (3)* | .60 | .60 |

Nativity, Sculpture by Pedro Duque Cornejo A338

**1966, Dec. 5 Photo. *Perf. 12½x13***

| | | | | | |
|---|---|---|---|---|---|
| 1391 | A338 | 1.50p | multicolored | .20 | .20 |

**Regional Costumes Issue**

Woman from Alava — A339

**1967 Photo. *Perf. 13***

| | | | | | |
|---|---|---|---|---|---|
| 1392 | A339 | 6p | shown | .20 | .20 |
| 1393 | A339 | 6p | Albacete | .20 | .20 |
| 1394 | A339 | 6p | Alicante | .20 | .20 |
| 1395 | A339 | 6p | Almeria | .20 | .20 |
| 1396 | A339 | 6p | Avila | .20 | .20 |
| 1397 | A339 | 6p | Badajoz | .20 | .20 |
| 1398 | A339 | 6p | Baleares | .20 | .20 |
| 1399 | A339 | 6p | Barcelona | .20 | .20 |
| 1400 | A339 | 6p | Burgos | .20 | .20 |
| 1401 | A339 | 6p | Caceres | .20 | .20 |
| 1402 | A339 | 6p | Cadiz | .20 | .20 |
| 1403 | A339 | 6p | Castellon de la Plana | .20 | .20 |
| | | | *Nos. 1392-1403 (12)* | 2.40 | 2.40 |

**1968**

| | | | | | |
|---|---|---|---|---|---|
| 1404 | A339 | 6p | Ciudad Real | .20 | .20 |
| 1405 | A339 | 6p | Cordoba | .20 | .20 |
| 1406 | A339 | 6p | Coruna | .20 | .20 |
| 1407 | A339 | 6p | Cuenca | .20 | .20 |
| 1408 | A339 | 6p | Fernando Po | .20 | .20 |
| 1409 | A339 | 6p | Gerona | .20 | .20 |
| 1410 | A339 | 6p | Gran Canaria, Las Palmas | .20 | .20 |
| 1411 | A339 | 6p | Granada | .20 | .20 |
| 1412 | A339 | 6p | Guadalajara | .20 | .20 |
| 1413 | A339 | 6p | Guipuzcoa | .20 | .20 |
| 1414 | A339 | 6p | Huelva | .20 | .20 |
| 1415 | A339 | 6p | Huesca | .20 | .20 |
| | | | *Nos. 1404-1415 (12)* | 2.40 | 2.40 |

**1969**

| | | | | | |
|---|---|---|---|---|---|
| 1416 | A339 | 6p | Ifni | .20 | .20 |
| 1417 | A339 | 6p | Jaen | .20 | .20 |
| 1418 | A339 | 6p | Leon | .20 | .20 |
| 1419 | A339 | 6p | Lerida | .20 | .20 |
| 1420 | A339 | 6p | Logroño | .20 | .20 |
| 1421 | A339 | 6p | Lugo | .20 | .20 |
| 1422 | A339 | 6p | Madrid | .20 | .20 |
| 1423 | A339 | 6p | Malaga | .20 | .20 |
| 1424 | A339 | 6p | Murcia | .20 | .20 |
| 1425 | A339 | 6p | Navarra | .20 | .20 |
| 1426 | A339 | 6p | Orense | .20 | .20 |
| 1427 | A339 | 6p | Oviedo | .20 | .20 |
| | | | *Nos. 1416-1427 (12)* | 2.40 | 2.40 |

**1970**

| | | | | | |
|---|---|---|---|---|---|
| 1428 | A339 | 6p | Palencia | .20 | .20 |
| 1429 | A339 | 6p | Pontevedra | .20 | .20 |
| 1430 | A339 | 6p | Sahara | .20 | .20 |
| 1431 | A339 | 6p | Salamanca | .20 | .20 |
| 1432 | A339 | 6p | Santa Cruz de Tenerife | .20 | .20 |
| 1433 | A339 | 6p | Santander | .20 | .20 |
| 1434 | A339 | 6p | Segovia | .20 | .20 |
| 1435 | A339 | 6p | Seville | .20 | .20 |
| 1436 | A339 | 6p | Soria | .20 | .20 |
| 1437 | A339 | 6p | Tarragona | .20 | .20 |
| 1438 | A339 | 6p | Teruel | .20 | .20 |
| 1439 | A339 | 6p | Toledo | .20 | .20 |
| | | | *Nos. 1428-1439 (12)* | 2.40 | 2.40 |

**1971**

| | | | | | |
|---|---|---|---|---|---|
| 1440 | A339 | 6p | Valencia | .20 | .20 |
| 1441 | A339 | 8p | Valladolid | .20 | .20 |
| 1442 | A339 | 8p | Vizcaya | .20 | .20 |
| 1443 | A339 | 8p | Zamora | .20 | .20 |
| 1444 | A339 | 8p | Zaragoza | .20 | .20 |
| | | | *Nos. 1440-1444 (5)* | 1.00 | 1.00 |
| | | | *Nos. 1392-1444 (53)* | 10.60 | 10.60 |

Archers A340

Ornament — A341

50c, Boar hunt. 1.20p, Bison. 1.50p, Hands. 2p, Warrior. 2.50p, Deer. 3.50p, Archers. 4p, Hunters & gazelle. 6p, Hunters & deer herd.

**1967, Mar. 27 Photo. *Perf. 13***
**Gold Frame**

| | | | | | |
|---|---|---|---|---|---|
| 1449 | A340 | 40c | ocher & car rose | .20 | .20 |
| 1450 | A340 | 50c | gray & dk red | .20 | .20 |
| 1451 | A341 | 1p | ocher & org ver | .20 | .20 |
| 1452 | A340 | 1.20p | gray & rose brn | .20 | .20 |
| 1453 | A340 | 1.50p | gray & red | .20 | .20 |
| 1454 | A341 | 2p | lt brn & dk car rose | .20 | .20 |
| 1455 | A341 | 2.50p | sky bl & rose brn | .20 | .20 |
| 1456 | A340 | 3.50p | yellow & blk | .20 | .20 |
| 1457 | A341 | 4p | citron & red | .20 | .20 |
| 1458 | A341 | 6p | olive & red | .20 | .20 |
| | | | *Nos. 1449-1458 (10)* | 2.00 | 2.00 |

Issued for Stamp Day, 1967. The designs are from paleolithic and mesolithic wall paintings found in Spanish caves.

For other art types see A236-A237, A240a, A246a, A257, A272, A285a, A300, A310, A324, A360, A371 and footnote following No. 1606.

Palma Cathedral and Conference Emblem — A342

**1967, Mar. 28**

| | | | | | |
|---|---|---|---|---|---|
| 1459 | A342 | 1.50p | brt blue grn | .20 | .20 |

Issued to publicize the Congress of the Interparliamentary Union, Palma de Mallorca.

W. K. Röntgen, X-ray Tube and Atom — A343

**1967, Apr. 3 Photo. *Perf. 13***

| | | | | | |
|---|---|---|---|---|---|
| 1460 | A343 | 1.50p | green | .20 | .20 |

7th Cong. of Latin Radiologists and 1st Cong. of European Radiologists, Barcelona, Apr. 2-8.

Averroes (1120-1198), Physician and Philosopher — A344

Portraits: 3.50p, José de Acosta (1539-1600), Jesuit, historian, poet. 4p, Moses ben Maimonides (1135-1204), Jewish philosopher and physician. 25p, Andres Laguna, 16th century physician.

**1967, Apr. 6 Engr. *Perf. 13x12½***

| | | | | | |
|---|---|---|---|---|---|
| 1461 | A344 | 1.20p | lil & dl vio | .20 | .20 |
| 1462 | A344 | 3.50p | mag & dl pur | .20 | .20 |
| 1463 | A344 | 4p | brn & sep | .20 | .20 |
| 1464 | A344 | 25p | dl bl & blk | .25 | .20 |
| | | | *Nos. 1461-1464 (4)* | .85 | .80 |

**Europa Issue, 1967**
Common Design Type

**1967, May 2 Photo. *Perf. 13***
**Size: 25x31mm**

| | | | | | |
|---|---|---|---|---|---|
| 1465 | CD10 | 1.50p | sl grn, red brn & dl red | .20 | .20 |
| 1466 | CD10 | 6p | vio, brt bl & brn | .20 | .20 |

Exhibition Building and Fountain, Valencia — A345

**1967, May 3**

| | | | | | |
|---|---|---|---|---|---|
| 1467 | A345 | 1.50p | gray grn | .20 | .20 |

International Fair at Valencia, 50th anniv.

Numeral Postmark No. 3 of 1850 — A346

Guardian Angel Over Indigent Sleeper — A347

Designs: 1.50p, No. 2, 12c stamp of 1850 with crowned M postmark of Madrid. 6p, No. 4, 6r stamp of 1850 with 1r postmark.

**1967, May 6**

| | | | | | |
|---|---|---|---|---|---|
| 1468 | A346 | 40c | brn org, dl bl & blk | .20 | .20 |
| 1469 | A346 | 1.50p | brn, grn & blk | .20 | .20 |
| 1470 | A346 | 6p | bl, red & blk | .20 | .20 |
| | | | *Nos. 1468-1470 (3)* | .60 | .60 |

Intl. Stamp Day, 1967. See #1527-1528.

**1967, May 16 *Perf. 13***

| | | | | | |
|---|---|---|---|---|---|
| 1471 | A347 | 1.50p | bl, blk, brn & red | .20 | .20 |

Issued for National Caritas Day to honor Caritas, Catholic welfare organization.

Betanzos Church, Coruña — A348

International Tourist Year Emblem A349

Tourism: 1p, Tower of St. Miguel Church, Palencia. 1.50p, Human pyramid (Castellers). 2.50p, Columbus monument, Huelva. 5p, The Enchanted City, Cuenca. 6p,Church of Our Lady, Sanlucar, Cadiz.

**1967, July 26 Engr. *Perf. 13***

| | | | | | |
|---|---|---|---|---|---|
| 1472 | A348 | 10c | ultra & blk | .20 | .20 |
| 1473 | A348 | 1p | dl bl & blk | .20 | .20 |
| 1474 | A348 | 1.50p | lt brn & blk | .20 | .20 |
| 1475 | A348 | 2.50p | grnsh bl & dk bl | .20 | .20 |
| 1476 | A349 | 3.50p | dl pur & dk bl | .20 | .20 |
| 1477 | A348 | 5p | yel grn & dk grn | .20 | .20 |
| 1478 | A348 | 6p | red lil & dl lil | .20 | .20 |
| | | | *Nos. 1472-1478 (7)* | 1.40 | 1.40 |

Balsareny Castle — A350

Castles: 1p, Jarandilla. 1.50p, Almodovar. 2p, Ponferrada, vert. 2.50p, Peniscola. 5p, Coca. 6p, Loarre. 10p, Belmonte.

**1967, Aug. 11 Engr.**

| | | | | | |
|---|---|---|---|---|---|
| 1479 | A350 | 50c | gray & lt brn | .20 | .20 |
| 1480 | A350 | 1p | bl gray & dl pur | .20 | .20 |
| 1481 | A350 | 1.50p | bl gray & sage grn | .20 | .20 |
| 1482 | A350 | 2p | brick red & bis brn | .20 | .20 |
| 1483 | A350 | 2.50p | grnsh bl & sep | .20 | .20 |
| 1484 | A350 | 5p | rose vio & vio bl | .20 | .20 |
| 1485 | A350 | 6p | bis brn & gray brn | .20 | .20 |
| 1486 | A350 | 10p | aqua & slate | .20 | .20 |
| | | | *Nos. 1479-1486 (8)* | 1.60 | 1.60 |

Globe, Snowflake and Thermometer A351

Galleon, Map of Americas, Spain and Philippines A352

**1967, Aug. 30** **Photo.**

**1487** A351 1.50p bright blue .20 .20

12th Intl. Refrigeration Cong., Madrid, Sept. 4-8.

**1967, Oct. 10** **Photo.** ***Perf. 13***

**1488** A352 1.50p red lilac .20 .20

4th Congress of Spanish, Portuguese, American & Philippine Municipalities, Barcelona, Oct. 6-12.

### Builders of the New World

Type of 1961 and

Nootka Settlement A353

Designs: 40c, Francisco de la Bodega. 50c, Old map of Nootka coast, vert. 1p, Francisco Antonio Mourelle. 1.50p, Esteban José Martinez. 3p, Old maps of coast of Northern California. 3.50p, Cayetano Valdes. 6p, Ships, San Elias, Alaska.

**1967, Oct. 12**

**1489** A265 40c pink & grnsh gray .20 .20
**1490** A353 50c dk brn .20 .20
**1491** A265 1p pale bl & red lil .20 .20
**1492** A353 1.20p dk ol grn .20 .20
**1493** A265 1.50p pale pink & bl grn .20 .20
**1494** A353 3p buff & vio blk .20 .20
**1495** A265 3.50p pale pink & bl .25 .25
**1496** A353 6p red brn, *bluish* .20 .20
*Nos. 1489-1496 (8)* 1.65 1.65

Issued to honor the explorers of the Northwest coast of North America.

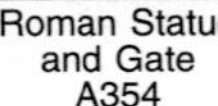

Roman Statue and Gate A354

José Bethencourt A355

Designs: 3.50p, Ancient plower with ox team, horiz. 6p, Roman coins of Caceres.

**1967, Oct. 31** **Photo.** ***Perf. 13***

**1497** A354 1.50p multi .20 .20
**1498** A354 3.50p multi .20 .20
**1499** A354 6p multi .20 .20
*Nos. 1497-1499 (3)* .60 .60

Founding of Caceres by the Romans, 2000th anniv.

**1967, Nov. 15**

1.50p, Enrique Granados (composer). 3.50p, Ruben Dario (poet). 6p, St. Ildefonso.

**1500** A355 1.20p gray & red brn .20 .20
**1501** A355 1.50p blk & grn .20 .20
**1502** A355 3.50p brn & pur .20 .20
**1503** A355 6p blk & slate .20 .20
*Nos. 1500-1503 (4)* .80 .80

Issued to honor famous Spanish men. See design A336.

Santa Maria de Veruela Monastery A356

St. José Receiving Last Unction, by Goya A357

Designs: 3.50p, Aerial view of monastery, horiz. 6p, Inside view, horiz.

**1967, Nov. 24** **Engr.** ***Perf. 13***

**1504** A356 1.50p ultra & ind .20 .20
**1505** A356 3.50p grn & blk .20 .20
**1506** A356 6p rose vio & bis brn .20 .20
*Nos. 1504-1506 (3)* .60 .60

**1967, Nov. 27** **Photo.**

**1507** A357 1.50p multi .20 .20

200th anniversary of the canonization of St. José de Calasanz (1556-1648), founder of the first Christian Schools in Rome.

Nativity, by Francisco Salzillo — A358

**1967, Dec. 5**

**1508** A358 1.50p multi .20 .20

Christmas, 1967.

Slalom A359

3.50p, Bobsled, vert. 6p, Ice hockey.

**1968, Feb. 6** **Photo.** ***Perf. 13***

**1509** A359 1.50p multi .20 .20
**1510** A359 3.50p multi .20 .20
**1511** A359 6p multi .20 .20
*Nos. 1509-1511 (3)* .60 .60

Issued to commemorate the 10th Winter Olympic Games, Grenoble, France, Feb. 6-18.

Mariano Fortuny, Self-portrait A360

Fortuny Paintings: 40c, The Vicariate, horiz. 50c, "Fantasy" (pianist). 1p, "Idyll" (piper and sheep). 1.20p, The Print Collector, horiz. 2p, Old Man in the Sun. 2.50p, Calabrian Man. 3.50p, Lady with Fan. 4p, Battle of Tetuan, 1860. 6p, Queen Christina in Carriage, horiz.

**1968, Mar. 25** **Photo.** ***Perf. 13***

**Gold Frame**

**1512** A360 40c dp red lil .20 .20
**1513** A360 50c dk bl grn .20 .20
**1514** A360 1p brown .20 .20
**1515** A360 1.20p dp vio .20 .20
**1516** A360 1.50p dp grn .20 .20
**1517** A360 2p org brn .20 .20
**1518** A360 2.50p car rose .20 .20
**1519** A360 3.50p dk red brn .20 .20
**1520** A360 4p dk ol .20 .20
**1521** A360 6p brt bl .20 .20
*Nos. 1512-1521 (10)* 2.00 2.00

Issued to honor Mariano Fortuny y Carbo (1838-74), and for Stamp Day.

For other art types see A236-A237, A240a, A246a, A257, A272, A285a, A300, A310, A324, A340-A341, A371 and footnote following No. 1606.

Beatriz Galindo A361

Famous Women: 1.50p, Agustina de Aragon. 3.50p, Maria Pacheco. 6p, Rosalia de Castro.

**1968, Apr. 8** **Engr.** ***Perf. 12½x13***

**1522** A361 1.20p yel brn & blk brn .20 .20
**1523** A361 1.50p bl grn & dk bl .20 .20
**1524** A361 3.50p lt vio & dk vio .20 .20
**1525** A361 6p gray bl & blk .20 .20
*Nos. 1522-1525 (4)* .80 .80

### Europa Issue, 1968

Common Design Type

**1968, Apr. 29** **Photo.** ***Perf. 13***

**Size: 38x22mm**

**1526** CD11 3.50p brt bl, gold & brn .20 .20

Spain No. 1 with Galicia Puebla Postmark — A362

Map of León and Seal — A363

Stamp Day: 3.50p, Spain No. 4 with Serena postmark.

**1968, May 6** **Photo.** ***Perf. 13***

**1527** A362 1.50p blk, bl & ocher .20 .20
**1528** A362 3.50p bl, dk grn & blk .20 .20

See Nos. 1568-1569, 1608, 1677, 1754.

***Perf. 13x12½, 12½x13***

**1968, June 15** **Photo.**

Designs: 1.50p, Roman legionary. 3.50p, Emperor Galba coin, horiz.

**Size: 25x38½mm**

**1529** A363 1p lil, red brn & yel .20 .20

**Size: 25x47½mm**

**1530** A363 1.50p brn, dk brn & buff .20 .20

**Size: 37½x26mm**

**1531** A363 3.50p ocher & sl grn .25 .25
*Nos. 1529-1531 (3)* .65 .65

1900th anniversary of the founding of León by the Roman Legion VII Gemina.

Human Rights Emblem A364

Benavente Palace, Baeza A365

**1968, June 25** **Photo.** ***Perf. 13x12½***

**1532** A364 3.50p bl, red & grn .20 .20

International Human Rights Year, 1968.

**1968, July 15** **Engr.** ***Perf. 13***

Tourism: 1.20p, View of Salamanca with Tormes River Bridge, horiz. 1.50p, Statuary group from St. Vincent's Church, Avila (The Adoration of the Magi). 2p, Tomb of Martin Vazquez de Arce, Cathedral of Sigüenza, horiz. 3.50p, Portal of St. Mary's Church, Sangüesa, Navarre.

**1533** A365 50c dp rose & brn .20 .20
**1534** A365 1.20p emer & sl grn .20 .20
**1535** A365 1.50p dp grn & ind .20 .20
**1536** A365 2p lil rose & blk .20 .20
**1537** A365 3.50p brt lil & rose lil .20 .20
*Nos. 1533-1537 (5)* 1.00 1.00

Escalona Castle, Toledo — A366

Castles: 1.20p, Fuensaldaña, Valladolid. 1.50p, Peñafiel, Valladolid. 2.50p, Vilasobroso, Pontevedra. 6p, Frias, Burgos, vert.

**1968, July 29** **Engr.** ***Perf. 13***

**1538** A366 40c dk bl & sepia .20 .20
**1539** A366 1.20p vio brn & vio blk .20 .20
**1540** A366 1.50p ol & blk .20 .20
**1541** A366 2.50p ol grn & blk .20 .20
**1542** A366 6p vio bl & bl grn .20 .20
*Nos. 1538-1542 (5)* 1.00 1.00

Rifle Shooting A367

Designs: 1.50p, Horse jumping. 3.50p, Bicycling. 6p, Sailing, vert.

***Perf. 12½x13, 13x12½***

**1968, Sept. 24** **Photo.**

**1543** A367 1p multi .20 .20
**1544** A367 1.50p multi .20 .20
**1545** A367 3.50p multi .20 .20
**1546** A367 6p multi .20 .20
*Nos. 1543-1546 (4)* .80 .80

19th Olympic Games, Mexico City, 10/12-27.

### Builders of the New World

Type of 1961 and

Map of Capuchin Missions along Orinoco River, 1732 — A368

1p, Diego de Losada. 1.50p, Losada family coat of arms. 3.50p, Diego de Henares. 6p, Map of Caracas, drawn by Diego de Henares, 1578, horiz.

**1968, Oct. 12** **Photo.** ***Perf. 13***

**1547** A368 40c grnsh bl, *bluish* .20 .20
**1548** A265 1p red lil, *gray* .20 .20
**1549** A368 1.50p sl, *pale rose* .20 .20
**1550** A265 3.50p dk bl, *pnksh* .20 .20
**1551** A368 6p dk ol bis .20 .20
*Nos. 1547-1551 (5)* 1.00 1.00

Christianization of Venezuela and the founding of Caracas.

St. Maria del Parral Monastery, Segovia — A369

3.50p, Monastery, inside view. 6p, Madonna & Child, statue from main altar.

**1968, Nov. 25 Engr. *Perf. 13***
**1552** A369 1.50p gray bl & rose vio .20 .20
**1553** A369 3.50p brn & red brn .20 .20
**1554** A369 6p rose claret & brn .20 .20
*Nos. 1552-1554 (3)* .60 .60

Nativity, by Federico Fiori da Urbino — A370

Alonso Cano by Velázquez A371

**1968, Dec. 2 Photo. *Perf. 13x12½***
**1555** A370 1.50p gold & multi .20 .20

Christmas, 1968.

**1969, Mar. 24 Photo. *Perf. 13***

Cano Paintings: 40c, St. Agnes. 50c, St. John. 1p, Jesus and Angel. 2p, Holy Family. 2.50p, Circumcision of Jesus. 3p, Jesus and the Samaritan Woman. 3.50p, Madonna and Child. 4p, Sts. John Capistrano and Bernardino, horiz. 6p, Vision of St. John the Baptist.

**Gold Frame**

**1556** A371 40c deep plum .20 .20
**1557** A371 50c green .20 .20
**1558** A371 1p sepia .20 .20
**1559** A371 1.50p slate grn .20 .20
**1560** A371 2p red brown .20 .20
**1561** A371 2.50p dp red lil .20 .20
**1562** A371 3p ultra .20 .20
**1563** A371 3.50p dk rose brn .20 .20
**1564** A371 4p dull lilac .20 .20
**1565** A371 6p slate blue .20 .20
*Nos. 1556-1565 (10)* 2.00 2.00

Alonso Cano (1601-1667), and Stamp Day.
For other art types see A236-A237, A240a, A246a, A257, A272, A285a, A300, A310, A324, A340-A341, A360 and footnote following No. 1606.

DNA (Genetic Code) Molecule and Chart A372

**1969, Apr. 7 Photo. *Perf. 13***
**1566** A372 1.50p gray & multi .20 .20

Issued to publicize the 6th European Congress of Biochemistry, Madrid, Apr. 7-11.

**Europa Issue, 1969**
Common Design Type

**1969, Apr. 28**
**Size: 38x22mm**
**1567** CD12 3.50p multi .20 .20

Stamp Day Type of 1968

1.50p, Spain #6 with crowned M postmark. 3.50p, Spain #11 with Corvera postmark.

**1969, May 6 Photo. *Perf. 13***
**1568** A362 1.50p blk, red & grn .20 .20
**1569** A362 3.50p grn, bl & red .20 .20

Issued for Stamp Day, 1969.

Spectrum A373

**1969, May 26**
**1570** A373 1.50p blk & multi .20 .20

Issued to publicize the 15th International Spectroscopy Colloquium, Madrid, May 26-30.

World Map, Red Crescent, Cross, Lion and Sun Emblems A374

**1969, May 30**
**1571** A374 1.50p multi .20 .20

League of Red Cross Societies, 50th anniv.

Last Supper, Finial from Lugo Cathedral — A375

**1969, June 4**
**1572** A375 1.50p grn, brn & blk .20 .20

300th anniversary of the dedication of Galicia Province to the reign of Jesus.

Turegano Castle, Segovia A376

Father Junipero Serra — A377

Castles: 1.50p, Villalonso, Zamora. 2.50p, Velez Blanco, Almeria. 3.50p, Castilnovo, Segovia. 6p, Torrelobaton, Valladolid.

**1969, June 24 Engr. *Perf. 13***
**1573** A376 1p dl grn & sl .20 .20
**1574** A376 1.50p bluish lil & dk bl .20 .20
**1575** A376 2.50p bl vio & bluish lil .20 .20
**1576** A376 3.50p red brn & ol grn .20 .20
**1577** A376 6p gray grn & dl brn .20 .20
*Nos. 1573-1577 (5)* 1.00 1.00

**1969, July 16 Photo. *Perf. 13***
**1578** A377 1.50p multi .20 .20

Bicentenary of San Diego, Calif.

Rock of Gibraltar — A378

Dama de Elche — A379

2p, View of Gibraltar across the Bay of Algeciras.

**1969, July 18**
**1579** A378 1.50p bl grn .20 .20
**1580** A378 2p brt rose lil .20 .20

**1969, July 23 Engr. *Perf. 13***

Tourism: 1.50p, Alcañiz Castle, Teruel, horiz. 3p, Murcia Cathedral. 6p, St. Maria de la Redonda, Logrono.

**1581** A379 1.50p dl grn & blk .20 .20
**1582** A379 3p yel grn & bl grn .20 .20
**1583** A379 3.50p gray bl & dk bl .20 .20
**1584** A379 6p yel grn & vio blk .20 .20
*Nos. 1581-1584 (4)* .80 .80

**Builders of the New World**
Type of 1961 and

Santo Domingo Church, Santiago, Chile — A380

1.50p, Casa de Moneda de Chile, horiz. 2p, Ambrosio O'Higgins. 3.50p, Pedro de Valdivia. 6p, First large bridge over Mapocho River, horiz.

**1969, Oct. 12 Photo. *Perf. 13***
**1585** A380 40c lt bl & dk red brn .20 .20
**1586** A380 1.50p pale rose & dk vio .20 .20
**1587** A265 2p pale pink & ol .20 .20
**1588** A265 3.50p pale yel & dk Prus grn .35 .30
**1589** A380 6p pale yel & blk brn .25 .20
*Nos. 1585-1589 (5)* 1.20 1.10

Exploration and development of Chile. See Nos. 1630-1631, 1634.

Adoration of the Magi, by Juan Bautista Mayno — A381

Christmas: 2p, Nativity, bas-relief from altar of Cathedral of Gerona.

**1969, Nov. 3**
**1590** A381 1.50p multi .20 .20
**1591** A381 2p multi .20 .20

Tomb of Alfonso VIII and Wife, Las Huelgas Monastery, Burgos — A382

Designs: 1.50p, Las Huelgas Monastery. 6p, Inside view, vert.

**1969, Nov. 22 Engr.**
**1592** A382 1.50p lt bl grn & indigo .25 .20
**1593** A382 3.50p ultra & vio bl .40 .35
**1594** A382 6p olive & yel grn .20 .20
*Nos. 1592-1594 (3)* .85 .75

See Nos. 1639-1641.

St. Juan de Avila, by El Greco — A383

St. Stephen, by Luis de Morales — A384

Design: 50p, Bishop Rodrigo Ximenez de Rada, Juan de Borgona mural.

**1970, Feb. 25 Engr. *Perf. 13***
**1595** A383 25p pale pur & ind 4.00 .20
**1596** A383 50p brn org & brn 1.60 .20

**1970, Mar. 24 Photo. *Perf. 13***

Morales Paintings: 1p, Annunciation. 1.50p, Madonna and Child with St. John. 2p, Madonna and Child. 3p, Presentation at the Temple. 3.50p, St. Jerome. 4p, St. John de Ribera. 5p, Ecce Homo. 6p, Pieta. 10p, St. Francis of Assisi.

**1597** A384 50c gold & multi .20 .20
**1598** A384 1p gold & multi .20 .20
**1599** A384 1.50p gold & multi .20 .20
**1600** A384 2p gold & multi .20 .20
**1601** A384 3p gold & multi .20 .20
**1602** A384 3.50p gold & multi .20 .20
**1603** A384 4p gold & multi .20 .20
**1604** A384 5p gold & multi .20 .20
**1605** A384 6p gold & multi .20 .20
**1606** A384 10p gold & multi .20 .20
*Nos. 1597-1606 (10)* 2.00 2.00

Issued to honor Luis de Morales, "El Divino" (1509-1586), and for Stamp Day.
For other art types see A397, A410, A431, A448, A473, A501, A522, A538, A558 and footnote following No. 876.

**Europa Issue, 1970**
Common Design Type

**1970, May 4 Photo. *Perf. 13x12½***
**Size: 37½x22mm**
**1607** CD13 3.50p brt bl & gold .20 .20

Stamp Day Type of 1968

Stamp Day: 2p, Spain No. 51 with "Ferro Carril de Langreo" postmark.

**1970, May 4 *Perf. 13x12½***
**1608** A362 2p dl red, grn & blk .20 .20

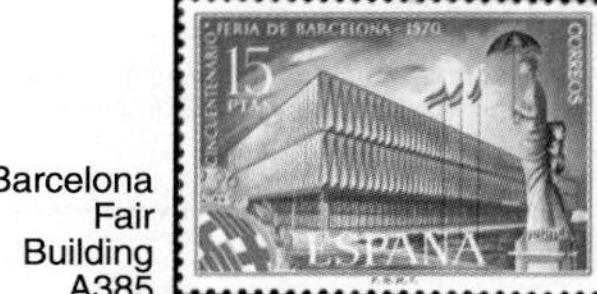


Barcelona Fair Building A385

**1970, May 27 *Perf. 13***
**1609** A385 15p multi .25 .20

Barcelona Trade Fair, 50th anniversary.

Miguel Primo de Rivera — A386

**1970, June 6 Photo. *Perf. 13***
**1610** A386 2p buff, brn & ol grn .20 .20

Gen. Miguel Primo de Rivera (1870-1930), Spanish dictator, 1923-1930.

Valencia de Don Juan Castle — A387

Castles: 1.20p, Monterrey. 3.50p, Mombeltran. 6p, Sadaba. 10p, Bellver.

**1970, June 24** **Engr.**

| | | | | | |
|---|---|---|---|---|---|
| **1611** | A387 | 1p | blk & dl bl | .35 | .20 |
| **1612** | A387 | 1.20p | lt grnsh bl & vio | .20 | .20 |
| **1613** | A387 | 3.50p | pale grn & brn | .20 | .20 |
| **1614** | A387 | 6p | sep & dl pur | .20 | .20 |
| **1615** | A387 | 10p | fawn & sepia | .80 | .20 |
| | | | *Nos. 1611-1615 (5)* | 1.75 | 1.00 |

Alcazaba Castle, Almeria A388

Tourism: 1p, Malaga Cathedral. 1.50p, St. Mary of the Assumption, Lequemo, vert. 2p, Cloister of St. Francis of Orense. 3.50p, Market (Lonja), Zaragoza, vert. 5p, The Gate of Vitoria, vert.

**1970, July 23** **Engr.** ***Perf. 13***

| | | | | | |
|---|---|---|---|---|---|
| **1616** | A388 | 50c | bluish gray & dl pur | .20 | .20 |
| **1617** | A388 | 1p | red brn & ocher | .20 | .20 |
| **1618** | A388 | 1.50p | bluish gray & sl grn | .20 | .20 |
| **1619** | A388 | 2p | sl & dk bl | .40 | .20 |
| **1620** | A388 | 3.50p | pur & vio bl | .20 | .20 |
| **1621** | A388 | 5p | gray grn & red brn | .80 | .20 |
| | | | *Nos. 1616-1621 (6)* | 2.00 | 1.20 |

Tailor, from Book Published in Madrid, 1589 A389

**1970, Aug. 18** **Photo.** ***Perf. 13***

**1622** A389 2p mag, brn & dl vio .20 .20

14th Intl. Tailoring Congress, Madrid.

Diver and Map of Europe A390

**1970, Aug. 25**

**1623** A390 2p grn & brt bl .20 .20

12th European Championships in Swimming, Diving and Water Polo, Barcelona.

Concha Espina — A391

1p, Guillen de Castro. 1.50p, Juan Ramon Jimenez. 2p, Gustavo Adolfo Becquer. 2.50p, Miguel de Unamuno. 3.50p, José M. Gabriel y Galan.

**1970, Sept. 21** **Photo.** ***Perf. 13x12½***

| | | | | | |
|---|---|---|---|---|---|
| **1624** | A391 | 50c | brn, vio bl & pale rose | .20 | .20 |
| **1625** | A391 | 1p | sl grn, dp rose lil & gray | .20 | .20 |
| **1626** | A391 | 1.50p | dk bl, brt grn & gray | .20 | .20 |
| **1627** | A391 | 2p | grn, dk ol & buff | .20 | .20 |
| **1628** | A391 | 2.50p | pur, rose lake & buff | .20 | .20 |
| **1629** | A391 | 3.50p | brn, dk red & gray | .20 | .20 |
| | | | *Nos. 1624-1629 (6)* | 1.20 | 1.20 |

Issued to honor Spanish writers.

**Builders of the New World**

Portrait Type of 1961 and Building Type of 1969

40c, Ecala House, Queretaro, Mexico. 1.50p, Mexico Cathedral, horiz. 2p, Vasco de Quiroga. 3.50p, Brother Juan de Zumarraga. 6p, Cathedral Towers, Morelia, Mexico.

**1970, Oct. 12** **Photo.** ***Perf. 13***

| | | | | | |
|---|---|---|---|---|---|
| **1630** | A380 | 40c | lt bl & ol gray | .20 | .20 |
| **1631** | A380 | 1.50p | lt bl & brn | .20 | .20 |
| **1632** | A265 | 2p | buff & dk vio | .50 | .20 |
| **1633** | A265 | 3.50p | pale grn & dk grn | .20 | .20 |
| **1634** | A380 | 6p | pale pink & Prus bl | .25 | .20 |
| | | | *Nos. 1630-1634 (5)* | 1.35 | 1.00 |

Exploration and development of Mexico.

Map of Western Mediterranean — A392

**1970, Oct. 20** **Photo.** ***Perf. 13***

**1635** A392 2p multi .20 .20

Geographical and Statistical Institute, cent.

Adoration of the Shepherds, by El Greco — A393

Christmas: 2p, Adoration of the Shepherds, by Murillo.

**1970, Oct. 30**

| | | | | | |
|---|---|---|---|---|---|
| **1636** | A393 | 1.50p | multi | .20 | .20 |
| **1637** | A393 | 2p | multi | .20 | .20 |

UN Emblem and Headquarters — A394

**1970, Nov. 3**

**1638** A394 8p multi .20 .20

25th anniversary of the United Nations.

Monastery Type of 1969

Ripoll Monastery: 2p, Portal. 3.50p, View of monastery. 5p, Inside court.

**1970, Nov. 12** **Engr.**

| | | | | | |
|---|---|---|---|---|---|
| **1639** | A382 | 2p | vio & pur | .45 | .20 |
| **1640** | A382 | 3.50p | org & mar | .20 | .20 |
| **1641** | A382 | 5p | Prus grn & yel grn | .90 | .20 |
| | | | *Nos. 1639-1641 (3)* | 1.55 | .60 |

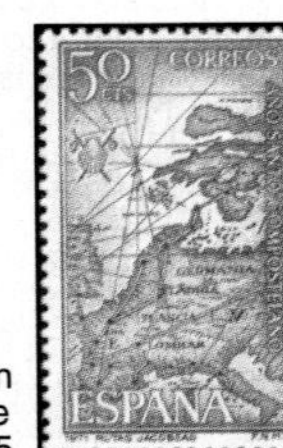

Map with Main European Pilgrimage Routes — A395

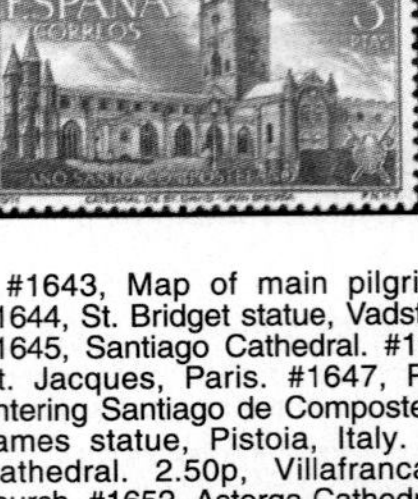

Cathedral of St. David, Wales A396

#1643, Map of main pilgrimage routes. #1644, St. Bridget statue, Vadstena, Sweden. #1645, Santiago Cathedral. #1646, Tower of St. Jacques, Paris. #1647, Pilgrim before entering Santiago de Compostela. #1648, St. James statue, Pistoia, Italy. #1649, Lugo Cathedral. 2.50p, Villafranca del Bierzo church. #1652, Astorga Cathedral. 3.50p, San Marcos de León. #1654, Charlemagne, bas-relief, Aachen Cathedral, Germany. #1655, San Tirso de Sahagun. 5p, San Martín de Fromista. 6p, Bas-relief, King's Hospital, Burgos. 7p, Portal of Santo Domingo de la Calzada. 7.50p, Cloister, Najera. 8p, Puente de la Reina (Christ on the Cross and portal). 9p, Santa Maria de Eunate. 10p, Cross of Roncesvalles.

**1971** **Engr.** ***Perf. 13***

| | | | | | |
|---|---|---|---|---|---|
| **1642** | A395 | 50c | grnsh bl & sep | .20 | .20 |
| **1643** | A396 | 50c | bl & dl vio | .20 | .20 |
| **1644** | A395 | 1p | brn & sl grn | .20 | .20 |
| **1645** | A395 | 1p | grn & sl grn | .20 | .20 |
| **1646** | A395 | 1.50p | dl grn & dp plum | .25 | .20 |
| **1647** | A396 | 1.50p | vio bl & lil | .20 | .20 |
| **1648** | A395 | 2p | dk pur & blk | .25 | .20 |
| **1649** | A395 | 2p | sl grn & dk bl | .80 | .20 |
| **1650** | A396 | 2.50p | vio brn & dl vio | .20 | .20 |
| **1651** | A396 | 3p | ultra & dk bl | .25 | .20 |
| **1652** | A395 | 3p | dl red & rose lil | .40 | .20 |
| **1653** | A396 | 3.50p | dp org & gray grn | .20 | .20 |
| **1654** | A396 | 4p | ol grn | .35 | .20 |
| **1655** | A395 | 4p | grnsh bl & brn | .20 | .20 |
| **1656** | A396 | 5p | lt grn & blk | .35 | .20 |
| **1657** | A395 | 6p | lt ultra | .20 | .20 |
| **1658** | A395 | 7p | lil & dl vio | .45 | .20 |
| **1659** | A396 | 7.50p | car lake & dl vio | .20 | .20 |
| **1660** | A395 | 8p | grn & vio blk | .25 | .25 |
| **1661** | A396 | 9p | grn & vio | .25 | .25 |
| **1662** | A395 | 10p | grn & brn | .40 | .20 |
| | | | *Nos. 1642-1662 (21)* | 6.00 | 4.30 |

Holy Year of Compostela, 1971.

Ignacio Zuloaga, Self-portrait A397

Amadeo Vives, Composer A398

Zuloaga Paintings: 50c, "My Uncle Daniel." 1p, View of Segovia, horiz. 1.50p, Countess of Alba. 3p, Juan Belmonte. 4p, Countess of Noailles. 5p, Pablo Uranga. 8p, Cobblers' Houses at Lerma, horiz.

**1971, Mar. 24** **Photo.** ***Perf. 13***

| | | | | | |
|---|---|---|---|---|---|
| **1663** | A397 | 50c | gold & multi | .20 | .20 |
| **1664** | A397 | 1p | gold & multi | .20 | .20 |
| **1665** | A397 | 1.50p | gold & multi | .20 | .20 |
| **1666** | A397 | 2p | gold & multi | .20 | .20 |
| **1667** | A397 | 3p | gold & multi | .20 | .20 |
| **1668** | A397 | 4p | gold & multi | .20 | .20 |
| **1669** | A397 | 5p | gold & multi | .20 | .20 |
| **1670** | A397 | 8p | gold & multi | .20 | .20 |
| | | | *Nos. 1663-1670 (8)* | 1.60 | 1.60 |

Ignacio Zuloaga (1870-1945). Stamp Day.

For other art types see A384, A410, A431, A448, A473, A501, A522, A538, A558 and footnote following No. 876.

**1971, Apr. 20**

2p, St. Teresa of Avila. 8p, Benito Perez Galdos, writer. 15p, Ramon Menendez Pidal, writer.

| | | | | | |
|---|---|---|---|---|---|
| **1671** | A398 | 1p | multicolored | .20 | .20 |
| **1672** | A398 | 2p | multicolored | .20 | .20 |
| **1673** | A398 | 8p | multicolored | .20 | .20 |
| **1674** | A398 | 15p | multicolored | .20 | .20 |
| | | | *Nos. 1671-1674 (4)* | .80 | .80 |

**Europa Issue, 1971**

Common Design Type

**1971, Apr. 29** **Photo.** ***Perf. 13***

**Size: 37x26mm**

| | | | | | |
|---|---|---|---|---|---|
| **1675** | CD14 | 2p | lt bl, brn & vio bl | *.45* | .20 |
| **1676** | CD14 | 8p | lt grn, dk brn & dk grn | *.30* | *.30* |

Stamp Day Type of 1968

Spain No. 1 with blue "A" cancellation.

**1971, May 6**

**1677** A362 2p black, bl & olive .20 .20

Gymnast — A399

Design: 2p, Gymnast on bar.

**1971, May 14**

| | | | | | |
|---|---|---|---|---|---|
| **1678** | A399 | 1p | ocher & multi | .20 | .20 |
| **1679** | A399 | 2p | lt blue & multi | .20 | .20 |

9th European Gymnastic Championships for Men, Madrid, May 14-15.

Great Bustard A400

Designs: 2p, Pardine lynx. 3p, Brown bear. 5p, Red-legged partridge, vert. 8p, Spanish ibex, vert.

**1971, May 24**

| | | | | | |
|---|---|---|---|---|---|
| **1680** | A400 | 1p | multicolored | .20 | .20 |
| **1681** | A400 | 2p | multicolored | .20 | .20 |
| **1682** | A400 | 3p | multicolored | .20 | .20 |
| **1683** | A400 | 5p | multicolored | .35 | .25 |
| **1684** | A400 | 8p | multicolored | .35 | .35 |
| | | | *Nos. 1680-1684 (5)* | 1.30 | 1.20 |

Legionnaires — A401

2p, Legionnaires on dress parade. 5p, Memorial service. 8p, Desert fighter and tank column.

**1971, June 21** **Photo.** ***Perf. 13***

| | | | | | |
|---|---|---|---|---|---|
| **1685** | A401 | 1p | multicolored | .20 | .20 |
| **1686** | A401 | 2p | multicolored | .20 | .20 |
| **1687** | A401 | 5p | multicolored | .20 | .20 |
| **1688** | A401 | 8p | multicolored | .30 | .30 |
| | | | *Nos. 1685-1688 (4)* | .90 | .90 |

50th anniversary of the Legion, a voluntary military organization.

UNICEF Emblem, Children of Various Races — A402

**1971, Sept. 10**

**1689** A402 8p multicolored .20 .20

25th anniv. of UNICEF.

Don Juan of Austria, Fleet Commander A403

Hockey Players, Hockey League and Games Emblems — A404

Designs: 5p, Battle of Lepanto, horiz. 8p, Holy League banner in Cathedral.

**1971, Oct. 7 Engr. *Perf. 13***

**1690** A403 2p sepia & slate grn .40 .20
**1691** A403 5p chocolate .75 .20
**1692** A403 8p rose car & vio bl .60 .60
*Nos. 1690-1692 (3)* 1.75 1.00

400th anniversary of the Battle of Lepanto against the Turks.

**1971, Oct. 15 Photo.**

**1693** A404 5p multicolored .50 .20

First World Hockey Cup, Barcelona, Oct. 15-24.

De Havilland DH-9 over Seville A405

Design: 15p, Boeing 747 over Plaza de la Cibeles, Madrid.

**1971, Oct. 25**

**1694** A405 2p multicolored .25 .20
**1695** A405 15p multicolored .25 .20

50th anniversary of Spanish air mail service.

Nativity, Avia Altarpiece A406

Emilia Pardo Bazan — A407

Christmas: 8p, Nativity, Sagas altarpiece.

**1971, Nov. 4 *Perf. 12½x13***

**1696** A406 2p multicolored .20 .20
**1697** A406 8p multicolored .20 .20

**1972, Jan. 27 Engr. *Perf. 13***

Portraits: 25p, José de Espronceda. 50p, King Fernan Gonzalez.

**1698** A407 15p brown & slate grn .20 .20
**1699** A407 25p lt grn & slate grn .25 .20
**1700** A407 50p claret & dp brn .55 .20
*Nos. 1698-1700 (3)* 1.00 .60

Honoring Emilia Pardo Bazan (1852-1921), novelist (15p); José de Espronceda (1808-1842), poet (25p); Fernan Gonzalez (910-970), first King of Castile (50p).

Figure Skating — A408

Don Quixote Title Page, 1605 — A409

Design: 2p, Ski jump and Sapporo Olympic emblem, horiz.

**1972, Feb. 10 Photo.**

**1701** A408 2p gray & multi .35 .20
**1702** A408 15p blue & multi .20 .20

11th Winter Olympic Games, Sapporo, Japan, Feb. 3-13.

**1972, Feb. 24 Engr. *Perf. 13x12½***

**1703** A409 2p brown & claret .20 .20

International Book Year 1972.

A410

A411

Gutierrez Solana Paintings: 1p, Clowns, horiz. 2p, José Gutierrez Solana with wife and child. 3p, Balladier. 4p, Fisherman. 5p, Mask makers. 7p, The book collector. 10p, Merchant marine captain. 15p, Afterdinner speaker, horiz.

**1972, Mar. 24 Photo. *Perf. 13***

**1704** A410 1p gold & multi .20 .20
**1705** A410 2p gold & multi .35 .20
**1706** A410 3p gold & multi .40 .20
**1707** A410 4p gold & multi .20 .20
**1708** A410 5p gold & multi 1.25 .35
**1709** A410 7p gold & multi .55 .20
**1710** A410 10p gold & multi .55 .20
**1711** A410 15p gold & multi .55 .25
*Nos. 1704-1711 (8)* 4.05 1.80

José Gutierrez Solana (1886-1945). Stamp Day 1972.

For other art types see A384, A397, A431, A448, A473, A501, A522, A538, A558 and footnote following No. 876.

**1972, Apr. 21**

**1712** A411 1p Fir .20 .20
**1713** A411 2p Strawberry tree .35 .20
**1714** A411 3p Cluster pine .40 .20
**1715** A411 5p Evergreen oak .55 .20
**1716** A411 8p Juniper .35 .30
*Nos. 1712-1716 (5)* 1.85 1.10

Europeans Interlocking A412

Pre-stamp Cordoba Postmark (1824-42) A413

**Europa, 1972**

Common Design Type and Type A412

**1972, May 2**

**1717** A412 2p dull grn & ocher *1.40* .20

**Size: 25x38mm**

**1718** CD15 8p multicolored *.50 .40*

**1972, May 6 *Perf. 12½x13***

**1719** A413 2p dull yel, blk & car .20 .20

Stamp Day 1972.

Santa Catalina Castle, Jaen — A414

Castles: 1p, Sajazarra, Rioja, vert. 3p, Biar, Alicante. 5p, San Servando, Toledo. 10p, Pedraza, Segovia.

**1972, June 22 Engr. *Perf. 13***

**1720** A414 1p dull bl grn & brn .45 .35
**1721** A414 2p gray olive & grn .85 .20
**1722** A414 3p rose car & red brn .85 .20
**1723** A414 5p vio bl & dull grn .85 .20
**1724** A414 10p slate & lilac 2.50 .20
*Nos. 1720-1724 (5)* 5.50 1.15

Weight Lifting, Olympic Emblems — A415

**1972, Aug. 26 Photo. *Perf. 13***

**1725** A415 1p Olympic emblems, fencing, horiz. .20 .20
**1726** A415 2p shown .25 .20
**1727** A415 5p Sculling .20 .20
**1728** A415 8p Pole vaulting .25 .25
*Nos. 1725-1728 (4)* .90 .85

20th Olympic Games, Munich, 8/26-9/11.

Egyptian Mongoose A416

**1972, Sept. 14**

**1729** A416 1p Aquatic mole, vert. .20 .20
**1730** A416 2p Chamois .20 .20
**1731** A416 3p Wolf .25 .20
**1732** A416 5p shown .50 .20
**1733** A416 7p Spotted genet .40 .20
*Nos. 1729-1733 (5)* 1.55 1.00

Brigadier M.A. de Ustariz — A417

San Juan, 1870 A418

**1972, Oct. 12 Photo. *Perf. 13***

**1734** A417 1p shown .20 .25
**1735** A418 2p shown .25 .20
**1736** A418 5p San Juan, 1625 .40 .20
**1737** A418 8p Map of Plaza and Bay, 1792 .40 .30
*Nos. 1734-1737 (4)* 1.25 .95

450th anniversary of San Juan.

St. Tomas Monastery, Avila — A419

8p, Inside view. 15p, Cloister, horiz.

**1972, Oct. 26 Engr.**

**1738** A419 2p Prus bl & gray grn .80 .20
**1739** A419 8p gray & claret .65 .30
**1740** A419 15p violet & red lil .50 .20
*Nos. 1738-1740 (3)* 1.95 .70

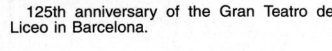

Teatro del Liceo, Barcelona A420

**1972, Nov. 7 *Perf. 12½x13***

**1741** A420 8p ultra & sepia .25 .20

125th anniversary of the Gran Teatro del Liceo in Barcelona.

Annunciation — A421

Christmas: 8p, Angel and shepherds. Designs are from Romanesque murals in the Collegiate Basilica of San Isidro, Leon.

**1972, Nov. 14 Photo. *Perf. 13***

**1742** A421 2p gold & multi .20 .20
**1743** A421 8p gold & multi .20 .20

Juan de Herrera and Escorial A422

Great Spanish Architects: 10p, Juan de Villanueva and Prado. 15p, Ventura Rodriguez and Apollo Fountain.

**1973, Jan. 29 Engr. *Perf. 12½x13***

**1744** A422 8p sepia & slate grn .50 .20
**1745** A422 10p blk brn & bluish blk 1.60 .20
**1746** A422 15p brt green & indigo .40 .20
*Nos. 1744-1746 (3)* 2.50 .60

Myrica Faya — A423 Europa, Roman Mosaic — A424

Designs: Flora of Canary Islands.

**1973, Mar. 21 Photo. *Perf. 13***

**1747** A423 1p Apollonias canariensis, horiz. .20 .20
**1748** A423 2p shown .55 .20
**1749** A423 4p Palms .20 .20
**1750** A423 5p Holly .55 .20
**1751** A423 15p Dracaena draco .30 .20
*Nos. 1747-1751 (5)* 1.80 1.00

**Europa Issue**

Common Design Type and A424

**1973, Apr. 30 Photo. *Perf. 13***

**1752** A424 2p multicolored *.40* .20

**Size: 37x26mm**

**1753** CD16 8p lt blue, blk & red *.35 .25*

Stamp Day Type of 1968

Stamp Day: 2p, Spain No. 23 with red Madrid, 1853, cancellation.

**1973, May 5**

**1754** A362 2p black, blue & red .20 .20

Iznajar Dam on Genil River — A425

**1973, June 9 Photo. *Perf. 12½x13***

**1755** A425 8p multicolored .20 .20

11th Congress of the International Commission on High Dams, Madrid, June 11-15.

Oñate University, Guipuzcoa A426

Designs: 2p, Plaza del Campo and fountain, Lugo. 3p, Plaza de Llerena and fountain, Badajoz, vert. 5p, House of Columbus, Las Palmas. 8p, Windmills, La Mancha.

**1973, June 11 Engr. *Perf. 13***

**1756** A426 1p gray & sepia .20 .20
**1757** A426 2p brt grn & sl grn .55 .20
**1758** A426 3p dk brn & org brn .55 .20
**1759** A426 5p dk gray & vio blk 1.40 .20
**1760** A426 8p dk gray & car .60 .20
*Nos. 1756-1760 (5)* 3.30 1.00

Azure-winged Magpie — A427

Knight, Holy Fraternity of Castile, 1488 — A428

Birds: 1p, Black-bellied sand grouse, horiz. 2p, Black stork, horiz. 7p, Imperial eagle, horiz. 15p, Red-crested pochard.

**1973, July 3 Photo. *Perf. 13***

**1761** A427 1p multicolored .20 .20
**1762** A427 2p multicolored .35 .20
**1763** A427 5p multicolored .50 .40
**1764** A427 7p multicolored .60 .20
**1765** A427 15p multicolored .25 .25
*Nos. 1761-1765 (5)* 1.90 1.25

**1973, July 17**

Uniforms: 2p, Knight, Castile, 1493, horiz. 3p, Harquebusier, 1534. 7p, Mounted rifleman, 1560. 8p, Infantry sergeants, 1567.

**1766** A428 1p multicolored .20 .20
**1767** A428 2p multicolored .50 .20
**1768** A428 3p multicolored .50 .20
**1769** A428 7p multicolored .40 .20
**1770** A428 8p multicolored .40 .25
*Nos. 1766-1770 (5)* 2.00 1.05

See Nos. 1794-1798, 1824-1828, 1869-1873, 1902-1906, 1989-1993, 2020-2024, 2051-2055, 2078-2082.

Fish in Net A429

**1973, Sept. 12 Photo. *Perf. 13***

**1771** A429 2p multicolored .20 .20

6th Intl. Fishing Exhibition, Vigo, Sept. 12-19.

Conference Hall — A430

**1973, Sept. 14**

**1772** A430 8p multicolored .20 .20

Plenipotentiary Conf. of the Intl. Telecommunications Union, Torremolinos, Sept. 1973.

Vicente López, Self-portrait A431

Stamp Day (Paintings by Vicente López y Portana (1772-1850)): 1p, King Ferdinand VII. 3p, Señora de Carvallo. 4p, Marshal Castelldosrrius. 5p, Queen Isabella II. 7p, Francisco Goya. 10p, Maria Amalia de Sajonia. 15p, The organist Felix López.

**1973, Sept. 29 Photo. *Perf. 13***

**1773** A431 1p gold & multi .20 .20
**1774** A431 2p gold & multi .25 .20
**1775** A431 3p gold & multi .25 .20
**1776** A431 4p gold & multi .20 .20
**1777** A431 5p gold & multi .20 .20
**1778** A431 7p gold & multi .20 .20
**1779** A431 10p gold & multi .25 .20
**1780** A431 15p gold & multi .25 .20
*Nos. 1773-1780 (8)* 1.80 1.60

For other art types see A384, A397, A410, A448, A473, A501, A522, A538, A558 and footnote following No. 876.

Leon Cathedral, Nicaragua A432

Designs: 2p, Subtiava Church. 5p, Portal of Governor's House, vert. 8p, Rio San Juan Castle.

**1973, Oct. 12**

**1781** A432 1p multicolored .20 .20
**1782** A432 2p multicolored .30 .20
**1783** A432 5p multicolored .50 .25
**1784** A432 8p multicolored .50 .20
*Nos. 1781-1784 (4)* 1.50 .85

Hispanic-American buildings in Nicaragua.

Pope Gregory XI and Pedro Fernandez Pecha — A433

**1973, Oct. 26**

**1785** A433 2p multicolored .20 .20

600th anniversary of the founding of the Order of the Hermites of St. Jerome by Pedro Fernandez Pecha.

St. Domingo de Silos Monastery A434 Nativity, Column Capital, Silos Church A435

Designs: 8p, Cloister walk, horiz. 15p, Three saints, sculpture.

***Perf. 13x12½, 12½x13***

**1973, Oct. 26 Engr.**

**1786** A434 2p brn & rose mag .45 .20
**1787** A434 8p dk blue & purple .20 .20
**1788** A434 15p Prus grn & indigo .25 .20
*Nos. 1786-1788 (3)* .90 .60

St. Domingo de Silos Monastery, Burgos.

**1973, Nov. 6 Photo. *Perf. 13***

Christmas: 8p, Adoration of the Kings, Butrera Church, horiz.

**1789** A435 2p multicolored .20 .20
**1790** A435 8p multicolored .20 .20

Map of Spain and Americas with Dates of First Printings A436

500 years of Spanish Printing: 7p, Teacher and Pupils, woodcut from "Libros de los Suenos," Valencia, 1474, vert. 15p, Title page from "Los Sinodales," Segovia, 1472.

**1973, Dec. 11 Engr. *Perf. 13***

**1791** A436 1p ind & slate grn .30 .20
**1792** A436 7p violet bl & purple .20 .20
**1793** A436 15p purple & black .25 .20
*Nos. 1791-1793 (3)* .75 .60

Uniform Type of 1973

Uniforms: 1p, Harquebusier on horseback, 1603. 2p, Harquebusiers, 1632. 3p, Cuirassier, 1635. 5p, Mounted drummer of the Dragoons, 1677. 9p, Two Musketeers, 1694.

**1974, Jan. 5 Photo. *Perf. 13***

**1794** A428 1p multicolored .20 .20
**1795** A428 2p multicolored .50 .20
**1796** A428 3p multicolored .70 .20
**1797** A428 5p multicolored .90 .25
**1798** A428 9p multicolored .25 .25
*Nos. 1794-1798 (5)* 2.55 1.10

Nautical Chart of Western Europe and North Africa — A437

**1974, Jan. 26**

**1799** A437 2p multicolored .20 .20

50th anniv. of the Superior Geographical Council of Spain. The chart is from a 14th cent. Catalan atlas.

M. Biada and Steam Engine A438

**1974, Apr. 2 Photo. *Perf. 13***

**1800** A438 2p multicolored .20 .20

Barcelona-Mataro Railroad, 125th anniv.

Young Collector, Album, Magnifier A439

Exhibition Emblem — A440

Design: 8p, Emblem, globe and arrows.

**1974, Apr. 4 *Perf. 13***

**1801** A439 2p lilac rose & multi .20 .20

***Perf. 12½***

**1802** A440 5p buff, blk & dull bl .35 .30
**1803** A440 8p dull green & multi .30 .25
*Nos. 1801-1803 (3)* .85 .75

Espana 75, International Philatelic Exhibition, Madrid, Apr. 4-13, 1975.

Woman with Offering — A441

Europa: 8p, Woman from Baza, painted sculpture.

**1974, Apr. 29 Photo. *Perf. 13***

**1804** A441 2p multicolored *.45* .20
**1805** A441 8p multicolored *.25 .25*

No. 28 and 1854 Seville Cancel A442

**1974, May 6**

**1806** A442 2p black, blue & red .20 .20

World Stamp Day.

Father Jaime Balmes A443

Designs: 10p, Father Pedro Poveda. 15p, Jorge Juan y Santacilla.

**1974, May 28 Engr. *Perf. 13***

**1807** A443 8p blue gray & sepia .20 .20
**1808** A443 10p red brn & dk brn .60 .20
**1809** A443 15p brown & slate .20 .20
*Nos. 1807-1809 (3)* 1.00 .60

Famous Spaniards: Jaime Balmes (1810-1848), mathematician; death centenary of Pedro Poveda, pedagogue; Don Jorge Juan (1712-1773), explorer and writer.

Templeto, by Bramante, Rome — A444

**1974, June 4 Photo.**

**1810** A444 5p multicolored .20 .20

Cent. of the Spanish Academy of Fine Arts, Rome.

Aqueduct, Segovia A445

Designs: 2p, Tajo Bridge, Alcantara. 3p, Marcus Valerius Martial lecturing. 4p, Triumphal Arch, Tarragona, vert. 5p, Theater, Merida. 7p, Bishop Ossius of Cordoba preaching. 8p, Tribunal Arch, Talavera Forum, vert. 9p, Emperor Trajan, vert.

**1974, June 25 Engr.**

**1811** A445 1p brown & black .20 .20
**1812** A445 2p gray grn & sepia .30 .20
**1813** A445 3p lt & dk brown .20 .20
**1814** A445 4p green & indigo .20 .20
**1815** A445 5p gray bl & choc .20 .20
**1816** A445 7p gray grn & lilac .20 .20
**1817** A445 8p dk brown & green .20 .20
**1818** A445 9p brt red lil & cl .20 .20
*Nos. 1811-1818 (8)* 1.70 1.60

Roman architecture and history in Spain.

Greek Tortoise A446

Reptiles: 2p, Common chameleon. 5p, Wall gecko. 7p, Emerald lizard. 15p, Blunt-nosed viper.

**1974, July 3 Photo.**

**1819** A446 1p multicolored .20 .20
**1820** A446 2p multicolored .30 .20
**1821** A446 5p multicolored .60 .50
**1822** A446 7p multicolored .40 .25
**1823** A446 15p multicolored .20 .20
*Nos. 1819-1823 (5)* 1.70 1.35

Uniform Type of 1973

Uniforms: 1p, Hussar and horse, 1705. 2p, Artillery officers, 1710. 3p, Piper and drummer, Granada Regiment, 1734. 7p, Mounted standard-bearer, Numancia Dragoons, 1737. 8p, Standard-bearer and soldier, Zamora Regiment, 1739.

**1974, July 17**

**1824** A428 1p multicolored .20 .20
**1825** A428 2p multicolored .40 .20
**1826** A428 3p multicolored .40 .20
**1827** A428 7p multicolored .30 .20
**1828** A428 8p multicolored .20 .20
*Nos. 1824-1828 (5)* 1.50 1.00

Life Saving A447

**1974, Sept. 5 Photo. *Perf. 13***

**1829** A447 2p multicolored .20 .20

18th World Life Saving Championships, Barcelona, Sept. 1974.

Eduardo Rosales, by Federico Madrazo — A448

Stamp Day (Eduardo Rosales, 1836-73, Paintings): 1p, Tobias and the Angel. 3p, The Last Will of Isabella the Catholic. 4p, Nena (little girl). 5p, Presentation of John of Austria to Charles I. 7p, The First Step. 10p, St. John the Evangelist. 15p, St. Matthew.

**1974, Sept. 29 Photo. *Perf. 13***

**1830** A448 1p gold & multi .20 .20
**1831** A448 2p gold & multi .20 .20
**1832** A448 3p gold & multi, horiz. .20 .20
**1833** A448 4p gold & multi .20 .20
**1834** A448 5p gold & multi, horiz. .20 .20
**1835** A448 7p gold & multi, horiz. .20 .20
**1836** A448 10p gold & multi .30 .20
**1837** A448 15p gold & multi .20 .20
*Nos. 1830-1837 (8)* 1.70 1.60

For other art types see A384, A397, A410, A431, A473, A501, A522, A538, A558 and footnote following No. 876.

"International Mail" — A449

UPU Monument, Bern — A450

**1974, Oct. 9**

**1838** A449 2p dark blue & multi .20 .20
**1839** A450 8p red & multi .20 .20

Centenary of Universal Postal Union.

Sobremonte House, Cordoba, Argentina — A451

Ruins of San Ignacio de Mini, 18th Century — A452

The Gaucho Martin Fierro — A453

Design: 2p, Municipal Council Building, Buenos Aires, 1829.

**1974, Oct. 12**

**1840** A451 1p multicolored .20 .20
**1841** A451 2p multicolored .40 .20
**1842** A452 5p multicolored .30 .20
**1843** A453 10p multicolored .25 .20
*Nos. 1840-1843 (4)* 1.15 .80

Cultural ties with Latin America.

Nativity, Valdavia Church A454

Adoration of the Kings, Valcobero Church — A455

**1974 Photo. *Perf. 13***

**1844** A454 2p multicolored .20 .20
**1845** A455 3p lt blue & multi .20 .20
**1846** A455 8p olive & multi .20 .20
*Nos. 1844-1846 (3)* .60 .60

Christmas 1974.
Issue dates: 2p, 8p, Nov. 4; 3p, Dec. 2.

Teucriun Lanigerum A456

Flowers: 2p, Hypericum ericoides. 4p, Thymus longiflorus. 5p, Anthyllis onobrychioides. 8p, Helianthemun paniculatum.

**1974, Nov. 8**

**1847** A456 1p multicolored .20 .20
**1848** A456 2p multicolored .20 .20
**1849** A456 4p multicolored .20 .20
**1850** A456 5p multicolored .25 .20
**1851** A456 8p multicolored .20 .20
*Nos. 1847-1851 (5)* 1.05 1.00

Franco Type of 1954-56
Imprint: "F.N.M.T."

**1974-75 Photo. *Perf. 12½x13***

**1852** A221 4p rose car ('75) .20 .20
**1853** A221 7p brt ultra .20 .20
**1854** A221 12p blue green .20 .20
**1855** A221 20p rose carmine .25 .20
*Nos. 1852-1855 (4)* .85 .80

Leyre Monastery A457

8p, Column and bas-relief, vert. 15p, Crypt.

**1974, Dec. 10 Engr. *Perf. 12½x13***

**1862** A457 2p slate grn & bl gray .45 .20
**1863** A457 8p carmine .20 .20
**1864** A457 15p grnsh black .35 .20
*Nos. 1862-1864 (3)* 1.00 .60

Leyre Monastery, Navarre.

Spain Nos. 1 and 1802 — A458

Mail Coach, 1850 A459

Designs: 8p, Mail ship of Indian Service. 10p, Chapel of St. Mark.

***Perf. 12½x13, 13x12½***

**1975, Jan. 2 Engr.**

**1865** A458 2p slate blue .35 .30
**1866** A459 3p olive & brown .45 .40
**1867** A459 8p lilac & slate bl 1.00 .50
**1868** A458 10p brn & slate grn .50 .40
*Nos. 1865-1868 (4)* 2.30 1.60

125th anniversary of Spanish postage stamps.

Uniform Type of 1973

1p, Sergeant and grenadier, Toledo Regiment, 1750. 2p, Royal Artillery, 1762. 3p, Queen's Regiment, 1763. 5p, Fusiliers, Vitoria Regiment, 1766. 10p, Dragoon, Sagunto Regiment, 1775.

**1975, Jan. 7 Photo. *Perf. 13***

**1869** A428 1p multicolored .20 .20
**1870** A428 2p multicolored .20 .20
**1871** A428 3p multicolored 1.60 .25
**1872** A428 5p multicolored .50 .20
**1873** A428 10p multicolored 1.40 .25
*Nos. 1869-1873 (5)* 3.90 1.10

Antonio Gaudi A460

Designs: 10p, Antonio Palacios and Casa Guell, Barcelona. 15p, Secundino Zuazo.

**1975, Feb. 25 Engr. *Perf. 13***

**1874** A460 8p green & black .20 .20
**1875** A460 10p carmine & dp claret .40 .20
**1876** A460 15p brown & black .20 .20
*Nos. 1874-1876 (3)* .80 .60

Contemporary Spanish architects.

Souvenir Sheets

Spanish Goldsmiths' Works — A461

Designs: 2p, Agate box, 9th cent. 3p, Votive crown of Recesvinto. 8p, Cover of Evangelistary, Roncesvalles Collegiate Church, 12th cent. 10p, Chalice of Infanta Donna Urraca, 11th cent. 12p, Processional monstrance, St. Domingo de Silos, 16th cent. 15p, Sword of Boabdil, 15th cent. 25p, Sword and head of Charles V (Carlos I of Spain). 50p, Earring and bracelet from Aliseda, 6th-4th centuries B.C. 3p, 10p, 12p, 25p vertical (No. 1878).

**1975, Apr. 4 Engr. *Perf. 13***

| | | | | |
|---|---|---|---|---|
| **1877** | A461 | Sheet of 4 | 8.00 | 8.00 |
| *a.* | | 2p gray & Prussian blue | 2.00 | 2.00 |
| *b.* | | 8p brown & Prus blue | 2.00 | 2.00 |
| *c.* | | 15p gray & dark carmine | 2.00 | 2.00 |
| *d.* | | 50p dark carmine & gray | 2.00 | 2.00 |
| **1878** | A461 | Sheet of 4 | 8.00 | 8.00 |
| *a.* | | 3p slate green & gray | 2.00 | 2.00 |
| *b.* | | 10p sepia & slate | 2.00 | 2.00 |
| *c.* | | 12p gray & bluish black | 2.00 | 2.00 |
| *d.* | | 25p sepia & bluish black | 2.00 | 2.00 |

Espana 75 Intl. Phil. Exhib., Madrid, 4/4-13.

Pomegranates A462

Woman Gathering Honey, Arana Cave — A463

**1975, Apr. 21 Photo.**

| | | | | |
|---|---|---|---|---|
| **1879** | A462 | 1p Almonds, nuts and blossoms, horiz. | .20 | .20 |
| **1880** | A462 | 2p shown | .25 | .20 |
| **1881** | A462 | 3p Oranges | .25 | .20 |
| **1882** | A462 | 4p Chestnuts | .20 | .20 |
| **1883** | A462 | 5p Apples | .20 | .20 |
| | | *Nos. 1879-1883 (5)* | 1.10 | 1.00 |

**1975, Apr. 28 Photo. *Perf. 13***

Europa: 12p, Horse, wall painting from Tito Bustillo Cave, horiz.

| | | | | |
|---|---|---|---|---|
| **1884** | A463 | 3p brown & multi | *.25* | .20 |
| **1885** | A463 | 12p brown & multi | *.35* | .20 |

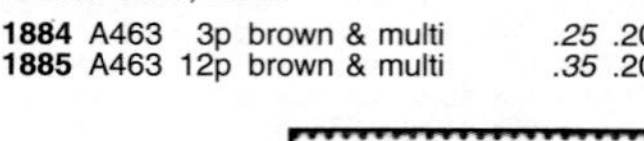

Pre-stamp León Cancellation A464

**1975, May 6 *Perf. 12½x13***

| | | | | |
|---|---|---|---|---|
| **1886** | A464 | 3p multicolored | .20 | .20 |

World Stamp Day.

World Tourism Organization Emblem — A465

**1975, May 12 Photo. *Perf. 13***

| | | | | |
|---|---|---|---|---|
| **1887** | A465 | 3p dark blue | .20 | .20 |

First General Assembly of the World Tourism Organization, Madrid, May 1975.

Fair Emblem, Agricultural Symbols — A466

**1975, May 14**

| | | | | |
|---|---|---|---|---|
| **1888** | A466 | 3p multicolored | .20 | .20 |

25th Agricultural Fair.

Equality Between Men and Women A467

**1975, June 3**

| | | | | |
|---|---|---|---|---|
| **1889** | A467 | 3p multicolored | .20 | .20 |

International Women's Year.

Virgin of Cabeza Sanctuary A468

**1975, June 18 Photo. *Perf. 13***

| | | | | |
|---|---|---|---|---|
| **1890** | A468 | 3p multicolored | .20 | .20 |

Virgin of Cabeza Sanctuary, site of siege during Civil War, 1937.

Cervantes' Prison Cell, Argamasilla de Alba — A469

Tourism: 2p, Bridge of St. Martin, Toledo. 3p, Church of St. Peter, Tarrasa. 4p, Arch, Alhambra, Granada, vert. 5p, Street, Mijas, Malaga, vert. 7p, Church of St. Mary, Tarrasa, vert.

**1975, June 25 Engr. *Perf. 13***

| | | | | |
|---|---|---|---|---|
| **1891** | A469 | 1p purple & black | .20 | .20 |
| **1892** | A469 | 2p red brn & brn | .20 | .20 |
| **1893** | A469 | 3p slate & sepia | .20 | .20 |
| **1894** | A469 | 4p orange & claret | .20 | .20 |
| **1895** | A469 | 5p slate grn & indigo | .20 | .20 |
| **1896** | A469 | 7p violet bl & indigo | .40 | .20 |
| | | *Nos. 1891-1896 (6)* | 1.40 | 1.20 |

Salamander — A470

**1975, July 9 Photo. *Perf. 13***

| | | | | |
|---|---|---|---|---|
| **1897** | A470 | 1p shown | .20 | .20 |
| **1898** | A470 | 2p Newt | .25 | .20 |
| **1899** | A470 | 3p Tree toad | .25 | .20 |
| **1900** | A470 | 6p Midwife toad | .20 | .20 |
| **1901** | A470 | 7p Leaf frog | .20 | .20 |
| | | *Nos. 1897-1901 (5)* | 1.10 | 1.00 |

Uniform Type of 1973

1p, Cavalry officer, 1788. 2p, Fusilier, Asturias Regiment, 1789. 3p, Infantry Colonel, 1802. 4p, Artillery standard-bearer, 1803. 7p, Sapper, 1809.

**1975, July 17**

| | | | | |
|---|---|---|---|---|
| **1902** | A428 | 1p multicolored | .20 | .20 |
| **1903** | A428 | 2p multicolored | .50 | .20 |
| **1904** | A428 | 3p multicolored | .20 | .20 |
| **1905** | A428 | 4p multicolored | .20 | .20 |
| **1906** | A428 | 7p multicolored | .20 | .20 |
| | | *Nos. 1902-1906 (5)* | 1.30 | 1.00 |

Infant and Children Playing A471

**1975, Sept. 9 Photo. *Perf. 13***

| | | | | |
|---|---|---|---|---|
| **1907** | A471 | 3p multicolored | .20 | .20 |

"Defend Life."

Scroll and Emblem A472

**1975, Sept. 25**

| | | | | |
|---|---|---|---|---|
| **1908** | A472 | 3p multicolored | .20 | .20 |

13th International Congress of Latin Notaries, Barcelona, Sept. 26-Oct. 4.

Blessing of the Birds A473

Scenes from Apocalypse: 2p, Angel at River of Life. 3p, Angel Guarding Gate of Paradise. 4p, Fox carrying cock. 6p, Daniel with wild bulls. 7p, The Last Judgment. 10p, Four horsemen of the Apocalypse. 12p, Bird holding snake.

**1975, Sept. 29**

| | | | | |
|---|---|---|---|---|
| **1909** | A473 | 1p gold & multi | .20 | .20 |
| **1910** | A473 | 2p gold & multi, vert. | .20 | .20 |
| **1911** | A473 | 3p gold & multi, vert. | .20 | .20 |
| **1912** | A473 | 4p gold & multi | .20 | .20 |
| **1913** | A473 | 6p gold & multi | .20 | .20 |
| **1914** | A473 | 7p gold & multi, vert. | .25 | .25 |
| **1915** | A473 | 10p gold & multi, vert. | .20 | .20 |
| **1916** | A473 | 12p gold & multi, vert. | .20 | .20 |
| | | *Nos. 1909-1916 (8)* | 1.65 | 1.65 |

Millenium Gerona Cathedral.

For other art types see A384, A397, A410, A431, A448, A501, A522, A538, A558 and footnote following No. 876.

Symbols of Industry A474

**1975, Oct. 7 Engr. *Perf. 13***

| | | | | |
|---|---|---|---|---|
| **1917** | A474 | 3p violet & lilac | .20 | .20 |

Spanish industrialization.



Pioneers' Covered Wagon A475

Designs: 1p, El Cabildo, meeting house of 1st Uruguayan Government. 3p, Fort St. Theresa over River Plate. 8p, Montevideo Cathedral, vert.

**1975, Oct. 12 Photo.**

| | | | | |
|---|---|---|---|---|
| **1918** | A475 | 1p multicolored | .20 | .20 |
| **1919** | A475 | 2p multicolored | .20 | .20 |
| **1920** | A475 | 3p multicolored | .25 | .20 |
| **1921** | A475 | 8p multicolored | .20 | .20 |
| | | *Nos. 1918-1921 (4)* | .85 | .80 |

Cultural ties with Latin America; sesquicentennial of Uruguay's independence.

Ruined Columns, San Juan de la Peña — A476

Madonna, Mosaic, Navarra Cathedral — A477

3p, Monastery, horiz. 8p, Cloister, horiz.

***Perf. 13x12½, 12½x13***

**1975, Oct. 28 Engr.**

| | | | | |
|---|---|---|---|---|
| **1922** | A476 | 3p slate grn & brn | .30 | .20 |
| **1923** | A476 | 8p violet & brt lil | .20 | .20 |
| **1924** | A476 | 10p dp magenta & car | .25 | .20 |
| | | *Nos. 1922-1924 (3)* | .75 | .60 |

San Juan de la Pena Monastery.

**1975, Nov. 4 Photo. *Perf. 13***

Christmas: 12p, Flight into Egypt, carved capital, Navarra Cathedral, horiz.

| | | | | |
|---|---|---|---|---|
| **1925** | A477 | 3p multicolored | .20 | .20 |
| **1926** | A477 | 12p multicolored | .20 | .20 |

King Juan Carlos I — A478

Queen Sofia and King — A479

Designs: No. 1928, Queen Sofia.

**1975, Dec. 29 Photo. *Perf. 13x12½***

| | | | | |
|---|---|---|---|---|
| **1927** | A478 | 3p multicolored | .20 | .20 |
| **1928** | A478 | 3p multicolored | .20 | .20 |

***Perf. 12½***

| | | | | |
|---|---|---|---|---|
| **1929** | A479 | 3p multicolored | .20 | .20 |
| **1930** | A479 | 12p multicolored | .20 | .20 |
| | | *Nos. 1927-1930 (4)* | .80 | .80 |

King Juan Carlos I, accession to the throne.

Pilgrim Virgin, Pontevedra A480

Mountains and Center Emblem A481

**1976, Jan. 2 Engr. *Perf. 13***

**1931** A480 3p rose & brown .20 .20

Holy Year of St. James of Compostela, patron saint of Spain.

**1976, Feb. 10 Photo.**

**1932** A481 6p multicolored .20 .20

Catalunya Excursion Center, centenary.

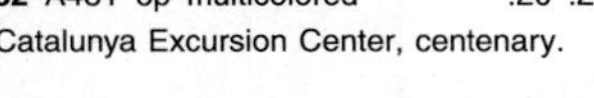

Cosme Damian Churruca — A482

Navigators: 12p, Luis de Requesens. 50p, Juan Sebastian Elcano, horiz.

**1976, Mar. 1 Engr. *Perf. 13***

**1933** A482 7p vio brn & grnsh blk 1.50 .25
**1934** A482 12p lt blue & violet .20 .20
**1935** A482 50p dp brn & gray ol .55 .20
*Nos. 1933-1935 (3)* 2.25 .65

A. G. Bell, Radar and Telephone A483

**1976, Mar. 10 Photo.**

**1936** A483 3p multicolored .20 .20

Centenary of first telephone call by Alexander Graham Bell, March 10, 1876.

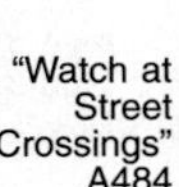

"Watch at Street Crossings" A484

Road Safety: 3p, "Don't pass when in doubt," vert. 5p, "Wear seat belts."

**1976, Apr. 6 Photo. *Perf. 13***

**1937** A484 1p orange & multi .20 .20
**1938** A484 3p gray & multi .35 .20
**1939** A484 5p lilac & multi .20 .20
*Nos. 1937-1939 (3)* .75 .60

St. George, Alcoy Cathedral A485

**1976, Apr. 23**

**1940** A485 3p multicolored .20 .20

7th centenary of the apparition of St. George in Alcoy.

Talavera Pottery A486

Europa: 12p, Lace making.

**1976, May 3 Photo. *Perf. 13***

**1941** A486 3p multicolored *.65* .20
**1942** A486 12p multicolored *.80* .30

17th Conference of European Postal and Telecommunications Administrations.

6r Stamp of 1851 with Coruna Cancel — A487

**1976, May 6**

**1943** A487 3p blue, org & blk .20 .20

World Stamp Day.

Coin of Caesar Augustus A488

7p, Map of Roman camp on banks of Ebro, and coin. 25p, Orpheus, mosaic from Roman era, vert.

**1976, May 26 Engr. *Perf. 13***

**1944** A488 3p dk brn & mar 1.90 .20
**1945** A488 7p dk brown & blue 1.00 .30
**1946** A488 25p brown & black .50 .20
*Nos. 1944-1946 (3)* 3.40 .70

Founding of Saragossa, 2000th anniv.

Spanish-made Rifle, 1757 — A489

Designs (Bicentennial Emblem and): 3p, Bernardo de Galvez, Spanish governor. 5p, Dollar bank note, Richmond, 1861. 12p, Spanish capture of Pensacola from English.

**1976, May 29**

**1947** A489 1p dk brn & vio bl .20 .20
**1948** A489 3p sl grn & dk brn .90 .20
**1949** A489 5p dk brn & sl grn .40 .20
**1950** A489 12p sl grn & dk brn .40 .30
*Nos. 1947-1950 (4)* 1.90 .90

American Bicentennial.

Old Customs House, Cadiz A490

Customs Houses: 3p, Madrid. 7p, Barcelona.

**1976, June 9**

**1951** A490 1p black & maroon .20 .20
**1952** A490 3p sepia & green .55 .20
**1953** A490 7p red brn & vio brn 1.10 .35
*Nos. 1951-1953 (3)* 1.85 .75

Postal Savings Box with Symbols — A491

Railroad Post Office — A492

Rural Mailman in Winter A493

Postal Service: 10p, Automatic letter sorting machine.

**1976, June 16 Photo.**

**1954** A491 1p multicolored .20 .20
**1955** A492 3p multicolored .35 .20
**1956** A493 6p multicolored .20 .20
**1957** A493 10p multicolored .25 .20
*Nos. 1954-1957 (4)* 1.00 .80

King and Queen, Map of Americas A494

**1976, June 25**

**1958** A494 12p multicolored .25 .20

Visit of King Juan Carlos I and Queen Sofia to the Americas, June 1976.

San Marcos, León — A495

Greco-Roman Wrestling — A496

Tourism (Famous Hotels): 2p, Las Cañadas, Tenerife. 3p, Portal of R. R. Catolicos, Santiago, vert. 4p, Cruz de Tejeda, Las Palmas. 7p, Gredos, Avila. 12p, La Arruzafa, Cordoba.

**1976, June 30 Engr. *Perf. 13***

**1959** A495 1p slate & sepia .20 .20
**1960** A495 2p green & indigo .65 .20
**1961** A495 3p brn & red brn .45 .20
**1962** A495 4p sepia & slate .25 .20
**1963** A495 7p slate & sepia .85 .35
**1964** A495 12p rose brn & pur 1.00 .25
*Nos. 1959-1964 (6)* 3.40 1.40

**1976, July 9 Photo.**

Montreal Olympic Emblem and: 1p, Men's rowing, horiz. 2p, Boxing, horiz. 12p, Basketball.

**1965** A496 1p multicolored .20 .20
**1966** A496 2p lilac & multi .35 .20
**1967** A496 3p multicolored .25 .20
**1968** A496 12p multicolored .25 .20
*Nos. 1965-1968 (4)* 1.05 .80

21st Olympic Games, Montreal, Canada, July 17-Aug. 1.

King Juan Carlos I — A497

**1976-77 Photo. *Perf. 13***

**1969** A497 10c orange ('77) .20 .20
**1970** A497 25c apple grn ('77) .20 .20
**1971** A497 30c dp blue ('77) .20 .20
**1972** A497 50c purple ('77) .20 .20
**1973** A497 1p emerald ('77) .20 .20
**1974** A497 1.50p scarlet .20 .20
**1975** A497 2p dp blue .20 .20
**1976** A497 3p dp green .20 .20
**1977** A497 4p blue grn ('77) .20 .20
**1978** A497 5p dp car rose .20 .20
**1979** A497 6p brt green ('77) .20 .20
**1980** A497 7p olive .20 .20
**1982** A497 8p brt blue ('77) .20 .20
**1983** A497 10p lilac rose ('77) .20 .20
**1984** A497 12p golden brown .25 .20
**1985** A497 15p vio blue ('77) .30 .20
**1986** A497 20p brt red lil ('77) .35 .20
*Nos. 1969-1986 (17)* 3.70 3.40

Nos. 1976, 1978-1980, 1982-1983 also issued as coils with number on back of every fifth stamp.

See Nos. 2185-2194, 2268-2270.

Nos. 1969-1970, 1972-1973, 1975-1983, 1985-1986, 2185-2194 and 2268-2270 also printed on prephosphored paper. Value, mint set of 27 values, $40.

### Uniform Type of 1973

Uniforms: 1p, Trumpeter, Alcantara Regiment, 1815. 2p, Sapper, 1821. 3p, Engineer in dress uniform, 1825. 7p, Artillery infantry, 1828. 25p, Infantry riflemen, 1830.

**1976, July 17**

**1989** A428 1p multicolored .20 .20
**1990** A428 2p multicolored .80 .20
**1991** A428 3p multicolored .30 .20
**1992** A428 7p multicolored .25 .25
**1993** A428 25p multicolored .30 .20
*Nos. 1989-1993 (5)* 1.85 1.05

Blood Donors A498

Mosaic, Batitales A499

**1976, Sept. 7 Engr. *Perf. 13***

**1994** A498 3p carmine & black .20 .20

Give blood, save a life!

**1976, Sept. 22**

Designs: 3p, Lugo city wall. 7p, Obverse and reverse of Roman 1st Legion coin.

**1995** A499 1p black & purple .20 .20
**1996** A499 3p black & dp brn .25 .20
**1997** A499 7p green & magenta .45 .20
*Nos. 1995-1997 (3)* .90 .60

2000th anniversary of Lugo City.

Parliament, Madrid A500

**1976, Sept. 23**
**1998** A500 12p green & sepia .20 .20

63rd Conference of Inter-parliamentary Union, Madrid.

Still Life, by L. E. Menendez — A501

St. Christopher Carrying Christ Child — A502

Luis Eugenio Menendez Paintings: 2p, Peaches and jar. 3p, Pears, melon and barrel. 4p, Brace of pigeons and basket. 6p, Sea bream and oranges, horiz. 7p, Water melon and bread, horiz. 10p, Figs, bread and jug, horiz. 12p, Various fruits, horiz.

**1976, Sept. 29 Photo. *Perf. 13***
**1999** A501 1p gold & multi .20 .20
**2000** A501 2p gold & multi .20 .20
**2001** A501 3p gold & multi .20 .20
**2002** A501 4p gold & multi .20 .20
**2003** A501 6p gold & multi .20 .20
**2004** A501 7p gold & multi .30 .25
**2005** A501 10p gold & multi .25 .20
**2006** A501 12p gold & multi .30 .25
*Nos. 1999-2006 (8)* 1.85 1.70

Luis Eugenio Menendez (1716-1780). Stamp Day 1976.
For other art types see A384, A397, A410, A431, A448, A473, A522, A538, A558 and footnote following No. 876.

**1976, Oct. 8**

Christmas: 3p, Nativity, horiz. Both designs after painted wood carvings.

**2007** A502 3p multicolored .75 .20
**2008** A502 12p multicolored 1.50 .50

Nicoya Church, Costa Rica — A503

Juan Vazquez de Coronado — A504

Designs: 3p, Orosi Mission, Costa Rica, horiz. 12p, Tomas de Acosta.

**1976, Oct. 12**
**2009** A503 1p multicolored .20 .20
**2010** A504 2p multicolored .25 .20
**2011** A503 3p multicolored .20 .20
**2012** A504 12p multicolored .25 .20
*Nos. 2009-2012 (4)* .90 .80

Spain's link with Costa Rica.

Map of South and Central America, Santa Maria, King and Queen A505

**1976, Oct. 12**
**2013** A505 12p multicolored .20 .20

Visit of King Juan Carlos I and Queen Sofia to Latin America.

St. Peter of Alcantara Monastery A506

Tomb of Peter of Alcantara A507

St. Peter of Alcantara A508

**1976, Oct. 29 Engr. *Perf. 13***
**2014** A506 3p dp brown & sepia .30 .20
**2015** A507 7p dk purple & blk .20 .20
**2016** A508 20p brown & dk brown .30 .20
*Nos. 2014-2016 (3)* .80 .60

St. Peter of Alcantara (1499-1562), Franciscan reformer.

Hand Releasing Doves A509

**1976, Nov. 23 Litho. *Perf. 13***
**2017** A509 3p multicolored .20 .20

11th Philatelic Exhibition of the National Association of the Handicapped.

Casals and Cello A510

Design: 5p, Manuel de Falla and Fire Dance from El Amor Brujo.

**1976, Dec. 29 Engr. *Perf. 13***
**2018** A510 3p black & vio bl .20 .20
**2019** A510 5p slate grn & car .20 .20

Birth centenaries of Pablo Casals (1876-1973), cellist and composer, and of Manuel de Falla (1876-1946), composer.

Uniform Type of 1973

Uniforms: 1p, Outrider, Calatrava Lancers, 1844. 2p, Sapper, 1850. 3p, Corporal, Light Infantry, 1861. 4p, Drum Major, 1861. 20p, Artillery Captain, Mounted, 1862.

**1977, Jan. 5 Photo. *Perf. 13***
**2020** A428 1p multicolored .20 .20
**2021** A428 2p multicolored .35 .20
**2022** A428 3p multicolored .20 .20
**2023** A428 4p multicolored .20 .20
**2024** A428 20p multicolored .25 .20
*Nos. 2020-2024 (5)* 1.20 1.00

King James I A511

**1977, Feb. 10 Engr. *Perf. 13***
**2025** A511 4p purple & ocher .20 .20

James I, El Conquistador (1208-1276), King of Aragon, 700th death anniversary.

Jacinto Verdaguer — A512

Portraits: 7p, Miguel Servet. 12p, Pablo Sarasate. 50p, Francisco Tarrega.

**1977, Feb. 22**
**2026** A512 5p purple & dk red .25 .20
**2027** A512 7p olive & slate grn .20 .20
**2028** A512 12p dk blue & bl grn .20 .20
**2029** A512 50p lt green & brown .55 .20
*Nos. 2026-2029 (4)* 1.20 .80

Honoring Jacinto Verdaguer (1845-1902), Catalan poet; Miguel Servet (1511-1553), physician and theologian; Pablo Sarasate (1844-1908), violinist and composer; Francisco Tarrega (1854-1909), creator of modern Spanish guitar music.

Marquis de Penaflorida — A513

**1977, Feb. 24 Engr. *Perf. 13***
**2030** A513 4p dull green & brn .20 .20

Bicentenary of the Economic Society of the Friends of the Land (agricultural improvements).

Trout A514

**1977, Mar. 8 Photo.**
**2031** A514 1p Salmon, vert. .20 .20
**2032** A514 2p shown .20 .20
**2033** A514 3p Eel .20 .20
**2034** A514 4p Carp .20 .20
**2035** A514 6p Barbel .20 .20
*Nos. 2031-2035 (5)* 1.00 1.00

Slalom A515

**1977, Mar. 24 Engr. *Perf. 13***
**2036** A515 5p multicolored .20 .20

World Ski Championships, Granada, Sierra Nevada, Mar. 24-27.

La Cuadra, 1900 A516

Spanish Pioneer Automobiles: 4p, Hispano Suiza, 1916. 5p, Elizalde, 1915. 7p, Abadal, 1914.

**1977, Apr. 23 Photo. *Perf. 13***
**2037** A516 2p multicolored .20 .20
**2038** A516 4p multicolored .20 .20
**2039** A516 5p multicolored .20 .20
**2040** A516 7p multicolored .20 .20
*Nos. 2037-2040 (4)* .80 .80

Ordesa National Park A517

Europa: 3p, Tree in Doñana National Park.

**1977, May 2 Litho.**
**2041** A517 3p multicolored .20 .20
**2042** A517 12p multicolored *.25* .20

Plaza Mayor, Spanish Stamps, Tongs A518

**1977, May 7 Engr. *Perf. 13***
**2043** A518 3p multicolored .20 .20

50th anniversary of Philatelic Market on Plaza Mayor, Madrid.

Enrique de Osso, St. Theresa and Book A519

**1977, June 7 Photo. *Perf. 13***
**2044** A519 8p multicolored .20 .20

Centenary of the founding by Enrique de Osso of the Society of St. Theresa of Jesus.

Toledo Gate, Ciudad Real — A520

Tourism: 2p, Roman aqueduct, Almuñecar. 3p, Cathedral, Jaen, vert. 4p, Ronda Gorge,

Malaga, vert. 7p, Ampudia Castle, Palencia. 12p, Bisagra Gate, Toledo.

**1977, June 24 Engr. *Perf. 13***

**2045** A520 1p orange & brown .20 .20
**2046** A520 2p sepia & slate .20 .20
**2047** A520 3p violet & purple .20 .20
**2048** A520 4p brt & dk green .20 .20
**2049** A520 7p brown & black .20 .20
**2050** A520 12p vio & org brn .20 .20
*Nos. 2045-2050 (6)* 1.20 1.20

### Uniform Type of 1973

Uniforms: 1p, Military Administration official, 1875. 2p, Cavalry lancers, 1883. 3p, General Staff Commander, 1884. 7p, Trumpeter, Divisional Artillery, 1887. 25p, Medical Corps official, 1895.

**1977, July 16 Photo.**

**2051** A428 1p multicolored .20 .20
**2052** A428 2p multicolored .20 .20
**2053** A428 3p multicolored .20 .20
**2054** A428 7p multicolored .20 .20
**2055** A428 25p multicolored .30 .20
*Nos. 2051-2055 (5)* 1.10 1.00

A521

A522

St. Emilian Cuculatus and earliest known Catalan manuscript.

**1977, Sept. 9 Engr. *Perf. 13***

**2056** A521 5p violet, grn & brn .20 .20

Millennium of Catalan language.

**1977, Sept. 29 Photo. *Perf. 13***

Federico Madrazo (1815-94) Portraits: 1p, The Boy Florez. 2p, Duke of San Miguel. 3p, Senora Coronado. 4p, Campoamor. 6p, Marquesa de Montelo. 7p, Rivadeneyra. 10p, Countess de Vilches. 15p, Senora Gomez de Avellaneda.

**2057** A522 1p gold & multi .20 .20
**2058** A522 2p gold & multi .20 .20
**2059** A522 3p gold & multi .20 .20
**2060** A522 4p gold & multi .20 .20
**2061** A522 6p gold & multi .20 .20
**2062** A522 7p gold & multi .20 .20
**2063** A522 10p gold & multi .20 .20
**2064** A522 15p gold & multi .20 .20
*Nos. 2057-2064 (8)* 1.60 1.60

For other art types see A384, A397, A410, A431, A448, A473, A501, A538, A558 and footnote following No. 876.

Sailing Ship and Mail Routes, 18th Century — A523

**1977, Oct. 7 Engr.**

**2065** A523 15p black, brn & grn .30 .30

ESPAMER '77 Philatelic Exhibition, Barcelona, Oct. 7-13, and for the Bicentenary for regular mail routes to the Indies (Central and South America). No. 2065 issued in sheets of 8 stamps and 8 labels showing exhibition emblem.

Church of St. Francis, Guatemala City
A524

Designs (Guatemala City): 3p, Modern buildings. 7p, Government Palace. 12p, Columbus Square and monument.

**1977, Oct. 12 Photo. *Perf. 13***

**2066** A524 1p multicolored .20 .20
**2067** A524 3p multicolored .20 .20
**2068** A524 7p multicolored .20 .20
**2069** A524 12p multicolored .20 .20
*Nos. 2066-2069 (4)* .80 .80

Spain's link with Guatemala.

San Pedro Monastery, Cardeña
A525

Designs: 7p, Cloister. 20p, Tomb of El Cid and Dona Gimena.

**1977, Oct. 28 Engr.**

**2070** A525 3p vio blue & slate .20 .20
**2071** A525 7p brown & maroon .20 .20
**2072** A525 20p green & slate .25 .20
*Nos. 2070-2072 (3)* .65 .60

San Pedro Monastery, Cardena, Burgos.

Adoration of the Kings
A526

Christmas: 12p, Flight into Egypt, vert. Designs from Romanesque paintings in Jaca Cathedral Museum.

**1977, Nov. 3 Photo.**

**2073** A526 5p multicolored .20 .20
**2074** A526 12p multicolored .20 .20

Old and New Iberia Planes
A527

**1977, Nov. 3**

**2075** A527 12p multicolored .20 .20

IBERIA, Spanish Airlines, 50th anniversary.

Felipe de Borbon, Prince of Asturias — A528

Judo, Games Emblem — A529

**1977, Dec. 22 Photo. *Perf. 13***

**2076** A528 5p multicolored .20 .20

Felipe de Borbon, Spanish crown prince.

**1977, Dec. 29**

**2077** A529 3p multicolored .20 .20

10th World Judo Championships, Taiwan.

### Uniform Type of 1973

Uniforms: 1p, Flag bearer, 1908. 2p, Lieutenant Colonel, Hussar, 1909. 3p, Mounted artillery lieutenant, 1912. 5p, Engineers' captain, 1921. 12p, Captain General, 1925.

**1978, Jan. 5**

**2078** A428 1p multicolored .20 .20
**2079** A428 2p multicolored .20 .20
**2080** A428 3p multicolored .20 .20
**2081** A428 5p multicolored .20 .20
**2082** A428 12p multicolored .20 .20
*Nos. 2078-2082 (5)* 1.00 1.00

Hilarión Eslava and Score
A530

8p, José Clara and sculpture. 25p, Pio Baroja and farm. 50p, Antonio Machado Ruiz and castle.

**1978, Feb. 20 Engr. *Perf. 13***

**2083** A530 5p black & dk pur .20 .20
**2084** A530 8p blue grn & blk .20 .20
**2085** A530 25p yel grn & blk .30 .20
**2086** A530 50p dk pur & dk brn .55 .20
*Nos. 2083-2086 (4)* 1.25 .80

Miguel Hilarión Eslava (1807-1878), composer; José Clara, sculptor; Pio Baroja (1872-1956), author and physician; Antonio Machado Ruiz (1875-1939), poet and playwright.

Burial of Christ, by de Juni — A531

Detail from Burial of Christ — A532

Designs: No. 2089, Juan de Juni. No. 2090, Rape of Sabine Women, by Rubens. No. 2091, Rape (detail) and Rubens portrait. No. 2092, Rubens signature and palette. No. 2093, Judgment of Paris, by Titian. No. 2094, Judgment and Titian portrait. No. 2095, Initial "TF" and palette.

**1978, Mar. 28 Engr. *Perf. 12½x13***

**2087** A532 3p multicolored .20 .20
**2088** A531 3p multicolored .20 .20
**2089** A532 3p multicolored .20 .20
*a.* Strip of 3, #2087-2089 .25 .25
**2090** A532 5p multicolored .20 .20
**2091** A531 5p multicolored .20 .20
**2092** A532 5p multicolored .20 .20
*a.* Strip of 3, #2090-2092 .25 .25
**2093** A532 8p multicolored .20 .20
**2094** A531 8p multicolored .20 .20
**2095** A532 8p multicolored .20 .20
*a.* Strip of 3, #2093-2095 .25 .25

Juan de Juni (1507-77), sculptor, (3p); Peter Paul Rubens (1577-1640), painter, (5p); Titian (1477-1576), painter, (8p).

Edelweiss in Pyrenees — A533

Designs: 5p, Fish and duck, wetlands. 7p, Forest, and forest destroyed by fire. 12p, Waves, oil rig, tanker and city. 20p, Sea gulls and seals, vert.

**1978, Apr. 4 Photo. *Perf. 13***

**2096** A533 3p multicolored .20 .20
**2097** A533 5p multicolored .20 .20
**2098** A533 7p multicolored .20 .20
**2099** A533 12p multicolored .20 .20
**2100** A533 20p multicolored .25 .20
*Nos. 2096-2100 (5)* 1.05 1.00

Protection of the environment.

Palace of Charles V, Granada
A534

Europa: 12p, The Lonja, Seville.

**1978, May 2 Engr. *Perf. 13***

**2101** A534 5p dull grn & sl grn .20 .20
**2102** A534 12p dull grn & car rose .20 .20

"España" — A535

**1978, May 5 Photo. *Perf. 12½***

**2103** A535 12p multicolored .20 .20

Spain's admission to the Council of Europe.

Symbols and Emblems of Postal Service
A536

**1978, June 27 Engr. *Perf. 13***

**2104** A536 5p slate green .20 .20

Stamp Day.

Map of Las Palmas, 16th Century
A537

5p, Hermitage of Columbus Church, vert. 12p, View of Las Palmas, 16th century.

**1978, June 23 Photo.**

**2105** A537 3p multicolored .20 .20
**2106** A537 5p multicolored .20 .20
**2107** A537 12p multicolored .20 .20
*Nos. 2105-2107 (3)* .60 .60

Founding of Las Palmas, 500th anniv.

Pablo Picasso, Self-portrait A538

Picasso Paintings: 3p, Señora Canals. 8p, Jaime Sabartes. 10p, End of the Act (actress). 12p, Science and Charity (woman patient, doctor, nurse and child), horiz. 15p, "Las Meninas" (blue period), horiz. 20p, The Sparrows. 25p, The Painter and his Model, horiz.

**1978, Sept. 29 Photo. *Perf. 13***

**2108** A538 3p gold & multi .20 .20
**2109** A538 5p gold & multi .20 .20
**2110** A538 8p gold & multi .20 .20
**2111** A538 10p gold & multi .20 .20
**2112** A538 12p gold & multi .20 .20
**2113** A538 15p gold & multi .20 .20
**2114** A538 20p gold & multi .25 .20
**2115** A538 25p gold & multi .30 .20
*Nos. 2108-2115 (8)* 1.75 1.60

Pablo Picasso (1881-1973). Stamp Day 1978.

A 7p stamp like No. 2111 was not issued.

For other art types see A384, A397, A410, A431, A448, A473, A501, A522, A558 and footnote following No. 876.

José de San Martin A539

Design: 12p, Simon Bolivar.

**1978, Oct. 12 Engr. *Perf. 13***

**2116** A539 7p sepia & car .20 .20
**2117** A539 12p violet & car .20 .20

José de San Martin (1778-1850) and Simon Bolivar (1783-1830), South American liberators.

Flight into Egypt, Capital from St. Mary de Nieva A540

Christmas: 12p, Annunciation, capital from St. Mary de Nieva.

**1978, Nov. 3 Photo. *Perf. 13***

**2118** A540 5p multicolored .20 .20
**2119** A540 12p multicolored .20 .20

Mexican Calendar Stone A541

Designs (King Juan Carlos I, Queen Sofia and): No. 2121, Machu Picchu. No. 2122, Calchaqui jars from Tucuman and Angalgala.

**1978**

**2120** A541 5p multicolored .20 .20
**2121** A541 5p multicolored .20 .20
**2122** A541 5p multicolored .20 .20
*Nos. 2120-2122 (3)* .60 .60

Royal visits to Mexico, Peru and Argentina.

Issued: #2120 (Mexico), Nov. 17; #2121 (Peru), Nov. 22; #2122 (Argentina), Nov. 26.

King Philip V — A542

Rulers of Spain: No. 2124, Louis I. 8p, Ferdinand VI. 10p, Carlos III. 12p, Carlos IV. 15p, Ferdinand VII. 20p, Isabella II. 25p, Alfonso XII. 50p, Alfonso XIII. 100p, Juan Carlos I.

**1978, Nov. 22 Engr. *Perf. 13***

**2123** A542 5p dk blue & rose red .20 .20
**2124** A542 5p olive & dull grn .20 .20
**2125** A542 8p vio bl & red brn .20 .20
**2126** A542 10p blue grn & blk .20 .20
**2127** A542 12p brown & mar .20 .20
**2128** A542 15p black & indigo .20 .20
**2129** A542 20p olive & indigo .25 .20
**2130** A542 25p ultra & vio brn .30 .20
**2131** A542 50p vermilion & brn .55 .25
**2132** A542 100p ultra & vio blk 1.10 .35
*Nos. 2123-2132 (10)* 3.40 2.20

Spanish Flag, Preamble to Constitution, Parliament — A543

**1978, Dec. Photo. *Perf. 13***

**2133** A543 5p multicolored .20 .20

Proclamation of New Constitution.

Illuminated Pages from Bible and Codex — A544

**1978, Dec. 27**

**2134** A544 5p multicolored .20 .20

Millennium of the consecration of the Basilica of Santa Maria de Ripoll.

Car and Drop of Oil — A545

Designs: 8p, Insulated house and thermometer. 10p, Hand pulling plug.

**1979, Jan. 24 Photo. *Perf. 13***

**2135** A545 5p multicolored .20 .20
**2136** A545 8p multicolored .20 .20
**2137** A545 10p multicolored .20 .20
*Nos. 2135-2137 (3)* .60 .60

Energy conservation.

De La Salle, Students A546

**1979, Feb. 14 Photo. *Perf. 13***

**2138** A546 5p multicolored .20 .20

Institute of Christian Brothers, founded by Jean-Baptiste de la Salle, centenary.

Jorge Manrique — A547

Portraits: 8p, Fernan Caballero (pen name of Cecilia Böhl de Faber). 10p, Francisco Villaespesa. 20p, Gregorio Marañon.

**1979, Feb. 28 Engr.**

**2139** A547 5p green & brown .20 .20
**2140** A547 8p dark red & blue .20 .20
**2141** A547 10p brown & purple .20 .20
**2142** A547 20p green & olive .25 .20
*Nos. 2139-2142 (4)* .85 .80

Jorge Manrique, poet, 500th death anniversary; Fernan Caballero, Francisco Villaespesa, and Gregorio Marañon, writers, birth centenaries.

Running and Jumping A548

Sport for All: 8p, Children kicking ball and skipping rope, jogging and bicycling. 10p, Family jogging, and dog.

**1979, Mar. 14 Photo. *Perf. 13***

**2143** A548 5p multicolored .20 .20
**2144** A548 8p multicolored .20 .20
**2145** A548 10p multicolored .20 .20
*Nos. 2143-2145 (3)* .60 .60

Children in Library A549

**1979, Apr. 27 Photo. *Perf. 13***

**2146** A549 5p multicolored .20 .20

International Year of the Child.

Manuel Ysasi (1810-1855) Postal Reformer — A550

Europa: 5p, Mounted messenger and postilion, 1761 engraving, vert.

**1979, Apr. 30 Engr.**

**2147** A550 5p brown & sepia .20 .20
**2148** A550 12p red brn & sl grn .20 .20

Radar and Satellite A551

5p, Symbolic people and cables, vert.

**1979, May 17 Photo. *Perf. 13***

**2149** A551 5p multicolored .20 .20
**2150** A551 8p multicolored .20 .20

World Telecommunications Day, May 17.

Bulgaria No. 1, Sofia Opera House, Housing Development — A552

**1979, May 18**

**2151** A552 12p multicolored .20 .20

Philaserdica '79, International Philatelic Exhibition, Sofia, Bulgaria, May 18-27.

Tank, Jet and Destroyer A553

**1979, May 25**

**2152** A553 5p multicolored .20 .20

Armed Forces Day.

Messenger Handing Letter to King — A554

**1979, June 15 Litho. & Engr.**

**2153** A554 5p multicolored .20 .20

Stamp Day 1979.

Daroca Gate, Zaragoza — A555

Architecture: 8p, Gerona Cathedral. 10p, Interior, Carthusian Monastery Church, Granada. 20p, Portal, Palace of the Marques de Dos Aguas, Valencia.

**1979, June 27 Engr.**

**2154** A555 5p vio bl & lilac brn .20 .20
**2155** A555 8p dk blue & sepia .20 .20
**2156** A555 10p black & green .20 .20
**2157** A555 20p brown & sepia .25 .20
*Nos. 2154-2157 (4)* .85 .80

Turkey Sponge A556

Fauna: 7p, Crayfish. 8p, Scorpion. 20p, Starfish. 25p, Sea anemone.

**1979, July 11 Photo. *Perf. 13***

**2158** A556 5p multicolored .20 .20
**2159** A556 7p multicolored .20 .20
**2160** A556 8p multicolored .20 .20
**2161** A556 20p multicolored .25 .20
**2162** A556 25p multicolored .30 .20
*Nos. 2158-2162 (5)* 1.15 1.00

Gen. Antonio Gutierrez and Battle
A557

**1979, Aug.** **Engr.**
**2163** A557 5p multicolored .20 .20

Naval defense of Tenerife, 18th century.

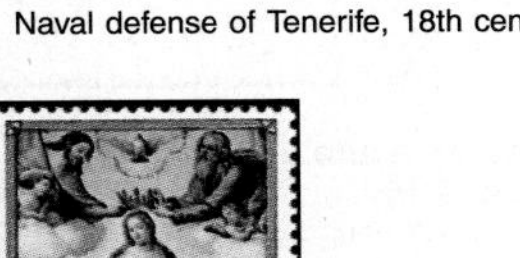
A558

A559

Juan de Juanes Paintings: 8p, Immaculate Conception. 10p, Holy Family. 15p, Ecce Homo. 20p, St. Stephen in the Synagogue. 25p, The Last Supper, horiz. 50p, Adoration of the Mystic Lamb, horiz.

**1979, Sept. 28** **Photo.** ***Perf. 13x13½***
**2164** A558 8p multicolored .20 .20
**2165** A558 10p multicolored .20 .20
**2166** A558 15p multicolored .20 .20
**2167** A558 20p multicolored .25 .20
**2168** A558 25p multicolored .30 .20
**2169** A558 50p multicolored .55 .20
*Nos. 2164-2169 (6)* 1.70 1.20

For other art types see A384, A397, A410, A431, A448, A473, A501, A522, A538 and footnote following No. 876.

**1979, Oct. 3** **Photo.** ***Perf. 13x13½***

Zaragoza Cathedral, Mother and Child statue.

**2170** A559 5p multicolored .20 .20

8th Mariology and 15th International Marianist Congresses, Zaragoza, Oct. 3-12.

Felipe de Borbon, Hospital
A560

**1979, Oct.** ***Perf. 13½x13***
**2171** A560 5p multicolored .20 .20

Hospital of the Child Jesus, centenary.

St. Bartholomew College, Bogota — A561

Hispanidad 79: 12p, University of St. Mark, Lima, coat of arms.

**1979, Oct. 12** **Engr.** ***Perf. 13***
**2172** A561 7p multicolored .20 .20
**2173** A561 12p multicolored .20 .20

Clasped Hands, Badge, Governor's Palace
A562

Design: No. 2175, Statute book, vert.

**Lithographed and Engraved**

**1979, Oct. 27** ***Perf. 13***
**2174** A562 8p multicolored .20 .20
**2175** A562 8p multicolored .20 .20

Catalonian and Basque autonomy statute.

Type A54, Barcelona Coat of Arms
A563

**Photogravure and Engraved**

**1979, Nov. 6** ***Perf. 13½x13***
**2176** A563 5p multicolored .20 .20

Barcelona Philatelic Congress and Exhibition, 50th anniversary.

Nativity, Capital from St. Peter the Elder
A564

Christmas 1979: 19p, Flight into Egypt, column from St. Peter the Elder, Huesca.

**1979, Nov. 14** **Photo.**
**2177** A564 8p multicolored .20 .20
**2178** A564 19p multicolored .25 .20

Carlos I, Coat of Arms
A565

Kings of the House of Austria (Hapsburg Dynasty): 20p, Philip II. 25p, Philip III. 50c, Philip IV. 100p, Carlos II.

**1979, Nov. 22** **Engr.** ***Perf. 13***
**2179** A565 15p sl grn & dk bl .20 .20
**2180** A565 20p dk blue & mag .25 .20
**2181** A565 25p violet & yel bis .30 .20
**2182** A565 50p brown & sl grn .55 .20
**2183** A565 100p magenta & brn 1.10 .30
*Nos. 2179-2183 (5)* 2.40 1.10

2nd International Olive Oil Year — A566

**1979, Dec. 4** **Photo.** ***Perf. 13½x13***
**2184** A566 8p multicolored .20 .20

King Juan Carlos I Type of 1976

**1980-84** **Photo.** ***Perf. 13***
**2185** A497 13p dk red brn ('81) .25 .20
**2186** A497 14p red orange ('82) .25 .20
**2187** A497 16p sepia .30 .20
**2188** A497 17p bluish gray ('84) .25 .20
**2189** A497 19p orange .35 .20
**2190** A497 30p dk green ('81) .40 .20
**2191** A497 50p org ver ('81) .90 .20
**2192** A497 60p blue ('81) .80 .20
**2193** A497 75p brt yel grn ('81) 1.00 .30
**2194** A497 85p gray ('81) 1.25 .45
*Nos. 2185-2194 (10)* 5.75 2.35

No. 2186 and 2187 also issued as coil with number on back of every fifth stamp.

Train and People
A567

**1980, Feb. 20** **Engr.** ***Perf. 13½***
**2200** A567 3p shown .20 .20
**2201** A567 4p Bus .20 .20
**2202** A567 5p Subway .20 .20
*Nos. 2200-2202 (3)* .60 .60

Public transportation.

Steel Export
A568

**1980, Mar. 15** **Photo.** ***Perf. 13½x13***
**2203** A568 5p shown .20 .20
**2204** A568 8p Ships .20 .20
**2205** A568 13p Shoes .20 .20
**2206** A568 19p Machinery .25 .20
**2207** A568 25p Technology .30 .20
*Nos. 2203-2207 (5)* 1.15 1.00

Federico Garcia Lorca (1899-1936) — A569

Europa: 19p, José Ortega y Gasset (1883-1955), philosopher and statesman.

**1980, Apr. 28** **Engr.** ***Perf. 13½***
**2208** A569 8p violet & ol grn .20 .20
**2209** A569 19p brown & dk grn .25 .20

Armed Forces Day
A570

**1980, May 24** **Photo.** ***Perf. 13½x13***
**2210** A570 8p multicolored .20 .20

Soccer Players
A571

**1980, May 23**
**2211** A571 8p shown .20 .20
**2212** A571 19p Soccer ball, flags .25 .20

World Soccer Cup 1982.

Bourbon Arms, Ministry of Finance
A572

**1980, June 9** **Engr.** ***Perf. 13½***
**2213** A572 8p dark brown .20 .20

Public Finances in Bourbon Spain Exhibition.

Helen Keller, Sign Language
A573

**1980, June 27**
**2214** A573 19p dk yel grn & rose lake .25 .20

Helen Keller (1880-1968), deaf mute writer and lecturer.

Mounted Postman, 12th Century Panel, Barcelona — A574

**Lithographed and Engraved**

**1980, June 28** ***Perf. 13x12½***
**2215** A574 8p multicolored .20 .20

Stamp Day.

King Alfonso and Count of Maceda at 1930 National Exhibition
A575

**1980, July 1** **Photo.** ***Perf. 13½***
**2216** A575 8p multicolored .20 .20

1st Natl. Stamp Exhibition, Barcelona, 50th anniv.

A576

A577

Altar of the Virgin, La Palma Cathedral.

**1980, July 12** **Engr.** ***Perf. 13***
**2217** A576 8p black & brown .20 .20

Appearance of the Virgin of the Snow at La Palma, 300th anniversary.

**1980, Aug. 9** **Engr.** ***Perf. 13***
**2218** A577 100p slate & sepia 1.10 .20

Ramon Perez de Ayala (1881-1962), novelist and diplomat.

Souvenir Sheet

La Atlantida Ruins, Mexican Bonampak Musicians — A578

Designs: b, Sun Gate, Tiahuanaco; Roman arch, Medinaceli. c, Alonso de Ercilla, Garcilaso de la Vega; title pages from La Arauca and Commentario Reales. d, Virgin of Quito, Virgin of Seafarers.

**1980, Oct. 3** **Engr.** ***Perf. 13***

**2219** A578 Sheet of 4 + 2 labels 2.25 2.25
*a.* 25p multicolored .30 .30
*b.* 25p multicolored .30 .30
*c.* 50p multicolored .55 .45
*d.* 100p multicolored 1.10 .85

ESPAMER '80 Stamp Exhib., Madrid, Oct. 3-12.

400th Anniversary of Buenos Aires — A579

**1980, Oct. 24**

**2220** A579 19p multicolored .25 .20

Miniature Sheet

The Creation, Tapestry, Gerona Cathedral — A580

**1980, Nov.** **Litho.** ***Perf. 13½x13***

**2221** A580 Sheet of 6 2.50 2.00
*a.-c.* 25p, any single .25 .20
*d.-f.* 50p, any single .55 .25

Conference Building, Flags of Participants A581

Holy Family Church of Santa Maria, Cuina — A582

**1980, Nov. 11** **Photo.** ***Perf. 13½***

**2222** A581 22p multicolored .25 .20

**1980, Nov. 12**

Christmas 1980, 22p, Adoration of the Kings, portal, Church of Santa Maria, Cuina, horiz.

**2223** A582 10p multicolored .20 .20
**2224** A582 22p multicolored .25 .20

Pedro Vives and His Airplane A583

Designs: Aviation pioneers.

**1980, Dec. 10**

**2225** A583 5p shown .20 .20
**2226** A583 10p Benito Loygorri .20 .20
**2227** A583 15p Alfonso De Orleans .20 .20
**2228** A583 22p Alfredo Kindelan .25 .20
*Nos. 2225-2228 (4)* .85 .80

Winter University Games A584

**1981, Mar. 4** ***Perf. 13½x13***

**2229** A584 30p multicolored .35 .20

Picasso's Birth Centenary Emblem, by Joan Miro — A585

**1981, Mar. 27** ***Perf. 13***

**2230** A585 100p multicolored 1.00 .25

Pablo Picasso (1881-1973).

Galician Autonomy — A586

**1981, Mar. 27** **Photo.** ***Perf. 13***

**2231** A586 12p multicolored .20 .20

Homage to the Press A587

**1981, Apr. 8** **Photo.** ***Perf. 13½x13***

**2232** A587 12p multicolored .20 .20

International Year of the Disabled — A588

**1981, Apr. 29** **Litho.**

**2233** A588 30p multicolored .35 .20

Soccer Players A589

**1981, May 2** **Photo.**

**2234** A589 12p Soccer players, diff., vert. .20 .20
**2235** A589 30p shown .35 .20

1982 World Cup Soccer.

**Europa Issue 1981**

La Jota Folkdance A590

**1981, May 4** **Engr.**

**2236** A590 12p shown .20 .20
**2237** A590 30p Virgin of Rocio procession .35 .20

Armed Forces Day — A591

Gabriel Miro (1879-1930), Writer — A592

**1981, May 29** **Photo.** ***Perf. 13x13½***

**2238** A591 12p multicolored .20 .20

**1981, June 17** **Engr.**

Famous Men: 12p, Francisco de Quevedo (1580-1645), writer. 30p, St. Benedict (480-543), patron saint of Europe.

**2239** A592 6p purple & dk grn .20 .20
**2240** A592 12p brown & purple .20 .20
**2241** A592 30p dk green & brown .35 .20
*Nos. 2239-2241 (3)* .75 .60

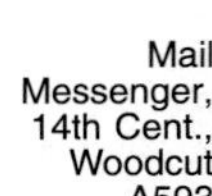


Mail Messenger, 14th Cent., Woodcut A593

**Photogravure and Engraved**

**1981, June 19** ***Perf. 12½x13***

**2242** A593 12p multicolored .20 .20

Stamp Day.

Map of Balearic Islands, Diego Homem's Atlas, 1563 — A594

**1981, July 8** **Photo.** ***Perf. 13x12½***

**2243** A594 7p shown .20 .20
**2244** A594 12p Canary Islds., Prunes map, 1563 .20 .20

Kings Alfonso XII and Juan Carlos, Advocates Arms A595

**1981, July 27** **Engr.** ***Perf. 13½x13***

**2245** A595 50p multicolored .55 .20

Chamber of Advocates of State (Public Prosecutor) centenary.

King Sancius VI of Navarre with City Charter, 12th Cent. Miniature A596

**1981, Aug. 5** **Photo.** ***Perf. 12½x13***

**2246** A596 12p multicolored .20 .20

Vitoria, 800th anniv.

Exports A597

**1981, Sept. 30** **Photo.** ***Perf. 13½x13***

**2247** A597 6p Fruit .20 .20
**2248** A597 12p Wine .20 .20
**2249** A597 30p Vehicles .35 .20
*Nos. 2247-2249 (3)* .75 .60

Congress Palace, Buenos Aires A598

**1981, Oct. 12 Engr. *Perf. 13½x13***
**2250** A598 12p dk bl & car rose .20 .20

ESPAMER '81 Intl. Stamp Exhibition, Buenos Aires, Nov. 13-22.

World Food Day A599

**1981, Oct. 16**
**2251** A599 30p multicolored .35 .20

Souvenir Sheet

Guernica, by Pablo Picasso (1881-1973) — A600

**1981, Oct. 25 Photo.**
**2252** A600 200p multicolored 2.25 2.25

Control number comes in two types.

A601

Christmas 1981: 12p, Adoration of the Kings, Cervera de Pisuerga, Palencia. 30p, Nativity, Paredes de Nava.

**1981, Nov. 18 Litho. *Perf. 13***
**2253** A601 12p shown .20 .20
**2254** A601 30p multicolored .35 .20

A602

**1981, Oct. 21 Engr. *Perf. 13x12½***

King Juan Carlos I.

**2268** A602 100p brown 1.25 .20
**2269** A602 200p dark green 2.60 .20
**2270** A602 500p dark blue 6.25 .55
*Nos. 2268-2270 (3)* 10.10 .95

Postal Museum, Madrid A603

**1981, Nov. 30 Engr. *Perf. 13***
**2273** A603 7p Telegrapher .20 .20
**2274** A603 12p Coach .20 .20

Souvenir Sheet

**2275** Sheet of 4 1.90 1.90
*c.* A603 50p Emblem .55 .50
*d.* A603 100p Cap, posthorn, pouch 1.10 1.00

No. 2275 also contains Nos. 2273, 2274.

Royal Mint Building, Seville A604

**1981, Dec. 4 Engr. *Perf. 13***
**2276** A604 12p black & brown .20 .20

Spanish Administration of the Bourbons in the Indies.

A605

12p, Iparraguirre (1820-81). 30p, Juan Ramon Jimenez (1881-1958), writer. 50p, Pedro Calderon (1600-81), playwright.

**1981-82**
**2277** A605 12p black & dk bl .20 .20
**2278** A605 30p dk bl & dk grn .35 .20
**2279** A605 50p black & violet .55 .20
*Nos. 2277-2279 (3)* 1.10 .60

Issued: 12p, 12/16; 30p, 50p, 3/10/82.

A606

**1982, Feb. 24 Photo.**
**2280** A606 14p Poster by Joan Miro .20 .20
**2281** A606 33p Cup, emblem .40 .20

Espana '82 World Cup Soccer.

A607

A608

**1982, Mar. 10 Engr.**
**2282** A607 30p grn & dk grn .35 .20

Andres Bello (1782-1865), writer.

**1982, Mar. 31 Photo. *Perf. 13***
**2283** A608 14p St. John of Compostelo .20 .20

Holy Year of Compostelo.

A609-A610

Operetta composers and scenes from their works: #2284, Manuel Fernandez Caballero (1835-1906). #2285, Gigantes and Cabezudos. #2286, Amadeo Vives Roig (1871-1932). #2287, Dona Francisquita. #2288, Tomas Breton Hernandez (1850-1923). #2289, Verbena of Paloma.

**Lithographed and Engraved**

**1982, Apr. 28 *Perf. 13***
**2284** A609 3p multicolored .20 .20
**2285** A610 3p multicolored .20 .20
*a.* Pair, #2284-2285 .20 .20
**2286** A609 6p multicolored .20 .20
**2287** A610 6p multicolored .20 .20
*a.* Pair, #2284-2285 .20 .20
**2288** A609 8p multicolored .20 .20
**2289** A610 8p multicolored .20 .20
*a.* Pair, #2284-2285 .25 .20

See Nos. 2319-2324, 2378-2383.

Europa 1982 — A611

**1982, May 3 Engr. *Perf. 12½***
**2290** A611 14p Unification, 1512 .20 .20
**2291** A611 33p Discovery of New World, 1492 .40 .20

Armed Forces Day — A612

**1982, May 28 Photo. *Perf. 13***
**2292** A612 14p multicolored .20 .20

1982 World Cup A613

Designs: Soccer players.

**1982, June 13 *Perf. 13***
**2293** A613 14p multicolored .20 .20
**2294** A613 33p multicolored .40 .20

**Souvenir Sheets**

**2295** Sheets of 4, #2293-2294, 9p, 100p, each 1.75 1.75
*a.* A613 9p Captains' handshake .20 .20
*b.* A613 100p Player holding cup 1.10 1.10

#2295 has two types of margin, each showing 7 arms of the 14 host cities. One sheet has 3 blue coats of arms, the other has 2.

Stamp Day — A614

**1982, July 16 Litho. *Perf. 12½***
**2296** A614 14p Map, postal code .20 .20

Organ Transplants A615

**1982, July 28 Photo. *Perf. 13***
**2297** A615 14p Symbolic organs .20 .20

Storks and Express Train — A616

Locomotive, 1850 — A617

***Perf. 12½, 13 (A617)***

**1982, Sept. 27 Photo.**
**2298** A616 9p shown .20 .20
**2299** A617 14p shown .20 .20
**2300** A617 33p Santa Fe locomotive .40 .20
*Nos. 2298-2300 (3)* .80 .60

23rd Intl. Railways Congress, Malaga.

ESPAMER '82 Intl. Stamp Exhibition, San Juan, Oct. 12-17 A618

**1982, Oct. 12 Engr. *Perf. 13½x13***
**2301** A618 33p dk blue & pur .40 .20

St. Teresa of Avila (1515-1582) — A619

**1982, Oct. 15**
**2302** A619 33p Statue by Gregorio Hernandez .40 .20

Visit of Pope John Paul II, Oct. 31-Nov. 9 — A620

**1982, Oct. 31 Engr. *Perf. 12½***
**2303** A620 14p multicolored .20 .20

Water Wheel, Alcantarilla A621

Landscapes and Monuments: 6p, Bank of Spain, 19th cent., horiz. 9p, Crucifixion. 14p, St. Martin's Tower, Teruel. 33p, St. Andrew's Gate, Zamora.

**1982, Nov. 5** ***Perf. 13x12½, 12½x13***

| | | | | | |
|---|---|---|---|---|---|
| **2304** | A621 | 4p | gray & dk blue | .20 | .20 |
| **2305** | A621 | 6p | dk blue & gray | .20 | .20 |
| **2306** | A621 | 9p | brt blue & vio | .20 | .20 |
| **2307** | A621 | 14p | brt blue & vio | .20 | .20 |
| **2308** | A621 | 33p | claret & brown | .40 | .20 |
| | | | *Nos. 2304-2308 (5)* | 1.20 | 1.00 |

Christmas 1982 A622

**1982, Nov. 17** **Photo.** ***Perf. 13½***

| | | | | | |
|---|---|---|---|---|---|
| **2309** | A622 | 14p | Nativity, wood carving, by Gil de Siloe | .20 | .20 |
| **2310** | A622 | 33p | Flight into Egypt | .40 | .20 |

Pablo Gargallo, Sculptor, Birth Centenary A623

Salesian Fathers in Spain, Centenary A624

**1982, Dec. 9** **Engr.** ***Perf. 13***
**2311** A623 14p blue & dk grn .20 .20

**1982, Dec. 16** **Photo.** ***Perf. 12½x13***
**2312** A624 14p multicolored .20 .20

Arms of King Juan Carlos I A625

**1983, Feb. 9** **Photo.** ***Perf. 12½***
**2313** A625 14p multicolored .20 .20

Andalusia Autonomy Statute A626

**1983** **Litho.** ***Perf. 13½***

| | | | | | |
|---|---|---|---|---|---|
| **2314** | A626 | 14p | shown | .25 | .20 |
| **2315** | A626 | 14p | Cantabria | .25 | .20 |

Issued: #2314, Feb. 28; #2315, Mar. 15.

State Security Forces A627

**1983, Mar. 23** **Photo.**

| | | | | | |
|---|---|---|---|---|---|
| **2316** | A627 | 9p | Natl. Police Force | .20 | .20 |
| **2317** | A627 | 14p | Civil Guard | .20 | .20 |
| **2318** | A627 | 33p | Superior Police Corps | .40 | .20 |

Operetta Type of 1982

Designs: #2319, Scene from La Parranda. Francisco Alonso Lopez (1887-1948). #2320, Francisco Alonso Lopez (1887-1948). #2321, Jacinto Guerrero y Torres (1895-1951). #2322, Scene from La Rosa del Azafran. #2323, Jesus de Guridi Bidaola (1886-1961). #2324, Scene from El Caserio.

**Lithographed and Engraved**

**1983, Apr. 22** ***Perf. 13***

| | | | | | |
|---|---|---|---|---|---|
| **2319** | A610 | 4p | multicolored | .20 | .20 |
| **2320** | A609 | 4p | multicolored | .20 | .20 |
| *a.* | | | Pair, #2319-2320 | .20 | .20 |
| **2321** | A609 | 6p | multicolored | .20 | .20 |
| **2322** | A610 | 6p | multicolored | .20 | .20 |
| *a.* | | | Pair, #2321-2322 | .25 | .25 |
| **2323** | A609 | 9p | multicolored | .20 | .20 |
| **2324** | A610 | 9p | multicolored | .20 | .20 |
| *a.* | | | Pair, #2323-2324 | .35 | .35 |

Europa 1983 — A628

Designs: 16p, Scene from Don Quixote, by Miguel Cervantes. 38p, L. Torres Quevaedo's Niagara Spanish aerocar.

**1983, May 5** **Engr.** ***Perf. 13x12½***
**Granite Paper**

| | | | | | |
|---|---|---|---|---|---|
| **2325** | A628 | 16p | dk grn & brn red | .20 | .20 |
| **2326** | A628 | 38p | brown | .45 | .20 |

Francisco Salzillo Alvarez (1707-83), Painter — A629

World Communications Year — A630

Designs: 38p, Antonio Soler Ramos (1729-1783), composer. 50p, Joaquin Turina Perez (1882-1949), composer. 100p, St. Isidro Labrador (1082-1170), patron saint of Madrid.

**1983, May 14** ***Perf. 13***

| | | | | | |
|---|---|---|---|---|---|
| **2327** | A629 | 16p | purple & dk grn | .20 | .20 |
| **2328** | A629 | 38p | blue & brown | .45 | .20 |
| **2329** | A629 | 50p | bl grn & dk brn | .55 | .20 |
| **2330** | A629 | 100p | red brn & pur | 1.10 | .25 |
| | | | *Nos. 2327-2330 (4)* | 2.30 | .85 |

**1983, May 17** **Photo.** ***Perf. 13***
**2331** A630 38p multicolored .45 .20

Rioja Autonomous Region — A631

**Lithographed and Engraved**

**1983, May 25** ***Perf. 13***
**2332** A631 16p multicolored .25 .20

Armed Forces Day — A632

**1983, May 26** **Photo.**
**2333** A632 16p multicolored .20 .20

Intl. Canine Exhibition, Madrid, June 1984 A633

**Lithographed and Engraved**

**1983, June 8** ***Perf. 13½***

| | | | | | |
|---|---|---|---|---|---|
| **2334** | A633 | 10p | Pointer | .20 | .20 |
| **2335** | A633 | 16p | Mastiff | .20 | .20 |
| **2336** | A633 | 26p | Iberian hound | .35 | .25 |
| **2337** | A633 | 38p | Navarro pointer | .50 | .20 |
| | | | *Nos. 2334-2337 (4)* | 1.25 | .85 |

Discovery of Tungsten Bicentenary — A634

Scouting Year A635

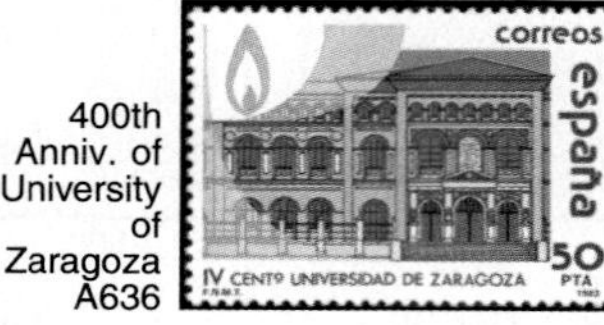
400th Anniv. of University of Zaragoza A636

**1983, June 22** **Photo.** ***Perf. 13***

| | | | | | |
|---|---|---|---|---|---|
| **2338** | A634 | 16p | Elhuyar brothers | .20 | .20 |
| **2339** | A635 | 38p | multicolored | .45 | .20 |
| **2340** | A636 | 50p | multicolored | .60 | .20 |
| | | | *Nos. 2338-2340 (3)* | 1.25 | .60 |

Murcia Autonomous Region — A637

**Photogravure and Engraved**

**1983, July 8** ***Perf. 13½***
**2341** A637 16p Arms .25 .20

Asturias Autonomous Region — A638

**Lithographed and Engraved**

**1983, Sept. 8** ***Perf. 13***
**2342** A638 14p Victory Cross, Covadonga Basilica .25 .20

Intl. Institute of Statistics, 44th Congress, Madrid, Sept. 12-22 A639

**1983, Sept. 12** **Photo.** ***Perf. 13***
**2343** A639 38p Institute building .45 .20

Stamp Day — A640

**Lithographed and Engraved**

**1983, Oct. 8** ***Perf. 13x12½***
**2344** A640 16p Roman mail cart .35 .30

No. 2344 se-tenant with label publicizing ESPANA '84 Philatelic Exhibition, April 27-May 6, 1984.

Valencia Autonomy Statute, 1st Anniv. A641

**1983, Oct. 10** ***Perf. 13***
**2345** A641 16p multicolored .25 .20

View of Seville, 16th cent. — A642

**1983, Oct. 12** **Engr.** ***Perf. 12½x13***
**2346** A642 38p multicolored .45 .20

Spanish-American trade in 17th century.

Stained-glass Windows A643

Designs: 10p King, Leon Cathedral. 16p, Epiphany, Gerona Cathedral. 38p, Apostle Santiago, Royal Hospital Chapel, Santiago.

**Lithographed and Engraved**

**1983, Oct. 28** *Perf. 12½x13*

**2347** A643 10p multicolored .20 .20
**2348** A643 16p multicolored .25 .20
**2349** A643 38p multicolored .45 .20
*Nos. 2347-2349 (3)* .90 .60

Church at Llivia, Gerona — A644

Designs: 6p, Temple, Santa Maria del Mar, Barcelona. 16p, Cathedral, Ceuta. 38p, Gate of the Santiago Bridge, Melilla. 50p, Charity Hospital, Seville.

**1983, Nov. 9** **Engr.** *Perf. 13x12½*

**2350** A644 3p dk bl gray & grn .20 .20
**2351** A644 6p dark blue gray .20 .20
**2352** A644 16p red brn & dull vio .20 .20
**2353** A644 38p bis brn & rose car .45 .25
**2354** A644 50p brown & org red .55 .20
*Nos. 2350-2354 (5)* 1.60 1.05

Christmas 1983 — A645

Indalecio Prieto (1883-1962), Patriot — A646

**1983, Nov. 23** **Photo.** *Perf. 13x13½*

**2355** A645 16p The Nativity, Tortosa .20 .20
**2356** A645 38p The Adoration, Vich .45 .20

**1983, Dec. 14** **Engr.** *Perf. 13*

**2357** A646 16p red brn & blk .20 .20

Industrial Accident Prevention A647

**1984, Jan. 25** **Photo.** *Perf. 13½*

**2358** A647 7p Construction worker .20 .20
**2359** A647 10p Fire .20 .20
**2360** A647 16p Electrical plug, pliers .20 .20
*Nos. 2358-2360 (3)* .60 .60

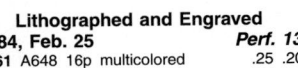

Extremadura Statute of Autonomy, First Anniv. — A648

**Lithographed and Engraved**

**1984, Feb. 25** *Perf. 13*

**2361** A648 16p multicolored .25 .20

1500th Anniv. of City of Burgos A649

**1984, Mar. 1** **Engr.**

**2362** A649 16p multicolored .20 .20

Carnivals A650

**1984** **Photo.** *Perf. 13½x13*

**2363** A650 16p Santa Cruz de Tenerife .25 .20
**2364** A650 16p Valencia Fallas .25 .20

Issued: #2363, Mar. 5; #2364, Mar. 16.

Man and the Biosphere A651

**1984, Apr. 11**

**2365** A651 38p da Vinci's Study of Man .45 .25

Aragon Statute of Autonomy, 2nd Anniv. A652

**Lithographed and Engraved**

**1984, Apr. 23** *Perf. 13x13½*

**2366** A652 16p Map .25 .20

Juan Carlos — A653

Souvenir Sheet

Espana '84 (Spanish Royal Family): b, Sofia of Greece. c, Cristina de Borbon. d, Prince of Asturias Felipe de Borbon. e, Elene de Borbon.

**1984, Apr. 27** *Perf. 12½x13*

**2367** A653 Sheet of 5 3.25 3.25
*a.-e.* 38p, any single .65 .65

Congress Emblem — A654

**1984, May 3** **Engr.** *Perf. 13x13½*

**2368** A654 38p purple & red .45 .20

World Philatelic Federation, 53rd Congress, Madrid, May 7-9.

Europa (1959-84) A655

**1984, May 5**

**2369** A655 16p orange .20 .20
**2370** A655 38p dark blue .45 .25

Armed Forces Day A656

Design: 17p, Monument to Hunters Regiment of Caceres, by Mariano Benlliure.

**1984, May 19** **Photo.** *Perf. 13½x13*

**2371** A656 17p multicolored .25 .20

Canary Islds. Statute of Autonomy — A657

Castilla-La Mancha Statute of Autonomy — A658

**Lithographed and Engraved**

**1984, May 29** *Perf. 13*

**2372** A657 16p Arms, map .25 .20

**1984, May 31** *Perf. 13*

**2373** A658 17p Arms .25 .20

King Alfonso X (1252-84) A659

Design: 38p, Ignacio Barroquer (1884-1965), ophthalmologist

**1984, June 20** **Engr.** *Perf. 13*

**2374** A659 16p multicolored .25 .20
**2375** A659 38p multicolored .45 .20

Balearic Islands Statute of Autonomy — A660

**1984, June 29** **Litho. & Engr.**

**2376** A660 17p multicolored .25 .20

Feast of San Fermin of Pamplona A661

**1984, July 5** **Photo.**

**2377** A661 17p Bull runners .25 .20

Operetta Type of 1982

#2378, El Nino Judio. #2379, Pablo Luna (1880-1942). #2380, Ruperto Chapi (1851-1909). #2381, La Revoltosa. #2382, La Reina Mora. #2383, Jose Serrano (1873-1941).

**Lithographed and Engraved**

**1984, July 20** *Perf. 13*

**2378** A610 6p multicolored .20 .20
**2379** A609 6p multicolored .20 .20
*a.* Pair, #2378-2379 .20 .20
**2380** A609 7p multicolored .20 .20
**2381** A610 7p multicolored .20 .20
*a.* Pair, #2380-2381 .20 .20
**2382** A610 10p multicolored .20 .20
**2383** A609 10p multicolored .20 .20
*a.* Pair, #2382-2383 .30 .30

1984 Summer Olympics A662

Greek or Roman sculptures.

**1984, July 27** **Photo.**

**2384** A662 1p Chariot race .20 .20
**2385** A662 2p Diving, vert. .20 .20
**2386** A662 5p Wrestling .20 .20
**2387** A662 8p Discus, vert. .20 .20
*Nos. 2384-2387 (4)* .80 .80

Navarra Statute of Autonomy A663

**Lithographed and Engraved**

**1984, Aug. 16** *Perf. 13*

**2388** A663 17p multicolored .25 .20

Intl. Bicycling Championship, Barcelona, Aug. 27-Sept. 2 — A664

**1984, Aug. 27** **Photo.**

**2389** A664 17p multicolored .20 .20

Castilla and Leon Statute of Autonomy A665

**1984, Sept. 5** **Litho. & Engr.**

**2390** A665 17p multicolored .25 .20

Jerez Vintage Feast — A666

**1984, Sept. 20** **Photo.** ***Perf. 13***
**2391** A666 17p Women picking grapes .25 .20

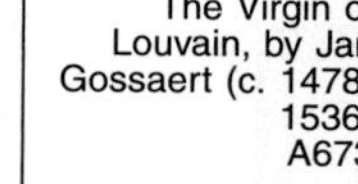

Journey to the Holy Land by Sister Egeria, 1600th Anniv. — A667

**1984, Sept. 26**
**2392** A667 40p Map, Sister Egeria .45 .25

Stamp Day — A668

**1984, Oct. 5** **Litho. & Engr.**
**2393** A668 17p Arab postrider .20 .20

Father Junipero Serra (1713-84), Mission Founder in California A669

**1984, Oct. 12** **Engr.** ***Perf. 13***
**2394** A669 40p Map, Serra, mission .45 .20

Christmas 1984 A670

**1984, Nov. 21** **Photo.**
**2395** A670 17p Nativity .20 .20
**2396** A670 40p Adoration of the Kings, vert. .45 .20

Madrid Autonomy Statue A671

**1984, Nov. 28** **Litho. & Engr.**
**2397** A671 17p Arms, buildings .25 .20

Andean Pact, 15th Anniv. A672

Condor, Flags of Bolivia, Colombia, Ecuador, Peru and Venezuela.

**1985, Jan. 16** **Photo.** ***Perf. 13***
**2398** A672 17p multicolored .20 .20

The Virgin of Louvain, by Jan Gossaert (c. 1478-1536) A673

Santa Cruz College, Valladolid University, 500th Anniv. — A674

**1985, Jan. 21** ***Perf. 13½***
**2399** A673 40p multicolored .45 .20

EUROPALIA '85. See Belgium No. 1185.

**1985, Feb. 20** **Litho. & Engr.**
**2400** A674 17p Main gateway .20 .20

OLYMPHILEX '85, Lausanne, Switz. — A675

**1985, Mar. 18** **Photo.**
**2401** A675 40p multicolored .45 .20

ESPAMER '85, Cuba A676

**1985, Mar. 20** **Engr.**
**2402** A676 40p Cathedral, Havana .45 .25

Fairs A677

***Perf. 13½, 13½x14 (#2405)***

**1985** **Photo.**
**2403** A677 17p Seville .25 .20
**2404** A677 17p Alcoy .25 .20
**2405** A677 17p Arriondas-Ribadesella .25 .20
**2406** A677 18p Toledo, vert. .25 .20
*Nos. 2403-2406 (4)* 1.00 .80

Issued: #2403, Apr. 16; #2404, Apr. 22; #2405, Aug. 2; #2406, June 6.

Intl. Youth Year — A678

**1985, Apr. 17** **Engr.** ***Perf. 13½***
**2407** A678 17p blk, hn brn & dk grn .20 .20

Europa '85 A680

Designs: 18p, Antonio de Cabezon (1510-1566), organist and composer, court Musician to Felipe II. 45p, Natl. Youth Orchestra.

**1985, May 3** **Engr.**
**2408** A680 18p dk bl, dk red & blk, *buff* *.25* .20
**2409** A680 45p ol grn, dk red & blk, *buff* *.45* *.25*

Armed Forces Day A681

**1985, May 24** **Photo.**
**2410** A681 18p multicolored .25 .20

Natl. Flag Bicent. — A682

#2411, Arms of King Carlos III, text of 1785 Decree, sailing ship Santisima Trinidad. #2412, Natl. arms, Article No. 4 from 1978 Constitution, lion ornament from Chamber of Deputies Building.

**Lithographed and Engraved**

**1985, May 28** ***Perf. 13x13½***
**2411** 18p multicolored .25 .20
**2412** 18p multicolored .25 .20
*a.* A682 Pair, #2411-2412 .45 .45

Intl. Environment Day — A683

**1985, June 5** **Photo.**
**2413** A683 17p multicolored .20 .20

Juan Carlos — A684

| **1985-92** | | **Photo.** | | ***Perf. 14*** | |
|---|---|---|---|---|---|
| **2414** | A684 | 10c | indigo | .20 | .20 |
| **2415** | A684 | 50c | lt blue green | .20 | .20 |
| **2416** | A684 | 1p | brt blue | .20 | .20 |
| **2417** | A684 | 2p | dark green | .20 | .20 |
| **2418** | A684 | 3p | chestnut brn | .20 | .20 |
| **2419** | A684 | 4p | olive green | .20 | .20 |
| **2420** | A684 | 5p | brt rose lilac | .20 | .20 |
| **2421** | A684 | 6p | brown black | .20 | .20 |
| **2422** | A684 | 7p | brt violet | .20 | .20 |
| **2423** | A684 | 7p | apple grn | .20 | .20 |
| **2424** | A684 | 8p | gray black | .20 | .20 |
| **2425** | A684 | 10p | lake | .20 | .20 |
| **2426** | A684 | 12p | red | .20 | .20 |
| **2427** | A684 | 13p | Prus blue | .20 | .20 |
| **2428** | A684 | 15p | emerald | .20 | .20 |
| **2429** | A684 | 17p | yellow bis | .20 | .20 |
| **2430** | A684 | 18p | brt grnsh bl | .25 | .20 |
| **2431** | A684 | 19p | violet brn | .25 | .20 |
| *a.* | Booklet pane of 6 | | | 1.50 | |
| **2432** | A684 | 20p | brt pink | .25 | .20 |
| **2433** | A684 | 25p | olive green | .30 | .20 |
| **2434** | A684 | 27p | deep rose lil | .35 | .20 |
| **2435** | A684 | 30p | ultra | .35 | .20 |
| **2436** | A684 | 45p | brt green | .50 | .20 |
| **2437** | A684 | 50p | violet blue | .55 | .20 |
| **2438** | A684 | 55p | black brown | .60 | .20 |
| **2439** | A684 | 60p | dark orange | .65 | .25 |
| **2440** | A684 | 75p | deep rose lil | .80 | .30 |
| | *Nos. 2414-2440 (27)* | | | 8.05 | 5.55 |

Issued: 1p, 5p, 8p, 12p, 18p, 45p, 6/12; #2422, 17p, 7/16; #2423, 1/86; 2p, 3p, 4p, 10p, 4/3/86; 19p, 9/27/86; 6p, 20p, 30p, 1/26/87; 50p, 60p, 75p, 4/24/89; 10c, 50c, 13p, 15p, 5/16/89; 25p, 55p, 12/14/90; 27p, 2/92.

Astrophysical Observatory Opening, La Palma, Canary Islands — A685

**1985, June 25** **Photo.** ***Perf. 14***
**2441** A685 45p multicolored .50 .20

European Music Year — A686

Designs: 12p, Ataulfo Argenta, conductor. 17p, Tomas Luis de Victoria, composer. 45p, Fernando Sor, composer.

**Litho. & Engr.**

**1985, June 26** ***Perf. 13***
**2442** A686 12p multicolored .20 .20
**2443** A686 17p multicolored .25 .20
**2444** A686 45p multicolored .50 .20
*Nos. 2442-2444 (3)* .95 .60

Bernal Diaz del Castillo (1492-1585), Historian — A687

Famous men: 12p, Esteban Terradas (1883-1950), mathematician. 17p, Vicente Aleixandre (1898-1984), 1977 Nobel laureate in literature. 45p, Leon Felipe Camino (1884-1968), poet.

**1985, July 24** **Engr.** ***Perf. 13½***
**2445** A687 7p dk red, blk & dk grn, *buff* .20 .20
**2446** A687 12p brt ver, dk bl & blk, *buff* .20 .20
**2447** A687 17p blk, dk grn & dk red, *buff* .25 .20
**2448** A687 45p bis, blk & dk grn, *buff* .55 .20
*Nos. 2445-2448 (4)* 1.20 .80

Monastic Mail Delivery, 1122 — A688

**Lithographed and Engraved**

**1985, Sept. 27** *Perf. 13*
**2449** A688 17p multicolored .25 .20

Stamp Day 1985.

12th Rhythmic Gymnastics World Championships, Valladolid — A689

**1985, Oct. 9 Photo.** *Perf. 13x13½*
**2450** A689 17p Ribbon exercise .20 .20
**2451** A689 45p Hoop exercise .50 .25

Souvenir Sheet

Prado Museum, La Alcachofa Fountain — A690

**Lithographed and Engraved**

**1985, Oct. 18** *Perf. 13*
**2452** A690 17p multicolored .50 .50

EXFILNA '85, Madrid, Oct. 18-27.

Virgin and Child, Seville Cathedral A691

Stained glass windows: 12p, Monk, by Peter Boniface, Toledo Cathedral. 17p, King Henry II of Castile, Alcazar of Segovia.

**1985, Oct. 24** *Perf. 12½x13*
**2453** A691 7p multicolored .20 .20
**2454** A691 12p multicolored .20 .20
**2455** A691 17p multicolored .20 .20
*Nos. 2453-2455 (3)* .60 .60

Christmas 1985 A692

14th-15th century paintings in the Episcopal Museum, Vich: 17p, Nativity, Guimera Altarpiece retable, 14th cent., by Ramon de Mur. 45p, Epiphany, from an embroidered frontal, 15th cent.

**1985, Nov. 27 Photo.** *Perf. 13½*
**2456** A692 17p multicolored .20 .20
**2457** A692 45p multicolored .50 .20

Birds — A693

**1985, Dec. 4 Litho. & Engr.**
**2458** A693 6p Sylvia cantillans .20 .20
**2459** A693 7p Monticola saxatilis .20 .20
**2460** A693 12p Sturnus unicolor .25 .20
**2461** A693 17p Panurus biarmicus .35 .20
*Nos. 2458-2461 (4)* 1.00 .80

Wildlife conservation.

Count of Penaflorida (1729-1785) — A694

**1985, Dec. 11 Engr.** *Perf. 13½*
**2462** A694 17p dark blue .20 .20

Francisco Javier de Munibe e Idiaquez, founded Natl. Economic Society of Friends in 1765.

Government Palace, Madrid, and Accession Agreement Text — A695

17p, Map and flags of EEC countries. 30p, Hall of Columns, Royal Palace. 45p, Member flags.

**1986, Jan 7. Litho.** *Perf. 13½x13*
**2463** A695 7p multicolored .20 .20
**2464** A695 17p multicolored .20 .20
**2465** A695 30p multicolored .35 .20
**2466** A695 45p multicolored .60 .20
*a.* Bklt. pane of 4, #2463-2466 3.25
*Nos. 2463-2466 (4)* 1.35 .80

Admission of Spain and Portugal to European Economic Community. See Portugal Nos. 1661-1662.

Tourism — A696

Historic sites: 12p, Inner courtyard, La Lupiana Monastery, Guadalajara. 35p, Balcony of Europe, Nerja.

**1986, Jan. 20 Engr.** *Perf. 13x12½*
**2467** A696 12p dk rose, brn & gray brn .20 .20
**2468** A696 35p brt blue & sep .45 .20

2nd World Conference on Merino Sheep — A697

**1986, Jan. 27 Photo.** *Perf. 13½*
**2469** A697 45p multicolored .50 .25

Masquerade, 19th Cent., by F. Hohenleiter — A698

**1986, Feb. 5**
**2470** A698 17p multicolored .25 .20

Cadiz Carnival.

Intl. Peace Year — A699

**Lithographed and Engraved**

**1986, Feb. 12** *Perf. 13x13½*
**2471** A699 45p multicolored .50 .25

Festival of Religious Music, Cuenca A700

**1986, Mar. 26 Photo.** *Perf. 13½*
**2472** A700 17p multicolored .25 .20

Chamber of Commerce, Cent. — A701

Painting detail: Swearing in of the Regent, Queen Maria Christina, Before the Spanish Parliament, 1886, by Francisco Jover and Joaquin Sorolla y Bastida, Senate Palace, Madrid.

**1986, Apr. 9 Engr.** *Perf. 13½*
**2473** A701 17p sage grn & grnsh blk .20 .20

Emigration of Spaniards — A702

**1986, Apr. 22 Photo.**
**2474** A702 45p multicolored .50 .25

Europa 1986 — A703

**Lithographed and Engraved**

**1986, May 5** *Perf. 13x13½*
**2475** A703 17p Youth feeding birds .25 .20
**2476** A703 45p Girl watering tree .55 .25

Our Lady of the Dew Festival, Almonte A704

**1986, May 14 Photo.** *Perf. 13½x13*
**2477** A704 17p multicolored .25 .20

Army Day A705

Captains-General Building, Canary Islands.

**1986, May 16 Engr.** *Perf. 13½*
**2478** A705 17p pale yel brn, sep & red .20 .20

Rodrigo City Cathedral A706

Design: 35p, Calella Lighthouse.

**1986, June 16** *Perf. 12½x13½*
**2479** A706 12p blue & black .20 .20
**2480** A706 35p multicolored .55 .20

10th World Basketball Championships, July 5-20 — A707

**1986, July 4 Photo.** *Perf. 12½*
**2481** A707 45p multicolored .50 .20

Famous Men — A708

Mystery of the Virgin's Death Festival Elche — A709

Designs: 7p, Francisco Loscos Bernal (1823-1886), botanist. 11p, Salvador Espriu (1913-1985), author. 17p, Jose Martinez Ruiz (Azorin, 1873-1967), writer. 45p, Jose Vitoriano Gonzalez (Juan Gris, 1887-1927), painter.

**1986, July 16 Engr. *Perf. 13***

**2482** A708 7p olive grn & bl .20 .20
**2483** A708 11p brt rose & blk .20 .20
**2484** A708 17p dk brn vio & blk .20 .20
**2485** A708 45p org, red vio & blk .50 .25
*Nos. 2482-2485 (4)* 1.10 .85

**1986, Aug. 11 Photo. *Perf. 13x13½***

**2486** A709 17p Angels carrying soul .25 .20

5th World Swimming, Water Polo, Diving and Synchronized Swimming Championships — A710

**1986, Aug. 13 Engr. *Perf. 13½***

**2487** A710 45p multicolored .50 .25

10th World Pelota Championships — A711

**1986, Sept. 12**

**2488** A711 17p multicolored .25 .20

Stamp Day — A712

Messenger, The Husband's Return, Song 63, TI1 Codex, 1979 edition, Spanish Royal Academy.

**1986, Sept. 27 Litho. *Perf. 13x12½***

**2489** A712 17p multicolored .20 .20

Souvenir Sheet

EXFILNA '86, Cordova, Oct. 9-18 — A713

**1986, Oct. 7 Litho. & Engr.**

**2490** A713 17p Man, Cordova "Mosque" .25 .25

Discovery of America, 500th Anniv. (in 1992) — A714

Men and text: 7p, Aristotle, text from De Cielo et Mundo. 12p, Seneca, text from Medea. 17p, San Isidoro, text from Etimologias. 30p, Pedro de Ailly, text from Imago Mundi. 35p, Mayan, prophesy from Libros de Chilam Balam. 45p, European, prophesy from Libros de Chilam Balam.

**Lithographed and Engraved**

**1986, Oct. 15 *Perf. 13x13½***

**2491** A714 7p multicolored .20 .20
**2492** A714 12p multicolored .20 .20
**2493** A714 17p multicolored .20 .20
**2494** A714 30p multicolored .35 .20
**2495** A714 35p multicolored .40 .20
**2496** A714 45p multicolored .50 .20
*a.* Bklt. pane of 6, #2491-2496 1.90
*Nos. 2491-2496 (6)* 1.85 1.20

Caspar de Portola y Rovira (1717-1786), Pioneer of California — A715

**1986, Nov. 6 *Perf. 13½***

**2497** A715 22p multicolored .25 .20

Christmas A716

Wood carving details: 19p, The Holy Family, by Diego de Siloe (c. 1495-1563), Natl. Sculpture Museum, Valladolid, vert. 48p, Nativity, Toledo Cathedral altarpiece, by Felipe de Borgona (c. 1475-1543).

**1986, Nov. 19 Photo. *Perf. 13½***

**2498** A716 19p multicolored .25 .20
**2499** A716 48p multicolored .55 .20

Spanish-Islamic Cultural Heritage — A717

Famous men: 7p, Abd Al Rahman II (792-852), 4th independent emir of Cordoba. 12p, Ibn Hazm (994-1064), scholar. 17p, Al-Zarqali (1061-1100), astronomer. 45p, Alfonso VII, scholar, Toledo School of Translators.

**1986, Dec. 3 Engr.**

**2500** A717 7p org red & dk red brn .20 .20
**2501** A717 12p brn blk & red org .20 .20
**2502** A717 17p black & dk blue .25 .20
**2503** A717 45p green & black .50 .20
*Nos. 2500-2503 (4)* 1.15 .80

Alfonso R. Castelao (1886-1950), Artist, Writer — A718

**Lithographed and Engraved**

**1986, Dec. 11 *Perf. 13x13½***

**2504** A718 32p El Buen Cura, 1917 .40 .20

Globe, Chateau de la Muette A719

**1987, Jan. 14 *Perf. 14***

**2505** A719 48p multicolored .55 .20

Organization for Economic Cooperation and Development, OECD, 25th anniv.

EXPO '92, Seville A720

**1987, Jan. 21 Photo.**

**2506** A720 19p Geometric shapes .35 .20
**2507** A720 48p Earth, Moon's surface .95 .20

See Nos. 2540-2541, 2550-2551.

Portrait of Vitoria, by Vera Fajardo A721

**1987, Feb. 11 Engr.**

**2508** A721 48p dark rose brown .55 .20

Francisco de Vitoria (c. 1486-1546), theologian, teacher and a founder of intl. law.

Marine Corps, 450th Anniv. A722

Design: 18th Cent. 74-gun man-of-war, period standard bearer, corps insignia.

**1987, Feb. 25**

**2509** A722 19p multicolored .25 .20

Deusto University, Cent. — A723

**1987, Feb. 26 Engr. *Perf. 14x13½***

**2510** A723 19p blk, hn brn & dk grn .25 .20

UN Child Survival Campaign A724

**1987, Mar. 4 *Perf. 13½x14***

**2511** A724 19p red brown & blk .25 .20

Constitution of Cadiz, 175th Anniv. — A725

Nos. 2512a-2512c in a continuous design: The Promulgation of 1812, by Salvador Viniegra. No. 2512d, Anniv. emblem.

**1987, Mar. 18 Litho. *Perf. 13½***

**2512** Strip of 4 1.25 1.25
*a.-d.* A725 25p, any single .30 .20

Ceramicware A726

Designs: 7p, Pharmaceutical jar, 15th cent., Manises of Valencia. 14p, Abstract figurine, 20th cent., Sargadelos of Galicia. 19p, Neo-classical lidded urn, 18th cent., Buen Retiro of Madrid. 32p, Water jar, 20th cent., Salvatierra of Extremadura. 40p, Pitcher, 18th cent., Talavera of Toledo. 48p, Pitcher, 18th-19th cent., Granada of Andalucia.

**Lithographed and Engraved**

**1987, Mar. 20 *Perf. 12½x13***

**2513** Block of 6 + 3 labels 2.25 2.25
*a.* A726 7p multicolored .20 .20
*b.* A726 14p multicolored .20 .20
*c.* A726 19p multicolored .30 .20
*d.* A726 32p multicolored .45 .30
*e.* A726 40p multicolored .50 .30
*f.* A726 48p multicolored .60 .30

See No. 2552.

Passion Week in Zamora and Seville A727

Paintings: 19p, The Amanecer Procession, by Gallego Marquina, vert. 48p, Jesus Carrying the Cross, by Martinez Montanes, and the Gate of Forgiveness, Seville Cathedral.

**1987, Apr. 13 Photo. *Perf. 14x13½***

**2514** A727 19p multicolored .25 .20
**2515** A727 48p multicolored .55 .20

Tourism A728

14p, Rock of Ifach, Calpe. 19p, Nave of Santa Marina d'Ozo Church, Pontevedra, before restoration. 40p, Sonanes Palace, Villacarriedo. 48p, Monastery of St. Joan de les Abadesses, Gerona, vert.

**1987 Engr. *Perf. 12½x13***

**2515A** A728 14p dp bl & sage grn .25 .20
**2516** A728 19p dp grn & grnsh blk .30 .20
**2516A** A728 40p dp claret .50 .20
**2517** A728 48p black .60 .20
*Nos. 2515A-2517 (4)* 1.65 .80

Issued: 19p, 48p, 4/21; 14p, 40p, 6/10.

Europa 1987 A729

Modern architecture: 19p, Bilbao Bank, Madrid, designed by Saenz de Oiza, vert. 48p, Natl. Museum of Roman Art, Merida, designed by Rafael Moneo.

**Lithographed and Engraved**

**1987, May 4** *Perf. 14x13½*
**2518** A729 19p multicolored .25 .20
**2519** A729 48p multicolored .55 .20

Horse Fair, Jerez de La Frontera A730

**1987, May 6 Photo.** *Perf. 13½x14*
**2520** A730 19p multicolored .25 .20

Ramon Carande (1887-1986), Historian — A731

**1987, May 29 Engr.**
**2521** A731 40p blk & dk vio brn .45 .20

Postal Code Inauguration — A732

**1987, June 1 Litho.** *Perf. 14*
**2522** A732 19p multicolored .25 .20

Eibar Weaponry School, 75th Anniv. A733

**1987, July 2 Litho.** *Perf. 14*
**2523** A733 20p multicolored .25 .20

1992 Summer Olympics, Barcelona A734

**1987, July 15 Photo.**
**2524** A734 32p Casa de Battlo masonry .50 .20
**2525** A734 65p Athletes 1.00 .20

25th Folk Festival of the Pyrenees, Jaca — A735

**1987, July 22**
**2526** A735 50p multicolored .55 .20

Monturiol and Submarine Designs A736

**1987, Sept. 9 Engr.** *Perf. 13½x14*
**2527** A736 20p black brown .25 .20

Narcis Monturiol (d. 1887), builder of the submarine Ictineos.

Stamp Day — A737

Illuminated codex from *Constitutiones Jacobi II Regis Majoricum,* 14th cent., King Albert I Royal Library, Brussels.

**Litho & Engr.**

**1987, Sept. 16** *Perf. 13*
**2528** A737 20p multicolored .25 .20

Postal service of Mallorca under James II.

ESPAMER '87 — A738

Designs: 8p, Handstamped letter that traveled from La Coruna to Havana, Cuba, 18th cent. 12p, La Coruna Harbor, 19th cent., engraving. 20p, Illustration of Havana harbor from *Viaje Alrededor da La Isla de Cuba,* by Francisco Mialche, 18th cent. 50p, West Indies packets.

**1987, Oct. 2 Litho. & Engr.** *Perf. 13*
**2529** A738 Sheet of 4 3.25 3.25
*a.* 8p blk, brt blue & red .30 .30
*b.* 12p brt blue, red & blk .45 .45
*c.* 20p blk, brt blue & red .75 .75
*d.* 50p blk, brt blue & red 1.75 1.75

No. 2529 printed se-tenant (rouletted between) with ESPAMER entrance ticket. Sold for 180p. Size: 150x83mm (including ticket).

Souvenir Sheet

EXFILNA '87, Gerona, Oct. 24-Nov. 1 — A739

Greek statue, Emporion, Olympic torch-bearer.

**1987, Oct. 24 Photo.** *Perf. 13x12½*
**2530** A739 20p multicolored .25 .25

Discovery of America, 500th Anniv. (in 1992) — A740

Ships and: 14p, Amerigo Vespucci (1454-1512), Italian navigator. 20p, Ferdinand and Isabella. 32p, Friar Juan Perez, Queen's confessor. 40p, Juan de la Cosa (c. 1460-1510), master of the Santa Maria, cartographer who made first map of the New World. 50p, Christopher Columbus. 65p, Vicente Yanez Pinzon (c. 1460-1523) and Martin Alonso Pinzon (c. 1441-1493), brothers, navigators and ship owners, accompanied Columbus on voyage.

**Litho. & Engr.**

**1987, Oct. 30** *Perf. 13*
**2531** A740 14p multicolored .20 .20
**2532** A740 20p multicolored .25 .20
**2533** A740 32p multicolored .40 .20
**2534** A740 40p multicolored .45 .20
**2535** A740 50p multicolored .55 .20
**2536** A740 65p multicolored .75 .30
*a.* Bklt. pane of 6, #2531-2536 3.00
*Nos. 2531-2536 (6)* 2.60 1.30

Christmas — A741

Self-portrait, Sculpture by Victorio Macho (1887-1966) A742

**1987, Nov. 17 Photo.** *Perf. 14x13½*
**2537** A741 20p Ornaments .30 .20
**2538** A741 50p Zambomba, tambourine .60 .20

**1987, Dec. 23 Engr.**
**2539** A742 50p brown black .55 .20

EXPO '92 Type of 1987

**1987, Dec. 29 Photo.** *Perf. 13½x14*
**2540** A720 20p like No. 2506 .30 .20
**2541** A720 50p like No. 2507 .55 .20

HRH Sofia and Juan Carlos, 50th Birth Annivs. — A743

**1988, Jan. 5** *Perf. 13x13½*
**2542** A743 20p Sofia .30 .20
**2543** A743 20p Juan Carlos .30 .20
*a.* Pair, #2542-2543 + label .60 .50

Clara Campoamor (b. 1888), Suffragette — A744

**1988, Feb. 12 Photo.** *Perf. 14*
**2544** A744 20p multicolored .25 .20

1988 Winter Olympics, Calgary — A745

Passion Week in Valladolid and Malaga — A746

**1988, Feb. 15** *Perf. 14*
**2545** A745 45p Speed skater .60 .20

**1988, Mar. 30 Photo.** *Perf. 14*

Designs: 20p, Valladolid Cathedral and 17th cent. statue of Christ at the column by Gregorio Fernandez. 50p, Christ carrying the cross along Malaga procession route.

**2546** A746 20p multicolored .30 .20
**2547** A746 50p multicolored .60 .20

Tourism A747

**1988, Apr. 7**
**2548** A747 18p Paella pan, ingredients .25 .20
**2549** A747 45p Covadonga Natl. Park .50 .20

EXPO '92 Type of 1987

Era of Discoveries: 8p, Road to globe, rays of light, vert. 45p, Compass rose, globe.

**1988, Apr. 12**
**2550** A720 8p multicolored .20 .20
**2551** A720 45p multicolored .50 .20

Art Type of 1987

Glassware: a, Chalice, Valencia, 18th cent. b, Cadalso de los Vidrios, Madrid, 18th cent. c, Candy dish, La Granja de San Ildefonso, 18th cent. d, Castril double-handled jar, Andalucia, 18th cent. e, Jug, Catalina, 17th cent. f, Bottle, Baleares, 20th cent.

**Litho. & Engr.**

**1988, Apr. 13** *Perf. 12½x13*
**2552** Block of 6 + 6 labels 1.75 1.75
*a.-f.* A726 20p any single .25 .20

Stamp Day 1988 — A748

Francis of Taxis, postmaster by royal appointment (1505) in charge of establishing communications between Spain, France, Germany, Rome, Naples.

**1988, Apr. 29 Engr. *Perf. 12½x13***
**2553** A748 20p dk violet & dk brn .25 .20

General Workers' Union (UGT), Cent. A749

Emblem and Pablo Iglesias, union pioneer.

**1988, May 1 Photo. *Perf. 14***
**2554** A749 20p multicolored .25 .20

Europa 1988 — A750

Transport and communication: 20p, Locomotive made in Spain and operated in Cuba, 1837. 50p, Spanish telegraph in the Philippines linking Plaza de Manila and Bagumbayan Camp, 1818.

**1988, May 5 Engr. *Perf. 13***
**2555** A750 20p black & dk red *.25* .20
**2556** A750 50p black & dk grn *.50* .20

Jean Monnet (1888-1979), Economist A751

**1988, May 9 *Perf. 14x13½***
**2557** A751 45p blue black .50 .20

Universal Exposition, Barcelona, Cent. A752

**1988, May 31 Photo. *Perf. 13½x14***
**2558** A752 50p multicolored .55 .20

Intl. Music and Dance Festival, Granada — A753

**1988, June 1 *Perf. 14x13½***
**2559** A753 50p multicolored .55 .20

World Expo '88, Brisbane, Australia A754

**1988, June 14 *Perf. 13½x14***
**2560** A754 50p Bull .55 .20

Coronation of the Virgin of Hope — A755

**1988, June 18 *Perf. 14x13½***
**2561** A755 20p multicolored .25 .20

Holy Week in Malaga.

Souvenir Sheet

EXFILNA '88, June 25-July 3, Madrid — A756

**1988, June 25 *Perf. 13x12½***
**2562** A756 20p Ciudadela Fortress floor plan .25 .25

Tourism A757

**1988, July 11 Engr. *Perf. 13½x14***
**2563** A757 18p Cantabrian Coast storehouse .30 .20
**2564** A757 45p Dulzaina (wind instrument) .60 .20

28th World Roller Hockey Championships, La Coruna — A758

**1988, Sept. 7 Photo. *Perf. 13½x14***
**2565** A758 20p multicolored .25 .20

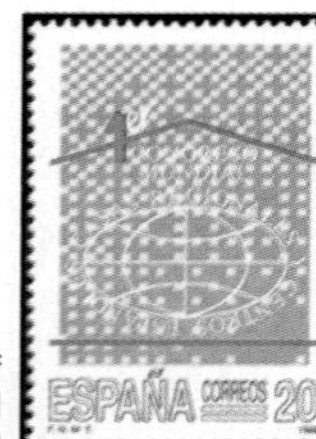
1st World Cong. of Spanish Regional Shelters — A759

1988 Summer Olympics, Seoul — A760

**1988, Sept. 9 *Perf. 14***
**2566** A759 20p multicolored .25 .20

**1988, Sept. 10 Litho.**
**2567** A760 50p Yachting .55 .20

Catalonia Millennium — A761

**1988, Sept. 21 Photo. *Perf. 12½***
**2568** A761 20p multicolored .25 .20

1st Call to Session of the Leon Court, 800th Anniv. — A762

Illumination & seal of Alfonso IX, King of Leon.

**1988, Sept. 26 Photo. *Perf. 12½x13***
**2569** A762 20p multicolored .25 .20

Federation of Spanish Philatelic Societies, 25th Anniv. A763

**1988, Sept. 27 *Perf. 14x13½***
**2570** A763 20p multicolored .25 .20

1992 Summer Olympics, Barcelona A764

**1988, Oct. 3 Photo. *Perf. 14***
**2571** A764 8p multicolored .20 .20

See Nos. B139-B141.

A765

A766

Design: Castle in Valencia and royal seal of James I, 13th cent.

**1988, Oct. 7 *Perf. 14x13½***
**2572** A765 20p multicolored .25 .20

Reconquest of Valencia by King James I, 750th anniv.

**1988, Oct. 10 *Perf. 13x13½***
**2573** A766 20p multicolored .25 .20

Civil Law, cent.

Discovery of America (in 1992), 500th Anniv. — A767

Conquerors, exporers and symbols: No. 2574, Hernando Cortez, conqueror of Mexico, and serpent Quetzalcoatl. No. 2575, Vasco Nunez de Balboa, discoverer of the Pacific Ocean, and sun setting over sea. No. 2576, Francisco Pizarro, conqueror of Peru, and llama. No. 2577, Portuguese navigator Ferdinand Magellan, Juan de Elcano (c. 1476-1526) and globe symbolizing circumnavigation of the world. No. 2578, Alvar Nunez Cabeza de Vaca (c. 1490-1560), explorer, and sunrise. No. 2579, Andres de Urdaneta (1498-1568), and symbol of the west-to-east route between the Philippines and America that he discovered.

**1988, Oct. 13 Engr. *Perf. 13x13½***
**2574** A767 10p multicolored .20 .20
**2575** A767 10p multicolored .20 .20
**2576** A767 20p multicolored .25 .20
**2577** A767 20p multicolored .25 .20
**2578** A767 50p multicolored .55 .20
**2579** A767 50p multicolored .55 .20
*a.* Bklt. pane of 6, #2574-2579 2.25
*Nos. 2574-2579 (6)* 2.00 1.20

Henry III of Castile, 1st Prince of Asturias — A768

**1988, Oct. 26 Photo. *Perf. 13***
**2580** A768 20p multicolored .25 .20

1st Bestowal of the title Prince of Asturias, 600th anniv., guaranteeing that the throne would continue to be inherited according to primogeniture.

Christmas — A769

**1988, Nov. 24 Photo. *Perf. 14***

**2581** A769 20p Snowflakes .25 .20
**2582** A769 50p Shepherd, horiz. .55 .20

Sites and Cities Appearing on the UNESCO World Heritage List — A770

**1988, Dec. 1 Engr. *Perf. 12½x13***

**2583** A770 18p Mosque de Cordoba, vert. .25 .20
**2584** A770 20p Burgos Cathedral, vert. .30 .20
**2585** A770 45p El Escorial Monastery .55 .20
**2586** A770 50p The Alhambra, Granada .65 .20
*Nos. 2583-2586 (4)* 1.75 .80

Natl. Constitution, 10th Anniv. — A771

**1988, Dec. 7 Photo. *Perf. 14***

**2587** A771 20p multicolored .25 .20

Souvenir Sheet

Charles III (1759-1788) and the Enlightenment — A772

**1988, Dec. 14 Engr. *Perf. 13x12½***

**2588** A772 45p black & dk grn .55 .55

Natl. Organization for the Blind, 50th Anniv. — A773

**1988, Dec. 27 Photo. *Perf. 14***

**2589** A773 20p multicolored .25 .20

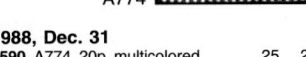

Fr. Luis de Granada (1504-1588) A774

**1988, Dec. 31**

**2590** A774 20p multicolored .25 .20

1992 Summer Olympics, Barcelona A775

**1989, Jan. 3**

**2591** A775 20p multicolored .25 .20

Stamp Collecting — A776

**1989, Jan. 3**

**2592** A776 20p multicolored .25 .20

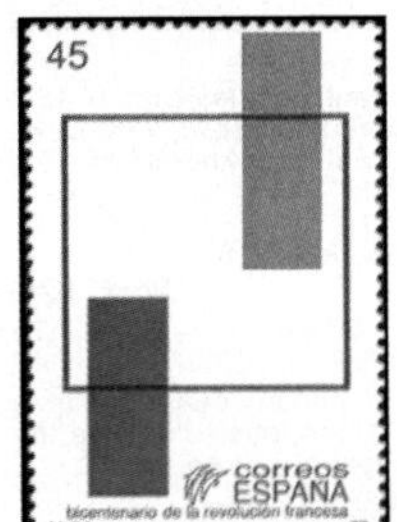

French Revolution, Bicent. — A777

**1989, Jan. 24 Photo. *Perf. 13***

**2593** A777 45p multicolored .50 .20

Maria de Maeztu (b. 1882), Educator A778

**1989, Feb. 7 Photo. *Perf. 14x13½***

**2594** A778 20p multicolored .25 .20

Postal Service, Cent. A779

**Litho. & Engr.**

**1989, Mar. 11 *Perf. 13½x14***

**2595** A779 20p Uniform, 1889 .25 .20

Stamp Day — A780

Design: Intl. postal treaty negotiated with France and Italy by Franz von Taxis, 1601.

**1989, Apr. 4 Engr. *Perf. 13***

**2596** A780 20p black .25 .20

A781

A782

**1989, Apr. 22 *Perf. 14x13½***

**2597** A781 20p black .25 .20

Casa del Cordon, Burgos.

**1989, May 5 Photo. *Perf. 13x13½***

Europa: Children's toys.

**2598** A782 40p shown *.40* .20
**2599** A782 50p Top *.50* .20

Spain's Presidency of the European Economic Community A783

**1989, May 9 *Perf. 13½x14***

**2600** A783 45p multicolored .50 .20

Souvenir Sheet

*Holy Family with St. Anne,* by El Greco — A784

**1989, May 20 Litho. *Perf. 14x13½***

**2601** A784 20p multicolored .25 .25

EXFILNA '89. Exists imperf in different colors.

Gabriela Mistral (1889-1957), Chilean Poet Awarded 1945 Nobel Prize for Literature — A785

**Litho. & Engr.**

**1989, June 1 *Perf. 14x13½***

**2602** A785 50p multicolored .60 .20

European Parliament 3rd Elections — A786

**1989, June 12 Photo. *Perf. 13x13½***

**2603** A786 45p multicolored .50 .20

Lace A787

Lace produced in: a, Catalonia. b, Andalusia. c, Extremadura. d, Canary Isls. e, Castile-La Mancha. f, Galicia.

**Litho. & Engr.**

**1989, June 20 *Perf. 13x12½***

**2604** Block of 6 + 3 labels 1.40 1.40
***a.-f.*** A787 20p any single .25 .20

Three center labels printed in a continuous design and picture lace-making.

Pope John Paul II at the Intl. Catholic Youth Forum, Santiago — A788

**1989, Aug. 19 Engr. *Perf. 13x12½***

**2605** A788 50p myrtle grn, dk red brn & blk .55 .20

Athletics World Cup, Barcelona A789

**1989, Sept. 1 Photo. *Perf. 13½x14***

**2606** A789 50p multicolored .55 .20

A790

Type A34 — A791

**Litho. & Engr.**

**1989, Sept. 19** ***Perf. 14x13½***
**2607** A790 50p multicolored .55 .20

Charlie Chaplin (1889-1977), English comedian and actor.

**1989, Oct. 2 Photo. *Perf. 14x13½***
**2608** A791 50p gray, ver & blk .55 .20

Cent. of the 1st Alfonso XIII issue.

A792

A793

Fr. Andres Manjon (d. 1923), teacher.

**1989, Oct. 13**
**2609** A792 20p multicolored .25 .20

Founding of the Ave Maria Schools by Fr. Manjon, cent.

**1989, Nov. 7 Litho. & Engr.**

UPAE emblem and "Irrigating Corn Field in November, 17th Cent.," an illustration from the *New Chronicle and Good Government,* by Guaman Poma de Ayala.

**2610** A793 50p multicolored .55 .20

America issue.

Christmas A794

***Perf. 14x13½, 13½x14***

**1989, Nov. 29 Photo.**
**2611** A794 20p Star, "NAVIdAd 89," vert. .25 .20
**2612** A794 45p shown .50 .20

Sites on the UNESCO World Heritage List — A795

**Litho. & Engr.**

**1989, Dec. 5** ***Perf. 13x12½***
**2613** A795 20p Altamira Caverns .25 .20
**2614** A795 20p Santiago de Compostela .25 .20
**2615** A795 20p Roman aqueduct, Segovia .25 .20
**2616** A795 20p Guell Park and palace, Mila House .25 .20
*Nos. 2613-2616 (4)* 1.00 .80

Souvenir Sheet

Sites on the World Heritage List — A796

Royal palaces: a, El Escorial. b, Aranjuez. c, Summer palace, La Granja, San Ildefonso. e, Madrid.

**1989, Dec. 20 Engr. *Perf. 13x13½***
**2617** Sheet of 4 2.00 2.00
***a.-d.*** A796 45p any single .30 .30

Illustration by Daniel Garcia Perez, Winner of the 2nd Youth Stamp Design Contest — A797

**1990, Jan. 29 Photo. *Perf. 14x13½***
**2618** A797 20p multicolored .25 .20

1992 Summer Olympics, Barcelona.

A798

A799

**1990, Feb. 2**
**2619** A798 20p multicolored .25 .20

World Cycle Cross Championship, Getzu.

**1990, Feb. 12 Engr.**
**2620** A799 20p dark purple .25 .20

Victoria Kent (1897-1987), prisons directer, reformer.

Honorary Postman Rafael Alvarez Sereix and Cancel — A800

**Litho. & Engr.**

**1990, Apr. 18** ***Perf. 13***
**2621** A800 20p sepia, buff & dull grn .25 .20

Stamp Day.

Europa 1990 A801

Post offices.

***Perf. 13½x14, 14x13½***

**1990, May 4 Photo.**
**2622** A801 20p Vitoria *.25* .20
**2623** A801 50p Malaga, vert. *.50* .20

Intl. Telecommunications Union, 125th Anniv. — A802

**1990, May 17** ***Perf. 13½x14***
**2624** A802 8p multicolored .20 .20

Wrought Iron — A803

Designs: a, 15th Cent. door knocker. b, 16th cent. lyre-shaped door knocker. c, 17th Cent. pistol. d, 17th-18th Cent. door knocker. e, 19th Cent. lock. f, Fire iron.

**Litho. & Engr.**

**1990, May 18** ***Perf. 12½***
**2625** Block of 6 + 3 labels 1.75 1.75
***a.-f.*** A803 20p any single .25 .20

Nos. 2625a-2625f printed se-tenant in a continuous design. Three labels continue the design and contain text or picture a forge.

Souvenir Sheet

Patio de La Infanta, Zaporta Palace, Zaragoza — A804

Illustration reduced.

**1990, May 25 Engr. *Perf. 14x13½***
**2626** A804 20p red brown .25 .25

EXFILNA '90.

Charity, by Lopez Alonso — A805

**1990, June 19 Litho. *Perf. 13½x13***
**2627** A805 8p multicolored .20 .20

Daughters of Charity in Spain, bicentennial.

Jose Padilla, Composer, Birth Centenary — A806

**1990, June 19 Photo. *Perf. 13x12½***
**2628** A806 20p multicolored .30 .20

Town of Estella, 900th Anniv. — A807

**1990, June 19 Litho. & Engr.**
**2629** A807 45p multicolored .60 .20

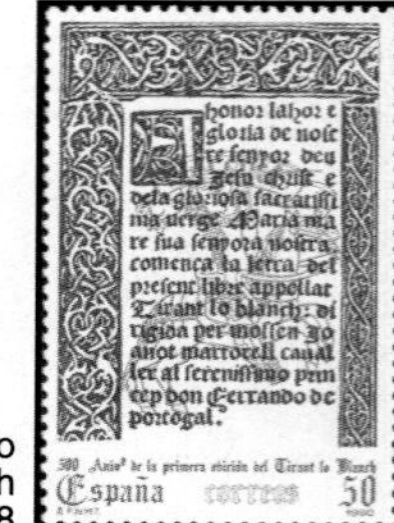

Novel, "Tirant lo Blanch," 500th Anniv. — A808

**1990, June 19** ***Perf. 12½x13***
**2630** A808 50p multicolored .65 .20

Souvenir Sheet

Crypt, Palencia Cathedral — A809

Illustration reduced.

**1990, June 22 Engr. *Perf. 13½x14***
**2631** A809 20p red brown .25 .25

Topical philatelic exposition.

A810

A811

**1990, Aug. 27 Photo. *Perf. 14x13½***
**2632** A810 50p multicolored .55 .20

17th Intl. Congress of Historical Sciences.

**Litho. & Engr.**
**1990, Nov. 14** ***Perf. 14***

America Issue: UPAE emblem and Caribean fauna.

**2633** A811 50p multicolored .55 .20

A812

A813

Christmas: Scenes from the film "Cosmic Poem" by Jose Antonio Sistiaga.

**1990, Nov. 22** **Photo.**
**2634** A812 25p multicolored .30 .20
**2635** A812 45p multi, horiz. .50 .20

**Litho. & Engr.**
**1990, Nov. 28** ***Perf. 13***

Tapestries in Monastery of San Lorenzo: a, The Crucifixion by Jan van Roome and Bernard van Orley. b, Flamenco Soldiers by Philip Wouvermans. c, Shipwreck of the Telemac by Miguel Angel Houasse. d, Flowers by Francisco Goya.

**2636** Sheet of 4 1.00 1.00
***a.-d.*** A813 20p any single .25 .20

European Tourism Year — A814

**1990, Dec. 1 Photo. *Perf. 14***
**2637** A814 45p multicolored .50 .20

World Heritage List — A815

Designs: No. 2638, Church of San Vicente, Avila. No. 2639, Tower of San Pedro, Teruel, vert. No. 2640, Church of San Miguel de Lillo, Oviedo, vert. No. 2641, Tower of Bujaco, Caceres.

**Litho. & Engr.**
**1990, Dec. 10** ***Perf. 13***
**2638** A815 20p multicolored .30 .20
**2639** A815 20p multicolored .30 .20
**2640** A815 20p multicolored .30 .20
**2641** A815 20p multicolored .30 .20
*Nos. 2638-2641 (4)* 1.20 .80

Natl. Orchestra of Spain A816

**1990, Dec. 20 Photo. *Perf. 13½x14***
**2642** A816 25p grn, yel grn & blk .30 .20

Maria Moliner (1900-1981), Spanish Linguist — A817

**1991, Jan. 21 Photo. *Perf. 14x13½***
**2643** A817 25p multicolored .35 .20

Souvenir Sheet

Santa Fe, 500th Anniv. — A818

Illustration reduced.

**Litho. & Engr.**
**1991, Apr. 19** ***Perf. 13½x14***
**2644** A818 25p brown & purple .35 .35

World Philatelic Exhibition, Granada '92.

Child's Drawing — A819

**1991, Apr. 12 Photo. *Perf. 14x13½***
**2645** A819 25p Olympic rings, sailboats .35 .20

Juan de Tassis y Peralta (1582-1622), Postal Reformer A820

**1991, Apr. 26 Engr. *Perf. 12½***
**2646** A820 25p black .35 .20

Stamp Day.

Souvenir Sheet

Porcelain and Ceramics — A821

a, Apothecary jar, 17th cent. b, Figurine, 18th cent. c, Vase, 19th cent. d, Plate, 19th cent.

**1991, May 3 Litho. & Engr. *Perf. 13***
**2647** A821 25p Sheet of 4, #a.-d. 1.50 1.50
***a.-d.*** Any single .30 .25

See No. 2692.

Europa A822

**1991, May 28 Litho. *Perf. 13½x14***
**2648** A822 25p INTA-NASA ground station *.35* .20
**2649** A822 45p Olympus I satellite *.55* .20

St. John of the Cross (1651-1695), Mystic — A823

Anniversaries: No. 2651, Fr. Luis de Leon (1527-1591), Augustinian writer, vert. No. 2652, Abd Al Rahman III (891-961), Moslem caliph, vert. No. 2653, St. Ignatius of Loyola (1451-1556), founder of Society of Jesus, vert.

***Perf. 13½x14, 14x13½***
**1991, June 6** **Litho.**
**2650** A823 15p multicolored .20 .20
**2651** A823 15p multicolored .20 .20
**2652** A823 25p multicolored .35 .20
**2653** A823 25p multicolored .35 .20
*Nos. 2650-2653 (4)* 1.10 .80

Antique Furniture A824

Designs: a, Wedge top armoire, 18th cent. b, Hutch cabinet, c. 19th cent. c, Ladder-back cane chair, c. 19th cent. d, Baby cradle, 19th cent. e, Round-top trunk, c. 19th cent. f, Ornate chest, c. 18th cent.

**Litho. & Engr.**
**1991, Sept. 9** ***Perf. 12½x13***
**2654** Block of 6 + 3 labels 1.90 1.90
***a.-f.*** A824 25p any single .30 .20

Orfeo Catala (Catalan Choral Society), Cent. — A825

Intl. Fishing Exposition, Vigo — A826

**1991, Sept. 6 Litho. *Perf. 14x13½***
**2655** A825 25p multicolored .35 .20

**1991, Sept. 10**
**2656** A826 55p multicolored .65 .20

America Issue — A827

Christmas — A828

**Litho. & Engr.**
**1991, Nov. 4** ***Perf. 14x13½***
**2657** A827 55p Nocturlabe .65 .20

**1991, Nov. 22 Photo. *Perf. 14x13½***

25p, The Nativity, illustration from 17th cent. book. 45p, The Birth of Christ, 16th cent. icon.

**2658** A828 25p multicolored .35 .20
**2659** A828 45p multicolored .55 .20

Souvenir Sheet

The Meadowlands of St. Isidro by Goya — A829

**Litho. & Engr.**

**1991, Dec. 12** ***Perf. 13½x14***
**2660** A829 25p multicolored .35 .35

EXFILNA '91, Madrid.

Sites on UNESCO World Heritage List — A830

#2661, Giralda bell tower, Seville Cathedral. #2662, Alcantara Gate, Toledo, vert. #2663, Casa de las Conchas, Salamanca, vert. #2664, Garajonay Natl. Park, Gomera, Canary Islands.

***Perf. 12½x13, 13x12½***

**1991, Dec. 16** **Engr.**
**2661** A830 25p brown & blue .40 .20
**2662** A830 25p red brn & brn .40 .20
**2663** A830 25p red brn & blk .40 .20
**2664** A830 25p violet & dk grn .40 .20
*Nos. 2661-2664 (4)* 1.60 .80

See Nos. 2756, 2830.

Carlos Ibanez de Ibero (1825-1891), Cartographer A831

Antarctic Treaty, Research Ship A52 — A832

**1991, Dec. 27** **Litho.** ***Perf. 14x13½***
**2665** A831 25p multicolored .35 .20
**2666** A832 55p multicolored .65 .20

Margarita Xirgu (1889-1969), Actress — A833

**1992, Jan. 20** ***Perf. 14***
**2667** A833 25p lake & gold .35 .20

Child's Drawing A834

**1992, Feb. 14** ***Perf. 13½x14***
**2668** A834 25p multicolored .35 .20

EXPO 92.

Pedro Rodriguez Campomanes (1723-1802), Historian, Postal Administrator — A835

**1992, Feb. 21** ***Perf. 13x12½***
**2669** A835 27p multicolored .45 .20

Expo '92, Seville A836

**1992, Feb. 28** ***Perf. 13½x14***
**2670** A836 27p gray, blk & brn .40 .20

Columbus Types of 1930
Souvenir Sheet

**1992, Apr. 24** **Engr.** ***Perf. 14***
**2671** Sheet of 2 10.00 10.00
*a.* A65 250p black 4.50 2.50
*b.* A67 250p brown 4.50 2.50

Intl. Philatelic Exhibition, Granada '92.

Miniature Sheets

Expo '92, Seville A837

#2672: a, Expo '92 World Trade Center. b, Aerial tram. c, Avenue 4. d, Barqueta Gate. e, Nature pavilion. f, Biosphere. g, Alamillo Bridge. h, Press center. i, 15th Century pavilion. j, Expo harbor. k, Tourist train. l, One day entrance ticket.

#2673: a, Cartuja Monastery. b, Arena. c, Monorail train. d, Europe Avenue. e, Discovery pavilion. f, Auditorium. g, Avenue 1. h, Plaza of the Future. i, Gate to Italy's exhibit. j, Terminal. k, Expo theater. l, Expo Mascot, Curro.

**1992, Apr. 21** **Litho.** ***Perf. 13½x14***
**2672** A837 Sheet of 12 + 4 labels 5.00 5.00
*a.-l.* 17p any single .40 .25
**2673** A837 Sheet of 12 + 4 labels 8.50 8.50
*a.-l.* 27p any single .60 .30

See No. B195.

1992 Paralympics, Barcelona — A838

**1992, Apr. 22** **Photo.** ***Perf. 14***
**2674** A838 27p multicolored .60 .20

Discovery of America, 500th Anniv. A839

Europa: 17p, Preparation Before Departing from Palos, by R. Espejo. 45p, Globe, ships, and buildings at La Rabida.

**1992, May 5** **Photo.** ***Perf. 14***
**2675** A839 17p multicolored .75 .20
**2676** A839 45p multicolored 1.50 .20

Souvenir Sheets

Voyages of Columbus — A840

#2677, Columbus in sight of land. #2678, Landing of Columbus. #2679, Columbus soliciting aid from Isabella. #2680, Columbus welcomed at Barcelona. #2681, Columbus presenting natives. #2682, Columbus.

Borders on Nos. 2677-2682 are lithographed. Nos. 2677-2682 are similar in design to US Nos. 230-231, 234-235, 237, 245.

**Litho. & Engr.**

**1992, May 22** ***Perf. 14***
**2677** A840 60p blue 1.25 1.10
**2678** A840 60p brown violet 1.25 1.10
**2679** A840 60p chocolate 1.25 1.10
**2680** A840 60p purple 1.25 1.10
**2681** A840 60p black brown 1.25 1.10
**2682** A840 60p black 1.25 1.10
*Nos. 2677-2682 (6)* 7.50 6.60

See US Nos. 2624-2629, Italy Nos. 1883-1888 and Portugal Nos. 1918-1923.

1992 Winter & Summer Olympics, Albertville & Barcelona A841

**1992, June 19** **Photo.** ***Perf. 14***
**2683** A841 45p multicolored .60 .20

A842 A843

**1992, June 5** **Photo.** ***Perf. 14x13½***
**2684** A842 27p blue & yellow .40 .20

World Environment Day.

**1992, Oct. 29** **Litho.** ***Perf. 14x13½***
**2685** A843 17p multicolored .25 .20

Juan Luis Vives (1492-1540), Philosopher.

Pamplona Choir, Cent. A844

**1992, Oct. 29** ***Perf. 13½x14***
**2686** A844 27p multicolored .35 .20

Unified Europe — A845

**1992, Nov. 4** **Photo.** ***Perf. 14x13½***
**2687** A845 45p multicolored .60 .20

Christmas A846

**1992, Nov. 5** ***Perf. 13½x14***
**2688** A846 27p multicolored .40 .20

1992 Special Olympics, Madrid A847

**1992, Sept. 7** **Photo.** ***Perf. 13½x14***
**2689** A847 27p brown & blue .35 .20

Souvenir Sheet

St. Paul's Church, Valladolid — A848

**Litho. & Engr.**

**1992, Oct. 9** ***Perf. 14x13½***
**2690** A848 27p multicolored .35 .35

Exfilna '92, Natl. Philatelic Exhibition, Valladolid.

Discovery of America, 500th Anniv. A849

**1992, Oct. 15** ***Perf. 13½x140***
**2691** A849 60p dk brn, lt brn & bis .75 .20

**Natl. Heritage Type of 1991**
Miniature Sheet

Codices: a, Veitia, 18th cent. b, Trujillo of Peru, 18th cent. c, The Chess Book, 13th cent. d, General History of New Spain, 16th cent.

**Litho. & Engr.**

**1992, Dec. 10** ***Perf. 13***
**2692** A821 27p Sheet of 4, #a.-d. 1.75 1.40

Road Safety A850

Environmental Protection A851

Health and Sanitation — A852

**1993 Photo. *Perf. 14x13½***

**2693** A850 17p green & red .35 .20
**2694** A851 28p green & blue .40 .20
**2695** A852 65p blue & green .90 .20
*Nos. 2693-2695 (3)* 1.65 .60

Issued: 17p, 4/20; 28p, 1/4; 65p, 2/12.

Maria Zambrano (1904-1991), Writer — A854

**1993, Jan. 18 Photo. *Perf. 14***

**2697** A854 45p buff, lil rose & brn .65 .25

Andres Segovia (1893-1987), Guitarist — A855

**1993, Feb. 19 Engr. *Perf. 14x13½***

**2698** A855 65p black & brown .90 .25

1908 Mailbox, Madrid Postal Museum A856

**Litho. & Engr.**

**1993, Mar. 12 *Perf. 13½x14***

**2699** A856 28p multicolored .45 .20

Stamp Day.

Mushrooms — A857

**1993, Mar. 18 Photo. *Perf. 14***

**2700** A857 17p Amanita caesarea .35 .20
**2701** A857 17p Lepiota procera .35 .20
**2702** A857 28p Lactarius sanguifluus .40 .20
**2703** A857 28p Russula cyanoxantha .40 .20
*Nos. 2700-2703 (4)* 1.50 .80

See Nos. 2759-2762.

Souvenir Sheet

Holy Week Celebration — A858

**1993, Apr. 2 Litho. *Perf. 14x13½***

**2704** A858 100p multicolored 1.40 1.40

Exfilna '93, Alcaniz. Margin of No. 2704 is Litho. & Engr.

Fusees, by Joan Miro A859

Europa: 65p, La Bague d'Aurore, by Miro, vert.

***Perf. 13½x14, 14x13½***

**1993, May 5 Litho.**

**2705** A859 45p blue & black .90 .20

**Litho. & Engr.**

**2706** A859 65p multicolored 1.40 .20

Year of St. James A860

Designs: 17p, Transfer of St. James' body by boat. 28p, Discovery of tomb of St. James. 45p, St. James on horseback.

**1993, May 13 Photo. *Perf. 13½x14***

**2707** A860 17p multicolored .35 .20
**2708** A860 28p multicolored .40 .20
**2709** A860 45p multicolored .60 .25
*Nos. 2707-2709 (3)* 1.35 .65

World Telecommunications Day — A861

**1993, May 17**

**2710** A861 28p multicolored .40 .20

Compostela '93 — A862

Stylized designs: 28p, Pilgrims paying homage to Saint James. 100p, Pilgrim under star tree while on way to Santiago de Campostela, vert.

**1993, May 18 Photo. *Perf. 13½x14***

**2711** A862 28p multicolored .45 .20

**Souvenir Sheet**

***Perf. 14x13½***

**2712** A862 100p multicolored 3.00 1.75

World Environment Day — A863

**1993, June 4 Litho. *Perf. 14x13½***

**2713** A863 28p multicolored .40 .20

King Juan Carlos — A864a
A864 2738

**1993-98 Photo. *Perf. 14x13½***

**A864 Gold and:**

| | | | | | |
|---|---|---|---|---|---|
| **2714** | A864 | 1p | prussian bl | .20 | .20 |
| **2715** | A864 | 2p | green | .20 | .20 |
| **2716** | A864 | 10p | magenta | .20 | .20 |
| **2717** | A864 | 15p | green | .20 | .20 |
| **2718** | A864 | 16p | brn lake | .20 | .20 |
| **2719** | A864 | 17p | yel org | .25 | .20 |
| **2720** | A864 | 18p | grn bl | .20 | .20 |
| **2721** | A864 | 19p | brown | .25 | .20 |
| **2722** | A864 | 20p | lil rose | .25 | .20 |
| **2723** | A864 | 21p | dark grn | .25 | .20 |
| **2724** | A864 | 28p | vio brn | .35 | .20 |
| **2725** | A864 | 29p | olive | .40 | .20 |
| **2726** | A864 | 30p | ultramarine | .40 | .20 |
| **2727** | A864 | 32p | green | .45 | .20 |
| **2728** | A864 | 35p | red | .40 | .25 |
| **2729** | A864 | 45p | bluish grn | .55 | .20 |
| **2730** | A864 | 55p | sepia | 3.00 | .50 |
| *a.* | Block of 4, #2714, 2720, 2725, 2730 + 2 labels | | | 3.00 | .50 |
| **2731** | A864 | 60p | org brn | 1.00 | .50 |
| *a.* | Block of 4, #2716, 2721, 2726, 2731 + 2 labels | | | 2.50 | 1.25 |
| **2732** | A864 | 65p | red org | .70 | .20 |
| *a.* | Block of 4, #2719, 2724, 2729, 2732 + 2 labels | | | 2.50 | 2.00 |
| **2733** | A864 | 70p | vermilion | .90 | .45 |

**Engr.**

| | | | | | |
|---|---|---|---|---|---|
| **2734** | A864a | 100p | brown | 2.50 | .30 |
| **2735** | A864a | 200p | green | 6.25 | .60 |
| **2736** | A864a | 300p | maroon | 11.00 | .90 |
| **2737** | A864a | 500p | blue | 17.50 | 1.50 |
| **2738** | A864a | 1000p | vio blk | 35.00 | 4.00 |
| | *Nos. 2714-2738 (25)* | | | 82.60 | 12.20 |

Issued: 17p, 28p, 45p, 65p, 5/21/93; 1p, 18p, 29p, 1/31/94; 19p, 30p, 1994; 19p, 30p, 1/3/95; 10p, 60p, 6/5/95; 1000p, 11/24/95; 100p, 200p, 300p, 500p, 12/12/96; 21p, 32p, 1/27/97; 2p, 16p, 5/19/97; 15p, 3/6/98; 35p, 2/13/98; 70p, 1/30/98. 20p, 11/20/00.

Don Juan de Borbon (1913-1993), Count of Barcelona — A865

**1993, June 20 Photo. *Perf. 14x13½***

**2744** A865 28p multicolored .35 .20

Igualada-Martorell Railway, Cent. — A866

**1993, July 4 Engr. *Perf. 13½x14***

**2745** A866 45p black & green .60 .20

Natl. Mint (F.N.M.T.), Cent. A867

**1993, Sept. 13**

**2746** A867 65p dark blue .90 .20

Explorers A868

Designs: 45p, Alejandro Malaspina (1754-1809), Italian explorer of South America. 65p, Jose Celestino Mutis (1732-1808), Spanish naturalist in the Americas, vert.

***Perf. 13½x14, 14x13½***

**1993, Sept 20 Litho.**

**2747** A868 45p multicolored .60 .20
**2748** A868 65p multicolored .90 .20

Ciconia Nigra A869

Endangered birds: No. 2750, Gypaetus barbatus (Quebrantahuesos).

**Litho. & Engr.**

**1993, Oct. 11 *Perf. 13½x14***

**2749** A869 65p pink & black .90 .20
**2750** A869 65p orange & black .90 .20

Child's Painting — A870

**1993, Oct. 2 Litho. *Perf. 14x13½***

**2751** A870 45p multicolored .60 .20

European Year of the Elderly A871

**1993, Oct. 29 Photo. *Perf. 14***

**2752** A871 45p multicolored .60 .20

A872

Christmas — A873

*Perf. 13½x14, 14x13½*

**1993, Nov. 23** **Photo.**
**2753** A872 17p multicolored .25 .20

**Litho., Photo. & Engr.**
**2754** A873 28p multicolored .40 .20

Jorge Guillen (1893-1984), Poet — A874

**1993, Nov. 29** **Engr.** ***Perf. 14x13½***
**2755** A874 28p green .40 .20

UNESCO World Heritage Type of 1991

Design: 50p, Monastery of Santa Maria of Poblet, Tarragona.

**1993, Dec. 3** **Engr.** ***Perf. 13x12½***
**2756** A830 50p multicolored .65 .20

Spanish Film Industry A875

29p, Luis Bunuel (1900-83), director. 55p, Segundo de Chomon (1871-1929), film pioneer.

**1994, Jan. 28** **Photo.** ***Perf. 14***
**2757** A875 29p multicolored .40 .20
**2758** A875 55p multicolored .75 .20

Mushroom Type of 1993

**1994, Feb. 18** **Photo.** ***Perf. 14***
**2759** A857 18p Boletus satanas .20 .20
**2760** A857 18p Boletus edulis .20 .20
**2761** A857 29p Amanita phalloides .35 .20
**2762** A857 29p Lactarius deliciosus .35 .20
*Nos. 2759-2762 (4)* 1.10 .80

Minerals A876

a, Cinnabar. b, Sphalerite. c, Pyrite. d, Galena.

**1994, Feb. 25**
**2763** A876 29p Block of 4, #a.-d., + 2 labels 2.75 2.00

Barrister's Mailbox A877

**Litho. & Engr.**

**1994, Mar. 9** ***Perf. 13½x14***
**2764** A877 29p light & dark brn .40 .20

Stamp Day.

ILO, 75th Anniv. A878

**1994, Apr. 7** **Photo.** ***Perf. 13½x14***
**2765** A878 65p multicolored .85 .20

Art of Salvador Dali (1904-89) A879

Paintings: #2766, Retrato de Gala. #2767, Poesia de America. #2768, El Gran Masturbador. #2769, Port Alguer. #2770, Self portrait. #2771, Cesta del Pan. #2772, El Enigma Sin Fin. #2173, Galatea de las Esferas.

**1994, Apr. 22** ***Perf. 13½x14, 14x13½***
**2766** A879 18p multi .25 .20
**2767** A879 18p multi, vert. .25 .20
**2768** A879 29p multi .40 .20
**2769** A879 29p multi, vert. .40 .20
**2770** A879 55p multi, vert. .80 .20
**2771** A879 55p multi, vert. .80 .20
**2772** A879 65p multi 1.00 .20
**2773** A879 65p multi, vert. 1.00 .20
*Nos. 2766-2773 (8)* 4.90 1.60

Josep Pla (1897-1981), Writer — A880

**1994, Apr. 23** **Engr.** ***Perf. 13½x14***
**2774** A880 65p dark grn & lake .85 .20

A881

A882

A883

Painting: Martyrdom of St. Andrew, by Rubens.

**1994, Apr. 29** **Photo.** ***Perf. 14***
**2775** A881 55p multicolored .70 .20

Carlos de Amberes Foundation, 400th anniv.

**1994, May 3** **Photo.**
**2776** A882 18p multicolored .25 .20

**Litho., Photo. & Engr.**
**2777** A883 29p multicolored .40 .20

Santa Cruz de Tenerife, 400th anniv. (#2776). Complutense University of Madrid, 700th Anniv. (#2777).

Europa A884

Designs: 55p, Severo Ochoa (1905-93), 1959 Nobel Laureate in Medicine. 65p, Miguel Angel Catalan (1894-1957), physicist.

**1994, May 5** **Litho. & Engr.**
**2778** A884 55p multicolored *.65* .20
**2779** A884 65p multicolored *.80* .20

Spanish Literature A885

Novels by Camilo Jose Cela: 18p, The Family of Pascual Duarte. 29p, Journey to Alcarria.

**1994, May 11** **Photo.**
**2780** A885 18p multicolored .25 .20
**2781** A885 29p multicolored .55 .20

King Sancho Ramirez, 900th Death Anniv. — A886

Treaty of Tordesillas, 500th Anniv. — A887

Design: 55p, Natl. Archives, Simancas.

**Litho. & Engr.**

**1994, June 7** ***Perf. 14***
**2782** A886 18p multicolored .20 .20
**2783** A887 29p multicolored .35 .20
**2784** A887 55p multicolored .70 .20
*Nos. 2782-2784 (3)* 1.25 .60

Souvenir Sheet

Cathedral of St. Anne, Las Palmas, Grand Canary Island — A888

Illustration reduced.

**1994, July 1** ***Perf. 13½x14***
**2785** A888 100p multicolored 2.00 1.50

Exfilna '94, Natl. Philatelic Exhibition, Grand Canary Island.

Yachts — A889

**1994, July 15** **Photo.** ***Perf. 14x13½***
**2786** A889 16p Giralda .20 .20
**2787** A889 29p Saltillo .35 .20

Roman City of Augusta Emerita (Merida), Badajoz — A890

**Litho. & Engr.**

**1994, Sept. 8** ***Perf. 13***
**2788** A890 55p lake, brn & buff .80 .20

UNESCO World Heritage list.

Museum of Cards, Alava — A891

Antique cards: 18p, Horse of Spades. 29p, Jack of Diamonds. 55p, King of Hearts. 65p, War god, Mars, of Diamonds.

**1994, Sept. 20** **Photo.** ***Perf. 14x13½***
**2789** A891 18p multicolored .20 .20
**2790** A891 29p multicolored .35 .20
**2791** A891 55p multicolored .70 .20
**2792** A891 65p multicolored .90 .20
*Nos. 2789-2792 (4)* 2.15 .80

Postal Transportation — A892

**1994, Oct. 11** **Litho.** ***Perf. 13½***
**2793** A892 65p DC-8 .90 .20

Public Transit — A893

Civil Guard A894

**1994, Oct. 17** **Photo.** ***Perf. 14x13½***
**2794** A893 18p multicolored .20 .20

***Perf. 13½x14***
**2795** A894 29p multicolored .40 .20

Western European Union A895

**1994, Oct. 21** *Perf. 13½x14*
**2796** A895 55p multicolored .75 .20

Olympic Venues A896

Designs: a, Track. b, Skiing. c, Equestrian. d, Wrestling. e, Archery. f, Cycling. g, Soccer. h, Field hockey. i, Swimming. j, Sailing.

**1994, Oct. 27**
**2797** Block of 10 + 10 labels 6.00 5.00
*a.-j.* A896 29p any single .50 .40

Labels inscribed with names of Spanish gold medalists and Intl. Olympic Committee cent.
See Nos. 2822, 2850.

Christmas — A897

**1994, Nov. 18** *Perf. 14x13½*
**2798** A897 29p multicolored .40 .20

Spanish Motion Pictures A898

Designs: 30p, Belle Epoque, by Fernando Trueba. 60p Volver A Empezar (Begin the Beguine), by Jose Luis Garci.

**1995, Jan. 20** **Photo.** *Perf. 14*
**2799** A898 30p multicolored .40 .20
**2800** A898 60p multicolored .85 .20

City of Logrono, 900th Anniv. A899

**1995, Jan. 25**
**2801** A899 30p multicolored .40 .20

Souvenir Sheet

SIERRA NEVADA '95, Granada — A900

Illustration reduced.

**1995, Jan. 30**
**2802** A900 130p White star flower 1.75 1.75

World Alpine Skiing Championships.

Mushrooms — A901

**1995, Feb. 9** **Photo.** *Perf. 13½x14*
**2803** A901 19p Coprinus comatus .25 .20
**2804** A901 30p Dermocybe cinnamomea .40 .20

Minerals A902

Designs: a, Dolomite. b, Technical School for Mining Engineers, Madrid. c, Aragonite.

**1995, Feb. 24**
**2805** Strip of 3 1.25 1.25
*a.-c.* A902 30p any single .40 .20

Stamp Day A903

**1995, Mar. 9** **Engr.**
**2806** A903 30p Bronze lion's head .40 .20

Alejandro Goicoechea Omar, TALGO Train — A904

Design: 60p, Young Omar, early train.

**1995, Mar. 17** **Photo.** *Perf. 14*
**2807** A904 30p multicolored .40 .20
**2808** A904 60p multicolored .85 .20

A905

A906

**1995, Apr. 6**
**2809** A905 60p multicolored .85 .20

Nature conservation in Europe.

**Litho. & Engr.**
**1995, Apr. 7** *Perf. 14*

18th Century Sailing Ships: 19p, San Juan Nepomuceno. 30p, San Telmo.

**2810** A906 19p multicolored .30 .20
*a.* Miniature sheet of 4 1.00 1.00
**2811** A906 30p multicolored .70 .20
*a.* Miniature sheet of 4 1.60 1.60

Lebaniego Celebration Year — A907

60p, Mountains, St. Toribio Monastery.

**1995, Apr. 21** **Photo.** *Perf. 12½*
**2812** A907 30p multicolored .40 .20
**2813** A907 60p multicolored .85 .20

Spanish Literature A908

Designs: 19p, El Nino Yuntero, by Miguel Hernandez (1910-42). 30p, Juanita la Larga, by Juan Valera (1824-1905), vert.

**Litho. & Engr.**
**1995, Apr. 27** *Perf. 14*
**2814** A908 19p multicolored .25 .20

**Engr.**
**2815** A908 30p green & blue .40 .20

Jose Marti (1853-95), Cuban Writer A909

**1995, Apr. 28** **Photo.**
**2816** A909 60p multicolored .85 .20

Spanish Cartoon Characters A910

**1995, May 4** **Photo.** *Perf. 14*
**2817** A910 30p Captain Trueno .45 .20
**2818** A910 60p Carpanta, vert. .90 .20

See Nos. 2854-2855.

Europa A911

**1995, May 5**
**2819** A911 60p multicolored .90 .20

Motion Pictures, Cent. A912

19p, Auguste and Louis Lumiere, early camera.

**1995, May 12** **Engr.** *Perf. 14*
**2820** A912 19p brownish black .25 .20

Press Assoc. of Madrid, Cent. A913

**1995, May 12** **Litho.**
**2821** A913 30p multicolored .45 .20

Olympic Venue Type of 1994

Designs: a, Track. b, Basketball. c, Boxing. d, Soccer. e, Gymnastics. f, Equestrian. g, Field hockey. h, Canoeing. i, Polo. j, Two-man rowing. k, Tennis. l, Shooting. m, Sailing. n, Water polo.

**1995, June 2** **Photo.** *Perf. 14*
**2822** Block of 14 + 6 labels 6.25 6.25
*a.-n.* A896 30p any single .45 .20

Labels are inscribed with names of Spanish silver medallists.

UN, 50th Anniv. A914

FAO, 50th Anniv. — A915

World Tourism Organization, 20th Anniv. — A916

**1995, June 26**
**2823** A914 60p multicolored .90 .20
**2824** A915 60p multicolored .90 .20
**2825** A916 60p multicolored .90 .20
*Nos. 2823-2825 (3)* 2.70 .60

A917

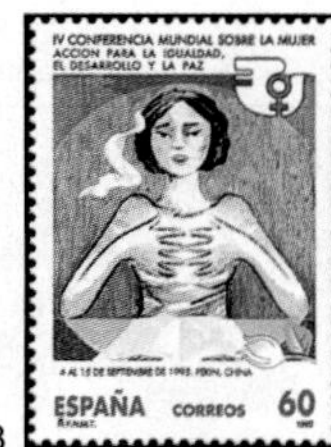
A918

**1995, July 1**
**2826** A917 60p multicolored .90 .20

Spanish Presidentcy of the European Community Council of Ministers.

**1995, Sept. 4** **Photo.** *Perf. 14*
**2827** A918 60p multicolored .90 .20

4th World Conference on Women, Beijing.

Souvenir Sheet

17th Intl. Conference of Cartography, Barcelona — A919

Illustration reduced.

**1995, Sept. 5**
**2828** A919 130p multicolored 2.75 2.25

Santiago de Compostela University, 500th Anniv. — A920

**1995, Sept. 15**
**2829** A920 30p multicolored .45 .20

UNESCO World Heritage Type of 1991 and

A921

#2830, Royal Monastery of Santa Maria de Guadalupe, vert. #2831, Map of Santiago de Compostela's 9th cent. route through northern Spain.

**1995, Sept. 29 Engr. *Perf. 12½***
**2830** A830 60p dark brown 1.00 .20

**Photo. & Engr.**
**2831** A921 60p multicolored 1.00 .20

Ecological Protection System, Lagunas Manchegas — A922

Ducks: 60p, Anade real, pato colorado.

**1995, Oct. 11 Photo. *Perf. 14***
**2832** A922 60p multicolored .90 .20

America Issue.

Souvenir Sheet

EXFILNA '95, Nat. Philatelic Exhibition, Malaga — A923

Illustration reduced.

**Litho. & Engr.**

**1995, Oct. 6 *Perf. 14x13½***
**2833** A923 130p dark green 2.00 2.00

Archaeology — A924

#2834, Cave of Menga, Antequera, Malaga. #2835, Ruins of Torralba, Minorca.

**1995, Oct. 20 Photo.**
**2834** A924 30p multicolored .50 .20
**2835** A924 30p multicolored .50 .20

Souvenir Sheet

The Contemporary Poets, by Antonio Maria Esquivel (1806-57) — A925

Group of poets: a, Seated at left. b, One reading from paper. c, Four standing. d, Standing, seated at right.
Illustration reduced.

**1995, Oct. 27**
**2836** A925 Sheet of 4 3.25 3.25
*a.* 19p multicolored .30 .25
*b.* 30p multicolored .55 .45
*c.-d.* 60p any single 1.25 .90

Christmas A926

Design: 30p, Capital sculpture of "Adoration of the Magi," Collegiate Church of San Martin de Elines, Cantabria.

**1995, Nov. 17 Photo. *Perf. 14***
**2837** A926 30p multicolored .45 .20

Espamer '96, Aviation & Space Philatelic Exhibitions, Seville — A927

#2838, Sevilla-Plaza de Armas Railway Station. #2839, Lorenzo Galindez de Carvajal, Master Courier, King Fernando's Court, vert.

**1995, Dec. 20 Photo. *Perf. 13***
**2838** A927 60p multicolored .90 .20
**2839** A927 60p multicolored .90 .20

Spanish Motion Pictures, Cent. A928

Designs: 30p, Scene from first Spanish motion picture, "Salida de los Fieles del Pilar de Zaragoza." 60p, Poster for 1952 motion picture, "Bienvenido, Mister Marshall."

**1996, Jan. 30 Photo. *Perf. 14***
**2840** A928 30p multicolored .45 .20
**2841** A928 60p multicolored .90 .20

Spanish Mining — A929

Designs: 30p, Miner's lamp from Museum of Mining and Industry, mine shaft. 60p, Fluorite.

**1996, Feb. 7**
**2842** A929 30p multicolored .45 .20
**2843** A929 60p multicolored .90 .20

Madrid-Irun Visual Telegraph Line, 150th Anniv. — A930

**1996, Mar. 8 Engr. *Perf. 14***
**2844** A930 60p lake & gray grn .90 .20

Stamp Day.

Barcelona, 10th Anniv. of Urban Transformation — A931

**1996, Mar. 22**
**2845** A931 30p multicolored .45 .20

Endangered Wildlife — A932

**1996, Mar. 27 Photo.**
**2846** A932 30p Ursus arctos .45 .20

18th Cent. Sailing Ship Type of 1995

Designs: 30p, King Phillip. 60p, Catalán.

**Litho. & Engr.**

**1996, Apr. 19 *Perf. 14x13½***
**2847** A906 30p multicolored .50 .20
*a.* Miniature sheet of 4 2.50 2.50
**2848** A906 60p multicolored 1.00 .20
*a.* Miniature sheet of 4 4.50 4.50

Nos. 2847-2848 printed in miniature sheets of 4.

Madrid Bar Assoc., 400th Anniv. A933

**1996, Apr. 23 Photo. *Perf. 14***
**2849** A933 19p multicolored .30 .20

Olympic Venue Type of 1994

Symbols of Olympic venues, bronze ribbon: a, like #2797a. b, like #2822c. c, like #2797b. d, like 2797h. e, like #2797i. f, like 2822h. g, like #2822k. h, like #2822 l. i, like #2797j.

**1996, Apr. 26 Photo. *Perf. 14***
**2850** Block of 9 + 6 labels 5.00 4.50
*a.-i.* A896 30p Any single .50 .20

Labels are inscribed with names of Spanish bronze medalists.

Souvenir Sheets

A934

Royal Family — A935

Espamer '96 Philatelic Exhibition, World Aviation and Space Exposition: No. 2851a, Map of Seville-Larache Air Route, 1921. b, Zeppelin cover, Seville, 1930. c, Rocket launch. d, Hispano HA 200 SAETA aircraft.
Illustration reduced (A935).

**1996, May 4**
**2851** Sheet of 4 7.00 6.50
*a.-d.* A934 100p any single 1.60 1.40
**2852** A935 400p multicolored 7.00 6.50

Carmen Amaya, Flamenco Dancer — A936

**1996, May 6 *Perf. 14x13½***
**2853** A936 60p multicolored .90 .20

Europa.

Cartoon Characters Type of 1995

**1996, May 10 *Perf. 14x13½, 13½x14***
**2854** A910 19p El Jabato, vert. .35 .20
**2855** A910 30p El Reporter Tribulete .65 .20

Paintings by Francisco de Goya Y Lucientes (1746-1828) — A937

19p, Gen. Don Antonio Ricardos, vert. 30p, Dairymaid of Bordeaux, vert. 60p, Boys with a Mastiff. 130p, The 3rd of May, 1808.

**1996, May 31 Photo. *Perf. 14x13½***
**2856** A937 19p multicolored .35 .20
**2857** A937 30p multicolored .60 .20

***Perf. 13½x14***
**2858** A937 60p multicolored 1.10 .20
**2859** A937 130p multicolored 2.00 .40
*Nos. 2856-2859 (4)* 4.05 1.00

Philatelic Service, 50th Anniv. A938

**1996, June 4 *Perf. 13½x14***
**2860** A938 30p multicolored .65 .20

Popular Personalities — A939

Designs: 19p, José Monge Cruz, singer, vert. 30p, Lola Flores, movie star.

***Perf. 14x13½, 13½x14***

**1996, June 14**

| | | |
|---|---|---|
| **2861** A939 19p multicolored | .25 | .20 |
| **2862** A939 30p multicolored | .45 | .20 |

Lanuza Central Market, Zaragoza A940

**1996, July 5 Photo. *Perf. 13½x14***

| | | |
|---|---|---|
| **2863** A940 30p multicolored | .65 | .20 |

19th Intl. Congress of Architects, Barcelona.

Gerardo Diego (1896-1987), Poet — A941

Joaquín Costa (1846-1911), Lawyer, Teacher — A942

**1996, Sept. 13 Engr.**

| | | |
|---|---|---|
| **2864** A941 19p red, black & vio | .30 | .20 |

**Litho. & Engr.**

| | | |
|---|---|---|
| **2865** A942 30p multicolored | .60 | .20 |

UNICEF, 50th Anniv. — A943

**1996, Sept. 13 Photo.**

| | | |
|---|---|---|
| **2866** A943 60p blue, black & red | 1.00 | .20 |

Archaeological Finds — A944

Designs: No. 2867, Naveta Des Tudons, tomb, 2000-1500BC. No. 2868, Cabezo de Alcala, reamains of Roman temple, 54-49BC.

**1996, Sept. 27 Photo.**

| | | |
|---|---|---|
| **2867** A944 30p multicolored | .50 | .20 |
| **2868** A944 30p multicolored | .50 | .20 |

Souvenir Sheet

Exfilna '96, Natl. Philatelic Exhibition, Vitoria-Gasteiz — A945

Painting of Vitoria-Gasteiz, capital of Alava Province, by Ignacio Diaz Ruiz de Olano (1860-1937). Illustration reduced.

**1996, Oct. 11 Engr. *Perf. 14x13½***

| | | |
|---|---|---|
| **2869** A945 130p rose carmine | 2.25 | 2.00 |

Sheet margin is litho.

America Issue — A946

Traditional costume of Charro Region, Salamanca.

**1996, Oct. 15 Photo. *Perf. 14***

| | | |
|---|---|---|
| **2870** A946 60p multicolored | .85 | .20 |

Sites on UNESCO World Heritage List — A947

Designs: 19p, Albaicin, old Muslim quarter, Granada, vert. 30p, Gateway to Tiberiades Square, statue of Maimonides. 60p, Deer, De Donana Natl. Park, Huelva province, vert.

***Perf. 12½x13, 13x12½***

**1996, Oct. 25 Engr.**

| | | |
|---|---|---|
| **2871** A947 19p dark blue violet | .35 | .20 |
| **2872** A947 30p deep claret | .55 | .20 |
| **2873** A947 60p dark blue | 1.10 | .20 |
| *Nos. 2871-2873 (3)* | 2.00 | .60 |

Spanish Literature A948

Designs: 30p, "La Regenta," by Leopoldo Garcia-Alas Ureña (1852-1901), vert. 60p, Don Juan Tenorio, by José Zorrilla Moral (1817-93).

***Perf. 14x13½, 13½x14***

**1996, Nov. 13 Engr.**

| | | |
|---|---|---|
| **2874** A948 30p bl, dep mag & dp vio | .40 | .20 |
| **2875** A948 60p dp blue & dp brn | .80 | .20 |

Christmas — A949

Birth of Christ, by Fernando Gallego.

**1996, Nov. 22 Photo. *Perf. 14***

| | | |
|---|---|---|
| **2876** A949 30p multicolored | .40 | .20 |

Souvenir Sheet

Official Map of Spain and Its Provinces — A950

Illustration reduced.

**1996, Dec. 5**

| | | |
|---|---|---|
| **2877** A950 130p multicolored | 2.25 | 2.00 |

A951

A952

Endangered species.

**1997, Jan. 30 Photo. *Perf. 14x13½***

| | | |
|---|---|---|
| **2878** A951 32p Genetta genetta | .45 | .20 |

See Nos. 2928, 2978-2980.

**1997, Feb. 28 Photo. *Perf. 14x13½***

| | | |
|---|---|---|
| **2879** A952 32p multicolored | .40 | .20 |

Juvenia '97, Natl. Juvenile Philatelic Exhibition.

Stamp Day A953

**1997, Mar. 7 Engr. *Perf. 14***

| | | |
|---|---|---|
| **2880** A953 65p Antique letter box | 1.00 | .20 |

Spanish Motion Pictures — A954

**1997, Mar. 12 Photo.**

| | | |
|---|---|---|
| **2881** A954 21p "Trip to Nowhere" | .25 | .20 |
| **2882** A954 32p "The South" | .40 | .20 |

World Day of Water — A955

19th Cent. Sailing Ships — A956

**1997, Mar. 22 *Perf. 14x13½***

| | | |
|---|---|---|
| **2883** A955 65p multicolored | .80 | .20 |

**1997, Apr. 16 *Litho. & Engr.***

| | | |
|---|---|---|
| **2884** A956 21p Frigate Asturias | .40 | .20 |
| *a.* Miniature sheet of 4 | 1.50 | 1.50 |
| **2885** A956 32p Spanish Brigantine | .60 | .20 |
| *a.* Miniature sheet of 4 | 3.00 | 3.00 |

Nos. 2884-2885 were each issued in sheets of 4.

Bilbao School of Engineering, Cent., — A957

194p, Atocha Station, High-Speed Spanish Train (AVE), 5th Anniv.

**1997, Apr. 22 Photo. *Perf. 14x13½***

| | | |
|---|---|---|
| **2886** A957 32p multicolored | .75 | .20 |
| **2887** A957 194p multicolored | 3.00 | .70 |

Stories and Legends — A959

Dr. Josep Trueta (1897-1977), Orthopedic Surgeon — A958

**1997, Apr. 30 *Perf. 14***

| | | |
|---|---|---|
| **2888** A958 32p multicolored | .40 | .20 |

Europa: Princess, Prince, gnome, castle.

**1997, May 5 Photo. *Perf. 14x13½***

| | | |
|---|---|---|
| **2889** A959 65p multicolored | 1.25 | .20 |

Fictional Characters A960

Designs: 21p, "El Lazarillo de Tormes," vert. 32p, "El Séneca," by José María Pemán.

**1997, May 8 Engr. *Perf. 14***

**2890** A960 21p green & black .30 .20
**2891** A960 32p black & blue .60 .20

Anxel Fole (1903-86), Poet, Writer A961

**1997, May 17 Photo.**

**2892** A961 65p multicolored 1.00 .20

Comics A962

**1997, May 30**

**2893** A962 21p The Ulysses Family .30 .20
**2894** A962 32p The Masked Warrior .65 .20

Popular Personalities — A963

32p, Manuel Rodríguez Sánchez (Manolete) (1917-47), bullfighter. 65p, Charlie Rivel (Josep Andreu i Lasserre) (1896-1983), circus clown.

**1997, June 5 Photo. *Perf. 14***

**2895** A963 32p multicolored .50 .20
**2896** A963 65p multicolored 1.25 .20

A964

A965

"The Age of Man" Cultural Exhibition: a, 21p, Painting, "The Annunciation," from Church of Nuestra Señora de la Peña, Agreda. b, 32p, Cathedral of El Burgo de Osma. c, 65p, Miniature from Codex titled "Commentary on the Apocalypse," by Beatus of Liebana, 786AD. d, 140p, Statue of Santo Domingo de Silos.

**1997, June 13 *Perf. 13***

**2897** A964 Sheet of 4, #a.-d. 4.50 4.00

**1997, June 24 *Perf. 14***

**2898** A965 65p multicolored .80 .20

30th European Men's Basketball Championships.

NATO Summit, Madrid — A966

**1997, July 8 *Perf. 13***

**2899** A966 65p multicolored 1.25 .20

A967

A968

Design: Natl. monument to honor grape harvesting, Requena.

**1997, July 11 Litho. *Perf. 14***

**2900** A967 32p multicolored .40 .20

**1997, July 24 Photo.**

Anniversaries: 21p, Don Antonio Canovas del Castillo (1828-97), politician. 32p, Roman colony of Elche, 2000th anniv. 65p, Naval defense of Tenerife, bicent.

**2901** A968 21p multicolored .25 .20
**2902** A968 32p multicolored .40 .20
**2903** A968 65p multicolored .80 .25
*Nos. 2901-2903 (3)* 1.45 .65

Peace in Basque Region — A969

Spanish Artists — A970

**1997, July 30 Photo. *Perf. 14***

**2904** A969 32p multicolored .35 .20

**1997, Sept. 12**

Designs: 32p, Mariano Benlliure Gil (1862-1947), sculptor. 65p, Photograph of Remero Vasco, by José Ortíz Echagüe (1886-1980).

**2905** A970 32p multicolored .50 .20
**2906** A970 65p black & beige 1.00 .20

VIGO '97, World Exposition on Fisheries A971

**1997, Sept. 17 Litho.**

**2907** A971 32p multicolored .35 .20

Anniversaries — A972

21p, City of Melilla, 500th anniv., vert. 32p, Declaration of St. Pascual Baylon as patron saint of World Eucharistic Congress, cent., vert. 65p, Ausias March (1397-1459), writer.

**1997, Sept. 24 Photo.**

**2908** A972 21p multicolored .25 .20
**2909** A972 32p multicolored .50 .20

**Engr.**

**2910** A972 65p multicolored 1.00 .20
*Nos. 2908-2910 (3)* 1.75 .60

Sites on UNESCO World Heritage List — A973

Churches in Oviedo: 21p, San Julian de los Prados. 32p, Santa Cristina de Lena.

**1997, Sept. 26 Engr. *Perf. 13***

**2911** A973 21p multicolored .50 .20
**2912** A973 32p multicolored .75 .20

29th Intl. Congress of Transport and Communications Museums, Madrid — A974

**1997, Oct. 1 Litho. *Perf. 14x13½***

**2913** A974 140p multicolored 2.00 .65

Souvenir Sheet

Monument to Don Pelayo, Revillagigedo Palace, Gijón — A975

Illustration reduced.

**1997, Oct. 4 Litho. & Engr. *Perf. 14***

**2914** A975 140p multicolored 2.50 2.00

Exfilna '97, Natl. Stamp Exhibition, Gijón, Asturias

Opening of Royal Theater, Madrid — A976

Designs: 21p, Miguel Fleta (1897-1938), opera singer. 32p, Outside view of theater.

**1997, Oct. 11 Engr. *Perf. 14x13½***

**2915** A976 21p violet brown .25 .20
**2916** A976 32p gray brown .40 .20

America Issue — A977

Foundation of St. Cristobal de La Laguna, 500th Anniv. — A978

**1997, Oct. 10 Photo.**

**2917** A977 65p Postman .80 .30

**1997, Oct. 17 Litho. & Engr.**

**2918** A978 32p multicolored .40 .20

6th World Conference on Down Syndrome, Madrid — A979

**1997, Oct. 23 Photo. *Perf. 13½x14***

**2919** A979 65p blue & yellow .80 .30

Veterinary College, Cordoba, 150th Anniv. A980

**1997, Nov. 14 Engr. *Perf. 14***

**2920** A980 21p green & blue .25 .20

Christmas — A981

Painting, Adoration of the Kings, by Pedro Berruguete.

**1997, Nov. 20** **Photo.**
**2921** A981 32p multicolored .40 .20

Jewish Heritage in Spain A982

Designs: 21p, Porta Nova, Ourense. No. 2923, Women's Gallery, Cordoba Synagogue. No. 2924, Jewish quarter, Caceres, 15th cent. 65p, Jewish Museum, Girona.

**1997, Nov. 28** **Engr.** ***Perf. 13½x14***
**2922** A982 21p black & brown .30 .20
**2923** A982 32p black & violet .50 .20
**2924** A982 32p black & brown .50 .20
**2925** A982 65p black & violet 1.00 .30
*a.* Strip of 4, #2922-2925 3.00 1.25

See Nos. 2969-2972.

Spanish Sports Accomplishments — A983

**1997, Dec. 5** **Photo.**
**2926** A983 32p multicolored 1.25 .20

XACOBEO 99 — A984

**1998, Jan. 12** **Photo.** ***Perf. 14x13½***
**2927** A984 35p blk, org & gray .60 .25

Endangered Fauna — A985

**1998, Feb. 5**
**2928** A985 35p Lynx pardina .90 .25

Bilbao Athletic Club, Cent. A986

**1998, Feb. 10** ***Perf. 13½x14***
**2929** A986 35p multicolored .45 .25

Comic Book Characters A987

Designs: 35p, Mortadelo and Filemón, by Ibáñez, vert. 70p, Zipi & Zape, by Escobar.

***Perf. 14x13½, 13½x14***
**1998, Feb. 26** **Photo.**
**2930** A987 35p multicolored .50 .25
**2931** A987 70p multicolored 1.10 .45

See Nos. 2998-2999.

Gredos State Hotel A988

**1998, Mar. 12** **Photo.** ***Perf. 13½x14***
**2932** A988 35p multicolored .45 .25

Self-Government Statutes for Melilla and Ceuta — A989

**1998, Mar. 16** ***Perf. 13½x14, 14x13½***
**2933** A989 150p Melilla 1.90 1.00
**2934** A989 150p Ceuta, vert. 1.90 1.00

"Generation of '98" Authors — A990

Design: Azorín (José Martinez Ruiz) (1873-1967), Pío Baroja (1872-1956), Miguel de Unamuno (1864-1936), Ramiro de Maetzu (1874-1936), Antonio Machado (1875-1939), Ramon Valle Inclán (1866-1936).

**1998, Apr. 3** **Photo.** ***Perf. 14***
**2935** A990 70p multicolored 1.10 .45

A991

A992

Design: Pedro Abarca de Bolea, Count of Aranda (1719-98), soldier, politician.

**1998, Apr. 17**
**2936** A991 35p multicolored .45 .25

**1998, Apr. 29** **Engr.** ***Perf. 14x13½***

Literary characters from: 35p, Fernando de Rojas' "Le Celestina." 70p, Benito Perez Galdos' "Fortunata and Jacinta."

**2937** A992 35p multicolored .55 .25
**2938** A992 70p multicolored 1.10 .45

Ships A993

**1998, Apr. 30** **Litho.** ***Perf. 14***
**2939** A993 35p Embarcación real .45 .25
**2940** A993 70p Jabeque tajo .90 .45

Popular Festivals — A994

**1998, May 5** **Photo.**
**2941** A994 70p Bonfire of St. John .90 .45

Europa.

College of Medicine, Madrid, Cent. A995

Dr. D. Carlos Jiménez Díaz (1898-1967).

**1998, May 18** ***Perf. 13½x14***
**2942** A995 35p multicolored .45 .25

Popular Personalities — A996

35p, Félix Rodríguez de la Fuente (b. 1928), wildlife activist. 70p, Alfonso Aragón Bermúdez ("Fofó") (1923-76), circus comic, vert.

**1998, May 28** ***Perf. 13½x14, 14x13½***
**2943** A996 35p multicolored .55 .25
**2944** A996 70p multicolored 1.10 .45

A997

A998

Design: King Philip II (1527-98).

**1998, June 1** **Photo.** ***Perf. 14x13½***
**2945** A997 35p multicolored .45 .25

**1998, June 2** **Litho. & Engr.**

Fedrico Garcia Lorca (1898-1936), poet, dramatist.

**2946** A998 35p multicolored .85 .25

Spanish Stamp Engravers A999

35p, Antonio Manso (1934-93), Spain #2129. 70p, J.L.L. Sánchez Toda (1901-), Spain #546.

**1998, June 5** ***Perf. 14***
**2947** A999 35p multicolored .45 .25
**2948** A999 70p multicolored .90 .45

Philippine Independence, Cent. — A1000

Design: Spanish flag, Basilica of Cebu, Holy Child of Cebu, Philippine flag.

**1998, June 12** **Photo.** ***Perf. 13½x14***
**2949** A1000 70p multicolored .95 .50

See Philippines No. 2539.

Sculpture, "Foster Brothers," by Aniceto Marinas (1866-1953) A1000a

**1998, July 10** **Photo.** ***Perf. 14***
**2949A** A1000a 35p multi .50 .25

Expo '98, Lisbon A1001

**1998, Sept. 4**
**2950** A1001 70p multicolored 1.00 .50

Letter Writing — A1002

Scenes from "Don Quixote" — #2951: a, "En un lugas de la Mancha." b, "Llenósele la fantasía." c, "Armado caballero." d, "La del alba sería." e, "Le molió como cibera." f, "El donoso escrutinio." g, "Has de saber, amigo Sancho." h, "Los gigantes." i, "Viole bajar y subir con tanta gracia." j, "El escuadrón de ovejas." k, "Los galeotes." l, "Los cueros."

No. 2952: a, "El encantamiento." b, "Oh princesa del toboso." c, "El caballero de los espejos." d, "El leon." e, "La cueva de montesinos." f, "Clavileño." g, "Sancho gobernador." h, "Doña Rodríguez." i, "Compañero mío." j, "Parecioles espaciosísimo." k, "El caballero de la blanca luna." l, "La vuelta a casa."

**1998, Sept. 25** ***Perf. 13***
**2951** Sheet of 12 4.50 4.50
*a.-l.* A1002 20p any single .30 .20
**2952** Sheet of 12 4.50 4.50
*a.-l.* A1002 20p any single .30 .20

See #3016, 3053-3954, 3121, 3175.

20th Intl. Conference on Data Protection, Santiago de Compostela — A1003

**1998, Sept. 16 Litho. *Perf. 14***

**2953** A1003 70p multicolored .90 .45

Souvenir Sheet

EXFILNA '98 Natl. Philatelic Exhibition — A1004

**Litho. & Engr.**

**1998, Sept. 18 *Perf. 14***

**2954** A1004 150p Cathedral of Barcelona 2.75 2.25

UNESCO World Heritage Sites — A1005

Designs: 35p, Walled city of Cuenca. 70p, Silk Exchange, Valencia.

**1998, Sept. 19 Engr. *Perf. 13***

**2955** A1005 35p blue & brown .60 .25

**2956** A1005 70p red & brown 1.40 .45

Angel Ganivet (1865-98), Writer A1006

**1998, Oct. 6 Engr. *Perf. 14***

**2957** A1006 35p brown & purple .50 .25

A1007

A1008

**1998, Oct. 6**

**2958** A1007 70p multicolored 1.00 .50

The Giralda of Seville, 800th Anniv.

**1998, Oct. 8 Engr. *Perf. 14***

**2959** A1008 35p brn & yel grn .50 .25

Aga Khan Architecture Award, Alhambra of Granada.

Stamp Day A1009

**1998, Oct. 9 Photo.**

**2960** A1009 70p multicolored 1.00 .50

María Guerrero (1867-1928), Theater Actress — A1010

**1998, Oct. 13**

**2961** A1010 70p multicolored 1.00 .50

America Issue.

Spanish Railroads, 150th Anniv. A1011

**1998, Oct. 28 Engr.**

**2962** A1011 35p multicolored .50 .25

Juan Carlos I Antarctic Base A1012

**1998, Nov. 6 Photo.**

**2963** A1012 35p multicolored .50 .25

A1013

Christmas (Works of art): 35p, Chestnut Seller, by Rafael Seco. 70p, Marriage of the Virgin and St. Joseph, Cathedral of Oviedo.

**1998, Nov. 13**

**2964** A1013 35p multicolored .50 .25

**2965** A1013 70p multicolored 1.00 .50

Souvenir Sheet

A1014

**1998, Nov. 11 Photo. *Perf. 14***

The Cathedral of San Salvador, Zaragoza (Details from Altarpiece: a, Holding cross, angel. b, Holy family.

**2966** A1014 35p Sheet of 2, a.-b. 1.50 1.25

Founding of New Mexico, 400th Anniv. A1015

Designs: 35p, Expedition of Juan de Oñate. 70p, Early map of Nueva Espana (Mexico) and Nuevo Mexico.

**1998, Nov. 20**

**2967** A1015 35p multicolored .50 .25

**2968** A1015 70p multicolored 1.00 .50

Jewish Heritage in Spain Type of 1997

Designs: No. 2969, Bust of Benjamin de Tudela, Tudela Commune, Navarre. No. 2970, Residence, Hervás Community, Cáceres. No. 2971, Courtyard, Corpus Christi Church, Segovia. No. 2972, Santa Maria la Blanca Synagogue, Toledo.

**1998, Nov. 23 Engr.**

**2969** A982 35p dp blue & dp ol .60 .25

**2970** A982 35p dp blue & dp cl .60 .25

**2971** A982 70p dp blue & dp cl 1.10 .50

**2972** A982 70p dp blue & dp ol 1.10 .50

*a.* Strip of 4, #2969-2972 4.00 4.00

Nos. 2969, 2971 have Star of David. Nos. 2970, 2972 have menorah.

UNESCO Biosphere Reserve, Minorca A1016

**1998, Dec. 2 Photo.**

**2973** A1016 35p multicolored .50 .25

Spanish Olympic Academy, 30th Anniv. A1017

**1998, Dec. 9**

**2974** A1017 70p Bust of Plato, amphora 1.00 .50

Universal Declaration of Human Rights, 50th Anniv.
A1018 A1019

Designs: 35p, Angel Sanz Briz (1910-80), Spanish ambassador. 70p, Fingerprints.

**1998, Dec. 10**

**2975** A1018 35p multicolored .50 .25

**2976** A1019 70p multicolored 1.00 .50

Carthusian Horses — A1020

Designs: a, 100p, Mare standing with colt. b, 185p, Two with heads together. c, 35p, Adult standing in grass. d, 150p, Adult standing in flowers. e, 20p, Colt lying down, mare eating grass. f, 70p, Head of adult, silhouette.

**1998, Dec. 29**

**2977** A1020 Block of 6, #a.-f. 25.00 25.00

España 2000, Intl. Philatelic Exhibition.

Issued in sheets of two blocks, the lower one in a different order. Two of the devices shown on the coat of arms appear on each block at the intersection of the perfs. On the top block the crown is on a.-b., d.-e., while the "H" is on b.-c., e.-f. On the bottom block the location of these devices is reversed, giving all the stamps in the sheet a slightly different design.

See #3019, 3052.

Endangered Fauna Type of 1997

Gallotia simonyi machadoi A1020a

Pandion haliaetus

Puffinus puffinus

**1999, Jan. 28 Photo. *Perf. 14***

**2978** A1020a 35p multicolored .50 .25

**2979** A1020b 70p multicolored 1.00 .50

**2980** A1020c 100p multicolored 1.40 .70

*Nos. 2978-2980 (3)* 2.90 1.45

Xacobeo '99 A1021

Designs: 35p, Stone cross of Paradela, vert. 70p, Sculpture of St. James, door on Church of St. James, Sangüesa. 100p, Stone cross, Cizur Bridge, Pamplona, vert. 185p, Jurisdictional stone pillar, Boadilla del Camino, vert.

**Litho. & Engr.**

**1999, Feb. 22** *Perf. 13¾*
**2981** A1021 35p multicolored .60 .25
**2982** A1021 70p multicolored 1.25 .45
**2983** A1021 100p multicolored 1.50 .65
**2984** A1021 185p multicolored 2.75 1.10
*Nos. 2981-2984 (4)* 6.10 2.45

Barcelona Soccer Club, Cent. — A1022

**1999, Mar. 11** **Photo.** *Perf. 14*
**2985** A1022 35p multicolored .45 .25

Juvenia '99, Natl. Junior Philatelic Exhibition A1023

**1999, Mar. 12** **Litho.** *Perf. 14*
**2986** A1023 35p multicolored .50 .25

Spanish Police Force, 175th Anniv. A1024

**1999, Mar. 26**
**2987** A1024 35p multicolored .50 .25

Souvenir Sheet

Palace of Alfonso I el Batallador, Zaragoza — A1025

Illustration reduced.

**Litho. & Engr.**

**1999, Apr. 9** *Perf. 14x13½*
**2988** A1025 185p multicolored 3.00 2.75

Exfilna '99, Zaragoza.

Spanish Amateur Radio Union, 50th Anniv. A1026

**1999, Apr. 16** **Photo.** *Perf. 14*
**2989** A1026 70p multicolored .95 .50

7th World Track & Field Championships, Seville — A1027

**1999, Apr. 30** **Photo.** *Perf. 14x13½*
**2990** A1027 70p multicolored .90 .45

Monfragüe Nature Park A1028

**Litho. & Engr.**

**1999, May 5** *Perf. 13½x14*
**2991** A1028 70p multicolored *.90 .45*

Europa.

Barcelona Subway System, 75th Anniv. A1029

**1999, May 7** **Photo.** *Perf. 14*
**2992** A1029 70p multicolored .90 .45

Spanish Art — A1030

Designs: 35p, Portrait of King Solomon. 70p, Artifact from cathedral, Palencia.

**1999, May 14**
**2993** A1030 35p multicolored .50 .25
**2994** A1030 70p multicolored 1.00 .45

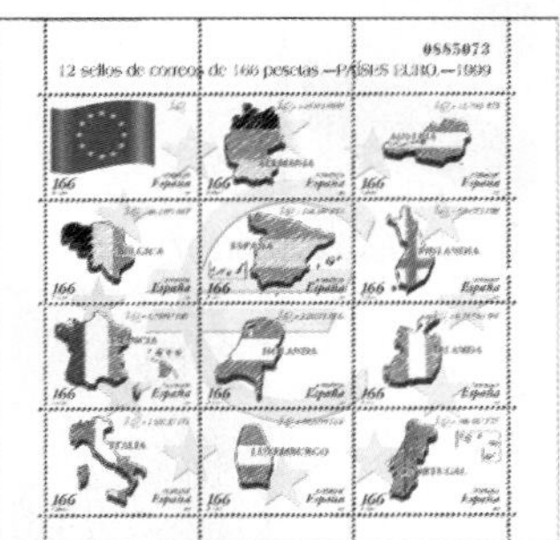

Introduction of the Euro — A1031

Design: a, European Union flag. Maps: b, Germany. c, Austria. d, Belgium e, Spain. f, Finland. g, France. h, Netherlands. i, Ireland. j, Italy. k, Luxembourg. l, Portugal.

**1999, May 28** *Perf. 13½x14*
**2995** A1031 166p Sheet of 12, #a.-l. 35.00 30.00

Denomination is shown in both pesetas and euros. Each stamp shows the equivilent of 1 euro in the currency of the represented country.

Royal Recreation Club of Huelva A1032

**1999, June 7**
**2996** A1032 35p multicolored .45 .25

Souvenir Sheet

Palma '99, Natl. Topical Philatelic Exhibition — A1033

Illustration reduced.

**1999, June 18** *Perf. 14x13½*
**2997** A1033 185p multicolored 3.00 3.00

**Comic Book Character Type**

35p, Dona Urraca, by Jorge, vert. 70p, El Coyote, by José Mallorquí Figuerola, vert.

**1999, June 11** **Photo.** *Perf. 13¾*
**2998** A987 35p multicolored .50 .25
**2999** A987 70p multicolored 1.00 .45

Defense of Las Palmas de Gran Canaria, 400th Anniv. A1034

**1999, June 25** **Litho. & Engr.**
**3000** A1034 70p multicolored .90 .45

A1035

A1036

**1999, July 2** **Photo.** *Perf. 13¾*
**3001** A1035 35p multicolored .45 .25

San Pedro de Villanueva Benedictine Monastery.

**1999, July 12**
**3002** A1036 35p multicolored .45 .25

Village of Balmaseda, 800th anniv.

Carlos Buigas (b. 1898), Graphic Designer A1037

**1999, July 12**
**3003** A1037 70p multicolored .90 .45

General Society of Authors and Editors, Cent. — A1038

**1999, July 12**
**3004** A1038 70p multicolored .90 .45

Spanish Mining Institute, 150th Anniv. A1039

**1999, July 12**
**3005** A1039 150p multicolored 1.90 .95

El Cid (Rodrigo Diaz de Vivar) (1040-99) A1040

**1999, July 16** **Photo.** *Perf. 13¾*
**3006** A1040 35p multicolored .45 .25

Paintings by Jose Vela Zanetti (1913-99) A1041

70p, "Winter." 150p, "The Harvest."

**1999, Sept. 10** **Photo.** *Perf. 13¾*
**3007** A1041 70p multi 1.25 .45
**3008** A1041 150p multi, vert. 2.25 .95

Diego Velazquez (1599-1660), Painter — A1042

Paintings: 35p, Sebastián de Morra. 70p, Sibyl.

**1999, Sept. 24**
**3009** A1042 35p multicolored .45 .25
**3010** A1042 70p multicolored .90 .45

Intl. Year of Older Persons A1043

**1999, Sept. 30**
**3011** A1043 35p multicolored .45 .25

Oix Castle, Lower Pyrenees A1044

**1999, Oct. 1 Engr. *Perf. 13½x14***
**3012** A1044 70p blue & vio brn .90 .45

World Heritage Sites — A1045

Designs: 35p, San Millán de Yuso Monastery. 70p, San Millán de Suso Monastery.

**1999, Oct. 8 *Perf. 13x12½***
**3013** A1045 35p multicolored .75 .25
**3014** A1045 70p multicolored 1.50 .45

UPU, 125th Anniv. A1046

**1999, Oct. 9 Photo. *Perf. 13¾***
**3015** A1046 70p multicolored .90 .45

**Letter Writing Type of 1998**

Designs: a, "Cumplimos 150 años." b, "Recorremos el mundo." c, "Llegamos juntos." d, "Escríbeme." e, "Ama la lectura." f, "Vive la naturaleza." g, "Te mostramos el patrimonio." h, "Te acercamos a la pintura." i, "Jugamos contigo." j, "Sentimos la musica." k, "Y además nos coleccionan." l, "Os esperamos."

**1999, Oct. 13 Photo. *Perf. 13x12½***
**3016** Sheet of 12 4.50 4.50
***a.-l.*** A1002 20p any single .30 .20

America Issue, A new Millennium Without Arms — A1047

**1999, Oct. 15 *Perf. 13¾***
**3017** A1047 70p multicolored .90 .45

Intl. Congress of Money Museums, Madrid — A1048

**1999, Oct. 18 Engr. *Perf. 13x12½***
**3018** A1048 70p blue & brown .90 .45

**Carthusian Horse Type of 1998**

Designs: a, 185p, White horse, six men. b, 70p, Espana Intl. Philatelic Exhibition emblem. c, 100p, Two white horses. d, 150p, Two white horses, one with leg raised. e, 35p, Emblem, exhibition dates. f, 20p, Horse, handler.

**1999, Nov. 3 Photo. *Perf. 13¾***
**3019** A1020 Block of 6, #a.-f. 14.00 14.00

See footnote following No. 2977.

Christmas A1049

35p, Adoration of the Magi, Toledo Cathedral retable. 70p, Child, statue, candles.

**1999, Nov. 5**
**3020** A1049 35p multi, vert. .60 .25
**3021** A1049 70p multi 1.25 .45

Spanish Postage Stamps, 150th Anniv. A1050

a, King Juan Carlos, altered 12c design A2. b, King, altered 6c design A1. c, King, altered 5r design A2. d, King, altered 6r design A2. e, 150th anniv. emblem, altered 6c design A1. f, King, altered 10r design A2. g, King, coat of arms.

**Litho. & Engr.**

**2000, Jan. 3 *Perf. 13¾x14***
**3022** Sheet of 12 7.00 6.50
***a.-g.*** A1050 35p any single .60 .25

#3022 contains 2 ea #3022a-3022d, 3022f, 1 ea #3022e, 3022g.

Endangered Butterflies — A1051

Designs: 35p, Parnassius apollo. 70p, Agriades zullichi.

**2000, Jan. 31 Photo. *Perf. 13¾***
**3023** A1051 35p multi .60 .25
**3024** A1051 70p multi 1.25 .45

First Printing at Montserrat Monastery, 500th Anniv. — A1052

**2000, Feb. 4 Photo. *Perf. 13¾***
**3025** A1052 35p multi .45 .25

Holy Roman Emperor Charles V (1500-58) A1053

**2000, Feb. 24 *Perf. 12¾x13***
**3026** A1053 35p shown .60 .25
**3027** A1053 70p At age 40 1.25 .45

**Souvenir Sheet**

***Perf. 13¼x12¾***
**3028** A1053 150p In armor 2.75 1.75

No. 3028 contains one 40x49mm stamp. See Belgium Nos. 1791-1793.

"Age of Man" Exhibition, Astorga — A1054

Designs: 70p, Carving of the Virgin Mary. 100p, Cross, Arab perfume bottle.

**2000, Mar. 24 Photo. *Perf. 14x13¾***
**3029** A1054 70p multi .75 .40
**3030** A1054 100p multi 1.10 .55

Ferdinand of Aragon Inn, Sos A1055

**2000, Apr. 7 *Perf. 13¾x14***
**3031** A1055 35p multi .60 .20

University Anniversaries — A1056

35p, Lleida, 700th anniv. 70p, Valencia, 500th anniv. ( in 1999).

**2000, Apr. 12 Engr. *Perf. 13¾x14***
**3032** A1056 35p red lil & brown .50 .20
**3033** A1056 70p blue & choc 1.00 .40

A1057

A1058

**2000, Apr. 28 Photo. *Perf. 14x13¾***
**3034** A1057 35p multi .60 .20

Royal Barcelona Sports Club, soccer team, cent.

**2000, May 4**
**3035** A1058 35p multi .60 .20

María de las Mercedes de Borbón y Orleáns (1910-2000), mother of King Juan Carlos.

**Europa Issue**

Common Design Type

**2000, May 9**
**3036** CD17 70p multi *.75 .40*

Royal Academy of Medicine, Seville, 300th Anniv. A1060

Julio Rey Pastor (1888-1962), Mathematician — A1061

Pharmacy College of Granada, 150th Anniv. — A1062

Valencia, City of Arts and Sciences A1063

**2000, May 25 *Perf. 13¾x14, 14x13¾***
**3037** A1060 35p multi .60 .20
**3038** A1061 70p multi 1.00 .40
**3039** A1062 100p multi 1.50 .55
**3040** A1063 185p multi 3.00 1.00
*Nos. 3037-3040 (4)* 6.10 2.15

Intl. Mathematics Year (No. 3038).

Comic Strips A1064

Designs: 35p, Las Hermanas Gilda, by Manuel Vázquez. 70p, Roberto Alcázar y Pedrín, by Eduardo Vañó, vert.

**2000, May 26 *Perf. 13¾x14, 14x13¾***
**3041** A1064 35p multi .60 .20
**3042** A1064 70p multi 1.25 .40

Guggenheim Museum, Bilbao — A1065

**2000, June 2 Photo. *Perf. 13¾x14***
**3043** A1065 70p multi 1.00 .40

Bilbao, 700th anniv.

Angel From Prayer in the Garden, Sculpture by Francisco Salzillo (1707-73) A1066

**2000, June 9 Photo. *Perf. 14x13¼***
**3044** A1066 70p multi 1.10 .40

Souvenir Sheet

Fountains of San Francisco, Aviles — A1067

Illustration reduced.

**Litho. & Engr.**
**2000, June 16 *Perf. 14x13¾***
**3045** A1067 185p multi 3.50 2.50

Exfilna 2000 Philatelic Exhibition, Aviles.

Trees A1068

Designs: 70p, Pinus sylvestris. 150p, Quercus ilex (encina).

***Perf. 12¾x12½***
**2000, June 19 Photo.**
**3046-3047** A1068 Set of 2 3.50 1.10

Local Festivals A1069

Designs: 35p, Fire Walking Festival, San Pedro Manrique. 70p, Chivalry Festival of San Juan, Ciudadela.

**2000, June 23 *Perf. 13¾x14***
**3048-3049** A1069 Set of 2 1.60 .55

Josemaria Escrivá de Balaguer (1902-75), Founder of Opus Dei. A1070

**Litho. & Engr.**
**2000, June 26 *Perf. 13¾x14***
**3050** A1070 70p black & orange 1.10 .40

Souvenir Sheet

World Map of Juan de la Cosa, 500th Anniv. — A1071

**2000, July 14 Photo. *Perf. 13¾x14***
**3051** A1071 150p multi 2.50 1.50

**Carthusian Horses Type of 1998**

No. 3052: a, 20p, Head of horse, five horses. b, 35p, White horse, sun partially obscured by clouds. c, 70p, Horse's head, two horses galloping. d, 100p, Heads of two horses. e, 150p, Horse's head, horse in lilac. f, 185p, Horse with bridle.

**2000, July 28**
**3052** A1020 Block of 6, #a-f 13.00 13.00

See note following No. 2977.

**Letter Writing Type of 1998**

No. 3053: a, Atapuerca Man, 800,000 B.C. b, Cave paintings of Altamira, 12,000 B.C. c, Phoenecians, 1100 B.C. d, Tartessians, 800 B.C. e, Iberians and Celts, 500 B.C. f, Lady of Elche, Iberian statue, 480 B.C. g, Carthaginians, 237 B.C. h, Roman Spain, 197 B.C. i, Viriathus, Lusitanian war leader against Romans, 147 B.C. j, Siege of Numantia, 133 B.C. k, Segovia aqueduct, A.D. 50. l, Vandals, Suebis, and Alanis, 409.

No. 3054: a, Visigoths, 415. b, Conversion of Recared to Catholicism, 589. c, Arabs, 711. d, Victory over Arabs by Asturian King, Pelayo, 722. e, Discovery of alleged tomb of St. James, 813. f, Collapse of the caliphate, 1031. g, Death of El Cid, 1099. h, Alfonso VIII's victory at Las Navas de Tolosa, 1212. i, Alfonso X (the Wise) becomes King, 1252. j, Trastámara Dynasty, 1369. k, Spanish Inquisition, 1478. l, Union of Aragon and Castile, 1479.

**2000, Sept. 22 *Perf. 13x12¾***
**3053** Sheet of 12 2.50 2.50
*a.-l.* A1002 20p Any single .20 .20
**3054** Sheet of 12 2.50 2.50
*a.-l.* A1002 20p Any single .20 .20

World Heritage Sites — A1072

Designs: 35p, Las Médulas. 70p, Pyrénées — Mt. Perdido, vert. 150p, Catalan Music Palace, Barcelona.

***Perf. 13x12¾(35p), 12¾***
**2000, Sept. 21 Litho. (35p), Engr.**
**3055-3057** A1072 Set of 3 2.75 1.40

Souvenir Sheets

España 2000 Intl. Philatelic Exhibition — A1073

Designs: No. 3058, Hand of Julio Iglesias, singer. No. 3059, Signature of Alejandro Sanz, singer. No. 3060, Signature of Antonio Banderas, movie star. No. 3061, Mannequin, signature of Jesús del Pozo, fashion designer. No. 3062, Signature of Miguel Induráin, cyclist. No. 3063, Soccer ball, signature of Raúl González, soccer player. No. 3064, Hands of Joaquín Cortés, dancer. No. 3065, Feet of Sara Baras, dancer. No. 3066, Emblem of TVE 1 television network. No. 3067, Radio and antenna. No. 3068, Newspaper mastheads.

Illustration reduced.

***Perf. 13 (round stamps), 13¾x14***
**2000 Photo.**
**3058-3068** A1073 200p Set of 11 35.00 35.00

150th anniv. of Spanish stamps, #3066.
Nos. 3060-3061, 3064-3068 each contain one 41x28mm rectangular stamp.
Exist imperf. Value $65.
Issued: #3058-3059, 10/6; #3060, 10/7; #3061, 10/8; #3062-3063, 10/9; #3064-3065, 10/10; #3066, 10/11; #3067, 10/12; #3068, 10/13.

Alfredo Kraus (1927-99), Operatic Tenor — A1074

**2000, Oct. 27 *Perf. 14x13¾***
**3069** A1074 70p multi 1.00 .40

America Issue, Fight Against AIDS — A1075

**2000, Oct. 19 Photo. *Perf. 14x13¾***
**3070** A1075 70p multi 1.00 .40

Christmas A1076

Designs: 35p, Nativity scene. 70p, Birth of Christ, by Conrad von Soest.

**2000, Nov. 9 *Perf. 12¾***
**3071-3072** A1076 Set of 2 1.50 .55

See Germany No. B878-B879.

Santa María la Real Church, Aranda de Duero — A1077

**2000, Nov. 10 Engr. *Perf. 14x13¾***
**3073** A1077 35p brown .50 .25

Spanish Literature A1078

Designs: 35p, Entre Naranjos, by Vicente Blasco Ibáñez. 70p, La Venganza de Don Mendo, by Pedro Muñoz Seca. 100p, El Alcalde Zalamea, by Pedro Calderón de la Barca.

**Photo., Engr. (100p)**
**2000, Nov. 17 *Perf. 13¾x14***
**3074-3076** A1078 Set of 3 3.25 1.50

Commercial Agents College, 75th Anniv. — A1079

**2001, Jan. 8 Photo. *Perf. 14x13¾***
**3077** A1079 40p multi .60 .25

Fire Fighters — A1080

**2001, Jan. 19**
**3078** A1080 75p multi 1.10 .45

Infantry College, Toledo, 150th Anniv. A1081

**2001, Feb. 16 *Perf. 13¾x14***
**3079** A1081 120p multi 2.00 .65

Intl. Campaign Against Domestic Violence — A1082

**2001, Feb. 22 *Perf. 14x13¾***
**3080** A1082 155p multi 2.25 .85

First Spanish Mail Box, Mayorga A1083

**2001, Mar. 2 Engr. *Perf. 13¾x14***
**3081** A1083 155p black 2.25 .85

Stamp Day.

Juvenia 2001, Natl. Youth Philatelic Exhibition A1084

**2001, Mar. 9 Photo.**
**3082** A1084 120p multi 1.75 .70

Placencia Inn — A1084a

**2001, Mar. 16** ***Perf. 14x13¾***
**3083** A1084a 40p multicolored .60 .20

Famous People A1085

Designs: 40p, Joaquín Rodrigo (1901-99), musician. 75p, Rafael Alberti (1902-99), writer.

**2001, Mar. 22 Engr.** ***Perf. 13¾x14***
**3084-3085** A1085 Set of 2 1.75 .60

Castles A1086

Designs: 40p, Zuda, Tortosa, vert. 75p, Cid, Jadraque. 155p, San Fernando, Figueres. 260p, Montesquiu, Montesquiu.

**2001, Apr. 20** ***Perf. 14x13¾, 13¾x14***
**3086-3089** A1086 Set of 4 8.00 3.00

Book Day — A1087

**2001, Apr. 23 Photo.** ***Perf. 14x13¾***
**3090** A1087 40p multi .60 .20

Souvenir Sheet

First Flights, 75th Anniv. — A1088

No. 3091: a, 40p, Spain-Argentina. b, 75p, Spain-Philippines. c, 155p, Spain-Equatorial Guinea. d, 260p, Commemorative flight.

**2001, Apr. 26** ***Perf. 13¾x14***
**3091** A1088 Sheet of 4, #a-d 8.00 3.00

Grand Theater, Liceu — A1089

**2001, Apr. 27** ***Perf. 14x13¾***
**3092** A1089 120p multi 1.75 .65

King Juan Carlos — A1091

**2001 Photo.** ***Perf. 12¾x13¼***
**3093** A1091 5p sil & lil rose .20 .20
**3094** A1091 40p sil & yel grn .60 .25
**3095** A1091 75p sil & bl vio 1.10 .40
**3096** A1091 100psil & lt red brn 1.50 .55
*Nos. 3093-3096 (4)* 3.40 1.40

Issued: 40p, 5/4; 5p, 75p, 6/28; 100p, 7/15.

Europa — A1092

**2001, May 9 Photo.** ***Perf. 14x13¾***
**3097** A1092 75p multi *.80 .40*

Architecture A1093

Designs: 40p, San Martiño Church, Noia. 75p, Santa Maria Cathedral, Tui. 155p, Villaconcha dovecote, Frechilla.

**Engr., Photo. (75p)**
**2001, May 17** ***Perf. 14x13¾***
**3098-3100** A1093 Set of 3 4.00 1.50

Luarca Harbor A1094

**2001, May 26 Photo.** ***Perf. 13¾x14***
**3101** A1094 40p multi .60 .25

Cardinal Rodrigo de Castro (1523-1600) — A1095

**2001, June 1**
**3102** A1095 40p multi .60 .25

Leopoldo Alas, "Clarín," (1852-1901), Writer — A1096

**2001, June 13**
**3103** A1096 75p multi 1.10 .40

Trees A1097

Designs: 40p, Olive. 75p, Beech.

**2001, June 22** ***Perf. 12¾***
**3104-3105** A1097 Set of 2 1.75 .60

King's Soccer Cup, 25th Anniv. A1098

**2001, July 6 Litho.** ***Perf. 13¾x14***
**3106** A1098 40p multi .60 .25

Issued in sheets of 8 + 4 labels.

Local Festivals A1099

Designs: 40p, Cipotegato, Tarazona. 120p, Giants of Pí, Barcelona, vert.

***Perf. 13¾x14, 14x13¾***
**2001, July 10 Photo.**
**3107-3108** A1099 Set of 2 2.40 .80

Baltasar Gracian (1601-58), Writer A1100

**2001, July 13** ***Perf. 13¾x14***
**3109** A1100 120p multi 1.75 .60

"Age of Man" Exhibition — A1101

Designs: 120p, Our Lady of La Calva. 155p, Cathedral dome, Zamora.

**2001, July 20 Engr.** ***Perf. 14x13¾***
**3110-3111** A1101 Set of 2 4.00 1.50

Grandparent's Day — A1102

Siervas de Jesús de la Caridad A1103

***Perf. 14x13¾, 13¾x14***
**2001, July 26 Photo.**
**3112** A1102 40p multi .60 .25
**3113** A1103 75p multi 1.10 .40

Salamanca, European City of Culture — A1104

Illustration reduced.

**2001, Sept. 5 Photo.** ***Perf. 13x13¼***
**3114** A1104 75p multi 1.10 .40

Covadonga Basilica, Cent. of Consecration — A1105

**2001, Sept. 7** ***Perf. 13¾x14***
**3115** A1105 40p multi .60 .25

Emblem of Privatized Postal System A1106

**2001, Sept. 15**
**3116** A1106 40p multi .60 .25

Souvenir Sheet

Exfilna 2001 Natl. Philatelic Exhibition, Vigo — A1107

**Engr. (Litho. Margin)**
**2001, Sept. 21**
**3117** A1107 260p multi 4.00 4.00

St. Dominic of Silos (c. 1000-73) — A1108

**Litho. & Engr.**
**2001, Oct. 4** ***Perf. 14x13¾***
**3118** A1108 40p multi .60 .25
*a.* Souvenir sheet of 1 with margin like stamp design .60 .60
*b.* Souvenir sheet of 1 with margin differing .60 .60

Year of Dialogue Among Civilizations
A1109

**2001, Oct. 9** **Photo.**
**3119** A1109 120p multi 1.75 .70

Stamp Day.

Posidonia Oceanica, Ses Salines Nature Reserve
A1110

**2001, Oct. 15** ***Perf. 13¾x14***
**3120** A1110 155p multi 2.25 .85

America issue — UNESCO World Heritage Sites.

**Letter Writing Type of 1998**

No. 3121: a, Christopher Columbus, 1492. b, Treaty of Tordesillas, 1494. c, Election of King Charles I as Holy Roman Emperor Charles V, 1519. d, Conquest of Mexico by Hernán Cortés, 1519. e, Circumnavigation by Juan Sebastián Elcano, 1522. f, Campaign against Incas by Francisco Pizarro, 1532. g, Ascension to throne of King Philip II, 1556. h, Start of construction of El Escorial Monastery, 1563. i, Battle of Lepanto, 1571. j, Saints John of the Cross, Teresa of Jesus and painter El Greco, 1580. k, First play by Lope de Vega, 1593. l, Ascension to throne of King Philip III, 1598.

**2001, Oct. 19** ***Perf. 13x12½***
**3121** Sheet of 12 5.25 5.25
*a.-l.* A1002 25p Any single .40 .20

**Souvenir Sheet**

Bullfighter Curro Romero — A1111

**2001, Oct. 25** ***Perf. 14x13¾***
**3122** A1111 260p multi 4.00 4.00

Christmas
A1112

Designs: 40p, Virgin With Child, by Alfredo Roldan. 75p, Adoration of the Shepherds, by José Ribera.

**2001, Nov. 8** ***Perf. 12¾***
**3123-3124** A1112 Set of 2 1.75 .60
*a.* Souvenir sheet, # 3123-3124, Germany #B895-B896, litho., perf. 13¼ 6.00 5.50

See Germany No. B896a.

Score of "El Sombrero de Tres Picos," by Manuel de Falla (1876-1946) — A1113

**2001, Nov. 14** **Photo.** ***Perf. 13¾x14***
**3125** A1113 75p multi 1.10 .40

Comic Strips
A1114

Designs: 40p, Cartoon by Josep Coll i Coll. 75p, Rompetechos, by Francisco Ibañez.

**2001, Nov. 20**
**3126-3127** A1114 Set of 2 1.75 .60

Carlos Cano (1946-2000), Singer — A1115

**2001, Nov. 23** ***Perf. 14x13¾***
**3128** A1115 40p black .60 .25

Intl. Volunteer Day for Economic and Social Development
A1116

**2001, Nov. 27**
**3129** A1116 120p multi 1.75 .70

World Heritage Sites — A1117

No. 3130: a, Catalan Romanesque Churches of the Vall de Boí. b, The Mystery of Elx (Elche). c, Hospital de Sant Pau, Barcelona. d, San Cristóbal de La Laguna. e, Archaeological Site of Atapuerca. f, Palmeral of Elche. g, Monuments of Oviedo. h, Roman Walls of Lugo. i, Rock Art of the Mediterranean Basin. j, Ibiza, Biodiversity and Culture. k, Archaeological Ensemble of Tarraco. l, University and Historic Precinct of Alcalá de Henares.

**2001, Nov. 30** ***Perf. 12¾***
**3130** Sheet of 12 7.00 7.00
*a.-l.* A1117 40p Any single .60 .25

**Souvenir Sheet**

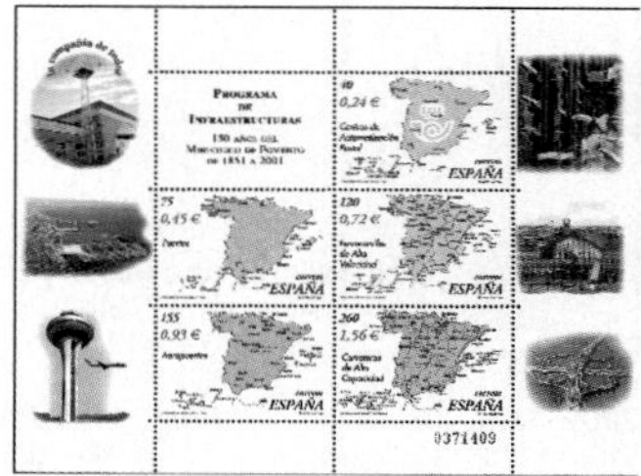

Ministry of Development, 150th Anniv. — A1118

No. 3131 — Maps showing: a, 40p, Automated postal centers. b, 75p, Ports. c, 120p, High-speed train lines. d, 155p, Airports. e, 260p, Highways.

**2001, Dec. 11**
**3131** A1118 Sheet of 5, #a-e, + label 11.00 10.00

**Souvenir Sheet**

King Juan Carlos, 25th Anniv. of Reign — A1119

No. 3132: a, 40p, Crown Prince Felipe. b, 40p, Princess Elena (patterned dress). c, 40p, Royal arms. d, 40p, Princess Cristina (black dress). e, 75p, King Juan Carlos. f, 75p, Queen Sofia. g, 260p, Royal palace, Madrid (49x28mm).

**2001, Dec. 14** ***Perf. 12¾x13¼***
**3132** A1119 Sheet of 7, #a-g 10.00 10.00

100 Cents = 1 Euro (€)

**King Juan Carlos Type of 2001 With Euro Denominations Only**

**2002, Jan. 2** **Photo.** ***Perf. 13¾x14***
**3133** A1091 1c sil & black .20 .20
**3134** A1091 5c sil & brt blue .20 .20
**3135** A1091 10c sil & gray blue .20 .20
**3136** A1091 25c sil & claret .60 .20
**3137** A1091 50c sil & gray 1.25 .35
**3138** A1091 75c sil & red lil 1.90 .55

***Perf. 12¾x13¼***
**3139** A1091 €1 sil & green 2.50 .75
**3140** A1091 €2 sil & ver 5.00 1.50
*Nos. 3133-3140 (8)* 11.85 3.95

Spain's Presidency of European Union
A1120

Color of star at UR: 25c, Orange. 50c, White.

**2002, Jan. 2** **Photo.** ***Perf. 13¾x14***
**3141-3142** A1120 Set of 2 1.90 .65

Trees
A1121

Designs: 50c, Savin (sabina). 75c, Elm (olmo).

**2002, Jan. 25** ***Perf. 12¾***
**3143-3144** A1121 Set of 2 3.00 1.10

A1122 A1123

A1124 A1125

A1126 A1127

Flowers
A1128 A1129

***Die Cut Perf. 13***

**2002, Feb. 20** **Litho.**

**Self-Adhesive**

**3145** Booklet of 8 5.50
*a.* A1122 25c multi .60 .25
*b.* A1123 25c multi .60 .25
*c.* A1124 25c multi .60 .25
*d.* A1125 25c multi .60 .25
*e.* A1126 25c multi .60 .25
*f.* A1127 25c multi .60 .25
*g.* A1128 25c multi .60 .25
*h.* A1129 25c multi .60 .25

España 2002 Youth Philatelic Exhibition, Salamanca
A1130

Designs: 50c, Exhibition emblem. €1.80, Emblem and New Cathedral, vert.

**2002, Feb. 22** **Photo.** ***Perf. 13¾x14***
**3146** A1130 50c multi 1.25 .45

**Souvenir Sheet**

***Perf. 14x13¾***

**3147** A1130 €1.80 multi 5.00 4.50

See No. 3183.

Father Francisco Piquer, Founder of Pawn Brokerage
A1131

**2002, Feb. 25** **Litho.** ***Perf. 14x13¾***
**3148** A1131 25c multi .60 .25

Caja Madrid Savings Bank, 300th anniv.

Real Madrid Soccer Team, Cent. A1132

**2002, Feb. 25** ***Perf. 13¾x14***
**3149** A1132 75c yel & gray 1.90 .65

Souvenir Sheet

Tarazona Town Hall Portico — A1133

**2002, Feb. 26**
**3150** A1133 €2.10 multi 5.25 5.25

Philaiberia '02, Tarazona.

Alejandro Mon (1801-82), Politician — A1134

**2002, Feb. 27** ***Perf. 14x13¾***
**3151** A1134 25c multi .60 .25

Retirement of Peseta Currency — A1135

**2002, Feb. 28** **Litho.**
**3152** A1135 25c multi .60 .25

Sil Canyons, Ribiera Sacra — A1136

Cabo de Gata Natl. Park A1137

**2002, Mar. 8** ***Perf. 14x13¾, 13¾x14***
**3153** A1136 75c multi 2.00 .65
**3154** A1137 €2.10 multi 5.50 2.75

Zaragoza Military Academy, 75th Anniv. — A1138

**2002, Mar. 15** ***Perf. 14x13¾***
**3155** A1138 25c multi .60 .25

Real Unión Soccer Team, Cent. — A1139

**2002, Mar. 22**
**3156** A1139 50c multi 1.25 .45

Stamp Day A1140

**2002, Mar. 25** ***Perf. 13¾x14***
**3157** A1140 25c multi .60 .25

**Castle Type of 2001**

Designs: 25c, Banyeres de Mariola. 50c, Soutomaior. 75c, Catalorao.

**2002, Apr. 8** **Engr.** ***Perf. 13¾x14***
**3158-3160** A1086 Set of 3 3.75 1.40

Tudela, 1200th Anniv. A1141

**2002, Apr. 12** **Photo.**
**3161** A1141 75c multi 1.90 .70

Monastery of Sant Cugat, 1000th Anniv. A1142

**2002, Apr. 12**
**3162** A1142 €1.80 multi 4.50 2.25

Luis Cernuda (1902-63), Poet A1143

**2002, May 8**
**3163** A1143 50c multi .90 .45

Dr. Federico Rubio (1827-1902) — A1144

**2002, May 8**
**3164** A1144 50c multi 1.25 .45

Europa A1145

**2002, May 9**
**3165** A1145 50c multi 1.25 .45

Reincorporation of Menorca to Spanish Crown, Bicent. — A1146

**2002, May 10**
**3166** A1146 50c multi 1.25 .45

World Equestrian Games — A1147

No. 3167: a, Carriage driving. b, Endurance (Raid). c, Dressage (Doma). d, Reining. e, Vaulting (Volteo). f, Jumping (Saltos). g, Three-day event (Completo).

Illustration reduced.

**2002, May 11** ***Perf. 12¾x13¼***
**3167** Sheet of 7 + 2 labels 9.50 9.50
***a.-e.*** A1147 25c Any single .60 .25
***f.*** A1147 75c multi 1.90 .70
***g.*** A1147 €1.80 multi 4.50 2.25

Dolores Peinado (1819-94), Character From Folk Song "La Dolores" A1148

**2002, May 31** ***Perf. 13¾x14***
**3168** A1148 50c multi 1.25 .50

Souvenir Sheet

Exfilna 2002 Natl. Philatelic Exhibition, Salamanca — A1149

No. 3169 — Plaza Mayor, Salamanca: a, 25c, West facade. b, 25c, City Hall. c, 25c, Royal Pavilion. d, €1.80, Aerial view.

**Engr. (#a-c), Litho. (#d, margin)**
**2002, July 7** ***Perf. 13¾x14***
**3169** A1149 Sheet of 4, #a-d 6.25 6.25

Iberian Airlines, 75th Anniv. A1150

Airplanes: 25c, Rohrbach R-VIII Roland. 50c, Boeing 747.

**2002, June 10** **Photo.** ***Perf. 13¾x14***
**3170-3171** A1150 Set of 2 1.90 .75

Wine Producing Regions — A1151

Grapes and map of: 25c, Rias Baixas region. 50c, Rioja region. 75c, Manzanilla — Sanlúcar de Barrameda region.

**2002** ***Perf. 14x13¼***
**3172-3174** A1151 Set of 3 3.75 1.50

Issued: 25c, 7/27; 50c, 75c, 9/20.

**Letter Writing Type of 1998**

No. 3175: a, Publication of *Don Quixote,* by Miguel de Cervantes, 1605. b, Accession to throne of King Philip IV and rise in power of Conde-Duque de Olivares, 1621. c, Rivalry of poets Francisco de Quevedo and Luis de Góngora, 1620. d, Painting of "Las Meninas" by Diego Velázquez, 1656. e, Accession to throne of King Charles II, 1665. f, Accession to throne of King Philip V, 1701. g, Accesstion to throne of Kign Ferdinand VI, 1746. h, Accession to throne of King Charles III, 1759. i, Squillaci Riots, 1766. j, Gaspar Melchor de Jovellanos, 1787. k, Accession to throne of King Charles IV, 1788. l, Appointment of Manuel de Godoy as prime minister, 1792.

**2002, Sept. 27** ***Perf. 12¾***
**3175** Sheet of 12 4.50 4.50
***a.-l.*** A1002 10c Any single .30 .20

Expiatory Temple of the Holy Family, by Architect Antonio Gaudí (1852-1926) A1152

**2002, Sept. 27** **Litho.** ***Perf. 14x13¾***
**3176** A1152 50c blue & black 1.25 .50

A1153

A1154

A1155

A1156

A1157

A1158

A1159

Paintings With Musical Instruments by Goyo Domínguez A1160

**2002, Sept. 30** ***Die Cut Perf. 13***

**Self-Adhesive**

| | | | |
|---|---|---|---|
| **3177** | Booklet pane of 8 | 5.00 | |
| *a.* | A1153 25c multi | .60 | .25 |
| *b.* | A1154 25c multi | .60 | .25 |
| *c.* | A1155 25c multi | .60 | .25 |
| *d.* | A1156 25c multi | .60 | .25 |
| *e.* | A1157 25c multi | .60 | .25 |
| *f.* | A1158 25c multi | .60 | .25 |
| *g.* | A1159 25c multi | .60 | .25 |
| *h.* | A1160 25c multi | .60 | .25 |

America Issue — Youth, Education and Literacy A1161

**2002, Oct. 14** **Photo.** ***Perf. 13¾x14***

**3178** A1161 75c multi 1.90 .75

Almanzor (Muhammad ibn Abu Amir al-Mansur, c. 938-1002), Caliph of Córdoba — A1162

**2002, Oct. 25**

**3179** A1162 75c multi 1.90 .75

Dijous Bó Fair, Mallorca — A1163

**2002, Nov. 4** ***Perf. 14x13¾***

**3180** A1163 75c multi 1.90 .75

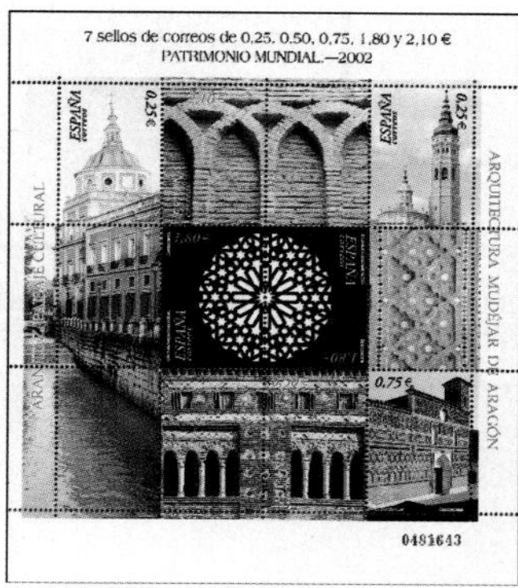
UNESCO World Heritage Sites — A1164

No. 3181 — Architectural details of: a, Aranjuez. b, Santa Maria Church, Calatayud. c, San Martin Church, Teruel. d, Santa Maria Church, Tobed. e, Santa Tecla Church, Cervera de la Cañada. f, San Pablo Church, Zaragoza.

**2002, Nov. 8**

| | | | |
|---|---|---|---|
| **3181** | A1164 Sheet of 7, #a-d, f, 2 #e, + 5 labels | 19.00 | 19.00 |
| *a.-b.* | 25c Either single | .60 | .25 |
| *c.* | 50c multi | 1.25 | .50 |
| *d.* | 75c multi | 1.90 | .75 |
| *e.* | €1.80 multi | 4.50 | 2.25 |
| *f.* | €2.10 multi | 5.25 | 2.75 |

The two examples of No. 3181e are tete-beche in the sheet.

Alcañiz Inn — A1164a

**2002, Nov. 15** ***Perf. 13¾x14***

**3182** A1164a 25c multicolored .60 .25

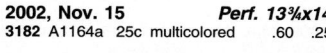

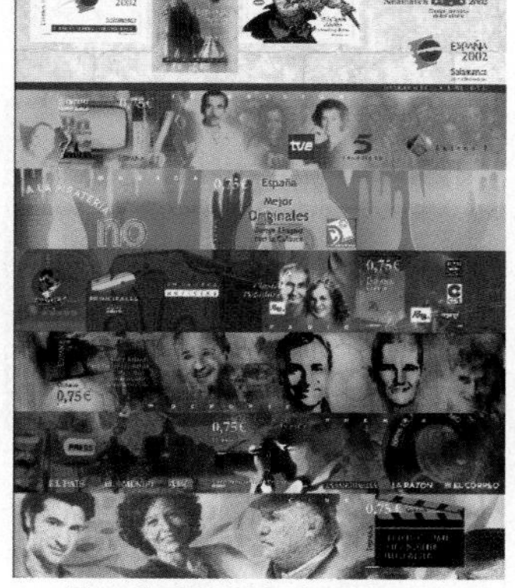
España 2002 Youth Philatelic Exhibition, Salamanca — A1165

Designs: No. 3183a, 50c, Like #3146. Nos. 3183b, 3190, 75c, Character from comic Strip "El Capitan Alatriste," by Arturo Pérez-Reverte. Nos. 3183c, 3185, 75c, Television and names of television shows. Nos. 3183d, 3189, 75c, Hand and compact disc. Nos. 3183e, 3187, 75c, Radio, musical notes and logos of Spanish radio stations. Nos. 3183f, 3188, 75c, Skier, race car, soccer ball, bicyclist and names of Spanish sports stars. Nos. 3183g, 3186, 75c, Photojournalist. Nos. 3183h, 3184, 75c, Clapboard and names of Spanish film personalities. No. 3183i, €1.80, Like #3147, vert.

**2002** **Litho.** ***Die Cut Perf. 13***

**Self-Adhesive (#3183)**

| | | | |
|---|---|---|---|
| **3183** | A1165 Sheet of 9 | 19.00 | 19.00 |
| *a.* | 50c multi | 1.25 | .50 |
| *b.-h.* | 75c Any single | 1.90 | .75 |
| *i.* | €1.80 multi | 4.50 | 2.25 |

**Souvenir Sheets**

***Perf. 13¾x14***

**3184-3190** A1165 Set of 7 11.50 11.50

Issued: No. 3183, 11/17; No. 3184, 11/18; No. 3185, 11/19; No. 3186, 11/20; No. 3187, 11/21; No. 3188, 11/22; No. 3189, 11/23; No. 3190, 11/24.

No. 3183 exists with at least three different pictures on backing paper.

San Jorge Church, Alcoy — A1166

**Litho. & Engr.**

**2002, Nov. 25** ***Perf. 14x13¾***

**3191** A1166 75c multi 1.90 .75

Compludo Forge, León A1167

**2002, Nov. 27** ***Perf. 13¾x14***

**3192** A1167 50c multi 1.25 .50

Souvenir Sheet

Stained Glass Window, Santa Maria Cathedral, Vitoria-Gasteiz — A1168

**2002, Nov. 27** ***Perf. 14x13¾***

**3193** A1168 50c multi 1.50 1.00

Crucifix, Hío A1169

Christmas A1170

**2002, Nov. 29**

**3194** A1169 25c multi .60 .25

**2002, Nov. 29** **Photo.**

Designs: 25c, Adoration of the Magi, from church altarpiece, Calzadilla de los Barros. 50c, Maternity, by Goyo Dominguez.

**3195-3196** A1170 Set of 2 1.90 .75

Opening of Somport Tunnel A1171

**2003, Jan. 17** **Photo.** ***Perf. 13¾x14***

**3197** A1171 51c multi 1.10 .55

Traditional Dress from Ansó Valley — A1172

**2003, Jan. 20** ***Perf. 14x13¾***

**3198** A1172 76c multi 1.75 .85

World Leprosy Day, 50th Anniv. — A1173

**2003, Jan. 21**

**3199** A1173 26c multi .55 .30

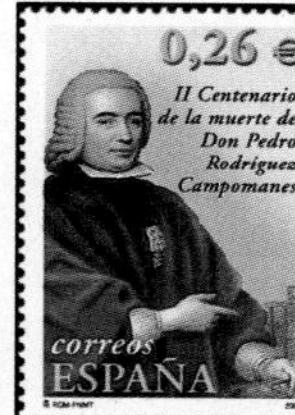
Pedro Rodríguez de Campomanes (1723-1802), Jurist — A1174

**2003, Feb. 14**

**3200** A1174 26c multi .55 .30

Juvenia 2003 Natl. Youth Philatelic Exhibition, Benissa A1175

**2003, Feb. 21** ***Perf. 13¾x14***

**3201** A1175 51c multi 1.10 .55

Práxedes Mateo Sagasta (1825-1903), Politician — A1176

**2003, Mar. 11**

**3202** A1176 26c multi .55 .30

ABC Newspaper, Cent. A1177

**2003, Mar. 17**

**3203** A1177 €2.15 multi 4.50 2.25

Nobel Prize Winners For Physiology or Medicine From Spain — A1178

No. 3204: a, Santiago Ramón y Cajal, 1906. b, Severo Ochoa, 1959.

Illustration reduced.

**Litho. & Engr.**

**2003, Mar. 20** ***Perf. 13x12¾***

| | | | | |
|---|---|---|---|---|
| **3204** | A1178 | Horiz. pair | 3.25 | 3.25 |
| *a.* | | 51c multi | 1.25 | .55 |
| *b.* | | 76c multi | 1.90 | .80 |

See Sweden No. 2460.

School of Civil Engineering, Madrid, Bicent. — A1179

Designs: 26c, Tui Bridge.
No. 3206: a, Estrecho de Puentes Dam. b, El Musel Port.

**2003, Mar. 21** **Photo.** ***Perf. 13¾x14***

**3205** A1179 26c multi .55 .30

**Souvenir Sheet**

| | | | |
|---|---|---|---|
| **3206** | Sheet of 3, #3205, 3206a, 3206b | 4.00 | 2.00 |
| *a.* | A1179 51c multi | 1.25 | .55 |
| *b.* | A1179 76c multi | 1.75 | .80 |

La Verdad Newspaper, Cent. A1180

**2003, Mar. 26**

**3207** A1180 26c multi .55 .30

Paintings by Chico Montilla A1181

No. 3208: a, La Hoz de Priego. b, Fields of Gold. c, Desfiladero de los Tornos. d, Campos de Pastrana. e, Campos de Armilla. f, Nenúfar. g, De qué Color es el Vento? h, Flores Tempranas.

***Die Cut Perf. 13***

**2003, Mar. 28** **Litho.**

**Self-Adhesive**

| | | | |
|---|---|---|---|
| **3208** | Booklet pane of 8 | 4.50 | |
| *a.-h.* | A1181 26c Any single | .55 | .30 |

Ramón José Sender (1901-82), Writer A1182

**Litho. & Engr.**

**2003, Mar. 31** ***Perf. 13½x14***

**3209** A1182 €2.15 multi 4.75 2.40

Rural Schools A1183

**2003, Apr. 3** **Photo.** ***Perf. 13¾x14***

**3210** A1183 26c multi .55 .30

Souvenir Sheet

EXFILNA 2003 Natl. Philatelic Exhibition, Granada — A1184

**Litho. (margin) & Engr. (stamp)**

**2003, Apr. 7**

**3211** A1184 €2.15 multi 4.75 2.40

Aviles, 1000th Anniv. A1185

**2003, Apr. 11** **Photo.**

**3212** A1185 51c multi 1.10 .55

Stamp Day A1186

**2003, Apr. 11**

**3213** A1186 €1.85 multi 4.00 2.00

Europa A1187

**2003, Apr. 24**

**3214** A1187 76c multi 1.75 .85

Atlético de Madrid Soccer Team, Cent. — A1188

**2003, Apr. 25** ***Perf. 14x13¾***

**3215** A1188 26c red & blue .60 .30

Roman Theater, Zaragoza A1189

**2003, May 5** ***Perf. 13¾x14***

**3216** A1189 €1.85 multi 4.25 2.10

European Year of the Disabled A1190

**2003, May 8** **Photo. & Embossed**

**3217** A1190 76c multi 1.75 .85

Castles A1191

Designs: 26c, San Felipe Castle, Ferrol. 51c, Cuellar Castle, Segovia. 76c, Montilla Castle, Córdoba.

**2003, May 17** **Engr.** ***Perf. 13¾x14***

**3218-3220** A1191 Set of 3 3.75 1.90

Battles of Ceriñola and Garellano, 500th anniv. (No. 3220).

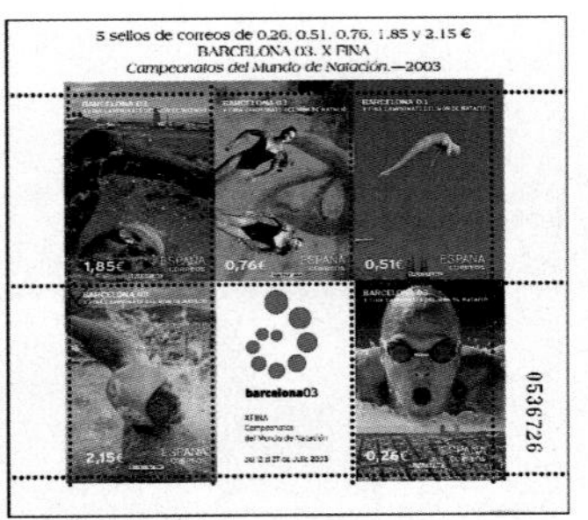

World Swimming Championships, Barcelona — A1192

**2003, May 23** **Photo.** ***Perf. 14x13¾***

| | | | | |
|---|---|---|---|---|
| **3221** | A1192 | Sheet of 5 + label | 13.00 | 6.50 |
| *a.* | | 26c Breaststroke | .60 | .30 |
| *b.* | | 51c Diving | 1.25 | .60 |
| *c.* | | 76c Synchronized swimming | 1.75 | .85 |
| *d.* | | €1.85 Freestyle | 4.25 | 2.10 |
| *e.* | | €2.15 Water polo | 5.00 | 2.50 |

Max Aub (1903-72), Writer — A1193

**2003, June 2** **Engr.**

**3222** A1193 76c black & red 1.75 .85

Sabadell Soccer Team, Cent. — A1194

**2003, June 4** **Photo.**

**3223** A1194 76c multi 1.75 .85

Juan Bravo Murillo (1803-73), Prime Minister — A1195

**2003, June 9**

**3224** A1195 51c multi 1.25 .60

Diario de Cadiz Newspaper, 136th Anniv. — A1196

**2003, June 16**

**3225** A1196 26c multi .60 .30

Souvenir Sheet

Royal Automobile Club of Spain, Cent. — A1197

**2003, June 27** ***Perf. 13¾x14***

| | | | | |
|---|---|---|---|---|
| **3226** | A1197 | Sheet of 4 | 7.75 | 4.00 |
| *a.* | | 26c 1967 Dodge Dart Barreiros | .60 | .30 |
| *b.* | | 51c 1957-73 Seat 600 | 1.10 | .55 |
| *c.* | | 76c 1907 Hispano-Suiza 20/30 HP | 1.75 | .85 |
| *d.* | | €1.85 1953 Pegaso Z-102 Berlinetta | 4.25 | 2.10 |

Chilean Postage Stamps, 150th Anniv. — A1198

**2003, July 1** **Photo.** ***Perf. 14x13¾***

**3227** A1198 76c Chile Type A1 1.75 .85

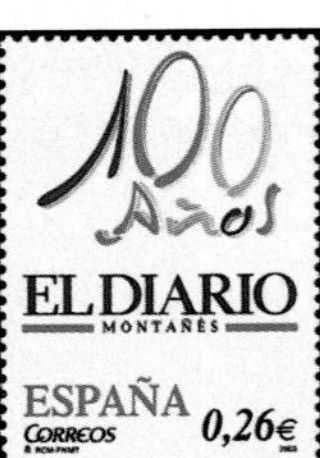

El Diario Montañés Newspaper, Cent. — A1199

**2003, July 4**

**3228** A1199 26c multi .60 .30

Santa Catalina Inn, Jaén — A1200

Illustration reduced.

**2003, July 9** ***Perf. 13x13¼***
**3229** A1200 76c multi + label 1.75 .85

Diario de Navarra Newspaper, Cent. — A1201

**2003, July 11** ***Perf. 13¾x14***
**3230** A1201 26c multi .60 .30

Seu Vella, Lleida, 800th Anniv. A1202

**2003, July 22 Engr.** ***Perf. 13¾x14***
**3231** A1202 €1.85 pur & brn blk 4.25 2.10

El Adelanto de Salamanca Newspaper, 120th Anniv. — A1203

**2003, July 24 Photo.** ***Perf. 14x13¾***
**3232** A1203 26c multi .60 .30

A1204

A1205

A1206

A1207

A1208

A1209

Paintings by Alfredo Roldán
A1210 A1211

***Die Cut Perf. 13***
**2003, July 28** **Litho.**
**Self-Adhesive**

| | | | |
|---|---|---|---|
| **3233** | Booklet pane of 8 | 5.00 | |
| *a.* | A1204 A multi | .60 | .30 |
| *b.* | A1205 A multi | .60 | .30 |
| *c.* | A1206 A multi | .60 | .30 |
| *d.* | A1207 A multi | .60 | .30 |
| *e.* | A1208 A multi | .60 | .30 |
| *f.* | A1209 A multi | .60 | .30 |
| *g.* | A1210 A multi | .60 | .30 |
| *h.* | A1211 A multi | .60 | .30 |

Nos. 3233a-3233g each sold for 26c on day of issue.

El Correo Gallego Newspaper, 125th Anniv. — A1212

**2003, Aug. 1 Photo.** ***Perf. 13¾x14***
**3234** A1212 26c multi .60 .30

El Comercio de Gijón Newspaper, 125th Anniv. — A1213

**2003, Sept. 2**
**3235** A1213 26c multi .60 .30

Holy Cross of Caravaca A1214

**2003, Sept. 4** ***Perf. 14x13¾***
**3236** A1214 76c multi 1.75 .85

Holy Year 2003.

World Sailing Championships, Gulf of Cádiz — A1215

**2003, Sept. 9** ***Perf. 13¾x14***
**3237** A1215 76c multi 1.75 .85

Wine of Penedés Region — A1216

Wine of Montilla-Moriles Region — A1217

Wine of Valdepeñas Region — A1218

Wine of Bierzo Region — A1219

**2003** ***Perf. 14x13¾***

| | | | | |
|---|---|---|---|---|
| **3238** | A1216 | 26c multi | .60 | .30 |
| **3239** | A1217 | 51c multi | 1.25 | .60 |
| **3240** | A1218 | 76c multi | 1.75 | .90 |
| **3241** | A1219 | €1.85 multi | 4.50 | 2.25 |
| | *Nos. 3238-3241 (4)* | | 8.10 | 4.05 |

Issued: 26c, 10/30; others, 9/22.

Academy of Military Engineering, Bicent. — A1220

**2003, Sept. 24** ***Perf. 13¾x14***
**3242** A1220 51c multi 1.25 .60

Souvenir Sheet

Santa María Cathedral, León, 700th Anniv — A1221

**2003, Sept. 26** **Litho. & Engr.**
**3243** A1221 76c multi 2.00 1.00

Souvenir Sheet

Royal Geographical Society, Cent. — A1222

**2003, Oct. 1**
**3244** A1222 €1.85 multi 4.75 2.50

Trees — A1223

Designs: 26c, Ficus macrophylla. 51c, Quercus rober.

**2003, Oct. 3 Photo.** ***Perf. 14x13¾***
**3245-3246** A1223 Set of 2 1.90 .95

School of Aeronautical Engineering, Madrid, 75th Anniv. — A1224

**2003, Oct. 6** ***Perf. 13¾x14***
**3247** A1224 51c multi 1.25 .60

America Issue - Rail Transport A1225

**2003, Oct. 14**
**3248** A1225 76c multi 1.75 .90

El Viejo y el Pájaro, by Luis Seoane (1910-79) A1226

**2003, Oct. 17** ***Perf. 14x13¾***
**3249** A1226 €1.85 multi 4.50 2.25

El Correo de Andalucia Newspaper, Cent. — A1227

Faro de Vigo Newspaper, 150th Anniv. — A1228

La Voz de Galicia Newspaper, 121st Anniv. — A1229

**2003, Nov. 3** ***Perf. 13¾x14***

**3250** A1227 26c multi .60 .30
**3251** A1228 26c multi .60 .30
**3252** A1229 26c multi .60 .30
*Nos. 3250-3252 (3)* 1.80 .90

Camilo José Cela (1916-2002), 1989 Nobel Laureate in Literature A1230

**2003, Nov. 10** ***Perf. 14x13¾***

**3253** A1230 26c multi .65 .30

Parade of the Magi — A1231

Nativity, by Raquel Fariñas — A1232

**2003, Nov. 10**

**3254** A1231 26c multi .65 .30
**3255** A1232 51c multi 1.25 .60

Christmas.

España 2004 Intl. Philatelic Exhibition A1233

Designs: 76c, Exhibition emblem. €1.85, Exhibition venue, Valencia.

**2003, Nov. 14** ***Perf. 13¾x14***

**3256** A1233 76c multi 1.90 .95

**Souvenir Sheet**

**3257** A1233 €1.85 multi 4.50 2.25

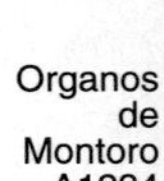

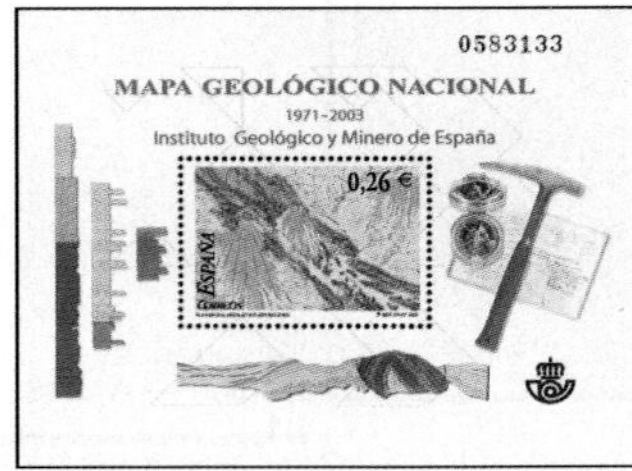


Organos de Montoro A1234

**2003, Nov. 17**

**3258** A1234 51c multi 1.25 .60

Souvenir Sheet

Completion of National Geological Map — A1235

**2003, Nov. 24**

**3259** A1235 26c multi .65 .30

Souvenir Sheets

Constitution, 25th Anniv. — A1236

Various photos or paintings with inscriptions in lower left corner of: No. 3260, 26c, RCM-FNMT. No. 3261, 26c, Miguel Torner. No. 3262, 26c, R. Seco. No. 3263, 26c, Araceli Alarcón. No. 3264, 26c, Galicia. No. 3265, 26c, Fesanpe. No. 3266, 26c, J. Carrero. No. 3267, 26c, J. Carrero, vert. No. 3268, 26c, Goyo Domínguez, vert. No. 3269, 26c, Juan Bautista Nieto, vert.

**2003, Dec. 5** ***Perf. 13¾x14, 14x13¾***

**3260-3269** A1236 Set of 10 6.50 3.25

Powered Flight, Cent. A1237

**2003, Dec. 17 Engr.** ***Perf. 13¾x14***

**3270** A1237 76c blue & brown 1.90 .95

**King Juan Carlos Type of 2001 With Euro Denominations Only**

**2004, Jan. 2 Photo.** ***Perf. 12¾x13¼***

**3271** A1091 2c sil & brt pink .20 .20
**3272** A1091 27c sil & blue .70 .35
*a.* Sheet of 4 + label 2.80 2.80
**3273** A1091 52c sil & bister brn 1.25 .65
**3274** A1091 77c sil & dull grn 1.90 .95
*Nos. 3271-3274 (4)* 4.05 2.15

No. 3272a issued 5/25.

Roman Art of Jaca — A1238

No. 3275: a, Grate. b, Huesca Cathedral Bible page. c, Painting of two apostles. d, Cloister, Monastery of San Juan de la Peña. e, Coins. f, Capital, Church of Santiago de Jaca. g, Detail of sarcophagus of Doña Sancha. h, Wooden carved crucifix.

***Serpentine Die Cut 13***

**2004, Jan. 16 Litho.**

**Self-Adhesive**

**3275** Booklet pane of 8 5.75
*a.-h.* A1238 A Any single .70 .35

Nos. 3275a-3275h each sold for 27c on day of issue.

Souvenir Sheets

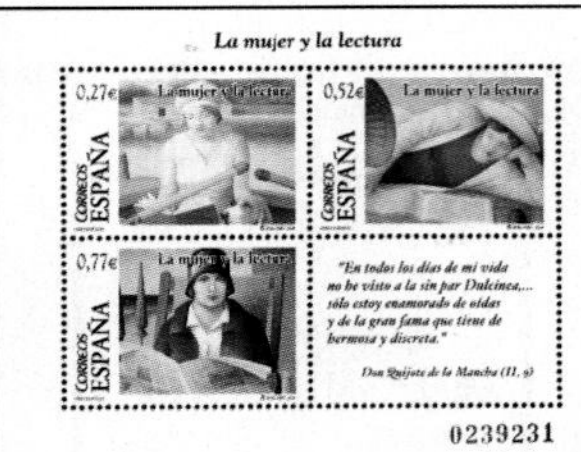


Paintings of Women Reading by Fabio Hurtado (1960- ) — A1239

No. 3276: a, 27c, Woman reading book in rowboat. b, 52c, Woman with head on hand reading book. c, 77c, Woman reading newspaper.

No. 3277: a, 27c, Woman with legs crossed reading book. b, 52c. Woman on back reading book. c, 77c, Woman with black hat reading book.

**2004, Jan. 23 Photo.** ***Perf. 13¾x14***

**Sheets of 3, #a-c, + label**

**3276-3277** A1239 Set of 2 8.00 4.50

Campaign Against Cancer A1240

**2004, Feb. 2**

**3278** A1240 27c multi .70 .35

"La Terrona" Oak Tree, Zarza de Montánchez A1241

**2004, Feb. 6** ***Perf. 14x13¾***

**3279** A1241 52c multi 1.40 .70

World Rowing Championships, Banyoles — A1242

**2004, Feb. 9** ***Perf. 13¾x14***

**3280** A1242 77c multi 1.90 .95

School Letter Writing Campaign — A1243

No. 3281 — Scenes from comic strip Trazo de Tiza, by Miguelanxo Prado: a, Woman on cliff. b, Sailboat. c, Woman near injured gull. d, Aerial view of lighthouse.

**2004, Feb. 10**

**3281** A1243 27c Sheet of 4, #a-d, + 12 labels 2.75 1.40

Souvenir Sheet

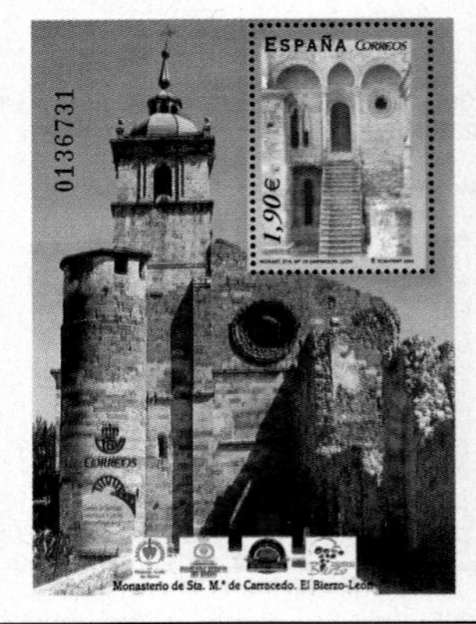


Santa María de Carracedo Monastery, Bierzo — A1244

**2004, Mar. 8** ***Perf. 14x13¾***

**3282** A1244 €1.90 multi 4.75 2.40

36th Chess Olympiad A1245

**2004, Mar. 18** ***Perf. 13¾x14***

**3283** A1245 77c multi 1.90 .95

Clocks — A1246

No. 3284: a, 27c, Clock with Muse Calliope, 19th cent. b, 52c, Clock with Cupid, 18th cent. c, 77c, Clock with Empress María Luisa, child and harp, 19th cent. d, €1.90, Clock with Venus and Cupid, 18th cent.

*Perf. 13¼x12¾*

**2004, Mar. 31 Litho. & Engr.**

**3284** A1246 Sheet of 4, #a-d 8.50 4.25

Diario de Burgos Newspaper, 113th Anniv. — A1247

**2004, Apr. 1 Photo. *Perf. 14x13¾***

**3285** A1247 27c multi .65 .35

March 11, 2004 Terrorist Attacks — A1248

**2004, Apr. 2 Litho. *Perf. 14x13¾***

**3286** A1248 27c black & gray .65 .35

**Booklet Stamp**

**Self-Adhesive**

**Size: 22x33mm**

***Serpentine Die Cut 13***

**3287** A1248 A black & gray .65 .35

*a.* Booklet pane of 8 5.25

No. 3287 sold for 27c on day of issue.

Egg Painting Festival, Pola de Siero A1249

**2004, Apr. 5 Photo. *Perf. 13¾***

**3288** A1249 27c multi .65 .35

Miniature Sheet

Paintings of Shawls, by Soledad Fernández — A1250

**2004, Apr. 7 *Perf. 14x13¾***

**3289** A1250 Sheet of 4 8.50 8.50

*a.* 27c Shawl, shell .65 .35

*b.* 52c Shawl, hands 1.25 .65

*c.* 77c Shawl, flowers 1.90 .95

*d.* €1.90 Shawl on chair 4.50 2.25

Department of Technical Engineering of Public Works, 150th Anniv. — A1251

**2004, Apr. 15 *Perf. 13¾x14***

**3290** A1251 52c multi 1.25 .60

Cable Inglés Loading Pier, Almadrabillas, Cent. — A1252

**2004, Apr. 27**

**3291** A1252 52c multi 1.25 .60

Europa — A1253

**2004, Apr. 29 *Perf. 14x13¾***

**3292** A1253 77c multi 1.90 .95

Expansion of the European Union A1254

**2004, May 3 *Perf. 13¾x14***

**3293** A1254 52c multi 1.25 .60

Self-Portrait with the Neck of Rafael, by Salvador Dali (1904-89) — A1255

**2004, May 11 Photo.**

**3294** A1255 77c multi 1.90 .95

FIFA (Fédération Internationale de Football Association), Cent. — A1256

**2004, May 21**

**3295** A1256 77c multi 1.90 .95

Wedding of Prince Felipe and Letizia Ortiz Rocasolano — A1257

**2004, May 22**

**3296** A1257 27c multi .65 .30

España 2004 Intl. Philatelic Exhibition — A1258

No. 3297 — Music: a, Vicente Martín y Soler (1754-1806), opera composer. b, Band instruments.

Illustration reduced.

**2004, May 23 Photo. *Perf. 13¾x14***

**3297** A1258 Horiz. pair + central label 1.90 1.90

*a.* 27c multi .65 .30

*b.* 52c multi 1.25 .60

Miniature Sheet

España 2004 Intl. Philatelic Exhibition — A1259

No. 3298 — Royalty: a, Prince Felipe and Letizia Ortiz Rocasolano. b, Prince Felipe. c, King Juan Carlos and Queen Sofia.

**Litho., Litho. & Engr. (#3298c)**

**2004, May 24 *Perf. 13¾x14***

**3298** A1259 Sheet of 3 + 3 labels 17.00 17.00

*a.* 27c multi .65 .30

*b.* 77c multi 1.90 .95

*c.* €6 multi 14.00 7.00

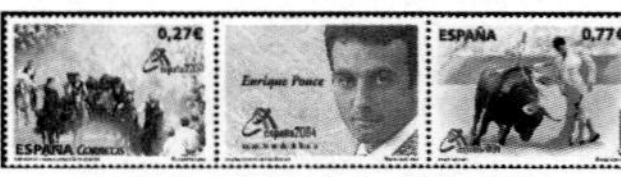

España 2004 Intl. Philatelic Exhibition — A1260

No. 3299 — Festival of the Bulls, Valencia: a, Running of the bulls. b, Bullfighter.

Illustration reduced.

**2004, May 26 Photo. *Perf. 13¾x14***

**3299** A1260 Horiz. pair + central label 2.50 2.50

*a.* 27c multi .60 .30

*b.* 77c multi 1.90 .95

Miniature Sheet

España 2004 Intl. Philatelic Exhibition — A1261

No. 3300 — Sports: a, Tennis. b, Motorcycle racing. c, Golf.

**2004, May 27 *Perf. 12¾x13***

**3300** A1261 Sheet of 3 + 3 labels 7.00 7.00

*a.* 35c multi .85 .40

*b.* 52c multi 1.25 .65

*c.* €1.90 multi 4.50 2.25

España 2004 Intl. Philatelic Exhibition — A1262

No. 3301 — The Sea: a, Yacht Bravo España. b, Valencia skyline.

Illustration reduced.

**2004, May 28 Photo. *Perf. 13¾x14***

**3301** A1262 Horiz. pair + central label 3.25 3.25

*a.* 52c multi 1.25 .65

*b.* 77c multi 1.90 .95

Diario de Valencia Newspaper, 214th Anniv. — A1263

**2004, May 29**

**3302** A1263 27c multi .65 .30

Jacobean Holy Year — A1264

**2004, June 11 *Perf. 14x13¾***

**3303** A1264 52c multi 1.25 .65

Lerma Inn A1265

**2004, July 18 *Perf. 13¾x14***

**3304** A1265 52c multi 1.25 .65

Castles A1266

Designs: 27c, Granadilla Fortress, Granadilla. 52c, Aguas Mansas Castle, Agoncillo. 77c, Mota Fortress, Alcalá la Real. €1.90, Villafuerte de Esgueva Castle, Villafuerte de Esgueva, vert.

**2004 Engr. *Perf. 13¾x14, 14x13¾***

**3305-3308** A1266 Set of 4 8.50 4.25

Issued: 27c, 77c, 7/1; 52c, €1.90, 7/19.

Anchor Museum, Salinas — A1267

**2004, July 16 Photo. *Perf. 14x13¾***

**3309** A1267 €1.90 multi 4.75 2.40

Ceramics in Paintings by Antonio Miguel González — A1268

No. 3310: a, Jar with two handles and lid, oranges. b, Goblet, amphora and jar. c, Pitcher with handle at top, bread, garlic. d, Decorated pitcher with side handle. e, Pitcher with handle at top, pentagonal dodecahedron, bread, tomatoes. f, Vase. g, Pitcher with side handle, plate of pears, grapes. h, Jar with flower design and lid.

***Serpentine Die Cut 13***

**2004, July 22** **Litho.**

**Self-Adhesive**

| | | | |
|---|---|---|---|
| **3310** | Booklet pane of 8 | 5.25 | |
| *a.-h.* | A1268 A Any single | .65 | .35 |

Nos. 3310a-3310h sold for 27c on day of issue.

Círculo Oscense Building, Huesca, Cent. — A1269

**2004, July 23** **Photo.** ***Perf. 13¾x14***
**3311** A1269 52c multi 1.25 .65

Our Lady of the Snows Festival, Vitoria-Gasteiz, 50th Anniv. — A1270

**2004, July 30** ***Perf. 14x13¾***
**3312** A1270 27c multi .65 .30

Ribeiro Wine Grapes — A1271

Wine of Malaga — A1272

**2004, Sept. 1** ***Perf. 14x13¾***
**3313** A1271 27c multi .70 .35
**3314** A1272 52c multi 1.25 .65

First Philippines Stamp, 150th Anniv. — A1273

**2004, Sept. 6** ***Perf. 13¾x14***
**3315** A1273 77c Philippines #1 1.90 .95

Heraldo de Aragón Newspaper, 109th Anniv. — A1274

**2004, Sept. 20** ***Perf. 14x13¾***
**3316** A1274 27c multi .70 .35

Nautical Astronomy, 250th Anniv. — A1275

**2004, Sept. 24** ***Perf. 13¾x14***
**3317** A1275 €1.90 multi 4.75 2.40

Souvenir Sheet

EXFILNA 2004 National Philatelic Exhibition, Valladolid — A1276

**Litho. & Engr.**

**2004, Oct. 1** ***Perf. 14x13¾***
**3318** A1276 €1.90 multi 4.75 4.75

Buildings in China and Spain — A1277

Designs: 52c, Park Guell, Barcelona. 77c, Jinmao Tower, Shanghai.

**2004, Oct. 8** **Photo.**
**3319-3320** A1277 Set of 2 3.25 1.60

See People's Republic of China Nos. 3406-3407.

America Issue — Environmental Protection — A1278

**2004, Oct. 14** ***Perf. 13¾x14***
**3321** A1278 77c multi 2.00 1.00

CERN (European Organization for Nuclear Research), 50th Anniv. — A1279

**2004, Oct. 19**
**3322** A1279 €1.90 multi 5.00 2.50

Nature — A1280

Designs: 27c, Cíes Islands. 52c, Ebro Delta Natural Park, horiz. 77c, Taburiente Caldera National Park, horiz.

**2004, Oct. 21** ***Perf. 14x13¾, 13¾x14***
**3323-3325** A1280 Set of 3 4.25 2.10

Taburiente Caldera National Park, 50th anniv. (#3325).

First Registered Letter, 400th Anniv. — A1281

**2004, Oct. 22** ***Perf. 13¾x14***
**3326** A1281 77c multi 2.00 1.00

Stamp Day.

Ebre Observatory, Cent. — A1282

**2004, Nov. 5**
**3327** A1282 €1.90 multi 5.00 2.50

Start of Reign of Alfonso I, King of Aragon, 900th Anniv. — A1283

**Litho. & Engr.**

**2004, Nov. 12** ***Perf. 14x13¾***
**3328** A1283 €1.90 multi 5.00 2.50

Christmas A1284

Designs: 27c, Birth of Christ, 18th cent. Neapolitan nativity scene. 52c, Nativity, by Juan Manuel Cossío.

**2004, Nov. 17** **Photo.**
**3329-3330** A1284 Set of 2 2.25 1.10

Queen Isabella I (1451-1504) A1285

**2004, Nov. 26**
**3331** A1285 €2.19 multi 6.00 3.00

Royal Expedition for Smallpox Vaccination in Latin America and Philippines, Bicent. — A1286

**2004, Nov. 30** **Engr.** ***Perf. 13¾x14***
**3332** A1286 77c brown 2.10 1.10

Souvenir Sheet

Stained Glass, Toledo Cathedral — A1287

**Litho. & Engr.**

**2004, Dec. 3** ***Perf. 14x13¾***
**3333** A1287 €1.90 multi 5.25 5.25

Arms of the Prince of Asturias A1288

**2004, Dec. 23** **Photo.** ***Perf. 13¾x14***
**3334** A1288 27c multi .75 .40

Best wishes for Prince Felipe's marriage to Letizia Ortiz Rocasolano on May 22, 2004.

A1289

A1290

A1291

A1292

A1293 A1294

Paintings of Circus Performers by Manolo Elices
A1295 A1296

**2005, Jan. 3 Litho. *Die Cut Perf. 13***
**Self-Adhesive**

| | | | | |
|---|---|---|---|---|
| **3335** | | Booklet pane of 8 | 6.00 | |
| *a.* | A1289 | A multi | .75 | .35 |
| *b.* | A1290 | A multi | .75 | .35 |
| *c.* | A1291 | A multi | .75 | .35 |
| *d.* | A1292 | A multi | .75 | .35 |
| *e.* | A1293 | A multi | .75 | .35 |
| *f.* | A1294 | A multi | .75 | .35 |
| *g.* | A1295 | A multi | .75 | .35 |
| *h.* | A1296 | A multi | .75 | .35 |

Nos. 3335a-3335h each sold for 28c on day of issue.

Signing of European Union Constitutional Treaty — A1297

**2005, Jan. 12 Photo. *Perf. 13¾x14***

| | | | | |
|---|---|---|---|---|
| **3336** | A1297 | 28c multi | .75 | .35 |

**King Juan Carlos Type of 2001 With Euro Denominations Only**

**2005, Jan. 14 Photo. *Perf. 13***

| | | | | | |
|---|---|---|---|---|---|
| **3337** | A1091 | 28c | sil & ol grn | .75 | .35 |
| **3338** | A1091 | 35c | sil & orange | .90 | .45 |
| **3339** | A1091 | 40c | sil & blue gray | 1.00 | .50 |
| **3340** | A1091 | 53c | sil & dull pur | 1.40 | .70 |
| **3341** | A1091 | 78c | sil & red | 2.00 | 1.00 |
| **3342** | A1091 | €1.95 | sil & yel brn | 5.00 | 2.50 |
| **3343** | A1091 | €2.21 | sil & ol brn | 5.75 | 2.75 |
| | *Nos. 3337-3343 (7)* | | | 16.80 | 8.25 |

Ahuehuete Tree, Retiro Park, Madrid — A1298

**2005, Jan. 17 Photo. *Perf. 14x13¾***

| | | | | |
|---|---|---|---|---|
| **3344** | A1298 | 78c multi | 2.00 | 1.00 |

Road Safety A1299

Blood Donation A1300

**2005, Jan. 26 *Perf. 13¾x14***

| | | | | |
|---|---|---|---|---|
| **3345** | A1299 | 28c multi | .75 | .35 |
| **3346** | A1300 | 53c multi | 1.40 | .70 |

University of Seville, 500th Anniv. — A1301

**2005, Feb. 3 Engr. *Perf. 14x13¾***

| | | | | |
|---|---|---|---|---|
| **3347** | A1301 | 28c brn & claret | .75 | .35 |

First Royal Spanish Pharmacopoeia, 500th Anniv. — A1302

**2005, Feb. 3 Litho. & Engr.**

| | | | | |
|---|---|---|---|---|
| **3348** | A1302 | 28c multi | .75 | .35 |

Miniature Sheet

Children's Songs and Stories — A1303

No. 3349: a, Al Levantar una Lancha. b, Aquí te Espero. c, Estaba la Pájara Pinta. d, Cuatro Esquinitas. e, El Patio de mi Casa. f, Pero Mira Cómo Beben. g, Los Pollitos Cantan. h, Para Entrar en Clase.

**2005, Feb. 14 Photo.**

| | | | | |
|---|---|---|---|---|
| **3349** | A1303 | Sheet of 8 | 11.00 | 11.00 |
| *a.-c.* | | 28c Any single | .75 | .40 |
| *d.-f.* | | 53c Any single | 1.40 | .70 |
| *g.-h.* | | 78c Either single | 2.10 | 1.10 |

Juvenia 2005 Youth Stamp Exhibition, Tordera — A1304

**2005, Feb. 25 *Perf. 14x13¾***

| | | | | |
|---|---|---|---|---|
| **3350** | A1304 | 28c multi | .75 | .35 |

Sevilla FC (Seville Soccer Team), Cent. A1305

Real Sporting de Gijón Soccer Team, Cent. — A1306

15th Mediterranean Games, Almería — A1307

**2005, Mar. 1 *Perf. 13¾x14***

| | | | | |
|---|---|---|---|---|
| **3351** | A1305 | 35c red | .95 | .45 |

***Perf. 14x13¾***

| | | | | |
|---|---|---|---|---|
| **3352** | A1306 | 40c multi | 1.10 | .55 |
| **3353** | A1307 | 78c multi | 2.10 | 1.10 |
| | *Nos. 3351-3353 (3)* | | 4.15 | 2.10 |

Europa A1308

**2005, Apr. 15 *Perf. 13¾x14***

| | | | | |
|---|---|---|---|---|
| **3354** | A1308 | 53c multi | 1.40 | .70 |

Juan Valera (1824-1905), Writer and Diplomat A1309

**2005, Apr. 18 Engr. *Perf. 14x13¾***

| | | | | |
|---|---|---|---|---|
| **3355** | A1309 | €2.21 vio brn & blue | 5.75 | 2.75 |

Souvenir Sheet

Publication of Don Quixote, 400th Anniv. — A1310

Various scenes from book.

**2005, Apr. 22**

| | | | | |
|---|---|---|---|---|
| **3356** | A1310 | Sheet of 4 | 10.00 | 10.00 |
| *a.* | | 28c black | .75 | .35 |
| *b.* | | 53c black | 1.40 | .70 |
| *c.* | | 78c black | 2.00 | 1.00 |
| *d.* | | €2.21 black | 5.75 | 2.75 |

Telegraphy in Spain, 150th Anniv. — A1311

**2005, Apr. 26 Photo. *Perf. 13¾x14***

| | | | | |
|---|---|---|---|---|
| **3357** | A1311 | 28c multi | .75 | .35 |

Intl. Year of Physics — A1312

***Die Cut Perf. 13¼***

**2005, Apr. 28 Litho.**

**Self-Adhesive**

| | | | | |
|---|---|---|---|---|
| **3358** | A1312 | 28c multi | .75 | .35 |

Souvenir Sheet

Fans — A1313

No. 3359 — Fan depicting: a, Flowers. b, Madrid street scene. c, Nymphs.

**2005, May 9 Photo. *Perf. 13¾***

| | | | | |
|---|---|---|---|---|
| **3359** | A1313 | Sheet of 3 + label | 4.00 | 4.00 |
| *a.* | | 28c multi | .70 | .35 |
| *b.* | | 53c multi | 1.40 | .70 |
| *c.* | | 78c multi | 1.90 | .95 |

Diario Palentino Newspaper, 124th Anniv. — A1314

Ultima Hora Newspaper, 112th Anniv. — A1315

Diario de Ibiza Newspaper, 112th Anniv. — A1316

**2005, May 16** *Perf. 14x13¾*
**3360** A1314 78c multi 1.90 .95

*Perf. 13¾x14*

**3361** A1315 €1.95 multi 4.75 2.40
**3362** A1316 €2.21 multi 5.50 2.75
*Nos. 3360-3362 (3)* 12.15 6.10

Inn, Oropesa A1317

**2005, June 13 Engr.** *Perf. 13¾x14*
**3363** A1317 €1.95 brown 4.75 2.40

Souvenir Sheet

EXFILNA 2005, Alicante — A1318

**Litho. & Engr.**

**2005, June 20** *Perf. 14x13¾*
**3364** A1318 €2.21 multi 5.50 2.75

Castles A1319

Designs: 78c, Alcaudete Castle. €1.95, Valderrobres Castle. €2.21, Molina de Aragón Castle.

**2005, July 4 Engr.** *Perf. 13¾x14*
**3365-3367** A1319 Set of 3 12.00 6.00

Fingerprint Registration for Newborns — A1320

**2005, July 11** **Photo.**
**3368** A1320 28c multi .70 .35

Stamp Day — A1321

*Die Cut Perf. 13*

**2005, Sept. 1** **Litho.**

**Self-Adhesive**

**3369** A1321 28c multi .70 .35

Nuestra Señora de la Asuncion Church, Pont de Suert A1322

**2005, Sept. 7 Photo.** *Perf. 13¾x14*
**3370** A1322 28c multi .70 .35

Lunnispark Building A1323

Lucho A1324

Lupita in Bed — A1325

*Die Cut Perf. 13*

**2005, Sept. 16** **Litho.**

**Self-Adhesive**

| | | | |
|---|---|---|---|
| **3371** | Booklet pane of 8 | 5.75 | |
| *a.* | A1323 28c shown | .70 | .35 |
| *b.* | A1324 28c shown | .70 | .35 |
| *c.* | A1323 28c Green building | .70 | .35 |
| *d.* | A1324 28c Lulila | .70 | .35 |
| *e.* | A1324 28c Lupita | .70 | .35 |
| *f.* | A1325 28c shown | .70 | .35 |
| *g.* | A1324 28c Lubliú | .70 | .35 |
| *h.* | A1323 28c Orange building | .70 | .35 |

Los Lunnis children's television show.

World Cycling Championships, Madrid — A1326

**2005, Sept. 20 Photo.** *Perf. 13¾x14*
**3372** A1326 78c multi 1.90 .95

España 2006 World Philatelic Exhibition, Malaga A1327

**2005 Photo.** *Perf. 13¾x14*
**3373** A1327 53c multi 1.40 .70

Gardens A1328

No. 3374: a, Gardens of La Granja de San Ildefonso, Segovia. b, Bagh-e-Shahzadeh Garden, Kerman, Iran.

**2005, Oct. 10**

| | | | |
|---|---|---|---|
| **3374** | Horiz. pair + central label | 7.25 | 3.75 |
| *a.* | A1328 78c multi | 1.90 | .95 |
| *b.* | A1328 €2.21 multi | 5.25 | 2.60 |

See Iran No. 2912.

15th Iberoamerican Summit, Salamanca — A1329

**2005, Oct. 13**
**3375** A1329 78c multi 1.90 .95

America Issue, Fight Against Poverty A1330

**2005, Oct. 14** *Perf. 12¾*
**3376** A1330 78c multi 1.90 .95

La Orotava, 500th Anniv. — A1331

**2005, Oct. 20** *Perf. 14x13¾*
**3377** A1331 €2.21 multi 5.50 2.75

Colonial Postage Stamps for Cuba and Philippines, 150th Anniv. — A1332

**2005, Oct. 20** *Perf. 13¾x14*
**3378** A1332 €2.21 multi 5.50 2.75

Prince of Asturias Awards, 25th Anniv. — A1333

Illustration reduced.

**2005, Oct. 20** *Perf. 13¼x13*
**3379** A1333 28c multi + label .70 .35

Printed in sheets of 8 stamps + 8 different labels.

Miniature Sheet

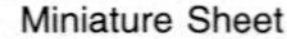

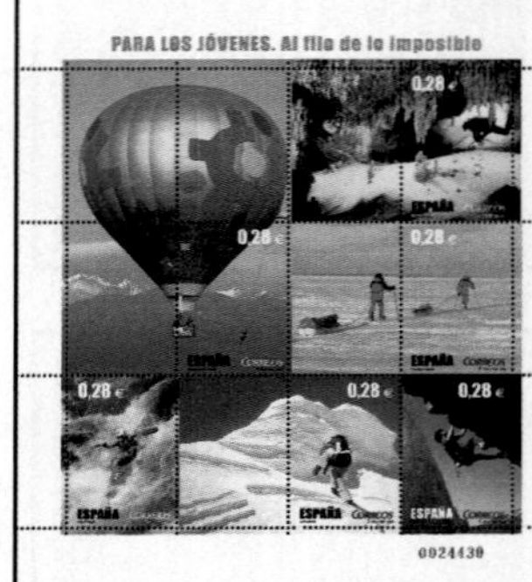

Scenes from Television Show "Al Filo de lo Imposible" — A1334

No. 3380: a, Underwater cave explorers. b, Hot-air balloon with man on rope outside of gondola. c, Man pulling sled. d, Kayaker. e, Climber on snowy mountain. f, Rock climber.

**2005, Oct. 24** *Perf. 14x13¾*

| | | | |
|---|---|---|---|
| **3380** | A1334 Sheet of 6 + 6 labels | 4.25 | 2.10 |
| *a.-f.* | 28c Any single | .70 | .35 |

See No. 3398.

A1335

Christmas A1336

**2005, Oct. 31**
**3381** A1335 28c multi .70 .35
**3382** A1336 53c multi 1.25 .65

Souvenir Sheet

Stained Glass Window, Avila Cathedral — A1337

**2005, Nov. 2** **Litho. & Engr.**
**3383** A1337 €2.21 multi 5.25 2.60

Euromediterranean Summit, Barcelona — A1338

**2005, Nov. 3 Photo. *Perf. 13¾x14***

**3384** A1338 53c multi 1.25 .65

Queen Juana of Castile (1479-1555) A1339

**2005, Nov. 4 *Perf. 14x13¾***

**3385** A1339 28c multi .70 .35

Parliament of Toro, 500th anniv.

Toys — A1340

No. 3386: a, Marionettes. b, Tops. c, Toy car. d, Toy truck. e, Doll. f, Container of marbles. g, Toy horse and cart. h, Toy motorcycle.

**2006, Jan. 2 Litho. *Die Cut Perf. 13***

**Self-Adhesive**

| | | | |
|---|---|---|---|
| **3386** | Booklet pane of 8 | 5.50 | |
| ***a.-h.*** | A1340 A Any single | .65 | .35 |

Nos. 3386a-3386h each sold for 28c on day of issue.

**King Juan Carlos Type of 2001 With Euro Denominations Only**

**2006 Photo. *Perf. 12¾x13¼***

| | | | | |
|---|---|---|---|---|
| **3387** | A1091 | 29c sil & brown | .70 | .35 |
| **3388** | A1091 | 57c sil & org | 1.40 | .70 |
| **3389** | A1091 | €2.26 sil & pur | 5.50 | 2.75 |
| **3390** | A1091 | €2.33 sil & claret | 5.50 | 2.75 |
| **3391** | A1091 | €2.39 sil & dull grn | 5.75 | 2.75 |
| | | *Nos. 3387-3391 (5)* | 18.85 | 9.30 |

Issued: 29c, 57c, 2/1; €2.26, 1/5; €2.33, €2.39, 2/13.

Carnation — A1341

***Die Cut Perf. 13***

**2006, Jan. 20 Litho.**

**Self-Adhesive**

**3392** A1341 28c multi .70 .35

No. 3392 was printed in sheets of 10, which were bound in booklets of 10 sheets.

Bank of Spain, 150th Anniv. — A1342

**2006, Jan. 27 Engr. *Perf. 14x13¾***

**3393** A1342 78c brown & black 1.90 .95

Cypress Tree, La Anunciada Convent, Villafranca del Bierzo — A1343

**2006, Jan. 30 Photo.**

**3394** A1343 53c multi 1.40 .70

Sparrow — A1344

***Die Cut Perf. 13***

**2006, Feb. 1 Litho.**

**Self-Adhesive**

**3395** A1344 A multi .70 .35

No. 3395 sold for 29p on day of issue, and was printed in sheets of 10 which were bound in booklets of 10 sheets.

Intl. Year of Deserts and Desertification — A1345

**2006, Feb. 6 Photo. *Perf. 13¾x14***

**3396** A1345 29c multi .70 .35

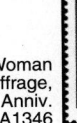

Woman Suffrage, 75th Anniv. A1346

**2006, Mar. 8**

**3397** A1346 29c blue & sepia .70 .35

**"Al Filo de lo Imposible" Type of 2005**

No. 3398: a, Cyclists. b, Man in desert. c, Parachutist. d, Kayakers. e, Rafters. f, Waterfall rock climbers.

**2006, Mar. 22 *Perf. 14x13¾***

| | | | |
|---|---|---|---|
| **3398** A1334 | Sheet of 6 + 6 labels | 12.00 | 6.00 |
| ***a.*** | 29c multi | .70 | .35 |
| ***b.*** | 38c multi | .95 | .45 |
| ***c.*** | 41c multi | 1.00 | .50 |
| ***d.*** | 57c multi | 1.40 | .70 |
| ***e.*** | 78c multi | 1.90 | .95 |
| ***f.*** | €2.39 multi | 6.00 | 3.00 |

Goldfinch A1347 — Strelitzia Flower A1348

**2006, Apr. 1 Litho. *Die Cut Perf. 13***

| | | | | |
|---|---|---|---|---|
| **3399** | A1347 | 29c multi | .70 | .35 |
| **3400** | A1348 | 38c multi | .95 | .45 |

Nos. 3399-3400 were each printed in sheets of 10, which were bound in booklets of 10 sheets.

Civic Values — A1349

Designs: No. 3401, 29c, Water conservation. No. 3402, 29c, Man with "No Drugs" balloons. 38c, Social Security and Labor inspectors, cent., horiz. 57c, Fight against human trafficking, horiz.

***Perf. 14x13¾, 13¾x14***

**2006, Apr. 4 Photo.**

**3401-3404** A1349 Set of 4 3.75 1.90

Diario de Pontevedra Newspaper, 117th Anniv. — A1350

Diario de Léon Newspaper, Cent. — A1351

Diario de Avila Newspaper, 108th Anniv. — A1352

El Norte de Castilla Newspaper, 150th Anniv. — A1353

Levante-El Mercantil Valenciano Newspaper, 134th Anniv. — A1354

**2006, Apr. 20 *Perf. 13¾x14, 14x13¾***

| | | | | |
|---|---|---|---|---|
| **3405** | A1350 | 41c multi | 1.10 | .55 |
| **3406** | A1351 | 41c multi | 1.10 | .55 |
| **3407** | A1352 | 41c multi | 1.10 | .55 |
| **3408** | A1353 | 41c red & blk | 1.10 | .55 |
| **3409** | A1354 | 41c multi | 1.10 | .55 |
| | | *Nos. 3405-3409 (5)* | 5.50 | 2.75 |

Souvenir Sheet

Christopher Columbus (1451-1506), Explorer — A1355

**2006, Apr. 24 *Perf. 14x13¾***

**3410** A1355 €2.39 multi 6.25 3.00

Coronation of Santa Maria de Los Remedios Icon, Cent. — A1356

**2006, Apr. 27**

**3411** A1356 €2.33 multi 6.00 3.00

Souvenir Sheet

Exfilna 2006 Philatelic Exhibition, Algeciras — A1357

**Litho. & Engr.**

**2006, May 5 *Perf. 13¾x14***

**3412** A1357 €2.39 multi 6.25 3.00

Inauguration of Taxis Family Postal System in Spain, 500th Anniv. — A1358

**2006, May 9 Photo.**

**3413** A1358 29c multi .75 .35

Internet Day A1359

25th Intl. Mathematics Conference, Madrid — A1360

*Die Cut Perf. 13*

**2006, May 17** **Litho.**

| | | | |
|---|---|---|---|
| **3414** A1359 29c multi | .75 | .35 |
| **3515** A1360 57c multi | 1.50 | .75 |

Socialist Youth In Spain, Cent. A1361

**2006, May 23 Photo.** ***Perf. 13¾x14***

**3416** A1361 78c multi 2.00 1.00

Souvenir Sheet

España 06 Intl. Philatelic Exhibition, Málaga — A1362

**2006, May 29**

**3417** A1362 78c multi 2.00 1.00

San Pedro and San Marcial Festivals, Irún — A1363

**2006, June 5** ***Perf. 14x13¾***

**3418** A1363 29c multi .75 .35

Architecture A1364

Designs: 29c, Casa Battló, Barcelona. 38c, Vapor Aymerich, Amt y Jover, Terrassa. 41c, Depósitos del Sol Library, Albacete. 57c, Campos Eliseos Theater, Bilbao. 78c, Alfredo Kraus Auditorium, Las Palmas, horiz. €2.33, Bus station, Casar de Cáceres, horiz.

**Engr., Photo. (41c, 78c, €2.33)**

**2006, June 8** ***Perf. 14x13¾, 13¾x14***

**3419-3424** A1364 Set of 6 12.00 6.00

Al-Idrisi (c. 1100-65), Geographer A1365

**2006, June 15 Photo.** ***Perf. 14x13¾***

**3425** A1365 78c multi 2.00 1.00

Greenfinch A1366 — Iris A1367

**2006, July 5 Litho.** ***Die Cut Perf. 13***

**Self-Adhesive**

| | | | |
|---|---|---|---|
| **3426** A1366 29c multi | .75 | .35 |
| **3427** A1367 41c multi | 1.10 | .55 |

Nos. 3426-3427 were each printed in sheets of 10 which were bound in booklets of 10 sheets.

Sanlúcar de Barrameda Horse Race A1368

**2006, July 6 Photo.** ***Perf. 13¾x14***

**3428** A1368 €2.33 multi 6.00 3.00

Archaeology A1369

Designs: 29c, Los Millares archaeological site. 57c, Art on vase from L'Alcudia archaeological site, horiz. 78c Moixent Warrior, bronze sculpture.

**2006, July 6** ***Perf. 14x13¾, 13¾x14***

**3429-3431** A1369 Set of 3 4.25 2.10

Earth Sciences A1370

Designs: No. 3432, 29c, Derived cartography. No. 3433, 29c, Vulcanology and seismology.

**2006, July 13** ***Perf. 13¾x14***

**3432-3433** A1370 Set of 2 1.50 .75

Benavides Thursday Market, Orbigo, 700th Anniv. A1371

Aragon-Cataluña Canal, Cent. — A1372

**2006, July 20**

| | | | |
|---|---|---|---|
| **3434** A1371 38c multi | 1.00 | .50 |
| **3435** A1372 38c multi | 1.00 | .50 |

Diplomatic Relations Between Spain and Israel, 20th Anniv. A1373

**2006, Sept. 1**

**3436** A1373 78c multi 2.00 1.00

Castles A1374

Designs: 29c, Baños de la Encina Castle. €2.39, Torroella de Montgri.

**2006, Sept. 8** **Engr.**

**3437-3438** A1374 Set of 2 6.75 3.50

A1375

Europa — A1376

**2006, Sept. 12 Photo.** ***Perf. 14x13¾***

| | | | |
|---|---|---|---|
| **3439** A1375 29c multi | .75 | .35 |
| **3440** A1376 57c multi | 1.50 | .75 |

Bridges Between Spain and Portugal — A1377

No. 3441: a, Ayamonte International Bridge (Vila Real de Santo António). b, Alcántara Bridge.

Illustration reduced.

**2006, Sept. 14** ***Perf. 13x13¼***

| | | | |
|---|---|---|---|
| **3441** Horiz. pair | 2.25 | 1.10 |
| *a.* A1377 29c multi | .75 | .35 |
| *b.* A1377 57c multi | 1.50 | .75 |

See Portugal Nos. 2855-2856.

Rioja Grape Harvest Festival A1378

**2006, Sept. 21** ***Perf. 13¾x14***

**3442** A1378 29c multi .75 .35

Real Club Deportivo La Coruna Soccer Team, Cent. A1379

**2006, Sept. 25**

**3443** A1379 57c multi 1.50 .75

Souvenir Sheet

Victory of Spanish Team at 2006 World Basketball Championships — A1380

**2006, Oct. 2 Photo.** ***Perf. 13¾x14***

**3444** A1380 29c multi .75 .35

Swallow A1381

Poinsettia A1382

**2006, Oct. 4 Litho.** ***Die Cut Perf. 13***

**Self-Adhesive**

| | | | |
|---|---|---|---|
| **3445** A1381 29c multi | .75 | .35 |
| **3446** A1382 29c multi | .75 | .35 |

Souvenir Sheets

España 06 World Philatelic Exhibition, Malaga — A1383

Exhibition emblem and: No. 3447, €2.33, Emblem of Vitorio & Lucchino, fashion designers. No. 3448, €2.33, Silhouette of hat and hand (cinema), vert. No. 3449, €2.33, Musical notes and staff. No. 3450, €2.33, Guitarist, vert. No. 3451, €2.33, Hand (flamenco dancing). No. 3452, €2.33, Tennis racquet and basketball, vert. No. 3453, €2.33, Pablo Picasso (1881-1973), artist.

**2006 Photo.** ***Perf. 13¾x14, 14x13¾***
**3447-3453** A1383 Set of 7 42.00 21.00

Issued: No. 3447, 10/8; No. 3448, 10/9; Nos. 3449-3450, 10/10; No. 3451, 10/11; No. 3452, 10/12; No. 3453, 10/13.

America Issue, Energy Conservation — A1384

**2006, Oct. 14** ***Perf. 13¾***
**3454** A1384 78c multi 2.00 1.00

Appointment of First Spanish Postmen, 250th Anniv. — A1385

***Die Cut Perf. 13***
**2006, Oct. 25 Litho.**
**Self-Adhesive**
**3455** A1385 29c multi .75 .35

Stamp Day.

Ramón Rubial (1906-99), Politician A1386

**2006, Oct. 27 Engr.** ***Perf. 14x13¾***
**3456** A1386 57c multi 1.50 .75

A1387

Christmas A1388

***Die Cut Perf. 13***
**2006, Nov. 2 Litho.**
**Self-Adhesive**
**3457** A1387 29c multi .75 .35
**3458** A1388 57c multi 1.50 .75

Souvenir Sheet

Stained Glass Window, School of Architecture, Polytechnic University of Madrid — A1389

**Litho. & Engr.**
**2006, Nov. 3** ***Perf. 14x13¾***
**3459** A1389 €2.39 multi 6.25 3.25

St. Francis Xavier (1506-52) A1390

**2006, Nov. 7** ***Perf. 13¾x14***
**3460** A1390 29c multi .80 .40

Television Broadcasting in Spain, 50th Anniv. — A1391

**2006, Nov. 8 Photo.**
**3461** A1391 29c multi .80 .40

La Vanguardia Newspaper, 125th Anniv. — A1392

**2006, Nov. 9** ***Perf. 14x13¾***
**3462** A1392 29c multi .80 .40

Pío Baroja (1872-1956), Writer — A1393

**2006, Nov. 23**
**3463** A1393 29c multi .80 .40

Revision of Spanish Coat of Arms, 25th Anniv. — A1394

**2006, Nov. 23**
**3464** A1394 29c multi .80 .40

A1395

Historical Memory Year A1396

**2006, Nov. 30** ***Perf. 13¾x14***
**3465** A1395 29c multi .80 .40
**3466** A1396 29c multi .80 .40

Toys — A1397

No. 3467: a, Tricycle. b, Bus. c, Train. d, Bowling game. e, Baby carriage. f, Seaplane. g, Printing kit. h, Firetruck.

**2007, Jan. 2 Litho.** ***Die Cut Perf. 13***
**Self-Adhesive**
**3467** Booklet pane of 8 6.50
***a.-h.*** A1397 A Any single .80 .40

Nos. 3467a-3467h each sold for 30p on day of issue.

King Juan Carlos — A1398

**2007, Jan. 13 Photo.** ***Perf. 13***
**Color of Portrait**
**3468** A1398 30c blue .80 .40
**3469** A1398 58c olive grn 1.50 .75
**3470** A1398 €2.43 org brn 6.25 3.25
**3471** A1398 €2.49 rose pink 6.50 3.25
*Nos. 3468-3471 (4)* 15.05 7.65

Hoopoe A1399

Red Rose A1400

***Die Cut Perf. 13***
**2007, Jan. 20 Litho.**
**Self-Adhesive**
**3472** A1399 30c multi .80 .40
**3473** A1400 39c multi 1.00 .50

Nos. 3472-3473 each were printed in sheets of 10, which were bound in booklets of 10 sheets.

Teacher and Pupils A1401

**2007, Jan. 23**
**Self-Adhesive**
**3474** A1401 58c multi 1.50 .75

Las Provincias Newspaper, 140th Anniv. (in 2006) — A1402

**2007, Jan. 31 Photo.** ***Perf. 13¾x14***
**3475** A1402 42c multi 1.10 .55

Stylized Periodic Table of Elements A1403

Gregorian Calendar, 425th Anniv. — A1404

***Die Cut Perf. 13***
**2007, Feb. 2 Litho.**
**Self-Adhesive**
**3476** A1403 30c multi .80 .40
**3477** A1404 42c multi 1.10 .55

Institute of Catalan Studies, Cent. A1405

**2007, Feb. 5 Photo.** ***Perf. 13¾x14***
**3478** A1405 30c multi .80 .40

2007 America's Cup Challenger Races — A1406

**2007, Feb. 8**
**3479** A1406 30c multi .80 .40

Earth and Space Sciences A1407

Designs: 30c, Map (cartography). 78c, Yebes Astronomical Center radio telescope.

***Die Cut Perf. 13***
**2007, Feb. 16 Litho.**
**Self-Adhesive**
**3480-3481** A1407 Set of 2 3.00 1.50

Fuentepiña Pine Tree — A1408

**2007, Mar. 5 Photo.** ***Perf. 13¾x14***

| | | | | |
|---|---|---|---|---|
| **3482** | A1408 | 78c multi | 2.10 | 1.10 |

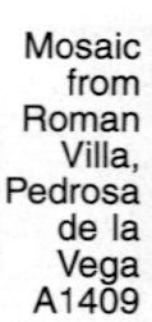

Mosaic from Roman Villa, Pedrosa de la Vega A1409

Roman Baths, Campo Valdés A1410

**2007, Mar. 8**

| | | | | |
|---|---|---|---|---|
| **3483** | A1409 | 30c multi | .80 | .40 |
| **3484** | A1410 | 30c multi | .80 | .40 |

European Economic Community, 50th Anniv. — A1411

**2007, Mar. 23** ***Perf. 14x13¾***

| | | | | |
|---|---|---|---|---|
| **3485** | A1411 | 58c multi | 1.60 | .80 |

## SEMI-POSTAL STAMPS

### Red Cross Issue

Princesses María Cristina and Beatrice SP1

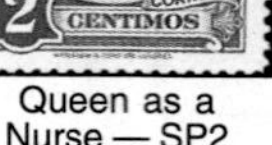

Queen as a Nurse — SP2

Queen Victoria Eugénia — SP3

Prince of Asturias — SP4

King Alfonso XIII — SP5

***Perf. 12½***

**1926, Sept. 15 Unwmk. Engr.**

| | | | | |
|---|---|---|---|---|
| **B1** | SP1 | 1c black | 2.00 | 1.90 |
| **B2** | SP2 | 2c ultra | 2.00 | 1.90 |
| **B3** | SP3 | 5c violet brn | 4.50 | 3.25 |
| **B4** | SP4 | 10c green | 3.75 | 3.25 |
| **B5** | SP1 | 15c indigo | 1.50 | 1.25 |
| **B6** | SP4 | 20c dull violet | 1.50 | 1.25 |
| *a.* | | 20c violet brown (error) | 500.00 | 375.00 |
| **B7** | SP5 | 25c rose red | .25 | .25 |
| **B8** | SP1 | 30c blue green | 35.00 | 32.50 |
| **B9** | SP3 | 40c dark blue | 20.00 | 17.50 |
| **B10** | SP2 | 50c red orange | 20.00 | 17.00 |
| **B11** | SP4 | 1p slate | 1.50 | .90 |
| **B12** | SP3 | 4p magenta | 1.10 | .65 |
| **B13** | SP5 | 10p brown | 1.10 | .90 |
| | | *Nos. B1-B13,EB1 (14)* | 102.95 | 91.25 |
| | | Set, never hinged | 185.00 | |

The 20c was printed in violet brown for use in the colonies (Cape Juby, Spanish Guinea, Spanish Morocco and Spanish Sahara). No. B6a, the missing overprint error, is listed here because it is not known to which colony it belongs.

For overprints see Nos. B19-B46.

Airplane and Map of Madrid-Manila Flight — SP6

**1926, Sept. 15**

| | | | | |
|---|---|---|---|---|
| **B14** | SP6 | 15c dp ultra & org | .30 | .30 |
| **B15** | SP6 | 20c car & yel grn | .30 | .30 |
| **B16** | SP6 | 30c dk brn & ultra | .30 | .30 |
| **B17** | SP6 | 40c dk grn & brn org | .30 | .30 |
| **B18** | SP6 | 4p magenta & yel | 82.50 | 82.50 |
| | | *Nos. B14-B18,CB1-CB5 (10)* | 91.20 | 91.20 |
| | | Set, never hinged | 160.00 | |

Madrid to Manila flight of Captains Eduardo G. Gallarza and Joaquim Loriga y Taboada.

Nos. B1-B18, CB1-CB5 and EB1 were used for regular postage on Sept. 15, 16, 17, 1926. Subsequently the unsold stamps were given to the Spanish Red Cross Society, by which they were sold uncanceled but they then had no franking power.

For overprints see Nos. B47-B53.

### Coronation Silver Jubilee Issue

Red Cross Stamps of 1926 Overprinted "ALFONSO XIII," Dates and Ornaments in Various Colors

**1927, May 27**

| | | | | |
|---|---|---|---|---|
| **B19** | SP1 | 1c black (R) | 4.50 | 4.00 |
| **B20** | SP2 | 2c ultra (Bl) | 7.75 | 7.75 |
| **B21** | SP3 | 5c vio brn (R) | 1.90 | 1.90 |
| *a.* | | Double overprint | 37.50 | |
| **B22** | SP4 | 10c green (Bl) | 55.00 | 55.00 |
| **B23** | SP1 | 15c indigo (R) | 1.60 | 1.60 |
| **B24** | SP4 | 20c dull vio (Bl) | 3.00 | 3.00 |
| **B25** | SP5 | 25c rose red (Bl) | .45 | .45 |
| **B26** | SP1 | 30c blue grn (Bl) | .85 | .85 |
| **B27** | SP3 | 40c dk blue (R) | .85 | .85 |
| **B28** | SP2 | 50c red org (Bl) | .85 | .85 |
| **B29** | SP4 | 1p slate (R) | 1.60 | 1.60 |
| **B30** | SP3 | 4p magenta (Bl) | 8.25 | 8.25 |
| **B31** | SP5 | 10p brown (G) | 32.50 | 32.50 |
| | | *Nos. B19-B31 (13)* | 119.10 | 118.60 |
| | | Set, never hinged | 240.00 | |

### Same with Additional Surcharges of New Values

| | | | | |
|---|---|---|---|---|
| **B32** | SP2 | 3c on 2c (G) | 9.50 | 9.50 |
| **B33** | SP2 | 4c on 2c (Bk) | 9.50 | 9.50 |
| **B34** | SP5 | 10c on 25c (Bk) | .55 | .55 |
| **B35** | SP5 | 25c on 25c (Bl) | .55 | .55 |
| **B36** | SP2 | 55c on 2c (R) | 1.00 | 1.00 |
| **B37** | SP4 | 55c on 10c (Bk) | 55.00 | 55.00 |
| **B38** | SP4 | 55c on 20c (Bk) | 55.00 | 55.00 |
| **B39** | SP1 | 75c on 15c (R) | .70 | .70 |
| **B40** | SP1 | 75c on 30c (R) | 140.00 | 140.00 |
| **B41** | SP3 | 80c on 5c (R) | 52.50 | 50.00 |
| **B42** | SP3 | 2p on 40c (R) | 1.00 | 1.00 |
| **B43** | SP4 | 2p on 1p (R) | 1.00 | 1.00 |
| **B44** | SP2 | 5p on 50c (G) | 1.90 | 1.90 |
| **B45** | SP3 | 5p on 4p (Bk) | 3.25 | 3.25 |
| **B46** | SP5 | 10p on 10p (G) | 27.50 | 27.50 |
| | | *Nos. B32-B46 (15)* | 358.95 | 356.45 |
| | | Set, never hinged | 625.00 | |

Nos. B14-B18 Overprinted

| | | | | |
|---|---|---|---|---|
| **B47** | SP6 | 15c (Br) | .40 | .40 |
| *a.* | | Double overprint | 30.00 | |
| **B48** | SP6 | 20c (Bl) | .40 | .40 |
| *a.* | | Brown overprint (error) | 65.00 | |
| *b.* | | Inverted overprint | 30.00 | |
| **B50** | SP6 | 30c (R) | .40 | .40 |
| *a.* | | Blue overprint (error) | 65.00 | |
| *b.* | | Double overprint | 30.00 | |
| **B52** | SP6 | 40c (Br) | .40 | .40 |
| *a.* | | Inverted overprint | 30.00 | |
| *b.* | | Double ovpt. (Bl + Br) | 95.00 | |
| **B53** | SP6 | 4p (Bl) | 95.00 | 95.00 |
| *a.* | | Inverted overprint | 160.00 | |

### Semi-Postal Special Delivery Stamp Overprinted "ALFONSO XIII," Dates and Ornaments in Violet

| | | | | |
|---|---|---|---|---|
| **B54** | SPSD1 | 20c | 5.50 | 5.50 |
| | | *Nos. B47-B54 (6)* | 102.10 | 102.10 |

Nos. CB1-CB5 Overprinted in Various Colors

| | | | | |
|---|---|---|---|---|
| **B55** | SPAP1 | 5c (R) | 1.90 | 1.60 |
| *a.* | | Inverted overprint | 30.00 | |
| **B56** | SPAP1 | 10c (R) | 2.25 | 2.25 |
| *a.* | | Inverted overprint | 30.00 | |
| **B57** | SPAP1 | 25c (Bl) | .40 | .40 |
| **B58** | SPAP1 | 50c (Bl) | .40 | .40 |
| *a.* | | Double ovpt., one invtd. | 72.50 | |
| **B59** | SPAP1 | 1p (R) | 2.50 | 2.50 |
| *a.* | | Inverted overprint | 95.00 | |

### Same with Additional Surcharges of New Values

| | | | | |
|---|---|---|---|---|
| **B60** | SPAP1 | 75c on 5c (R) | 4.50 | 3.25 |
| *a.* | | Inverted surcharge | 30.00 | |
| **B61** | SPAP1 | 75c on 10c (R) | 17.00 | 13.00 |
| *a.* | | Inverted surcharge | 30.00 | |
| **B62** | SPAP1 | 75c on 25c (Bl) | 32.50 | 27.50 |
| *a.* | | Double surcharge | 55.00 | |
| **B63** | SPAP1 | 75c on 50c (Bl) | 15.00 | 13.00 |
| | | *Nos. B55-B63 (9)* | 76.45 | 63.90 |
| | | Set, never hinged | 225.00 | |

Nos. B54-B63 were available for ordinary postage.

Stamps of Spanish Offices in Morocco and Spanish Colonies, 1926 (Spain Types SP3, SP5) Surcharged in Various Colors with New Values and

### On Spanish Morocco

| | | | | |
|---|---|---|---|---|
| **B64** | SP3 | 55c on 4p bis (Bl) | 21.00 | 17.50 |
| **B65** | SP5 | 80c on 10p vio (Br) | 21.00 | 17.50 |

### On Spanish Tangier

| | | | | |
|---|---|---|---|---|
| **B66** | SP5 | 1p on 10p vio (Br) | 110.00 | 90.00 |
| **B67** | SP3 | 4p bis (G) | 37.50 | 32.50 |

### On Cape Juby

| | | | | |
|---|---|---|---|---|
| **B68** | SP3 | 5p on 4p bis (R) | 70.00 | 57.50 |
| **B69** | SP5 | 10p on 10p vio (R) | 37.50 | 32.50 |

### On Spanish Guinea

| | | | | |
|---|---|---|---|---|
| **B70** | SP5 | 1p on 10p vio (Bl) | 21.00 | 17.50 |
| **B71** | SP3 | 2p on 4p bis (G) | 21.00 | 17.50 |

### On Spanish Sahara

| | | | | |
|---|---|---|---|---|
| **B72** | SP5 | 80c on 10p vio (R) | 32.50 | 27.50 |
| **B73** | SP3 | 2p on 4p bis (R) | 21.00 | 17.50 |
| | | *Nos. B64-B73 (10)* | 392.50 | 327.50 |
| | | Set, never hinged | 800.00 | |

Nos. B64-B73 were available for postage in Spain only.

Nos. B19-B73 were for the 25th year of the reign of King Alfonso XIII.

Counterfeits of Nos. B64-B73 abound.

### Catacombs Restoration Issues

Pope Pius XI and King Alfonso XIII SP7

**1928, Dec. 23 Engr.** ***Perf. 12½***

#### Santiago Issue

| | | | | |
|---|---|---|---|---|
| **B74** | SP7 | 2c violet & blk | .25 | .25 |
| **B75** | SP7 | 2c lake & blk | .30 | .30 |
| **B76** | SP7 | 3c bl blk & vio | .25 | .25 |
| **B77** | SP7 | 3c dl bl & vio | .30 | .30 |
| **B78** | SP7 | 5c ol grn & vio | .65 | .65 |
| **B79** | SP7 | 10c yel grn & blk | 1.10 | 1.10 |
| **B80** | SP7 | 15c bl grn & vio | 3.75 | 3.75 |
| **B81** | SP7 | 25c dp rose & vio | 3.75 | 3.75 |
| **B82** | SP7 | 40c ultra & blk | .25 | .25 |
| **B83** | SP7 | 55c ol brn & vio | .25 | .25 |
| **B84** | SP7 | 80c red & blk | .25 | .25 |
| **B85** | SP7 | 1p gray blk & vio | .25 | .25 |
| **B86** | SP7 | 2p red brn & blk | 5.25 | 5.25 |
| **B87** | SP7 | 3p pale rose & vio | 5.25 | 5.25 |
| **B88** | SP7 | 4p vio brn & blk | 5.25 | 5.25 |
| **B89** | SP7 | 5p grnsh blk & vio | 5.25 | 5.25 |

#### Toledo Issue

| | | | | |
|---|---|---|---|---|
| **B90** | SP7 | 2c bl blk & car | .25 | .25 |
| **B91** | SP7 | 2c ultra & car | .30 | .30 |
| **B92** | SP7 | 3c bis brn & ultra | .25 | .25 |
| **B93** | SP7 | 3c ol grn & ultra | .30 | .30 |
| **B94** | SP7 | 5c red vio & car | .65 | .65 |
| **B95** | SP7 | 10c yel grn & ultra | 1.10 | 1.10 |
| **B96** | SP7 | 15c slate bl & car | 3.75 | 3.75 |
| **B97** | SP7 | 25c red brn & ultra | 3.75 | 3.75 |
| **B98** | SP7 | 40c ultra & car | .25 | .25 |
| **B99** | SP7 | 55c dk brn & ultra | .25 | .25 |
| **B100** | SP7 | 80c black & car | .25 | .25 |
| **B101** | SP7 | 1p yellow & car | .25 | .25 |
| **B102** | SP7 | 2p dk gray & ultra | 5.25 | 5.25 |
| **B103** | SP7 | 3p violet & car | 5.25 | 5.25 |
| **B104** | SP7 | 4p vio brn & car | 5.25 | 5.25 |
| **B105** | SP7 | 5p bister & ultra | 5.25 | 5.25 |
| | | *Nos. B74-B105 (32)* | 64.70 | 64.70 |
| | | Set, never hinged | 105.00 | |

Nos. B74-B105 replaced regular stamps from Dec. 23, 1928 to Jan. 6, 1929. The proceeds from their sale were given to a fund to restore the catacombs of Saint Damasus and Saint Praetextatus at Rome.

Nos. B74-B105 exist imperforate. Value set, $325 hinged, $375 never hinged.

### Issues of the Republic

SP13

**1938, Apr. 15** ***Perf. 11½***

| | | | | |
|---|---|---|---|---|
| **B106** | SP13 | 45c + 2p bl & grnsh bl | .75 | .65 |
| *a.* | | Imperf., pair | 15.00 | 12.50 |
| *b.* | | Souv. sheet of 1 | 22.50 | 22.50 |
| *c.* | | Souv. sheet of 1, imperf. | 625.00 | 575.00 |
| | | Never hinged | 775.00 | |

Surtax for the defenders of Madrid.

For overprint and surcharge see Nos. B108, CB6.

Nurse and Orderly Carrying Wounded Soldier — SP14

**1938, June 1 Engr.** ***Perf. 10***

| | | | | |
|---|---|---|---|---|
| **B107** | SP14 | 45c + 5p cop red | .55 | .55 |
| *a.* | | Imperf., pair | 220.00 | |

For surcharge see No. CB7.

No. B106 Overprinted in Black

**1938, Nov. 7** ***Perf. 11½***

**B108** SP13 45c + 2p 3.25 3.25
Never hinged 5.00

Defense of Madrid, 2nd anniversary.
A similar but larger overprint was applied to cover blocks of four. Value never hinged, $30.

Values for souvenir sheets of 1937-38 are for copies with some faults. Undamaged sheets are very hard to find.

**Spanish State**
Souvenir Sheets

Alcazar, Toledo SP15

Design: No. B108C, A patio of Alcazar after Civil War fighting.

**1937 Unwmk. Photo.** ***Perf. 11½***
**Control Numbers on Back**

| | | | |
|---|---|---|---|
| **B108A** | SP15 2p org brn | 19.00 | 19.00 |
| *b.* | Imperf. | 450.00 | 400.00 |
| **B108C** | SP15 2p dark green | 19.00 | 19.00 |
| *d.* | Imperf. | 450.00 | 400.00 |
| | Set, never hinged | 95.00 | |
| | Set, B108Ab, B108Cd, never hinged | 1,100. | |

Nos. B108A-B108C sold for 4p each.

SP16

Designs: 20c, Covadongas Cathedral. 30c, Palma Cathedral, Majorca. 50c, Alcazar of Segovia. 1p, Leon Cathedral.

**1938 Unwmk. Photo.** ***Perf. 12½***
**Control Numbers on Back**

| | | | |
|---|---|---|---|
| **B108E** | SP16 Sheet of 4 | 42.50 | 42.50 |
| *f.* | 20c dull violet | 5.00 | 5.00 |
| *g.* | 30c rose red | 5.00 | 5.00 |
| *h.* | 50c bright blue | 5.00 | 5.00 |
| *i.* | 1p greenish gray | 5.00 | 5.00 |
| *j.* | Imperf. sheet | 72.50 | 65.00 |
| | Never hinged | 115.00 | |

Each sheet sold for 4p.

SP17

Designs, alternating in sheet: Flag bearer. Battleship "Admiral Cervera." Soldiers in trenches. Moorish guard.

**1938, July 1 Unwmk.** ***Perf. 13***
**Control Numbers on Back**

| | | | |
|---|---|---|---|
| **B108K** | SP17 Sheet of 20 | 35.00 | 35.00 |
| | Never hinged | 45.00 | |
| *l.* | Imperf. sheet | 160.00 | 160.00 |
| | Never hinged | 210.00 | |

Sheet measures 175x132mm. Consists of five vertical rows of four 2c violet, 3c deep blue, 5c olive gray, 10c deep green and 30c red orange, with each denomination appearing in two different designs. Marginal inscription: "Homenaje al Ejercito y a la Marina" (Honoring the Army and Navy). Sold for 4p, or double face value.

Souvenir Sheets

Don Juan of Austria — SP18

Battle of Lepanto SP19

***Perf. 12½***
**1938, Dec. 15 Unwmk. Engr.**
**Control Numbers on Back**

| | | | |
|---|---|---|---|
| **B108M** | SP18 30c dk car | 22.50 | 22.50 |
| **B108N** | SP19 50c blue black | 22.50 | 22.50 |
| | *Nos. B108M-B108N (2)* | 45.00 | 45.00 |
| | Set, never hinged | 77.50 | |

***Imperf***

| | | | |
|---|---|---|---|
| **B108O** | SP18 30c black vio | 550.00 | 550.00 |
| **B108P** | SP19 50c dk sl grn | 550.00 | 550.00 |
| | *Nos. B108O-B108P (2)* | 1,100. | 1,100. |
| | Set, never hinged | 1,300. | |

Victory over the Turks in the Battle of Lepanto, 1571.
Nos. B108M-B108P contain one stamp. The dates "1571-1938" appear in the lower sheet margin. Size: 89x74mm. Sold for 10p a pair.

LOCAL CHARITY STAMPS
Hundreds of different charity stamps were issued by local organizations and cities during the Civil War, 1936-39. Some had limited franking value, but most were simply charity labels. They are of three kinds: 1. Local semipostals. 2. Obligatory surtax stamps. 3. Propaganda or charity labels.

Ruins of Belchite SP20

Miracle of Calanda — SP21

Designs: 10c+5c, 70c+20c, Ruins of Belchite. 15c+10c, 80c+20c, The Rosary. 20c+10c, 1.50p+50c, El Pilar Cathedral. 25c+10c, 1p+30c, Mother Raffols praying. 40c+10c, 2.50p+50c, The Little Chamber. 45c+15c, 1.40p+40c, Oath of the Besieged. 10p+4p, The Apparition.

***Perf. 10½, 11½x10½, 11½***
**1940, Jan. 29 Litho. Unwmk.**
**Design SP20**

| | | | |
|---|---|---|---|
| **B109** | 10c + 5c dp bl & vio brn | .20 | .20 |
| **B110** | 15c + 10c rose vio & dk grn | .25 | .25 |
| **B111** | 20c + 10c vio & dp bl | .25 | .25 |
| **B112** | 25c + 10c dp rose & vio brn | .25 | .25 |
| **B113** | 40c + 10c sl grn & rose vio | .20 | .20 |
| **B114** | 45c + 15c vio & dp rose | .30 | .30 |
| **B115** | 70c + 20c multi | .30 | .30 |
| **B116** | 80c + 20c dp rose & vio | .40 | .40 |
| **B117** | 1p + 30c dk sl grn & pur | .40 | .40 |
| **B118** | 1.40p + 40c pur & gray blk | 32.50 | 32.50 |
| **B119** | 1.50p + 50c lt bl & brn vio | .50 | .50 |
| **B120** | 2.50p + 50c choc & bl | .50 | .50 |

**Design SP21**

| | | | |
|---|---|---|---|
| **B121** | 4p + 1p rose lil & sl grn | 11.00 | 11.00 |
| **B122** | 10p + 4p ultra & chnt | 160.00 | 160.00 |
| | *Nos. B109-B122,CB8-CB17,EB2 (25)* | 444.35 | 444.25 |
| | Set, never hinged | 850.00 | |

19th centenary of the Virgin of the Pillar.
The surtax was used to help restore the Cathedral at Zaragoza, damaged during the Civil War.
No. B121 exists in violet & slate green, No. B122 in ultramarine & brown violet. Value, $42.50 each.
Nos. B109-B122 exist imperf. Value, $750.
See No. 743, CB8-CB17.

General Franco — SP23

Knight and Lorraine Cross — SP24

**1940, Dec. 23 Unwmk.** ***Perf. 10***

| | | | |
|---|---|---|---|
| **B123** | SP23 20c + 5c dk grn & red | .65 | .65 |
| **B124** | SP23 40c + 10c dk bl & red | .90 | .40 |
| | Set, never hinged | 3.25 | |

The surtax was for the tuberculosis fund.
See Nos. RA15, RAC1.

Stamps of 10c denomination, types SP23 to SP28, are postal tax issues.

**1941, Dec. 23**

| | | | |
|---|---|---|---|
| **B125** | SP24 20c + 5c bl vio & red | .50 | .30 |
| **B126** | SP24 40c + 10c sl grn & red | .50 | .25 |
| | Set, never hinged | 1.25 | |

The surtax was used to fight tuberculosis.
See Nos. RA16, RAC2.

Cross of Lorraine
SP25 SP26

**1942, Dec. 23 Litho.**

| | | | |
|---|---|---|---|
| **B127** | SP25 20c + 5c pale brn & rose red | 1.40 | 1.25 |
| **B128** | SP25 40c + 10c lt bluish grn & rose red | .80 | .45 |
| | Set, never hinged | 3.50 | |

The surtax was used to fight tuberculosis.
See Nos. RA17, RAC3.

**1943, Dec. 23 Photo.** ***Perf. 11½***

| | | | |
|---|---|---|---|
| **B129** | SP26 20c + 5c dl sl grn & dl red | 3.25 | 1.40 |
| **B130** | SP26 40c + 10c brt bl & dl red | 2.00 | 1.10 |
| | Set, never hinged | 11.00 | |

The surtax was used to fight tuberculosis.
See Nos. RA18, RAC4.

Dragon Slaying — SP27

St. George Slaying the Dragon — SP28

***Perf. 9½x10***
**1944, Dec. 23 Litho. Unwmk.**

| | | | |
|---|---|---|---|
| **B131** | SP27 20c + 5c sl grn & red | .25 | .25 |
| **B132** | SP27 40c + 10c dl vio & red | .50 | .50 |
| **B133** | SP27 80c + 10c ultra & rose | 7.75 | 7.75 |
| | *Nos. B131-B133 (3)* | 8.50 | 8.50 |
| | Set, never hinged | 14.50 | |

The surtax was used to fight tuberculosis.
See Nos. RA19, RAC5.

**1945, Dec. 23**
**Lorraine Cross in Red**

| | | | |
|---|---|---|---|
| **B134** | SP28 20c + 5c dl gray grn | .25 | .20 |
| **B135** | SP28 40c + 10c vio | .30 | .20 |
| **B136** | SP28 80c + 10c ultra | 8.00 | 7.50 |
| | *Nos. B134-B136 (3)* | 8.55 | 7.90 |
| | Set, never hinged | 14.00 | |

The surtax was used to fight tuberculosis.
See Nos. RA20, RAC6.

Nos. 753 and 768 Surcharged in Blue

VISITA
DEL
CAUDILLO
A CANARIAS
OCTUBRE 1950
SOBRETASA:
DIEZ CTS

**1950, Oct. 23**

| | | | |
|---|---|---|---|
| **B137** | A195 50c + 10c | 32.50 | 32.50 |
| *a.* | "Caudillo" 14¾mm wide | 95.00 | 97.50 |
| **B138** | A195 1p + 10c | 32.50 | 32.50 |
| *a.* | "Caudillo" 14¾mm wide | 95.00 | 97.50 |
| | Set, never hinged | 100.00 | |
| *a* | #B137a-B138a, never hinged | 225.00 | |

Visit of General Franco to Canary Islands. First printing, brighter colors and pale blue surcharge, was issued in Canary Islands. Value, $200 hinged, $300 never hinged, $200 used. Second printing was issued in Madrid Feb. 22, 1951. See No. CB18.

**Catalogue values for unused stamps in this section, from this point to the end of the section, are for Never Hinged items.**

1992 Summer Olympics, Barcelona SP29

**1988, Oct. 3 Photo.** ***Perf. 14***

| | | | |
|---|---|---|---|
| **B139** | SP29 20p +5p Track and field | .35 | .35 |
| **B140** | SP29 45p +5p Badminton | .60 | .60 |
| **B141** | SP29 50p +5p Basketball | .70 | .70 |
| | *Nos. B139-B141 (3)* | 1.65 | 1.65 |

See Nos. B146-B152, B163-B168, B177-B179, B184-B186, B191-B193.

EXPO '92, Seville — SP30

Globes and sites of previous exhibitions: No. B142, Crystal Palace, London, 1851. No. B143, Eiffel Tower, Paris, 1889. No. B144, "The Atom," Brussels, 1958. No. B145, Monument, Osaka, 1970.

**1989, Feb. 9 Photo. *Perf. 14x13½***
**B142** SP30 8p +5p multi .20 .20
**B143** SP30 8p +5p multi .20 .20
**B144** SP30 20p +5p multi .30 .30
**B145** SP30 20p +5p multi .30 .30
*Nos. B142-B145 (4)* 1.00 1.00

1992 Summer Olympics Type of 1988

**1989, Mar. 7 Photo. *Perf. 14***
**B146** SP29 8p +5p Handball .25 .25
**B147** SP29 18p +5p Boxing .35 .35
**B148** SP29 20p +5p Cycling .35 .35
**B149** SP29 45p +5p Equestrian .60 .60
*Nos. B146-B149 (4)* 1.55 1.55

**1989, Oct. 3 Photo. *Perf. 13½x14***
**B150** SP29 18p +5p Fencing .65 .65
**B151** SP29 20p +5p Soccer .65 .65
**B152** SP29 45p +5p Pommel horse 1.25 1.25
*Nos. B150-B152 (3)* 2.55 2.55

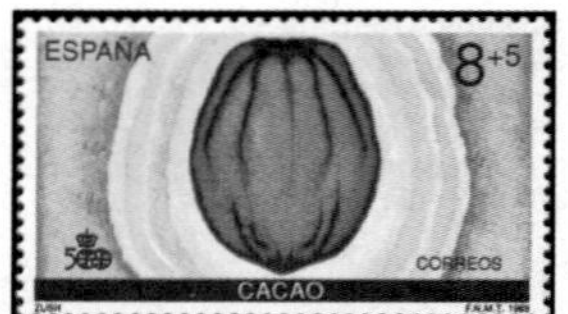

500th Anniv. Emblem and Produce or Fauna Indigenous to the Americas — SP31

**1989, Oct. 16 Litho. *Perf. 13x13½***
**B153** SP31 8p +5p Cocoa .20 .20
**B154** SP31 8p +5p Corn .20 .20
**B155** SP31 20p +5p Tomato .30 .30
**B156** SP31 20p +5p Horse .30 .30
**B157** SP31 50p +5p Potato .60 .60
**B158** SP31 50p +5p Turkey .60 .60
*a.* Bklt. pane of 6, #B153-B158 2.25
*Nos. B153-B158 (6)* 2.20 2.20

Discovery of America, 500th anniv.

EXPO '92, Seville SP32

Curro, the character trademark, and symbols of development in Spain.

**1990, Feb. 22 Photo. *Perf. 14***
**B159** SP32 8p +5p multi .20 .20
**B160** SP32 20p +5p multi, diff. .30 .30
**B161** SP32 45p +5p multi, diff. .60 .60
**B162** SP32 50p +5p multi, diff. .70 .70
*Nos. B159-B162 (4)* 1.80 1.80

1992 Summer Olympics Type of 1988

**1990, Mar. 7 Photo. *Perf. 13½x14***
**B163** SP29 18p +5p Weight lifting .30 .30
**B164** SP29 20p +5p Field hockey .30 .30
**B165** SP29 45p +5p Judo .55 .55
*Nos. B163-B165 (3)* 1.15 1.15

**1990, Oct. 3 Photo. *Perf. 13½x14***
**B166** SP29 8p +5p Wrestling .20 .20
**B167** SP29 18p +5p Swimming .40 .40
**B168** SP29 20p +5p Baseball .50 .50
*Nos. B166-B168 (3)* 1.10 1.10

Discovery of America, 500th Anniv. (in 1992) — SP33

Drawings of sailing ships.

**1990, Oct. 15 Litho. *Perf. 13***
**B169** SP33 8p +5p "Viajes-A" .20 .20
**B170** SP33 8p +5p "Viajes-B" .20 .20
**B171** SP33 20p +5p "Viajes-C" .30 .30
**B172** SP33 20p +5p "Viajes-D" .30 .30
*a.* Bklt. pane of 4, #B169-B172 1.00
*Nos. B169-B172 (4)* 1.00 1.00

Expo '92, Seville SP34

Designs: 15p+5p, La Cartuja, Monastery of Santa Maria de las Cuevas. 25p+5p, Amphitheater. 45p+5p, La Cartuja Bridge. 55p+5p, La Barqueta Bridge.

**Litho. & Engr.**

**1991, Feb. 12 *Perf. 14***
**B173** SP34 15p +5p multi .30 .30
**B174** SP34 25p +5p multi .40 .40
**B175** SP34 45p +5p multi .65 .65
**B176** SP34 55p +5p multi .80 .80
*Nos. B173-B176 (4)* 2.15 2.15

Summer Olympics Type of 1988

**1991, Mar. 7 Litho. *Perf. 13½x14***
**B177** SP29 15p + 5p Five athletes .30 .30
**B178** SP29 25p + 5p Kayaking .40 .40
**B179** SP29 45p + 5p Rowing .65 .65
*Nos. B177-B179 (3)* 1.35 1.35

Madrid, European City of Culture, 1992 SP35

Designs: 15p+5p, Fountain of Apollo. 25p+5p, Statue of Alvaro de Bazan. 45p+5p, Bank of Spain. 55p+5p, St. Isidore's Institute.

**1991, July 29 Photo. *Perf. 13½x14***
**B180** SP35 15p + 5p multi .30 .30
**B181** SP35 25p + 5p multi .40 .40
**B182** SP35 45p + 5p multi .60 .60
**B183** SP35 55p + 5p multi .75 .75
*Nos. B180-B183 (4)* 2.05 2.05

1992 Summer Olympics Type of 1988

**1991, Oct. 3 Litho. *Perf. 14***
**B184** SP29 15p +5p Tennis .45 .45
**B185** SP29 25p +5p Table tennis .60 .60
**B186** SP29 55p +5p Shooting 1.25 1.25
*Nos. B184-B186 (3)* 2.30 2.30

Discovery of America, 500th Anniv., 1992 — SP36

15p+5p, Garcilaso Gomez Suarez de Figueroa, the Inca, poet. 25p+5p, Pope Alexander VI. 45p+5p, Luis de Santangel, banker. 55p+5p, Friar Toribio de Paredes, monk.

**1991, Oct. 15 Photo. *Perf. 13x13½***
**B187** SP36 15p +5p multi .30 .30
**B188** SP36 25p +5p multi .40 .40
**B189** SP36 45p +5p multi .60 .60
**B190** SP36 55p +5p multi .75 .75
*a.* Bklt. pane of 4, #B187-B190 2.00
*Nos. B187-B190 (4)* 2.05 2.05

1992 Summer Olympics Type of 1988

**1992, Mar. 6 Photo. *Perf. 13½x14***
**B191** SP29 15p +5p Archery .40 .40
**B192** SP29 25p +5p Sailing .55 .55
**B193** SP29 55p +5p Volleyball 1.10 1.10
*Nos. B191-B193 (3)* 2.05 2.05

Columbus Type of 1930
Souvenir Sheet

**1992, Mar. 31 Engr. *Perf. 14***
**B194** Sheet of 3 1.00 1.00
*a.* A65 17p +5p dark red .30 .30
*b.* A65 17p +5p ultramarine .30 .30
*c.* A65 17p +5p black .30 .30

Discovery of America, 500th anniv.

Expo '92 Type

Design: No. B195, Seville, 16th cent.

**1992, Apr. 21 Litho. *Perf. 13½x14***
**Souvenir Sheet**
**B195** A837 17p +5p multi .35 .35

1992 Summer Olympics, Barcelona — SP37

***Perf. 14x13½, 13½x14***

**1992, July 16 Photo.**
**B196** SP37 17p +5p Mascot COBI .40 .40
**B197** SP37 17p +5p Hand holding torch, horiz. .40 .40
**B198** SP37 17p +5p "25 Jul" .40 .40
*Nos. B196-B198 (3)* 1.20 1.20

1992 Summer Olympics, Barcelona SP38

Designs: a, Olympic Stadium. b, San Jordi Sports Palace. c, INEF Sports University.

**1992, July 25 *Perf. 13½x14***
**B199** SP38 27p +5p Triptych, #a.-c. 1.40 1.40

1992 Summer Olympics, Barcelona
SP39 SP40

#B200, Olympic mascot as stamp collector. #B201, Sagrada Family Church, Barcelona.

**1992, July 29 Photo. *Perf. 14x13½***
**B200** SP39 17p +5p multi .35 .35
**B201** SP40 17p +5p multi .35 .35

Olymphilex '92 (#B201).

Madrid, European City of Culture — SP41

#B202, Municipal Museum. #B203, Royal Theater. #B204, The Prado Museum. #B205, Queen Sofia Natl. Center for the Arts.

**1992, Nov. 24 Photo. *Perf. 14x13½***
**B202** SP41 17p +5p multi .35 .30
**B203** SP41 17p +5p multi .35 .30
**B204** SP41 17p +5p multi .35 .30
**B205** SP41 17p +5p multi .35 .30
*Nos. B202-B205 (4)* 1.40 1.20

## AIR POST STAMPS

Regular Issue of 1909-10 Overprinted in Red or Black

***Perf. 13x12½, 14***

**1920, Apr. 4 Unwmk.**
**C1** A46 5c green (R) 1.25 .80
*a.* Imperf., pair 105.00 105.00
*b.* Double overprint 35.00 35.00
*c.* Inverted overprint 90.00 90.00
*d.* Double ovpt., one invtd. 35.00 35.00
*e.* Triple overprint 35.00 35.00
**C2** A46 10c car (Bk) 1.50 1.00
*a.* Imperf., pair 105.00 105.00
*b.* Double overprint 35.00 35.00
*d.* Double ovpt., one invtd. 35.00 35.00
**C3** A46 25c dp blue (R) 2.75 1.40
*a.* Inverted overprint 90.00 90.00
*b.* Double overprint 35.00 35.00
**C4** A46 50c sl blue (R) 11.00 5.00
*a.* Imperf., pair 105.00 105.00
**C5** A46 1p lake (Bk) 35.00 19.00
*a.* Imperf., pair 385.00 385.00
*Nos. C1-C5 (5)* 51.50 27.20
Set, never hinged 110.00

Dangerous counterfeits are plentiful.
A 30c green was authorized, but not issued. Value: hinged $550; never hinged $750.
For overprints see Nos. C58-C61.

"Spirit of St. Louis" over Coast of Europe — AP1
Plane and Congress Seal — AP2

**Seville-Barcelona Exposition Issue**
Control Numbers on Back

**1929, Feb. 15 Engr. *Perf. 11***
**C6** AP1 5c brown 5.00 5.00
**C7** AP1 10c rose 5.00 5.00
**C8** AP1 25c dark blue 5.50 5.50
**C9** AP1 50c purple 5.75 5.75
**C10** AP1 1p green 30.00 25.00
**C11** AP1 4p black 21.00 20.00
*Nos. C6-C11 (6)* 72.25 66.25
Set, never hinged 175.00

Nos. C6 to C11 exist imperforate. Value, $575.

The so-called errors of color of Nos. C10, C18-C21, C23-C24, C28-C31, C37, C40, C42, C44, C46, C48, C50, C52, C55, C62-C67 are believed to have been irregularly produced.

**Railway Congress Issue**
Control Numbers on Back

**1930, May 10 Litho. *Perf. 14***
**C12** AP2 5c bister brn 5.25 5.25
**C13** AP2 10c rose 5.25 5.25
**C14** AP2 25c dark blue 5.25 5.25
**C15** AP2 50c purple 13.50 13.50
*a.* Vert. pair, imperf. between 300.00
Never hinged *600.00*
**C16** AP2 1p yellow green 27.50 27.50
**C17** AP2 4p black 27.50 27.50
*Nos. C12-C17 (6)* 84.25 84.25
Set, never hinged 175.00

The note after No. 385 will apply here also. Dangerous counterfeits exist.

### Goya Issue

Fantasy of Flight AP3

Asmodeus and Cleofas — AP4

Fantasy of Flight AP5

Fantasy of Flight — AP6

**1930, June 15 Engr. *Perf. 12½***

| | | | | |
|---|---|---|---|---|
| **C18** | AP3 | 5c brn red & yel | .20 | .20 |
| **C19** | AP3 | 15c blk & red org | .20 | .20 |
| **C20** | AP3 | 25c brn car & dp red | .20 | .20 |
| **C21** | AP4 | 5c ol grn & grnsh bl | .20 | .20 |
| **C22** | AP4 | 10c sl grn & yel grn | .20 | .20 |
| **C23** | AP4 | 20c ultra & rose red | .20 | .20 |
| **C24** | AP4 | 40c vio bl & lt bl | .30 | .30 |
| **C25** | AP5 | 30c brown & vio | .30 | .30 |
| **C26** | AP5 | 50c ver & grn | .30 | .30 |
| **C27** | AP5 | 4p brn car & blk | 2.10 | 2.10 |
| **C28** | AP6 | 1p vio brn & vio | .30 | .30 |
| **C29** | AP6 | 4p bl blk & sl grn | 2.10 | 2.10 |
| **C30** | AP6 | 10p blk brn & bis brn | 7.75 | 7.75 |
| | | *Nos. C18-C30,CE1 (14)* | 14.55 | 14.55 |
| | | Set, never hinged | 22.50 | |

Exist imperf. Value, set $150.

### Christopher Columbus Issue

La Rábida Monastery — AP7

Martín Alonso Pinzón — AP8

Vicente Yanez Pinzón — AP9

Columbus in His Cabin — AP10

**1930, Sept. 29 Litho.**

| | | | | |
|---|---|---|---|---|
| **C31** | AP7 | 5c lt red brn | .25 | .20 |
| **C32** | AP7 | 5c olive bister | .25 | .20 |
| **C33** | AP7 | 10c blue green | .25 | .20 |
| **C34** | AP7 | 15c dark violet | .25 | .20 |
| **C35** | AP7 | 20c ultra | .25 | .20 |

**Engr.**

| | | | | |
|---|---|---|---|---|
| **C36** | AP8 | 25c carmine rose | .25 | .20 |
| **C37** | AP9 | 30c dp red brn | 1.75 | 1.75 |
| **C38** | AP8 | 40c indigo | 1.75 | 1.75 |
| **C39** | AP9 | 50c orange | 1.75 | 1.75 |
| **C40** | AP8 | 1p dull violet | 1.75 | 1.75 |
| **C41** | AP10 | 4p olive green | 1.75 | 1.75 |
| **C42** | AP10 | 10p light brown | 10.00 | 11.00 |
| | | *Nos. C31-C42 (12)* | 20.25 | 20.95 |
| | | Set, never hinged | 30.00 | |

Exist imperf. Value, set $190.

### Spanish-American Issue

AP11

Columbus AP12

Columbus and Pinzón Brothers AP13

**1930, Sept. 29 Litho.**

| | | | | |
|---|---|---|---|---|
| **C43** | AP11 | 5c lt red | .20 | .20 |
| **C44** | AP11 | 10c dull green | .20 | .20 |

**Engr.**

| | | | | |
|---|---|---|---|---|
| **C45** | AP12 | 25c scarlet | .20 | .20 |
| **C46** | AP12 | 50c slate gray | 2.25 | 1.90 |
| **C47** | AP12 | 1p fawn | 2.25 | 1.90 |
| **C48** | AP13 | 4p slate blue | 2.25 | 1.90 |
| **C49** | AP13 | 10p brown violet | 10.00 | 9.25 |
| | | *Nos. C43-C49 (7)* | 17.35 | 15.55 |
| | | Set, never hinged | 27.50 | |

Exist imperf. Value, set $160.

### Spanish-American Exhibition Issue

Santos-Dumont and First Flight of His Airplane — AP14

Teodoro Fels and His Airplane AP15

Dagoberto Godoy and Pass over Andes — AP16

Sacadura Cabral and Gago Coutinho and Their Airplane AP17

Sidar of Mexico and Map of South America — AP18

Ignacio Jiménez and Francisco Iglesias — AP19

Charles A. Lindbergh, Statue of Liberty, Spirit of St. Louis and Cat AP20

Santa Maria, Plane and Torre del Oro, Seville AP21

**1930, Oct. 10 Photo. *Perf. 14***

| | | | | |
|---|---|---|---|---|
| **C50** | AP14 | 5c gray black | .80 | .50 |
| **C51** | AP15 | 10c dk olive grn | .80 | .50 |
| **C52** | AP16 | 25c ultra | .80 | .50 |
| **C53** | AP17 | 50c blue gray | 1.75 | 1.25 |
| **C54** | AP18 | 50c black | 1.75 | 1.25 |
| **C55** | AP19 | 1p car lake | 3.75 | 2.75 |
| ***a.*** | | 1p brown violet | 65.00 | 65.00 |
| | | Never hinged | 140.00 | |
| **C56** | AP20 | 1p deep green | 3.75 | 2.75 |
| **C57** | AP21 | 4p slate blue | 6.75 | 5.00 |
| | | *Nos. C50-C57 (8)* | 20.15 | 14.50 |
| | | Set, never hinged | 75.00 | |

Exist imperf. Value, set $110.

Note after No. 432 also applies to Nos. C31-C57.

*Reprints of Nos. C50-C57 have blurred impressions, yellowish paper. Value: one-tenth of originals.*

Nos. C1-C4 Overprinted in Red or Black

**1931 *Perf. 13x12½***

| | | | | |
|---|---|---|---|---|
| **C58** | A46 | 5c green (R) | 11.00 | 10.00 |
| **C59** | A46 | 10c carmine (Bk) | 11.00 | 10.00 |
| **C60** | A46 | 25c deep blue (R) | 15.00 | 14.50 |
| **C61** | A46 | 50c slate blue (R) | 30.00 | 22.50 |
| | | *Nos. C58-C61 (4)* | 67.00 | 57.00 |
| | | Set, never hinged | 140.00 | |

Counterfeits of overprint exist.

The status of Nos. C58-C61 has been questioned.

Plane and Royal Palace, Madrid AP22

Madrid Post Office and Cibeles Fountain AP23

Plane over Calle de Alcalá, Madrid AP24

**1931, Oct. 10 Engr. *Perf. 12***

| | | | | |
|---|---|---|---|---|
| **C62** | AP22 | 5c brown violet | .20 | .30 |
| **C63** | AP22 | 10c deep green | .20 | .30 |
| **C64** | AP22 | 25c dull red | .20 | .30 |
| **C65** | AP23 | 50c deep blue | .40 | .45 |
| **C66** | AP23 | 1p deep violet | .60 | .55 |
| **C67** | AP24 | 4p black | 7.75 | 10.00 |
| | | *Nos. C62-C67 (6)* | 9.35 | 11.90 |
| | | Set, never hinged | 13.00 | |

3rd Pan-American Postal Union Congress, Madrid.

Exist imperf. Value, set $45.

For overprints see Nos. CO1-CO6.

### Montserrat Issue

Plane over Montserrat Pass — AP25

**1931, Dec. 9 *Perf. 11½***

**Control Number on Back**

| | | | | |
|---|---|---|---|---|
| **C68** | AP25 | 5c black brown | .50 | .50 |
| **C69** | AP25 | 10c yellow green | 2.25 | 2.25 |
| **C70** | AP25 | 25c deep rose | 9.00 | 9.00 |
| **C71** | AP25 | 50c orange | 32.50 | 32.50 |
| **C72** | AP25 | 1p gray black | 22.50 | 22.50 |
| | | *Nos. C68-C72 (5)* | 66.75 | 66.75 |
| | | Set, never hinged | 85.00 | |

***Perf. 14***

| | | | | |
|---|---|---|---|---|
| *C68a* | AP25 | 5c | 6.75 | *13.00* |
| *C69a* | AP25 | 10c | 37.50 | 40.00 |
| *C70a* | AP25 | 25c | 67.50 | 67.50 |
| *C71a* | AP25 | 50c | 67.50 | 67.50 |
| *C72f* | AP25 | 1p | 67.50 | 67.50 |
| | | *Nos. C68a-C72f (5)* | 246.75 | 255.50 |
| | | Set, never hinged | 275.00 | |

900th anniv. of Montserrat Monastery.

Nos. C68-C72 exist imperf. Value, $525.

Autogiro over Seville — AP26

**1935-39** ***Perf. 11½***

C72A AP26 2p gray blue 20.00 4.50
  g. Imperf., pair 300.00

**Re-engraved**

C72B AP26 2p dk blue ('38) .65 .25
  c. Imperf., pair 20.00
  d. Perf. 10 ('39) 1.50 1.10
  Set, #C72A-C72B, never hinged 42.50

The sky has heavy horizontal lines of shading. Entire design is more heavily shaded than No. C72A.

No. C72B exists privately perforated 14. Value, $9 unused, $9 used.

For overprints see Nos. 7LC14, 7LC19, 14L26.

Eagle and Newspapers — AP27

Press Building, Madrid — AP28

Don Quixote and Sancho Panza Flying on the Wooden Horse — AP29

Design: 15c, 30c, 50c, 1p, Autogiro over House of Nazareth.

**1936, Mar. 11** **Photo.** ***Perf. 12½***

C73 AP27 1c rose car .20 .20
C74 AP28 2c dark brown .20 .20
C75 AP27 5c black brown .20 .20
C76 AP28 10c dk yellow grn .20 .20
C77 AP28 15c Prus blue .20 .20
C78 AP27 20c violet .20 .20
C79 AP28 25c magenta .20 .20
C80 AP28 30c red orange .20 .20
C81 AP27 40c orange .50 .20
C82 AP28 50c light blue .30 .20
C83 AP28 60c olive green .65 .40
C84 AP28 1p brnsh black .65 .45
C85 AP29 2p brt ultra 5.00 2.25
C86 AP29 4p lilac rose 5.00 2.75
C87 AP29 10p violet brown 14.00 11.00
  *Nos. C73-C87 (15)* 27.70 18.85
  Set, never hinged 37.50

Madrid Press Association, 40th anniv.

Exist imperf. Value, set $250 hinged and $325 never hinged.

See note after No. 432.

Types of Regular Postage of 1936 Overprinted in Blue or Red

**1936** ***Imperf.***

C88 A125 10c dk red (Bl) 150.00 150.00
C89 A125 15c dk blue (R) 150.00 150.00
  Set, never hinged 500.00

1st National Philatelic Exhibition which opened in Madrid, Apr. 2, 1936.

No. 577 Overprinted in Black

**1936, Aug. 1** ***Perf. 11½***

C90 A128 30c rose red 3.00 3.75
  Never hinged 6.00
  b. Imperf., pair 140.00

Issued in commemoration of the flight of aviators Antonio Arnaiz and Juan Calvo from Manila to Spain.

Counterfeit overprints exist.

Exists privately perforated 14. Value, $50 unused, $50 used.

No. 288 Surcharged in Black

**1938, Apr. 13** ***Perf. 14***

C91 A36 2.50p on 10c 80.00 72.50
  Never hinged 150.00

7th anniversary of the Republic.

Values are for examples with perforations nearly touching the design on one or two sides.

No. 507 Surcharged in Various Colors

**1938, Aug.** ***Perf. 11½***

C92 A92 50c on 25c (Bk) 25.00 25.00
C93 A92 1p on 25c (G) 1.90 1.40
C94 A92 1.25p on 25c (R) 1.90 1.40
C95 A92 1.50p on 25c (Bl) 1.90 1.40
C96 A92 2p on 25c (Bk & R) 35.00 30.00
  *Nos. C92-C96 (5)* 65.70 59.20
  Set, never hinged 110.00

No. 585 Surcharged

**1938, June 1** ***Perf. 11***

C97 A132 5p on 1p multi 250.00 250.00
  Never hinged 375.00
  a. Imperf., pair 550.00 550.00
  b. Inverted surcharge 350.00 350.00
  c. Souvenir sheet 3,000. 3,000.
  Never hinged 6,000.
  d. As "c," imperf. 6,500. 6,500.
  e. As "c," inverted surcharge 6,000. 6,000.

Counterfeit overprints exist.

Type of 1938-39 Overprinted in Red or Carmine



**1938, May** ***Perf. 10, 10½***

C98 A163 50c indigo (R) .70 .55
C99 A163 1p dk blue (C) 3.00 .70
  Set, never hinged 4.50

Exist imperf. Value, each $100.

Copies without overprint are proofs.

Juan de la Cierva and his Autogiro over Madrid AP30

**1939, Jan.** **Unwmk.** **Litho.** ***Perf. 11***

C100 AP30 20c red orange .60 .40
C101 AP30 25c dk carmine .45 .20
C102 AP30 35c brt violet .65 .40
C103 AP30 50c dk brown .65 .25
C105 AP30 1p blue .65 .25
C107 AP30 2p green 3.25 1.75
C108 AP30 4p dull blue 5.00 2.75
  *Nos. C100-C108 (7)* 11.25 6.00
  Set, never hinged 19.00

Exist imperf. Value, set $325.

**1941-47** ***Perf. 10***

C109 AP30 20c dk red orange .20 .20
C110 AP30 25c redsh brown .20 .20
C111 AP30 35c lilac rose 1.60 .50
C112 AP30 50c brown .45 .20
C113 AP30 1p chalky blue 1.40 .20
C114 AP30 2p lt gray grn 1.60 .20
C115 AP30 4p gray blue 5.00 .30
C116 AP30 10p brt purple ('47) 3.75 .65
  *Nos. C109-C116 (8)* 14.20 2.45
  Set, never hinged 26.00

Issued in honor of Juan de la Cierva (1895-1936), inventor of the autogiro.

Nos. C109-C115 exist imperf. Value, set $300.

The overprint "EXPOSICION NACIONAL DE FILATELIA 1948 SAN SEBASTIAN" multiple, in parallel horizontal lines, on Nos. C109 to C113 and other airmail stamps, was privately applied.

---

Correo Aéreo

Correo Aéreo

Nos. 625-634, 660, 676 and 677 with either of these overprints have not been established as issues of the Spanish government.

---

Mariano Pardo de Figueroa (Dr. Thebussem) AP31

**1944, Oct. 12** **Engr.** ***Perf. 10***

C117 AP31 5p brt ultra 15.00 13.00
  Never hinged 23.00

"Stamp Day" and "Day of the Race," Oct. 12, 1944. Valid for franking air mail correspondence one day only.

Mail Coach, Plane and Count of St. Louis AP32

**1945, Oct. 12** **Unwmk.**

C118 AP32 10p yellow green 17.50 *19.00*
  Never hinged 25.00

"Stamp Day" and "Day of the Race," Oct. 12, 1945, and to honor Luis José Sartorius, Count of St. Louis, who issued the decree for Spain's 1st postage stamps. No. C118 was valid for franking air mail correspondence one day only.

C118 exists imperf. Value, $800.

Maj. Joaquin Garcia Morato AP33

**1945, Nov. 27**

C119 AP33 10p deep claret 13.50 5.50
  Never hinged 32.50

C119 exists imperf. Value, $275 hinged, $425 never hinged.

Capt. Carlos Haya Gonzalez AP34

Bartolomé de las Casas AP35

**1945, Dec. 14**

C120 AP34 4p red 5.50 4.50
  Never hinged 12.50

C120 exists imperf. Value, $375 hinged and $500 never hinged.

**1946, Oct. 12** ***Perf. 11½x11***

C121 AP35 5.50p green 1.90 2.50
  Never hinged 3.00

Stamp Day and Day of the Race. Exists imperf. Value $16.

Don Quixote and Sancho Panza Astride Clavileno AP36

**1947, Oct. 9** ***Perf. 10***

C122 AP36 5.50p purple 4.00 4.00
  Never hinged 6.00

Stamp Day and the 400th anniversary of the birth of Miguel de Cervantes Saavedra.

C122 exists imperf. Value, $500.

Manuel de Falla — AP37

Ignacio Zuloaga — AP38

**1947, Dec. 1** ***Perf. 9½x10½***

**Control Number on Back**

C123 AP37 25p dk vio brn 27.50 15.00
C124 AP38 50p dk carmine 110.00 40.00
  Set, never hinged 250.00

For overprint see No. CB18.

C124 exists imperf. Value, $925.

Train and Plane — AP39

**1948, Oct. 9** **Litho.** ***Perf. 13x12½***

C125 AP39 2p scarlet 1.50 1.50
  Never hinged 2.25

Cent. of Spanish railroads and Stamp Day.

**UPU Type of Regular Issue with Pedestal and Propeller Added**

**1949, Oct. 9** ***Perf. 12½x13***

**C126** A202 4p dk olive green .20 .45
Never hinged .40

Stamp Day and the 75th anniv. of the UPU.

Stamp of 1850
AP40

Map of Western Hemisphere
AP41

**1950, Oct. 12** **Engr.** ***Imperf.***

**C127** AP40 1p rose brn 4.50 6.50
**C128** AP40 2.50p brown org 4.50 6.50
**C129** AP40 20p dark blue 80.00 87.50
**C130** AP40 25p green 80.00 87.50
*Nos. C127-C130 (4)* 169.00 188.00
Set, never hinged 290.00

Centenary of Spanish postage stamps.

**1951, Apr. 16** **Photo.** ***Perf. 12½***

**C131** AP41 1p blue 4.50 2.25
Never hinged 6.25

6th Congress of the Postal Union of the Americas and Spain.

Isabella I
AP42

**1951, Oct. 12** **Engr.** ***Perf. 13***

**C132** AP42 60c dk gray grn 6.50 .40
**C133** AP42 90c orange .80 .55
**C134** AP42 1.30p plum 5.00 4.00
**C135** AP42 1.90p sepia 4.50 4.00
**C136** AP42 2.30p dk blue 2.75 2.75
*Nos. C132-C136 (5)* 19.55 11.70
Set, never hinged 27.50

Stamp Day and 500th anniv. of the birth of Queen Isabella I.

"The Eucharist" by Tiepolo — AP43

St. Francis Xavier — AP44

**1952, May 26** **Photo.** ***Perf. 12½x13***

**C137** AP43 1p gray green 3.00 .60
Never hinged 3.50

35th International Encharistic Congress, Barcelona, 1952.

**1952, July 3** **Engr.**

**C138** AP44 2p deep blue 30.00 14.00
Never hinged 50.00

400th anniv. of the death of St. Francis Xavier.

Ferdinand the Catholic and Columbus Presenting Natives
AP45

**1952, Oct. 12**

**C139** AP45 60c dull green .25 .20
**C140** AP45 90c orange .25 .20
**C141** AP45 1.30p plum .45 .30
**C142** AP45 1.90p sepia 2.00 2.00
**C143** AP45 2.30p deep blue 10.00 9.50
*Nos. C139-C143 (5)* 12.95 12.20
Set, never hinged 17.50

500th anniversary of the birth of Ferdinand the Catholic and to publicize Stamp Day.

Joaquin Sorolla y Bastida
AP46

Miguel Lopez de Legazpi
AP47

**1953, Oct. 9** ***Perf. 13x12½***

**C144** AP46 50p dark violet 300.00 22.50
Never hinged 675.00

Issued to honor Joaquin Sorolla y Bastida (1863-1923), impressionist painter.

**1953, Nov. 5**

**C145** AP47 25p gray black 57.50 27.50
Never hinged 125.00

Spanish-Philippine Postal Convention of 1951.

Leonardo Torres Quevedo (1852-1939), Mathematician and Inventor — AP48

***Perf. 13x12½***

**1955, Sept. 6** **Engr.** **Unwmk.**

**C146** AP48 50p bluish gray & blk 5.00 .90
Never hinged 11.00

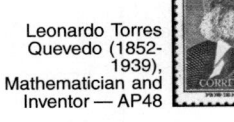

Plane and Caravel
AP49

**1955-56** **Photo.** ***Perf. 12½x13***

**C147** AP49 20c gray grn ('56) .20 .20
**C148** AP49 25c gray violet .20 .20
**C149** AP49 50c ol gray ('56) .20 .20
**C150** AP49 1p red orange .20 .20
**C151** AP49 1.10p emer ('56) .20 .20
**C152** AP49 1.40p rose car .20 .20
**C153** AP49 3p brt blue ('56) .20 .20
**C154** AP49 4.80p yellow .20 .20
**C155** AP49 5p redsh brown 1.50 .20
**C156** AP49 7p lilac ('56) .45 .20
**C157** AP49 10p lt ol grn ('56) .50 .25
*Nos. C147-C157 (11)* 2.25
Set, never hinged 4.00

Mariano Fortuny y Carbo (1838-1874), Painter — AP50

**1956, Jan. 10** **Engr.** ***Perf. 13x12½***

**C158** AP50 25p grnsh black 14.00 .90
Never hinged 30.00

**Catalogue values for unused stamps in this section, from this point to the end of the section, are for Never Hinged items.**

**Bullfight Type of Regular Issue**

25c, Small town arena. 50c, Fighting with cape. 1p, Dedication of the bull. 5p, Bull ring.

***Perf. 13x12½, 12½x13***

**1960, Feb. 29** **Engr.** **Unwmk.**

**C159** A246 25c brn car & dl lil .20 .20
**C160** A245 50c blue .20 .20
**C161** A246 1p red & dull red .20 .20
**C162** A245 5p red lilac & vio .55 .40
*Nos. C159-C162 (4)* 1.15 1.00

Jai Alai
AP51

**1960, Mar. 27** **Photo.** ***Perf. 12½x13***

**C163** AP51 1p brt red & dk brn 4.75 3.25
**C164** AP51 5p dull brn & mag 4.75 3.25
**C165** AP51 6p vio blk & mag 4.75 3.25
**C166** AP51 10p grn, mag & dk brn 4.75 3.25
*Nos. C163-C166 (4)* 19.00 13.00

1st Intl. Cong. of Philately, Barcelona, Mar. 26-Apr. 5. Nos. C163-C166 could be bought at the exhibition upon presentation of 5p entrance ticket.

**Sport Type of Regular Issue**

Sports: 1.25p, 6p, Steeplechase, horiz. 1.50p, 10p, Basque ball game.

***Perf. 12½x13, 13x12½***

**1960, Oct. 31** **Unwmk.**

**C167** A251 1.25p choc & car .30 .20
**C168** A251 1.50p pur, brn & blk .30 .20
**C169** A251 6p vio blk & car .95 .55
**C170** A251 10p ol grn, red & blk 1.25 .55
*Nos. C167-C170 (4)* 2.80 1.50

**Rosary Type of Regular Issue**

Mysteries of the Rosary: 25c, The Ascension, Bayeu. 1p, The Descent of the Holy Ghost, El Greco. 5p, The Assumption, Mateo Cerezo. 10p, The Coronation of the Virgin Mary, El Greco.

**1962, Oct. 26** **Engr.** ***Perf. 13***

**C171** A280 25c vio & dl gray vio .25 .20
**C172** A280 1p olive & brown .35 .20
**C173** A280 5p brn & rose cl .60 .25
**C174** A280 10p bluish grn & yel grn 1.40 .50
*Nos. C171-C174 (4)* 2.60 1.15

Recaredo I, Visigothic King, 586-601 — AP52

Portrait: 50p, Francisco Cardinal Jimenez de Cisneros (1436-1517).

**1963, Dec. 5** **Engr.** ***Perf. 13x12½***

**C175** AP52 25p dull purple 1.10 .40
**C176** AP52 50p green & black 1.90 .55

**1966, Feb. 26**

Portraits: 25p, Seneca (4 B.C.-65 A.D.). 50p, Pope St. Damasus I (304?-384).

**C177** AP52 25p yel grn & dk grn 1.75 .20
**C178** AP52 50p sky bl & gray bl 2.75 .55

Plaza de Espana, Seville
AP53

**1981, Nov. 26** **Engr.** ***Perf. 13***

**C179** AP53 13p shown .20 .20
**C180** AP53 20p Rande River Bridge, Pontevedra .25 .20

St. Thomas, by El Greco — AP54

**1982, July 7** **Photo.** ***Perf. 13***

**C181** AP54 13p Sts. Andrew and Francis .20 .20
**C182** AP54 20p shown .20 .20

Bowling
AP55

**1983, Apr. 13** **Photo.** ***Perf. 13***

**C183** AP55 13p Bicycling, vert. .20 .20
**C184** AP55 20p shown .20 .20

---

**AIR POST SEMI-POSTAL STAMPS**

**Red Cross Issue**

Ramon Franco's Plane Plus Ultra
SPAP1

***Perf. 12½, 13***

**1926, Sept. 15** **Engr.** **Unwmk.**

**CB1** SPAP1 5c black & vio 1.40 1.40
**CB2** SPAP1 10c ultra & blk 3.00 3.00
**CB3** SPAP1 25c carmine & blk .30 .30
**CB4** SPAP1 50c red org & blk .30 .30
**CB5** SPAP1 1p black & green 2.50 2.50
*Nos. CB1-CB5 (5)* 7.50 7.50
Set, never hinged 10.00

For overprints and surcharges see Nos. B55-B63.

No. B106 Surcharged in Black

**1938, Apr. 15** ***Perf. 11½***

**CB6** SP13 45c + 2p + 5p 250.00 225.00
Never hinged 450.00
*a.* Imperf., pair 1,150. 900.00
*b.* Souvenir sheet of 1 4,500. 4,500.
*c.* Souvenir sheet, imperf. 6,000. 6,000.
*d.* Souv. sheet, surch. invtd. 6,500. 5,750.

The surtax was used to benefit the defenders of Madrid.

This issue has been extensively counterfeited.

No. B107 Surcharged

**1938, June 1** ***Perf. 10***

**CB7** SP14 45c + 5p + 3p 10.00 9.75
Never hinged 17.50

Monument SPAP2

Dome Fresco by Goya, Cathedral of Zaragoza SPAP3

#CB8, CB11, Monument. #CB9, CB14, Caravel Santa Maria. #CB10, CB12, The Ascension. #CB13, CB15, The Coronation. #CB17, Bombardment of Cathedral of Zaragoza.

***Perf. 10½, 11½x10½, 11½***

**1940, Jan. 29 Litho. Unwmk.**

**Bicolored**

| | | | | |
|---|---|---|---|---|
| **CB8** | SPAP2 | 25c + 5c | .25 | .25 |
| **CB9** | SPAP2 | 50c + 5c | .25 | .25 |
| **CB10** | SPAP2 | 65c + 15c | .25 | .25 |
| **CB11** | SPAP2 | 70c + 15c | .25 | .25 |
| **CB12** | SPAP2 | 90c + 20c | .25 | .25 |
| **CB13** | SPAP2 | 1.20p + 30c | .25 | .25 |
| **CB14** | SPAP2 | 1.40p + 40c | .25 | .25 |
| **CB15** | SPAP2 | 2p + 50c | .40 | .40 |
| **CB16** | SPAP3 | 4p + 1p sl grn & rose lil | 9.75 | 9.75 |
| **CB17** | SPAP3 | 10p + 4p chnt & ultra | 225.00 | 225.00 |
| | | *Nos. CB8-CB17 (10)* | 236.90 | 236.90 |
| | | Set, never hinged | 350.00 | |

19th centenary of the Pillar Virgin. The surtax was used to help restore the Cathedral at Zaragoza, damaged during the Civil War.

No. CB16 exists in slate green & violet, No. CB17 in red violet & ultramarine. Value, $32.50 each.

Exist imperf. Value, set $350.

No. C123 Surcharged in Black

**1950-51** ***Perf. 9½x10½***

**Control Number on Back**

**CB18** AP37 25p + 10c 275.00 225.00
Never hinged 550.00
*a.* Without control number *3,250.* *1,250.*
Without control number, never hinged *5,000.*

Visit of Gen. Franco to the Canary Islands, Oct., 1950.

The control number was printed on the gum, and regummed copies of No. CB18 are frequently offered as No. CB18a.

Counterfeit surcharges exist.

Issued: #CB18a, 10/23/50; #CB18 2/22/51.

---

### AIR POST SPECIAL DELIVERY STAMP

#### Goya Commemorative Issue

Type of Air Post Stamp of 1930 Overprinted

**1930 Unwmk.** ***Perf. 12½***

**CE1** AP4 20c bl blk & lt brn (Bk) .20 .20
Never hinged .25
*a.* Blue overprint 15.00 7.75
Never hinged 21.00
*b.* Overprint omitted 15.00 22.50
Never hinged 25.00

See note after No. 432.

---

### AIR POST OFFICIAL STAMPS

#### Pan-American Postal Union Congress Issue

Types of Air Post Stamps of 1931 Overprinted in Red or Blue

**1931 Unwmk.** ***Perf. 12***

| | | | | |
|---|---|---|---|---|
| **CO1** | AP22 | 5c red brown (R) | .20 | .20 |
| **CO2** | AP22 | 10c blue grn (Bl) | .20 | .20 |
| **CO3** | AP22 | 25c rose (Bl) | .20 | .20 |
| **CO4** | AP23 | 50c lt blue (R) | .20 | .20 |
| **CO5** | AP23 | 1p violet (R) | .20 | .20 |
| **CO6** | AP24 | 4p gray blk (R) | 3.25 | 3.25 |
| | | *Nos. CO1-CO6 (6)* | 4.25 | 4.25 |
| | | Set, never hinged | 5.75 | |

Shades exist.

Exist imperf. Value, set $22.50.

---

### SPECIAL DELIVERY STAMPS

Pegasus and Coat of Arms — SD1

**1905-25 Unwmk. Typo.** ***Perf. 14***

**Control Number on Back**

**E1** SD1 20c deep red 40.00 .30
Never hinged 75.00
*a.* 20c rose red, litho. ('25) 35.00 .30
*b.* Imperf., pair 275.00
*c.* As "a," imperf., pair 275.00

Gazelle SD2

Pegasus — SD3

**1929 Engr.** ***Perf. 11***

**Control Number on Back**

**E2** SD2 20c dull red 17.50 20.00
Never hinged 32.50
*a.* Perf. 14 29.00 32.50
Never hinged 55.00

Seville and Barcelona Exhibitions. See note after No. 432.

**1929-32** ***Perf. 13½x12½, 11½***

**Control Number on Back**

**E3** SD3 20c red 19.00 3.75
Never hinged 37.50
*a.* Imperf., pair 375.00
*b.* Without control number, perf. 11½ ('32) 55.00 1.40
Never hinged 87.50
*c.* As "b," imperf., pair *875.00*

#### No. E3 Overprinted like Nos. 358-370

**E4** SD3 20c red (Bl) 12.00 25.00
Never hinged 25.00

League of Nations 55th assembly.

For overprints see Nos. E5, E10-E12.

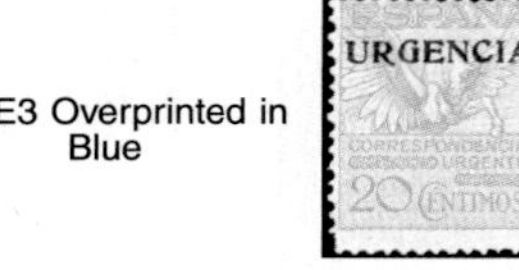

No. E3 Overprinted in Blue

**1930** ***Perf. 13½x12½, 11½***

**E5** SD3 20c red 12.00 .65
Never hinged 32.50

#### Railway Congress Issue

Electric Locomotive — SD4

**1930, May 10 Litho.** ***Perf. 14***

**Control Number on Back**

**E6** SD4 20c brown orange 50.00 50.00
Never hinged 95.00

See note after No. 385.

#### Goya Issue

Type of Regular Issue of 1930 Overprinted

**1930** ***Perf. 12½***

**E7** A57 20c lilac rose .20 .30
Never hinged .40

#### Christopher Columbus Issue

Type of Regular Issue of 1930 Overprinted

**1930 Sept. 29**

**E8** A64 20c brown violet 1.75 1.75
Never hinged 2.75

See note after No. 432.

#### Spanish-American Exhibition Issue

View of Seville Exhibition — SD5

**1930, Oct. 10 Photo.** ***Perf. 14***

**E9** SD5 20c orange .40 .25
Never hinged .55

See note after No. 432.

#### Madrid Issue

No. E5 Overprinted in Green

**1931** ***Perf. 11½***

**E10** SD3 20c red 4.50 4.50
Never hinged 7.25

The status of No. E10 has been questioned.

#### Barcelona Issue

No. E3 Overprinted

**E11** SD3 20c red 5.00 5.00
Never hinged 11.00

No. E11 also exists with accent over "U." The status of No. E11 has been questioned.

No. E3 Overprinted in Blue

**E12** SD3 20c red 5.50 1.00
Never hinged 19.00

#### Montserrat Issue

Pegasus — SD6

**1931 Engr.** ***Perf. 11***

**Control Number on Back**

**E13** SD6 20c vermilion 22.50 22.50
Never hinged 35.00
*a.* Perf. 14 55.00 60.00

SD7

**1934** ***Perf. 10***

**E14** SD7 20c vermilion .20 .20
Never hinged .20
*a.* Imperf., pair 32.50

For overprints see #10LE1, 11LE1-11LE4, 14LE1.

Newsboy — SD8

Pegasus SD9

**1936 Photo. *Perf. 12½***

**E15** SD8 20c rose carmine .25 .30
Never hinged .40

Madrid Press Association, 40th anniv.
See note after No. 432.

### Spanish State

**1937-38 Unwmk. Litho. *Perf. 11***
**With imprint "Hija. de B Fournier-Burgos"**

**E16** SD9 20c violet brn 7.75 4.50
Never hinged 11.00
*a.* Imperf., pair 77.50

**Without Imprint**

**E17** SD9 20c dk vio brn ('38) 1.50 .30
Never hinged 2.75
*a.* Imperf., pair 50.00

No. 645 Overprinted in Black

**1937**

**E18** A162 20c dark violet 11.00 11.00
Never hinged 14.50

Pegasus SD10

**1939-42 *Perf. 10½***
**Imprint: "SANCHEZ TODA"**

**E19** SD10 25c carmine 4.50 .70
Never hinged 6.25
*a.* Imperf., pair 50.00

**Without Imprint**
***Perf. 10***

**E20** SD10 25c carmine ('42) .20 .20
Never hinged .30

**Catalogue values for unused stamps in this section, from this point to the end of the section, are for Never Hinged items.**

"Flight" SD11

Centaur — SD12

***Perf. 12½x13, 13x12½***
**1956, Feb. 12 Photo. Unwmk.**

**E21** SD11 2p scarlet .20 .20
**E22** SD12 4p black & magenta .20 .20

**1965-66**

**E23** SD11 3p dp car .20 .20
**E24** SD11 5p dp org ('66) .20 .20
**E25** SD12 6.50p dk vio & rose brn ('66) .20 .20
*Nos. E21-E25 (5)* 1.00 1.00

Chariot SD13

Mail Circling Globe — SD14

**1971, June 1 Photo. *Perf. 13***

**E26** SD13 10p red & yel grn .20 .20
**E27** SD14 15p red, bl & blk .20 .20

Communications — SD15

**1993, Apr. 20 Photo. *Perf. 14x13½***

**E28** SD15 180p red & yellow 2.50 .35

### SEMI-POSTAL SPECIAL DELIVERY STAMPS

**Red Cross Issue**

Royal Family Group SPSD1

**1926 Unwmk. Engr. *Perf. 12½, 13***

**EB1** SPSD1 20c red vio & vio brn 8.75 8.75
Never hinged 17.00

See notes after Nos. 432 and B18.
For overprint see No. B54.

Motorcyclist and Zaragoza Cathedral SPSD2

**1940 Litho. *Perf. 11½***

**EB2** SPSD2 25c + 5c rose red & buff .40 .30

19th cent. of the Pillar Virgin. The surtax was used to help restore the Cathedral at Zaragoza, damaged during the Civil War.

### DELIVERY TAX STAMPS

D1

**1931 Unwmk. Litho. *Perf. 11½***

**ER1** D1 5c black 7.25 .20
Never hinged 12.00

For overprints see Nos. ER2-ER3, 7LE5-7LE6.

No. ER1 Overprinted in Red

**1931**

**ER2** D1 5c black 1.25 1.40
Never hinged 2.25

No. ER2 also exists with accent over "U."

No. ER1 Overprinted in Red

**ER3** D1 5c black 3.00 3.00
Never hinged 5.50

These stamps were originally issued for Postage Due purpose but were later used as regular postage stamps.

### WAR TAX STAMPS

These stamps did not pay postage but represented a fiscal tax on mail matter in addition to the postal fees. Their use was obligatory.

Coat of Arms
WT1 WT2

**Unwmk.**
**1874, Jan. 1 Typo. *Perf. 14***

**MR1** WT1 5c black 9.50 .95
*a.* Imperf. pair 14.00
**MR2** WT1 10c pale blue 10.50 1.60
*a.* Imperf., pair 62.50

**1875, Jan. 1**

**MR3** WT2 5c green 5.25 .60
*a.* Imperf., pair 27.50
**MR4** WT2 10c lilac 11.00 2.75
*a.* Imperf., pair 55.00

King Alfonso XII
WT3 WT4

**1876, June 1**

**MR5** WT3 5c pale green 6.25 1.00
**MR6** WT3 10c blue 6.25 1.00
*a.* Cliche of 5c in plate of 10c 125.00
**MR7** WT3 25c black 50.00 17.00
**MR8** WT3 1p lilac 475.00 110.00
**MR9** WT3 5p rose 775.00 300.00

Nos. MR5-MR9 exist imperforate. Value, $1,100.

**1877, Sept. 1**

**MR10** WT4 15c claret 27.50 1.00
*a.* Imperf., pair 100.00
**MR11** WT4 50c yellow 775.00 110.00

WT5

WT6

**1879**

**MR12** WT5 5c blue 42.00
**MR13** WT5 10c rose 25.00
**MR14** WT5 15c violet 15.50
**MR15** WT5 25c brown 25.00
**MR16** WT5 50c olive green 15.50
**MR17** WT5 1p bister 25.00
**MR18** WT5 5p gray 90.00
*Nos. MR12-MR18 (7)* 238.00

Nos. MR12-MR18 were never placed in use.
Nos. MR17 and MR18 exist imperf. Value, $225.

Inscribed "1897 A 1898"

**1897 *Perf. 14***

**MR19** WT6 5c green 3.00 1.90
**MR20** WT6 10c green 3.00 1.90
**MR21** WT6 15c green 450.00 190.00
**MR22** WT6 20c green 7.50 3.00

Nos. MR19-MR22 exist imperf. Value for set $825.

Inscribed "1898-99"

**1898**

**MR23** WT6 5c black 2.25 1.75
**MR24** WT6 10c black 2.25 1.75
**MR25** WT6 15c black 50.00 9.50
**MR26** WT6 20c black 3.50 3.00
*Nos. MR23-MR26 (4)* 58.00 16.00

Nos. MR23-MR26 exist imperf. Value about $275 a pair.

King Alfonso XIII — WT7

**1898**

**MR27** WT7 5c black 7.50 .60
*a.* Imperf., pair 85.00

### OFFICIAL STAMPS

Coat of Arms
O1 O2

**Unwmk.**
**1854, July 1 Typo. *Imperf.***

**O1** O1 ½o blk, *yellow* 2.10 2.75
**O2** O1 1o blk, *rose* 2.75 3.25
*a.* 1o black, *blue* 29.00
**O3** O1 4o blk, *green* 7.50 9.25
**O4** O1 1 l blk, *blue* 52.50 60.00
*Nos. O1-O4 (4)* 64.85 75.25

**1855-63**

**O5** O2 ½o blk, *yellow* 1.50 1.75
*a.* ½o black, *straw* ('63) 1.75 1.90
**O6** O2 1o blk, *rose* 1.50 1.75
*a.* 1o black, *salmon rose* 3.25 1.90
**O7** O2 4o blk, *green* 3.25 1.90
*a.* 4o black, *yellow green* 8.75 1.90
**O8** O2 1 l blk, *gray blue* 14.50 17.50
*Nos. O5-O8 (4)* 20.75 22.90

The "value indication" on Nos. O1-O8 actually is the weight of the mail in onzas (ounces, "o") and libras (pounds, "l") for which they were valid.

Type of Regular Issue of 1889

**1895 *Perf. 14***

**O9** A34 15c yellow 10.00 6.00
*a.* Imperf., pair 250.00

Coat of Arms — O5

**1896-98**

**O10** O5 rose 5.25 1.75
*a.* Imperf., pair 87.50
**O11** O5 dk blue ('98) 17.50 6.00

**Cervantes Issue**

Chamber of Deputies O6

Statue of Cervantes — O7

Cervantes — O9

National Library O8

**1916, Apr. 22 Engr. *Perf. 12***

**For the Senate**

| | | | | |
|---|---|---|---|---|
| **O12** | O6 | green & blk | 1.10 | .90 |
| **O13** | O7 | brown & blk | 1.10 | .90 |
| **O14** | O8 | carmine & blk | 1.10 | .90 |
| **O15** | O9 | brown & blk | 1.10 | .90 |

**For the Chamber of Deputies**

| | | | | |
|---|---|---|---|---|
| **O16** | O6 | violet & blk | 1.10 | .90 |
| **O17** | O7 | carmine & blk | 1.10 | .90 |
| **O18** | O8 | green & blk | 1.10 | .90 |
| **O19** | O9 | violet & blk | 1.10 | .90 |
| | | *Nos. O12-O19 (8)* | 8.80 | 7.20 |

Exist imperf. Value set of pairs, $110.

Exist with centers inverted. Value for set, $87.50.

### Pan-American Postal Union Congress Issue

Types of Regular Issue of 1931 Overprinted in Red or Blue

**1931 *Perf. 12½***

| | | | | |
|---|---|---|---|---|
| **O20** | A84 | 5c dk brown (R) | .40 | .20 |
| **O21** | A85 | 10c brt green (Bl) | .40 | .20 |
| **O22** | A86 | 15c dull violet (R) | .40 | .20 |
| **O23** | A85 | 25c deep rose (Bl) | .40 | .20 |
| **O24** | A87 | 30c olive green (Bl) | .40 | .20 |
| **O25** | A84 | 40c ultra (R) | .55 | .50 |
| **O26** | A85 | 50c deep orange (Bl) | .55 | .50 |
| **O27** | A86 | 1p blue black (R) | .55 | .50 |
| **O28** | A88 | 4p magenta (Bl) | 12.50 | 12.50 |
| **O29** | A88 | 10p lt brown (R) | 22.50 | 22.50 |
| | | *Nos. O20-O29 (10)* | 38.65 | 37.50 |
| | | Set, never hinged | 55.00 | |

Nos. O22-O29 exist imperf. Values about 3 times those quoted.

Mail Coach O30

Decorative Mailbox Opening O10

Mail Pouch O11

Bicycle for Mail Delivery O12

**1999 Photo. *Perf. 13¾x14***

| | | | |
|---|---|---|---|
| **O30** | O9 | multi | — |
| **O31** | O10 | multi | — |
| **O32** | O11 | multi | — |
| **O33** | O12 | multi | — |
| *a.* | | Horiz. strip, #O30-O33 | — |

For use by the Philatelic Service to any address. Not normally available unused.

## POSTAL TAX STAMPS

PT5

PT6

***Perf. 10½x11½***

**1937, Dec. 23 Litho.**

| | | | | |
|---|---|---|---|---|
| **RA11** | PT5 | 10c blk, pale bl & red | 7.25 | 4.50 |
| | | Never hinged | 19.00 | |
| *a.* | | Imperf. pair | 72.50 | |
| | | Never hinged | 110.00 | |

The tax was for the tuberculosis fund.

**1938, Dec. 23 *Perf. 11½***

| | | | | |
|---|---|---|---|---|
| **RA12** | PT6 | 10c multicolored | 4.50 | 1.75 |
| | | Never hinged | 10.00 | |
| *a.* | | Imperf. pair | 45.00 | |
| | | Never hinged | 55.00 | |

The tax was for the tuberculosis fund.

"Spain" Holding Wreath of Peace over Marching Soldiers PT7

**1939, July 18 *Perf. 11***

| | | | | |
|---|---|---|---|---|
| **RA13** | PT7 | 10c blue | .20 | .20 |
| | | Never hinged | .25 | |
| *a.* | | Imperf. pair | 65.00 | |
| | | Never hinged | 82.50 | |

Type of Regular Issue, 1939 Without Imprint

**Unwmk.**

**1939, Dec. 23 Litho. *Imperf.***

| | | | | |
|---|---|---|---|---|
| **RA14** | A166 | 10c dull claret | .20 | .20 |
| | | Never hinged | .25 | |

### Tuberculosis Fund Issues

Types of Corresponding Semi-Postal Stamps

**1940, Dec. 23 *Perf. 10***

| | | | | |
|---|---|---|---|---|
| **RA15** | SP23 | 10c violet & red | .20 | .20 |
| | | Never hinged | .25 | |

**1941, Dec. 23**

| | | | | |
|---|---|---|---|---|
| **RA16** | SP24 | 10c black & red | .20 | .20 |
| | | Never hinged | .25 | |

**1942, Dec. 23**

| | | | | |
|---|---|---|---|---|
| **RA17** | SP25 | 10c dl sal & rose red | .20 | .20 |
| | | Never hinged | .25 | |

**1943, Dec. 23 Photo. *Perf. 11***

| | | | | |
|---|---|---|---|---|
| **RA18** | SP26 | 10c purple & dl red | .30 | .25 |
| | | Never hinged | .50 | |

***Perf. 9½x10***

**1944, Dec. 23 Litho. Unwmk.**

| | | | | |
|---|---|---|---|---|
| **RA19** | SP27 | 10c salmon & rose | .20 | .20 |
| | | Never hinged | .25 | |

**1945, Dec. 23**

| | | | | |
|---|---|---|---|---|
| **RA20** | SP28 | 10c salmon & car | .20 | .20 |
| | | Never hinged | .25 | |

Mother and Child — PT8

**1946, Dec. 22 Litho. *Perf. 9½x10½***

| | | | | |
|---|---|---|---|---|
| **RA21** | PT8 | 5c violet & red | .20 | .20 |
| **RA22** | PT8 | 10c green & red | .20 | .20 |
| | | Set, never hinged | .40 | |

See No. RAC7.

Lorraine Cross PT9

Tuberculosis Sanatorium PT10

***Perf. 9½x10½***

**1947, Dec. 22 Unwmk.**

| | | | | |
|---|---|---|---|---|
| **RA23** | PT9 | 5c dk brown & red | .20 | .20 |
| **RA24** | PT10 | 10c vio bl & red | .20 | .20 |
| | | Set, never hinged | .40 | |

See No. RAC8.

Aesculapius PT11

"El Cid" PT11a

**Photogravure; Cross Engraved**

**1948, Dec. 22 Unwmk. *Perf. 12½***

| | | | | |
|---|---|---|---|---|
| **RA25** | PT11 | 5c brown & car | .20 | .20 |
| **RA26** | PT11 | 10c dp green & car | .20 | .20 |
| | | Set, never hinged | .40 | |

The tax on Nos. RA15-RA26 was used to fight tuberculosis. See Nos. RAB1, RAC9.

**1949, Feb. 1 Litho. *Perf. 10½x9½***

| | | | | |
|---|---|---|---|---|
| **RA27** | PT11a | 5c violet | .20 | .20 |
| | | Never hinged | .25 | |

The tax aided displaced children. Valid for ordinary postage after Dec. 24, 1949.

### Tuberculosis Fund Issues

Galleon and Lorraine Cross — PT12

Pine Branch and Candle — PT13

**Photogravure; Cross Engraved**

**1949, Dec. 22 *Perf. 12½***

| | | | | |
|---|---|---|---|---|
| **RA28** | PT12 | 5c violet & red | .20 | .20 |
| **RA29** | PT12 | 10c yel grn & red | .20 | .20 |
| | | Set, never hinged | .40 | |

See Nos. RAB2, RAC10.

**1950, Dec. 22**

**Cross in Carmine**

| | | | | |
|---|---|---|---|---|
| **RA30** | PT13 | 5c rose violet | .20 | .20 |
| **RA31** | PT13 | 10c deep green | .20 | .20 |
| | | Set, never hinged | .35 | |

See Nos. RAB3, RAC11.

Children at Seashore PT14

Nurse and Baby PT15

**1951, Oct. 1**

**Cross in Carmine**

| | | | | |
|---|---|---|---|---|
| **RA32** | PT14 | 5c rose brown | .20 | .20 |
| **RA33** | PT14 | 10c dull green | .35 | .20 |
| | | Set, never hinged | .75 | |

See No. RAC12.

**1953, Oct. 1**

**Cross in Carmine**

| | | | | |
|---|---|---|---|---|
| **RA34** | PT15 | 5c carmine lake | .30 | .20 |
| **RA35** | PT15 | 10c gray blue | .80 | .20 |
| | | Set, never hinged | 2.25 | |

The tax on RA28-RA35 was used to fight tuberculosis. See No. RAC13.

## POSTAL TAX SEMI-POSTAL STAMPS

Types of Corresponding Postal Tax Stamps

**Photogravure; Cross Engraved**

**1948 Unwmk. *Perf. 12½***

| | | | | |
|---|---|---|---|---|
| **RAB1** | PT11 | 50c + 10c red brn & car | .80 | .75 |
| | | Never hinged | 1.25 | |

**1949**

| | | | | |
|---|---|---|---|---|
| **RAB2** | PT12 | 50c + 10c dk ol bis & red | .50 | .25 |
| | | Never hinged | .80 | |

**1950**

| | | | | |
|---|---|---|---|---|
| **RAB3** | PT13 | 50c + 10c brn & car | 1.25 | 1.25 |
| | | Never hinged | 2.25 | |

The surtax on Nos. RAB1-RAB3 was used to fight tuberculosis. Combines domestic letter rate and tax obligatory Dec. 22-Jan. 3.

## POSTAL TAX AIR POST STAMPS

### Tuberculosis Fund Issues

Franco Type of Semi-Postal Stamps

**Unwmk.**

**1940, Dec. 23 Litho. *Perf. 10***

| | | | | |
|---|---|---|---|---|
| **RAC1** | SP23 | 10c bright pink & red | .90 | .90 |
| | | Never hinged | 2.50 | |

Knight and Lorraine Cross — PTAP2

**1941, Dec. 23**

| | | | | |
|---|---|---|---|---|
| **RAC2** | PTAP2 | 10c blue & red | .25 | .25 |
| | | Never hinged | .50 | |

Lorraine Cross and Doves PTAP3

**1942, Dec. 23**

| | | | | |
|---|---|---|---|---|
| **RAC3** | PTAP3 | 10c dl sal & rose | .80 | .50 |
| | | Never hinged | 1.25 | |

Cross of Lorraine — PTAP4

Tuberculosis Sanatorium PTAP5

**1943, Dec. 23 Photo. *Perf. 11***

**RAC4** PTAP4 10c vio & dl red .90 1.00
Never hinged 1.60

**1944, Dec. 23 Litho. *Perf. 10x9½***

**RAC5** PTAP5 25c salmon & rose 3.75 3.75
Never hinged 5.50

Lorraine Cross and Eagle — PTAP6

**1945, Dec. 23 *Perf. 10***

**RAC6** PTAP6 25c red & car 1.40 1.25
Never hinged 1.75

Eagle — PTAP7

**1946, Dec. 22**

**RAC7** PTAP7 25c red & car .20 .20
Never hinged .40

Tuberculosis Sanatorium PTAP8

Plane over Sanatorium PTAP9

**1947, Dec. 22 *Perf. 11½***

**RAC8** PTAP8 25c red vio .20 .20
Never hinged .40

**Photogravure; Cross Engraved**

**1948, Dec. 22 *Perf. 12½***

**RAC9** PTAP9 25c ultra & car .30 .25
Never hinged .60

Bell and Lorraine Cross PTAP10

Dove and Flowers PTAP11

**1949, Dec. 22**

**RAC10** PTAP10 25c maroon & red .20 .20
Never hinged .25

**1950, Dec. 22**

**RAC11** PTAP11 25c dk bl & car .30 .30
Never hinged .60

Mother and Child PTAP12

Tobias and Archangel PTAP13

**1951, Oct. 1**

**RAC12** PTAP12 25c brn & car .50 .20
Never hinged .80

**1953, Oct. 1**

**RAC13** PTAP13 25c brn & car 3.50 5.50
Never hinged 6.50

## FRANCHISE STAMPS

F1

F2

**1869 Unwmk. Litho. *Imperf.***

**S1** F1 blue 47.50 35.00
*a.* Tête bêche pair 125.00 110.00

The franchise of No. S1 was granted to Diego Castell to use in distributing his publications on Spanish postal history.

**1881**

**S2** F2 black, *buff* 32.50 14.00

The franchise of No. S2 was granted to Antonio Fernandez Duro for his book, "Resena histórico-descriptiva de los sellos correos de Espana."

*Reprints of No. S2 have been made on carmine, blue, gray, fawn and yellow paper.*

## CARLIST STAMPS

From the beginning of the Civil War (April 21, 1872) until separate stamps were issued on July 1, 1873, stamps of France were used on all mail from the provinces under Carlist rule.

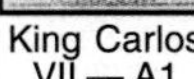
King Carlos VII — A1

Tilde on N — A1a

**Unwmk.**

**1873, July 1 Litho. *Imperf.***

**X1** A1 1r blue 550.00
**X2** A1a 1r blue 450.00 300.00

*These stamps were reprinted three times in 1881 and once in 1887. The originals have 23 white lines and dots in the lower right spandrel. They are thin and of even width and spacing. The first reprint has 17 to 20 lines in the spandrel, most of them thick and of irregular width and length. The second and third reprints have 21 very thin lines, the second from the bottom being almost invisible. In the fourth reprint the lower right spandrel is an almost solid spot of color.*

*Originals of type A1 have the curved line above "ESPANA" broken at the left of the "E." All reprints of this type have the curved line continuous.*

*The reprints exist in various shades of blue, rose, red, violet and black.*

King Carlos VII
A2 A3

A4

A5

**1874**

**X3** A2 1r violet 240.00 240.00
**X4** A3 16m rose 4.75 *72.50*
**X5** A4 ½r rose 100.00 100.00

Nos. X3 and X6-X7 were for use in the Basque Provinces and Navarra; No. X4 in Catalonia, and No. X5 in Valencia.

Two types of No. X5, alternating in each sheet.

No. X4 with favor cancellation (lozenge of dots) sells for same price as unused.

**1875**

**White Paper**

**X6** A5 50c green 8.00 *82.50*
*a.* 50c blue green 25.00 *100.00*
*b.* Bluish paper 50.00
**X7** A5 1r brown 8.00 *82.50*
*a.* Bluish paper 50.00
Set, #X6-X7, never hinged 24.00

Fake cancellations exist on Nos. X1-X7.

## REVOLUTIONARY OVERPRINTS

### Issued by the Nationalist (Revolutionary) Forces

Many districts or cities made use of the stamps of the Republic overprinted in various forms. Most such overprinting was authorized by military or postal officials but some were without official sanction. These overprints were applied in patriotic celebration and partly as a protection from the use of unoverprinted stamps seized or stolen by soldiers.

## BURGOS AIR POST STAMPS

RAP1

Revenue Stamps Overprinted in Red, Blue or Black

**1936, Dec. 1 Unwmk. *Perf. 11½***

**Control Number on Face of Stamp**

**7LC1** RAP1 25c gray grn & blk (R) 42.50 42.50
*a.* Blue overprint 42.50 42.50
**7LC2** RAP1 1.50p bl & blk (R) 5.50 5.50
**7LC3** RAP1 3p rose & blk (Bl) 5.50 5.50
*Nos. 7LC1-7LC3 (3)* 53.50 53.50
Set, never hinged 95.00

RAP2

RAP4

***Perf. 13½***

**Blue Control Number on Back**

**7LC4** RAP2 15c green (R) 3.75 3.75
**7LC5** RAP2 25c blue (R) 27.50 27.50
Set, never hinged 45.00

***Perf. 11½***

**Without Control Number**

**Overprint in Black**

**7LC6** RAP4 1.50p dk blue 6.50 6.50
**7LC7** RAP4 3p carmine 6.50 6.50
Set, never hinged 21.00

RAP5

RAP6

**Overprint in Black**

***Perf. 13½, 11½***

**7LC8** RAP5 1.20p green 25.00 25.00
Never hinged 37.50

***Perf. 14***

**Control Number on Back**

**7LC9** RAP6 1.20p green 25.00 25.00
**7LC10** RAP6 2.40p green 25.00 25.00
Set #7LC9-7LC10, never hinged 70.00

No. 7LC9 is inscribed "CLASE 8a."

RAP7

**1937 Unwmk. *Perf. 11½***

**Control Number on Back**

**7LC11** RAP7 25c ultra (R) 225.00 225.00

Stamps of Spain, 1931-36, Overprinted in Red or Black (10p)

***Perf. 11, 11½, 11x11½***

**1937 Unwmk.**

**Overprint 13mm high**

**7LC12** A100 40c blue 1.10 1.10
*a.* Ovpt. 15mm high 1.10 1.10
**7LC13** A97 50c dark blue 1.40 1.40
*a.* Ovpt. 15mm high 1.40 1.40
**7LC14** A130 50c dark blue 1.75 1.75
*a.* Ovpt. 15mm high 1.75 1.75
**7LC15** A100 60c apple green 2.50 2.50
*a.* Ovpt. 15mm high 2.50 2.50
**7LC16** AP26 2p gray blue 32.50 32.50
*a.* Ovpt. 15mm high 32.50 32.50
**7LC17** A49a 10p brown 82.50 82.50
*a.* Ovpt. 15mm high 82.50 82.50
*Nos. 7LC12-7LC17 (6)* 121.75 121.75

Issue dates: Nos. 7LC12-7LC17, 4/1. Nos. 7LC12a-7LC17a, 5/1.

Spain Nos. 576, 578 and 541b overprinted in Blue or Black

Nos. 7LC18, 7LC19

Nos. 7LC20, 7LC21

***Perfs as on Basic Stamps***

**1937, May**

**7LC18** A127 30c carmine (Bk) 1.40 1.40
**7LC19** A127 30c carmine (Bl) .70 .70
**7LC20** A129 30c car rose (Bk) 1.40 1.40

**7LC21** A129 30c car rose (Bl) .70 .70
**7LC22** A107 10p dp brn (Bk) 11.00 11.00
*Nos. 7LC18-7LC22 (5)* 15.20 15.20

Spain Nos. 539b and 540b, the 1p and 4p values, were prepared with this overprint in January, 1938, but were not issued. Value, each $4.50.

### BURGOS ISSUE SPECIAL DELIVERY STAMPS

Pair of Spain No. 546 Overprinted in Black

**1936 Unwmk. *Perf. 11½x11***
**7LE3** A110 20c (10c+10c) emer 4.50 4.50
Never hinged 9.00
*a.* Overprint inverted 14.00

Type of Regular Stamp of 1931 Overprinted in Red

**7LE4** A95 20c dark violet 10.00 10.00

Type of Delivery Tax Stamp of 1931 Overprinted in Red on four 5c stamps

***Perf. 11½***
**7LE5** D1 20c black 8.75 8.00
Never hinged 13.50

Same Overprinted in Red on four 5c stamps

**7LE6** D1 20c black 30.00 25.00
Never hinged 50.00

SD1

**1936 Unwmk. *Perf. 11½***
**7LE7** SD1 20c green & blk 7.25 5.50
**7LE8** SD1 20c green & red 7.25 5.50
Set, never hinged 25.00

Nos. 7LE7-7LE8 exist with control number on back. Value $42.50 each.

### CADIZ ISSUE SEMI-POSTAL STAMPS

Stamps of Spain, 1931-36, Surcharged in Black or Red

**1936 Unwmk. *Imperf.***
**8LB1** A108 1c + 5c blue grn .20 .20

***Perf. 11½x11, 11½***
**8LB2** A108 2c + 5c orange brn .20 .20
**8LB3** A103 5c + 5c choc (R) .45 .45
**8LB4** A110 10c + 5c green .45 .45
**8LB5** A111 15c + 5c Prus grn (R) 2.75 2.75
**8LB6** A95 20c + 5c dk vio (R) 3.25 3.25
**8LB7** A104 25c + 5c lake 2.50 2.50
**8LB8** A113 30c + 5c rose red 1.40 1.40
**8LB9** A100 40c + 5c dk blue (R) 3.25 3.25
**8LB10** A97 50c + 5c dk blue (R) 6.50 6.50
*Nos. 8LB1-8LB10 (10)* 20.95 20.95

### CANARY ISLANDS AIR POST STAMPS

**Issued for Use via the Lufthansa Service**

Stamps of Spain, 1932-34, Surcharged in Blue

VIVA ESPAÑA
18 JULIO 1936
HABILITADO
AVIÓN
Pts. 0'50

**1936, Oct. 27 Unwmk. *Imperf.***
**9LC1** A108 50c on 1c bl grn 27.50 17.50

***Perf. 11½x11***
**9LC2** A108 80c on 2c buff 14.50 6.50
**9LC3** A103 1.25p on 5c choc 30.00 17.50
*Nos. 9LC1-9LC3 (3)* 72.00 41.50
Set, never hinged 82.50

The date July 18, 1936, in the overprints of Nos. 9LC1-9LC22 marks the beginning of the Franco insurrection.

Spain Nos. 542, 543, 528 and 641 Surcharged in Black, Red or Green

The surcharge on Nos. 9LC4 and 9LC6 exists in two types: Type I, 2½-3mm space between numerals and "Cts.". Type II, 1½-2mm space between numerals and "Cts."

**1936-37 *Imperf.***
**9LC4** A108 50c on 1c bl grn (I) 4.50 2.75
*a.* Overprint type II 11.00 7.75
**9LC5** A108 50c on 1c bl grn (R) ('37) 4.50 2.75

***Perf. 11, 11½x11***
**9LC6** A108 80c on 2c buff (I) 2.25 1.60
*a.* Overprint type II 5.50 3.25
**9LC7** A108 80c on 2c buff (G) ('37) 3.25 1.60
**9LC8** A103 1.25 Pts on 5c choc (R) 6.25 4.50
**9LC9** A103 Pts 1.25 on 5c choc (R) ('37) 17.00 11.00
**9LC10** A161 1.25p on 5c brn (G) ('37) 3.25 1.40
*Nos. 9LC4-9LC10 (7)* 41.00 25.60
Set, never hinged 65.00

Issued: Nos. 9LC4, 9LC6, 11/28/36; No. 9LC8, 1/7/37; Nos. 9LC4a, 9LC6a, 9LC9, 2/12/37; Nos. 9LC5, 9LC7, 9LC10, 3/2/37.

Spain Nos. 542, 543 and 641 Surcharged in Blue

CANARIAS
A
FRANCO
18 JULIO 1936
AVIÓN
50 Cts.

**1937, Mar. 31 *Imperf.***

The surcharge on Nos. 9LC11-9LC13 exists in two types: Type I, 18mm tall. Type II, 20mm tall.

**9LC11** A108 50c on 1c bl grn (I) 11.00 5.50
*a.* Overprint type II 4.50 2.25

***Perf. 11***
**9LC12** A108 80c on 2c buff (I) 11.00 4.50
*a.* Overprint type II 2.75 1.10
**9LC13** A161 1.25p on 5c brown (I) 3.25 1.10
*Nos. 9LC11-9LC13 (3)* 25.25 11.10
Set, never hinged 40.00

Type II overprints issued 4/17/37.

Stamps of Spain, 1931-1936, Surcharged in Blue or Red (#9LC17, 9LC19)

The surcharge on Nos. 9LC15 and 9LC18 exists in two types: Type I, 2mm space between "+" and denomination. Type II, "+" abuts surcharged denomination. Other values are Type I.

**1937**
**9LC14** A104 25c + 50c lake 50.00 10.00
**9LC15** A162 30c + 80c rose 17.50 7.75
*a.* Overprint type II 17.50 7.75
**9LC16** A162 30c + 1.25p rose 22.50 8.25
**9LC17** A97 50c + 1.25p dp bl 29.00 11.00
**9LC18** A100 60c + 80c ap grn 22.50 8.75
*a.* Overprint type II 25.00 10.00
**9LC19** A105 1p + 1.25p bl blk 72.50 22.50
*Nos. 9LC14-9LC19 (6)* 214.00 68.25
Set, never hinged 300.00

The surcharge represents the airmail rate and the basic stamp the postage rate.

Issued: 9LC15a, 9LC18a, 4/15. 9LC14-9LC19, 5/5.

Spain Nos. 542, 624 and 641 Surcharged in Black

**1937, May 25 Unwmk. *Imperf.***
**9LC20** A108 50c on 1c bl grn 7.75 4.50

***Perf. 11½, 11½x11***
**9LC21** A143 80c on 2c org brn 6.50 2.25
**9LC22** A161 1.25p on 5c gray brn 6.50 2.25
*Nos. 9LC20-9LC22 (3)* 20.75 9.00
Set, never hinged 30.00

Stamps and Type of Spain, 1933-36, Surcharged in Black

**1937, July *Perf. 13½x13, 11, 11½***
**9LC23** A143 50c on 2c org brn 3.25 2.25
**9LC24** A126 80c on 2c org brn 325.00 180.00
**9LC25** A161 80c on 5c gray brn 3.25 2.25
**9LC26** A108 1.25p on 1c bl grn 3.75 2.25
**9LC27** A161 2.50p on 10c grn 14.50 8.75

Spain Nos. 647, 650 and 652 Surcharged in Black or Red

***Perf. 11***
**9LC28** A162 30c + 80c rose 2.75 1.40
**9LC29** A162 50c + 1.25p dk bl (R) 9.50 5.00
**9LC30** A162 1p + 1.25p bl (R) 14.50 8.75
*Nos. 9LC23-9LC30 (8)* 376.50 210.65
Set, never hinged 375.00

See note after No. 9LC19.

AP1

***Perf. 14x13½***
**1937, July 16 Wmk. 116**
**Surcharge in Various Colors**
**9LC31** AP1 50c on 5c ultra (Br) 2.75 2.50
**9LC32** AP1 80c on 5c ultra (G) 1.90 1.75
**9LC33** AP1 1.25p on 5c ultra (V) 2.25 2.25
*Nos. 9LC31-9LC33 (3)* 6.90 6.50
Set, never hinged 10.00

Spain Nos. 641, 643 and 640 Surcharged in Green or Orange

**1937, Oct. 29 Unwmk. *Perf. 11***
**9LC34** A161 50c on 5c (G) 8.50 3.75
**9LC35** A161 80c on 10c (O) 5.25 2.75
**9LC36** A160 1.25p on 2c (G) 9.50 7.25
*Nos. 9LC34-9LC36 (3)* 23.25 13.75
Set, never hinged 35.00

Spain Nos. 638, 640 and 643 Surcharged in Red, Blue or Violet

**1937, Dec. 23 *Imperf.***
**9LC37** A159 50c on 1c (R) 9.50 4.50

***Perf. 11, 11x11½***
**9LC38** A160 80c on 2c (Bl) 3.75 2.75
**9LC39** A161 1.25p on 10c (V) 8.50 3.50
*Nos. 9LC37-9LC39 (3)* 21.75 10.75
Set, never hinged 32.50

Spain Nos. 647, 650 to 652 Surcharged in Black, Green or Brown



**1937, Dec. 29**
**9LC40** A162 30c + 30c rose 4.50 3.75
**9LC41** A162 50c + 2.50p dk bl (G) 29.00 21.00
**9LC42** A162 60c + 2.30p yel (G) 29.00 21.00
**9LC43** A162 1p + 5p bl (Br) 35.00 21.00
*Nos. 9LC40-9LC43 (4)* 97.50 66.75
Set, never hinged 110.00

See note after No. 9LC19.

Stamps of Spain, 1936, Surcharged in Black, Green, Blue or Red

**1938, Feb. 2 *Perf. 11, 11½, 11x11½***
**9LC44** A160 50c on 2c brn 5.00 3.75
**9LC45** A161 80c on 5c brn (G) 3.75 3.25
**9LC46** A162 80c on 30c rose (Bl) 4.50 2.50
**9LC47** A161 1.25p on 10c grn (Bl) 4.50 3.25
**9LC48** A162 1.25p on 50c dk bl (R) 4.50 2.75
*Nos. 9LC44-9LC48 (5)* 22.25 15.50
Set, never hinged 27.50

Spain Nos. 645, 646 and 649 Surcharged in Brown, Green or Violet

**1938, Feb. 14**

| | | | | |
|---|---|---|---|---|
| **9LC51** | A162 | 2.50p on 20c (Br) | 50.00 | 25.00 |
| **9LC52** | A162 | 5p on 25c (G) | 50.00 | 25.00 |
| **9LC53** | A162 | 10p on 40c (V) | 50.00 | 25.00 |
| | | *Nos. 9LC51-9LC53 (3)* | 150.00 | 75.00 |
| | | Set, never hinged | 175.00 | |

### MALAGA ISSUE

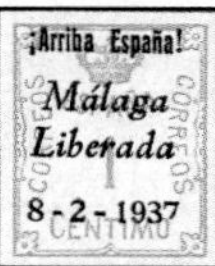


Stamps of 1920-36 Overprinted in Black or Red

**1937 Unwmk. *Imperf.***

| | | | | |
|---|---|---|---|---|
| **10L1** | A47 | 1c blue green | .20 | .20 |
| **10L2** | A108 | 1c blue green | .20 | .20 |
| **10L3** | A108 | 1c lt green (R) | .20 | .20 |

***Perf. 13½, 13½x13, 11, 11½x11***

| | | | | |
|---|---|---|---|---|
| **10L4** | A108 | 2c orange brn | 14.50 | 14.50 |
| **10L5** | A126 | 2c orange brn | .20 | .20 |
| **10L6** | A103 | 5c chocolate (R) | .20 | .20 |
| **10L7** | A96 | 10c yellow green | 12.00 | 12.00 |
| **10L8** | A110 | 10c emerald | .30 | .30 |
| **10L9** | A111 | 15c Prus grn (R) | .55 | .55 |
| **10L10** | A97 | 15c blue grn (R) | .55 | .55 |
| **10L11** | A95 | 20c dk violet (R) | .50 | .50 |
| **10L12** | A99 | 25c lake | 1.50 | 1.50 |
| **10L13** | A104 | 25c lake | .50 | .50 |
| **10L14** | A113 | 30c carmine | .50 | .50 |
| **10L15** | A129 | 30c carmine rose | 2.50 | 2.50 |
| **10L16** | A100 | 40c blue (R) | .45 | .45 |
| **10L17** | A97 | 50c dk blue (R) | 2.50 | 2.50 |
| **10L18** | A100 | 60c apple green | 1.40 | 1.40 |
| **10L19** | A105 | 1p black (R) | 2.75 | 2.75 |
| | | *Nos. 10L1-10L19 (19)* | 41.50 | 41.50 |

Stamps of 1932-35 Overprinted in Red or Black in panes of 25, reading down. "8.2.37" and "!Arriba Espana!" form the lower half of all overprints. The upper half varies.

Overprint a (1st and 2nd rows): "MALAGA AGRADECIDA A TRANQUILLO-BIANCHI"
Overprint b (3rd row): "MALAGA A SU SALVADOR QUEIPO DE LLANO"
Overprint c (4th and 5th rows): "MALAGA A SU CAUDILLO FRANCO"
Values are for vertical strips of 3 containing examples of each overprint type.

**1937 *Perf. 11½***

| | | | | |
|---|---|---|---|---|
| **10L20** | A111 | 15c Prus grn (R) | 5.50 | 5.50 |
| *a.* | | 15c single stamp, ovpt. a | .85 | .85 |
| *b.* | | 15c single stamp, ovpt. b | 1.60 | 1.60 |
| *c.* | | 15c single stamp, ovpt. c | .85 | .85 |
| **10L21** | A113 | 30c rose red (Bk) | 5.50 | 5.50 |
| *a.* | | 30c single stamp, ovpt. a | .85 | .85 |
| *b.* | | 30c single stamp, ovpt. b | 1.60 | 1.60 |
| *c.* | | 30c single stamp, ovpt. c | .85 | .85 |
| **10L22** | A97 | 50c dk blue (R) | 8.75 | 8.75 |
| *a.* | | 50c single stamp, ovpt. a | 1.60 | 1.60 |
| *b.* | | 50c single stamp, ovpt. b | 3.25 | 3.25 |
| *c.* | | 50c single stamp, ovpt. c | 1.60 | 1.60 |
| **10L23** | A100 | 60c apple grn (Bk) | 11.00 | 11.00 |
| *a.* | | 60c single stamp, ovpt. a | 1.60 | 1.60 |
| *b.* | | 60c single stamp, ovpt. b | 3.25 | 3.25 |
| *c.* | | 60c single stamp, ovpt. c | 1.60 | 1.60 |
| | | *Nos. 10L20-10L23 (4)* | 30.75 | 30.75 |

### SPECIAL DELIVERY STAMP

Overprinted like Nos. 10L1-10L19 on Type of Special Delivery Stamp of 1934

**1937 *Perf. 10***

| | | | | |
|---|---|---|---|---|
| **10LE1** | SD7 | 20c rose red (Bk) | .45 | .45 |

### ORENSE ISSUE

Stamps of 1931-36 Overprinted in Red, Blue or Black

**1936 *Imperf.***

| | | | | |
|---|---|---|---|---|
| **11L1** | A108 | 1c blue grn (Bl) | .45 | .45 |
| *a.* | | Red overprint | 1.10 | 1.10 |

***Perf. 11½, 13½x13***

| | | | | |
|---|---|---|---|---|
| **11L2** | A108 | 2c org brn (Bk) | 3.50 | 3.25 |
| **11L3** | A126 | 2c org brn (Bk) | .65 | .65 |
| **11L4** | A103 | 5c brown (R) | 1.50 | 1.50 |
| **11L5** | A110 | 10c lt green (Bl) | 2.25 | 2.25 |
| *a.* | | Red overprint | 11.00 | 11.00 |
| **11L6** | A111 | 15c Prus grn (R) | 3.25 | 3.25 |
| **11L7** | A95 | 20c violet (Bl) | 3.25 | 3.25 |
| **11L8** | A104 | 25c lake (Bk) | 3.75 | 3.75 |
| **11L9** | A113 | 30c rose red (Bl) | 2.75 | 2.75 |
| *a.* | | Black overprint | 5.50 | 5.50 |
| **11L10** | A100 | 40c blue (R) | 3.75 | 3.75 |
| *a.* | | Imperf, pair | 50.00 | |
| **11L11** | A97 | 50c dark blue (R) | 6.50 | 6.50 |
| **11L12** | A100 | 60c apple grn (Bk) | 4.75 | 4.75 |
| *a.* | | Red overprint | 17.00 | 17.00 |
| *b.* | | As "a," imperf, pair | 50.00 | |
| | | *Nos. 11L1-11L12 (12)* | 36.35 | 36.10 |

### SEMI-POSTAL STAMPS

Stamps of Spain, 1931-36, Surcharged in Blue on front and on back of stamp

**1936-37 Unwmk. *Imperf.***

| | | | | |
|---|---|---|---|---|
| **11LB1** | A47 | 1c + 5c bl grn | 2.25 | 2.25 |
| **11LB2** | A108 | 1c + 5c green | .40 | .40 |

***Perf. 13½x13, 11½, 11½x11***

| | | | | |
|---|---|---|---|---|
| **11LB3** | A108 | 2c + 5c org brn | .45 | .45 |
| **11LB4** | A126 | 2c + 5c red brn | .45 | .45 |
| **11LB5** | A103 | 5c + 5c choc | .65 | .65 |
| **11LB6** | A110 | 10c + 5c emer | .65 | .65 |
| **11LB7** | A111 | 15c + 5c Prus grn | .95 | .95 |
| **11LB8** | A95 | 20c + 5c violet | .65 | .65 |
| **11LB9** | A104 | 25c + 5c lake | .95 | .95 |
| **11LB10** | A113 | 30c + 5c rose red | 2.75 | 2.75 |
| **11LB11** | A117 | 30c + 5c rose red | 42.50 | 42.50 |
| **11LB12** | A100 | 60c + 5c apple grn | 190.00 | 190.00 |
| | | *Nos. 11LB1-11LB12 (12)* | 242.65 | 242.65 |

### SPECIAL DELIVERY STAMPS

Type of Special Delivery Stamp of 1934 Overprinted "!VIVA ESPANA!" in Blue or Black

**1936 *Perf. 10***

| | | | | |
|---|---|---|---|---|
| **11LE1** | SD7 | 20c rose red (Bl) | 1.90 | 1.90 |
| **11LE2** | SD7 | 20c rose red (Bk) | 4.25 | 4.25 |

**Same with Surcharge "+ 5 cts."**

| | | | | |
|---|---|---|---|---|
| **11LE3** | SD7 | 20c + 5c rose red | 1.00 | 1.00 |

**Same Surcharge, Overprint Repeated at Right**

| | | | | |
|---|---|---|---|---|
| **11LE4** | SD7 | 20c + 5c rose red | 1.10 | 1.10 |
| | | *Nos. 11LE1-11LE4 (4)* | 8.25 | 8.25 |

### SAN SEBASTIAN ISSUE

**For Use in Province of Guipuzcoa**

Stamps of 1931-36 Overprinted in Red or Blue

**1937 Unwmk. *Imperf.***

| | | | | |
|---|---|---|---|---|
| **12L1** | A108 | 1c bl grn (R) | .65 | .65 |

***Perf. 11, 13½***

| | | | | |
|---|---|---|---|---|
| **12L2** | A108 | 2c buff (Bl) | 1.00 | 1.50 |
| **12L3** | A126 | 2c org brn (Bl) | 2.10 | 2.10 |
| **12L4** | A95 | 5c chocolate (R) | 5.00 | 5.00 |
| **12L5** | A103 | 5c chocolate (R) | 1.75 | 1.75 |
| **12L6** | A110 | 10c emerald (R) | 1.75 | 1.75 |
| **12L7** | A111 | 15c Prus grn (R) | 2.10 | 2.10 |
| **12L8** | A95 | 20c dk violet (R) | 2.75 | 2.75 |
| **12L9** | A104 | 25c car lake (Bl) | 2.75 | 2.75 |
| **12L10** | A113 | 30c rose red (Bl) | 2.75 | 2.75 |
| **12L11** | A100 | 40c blue (R) | 5.50 | 5.50 |
| **12L12** | A97 | 50c dark blue (R) | 5.50 | 5.50 |
| | | *Nos. 12L1-12L12 (12)* | 33.60 | 34.10 |

### SANTA CRUZ DE TENERIFE ISSUE

Stamps of Spain, 1931-36 Overprinted in Black or Red

**1936 Unwmk. *Imperf.***

| | | | | |
|---|---|---|---|---|
| **13L1** | A108 | 1c bl grn (R) | .75 | .75 |
| **13L2** | A108 | 1c bl grn (Bk) | 2.75 | 2.75 |

***Perf. 11, 13½***

| | | | | |
|---|---|---|---|---|
| **13L3** | A108 | 2c buff (Bk) | 5.50 | 5.50 |
| **13L4** | A126 | 2c org brn (Bk) | .95 | .95 |
| **13L5** | A103 | 5c choc (R) | 3.00 | 3.00 |
| **13L6** | A110 | 10c green (R) | 3.00 | 3.00 |
| **13L7** | A104 | 25c lake (Bk) | 11.00 | 11.00 |
| **13L8** | A100 | 40c dk blue (R) | 3.25 | 3.25 |
| **13L9** | A107 | 10p dp brn (Bk) | 225.00 | 225.00 |
| | | *Nos. 13L1-13L9 (9)* | 255.20 | 255.20 |

Many forgeries of #13L9 exist.

### SEVILLE ISSUE

Stamps of Spain, 1931-36, Overprinted in Black or Red

**1936 *Imperf.***

| | | | | |
|---|---|---|---|---|
| **14L1** | A108 | 1c blue grn (Bk) | .25 | .25 |

***Perf. 13½x13, 11, 11½x11***

| | | | | |
|---|---|---|---|---|
| **14L2** | A126 | 2c org brn (Bk) | .30 | .30 |
| **14L3** | A103 | 5c chocolate (R) | .40 | .40 |
| **14L4** | A110 | 10c emerald (Bk) | .50 | .50 |
| **14L5** | A111 | 15c Prus grn (R) | 1.25 | 1.25 |
| **14L6** | A95 | 20c violet (R) | 1.25 | 1.25 |
| **14L7** | A104 | 25c lake (Bk) | 1.25 | 1.25 |
| **14L8** | A113 | 30c carmine (Bk) | 1.25 | 1.25 |
| **14L9** | A128 | 30c rose red (Bk) | 7.50 | 7.50 |
| **14L10** | A100 | 40c blue (R) | 5.00 | 5.00 |
| **14L11** | A97 | 50c dk blue (R) | 5.00 | 5.00 |
| **14L12** | A100 | 60c apple grn (Bk) | 6.00 | 6.00 |
| | | *Nos. 14L1-14L12 (12)* | 29.95 | 29.95 |

Stamps of Spain, 1931-36, Handstamped in Black

***Imperf***

| | | | | |
|---|---|---|---|---|
| **14L13** | A108 | 1c blue grn | .25 | .25 |

***Perf. 13½x13, 11, 11x11½, 11½x11***

| | | | | |
|---|---|---|---|---|
| **14L14** | A126 | 2c orange brn | .40 | .40 |
| **14L15** | A103 | 5c chocolate | .40 | .40 |
| **14L16** | A110 | 10c emerald | .40 | .40 |
| **14L17** | A111 | 15c Prus green | .50 | .50 |
| **14L18** | A95 | 20c violet | .50 | .50 |
| **14L19** | A104 | 25c lake | .50 | .50 |
| **14L20** | A113 | 30c carmine | .50 | .50 |
| **14L21** | A128 | 30c rose red | 2.75 | 2.75 |
| **14L22** | A100 | 40c blue | .95 | .95 |
| **14L23** | A97 | 50c dk blue | 2.75 | 2.75 |
| **14L24** | A100 | 60c apple grn | .90 | .90 |
| **14L25** | A105 | 1p black | 2.75 | 2.75 |
| **14L26** | AP26 | 2p gray blue | 12.00 | 12.00 |
| **14L27** | A106 | 4p magenta | 6.50 | 6.50 |
| **14L28** | A107 | 10p deep brown | 9.50 | 9.50 |
| | | *Nos. 14L13-14L28,14LE1 (17)* | 42.00 | 42.00 |

The date "Julio-1936" in the overprints of Nos. 14L1-14L28 and 14LE1 marks the beginning of the Franco insurrection.

### SPECIAL DELIVERY STAMP

Overprinted like Nos. 14L13-14L25 on Type of Special Delivery Stamp of 1934

**1936 *Perf. 10***

| | | | | |
|---|---|---|---|---|
| **14LE1** | SD7 | 20c rose red | 1.75 | 1.75 |

## SPANISH GUINEA

'spa-nish 'gi-nē

LOCATION — In western Africa, bordering on the Gulf of Guinea
GOVT. — Spanish Colony
AREA — 10,852 sq. mi.
POP. — 212,000 (est. 1957)
CAPITAL — Santa Isabel

Spanish Guinea 1-84 were issued for and used only in the continental area later called Rio Muni. From 1909 to 1960, Spanish Guinea also included Fernando Po, Elobey, Annobon and Corisco.

Fernando Po and Rio Muni united in 1968 to become the Republic of Equatorial Guinea.

100 Centimos = 1 Peseta

**Catalogue values for unused stamps in this country are for Never Hinged items, beginning with Scott 319 in the regular postage section, Scott B13 in the semi-postal section, and Scott C13 in the airpost section.**

King Alfonso XIII
A1 A2

**1902 Unwmk. Typo. *Perf. 14***
**Blue Control Numbers on Back**

| No. | Type | Description | Unused | Used |
|---|---|---|---|---|
| **1** | A1 | 5c dark green | 11.00 | 6.25 |
| **2** | A1 | 10c indigo | 11.00 | 6.25 |
| **3** | A1 | 25c claret | 82.50 | 47.50 |
| **4** | A1 | 50c deep brown | 82.50 | 47.50 |
| **5** | A1 | 75c violet | 82.50 | 47.50 |
| **6** | A1 | 1p carmine rose | 120.00 | 47.50 |
| **7** | A1 | 2p olive green | 155.00 | 100.00 |
| **8** | A1 | 5p dull red | 250.00 | 175.00 |
| | | *Nos. 1-8 (8)* | 794.50 | 477.50 |
| | | Set, never hinged | 1,400. | |

Exists imperf, value set $1,750.

Revenue Stamps Surcharged

**1903 *Imperf.***
**Blue or Black Control Numbers on Back**

| No. | Type | Description | Unused | Used |
|---|---|---|---|---|
| **8A** | | 10c on 25c blk (R) | 550.00 | 210.00 |
| **8B** | | 10c on 50c org (Bl) | 125.00 | 35.00 |
| **8D** | | 10c on 1p 25c car (Bk) | 750.00 | 350.00 |
| **8F** | | 10c on 2p cl (Bk) | 800.00 | 550.00 |
| *g.* | | Blue surcharge | 1,300. | 750.00 |
| **8H** | | 10c on 2p 50c red brn (Bl) | 1,250. | 675.00 |
| **8J** | | 10c on 5p ol blk (R) | 1,500. | 475.00 |

Nos. 8A-8J are surcharged on stamps inscribed "Posesiones Espanolas de Africa Occidental" and "1903," with arms at left.

This surcharge was also applied to revenue stamps of 10, 15, 25, 50, 75 and 100 pesetas and in other colors.

See Nos. 98-101C.

**1903 Typo. *Perf. 14***
**Blue Control Numbers on Back**

| No. | Type | Description | Unused | Used |
|---|---|---|---|---|
| **9** | A2 | ¼c black | 1.25 | .75 |
| **10** | A2 | ½c blue green | 1.25 | .75 |
| **11** | A2 | 1c claret | 1.25 | .65 |
| **12** | A2 | 2c dark olive | 1.25 | .65 |
| **13** | A2 | 3c dark brown | 1.25 | .65 |
| **14** | A2 | 4c vermilion | 1.25 | .65 |
| **15** | A2 | 5c black brown | 1.25 | .65 |
| **16** | A2 | 10c red brown | 2.00 | .75 |
| **17** | A2 | 15c dark blue | 7.00 | 5.75 |
| **18** | A2 | 25c orange buff | 7.00 | 5.75 |
| **19** | A2 | 50c carmine lake | 13.00 | 12.50 |
| **20** | A2 | 75c violet | 17.50 | 12.50 |
| **21** | A2 | 1p blue green | 30.00 | 20.00 |
| **22** | A2 | 2p dark green | 30.00 | 20.00 |
| **23** | A2 | 3p scarlet | 80.00 | 26.00 |
| **24** | A2 | 4p dull blue | 92.50 | 45.00 |
| **25** | A2 | 5p dark violet | 175.00 | 65.00 |
| **26** | A2 | 10p carmine rose | 240.00 | 90.00 |
| | | *Nos. 9-26 (18)* | 702.75 | 308.00 |
| | | Set, never hinged | 1,300. | |

**1905**
**Same, Dated "1905"**
**Blue Control Numbers on Back**

| No. | Type | Description | Unused | Used |
|---|---|---|---|---|
| **27** | A2 | 1c black | .20 | .20 |
| **28** | A2 | 2c blue grn | .20 | .20 |
| **29** | A2 | 3c claret | .20 | .20 |
| **30** | A2 | 4c bronze grn | .20 | .20 |
| **31** | A2 | 5c dark brown | .20 | .20 |
| **32** | A2 | 10c red | 1.10 | .65 |
| **33** | A2 | 15c black brown | 3.25 | 2.25 |
| **34** | A2 | 25c chocolate | 3.25 | 2.25 |
| **35** | A2 | 50c dark blue | 7.25 | 5.25 |
| **36** | A2 | 75c orange buff | 7.75 | 5.25 |
| **37** | A2 | 1p carmine rose | 7.75 | 5.25 |
| **38** | A2 | 2p violet | 19.00 | 11.00 |
| **39** | A2 | 3p blue green | 50.00 | 22.50 |
| **40** | A2 | 4p dark green | 50.00 | 32.50 |
| **40A** | A2 | 5p vermilion | 80.00 | 35.00 |
| **41** | A2 | 10p dull blue | 140.00 | 110.00 |
| | | *Nos. 27-41 (16)* | 370.35 | 232.90 |
| | | Set, never hinged | 675.00 | |

Stamps of Elobey, 1905, Overprinted in Violet or Blue

**1906**

| No. | Type | Description | Unused | Used |
|---|---|---|---|---|
| **42** | A1 | 1c rose | 3.25 | 1.90 |
| **43** | A1 | 2c deep violet | 3.25 | 1.90 |
| **44** | A1 | 3c black | 3.25 | 1.90 |
| **45** | A1 | 4c orange red | 3.25 | 1.90 |
| **46** | A1 | 5c deep green | 3.25 | 1.90 |
| **47** | A1 | 10c blue green | 7.25 | 4.25 |
| **48** | A1 | 15c violet | 12.50 | 7.50 |
| **49** | A1 | 25c rose lake | 12.50 | 7.50 |
| **50** | A1 | 50c orange buff | 17.50 | 10.50 |
| **51** | A1 | 75c dark blue | 21.00 | 12.00 |
| **52** | A1 | 1p red brown | 37.50 | 21.00 |
| **53** | A1 | 2p black brown | 55.00 | 32.50 |
| **54** | A1 | 3p vermilion | 77.50 | 45.00 |
| **55** | A1 | 4p dark brown | 350.00 | 210.00 |
| **56** | A1 | 5p bronze green | 350.00 | 210.00 |
| **57** | A1 | 10p claret | *1,400.* | *850.00* |
| | | *Nos. 42-54 (13)* | 257.00 | 149.75 |

King Alfonso XIII
A3 A4

**1907 Typo.**
**Blue Control Numbers on Back**

| No. | Type | Description | Unused | Used |
|---|---|---|---|---|
| **58** | A3 | 1c dark green | .60 | .20 |
| **59** | A3 | 2c dull blue | .60 | .20 |
| **60** | A3 | 3c violet | .60 | .20 |
| **61** | A3 | 4c yellow grn | .60 | .20 |
| **62** | A3 | 5c carmine lake | .60 | .20 |
| **63** | A3 | 10c orange | 3.25 | 1.00 |
| **64** | A3 | 15c brown | 2.50 | .65 |
| **65** | A3 | 25c dark blue | 2.50 | .65 |
| **66** | A3 | 50c black brown | 2.50 | .65 |
| **67** | A3 | 75c blue green | 2.50 | .65 |
| **68** | A3 | 1p red | 4.75 | 1.10 |
| **69** | A3 | 2p dark brown | 8.00 | 5.00 |
| **70** | A3 | 3p olive gray | 8.00 | 5.00 |
| **71** | A3 | 4p maroon | 10.50 | 5.00 |
| **72** | A3 | 5p green | 11.00 | 7.50 |
| **73** | A3 | 10p red violet | 16.50 | 9.75 |
| | | *Nos. 58-73 (16)* | 75.00 | 37.95 |
| | | Set, never hinged | 135.00 | |

Issue of 1907 Surcharged in Black or Red

**1908-09**

| No. | Type | Description | Unused | Used |
|---|---|---|---|---|
| **74** | A3 | 05c on 1c dk grn (R) | 2.75 | 1.50 |
| **75** | A3 | 05c on 2c blue (R) | 2.75 | 1.50 |
| **76** | A3 | 05c on 3c violet | 2.75 | 1.50 |
| **77** | A3 | 05c on 4c yel grn | 2.75 | 1.50 |
| **78** | A3 | 05c on 10c orange | 2.75 | 1.50 |
| *a.* | | Red surcharge | 5.00 | 2.75 |
| **84** | A3 | 15c on 10c orange | 13.50 | 9.00 |
| | | *Nos. 74-84 (6)* | 27.25 | 16.50 |

Many stamps of this issue are found with the surcharge inverted, sideways, double and in both black and red. Other stamps of the 1907 issue are known with this surcharge but are not believed to have been put in use. Value, each $17.

**1909 Typo. *Perf. 14½***
**Blue Control Numbers on Back**

| No. | Type | Description | Unused | Used |
|---|---|---|---|---|
| **85** | A4 | 1c orange brown | .20 | .20 |
| **86** | A4 | 2c rose | .20 | .20 |
| **87** | A4 | 5c dark green | 1.00 | .20 |
| **88** | A4 | 10c vermilion | .30 | .20 |
| **89** | A4 | 15c dark brown | .30 | .20 |
| **90** | A4 | 20c violet | .55 | .25 |
| **91** | A4 | 25c dull blue | .55 | .25 |
| **92** | A4 | 30c chocolate | .65 | .20 |
| **93** | A4 | 40c lake | .40 | .20 |
| **94** | A4 | 50c dark violet | .40 | .20 |
| **95** | A4 | 1p blue green | 11.00 | 5.50 |
| **96** | A4 | 4p orange | 2.75 | 3.25 |
| **97** | A4 | 10p red | 2.75 | 3.25 |
| | | *Nos. 85-97 (13)* | 21.05 | 14.10 |
| | | Set, never hinged | 37.50 | |

For overprints see Nos. 102-114.

Revenue Stamps Surcharged like Nos. 8A-8J in Black

**1909 *Imperf.***
**With or Without Control Numbers on Back**

| No. | Type | Description | Unused | Used |
|---|---|---|---|---|
| **98** | | 10c on 50c bl grn | 80.00 | 52.50 |
| *a.* | | Red or violet surcharge | 100.00 | 72.50 |
| **99** | | 10c on 1p 25c violet | 100.00 | 72.50 |
| **100** | | 10c on 2p dk brn | 550.00 | 325.00 |
| **100A** | | 10c on 5p dk vio | 550.00 | 325.00 |
| **101** | | 10c on 25p red brn | *725.00* | *525.00* |
| **101A** | | 10c on 50p brn lil | *2,500.* | *1,450.* |
| **101B** | | 10c on 75p carmine | *2,500.* | *1,450.* |
| **101C** | | 10c on 100p orange | *2,500.* | *1,450.* |

Nos. 98-101C are surcharged on undated stamps, arms centered. Stamps inscribed: "Territorios Espanoles del Africa Occidental." Basic revenue stamps similar to Rio de Oro type A3.

Stamps of 1909 Overprinted with Handstamp in Black, Blue, Green or Red

**1911**

| No. | Type | Description | Unused | Used |
|---|---|---|---|---|
| **102** | A4 | 1c orange brn (Bl) | .25 | .20 |
| **103** | A4 | 2c rose (G) | .25 | .20 |
| **104** | A4 | 5c dk green (R) | 1.25 | .20 |
| **105** | A4 | 10c vermilion | .70 | .30 |
| **106** | A4 | 15c dk brown (R) | 1.25 | .50 |
| **107** | A4 | 20c violet | 1.50 | .70 |
| **108** | A4 | 25c dull blue (R) | 1.75 | 1.60 |
| **109** | A4 | 30c choc (Bl) | 2.50 | 2.25 |
| **110** | A4 | 40c lake (Bl) | 2.75 | 2.25 |
| **111** | A4 | 50c dark violet | 4.50 | 3.25 |
| **112** | A4 | 1p blue grn (R) | 37.50 | 27.50 |
| **113** | A4 | 4p orange (R) | 19.00 | 15.00 |
| **114** | A4 | 10p red (G) | 25.00 | 27.50 |
| | | *Nos. 102-114 (13)* | 98.20 | 81.45 |
| | | Set, never hinged | 180.00 | |

The date "1911" is missing from the overprint on the first stamp in each row, or ten times in each sheet of 100 stamps. This variety occurs on all stamps of the series. Value, set $450.

King Alfonso XIII
A5 A6

**1912 Typo. *Perf. 13½***
**Blue Control Numbers on Back**

| No. | Type | Description | Unused | Used |
|---|---|---|---|---|
| **115** | A5 | 1c black | .20 | .20 |
| **116** | A5 | 2c dark brown | .20 | .20 |
| **117** | A5 | 5c deep green | .20 | .20 |
| **118** | A5 | 10c red | .20 | .20 |
| **119** | A5 | 15c claret | .20 | .20 |
| **120** | A5 | 20c red | .30 | .20 |
| **121** | A5 | 25c dull blue | .20 | .20 |
| **122** | A5 | 30c lake | 2.50 | 1.40 |
| **123** | A5 | 40c car rose | 1.60 | .75 |
| **124** | A5 | 50c brown org | 1.40 | .25 |
| **125** | A5 | 1p dark violet | 1.60 | .95 |
| **126** | A5 | 4p lilac | 3.75 | 1.90 |
| **127** | A5 | 10p blue green | 7.75 | 7.00 |
| | | *Nos. 115-127 (13)* | 20.10 | 13.65 |
| | | Set, never hinged | 32.50 | |

For overprints and surcharges see Nos. 141-157.

**1914 *Perf. 13***
**Blue Control Numbers on Back**

| No. | Type | Description | Unused | Used |
|---|---|---|---|---|
| **128** | A6 | 1c dull violet | .20 | .20 |
| **129** | A6 | 2c car rose | .20 | .20 |
| **130** | A6 | 5c deep green | .20 | .20 |
| **131** | A6 | 10c vermilion | .20 | .20 |
| **132** | A6 | 15c dark violet | .20 | .20 |
| **133** | A6 | 20c dark brown | .70 | .40 |
| **134** | A6 | 25c dark blue | .30 | .20 |
| **135** | A6 | 30c brown orange | 1.10 | .40 |
| **136** | A6 | 40c blue green | 1.10 | .40 |
| **137** | A6 | 50c dp claret | .55 | .25 |
| **138** | A6 | 1p vermilion | 1.25 | 1.50 |
| **139** | A6 | 4p maroon | 5.00 | 3.25 |
| **140** | A6 | 10p olive black | 5.50 | 6.00 |
| | | *Nos. 128-140 (13)* | 16.50 | 13.40 |
| | | Set, never hinged | 25.00 | |

Stamps with these or similar overprints are unauthorized and fraudulent.

Stamps of 1912 Overprinted

**1917 *Perf. 13½***

| No. | Type | Description | Unused | Used |
|---|---|---|---|---|
| **141** | A5 | 1c black | 90.00 | 60.00 |
| **142** | A5 | 2c dark brown | 90.00 | 60.00 |
| **143** | A5 | 5c deep green | .25 | .20 |
| **144** | A5 | 10c red | .25 | .20 |
| **145** | A5 | 15c claret | .25 | .20 |
| **146** | A5 | 20c red | .25 | .20 |
| **147** | A5 | 25c dull blue | .20 | .20 |
| **148** | A5 | 30c lake | .25 | .20 |
| **149** | A5 | 40c carmine rose | .50 | .25 |
| **150** | A5 | 50c brown orange | .25 | .20 |
| **151** | A5 | 1p dark violet | .50 | .25 |
| **152** | A5 | 4p lilac | 6.25 | 3.00 |
| **153** | A5 | 10p blue green | 6.25 | 3.00 |
| | | *Nos. 141-153 (13)* | 195.20 | 127.90 |
| | | Set, never hinged | 260.00 | |

Nos. 143-153 exist with overprint double, inverted, in dark blue, reading "9117" and in pairs one without overprint.

Stamps of 1917 Surcharged

**1918**

| No. | Type | Description | Unused | Used |
|---|---|---|---|---|
| **154** | A5 | 5c on 40c car rose | 27.50 | 11.00 |
| **155** | A5 | 10c on 4p lilac | 27.50 | 11.00 |
| **156** | A5 | 15c on 20c red | 50.00 | 19.00 |
| **157** | A5 | 25c on 10p bl grn | 50.00 | 19.00 |
| *a.* | | "52" for "25" | 375.00 | 325.00 |
| | | *Nos. 154-157 (4)* | 155.00 | 60.00 |
| | | Set, never hinged | 260.00 | |

The varieties "Gents" and "Censt" occur on Nos. 154-157. Values 50 percent more.

King Alfonso XIII
A7 A8

**1919 Typo. *Perf. 13***

**Blue Control Numbers on Back**

**158** A7 1c lilac .85 .25
**159** A7 2c rose .85 .25
**160** A7 5c vermilion .85 .25
**161** A7 10c violet 1.40 .25
**162** A7 15c brown 1.40 .40
**163** A7 20c blue 1.40 .65
**164** A7 25c green 1.40 .65
*a.* 25c blue (error) 52.50
**165** A7 30c orange 1.75 .65
**166** A7 40c orange 3.75 .65
**167** A7 50c red 3.75 .65
**168** A7 1p light green 3.75 2.25
**169** A7 4p claret 8.25 8.50
**170** A7 10p brown 17.00 16.00
*Nos. 158-170 (13)* 46.40 31.40
Set, never hinged 60.00

**1920**

**Blue Control Numbers on Back**

**171** A8 1c brown .20 .20
**172** A8 2c dull rose .20 .20
**173** A8 5c gray green .20 .20
**174** A8 10c dull rose .20 .20
**175** A8 15c orange .20 .20
**176** A8 20c yellow .20 .20
**177** A8 25c dull blue .75 .20
**178** A8 30c greenish blue 27.50 17.50
**179** A8 40c lt brown 1.25 .20
**180** A8 50c lilac 1.40 .20
**181** A8 1p light red 1.40 .20
**182** A8 4p bright rose 4.50 4.50
**183** A8 10p gray lilac 6.50 8.75
*Nos. 171-183 (13)* 44.50 32.75
Set, never hinged 72.50

A9

Nipa House — A10

**1922**

**Blue Control Numbers on Back**

**184** A9 1c dark brown .50 .20
**185** A9 2c claret .50 .20
**186** A9 5c blue green .50 .20
**187** A9 10c pale red 3.50 .95
**188** A9 15c orange .50 .20
**189** A9 20c lilac 2.25 .85
**190** A9 25c dark blue 3.75 1.00
**191** A9 30c violet 3.50 1.10
**192** A9 40c turq blue 2.50 .55
**193** A9 50c deep rose 2.50 .55
**194** A9 1p myrtle green 2.50 .55
**195** A9 4p red brown 10.50 10.50
**196** A9 10p yellow 21.00 20.00
*Nos. 184-196 (13)* 54.00 36.85
Set, never hinged 85.00

**1924**

**Blue Control Numbers on Back**

**197** A10 5c choc & bl .20 .20
**198** A10 10c gray grn & bl .20 .20
**199** A10 15c rose & blk .20 .20
**200** A10 20c violet & blk .20 .20
**201** A10 25c org red & blk .40 .25
**202** A10 30c orange & blk .40 .20
**203** A10 40c dl bl & blk .40 .20
**204** A10 50c claret & blk .40 .20
**205** A10 60c red brn & blk .40 .20
**206** A10 1p dk vio & blk 1.60 .20
*a.* Center inverted 275.00 125.00
**207** A10 4p brt bl & blk 3.75 2.25
**208** A10 10p bl grn & blk 8.75 4.50
*Nos. 197-208 (12)* 16.90 8.80
Set, never hinged 25.00

Seville-Barcelona Issue of Spain, 1929, Overprinted in Red or Blue

**1929 *Perf. 11***

**209** A52 5c rose lake .25 .30
**210** A53 10c green (R) .25 .30
**211** A50 15c Prus bl (R) .25 .30
**212** A51 20c purple (R) .25 .30
**213** A50 25c brt rose .25 .30
**214** A52 30c black brn .25 .30
**215** A53 40c dk blue (R) .50 .45
**216** A51 50c dp orange .50 .45
**217** A52 1p blue blk (R) 8.50 4.50
**218** A53 4p deep rose 17.50 8.75
**219** A53 10p brown 32.50 17.00
*Nos. 209-219 (11)* 61.00 32.95
Set, never hinged 120.00

Porter A11

Drummers A12

King Alfonso XIII and Queen Victoria — A13

**1931 Engr. *Perf. 14***

**220** A11 1c blue green .20 .20
**221** A11 2c red brown .20 .20

**Blue Control Numbers on Back**

**222** A11 5c brown black .20 .20
**223** A11 10c light green .20 .20
**224** A11 15c dark green .20 .20
**225** A11 20c deep violet .20 .20
**226** A12 25c carmine .20 .20
**227** A12 30c lake .30 .20
**228** A12 40c dark blue .70 .55
**229** A12 50c red orange 1.50 1.10
**230** A13 80c blue violet 2.50 1.60
**231** A13 1p black 4.50 4.50
**232** A13 4p violet rose 30.00 17.00
**233** A13 5p dark brown 13.00 12.00
*Nos. 220-233 (14)* 53.90 38.35
Set, never hinged 110.00

Exist imperf. Value for set, $300.

See Nos. 262-271. For overprints and surcharges see Nos. 234-277, 282-283, 298.

Stamps of 1931 Overprinted

**1931**

**234** A11 1c blue green .20 .20
**235** A11 2c red brown .20 .20
**236** A11 5c brown black .20 .20
**237** A11 10c light green .20 .20
**238** A11 15c dark green .20 .20
**239** A11 20c deep violet .20 .20
**240** A12 25c carmine .20 .20
**241** A12 30c lake .40 .20
**242** A12 40c dark blue 1.40 .45
**243** A12 50c red orange 9.75 5.50
**244** A13 80c blue violet 3.00 1.60
**245** A13 1p black 10.00 3.50
**246** A13 4p violet rose 17.50 10.50
**247** A13 5p dark brown 17.50 10.50
*Nos. 234-247 (14)* 60.95 33.65
Set, never hinged 100.00

Stamps of 1931 Overprinted in Red or Blue

**1933**

**248** A11 1c blue grn (R) .20 .20
**249** A11 2c red brown (Bl) .20 .20
**250** A11 5c brown blk (R) .20 .20
**251** A11 10c lt green (Bl) .20 .20
**252** A11 15c dk green (R) .20 .20
**253** A11 20c dp violet (R) .40 .20
**254** A12 25c carmine (Bl) .40 .20
**255** A12 30c lake (Bl) .45 .20
**256** A12 40c dk blue (R) 2.75 .70
**257** A12 50c red orange (Bl) 17.00 3.50
**258** A13 80c blue vio (R) 5.50 3.00
**259** A13 1p black (R) 19.00 3.25
**260** A13 4p violet rose (Bl) 35.00 15.00
**261** A13 5p dk brown (Bl) 35.00 15.00
*Nos. 248-261 (14)* 116.50 42.05
Set, never hinged 175.00

Types of 1931
Without Control Number

**1934-35 Engr. *Perf. 10***

**262** A11 1c blue green ('35) 8.25 .20
**263** A11 2c red brown ('35) 8.25 .20
**264** A11 5c black brn 1.50 .20
**265** A11 10c light green 1.50 .20
**266** A11 15c dark green 2.75 .20
**267** A12 30c rose red 3.25 .20
**268** A12 50c indigo ('35) 7.25 .70
*Nos. 262-268 (7)* 32.75 1.90
Set, never hinged 47.50

Types of 1931

**1941 Litho. Unwmk.**

**269** A11 5c olive gray 2.10 .20
**270** A11 20c violet 2.10 .20
**271** A12 40c gray green .85 .20
*Nos. 269-271 (3)* 5.05 .60
Set, never hinged 6.25

Stamps of 1931-33 Surcharged in Black

a

1
peseta.
b

**1936-37 *Perf. 10, 14***

**272** A12 30c on 40c (#228) 3.75 2.25
**273** A12 30c on 40c (#242) 15.00 3.50
**274** A12 30c on 40c (#256) 57.50 17.50
*Nos. 272-274 (3)* 76.25 23.25
Set, never hinged 110.00

The surcharge on Nos. 272-274 exists in two types, differing in the "3" which is scarcer in italic.

No. 268 Surcharged Type "b" in Red

**275** A12 1p on 50c indigo 22.50
**276** A12 4p on 50c indigo 72.50
**277** A12 5p on 50c indigo 42.50
*Nos. 275-277 (3)* 137.50

Nos. 275-277 were not issued.

Stamps of Spain, 1936, Overprinted in Black or Carmine

**1938 *Perf. 11***

**278** A161 10c gray green 1.50 .45
**279** A162 15c gray black (C) 1.50 .45
**280** A162 20c dark violet 3.50 1.40
**281** A162 25c brown lake 3.50 1.40
*Nos. 278-281 (4)* 10.00 3.70
Set, never hinged 13.00

Nos. 278-281 exist imperf. Value $175.

Stamps of 1931-33, Surcharged in Black

**1939**

**282** A13 40c on 80c (#244) 11.00 7.25
**283** A13 40c on 80c (#258) 11.00 4.50
Set, never hinged 30.00

A14

A15

Revenue Stamps Surcharged in Black

**1940-41 *Perf. 11½***

**284** A14 5c on 35c pale grn 5.75 1.90
**285** A14 25c on 60c org brn 5.75 2.25
**286** A14 50c on 75c blk brn 8.00 2.50
*Nos. 284-286 (3)* 19.50 6.65

**Red Surcharge**

**287** A15 10c on 75c blk brn 8.00 2.50
**288** A15 15c on 1.50p lt vio 5.75 2.25
**289** A15 25c on 60c org brn 10.00 3.25
*Nos. 287-289 (3)* 23.75 8.00

A16

A17

**Black or Carmine Surcharge**
***Perf. 11***

**290** A16 1p on 17p deep red 45.00 13.50
**291** A17 1p on 40p yel grn (C) 11.00 3.50

See No. C1.

A18

A19

**Black Surcharge**
***Perf. 11, 13x12½***

**292** A18 5c carmine 5.50 1.40
**293** A19 1p yellow 87.50 32.50

A20

General Francisco Franco — A21

**Black Surcharge**

**294** A20 1p on 15c gray grn 9.50 3.25

**1940 *Perf. 11½, 13½***

**295** A21 5c olive brown 2.50 .40
**296** A21 40c blue 3.75 .40
**297** A21 50c green 4.50 .40
*a.* 50c greenish gray 19.00 7.25
*Nos. 295-297 (3)* 10.75 1.20
Set, never hinged 24.50

Nos. 295-297 exist imperf. Value $45.

No. 270 Surcharged in Black

**1942**

**298** A11 3p on 20c vio 8.75 1.25

Spain, Nos. 702 and 704 Overprinted in Carmine or Black

**1942 *Perf. 9½x10½***

**299** A166 1p gray blk (C) .45 .20
**300** A166 4p dl rose (Bk) 6.50 .65

The overprint on No. 299 exists in two types: Spacing between lines of 2mm, and spacing of 3mm. The 3mm spacing sells for about twice as much.

For surcharges and overprint see #302-303, C3.

Spain, No. 703 Overprinted in Carmine

**1943**

**301** A166 2p dull brown .85 .20

Nos. 299 and 301 Surcharged in Green

Habilitado para quince cts.

**1949 Unwmk. *Perf. 9½x10½***

**302** A166 5c (cinco) on 1p gray blk .25 .20
**303** A166 15c on 2p dl brn .25 .20

The two types of No. 299, described in footnote, also exist on No. 302.

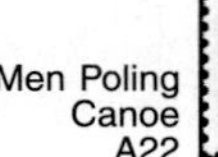

Men Poling Canoe A22

**1949, Oct. 9 Litho. *Perf. 12½x13***

**304** A22 4p dk vio .85 .65
Never hinged 1.25

UPU, 75th anniversary.

San Carlos Bay — A23

Designs: Various Views

**1949-50 *Perf. 12½x13***

| | | | | |
|---|---|---|---|---|
| **305** | A23 | 2c brown | .20 | .20 |
| **306** | A23 | 5c rose vio | .20 | .20 |
| **307** | A23 | 10c Prussian bl | .20 | .20 |
| **308** | A23 | 15c dp ol gray | .25 | .20 |
| **309** | A23 | 25c red brown | .25 | .20 |
| **309A** | A23 | 30c brt yel ('50) | .20 | .20 |
| **310** | A23 | 40c olive gray | .20 | .20 |
| **311** | A23 | 45c rose lake | .20 | .20 |
| **312** | A23 | 50c brn orange | .20 | .20 |
| **312A** | A23 | 75c ultra ('50) | .20 | .20 |
| **313** | A23 | 90c dl bl grn | .25 | .20 |
| **314** | A23 | 1p gray | .90 | .20 |
| **315** | A23 | 1.35p violet | 3.50 | 1.00 |
| **316** | A23 | 2p sepia | 9.50 | 2.00 |
| **317** | A23 | 5p lilac rose | 13.00 | 5.00 |
| **318** | A23 | 10p light brn | 52.50 | 20.00 |
| | | *Nos. 305-318 (16)* | 81.75 | 30.40 |
| | | Set, never hinged | 125.00 | |

**Catalogue values for unused stamps in this section, from this point to the end of the section, are for Never Hinged items.**

Surveyor A24

**1951, Dec. 5**

**319** A24 50c orange .40 .20
**320** A24 5p indigo 7.50 1.25

Intl. Conference of West Africans, 1951.

Drummer A25

**1952, Mar. 10**

**321** A25 5c red brown .20 .20
**322** A25 50c olive gray .35 .20
**323** A25 5p violet 2.25 .20
*Nos. 321-323 (3)* 2.80 .60

Musician A26

Design: 60c, Musician facing right.

**1953, July 1 Photo.**

**324** A26 15c sepia .25 .20
**325** A26 60c brown .25 .20
*Nos. 324-325,B25-B26 (4)* 1.00 .80

Woman and Dove A27

Drummer A28

**1953, Sept. 5 *Perf. 13x12½***

**326** A27 5c orange .20 .20
**327** A27 10c brt lilac rose .20 .20
**328** A27 60c brown .20 .20
**329** A28 1p dull purple 1.50 .20
**330** A28 1.90p greenish blk 2.25 .30
*Nos. 326-330 (5)* 4.35 1.10

Tragocephala Nobilis — A29

Butterfly: 60c, Papilio antimachus.

**1953, Nov. 23**

**331** A29 15c dark green .35 .20
**332** A29 60c brown .40 .20
*Nos. 331-332,B27-B28 (4)* 1.25 .80

Colonial Stamp Day.

Hunter A30

Design: 60c, Hunter and elephant.

**1954, June 10 *Perf. 12½x13***

**333** A30 15c dark gray green .35 .20
**334** A30 60c dark brown .45 .20
*Nos. 333-334,B29-B30 (4)* 1.30 .80

Swimming Turtle A31

**1954, Nov. 23**

**335** A31 15c shown .30 .20
**336** A31 60c Shark .70 .20
*Nos. 335-336,B31-B32 (4)* 1.60 .80

Colonial Stamp Day.

Manuel Iradier y Bulfy, Birth Cent. (in 1954) A32

**1955, Jan. 18**

**337** A32 60c orange brown .50 .20
**338** A32 1p dark violet 3.00 .30

Priest Saying Mass — A33

**1955, June 1 Photo. *Perf. 13x12½***

**339** A33 50c olive gray .30 .20
*Nos. 339,B33-B34 (3)* .90 .60

Centenary of the establishment of an Apostolic Prefecture at Fernando Po.

Palace of Pardo A34

**1955, July 18 *Perf. 12½x13***

**340** A34 5c ol brn .30 .20
**341** A34 15c brn lake .30 .20
**342** A34 80c Prus grn .30 .20
*Nos. 340-342 (3)* .90 .60

Treaty of Pardo, 1778.

Red-eared Guenons — A35

Orchid — A36

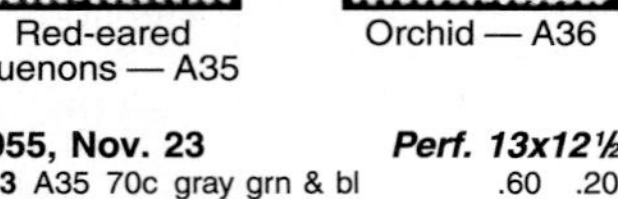

**1955, Nov. 23 *Perf. 13x12½***

**343** A35 70c gray grn & bl .60 .20
*Nos. 343,B35-B36 (3)* 1.10 .60

Colonial Stamp Day.

**1956, June 1 Unwmk.**

Flower: 50c, Strophantus Kombe.

**344** A36 20c bluish green .25 .20
**345** A36 50c brown .25 .20
*Nos. 344-345,B37-B38 (4)* 1.00 .80

See Nos. 360-361, B53-B54.

Arms of Santa Isabel — A37

African Gray Parrot — A38

**1956, Nov. 23 *Perf. 13x12½***

**346** A37 70c light olive green .20 .20
*Nos. 346,B39-B40 (3)* .60 .60

Colonial Stamp Day.

**1957, June 1 Photo.**

**347** A38 70c olive green .40 .20
*Nos. 347,B41-B42 (3)* .90 .60

Elephants A39

Design: 70c, Elephant, vert.

***Perf. 12½x13, 13x12½***

**1957, Nov. 23**

**348** A39 20c blue green .35 .20
**349** A39 70c emerald .40 .20
*Nos. 348-349,B43-B44 (4)* 1.35 .80

Colonial Stamp Day.

Boxing A40

Basketball A41

Preaching Missionary A42

Various Sports: 15c, 2.30p, Jumping. 80c, 3p, Runner at finish line.

**1958, Apr. 10 Photo. Unwmk.**

| | | | | |
|---|---|---|---|---|
| **350** | A40 | 5c violet brn | .20 | .20 |
| **351** | A41 | 10c orange brn | .20 | .20 |
| **352** | A40 | 15c brown | .20 | .20 |
| **353** | A41 | 80c green | .20 | .20 |
| **354** | A40 | 1p orange red | .25 | .20 |
| **355** | A41 | 2p rose lilac | .30 | .20 |
| **356** | A40 | 2.30p dl violet | .35 | .20 |
| **357** | A41 | 3p brt blue | .40 | .20 |
| | | *Nos. 350-357 (8)* | 2.10 | 1.60 |

**1958, June 1 *Perf. 13x12½***

Design: 70c, Crucifix and missal.

**358** A42 20c blue green .30 .20
**359** A42 70c green .30 .20
*Nos. 358-359,B48-B49 (4)* 1.20 .80

Catholic missions in Spanish Guinea, 75th anniv.

Type of 1956 Inscribed: "Pro-Infancia 1959"

**1959, June 1 *Perf. 13x12½***

**360** A36 20c Castor bean .25 .20
**361** A36 70c Digitalis .25 .20
*Nos. 360-361,B53-B54 (4)* 1.00 .80

Promoting child welfare.

Stamps of Spanish Guinea were succeeded by those of Fernando Po and Rio Muni in 1960.

---

## SEMI-POSTAL STAMPS

### Red Cross Issue

Types of Semi-Postal Stamps of Spain, 1926, Overprinted in Black or Blue

B1ovpt

**1926 Unwmk. *Perf. 12½, 13***

**B1** SP3 5c black brown 9.50 6.25
**B2** SP4 10c dark green 9.50 6.25
**B3** SP1 15c dark vio (Bl) 2.10 1.40

**B4** SP4 20c violet brown 2.10 1.40
**B5** SP5 25c deep carmine 2.10 1.40
**B6** SP1 30c olive green 2.10 1.40
**B7** SP3 40c ultra .45 .20
**B8** SP2 50c red brown .45 .20
**B9** SP5 60c myrtle green .45 .20
**B10** SP4 1p vermilion .45 .20
**B11** SP3 4p bister 1.75 1.25
**B12** SP5 10p light violet 6.25 4.25
*Nos. B1-B12 (12)* 37.20 24.40
Set, never hinged 52.50

See Spain No. B6a for No. B4 without overprint. For surcharges see Spain Nos. B70-B71.

**Catalogue values for unused stamps in this section, from this point to the end of the section, are for Never Hinged items.**

Allegory — SP1

Leopard — SP2

**1950, Dec. 1 Photo. *Perf. 13x12½***
**B13** SP1 50c + 10c ultra .25 .20
**B14** SP1 1p + 25c dk grn 10.00 3.50
**B15** SP1 6.50p + 1.65p dp org 2.50 1.60
*Nos. B13-B15 (3)* 12.75 5.30

The surtax was to help the native population.

**1951, Nov. 23**
**B16** SP2 5c + 5c brown .20 .20
**B17** SP2 10c + 5c red orange .20 .20
**B18** SP2 60c + 15c olive brn .30 .20
*Nos. B16-B18 (3)* .70 .60

Colonial Stamp Day, Nov. 23.

Love Lily — SP3

Brown-cheeked Hornbill — SP4

**1952, June 1**
**B19** SP3 5c + 5c brown .20 .20
**B20** SP3 50c + 10c gray .20 .20
**B21** SP3 2p + 30c blue 1.25 .90
*Nos. B19-B21 (3)* 1.65 1.30

The surtax was to help the native population.

**1952, Nov. 23 *Perf. 12½***
**B22** SP4 5c + 5c brown .20 .20
**B23** SP4 10c + 5c brown car .20 .20
**B24** SP4 60c + 15c dk green .40 .25
*Nos. B22-B24 (3)* .80 .65

Colonial Stamp Day, Nov. 23.

Music Type of Regular Issue

**1953, July 1 *Perf. 12½x13***
**B25** A26 5c + 5c like #324 .25 .20
**B26** A26 10c + 5c like #325 .25 .20

The surtax was to help the native population.

Insect Type of Regular Issue

**1953, Nov. 23 *Perf. 13x12½***
**B27** A29 5c + 5c like #331 .25 .20
**B28** A29 10c + 5c like #332 .25 .20

Hunter Type of Regular Issue

**1954, June 10 *Perf. 12½x13***
**B29** A30 5c + 5c like #333 .25 .20
**B30** A30 10c + 5c like #334 .25 .20

The surtax was to help the native population.

Type of Regular Issue

**1954, Nov. 23**
**B31** A31 5c + 5c like #335 .30 .20
**B32** A31 10c + 5c like #336 .30 .20

Type of Regular Issue and

Baptism — SP5

***Perf. 13x12½***
**1955, June 1 Photo. Unwmk.**
**B33** A33 10c + 5c like #339 .30 .20
**B34** SP5 25c + 10c shown .30 .20

Type of Regular Issue and

Red-eared Guenons SP6

***Perf. 13x12½, 12½x13***
**1955, Nov. 23**
**B35** A35 5c + 5c like #343 .25 .20
**B36** SP6 15c + 5c shown .25 .20

Flower Type of Regular Issue

**1956, June 1 *Perf. 13x12½***
**B37** A36 5c + 5c like #344 .25 .20
**B38** A36 15c + 5c like #345 .25 .20

The tax was for native welfare work.

Type of Regular Issue and

Drummers and Arms of Bata SP7

***Perf. 13x12½, 12½x13***
**1956, Nov. 23**
**B39** A37 5c + 5c like #346 .20 .20
**B40** SP7 15c + 5c shown .20 .20

Type of Regular Issue and

African Gray Parrot SP8

***Perf. 13x12½, 12½x13***
**1957, June 1 Photo. Unwmk.**
**B41** A38 5c + 5c like #347 .25 .20
**B42** SP8 15c + 5c shown .25 .20

The surtax was for child welfare.

Type of Regular Issue, 1957
***Perf. 12½x13, 13x12½***
**1957, Nov. 23**
**B43** A39 10c + 5c like #348 .30 .20
**B44** A39 15c + 5c like #349 .30 .20

Pigeons and Arms of Valencia and Santa Isabel SP9

**1958, Mar. 6 *Perf. 12½x13***
**B45** SP9 10c + 5c org brn .20 .20
**B46** SP9 15c + 10c bister .20 .20
**B47** SP9 50c + 10c ol gray .20 .20
*Nos. B45-B47 (3)* .60 .60

The surtax was to aid the victims of the Valencia flood, Oct., 1957.

Type of Regular Issue, 1958

**1958, June 1 Photo. *Perf. 13x12½***
**B48** A42 10c + 5c like #358 .30 .20
**B49** A42 15c + 5c like #359 .30 .20

The surtax was to help the native population.

Butterflies SP10

Early Bicycle SP11

Stamp Day: Various butterflies.

**1958, Nov. 23 Unwmk.**
**B50** SP10 10c + 5c brown red .35 .20
**B51** SP10 25c + 10c brt pur .35 .20
**B52** SP10 50c + 10c gray olive .35 .20
*Nos. B50-B52 (3)* 1.05 .60

Type of Regular Issue 1956 Inscribed: "Pro-Infancia 1959"

**1959, June 1 Photo. *Perf. 13x12½***
**B53** A36 10c + 5c like #361 .25 .20
**B54** A36 15c + 5c like #360 .25 .20

The surtax was for child welfare.

**1959, Nov. 23**

Designs: 20c+5c, Bicycle race. 50c+20c, Bicyclist winning race.

**B55** SP11 10c + 5c lt rose brn .25 .20
**B56** SP11 20c + 5c turq blue .25 .20
**B57** SP11 50c + 20c olive gray .25 .20
*Nos. B55-B57 (3)* .75 .60

Stamp Day.

---

## AIR POST STAMPS

AP1

Revenue Stamp Surcharged "Habilitado para / Correo Aéreo / Intercolonial / Una Peseta"

Type I — "Correo Aereo," 20½mm.
Type II — "Correo Aereo," 22mm.

**1941 Unwmk. *Perf. 11***
**C1** AP1 1p on 17p dp red, I 30.00 6.50
*a.* Type II 40.00 9.25

Spain No. C113 Overprinted in Red — Golfo de Guinea.

**1942, June 23**
**C2** AP30 1p chalky blue 1.60 .25

No. 300 Overprinted in Green — Correo Aéreo / Viaje Ministerial / 10-19 Enero 1948

**1948, Jan. 15 *Perf. 10½x9½***
**C3** A166 4p dull rose 7.50 2.25
Never hinged 12.00

The overprint exists in two types: I — The numeral 1's are lower case L's. II — The numeral 1's are actual ones.

Count of Argelejo and Frigate Catalina at Fernando Po, 1778
AP2

**1949, Nov. 23 Photo. *Perf. 12½x13***
**C4** AP2 5p dark slate green .85 .65
Never hinged 1.25

Stamp Day, Nov. 23, 1949.

Manuel Iradier and Native Products — AP3

Woman Holding Dove — AP5

Benito Rapids AP4

**1950, Nov. 23 Unwmk. *Perf. 12½***
**C5** AP3 5p dk brn 2.10 .85
Never hinged 3.00

Stamp Day, Nov. 23, 1950.

**1951, Mar. 1 Litho. *Perf. 12½x13***

Various views.

**C6** AP4 25c ocher .20 .20
**C7** AP4 50c lilac rose .20 .20
**C8** AP4 1p green .20 .20
**C9** AP4 2p bright blue .20 .20
**C10** AP4 3.25p rose lilac .40 .20
**C11** AP4 5p gray brown 3.50 1.50
**C12** AP4 10p rose red 13.50 5.50
*Nos. C6-C12 (7)* 18.20 8.00
Set, never hinged 27.50

**Catalogue values for unused stamps in this section, from this point to the end of the section, are for Never Hinged items.**

**1951, Apr. 22 Engr. *Perf. 10***
**C13** AP5 5p dark blue 19.00 2.50

500th birth anniv. of Queen Isabella I.

Ferdinand the Catholic — AP6

Soccer Players — AP7

**1952, July 18 Photo. *Perf. 13x12½***
**C14** AP6 5p red brown 25.00 6.00

500th birth anniv. of Ferdinand the Catholic of Spain.

**1955-56 Unwmk.**
**C15** AP7 25c blue vio ('56) .20 .20
**C16** AP7 50c olive ('56) .20 .20
**C17** AP7 1.50p brown ('56) .85 .20
**C18** AP7 4p rose car ('56) 2.75 .35
**C19** AP7 10p yellow grn 1.50 .35
*Nos. C15-C19 (5)* 5.50 1.30

Planes and Arm Holding Spear — AP8

**1957, Sept. 19** *Perf. 13x12½*

| | | | | |
|---|---|---|---|---|
| C20 | AP8 | 25p bister & sepia | 6.75 | .75 |

30th anniv. of the Atlantida Squadron flight to Spanish Guinea.

### SPECIAL DELIVERY STAMP

View of Fernando Po — SD1

*Perf. 12½x13*

**1951, Mar. 1** **Litho.** **Unwmk.**

| | | | | |
|---|---|---|---|---|
| E1 | SD1 | 25c rose carmine | .20 | .20 |
| | | Never hinged | .25 | |

## SPANISH MOROCCO

ˈspa-nish mə-ˈrä-ˌkō

LOCATION — Northwest coast of Africa
GOVT. — Spanish Protectorate
AREA — 17,398 sq. mi. (approx.)
POP. — 1,010,117 (1950)
CAPITAL — Tetuán

Spanish Morocco was a Spanish Protectorate until 1956 when it, along with the French and Tangier zones of Morocco, became the independent country, Morocco.

100 Centimos = 1 Peseta

**Catalogue values for unused stamps in this country are for Never Hinged items, beginning with Scott 280 in the regular postage section, Scott B27 in the semi-postal section, Scott C24 in the airpost section, and Scott E11 in special delivery section.**

### Spanish Offices in Morocco

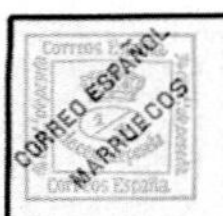
Spain No. 221A Overprinted in Carmine

**1903-09** **Unwmk.** *Imperf.*

| | | | | |
|---|---|---|---|---|
| 1 | A21 | ¼c blue green | .50 | .20 |
| a. | | Complete 1c (block 4 ¼c) | 1.90 | 1.25 |

See Nos. 26, 39, 52, Tetuan 1, 7.

Stamps of Spain Overprinted in Carmine or Blue

a

On Stamps of 1900
*Perf. 14*

| | | | | |
|---|---|---|---|---|
| 2 | A35 | 2c bister brown | 1.40 | 1.10 |
| 3 | A35 | 5c green | 1.60 | .60 |
| 4 | A35 | 10c rose red (Bl) | 1.75 | .25 |
| 5 | A35 | 15c brt violet | 2.50 | .60 |
| 6 | A35 | 20c grnsh black | 10.00 | 2.75 |
| 7 | A35 | 25c blue | .80 | .65 |
| 8 | A35 | 30c blue green | 6.00 | 2.75 |
| 9 | A35 | 40c rose (Bl) | 10.00 | 4.75 |
| 10 | A35 | 50c slate grn | 6.00 | 4.50 |
| 11 | A35 | 1p lake (Bl) | 12.00 | 6.25 |
| 12 | A35 | 4p dull violet | 32.50 | 11.00 |
| 13 | A35 | 10p brown org (Bl) | 32.50 | 27.50 |
| | | *Nos. 1-13 (13)* | 117.55 | 62.90 |
| | | Set, never hinged | 175.00 | |

Many varieties of overprint exist. Nos. 7-13 exist imperf. Value, $500.
See Tetuan Nos. 2-6, 8-15.

On Stamps of 1909-10

**1909-10** *Perf. 13x12½, 14*

| | | | | |
|---|---|---|---|---|
| 14 | A46 | 2c dark brown | .55 | .20 |
| 15 | A46 | 5c green | 2.75 | .20 |
| 16 | A46 | 10c carmine (Bl) | 3.25 | .20 |
| 17 | A46 | 15c violet | 7.50 | .45 |
| 18 | A46 | 20c olive green | 19.00 | .95 |
| 19 | A46 | 25c deep blue | 65.00 | |
| 20 | A46 | 30c blue green | 6.00 | .45 |
| 21 | A46 | 40c rose (Bl) | 6.00 | .45 |
| 22 | A46 | 50c slate blue | 10.50 | 10.00 |
| 23 | A46 | 1p lake (Bl) | 25.00 | 21.00 |
| 24 | A46 | 4p deep violet | 65.00 | |
| 25 | A46 | 10p orange (Bl) | 65.00 | |
| | | *Nos. 14-18,20-23 (9)* | 80.55 | 33.90 |
| | | Set, never hinged | 110.00 | |
| | | *Nos. 14-25 (12)* | 275.55 | |

The stamps overprinted "Correo Espanol Marruecos" were used in all Morocco until the year 1914. After the issue of special stamps for the Protectorate the "Correo Espanol" stamps were continued in use solely in the city of Tangier.
Many varieties of overprint exist.
Nos. 19, 24 and 25 were not regularly issued.
See Nos. 27-38, 40-51, 53-67, 75-76, 78.

### Spanish Morocco

Spain No. 221A Overprinted in Carmine

**1914** *Imperf.*

| | | | | |
|---|---|---|---|---|
| 26 | A21 | ¼c green | .20 | .20 |
| a. | | Complete 1c (block 4 ¼c) | 1.25 | .90 |

Stamps of Spain 1909-10 Overprinted in Carmine or Blue

*Perf. 13x12½, 14*

| | | | | |
|---|---|---|---|---|
| 27 | A46 | 2c dark brown (C) | .20 | .20 |
| 28 | A46 | 5c green (C) | .20 | .20 |
| 29 | A46 | 10c carmine (Bl) | .20 | .20 |
| 30 | A46 | 15c violet (C) | 1.10 | .75 |
| 31 | A46 | 20c olive grn (C) | 2.10 | 1.50 |
| 32 | A46 | 25c deep blue (C) | 2.10 | 1.10 |
| 33 | A46 | 30c blue grn (C) | 4.25 | 2.10 |
| 34 | A46 | 40c rose (Bl) | 9.75 | 3.00 |
| 35 | A46 | 50c slate blue (C) | 5.00 | 2.10 |
| 36 | A46 | 1p lake (Bl) | 5.00 | 3.00 |
| 37 | A46 | 4p dp violet (C) | 25.00 | 21.00 |
| 38 | A46 | 10p orange (Bl) | 37.50 | 27.50 |
| | | *Nos. 26-38,E1 (14)* | 96.35 | 64.60 |
| | | Set, never hinged | 165.00 | |

Many varieties of overprint exist, including inverted.
#27-38 exist imperf. Value for set, $525.

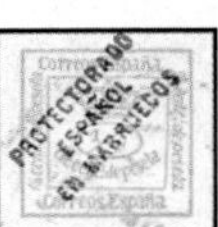
Stamps of Spain 1876 and 1909-10 Overprinted in Red or Blue

**1915** *Imperf.*

| | | | | |
|---|---|---|---|---|
| 39 | A21 | ¼c blue grn (R) | .20 | .20 |
| a. | | Complete 1c (block 4 ¼c) | 1.25 | .95 |

*Perf. 13x12½, 14*

| | | | | |
|---|---|---|---|---|
| 40 | A46 | 2c dk brown (R) | .20 | .25 |
| 41 | A46 | 5c green (R) | .25 | .25 |
| 42 | A46 | 10c carmine (Bl) | .25 | .25 |
| 43 | A46 | 15c violet (R) | .25 | .25 |
| 44 | A46 | 20c olive grn (R) | .95 | .25 |
| 45 | A46 | 25c deep blue (R) | .95 | .40 |
| 46 | A46 | 30c blue grn (R) | 1.10 | .45 |
| 47 | A46 | 40c rose (Bl) | 3.00 | .45 |
| 48 | A46 | 50c slate blue (R) | 5.00 | .40 |
| 49 | A46 | 1p lake (Bl) | 5.00 | .45 |
| 50 | A46 | 4p deep violet (R) | 32.50 | 21.00 |
| 51 | A46 | 10p orange (Bl) | 47.50 | 22.50 |
| | | *Nos. 39-51,E2 (14)* | 99.65 | 48.50 |
| | | Set, never hinged | 155.00 | |

One stamp in the setting on Nos. 39-51 has the first "R" of "PROTECTORADO" inverted. Many other varieties of overprint exist, including double and inverted.
Nos. 40-51 exist imperf. Value, set $650.

Stamps of Spain 1877 and 1909-10 Overprinted in Red or Blue

b

**1916-18** *Imperf.*

| | | | | |
|---|---|---|---|---|
| 52 | A21 | ¼c blue grn (R) | 1.10 | .20 |
| a. | | Complete 1c (block 4 ¼c) | 1.75 | 1.25 |

*Perf. 13x12½, 14*

| | | | | |
|---|---|---|---|---|
| 53 | A46 | 2c dk brown (R) | 1.10 | .20 |
| 54 | A46 | 5c green (R) | 5.00 | .20 |
| 55 | A46 | 10c carmine (Bl) | 5.50 | .20 |
| 56 | A46 | 15c violet (R) | 125.00 | |
| 57 | A46 | 20c olive grn (R) | 125.00 | |
| 58 | A46 | 25c dp blue (R) | 19.00 | 3.00 |
| 59 | A46 | 30c blue grn (R) | 25.00 | 20.00 |
| 60 | A46 | 40c rose (Bl) | 26.00 | .45 |
| 61 | A46 | 50c slate blue (R) | 12.00 | .20 |
| 62 | A46 | 1p lake (Bl) | 30.00 | 2.10 |
| 63 | A46 | 4p dp violet (R) | 50.00 | 29.00 |
| 64 | A46 | 10p orange (Bl) | 100.00 | 65.00 |
| | | *Nos. 52-55,58-64 (11)* | 274.70 | 120.55 |
| | | Set, never hinged | 400.00 | |
| | | *Nos. 52-64 (13)* | 524.70 | |
| | | Set, never hinged | 1,000. | |

Nos. 56-57 were not regularly issued.
Varieties of overprint, including double and inverted, exist for several denominations.
The 5c exists in olive brown. Value $525.

Same Overprint on Spain No. 310

**1920**

| | | | | |
|---|---|---|---|---|
| 65 | A46 | 15c ocher (Bl) | 5.50 | .30 |

Exists imperf.; also with overprint inverted.

Nos. 44, 46 Perforated through the middle and each half Surcharged "10 céntimos" in Red

**1920**

| | | | | |
|---|---|---|---|---|
| 66 | A46 | 10c on half of 20c | 5.00 | 1.90 |
| 67 | A46 | 15c on half of 30c | 11.00 | 7.25 |

**No. E2 Divided and Surcharged in Black**

| | | | | |
|---|---|---|---|---|
| 68 | SD1 | 10c on half of 20c | 12.00 | 7.75 |
| a. | | "10/cts." surcharge added | 145.00 | 45.00 |
| | | *Nos. 66-68 (3)* | 28.00 | 16.90 |

Values of Nos. 66-68 are for pairs, both halves of the stamp. Varieties were probably made deliberately.

"Justice" — A1

Revenue Stamps Perforated through the Middle and each half Surcharged with New Value in Red or Green

**1920** *Perf. 11½*

| | | | | |
|---|---|---|---|---|
| 69 | A1 | 5c on 5p lt bl | 9.50 | 1.90 |
| 70 | A1 | 5c on 10p green | .40 | .20 |
| 71 | A1 | 10c on 25p dk grn | .40 | .20 |
| a. | | Inverted surcharge | 11.00 | 10.00 |
| 72 | A1 | 10c on 50p indigo | .45 | .30 |
| 73 | A1 | 15c on 100p red (G) | .45 | .30 |
| 74 | A1 | 15c on 500p cl (G) | 12.50 | 6.50 |
| | | *Nos. 69-74 (6)* | 23.70 | 9.40 |
| | | Set, never hinged | 37.50 | |

Values of Nos. 69-74 are for pairs, both halves of the stamp.

Stamps of Spain 1917-20 Overprinted Type "a" in Blue or Red

**1921-24** *Perf. 13*

| | | | | |
|---|---|---|---|---|
| 75 | A46 | 15c ocher (Bl) | 1.25 | .20 |
| 76 | A46 | 20c violet (R) | 1.90 | .20 |

**Stamps of Spain 1920-21 Overprinted Type "b" in Red**

*Imperf*

| | | | | |
|---|---|---|---|---|
| 77 | A47 | 1c blue green | 1.40 | .20 |

**Engr.**
*Perf. 13*

| | | | | |
|---|---|---|---|---|
| 78 | A46 | 20c violet | 10.00 | .20 |

See No. 92.

Stamps of Spain, 1922 Overprinted Type "a" in Red or Blue

**1923-28** *Perf. 13½x12½*

| | | | | |
|---|---|---|---|---|
| 79 | A49 | 2c olive green (R) | 3.50 | .20 |
| 80 | A49 | 5c red violet (Bl) | 3.50 | .20 |
| 81 | A49 | 10c yellow green (R) | 4.25 | .20 |
| 82 | A49 | 20c violet (R) | 6.00 | .90 |
| | | *Nos. 79-82 (4)* | 17.25 | 1.50 |

Same Overprinted Type "b"

**1923-25**

| | | | | |
|---|---|---|---|---|
| 83 | A49 | 2c olive green (R) | .65 | .20 |
| 84 | A49 | 5c red violet (Bl) | .65 | .20 |
| 85 | A49 | 10c yellow grn (R) | 2.75 | .20 |
| 86 | A49 | 15c blue (R) | 2.75 | .20 |
| 87 | A49 | 20c violet (R) | 6.00 | .20 |
| 88 | A49 | 25c carmine (Bl) | 12.00 | 1.40 |
| 89 | A49 | 40c deep blue (R) | 12.50 | 4.50 |
| 90 | A49 | 50c orange (Bl) | 32.50 | 7.75 |
| 91 | A49a | 1p blue black (R) | 50.00 | 4.50 |
| | | *Nos. 83-91,E3 (10)* | 130.30 | 27.40 |
| | | Set, never hinged | 210.00 | |

Spain No. 314 Overprinted Type "a" in Red

**1927** *Imperf.*

| | | | | |
|---|---|---|---|---|
| 92 | A47 | 1c blue green | .20 | .20 |

Mosque of Alcazarquivir A2

Moorish Gateway at Larache A3

Well at Alhucemas A4

View of Xauen — A5

View of Tetuan — A6

**1928-32** **Engr.** *Perf. 14, 14½*

| | | | | |
|---|---|---|---|---|
| 93 | A2 | 1c red ("Cs") | .20 | .20 |
| 94 | A2 | 1c car rose ("Ct") ('32) | .30 | .30 |
| 95 | A2 | 2c dark violet | .20 | .20 |
| 96 | A2 | 5c deep blue | .20 | .20 |
| 97 | A2 | 10c dark green | .20 | .20 |
| 98 | A2 | 15c orange brown | .50 | .20 |
| 99 | A3 | 20c olive green | .50 | .20 |
| 100 | A3 | 25c copper red | .50 | .20 |
| 102 | A3 | 30c black brown | 1.75 | .20 |
| 103 | A3 | 40c dull blue | 2.25 | .20 |
| 104 | A3 | 50c brown violet | 4.75 | .20 |
| 105 | A4 | 1p yellow green | 7.00 | .25 |
| 106 | A5 | 2.50p red violet | 22.00 | 7.50 |
| 107 | A6 | 4p ultra | 16.50 | 4.50 |
| | | *Nos. 93-107,E4 (15)* | 61.10 | 15.95 |
| | | Set, never hinged | 85.00 | |

For surcharges see Nos. 164-167.

### Seville-Barcelona Issue of Spain, 1929, Overprinted in Red or Blue

**1929** *Perf. 11, 14*

| No. | Type | Value | Color | Unused | Used |
|---|---|---|---|---|---|
| **108** | A50 | 1c | greenish blue | .25 | .25 |
| **109** | A51 | 2c | pale yel grn | .25 | .25 |
| **110** | A52 | 5c | rose lake (Bl) | .25 | .25 |
| **111** | A53 | 10c | green | .25 | .25 |
| **112** | A50 | 15c | Prussian blue | .25 | .25 |
| **113** | A51 | 20c | purple | .25 | .25 |
| **114** | A50 | 25c | bright rose (Bl) | .25 | .25 |
| **115** | A52 | 30c | black brown (bl) | .70 | .55 |
| **116** | A53 | 40c | dark blue | .70 | .55 |
| **117** | A51 | 50c | deep orange (Bl) | .70 | .55 |
| **118** | A52 | 1p | blue black | 5.75 | 4.25 |
| **119** | A53 | 4p | deep rose (Bl) | 12.50 | 9.75 |
| **120** | A53 | 10p | brown (Bl) | 27.50 | 21.00 |
| | | | *Nos. 108-120 (13)* | 49.60 | 38.40 |
| | | | Set, never hinged | 87.50 | |

See Nos. L1-L11.

### Stamps of Spain, 1922-31, Overprinted Type "a" in Black, Blue or Red

**1929-34** *Perf. 11½, 13x12½*

| No. | Type | Value | Color | Unused | Used |
|---|---|---|---|---|---|
| **121** | A49 | 5c | claret (Bk) | 3.25 | .20 |
| **122** | A61 | 10c | green (R) | 2.75 | .40 |
| **123** | A61 | 15c | slate grn (R) | 97.50 | 1.00 |
| **124** | A61 | 20c | violet (R) | 2.75 | .45 |
| **125** | A61 | 30c | brown lake (Bl) | 3.00 | 1.00 |
| **126** | A61 | 40c | dark blue (R) | 11.00 | 5.00 |
| **127** | A49 | 50c | orange (Bl) | 27.50 | 4.75 |
| **128** | A49a | 10p | brown (Bl) | 2.75 | 4.25 |
| | | | *Nos. 121-128 (8)* | 150.50 | 17.05 |
| | | | Set, never hinged | 210.00 | |

Stamps of Spain, 1922-26, overprinted diagonally as above, and with no control number, or with "A000,000" on back, were not issued but were presented to the delegates at the 1929 UPU Congress in London. Value of complete set of 16, $3,250.

### Stamps of Spain 1931-32, Overprinted in Black

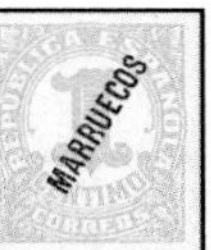


**1933-34** *Imperf.*

| No. | Type | Value | Color | Unused | Used |
|---|---|---|---|---|---|
| **130** | A108 | 1c | blue green | .20 | .20 |
| | | | ***Perf. 11½*** | | |
| **131** | A108 | 2c | buff | .20 | .20 |
| **132** | A95 | 5c | brnsh black | .20 | .20 |
| **133** | A96 | 10c | yellow green | .20 | .20 |
| **134** | A97 | 15c | slate green | .20 | .20 |
| **135** | A95 | 20c | dark violet | .20 | .20 |
| **136** | A104 | 25c | lake | .20 | .20 |
| **137** | A99 | 30c | carmine rose | 50.00 | 5.00 |
| **138** | A100 | 40c | dark blue | .50 | .20 |
| **139** | A97 | 50c | orange | .95 | .20 |
| **140** | A100 | 60c | apple green | .95 | .20 |
| **141** | A105 | 1p | blue black | .95 | .40 |
| **142** | A106 | 4p | magenta | 2.10 | 2.10 |
| **143** | A107 | 10p | deep brown | 3.00 | 4.75 |
| | | | *Nos. 130-143,E7 (15)* | 61.10 | 14.45 |
| | | | Set, never hinged | 100.00 | |

Street Scene in Tangier — A7

View of Xauen A8

Gate in Town Wall, Arzila — A9

Street Scene in Tangier A10

Mosque of Alcazarquivir A11

Caliph and His Guard A12

View of Tangier A13

### Green Control Numbers Printed on Gum

**1933-35** **Photo.** *Perf. 14, 13½*

| No. | Type | Value | Color | Unused | Used |
|---|---|---|---|---|---|
| **144** | A7 | 1c | brt rose | .20 | .20 |
| **145** | A8 | 2c | green ('35) | .20 | .20 |
| **146** | A9 | 5c | magenta ('35) | .20 | .20 |
| **147** | A10 | 10c | dark green | .30 | .20 |
| **148** | A11 | 15c | yellow ('35) | 1.90 | .20 |
| **149** | A7 | 20c | slate green | .80 | .20 |
| **150** | A12 | 25c | crimson ('35) | 20.00 | .20 |
| **151** | A10 | 30c | red brown | 6.00 | .20 |
| **152** | A13 | 40c | deep blue | 9.25 | .20 |
| **153** | A13 | 50c | red orange | 30.00 | 3.75 |
| **154** | A8 | 1p | slate blk ('35) | 13.00 | .20 |
| **155** | A9 | 2.50p | brown ('35) | 22.50 | 3.75 |
| **156** | A11 | 4p | yel grn ('35) | 22.50 | 3.75 |
| **157** | A12 | 5p | black ('35) | 30.00 | 3.75 |
| | | | *Nos. 144-157,E5 (15)* | 157.85 | 17.20 |
| | | | Set, never hinged | 230.00 | |

For surcharge see No. CB1.

Mosque — A14

Landscape A15

### Green Control Numbers Printed on Gum

**1935**

| No. | Type | Value | Color | Unused | Used |
|---|---|---|---|---|---|
| **158** | A14 | 25c | violet | .85 | .20 |
| **159** | A15 | 30c | crimson | 12.00 | .20 |
| **160** | A14 | 40c | orange | 6.00 | .20 |
| **161** | A15 | 50c | bright blue | 6.00 | .20 |
| **162** | A14 | 60c | dk blue green | 6.00 | .20 |
| **163** | A15 | 2p | brown lake | 30.00 | 4.25 |
| | | | *Nos. 158-163 (6)* | 60.85 | 5.25 |
| | | | Set, never hinged | 87.50 | |

See No. 174.

### Regular Issue and Special Delivery Stamp of 1928, Surcharged in Blue, Green or Red with New Values and Ornaments

**1936**

| No. | Type | Value | Color | Unused | Used |
|---|---|---|---|---|---|
| **164** | A6 | 1c | on 4p ultra (Bl) | .25 | .20 |
| **165** | A5 | 2c | on 2.50p red vio (G) | .25 | .20 |
| **166** | A3 | 5c | on 25c cop red (R) | .20 | .20 |
| **167** | A4 | 10c | on 1p yel grn (G) | 8.50 | 3.50 |
| **168** | SD2 | 15c | on 20c blk (Bl) | 6.50 | 1.75 |
| | | | *Nos. 164-168 (5)* | 15.70 | 5.85 |
| | | | Set, never hinged | 20.00 | |

Caliph and Viziers — A16

View of Bokoia A17

View of Alcazarquivir — A18

Sidi Saida Mosque A19

Caliph and Procession A20

### Without Control Numbers

**1937** **Photo.** *Perf. 13½*

| No. | Type | Value | Color | Unused | Used |
|---|---|---|---|---|---|
| **169** | A16 | 1c | green | .20 | .20 |
| **170** | A17 | 2c | red violet | .20 | .20 |
| **171** | A18 | 5c | orange | .20 | .20 |
| **172** | A16 | 15c | violet | .20 | .20 |
| **173** | A19 | 30c | red | .60 | .20 |
| *a.* | | | Souvenir sheet of 4, #170-173 | 18.00 | 10.00 |
| **174** | A14 | 1p | ultra | 6.00 | .20 |
| *a.* | | | Souv. sheet of 4, #169-171, 174 | 18.00 | 10.00 |
| **175** | A20 | 10p | brown | 50.00 | 15.00 |
| | | | *Nos. 169-175 (7)* | 57.40 | 16.20 |
| | | | Set, never hinged | 75.00 | |

Nos. 173a, 174a for 1st year of the Spanish Civil War.

Nos. 173a, 174a were privately overprinted "TANGER" in black on each stamp in the sheet for "use" in the International City of Tangier, and "GUINEA" for "use" in Spanish Guinea.

Harkeno Rifleman — A21

Troops Marching A22

Designs: 2c, Legionnaires. 5c, Cavalryman leading his mount. 10c, Moroccan phalanx. 15c, Legion flag-bearer. 20c, Colonial soldier. 25c, Ifni sharpshooters. 30c, Mounted trumpeters. 40c, Cape Juby Dromedary Corps. 50c, Regular infantry. 60c, Caliphate guards. 1p, Orderly on guard. 2p, Sentry. 2.50p, Regular cavalry. 4p, Orderly.

**1937** *Perf. 13½*

| No. | Type | Value | Color | Unused | Used |
|---|---|---|---|---|---|
| **176** | A21 | 1c | dull blue | .20 | .20 |
| **177** | A21 | 2c | orange brn | .20 | .20 |
| **178** | A21 | 5c | cerise | .20 | .20 |
| **179** | A21 | 10c | emerald | .20 | .20 |
| **180** | A21 | 15c | brt blue | .20 | .20 |
| **181** | A21 | 20c | red brown | .20 | .20 |
| **182** | A21 | 25c | magenta | .20 | .20 |
| **183** | A21 | 30c | red orange | .20 | .20 |
| **184** | A21 | 40c | orange | .20 | .20 |
| **185** | A21 | 50c | ultra | .20 | .20 |
| **186** | A21 | 60c | yellow grn | .20 | .20 |
| **187** | A21 | 1p | blue violet | .20 | .20 |
| **188** | A21 | 2p | Prus blue | 8.50 | 3.50 |
| **189** | A21 | 2.50p | gray black | 8.50 | 3.50 |
| **190** | A21 | 4p | dark brown | 8.50 | 3.50 |
| **191** | A22 | 10p | black | 8.50 | 3.50 |
| | | | *Nos. 176-191,E6 (17)* | 36.60 | 16.60 |
| | | | Set, never hinged | 52.50 | |

First Year of Spanish Civil War.

Exists imperf. Value, set $250.

For overprints see Nos. 214-229.

Spanish Quarter — A25

Designs: 10c, Moroccan quarter. 15c, Street scene, Larache. 20c, Tetuan.

**1939** **Unwmk.** **Photo.** *Perf. 13½*

| No. | Type | Value | Color | Unused | Used |
|---|---|---|---|---|---|
| **194** | A25 | 5c | orange | .20 | .20 |
| **195** | A25 | 10c | brt blue grn | .20 | .20 |
| **196** | A25 | 15c | golden brown | .40 | .20 |
| **197** | A25 | 20c | brt ultra | .40 | .20 |
| | | | *Nos. 194-197 (4)* | 1.20 | .80 |

Postman — A26

Mail Box — A27

Landscape A28

Street Scene, Alcazarquivir A29

View of Xauen — A30

Sentry Guarding Palace at Sat — A31

The Chieftain — A32

Market Place, Larache — A33

Tetuán — A34

Ancient Gateway at Xauen — A35

Scene in Alcazarquivir A36

Post Office A37

Spanish War Veterans — A38

Victory Flag Bearers — A39

Cavalry — A40

Day of Court — A41

**1940 Unwmk. Photo. *Perf. 11½x11***

| No. | Type | Value | Color | Unused | Used |
|---|---|---|---|---|---|
| 198 | A26 | 1c | dark brown | .20 | .20 |
| 199 | A27 | 2c | olive grn | .20 | .20 |
| 200 | A28 | 5c | dk blue | .20 | .20 |
| 201 | A29 | 10c | dk red lilac | .20 | .20 |
| 202 | A30 | 15c | dk green | .25 | .20 |
| 203 | A31 | 20c | purple | .20 | .20 |
| 204 | A32 | 25c | black brown | .20 | .20 |
| 205 | A33 | 30c | brt green | .20 | .20 |
| 206 | A34 | 40c | slate green | 1.75 | .20 |
| 207 | A35 | 45c | orange ver | .70 | .20 |
| 208 | A36 | 50c | brown orange | .70 | .20 |
| 209 | A37 | 70c | sapphire | .70 | .20 |
| 210 | A38 | 1p | indigo & brn | 2.00 | .20 |
| 211 | A39 | 2.50p | choc & dk grn | 12.00 | 3.00 |
| 212 | A40 | 5p | dk cerise & sep | 2.25 | .20 |
| 213 | A41 | 10p | dk ol grn & brn org | 20.00 | 5.00 |
| | | | *Nos. 198-213,E8 (17)* | 42.35 | 11.00 |
| | | | Set, never hinged | 70.00 | |

"ZONA" printed in black on back.
Exists imperf. Value, set $250.

Stamps of 1937 Overprinted in Various Colors

**1940 Unwmk. *Perf. 13½***

| No. | Type | Value | Color | Unused | Used |
|---|---|---|---|---|---|
| 214 | A21 | 1c | dull blue (Bk) | .70 | .55 |
| 215 | A21 | 2c | org brn (Bk) | .70 | .55 |
| 216 | A21 | 5c | cerise (Bk) | .70 | .55 |
| 217 | A21 | 10c | emerald (Bk) | .70 | .55 |
| 218 | A21 | 15c | brt blue (Bk) | .70 | .55 |
| 219 | A21 | 20c | red brn (Bk) | .70 | .55 |
| 220 | A21 | 25c | mag (Bk) | .70 | .55 |
| 221 | A21 | 30c | red org (V) | .70 | .55 |
| 222 | A21 | 40c | orange (V) | 1.25 | 1.00 |
| 223 | A21 | 50c | ultra (Bk) | 1.25 | 1.00 |
| 224 | A21 | 60c | yel grn (Bk) | 1.25 | 1.00 |
| 225 | A21 | 1p | blue vio (V) | 1.25 | 1.00 |
| 226 | A21 | 2p | Prus bl (Bl) | 38.00 | 38.00 |
| 227 | A21 | 2.50p | gray blk (V) | 38.00 | 38.00 |
| 228 | A21 | 4p | dk brn (Bl) | 38.00 | 38.00 |
| 229 | A22 | 10p | black (R) | 38.00 | 38.00 |
| | | | *Nos. 214-229,E10 (17)* | 172.10 | 167.65 |
| | | | Set, never hinged | 290.00 | |

4th anniversary of Spanish Civil War.

Larache A42

Alcazarquivir A43

Market Place, Larache — A44

Tangier

A45 A46

**1941 Unwmk. Photo. *Perf. 10½***

| No. | Type | Value | Color | Unused | Used |
|---|---|---|---|---|---|
| 230 | A42 | 5c | dk brn & brn | .20 | .20 |
| 231 | A43 | 10c | dp rose & ver | .20 | .20 |
| 232 | A44 | 15c | sl grn & yel grn | .20 | .20 |
| 233 | A45 | 20c | vio bl & dp bl | .45 | .20 |
| 234 | A46 | 40c | dp plum & claret | 1.25 | .20 |
| | | | *Nos. 230-234 (5)* | 2.30 | 1.00 |

Exists imperf. Value, set $125.

**1943 *Perf. 12x12½***

| No. | Type | Value | Color | Unused | Used |
|---|---|---|---|---|---|
| 234A | A43 | 5c | dark blue | .20 | .20 |
| 235 | A44 | 40c | dull violet brn | 55.00 | .20 |

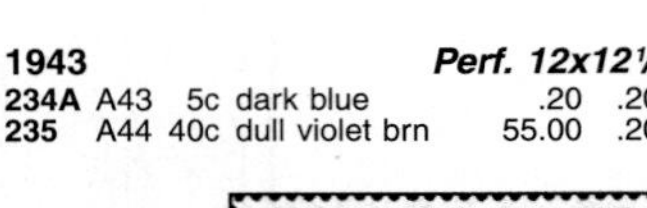

Plowing A47

Harvesting A48

Returning from Work A49

Transporting Wheat — A50

Vegetable Garden A51

Picking Oranges A52

Goat Herd — A53

**1944 Unwmk. Photo. *Perf. 12½***

| No. | Type | Value | Color | Unused | Used |
|---|---|---|---|---|---|
| 236 | A47 | 1c | choc & lt bl | .20 | .20 |
| 237 | A48 | 2c | sl grn & lt grn | .20 | .20 |
| 238 | A49 | 5c | choc & grnsh blk | .20 | .20 |
| 239 | A50 | 10c | brt ultra & red org | .20 | .20 |
| 240 | A51 | 15c | sl grn & lt grn | .20 | .20 |
| 241 | A52 | 20c | dp cl & blk | .20 | .20 |
| 242 | A53 | 25c | lt bl & choc | .20 | .20 |
| 243 | A47 | 30c | yel grn & brt ultra | .20 | .20 |
| 244 | A48 | 40c | choc & red vio | .20 | .20 |
| 245 | A49 | 50c | brt ultra & red brn | .60 | .20 |
| 246 | A50 | 75c | yel grn & brt ultra | .80 | .20 |
| 247 | A51 | 1p | brt ultra & choc | .80 | .20 |
| 248 | A52 | 2.50p | blk & brt ultra | 7.00 | 1.60 |
| 249 | A53 | 10p | sal & gray blk | 10.50 | 3.25 |
| | | | *Nos. 236-249 (14)* | 21.50 | 7.25 |
| | | | Set, never hinged | 30.00 | |

Exists imperf. Value, set $100.

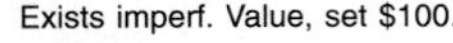

Potters A54

Dyers A55

Blacksmiths A56

Cobblers A57

Weavers A58

Metal Workers A59

**1946 Unwmk. Litho. *Perf. 10½x10***

| No. | Type | Value | Color | Unused | Used |
|---|---|---|---|---|---|
| 250 | A54 | 1c | purple & brn | .20 | .20 |
| 251 | A55 | 2c | dk Prus grn & vio blk | .20 | .20 |
| 252 | A54 | 10c | dp org & vio bl | .20 | .20 |
| 253 | A55 | 15c | dk bl & bl grn | .20 | .20 |
| 254 | A54 | 25c | yel grn & ultra | .20 | .20 |
| 255 | A56 | 40c | dk bl & brn, perf. 12½ | .20 | .20 |
| 256 | A55 | 45c | black & rose | .50 | .20 |
| 257 | A57 | 1p | dk Prus grn & dp bl | .60 | .20 |
| 258 | A58 | 2.50p | dp org & gray | 1.75 | .65 |
| 259 | A59 | 10p | dk bl & gray | 3.00 | 1.50 |
| | | | *Nos. 250-259 (10)* | 7.05 | 3.75 |
| | | | Set, never hinged | 9.50 | |

Control letter "Z" in circle in black on back.
Exists imperf. Value, set $80.

A60

Sanitorium — A61

**1946, Sept. 1 *Perf. 11½x10½, 10½***

| No. | Type | Value | Color | Unused | Used |
|---|---|---|---|---|---|
| 260 | A60 | 10c | crim & bl grn | .20 | .20 |
| 261 | A61 | 25c | crimson & brn | .20 | .20 |
| | | | *Nos. 260-261,B14-B16 (5)* | 1.65 | 1.05 |

Issued to aid anti-tuberculosis work.

A62

A63

**1947 *Perf. 10***

| No. | Type | Value | Color | Unused | Used |
|---|---|---|---|---|---|
| 262 | A62 | 10c | carmine & blue | .20 | .20 |
| 263 | A63 | 25c | red & chocolate | .20 | .20 |
| | | | *Nos. 262-263,B17-B19 (5)* | 1.65 | 1.30 |

Issued to aid anti-tuberculosis work.

Commerce by Railroad A64

Commerce by Truck A65

Urban Market A66

Country Market A67

Caravan A68

Maritime Commerce A69

**1948** **Litho.** ***Perf. 10, 10x10½***

| | | | | |
|---|---|---|---|---|
| **264** | A64 | 2c purple & brn | .20 | .20 |
| **265** | A65 | 5c dp cl & vio | .20 | .20 |
| **266** | A66 | 15c brt ultra & bl grn | .20 | .20 |
| **267** | A67 | 25c blk & Prus grn | .20 | .20 |
| **268** | A65 | 35c brt ultra & gray blk | .20 | .20 |
| **269** | A68 | 50c red & violet | .20 | .20 |
| **270** | A66 | 70c dk gray grn & ultra | .20 | .20 |
| **271** | A67 | 90c cer & dk gray grn | .20 | .20 |
| **272** | A68 | 1p brt ultra & vio | .60 | .20 |
| **273** | A64 | 2.50p vio brn & sl grn | 1.50 | .45 |
| **274** | A69 | 10p blk & dp ultra | 2.75 | 1.25 |
| | | *Nos. 264-274 (11)* | 6.45 | 3.50 |
| | | Set, never hinged | 9.50 | |

Exists imperf. Value, set $80.

Emblem of Tuberculosis Association
A70 A71

Design: 25c, Plane over sanatorium.

**1948, Oct. 1** ***Perf. 10***

| | | | | |
|---|---|---|---|---|
| **275** | A70 | 10c car & green | .20 | .20 |
| **276** | A70 | 25c car & grnsh gray | 1.50 | .60 |
| | | *Nos. 275-276,B20-B23 (6)* | 24.70 | 8.40 |

See No. B39.

**1949**

10c, Road of Health. 25c, Minaret and Palm.

**Black Control Number on Back**

| | | | | |
|---|---|---|---|---|
| **277** | A71 | 5c car & green | .20 | .20 |
| **278** | A71 | 10c car & dk vio | .20 | .20 |
| **279** | A71 | 25c car & black | .60 | .25 |
| | | *Nos. 277-279,B25-B26 (5)* | 2.10 | 1.10 |

**Catalogue values for unused stamps in this section, from this point to the end of the section, are for Never Hinged items.**

Mail Transport, 1890 — A72

Herald — A73

Designs: 5c, 50c, 90c, Mail transport, 1890. 10c, 45c, 1p, Mail transport, 1906. 15c, 1.50p, Mail transport, 1913. 35c, 75c, 5p, Mail transport, 1914. 10p, Mail transport, 1918.

**1950** **Litho.** ***Perf. 10½***

| | | | | |
|---|---|---|---|---|
| **280** | A72 | 5c choc & vio bl | .20 | .20 |
| **281** | A72 | 10c deep bl & sep | .20 | .20 |
| **282** | A72 | 15c grnsh blk & emer | .20 | .20 |
| **283** | A72 | 35c pur & gray blk | .20 | .20 |
| **284** | A72 | 45c dp car & rose lil | .20 | .20 |
| **285** | A72 | 50c emer & dk brn | .20 | .20 |
| **286** | A72 | 75c dk vio bl & bl | .20 | .20 |
| **287** | A72 | 90c grnsh blk & rose car | .20 | .20 |
| **288** | A72 | 1p blk brn & gray | .20 | .20 |
| **289** | A72 | 1.50p carmine & blue | .70 | .20 |
| **290** | A72 | 5p black & vio brn | 1.25 | .20 |
| **291** | A72 | 10p purple & blue | 26.00 | 10.00 |
| | | *Nos. 280-291,E11 (13)* | 53.75 | 21.20 |

UPU, 75th anniv. (in 1949).
Nos. 280-291 exist imperf. Value $350.

**1950** **Unwmk.** ***Perf. 10***
**Frame and Device in Carmine**
**Black Control Number on Back**

| | | | | |
|---|---|---|---|---|
| **292** | A73 | 5c gray black | .20 | .20 |
| **293** | A73 | 10c Old fort | .20 | .20 |
| **294** | A73 | 25c Sanatorium | .50 | .30 |
| | | *Nos. 292-294,B27-B28 (5)* | 1.65 | 1.20 |

Boar Hunt A74

10c, 1p, Hunters and hounds. 50c, Boar hunt. 5p, Fishermen. 10p, Moorish fishing boat.

**1950, Dec. 30** ***Perf. 10½x10***
**Black Control Number on Back**

| | | | | |
|---|---|---|---|---|
| **295** | A74 | 5c dk brn & rose vio | .20 | .20 |
| **296** | A74 | 10c carmine & gray | .20 | .20 |
| **297** | A74 | 50c green & sepia | .20 | .20 |
| **298** | A74 | 1p bl vio & claret | .45 | .20 |
| **299** | A74 | 5p dp claret & bl vio | .70 | .25 |
| **300** | A74 | 10p grnsh blk & dp cl | 2.25 | .40 |
| | | *Nos. 295-300 (6)* | 4.00 | 1.45 |

Emblem — A75

Worship — A77

Armed Attack A76

10c, Patients expressing gratitude. 25c, Plane in the Clouds.

Dated "1951"

**1951** **Litho.** ***Perf. 12***
**Frame and Device in Carmine**
**Black Control Number on Back**

| | | | | |
|---|---|---|---|---|
| **301** | A75 | 5c green | .20 | .20 |
| **302** | A75 | 10c blue violet | .20 | .20 |
| **303** | A75 | 25c gray black | .85 | .30 |
| | | *Nos. 301-303,B29-B32 (7)* | 13.55 | 5.00 |

Issued to aid anti-tuberculosis work.

**1952** ***Perf. 11***

Designs: 10c, Horses on parade. 15c, Holiday procession. 20c, Road to market. 25c, "Brother-hoods." 35c, "Offering." 45c, Soldiers. 50c, On the rooftop. 75c, Teahouse. 90c, Wedding. 1p, Pilgrimage. 5p, Storyteller. 10p, Market corner.

**Black Control Number on Back**

| | | | | |
|---|---|---|---|---|
| **304** | A76 | 5c dk blue & brn | .20 | .20 |
| **305** | A76 | 10c dk brn & lil rose | .20 | .20 |
| **306** | A76 | 15c black & emer | .20 | .20 |
| **307** | A76 | 20c ol grn & red vio | .20 | .20 |
| **308** | A76 | 25c red & lt blue | .20 | .20 |
| **309** | A76 | 35c olive & orange | .20 | .20 |
| **310** | A76 | 45c red & rose red | .20 | .20 |
| **311** | A76 | 50c rose car & gray grn | .20 | .20 |
| **312** | A76 | 75c purple & ultra | .20 | .20 |
| **313** | A76 | 90c dk bl & rose vio | .20 | .20 |
| **314** | A76 | 1p dk bl & red brn | .20 | .20 |
| **315** | A76 | 5p red & blue | 1.25 | .25 |
| **316** | A76 | 10p dk grn & gray blk | 1.75 | .40 |
| | | *Nos. 304-316,E12 (14)* | 5.40 | 3.05 |

**1952, Oct. 1** **Dated "1952"**

10c, Distributing alms. 25c, Prickly pear.

**Black Control Number on Back**

| | | | | |
|---|---|---|---|---|
| **317** | A77 | 5c car & dk ol grn | .20 | .20 |
| **318** | A77 | 10c car & dk brown | .20 | .20 |
| **319** | A77 | 25c car & dp blue | .35 | .20 |
| | | *Nos. 317-319,B33-B37 (8)* | 9.35 | 3.80 |

Semi-Postal Types of 1948-49 Dated "1953"

**1953** **Litho.** ***Perf. 10***
**Black Control Number on Back**

| | | | | |
|---|---|---|---|---|
| **320** | SP7 | 5c shown | .20 | .20 |
| **321** | SP9 | 10c like #B26 | .20 | .20 |
| **322** | SP7 | 25c like #B23 | .85 | .35 |
| | | *Nos. 320-322,B38-B42 (8)* | 14.90 | 5.35 |

Issued to aid anti-tuberculosis work.

A78

**1953, Nov. 15**
**Black Control Number on Back**

| | | | | |
|---|---|---|---|---|
| **323** | A78 | 5c red | .20 | .20 |
| **324** | A78 | 10c gray green | .20 | .20 |

Mountain Women — A79

Zauia — A80

50c and 2.50p, Water carrier. 90c and 2p, Mountaineers and donkey. 1p and 4.50p, Moorish women and child. 10p, Mounted dignitary.

**1953, Dec. 15** **Photo.**
**Black Control Number on Back**

| | | | | |
|---|---|---|---|---|
| **334** | A79 | 35c grn & rose vio | .20 | .20 |
| **335** | A79 | 50c red & green | .20 | .20 |
| **336** | A79 | 90c dk bl & org | .20 | .20 |
| **337** | A79 | 1p dk brn & grn | .20 | .20 |
| **338** | A79 | 1.25p dk grn & car rose | .20 | .20 |
| **339** | A79 | 2p dk rose vio & bl | .25 | .20 |
| **340** | A79 | 2.50p black & orange | .65 | .25 |
| **341** | A79 | 4.50p brt car rose & dk grn | 3.25 | .35 |
| **342** | A79 | 10p green & black | 4.25 | .65 |
| | | *Nos. 334-342,E13 (10)* | 9.60 | 2.65 |

25th anniv. of Spanish Morocco's first definitive postage stamps.

**1954, Nov. 1** **Dated "1954"**

10c, "The Family." 25c, Plane, Spanish coast.

**Black Control Number on Back**

| | | | | |
|---|---|---|---|---|
| **343** | A80 | 5c car & bl grn | .20 | .20 |
| **344** | A80 | 10c car & dk brn | .20 | .20 |
| **345** | A80 | 25c car & blue | .20 | .20 |
| | | *Nos. 343-345,B43-B45 (6)* | 7.50 | 4.40 |

Queen's Gate — A81

Honor Guard — A82

**1955** **Litho.** ***Perf. 11***
**Black Control Number on Back**
**Frames in Black**

| | | | | |
|---|---|---|---|---|
| **346** | A81 | 15c shown | .20 | .20 |
| **347** | A81 | 25c Saida | .20 | .20 |
| **348** | A81 | 80c like #346 | .20 | .20 |
| **349** | A81 | 1p like #347 | .20 | .20 |
| **350** | A81 | 15p Ceuta | 3.00 | .65 |
| | | *Nos. 346-350,E14 (6)* | 4.00 | 1.65 |

***Perf. 13x12½***
**1955, Nov. 8** **Photo.** **Unwmk.**

Designs: 25c, 80c, 3p, Caliph Moulay Hassan ben el-Medi. 30c, 1p, 5p, Caliph and procession. 15p, Coat of arms.

| | | | | |
|---|---|---|---|---|
| **351** | A82 | 15c ol brn & ol | .20 | .20 |
| **352** | A82 | 25c lil & dp rose | .20 | .20 |
| **353** | A82 | 30c brn blk & Prus grn | .20 | .20 |
| **354** | A82 | 70c Prus grn & yel grn | .20 | .20 |
| **355** | A82 | 80c ol & ol brn | .20 | .20 |
| **356** | A82 | 1p dk bl & redsh brn | .20 | .20 |
| **357** | A82 | 1.80p black & bl vio | .20 | .20 |
| **358** | A82 | 3p blue & gray | .20 | .20 |
| **359** | A82 | 5p dk grn & brn | 1.25 | .45 |

**Engr.**

| | | | | |
|---|---|---|---|---|
| **360** | A82 | 15p red brn & yel grn | 2.75 | 1.65 |
| | | *Nos. 351-360 (10)* | 5.60 | 3.70 |

30th anniv. of accession to throne by Caliph Moulay Hassan ben el-Medi ben Ismail.

Succeeding issues, released under the Kingdom, are listed under Morocco.

## SEMI-POSTAL STAMPS

Types of Semi-Postal Stamps of Spain, 1926, Overprinted in Black or Blue

**1926** **Unwmk.** ***Perf. 12½, 13***

| | | | | |
|---|---|---|---|---|
| **B1** | SP1 | 1c orange | 7.00 | 4.50 |
| **B2** | SP2 | 2c rose | 10.00 | 8.25 |
| **B3** | SP3 | 5c black brn | 3.50 | 3.00 |
| **B4** | SP4 | 10c dark grn | 3.50 | 3.00 |
| **B5** | SP1 | 15c dk violet (Bl) | .65 | .55 |
| **B6** | SP4 | 20c violet brn | .65 | .55 |
| **B7** | SP5 | 25c deep carmine | .65 | .55 |
| **B8** | SP1 | 30c olive grn | .65 | .55 |
| **B9** | SP3 | 40c ultra | .20 | .20 |
| **B10** | SP2 | 50c red brown | .20 | .20 |
| **B11** | SP4 | 1p vermilion | .20 | .20 |
| **B12** | SP3 | 4p bister | .65 | .55 |
| **B13** | SP5 | 10p light violet | 2.75 | 2.25 |
| | | *Nos. B1-B13,EB1 (14)* | 33.10 | 26.45 |
| | | Set, never hinged | 57.50 | |

See Spain No. B6a for No. B6 without overprint. For surcharges see Spain Nos. B64-B65.

### Tuberculosis Fund Issues

SP1

SP2

SP3

***Perf. 10½, 11½x10½***

**1946, Sept. 1 Litho. Unwmk.**

**B14** SP1 25c + 5c crim & rose vio .20 .20
**B15** SP2 50c + 10c crim & blue .30 .20
**B16** SP3 90c + 10c crim & gray brn .75 .25
*Nos. B14-B16 (3)* 1.25 .65

Medical Center — SP4

Nurse and Children — SP5

Herald SP7

"Protection" SP6

**1947** ***Perf. 10***

**B17** SP4 25c + 5c red & violet .20 .20
**B18** SP5 50c + 10c red & blue .30 .20
**B19** SP6 90c + 10c red & sepia .75 .50
*Nos. B17-B19 (3)* 1.25 .90

**1948, Oct. 1**

Designs: No. B21, Protection. No. B22, Sun bath. No. B23, Plane over Ben Karrich.

**B20** SP7 50c + 10c car & dk vio .25 .20
**B21** SP7 90c + 10c car & dk gray 1.25 .40
**B22** SP7 2.50p + 50c car & brn 8.50 2.75
**B23** SP7 5p + 1p car & vio bl 13.00 4.25
*Nos. B20-B23 (4)* 23.00 7.60

See Nos. 320, 322.

Moulay Hassan ben el-Medi ben Ismail — SP8

Flag — SP9

**1949, May 15**

**B24** SP8 50c + 10c lilac rose .25 .20

Wedding of the Caliph at Tetuan, June 5.

### Tuberculosis Fund Issues

Design: No. B26, Fight with dragon.

**1949**

**Black Control Numbers on Back**

**B25** SP9 50c + 10 car & brown .25 .20
**B26** SP9 90c + 10 car & grnsh gray .85 .25

See No. 321.

**Catalogue values for unused stamps in this section, from this point to the end of the section, are for Never Hinged items.**

Crowd at Fountain of Life — SP10

Warrior — SP11

90c+10c, Mohammedan hermit's tomb.

**1950, Oct. 1 Litho.** ***Perf. 10***

**Black Control Numbers on Back**

**Frame and Cross in Carmine**

**B27** SP10 50 + 10c dk brown .20 .20
**B28** SP10 90 + 10c dk green .55 .30

**1951 Unwmk.** ***Perf. 12***

Designs: 90c+10c, Fort. 1p+5p, Port of Salvation. 1.10p+25c, Road to market.

**Black Control Numbers on Back**

**B29** SP11 50c + 10c car & brn .20 .20
**B30** SP11 90c + 10c car & bl .35 .20
**B31** SP11 1p + 5p car & gray 7.50 2.50
**B32** SP11 1.10p + 25p car & gray 4.25 1.40
*Nos. B29-B32 (4)* 12.30 4.30

See No. B40.

Pilgrimage SP12

Armed Horseman in Action SP13

Designs: 60c+25c, Palmettos. 90c+10c, Fort. 1.10p+25c, Agave. 5p+2p, Warrior.

**1952** ***Perf. 11***

**Black Control Numbers on Back**

**B33** SP12 50 + 10c car & gray .20 .20
**B34** SP12 60 + 25c car & dk grn .70 .35
**B35** SP12 90 + 10c car & vio brn .70 .35
**B36** SP12 1.10p + 25p car & pur 2.00 .70
**B37** SP12 5p + 2p car & gray 5.00 1.60
*Nos. B33-B37 (5)* 8.60 3.20

**1953** ***Perf. 10***

#B39, As #276. #B42, Plane & clouds.

**Black Control Numbers on Back**

**B38** SP13 50c + 10c car & vio .20 .20
**B39** A70 60c + 25c car & brn 2.10 .65
**B40** SP11 90c + 10c car & blk .60 .25
**B41** SP13 1.10p + 25c car & vio brn 3.00 1.00
**B42** A73 5p + 2p car & bl 7.75 2.50
*Nos. B38-B42 (5)* 13.65 4.60

Stork — SP14

50c+10c, Father & Child. 5p+2p, Tomb.

**1954 Photo.**

**Black Control Numbers on Back**

**B43** SP14 5c + 5c car & rose vio .20 .20
**B44** SP14 50c + 10c car & gray grn .70 .35
**B45** SP14 5p + 2p car & gray 6.00 3.25
*Nos. B43-B45 (3)* 6.90 3.80

## AIR POST STAMPS

Mosque de Baja and Plane — AP1

View of Tetuán and Plane AP2

10c, Stork of Alcazar. 25c, Shore scene, plane. 40c, Desert tribesmen watching plane. 75c, View of shoreline at Larache. 1p, Arab mailman, plane above. 1.50p, Arab farmers, stork. 2p, Plane at twilight. 3p, Shadow of plane over city.

**1938 Unwmk. Photo.** ***Perf. 13½***

**C1** AP1 5c red brown .20 .20
**C2** AP1 10c emerald .20 .20
**C3** AP1 25c crimson .20 .20
**C4** AP1 40c dull blue 1.75 .50
**C5** AP2 50c cerise .20 .20
**C6** AP2 75c ultra .20 .20
**C7** AP1 1p dark brown .20 .20
**C8** AP1 1.50p purple .60 .30
**C9** AP1 2p brown lake .35 .20
**C10** AP1 3p gray black 1.60 .20
*Nos. C1-C10 (10)* 5.50 2.40

Exist imperf. Value, set $140.
For surcharge see No. C32.

Landscape, Ketama — AP3

Mosque, Tangier — AP4

Velez — AP5

Sanjurjo — AP6

Strait of Gibraltar
AP7 AP8

**1942** ***Perf. 12½***

**C11** AP3 5c deep blue .20 .20
**C12** AP4 10c orange brn .20 .20
**C13** AP5 15c grnsh black .20 .20
**C14** AP6 90c dark rose .20 .20
**C15** AP7 5p black 1.25 .75
*Nos. C11-C15 (5)* 2.05 1.55

Exist imperf. Value, set $45.

**1949 Litho.** ***Perf. 10***

Designs: 5c, 1.75p, Strait of Gibraltar. 10c, 3p, Market day. 30c, 4p, Kebira Fortress. 6.50p, Airmail arrival. 8p, Horseman.

**C16** AP8 5c vio brn & brt grn .20 .20
**C17** AP8 10c blk & rose lil .20 .20
**C18** AP8 30c dk vio bl & grnsh gray .20 .20
**C19** AP8 1.75p car & bl vio .20 .20
**C20** AP8 3p dk blue & gray .20 .20
**C21** AP8 4p grnsh blk & car rose .25 .20
**C22** AP8 6.50p brt grn & brn .85 .20
**C23** AP8 8p rose lil & bl vio 1.40 .40
*Nos. C16-C23 (8)* 3.50 1.80

Exist imperf. Value, set $80.

**Catalogue values for unused stamps in this section, from this point to the end of the section, are for Never Hinged items.**

Road to Tetuan — AP9

Designs: 4p, Arrival of mail from Spain. 8p, Greeting plane. 16p, Shadow of plane.

**1952** ***Perf. 11***

**Black Frames and Inscriptions**

**Black Control Numbers on Back**

**C24** AP9 2p brt blue .20 .20
**C25** AP9 4p scarlet .25 .20
**C26** AP9 8p dk olive green .40 .20
**C27** AP9 16p violet brown 2.00 .85
*Nos. C24-C27 (4)* 2.85 1.45

Part of the proceeds was used toward the establishment of a postal museum at Tetuan.

Plane over Boat — AP10

Designs: 60c, Mosques, Sidi Saidi. 1.10p, Plowing. 4.50p, Fortress, Xauen.

**1953** *Perf. 10*

**C28** AP10 35c dp bl & car rose .20 .20
**C29** AP10 60c dk car & sl grn .20 .20
**C30** AP10 1.10p dp blue & blk .20 .20
**C31** AP10 4.50p dk car & dk brn 1.00 .30
*Nos. C28-C31 (4)* 1.60 .90

Exist imperf. Value, set $75.

No. C6 Surcharged with New Value in Black

Type I

Type II

**1953** *Perf. 13½*

**C32** AP2 50c on 75c ultra (I) .45 .20
*a.* 50c on 75c ultra (II) .45 .20
*b.* Vert. gutter pair, types I and II 2.50

Sheets of 2 panes, 25 stamps each, with gutter between. Upper pane surcharged type I, lower type II.

## AIR POST SEMI-POSTAL STAMPS

No. 150 Surcharged in Black

**1936** **Unwmk.** *Perf. 14*

**CB1** A12 25c + 2p on 25c 11.00 4.50
Never hinged 25.00
*a.* Bars at right omitted 45.00 32.50
*b.* Blue surcharge 35.00 11.50

25c was for postage, 2p for air post.

Nos. C1-C10 surcharged "Lucha Antituberculosa," a Lorraine cross and surtax are stated to be bogus.

Crowd at Palace — SPAP1

**1949, May 15** **Unwmk.** *Perf. 10*

**CB2** SPAP1 1p + 10c gray black .70 .30

Wedding of the Caliph at Tetuan, June 5.

## SPECIAL DELIVERY STAMPS

Special Delivery Stamp of Spain Overprinted in Blue

**1914** **Unwmk.** *Perf. 14*

**E1** SD1 20c red 3.75 1.75

Special Delivery Stamp of Spain Overprinted in Blue

**1915**

**E2** SD1 20c red 2.50 1.40

For bisected surcharge see No. 68.

Special Delivery Stamp of Spain Overprinted in Blue

**1923**

**E3** SD1 20c red 10.50 8.25

Mounted Courier SD2

**1928** **Engr.** *Perf. 14, 14½*

**E4** SD2 20c black 4.25 1.40

For surcharge see No. 168.

Moorish Postman — SD3 Mounted Courier — SD4

**1935** **Photo.** *Perf. 14*

**Green Control Number on Back**

**E5** SD3 20c vermilion 1.00 .20

See No. E9.

**1937** *Perf. 13½*

**E6** SD4 20c bright carmine .20 .20

1st Year of the Spanish Civil War.
For surcharge see No. E10.

Spain No. E14 Overprinted in Black

**1938** *Perf. 10*

**E7** SD7 20c vermilion 1.25 .20

Arab Postman SD5

Airmail 1935 SD6

**1940** **Photo.** *Perf. 11½x11*

**E8** SD5 25c scarlet .60 .20

"ZONA" printed on back in black.

Type of 1935

**1940** **Litho.** *Perf. 10*

**E9** SD3 20c black brown 1.40

No. E9 was prepared but not issued.

No. E6 Surcharged with New Value, Bars and

**1940** *Perf. 13½*

**E10** SD4 25c on 20c brt car 9.50 7.25

4th anniversary of Spanish Civil War.

**Catalogue values for unused stamps in this section, from this point to the end of the section, are for Never Hinged items.**

**1950** **Unwmk.** **Litho.** *Perf. 10½*

**E11** SD6 25c carmine & gray 24.00 9.00

UPU, 75th anniv. (in 1949).

Moorish Postrider SD7

**1952** *Perf. 11*

**Black Control Number on Back**

**E12** SD7 25c car & rose car .20 .20

Rider with Special Delivery Mail — SD8

Gate of Tangier — SD9

**1953** **Photo.** *Perf. 10*

**Black Control Number on Back**

**E13** SD8 25c dk bl & car rose .20 .20

25th anniv. of Spanish Morocco's first definitive postage stamps.

**1955** **Litho.** *Perf. 11*

**Black Control Number on Back**

**E14** SD9 2p violet & black .20 .20

## SEMI-POSTAL SPECIAL DELIVERY STAMP

Type of Semi-Postal Special Delivery Stamp of Spain, 1926, Overprinted like #B1-B13

**1926** **Unwmk.** *Perf. 12½, 13*

**EB1** SPSD1 20c ultra & black 2.50 2.10

## POSTAL TAX STAMPS

General Francisco Franco — PT1

**1937-39** **Unwmk.** **Photo.** *Perf. 12½*

**RA1** PT1 10c sepia .45 .20
*a.* Sheet of 4, imperf. 4.00 1.60
**RA2** PT1 10c copper brn ('38) .45 .20
*a.* Sheet of 4, imperf. 4.00 1.60
**RA3** PT1 10c blue ('39) .45 .20
*a.* Sheet of 4, imperf. 4.00 1.60
*Nos. RA1-RA3 (3)* 1.35 .60
Set, never hinged 1.75
Set, RA1a-RA3a 12.00

The tax was used for the disabled soldiers in North Africa.

Soldiers PT2

**1941** **Litho.** *Perf. 13½*

**RA4** PT2 10c brt grn 3.75 .20
**RA5** PT2 10c rose pink 3.75 .20
**RA6** PT2 10c henna brn 3.75 .20
**RA7** PT2 10c ultra 3.75 .20
*Nos. RA4-RA7 (4)* 15.00 .80
Set, never hinged 22.50

The tax was used for the disabled soldiers in North Africa.
Exist imperf. Value, set $60.

General Francisco Franco — PT3

**1943** **Photo.** *Perf. 10*

**RA8** PT3 10c chalky blue 7.50 .20
**RA9** PT3 10c slate blue 7.50 .20
**RA10** PT3 10c dl gray brn 7.50 .20
**RA11** PT3 10c blue violet 7.50 .20
*Nos. RA8-RA11 (4)* 30.00 .80
Set, never hinged 42.50

Exists imperf. Value, set $125.

**1944** *Perf. 12*

**RA12** PT3 10c dp mag & brn 5.50 .20
**RA13** PT3 10c dp org & dk grn 5.50 .20
Set, never hinged 14.50

Exists imperf. Value, set $45.00.

**1946** **Litho.**

**RA14** PT3 10c ultra & brown 6.00 .20
**RA15** PT3 10c gray blk & rose lil 6.00 .20
Set, never hinged 16.00

Exists imperf. Value, set $45.00.

## TANGIER

**For the International City of Tangier**

Seville-Barcelona Issue of Spain, 1929, Overprinted in Blue or Red

TANGER

**1929** *Perf. 11*

| | | | | | |
|---|---|---|---|---|---|
| **L1** | A52 | 5c rose lake | .25 | .25 |
| **L2** | A53 | 10c green (R) | .25 | .25 |
| **L3** | A50 | 15c Prus blue (R) | .25 | .25 |
| **L4** | A51 | 20c purple (R) | .25 | .25 |
| **L5** | A50 | 25c brt rose | .25 | .25 |
| **L6** | A52 | 30c black brn | .25 | .25 |
| **L7** | A53 | 40c dk blue (R) | .65 | .65 |
| **L8** | A51 | 50c deep org | .65 | .65 |
| **L9** | A52 | 1p blue blk (R) | 7.00 | 7.00 |
| **L10** | A53 | 4p deep rose | 19.00 | 19.00 |
| **L11** | A53 | 10p brown | 27.50 | 27.50 |
| | | *Nos. L1-L11 (11)* | 56.30 | 56.30 |
| | | Never hinged | 95.00 | |

Overprints of 1937-39

The following overprints on stamps of Spain exist in black or in red:

"TANGER" vertically on Nos. 517-518, 522-523, 528, 532, 534, 539-543, 549.

"Correo Espanol Tanger" horizontally or vertically in three lines on Nos. 540, 592-597 (gray paper), 598-601.

"Tanger" horizontally on Nos. 539-541, 592-601.

"Correo Tanger" horizontally in two lines on five consular stamps.

Woman — A1

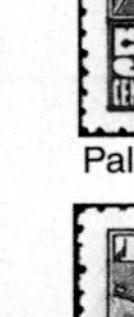
Palm Tree — A2

Man — A3

Old Map of Tangier — A4

Tangier Street — A5

Moroccan Women — A6

Head of Moor — A7

***Perf. 9½x10½, 12½x13 (1c, 2c, 10c, 20c)***

**1948-51** **Photo.** **Unwmk.**

| | | | | |
|---|---|---|---|---|
| **L12** | A1 | 1c blue grn ('51) | .20 | .20 |
| **L13** | A1 | 2c red org ('51) | .20 | .20 |

**Engr.**

| | | | | |
|---|---|---|---|---|
| **L14** | A2 | 5c vio brn ('49) | .20 | .20 |
| **L15** | A3 | 10c deep blue ('51) | .20 | .20 |
| **L16** | A3 | 20c gray ('51) | .20 | .20 |
| **L17** | A2 | 25c green ('51) | .20 | .20 |
| **L18** | A4 | 30c dk slate grn | .30 | .20 |
| **L19** | A5 | 45c car rose | .30 | .20 |
| **L20** | A6 | 50c dp claret | .30 | .20 |
| **L21** | A7 | 75c deep blue | .60 | .20 |
| **L22** | A7 | 90c green | .50 | .20 |
| **L23** | A4 | 1.35p org ver | 1.90 | .30 |
| **L24** | A6 | 2p purple | 3.50 | .30 |
| **L25** | A5 | 10p dk grnsh bl ('49) | 4.75 | .55 |
| | | *Nos. L12-L25,LE1 (15)* | 14.10 | 3.65 |
| | | Never hinged | 22.50 | |

Nos. L18-L25, LE1 exist imperf. Value, set $275.

## TANGIER SEMI-POSTAL STAMPS

Types of Semi-Postal Stamps of Spain, 1926, Overprinted

**1926** ***Perf. 12½, 13***

| | | | | |
|---|---|---|---|---|
| **LB1** | SP1 | 1c orange | 6.00 | 6.50 |
| **LB2** | SP2 | 2c rose | 6.00 | 6.50 |
| **LB3** | SP3 | 5c black brn | 3.00 | 3.25 |
| **LB4** | SP4 | 10c dk green | 3.00 | 3.25 |
| **LB5** | SP1 | 15c dk violet | 1.00 | 1.25 |
| **LB6** | SP4 | 20c violet brn | 1.00 | 1.25 |
| **LB7** | SP5 | 25c dp carmine | 1.00 | 1.25 |
| **LB8** | SP1 | 30c olive grn | 1.00 | 1.25 |
| **LB9** | SP3 | 40c ultra | .25 | .25 |
| **LB10** | SP2 | 50c red brn | .25 | .25 |
| **LB11** | SP4 | 1p vermilion | .60 | .60 |
| **LB12** | SP3 | 4p bister | .60 | .60 |
| **LB13** | SP5 | 10p lt violet | 2.75 | 3.00 |
| | | *Nos. LB1-LB13,LEB1 (14)* | 29.70 | 32.45 |
| | | Never hinged | 50.00 | |

For overprints & surcharges see Spain Nos. B66-B67.

## TANGIER AIR POST STAMPS

Overprints of 1939

The following overprints on stamps of Spain exist in black or in red:

"Correo Aereo Tanger" in two lines on Nos. 539-541, 596 (gray paper), 600, C72B.

"Via Aerea Tanger" in three lines on Nos. 539-540, 592-597 (gray paper), 599, 601, E14.

"Correo Aereo Tanger" in three lines on four consular stamps.

"Correo Espanol Tanger" in three lines on No. C72B.

"Tanger" on No. C72B.

Plane over Shore — AP1

Twin-Engine Plane — AP2

Passenger Plane in Flight — AP3

***Perf. 11x11½, 11½***

**1949-50** **Engr.** **Unwmk.**

| | | | | |
|---|---|---|---|---|
| **LC1** | AP1 | 20c violet brn ('50) | .25 | .20 |
| **LC2** | AP2 | 25c bright red | .25 | .20 |
| **LC3** | AP3 | 35c dull green | .25 | .20 |
| **LC4** | AP1 | 1p violet ('50) | .80 | .20 |
| **LC5** | AP2 | 2p deep blue | 1.50 | .25 |
| **LC6** | AP3 | 10p brown violet | 2.75 | 1.00 |
| | | *Nos. LC1-LC6 (6)* | 5.80 | 2.05 |
| | | Never hinged | 8.50 | |

Nos. LC1, LC4-LC6 exist imperf. Value $50 each.

## TANGIER SPECIAL DELIVERY STAMP

Arab Postrider — SD1

**1949** **Unwmk.** **Engr.** ***Perf. 13***

| | | | | |
|---|---|---|---|---|
| **LE1** | SD1 | 25c red | .75 | .30 |
| | | Never hinged | 1.25 | |

## TANGIER SEMI-POSTAL SPECIAL DELIVERY STAMP

Types of Semi-Postal Special Delivery Stamp of Spain, 1926, Overprinted like #LB1-LB13

**1926** **Unwmk.** ***Perf. 12½, 13***

| | | | | |
|---|---|---|---|---|
| **LEB1** | SPSD1 | 20c ultra & black | 3.25 | 3.25 |
| | | Never hinged | 5.50 | |

## TETUAN

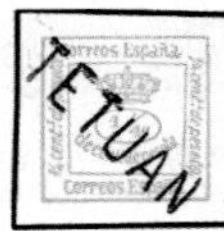
Stamps of Spanish Offices in Morocco, 1903-09, Handstamped in Black, Blue or Violet

**1908** **Unwmk.** ***Imperf.***

| | | | | |
|---|---|---|---|---|
| **1** | A21 | ¼c blue green | 13.00 | 10.00 |

***Perf. 14***

| | | | | |
|---|---|---|---|---|
| **2** | A35 | 2c bister brown | 150.00 | 60.00 |
| **3** | A35 | 5c green | 140.00 | 35.00 |
| **4** | A35 | 10c rose red | 140.00 | 35.00 |
| **5** | A35 | 20c grnsh black | 300.00 | 125.00 |
| **6** | A35 | 25c blue | 100.00 | 35.00 |
| | | *Nos. 1-6 (6)* | 843.00 | 300.00 |

Same Handstamp On Stamps of Spain, 1876 and 1900-05, in Black, Blue or Violet

**1908** ***Imperf.***

| | | | | |
|---|---|---|---|---|
| **7** | A21 | ¼c deep green | 7.50 | 3.25 |

***Perf. 14***

| | | | | |
|---|---|---|---|---|
| **8** | A35 | 2c bister brn | 40.00 | 13.00 |
| **9** | A35 | 5c dark green | 55.00 | 22.50 |
| **10** | A35 | 10c rose red | 52.50 | 22.50 |
| **11** | A35 | 15c purple | 52.50 | 25.00 |
| **12** | A35 | 20c grnsh black | 150.00 | 110.00 |
| **13** | A35 | 25c blue | 80.00 | 35.00 |
| **14** | A35 | 30c blue green | 175.00 | 60.00 |
| **15** | A35 | 40c olive bister | 225.00 | 110.00 |
| | | *Nos. 7-15 (9)* | 837.50 | 401.25 |

Counterfeits of this overprint are plentiful.

# SPANISH SAHARA

'spa-nish sə-'har-ə

## (Spanish Western Sahara)

LOCATION — Northwest Africa, bordering on the Atlantic
GOVT. — Spanish possession
AREA — 102,703 sq. mi.
POP. — 76,425 (1970)
CAPITAL — Aaiún

Spanish Sahara was a subdivision of Spanish West Africa. It included the colony of Rio de Oro and the territory of Saguiet el Hamra. Spanish Sahara was formerly known as Spanish Western Sahara, which superseded the older title of Rio de Oro.

In 1976, Spanish Sahara was divided between Morocco and Mauritania.

100 Centimos = 1 Peseta

**Catalogue values for unused stamps in this country are for Never Hinged items, beginning with Scott 51 in the regular postage section, Scott B13 in the semi-postal section, Scott C8 in the air-post section, and Scott E1 in the special delivery section.**

Tuareg and Camel — A1

**1924** **Unwmk.** **Typo.** ***Perf. 13***

**Control Number on Back**

| | | | | |
|---|---|---|---|---|
| **1** | A1 | 5c blue green | 2.25 | .70 |
| **2** | A1 | 10c gray green | 2.25 | .70 |
| **3** | A1 | 15c turq blue | 2.25 | .70 |
| **4** | A1 | 20c dark violet | 2.25 | 1.00 |
| **5** | A1 | 25c red | 2.25 | 1.00 |
| **6** | A1 | 30c red brown | 2.25 | 1.00 |
| **7** | A1 | 40c dark blue | 2.25 | 1.00 |
| **8** | A1 | 50c orange | 2.25 | 1.00 |
| **9** | A1 | 60c violet | 2.25 | 1.00 |
| **10** | A1 | 1p rose | 12.00 | 5.50 |
| **11** | A1 | 4p chocolate | 55.00 | 27.50 |
| **12** | A1 | 10p claret | 140.00 | 85.00 |
| | | *Nos. 1-12 (12)* | 227.25 | 126.10 |
| | | Set, never hinged | 300.00 | |

#1-12 were for use in La Aguera & Rio de Oro.

An unissued set of 10, similar to Nos. 3-12, exists perf. 10 or imperf, and no control number except on 50c. The set also exists perf 14. Value, $300.

Nos. 1-12 also exist perf 14. Value, unused $350.

For overprints see Nos. 24-35.

Seville-Barcelona Issue of Spain, 1929 Overprinted in Blue or Red

**1929** ***Perf. 11***

| | | | | |
|---|---|---|---|---|
| **13** | A52 | 5c rose lake | .25 | .25 |
| **14** | A53 | 10c green (R) | .25 | .25 |
| **15** | A50 | 15c Prus blue (R) | .25 | .25 |
| **16** | A51 | 20c purple (R) | .25 | .25 |
| **17** | A50 | 25c bright rose | .25 | .25 |
| **18** | A52 | 30c black brown | .25 | .25 |
| **19** | A53 | 40c dark blue (R) | .60 | .40 |
| **20** | A51 | 50c deep orange | .60 | .40 |
| **21** | A52 | 1p blue black (R) | 2.50 | 1.60 |
| **22** | A53 | 4p deep rose | 20.00 | 15.00 |
| **23** | A53 | 10p brown | 37.50 | 30.00 |
| | | *Nos. 13-23 (11)* | 62.70 | 48.90 |
| | | Set, never hinged | 90.00 | |

Stamps of 1924 Overprinted in Red or Blue

**1931** ***Perf. 13***

| | | | | |
|---|---|---|---|---|
| **24** | A1 | 5c blue grn (R) | .70 | .55 |
| **25** | A1 | 10c gray grn (R) | .70 | .55 |
| **26** | A1 | 15c turq blue (R) | .70 | .55 |
| **27** | A1 | 20c dark violet (R) | .70 | .55 |
| **28** | A1 | 25c red | .75 | .55 |
| **29** | A1 | 30c red brown | .75 | .55 |
| **30** | A1 | 40c dark blue (R) | 3.50 | .75 |
| **31** | A1 | 50c orange | 3.50 | 1.90 |
| **32** | A1 | 60c violet | 3.50 | 1.90 |
| **33** | A1 | 1p rose | 3.50 | 1.90 |

**34** A1 4p chocolate 37.50 19.00
**35** A1 10p claret 72.50 42.50
*Nos. 24-35 (12)* 128.30 71.25
Set, never hinged 175.00

The stamps of the 1931 issue exist with the overprint reading upward, downward or horizontally. Some values also exist with double overprint, double overprint, one inverted and diagonal overprint.

Stamps of Spain, 1936-40, Overprinted in Carmine or Blue

**1941-46 Unwmk. *Imperf.***
**36** A159 1c green 1.60 1.50

***Perf. 10 to 11***
**37** A160 2c org brn (Bl) 1.60 1.50
**38** A161 5c gray brown .50 .45
**39** A161 10c dk car (Bl) 1.60 1.50
**40** A161 15c dark green .50 .45
**41** A166 20c bright violet .50 .45
**42** A166 25c deep claret 1.20 .90
**43** A166 30c light blue 1.20 1.10
**44** A166 40c Prus grn .50 .45
**45** A166 50c indigo 15.00 1.25
**46** A166 70c blue 10.00 1.90
**47** A166 1p gray black 19.00 2.75
**48** A166 2p dull brown 110.00 60.00
**49** A166 4p dull rose (Bl) 275.00 160.00
**50** A166 10p lt brown 850.00 250.00
*Nos. 36-50 (15)* 1,288. 484.20
Set, never hinged 1,950.

Counterfeit overprints exist.

**Catalogue values for unused stamps in this section, from this point to the end of the section, are for Never Hinged items.**

Dorcas Gazelles — A2

Designs: 2c, 20c, 45c, 3p, Caravan. 5c, 75c, 10p, Camel troops.

**1943 Unwmk. *Perf. 12½***
**51** A2 1c brown & lil rose .20 .20
**52** A2 2c yel grn & sl bl .20 .20
**53** A2 5c magenta & vio .20 .20
**54** A2 15c slate grn & grn .20 .20
**55** A2 20c violet & red brn .20 .20
**56** A2 40c rose vio & vio .20 .20
**57** A2 45c brn vio & red .35 .20
**58** A2 75c indigo & blue .35 .20
**59** A2 1p red & brown 1.25 .70
**60** A2 3p bl vio & sl grn 2.75 1.40
**61** A2 10p black brn & blk 37.50 19.00
*Nos. 51-61,E1 (12)* 44.65 23.45

Nos. 51-61, El exist imperf. Value for set, $80.

Gen. Franco and Desert Scene A5

**1951 Photo. *Perf. 12½x13***
**62** A5 50c deep orange .20 .20
**63** A5 1p chocolate .30 .25
**64** A5 5p blue green 27.50 11.00
*Nos. 62-64 (3)* 28.00 11.45

Visit of Gen. Francisco Franco, 1950.

Allegorical Figure and Globe — A6

Woman Musician — A7

**1953, Mar. 2 *Perf. 13x12½***
**65** A6 5c red orange .20 .20
**66** A6 35c dk slate green .20 .20
**67** A6 60c brown .25 .20
*Nos. 65-67 (3)* .65 .60

75th anniv. of the founding of the Royal Geographical Society.

**1953, June 1**

Design: 60c, Man musician.

**68** A7 15c olive gray .20 .20
**69** A7 60c brown .20 .20
*Nos. 68-69,B25-B26 (4)* .80 .80

Orange Scorpionfish — A8

Fish: 60c, Banded sargo.

**1953, Nov. 23 *Perf. 12½x13***
**70** A8 15c dk olive green .25 .20
**71** A8 60c orange .35 .20
*Nos. 70-71,B27-B28 (4)* 1.00 .80

Colonial Stamp Day.

Hurdlers A9

Runner — A10

**1954, June 1 *Perf. 12½x13, 13x12½***
**72** A9 15c gray green .20 .20
**73** A10 60c brown .25 .20
*Nos. 72-73,B29-B30 (4)* .85 .80

Atlantic Flyingfish A11

**1954, Nov. 23 *Perf. 12½x13***
**74** A11 15c shown .25 .20
**75** A11 60c Gilthead .35 .20
*Nos. 74-75,B31-B32 (4)* 1.00 .80

Colonial Stamp Day.

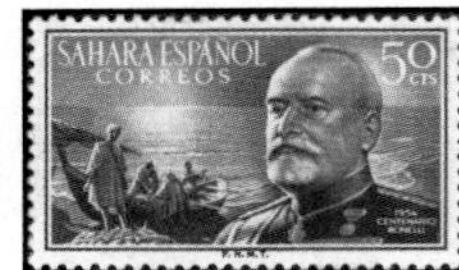

Emilio Bonelli A12

**1955, June 1 Photo. Unwmk.**
**76** A12 50c olive gray .20 .20
*Nos. 76,B33-B34 (3)* .60 .60

Birth cent. of Emilio Bonelli, explorer.

Scimitar-horned Oryx — A13

**1955, Nov. 23**
**77** A13 70c green .20 .20
*Nos. 77,B35-B36 (3)* .60 .60

Colonial Stamp Day.

Antirrhinum Romosissimum A14

Design: 50c, Sesiviun portulacastrum.

**1956, June 1 *Perf. 13x12½***
**78** A14 20c bluish green .20 .20
**79** A14 50c brown .30 .20
*Nos. 78-79,B37-B38 (4)* .90 .80

Arms of Aaiun and Camel Rider A15

**1956, Nov. 23 *Perf. 12½x13***
**80** A15 70c olive grn & sepia .20 .20
*Nos. 80,B39-B40 (3)* .60 .60

Colonial Stamp Day.

Dromedaries A16

Golden Eagle A17

15c, 80c, Ostrich. 50c, 1.80p, Mountain gazelle.

**1957, Apr. 10 *Perf. 13x12½***
**81** A16 5c purple .20 .20
**82** A16 15c bister .20 .20
**83** A16 50c dark olive .20 .20
**84** A16 70c yellow green .65 .20
**85** A16 80c blue green .65 .20
**86** A16 1.80p lilac rose .65 .20
*Nos. 81-86 (6)* 2.55 1.20

**1957, June 1 Photo. Unwmk.**
**87** A17 70c dark green .20 .20
*Nos. 87,B41-B42 (3)* .60 .60

Striped Hyena — A18

Design: 70c, Striped Hyena, horiz.

***Perf. 13x12½, 12½x13***
**1957, Nov. 23**
**88** A18 20c slate green .20 .20
**89** A18 70c yellowish green .20 .20
*Nos. 88-89,B43-B44 (4)* .80 .80

Stamp Day.

Don Quixote and the Lion A19

Cervantes A20

Gray Heron A21

**1958, June 1 *Perf. 12½x13, 13x12½***
**90** A19 20c bister brn & grn .20 .20
**91** A20 70c dk grn & yel grn .25 .20
*Nos. 90-91,B48-B49 (4)* .85 .80

Cervantes Type of 1958

Designs: 20c, Actor as "Peribanez," by Lope de Vega. 70c, Lope de Vega.

**1959, June Photo. *Perf. 13x12½***
**92** A20 20c lt green & brn .20 .20
**93** A20 70c yel grn & slate grn .25 .20
*Nos. 92-93,B53-B54 (4)* .85 .80

Promoting child welfare.

**1959, Oct. 15 *Perf. 13x12½***

Birds: 50c, 1.50p, 5p, Sparrowhawk. 75c, 2p, 10p, Sea gull.

**94** A21 25c dull violet .20 .20
**95** A21 50c dark olive .20 .20
**96** A21 75c dark brown .20 .20
**97** A21 1p red orange .20 .20
**98** A21 1.50p brt green .25 .20
**99** A21 2p brt red lilac .90 .20
**100** A21 3p blue .95 .20
**101** A21 5p red brown 1.60 .25
**102** A21 10p olive green 9.00 4.00
*Nos. 94-102 (9)* 13.50 5.65

Scene from "The Pilferer Don Pablos" by Quevedo — A22

Francisco Gomez de Quevedo A23

**1960, June *Perf. 13x12½, 12½x13***
**103** A22 35c slate green .20 .20
**104** A23 80c Prussian green .20 .20
*Nos. 103-104,B58-B59 (4)* .80 .80

Francisco Gomez de Quevedo, writer.

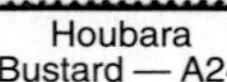

Houbara Bustard — A24

Map of Spanish Sahara — A25

Gen. Franco and Camel Rider A26

Design: 50c, 1p, 2p, 5p, Doves.

**1961, Apr. 18 Photo. *Perf. 13x12½***

**105** A24 25c blue violet .20 .20
**106** A24 50c olive gray .20 .20
**107** A24 75c brown violet .20 .20
**108** A24 1p orange ver .20 .20
**109** A24 1.50p blue green .20 .20
**110** A24 2p magenta .70 .20
**111** A24 3p dark blue .85 .20
**112** A24 5p red brown 1.00 .30
**113** A24 10p olive 2.75 1.40
*Nos. 105-113 (9)* 6.30 3.10

**1961, Oct. 1 *Perf. 13x12½, 12½x13***

Design: 70c, Chapel of Aaiun.

**114** A25 25c gray violet .20 .20
**115** A26 50c olive brown .20 .20
**116** A25 70c brt green .20 .20
**117** A26 1p red orange .20 .20
*Nos. 114-117 (4)* .80 .80

25th anniv. of the nomination of Gen. Francisco Franco as Chief of State.

Neurada Procumbres A27

Clock Fish A28

50c, 1.50p, 10p, Anabasis articulata, flower. 70c, 2p, Euphorbia resinifera, cactus.

**1962, Feb. 26 *Perf. 13x12½***

**118** A27 25c black violet .20 .20
**119** A27 50c dark brown .20 .20
**120** A27 70c brt green .20 .20
**121** A27 1p orange ver .20 .20
**122** A27 1.50p blue green .30 .20
**123** A27 2p red lilac 1.00 .20
**124** A27 3p slate 1.75 .25
**125** A27 10p olive 4.00 1.40
*Nos. 118-125 (8)* 7.85 2.85

***Perf. 13x12½, 12½x13***

**1962, July 10 Photo.**

Design: 50c, Avia fish, horiz.

**126** A28 25c violet black .20 .20
**127** A28 50c dark green .20 .20
**128** A28 1p orange brown .20 .20
*Nos. 126-128 (3)* .60 .60

Goats A29

Stamp Day: 35c, Sheep.

**1962, Nov. 23 *Perf. 12½x13***

**129** A29 15c yellow green .20 .20
**130** A29 35c magenta .20 .20
**131** A29 1p orange brown .20 .20
*Nos. 129-131 (3)* .60 .60

Seville Cathedral Tower — A30

**1963, Jan. 29 *Perf. 13x12½***

**132** A30 50c olive .20 .20
**133** A30 1p brown orange .20 .20

Issued to help Seville flood victims.

Camel Riders — A31

Hands Releasing Dove and Arms — A32

Design: 50c, Tuareg and camel.

**1963, June 1 Unwmk.**

**134** A31 25c deep violet .20 .20
**135** A31 50c gray .20 .20
**136** A31 1p orange red .20 .20
*Nos. 134-136 (3)* .60 .60

Issued for child welfare.

**1963, July 12**

**137** A32 50c Prussian green .20 .20
**138** A32 1p orange brown .20 .20

Issued for Barcelona flood relief.

John Dory A33

Fish: 50c, Plain bonito, vert.

***Perf. 12½x13, 13x12½***

**1964, Mar. 6 Photo.**

**139** A33 25c purple .20 .20
**140** A33 50c olive green .20 .20
**141** A33 1p brown red .40 .20
*Nos. 139-141 (3)* .80 .60

Issued for Stamp Day 1963.

Moth and Flowers A34

Design: 50c, Two moths, vert.

***Perf. 12½x13, 13x12½***

**1964, June 1 Unwmk.**

**142** A34 25c dull violet .20 .20
**143** A34 50c brown black .20 .20
**144** A34 1p orange red .40 .20
*Nos. 142-144 (3)* .80 .60

Issued for child welfare.

Camel Rider and Microphone A35

Squirrel A36

Designs: 50c, 1.50p, 3p, Boy with flute and camels. 70c, 2p, 10p, Woman with drum.

**1964, Sept. Photo. *Perf. 13x12½***

**145** A35 25c dull purple .20 .20
**146** A35 50c olive .20 .20
**147** A35 70c green .20 .20
**148** A35 1p dull red brn .20 .20
**149** A35 1.50p bright green .20 .20
**150** A35 2p Prus green .20 .20
**151** A35 3p dark blue .25 .20
**152** A35 10p carmine lake 1.25 .60
*Nos. 145-152 (8)* 2.70 2.00

**1964, Nov. 23 Unwmk.**

Stamp Day: 1p, Squirrel's head, horiz.

**153** A36 50c olive gray .20 .20
**154** A36 1p brown carmine .20 .20
**155** A36 1.50p green .20 .20
*Nos. 153-155 (3)* .60 .60

Tuareg Girl — A37

Wellhead and Camel Rider — A38

25 Years of Peace: 1p, Physician examining patient, horiz.

***Perf. 13x12½, 12½x13***

**1965, Feb. 22 Photo.**

**156** A37 50c black brown .20 .20
**157** A38 1p dark red .20 .20
**158** A38 1.50p deep blue .20 .20
*Nos. 156-158 (3)* .60 .60

Anthia Sexmaculata — A39

1p, 3p, Blepharopsis mendica, vert.

***Perf. 12½x13, 13x12½***

**1965, June 1 Photo. Unwmk.**

**159** A39 50c slate blue .20 .20
**160** A39 1p blue green .20 .20
**161** A39 1.50p brown .25 .20
**162** A39 3p dark blue 1.10 .50
*Nos. 159-162 (4)* 1.75 1.10

Issued for child welfare.

Basketball A40

Arms and Camels A41

**1965, Nov. 23 *Perf. 13x12½***

**163** A40 50c rose claret .20 .20
**164** A41 1p deep magenta .20 .20
**165** A40 1.50p slate blue .20 .20
*Nos. 163-165 (3)* .60 .60

Issued for Stamp Day.

Ship "Rio de Oro" A42

Design: 1.50p, S.S. Fuerte Ventura.

**1966, June 1 Photo. *Perf. 12½x13***

**166** A42 50c olive .20 .20
**167** A42 1p dark red brown .20 .20
**168** A42 1.50p blue green .25 .20
*Nos. 166-168 (3)* .65 .60

Issued for child welfare.

Ocean Sunfish — A43

A44

Designs: 10c, 1.50p, Bigeye tuna, horiz.

**1966, Nov. 23 Photo. *Perf. 13***

**169** A43 10c bl gray & cit .20 .20
**170** A43 40c slate & pink .20 .20
**171** A43 1.50p brown & olive .25 .20
**172** A43 4p rose vio & gray .40 .20
*Nos. 169-172 (4)* 1.05 .80

Issued for Stamp Day.

**1967, June 1 Photo. *Perf. 13***

Designs: 40c, 4p, Flower and leaves.

**173** A44 10c blk, ocher & gray grn .20 .20
**174** A44 40c emerald & lilac .20 .20
**175** A44 1.50p dk grn & yel grn .20 .20
**176** A44 4p brt blue & org .25 .20
*Nos. 173-176 (4)* .85 .80

Issued for child welfare.

Aaiun Harbor A45

Design: 4p, Villa Cisneros Harbor.

**1967, Sept. 28 Photo. *Perf. 12½x13***

**177** A45 1.50p brt bl & red brn .20 .20
**178** A45 4p brt bl & bis brn .20 .20

Modernization of harbor installations.

Ruddy Sheldrake A46

Stamp Day: 1.50p, Flamingo, vert. 3.50p, Rufous bush robin.

**1967, Nov. 23 Photo. *Perf. 13***

**179** A46 1p bister brn & grn .20 .20
**180** A46 1.50p brt rose & gray .25 .20
**181** A46 3.50p brn red & sep .40 .20
*Nos. 179-181 (3)* .85 .60

Scorpio — A47

Mailman — A48

**Zodiac Issue**

1.50p, Aries. 2.50p, Virgo.

**1968, Apr. 25 Photo. *Perf. 13***

| | | | | | |
|---|---|---|---|---|---|
| **182** | A47 | 1p | brt mag, *lt yel* | .20 | .20 |
| **183** | A47 | 1.50p | brown, *pink* | .20 | .20 |
| **184** | A47 | 2.50p | dk vio, *yel* | .35 | .20 |
| | | | *Nos. 182-184 (3)* | .75 | .60 |

Issued for child welfare.

**1968, Nov. Photo. *Perf. 13x12½***

Stamp Day: 1p, Post horn, pigeon, letter and Spain No. 1. 1.50p, Letter, canceller and various stamps of Spain and Ifni.

| | | | | | |
|---|---|---|---|---|---|
| **185** | A48 | 1p | dp lil rose & dk bl | .20 | .20 |
| **186** | A48 | 1.50p | green & sl grn | .25 | .20 |
| **187** | A48 | 2.50p | dp org & dk bl | .40 | .20 |
| | | | *Nos. 185-187 (3)* | .85 | .60 |

Dorcas Gazelle — A49

Designs: 1.50p, Doe and fawn. 2.50p, Gazelle and camel. 6p, Leaping gazelle.

**1969, June 1 Photo. *Perf. 13***

| | | | | | |
|---|---|---|---|---|---|
| **188** | A49 | 1p | gldn brn & blk | .20 | .20 |
| **189** | A49 | 1.50p | gldn brn & blk | .20 | .20 |
| **190** | A49 | 2.50p | gldn brn & blk | .25 | .20 |
| **191** | A49 | 6p | gldn brn & blk | .45 | .25 |
| | | | *Nos. 188-191 (4)* | 1.10 | .85 |

Child welfare. See Nos. 196-199, 209-212.

Woman Playing Drum — A50

Stamp Day: 1.50p, Man with flute. 2p, Drum and camel rider, horiz. 25p, Flute, horiz.

**1969, Nov. 23 Photo. *Perf. 13***

| | | | | | |
|---|---|---|---|---|---|
| **192** | A50 | 50c | brn red & lt ol | .20 | .20 |
| **193** | A50 | 1.50p | dk bl grn & grnsh gray | .20 | .20 |
| **194** | A50 | 2p | indigo & bis brn | .25 | .20 |
| **195** | A50 | 25p | brn & lt bl grn | .90 | .25 |
| | | | *Nos. 192-195 (4)* | 1.55 | .85 |

**Animal Type of 1969**

Fennec: 50c, Sitting. 2p, Running. 2.50p, Head. 6p, Vixen and pups.

**1970, June 1 Photo. *Perf. 13***

| | | | | | |
|---|---|---|---|---|---|
| **196** | A49 | 50c | dp bister & blk | .20 | .20 |
| **197** | A49 | 2p | org brn & blk | .20 | .20 |
| **198** | A49 | 2.50p | dp bister & blk | .25 | .20 |
| **199** | A49 | 6p | dp bister & blk | .45 | .20 |
| | | | *Nos. 196-199 (4)* | 1.10 | .80 |

Issued for child welfare.

Grammodes Boisdeffrei — A51

Designs: 1p, like 50c. 2p, 5p, Danaus chrysippus. 8p, Celerio euphorbiae.

**1970, Nov. 23 Photo. *Perf. 12½***

| | | | | | |
|---|---|---|---|---|---|
| **200** | A51 | 50c | red & multi | .20 | .20 |
| **201** | A51 | 1p | carmine & multi | .20 | .20 |
| **202** | A51 | 2p | green & multi | .25 | .20 |
| **203** | A51 | 5p | Prus bl & multi | .35 | .20 |
| **204** | A51 | 8p | dk blue & multi | .65 | .30 |
| | | | *Nos. 200-204 (5)* | 1.65 | 1.10 |

Issued for Stamp Day. See Nos. 233-234.

Gazelle, Arms of Aaiun — A52

Smara Mosque — A53

Designs: 2p, Inn, horiz. 5p, Assembly building, Aaiun, horiz.

***Perf. 12½x13, 13x12½***

**1971, June 1 Photo.**

| | | | | | |
|---|---|---|---|---|---|
| **205** | A52 | 1p | multicolored | .20 | .20 |
| **206** | A53 | 2p | gray grn & ol | .20 | .20 |
| **207** | A53 | 5p | lt bl & lt red brn | .25 | .20 |
| **208** | A53 | 25p | lt bl & grnsh gray | .85 | .30 |
| | | | *Nos. 205-208 (4)* | 1.50 | .90 |

Issued for child welfare.

**Animal Type of 1969**

Birds: 1.50p, 2p, Trumpeter bullfinch. 5p, Cream-colored courser. 24p, Lanner (falcon).

**1971, Nov. 23 Photo. *Perf. 12½***

| | | | | | |
|---|---|---|---|---|---|
| **209** | A49 | 1.50p | black & multi | .20 | .20 |
| **210** | A49 | 2p | blue & multi | .20 | .20 |
| **211** | A49 | 5p | green & multi | .25 | .20 |
| **212** | A49 | 24p | black & multi | .80 | .30 |
| | | | *Nos. 209-212 (4)* | 1.45 | .90 |

Stamp Day.

Saharan Woman — A55

Tuareg Woman — A56

1.50p, 2p, Saharan man. 8p, 10p, Man's head. 12p, Woman. 15p, Soldier. 24p, Dancer.

**1972, Feb. 18 Photo. *Perf. 13***

| | | | | | |
|---|---|---|---|---|---|
| **213** | A55 | 1p | blue, pink & brn | .20 | .20 |
| **214** | A55 | 1.50p | brn, lil & blk | .20 | .20 |
| **215** | A55 | 2p | green, buff & sep | .20 | .20 |
| **216** | A55 | 5p | green, pur & vio brn | .20 | .20 |
| **217** | A55 | 8p | black, lt grn & vio | .20 | .20 |
| **218** | A55 | 10p | black, gray & Prus bl | .25 | .20 |
| **219** | A55 | 12p | multicolored | .30 | .25 |
| **220** | A55 | 15p | multicolored | .40 | .35 |
| **221** | A55 | 24p | multicolored | .85 | .50 |
| | | | *Nos. 213-221 (9)* | 2.80 | 2.30 |

**1972, June 1 Photo. *Perf. 13***

| | | | | | |
|---|---|---|---|---|---|
| **222** | A56 | 8p | shown | .25 | .20 |
| **223** | A56 | 12p | Tuareg man | .35 | .20 |

Child welfare.

Mother and Child — A57

**1972, Nov. 23 Photo. *Perf. 13***

| | | | | | |
|---|---|---|---|---|---|
| **224** | A57 | 4p | shown | .20 | .20 |
| **225** | A57 | 15p | Saharan man | .40 | .20 |

Stamp Day. See No. 229.

Dunes A58

Design: 7p, Old Market and Gate, Aaiun.

**1973, June 1 Photo. *Perf. 13***

| | | | | | |
|---|---|---|---|---|---|
| **226** | A58 | 2p | multicolored | .20 | .20 |
| **227** | A58 | 7p | multicolored | .20 | .20 |

Child welfare.

Type of 1972 and

View of Villa Cisneros A59

**1973, Nov. 23 Photo. *Perf. 13***

| | | | | | |
|---|---|---|---|---|---|
| **228** | A59 | 2p | shown | .20 | .20 |
| **229** | A57 | 7p | Tuareg man | .20 | .20 |

Stamp Day.

UPU Monument, Bern — A60

Gate, Smara Mosque — A61

**1974, May Photo. *Perf. 13***

| | | | | | |
|---|---|---|---|---|---|
| **230** | A60 | 15p | multicolored | .45 | .20 |

Centenary of the Universal Postal Union.

**1974, May**

2p, Court and Minaret, Villa Cisneros Mosque.

| | | | | | |
|---|---|---|---|---|---|
| **231** | A61 | 1p | multicolored | .20 | .20 |
| **232** | A61 | 2p | multicolored | .20 | .20 |

Child welfare.

**Animal Type of 1970**

**1974, Nov. Photo. *Perf. 13***

| | | | | | |
|---|---|---|---|---|---|
| **233** | A51 | 2p | Desert eagle owl | .20 | .20 |
| **234** | A51 | 5p | Lappet-faced vulture | .20 | .20 |

Stamp Day.

Espana 75 Emblem, Spain No. 1084 — A63

Old Man — A65

Children A64

**1975, Apr. 4 Photo. *Perf. 13***

| | | | | | |
|---|---|---|---|---|---|
| **235** | A63 | 8p | olive, blk & bl | .20 | .20 |

Espana 75 Intl. Phil. Exhib., Madrid, 4/4-13.

**1975 Photo. *Perf. 13***

| | | | | | |
|---|---|---|---|---|---|
| **236** | A64 | 1.50p | shown | .20 | .20 |
| **237** | A64 | 3p | Children's village | .20 | .20 |

Child welfare.

**1975, Nov. 7 Photo. *Perf. 13***

| | | | | | |
|---|---|---|---|---|---|
| **238** | A65 | 3p | blk, lt grn & mar | .20 | .20 |

## SEMI-POSTAL STAMPS

**Red Cross Issue**

Types of Semi-Postal Stamps of Spain, 1926, Overprinted

**1926 Unwmk. *Perf. 12½, 13***

| | | | | | |
|---|---|---|---|---|---|
| **B1** | SP3 | 5c | black brown | 8.00 | 8.00 |
| **B2** | SP4 | 10c | dark green | 8.00 | 8.00 |
| **B3** | SP1 | 15c | dark violet | 2.50 | 2.50 |
| **B4** | SP4 | 20c | violet brown | 2.50 | 2.50 |
| **B5** | SP5 | 25c | deep carmine | 2.50 | 2.50 |
| **B6** | SP1 | 30c | olive green | 2.50 | 2.50 |
| **B7** | SP3 | 40c | ultra | .20 | .20 |
| **B8** | SP2 | 50c | red brown | .20 | .20 |
| **B9** | SP5 | 60c | myrtle green | .20 | .20 |
| **B10** | SP4 | 1p | vermilion | .20 | .20 |

B11 SP3 4p bister 2.50 1.90
B12 SP5 10p light violet 6.50 5.50
*Nos. B1-B12 (12)* 35.80 34.20
Set, never hinged 52.50

See Spain No. B6a for No. B4 without overprint. For surcharges see Spain #B72-B73.

**Catalogue values for unused stamps in this section, from this point to the end of the section, are for Never Hinged items.**

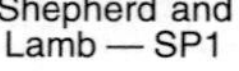
Shepherd and Lamb — SP1

Dromedary and Calf — SP2

**1950, Oct. 20 Photo. *Perf. 13x12½***
B13 SP1 50c + 10c brown .25 .20
B14 SP1 1p + 25c rose brn 12.00 5.50
B15 SP1 6.50p + 1.65p dk gray grn 6.50 1.60
*Nos. B13-B15 (3)* 18.75 7.30

The surtax was for child welfare.

**1951, Nov. 23**
B16 SP2 5c + 5c brown .20 .20
B17 SP2 10c + 5 red org .20 .20
B18 SP2 60c + 15c olive brn .40 .20
*Nos. B16-B18 (3)* .80 .60

Colonial Stamp Day, Nov. 23.

Child and Protector SP3

Ostrich SP4

**1952, June 1**
B19 SP3 5c + 5c brown .20 .20
B20 SP3 50c + 10c gray .20 .20
B21 SP3 2p + 30c blue 1.40 .95
*Nos. B19-B21 (3)* 1.80 1.35

The surtax was for child welfare.

**1952, Nov. 23 *Perf. 12½***
B22 SP4 5c + 5c brn .20 .20
B23 SP4 10c + 5c brn car .20 .20
B24 SP4 60c + 15c dk grn .30 .20
*Nos. B22-B24 (3)* .70 .60

Colonial Stamp Day, Nov. 23.

### Musician Type of Regular Issue

**1953, June 1 *Perf. 13x12½***
B25 A7 5c + 5c like #68 .20 .20
B26 A7 10c + 5c like #69 .20 .20

The surtax was for child welfare.

### Fish Type of Regular Issue

**1953, Nov. 23 *Perf. 12½x13***
B27 A8 5c + 5c like #70 .20 .20
B28 A8 10c + 5c like #71 .20 .20

### Athlete Types of Regular Issue

**1954, June 1 *Perf. 12½x13, 13x12½***
B29 A9 5c + 5c brn org .20 .20
B30 A10 10c + 5c purple .20 .20

The surtax was to help the native population.

### Fish Type of Regular Issue

**1954, Nov. 23 *Perf. 12½x13***
B31 A11 5c + 5c like #74 .20 .20
B32 A11 10c + 5c like #75 .20 .20

Type of Regular Issue and

Emilio Bonelli SP5

**1955, June 1 Photo. Unwmk.**
B33 A12 10c + 5c red vio .20 .20
B34 SP5 25c + 10c violet .20 .20

The surtax was for child welfare.

### Antelope Type of Regular Issue

15c+5c, Head of scimitar-horned oryx.

**1955, Nov. 23 *Perf. 12½x13***
B35 A13 5c + 5c org brn .20 .20
B36 A13 15c + 5c olive bister .20 .20

### Flower Type of Regular Issue

**1956, June 1 *Perf. 13x12½***
B37 A14 5c + 5c like #78 .20 .20
B38 A14 15c + 5c like #79 .20 .20

The tax was for the children.

Aaiun Type of Regular Issue and

Arms of Villa Cisneros and Man — SP6

***Perf. 12½x13, 13x12½***
**1956, Nov. 23 Unwmk.**
B39 A15 5c + 5c pur & blk .20 .20
B40 SP6 15c + 5c bis & grn .20 .20

### Eagle Type of Regular Issue

15c+5c, Lesser spotted eagle in flight.

**1957, June 1 *Perf. 13x12½***
B41 A17 5c + 5c red brown .20 .20
B42 A17 15c + 5c golden brn .20 .20

The surtax was for child welfare.

### Hyena Type of Regular Issue

***Perf. 13x12½, 12½x13***
**1957, Nov. 23**
B43 A18 10c + 5c like #88 .20 .20
B44 A18 15c + 5c like #89 .20 .20

Stork and Arms of Valencia and Aaiun SP7

**1958, Mar. 6 Photo. *Perf. 12½x13***
B45 SP7 10c + 5c org brn .20 .20
B46 SP7 15c + 10c bister .20 .20
B47 SP7 50c + 10c brn olive .20 .20
*Nos. B45-B47 (3)* .60 .60

The surtax was to aid the victims of the Valencia flood, Oct. 1957.

### Cervantes Type of Regular Issue

15c+5c, Don Quixote & Sancho Panza.

**1958, June 1 *Perf. 13x12½***
B48 A20 10c + 5c hn brn & chnt brn .20 .20
B49 A20 15c + 5c dp org & slate grn .20 .20

The surtax was for child welfare.

Hoopoe Lark — SP8

Mailman — SP9

25c+10c, Hoopoe larks, horiz. 50c+10c, Bird.

***Perf. 13x12½, 12½x13***
**1958, Nov. 23 Photo. Unwmk.**
B50 SP8 10c + 5c brn red .20 .20
B51 SP8 25c + 10c brt pur .20 .20
B52 SP8 50c + 10c olive .20 .20
*Nos. B50-B52 (3)* .60 .60

### Cervantes Type of Regular Issue

10c+5c, Lope de Vega. 15c+5c, Actress from "Star of Seville," by Lope de Vega.

**1959, June *Perf. 13x12½***
B53 A20 10c + 5c org brn & ol gray .20 .20
B54 A20 15c + 5c dp ocher & choc .20 .20

The surtax was for child welfare.

**1959, Nov. 23 Photo.**

Stamp Day: 20c+5c, Mailman. 50c+20c, Mailman on camel.

B55 SP9 10c + 5c rose & brn .20 .20
B56 SP9 20c + 5c lt grn & brn .20 .20
B57 SP9 50c + 20c ol gray & slate .20 .20
*Nos. B55-B57 (3)* .60 .60

### Quevedo Type of Regular Issue

Designs: 10c+5c, Francisco Gomez de Quevedo. 15c+5c, Winged wheel and hour-glass, symbolic of "Hora de Todas."

**1960, June 1 *Perf. 12½x13, 13x12½***
B58 A23 10c + 5c maroon .20 .20
B59 A22 15c + 5c bister brown .20 .20

The surtax was for child welfare.

Leopard SP10

Alonso Fernandez de Lugo SP11

Stamp Day: 20c+5c, Desert fox. 30c+10c, Eagle and leopard. 50c+20c, Sand fox.

**1960, Nov. 23 Photo. *Perf. 13x12½***
B60 SP10 10c + 5c rose lilac .20 .20
B61 SP10 20c + 5c dk slate grn .20 .20
B62 SP10 30c + 10c chocolate .20 .20
B63 SP10 50c + 20c olive gray .30 .20
*Nos. B60-B63 (4)* .90 .80

### Animal Type of 1961 inscribed: "Pro-Infancia 1961"

Designs: Various Mountain Gazelles.

**1961, June 21 Unwmk.**
B64 SP10 10c + 5c rose brn .20 .20
B65 SP10 25c + 10c gray vio .20 .20
B66 SP10 80c + 20c dk grn .30 .20
*Nos. B64-B66 (3)* .70 .60

The surtax was for child welfare.

**1961, Nov. 23 *Perf. 13x12½***

Stamp Day: #B68, B70, Diego de Herrera.

B67 SP11 10c + 5c org red .20 .20
B68 SP11 25c + 10c dk pur .20 .20
B69 SP11 30c + 10c dk red brn .20 .20
B70 SP11 1p + 10c red org .30 .20
*Nos. B67-B70 (4)* .90 .80

## AIR POST STAMPS

In 1942, seven air post stamps of Spain, Nos. C100-C108, were overprinted "SAHARA ESPANOL", but satisfactory information regarding their status is not available.

**Catalogue values for unused stamps in this section are for Never Hinged items.**

Ostriches — AP1

Desert Scene — AP2

**1943 Unwmk. Litho. *Perf. 12½***
C8 AP1 5c cer & vio brn .20 .20
C9 AP2 25c yel grn & ol grn .20 .20
C10 AP1 50c ind & turq grn .20 .20
C11 AP2 1p pur & grnsh bl .20 .20
C12 AP1 1.40p gray grn & bl .20 .20
C13 AP2 2p mag & org brn 1.75 1.10
C14 AP1 5p brown & purple 2.40 1.10
C15 AP2 6p brt bl & gray grn 42.50 19.00
*Nos. C8-C15 (8)* 47.65 22.20

Nos. C8-C15 exist imperf. Value of set $90.

Diego Garcia de Herrera AP3

**1950, Nov. 23 Photo.**
C16 AP3 5p rose violet 2.50 1.00

Stamp Day.

Woman Holding Dove — AP4

**1951, Apr. 22 Engr. *Perf. 10***
C17 AP4 5p deep green 22.50 6.50

500th birth anniv. of Queen Isabella I. No. C17 is valued in the grade of fine.

Helmet and Trappings AP5

Plane and Camel Rider AP6

**1952, July 18 Photo. *Perf. 13x12½***
C18 AP5 5p brown 27.50 6.50

500th birth anniv. of Ferdinand the Catholic, of Spain.

**1961, May 16 Unwmk.**
C19 AP6 25p gray brown 2.50 .80

### SPECIAL DELIVERY STAMPS

**Catalogue value for unused stamps in this section are for Never Hinged items.**

Type A2 Inscribed "URGENTE"

**1943 Unwmk. *Perf. 12½***

| | | | | |
|---|---|---|---|---|
| **E1** | A2 | 25c Camel troops | 1.25 | .75 |

Messenger on Motorcycle — SD1

**Unwmk.**

**1971, Sept. 6 Photo. *Perf. 13***

| | | | | |
|---|---|---|---|---|
| **E2** | SD1 | 10p bright rose & olive | .65 | .30 |

## SPANISH WEST AFRICA

'spa-nish 'west 'a-fri-kə

LOCATION — Northwest Africa bordering on the Atlantic Ocean
GOVT. — Spanish administration
AREA — 117,000 sq. mi.
POP. — 95,000 (1950)
CAPITAL — Sidi Ifni

Spanish West Africa was the major political division of Spanish areas in northwest Africa. It included Spanish Sahara (Rio de Oro and Saguiet el Hamra) Ifni and, for administrative purposes, Southern Morocco. Separate stamp issues have been used for Rio de Oro, Ifni and La Aguera.

**Catalogue values for all unused stamps in this country are for Never Hinged items.**

Native — A1

***Perf. 13x12½***

**1949, Oct. Litho. Unwmk.**

| | | | | |
|---|---|---|---|---|
| **1** | A1 | 4p dark gray green | 2.10 | .90 |

UPU, 75th anniversary.

Nomad Camp A2

5c, 30c, 75c, 2p, Tinzgarrentz Oasis. 10c, 40c, 90c, 5p, Desert well. 15c, 45c, 1p, Caravan.

**1950, June 5 *Perf. 12½x13***

| | | | | |
|---|---|---|---|---|
| **2** | A2 | 2c brown | .20 | .20 |
| **3** | A2 | 5c rose violet | .20 | .20 |
| **4** | A2 | 10c Prussian blue | .20 | .20 |
| **5** | A2 | 15c deep olive gray | .20 | .20 |
| **6** | A2 | 25c red brown | .20 | .20 |
| **7** | A2 | 30c bright yellow | .20 | .20 |
| **8** | A2 | 40c olive gray | .20 | .20 |
| **9** | A2 | 45c rose lake | .20 | .20 |
| **10** | A2 | 50c brown orange | .20 | .20 |
| **11** | A2 | 75c ultramarine | .20 | .20 |
| **12** | A2 | 90c dull blue grn | .20 | .20 |
| **13** | A2 | 1p gray | .20 | .20 |
| **14** | A2 | 1.35p violet | .70 | .45 |
| **15** | A2 | 2p sepia | 1.25 | 1.00 |
| **16** | A2 | 5p lilac rose | 11.50 | 3.50 |
| **17** | A2 | 10p light brown | 27.50 | 20.00 |
| | | *Nos. 2-17 (16)* | 43.35 | 27.35 |

### AIR POST STAMPS

Isabella the Catholic, Queen of Castile — AP1

***Perf. 13x12½***

**1949, Nov. 23 Photo. Unwmk.**

| | | | | |
|---|---|---|---|---|
| **C1** | AP1 | 5p yellow brown | 2.00 | .90 |

Stamp Day, Nov. 23, 1949.

Desert Camp AP2

Designs: Various Desert Scenes.

**1951, Mar. 1 Litho. *Perf. 12½x13***

| | | | | |
|---|---|---|---|---|
| **C2** | AP2 | 25c ocher | .20 | .20 |
| **C3** | AP2 | 50c lilac rose | .20 | .20 |
| **C4** | AP2 | 1p green | .25 | .20 |
| **C5** | AP2 | 2p bright blue | .50 | .20 |
| **C6** | AP2 | 3.25p rose lilac | 1.00 | .75 |
| **C7** | AP2 | 5p gray brown | 11.00 | 2.75 |
| **C8** | AP2 | 10p rose red | 20.00 | 17.50 |
| | | *Nos. C2-C8 (7)* | 33.15 | 21.80 |

### SPECIAL DELIVERY STAMP

Tilimenzo Pass and Franco SD1

***Perf. 12½x13***

**1951, Mar. 1 Litho. Unwmk.**

| | | | | |
|---|---|---|---|---|
| **E1** | SD1 | 25c rose carmine | .30 | .25 |

## SRI LANKA

ˌsrē 'läŋ-kə

LOCATION — Indian Ocean south of India
GOVT. — Democratic Socialist Republic
AREA — 26,244 sq. mi.
POP. — 19,144,875 (1999 est.)
CAPITAL — Colombo

Sri Lanka was named Ceylon until May 22, 1972. Issues inscribed "Ceylon" are listed under that name in Volume 2.

100 Cents = 1 Rupee

**Catalogue values for all unused stamps in this country are for Never Hinged items.**

**Watermark**

Wmk. 385 — CARTOR

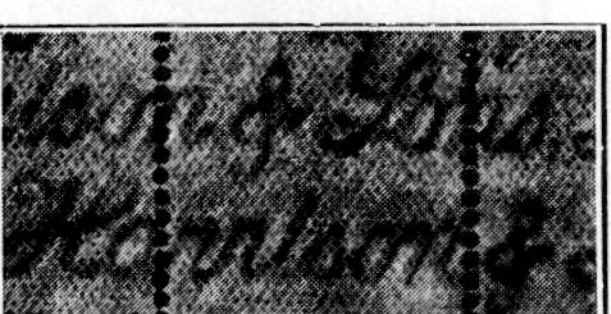

Wmk. 233 — "Harrison & Sons, London" in Script

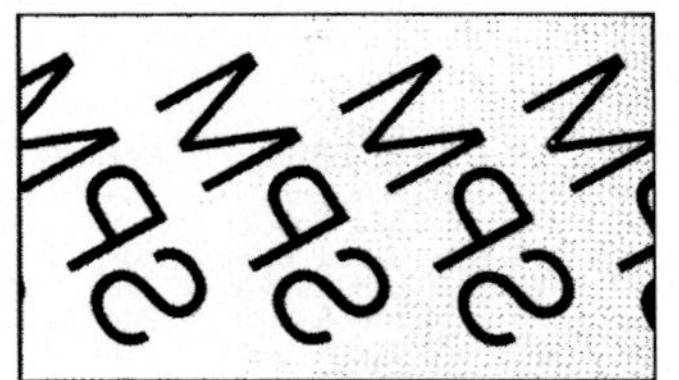

Wmk. 388 — Multiple "SPM"

Lotus and Sunrise over Adam's Peak — A162

**1972, May 22 Litho. *Perf. 13½x13***

| | | | | |
|---|---|---|---|---|
| **470** | A162 | 15c blue & multi | .35 | .35 |

Inauguration of Ceylon as Republic of Sri Lanka.

A162a

Overprinted "1972" in Red

**1972, May 26 *Perf. 14x13½***

| | | | | |
|---|---|---|---|---|
| **471** | A162a | 5c orange brn & multi | .35 | .35 |

World Fellowship of Buddhists, Sri Lanka, May 22-28.

Supposedly not issued without overprint, copies sell for 25-cents.

Book Year Emblem, Oil Lamp — A163

**1972, Sept. 8 Photo. *Perf. 13***

| | | | | |
|---|---|---|---|---|
| **472** | A163 | 20c yellow & dk brn | .25 | .25 |

International Book Year 1972.

Imperial Angelfish A164

Tropical Fish: 3c, Green chromide. 30c, Skipjack bonito. 2r, Black ruby barbs.

***Perf. 14x13½***

**1972, Oct. 12 Litho. Unwmk.**

| | | | | |
|---|---|---|---|---|
| **473** | A164 | 2c ultra & multi | .20 | *1.00* |
| **474** | A164 | 3c dp orange & multi | .20 | *1.00* |
| **475** | A164 | 30c brt green & multi | 1.90 | .35 |
| **476** | A164 | 2r dp green & multi | 5.50 | *5.75* |
| | | *Nos. 473-476 (4)* | 7.80 | 8.10 |

3rd Session of Indian Ocean Fisheries Commission, Colombo, Oct. 9-14.

Bandaranaike Memorial Hall — A165

**1973, May 17 Litho. *Perf. 14***

| | | | | |
|---|---|---|---|---|
| **477** | A165 | 15c lt ultra & vio blue | .35 | .35 |

Opening of Bandaranaike Memorial International Conference Hall.

Women Holding Lotus A166

Rock and Temple Paintings: 35c, King giving away his children, Degaldoruwa Temple, near Kandy, 18th cent. 50c, Prince and gravedigger, Polonaruwa, 12th cent. 90c, Holy man holding lotus, Polonaruwa, 12th cent. Design of 1.55r is from Sigiriya, 5th cent.

**1973, Sept. 3 *Perf. 13½x14***

| | | | | |
|---|---|---|---|---|
| **478** | A166 | 35c lt gray & multi | .40 | .20 |
| **479** | A166 | 50c gray & multi | .50 | .20 |
| **480** | A166 | 90c slate & multi | .75 | .75 |
| **481** | A166 | 1.55r brown & multi | .90 | .90 |
| *a.* | | Souvenir sheet of 4, #478-481 | 4.00 | 4.00 |
| | | *Nos. 478-481 (4)* | 2.55 | 2.05 |

For surcharges see Nos. 538-540.

Bandaranaike Conference Hall — A167

**1974, Sept. 6 Litho. *Perf. 14***

| | | | | |
|---|---|---|---|---|
| **482** | A167 | 85c multicolored | .35 | .35 |

20th Commonwealth Parliamentary Conference, Sri Lanka, Sept. 1-15.

S.W.R.D. Bandaranaike A168

"UPU," "100" and UPU Emblem A170

**1974, Sept. 25 Photo. *Perf. 14½***

| | | | | |
|---|---|---|---|---|
| **486** | A168 | 15c ultra & multi | .20 | .20 |

For surcharge see No. 541.

**1974, Oct. 9 Litho. *Perf. 13***

| | | | | |
|---|---|---|---|---|
| **490** | A170 | 50c multicolored | 1.25 | 1.00 |

Parliament, Colombo
A171

**1975, Apr. 1 Litho. *Perf. 13½***
**491** A171 1r multicolored .35 .35

Interparliamentary Union, Spring Meeting at Bandaranaike Memorial International Conference Hall, Sri Lanka, Mar. 31-Apr. 5.

Ponnambalam Ramanathan
A172

D. J. Wimalasurendra
A173

**1975, Sept. 4 Litho. *Perf. 13½***
**492** A172 75c multicolored .35 .35

Sir Ponnambalam Ramanathan (1851-1930), lawyer and educator.

**1975, Sept. 17**
**493** A173 75c ultra & blue blk .35 .35

Devapura Jayasena Wimalasurendra (1874-1953), engineer and irrigation specialist.

Map, Mrs. Bandaranaike, Dove — A174

**1975, Dec. 22 Litho. *Perf. 13½***
**494** A174 1.15r blue & multi 2.90 1.50

International Women's Year 1975.

Rhododendron Zeylanicum
A175

Flowers: 50c, Exacum trinerve. 75c, Daffodil orchid. 10r, Wormia triquetra.

**1976, Jan. 1 Litho. *Perf. 13***
**495** A175 25c blue & multi .20 .20
**496** A175 50c ocher & multi .20 .20
**497** A175 75c black & multi .25 .25
**498** A175 10r black & multi 4.00 4.00
*a.* Souvenir sheet of 4, #495-498 15.00 15.00
*Nos. 495-498 (4)* 4.65 4.65

Mahaveli-ganga Sluice — A176

**1976, Jan. 8 Litho. *Perf. 13x12½***
**499** A176 85c lt blue, lt grn & lil .35 .50

Mahaveli-ganga River diversion.

Radar Station — A177

**1976, May 6 Litho. *Perf. 14***
**500** A177 1r blue & multi .85 .85

Opening of Satellite Earth Station, Padukka.

Prince Siddhartha as White Elephant and Sleeping Queen — A178

Birth of Buddha: 10c, King consulting astrologers. 1.50r, King entertaining astrologers at banquet. 2r, Queen taken in procession to her parents. 2.25r, Flag bearers, musicians in procession. 5r, Queen giving birth to Prince Siddhartha, the Buddha. Designs taken from 18th cent. wall paintings in Dambawa Vihara Temple.

**1976, May 7 Litho. *Perf. 13½***
**501** A178 5c blue & multi .20 *.50*
**502** A178 10c blue & multi .20 *.50*
**503** A178 1.50r blue & multi 1.00 1.00
**504** A178 2r blue & multi 1.00 1.00
**505** A178 2.25r blue & multi 2.00 *2.00*
**506** A178 5r blue & multi 5.00 *5.00*
*a.* Souvenir sheet of 6, #501-506 12.00 12.00
*Nos. 501-506 (6)* 9.40 *10.00*

Blue Sapphire
A179

Gems of Sri Lanka: 1.15r, Cat's-eye. 2r, Star sapphire. 5r, Ruby.

**1976, June 16 *Perf. 12x12½***
**507** A179 60c multicolored 5.50 .35
**508** A179 1.15r multicolored 9.25 2.00
**509** A179 2r multicolored 10.50 4.25
**510** A179 5r multicolored 14.00 14.00
*a.* Souv. sheet of 4, #507-510 45.00 35.00
*Nos. 507-510 (4)* 39.25 20.60

Prime Minister Sirimavo Bandaranaike
A180

Statue of Liberty
A181

**1976, Aug. 3 Photo. *Perf. 14¼x14½***
**511** A180 1.15r pink & multi .35 .35
**512** A180 2r pink & multi .60 .60

5th Summit Conference of Non-aligned Countries, Colombo, Aug. 9-19.

**1976, Nov. 29 Litho. *Perf. 14***
**513** A181 2.25r lt blue & indigo .85 1.00

American Bicentennial.

A. G. Bell, Telephone and Telephone Line
A182

Maitreya Bodhisattva
A183

**1976, Dec. 21 Litho. *Perf. 13x13½***
**514** A182 1r orange & multi .80 .30

Centenary of first telephone call by Alexander Graham Bell, Mar. 10, 1876.

**1977, Jan. 1 Litho. *Perf. 12½x13***

Bronze Statues: 1r, Sundara Murti Swami, 11th century. 5r, Goddess Tara.

**515** A183 50c multicolored .35 .35
**516** A183 1r multicolored .35 .35
**517** A183 5r multicolored 2.90 2.90
*Nos. 515-517 (3)* 3.60 3.60

Colombo Museum, centenary.

Kandyan Crown, 1737-1815
A184

2r, Kandyan throne and footstool, 1693-1815.

**1977, Jan. 18**
**518** A184 1r multicolored .50 .50
**519** A184 2r multicolored 1.50 1.50

Rahula Thero — A185

Brass Lamps — A186

No. 521, Ponnambalam Arunachalam.

**1977 Litho. *Perf. 13½***
**520** A185 1r multicolored 1.00 1.00
**521** A185 1r multicolored .65 .65

Sri Rahula Thero, 15th cent. poet and scholar, and Sir Ponnambalam Arunachalam (1851-1930), 1st president of Ceylon University Assoc., member of Congress.
Issue dates: #520, Feb. 23; #521, Mar. 10.

**1977, Apr. 7 *Perf. 13***

Handicrafts: 25c, Jewelry box and jewelry. 50c, Caparisoned ivory elephant. 5r, Sinhala wooden mask.

**522** A186 20c multicolored .20 .20
**523** A186 25c multicolored .20 .20
**524** A186 50c multicolored .45 .45
**525** A186 5r multicolored 2.50 2.75
*a.* Souvenir sheet of 4, #522-525 5.00 5.00
*Nos. 522-525 (4)* 3.35 3.60

Mohammed Cassim Siddi Lebbe — A187

**1977, June 11 Litho. *Perf. 13***
**526** A187 1r multicolored .35 .50

Lebbe (1838-98), lawyer, educator and Moslem journalist.

Girl Guide
A188

**1977, Dec. 13 Litho. *Perf. 15***
**527** A188 75c multicolored .85 .35

60th anniversary of Sri Lanka Girl Guides.

Parliament and Wheel of Life — A189

Runners — A190

**1978, Feb. 4 Photo. *Perf. 12x12½***
**528** A189 15c green & gold .25 .20

J.R. Jayewardene, first elected president, assumption of office.
See Nos. 559, 611-611A, 847. For surcharges see Nos. 542, 572, 698A-698B.

**1978, Apr. 27 Litho. *Perf. 15***
**529** A190 15c multicolored .35 .35

National Youth Service Council.
For surcharge see No. 543.

Bodhisattva in Royal Attire in Lotus Position
A191

Vesak Festival: 50c, Bodhisattva without royal attire cutting off his hair with sword. Both designs from rock carvings in Borobudur Temple, Java.

**1978, May 16 *Perf. 13***
**530** A191 15c multicolored 1.00 1.00
**531** A191 50c multicolored 1.25 1.25

Veera Puran Appu and his Flag — A192

Birdwing Butterfly — A193

**1978, Aug. 8 Litho. *Perf. 13***
**532** A192 15c multicolored .30 .20

Veera Puran Appu (1848-1908), revolutionist, 130th birth anniversary.

**1978, Nov. 28 Litho. *Perf. 14x13½***

Butterflies: 50c, Tamil lacewing. 5r, Blue oakleaf. 10r, Blue mormon.

**534** A193 25c multicolored .75 .20
**535** A193 50c multicolored 1.25 .20
**536** A193 5r multicolored 2.25 1.50
**537** A193 10r multicolored 2.25 2.25
*a.* Souvenir sheet of 4, #534-537 16.00 12.50
*Nos. 534-537 (4)* 6.50 4.15

Nos. 478, 480-481 Surcharged with New Value and Bar

**1978 Litho. *Perf. 13½x14***
**538** A166 5c on 90c multi 2.50 2.50
**539** A166 10c on 35c multi .65 .65
**540** A166 1r on 1.55r multi 1.50 1.50
*Nos. 538-540 (3)* 4.65 4.65

Nos. 486, 528 Surcharged with New Value and 2 Bars; No. 529 with New Value on Pink Panel

***Perf. 14½, 12x12½, 15***
**1979, Jan. Litho.; Engr.**
**541** A168 25c on 15c multi 5.25 5.25
**542** A189 25c on 15c multi 5.25 5.25
**543** A190 25c on 15c multi 5.25 5.25
*Nos. 541-543 (3)* 15.75 15.75

Ceylon No. 390 Overprinted Vertically "SRI LANKA" in Green and Surcharged in Black

**1979, Mar. 22 Photo. *Perf. 11½***
**Granite Paper**
**544** A118 15c on 10c brt green 3.50 2.25

Arrival of Sacred Tooth — A194

Wrestlers — A195

Wall Paintings from Kelaniya Temple: 25c, Prince Danta and Princess Hema Mala bringing Sacred Tooth from Kalinga, 4th century A.D. 1r, Princess Theri Sanghamitta bringing, by ship, the bodhi tree branch, 3rd century B.C. 10r, King Kirti offering fan of authority to supreme patriarch, 18th century.

**1979, May 3 Litho. *Perf. 13½***
**546** A194 25c multicolored .20 .20
**547** A194 1r multicolored .20 .20
**548** A194 10r multicolored 2.00 *2.00*
*a.* Souvenir sheet of 3, #546-548 3.25 3.25
*Nos. 546-548 (3)* 2.40 2.40

2523rd Vesak Festival, May 11.

**1979, May 18 Litho. *Perf. 14***

Design: 50r, Dancer. Woodcarvings from Embekke Temple.

**549** A195 20r multicolored 1.40 .90
**550** A195 50r multicolored 3.50 3.00

Piyadasa Sirisena A196

Dudley S. Senanayake A197

**1979, May 22 *Perf. 13x13½***
**551** A196 1.25r deep green .50 .50

Piyadasa Sirisena (1875-1946), patriot, journalist, novelist and poet.

**1979, June 19 Photo.**
**552** A197 1.25r deep green .20 .20

27th death anniversary of Prime Minister Dudley S. Senanayake.

Mother Feeding Child, IYC Emblem A198

Designs: 3r, Faces and IYC emblem. 5r, Children with rope and ball, IYC emblem.

**1979, July 31 Litho. *Perf. 12½***
**553** A198 5c multicolored .20 .20
**554** A198 3r multicolored .45 .45
**555** A198 5r multicolored .50 .50
*Nos. 553-555 (3)* 1.15 1.15

International Year of the Child.

Ceylon No. 2, Rowland Hill — A199

Airlanka Emblem — A200

**1979, Aug. 27 Litho. *Perf. 13½***
**556** A199 3r multicolored .35 .50

Sir Rowland Hill (1795-1879), originator of penny postage.

**1979, Sept. 1 Litho. *Perf. 12½***
**557** A200 3r red, dk grn & blk 1.00 1.00

Airlanka National Airline, inaugural flight, Colombo-Bangkok.

Coconut Palm — A201

**1979, Oct. 9 Litho. *Perf. 13½***
**558** A201 2r multicolored 1.10 1.10

Asian and Pacific Coconut Community, 10th anniversary.

No. 528 Redrawn Without Date

**1979, Oct. 9 Photo. *Perf. 13***
**Size: 20x24mm**
**559** A189 25c green & gold .35 .20

Family in Cogwheel, Parliament A202

**1979, Oct. Litho. *Perf. 13½***
**560** A202 2r multicolored 1.10 1.10

Intl. Conf. of Parliamentarians on Population & Development, Colombo, Aug. 28-Sept. 1.

Swami Vipulananda (1892-1947), Philosopher & Theologian — A203

**1979, Nov. 18 *Perf. 12½***
**561** A203 1.25r multicolored .35 .35

Text and Crescent A204

**1979, Nov. 22**
**562** A204 3.75r multicolored .50 .80

Hegira (pilgrimage year).

Institute Emblem A205

Blue Magpie A206

**1979, Nov. 29 *Perf. 13***
**563** A205 15c multicolored .35 .35

Ayurveda Medical Institute, 50th anniversary.

**1979, Dec. 13 Litho. *Perf. 14***
**564** A206 10c shown .20 *.20*
**565** A206 15c Lorikeet .20 .20
**566** A206 75c Arrenga .20 .20
**567** A206 1r Spurfowl .20 .20
**568** A206 5r Yellow-fronted barbet 1.00 1.00
**569** A206 10r Yellow-eared bulbul 1.25 *1.25*
*a.* Souvenir sheet of 6, #564-569 6.50 6.50
*Nos. 564-569 (6)* 3.05 *3.05*

For surcharge see No. 1062B.

Rotary Emblem, Map of Sri Lanka A207

**1979, Dec. 27 Litho. *Perf. 14½***
**570** A207 1.50r multicolored .95 1.10

Rotary International, 75th anniversary.

A. Ratnayake, Educator and Pres. of Senate — A208

**1980, Jan. 7 Photo. *Perf. 14x13½***
**571** A208 1.25r slate green .25 .25

No. 559 Surcharged

**1980, Mar. 17 Photo. *Perf. 13***
**572** A189 35c on 25c multi .20 .20

One position has ".33" instead of ".35."

Leaf, Wheel, Fan (Buddhist Symbols) A209

**1980, Mar. 25 Photo. *Perf. 13½x14***
**573** A209 10c Steeple .30 .60
**574** A209 35c shown .30 .25

All Ceylon Buddhist Cong., 60th anniv.

Col. Henry Olcott, Buddhist Emblem — A210

Journey of Patachara, Temple Painting — A211

**1980, May 17 Litho. *Perf. 14***
**575** A210 2r multicolored .95 1.00

Col. Henry S. Olcott (1832-1907), American theosophist and Buddhist lecturer, centenary of arrival in Sri Lanka.

**1980, May 23 *Perf. 13½x14***

Vesak Festival (Paintings, life of Buddha): 1.60r, Patachara crossing river.

**576** A211 35c multicolored .35 .35
**577** A211 1.60r multicolored 1.40 1.40

George E. De Silva — A212

**1980, June 8 *Perf. 13x13½***
**578** A212 1.60r multicolored .35 .35

George E. de Silva (1879-1950), politician.

Siva Temples, Polonnaruwa — A213

**1980, Aug. 25 Litho. *Perf. 13½***
**579** A213 35c shown .20 *.30*
**580** A213 35c Cave Temples, Dambulla .20 *.30*
**581** A213 35c Sacred Tooth Temple, Kandy .20 *.30*
**582** A213 1.60r Abhayagiri Hill .50 *.90*
**583** A213 1.60r Jetavanarama Hill .50 *.90*

**584** A213 1.60r Sigiri .50 *.90*
*a.* Souvenir sheet of 6, #579-584 2.75 2.25
*Nos. 579-584 (6)* 2.10 *3.60*

UNESCO "Cultural Triangle" Project.

Department of Cooperative Development, 50th Anniversary A214

**1980, Oct. 1 Litho. *Perf. 13½***
**585** A214 20c multicolored .20 .25

Women's Movement Emblem A215

**1980, Oct. 16 Photo. *Perf. 14x13½***
**586** A215 35c multicolored .20 .30

Mahila Samiti (Rural Women's Movement), 50th anniversary.

Nativity — A216

**1980, Nov. 20 Litho. *Perf. 13½***
**587** A216 35c shown .20 .20
**588** A216 3.75r Three kings .65 .75
*a.* Souvenir sheet of 2, #587-588 1.40 1.40

Christmas 1980/Year of the family.

Colombo Public Library Opening A217

**1980, Dec. 17 *Perf. 12x12½***
**589** A217 35c multicolored .20 .20

Peacock Banner A218

Designs: Ancient flags.

**1980, Dec. 18 *Perf. 13***
**590** A218 10c shown .20 .20
**591** A218 25c Elephant banner .20 .20
**592** A218 1.60r Sinhalese royal flag .25 .25
**593** A218 20r Kings Civil Standard 1.90 1.90
*a.* Souvenir sheet of 4, #590-593 2.40 2.40
*Nos. 590-593 (4)* 2.55 2.55

Fishing Cat — A219

**1981, Feb. 10 Litho. *Perf. 14***
**594** A219 2.50r on 1.60r, shown .55 .20
**595** A219 3r on 1.50r, Golden palm cat .55 .25
**596** A219 4r on 2r, Mouse deer .55 .45
**597** A219 5r on 3.75r, Rusty-spotted cat .85 .60
*a.* Souvenir sheet of 4, #594-597 3.00 3.00
*Nos. 594-597 (4)* 2.50 1.50

See #728-730A, 928. For surcharge see #731.

Population and Housing Census — A220

**1981, Mar. 2 Litho. *Perf. 12½x12***
**598** A220 50c multicolored .85 .85

Ceylon Light Infantry Centenary A221

**1981, Apr. 1 Litho. *Perf. 12***
**599** A221 2r multicolored 1.25 1.25

The Death of Buddha, Carved Panel, 1st Cent. — A222

**1981, May 5 *Perf. 13x13½***
**600** A222 35c shown .20 .20
**601** A222 50c Silk banner .20 .20
**602** A222 7r Statuette 2.00 1.75
*a.* Souvenir sheet of 3, #600-602 5.25 5.25
*Nos. 600-602 (3)* 2.40 2.15

Vesak Festival.

St. John Baptist de la Salle A223

**1981, May 15 Litho. *Perf. 12½x12***
**603** A223 2r multicolored 1.75 1.75

De la Salle Brothers Order, 300th anniv.

Polwatte Sri Buddadatta A224

Intl. Year of the Disabled — A225

Famous Men: No. 605, Mohottiwatte Gunananda, Buddhist leader. No. 606, Gnanapra Kasar, Catholic missionary. No. 607, Al-Haj T.B. Jayah, Muslim teacher. No. 608, James Peiris. No. 609, N.M. Perera, founded first Marxist Party in Sri Lanka, 1935.

**1981 Photo. *Perf. 12***
**604** A224 50c olive bister .75 .75
**605** A224 50c dull red brown .75 .75
**606** A224 50c lilac .75 .75
**607** A224 50c gray green .75 .75
**608** A224 50c brown .75 .75
**609** A224 50c crimson rose .75 .75
*Nos. 604-609 (6)* 4.50 4.50

Issued: #604-606, 5/22; #607, 5/31; #609, 6/6; #608, 12/20.
See #623-624, 640-642, 646, 672-676, 713-717.

**1981, June 19 Litho. *Perf. 12x12½***
**610** A225 2r multicolored 1.40 1.40

No. 528 Redrawn with Denomination in Upper Right Corner

**1981-83 Photo. *Perf. 13***
**Size: 20x24mm**
**611** A189 50c green & gold 3.00 .20
**611A** A189 60c green & gold 10.00 1.40

Issued: 50c, June 6; 60c, Dec. 30, 1983.
For surcharges see Nos. 698A-698B.

Hand Putting Ballot in Box A226

***Perf. 12½x12, 12x12½***
**1981, July 7 Litho.**
**612** A226 50c shown .25 .25
**613** A226 7r Ballot box on map, vert. 2.00 1.90

Universal Franchise, 50th anniv.

Rhys Davids (Society Founder) A227

**1981, July 14 *Perf. 12½x12***
**614** A227 35c multicolored .75 .35

All Ceylon Buddhist Students' Federation, 25th Anniv. A228

**1981, July 21 Litho. *Perf. 13½***
**615** A228 2r multicolored 1.10 1.10

Family Planning — A229

7th World Acupuncture Cong. — A230

**1981, Sept. 25**
**616** A229 50c multicolored 1.10 1.10

**1981, Oct. 20 Litho. *Perf. 12x12½***
**617** A230 2r multicolored 3.25 3.25

Visit of Queen Elizabeth II, Oct. A231

Designs: Flags of Gt. Britain and Sri Lanka.

**1981, Oct. 21 *Perf. 14***
**618** A231 50c multicolored .50 .50
**619** A231 5r multicolored 1.75 1.75
*a.* Souvenir sheet of 2, #618-619 3.00 3.00

Forest Conservation A232

**1981, Nov. 27 *Perf. 13½x13***
**620** A232 35c Forest .20 .20
**621** A232 50c Tree planting .25 .25
**622** A232 5r Jack tree 1.75 2.00
*a.* Souvenir sheet of 3, #620-622, perf. 14x13 2.25 3.00
*Nos. 620-622 (3)* 2.20 2.45

Famous Men Type of 1981

Designs: No. 623, F.R. Senanayaka (1882-1926), lawyer and politician. No. 624, Philip Gunawardhane, politician, 10th death anniv.

**1982 Litho. *Perf. 14***
**623** A224 50c brown .75 .75
**624** A224 50c bright rose .75 .75

Issue dates: #623, Jan. 1; #624, Jan. 11.

Dept. of Inland Revenue, 50th Anniv. A233

Natl. Television Inauguration A234

**1982, Feb. 9 Litho. *Perf. 14***
**625** A233 50c multicolored .75 .75

**1982, Feb. 15**
**626** A234 2.50r multicolored 3.00 3.00

Sesquicentennial of Cricket Introduction and Centenary of Sri Lanka vs. England Match — A235

**1982, Feb. 17**
**627** A235 2.50r multicolored 5.50 5.50

Osbeckia Wightiana A236

**1982, Apr. 1** ***Perf. 12***
**628** A236 35c shown .20 .20
**629** A236 2r Mesua nagassarium .35 .25
**630** A236 7r Rhodomyrtus tomentosa .80 .85
**631** A236 20r Phaius tancarvilleae 2.25 2.25
*a.* Souvenir sheet of 4, #628-631 8.50 9.00
*Nos. 628-631 (4)* 3.60 3.55

Food and Nutrition Planning A237

World Hindu Conference A238

**1982, Apr. 6 Litho.** ***Perf. 13***
**632** A237 50c multicolored 1.75 1.75

**1982, Apr. 21** ***Perf. 14x14½***
**633** A238 50c multicolored 1.10 1.10

Vesak Festival 1982 A239

Scenes from Jataka Story (Pre-incarnation of Buddha), Cloth Painting, 3rd cent. B.C., Hanguranketa Temple (King Vessantara and): 35c, Giving away white elephant. 50c, Royal Family in Vankagiri Forest. 2.50r, Giving away his children to a Brahmin. 5r, Royal family in chariot.

**1982, Apr. 23** ***Perf. 14***
**634** A239 35c multicolored .70 .20
**635** A239 50c multicolored .85 .20
**636** A239 2.50r multicolored 3.00 2.50
**637** A239 5r multicolored 4.00 *4.00*
*a.* Souvenir sheet of 4, #634-637 9.75 9.75
*Nos. 634-637 (4)* 8.55 6.90

New Parliament Building Opening A240

**1982, Apr. 29**
**638** A240 50c multicolored 1.10 1.10

Scouting Year A241

**1982, May 24 Litho.** ***Perf. 12½x12***
**639** A241 50c multicolored 2.25 2.00

Famous Men Type of 1981

**1982** ***Perf. 12x12½***
**640** A224 50c C.W.W. Kannangara 1.10 1.10
**641** A224 50c G.P. Malalasekara 1.10 1.10
**642** A224 50c John Kotelawala 1.10 1.10
*Nos. 640-642 (3)* 3.30 3.30

Issued: #640, 5/22; #641, 5/26; #642, 6/8.

World Buddhist Leaders Conference — A242

**1982, June 10** ***Perf. 12½x12***
**643** A242 50c multicolored 1.10 1.10

World Environment Day — A243

**1982, June 5**
**644** A243 50c multicolored 2.10 1.75

YMCA Centenary — A244

**1982, June 24 Photo.** ***Perf. 11½***
**645** A244 2.50r multicolored 3.75 3.75

Famous Men Type of 1981

**1982, June 14 Litho.** ***Perf. 12x12½***
**646** A224 50c Waitialingam Duraiswamy 1.10 1.10

Weliwita Saranankara Sangharaja A245

**1982, July 5**
**647** A245 50c orange & black 1.10 1.10

25th Anniv. of Sasana Sevaka Samithiya A246

**1982, Aug. 8**
**648** A246 50c multicolored 1.50 1.50

TB Bacillus Centenary A247

**1982, Sept. 21**
**649** A247 50c Koch, microscope, bacillus 2.25 1.75

Eye Donation Society — A248

**1982, Nov. 16 Litho.** ***Perf. 12x12½***
**650** A248 2.50r Emblems, map 3.75 *4.00*

125th Anniv. of Ceylon Postage Stamps — A249

**1982, Dec. 1 Litho.** ***Perf. 13½***
**651** A249 50c Ceylon #5, 302 .55 .55
**652** A249 2.50r Ceylon #12, #611 2.25 2.25
*a.* Souv. sheet, #651-652, perf. 12 3.25 3.25

Natl. Stamp Exhibition.

Sir Oliver Goonetilleke A250

**1982, Dec. 17 Litho.** ***Perf. 12x12½***
**653** A250 50c black & brown .75 .75

25th Anniv. of Sarvodaya Social Movement A251

**1983, Jan. 1** ***Perf. 13½***
**654** A251 50c multicolored 1.00 1.00

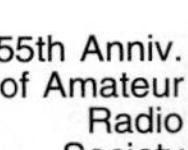

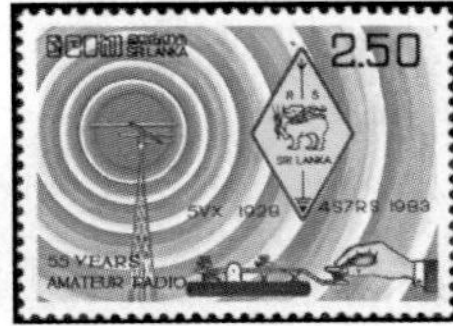

55th Anniv. of Amateur Radio Society A252

**1983, Jan. 17**
**655** A252 2.50r multicolored 4.00 4.00

Customs Cooperation Council and First Intl. Customs Day — A253

**1983, Jan. 26 Litho.** ***Perf. 12***
**656** A253 50c orange & multi .55 .55
**657** A253 5r green & multi 3.50 3.75

Bottlenose Dolphin A254

**1983, Feb. 22** ***Perf. 14½x14***
**658** A254 50c shown .75 .20
**659** A254 2r Dugongs 1.25 .75
**660** A254 2.50r Humpback whale 3.50 2.25
**661** A254 10r Great sperm whale 8.00 8.00
*Nos. 658-661 (4)* 13.50 11.20

Ceylon Shipping Corp. A255

**1983, Mar. 1** ***Perf. 12x12½***
**662** A255 50c Container ship .30 .20
**663** A255 2.50r Liner services map 1.10 .65
**664** A255 5r Conventional ship 1.60 1.50
**665** A255 20r Oil tanker 2.50 3.00
*Nos. 662-665 (4)* 5.50 5.35

Intl. Women's Day — A256

**1983, Mar. 8** ***Perf. 13½***
**666** A256 50c Woman, flag .25 .20
**667** A256 5r Woman, map .90 1.25

Commonwealth Day — A257

**1983, Mar. 14**
**668** A257 50c Waterfall .20 .20
**669** A257 2.50r Tea picking .20 .20
**670** A257 5r Harvesting .35 .50
**671** A257 20r Cultural pageant 1.40 1.40
*Nos. 668-671 (4)* 2.15 2.30

Famous Men Type of 1981

**1983 Litho. *Perf. 12***

**672** A224 50c Henry W. Amarasuriya .35 .50

**Size: 29x40mm**

**673** A224 50c Charles A. Lorenz .35 .50
**674** A224 50c Simon G. Perera .35 .50
**675** A224 50c Nordeen H.M. Abdul Cader .35 .50
**676** A224 50c C.W. Tamotherampillai 1.10 1.10
*Nos. 672-676 (5)* 2.50 3.10

No. 676 shows Tamotherampillai looking towards the right of the stamp. A version that was to be issued May 22, showed someone labeled C. W. Tamotherampillai looking straight ahead.

Issued: No. 676, Oct. 1; others, May 22.

25th Anniv. of Lions Club A258

**1983, May 7 Litho. *Perf. 14***

**677** A258 2.50r multicolored 3.75 2.50

Vesak Festival 1983 — A259

Various Colombo murals.

**1983, May 13 *Perf. 12½x12***

**678** A259 35c multicolored .20 .20
**679** A259 50c multicolored .20 .20
**680** A259 5r multicolored .95 .95
**681** A259 10r multicolored 1.50 1.50
*a.* Souvenir sheet of 4, #678-681 3.25 3.25
*Nos. 678-681 (4)* 2.85 2.85

125th Anniv. of Telecommunication Service — A260

**1983, May 17 *Perf. 12x12½***

**682** A260 2r shown .80 *.60*
**683** A260 10r World Communications Year 2.50 *3.00*

Gam Udawa Village Re-awakening Movement — A261

**1983, June 23 Litho. *Perf. 12x12½***

**684** A261 50c Family .20 .25
**685** A261 5r Village .65 1.00

Cattle Transport A262

**1983, Aug. 1 Litho. *Perf. 12***

**686** A262 35c shown .20 .20
**687** A262 2r Train 2.25 2.25
**688** A262 2.50r Cattle cart 1.10 1.10
**689** A262 5r Model T Ford 2.50 2.50
*Nos. 686-689 (4)* 6.05 6.05

Sir Tikiri Banda Panabokke, 20th Death Anniv. — A263

**1983, Sept. 2 Litho. *Perf. 13½x14***

**690** A263 50c dark red 1.10 1.10

Ceylon Wood Pigeon A264

**1983, Dec. 1 Litho. *Perf. 14½***

**691** A264 25c shown .75 .75
**692** A264 35c Ceylon white-eye .75 .75
**693** A264 2r Dusky-blue flycatcher 1.10 1.10
**694** A264 20r Ceylon coucal 1.75 1.75
*a.* Souvenir sheet of 4, #691-694 6.00 6.00
*Nos. 691-694 (4)* 4.35 4.35

See No. 877. For surcharge see No. 780A.

Christmas, Stone Carvings — A265

**1983, Dec. 5 Litho. *Perf. 12½x13***

**695** A265 50c multicolored .20 .20
**696** A265 5r ultra & bister .50 .50
*a.* Souv. sheet, #695-696+label .85 1.75

A266

A267

**1983, Nov. 25 Litho. *Perf. 14x15***

**697** A266 50c brown 1.75 1.75

Rev. Pelene Thero (1878-1955), Buddhist leader.

**1983 Litho. *Perf. 13½***

**698** A267 50c Ahamed Orabi Al-Misri 1.10 1.10

#611 Surcharged with Four Bars, #611A with Three Bars and New Denomination in Black or Green

**1983-85 Photo. *Perf. 13***

**698A** A189 60c on 50c ('83) 4.00 2.00

**Size: 20x24mm**

**698B** A189 75c on 60c (G) ('85) .20 .20

Ovpt. on No. 698A also exists with two bars. Value, $6.50.

Issue dates: both Dec. 1.

World Food Day (Oct. 16) A268

**1984, Jan. 2 *Perf. 12½x12***

**699** A268 3r Rice paddy .40 .75

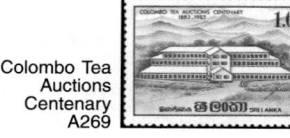


Colombo Tea Auctions Centenary A269

**1984, Jan. 31**

**700** A269 1r Auction House .25 .20
**701** A269 2r Emblem .45 .45
**702** A269 5r Tea picker 1.10 1.25
**703** A269 10r Auction 2.25 2.50
*Nos. 700-703 (4)* 4.05 4.40

Mahapola Anniversary (Educational System) — A270

**1984, Feb. 10 *Perf. 12***

**704** A270 60c Students .20 .20
**705** A270 1r Classroom .20 .20
**706** A270 5.50r Student in library, lab .35 .75
**707** A270 6r Emblem .40 .75
*Nos. 704-707 (4)* 1.15 1.90

Vesak Festival 1984 A271

Wooden Casket Paintings, Temple Godapitiya Rajamaha Vihara, Akuressa: Scenes from Daham Sonda Jathaka legend.

**1984, Apr. 27 Litho. *Perf. 14***

**708** A271 35c multicolored .20 .20
**709** A271 60c multicolored .65 .55
**710** A271 5r multicolored 1.50 1.60
**711** A271 10r multicolored 2.00 2.00
*a.* Souv. sheet of 4, #708-711, perf. 13x13½ 2.50 2.50
*Nos. 708-711 (4)* 4.35 4.35

Lions Club Intl., District 306A — A272

**1984, May 5 Litho. *Perf. 14x14½***

**712** A272 60c multicolored 1.60 1.10

Famous Men Type of 1981

Designs: No. 713, K. Balasingham, lawyer. No. 714, Mohamed Macan Markar (1879-1952), Muslim politician. No. 715, W. Arthur de Silva (d. 1942), industrialist. No. 716, Tissa Mahanayake Thero (1826-1907), Buddhist educator. No. 717, G.P. Wickremarachchi, medical pioneer.

**1984, May 22 Litho. *Perf. 12x12½***

**713** A224 60c brown .30 .50
**714** A224 60c green .30 .50
**715** A224 60c orange red .30 .50
**716** A224 60c bister .30 .50
**717** A224 60c yellow green .30 .50
*Nos. 713-717 (5)* 1.50 2.50

Public Service Mutual Provident Assoc. Centenary A273

**1984, June 16 *Perf. 13x13½***

**718** A273 4.60r Emblem .75 1.25

Village Re-awakening Movement A274

**1984, June 23 *Perf. 12x12½***

**719** A274 60c "One Million Houses" .50 .50

Asia-Pacific Broadcasting Union, 20th Anniv. — A275

**1984, June 30 *Perf. 12½x12***

**720** A275 7r Map 2.75 2.75

For surcharge see No. 776.

Cultural Pageant A276

Procession: a, Drummers, elephant. b, Torch bearers, 3 elephants (green or red masks). c, Torch bearers, 3 elephants (orange or yellow masks). d, Dancers. Continuous design.

**1984, Aug. 11 Litho. *Perf. 12½x12***

**721** Strip of 4 5.75 5.75
*a.-d.* A276 4.60r any single 1.25 1.25
*e.* Souvenir sheet of 4 5.75 5.75

Orchid Circle of Sri Lanka, 50th Anniversary A277

**1984, Aug. 31 *Perf. 14***

**722** A277 60c Vanda memoria 1.50 1.50
**723** A277 4.60r Acanthephippium bicolor 3.00 3.00

724 A277 5r Vanda Tesselata 2.00 2.00
725 A277 10r Anoectochillus setaceus 6.50 6.50
*a.* Souvenir sheet of 4, #722-725 12.50 *12.50*
*Nos. 722-725 (4)* 13.00 13.00

Wildlife Type of 1981

**1982-89 Litho. *Perf. 14***

728 A219 2.50r Felis viverrina .30 .25
729 A219 3r Paradoxurus zeylonensis 4.25 4.25
730 A219 4r Tragulus meminna .30 .30
730A A219 5r Felis rubiginosa ('89) .40 .30
*Nos. 728-730A (4)* 5.25 5.10

No. 729 has brown inscriptions. See No. 928 for black inscriptions.

No. 728 is unwatermarked.

Issued: 2.50r, 6/1/83; 3r, 6/21/83; 4r, 11/16/82; 5r, 12/1/89.

No. 728 Surcharged in Brown

**1985, Dec. 1 Litho. *Perf. 14***

731 A219 5.75r on 2.50r multi 4.00 1.75

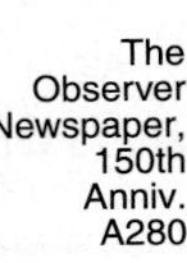

The Observer Newspaper, 150th Anniv. A280

**1984, Aug. 31 Litho. *Perf. 13x13½***

732 A280 4.60r Publisher, Colombo 2.90 2.90

Natl. School Games — A281

**1984, Oct. 5 *Perf. 13½x13***

733 A281 60c blue, gray & blk 2.50 2.00

D. S. Senanayake (1884-1952), Prime Minister — A282

**1984, Oct. 20 *Perf. 14½x14***

734 A282 35c Irrigated field .20 .20
735 A282 60c Statue .20 .20
736 A282 4.60r Reservoir .30 .30
737 A282 6r Parliament House, Colombo .45 .45
*Nos. 734-737 (4)* 1.15 1.15

World Food Program — A284

Baari Arabic College, Weligama, Cent. — A285

**1984, Dec. 10 Litho. *Perf. 13x13½***

738 A284 7r Globe, Sri Lankans working field 1.90 1.40

**1984, Dec. 24 *Perf. 13x12½***

739 A285 4.60r dull bl grn & blk 1.50 1.50

Intl. Youth Year — A286

World Religion Day — A287

**1985, Jan. 1 *Perf. 12½x13***

740 A286 4.60r multicolored .80 .60
741 A286 20r multicolored 2.50 2.50

For surcharge see No. 790.

**1985, Jan. 20 *Perf. 12***

Design: Emblems of World religions.

742 A287 4.60r multicolored 2.50 2.50

Royal College, Colombo, 150th Anniv. — A288

Mahapola Scholarship Program for Development & Education, 5th Anniv. — A289

**1985, Jan. 29 *Perf. 13x12½***

743 A288 60c College crest .20 .25
744 A288 7r Campus 2.25 2.25

**1985, Feb. 7 *Perf. 14***

745 A289 60c Diplomas, freighter, office buildings 1.00 1.00

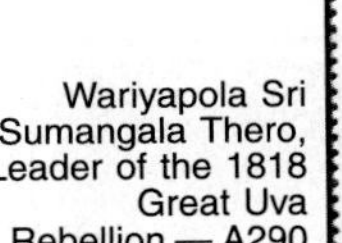

Wariyapola Sri Sumangala Thero, Leader of the 1818 Great Uva Rebellion — A290

**1985, Mar. 2 *Perf. 13x13½***

746 A290 60c brown & yellow .80 .80

Victoria Project A291

***Perf. 12½x12, 12x12½***

**1985, Apr. 12 Litho.**

747 A291 60c Victoria Dam .90 .90
748 A291 7r Dam, map, vert. 5.25 5.25

Vesak Festival 1985 — A292

Natl. Heroes — A293

Designs: 35c, Frontispiece of the Buddhist Annual golden jubilee issue. 60c, Women worshiping at temple, Vesak Poya Holiday cent. 6r, Bauddha Mandiraya, Colombo. 9r, Buddhist flag cent.

**1985, Apr. 26 *Perf. 13x12½***

749 A292 35c multicolored .20 .20
750 A292 60c multicolored .20 .20
751 A292 6r multicolored .70 .70
752 A292 9r multicolored 1.40 1.40
*a.* Souvenir sheet of 4, #749-752 6.25 6.25
*Nos. 749-752 (4)* 2.50 2.50

**1985, May 22 *Perf. 13x12½***

#753,753, Waskaduwe Sri Subhuthi Thero (1835-1917), Pali scholar, philologist responsible for the Sinhala dictionary. #754, Rev. Fr. Peter A. Pillai (1904-64), educational & social reformer. #755, Dr. Senarath Paranavitane (c. 1900-72), epigraphist. #756, A.M. Wapche Marikar (1829-1925), educational reformer, architect.

Pale Yellow Orange and

753 A293 60c tan .35 .35
754 A293 60c brt rose lilac .35 .35
755 A293 60c brown .35 .35
756 A293 60c emerald .35 .35
*Nos. 753-756 (4)* 1.40 1.40

Gam Udawa — Yovur Udanaya Village Reformation Movement A294

**1985, June 23 *Perf. 13½x13***

757 A294 60c multicolored 1.25 1.25

Colombo Young Poets Assoc., 50th Anniv. — A295

**1985, June 25 *Perf. 14***

758 A295 60c Emblem 1.40 1.40

Kothmale Project Commission — A296

**1985, Aug. 24**

759 A296 60c Dam, lake .85 .85
760 A296 6r Hydro-electric power station 4.00 4.00

A297

A298

Child Survival: 35c, Mother breastfeeding. 60c, Infant, oral inoculant. 6r, Weighing toddler. 9r, Infant, intravenous inoculant.

**1985, Sept. 1 Wmk. 385 *Perf. 13½***

761 A297 35c multicolored .35 .20
762 A297 60c multicolored .50 .30
763 A297 6r multicolored 2.25 *2.50*
764 A297 9r multicolored 2.75 *3.00*
*a.* Souvenir sheet of 4, #761-764 6.00 6.00
*Nos. 761-764 (4)* 5.85 6.00

**1985, Sept. 2 Unwmk. *Perf. 14***

765 A298 7r Womb, infant 4.75 4.75

10th Asian & Oceanic Congress of Obstetrics & Gynecology.

World Tourism Org., 10th Anniv. A299

**1985, Sept. 27 Litho. *Perf. 14***

766 A299 1r Conch shell horn .40 .20
767 A299 6r Parliament complex 1.00 1.00
768 A299 7r Tea plantation 1.25 1.25
769 A299 10r Buddhist monastery, Ruwanveliseya 1.75 1.75
*a.* Souv. sheet of 4, #766-769, perf. 13½ 7.00 7.00
*Nos. 766-769 (4)* 4.40 4.20

Land Development Ordinance, 50th Anniv. — A300

Sinhal Translation, Koran — A301

**1985, Oct. 15 *Perf. 14x15***

770 A300 4.60r Deeds presentation 3.00 3.25

**1985, Oct. 17 Wmk. 385 *Perf. 13½***

771 A301 60c violet & gold 2.00 1.75

Christmas — A302

**1985, Nov. 5 *Perf. 12***

772 A302 60c Our Lady of Matara .35 .20
773 A302 9r Our Lady of Madhu 1.75 2.00
*a.* Souvenir sheet of 2, #772-773 8.00 8.50

SAARC 1st Summit, Dec. 7-8 A303

**1985, Dec. 8 *Perf. 14½x14***

774 A303 60c shown 4.25 *4.25*
775 A303 5.50r Flags on UN emblem 4.25 *4.25*

No. 720 Surcharged in Intense Blue

**1986, Jan. 20 *Perf. 12½x12***

776 A275 1r on 7r Map 8.50 3.50

Viceroy Special Train A304

**1986, Feb. 2** ***Perf. 12½x13***

**777** A304 1r multicolored 1.75 1.50

Colombo-Kandy line inauguration.

Students A305

**1986, Feb. 14** ***Perf. 14***

**778** A305 75c multicolored .65 .65

Mahapola Scholarship Program for development and education, 6th anniv.

Don Richard Wijewardene (1886-1950), Newspaper Publisher — A306

Welitara Gnanatillake Mahanayake Thero (1858-1941), Scientist — A307

**1986, Feb. 23** ***Perf. 14x15***

**779** A306 75c sage grn & brn .35 .40

**1986, Feb. 26** **Wmk. 385** ***Perf. 13½***

**780** A307 75c multicolored .85 .90

No. 692 Surcharged

**1986, Mar. 10** **Litho.** ***Perf. 14½***

**780A** A264 7r on 35c 6.50 1.50

Natl. Red Cross Society, 50th Anniv. A308

**1986, Mar. 31** ***Perf. 12½x13***

**781** A308 75c multicolored 2.75 2.25

Halley's Comet A309

**1986, Apr. 5** ***Perf. 12½***

**782** A309 50c Comet is not an omen .20 .20
**783** A309 75c Constellations .20 .20
**784** A309 6.50r Trajectory diagrams .40 *1.00*
**785** A309 8.50r Edmond Halley .55 *1.50*
*a.* Souvenir sheet of 4, #782-785, perf. 12½x13 6.00 *7.75*
*Nos. 782-785 (4)* 1.35 2.90

Sinhalese and Tamil New Year — A310

Designs: 50c, Woman lighting lamp. 75c, Woman, holiday foods. 6.50r, Women celebrating around table. 8.50r, Food preparation, feast, anointment ritual.

**1986, Apr. 10**

**786** A310 50c multicolored .20 .20
**787** A310 75c multicolored .20 .20
**788** A310 6.50r multicolored .30 .80
**789** A310 8.50r multicolored .50 1.00
*a.* Souvenir sheet of 4, #786-789, perf. 13x12½ 5.00 5.00
*Nos. 786-789 (4)* 1.20 2.20

No. 740 Surcharged

**1986, Apr. 29** ***Perf. 12½x13***

**790** A286 1r on 4.60r multi 6.50 3.25

Vesak Festival A311

Jathaka Story frescoes from the house Samudragiri Vihara, Mirissa, recounting the life of Siddhartha (583-463 B.C.): 50c, King Kurudhamma Jathakaya gives elephant to the brahman. 75c, Vasavarthi heaven. 5r, Sujatha's milk rice offering. 10d, Thapassu and Bhalluka's parched corn and honey offering.

**1986, May 16**

**791** A311 50c multicolored .20 .20
**792** A311 75c multicolored .20 .20
**793** A311 5d multicolored .60 *1.50*
**794** A311 10d multicolored .70 *2.00*
*Nos. 791-794 (4)* 1.70 3.90

Natl. Heroes — A312

Natl. Cooperative Movement, 75th Anniv. — A313

#795, Kalukondayave Sri Prajnasekhara Mahanayaka Thero (1895-1977), theologian. #796, Brahmachari Walisinghe Harischandra (1876-1913), historian, social reformer. #797, Martin Wickramasinghe (1890-1970), author. #798, Ganapathipillai Gangaser Ponnambalam (1901-72), diplomat. #799, Aboobucker Mohammed Abdul Azeez (1911-73), scholar.

**1986, May 22** ***Perf. 13x12½***

**795** A312 75c multicolored .20 .45
**796** A312 75c multicolored .20 .45
**797** A312 75c multicolored .20 .45
**798** A312 75c multicolored .20 .45
**799** A312 75c multicolored .20 .45
*Nos. 795-799 (5)* 1.00 2.25

**1986, June 23**

**800** A313 1r multicolored 1.50 1.75

Gam Udawa, Intl. Year of Housing A314

**1986, June 23** ***Perf. 13½x13***

**801** A314 75c multicolored 1.90 1.90

Arthur V. Dias — A315

**1986, July 31** ***Perf. 14x15***

**802** A315 1r multicolored 1.90 2.00

World Wildlife Fund A316

Elephants: a, Adult with tusks. b, Adult, calf. c, Adult. d, Family in river.

**1986, Aug. 5** ***Perf. 15x14***

**803** Strip of 4 *62.50 35.00*
*a.-d.* A316 5r any single *13.50 8.50*

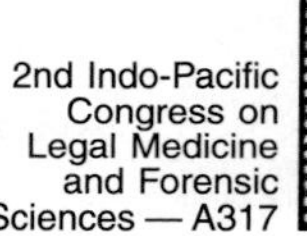

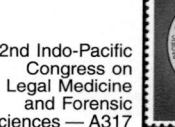

2nd Indo-Pacific Congress on Legal Medicine and Forensic Sciences — A317

**1986, Aug. 14** ***Perf. 13½x13***

**804** A317 8.50r multicolored 3.50 3.50

Submarine Cable — A318

**1986, Sept. 8** ***Perf. 13½x14***

**805** A318 5.75r Handset, map 5.25 3.50

South-East Asia, Middle East, Western Europe Submarine Cable System.

Dag Hammarskjold Award — A320

Second Natl. School Games, Sept. 22-27 — A321

**1986, Sept. 20** **Litho.** ***Perf. 13x12½***

**808** A320 2r multicolored 1.40 1.10

**1986, Sept. 22** ***Perf. 12***

**809** A321 1r multicolored 3.50 2.00

Natl. Surveyor's Institute, 60th Anniv. — A322

**1986, Sept. 27** ***Perf. 13½x13***

**810** A322 75c multicolored .70 .80

Ananda College, Cent. A323

College crest and: 75c, College. 5r, Athletic field. 5.75r, Founders Migettuwatte Gunananda, Hikkaduwe Sumangala and Col. H.S. Olcott, Buddhist flag and College, 1886, 1986. 6r, Crest on flag.

**1986, Nov. 1** ***Perf. 12***

**811** A323 75c multicolored .20 .20
**812** A323 5r multicolored .30 .40
**813** A323 5.75r multicolored .35 .40
**814** A323 6r multicolored .45 .55
*Nos. 811-814 (4)* 1.30 1.55

Wildlife Conservation — A324

**1986, Nov. 11**

**815** A324 35c Mangrove habitat 1.00 1.00
**816** A324 50c Rhizophora apiculata 1.10 1.10
**817** A324 75c Germinating flower 1.25 1.25
**818** A324 6r Fiddler crab 9.00 9.00
*Nos. 815-818 (4)* 12.35 12.35

Preservation of mangrove habitats.

Intl. Year of Shelter for the Homeless A325

**1987, Jan. 1** **Litho.** ***Perf. 13x13½***

**819** A325 75c multicolored 2.40 .75

A.I. Thero, 19th Cent. Theologian A326

Proctor John De Silva (b. 1854), Lawyer and Playwright A327

**1987, Jan. 29** *Perf. 12*
**820** A326 5.75r multicolored 3.75 1.10

**1987, Jan. 31**
**821** A327 5.75r multicolored .85 .85

Mahapola Educational Plan, 7th Anniv. — A328

**1987, Feb. 6**
**822** A328 75c multicolored .85 .85

Dr. R.L. Brohier, Historian — A329

**1987, Feb. 14**
**823** A329 5.75r multicolored 3.25 1.50

Sri Lanka Tire Corp., 25th Anniv. A330

**1987, Mar. 23** *Perf. 14*
**824** A330 5.75r multicolored .70 .70

Sri Lanka Medical Assoc., Cent. A331

**1987, Mar. 24** *Perf. 13x13½*
**825** A331 5.75r multicolored 3.00 3.25

Farmers' Pension and Social Security Plan — A332

AGRO MAHAWELI '87 Agricultural Exposition A333

**1987, Mar. 29** *Perf. 14*
**826** A332 75c multicolored 1.10 1.10

**1987, Apr. 2** *Perf. 12*
**827** A333 75c multicolored .50 .50

Child Immunization Program — A334

**1987, Apr. 7** *Perf. 13½*
**828** A334 1r multicolored 3.25 1.10

World Health Day.

Sinhalese and Tamil New Year — A335

**1987, Apr. 9** *Perf. 12*
**829** A335 75c Three girls, swing .20 .20
**830** A335 5r Lamp, women .60 .60

Vesak Festival Lanterns A336

**1987, May 4** *Perf. 12*
**831** A336 50c Lotus .20 .20
**832** A336 75c Octagonal .20 .20
**833** A336 5r Star .40 .40
**834** A336 10r Gok .60 .60
*a.* Souvenir sheet of 4, #831-834 1.50 1.50
*Nos. 831-834 (4)* 1.40 1.40

Natl. Olympic Committee, 50th Anniv. — A337

**1987, May 8** *Perf. 13½*
**835** A337 10r multicolored 3.25 1.40

Birds A338

**1987, May 18** *Perf. 14*
**836** A338 50c Layard's parakeet .65 .20
**837** A338 1r Legge's flowerpecker .95 .20
**838** A338 5r Sri Lanka white-headed starling 1.40 1.50
**839** A338 10r Sri Lanka rufous babbler 1.75 1.90
*a.* Souvenir sheet of 4, #836-839 7.50 7.50
*Nos. 836-839 (4)* 4.75 3.80

#839 exists dated "1990."

Natl. Heroes — A339

#840, Heenatiyana Sri Dhammaloka Thero, 20th cent. theologian. #841, P. de S. Kularatne, educator. #842, M.C. Abdul Rahuman, politician.

**1987, May 22** *Perf. 12*
**840** A339 75c multicolored .50 .35
**841** A339 75c multicolored .50 .35
**842** A339 75c multicolored .50 .35
*Nos. 840-842 (3)* 1.50 1.05

Gam Udawa A340

**1987, June 23**
**843** A340 75c multicolored .35 .35

Village reformation movement.

Natl. Forestry Agency, Cent. A341

**1987, June 25**
**844** A341 75c Mesua nagassarium .25 .25
**845** A341 5r Elephants in forest 1.75 1.75

Founder H.S. Olcott and College A342

**1987, June 30**
**846** A342 75c multicolored 2.50 .40

Dharmaraja College, cent.

No. 528 Redrawn with Denomination in Upper Right Corner

**1987, July 1 Photo.** *Perf. 13x13½*
**Size: 20x24mm**
**847** A189 75c green & gold .25 .20

Youth Services Emblem A343

**1987, July 15 Litho.** *Perf. 12*
**848** A343 75c multicolored .30 .30

Natl. Youth Services Act, 20th anniv.

Mahaweli Games — A344

Ceylon Bible Society, 175th Anniv. — A345

**1987, Sept. 5 Litho.** *Perf. 12*
**849** A344 75c multicolored 3.50 1.75

**1987, Oct. 2**
**850** A345 5.75r multicolored .70 .70

Kandy Friend-in-Need Society, 150th Anniv. — A346

**1987, Nov. 4** *Perf. 13½x13*
**851** A346 75c multicolored .35 .35

Christmas 1987 — A347

Sir Ernest de Silva (1887-1957), Banker, Philatelist — A348

**1987, Nov. 25 Litho.** *Perf. 12*
**852** A347 75c Mother and Child .20 .20
**853** A347 10r Infant, star, dove .50 .50
*a.* Souvenir sheet of 2, #852-853 1.50 1.50

**1987, Nov. 25** *Perf. 13x13½*
**854** A348 75c multicolored .35 .35

1st Convocation Ceremony at Buddhist and Pali University — A349

Missionary Work of Fr. Joseph Vaz (1651-1711), 300th Anniv. — A350

**1987, Dec. 14** *Perf. 12*
**855** A349 75c yel, lake & org yel .35 .35

**1987, Dec. 15**
**856** A350 75c multicolored .35 .35

Buddhist Publication Soc., Kandy, 30th Anniv. — A351

Design: Wheel of Life, dagaba (temple cupola) and Bo (Tree of Life) leaf.

**1988, Jan. 1** **Litho.** *Perf. 12*
**857** A351 75c multicolored .35 .35

Mahapola Dharmayatra, 5th Anniv. A352

**1988, Jan. 4** *Perf. 13½x13*
**858** A352 75c multicolored .50 .50

Ceylon Arts Soc., Cent. — A353

**1988, Jan. 8** *Perf. 12*
**859** A353 75c multicolored .85 .75

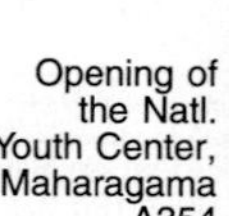

Opening of the Natl. Youth Center, Maharagama A354

**1988, Jan. 31** *Perf. 13½x13*
**860** A354 1r multicolored 3.50 .50

Natl. Independence, 40th Anniv. — A355

Mahapola Movement, 8th Anniv. — A356

**1988, Feb. 4** *Perf. 12*
**861** A355 75c shown .20 .20
**862** A355 8.50r Heraldic lion, "40" .90 .90

**1988, Feb. 11**
**863** A356 75c Youth Education Services .25 .25

Transportation Board, 30th Anniv. — A357

**1988, Feb. 19**
**864** A357 5.75r multicolored .70 .70

Weligama Sri Sumangala Maha Nayake Thero (1825-1905), Buddhist Monk, Sanskrit Scholar — A358

**1988, Mar. 13**
**865** A358 75c multicolored .25 .25

Artillery Regiment, Cent. A359

**1988, Apr. 20**
**866** A359 5.75r multicolored 3.00 .90

Chevalier I.X. Pereira (1888-1951), Politician — A360

**1988, Apr. 26** **Litho.** *Perf. 12*
**867** A360 5.75r multicolored .35 .35

Vesak Festival A361

Paintings in Suriyagoda Sri Narendraramaya Viharaya temple, Kandy District: 50c, Buddha inviting deities and brahmas to be born into the world as Buddhists. 75c, Buddha walking seven steps on seven lotus flowers, followers paying homage.

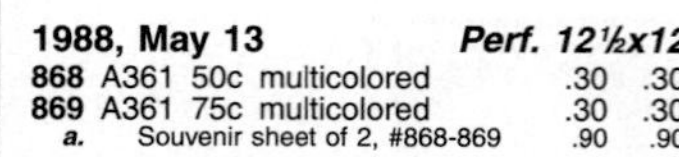

**1988, May 13** *Perf. 12½x12*
**868** A361 50c multicolored .30 .30
**869** A361 75c multicolored .30 .30
*a.* Souvenir sheet of 2, #868-869 .90 .90

Natl. Heroes — A362

Designs: No. 870, Rev.-Father Ferdinand Bonnel (1873-1945), Jesuit priest who founded St. Michael's College, Batticaloa. No. 871, Sir Razik Fareed (1893-1984), political and social reformer. No. 872, W.F. Gunawardhana (b. 1861), founder of the Oriental Studies Soc. No. 873, Edward Alexander Nugawela (1898-1972), politician. No. 874, Sir Edwin Arthur Lewis Wijeyewardene (b. 1887), first Ceylonese chief justice, attorney general.

**1988, May 22** *Perf. 12x12½*
**870** A362 75c multicolored .25 .25
**871** A362 75c multicolored .25 .25
**872** A362 75c multicolored .25 .25
**873** A362 75c multicolored .25 .25
**874** A362 75c multicolored .25 .25
*Nos. 870-874 (5)* 1.25 1.25

Gam Udawa, 10th Anniv. A363

**1988, June 23** **Litho.** *Perf. 12*
**875** A363 75c multicolored .50 .25

Village reformation movement.

Maliyadeva College, Cent. — A364

**1988, June 30** *Perf. 13½x13*
**876** A364 75c multicolored .50 .25

Bird Type of 1983

**1988, Sept. 28** **Litho.** *Perf. 14½*
**877** A264 7r like No. 692 .55 .55

Mohamed J.M. Lafir (1929-1980), World Amateur Billiards Champion — A365

**1988, July 5** **Litho.** *Perf. 12½x12*
**878** A365 5.75r multicolored .50 .50

Australia Bicentennial — A366

**1988, July 19** **Litho.** *Perf. 12*
**879** A366 8.50r multicolored .85 .60

A367

A368

**1988, Aug. 11** *Perf. 12x12½*
**880** A367 75c multicolored .40 .25

Gunaratna Maha Nayake Thero (1752-1832), Buddhist and Sinhalese language scholar.

**1988, Sept. 3** *Perf. 12*
**881** A368 75c multicolored .40 .25

Mahaweli games.

1988 Summer Olympics, Seoul — A369

WHO, 40th Anniv. — A370

**1988, Sept. 6** *Perf. 12x12½*
**882** A369 75c Running .20 .20
**883** A369 1r Swimming .20 .20
**884** A369 5.75r Boxing .45 .45
**885** A369 8.50r Handshake, map, emblems .75 .75
*a.* Souvenir sheet of 4, #882-885 2.25 2.25
*Nos. 882-885 (4)* 1.60 1.60

**1988, Sept. 12** *Perf. 12*
**886** A370 75c multicolored .35 .35

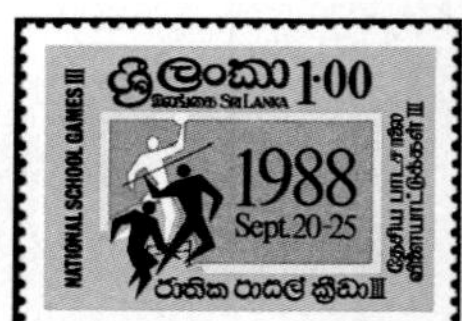

3rd Natl. School Games, Sept. 20-25 A371

**1988, Sept. 20**
**887** A371 1r multicolored 3.50 .50

Mahatma Gandhi — A372

**1988, Oct. 2** ***Perf. 12***
**888** A372 75c multicolored 1.25 .40

Transportation and Communication Decade, 1978-88 — A373

Modes of transportation and: 75c, Globe. 5.75r, Communication tower.

**1988, Oct. 24 Litho.** ***Perf. 12½x12***
**889** A373 75c multicolored .55 .20
**890** A373 5.75r multicolored 2.90 1.75

Randenigala Project — A374

**1988, Oct. 31** ***Perf. 12***
**891** A374 75c Woman, dam, power station .20 .20
**892** A374 5.75r Hydrelectric dam .65 .65

Some copies were distributed at the time the set was originally planned to be issued in 1986.

A375

Christmas — A376

**1988, Nov. 17 Litho.** ***Perf. 13½***
**893** A375 75c multicolored .35 .35

Opening of Gramodaya Folk Art Center.

**1988, Nov. 25** ***Perf. 12x12½***
**894** A376 75c shown .20 .20
**895** A376 8.50r Shepherds see star .70 .70
*a.* Souvenir sheet of 2, #894-895 2.50 2.50

A377

Waterfalls — A378

**1988, Dec. 28** ***Perf. 12***
**896** A377 75c multicolored .20 .20

E.W. Adikaram (1905-85), educator.

**1989, Aug. 11 Litho.** ***Perf. 12***
**897** A378 75c Dunhinda .20 .20
**898** A378 1r Rawana .20 .20
**899** A378 5.75r Laxapana 1.00 1.00
**900** A378 8.50r Diyaluma 1.25 1.25
*Nos. 897-900 (4)* 2.65 2.65

Free Distribution of School Text Books, 10th Anniv. A379

**1989, Jan. 23 Litho.** ***Perf. 13½x13***
**901** A379 75c multicolored .25 .25

Poets — A380

**1989, Jan. 27** ***Perf. 13***
**902** A380 75c Wimalaratne Kumaragama .25 .25
**903** A380 75c G.H. Perera .25 .25
**904** A380 75c Sagara Palansuriya .25 .25
**905** A380 75c P.B. Alwis Perera .25 .25
*Nos. 902-905 (4)* 1.00 1.00

Mahapola Educational Plan, 8th Anniv. — A381

**1989, Feb.** ***Perf. 13½***
**906** A381 75c multicolored .25 .20

Chamber of Commerce, 150th Anniv. — A382

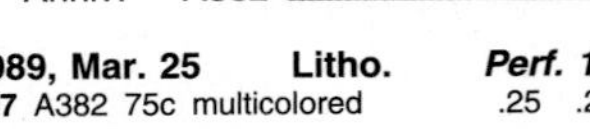
**1989, Mar. 25 Litho.** ***Perf. 12***
**907** A382 75c multicolored .25 .20

AGRO Mahaweli A383

**1989, Sept. 2 Litho.** ***Perf. 12***
**908** A383 75c multicolored .25 .20

Famous Men A384

**1989, May 22**
**909** A384 75c Simon Casie Chitty .25 .25
**910** A384 75c Parawahera Sri Vajiragnana Thero .25 .25
**911** A384 75c Fr. Maurice Le Goc .25 .25
**912** A384 75c Hemapala Munidasa .25 .25
**913** A384 75c Ananda Samarakoon .25 .25
*Nos. 909-913 (5)* 1.25 1.25

Nos. 910-913 vert.

Hartley College, 150th Anniv. (in 1988) — A385

**1989, June 5**
**914** A385 75c multicolored .25 .20

Vesak Festival A386

Various paintings in Medawala Viharaya, Harispattuwa.

**1989, May 15 Litho.** ***Perf. 12½x12***
**915** A386 50c multicolored .20 .20
**916** A386 75c multicolored .25 .20
**917** A386 5r multicolored .55 .40
**918** A386 5.75r multicolored .65 .50
*a.* Souvenir sheet of 4, #915-918 1.90 1.90
*Nos. 915-918 (4)* 1.65 1.30

For surcharge see No. 953A.

Pres. Premadasa's Declaration Establishing the Ministry of Buddha Sasana — A387

**1989, June 18 Litho.** ***Perf. 12½x12***
**919** A387 75c multicolored .35 .35

Gam Udawa, 11th Anniv. A388

**1989, June 23**
**920** A388 75c multicolored .35 .25

Village reformation movement.

French Revolution, Bicent. A389

**1989, Aug. 26 Litho.** ***Perf. 13½x13***
**921** A389 8.50r rose & deep blue 1.25 1.25

Bank of Ceylon, 50th Anniv. A390

**1989, Aug. 31**
**922** A390 75c Old, new headquarters .20 .20
**923** A390 5r Emblem, flowers .65 .50

Jana Saviya Grants A391

**1989, June 23 Litho.** ***Perf. 12x11½***
**924** A391 75c multicolored .35 .35

Development program to eliminate poverty and improve the standard of living through education and by providing food, health care, shelter and clothing.

See No. 953. For surcharge see No. 955.

Baptist Mission, 177th Anniv. A392

**1989, Aug. 19** ***Perf. 12½x12***
**925** A392 5.75r James Chater, church, 1812 .35 .35

State Literary Festival — A393

Wilhelm Geiger — A394

**1989, Sept. 22** *Perf. 12x11½*
**926** A393 75c multicolored .35 .25

**1989, Sept. 30** *Perf. 13x13½*
**927** A394 75c multicolored .35 .25

Wilhelm Geiger (1856-1943), German philologist who studied Sinhalese.

Wildlife Type of 1981

**1989, Oct. 11** *Perf. 14*
**928** A219 3r like No. 595 3.50 .35

No. 928 has black inscriptions and is dated "1989." See No. 729 for brown inscriptions.

Famous Lawyers — A395

Sir Cyril de Zoysa — A396

**1989, Oct. 16** *Perf. 12x11½*
**929** A395 75c H.V. Perera (1890-1969) .25 .25
**930** A395 75c Sir Ivor Jennings (1903-1965) .25 .25

**1989, Oct. 26** *Perf. 13x13½*
**931** A396 75c multicolored .35 .25

Sir Cyril de Zoysa (1896-1978), key figure in the Buddhist cultural reformation.

Asia-Pacific Telecommunity, 10th Anniv. — A397

**1989, Nov. 1** *Perf. 12x12½*
**932** A397 5.75r multicolored .80 .55

Sri Sucharitha Viyaparaya Oratory Children's Soc., 50th Anniv. A398

**1989, Nov. 9** *Perf. 13*
**933** A398 75c multicolored .50 .50

1st Moon Landing, 20th Anniv. — A399

Christmas — A400

**1989, Nov. 10** *Perf. 12x12½*
**934** A399 75c Apollo 11 liftoff, crew .20 .20
**935** A399 1r Astronaut descending ladder .25 .20
**936** A399 2r Astronaut on lunar surface .45 .40
**937** A399 5.75r Lunar surface, view of Earth 1.25 .70
*a.* Souvenir sheet of 4, #934-937 2.50 2.50
*Nos. 934-937 (4)* 2.15 1.50

**1989, Nov. 21** *Perf. 13½*
**938** A400 75c Adoration of the Shepherds .20 .20
**939** A400 8.50r Adoration of the Magi .65 .65
*a.* Souvenir sheet of 2, #938-939 1.75 1.75

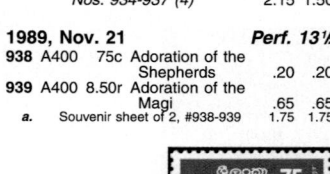

Devananda Nayake Thero — A401

**1989, Nov. 25** *Perf. 12x11½*
**940** A401 75c multicolored .35 .35

Devananda Nayake Thero (1921-1983), religious scholar, educator, reformer.

Rev. William Ault, College and Crest A402

**1989, Nov. 29** *Perf. 11½x12*
**941** A402 75c multicolored .35 .25

Batticaloa Methodist Central College, 175th anniv.

Nuwara Eliya Golf Club, Cent. A403

**1989, Dec. 8** *Perf. 14x13½*
**942** A403 75c shown 2.75 .35
**943** A403 8.50r Course, golf house 8.00 6.75

Raja — A404

**1989, Dec. 12** *Perf. 13x13½*
**944** A404 75c multicolored 6.00 1.00

Raja (1913-1988), the royal tusker of the Sri Dalada Maligawa that carried the relic casket in the Kandy Esala Procession.

Gampaha Wickamarachchi Ayurveda Medical College, 60th Anniv. — A405

**1989, Dec. 14** *Perf. 13½x13*
**945** A405 75c Founder, institute .60 .35

Udunuwara Sri Sarananda Mahanayake Thero (1867-1947), Educator — A406

**1989, Dec. 20** *Perf. 12x12½*
**946** A406 75c multicolored .35 .25

Railway Dept., 125th Anniv. A407

**1989, Dec. 27** *Perf. 11½x12, 13 (3r)*
**947** A407 75c Train, viaduct .75 .25
**948** A407 2r Train, light signal, Maradana Station 1.75 .40
**949** A407 3r Steam locomotive, semaphore signal 1.75 .70
**950** A407 7r 1st train in Sri Lanka 3.50 1.40
*Nos. 947-950 (4)* 7.75 2.75

A408

A409

**1989, Dec. 28** *Perf. 13x13½*
**951** A408 75c multicolored 2.00 .35

Thomas Cooray (1901-88), 1st native Sri Lankan Cardinal.

**1990, Jan. 14** *Perf. 12x12½*
**952** A409 1r multicolored 3.00 .30

Justin Wijayawardena (1904-82), educator, politician.

Jana Saviya Grants Type of 1989

**1990, Jan. 31 Litho.** *Perf. 12x11½*
**953** A391 1r multicolored .25 .25

No. 918 Surcharged

**.25**

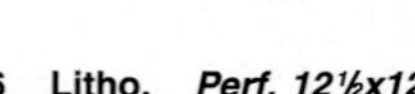

**1990, Feb. 16 Litho.** *Perf. 12½x12*
**953A** A386 25c on 5.75r multi 1.20 .25

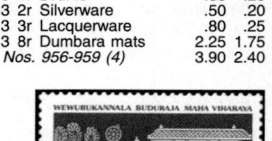

Induruwe Uttarananda Mahanayake Thero — A411

**1990, Mar. 15 Litho.** *Perf. 12*
**954** A411 1r multicolored 2.00 1.40

No. 924 Surcharged **1.00**

**1990, Mar. 22 Litho.** *Perf. 12x11½*
**955** A391 1r on 75c multi 2.50 1.40

Silver Jubilee of Laksala A413

Traditional handicrafts.

**1990, Apr. 2 Litho.** *Perf. 12*
**956** A413 1r Drums .35 .20
**957** A413 2r Silverware .50 .20
**958** A413 3r Lacquerware .80 .25
**959** A413 8r Dumbara mats 2.25 1.75
*Nos. 956-959 (4)* 3.90 2.40

Vesak Festival A414

Various paintings in Wewurukannala Buduraja Maha Viharaya.

**1990, May 2** *Perf. 12½x12*
**960** A414 75c multicolored .20 .20
**961** A414 1r multicolored .20 .20
**962** A414 2r multicolored .25 .25

**963** A414 8r multicolored .85 .85
*a.* Souvenir sheet of 4, #960-963 2.00 2.00
*Nos. 960-963 (4)* 1.50 1.50

A415

Famous Men — A416

**1990, May 22** ***Perf. 12***
**964** A415 1r Rev. T.M.F. Long .50 .30

**Size: 25x39mm**

***Perf. 12x12½***
**965** A416 1r D.P.A. Wijewardene .50 .30
**966** A416 1r L.T.P. Manjusri .50 .30
**967** A416 1r M.D. Ratnasuriya .50 .30
*Nos. 964-967 (4)* 2.00 1.20

Gam Udawa Program, 12th Anniv. A417

**1990, June 23** ***Perf. 12½x12***
**968** A417 1r multicolored 2.25 .50

Dept. of Archaeology, Cent. — A418

1r, Gold reliquary from Delivala Temple, c. 200 B.C. 2r, Statuette of Ganesha (the Elephant God) from Polonnaruwa. 3r, Terrace of the Bodhi-tree at Isurumuni Vihara. 8r, Stone seat with inscription of King Nissankamalle, 12th cent. A.D.

**1990, July 7** ***Perf. 12***
**969** A418 1r black & orange .35 .20
**970** A418 2r black & gray .60 .20
**971** A418 3r black, yel grn & gold .80 .35
**972** A418 8r black & gold 2.00 1.40
*Nos. 969-972 (4)* 3.75 2.15

Sri Lanka Tennis Assoc., 75th Anniv. A419

**1990, Aug. 14** ***Perf. 13½***
**973** A419 1r Player ready to volley .80 .80
**974** A419 1r Player receiving volley .80 .80
*a.* Pair, #973-974 1.75 1.75
**975** A419 8r Men players 2.75 2.75
**976** A419 8r Women players 2.75 2.75
*a.* Pair, #975-976 6.25 6.25
*Nos. 973-976 (4)* 7.10 7.10

Fish — A420

**1990, Sept. 14** ***Perf. 11½***
**977** A420 25c Spotted loach .30 .30
**978** A420 2r Ornate paradise fish .45 .45
**979** A420 8r Mountain labeo 1.10 1.10
**980** A420 20r Cherry barb 2.25 2.25
*a.* Souvenir sheet of 4, #977-980 5.00 5.00
*Nos. 977-980 (4)* 4.10 4.10

A421

A422

**1990, Dec. 26** ***Perf. 12***
**981** A421 1r Letter box, 1904 .65 .45
**982** A421 2r Mail runner, 1815 1.25 .65
**983** A421 5r Mail coach, 1832 2.50 2.10
**984** A421 10r Nuwara-Eliya Post Office, 1894 3.25 3.25
*Nos. 981-984 (4)* 7.65 6.45

Sri Lanka Postal Service, 175th anniv.

**1990, Oct. 28** **Litho.** ***Perf. 12***
**985** A422 1r multicolored 4.50 1.25

Rukmani Devi (1923-78), actress.

Christmas A423

**1990, Nov. 28** ***Perf. 13***
**986** A423 1r Mary, Joseph at inn .50 .30
**987** A423 10r Adoration of the Magi 4.50 4.00
*a.* Souv. sheet of 2, #986-987, perf. 12 6.00 6.00

World AIDS Day A424

**1990, Nov. 30**
**988** A424 1r multicolored 1.00 .20
**989** A424 8r AIDS Virus 5.00 3.25

A425

A426

**1990, Dec. 8** ***Perf. 12***
**990** A425 1r multicolored 3.00 1.40

Dharmapala College, 50th anniv.

**1990, Dec. 14** **Litho.** ***Perf. 12***
**991** A426 1r olive green & brown 4.00 1.40

Peri Sunderam (b. 1890), political & social reformer.

Ceylon Institute of Chemistry, 50th anniv. — A427

**1991, Jan. 25** **Litho.** ***Perf. 12***
**992** A427 1r multicolored 3.75 1.40

Vesak Festival A428

Various scenes from Buddha's life.

**1991, May 17** **Litho.** ***Perf. 12***
**993** A428 75c multicolored .40 .20
**994** A428 1r multicolored .40 .20
**995** A428 2r multicolored .70 .35
**996** A428 11r multicolored 3.50 3.00
*a.* Souvenir sheet of 4, #993-996 5.50 5.50
*Nos. 993-996 (4)* 5.00 3.75

A429

A430

**1991, May 31** ***Perf. 12***
**997** A429 1r multicolored 1.75 1.00

Mahabodhi Society, cent.

**1991, May 22** **Litho.** ***Perf. 12x12½***

Famous men.

**998** A430 1r Narada Thero .65 .55
**999** A430 1r Sir Muttu Coomaraswamy .65 .55
**1000** A430 1r Dr. Andreas Nell .65 .55
**1001** A430 1r W.A. Silva .65 .55
*Nos. 998-1001 (4)* 2.60 2.20

Gam Udawa, 13th Anniv. A431

**1991, June 23** **Litho.** ***Perf. 12½***
**1002** A431 1r multicolored 3.00 .85

Henpitagedera Gnanaseeha Nayake Thero (1909-1981), Religious Leader — A432

**1991, Aug. 1**
**1003** A432 1r multicolored 2.25 .85

Colombo Plan, 40th Anniv. A433

**1991, July 1** **Litho.** ***Perf. 12***
**1004** A433 1r multicolored 2.25 .85

Survey Dept., 190th Anniv. A434

**1991, Aug. 2** ***Perf. 12½***
**1005** A434 1r multicolored 2.25 .85

Police Service, 125th Anniv. A435

**1991, Sept. 3** **Litho.** ***Perf. 12½***
**1006** A435 1r multicolored 1.60 .60

6th SAARC Summit A436

**1991, Dec. 21** **Litho.** ***Perf. 12½***
**1007** A436 1r shown .20 .20
**1008** A436 8r Flags encircling bldg. .60 .50

Kingswood College, Cent. — A437

**1991, Oct. 26** *Perf. 12½x12*
**1009** A437 1r multicolored .80 .40

Christmas — A439

**1991, Nov. 19 Litho.** *Perf. 12½*
**1014** A439 1r The Annunciation .30 .20
**1015** A439 10r Nativity scene 1.25 1.25
*a.* Sheet of 2, #1014-1015 1.90 1.90

A440

**1991, Nov. 23**

Telecommunications: 1r, Early telephone network. 2r, Switchboard operations. 8r, Satellite transmitters, cable network. 10r, Telephone, fiber optic cable, computer, cordless telephone, FAX machine.

**1016** A440 1r multicolored .25 .20
**1017** A440 2r multicolored .30 .20
**1018** A440 8r multicolored .90 .90
**1019** A440 10r multicolored .90 .90
*Nos. 1016-1019 (4)* 2.35 2.20

5th South Asian Federation Games A441

**1991, Dec. 22** *Perf. 14*
**1020** A441 1r Mascot .30 .20
**1021** A441 2r Emblem .55 .25
**1022** A441 4r Stadium, Colombo 1.00 1.00
**1023** A441 11r Globe and flags 2.10 2.25
*Nos. 1020-1023 (4)* 3.95 3.70

Year of Exports A442

**1992, Jan. 13 Litho.** *Perf. 11½x12*
**1024** A442 1r multicolored 2.00 .85

Mahinda College, Cent. A443

**1992, Mar. 2 Litho.** *Perf. 11½x12*
**1025** A443 1r multicolored .25 .25

General Ranjan Wijeratne (1931-1991) A444

**1992, Mar. 2 Litho.** *Perf. 12x12½*
**1026** A444 1r multicolored .35 .20

Tea Production, 125th Anniv. A445

Field of tea and: 1r, Tea picker. 2r, Family, cup and glass of tea. 5r, Package of tea. 10r, James Taylor.

**1992, Feb. 12** *Perf. 13½*
**1027** A445 1r multicolored .55 .20
**1028** A445 2r multicolored 1.10 .25
**1029** A445 5r multicolored 2.75 2.40
**1030** A445 10r multicolored 3.75 3.25
*Nos. 1027-1030 (4)* 8.15 6.10

Newstead College, 175th Anniv. (in 1991) A446

**1992, Mar. 13 Litho.** *Perf. 11½x12*
**1031** A446 1r multicolored .25 .25

Dated 1991.

Mahapola Scholarship Fund, 11th Anniv. — A447

**1992, Mar. 30** *Perf. 12*
**1032** A447 1r multicolored .25 .25

Vesak Festival A448

Mural paintings from Kottimbulwala Rajamaha Vihara: 75c, Dukula and Parika retiring to forest. 1r, Sama and parents living in forest. 8r, Sama directing blind parents to hermitage. 11r, Sama's parents approach wounded son.

**1992, May 5 Litho.** *Perf. 11½x12*
**1033** A448 75c multicolored .20 .20
**1034** A448 1r multicolored .25 .20
**1035** A448 8r multicolored 1.25 1.25
**1036** A448 11r multicolored 1.75 1.75
*a.* Souvenir sheet, #1033-1036 3.25 3.25
*Nos. 1033-1036 (4)* 3.45 3.40

A449

A450

National Heroes: No. 1037, Wadeebhasinha Dewamottawe Amarawansa Thero. No. 1038, R. A. Mirando. No. 1039, Gate Mudaliyar N. Canaganayagam. No. 1040, I.L.M. Abdul Azeez.

**1992, May 22** *Perf. 14*
**1037** A449 1r multicolored .20 .20
**1038** A449 1r multicolored .20 .20
**1039** A449 1r multicolored .20 .20
**1040** A449 1r multicolored .20 .20
*Nos. 1037-1040 (4)* .80 .80

**1992, June 14 Litho.** *Perf. 12x12½*
**1041** A450 1r multicolored .25 .25

Introduction of Buddhism on Sri Lanka by Anubudu Mihindu Jayanthi, 2300th anniv.

Gam Udawa, 14th Anniv. A451

**1992, June 23** *Perf. 12*
**1042** A451 1r multicolored .25 .25

Postal Excellence Service Awards A452

Designs: 1r, Award presentation, postal work. 10r, Award of excellence medals, No. 1043 canceled on envelope.

**1992, July 11 Litho.** *Perf. 14*
**1043** A452 1r multicolored .35 .35
**1044** A452 10r multicolored 3.00 3.00

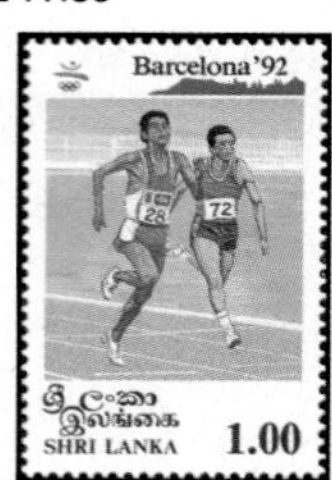

A454

A453

Masks of Sri Lanka.

**1992, Aug. 19 Litho.** *Perf. 13*
**1045** A453 1r Narilata .35 .20
**1046** A453 2r Mudali .45 .35
**1047** A453 5r Queen .90 .65
**1048** A453 10r King 1.50 1.50
*a.* Souvenir sheet, #1045-1048 3.50 3.50
*Nos. 1045-1048 (4)* 3.20 2.70

**1992, Sept. 15 Litho.** *Perf. 14*
**1049** A454 1r Running .30 .20
**1050** A454 11r Rifle shooting 2.00 2.00
**1051** A454 13r Swimming 2.50 2.50
**1052** A454 15r Weight lifting 2.75 2.75
*a.* Souvenir sheet, #1049-1052 10.00 10.00
*Nos. 1049-1052 (4)* 7.55 7.45

1992 Summer Olympics, Barcelona.

Cricket in Sri Lanka, 160th Anniv. A455

**1992, Sept. 8 Litho.** *Perf. 13*
**1053** A455 5r multicolored 4.25 3.00

Vijaya Kumaratunga, Entertainer and Political Leader, Birth Anniv. — A456

**1992, Oct. 9**
**1054** A456 1r multicolored .35 .30

Al-Bahjathul Ibraheemiyyah Arabic College, Cent. — A457

**1992, Oct. 24** *Perf. 12*
**1055** A457 1r multicolored .35 .30

A458

Christmas A459

**1992, Oct. 25 Litho.** *Perf. 12x11½*
**1056** A458 1r multicolored 1.25 .50

Dutch Reformed Church in Sri Lanka, 350th anniv.

**1992, Nov. 17 Litho.** *Perf. 12x11½*
**1057** A459 1r Holy Family .30 .20
**1058** A459 9r Church, family 1.90 1.90
*a.* Souvenir sheet, #1057-1058 2.50 2.50

Discovery of America, 500th Anniv. A460

Designs: 1r, Ships at sea, Aug. 1492. 11r, First landing in the Americas, Oct. 1492. 13r, Santa Maria aground, Dec. 1492. 15r, Return to Spain, Apr. 1493.

**1992, Dec. 1** ***Perf. 14***

**1059** A460 1r multicolored .60 .25
**1060** A460 11r multicolored 1.50 1.50
**1061** A460 13r multicolored 2.25 2.25
**1062** A460 15r multicolored 2.25 2.25
*a.* Souvenir sheet, #1059-1062 6.75 6.75
*Nos. 1059-1062 (4)* 6.60 6.25

No. 564 Surcharged 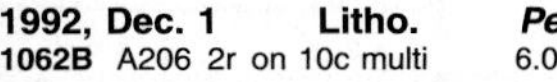


**1992, Dec. 1** **Litho.** ***Perf. 14***

**1062B** A206 2r on 10c multi 6.00 .75

Dambagasare Sri Sumedhankara Maha Nayake Thero (1892-1984), Buddhist Monk — A461

**1992, Dec. 10** **Litho.** ***Perf. 12***

**1063** A461 1r multicolored .25 .25

University Education in Sri Lanka A462

**1992, Dec. 12** **Litho.** ***Perf. 12***

**1064** A462 1r multicolored .25 .25

No. 1064 was not available until Dec. 1993.

University of Colombo, 50th Anniv. (in 1992) A463

**1993, Mar. 23** **Litho.** ***Perf. 13***

**1065** A463 1r multicolored .95 .30

Zahira College, Cent. A464

**1993, Apr. 7**

**1066** A464 1r multicolored 1.10 .35

Vesak Festival — A465

Designs based on verses from the Dhammapada (sermons of Buddha): 75c, Magandiya being presented to Buddha. 1r, Kisa Gotami carrying dead child. 3r, Patachara, dead family members. 10r, Conversion of Angulimala, the murderer.

**1993, Apr. 30** ***Perf. 12x12½***

**1067** A465 75c multicolored .20 .20
**1068** A465 1r multicolored .30 .30
**1069** A465 3r multicolored .60 .60
**1070** A465 10r multicolored 1.40 1.40
*a.* Souvenir sheet, #1067-1070 2.25 2.25
*Nos. 1067-1070 (4)* 2.50 2.50

A466

A467

**1993, May 10** ***Perf. 12***

**1071** A466 1r Guide, tent, emblem .55 .25
**1072** A466 5r Activities, map 2.00 1.75

Girl Guides in Sri Lanka, 75th Anniv. (in 1992).

**1993, May 22** ***Perf. 14***

National Heroes: No. 1073, Yagirala Sri Pagnananda Maha Nayaka Thero. No. 1074, C.P. De Silva. No. 1075, Wilmot A. Perera. No. 1076, N.D.H. Abdul Caffoor.

**1073** A467 1r multicolored .35 .35
**1074** A467 1r multicolored .35 .35
**1075** A467 1r multicolored .35 .35
**1076** A467 1r multicolored .35 .35
*Nos. 1073-1076 (4)* 1.40 1.40

Gam Udawa, 15th Anniv. A468

**1993, June 23** **Litho.** ***Perf. 12½***

**1077** A468 1r multicolored 1.60 .40

Co-operative Consumer Service, 50th Anniv. — A469

**1993, July 3** ***Perf. 13***

**1078** A469 1r multicolored 2.00 .40

Birds A470

Designs: 3r, Ashy-headed laughing thrush. 4r, Ceylon brown-capped babbler. 5r, Red-faced malkoha. 10r, Ceylon hill-mynah.

**1993, July 14** ***Perf. 12½x12***

**1079** A470 3r multicolored .40 .40
**1080** A470 4r multicolored .40 .40
**1081** A470 5r multicolored .55 .55
**1082** A470 10r multicolored 1.00 1.00
*a.* Souvenir sheet, #1079-1082 3.25 3.25
*Nos. 1079-1082 (4)* 2.35 2.35

Talawila Church, 150th Anniv. A471

**1993, July 26** ***Perf. 13***

**1083** A471 1r multicolored 1.25 .40

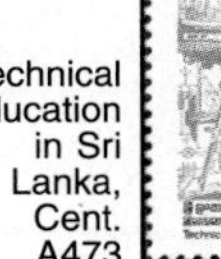


Postal Excellence Service Awards — A472

**1993, Aug. 22**

**1084** A472 1r multicolored 1.25 .35

Technical Education in Sri Lanka, Cent. A473

**1993, Dec. 17**

**1085** A473 1r multicolored 1.25 .35

Musaeus College, Cent. — A474

**1993, Nov. 15**

**1086** A474 1r multicolored 2.25 .40

Christmas A475

Designs: 1r, Presentation of infant Jesus in Temple of Jerusalem. 17r, Boy Jesus in Temple.

**1993, Nov. 30** **Litho.** ***Perf. 14x13½***

**1087** A475 1r multicolored .30 .20
**1088** A475 17r multicolored 1.25 1.25
*a.* Souvenir sheet, #1087-1088 2.00 2.00

Youth and Health — A476

**1993, Dec. 16** ***Perf. 14***

**1089** A476 1r multicolored .70 .35

Old Boy's Assoc., Trinity College, Kandy, Cent. — A478

**1994, Feb. 11** **Litho.** ***Perf. 12½***

**1091** A478 1r multicolored .35 .30

St. Thomas College, Matara, 150th Anniv. A479

**1994, Mar. 10** **Litho.** ***Perf. 13***

**1092** A479 1r multicolored .35 .30

St. Joseph's College, 125th Anniv. A480

**1994, Apr. 4** **Litho.** ***Perf. 12½***

**1093** A480 1r multicolored .50 .30

Siyambalangamuwe Sri Gunaratana Thero — A481

**1994, Apr. 2** **Litho.** ***Perf. 13***

**1094** A481 1r multicolored 2.00 .35



ILO, 75th Anniv. — A482

**1994, May. 12**

**1095** A482 1r multicolored 1.50 .40

Vesak Festival A483

Designs show actions by Bodhisatva in four of ten perfections: 1r, Dana, displaying generosity. 2r, Sila, morality. 5r, Nekkhamma, ascetic surrounded by worshippers. 17r, Panna, wisdom dispensed by Bodhisatva to others.

**1994, May 7 Litho. *Perf. 12½***

| | | | | |
|---|---|---|---|---|
| **1096** | A483 | 1r multicolored | .25 | .20 |
| **1097** | A483 | 2r multicolored | 1.10 | 1.10 |
| **1098** | A483 | 5r multicolored | 1.10 | 1.10 |
| **1099** | A483 | 17r multicolored | 2.10 | 2.10 |
| *a.* | | Souvenir sheet, #1096-1099 | 5.00 | 5.00 |
| | | *Nos. 1096-1099 (4)* | 4.55 | 4.50 |

Famous People A484

Designs: No. 1100, Pres. Ranasinghe Premadasa. No. 1101, Ven. Mihiripanne Dhammaratana Thero. No. 1102, E. Periyathambipillai, poet. No. 1103, Dr. Colvin R. De Silva, politician.

**1994, May 22 Litho. *Perf. 14***

| | | | | |
|---|---|---|---|---|
| **1100** | A484 | 1r multicolored | .25 | .20 |
| **1101** | A484 | 1r multicolored | .25 | .20 |
| **1102** | A484 | 1r multicolored | .25 | .20 |
| **1103** | A484 | 1r multicolored | .25 | .20 |
| | | *Nos. 1100-1103 (4)* | 1.00 | .80 |

World Conference of Intl. Federation of Social Workers, Colombo A485

**1994, July 9 Litho. *Perf. 12½***

**1104** A485 8r blue, lt blue & blk 3.00 3.00

Bellanwila Sri Somaratana Nayake Thero — A486

**1994, Aug. 2 Litho. *Perf. 12½***

**1105** A486 1r multicolored 2.60 .40

Infotel Lanka '94 A487

**1994, Sept. 8**

**1106** A487 10r multicolored 3.00 3.00

Intl. Year of Indigenous People — A488

Designs: 1r, Veddah man making bow. 17r, Veddah man seated by rock art paintings.

**1994, Sept. 12 Litho. *Perf. 12***

| | | | | |
|---|---|---|---|---|
| **1107** | A488 | 1r multicolored | .35 | .35 |
| **1108** | A488 | 17r multicolored | 4.50 | 3.50 |

Natl. Wildlife & Nature Protection Society, Cent. A489

**1994, Nov. 24 Litho. *Perf. 12½***

| | | | | |
|---|---|---|---|---|
| **1109** | A489 | 1r Emblem | .25 | .20 |
| **1110** | A489 | 2r Rhino-horned lizard | .65 | .65 |
| **1111** | A489 | 10r Giant squirrel | 1.90 | 1.90 |
| **1112** | A489 | 17r Sloth bear | 2.75 | 2.75 |
| *a.* | | Souvenir sheet, #1109-1112 | 5.50 | 5.50 |
| | | *Nos. 1109-1112 (4)* | 5.55 | 5.50 |

Gam Udawa, 16th Anniv. A490

**1994, Sept. Litho. *Perf. 13***

**1113** A490 1r multicolored .75 .20

A491

A492

**1994, Oct. 11 Litho. *Perf. 12½***

**1114** A491 1r multicolored 2.25 .40

Double entry bookkeeping, 500th anniv.

**1995, Feb. 22 *Perf. 14***

**1115** A492 1r Water lily 1.00 .20

Richmond College Old Boys Assoc., Cent. A493

**1994 *Perf. 12½***

**1116** A493 1r multicolored .25 .20

ICAO, 50th Anniv. A494

**1994, Dec. 7 Litho. *Perf. 13***

**1117** A494 10r multicolored 4.00 2.00

Christmas A495

Designs: 1r, Nativity. 17r, Jesus growing up, at home with Joseph and Mary.

**1994, Dec. 8 Litho. *Perf. 13***

| | | | | |
|---|---|---|---|---|
| **1118** | A495 | 1r multicolored | .30 | .20 |
| **1119** | A495 | 17r multicolored | 3.50 | 3.00 |
| *a.* | | Souvenir sheet, #1118-1119 | 4.00 | 4.00 |

Assoc. for Advancement of Science, 50th Anniv. — A496

**1994, Dec. 19 Litho. *Perf. 13***

**1120** A496 1r multicolored 3.00 .55

Orchid Circle of Ceylon, 60th Anniv. — A498

Orchids: 50c, Dendrobium maccarthiae. 1r, Cottonia peduncularis. 5r, Bulbophyllum wightii. 17r, Habenaria crinifera.

**1994, Dec. 27 Litho. *Perf. 13***

| | | | | |
|---|---|---|---|---|
| **1122** | A498 | 50c multicolored | .25 | .20 |
| **1123** | A498 | 1r multicolored | .35 | .25 |
| **1124** | A498 | 5r multicolored | .60 | .55 |
| **1125** | A498 | 17r multicolored | 1.40 | 1.25 |
| *a.* | | Souvenir sheet, #1122-1125 | 3.50 | 3.50 |
| | | *Nos. 1122-1125 (4)* | 2.60 | 2.25 |

Visit of Pope John Paul II, Beatification of Fr. Joseph Vaz — A499

**1995, Jan. 20**

**1126** A499 1r multicolored 3.50 .50

St. Joseph's College, Colombo, Cent. A500

**1995, Mar. 2 Litho. *Perf. 13***

**1127** A500 1r multicolored 1.40 .25

Royal Asiatic Society of Sri Lanka, 150th Anniv. — A501

**1995, Apr. 4**

**1128** A501 1r multicolored 3.00 .75

Sirimavo Bandaranaike, World's First Woman Prime Minister — A502

**1995, Apr. 17 Litho. *Perf. 12***

**1129** A502 2r multicolored 2.00 .85

A503

A504

Vesak Festival (Designs show actions by a Bodhisatva in four of ten perfections): 1r, Endeavor, standing on shore. 2r, Forebearance, one holding another. 10r, Veracity, two people listening to truths. 17r, Resolution, man holding hoe.

**1995, May 5 *Perf. 12x12½***

| | | | | |
|---|---|---|---|---|
| **1130** | A503 | 1r multicolored | .35 | .20 |
| **1131** | A503 | 2r multicolored | .45 | .20 |
| **1132** | A503 | 10r multicolored | 1.25 | 1.00 |
| **1133** | A503 | 17r multicolored | 2.25 | 2.00 |
| *a.* | | Souvenir sheet, #1130-1133 | 4.50 | 4.50 |
| | | *Nos. 1130-1133 (4)* | 4.30 | 3.40 |

**1995, June 3 *Perf. 11***

**1134** A504 2r M. C. Abdul Cader 2.00 .90

St. Aloysius College, Galle, Cent. A506

**1995, June 21 Litho. *Perf. 12½x12***

**1136** A506 2r multicolored 2.00 .85

T.B. Ilangaratna (1913-92), Politician A507

**1995, July 7 Litho. *Perf. 13***

**1137** A507 2r multicolored 2.00 .85

Dhamma School, Cent. A508

**1995, Aug. 3**

**1138** A508 2r multicolored 2.00 .85

General Post Office, Colombo, Cent. A509

**1995, Aug. 22 Litho. *Perf. 13½***

**1139** A509 1r multicolored 1.50 .35

Help the Elderly — A510

**1995, Oct. 1 Litho. *Perf. 14x13½***
1140 A510 2r multicolored 2.25 .85

41st Commonwealth Parliamentary Conference — A511

**1995, Oct. 9 Litho. *Perf. 14x13½***
1141 A511 2r multicolored 2.25 .85

UN, 50th Anniv. — A512

World Thrift Day — A513

**1995, Oct. 24 *Perf. 13½x14***
1142 A512 2r multicolored 2.25 1.00

**1995, Oct. 15**
1143 A513 2r multicolored 2.25 .85

Christmas A514

Designs: 2r, Arms of Colombo and Kurunegla, Persian cross from Anuradhapura, Christian church. 20r, Clasping arms, nativity scene.

**1995, Nov. 10 Litho. *Perf. 13***
1144 A514 2r multicolored .50 .20
1145 A514 20r multicolored 2.50 2.00
a. Souvenir sheet, #1144-1145 3.50 3.50

A515

A516

**1995, Dec. 8**
1146 A515 2r multicolored 2.75 1.00

SAARC, 10th anniv.

**1996, Jan. 22 Litho. *Perf. 12***
1147 A516 50c Little Basses .60 .30
1148 A516 75c Great Basses .60 .30
1149 A516 2r Devinuwara 1.40 .75
1149A A516 2.50r like #1149 .60 .30
1150 A516 20r Galle 4.00 2.25
a. Souv. sheet, #1147-1149, 1150 8.00 8.00
*Nos. 1147-1150 (5)* 7.20 3.90

Lighthouses of Sri Lanka.
For surcharges see Nos. 1191-1193.

Vincent High School, Batticaloa, 175th Anniv. — A517

**1996, Jan. 17 Litho. *Perf. 13***
1151 A517 2r multicolored 2.00 .85

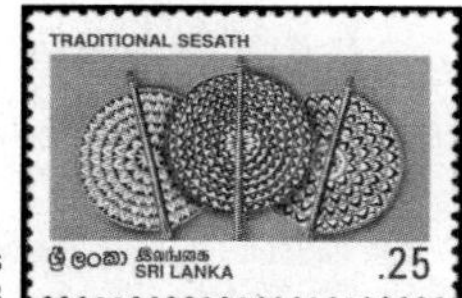

Handicrafts A518

**1996, Mar. 13 *Perf. 12***
1152 A518 25c Traditional sesath .20 .20
1153 A518 8.50r Pottery .45 .40
1154 A518 10.50r Mats .65 .55
1155 A518 17r Lace .95 .95
a. Souvenir sheet, #1152-1155 1.90 1.90
*Nos. 1152-1155 (4)* 2.25 2.10

For surcharges see Nos. 1189-1190.

A519

A520

**1996, Mar. 21**
1156 A519 2r multicolored 2.00 .85

Chundikuli Girls' College, Jaffna, cent.

**1996, Apr. 30 Litho. *Perf. 12***

Vesak Festival: 1r, Capa cradling her son, teasing her husband. 2r, Dantika, mahout, elephant. 5r, Subha holding her eye in her hand, man of low morals. 10r, Punna explaining purification by water to Brahmin.

1157 A520 1r multicolored .20 .20
1158 A520 2r multicolored .45 .45
1159 A520 5r multicolored .60 .60
1160 A520 10r multicolored 1.00 1.00
a. Souvenir sheet, #1157-1160 2.75 2.75
*Nos. 1157-1160 (4)* 2.25 2.25

1996 Summer Olympic Games, Atlanta A521

**1996, July 22 Litho. *Perf. 13½***
1161 A521 1r Diving, vert. .30 .20
1162 A521 2r Volleyball, vert. 1.00 .45
1163 A521 5r Shooting 1.25 1.25
1164 A521 17r Running 2.50 2.50
*Nos. 1161-1164 (4)* 5.05 4.40

Sri Lanka, 1996 World Cup Cricket Champions — A522

**1996, Aug. 18**
1165 A522 2r Bowler .45 .45
1166 A522 10.50r Wicketkeeper 1.00 1.00
1167 A522 17r Batsman 1.50 1.50
1168 A522 20r Trophy 1.60 1.60
a. Souvenir sheet, #1165-1168 4.50 4.50
*Nos. 1165-1168 (4)* 4.55 4.55

No. 1168a contains two se-tenant pairs.

Jaffna Central College, 180th Anniv. A523

**1996, Sept. 7 Litho. *Perf. 13½***
1169 A523 2r multicolored 2.25 .85

A524

A525

**1996, Nov. 4 Litho. *Perf. 13½x14***
1170 A524 2r multicolored 2.75 1.00

UNESCO, 50th anniv.

**1996, Dec. 2 *Perf. 13½x13***

Christmas (Scenes of parables from murals, Trinity College Chapel): 2r, Washing of the feet. 17r, Good Samaritan.

1171 A525 2r multicolored .25 .20
1172 A525 17r multicolored 1.75 1.50
a. Souvenir sheet, #1171-1172 2.00 2.00

UNICEF, 50th Anniv. — A526

Swami Vivekananda A527

**1996, Dec. 12 Litho. *Perf. 13½x14***
1173 A526 5r multicolored 1.00 .70

**1997, Jan. 15 *Perf. 13½x13***
1174 A527 2.50r multicolored 1.50 .70

Personalities A528

Vesak Festival — A529

Designs: No. 1175, Lt. Gen. Denzil Kobbekaduwa. No. 1176, Ven. Welivitiye Serata Thero. No. 1177, Dr. S.A. Wickremasinghe.

**1997, Apr. 4 Litho. *Perf. 13½x13***
1175 A528 2r multicolored .50 .30
1176 A528 2r multicolored .50 .30
1177 A528 2r multicolored .50 .30
*Nos. 1175-1177 (3)* 1.50 .90

**1997, May 7 *Perf. 12x12½***

Cemeteries, monuments to the dead: 1r, Thuparama. 2.50r, Ruwanvalisaya. 3r, Abhayagiri Dagaba. 17r, Jetavana Dagaba.

1178 A529 1r multicolored .20 .20
1179 A529 2.50r multicolored .20 .20
1180 A529 3r multicolored .20 .20
1181 A529 17r multicolored .90 .90
a. Souvenir Sheet of 4, #1178-1181 2.75 2.75
*Nos. 1178-1181 (4)* 1.50 1.50

D.J. Kumarage, Birth Cent. — A530

**1997, Apr. 4 Litho. *Perf. 13½x14***
1182 A530 2.50r multicolored 1.50 .70

Medicinal Herbs — A531

2.40r, Munronia pinnata. 14r, Rauvolfia serpentina.

**1997, July 22 Litho. *Perf. 13½x14***
1183 A531 2.50r multicolored .25 .20
1184 A531 14r multicolored 1.25 .90

Tourism A532

**1997, Sept. 11** ***Perf. 12***
**1185** A532 20r multicolored 3.00 2.00

St. Servatius College, Matara, Cent. A533

**1997, Nov. 1** ***Perf. 12½x12***
**1186** A533 2.50r multicolored .80 .25

Mahagama Sekera — A534

**1997, Apr. 4** **Litho.** ***Perf. 13½x13***
**1187** A534 2r multicolored .75 .35

Asterisks obliterate portions of Mahagama Sekera's name.

Sri Jayawardenapura Vidalaya, Kotte, 175th Anniv. — A535

**1997, Jan. 28** ***Perf. 12½***
**1188** A535 2.50r multicolored .50 .25

Nos. 1153-1154 Surcharged

**1997, May 6** **Litho.** ***Perf. 12***
**1189** A518 1r on 8.50r, #1153 4.00 .50
**1190** A518 11r on 10.50r, #1154 (a) 3.25 3.25
*a.* Surcharge type b 3.25 3.25

Surcharge Type a on #1190 is 2½mm high. Type b surcharge is 3mm high.

No. 1149 Surcharged

c

d

e

**1997, Feb. 12** **Litho.** ***Perf. 12***
**1191** A516(c) 2.50r on 2r *3.00 3.00*
**1192** A516(d) 2.50r on 2r *3.00 3.00*
**1193** A516(e) 2.50r on 2r *3.00 3.00*
*Nos. 1191-1193 (3)* *9.00 9.00*

A number has been reserved additional surcharge on No. 1149.

Reptiles A537

2.50r, Lyre head lizard. 5r, Boie's roughside. 17r, Common Lanka skink. 20r, Great forest gecko.

**1997, Oct. 18** **Litho.** ***Perf. 12***
**1195** A537 2.50r multicolored .25 .25
**1196** A537 5r multicolored .35 .35
**1197** A537 17r multicolored .70 .70
**1198** A537 20r multicolored .75 .75
*a.* Souvenir sheet, #1195-1198 2.25 2.25
*Nos. 1195-1198 (4)* 2.05 2.05

A538

A539

Christmas: 2.50r, Holy Family. 20r, Adoration of the Magi.

**1997, Nov. 20** ***Perf. 12½x13***
**1199** A538 2.50r multicolored .25 .20
**1200** A538 20r multicolored 1.40 .85
*a.* Souvenir sheet, #1199-1200 1.75 1.75

**1997, Nov. 11** **Litho.** ***Perf. 12½***

Personalities: #1201, Hegoda Sri Indasara Thero (1932-87), religious leader. #1202, Abdul Aziz (d. 1990), politician. #1203, Subramaniam Vithiananthan (b. 1924), teacher, writer. #1204, Vivienne Goonewardene (1916-96), politician.

**1201** A539 2.50r multicolored .20 .20
**1202** A539 2.50r multicolored .20 .20
**1203** A539 2.50r multicolored .20 .20
**1204** A539 2.50r multicolored .20 .20
*a.* Block of 4, #1201-1204 1.10 1.10

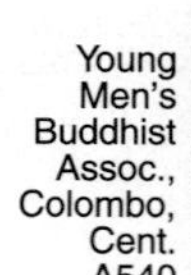

Young Men's Buddhist Assoc., Colombo, Cent. A540

**1998, Jan. 1** **Litho.** ***Perf. 12½***
**1205** A540 2.50r multicolored .55 .30

Traditional Jewelry and Crafts — A541

Designs: 2.50r, Chunam box. 5r, Necklace of agate. 10r, Bangle and hairpin. 17r, Sigiri earrings.

**1998, Apr. 24** **Litho.** ***Perf. 13½***
**1206** A541 2.50r multicolored .25 .20
**1207** A541 5r multicolored .40 .20
**1208** A541 10r multicolored .75 .75
**1209** A541 17r multicolored 1.25 1.25
*a.* Souvenir sheet, #1206-1209 3.00 3.00

Independence, 50th Anniv. — A542

Natl. flag and: 2r, People holding up arms, letters and symbols. No. 1211, Ceylon #300. No. 1212, People standing, images of industry and technology. 5r, People playing musical instruments, book, pen, television, musical instruments. 10r, People holding up items, symbols of religion, government.

***Perf. 13, 13½ (#1211)***

**1998, Feb. 4** **Litho.**
**1210** A542 2r multicolored .40 .20
**1211** A542 2.50r multicolored .70 .45
**1212** A542 2.50r multicolored .70 .45
**1213** A542 5r multicolored .70 .50
**1214** A542 10r multicolored 1.00 .75
*Nos. 1210-1214 (5)* 3.50 2.35

No. 1211 is 28x38mm.

William Gopallawa, 1st President A543

**1998** **Litho.** ***Perf. 13½***
**1215** A543 2.50r multicolored .55 .20

5th Natl. Scout Jamboree A544

Designs: 2.50r, Scouts holding flag, emblem, campground. 17r, Campground, flag, emblems, scout saluting.

**1998, Feb. 18**
**1216** A544 2.50r multicolored .75 .50
**1217** A544 17r multicolored 2.75 2.25

World Health Organization, 50th Anniv. — A545

**1998, Apr. 7** **Litho.** ***Perf. 13x12½***
**1218** A545 2.50r multicolored .60 .20

St. John's College, Jaffna, 175th Anniv. — A546

**1998, May 7** **Litho.** ***Perf. 14½x14***
**1219** A546 2.50r multicolored .25 .20

Elephas Maximus Ceylonensis — A547

Designs: 2.50r, Wading in lake. 10r, Female, calf. 17r, Three standing in plains. 50r, Large bull.

**1998, May 28** ***Perf. 13***
**1220** A547 2.50r multicolored .70 .50
**1221** A547 10r multicolored 1.00 .80
**1222** A547 17r multicolored 1.50 1.10
**1223** A547 50r multicolored 2.50 2.00
*a.* Souvenir sheet, #1220-1223 6.00 6.00
*Nos. 1220-1223 (4)* 5.70 4.40

Vesak Festival — A548

Kelaniya Rajamaha Vihara paintings: 1r, Waterfalls, tree. 2.50r, Procession of people, elephant with rider. 4r, Looking at mother with newborn baby. 17r, Presenting child for ceremony, laying stone.

**1998, Apr. 30** **Litho.** ***Perf. 12½***
**1224** A548 1r multicolored .25 .20
**1225** A548 2.50r multicolored .25 .20
**1226** A548 4r multicolored .50 .30
**1227** A548 17r multicolored 1.00 .45
*a.* Souvenir sheet, #1224-1228 2.25 2.25
*Nos. 1224-1227 (4)* 2.00 1.15

SAARC Summit, Colombo — A549

**1998** **Litho.** ***Perf. 14½x14***
**1228** A549 2.50r multicolored .80 .30

1998, Year of Information Technology A550

**1998** **Litho.** ***Perf. 13½***
**1229** A550 2.50r multicolored .55 .20

Personalities A551

#1230, Ven. Pannakitti Nayake Thero. #1231, Sir Nicholas Attygalle. #1232, Dr. Samuel Fisk Green. #1233, Prof. Ediriweera Sarachchandra.

**1998** ***Perf. 13***
**1230** A551 2.50r multicolored .35 .25
**1231** A551 2.50r multicolored .35 .25
**1232** A551 2.50r multicolored .35 .25
**1233** A551 2.50r multicolored .35 .25
*Nos. 1230-1233 (4)* 1.40 1.00

Meteorological Dept., 50th Anniv. — A552

**1998** **Litho.** ***Perf. 14x13½***
**1234** A552 2.50r multicolored .90 .25

26th Forum of South Asia, Africa & Middle East Lions Clubs Intl. — A553

**1998, Nov. 20** **Litho.** ***Perf. 14x14½***
**1235** A553 2.50r multicolored 2.00 .65

Christmas A554

**1998, Dec. 10** ***Perf. 13½x14***
**1236** A554 2.50r Nativity .25 .20
**1237** A554 20r Annunciation 1.40 .90
*a.* Souvenir sheet, #1236-1237 1.75 1.75

A555

Kandyan Dancer — A556

S.W.R.D. Bandaranaike, Birth Cent.: No. 1238, Wearing white scarf. No. 1239, Wearing blue scarf.

**1999, Jan. 8** **Litho.** ***Perf. 12***
**1238** A555 3.50r multicolored .80 .45
**1239** A555 3.50r multicolored .80 .45
*a.* Souvenir sheet, #1238-1239, perf. 12½ 1.75 1.75

**1999, Feb. 3** **Photo.** ***Perf. 12***
**1240** A556 1r brown .20 .20
**1241** A556 2r green blue .20 .20
**1242** A556 3r plum .20 .20
**1243** A556 3.50r blue .20 .20
**1244** A556 4r dark red .20 .20

**Size: 21x26mm**

**1245** A556 5r green .20 .20
**1246** A556 10r violet .30 .25
**1247** A556 13.50r bright red .40 .35
**1248** A556 17r blue green .50 .40
**1249** A556 20r olive bister .60 .50
*Nos. 1240-1249 (10)* 3.00 2.70

Telecommunications, 50th Anniv. — A557

Portraits of Sir Arthur C. Clarke, diagrams of Orbital Concept: a, Rocket launch, satellites, space shuttle. b, Satellites, earth from outer space, space capsule.

**1999, Feb. 10** **Litho.** ***Perf. 12***
**1250** A557 3.50r Pair, #a.-b. 2.00 2.00

Dated 1998.

Salvation Army, 116th Anniv. A558

**1999, Apr. 28** **Litho.** ***Perf. 11¾x12***
**1251** A558 3.50r multicolored .80 .40

British Council, 50th Anniv. — A559

**1999, May 20** ***Perf. 12***
**1252** A559 3.50r multicolored .70 .25

Sumithrayo Organization Suicide Hot Line, 25th Anniv. — A560

**1999, June 14** ***Perf. 12½***
**1253** A560 3.50r multicolored .55 .30

Vesak Festival — A561

Designs: 2r, Flowers. 3.50r, Leaf, wheel. 13.50r, Nut, flower. 17r, Young people with traditional lanterns.

**Unwmk.**

**1999, May 25** **Litho.** ***Perf. 12***
**1254** A561 2r multicolored .20 .20
**1255** A561 3.50r multicolored .20 .20
**1256** A561 13.50r multicolored .60 .30
**1257** A561 17r multicolored .75 .40
*Nos. 1254-1257 (4)* 1.75 1.10

**Souvenir Sheet**

**Wmk. 388**

***Perf. 12½***

**1258** Sheet of 4 2.00 2.00
*a.* A561 2r like #1254 .20 .20
*b.* A561 3.50r like #1255 .20 .20
*c.* A561 13.50r like #1256 .60 .30
*d.* A561 17r like #1257 .75 .40

Independent Television Network, 20th Anniv. — A562

**1999, June 5** **Unwmk.** ***Perf. 12¾***
**1259** A562 3.50r multicolored .55 .30

Vidyodaya Pirivena, 125th Anniv. A563

***Perf. 12¾***

**1999, Sept. 17** **Litho.** **Unwmk.**
**1260** A563 3.50r multicolored .55 .30

Sri Lankan Cinema, 50th Anniv. — A564

**1999, Sept. 17** **Litho.** ***Perf. 12¾***
**1261** A564 3.50r Handaya, 1979 .20 .20
**1262** A564 4r Nidhanaya, 1972 .30 .25
**1263** A564 10r Gam Peraliya, 1963 .40 .30
**1264** A564 17r Kadawunu Poronduwa, 1947 1.20 1.00
*a.* Souvenir sheet, #1261-1264 2.25 2.25
*Nos. 1261-1264 (4)* 2.10 1.75

Bhakthi Prabodanaya Magazine, Cent. — A565

**1999, Sept.** **Litho.** ***Perf. 12x12¼***
**1265** A565 3.50r multicolored .55 .30

Hector Kobbekaduwa, Politician — A566

***Perf. 12¾x12½***

**1999, Sept. 19** **Wmk. 388** **Litho.**
**1266** A566 3.50r multicolored .55 .30

National Army, 50th Anniv. — A567

**1999, Oct. 10** **Unwmk.** ***Perf. 12¾***
**1267** A567 3.50r multicolored .70 .30

Convention on the Rights of the Child, 10th Anniv. — A568

**1999, Nov. 20** ***Perf. 12¾x12½***
**1268** A568 3.50r multicolored 1.10 .50

A569

A570

**1999, Nov. 26** ***Perf. 12¾***
**1269** A569 3.50r multicolored .55 .30

Balangoda Ananda Maitreya Mahanyake Thero (b. 1895), Buddhist priest.

**1999, Dec. 12** ***Perf. 12¾***

Paintings.

**1270** A570 3.50r By David Paynter .20 .20
**1271** A570 4r By Justin Daraniyagala .20 .20
**1272** A570 17r By Ivan Peries .50 .45
**1273** A570 20r By Solias Mendis .60 .55
*a.* Souvenir sheet of 4, #1270-1273 2.00 2.00
*Nos. 1270-1273 (4)* 1.50 1.40

Athletic Accomplishments — A571

Designs: 1r, Kumar Anandan's swim across Palk Strait. 3.50r, World champions in cricket. 13.50r, International fame in track and field.

**1999** *Perf. 12¾*

**1274** A571 1r multicolored .25 .20
**1275** A571 3.50r multicolored .55 .50
**1276** A571 13.50r multicolored 1.20 1.00
*Nos. 1274-1276 (3)* 2.00 1.70

Natl. Commission for UNESCO, 50th Anniv. — A572

*Perf. 12¾x12½*

**1999, Nov. 16 Litho. Wmk. 388**

**1277** A572 13.50r multi 2.75 2.00

Christmas A573

**1999, Nov. 30** *Perf. 12½x12¾*

**1278** A573 3.50r shown .25 .20
**1279** A573 20r Magi 1.00 .75
*a.* Souvenir sheet, #1278-1279 1.50 1.50

Famous People — A574

Designs: No. 1280, Dr. Pandithamani S. Kanapathipillai, Tamil scholar. No. 1281, Sunil Santha, musician. No. 1282, Dr. Al Haj Badi-udin Mahmud, Education minister.

**1999, Dec. 3** *Perf. 12¾x12½*

**1280** A574 3.50r multi 1.00 .40
**1281** A574 3.50r multi 1.50 .65
**1282** A574 3.50r multi .90 .35
*Nos. 1280-1282 (3)* 3.40 1.40

No. 1149A Surcharged

**1999, Dec. 3 Litho.** *Perf. 12*

**1282A** A516 2r on 2.50r multi 4.50 .80

Butterflies — A575

Designs: 3.50r, Striped albatross. 13.50r, Ceylon tiger. 17r, Three-spot grass yellow. 20r, Great orange tip.

*Perf. 12x11¾*

**1999, Dec. 30 Unwmk.**

**Granite Paper**

**1283** A575 3.50r multi .45 .25
**1284** A575 13.50r multi 1.00 .80
**1285** A575 17r multi 1.20 .90
**1286** A575 20r multi 1.40 1.00
*a.* Souvenir sheet, #1283-1286 4.25 4.25
*Nos. 1283-1286 (4)* 4.05 2.95

Corals A576

**1999, Dec. 30** *Perf. 11¾x12*

**Granite Paper**

**1287** A576 3.50r Boulder .25 .35
**1288** A576 13.50r Blue-tipped 1.20 .90
**1289** A576 14r Brain-boulder 1.20 .90
**1290** A576 22r Elkhorn 1.40 1.10
*a.* Souvenir sheet, #1287-1290 1.75 1.75
*Nos. 1287-1290 (4)* 4.05 3.25

Auditor General's Department, Bicent. — A576a

*Perf. 12½x12¾*

**1999, Dec. Litho. Unwmk.**

**1290B** A576a 3.50r multi .55 .40

Year 2000 — A577

Satellite and: 10r, Birds, religious symbols. No. 1292, Scales, girl, Red Cross, computer. No. 1293, airplane, satellite dish, man at computer. No. 1294, Hands, symbols of women's equality, crippled and blind.

**2000, Jan. 1** *Perf. 11¾*

**Granite Paper**

**1291** A577 10r multi .25 .25
**1292** A577 100r multi 3.00 3.00
**1293** A577 100r multi 3.00 3.00
**1294** A577 100r multi 3.00 3.00
*a.* Souvenir sheet, #1291-1294 9.25 9.25
*Nos. 1291-1294 (4)* 9.25 9.25

Kurunagala Diocese, 50th Anniv. A578

**Unwmk.**

**2000, Feb. 2 Litho.** *Perf. 12*

**1295** A578 13.50r multi .55 .55

Wesley College, Colombo, 125th Anniv. A579

**2000, Mar. 2** *Perf. 11¾x12*

**1296** A579 3.50r multi .55 .30

Panadura Pinwatte Saddharmakara Vidyayathana Pirivena, Cent. — A580

**2000, Mar. 12**

**1297** A580 3.50r multi .55 .30

Vesak Festival — A581

2r, Arrival of Jaya Sri Maha Bodhi sapling. 3.50r, King Devanampiyatissa carrying sapling on his head. 10r, Venerating sapling. 13.50r, Royal tree planting, Anuradhapura.

**2000, Apr. 28 Litho.** *Perf. 12¾x12½*

**1298-1301** A581 Set of 4 2.00 1.50
*1301a* Souvenir sheet, #1298-1301 2.25 2.25

Sri Lanka Bar Association, 25th Anniv. (in 1999) — A582

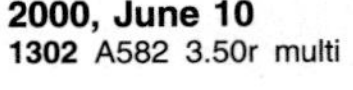

**2000, June 10** *Perf. 12*

**1302** A582 3.50r multi .55 .30

Co-operative Wholesale Establishment, 50th Anniv. — A583

**2000, July 1** *Perf. 12¾*

**1303** A583 3.50r multi .55 .30

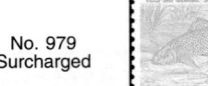

No. 979 Surcharged

**2000, July 21 Litho.** *Perf. 11½*

**1303A** A420 50c on 8r multi 3.00 2.00

St. Patrick's College, Jaffna, 150th Anniv. A584

**2000, July 21**

**1304** A584 3.50r multi 1.00 .40

Survey Dept., 200th Anniv. A585

**2000, Aug. 2**

**1305** A585 3.50r multi .55 .30

Central Bank of Sri Lanka, 50th Anniv. — A586

**2000, Aug. 27** *Perf. 13¼*

**1306** A586 3.50r multi .55 .30

Dr. Maria Montessori (1870-1952), Educator — A587

**2000, Aug. 31** *Perf. 11¾*

**1307** A587 3.50r multi .55 .30

2000 Summer Olympics, Sydney — A588

Sydney Olympic Games emblem and: a, Hurdler, map. b, Shooter, runners. c, Runners. d, Hurdlers, swimmer.

**2000, Sept. 7**

**1308** A588 10r Horiz. strip of 4, #a-d 2.25 2.25
*e.* Souvenir sheet, #1308 2.50 2.50

All Ceylon Young Men's Muslim Association Conference, 50th Anniv. — A589

**2000, Sept. 16**

**1309** A589 3.50r multi .55 .30

Hotel Industry, 25th Anniv. A590

**2000. Sept. 18** ***Perf. 12¾***
**1310** A590 10r multi 2.25 1.00

Immigration and Emigration Dept., 50th Anniv. A591

**2000, Oct. 2** ***Perf. 11¾***
**1311** A591 3.50r multi .60 .30

Traditional Dancer — A592

***Perf. 13½x13 Syncopated***

**2000, Oct. 5** **Litho.**
**1312** A592 50r multi 1.75 1.75
**1313** A592 100r multi 3.50 3.50
**1314** A592 200r multi 6.75 6.75
*Nos. 1312-1314 (3)* 12.00 12.00

All-Ceylon Buddhist Congress Natl. Awards Ceremony A593

**2000, Aug. 27** **Litho.** ***Perf. 12¾***
**1315** A593 3.50r multi .55 .30

Saumiyamoorthy Thondaman, Government Minister — A594

**2000, Oct. 30**
**1316** A594 3.50r multi .55 .30

Famous People — A595

Designs: No. 1317, 3.50r, Most Ven. Baddegama Siri Piyaratana Nayake Thero, educator. No. 1318, 3.50r, Aluthgamage Simon de Silva (1874-1920), writer. No. 1319, 3.50r, Desigar Ramanujam (1907-68), politician.

***Perf. 12x12¼ (#1317), 12¾x12½***

**2000, Nov. 14**
**1317-1319** A595 Set of 3 1.00 .60

Christmas A596

Designs: 2r, Joseph, Mary, donkey. 17r, Holy family.

**2000, Nov. 23** ***Perf. 12¾x12½***
**1320-1321** A596 Set of 2 2.00 1.50
*1321a* Souvenir sheet, #1320-1321, perf. 12 2.00 2.00

Lalith Athulathmudali (1936-93), Politician — A597

**2000, Nov. 30** ***Perf. 12½x12¾***
**1322** A597 3.50r multi .55 .30

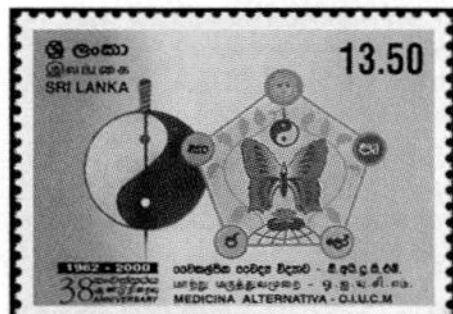

Medicina Alternativa Medical Society, 38th Anniv. A598

**2000, Dec. 1** ***Perf. 12¾***
**1323** A598 13.50r multi 1.50 1.00

Ladies' College, Cent. — A599

**2000, Dec. 7**
**1324** A599 3.50r multi .55 .30

Navy, 50th Anniv. A600

**2000, Dec. 9**
**1325** A600 3.50r multi .90 .40

Peliyagoda Vidyalankara Pirivena, 125th Anniv. — A601

**2000, Dec. 30** ***Perf. 12x12¼***
**1326** A601 3.50r multi .55 .30

Bishop's College, 125th Anniv. A602

**2001, Jan. 19** **Litho.**
**1327** A602 3.50r multi .55 .30

St. Thomas' College, 150th Anniv. A603

**2001, Feb. 3** ***Perf. 12¾***
**1328** A603 3.50r multi .55 .30

Lanka Mahila Samiti Women's Training Society, 70th Anniv. A604

**2001, Feb. 15**
**1329** A604 3.50r multi .55 .30

Air Force, 50th Anniv. A605

**2001, Mar. 9**
**1330** A605 3.50r multi .90 .40

St. Lawrence's School, Cent. A606

**2001, Mar. 15**
**1331** A606 3.50r multi .55 .30

Bernard Soysa (1914-97), Politician — A607

**2001, Mar. 20** ***Perf. 12¾***
**1332** A607 3.50r multi .55 .30

Vesak Festival — A608

Designs: 2r, Sri Nagadeepa Chaithya, Jaffna. 3,50r, Muthiyangana Chaithya, Badulla. 13.50r, Kirivehera, Kataragama. 17r, Sri Dalada Maligawa, Kandy.

**2001, Apr. 7** **Litho.** ***Perf. 13½x13¾***
**1333** A608 2r multi .20 .20
*a.* Perf. 14¼ .20 .20

***Perf. 14¼***

**1334** A608 3.50r multi .20 .20
*a.* Perf. 13½x13¾ .20 .20
**1335** A608 13.50r multi .75 .75
**1336** A608 17r multi 1.00 1.00
*a.* Souvenir sheet, #1333a, 1334-1336 2.00 2.00

Hansa Jataka, by George Keyt (1901-93) — A609

Illustration reduced.

**2001, Apr. 24** ***Perf. 13¼***
**1337** A609 13.50r multi 1.25 1.00

Coins A610

Designs: 3.50r, Kahavanu gold coin, 9th cent. 13.50r, Vijayabahu I silver coin, 1055-1111. 17r, Sethu copper coin, 13th-14th cent. 20r, Buddha Jayanthi 5r commemorative silver coin, 1957.

***Perf. 13¾x13½, 14¼ (17r)***

**2001, June 18**
**1338** A610 3.50r multi .25 .20
**1339** A610 13.50r multi .80 .55
**1340** A610 17r multi 1.00 .85
*a.* Perf. 13¾x13½x14¼x13½ 1.00 .85
**1341** A610 20r multi 1.25 1.25
*a.* Perf. 13¾x13½x14¼x13½ 1.25 1.25
*b.* Souvenir sheet, #1338-1339, 1340a, 1341a 3.25 3.25

Colombo Plan, 50th Anniv. — A611

**2001, July 2** ***Perf. 13½x13¾***
**1342** A611 10r multi .90 .50

US-Sri Lankan Diplomatic Relations, 150th Anniv. A612

**2001, July 3** ***Perf. 12¾***
**1343** A612 10r multi .90 .50

Lance Corporal Gamini Kularatne (1966-91), Military Hero — A613

**2001, July 14** ***Perf. 13¾x13½***
**1344** A613 3.50r multi .55 .30

Prince and Princess of Wales College, Moratuwa, 125th Anniv. A614

**2001, Sept. 14** ***Perf. 13¼***
**1345** A614 3.50r multi .55 .30

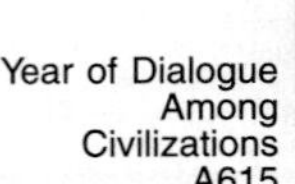

Year of Dialogue Among Civilizations A615

**2001, Oct. 9** *Perf. 13x13½*

**1346** A615 10r multi .70 .50

No. 511 Surcharged

**2001, July 9 Photo.** *Perf. 14¼x14½*

| | | | | |
|---|---|---|---|---|
| **1347** | A180 | 5r on 1.15r multi | 2.50 | 2.50 |
| **1348** | A180 | 10r on 1.15r multi | 2.50 | 2.50 |

An additional surcharge was released in this set. The editors would like to examine it.

13th Meeting of Parties to the Montreal Protocol — A616

**2001, Oct. 18 Litho.** *Perf. 13x13¼*

**1349** A616 13.50r multi .80 .65

Ramakrishna Mission Students' Home, Batticaloa, 75th Anniv. — A617

**2001, Oct. 19** *Perf. 12¾*

**1350** A617 3.50r multi .55 .30

Drummer — A618

Drummer from: 1r, 2r, 3r, 3.50r, Daul. 4r, 5r, 10r, Kandy. 13.50r, 17r, 20r, Low country.

**2001, Nov. 8 Litho.** *Perf. 12½x13¼*

| | | | | |
|---|---|---|---|---|
| **1351** | A618 | 1r rose | .20 | .20 |
| **1352** | A618 | 2r emerald | .20 | .20 |
| **1353** | A618 | 3r fawn | .20 | .20 |
| **1354** | A618 | 3.50r dark blue | .20 | .20 |

**Size: 23x28mm**

*Perf. 13¼x12½*

| | | | | |
|---|---|---|---|---|
| **1355** | A618 | 4r pink | .30 | .20 |
| **1356** | A618 | 5r orange | .30 | .20 |
| **1357** | A618 | 10r violet | .60 | .25 |
| **1358** | A618 | 13.50r dull purple | .80 | .35 |
| **1359** | A618 | 17r yel orange | 1.00 | .40 |
| **1360** | A618 | 20r Prus blue | 1.25 | .50 |
| | | *Nos. 1351-1360 (10)* | 5.05 | 2.70 |

S.W.R.D. Bandaranaike Natl. Memorial Foundation, 25th Anniv. — A619

**2001, Nov. 27** *Perf. 13¾x13¼*

**1361** A619 3.50r multi .55 .30

Christmas A620

Designs: 3.50r, Jesus and children. 17r, The Annunciation.

**2001, Nov. 28** *Perf. 13*

| | | | | |
|---|---|---|---|---|
| **1362-1363** | A620 | Set of 2 | .90 | .70 |
| *1363a* | | Souvenir sheet, #1362-1363 | 1.10 | 1.10 |

Frogs A621

Designs: 3.50r, Conical wart pygmy tree frog. 13.50r, Sharp-snout saddle tree frog. 17r, Round-snout pygmy tree frog. 20r, Sri Lanka wood frog.

**2001, Dec. 3** *Perf. 13¼x13*

| | | | | |
|---|---|---|---|---|
| **1364-1367** | A621 | Set of 4 | 2.75 | 2.25 |
| *1367a* | | Souvenir sheet, #1364-1367 | 2.75 | 2.75 |

St. Bridget's Convent, Cent. A622

**2002, Feb. 1**

**1368** A622 3.50r multi .55 .20

Ceylon Government Gazette, 200th Anniv. — A623

**2002, Mar. 15 Litho.** *Perf. 13¾x14*

**1369** A623 3.50r multi .55 .20

D. S. Senanayake (1884-1952), Prime Minister — A624

**2002, Mar. 22** *Perf. 14x13¾*

**1370** A624 3.50r multi .55 .20

Gamini Dissanayake (1942-94), Assassinated Government Minister — A625

**2002, Mar. 27** *Perf. 13¾x14*

**1371** A625 3.50r multi .55 .20

Lester James Peries (b. 1919), Film Director A626

**2002, Apr. 5** *Perf. 13¼x13*

**1372** A626 3.50r multi .55 .20

Natural Beauty of Sri Lanka — A627

Designs: 5r, Sinharaja Forest Reserve. 10r, Horton Plains National Park. 13.50r, Knuckles Range. 20r, Rumassala Cliff and Bonavista Coral Reef.

**2002, Apr. 10** *Perf. 13x13¼*

**1373-1376** A627 Set of 4 1.75 1.10

Pres. Ranasinghe Premadasa (1924-93) A628

**2002, Apr. 29** *Perf. 13¾x14*

**1377** A628 4.50r multi .55 .20

Sri Lanka - Japan Diplomatic Relations, 50th Anniv. — A629

**2002, Apr. 29** *Perf. 14x13¾*

**1378** A629 16.50r multi .90 .70

Vesak Festival A630

Dambulla Raja Maha Vihara rock paintings: 3r, Queen Mahamaya's dream. 4.50r, Birth of Prince Siddhartha. 16.50r, Siddhartha's exhibition of archery talents. 23r, Ordination of Prince Siddhartha.

**2002, May 17** *Perf. 13¾x14*

| | | | | |
|---|---|---|---|---|
| **1379-1382** | A630 | Set of 4 | 1.75 | 1.25 |
| *1382a* | | Souvenir sheet, #1379-1382 | 1.75 | 1.75 |

Most Venerable Madihe Pannasiha Maha Nayaka Thera, Religious Leader, 90th Birthday — A631

**2002, June 23** *Perf. 14x13¾*

**1383** A631 4.50r multi .55 .20

Sri Lanka Oriental Studies Society, Cent. A632

**2002, July 24** *Perf. 13¾x14*

**1384** A632 4.50r multi .60 .20

Rifai Thareeq Association, 125th Anniv. — A633

**2002, July 26**

**1385** A633 4.50r multi .60 .20

14th Asian Track and Field Championships, Colombo — A634

Designs: 4.50r, Discus thrower. 16.50r, Sprinter. 23r, Hurdler. 26r, Long jumper.

**2002, Aug. 8**

**1386-1389** A634 Set of 4 2.75 2.00

National Museum, 125th Anniv. — A635

No. 1390: a, Carved lion (sitting). b, Carved lion (standing with head turned).

Illustration reduced.

**2002, Aug. 27**

**1390** A635 4.50r Horiz. pair, #a-b 1.75 1.75

Woman's Hand Holding Flower — A636

**2002, Aug. 28** *Perf. 14x13¾*

**1391** A636 10r multi .90 .40

Tourism promotion.

Dr. A. C. S. Hameed (1929-99), Government Minister — A637

**2002, Sept. 3**
**1392** A637 4.50r multi .60 .20

Freemasons' Hall, Colombo, Cent. — A638

**2002, Sept. 5** ***Perf. 13¾x14***
**1393** A638 4.50r multi .60 .20

Holy Cross College, Kalutara, Cent. A639

**2002, Sept. 13**
**1394** A639 4.50r multi .60 .20

German Dharmaduta Society, 50th Anniv. — A640

**2002, Sept. 21** ***Perf. 14x13¾***
**1395** A640 4.50r multi .60 .20

Intl. Children's Day — A641

**2002, Oct. 1**
**1396** A641 4.50r multi .60 .20

Dr. M. C. M. Kaleel (1899-1995), Government Minister — A642

**2002, Oct. 18**
**1397** A642 4.50r green .60 .20

Dr. Wijayananda Dahanayake (1902-97), Prime Minister — A644

**2002, Oct. 22 Litho.** ***Perf. 14x13¾***
**1399** A644 4.50r brown .60 .20

Sri Lanka - Netherlands Relations, 400th Anniv. — A645

**2002, Nov. 22** ***Perf. 13¾x14***
**1400** A645 16.50r multi .90 .55

Christmas — A646

Designs: 4.50r, Madonna and Child. 26r, Holy Family.

**2002, Dec. 15** ***Perf. 13x13¼***
**1401-1402** A646 Set of 2 1.75 1.40
*1402a* Souvenir sheet, #1401-1402 1.75 1.75

Sri Lanka - China Rubber and Rice Pact, 50th Anniv. A647

**2002, Dec. 20** ***Perf. 13¾x14***
**1403** A647 4.50r multi .60 .20

Kopay Christian College, 150th Anniv. A648

**2002, Dec. 28**
**1404** A648 4.50r multi .60 .20

No. 925 Surcharged

**2002 ? Litho.** ***Perf. 12½x12***
**1405** A392 25c on 5.75r multi — —

No. 1354 Surcharged

**2002 ? Litho.** ***Perf. 12½x13¼***
**1406** A618 4.50r on 3.50r dk bl — —

Teachers' College, Maharagama, Cent. — A649

**2003, Jan. 21** ***Perf. 13¾x14***
**1407** A649 4.50r multi .60 .20

Holy Family Convent, Bambalapitiya, Cent. — A650

**2003, Feb. 3** ***Perf. 14x13¾***
**1408** A650 4.50r multi .60 .20

**Drummer Type of 2001 and**

No. 1359 Surcharged

Drummer from: 16.50r, Low country.

***Perf. 13¼x12½***
**2003, Feb. 17 Litho.**
**1409** A618 50c on 5r org yel .30 .25
**1410** A618 16.50r purple .70 .50

M. D. Banda (1914-74), Government Minister — A651

**2003, Mar. 14** ***Perf. 13¾x14***
**1411** A651 4.50r multi .60 .20

Balagalle Saraswati Maha Pirivena, Cent. A652

**2003, Apr. 3**
**1412** A652 4.50r multi .60 .20

D. B. Welagedara, Politician — A653

**2003, Apr. 22** ***Perf. 14x13¾***
**1413** A653 4.50r multi .60 .20

Vesak Festival — A654

Designs: 2.50r, Paying obeisance to parents. 3r, Dhamma school. 4.50r, Going on alms round. 23r, Meditation.

**2003, Apr. 26**
**1414-1417** A654 Set of 4 1.40 1.00
*1417a* Souvenir sheet, #1414-1417 1.60 1.60

Dagoba Construction Features — A655

Designs: 4.50r, Stupa. 16.50r, Guard stone, horiz. (58x28mm). 50r, Moonstone, horiz.

**2003, Apr. 28** ***Perf. 13x13¼, 13¼x13***
**1418-1420** A655 Set of 3 2.25 1.75
*1420a* Souvenir sheet, #1418-1420 2.25 2.25

Second World Hindu Conference, Colombo — A656

**2003, May 2** ***Perf. 14x13¾***
**1421** A656 4.50r multi .55 .20

International Nursing Day — A657

**2003, May 12** ***Perf. 13¾x14***
**1422** A657 4.50r multi .55 .20

Sirimavo Bandaranaike Memorial Exhibition Center — A658

**2003, May 17** ***Perf. 13¼x12***
**1423** A658 4.50r multi .55 .20

Al-Haj H. S. Ismail (1901-73), Parliament Speaker — A659

**2003, May 18** ***Perf. 14x13¾***
**1424** A659 4.50r multi .55 .20

Board of Investment, 25th Anniv. — A660

**2003, May 21** ***Perf. 13¾x12***
**1425** A660 4.50r multi .55 .20

World Biodiversity Day — A661

Designs: 4r, Pidurutalagal Mountain Range. 4.50r, Seven Maidens Mountain Range. 16.50r, Kirigalpoththa Mountain. 23r, Ritigala Mountain.

**2003, May 22** ***Perf. 13¾x12***
**1426-1429** A661 Set of 4 1.75 1.25

Saralankara College, Gonapinuwala, Cent. — A662

**2003, June 6** ***Perf. 13¾x14***
**1430** A662 4.50r multi .55 .20

A663

A664

First Arab settlement, Beruwala: 4.50r, Masjidul Abrar. 23r, Masjidul Abrar, horiz. (57x22mm).

***Perf. 14x13¾, 13¼x12 (23r)***

**2003, June 8**
**1431-1432** A663 Set of 2 1.00 .75

**2003, June 23** ***Perf. 14x13¾***
**1433** A664 4.50r multi .55 .20

Anti-narcotics Week.

Syamopali Maha Nikaya, 250th Anniv. A665

Designs: No. 1434, 4.50r, Asgiri Maha Viharaya. No. 1435, 4.50r, Malwathu Maha Viharaya.

**2003, July 13** ***Perf. 13¾x14***
**1434-1435** A665 Set of 2 .90 .40

Lanka Philex Intl. Stamp Exhibition, Colombo — A666

**2003, July 31** ***Perf. 13¼x12***
**1436** A666 16.50r multi .60 .35
*a.* Souvenir sheet of 1 1.00 1.00

Dr. Ananda Tissa de Alwis, Government Minister — A667

**2003, Aug. 21** ***Perf. 13¾x14***
**1437** A667 4.50r multi .60 .20

Panadura Controversy, 130th Anniv. — A668

**2003, Aug. 24** ***Perf. 14x13¾***
**1438** A668 4.50r multi .60 .20

Venerable Haldanduwana Dhammarakkhitha Thero — A669

**2003, Sept. 3** **Litho.**
**1439** A669 4.50r multi .60 .20

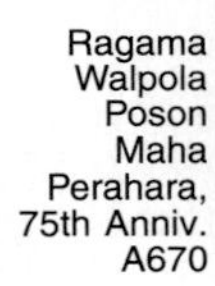

Ragama Walpola Poson Maha Perahara, 75th Anniv. A670

**2003, Sept. 10** ***Perf. 13¾x14***
**1440** A670 4.50r multi .60 .20

M. H. M. Ashraff (1948-2000), Government Minister — A671

**2003, Sept. 18** ***Perf. 14x13¾***
**1441** A671 4.50r multi .60 .20

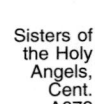

Sisters of the Holy Angels, Cent. A672

**2003, Sept. 27** ***Perf. 13¾x14***
**1442** A672 4.50r multi .60 .20

Birds — A673

No. 1443: a, Black-necked stork. b, Purple swamphen. c, Gray heron. d, White-throated kingfisher. e, Black-crowned night heron. f, Scarlet minivet. g, White-rumped shama. h, Malabar trogon. i, Asian paradise flycatcher. j, Little green bee-eater. k, Brown wood owl. l, Crested serpent eagle. m, Crested goshawk. n, Jungle owlet. o, Rufous-bellied eagle. p, Black-headed munia. q, Pompadour green pigeon. r, Plum-headed parakeet. s, Coppersmith barbet. t, Emerald dove. u, Blue-faced malkoha. v, Scimitar babbler. w, Painted francolin. x, Red-backed woodpecker. y, Malabar pied hornbill.

**2003, Sept. 27** ***Perf. 14x13¾***
**1443** A673 4.50r Sheet of 25, #a-y 10.00 10.00

World Habitat Day — A674

**2003, Oct. 6** ***Perf. 13***
**1444** A674 4.50r multi .60 .20

World Post Day A675

Blue Sapphire A676

**2003, Oct. 9** ***Perf. 14x13¾***
**1445** A675 23r multi 1.50 .80

**2003, Oct. 21** ***Perf. 12x13½***
**1446** A676 4.50r multi .60 .20

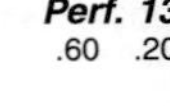

Ponificate of Pope John Paul II, 25th Anniv. — A677

**2003, Oct. 22** ***Perf. 13***
**1447** A677 4.50r multi .60 .20

Deepavali Festival — A678

**2003, Oct. 23**
**1448** A678 4.50r multi .60 .20

Pinnawala Elephant Orphanage A679

Designs: 4.50r, Two adult and two young elephants. 16.50r, Elephants and caretaker. 23r, Two adult elephants. 26r, Elephants in water.

**2003, July 13** **Litho.** ***Perf. 13½x13***
**1449-1452** A679 Set of 4 2.50 2.00
*1452a* Souvenir sheet, #1449-1452 2.75 2.75

Waterfalls — A680

Designs: 2.50r, Ramboda. 4.50r, Saint Clair. 23r, Bopath Ella. 50r, Devon.

**2003, Nov. 11** ***Perf. 14x13¾***
**1453-1456** A680 Set of 4 2.25 1.75

Ukku Banda Wanninayake (1905-73), Finance Minister — A681

**2003, Nov. 23** ***Perf. 13***
**1457** A681 4.50r multi .55 .20

Christmas A682

Designs: 4.50r, Church. 16.50r, Shepherds and angel, vert.

**2003, Nov. 30**
**1458-1459** A682 Set of 2 .70 .50

Pandith W. D. Amaradeva, Musician, 76th Birthday — A683

**2003, Dec. 5**
**1460** A683 4.50r multi .55 .20

Gangarama Seemamalakaya — A684

**2003, Dec. 20**
**1461** A684 4.50r multi .55 .20

Daham Pahana, Sri Pushparamaya, Malegoda — A685

**2003, Dec. 31**
**1462** A685 4.50r multi .55 .20

Shazuliyathul Fassiya Tharika — A686

**2004, Jan. 6**
**1463** A686 18r multi .60 .40

Chavakachcheri Hindu College, Cent. — A687

**2004, Jan. 30** ***Perf. 12x13½***
**1464** A687 4.50r multi .55 .20

Royal-Thomian Cricket Match, 125th Anniv. — A688

**2004, Jan. 30** ***Perf. 13***
**1465** A688 4.50r multi .55 .20

Pres. Dingiri Banda Wijetunga A689

**2004, Feb. 15 Litho.** ***Perf. 13***
**1466** A689 4.50r multi .55 .20

Planters Association of Ceylon, 150th Anniv. — A690

**2004, Feb. 17** ***Perf. 13¾x14***
**1467** A690 4.50r multi .55 .20

Kalashuri Most Venerable Mapalagama Vipulasara Thero, Religious Leader — A691

Maithripala Senanayeke A692

Cathiravelu Sittampalam (1898-1964), First Posts and Telecommunications Minister — A693

M. G. Mendis, Communist Leader — A694

**2004, Feb. 28** ***Perf. 13x13¼***
**1468** A691 3.50r multi .35 .20
**1469** A692 3.50r multi .35 .20
**1470** A693 3.50r multi .35 .20
**1471** A694 3.50r multi .35 .20
*Nos. 1468-1471 (4)* 1.40 .80

Nos. 1468-1471 are dated 2002. They were made available then, but not issued.

75th Ananda-Nalanda Cricket Match — A695

**2004, Mar. 7** ***Perf. 12x13¼***
**1472** A695 4.50r multi .20 .20

St. Anthony's College, Kandy, 150th Anniv. — A696

**2004, Mar. 12** ***Perf. 13½x12***
**1473** A696 4.50r multi .20 .20

Vesak Festival — A697

Various scenes of Sittara painting on wooden casket (with white borders on top and bottom): 4r, 4.50r, 16.50r, 20r.
26r, Scene of Sittara painting (no white borders).

**2004, Apr. 30**
**1474-1477** A697 Set of 4 .95 .95

**Souvenir Sheet**

**1478** A697 26r multi .55 .55

Gongalegoda Banda (1809-49), Leader of 1848 Rebellion — A698

**2004, May 22** ***Perf. 14x13¾***
**1479** A698 4.50r multi .20 .20

World Blood Donor Day — A699

**2004, June 15** ***Perf. 13***
**1480** A699 4.50r multi .20 .20

2004 Summer Olympics, Athens — A700

Designs: 4.50r, Swimming. 16.50r, Women's track. 17r, Shooting. 20r, Men's track.

**2004, Aug. 6** **Litho.**
**1481-1484** A700 Set of 4 1.10 1.10

Sri Siddhartha Buddharakkhita, 18th Cent. Religious Leader — A701

**2004, Aug. 16**
**1485** A701 4.50r brown .20 .20

Robert Gunawardena, Communist Leader — A702

**2004, Aug. 23** ***Perf. 14x13¾***
**1486** A702 4.50r multi .20 .20

Pres. Junius Richard Jayewardene (1906-96) A703

**2004, Sept. 27** ***Perf. 13***
**1487** A703 4.50r multi .20 .20

Intl. Day of Peace — A704

**2004, Sept. 21**
**1488** A704 4.50r multi .20 .20

Sri Chandrarathna Manawasinghe, Writer — A705

**2004, Oct. 6** ***Perf. 12x13¼***
**1489** A705 4.50r multi .20 .20

Government Service Buddhist Association, 50th Anniv. — A706

**2004, Oct. 7** ***Perf. 13***
**1490** A706 4.50r multi .20 .20

World Post Day — A707

**2004, Oct. 9** ***Perf. 12x13½***
**1491** A707 4.50r multi .20 .20

Raddelle Sri Pannaloka Anunayaka Thero, Religious Leader — A708

**2004, Oct. 20** ***Perf. 13***
**1492** A708 4.50r multi .20 .20

Christmas A709

**2004, Nov. 27** ***Perf. 14x13¾***
**1493** A709 5r multi .20 .20

Fathers Jacome Gonsalves and Edmond Peiris — A710

**2004, Nov. 27** ***Perf. 13¼x12***
**1494** A710 20r multi .40 .40

Information and Communication Technology Week — A711

**2004, Nov. 29** ***Perf. 13¾x14***
**1495** A711 5r multi .20 .20

De Soysa Hospital for Women, Colombo, 125th Anniv. A712

**2004, Dec. 11** ***Perf. 13½x14***
**1496** A712 5r multi .20 .20

**Blue Sapphire Type of 2003**

**2004, Dec. 14 Litho.** ***Perf. 12x13½***
**1497** A676 5r multi .20 .20

Most Venerable Talalle Siri Dhammananda Maha Nayaka Thero, Educator — A713

**2005, Mar. 13** ***Perf. 14x13¾***
**1498** A713 5r multi .20 .20

Most Venerable Hammalawa Saddhatissa Nayaka Maha Thero (1914-90), Monk — A714

**2005, Mar. 22**
**1499** A714 5r multi .20 .20

T. B. Tennakoon, Politician — A715

**2005, Mar. 25**
**1500** A715 5r multi .20 .20

D. A. Rajapaksa (1905-67), Politician A716

**2005, Mar. 25** ***Perf. 13¾x14***
**1501** A716 5r multi .20 .20

Vesak Festival — A717

Designs: 4.50r, Ambulatory meditation. 5r, Spiritual bliss through Buddhism. 10r, Meditation in standing posture. 50r, Sedentary meditation.

**2005, May 12** ***Perf. 14x13¾***
**1502-1505** A717 Set of 4 1.40 1.40
*1505a* Sheet, #1502-1505 1.40 1.40

Compare with Type A723.

Rev. Marcelline Jayakody (1902-98) A718

**2005, June 3** ***Perf. 13***
**1506** A718 20r multi .40 .40

Rana Viru Day — A719

**2005, June 7** ***Perf. 14x13¾***
**1507** A719 50r multi 1.00 1.00

Deshamanya M. A. Bakeer Markar (1917-96), Parliament Speaker — A720

**2005, July 20**
**1508** A720 5r multi .20 .20

Most Venerable Matara Kithalagama Sri Seelalankara Nayaka Thero — A721

**2005, July 21**
**1509** A721 25r multi .50 .50

South Asia Tourism Year — A722

**2005, July 29** ***Perf. 13***
**1510** A722 100r multi 2.00 2.00

Kalutara Bodhi Trust A723

**2005, Aug. 6** ***Perf. 13¾x14***
**1511** A723 5r multi .20 .20

No. 1352 Surcharged Like No. 1409 and Nos. 564, 815, 818 and 937 Surcharged

**Methods and Perfs As Before**

**2005**

| | | | | |
|---|---|---|---|---|
| **1512** | A206 | 50c on 10c #564 | .20 | .20 |
| **1513** | A324 | 50c on 35c #815 | .20 | .20 |
| **1514** | A618 | 50c on 2r #1352 | .20 | .20 |
| **1515** | A399 | 50c on 5.75r #937 | .20 | .20 |
| **1516** | A324 | 50c on 6r #818 | .20 | .20 |
| | | *Nos. 1512-1516 (5)* | 1.00 | 1.00 |

Issued: No. 1514, 9/16; others, 3/21.

Postal Headquarters — A725

**2005, Sept. 12 Litho.** ***Perf. 13½x14***
**1518** A725 5r multi .20 .20

Ampitiya National Seminary A726

**2005, Oct. 1**
**1519** A726 10r multi .20 .20

World Post Day A727

**2005, Oct. 9**
**1520** A727 5r multi .20 .20

General Sir John Kotelawala Defense Academy, 25th Anniv. — A728

**2005, Oct. 11** **Litho.** ***Perf. 13***
**1521** A728 5r multi .20 .20

Christmas A729

Cross of Blessed Joseph Vaz, Madonna and Child and: 5r, Angel. 30r, Star of Bethlehem.

**2005, Dec. 3** **Litho.** ***Perf. 13¾x14***
**1522-1523** A729 Set of 2 .70 .70
*1523a* Souvenir sheet, #1522-1523 .70 .70

Admission to the UN, 50th Anniv. — A730

**2005, Dec. 13** **Litho.** ***Perf. 14x13½***
**1524** A730 20r multi .40 .40

Amarapura Maha Nikaya, Bicent. A731

**2005, Dec. 20** ***Perf. 13½x14***
**1525** A731 10r multi .20 .20

Ancient Sri Lanka — A732

Designs: 5r, Minhagalkanda and stone tools. 20r, Extinct animals in Ratnapura gem gravels and rhinoceros and hippopotamus bone fragments. 25r, Kuruwita, Batadombalena and human skull from Bellan-bandi Palassa. 30r, Agriculture on the Horton Plains, fossilized barley pollen grain.

**2005, Dec. 21** ***Perf. 13¼x12***
**1526-1529** A732 Set of 4 1.60 1.60

Damage From Dec. 26, 2004 Tsunami A733

Designs: 5r, Damaged Kalmunai Post Office, vehicles. 20r, Train derailed near Telwatte. 30r, Giant wave breaking along coast. 33r, Lighthouse and tsunami wave.

**2005, Dec. 26** **Litho.** ***Perf. 13¾x14***
**1530-1533** A733 Set of 4 1.75 1.75
*1533a* Souvenir sheet, #1530-1533 1.75 1.75

Animals of Wilpattu National Park — A734

Designs: 5r, Barking deer. 10r, White-bellied sea eagle. 20r, Sloth bear. 50r, Leopard.

**2006, Jan. 4** **Litho.** ***Perf. 13½x12***
**1534** A734 5r multi .20 .20
*a.* Souvenir sheet of 1 .20 .20
**1535** A734 10r multi .20 .20
*a.* Souvenir sheet of 1 .20 .20
**1536** A734 20r multi .40 .40
*a.* Souvenir sheet of 1 .40 .40
**1537** A734 50r multi 1.00 1.00
*a.* Souvenir sheet of 1 1.00 1.00
*Nos. 1534-1537 (4)* 1.80 1.80

Institution of Engineers Sri Lanka, Cent. — A735

**2006, Jan. 6** **Litho.** ***Perf. 12x13¼***
**1538** A735 5r black & blue .20 .20

Europa Stamps, 50th Anniv. — A736

Sri Lanka flag and: 100r, Ceylon #336. 500r, Ship, maps of Europe and Sri Lanka.

**2006, Feb. 2** ***Perf. 12¾x13¼***
**1539-1540** A736 Set of 2 12.00 12.00
*1540a* Souvenir sheet, #1539-1540 12.00 12.00

Most Venerable Madithiyawala Vijithasena Anunayake Thero — A737

**2006, Mar. 5** **Litho.** ***Perf. 14x13¾***
**1541** A737 17r multi .35 .35

100th Kingswood-Dharmaraja Cricket Match — A738

**2006, Mar. 24** ***Perf. 13¾x14***
**1542** A738 4.50r multi .20 .20

Vesak — A739

No. 1543: a, Wall painting depicting a plea to the Master to descend from heaven, Tivamka Image House, Polonnaruva (1/50). b, Bas-relief of Queen Mahamaya on her way to visit her parents, Jetavana Vihara, Anuradhapura (2/50). c, Wall painting depicting birth of Prince Siddhartha, Shailabimbarama Vihara, Dodanduwa (3/50). d, Wall painting of royal teacher Asita visiting Prince Siddhartha, Purwarama Viharaya, Kataluva (4/50). e, Bas-relief of Great Renunciation, Girihandu Vihara, Ambalantota (5/50). f, Rock painting depicting defeat of evils by the Master, Hindagala Vihara, Hindagala (6/50). g, Rock painting depicting first sermon of Dhammachakka, Rangiri Dambulu Vihara, Dambulla (7/50). h, Wall painting depicting conversion of Alavaka, Sapugoda Vihara, Beruvala (8/50). i, Wall painting depicting funeral pyre of the Master, Veheragalla Samudragiri Vihara, Mirissa (9/50). j, Tapassu and Bhalluka arriving in Sri Lanka with relics of the Master, Girihandu Seya, Tiriyaya (10/50). k, Wall painting depicting perfection of generosity, Bodhirukkharama Vihara, Eluvapitiya (11/50). l, Rock painting depicting perfection of wisdom, Kaballelena Vihara, Wariyapola (12/50). m, Wall painting depicting perfection of reunification, Degaldoruva Vihara, Kandy (13/50). n, Wall painting depicting perfection of equanimity, Paramakanda Vihara, Anamaduwa (14/50). o, Wall painting depicting perfection of loving kindness, Sunandarama Vihara, Ambalangoda (15/50). p, Recitation of Chullahastpadopama Sutta by Arhat Mahinda, Stupa, Mihintale (16/50). q, Establishment of Buddhism in Sri Lanka, Rajagiri Lena, Mihintale (17/50). r, Sri Maha Bodhi entering city, Sri Maha Bodhi, Anuradhapura (18/50). s, Writing Dhamma on ola leaves, Alu Vihara, Matale (19/50). t, Arrival of tooth relic of the Master, Lankapattana, Trincomalee (20/50). u, Practice of aranyaka, Situlpavuva Vihara (21/50). v, Symbols of three traditions, Lovamahapaya, Abhayagiri Vihara, Vajra symbol and lotus (22/50). w, Emergence of katikavatas, Vatadage, Polonnaruva (23/50). x, Buddhist discourse between Sri Lanka and Southeast Asia, Tooth Relic Temple, Kandy (24/50). y, Translation of the Tripitaka into Sinhala, Buddhajayanti Vihara, Colombo (25/50). z, Vesak festival scene, Deepaduttarama Vihara, Kotahena (26/50). aa, Serving of food to Buddhist clergy, Refectory at Abhayagiriya, Anuradhapura (27/50). ab, Chanting Paritta, Nishshanka Lata Mandapa, Polonnaruva (28/50). ac, Combination with village, temple tank and stupa, Tissamaharama Stupa (29/50). ad, Veneration of Bodhi tree, Bodhighara, Nillakgama (30/50). ae, Hatthikuchchi Vihara, Galgamuva, Padhanaghara, Anuradhapura (31/50). af, Ritual performance for tooth relic, Atadage, Polonnaruva (32/50). ag, Perahara, Subodharma Vihara, Karagampitiya (33/50). ah, Wall painting of a street market, Mulgirigala Vihara, local coin (34/50). ai, Sanctity of the temple, Namal Uyana, Ranava (35/50). aj, Ruvanvalisaya and Thuparama Stupas, Anuradhapura (36/50). ak, Kirivehera Stupa, Kataragama, Seruvila Stupa (37/50). al, Mahiyangana and Nagadipa Stupas, Jaffna (38/50). am, Kelaniya Stupa and Samantakuta (39/50). an, Mutiyangana Stupa, Badulla, and Deeghavapi Stupa (40/50). ao, Painted stupa, Hanguranketa Raja Maha Vihara, ancient stupas at Kandarodai, Jaffna (41/50). ap, Facade of Mihintale Stupa, bas-relief of Bahiravas (42/50). aq, Twin pond, Anuradhapura, Punkalasa lotus pond, Polonnaruva (43/50). ar, Moonstone, Mangul Maha Vihara, Lahugala (44/50). as, Bodhisattva Avalokiteshvara, Muhudumaha Vihara, Potuvil (45/50). at, Nalanda Gedige, Naula, Satmahal Prasada, Polonnaruva (46/50). au, Bas-relief of Vimana, Lankatilaka Vihara, Polonnaruva (47/50). av, Thuparama Image House, Polonnaruva, Tampita Vihara, Menikkadawara (48/50). aw, Wall painting depicting Buddhist cosmos, Omalpe Vihara, Kolonne (49/50). ax, Depiction of time in the motif of Makara, Madanvala Vihara, Hanguranketa (50/50).

**2006, May 5** **Litho.** ***Perf. 13¼x12***
**1543** Sheet of 50 7.75 7.75
*a.-j.* A739 2.50r Any single .20 .20
*k.-t.* A739 4.50r Any single .20 .20
*u.-ad.* A739 5r Any single .20 .20
*ae.-an.* A739 10r Any single .20 .20
*ao.-ax.* A739 17r Any single .30 .30

Sinhala Bauddhaya Newspaper, Cent. — A740

**2006, May 7** ***Perf. 13¾x14***
**1544** A740 5r multi .20 .20

Natl. Cadet Corps, 125th Anniv. — A741

**2006, May 18** ***Perf. 12x13¼***
**1545** A741 2r multi .20 .20

Kotte Sri Kalyani Samagridharma Maha Sanga Sabha, 150th Anniv. — A742

**2006, June 25** ***Perf. 13¾x14***
**1546** A742 4.50r multi .20 .20

Sri Lanka Ramanna Maha Nikaya — A743

**2006, June 29** ***Perf. 14x13¾***
**1547** A743 4.50r multi .20 .20

Nos. 592, 1154, and 1353 Surcharged

**Methods and Perfs As Before**

**2006**
**1548** A518 10r on 10.50r #1154 .20 .20
**1549** A618 20r on 3r #1353 .40 .40
**1550** A218 50r on 1.60r #592 .95 .95
*Nos. 1548-1550 (3)* 1.55 1.55

Size, location and style of surcharges vary.

### POSTAL-FISCAL STAMP

The editors believe that seven additional revenue stamps were authorized for postal use during 1979-98 and would like to examine them.

National Coat of Arms — PF1

*Perf. 14½x14*

**1984** **Engr.** **Wmk. 233**

| No. | Type | Value | Unused | Used |
|---|---|---|---|---|
| **AR6** | PF1 | 50r vermilion | 1.50 | 1.50 |
| **AR7** | PF1 | 100r deep claret | 3.00 | 3.00 |

A lithographed 500r value exists but was not authorized for postal use.

## STELLALAND

ˈste-lə-ˌland

LOCATION — South Africa
GOVT. — Republic
AREA — 5,000 sq. mi. (approx.)
CAPITAL — Vryburg

This short-lived republic was set up by the Boers in an effort to annex territory ruled by the Bechuana chiefs. Great Britain refused to recognize it and in 1885 sent an expeditionary force which ended the political career of the country.

Stellaland was annexed by Great Britain in 1885 and became a part of British Bechuanaland.

12 Pence = 1 Shilling

Coat of Arms
A1 A2

**1884, Feb.** **Unwmk.** **Typo.** ***Perf. 12***

| No. | Type | Description | Unused | Used |
|---|---|---|---|---|
| **1** | A1 | 1p red | 225.00 | *375.00* |
| *a.* | | Horiz. pair, imperf. vert. | 4,250. | |
| *b.* | | Vert. pair, imperf. horiz. | 4,600. | |
| **2** | A1 | 3p orange | 25.00 | *375.00* |
| *a.* | | Horiz. pair, imperf. vert. | 800.00 | |
| *b.* | | Vert. pair, imperf. horiz. | 1,450. | |
| **3** | A1 | 4p gray | 24.00 | *400.00* |
| *a.* | | Horiz. pair, imperf. vert. | 750.00 | |
| *b.* | | Vert. pair, imperf. horiz. | *1,900.* | |
| **4** | A1 | 6p lilac | 25.00 | *400.00* |
| *a.* | | Horiz. pair, imperf. vert. | 1,400. | |
| *b.* | | Vert. pair, imperf. horiz. | 1,600. | |
| **5** | A1 | 1sh green | 62.50 | *750.00* |
| | | *Nos. 1-5 (5)* | 361.50 | 2,300. |

Imperf. varieties are believed to be proofs.

No. 3 Handstamped "Twee" in Blackish Violet

**1885**

| No. | Type | Description | Unused | Used |
|---|---|---|---|---|
| **6** | A2 | 2p on 4p gray | *4,000.* | |

The status of No. 6 has long been questioned.

## STRAITS SETTLEMENTS

ˈstrāts ˈse-təl-mənt

LOCATION — Malay Peninsula in southeastern Asia
GOVT. — British Colony
AREA — 1,356 sq. mi.
POP. — 1,435,895 (estimated)
CAPITAL — Singapore

The colony comprised the settlements of Malacca, Singapore and Penang, which were incorporated under one government in 1826 and the administration transferred from India to the Secretary of State for the Colonies in 1867.

The colony was dissolved in 1946 when Singapore became a separate crown colony. Malacca and Penang were incorporated into the Malayan Union, which became the Federation of Malaya in 1948.

Stamps of India were used in Malacca, Penang and Singapore, 1854-67.

See Malaya for stamps of the Federated Malay States, the Federation of Malaya, Johore, Kedah, Kelantan, Malacca, Negri Sembilan, Pahang, Penang, Perak, Perlis, Selangor, Sungei Ujong and Trengganu.

100 Cents = 1 Dollar

Stamps of India Surcharged in Red, Blue, Black Violet or Green:

Nos. 1-7

24 CENTS
Nos. 8-9

**1867, Sept. 1** **Wmk. 38** ***Perf. 14***

| No. | Type | Description | Unused | Used |
|---|---|---|---|---|
| **1** | A7 | 1½c on ½a bl (R) | 97.50 | *190.00* |
| **2** | A7 | 2c on 1a brn (R) | 130.00 | 75.00 |
| **3** | A7 | 3c on 1a brn (Bl) | 140.00 | 80.00 |
| **4** | A7 | 4c on 1a brn (Bk) | 275.00 | *250.00* |
| **5** | A7 | 6c on 2a yel (V) | 625.00 | 225.00 |
| **6** | A7 | 8c on 2a yel (G) | 200.00 | 40.00 |
| **7** | A9 | 12c on 4a grn (R) | 1,050. | 275.00 |
| *a.* | | Double surcharge | 2,250. | |
| **8** | A7 | 24c on 8a rose (Bl) | 450.00 | 72.50 |
| **9** | A7 | 32c on 2a yel (Bk) | 375.00 | 80.00 |

**Manuscript Surcharge, Pen Bar Across "THREE HALF" of No. 1**

| No. | Type | Description | Unused | Used |
|---|---|---|---|---|
| **9A** | A7 | 2(c) on 1½c on ½a | *10,500.* | *5,000.* |

Values for Nos. 1-9A are for stamps with perforations touching the frame line on one or two sides. Used values for Nos. 1-9 are for stamps with company chops in addition to postal cancellations. Examples with postal cancels only sell for somewhat lower prices.

A2 A3

A4 A5

**1867-72** **Typo.** **Wmk. 1** ***Perf. 14***

| No. | Type | Description | Unused | Used |
|---|---|---|---|---|
| **10** | A2 | 2c bister brown | 30.00 | 4.50 |
| **11** | A2 | 4c rose | 50.00 | 7.75 |
| **12** | A2 | 6c violet | 87.50 | 16.50 |
| **13** | A3 | 8c yellow | 150.00 | 10.00 |
| *a.* | | 8c orange | 150.00 | 11.00 |
| **14** | A3 | 12c blue | 125.00 | 10.00 |
| **15** | A3 | 24c green | 125.00 | 5.75 |
| **16** | A4 | 30c claret ('72) | 225.00 | 12.50 |
| **17** | A5 | 32c pale red | 500.00 | 75.00 |
| **18** | A5 | 96c olive gray | 300.00 | 45.00 |
| | | *Nos. 10-18 (9)* | 1,592. | 187.00 |

Corner ornaments of types A2, A3 and A5 differ for each value.

See Nos. 19, 40-44, 48-50, 52-57. For surcharges see Nos. 20-35, 58-59, 61-66, 73-82, 91. For overprints see Malaya, Johore No. 1, Perak Nos. 1, O1-O2, Selangor Nos. 1-2, Sungei Ujong Nos. 2-3.

See the *Scott Classic Catalogue* for other shades.

**Stamps of Straits Settlements, 1867-82, overprinted "B" are listed under Bangkok.**

**1871** ***Perf. 12½***

| No. | Type | Description | Unused | Used |
|---|---|---|---|---|
| **19** | A5 | 96c olive gray | 2,300. | 275.00 |

Stamps of 1867-72 Surcharged:

**1879, May** ***Perf. 14***

| No. | Type | Description | Unused | Used |
|---|---|---|---|---|
| **20** | A3 | 5c on 8c yellow | 100.00 | 160.00 |
| *a.* | | No period after "CENTS" | 825.00 | 875.00 |
| **21** | A5 | 7c on 32c pale red | 125.00 | 150.00 |
| *a.* | | No period after "CENTS" | 1,100. | 1,200. |

No. 16 Surcharged:

e f g

10 10 10 10
j k m h

**1880**

| No. | Type | Description | Unused | Used |
|---|---|---|---|---|
| **22** | A4(e) | 10c on 30c | 175.00 | 55.00 |
| **23** | A4(f) | 10c on 30c | 550.00 | 125.00 |
| **24** | A4(g) | 10c on 30c | 190.00 | 55.00 |
| **25** | A4(h) | 10c on 30c | — | |
| **25A** | A4(j) | 10c on 30c | 3,800. | 925.00 |
| **25B** | A4(k) | 10c on 30c | 3,800. | 925.00 |
| **25C** | A4(m) | 10c on 30c | 3,800. | 925.00 |

Surcharges e & f and g, h, j & m are virtually identical. These must have an expert certificate identifying them. Values can be suspect because of misidentifications.

Unused examples are valued without gum.

With Additional Surcharge *cents*

| No. | Type | Description | Unused | Used |
|---|---|---|---|---|
| **26** | A4(e) | 10c on 30c | 325.00 | 82.50 |
| **27** | A4(f) | 10c on 30c | 4,750. | 700.00 |
| **27A** | A4(g) | 10c on 30c | 3,000. | 500.00 |
| **28** | A4(h) | 10c on 30c | *8,750.* | 1,425. |
| **28A** | A4(j) | 10c on 30c | *8,750.* | 1,425. |
| **28B** | A4(k) | 10c on 30c | *8,750.* | 1,425. |
| **28C** | A4(m) | 10c on 30c | *8,750.* | 1,425. |

Unused examples are valued without gum.

No. 13 Surcharged:

n o p

**1880**

| No. | Type | Description | Unused | Used |
|---|---|---|---|---|
| **29** | A3(n) | 5c on 8c yellow | 125.00 | *150.00* |
| **30** | A3(o) | 5c on 8c yellow | 450.00 | 525.00 |
| **31** | A3(p) | 5c on 8c yellow | 130.00 | *160.00* |

No. 11 Surcharged *5 cents.*

**1882, Jan.**

| No. | Type | Description | Unused | Used |
|---|---|---|---|---|
| **32** | A2 | 5c on 4c rose | 275.00 | *300.00* |

Nos. 12, 14a, 16 Surcharged

**1880-81**

| No. | Type | Description | Unused | Used |
|---|---|---|---|---|
| **33** | A2 | 10c on 6c violet ('81) | 65.00 | 7.50 |
| *a.* | | Double surcharge | | 2,100. |
| **34** | A3 | 10c on 12c blue ('81) | 52.50 | 12.00 |
| **35** | A4 | 10c on 30c claret | 400.00 | 97.50 |
| | | *Nos. 33-35 (3)* | 517.50 | 117.00 |

A6 A7

**1882, Jan.** **Typo.** ***Perf. 14***

| No. | Type | Description | Unused | Used |
|---|---|---|---|---|
| **38** | A6 | 5c violet brown | 87.50 | 100.00 |
| **39** | A7 | 10c slate | 400.00 | 75.00 |

See Nos. 45-47, 51. For surcharges see Nos. 60, 67-72, 89-92.

**1882-99** **Wmk. Crown and C A (2)**

| No. | Type | Description | Unused | Used |
|---|---|---|---|---|
| **40** | A2 | 2c bister brown | 250.00 | 45.00 |
| **41** | A2 | 2c car rose ('83) | 7.00 | 1.00 |
| *a.* | | 2c rose | 40.00 | 4.00 |
| **42** | A2 | 4c rose | 125.00 | 6.00 |
| **43** | A2 | 4c car rose ('99) | 5.25 | 1.40 |
| **44** | A2 | 4c bister brn ('83) | 27.50 | 1.50 |
| **45** | A6 | 5c ultra ('83) | 13.00 | 1.10 |
| **46** | A6 | 5c brown ('94) | 5.50 | 1.10 |
| **47** | A6 | 5c magenta ('99) | 2.75 | *2.40* |
| **48** | A2 | 6c violet | 2.25 | *4.00* |
| **49** | A3 | 8c orange | 3.50 | 1.10 |
| **50** | A3 | 8c ultra ('94) | 5.25 | .60 |
| **51** | A7 | 10c slate | 5.50 | 1.50 |
| **52** | A3 | 12c vio brn ('83) | 70.00 | 12.00 |
| **53** | A3 | 12c claret ('94) | 12.00 | *9.75* |
| **54** | A3 | 24c blue grn ('83) | 4.75 | *4.50* |
| *a.* | | 24c yellow green ('84) | 77.50 | 7.00 |
| **55** | A4 | 30c claret ('91) | 10.00 | 11.00 |
| **56** | A5 | 32c red org ('87) | 8.00 | 3.00 |
| **57** | A5 | 96c olive gray ('88) | 82.50 | 52.50 |
| | | *Nos. 40-57 (18)* | 639.75 | 159.45 |

For overprints see Malaya, Perak #O3-O9, Selangor #3-4, Sungei Ujong #6-7, 11.

Preceding Issues Surcharged

Surcharged Vertically

**1883-84** **Wmk. 2, 1**

| No. | Type | Description | Unused | Used |
|---|---|---|---|---|
| **58** | A3 | 2c on 8c orange | 125.00 | 77.50 |
| *a.* | | Double surcharge | *2,750.* | *1,100.* |
| **59** | A5 | 2c on 32c pale red | 650.00 | 190.00 |
| *a.* | | Double surcharge | | |
| **60** | A6 | 2c on 5c ultra ('84) | 130.00 | 140.00 |
| *a.* | | Pair, one without surcharge | | |
| *b.* | | Double surcharge | | |
| | | *Nos. 58-60 (3)* | 905.00 | 407.50 |

Five types of surcharge on No. 58, two types on No. 59 and three types on No. 60.

Surcharged in Black

**1883** **Wmk. 2**

| No. | Type | Description | Unused | Used |
|---|---|---|---|---|
| **61** | A2 | 2c on 4c rose | 85.00 | *97.50* |
| *b.* | | "s" of "Cents." inverted | 1,325. | 1,425. |

**Wmk. 1**

| No. | Type | Description | Unused | Used |
|---|---|---|---|---|
| **62** | A3 | 2c on 12c blue | 275.00 | 140.00 |
| *a.* | | "s" of "Cents." inverted | 4,000. | 2,000. |

Surcharged in Black or Blue *8 Cents*

**1884**

| No. | Type | Description | Unused | Used |
|---|---|---|---|---|
| **63** | A3 | 8c on 12c blue | 475.00 | 130.00 |

**Wmk. 2**

| No. | Type | Description | Unused | Used |
|---|---|---|---|---|
| **64** | A3 | 8c on 12c vio brn | 325.00 | 130.00 |

With Additional Surcharge Handstamped in Red

8

| No. | Type | Description | Unused | Used |
|---|---|---|---|---|
| **65** | A3 | 8c on 8c on 12c vio brn (R + Bk) | 275.00 | 300.00 |
| **66** | A3 | 8c on 8c on 12c vio brn (R + Bl) | 7,250. | |

Surcharged in Black or Red — 4 Cents

**1884**

**67** A6 4c on 5c ultra (Bk) 3,250. *4,250.*
**68** A6 4c on 5c ultra (R) 125.00 110.00

No. 68 Surcharged in Red — 4

**69** A6 4c on 4c on 5c ultra *24,000.*

No. 69 may be a trial printing. "Usage" seems to be restricted to less than 10 letters known sent from the Postmaster General to his wife.

Surcharged in Black

**1885-87**

**70** A6 3c on 5c ultra 125.00 *250.00*
*a.* Double surcharge 2,500.

Surcharged in Black — 3 cents

**71** A6 3c on 5c vio brn ('86) 210.00 *225.00*

Surcharged

**72** A6 2c on 5c ultra ('87) 25.00 *70.00*
*a.* Double surcharge 1,200. 1,100.
*b.* "C" omitted *3,000.*

In the surcharged issues of 1883 to 1887, Nos. 59, 62, 63 and 71 are on stamps watermarked Crown and C C, the others are watermarked Crown and C A.

Surcharged

**1885-94 Wmk. Crown and C A (2)**

**73** A5 3c on 32c magenta 1.50 1.10
**74** A5 3c on 32c rose ('94) 2.75 .85
*a.* Without surcharge *4,000.*

No. 74a value is for copy with perfs touching frame line.

Surcharged

**1891**

**75** A3 10c on 24c green 3.50 1.40
*a.* Narrow "0" in "10" 32.50 32.50

Surcharged

**76** A5 30c on 32c red orange 8.25 4.25

Surcharged

**1892**

**77** A2 1c on 2c rose 2.25 *4.25*
**78** A2 1c on 4c bister brn 5.75 *6.25*
*a.* Double surcharge 1,300.
**79** A2 1c on 6c violet 1.60 *5.50*
*a.* Dbl. surch., one invtd. 1,425. 1,325.
**80** A3 1c on 8c orange 1.25 1.50
**81** A3 1c on 12c vio brown 5.75 *10.50*
*Nos. 77-81 (5)* 16.60 28.00

Surcharged

**82** A3 1c on 8c gray green 1.10 *1.75*

Queen Victoria — A13

**1892-99 Typo.**

**83** A13 1c gray green 3.75 .80
**84** A13 3c car rose ('95) 12.50 .55
**85** A13 3c brown ('99) 6.50 .70
**86** A13 25c dk vio & grn 26.00 7.50
**87** A13 50c ol grn & car 22.50 3.00
**88** A13 $5 org & car ('98) 500.00 275.00
*Nos. 83-88 (6)* 571.25 287.55

Denomination of $5, is in color on plain tablet.

Stamps of 1883-94 Surcharged

**1899**

**89** A6 4c on 5c ultra 4.00 *15.00*
*a.* Double surcharge 1,400.
**90** A6 4c on 5c brown 3.25 *5.25*
**91** A3 4c on 8c brt blue 1.50 *1.25*
*b.* Double surcharge *1,100. 1,000.*
*Nos. 89-91 (3)* 8.75 *21.50*

Type of 1882 Issue Surcharged

**92** A6 4c on 5c rose .85 .40
*a.* Without surcharge *30,000.*

King Edward VII — A14

Numerals of 5c, 8c, 10c, 30c, $1 and $5, type A14, are in color on plain tablet.

**1902 Wmk. 2 Typo.**

**93** A14 1c green 3.25 *3.50*
**94** A14 3c vio & org 4.00 .25
**95** A14 4c violet, *red* 5.50 .35
**96** A14 5c violet 6.25 .95
**97** A14 8c violet, *blue* 4.50 .30
**98** A14 10c vio & blk, *yel* 29.00 1.75
**99** A14 25c violet & grn 14.00 7.00
**100** A14 30c gray & car rose 21.00 9.25
**101** A14 50c grn & car rose 22.50 22.50
**102** A14 $1 green & blk 25.00 *75.00*
**103** A14 $2 violet & blk 80.00 80.00
**104** A14 $5 grn & brn org 225.00 190.00
**104A** A14 $100 dl vio & grn, *yel* *11,000.*
*Nos. 93-104 (12)* 440.00 390.85

High values of the 1902 and 1904 issues with revenue cancellations are of minimal value. No. 104A is inscribed "Postage & Revenue" but the limit of weight probably precluded its use postally.

See Nos. 113, 115-128B, 133.

A15 A16

A17 A18

**1903-04**

**105** A15 1c gray green 2.00 9.25
**106** A16 3c dull violet 12.50 5.25
**107** A17 4c violet, *red* 5.50 .35
**108** A18 8c violet, *blue* 55.00 1.50
*Nos. 105-108 (4)* 75.00 16.35

See Nos. 109-112, 114, 129-132, 134.

**1904-11 Wmk. 3**

**Chalky Paper**

**109** A15 1c gray green 3.25 .20
**110** A16 3c dull violet 2.75 .35
**111** A17 4c violet, *red* 11.50 .85
**112** A17 4c dull vio ('08) 6.25 .20
**113** A14 5c violet ('06) 12.50 2.75
**114** A18 8c violet, *bl* 32.50 1.75
**115** A14 10c vio & blk, *yel* 9.25 .90
**116** A14 10c vio, *yel* ('08) 8.50 1.10
**117** A14 25c vio & grn 37.50 24.00
**118** A14 25c violet ('09) 16.00 8.00
**119** A14 30c gray & car rose 55.00 3.00
**120** A14 30c vio & org ('09) 45.00 4.50
**121** A14 50c grn & car rose 62.50 17.50
**122** A14 50c blk, *grn* ('10) 5.75 *5.50*
**123** A14 $1 green & blk *62.50 21.00*
**124** A14 $1 blk & red, *bl* ('11) 17.00 5.75
**125** A14 $2 violet & blk 110.00 97.50
Revenue cancel 12.00
**126** A14 $2 grn & red, *yel* ('09) 27.50 27.50
**127** A14 $5 grn & brn org 225.00 160.00
**128** A14 $5 grn & red, *grn* ('10) 140.00 85.00
Revenue cancel 5.00
**128A** A14 $25 green & blk 1,725. 1,600.
Revenue cancel 55.00
**128B** A14 $100 dl vio & grn, *yel* *12,650.*
Revenue cancel 200.00
*Nos. 109-128 (20)* 890.25 467.35

Nos. 125, 128A and 128B are on chalky paper, the other values are on both ordinary and chalky. The note about No. 104A will apply to No. 128B.

**1906-11**

**Ordinary Paper**

**129** A15 1c blue grn ('10) 26.00 1.25
**130** A16 3c carmine ('08) 3.75 .20
**131** A17 4c carmine ('07) 6.25 3.00
**132** A17 4c lake ('11) 2.25 .95
**133** A14 5c orange ('09) 3.25 2.25
**134** A18 8c ultra ('06) 4.00 .60
*Nos. 129-134 (6)* 45.50 8.25

Stamps of Labuan 1902-03, Overprinted or Surcharged in Red or Black

a

b

c

***Perf. 12½ to 16 and Compound***

**1907 Unwmk.**

**134A** A38(a) 1c violet & blk 70.00 *200.00*
**135** A38(a) 2c grn & blk 350.00 *350.00*
**136** A38(a) 3c brn & blk 22.50 *97.50*
**137** A38(c) 4c on 12c yel & blk 2.75 *7.00*
*a.* No period after "CENTS" 350.00 —
**138** A38(c) 4c on 16c org brn & grn (Bk) 5.25 *9.25*
*a.* With additional name in red 750.00 800.00
**139** A38(c) 4c on 18c bis & blk 3.25 *7.50*
*a.* No period after "CENTS" 325.00 —
*b.* "FOUR CENTS." & bar double 8,650.
**140** A38(a) 8c org & blk 3.50 *9.25*
**141** A38(b) 10c sl bl & brn 8.50 *8.00*
*a.* No period after "Settlements" 375.00
**142** A38(a) 25c grnsh bl & grn 17.00 *45.00*
**143** A38(a) 50c gray lil & vio 18.00 *80.00*
**144** A38(a) $1 org & red brn 52.50 *125.00*
*Nos. 134A-144 (11)* 553.25 *938.50*

A19

A20

**1908-11 Typo. Wmk. 3 *Perf. 14***

**Chalky Paper**

**145** A19 $25 bl & vio, *bl* ('11) 1,600. 1,250.
**146** A19 $500 violet & org *92,000.*
Revenue cancel 275.

No. 146 is inscribed "Postage-Revenue" but was probably used only for revenue.
Excellent forgeries of No. 146 exist.

**1910**

**Chalky Paper**

**147** A20 21c maroon & vio 7.50 *40.00*
**148** A20 45c black, *green* 3.00 4.50

King George V
A21 A22

A23

A24

A25

A26

Die I (Type A24).

For description of dies I and II see "Dies of British Colonial Stamps" in Table of Contents.
The 25c, 50c and $2 denominations of type A24 show the numeral on horizontally-lined tablet.

**1912-18 Chalky Paper Wmk. 3**

**149** A21 1c green 7.00 1.50
**150** A21 1c black ('18) 1.75 *1.10*
**151** A25 2c dp green ('18) 1.10 .60
**152** A22 3c scarlet 2.50 .40
*a.* 3c carmine 3.25 1.00
**153** A23 4c gray violet 1.75 .40
**154** A23 4c scarlet ('18) 2.75 .20
*a.* Booklet pane of 1
*b.* Booklet pane of 12
*c.* 4c carmine ('18) 2.75 .20
**155** A24 5c orange 2.00 .60
**156** A25 6c claret ('18) 2.00 .60
**157** A25 8c ultra 2.25 .90
**158** A24 10c violet, *yel* 1.75 .60
**159** A24 10c ultra ('18) 7.00 .60
**160** A26 21c maroon & vio 5.75 *11.00*
**161** A24 25c vio & red vio 14.00 9.75
**162** A24 30c vio & org ('14) 9.25 2.25
**163** A26 45c blk, *bl grn,* ol back ('14) 3.75 *22.50*
*a.* 45c black, *emerald* ('17) 3.75 *15.00*
**164** A24 50c black, *grn* ('14) 6.50 3.25
*a.* 50c blk, *bl grn,* olive back 21.00 8.50
*b.* 50c black, *emerald* 14.00 11.00
*c.* Die II 3.50 4.50
**165** A24 $1 blk & red, *bl* ('14) 10.50 9.75
**166** A24 $2 grn & red, *yel* ('15) 11.50 50.00
**167** A24 $5 grn & red, *grn* ('15) 92.50 70.00
*a.* $5 grn & red, *bl grn,* ol back 175.00 97.50
*b.* $5 grn & red, *emer* ('15) 92.50 110.00
*c.* Die II 110.00 75.00
*Nos. 149-167 (19)* 185.60 186.00

The 1c, 3c, 5c and 8c are on ordinary paper.

**Surface-colored Paper**

**168** A24 10c violet, *yel* 1.75 1.10
**169** A26 45c black, *grn* ('14) 7.50 *21.00*
**170** A24 $2 grn & red, *yel* ('14) 9.75 *50.00*
**171** A24 $5 grn & red, *grn* 92.50 50.00
*Nos. 168-171 (4)* 111.50 *122.10*

See Nos. 179-201. For surcharges see Nos. B1-B2.

A27

**1915**

**172** A27 $25 bl & vio, *bl* 1,400. 500.00
Revenue cancel 5.75
**173** A27 $100 red & blk, *bl* *5,750.*
Revenue cancel 90.00
**174** A27 $500 org & dl vio *46,000.*
Revenue cancel 200.00

Although Nos. 173 and 174 were available for postage, it is probable that they were used only for fiscal purposes.
See Nos. 202-204.

Die II (Type A24)

**1921-32 Wmk. 4**

**Ordinary Paper**

**179** A21 1c black .60 .20
**180** A25 2c green .60 .20
**181** A25 2c brown 8.00 3.00
**182** A22 3c green 1.75 .90
**183** A23 4c scarlet 2.25 *4.75*
**184** A23 4c dp violet ('25) .70 .20
**185** A23 4c orange ('29) 1.10 .20
**186** A24 5c orange ('23) 2.75 1.50
*a.* Die I 1.75 .20
**187** A24 5c dk brown ('32) 3.25 .20
*a.* Die I ('32) 5.75 .20
**188** A25 6c claret 2.25 .25
**189** A25 6c scarlet ('27) 3.00 .20
*a.* 6c rose red ('25) 22.50 11.00
**190** A24 10c ultra (I) 2.00 3.00

**Chalky Paper**

**191** A24 10c vio, *yel* ('27) 2.25 .35
*a.* Die I ('25) 3.00 *7.50*
**192** A25 12c ultra 1.10 .20
**193** A26 21c mar & vio 7.00 *55.00*
**194** A24 25c vio & red vio 5.75 *2.00*
*a.* Die I 32.50 80.00
**195** A24 30c violet & org 2.25 *1.50*
*a.* Die I 26.00 40.00
**196** A26 35c orange & vio 14.00 7.00
**197** A26 35c vio & car ('31) 11.50 8.00
**198** A24 50c blk, *emerald* 2.00 .45
**199** A24 $1 blk & red, *bl* 7.00 .75
**200** A24 $2 grn & red, *yel* 11.50 9.25
**201** A24 $5 grn & red, *grn* 100.00 37.50
**202** A27 $25 bl & vio, *bl* 800.00 140.00
**203** A27 $100 red & blk, *bl* 4,600. 1,900.
**204** A27 $500 org & dl vio *37,000.*
*Nos. 179-201 (23)* 192.60 136.60

No. 192 is on ordinary paper.
Nos. 203 and 204 were probably used only for fiscal purposes.

Stamps of 1912-21 Overprinted in Black:

"MALAYA-BORNEO EXHIBITION," in Three Lines

**1922 Wmk. 3**

*151d* A25 2c deep green 32.50 *85.00*
*154d* A23 4c scarlet 8.50 *26.00*
*155d* A24 5c orange 5.75 *22.50*
*157d* A25 8c ultra 2.00 *8.50*
*161d* A24 25c vio & red vio 3.75 *35.00*
*163d* A26 45c blk, *bl grn,* ol back 3.50 *30.00*
*165d* A24 $1 blk & red, *bl* 225.00 *800.00*
*166d* A24 $2 grn & red, *yel* 30.00 *125.00*
*167d* A24 $5 grn & red, *grn* 275.00 *450.00*

**Wmk. 4**

*179d* A21 1c black 3.50 *14.00*
*180d* A25 2c green 2.75 *16.00*
*183d* A23 4c scarlet 4.00 *30.00*
*186d* A24 5c orange (II) 3.25 *45.00*
*190d* A24 10c ultra 2.75 *29.00*
*199d* A24 $1 blk & red, *bl* 22.50 *140.00*
*Nos. 151d-199d (15)* 624.75 *1,856.*

Industrial fair at Singapore, Mar. 31-Apr. 15, 1922.

**Common Design Types**

pictured following the introduction.

**Silver Jubilee Issue**

Common Design Type

**1935, May 6 Engr. *Perf. 11x12***

**213** CD301 5c black & ultra 3.50 .35
**214** CD301 8c indigo & green 3.75 *3.50*
**215** CD301 12c ultra & brown 3.75 4.25
**216** CD301 25c brown vio & ind 4.00 *5.75*
*Nos. 213-216 (4)* 15.00 *13.85*
Set, never hinged 24.00

George V
A28

George VI
A29

**1936-37 Typo. *Perf. 14***

**Chalky Paper**

**217** A28 1c black ('37) .90 .20
**218** A28 2c green 1.00 .80
**220** A28 4c orange brn 2.00 .80
**221** A28 5c brown .80 .35
**222** A28 6c rose red 1.10 1.25
**223** A28 8c gray 1.50 .80
**224** A28 10c dull vio 1.75 .70
**225** A28 12c ultra 2.00 3.00
**226** A28 25c rose red & vio 1.60 .60
**227** A28 30c org & dk vio 1.10 3.50
**229** A28 40c dk vio & car 1.10 2.75
**230** A28 50c blk, *emerald* 4.00 1.40
**232** A28 $1 red & blk, *blue* 17.00 1.90
**233** A28 $2 rose red & gray grn 37.50 11.50
**234** A28 $5 grn & red, *grn* ('37) 80.00 11.50
*Nos. 217-234 (15)* 153.35 41.05
Set, never hinged 290.00

**Coronation Issue**

Common Design Type

**1937, May 12 Engr. *Perf. 13½x14***

**235** CD302 4c deep orange .20 .20
**236** CD302 8c gray black .30 .20
**237** CD302 12c bright ultra .50 .65
*Nos. 235-237 (3)* 1.00 1.05
Set, never hinged 2.00

Two Dies

Die I. Printed in two operations. Lines of background touch outside of central oval. Foliage of palms touches outer frame line. Palm frond in front of King's eye has two points.
Die II. Printed from a single plate. Lines of background separated from central oval by a white line. Foliage of palms does not touch outer frame line. Palm frond in front of King's eye has one point.

**1937-41 Typo. *Perf. 14***

**238** A29 1c black (I) 2.75 .20
**239** A29 2c green (I) 9.00 .25
*c.* Die II ('38) 35.00 .45
**239A** A29 2c brown org ('41) (II) 1.25 *5.00*
**239B** A29 3c green ('41) (II) 2.25 3.00
**240** A29 4c brown org (I) 8.00 .25
*a.* Die II ('38) 50.00 .25
**241** A29 5c brown (I) 10.00 .35
*a.* Die II ('39) 27.50 .20
**242** A29 6c rose red ('38) (I) 5.50 .50
**243** A29 8c gray ('38) (I) 19.00 .25
**244** A29 10c dull vio (I) 4.00 .20
**245** A29 12c ultra ('38) (I) 8.00 .35
**245A** A29 15c ultra ('41) (II) 3.25 *6.25*
**246** A29 25c rose red & vio (I) 40.00 1.10
**247** A29 30c org & vio (I) 25.00 2.00
**248** A29 40c dk vio & rose red (I) 10.00 2.25
**249** A29 50c blk, *emer* ('38) (I) 10.00 .45
**250** A29 $1 red & blk, *bl* ('38) (I) 15.00 .40
**251** A29 $2 rose red & gray grn ('38) (I) 30.00 4.25
**252** A29 $5 grn & red, *grn* ('38) (I) 25.00 4.50
*Nos. 238-252 (18)* 228.00 31.55
Set, never hinged 375.00

For overprints see #256-271, N1-N29 and Malaya, Malacca #N1-N14, Penang #N1-N26.

Stamps and Type of 1937-41 Overprinted in Red or Black

**1945-48**

**256** A29 1c black (R) .20 .20
**257** A29 2c brown org (II) .25 .20
*a.* Die I ('46) 7.50 *3.75*
**258** A29 3c green .25 .25
**259** A29 5c brown .75 .60
**260** A29 6c gray .25 .20
**261** A29 8c rose red .25 .20
**262** A29 10c dull vio (I) .30 .20
*a.* 10c claret (II) ('48) *10.00* 1.25
**263** A29 12c ultra 1.75 *3.25*
**264** A29 15c ultra (Bk) 2.25 *4.75*
**265** A29 15c ultra (R) .25 .20
**266** A29 25c rose red & vio 1.40 .25
*a.* Double overprint 400.00
**267** A29 50c blk, *emer* (R) .60 .20
**268** A29 $1 rose red & blk 2.00 .25
**269** A29 $2 rose red & gray grn 2.50 .65
**270** A29 $5 grn & red, *grn* 72.50 72.50
**271** A29 $5 brn org & vio 3.75 2.75
*Nos. 256-271 (16)* 89.25 86.65
Set, never hinged 140.00

The letters "B M A" are initials of "British Military Administration".
An 8c gray with BMA overprint was prepared but not issued. Value $5.
The 6c gray, 8c rose red and $5 brown orange & violet exist without BMA overprint, but were issued only with it.
No. 262a does not exist without overprint. No. 262 exists in at least three shades.

## SEMI-POSTAL STAMPS

Nos. 152-153 Surcharged

**1917 Wmk. 3 *Perf. 14***

**B1** A22 3c + 2c scarlet 3.00 *29.00*
*a.* No period after "C" 375.00 *575.00*
**B2** A23 4c + 2c gray violet 4.00 *29.00*
*a.* No period after "C" 400.00 *575.00*

## POSTAGE DUE STAMPS

D1

**1924-26 Typo. Wmk. 4 *Perf. 14***

**J1** D1 1c violet 5.75 *7.50*
**J2** D1 2c black 3.75 1.50
**J3** D1 4c green ('26) 2.25 *5.50*
**J4** D1 8c red 5.25 .60
**J5** D1 10c orange 7.00 .95
**J6** D1 12c ultramarine 8.00 .75
*Nos. J1-J6 (6)* 32.00 *16.80*
Set never hinged 55.00

## OCCUPATION STAMPS

**Issued Under Japanese Occupation**

Straits Settlements Nos. 238, 239A, 239B, 243 and 245A Handstamped in Red

**1942, Mar. 16 Wmk. 4 *Perf. 14***

**N1** A29 1c black 16.00 20.00
**N2** A29 2c brown orange 16.00 16.00
**N3** A29 3c green 70.00 *85.00*

**N4** A29 8c gray 27.50 22.50
**N5** A29 15c ultra 20.00 20.00
*Nos. N1-N5 (5)* 149.50 163.50
Set never hinged 200.00

Other denominations with this handstamp are believed to be proofs.
The handstamp reads: "Seal of Post Office of Malayan Military Department."

Stamps of Straits Settlements, 1937-41, Handstamped in Red, Black, Violet or Brown

**1942, Apr. 3**

| | | | | |
|---|---|---|---|---|
| **N6** | A29 | 1c black | 4.00 | 4.00 |
| **N6A** | A29 | 2c green (V) | 2,875. | 500.00 |
| **N7** | A29 | 2c brown org | 3.50 | 3.50 |
| **N8** | A29 | 3c green | 3.25 | 3.50 |
| **N9** | A29 | 5c brown | 25.00 | 30.00 |
| **N10** | A29 | 8c gray | 5.00 | 3.50 |
| **N11** | A29 | 10c dull violet | 55.00 | 45.00 |
| **N12** | A29 | 12c ultra | 92.50 | 90.00 |
| **N13** | A29 | 15c ultra | 4.50 | 4.00 |
| **N14** | A29 | 30c orange & vio | 2,200. | 350.00 |
| **N15** | A29 | 40c dk vio & rose red | 100.00 | 125.00 |
| **N16** | A29 | 50c blk, *emerald* | 60.00 | 60.00 |
| **N17** | A29 | $1 red & blk, *bl* | 87.50 | 80.00 |
| **N18** | A29 | $2 rose red & gray grn | 150.00 | 150.00 |
| **N19** | A29 | $5 grn & red, *grn* | 200.00 | 165.00 |

Nos. N6-N7, N9, N11-N12, N15-N19 with red handstamp were used in Sumatra. The 2c green with red handstamp was not regularly issued.

Straits Settlements Nos. 239A, 239B, 243 and 245A Overprinted in Black

**1942**

| | | | | |
|---|---|---|---|---|
| **N20** | A29 | 2c brown orange | 2.00 | 6.00 |
| *a.* | | Inverted overprint | 11.50 | 21.00 |
| *b.* | | Dbl. ovpt., one invtd. | 55.00 | 70.00 |
| **N21** | A29 | 3c green | 57.50 | *62.50* |
| **N22** | A29 | 8c gray | 5.75 | 2.75 |
| *a.* | | Inverted overprint | 17.00 | 32.50 |
| **N23** | A29 | 15c ultra | 15.00 | 9.25 |
| | | *Nos. N20-N23 (4)* | 80.25 | 80.50 |
| | | Set never hinged | 100.00 | |

Straits Settlements Nos. 239A and 243 Overprinted in Black

**1942, Nov. 3**

| | | | | |
|---|---|---|---|---|
| **N24** | A29 | 2c brown orange | 14.00 | *25.00* |
| *a.* | | Inverted overprint | 375.00 | 375.00 |
| **N25** | A29 | 8c gray | 15.00 | *20.00* |
| *a.* | | Inverted overprint | 375.00 | 375.00 |

Agricultural-Horticultural Exhibition held at Kuala Lumpur, Selangor, Nov. 1-2, 1942. Sold only at a temporary post office at the exhibition.

Straits Settlements Nos. 243, 245 and 248 Overprinted in Black or Red

**1943**

| | | | | |
|---|---|---|---|---|
| **N26** | A29 | 8c gray (Bk) | 1.60 | .60 |
| *a.* | | Inverted overprint | 52.50 | 62.50 |
| **N27** | A29 | 8c gray (R) | 2.50 | 3.00 |
| **N28** | A29 | 12c ultramarine | 1.40 | 10.50 |
| **N29** | A29 | 40c dk vio & rose red | 2.00 | 4.50 |
| | | *Nos. N26-N29 (4)* | 7.50 | 18.60 |
| | | Set never hinged | 10.00 | |

The Japanese characters read: "Japanese Postal Service."

## SUDAN

sü-'dan

LOCATION — Northeastern Africa, south of Egypt
GOVT. — Republic
AREA — 967,500 sq. mi.
POP. — 27,953,000 (1997 est.)
CAPITAL — Khartoum

10 Milliemes = 1 Piaster
100 Piasters = 1 Egyptian Pound
Dinar (1992)

**Catalogue values for unused stamps in this country are for Never Hinged items, beginning with Scott 79 in the regular postage section, Scott C35 in the air post section, Scott CO1 in the air post official section, Scott J12 in the postage due section, and Scott O28 in the officials section.**

**Watermarks**

Wmk. 71 — Rosette

Wmk. 179 — Multiple Crescent and Star

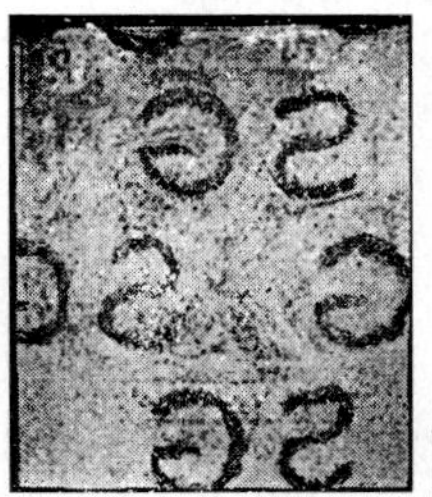
Wmk. 214 — Multiple S G

Wmk. 334 — Rectangles

Wmk. 345 — Rhinoceros

Egyptian Stamps of 1884-93 Overprinted in Black

**1897, Mar. 1 Wmk. 119 *Perf. 14***

| | | | | |
|---|---|---|---|---|
| **1** | A18 | 1m brown | 2.50 | *2.00* |
| *a.* | | Inverted overprint | 300.00 | |
| **2** | A19 | 2m green | 2.50 | *2.25* |
| **3** | A21 | 3m orange | 1.75 | *1.75* |
| **4** | A22 | 5m carmine rose | 2.25 | 1.50 |
| *a.* | | Inverted overprint | 300.00 | |
| **5** | A14 | 1p ultra | 9.00 | 2.00 |
| **6** | A15 | 2p orange brown | 55.00 | 15.00 |
| **7** | A16 | 5p gray | 45.00 | 17.50 |
| *a.* | | Double overprint | *4,500.* | |
| **8** | A22 | 10p violet | 32.50 | *40.00* |
| | | *Nos. 1-8 (8)* | 150.50 | 82.00 |

Counterfeits of Nos. 1-8 are plentiful.

Camel Post — A1

**1898, Mar. 1 Typo. Wmk. 71**

| | | | | |
|---|---|---|---|---|
| **9** | A1 | 1m rose & brn | 1.00 | 1.25 |
| **10** | A1 | 2m brown & grn | 2.50 | 1.75 |
| **11** | A1 | 3m green & vio | 2.75 | 2.00 |
| **12** | A1 | 5m black & rose | 2.25 | .75 |
| **13** | A1 | 1p yel brn & ultra | 6.00 | 3.50 |
| **14** | A1 | 2p ultra & blk | 25.00 | 6.75 |
| **15** | A1 | 5p grn & org brn | 30.00 | 16.00 |
| **16** | A1 | 10p dp vio & blk | 27.50 | 2.50 |
| | | *Nos. 9-16 (8)* | 97.00 | 34.50 |

See Nos. 17-27, 43-50. For overprints see Nos. C3, MO1-MO15, O1-O9, O17-O24. For surcharges see Nos. 28, 62, C16.

**1902-21 Wmk. 179**

| | | | | |
|---|---|---|---|---|
| **17** | A1 | 1m car rose & brn ('05) | 1.50 | .50 |
| **18** | A1 | 2m brown & grn | 2.00 | .20 |
| **19** | A1 | 3m grn & vio ('03) | 2.75 | .30 |
| **20** | A1 | 4m ol brn & bl ('07) | 2.00 | *2.50* |
| **21** | A1 | 4m brn & red ('07) | 2.00 | .80 |
| **22** | A1 | 5m blk & rose red ('03) | 2.50 | .20 |
| **23** | A1 | 1p brn & ultra ('03) | 3.00 | .30 |
| **24** | A1 | 2p ultra & blk ('08) | 27.50 | 2.00 |
| **25** | A1 | 2p org & vio brn ('21) | 5.00 | *10.00* |
| **26** | A1 | 5p grn & org brn ('08) | 25.00 | .35 |
| **27** | A1 | 10p dp vio & blk ('11) | 25.00 | 4.00 |
| | | *Nos. 17-27 (11)* | 98.25 | 21.15 |

No. 15 Surcharged in Black

**1903, Sept. Wmk. 71**

| | | | | |
|---|---|---|---|---|
| **28** | A1 | 5m on 5p | 8.00 | *10.00* |
| *a.* | | Inverted surcharge | 325.00 | *260.00* |

A2

**1921-22 Typo. Wmk. 179**

| | | | | |
|---|---|---|---|---|
| **29** | A2 | 1m orange & blk ('22) | 1.25 | *4.50* |
| **30** | A2 | 2m dk brn & org ('22) | 11.00 | *12.00* |
| **31** | A2 | 3m green & vio ('22) | 3.00 | *10.00* |
| **32** | A2 | 4m brown & grn ('22) | 7.00 | 5.50 |
| **33** | A2 | 5m blk & ol brn ('22) | 3.00 | .20 |
| **34** | A2 | 10mblack & car ('22) | 5.00 | .20 |
| **35** | A2 | 15morg brn & ultra | 4.00 | 1.25 |
| | | *Nos. 29-35 (7)* | 34.25 | 33.65 |

See Nos. 36-42. For overprints see Nos. C1-C2, O10-O16.
For surcharges see Nos. 60-61.

**1927-40 Wmk. 214**

| | | | | |
|---|---|---|---|---|
| **36** | A2 | 1m org yel & blk | 1.00 | .20 |
| **37** | A2 | 2m dk brn & org | .90 | .20 |
| **38** | A2 | 3m green & violet | 1.00 | .20 |
| **39** | A2 | 4m brown & green | .90 | .20 |
| **40** | A2 | 5m blk & ol brn | .75 | .20 |
| *a.* | | Booklet pane of 4 | | |
| **41** | A2 | 10m black & car | 2.00 | .20 |
| **42** | A2 | 15m org brn & ultra | 2.00 | .20 |
| **43** | A1 | 2p orange & vio brn | 2.00 | .20 |
| **44** | A1 | 3p dk bl & red brn ('40) | 3.00 | .20 |
| **45** | A1 | 4p black & ultra ('36) | 3.50 | .20 |
| **46** | A1 | 5p dk grn & org brn | 1.75 | .20 |
| **47** | A1 | 6p blk & pale bl ('36) | 6.00 | 1.00 |
| **48** | A1 | 8p blk & pck grn ('36) | 7.00 | 2.50 |
| **49** | A1 | 10p dp vio & blk | 4.00 | .20 |
| **50** | A1 | 20p bl & lt bl ('35) | 4.00 | .20 |
| | | *Nos. 36-50 (15)* | 39.80 | 6.10 |

Charles George Gordon — A3

Gordon Memorial College A4

Memorial Service at Khartoum — A5

**1935, Jan. 1 Engr. *Perf. 13½x14***

| | | | | |
|---|---|---|---|---|
| **51** | A3 | 5m deep green | .50 | .20 |
| **52** | A3 | 10m brown | .90 | .20 |
| **53** | A3 | 13m ultra | 2.00 | *11.00* |
| **54** | A3 | 15m carmine | 1.50 | .20 |

**55** A4 2p deep blue 1.50 .20
**56** A4 5p orange 1.75 .35
**57** A4 10p dull violet 8.00 *8.00*
**58** A5 20p black 30.00 *50.00*
**59** A5 50p red brown 90.00 *110.00*
*Nos. 51-59 (9)* 136.15 180.15

50th anniv. of the death of Gen. Charles George ("Chinese") Gordon (1833-85).

No. 41 Surcharged in Black

**Wmk. Multiple S G (214)**

**1940, Feb. 25 Typo. *Perf. 14***
**60** A2 5m on 10m black & car .75 .50

Nos. 40 and 48 Surcharged in Black

a

b

**1940-41**
**61** A2(a) 4½p on 5m ('41) 55.00 4.50
**62** A1(b) 4½p on 8p 45.00 7.50

Sudan Landscape A6

***Perf. 13½, 14x13½***
**1941 Litho. Unwmk.**
**Size: 21½x17½mm**
**63** A6 1m orange & slate bl 1.10 *4.00*
**64** A6 2m chocolate & org 1.10 *4.00*
**65** A6 3m grn & rose vio 1.10 .20
**66** A6 4m choc & bl grn .55 .50
**67** A6 5m indigo & ol bis .20 .20
**68** A6 10m indigo & rose pink 5.50 2.00
**69** A6 15m chestnut & ultra .75 .20
**Size: 29x25mm**
**71** A6 2p orange & claret 4.00 .60
**72** A6 3p dk blue & fawn .75 .20
**73** A6 4p blk & brt ultra .90 .20
**74** A6 5p dk grn & brn org 3.50 *9.00*
**75** A6 6p ind & turq bl 13.00 .40
**76** A6 8p black & green 10.00 .50
**77** A6 10p rose vio & gray 40.00 .75
**78** A6 20p dk & lt blue 35.00 35.00
*Nos. 63-78 (15)* 117.45 57.75
Set, never hinged 200.00

**Catalogue values for unused stamps in this section, from this point to the end of the section, are for Never Hinged items.**

Types of 1898-1940 with Changed Arabic Wording Below Camel

A7

A8

**Wmk. 214**
**1948, Jan. 1 Typo. *Perf. 14***
**79** A7 1m dk orange & blk .40 *3.00*
**80** A7 2m chocolate & org .90 *4.00*
**81** A7 3m green & rose lilac .30 *4.25*
**82** A7 4m choc & sl grn .60 .50
**83** A7 5m black & ol brn 6.00 1.75
**84** A7 10m black & car 6.00 .20
*a.* Center inverted —
**85** A7 15m org brn & ultra 5.50 .20
**86** A8 2p org yel & vio brn 8.50 2.25
**87** A8 3p dk bl & red brn 7.50 .35
**88** A8 4p black & ultra 4.00 1.60
**89** A8 5p dk grn & org 4.00 2.75
**90** A8 6p blk & pale bl 4.75 3.00
**91** A8 8p blk & peacock grn 5.00 3.00
**92** A8 10p dp rose lil & blk 11.50 4.50
**93** A8 20p dk blue & blue 4.75 .35
*a.* Perf. 13 55.00 *175.00*
**94** A8 50p ultra & carmine 7.00 2.50
*Nos. 79-94 (16)* 76.70 34.20

Arabic inscription, types A7 and A8: "Berid es-Sudan"; types A1 and A2; "Postai-Sudaniye."

For overprints see Nos. O28-O43.

Stamp of 1898 — A9

**1948, Oct. 1 *Perf. 12½x13***
**95** A9 2p dull blue & gray blk .50 .20

50th anniv. of Sudan's 1st postage stamp.

A10

**1948, Dec. 19 *Perf. 13***
**96** A10 10m black & carmine .50 .20
**97** A10 5p dk green & orange 1.00 1.00

Legislative Assembly opening, Dec., 1948.

Nubian Ibex — A11

Cotton Picking — A12

Camel Post — A13

Designs: 2m, Shoebill. 3m, Giraffe. 4m, Baggara girl. 5m, Shilluk warrior. 10m, Hadendowa. 15m, Sudan policeman. 3p, Ambatch canoe. 3½p, Nuba wrestlers. 4p, Weaving. 5p, Saluka farming. 6p, Gum tapping. 8p, Darfur chief. 10p, Stack laboratory. 20p, Nile lechwe.

**1951, Sept. 1 Typo. *Perf. 14***
**Center in Black (#98-104)**
**98** A11 1m orange 1.75 1.50
**99** A11 2m ultra 1.75 .90
**100** A11 3m dark green 6.25 3.25
**101** A11 4m emerald 1.75 *3.25*
**102** A11 5m plum 2.25 .20
**103** A11 10m light blue .35 .20
**104** A11 15m dp orange brn 3.75 .20
***Perf. 13***
**105** A12 2p lt blue & dk blue .25 .20
**106** A12 3p vio blue & brn 8.75 .20
**107** A12 3½p brown & bl grn 2.25 .20
**108** A12 4p black & dp blue 1.40 .20
**109** A12 5p emer & org brn .55 .20
**110** A12 6p black & blue 8.50 2.50
**111** A12 8p brown & dp bl 15.00 3.50
**112** A12 10p green & black 1.50 .20
**113** A12 20p black & blue grn 5.75 2.00
**114** A13 50p black & carmine 13.50 2.00
*Nos. 98-114 (17)* 75.30 20.70

See #159. For overprints see #O44-O61, O75.

Camel Post — A14

**1954, Jan. 9 *Perf. 12½x13***
**115** A14 15m emerald & brn org .55 *.85*
**116** A14 3p black & blue .65 *1.40*
**117** A14 5p red violet & blk .80 *1.00*
*Nos. 115-117 (3)* 2.00 3.25

Self-government in the Sudan.

A quantity of these sets inscribed "1953" was sold in London. They were not valid for postage. Value, set $25.

**Independent Republic**

Map of Sudan and Sun — A15

Rhinoceros Carrying Globe — A16

**Wmk. 214**
**1956, Sept. 15 Engr. *Perf. 14***
**118** A15 15m rose lilac & org .60 *.80*
**119** A15 3p dk blue & org .60 *1.25*
**120** A15 5p green & org .60 *.95*
*Nos. 118-120 (3)* 1.80 3.00

Independence Day, Jan. 1, 1956.

**1958, Aug. 2**
**Center in Orange**
**121** A16 15m plum .50 .20
**122** A16 3p blue .75 .35
**123** A16 5p green 1.00 .60
*Nos. 121-123 (3)* 2.25 1.15

APU Cong., Khartoum, Aug. 2, 1958.

Soldier, Farmer and Map of Nile — A17

**Lithographed and Engraved**
**1959, Nov. 17 Unwmk. *Perf. 14***
**124** A17 15m brown, yel & ultra .30 .20
**125** A17 3p multicolored .65 .30
**126** A17 55m multicolored .75 .40
*Nos. 124-126 (3)* 1.70 .90

Sudanese army revolution, 1st anniv.

Arab League Center A17a

***Perf. 13x13½***
**1960, Mar. 22 Photo. Wmk. 328**
**127** A17a 15m dull green & blk .40 .20

Opening of the Arab League Center and the Arab Postal Museum in Cairo.

Uprooted Oak Emblem, Refugee Man and Child — A18

**Wmk. 214**
**1960, Apr. 7 Litho. *Perf. 14***
**128** A18 15m black, buff & ultra .25 .20
**129** A18 55m black, beige & org .70 .50

World Refugee Year, 7/1/59-6/30/60.

Soccer Player — A19

Forest — A20

**1960, Aug. 25 Wmk. 214 *Perf. 14***
**130** A19 15m ultra, blk & yel .25 .20
**131** A19 3p yellow, blk & grn .55 .45
**132** A19 55m emerald, blk & yel .80 .60
*Nos. 130-132 (3)* 1.60 1.25

17th Olympic Games, Rome, 8/25-9/11.

**1960, Sept. 6**
**133** A20 15m multicolored .30 .20
**134** A20 3p multicolored .60 .20
**135** A20 55m multicolored .75 .35
*Nos. 133-135 (3)* 1.65 .75

5th World Forestry Cong., Seattle, WA, Aug. 29-Sept. 10.

King Tirhaqah, 689-663 B.C. — A21

Girl with Book — A22

**Unwmk.**
**1961, Mar. 1 Engr. *Perf. 14***
**136** A21 15m yellow grn & brown .25 .20
**137** A21 3p salmon & violet .55 .30
**138** A21 55m lt blue & red brown .85 .40
*Nos. 136-138 (3)* 1.65 .90

Save historic monuments in Nubia.

An imperf. souvenir sheet exists, not sold at post offices, containing one each of Nos. 136-138. Size: 154x97mm. The sheet was not issued for postal purposes and cancellation requests are declined. Value $8.

**1961, Nov. 17 Litho. Wmk. 214**
**139** A22 15m violet, claret & pink .30 .20
**140** A22 3p orange, blk & blue .55 .30
**141** A22 55m gray grn, blk & och .65 .40
*Nos. 139-141 (3)* 1.50 .90

50 years of girls' education in the Sudan.

Malaria Eradication Emblem — A23

Arab League Building, Cairo — A24

**1962, Apr. 7 Unwmk. *Perf. 14***

| | | | | |
|---|---|---|---|---|
| 142 | A23 | 15m black, pur & blue | .50 | .20 |
| 143 | A23 | 55m dk brown & green | .75 | .50 |

WHO drive to eradicate malaria.

**1962, Apr. 22 Photo. *Perf. 13½x13***

| | | | | |
|---|---|---|---|---|
| 144 | A24 | 15m deep orange | .40 | .20 |
| 145 | A24 | 55m blue green | .55 | .40 |

Arab League Week, Mar. 22-28.

Type of 1951 and

Palace of the Republic, Khartoum — A25

Cotton Picker — A26

Designs: 15m, Straw cover. 35m, 4p, Wild animals. 55m, 6p, Cattle. 8p, Date palms. 10p, Sailboat. 20p, Bohein Temple, 1500 B.C. 50p, Sennar Dam. £1, Camel Post (A13 redrawn).

***Perf. 14½x14, 14x14½***

**1962, Oct. 1 Litho. Wmk. 345**

**Size: 23x19mm, 19x23mm**

| | | | | |
|---|---|---|---|---|
| 146 | A25 | 5m blue | .20 | .20 |
| 147 | A26 | 10m blue & lilac | .20 | .20 |
| 148 | A25 | 15m multicolored | .20 | .20 |
| 149 | A25 | 2p lt purple | .20 | .20 |
| 150 | A26 | 3p bl grn, red brn & brn | .35 | .20 |
| 151 | A26 | 35m yel grn, brn & org brn | .65 | .20 |
| 152 | A26 | 4p red, lt bl & lil | .65 | .20 |
| 153 | A25 | 55m gray & yel ol | .65 | .20 |
| 154 | A25 | 6p brown & lt blue | .85 | .20 |
| 155 | A25 | 8p green | .85 | .20 |

***Perf. 14x14½, 13x13½, 14x13½, 13½x14***

**Size: 24½x30mm, 30x24½mm**

| | | | | |
|---|---|---|---|---|
| 156 | A26 | 10p lt bl, red brn & blk | .95 | .40 |
| 157 | A25 | 20p gray ol & yel grn | 2.25 | .75 |
| 158 | A25 | 50p dk gray, ol & bl | 5.50 | 1.25 |

**Engr.**

| | | | | |
|---|---|---|---|---|
| 159 | A13 | £1 green & brn org | 10.50 | 5.00 |
| | | *Nos. 146-159 (14)* | 24.00 | 9.40 |

The frame of No. 159 has been altered with Arabic inscription on top and English at bottom.

See Nos. 420, 427-428. For surcharge and overprints see Nos. 430, O62-O74, O92, O99-O100.

**1975-79 Unwmk.**

**Perfs, Sizes and Printing Methods as Before**

| | | | | |
|---|---|---|---|---|
| 146a | A25 | 5m ('76) | .20 | .20 |
| 147a | A26 | 10m ('76) | .20 | .20 |
| 148a | A25 | 15m | .20 | .20 |
| 149a | A25 | 2p | .20 | .20 |
| 150a | A26 | 3p ('76) | .20 | .20 |
| 151a | A26 | 35m | .20 | .20 |
| 152a | A26 | 4p | .20 | .20 |
| 153a | A25 | 55m ('79) | .40 | .20 |
| 154a | A25 | 6p | .40 | .20 |
| 155a | A25 | 8p ('77) | .50 | .20 |
| 156a | A26 | 10p | .60 | .20 |
| 157a | A25 | 20p | 1.25 | .40 |
| 158a | A25 | 50p | 3.00 | .60 |
| 159a | A13 | £1 | | |
| | | *Nos. 146a-158a (13)* | 7.55 | 3.20 |

Corn and Millet — A27

Centenary Emblem and Medals — A28

**1963, Mar. 21 Litho. Wmk. 345**

| | | | | |
|---|---|---|---|---|
| 160 | A27 | 15m. emerald, gray & brn | .30 | .20 |
| 161 | A27 | 55m violet, lt & dk blue | .65 | .30 |

FAO "Freedom from Hunger" campaign.

**1963, Oct. 1 *Perf. 14***

| | | | | |
|---|---|---|---|---|
| 162 | A28 | 15m blk, red, gray & gold | .45 | .20 |
| 163 | A28 | 55m grn, gray, red & gold | .90 | .40 |

Centenary of the International Red Cross.

Melchior — A29

Khashm El Girba Dam — A30

Designs: 30m, St. Joseph seated, with cross and manuscript, horiz. 55m, Archangel with cross. Designs from frescoes in excavated Faras Church.

**1964, Mar. 8 Litho. *Perf. 14***

| | | | | |
|---|---|---|---|---|
| 164 | A29 | 15m multicolored | .40 | .20 |
| 165 | A29 | 30m red brn, blk & brn | .60 | .30 |
| 166 | A29 | 55m red brn, blk & brn | 1.25 | .75 |
| | | *Nos. 164-166 (3)* | 2.25 | 1.25 |

UNESCO world campaign to save historic monuments in Nubia.

***Perf. 14x14½, 14½x14***

**1964, Apr. 22 Wmk. 345**

New York World's Fair, 1964-65: 3p, Pavilion. 55m, Illustrated map of Sudan, vert.

| | | | | |
|---|---|---|---|---|
| 167 | A30 | 15m lt vio bl & vio brn | .25 | .20 |
| 168 | A30 | 3p multicolored | .25 | .20 |
| 169 | A30 | 55m multicolored | .70 | .25 |
| | | *Nos. 167-169 (3)* | 1.20 | .65 |

Eleanor Roosevelt and People Breaking Chains — A31

Arab Postal Union Emblem — A32

**1964, Dec. 10 *Perf. 14***

| | | | | |
|---|---|---|---|---|
| 170 | A31 | 15m grnsh blue & blk | .25 | .20 |
| 171 | A31 | 3p violet & black | .40 | .20 |
| 172 | A31 | 55m orange brn & blk | .60 | .30 |
| | | *Nos. 170-172 (3)* | 1.25 | .70 |

Eleanor Roosevelt (1884-1962), on the 16th anniv. of the Universal Declaration of Human Rights.

**1964, Dec. 30 Litho.**

| | | | | |
|---|---|---|---|---|
| 173 | A32 | 15m brick red, blk & gold | .25 | .20 |
| 174 | A32 | 3p gray green, blk & gold | .40 | .20 |
| 175 | A32 | 55m violet, blk & gold | .60 | .30 |
| | | *Nos. 173-175 (3)* | 1.25 | .70 |

10th anniv. of the Permanent Office of the Arab Postal Union.

ITU Emblem, Old and New Communication Equipment — A33

**1965, May 17 Wmk. 345 *Perf. 13½***

| | | | | |
|---|---|---|---|---|
| 176 | A33 | 15m brown & gold | .30 | .20 |
| 177 | A33 | 3p black & gold | .45 | .20 |
| 178 | A33 | 55m green & gold | .75 | .30 |
| | | *Nos. 176-178 (3)* | 1.50 | .70 |

Cent. of the ITU.

"Gurashi" and Revolutionists — A34

**1965, Nov. 10 Litho. *Perf. 12***

| | | | | |
|---|---|---|---|---|
| 179 | A34 | 15m deep ocher & black | .25 | .20 |
| 180 | A34 | 3p bright red & black | .40 | .20 |
| 181 | A34 | 55m dark gray & black | .60 | .30 |
| | | *Nos. 179-181 (3)* | 1.25 | .70 |

1st anniv. of the October 21st Revolution and to honor "Gurashi," one of its heroes.

ICY Emblem — A35

El Siddig el Mahdi — A36

***Perf. 14½x14***

**1965, Dec. 10 Litho. Wmk. 345**

| | | | | |
|---|---|---|---|---|
| 182 | A35 | 15m violet & blk | .30 | .20 |
| 183 | A35 | 3p yellow green & blk | .45 | .20 |
| 184 | A35 | 55m vermilion & blk | .75 | .30 |
| | | *Nos. 182-184 (3)* | 1.50 | .70 |

International Cooperation Year, 1965.

**1966, Jan. 1 *Perf. 13***

| | | | | |
|---|---|---|---|---|
| 185 | A36 | 15m lt blue & vio blue | .40 | .20 |
| 186 | A36 | 3p orange & brown | .60 | .25 |
| 187 | A36 | 55m gray & red brown | 1.25 | .65 |
| | | *Nos. 185-187 (3)* | 2.25 | 1.10 |

El Siddig el Mahdi (1911-61), imam of Ansar region and political leader.

Mubarak Zaroug A37

**1966, Jan. 1 Litho.**

| | | | | |
|---|---|---|---|---|
| 188 | A37 | 15m pink & lt olive grn | .35 | .20 |
| 189 | A37 | 3p brt yel grn & dk grn | .60 | .35 |
| 190 | A37 | 55m orange brn & dk brn | 1.25 | .60 |
| | | *Nos. 188-190 (3)* | 2.20 | 1.15 |

Issued in memory of Mubarak Zaroug (1917-65), lawyer and political leader.

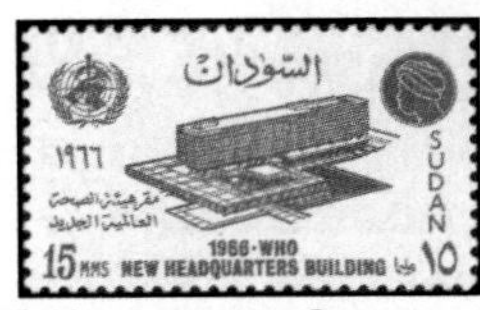

WHO Headquarters, Geneva — A38

**1966, June 11 Photo. *Perf. 11½x11***

| | | | | |
|---|---|---|---|---|
| 191 | A38 | 15m blue | .30 | .20 |
| 192 | A38 | 3p magenta | .40 | .20 |
| 193 | A38 | 55m brown | .75 | .25 |
| | | *Nos. 191-193 (3)* | 1.45 | .65 |

Inauguration of WHO Headquarters, Geneva.

Map of Sudan and Crests of Upper Nile, Blue Nile and Kassala Provinces — A39

Designs: 3p, Map of Sudan and crests of Equatoria, Kordofan and Khartoum Provinces. 55m, Map of Sudan and crests of Bahr El Gazal, Darfur and Northern Provinces.

**1967, Apr. 1 Litho. *Perf. 14***

| | | | | |
|---|---|---|---|---|
| 194 | A39 | 15m org, pur & lt blue grn | .20 | .20 |
| 195 | A39 | 3p dp org, vio & lt blue | .35 | .30 |
| 196 | A39 | 55m yel, dp claret & yel grn | 1.25 | .60 |
| | | *Nos. 194-196 (3)* | 1.80 | 1.10 |

Month of the South.

Giraffe and ITY Emblem — A40

Clasped Hands and Arab League Emblem — A41

***Perf. 12½x13***

**1967, Aug. 15 Litho. Wmk. 345**

| | | | | |
|---|---|---|---|---|
| 197 | A40 | 15m multicolored | .45 | .20 |
| 198 | A40 | 3p multicolored | .90 | .40 |
| 199 | A40 | 55m multicolored | 1.25 | .40 |
| | | *Nos. 197-199 (3)* | 2.60 | 1.00 |

International Tourist Year 1967.

***Perf. 11x11½***

**1967, Aug. 29 Photo. Unwmk.**

| | | | | |
|---|---|---|---|---|
| 200 | A41 | 15m orange & ultra | .35 | .20 |
| 201 | A41 | 3p brown org & emer | .45 | .35 |
| 202 | A41 | 55m lemon & violet | .80 | .70 |
| | | *Nos. 200-202 (3)* | 1.60 | 1.25 |

Arab League Summit Conference.

Emblem of Palestine Liberation Organization — A42

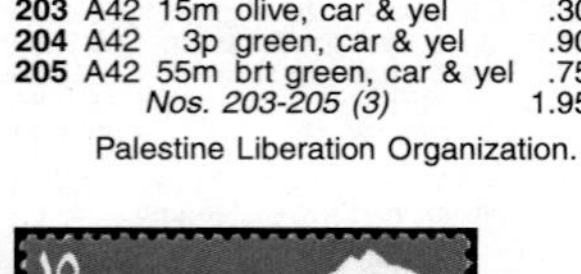

**1967, Aug. 29** ***Perf. 11½x11***

**203** A42 15m olive, car & yel .30 .20
**204** A42 3p green, car & yel .90 .25
**205** A42 55m brt green, car & yel .75 .30
*Nos. 203-205 (3)* 1.95 .75

Palestine Liberation Organization.

Abdullahi el Fadil el Mahdi A43

***Perf. 11½x11***

**1968, Feb. 15 Photo. Unwmk.**

**206** A43 15m ultra & brt purple .40 .20
**207** A43 3p dp ultra & brt grn .60 .30
**208** A43 55m orange & green 1.25 .55
*Nos. 206-208 (3)* 2.25 1.05

Issued in memory of Abdullahi el Fadil el Mahdi (1892-1966), political leader.

Mohammed Nur el Din — A44

**1968, Feb. 15**

**209** A44 15m sl blue & apple grn .40 .20
**210** A44 3p blue & olive .60 .30
**211** A44 55m blue & violet blue 1.25 .55
*Nos. 209-211 (3)* 2.25 1.05

Issued in memory of Mohammed Nur el Din (1898-1964), political leader.

Ahmed Yousif Hashim A45

***Perf. 11½x11***

**1968, Mar. 5 Photo. Unwmk.**

**212** A45 15m green & brown .40 .20
**213** A45 3p brt blue & sepia .60 .30
**214** A45 55m indigo & violet 1.25 .55
*Nos. 212-214 (3)* 2.25 1.05

Ahmed Yousif Hashim (1906-1958), journalist.

Mohammed Ahmed el Mardi (1905-1966), Political Leader — A46

***Perf. 11x11½***

**1968, Mar. 5 Photo. Unwmk.**

**215** A46 15m Prus bl & vio bl .60 .20
**216** A46 3p ultra, och & dl rose .85 .30
**217** A46 55m dk blue & brown 1.50 .55
*Nos. 215-217 (3)* 2.95 1.05

DC-3 A47

20th anniv. of Sudan Airways: 2p, De Havilland Dove. 3p, Fokker Friendship. 55m, De Havilland Comet 4C.

**1968, Dec. 15 Litho.** ***Perf. 13½x13***

**218** A47 15m multicolored .45 .20
**219** A47 2p multicolored .75 .20
**220** A47 3p multicolored 1.00 .20
**221** A47 55m multicolored 1.25 .30
*Nos. 218-221 (4)* 3.45 .90

African Development Bank Emblem (right) — A48

**Wmk. Rectangles (334)**

**1969, Dec. 20 Photo.** ***Perf. 13***

**222** A48 2p black, gray & gold .45 .20
**223** A48 4p dark red & gold .45 .20
**224** A48 65m green & gold .65 .25
*Nos. 222-224 (3)* 1.55 .65

5th anniv. of the African Development Bank.

ILO Emblem A49

**Unwmk.**

**1969, Dec. 27 Litho.** ***Perf. 14***

**225** A49 2p blue, blk & pink .35 .20
**226** A49 4p yellow, blk & silver .35 .20
**227** A49 65m green, blk & lilac .55 .25
*Nos. 225-227 (3)* 1.25 .65

50th anniv. of the ILO.

Citizens A50

**1970, May 25** ***Perf. 11½x11***

**228** A50 2p multicolored
**228A** A50 4p multicolored
**228B** A50 65m multicolored
Set, 228-228B 75.00 —

First anniv. of May 25th Revolution.

This set was withdrawn on day of issue; 1721 sets of the 2p, 4p and 65m stamps in same design were sold through the Philatelic service. A few copies of No. 228 were sold at Post offices. Nos. 229-231 were issued in October to replace this set.

Citizens A51

**1970, Oct. 21 Photo.** ***Perf. 11½x11***

**229** A51 2p brown, olive & red .25 .20
**230** A51 4p lt blue, olive & red .50 .20
**231** A51 65m olive, dk blue & red .65 .25
*Nos. 229-231 (3)* 1.40 .65

1st anniv. of the May 25th Revolution.

Map and Flags of UAR, Libya, Sudan A52

**1971, Jan. 2 Unwmk.** ***Perf. 11½***

**232** A52 2p lt green, car & blk .40 .20

Signing of the Charter of Tripoli affirming the unity of UAR, Libya and the Sudan, Dec. 27, 1970.

Education Year Emblem — A53

Emblem — A54

**1971, May 2 Photo.** ***Perf. 11x11½***

**233** A53 2p blue, blk & brn .35 .20
**234** A53 4p carmine, blk & brn .35 .20
**235** A53 65m vio brn, blk & brn .60 .25
*Nos. 233-235 (3)* 1.30 .65

International Education Year.

**1971, Nov. 10** ***Perf. 11x11½***

**236** A54 2p yellow, grn & blk .30 .20
**237** A54 4p blue, grn & blk .45 .30
**238** A54 10½p gray, grn & blk 1.00 .75
*Nos. 236-238 (3)* 1.75 1.25

2nd anniversary of May 25th Revolution.

Arab League and Sudanese Emblems — A55

UN Emblem — A56

**1972, Feb. 10 Photo.** ***Perf. 11x11½***

**239** A55 2p yellow, grn & blk .30 .20
**240** A55 4p orange, bl & blk .50 .20
**241** A55 10½p orange, brn & blk 1.00 .45
*Nos. 239-241 (3)* 1.80 .85

25th anniv. (in 1971) of the Arab League.

**1972, Mar. 12 Photo.** ***Perf. 11x11½***

**242** A56 2p emer, rose red & org .30 .20
**243** A56 4p ultra, rose red & org .50 .20
**244** A56 10½p blk, rose red & org 1.00 .55
*Nos. 242-244 (3)* 1.80 .95

25th anniv. (in 1970) of the UN.

Emblems and Measure A57

**1972, Apr. 22 Photo.** ***Perf. 11½x11***

**245** A57 2p multicolored .30 .20
**246** A57 4p lt blue & multi .55 .20
**247** A57 10½p pink & multi 1.25 .60
*Nos. 245-247 (3)* 2.10 1.00

World Standards Day, Oct. 14, 1970.

Pres. Nimeiry and Arms of Sudan A58

**1972, May 2 Litho.** ***Perf. 13x13½***

**248** A58 2p vio bl, blk & gold .30 .20
**249** A58 4p dp org, blk & gold .50 .20
**250** A58 10½p ol grn, blk & gold 1.00 .55
*Nos. 248-250 (3)* 1.80 .95

Election of Gaafar al-Nimeiry as President, Oct. 1971.

Arms of Sudan and Congress Emblem A59

**1972, Oct. 15 Photo.** ***Perf. 11½x11***

**251** A59 2p blue & multi .30 .20
**252** A59 4p multicolored .35 .20
**253** A59 10½p lt olive & multi .90 .30
*Nos. 251-253 (3)* 1.55 .70

Founding Congress of the Sudanese Socialist Union.

Letter and African Postal Union Emblem A60

**1972, Dec. 16**

**254** A60 2p yellow & multi .30 .20
**255** A60 4p multicolored .35 .20
**256** A60 10½p blue & multi 1.00 .40
*Nos. 254-256 (3)* 1.65 .80

10th anniv. (in 1971) of the APU.

Emblems of Sudanese Provinces A61

Designs: 4p, Governing Council of Sudan. 10½p, Nat'l Coat of Arms and Unity emblem, vert.

**1973, Jan. 1 Litho.** ***Perf. 13***

**257** A61 2p gold & multi .30 .20
**258** A61 4p dk red brn & blk .40 .20
**259** A61 10½p silver, org & grn 1.00 .40
*Nos. 257-259 (3)* 1.70 .80

National Unity Day, March 3, 1972.

Emperor Haile Selassie — A62

**1973, June 25 Unwmk.** ***Perf. 13***

**260** A62 2p tan & multi .35 .20
**261** A62 4p silver & multi .75 .25
**262** A62 10½p gold & multi 1.50 .45
*Nos. 260-262 (3)* 2.60 .90

80th birthday of Haile Selassie, Emperor of Ethiopia.

Nasser and Crowd A63

**1973, July 15 Photo.** ***Perf. 11½x11***

**263** A63 2p black .35 .20
**264** A63 4p pale green & blk .55 .20
**265** A63 10½p lilac & blk .85 .40
*Nos. 263-265 (3)* 1.75 .80

Gamal Abdel Nasser (1918-70), President of Egypt.

UN and FAO Emblems, Portal and Map of Resettlement Project — A64

**1973, Dec. 30 Litho. *Perf. 13***

| | | | | |
|---|---|---|---|---|
| **266** | A64 | 2p multicolored | .30 | .20 |
| **267** | A64 | 4p multicolored | .40 | .20 |
| **268** | A64 | 10½p multicolored | 1.00 | .45 |
| | | *Nos. 266-268 (3)* | 1.70 | .85 |

World Food Program, 10th anniversary.

Scout Emblem, Knotted Rope and Stave — A65

**1974, Jan. 15**

| | | | | |
|---|---|---|---|---|
| **269** | A65 | 2p multicolored | .50 | .20 |
| **270** | A65 | 4p multicolored | .75 | .20 |
| **271** | A65 | 10½p multicolored | 1.50 | .50 |
| | | *Nos. 269-271 (3)* | 2.75 | .90 |

24th World Boy Scout Conference.

INTERPOL Emblem A66

**1974, Feb. 16 Litho. *Perf. 13x13½***

| | | | | |
|---|---|---|---|---|
| **272** | A66 | 2p orange & multi | .50 | .20 |
| **273** | A66 | 4p gray & multi | .75 | .20 |
| **274** | A66 | 10½p lt blue & multi | 1.00 | .40 |
| | | *Nos. 272-274 (3)* | 2.25 | .80 |

50th anniv. of Intl. Criminal Police Organ.

K.S.M. Building A67

**1974, July 1 Litho. *Perf. 13x13½***

| | | | | |
|---|---|---|---|---|
| **275** | A67 | 2p lilac rose & multi | .40 | .20 |
| **276** | A67 | 4p lt green & multi | .80 | .20 |
| **277** | A67 | 10½p vermilion & multi | 1.50 | .40 |
| | | *Nos. 275-277 (3)* | 2.70 | .80 |

50th anniversary of the Faculty of Medicine, University of Khartoum.

African Postal Union and UPU Emblems — A68

4p, Letters, Arab Postal Union and UPU emblems. 10½p, Letters, UPU and African Postal Union emblems.

**1974, Sept. 9 Litho. *Perf. 13½***

| | | | | |
|---|---|---|---|---|
| **278** | A68 | 2p multicolored | .25 | .20 |
| **279** | A68 | 4p lt blue & multi | .30 | .20 |
| **280** | A68 | 10½p lilac & multi | .85 | .40 |
| | | *Nos. 278-280 (3)* | 1.40 | .80 |

Centenary of Universal Postal Union.

Ali Abdel Latif, Abdel Fadil Elmaz, Revolutionary Flag and Nile — A69

**1975, July 26 Litho. *Perf. 14x13½***

| | | | | |
|---|---|---|---|---|
| **281** | A69 | 2½p green & vio blue | .25 | .20 |
| **282** | A69 | 4p rose & vio blue | .50 | .20 |
| **283** | A69 | 10½p sepia & vio blue | .90 | .40 |
| | | *Nos. 281-283 (3)* | 1.65 | .80 |

50th anniversary of 1924 revolution. Portraits show political and military leaders of the revolution.

ADB Emblem with Map of Africa A70

**1975, July 26**

| | | | | |
|---|---|---|---|---|
| **284** | A70 | 2½p multicolored | .25 | .20 |
| **285** | A70 | 4p multicolored | .45 | .20 |
| **286** | A70 | 10½p multicolored | .90 | .40 |
| | | *Nos. 284-286 (3)* | 1.60 | .80 |

African Development Bank, 10th anniv.

Radar Station and Camel Rider — A71

**1976, Feb. 2 Litho. *Perf. 13½x14***

| | | | | |
|---|---|---|---|---|
| **287** | A71 | 2½p lt green & multi | .25 | .20 |
| **288** | A71 | 4p lilac & multi | .35 | .20 |
| **289** | A71 | 10½p vio blue & multi | .85 | .40 |
| | | *Nos. 287-289 (3)* | 1.45 | .80 |

Umm Haraz Satellite Station.

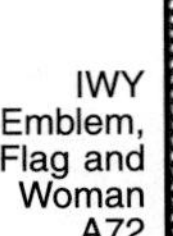

IWY Emblem, Flag and Woman A72

**1976, May 10 Litho. *Perf. 14x13½***

| | | | | |
|---|---|---|---|---|
| **290** | A72 | 2½p multicolored | .20 | .20 |
| **291** | A72 | 4p multicolored | .30 | .20 |
| **292** | A72 | 10½p dk blue & multi | .80 | .40 |
| | | *Nos. 290-292 (3)* | 1.30 | .80 |

International Women's Year 1975.

Arms of Sudan, Olympic Rings, Track — A73

**1976, July 17 Litho. *Perf. 13½x14***

| | | | | |
|---|---|---|---|---|
| **293** | A73 | 2½p green & multi | .45 | .20 |
| **294** | A73 | 4p green & multi | .50 | .25 |
| **295** | A73 | 10½p green & multi | 1.25 | .55 |
| | | *Nos. 293-295 (3)* | 2.20 | 1.00 |

21st Olympic Games, Montreal, Canada, July 17-Aug. 1.

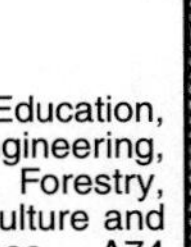

Education, Engineering, Forestry, Agriculture and Defense — A74

**1977, July 20 Litho. *Perf. 13½x14***

| | | | | |
|---|---|---|---|---|
| **296** | A74 | 2½p multicolored | .20 | .20 |
| **297** | A74 | 4p multicolored | .25 | .20 |
| **298** | A74 | 10½p multicolored | .75 | .40 |
| | | *Nos. 296-298 (3)* | 1.20 | .80 |

5th anniversary of national unity.

Archbishop Capucci — A75

**1977, Oct. 22 Photo. *Perf. 11x11½***

| | | | | |
|---|---|---|---|---|
| **299** | A75 | 2½p black | .75 | .20 |
| **300** | A75 | 4p black & green | 1.00 | .40 |
| **301** | A75 | 10½p black & red | 1.25 | .60 |
| | | *Nos. 299-301 (3)* | 3.00 | 1.20 |

Palestinian Archbishop Hilarion Capucci, jailed by Israel in 1974.

Fair Emblem, Sudanese Flag A76

***Perf. 11½x 11***

**1978, Jan. 19 Photo. Wmk. 342**

| | | | | |
|---|---|---|---|---|
| **302** | A76 | 3p multicolored | .25 | .20 |
| **303** | A76 | 4p multicolored | .40 | .20 |
| **304** | A76 | 10½p multicolored | .65 | .40 |
| | | *Nos. 302-304 (3)* | 1.30 | .80 |

International Khartoum Fair, Jan. 19-27.

APU Emblem A77

**1978, Mar. 8 Litho. *Perf. 14x13½***

| | | | | |
|---|---|---|---|---|
| **305** | A77 | 3p black, car & sil | .25 | .20 |
| **306** | A77 | 4p dk green, blk & sil | .30 | .20 |
| **307** | A77 | 10½p ultra, blk & sil | .75 | .40 |
| | | *Nos. 305-307 (3)* | 1.30 | .80 |

APU, 25th anniv. (in 1977).

Jinnah and Sudanese Flag A78

**1978, May 6 Litho. *Perf. 13***

| | | | | |
|---|---|---|---|---|
| **308** | A78 | 3p multicolored | .20 | .20 |
| **309** | A78 | 4p multicolored | .40 | .20 |
| **310** | A78 | 10½p multicolored | .65 | .40 |
| | | *Nos. 308-310 (3)* | 1.25 | .80 |

Mohammed Ali Jinnah (1876-1948), first Governor General of Pakistan.

Desert A79

**1978, May 6 *Perf. 14x13½***

| | | | | |
|---|---|---|---|---|
| **311** | A79 | 3p multicolored | .20 | .20 |
| **312** | A79 | 4p multicolored | .40 | .20 |
| **313** | A79 | 10½p multicolored | .90 | .45 |
| | | *Nos. 311-313 (3)* | 1.50 | .85 |

UN Desertification Conference.

Lion God Apedemek, African Unity Emblems — A80

**1978, July 18 Litho. *Perf. 13½x14***

| | | | | |
|---|---|---|---|---|
| **314** | A80 | 3p multicolored | .25 | .20 |
| **315** | A80 | 4p multicolored | .35 | .20 |
| **316** | A80 | 10½p multicolored | .75 | .35 |
| | | *Nos. 314-316 (3)* | 1.35 | .75 |

15th African Summit Conference, Khartoum, July 18-21.

A81

A82

**1979, Oct. 1 Litho. *Perf. 13½x14***

| | | | | |
|---|---|---|---|---|
| **317** | A81 | 3½p multicolored | .30 | .20 |
| **318** | A81 | 6p multicolored | .50 | .20 |
| **319** | A81 | 13p multicolored | .75 | .35 |
| | | *Nos. 317-319 (3)* | 1.55 | .75 |

May Revolution, 10th Anniversary.

**1980, Jan. 19 Litho. *Perf. 13½x14***

| | | | | |
|---|---|---|---|---|
| **320** | A82 | 4½p orange & black | .30 | .20 |
| **321** | A82 | 8p olive green & blk | .75 | .20 |
| **322** | A82 | 15½p blue & black | 1.25 | .45 |
| | | *Nos. 320-322 (3)* | 2.30 | .85 |

UNESCO emblem, children holding globe.

IYC Emblem, Hands Protecting Child A83

**1980, Mar. 15** *Perf. 14x13½*

**323** A83 4½p multicolored .30 .20
**324** A83 8p multicolored .55 .30
**325** A83 15½p multicolored 1.00 .45
*Nos. 323-325 (3)* 1.85 .95

International Year of the Child (1979).

25th Anniv. of Independence — A84

**1982, Mar. 4** **Photo.** *Perf. 11½*

**326** A84 60m multicolored .50 .20
**327** A84 120m multicolored 1.00 .30
**328** A84 250m multicolored 1.75 .75
*Nos. 326-328 (3)* 3.25 1.25

World Food Day, Oct. 16, 1981 A85

**1983, Jan. 15** **Photo.** *Perf. 11½*

**329** A85 60m Emblem on map, reaching hands .30 .20
**330** A85 120m Produce .75 .20
**331** A85 250m Map, grain 1.25 .50
*Nos. 329-331 (3)* 2.30 .90

A86

A87

**1984, Feb. 20** **Litho.** *Perf. 13½*

**332** A86 10p pink & silver .20 .20
**333** A86 25p lt blue & silver .60 .40
**334** A86 40p green & silver 1.10 .65
*Nos. 332-334 (3)* 1.90 1.25

25th Anniv. of Economic Commission for Africa (1983).

**1984, June 16** **Litho.** *Perf. 14*

**335** A87 10p multicolored .25 .20
**336** A87 25p multicolored .75 .40
**337** A87 40p multicolored 1.10 .55
*Nos. 335-337 (3)* 2.10 1.15

Cent. of Shaykan Battle, Kordofan (1983).

Olympic Week A88

**1984, Dec. 1** **Litho.** *Perf. 14*

**338** A88 10p multicolored .40 .20
**339** A88 25p multicolored .80 .35
**340** A88 40p multicolored 1.50 .60
*Nos. 338-340 (3)* 2.70 1.15

Sudan-Egypt Integration Charter, 2nd Anniv. — A89

Bakht Erruda, Teacher Training Institute — A90

**1985, Mar. 16** **Photo.** *Perf. 13½x13*

**341** A89 10p multicolored .25 .20
**342** A89 25p multicolored .75 .40
**343** A89 40p multicolored 1.25 .60
*Nos. 341-343 (3)* 2.25 1.20

**1985, Apr. 1**

**344** A90 10p multicolored .40 .20
**345** A90 25p multicolored .60 .20
**346** A90 40p multicolored 1.00 .40
*Nos. 344-346 (3)* 2.00 .80

April 6 Uprising, 1st Anniv. A91

**1986, Apr. 1** **Litho.** *Perf. 14*

**347** A91 5p multicolored .25 .20
**348** A91 25p multicolored .65 .40
**349** A91 40p multicolored 1.25 .60
*Nos. 347-349 (3)* 2.15 1.20

World Food Day 1986 A92

***Perf. 13x13½, 13½x13 (30p), 14 (50p)***

**1988, Jan. 1** **Litho.**

**350** A92 25p Net fishermen .45 .20
**351** A92 30p Two fish, vert. .45 .20
**352** A92 50p Globe .60 .40
**353** A92 75p Stylized fish on wave 1.00 .50
**354** A92 300p Fish in sea 3.75 1.50
*Nos. 350-354 (5)* 6.25 2.80

**Souvenir Sheet**

***Imperf***

**354A** A92 75p like 25p 1.50 1.50

Child Survival — A93

***Perf. 14, Imperf. (No. 357)***

**1988, Mar. 15** **Litho.**

**355** A93 50p Breast-feeding, vert. .50 .20
**356** A93 75p Oral rehydration 1.00 .40
**357** A93 75p like 50p, vert. 1.25 1.25
**358** A93 100p Oral vaccine 1.25 .50
**359** A93 150p Growth monitoring 1.50 .85
*Nos. 355-359 (5)* 5.50 3.20

No. 357 issued without gum. Size: 63x84mm.

Red Crescent in Sudan, 30th Anniv. (in 1987) — A94

World Food Day, Oct. 16, 1987, and the Small Farmer — A95

Designs: 100p, Crescent, candle. 150p, Crescent, stylized figure of a man.

**1988, Oct. 31** **Litho.** *Perf. 14*

**360** A94 40p org yel, blk & dk red .45 .20
**361** A94 100p blk, blue grn & dk red 1.00 .50
**362** A94 150p blk, brt blue & dk red 1.40 .85
*Nos. 360-362 (3)* 2.85 1.55

Nos. 361-362 horiz.

**1988, Oct. 31** *Perf. 13x13½, 13½x13*

FAO emblem and: 40p, Early farming tools, horiz. 100p, Ox-drawn plow. 150p, Crude public water supply.

**363** A95 40p multicolored .45 .20
**364** A95 100p shown 1.00 .50
**365** A95 150p multicolored 1.40 .75
*Nos. 363-365 (3)* 2.85 1.45

Khartoum Bank, 75th Anniv. A96

Designs: 40p, Anniv. emblem. 100p, Spheres, emblem, medallion on ribbon. 150p, Text, emblem.

**1988, Oct. 31** *Perf. 14*

**366** A96 40p multicolored .45 .20
**367** A96 100p multicolored 1.00 .50
**368** A96 150p multicolored 1.50 .75
*Nos. 366-368 (3)* 2.95 1.45

Declaration of Palestinian State, 1st Anniv. — A97

#370, 372, 374, Crowd of demonstrators.

**1989, Dec. 10** **Litho.** *Perf. 14*

**369** A97 100p yellow grn & multi .95 .60
**370** A97 100p buff & multi .95 .60
**371** A97 150p lt vio & multi 1.40 .95
**372** A97 150p lt blue & multi 1.40 .95
**373** A97 200p pink & multi 1.90 1.25
**374** A97 200p lt green & multi 1.90 1.25
*Nos. 369-374 (6)* 8.50 5.60

Palestinian Uprising (Nos. 370, 372, 374).

African Development Bank, 25th Anniv. — A99

**1989, Dec. 28** *Perf. 13x13½*

**375** A99 100p yel grn, blk & sil .95 .60
**376** A99 150p blue, blk & sil 1.40 .95
**377** A99 200p plum, blk & sil 1.90 1.25
*Nos. 375-377 (3)* 4.25 2.80

Independence, 33rd Anniv. (in 1989) — A100

**1990, Jan. 22** **Litho.** *Perf. 13½x13*

**378** A100 50p blue & yellow .35 .20
**379** A100 100p deep claret & yel .75 .45
**380** A100 150p brt rose & yel 1.00 .70
**381** A100 200p dp rose lil & yel 1.40 .90
*Nos. 378-381 (4)* 3.50 2.25

Mammals A101

**1990, Feb. 20** *Perf. 13x13½*

**382** A101 25p Leopard .30 .20
**383** A101 50p Elephant .50 .20

***Perf. 14***

**384** A101 75p Giraffe, vert. .75 .35
**385** A101 100p White rhinoceros 1.00 .45
**386** A101 125p Addax, vert. 1.25 .60
*Nos. 382-386 (5)* 3.80 1.80

No. 385 inscribed "Rino."

Birds — A102

**1990, Mar. 25** *Perf. 13½x13*

**387** A102 25p Zande hornbill .30 .20
**388** A102 50p Marabou stork .75 .20
**389** A102 75p Buff-crested bustard 1.10 .45
**390** A102 100p Saddle-bill 1.50 .55

***Perf. 14***

**391** A102 150p Bald-headed ibis 2.00 .75
*Nos. 387-391 (5)* 5.65 2.15

Traditional Dances A103

***Perf. 13x13½, 13½x13***

**1990, May 10** **Litho.**

**392** A103 25p Mardoum .20 .20
**393** A103 50p Zandi, vert. .45 .25
**394** A103 75p Kambala, vert. .60 .45
**395** A103 100p Nubian, vert. .75 .60
**396** A103 125p Sword .85 .75
*Nos. 392-396 (5)* 2.85 2.25

Natl. Salvation Revolution, 1st Anniv. — A104

**1991, Apr. 14 Litho. *Perf. 13***

**399** A104 150p multicolored 1.00 .70
**400** A104 200p multicolored 1.40 .90
**401** A104 250p multicolored 1.75 1.10
**402** A104 £5 multicolored 3.50 2.25
**403** A104 £10 multicolored 7.00 4.50
*Nos. 399-403 (5)* 14.65 9.45

For surcharge see No. 438.

Type of 1962 and:

Shoebill A105 Camel Postman A109

**1991, July 1 *Perf. 13½x13***

**404** A105 25p shown .20 .20
**405** A105 50p Sunflower .35 .20
**406** A105 75p Gum Arabic .50 .35
**407** A105 100p Cotton .70 .45
**408** A105 125p Crowned crane .90 .60

**Size: 30x24mm**

***Perf. 14x14½, 13½x14***

**409** A105 150p Kenana Sugar Co., horiz. 1.00 .70
**410** A105 175p Secretary bird 1.25 .80
**411** A105 £2 Atbara cement factory, horiz. 1.40 .90

**Size: 26x37mm**

***Perf. 14***

**412** A105 250p King Taharqa statue 1.75 1.10
**413** A105 £3 Republican palace 2.10 1.40

**Size: 24x30mm**

***Perf. 13½x14***

**414** A105 £4 Hug jar 2.75 1.90
**415** A105 £5 Gabana coffee pot 3.50 2.25

**Size: 36x27mm**

**Litho. & Engr.**

***Perf. 14***

**Wmk. 334**

**416** A109 £8 Pterois volitans, horiz. 5.50 3.75
**417** A109 £10 Animal wealth, horiz. 7.00 4.50
**418** A109 £15 Nubian ibex 10.50 6.75
**419** A109 £20 shown 14.00 9.00
*Nos. 404-419 (16)* 53.40 34.85

**1992 Litho. Unwmk. *Perf. 14½x14***

**420** A25 25p Cattle .20 .20

**1990 Unwmk. *Perf. 14x13½***

**427** A25 £5 Bohein Temple 3.50 2.25

***Perf. 13½x14***

**428** A26 £10 Sailboat 7.00 4.50

This is an expanding set. Numbers will change if necessary.

See Nos. O76-O100. For surcharges see Nos. 430, 436-453, O104-O111.

No. 156a Handstamp Surcharged in Blue Violet

**1990, Sept. *Perf. 13½x14***

**430** A26 £1 on 10p #156a — 2.00

Surcharge on No. 430 is often incomplete.

Pan-African Rinderpest Campaign A114

***Perf. 13½x13***

**1991, July 27 Litho. Unwmk.**

**431** A114 £1 black & brt grn .70 .45
**432** A114 £2 dp violet & emer 1.40 .90
**433** A114 £5 orange & blue grn 3.50 2.25
*Nos. 431-433 (3)* 5.60 3.60

Nos. 404, 407, 411, 413-414 Surcharged in Black or Blue Violet

Nos. 406, 409, 420 Surcharged

Nos. 405//420 Surcharged

5d

No. 409 Surcharged in Black

No. 406 Surcharged in Black

No. 412 Surcharged in Red

35d

No. 408 Surcharged

**1992?-97**

**Perfs. & Printing Methods as Before**

**436** A105 1d on 100p #407 (Blk) 3.75 2.50
**437** A105 2d on £2 #411 7.25 4.75
**438** A104 2.50d on 25p #404 9.00 5.75
**438A** A105 2.50d on 25p #420 2.50 1.75
**439** A105 3d on £3 #413 11.00 7.00
**440** A105 4d on £4 #414 14.50 9.50
**441** A105 5d on 50p #405 2.75 .90
**443** A105 7.50d on 75p #406 7.50 5.00
**446** A105 1.50d on 150p #409 1.50 1.00
**447** A105 15d on 150p #409 — —
**448** A105 25d on 75p #406 — —
**449** A105 25d on 250p #412 — —
**451** A105 35d on £8 #416 4.75 1.60
*a.* Inverted surcharge — —
**452** A105 100d on 125p #408 5.75 5.75
**453** A105 100d on 125p #408 (R) — —
*Nos. 436-453 (11)* 70.25 45.50

This is an expanding set. Numbers will change if necessary.

Intl. Human Rights Day — A115

Fung Sultanate, 5th Cent. — A116

Designs: £5, Chain links, rainbow of colors, horiz. 750p, Trellis, rose, inscription.

**1993, Dec. 20 Litho. *Perf. 14***

**454** A115 £4 multicolored .75 .50
**455** A115 £5 multicolored 1.00 .65
**456** A115 750p multicolored 1.50 1.00
*Nos. 454-456 (3)* 3.25 2.15

**1993, Dec. 20**

Designs: £5, Inscription on tablet. 750p, Inscription in circle, helmet, horiz.

**457** A116 £4 multicolored .80 .50
**458** A116 £5 multicolored 1.00 .65
**459** A116 750p multicolored 1.50 1.00
*Nos. 457-459 (3)* 3.30 2.15

Wild Ass — A117

A118

**1994, July 15 Litho. *Perf. 14½***

**460** A117 4d With young .75 .40
**461** A117 8d Standing 1.25 .75
**462** A117 10d Running 1.75 1.00
**463** A117 15d Up close 2.75 1.50
*Nos. 460-463 (4)* 6.50 3.65

**1994, Aug. 1 Litho. *Perf. 14***

**464** A118 5d vermilion & multi .25 .20
**465** A118 7d green & multi .40 .25
**466** A118 15d gray & multi .85 .55
*Nos. 464-466 (3)* 1.50 1.00

Intl. Olympic Committee, cent.

A119

A120

**1994, Dec. 7 Litho. *Perf. 13½***

**467** A119 5d lilac & multi .25 .20
**468** A119 7d brown & multi .35 .20
**469** A119 15d blue & multi .80 .50
*Nos. 467-469 (3)* 1.40 .90

ICAO, 50th anniv.

**1995, July 15 Litho. *Perf. 14***

1994 World Cup Soccer Championships, US: 4d, Goalie, green vest. 5d, Like 4d, blue vest. 7d, Player about to kick ball, green shirt. 8d, Like 7d, brown shirt. 10d, Player, long-sleeved shirt. 15d, Player, yellow shirt. 20d, Player, magenta & blue background. 25d, Player, white shirt & pants. 35d, Like 20d, blue & green background.

75d, Goalie, orange shirt, horiz. 100d, Player kicking ball, horiz.

**470** A120 4d multicolored .20 .20
**471** A120 5d multicolored .20 .20
**472** A120 7d multicolored .25 .20
**473** A120 8d multicolored .30 .20
**474** A120 10d multicolored .40 .25
**475** A120 15d multicolored .60 .40
**476** A120 20d multicolored .75 .50
**477** A120 25d multicolored .95 .60
**478** A120 35d multicolored 1.25 .80
*Nos. 470-478 (9)* 4.90 3.35

**Souvenir Sheets**

**479** A120 75d multicolored 5.50 3.75
**480** A120 100d multicolored 7.50 5.00

A121

A122

**1995, Dec. 16 Litho. *Perf. 13½***

**481** A121 15d apple grn & blk 1.25 .80
**482** A121 25d blue & black 2.00 1.25
**483** A121 30d purple & black 2.40 1.60
*Nos. 481-483 (3)* 5.65 3.65

Arab League, 50th anniv.

**1996, May 4 Litho. *Perf. 13½***

**484** A122 15d orange & multi .30 .20
**485** A122 25d apple grn & multi .50 .35
**486** A122 30d purple & multi .60 .60
*Nos. 484-486 (3)* 1.40 1.15

Common Market for East and South Africa (COMESA).

A123

A124

**1997, Jan. 22 Photo. *Perf. 13½***

**487** A123 25d black & violet .35 .20
**488** A123 35d black & red brown .50 .35
**489** A123 50d black & brown .70 .45
*Nos. 487-489 (3)* 1.55 1.00

Abdel Rahman el Mahdi (1885-1959).

**1997, June 1 Photo. *Perf. 13½x13***

**490** A124 5d multicolored .20 .20

Waiting For Peace.

A125

A126

**1997, Oct. 15 Photo. *Perf. 13½***

**491** A125 25d lilac & multi 1.10 .75
**492** A125 35d apple grn & multi 1.50 1.00
**493** A125 50d green, black & sil 2.25 1.50
*Nos. 491-493 (3)* 4.85 3.25

Police Commanders, Arab Security Conference, 25th anniv.

**1997, Nov. 1**

Al-Shaykh Qaribulla's Mosque:Various views of mosque.

**494** A126 25d blue & multi 1.10 .75
**495** A126 35d yellow & multi 1.50 1.00
**496** A126 50d buff & multi, vert. 2.25 1.50
*Nos. 494-496 (3)* 4.85 3.25

A127

A128

**1998, Jan. 18 Litho. *Perf. 13½***

**497** A127 25d multicolored .30 .20
**498** A127 35d violet & multi .45 .30
**499** A127 50d multicolored .65 .40
*Nos. 497-499 (3)* 1.40 .90

Pan African Postal Union, 18th anniv.

**1998, Jan. 25 *Perf. 13½x13, 13x13½***

Sudanese Archeology: No. 500, Kerma pottery, 2500 BC. No. 501, Fresco, Faras church, 11th cent. No. 502, Close-up of fresco, Faras Church, 11th cent. 60d, C Group pottery, 2000 BC. No. 504, Meroe pottery, 4000 BC. No. 505, Tomb of Natakamani Meroitic king, 1st cent. BC, vert. 100d, C Group pottery, 2000 BC, diff.

**500** A128 50d multicolored .65 .40
**501** A128 50d multicolored .65 .40
**502** A128 50d multicolored .65 .40
**503** A128 60d multicolored .75 .50
**504** A128 75d multicolored .95 .65
**505** A128 75d multicolored .95 .65
**506** A128 100d multicolored 1.25 .85
*Nos. 500-506 (7)* 5.85 3.85

A129

A130

**1998, Mar. 1 *Perf. 13x13½***

**507** A129 100d Ruins, Camel Post rider 1.25 .85

First Sudanese Postage Stamp, cent.

**1999, May 15 Litho. *Perf. 13¼x13½***

**508** A130 75d multicolored *2.25 1.50*
**509** A130 100d green & multi *3.00 2.00*
**510** A130 150d blue & multi *4.50 3.00*
*Nos. 508-510 (3)* *9.75 6.50*

Battle of Kerreri, cent.

American Bombing of Elshifa Pharmaceuticals Factory, Aug. 20, 1998 — A131

75d, Bomb damage. 100d, Company emblem, falling bombs. 150d, Casualties.

***Perf. 13¾x13½, 13¾x13¼***
**1999, July 1 Litho.**

**511** A131 75d multi *1.75 1.75*
**512** A131 100d multi, vert. *2.25 2.25*
**513** A131 150d multi *3.50 3.50*
*Nos. 511-513 (3)* *7.50 7.50*

A132

A133

***Perf. 13¼x13½, 13½x13¼***
**1999, Oct. 20 Litho.**

**514** A132 75d shown *2.40 2.40*
**515** A133 100d shown *3.00 3.00*
**516** A132 150d 7 people *4.75 4.75*
*Nos. 514-516 (3)* *10.15 10.15*

Intl. Year of the Elderly.

SOS Children's Villages, 50th Anniv. — A134

**1999, Oct. 31 *Perf. 13½x13¼***

**517** A134 75d brn & multi *2.40 2.40*
**518** A134 100d grn & multi *3.00 3.00*
**519** A134 150d blue & multi *4.75 4.75*
*Nos. 517-519 (3)* *10.15 10.15*

UPU, 125th Anniv. (in 1999) — A134a

**2000, Mar. 1 Litho. *Perf. 13½x13¼***
**Denomination Color**

**519A** A134a 75d red 3.50 3.50
**519B** A134a 100d violet 4.75 4.75
**519C** A134a 150d black 7.00 7.00
*Nos. 519A-519C (3)* 15.25 15.25

Common Market for Eastern and Southern Africa Free Trade Area — A135

Panel color: 100d, White. 150d, Pink. 200d, Yellow.

**2000, Oct. 31 Litho. *Perf. 13¼x13¾***

**520-522** A135 Set of 3 — —

UN High Commissioner for Refugees, 50th Anniv. — A136

Frame color: 100d, Green. 150d, Red. 200d, Violet.

***Perf. 13¼x13½***
**2001, Aug. 15 Litho.**

**523-525** A136 Set of 3 — —

Al-Zubair Prize for Innovation and Scientific Excellence A137

Frame color: 100d, Yellow. 150d, Red. 200d, Green.

**2002, Feb. 14 *Perf. 13¼***

**526-528** A137 Set of 3 — —

Association for the Promotion of Scientific Innovation — A138

Frame color: 100d, Black. 150d, Red. 200d, Green.

**2002, Feb. 14**

**529-531** A138 Set of 3 — —

Year of Dialogue Among Civilizations A139

Country name in: 100d, Red. 150d, Orange. 200d, Black.

**2002, Jan. 28 Litho. *Perf. 13¼x13¾***

**532-534** A139 Set of 3 — —

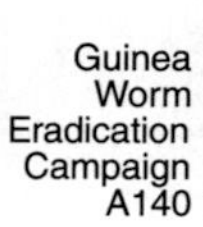
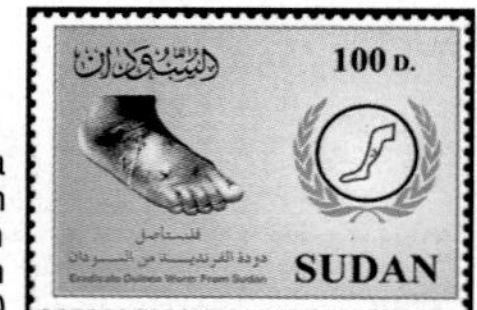

Guinea Worm Eradication Campaign A140

Designs: 100d, Infested foot, campaign emblem. 150d, Campaign emblem. 200d, Child, campaign emblem.

**2002, Mar. 3 Litho. *Perf. 13¼***

**535-537** A140 Set of 3 — —

Palestinian Intifada — A141

Country name in: 100d, Green. 150d, Red. 200d, Black.

***Perf. 13½x13¼***
**2002, Feb. 14 Litho.**

**538-540** A141 Set of 3 — —

Sudanese postal officials have declared as illegal the following items:
Sheets of six stamps depicting Pope John Paul II (2 different)
Miniature sheet of two stamps depicting Pope John Paul II (2 different).

Association of African Banknote and Security Document Printers 11th Annual Conference — A142

Conference emblem and: 100d, Association emblem, circular design. 150d, Banknote rosettes. 200d, Archaeological ruins.

**2003, May 10 Litho. *Perf. 13½x13¼***

**541-543** A142 Set of 3 *6.25 6.25*

Mango — A143

Nile Perch — A144

Cattle — A145

Soldiers — A146

Muhammad Ahmad (Al-Mahdi, 1844-85), Religious Leader — A147

Butterflyfish — A148

Temple of Amun Ra — A149

Baobab Tree — A150

Doum Palm Tree — A151

Sheep — A152

Grapefruit A153

Sudan Petrol
SUDAN 200D.
Oil Rigs A154

Tomb of Sheikh El-Mursi
A155

Camel Postman
A156

*Perf. 13½x13¼, 13¼x13½*

**2003, July 15**

| | | | | |
|---|---|---|---|---|
| **544** | A143 | 50d multi | .70 | .70 |
| **545** | A144 | 50d multi | .70 | .70 |
| **546** | A145 | 75d multi | 1.00 | 1.00 |
| **547** | A146 | 100d multi | 1.40 | 1.40 |
| **548** | A147 | 100d multi | 1.40 | 1.40 |
| **549** | A148 | 125d multi | 1.75 | 1.75 |
| **550** | A149 | 150d multi | 2.10 | 2.10 |
| **551** | A150 | 150d multi | 2.10 | 2.10 |
| **552** | A151 | 150d multi | 2.10 | 2.10 |
| **553** | A152 | 150d multi | 2.10 | 2.10 |
| **554** | A153 | 200d multi | 2.75 | 2.75 |
| **555** | A154 | 200d multi | 2.75 | 2.75 |
| **556** | A155 | 300d multi | 4.25 | 4.25 |
| **557** | A156 | 500d multi | 7.00 | 7.00 |
| *a.* | | Souvenir sheet, #544-557, imperf. | 32.50 | 32.50 |
| | | *Nos. 544-557 (14)* | 32.10 | 32.10 |

Parliament, 50th Anniv. — A157

Panel colors: 100d, Lilac. 200d, Yellow orange. 250d, Pink.

**2004, Jan. 5** *Perf. 13½x13¼*
**558-560** A157 Set of 3 6.25 6.25

General Secretariat for Council of Ministers, 50th Anniv. — A158

Panel colors: 100d, Light blue. 200d, Yellow. 250d, Pink.

**2004, Jan. 8**
**561-563** A158 Set of 3 6.25 6.25

Rural Women's Innovation — A159

Panel colors: 100d, Light blue. 200d, Yellow. 250d, Lilac.

**2004, Jan. 26**
**564-566** A159 Set of 3 6.25 6.25

Armed Forces, 50th Anniv. — A160

Background color: 100d, Orange. 200d, Red. 250d, Purple.

*Perf. 13¼x13½*

**2004, Aug. 14** **Litho.**
**567-569** A160 Set of 3 10.00 10.00

Peace — A161

Background color: 200d, Dark blue. 300d, Green and yellow, 400d, Light blue.

**2005, Jan. 9** *Perf. 13½x13¼*
**570-572** A161 Set of 3 15.50 15.50

7th Conference of Sudanese Women's General Union — A162

Panel color: 200d, White. 300d, Lilac. 400d, Light blue.

*Perf. 13½x13¼*

**2005, June 29** **Litho.**
**573-575** A162 Set of 3 — —

Merowe Dam Project — A163

Background color: 200d, Light blue. 300d, Light green. 400d, Lilac.

**2005, June 30**
**576-578** A163 Set of 3 — —

World Summit on the Information Society, Tunis — A164

Background color: 200d, Yellow green. 300d, Blue. 400d, Yellow orange.

**2005, Sept. 24**
**579-581** A164 Set of 3 — —

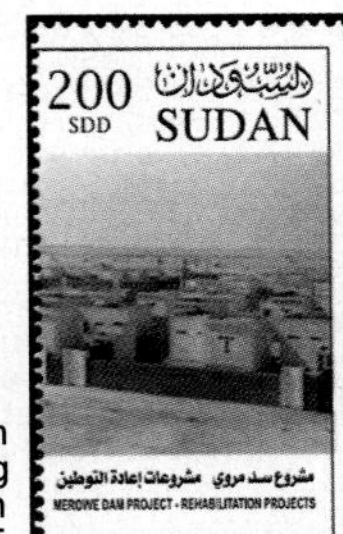
Merowe Dam Housing Rehabilitation Projects — A165

Denomination in: 200d, Black. 300d, Green. 400d, Red.

**2005, Oct. 1** **Litho.** *Perf. 13¼x13¾*
**582-584** A165 Set of 3 9.00 9.00

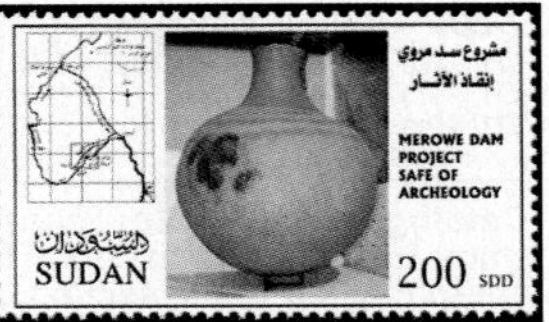
Merowe Dam Archaeology Project — A166

Map and clay pot: 200d, Shown. 300d, With blue panel. 400d, With peach panel.

**2005, Dec. 20** *Perf. 13¾x13¼*
**585-587** A166 Set of 3 9.00 9.00

A167

A168

Independence, 50th Anniv. — A169

*Perf. 13¼x13¾, 13¾x13¼*

**2006, Jan. 15**

| | | | | |
|---|---|---|---|---|
| **588** | A167 | 200d multi | 2.00 | 2.00 |
| **589** | A168 | 300d multi | 3.00 | 3.00 |
| **590** | A169 | 400d multi | 4.00 | 4.00 |
| | | *Nos. 588-590 (3)* | 9.00 | 9.00 |

OPEC Intl. Development Fund, 30th Anniv. — A170

Background color: 200d, Red. 300d, Green. 400d, Blue.

**2006, Oct. 12** **Litho.** *Perf. 13¾x13½*
**591-593** A170 Set of 3 8.50 8.50

## AIR POST STAMPS

Nos. 40-41, 43 Overprinted in Black

Nos. C1-C2

No. C3

**1931** **Wmk. 214** *Perf. 11½x12½, 14*

| | | | | |
|---|---|---|---|---|
| **C1** | A2 | 5m blk & olive brown | .75 | 1.00 |
| **C2** | A2 | 10m blk & carmine | 1.25 | 4.00 |
| **C3** | A1 | 2p org & vio brown | 2.00 | 3.50 |
| | | *Nos. C1-C3 (3)* | 4.00 | 8.50 |

Statue of Gen. C. G. Gordon AP3

**1931-35** **Engr.** *Perf. 14*

| | | | | |
|---|---|---|---|---|
| **C4** | AP3 | 3m dk brn & grn ('33) | 3.00 | 6.00 |
| **C5** | AP3 | 5m grn & blk | 1.10 | .20 |
| **C6** | AP3 | 10m car rose & blk | 1.10 | .25 |
| **C7** | AP3 | 15m dk brn & brn | .45 | .20 |
| **C8** | AP3 | 2p org & blk | .40 | .20 |
| **C9** | AP3 | 2½p bl & red vio ('33) | 3.25 | .20 |
| **C10** | AP3 | 3p gray & blk | .65 | .20 |
| **C11** | AP3 | 3½p dl vio & blk | 1.50 | .90 |
| **C12** | AP3 | 4½p gray & brn | 11.00 | 16.00 |
| **C13** | AP3 | 5p ultra & blk | 1.10 | .35 |
| **C14** | AP3 | 7½p pck grn & dk grn ('35) | 10.00 | 6.00 |
| **C15** | AP3 | 10p peacock bl & sep ('35) | 10.00 | .75 |
| | | *Nos. C4-C15 (12)* | 43.55 | 31.25 |

See Nos. C23-C30. For surcharges see Nos. C17-C22, C31-C34.

No. 43 Surcharged in Black

**1932, July 18** **Typo.**
**C16** A1 2½p on 2p 2.00 4.00

Nos. C6, C4-C5, C12 Surcharged

**1935** **Engr.** *Perf. 14*

| | | | | |
|---|---|---|---|---|
| **C17** | AP3 | 15m on 10m | .45 | .20 |
| *a.* | | Double surcharge | 700.00 | 775.00 |
| *b.* | | Arabic characters omitted | 650.00 | |
| **C18** | AP3 | 2½p on 3m | .95 | 6.00 |
| *a.* | | "½" 2¼mm high instead of 3mm | 2.50 | 20.00 |
| *b.* | | Second Arabic character of surcharge omitted | 55.00 | 125.00 |
| **C19** | AP3 | 2½p on 5m | .50 | 1.75 |
| *a.* | | "½" 2¼mm high instead of 3mm | 1.50 | 9.00 |
| *b.* | | Second Arabic character of surcharge omitted | 30.00 | 60.00 |
| *c.* | | Inverted surcharge | 900.00 | 900.00 |
| *d.* | | As "a," inverted | 4,000. | |
| *e.* | | As "b," inverted | 1,500. | 1,600. |
| *f.* | | Pair, C19c and C19d | 5,750. | |
| **C20** | AP3 | 3p on 4½p | 2.00 | 10.00 |
| **C21** | AP3 | 7½p on 4½p | 6.50 | 45.00 |
| *a.* | | "7¼" instead of "7½" | | |
| **C22** | AP3 | 10p on 4½p | 6.50 | 45.00 |
| | | *Nos. C17-C22 (6)* | 16.90 | 107.95 |

Type of 1931-35

**1936-37** *Perf. 11½x12½*

| | | | | |
|---|---|---|---|---|
| **C23** | AP3 | 15m dk brn & brn ('37) | 4.00 | .20 |
| **C24** | AP3 | 2p org & blk ('37) | 5.00 | 15.00 |
| **C25** | AP3 | 2½p bl & red vio | 3.00 | .20 |
| **C26** | AP3 | 3p gray & blk ('37) | 1.00 | .40 |
| **C27** | AP3 | 3½p dl vio & blk ('37) | 2.50 | 12.00 |
| **C28** | AP3 | 5p ultra & blk ('37) | 4.00 | .40 |
| **C29** | AP3 | 7½p pck grn & dk grn ('37) | 4.50 | 10.00 |
| **C30** | AP3 | 10p pck bl & sep ('37) | 4.50 | 20.00 |
| | | *Nos. C23-C30 (8)* | 28.50 | 58.20 |

Nos. C25, C11, C14 and C15 Surcharged as in 1935

**1938 Wmk. 214 *Perf. 11½x12½, 14***

**C31** AP3 5m on 2½p 1.00 .25
**C32** AP3 3p on 3½p 15.00 *30.00*
*a.* On No. C27 400.00 *500.00*
**C33** AP3 3p on 7½p 6.00 *6.00*
*a.* On No. C29 400.00 *500.00*
**C34** AP3 5p on 10p 1.00 *5.00*
*a.* On No. C30 400.00 *500.00*
*Nos. C31-C34 (4)* 23.00 41.25

**Catalogue values for unused stamps in this section, from this point to the end of the section, are for Never Hinged items.**

Bridge Over Blue Nile, Khartoum AP4

Designs: 2½p, Kassala Jebel. 3p, Water wheel. 3½p, Port Sudan. 4p, Gordon Memorial College. 4½p, Nile post boat. 6p, Suakin. 20p, General Post Office, Khartoum.

**1950, July 1 Engr. *Perf. 12***

**C35** AP4 2p dk bl grn & blk 5.00 .65
**C36** AP4 2½p red org & bl .40 .85
**C37** AP4 3p dp bl & plum 2.75 .35
**C38** AP4 3½p chnt & choc .90 *2.10*
**C39** AP4 4p bl & brn .90 *1.50*
**C40** AP4 4½p ultra & blk 2.50 *3.00*
**C41** AP4 6p car & blk 2.00 *1.75*
**C42** AP4 20p plum & blk 2.00 *3.25*
*Nos. C35-C42 (8)* 16.45 *13.45*

For overprints see Nos. CO1-CO8.

### AIR POST OFFICIAL

**Catalogue values for unused stamps in this section are for Never Hinged items.**

Nos. C35 to C42 Overprinted in Carmine or Black

**1950, July 1 Wmk. 214 *Perf. 12***

**CO1** AP4 2p dk bl grn & blk (C) 13.00 2.50
**CO2** AP4 2½p red org & bl 1.40 *1.50*
**CO3** AP4 3p dp bl & plum .75 *1.00*
**CO4** AP4 3½p chnt & choc .75 *5.50*
**CO5** AP4 4p bl & brn .75 *4.75*
**CO6** AP4 4½p ultra & blk (C) 3.50 *13.00*
**CO7** AP4 6p car & blk (C) .95 *3.75*
**CO8** AP4 20p plum & blk (C) 4.75 *11.00*
*Nos. CO1-CO8 (8)* 25.85 43.00

### POSTAGE DUE STAMPS

Postage Due Stamps of Egypt, 1889, Overprinted in Black

**1897 Wmk. 119 *Perf. 14***

**J1** D3 2m green 1.50 *5.00*
**J2** D3 4m maroon 1.50 *5.00*
**J3** D3 1p ultra 10.00 *4.00*
**J4** D3 2p orange 10.00 *8.50*
*Nos. J1-J4 (4)* 23.00 22.50

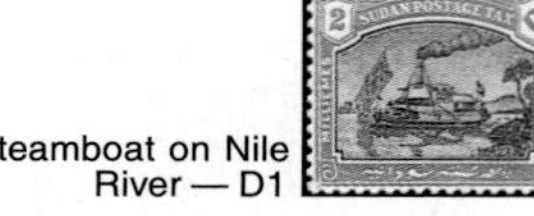

Steamboat on Nile River — D1

**1901 Typo. Wmk. 179**

**J5** D1 2m orange brn & blk .70 .50
**J6** D1 4m blue green & brn 2.00 1.00
**J7** D1 10m blue vio & blue grn 4.00 3.50
**J8** D1 20m car rose & ultra 3.75 3.75
*Nos. J5-J8 (4)* 10.45 8.75

**1927-30 Wmk. Multiple S G (214)**

**J9** D1 2m org brn & blk ('30) 2.50 2.50
**J10** D1 4m blue grn & brn 1.00 .75
**J11** D1 10m violet & blue grn 1.50 *1.60*
*Nos. J9-J11 (3)* 5.00 4.85

**Catalogue values for unused stamps in this section, from this point to the end of the section, are for Never Hinged items.**

Redrawn

Bottom inscription altered — D2

**1948, Jan. 1**

**J12** D2 2m dp orange & blk 1.00 *21.00*
**J13** D2 4m blue grn & choc 2.25 *21.00*
**J14** D2 10m rose lil & bl grn 17.00 *13.00*
*a.* Wmk. 345 ('71?)
**J15** D2 20m brt car rose & ultra 18.00 *24.00*
*a.* Wmk. 345 ('73)
*Nos. J12-J15 (4)* 38.25 *79.00*

### ARMY OFFICIAL STAMPS

Regular Issues of 1898 and 1902-08 Overprinted in Black:

Nos. MO1, MO3 and MO2, MO4

**1905 Wmk. 71 *Perf. 14***

**MO1** A1 1m rose & brown 150.00 125.00
*a.* "OFFICIAL" 3,250. 1,750.
*b.* Pair, #MO1 and #MO2 2,750.
**MO2** A1 1m rose & brown 1,800. *1,800.*

**Wmk. 179**

**MO3** A1 1m car rose & brn 3.00 2.00
*a.* "OFFICIAL" 45.00 30.00
*b.* Inverted overprint 70.00 60.00
*c.* Horizontal overprint 375.00
**MO4** A1 1m car rose & brn 40.00 24.00
*a.* Inverted overprint 350.00 375.00

Regular Issues of 1902-11 Overprinted in Black

**1906-11**

**MO5** A1 1m car rose & brn 1.25 .30
*a.* "Army" and "Service" 14mm apart 275.00 200.00
*b.* Inverted overprint 425.00 *450.00*
*c.* Pair, one without ovpt. *3,750.*
*d.* Double overprint 800.00
*e.* "Service" omitted *3,750.*
**MO6** A1 2m brn & grn 10.00 .95
*a.* Pair, one without ovpt. *2,500.*
*b.* "Army" omitted *3,000.*
**MO7** A1 3m green & violet 16.00 .40
*a.* Inverted overprint *2,000.*
**MO8** A1 5m blk & rose red 1.40 .20
*a.* Inverted overprint 225.00
*b.* Double overprint 225.00 225.00
*c.* Double ovpt., one invtd. 875.00 400.00
**MO9** A1 1p yel brn & ultra 12.00 .40
*a.* "Army" omitted 2,000. 2,000.
**MO10** A1 2p ultra & blk ('09) 45.00 12.50
*a.* Double overprint —
**MO11** A1 5p grn & org brn ('08) 100.00 60.00
**MO12** A1 10p dp vio & blk ('11) 600.00 *600.00*
*Nos. MO5-MO12 (8)* 785.65 674.75

**Same Overprint On Regular Issue of 1898**

**Wmk. 71**

**MO13** A1 2p ultra & black 60.00 10.00
*a.* Inverted overprint
**MO14** A1 5p grn & org brn 95.00 *175.00*
**MO15** A1 10p dp vio & blk 140.00 *375.00*

There are two types of this overprint which may be distinguished by the size and shape of the "y."

### OFFICIAL STAMPS

Regular Issue of 1898 Overprinted in Black

**1902-06 Wmk. 71 *Perf. 14***

**O1** A1 1m rose & brown 2.00 *7.50*
*a.* Inverted overprint 325.00 *400.00*
*b.* Round periods 7.50 *30.00*
*c.* Double overprint 650.00
*d.* Oval "O" in overprint 90.00
*e.* As "d," inverted overprint 5,500.
**O2** A1 10p dp vio & blk ('06) 13.00 *20.00*

Same Ovpt. on Stamps of 1902-11

**1903-12 Wmk. 179**

**O3** A1 1m car rose & brn ('04) .45 .20
*a.* Double overprint
**O4** A1 3m grn & vio ('04) 2.25 .20
*a.* Double overprint
**O5** A1 5m blk & rose red 2.25 .20
**O6** A1 1p yel brn & ultra 2.25 .20
**O7** A1 2p ultra & blk 20.00 .20
**O8** A1 5p grn & org brn 1.75 .25
**O9** A1 10p dp vio & blk 3.75 47.50
*Nos. O3-O9 (7)* 32.70 48.75

Regular Issue of 1927-40 Overprinted in Black

***Perf. 14, 13½x 14***

**1936-46 Wmk. 214**

**O10** A2 1m dk org & int blk ('46) .75 *3.50*
**O11** A2 2m dk brn & dk org ('45) .25 .20
**O12** A2 3m green & vio ('37) 1.25 .20
**O13** A2 4m brown & green 1.60 .20
**O14** A2 5m blk & ol brn ('40) .35 .20
**O15** A2 10m blk & car ('46) .35 .20
**O16** A2 15m org brn & ultra ('37) 3.00 .20

**O17** A1 2p org & vio brn ('37) 5.00 .20
**O18** A1 3p dk bl & red brn ('46) 2.75 .50
**O19** A1 4p blk & ultra ('46) 12.50 1.00
**O20** A1 5p dk grn & org brn 6.75 .20
**O21** A1 6p blk & pale bl ('46) 4.00 2.00
**O22** A1 8p blk & pck grn ('46) 2.75 9.00
**O23** A1 10p dp vio & blk ('37) 15.00 2.50
**O24** A1 20p bl & lt bl ('46) 13.00 9.00
*Nos. O10-O24 (15)* 69.30 29.10

**Catalogue values for unused stamps in this section, from this point to the end of the section, are for Never Hinged items.**

#79-85 Overprinted Like #O10-O16

**1948, Jan. 1**

**O28** A7 1m dk org & blk .25 1.50
**O29** A7 2m choc & org 1.00 .20
**O30** A7 3m grn & rose lil 1.75 3.00
**O31** A7 4m choc & sl grn 1.75 1.00
**O32** A7 5m blk & ol brn 1.75 .20
**O33** A7 10m blk & car 1.50 .35
**O34** A7 15m org brn & ultra 1.75 .20

**Nos. 86-94 Overprinted Like Nos. O17-O24**

**O35** A8 2p org yel & vio brn 1.75 .20
**O36** A8 3p dk bl & red brn 1.75 .20
**O37** A8 4p blk & ultra 1.75 .20
*a.* Perf. 13 14.00 16.00
**O38** A8 5p dk grn & org 2.25 .20
**O39** A8 6p blk & pale bl 1.75 .20
**O40** A8 8p blk & pck grn 1.75 1.25
**O41** A8 10p dp rose lil & blk 2.50 .20
**O42** A8 20p dk bl & bl 3.75 1.00
*a.* Perf. 13
**O43** A8 50p ultra & car 55.00 25.00
*Nos. O28-O43 (16)* 82.00 34.90

Nos. 98-104 Overprinted Liked Nos. O10-O16 in Red

**1951, Sept. 1 Wmk. 214 *Perf. 14***

**Center in Black**

**O44** A11 1m orange .20 .20
**O45** A11 2m ultra .20 .20
**O46** A11 3m dk grn .60 .60
**O47** A11 4m emerald .20 .20
**O48** A11 5m plum .20 .20
**O49** A11 10m light blue .20 .20
**O50** A11 15m dp org brn .20 .20

**Nos. 105-114 Overprinted Like Nos. O17-O24 in Black or Red**

***Perf. 13***

**O51** A12 2p lt bl & dk bl .20 .20
*a.* Inverted overprint 350.00
**O52** A12 3p vio bl & brn .60 .20
**O53** A12 3½p brn & bl grn .80 .40
**O54** A12 4p blk & dp bl .80 .20
**O55** A12 5p emer & org brn .85 .20
**O56** A12 6p blk & bl 1.00 .35
**O57** A12 8p brn & dp bl 1.40 .35
**O58** A12 10p grn & blk (R) 1.75 .35
**O59** A12 20p blk & bl grn 2.75 1.25
*a.* Inverted overprint 700.00
**O60** A13 50p blk & car 8.50 4.00
*Nos. O44-O60 (17)* 20.45 9.30

No. 112 Overprinted Like Nos.O17-O24 in Black

**1958**

**O61** A12 10p green & black .65 .20

Nos. 146-159 Overprinted

***Perf. 14½x14, 14x14½***

**1962, Oct. 1 Litho. Wmk. 345**

**Size: 23x19mm, 19x23mm**

**O62** A25 5m blue .20 .20
**O63** A26 10m blue & lilac .20 .20
**O64** A25 15m yel, vio, org & brn .20 .20
**O65** A25 2p lt pur .25 .20
**O66** A26 3p bl grn, red brn & brn .35 .20
**O67** A26 35m yel grn, brn & org brn .40 .20
**O68** A26 4p red, lt bl & lil .45 .25
**O69** A25 55m gray & yel ol .75 .45
**O70** A25 6p brn & lt bl .85 .45
**O71** A25 8p green 1.10 .55

**Size: 24½x30mm, 30x24½mm**

**O72** A26 10p lt bl, red brn & blk 1.50 .65
**O73** A25 20p gray ol & yel grn 3.00 1.40
*a.* Perf. 13½x12½ 2.75 1.10
**O74** A25 50p dk gray, ol & bl 7.50 3.50
*a.* Perf. 13½x14 6.50 3.25

**Engr.**

**O75** A13 £1 grn & brn org 19.00 12.50
*Nos. O62-O75 (14)* 35.75 20.95

The overprint measures 12x4½mm on Nos. O62-O71; 16x6mm on Nos. O72-O75.

**1975-79 Unwmk.**

**Same Perfs., Sizes and Printing Methods as Before**

*O62a* A25 5m .20 .20
*O63a* A26 10m ('76) .20 .20
*O64a* A25 15m .20 .20
*O65a* A25 2p .20 .20
*O66a* A26 3p .35 .25
*O67a* A26 35m .40 .25
*O68a* A26 4p .45 .25
*O69a* A25 55m .75 .45
*O70a* A25 6p ('76) .80 .45
*O71a* A25 8p 1.10 .55
*O72a* A26 10p 1.50 .70
*O73b* A25 20p 2.50 1.25
*O74b* A25 50p 2.50 1.25
*O75a* A13 £1 ('79) 19.00 12.50
*Nos. O62a-O75a (14)* 30.15 18.70

Nos. 404-419 Overprinted

*Perf. 13½x13*

**1991, July 1 Litho. Unwmk.**

| No. | Type | Description | Unused | Used |
|---|---|---|---|---|
| **O76** | A105 | 25p on #404 | .20 | .20 |
| **O77** | A105 | 50p on #405 | .20 | .20 |
| **O78** | A105 | 75p on #406 | .35 | .20 |
| **O79** | A105 | 100p on #407 | .45 | .30 |
| **O80** | A105 | 125p on #408 | .55 | .35 |
| | | **Size: 30x24mm** | | |
| | | ***Perf. 14x14½, 13½x14*** | | |
| **O81** | A105 | 150p on #409 | .65 | .40 |
| **O82** | A105 | 175p on #410 | .80 | .50 |
| **O83** | A105 | £2 on #411 | .90 | .60 |
| | | **Size: 26x37mm** | | |
| | | ***Perf. 14*** | | |
| **O84** | A105 | 250p on #412 | 1.10 | .70 |
| **O85** | A105 | £3 on #413 | 1.35 | .90 |
| | | **Size: 24x30mm** | | |
| | | ***Perf. 13½x14*** | | |
| **O86** | A105 | £4 on #414 | 1.75 | 1.10 |
| **O87** | A105 | £5 on #415 | 2.20 | 1.40 |
| | | **Size: 36x27mm** | | |
| | | ***Perf. 14*** | | |
| | | **Wmk. 334** | | |
| **O88** | A105 | £8 on #416 | 3.50 | 2.25 |
| **O89** | A105 | £10 on #417 | 4.40 | 5.00 |
| **O90** | A105 | £15 on #418 | 6.60 | 4.25 |
| **O91** | A105 | £20 on #419 | 8.80 | 5.75 |
| | | *Nos. O76-O91 (16)* | 33.80 | 24.10 |

For surcharges see Nos. O104-O111.

Nos. 420, 427-428 Overprinted

**1992 Litho. Unwmk.** ***Perf. 14½***

| No. | Type | Description | Unused | Used |
|---|---|---|---|---|
| **O92** | A25 | 25p on #420 | .25 | .20 |
| | | ***Perf. 14x13½, 13½x14*** | | |
| **O99** | A25 | £5 on #427 | 2.50 | 1.75 |
| **O100** | A25 | £10 on #428 | 5.25 | 3.50 |
| | | *Nos. O92-O100 (3)* | 8.00 | 5.45 |

Nos. O79, O81, O83, O85-O87 Surcharged in Blue Violet or Black

*Perf. 13½x13*

**1993? Litho. Unwmk.**

| No. | Type | Description | Unused | Used |
|---|---|---|---|---|
| **O104** | A105 | 1d on 100p #O79 | 1.00 | .65 |
| | | ***Perf. 13½x14*** | | |
| **O105** | A105 | 1.50d on 150p #O81 | 1.50 | 1.00 |
| **O107** | A105 | 2d on £2 #O83 | 2.00 | 1.25 |
| | | ***Perf. 14*** | | |
| **O109** | A105 | 3d on £3 #O85 | 3.00 | 2.00 |
| | | ***Perf. 14½x14*** | | |
| **O110** | A105 | 4d on £4 #O86 | 4.00 | 2.75 |
| | | ***Perf. 13½x14*** | | |
| **O111** | A105 | 5d on £5 #O87 (Blk) | 5.00 | 3.25 |
| | | ***Perf. 14*** | | |
| | | **Size: 36x27mm** | | |
| **O112** | A109 | 35d on £8 #O88 | 14.50 | 14.50 |
| | | *Nos. O104-O112 (7)* | 31.00 | 25.40 |

Coat of Arms — O1

**2003 Litho.** ***Perf. 13½x13¼***

| No. | Type | Description | Unused | Used |
|---|---|---|---|---|
| **O113** | O1 | 50d multi | .50 | .50 |
| **O114** | O1 | 100d multi | .95 | .95 |
| **O115** | O1 | 200d multi | 1.90 | 1.90 |
| **O116** | O1 | 300d multi | 3.00 | 3.00 |
| | | *Nos. O113-O116 (4)* | 6.35 | 6.35 |

## SURINAM

'sur-ə-ˌnam

(Dutch Guiana)

LOCATION — On the northeast coast of South America, bordering on the Atlantic Ocean
GOVT. — Republic
AREA — 63,234 sq. mi.
POP. — 431,156 (1999 est.)
CAPITAL — Paramaribo

The Dutch colony of Surinam became an integral part of the Kingdom of the Netherlands under the Constitution of 1954. It became an independent state November 25, 1975.

100 Cents = 1 Gulden (Florin)
100 Cents = 1 Dollar (2004)

**Catalogue values for unused stamps in this country are for Never Hinged items, beginning with Scott 168 in the regular postage section, Scott B34 in the semi-postal section, Scott C23 in the airpost section, Scott CB1 in the airpost semi-postal section, and Scott J33 in the postage due section.**

**Watermark**

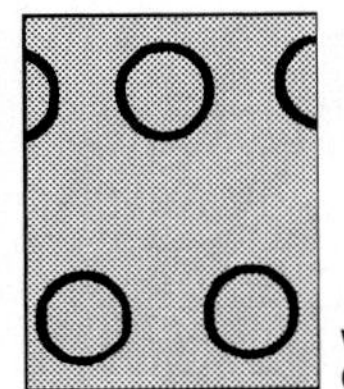

Wmk. 202 — Circles

Early issues of Surinam were sent to the colony without gum. Many of these were subsequently gummed locally.

King William III — A1

Numeral of Value — A2

***Perf. 11½, 11½x12, 12½x12, 13½, 14***

**1873-89 Typo. Unwmk.**

**Without Gum**

| No. | Type | Description | Unused | Used |
|---|---|---|---|---|
| **1** | A1 | 1c lil gray ('85) | 2.10 | 2.40 |
| **2** | A1 | 2c yellow ('85) | 1.40 | 1.40 |
| **3** | A1 | 2½c rose | 1.40 | 1.40 |
| **4** | A1 | 3c green | 17.50 | 15.00 |
| **5** | A1 | 5c dull violet | 15.00 | 4.75 |
| **6** | A1 | 10c bister | 3.25 | 2.25 |
| **7** | A1 | 12½c sl bl ('85) | 17.00 | 6.75 |
| **8** | A1 | 15c gray ('89) | 20.00 | 6.75 |
| **9** | A1 | 20c green ('89) | 30.00 | 27.50 |
| **10** | A1 | 25c grnsh blue | 70.00 | 8.00 |
| **11** | A1 | 25c ultra | 240.00 | 20.00 |
| **12** | A1 | 30c red brn ('88) | 30.00 | 32.50 |
| **13** | A1 | 40c dk brn ('89) | 27.50 | 26.00 |
| **14** | A1 | 50c brown org | 26.00 | 17.00 |
| **15** | A1 | 1g red brn & gray ('89) | 42.50 | 42.50 |
| **16** | A1 | 2.50g grn & org ('79) | 65.00 | 57.50 |
| | | *Nos. 1-16 (16)* | 608.65 | 271.70 |
| | | ***Perf. 14, Small Holes*** | | |
| *3b* | A1 | 2½c rose | 10.00 | 11.50 |
| *4b* | A1 | 3c green | 18.00 | 24.00 |
| *5b* | A1 | 5c dull violet | 18.00 | 15.00 |
| *6b* | A1 | 10c bister | 17.00 | 20.00 |
| *11b* | A1 | 25c ultra | 225.00 | 60.00 |
| *14b* | A1 | 50c brown org | 47.50 | 40.00 |
| | | *Nos. 3b-14b (6)* | 335.50 | 170.50 |

The paper of Nos. 3-6, 11 and 14 sometimes has an accidental bluish tinge of varying strength. During its manufacture a chemical whitener (bluing agent) was added in varying quantities. No particular printing was made on bluish paper.

"Small hole" varieties have the spaces between the holes wider than the diameter of the holes.

Nos. 1-16 and 3b-14b exist with gum.

For surcharges see Nos. 23, 31-35, 39-42.

**1890** ***Perf. 11½x11, 12½***

**Without Gum**

| No. | Type | Description | Unused | Used |
|---|---|---|---|---|
| **17** | A2 | 1c gray | 1.60 | 1.10 |
| **18** | A2 | 2c yellow brn | 2.50 | 2.00 |
| **19** | A2 | 2½c carmine | 2.00 | 1.60 |
| **20** | A2 | 3c green | 4.75 | 3.25 |
| **21** | A2 | 5c ultra | 21.00 | 1.10 |
| | | *Nos. 17-21 (5)* | 31.85 | 9.05 |

Nos. 17-21 exist with gum.

For surcharges see Nos. 63-64.

A3

**1892, Aug. 11** ***Perf. 10½***

**Without Gum**

| No. | Type | Description | Unused | Used |
|---|---|---|---|---|
| **22** | A3 | 2½c black & org | 1.50 | 1.00 |
| *a.* | | First and fifth vertical words have fancy "F" | 22.50 | 14.00 |
| *b.* | | Imperf. | 2.00 | |
| *c.* | | As "a," imperf. | 27.50 | |

No. 14 Surcharged in Black

2½ CENT.

**1892, Aug. 1** ***Perf. 14***

**Without Gum**

| No. | Type | Description | Unused | Used |
|---|---|---|---|---|
| **23** | A1 | 2½c on 50c | 210.00 | 10.00 |
| *a.* | | Perf. 12½x12 | 300.00 | 9.00 |
| *b.* | | Perf. 11½x12 | 350.00 | 12.50 |
| *c.* | | Double surcharge | 300.00 | 225.00 |
| *d.* | | Perf. 14, small holes | 225.00 | 12.50 |

Nos. 23-23c were issued without gum.

Queen Wilhelmina — A5

**1892-93 Typo.** ***Perf. 12½***

**Without Gum**

| No. | Type | Description | Unused | Used |
|---|---|---|---|---|
| **25** | A5 | 10c bister | 35.00 | 2.75 |
| **26** | A5 | 12½c rose lilac | 40.00 | 4.75 |
| **27** | A5 | 15c gray | 3.25 | 2.25 |
| **28** | A5 | 20c green | 3.75 | 2.75 |
| **29** | A5 | 25c blue | 8.25 | 4.75 |
| **30** | A5 | 30c red brown | 4.75 | 4.00 |
| | | *Nos. 25-30 (6)* | 95.00 | 21.25 |

Nos. 25-30 exist with gum.

For surcharges see Nos. 65-66.

Nos. 7-12 Surcharged

**1898** ***Perf. 11½x12, 12½x12, 13½***

**Without Gum**

| No. | Type | Description | Unused | Used |
|---|---|---|---|---|
| **31** | A1 | 10c on 12½c sl bl | 22.50 | 3.25 |
| **32** | A1 | 10c on 15c gray | 52.50 | 45.00 |
| **33** | A1 | 10c on 20c green | 4.25 | 4.25 |
| **34** | A1 | 10c on 25c grnsh bl | 9.00 | 5.25 |
| *c.* | | Perf. 11½x12 | 10.00 | 10.00 |
| **34A** | A1 | 10c on 25c ultra | 475.00 | 425.00 |
| *b.* | | Perf. 11½x12 | 550.00 | 475.00 |
| **35** | A1 | 10c on 30c red brn | 4.25 | 4.25 |
| *a.* | | Double surcharge | 275.00 | |

Dangerous counterfeits exist.

Netherlands Nos. 80, 83-84 Surcharged

50 C^T^

SURINAME

No. 36

Nos. 37-38

**1900, Jan. 8** ***Perf. 12½***

**Without Gum**

| No. | Type | Description | Unused | Used |
|---|---|---|---|---|
| **36** | A11 | 50c on 50c | 22.50 | 8.50 |
| | | **Engr.** | | |
| | | ***Perf. 11½x11*** | | |
| **37** | A12 | 100c on 1g dk grn | 22.50 | 13.50 |
| **38** | A12 | 2.50g on 2½g brn lil | 20.00 | 12.50 |
| | | *Nos. 36-38 (3)* | 65.00 | 34.50 |

For surcharge see No. 67.

Nos. 13-16 Surcharged

***Perf. 11½, 11½x12, 12½x12, 14***

**1900 Typo.**

**Without Gum**

| No. | Type | Description | Unused | Used |
|---|---|---|---|---|
| **39** | A1 | 25c on 40c | 5.00 | 3.50 |
| **40** | A1 | 25c on 50c | 5.00 | 3.50 |
| *a.* | | Perf. 14, small holes | 110.00 | 125.00 |
| *b.* | | Perf. 11½x12 | 3.75 | 3.75 |
| **41** | A1 | 50c on 1g | 40.00 | 35.00 |
| **42** | A1 | 50c on 2.50g | 140.00 | 160.00 |
| | | *Nos. 39-42 (4)* | 190.00 | 202.00 |

Counterfeits of No. 42 exist.

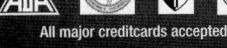

A9

Queen Wilhelmina
A10 A11

**1902-08 Typo. *Perf. 12½***
**Without Gum**

44 A9 ½c violet 1.00 .90
45 A9 1c olive grn 2.10 1.25
46 A9 2c yellow brn 11.50 4.50
47 A9 2½c blue grn 5.00 .45
48 A9 3c orange 8.25 5.25
49 A9 5c red 8.25 .45
50 A9 7½c gray ('08) 18.00 8.25
51 A10 10c slate 12.00 .95
52 A10 12½c deep blue 4.50 .45
53 A10 15c dp brown 30.00 10.50
54 A10 20c olive grn 27.50 5.25
55 A10 22½c brn & ol grn 24.00 13.00
56 A10 25c violet 20.00 1.25
57 A10 30c orange brn 47.50 15.00
58 A10 50c lake brown 37.50 9.25

**Engr.**
***Perf. 11***

59 A11 1g violet 60.00 20.00
60 A11 2½g slate blue 60.00 65.00
*Nos. 44-60 (17)* 377.10 161.70

Nos. 44-60 exist with gum.

A12

**1909 Typeset *Serrate Roulette 13½***
**Without Gum**

61 A12 5c red 13.50 11.50
a. Tête bêche pair 190.00 175.00

***Perf. 11½x10½***

62 A12 5c red 14.50 12.00
a. Tête bêche pair 140.00 140.00

Nos. 17-18, 29-30, 38 Surcharged in Red

Nos. 63-64

Nos. 65-66

No. 67

**1911, July 15 Typo. *Perf. 12½***
**Without Gum**

63 A2 ½c on 1c 1.75 1.10
64 A2 ½c on 2c 12.25 9.00
65 A5 15c on 25c 75.00 57.50
66 A5 20c on 30c 14.00 9.50

**Engr.**
***Perf. 11½x11***

67 A12 30c on 2.50g on 2½g 125.00 110.00
*Nos. 63-67 (5)* 228.00 187.10

A13

**1912, July Typeset *Perf. 11½***
**Without Gum**

70 A13 ½c lilac .95 .95
a. Horiz. pair, imperf. btwn. 200.00
71 A13 2½c dk green .95 .95
72 A13 5c pale red 8.75 8.75
a. Vert. pair, imperf. btwn. 240.00
73 A13 12½c deep blue 11.00 11.00
*Nos. 70-73 (4)* 21.65 21.65

Numeral of Value — A14

Queen Wilhelmina
A15 A16

**1913-31 Typo. *Perf. 12½***

74 A14 ½c violet .40 .25
75 A14 1c olive green .40 .20
76 A14 1½c blue, perf 11½ ('21) .40 .20
a. Perf. 12½ ('32) 1.10 .85
77 A14 2c yellow brn 1.60 1.10
78 A14 2½c green .95 .20
79 A14 3c yellow .80 .65
80 A14 3c green ('26) 3.25 2.50
81 A14 4c chlky bl ('26) 8.25 5.00
82 A14 5c rose 1.60 .20
83 A14 5c green ('22) 2.00 1.00
84 A14 5c lilac ('26) 1.60 .20
85 A14 6c bister ('26) 2.75 2.50
86 A14 6c red org ('31) 2.25 .50
87 A14 7½c drab 1.00 .40
a. Perf. 11x11½ 1.40 .65
88 A14 7½c orange ('27) 1.40 .40
89 A14 7½c yellow ('31) 9.25 9.25
90 A14 10c violet ('22) 5.00 5.00
91 A14 10c rose ('26) 4.00 .55
92 A15 10c car rose 1.40 .65
93 A15 12½c blue 1.90 .65
94 A15 12½c red ('22) 2.00 2.25
95 A15 15c olive grn .55 .70
96 A15 15c lt blue ('26) 7.75 4.75
97 A15 20c green 3.50 3.25
98 A15 20c blue ('22) 2.50 2.00
99 A15 20c ol grn ('26) 3.50 2.75
100 A15 22½c orange 2.50 2.50
101 A15 25c red violet 4.00 .40
102 A15 30c slate 5.00 1.10
103 A15 32½c vio & org ('22) 15.00 17.50
104 A15 35c sl & red ('26) 5.00 5.00

***Perf. 11, 11½, 11½x11, 12½***
**Engr.**

105 A16 50c green 4.00 .85
a. Perf. 12½ ('32) 14.00 1.60
106 A16 1g brown 5.50 .50
a. Perf. 12½ ('32) 15.00 1.00
107 A16 1½g dp vio ('26) 35.00 35.00
108 A16 2½g carmine ('23) 30.00 26.00
a. Perf. 11½x11 35.00 32.50
*Nos. 74-108 (35)* 176.00 135.95

Nos. 74, 75, 77-79, 82, 87, 105, 106 and 108 were issued both with and without gum.

Early printings of Nos. 74-104 had water soluble ink.

For surcharges see Nos. 116-120, 139.

Queen Wilhelmina — A17

**1923, Oct. 5 *Perf. 11, 11x11½, 11½***

109 A17 5c green 1.10 .70
110 A17 10c car rose 1.75 1.50
111 A17 20c indigo 3.50 3.00
112 A17 50c brown org 19.00 19.00
113 A17 1g brown vio 26.00 17.00
114 A17 2½g gray blk 75.00 *200.00*
115 A17 5g brown 100.00 *240.00*
*Nos. 109-115 (7)* 226.35 *481.20*

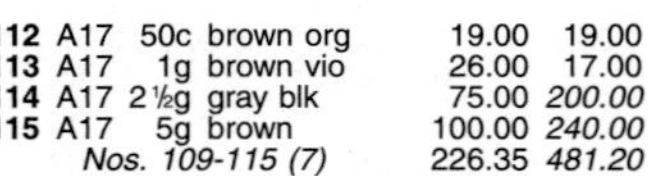

25th anniv. of the assumption of the government of the Netherlands by Queen Wilhelmina, at age 18.

Values for Nos. 114-115 used are for copies clearly dated before July 15, 1924.

Nos. 83, 93-94, 98 Surcharged in Black or Red:

j

k

m

**1925, Dec. 19 Typo. *Perf. 12½***

116 A14 3c on 5c green 1.10 1.10
117 A15 10c on 12½c red 2.25 2.25
118 A15 15c on 12½c blue (R) 1.60 1.60
119 A15 15c on 20c blue 1.60 1.60
*Nos. 116-119 (4)* 6.55 6.55

No. 100 Surcharged in Blue

**1926, Jan. 1**

120 A15 12½c on 22½c org 27.50 27.50

Postage Due Stamps Nos. J14 and J29 Surcharged in Blue or Black:

o

Frankeerzegel
12½
CENT
SURINAME
p

121 D2(o) 12½c on 40c (Bl) 3.25 3.25
122 D2(p) 12½c on 40c (Bk) 30.00 30.00
*Nos. 120-122 (3)* 60.75 60.75

No. 121 issued without gum.

Queen Wilhelmina — A21

**1927-30 Engr. *Perf. 11½***

123 A21 10c carmine 1.00 .40
124 A21 12½c red orange 1.75 1.90
125 A21 15c dark blue 2.00 .60
126 A21 20c indigo 2.00 .80
127 A21 21c dk brown ('30) 19.00 19.00
128 A21 22½c brown ('28) 8.00 9.75
129 A21 25c dk violet 3.00 .70
130 A21 30c dk green 3.00 1.10
131 A21 35c black brown 3.00 3.00
*Nos. 123-131 (9)* 42.75 37.25

Types of Netherlands Marine Insurance Stamps Inscribed "SURINAME" and Surcharged

**1927, Oct. 26**

132 MI1 3c on 15c dk grn .65 .65
133 MI1 10c on 60c car rose .65 .65
134 MI1 12½c on 75c gray brn .65 .65
135 MI2 15c on 1.50 dk blue 2.75 2.75
136 MI2 25c on 2.25g org brn 7.25 7.25
137 MI3 30c on 4½g black 9.00 7.25
138 MI3 50c on 7½g red 7.25 7.25
*Nos. 132-138 (7)* 28.20 26.45

Nos. 135-137 have "FRANKEERZEGEL" in small capitals in one line. Nos. 135 and 136 have a heavy bar across the top of the stamp.

No. 88 Surcharged

**1930, Mar. 1 Typo. *Perf. 12½***

139 A14 6c on 7½c orange 1.90 1.00

Prince William I (Portrait by Van Key) — A22

**1933, Apr. 24 Photo.**

141 A22 6c deep orange 6.75 1.90

400th birth anniv. of Prince William I, Count of Nassau and Prince of Orange, frequently referred to as William the Silent.

Van Walbeeck's Ship
A23

Queen Wilhelmina
A24

**1936-41 Litho. *Perf. 13½x12½***

142 A23 ½c yellow brn .30 .30
143 A23 1c lt yellow grn .40 .20
144 A23 1½c brt blue .55 .40
145 A23 2c black brown .60 .25
146 A23 2½c green .25 .20
a. Perf. 13 ('41) 9.00 3.25
147 A23 3c dark ultra .60 .40
148 A23 4c orange .60 .75
149 A23 5c gray .60 .20
150 A23 6c red 2.50 2.00
151 A23 7½c red violet .25 .20
a. 7½c plum, perf. 13 ('41) 3.00 .25

**Engr.**
***Perf. 14, 12½***
**Size: 20x30mm**

152 A24 10c vermilion .85 .20
a. Perf. 12½ ('39) 60.00 11.50
153 A24 12½c dull green 3.50 1.25
154 A24 15c dark blue 1.25 .60
155 A24 20c yellow org 2.10 .60
156 A24 21c dk gray 3.25 3.00
a. Perf. 12½ ('39) 3.75 3.75
157 A24 25c brown lake 2.40 1.00
158 A24 30c brown vio 3.75 1.00
159 A24 35c olive brown 4.00 4.00

***Perf. 12½x14***
**Size: 22x33mm**

160 A24 50c dull yel grn 4.00 2.00
161 A24 1g dull blue 8.25 3.00
162 A24 1.50g black brown 22.50 18.00
163 A24 2.50g rose lake 13.50 9.50
*Nos. 142-163 (22)* 76.00 49.05

For surcharges see Nos. 181-183, 209-210, B37-B40.

Queen Wilhelmina — A25

***Perf. 12½x12***

**1938, Aug. 30 Photo. Wmk. 202**

**164** A25 2c dull purple .50 .30
**165** A25 7½c red orange 1.50 1.25
**166** A25 15c royal blue 3.00 3.00
*Nos. 164-166 (3)* 5.00 4.55

Reign of Queen Wilhelmina, 40th anniv.

**Catalogue values for unused stamps in this section, from this point to the end of the section, are for Never Hinged items.**

Van Walbeeck's Ship A26

Queen Wilhelmina A27

**1941 Unwmk. Typo. *Perf. 12***

**168** A26 1c lt yellow grn .80 .20
**169** A26 2c black brown 1.90 1.90

Type A26 is similar to type A23 except for the white side frame lines which extend to the base.
For surcharges see No. 180.

**1941-46 Photo. *Perf. 13½x12½***
**Size: 18x22½mm**

**174** A27 12½c royal blue ('46) .25 .20

***Perf. 12½***

**175** A27 15c ultra 22.50 8.25

Royal Family — A28

**1943, Nov. 2 Engr. *Perf. 13½x13***

**176** A28 2½c deep orange .25 .35
**177** A28 7½c red .25 .20
**178** A28 15c black 2.50 2.10
**179** A28 40c deep blue 3.00 2.50
*Nos. 176-179 (4)* 6.00 5.15

Birth of Princess Margriet Francisca of the Netherlands.

Nos. 168, 151, 152 Surcharged with New Values and Bars in Black

**1945 Unwmk. *Perf. 13, 14, 12***

**180** A26 ½c on 1c .20 .20
**181** A23 2½c on 7½c 2.00 1.75
**182** A24 5c on 10c .70 .40
**183** A24 7½c on 10c .80 .40
*a.* Double surcharge 225.00 190.00
*Nos. 180-183 (4)* 3.70 2.75

Bauxite Mine, Moengo A29

Queen Wilhelmina
A30 A31

Designs: 1½c, Bush Negroes on Cottica River near Moengo. 2c, Waterfall in interior. 2½c, Road scene, Coronie District. 3c, Surinam River near Berg en Dahl Plantation. 4c, Government Square, Paramaribo. 5c, Mining gold. 6c, Street in Paramaribo. 7½c, Sugar cane train.

**1945, Nov. 5 Engr. *Perf. 12***

**184** A29 1c rose carmine .25 .25
**185** A29 1½c rose lake 1.25 1.25
**186** A29 2c violet .55 .40
**187** A29 2½c olive brn .55 .40
**188** A29 3c dull green 1.25 .70
**189** A29 4c brown 1.25 .75
**190** A29 5c blue 1.25 .25
**191** A29 6c olive 2.25 1.60
**192** A29 7½c deep orange .80 .35
**193** A30 10c blue 1.60 .20
**194** A30 15c brown 2.00 .25
**195** A30 20c dull green 3.25 .20
**196** A30 22½c gray 3.75 .90
**197** A30 25c carmine 10.00 4.50
**198** A30 30c olive green 10.00 .55
**199** A30 35c brt blue grn 17.00 7.25
**200** A30 40c rose lake 9.75 .25
**201** A30 50c red orange 9.75 .25
**202** A30 60c violet 9.75 .80
**203** A31 1g red brown 12.00 .35
**204** A31 1.50g lilac 10.00 .80
**205** A31 2.50g olive brn 20.00 .95
**206** A31 5g rose carmine 45.00 12.50
**207** A31 10g red orange 77.50 19.00
*Nos. 184-207 (24)* 250.75 54.70

For surcharges see #240, B41-B46, CB2-CB3.

Nos. 151 and 152 Surcharged with New Value and Bar in Blue or Black

**1947 *Perf. 13½x12½, 14***

**209** A23 1½(c) on 7½c (Bl) .20 *.20*
*a.* Double surcharge 200.00
**210** A24 2½c on 10c (Bk) .90 .30

Numeral A32

Queen Wilhelmina A33

***Perf. 12½x13½***

**1948, July 21 Unwmk. Photo.**

**211** A32 1c dark red .20 .20
**212** A32 1½c plum .20 .20
**213** A32 2c purple .20 .20
**214** A32 2½c olive grn 1.25 .20
**215** A32 3c dark green .20 .20
**216** A32 4c red brown .20 .20

***Perf. 13½x12½***

**217** A33 5c deep blue .35 .20
**218** A33 6c dark olive .85 .65
**219** A33 7½c scarlet .35 .20
**220** A33 10c blue .50 .20
**221** A33 12½c dark blue 1.10 1.00
**222** A33 15c henna brown 1.50 .40
**223** A33 17½c dk vio brn 1.60 1.25
**224** A33 20c dk blue grn 1.40 .20
**225** A33 22½c slate blue 1.40 .65
**226** A33 25c crimson 1.40 .30
**227** A33 27½c car lake 1.40 .20
**228** A33 30c olive green 1.60 .20
**229** A33 37½c olive brn 2.75 1.90
**230** A33 40c lilac rose 1.90 .30
**231** A33 50c red orange 1.90 .30
**232** A33 60c purple 2.10 .40
**233** A33 70c black 2.50 .65
*Nos. 211-233 (23)* 26.85 10.20

See Nos. 241-242.

Wilhelmina - Juliana
A34 A35

**1948, Aug. 30 Engr. *Perf. 12½x14***

**234** A34 7½c vermilion .85 .85
**235** A34 12½c deep blue .85 .85

Reign of Queen Wilhelmina, 50th anniv.

***Perf. 14x13***

**1948, Sept. 10 Wmk. 202 Photo.**

**236** A35 7½c deep orange 3.50 3.50
**237** A35 12½c ultra 3.50 3.50

Investiture of Queen Juliana, Sept. 6, 1948.
For surcharges see Nos. B53-B54.

Post Horns Entwined — A36

**1949, Oct. 1 Unwmk. *Perf. 11½x12***

**238** A36 7½c brown red 7.00 3.75
**239** A36 27½c dull blue 7.00 2.75

UPU, 75th anniversary.

No. 192 Surcharged with New Value, Square and Bar in Black

**1950, Aug. 9 *Perf. 12***

**240** A29 1c on 7½c dp org .60 .60

Numeral Type of 1948

**1951, Apr. 5 *Perf. 12½x13½***

**241** A32 5c deep blue 1.25 .20
**242** A32 7½c deep orange 3.00 1.60

A37

Queen Juliana — A38

**1951, Apr. 5 *Perf. 13½x13***

**243** A37 10c blue .45 .20
**244** A37 15c henna brn 1.00 .20
**245** A37 20c dk blue grn 2.40 .20
**246** A37 25c crimson 1.50 .40
**247** A37 27½c carmine lake 1.50 .20
**248** A37 30c olive green 1.50 .40
**249** A37 35c olive brown 1.90 1.60
**250** A37 40c lilac rose 2.10 .40
**251** A37 50c red orange 2.50 .45

**Engr.**

***Perf. 12½x12***

**252** A38 1g red brown 27.50 .50
*Nos. 243-252 (10)* 42.35 4.55

For surcharge see No. 271.

Shooting Fish A39

Fisherman A40

Designs: 5c, Bauxite mining. 6c, Log raft. 7½c, Plowing with Water Buffalo. 10c, Woman picking fruit. 12½c, Armored catfish. 15c, Macaw. 17½c, Armadillo. 20c, Poling canoe. 25c, Common iguana.

**1953-55 Photo. *Perf. 14x13, 13x14***

**253** A39 2c olive green .20 .20
**254** A40 2½c blue green .30 .20
**255** A40 5c gray .50 .20
**256** A40 6c bright blue 2.50 1.75
**257** A40 7½c purple .20 .20
**258** A40 10c bright red .20 .20
**259** A40 12½c dk gray blue 3.25 2.10
**260** A40 15c crimson 1.10 .20
**261** A40 17½c red brown 5.00 3.00
**262** A40 20c Prus green .90 .20
**263** A40 25c olive green 4.50 1.25
*a.* Min. sheet of 4, #259-261, 263 90.00 90.00
*Nos. 253-263 (11)* 18.65 9.50

Issued: 2c, 7½c, 10c, 20c, 5/9/53; #263a, 2/14/55;.others, 12/1/54.

Queen Juliana — A41

Harvesting Bananas — A46

**1954, Dec. 15 *Perf. 13½***

**264** A41 7½c dark red brown .90 .90

Charter of the Kingdom, adopted Dec. 15, 1954.

**1955, May 12 *Perf. 14x13***

Designs: 7½c, Pounding rice. 10c, Preparing cassava. 15c, Fishing.

**265** A46 2c dark green 2.10 2.10
**266** A46 7½c dull yellow 3.25 3.00
**267** A46 10c orange brown 3.25 3.00
**268** A46 15c ultra 3.25 3.00
*Nos. 265-268 (4)* 11.85 11.10

4th anniv. of the establishment of the Caribbean Tourist Assoc.

Globe and Mercury's Rod A47

Flags and Map of Caribbean A48

**1955, Sept. 19 Unwmk. *Perf. 13x12***

**269** A47 5c bright ultra .50 .45

Paramaribo Trade Fair, Oct. 1955.

**1956, Dec. 6 Litho. *Perf. 13x14***

**270** A48 10c lt blue & red .40 .35

10th anniv. of Caribbean Commission.

No. 247 Surcharged

**1958, Nov. 11 Photo. *Perf. 13½x13***

**271** A37 8c on 27½c car lake .20 .20

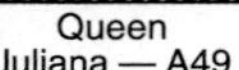

Queen Juliana — A49

Symbolic Flowers — A50

*Perf. 12½x12*

**1959, Oct. 15 Unwmk. Litho.**

| | | | | |
|---|---|---|---|---|
| **272** | A49 | 1g magenta | 2.00 | .20 |
| **273** | A49 | 1.50g olive bister | 3.25 | .80 |
| **274** | A49 | 2.50g dk carmine | 4.75 | .50 |
| **275** | A49 | 5g dull blue | 9.00 | .50 |
| | | *Nos. 272-275 (4)* | 19.00 | 2.00 |

**1959, Dec. 15 Photo. *Perf. 12½x13***

**276** A50 20c multicolored 3.75 2.75

5th anniv. of the constitution. Flowers in design symbolize Netherlands, Surinam and Netherlands Antilles.

Charles Lindbergh's Plane — A51

10c, De Snip plane. 15c, Cessna 170B. 20c, Super Constellation. 40c, Boeing 707 Jet.

**1960, Mar. 12 *Perf. 12½***

| | | | | |
|---|---|---|---|---|
| **277** | A51 | 8c chalky blue | 1.25 | 1.40 |
| **278** | A51 | 10c bright green | 1.75 | 2.00 |
| **279** | A51 | 15c rose red | 1.75 | 2.00 |
| **280** | A51 | 20c pale violet | 2.00 | 2.40 |
| **281** | A51 | 40c light brown | 3.00 | 3.25 |
| | | *Nos. 277-281 (5)* | 9.75 | 11.05 |

Inauguration of Zanderij Airport, Mar. 12. Nos. 277-281 show 25 years of Surinam's civil aviation.

Flag of Surinam and Map — A52

Arms of Surinam — A53

**1960, July 1 Litho. *Perf. 12½x13***

**282** A52 10c multicolored .70 .70

***Perf. 13x12½***

**283** A53 15c multicolored .70 .70

Day of Freedom, July 1.

Bananas — A54

Finance Building — A55

**1961, Mar. 1 Litho. *Perf. 13½***

| | | | | |
|---|---|---|---|---|
| **284** | A54 | 1c shown | .25 | .25 |
| **285** | A54 | 2c Citrus fruit | .25 | .25 |
| **286** | A54 | 3c Cacao | .25 | .25 |
| **287** | A54 | 4c Sugar cane | .25 | .25 |
| **288** | A54 | 5c Coffee | .25 | .25 |
| **289** | A54 | 6c Coconuts | .25 | .25 |
| **290** | A54 | 8c Rice | .25 | .25 |
| | | *Nos. 284-290 (7)* | 1.75 | 1.75 |

**1961 *Perf. 13½x14, 14x13½***

Buildings: 15c, Court of Justice. 20c, Concordia Lodge (Masons). 25c, Neve Shalom Synagogue, Paramaribo, horiz. 30c, Old Dutch lock in New Amsterdam. 35c, Government office, horiz. 40c, Governor's palace, horiz. 50c, Legislative Council, horiz. 60c, Old Dutch Reformed Church, horiz. 70c, Zeelandia Fortress, horiz.

| | | | | |
|---|---|---|---|---|
| **291** | A55 | 10c multi | .20 | .20 |
| **292** | A55 | 15c multi | .20 | .20 |
| **293** | A55 | 20c multi | .30 | .30 |
| **294** | A55 | 25c multi | .65 | .65 |
| **295** | A55 | 30c multi | 1.75 | 1.75 |
| **296** | A55 | 35c multi | 1.75 | 1.75 |
| **297** | A55 | 40c multi | .90 | .90 |
| **298** | A55 | 50c multi | .90 | .90 |
| **299** | A55 | 60c multi | 1.00 | 1.00 |
| **300** | A55 | 70c multi | 1.10 | 1.10 |
| | | *Nos. 291-300 (10)* | 8.75 | 8.75 |

Issued: 10c, 20c, 25c, 50c, 70c, 4/1; others, 5/15.

Dag Hammarskjold (1905-1961) A56

**1962, Jan. 2 Litho. *Perf. 11½, 12½***

**301** A56 10c brt blue & blk .20 .20
**302** A56 20c lilac & blk .20 .20

Dag Hammarskjold, Secretary General of the United Nations, 1953-61.

Sheets of both perfs. exist either with or without extension of perforations through the margins.

A56a

A57

**1962, Feb. 1 Photo. *Perf. 14x13***

**303** A56a 20c olive green .35 .35

Silver wedding anniversary of Queen Juliana and Prince Bernhard.

**1962, May 2 Litho. *Perf. 13x14***

Malaria eradication emblem.

**304** A57 8c bright red .20 .20
**305** A57 10c blue .20 .20

WHO drive to eradicate malaria.

Stoelmans Guesthouse — A58

Design: 15c, Torarica Hotel.

**1962, July 4 *Perf. 14x13½***

**306** A58 10c multicolored .40 .40
**307** A58 15c multicolored .40 .40

Opening of the Torarica Hotel in Paramaribo and Stoelmans Guesthouse on Stoelman Island.

Deaconess Residence and Recreation Area — A59

Design: 20c, Deaconess Hospital.

**1962, Nov. 30**

**308** A59 10c multicolored .40 .40
**309** A59 20c multicolored .40 .40

Hands Holding Wheat Emblem A60

20c, Farmer harvesting & wheat emblem, vert.

***Perf. 14x13, 13x14***

**1963, Mar. 21 Photo.**

**310** A60 10c deep carmine .20 .20
**311** A60 20c dark blue .20 .20

FAO "Freedom from Hunger" campaign.

Broken Chain — A61

**1963, June 28 Litho. *Perf. 14x13***

**312** A61 10c red & blk .20 .20
**313** A61 20c green & blk .20 .20

Centenary of emancipation of the slaves.

Prince William of Orange Landing at Scheveningen A61a

Faja Lobbi Wreath A62

**1963, Nov. 21 Photo. *Perf. 13½x14***
**Size: 26x26mm**

**314** A61a 10c dull bl, blk & brn .20 .20

Founding of the Kingdom of the Netherlands, 150th anniv.

**1964, Dec. 15 Litho. *Perf. 12½x13***

**315** A62 25c multicolored .40 .40

Charter of the Kingdom of the Netherlands, 10th anniv.

Abraham Lincoln (1809-1865) — A63

**1965, Apr. 14 Litho. *Perf. 12½x13***

**316** A63 25c olive bister & brn .20 .20

ICY Emblem A64

**1965, May 26 *Perf. 13x12½***

**317** A64 10c orange & blue .20 .20
**318** A64 15c red & violet bl .20 .20

International Cooperation Year.

Bauxite Mine, Moengo A65

Red-breasted Blackbird — A66

Designs: 15c, Alum Pottery Works, Paranam. 20c, Hydroelectric plant, Afobaka. 25c, Aluminum smeltery, Paranam.

**1965, Oct. 9 Photo. Unwmk.**

| | | | | |
|---|---|---|---|---|
| **319** | A65 | 10c ocher | .55 | .55 |
| **320** | A65 | 15c dark green | .55 | .55 |
| **321** | A65 | 20c dark blue | .55 | .55 |
| **322** | A65 | 25c carmine | .55 | .55 |
| | | *Nos. 319-322 (4)* | 2.20 | 2.20 |

Opening of the Brokopondo Power Station.

**1966, Feb. 16 Litho. *Perf. 13x14***

2c, Great kiskadee. 3c, Silver-beaked tanager. 4c, Ruddy ground dove. 5c, Blue-gray tanager. 6c, Glittering-throated emerald (hummingbird). 8c, Turquoise tanager. 10c, Pale-breasted robin.

| | | | | |
|---|---|---|---|---|
| **323** | A66 | 1c brt grn, blk & red | .35 | .35 |
| **324** | A66 | 2c lt ultra, yel & brn | .35 | .35 |
| **325** | A66 | 3c multi | .35 | .35 |
| **326** | A66 | 4c lt ol grn, red brn & blk | .35 | .35 |
| **327** | A66 | 5c org, ultra & blk | .35 | .35 |
| **328** | A66 | 6c multi | .35 | .35 |
| **329** | A66 | 8c gray, vio bl & blk | .35 | .35 |
| **330** | A66 | 10c multi | .35 | .35 |
| | | *Nos. 323-330 (8)* | 2.80 | 2.80 |

Central Hospital A67

Design: 15c, Hospital, side view.

**1966, Mar. 9 Litho. *Perf. 13x12½***

**331** A67 10c multi .20 .20
**332** A67 15c multi .20 .20

Opening of Central Hospital, Paramaribo.

Father Petrus Donders — A68

Designs: 10c, Church and parsonage, Batavia. 15c, Msgr. Joannes B. Swinkels. 25c, Cathedral, Paramaribo.

**1966, Mar. 26 Photo.** ***Perf. 12½x13***
**333** A68 4c org brn & blk .20 .20
**334** A68 10c rose brn & blk .20 .20
**335** A68 15c yel brn & blk .20 .20
**336** A68 25c lt vio & blk .20 .20
*Nos. 333-336 (4)* .80 .80

Centenary of the Redemptorist Mission in Surinam (Congregation of the Most Holy Redeemer).

100-Year-Old Tree — A69

**1966, May 9 Litho.** ***Perf. 13x12½***
**337** A69 25c grn, dp org & blk .20 .20
**338** A69 30c red org, grn & blk .20 .20

Centenary of the Surinam Parliament.

Television Transmitter, Eye and Globe — A70

**1966, Oct. 20 Litho.** ***Perf. 12½x13***
**339** A70 25c dk bl & ver .20 .20
**340** A70 30c brn & ver .20 .20

Inauguration of television service.

Bauxite Industry, 1916 — A71

Design: 25c, Bauxite industry, 1966.

**1966, Dec. 19 Litho.** ***Perf. 13x12½***
**341** A71 20c yel, org & blk .20 .20
**342** A71 25c org, bl & blk .20 .20

50th anniversary of bauxite industry.

Central Bank, Paramaribo A72

Design: 25c, Central Bank, different view.

**1967, Apr. 1 Litho.** ***Perf. 13x12½***
**343** A72 10c dp yel & blk .20 .20
**344** A72 25c lil & blk .20 .20

Central Bank of Surinam, 10th anniv.

Amelia Earhart, Lockheed Electra and Paramaribo A73

**1967, June 3 Photo.** ***Perf. 13x12½***
**345** A73 20c yel & dk car .20 .20
**346** A73 25c yel & grn .20 .20

30th anniv. of Amelia Earhart's visit to Surinam, June 3-4, 1937.

Siva Nataraja, God of Dance, and Ballerina's Foot — A74

Design: 25c, Drummer's mask "Bashi Lele," and scroll of violin.

**1967, June 21 Litho.** ***Perf. 12½x13***
**347** A74 10c yel grn & bl .20 .20
**348** A74 25c yel grn & brn .20 .20

20th anniv. of the Surinam Cultural Center Foundation.

New Amsterdam, 1660 (New York City) — A75

Designs after 17th Century Engravings: 10c, Fort Zeelandia, Paramaribo, 1670. 25c, Breda Castle, Netherlands, 1667.

**1967, July 31 Litho.** ***Perf. 13½x13***
**349** A75 10c yel, blk & bl .30 .30
**350** A75 20c red brn, yel & blk .30 .30
**351** A75 25c bl grn, yel & blk .30 .30
*Nos. 349-351 (3)* .90 .90

300th anniv. of the Treaty of Breda between Britain, France and the Netherlands.

WHO Emblem A76

**1968, Apr. 7 Litho.** ***Perf. 13x12½***
**352** A76 10c magenta & dk bl .20 .20
**353** A76 25c bl & dk pur .50 .50

WHO, 20th anniversary.

Chandelier and Christian Symbols A77

15c, like 10c, reversed. Brass chandelier from the Reformed Church, Paramaribo.

**1968, May 29 Litho.** ***Perf. 13x12½***
**354** A77 10c dark blue .20 .20
**355** A77 25c dp yel grn .50 .50

Reformed Church of Paramaribo, 300th anniv.

Missionary Store, 1768 — A78

Designs: 25c, Main Church and store, Paramaribo, 1868. 30c, C. Kersten & Co., 1968.

**1968, June 29 Litho.** ***Perf. 13x12½***
**356** A78 10c yel & blk .20 .20
**357** A78 25c lt grnsh bl & blk .20 .20
**358** A78 30c lilac rose & blk .20 .20
*Nos. 356-358 (3)* .60 .60

200th anniv. of C. Kersten & Co., which is partially owned by the Evangelical Brotherhood Missionary Society.

Joden Savanne Synagogue A79

Mahatma Gandhi A81

Spectacled Caiman A80

Designs: 20c, Map of Joden Savanne and Surinam River. 30c, Gravestone, 1733. The Hebrew inscriptions are quotations from the Bible: 20c, Joshua 24:2; 25c, Isaiah 56:7; 30c, Genesis 31:52.

**1968, Aug. 28** ***Perf. 12½x13***
**359** A79 20c multi .35 .35
**360** A79 25c multi .50 .50
**361** A79 30c multi .50 .50
*Nos. 359-361 (3)* 1.35 1.35

Founding of the first synagogue in the Western Hemisphere in 1685 in Joden Savanne, Surinam.

***Perf. 13x12½, 12½x13***
**1969, Aug. 20 Litho.**

20c, Squirrel monkey, vert. 25c, Armadillo.

**362** A80 10c grn & multi .90 .75
**363** A80 20c bl gray & multi .90 .75
**364** A80 25c vio & multi .90 .75
*Nos. 362-364 (3)* 2.70 2.25

**1969, Oct. 2 Litho.** ***Perf. 12½x13***
**365** A81 25c red & blk .35 .35

Mohandas K. Gandhi (1869-1948), leader in India's fight for independence.

ILO Emblem A82

**1969, Oct. 29 Litho.** ***Perf. 13x12½***
**366** A82 10c brt bl grn & blk .20 .20
**367** A82 25c red & blk .40 .40

ILO, 50th anniversary.

Queen Juliana and Rising Sun — A82a

**1969, Dec. 15 Photo.** ***Perf. 14x13***
**368** A82a 25c blue & multi .50 .50

15th anniv. of the Charter of the Kingdom of the Netherlands. Phosphorescent paper.

"1950-1970" A83

**1970, Apr. 3 Litho.** ***Perf. 13x12½***
**369** A83 10c brn, grn & org .20 .20
**370** A83 25c emer, dk bl & org .40 .40

20th anniv. of secondary education in Surinam.

Inauguration of UPU Headquarters, Bern — A84

Design: 25c, UPU Headquarters, sideview and UPU emblem.

**1970, May 20 Litho.** ***Perf. 13x12½***
**371** A84 10c sky bl & dk pur .20 .20
**372** A84 25c red & blk .50 .50

"UNO" A85

Plane over Paramaribo A86

**1970, June 26 Litho.** ***Perf. 12½x13***
**373** A85 10c ocher & yel .20 .20
**374** A85 25c dp bl & ultra .50 .50

25th anniversary of the United Nations.

**1970, July 15**

Designs: 20c, Plane over map of Totness, 25c, Plane over Nieuw-Nickerie.

**375** A86 10c bl, vio bl & gray .35 .35
**376** A86 20c yel, red & gray .35 .35
**377** A86 25c pink, dk red & gray .35 .35
*Nos. 375-377 (3)* 1.05 1.05

40th anniv. of domestic airmail service.

Plan of Soccer Field and Ball — A87

Morse Key — A89

Cocoi Heron A88

Plan of soccer field with ball in different positions.

**1970, Oct. 1**
**378** A87 4c yel, red brn & blk .20 .20
**379** A87 10c pale lem, red brn & blk .20 .20
**380** A87 15c lt yel grn, red brn & blk .20 .20
**381** A87 25c lt grn, red brn & blk .60 .60
*Nos. 378-381 (4)* 1.20 1.20

50th anniv. of the Soccer Assoc. of Surinam.

**1971, Feb. 14 Litho.** ***Perf. 13x12½***

Birds in Flight: 20c, Flamingo. 25c, Scarlet macaw.

**382** A88 15c gray & multi 1.25 1.25
**383** A88 20c ultra & multi 1.25 1.25
**384** A88 25c pale grn & multi 1.25 1.25
*Nos. 382-384 (3)* 3.75 3.75

25th anniversary of regular air service between the Netherlands, Surinam and Netherlands Antilles.

**1971, May 17 Photo. *Perf. 12½x13***

Designs: 20c, Telephone. 25c, Lunar landing module, telescope.

**385** A89 15c light green & multi .45 .40
**386** A89 20c blue & multi .55 .55
**387** A89 25c lilac & multi .75 .60
*Nos. 385-387 (3)* 1.75 1.55

3rd World Telecommunications Day.

Prince Bernhard, Fokker F27, Boeing 747B — A89a

Map of Surinam, Population Chart — A90

**1971, June 29 Photo. *Perf. 13x14***
**388** A89a 25c multi .60 .50

60th birthday of Prince Bernhard.

**1971, July 31 Litho. *Perf. 12½x13***

Design: 30c, Map of Surinam and individual representing population.

**389** A90 15c gray bl, blk & ver .20 .20
**390** A90 30c ver, gray bl & blk .25 .25

50th anniv. of the first census; introduction of civil registration in Surinam.

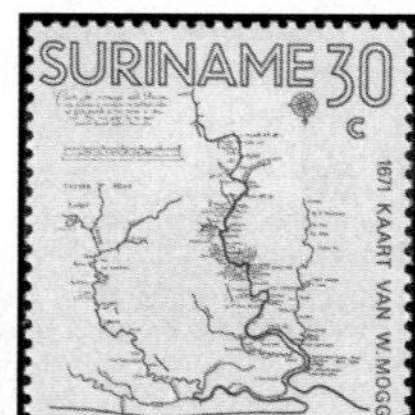


William Mogge's Map of Surinam A91

**1971, Oct. 27 *Perf. 11½x11***
**391** A91 30c dull yel & dk brn .80 .85

300th anniv. of the first map of Surinam.

Map of Albina A92

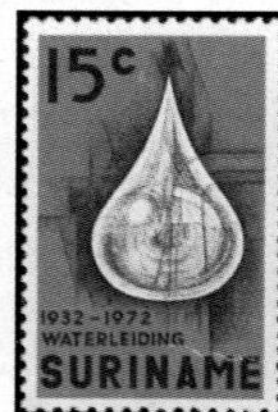


August Kappler — A93

Drop of Water — A94

20c, View of Albina from Maroni River.

**1971, Dec. 13 *Perf. 13x12½, 12½x13***
**392** A92 15c sapphire & blk .55 .55
**393** A92 20c brt grn & blk .60 .60
**394** A93 25c yel & blk .60 .60
*Nos. 392-394 (3)* 1.75 1.75

125th anniv. of the founding of Albina by August Kappler (1815-1887).

**1972, Feb. 2 *Perf. 12½x13***

Design: 30c, Faucet and water tower.

**395** A94 15c vio & blk .60 .60
**396** A94 30c bl & blk .75 .75

Surinam water works, 40th anniversary.

Air Mail Envelope A95

**1972, Aug. 2 Litho. *Perf. 13x12½***
**397** A95 15c red & blue .20 .20
**398** A95 30c blue & red .25 .25

Arrival of the 1st airmail in Surinam, carried by Capt. Dutertre from French Guiana, 50th anniv.

Giant Tree — A96

Hindu Woman in Rice Field — A97

Designs: 20c, Wood transport by air lift. 30c, Hands tending seedling.

**1972, Dec. 20 Photo. *Perf. 12½x13***
**399** A96 15c yel & dk brn .20 .20
**400** A96 20c bl & dp brn .20 .20
**401** A96 30c brt grn & dp brn .95 .95
*Nos. 399-401 (3)* 1.35 1.35

Surinam Forestry Commission, 25th anniv.

**1973, June 5 Litho. *Perf. 13½x14***

25c, J. F. A. Cateau van Rosevelt with map of Surinam, ship "Lalla Rookh." 30c, Symbolic bird, flower, sun, flag, factories.

**402** A97 15c purple & yel .45 .45
**403** A97 25c maroon & gray .45 .20
**404** A97 30c yel & light blue .50 .50
*Nos. 402-404 (3)* 1.40 1.15

1st immigrants from India, cent.

Queen Juliana, Surinam and House of Orange Colors A97a

**Engr. & Photo.**

**1973, Sept. 4 *Perf. 12½x12***
**405** A97a 30c sil, blk & org .80 .80

25th anniversary of reign of Queen Juliana.

INTERPOL Emblem — A98

Mailman — A99

Design: 30c, INTERPOL emblem, Surinam visa handstamp.

**1973, Nov. 7 Litho. *Perf. 14x14½***
**406** A98 15c vio bl & multi .20 .20
**407** A98 30c lt bl, lil & blk .80 .80

50th anniv. of Intl. Criminal Police Org.

**1973, Dec. 12 Litho. *Perf. 12½x13***

15c, Pigeons carrying Letters. 30c, Map of Surinam, plane, ship, train and truck.

**408** A99 15c lt yel grn & bl .20 .20
**409** A99 25c sal, blk & bl .35 .35
**410** A99 30c ver & multi .60 .60
*Nos. 408-410 (3)* 1.15 1.15

Centenary of stamps of Surinam.

Patient and Blood Transfusion A100

30c, Cross section of tissue and oscilloscope.

**1974, June 1 Litho. *Perf. 14½x14***
**411** A100 15c red brn & multi .20 .20
**412** A100 30c lemon & multi .25 .25

75th anniversary of the Medical College.

Crop Dusting A101

**1974, July 17 Litho. *Perf. 13½***
**413** A101 15c shown .20 .20
**414** A101 30c Fertilizer plant .25 .25

Foundation for Development of Mechanical Agriculture in Surinam, 25th anniv.

Old Title Page — A102

**1974, July 31 *Perf. 14x14½***
**415** A102 15c multicolored .20 .20
**416** A102 30c multicolored .25 .25

"Weekly Wednesday Surinam Newspaper," bicent. 1st editor was Beeldsnijder Matroos.

Paramaribo Main Post Office A103

Design: 30c, Post Office, different view.

**1974, Sept. 11 Litho. *Perf. 14½x14***
**417** A103 15c brown & blk .20 .20
**418** A103 30c blue & blk .70 .70

Centenary of Universal Postal Union.

Gold Panner A104

Design: 30c, Modern excavator.

**1975, Feb. 5 Litho. *Perf. 13x12½***
**419** A104 15c brown & olive bis .20 .20
**420** A104 30c vermilion & maroon .50 .50

Centenary of prospecting policy granting concessions for winning of raw materials.

Symbolic Design A105

**1975, June 25 Litho. *Perf. 13x12½***
**421** A105 15c green & multi .55 .55
**422** A105 25c blue & multi .60 .60
**423** A105 30c red & multi .60 .60
*Nos. 421-423 (3)* 1.75 1.75

Cent. of Intl. Meter Convention, Paris, 1875.

Hands Holding Saw — A106

Designs: 50c, Book with notes and letter "a." 75c, Hands holding ball.

**1975, Nov. 25 Litho. *Perf. 13½x14***
**424** A106 25c yellow, red & brn .60 .60
**425** A106 50c yellow, red & pur 1.40 1.40
**426** A106 75c dk bl, org & emer 2.00 2.00
*Nos. 424-426 (3)* 4.00 4.00

Independence. Sheets of 10 (5x2) with ornamental margins.

Oncidium Lanceanum A107

Central Bank, Paramaribo A109

Orchids: 2c, Epidendrum stenopetalum. 3c, Brassia lanceana. 4c, Epidendrum ibaguense. 5c, Epidendrum fragrans.

**1975-76 Litho. *Perf. 14½x13½***
**427** A107 1c multicolored .35 .35
**428** A107 2c multicolored .35 .35
**429** A107 3c multicolored .35 .35
**430** A107 4c multicolored .35 .35
**431** A107 5c multicolored .35 .35

***Perf. 14x13½***

**436** A109 1g rose lil & blk 1.75 .35
**437** A109 1½g brn, dp org & blk 3.00 .35
**438** A109 2½g red brn, org red & blk 4.50 .35
**439** A109 5g grn, yel grn & blk 8.50 .35
**440** A109 10g dk vio bl & blk 19.00 .95
*Nos. 427-431,436-440 (10)* 38.50 4.10

Issued: #436-439, Nov. 25, 1975; #427-431, Feb. 18, 1976; #440, May 5, 1976.

For surcharges see Nos. 772-774, 810.

Flag of Surinam — A110

Design: 35c, Coat of Arms.

**1976, Mar. 3 *Perf. 14x13½***
**445** A110 25c emerald & multi .65 .65
**446** A110 35c red orange & multi .85 .85

Sheets of 12 (6x2) with ornamental margins.

Pomacanthus Semicirculatus — A111

Fish: 2c, Adioryx diadema. 3c, Pogonoculius zebra. 4c, Balistes vetula. 5c, Myripristis jacobus.

**1976, June 2 Litho. *Perf. 12½x13***
**447** A111 1c multicolored .20 .20
**448** A111 2c multicolored .20 .20
**449** A111 3c multicolored .20 .20

**450** A111 4c multicolored .20 .20
**451** A111 5c multicolored .25 .20
*Nos. 427-431,C55-C57 (8)* 7.25 4.60

See #471-475, 504-508, C72-C74, C85-C87.

19th Century Switchboard and Telephone — A112

35c, Satellite, globe and 1976 telephone.

**1976, Aug. 5 Litho. *Perf. 13½x14***
**452** A112 20c yellow & multi .45 .45
**453** A112 35c ultra & multi .90 .90

Centenary of first telephone call by Alexander Graham Bell, Mar. 10, 1876.

The Story of Anansi Tori, by A. Baag — A113

Designs: 30c, "Surinam Now" (young people), by R. Chang. 35c, Lamentation, by Nola Hatterman, vert. 50c, Chess Players, by Q. Jan Telting.

***Perf. 13½x14, 14x13½***
**1976, Sept. 29 Photo.**
**454** A113 20c multicolored .40 .40
**455** A113 30c multicolored .70 .60
**456** A113 35c multicolored .90 .70
**457** A113 50c multicolored 1.25 1.25
*Nos. 454-457 (4)* 3.25 2.95

Paintings by Surinam artists.

Franklin's Divided Snake Poster, 1754 — A114

**1976, Nov. 10 Litho. *Perf. 13½x14***
**458** A114 20c green & blk .65 .65
**459** A114 60c orange & blk 2.10 2.10

American Bicentennial.

Ionopsis Utricularioides A115

Surinam Costume A116

Orchids: 30c, Rodiguezia secunda. 35c, Oncidium pusillum. 55c, Sobralia sessilis. 60c, Octomeria surinamensis.

**1977, Jan. 19 Litho. *Perf. 14½x13½***
**460** A115 20c vermilion & multi .45 .20
**461** A115 30c ultra & multi .65 .25
**462** A115 35c magenta & multi .65 .50
**463** A115 55c yellow & multi 1.25 .90
**464** A115 60c green & multi 1.25 1.00
*Nos. 460-464 (5)* 4.25 2.85

**1977, Mar. 2 Litho. *Perf. 14x13½***

Various Surinamese women's costumes.

**465** A116 10c brt blue & multi .35 .35
**466** A116 15c green & multi .35 .35
**467** A116 35c violet & multi .45 .45
**468** A116 60c orange & multi 1.00 1.00
**469** A116 75c ultra & multi 1.25 1.25
**470** A116 1g yellow & multi 1.60 1.60
*Nos. 465-470 (6)* 5.00 5.00

Fish Type of 1976

Tropical Fish: 1c, Liopropoma carmabi. 2c, Holacanthus ciliaris. 3c, Opistognathus aurifrons. 4c, Anisotremus virginicus. 5c, Gramma loreto.

**1977, June 8 Litho. *Perf. 13x13½***
**471** A111 1c multicolored .20 .20
**472** A111 2c multicolored .20 .20
**473** A111 3c multicolored .20 .20
**474** A111 4c multicolored .20 .20
**475** A111 5c multicolored .20 .20
*Nos. 471-475,C72-C74 (8)* 6.25 4.80

Edison's Phonograph, 1877 — A117

Design: 60c, Modern turntable.

**1977, Aug. 24 Litho. *Perf. 13½x14***
**476** A117 20c multicolored .25 .25
**477** A117 60c multicolored .60 .60

Invention of the phonograph, cent.

Packet Curacao, 1827 A118

Designs: 15c, Hellevoetsluis Harbor and postmark, 1827. 30c, Sea chart and technical details of packet Curacao. 35c, Logbook and compass rose. 60c, Map of Paramaribo harbor and 1852 postmark. 95c, Modern liner Stuyvesant.

**1977, Sept. 28 Litho. *Perf. 14x13½***
**478** A118 5c grnsh bl & dk bl .25 .25
**479** A118 15c orange & mar .25 .25
**480** A118 30c lt brn & blk .25 .25
**481** A118 35c olive & blk .25 .25
**482** A118 60c lilac & blk .30 .30
**483** A118 95c yel grn & dk grn .70 .70
*Nos. 478-483 (6)* 2.00 2.00

Regular steamer connection between the Netherlands and Surinam, 150th anniversary.

Passiflora Quad-rangularis A119

Javanese Costume A120

Flowers: 30c, Centropogon surinamensis. 55c, Gloxinia perennis. 60c, Hydrocleis nymphoides. 75c, Clusia grandiflora.

**1978, Feb. 8 Litho. *Perf. 13x14***
**484** A119 20c multicolored .60 .60
**485** A119 30c multicolored .60 .60
**486** A119 55c multicolored .95 .75
**487** A119 60c multicolored 1.10 .95
**488** A119 75c multicolored 1.25 1.10
*Nos. 484-488 (5)* 4.50 4.00

**1978, Mar. 1 Litho. *Perf. 13x14***

People of Surinam, Costumes: 20c, Forest black. 35c, Chinese. 60c, Creole. 75c, Aborigine Indian. 1g, Hindustani.

**489** A120 10c multicolored .35 .35
**490** A120 20c multicolored .35 .35
**491** A120 35c multicolored .35 .35
**492** A120 60c multicolored .55 .55
**493** A120 75c multicolored .65 .65
**494** A120 1g multicolored 1.00 1.00
*Nos. 489-494 (6)* 3.25 3.25

Air Post Stamps of 1972 Surcharged

**1977, Nov. 15 Litho. *Perf. 13½x14***
**495** AP6 1c on 25c #C44 .25 .25
**496** AP6 4c on 15c #C42 .25 .25
**497** AP6 4c on 30c #C45 .25 .25
**498** AP6 5c on 40c #C47 .35 .25
**499** AP6 10c on 75c #C54 .45 .25
*Nos. 495-499 (5)* 1.55 1.25

"Luchtpost" obliterated with 2 bars.

Old Municipal Church A121

Johannes King — A122

Designs: 55c, New Municipal Church. 60c, Johannes Raillard.

**1978, May 31 Litho. *Perf. 14x13***
**500** A121 10c blue, blk & gray .25 .25
**501** A122 20c gray & blk .25 .25
**502** A121 55c rose lil & blk .40 .40
**503** A122 60c orange & blk .45 .45
*Nos. 500-503 (4)* 1.35 1.35

Evangelical Brothers Community Church, Paramaribo, bicentenary.

Tropical Fish Type of 1976

Tropical Fish: 1c, Nannacara Anomala. 2c, Leporinus fasciatus. 3c, Pristella riddlei. 4c, Nannostomus beckfordi. 5c, Rivulus agilae.

**1978, June 21 *Perf. 12½x13½***
**504** A111 1c multicolored .20 .20
**505** A111 2c multicolored .20 .20
**506** A111 3c multicolored .20 .20
**507** A111 4c multicolored .20 .20
**508** A111 5c multicolored .20 .20
*Nos. 504-508,C85-C87 (8)* 5.85 4.20

Souvenir Sheet

Commewijne River Development A124

Development: 60c, Map of Surinam and dam. 95c, Planes and world map.

**1978, Oct. 18 Litho. *Perf. 14x13***
**509** Sheet of 3 2.75 2.75
*a.* A124 20c multi .20 .20
*b.* A124 60c multi .35 .35
*c.* A124 95c multi .50 .50

Coconuts A125

Wright Brothers' Flyer 1 A126

**1978-85 Litho. *Perf. 13½x13***
**510** A125 5c shown .20 .20
*a.* Bklt. pane, 4 #510, 3 #511, 5 #515 ('80) 2.00
**511** A125 10c Oranges .20 .20
**512** A125 15c Papayas .20 .20
*a.* Bklt. pane, 5 #512, 6 #514 + label ('79) 2.00
**513** A125 20c Bananas .20 .20
**514** A125 25c Soursop .20 .20
**514A** A125 30c Cocoa beans ('85) .85 .85
*b.* Bklt. pane, 6 #514A, 1 #513 = label ('85) 3.25 3.25
**515** A125 35c Watermelon .55 .55
*Nos. 510-515 (7)* 2.40 2.40

***Perf. 13x14, 14x13***
**1978, Dec. 13 Litho.**

Designs: 20c, Daedalus and Icarus, vert. 95c, DC 8. 125c, Concorde.

**516** A126 20c multicolored .40 .40
**517** A126 60c multicolored .95 .95
**518** A126 95c multicolored 1.40 1.40
**519** A126 125c multicolored 1.75 1.75
*Nos. 516-519 (4)* 4.50 4.50

75th anniversary of 1st powered flight.

Rodriguezia Candida A127

Javanese Dancer A128

Flowers: 20c, Stanhopea grandiflora. 35c, Scuticaria steelei. 60c, Bollea violacea.

**1979, Feb. 7 Litho. *Perf. 13x14***
**520** A127 10c multicolored .45 .45
**521** A127 20c multicolored .45 .45
**522** A127 35c multicolored .85 .60
**523** A127 60c multicolored 1.10 .90
*Nos. 520-523 (4)* 2.85 2.40

**1979, Feb. 28**

Dancing Costumes: 10c, Forest Negro. 15c, Chinese. 20c, Creole. 25c, Aborigine Indian. 35c, Hindustani.

**524** A128 5c multicolored .20 .20
**525** A128 10c multicolored .20 .20
**526** A128 15c multicolored .20 .20
**527** A128 20c multicolored .20 .20
**528** A128 25c multicolored .20 .20
**529** A128 35c multicolored .70 .70
*Nos. 524-529 (6)* 1.70 1.70

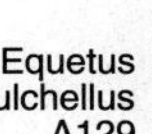

Equetus Pulchellus A129

Tropical Fish: 2c, Apogon binotatus. 3c, Anisotremus virginicus. 5c, Bodianus rufus. 35c, Microspathodon chrysurus.

**1979, May 30 Photo. *Perf. 14x13***
**530** A129 1c multicolored .20 .20
**531** A129 2c multicolored .20 .20
**532** A129 3c multicolored .20 .20
**533** A129 5c multicolored .20 .20
**534** A129 35c multicolored .45 .30
*Nos. 530-534,C89-C91 (8)* 5.00 3.70

See Nos. 557-561, C92-C94.

Javanese Wooden Head — A130

Folkart: 35c, Head ornament, Indian. 60c, Horse's head, Javanese.

**1979, Aug. 29 Litho. *Perf. 14x13***
**535** A130 20c multicolored .30 .30
**536** A130 35c multicolored .50 .50
**537** A130 60c multicolored .85 .85
*Nos. 535-537 (3)* 1.65 1.65

Sir Rowland Hill A131 — Javanese Girl's Costume A133

SOS Emblem, House A132

**1979, Oct. 3 Litho. *Perf. 13x14***
**538** A131 1g yellow & olive 1.50 1.00

Sir Rowland Hill (1795-1879), originator of penny postage.

**1979, Oct. 3 *Perf. 13x14***

Design: 60c, SOS emblem and buildings.

**539** A132 20c multicolored .35 .35
**540** A132 60c multicolored .80 .80

Intl. Year of the Child; SOS Children's Villages, 30th anniv.

**1980, Feb. 6 Photo. *Perf. 13x14***
**541** A133 10c Javanese girl .40 .40
**542** A133 15c Forest Black boy .40 .40
**543** A133 25c Chinese girl .40 .40
**544** A133 60c Creole girl .95 .65
**545** A133 90c Indian girl 1.10 .95
**546** A133 1g Hindustani boy 1.25 1.00
*Nos. 541-546 (6)* 4.50 3.80

Rotary Intl., 75th Anniversary A134

20c, Handshake, Rotary emblem, vert.

***Perf. 13x14, 14x13***

**1980, Feb. 23 Litho.**
**547** A134 20c ultra & yellow .30 .30
**548** A134 60c ultra & yellow .85 .65

Rowland Hill — A135 — Weight Lifting — A136

**1980, May 6 Litho. *Perf. 13x14***
**549** A135 50c Mailcoach .50 .50
**550** A135 1g shown 1.25 1.25
*a.* Souvenir sheet 1.10 1.10
**551** A135 2g People mailing letters 2.75 2.75
*Nos. 549-551 (3)* 4.50 4.50

London 1980 Intl. Stamp Exhibition, May 6-14. No. 550a contains No. 550 in changed colors. Blue and black margin shows designs of Nos. 549, 551, London 1980 emblem. (No. 550 in lilac rose and multicolored; stamps of No. 550a in light green and multicolored).

**1980, June 17**
**552** A136 20c shown .25 .25
**553** A136 30c Diving .45 .45
**554** A136 50c Gymnast .55 .55
**555** A136 75c Basketball 1.00 1.00
**556** A136 150c Running 2.00 2.00
*a.* Souvenir sheet of 3, #554-556 3.75 3.75
*Nos. 552-556 (5)* 4.25 4.25

22nd Summer Olympic Games, Moscow, July 19-Aug. 3.

Fish Type of 1979

Tropical Fish: 10c, Osteoglossum bicirrhosum. 15c, Colossoma species. 25c, Hemigrammus pulcher. 30c, Petitella georgiae. 45c, Copeina guttata.

**1980, Sept. 10 Photo. *Perf. 14x13***
**557** A129 10c multicolored .20 .20
**558** A129 15c multicolored .20 .20
**559** A129 25c multicolored .20 .20
**560** A129 30c multicolored .20 .20
**561** A129 45c multicolored .70 .70
*Nos. 557-561,C92-C94 (8)* 5.50 4.55

Open Hands (Reflection) A137 — Passiflora Laurifolia A138

Souvenir Sheet

**1980, Nov. 19 Litho. *Perf. 13x14***
**562** Sheet of 3 8.00 8.00
*a.* A137 50c shown .50 .50
*b.* A137 1g Shaking hands (cooperation) .90 .90
*c.* A137 2g Victory sign 1.75 1.75

5th anniv. of independence.

**1981, Jan. 14 Litho. *Perf. 13x14***

Designs: Flower paintings by Maria Sibylle Merian (1647-1717).

**563** A138 20c shown .30 .30
**564** A138 30c Aphelandra pectinata .40 .40
**565** A138 60c Caesalpinia pulcherrima .90 .90
**566** A138 75c Hibiscus mutabilis 1.00 1.00
**567** A138 1.25g Hippeastrum puniceum 1.90 1.90
*Nos. 563-567 (5)* 4.50 4.50

Renovation of the Economic Order — A139

**1981, Feb. 25 *Perf. 14x13***
**568** A139 30c shown .25 .25
**569** A139 60c Educational Order .50 .50
**570** A139 75c Social Order .55 .55
**571** A139 1g Political Order .80 .80
*a.* Souvenir sheet of 2, #569, 571 3.00 3.00
*Nos. 568-571 (4)* 2.10 2.10

Government renovation.

Miniature Sheet

Youths — A140

**1981, Apr. 29 Litho. *Perf. 14x13½***
**572** A140 Sheet of 2 2.75 2.75
*a.* 1g shown .95 .95
*b.* 1.50g Youths, diff. .95 .95

Youth and its future. Entire sheet in continuous design.

Souvenir Sheet

No. 424, Exhibition Hall — A141

**1981, May 22 Litho. *Perf. 13½x14***
**573** Sheet of 3 5.00 5.00
*a.* A141 50c shown .55 .60
*b.* A141 1g Penny Black 1.10 1.10
*c.* A141 2g Austria #5 2.10 2.25

WIPA '81 Intl. Philatelic Exhibition, Vienna, May 22-31.

Leptodactylus Pentadactylus A142

**1981, June 24 Photo. *Perf. 14x13***
**574** A142 40c Phyllomedusa hypochondrialis .75 .35
**575** A142 50c shown .95 .50
**576** A142 60c Hyla boans 1.10 .65
*Nos. 574-576,C95-C97 (6)* 9.00 4.80

Child Wearing Earphones A143

**1981, Sept. 16 Litho. *Perf. 14x13***
**580** A143 50c shown .60 .60
**581** A143 100c Child reading Braille 1.50 1.50
**582** A143 150c Woman in wheelchair 2.40 2.40
*Nos. 580-582 (3)* 4.50 4.50

Intl. Year of the Disabled.

Planter's House on Parakreek River — A144

Designs: Illustrations from Voyage to Surinam, by P.I. Benoit.

**1981, Oct. 21 Photo. *Perf. 14x13***
**583** A144 20c shown .20 .20
**584** A144 30c Sarameca St., Paramaribo .40 .40
**585** A144 75c Negro Hamlet, Paramaribo 1.00 1.00
**586** A144 1g Fish Market, Paramaribo 1.40 1.40
*a.* Miniature sheet of 1, perf 13½x13 1.60 1.60
**587** A144 1.25g Blaauwe Berg Cascade 2.00 2.00
*Nos. 583-587 (5)* 5.00 5.00

Research and Peaceful Uses of Space A145

**1982, Jan. 13 Litho.**
**588** A145 35c Satellites .55 .55
**589** A145 65c Columbia space shuttle 1.00 1.00
**590** A145 1g Apollo-Soyuz 1.50 1.50
*Nos. 588-590 (3)* 3.05 3.05

Caretta Caretta A146

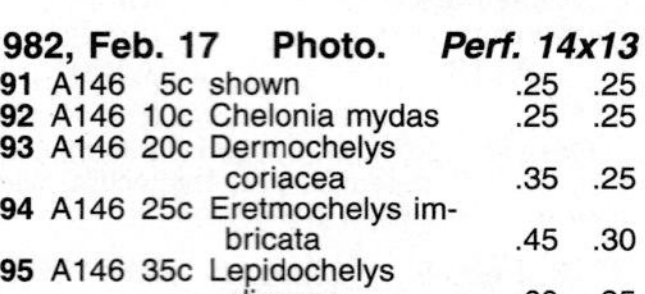

**1982, Feb. 17 Photo. *Perf. 14x13***
**591** A146 5c shown .25 .25
**592** A146 10c Chelonia mydas .25 .25
**593** A146 20c Dermochelys coriacea .35 .25
**594** A146 25c Eretmochelys imbricata .45 .30
**595** A146 35c Lepidochelys olivacea .60 .35
*Nos. 591-595,C98-C100 (8)* 6.15 4.25

25th Anniv. of Lions Intl. in Surinam A147

**1982, May 7 Litho.**
**596** A147 35c multicolored .65 .65
**597** A147 70c multicolored 1.25 1.25

A148 — A149

**1982, May 18 Litho. *Perf. 13x14***
**598** A148 35c Helping the sick .75 .75
**599** A148 65c Birthplace, map 1.50 1.50
*a.* Souvenir sheet 1.75 1.75

Beatification of Father Petrus Donders, May 23.

**1982, June 9 Litho. *Perf. 13x14***
**600** A149 50c Stamp designing .75 .75
**601** A149 100c Printing 1.50 1.50
**602** A149 150c Collecting 2.25 2.25
*a.* Souvenir sheet of 3, #600-602 5.00 5.00
*Nos. 600-602 (3)* 4.50 4.50

PHILEXFRANCE '82 Stamp Exhibition, Paris, June 11-21. Nos. 600-602 in continuous design.

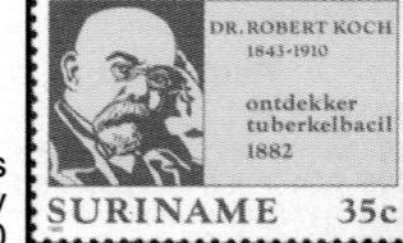


TB Bacillus Centenary A150

**1982, Sept. 15 Litho. *Perf. 14x13***
**603** A150 35c Text .40 .40
**604** A150 65c Microscope 1.10 1.10
**605** A150 150c Bacillus 3.00 3.00
*Nos. 603-605 (3)* 4.50 4.50

Marienburg Sugar Co. Centenary A151

**1982, Oct. 20**
**606** A151 35c Mill .50 .50
**607** A151 65c Gathering cane .90 .90
**608** A151 100c Rail transport 1.60 1.60
**609** A151 150c Gears 2.50 2.50
*Nos. 606-609 (4)* 5.50 5.50

A152 — Inga Edulis — A153

EBG Missionaries, 250th Anniv. in Caribbean: 35c, Municipal Church, horiz. 65c, St. Thomas Monastery, horiz. 150c, Johan Leonhardt Dober (1706-1766).

***Perf. 14x13, 13x14***

**1982, Dec. 13 Litho.**
**610** A152 35c multicolored .50 .50
**611** A152 65c multicolored .95 .95
**612** A152 150c multicolored 2.50 2.50
*Nos. 610-612 (3)* 3.95 3.95

**1983, Jan. 12**

Flower Paintings by Maria Sibylle Merian (1647-1717). Nos. 613-618 horiz.

**613** A153 1c Erythrina fusca .25 .25
**614** A153 2c Ipomoea acuminata .25 .25
**615** A153 3c Heliconia psittacorum .25 .25
**616** A153 5c Ipomoea .25 .25
**617** A153 10c Herba non denominata .25 .25
**618** A153 15c Anacardium occidentale .45 .45
**619** A153 20c shown .55 .55
**620** A153 25c Abelmoschus moschatus .80 .80
**621** A153 30c Argemone mexicana 1.00 1.00
**622** A153 35c Costus arabicus 1.10 1.10
**623** A153 45c Muellera frutescens 1.25 1.25
**624** A153 65c Punica granatum 2.10 2.10
*Nos. 613-624 (12)* 8.50 8.50

Scouting Year — A154

500th Birth Anniv. of Raphael — A155

**1983, Feb. 22 Litho. *Perf. 13x14***
**625** A154 40c Anniv. emblem 1.00 1.00
**626** A154 65c Baden-Powell 1.50 1.50
**627** A154 70c Tent, campfire 1.60 1.60
**628** A154 80c Ax in log 1.75 1.75
*Nos. 625-628 (4)* 5.85 5.85

**1983, Apr. 13 Photo.**

Crayon sketches.

**629** A155 5c multicolored .30 .30
**630** A155 10c multicolored .30 .30
**631** A155 40c multicolored .80 .80
**632** A155 65c multicolored 1.25 1.25
**633** A155 70c multicolored 1.25 1.25
**634** A155 80c multicolored 1.50 1.50
*Nos. 629-634 (6)* 5.40 5.40

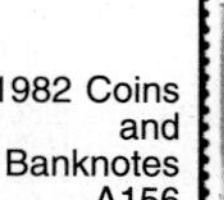

1982 Coins and Banknotes A156

**1983, June 1 Litho. *Perf. 14x13***
**635** A156 5c 1-cent coin .25 .25
**636** A156 10c 5-cent coin .25 .25
**637** A156 40c 10-cent coin .65 .65
**638** A156 65c 25-cent coin 1.10 1.10
**639** A156 70c 1g note 1.25 1.25
**640** A156 80c 2.50g note 1.50 1.50
*Nos. 635-640 (6)* 5.00 5.00

For surcharge & overprints see Nos. 751, J59-J60.

25th Anniv. of Dept. of Construction A157

Manned Ballooning, 200th Anniv. A159

Local Butterflies A158

**1983, June 15 Litho. *Perf. 13x14***
**641** A157 25c Map .40 .40
**642** A157 50c Map, bulldozers .85 .85

***Perf. 13x14, 14x13***
**1983, Sept. 14 Litho.**

Drawings by Maria Sibylle Merian (1647-1717). Nos. 643-648 vert.

**643** A158 1c Papile anchisiades esper .25 .25
**644** A158 2c Urania leilus .25 .25
**645** A158 3c Morpho deidamia .25 .25
**646** A158 5c Thysania aguippina .25 .25
**647** A158 10c Morpho sp. .30 .25
**648** A158 15c Metamorpha dido .45 .30
**649** A158 20c Morpho menelaus .60 .40
**650** A158 25c Manduca rustica .85 .55
**651** A158 30c Rothschildia sp. 1.00 .55
**652** A158 35c Catopsilia ebule 1.25 .80
**653** A158 45c Pailio androgeos 1.60 1.10
**654** A148 65c Eumorpha vitis 2.40 1.60
*Nos. 643-654 (12)* 9.45 6.55

**1983, Oct. 19 Litho. *Perf. 13x14***

Designs: 5c, 1783, sheep, cock and duck. 10c, first manned flight, d'Arlandes and Pilatre de Rozier. 40c, first hydrogen balloon, Jacques Charles. 65c, 1870, Paris flight, minister Gambetta. 70c, Double Eagle II, transatlantic flight. 80c, Intl. Balloon Festival, Albuquerque.

**655** A159 5c multicolored .20 .20
**656** A159 10c multicolored .20 .20
**657** A159 40c multicolored .95 .95
**658** A159 65c multicolored 1.40 1.40
**659** A159 70c multicolored 1.50 1.50
**660** A159 80c multicolored 2.00 2.00
*Nos. 655-660 (6)* 6.25 6.25

Martin Luther, 500th Birth Anniv. — A160

**1983, Dec. 7 Litho.**
**661** A160 25c Portrait .50 .50
**662** A160 50c Engraving 1.25 1.10

Local Flowers A161

Local Seashells A162

**1984, Jan. 11 Litho.**
**663** A161 5c Catasetum discolor .20 .20
**664** A161 10c Menadenium labiosum .20 .20
**665** A161 40c Comparettia falcata .95 .95
**666** A161 50c Rodriquezia decora 1.40 1.25
**667** A161 70c Oncidium papilio 1.60 1.40
**668** A161 75c Epidendrum porpax 1.90 1.50
*Nos. 663-668 (6)* 6.25 5.50

**1984, Feb. 22 Litho.**
**669** A162 40c Arca zebra .95 .65
**670** A162 65c Trachycardium egmontianum 1.60 1.10
**671** A162 70c Tellina radiata 1.60 1.10
**672** A162 80c Vermicularia knorrii 2.00 1.25
*Nos. 669-672 (4)* 6.15 4.10

Intl. Civil Aviation Org., 40th Anniv. A163

**1984, May 16 Litho. *Perf. 14x13***
**673** A163 35c Sea plane .65 .65
**674** A163 65c Surinam Airways jet 1.50 1.50

A164

A165

Greek Art and Artifacts: Ancient Games.

**1984, June 13 *Perf. 13x14***
**675** A164 2c Running .20 .20
**676** A164 3c Javelin, discus, long jump .20 .20
**677** A164 5c Massage .20 .20
**678** A164 10c Ointment massage .20 .20
**679** A164 15c Wrestling .20 .20
**680** A164 20c Boxing .20 .20
**681** A164 30c Horse racing .60 .60
**682** A164 35c Chariot racing .65 .65
**683** A164 45c Temple of Olympia .85 .85
**684** A164 50c Crypt entrance .95 .95
**685** A164 65c Olympia Stadium 1.50 1.50
**686** A164 75c Zeus (bust) 1.50 1.50
*a.* Min. sheet of 3, #675, 682, 686 2.75 2.75
*Nos. 675-686 (12)* 7.25 7.25

1984 Summer Olympics.
For overprint see No. 843.

**1984, Sept. 18 Litho. *Perf. 13x14***
**687** A165 50c Ball, net 1.25 1.10
**688** A165 90c Ball in net 2.00 1.90

Intl. Council of Military Sports basketball championship.

World Chess Championship, Moscow — A166

**1984, Oct. 10 Litho. *Perf. 14x13***
**689** A166 10c Red Square .35 .35
**690** A166 15c Knight, king, pawn .35 .35
**691** A166 30c Kasparov .65 .65
**692** A166 50c Board 1.10 1.10
**693** A166 75c Karpov 1.75 1.75
*a.* Souv. sheet of 3 (30c, 50c, 75c), perf 13½x13 4.75 4.75
**694** A166 90c Game 2.00 2.00
*Nos. 689-694 (6)* 6.20 6.20

For overprints see Nos. 742, 796.

World Food Day, Oct. 16 — A167

**1984, Oct. 10**
**695** A167 50c Children receiving milk 1.25 1.25
**696** A167 90c Food 2.00 2.00

A168

A169

Cacti.

**1985, Jan. 9 Litho. *Perf. 13x14***
**697** A168 5c Leaf .25 .25
**698** A168 10c Melon .25 .25
**699** A168 30c Pillar .95 .95
**700** A168 50c Fig 1.40 1.40
**701** A168 75c Nightqueen 2.25 2.25
**702** A168 90c Segment 2.40 2.40
*Nos. 697-702 (6)* 7.50 7.50

**1985, Feb. 22**

Independence, 5th Anniv.: 5c, Star, red stripe from national flag. 30c, Unified labor. 50c, Perpetual flowering plant. 75c, Growth of agriculture. 90c, Peace dove and plant.

**703** A169 5c multicolored .20 .20
**704** A169 30c multicolored .60 .60
**705** A169 50c multicolored 1.00 1.00
*a.* Min. sheet of 3, 2 #703, #705 3.00
**706** A169 75c multicolored 1.60 1.60
**707** A169 90c multicolored 2.10 2.10
*Nos. 703-707 (5)* 5.50 5.50

Chamber of Commerce and Industry, 75th Anniv. A170

UN Emblem, Natl. Coat of Arms — A171

**1985, Apr. 17 Litho. *Perf. 14x13***
**708** A170 50c Chamber emblem .75 .75
**709** A170 90c Chamber, factories 1.50 1.50

**1985, Apr. 29 Litho. *Perf. 13x14***
**710** A171 50c multicolored .75 .75
**711** A171 90c multicolored 1.40 1.40

UN, 40th anniv.

Trains — A172

**1985, June 5 Litho. *Perf. 13½***
**712** A172 5c No. 192 .20 .20
**713** A172 5c Monaco, No. J50 .20 .20
*a.* Pair, #712-713 .40 .40
**714** A172 10c Locomotive "Dam" .20 .20
**715** A172 10c Diesel locomotive .20 .20
*a.* Pair, #714-715 .60 .60
**716** A172 20c Steam locomotive "No. 3737" .50 .50
**717** A172 20c Netherlands locomotive "IC III" .50 .50
*a.* Pair, #716-717 1.00 1.00
**718** A172 30c Stephenson's locomotive "Rocket" .85 .85
**719** A172 30c French Railways high-speed TGV .85 .85
*a.* Pair, #716-717 1.60 1.60
**720** A172 50c Stephenson's locomotive "Adler" 1.25 1.25
**721** A172 50c French Railways commuter train 1.25 1.25
*a.* Pair, #720-721 2.75 2.75
**722** A172 75c Locomotive "General" 2.00 2.00
**723** A172 75c Japanese bullet train "Shinkansen" 2.00 2.00
*a.* Pair, #722-723 4.00 4.00
*Nos. 712-723 (12)* 10.00 10.00

For surcharges see Nos. 749-750, 808-809, 928-929.

Birds — A173

**1985-95 Litho. *Perf. 14x13***
**724** A173 10c Toucan .20 .20
**725** A173 1g American purple fowl 1.10 1.10
*a.* Miniature sheet of 1 3.75 3.75
**726** A173 1.50g Tiger bird 1.90 1.90
**727** A173 2.50g Red ibis 3.00 3.00

**728** A173 5g Guyana red cockerel 5.75 5.75
**729** A173 10g Harpy eagle *11.50 11.50*
**730** A173 15g Parrot *22.50 22.50*
**731** A173 25g Owl *35.00 35.00*
**732** A173 1300g Rose lepelaar *32.50 32.50*
**733** A173 1780g Toucan *9.25 9.25*
**734** A173 2225g Hummingbird *11.50 11.50*
**735** A173 2995g Hoatzin *16.00 16.00*
*Nos. 724-735 (12)* *150.20 150.20*

Nos. 724, 730 inscribed 1990.

Issued: 1g, 1.50g, 2.50g, 8/21; #725a, 5g, 1/2/86; 10g, 10/1/86; 10c, 15g, 1/30/91; 25g, 1/20/93; 1300g, 3/31/94; 1780g, 2225g, 2995g, 9/6/95.

See #1040, 1053-1055, 1108-1111, 1136-1138, 1160, 1194-1195, 1220-1221. For surcharges & overprint see #963-964, J63.

Mailboxes — A174

**1985, Oct. 2 Litho. *Perf. 13x14***
**736** A174 15c Germany, 1900 .35 .35
**737** A174 30c France, 1900 .55 .55
**738** A174 50c England, 1932 .95 .95
**739** A174 90c Netherlands, 1850 1.90 1.90
*Nos. 736-739 (4)* 3.75 3.75

Natl. Independence, 10th Anniv. — A175

**1985, Nov. 22**
**740** A175 50c Agriculture 1.25 1.25
**741** A175 90c Industry 2.00 2.00
*a.* Miniature sheet of 2, #740-741 3.25 3.25

No. 691 Ovptd. in Red

**1985, Nov. 22 Litho. *Perf. 14x13***
**742** A166 30c multi 2.25 2.25

Orchids, World Wildlife Fund — A177

**1986, Feb. 19 Litho. *Perf. 14x13***
**743** A177 5c Epidendrum ciliare 3.00 3.00
**744** A177 15c Cycnoches chlorochilon 7.50 7.50
**745** A177 30c Epidendrum anceps 15.00 15.00
**746** A177 50c Epidendrum vespa 24.00 24.00
*Nos. 743-746 (4)* 49.50 49.50

Halley's Comet A178

Designs: 50c, The Bayeux Tapestry, c. 1092, France. 110c, Halley's Comet.

**1986, Mar. 5 Litho. *Perf. 14x13***
**747** A178 50c multi .85 .85
**748** A178 110c multi 1.75 1.75

Nos. 720-721 Surcharged in Red

**1986, May 28 Litho. *Perf. 13½***
**749** A172 15c on 50c #720 1.50 1.50
**750** A172 15c on 50c #721 1.50 1.50
*a.* Pair, #749-750 3.50 3.50

No. 639 Surcharged

**1986, June 25 Litho. *Perf. 14x13***
**751** A156 30c on 70c multi 2.10 2.10

Finance Building, Paramaribo, 150th anniv.

Surinam Shipping Co., 50th Anniv. A179

**1986, Sept. 1 Litho. *Perf. 14x13***
**752** A179 50c Emblem .70 .70
**753** A179 110c Freighter Saramacca 2.00 2.00

Monkeys A180

**1987, Jan. 7 Litho.**
**755** A180 35c Alouatta .60 .60
**756** A180 60c Aotus 1.00 1.00
**757** A180 110c Saimiri 2.00 2.00
**758** A180 120c Cacajao 2.25 2.25
*Nos. 755-758 (4)* 5.85 5.85

Esperanto, Cent. — A181

**1987, Feb. 4 Litho.**
**759** A181 60c shown 1.00 1.00
**760** A181 110 World map, doves 1.90 1.90
**761** A181 120c L.L. Zamenhof 2.10 2.10
*Nos. 759-761 (3)* 5.00 5.00

10th Pan-American Games, Indianapolis, July 23 — A182

Forestry Commission, 40th Anniv. — A183

**1987, June 3 Litho. *Perf. 13x14***
**763** A182 90c Soccer 1.50 1.50
**764** A182 110c Swimming 1.75 1.75
**765** A182 150c Basketball 2.25 2.25
*Nos. 763-765 (3)* 5.50 5.50

**1987, July 21 Litho. *Perf. 13x14***
**766** A183 90c Emblem 1.50 1.50
**767** A183 120c Logging 2.00 2.00
**768** A183 150c Parrot in virgin forest 2.75 2.75
*Nos. 766-768 (3)* 6.25 6.25

Intl. Year of Shelter for the Homeless A184

**1987, Sept. 2 Litho. *Perf. 14x13***
**769** A184 90c Distressed boy, encampment 1.40 1.40
**770** A184 120c Man, ghetto 2.10 2.10

Founders Catherine and William Booth — A185

**1987, Sept. 2 *Perf. 14x13***
**771** A185 150c multi 2.25 2.25

Salvation Army in the Caribbean, cent.

Nos. 436-438 Surcharged

**1986, Dec. 29 Litho. *Perf. 13½x13***
**772** A109 35c on 1g 2.25 2.25
**773** A109 50c on 1.50g 3.50 3.50
**774** A109 60c on 2.50g 4.50 4.50
*Nos. 772-774 (3)* 10.25 10.25


Fruits — A186

**1987, Oct. 14 Litho. *Perf. 13x13½***
**775** A186 10c Bananas .20 .20
**776** A186 15c Cacao .20 .20
**777** A186 20c Pineapple .20 .20
**778** A186 25c Papaya .30 .30
**779** A186 35c Oranges .40 .40
*Nos. 775-779 (5)* 1.30 1.30

Aircraft and Aircraft on Stamps — A187

**1987, Oct. 14 Litho. *Perf. 13½***
**784** A187 25c Degen, 1808 .25 .25
**785** A187 25c Ultra Light .25 .25
*a.* Pair, #784-785 .90 .90
**786** A187 35c J.C.H. Ellehammer, 1906 .55 .55
**787** A187 35c Concorde jet .55 .55
*a.* Pair, #786-787 1.25 1.25
**788** A187 60c Fokker F7, 1924 .90 .90
**789** A187 60c Fokker F28 jet .90 .90
*a.* Pair, #788-789 2.10 2.10
**790** A187 90c Spin Fokker, 1910 1.40 1.40
**791** A187 90c DC-10 1.40 1.40
*a.* Pair, #790-791 3.00 3.00
**792** A187 110c Orion, 1932 1.75 1.75
**793** A187 110c Boeing 747 1.75 1.75
*a.* Pair, #792-793 3.75 3.75
**794** A187 120c No. 346 1.90 1.90
**795** A187 120c No. 518 1.90 1.90
*a.* Pair, #794-795 4.00 4.00
*Nos. 784-795 (12)* 13.50 13.50

No. 693a Overprinted "3e match sevilla 1987" on Stamps in 3 or 4 Lines and with Bar and "sevilla 1987" in Sheet Margin

**1987, Nov. 2 Litho. *Perf. 13½x13***
**Souvenir Sheet**
**796** Sheet of 3 *32.50*
*a.* A166 30c Kasparov *3.50*
*b.* A166 50c Board *6.00*
*c.* A166 75c Karpov *9.00*

Alligators and Crocodiles A188

**1988, Jan. 20 Litho. *Perf. 14x13***
**797** A188 50c Gavialis gangeticus .80 .80
**798** A188 60c Crocodylus niloticus 1.10 1.10
**799** A188 90c Melanosuchus niger 1.50 1.50
**800** A188 110c Mississippi alligator 2.10 2.10
*Nos. 797-800 (4)* 5.50 5.50

Traditional Wedding Costumes — A189

**1988, Feb. 24 Litho. *Perf. 13x14***
**801** A189 35c Javanese .50 .50
**802** A189 60c Bushman .95 .95
**803** A189 80c Chinese 1.10 1.10
**804** A189 110c Creole 1.60 1.60
**805** A189 120c Indian 1.75 1.75
**806** A189 130c Hindustan 2.10 2.10
*Nos. 801-806 (6)* 8.00 8.00

Nos. 722-723 and 440 Surcharged in Black or Silver

***Perf. 13½x13, 13½***
**1988, Mar. 23 Litho.**
**808** A172 60c on 75c #722 *5.50*
**809** A172 60c on 75c #723 *5.50*
*a.* Pair, #808-809 *11.00*
**810** A109 125c on 10g #440 (S) *12.00*
*Nos. 808-810 (3)* *23.00*

1988 Summer Olympics, Seoul — A190

Abolition of Slavery, 125th Anniv. — A191

**1988, May 4 Litho. *Perf. 13x14***
**812** A190 90c Relay 1.10 1.10
**813** A190 110c Soccer 1.75 1.75
**814** A190 120c Pole vault 1.90 1.90
*a.* Souvenir sheet of 3, #812-814 5.00 5.00
**815** A190 250c Women's tennis 4.25 4.25
*Nos. 812-815 (4)* 9.00 9.00

**1988, June 29 Litho.**
**816** A191 50c Abaisa Monument .65 .65
**817** A191 110c Kwakoe Monument 1.75 1.75
**818** A191 120c Home of Anton de Kom 2.10 2.10
*Nos. 816-818 (3)* 4.50 4.50

See Netherlands Antilles Nos. 597-598.

Intl. Fund for Agricultural Development (IFAD), 10th Anniv. A192

**1988, Sept. 21** ***Perf. 14x13***

**819** A192 105c Crop harvest 1.75 1.75
**820** A192 110c Net fishing 1.75 1.75
**821** A192 125c Agricultural research 2.25 2.25
*Nos. 819-821 (3)* 5.75 5.75

FILACEPT '88, The Netherlands, Oct. 18-23 — A193

**1988, Oct. 18** **Litho.** ***Perf. 13x14***

**822** A193 120c Egypt #49 1.50 1.50
**823** A193 150c Netherlands #334 2.25 2.25
**824** A193 250c Surinam #238 3.50 3.50
*Nos. 822-824 (3)* 7.25 7.25

**Souvenir Sheet**

**Same Types, Colors Changed (120c, 150c)**

**825** Sheet of 3 10.00 10.00
*a.* A193 120c Egypt Type A23 (4m green) 1.10 1.10
*b.* A193 150c Netherlands Type A81 (10c red brown) 1.40 1.40
*c.* A193 250c Surinam No. 239 2.40 2.40

Stylized Butterfly Stroke A194

**1988, Nov. 1** **Litho.** ***Perf. 14x13***

**826** A194 110c multi 1.60 1.60

Anthony Nesty, swimmer and 1st Olympic gold medalist from Surinam.

Otters A195

**1989, Jan. 18** **Litho.** ***Perf. 14x13***

**827** A195 10c Otter .20 .20
**828** A195 20c Two on land .20 .20
**829** A195 25c Two crossing log .50 .50
**830** A195 30c Fishing .60 .60
*Nos. 827-830,C107 (5)* 4.50 4.50

Classic and Modern Automobiles — A196

**1989, June 7** **Litho.** ***Perf. 13½***

**Design A196**

**831** 25c 1930 Mercedes Tourenwagen .60 .60
**832** 25c 1985 Mercedes-Benz 300E .60 .60
*a.* Pair, #831-832 1.00 1.00
**833** 60c 1897 Daimler 1.25 1.25
**834** 60c 1986 Jaguar Sovereign 1.25 1.25
*a.* Pair, #833-834 2.50 2.50
**835** 90c 1898 Renault Voiturette 2.00 2.00
**836** 90c 1989 Renault 25TX 2.00 2.00
*a.* Pair, #835-836 3.75 3.75
**837** 105c 1927 Volvo Jacob 2.25 2.25
**838** 105c 1989 Volvo 440 2.25 2.25
*a.* Pair, #837-838 4.50 4.50
**839** 110c Left half of Monaco #484 2.40 2.40
**840** 110c Right half of Monaco #484 2.40 2.40
*a.* Pair, #839-840 5.00 5.00
**841** 120c 1936 Toyota AA 2.75 2.75
**842** 120c 1988 Toyota Corolla sedan 2.75 2.75
*a.* Pair, #841-842 5.75 5.75
*Nos. 831-842 (12)* 22.50 22.50

No. 686a Ovptd. "PHILEXFRANCE 7t/m 17 juli 1989" on Margin, with Exhibition Emblem on Stamps in Gold

**1989, July 7** **Litho.** ***Perf. 13x14***

**Miniature Sheet**

**843** Sheet of 3 6.25 6.25
*a.* A164 2c on No. 675 .20 .20
*b.* A164 35c on No. 682 .40 .40
*c.* A164 75c on No. 686 .95 .95

PHILEXFRANCE '89.

Photography, 150th Anniv. A197

**1989, Sept. 6** **Litho.** ***Perf. 14x13***

**844** A197 60c Joseph Niepce 1.00 1.00
**845** A197 110c Daguerreotype camera 1.90 1.90
**846** A197 120c Louis Daguerre 2.10 2.10
*Nos. 844-846 (3)* 5.00 5.00

America Issue — A198

UPAE emblem and pre-Columbian amulets.

**1989, Oct. 12** **Litho.** ***Perf. 13x14***

**847** A198 60c Amazon or Jade Stones 2.10 2.10
**848** A198 110c Bisque fertility statue 4.00 4.00

The White House, Washington, DC, and Stamps on Stamps A199

***Perf. 13x14, 14x13***

**1989, Nov. 17** **Litho.**

**849** A199 110c No. 445, vert. 2.00 2.00
**850** A199 150c US No. 990 2.50 2.50
**851** A199 250c No. 459 4.00 4.00
*a.* Souv. sheet, #849-851, perf 13x14, 14 8.75 8.75
*Nos. 849-851 (3)* 8.50 8.50

World Stamp Expo '89 and 20th UPU Congress, Washington, DC.

UNESCO Intl. Literacy Year — A200

Arya Dewaker Temple, 60th Anniv. — A201

**1990, Jan. 19** **Photo.** ***Perf. 13x14***

**852** A200 60c shown 1.10 1.10
**853** A200 110c Emblems 2.10 2.10
**854** A200 120c Emblems, youth reading 2.25 2.25
*Nos. 852-854 (3)* 5.45 5.45

**1990, Feb. 14** **Litho.**

**855** A201 60c dk red brn, blk & red 1.10 1.10
**856** A201 110c vio blue & blk 2.10 2.10
**857** A201 200c emer grn & blk 3.50 3.50
*Nos. 855-857 (3)* 6.70 6.70

A202

A203

**1990, May 4**

**858** A202 110c Surinam #C1 1.75 1.75
**859** A202 200c Great Britain #1 3.00 3.00
**860** A202 250c Great Britain #208 4.25 4.25
*a.* Souvenir sheet of 3, #858-860 11.00 11.00
*Nos. 858-860 (3)* 9.00 9.00

Penny Black, 150th anniv. Stamps World London '90.

**1990, Aug. 9**

**861** A203 60c Couple carrying baskets 1.00 1.00
**862** A203 110c Woman carrying bundle 1.90 1.90
**863** A203 120c Man carrying baskets 2.10 2.10
*Nos. 861-863 (3)* 5.00 5.00

Javanese Immigration, cent.

Flowers — A204

**1990, Sept. 5** ***Perf. 13½***

**864** A204 25c Punica granatum .45 .45
**865** A204 25c Passiflora laurifolia .45 .45
*a.* Pair, #864-865 .80 .80
**866** A204 35c Hippeastrum puniceum .55 .55
**867** A204 35c Ipomaea batatas .55 .55
*a.* Pair, #866-867 1.10 1.10
**868** A204 60c Hibiscus syriacus 1.00 1.00
**869** A204 60c Jasminum officinale 1.00 1.00
*a.* Pair, #868-869 2.10 2.10
**870** A204 105c Musa serapionis 1.75 1.75
**871** A204 105c Hibiscus mutabilis 1.75 1.75
*a.* Pair, #870-871 3.50 3.50
**872** A204 110c Plumiria rubra 1.75 1.75
**873** A204 110c Hibiscus diversifolius 1.75 1.75
*a.* Pair, #872-873 3.50 3.50
**874** A204 120c Bixa orellana 2.00 2.00
**875** A204 120c Ceasalpinia pulcherima 2.00 2.00
*a.* Pair, #874-875 4.00 4.00
*Nos. 864-875 (12)* 15.00 15.00

America Issue — A205

**1990, Oct. 10** **Litho.** ***Perf. 14x13***

**876** A205 60c bluish grn & blk 1.60 1.60
**877** A205 110c brn & blk 3.25 3.25

Organization of American States, Cent. — A206

**1990, Oct. 10**

**878** A206 110c multicolored 1.60 1.60

Independence, 15th Anniv. — A207

**1990, Nov. 21** **Litho.** ***Perf. 13x14***

**879** A207 10c shown .20 .20
**880** A207 60c Passion flower .95 .95
**881** A207 110c Dove with olive branch 2.10 2.10
*Nos. 879-881 (3)* 3.25 3.25

Architecture A208

Buildings: 35c, Waterfront warehouse. 60c, Upper class residence. 75c, Labor inspection building. 105c, Plantation supervisor's residence. 110c, Ministry of Labor. 200c, Small residences.

**1991, May 15** **Litho.** ***Perf. 14x13***

**882** A208 35c multicolored .80 .80
**883** A208 60c multicolored 1.10 1.10
**884** A208 75c multicolored 1.50 1.50
**885** A208 105c multicolored 2.10 2.10
**886** A208 110c multicolored 2.25 2.25
**887** A208 200c multicolored 4.00 4.00
*Nos. 882-887 (6)* 11.75 11.75

Nos. 714-715, 720-721 Surcharged

**Methods and Perfs as Before**

**1991**

**888** A172 2c on 10c #714 1.00 1.00
**889** A172 2c on 10c #715 1.00 1.00
*a.* Pair, #888-889 2.25 2.25
**890** A172 3c on 50c #720 1.00 1.00
**891** A172 3c on 50c #721 1.00 1.00
*a.* Pair, #890-891 2.25 2.25

Puma Concolor A209

Various pictures of pumas.

***Perf. 13x14, 14x13***

**1991, Sept. 12** **Litho.**

**892** A209 10c multi, vert. .20 .20
**893** A209 20c multi, vert. .25 .25
**894** A209 25c multi, vert. .40 .40
**895** A209 30c multi, vert. .50 .50
**896** A209 125c multi 1.90 1.90
**897** A209 500c multi 6.75 6.75
*Nos. 892-897 (6)* 10.00 10.00

Nos. 896-897 are airmail.

Discovery of America, 500th Anniv. (in 1991) — A210

Diagram showing Columbus' route: 60c, Western Atlantic and Caribbean Sea. 110c, Eastern Atlantic.

**1991, Oct. 11** *Perf. 13x14*

**898** 60c lt bl, red & blk 1.50 1.50
**899** 110c lt bl, red & blk 3.00 3.00
*a.* A210 Pair, #898-899 5.00 5.00

UPAEP. No. 899a has continous design.

Snakes — A211

#900, Corallus enydris. #901, Corallus caninus. #902, Lachesis muta. #903, Boa constrictor. #904, Micrurus surinamensis. #905, Crotalus durissus. #906, Eunectes murinus. #907, Clelia cloelia. #908, Epicrates cenchris. #909, Chironius carinatus. #910, Oxybelis argentieus. #911, Spilotes pullatus.

**1991, Nov. 14** *Perf. 13½*

**900** A211 25c multicolored .30 .30
**901** A211 25c multicolored .30 .30
*a.* Pair, #900-901 .80 .80
**902** A211 35c multicolored .55 .55
**903** A211 35c multicolored .55 .55
*a.* Pair, #902-903 1.10 1.10
**904** A211 60c multicolored .90 .90
**905** A211 60c multicolored .90 .90
*a.* Pair, #904-905 2.10 2.10
**906** A211 75c multicolored 1.25 1.25
**907** A211 75c multicolored 1.25 1.25
*a.* Pair, #906-907 2.50 2.50
**908** A211 110c multicolored 1.75 1.75
**909** A211 110c multicolored 1.75 1.75
*a.* Pair, #908-909 3.75 3.75
**910** A211 200c multicolored 3.25 3.25
**911** A211 200c multicolored 3.25 3.25
*a.* Pair, #910-911 6.75 6.75
*Nos. 900-911 (12)* 16.00 16.00

Orchids — A212

A213

Designs: 50c, Cycnoches haagii. 60c, Lycaste cristata. 75c, Galeandra dives, horiz. 125c, Vanilla mexicana. 150c, Cyrtopodium glutiniferum. 250c, Gongora quinquenervis.

**1992, Feb. 12** *Perf. 13x14, 14x13*

**912** A212 50c multicolored .65 .65
**913** A212 60c multicolored .85 .85
**914** A212 75c multicolored 1.00 1.00
**915** A212 125c multicolored 2.00 2.00
**916** A212 150c multicolored 2.50 2.50
**917** A212 250c multicolored 4.00 4.00
*Nos. 912-917 (6)* 11.00 11.00

Souvenir Sheet

Designs: a, 75c, #847. b, 125c, #848. c, 150c, #898. d. 250c, #899.

**1992, Mar. 24 Litho.** *Perf. 13x13½*

**918** A213 Sheet of 4, #a.-d. 11.00 11.00

Granada '92, Intl. Philatelic Exibition.

1992 Summer Olympics, Barcelona — A214

**1992, Apr. 8 Litho.** *Perf. 13x14*

**919** A214 35c Basketball .55 .55
**920** A214 60c Volleyball .95 .95
**921** A214 75c Running 1.10 1.10
**922** A214 125c Soccer 1.90 1.90
**923** A214 150c Cycling 2.25 2.25
**924** A214 250c Swimming 4.25 4.25
*a.* Souvenir sheet of 3, #921, 922, 924, perf 13x13½ 7.50 7.50
*Nos. 919-924 (6)* 11.00 11.00

YWCA, 50th Anniv. A215

**1992, June 12 Litho.** *Perf. 14x13*

**925** A215 60c red brown & multi 1.00 1.00
**926** A215 250c purple & multi 4.00 4.00

Expulsion of Jews from Spain, 500th Anniv. A216

**1992, Aug. 17**

**927** A216 250c multicolored 4.00 4.00

Nos. 712-713 Surcharged

**1992, Aug. 17** *Perf. 13½*

**928** A172 1c on 5c multi .40 .40
**929** A172 1c on 5c multi .40 .40
*a.* Pair, #928-929 .90 .90

A217

A218

**1992, Sept. 15** *Perf. 13x14*

**930** A217 60c green & multi 1.00 1.00
**931** A217 250c pink & multi 4.00 4.00

Jan E. Matzeliger (1852-1889), inventor of shoe lasting machine.

**1992, Oct. 12**

**932** A218 60c blue grn & multi 1.00 1.00
**933** A218 250c dp org & multi 4.00 4.00

Discovery of America, 500th anniv.

Christmas — A219

Various abstract designs.

**1992, Nov. 15**

**934** A219 10c multicolored .50 .50
**935** A219 60c multicolored 1.00 1.00
**936** A219 250c multicolored 3.50 3.50
**937** A219 400c multicolored 6.00 6.00
*Nos. 934-937 (4)* 11.00 11.00

Medicinal Plants A220

Designs: 50c, Costus arabicus, vert. 75c, Quassia amara, vert. 125c, Combretum rotundifolium. 500c, Bixa orellana.

*Perf. 13x14, 14x13*

**1993, Feb. 3 Litho.**

**938** A220 50c multicolored .85 .85
**939** A220 75c multicolored 1.40 1.40
**940** A220 125c multicolored 2.25 2.25
**941** A220 500c multicolored 9.00 9.00
*Nos. 938-941 (4)* 13.50 13.50

Beetles and Grasshoppers — A221

Designs: No. 942, Macrodontia cervicornis. No. 943, Acrididae. No. 944, Curculionidae. No. 945, Acrididae, diff. No. 946, Euchroma gigantea. No. 947, Tettigonidae. No. 948, Tettigonidae. No. 949, Phanaeus festivus. No. 950, Gryllidae. No. 951, Phanaeus lancifer. No. 952, Tettigonidae. No. 953, Batus barbicornis.

**1993, June 30 Litho.** *Perf. 13½*

**942** A221 25c multicolored .40 .40
**943** A221 25c multicolored .40 .40
*a.* Pair, #942-943 .90 .90
**944** A221 35c multicolored .50 .50
**945** A221 35c multicolored .50 .50
*a.* Pair, #944-945 1.60 1.60
**946** A221 50c multicolored .70 .70
**947** A221 50c multicolored .70 .70
*a.* Pair, #946-947 2.00 2.00
**948** A221 100c multicolored 1.40 1.40
**949** A221 100c multicolored 1.40 1.40
*a.* Pair, #948-949 3.75 3.75
**950** A221 175c multicolored 2.75 2.75
**951** A221 175c multicolored 2.75 2.75
*a.* Pair, #950-951 6.75 6.75
**952** A221 220c multicolored 3.25 3.25
**953** A221 220c multicolored 3.25 3.25
*a.* Pair, #952-953 8.50 8.00
*Nos. 942-953 (12)* 18.00 18.00

A222

A223

#956b, 250c, like #955. #956c, 500c, like #956.

**1993, July 30** *Perf. 13x14*

**954** A222 50c Brazil No. 3 .75 .75
**955** A222 250c Brazil No. 2 3.75 3.75
**956** A222 500c Brazil No. 1 8.00 8.00
*Nos. 954-956 (3)* 12.50 12.50

**Souvenir Sheet**

**956A** A222 Sheet of 2, #b.-c. 10.00 10.00

1st Brazilian postage stamps, 150th Anniv. Brasiliana '93 (#956A).
Nos. 956b-956c have purple border.

**1993, Oct. 12** *Perf. 14x13*

America issue: Paleosuchus palpebrosus.

**957** A223 50g brown & multi 1.90 1.90
**958** A223 100g green & multi 4.00 4.00

Christmas Angels — A224

25g, African angel with drum. 45g, Asian angel holding lamp. 50g, Oriental angel holding lantern. 150g, American Indian angel holding wand.

**1993, Nov. 15 Litho.** *Perf. 13x14*

**959** A224 25g multicolored 1.00 1.00
**960** A224 45g multicolored 1.75 1.75
**961** A224 50g multicolored 2.00 2.00
**962** A224 150g multicolored 6.25 6.25
*Nos. 959-962 (4)* 11.00 11.00

The foreign exchange rate of the Surinam florin was allowed to float freely against foreign currencies on Oct. 19, 1994. The florin's value against the dollar has fluctuated dramatically. Stamps may sell for values significantly different from those quoted in the Scott listings.

Nos. 729-730 Surcharged

**1993 Litho.** *Perf. 14x13*

**963** A173 5g on 10g Harpy eagle *1.90* .20
**964** A173 5g on 15g Parrot 1.90 1.90

Surchanges differ slightly. Issued: #963, 12/16. #964, 12/28.

Traditional Musical Instruments — A225

**1994, Feb. 16 Litho.** *Perf. 13x14*

**965** A225 25g Indian drum 1.50 1.50
**966** A225 50g Bosland Creooise drum 3.00 3.00
**967** A225 75g Tambourine 5.00 5.00
**968** A225 100g Hindu drum 6.50 6.50
*Nos. 965-968 (4)* 16.00 16.00

Environmental Protection A226

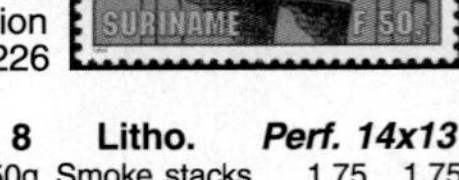

**1994, June 8 Litho.** *Perf. 14x13*

**969** A226 50g Smoke stacks 1.75 1.75
**970** A226 350g Dying fish 12.50 12.50

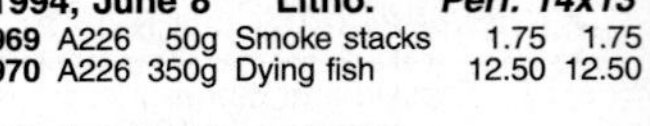

Intl. Olympic Committee, Cent. — A227

**1994, July 4 Litho.** *Perf. 14x13*

**971** A227 250g multicolored 7.75 7.75

1994 World Cup Soccer Championships, U.S. — A228

**1994, July 4** *Perf. 13x14*

**972** A228 100g Goalkeeper's hands 3.00 3.00
**973** A228 250g Soccer shoe 7.75 7.75
**974** A228 300g Goal 9.00 9.00
*a.* Souvenir sheet of 2, #973-974 17.00 17.00
*Nos. 972-974 (3)* 19.75 19.75

Butterflies — A229

**1994, Sept. 7** **Litho.** *Perf. 13½*

**975** A229 25g Dulcedo .45 .45
**976** A229 25g Ithomia .45 .45
*a.* Pair, #975-976 .90 .90
**977** A229 30g Danaus .50 .50
**978** A229 30g Danaus, diff. .50 .50
*a.* Pair, #977-978 1.00 1.00
**979** A229 45g Echenais .75 .75
**980** A229 45g Bithijs .75 .75
*a.* Pair #979-980 1.50 1.50
**981** A229 75g Junonia evarette 1.25 1.25
**982** A229 75g Anartia jatrophae 1.25 1.25
*a.* Pair, #981-982 2.50 2.50
**983** A229 250g Heliconius 4.00 4.00
**984** A229 250g Heliconius erato 4.00 4.00
*a.* Pair, #983-984 8.25 8.25
**985** A229 300g Eurytides 5.00 5.00
**986** A229 300g Parides 5.00 5.00
*a.* Pair, #985-986 10.00 10.00
*Nos. 975-986 (12)* 23.90 23.90

For surcharges see #1088-1091.

FEPAPOST '94 — A230

**1994, Oct. 1** **Litho.** *Perf. 14x13*

**987** A230 250g Netherlands #B148 6.25 6.25
**988** A230 300g #168 7.75 7.75
*a.* Souvenir sheet of 2, #987-988, perf. 13½x13 14.00 14.00

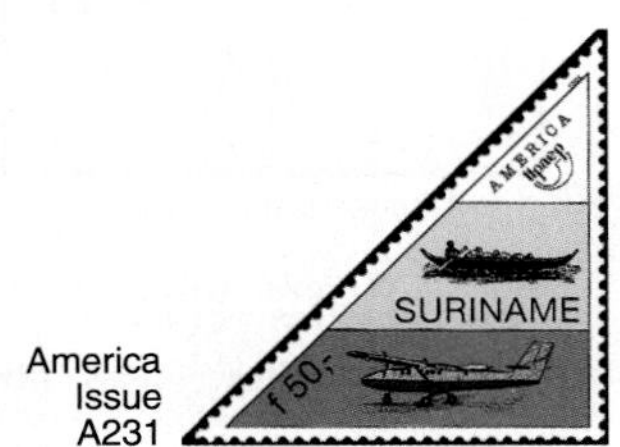


America Issue A231

Post vehicles: 50g, Airplane, canoe. 400g, Van, donkey cart.

**1994, Oct. 12** **Litho.** *Perf. 13½*

**989** A231 50g multicolored 1.40 1.40
**990** A231 400g multicolored 12.00 12.00

A232

A233

Christmas: (A), Angel in sky. 250g, Mother reading to children. 625g, Woman kneeling in prayer.

**1994, Nov. 22** *Perf. 13x14*

**991** A232 (A) multicolored .60 .60
**992** A232 250g multicolored 1.90 1.90
**993** A232 625g multicolored 5.00 5.00
*a.* Souvenir sheet, #992-993 13.50 13.50
*Nos. 991-993 (3)* 7.50 7.50

No. 991 sold for 37g on day of issue.

**1995, Jan. 31**

**994** A233 375g shown 3.25 3.25
**995** A233 650g Volleyballs 5.25 5.50
*a.* Souvenir sheet, #994-995 9.00 9.00

Volleyball, cent.

Medicinal Plants — A234

Designs: No. 998, Stachytarpheta jamaicense. No. 999, Ruellia tuberosa. No. 1000, Peperomia pellucida. No. 1001, Ocimum sanctum. No. 1002, Phyllanthus amarus. No. 1003, Portulaca oleracea. No. 1004, Wulffia baccata. No. 1005, Sesamum indicum. No. 1006, Ascelepias curassavica. No. 1007, Heliotropium indicum. No. 1008, Wedelia trilobata. No. 1009, Lantana camara.

**1995, Mar. 31** **Litho.** *Perf. 13½*

**998** A234 30g multicolored .35 .35
**999** A234 30g multicolored .35 .35
*a.* Pair, #998-999 .50 .50
**1000** A234 50g multicolored .50 .50
**1001** A234 50g multicolored .50 .50
*a.* Pair, #1000-1001 .80 .80
**1002** A234 75g multicolored .75 .75
**1003** A234 75g multicolored .75 .75
*a.* Pair, #1002-1003 1.40 1.40
**1004** A234 250g multicolored 2.40 2.40
**1005** A234 250g multicolored 2.40 2.40
*a.* Pair, #1004-1005 4.75 4.75
**1006** A234 500g multicolored 4.75 4.75
**1007** A234 500g multicolored 4.75 4.75
*a.* Pair, #1006-1007 9.50 9.50
**1008** A234 600g multicolored 5.75 5.75
**1009** A234 600g multicolored 5.75 5.75
*a.* Pair, #1008-1009 12.00 12.00
*Nos. 998-1009 (12)* 29.00 29.00

World Wildlife Fund — A235

25g, Herpailurus yaguarondi. 30g, same up close. 50g, Leopardus tigrinus. 100g, same up close. 1000g, Leopardus wiedi. 1200g, same up close.

**1995, May 31** *Perf. 14x13*

**1010** A235 25g multicolored .90 .40
**1011** A235 30g multicolored .90 .40
**1012** A235 50g multicolored .90 .40
**1013** A235 100g multicolored 2.25 1.25
**1014** A235 1000g multicolored 5.75 5.75
**1015** A235 1200g multicolored 7.00 7.00
*Nos. 1010-1015 (6)* 17.70 15.20

Nos. 1014-1015 are airmail and do not contain WWF emblem.

UN, 50th Anniv. — A236

**1995, June 26** **Litho.** *Perf. 13x14*

**1016** A236 135g green & multi .75 .75
**1017** A236 740g blue & multi 5.00 5.00

Surinam Police Force, Cent. — A237

**1995, June 21** *Perf. 14x13*

**1018** A237 875g multicolored 9.00 9.00

Nilom Junior Chamber, 25th Anniv. A238

**1995, Sept. 6** **Litho.** *Perf. 14x13*

**1019** A238 700g multicolored 3.75 3.75

Environmental Protection A239

**1995, Oct. 12**

**1020** A239 135f multicolored 1.00 1.00
**1021** A239 1500f multicolored 11.50 11.50

America issue.

A240

A241

Christmas: 70g, Shepherds, star. 135g, Flight into Egypt. 295g, Magi. 1000g, Nativity, horiz.

**1995, Nov. 15** *Perf. 13x14, 14x13*

**1022** A240 70g multicolored .35 .35
**1023** A240 135g multicolored .75 .75
**1024** A240 295g multicolored 1.50 1.50
**1025** A240 1000g multicolored 6.25 6.25
*a.* Souvenir sheet of 1 4.75 4.75
*Nos. 1022-1025 (4)* 8.85 8.85

For surcharges see #1065A-1065B.

**1995, Dec. 5** *Perf. 13x14*

Paintings of Jesters, by Corneille.

**1026** A241 135f With bird 1.00 1.00
**1027** A241 615f With cat 4.75 4.75

Orchids — A242

#1028, Cyrtopodium cristatum. #1029, Epidendrum cristatum. #1030, Otostylis lepida. #1031, Cochleanthes guianensis. #1032, Rudolfiella aurantiaca. #1033, Catasetum longifolium. #1034, Maxillaria splendens. #1035, Encyclia granitica. #1036, Catasetum macrocarpum. #1037, Brassia caudata. #1038, Vanilla grandiflora. #1039, Maxillaria rufescens.

**1996, Feb. 29** **Litho.** *Perf. 13½*

**1028** A242 10g multicolored .20 .20
**1029** A242 10g multicolored .20 .20
*a.* Pair, #1028-1029 .25 .25
**1030** A242 75g multicolored .50 .50
**1031** A242 75g multicolored .50 .50
*a.* Pair, #1030-1031 .90 .90
**1032** A242 135g multicolored .85 .85
**1033** A242 135g multicolored .85 .85
*a.* Pair, #1032-1033 1.60 1.60
**1034** A242 250g multicolored 1.60 1.60
**1035** A242 250g multicolored 1.60 1.60
*a.* Pair, #1034-1035 3.25 3.25
**1036** A242 300g multicolored 2.00 2.00
**1037** A242 300g multicolored 2.00 2.00
*a.* Pair, #1036-1037 4.00 4.00
**1038** A242 750g multicolored 4.75 4.75
**1039** A242 750g multicolored 4.75 4.75
*a.* Pair, #1038-1039 10.00 10.00
*Nos. 1028-1039 (12)* 19.80 19.80

Bird Type of 1985

**1996, Apr. 16** **Litho.** *Perf. 14x13*

**1040** A173 2000f Kraagpapegaai 12.50 12.50

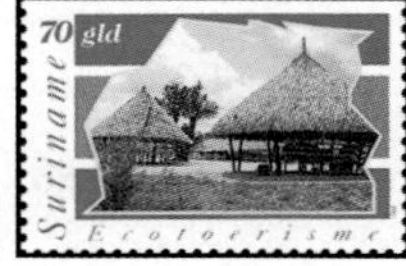


Ecotourism A243

Designs: No. 1041, Traditional huts. No. 1042, Butterfly in rain forest. No. 1043, Two natives. No. 1044, Native woman.

*Perf. 13½x13 on 3 Sides*

**1996, Apr. 30** **Litho.**

**Booklet Stamps**

**1041** A243 70g multicolored .30 .30
**1042** A243 70g multicolored .30 .30
**1043** A243 135g multicolored .60 .60
**1044** A243 135g multicolored .60 .60
*a.* Booklet pane of 4, #1041-1044 2.75
Complete booklet, #1044a 5.75

Radio, Cent. — A244

135g, First wireless radio communication device, vert. 615g, Guglielmo Marconi.

*Perf. 13x14, 14x13*

**1996, May 17** **Litho.**

**1045** A244 135g multicolored 1.00 1.00
**1046** A244 615g multicolored 4.50 4.50

1996 Summer Olympic Games, Atlanta — A245

Olymphilex '96, Atlanta — A245a

Stamp on stamp: b, 135f, #678. c, 865f, #683.
Illustration A254a reduced.

**1996, June 27** **Litho.** *Perf. 13x14*

**1047** A245 70g Basketball .50 .50
**1048** A245 135g Athletics .95 .95
**1049** A245 195g Badminton 1.40 1.40
**1050** A245 200g Swimming 1.60 1.60
**1051** A245 900g Cycling 7.00 7.00
**1052** A245 1000g Hurdles 7.50 7.50
*Nos. 1047-1052 (6)* 18.95 18.95

**Souvenir Sheet**

**1052A** A245a Sheet of 2, #b.-c. 9.00 9.00

Bird Type of 1985

Designs: 75f, Fisman. 160f, Fremusu-aka. 1765f, Roodpoot honingzuiger.

**1996, Oct. 2** **Litho.** *Perf. 14x13*

**1053** A173 75f multicolored .45 .45
**1054** A173 160f multicolored 1.00 1.00
**1055** A173 1765f multicolored 11.00 11.00
*Nos. 1053-1055 (3)* 12.45 12.45

A246

Women's Traditional Costumes: Various styles.

**1996, Oct. 9 Litho. *Perf. 13x14***

**1056** 135f multicolored *1.25 1.25*
**1057** 990f multicolored *7.75 7.75*
*a.* A246 Pair, #1056-1057 *10.00 10.00*

America issue.

A247

**1996, Oct. 30 Litho. *Perf. 13x14***

Christmas: Various stylized designs of Madonna and Child.

**1058** A247 10f multicolored *.20 .20*
**1059** A247 70f multicolored *.50 .50*
**1060** A247 135f multicolored *.90 .90*
**1061** A247 285f multicolored *2.40 2.40*
**1062** A247 750f multicolored *6.00 6.00*
*a.* Souvenir sheet, #1062 *6.25 6.25*
*Nos. 1058-1062 (5)* *10.00 10.00*

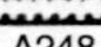
A248

A249

Youth Care: Paintings, by Jan Telting: 135f, Brown dog, child. 865f, White dog, child.

**1996, Dec. 4 Litho. *Perf. 13x14***

**1063** A248 135f multicolored *1.00 1.00*
**1064** A248 865f multicolored *6.75 6.75*

**1996, Dec. 13**

City of Albina, 150th Anniv.: August Kappler (1815-87), founder.

**1065** A249 875f multicolored *7.25 7.25*

Nos. 1024, 1025 Surcharged in Black or Silver

**Methods and perfs as before**

**1996, Dec. 16**

**1065A** A240 (125g) on 295g *2.40 2.40*
**1065B** A240 (125g) on 1000g (S) *2.40 2.40*

SURALCO (Surinam Aluminum Co.) — A250

10f, Opening of aluminum smelter, Paranam, 1965. 70f, Drilling blasting holes for ore exploration, Moengo, 1947. 130f, Workers' housing, Moengo, 1919. 150f, Dust-free loading of alumina, Paranam dock, 1995. 160f, Constructing dam, power station, 1960. 730f, Schooner Moengo, 1922.

***Perf. 13½x13 on 2 or 3 Sides***

**1996, Dec. 18**

**Booklet Stamps**

**1066** A250 10f multicolored *.20 .20*
**1067** A250 70f multicolored *.45 .45*
**1068** A250 130f multicolored *.80 .80*
**1069** A250 150f multicolored *.90 .90*
**1070** A250 160f multicolored *1.00 1.00*
**1071** A250 730f multicolored *4.50 4.50*
*a.* Booklet pane, #1066-1071 + label *9.75*
Complete booklet, #1071a *11.50*

Heinrich von Stephan (1831-97) — A251

**1997, Jan. 31 Litho. *Perf. 13x14***

**1072** A251 275f brown & multi 2.40 2.40
**1073** A251 475f dk blue & multi 3.75 3.75

Fauna — A252

#1074, Cebus nigrivittatus. #1075, Cebus apella. #1076, Saguinus midas. #1077, Ateles paniscus. #1078, Ateles geoffroyi panamensis. #1079, Ateles geoffroyi frontatus. #1080, Cacajao calvus. #1081, Lagothrix flavicauda. #1082, Saguinus bicolor. #1083, Saguinus oedipus. #1084, Alouatta seniculus. #1085, Saimiri sciureus.

**1997, Feb. 12 Litho. *Perf. 13½***

**1074** A252 25f multicolored .20 .20
**1075** A252 25f multicolored .20 .20
*a.* Pair, #1074-1075 .35 .35
**1076** A252 75f multicolored .55 .55
**1077** A252 75f multicolored .55 .55
*a.* Pair, #1076-1077 1.10 1.10
**1078** A252 100f multicolored .75 .75
**1079** A252 100f multicolored .75 .75
*a.* Pair, #1078-1079 1.50 1.50
**1080** A252 275f multicolored 2.00 2.00
**1081** A252 275f multicolored 2.00 2.00
*a.* Pair, #1080-1081 4.00 4.00
**1082** A252 300f multicolored 2.50 2.50
**1083** A252 300f multicolored 2.50 2.50
*a.* Pair, #1082-1083 4.75 4.75
**1084** A252 725f multicolored 5.25 5.25
**1085** A252 725f multicolored 5.25 5.25
*a.* Pair, #1084-1085 11.00 11.00
*Nos. 1074-1085 (12)* 22.50 22.50

Retracing and Completion of Amelia Earhart's Trans-Global Flight by Linda Finch — A253

**1997, Mar. 30 Litho. *Perf. 14x13***

**1086** A253 275f multicolored 2.10 2.10

Surinam Museum, 50th Anniv. A254

**1997, Apr. 3**

**1087** A254 625f multicolored 4.75 4.75

Nos. 983-986 Surcharged in Black or Silver

**1996-97 Litho. *Perf. 13½***

**1088** A229 50f on 250g #983 1.40 1.40
**1089** A229 50f on 250g #984 1.40 1.40
*a.* Pair, #1088-1089 5.75 5.75
**1090** A229 100f on 300g #985 (S) 2.75 2.75
**1091** A229 100f on 300g #986 (S) 2.75 2.75
*a.* Pair, #1090-1091 6.25 6.25
*Nos. 1088-1091 (4)* 8.30 8.30

Issued; #1089a, 11/1; #1091a, 1/1/97.

Orchids — A255

Designs: 25f, Selenipedium steyermarkii. 50f, Phragmipedium schlimii. 75f, Criosantes arietina. 200f, Cypripedium margaritaceum. 775f, Paphiopedilum gratrixianum.

**1997, Apr. 3 Litho. *Perf. 13x14***

**1092** A255 25f multicolored .20 .20
**1093** A255 50f multicolored .40 .40
**1094** A255 75f multicolored .55 .55
**1095** A255 200f multicolored 1.60 1.60
**1096** A255 775f multicolored 6.00 6.00
*Nos. 1092-1096 (5)* 8.75 8.75

Souvenir Sheet

PACIFIC 97, San Francisco — A256

Illustration reduced.

**1997, May 29 Litho. *Perf. 13½x13***

**1097** A256 675f #458-459 5.00 5.00

A257

A258

Mosques: 50f, Great Mosque, Isfahan, Iran. 125f, Dome of the Rock, Jerusalem. 175f, Madrasa of Ulugh beg, Samarkand. 225f, Taj Mahal, Agra, India. 275f, Kaiser St. Mosque, Paramaribo. 325f, Sülcjamiye, Istanbul.

**1997, July 7 *Perf. 13x14***

**Background Color**

**1098** A257 50f pink .35 .35
**1099** A257 125f olive .90 .90
**1100** A257 175f blue 1.25 1.25
**1101** A257 225f purple 1.60 1.60
**1102** A257 275f green 2.10 2.10
**1103** A257 325f brown 2.50 2.50
*a.* Souvenir sheet of 1 2.75 2.75
*Nos. 1098-1103 (6)* 8.70 8.70

***Perf. 13x13½ on 3 Sides***

**1997, Aug. 16 Litho.**

State Oil Co. Refinery, Saramacca: 50f, Pumping station. 125f, Derrick, butterfly. #1106, Storage tanks. #1107, Gauge, testing mechanism.

**Booklet Stamps**

**1104** A258 50f multicolored .25 .25
**1105** A258 125f multicolored .75 .75
**1106** A258 275f multicolored 1.75 1.75
**1107** A258 275f multicolored 1.75 1.75
*a.* Booklet pane, #1104-1107 5.50
Complete booklet, #1107a 9.75

Bird Type of 1985

**1997, Sept. 17 Litho. *Perf. 14x13***

**1108** A173 50f Krabu-owrukuku .50 .50
**1109** A173 125f Mangrodoifi 1.50 1.50
**1110** A173 275f Peprefowru 2.00 2.00
**1111** A173 3150f Kroonvink 25.00 25.00
*Nos. 1108-1111 (4)* 29.00 29.00

A259

A260

Child Care: 50f, Right side of boy's face. 100f, Left side of boy's face, 175f, Right side of girl's face. 225f, Left side of girl's face. 350f, 675f, Boy's face upside down, girl's face.

**1997, Dec. 4 Litho. *Perf. 13x14***

**1112** A259 50f multicolored .40 .40
**1113** A259 100f multicolored .75 .75
**1114** A259 175f multicolored 1.25 1.25
**1115** A259 225f multicolored 1.75 1.75
**1116** A259 350f multicolored 2.75 2.75
*Nos. 1112-1116 (5)* 6.90 6.90

**Souvenir Sheet**

**1117** A259 675f multicolored 5.00 5.00

**1997, Dec. 4**

Christmas: 125f, Madonna and Child. 225f, Children looking at baby. 450f, Angel.
675f, Children singing, horiz.

**1118** A260 125f multicolored 1.00 1.00
**1119** A260 225f multicolored 1.75 1.75
**1120** A260 450f multicolored 3.50 3.50
*Nos. 1118-1120 (3)* 6.25 6.25

**Souvenir Sheet**

**1121** A260 675f multicolored 5.00 5.00

America Issue — A261

Designs: 170f, Postal worker, motorcycle. 230f, Postal worker carrying package.

**1997, Dec. 10 Litho. *Perf. 13x14***

**1122** 170f multicolored 1.00 1.00
**1123** 230f multicolored 1.40 1.40
*a.* A261 Pair, #1122-1123 3.25 3.25

Moths & Butterflies — A262

**1998, Jan. 26 *Perf. 13½***

**1124** A262 50f Alcandor .30 .30
**1125** A262 50f Achilles .30 .30
*a.* Pair, #1124-1125 .85 .85
**1126** A262 75f Alphenor .45 .45
**1127** A262 75f Ceres .45 .45
*a.* Pair, #1126-1127 1.25 1.25
**1128** A262 100f Cecropia .60 .60
**1129** A262 100f Helenor .60 .60
*a.* Pair, #1128-1129 1.60 1.60

**1130** A262 175f Promothea 1.00 1.00
**1131** A262 175f Cassiae 1.00 1.00
*a.* Pair, #1130-1131 2.75 2.75
**1132** A262 275f Ino 2.10 2.10
**1133** A262 275f Phidippus 2.10 2.10
*a.* Pair, #1132-1133 5.00 5.00
**1134** A262 725f Palamedes 5.50 5.50
**1135** A262 725f Helenor, diff. 5.50 5.50
*a.* Pair, #1134-1135 12.50 12.50
*Nos. 1124-1135 (12)* 19.90 19.90

Bird Type of 1985

**1998, Mar. 12** ***Perf. 14x13, 13x14***
**1136** A173 50f Marjrietje .40 .40
**1137** A173 225f Aka 1.75 1.75
**1138** A173 2425f Timmerman, vert. 19.00 19.00
*Nos. 1136-1138 (3)* 21.15 21.15

Hindustani Immigration, 125th Anniv. A263

Designs: 175f, Painting showing first immigrants from boat, "Lala Rooch." 200f, Statue of Baba and Mai, first immigrants from India.

**1998, June 4** **Litho.** ***Perf. 14x13***
**1139** A263 175f multicolored 1.25 1.25
**1140** A263 200f multicolored 1.60 1.60

Temples A264

Designs: 50f, Sri Lanka. 75f, Golden Pagoda, Burma, vert. 275f, Swayambhunath, Nepal, vert. 325f, Borobudur, Indonesia. 400f, Wat Phra Kaew, Thailand, vert. 450f, Peking Temple, China, vert.
675f, Statue, Borobudur, Indonesia, vert.

***Perf. 13½x12½, 12½x13½***

**1998, June 4**
**1141** A264 50f multicolored .35 .35
**1142** A264 75f multicolored .55 .55
**1143** A264 275f multicolored 2.00 2.00
**1144** A264 325f multicolored 2.40 2.40
**1145** A264 400f multicolored 2.75 2.75
**1146** A264 450f multicolored 3.50 3.50
*Nos. 1141-1146 (6)* 11.55 11.55

**Souvenir Sheet**

**1147** A264 675f multicolored 5.00 5.00

No. 1147 is a continuous design.

Ferry Boat A265

**1998, Oct. 31** ***Perf. 13½x14***
**1148** A265 275f blue & multi 2.00 2.00
**1149** A265 400f sepia & multi 3.00 3.00

America Issue — A266

Outstanding women: 400f, Sophie Redmond (1907-55). 1000f, Grace Ruth Schneiders-Howard (1869-1968).

**1998, Oct. 8** **Litho.** ***Perf. 13x14***
**1150** A266 400f multicolored 3.00 3.00
**1151** A266 1000f multicolored 7.50 7.50

World Stamp Exhibition, The Hague, Netherlands A267

Designs: 400f, #245, portions of #174, #141. 800f, #174, portions of #245, #141.
2400f, #141, portions of #245, #174.

**1998, Oct.** **Litho.** ***Perf. 14x13***
**1152** A267 400f multicolored 3.00 3.00
**1153** A267 800f multicolored 5.75 5.75

**Souvenir Sheet**

**1154** A267 2400f multicolored 20.00 20.00

A268

A269

Christmas: Various nativity scenes.

**1998, Nov. 1** ***Perf. 13x14***
**1155** A268 50f multicolored .40 .40
**1156** A268 325f multicolored 1.60 1.60
**1157** A268 400f multicolored 2.00 2.00
**1158** A268 1225f multicolored 7.00 7.00
*Nos. 1155-1158 (4)* 11.00 11.00

**Souvenir Sheet**

**1159** A268 1400f multicolored 8.00 8.00

Bird Type of 1985

**1998, Nov. 16** **Litho.** ***Perf. 14x13***
**1160** A173 3800f Butarides striatus 16.00 16.00

**1998, Dec. 4** **Litho.** ***Perf. 13x14***
**1161** A269 400f Mother, child, foods 2.10 2.10
**1162** A269 1000f Mother, child, flower 5.50 5.50

World Health Organization, 50th anniv.

Child Care — A270

**1998, Dec. 4** **Litho.** ***Perf. 14x13***
**1163** A270 375f shown 2.00 2.00
**1164** A270 400f Flying kite, diff. 2.00 2.00
**1165** A270 1225f Holding kite 7.00 7.00
*Nos. 1163-1165 (3)* 11.00 11.00

Heliconia — A271

#1166, Caribaea kawauchi. #1167, Pastazae. #1168, Rostrata. #1169, Sexy pink. #1170, Collinsiana. #1171, Wagneriana. #1172, Bihai-nappi. #1173, Jaded forest. #1174, Golden torch. #1175, Latispatha-red yellow gyro. #1176, Sexy pink, diff. #1177, Nappi yellow.

**1999, Jan. 27** **Litho.** ***Perf. 13½***
**1166** A271 50f multicolored .20 .20
**1167** A271 50f multicolored .20 .20
*a.* Pair, #1166-1167 .30 .30
**1168** A271 200f multicolored .65 .65
**1169** A271 200f multicolored .65 .65
*a.* Pair, #1168-1169 1.25 1.25
**1170** A271 300f multicolored 1.00 1.00
**1171** A271 300f multicolored 1.00 1.00
*a.* Pair, #1170-1171 2.00 2.00
**1172** A271 400f multicolored 1.25 1.25
**1173** A271 400f multicolored 1.25 1.25
*a.* Pair, 1172-1173 2.50 2.50
**1174** A271 750f multicolored 2.50 2.50
**1175** A271 750f multicolored 2.50 2.50
*a.* Pair, #1174-1175 5.00 5.00
**1176** A271 1300f multicolored 4.25 4.25
**1177** A271 1300f multicolored 4.25 4.25
*a.* Pair, #1176-1177 8.50 8.50
*Nos. 1166-1177 (12)* 19.70 19.70

Old Plantation Houses A272

**1999, Mar. 17** **Litho.** ***Perf. 14x13***
**1178** A272 75f Katwijk .25 .25
**1179** A272 300f Sorgvliet 1.00 1.00
**1180** A272 400f Peperpot 1.25 1.25
**1181** A272 2225f Spieringshoek 7.25 7.25
*Nos. 1178-1181 (4)* 9.75 9.75

Endangered Species — A273

**1999, June 30** **Litho.** ***Perf. 13x14***
**1182** A273 75f Flamingo *.20 .20*
**1183** A273 375f Orangutan *.75 .75*
**1184** A273 450f Elephant *.90 .90*
**1185** A273 500f Whale *.95 .95*
**1186** A273 850f Frog *1.60 1.60*
**1187** A273 900f Rhinoceros *1.75 1.75*
**1188** A273 1600f Giant panda *3.00 3.00*
**1189** A273 7250f Tiger *14.00 14.00*
*Nos. 1182-1189 (8)* *23.15 23.15*

Coppename Bridge A274

**1999, June 30** ***Perf. 14x13***
**1190** A274 850f black & green *1.60 1.60*
**1191** A274 2250f black & blue *4.25 4.25*

A275

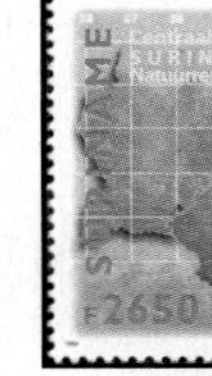

A276

**1999, July 9** ***Perf. 13x14***
**1192** A275 850f multicolored *1.40 1.40*
**1193** A276 2650f multicolored *4.25 4.25*
*a.* Souvenir sheet, #1192-1193, perf. 13x13½ *5.75 5.75*

Surinam Conservation Foundation, 30th anniv. (No. 1192), Central Surinam Nature Preserve, 1st anniv. (No. 1193).

**Bird Type of 1985-95**

**1999, Aug. 21** ***Perf. 14x13***
**1194** A173 1000f Blauwtje *1.90 1.90*
**1195** A173 5500f Kepanki *8.75 8.75*

A277

**1999, Oct. 9** ***Perf. 13x14***
**1196** A277 950f Earth *1.75 1.75*
**1197** A277 1000f Saturn *1.90 1.90*

UPU, 125th anniv.

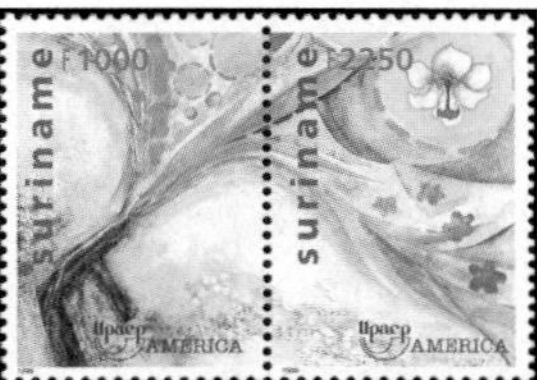


A278

**1999, Oct. 9**
**1198** 1000f Gun *1.75 1.75*
**1199** 2250f Flower *3.50 3.50*
*a.* A278 Pair, #1198-1199 *6.00 6.00*

America issue, A New Millennium Without Arms.

Christmas — A279

**1999, Nov. 3** ***Perf. 13x14***
**1200** A279 500f Star, stable *.80 .80*
**1201** A279 850f Christmas tree *1.40 1.40*
**1202** A279 900f Angel *1.50 1.50*
**1203** A279 1000f Candle *1.60 1.60*
*Nos. 1200-1203 (4)* *5.30 5.30*

**Souvenir Sheet**

**1204** A279 2275f Mother and child *4.25 4.25*

Children's Pictures A280

**1999, Dec. 3** **Litho.** ***Perf. 14x13***
**1205** A280 1100f multi *1.75 1.75*
**1206** A280 1400f multi, diff. *2.25 2.25*
**1207** A280 1600f multi, diff. *2.50 2.50*
*a.* Souvenir sheet of 1 *2.75 2.75*
*Nos. 1205-1207 (3)* *6.50 6.50*

Children's Drawings A281

**2000, Jan. 3** **Litho.** ***Perf. 14x13***
**1208** A281 1000f By Tahirih van Kanten *1.75 1.75*
**1209** A281 2500f By Tirsa Braaf *4.25 4.25*

See No. 1224.

Traffic Signs — A282

**2000** ***Perf. 13x14***
**1210** A282 2000f Turn right *4.00 4.00*
**1211** A282 2000f No passing *4.00 4.00*
**1212** A282 2000f Sharp turns *4.00 4.00*
**1213** A282 2000f Traffic circle *4.00 4.00*
*Nos. 1210-1213 (4)* *16.00 16.00*

Issued: #1210, 1/3; #1211, 4/3; #1212, 5/18. #1213, 9/29.

Fruits A283

No. 1214, 50f: a, Citrullus vulgaris. b, Carica papaya.
No. 1215, 175f: a, Mangifera indica. b, Garcinia mangostana.
No. 1216, 200f: a, Musa nana. b, Citrus paradisi.
No. 1217, 250f: a, Punika granatum. b, Ananas comosus.
No. 1218, 325f: a, Cocos nucifera. b, Passiflora quadrangularis.
No. 1219, 5000f: a, Citrus sinensis. b, Persea gratissima.

**2000, Feb. 29 Litho. *Perf. 13¼***
**Pairs, #a-b**
**1214-1219** A283 Set of 6 *18.00 18.00*
No. 1219 is airmail.

**Bird Type of 1985**

Designs: 1100f, Dendrocygna autumnalis. 4425f, Ceryle torquata.

**2000, Apr. 3 *Perf. 14x13***
**1220** A173 1100f multi *1.75 1.75*
**1221** A173 4425f multi *7.50 7.50*

Surinam River Bridge A284

Lettering in: 1100f, Red. 1700f, Blue.

**2000, May 18**
**1222-1223** A284 Set of 2 *4.75 4.75*

**Children's Drawings Type**
Souvenir Sheet

**2000 *Perf. 13¼x13***
**1224** A281 3575f #1208, 1209 5.50 5.50

World Stamp Expo 2000, Anaheim, Stampin' the Future children's stamp design contest.

2000 Summer Olympic, Sydney A285

No. 1225, 1100f: a, Soccer. b, Track and field.
No. 1226, 3900f: a, Tennis. b, Swimming.
No. 1227: a, Soccer, diff. b, Swimming, diff.

**2000, Aug. 8 Litho. *Perf. 13¼***
**Pairs, #a-b**
**1225-1226** A285 Set of 2 *14.50 14.50*
**Souvenir Sheet**
**1227** A285 2500f Sheet of 2, #a-b *7.25 7.25*

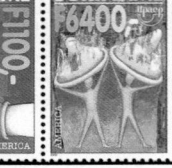

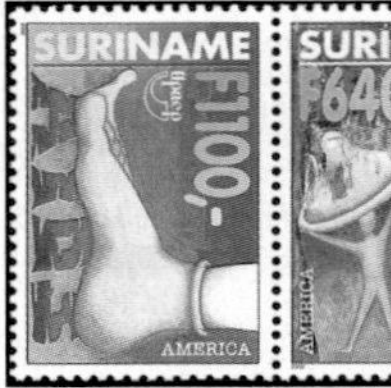

America Issue, Fight Against AIDS — A286

No. 1228: a, 1100f, Foot with condom stamping out AIDS, horiz. b, 6400f, People holding condoms.

**2000 *Perf. 13x14***
**1228** A286 Pair, #a-b *10.50 10.50*

25th Anniv. of International Agencies Ltd. as Philatelic and Numismatic Agent — A287

Designs: 125f, Paper money. 5900f, Stamps.

**2000, Nov. 24**
**1229-1230** A287 Set of 2 *7.00 7.00*
*1230a* Souvenir sheet, #1229-1230 *7.25 7.25*

Children — A288

Child: 1100f, Walking. 3900f, Breastfeeding. 2000f, With umbilical cord, horiz.

**2000, Dec. 5 *Perf. 13x14***
**1231-1232** A288 Set of 2 *6.00 6.00*
**Souvenir Sheet**
***Perf. 14x13***
**1233** A288 2000f multi *2.25 2.25*

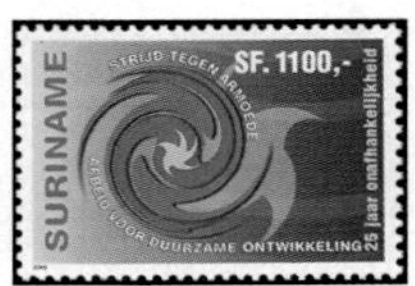
Fight Against Poverty A289

Country name in: 1100f, Green. 4900f, Red.

**2000 *Perf. 14x13***
**1234-1235** A289 Set of 2 *4.50 4.50*

Christmas — A290

Designs: 1100f, Star of Bethlehem. 3900f, Madonna and Child.
3000f, Magi with gifts, horiz.

**2000 *Perf. 13x14***
**1236-1237** A290 Set of 2 *6.75 6.75*
**Souvenir Sheet**
***Perf. 14x13***
**1238** A290 3000f multi *4.25 4.25*

No. 945a Surcharged

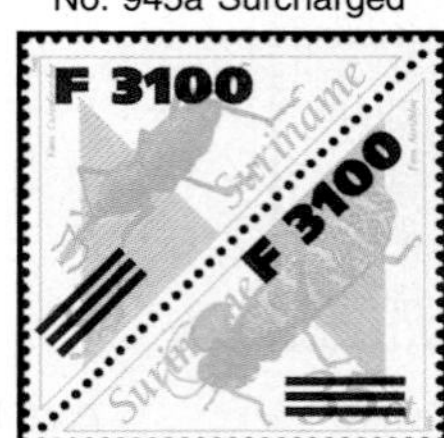

**Methods and Perfs as Before**

**2000 (?)**
**1238A** Pair 2.50 2.50
*b.* A221 1000f on 25c No. 942 .95 .95
*c.* A221 1000f on 25c No. 943 .95 .95

**1239** Pair *6.75 6.75*
*a.* A221 3100f on 35c No. 944 *2.50 2.50*
*b.* A221 3100f on 35c No. 945 *2.50 2.50*

Birds A291

No. 1240, 50f: a, Rood zwart vink tagara. b, Tyarman.
No. 1241, 175f: a, Sabaku. b, Kolibrie.
No. 1242, 200f: a, Aka. b, Timmerman.
No. 1243, 250f: a, Paarskeel cotinga. b, Zwarte kraag donfowru.
No. 1244, 825f: a, Kees. b, Stonkuyake.
No. 1245, 7500f: a, Guyanese rood cotinga. b, Butabuta.

**2001, Jan. 31 Litho. *Perf. 13¼***
**Pairs, #a-b**
**1240-1245** A291 Set of 6 *18.00 18.00*
No. 1245 is airmail.

**Traffic Signs Type of 2000**

**2001 Litho. *Perf. 13x14***
**1246** A282 2000f No parking 1.90 1.90
**1247** A282 4000f Drawbridge 3.75 3.75
**1248** A282 4000f Tractor, No entry 3.75 3.75

Issued: 2000f, 3/8; No. 1247, 4/25; No. 1248, 9/12.

UN Women's Human Rights Campaign A292

Youth Philately A293

Designs: 1400f, Female and male symbols. 4600f, Woman.

**2001, Mar. 15 Litho. *Perf. 13x14***
**1249-1250** A292 Set of 2 6.00 6.00

**2001, Apr. 25**

Children's art by: 650f, Bhoelai Surender Kumar. 5350f, Sharon Cameron.

**1251-1252** A293 Set of 2 6.00 6.00

**Bird Type of 1985**

Designs: 4500f, Charadrius collaris. 9000f, Bubo virginianus.

**2001, May 10 *Perf. 14x13***
**1253** A173 4500f multi 5.25 5.25
**1254** A173 9000f multi 10.50 10.50

Fruit — A294

Designs: 150f, Sapotille. 200f, Noni vrucht. 800fr, Baby bananas. 1200f, Mope. 1700f, Pommerak.

**2001, July 20 Litho. *Perf. 12¾x13½***
**1255-1259** A294 Set of 5 3.75 3.75

America Issue — A295

Paramaribo buildings: Nos. 1260a, 1261a, 1700f, Bishop's house. Nos. 1260b, 1261b, 7300f, Presidential palace.
Illustration reduced.

**2001, Sept. 12 Litho. *Perf. 14x13***
**Country Name in Red**
**1260** A295 Pair, #a-b 9.75 9.75
**Souvenir Sheet**
**Country Name in Green**
***Perf. 13¼x13***
**1261** A295 Sheet of 2, #a-b 9.75 9.75

Stamp Day — A296

Designs: No. 1262a, 3750f, #648 (green background). No. 1262b, 5250f, #29 (red background).
No. 1263a, 3750f, #648 (red background). No. 1263b, 5250f, #29 (orange background).

**2001, Oct. 19 *Perf. 13x14***
**1262** A296 Pair, #a-b 9.75 9.75
**Souvenir Sheet**
***Perf. 13x13¼***
**1263** A296 Sheet of 2, #a-b 9.75 9.75

Christmas A297

Children's Sports — A298

**2001, Nov. 2 *Perf. 13¼***
**1264** A297 1700f blue & multi 1.50 1.50
***Perf. 14x13***
**1265** A298 5000f red & multi 4.50 4.50
**Souvenir Sheet**
***Perf. 13¼x13***
**1266** Sheet of 2 6.00 6.00
*a.* A297 1700f green & multi 1.50 1.50
*b.* A298 5000f blue & multi 4.50 4.50

No. 947a Surcharged in Gold

**2001, Dec. 7 Litho. *Perf. 13½***
**1266C** Pair 4.50 4.50
*d.* A221 2500f on 50c No. 946 2.25 2.25
*e.* A221 2500f on 50c No. 947 2.25 2.25

**Traffic Signs Type of 2000**

**2001-02 *Perf. 13x14***
**1267** A282 4000f Pedestrian crossing 3.75 3.75
**1268** A282 4000f Yield 3.75 3.75

Issued: No. 1267, 12/7/01; No. 1268, 2/13/02.

Parrots
A299

No. 1269, 150f: a, Deroptyus acciptrinus. b, Amazona achrocephala.
No. 1270, 200f: a, Ara manilata. b, Amazona dufresniana.
No. 1271, 800f: a, Ara severa. b, Pionites melanocephala.
No. 1272, 1200f: a, Ara nobilis. b, Pionus fiscus.
No. 1273, 1700f: a, Ara chloroptera. b, Pionopsitta caicca.
No. 1274, 5325f: a, Ara macao. b, Amazona farinosa.

**2002, Jan. 9** ***Perf. 13¼***

**Pairs, #a-b**

**1269-1274** A299 Set of 6 17.50 17.50

No. 1274 is airmail.

### Traffic Signs Type of 2000

**2002, Apr. 17 Litho.** ***Perf. 13x14***

**1275** A282 4000f U turn 3.75 3.75

### Traffic Signs Type of 2000

**2002-03 Litho.** ***Perf. 12¾x14***

**1276** A282 4000f Pedestrian path 3.75 3.75
**1277** A282 4000f Train crossing without barriers 3.75 3.75
**1278** A282 4000f Motorcycles 3.75 3.75
*Nos. 1276-1278 (3)* 11.25 11.25

Issued: No. 1276, 6/19/02; No. 1277, 9/20/02; No. 1278, 2/13/03.

Costumes
A300

Birds
A301

Costumes of: Nos. 1279a, 1279c, 1279e, 1279g, 1279i, 1279k, Various men. Nos. 1279b, 1279d, 1279f, 1279h, 1279j, 1279l, Various women.

**2002, May 15** ***Perf. 12¾x13¼***

**1279** Horiz. strip of 12 17.00 17.00
*a.-b.* A300 150f Either single .20 .20
*c.-d.* A300 200f Either single .20 .20
*e.-f.* A300 800f Either single .75 .75
*g.-h.* A300 1200f Either single 1.10 1.10
*i.-j.* A300 1700f Either single 1.60 1.60
*k.-l.* A300 4950f Either single 4.50 4.50

**2002, June 19** ***Perf. 12¾x14***

**1280** A301 5000f Royal flycatcher 4.75 4.75
**1281** A301 8500f Swampufowru 7.75 7.75

Amphilex 2002 Intl. Stamp Exhibition, Amsterdam — A302

No. 1282: a, 1700f, Netherlands #244 (yellow background). b, 6800f, Netherlands #103 (maroon background).
No. 1283: a, 1700f, Like No. 1282a (maroon background). b, 6800f, Like No. 1282b (yellow background).
Illustration reduced.

**2002, Aug. 30** ***Perf. 13¼x12¾***

**1282** A302 Horiz. pair, #a-b 7.75 7.75

**Souvenir Sheet**

**1283** A302 Sheet of 2, #a-b 7.75 7.75

Souvenir Sheet
No. 1230a Overprinted in Gold

**2002, Aug. 30 Litho.** ***Perf. 13x14***

**1284** A287 Sheet of 2 5.75 5.75
*a.* 250f on 125f #1229 .25 .25
*b.* 5900f #1230 overprinted 5.50 5.50

America Issue - Youth, Education and Literacy — A303

No. 1285 — Letters, numbers and: a, 1700f, Stylized head and question mark. b, 7300f, "X" in signature box.

**2002, Sept. 20** ***Perf. 13¼x12¾***

**1285** A303 Horiz. pair, #a-b 8.25 8.25

Christmas
A304

Designs: No. 1286, 1700f, Unclothed Santa Claus and clothing (light blue background). No. 1287, 5000f, Christmas tree, decorations and gifts (green background).
No. 1288: a, 1700f, Like No. 1286 (yellow background). b, 5000f, Like No. 1287 (blue background).

**2002, Nov. 6**

**1286-1287** A304 Set of 2 6.25 6.25

**Souvenir Sheet**

**1288** A304 Sheet of 2, #a-b 6.25 6.25

### Nos. 949a, 953a Surcharged Like No. 1266C in Gold or Silver

**2002 ? Litho.** ***Perf. 13½***

**1289** Pair 4.75 4.75
*a.* A221 2500f on 100c #948 2.25 2.25
*b.* A221 2500f on 100c #949 2.25 2.25
**1290** Pair 7.00 7.00
*a.* A221 3750f on 220c #952 (S) 3.50 3.50
*b.* A221 3750f on 220c #953 (S) 3.50 3.50

Birds — A305

No. 1291: a, Falco deiroleucus. b, Lophornis ornatus. c, Touit purpurata. d, Thanlurania furcata. e, Myrmeciza ferruginea. f, Pteroglossus aracari. g, Cotinga cotinga. h, Granatellus pelzelni. i, Euphonia musica. j, Pitangus lictor. k, Cacicus haemorrhous. l, Columba speciosa.

**2003, Jan. 9** ***Perf. 13¼x14***

**1291** Block of 12 17.00 17.00
*a.-b.* A305 150f Either single .20 .20
*c.-d.* A305 200f Either single .20 .20
*e.-f.* A305 800f Either single .75 .75
*g.-h.* A305 1200f Either single 1.10 1.10
*i.-j.* A305 1700f Either single 1.60 1.60
*k.-l.* A305 4950f Either single 4.50 4.50

### No. 951a Surcharged in Silver Like No. 1266C

**2002, Dec. 30 Litho.** ***Perf. 13½***

**1292** Pair 5.00 5.00
*a.* A221 2750f on 175c #950 2.50 2.50
*b.* A221 2750f on 175c #951 2.50 2.50

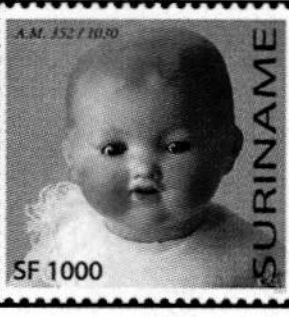


Dolls — A306

No. 1293: a, A. M. 352/1030. b, S&H 1079, 1892. c, Jumeau, 1895 (denomination in white). d, Jumeau, 1895 (denomination in red). e, A. M. 390, 1900. f, Minerva, 1900. g, K&R 126, 1905. h, K&R, 1905. i, Handwerck, 1905. j, SFBJ, 1907. k, A. M. 980, 1920. l, K&R, 1910.

**2003, May 12** ***Perf. 13½x14***

**1293** Block of 12 9.75 9.75
*a.-l.* A306 1000f Any single .80 .80

A307

SURINAME
F5400

A308

Designs: 150f, Izaak Enschedé. 800f, Old building of Johann Enschedé Printers, horiz. 1700f, Surinam #7. 3850f, First Surinam banknote printed by Enschedé, horiz.
7500f, Like 150f.

***Perf. 12¾x13½, 13½x12¾***

**2003, June 3**

**1294-1297** A307 Set of 4 5.25 5.25

**Souvenir Sheet**

**1298** A307 7500f multi 6.00 6.00

Johann Enschedé and Sons, printers, 300th anniv.

**2003, Sept. 3** ***Perf. 12¾x14***

Birds: 5400f, Anthracothorax viridigula. 6600f, Campephilus melanoleucos.

**1299** A308 5400f multi 4.25 4.25
**1300** A308 6600f multi 5.25 5.25

### Traffic Signs Type of 2000

**2003, Sept. 3 Litho.** ***Perf. 12¾x14***

**1301** A282 4000f 10% grade 3.25 3.25

America Issue - Flora and Fauna — A309

No. 1302: a, 1700f, Faya lobi. b, 8500f, Puma.
Illustration reduced.

**2003, Sept. 20 Litho.** ***Perf. 14x12¾***

**1302** A309 Horiz. pair, #a-b 8.25 8.25
*c.* Souvenir sheet, #1302 8.25 8.25

Nos. 889a, 929a Surcharged

### Methods and Perfs as Before

**2003**

**1303** Pair 5.50 5.50
*a.* A172 3500f on 1c on 5c #928 2.75 2.75
*b.* A172 3500f on 1c on 5c #929 2.75 2.75
**1304** Pair 5.50 5.50
*a.* A172 3500f on 2c on 10c #888 2.75 2.75
*b.* A172 3500f on 2c on 10c #889 2.75 2.75

Issued: No. 1303, 11/1; No. 1304, 12/1.

Christmas — A310

Designs: 1700f, Children, dog, toy horse. 5300f, Woman holding candle.

**2003, Nov. 6 Litho.** ***Perf. 12¾x14***

**1306** A310 1700f multi 1.40 1.40
**1307** A310 5300f multi 4.25 4.25
*a.* Horiz. pair, #1306-1307 + central label 5.75 5.75
*b.* Souvenir sheet, #1306-1307 5.75 5.75

Powered Flight, Cent.
A311

Designs: 1700f, Santos-Dumont 14bis, first European flight, 1906. 5300f, Replica of 1903 aircraft by Richard Pearse, New Zealand.

**2003, Dec. 13** ***Perf. 14x12¾***

**1308** A311 1700f multi 1.40 1.40
**1309** A311 5300f multi 4.25 4.25
*a.* Souvenir sheet, #1308-1309 5.75 5.75

The Surinam dollar replaced the florin in January 2004 at an exchange rate of 1000 florins to 1 dollar. Nos. 1310-1313, though issued after the introduction of the new currency, have denominations expressed in florins.

Butterflies
A312

No. 1310: a, Anartia amathea. b, Vanessa carye. c, Papilio demetrius. d, Precis octavia. e, Papilio blumei. f, Papilio aritodemus ponceanus. g, Zerynthia rumina. h, Parides gundlachianus. i, Ornithoptera priamus. j, Lyropteryx apollonia. k, Agrias narcissus. l, Elzunia bonplandii.

**2004, Jan. 12** ***Perf. 12¾x14***

**1310** Block of 12 22.00 22.00
*a.-b.* A312 150f Either single .20 .20
*c.-d.* A312 200f Either single .20 .20
*e.-f.* A312 800f Either single .65 .65
*g.-h.* A312 1200f Either single .95 .95
*i.-j.* A312 1700f Either single 1.40 1.40
*k.-l.* A312 L Either single 7.50 7.50

Nos. 1310k-1310l sold for 9500f on day of issue.

### Traffic Signs Type of 2000

**2004 Litho.** ***Perf. 12¾x14***

**1311** A282 4000f Horse and rider crossing 3.25 3.25
**1312** A282 4000f Large vehicles prohibited 3.25 3.25
*a.* Souvenir sheet, #1278, 1301, 1311, 1312 13.00 13.00

Issued: Nos. 1311-1312, 3/31; No. 1312a, 10/1.

Mailboxes of the World — A313

No. 1313: a, Indonesia. b, Brazil. c, Macao. d, Germany. e, Uruguay. f, Republic of Korea. g, Oman. h, Mexico. i, Australia. j, Switzerland. k, Hong Kong. l, United States.

**2004, May 6**

| | | | |
|---|---|---|---|
| **1313** | Block of 12 | 25.00 | 25.00 |
| *a.-b.* | A313 150f Either single | .20 | .20 |
| *c.-d.* | A313 200f Either single | .20 | .20 |
| *e.-f.* | A313 800f Either single | .65 | .65 |
| *g.-h.* | A313 1200f Either single | .95 | .95 |
| *i.-j.* | A313 1700f Either single | 1.40 | 1.40 |
| *k.-l.* | A313 K Either single | 9.00 | 9.00 |

Nos. 1313k-1313l each sold for 11,500f ($11.50) on day of issue.

Greek Amphorae — A314

No. 1314 — Inscriptions: a, Athena en Poseidon. b, Wedren. c, Athena Promachus, 363/62 v. C. d, Hippodamia ontvoerd door Pelops, 415 v. C. e, Winnaar muziekconcours, 440-430 v. C. f, Wedren 485-470 v. C. g, Vaashals: speer-en discuswerpers. h, Wedren vier paarden. i, Heracles met leeuw van Nemea, 520 v. C. j, Amfoor, 566 v. C. k, Winnaar muziekconcours (no handles). l, Winnaar muziekconcours (with handles).

No. 1315 — Portions of an amphora: a, $2, Left. b, $3, Center. c, $5, Right.

**2004, July 1**

| | | | |
|---|---|---|---|
| **1314** | Block of 12 | 28.00 | 28.00 |
| *a.-b.* | A314 5c Either single | .20 | .20 |
| *c.-d.* | A314 15c Either single | .20 | .20 |
| *e.-f.* | A314 20c Either single | .20 | .20 |
| *g.-h.* | A314 45c Either single | .35 | .35 |
| *i.-j.* | A314 80c Either single | .60 | .60 |
| *k.-l.* | A314 M Either single | 12.50 | 12.50 |

**Souvenir Sheet**

**1315** A314 Sheet of 3, #a-c 8.00 8.00

2004 Summer Olympics, Athens (No. 1315). Nos. 1314k-1314l each sold for $16 on day of issue, and are airmail.

America Issue - Birds — A315

Designs: $1.70, Duck. $12, Parrots.

**2004, Sept. 16** ***Perf. 14x12¾***

| | | | |
|---|---|---|---|
| **1316-1317** | A315 Set of 2 | 11.00 | 11.00 |
| *1317a* | Souvenir sheet, #1316-1317 | 11.00 | 11.00 |

Birds — A316

No. 1318: a, Chloroceryle inda. b, Brotogeris chrysopterus. c, Buteo magnirostris. d, Buteo albicaudatus. e, Calliphlox amethystina (facing left). f, Calliphlox amethystina (facing right). g, Harpagus diodon. h, Aratinga pertinax. i, Chlorocersyle amazona. j, Galbula galbula. k, Buteogallus aequinoctialis. l, Polyborus plancus.

**2004, Oct. 21** ***Perf. 12¾x14***

| | | | |
|---|---|---|---|
| **1318** | Block of 12 | 28.00 | 28.00 |
| *a.-b.* | A316 5c Either single | .20 | .20 |
| *c.-d.* | A316 15c Either single | .20 | .20 |
| *e.-f.* | A316 20c Either single | .20 | .20 |
| *g.-h.* | A316 45c Either single | .35 | .35 |
| *i.-j.* | A316 80c Either single | .60 | .60 |
| *k.-l.* | A316 M Either single | 12.50 | 12.50 |

Nos. 1318k-1318l each sold for $16 on day of issue, and are airmail.

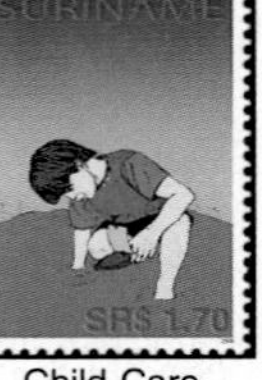
Child Care A317

Christmas A318

**2004, Nov. 18 Litho.** ***Perf. 12¾x14***

| | | | |
|---|---|---|---|
| **1319** | A317 $1.70 multi | 1.40 | 1.40 |
| **1320** | A318 $7.70 multi | 6.25 | 6.25 |
| *a.* | Souvenir sheet, #1319-1320 | 7.75 | 7.75 |

Teddy Bears — A319

No. 1321: a, Bing, 1919. b, Steiff "Teddy Clown," 1926. c, Steiff "Teddy Girl," 1905. d, Steiff, 1905. e, Steif "Elliot," 1907. f, Ideal "Aloysius," 1907. g, Steiff, 1936. h, Steif "Zotty," 1951. i, Steiff, 1910. j, Steiff "Titanic," 1912. k, Steiff "Berlin," 1985. l, Aux Nations, 1903.

No. 1322: a, Blue mohair, 1938-52. b, Musical bear, 1937. c, Red mohair, 1908. d, Shaggy beige mohair, 1908. e, Ally bear, 1916. f, National bear, 1917. g, Cowboy, 1940s. h, Coronation bear, 1953. i, Tumbling bear, 1920-30s. j, Messenger bear, 1923. k, Bear on a tricycle, 1958. l, Michi Takahashi, 1999.

**2004-05 Litho.** ***Perf. 12¾x14***

| | | | |
|---|---|---|---|
| **1321** | Block of 12 | 21.00 | 21.00 |
| *a.-b.* | A319 5c Either single | .20 | .20 |
| *c.-d.* | A319 15c Either single | .20 | .20 |
| *e.-f.* | A319 20c Either single | .20 | .20 |
| *g.-h.* | A319 45c Either single | .35 | .35 |
| *i.-j.* | A319 80c Either single | .65 | .65 |
| *k.-l.* | A319 K Either single | 9.00 | 9.00 |
| **1322** | Block of 12 | 30.00 | 30.00 |
| *a.-b.* | A319 5c Either single | .20 | .20 |
| *c.-d.* | A319 15c Either single | .20 | .20 |
| *e.-f.* | A319 20c Either single | .20 | .20 |
| *g.-h.* | A319 45c Either single | .35 | .35 |
| *i.-j.* | A319 80c Either single | .65 | .65 |
| *k.-l.* | A319 N Either single | 13.50 | 13.50 |

Issued: No. 1321, 2004; No. 1322, 3/1/05. Nos. 1321k-1321l each sold for $11.50 on day of issue, and are airmail. Nos. 1322k-1322l each sold for $17 on day of issue, and are airmail.

Butterflies — A320

No. 1323: a, Papilio chikae. b, Iphiclides podalirius. c, Paraphnaeus. d, Morpho didius. e, Delias eucharis. f, Parides sesostris. g, Baronia brevicornis. h, Graphium agamemnon. i, Papilio palinurus. j, Ornithoptera meridionalis. k, Battus bhilenor. l, Eurytides bellerophon.

**2005, Jan. 5**

| | | | |
|---|---|---|---|
| **1323** | Block of 12 | 30.00 | 30.00 |
| *a.-b.* | A320 5c Either single | .20 | .20 |
| *c.-d.* | A320 15c Either single | .20 | .20 |
| *e.-f.* | A320 20c Either single | .20 | .20 |
| *g.-h.* | A320 45c Either single | .35 | .35 |
| *i.-j.* | A320 80c Either single | .60 | .60 |
| *k.-l.* | A320 N Either single | 13.50 | 13.50 |

Nos. 1323k-1323l each sold for $17 on day of issue, and are airmail.

Ships A321

No. 1324: a, Louis Roux, Altana. b, Fanerom Eni. c, Nafsika. d, Aristeidis Glykas. e, G. D'Esposito. f, G. D'Esposito, diff.

**2005, May 4 Litho.** ***Perf. 14x12¾***

| | | | |
|---|---|---|---|
| **1324** | Block of 6 | 17.00 | 17.00 |
| *a.* | A321 5c multi | .20 | .20 |
| *b.* | A321 15c multi | .20 | .20 |
| *c.* | A321 20c multi | .20 | .20 |
| *d.* | A321 80c multi | .60 | .60 |
| *e.* | A321 $1.70 multi | 1.40 | 1.40 |
| *f.* | A321 P multi | 14.00 | 14.00 |

No. 1324f is airmail and sold for $18 on day of issue.

Orchids — A322

No. 1325: a, Vanda hybrid. b, Phalaenopsis hybrid, dark pink flowers. c, Dendrobium hybrid, pink flowers. d, Dendrobium hybrid, dark red flowers with foliage in background. e, Vanda hybrid, diff. f, Peristeria elata. g, Spathoglottis hybrid. h, Dendrobium hybrid, yellow orange flowers. i, Vanda sanderiana. j, Phalaenopsis hybrid, peach flowers. k, Phalaenopsis hybrid, pink flowers. l, Phalaenopsis hybrid, white flowers.

**2005, June 29** ***Perf. 12¾x14***

| | | | |
|---|---|---|---|
| **1325** | Block of 12 | 22.50 | 22.50 |
| *a.-b.* | A322 5c Either single | .20 | .20 |
| *c.-d.* | A322 15c Either single | .20 | .20 |
| *e.-f.* | A322 20c Either single | .20 | .20 |
| *g.-h.* | A322 45c Either single | .35 | .35 |
| *i.-j.* | A322 80c Either single | .60 | .60 |
| *k.-l.* | A322 Q Either single | 10.00 | 10.00 |

Nos. 1325k and 1325 l are airmail and each sold for $12.50 on day of issue. See No. 1337.

America Issue, Fight Against Poverty A323

Designs: $1.70, Teacher and children. $14.50, Farmer, oxen and plow.
$14, Teacher and children, diff.

**2005** ***Perf. 14x12¾, 12¾x14***

**1326-1327** A323 Set of 2 13.00 13.00

**Souvenir Sheet**

***Perf. 12¾x13¼***

**1328** A323 $14 multi 11.50 11.50

Issued: Nos. 1326-1327, 9/14; No. 1328, 9/17.

**Birds Type of 2004**

No. 1329: a, Porphyrula flavirostris. b, Asio clamator. c, Herpetotheres cashinnans. d, Jacana jacana. e, Touit batavica. f, Dendrocygna autumnalis. g, Coccyzus minor. h, Busarellus nigricollis. i, Lophostrix cristata. j, Otus choliba. k, Chrysolampis mosquitus. l, Pyrrhula picta.

**2005, Oct. 19** ***Perf. 12¾x14***

| | | | |
|---|---|---|---|
| **1329** | Block of 12 | 35.00 | 35.00 |
| *a.-b.* | A316 5c Either single | .20 | .20 |
| *c.-d.* | A316 15c Either single | .20 | .20 |
| *e.-f.* | A316 20c Either single | .20 | .20 |
| *g.-h.* | A316 80c Either single | .65 | .65 |
| *i.-j.* | A316 $1.80 Either single | 1.40 | 1.40 |
| *k.-l.* | A316 P Either single | 14.50 | 14.50 |

Nos. 1329k and 1329 l are airmail and each sold for $18 on day of issue.

Children — A324

Designs (country name in red): 80c, Girl jumping rope. $9.50, Boy on swing.

No. 1332 — Country name in white: a, Girl jumping rope, diff. b, Boy on swing, diff.

**2005, Nov. 16** ***Perf. 12¾x13¼***

**1330-1331** A324 Set of 2 7.50 7.50

**Souvenir Sheet**

**1332** A324 $5 Sheet of 2, #a-b 7.50 7.50

No. 891a Surcharged

**Methods and Perfs as Before**

**2005, Dec. 1**

| | | | |
|---|---|---|---|
| **1333** | Pair | 5.25 | 5.25 |
| *a.* | A172 $3.50 on 3c on 50c #891a | 2.60 | 2.60 |
| *b.* | A172 $3.50 on 3c on 50c #891b | 2.60 | 2.60 |

Europa Stamps, 50th Anniv. — A325

Designs: $1, Netherlands #379. $2, Netherlands #369. $9, Netherlands #375.

**2006, Jan. 4 Litho.** ***Perf. 12¾x13¼***

| | | | |
|---|---|---|---|
| **1334-1336** | A325 Set of 3 | 8.75 | 8.75 |
| *1336a* | Souvenir sheet, #1334-1336 | 8.75 | 8.75 |

**Orchids Type of 2005**

No. 1337: a, Dendrobium hybrid, yellow flowers. b, Dendrobium hybrid, white flowers. c, Phalaenopsis hybrid, light purple flowers. d, Phalaenopsis hybrid, pink flowers. e, Vanda hybrid, white flowers. f, Vanda hybrid, purple flowers. g, Dendrobium hybrid, purple and white flowers. h, Arachnis hybrid. i, Vanda hybrid, light orange flowers. j, Vanda hybrid, speckled purple flowers. k, Complex hybrid, orange flowers. l, Vanda hybrid, purple and white flowers.

**2006, Feb. 15** ***Perf. 12¾x14***

| | | | |
|---|---|---|---|
| **1337** | Block of 12 | 28.00 | 28.00 |
| *a.-b.* | A322 5c Either single | .20 | .20 |
| *c.-d.* | A322 15c Either single | .20 | .20 |
| *e.-f.* | A322 20c Either single | .20 | .20 |
| *g.-h.* | A322 45c Either single | .35 | .35 |
| *i.-j.* | A322 80c Either single | .60 | .60 |
| *k.-l.* | A322 Q Either single | 12.50 | 12.50 |

Nos. 1337k and 1337 l are airmail and each sold for $17.50 on day of issue.

Birds — A326

No. 1338: a, Phaethornis ruber. b, Threnetes leucurus. c, Podager nacunda. d, Columbina passerina. e, Leptotila rufaxilla. f, Claravis pretiosa. g, Campylopterus largipennis. h, Otus choliba. i, Porzana albicollis. j, Amazilia fimbriata. k, Ciccata virgata. l, Nyctidromus albicollis.

**2006, May 15 Litho.** ***Perf. 14x12¾***

| | | | |
|---|---|---|---|
| **1338** | Block of 12 | 28.00 | 28.00 |
| *a.-b.* | A326 5c Either single | .20 | .20 |
| *c.-d.* | A326 15c Either single | .20 | .20 |
| *e.-f.* | A326 20c Either single | .20 | .20 |
| *g.-h.* | A326 45c Either single | .30 | .30 |
| *i.-j.* | A326 80c Either single | .55 | .55 |
| *k.-l.* | A326 Q Either single | 12.50 | 12.50 |

Nos. 1338k-1338l each sold for $17.50, and are airmail.

Nobel Laureates — A327

No. 1339: a, Aung San Suu Kyi, Peace, 1991. b, Milton Friedman, Economics, 1976. c, Marie Curie, Chemistry, 1911. d, Johannes Diderik van der Waals, Physics, 1910. e, Selma Lagerlöf, Literature, 1909. f, Gary S. Becker, Economics, 1992.

**2006, June 26** *Perf. 12¾x13¼*

| | | | |
|---|---|---|---|
| **1339** | Block of 6 | 8.50 | 8.50 |
| *a.* | A327 20c multi | .20 | .20 |
| *b.* | A327 $1.20 multi | .85 | .85 |
| *c.* | A327 $1.70 multi | 1.25 | 1.25 |
| *d.* | A327 $2 multi | 1.40 | 1.40 |
| *e.* | A327 $3 multi | 2.25 | 2.25 |
| *f.* | A327 $3.50 multi | 2.50 | 2.50 |

America Issue, Energy Conservation A328

Designs: 80c, Solar-powered airplane. $16.20, Windmill.

No. 1342: a, $3.50, Glider. b, $12.50, Windmills.

**2006, Sept. 15** *Perf. 14*

**1340-1341** A328 Set of 2 12.50 12.50

**Souvenir Sheet**

**1342** A328 Sheet of 2, #a-b 12.00 12.00

Fish — A329

No. 1343: a, Crown betta. b, Barbus barilioides. c, Macropodus opercularis. d, Xiphophorus maculatus. e, Acanthurus lineatus. f, Carassius auratus.

**2006, Oct. 15** *Perf. 13¼x12¾*

| | | | |
|---|---|---|---|
| **1343** | Block of 6 | 14.50 | 14.50 |
| *a.* | A329 $1.20 multi | .85 | .85 |
| *b.* | A329 $1.70 multi | 1.25 | 1.25 |
| *c.* | A329 $2 multi | 1.40 | 1.40 |
| *d.* | A329 $3 multi | 2.25 | 2.25 |
| *e.* | A329 $3.50 multi | 2.50 | 2.50 |
| *f.* | A329 $8.60 multi | 6.25 | 6.25 |

Child Care — A330

Christmas A331

**2006, Nov. 6** *Perf. 14*

**1344** A330 $4 shown 3.00 3.00
**1345** A331 $9.20 shown 6.75 6.75

**Souvenir Sheet**

| | | | |
|---|---|---|---|
| **1346** | Sheet of 2 | 5.00 | 5.00 |
| *a.* | A330 80c Children with ball | .60 | .60 |
| *b.* | A331 $6 Stained glass, diff. | 4.25 | 4.25 |

No. 447 Surcharged in Brown

**Methods and Perfs As Before**

**2006, Dec. 1**

**1347** A111 $3.25 on 1c #447 2.40 2.40
**1348** A111 $3.75 on 1c #447 2.75 2.75

Primates — A332

No. 1349: a, Hylobates lar. b, Leontopithecus rosalia. c, Saguinus imperator. d, Callithrix geoffroyi. e, Callithrix argentata. f, Pygathrix nemaeus nemaeus. g, Saimiri sciureus. h, Douc langur. i, Cercopithecus neglectus. j, Alouatta caraya. k, Verreaux sitaka. l, Pan troglodytes.

**2006, Dec. 13** *Perf. 12¾x13¼*

| | | | |
|---|---|---|---|
| **1349** | Block of 12 | 24.00 | 24.00 |
| *a.* | A332 R multi | .20 | .20 |
| *b.* | A332 20c multi | .20 | .20 |
| *c.* | A332 45c multi | .35 | .35 |
| *d.* | A332 80c multi | .60 | .60 |
| *e.* | A332 $1.20 multi | .90 | .90 |
| *f.* | A332 $1.70 multi | 1.25 | 1.25 |
| *g.* | A332 $2 multi | 1.40 | 1.40 |
| *h.* | A332 $3 multi | 2.25 | 2.25 |
| *i.* | A332 $3.50 multi | 2.50 | 2.50 |
| *j.* | A332 $4 multi | 3.00 | 3.00 |
| *k.* | A332 $5 multi | 3.75 | 3.75 |
| *l.* | A332 $10 multi | 7.25 | 7.25 |

No. 1349a sold for 15c on day of issue.

**Bird Type of 2004**

**2006, Dec. 20** *Perf. 12¾x14*

**1350** A316 $10 Phaethornis superciliosus 7.25 7.25

Printed in sheets of 2 + label.

Orchids — A333

No. 1351: a, Cattleya labiata. b, Vuylstekeara. c, Cymbidium. d, Odontoglossum pestcatorei. e, Odontocidium f, Odontioda. g, Vanda. h, Cattleya. i, Paphiopedilum insigne. j, Phalaenopsis. k, Thunia. l, Oncidium.

**2007, Jan. 3** *Perf. 12¾x13¼*

| | | | |
|---|---|---|---|
| **1351** | Block of 12 | 24.00 | 24.00 |
| *a.* | A333 S multi | .20 | .20 |
| *b.* | A333 20c multi | .20 | .20 |
| *c.* | A333 45c multi | .35 | .35 |
| *d.* | A333 80c multi | .60 | .60 |
| *e.* | A333 $1.20 multi | .90 | .90 |
| *f.* | A333 $1.70 multi | 1.25 | 1.25 |
| *g.* | A333 $2 multi | 1.40 | 1.40 |
| *h.* | A333 $3 multi | 2.25 | 2.25 |
| *i.* | A333 $3.50 multi | 2.50 | 2.50 |
| *j.* | A333 $4 multi | 3.00 | 3.00 |
| *k.* | A333 $5 multi | 3.75 | 3.75 |
| *l.* | A333 $10 multi | 7.25 | 7.25 |

No. 1351a sold for 10c on day of issue.

Butterflies A334

No. 1352: a, Great spangled fritillary. b, Peacock pansy. c, Viceroy. d, Unidentified taxco. e, Tropical buckeye. f, Limenitis popul.

**2007, Feb. 14** *Perf. 14*

| | | | |
|---|---|---|---|
| **1352** | Block of 6 | 9.00 | 9.00 |
| *a.* | A334 T multi | .20 | .20 |
| *b.* | A334 $1.20 multi | .85 | .85 |
| *c.* | A334 $1.70 multi | 1.25 | 1.25 |
| *d.* | A334 $2 multi | 1.40 | 1.40 |
| *e.* | A334 $3 multi | 2.25 | 2.25 |
| *f.* | A334 $4 multi | 3.00 | 3.00 |

No. 1352a sold for 5c on day of issue.

## SEMI-POSTAL STAMPS

SP1

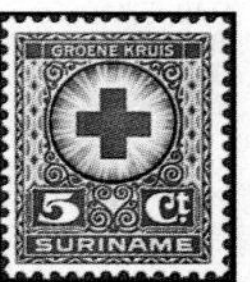


SP2

Green Cross — SP3

*Perf. 12½*

**1927, Aug. 1** **Unwmk.** **Photo.**

**B1** SP1 2c (+ 2c) bl blk & grn 1.10 1.00
**B2** SP2 5c (+ 3c) vio & grn 1.10 1.00
**B3** SP3 10c (+ 3c) ver & grn 2.00 1.75
*Nos. B1-B3 (3)* 4.20 3.75
Set, never hinged 10.50

Surtax was given to the Green Cross Society, which promotes public health services.

Nurse and Patient SP4

Good Samaritan SP5

**1928, Dec. 1** *Perf. 11½*

**B4** SP4 1½c (+ 1½c) ultra 4.50 4.50
**B5** SP4 2c (+ 2c) bl grn 4.50 4.50
**B6** SP4 5c (+ 3c) vio 4.50 4.50
**B7** SP4 7½c (+ 2½c) ver 4.50 4.50
*Nos. B4-B7 (4)* 18.00 18.00
Set, never hinged 67.50

The surtax on these stamps was for a fund to combat indigenous diseases.

**1929, Dec. 1** *Perf. 12½*

**B8** SP5 1½c (+ 1½c) grn 6.75 6.75
**B9** SP5 2c (+ 2c) scar 6.75 6.75
**B10** SP5 5c (+ 3c) ultra 6.75 6.75
**B11** SP5 6c (+ 4c) blk 6.75 6.75
*Nos. B8-B11 (4)* 27.00 27.00
Set, never hinged 72.50

Surtax for the Green Cross Society.

Surinam Mother and Child — SP6

**1931, Dec. 14**

**B12** SP6 1½c (+ 1½c) blk 4.75 4.75
**B13** SP6 2c (+ 2c) car rose 4.75 4.75
**B14** SP6 5c (+ 3c) ultra 4.75 4.75
**B15** SP6 6c (+ 4c) dp grn 4.75 4.75
*Nos. B12-B15 (4)* 19.00 19.00
Set, never hinged 45.00

The surtax was for Child Welfare Societies.

Designs Symbolical of the Creed of the Moravians
SP7 SP8

**1935, Aug. 1** *Perf. 13x14*

**B16** SP7 1c (+ ½c) dk brn 6.00 6.00
**B17** SP7 2c (+ 1c) dp ultra 6.00 6.00
**B18** SP8 3c (+ 1½c) grn 7.50 7.50
**B19** SP8 4c (+ 2c) red org 7.50 7.50
**B20** SP8 5c (+ 2½c) blk brn 9.00 9.00
**B21** SP7 10c (+ 5c) car 9.00 9.00
*Nos. B16-B21 (6)* 45.00 45.00
Set, never hinged 90.00

200th anniv. of the founding of the Moravian Mission in Surinam.

Surinam Child — SP9

**1936, Dec. 14** *Perf. 12½*

**B22** SP9 2c (+ 1c) dk grn 2.75 2.75
**B23** SP9 3c (+ 1½c) dk bl 2.75 2.75
**B24** SP9 5c (+ 2½c) brn blk 4.00 4.00
**B25** SP9 10c (+ 5c) lake 4.00 4.00
*Nos. B22-B25 (4)* 13.50 13.50
Set, never hinged 26.50

Surtax for baby food and the Green Cross Society.

"Emancipation" SP10

Surinam Girl SP11

**1938, June 1** **Litho.** *Perf. 12½x12*

**B26** SP10 2½c (+ 2c) dk bl grn 2.40 1.90

**Photo.**

**B27** SP11 3c (+ 2c) vio blk 2.40 1.90
**B28** SP11 5c (+ 3c) dk brn 2.60 2.25
**B29** SP11 7½c (+ 5c) indigo 2.60 2.25
*Nos. B26-B29 (4)* 10.00 8.30
Set, never hinged 20.00

75th anniv. of the abolition of slavery in Surinam. Surtax to Slavery Remembrance Committee.

Creole Woman — SP12

Javanese Woman — SP13

Hindustani Woman — SP14

American Indian Woman — SP15

**1940, Jan. 8** **Engr.** *Perf. 13x14*

**B30** SP12 2½c (+ 2c) dk grn 3.00 3.00
**B31** SP13 3c (+ 2c) red org 3.00 3.00
**B32** SP14 5c (+ 3c) dp bl 3.00 3.00
**B33** SP15 7½c (+ 5c) henna brn 3.00 3.00
*Nos. B30-B33 (4)* 12.00 12.00
Set, never hinged 25.00

Surtax to leper care and baby food.

**Catalogue values for unused stamps in this section, from this point to the end of the section, are for Never Hinged items.**

Netherlands Coat of Arms and Inscription, "Netherlands Shall Rise Again" — SP16

**1941, Aug. 30 Litho. *Perf. 12½***

**B34** SP16 7½c + 7½c dp org, ultra & blk 3.75 3.00
**B35** SP16 15c + 15c scar, ultra & blk 3.75 3.00
**B36** SP16 1g + 1g gray & ultra 26.00 22.50
*Nos. B34-B36 (3)* 33.50 28.50

The surtax was used to buy fighters for Dutch pilots in the Royal Air Force of Great Britain.

Nos. 145, 169, 146, 151 Surcharged in Red:

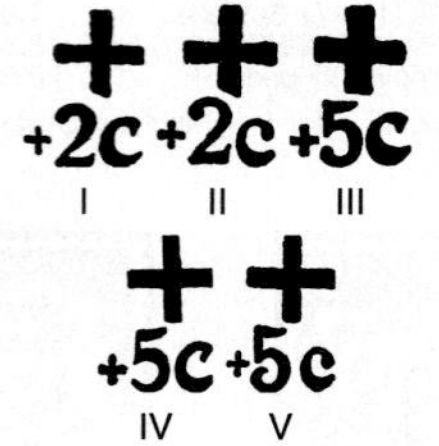

**1942, Jan. 2**

**B37** A23 2c + 2c blk brn, I 2.50 2.50
*a.* Type II 2.50 2.50
**B38** A26 2c + 2c blk brn, I 67.50 67.50
*a.* Type II 67.50 67.50
**B39** A23 2½c + 2c green, I 2.50 2.50
*a.* Type II 2.50 2.50
**B40** A23 7½c + 5c red vio, III 2.50 2.50
*a.* Type IV 8.00 8.00
*b.* Type V 20.00 20.00
*Nos. B37-B40,CB1 (5)* 77.50 77.50

The surtax was for the Red Cross.

In type III, the "c" may be "large," as illustrated, or "small," as in type II. Value is the same.

The distinctive feature of type IV is the pointed ending of the lower part of the "5."

Types of Regular Issue of 1945 Surcharged in Black

**Unwmk.**

**1945, July 23 Engr. *Perf. 12***

**B41** A29 7½c + 5c dp org 3.75 2.50
**B42** A30 15c + 10c brn 3.00 2.50
**B43** A30 20c + 15c dl grn 3.00 2.50
**B44** A30 22½c + 20c gray 3.00 2.50
**B45** A30 40c + 35c rose lake 3.00 2.50
**B46** A30 60c + 50c vio 3.00 2.50
*Nos. B41-B46 (6)* 18.75 15.00

Surtax for the National Welfare Fund.

Star — SP17

Marie Curie — SP18

**1947, Dec. 16 Photo. *Perf. 13½x13***

**B47** SP17 7½c + 12½c red org 2.75 2.25
**B48** SP17 12½c + 37½c blue 2.75 2.25
*Nos. B47-B48,CB4-CB5 (4)* 10.00 8.00

The surtax was used to combat leprosy.

**1950, May 15 *Perf. 14x13***

7½c+22½c, 27½c+12½c, Wm. Roentgen.

**B49** SP18 7½c + 7½c 17.50 10.50
**B50** SP18 7½c + 22½c 17.50 10.50
**B51** SP18 27½c + 12½c 17.50 10.50
**B52** SP18 27½c + 97½c 17.50 10.50
*Nos. B49-B52 (4)* 70.00 42.00

The surtax was used to combat cancer.

Nos. 236-237 Surcharged in Black (#B53) or Red (#B54)

**1953, Feb. 18 Wmk. 202**

**B53** A35 12½c + 7½c on 7½c 2.75 2.75
**B54** A35 20c + 10c on 12½c 2.75 2.75

The surtax was for flood relief in the Netherlands.

Stadium, Paramaribo — SP19

**1953, Aug. 29 Unwmk. *Perf. 13½***

**B55** SP19 10c + 5c claret 11.50 8.25
**B56** SP19 15c + 7½c brn 11.50 8.25
**B57** SP19 30c + 15c dk grn 11.50 8.25
*Nos. B55-B57 (3)* 34.50 24.75

Opening of the new stadium.

Surinam Children — SP20

Doves — SP21

**1954, Nov. 1 *Perf. 13x14***

**B58** SP20 7½c + 3c sepia 6.00 4.75
**B59** SP20 10c + 5c bl grn 6.00 4.75
**B60** SP20 15c + 7½c red brn 6.00 4.75
**B61** SP20 30c + 15c blue 6.00 4.75
*Nos. B58-B61 (4)* 24.00 19.00

Surtax for the youth center of the Moravian Church.

**1955, May 5 *Perf. 14x13***

**B62** SP21 7½c + 3½c brt red 2.75 3.00
**B63** SP21 15c + 8c ultra 2.75 3.00

The Netherlands' liberation, 10th anniv.

Queen Juliana and Prince Bernhard SP22

**1955, Oct. 27 Unwmk.**

**B64** SP22 7½c + 2½c dk olive .55 .55

Royal visit to Surinam, 1955. Surtax for the Royal present.

Theater, 1837 — SP23

Designs: 10c+5c, Theater and car, circa 1920. 15c+7½c, Theater and car, circa 1958. 20c+10c, Theater interior.

**1958, Feb. 15 Litho. *Perf. 13x12½***

**B65** SP23 7½c + 3c lt bl & blk .45 .45
**B66** SP23 10c + 5c rose lil & blk .45 .45
**B67** SP23 15c + 7½c lt grn & blk .45 .45
**B68** SP23 20c + 10c org & blk .45 .45
*Nos. B65-B68 (4)* 1.80 1.80

120th anniv. of the "Thalia" theatrical society.

Carved Eating Utensils and Map of South America SP24

Native Art (Map of So. America and): 10c+5c, Feather headgear. 15c+7c, Clay pottery. 20c+10c, Carved wooden stool.

**1960, Jan. 15**

**B69** SP24 8c + 4c multi .90 .90
**B70** SP24 10c + 5c salmon, red & bl .90 .90
**B71** SP24 15c + 7c red org, grn & sepia .90 .90
**B72** SP24 20c + 10c lt bl, ultra & bis .90 .90
*Nos. B69-B72 (4)* 3.60 3.60

SP25

SP26

Design: Uprooted Oak emblem of WRY.

**1960, Apr. 7 *Perf. 13x14***

**B73** SP25 8c + 4c choc & grn .20 .20
**B74** SP25 10c + 5c vio bl & ol grn .20 .20

World Refugee Year, July 1, 1959-June 30, 1960. The surtax was for aid to refugees.

**1960, Aug. 10 Litho. *Perf. 14x13***

**B75** SP26 8c + 4c Shot put .55 .55
**B76** SP26 10c + 5c Basketball .55 .55
**B77** SP26 15c + 7c Runner .85 .85
**B78** SP26 20c + 10c Swimmer .85 .85
**B79** SP26 40c + 20c Soccer .85 .85
*Nos. B75-B79 (5)* 3.65 3.65

17th Olympic Games, Rome, 8/25-9/11. Surtax for Olympic Committee.

Girl Scout Signaling SP27

Designs: 10c+3c, Scout Saluting, vert. 15c+4c, Brownies around toadstool. 20c+5c, Scouts around campfire, vert. 25c+6c, Scouts cooking outdoors.

***Perf. 14x13, 13x14***

**1961, Aug. 19 Litho.**

**Multicolored Designs**

**B80** SP27 8c + 2c blue .30 .30
**B81** SP27 10c + 3c lilac .35 .35
**B82** SP27 15c + 4c yellow .35 .35
**B83** SP27 20c + 5c brn red .40 .40
**B84** SP27 25c + 6c aqua .40 .40
*Nos. B80-B84 (5)* 1.80 1.80

Caribbean Girl Scout Jamborette. Surtax for various charities.

Hibiscus SP28

Flowers: 10c+5c, Caesalpinia pulcherrima. 15c+6c, Heliconia psittacorum. 20c+10c, Lochnera rosea. 25c+12c, Ixora macrothyrsa.

**1962, Mar. 7 Photo. *Perf. 14x13***

**Cross in Red**

**B85** SP28 8c + 4c dk ol & scar .32 .30
**B86** SP28 10c + 5c dk bl & org .32 .30
**B87** SP28 15c + 6c multi .32 .30
**B88** SP28 20c + 10c multi .32 .30
**B89** SP28 25c + 12c dk bl grn, red & yel .32 .30
*Nos. B85-B89 (5)* 1.60 1.50

The surtax was for the Red Cross.

Hands Protecting Duck — SP29

American Indian Girl — SP30

**1962, Dec. 15 Litho. *Perf. 13x14***

**B90** SP29 2c + 1c shown .20 .20
**B91** SP29 8c + 2c Dog .20 .20
**B92** SP29 10c + 3c Donkey .20 .20
**B93** SP29 15c + 4c Horse .25 .25
*Nos. B90-B93 (4)* .85 .85

The surtax was for the Organization for Animal Protection.

**1963, Oct. 30 Photo. Unwmk.**

Girls: 10c+4c, Negro. 15c+10c, East Indian. 20c+10c, Indonesian. 40c+20c, Caucasian.

**B94** SP30 8c + 3c Prus grn .20 .20
**B95** SP30 10c + 4c red brn .20 .20
*a.* Min. sheet, 2 each #B94-B95 1.25 1.25
**B96** SP30 15c + 10c dp blue .25 .25
**B97** SP30 20c + 10c brn red .25 .25
**B98** SP30 40c + 20c red vio .35 .35
*Nos. B94-B98 (5)* 1.25 1.25

The surtax was for Child Welfare.

X-15 SP31

Designs: 8c+4c, Flag of the Aeronautical and Astronautical Foundation. 10c+5c, 20c+10c, Agena B Ranger rocket.

**1964, Apr. 15 *Perf. 13x12½***

**B99** SP31 3c + 2c blk & rose lake .20 .20
**B100** SP31 8c + 4c blk, ultra & lt ultra .20 .20
**B101** SP31 10c + 5c blk & grn .20 .20
**B102** SP31 15c + 7c blk & yel brn .20 .20
**B103** SP31 20c + 10c blk & vio .20 .20
*Nos. B99-B103 (5)* 1.00 1.00

Surtax for the Aeronautical and Astronautical Foundation of Surinam.

Stylized Campfire amid Trees — SP32

Girls Skipping Rope — SP33

**1964, July 29 Litho. *Perf. 13x14***

B104 SP32 3c + 1c brn ol, yel bis & lem .20 .20
B105 SP32 8c + 4c bluish blk, vio bl & yel bis .20 .20
B106 SP32 10c + 5c dk red, red & yel bis .20 .20
B107 SP32 20c + 10c grnsh blk, ol grn & yel bis .20 .20
*Nos. B104-B107 (4)* .80 .80

Jamborette at Paramaribo, Aug. 20-30, marking the 40th anniv. of the Surinam Boy Scout Association.

Surtax for various charities.

**1964, Nov. 30 Photo. *Perf. 14x13***

10c+4c, Children on swings. 15c+9c, Girl on scooter. 20c+10c, Boy rolling hoop.

B108 SP33 8c + 3c dk blue .20 .20
B109 SP33 10c + 4c red .20 .20
a. Min. sheet, 2 each #B108-B109 .55 .55
B110 SP33 15c + 9c olive grn .20 .20
B111 SP33 20c + 10c magenta .20 .20
*Nos. B108-B111 (4)* .80 .80

Issued for Child Welfare.

Mother and Child — SP34

Designs: 4c+2c, Pregnant woman. 15c+7c, Child. 25c+12c, Old man.

**1965, Feb. 27 Photo. *Perf. 13x14***

B112 SP34 4c + 2c green .20 .20
B113 SP34 10c + 5c brn & grn .20 .20
B114 SP34 15c + 7c Prus bl & grn .20 .20
B115 SP34 25c + 12c brt pur & grn .20 .20
*Nos. B112-B115 (4)* .80 .80

50th anniv. of the Green Cross Assoc. which promotes public health services.

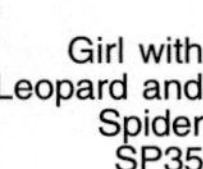

Girl with Leopard and Spider SP35

Designs: 10c+5c, Boy with monkey and spider. 15c+7c, Girl with tortoise and spider. 25c+10c, Boy with rabbit and spider.

***Perf. 13x12½***

**1965, Nov. 26 Litho. Unwmk.**

B116 SP35 4c + 4c lt grn & blk .20 .20
B117 SP35 10c + 5c ocher & blk .20 .20
B118 SP35 15c + 7c dp org & blk .20 .20
a. Min. sheet, 2 each #B116, B118 .55 .55
B119 SP35 25c + 10c lt ultra & blk .20 .20
*Nos. B116-B119 (4)* .80 .80

Issued for Child Welfare.

"Help them to a safe haven" SP35a

**1966, Jan. 31 Photo. *Perf. 14x13***

B120 SP35a 10c + 5c blk & grn .20 .20
B121 SP35a 25c + 10c blk & rose brn .20 .20
a. Min. sheet of 3, 2 #B120, B121 .45 .45

The surtax was for the Intergovernmental Committee for European Migration (ICEM). The message on the stamps was given and signed by Queen Juliana.

Mary Magdalene, Disciples and "Round Table" Emblem SP36

"New Year's Eve" Boys with Bamboo Gun SP37

Mary Magdalene (John 20:18), and Service Club Emblems: 15c+8c, Toastmasters Intl. 20c+10c, Junior Chamber, Surinam. 25c+12c, Rotary Intl. 30c+15c, Lions Intl.

**1966, Apr. 13 Photo. *Perf. 12½x13***

B122 SP36 10c + 5c dp crim, blk & gold .20 .20
B123 SP36 15c + 8c dp vio, blk & bl .20 .20
B124 SP36 20c + 10c yel org, blk & ultra .20 .20
B125 SP36 25c + 12c grn, blk & gold .20 .20
B126 SP36 30c + 15c ultra, blk & gold .20 .20
*Nos. B122-B126 (5)* 1.00 1.00

Easter charities.

**1966, Nov. 25 Litho. *Perf. 12½x13***

Designs: 15c+8c, "The End of Lent," boys pouring paint over each other. 20c+10c, "Liberation Day," parading children. 25c+12c, "Queen's Birthday," children on hobbyhorses. 30c+15c, "Christmas," Children decorating room with star.

B127 SP37 10c + 5c multi .20 .20
B128 SP37 15c + 8c multi .20 .20
B129 SP37 20c + 10c multi .20 .20
a. Min. sheet of 3, 2 #B127, B129 .35 .35
B130 SP37 25c + 12c multi .20 .20
B131 SP37 30c + 15c multi .20 .20
*Nos. B127-B131 (5)* 1.00 1.00

Child welfare.

Good Samaritan Giving His Coat SP38

Children Stilt-walking SP39

The Good Samaritan: 15c+8c, Dressing the wounds. 20c+10c, Feeding the poor man. 25c+12c, Poor man riding Samaritan's horse. 30c+15c, Samaritan taking poor man to the inn.

**1967, Mar. 22**

B132 SP38 10c + 5c yellow & blk .20 .20
B133 SP38 15c + 8c lt blue & blk .20 .20
B134 SP38 20c + 10c buff & blk .20 .20
B135 SP38 25c + 12c pale rose & blk .20 .20
B136 SP38 30c + 15c grn & blk .20 .20
*Nos. B132-B136 (5)* 1.00 1.00

Easter charities.

**1967, Nov. 21 Litho. *Perf. 12½x13***

Children's Games: 15c+8c, Boys playing with marbles. 20c+10c, Girl playing dibs (five stones). 25c+12c, Boy making kite. 30c+15c, Girls play-cooking.

B137 SP39 10c + 5c multi .20 .20
B138 SP39 15c + 8c multi .20 .20
B139 SP39 20c + 10c multi .20 .20
a. Min. sheet, #B139, 2 #B137 .45 .45
B140 SP39 25c + 12c multi .20 .20
B141 SP39 30c + 15c multi .20 .20
*Nos. B137-B141 (5)* 1.00 1.00

Child welfare.

Cross, Ash Wednesday SP40

Hopscotch SP41

Easter Symbols: 15c+8c, Palms, Palm Sunday. 20c+10c, Bread and Wine, Maundy Thursday. 25c+12c, Cross, Good Friday. 30c+15c, Chrismon, Easter Sunday.

**1968, Mar. 27 Litho. *Perf. 12½x13***

B142 SP40 10c + 5c lilac & gray .20 .20
B143 SP40 15c + 8c brick red & grn .20 .20
B144 SP40 20c + 10c yellow & dk grn .20 .20
B145 SP40 25c + 12c gray & blk .20 .20
B146 SP40 30c + 15c brt yel & brn .20 .20
*Nos. B142-B146 (5)* 1.00 1.00

Easter charities.

**1968, Nov. 22 Litho. *Perf. 12½x13***

15c+8c, Balancing pyramid. 20c+10c, Handball. 25c+12c, Handicraft. 30c+15c, Tug-of-war.

B147 SP41 10c + 5c fawn & blk .20 .20
B148 SP41 15c + 8c lt ultra & blk .20 .20
B149 SP41 20c + 10c pink & blk .20 .20
a. Min. sheet, #B149, 2 #B147 .50 .50
B150 SP41 25c + 12c yel grn & blk .25 .25
B151 SP41 30c + 15c bluish lil & blk .30 .30
*Nos. B147-B151 (5)* 1.15 1.15

Child welfare.

Globe with Map of South America SP42

Pillow Fight SP43

**1969, Apr. 2 Litho. *Perf. 12½x13***

B152 SP42 10c + 5c bl & lt bl .25 .25
B153 SP42 15c + 8c sl grn & yel .25 .25
B154 SP42 20c + 10c sl grn & gray grn .25 .25
B155 SP42 25c + 12c brn & bis .25 .25
B156 SP42 30c + 15c vio & gray .25 .25
*Nos. B152-B156 (5)* 1.25 1.25

Easter charities.

**1969, Nov. 21 Litho. *Perf. 12½x13***

15c+8c, Eating contest. 20c+10c, Pole climbing. 25c+12c, Sack race. 30c+15c, Obstacle race.

B157 SP43 10c + 5c lt ultra & mag .20 .20
B158 SP43 15c + 8c yel & brn .25 .25
B159 SP43 20c + 10c gray & dp bl .20 .20
a. Min. sheet, #B159, 2 B157 .80 .80
B160 SP43 25c + 12c pink & brt bl .25 .25
B161 SP43 30c + 15c emer & brn .25 .25
*Nos. B157-B161 (5)* 1.15 1.15

Child welfare.

Butterfly SP44

Ludwig van Beethoven, 1786 SP45

Designs: 10c+5c, Flower. 20c+10c, Flying bird. 25c+12c, Sun. 30c+15c, Star.

**1970, Mar. 25 Litho. *Perf. 12½x13***

B162 SP44 10c + 5c multi .50 .50
B163 SP44 15c + 8c multi .50 .50
B164 SP44 20c + 10c multi .50 .50
B165 SP44 25c + 12c multi .50 .50
B166 SP44 30c + 15c multi .50 .50
*Nos. B162-B166 (5)* 2.50 2.50

Easter.

**1970, Nov. 25 Litho. *Perf. 12½x13***

Various Portraits of Beethoven: 15c+8c, In 1804. 20c+10c, In 1812. 25c+12c, In 1814. 30c+15c, In 1827 (death mask).

**Portrait and Inscription in Gray and Ocher**

B167 SP45 10c + 5c green .50 .50
B168 SP45 15c + 8c scarlet .50 .50
B169 SP45 20c + 10c blue .50 .50
a. Min. sheet, #B169, 2 #B167 1.60 1.60
B170 SP45 25c + 12c red org .50 .50
B171 SP45 30c + 15c purple .50 .50
*Nos. B167-B171 (5)* 2.50 2.50

Ludwig van Beethoven (1770-1827), composer. The surtax was for child welfare.

Donkey and Palm — SP46

Leapfrog, by Peter Brueghel — SP47

Easter: 15c+8c, Cock. 20c+10c, Lamb of God. 25c+12c, Cross and Crown of Thorns. 30c+15c, Sun.

**1971, Apr. 7 Litho. *Perf. 12½x13***

B172 SP46 10c + 5c multi .50 .50
B173 SP46 15c + 8c blue & multi .50 .50
B174 SP46 20c + 10c multi .50 .50
B175 SP46 25c + 12c multi .50 .50
B176 SP46 30c + 15c multi .50 .50
*Nos. B172-B176 (5)* 2.50 2.50

Easter charities.

**1971, Nov. 24 Photo. *Perf. 13x14***

Children's Games, by Peter Brueghel: 15c+8c, Girl strewing flowers. 20c+10c, Spinning the hoop. 25c+12c, Ball players. 30c+15c, Stilt walker.

B177 SP47 10c + 5c multi .60 .60
B178 SP47 15c + 8c multi .60 .60
B179 SP47 20c + 10c multi .60 .60
a. Min. sheet, #B179, 2 #B177 2.00 2.00
B180 SP47 25c + 12c multi .60 .60
B181 SP47 30c + 15c multi .60 .60
*Nos. B177-B181 (5)* 3.00 3.00

Child welfare.

Easter Candle — SP48

Toys — SP49

Easter: 15c+8c, Christ teaching Apostles, and crosses. 20c+10c, Cup and folded hands. 25c+12c, Fish in net. 30c+15c, Judas' bag of silver.

**1972, Mar. 29 Litho. *Perf. 12½x13***

**B182** SP48 10c + 5c multi .45 .45
**B183** SP48 15c + 8c multi .45 .45
**B184** SP48 20c + 10c multi .45 .45
**B185** SP48 25c + 12c multi .45 .45
**B186** SP48 30c + 15c multi .45 .45
*Nos. B182-B186 (5)* 2.25 2.25

Easter charities.

**1972, Nov. 29 Litho. *Perf. 12½x13***

Designs: 15c+8c, Abacus and clock. 20c+10c, Pythagorean theorem. 25c+12c, Model of molecule. 30c+15c, Monkey wrench and drill. Each design represents a different stage of education.

**B187** SP49 10c + 5c multi .50 .50
**B188** SP49 15c + 8c multi .50 .50
**B189** SP49 20c + 10c multi .50 .50
*a.* Min. sheet, #B189, 2 #B187 1.50 1.50
**B190** SP49 25c + 12c multi .50 .50
**B191** SP49 30c + 15c multi .50 .50
*Nos. B187-B191 (5)* 2.50 2.50

Child welfare.

Jesus Calming the Waves — SP50

Easter: 15c+8c, The washing of the feet. 20c+10c, Jesus carrying Cross. 25c+12c, Cross and "ELI, ELI, LAMA SABACHTHANI?" 30c+15c, on the road to Emmaus.

**1973, Apr. 4 Litho. *Perf. 12½x13***

**B192** SP50 10c + 5c multi .45 .45
**B193** SP50 15c + 8c multi .45 .45
**B194** SP50 20c + 10c multi .45 .45
**B195** SP50 25c + 12c multi .45 .45
**B196** SP50 30c + 15c multi .45 .45
*Nos. B192-B196 (5)* 2.25 2.25

Easter charities.

Red Cross and Florence Nightingale SP51

**1973, Oct. 3 Litho. *Perf. 14½x14***

**B197** SP51 30c + 10c multi .90 .90

30th anniversary of Surinam Red Cross.

Flower SP52

Bitterwood SP53

**1973, Nov. 28 Litho. *Perf. 14x14½***

**B198** SP52 10c + 5c shown .25 .25
**B199** SP52 15c + 8c Tree .45 .45
**B200** SP52 20c + 10c Dog .40 .40
*a.* Min. sheet, #B200, 2 #B198 1.25 1.25
**B201** SP52 25c + 12c House .60 .60
**B202** SP52 30c + 15c Girl .60 .60
*Nos. B198-B202 (5)* 2.30 2.30

Child welfare.

**1974, Apr. 3 Litho. *Perf. 14x14½***

Tropical Flowers: 15c+8c, Passion flower. 20c+10c, Wild angelica. 25c+12c, Candlestick senna. 30c+15c, Blood flower.

**B203** SP53 10c + 5c multi .45 .45
**B204** SP53 15c + 8c multi .45 .45
**B205** SP53 20c + 10c multi .45 .45
**B206** SP53 25c + 12c multi .45 .45
**B207** SP53 30c + 15c multi .45 .45
*Nos. B203-B207 (5)* 2.25 2.25

Easter charities.

Boy Scout, Tent and Trees — SP54

Designs: 15c+8c, 5th Caribbean Jamboree emblem. 20c+10c, Scouts and emblem.

**1974, Aug. 21 Litho. *Perf. 14x14½***

**B208** SP54 10c + 5c multi .40 .40
**B209** SP54 10c + 8c multi .40 .40
**B210** SP54 20c + 10c multi .40 .40
*Nos. B208-B210 (3)* 1.20 1.20

50th anniversary of Surinam Boy Scouts.

Fruit — SP55

Designs: 15c+8c, Children, birds and nest (security). 20c+10c, Flower, mother and child (protection). 25c+12c, Child and corn (good food). 30c+15c, Dancing children (child care).

**1974, Nov. 27 Litho. *Perf. 14½x14***

**B211** SP55 10c + 5c multi .25 .25
**B212** SP55 15c + 8c multi .35 .35
**B213** SP55 20c + 10c multi .35 .35
*a.* Min. sheet, #B213, 2 #B211 1.00 1.00
**B214** SP55 25c + 12c multi .55 .55
**B215** SP55 30c + 15c multi .60 .60
*Nos. B211-B215 (5)* 2.10 2.10

Child welfare.

The Good Shepherd SP56

Woman and IWY Emblem SP57

Designs: 20c+10c, Peter's denial. 30c+15c, The Women at the Tomb. 35c+20c, Jesus showing His wounds to Thomas.

**1975, Mar. 26 Litho. *Perf. 12½x13***

**B216** SP56 15c + 5c yel grn & grn .45 .45
**B217** SP56 20c + 10c org & dk bl .60 .60
**B218** SP56 30c + 15c yel & red .60 .60
**B219** SP56 35c + 20c bl & pur .60 .60
*Nos. B216-B219 (4)* 2.25 2.25

Easter charities.

**1975, May 14 Litho. *Perf. 12½x13***

**B220** SP57 15c + 5c multi .65 .65
**B221** SP57 30c + 15c multi .65 .65

International Women's Year.

Carib Indian Water Jug — SP58

Feeding the Hungry — SP59

Designs: 20c+10c, 35c+20c, Indian arrow head, diff. 30c+15c, Wayana board with animal figures.

**1975, Nov. 12 Litho. *Perf. 12½x13***

**B222** SP58 15c + 5c multi .20 .20
**B223** SP58 20c + 10c multi .55 .55
*a.* Min. sheet, #B223, 2 #B222 1.50 1.50
**B224** SP58 30c + 15c multi .90 .90
**B225** SP58 35c + 20c multi .90 .90
*Nos. B222-B225 (4)* 2.55 2.55

Child welfare.

***Perf. 14½x13½***

**1976, Apr. 14 Photo.**

Paintings: 25c+15c, Visiting the Sick. 30c+15c, Clothing the Naked. 35c+15c, Burying the Dead. 50c+25c, Giving Water to the Thirsty. Designs after panels in Alkmaar Church, 1504.

**B226** SP59 20c + 10c multi .65 .65
**B227** SP59 25c + 15c multi .80 .80
**B228** SP59 30c + 15c multi 1.10 1.10
*a.* Souv. sheet, #B228, 2 #B226 3.25 3.25
**B229** SP59 35c + 15c multi 1.10 1.10
**B230** SP59 50c + 25c multi 1.60 1.60
*Nos. B226-B230 (5)* 5.25 5.25

Easter.

Pekingese and Boy's Head — SP60

25c+10c, German shepherd. 30c+15c, Dachshund. 35c+15c, Retriever. 50c+25c, Terrier.

**1976 Litho. *Perf. 13½***

**B231** SP60 20c + 10c multi .75 .50
**B232** SP60 25c + 10c multi 1.00 .70
**B233** SP60 30c + 15c multi 1.25 .80
*a.* Min. sheet, #B233, 2 #B231 6.75 5.50
**B234** SP60 35c + 15c multi 1.25 .85
**B235** SP60 50c + 25c multi 2.00 1.25
*Nos. B231-B235 (5)* 6.25 4.10

Surtax was for child welfare.

St. Veronica's Veil — SP61

Descent from the Cross — SP62

Easter: Religious scenes, side panels, front and back, from triptych by Jan Mostaert (1473-1555).

**1977, Apr. 6 Litho. *Perf. 13½x14***

**B236** SP61 20c + 10c multi .25 .25
**B237** SP61 25c + 15c multi .40 .40
**B238** SP61 30c + 15c multi .45 .45
**B239** SP62 35c + 15c multi .55 .55
**B240** SP61 50c + 25c multi .65 .65
*Nos. B236-B240 (5)* 2.30 2.30

Dog and Girl's Head — SP63

Crosses, Luke 23:43 — SP64

Child's Head and: 25c+15c, Monkey. 30c+15c, Rabbit. 35c+15c, Cat. 50c+25c, Parrot.

**1977, Nov. 23 Litho. *Perf. 13x14***

**B241** SP63 20c + 10c multi .45 .45
**B242** SP63 25c + 15c multi .55 .55
**B243** SP63 30c + 15c multi .65 .65
*a.* Min. sheet, #B243, 2 #B241 1.60 1.60
**B244** SP63 35c + 15c multi .75 .75
**B245** SP63 50c + 25c multi 1.10 1.10
*Nos. B241-B245 (5)* 3.50 3.50

Surtax was for child welfare.

**1978, Mar. 22 Litho. *Perf. 12½x14***

Easter: 25c+15c, Serpent and Cross, John 3:14. 30c+15c, Lamb and blood, Exodus 12:13. 35c+15c, Passover plate, chalice and bread. 60c+30c, Cross and solar eclipse.

**B246** SP64 20c + 10c multi .25 .25
**B247** SP64 25c + 15c multi .35 .35
**B248** SP64 30c + 15c multi .40 .40
**B249** SP64 35c + 15c multi .45 .45
**B250** SP64 60c + 30c multi .90 .90
*Nos. B246-B250 (5)* 2.35 2.35

Child's Head and White Cat — SP65

Church, Cross and Chalice — SP66

Child's head and cats in various positions.

**1978, Nov. 22 Litho. *Perf. 14x13***

**B251** SP65 20c + 10c multi .25 .25
**B252** SP65 25c + 15c multi .40 .30
**B253** SP65 30c + 15c multi .45 .35
*a.* Min. sheet, #B253, 2 #B251 1.40 1.40
**B254** SP65 35c + 15c multi .50 .40
**B255** SP65 60c + 30c multi .85 .70
*Nos. B251-B255 (5)* 2.45 2.00

Surtax was for child welfare.

**1979, Apr. 11 Litho. *Perf. 13x14***

Easter: Cross, chalice and various churches.

**B256** SP66 20c + 10c multi .20 .20
**B257** SP66 30c + 15c multi .35 .35
**B258** SP66 35c + 15c multi .45 .45
**B259** SP66 40c + 20c multi .55 .55
**B260** SP66 60c + 30c multi .80 .80
*Nos. B256-B260 (5)* 2.35 2.35

Boy, Bird, Red Cross, Blood Transfusion Bottle — SP67

**1979, Nov. 21 Litho. *Perf. 13x14***

**B261** SP67 20c + 10c multi .20 .20
**B262** SP67 30c + 15c multi .35 .35
**B263** SP67 35c + 15c multi .45 .45
*a.* Min. sheet, #B263, 2 #B261 1.90 1.90
**B264** SP67 40c + 20c multi .55 .55
**B265** SP67 60c + 30c multi .80 .80
*Nos. B261-B265 (5)* 2.35 2.35

Surtax was for child welfare.

Cross — SP68

Anansi — SP69

Easter: Various symbols.

**1980, Mar. 26 Litho. *Perf. 13x14***

**B266** SP68 20c + 10c multi .30 .30
**B267** SP68 30c + 15c multi .45 .45
**B268** SP68 40c + 20c multi .55 .55
**B269** SP68 50c + 25c multi .70 .70
**B270** SP68 60c + 30c multi .80 .80
*Nos. B266-B270 (5)* 2.80 2.80

**1980, Nov. 5 Litho. *Perf. 13x14***

Characters from Anansi and His Creditors.

**B271** SP69 20c + 10c shown .25 .25
**B272** SP69 25c + 15c Ba Tigri .35 .35
**B273** SP69 30c + 15c Kakafowroe .40 .40
**B274** SP69 35c + 15c Ontiman .45 .45
**B275** SP69 60c + 30c Mat Kalaka .80 .80
a. Min. sheet, #B275, 2 #B271 1.40 1.40
*Nos. B271-B275 (5)* 2.25 2.25

Surtax was for child welfare.

Woman Reading SP70

**1980, Dec. 10 *Perf. 14x13***

**B276** SP70 25c + 10c shown .30 .30
**B277** SP70 50c + 15c Gardening .55 .55
**B278** SP70 75c + 20c With grandchildren .80 .80
*Nos. B276-B278 (3)* 1.65 1.65

Surtax was for the elderly.

Crucifixion SP71

Indian Girl SP72

Easter: Scenes from the Passion of Christ.

**1981, Apr. 8 Litho. *Perf. 13x14***

**B279** SP71 20c + 10c multi .25 .25
**B280** SP71 30c + 15c multi .40 .40
**B281** SP71 50c + 25c multi .70 .70
**B282** SP71 60c + 30c multi .75 .75
**B283** SP71 75c + 35c multi .90 .90
*Nos. B279-B283 (5)* 3.00 3.00

Surtax was for the elderly.

**1981, Nov. 26 Litho.**

**B284** SP72 20c + 10c shown .25 .25
**B285** SP72 30c + 15c Black .45 .45
**B286** SP72 50c + 25c Hindustani .75 .75
**B287** SP72 60c + 30c Javanese .80 .80
**B288** SP72 75c + 35c Chinese .90 .90
a. Souv. sheet, #B288, 2 #B285 2.50 2.50
*Nos. B284-B288 (5)* 3.15 3.15

Surtax was for child welfare.

Easter SP73

Man Pushing Wheelbarrow SP74

Designs: Stained-glass windows, Sts. Peter and Paul Church, Paramaribo.

**1982, Apr. 7 Litho. *Perf. 13x14***

**B289** SP73 20c + 10c multi .35 .35
**B290** SP73 35c + 15c multi .65 .65
**B291** SP73 50c + 25c multi 1.00 1.00
**B292** SP73 65c + 30c multi 1.00 1.00
**B293** SP73 75c + 35c multi 1.25 1.25
*Nos. B289-B293 (5)* 4.25 4.25

**1982, Nov. 17 Litho.**

Children's Drawings of City Cleaning Activities.

**B294** SP74 20c + 10c multi .35 .35
**B295** SP74 35c + 15c multi .65 .65
**B296** SP74 50c + 25c multi 1.00 1.00
**B297** SP74 65c + 30c multi 1.00 1.00
**B298** SP74 75c + 35c multi 1.25 1.25
a. Souv. sheet, #B298, 2 #B295 3.00 3.00
*Nos. B294-B298 (5)* 4.25 4.25

Surtax was for child welfare.

Easter — SP75

Pitcher — SP76

Mosaic Symbols.

**1983, Mar. 23 Litho. *Perf. 13x14***

**B299** SP75 10c + 5c Dove .20 .20
**B300** SP75 15c + 5c Bread .35 .35
**B301** SP75 25c + 10c Fish .65 .65
**B302** SP75 50c + 25c Eye 1.40 1.40
**B303** SP75 65c + 30c Wine cup 1.60 1.60
*Nos. B299-B303 (5)* 4.20 4.20

**1983, Nov. 16 Litho. *Perf. 13x14***

**B304** SP76 10c + 5c shown .30 .30
**B305** SP76 15c + 5c Headdress .30 .30
**B306** SP76 25c + 10c Medicine rattle .55 .55
**B307** SP76 50c + 25c Sieve 1.50 1.50
**B308** SP76 65c + 30c Basket 1.75 1.75
a. Min. sheet, #B305, B306, B308 3.00 3.00
*Nos. B304-B308 (5)* 4.40 4.40

Easter — SP77

SP78

**1984, Apr. 4 Litho. *Perf. 13x14***

**B309** SP77 10c + 5c Cross, rose .30 .30
**B310** SP77 15c + 5c Cemetery .30 .30
**B311** SP77 25c + 10c Candles .55 .55
**B312** SP77 50c + 25c Cross, crown of thorns 1.50 1.50
**B313** SP77 65c + 30c Candle 1.75 1.50
*Nos. B309-B313 (5)* 4.40 4.15

**1984, Aug. 15 Litho. *Perf. 13x14***

Boy Scouts in Surinam, 60th Anniv.: 30c+10c, 8th Caribbean Jamboree emblem. 35c+10c, Salute. 50c+10c, Gardening. 90c+10c, Campfire in map of Surinam. Surtax was for Boy Scouts.

**B314** SP78 30c + 10c multi .90 .90
**B315** SP78 35c + 10c multi 1.10 1.10
**B316** SP78 50c + 10c multi 1.40 1.40
**B317** SP78 90c + 10c multi 2.25 2.25
*Nos. B314-B317 (4)* 5.65 5.65

Children's Games — SP79

Easter — SP80

**1984, Nov. 14 Litho. *Perf. 13x14***

**B318** SP79 5c + 5c Kites .30 .30
**B319** SP79 10c + 5c Kites, diff. .30 .30
**B320** SP79 30c + 10c Pingi-pingi-kasi .70 .70
**B321** SP79 50c + 25c Cricket 1.40 1.40
a. Souv. sheet of 3, #B319-B321 2.50 2.50
**B322** SP79 90c + 30c Peroen, peroen 2.10 2.10
*Nos. B318-B322 (5)* 4.80 4.80

Surtax was for child welfare.

**1985, Mar. 27 Litho. *Perf. 12½x14***

**B323** SP80 5c + 5c multi .25 .25
**B324** SP80 10c + 5c multi .25 .25
**B325** SP80 30c + 15c multi .65 .65
**B326** SP80 50c + 25c multi 1.10 1.10
**B327** SP80 90c + 30c multi 1.75 1.75
*Nos. B323-B327 (5)* 4.00 4.00

Surtax for child welfare.

Map, Emblem SP81

Literacy SP82

**1985, Oct. 22 Litho. *Perf. 13x14***

**B328** SP81 30c + 10c shown .75 .75
**B329** SP81 50c + 10c Crucifix, missionaries 1.10 1.10
**B330** SP81 90c + 20c Scroll 1.90 1.90
*Nos. B328-B330 (3)* 3.75 3.75

Evangelical Brotherhood Mission in Surinam, 250th anniv. Surtax for mission medical and social work.

**1985, Nov. 6**

**B331** SP82 5c + 5c Boy reading .35 .35
**B332** SP82 10c + 5c Learning alphabet .35 .35
**B333** SP82 30c + 10c Writing .60 .60
**B334** SP82 50c + 25c Girl reading 1.25 1.25
a. Min. sheet of 3, #B332-B334 2.50 2.50
**B335** SP82 90c + 30c Studying 2.25 2.25
*Nos. B331-B335 (5)* 4.80 4.80

Surtax for child welfare.

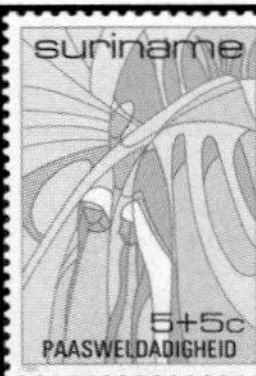

Easter — SP83

Sts. Peter and Paul Cathedral, Cent. — SP84

**1986, Mar. 19 Litho. *Perf. 13x14***

**B336** SP83 5c + 5c multi .25 .25
**B337** SP83 10c + 5c multi .25 .25
**B338** SP83 30c + 15c multi .65 .65
**B339** SP83 50c + 25c multi 1.10 1.10
**B340** SP83 90c + 30c multi 1.60 1.60
*Nos. B336-B340 (5)* 3.85 3.85

**1986, May 28 Litho.**

**B341** SP84 30c + 10c Exterior .55 .55
**B342** SP84 50c + 10c Saints, bas-relief .80 .80
**B343** SP84 110c + 30c Baptismal font 2.00 2.00
*Nos. B341-B343 (3)* 3.35 3.35

Ancient Order of Foresters Court Charity, Cent. — SP85

**1986, July 29 Litho. *Perf. 14x13***

**B344** SP85 50c + 20c Foresters emblem .90 .90
**B345** SP85 110c + 30c Court building 2.00 2.00

Youth Activities SP86

**1986, Nov. 5 Litho. *Perf. 14x13***

**B346** SP86 5c + 5c Hopscotch .30 .30
**B347** SP86 10c + 5c Ballet .30 .30
**B348** SP86 30c + 10c Mobile library .60 .60
**B349** SP86 50c + 25c Crafts 1.10 1.10
a. Min. sheet of 3, #B347-B349 2.25 2.25
**B350** SP86 110c + 30c Education 2.40 2.40
*Nos. B346-B350 (5)* 4.70 4.70

Surtax for Children's Charities.

Easter — SP87

Natl. Girl Guides Movement, 40th Anniv. — SP88

Stations of the cross.

**1987, Apr. 8 Litho. *Perf. 13x14***

**B351** SP87 5c + 5c Crucifixion .20 .20
**B352** SP87 10c + 5c Christ on cross .20 .20
**B353** SP87 35c + 15c Descent from cross .60 .60
**B354** SP87 60c + 30c Funeral procession 1.10 1.10
**B355** SP87 110c + 50c Entombment 1.90 1.90
*Nos. B351-B355 (5)* 4.00 4.00

Surtax for annual Easter Charity programs.

**1987, May 7 Litho.**

Designs: 15c+10c, Mushroom, Brownie's emblem. 60c+10c, Clover, Guides' emblem. 110c+10c, Campfire, Rangers' emblem. 120c+10c, Ivy, Captain's emblem.

**B356** SP88 15c + 10c multi .50 .50
**B357** SP88 60c + 10c multi 1.10 1.10
**B358** SP88 110c + 10c multi 2.00 2.00
**B359** SP88 120c + 10c multi 2.25 2.25
*Nos. B356-B359 (4)* 5.85 5.85

Surtax for the Surinam Girl Guides.

Caribbean Manari — SP89

Easter — SP90

**1987, Nov. 4 Litho. *Perf. 13x14***

**B360** SP89 50c + 25c Herring bone .95 .95
**B361** SP89 60c + 30c Tortoise-back 1.00 1.00
**B362** SP89 110c + 50c Whirlpool (squares) 1.90 1.90
a. Min. sheet of 2, #B360, B362 2.75 2.75
*Nos. B360-B362 (3)* 3.85 3.85

Surtax to benefit child welfare organizations.

**1988, Mar. 23 *Perf. 13x13½***

**B363** SP90 50c + 25c multi .80 .80
**B364** SP90 60c + 30c multi 1.10 1.10
**B365** SP90 110c + 50c multi 2.00 2.00
*Nos. B363-B365 (3)* 3.90 3.90

Surtax for annual Easter Charity programs.

Intl. Red Cross and Red Crescent Organizations, 125th Annivs. — SP91

#B367, Anniv. & blood donation emblems.

**1988, Oct. 26 Litho. *Perf. 13x14***

**B366** SP91 60c + 30c multi 1.25 1.25
**B367** SP91 120c + 60c multi 2.40 2.40

Children's Drawings SP92

**1988, Dec. 5 Litho. *Perf. 14x13***

**B368** SP92 50c + 25c Man and animal 1.00 1.00
**B369** SP92 60c + 30c Children and nature 1.10 1.10
**B370** SP92 110c + 50c Stop drugs 2.25 2.25
*a.* Souv. sheet of 3, #B368-B370, perf 13½x13 3.75 3.75
*Nos. B368-B370 (3)* 4.35 4.35

Surtax to benefit children's charities.

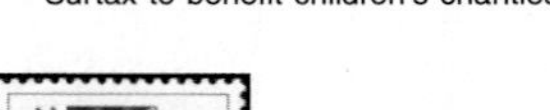

Easter 1989 — SP93

Details from Hungarian altarpieces: 60c+30c, Scenes of the Passion, by M.S., 1506. 105c+50c, Crucifixion, by Tamas of Koszvar, 1427. 110c+55c, Miracles, by Tamas of Koszvar, 1427.

**1989, Mar. 21 Litho. *Perf. 13½***
**Size: No. B372, 28½x36½mm**

**B371** SP93 60c + 30c multi 1.10 1.10
**B372** SP93 105c + 50c multi 2.00 2.00
**B373** SP93 110c + 55c multi 2.25 2.25
*Nos. B371-B373 (3)* 5.35 5.35

Surtax for annual East Charity programs.

Children's Drawings SP94

No. B374, Helping each other. No. B375, Child and nature. No. B376, In the school bus.

**1989, Dec. 6 Litho. *Perf. 14x13***

**B374** SP94 60c +30c multi 1.40 1.40
**B375** SP94 105c +50c multi 2.40 2.40
**B376** SP94 110c +55c multi 2.50 2.50
*a.* Souv. sheet of 2, #B374, B376 3.75 3.75
*Nos. B374-B376 (3)* 6.30 6.30

Surtax for children's charities.

Easter — SP95

Designs: No. B377, Mother holding Christ child. No. B378, Christ, follower. No. B379, Mary holding martyred Christ.

**1990, Mar. 28 Litho. *Perf. 13x14***

**B377** SP95 60c +30c multi 1.00 1.00
**B378** SP95 105c +50c multi 1.75 1.75
**B379** SP95 110c +55c multi 1.90 1.90
*Nos. B377-B379 (3)* 4.65 4.65

Children's Drawings SP96

**1990, Dec. 4 Litho. *Perf. 14x13***

**B380** SP96 60c +30c Children, hammock 1.25 1.25
**B381** SP96 105c +50c Child, animal, palm tree 2.00 2.00
**B382** SP96 110c +55c Child, bird in tree 2.25 2.25
*a.* Souv. sheet of 2, #B380, B382, perf. 13½x13 3.00 3.00
*Nos. B380-B382 (3)* 5.50 5.50

SP97

SP98

Easter: 60c+30c, Christ carrying cross. 105c+50c, The Crucifixion. 110c+55c, Woman cradling Christ's body.

**1991, Mar. 20 Litho. *Perf. 13x14***

**B383** SP97 60c +30c multi 1.10 1.10
**B384** SP97 105c +50c multi 1.25 1.25
**B385** SP97 110c +55c multi 2.00 2.00
*a.* Souv. sheet of 2, #B383, B385 3.25 3.25
*Nos. B383-B385 (3)* 4.35 4.35

**1991, Dec. 4 Litho. *Perf. 13x14***

Children's Drawings: 60c+30c, Child in wheelchair. 105c+50c, Child beside trees. 110c+55c, Children playing outdoors.

**B386** SP98 60c +30c multi 1.00 1.00
**B387** SP98 105c +50c multi 1.75 1.75
**B388** SP98 110c +55c multi 1.90 1.90
*a.* Souv. sheet of 2, #B386, B388 3.00 3.00
*Nos. B386-B388 (3)* 4.65 4.65

SP99

SP100

Easter: 60c+30c, Crucifixion. 105c+50c, Taking away body of Christ. 110c+55c, Resurrection.

**1992, Mar. 18**

**B389** SP99 60c +30c multi 1.00 1.00
**B390** SP99 105c +50c multi 1.75 1.75
**B391** SP99 110c +55c multi 1.90 1.90
*Nos. B389-B391 (3)* 4.65 4.65

**1992, Dec. 3 Litho. *Perf. 13x14***

Children's Drawings: 60c + 30c, Child as tree. 105c + 50c, Face as tree. 110c, + 55c, Boy and girl hanging from tree.

**B392** SP100 60c +30c multi 1.00 1.00
**B393** SP100 105c +50c multi 1.75 1.75
**B394** SP100 110c +55c multi 1.90 1.90
*a.* Souv. sheet, #B392, B394 3.00 3.00
*Nos. B392-B394 (3)* 4.65 4.65

Surtax for Child Welfare.

SP101

SP102

Easter: 60c+30c, Message from Christ. 110c+50c, Crucifixion. 125c+60c, Resurrection.

**1993, Mar. 31 Litho. *Perf. 13x14***

**B395** SP101 60c +30c multi 1.10 1.10
**B396** SP101 110c +50c multi 1.75 1.75
**B397** SP101 125c +60c multi 2.10 2.10
*Nos. B395-B397 (3)* 4.95 4.95

**1993, Dec. 3**

Children Playing Hopscotch: 25c+10c, 2 children. 35c+10c, 3 children. 50c+25c, 8 children. 75c+25c, 7 children.

**B398** SP102 25c +10c grn & multi .95 .95
**B399** SP102 35c +10c bl & multi 1.25 1.25
**B400** SP102 50c +25c grn & multi 2.10 2.10
*a.* Souvenir sheet of 2, #B399-B400 4.50 4.50
**B401** SP102 75c +25c bl & multi 2.75 2.75
*Nos. B398-B401 (4)* 7.05 7.05

Surtax for Child Welfare.

Stamps in No. B400a do not have the 1993 date in lower left corner.

## AIR POST STAMPS

Allegory of Flight — AP1

***Perf. 12½***

**1930, Sept. 3 Unwmk. Engr.**

**C1** AP1 10c dull red 3.75 .50
**C2** AP1 15c ultra 3.75 .75
**C3** AP1 20c dull green .20 .20
**C4** AP1 40c orange .20 .35
**C5** AP1 60c brown violet .55 .40
**C6** AP1 1g gray black 1.60 1.75
**C7** AP1 1½g deep brown 1.75 1.90
*Nos. C1-C7 (7)* 11.80 5.85

Nos. C1-C7 Overprinted in Black or Red

**1931, Aug. 8**

**C8** AP1 10c red (Bk) 19.00 15.00
*a.* Double overprint 425.00
**C9** AP1 15c ultra (Bk) 19.00 15.00
**C10** AP1 20c dull grn (R) 19.00 15.00
**C11** AP1 40c orange (Bk) 29.00 22.50
*a.* Double overprint 425.00
**C12** AP1 60c brn vio (R) 62.50 52.50
**C13** AP1 1g gray blk (R) 72.50 65.00
**C14** AP1 1½g deep brn (Bk) 72.50 67.50
*Nos. C8-C14 (7)* 293.50 252.50

The variety with period omitted after "Do" occurs twice on each sheet.

**Warning:** The red overprint may dissolve in water.

Type of 1930
Thick Paper

**1941, Sept. 25 Litho. *Perf. 13***

**C15** AP1 20c lt green 1.25 .90
**C16** AP1 40c lt orange 7.50 5.25
**C17** AP1 2½g yellow 7.50 12.50
**C18** AP1 5g blue green 300.00 350.00
**C19** AP1 10g lt bister 17.50 52.50
*Nos. C15-C19 (5)* 333.75 421.15

The lines of shading on Nos. C15 and C16 are not as heavy as on Nos. C3 and C4. For surcharges see Nos. C24-C25.

Type of 1930
Redrawn

**1941 Engr. *Perf. 12***

**C20** AP1 10c light red 1.50 .35
**C21** AP1 60c dl brn vio .85 .45
**C22** AP1 1g black 19.00 22.50
*Nos. C20-C22 (3)* 21.35 23.30

Redrawn stamps have three horizontal lines through post horn and many minor variations. For surcharges see Nos. C23, CB1.

**Catalogue values for unused stamps in this section, from this point to the end of the section, are for Never Hinged items.**

Nos. C21, C17, C19 Surcharged with New Values and Bars in Carmine

**1945, Mar. 12 *Perf. 13, 12***

**C23** AP1 22½c on 60c .45 .70
*a.* Inverted surcharge 250.00 250.00
**C24** AP1 1g on 2½g 15.00 15.00
**C25** AP1 5g on 10g 22.50 22.50
*Nos. C23-C25 (3)* 37.95 38.20

Women of Netherlands and Surinam — AP2

Globe and Winged Post Horn — AP3

***Perf. 12x12½***

**1949, May 10 Photo. Unwmk.**

**C26** AP2 27½c henna brown 5.75 2.75

Valid only on first flight of Paramaribo-Amsterdam service.

**1954, Sept. 25 *Perf. 13½x12½***

**C27** AP3 15c dp ultra & ultra 1.40 1.25

Establishment of airmail service in Surinam, 25th anniv.

Redstone Mercury Rocket and Comdr. Alan B. Shepard, Jr. — AP4

15c, Cosmonaut Gagarin in capsule and globe.

**1961, July 3 Litho. *Perf. 12***

**C28** AP4 15c multicolored .85 .85
**C29** AP4 20c multicolored .85 .85

"Man in Space," Major Yuri A. Gagarin, USSR, and Comdr. Alan B. Shepard, Jr., US.

Printed in sheets of 12 (4x3) with ornamental borders and inscriptions. Two printings differ in shades and selvage perforations.

Water Tower — AP5

Eucyane Bicolor — AP6

Designs: 15c, 65c, Brewery. 20c, Boat on lake. 25c, 75c, Wood industry. 30c, Bauxite mine. 35c, 50c, Poelepantje bridge. 40c, Ship in harbor. 45c, Wharf.

**1965, July 31 Photo. *Perf. 14x13½***
**Size: 25x18mm**

**C30** AP5 10c olive grn .20 .20
**C31** AP5 15c ocher .20 .20
**C32** AP5 20c slate grn .20 .20
**C33** AP5 25c violet blue .20 .20
**C34** AP5 30c blue green .20 .20
**C35** AP5 35c red orange .25 .25
**C36** AP5 40c orange .25 .25
**C37** AP5 45c dk carmine .25 .25
**C38** AP5 50c vermilion .25 .25
**C39** AP5 55c emerald .25 .25
**C40** AP5 65c bister .30 .30
**C41** AP5 75c blue .30 .30
*Nos. C30-C41 (12)* 2.85 2.85

See Nos. C75-C82.

**1972, July 26 Litho. *Perf. 13½x14***

**C42** AP6 15c shown .20 .20
**C43** AP6 20c Helicopis cupido .25 .20
**C44** AP6 25c Papilio thoas thoas .25 .20
**C45** AP6 30c Urania leilus .30 .20
**C46** AP6 35c Stalachtis calliope .30 .40
**C47** AP6 40c Stalachtis phlegia .35 .30
**C48** AP6 45c Victorina steneles .45 .20
**C49** AP6 50c Papilio neophilus .50 .20
**C50** AP6 55c Anartia amathea .60 .65
**C51** AP6 60c Adelpha cytherea .65 .95
**C52** AP6 65c Heliconius doris metharmina .65 .65
**C53** AP6 70c Nessaea obrinus .75 .75
**C54** AP6 75c Agreonia feronia .75 .60
*Nos. C42-C54 (13)* 6.00 5.50

Surinam butterflies. Valid for regular postage also. For surcharges, see Nos. 495-499.

#C42, C45 exist perf 14 with redrawn design.

### Fish Type of 1976

Fish: 35c, Chaetodon unimaculatus. 60c, Centropyge loriculus. 95c, Caetodon collare.

**1976, June 2 Litho.** ***Perf. 12½x13***
**C55** A111 35c multicolored 1.00 .55
**C56** A111 60c multicolored 1.75 .90
**C57** A111 95c multicolored 2.75 1.40
*Nos. C55-C57 (3)* 5.50 2.85

Black-headed Sugarbird
AP7

Birds of Surinam: 20c, Leistes militaris. 30c, Paradise tangara. 40c, Whippoorwill. 45c, Hemitraupis flavicollis. 50c, White-tailed gold-throated hummingbird. 55c, Saberwing. 60c, Blackcap parrot, vert. 65c, Toucan, vert. 70c, Manakin, vert. 75c, Collared parrot, vert. 80c, Cayenne cotinga, vert. 85c, Trogon, vert. 95c, Black-striped tropical tree owl, vert.

**1977 Litho.** ***Perf. 14x13, 13x14***
**C58** AP7 20c multi .25 .20
**C59** AP7 25c multi .35 .20
**C60** AP7 30c multi .40 .20
*a.* Min. sheet of 4, 2 each #C59-C60, perf. 13½x14 3.75 2.00
**C61** AP7 40c multi .70 .40
**C62** AP7 45c multi .70 .40
**C63** AP7 50c multi .80 .50
**C64** AP7 55c multi .95 .55
**C65** AP7 60c multi 1.00 .65
**C66** AP7 65c multi 1.10 .70
**C67** AP7 70c multi 1.25 .70
**C68** AP7 75c multi 1.25 .80
**C69** AP7 80c multi 1.25 .80
**C70** AP7 85c multi 1.40 .95
**C71** AP7 95c multi 1.75 1.10
*Nos. C58-C71 (14)* 13.15 8.15

A souv. sheet of 4 with same stamps and perf. as No. C60a has marginal inscription "Amphilex 77" with magnifier over No. 424. Sold in folder at phil. exhib. in Amsterdam May 26-June 5, 1977. Value $5.75.

Issued: 25c, 30c, 50c, 60c, 75c, 80c, 95c, Apr. 27; #C60a, May 26; others, Aug. 24.

See Nos. C88, C101. For surcharges and overprints see Nos. C102-C105, C108-C111, J58, J62.

### Tropical Fish Type of 1976

60c, Chaetodon striatus. 90c, Bodianus pulchellus. 120c, Centropyge argi.

**1977, June 8 Litho.** ***Perf. 13x13½***
**C72** A111 60c multi 1.00 .80
**C73** A111 90c multi 1.75 1.10
**C74** A111 120c multi 2.50 1.90
*Nos. C72-C74 (3)* 5.25 3.80

### Type of 1965 Redrawn

Designs: 5c, Brewery. 10c, Water tower. 20c, Boat on lake. 25c, Wood industry. 30c, Bauxite mine. 35c, Poelepantje bridge. 40c, Ship in harbor. 60c, Wharf.

**1976-78 Photo.** ***Perf. 12½x13½***
**Size: 22x18mm**
**C75** AP5 5c ocher .20 .20
*a.* Bklt. pane, 4 #C75, 3 #C82 + label 2.50
**C76** AP5 10c olive green .55 .55
*a.* Bklt. pane, 1 #C76, 4 #C80 + label 2.75
**C77** AP5 20c slate green .20 .20
*a.* Bklt. pane, 2 ea #C77-C79 2.75
*b.* Bklt. pane, 6 #C77, 2 #C81 2.50
**C78** AP5 25c vio bl .55 .55
**C79** AP5 30c bl grn .65 .65
**C80** AP5 35c red org .55 .55
**C81** AP5 40c org .90 .90
**C82** AP5 60c dk car .75 .75
*Nos. C75-C82 (8)* 4.35 4.35

Nos. C75-C82 issued in booklets only. Nos. C75a and C77b have inscribed selvage the size of 4 stamps; Nos. C76a and C77a the size of 6 stamps.

Issued: 10c-35c, 12/8; 5c, 40c, 60c, #C77b, 1/11/78.

### Tropical Fish Type of 1976

60c, Astyanax species. 90c, Corydoras wotroi. 120c, Gasteropelecus sternicla.

**1978, June 21 Litho.** ***Perf. 13x13½***
**C85** A111 60c multi 1.00 .95
**C86** A111 90c multi 1.60 1.00
**C87** A111 120c multi 2.25 1.25
*Nos. C85-C87 (3)* 4.85 3.20

### Bird Type of 1977

Design: 5g, Crested curassow, vert.

**1979, Jan. 10 Engr.** ***Perf. 13x13½***
**C88** AP7 5g violet 6.00 3.00

### Tropical Fish Type of 1979

60c, Cantherinus macrocerus. 90c, Holocenthrus rufus. 120c, Holacanthus tricolor.

**1979, May 30 Photo.** ***Perf. 14x13***
**C89** A129 60c multi .75 .30
**C90** A129 90c multi 1.25 .90
**C91** A129 120c multi 1.75 1.40
*Nos. C89-C91 (3)* 3.75 2.60

### Tropical Fish Type of 1979

60c, Symphysodon discus. 75c, Aeqidens curviceps. 90c, Catoprion mento.

**1980, Sept. 10 Photo.** ***Perf. 14x13***
**C92** A129 60c multi 1.00 .80
**C93** A129 75c multi 1.50 1.00
**C94** A129 90c multi 1.50 1.25
*Nos. C92-C94 (3)* 4.00 3.05

### Frog Type of 1981

**1981, June 24** ***Perf. 13x14***
**C95** A142 75c Phyllomedusa burmeisteri, vert. 1.60 .80
**C96** A142 1g Dendrobates tinctorius, vert. 2.10 1.10
**C97** A142 1.25g Bufo guttatus, vert. 2.50 1.40
*Nos. C95-C97 (3)* 6.20 3.30

### Turtle Type of 1982

**1982, Feb. 17 Photo.** ***Perf. 14x13***
**C98** A146 65c Platemys platycephala 1.00 .65
**C99** A146 75c Phrynops gibba 1.25 .80
**C100** A146 125c Rhinoclemys punctularia 2.00 1.40
*Nos. C98-C100 (3)* 4.25 2.85

### Bird Type of 1977

**1985, Jan. 9 Litho.** ***Perf. 13x14***
**C101** AP7 90c Venezuelan Amazon, vert. 4.50 4.50

For overprint see No. J61.

No. C60 Surcharged

**1986, Oct. 1 Litho.** ***Perf. 14x13***
**C102** AP7 15c on 30c multi *3.75 3.75*

Nos. C70-C71 and C67 Surcharged

**1987, Mar. Litho.** ***Perf. 13x14***
**C103** AP7 10c on 85c No. C70 *1.90 1.90*
**C104** AP7 10c on 95c No. C71 *1.90 1.90*
**C105** AP7 25c on 70c No. C67 *5.00 5.00*
*Nos. C103-C105 (3)* *8.80 8.80*

Otter Type of 1989

**1989, Jan. 18 Litho.** ***Perf. 13x14***
**C107** A195 185c Otters, vert. 3.00 3.00

No. C63 Surcharged

**1993, Jan. 20 Litho.** ***Perf. 14x13***
**C108** AP7 35c on 50c multi .40 .40

Nos. C62, C64-C65 Surcharged

**1994, Apr. 11** ***Perf. 14x13, 13x14***
**C109** AP7 ( ) on 60c #C65 .20 .20
**C110** AP7 ( ) on 45c #C62 1.00 1.00
**C111** AP7 ( ) on 55c #C64 1.50 1.50
*Nos. C109-C111 (3)* 1.75 1.75

The face value of Nos. C109-C111 fluctuates with postal rate changes. Face values on day of issue were: No. C109, 2.50f; No. C110, 10f; No. C111, 25f. No. C109 paid the additional 5 grams letter rate to the Netherlands. No. C110 paid the basic rate to North and South America and the Caribbean. No. C111 paid the basic 10-gram letter rate to the Netherlands.

Size and location of surcharge varies.

---

## AIR POST SEMI-POSTAL STAMPS

**Catalogue values for unused stamps in this section are for Never Hinged items.**

No. C20 Surchd. in Red like No. B40

**Unwmk.**

**1942, Jan. 2 Engr.** ***Perf. 12***
**CB1** AP1 10c + 5c lt red, III 2.50 2.50
*a.* Type IV 4.25 5.25
*b.* Type V 11.50 14.00

The surtax was for the Red Cross.

See note on types III and IV below No. B40.

Nos. 193 and 194 Surcharged in Carmine

**1946, Feb. 24** ***Perf. 12***
**CB2** A30 10c + 40c blue 1.00 1.00
**CB3** A30 15c + 60c brown 1.00 1.00

The surtax was for the Red Cross.

Star Type of Semi-Postals

***Perf. 13½x12½***

**1947, Dec. 16 Photo.**
**CB4** SP17 22½c + 27½c gray 2.25 1.75
**CB5** SP17 27½c + 47½c grn 2.25 1.75

---

## POSTAGE DUE STAMPS

D1

D2

Type I — 34 loops. "T" of "BETALEN" over center of loop; top branch of "E" of "TE" shorter than lower branch.

Type II — 33 loops. "T" of "BETALEN" over space between two loops.

Type III — 32 loops. "T" of "BETALEN" slightly to the left of center of loop; top branch of first "E" of "BETALEN" shorter than lower branch.

Type IV — 37 loops and letters of "PORT" larger than in the other 3 types.

**Value in Black**

***Perf. 12½x12***

**1886-88 Typo. Unwmk.**

**Type III**

**J1** D1 2½c lilac 3.00 3.00
**J2** D1 5c lilac 9.00 9.00
**J3** D1 10c lilac 100.00 65.00
**J4** D1 20c lilac 9.00 9.00
**J5** D1 25c lilac 12.50 12.50
**J6** D1 30c lilac ('88) 2.50 2.50
**J7** D1 40c lilac 6.00 6.00
**J8** D1 50c lilac ('88) 3.00 3.00
*Nos. J1-J8 (8)* 145.00 110.00

**Type I**

*J1a* D1 2½c 6.00 6.00
*J2a* D1 5c 11.00 11.00
*J3a* D1 10c 125.00 90.00
*J4a* D1 20c 22.50 22.50
*J5a* D1 25c 19.00 19.00
*J6a* D1 30c 22.50 22.50
*J7a* D1 40c 12.50 12.50
*J8a* D1 50c 4.00 4.00
*Nos. J1a-J8a (8)* 222.50 187.50

**Type II**

*J1b* D1 2½c 5.00 5.00
*J2b* D1 5c 10.00 10.00
*J3b* D1 10c 1,250. 1,250.
*J4b* D1 20c 9.00 9.00
*J5b* D1 25c 300.00 300.00
*J6b* D1 30c 75.00 75.00
*J7b* D1 40c 350.00 350.00
*J8b* D1 50c 5.00 5.00

**Type IV**

*J3c* D1 10c 350.00 250.00
*J5c* D1 25c 160.00 150.00
*J7c* D1 40c 150.00 150.00
*Nos. J3c-J7c (3)* 660.00 550.00

Nos. J1-J16 were issued without gum. For surcharges see Nos. J15-J16.

**1892-96 Value in Black** ***Perf. 12½***

**Type III**

**J9** D2 2½c lilac .40 .40
**J10** D2 5c lilac 1.25 1.00
**J11** D2 10c lilac 24.00 22.50
**J12** D2 20c lilac 2.50 2.25
**J13** D2 25c lilac 10.00 10.00

**Type I**

*J9a* D2 2½c .40 .40
*J10a* D2 5c 2.00 2.00
*J11a* D2 10c 24.00 20.00
*J12a* D2 20c 5.00 5.00
*J13a* D2 25c 13.00 12.50
**J14** D2 40c ('96) 3.25 4.50

**Type II**

*J9b* D2 2½c .80 .80
*J10b* D2 5c 3.00 3.00
*J11b* D2 10c 40.00 42.50
*J12b* D2 20c 90.00 90.00
*J13b* D2 25c 100.00 100.00

For surcharges see Nos. 121-122.

Stamps of 1888 Surcharged in Red

**10 cent**

**1911, July 15**
**J15** D1 10c on 30c lil (III) 80.00 80.00
*a.* 10c on 30c lilac (I) 200.00 225.00
*b.* 10c on 30c lilac (II) *1,800. 1,800.*
**J16** D1 10c on 50c lil (III) 110.00 110.00
*a.* 10c on 50c lilac (I) 115.00 115.00
*b.* 10c on 50c lilac (II) 115.00 115.00

D3

Type I

**Value in Color of Stamp**

**1913-31** ***Perf. 12½, 13½x12½***
**J17** D2 ½c lilac ('30) .25 .25
**J18** D2 1c lilac ('31) .25 .35
**J19** D2 2c lilac ('31) .25 .25
**J20** D2 2½c lilac .25 .25
**J21** D2 5c lilac .25 .25
**J22** D2 10c lilac .25 .25
**J23** D2 12c lilac ('31) .25 .25
**J24** D2 12½c lilac ('22) .25 .25
**J25** D2 15c lilac ('26) .55 .45
**J26** D2 20c lilac .85 .45
**J27** D2 25c lilac .45 .25
**J28** D2 30c lilac ('26) .45 .60
**J29** D2 40c lilac 14.50 14.00
**J30** D2 50c lilac ('26) 1.25 1.25
**J31** D2 75c lilac ('26) 1.50 1.50
**J32** D3 1g lilac ('26) 1.75 1.50
*Nos. J17-J32 (16)* 23.30 22.10

**Catalogue values for unused stamps in this section, from this point to the end of the section, are for Never Hinged items.**

D4

**1945 Litho. *Perf. 12***

| | | | | |
|---|---|---|---|---|
| **J33** | D4 | 1c light brown violet | .20 | .30 |
| **J34** | D4 | 5c light brown violet | 3.00 | 2.50 |
| **J35** | D4 | 25c light brown violet | 7.00 | .50 |
| | | *Nos. J33-J35 (3)* | 10.20 | 3.30 |

D5

D6

***Perf. 13½x12½***

**1950 Unwmk. Photo.**

| | | | | |
|---|---|---|---|---|
| **J36** | D5 | 1c purple | 3.00 | 2.50 |
| **J37** | D5 | 2c purple | 4.50 | 2.25 |
| **J38** | D5 | 2½c purple | 3.75 | 2.50 |
| **J39** | D5 | 5c purple | 5.50 | .50 |
| **J40** | D5 | 10c purple | 3.00 | .50 |
| **J41** | D5 | 15c purple | 7.50 | 3.25 |
| **J42** | D5 | 20c purple | 2.50 | 4.50 |
| **J43** | D5 | 25c purple | 15.00 | .20 |
| **J44** | D5 | 50c purple | 25.00 | 1.90 |
| **J45** | D5 | 75c purple | 62.50 | 50.00 |
| **J46** | D5 | 1g purple | 22.50 | 9.25 |
| | | *Nos. J36-J46 (11)* | 154.75 | 77.35 |

**1956**

| | | | | |
|---|---|---|---|---|
| **J47** | D6 | 1c purple | .20 | .20 |
| **J48** | D6 | 2c purple | .50 | .45 |
| **J49** | D6 | 2½c purple | .50 | .45 |
| **J50** | D6 | 5c purple | .50 | .45 |
| **J51** | D6 | 10c purple | .50 | .45 |
| **J52** | D6 | 15c purple | .70 | .70 |
| **J53** | D6 | 20c purple | .70 | .70 |
| **J54** | D6 | 25c purple | .80 | .40 |
| **J55** | D6 | 50c purple | 2.10 | .50 |
| **J56** | D6 | 75c purple | 2.75 | 1.60 |
| **J57** | D6 | 1g purple | 4.00 | 1.25 |
| | | *Nos. J47-J57 (11)* | 13.25 | 7.15 |

Stamps of 1977-1985 Overprinted "TE BETALEN"

***Perf. 13x14, 14x13***

**1987, July Litho.**

| | | | | |
|---|---|---|---|---|
| **J58** | AP7 | 65c No. C66 | 2.25 | 2.25 |
| **J59** | A156 | 65c No. 638 | 2.25 | 2.25 |
| **J60** | A156 | 80c No. 640 | 2.75 | 2.75 |
| **J61** | AP7 | 90c No. C101 | 3.00 | 3.00 |
| **J62** | AP7 | 95c No. C71 | 3.50 | 3.50 |
| **J63** | A173 | 1g No. 725 | 3.75 | 3.75 |
| | | *Nos. J58-J63 (6)* | 17.50 | 17.50 |

## SWAZILAND

ˈswə-zē-ˌland

LOCATION — Southeast Africa bordered by the Transvaal and Zululand in South Africa and by Mozambique
GOVT. — Constitutional monarchy
AREA — 6,705 sq. mi.
POP. — 985,335 (1999 est.)
CAPITAL — Mbabane

An independent state in the 19th century, Swaziland was administered by Transvaal from 1894 to 1906, when the administration was transferred to the British High Commissioner for South Africa. In 1934 Swaziland and Bechuanaland Protectorate came under the administration of the British High Commissioner for Basutoland. The issuing of individual postage stamps had been resumed in 1933. Internal self-government was introduced in 1967. Independence was proclaimed September 6, 1968.

12 Pence = 1 Shilling
20 Shillings = 1 Pound
100 Cents = 1 Rand (1961)
100 Cents = 1 Emalangeni (1975)

**Catalogue values for unused stamps in this country are for Never Hinged items, beginning with Scott 38 in the regular postage section and Scott J1 in the postage due section.**

Coat of Arms — A1

George V — A2

Black Overprint

**1889 Unwmk. *Perf. 12½, 12½x12***

| | | | | |
|---|---|---|---|---|
| **1** | A1 | ½p gray | 10.50 | 21.00 |
| *a.* | | Inverted overprint | 925.00 | 725.00 |
| *b.* | | "Swazielan" | 1,350. | 850.00 |
| *c.* | | As "b," inverted overprint | | 5,000. |
| **2** | A1 | 1p rose | 20.00 | 19.00 |
| *a.* | | Inverted overprint | 800.00 | 750.00 |
| **3** | A1 | 2p olive bister | 20.00 | 18.00 |
| *a.* | | Inverted overprint | 900.00 | 525.00 |
| *b.* | | "Swazielan" | 550.00 | 475.00 |
| *c.* | | Perf. 12½x12 | 100.00 | 25.00 |
| *d.* | | As "c," "Swazielan" | 1,250. | 725.00 |
| *e.* | | As "d," inverted overprint | | 1,250. |
| *f.* | | As "b," inverted overprint | 5,100. | 4,600. |
| *g.* | | Double overprint | 2,600. | |
| **4** | A1 | 6p gray blue | 25.00 | 50.00 |
| **5** | A1 | 1sh green | 12.50 | 16.00 |
| *a.* | | Inverted overprint | 850.00 | 525.00 |
| **6** | A1 | 2sh6p yellow | 275.00 | 300.00 |
| **7** | A1 | 5sh slate | 175.00 | 225.00 |
| *a.* | | Inverted overprint | 1,900. | 2,500. |
| *b.* | | "Swazielan" | 5,250. | |
| *c.* | | As "b," inverted overprint | 5,750 | |
| **8** | A1 | 10sh lt brown | 5,750. | 3,750. |

**1892 Red Overprint**

| | | | | |
|---|---|---|---|---|
| **9** | A1 | ½p gray | 8.50 | 19.00 |
| *a.* | | Inverted overprint | 575.00 | |
| *b.* | | Double overprint | 525.00 | 525.00 |
| *c.* | | Pair, one without overprint | | 1,900. |

Beware of counterfeits.
*Reprints have a period after "Swazieland."*

Stamps of Swaziland were replaced by those of Transvaal in 1895. Swaziland issues were resumed in 1933.

***Perf. 14***

**1933, Jan. 2 Engr. Wmk. 4**

| | | | | |
|---|---|---|---|---|
| **10** | A2 | ½p green | .35 | .35 |
| **11** | A2 | 1p carmine | .35 | .25 |
| **12** | A2 | 2p lt brown | .35 | .50 |
| **13** | A2 | 3p ultra | .50 | 3.00 |
| **14** | A2 | 4p orange | 3.25 | 3.50 |
| **15** | A2 | 6p rose violet | 1.50 | 1.10 |
| **16** | A2 | 1sh olive green | 1.75 | 3.25 |
| **17** | A2 | 2sh6p violet | 17.50 | 25.00 |
| **18** | A2 | 5sh gray | 35.00 | 57.50 |
| **19** | A2 | 10sh black brown | 92.50 | 125.00 |
| | | *Nos. 10-19 (10)* | 153.05 | 219.45 |

Common Design Types pictured following the introduction.

### Silver Jubilee Issue

Common Design Type

**1935, May 4 *Perf. 11x12***

| | | | | |
|---|---|---|---|---|
| **20** | CD301 | 1p carmine & blue | .60 | 1.75 |
| **21** | CD301 | 2p black & ultra | .60 | 1.50 |
| **22** | CD301 | 3p ultra & brown | .65 | 5.75 |
| **23** | CD301 | 6p brown, vio & ind | .75 | 1.75 |
| | | *Nos. 20-23 (4)* | 2.60 | 10.75 |
| | | Set, never hinged | 5.00 | |

### Coronation Issue

Common Design Type

**1937, May 12 *Perf. 11x11½***

| | | | | |
|---|---|---|---|---|
| **24** | CD302 | 1p dark carmine | .35 | .55 |
| **25** | CD302 | 2p brown | .35 | .20 |
| **26** | CD302 | 3p deep ultra | .35 | .55 |
| | | *Nos. 24-26 (3)* | 1.05 | 1.30 |
| | | Set, never hinged | 1.60 | |

George VI — A3

**1938, Apr. 1 *Perf. 13, 13x13½***

| | | | | |
|---|---|---|---|---|
| **27** | A3 | ½p green | .25 | 1.50 |
| **28** | A3 | 1p rose carmine | .80 | 1.50 |
| **29** | A3 | 1½p light blue | .30 | .85 |
| *a.* | | Perf. 14 ('42) | 1.40 | 1.25 |
| | | Never hinged | 3.25 | |
| **30** | A3 | 2p brown | .30 | .45 |
| **31** | A3 | 3p ultra | 2.75 | 2.00 |
| **32** | A3 | 4p red orange | .40 | 1.60 |
| **33** | A3 | 6p rose violet | 3.50 | 1.75 |
| **34** | A3 | 1sh olive green | .95 | .75 |
| **35** | A3 | 2sh6p dark violet | 10.50 | 2.75 |
| **36** | A3 | 5sh gray | 20.00 | 15.00 |
| **37** | A3 | 10sh black brown | 4.75 | 6.50 |
| | | *Nos. 27-37 (11)* | 44.50 | 34.65 |
| | | Set, never hinged | 57.50 | |

**Catalogue values for unused stamps in this section, from this point to the end of the section, are for Never Hinged items.**

### Peace Issue

South Africa, Nos. 100-102 Overprinted

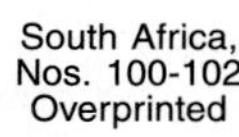

Basic stamps inscribed alternately in English and Afrikaans.

**1945, Dec. 3 Wmk. 201 *Perf. 14***

| | | | | |
|---|---|---|---|---|
| **38** | A42 | 1p rose pink & choc, pair | .55 | .85 |
| *a.* | | Single, English | .20 | .20 |
| *b.* | | Single, Afrikaans | .20 | .20 |
| **39** | A43 | 2p vio & sl blue, pair | .55 | .85 |
| *a.* | | Single, English | .20 | .20 |
| *b.* | | Single, Afrikaans | .20 | .20 |
| **40** | A43 | 3p ultra & dp ultra, pair | .55 | 2.75 |
| *a.* | | Single, English | .20 | .25 |
| *b.* | | Single, Afrikaans | .20 | .25 |
| | | *Nos. 38-40 (3)* | 1.65 | 4.45 |

World War II victory of the Allies.

### Royal Visit Issue

Type of Basutoland, 1947

***Perf. 12½***

**1947, Feb. 17 Wmk. 4 Engr.**

| | | | | |
|---|---|---|---|---|
| **44** | A3 | 1p red | .20 | .20 |
| **45** | A4 | 2p green | .20 | .20 |
| **46** | A5 | 3p ultramarine | .20 | .20 |
| **47** | A6 | 1sh dark violet | .20 | .20 |
| | | *Nos. 44-47 (4)* | .80 | .80 |

Visit of the British Royal Family, 3/25/47.

### Silver Wedding Issue

Common Design Types

**1948, Dec. 1 Photo. *Perf. 14x14½***

| | | | | |
|---|---|---|---|---|
| **48** | CD304 | 1½p bright ultra | .20 | .20 |

***Perf. 11½x11***

**Engraved; Name Typographed**

| | | | | |
|---|---|---|---|---|
| **49** | CD305 | 10sh violet brown | 50.00 | 30.00 |

### UPU Issue

Common Design Types

**Engr.; Name Typo. on 3p, 6p**

***Perf. 13½, 11x11½***

**1949, Oct. 10 Wmk. 4**

| | | | | |
|---|---|---|---|---|
| **50** | CD306 | 1½p blue | .35 | .20 |
| **51** | CD307 | 3p indigo | .65 | .65 |
| **52** | CD308 | 6p red lilac | .85 | .65 |
| **53** | CD309 | 1sh olive | .95 | .65 |
| | | *Nos. 50-53 (4)* | 2.80 | 2.15 |

### Coronation Issue

Common Design Type

**1953, June 3 Engr. *Perf. 13½x13***

| | | | | |
|---|---|---|---|---|
| **54** | CD312 | 2p yellow brown & blk | .20 | .20 |

Asbestos Mine — A4

Married Woman — A5

1p, 2sh 6p, Highveld view. 3p, 1sh 3p, Courting couple. 4½p, 5sh, Warrior. 6p, £1, Kudu. 1sh, Asbestos mine. 10sh, Married woman.

***Perf. 13x13½, 13½x13***

**1956, July 2 Engr. Wmk. 4**

**Center in Black, except Nos. 63-64**

| | | | | |
|---|---|---|---|---|
| **55** | A4 | ½p orange | .20 | .20 |
| **56** | A4 | 1p emerald | .20 | .20 |
| **57** | A5 | 2p redsh brown | .35 | .20 |
| **58** | A5 | 3p rose red | .25 | .20 |
| **59** | A5 | 4½p ultra | .70 | .20 |
| **60** | A5 | 6p magenta | .45 | .20 |
| **61** | A4 | 1sh gray olive | .35 | .20 |
| **62** | A5 | 1sh3p brown | 1.25 | 7.50 |
| **63** | A4 | 2sh6p car & brt grn | 1.25 | 1.10 |
| **64** | A5 | 5sh blue gray & vio | 8.00 | 2.00 |
| **65** | A5 | 10sh dull violet | 17.00 | 6.50 |
| **66** | A5 | £1 turquoise | 40.00 | 25.00 |
| | | *Nos. 55-66 (12)* | 70.00 | 43.50 |

Nos. 55-61 and 63-66 Surcharged with New Value

2½c 2½c 4c 4c
I II I II

5c 5c 25c 25c
I II I II

50c 50c 50c
I II III

R1 R1 R1 R2 R2
I II III I II

**1961**

| | | | | |
|---|---|---|---|---|
| **67** | A4 | ½c on ½p | 2.75 | 2.00 |
| *a.* | | Inverted surcharge | 500.00 | |
| **68** | A4 | 1c on 1p | .20 | .20 |
| *a.* | | "1c" at center | 27.50 | |
| *b.* | | Double surcharge | 500.00 | |
| **69** | A5 | 2c on 2p | .20 | .20 |
| **70** | A5 | 2½p on 2p | .20 | .20 |
| **71** | A5 | 2½c on 3p (I) | .20 | .20 |
| *a.* | | Type II | .20 | .25 |
| **72** | A5 | 3½c on 2p | .20 | .20 |
| **73** | A5 | 4c on 4½p (II) | .20 | .20 |
| *a.* | | Type I | .20 | .20 |
| **74** | A5 | 5c on 6p (II) | .20 | .20 |
| *a.* | | Type I | .20 | .20 |
| **75** | A4 | 10c on 1sh | 21.00 | 5.50 |
| *a.* | | Double surcharge | 550.00 | |
| **76** | A4 | 25c on 2sh6p (I) | .30 | .90 |
| *a.* | | Type II, "25c" centered | 1.25 | .60 |
| *b.* | | Type II, "25c" at lower left | 190.00 | 225.00 |
| **77** | A5 | 50c on 5sh (I) | .30 | 1.10 |
| *a.* | | Type II | 6.00 | 2.50 |
| *b.* | | Type III | 375.00 | 450.00 |
| **78** | A5 | 1r on 10sh (I) | 1.75 | 1.50 |
| *a.* | | Type II | 3.50 | 3.50 |
| *b.* | | Type III | 55.00 | 60.00 |
| **79** | A5 | 2r on £1 (II, "R2" at middle left) | 8.00 | 4.75 |
| *a.* | | Type I | 10.00 | 10.00 |
| *b.* | | Type II, "R2" at center bottom | 27.50 | 45.00 |
| | | *Nos. 67-79 (13)* | 35.50 | 17.15 |

The type II "25c" surcharge is nearly centered in the sky on No. 76a, and is at lower left touching the value tablet on No. 76b.

Surcharge types are numbered chronologically.

For surcharges see Nos. J3-J6.

Types of 1956

½c, 10c, Asbestos mine. 1c, 25c, Highveld view. 2c, 1r, Married woman. 2½c, 12½c, Courting couple. 4c, 50c, Warrior. 5c, 2r, Kudu.

***Perf. 13x13½, 13½x13***

**1961 Engr. Wmk. 4**

**Center in Black, except Nos. 88-89**

| | | | | |
|---|---|---|---|---|
| **80** | A4 | ½c orange | .20 | .70 |
| **81** | A4 | 1c emerald | .20 | .20 |
| **82** | A5 | 2c redsh brown | .20 | 2.10 |
| **83** | A5 | 2½c rose red | .20 | .20 |
| **84** | A5 | 4c ultra | .20 | .90 |
| **85** | A5 | 5c magenta | .40 | .20 |

**86** A4 10c gray olive .20 .20
**87** A5 12½c brown 1.50 .40
**88** A4 25c car & brt green 2.50 2.75
**89** A5 50c blue gray & vio 2.75 1.40
**90** A5 1r dull violet 5.25 *8.75*
**91** A5 2r turquoise 11.50 10.50
*Nos. 80-91 (12)* 25.10 28.30

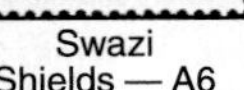
Swazi Shields — A6

Train and Railroad Map — A7

Designs: 1c, Battle axe. 2c, Forestry. 2½c, Ceremonial headdress. 3½c, Musical instrument. 4c, Irrigation. 5c, Widow bird. 7½c, Rock paintings. 10c, Secretary bird. 12½c, Pink arum lily. 15c, Married woman. 20c, Malaria control. 25c, Swazi warrior. 50c, Ground hornbill, horiz. 1r, Aloes. 2r, Msinsi (flame tree), horiz.

***Perf. 12½x14, 14x12½***

**1962, Apr. 24 Photo. Wmk. 314**
**92** A6 ½c ocher, blk & brn .20 .20
**93** A6 1c gray & orange .20 *.20*
**94** A6 2c lt yel grn, dk grn & blk .20 *1.00*
**95** A6 2½c vermilion & blk .20 .20
**96** A6 3½c gray & emerald .20 *.60*
**97** A6 4c aqua & black .20 .20
**98** A6 5c orange red & blk .80 .20
**99** A6 7½c dull ocher & brn .90 .35
**100** A6 10c lt blue & black 1.50 .20
**101** A6 12½c lt olive & dp car 1.10 *2.25*
**102** A6 15c red lilac & blk 1.60 1.00
**103** A6 20c emerald & blk .45 *1.25*
**104** A6 25c ultra & blk .55 *1.00*
**105** A6 50c rose red & dk brn 10.00 4.00
**106** A6 1r bister & emer 3.50 2.60
**107** A6 2r ultra & scar 14.00 9.00
*Nos. 92-107 (16)* 35.60 24.25

For surcharge & overprints see #138, 143-159.

**Freedom from Hunger Issue**
Common Design Type

**1963, June 4** ***Perf. 14x14½***
**108** CD314 15c lilac .50 .50

**Red Cross Centenary Issue**
Common Design Type

**1963, Sept. 2 Litho.** ***Perf. 13***
**109** CD315 2½c black & red .25 .25
**110** CD315 15c ultra & red .75 .75

***Perf. 11½x12***

**1964, Nov. 5 Engr. Wmk. 314**
**111** A7 2½c purple & brt grn .55 .20
**112** A7 3½c dk olive & blue .60 *1.00*
**113** A7 15c dk brown & orange .75 .65
**114** A7 25c dk blue & yellow .95 .75
*Nos. 111-114 (4)* 2.85 2.60

Opening of the Swaziland Railroad linking Ka Dake with Lourenco Marques.

**ITU Issue**
Common Design Type
***Perf. 11x11½***

**1965, May 17 Litho. Wmk. 314**
**115** CD317 2½c blue & bister .20 .20
**116** CD317 15c red lil & rose red .50 .50

**Intl. Cooperation Year Issue**
Common Design Type

**1965, Oct. 25** ***Perf. 14½***
**117** CD318 ½c bl grn & claret .20 .20
**118** CD318 15c lt violet & grn .50 .50

**Churchill Memorial Issue**
Common Design Type

**1966, Jan. 24 Photo.** ***Perf. 14***
**Design in Black, Gold and Carmine Rose**
**119** CD319 ½c brt blue .20 .50
**120** CD319 2½c green .30 .20
**121** CD319 15c brown .50 .40
**122** CD319 25c violet .75 .80
*Nos. 119-122 (4)* 1.75 1.90

**UNESCO Anniversary Issue**
Common Design Type

**1966, Dec. 1 Litho.** ***Perf. 14***
**123** CD323 2½c "Education" .20 .20
**124** CD323 7½c "Science" .30 .30
**125** CD323 15c "Culture" .65 .65
*Nos. 123-125 (3)* 1.15 1.15

King Sobhuza II and Map of Swaziland A8

Design: 7½c, 25c, King Sobhuza II, vert.

***Perf. 14½x14, 14x14½***

**1967, Apr. 25 Photo. Wmk. 314**
**126** A8 2½c multicolored .20 .20
**127** A8 7½c multicolored .20 .20
**128** A8 15c multicolored .20 .20
**129** A8 25c multicolored .30 .30
*Nos. 126-129 (4)* .90 .90

Attainment of internal self-government.

King Sobhuza II, University Buildings and Graduates — A9

***Perf. 14x14½***

**1967, Sept. 1 Photo. Unwmk.**
**130** A9 2½c yel, sepia & dp bl .20 .20
**131** A9 7½c blue, sepia & dp bl .20 .20
**132** A9 15c dl rose, sepia & dp bl .20 .20
**133** A9 25c lt vio, sepia & dp bl .30 .30
*Nos. 130-133 (4)* .90 .90

1st conferment of degrees by the University of Botswana, Lesotho and Swaziland at Roma, Lesotho.

Swazi Reed Dance (Umhlanga) — A10

Designs: 3c, 15c, Feast of the First Fruits, Incwala (bull, sun and king), horiz.

***Perf. 14½x14, 14x14½***

**1968, Jan. 5 Photo. Wmk. 314**
**134** A10 3c red, blk & silver .20 .20
**135** A10 10c brown, blk, org & sil .20 .20
**136** A10 15c red, blk & gold .20 .20
**137** A10 25c brown, blk, org & gold .30 .30
*Nos. 134-137 (4)* .90 .90

No. 98 Surcharged with New Value

**1968, May 1** ***Perf. 12½x14***
**138** A6 3c on 5c org red & blk .75 .45

**Independent Kingdom**

Plowing and King Sobhuza II A11

Designs: 4½c, Cable lift carrying asbestos. 17½c, Worker cutting sugar cane. 25c, Iron ore mining and map showing Swaziland railroad.

***Perf. 14x12½***

**1968, Sept. 6 Photo. Wmk. 314**
**139** A11 3c gold & multi .20 .20
**140** A11 4½c gold & multi .20 .20
**141** A11 17½c gold & multi .20 .20
**142** A11 25c slate & gold .50 .50
*a.* Strip of 4, #139-142 4.00 4.00
*Nos. 139-142 (4)* 1.10 1.10

Swaziland's independence.
Nos. 139-142 printed in sheets of 50. No. 142a printed in sheets of 20 (4x5).

Nos. 92-107 Overprinted; No. 96 Surcharged

**1968, Sept. 6** ***Perf. 12½x14, 14x12½***
**143** A6 ½c ocher, blk & brn .20 .20
**144** A6 1c gray & orange .20 .20
**145** A6 2c multicolored .20 .20
**146** A6 2½c vermilion & blk .80 *1.50*
**147** A6 3c on 2½c #146 .20 .20
**148** A6 3½c gray & emerald .20 .20
**149** A6 4c aqua & black .20 .20
**150** A6 5c org red & blk 3.75 .20
**151** A6 7½c dull ocher & brn .60 .20
**152** A6 10c lt blue & blk 4.00 .20
**153** A6 12½c lt olive & dp car .35 *.60*
**154** A6 15c red lilac & blk .35 *.75*
**155** A6 20c emerald & blk 1.00 *1.60*
**156** A6 25c ultra & blk .45 *.75*
**157** A6 50c rose red & dk brn 7.50 4.50
*a.* Wmk. sideways 3.00 3.00
**158** A6 1r bister & emerald 2.75 *4.50*
**159** A6 2r ultra & scarlet 5.25 *9.00*
*a.* Wmk. sideways 5.00 5.00
*Nos. 143-159 (17)* 28.00 25.00

Caracal (African Lynx) — A12

Waterbuck — A12a

1c, Cape porcupine. 2c, Crocodile. 3c, Lion. 3½c, African elephants. 5c, Bush pig. 7½c, Impalas. 10c, Chacma baboon. 12½c, Ratel (honey badger). 15c, Leopard. 20c, Blue wildebeest (brindled gnu). 25c, White (square-lipped) rhinoceros. 50c, Burchell's zebra. 2r, Giraffe.

***Perf. 13x12½, 12½x13***

**1969, Aug. 1 Litho. Wmk. 314**
**Size: 30½x21½mm**
**160** A12 ½c multicolored .20 .20
**161** A12 1c multicolored .20 .20
**162** A12 2c multicolored .20 .20
**Size: 35x25mm**
**163** A12 3c multicolored .50 .20
*a.* Wmk. upright ('75) 5.00 5.00
**164** A12 3½c multicolored .70 .20
**Size: 30½x21½mm, 21½x30½mm**
**165** A12 5c multicolored .35 .20
**166** A12 7½c multicolored .45 .20
**167** A12 10c multicolored .65 .20
**168** A12 12½c multicolored .80 3.50
**169** A12 15c multicolored 1.25 .75
**170** A12 20c multicolored 1.00 .65
**171** A12 25c multicolored 1.60 *1.75*
**172** A12 50c multicolored 2.10 *3.00*
**173** A12a 1r multicolored 5.25 *6.25*
**174** A12a 2r multicolored 10.50 *11.00*
*Nos. 160-174 (15)* 25.75 28.50

See #228-229. For surcharges see #259-260.

King Sobhuza II and Flags — A13

Designs: 7½c, 25c, UN emblem, UN Headquarters, NY, and King Sobhuza II.

**1969, Sept. 24 Litho.** ***Perf. 13½***
**175** A13 3c dp blue & multi .20 .20
**176** A13 7½c pink & multi .20 .20
**177** A13 12½c yellow & multi .25 .25
**178** A13 25c lt blue & multi .45 .45
*Nos. 175-178 (4)* 1.10 1.10

1st anniv. of admission to the UN.

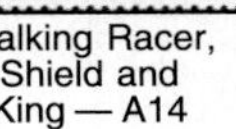
Walking Racer, Shield and King — A14

Bauhinia Galpinii and King — A15

Designs: 7½c, Runner. 12½c, Hurdler. 25c, Parade of Swaziland team with flag bearer.

***Perf. 14x14½***

**1970, July 16 Litho. Wmk. 314**
**179** A14 3c red org & multi .20 .20
**180** A14 7½c yellow & multi .20 .20
**181** A14 12½c lt blue & multi .25 .25
**182** A14 25c multicolored .40 .40
*Nos. 179-182 (4)* 1.05 1.05

Issued to publicize the 9th Commonwealth Games, Edinburgh, July 16-25.

***Perf. 14x14½***

**1971, Feb. 1 Litho. Wmk. 314**

Flowers of Swaziland: 10c, Crocosmia aurea. 15c, Gloriosa superba. 25c, Watsonia densiflora.

**183** A15 3c bister & multi .35 .20
**184** A15 10c pale salmon & multi .40 .20
**185** A15 15c pale green & multi .85 .50
**186** A15 25c multicolored 1.25 1.25
*Nos. 183-186 (4)* 2.85 2.15

King Sobhuza II — A16

Designs (King Sobhuza II): 3½c, In 1971. 7½c, In tribal costume at gathering of chiefs (Incwala). 25c, Opening Swazi parliament.

**1971, Dec. 22**
**187** A16 3c blue & multi .20 .20
**188** A16 3½c gold, blk, bl & brn .20 .20
**189** A16 7½c gold & multi .20 .20
**190** A16 25c lilac & multi .30 .30
*Nos. 187-190 (4)* .90 .90

50th anniv. of the reign of Sobhuza II.

UNICEF Emblem, King Sobhuza II — A17

**1972, Apr. 17** ***Perf. 14½x14***
**191** A17 15c violet & black .20 .20
**192** A17 25c olive & black .50 *.60*

25th anniv. (in 1971) of UNICEF.

Traditional Reed Dancers — A18

*Perf. 13½x14*

**1972, Sept. 11 Wmk. 314**

**193** A18 3½c shown .20 .20
**194** A18 7½c Swazi beehive hut .25 .25
**195** A18 15c Ezulwini Valley .55 .55
**196** A18 25c Usutu River fishing .90 .90
*Nos. 193-196 (4)* 1.90 1.90

Tourist publicity.

Mosquito Control A19

**1973, May 21 Litho. *Perf. 14½***

**197** A19 3½c shown .25 .20
**198** A19 7½c Anti-malaria vaccination .75 .50

25th anniv. of WHO.

Mpaka Coal Mines — A20

7½c, Oxen pulling plow. 15c, Weir over Komati River. 25c, Experimental rice plantation.

*Perf. 13½x14*

**1973, June 21 Wmk. 314**

**199** A20 3½c multicolored .60 .20
**200** A20 7½c multicolored .30 .20
**201** A20 15c multicolored .40 .25
**202** A20 25c multicolored .60 .60
*Nos. 199-202 (4)* 1.90 1.25

Development of natural resources.

Swaziland Coat of Arms — A21

10c, King Sobhuza II in dress uniform. 15c, Parliament. 25c, National Somhlolo Stadium.

**1973, Sept. 7 Litho. *Perf. 14***

**203** A21 3c brick red & black .20 .20
**204** A21 10c dull orange & multi .20 .20
**205** A21 15c blue & multi .40 *.50*
**206** A21 25c yellow & multi .50 *1.00*
*Nos. 203-206 (4)* 1.30 1.90

5th anniversary of independence.

Botswana, Lesotho, Swaziland Flags and Cap — A22

12½c, Kwaluseni Campus. 15c, Map of Africa & location of Botswana, Lesotho & Swaziland. 25c, Shield of University.

**1974, Mar. 29 Litho. *Perf. 14***

**207** A22 7½c orange & multi .25 .20
**208** A22 12½c emerald & multi .35 .20
**209** A22 15c yellow & multi .40 .30
**210** A22 25c ultra & multi .50 .45
*Nos. 207-210 (4)* 1.50 1.15

10th anniversary of the University of Botswana, Lesotho and Swaziland.

Sobhuza as Student at Lovedale College, South Africa — A23

**1974, July 22 Litho. *Perf. 13x11***

**211** A23 3c shown .20 .20
**212** A23 9c Sobhuza as middle-aged man .20 .20
**213** A23 50c As old man .85 .75
*Nos. 211-213 (3)* 1.25 1.15

75th birthday of King Sobhuza II.

Mail Carried by Overhead Cable A24

**1974, Oct. 9 *Perf. 14***

**214** A24 4c Post Office, Lobamba .20 .20
**215** A24 10c Mbabane temporary P.O., 1902 .25 .20
**216** A24 15c shown .45 .45
**217** A24 25c Mule-drawn mail coach .65 .65
*Nos. 214-217 (4)* 1.55 1.50

Centenary of Universal Postal Union.

Animal Type of 1969
"E" instead of "R"

Designs as before.

**1975, Jan. 2 Litho. *Perf. 12½x13***

**228** A12a 1e multicolored 3.75 3.00
**229** A12a 2e multicolored 7.50 6.00

Girl's Umcwasho Ceremony — A26

Swazi youth: 10c, Butimba, hunting ceremony. 15c, Lusekwane, ceremony of preparation, horiz. 25c, Gcina Regiment marching with flags.

**1975, Mar. 20 Wmk. 314 *Perf. 14***

**232** A26 3c lt green & multi .20 .20
**233** A26 10c lt violet & multi .25 .20
**234** A26 15c brown org & multi .45 .40
**235** A26 25c yellow & multi .65 .65
*Nos. 232-235 (4)* 1.55 1.45

Matsapa Airport Control Tower A27

5c, Fire brigade car and staff. 15c, Douglas C-47 Dakota. 25c, Hawker Siddeley 748.

**1975, Aug. 18 Litho. *Perf. 14½***

**236** A27 4c multicolored .40 .20
**237** A27 5c multicolored .80 .30
**238** A27 15c multicolored 1.75 1.50
**239** A27 25c multicolored 2.50 2.50
*Nos. 236-239 (4)* 5.45 4.50

10th anniversary of internal air service.

Women in Service — A28

Green Pigeon — A29

4c, Elephant with IWY emblem, horiz. 5c, Queen Labotsibeni, grandmother of King Sobhuza II, horiz. 15c, Handicrafts women.

**Wmk. 373**

**1975, Dec. 22 Litho. *Perf. 14***

**240** A28 4c ultra, blk & gray .20 .20
**241** A28 5c bister & multi .20 .20
**242** A28 15c multicolored .40 .40
**243** A28 25c multicolored .50 *.70*
*Nos. 240-243 (4)* 1.30 1.50

International Women's Year 1975.

**1976, Jan. 2 Wmk. 373 *Perf. 14***

Birds: 1c, Black-headed oriole, horiz. 3c, Melba finch, horiz. 4c, Plum-colored starling. 5c, Black-headed heron. 6c, Stonechat. 7c, Chorister robin. 10c, Gorgeous bush shrike. 15c, Black-collared barbet. 20c, Gray heron. 25c, Giant kingfisher. 30c, Black eagle. 50c, Red bishop. 1e, Pin-tailed whydah. 2e, Lilac-breasted roller, horiz.

**244** A29 1c orange & multi .75 1.50
**245** A29 2c lilac & multi .85 1.50
**246** A29 3c yel grn & multi 1.25 1.10
**247** A29 4c gray blue & multi .85 .85
**248** A29 5c orange & multi .95 1.25
**249** A29 6c orange & multi 1.75 1.60
**250** A29 7c orange & multi 1.75 1.60
**251** A29 10c slate & multi 1.75 1.75
**252** A29 15c lt green & multi 2.75 1.00
**253** A29 20c ocher & multi 4.00 3.50
**254** A29 25c orange & multi 4.25 3.75
**255** A29 30c orange & multi 4.25 3.75
**256** A29 50c sepia & multi 2.40 2.40
**257** A29 1e vermilion & multi 2.75 2.75
**258** A29 2e lt blue & multi 4.75 *5.00*
*Nos. 244-258 (15)* 35.05 33.30

Nos. 166 and 168 Surcharged in Ultramarine or Brown

**1976 Wmk. 314 *Perf. 13x12½***

**259** A12 3c on 7½c multi (U) 1.00 *1.25*
**260** A12 6c on 12½c multi (B) 1.75 1.75

Denomination at lower left on No. 260.

Blindness from Malnutrition — A30

Designs (WHO Emblem and): 10c, Retina, "Operation prevents blindness." 20c, Blind eye, "Blindness from trachoma." 25c, Medicine and syringe, "Medicine and rehabilitation."

**Wmk. 373**

**1976, June 15 Litho. *Perf. 14***

**261** A30 5c multicolored .20 .20
**262** A30 10c multicolored .30 .20
**263** A30 20c multicolored .60 .55
**264** A30 25c multicolored .65 .65
*Nos. 261-264 (4)* 1.75 1.60

World Health Day: Foresight prevents blindness.

Marathon Runner — A31

Soccer — A32

Designs (Olympic Rings and): 6c, Boxing. 20c, Soccer. 25c, Olympic torch and flame.

**1976, July 17 Litho. Wmk. 373**

**265** A31 5c lt blue & multi .20 .20
**266** A31 6c olive & multi .25 .25
**267** A31 20c lt violet & multi .50 .50
**268** A31 25c dull orange & multi .70 .70
*Nos. 265-268 (4)* 1.65 1.65

21st Olympic Games, Montreal, Canada, July 17-Aug. 1.

**1976, Sept. 13 Litho. *Perf. 14½***

Designs: 5c, Player heading ball. 20c, Goalkeeper catching ball. 25c, Player kicking ball.

**269** A32 4c blue & multi .20 .20
**270** A32 5c olive & multi .20 .20
**271** A32 20c red & multi .45 .40
**272** A32 25c multicolored .60 .55
*Nos. 269-272 (4)* 1.45 1.35

FIFA membership for Swaziland in 1976 (Federation Internationale de Football Associations).

A. G. Bell and 1976 Telephone — A33

Designs (A. G. Bell and Telephone): 5c, 1895. 10c, 1876. 15c, 1877. 20c, 1905.

**1976, Nov. 22 *Perf. 14***

**273** A33 4c multicolored .20 .20
**274** A33 5c multicolored .20 .20
**275** A33 10c multicolored .20 .20
**276** A33 15c multicolored .30 .30
**277** A33 20c multicolored .40 .40
*Nos. 273-277 (5)* 1.30 1.30

Centenary of first telephone call by Alexander Graham Bell, Mar. 10, 1876.

Elizabeth II and Sobhuza II — A34

Designs: 25c, Queen's coach at Admiralty Arch. 50c, Queen seated in coach.

**1977, Feb. 7 *Perf. 13½***

**278** A34 20c silver & multi .25 .25
**279** A34 25c silver & multi .30 .30
**280** A34 50c silver & multi .65 .65
*Nos. 278-280 (3)* 1.20 1.20

25th anniv. of the reign of Elizabeth II.

Matsapa College A35

10c, Men's & Women's uniforms & jeep. 20c, Police badge. 25c, Dog handler & dog.

**1977, May 2 Litho. *Perf. 14***

**281** A35 5c multi .35 .35
**282** A35 10c multi .55 .35
**283** A35 20c multi, vert. .85 .85
**284** A35 25c multi 1.40 1.25
*Nos. 281-284 (4)* 3.15 2.80

50 years of police training in Swaziland.

Various Animals A36

Rock Paintings: 10c, 20c, Groups of men. 15c, Cattle and herdsman.

***Perf. 14x14½***

**1977, Aug. 8 Wmk. 373**

**285** A36 5c multicolored .30 .20
**286** A36 10c multicolored .40 .35
**287** A36 15c multicolored .60 .55
**288** A36 20c multicolored .80 .75
*a.* Souvenir sheet of 4, #285-288 3.50 3.50
*Nos. 285-288 (4)* 2.10 1.85

Rock paintings from Highveld area, c. 1700-1850.

Evergreens, Timber, Map of Highveld — A37

Designs: 10c, Pineapple and map of Middleveld. 15c, Map of Lowveld, orange and lemon. 20c, Map of Lubombo and grazing cattle. No. 293, Map of Swaziland and produce, vert.: UL, Evergreens; UR, Orange and lemon; LL, Pineapple; LR, Cattle.

**1977, Oct. 17 Litho. *Perf. 13½***

**289** A37 5c multicolored .20 .20
**290** A37 10c multicolored .40 .40
**291** A37 15c multicolored .60 .60
**292** A37 20c multicolored .85 .85
*Nos. 289-292 (4)* 2.05 2.05

**Souvenir Sheet**

**293** Sheet of 4 2.50 2.50
*a.-d.* A37 25c single stamp .60 .60

Nos. 293a-293d are vertical.

Cussonia Spicata Thunb. — A38

Trees: 10c, Sclerocarya birrea. 20c, Pterocarpus angolensis. 25c, Erythrina lysistemon.

**1978, Jan. 12 Litho. Wmk. 373**

**294** A38 5c multicolored .20 .20
**295** A38 10c multicolored .30 .25
**296** A38 20c multicolored .55 .55
**297** A38 25c multicolored .70 *1.00*
*Nos. 294-297 (4)* 1.75 2.00

Rural Electrification, Lobamba — A39

Hydroelectric Power: 10c, Edwaleni Power Station. 20c, Switchgear, Maguduza Power Station. 25c, Hydroturbine hall, Edwaleni.

**1978, Mar. 6 Litho. *Perf. 13½***

**298** A39 5c black & ocher .20 .20
**299** A39 10c black & yel grn .20 .20
**300** A39 20c black & blue .30 .30
**301** A39 25c black & rose mag .55 *1.00*
*Nos. 298-301 (4)* 1.25 1.70

**Elizabeth II Coronation Anniversary Issue**

Souvenir Sheet

Common Design Types

**1978, Apr. 21 Unwmk. *Perf. 15***

**302** Sheet of 6 2.50 2.50
*a.* CD326 25c Queen's lion .40 .40
*b.* CD327 25c Elizabeth II .40 .40
*c.* CD328 25c African Elephant .40 .40

No. 302 contains 2 se-tenant strips of Nos. 302a-302c, separated by horizontal gutter with commemorative and descriptive inscriptions and showing central part of coronation procession with coach.

Clay Pots A40

Handicrafts: 10c, Basketwork. 20c, Wooden utensils. 30c, Wooden pot with lid.

**Wmk. 373**

**1978, June 26 Litho. *Perf. 13½***

**303** A40 5c multicolored .20 .20
**304** A40 10c multicolored .20 .20
**305** A40 20c multicolored .30 .30
**306** A40 30c multicolored .50 .50
*Nos. 303-306 (4)* 1.20 1.20

See Nos. 317-320.

Defense Force A41

Designs: 6c, King's Regiment. 10c, Tinkabi tractor and ox-drawn plow. 15c, Laying water pipe. 25c, Adult literacy class. 50c, Fire engine and ambulance.

**1978, Sept. 6 Litho. *Perf. 14***

**307** A41 4c multicolored .20 .20
**308** A41 6c multicolored .20 .20
**309** A41 10c multicolored .20 .20
**310** A41 15c multicolored .30 .20
**311** A41 25c multicolored .40 .35
**312** A41 50c multicolored 1.25 .70
*Nos. 307-312 (6)* 2.55 1.85

10th anniversary of independence.

Angel Appearing to the Shepherds — A42

Christmas: 10c, Adoration of the Kings. 15c, Angel warning Joseph in a dream. 25c, Flight into Egypt.

**1978, Dec. 12 Litho. *Perf. 14***

**313** A42 5c multicolored .20 .20
**314** A42 10c multicolored .20 .20
**315** A42 15c multicolored .25 .25
**316** A42 25c multicolored .45 .45
*Nos. 313-316 (4)* 1.10 1.10

Handicrafts Type of 1978

**1979, Jan. 10 *Perf. 13½***

**317** A40 5c Sisal bowls .20 .20
**318** A40 15c Clay pots .30 .30
**319** A40 20c Basketwork .35 .35
**320** A40 30c Hide shield .55 .55
*Nos. 317-320 (4)* 1.40 1.40

Prospecting at Phophonyane A43

15c, Early 3-stamp battery mill. 25c, Cyanide tanks at Piggs Peak. 50c, Pouring off molten gold.

**Wmk. 373**

**1979, Mar. 27 Litho. *Perf. 14***

**321** A43 5c blue & gold .35 .30
**322** A43 15c brown & gold .60 .50
**323** A43 25c green & gold .85 .80
**324** A43 50c red & gold 1.75 1.75
*Nos. 321-324 (4)* 3.55 3.35

Centenary of discovery of gold in Swaziland.

Girls at Piano, 1892, by Renoir A44

Paintings by Renoir: 15c, Madame Charpentier and her Children, 1878. 25c, Girls Picking Flowers, 1889. 50c, Girl with Watering Can, 1876.

**1979, May 8 *Perf. 13½***

**325** A44 5c multicolored .20 .20
**326** A44 15c multicolored .25 .25
**327** A44 25c multicolored .40 .40
**328** A44 50c multicolored .80 .80
*a.* Souvenir sheet of 4, #325-328 2.25 2.25
*Nos. 325-328 (4)* 1.65 1.65

International Year of the Child.

Swaziland No. 40 and Rowland Hill — A45

Rowland Hill and: 20c, Swaziland #18. 25c, Swaziland #142. 50c, Swaziland #60.

**1979, July 17 Litho. *Perf. 14½***

**329** A45 10c multicolored .20 .20
**330** A45 20c multicolored .35 .30
**331** A45 25c multicolored .40 .40
*Nos. 329-331 (3)* .95 .90

**Souvenir Sheet**

**332** A45 50c multicolored 1.25 1.25

Sir Rowland Hill (1795-1879), originator of penny postage.

5c Cupro-Nickel Coin — A46

Coins: 10c, King Sobhuza II and sugar cane. 20c, King and elephant head. 50c, Coat of arms. 1e, Mother and son.

***Perf. 13½x14***

**1979, Sept. 6 Litho. Wmk. 373**

**333** A46 5c multicolored .20 .20
**334** A46 10c multicolored .25 .20
**335** A46 20c multicolored .40 .25
**336** A46 50c multicolored .65 .65
**337** A46 1e multicolored 1.25 1.25
*Nos. 333-337 (5)* 2.75 2.55

Big Bend Post Office A47

15c, Mount Ntondozi microwave station, vert. 20c, Swaziland #53. 50c, Swaziland #217.

**1979, Nov. 22**

**338** A47 5c multicolored .20 .20
**339** A47 15c multicolored .20 .20
**340** A47 20c multicolored .25 .25
**341** A47 50c multicolored .55 .55
*Nos. 338-341 (4)* 1.20 1.20

25th anniv. of Post and Telecommunications service (5c, 15c); 10th anniv. of UPU membership (20c, 50c).

Rotary International, 75th Anniversary A48

**Wmk. 373**

**1980, Feb. 23 Litho. *Perf. 14***

**342** A48 5c shown .20 .20
**343** A48 15c Hospital equipment .25 .25
**344** A48 50c Rotary principles .90 .90
**345** A48 1e Headquarters, Evanston, IL 1.75 1.75
*Nos. 342-345 (4)* 3.10 3.10

Eucomis Autumnalis — A49

Flowers: 1c, Brunsvigia radulosa. 2c, Aloe suprafoliata. 3c, Haemanthus magificus. 4c, Aloe marlothii. 5c, Dicoma zeyheri. 6c, Aloe kniphofioides. 7c, Cyrtanthus bicolor. 15c, Leucospermum gerrardii. 20c, Haemanthus multiflorus. 30c, Acridocarpus natalitius. 50c, Adenium swazicum. 1e, Protea simplex. 2e, Calodendrum capense. 5e, Gladiolus ecklonii. All vert. except. 15c, 20c, 30c, 50c.

**1980, Apr. 28 Unwmk. *Perf. 13½***

**346** A49 1c multicolored .20 .20
**347** A49 2c multicolored .20 .20
**348** A49 3c multicolored .20 .20
**349** A49 4c multicolored .20 .20
**350** A49 5c multicolored .20 .20
**351** A49 6c multicolored .20 .20
**352** A49 7c multicolored .20 .20
**353** A49 10c multicolored .20 .20
**354** A49 15c multicolored .30 .30
**355** A49 20c multicolored .40 .40
**356** A49 30c multicolored .55 .55
**357** A49 50c multicolored .70 .70

**Size: 22x37½mm**

**358** A49 1e multicolored 1.40 1.40
**359** A49 2e multicolored 3.00 3.00
**360** A49 5e multicolored 7.00 7.00
*Nos. 346-360 (15)* 14.95 14.95

No. 348a does not have a date inscription below design.

For surcharges see Nos. 465-470.

**1983 *Perf. 12***

*346a* A49 1c 1.00 .75
*347a* A49 2c 1.00 .75
*348a* A49 3c *3.50 3.50*
*349a* A49 4c 1.25 1.25
*350a* A49 5c *4.00 2.50*
*351a* A49 6c 2.00 1.50
*353a* A49 10c 2.50 1.00
*355a* A49 20c 2.75 1.75
*Nos. 346a-355a (8)* *18.00 13.00*

Inscribed 1983. Nos. 348a, 350a do not have a date inscription below design.

Mail Runner, London 1980 Emblem A50

**1980, May 6 Wmk. 373 *Perf. 14***
**361** A50 10c shown .20 .20
**362** A50 20c Mail truck .30 .25
**363** A50 25c Mail sorting .40 .30
**364** A50 50c Mail ropeway .80 .80
*Nos. 361-364 (4)* 1.70 1.55

London 80 Intl. Stamp Exhib., May 6-14.

Yellow Fish A51

**1980, Aug. 25 Litho. *Perf. 14***
**365** A51 5c shown .35 .20
**366** A51 10c Silver barbel .35 .20
**367** A51 15c Tigerfish .50 .35
**368** A51 30c Squeaker fish .65 .60
**369** A51 1e Bream 2.10 2.10
*Nos. 365-369 (5)* 3.95 3.45

Oribi Antelope A52

**1980, Oct. 1 Litho. *Perf. 14***
**370** A52 5c shown .20 .20
**371** A52 10c Nile crocodile, vert. .40 .20
**372** A52 50c Pangolin .90 .85
**373** A52 1e Leopard, vert. 2.00 1.90
*Nos. 370-373 (4)* 3.50 3.15

Bus A53

**1981, Jan. 5 Litho. *Perf. 14½***
**374** A53 5c shown .20 .20
**375** A53 25c Jet .50 .50
**376** A53 30c Truck .55 .55
**377** A53 1e Train 1.90 1.90
*Nos. 374-377 (4)* 3.15 3.15

Mantenga Falls — A54

**1981, Apr. 16 Litho. *Perf. 14***
**378** A54 5c shown .20 .20
**379** A54 15c Mananga Yacht Club .25 .25
**380** A54 30c White rhinoceri, Mlilwane Game Sanctuary .50 .50
**381** A54 1e Gambling 1.65 1.65
*Nos. 378-381 (4)* 2.60 2.60

**Royal Wedding Issue**
Common Design Type
**Wmk. 373**

**1981, July 21 Litho. *Perf. 14***
**382** CD331 10c Bouquet .20 .20
**383** CD331 25c Charles .40 .40
**384** CD331 1e Couple 1.50 1.50
*Nos. 382-384 (3)* 2.10 2.10

Installation of King Sobhuza II, 1921 A55

60th Anniv. of King Sobhuza II's Reign (King and): 10c, Visit of Royal Family, 1947. 15c, Coronation of Queen Elizabeth II, 1953. 25c, Independence ceremony, 1968. 30c, Early portrait. 1e, Parliament buildings.

**Wmk. 373**
**1981, Aug. 24 Litho. *Perf. 14½***
**385** A55 5c multicolored .20 .20
**386** A55 10c multicolored .20 .20
**387** A55 15c multicolored .25 .25
**388** A55 25c multicolored .40 .40
**389** A55 30c multicolored .50 .50
**390** A55 1e multicolored 1.60 1.60
*Nos. 385-390 (6)* 3.15 3.15

Duke of Edinburgh's Awards, 25th Anniv. — A56

Intl. Year of the Disabled — A57

**1981, Nov. 5 Litho. *Perf. 14***
**391** A56 5c Basketball .20 .20
**392** A56 20c Compass reading .35 .35
**393** A56 50c Square .90 .90
**394** A56 1e Duke of Edinburgh 1.75 1.75
*Nos. 391-394 (4)* 3.20 3.20

**1981, Dec. 7 *Perf. 14x14½, 14½x14***
**395** A57 5c Men learning carpentry, horiz. .35 .25
**396** A57 15c Boy learning Braille .60 .40
**397** A57 25c Carpentry, diff. .90 .65
**398** A57 1e Driving, horiz. 2.75 2.75
*Nos. 395-398 (4)* 4.60 4.05

Papilio Demodocus — A58

**1982, Jan. 6 Litho. *Perf. 14***
**399** A58 5c shown .65 .20
**400** A58 10c Charaxes candiope .70 .35
**401** A58 50c Papilio nireus 2.50 2.40
**402** A58 1e Eurema desjardinsii 5.00 4.75
*Nos. 399-402 (4)* 8.85 7.70

A59

A60

**1982, Apr. 27 Litho. *Perf. 14***
**403** A59 5c Non-smoker, flowers .75 .70
**404** A59 10c Smoker, non-smoker .90 .85

First Intl. Conference on Smoking and Health, Apr. 25-29

***Perf. 13½x13***
**1982, June 16 Litho. Wmk. 373**

a, Female fishing owl. b, Pair. c, Owl in nest, egg. d, Adult and young owls. e, Male.

**405** Strip of 5, multi *125.00 85.00*
*a.-e.* A60 35c, any single *16.00 10.00*

**Princess Diana Issue**
Common Design Type

**1982, July 1 *Perf. 14½***
**406** CD333 5c Arms .30 .30
**407** CD333 20c Diana .55 .55
**408** CD333 50c Wedding 1.40 1.40
**409** CD333 1e Portrait 2.75 2.75
*Nos. 406-409 (4)* 5.00 5.00

Sugar Industry A61

**1982, Sept. 1 Litho.**
**410** A61 5c Planting sugar cane .20 .20
**411** A61 20c Harvesting cane .45 .45
**412** A61 30c Mhlume Mills .65 .65
**413** A61 1e Rail transport 2.25 2.25
*Nos. 410-413 (4)* 3.55 3.55

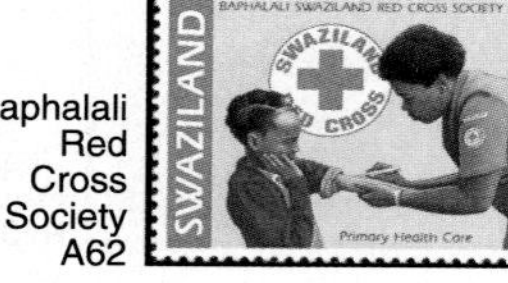

Baphalali Red Cross Society A62

**1982, Nov. 9 *Perf. 14***
**414** A62 5c Immunization .20 .20
**415** A62 20c Red Cross Juniors .35 .35
**416** A62 50c Disaster relief .90 .90
**417** A62 1e Red Cross founder Henry Dunant 1.75 1.75
*Nos. 414-417 (4)* 3.20 3.20

Scouting Year — A63

***Perf. 14½x14***
**1982, Dec. 6 Litho. Wmk. 373**
**418** A63 5c Reciting promise .20 .20
**419** A63 10c Hiking .25 .25
**420** A63 25c Community development .65 .65
**421** A63 75c Baden-Powell 1.90 1.90
*Nos. 418-421 (4)* 3.00 3.00

**Souvenir Sheet**
**422** A63 1e Emblem 3.25 3.25

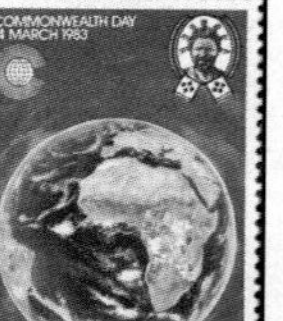

A64

Bearded Vulture — A65

**1983, Mar. 14 Litho. *Perf. 14***
**423** A64 6c Satellite view .20 .20
**424** A64 10c King Sobhuza II, flag .20 .20
**425** A64 50c Beehive huts, horiz. 1.00 1.00
**426** A64 1e Spraying sugar crop, horiz. 2.00 2.00
*Nos. 423-426 (4)* 3.40 3.40

Commonwealth Day.

***Perf. 13½x13***
**1983, May 16 Litho. Wmk. 373**

Designs: a, Male. b, Pair. c, Nest, egg. d, Female at nest. e, Adult, fledgeling.

**427** Strip of 5 22.50 22.50
*a.-e.* A65 35c, any single 3.00 3.00

Souvenir Sheets

Soccer Tour of Swaziland 1983 — A66

**1983, Aug. 20 Litho. *Perf. 14x13½***
**428** A66 75c Natl. team 1.40 1.40
**429** A66 75c Tottenham Hotspur 1.40 1.40
**430** A66 75c Manchester United 1.40 1.40
*Nos. 428-430 (3)* 4.20 4.20

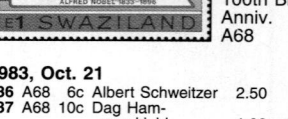

Manned Flight Bicentenary A67

**1983, Sept. 22 Litho. *Perf. 14***
**431** A67 5c Montgolfiere, 1783, vert. .20 .20
**432** A67 10c Wright brothers' plane .20 .20
**433** A67 25c Royal Swazi Fokker Fellowship .40 .40
**434** A67 50c Bell X-1 jet .85 .85
*Nos. 431-434 (4)* 1.65 1.65

**Souvenir Sheet**
**435** A67 1e Columbia space shuttle take-off, vert. 2.50 2.50

Alfred Nobel, 100th Birth Anniv. A68

**1983, Oct. 21**
**436** A68 6c Albert Schweitzer 2.50 .65
**437** A68 10c Dag Hammarskjold 1.00 1.00
**438** A68 50c Albert Einstein 3.25 3.25
**439** A68 1e shown 6.75 6.75
*Nos. 436-439 (4)* 13.50 11.65

World Food Program A69

**1983, Nov. 29**
**440** A69 6c Maize .20 .20
**441** A69 10c Rice .35 .30
**442** A69 50c Cattle 1.00 1.00
**443** A69 1e Tractor 1.90 1.90
*Nos. 440-443 (4)* 3.45 3.40

Women's College A70

**Wmk. 373**
**1984, Mar. 12 Litho. *Perf. 14***
**444** A70 5c shown .20 .20
**445** A70 15c Technical training school .30 .30
**446** A70 50c University .90 .90
**447** A70 1e Primary school 1.75 1.75
*Nos. 444-447 (4)* 3.15 3.15

Bald Ibis — A71

Designs: a, Male. b, Male, female. c, Nest, egg. d, Female at nest. e, Adult, fledgeling.

**1984, May 18 Litho. *Perf. 13½x13***
**448** Strip of 5 29.00 29.00
*a.-e.* A71 35c, any single 4.50 4.50

1984 UPU Congress — A72

Mail Coaches.

**1984, June 15 Litho. *Perf. 14½***
**449** A72 7c Mule-drawn coach .35 .20
**450** A72 15c Oxen-drawn post wagon .50 .30
**451** A72 50c Mule-drawn, diff. 1.10 .90
**452** A72 1e Bristol-London 1.75 1.75
*Nos. 449-452 (4)* 3.70 3.15

1984 Summer Olympics A73

**1984, July 28 *Perf. 14***
**453** A73 7c Running .20 .20
**454** A73 10c Swimming .25 .20
**455** A73 50c Shooting .90 .85
**456** A73 1e Boxing 1.75 1.75
*a.* Souvenir sheet of 4, #453-456 3.50 3.50
*Nos. 453-456 (4)* 3.10 3.00

Local Fungi A74

**1984, Sept. 19 Litho. *Perf. 14***
**457** A74 10c Suillus bovinus 1.75 .35
**458** A74 15c Langermannia gigantea, vert. 2.50 .60
**459** A74 50c Coriolus versicolor, vert. 2.75 2.00
**460** A74 1e Boletus edulis 3.75 3.75
*Nos. 457-460 (4)* 10.75 6.70

20th Anniv. of Swazi Railways A75

**1984, Nov. 5 Litho. Wmk. 373**
**461** A75 10c Opening ceremony .40 .20
**462** A75 25c Type 15A locomotive, Siweni Exchange Yard .75 .60
**463** A75 30c Container loading, Matsapha Station .90 .75
**464** A75 1e No. 268, Alto Tunnel 3.00 2.50
*a.* Souvenir sheet of 4, #461-464 6.25 6.25
*Nos. 461-464 (4)* 5.05 4.05

Nos. 346a, 346-349, 351-352 Surcharged

**1984, Dec. 15 Litho. *Perf. 12***
**465** A49 10c on 4c #349 .40 .20
*a.* Perf. 13½ *50.00 50.00*

***Perf. 13½, 12 (#469)***
**466** A49 15c on 7c #352 .50 .30
**467** A49 20c on 3c #348 .45 .25
*a.* Perf 12 —
**468** A49 25c on 6c #351 .50 .25
**469** A49 30c on 1c #346a .60 .30
**470** A49 30c on 2c #347 2.75 2.75
*Nos. 465-470 (6)* 5.20 4.05

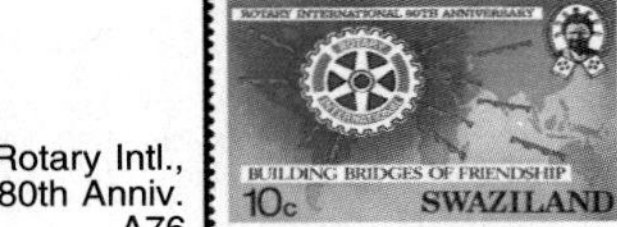
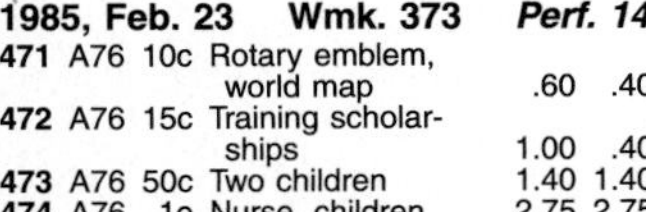

Rotary Intl., 80th Anniv. A76

**1985, Feb. 23 Wmk. 373 *Perf. 14***
**471** A76 10c Rotary emblem, world map .60 .40
**472** A76 15c Training scholarships 1.00 .40
**473** A76 50c Two children 1.40 1.40
**474** A76 1e Nurse, children 2.75 2.75
*Nos. 471-474 (4)* 5.75 4.95

Life Cycle of the Ground Hornbill — A77

Audubon birth bicentenary.

**1985, May 15 Wmk. 373**
**475** Strip of 5 16.00 16.00
*a.-e.* A77 25c, any single 2.25 2.25

**Queen Mother 85th Birthday**
Common Design Type
***Perf. 14½x14***

**1985, June 7 Litho. Wmk. 384**
**476** CD336 10c Visit to South Africa, 1947 .35 .20
**477** CD336 15c With Elizabeth II and Margaret .35 .20
**478** CD336 50c 75th birthday celebration .90 .60
**479** CD336 1e Holding Prince Henry 1.25 1.25
*Nos. 476-479 (4)* 2.85 2.25

**Souvenir Sheet**
**480** CD336 2e Greeting Prince Andrew 4.00 4.00

Classic Automobiles — A78

**Wmk. 373**
**1985, Sept. 16 Litho. *Perf. 14***
**481** A78 10c Buick Tourer .75 .75
**482** A78 15c Four-cylinder Rover .80 .75
**483** A78 50c De Dion Bouton 1.90 1.60
**484** A78 1e Ford Model-T 3.25 3.25
*Nos. 481-484 (4)* 6.70 6.35

Intl. Youth Year A79

**1985, Dec. 2**
**485** A79 10c Bridge-building .20 .20
**486** A79 20c Girl Guides camping .20 .20
**487** A79 50c Recreation .50 .45
**488** A79 1e Guides collecting branches .95 .90
*Nos. 485-488 (4)* 1.85 1.75

Girl Guide Movement, 20c, 1e. IYY, 10c, 50c.

Halley's Comet A80

**1986, Feb. 27 Wmk. 384 *Perf. 14½***
**489** A80 1.50e multicolored 4.25 4.25

**Queen Elizabeth II 60th Birthday**
Common Design Type

10c, Princess Anne's christening, 1950. 30c, Wedding of Prince Charles and Lady Diana, 1981. 45c, With George VI, the Dutchess of York and Sobhuza II at Nhlangano, 1947. 1e, At Windsor Polo Ground, 1984. 2e, Visiting Crown Agents' offices, 1983.

**1986, Apr. 21 *Perf. 14x14½***
**490** CD337 10c scar, blk & sil .20 .20
**491** CD337 30c ultra & multi .30 .30
**492** CD337 45c green, blk & sil .45 .45
**493** CD337 1e violet & multi .95 .95
**494** CD337 2e rose vio & multi 2.00 2.00
*Nos. 490-494 (5)* 3.90 3.90

For overprints see Nos. 527-530.

Coronation of Crown Prince Makhosetive A81

10c, Portrait, vert. 20c, Prince and King Sobhuza II at an Incwala ceremony. 25c, Prince at primary school. 30c, At school in England. 40c, Escorted from Matsapha Airport by Guard of Honor. 2e, Dancing the Simemo.

**1986, Apr. 25 *Perf. 14½***
**495** A81 10c multicolored .50 .50
**496** A81 20c multicolored .60 .60
**497** A81 25c multicolored .75 .75
**498** A81 30c multicolored .90 .90
**499** A81 40c multicolored 1.75 1.10
**500** A81 2e multicolored 5.75 5.75
*Nos. 495-500 (6)* 10.25 9.60

Assoc. of Round Tables in Central Africa, 50th Anniv. — A82

Club emblems.

**Wmk. 384**
**1986, Oct. 4 Litho. *Perf. 14***
**501** A82 15c Orbis .30 .20
**502** A82 25c Ehlanzeni 51 .40 .35
**503** A82 55c Mbabane 30 .85 .70
**504** A82 70c Bulembu 54 1.00 1.00
**505** A82 2e Manzini 44 2.50 2.50
*Nos. 501-505 (5)* 5.05 4.75

Butterflies — A83

**Unwmk.**
**1987, Mar. 17 Litho. *Perf. 14***
**506** A83 10c Yellow pansy .50 .50
**507** A83 15c Guineafowl .60 .50
**508** A83 20c Red forest charaxes .60 .30
**509** A83 25c Paradise skipper .60 .60
**510** A83 30c Broad-bordered acraea .60 .50
**511** A83 35c Veined swallowtail .60 .50
**512** A83 45c Large striped swordtail .65 .65
**513** A83 50c Eyed pansy .70 .50
**514** A83 55c Zebra white .70 .50
**515** A83 70c Gaudy commodore .90 1.25
**516** A83 1e Common dotted border 1.25 3.00
**517** A83 5e Queen purple tip 4.25 2.00
**518** A83 10e Natal barred blue 6.75 5.75
*Nos. 506-518 (13)* 18.70 16.55

See Nos. 600-611. For surcharges see Nos. 574-577. Compare with design A101.

White Rhinoceros A84

**1987, July 1 Wmk. 384 *Perf. 14½***
**519** A84 15c Two adults 2.50 1.10
**520** A84 25c Adult, calf 3.75 1.75
**521** A84 45c Adult walking 7.25 5.25
**522** A84 70c Adult in mud 8.75 5.75
*Nos. 519-522 (4)* 22.25 13.85

World Wildlife Fund.

Flowers — A85

**1987, Oct. 19 Litho. *Perf. 14½***
**523** A85 15c Blue moon 1.25 .85
**524** A85 35c Danse de feu 2.25 1.50
**525** A85 55c Odin 2.75 2.25
**526** A85 2e Lilium davidii 8.50 8.50
*Nos. 523-526 (4)* 14.75 13.10

Nos. 491-494 Ovptd. "40TH WEDDING ANNIVERSARY" in Silver
***Perf. 14x14½***

**1987, Dec. 9 Litho. Wmk. 384**
**527** CD337 30c ultra & multi .30 .30
**528** CD337 45c green, blk & sil .45 .45
**529** CD337 1e violet & multi 1.00 1.00
**530** CD337 2e rose vio & multi 2.00 2.00
*Nos. 527-530 (4)* 3.75 3.75

Insects A86

**Wmk. 384**
**1988, Mar. 14 Litho. *Perf. 14***
**531** A86 15c Zabalius aridus 1.75 .25
**532** A86 55c Callidea bohemani 3.25 1.00
**533** A86 1e Phymateus viridipes 5.50 5.50
**534** A86 2e Nomadacris septemfasciata 8.50 9.50
*Nos. 531-534 (4)* 19.00 16.25

1988 Summer Olympics, Seoul A87

**1988, Aug. 22 Litho. Wmk. 384**
**535** A87 15c Flag-bearer, stadium 1.00 .40
**536** A87 35c Tae kwon do 1.50 .80
**537** A87 1e Boxing 2.00 2.00
**538** A87 2e Tennis 4.00 4.00
*Nos. 535-538 (4)* 8.50 7.20

Intl. Tennis Federation, 75th anniv. (2e).

Small Mammals A88

**Wmk. 384**
**1989, Jan. 16 Litho. *Perf. 14***
**539** A88 35c Green monkey 1.75 .40
**540** A88 55c Rock dassie 2.50 .80
**541** A88 1e Zorilla 4.50 4.00
**542** A88 2e African wildcat 8.00 9.00
*Nos. 539-542 (4)* 16.75 14.20

Intl. Red Cross and Red Crescent Organizations, 125th Annivs. — A89

**Wmk. 373**

**1989, Sept. 21 Litho.** ***Perf. 12***

**543** A89 15c David Hynd .30 .20
**544** A89 60c First aid .75 .65
**545** A89 1e Sigombeni Clinic 1.25 1.25
**546** A89 2e Relief work 2.10 2.10
*Nos. 543-546 (4)* 4.40 4.20

21st Birthday of King Mswati III A90

King Mswati III: 15c, With Prince of Wales, 1987. 60c, With Pope John Paul II, 1988. 1e, Introduction to the nation while crown prince. 2e, With queen mother.

***Perf. 14½x14***

**1989, Nov. 15 Unwmk.**

**547** A90 15c multicolored .20 .20
**548** A90 60c multicolored .55 .55
**549** A90 1e multicolored .95 .95
**550** A90 2e multicolored 1.90 1.90
*Nos. 547-550 (4)* 3.60 3.60

African Development Bank, 25th Anniv. — A91

15c, Manzini-Mahamba Road. 60c, Mbabane microwave radio link. 1e, Mbabane Government Hospital. 2e, Ezulwini Power Switching Station.

***Perf. 14x14½***

**1989, Dec. 18 Wmk. 384**

**551** A91 15c multicolored .30 .20
**552** A91 60c multicolored .55 .40
**553** A91 1e multicolored .90 .90
**554** A91 2e multicolored 1.75 1.75
*Nos. 551-554 (4)* 3.50 3.25

Stamp World London '90 — A92

**Wmk. 384**

**1990, May 3 Litho.** ***Perf. 12½***

**555** A92 15c Intl. priority mail .30 .25
**556** A92 60c Facsimile service .65 .55
**557** A92 1e Post office 1.25 1.25
**558** A92 2e Ezulwini Earth Satellite Station 2.25 2.25
*Nos. 555-558 (4)* 4.45 4.30

**Souvenir Sheet**

**559** A92 2e Mail runner 6.75 6.75

150th anniv. of the Penny Black.

**Queen Mother, 90th Birthday**
Common Design Types

**1990, Aug. 4 Wmk. 384** ***Perf. 14x15***

**565** CD343 75c Queen Mother .70 .60

***Perf. 14½***

**566** CD344 4e King, Queen visiting Hatfield House 3.50 3.50

Intl. Literacy Year A94

**Wmk. 373**

**1990, Sept. 21 Litho.** ***Perf. 14***

**567** A94 15c shown .20 .20
**568** A94 75c Outdoor class .65 .65
**569** A94 1e Modern instruction .80 .80
**570** A94 2e Receiving diploma 1.60 1.60
*Nos. 567-570 (4)* 3.25 3.25

UN Development Program, 40th Anniv. — A95

***Perf. 13½x14***

**1990, Dec. 10 Litho. Wmk. 373**

**571** A95 60c Rural water supply .55 .55
**572** A95 1e Seed production .95 .95
**573** A95 2e Low cost housing 1.90 1.90
*Nos. 571-573 (3)* 3.40 3.40

Nos. 509-510, 512, 514 Surcharged

**Unwmk.**

**1990, Dec. 17 Litho.** ***Perf. 14***

**574** A83 10c on 25c multi .20 .20
**575** A83 15c on 30c multi .25 .25
**575A** A83 15c on 45c multi *50.00 30.00*
**576** A83 20c on 45c multi .35 .35
**577** A83 40c on 55c multi .70 .70

National Heritage A96

***Perf. 14x14½***

**1991, Feb. 11 Wmk. 233**

**578** A96 15c Lobamba Hot Spring .35 .20
**579** A96 60c Sibebe Rock .80 .60
**580** A96 1e Jolobela Falls 1.25 1.25
**581** A96 2e Mantjolo Sacred Pool 2.00 2.00
*Nos. 578-581 (4)* 4.40 4.05

**Souvenir Sheet**

***Perf. 14***

**581A** A96 2e Usushwana River 5.00 5.00

Coronation of King Mswati III, 5th Anniv. A97

***Perf. 14x13½***

**1991, Apr. 24 Litho. Wmk. 373**

**582** A97 15c King making radio address .30 .20
**583** A97 75c Butimba royal hunt 1.00 .80
**584** A97 1e King, schoolmates, 1986 1.10 1.10
**585** A97 2e King opening parliament 2.25 2.25
*Nos. 582-585 (4)* 4.65 4.35

**Elizabeth & Philip, Birthdays**
Common Design Types

**Wmk. 384**

**1991, June 17 Litho.** ***Perf. 14½***

**586** CD346 1e multicolored 1.25 1.25
**587** CD345 2e multicolored 2.00 2.00
*a.* Pair, #586-587 + label 3.75 3.75

Flowers — A98

Christmas — A99

**1991, Sept. 30 Wmk. 373** ***Perf. 14***

**588** A98 15c Xerophyta retinervis .50 .35
**589** A98 75c Bauhinia galpinii 1.25 1.00
**590** A98 1e Dombeya rotundifolia 1.50 1.50
**591** A98 2e Kigelia africana 2.75 2.75
*Nos. 588-591 (4)* 6.00 5.60

**Wmk. 373**

**1991, Dec. 18 Litho.** ***Perf. 13½***

**592** A99 20c Santa Claus, children .25 .20
**593** A99 70c Carolers .90 .80
**594** A99 1e Priest reading Bible 1.25 1.25
**595** A99 2e Nativity Scene 2.25 2.25
*Nos. 592-595 (4)* 4.65 4.50

Reptiles A100

**1992, Feb. 25**

**596** A100 20c Lubombo flat lizard 1.10 .25
**597** A100 70c Natal hinged tortoise 2.75 1.50
**598** A100 1e Swazi thick-toed gecko 3.50 3.50
**599** A100 2e Nile monitor 4.75 4.75
*Nos. 596-599 (4)* 12.10 10.00

Butterflies A101

**1992-2000 Litho.** ***Perf. 14***

**600** A101 5c Red tip .20 .20
**601** A101 10c like #506 .20 .20
**602** A101 15c like #507 .20 .20
**603** A101 20c like #508 .25 .20
**604** A101 25c like #509 .25 .20
**605** A101 30c like #510 .30 .20
**606** A101 35c like #511 .35 .30
**607** A101 45c like #512 .40 .35
**608** A101 50c like #513 .45 .40
**609** A101 55c like #514 .50 .45
**610** A101 70c like #515 .55 .55
**611** A101 1e like #516 1.00 1.00
**612** A101 5e Like #517 — —
**613** A101 10e Like #518 — —
*Nos. 600-611 (12)* 4.65 4.25

Issued: Nos. 600-611, 8/26/92. No. 612, 2000.

Nos. 600-611 dated 1991. Nos. 612 and 613 dated 2000.

Nos. 600-612 have different portrait of King Mswati III from Nos. 506-517.

A102

A103

Designs: 20c, Missionaries with royal family. 1e, Pioneer missionaries.

**1992, Dec. 16 Litho.** ***Perf. 13½x14***

**614** A102 20c multicolored .60 .50
**615** A102 1e multicolored 2.25 2.25

Evangelical Alliance Mission in Swaziland, cent.

**1993, Mar. 18 Litho.** ***Perf. 13½x14***

Cooking Utensils: 20c, Calabashes. 70c, Contemporary pottery for cooking. 1e, Wooden bowls. 2e, Quern for grinding seeds.

**616** A103 20c multicolored .55 .20
**617** A103 70c multicolored 1.25 .80
**618** A103 1e multicolored 1.75 1.75
**619** A103 2e multicolored 2.75 2.75
*Nos. 616-619 (4)* 6.30 5.50

A104

A105

King Mswati, 25th Birthday: 25c, King Mswati as baby with mother. 40c, King Mswati III addressing PTA meeting. 1e, King Sobhuza II receiving Instrument of Independence, 1968. 2e, King Mswati III delivering first speech on Coronation Day, 1986.

**1993, Sept. 6 Litho.** ***Perf. 13½x14***

**620** A104 25c multicolored .25 .20
**621** A104 40c multicolored .35 .25
**622** A104 1e multicolored .90 .90
**623** A104 2e multicolored 1.75 1.75
*Nos. 620-623 (4)* 3.25 3.10

Independence, 25th anniv.

**1993, Nov. 25** ***Perf. 13½***

Common Waxbill

**624** A105 25c Male & female .50 .25
**625** A105 40c Nest & eggs .75 .30
**626** A105 1e Incubating 1.75 1.75
**627** A105 2e Feeding nestlings 2.75 2.75
*Nos. 624-627 (4)* 5.75 5.05

A106

A107

**1994, Feb. 22 Litho.** ***Perf. 13½***

**628** A106 25c Education .35 .25
**629** A106 40c Rural services .45 .25
**630** A106 1e Swazi culture 1.75 1.75
**631** A106 2e People to people 2.00 2.00
*Nos. 628-631 (4)* 4.55 4.25

US Peace Corps, 25th anniv.

**1994, Sept. 15** ***Perf. 13½x14***

Mushrooms.

**632** A107 30c Horse mushroom 1.40 .60
**633** A107 40c Penny bun bolete 1.40 .60
**634** A107 1e Rusulla verdigris 3.00 2.00
**635** A107 2e Honey fungus 4.00 4.00
*Nos. 632-635 (4)* 9.80 7.20

ICAO, 50th Anniv. A108

**1994, Nov. 30 Litho.** ***Perf. 14***

**636** A108 30c Natl. airline .50 .20
**637** A108 40c Control tower .55 .30
**638** A108 1e Air rescue service 1.25 1.25
**639** A108 2e Air traffic control 1.75 1.75
*Nos. 636-639 (4)* 4.05 3.50

A109

A110

Traditional handicrafts.

**1995, Apr. 7** **Litho.** ***Perf. 13½***

**640** A109 35c Wooden bowls .20 .20
**641** A109 50c Chicken nests .30 .30
**642** A109 1e Leather crafts .55 .55
**643** A109 2e Wood carvings 1.10 1.10
*Nos. 640-643 (4)* 2.15 2.15

**1995, June 5** **Litho.** ***Perf. 13½***

FAO, 50th anniv.: 35c, Corn harvest. 50c, Planting vegetables. 1e, Herd of cattle. 2e, Sorghum harvest.

**644** A110 35c multicolored .20 .20
**645** A110 50c multicolored .35 .35
**646** A110 1e multicolored .70 .70
**647** A110 2e multicolored 1.40 1.40
*Nos. 644-647 (4)* 2.65 2.65

Lourie A111

**1995, Sept. 27** **Litho.** ***Perf. 13½x13***

**648** A111 35c Knysna lourie .65 .30
**649** A111 50c Lourie in flight .85 .50
**650** A111 1e Purple crested lourie 1.25 1.25
**651** A111 2e Gray lourie 1.75 1.75
*Nos. 648-651 (4)* 4.50 3.80

Reptiles A112

**1996, Jan. 17** **Litho.** ***Perf. 13½x13***

**652** A112 35c Chameleon .60 .25
**653** A112 50c Rock monitor .75 .40
**654** A112 1e African python 1.25 1.25
**655** A112 2e Tree agama 2.00 2.00
*Nos. 652-655 (4)* 4.60 3.90

Trees — A113

**1996, Apr. 23** **Litho.** ***Perf. 13***

**656** A113 40c Waterberry .30 .20
**657** A113 60c Sycamore fig .40 .35
**658** A113 1e Stem fruit .70 .70
**659** A113 2e Wild medlar 1.25 1.25
*Nos. 656-659 (4)* 2.65 2.50

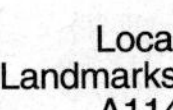
Local Landmarks A114

Designs: 40c, First church, Mahamba Methodist. 60c, Colonial Secretariat, Mbabane. 1e, King Sobhuza II Memorial Monument. 2e, First High Court Building, Hlatikulu.

**1996, Aug. 26** **Litho.** ***Perf. 13½x13***

**660** A114 40c multicolored .20 .20
**661** A114 60c multicolored .35 .35
**662** A114 1e multicolored .75 .75
**663** A114 2e multicolored 1.40 1.40
*Nos. 660-663 (4)* 2.70 2.70

UNICEF, 50th Anniv. A115

Designs: 40c, Basic education for all. 60c, Universal child immunization, vert. 1e, No more polio, vert. 2e, Children first, vert.

**1996, Dec. 31** **Litho.** ***Perf. 13½x14***

**664** A115 40c multicolored .20 .20

***Perf. 14x13½***

**665** A115 60c multicolored .40 .40
**666** A115 1e multicolored .55 .55
**667** A115 2e multicolored 1.25 1.25
*Nos. 664-667 (4)* 2.40 2.40

Wild Animals A116

50c, Klipspringer, vert. 70c, Gray duiker, vert. 1e, Antbear. 2e, Cape clawless otter.

***Perf. 14x13½, 13½x14***

**1997, Sept. 22** **Litho.**

**668** A116 50c multicolored .40 .30
**669** A116 70c multicolored .50 .40
**670** A116 1e multicolored .85 .85
**671** A116 2e multicolored 1.50 1.50
*Nos. 668-671 (4)* 3.25 3.05

Traditional Costumes — A117

**1997, Dec. 1** **Litho.** ***Perf. 13x13½***

**672** A117 50c Umgaco .20 .20
**673** A117 70c Sigeja .45 .45
**674** A117 1e Umdada .60 .60
**675** A117 2e Ligcebesha 1.25 1.25
*Nos. 672-675 (4)* 2.50 2.50

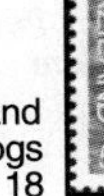
Toads and Frogs A118

**1998, June 1** **Litho.** ***Perf. 14***

**676** A118 55c Olive toad .35 .20
**677** A118 75c African bullfrog .50 .30
**678** A118 1e Water lily frog .80 .80
**679** A118 2e Bushveld rain frog 1.50 1.50
*Nos. 676-679 (4)* 3.15 2.80

Independence, 30th Anniv., King Mswati III, 30th Birthday — A119

55c, King Sobhuza II Memorial Park. 75c, King Mswati III taking oath. 1e, King Mswati III delivering 1st speech. 2e, King Sobhuza II receiving instrument of independence.

***Perf. 13½x14, 14x13½***

**1998, Sept. 3** **Litho.**

**680** A119 55c multicolored .20 .20
**681** A119 75c multicolored .45 .45
**682** A119 1e multicolored .65 .65
**683** A119 2e multicolored 1.10 1.10
*Nos. 680-683 (4)* 2.40 2.40

Traditional Utensils — A120

**1999, May 17** **Litho.** ***Perf. 13¾x13¼***

**684** A120 60c Grinding stone .20 .20
**685** A120 75c Stirring sticks .30 .30
**686** A120 80c Clay pot .30 .30
**687** A120 95c Swazi spoons .35 .35
**688** A120 1.75e Beer cup .75 .75
**689** A120 2.40e Mortar and pestle 1.00 1.00
*Nos. 684-689 (6)* 2.90 2.90

UPU, 125th Anniv. A121

***Perf. 13¾x13½***

**1999, Oct. 9** **Litho.** **Unwmk.**

**690** A121 60c Internet service, vert. .20 .20
**691** A121 80c Cellular phone service, vert. .30 .30

***Perf. 13½x13¾***

**692** A121 1e Intl. mail exchange .40 .40
**693** A121 2.40e Training school 1.00 1.00
*Nos. 690-693 (4)* 1.90 1.90

Wildlife A122

Designs: 65c, Lion, vert. 90c, Leopard. 1.50e, Rhinoceros. 2.50e, Buffalo, vert.

***Perf. 13½x13¼, 13¼x13½***

**2000. July 3** **Litho.** **Unwmk.**

**694** A122 65c multi .35 .20
**695** A122 90c multi .60 .30
**696** A122 1.50e multi 1.50 1.50
**697** A122 2.50e multi 1.25 1.25
*Nos. 694-697 (4)* 3.70 3.25

Worldwide Fund for Nature (WWF) — A123

Designs: 65c, Oribi with young. 90c, Oribi. 1.50e, Klipspringers. 2.50e, Klipspringers, diff.

**Wmk. 373**

**2001, Feb. 1** **Litho.** ***Perf. 14***

**698-701** A123 Set of 4 3.25 3.25
*701a* Sheet, 4 each #698-701 13.00 13.00

Environmental Protection — A124

Designs: 70c, Fighting forest fires. 95c, Tree planting. 2.05e Construction of Maguga Dam. 2.80e, Building embankment.

**2001, July 30** **Litho.** ***Perf. 14***

**702-705** A124 Set of 4 1.60 1.60

**Reign Of Queen Elizabeth II, 50th Anniv. Issue**

Common Design Type

Designs: Nos. 706, 710a, 70c, Princess Elizabeth, Princess Anne, Princes Philip and Charles, 1947. Nos. 707, 710b, 95c, Wearing purple hat. Nos. 708, 710c, 2.05e, Wearing crown. Nos. 709, 710d, 2.80e, Wearing yellow hat, 2001. No. 710e, 22.50e, 1955 portrait by Annigoni (38x50mm).

***Perf. 14¼x14½, 13¾ (#710e)***

**2002, Feb. 6** **Litho.** **Wmk. 373**

**With Gold Frames**

**706-709** CD360 Set of 4 4.50 4.50

**Souvenir Sheet**

**Without Gold Frames**

**710** CD360 Sheet of 5, #a-e 7.50 7.50

Tourism A125

Designs: 75c, Swazi chalets. 1e, King Mswati III facing lions, vert. 2.05e, Crocodile. 2.80e, Ostriches.

***Perf. 13¼x13¾, 13¾x13¼***

**2002, Dec. 23** **Litho.**

**711-714** A125 Set of 4 1.90 1.90

Musical Instruments — A126

Designs: 80c, Mouth organ, vert. 1.05e, Rattles. 2.35e, Kudu horn trumpet. 2.80e, Chordphone, vert.

**2003, Aug. 12** **Litho.** ***Perf. 14***

**715-718** A126 Set of 4 1.90 1.90

AIDS Prevention — A127

Designs: 85c, Community home-based care. 1.10e, Know your HIV status. 2.45e, Testing blood samples, vert. 3.35e, Unsterilized instruments can transmit HIV and AIDS, vert.

***Perf. 13¼x13¾, 13¾x13¼***

**2004, Mar. 9** **Litho.**

**719-722** A127 Set of 4 2.40 2.40

Global 2003 Smart Partnership International Dialogue, Ezulwini — A128

Designs: 85c, King Mswati III, Swaziland flag, map of Africa. 1.10e, Map of Africa, Swaziland flag, Smart Partnership International Movement emblems, horiz. 2.45e, Sharing ideas. 3.35e, Man, woman at microphone.

*Perf. 13¾x13¼, 13¼x13¾*

**2004, June 14** **Litho.**
**723-726** A128 Set of 4 2.40 2.40

Birds
A129

Designs: 85c, Purple-crested louries, national bird of Swaziland. 1.10e, Blue cranes, national bird of South Africa. 1.35e, Cattle egrets, national bird of Botswana. 1.90e, African fish eagles, national bird of Zimbabwe. 2e, African fish eagles, national bird of Namibia. 2.45e, Bar-tailed trogons. 3e, African fish eagles, national bird of Zambia. 3.35e, Peregrine falcons, national bird of Angola.

**2004, Oct. 11** **Litho.** ***Perf. 14***
**727-734** A129 Set of 8 5.00 5.00

**Sheet of 8**

No. 735: a, Cattle egrets, national bird of Botswana. b, African fish eagles, national bird of Namibia. c, Bar-tailed trogons. d, African fish eagles, national bird of Zambia. e, Peregrine falcons, national bird of Angola.

**2004, Oct. 11** **Litho.** ***Perf. 14***
**735** Sheet of 8, #727, 728, 730, #735a-735e *6.75 6.75*
***a.-b.*** A129 1.90e Either single *.90 .90*
***c.*** A129 2.25e multi *1.10 1.10*
***d.-e.*** A129 2.30e Either single *1.10 1.10*

See Angola No. , Botswana Nos. 792-793, Malawi No., Namibia No. 1052, South Africa No. 1342, Zambia No. 1033, and Zimbabwe No. 975.

Road Safety Council
A130

Inscriptions: 85c, Stop Killing Them In Traffic. 1.10e, Avoid Accidents. 2.45e, Safe Crossing. 3.35e, No Overloading.

**2005, Jan. 25** **Litho.** ***Perf. 13¼x13¾***
**736-739** A130 Set of 4 2.60 2.60

Snakes
A131

Designs: 85c, Black mamba. 1.10e, Python. 2.45e, Boomslang. 3.35e, Puff adder.

**2005, Apr. 5** **Litho.** ***Perf. 13¼x13¾***
**740-743** A131 Set of 4 2.50 2.50

Pope John Paul II (1920-2005)
A132

**2005, Aug. 18** **Litho.** ***Perf. 14***
**744** A132 4.50e multi 1.50 1.50

Locusts
A133

Designs: 85c, Schistocerca solitaria. 1.10e, Red locust. 2.45e, Southern Africa desert locust. 3.35e, African migratory locust.

**2005, Oct. 11** **Litho.** ***Perf. 13¼x13¾***
**745-748** A133 Set of 4 2.40 2.40

Queen Mothers — A134

Designs: 85c, Ntombi Tfwala. 1.10e, Dzeliwe Shongwe. 2e, Lomawa Ndwandwe. 2.45e, Labotsibeni Mdluli. 3.35e, Tibati Nkambule.

**2006, Jan. 10** ***Perf. 13¾x13¼***
**749-753** A134 Set of 5 3.25 3.25

Postal History
A135

Designs: 90c, Manzini District Office and Post Office, 1920s. 1.15e, Ox wagon. 2e, Bremersdorp Post Office, 1893. 2.55e, Mail runner, vert. 3.50e, Mbabane Temporary Post Office, 1902.

***Perf. 13¾***

**2006, May 8** **Litho.** **Unwmk.**
**754-758** A135 Set of 5 3.50 3.50

Waterfalls — A136

Designs: 90c, Mgubudla Falls. 1.15e, Phophonyane Falls. 1.40e, Mantenga Falls, horiz. 2e, Malolotja Falls. 2.55e, Mabhudlweni Falls. 3.50e, Manzamnyama Falls.

**2006, Sept. 26**
**759-764** A136 Set of 6 3.00 3.00

Trees
A137

Designs: 70c, Common cabbage tree. 85c, Broom cluster fig. 90c, Scented thorn. 1.05e, Natal mahogany. 1.15e, Marula. 1.40e, Stem fruit tree. 2e, Fever tree. 2.40e, Large-leaved coral tree. 2.55e, African teak. 3.50e, Red ivory. 5e, Common coral tree. 10e, Jacket-plum. 20e, Sausage tree.

**2007, Jan. 23** **Litho.** ***Perf. 13¼x13¾***

| | | | | |
|---|---|---|---|---|
| **765** | A137 70c multi | | .20 | .20 |
| **766** | A137 85c multi | | .25 | .25 |
| **767** | A137 90c multi | | .25 | .25 |
| **768** | A137 1.05e multi | | .30 | .30 |
| **769** | A137 1.15e multi | | .30 | .30 |
| **770** | A137 1.40e multi | | .40 | .40 |
| **771** | A137 2e multi | | .55 | .55 |
| **772** | A137 2.40e multi | | .65 | .65 |
| **773** | A137 2.55e multi | | .70 | .70 |
| **774** | A137 3.50e multi | | 1.00 | 1.00 |
| **775** | A137 5e multi | | 1.40 | 1.40 |
| **776** | A137 10e multi | | 2.75 | 2.75 |
| **777** | A137 20e multi | | 5.50 | 5.50 |
| | *Nos. 765-777 (13)* | | 14.25 | 14.25 |

## POSTAGE DUE STAMPS

**Catalogue values for unused stamps in this section are for Never Hinged items.**

D1

D2

**1933** **Typo.** **Wmk. 4** ***Perf. 14***
**J1** D1 1p carmine rose .30 *4.00*
***a.*** Wmk. 4a (error) 275.00
**J2** D1 2p violet 2.25 *15.00*

No. 57 Surcharged

I

II

**1961** **Engr.** ***Perf. 13½x13***

| | | | |
|---|---|---|---|
| **J3** | A5 (2d) on 2p, type I | 10.00 | *12.00* |
| ***a.*** | Type II | .40 | |
| **J4** | A5 1c on 2p, type I | 2.00 | *3.25* |
| ***a.*** | Type II | 1.50 | 1.50 |
| **J5** | A5 2c on 2p, type I | 2.00 | *3.25* |
| ***a.*** | Type II | 1.10 | 1.10 |
| **J6** | A5 5c on 2p, type I | 2.00 | *3.25* |
| ***a.*** | Type II | 1.75 | 1.75 |
| | *Nos. J3-J6 (4)* | 16.00 | 21.75 |
| | *Nos. J3a-J6a (4)* | 4.75 | |
| | *Nos. J4a-J6a (3)* | | 4.35 |

No. J3a was surcharged after decimal currency was introduced.

Type of 1933

**1961** **Typo.** ***Perf. 14***

| | | | |
|---|---|---|---|
| **J7** | D1 1c carmine rose | .20 | .20 |
| **J8** | D1 2c violet | .30 | .30 |
| **J9** | D1 5c green | .75 | 1.00 |
| | *Nos. J7-J9 (3)* | 1.25 | 1.50 |

**Wmk. 314**

**1971, Feb. 1** **Litho.** ***Perf. 11½***

| | | | |
|---|---|---|---|
| **J10** | D2 1c carmine rose | .30 | .35 |
| **J11** | D2 2c dull purple | .40 | .50 |
| **J12** | D2 5c green | .70 | .80 |
| | *Nos. J10-J12 (3)* | 1.40 | 1.65 |

**1977, Jan. 17** **Wmk. 373**

| | | | |
|---|---|---|---|
| *J10a* | D2 1c carmine rose | .30 | .30 |
| *J11a* | D2 2c dull purple | .40 | .40 |
| *J12a* | D2 5c green | .70 | .70 |
| | *Nos. J10a-J12a (3)* | 1.40 | 1.40 |

**1978-91** ***Perf. 15x14***

**Size: 17½x21mm**

| | | | |
|---|---|---|---|
| **J13** | D2 1c carmine lake | .20 | .20 |
| **J14** | D2 2c purple | .20 | .20 |
| **J15** | D2 5c green | .20 | .20 |
| **J16** | D2 10c sky blue | .20 | .20 |
| **J17** | D2 25c brown | .30 | .20 |
| | *Nos. J13-J17 (5)* | 1.10 | 1.00 |

Nos. J14-J15 reissued dated 1991. Issued: 1c-5c, 4/20; 10c-25c, 7/17/91.

# SWEDEN

'swē-dən

LOCATION — Northern Europe, occupying the eastern half of the Scandinavian Peninsula
GOVT. — Constitutional Monarchy
AREA — 173,341 sq. mi.
POP. — 8,911,296 (1999 est.)
CAPITAL — Stockholm

48 skilling banco = 1 riksdaler banco (until 1858)

100 öre = 1 riksdaler (1858 to 1874)
100 öre = 1 krona (since 1874)

**Catalogue values for unused stamps in this country are for Never Hinged items, beginning with Scott 358 in the regular postage section, and Scott B37 in the semi-postal section.**

### Watermarks

Wmk. 180 — Crown

Wmk. 307 — Crown and 1955

Wmk. 181 — Wavy Lines

Values for unused stamps are for examples with original gum as defined in the catalogue introduction except Nos. 1-5, including reprints, and LX1 which are valued without gum.

Coat of Arms
A1 A2

**1855 Unwmk. Typo. *Perf. 14***

1 A1 3s blue green 7,500. *3,000.*
*a.* 3s orange (error) *3,000,000.*
2 A1 4s lt blue 1,250. 70.00
3 A1 6s gray *8,000.* 975.00
*b.* Imperf. —
4 A1 8s orange 4,250. 550.00
*c.* Imperf. —
5 A1 24s dull red *6,500.* *1,500.*

*Nos. 1-5 were reprinted two or three times perf. 14, once perf. 13. Value of the lowest cost perf. 14 reprints, $375 each. Perf. 13, $325 each.*

*The reprints were made after Nos. 1-5 were withdrawn, but before being demonitized. Used copies are known.*

**1858-61 *Perf. 14***

6 A2 5o green 160.00 18.00
*a.* 5o deep green 575.00 140.00
7 A2 9o violet 350.00 225.00
*a.* 9o lilac 450.00 275.00
8 A2 12o blue 175.00 1.90
9 A2 12o ultra ('61) 310.00 12.50
10 A2 24o orange 400.00 27.50
*a.* 24o yellow 400.00 35.00
11 A2 30o brown 400.00 27.50
*a.* 30o red brown 450.00 45.00
12 A2 50o rose 500.00 90.00
*a.* 50o carmine 550.00 95.00
*Nos. 6-12 (7)* 2,295. 402.40

Nos. 6 and 8 exist with double impressions. No. 8 is known printed on both sides. No. 11 exists imperf.

*Nos. 6-8, 10-12 were reprinted in 1885, perf. 13. Value $100 each. Also reprinted in 1963, perf. 13½, with lines in stamp color crossing denominations, and affixed to book page. Value $12.50 each.*

Lion and Arms
A3 A4

**1862-69**

13 A3 3o bister brown 200.00 13.50
*a.* Printed on both sides *2,300.*
14 A4 17o red violet ('66) 600.00 160.00
15 A4 17o gray ('69) 650.00 650.00
16 A4 20o vermilion ('66) 225.00 16.00
*Nos. 13-16 (4)* 1,675. 839.50

*Nos. 13-15 were reprinted in 1885, perf. 13. Values $65, $100 and $65, respectively.*

Numeral of Value — A5

Coat of Arms — A6

**1872-77 *Perf. 14***

17 A5 3o bister brown 60.00 8.00
18 A5 4o gray ('76) 425.00 135.00
19 A5 5o blue green 310.00 4.50
*a.* 5o emerald 500.00 55.00
20 A5 6o violet 325.00 40.00
*a.* 6o dark violet 325.00 40.00
21 A5 6o gray ('74) 900.00 87.50
22 A5 12o blue 175.00 1.00
23 A5 20o vermilion 800.00 7.00
*a.* 20o dull org yel ('75) 3,500. 35.00
*b.* Double impression, dull yel & ver ('76) 3,250. 45.00
24 A5 24o orange 700.00 35.00
*a.* 24o yellow 700.00 35.00
25 A5 30o pale brown 600.00 9.25
*a.* 30o black brown 600.00 11.50
26 A5 50o rose 650.00 40.00
*a.* 50o carmine 750.00 40.00
27 A6 1rd bister & blue 800.00 75.00
*a.* 1rd bister & ultra 800.00 75.00
*Nos. 17-27 (11)* 5,745. 442.25

**1877-79 *Perf. 13***

28 A5 3o yellow brown 75.00 5.00
29 A5 4o gray ('79) 190.00 3.50
30 A5 5o dark green 125.00 1.00
31 A5 6o lilac 140.00 4.00
*a.* 6o red lilac 150.00 4.50
32 A5 12o blue 26.00 .80
33 A5 20o vermilion 225.00 1.00
*a.* "TRETIO" instead of "TJUGO" ('79) 8,250. 5,250.
34 A5 24o yellow ('78) 55.00 25.00
*a.* 24o lemon yellow ('83) 400.00 45.00
35 A5 30o pale brown 350.00 1.90
*a.* 30o black brown 400.00 2.50
36 A5 50o carmine ('78) 260.00 7.00
37 A6 1rd bister & blue 1,850. 400.00
38 A6 1k bister & bl ('78) 500.00 16.00
*Nos. 28-36,38 (10)* 1,946. 65.20

**Imperf., Pairs**

*28a* A5 3o 750.00
*29a* A5 4o 750.00
*30a* A5 5o 750.00
*31b* A5 6o 750.00
*32a* A5 12o 750.00
*33b* A5 20o 750.00
*34b* A5 24o 750.00
*35b* A5 30o 750.00 *2,900.*
*36a* A5 50o 750.00
*38a* A6 1k 750.00

See Nos. 40-44, 46-49. For surcharges see Nos. B1-B10, B22-B31.

*No. 37 has been reprinted in yellow brown and dark blue; perforated 13. Value, $325.*

King Oscar II — A7

**1885 Typo.**

39 A7 10o dull rose 190.00 .65
*a.* Imperf., pair *2,000.*

Numeral Type with Post Horn on Back

**1886-91**

40 A5 2o orange ('91) 2.10 *7.50*
*a.* Period before "FRIMARKE" 11.00 *22.50*
*b.* Imperf., pair 725.00
41 A5 3o yellow brn ('87) 11.00 *21.00*
42 A5 4o gray 25.00 1.40
43 A5 5o green 55.00 .65
44 A5 6o red lilac ('88) 27.50 *55.00*
*a.* 6o violet 30.00 *55.00*
45 A7 10o pink 77.50 .25
*a.* 10o rose 77.50 .25
*b.* Imperf. 1,750.
46 A5 20o vermilion 100.00 .65
47 A5 30o pale brown 175.00 1.50
48 A5 50o rose 150.00 4.25
49 A6 1k bister & dk bl 82.50 2.50
*a.* Imperf., pair 600.00
*Nos. 40-49 (10)* 705.60 94.70

Nos. 32, 34 with Blue Surcharge

**1889, Oct. 1**

50 A5 10o on 12o blue 3.25 *4.50*
51 A5 10o on 24o orange 11.00 *42.50*

A9

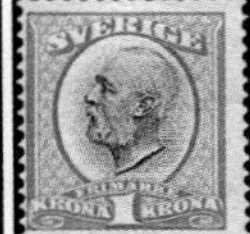


King Oscar II
A10 A11

**Wmk. 180**

**1891-1904 Typo. *Perf. 13***

52 A9 1o brown & ultra ('92) 1.40 .65
53 A9 2o blue & yellow org 3.25 .30
54 A9 3o brown & orange ('92) .55 1.50
55 A9 4o carmine & ultra ('92) 4.75 .30

**Engr.**

56 A10 5o yellow green 2.75 .20
*a.* 5o blue green 11.50 .20
*d.* 5o brown (error) *6,000.*
*e.* Booklet pane of 6 140.00
57 A10 8o red violet ('03) 3.25 1.25
58 A10 10o carmine 4.50 .20
*c.* Booklet pane of 6 240.00
59 A10 15o red brown ('96) 22.50 .30
60 A10 20o blue 22.50 .30
61 A10 25o red orange ('96) 27.50 .40
62 A10 30o brown 50.00 .30
63 A10 50o slate 80.00 .85
64 A10 50o olive gray ('04) 80.00 .85
65 A11 1k car & sl ('00) 140.00 2.25
*Nos. 52-65 (14)* 442.95 9.65

**Imperf., Pairs**

*52a* A9 1o 82.50
*53a* A9 2o *275.00*
*54a* A9 3o *275.00*
*55a* A9 4o 250.00
*56b* A10 5o No. 56 82.50
*c.* No. 56a 300.00
*57a* A10 8o 325.00
*58a* A10 10o 52.50
*59a* A10 15o 375.00
*60a* A10 20o 140.00
*61a* A10 25o 475.00
*62a* A10 30o 450.00
*63a* A10 50o 525.00
*64a* A10 50o 375.00
*65a* A11 1k 525.00

No. 56d may be a proof.

A booklet pane of 6 invalid stamps similar to No. 56 but with engraved lines through the denominations was released in 2004 to commemorate the 100th anniversary of the first Swedish booklet. This booklet pane is unwatermarked.

See Nos. 75-76.

Stockholm Post Office — A12

**1903, Oct. 26**

**66** A12 5k blue 225.00 25.00
*a.* Imperf., pair 1,900.

Opening of the new General Post Office at Stockholm.

For surcharge see No. B11.

Arms — A13

Gustaf V — A14

***Perf. 13, 13x13½***

**1910-14 Typo. Wmk. 180**

**67** A13 1o black ('11) .65 *1.50*
**68** A13 2o orange 1.75 *3.50*
**69** A13 4o violet 2.50 1.10

**Engr.**

**70** A14 5o green ('11) 14.00 *29.00*
**71** A14 10o carmine 9.50 .50
**72** A14 1k black, *yel* ('11) 87.50 .50
**73** A14 5k claret, *yel* ('14) 1.75 *3.00*
*Nos. 67-73 (7)* 117.65 *39.10*

See #77-98. For surcharges see #99-104, Q1-Q2.

**1911 Unwmk.**

**75** A10 20o blue 20.00 14.00
**76** A10 25o red orange 25.00 3.50

**1910-19**

**77** A14 5o green ('11) 1.90 .20
*a.* Booklet pane of 10 225.00
*b.* Booklet pane of 4 125.00
**78** A14 7o gray grn ('18) .20 .20
*a.* Booklet pane of 10 8.75
**79** A14 8o magenta ('12) .20 .20
**80** A14 10o carmine ('10) 1.90 .20
*a.* Booklet pane of 10 225.00
*b.* Booklet pane of 4 125.00
**81** A14 12o rose lake ('18) .25 .20
*a.* Booklet pane of 10 8.75
**82** A14 15o red brown ('11) 6.50 .20
*a.* Booklet pane of 10 325.00
**83** A14 20o deep blue ('11) 9.50 .20
*a.* Booklet pane of 10 350.00
**84** A14 25o orange red ('11) .25 .20
**85** A14 27o pale blue ('18) .40 .90
**86** A14 30o claret brn ('11) 20.00 .20
**87** A14 35o dk violet ('11) 17.00 .20
**88** A14 40o olive green ('17) 32.50 .20
**89** A14 50o gray ('12) 57.50 .20
**90** A14 55o pale blue ('18) *1,550.* *4,750.*
**91** A14 65o pale ol grn ('18) .65 1.90
**92** A14 80o black ('18) *1,550.* *4,750.*
**93** A14 90o gray green ('18) .60 .65
**94** A14 1k black, *yel* ('19) 92.50 .30
*Nos. 77-89,91,93-94 (16)* 241.85 6.15

Excellent forgeries of Nos. 90 and 92 exist.

**1911-19 Typo. Wmk. 181 *Perf. 13***

**95** A13 1o black .20 .20
**96** A13 2o orange .20 .20
**97** A13 3o pale brown ('19) .20 .20
**98** A13 4o pale violet .20 .20
*Nos. 95-98 (4)* .80 .80

Remainders of Nos. 95-98 received various private overprints, mostly as publicity for stamp exhibitions. They were not postally valid.

Unwatermarked Stamps with Watermarks

Stamps of these and later issues through the UPU Congress issue of 1924, are frequently found with watermark showing parts of the words "Kungl Postverket" in double-lined capitals. This watermark is normally located in the margins of the sheets of unwatermarked paper or paper watermarked wavy lines or crown.

Nos. 80, 84, 91, 90, 92 Surcharge:

a

b

**1918 Unwmk.**

**99** A14(a) 7o on 10o .20 .20
**100** A14(b) 12o on 25o 1.90 .40
*a.* Inverted surcharge 300.00 500.00
**101** A14(a) 12o on 65o .85 1.40
**102** A14(a) 27o on 55o .75 1.60
**103** A14(a) 27o on 65o 1.40 3.50
**104** A14(a) 27o on 80o .85 1.60
*Nos. 99-104 (6)* 5.95 8.70

Arms A15

Heraldic Lion Supporting Arms of Sweden A16

Two types each of 5o green, 5o copper red and 10o violet, type A16.

***Perf. 10 Vertically***

**1920-25 Engr. Unwmk.**

**115** A15 3o copper red .20 .30
**116** A16 5o green ('25) 3.75 .25
**117** A16 5o cop red ('21) 6.25 .25
**118** A16 10o green ('21) 21.00 .30
*a.* Tête bêche pair *1,550.* *2,500.*
**119** A16 10o violet ('25) 5.25 .20
**120** A16 25o orange ('21) 13.00 .40
**121** A16 30o brown .45 .45

**Wmk. 181**

**122** A16 5o green 2.50 .90
**123** A16 5o cop red ('21) 8.25 1.00
**124** A16 10o green ('21) 2.50 1.10
**125** A16 30o brown 8.25 16.00
*Nos. 115-125 (11)* 71.40 21.15

Coil Stamps

Unless part of a booklet pane any stamp perforated only horizontally or vertically is a coil stamp.

**1920-26 Unwmk. *Perf. 10***

**126** A16 5o green 4.00 1.00
*a.* Booklet pane of 10 80.00
**127** A16 10o green ('21) 11.50 3.50
*a.* Booklet pane of 10 225.00
**128** A16 10o violet ('25) 6.50 .85
*a.* Booklet pane of 10 180.00
**129** A16 30o brown 32.50 3.25

**Wmk. 181**

**130** A16 5o green 11.50 26.00
**131** A16 10o green ('21) 45.00 90.00
*a.* Booklet pane of 10 425.00

***Perf. 13 Vertically***

**Unwmk.**

**132** A16 5o green ('25) 16.00 8.50
**133** A16 5o cop red ('21) 425.00 140.00
**134** A16 10o violet ('26) 25.00 32.50

**Wmk. 181**

**135** A16 5o green ('25) 1.60 6.50
**136** A16 5o copper red ('22) 1.90 5.50
**137** A16 10o green ('24) 9.00 35.00
**138** A16 10o violet ('25) 8.00 22.50
*Nos. 126-138 (13)* 597.50 375.10

The paper used for the earlier printings of types A16, A17, A18, A18a and A20 is usually tinted by the color of the stamp. Printings of 1934 and later are on white paper in slightly different shades.

King Gustaf V — A17

**1920-21 Unwmk. *Perf. 10 Vertically***

**139** A17 10o rose 32.50 .35
**140** A17 15o claret .30 .45
**141** A17 20o blue 35.00 .50

***Perf. 10***

**142** A17 10o rose 12.50 5.50
**143** A17 20o blue ('21) 29.00 9.00
*a.* Booklet pane of 10 550.00
*Nos. 139-143 (5)* 109.30 15.80

**Wmk. 181**

**144** A17 20o blue *4,000.*

Crown and Post Horn — A18 A18a

See note after No. 138 regarding paper. There are 2 types of the 35, 40, 45 and 60o.

**1920-34 Unwmk. *Perf. 10 Vert.***

**145** A18 35o yellow ('22) 42.50 .75
**146** A18 40o olive green 32.50 .75
**147** A18 45o brown ('22) 1.25 .55
**148** A18 60o claret 19.00 .30
**149** A18 70o red brn ('22) .60 2.50
**150** A18 80o deep green .40 .25
**151** A18 85o myrtle grn ('29) 3.75 .45
**152** A18 90o lt blue ('25) 55.00 .30
**153** A18a 1kr dp org ('21) 7.75 .25
**154** A18 110o ultra .50 .40
**155** A18 115o red brn ('29) 9.00 .45
**156** A18 120o gray blk ('25) 62.50 .60
**157** A18 120o lil rose ('33) 14.00 .60
**158** A18 140o gray black .90 .30
**159** A18 145o brt grn ('30) 8.50 .55

**Wmk. 181**

**160** A18 35o yellow ('23) 60.00 7.50
**161** A18 60o red violet 95.00 *110.00*
**162** A18 80o blue green 8.25 15.00
**163** A18 110o ultra 3.50 3.75
*Nos. 145-163 (19)* 424.90 145.25

The value for #147 is for the 2nd type, issued in 1925.

Gustavus Adolphus A19

King Gustaf V A20

***Perf. 10 Vertically***

**1920, July 28 Unwmk.**

**164** A19 20o deep blue 2.25 .40

**Wmk. 181**

**165** A19 20o blue 150.00 32.50

**Unwmk.**

***Perf. 10***

**166** A19 20o blue 6.25 2.25
*a.* Booklet pane of 10 130.00
*Nos. 164-166 (3)* 158.50 35.15

Tercentenary of Swedish post which first ran between Stockholm and Hamburg.

**1921-36 Unwmk. *Perf. 10 Vert.***

See note after No. 138 regarding paper.

There are two types each of the 15o rose and 40o olive green.

**167** A20 15o violet ('22) 17.00 .30
**168** A20 15o rose ('28) 5.50 .45
**169** A20 15o brown ('36) 4.75 .45
**170** A20 20o violet .20 .20
**171** A20 20o rose ('22) 22.50 .50
**172** A20 20o orange ('25) .20 .35
**174** A20 25o rose red ('22) .55 1.50
**175** A20 25o dk bl ('25) 17.00 .20
**176** A20 25o ultra ('34) 17.00 .65
**177** A20 25o yel org ('36) 32.50 .45
**178** A20 30o blue ('23) 19.00 .45
**179** A20 30o brown ('25) 22.50 .35
**180** A20 30o lt ultra ('36) 6.00 .70
**181** A20 35o red vio ('30) 24.00 .45
**182** A20 40o blue .45 .70
**183** A20 40o ol grn ('29) 45.00 1.25
**184** A20 45o brown ('29) 5.00 .90
**185** A20 50o gray 1.75 1.00
**186** A20 85o myrtle grn ('25) 17.00 1.75
**187** A20 115o brn red ('25) 11.00 1.75
**188** A20 145o apple grn ('25) 8.25 1.75
*Nos. 167-188 (21)* 277.15 16.10

**Wmk. 181**

**189** A20 15o violet ('22) 2,650. 850.00
**189A** A20 20o violet *4,500.*

**1922-36 Unwmk. *Perf. 10***

**190** A20 15o violet 17.50 .70
*a.* Booklet pane of 10 400.00
**191** A20 15o rose red ('25) 22.50 .85
*a.* Booklet pane of 10 600.00
**192** A20 15o brown ('36) 5.75 1.25
*a.* Booklet pane of 10 175.00
**193** A20 20o violet ('22) .50 *1.50*
*a.* Booklet pane of 10 10.00
*Nos. 190-193 (4)* 46.25 4.30

Gustavus Vasa — A21

**1921, June *Perf. 10 Vertically***

**194** A21 20o violet 12.50 *25.00*
**195** A21 110o ultra 55.00 7.50
**196** A21 140o gray black 30.00 7.50
*Nos. 194-196 (3)* 97.50 40.00

400th anniversary of Gustavus Vasa's war of independence from the Danes.

**Universal Postal Union Congress**

Composite View of Stockholm's Skyline A22

King Gustaf V — A23

**1924, July 4 Unwmk. *Perf. 10***

**197** A22 5o red brown 1.60 *3.25*
**198** A22 10o green 1.60 *3.25*
**199** A22 15o dk violet 1.60 *2.50*
**200** A22 20o rose red 12.50 *17.00*
**201** A22 25o dp orange 15.00 *21.00*
**202** A22 30o deep blue 14.50 *21.00*
*a.* 30o greenish blue 87.50 125.00
**203** A22 35o black 19.00 *26.00*
**204** A22 40o olive green 29.00 *32.50*
**205** A22 45o deep brown 32.50 32.50
**206** A22 50o gray 32.50 32.50
**207** A22 60o violet brn 47.50 *55.00*
**208** A22 80o myrtle grn 35.00 35.00
**209** A23 1k green 57.50 *87.50*
**210** A23 2k rose red 140.00 *250.00*
**211** A23 5k deep blue 300.00 *450.00*

**Wmk. 181**

**212** A22 10o green 26.00 *55.00*
*Nos. 197-212 (16)* 765.80 *1,124.*
Set, never hinged 1,200.

Postrider Watching Airplane A24

Carrier Pigeon and Globe — A25

**1924, Aug. 16 Engr. Unwmk.**

| | | | | |
|---|---|---|---|---|
| **213** | A24 | 5o red brown | 2.75 | 4.50 |
| **214** | A24 | 10o green | 2.75 | 5.75 |
| **215** | A24 | 15o dk violet | 3.00 | 3.00 |
| **216** | A24 | 20o rose red | 21.00 | 32.50 |
| **217** | A24 | 25o deep orange | 26.00 | 32.50 |
| **218** | A24 | 30o deep blue | 26.00 | 32.50 |
| *a.* | | 30o greenish blue | 90.00 | 52.50 |
| **219** | A24 | 35o black | 32.50 | 47.50 |
| **220** | A24 | 40o olive green | 32.50 | 32.50 |
| **221** | A24 | 45o deep brown | 37.50 | 35.00 |
| **222** | A24 | 50o gray | 50.00 | 62.50 |
| **223** | A24 | 60o violet brown | 50.00 | 77.50 |
| **224** | A24 | 80o myrtle green | 37.50 | 35.00 |
| **225** | A25 | 1k green | 75.00 | 87.50 |
| **226** | A25 | 2k rose red | 140.00 | 75.00 |
| **227** | A25 | 5k deep blue | 275.00 | 210.00 |

**Wmk. 181**

| | | | | |
|---|---|---|---|---|
| **228** | A24 | 10o green | 22.50 | *60.00* |
| | | *Nos. 213-228 (16)* | 834.00 | 833.25 |
| | | Set, never hinged | 1,450. | |

Universal Postal Union issue.

Royal Palace at Stockholm A26

**1931, Nov. 26 Unwmk. *Perf. 10***

| | | | | |
|---|---|---|---|---|
| **229** | A26 | 5k dark green | 110.00 | 12.50 |
| | | Never hinged | 300.00 | |
| *a.* | | Booklet pane of 10 | 2,500. | |

Death of Gustavus Adolphus — A27

**1932, Nov. 1**

| | | | | |
|---|---|---|---|---|
| **230** | A27 | 10o dark violet | 2.50 | 5.50 |
| *a.* | | Booklet pane of 10 | 40.00 | |
| **231** | A27 | 15o dark red | 4.50 | 1.90 |
| *a.* | | Booklet pane of 10 | 110.00 | |

***Perf. 10 Vertically***

| | | | | |
|---|---|---|---|---|
| **232** | A27 | 10o dark violet | 1.90 | .20 |
| **233** | A27 | 15o dark red | 2.50 | .20 |
| **234** | A27 | 25o dark blue | 6.00 | .95 |
| **235** | A27 | 90o dark green | 22.50 | 2.25 |
| | | *Nos. 230-235 (6)* | 39.90 | 11.00 |
| | | Set, never hinged | 80.00 | |

300th anniv. of the death of King Gustavus Adolphus II who was killed on the battlefield of Lützen, Nov. 6, 1632.

Catching Sunlight in Bowl — A28

**1933, Dec. 6 *Perf. 10***

| | | | | |
|---|---|---|---|---|
| **236** | A28 | 5o green | 2.50 | 1.75 |
| *a.* | | Booklet pane of 10 | 60.00 | |

There are two types of No. 236.

***Perf. 10 Vertically***

| | | | | |
|---|---|---|---|---|
| **237** | A28 | 5o green | 2.50 | .30 |

***Perf. 13 Vertically***

| | | | | |
|---|---|---|---|---|
| **238** | A28 | 5o green | 3.50 | 7.25 |
| | | *Nos. 236-238 (3)* | 8.50 | 9.30 |
| | | Set, never hinged | 17.50 | |

Swedish Postal Savings Bank, 50th anniv.

The Old Law Courts — A29

The "Four Estates" and Arms of Engelbrekt A34

Designs: 10o, Stock exchange. 15o, Parish church (Storkyrkan). 25o, House of the Nobility. 35o, House of Parliament.

**1935, Jan. 10 *Perf. 10***

| | | | | |
|---|---|---|---|---|
| **239** | A29 | 5o green | 2.25 | 1.40 |
| *a.* | | Booklet pane of 10 | 55.00 | |
| **240** | A29 | 10o dull violet | 4.25 | *5.75* |
| *a.* | | Booklet pane of 10 | 60.00 | |
| **241** | A29 | 15o carmine | 4.75 | 1.10 |
| *a.* | | Booklet pane of 10 | 125.00 | |

***Perf. 10 Vertically***

| | | | | |
|---|---|---|---|---|
| **242** | A29 | 5o green | 1.25 | .20 |
| **243** | A29 | 10o dull violet | 5.75 | .20 |
| **244** | A29 | 15o carmine | 2.25 | .20 |
| **245** | A29 | 25o ultra | 6.00 | .60 |
| **246** | A29 | 35o deep claret | 12.00 | 2.25 |
| **247** | A34 | 60o deep claret | 17.50 | 2.50 |
| | | *Nos. 239-247 (9)* | 56.00 | 14.20 |
| | | Set, never hinged | 110.00 | |

500th anniv. of the Swedish Parliament.

Chancellor Axel Oxenstierna A35

Post Runner — A36

Mounted Courier — A37

Old Sailing Packet — A38

Mail Paddle Steamship A39

Mail Coach — A40

1855 Stamp Model — A41

Mail Train — A42

Postmaster General A. W. Roos — A43

Mail Truck and Trailer — A44

Modern Swedish Liner — A45

Junkers Plane with Pontoons — A46

**1936, Feb. 20 Engr. *Perf. 10***

| | | | | |
|---|---|---|---|---|
| **248** | A35 | 5o green | 1.75 | .85 |
| *a.* | | Booklet pane of 18 | 72.50 | |
| **249** | A36 | 10o dk violet | 2.10 | 2.75 |
| *a.* | | Booklet pane of 18 | 95.00 | |
| **250** | A37 | 15o dk carmine | 3.00 | .55 |
| *a.* | | Booklet pane of 18 | 250.00 | |

***Perf. 10 Vertically***

| | | | | |
|---|---|---|---|---|
| **251** | A35 | 5o green | 1.75 | .20 |
| **252** | A36 | 10o dk violet | 1.75 | .20 |
| **253** | A37 | 15o dk carmine | 3.25 | .20 |
| **254** | A38 | 20o lt blue | 8.25 | 5.00 |
| **255** | A39 | 25o lt ultra | 5.25 | .50 |
| **256** | A40 | 30o yellow brn | 17.50 | 3.25 |
| **257** | A41 | 35o plum | 5.50 | 1.25 |
| **258** | A42 | 40o olive grn | 5.75 | 2.75 |
| **259** | A43 | 45o myrtle grn | 7.75 | 1.50 |
| **260** | A44 | 50o gray | 22.50 | 2.75 |
| **261** | A45 | 60o maroon | 29.00 | .70 |
| **262** | A46 | 1k deep blue | 8.25 | 8.50 |
| | | *Nos. 248-262 (15)* | 123.35 | 30.95 |
| | | Set, never hinged | 300.00 | |

300th anniv. of the Swedish Postal Service.
See Nos. 946-950, B55-B56.

Airplane over Bromma Airport A47

Emanuel Swedenborg — A48

**1936, May 23 *Perf. 10 Vert.***

| | | | | |
|---|---|---|---|---|
| **263** | A47 | 50o ultra | 5.50 | 8.50 |
| | | Never hinged | 10.50 | |

Opening of Bromma Airport near Stockholm.

Swedish Booklets

Before 1940, booklets were handmade and usually held two panes of 10 stamps (2x5). About every third booklet contained one row of stamps with straight edges at right or left side. Se-tenant pairs may be obtained with one stamp perforated on 4 sides and one perforated on 3 sides.

Starting in 1940, booklet stamps have one or more straight edges.

**1938, Jan. 29 *Perf. 12½***

| | | | | |
|---|---|---|---|---|
| **264** | A48 | 10o violet | 1.50 | .35 |
| *a.* | | Perf. on 3 sides | 10.00 | 3.00 |
| | | Never hinged | 17.00 | |
| *b.* | | Booklet pane of 10 | 30.00 | |

***Perf. 12½ Vertically***

| | | | | |
|---|---|---|---|---|
| **266** | A48 | 10o violet | 1.10 | .20 |
| **267** | A48 | 100o green | 3.75 | 1.40 |
| | | *Nos. 264-267 (3)* | 6.35 | 1.95 |
| | | Set, never hinged | 12.00 | |

250th anniv. of the birth of Swedenborg, scientist, philosopher and religious writer.

Johann Printz and Indian Chief — A49

"Kalmar Nyckel" Sailing from Gothenburg A50

Symbolizing the Settlement of New Sweden — A51

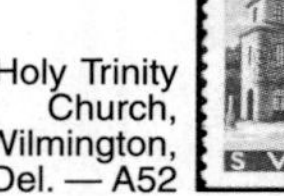

Holy Trinity Church, Wilmington, Del. — A52

Queen Christina — A53

**1938, Apr. 8** ***Perf. 12½ Vert.***

**268** A49 5o green .65 .20
**269** A50 15o brown .90 .20
**270** A51 20o red 1.60 .70
**271** A52 30o ultra 5.25 .85
**272** A53 60o brown lake 8.25 .35

***Perf. 12½***

**273** A49 5o green 1.60 1.00
*a.* Perf. on 3 sides 10.00 7.50
Never hinged 17.00
*b.* Booklet pane of 18 67.50
**274** A50 15o brown 2.75 .70
*a.* Perf. on 3 sides 17.00 4.75
Never hinged 26.00
*b.* Booklet pane of 18 115.00
*Nos. 268-274 (7)* 21.00 4.00
Set, never hinged 32.50

Tercentenary of the Swedish settlement at Wilmington, Del. See No. B54.

King Gustaf V — A54

**1938, June 16** ***Perf. 12½ Vert.***

**275** A54 5o green .65 .20
**276** A54 15(o) brown .75 .20
**277** A54 30(o) ultra 17.50 .75

***Perf. 12½***

**278** A54 5o green 1.40 .25
*a.* Perf. on 3 sides 13.00 5.50
Never hinged 22.50
*b.* Booklet pane of 10 45.00
**279** A54 15(o) brown 1.90 .30
*a.* Perf. on 3 sides 20.00 1.40
Never hinged 32.50
*b.* Booklet pane of 10 65.00
*Nos. 275-279 (5)* 22.20 1.70
Set, never hinged 29.00

80th birthday of King Gustaf V.

King Gustaf V — A55

Three Crowns — A56

**1939** ***Perf. 12½ Vertically***

**280** A55 10o violet .65 .20
**281** A55 20o carmine 2.25 .60
**282** A56 60o lake .65 .20
**283** A56 85o dk green .30 .20
**284** A56 90o peacock blue .30 .20
**285** A56 1k orange .30 .20
**286** A56 1.15k henna brn .30 .20
**287** A56 1.20k brt rose vio 1.60 .20
**288** A56 1.45k lt yel grn 2.25 .80

***Perf. 12½***

**289** A55 10o violet 1.60 3.00
*a.* Perf. on 3 sides 47.50 65.00
Never hinged 77.50
*b.* Bklt. pane of 10, perf. on 4 sides 30.00
*Nos. 280-289 (10)* 10.20 5.80
Set, never hinged 17.50

See Nos. 394-398, 416-417, 425-426, 431, 439-441, 473, 588-591, 656-664.

Per Henrik Ling — A57

**1939, Feb. 25** ***Perf. 12½ Vert.***

**290** A57 5o green .20 .20
**291** A57 25(o) brown 1.10 .40

***Perf. 12½***

**292** A57 5o green .90 .40
*a.* Perf. on 3 sides 14.00 3.75
Never hinged 29.00
*b.* Booklet pane of 10 37.50
*Nos. 290-292 (3)* 2.20 1.00
Set, never hinged 3.50

Centenary of the death of P. H. Ling, father of Swedish gymnastics.

J. J. Berzelius A58

Carl von Linné A59

***Perf. 12½ Vertically***

**1939, June 2** **Engr.**

**293** A58 10o violet 3.75 .30
**294** A59 15o fawn .20 .20
**295** A58 30o ultra 11.50 .45
**296** A59 50o gray 13.00 1.00

***Perf. 12½***

**297** A58 10o violet 2.10 .65
*a.* Perf. on 3 sides 72.50 19.00
Never hinged 125.00
*b.* Booklet pane of 10 65.00
**298** A59 15o fawn 3.00 .30
*a.* Perf. on 3 sides 11.50 .45
Never hinged 19.00
*b.* Booklet pane of 10 100.00
*c.* As "a," bklt. pane of 20 450.00
*Nos. 293-298 (6)* 33.55 2.90
Set, never hinged 60.00

200th anniv. of the founding of the Royal Academy of Science at Stockholm.

King Gustaf V — A60

**Type A55 Re-engraved**

**1939-46** ***Perf. 12½***

**299** A60 5o dp green ('46) .30 .20
*b.* Perf. on 3 sides ('41) .40 .20
Never hinged .50
*c.* As "b," bklt. pane of 20 12.00
**300** A60 10(o) violet ('46) .20 .20
*a.* Bklt. pane of 10, perf. on 4 sides 55.00
Never hinged 2.25
*c.* Perf. on 3 sides 2.25 .20
*i.* As "c," booklet pane of 20 50.00
**300D** A60 15(o) chestnut ('46) .20 .20
*f.* Perf. on 3 sides ('45) .40 .20
Never hinged .65
*j.* As "f," booklet pane of 20 7.75
**300G** A60 20(o) red ('42) .30 .20
*h.* Booklet pane of 20 6.50
*Nos. 299-300G (4)* 1.00 .80
Set, never hinged 1.40

No. 300 differs slightly from the original due to deeper engraving. No. 300G was issued only in booklets; all copies have one straight edge.

Nos. 299, 300, 300D exist in booklet panes of 20 made from sheets of stamps. These can be collected as booklets.

**1940-42** ***Perf. 12½ Vertically***

**301** A60 5o dp green ('41) .25 .20
**302** A60 10(o) violet .20 .20
**302A** A60 15(o) chestnut ('42) .20 .20
**303** A60 20(o) red .20 .20
**304** A60 25(o) orange 1.00 .20
**305** A60 30(o) ultra .40 .20
**306** A60 35(o) red vio ('41) .60 .20
**307** A60 40(o) olive grn .60 .20
**308** A60 45(o) dk brown .60 .20
**309** A60 50(o) gray blk ('41) 3.25 .20
*Nos. 301-309 (10)* 7.30 2.00
Set, never hinged 11.50

Numerals measure 4½mm high. Less shading around head gives a lighter effect. Horizontal lines only as background for "SVERIGE."

See Nos. 391-393, 399.

Carl Michael Bellman A61

Tobias Sergel A62

**1940, Feb. 4** **Engr.** ***Perf. 12½ Vert.***

**310** A61 5o green .25 .25
**311** A61 35(o) rose red 1.00 .40

***Perf. 12½***

**312** A61 5o green 1.25 .60
*a.* Perf. on 3 sides 10.00 .75
Never hinged 21.00
*b.* Booklet pane of 10 50.00
*c.* As "a," bklt. pane of 20 425.00
*Nos. 310-312 (3)* 2.50 1.25
Set, never hinged 3.00

Bellman (1740-95), lyric poet.

**1940, Sept. 5** ***Perf. 12½ on 3 Sides***

**313** A62 15o lt brown 7.50 .25
*a.* Booklet pane of 20 275.00

***Perf. 12½ Vertically***

**314** A62 15o lt brown 3.25 .20
**315** A62 50o gray black 17.00 1.20
*Nos. 313-315 (3)* 27.75 1.65
Set, never hinged 47.50

Bicentenary of birth of Johan Tobias von Sergel (1740-1814), sculptor.

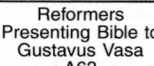

Reformers Presenting Bible to Gustavus Vasa A63

View of Skansen A64

**1941, May 11** ***Perf. 12½ on 3 Sides***

**316** A63 15o brown 2.75 .45
*a.* Booklet pane of 18 90.00

***Perf. 12½ Vertically***

**317** A63 15o brown .30 .20
**318** A63 90o ultra 19.00 .95
*Nos. 316-318 (3)* 22.05 1.60
Set, never hinged 35.00

400th anniv. of the 1st authorized version of the Bible in Swedish.

**1941, June 18** ***Perf. 12½ on 3 Sides***

**319** A64 10o violet 2.50 .65
*a.* Booklet pane of 20 85.00

***Perf. 12½ Vertically***

**320** A64 10o violet 3.00 .20
**321** A64 60o red lilac 8.00 .60
*Nos. 319-321 (3)* 13.50 1.45
Set, never hinged 25.00

50th anniv. of Skansen, an open air extension of the Nordic Museum.

Royal Palace at Stockholm A65

Artur Hazelius A66

**1941** ***Perf. 12½ on 3 Sides***

**322** A65 5k blue 1.50 .20
Never hinged 2.50
*a.* Perf. on 4 sides 29.00 1.00
Never hinged 57.50
*b.* Bklt. pane of 20, perf. 3 sides 50.00
*c.* Bklt. pane of 10, perf. 4 sides 575.00

For coil stamp see No. 537.

**1941, Aug. 30** ***Perf. 12½ on 3 Sides***

**323** A66 5o lt green 2.50 .55
*a.* Booklet pane of 20 100.00

***Perf. 12½ Vertically***

**324** A66 5o lt green .20 .20
**325** A66 1k lt orange 7.00 4.00
*Nos. 323-325 (3)* 9.70 4.75
Set, never hinged 22.50

Issued to honor Artur Hazelius, founder of Skansen, Nordic museum.

St. Bridget of Sweden — A67

***Perf. 12½ on 3 Sides***

**1941, Oct. 7** **Engr.**

**326** A67 15o deep brown 1.90 .40
*a.* Booklet pane of 18 60.00

***Perf. 12½ Horiz.***

**327** A67 15o deep brown .20 .20
**328** A67 1.20k red vio 21.00 10.50
*Nos. 326-328 (3)* 23.10 11.10
Set, never hinged 47.50

King Gustavus III — A68

K. G. Tessin, Architect — A69

**1942, June 29** ***Perf. 12½ on 3 Sides***

**329** A68 20o red 1.25 .45
*a.* Booklet pane of 20 45.00

***Perf. 12½ Vertically***

**330** A68 20o red .60 .20
**331** A69 40o olive green 14.00 1.25
*Nos. 329-331 (3)* 15.85 1.90
Set, never hinged 32.50

Sesquicentennial of the Swedish National Museum, Stockholm.

Torsten Rudenschold and Nils Mansson — A70

**1942, July 1** ***Perf. 12½ Horiz.***

**332** A70 10o magenta .25 .40
*a.* Booklet pane of 10 3.50

***Perf. 12½ Vertically***

**333** A70 10o magenta .25 .35
**334** A70 90o light blue 2.50 6.00
*Nos. 332-334 (3)* 3.00 6.75
Set, never hinged 5.00

Swedish Public School System, 100th anniv.

Carl Wilhelm Scheele A71

King Gustaf V A72

**1942, Dec. 9** ***Perf. 12½ on 3 Sides***

**335** A71 5o green 1.50 1.00
*a.* Booklet pane of 20 55.00

***Perf. 12½ Vertically***

**336** A71 5o green .20 .20
**337** A71 60o deep magenta 7.00 .60
*Nos. 335-337 (3)* 8.70 1.80
Set, never hinged 15.00

200th anniv. of the birth of Carl Wilhelm Scheele, chemist.

***Perf. 12½ Horizontally***

**1943, June 16**

**338** A72 20o red .60 .45
**339** A72 30o ultra .90 2.50
**340** A72 60o brt red vio 1.10 3.25

***Perf. 12½ on 3 Sides***

**341** A72 20o red 4.50 1.10
*a.* Booklet pane of 20 160.00
*Nos. 338-341 (4)* 7.10 7.30
Set, never hinged 12.00

85th birthday of King Gustaf V, June 16.

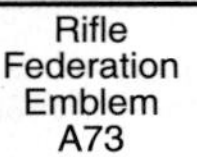

Rifle Federation Emblem A73

Oscar Montelius A74

**1943, July 22** ***Perf. 12½ Vert.***

**342** A73 10o rose violet .20 .20
**343** A73 90o dp ultra 3.75 .45

***Perf. 12½ on 3 Sides***

**344** A73 10o rose violet .40 .40
*a.* Booklet pane of 20 12.50
*Nos. 342-344 (3)* 4.35 1.05
Set, never hinged 8.00

50th anniversary of the Swedish Voluntary Rifle Associations.

**1943, Sept. 9 Engr.** ***Perf. 12½ Vert.***

**345** A74 5o green .20 .20
**346** A74 1.20k brt red vio 6.00 2.50

***Perf. 12½ on 3 Sides***

**347** A74 5o green .55 .40
*a.* Booklet pane of 20 19.00
*Nos. 345-347 (3)* 6.75 3.10
Set, never hinged 11.50

Montelius (1843-1921), archaeologist.

Johan Mansson's Chart of Baltic, 1644 — A75

***Perf. 12½ on 3 Sides***

**1944, Apr. 15 Engr. Unwmk.**

**348** A75 5o green .60 *.80*
*a.* Booklet pane of 20 25.00

***Perf. 12½ Vertically***

**349** A75 5o green .20 .20
**350** A75 60o lake 4.25 .80
*Nos. 348-350 (3)* 5.05 1.80
Set, never hinged 10.00

1st Swedish Marine Chart, tercentenary.

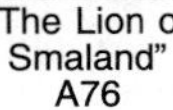

"The Lion of Smaland" A76

Clas Fleming A77

30o, "Kung Karl." 40o, "Gustaf V." 90o, Stern of "Amphion," Flagship of Gustavus III.

**1944, Oct. 13** ***Perf. 12½ Vert.***

**351** A76 10o purple .35 .35
**352** A77 20o red .30 .20
**353** A76 30o blue .50 *.80*
**354** A76 40o olive green .60 *1.25*
**355** A76 90o gray black 6.50 2.25

***Perf. 12½ on 3 Sides***

**356** A76 10o purple .60 *2.00*
*a.* Booklet pane of 20 24.00
**357** A77 20o red 2.25 .35
*a.* Booklet pane of 20 90.00
*Nos. 351-357 (7)* 11.10 7.20
Set, never hinged 21.00

Issued to honor the Swedish Fleet and mark the tercentenary of the Swedish naval victory at Femern, 1644.

See Nos. B53, B57-B58.

**Catalogue values for unused stamps in this section, from this point to the end of the section, are for Never Hinged items.**

Red Cross — A81

Torch and Quill Pen — A82

**1945, Feb. 27** ***Perf. 12½ Vert.***

**358** A81 20o red .60 .20

***Perf. 12½ on 3 Sides***

**359** A81 20o red 3.00 .40
*a.* Booklet pane of 20 65.00

Swedish Red Cross Society, 80th anniv.

**1945, May 29** ***Perf. 12½ Vert.***

**360** A82 5o green .20 .20
**361** A82 60o carmine rose 6.00 .45

***Perf. 12½ on 3 Sides***

**362** A82 5o green .35 .45
*a.* Booklet pane of 20 7.75
*Nos. 360-362 (3)* 6.55 1.10

Tercentenary of Swedish press.

Rydberg A83

Oak Tree A84

**1945, Sept. 21** ***Perf. 12½ Vert.***

**363** A83 20o red .35 .20
**364** A83 90o blue 7.00 .45

***Perf. 12½ on 3 Sides***

**365** A83 20o red 1.50 .45
*a.* Booklet pane of 20 32.50
*Nos. 363-365 (3)* 8.85 1.10

Viktor Rydberg (1828-95), author.

**1945, Oct. 27** ***Perf. 12½ Vert.***

**366** A84 10o violet .25 .35
**367** A84 40o olive 1.60 1.25

***Perf. 12½ on 3 Sides***

**368** A84 10o violet .40 *.70*
*a.* Booklet pane of 20 10.00
*Nos. 366-368 (3)* 2.25 2.30

125th anniv. of the Savings Bank movement.

Angel and Lund Cathedral A85

View of Lund Cathedral A86

***Perf. 12½ Vertically***

**1946, May 28 Unwmk.**

**369** A85 15o orange brn .70 .55
**370** A86 20o red .30 .20
**371** A85 90o ultra 8.25 .85

***Perf. 12½ on 3 Sides***

**372** A85 15o orange brn .95 1.10
*a.* Booklet pane of 20 19.00
**373** A86 20o red 2.25 .45
*a.* Booklet pane of 20 45.00
*Nos. 369-373 (5)* 12.45 3.15

Lund Cathedral, 800th anniversary.

Mare and Colt — A87

Esaias Tegner — A88

**1946, June 8** ***Perf. 12½ Vert.***

**374** A87 5o green .20 .20
**375** A87 60o carmine rose 7.25 .40

***Perf. 12½ on 3 Sides***

**376** A87 5o green .30 .45
*a.* Booklet pane of 20 6.50
*Nos. 374-376 (3)* 7.75 1.05

Centenary of Swedish agricultural shows.

***Perf. 12½ Vertically***

**1946, Nov. 2 Engr. Unwmk.**

**377** A88 10o deep violet .20 .20
**378** A88 40o dk olive grn 1.40 .45

***Perf. 12½ on 3 Sides***

**379** A88 10o dp violet .30 .20
*a.* Booklet pane of 20 6.00
*Nos. 377-379 (3)* 1.90 .85

Esaias Tegner (1782-1846), poet.

Nobel — A89

Geijer — A90

**1946, Dec. 10** ***Perf. 12½ Vert.***

**380** A89 20o red .80 .20
**381** A89 30o ultra 2.25 .60

***Perf. 12½ on 3 Sides***

**382** A89 20o red 1.90 .55
*a.* Booklet pane of 20 40.00
*Nos. 380-382 (3)* 4.95 1.35

50th anniversary of the death of Alfred Nobel, inventor and philanthropist.

**1947, Apr. 23** ***Perf. 12½ Vert.***

**383** A90 5o dk yellow grn .25 .20
**384** A90 90o ultra 4.25 .25

***Perf. 12½ on 3 Sides***

**385** A90 5o dk yellow grn .30 .45
*a.* Booklet pane of 20 7.00
*Nos. 383-385 (3)* 4.80 .90

Centenary of the death of Erik Gustaf Geijer, historian, philosopher and poet.

King Gustaf V — A91

**1947, Dec. 8 Engr.** ***Perf. 12½ Horiz.***

**386** A91 10o deep violet .20 .20
**387** A91 20o red .20 .20
**388** A91 60o red violet 1.40 1.40

***Perf. 12½ on 3 Sides***

**389** A91 10o deep violet .20 .30
*a.* Booklet pane of 20 4.00
**390** A91 20o red .40 .40
*a.* Booklet pane of 20 8.00
*Nos. 386-390 (5)* 2.40 2.50

40th anniv. of the reign of King Gustaf V.

**King and 3-Crown Types of 1939**

**1948 Unwmk.** ***Perf. 12½ Vertically***

**391** A60 5o orange .25 .20
**392** A60 10o green .30 .20
**393** A60 25o violet 1.50 .20
**394** A56 55o orange brown 1.40 .20
**395** A56 80o olive green .80 .20
**396** A56 1.10k violet 7.00 .20
**397** A56 1.40k dk blue green .80 .20
**398** A56 1.75k brt grnsh blue 12.50 6.75

***Perf. 12½ on 3 Sides***

**399** A60 10o green .25 .20
*a.* Booklet pane of 20 6.00
*Nos. 391-399 (9)* 24.80 8.35

Plowman, Early and Modern Buildings A92

August Strindberg A93

**1948, Apr. 26** ***Perf. 12½ Vert.***

**400** A92 15o orange brown .25 .20
**401** A92 30o ultra .50 .55
**402** A92 1k orange 1.50 1.25

***Perf. 12½ on 3 Sides***

**403** A92 15o orange brown .40 *.50*
*a.* Booklet pane of 20 8.50
*Nos. 400-403 (4)* 2.65 2.50

Centenary of the Swedish pioneers' settlement in the United States.

**1949, Jan. 22** ***Perf. 12½ Vert.***

**404** A93 20o red .45 .20
**405** A93 30o blue .80 .75
**406** A93 80o olive green 2.75 .45

***Perf. 12½ on 3 Sides***

**407** A93 20o red .80 .35
*a.* Booklet pane of 20 16.00
*Nos. 404-407 (4)* 4.80 1.75

Birth centenary of August Strindberg (1849-1912), author and playwright.

Girl and Boy Gymnasts — A94

***Perf. 12½ Horiz.***

**1949, July 27 Engr.**

**408** A94 5o ultra .30 *.45*
**409** A94 15o brown .35 .20

***Perf. 12½ on 3 Sides***

**410** A94 15o brown .45 .65
*a.* Booklet pane of 20 9.00
*Nos. 408-410 (3)* 1.10 1.30

2nd Lingiad or World Gymnastics Festival, Stockholm, July-August 1949.

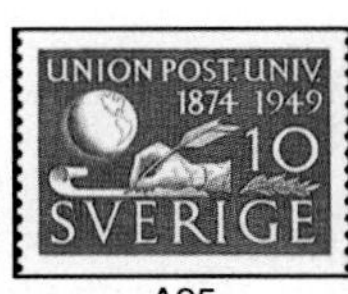

A95

Symbols of UPU — A96

**1949, Oct. 9** ***Perf. 12½ Vert.***

**411** A95 10o green .25 .20
**412** A95 20o red .30 .20

***Perf. 12½ Horizontally***

**413** A96 30o lt blue .40 .65

***Perf. 12½ on 3 sides***

**414** A95 10o green .20 .20
*a.* Booklet pane of 20 3.50
**415** A95 20o red .20 .20
*a.* Booklet pane of 20 4.00
*Nos. 411-415 (5)* 1.35 1.45

75th anniv. of the formation of the UPU.

**Three-Crown Type of 1939**

***Perf. 12½ Vertically***

**1949, Nov. 11 Unwmk.**

**416** A56 65o lt yellow grn .75 .30
**417** A56 70o peacock blue 4.00 1.25

Gustaf VI Adolf (Letters in color) A97

Christopher Polhem A98

**1951, June 6** ***Perf. 12½ Vert.***

**Without Imprint**

**418** A97 10o dull green .25 .20
**419** A97 15o chestnut brown .35 .20
**420** A97 20o carmine rose .35 .20
**421** A97 25o gray .65 .20
**422** A97 30o ultra .45 .20

***Perf. 12½ on 3 sides***

**423** A97 10o dull green .40 .20
*a.* Booklet pane of 20 8.00
**424** A97 25o gray .50 .25
*a.* Booklet pane of 20 12.00
*Nos. 418-424 (7)* 2.95 1.45

See Nos. 435-438, 442-443, 456-461, 502, 505-509, 515-517.

### Three-Crown Type of 1939

**1951, June 1** ***Perf. 12½ Vert.***

**425** A56 85o orange brown 5.75 1.60
**426** A56 1.70k red 1.25 .20

**1951, Aug. 30** ***Perf. 12½ Vert.***

**427** A98 25o gray 1.40 .20
**428** A98 45o brown .55 .40

***Perf. 12½ on 3 sides***

**429** A98 25o gray .45 .30
*a.* Booklet pane of 20 9.00
*Nos. 427-429 (3)* 2.40 .90

200th anniversary of the death of Christopher Polhem, engineer and technician.

Numeral (Lettering in color) A99

Olaus Petri Preaching A100

### Type A99 and 3-Crown Type of 1939

**1951, Nov.** **Engr.** ***Perf. 12½ Vert.***

**430** A99 5o rose carmine .25 .20
**431** A56 1.50k red violet 1.60 1.25

For other stamps similar to type A99, see type A115a, Nos. 503-504, 513-514, 570, 580, 666-667.

**1952, Apr. 19** ***Perf. 12½ Horiz.***

**432** A100 25o gray black .45 .20
**433** A100 1.40k brown 2.75 .80

***Perf. 12½ on 3 sides***

**434** A100 25o gray black 2.00 2.60
*a.* Booklet pane of 20 50.00
*Nos. 432-434 (3)* 5.20 3.60

Olaus Petri (1493-1552), Lutheran clergyman, historian and Bible translator.

### King and 3-Crown Types of 1951 and 1939

**1952** ***Perf. 12½ Vertically***

**Without Imprint**

**435** A97 20o gray .30 .20
**436** A97 25o car rose 1.25 .20
**437** A97 30o dk brown .50 .40
**438** A97 40o blue 1.00 .40
**439** A56 50o gray 1.75 .20
**440** A56 75o orange brown 2.75 .80
**441** A56 2k red violet .90 .20

***Perf. 12½ on 3 sides***

**442** A97 20o gray .55 .60
*a.* Booklet pane of 20 15.00
**443** A97 25o carmine rose 1.25 .40
*a.* Booklet pane of 20 27.50
*Nos. 435-443 (9)* 10.25 3.40

Ski Jump A101

Ice Hockey A102

40o, Woman throwing slingball. 1.40kr, Wrestlers.

***Perf. 12½ Vert. (V), Horiz. (H)***

**1953, May 27**

**444** A101 10o green (V) .50 .20
**445** A102 15o brown (H) .75 *1.10*
**446** A102 40o deep blue (H) 1.50 *1.60*
**447** A101 1.40k red violet (V) 4.50 1.25

***Perf. 12½ on 3 sides***

**448** A101 10o green .75 1.10
*a.* Booklet pane of 20 17.50
*Nos. 444-448 (5)* 8.00 5.25

50th anniv. of Swedish Athletic Association.

Old Stockholm A103

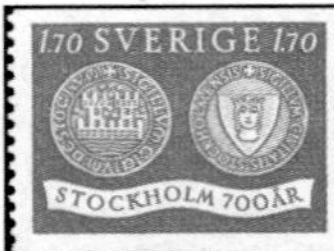


Original and Present Seals of Stockholm A104

**1953, June 17** ***Perf. 12½ Vert.***

**449** A103 25o blue .40 .20
**450** A104 1.70k red 2.75 .75

***Perf. 12½ on 3 sides***

**451** A103 25o blue .80 .30
*a.* Booklet pane of 20 17.50
*Nos. 449-451 (3)* 3.95 1.25

700th anniv. of the founding of Stockholm.

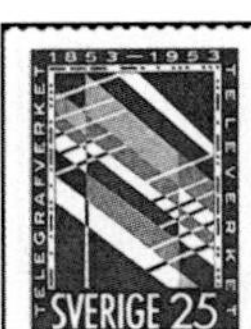


"Telephone" — A105

**1953, Nov. 2** ***Perf. 12½ Horiz.***

**452** A105 25o shown .30 .20
**453** A105 40o "Radio" 1.00 *1.60*
**454** A105 60o "Telegraph" 2.50 2.75

***Perf. 12½ on 3 sides***

**455** A105 25o shown .85 .50
*a.* Booklet pane of 20 20.00
*Nos. 452-455 (4)* 4.65 5.05

Centenary of the foundation of the Swedish Telegraph Service.

### King Type of 1951

**1954** ***Perf. 12½ Vertically***

**Without Imprint**

**456** A97 10o dark brown .20 .20
**457** A97 25o ultra .25 .20
**458** A97 30o red 9.00 .20
**459** A97 40o olive green .60 .20

***Perf. 12½ on 3 sides***

**460** A97 10o dark brown .25 .20
*a.* Booklet pane of 10 9.00
*b.* Booklet pane of 20 7.50
**461** A97 25o ultra .25 .20
*a.* Booklet pane of 4 10.00 11.00
*b.* Booklet pane of 8 100.00 —
*c.* Booklet pane of 20 10.00 —
*Nos. 456-461 (6)* 10.55 1.20

The booklet pane of 4 contains two copies of No. 461 which are perforated on two adjoining sides.

Skier A106

Anna Maria Lenngren A107

**1954, Feb. 13** ***Perf. 12½ Vert.***

**462** A106 20o shown .50 .45
**463** A106 1k Girl skier 8.50 1.25

***Perf. 12½ on 3 sides***

**464** A106 20o shown 1.25 *1.90*
*a.* Booklet pane of 20 35.00
*Nos. 462-464 (3)* 10.25 3.60

World Ski Championship Matches, 1954.

**1954, June 18** ***Perf. 12½ Horiz.***

**465** A107 20o gray .30 .30
**466** A107 65o dark brown 5.50 3.75

***Perf. 12½ on 3 sides***

**467** A107 20o gray 1.25 1.90
*a.* Booklet pane of 20 35.00
*Nos. 465-467 (3)* 7.05 5.95

200th anniversary of the birth of Anna Maria Lenngren, author.

Rock Carvings A108

Coat of Arms A109

**1954, Nov. 8** ***Perf. 12½ Vert.***

**468** A108 50o gray .30 .20
**469** A108 60o dp carmine .50 .20
**470** A108 65o dk olive grn 1.25 .20
**471** A108 75o dk brown 2.00 .20
**472** A108 90o dk blue .60 .20
*Nos. 468-472 (5)* 4.65 1.00

See Nos. 510-512, 655.

### Three-Crown Type of 1939

**1954, Dec. 10** ***Perf. 12½ Vert.***

**473** A56 2.10k dp ultra 7.50 .20

**1955, May 16** ***Perf. 12½ Vert.***

**474** A109 25o blue .20 .20
**475** A109 40o green 1.25 .35

***Perf. 12½ on 3 sides***

**476** A109 25o blue .20 .20
*a.* Booklet pane of 4 9.00 8.50
*b.* Booklet pane of 20 4.00 —
*Nos. 474-476 (3)* 1.65 .75

Centenary of Sweden's 1st postage stamps.

The booklet pane of 4 contains two copies of No. 476 which are perforated on two adjoining sides.

Crown and Flag — A110

A111

***Perf. 12½***

**1955, June 6** **Unwmk.** **Litho.**

**477** A110 10o green, bl & yel .20 .30
**478** A110 15o lake, bl & yel .30 .40

National Flag Day.

**Wmk. 307**

**1955, July 1** **Typo.** ***Perf. 13***

**479** A111 3o yellow green 2.25 *5.00*
**480** A111 4o blue 2.25 *5.00*
**481** A111 6o gray 2.25 *5.00*
**482** A111 8o orange yellow 2.25 *5.00*
**483** A111 24o salmon 2.25 *5.00*
*Nos. 479-483 (5)* 11.25 25.00

Cent. of the 1st Swedish postage stamps. Nos. 479-483 were printed in sheets of nine. They were sold in complete sets at the Stockholmia Philatelic Exhibition, July 1-10, 1955. A set cost 45 ore (face value) plus 2k (entrance fee).

Per Atterbom A112

Greek Horseman A113

***Perf. 12½ Horizontally***

**1955, July 21** **Engr.** **Unwmk.**

**484** A112 20o dark blue .40 .30
**485** A112 1.40k sepia 3.75 .80

***Perf. 12½ on 3 sides***

**486** A112 20o dark blue 1.25 *1.40*
*a.* Booklet pane of 20 35.00
*Nos. 484-486 (3)* 5.40 2.50

Cent. of the death of Per Daniel Amadeus Atterbom, poet.

**1956, Apr. 16** ***Perf. 12½ Vert.***

**487** A113 20o carmine .85 .60
**488** A113 25o ultra .85 .20
**489** A113 40o gray green 2.50 2.10

***Perf. 12½ on 3 sides***

**490** A113 20o carmine .40 *.70*
*a.* Booklet pane of 20 10.00
**491** A113 25o ultra .40 .20
*a.* Booklet pane of 20 10.00
*Nos. 487-491 (5)* 5.00 3.80

Issued to publicize the Olympic Equestrian Competitions, Stockholm, June 10-17, 1956.

### Northern Countries Issue

Whooper Swans — A113a

***Perf. 12½ Vertically***

**1956, Oct. 30** **Engr.** **Unwmk.**

**492** A113a 25o rose red .20 .20
**493** A113a 40o ultra .75 .65

See footnote after Norway No. 354.

Railroad Builders — A114

Designs: 25o, First Swedish locomotive and passenger car. 40o, Express train crossing Arsta bridge.

**1956, Dec. 1** ***Perf. 12½ Vert.***

**494** A114 10o olive green .60 .20
**495** A114 25o ultra .25 .20
**496** A114 40o orange 3.00 *3.00*

***Perf. 12½ on 3 sides***

**497** A114 10o olive green .45 .45
*a.* Booklet pane of 20 11.00
**498** A114 25o ultra .75 .45
*a.* Booklet pane of 20 18.00
*Nos. 494-498 (5)* 5.05 4.30

Centenary of Swedish railroads.

Ship in Distress and Lifeboat — A115

***Perf. 12½ Vertically***

**1957, June 1** **Engr.** **Unwmk.**

**499** A115 30o blue 3.75 .20
**500** A115 1.40k deep rose 4.50 1.25

***Perf. 12½ on 3 sides***

**501** A115 30o blue 1.60 1.25
*a.* Booklet pane of 20 45.00
*Nos. 499-501 (3)* 9.85 2.70

Swedish Life Saving Society, 50th anniv.

### King Type of 1951

**1957, June 1** ***Perf. 12½ Vert.***

**Without Imprint**

**502** A97 25o dark brown 1.10 *1.60*

Re-engraved Types of 1951 and 1954 with Imprint, and

Numeral (Letters in white) — A115a

**1957-64** ***Perf. 12½ Vertically***

**503** A115a 5o red ('61) .20 .20
*a.* 5o dark red .20 .20
**504** A115a 10o blue ('61) .20 .20
*a.* 10o dark blue .30 .25
**505** A97 15o dark red .30 .20
**506** A97 20o gray .25 .20
**507** A97 25o brown .60 .20
**508** A97 30o blue .45 .20
**509** A97 40o olive green 1.25 .20
**510** A108 55o vermilion 1.25 .20
**511** A108 70o orange .60 .20
**512** A108 80o yellow green .80 .20

***Perf. 12½ on 3 sides***

**513** A115a 5o red ('61) .20 .20
*a.* Bklt. pane of 20 ('64) 2.00
*b.* 5o dark red 5.00 1.00
*c.* Bklt. pane, 5 #513b, 5 #515 22.50

**514** A115a 10o blue ('61) .20 .20
*a.* 10o dark blue 20.00 2.50
*b.* Bklt. pane, #514a, 3 #517 37.50 18.00
**515** A97 15o dark red .60 .20
*a.* Bklt. pane of 20 12.00
**516** A97 20o gray 1.00 .60
*a.* Bklt. pane of 20 30.00
**517** A97 30o blue .75 .20
*a.* Bklt. pane of 20 35.00
*Nos. 503-517 (15)* 8.65 3.40

In the redrawn Numeral type A99, "Sverige, ore" and the "g" tail flourishes are white instead of in color.

Booklet pane including #513 is listed as #581b.

The booklet pane of 4, No. 514b, contains two copies of No. 517 which are imperf. on two adjoining sides. No. 514a was issued only in booklet pane No. 514b.

See Nos. 570, 580, 580a, 581b, 584b, 586b-586c, 666-667, 668a, 669b-669c.

Helicopter Mail Service — A116

***Perf. 12½ Vertically***
**1958, Feb. 10 Engr. Unwmk.**
**518** A116 30o blue .40 .20
**519** A116 1.40k brown 4.50 1.00

***Perf. 12½ on 3 sides***
**520** A116 30o blue .80 .55
*a.* Booklet pane of 20 20.00
*Nos. 518-520 (3)* 5.70 1.75

10th anniversary of helicopter mail service to the Stockholm archipelago, Feb. 10.

Modern and 17th Century Vessels — A117

**1958, Feb. 10** ***Perf. 12½ Vert.***
**521** A117 15o dark red .40 .25
**522** A117 40o gray olive 4.25 3.25

***Perf. 12½ on 3 sides***
**523** A117 15o dark red .50 .60
*a.* Booklet pane of 20 12.00
*Nos. 521-523 (3)* 5.15 4.10

3 centuries of transatlantic mail service.

Soccer Player — A118

**1958, May 8** ***Perf. 12½ Vert.***
**524** A118 15o vermilion .85 .20
**525** A118 20o yellow green .50 .20
**526** A118 1.20k dark blue 1.90 1.10

***Perf. 12½ on 3 sides***
**527** A118 15o vermilion .55 .45
*a.* Booklet pane of 20 9.00
**528** A118 20o yellow green .50 *.65*
*a.* Booklet pane of 20 12.00
*Nos. 524-528 (5)* 4.30 2.60

Issued to publicize the 6th World Soccer Championships, Stockholm, June 8-29.

Bessemer Converter A119

Selma Lagerlof A120

***Perf. 12½ Horizontally***
**1958, June 18 Engr. Unwmk.**
**529** A119 30o gray blue .35 .20
**530** A119 1.70k dull red brown 3.00 .95

***Perf. 12½ on 3 sides***
**531** A119 30o gray blue .65 .55
*a.* Booklet pane of 20 15.00
*Nos. 529-531 (3)* 4.00 1.70

Centenary of the first successful Bessemer blow in Sweden, July 18, 1858.

**1958, Nov. 20** ***Perf. 12½ Horiz.***
**532** A120 20o dark red .30 .30
**533** A120 30o blue .40 .20
**534** A120 80o olive green .75 .90

***Perf. 12½ on 3 Sides***
**535** A120 20o dark red .50 .75
*a.* Booklet pane of 20 13.00
**536** A120 30o blue .50 .60
*a.* Booklet pane of 20 16.00
*Nos. 532-536 (5)* 2.45 2.75

Selma Lagerlof, writer, birth cent.

**Palace Type of 1941**
**1958, Sept. 17** ***Perf. 12½ Vert.***
**537** A65 5k blue 2.75 .20

Electric Power Line — A121

Hydroelectric Plant and Dam — A122

***Perf. 12½ Horiz. (H), Vert. (V)***
**1959, Jan. 20 Unwmk.**
**538** A121 30o ultra (H) .45 .20
**539** A122 90o carmine rose (V) 3.25 2.40

***Perf. 12½ on 3 sides***
**540** A121 30o ultra .50 .50
*a.* Booklet pane of 20 14.00
*Nos. 538-540 (3)* 4.20 3.10

50th anniv. of the establishment of the State Power Board.

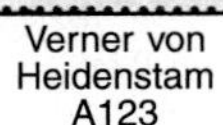
Verner von Heidenstam A123


Forest A124

***Perf. 12½ Horizontally***
**1959, July 6 Engr. Unwmk.**
**541** A123 15o rose carmine 1.00 .35
**542** A123 1k slate 3.00 .90

***Perf. 12½ on 3 Sides***
**543** A123 15o rose carmine .50 .95
*a.* Booklet pane of 20 13.00
*Nos. 541-543 (3)* 4.50 2.20

Verner von Heidenstam, poet, birth cent.

**1959, Sept. 4** ***Perf. 12½ Horiz.***

Design: 1.40k, Felling tree.

**544** A124 30o green 1.50 .20
**545** A124 1.40k brown red 3.50 .60

***Perf. 12½ on 3 sides***
**546** A124 30o green .90 *1.10*
*a.* Booklet pane of 20 25.00
*Nos. 544-546 (3)* 5.90 1.90

Administration of crown lands and forests, cent.

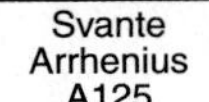
Svante Arrhenius A125

Anders Zorn A126

***Perf. 12½ Horizontally***
**1959, Dec. 10 Engr. Unwmk.**
**547** A125 15o dull red brown .25 .20
**548** A125 1.70k dark blue 3.50 .45

***Perf. 12½ on 3 sides***
**549** A125 15o dull red brown .45 .60
*a.* Booklet pane of 20 10.00
*Nos. 547-549 (3)* 4.20 1.25

Arrhenius (1859-1927), chemist and physicist.

**1960, Feb. 18** ***Perf. 12½ Horiz.***
**550** A126 30o gray .35 .20
**551** A126 80o sepia 3.50 2.25

***Perf. 12½ on 3 sides***
**552** A126 30o gray 1.60 .60
*a.* Booklet pane of 20 35.00
*Nos. 550-552 (3)* 5.45 3.05

Zorn (1860-1920), painter and sculptor.

Uprooted Oak Emblem A127

People of Various Races, WRY Emblem A128

***Perf. 12½ Vert. (V), Horiz. (H)***
**1960, Apr. 7 Engr. Unwmk.**
**553** A127 20o red brown (V) .20 .20
**554** A128 40o purple (H) .30 .30

***Perf. 12½ on 3 sides***
**555** A127 20o red brown .50 .60
*a.* Booklet pane of 20 12.00
*Nos. 553-555 (3)* 1.00 1.10

World Refugee Year, 7/1/59-6/30/60.

Target Shooting A129

Gustaf Froding A130

Design: 90o, Parade of riflemen.

**1960, June 30** ***Perf. 12½ Vert.***
**556** A129 15o rose carmine .30 .20
**557** A129 90o grnsh blue 2.50 2.00

***Perf. 12½ on 3 sides***
**558** A129 15o rose carmine .35 *.50*
*a.* Booklet pane of 20 9.00
*Nos. 556-558 (3)* 3.15 2.70

Centenary of the founding of the Voluntary Shooting Organization.

**1960, Aug. 22** ***Perf. 12½ Horiz.***
**559** A130 30o red brown .30 .20
**560** A130 1.40k slate green 2.60 .45

***Perf. 12½ on 3 sides***
**561** A130 30o red brown .45 .35
*a.* Booklet pane of 20 10.00
*Nos. 559-561 (3)* 3.35 1.00

Gustaf Froding (1860-1911), poet.

Common Design Types pictured following the introduction.

**Europa Issue, 1960**
Common Design Type
**1960, Sept. 19** ***Perf. 12½ Vert.***
**Size: 27x21mm**
**562** CD3 40o blue .20 .20
**563** CD3 1k red .80 .30

Hjalmar Branting (1860-1925), Labor Party Leader and Prime Minister — A131

***Perf. 12½ Horiz.***
**1960, Nov. 23 Engr.**
**564** A131 15o rose carmine .20 .20
**565** A131 1.70k slate blue 3.00 .55

***Perf. 12½ on 3 sides***
**566** A131 15o rose carmine .45 .35
*a.* Booklet pane of 20 4.50
*Nos. 564-566 (3)* 3.65 1.10

**SAS Issue**

DC-8 Airliner — A131a

***Perf. 12½ Vertically***
**1961, Feb. 24 Unwmk.**
**567** A131a 40o blue .30 .35

***Perf. 12½ on 3 sides***
**568** A131a 40o blue .85 *1.25*
*a.* Booklet pane of 10 10.00

Scandinavian Airlines System, SAS, 10th anniv.

**Numeral Type of 1957, Three-Crown Type of 1939 and**

Gustaf VI Adolf (Letters, numerals in white) A132

Rune Stone, Oland, 11th Century A133

**1961-65** ***Perf. 12½ Vert.***
**570** A115a 15o green ('62) .30 .20
**571** A132 15o red .35 .20
**572** A132 20o gray .35 .20
**573** A132 25o brown .65 .20
**574** A132 30o ultra 1.50 .20
**575** A132 30o lilac ('62) .55 .20
**576** A132 35o lilac .55 .20
**577** A132 35o ultra ('62) 1.10 .20
**578** A132 40o emerald 1.00 .20
**579** A132 50o gray grn ('62) .65 .20

***Perf. 12½ on 3 sides***
**580** A115a 15o grn ('65) .30 .30
*a.* Bklt. pane, 2 each #514, 580, 583 2.25
**581** A132 15o red .25 .20
*a.* Bklt. pane of 20 5.00
*b.* Bklt. pane, 5 #513, 5 #581 2.50
**582** A132 20o gray 1.25 .75
*a.* Bklt. pane of 20 27.50
**583** A132 25o brown ('62) .35 .20
*a.* Bklt. pane of 20 15.00
*b.* Bklt. pane of 4 2.25
**584** A132 30o ultra .65 .20
*a.* Bklt. pane of 20 15.00
*b.* Bklt. pane, #514 + 3 #584 4.00
**585** A132 30o lilac ('64) .65 .50
*a.* Bklt. pane of 20 14.00
**586** A132 35o ultra ('62) .55 .20
*a.* Bklt. pane of 20 12.50
*b.* Bklt. pane, 3 #514, 2 #586 + blank label 5.00 3.50
*c.* As "b," inscribed label 3.50 1.50

***Perf. 12½ Vertically***
**588** A56 1.05k Prus grn ('62) 1.10 .30
**589** A56 1.50k brown ('62) .80 .30
**590** A56 2.15k dk sl grn ('62) 4.00 .65
**591** A56 2.50k emerald 1.50 .20

***Perf. 12½ on 3 sides***
**592** A133 10k dl red brn 20.00 .50
*a.* Bklt. pane of 10 ('68) 250.00
*b.* Bklt. pane of 20 850.00
*Nos. 570-592 (22)* 38.40 6.30

Booklet panes of 4, 5 or 6 (Nos. 580a, 583b, 584b, 586b, 586c) contain two stamps which are imperf. on two adjoining sides.

Combination panes (Nos. 580a, 581b, 584b, 586b, 586c) come in different arrangements of the denominations.

The label of No. 586c is inscribed "ett brev / betyder / sa / mycket" ("a letter means so much"). The label inscription "nord 63 / 5-13 oktober / GÖTEBORG" was privately applied to No. 586b by the Gothenburg Philatelic Society to raise funds for Nord 63 Philatelic Exhibition in Gothenburg. The pane was sold for the equivalent of $1 US, 5 times face value.

See Nos. 648-654A, 666a, 668-672F.

K.-G. Pilo, Self-portrait
A134

Jonas Alstromer
A135

**1961, Apr. 17** ***Perf. 12½ Horiz.***
**594** A134 30o brown .35 .25
**595** A134 1.40k Prus blue 3.50 1.30

***Perf. 12½ on 3 sides***
**596** A134 30o brown 1.10 .45
*a.* Booklet pane of 20 30.00
*Nos. 594-596 (3)* 4.95 2.00

Karl-Gustaf Pilo (1711-1793), painter. Self-portrait from "The Coronation of Gustavus III."

**1961, June 2** ***Perf. 12½ Vert.***
**597** A135 15o dull claret .20 .20
**598** A135 90o grnsh blue 1.60 2.25

***Perf. 12½ on 3 sides***
**599** A135 15o dull claret .25 .40
*a.* Booklet pane of 20 7.00
*Nos. 597-599 (3)* 2.05 2.85

200th anniversary of the birth of Jonas Alstromer, pioneer of agriculture and industry.

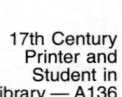

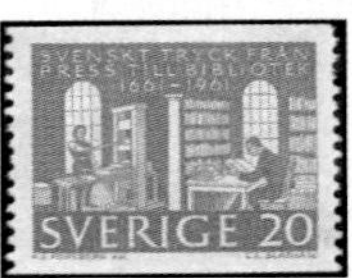
17th Century Printer and Student in Library — A136

***Perf. 12½ Vert.***
**1961, Sept. 22** **Engr.**
**600** A136 20o dark red .30 .30
**601** A136 1k blue 7.00 1.60

***Perf. 12½ on 3 sides***
**602** A136 20o dark red .30 .55
*a.* Booklet pane of 20 9.00
*Nos. 600-602 (3)* 7.60 2.45

300th anniversary of the regulation requiring copies of all Swedish printed works to be deposited in the Royal Library.

Roentgen, Prudhomme, von Behring, van't Hoff — A137

**1961, Dec. 9** ***Perf. 12½ Vertically***
**603** A137 20o vermilion .20 .20
**604** A137 40o blue .20 .20
**605** A137 50o green .50 .20

***Perf. 12½ on 3 sides***
**606** A137 20o vermilion .25 .20
*a.* Booklet pane of 20 6.00
*Nos. 603-606 (4)* 1.15 .80

Winners of the 1901 Nobel Prize; Wilhelm K. Roentgen, Rene Sully Prudhomme, Emil von Behring, Jacob van't Hoff.

See Nos. 617-619, 673-676, 689-692, 710-713, 769-772, 804-807.

A138

A139

Footsteps and postmen's badges.

**1962, Jan. 29** **Engr.** ***Perf. 12½ Vert.***
**607** A138 30o lilac .40 .20
**608** A138 1.70k rose red 3.50 .55

***Perf. 12½ on 3 sides***
**609** A138 30o lilac .50 .50
*a.* Booklet pane of 20 11.00
*Nos. 607-609 (3)* 4.40 1.25

Local mail delivery service in Sweden, cent.

**1962, Mar. 21** ***Perf. 12½ Horiz.***

Voting Tool (Budkavle), Codex of Law and Gavel

**610** A139 30o dark blue .35 .20
**611** A139 2k red 4.50 .35

***Perf. 12½ on 3 sides***
**612** A139 30o dark blue .40 .45
*a.* Booklet pane of 20 10.50
*Nos. 610-612 (3)* 5.25 1.00

Centenary of the municipal reform laws.

St. George, Great Church, Stockholm
A140

Skokloster Castle
A141

***Perf. 12½ Horiz. (H), Vert. (V)***
**1962, Sept. 24**
**613** A140 20o rose lake (H) .25 .20
**614** A141 50o dk slate grn (V) .55 .35

***Perf. 12½ on 3 sides***
**615** A140 20o rose lake .20 .30
*a.* Booklet pane of 20 6.00
**616** A141 50o dk slate grn .90 1.20
*a.* Booklet pane of 10 9.00
*Nos. 613-616 (4)* 1.90 2.05

Nobel Prize Winners Type of 1961

Designs: 25o, Theodor Mommsen and Sir Ronald Ross. 50o, Hermann Emil Fischer, Pieter Zeeman and Hendrik Antoon Lorentz.

**1962, Dec. 10** ***Perf. 12½ Vert.***
**617** A137 25o dark red .30 .30
**618** A137 50o blue .40 .40

***Perf. 12½ on 3 sides***
**619** A142 25o dark red .40 .65
*a.* Booklet pane of 20 10.00
*Nos. 617-619 (3)* 1.10 1.35

Winners of the 1902 Nobel Prize.

Ice Hockey — A143

**1963, Feb. 15** ***Perf. 12½ Horiz.***
**620** A143 25o green .40 .20
**621** A143 1.70k violet bl 3.00 .70

***Perf. 12½ on 3 sides***
**622** A143 25o green .25 .55
*a.* Booklet pane of 20 7.00
*Nos. 620-622 (3)* 3.65 1.45

1963 Ice Hockey World Championships.

Wheat Emblem and Stylized Hands — A144

**1963, Mar. 21** ***Perf. 12½ Vertically***
**623** A144 35o lilac rose .35 .20
**624** A144 50o violet .30 .35

***Perf. 12½ on 3 sides***
**625** A144 35o lilac rose .30 .40
*a.* Booklet pane of 20 6.00
*Nos. 623-625 (3)* .95 .95

FAO "Freedom from Hunger" campaign.

Engineering and Industry Symbols — A145

**1963, May 27** ***Perf. 12½ Vertically***
**626** A145 50o gray .50 .35
**627** A145 1.05k orange 3.25 2.75

***Perf. 12½ on 3 sides***
**628** A145 50o gray 2.60 2.75
*a.* Booklet pane of 10 27.50
*Nos. 626-628 (3)* 6.35 5.85

Gregoire François Du Reitz — A146

***Perf. 12½ Vertically***
**1963, Sept. 16** **Engr.** **Unwmk.**
**629** A146 25o brown .40 .45
**630** A146 35o dark blue .30 .20
**631** A146 2k dark red 4.00 .55

***Perf. 12½ on 3 sides***
**632** A146 25o brown .65 .75
*a.* Booklet pane of 20 16.00
**633** A146 35o dark blue .40 .30
*a.* Booklet pane of 20 10.00
*Nos. 629-633 (5)* 5.75 2.25

300th anniversary of the Swedish Board of Health. Dr. Du Rietz (1607-1682) was first president of the "Collegium Medicorum," forerunner of the Board of Health.

Hammarby, Home of Carl von Linné (Linnaeus) A147

**1963, Oct. 25** ***Perf. 12½ Vert.***
**634** A147 20o orange red .30 .20
**635** A147 50o yellow grn .30 .25

***Perf. 12½ on 3 sides***
**636** A147 20o orange red .30 .35
*a.* Booklet pane of 20 6.00
*Nos. 634-636 (3)* .90 .80

**Nobel Prize Winners Type of 1961**

Designs: 25o, Svante Arrhenius, Niels Finsen, Bjornstjerne Bjornson. 50o, Antoine Henri Becquerel, Pierre and Marie Curie.

***Perf. 12½ Vertically***
**1963, Dec. 10** **Engr.** **Unwmk.**
**637** A137 25o gray olive .75 .70
**638** A137 50o chocolate .40 .50

***Perf. 12½ on 3 sides***
**639** A137 25o gray olive .75 1.10
*a.* Booklet pane of 20 16.00
*Nos. 637-639 (3)* 1.90 2.30

Winners of the 1903 Nobel Prize.

A149

A150

"The Assumption of Elijah."

**1964, Feb. 3** ***Perf. 12½ Horiz.***
**640** A149 35o lt ultra .65 .20
**641** A149 1.05k dull red 3.75 3.75

***Perf. 12½ on 3 sides***
**642** A149 35o lt ultra .45 .35
*a.* Booklet pane of 20 10.00
*Nos. 640-642 (3)* 4.85 4.30

Erik Axel Karlfeldt (1864-1931), poet.

**1964, June 12** ***Perf. 12½ Horiz.***

Seal of Archbishop Stephen.

**643** A150 40o slate green .30 .30
**644** A150 60o orange brown .30 .35

***Perf. 12½ Vertically***
**645** A150 40o slate green .30 .30
*a.* Booklet pane of 10 3.50
**646** A150 60o orange brown .35 .55
*a.* Booklet pane of 10 4.00
*Nos. 643-646 (4)* 1.25 1.50

800th anniv. of the Archbishopric of Uppsala.

**Types of Regular Issues, 1939-61, and**

Post Horns — A151

Ship Grave, Skane (Bronze Age) — A152

**1964-71** **Engr.** ***Perf. 12½ Vert.***
**647** A151 20o sl bl & org yel ('65) .20 .20
**648** A132 35o gray .60 .20
**649** A132 40o ultra .60 .20
**650** A132 45o orange .60 .20
**651** A132 45o violet bl ('67) .60 .20
**652** A132 50o green ('68) .55 .20
**652A** A132 55o dark red ('69) .40 .20
**653** A132 60o rose car .65 .65
**653A** A132 65o dull grn ('71) .80 .20
**654** A132 70o lil rose ('67) .50 .20
**654A** A132 85o dp cl ('71) .80 .30
**655** A108 95o violet 3.00 4.00
**656** A56 1.20k lt blue 3.50 3.50
**657** A56 1.80k dk blue ('67) 1.25 .50
**658** A56 1.85k blue ('67) 3.00 1.00
**659** A56 2k dp car ('69) .75 .20
**660** A56 2.30k choc ('65) 5.50 .20
**661** A56 2.55k red 2.10 2.60
**662** A56 2.80k red ('67) 1.40 .20
**663** A56 2.85k orange ('65) 2.75 4.00
**664** A56 3k brt ultra 1.40 .20
**665** A152 3.50k grnsh gray ('66) 1.50 .20

***Perf. 12½ on 3 Sides***
**666** A115a 10o brown .20 .25
*a.* Bklt. pane, 2 each #666, 667, 583 3.00
**667** A115a 15o brown .50 .80
**668** A132 30o rose red ('66) .85 .85
*a.* Bklt. pane, 2 each #513, 580, 668 1.40
*b.* Perf. on 3 sides 1.10 1.10

No. 668 is perf. on 2 adjoining sides.

**669** A132 40o ultra .20 .20
*a.* Bklt. pane of 20 16.00
*b.* Bklt. pane, 2 ea #514, 669 1.50
*c.* Bklt. pane, 2 each #513-514, 580, 668b-669 4.00
**670** A132 45o org ('67) .65 .20
*a.* Bklt. pane of 20 14.00
**671** A132 45o vio bl ('67) .70 .20
*a.* Bklt. pane of 20 14.00
**672** A132 50o green ('69) .50 .60
*a.* Bklt. pane of 10 5.00
**672B** A132 55o dk red ('69) .50 .20
*c.* Bklt. pane of 10 5.00
**672D** A132 65o dull grn ('71) .85 .50
*e.* Bklt. pane of 10 9.00
**672F** A132 85o dp cl ('71) .90 1.25
*g.* Bklt. pane of 10 9.50
*Nos. 647-672F (32)* 38.30 24.40

Some combination booklet panes of 4, 6 or 10 contain two stamps which are imperf. on two adjoining sides. Combination panes come in different arrangements of the denominations.

Fluorescent Paper

Starting in 1967, fluorescent paper was used in printing both definitive and commemorative issues. Its use was gradually eliminated starting in 1976. Numerous definitives and a few commemoratives were printed on both ordinary and fluorescent paper.

**Nobel Prize Winners Type of 1961**

30o, José Echegaray y Eizaguirre, Frédéric Mistral and John William Strutt, Lord Rayleigh. 40o, Sir William Ramsey and Ivan Petrovich Pavlov.

***Perf. 12½ Vertically***
**1964, Dec. 10** **Engr.**
**673** A137 30o blue .45 .45
**674** A137 40o red .70 .25

***Perf. 12½ on 3 Sides***
**675** A137 30o blue .45 .75
*a.* Booklet pane of 20 12.00
**676** A137 40o red .75 .35
*a.* Booklet pane of 20 18.00
*Nos. 673-676 (4)* 2.35 1.80

Winners of the 1904 Nobel Prize.

Visby Town Wall A154

Antenna A155

**1965, Apr. 5** *Perf. 12½ Horiz.*
**677** A154 30o dk car rose .30 .20
**678** A154 2k brt ultra 4.25 .35

*Perf. 12½ on 3 Sides*
**679** A154 30o dk car rose .40 .35
*a.* Booklet pane of 20 9.00
*Nos. 677-679 (3)* 4.95 .90

**1965, May 17** *Perf. 12½ Horiz.*
**680** A155 60o lilac .45 .45
**681** A155 1.40k bluish blk 2.25 1.90

*Perf. 12½ on 3 Sides*
**682** A155 60o lilac 1.10 1.60
*a.* Booklet pane of 10 12.50
*Nos. 680-682 (3)* 3.80 3.95

Centenary of the ITU.

Prince Eugen — A156

**1965, July 5** *Perf. 12½ Horiz.*
**683** A156 40o black .20 .20
**684** A156 1k brown 2.10 .35

*Perf. 12½ on 3 Sides*
**685** A156 40o black .25 .25
*a.* Booklet pane of 20 7.00
*Nos. 683-685 (3)* 2.55 .80

Prince Eugen (1865-1947), painter and patron of the arts.

Fredrika Bremer (1801-65), Novelist — A157

*Perf. 12½ Vertically*
**1965, Oct. 25** **Engr.**
**686** A157 25o violet .20 .20
**687** A157 3k gray green 4.00 .35

*Perf. 12½ on 3 Sides*
**688** A157 25o violet .25 .20
*a.* Booklet pane of 20 5.00
*Nos. 686-688 (3)* 4.45 .75

**Nobel Prize Winners Type of 1961**

30o, Philipp von Lenard, Adolf von Baeyer. 40o, Robert Koch, Henryk Sienkiewicz.

*Perf. 12½ Vertically*
**1965, Dec. 10** **Unwmk.**
**689** A137 30o ultra .35 .45
**690** A137 40o dark red .40 .25

*Perf. 12½ on 3 Sides*
**691** A137 30o ultra .45 .75
*a.* Booklet pane of 20 11.00
**692** A137 40o dark red .85 .30
*a.* Booklet pane of 20 19.00
*Nos. 689-692 (4)* 2.05 1.75

Winners of the 1905 Nobel Prize.

Nathan Soderblom A158

Speed Skater A159

**1966, Jan. 15** *Perf. 12½ Horiz.*
**693** A158 60o brown .35 .20
**694** A158 80o green .85 .20

*Perf. 12½ on 3 Sides*
**695** A158 60o brown .75 .90
*a.* Booklet pane of 10 8.00
*Nos. 693-695 (3)* 1.95 1.30

Nathan Soderblom (1866-1931), Protestant theologian, who worked for the union of Christian churches and received 1930 Nobel Peace Prize.

*Perf. 12½ on 3 Sides*
**1966, Feb. 18** **Engr.**
**696** A159 5o rose red .20 .20
**697** A159 25o slate green .20 .20
**698** A159 40o dark blue .35 *.70*
*a.* Bklt. pane, 4 ea #696-697, 2 #698 2.25
*Nos. 696-698 (3)* .75 1.10

World Speed Skating Championships for Men, Gothenburg, Feb. 18-20, and 75th anniversary of World Skating Championships.

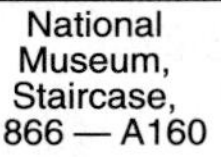

National Museum, Staircase, 1866 — A160

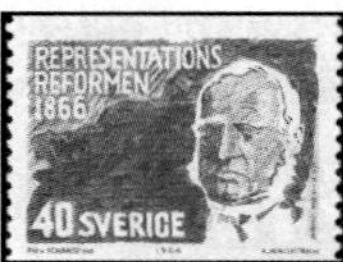

Baron Louis Gerhard De Geer — A161

**1966, Mar. 26** *Perf. 12½ Vert.*
**699** A160 30o violet .20 .25
*a.* Booklet pane of 10 2.50
**700** A160 2.30k olive green 1.40 1.50
*a.* Booklet pane of 10 13.00

National Gallery, Blasieholmen, Stockholm, cent. The design is from an 1866 woodcut showing the inauguration of the Museum.

**1966, May 12** *Perf. 12½ Vertically*
**701** A161 40o dark blue .25 .20
**702** A161 3k brown carmine 3.75 .65

*Perf. 12½ on 3 Sides*
**703** A161 40o dark blue .25 .35
*a.* Booklet pane of 20 8.00
*Nos. 701-703 (3)* 4.25 1.20

Cent. of the reform of the Representative Assembly under the leadership of Minister of Justice (1858-70) Baron Louis Gerhard De Geer (1818-96).

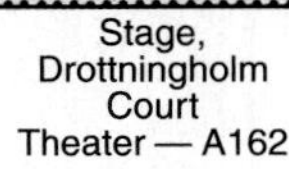

Stage, Drottningholm Court Theater — A162

Almqvist and Wild Rose — A163

*Perf. 12½ on 3 Sides*
**1966, June 15** **Engr.**
**Salmon Paper**
**704** A162 5o vermilion .20 .20
**705** A162 25o olive bister .20 .20
**706** A162 40o dark purple .40 .65
*a.* Bklt. pane, 4 ea #704-705, 2 #706 2.00
*Nos. 704-706 (3)* .80 1.05

Drottningholm Court Theater, 200th anniv.

*Perf. 12½ Horizontally*
**1966, Sept. 26** **Engr.**
**707** A163 25o magenta .25 .20
**708** A163 1k green 2.25 .30

*Perf. 12½ on 3 Sides*
**709** A163 25o magenta .20 .20
*a.* Booklet pane of 20 4.75
*Nos. 707-709 (3)* 2.70 .70

Carl Jonas Love Almqvist (1793-1866), writer and poet.

**Nobel Prize Winner Type of 1961**

Designs: 30o, Joseph John Thomson and Giosue Carducci. 40o, Henri Moissan, Camillo Golgi and Santiago Ramon y Cajal.

*Perf. 12½ Vertically*
**1966, Dec. 10** **Engr.**
**710** A137 30o rose lake .55 .20
**711** A137 40o dark green .50 .20

*Perf. 12½ on 3 Sides*
**712** A137 30o rose lake .55 .45
*a.* Booklet pane of 20 11.00
**713** A137 40o dark green .55 .45
*a.* Booklet pane of 20 12.00
*Nos. 710-713 (4)* 2.15 1.30

Winners of the 1906 Nobel Prize.

Field Ball Player A164

EFTA Emblem A165

**1967, Jan. 12** *Perf. 12½ Horiz.*
**714** A164 45o dk violet blue .20 .20
**715** A164 2.70k dp rose lilac 2.75 1.50

*Perf. 12½ on 3 Sides*
**716** A164 45o dk violet blue .25 .30
*a.* Booklet pane of 20 6.00
*Nos. 714-716 (3)* 3.20 2.00

World Field Ball Championships, Jan. 12-21.

**1967, Feb. 15** *Perf. 12½ Horiz.*
**717** A165 70o orange .45 .40

*Perf. 12½ on 3 Sides*
**718** A165 70o orange 1.10 1.25
*a.* Booklet pane of 10 15.00

European Free Trade Association. Tariffs were abolished Dec. 31, 1966, among EFTA members: Austria, Denmark, Finland, Great Britain, Norway, Portugal, Sweden, Switzerland.

"The Fjeld," by Sixten Lundbohm A166

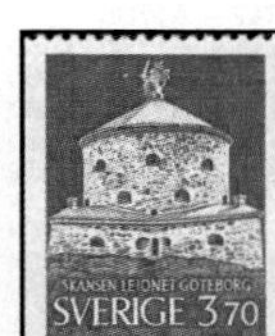

Lion Fortress, Gothenburg A167

Uppsala Cathedral A168

Gripsholm Castle A169

**1967** **Engr.** *Perf. 12½ Vert.*
**719** A166 35o dl bl & blk brn .20 .20

*Perf. 12½ Horiz.*
**720** A167 3.70k violet 2.10 .20
**721** A168 4.50k dull red 2.40 .20

*Perf. 12½ Vert.*
**722** A169 7k vio bl & rose red 3.25 .55

*Perf. 12½ on 3 Sides*
**723** A166 35o dl bl & blk brn .20 .20
*a.* Booklet pane of 10 2.50
*Nos. 719-723 (5)* 8.15 1.35

Issued: #719, 721, 723, 3/15; #720, 2/15; #722, 4/11.

Table Tennis — A170

**1967, Apr. 11** *Perf. 12½ Horiz.*
**724** A170 35o bright magenta .30 .20
**725** A170 90o greenish blue 1.30 .50

*Perf. 12½ on 3 Sides*
**726** A170 35o bright magenta .35 .40
*a.* Booklet pane of 20 7.00
*Nos. 724-726 (3)* 1.95 1.10

World Table Tennis Championships, Stockholm.

Man with Axe and Fettered Beast — A171

Double Mortise Corner — A172

Designs: 15o, Man fighting two bears. 30o, Warrior disguised as wolf pursuing enemy. 35o, Two warriors with swords and lances. The designs are taken from 6th century bronze plates (1¾in. x 2⅛in.) used to decorate helmets; now in Swedish Museum of National Antiquities.

*Perf. 12½ on 3 Sides*
**1967, May 17** **Engr.**
**727** A171 10o dk brown & dp bl .20 .20
**728** A171 15o dp blue & dk brn .20 .20
**729** A171 30o brt pink & dk brn .20 .20
**730** A171 35o dk brown & brt pink .20 .20
*a.* Bklt. pane, 4 #727, 2 ea #728-730 2.10 *2.75*
*Nos. 727-730 (4)* .80 .80

**Lithographed and Photogravure**
**1967, June 16** *Perf. 12½*
**731** A172 10o olive & multi .20 .20
**732** A172 35o dk blue multi .30 .30
*a.* Bklt. pane, 6 #731, 4 #732 1.75 *2.00*

Issued to honor generations of Finnish settlers in Sweden.

Right-hand Driving as Seen Through Windshield — A173

**1967, Sept. 2** **Engr.** *Perf. 12½ Vert.*
**733** A173 35o dp bl, ocher & blk .30 .35
**734** A173 45o yel grn, ocher & blk .35 .45

*Perf. 12½ Horiz.*
**735** A173 35o dp bl, ocher & blk .30 .45
*a.* Booklet pane of 10 3.00
**736** A173 45o yel grn, ocher & blk .20 .20
*a.* Booklet pane of 10 2.50
*Nos. 733-736 (4)* 1.15 1.45

Issued to publicize the introduction of right-hand driving in Sweden, Sept. 3, 1967.

Postrider A174

The Prodigal Son, 13th cent., Rada Church A174a

Griffin
A174b

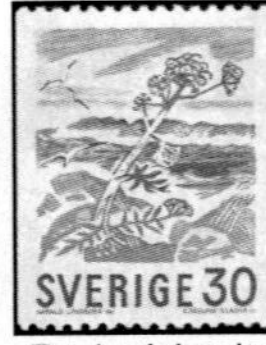
Rocky Isles in Bloom, by Harald Lindberg
A175

Dalsland Canal — A176

Log roller — A176a

Gothenburg Harbor — A176b

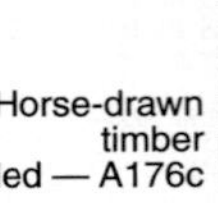

Horse-drawn timber sled — A176c

Nils Holgersson Riding Wild Goose — A176d

Windmills, Ölana Island — A176e

Steamer Storskar and Royal Palace, Stockholm
A176f

Elk — A177

Roe deer — A177a

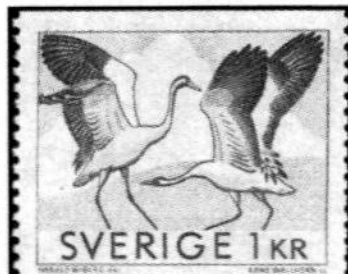
Dancing cranes — A177b

Mail Coach, by Eigil Schwab
A177c

Illustration from Lapponia, by Johannes Schefferus — A177d

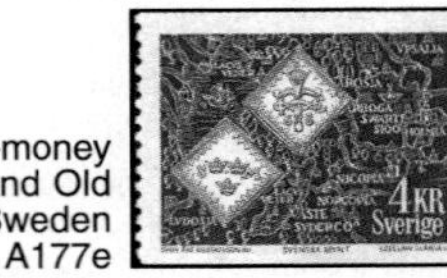
Blood-money Coins and Old Map of Sweden
A177e

Great Seal, 1439 (St. Erik with Banner and Shield) — A177f

10o, Merchant vessel in Oresund, 1661. 20o, St. Stephen as a boy tending horses, medallion from Dädesio Church. #742, Lion, from Grodinge tapestry, 15th cent. 2.55k, Seal of Magnus Ladulas, 1285 (King Magnus Birgersson on throne with lily scepter and orb). 3k, Seal of Duke Erik Magnusson, 1306 (Duke on horseback with standard of Folkunga dynasty). 6k, Gustavus Vasa's silver daler.

**1967-72** ***Perf. 12½ Horiz. or Vert.***

**737** A174 5o red & blk .20 .20
**738** A174 10o blue & blk .20 .20
**739** A174a 15o sl grn, *grnsh* ('71) .20 .20
**740** A174 20o sep, *buff* ('70) .20 .20
**741** A174b 25o bis & blk ('71) .20 .20
**742** A174b 25o blk & bis ('71) .20 .20
*a.* Pair, #741-742 .40 .50
**743** A175 30o ultra & ver .20 .20
**744** A176 40o blk, dk grn & ultra ('68) .30 .20
**745** A176a 45o bl & brn blk ('70) .30 .20
**746** A176b 55o bl & vio, vert. ('71) .40 .20
**747** A176c 60o black brn ('71) .30 .20
**747A** A176d 65o brt blue ('71) .30 .20
**748** A176e 75o slate grn ('71) .30 .20
**749** A176f 80o blue & blk ('71) .40 .20
**750** A177 90o sep & bl gray .55 .20
**750A** A177a 95o sepia ('72) .40 .20
**751** A177b 1k slate grn ('68) .55 .20
**751A** A177c 1.20k multi ('71) .65 .20
**751B** A177d 1.40k lt bl & red ('72) .75 .20
**752** A177f 2.55k brt blue ('70) 1.25 .65
**753** A177f 3k dk gray bl ('70) 1.25 .20
**754** A177e 4k black ('71) 1.60 .20
**755** A177f 5k Prus grn ('70) 2.00 .20
**755A** A177e 6k indigo ('72) 3.00 .20

***Perf. 12½ on 3 Sides***

**756** A174 5o red & blk .20 .20
*a.* Booklet pane of 20 .75
**757** A174 10o bl & blk ('69) .20 .20
*a.* Booklet pane of 20 2.10
**758** A175 30o ultra & ver .30 .30
*a.* Booklet pane of 10 3.25
**759** A176 40o blk, dk grn & ultra ('68) .20 .30
*a.* Booklet pane of 10 2.75
**760** A176a 45o bl & brn blk ('70) .20 .20
*a.* Booklet pane of 10 2.75
**761** A176b 55o bl & vio, perf. 12½ horiz. ('71) .35 .20
*a.* Booklet pane of 10 3.50
**762** A176d 65o brt blue ('71) .40 .40
*a.* Booklet pane of 10 4.00
**763** A176e 75o slate grn ('72) .50 .20
*a.* Booklet pane of 10 5.50
**764** A177 90o sepia & bl gray 1.00 1.00
*a.* Booklet pane of 10 10.00
*Nos. 737-764 (33)* 19.05 8.25

King Gustaf VI Adolf — A178

***Perf. 12½ Horiz.***

**1967, Nov. 11** **Engr.**

**765** A178 45o lt ultra .30 .20
**766** A178 70o green .30 .30

***Perf. 12½ on 3 Sides***

**767** A178 45o lt ultra .25 .25
*a.* Booklet pane of 20 4.50
**768** A178 70o green .65 .95
*a.* Booklet pane of 10 6.50
*Nos. 765-768 (4)* 1.50 1.70

85th birthday of King Gustaf VI Adolf.

### Nobel Prize Winners Type of 1961

35o, Eduard Buchner (Chemistry), Albert A. Michelson (Physics). 45o, Charles L. A. Laveran (Medicine), Rudyard Kipling (Literature).

**1967, Dec. 9** ***Perf. 12½ Vert.***

**769** A137 35o vermilion .65 .50
**770** A137 45o dark blue .55 .20

***Perf. 12½ on 3 Sides***

**771** A142 35o vermilion .70 *.95*
*a.* Booklet pane of 10 7.50
**772** A142 45o dark blue .45 *.50*
*a.* Booklet pane of 10 6.50
*Nos. 769-772 (4)* 2.35 2.15

Winners of the 1907 Nobel Prize.

Franz Berwald, Violin and His Music — A179

**1968, Apr. 3** ***Perf. 12½ Horiz.***

**773** A179 35o black & red .35 .20
**774** A179 2k blk, vio bl & org yel 3.00 .80

***Perf. 12½ on 3 Sides***

**775** A179 35o black & red .45 .60
*a.* Booklet pane of 10 4.50
*Nos. 773-775 (3)* 3.80 1.60

Franz Berwald (1796-1868), composer. Design includes opening bar of overture to his opera, "The Queen of Golconda."

National Bank Seal — A180

***Perf. 12½ Vertically***

**1968, May 15** **Engr.**

**776** A180 45o dull blue .25 .20
**777** A180 70o black, *pink* .30 .35

***Perf. 12½ on 3 Sides***

**778** A180 45o dull blue .35 *.50*
*a.* Booklet pane of 10 4.00
**779** A180 70o black, *pink* .55 *.85*
*a.* Booklet pane of 10 6.50
*Nos. 776-779 (4)* 1.45 1.90

300th anniv. of the National Bank of Sweden. Nos. 777, 779 are on non-fluorescent paper.

Seal of Lund University — A181

Butterfly Orchid — A182

**1968, June 4** ***Perf. 12½ on 3 sides***

**780** A181 10o deep blue .20 .20
**781** A181 35o red .30 *.50*
*a.* Bklt. pane, 6 #780, 4 #781 2.25 *2.75*

300th anniversary of University of Lund.

**1968, June 4**

Nordic Wild Flowers: No. 783, Wood anemone. No. 784, Dog rose. No. 785, Prune Cherry. No. 786, Lily of the valley.

**782** A182 45o slate green .90 .55
**783** A182 45o gray green .90 .55
**784** A182 45o sl grn & rose car .90 .55
**785** A182 45o gray green .90 .55
**786** A182 45o slate green .90 .55
*a.* Bklt. pane, 2 each #782-786 11.00
*Nos. 782-786 (5)* 4.50 2.75

World Council of Churches' Emblem
A183

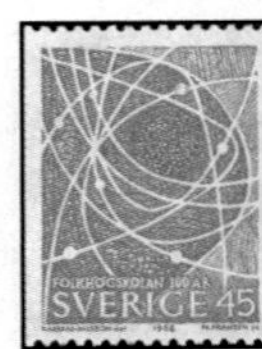
Electron Orbits
A184

**1968, July 4** ***Perf. 12½ Horiz.***

**787** A183 70o plum .55 *.60*
**788** A183 90o Prus green 1.00 .50

***Perf. 12½ on 3 Sides***

**789** A183 70o plum .65 *.95*
*a.* Booklet pane of 10 7.50
*Nos. 787-789 (3)* 2.20 2.05

4th General Assembly of the World Council of Churches, Uppsala, July 4-19.

***Perf. 12½ Horizontally***

**1968, Aug. 9** **Engr.**

**790** A184 45o rose carmine .55 .20
**791** A184 2k dark blue 2.90 .40

***Perf. 12½ on 3 Sides***

**792** A184 45o rose carmine .50 .45
*a.* Booklet pane of 10 5.00
*Nos. 790-792 (3)* 3.95 1.05

Establishment of the 1st 3 People's Colleges, cent.

"Orienteer" Finding Way through Forest — A185

"Fingerkrok" by Axel Petersson — A186

***Perf. 12½ Horizontally***

**1968, Sept. 5** **Engr.**

**793** A185 40o violet & red brn .35 .40
**794** A185 2.80k green & violet 3.00 3.00

***Perf. 12½ on 3 Sides***

**795** A185 40o violet & red brn .40 .65
*a.* Booklet pane of 10 5.00
*Nos. 793-795 (3)* 3.75 4.05

Issued to publicize the World Championships in Orienteering, Linkoping, Sept. 28-29.

***Perf. 12½ on 3 Sides***

**1968, Oct. 28** **Engr.**

**796** A186 5o green .20 .20
**797** A186 25o sepia 1.40 1.10
**798** A186 45o blk brn & red brn .20 .25
*a.* Bklt. pane, 3 #796, 2 #797, 3 #798 3.00
*Nos. 796-798 (3)* 1.80 1.55

Axel Petersson, called "Doderhultarn" (1868-1925), sculptor.

Black-backed Gull — A187

Designs: No. 799, Varying hare. No. 801, Red fox. No. 802, Hooded crows harassing golden eagle. No. 803, Weasel.

***Perf. 12½ on 3 Sides***

**1968, Nov. 9** **Engr.**

**799** A187 30o blue .65 *.80*
**800** A187 30o black .65 *.80*
**801** A187 30o dark brown .65 *.80*
**802** A187 30o black .65 *.80*
**803** A187 30o blue .65 *.80*
*a.* Bklt. pane, 2 each #799-803 6.50
*Nos. 799-803 (5)* 3.25 4.00

See Nos. 873-877.

### Nobel Prize Winners Type of 1961

35o, Elie Metchnikoff, Paul Ehrlich, Ernest Rutherford. 45o, Gabriel Lippmann, Rudolf Eucken.

**1968, Dec. 10** ***Perf. 12½ Vertically***

**804** A137 35o maroon .55 .50
**805** A137 45o dark green .50 .20

***Perf. 12½ on 3 Sides***

**806** A137 35o maroon .50 *1.15*
a. Booklet pane of 10 6.00
**807** A137 45o dark green .45 .50
a. Booklet pane of 10 5.00
*Nos. 804-807 (4)* 2.00 2.35

**Nordic Cooperation Issue**

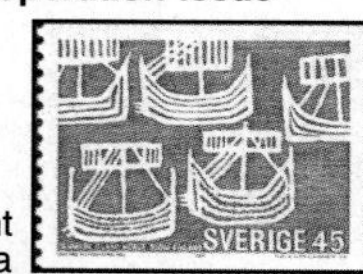

Five Ancient Ships — A187a

**1969, Feb. 28** **Engr.** ***Perf. 12½ Vert.***

**808** A187a 45o dark gray .35 .35
**809** A187a 70o blue .55 *.90*

***Perf. 12½ on 3 Sides***

**810** A187a 45o dark gray .50 *.85*
a. Booklet pane of 10 11.00
*Nos. 808-810 (3)* 1.40 2.10

See footnote after Norway No. 524.

Worker, by Albin Amelin — A188

***Perf. 12½ Horiz.***

**1969, Mar. 31** **Engr.**

**811** A188 55o dk carmine rose .45 .20
**812** A188 70o dk blue .70 .65

***Perf. 12½ on 3 Sides***

**813** A188 55o dk carmine rose .35 .20
a. Booklet pane of 10 4.00
*Nos. 811-813 (3)* 1.50 1.05

50th anniv. of the ILO.

**Europa Issue, 1969**

Common Design Type

**1969, Apr. 28** **Photo.** ***Perf. 14 Vert.***

**Size: 27x22mm**

**814** CD12 70o orange & multi *2.25* .50
**815** CD12 1k vio blue & multi *1.40* .45

***Perf. 14 on 3 Sides***

**816** CD12 70o orange & multi *2.25* *2.60*
a. Booklet pane of 10 *30.00*
*Nos. 814-816 (3)* 5.90 3.55

Not fluorescent.

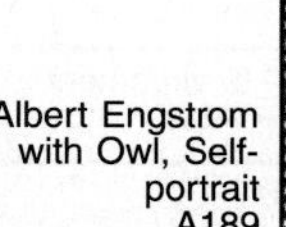

Albert Engstrom with Owl, Self-portrait A189

**1969, May 12** **Engr.** ***Perf. 12½ Vert.***

**817** A189 35o black brown .30 .20
**818** A189 55o blue gray .30 .20

***Perf. 12½ on 3 Sides***

**819** A189 35o black brown .35 .55
a. Booklet pane of 10 3.50
**820** A189 55o blue gray .30 .30
a. Booklet pane of 10 3.00
*Nos. 817-820 (4)* 1.25 1.25

Albert Engstrom (1869-1940), cartoonist.

Souvenir Sheet

Paintings by Ivan Agueli — A190

**1969, June 6** **Litho.** ***Perf. 13½***

**821** A190 Sheet of 6 2.50 *4.25*
a. 45o Landscape .40 *.45*
b. 45o Still life .40 *.45*
c. 45o Near East town .40 *.45*
d. 55o Young woman .40 *.45*
e. 55o Sunny landscape .40 *.45*
f. 55o Street at night .40 *.45*

Ivan Agueli (1869-1917), painter. Size: #821a-821c, 35x28mm. #821d-821e, 28x44mm. #821f, 48x44mm. Not fluorescent.

Tjorn Bridges — A191

Designs: 15o, 30o, Various bridges.

***Perf. 12½ on 3 Sides***

**1969, Sept. 3** **Engr.**

**Size: 20x19mm**

**Bluish Paper**

**822** A191 15o deep blue 1.10 .45
**823** A191 30o dk grn & blk 1.10 .45

**Size: 41x19mm**

**824** A191 55o blk & dp bl 1.10 .45
a. Bklt. pane, 2 each #822-824 8.00
*Nos. 822-824 (3)* 3.30 1.35

Tjorn highway bridges connecting the Islands of Orust and Tjorn in the Gothenburg Archipelago with the mainland.

Man's Head, Woodcarving — A192

Warship Wasa, 1628 — A193

Designs: No. 826, Crowned lion. No. 827, Great Swedish coat of arms. No. 828, Lion, front view. No. 829, Man's head (different from No. 825).

**1969, Sept. 3** ***Perf. 12½ on 3 Sides***

**825** A192 55o dark red .40 .20
**826** A192 55o brown .40 .20
**827** A193 55o dark blue .60 *.70*
**828** A192 55o brown .40 .20
**829** A192 55o dark red .40 .20
**830** A193 55o dark blue .60 *.70*
a. Bklt. pane, #827, #830, 2 each #825-826, 828-829 5.50
*Nos. 825-830 (6)* 2.80 2.20

Salvaging in 1961 of the warship Wasa, sunk on her maiden voyage, Aug. 10, 1628.

Soderberg A194

Bo Bergman A195

***Perf. 12½ Horiz.***

**1969, Oct. 13** **Engr.**

**831** A194 45o brown, *buff* .40 .30

***Perf. 12½ Vert.***

**832** A195 55o green, *grnsh* .40 .20

***Perf. 12½ on 3 Sides***

**833** A194 45o brown, *buff* .50 *.85*
a. Booklet pane of 10 5.00
**834** A195 55o green, *grnsh* .25 .40
a. Booklet pane of 10 4.00
*Nos. 831-834 (4)* 1.55 1.75

Hjalmar Soderberg (1869-1941), writer; Bo Bergman (1869-1967), poet.

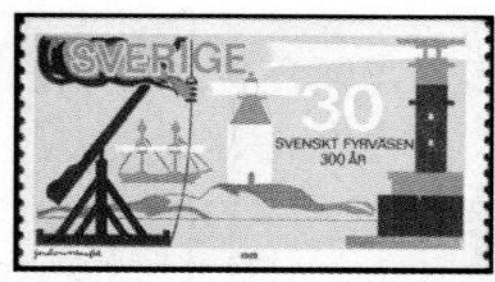

Lever Light, Lightship, Landsort and Svenska Lighthouses — A196

***Perf. 12½ Vert.***

**1969, Nov. 17** **Photo.**

**835** A196 30o gray, blk & pink .25 .20
**836** A196 55o lt bl, blk & brn .35 .20

300th anniversary of Swedish lighthouses.

Pelle's New Suit — A197

The Adventures of Nils — A198

Swedish Fairy Tales: No. 839, Pippi Longstocking (little girl, horse and monkey). No. 840, Vill-Vallareman (boy blowing horn). No. 841, Kattresan (child riding on back of cat).

***Perf. 12½ on 3 Sides***

**1969, Nov. 17** **Engr.**

**837** A197 35o org, red & dk brn 1.60 1.60
**838** A198 35o dark brown 1.60 1.60
**839** A197 35o org, red & dk brn 1.60 1.60
**840** A198 35o dark brown 1.60 1.60
**841** A197 35o org, red & dk brn 1.60 1.60
a. Bklt. pane, 2 each #837-841 20.00 22.50
*Nos. 837-841 (5)* 8.00 8.00

Issued for use in Christmas cards.

Dr. Emil T. Kocher and Wilhelm Ostwald — A199

55o, Selma Lagerlof, open book. 70o, Guglielmo Marconi, Carl Ferdinand Braun.

**1969, Dec. 10** ***Perf. 12½ Vert.***

**842** A199 45o dull green .75 .35
**843** A199 55o blk, *pale sal* .60 .20
**844** A199 70o black .75 1.25

***Perf. 12½ on 3 Sides***

**845** A199 45o dull green .45 .55
a. Booklet pane of 10 5.00
**846** A199 55o blk, *pale sal* .40 .30
a. Booklet pane of 10 4.50
*Nos. 842-846 (5)* 2.95 2.65

Winners of the 1909 Nobel Prize.

Weather Vane, Soderala Church A200

Door with Iron Fittings, Bjorksta Church, Vastmanland A201

Swedish Art Forgings: 10o, like 5o, facing right. 30o, Memorial cross, Ekshärad churchyard, Varmland.

***Perf. 12½ on 3 sides***

**1970, Feb. 9** **Engr.**

**847** A200 5o slate grn & brn .30 .20
**848** A200 10o slate grn & brn .30 .20
**849** A200 30o blk & slate grn .30 .20

***Perf. 12½ Vert.***

**850** A201 55o brn & slate grn .30 .20
a. Bklt. pane, 2 each #847-850 2.00 *3.75*
*Nos. 847-850 (4)* 1.20 .80

Ljusman River Rapids A202

**1970, May 11** **Engr.** ***Perf. 12½ Vert.***

**851** A202 55o black & multi .30 .20
**852** A202 70o black & multi .65 .45

European Nature Conservation Year, 1970.

Skiing — A203

"Around the Arctic Circle": No. 853, View of Kiruna. No. 855, Boat on mountain lake in Stora Sjofellet National Park. No. 856, Reindeer herd and herdsman. No. 857, Rocket probe under northern lights.

***Perf. 12½ Horiz.***

**1970, June 5** **Engr.**

**853** A203 45o sepia .50 *.85*
**854** A203 45o violet blue .50 *.85*
**855** A203 45o dull green .50 *.85*
**856** A203 45o sepia .50 *.85*
**857** A203 45o violet blue .50 *.85*
a. Bklt. pane, 2 each #853-857 5.50
*Nos. 853-857 (5)* 2.50 4.25

China Palace, Drottningholm Park, 1769 — A204

***Perf. 12½ Vert.***

**1970, Aug. 28** **Photo.**

**858** A204 2k yel, grn & pink 1.50 .25

Glimmingehus, Skane Province, 15th Century — A205

***Perf. 12½ Horiz.***

**1970, Aug. 28** **Engr.**

**859** A205 55o gray green .30 .20

***Perf. 12½ on 3 Sides***

**860** A205 55o gray green .35 .35
a. Booklet pane of 10 2.50

Timber Industry A206

Miner A208

Shipping Industry — A207

Designs: No. 863, Heavy industry (propeller). No. 864, Hydroelectric power (dam and diesel). No. 865, Mining (freight train and mine). No. 866, Technical research.

***Perf. 12½ on 3 sides***

**1970, Sept. 28** **Engr.**

**861** A206 70o indigo & lt brn 2.00 *2.50*
**862** A207 70o ind, lt brn & dp plum 2.00 *2.50*
**863** A206 70o ind & dp plum 2.00 *2.50*
**864** A206 70o ind & dp plum 2.00 *2.50*
**865** A207 70o ind & dp plum 2.00 *2.50*
**866** A206 70o dp plum & lt brn 2.00 *2.50*
*a.* Booklet pane of 6, #861-866 12.00 *15.00*
**867** A208 1k black, *buff* .40 .35
*a.* Booklet pane of 10 4.00

***Perf. 12½ Vertically***

**868** A208 1k black, *buff* .75 .30
*Nos. 861-868 (8)* 13.15 15.65

Swedish trade and industry.

"Love, Not War" A209

Design: 70o, Four-leaf clovers symbolizing efforts for equality and brotherhood.

**Engraved and Lithographed**

**1970, Oct. 24** ***Perf. 12½ Horiz.***

**869** A209 55o rose red, yel & blk .20 .40
*a.* Booklet pane of 4 1.00
**870** A209 70o emerald, yel & blk .40 .55
*a.* Booklet pane of 4 1.25

***Perf. 12½ Vert.***

**871** A209 55o rose red, yel & blk .35 .30
**872** A209 70o emerald, yel & blk .30 *.35*
*Nos. 869-872 (4)* 1.25 1.60

25th anniversary of the United Nations.

**Bird Type of 1968**

Birds: No. 873, Blackbird. No. 874, Great titmouse. No. 875, Bullfinch. No. 876, Greenfinch. No. 877, Blue titmouse.

***Perf. 12½ on 3 Sides***

**1970, Nov. 20** **Photo.**

**873** A187 30o blue grn & multi .85 .85
**874** A187 30o bister & multi .85 .85
**875** A187 30o blue & multi .85 .85
**876** A187 30o pink & multi .85 .85
**877** A187 30o org yel & multi .85 .85
*a.* Bklt. pane, 2 each #873-877 8.00 *12.50*
*Nos. 873-877 (5)* 4.25 4.25

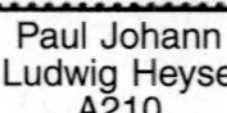

Paul Johann Ludwig Heyse A210

Kerstin Hesselgren A211

Designs: 55o, Otto Wallach and Johannes Diderik van der Waals. 70o, Albrecht Kossel.

***Perf. 12½ Horiz.***

**1970, Dec. 10** **Engr.**

**878** A210 45o violet .80 .40
**879** A210 55o slate blue .50 .30
**880** A210 70o gray 1.10 1.10

***Perf. 12½ on 3 Sides***

**881** A210 45o violet .60 *1.10*
*a.* Booklet pane of 10 6.50
**882** A210 55o slate blue .65 .35
*a.* Booklet pane of 10 6.50
*Nos. 878-882 (5)* 3.65 3.25

Winners of the 1910 Nobel Prize.

***Perf. 12½ Horiz.***

**1971, Feb. 19** **Engr.**

**883** A211 45o dp claret, *gray* .45 .40
**884** A211 1k dp brn, *buff* .65 .20

***Perf. 12½ on 3 Sides***

**885** A211 45o dp claret, *gray* .30 *.85*
*a.* Booklet pane of 10 3.25
*Nos. 883-885 (3)* 1.40 1.45

50th anniv. of woman suffrage; Kerstin Hesselgren, was 1st woman member of Swedish Upper House.

Terns in Flight A212

Abstract Music, by Ingvar Lidholm A213

**1971, Mar. 26** ***Perf. 13½ Vert.***

**886** A212 40o dark red .40 .35
**887** A212 55o violet blue .80 .20

***Perf. 12½ on 3 Sides***

**888** A212 55o violet blue .40 .20
*a.* Booklet pane of 10 4.50
*Nos. 886-888 (3)* 1.60 .75

Joint northern campaign for the benefit of refugees.

***Perf. 12½ Horiz.***

**1971, Aug. 27** **Engr.**

**889** A213 55o deep lilac .40 .20
**890** A213 85o green .45 .20

***Perf. 12½ on 3 Sides***

**891** A213 55o deep lilac .30 *.30*
*a.* Booklet pane of 10 3.00
*Nos. 889-891 (3)* 1.15 .70

The Three Kings, Grotlingbo Church — A214

Flight into Egypt, Stanga Church A215

Designs: 10o, Adam and Eve, Gammelgarn Church. 55o, Saint on horseback and Samson with the lion, Hogrän Church.

***Perf. 12½ on 3 Sides***

**1971, Sept. 28** **Engr.**

**892** A214 5o violet & brn .60 .45
**893** A214 10o violet & sl grn .60 .45

***Perf. 12½ Horiz.***

**894** A215 55o slate grn & brn .60 .40
**895** A215 65o brown & vio blk .30 .20
*a.* Bklt. pane, #892-894, 2 #895 2.50 *3.50*
*Nos. 892-895 (4)* 2.10 1.50

Art of medieval stonemasons in Gotland.

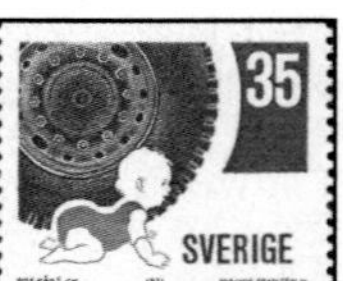

Toddler and Automobile Wheel — A216

**1971, Oct. 20** ***Perf. 12½ Vert.***

**896** A216 35o black & red .20 *.30*
**897** A216 65o dp blue & multi .60 .20

***Perf. 12½ on 3 Sides***

**898** A216 65o dp blue & multi .40 .35
*a.* Booklet pane of 10 5.75
*Nos. 896-898 (3)* 1.20 .85

Publicity for road safety.

King Gustavus Vasa's Sword, c. 1500 — A217

Swedish Crown Regalia: No. 900, Scepter. No. 901, Crown. No. 902, Orb (Scepter, crown and orb were made in 1561 for Erik XIV). No. 903, Karl IX's anointing horn, 1606.

***Perf. 12½ on 3 Sides***

**1971, Oct. 20** **Engr.**

**899** A217 65o lt blue & multi .50 .30
**900** A217 65o lt ol grn & multi .50 .30
**901** A217 65o dk blue & multi .50 .30
**902** A217 65o lt ol grn & multi .50 .30
**903** A217 65o lt blue & multi .50 .30
*a.* Bklt. pane, 2 each #899-903 5.50 *9.50*
*Nos. 899-903 (5)* 2.50 1.50

Christmas Elf and Goat Bringing Gifts — A218

Christmas Customs (Old Prints): No. 905, Christmas market. No. 906, Dancing children and father playing fiddle. No. 907, Ice-skating on frozen waterways in Stockholm. No. 908, Sleigh ride to church.

**1971, Nov. 10**

**904** A218 35o deep carmine 1.25 1.10
**905** A218 35o violet blue 1.25 1.10
**906** A218 35o violet brown 1.25 1.10
**907** A218 35o violet blue 1.25 1.10
**908** A218 35o slate green 1.25 1.10
*a.* Bklt. pane, 2 each #904-908 12.50 *14.00*
*Nos. 904-908 (5)* 6.25 5.50

Maurice Maeterlinck A219

Women Athletes A220

Designs: 65o, Wilhelm Wien and Allvar Gullstrand. 85o, Marie Sklodovska Curie.

**1971, Dec. 10** ***Perf. 12½ Horiz.***

**909** A219 55o orange .65 .55
**910** A219 65o green .65 .20
**911** A219 85o dk carmine .65 .60

***Perf. 12½ on 3 Sides***

**912** A219 55o orange .60 *.80*
*a.* Booklet pane of 10 6.00
**913** A219 65o green .65 .40
*a.* Booklet pane of 10 6.50
*Nos. 909-913 (5)* 3.20 2.55

Winners of the 1911 Nobel Prize.

**1972, Feb. 23** ***Perf. 12½ on 3 Sides***

**914** A220 55o Fencing .60 *.75*
**915** A220 55o Diving .60 *.75*
**916** A220 55o Gymnastics .60 *.75*
**917** A220 55o Tennis .60 *.75*
**918** A220 55o Figure skating .60 *.75*
*a.* Bklt. pane, 2 each #914-918 6.25 *10.00*
*Nos. 914-918 (5)* 3.00 3.75

Lars Johan Hierta, by Christian Eriksson — A221

Frans Michael Franzen, by Soderberg and Hultstrom — A222

Hugo Alfven, by Carl Milles — A223

Georg Stiernhielm, by David K. Ehrenstrahl — A224

**Photo., Perf 12½ Horiz. (35, 85o); Engr., Perf. 12½ Vert. (50, 65o)**

**1972 Feb. 23**

**919** A221 35o multicolored .30 *.25*
**920** A222 50o violet .40 .20
**921** A223 65o bluish black .40 .20
**922** A224 85o multicolored .50 *.55*
*Nos. 919-922 (4)* 1.60 1.20

Hierta (1801-72), journalist. Franzen (1772-1847), poet. Alfven (1872-1960), composer. Stiernhielm (1598-1672), poet, writer, scientist.

Lifting Molten Glass A225

Swedish Glassmaking: No. 924, Glass blower. No. 925, Decorating vase. No. 926, Annealing vase. No. 927, Polishing jug.

***Perf. 12½ Horiz.***

**1972, Mar. 22** **Engr.**

**923** A225 65o black .80 .75
**924** A225 65o violet blue .80 .75
**925** A225 65o carmine .80 .75
**926** A225 65o black .80 .75
**927** A225 65o violet blue .80 .75
*a.* Bklt. pane, 2 each #923-927 8.00
*Nos. 923-927 (5)* 4.00 3.75

Horses and Ruin of Borgholm Castle — A226

Designs: No. 929, Oland Island Bridge. No. 930, Kalmar Castle. No. 931, Salmon fishing. No. 932, Schooner Falken, Karlskrona.

**1972, May 8** ***Perf. 12½ Horiz.***

**928** A226 55o chocolate .65 *.85*
**929** A226 55o dk violet blue .65 *.85*
**930** A226 55o chocolate .65 *.85*
**931** A226 55o blue green .65 *.85*
**932** A226 55o dk violet blue .65 *.85*
*a.* Bklt. pane, 2 each #928-932 6.00
*Nos. 928-932 (5)* 3.25 4.25

Tourist attractions in Southeast Sweden.

"Only one Earth" Environment Emblem — A227

"Spring," Bror Hjorth — A228

**1972, June 5** **Engr.** ***Perf. 12½ Vert.***

**933** A227 65o blue & carmine .30 .20

***Perf. 12½ Horiz.***

**934** A227 65o blue & carmine .30 .30
*a.* Booklet pane of 10 3.00

***Perf. 12½ Vert.***

**935** A228 85o brown & multi .45 .30
*a.* Booklet pane of 4 1.80
*Nos. 933-935 (3)* 1.05 .80

UN Conference on Human Environment, Stockholm, June 5-16.

Junkers JU52 — A229

Historic Planes: 5o, Junkers F13. 25o, Friedrichshafen FF49. 75o, Douglas DC-3.

**1972, Sept. 8** ***Perf. 12½ on 3 Sides***

**Size: 20x19mm**

**936** A229 5o lilac .20 .20

**Size: 44x19mm**

**937** A229 15o blue .45 .50
**938** A229 25o blue .45 .50
**939** A229 75o gray green .30 .30
*a.* Bklt. pane, #937-938, 2 ea #936, 939 1.60 *3.00*
*Nos. 936-939 (4)* 1.40 1.50

Stockholm from the South, by Johan Fredrik Martin — A230

Amphion Figurehead, by Per Ljung — A231

Lady with Veil, by Alexander Roslin — A232

#941, Anchor Forge, by Pehr Hillestrom. #943, Quadriga, by Johan Tobias von Sergel. #945, (Queen) Sofia Magdalena, by Carl Gustaf Pilo.

**1972, Oct. 7 Engr.** ***Perf. 12½ Horiz.***

**940** A230 75o greenish black .40 *.50*
**941** A230 75o dark brown .40 *.50*

***Perf. 12½ on 3 Sides***

**942** A231 75o dark carmine .45 *.55*
**943** A231 75o dark carmine .45 *.55*

***Perf. 12½ on 2 Sides***

**944** A232 75o dk brn, blk & dk car .45 *.60*
**945** A232 75o dk brn, blk & dk car .45 *.60*
*a.* Booklet pane of 6, #940-945 2.75 *4.50*

18th century Swedish art.

**Types of 1936**

Imprint: "1972"

**1972, Oct. 7** ***Perf. 12½ on 3 Sides***

**946** A36 10o dark carmine .35 *.50*
**947** A37 15o yellow green .35 *.50*
**948** A42 40o deep blue .35 *.50*
**949** A44 50o deep claret .35 *.50*
**950** A45 60o deep blue .35 *.50*
*a.* Bklt. pane, 2 each #946-950 3.00 *7.00*
*Nos. 946-950 (5)* 1.75 2.50

Olle Hjortzberg (1872-1959), stamp designer. Booklet sold for 5k of which 1.50k was for Stockholmia 74, Intl. Phil. Exhib., Sept. 21-29, 1973.

Santa Claus — A233

St. Lucia Singers A234

***Perf. 14 on 3 Sides***

**1972, Nov. 6** **Photo.**

**951** A233 45o Candles .35 .25
**952** A233 45o shown .35 .25
*a.* Bklt. pane, 5 each #951-952 3.50

***Perf. 12½ Vert.***

**953** A234 75o gray & multi .55 .20
*Nos. 951-953 (3)* 1.25 .70

Christmas 1972 (children's drawings).

Horse — A235

Viking Ship — A236

Willows, by Peter A. Persson A237

Trosa, by Reinhold Ljunggren A238

Spring Birches, by Oskar Bergman A239

King Gustaf VI Adolf — A240

***Perf. 12½ Horiz. or Vert.***

**1972-73** **Engr.**

**954** A235 5o maroon ('73) .20 .20
**955** A236 10o dk blue ('73) .20 .20
**956** A237 40o sepia ('73) .20 .20
**957** A238 50o blk & brn ('73) .30 .20
**958** A239 55o yel grn ('73) .35 .20
**959** A240 75o indigo .40 .20
**960** A240 1k dp carmine .65 .20

**1973** ***Perf. 12½ on 3 Sides***

**961** A235 5o maroon .20 .20
*a.* Booklet pane of 20 .50
**962** A236 10o dark blue .20 .20
*a.* Booklet pane of 20 .60
**963** A240 75o indigo .40 .20
*a.* Booklet pane of 10 4.00
*Nos. 954-963 (10)* 3.10 2.00

King Gustaf VI Adolf — A245

Chinese Objects — A246

Designs: No. 983, King opening Parliament. No. 984, Etruscan vase and dish. No. 985, King with flowers.

**1972, Nov. 11** ***Perf. 12½ Vert.***

**981** A245 75o violet blue 1.25 *2.75*
**982** A246 75o slate green 1.25 *2.75*
**983** A245 75o maroon 1.25 *2.75*
**984** A246 75o violet blue 1.25 *2.75*
**985** A245 75o slate green 1.25 *2.75*
*a.* Bklt. pane of 5, #981-985 5.75 *15.00*

90th birthday of King Gustaf VI Adolf. Booklet sold for 4.75k of which 1k was for the King Gustaf VI Adolf Foundation for Swedish Cultural Activities.

Paul Sabatier and Victor Grignard — A247

Dr. Alexis Carrel — A248

75o, Nils Gustaf Dalen. 1k, Gerhart Hauptmann.

**1972, Dec. 8 Engr.** ***Perf. 12½ Vert.***

**986** A247 60o olive bister .60 .40

***Perf. 12½ Horiz.***

**987** A248 65o dark blue .70 .40
**988** A248 75o violet .90 .20
**989** A248 1k redsh brown 1.10 .30
*Nos. 986-989 (4)* 3.30 1.30

Winners of the 1912 Nobel Prize.

Mail Coach, 1923 — A249

Design: 70o, Postal autobus, 1972.

***Perf. 12½ on 3 Sides***

**1973, Jan. 18** **Engr.**

**990** A249 60o black, *yellow* .30 .25
*a.* Booklet pane of 10 3.00

***Perf. 12½ Vert.***

**991** A249 70o blue, orange & grn .45 .25

Tintomara, by Lars Johan Werle — A250

Orpheus and Eurydice, by Christoph W. Gluck — A251

**1973, Jan. 18** ***Perf. 12½ Horiz.***

**992** A250 75o green .55 .20

**Booklet Stamp**

**993** A251 1k red lilac .55 .35
*a.* Booklet pane of 5 3.00

Bicentenary of the Royal Theater in Stockholm. The 75o shows a stage setting by Bo-Ruben Hedwall for Tintomara, a new opera, performed for the bicentenary celebration. The 1k shows painting by Pehr Hillestrom of Orpheus and Eurydice, which was first opera performed in Royal Theater.

Vaasa Ski Race, Dalecarlia — A252

Designs: No. 995, "Going to Church in Mora" (church boats), by Anders Zorn. No. 996, Church stables, Rättvik. No. 997, Falun copper mine. No. 998, Midsummer Dance, by Bengt Nordenberg.

**1973, Mar. 2** ***Perf. 12½ Horiz.***

**994** A252 65o slate green .40 .40
**995** A252 65o slate green .40 .40
**996** A252 65o black .40 .40
**997** A252 65o slate green .40 .40
**998** A252 65o claret .40 .40
*a.* Bklt. pane, 2 each #994-998 4.00
*Nos. 994-998 (5)* 2.00 2.00

Tourist attractions in Dalecarlia.

Worker, Confederation Emblem — A253

**1973, Apr. 26** ***Perf. 12½ Vert.***

**999** A253 75o dark carmine .40 .20
**1000** A253 1.40k slate blue .75 .25

75th anniversary of the Swedish Confederation of Trade Unions (LO).

Observer Reading Temperature A254

Design: No. 1002, Clouds, photographed by US weather satellite.

**1973, May 24 Engr.** ***Perf. 12½ Vert.***

**1001** A254 65o slate green .75 .45
**1002** A254 65o black & ultra .75 .45
*a.* Pair, #1001-1002 1.50 *2.50*

Cent. of the Swedish Weather Organization and of Intl. Meteorological Cooperation.

**Nordic Cooperation Issue 1973**

Nordic House, Reykjavik A254a

**1973, June 26** ***Perf. 12½ Vert.***

**1003** A254a 75o multicolored .45 .20
**1004** A254a 1k multicolored .65 .20

A century of postal cooperation among Denmark, Finland, Iceland, Norway and Sweden and in connection with the Nordic Postal Conference, Reykjavik, Iceland.

Carl Peter Thunberg (1743-1828) — A255

Swedish Explorers: No. 1006, Anders Sparrman (1748-1820) and Polynesian double canoe. No. 1007, Nils Adolf Erik Nordenskjold (1832-1901) and ship in pack ice. No. 1008, Salomon August Andrée (1854-1897) and balloon on snow field. No. 1009, Sven Hedin (1865-1952) and camel riders.

**1973, Sept. 22** ***Perf. 12½ Horiz.***

**1005** A255 1k sl grn, bl & brn .95 *1.10*
**1006** A255 1k bl, sl grn & brn .95 *1.10*
**1007** A255 1k bl, sl grn & brn .95 *1.10*
**1008** A255 1k black & multi .95 *1.10*
**1009** A255 1k black & multi .95 *1.10*
*a.* Bklt. pane of 5, #1005-1009 5.00 *8.25*

Plower with Ox Team A256

Designs: No. 1011, Woman working flax brake. No. 1012, Farm couple planting potatoes. No. 1013, Women baking bread. No. 1014, Man with horse-drawn sower.

**1973, Oct. 24** ***Perf. 12½ Horiz.***
**1010** A256 75o grnsh black 1.00 .30
**1011** A256 75o red brown 1.00 .30
**1012** A256 75o grnsh black 1.00 .30
**1013** A256 75o plum 1.00 .30
**1014** A256 75o red brown 1.00 .30
*a.* Bklt. pane, 2 ea #1010-1014 10.00
*Nos. 1010-1014 (5)* 5.00 1.50

Centenary of Nordic Museum, Stockholm.

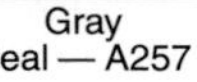

Gray Seal — A257

King Gustaf VI Adolf — A258

Protected Animals: 20o, Peregrine falcon. 25o, Lynx. 55o, Otter. 65o, Wolf. 75o, White-tailed sea eagle.

**1973, Oct. 24** ***Perf. 12½ on 3 Sides***
**1015** A257 10o slate green .20 .20
**1016** A257 20o violet .20 .20
**1017** A257 25o Prus green .20 .20
**1018** A257 55o Prus green .20 .20
**1019** A257 65o violet .20 .20
**1020** A257 75o slate green .35 .35
*a.* Bklt. pane, 2 each #1015-1020 2.50 *3.00*
*Nos. 1015-1020 (6)* 1.35 1.35

**1973, Oct. 24** ***Perf. 12½ Vert.***
**1021** A258 75o dk violet blue .30 .20
**1022** A258 1k purple .50 .20

King Gustaf VI Adolf (1882-1973).

The Three Kings A259

Charles XIV John A260

The Goosegirl, by Josephson A261

#1024, Merry country dance. #1026, Basket with stylized Dalecarlian gourd plant.

***Perf. 14 Horiz.***

**1973, Nov. 12** **Photo.**
**1023** A259 45o multicolored .35 .30
**1024** A259 45o multicolored .35 .30
*a.* Bklt. pane, 5 each #1023-1024 3.50

**Coil Stamps**

**1025** A260 75o multicolored 1.40 .20
**1026** A260 75o multicolored 1.40 .20
*a.* Pair, #1025-1026 3.00 *5.00*
*Nos. 1023-1026 (4)* 3.50 1.00

Christmas 1973. Designs are from Swedish peasant paintings.

***Perf. 12½ Horiz.***

**1973, Nov. 12** **Engr.**
**1027** A261 10k multicolored 4.50 .35

Ernst Josephson (1851-1906), painter.

Alfred Werner and Heike Kamerlingh-Onnes A262

Charles Robert Richet A263

Design: 1.40k, Rabindranath Tagore.

**1973, Dec. 10** **Engr.** ***Perf. 12½ Vert.***
**1028** A262 75o dark violet .55 .20

***Perf. 12½ Horiz.***

**1029** A263 1k dark brown .55 .30
**1030** A263 1.40k green .65 .20
*Nos. 1028-1030 (3)* 1.75 .70

Winners of 1913 Nobel Prize.

Ski Jump A264

Skiing: No. 1032, Cross-country race. No. 1033, Relay race. No. 1034, Slalom. No. 1035, Women's cross-country race.

***Perf. 12½ Horiz.***

**1974, Jan. 23** **Engr.**
**1031** A264 65o slate green .55 .65
**1032** A264 65o violet blue .55 .65
**1033** A264 65o slate green .55 .65
**1034** A264 65o dk carmine .55 .65
**1035** A264 65o violet blue .55 .65
*a.* Bklt. pane, 2 each #1031-1035 11.00
*Nos. 1031-1035 (5)* 2.75 3.25

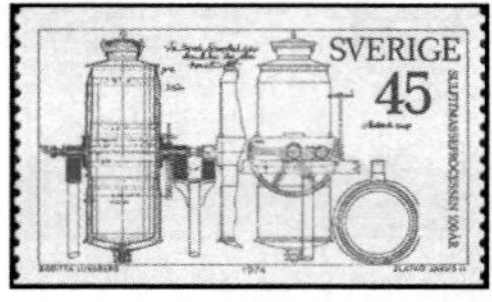

Drawing of First Industrial Digester A265

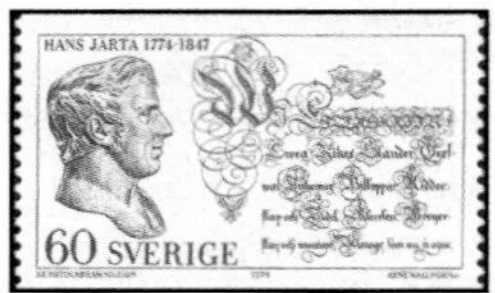

Hans Järta and Quotation from 1809 — A266

Samuel Owen and 19th Century Factory A267

**1974, Mar. 5** **Engr.** ***Perf. 12½ Vert.***
**1036** A265 45o sepia .20 .20
**1037** A266 60o green .30 .30
**1038** A267 75o dull red .45 .20
*Nos. 1036-1038 (3)* .95 .70

Centenary of sulphite pulp process (45o); Hans Järta (1774-1847), statesman responsible for the Instrument of Government Act of 1809 (60o); Samuel Owen (1774-1854), English-born industrialist who introduced new production methods (75o).

Stora Sjofallet (Great Falls) — A268

Street in Ystad — A269

**1974, Apr. 2** ***Perf. 12½ Horiz.***
**1039** A268 35o blue grn & blk .20 .20

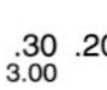

***Perf. 12½ on 3 Sides***

**1040** A269 75o dull claret .30 .20
*a.* Booklet pane of 10 3.00

UPU Type of 1924 A270

**1974** **Engr.** ***Perf. 12½ on 3 Sides***
**1041** A270 20o green .30 *.35*
**1042** A270 25o ultra .30 *.35*
**1043** A270 30o dark brown .30 *.35*
**1044** A270 35o dark red .30 *.35*
*a.* Bklt. pane, 2 each #1041-1044 2.50 *3.50*
*Nos. 1041-1044 (4)* 1.20 1.40

**Miniature Sheets**

***Perf. 12½***

**1045** Sheet of 4 2.00 *3.50*
*a.* A270 20o ocher, single stamp .40 *.75*
**1046** Sheet of 4 2.00 *3.50*
*a.* A270 25o dk vio, single stamp .40 *.75*
**1047** Sheet of 4 2.00 *3.50*
*a.* A270 30o dk red, single stamp .40 *.75*
**1048** Sheet of 4 2.00 *3.50*
*a.* A270 35o yel grn, single stamp .40 *.75*

Stockholmia 74 philatelic exhibition, Stockholm, Sept. 21-29. Booklet sold for 3k with surtax going toward financing the exhibition.

Nos. 1045-1048 sold during exhibition in folder with 5k entrance ticket.

Issued: #1041-1044, 4/2; #1045-1048, 9/21.

"Man in Storm," by Bror Marklund — A271

Europa: 1k, Sculpture by Picasso, Lake Vanern, Kristinehamm.

***Perf. 12½ Horiz.***

**1974, Apr. 29** **Engr.**
**1049** A271 75o violet brown 1.10 .30
**1050** A271 1k slate green 1.25 .30

King Carl XVI Gustaf — A272

**1974-78** **Engr.** ***Perf. 12½ Vert.***
**1068** A272 75o slate grn .40 .20
**1069** A272 90o brt blue ('75) .35 .20
**1070** A272 1k maroon .45 .20
**1071** A272 1.10k rose red ('75) .40 .20
**1072** A272 1.30k green ('76) .50 .20
**1073** A272 1.40k violet bl ('77) .60 .20
**1074** A272 1.50k red lilac ('80) .60 .20
**1075** A272 1.70k orange ('78) .75 .20
**1076** A272 2k dk brown ('80) .85 .20

***Perf. 12½ on 3 Sides***

**1077** A272 75o slate green .30 .20
*a.* Booklet pane of 10 3.00
**1078** A272 90o brt blue ('75) .30 .20
*a.* Booklet pane of 10 3.00
**1079** A272 1k maroon ('76) .40 .20
*a.* Booklet pane of 10 4.00
**1080** A272 1.10k rose red ('77) .40 .20
*a.* Booklet pane of 10 4.00
**1081** A272 1.30k green ('78) .50 .20
*a.* Booklet pane of 10 5.00
**1082** A272 1.50k red lilac ('80) .60 .20
*a.* Booklet pane of 10 6.00
*Nos. 1068-1082 (15)* 7.40 3.00

A273

Central Post Office, Stockholm A274

Mailman, Northernmost Rural Delivery Route — A275

***Perf. 12½ on 3 Sides***

**1974, June 7** **Engr.**
**1084** A273 75o violet brown .70 .30
**1085** A274 75o violet brown .70 .30
*a.* Bklt. pane, 5 ea #1084-1085 7.00

***Perf. 12½ Vert.***

**1086** A275 1k slate green .65 .20
*Nos. 1084-1086 (3)* 2.05 .80

Centenary of Universal Postal Union.

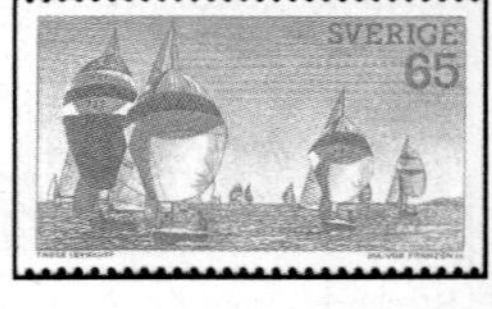

Regatta A276

Scenes from Sweden's West Coast: No. 1088, Vinga Lighthouse. No. 1089, Varberg Fortress. No. 1090, Seine fishing. No. 1091, Fishing village Mollosund.

**1974, June 7** ***Perf. 12½ Horiz.***
**1087** A276 65o crimson .55 .55
**1088** A276 65o blue .55 .55
**1089** A276 65o dk olive green .55 .55
**1090** A276 65o slate green .55 .55
**1091** A276 65o brown .55 .55
*a.* Bklt. pane, 2 each #1087-1091 4.50
*Nos. 1087-1091 (5)* 2.75 2.75

Mr. Simmons, by Axel Fridell — A277

Thread and Spool — A278

***Perf. 12½ on 3 Sides***

**1974, Aug. 28** **Engr.**
**1092** A277 45o black .25 .20
*a.* Booklet pane of 10 2.50

***Perf. 12½ Horiz.***

**1093** A277 1.40k deep claret .75 .20

Swedish Publicists' Club, centenary.

**1974, Aug. 28** ***Perf. 12½ Horiz.***

#1095, Sewing machines (abstract).

**1094** A278 85o deep violet .40 .30
**1095** A278 85o black & org .40 .30
*a.* Pair, #1094-1095 .90 *.80*

Swedish textile and clothing industries.

Tugs in Stockholm Harbor — A279

#1096, Tanker. #1097, Liner "Snow Storm." #1098, Ice breakers Tor and Atle. #1099, Skane Train Ferry, Trelleborg-Sassnitz.

**1974, Nov. 16** ***Perf. 12½ Horiz.***
**1096** A279 1k dark blue .70 *.75*
**1097** A279 1k dark blue .70 *.75*
**1098** A279 1k dark blue .70 *.75*
**1099** A279 1k dark blue .70 *.75*
**1100** A279 1k dark blue .70 *.75*
*a.* Bklt. pane of 5, #1096-1100 3.50 *6.00*

Swedish shipping industry.

Miniature Sheet

Quilt from Skepptuna Church — A280

Deer, Quilt from Hog Church — A281

Designs are from woolen quilts, 15th-16th centuries. Motifs shown on No. 1101 are stylized deer, griffins, lions, unicorn and horses.

**1974, Nov. 16 Photo. *Perf. 14***
1101 A280 Sheet of 10 9.50 *13.00*
a.-j. 45o, single stamp .95 1.00

***Perf. 13 Horiz.***
1102 A281 75o bl blk, red & yel .45 .20

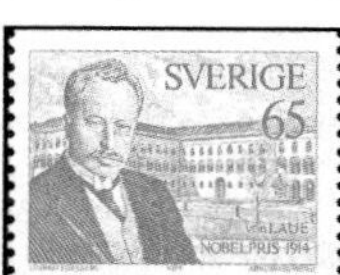

Max von Laue — A282

Designs: 70o, Theodore William Richards. 1k, Robert Bárány.

**1974, Dec. 10 Engr. *Perf. 12½ Vert.***
1103 A282 65o rose red .35 .20
1104 A282 70o slate .45 .30
1105 A282 1k indigo .95 .20
*Nos. 1103-1105 (3)* 1.75 .70

Winners of 1914 Nobel Prize.

A283

No. 1106, Sven Jerring's children's program. No. 1107, Televising parliamentary debate.

**1974, Dec. 10 *Perf. 12½ Vert.***
1106 75o dk blue & brn .65 .20
1107 75o brown & dk bl .65 .20
a. A283 Pair, #1106-1107 1.25 *2.00*

Swedish Broadcasting Corp., 50th anniv.

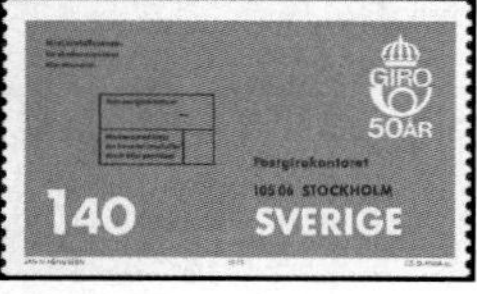

Account Holder's Envelope A285

**Photogravure and Engraved**

**1975, Jan. 21 *Perf. 14 Vert.***
1108 A285 1.40k ocher & blk .65 .35

Swedish Postal Giro Office, 50th anniv.

Male and Female Architects, New Parliament A286

Jenny Lind (1820-87), by J. O. Sodermark A287

**1975, Mar. 25 Engr. *Perf. 12½ Vert.***
1109 A286 75o slate green .40 .20

***Perf. 12½ Horiz.***
1110 A287 1k claret .60 .20

***Perf. 12½ on 3 Sides***
1111 A286 75o slate green .35 .20
a. Booklet pane of 10 3.50
*Nos. 1109-1111 (3)* 1.35 .60

International Women's Year 1975.

Horseman, Helmet Decoration A288

"Gold Men" A289

Designs: 15o, Scabbard and hilt. 20o, Shield buckle. 55o, Iron helmet.

**1975, Mar. 25 *Perf. 12½ on 3 sides***
1112 A288 10o dull red .20 .20
1113 A288 15o slate green .20 .20
1114 A288 20o violet .20 .20
1115 A288 55o violet brown .20 .20
a. Bklt. pane, 2 each #1112-1115 .75 *1.60*

***Perf. 12½ Horiz.***
1116 A289 25o deep yellow .20 .20
*Nos. 1112-1116 (5)* 1.00 1.00

Treasures from tombs of the Vendel period (550-800 A.D.), and "gold men" (25o) from Eketorp II excavations (400-700 A.D.).

**Europa Issue 1975**

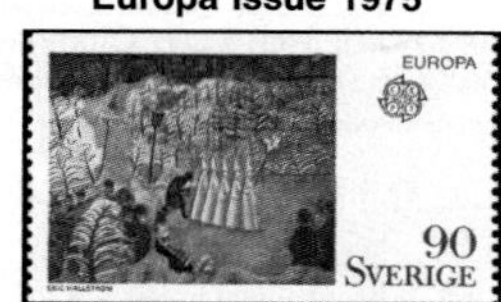

New Year's Eve at Skansen, by Eric Hallstrom — A290

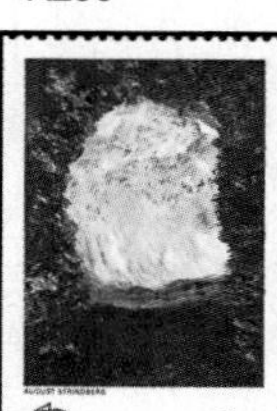

Inferno, by August Strindberg — A291

***Perf. 12½ Vert.***

**1975, Apr. 28 Photo.**
1117 A290 90o multi 1.10 .20

***Perf. 12½ Horiz.***
1118 A291 1.10k multi 1.10 .20

Capercaillie A292

Rok Stone, 9th Century A293

**1975, May 20 Engr. *Perf. 12½ Vert.***
1119 A292 170o indigo .70 .20

***Perf. 12½ Horiz.***
1120 A293 2k deep claret .85 .20

Metric Tape Measure — A294

Folke Filbyter Statue, by Milles — A296

Hernqvist by Per Krafft the Younger — A295

**1975, May 20 *Perf. 12½ Vert.***
1121 A294 55o deep blue .35 .30
1122 A295 70o yel brn & dk brn .40 .20

***Perf. 12½ Horiz.***
1123 A296 75o violet .40 .20
*Nos. 1121-1123 (3)* 1.15 .70

Cent. of Intl. Meter Convention, Paris, 1875; bicent. of Swedish veterinary medicine, founded by Peter Hernqvist (1726-1808); Carl Milles (1875-1955), sculptor.

Officers' Mess, Rommehed, 1798 — A297

No. 1124, Skelleftea Church Village, 17th cent. No. 1125, Foundry and furnace, Engelsberg, 18th cent. No. 1126, Gunpowder Tower, Visby. No. 1127, Falun Mine pithead gear, 1852.

**1975, June 13 *Perf. 12½ Horiz.***
1124 A297 75o black .50 *.65*
1125 A297 75o dk carmine .50 *.65*
1126 A297 75o black .50 *.65*
1127 A297 75o dk carmine .50 *.65*
1128 A297 75o violet blue .50 *.65*
a. Bklt. pane, 2 each #1124-1128 5.50
*Nos. 1124-1128 (5)* 2.50 3.25

European Architectural Heritage Year 1975.

Rescue at Sea: Helicopter over Ice-covered Tanker — A298

Designs: No. 1129, Fire fighters: firemen fighting fire. No. 1130, Customs narcotics service: trained dogs checking cargo. No. 1131, Police: Officer talking to boy on bridge. No. 1132, Hospital Service: patient arriving by ambulance.

**1975, Aug. 27 *Perf. 12½ Horiz.***
1129 A298 90o dk car rose .65 .45
1130 A298 90o dk bl .65 .45
1131 A298 90o dk car rose .65 .45
1132 A298 90o dk bl .65 .45
1133 A298 90o green .65 .45
a. Bklt. pane, 2 each #1129-1133 5.50
*Nos. 1129-1133 (5)* 3.25 2.25

Public service organizations watching, guarding, helping.

"Fryckstad" A299

"Gotland" A300

Design: 90o, "Prins August."

**1975, Aug. 27 *Perf. 12½ on 3 Sides***

**Size: 20x19mm**
1134 A299 5o green .20 .20
1135 A300 5o dark blue .20 .20

**Size: 45x19mm**
1136 A299 90o slate green .55 .20
a. Bklt. pane, 2 each #1134-1136 1.75 *2.50*
*Nos. 1134-1136 (3)* .95 .60

Scouts — A302

**1975, Oct. 11 Photo. *Perf. 14 Vert.***
1137 90o Around campfire .50 .20
1138 90o In canoes .50 .20
a. A301 Pair, #1137-1138 1.25 *2.00*

Nordjamb 75, 14th World Boy Scout Jamboree, Lillehammer, Norway, July 29-Aug. 7.

Hedgehog A303

Old Man Playing Key Fiddle — A304

Romeo and Juliet Ballet — A305

**1975, Oct. 11 Engr. *Perf. 12½ Vert.***
1139 A303 55o black .30 .20
1140 A304 75o dk red .55 .20

***Perf. 12½ Horiz.***
1141 A305 7k blue green 3.25 .20

***Perf. 12½ on 3 Sides***
1142 A303 55o black .25 .20
a. Booklet pane of 10 2.50
*Nos. 1139-1142 (4)* 4.35 .80

Virgin Mary, 12th Cent. Statue — A306

Chariot of the Sun, from 12th Cent. Altar — A307

Mourning Mary, c. 1280 — A308

Jesse at Foot of Genealogical Tree, c. 1510 — A309

Christmas: #1145, Nativity, from 12th cent. gilt-copper altar. #1148, like #1147.

***Perf. 14 Horiz.***

**1975, Nov. 11 Photo.**
1143 A306 55o multi .30 .20

***Perf. 12½ on 3 Sides***
1144 A307 55o gold & multi .35 .30
1145 A307 55o gold & multi .35 .30
a. Bklt. pane, 5 each #1144-1145 3.00

***Perf. 12½ Horiz.***

**Engr.**
1146 A308 90o brown .50 .20

***Perf. 12½ on 3 Sides***

**1147** A309 90o red .60 .30
**1148** A309 90o blue .60 .30
*a.* Bklt. pane, 5 ea #1147-1148 6.00
*Nos. 1143-1148 (6)* 2.70 1.60

No. 1145a was issued with top row of 5 either No. 1144 or No. 1145.

William H. and William L. Bragg — A310

Designs: 90o, Richard Willstätter. 1.10k, Romain Rolland.

**1975, Dec. 10 Engr.** ***Perf. 12½ Vert.***

**1149** A310 75o claret .40 *.45*
**1150** A310 90o violet blue .45 .20
**1151** A310 1.10k slate green .55 .35
*Nos. 1149-1151 (3)* 1.40 1.00

Winners of 1915 Nobel Prize.

Cave of the Winds, by Eric Grate — A311

**1976, Jan. 27** ***Perf. 12½ Vert.***

**1152** A311 1.90k slate green .90 .20

The sculpture by Eric Grate (b. 1896) stands in front of the Town Hall of Vasteras.

Razor-billed Auks and Black Guillemot A312

Bobbin Lace Maker from Vadstena A313

**1976, Mar. 10 Engr.** ***Perf. 12½ Vert.***

**1153** A312 85o dark blue .55 .20

***Perf. 12½ Horiz.***

**1154** A313 1k claret brn .45 .30

***Perf. 12½ on 3 Sides***

**1155** A312 85o dk bl .30 .30
*a.* Booklet pane of 10 3.00
**1156** A313 1k claret brn .40 .30
*a.* Booklet pane of 10 4.00
*Nos. 1153-1156 (4)* 1.70 1.10

Old and New Telephones, Relays — A314

**1976, Mar. 10** ***Perf. 12½ Vert.***

**1157** A314 1.30k brt violet .75 .20
**1158** A314 3.40k red 1.35 .45

Centenary of first telephone call by Alexander Graham Bell, March 10, 1876.

**Europa Issue 1976**

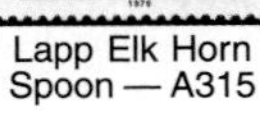

Lapp Elk Horn Spoon — A315

Tile Stove — A316

***Perf. 14½ Horiz.***

**1976, May 3** **Photo.**

**1159** A315 1k multi .85 .20
**1160** A316 1.30k multi .85 .45

Wheat and Cornflower Seeds — A317

Viable and Nonviable Seedlings A318

**1976, May 3 Engr.** ***Perf. 12½ Vert.***

**1161** A317 65o brown .30 .20
**1162** A318 65o choc & grn .30 .20
*a.* Pair, #1161-1162 .60 *.65*

Swedish seed testing centenary.

King Carl XVI Gustaf and Queen Silvia — A319

***Perf. 12½ Vert.***

**1976, June 19** **Engr.**

**1163** A319 1k rose car .30 .20
**1164** A319 1.30k slate grn .40 .20

***Perf. 12½ on 3 Sides***

**1165** A319 1k rose car .30 .20
*a.* Booklet pane of 10 3.00
*Nos. 1163-1165 (3)* 1.00 .60

Wedding of King Carl XVI Gustaf and Silvia Sommerlath.

View from Ringkallen, by Helmer Osslund — A320

Views in Angermanland Province: No. 1167, Tugboat pulling timber. No. 1168, Hay-drying racks. No. 1169, Granvagsnipan slope, Angerman River. No. 1170, Seine fishing.

**1976, June 19** ***Perf. 12½ Horiz.***

**1166** A320 85o slate grn .40 *.55*
**1167** A320 85o vio bl .40 *.55*
**1168** A320 85o dp brn .40 *.55*
**1169** A320 85o vio bl .40 *.55*
**1170** A320 85o brn red .40 *.55*
*a.* Bklt. pane, 2 each #1166-1170 4.50
*Nos. 1166-1170 (5)* 2.00 2.75

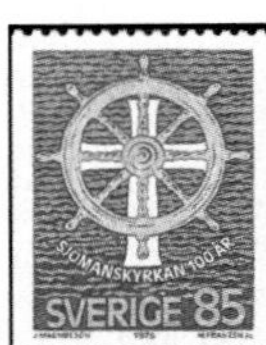


Roman Cross and Ship's Wheel — A321

**1976, June 19** ***Perf. 12½ Horiz.***

**1171** A321 85o brt bl & bl .45 *.30*

Swedish Seamen's Church, centenary.

Torgny Segerstedt and 1917 Page of Gothenburg Journal — A322

**1976, June 19** ***Perf. 12½ Vert.***

**1172** A322 1.90k brn & blk .80 .30

Torgny Segerstedt (1876-1945), editor in chief of the Gothenburg Journal of Commerce and Shipping, birth centenary.

Coiled Snake, Bronze Buckle — A323

Pilgrim's Badge, Adoration of the Magi — A324

Drinking Horn, 14th Century — A325

Chimney Sweep — A326

Girl's Head, by Bror Hjorth, 1922 — A327

***Perf. 12½ Horiz., Vert. (30o)***

**1976, Sept. 8** **Engr.**

**1173** A323 15o bister .20 .20
**1174** A324 20o green .20 .20
**1175** A325 30o dk rose brn .20 .20
**1176** A326 90o indigo .40 .20
**1177** A327 9k yel grn & sl grn 3.50 .25
*Nos. 1173-1177 (5)* 4.50 1.05

Inventors A328

#1178, John Ericsson (1803-1889), ship propeller and "Monitor". #1179, Helge Palmcrantz (1842-80) & reaper. #1180, Lars Magnus Ericsson (1846-1926) & switchboard. #1181, Sven Wingquist (1876-1953) & ball bearing. #1182, Gustaf de Laval (1845-1913) & milk separator.

**1976, Oct. 9 Engr.** ***Perf. 12½ Horiz.***

**1178** A328 1.30k multi .60 *.75*
**1179** A328 1.30k multi .60 *.75*
**1180** A328 1.30k multi .60 *.75*
**1181** A328 1.30k multi .60 *.75*
**1182** A328 1.30k multi .60 *.75*
*a.* Bklt. pane of 5, #1178-1182 3.75 *6.00*

Swedish inventors and their technological inventions.

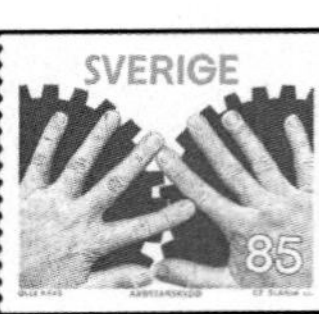


Hands and Cogwheels A329

**1976, Oct. 9** ***Perf. 12½ Vert.***

**1183** A329 85o org & dk vio .40 .20
**1184** A329 1k yel grn & brn .55 .20

Industrial safety.

Verner von Heidenstam, Lake Vattern — A330

**1976, Nov. 17** ***Perf. 12½ Vert.***

**1185** A330 1k yellow green .40 .20
**1186** A330 1.30k blue .55 .45

Verner von Heidenstam (1859-1940), Swedish poet, 1916 Nobel Prize winner.

Archangel Michael A331

Virgin Mary Visiting St. Elizabeth A332

Christmas: No. 1189, like No. 1187. No. 1190, St. Nicholas saving 3 children. No. 1191, like No. 1188. No. 1192, Illuminated page, prayer to Virgin Mary. 65o, stamps are from Flemish prayer book, c. 1500. 1k stamps are from Austrian prayer book, late 15th century.

***Perf. 12½ Horiz.***

**1976, Nov. 17** **Photo.**

**1187** A331 65o blue & multi .30 .20
**1188** A332 1k gold & multi .30 .20

***Perf. 12½ on 3 Sides***

**1189** A331 65o blue & multi .20 *.40*
**1190** A331 65o blue & multi .20 *.40*
*a.* Bklt. pane, 5 each #1189-1190 2.50

***Perf. 12½ Vert.***

**1191** A332 1k gold & multi .30 .20
**1192** A332 1k gold & multi .30 .20
*a.* Bklt. pane, 5 each #1191-1192 3.00
*Nos. 1187-1192 (6)* 1.60 1.60

Five Water Lilies — A333

**Photogravure and Engraved**

**1977, Feb. 2** ***Perf. 12½ Horiz.***

**1193** A333 1k brt grn & multi .45 .20
**1194** A333 1.30k ultra & multi .55 *.55*

Nordic countries cooperation for protection of the environment and 25th Session of Nordic Council, Helsinki, Feb. 19.

Tailor — A334

**1977, Feb. 24** ***Perf. 12½ Vert.***

**1195** A334 2.10k red brn .95 .20

Longdistance Skating — A335

*Perf. 12½ Horiz.*

**1977, Mar. 24** **Engr.**

| | | | | |
|---|---|---|---|---|
| **1196** | A335 | 95o shown | .45 | *.55* |
| **1197** | A335 | 95o Swimming | .45 | *.55* |
| **1198** | A335 | 95o Bicycling | .45 | *.55* |
| **1199** | A335 | 95o Jogging | .45 | *.55* |
| **1200** | A335 | 95o Badminton | .45 | *.55* |
| *a.* | | Bklt. pane, 2 each #1196-1200 | 4.50 | |
| | | *Nos. 1196-1200 (5)* | 2.25 | 2.75 |

Physical fitness.

Politeness, by "OA," 1905 — A336

**1977, Mar. 24** ***Perf. 12½ on 3 Sides***

| | | | | |
|---|---|---|---|---|
| **1201** | A336 | 75o black | .35 | .20 |
| *a.* | | Booklet pane of 10 | 3.50 | |

***Perf. 12½ Horiz.***

| | | | | |
|---|---|---|---|---|
| **1202** | A336 | 3.80k red | 1.75 | .45 |

Oskar Andersson (1877-1906), cartoonist.

Calle Schewen A337

No. 1204, Seagull. No. 1205, Dancers and accordionist. No. 1206, Fishermen in boat. No. 1207, Tree on shore at sunset.

Designs are illustrations for poem The Calle Schewen Waltz, by Evert Taube, and include bars of music of this song.

**1977, May 2** **Engr.** ***Perf. 12½ Horiz.***

| | | | | |
|---|---|---|---|---|
| **1203** | A337 | 95o slate grn | .45 | *.55* |
| **1204** | A337 | 95o vio bl | .45 | *.55* |
| **1205** | A337 | 95o grn & blk | .45 | *.55* |
| **1206** | A337 | 95o dark blue | .45 | *.55* |
| **1207** | A337 | 95o red | .45 | *.55* |
| *a.* | | Bklt. pane, 2 each #1203-1207 | 4.50 | |
| | | *Nos. 1203-1207 (5)* | 2.25 | 2.75 |

Tourist publicity for Roslagen (archipelago) and to honor Evert Taube (1890-1976), poet.

Gustavianum, Uppsala University A338

**1977, May 2** **Photo.** ***Perf. 12½ Vert.***

| | | | | |
|---|---|---|---|---|
| **1208** | A338 | 1.10k multi | .55 | .20 |

***Perf. 12½ on 3 Sides***

| | | | | |
|---|---|---|---|---|
| **1209** | A338 | 1.10k multi | .35 | .20 |
| *a.* | | Booklet pane of 10 | 3.50 | |

Uppsala University, 500th anniversary.

**Europa Issue 1977**

Forest in Snow A339

Rapadalen Valley — A340

**1977, May 2** ***Perf. 12½ Vert.***

| | | | | |
|---|---|---|---|---|
| **1210** | A339 | 1.10k multi | 1.10 | .30 |
| **1211** | A340 | 1.40k multi | 1.10 | .65 |

Owl — A341

Cast-iron Stove Decoration — A342

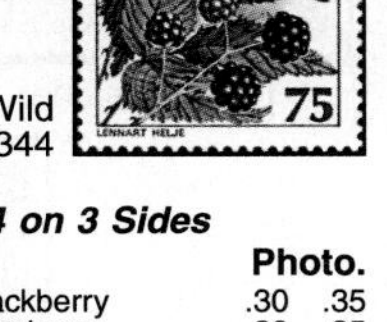

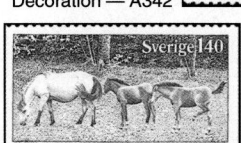

Gotland Ponies A343

**1977, Sept. 8** **Engr.** ***Perf. 12½ Vert.***

| | | | | |
|---|---|---|---|---|
| **1212** | A341 | 45o dk slate grn | .40 | .30 |

***Perf. 12½ Horiz.***

| | | | | |
|---|---|---|---|---|
| **1213** | A342 | 70o dk vio bl | .45 | .20 |

**Booklet Stamp**

| | | | | |
|---|---|---|---|---|
| **1214** | A343 | 1.40k brown | .55 | .35 |
| *a.* | | Booklet pane of 5 | 2.75 | |
| | | *Nos. 1212-1214 (3)* | 1.40 | .85 |

Wild Berries — A344

***Perf. 14 on 3 Sides***

**1977, Sept. 8** **Photo.**

| | | | | |
|---|---|---|---|---|
| **1215** | A344 | 75o Blackberry | .30 | .35 |
| **1216** | A344 | 75o Cranberry | .30 | .35 |
| **1217** | A344 | 75o Raspberry | .30 | .35 |
| **1218** | A344 | 75o Whortleberry | .30 | .35 |
| **1219** | A344 | 75o Alpine strawberry | .30 | .35 |
| *a.* | | Bklt. pane, 2 each #1215-1219 | 3.00 | *5.00* |
| | | *Nos. 1215-1219 (5)* | 1.50 | 1.75 |

Horse-drawn Trolley — A345

Designs: Public transportation.

**1977, Oct. 8** **Engr.** ***Perf. 12½ Horiz.***

| | | | | |
|---|---|---|---|---|
| **1220** | A345 | 1.10k shown | .55 | *.65* |
| **1221** | A345 | 1.10k Electric trolley | .55 | *.65* |
| **1222** | A345 | 1.10k Ferry | .55 | *.65* |
| **1223** | A345 | 1.10k Tandem bus | .55 | *.65* |
| **1224** | A345 | 1.10k Subway | .55 | *.65* |
| *a.* | | Bklt. pane of 5, #1220-1224 | 3.00 | *5.50* |

Putting up Sheaf for the Birds — A346

Preparing Dried Soaked Fish — A347

Traditional Christmas Preparations: No. 1227, Children baking ginger snaps. No. 1228, Bringing in Yule tree. No. 1229, Making straw goat. No. 1230, Candle dipping.

***Perf. 12½ Horiz.***

**1977, Nov. 17** **Engr.**

| | | | | |
|---|---|---|---|---|
| **1225** | A346 | 75o violet | .35 | .20 |
| **1226** | A347 | 1.10k yel grn | .55 | .20 |

***Perf. 12½ on 3 Sides***

| | | | | |
|---|---|---|---|---|
| **1227** | A346 | 75o ocher | .35 | .20 |
| **1228** | A346 | 75o slate grn | .35 | .20 |
| *a.* | | Bklt. pane, 5 each #1227-1228 | 2.50 | |
| **1229** | A347 | 1.10k dk red | .40 | .20 |
| **1230** | A347 | 1.10k dk bl | .40 | .20 |
| *a.* | | Bklt. pane, 5 each #1229-1230 | 4.00 | |
| | | *Nos. 1225-1230 (6)* | 2.40 | 1.20 |

Christmas 1977.

Henrik Pontoppidan, Karl Adolph Gjellerup A348

Design: 1.40k, Charles Glover Barkla.

**1977, Nov. 17** ***Perf. 12½ Vert.***

| | | | | |
|---|---|---|---|---|
| **1231** | A348 | 1.10k red brn | .60 | .30 |
| **1232** | A348 | 1.40k yel grn | .65 | *.65* |

1917 Nobel Prize winners: Henrik Pontoppidan (1857-1943) and Karl Adolph Gjellerup (1857-1919), Danish writers; Charles Glover Barkla (1877-1944), English X-ray pioneer.

Space Without Affiliation, by Arne Jones — A349

Brown Bear — A350

**1978, Jan. 25** ***Perf. 12½ Horiz.***

| | | | | |
|---|---|---|---|---|
| **1233** | A349 | 2.50k vio bl | 1.00 | .20 |

**1978, Apr. 11** ***Perf. 12½ Horiz.***

| | | | | |
|---|---|---|---|---|
| **1234** | A350 | 1.15k dark brown | .50 | .20 |

**Europa Issue 1978**

Örebro Castle — A351

Arch and Stairs — A352

**1978, Apr. 11** ***Perf. 12½ Vert.***

| | | | | |
|---|---|---|---|---|
| **1235** | A351 | 1.30k slate green | 1.35 | .20 |

***Perf. 12½ Horiz.***

| | | | | |
|---|---|---|---|---|
| **1236** | A352 | 1.70k dull red | 1.75 | .65 |

Pentecostal Preacher and Congregation A353

Free Churches: No. 1238, Swedish Missionary Society. No. 1239, Evangelical National Missionary Society. No. 1240, Baptist Society. No. 1241, Salvation Army.

**1978, Apr. 11** ***Perf. 12½ on 3 sides***

| | | | | |
|---|---|---|---|---|
| **1237** | A353 | 90o purple | .45 | .35 |
| **1238** | A353 | 90o slate | .45 | .35 |
| **1239** | A353 | 90o violet | .45 | .35 |
| **1240** | A353 | 90o slate | .45 | .35 |
| **1241** | A353 | 90o purple | .45 | .35 |
| *a.* | | Bklt. pane, 2 each #1237-1241 | 4.50 | 6.00 |
| | | *Nos. 1237-1241 (5)* | 2.25 | 1.75 |

Independent Christian Associations.

Brosarp Hills — A354

Grindstone Production A355

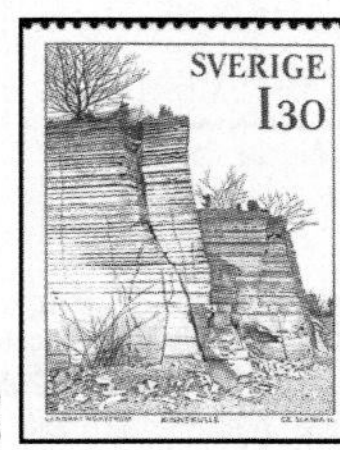

Red Limestone Cliff — A356

Designs: No. 1243, Avocets. No. 1245, Linnaea borealis (Linné's favorite flower.) No. 1247, Linné with Lapp drum, wearing Lapp clothes and Dutch doctor's hat.

***Perf. 12½ Horiz.***

**1978, May 23** **Engr.**

| | | | | |
|---|---|---|---|---|
| **1242** | A354 | 1.30k gray green | .65 | .40 |
| **1243** | A354 | 1.30k violet blue | .65 | .40 |

***Perf. 12½ on 3 Sides***

| | | | | |
|---|---|---|---|---|
| **1244** | A355 | 1.30k violet brown | .65 | .60 |
| **1245** | A355 | 1.30k brown red | .65 | .60 |

***Perf. 12½ on 2 Sides***

| | | | | |
|---|---|---|---|---|
| **1246** | A356 | 1.30k violet blue | .65 | .60 |
| **1247** | A356 | 1.30k violet brown | .65 | .60 |
| *a.* | | Bklt. pane of 6, #1242-1247 | 4.25 | *5.00* |

Travels of Carl von Linné (1707-1778), botanist.

Cranes, Lake Hornborgasjon — A357

Designs: No. 1248, Gliding School, Alleberg. No. 1250, Skara Church, Lacko Island. No. 1251, Ancient rock tomb, Luttra. No. 1252, Cloth merchants, sculpture by Nils Sjogren.

**1978, May 23** ***Perf. 12½ Horiz.***

| | | | | |
|---|---|---|---|---|
| **1248** | A357 | 1.15k dull green | .55 | .45 |
| **1249** | A357 | 1.15k maroon | .55 | .45 |
| **1250** | A357 | 1.15k violet blue | .55 | .45 |
| **1251** | A357 | 1.15k dk gray grn | .55 | .45 |
| **1252** | A357 | 1.15k brn & gray grn | .55 | .45 |
| *a.* | | Bklt. pane, 2 each #1284-1252 | 5.50 | |
| | | *Nos. 1248-1252 (5)* | 2.75 | 2.25 |

Tourist publicity for Vastergotland.

Laurel and Scroll — A358

**1978, May 23** ***Perf. 12½ Vert.***

| | | | | |
|---|---|---|---|---|
| **1253** | A358 | 2.50k gray & sl grn | 1.00 | .20 |

Stockholm University, centenary.

Homecoming, by Carl Kylberg — A359

Nude, by Karl Isakson A360

Self-portrait, by Ivar Arosenius A361

**1978, Sept. 5 Engr. *Perf. 12½ Vert.***

1254 A359 90o multicolored .40 .40

***Perf. 12½ Horiz.***

1255 A360 1.15k multi .55 .30
1256 A361 4.50k multi 1.75 .40
*Nos. 1254-1256 (3)* 2.70 1.10

Swedish painters: Carl Kylberg (1878-1952); Karl Isakson (1878-1922); Ivar Arosenius (1878-1909).

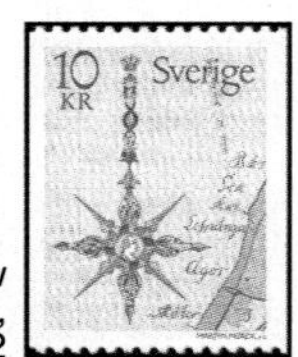
North Arrow (Compass Rose), Map, 1769 — A362

**1978, Sept. 5** ***Perf. 12½ Horiz.***

1257 A362 10k lilac 3.75 .20

Coronation Coach, 1699 — A363

**1978, Oct. 7 Engr. *Perf. 12½ Horiz.***

1258 A363 1.70k dk red, *yel* .80 .45
a. Booklet pane of 5 4.00

Orange Russula — A364

Designs: Edible mushrooms.

**1978, Oct. 7** ***Perf. 12½ on 3 Sides***

1259 A364 1.15k shown .50 *.65*
1260 A364 1.15k Lycoperdon perlatum .50 *.65*
1261 A364 1.15k Macrolepiota procera .50 *.65*
1262 A364 1.15k Cantharellus cibarius .50 *.65*
1263 A364 1.15k Boletus edulis .50 *.65*
1264 A364 1.15k Ramaria botrytis .50 *.65*
a. Bklt. pane of 6, #1259-1264 3.50 *6.50*

Toy Ferris Wheel — A365

Rider Drawing Water Cart — A366

Toys: No. 1266, Teddy bear. No. 1267, Dalecarlian wooden horse. No. 1268, Doll. No. 1269, Spinning tops.

***Perf. 12½ Horiz.***

**1978, Nov. 14 Engr.**

1265 A365 90o dk red & grn .45 .20
1266 A365 1.30k brt ultra .65 .20

***Perf. 12½ on 3 Sides***

**Photo.**

1267 A365 90o multicolored .35 .20
1268 A365 90o multicolored .35 .20
a. Bklt. pane, 5 each #1267-1268 3.50
1269 A366 1.30k multicolored .55 .20
1270 A366 1.30k multicolored .55 .20
a. Bklt. pane, 5 each #1269-1270 5.50
*Nos. 1265-1270 (6)* 2.90 1.20

Christmas 1978.

Fritz Haber — A367

Design: 1.70k, Max Planck.

**1978, Nov. 14 Engr. *Perf. 12½ Vert.***

1271 A367 1.30k dark brown .65 .50
1272 A367 1.70k dark violet bl .85 .65

1918 Nobel Prize winners: Fritz Haber (1868-1934), German chemist; Max Planck (1858-1947), German physicist.

See #1310-1312, 1341-1344, 1387-1389.

Bandy — A368

**1979, Jan. 25 Engr. *Perf. 12½ Vert.***

1273 A368 1.05k violet blue .45 .20
1274 A368 2.50k orange 1.10 .20

Child Wearing Gas Mask in Heavy Traffic — A369

**1979, Mar. 13** ***Perf. 12½ Vert.***

1275 A369 1.70k dark blue .85 .60

International Year of the Child.

Drill-weave Tapestry, c. 1855-1860 A370

Carrier Pigeon, Hand with Quill A371

**1979, Mar. 13** ***Perf. 12½ Horiz.***

1276 A370 4k gray & red 1.65 .20

***Perf. 14x14½ on 3 Sides***

**1979, Apr. 2 Photo.**

1277 A371 (1k) ultra & yel 1.50 .20
a. Booklet pane of 20 30.00

Price of booklet 20k.

DISCOUNT BOOKLETS

Every Swedish household received during Apr. 1979, 2 coupons for the purchase of 2 discount booklets, #1277a. The stamps were for use on post cards and letters within Sweden. The stamps are inscribed "INRIKES POST."

The program continued with numerous changes. The Inscription changed to "PRIVATPOST" in 1981, the same year that denominations were added. At some point the stamps could also be used to Denmark, Norway, Finland and Iceland. In 1991 the discount value of the stamps ended July, 1.

The last stamps inscribed "PRIVAT POST" were issued in 1993.

Mail Service by Boat, Grisslehamn to Echero A372

Europa: 1.70k, Hand on telegraph.

**1979, May 7 Engr. *Perf. 12½ Vert.***

1278 A372 1.30k slate grn & blk *2.25* .35
1279 A372 1.70k ocher & blk *2.25* .85

Woodcutter, Winter — A373

Designs: No. 1281, Sowing, spring. No. 1282, Grazing cattle, summer. No. 1283, Harvester, summer. No. 1284, Plowing, autumn.

**1979, May 7** ***Perf. 12½ Horiz.***

1280 A373 1.30k multicolored .55 .45
1281 A373 1.30k sl grn & dk brn .55 .45
1282 A373 1.30k dk brn & sl grn .55 .45
1283 A373 1.30k sl grn & ocher .55 .45
1284 A373 1.30k multicolored .55 .45
a. Bklt. pane, 2 each #1280-1284 5.75
*Nos. 1280-1284 (5)* 2.75 2.25

Tourist Steamer Juno — A374

Roller Bridge, Hajstorp — A375

Sailing Ship — A376

Gota Canal: No. 1286, Borenshult Lock. No. 1288, Hand-drawn gate. No. 1290, Rowboat in Forsvik lock.

**1979, May 7** ***Perf. 12½ Horiz.***

1285 A374 1.15k violet blue .55 *.60*
1286 A374 1.15k slate green .55 *.60*

***Perf. 12½ on 3 Sides***

1287 A375 1.15k dull purple .55 *.75*
1288 A375 1.15k carmine .55 *.75*

***Perf. 12½ on 2 Sides***

1289 A376 1.15k violet blue .55 *.75*
1290 A376 1.15k slate green .55 *.75*
a. Bklt. pane of 6, #1285-1290 3.50 *5.00*
*Nos. 1285-1290 (6)* 3.30 4.20

Strikers and Sawmill A377

Temperance Movement Banner — A378

Jons Jacob Berzelius A379

Johan Olof Wallin A380

**1979, Sept. 6 Engr. *Perf. 12½ Vert.***

1291 A377 90o car & dp brn .55 *.35*

***Perf. 12½ Horiz.***

**Litho.**

1292 A378 1.30k multi .55 .30

**Engr.**

1293 A379 1.70k brown & grn .75 .40
1294 A380 4.50k slate blue 1.75 .50
*Nos. 1291-1294 (4)* 3.60 1.55

Centenaries of Sundsvall strike and Swedish Temperance Movement; birth bicentennials of Jons Jacob Berzelius (1779-1848), physician and chemist; Johan Olof Wallin (1779-1839), Archbishop and poet.

Dragonfly A381

Green Spotted Toad A383

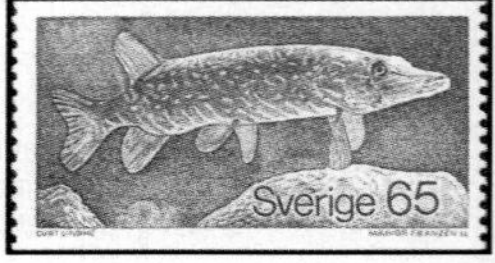
Pike A382

**1979, Sept. 6** ***Perf. 12½ Horiz.***

1295 A381 60o violet .40 .40

***Perf. 12½ Vert.***

1296 A382 65o gray .50 .35
1297 A383 80o olive green .50 .55
*Nos. 1295-1297 (3)* 1.40 1.30

Swedish Rococo — A384

Designs: 90o, Potpourri pot. 1.15k, Portrait, by Johan Henrik Scheffel. 1.30k, Silver coffee-pot. 1.70k, Bust of Carl Johan Cronstedt.

Souvenir Sheet

**Engraved and Photogravure**

**1979, Oct. 6** ***Perf. 12x12½***

1298 A384 Sheet of 4 2.40 *3.25*
a.-d. Any single .50 *.60*

No. 1298 sold for 6k; surtax was for philately.

Herrings, Age Determination — A386

Sea Research: No. 1300, Acoustic survey of sea bottom. No. 1301, Water bloom of algae in Baltic Sea. No. 1302, Computer map of herring distribution in South Baltic Sea. No. 1303, Research ship Argos.

**1979, Oct. 6 Engr. *Perf. 12½ Horiz.***

**1299** A386 1.70k multicolored .75 .75
**1300** A386 1.70k sepia .75 .75
**1301** A386 1.70k multicolored .75 .75
**1302** A386 1.70k sepia .75 .75
**1303** A386 1.70k multicolored .75 .75
*a.* Bklt. pane of 5, #1299-1303 3.75 *5.00*

Brooch from Jamtland A387

Ljusdal Costume A388

Christmas (Costumes and Jewelry from): #1305, Pendant, Smaland. #1307, Osteraker. #1308, Goinge. #1309, Mora.

***Perf. 12½ Horiz.***

**1979, Nov. 15 Engr.**

**1304** A387 90o dk Prus blue .40 .30
**1305** A387 1.30k dull red .40 .20

***Perf. 12½ on 3 Sides***

**Photo.**

**Size: 22x27mm**

**1306** A388 90o multicolored .30 .30
**1307** A388 90o multicolored .30 .30
*a.* Bklt. pane, 5 each #1306-1307 3.00

***Perf. 12½ Vert.***

**Size: 26x44mm**

**1308** A388 1.30k multicolored .45 .20
**1309** A388 1.30k multicolored .45 .20
*a.* Bklt. pane, 5 each #1308-1309 4.50
*Nos. 1304-1309 (6)* 2.30 1.50

**Nobel Prize Winner Type of 1978**

1919 Winners: 1.30k, Jules Bordet (1870-1961), Belgian bacteriologist. 1.70k, Johannes Stark (1874-1957), German physicist. 2.50k, Carl Spitteler (1845-1924), Swiss poet.

**1979, Nov. 15 Engr. *Perf. 12½ Vert.***

**1310** A367 1.30k lilac .50 .35
**1311** A367 1.70k ultra .75 *.85*
**1312** A367 2.50k olive green 1.00 .30
*Nos. 1310-1312 (3)* 2.25 1.50

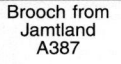

Wind Power — A389

Renewable Energy Sources: No. 1314, Biodegradable material. No. 1315, Solar energy. No. 1316, Geothermal energy. No. 1317, Hydro power.

**1980, Jan. 29 *Perf. 12½ on 3 sides***

**1313** A389 1.15k dark blue .65 .65
**1314** A389 1.15k dk grn & bis .65 .65
**1315** A389 1.15k yellow orange .65 .65
**1316** A389 1.15k dark green .65 .65
**1317** A389 1.15k dk bl & dk grn .65 .65
*a.* Bklt. pane, 2 each #1313-1317 6.50 *10.00*
*Nos. 1313-1317 (5)* 3.25 3.25

Crown Princess Victoria and King Carl XVI Gustaf — A390

**1980, Feb. 26 *Perf. 12½ on 3 sides***

**1318** A390 1.30k brt blue .40 .20
*a.* Booklet pane of 10 4.00

***Perf. 12½ Vert.***

**1319** A390 1.30k brt blue .55 .20
**1320** A390 1.70k carmine rose .75 .40
*Nos. 1318-1320 (3)* 1.70 .80

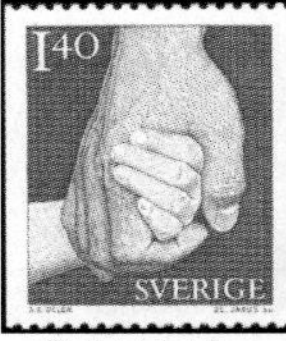

Child Holding Adult's Hand — A391

Hand Holding Cane — A392

**1980, Apr. 22 *Perf. 12½ Horiz.***

**1321** A391 1.40k red brown .65 .20
**1322** A392 1.60k slate green .75 .20

Parents' insurance system; care for the elderly.

Squirrel — A393

***Perf. 15 on 3 Sides***

**1980, May 12 Photo.**

**1323** A393 (1k) ultra & yellow 1.50 .20
*a.* Booklet pane of 20 30.00

See note after No. 1277.

Elise Ottesen-Jensen (1886-1973), Journalist A394

Europa: 1.70k, Joe Hill (1879-1915), member of American Workers' Movement and poet.

**1980, June 4 Engr. *Perf. 12½ Vert.***

**1324** A394 1.30k green 1.10 .20
**1325** A394 1.70k red 1.30 1.10

Banga Farm, Alfta, Halsingland Province — A395

Tourism (Halsingland Province): No. 1327, Iron Works, Iggesund. No. 1328, Blaxas Ridge, Forsa. No. 1329, Tybling farm, Tyby. No. 1330, Sunds Canal, Hudiksvall.

**1980, June 4 *Perf. 12½ Horiz.***

**1326** A395 1.15k red .55 *.65*
**1327** A395 1.15k dark blue .55 *.65*
**1328** A395 1.15k dark green .55 *.65*
**1329** A395 1.15k chocolate .55 *.65*
**1330** A395 1.15k dark blue .55 *.65*
*a.* Bklt. pane, 2 each #1326-1330 5.50
*Nos. 1326-1330 (5)* 2.75 3.25

Chair, Scania, 1831 — A396

Cradle, North Bothnia, 19th Century — A397

***Perf. 12½ Horiz.***

**1980, Sept. 9 Engr.**

**1331** A396 1.50k grnsh blue .65 .20

***Perf. 12½ Vert.***

**1332** A397 2k dk red brown .95 .45

Norden 80.

Scene from "Diagonal Symphony," 1924 — A398

**1980, Sept. 9 *Perf. 12½ Horiz.***

**1333** A398 3k dark blue 1.10 .30

Viking Eggeling (1880-1925), artist and film maker.

Souvenir Sheet

Gustaf Erikson's Carriage — A399

Swedish Automobile History: 90o, Gustaf Erikson's carriage. 1.15k, Vabis, 1909. 1.30k, Thulin, 1923. 1.40k, Scania, 1903. 1.50k, Tidaholm, 1917. 1.70k, Volvo, 1927.

**Photogravure and Engraved**

**1980, Oct. 11 *Perf. 12½***

**1334** A399 Sheet of 6 4.00 *5.00*
*a.-f.* Any single .65 *.65*

No. 1334 sold for 9k.

Bamse the Bear — A401

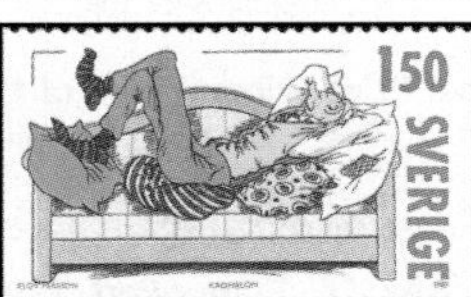

Farmer Kronblom — A402

Christmas 1980 (Comic Strip Characters): No. 1336, Mandel Karlsson, vert. No. 1337, Adamson, vert.

**1980, Oct. 11 Engr. *Perf. 12½ Vert.***

**1335** A401 1.15k multicolored .45 .30

***Perf. 12½ on 3 sides***

**Photo.**

**1336** A401 1.15k multicolored .40 .30
*a.* Booklet pane of 10 4.00

***Perf. 12½ Horiz.***

**Engr.**

**1337** A401 1.50k black .50 .20

**Photo.**

**1338** A402 1.50k multicolored .50 .20
*a.* Booklet pane of 10 5.00
*Nos. 1335-1338 (4)* 1.85 1.00

Angel Blowing Horn A403

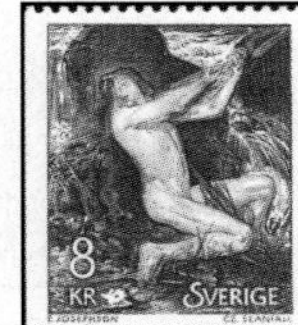

Necken, by Ernst Josephson A404

***Perf. on 3 Sides***

**1980, Nov. 18 Engr.**

**1339** A403 1.25k multicolored .50 .20
*a.* Booklet pane of 12 6.00

Christmas 1980.

**1980, Nov. 18 *Perf. 12½ Horiz.***

**1340** A404 8k multicolored 3.25 .20

**Nobel Prize Winner Type of 1978**

1920 Winners: #1341, Knut Hamsun (1859-1953), Norwegian writer. #1342, August Krogh (1874-1949), Danish Physiologist, #1343, Charles-Edouard Guillaume (1861-1938), French physicist. #1344, Walther Nernst (1864-1941), German chemist.

**1980, Nov. 18 *Perf. 13 on 3 Sides***

**1341** A367 1.40k dk blue gray .65 .30
**1342** A367 1.40k red .65 .30
*a.* Bklt. pane, 5 each #1341-1342 6.50
**1343** A367 2k green .85 .55
**1344** A367 2k brown .85 .55
*a.* Bklt. pane, 5 each #1343-1344 8.50
*Nos. 1341-1344 (4)* 3.00 1.70

Ernst Wigforss (1881-1977), Politician & Writer A405

Freya (Fertility Goddess) A406

**1981, Jan. 29 Engr. *Perf. 12½ Vert.***

**1345** A405 5k rose carmine 2.25 .35

**1981, Jan. 29 *Perf. 12½ on 3 Sides***

Norse Mythological Characters: 10o, Thor (thunder god). 15o, Heimdall (rainbow god). 50o, Frey (god of peace, fertility, weather). 1k, Odin.

**1346** A406 10o blue black .20 .20
**1347** A406 15o dk carmine .20 .20
**1348** A406 50o dk carmine .30 .20
**1349** A406 75o deep green .30 .20
**1350** A406 1k blue black .35 .20
*a.* Bklt. pane, 2 each #1346-1350 2.75
*Nos. 1346-1350 (5)* 1.35 1.00

Gyrfalcon A407

**1981, Feb. 26 Engr. *Perf. 12½ Vert.***

**1351** A407 50k multicolored 13.50 .75
*a.* Booklet pane of 4 55.00

Troll Chasing Boy — A408

Europa: 2k, Lady of the Woods.

**1981, Apr. 28 Engr.**

**1352** A408 1.50k dk blue & red 1.40 .30
**1353** A408 2k dk green & red 1.40 .40

Intl. Year of the Disabled — A409

**1981, Apr. 28**

**1354** A409 1.50k dk green .65 .20
**1355** A409 3.50k purple 1.60 .50

Arms of Oster-gotland Province
A410

Sail Boat, Bohuslan
A411

*Perf. 14½ on 3 Sides*

**1981, May 18** **Photo.**

**1356** A410 1.40k shown 1.50 .20
**1357** A410 1.40k Jamtland 1.50 .20
**1358** A410 1.40k Dalarna 1.50 .20
**1359** A410 1.40k Bohuslan 1.50 .20
*a.* Bklt. pane, 5 each #1356-1359 30.00
*Nos. 1356-1359 (4)* 6.00 .80

See note after No. 1277. See Nos. 1403-1406, 1456-1459, 1492-1495, 1534-1537, 1592-1595.

*Perf. 12½ on 3 Sides*

**1981, May 26** **Engr.**

**1360** A411 1.65k shown .65 .60
**1361** A411 1.65k Blekinge .65 .60
**1362** A411 1.65k Norrbotten .65 .60
**1363** A411 1.65k Halsingland .65 .60
**1364** A411 1.65k Gotland .65 .60
**1365** A411 1.65k Skane .65 .60
*a.* Bklt. pane of 6, #1360-1365 4.00 *6.50*

King Carl XVI Gustaf
A412

Queen Silvia
A413

**1981-84** ***Perf. 12½ Vert.***

**1366** A412 1.65k dark green .65 .20
**1367** A413 1.75k dark blue .75 .35
**1368** A412 1.80k dark blue ('83) .75 .20
**1369** A412 1.90k red ('84) .75 .20
**1370** A412 2.40k violet brn .95 .55
**1371** A413 2.40k grnsh black ('84) .95 .85
**1372** A412 2.70k brt lilac ('83) 1.20 1.10
**1373** A413 3.20k red ('83) 1.30 1.00
*Nos. 1366-1373 (8)* 7.30 4.45

Day and Night — A414

Scene from Par Lagerkvist's Autobiography Guest of Reality — A415

*Perf. 12½ on 3 Sides*

**1981, Sept. 9** **Engr.**

**1376** A414 1.65k dark blue .50 .20
*a.* Booklet pane of 10 5.00

**1981, Sept. 9** ***Perf. 12½ Horiz.***

**1377** A415 1.50k dark green .75 .20

Conductor Sixten Ehrling and Opera Singer Birgit Nilsson — A416

Bjorn Borg, Tennis Player
A417

Baker's Sign
A418

Designs: No. 1378, Electric locomotive. No. 1379, Trucks. No. 1381, Oil rig. No. 1383, Ingemar Stenmark, skier.

*Perf. 12½ on 2 (Type A416) or 3 (Type A417) sides*

**1981, Sept. 9**

**1378** A416 2.40k rose carmine 1.25 .75
**1379** A416 2.40k red 1.25 .75
**1380** A416 2.40k rose lilac 1.25 .75
**1381** A416 2.40k deep violet 1.25 .75
**1382** A417 2.40k dark blue 1.25 .75
**1383** A417 2.40k dark blue 1.25 .75
*a.* Bklt. pane of 6, #1378-1383 7.50 8.50

**1981, Sept. 9** ***Perf. 12½ Vert.***

**1384** A418 2.30k shown 1.50 .20
**1385** A418 2.30k Pewter shop sign 1.50 .20
*a.* Pair, #1384-1385 3.00 1.90

A419

Swedish Films: a, Olof Ahs in The Coachman. b, Ingrid Bergman and Gosta Ekman in Intermezzo. c, Greta Garbo in The Gosta Berling Saga, d, Stig Jarrel and Alf Kjellin in Persecution. e, Kari Sylwan and Harriet Andersson in Cries and Whispers

**Photogravure and Engraved**

**1981, Oct. 10** ***Perf. 13½***

**1386** A419 Sheet of 5 3.75 *5.50*
*a.-e.* Any single .75 *.90*

No. 1386 sold for 10k.

**Nobel Prize Winner Type of 1978**

1921 Winners: 1.35k, Albert Einstein (1879-1955), German physicist. 1.65k, Anatole France (1844-1924), French writer. 2.70k, Frederick Soddy (1877-1956), British chemist.

**1981, Nov. 24** **Engr.** ***Perf. 12½ Vert.***

**1387** A367 1.35k red .55 .30
**1388** A367 1.65k green .75 .20
**1389** A367 2.70k blue 1.10 .75
*Nos. 1387-1389 (3)* 2.40 1.25

Christmas 1981 — A421

Designs: Wooden birds.

**1981, Nov. 24** ***Perf. 12½ on 3 Sides***

**1390** A421 1.40k red .55 .20
**1391** A421 1.40k green .55 .20
*a.* Bklt. pane, 5 each #1390-1391 5.50

Knight on Horseback, by John Bauer
A422

John Bauer (1882-1918), Fairytale Illustrator: No. 1393, "What a Miserable Little Paleface, said the Troll Mother." No. 1394, Marsh Princess. No. 1395, Now the Dusk of the Night is already Upon Us.

*Perf. 12x12½ on 3 sides*

**1982, Feb. 16** **Engr.**

**1392** A422 1.65k multicolored .65 .55
**1393** A422 1.65k multicolored .65 .55
**1394** A422 1.65k multicolored .65 .55
**1395** A422 1.65k multicolored .65 .55
*a.* Bklt. pane of 4, #1392-1395 2.75 *3.50*

Impossible Figures — A423

Designs: Geometric figures.

**1982, Feb. 16** ***Perf. 12½ Horiz.***

**1396** A423 25o violet brown .20 .20
**1397** A423 50o brown olive .20 .20
**1398** A423 75o dark blue .30 .20
*Nos. 1396-1398 (3)* .70 .60

Newspaper Distributor, by Svenolov Ehren
A424

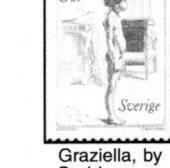

Graziella, by Carl Larsson
A425

**1982, Feb. 16**

**1399** A424 1.35k deep violet .70 .20
**1400** A425 5k violet brown 1.90 .20

**Europa Issue 1982**

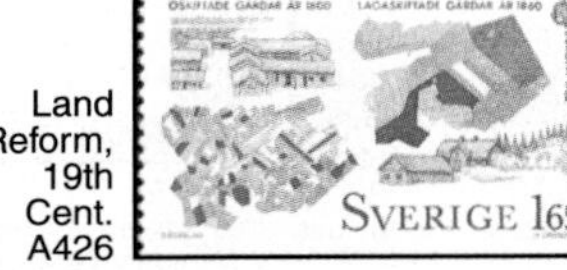

Land Reform, 19th Cent.
A426

Anders Celsius (1701-1744), Inventor of Temperature Scale — A427

**1982, Apr. 26** **Engr.** ***Perf. 12½ Vert.***

**1401** A426 1.65k dk olive grn 2.75 .20

*Perf. 12½ on 3 Sides*

**1402** A427 2.40k dark green 1.10 .65
*a.* Booklet pane of 6 6.50

**Provincial Arms Type of 1981**

*Perf. 14 on 3 Sides*

**1982, Apr. 26** **Photo.**

**1403** A410 1.40k Dalsland 1.50 .20
**1404** A410 1.40k Oland 1.50 .20
**1405** A410 1.40k Vastmandland 1.50 .20
**1406** A410 1.40k Halsingland 1.50 .20
*a.* Bklt. pane, 5 each #1403-1406 30.00
*Nos. 1403-1406 (4)* 6.00 .80

See note after No. 1277.

Elin Wagner (1882-1949), Writer — A428

*Perf. 12½ Horiz.*

**1982, June 3** **Engr.**

**1407** A428 1.35k Sketch by Siri Derkert .50 .35

Burgher House — A429

Embroidered Lace Ribbon, 19th Cent. — A430

**1982, June 3** ***Perf. 12½ Vert.***

**1408** A429 1.65k brown .75 .20

*Perf. 12½ Horiz.*

**1409** A430 2.70k bister 1.10 .80

Cent. of Museum of Cultural History, Lund.

1982 Intl. Buoyage System
A431

Designs: Various buoy signals.

**1982, June 3** ***Perf. 13 Horiz.***

**1410** A431 1.65k shown .60 .45
**1411** A431 1.65k Ferry .60 .45
**1412** A431 1.65k Six sailboats .60 .45
**1413** A431 1.65k One-globed buoy .60 .45
**1414** A431 1.65k Two-globed buoy .60 .45
*a.* Bklt. pane, 2 each #1410-1414 6.00
*Nos. 1410-1414 (5)* 3.00 2.25

Vietnamese Workers in Sweden — A432

Living Together: Swedish emigration and immigration.

**1982, Aug. 26** **Engr.** ***Perf. 13 Horiz.***

**1415** A432 1.65k Leaving Sweden, 1880 .65 .55
**1416** A432 1.65k shown .65 .55
**1417** A432 1.65k Local voting right .65 .55
**1418** A432 1.65k Girls .65 .55
*a.* Bklt. pane, 2 each #1415-1418 5.50
*Nos. 1415-1418 (4)* 2.60 2.20

Wild Orchids — A433

**Photogravure and Engraved**

**1982, Oct. 9** ***Perf. 12x13***

Wild Orchids: 1.65k (No. 1419a), Orchis mascula. 1.65k (No. 1419d), Cypripedium calcéolus. 2.40k, Epipactis palustris. 2.70k, Dactylorhiza sambucina.

**1419** A433 Sheet of 4 5.00 *6.00*
*a.-d.* Any single 1.10 1.30

Sold for 10k for benefit of stamp collecting.

Christmas 1982 — A434

Stained-glass Windows, Church at Lye, Gotland, 14th cent.

***Perf. 13 on 3 Sides***

**1982, Nov. 24** **Photo.**

**1420** A434 1.40k Angel .65 .40
**1421** A434 1.40k Child in the Temple .65 .40
**1422** A434 1.40k Adoration of the Kings .65 .40
**1423** A434 1.40k Tidings to the Shepherds .65 .40
**1424** A434 1.40k Birth of Christ .65 .40
*a.* Bklt. pane, 2 each #1420-1424 6.50 *7.50*
*Nos. 1420-1424 (5)* 3.25 2.00

Signature, Atomic Model — A435

Nobel Prizewinners in Physics (Quantum Mechanics). Various Atomic Models: No. 1425, Niels Bohr, Denmark, 1922. No. 1426, Erwin Schrodinger, Austria, 1933. No. 1427, Louis de Broglie, France, 1929. No. 1428, Paul Dirac, England, 1933. No. 1429, Werner Heisenberg, Germany, 1932.

**1982, Nov. 24** **Engr.** ***Perf. 13 Horiz.***

**1425** A435 2.40k multi 1.10 .85
**1426** A435 2.40k multi 1.10 .85
**1427** A435 2.40k multi 1.10 .85
**1428** A435 2.40k multi 1.10 .85
**1429** A435 2.40k multi 1.10 .85
*a.* Bklt. pane of 5, #1425-1429 6.00 *6.50*
*Nos. 1425-1429 (5)* 5.50 4.25

Fruit A436

Games A436a

Crown and Posthorn A436b

King Carl XVI Gustaf A436c

Queen Silvia A436d

Games A436e

**1983-85** **Engr.** ***Perf. 12½ Vert.***

**1430** A436 5o Horse chestnut .20 .20
**1431** A436 10o Norway maple .20 .20
**1432** A436 15o Dogrose .20 .20
**1433** A436 20o Sloe .20 .20
**1434** A436a 50o Fox and cheese .30 .20
**1435** A436a 60o Dominoes .30 .30
**1436** A436a 70o Ludo .30 .30
**1437** A436a 80o Chinese checkers .40 .30
**1438** A436a 90o Backgammon .45 .40
**1439** A436b 1.60k deep blue .75 .20
**1440** A436c 2k black .70 .20
**1441** A436b 2.50k bister .90 .30
**1442** A436c 2.70k dull red brn 1.10 1.00

***Perf. 12½ Horiz.***

**1443** A436e 3k Chess 1.40 .20

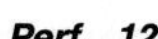

***Perf. 12½ Vert.***

**1444** A436d 3.20k brt blue 1.30 1.25
**1445** A436b 4k dp car 1.30 .20
*Nos. 1430-1445 (16)* 10.00 5.65

Issued: #1430-1433, 2/10/83; #1434-1438, 1443, 10/12/85; #1439-1442, 1444-1445, 1/24/85.

See Nos. 1567-1580, 1783.

Peace Movement Centenary A437

**1983, Feb. 10**

**1446** A437 1.35k blue .55 .35

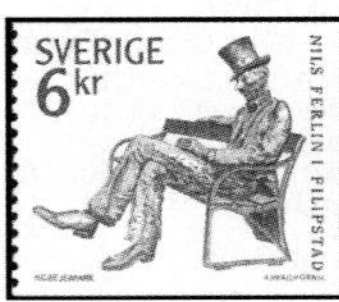

Nils Ferlin (1898-1961), Poet — A438

**1983, Feb. 10**

**1447** A438 6k dk grn 2.50 .20

500th Anniv. of Printing in Sweden A439

**1983, Feb. 10** ***Perf. 13 Horiz.***

**1448** A439 1.65k Lead type .65 .35
**1449** A439 1.65k Dialogus Creaturarum, 1483 .65 .35
**1450** A439 1.65k Carolus XII Bible, 1703 .65 .35
**1451** A439 1.65k ABC Books, 1760s .65 .35
**1452** A439 1.65k Laser photo composition .65 .35
*a.* Bklt. pane, 2 each #1448-1452 7.50
*Nos. 1448-1452 (5)* 3.25 1.75

Sweden-US Relations Bicentenary — A440

**1983, Mar. 24**

**1453** A440 2.70k Ben Franklin, Swedish Arms 1.10 .65
*a.* Booklet pane of 5 5.50

See US No. 2036.

Nordic Cooperation Issue — A441

***Perf. 12½ Horiz.***

**1983, Mar. 24** **Engr.**

**Size: 21x27mm**

**1454** A441 1.65k Bicycling .60 .35

***Perf. 13 Vert.***

**1455** A441 2.40k Sailing 1.00 .85

**Provincial Arms Type of 1981**

**1983, Apr. 25** **Photo.** ***Perf. 14½x14***

**1456** A410 1.60k Vastergotland 1.50 .20
**1457** A410 1.60k Medelpad 1.50 .20
**1458** A410 1.60k Gotland 1.50 .20
**1459** A410 1.60k Gastrikland 1.50 .20
*a.* Bklt. pane, 5 each #1456-1459 30.00
*Nos. 1456-1459 (4)* 6.00 .80

See note after No. 1277.

Europa — A442

***Perf. 12½ Horiz.***

**1983, Apr. 25** **Engr.**

**1460** A442 1.65k Swedish Ballet Co. 1.50 .35
**1461** A442 2.70k Sliding-jaw wrench 1.50 1.50

A443

Designs: 1k, 3k, 10-ore King Oscar II definitive essays, 1884. 2k, No. 39. 4k, No. 58.

**1983, May 25** ***Perf. 12½***

**1462** A443 1k blue .60 .50
**1463** A443 2k red .85 .55
**1464** A443 3k blue 1.10 .85
**1465** A443 4k green 1.25 1.00
*a.* Bklt. pane of 4, #1462-1465 4.25 *4.50*

STOCKHOLMIA Intl. Stamp Exhibition, Aug. 28-Sept. 7, 1986

Red Cross — A444

Greater Karlso — A445

**1983, Aug. 24** ***Perf. 12½ Horiz.***

**1466** A444 1.50k red .75 .20
**1467** A445 1.60k dk blue .75 .20

Planorbis Snail — A446

Arctic Fox — A447

**1983, Aug. 24** ***Perf. 12½ on 3 Sides***

**1468** A446 1.80k green .65 .20
*a.* Booklet pane of 10 6.50

***Perf. 12½ Horiz.***

**1469** A447 2.10k grnsh blk .75 .45

See Nos. 1488-1489, 1526-1527, 1623-1626, 1678-1680, 1762-1763.

Hjalmar Bergman (1883-1931), Writer — A448

**1983, Aug. 24** ***Perf. 13 Horiz.***

**1470** A448 1.80k Portrait .75 .20
**1471** A448 1.80k Jac the Clown illustration by Nisse Skoog .75 .20
*a.* Pair, #1470-1471 1.50 .95

View of Helgeandsholmen, Stockholm, by Franz Hogenberg, 1580 — A449

**1983, Aug. 24** ***Perf. 12½ Vert.***

**1472** A449 2.70k dl pur & dk bl 1.25 .70

A450

**Photogravure and Engraved**

**1983, Oct. 1** ***Perf. 13½***

**1473** A450 Sheet of 5 5.25 *6.00*
*a.* 1.80k Wilhelm Stenhammar, pianist .95 .75
*b.* 1.80k Aniara (opera) .95 .75
*c.* 1.80k Lars Gullin, jazz saxophonist .95 .75
*d.* 1.80k ABBA, pop music group .95 .75
*e.* 2.70k Hins Anders, violinist 1.20 1.20

Sold for 11.50k.

Christmas 1983 — A452

Postcard designs: No. 1474, Christmas Gnomes around the tree. No. 1475, on straw goats. No. 1476, Folk children, Christmas porridge and gingerbread. No. 1477, Gnomes carrying Christmas gifts on a pole.

***Perf. 12½ on 3 sides***

**1983, Nov. 22** **Photo.**

**1474** A452 1.60k multi .65 .30
**1475** A452 1.60k multi .65 .30
**1476** A452 1.60k multi .65 .30
**1477** A452 1.60k multi .65 .30
*a.* Bklt. pane, 3 each #1474-1477 7.50
*Nos. 1474-1477 (4)* 2.60 1.20

Chemistry, Nobel Prize Winners — A453

Designs: No. 1478, Arne Tiselius (1902-1971), Electrophoresis Studies. No. 1479, George De Hevesy (1885-1966), Radioactive isotope tracers. No. 1480 Svante Arrhenius (1859-1927), Theory of Electrolytic Dissociation. No. 1481, Theodor Svedberg (1884-1971), Colloid Studies. No. 1482, Hans Von Euler-Chelpin (1873-1964). Enzyme and Vitamin Structures.

**Photogravure and Engraved**

**1983, Nov. 22** ***Perf. 12½ Horiz.***

**1478** A453 2.70k slate 1.25 .85
**1479** A453 2.70k dp bl vio 1.25 .85
**1480** A453 2.70k red lilac 1.25 .85
**1481** A453 2.70k blue blk 1.25 .85
**1482** A453 2.70k grnsh blk 1.25 .85
*a.* Bklt. pane of 5, #1478-1482 6.50 *7.00*

Postal Savings Centenary — A454

Design: 100o, Three crowns.

**1984, Feb. 9 Engr.** ***Perf. 12½ Vert.***

**1483** A454 100o orange .45 .35
**1484** A454 1.60k purple .65 .55
**1485** A454 1.80k pink .75 .20
*Nos. 1483-1485 (3)* 1.85 1.10

Europa 1984 A455

Symbolic bridge of communications exchange.

**1984, Feb. 9** ***Perf. 12½ Horiz.***

**1486** A455 1.80k red .75 .25
*a.* Booklet pane of 10 7.50

***Perf. 13 Vert.***

**1487** A455 2.70k dp ultra 2.75 1.50

### Conservation Type of 1983 and

Angelica — A457

**1984, Mar. 27** ***Perf. 12½ on 3 Sides***

**1488** A447 1.90k Lemmings .60 .20
**1489** A447 1.90k Musk ox .60 .20
*a.* Bklt. pane, 5 each #1488-1489 6.00

***Perf. 12½ Horiz.***

**1490** A457 2k shown 1.00 .20
**1491** A457 2.25k Alpine birch 1.10 .75
*Nos. 1488-1491 (4)* 3.30 1.35

### Provincial Arms Type of 1981

**1984, Apr. 24 Photo.** ***Perf. 14½x14***

**1492** A410 1.60k Sodermanland 1.50 .20
**1493** A410 1.60k Blekinge 1.50 .20
**1494** A410 1.60k Vasterbotten 1.50 .20
**1495** A410 1.60k Skane 1.50 .20
*a.* Bklt. pane, 5 ea #1492-1495 30.00
*Nos. 1492-1495 (4)* 6.00 .80

See note after No. 1277.

A458

A459

Swedish Patent System Centenary: No. 1496, Paraffin stove, F.W. Lindqvist, 1892. No. 1497, Industrial robot ASEA-IRB 6. No. 1498, Fan suction vacuum cleaner, Axel Wennergren, 1912. No. 1499, Inboard-outboard motor, AQ-200, No. 1500, SLIC integrated electronic circuit. No. 1501, Tetrahedron container, 1948, 1951.

***Perf. 12½ on 3 Sides***

**1984, June 6 Engr.**

**1496** A458 2.70k red 1.10 .95
**1497** A458 2.70k sepia 1.10 .95
**1498** A458 2.70k green 1.10 .95
**1499** A458 2.70k green 1.10 .95
**1500** A458 2.70k sepia 1.10 .95
**1501** A458 2.70k blue 1.10 .95
*a.* Bklt. pane of 6, #1496-1501 6.75 8.50

### Lithographed and Engraved

**1984, June 6** ***Perf. 12½***

Stockholmia '86 (Famous Letters): 1k, Erik XIV's marriage proposal to Queen Elizabeth I, 1561. 2k, Erik Dahlbergh to Sten Bielke, 1684. 3k, Feather letter, 1834. 4k, August Strindberg to Harriet Bosse, 1905.

**1502** A459 1k multi .75 .60
**1503** A459 2k multi .85 .65
**1504** A459 3k multi 1.10 .85
**1505** A459 4k multi 1.25 1.10
*a.* Bklt. pane of 4, #1502-1505 4.25 *6.00*

Fredrika Bremer Assn. (Women's Rights) Centenary A460

***Perf. 12½ Vert.***

**1984, Aug. 28 Engr.**

**1506** A460 1.50k pink .60 .40
**1507** A460 6.50k red 2.50 .85

Medieval Towns A461

Engravings by E. Dahlbergh or M. Karl.

**1984, Aug. 28** ***Perf. 12½x13***

**1508** A461 1.90k Jonkoping .85 .75
**1509** A461 1.90k Karlstad .85 .75
**1510** A461 1.90k Gavle .85 .75
**1511** A461 1.90k Sigtuna .85 .75
**1512** A461 1.90k Norrkoping .85 .75
**1513** A461 1.90k Vadstena .85 .75
*a.* Bklt. pane of 6, #1508-1513 5.25 *6.00*

Viking Satellite, 1985 A462

**1984, Oct. 13** ***Perf. 12½ Vert.***

**1514** A462 1.90k Satellite .70 .30
**1515** A462 3.20k Receiving station 1.40 1.10

Souvenir Sheet

Swedish Aviation History — A463

Designs: a, Thulin D Two-Seater, 1915. b, SAAB-90 Scandia, 1946. c, Carl Gustaf Cederstrom (1867-1918, "The Flying Baron"), Bleriot, 1910. d, Tomten, 1927. e, Carl Nyberg's Flugan, 1900.

**1984, Oct. 13** ***Perf. 12½***

**1516** A463 Sheet of 5 5.75 5.75
*a.-d.* 1.90k, any single .90 .85
*e.* 2.70k, multi 1.10 1.00

Sold for 12k.

Christmas 1984 — A465

Birds.

### Lithographed and Engraved

**1984, Nov. 29** ***Perf. 12½ on 3 Sides***

**1517** A465 1.60k Coccothraustes coccothraustes .55 .35
**1518** A465 1.60k Bombycilla garrulus .55 .35
**1519** A465 1.60k Dendrocopos major .55 .35
**1520** A465 1.60k Sitta europaea .55 .35
*a.* Bklt. pane, 3 each #1517-1520 7.00
*Nos. 1517-1520 (4)* 2.20 1.40

Inner Ear A466

Nobel Prize Winners in Physiology or Medicine: No. 1521, Georg von Bekesy, 1961, hearing. No. 1522, John Eccles, Alan Hodgkin & Andrew Huxley, 1963, Nerve cell activation. No. 1523, Julius Axelrod, Bernard Katz & Ulf von Euler, 1970, nerve cell storage and release. No. 1524, Roger Sperry, 1981, brain functions. No. 1525, David Hubel, Torsten Wiesel, 1981, Visual information processing.

***Perf. 12½ Horiz.***

**1984, Nov. 29 Engr.**

**1521** A466 2.70k shown 1.10 .85
**1522** A466 2.70k Nerve, arrows 1.10 .85
**1523** A466 2.70k Nerve (front, side) 1.10 .85
**1524** A466 2.70k Brain halves 1.10 .85
**1525** A466 2.70k Eye 1.10 .85
*a.* Bklt. pane of 5, #1521-1525 6.00 *7.00*

### Conservation Type of 1983 and

A467

***Perf. 13 on 3 Sides***

**1985, Mar. 14 Engr.**

**1526** A447 2k Muscardinus avellanarius .75 .20
**1527** A447 2k Salvelinus salvelinus .75 .20
*a.* Bklt. pane, 5 each #1526-1527 7.50

World Wildlife Fund.

***Perf. 12½ Horiz.***

**1528** A467 2.20k Nigritella nigra .75 .20
**1529** A467 3.50k Nymphaea alba 1.50 .65
*Nos. 1526-1529 (4)* 3.75 1.25

World Table Tennis Championships A468

**1985, Mar. 14** ***Perf. 12½ Vert.***

**1530** A468 2.70k Jan-Ove Waldner, Sweden 1.30 .90
**1531** A468 3.20k Cai Zhenhua, China 1.60 1.20

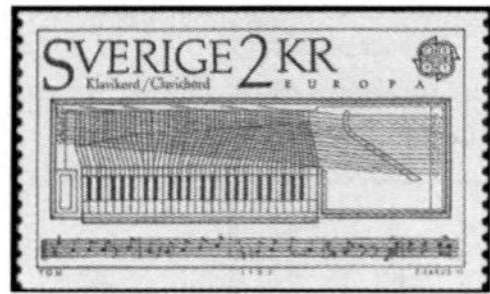


Clavichord — A469

Key Harp — A470

**1985, Apr. 24** ***Perf. 13 Vert.***

**1532** A469 2k bluish blk, *buff* 3.75 .25

***Perf. 13 on 3 Sides***

**1533** A470 2.70k dl red brn, *buff* .90 .75
*a.* Booklet pane of 6 5.50

Europa 1985.

### Provincial Arms Type of 1981

***Perf. 14½x14 on 3 Sides***

**1985, Apr. 24 Photo.**

**1534** A410 1.80k Narke 1.50 .20
**1535** A410 1.80k Angermanland 1.50 .20
**1536** A410 1.80k Varmland 1.50 .20
**1537** A410 1.80k Smaland 1.50 .20
*a.* Bklt. pane, 5 ea #1534-1537 30.00
*Nos. 1534-1537 (4)* 6.00 .80

See note after No. 1277.

St. Cnut's Land Grant to Lund Cathedral, 900th Anniv. — A471

Seal of St. Cnut and: No. 1538, Lund Cathedral. No. 1539, City of Helsingdorg.

***Perf. 12½ on 3 Sides***

**1985, May 21 Engr.**

**1538** A471 2k bluish blk & blk .75 .20
**1539** A471 2k blk & dk red .75 .20
*a.* Bklt. pane, 5 each, #1538-1539 8.50

See Denmark Nos. 777-778.

Stockholmia '86 — A472

Paintings of old Stockholm: No. 1540, A View of Slussen, by Sigrid Hjerten (1919). No. 1541, Skeppsholmen, Winter, by Gosta Adrian-Nilsson (1919). No. 1542, A Summer's Night by the Riddarholmen, by Hilding Linnqv©ist (1945). No. 1543, Klara Church Tower, by Otte Skold (1927).

### Lithographed and Engraved

**1985, May 21** ***Perf. 12½***

**1540** A472 2k multi 1.10 1.10
**1541** A472 2k multi 1.10 1.10
**1542** A472 3k multi 1.25 1.00
**1543** A472 4k multi 1.40 1.20
*a.* Bklt. pane of 4, #1540-1543 5.50 *7.50*

Swedish Touring Club Cent. — A473

#1544, Touring Club Syl Station (c. 1920). #1545, Af Chapman Hostel, Stockholm.

**1985, May 21 Engr.** ***Perf. 12½ Vert.***

**1544** 2k blk & dp bl .75 .35

**Size: 58x23mm**

**1545** 2k dp bl & blk .75 .35
*a.* A473 Pair, #1544-1545 1.75 1.25

Trade Signs — A474

***Perf. 12½ on 3 Sides***

**1985, Aug. 28 Engr.**

**1546** A474 10o Music Shop, Slottsgatan .20 .20
**1547** A474 20o Furrier, Stockholm .20 .20
**1548** A474 20o Coppersmith, Landskrona .20 .20
**1549** A474 50o Haberdasher, Stockholm .30 .20
**1550** A474 2k Shoemaker, Norrkoping .70 .20
*a.* Bklt. pane, #1546-1549, 2 #1550 2.00 *2.50*
*Nos. 1546-1550 (5)* 1.60 1.00

The Dying Spartan Hero, Otryades, 1779, by Johan Tobias Sergel — A475

Baron Carl Frederik Adelcrantz, Academy Pres., 1754, by Alexander Roslin (1718-1793) — A476

**1985, Aug. 28** ***Perf. 12½ Vert.***

**1551** A475 2k slate blue .85 .30

***Perf. 12½ Horiz.***

**1552** A476 7k dk red brn 2.75 .55

Royal Academy of Fine Arts, 250th anniv.

Intl. Youth Year — A477

Children's drawings: 2k, Participation, by Marina Karlsson. 2.70k, Development, by Madeleine Andersson. 3.20k, Peace, by Charlotta Ankar.

**Lithographed and Engraved**

**1985, Oct. 12** ***Perf. 12½x13***

**1553** A477 Sheet of 3 4.25 *5.25*
*a.* 2k multi 1.25 .80
*b.* 2.70k multi 1.25 1.10
*c.* 3.20k multi 1.50 1.30

Sold for 10k.

Prime Minister Per Albin Hansson (1885-1946) — A478

Birger Sjoberg (1885-1929), Journalist, Novelist, Poet — A479

**1985, Oct. 12** **Engr.** ***Perf. 12½ Vert.***

**1556** A478 1.60k black & red .65 *.65*

***Perf. 12½ Horiz.***

**1557** A479 4k dk blue grn 1.65 .45

Christmas 1985 — A480

15th cent. religious paintings by Albertus Pictor.

***Perf. 13x12½ on 3 Sides***

**1985, Nov. 21** **Engr.**

**1558** A480 1.80k Annunciation .75 .50
**1559** A480 1.80k Birth of Christ .75 .50
**1560** A480 1.80k Adoration of the Magi .75 .50
**1561** A480 1.80k Mary as the Apocalyptic Virgin .75 .50
*a.* Bklt. pane, 3 each #1558-1561 9.00
*Nos. 1558-1561 (4)* 3.00 2.00

Nobel Laureates in Literature — A481

Authors: No. 1562, William Faulkner (1897-1962), 1949, Southern United States. No. 1563, Halldor Kiljan Laxness (b.1902), 1955, Iceland. No. 1564, Miguel Angel Asturias (1899-1974), 1967, Guatemala. No. 1565, Yasunari Kawabata (1899-1972), 1968, Japan. No. 1566, Patrick White (b. 1912), 1973, Australia.

**Lithographed and Engraved**

**1985, Nov. 21** ***Perf. 13 Horiz.***

**1562** A481 2.70k myr grn 1.00 .95
**1563** A481 2.70k dp brn, chlky bl & myr grn 1.00 .95
**1564** A481 2.70k myr grn & tan 1.00 .95
**1565** A481 2.70k chlky bl & myr grn 1.00 .95
**1566** A481 2.70k chlky bl & ocher 1.00 .95
*a.* Blkt. pane of 5, #1562-1566 6.00 *6.25*

**Types of 1983-85**

**Engr., Litho. (1.80k, 3.20k, 6k)**

**1986-89** ***Perf. 12½ Vert.***

**1567** A436b 1.70k dk violet .65 .20
**1568** A436b 1.80k brt violet .65 .20
**1569** A436c 2.10k dk blue .80 .20
**1570** A436c 2.20k int blue .75 .20
**1571** A436c 2.30k dk ol grn .80 .20
**1572** A436b 2.80k emerald 1.10 .80
**1573** A436c 2.90k dk green 1.20 .60
**1574** A436c 3.10k dk brown 1.30 .65
**1575** A436b 3.20k yellow brn 1.25 .85
**1576** A436c 3.30k dk rose brn 1.25 1.00
**1577** A436d 3.40k dk red 1.40 .45
**1578** A436d 3.60k green 1.50 .60
**1579** A436d 3.90k violet blue 1.65 1.50
**1580** A436b 6k blue green 2.00 .35
*Nos. 1567-1580 (14)* 16.30 7.80

Issued: 2.10, 2.90, 3.40k, 1/23'; 1.70, 2.80k, 2/20; 1.80, 3.10, 3.20, 3.60, 6k, 1/27/87; 2.20k, 1/29/88; 2.30, 3.30, 3.90k, 4/20/89.

See No. 1796.

Waterbirds A484

***Perf. 13 on 2 or 3 Sides***

**1986, Jan. 23** **Engr.**

**1582** A484 2.10k Eider .75 .20
**1583** A484 2.10k Smaspov .75 .20
*a.* Bklt. pane, 5 each #1582-1583 7.50
**1584** A484 2.30k Storlom .85 .20
*Nos. 1582-1584 (3)* 2.35 .60

STOCKHOLMIA '86 — A485

**Lithographed and Engraved**

**1986, Jan. 23** ***Perf. 13***

**1585** A485 2k #33a, cancel .95 .95
**1586** A485 2k Stamp engraver .95 .95
**1587** A485 3k #268, 271, US #836 1.25 1.10
**1588** A485 4k Boy soaking stamps 1.50 1.40
*a.* Bklt. pane of 4, #1585-1588 4.75 *6.50*

See US Nos. 2198-2201a.

Swedish PO, 350th Anniv. A486

Sundial A487

**Lithographed and Engraved**

**1986, Feb. 20** ***Perf. 13x12½***

**1589** A486 2.10k org yel & dk bl .75 .20
*a.* Bklt pane of 8 6.00

**1986, Feb. 20** **Engr.** ***Perf. 13 Horiz.***

No. 1591, Motto of the Swedish Academy.

**1590** A487 1.70k dk bl & lake, *gray* .75 .60
**1591** A487 1.70k grn & dk red, *gray* .75 .60
*a.* Pair, #1590-1591 1.60 *1.50*

Royal Swedish Academy of Letters, History and Antiquities, and Swedish Academy, bicents.

**Provincial Arms Type of 1981**

***Perf. 15x14½ on 3 Sides***

**1986, Apr. 23** **Photo.**

**1592** A410 1.90k Harjedalen 1.50 .20
**1593** A410 1.90k Uppland 1.50 .20
**1594** A410 1.90k Halland 1.50 .20
**1595** A410 1.90k Lapland 1.50 .20
*a.* Bklt. pane, 5 each #1592-1595 30.00
*Nos. 1592-1595 (4)* 6.00 .80

See note after No. 1277.

King Carl XVI Gustaf — A488

Royal Cipher — A489

40th birthday: No. 1598, King presenting Nobel Prize for literature to Czeslaw Milosz, 1980. No. 1600, Royal family at Soldien palace

**Lithographed and Engraved**

**1986, Apr. 23** ***Perf. 12 on 3 Sides***

**1596** A488 2.10k grnsh blk & pale grn .95 .40
**1597** A489 2.10k dk bl, pink & gold .95 .40
**1598** A488 2.10k dk bl & pale bl .95 .40
**1599** A489 2.10k dk bl, pale grn & gold .95 .40
**1600** A488 2.10k blk & pale pink .95 .40
*a.* Bklt. pane, 2 each #1596-1600 10.00 *11.00*
*Nos. 1596-1600 (5)* 4.75 2.00

Olof Palme (1927-1986), Prime Minister — A490

***Perf. 13 on 3 Sides***

**1986, Apr. 11** **Engr.**

**1601** A490 2.10k dk lilac rose .95 .85
**1602** A490 2.90k grnsh black 1.25 1.10
*a.* Bklt. pane, 5 ea #1601-1602 12.50

Nordic Cooperation Issue — A491

Sister towns.

**1986, May 27** **Engr.** ***Perf. 13 Vert.***

**1603** A491 2.10k Uppsala .85 .30
**1604** A491 2.90k Eskilstuna 1.25 .75

Europa 1986 — A492

**1986, May 27** ***Perf. 13 Horiz.***

**1605** A492 2.10k Automotive pollutants 2.10 .40

***Perf. 13 on 3 Sides***

**1606** A492 2.90k Industrial pollutants 1.10 .85
*a.* Booklet pane of 6 6.75

STOCKHOLMIA '86 — A493

Designs: No. 1607, Mail handling terminal, Tomteboda, 1986. No. 1608, Railroad mail car, 19th cent. No. 1609, Post Office, 18th cent. No. 1610, Postman, 17th cent.

**Lithographed and Engraved**

**1986, Aug. 29** ***Perf. 13***

**1607** A493 2.10k multi 1.50 *3.00*
**1608** A493 2.10k multi 1.50 *3.00*
**1609** A493 2.90k multi 1.50 *3.00*
**1610** A493 2.90k multi 1.50 *3.00*
*a.* Bklt. pane of 4, #1607-1610 6.50 *16.00*

Bklt. sold for 40k, including 30k ticket to STOCKHOLMIA '86.

**Souvenir Sheet**

World Class Athletes in Track and Field — A494

Designs: a, Ann-Louise Skoglund, 400-meter hurdle, 1982. b, Dag Wennlund, 1986, and Eric Lemming, c. 1900, javelin. c, Standing high jumper and Patrik Sjoberg, high jump, 1985. d, Anders Garderud, 300-meter steeplechase record-holder.

**1986, Oct. 18** **Engr.** ***Perf. 12½***

**1611** A494 Sheet of 4 4.50 *6.00*
*a.-d.* 2.10k, any single 1.10 *1.10*

No. 1611 sold for 11k to benefit philatelic organizations.

Intl. Peace Year — A495

Amnesty Intl., 25th Anniv. — A496

**1986, Oct. 18** ***Perf. 13 Vert.***

**1612** A495 3.40k bluish blk & emer grn 1.50 1.50
**1613** A496 3.40k dk red & bluish blk 1.50 1.50
*a.* Pair, #1612-1613 3.00 *3.50*

Christmas — A497

Winter village scenes.

***Perf. 13x12½ on 3 Sides***

**1986, Nov. 25 Litho. & Engr.**

**1614** 1.90k Postal van .85 .35
**1615** 1.90k Postman on bicycle .85 .35
**1616** 1.90k Children, sled .85 .35
**1617** 1.90k Child mailing letter .85 .35
*a.* A497 Block of 4, #1614-1617 3.50 *4.00*
*b.* Bklt. pane of 12, 3 #1617a 10.00 —

Nobel Peace Prize Laureates — A498

#1618, Bertha von Suttner, 1905. #1619, Carl von Ossietzky, 1935. #1620, Albert Luthuli, 1960. #1621, Martin Luther King, Jr., 1964. #1622, Mother Teresa, 1979.

**1986, Nov. 25 Engr. *Perf. 13 Horiz.***

**1618** A498 2.90k brt bl, blk & hn brn 1.25 1.10
**1619** A498 2.90k blk & hn brn 1.25 1.10
**1620** A498 2.90k brt bl, blk & brn blk 1.25 1.10
**1621** A498 2.90k brn blk & hn brn 1.25 1.10
**1622** A498 2.90k blk, brt bl & hn brn 1.25 1.10
*a.* Bklt. pane of 5, #1618-1622 6.75 *7.50*

**Conservation Type of 1983**

***Perf. 13 on 3 Sides***

**1987, Mar. 10 Engr.**

**1623** A447 2.10k Parnassius mnemosyne .85 .20
**1624** A447 2.10k Gentianella campestris .85 .30
*a.* Booklet pane, 5 ea #1623-1624 8.50

***Perf. 13 Horiz.***

**1625** A447 2.50k Osmoderma eremita .85 .20
**1626** A447 4.20k Arnica montana 1.40 .30
*Nos. 1623-1626 (4)* 3.95 1.00

Swedish Aviation Industry A500

**1987, Mar. 10 *Perf. 13 Vert.***

**1627** A500 25k Saab SF340 10.00 .40

Europa 1987 — A501

Nos. 1628-1629, City Library, Asplund. No. 1630, Lewerentz Marcus Church.

**1987, May 14 Engr. *Perf. 13 Vert.***

**1628** A501 2.10k int blk & grn 2.75 .35

***Perf. 13 on 3 Sides***

**1629** A501 3.10k emer grn & red brn 1.10 .85
**1630** A501 3.10k emer grn & sep 1.10 .85
*a.* Bklt. pane, 3 each #1629-1630 7.00
*Nos. 1628-1630 (3)* 4.95 2.05

Illustrations from Children's Novels by Astrid Lindgren (b. 1907) — A502

***Perf. 13x12½ on 3 Sides***

**1987, May 14 Litho. & Engr.**

**1631** A502 1.90k Karlsson Pa Taket 2.00 .25
**1632** A502 1.90k Barnen and Bullerbyn 2.00 .25
**1633** A502 1.90k Madicken 2.00 .25
**1634** A502 1.90k Mio, Min Mio 2.00 .25
**1635** A502 1.90k Nils Karlsson-Pyssling 2.00 .25
**1636** A502 1.90k Emil and Lonneberga 2.00 .25
**1637** A502 1.90k Ronja Rovardotter 2.00 .25
**1638** A502 1.90k Pippi Longstocking 2.00 .25
**1639** A502 1.90k Broderna Lejonhjarta 2.00 .25
**1640** A502 1.90k Lotta Pa Brakmakargatan 2.00 .25
*a.* Bklt. pane, 2 ea #1631-1640 40.00
*Nos. 1631-1640 (10)* 20.00 2.50

See note after No. 1277.

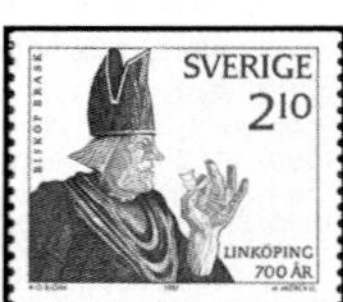


Medieval Towns — A503

#1641, Hans Brask, Bishop of Linkoping, 16th cent. #1642, Nykopingshus Castle.

**1987, May 14 Engr. *Perf. 12½ Vert.***

**1641** A503 2.10k blk, dk vio & yel bis .85 .55
**1642** A503 2.10k dk vio, blk & yel bis .85 .55
*a.* Pair, #1641-1642 1.75 *2.00*

Swedes in the Service of Mankind A504

Designs: No. 1643, Raoul Wallenberg, Swedish diplomat in Budapest during World War II. No. 1644, Dag Hammarskjold (1905-1961), UN secretary-general. No. 1645, Folke Bernadotte af Wisborg (1895-1948), organizer of the Red Cross operation that saved thousands from Nazi death camps.

***Perf. 12½ Horiz.***

**1987, Aug. 10 Engr.**

**1643** A504 3.10k blue 1.40 1.10
**1644** A504 3.10k green 1.40 1.10
**1645** A504 3.10k brown violet 1.40 1.10
*a.* Bklt. pane, 2 each #1643-1645 8.50
*Nos. 1643-1645 (3)* 4.20 3.30

Gripsholm Castle, 450th Anniv. — A505

Paintings from the Royal Castle Collection, Gripsholm: No. 1646, King Gustav I Vasa (d. 1560), artist unknown. No. 1647, Blue Tiger, 1673, favorite horse of King Charles XI, by D.K. Ehrenstrahl. No. 1648, Hedvig Charlotta Nordenflycht (1718-1763), poet, by Kopia J.H. Scheffel. No. 1649, Gripsholm Castle Outer Courtyard, 17th Cent., 19th cent. lithograph by C.J. Billmark.

**1987, Aug. 10 *Perf. 13 Vert.***

**1646** A505 2.10k multi .85 .40
**1647** A505 2.10k multi .85 .40
**1648** A505 2.10k multi .85 .40
**1649** A505 2.10k multi .85 .40
*a.* Bklt. pane of 8, 2 strips of #1646-1649 with gutter btwn. 7.00
*Nos. 1646-1649 (4)* 3.40 1.60

Botanical Gardens A506

Designs: No. 1650, Victoria cruziana (water lily), Victoria House, Bergian Garden, c. 1790, Stockholm University. No. 1651, Layout of baroque palace garden, by Carl Harleman (1700-1753), Uppsala University. No. 1652, White anemones, rock garden, Gothenberg Botanical Gardens, 1923. No. 1653, Tulip tree blossoms, Academy Garden, c. 1860, Lund University.

**1987, Oct. 10 Engr. *Perf. 13 Vert.***

**1650** A506 2.10k multi .85 .55
**1651** A506 2.10k multi .85 .55
**1652** A506 2.10k multi .85 .55
**1653** A506 2.10k multi .85 .55
*a.* Bklt. pane, 2 each #1650-1653 with gutter between 7.00
*Nos. 1650-1653 (4)* 3.40 2.20

The Circus in Sweden, Bicent. — A507

**Litho. & Engr.**

**1987, Oct. 10 *Perf. 13***

**1654** A507 2.10k Juggler, clown .95 *.95*
**1655** A507 2.10k High wire .95 *.95*
**1656** A507 2.10k Equestrian .95 *.95*
*a.* Bklt. pane of 3, #1654-1656 3.00 *4.00*

Stamp Day. Sold for 8k.

Christmas A508

Customs: No. 1657, Putting porridge in the stable for the gray Christmas elf. No. 1658, Watering horses at a north-running stream on Boxing Day. No. 1659, Sled-race home from church on Christmas Day. No. 1660, Hanging out sheaves of wheat to foretell a good harvest.

***Perf. 13 on 3 Sides***

**1987, Nov. 25 Litho.**

**1657** A508 2k multi .75 .30
**1658** A508 2k multi .75 .30
**1659** A508 2k multi .75 .30
**1660** A508 2k multi .75 .30
*a.* Bklt. pane, 3 each #1657-1660 9.50
*Nos. 1657-1660 (4)* 3.00 1.20

Nobel Prize Winners in Physics A509

Space and diagram or formula: No. 1661, Antony Hewish, Great Britain, 1974. No. 1662, Subrahmanyan Chandrasekhar, US, 1983. No. 1663, William Fowler, US, 1983. No. 1664, Arno Penzias and Robert Wilson, US, 1978. No. 1665, Martin Ryle, Great Britain, 1974.

**1987, Nov. 25 Engr. *Perf. 13***

**1661** A509 2.90k dark blue 1.25 1.25
**1662** A509 2.90k blk 1.25 1.25
**1663** A509 2.90k dark blue 1.25 1.25
**1664** A509 2.90k dark blue 1.25 1.25
**1665** A509 2.90k blk 1.25 1.25
*a.* Bklt. pane of 5, #1661-1665 7.50 *9.00*

Inland Boats A510

**1988, Jan. 29 Engr. *Perf. 13***

**1666** A510 3.10k Skiff, Lake Hjalmaren 1.25 1.25
**1667** A510 3.10k Village boat, Lake Vattern 1.25 1.25
**1668** A510 3.10k Rowboat, Byske 1.25 1.25
**1669** A510 3.10k Flat-bottomed rowboat, Asnen 1.25 1.25
**1670** A510 3.10k Ice boat, Lake Vanern 1.25 1.25
**1671** A510 3.10k Church boat, Lake Locknesjon 1.25 1.25
*a.* Bklt. pane of 6, #1666-1671 8.00 *8.75*

A511

A512

Settling of New Sweden, 350th Anniv. — A513

Designs: No. 1672, 17th Cent. European settlers negotiating with American Indians, map of New Sweden, the Swedish ships *Kalmar Nyckel* and *Fogel Grip*, based on an 18th cent. illustration from a Swedish book about the American Colonies. No. 1673, Bishop Hill and painter Olof Krans. No. 1674, Carl Sandburg (1878-1967), author, and Jenny Lind (1820-1867), opera singer known as the "Swedish Nightingale." No. 1675, Charles Lindbergh (1902-1974), and *The Spirit of St. Louis.* No. 1676, American astronaut with Swedish Hasselblad camera on the Moon. No. 1677, Swedish players in National Hockey League.

**Litho. & Engr., Engr. (#1674-1675)**

**1988, Mar. 29 *Perf. 13x12½ Horiz***

**1672** A511 3.60k multi 1.30 1.10
**1673** A511 3.60k multi 1.30 1.10

***Perf. 13x12½ on 3 Sides***

**1674** A512 3.60k brn 1.30 1.20
**1675** A512 3.60k dk bl & brn 1.30 1.20

***Perf. 13x12½ on 2***

**1676** A513 3.60k dk bl & yel 1.30 1.30
**1677** A513 3.60k dk red, dk bl & blk 1.30 1.30
*a.* Bklt. pane of 6, #1672-1677 8.00 *10.50*

See US No. C117 and Finland No. 768.

**Conservation Type of 1983**

Species Inhabiting Coastal Waters

*Perf. 13 on 3 Sides*

**1988, Mar. 29** **Engr.**

**1678** A447 2.20k Haliaetus albicilla .75 .30
**1679** A447 2.20k Halichoerus grypus .75 .30
*a.* Bklt. pane, 5 #1678, 5 #1679 8.00

*Perf. 13 Horiz.*

**1680** A446 4.40k Anguilla anguilla 2.10 .35
*Nos. 1678-1680 (3)* 3.60 .95

Midsummer Celebration A515

Skara Township Millennium A516

*Perf. 12½ on 3 Sides*

**1988, May 17** **Litho. & Engr.**

**1681** A515 2k Wildflowers in meadow 1.80 .25
**1682** A515 2k Rowing 1.80 .25
**1683** A515 2k Children making wreaths 1.80 .25
**1684** A515 2k Raising maypole 1.80 .25
**1685** A515 2k Fiddlers 1.80 .25
**1686** A515 2k Ferry 1.80 .25
**1687** A515 2k Dancing 1.80 .25
**1688** A515 2k Accordion player 1.80 .25
**1689** A515 2k Maypole, residence 1.80 .25
**1690** A515 2k Bouquet of flowers 1.80 .25
*a.* Bklt. pane, 2 ea #1681-1690 36.00
*Nos. 1681-1690 (10)* 18.00 2.50

See note after No. 1277.

**1988, May 17** ***Perf. 13 Horiz.***

Design: Detail from Creation, a Skara Cathedral stained-glass window by Bo Beskow, 20th cent.

**1691** A516 2.20k multi .90 .40

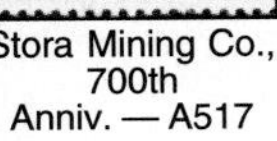

Stora Mining Co., 700th Anniv. — A517

Royal Dramatic Theater, Stockholm, Founded by King Gustav III in 1788 — A518

**1988, May 17** **Engr.**

**1692** A517 4.40k Mine, 18th cent. 1.65 .85

**1988, May 17**

Design: Scene fron *The Queen's Diamond Ornament,* about the murder of King Gustav III at the Royal Opera in 1792.

**1693** A518 8k grn, red & blk 3.00 1.60

Self-portrait, 1923, by Nils Dardel (1888-1943) A519

Paintings: No. 1695, *Old Age Home in Autumn,* c. 1930, by Vera Nilsson (1888-1979). No. 1696, *Self-portrait,* 1912, by Isaac Grunewald (1899-1979). No. 1697, *Visit of an Eccentric Lady,* 1921, by Dardel. No. 1698, *Soap Bubbles,* 1927, by Nilsson. No. 1699, *The Fair,* 1915, by Grunewald.

*Perf. 13 on 3 Sides*

**1988, Aug. 25** **Litho. & Engr.**

**Size: 33x35mm (Nos. 1695, 1698)**

**1694** A519 2.20k shown .95 .90
**1695** A519 2.20k multi .95 .90
**1696** A519 2.20k multi .95 .90
**1697** A519 2.20k multi .95 .90
**1698** A519 2.20k multi .95 .90
**1699** A519 2.20k multi .95 .90
*a.* Bklt. pane of 6, #1694-1699 5.75 *7.50*

Europa — A520

Transport and communication.

**1988, Aug. 25** **Engr.** ***Perf. 13 Vert.***

**1700** A520 2.20k like No. 1701 2.75 .65

*Perf. 13 on 3 Sides*

**1701** A520 3.10k X2 high-speed train 1.25 1.10
**1702** A520 3.10k Steam locomotive, 1887 1.25 1.10
*a.* Bklt. pane, 3 each #1701-1702 7.50
*Nos. 1700-1702 (3)* 5.25 2.85

Common Swift — A521

**1988, Aug. 25** ***Perf. 12½ Vert.***

**1703** A521 20k brt vio & dk vio 6.50 .35

Dan Andersson (1888-1920), Poet, and Manuscript A522

Forest and Pond, Finnmarken — A523

**1988, Oct. 8** **Engr.** ***Perf. 13 Vert.***

**1704** A522 2.20k vio, dk bl & dk bl grn .90 .45
**1705** A523 2.20k vio, dk bl & dk bl grn .90 .45
*a.* Pair, #1704-1705 1.90 1.50

Soccer — A524

Match scenes: No. 1706, Dribble (Torbjorn Nilsson representing local club matches). No. 1707, Heading the ball (Ralf Edstrom of the national league). No. 1708, Kick (Pia Sundhage, women's soccer).

**1988, Oct. 8** **Litho. & Engr.** ***Perf. 13***

**1706** A524 2.20k multi 1.25 1.00
**1707** A524 2.20k multi 1.25 1.00
**1708** A524 2.20k multi 1.25 1.00
*a.* Bklt. pane of 3, #1706-1708 3.75 4.25

No. 1708a sold for 8.50k; surtax benefited stamp collecting.

Nobel Laureates in Chemistry A525

Christmas A526

Designs: No. 1709, Willard F. Libby, US, 1960, carbon-14 method of dating artifacts. No. 1710, Karl Ziegler, West Germany, and Guilio Natta, Italy, 1963, catalysts. No. 1711, Aaron Klug, South Africa, 1982, electron microscopy. No. 1712, Ilya Prigogine, Belgium, 1977, proof that molecular order can occur spontaneously out of chaos.

**1988, Nov. 29** ***Perf. 12½ Vert.***

**1709** A525 3.10k multi 1.25 1.10
**1710** A525 3.10k multi 1.25 1.10
**1711** A525 3.10k multi 1.25 1.10
**1712** A525 3.10k multi 1.25 1.10
*a.* Bklt. pane, 2 each #1709-1712 10.00
*Nos. 1709-1712 (4)* 5.00 4.40

*Perf. 12½x13 on 3 Sides*

**1988, Nov. 29**

Story of Christ's birth according to Luke (2:7-20): No. 1713, Angels appear to inform shepherds of Christ's birth. No. 1714, Star of Bethlehem, angel, horse. No. 1715, Birds singing. No. 1716, Magi offering gifts. No. 1717, Holy family. No. 1718, Shepherds with palm offering.

**1713** A526 2k multi .75 .55
**1714** A526 2k multi .75 .55
**1715** A526 2k multi .75 .55
**1716** A526 2k multi .75 .55
**1717** A526 2k multi .75 .55
**1718** A526 2k multi .75 .55
*a.* Bklt. pane, 2 each #1713-1718 9.00
*Nos. 1713-1718 (6)* 4.50 3.30

Nos. 1713 and 1716, 1714 and 1717, 1715 and 1718 have continuous designs.

Lighthouses A527

Designs: 1.90k, Twin masonry lighthouses, 1832, and concrete lighthouse, 1946, Nidingen, Kattegat Is. 2.70k, Soderarm, Uppland, 1839. 3.80k, Sydostbrotten, Gulf of Bothnia, 1963. 3.90k, Sandhammaren, Skane, c. 1860.

**1989, Jan. 31** **Engr.** ***Perf. 13 Vert.***

**1719** A527 1.90k multi .85 .35
**1720** A527 2.70k multi 1.25 .85
**1721** A527 3.80k multi 1.60 .75
**1722** A527 3.90k multi 1.75 .85
*Nos. 1719-1722 (4)* 5.45 2.80

Endangered Species — A528

**1989, Jan. 31** ***Perf. 13 on 3 Sides***

**1723** A528 2.30k *Gulo gulo* .85 .25
**1724** A528 2.30k *Strix uralensis* .85 .25
*a.* Bklt. pane, 5 each #1723-1724 8.50

*Perf. 13 Horiz.*

**1725** A528 2.40k *Dendrocopos minor* .90 .25
**1726** A528 2.60k *Calidris alpina schinzii* 1.25 .85
**1727** A528 3.30k *Hyla arborea* 1.40 1.10
**1728** A528 4.60k *Ficedula parva* 2.25 .50
*Nos. 1723-1728 (6)* 7.50 3.20

Opening of The Globe Arena, Stockholm — A529

*Perf. 13 Horiz.*

**1989, Apr. 14** **Litho. & Engr.**

**1729** A529 2.30k Exterior .95 .55
**1730** A529 2.30k Ice hockey .95 .55
**1731** A529 2.30k Gymnastics .95 .55
**1732** A529 2.30k Concert .95 .55
*a.* Bklt. pane of 4, #1729-1732 4.00

Nordic Cooperation Issue — A530

Folk costumes.

*Perf. 13 Horiz.*

**1989, Apr. 20** **Litho. & Engr.**

**1733** A530 2.30k Woman's wool waist 1.10 .40
**1734** A530 3.30k Belt pouch 1.60 .80

Natl. Labor Movement, Cent. — A531

**1989, May 17** **Engr.** ***Perf. 13 Horiz.***

**1735** A531 2.30k dk red & blk 1.10 .45

Europa 1989 — A532

Children's games: 2.30k, No. 1738, Sailing toy boats. No. 1737, Kick-sledding.

**1989, May 17** ***Perf. 13 Vert.***

**1736** A532 2.30k car lake 3.25 .45

*Perf. 13*

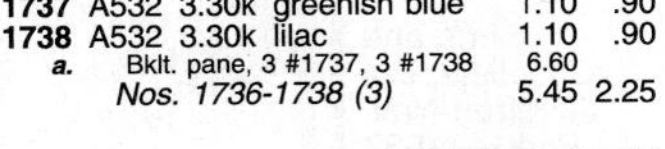

**1737** A532 3.30k greenish blue 1.10 .90
**1738** A532 3.30k lilac 1.10 .90
*a.* Bklt. pane, 3 #1737, 3 #1738 6.60
*Nos. 1736-1738 (3)* 5.45 2.25

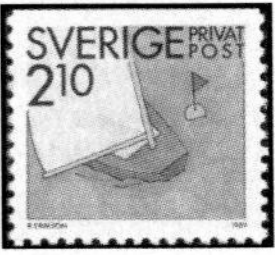

Summer — A533

*Perf. 13 on 3 Sides*

**1989, May 17** **Litho.**

**1739** A533 2.10k Sailing 1.90 .35
**1740** A533 2.10k Beach ball 1.90 .35
**1741** A533 2.10k Cycling 1.90 .35
**1742** A533 2.10k Canoeing 1.90 .35
**1743** A533 2.10k Angling 1.90 .35
**1744** A533 2.10k Camping 1.90 .35
**1745** A533 2.10k Croquet 1.90 .35
**1746** A533 2.10k Badminton 1.90 .35
**1747** A533 2.10k Gardening 1.90 .35
**1748** A533 2.10k Sand sculpture 1.90 .35
*a.* Bklt. pane, 2 ea #1739-1748 38.00
*Nos. 1739-1748 (10)* 19.00 3.50

See note after No. 1277.

Polar Exploration
A534

Swedish polar techniques used in the Arctic (Nos. 1749-1751) and Antarctic: No. 1749, Aircraft, temperature experiment. No. 1750, Settlement, Arctic pass. No. 1751, Icebreaker, experiment. No. 1752, Penguins, tall ship and longboat. No. 1753, Antarctic transports, helicopter. No. 1754, Surveying, albatross.

***Perf. 13 on 3 Sides***

**1989, Aug. 22 Litho. & Engr.**

**Size: 40x43mm (Nos. 1750, 1753)**

**1749** A534 3.30k multi 1.40 1.25
**1750** A534 3.30k multi 1.40 1.25
**1751** A534 3.30k multi 1.40 1.25
**1752** A534 3.30k multi 1.40 1.25
**1753** A534 3.30k multi 1.40 1.25
**1754** A534 3.30k multi 1.40 1.25
*a.* Bklt. pane of 6, #1749-1754 8.50 *11.00*

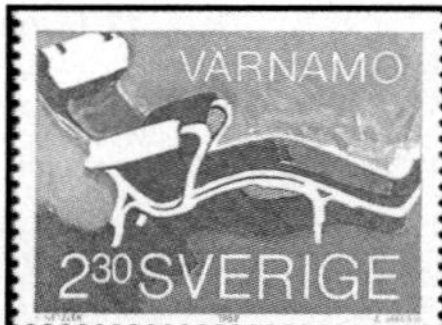

Smaland Businesses A535

***Perf. 12½x12 on 3 Sides***

**1989, Aug. 22 Engr.**

**1755** A535 2.30k Furniture 1.15 .85
**1756** A535 2.30k Assembly equipment 1.15 .85
**1757** A535 2.30k Sewing machines 1.15 .85
**1758** A535 2.30k Glassware 1.15 .85
**1759** A535 2.30k Metal springs 1.15 .85
**1760** A535 2.30k Matchsticks 1.15 .85
*a.* Bklt. pane of 6, #1755-1760 7.50 *9.00*

Eagle Owl, *Bubo bubo* A536

**1989, Aug. 22** ***Perf. 13 Vert.***

**1761** A536 30k vio, blk & grn blk 8.25 .40

**Conservation Type of 1983 and**

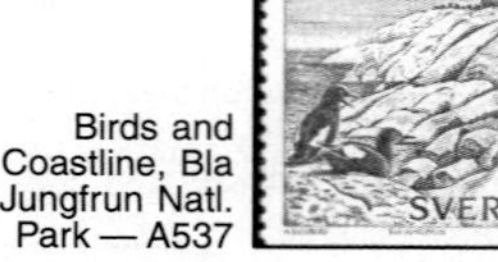

Birds and Coastline, Bla Jungfrun Natl. Park — A537

***Perf. 13x12½ on 3 Sides***

**1989, Sept. 12 Engr.**

**1762** A447 2.40k *Rhododendron lapponicum* .90 .25
**1763** A447 2.40k *Calypso bulbosa* .90 .25
*a.* Bklt. pane, 5 ea #1762-1763 9.00

***Perf. 12½ Vert.***

**1764** A537 4.30k dark blue, blk & brn vio 2.10 1.10
*Nos. 1762-1764 (3)* 3.90 1.60

See Nos. 1776-1780.

Swedish Kennel Club, Cent. — A538

a, Large spitz. b, Fox hound. c, Small spitz.

**1989, Oct. 7 Litho.** ***Perf. 13x12½***

**1765** A538 Bklt. pane of 3 3.50 *4.50*
*a.-c.* 2.40k any single 1.10 1.00

Sold for 9.50k.

Christmas — A539

Holiday symbols: No. 1766, Top of Christmas tree, wreath. No. 1767, Candelabrum, foods. No. 1768, Star, poinsettia plant, grot pot. No. 1769, Bottom of tree, straw goat, gifts. No. 1770, Gifts, television, girl. No. 1771, Boy, grandfather, girl opening gift.

***Perf. 12½x13 on 3 Sides***

**1989, Nov. 24 Litho.**

**1766** A539 2.10k multi .85 .50
**1767** A539 2.10k multi .85 .50
**1768** A539 2.10k multi .85 .50
**1769** A539 2.10k multi .85 .50
**1770** A539 2.10k multi .85 .50
**1771** A539 2.10k multi .85 .50
*a.* Bklt. pane, 2 each #1766-1771 10.50
*Nos. 1766-1771 (6)* 5.10 3.00

Nobel Laureates in Physiology A540

Genetics: No. 1772, Thomas Morgan (1866-1945), US, 1933, chromosomal study of fruit flies to determine laws and mechanism of heredity. No. 1773, James Watson, US, and Francis Crick with Maurice Wilkins, Great Britain, 1962, molecular structure of DNA. No. 1774, Werner Arber, Switzerland, Daniel Nathans and Hamilton Smith, US, 1978, enzymatic cutting of nucleotides to create gene hybrids. No. 1775, Barbara McClintock, botanist, US, 1983, corn color studies that led to theory of gene jumping.

***Perf. 12½ Vert.***

**1989, Nov. 24 Litho. & Engr.**

**1772** A540 3.60k multi 1.50 1.10
**1773** A540 3.60k multi 1.50 1.10
**1774** A540 3.60k multi 1.50 1.10
**1775** A540 3.60k multi 1.50 1.10
*a.* Bklt. pane, 2 each #1772-1775 with gutter between 12.00
*Nos. 1772-1775 (4)* 6.00 4.40

**Natl. Parks Type of 1989**

Designs: No. 1776, Campground, sailboat on lake, Angso Park. No. 1777, Hiking, Pieljekaise Park. 3.70k, Three whooper swans over wetlands, Muddus Park. 4.10k, Deer, lake, Padjelanta Park. 4.80k, Bears, forest, Sanfjallet Park.

***Perf. 13 on 3 Sides***

**1990, Jan. 26 Engr.**

**1776** A537 2.50k multicolored .95 .20
**1777** A537 2.50k multicolored .95 .20
*a.* Bklt. pane, 5 each #1776-1777 9.50

***Perf. 13 Vert.***

**1778** A537 3.70k multicolored 1.50 .30
**1779** A537 4.10k multicolored 2.10 1.30
**1780** A537 4.80k multicolored 2.10 1.25
*Nos. 1776-1780 (5)* 7.60 3.25

**King and Queen Types of 1985-86 and**

Queen Silvia — A541

King Carl XVI Gustaf — A542

King Carl XVI Gustav A543

Queen Silvia A544

King Carl XVI Gustaf — A545

***Perf. 12½ Vert., Horiz. (A541, A542, A545)***

**1990-97 Engr.**

**1783** A436c 2.50k deep claret 1.00 .20
**1784** A542 2.80k dk blue 1.10 .20
**1785** A542 2.90k deep green 1.30 .25
**1786** A542 3.20k violet 1.50 .20
**1787** A543 3.70k dark red brown 1.50 .20
**1788** A543 3.85k black 1.75 .30
**1789** A436d 4.60k bright org 1.75 1.50
**1790** A541 5k deep rose vio 2.00 .40
**1791** A545 (5k) deep blue 2.10 .30
**1792** A541 6k deep claret 2.25 .60
**1793** A544 6k dark green 2.75 .95
**1794** A541 6.50k purple 3.50 1.25
**1795** A544 7.50k purple 3.10 1.65
**1796** A544 8k brown red 3.10 1.00
*Nos. 1783-1796 (14)* 28.70 9.00

Issued: 2.50k, 4.60k, 1/26; 5k, 3/20/91; 2.80k, 11/20/91; 2.90k, #1792, 1/2/93; 3.20k, 1/17/94; 6.50k, 3/18/94; 3.70k, #1793, 1/2/95; 3.85k, 7.50k, 1/2/96; (5k), 8k, 2/28/97.

No. 1791 is inscribed "BREV."

Viking Heritage A546

Designs: No. 1801, Viking head of carved bone, dragon carving from a molding found in Birka. No. 1802, Three viking longships. No. 1803, Viking town. No. 1804, Bronze statue of pagan fertility god, silver filigree cross. No. 1805, Bishop's crosier, southern Russian carved statue of a deer. No. 1806, Viking longship (stern). No. 1807, Viking longship (bow), horsemen, woman, warrior, wolf. No. 1808, Sword hilts.

***Perf. 12x13 on 3 Sides***

**1990, Mar. 28 Litho. & Engr.**

**1801** A546 2.50k multicolored 1.10 .85
**1802** A546 2.50k multicolored 1.10 .85
**1803** A546 2.50k multicolored 1.10 .85
**1804** A546 2.50k multicolored 1.10 .85
**1805** A546 2.50k multicolored 1.10 .85
**1806** A546 2.50k multicolored 1.10 .85
**1807** A546 2.50k multicolored 1.10 .85
**1808** A546 2.50k multicolored 1.10 .85
*a.* Bklt. pane of 8, #1801-1808 9.00 *10.00*

Nos. 1802-1803, 1806-1807 printed in a continuous design.

Swedish Industrial Safety, Cent. — A547

**1990, Mar. 28 Engr.** ***Perf. 13 Horiz.***

**1809** A547 2.50k Lumberjack 1.10 .30

Europa 1990 — A548

Post offices.

**1990, Mar. 28** ***Perf. 13 Vert.***

**1810** A548 2.50k Postal Museum, 1720 3.25 .45

***Perf. 13 on 3 Sides***

**1811** A548 3.80k Sollebrunn, 1985 1.50 1.10
**1812** A548 3.80k Vasteras, 1956 1.50 1.10
*a.* Bklt. pane, 3 each #1811-1812 9.00
*Nos. 1810-1812 (3)* 6.25 2.65

World Equestrian Games, Stockholm A549

**Litho. & Engr.**

**1990, May 15** ***Perf. 12½x13***

**1813** A549 3.80k Endurance riding 1.60 1.40
**1814** A549 3.80k Combined training 1.60 1.40
**1815** A549 3.80k Show jumping 1.60 1.40
**1816** A549 3.80k Dressage 1.60 1.40
**1817** A549 3.80k Volting 1.60 1.40
**1818** A549 3.80k Four-in-hand 1.60 1.40
*a.* Bklt. pane of 6, #1813-1818 10.00 *11.50*

Apiculture — A550

#1819, Worker bee collecting nectar. #1820, Bee, bilberry flower. #1821, Worker bee. #1822, Apiary hive. #1823, Two bees in honeycomb. #1824, Drone, 7 cells, blue green panel. #1825, Queen bee, 7 cells, yellow panel. #1826, Swarm hanging from tree. #1827, Beekeeper. #1828, Honey.

**1990, May 15 Litho.**

**1819** A550 2.30k multicolored 1.80 .40
**1820** A550 2.30k multicolored 1.80 .40
**1821** A550 2.30k multicolored 1.80 .40
**1822** A550 2.30k multicolored 1.80 .40
**1823** A550 2.30k multicolored 1.80 .40
**1824** A550 2.30k multicolored 1.80 .40
**1825** A550 2.30k multicolored 1.80 .40
**1826** A550 2.30k multicolored 1.80 .40
**1827** A550 2.30k multicolored 1.80 .40
**1828** A550 2.30k multicolored 1.80 .40
*a.* Bklt. pane, 2 ea #1819-1828 36.00
*Nos. 1819-1828 (10)* 18.00 4.00

See note after No. 1277.

Wasa Nautical Museum — A551

Man-of-war *Wasa:* 2.50k, Bow. 4.60k, Stern.

**1990, May 15 Engr.** ***Perf. 13 Vert.***

**1829** A551 2.50k org & blk 1.10 .45
**1830** A551 4.60k dk bl & org 2.00 1.25

Dearest Brothers, Sisters and Friends — A552

Proud City A553

Allusions to poetry verses of Carl Michael Bellman (No. 1833) and Evert Taube: No. 1833, Fredmen in the gutter. No. 1834, Happy baker in San Remo. No. 1835, At sea. No. 1836, Violava.

***Perf. 13 on 3 Sides***

**1990, Aug. 8** **Litho. & Engr.**

**1831** A552 2.50k multicolored 1.75 1.20
**1832** A553 2.50k multicolored 1.75 1.20
**1833** A552 2.50k multicolored 1.75 1.20
**1834** A552 2.50k multicolored 1.75 1.20
**1835** A553 2.50k multicolored 1.75 1.20
**1836** A552 2.50k multicolored 1.75 1.20
*a.* Bklt. pane of 6, #1831-1836 7.50 *11.00*

Paper Production A554

#1837, Paper production c. 1600. #1838, Watermark. #1839, Newspaper mastheads. #1840, Modern paper production.

**1990, Aug. 8** ***Perf. 12½ Vert.***

**1837** A554 2.50k multicolored 1.10 .45
**1838** A554 2.50k multicolored 1.10 .45
**1839** A554 2.50k multicolored 1.10 .45
**1840** A554 2.50k multicolored 1.10 .45
*a.* Bklt. pane, 2 each #1837-1840 with gutter between 9.00
*Nos. 1837-1840 (4)* 4.40 1.80

Ovedskloster Palace — A555

**1990, Aug. 8** **Engr.** ***Perf. 13 Vert.***

**1841** A555 40k multicolored 11.00 .30

See Nos. 1874-1877.

Photography A556

**Litho. & Engr.**

**1990, Oct. 6** ***Perf. 12½***

**1842** A556 2.50k Bellows camera 1.10 1.25
**1843** A556 2.50k August Strindberg 1.10 1.25
**1844** A556 2.50k 35mm camera 1.10 1.25
*a.* Bklt. pane of 3, #1842-1844 3.30 *5.00*

Stamp Day. Booklet of two panes sold for 20k. Surtax benefited stamp collecting.

Clouds — A557

A558

**1990, Oct. 6** **Engr.** ***Perf. 12½ Horiz.***

**1845** A557 4.50k Cumulus 2.00 .45
**1846** A557 4.70k Cumulonimbus 2.25 1.25
**1847** A557 4.90k Cirrus 2.50 1.25
**1848** A557 5.20k Alto cumulus 2.75 1.50
*Nos. 1845-1848 (4)* 9.50 4.45

**1990, Oct. 6** ***Perf. 12½ Vert.***

**1849** A558 2.50k shown 1.20 .50
**1850** A558 2.50k Women bathing 1.20 .50
*a.* Pair, #1849-1850 2.50 2.25

Moa Martinson (1890-1964), author.

Nobel Laureates in Literature — A559

***Perf. 13 on 2 Sides***

**1990, Nov. 27** **Engr.**

**1851** A559 3.80k Par Lagerkvist, 1951 1.50 1.40
**1852** A559 3.80k Ernest Hemingway, 1954 1.50 1.40
**1853** A559 3.80k Albert Camus, 1957 1.50 1.40
**1854** A559 3.80k Boris Pasternak, 1958 1.50 1.40
*a.* Bklt. pane, 2 each #1851-1854 with gutter between 13.00
*Nos. 1851-1854 (4)* 6.00 5.60

See Nos. 1914-1917.

Christmas — A560

Flowers.

***Perf. 13 on 3 Sides***

**1990, Nov. 27** **Litho.**

**1855** A560 2.30k Schlumbergera x buckleyi 1.00 .55
**1856** A560 2.30k Helleborus niger 1.00 .55
**1857** A560 2.30k Rhododendron simsii 1.00 .55
**1858** A560 2.30k Hippeastrum x hortorum 1.00 .55
**1859** A560 2.30k Hyacinthus orientalis 1.00 .55
**1860** A560 2.30k Euphorbia pulcherrima 1.00 .55
*a.* Bklt. pane, 2 each #1855-1860 12.00
*Nos. 1855-1860 (6)* 6.00 3.30

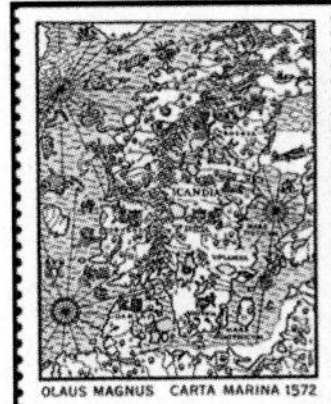

Carta Marina by Olaus Magnus, 1572 — A561

Scandanavia by A. Bureas and J. Blaeus, 1662 — A562

Maps: No. 1863, Celestial globe by Anders Akerman, 1759. No. 1864, Contour map, 1938. No. 1865, Stockholm, 1989. No. 1866, Bedrock Map, Geological Survey, 1984.

***Perf. 13 on 3 Sides***

**1991, Jan. 30** **Litho. & Engr.**

**1861** A561 5k multicolored 2.40 1.60
**1862** A562 5k multicolored 2.40 1.60
**1863** A561 5k multicolored 2.40 1.60
**1864** A561 5k multicolored 2.40 1.60
**1865** A562 5k multicolored 2.40 1.60
**1866** A561 5k multicolored 2.40 1.60
*a.* Bklt. pane of 6, #1861-1866 15.00 *18.00*

Fish — A563 A564

***Perf. 13 on 3 Sides***

**1991, Jan. 30** **Engr.**

**1867** A563 2.50k shown 1.00 .25
**1868** A563 2.50k Siluris glanis, diff. 1.00 .25
*b.* Bklt. pane, 5 each #1867-1868 10.00

***Perf. 13 Vert.***

**1869** A563 5k Cobitis taenia 1.75 .20
**1870** A563 5.40k Gobio gobio 2.50 2.50
**1871** A563 5.50k Noemacheilus barbatulus 2.40 .25
**1872** A563 5.60k Leucaspius delineatus 2.40 1.40
*Nos. 1867-1872 (6)* 11.05 4.85

Palace Type of 1990

Designs: 10k, Stromsholm Castle. 20k, Karlberg Castle. 25k, Drottningholm Palace.

**1991-92** **Engr.** ***Perf. 13 Vert.***

**1874** A555 10k blk & olive brn 4.00 .25
**1876** A555 20k multicolored 6.50 .75

**Size: 58x23mm**

**1877** A555 25k multicolored 7.00 .75
*Nos. 1874-1877 (3)* 17.50 1.75

Issued: 10k, 4/27; 25k, 3/20; 20k, 5/21/92.

***Perf. 12½x13 on 3 Sides***

**1991, May 15** **Litho.**

**1883** A564 2.40k Seglora church .95 .25
**1884** A564 2.40k Flag above park .95 .25
**1885** A564 2.40k Wedding .95 .25
**1886** A564 2.40k Animals .95 .25
*b.* Bklt. pane, 5 ea #1883-1886 19.00
*Nos. 1883-1886 (4)* 3.80 1.00

Skansen Park, Stockholm, 100th anniv.

See note after No. 1277. Complete booklet of 20 stamps sold for 46k.

Kolmarden Zoological Park, Ostergotland A565

***Perf. 12½ Horiz.***

**1991, May 15** **Engr.**

**1887** A565 2.50k Polar bears 1.10 .25
**1888** A565 4k Dolphin show 1.75 1.10

Norden '91.

A566

Public Parks, cent.: #1890, Dancing in park.

**1991, May 15** ***Perf. 13 Vert.***

**1889** A566 2.50k dark blue 1.10 .50
**1890** A566 2.50k dark blue 1.10 .50
*a.* Pair, #1889-1890 2.25 2.25

Europa — A567

**Litho. & Engr.**

**1991, May 15** ***Perf. 13***

**1891** A567 4k Hermes space plane 2.00 1.75
**1892** A567 4k Freja satellite 2.00 1.75
**1893** A567 4k Tele-X satellite 2.00 1.75
*a.* Bklt. pane of 3, #1891-1893 7.00 *8.50*

Olympic Champions A568

Designs: No. 1894, Magda Julin, figure skating, Antwerp, 1920. No. 1895, Toini Gustaffson, cross country skiing, Grenoble, 1968. No. 1896, Agneta Andersson, Anna Olsson, two-person kayak, Los Angeles, 1984. No. 1897, Ulrika Knape, diving, Munich, 1972.

***Perf. 12x13 on 3 Sides***

**1991, Aug. 27** **Litho. & Engr.**

**1894** A568 2.50k multicolored 1.10 .70
**1895** A568 2.50k multicolored 1.10 .70
**1896** A568 2.50k multicolored 1.10 .70
**1897** A568 2.50k multicolored 1.10 .70
*a.* Bklt. pane, 2 each #1894-1897 9.00
*Nos. 1894-1897 (4)* 4.40 2.80

See Nos. 1937-1940, 1953-1956.

Iron Mining — A569

#1898, Spetal Mine, Norberg. #1899, Forsmark Mill. #1900, Ironworks forge. #1901, Forge welding. #1902, Dannemora Mine. #1903, Blast furnace, Pershyttan.

***Perf. 13 on 2 or 3 Sides***

**1991, Aug. 27** **Engr.**

**1898** A569 2.50k multicolored 1.25 .85
**1899** A569 2.50k multicolored 1.25 .85

**Size: 31x26mm**

**1900** A569 2.50k multicolored 1.25 *1.10*
**1901** A569 2.50k multicolored 1.25 *1.10*

**Size: 31x40mm**

**1902** A569 2.50k multicolored 1.25 *1.10*
**1903** A569 2.50k multicolored 1.25 *1.10*
*a.* Bklt. pane of 6, #1898-1903 7.50 6.75

Coronation of King Gustavus III, by Carl Gustaf Pilo — A570

Details from painting: No. 1904, King Gustavus III. No. 1905, Gustavus with crown held above head. No. 1906, Chancellor Arvid Horn, Archbishop Mattias Beronius holding crown above Gustavus III.

**1991, Oct. 5 Engr. *Perf. 13***

| | | | | |
|---|---|---|---|---|
| **1904** | A570 10k blue | | 4.00 | 3.50 |
| **1905** | A570 10k violet | | 4.00 | 3.50 |

**Size: 76x44mm**

| | | | |
|---|---|---|---|
| **1906** | A570 10k greenish black | 5.00 | 5.00 |
| *a.* | Bklt. pane of 3, #1904-1906 | 13.00 | 13.00 |

Czeslaw Slania, engraver, 70th birthday. No. 1906a sold for 35k to benefit stamp collecting.

Rock Musicians A571

**1991, Oct. 5 Litho. & Engr.**

| | | | |
|---|---|---|---|
| **1907** | A571 2.50k Lena Philipsson | 1.75 | .85 |
| **1908** | A571 2.50k Roxette | 1.75 | .85 |
| **1909** | A571 2.50k Jerry Williams | 1.75 | .85 |
| *a.* | Bklt. pane of 3, #1907-1909 | 7.50 | *4.25* |

A572

A573

Christmas: No. 1910, Boy with star, girl with snacks. No. 1911, Family dancing around Christmas tree. No. 1912, Cat beside tree. No. 1913, Child beside bed.

***Perf. 12½x13 on 3 Sides***

**1991, Nov. 20 Litho.**

| | | | |
|---|---|---|---|
| **1910** | A572 2.30k multicolored | .95 | .45 |
| **1911** | A572 2.30k multicolored | .95 | .45 |
| **1912** | A572 2.30k multicolored | .95 | .45 |
| **1913** | A572 2.30k multicolored | .95 | .45 |
| *b.* | Bklt. pane, 3 ea #1910-1913 | 12.00 | |
| | *Nos. 1910-1913 (4)* | 3.80 | 1.80 |

### Nobel Laureates Type of 1990

Nobel Peace Prize Winners: No. 1914, Jean Henri Dunant, founder of Red Cross. No. 1915, Albert Schweitzer, physician and theologian. No. 1916, Alva Myrdal, disarmament negotiator. No. 1917, Andrei Sakharov, physicist.

**1991, Nov. 20 Engr. *Perf. 13 Horiz.***

| | | | |
|---|---|---|---|
| **1914** | A559 4k carmine | 1.60 | 1.60 |
| **1915** | A559 4k dk green | 1.60 | 1.60 |
| **1916** | A559 4k dk ultra | 1.60 | 1.60 |
| **1917** | A559 4k dk violet | 1.60 | 1.60 |
| *a.* | Bklt. pane, 2 each #1914-1917 with gutter between | 13.00 | |
| | *Nos. 1914-1917 (4)* | 6.40 | 6.40 |

**1992, Jan. 30 Engr. *Perf. 13 Horiz.***

| | | | |
|---|---|---|---|
| **1918** | A573 2.30k red, grn & blk | 1.10 | .35 |

Outdoor Life Assoc., cent.

A574

Wild Animals — A575

**1992-96 Engr. *Perf. 13 on 3 Sides***

| | | | |
|---|---|---|---|
| **1920** | A574 2.80k Capreolus capreolus | 1.00 | .20 |
| **1921** | A574 2.80k Capreolus capreolus (with fawn) | 1.00 | .20 |
| *b.* | Bklt. pane, 5 ea #1920-1921 | 10.00 | |
| **1922** | A574 2.90k Ursus arctos (2 cubs) | 1.10 | .30 |
| **1923** | A574 2.90k Ursus arctos (adult) | 1.10 | .30 |
| *b.* | Bklt. pane, 5 ea #1922-1923 | 11.00 | |
| **1924** | A574 3.85k Mustela erminea | 1.00 | .25 |
| **1925** | A574 3.85k Lutra lutra | 1.00 | .25 |
| *a.* | Bklt. pane, 5 ea #1924-1925 | 16.00 | |
| | Complete booklet, 1 #1925a | 16.00 | |

***Perf. 13 Vert. (A574), Horiz. (A575)***

| | | | |
|---|---|---|---|
| **1926** | A574 1k Erinaeceus eropaeus | .40 | .30 |
| **1927** | A574 2.80k like #1921 | 1.00 | .20 |
| **1928** | A574 2.90k like #1922 | 1.25 | .20 |
| **1929** | A574 3k Mustela putorius | 1.25 | .45 |
| **1930** | A575 3.20k Castor fiber | 1.50 | 1.25 |
| **1931** | A574 3.85k like #1924 | 1.50 | .35 |
| **1932** | A574 5.80k Canis lupus | 2.75 | .40 |
| **1933** | A575 6k Sciurus vulgaris | 2.50 | .50 |
| **1934** | A575 7k Alces alces | 2.75 | .50 |
| **1935** | A574 7.70k Vulpes vulpes | 3.00 | .60 |
| **1936** | A575 12k Lynx lynx | 3.75 | .85 |
| | *Nos. 1920-1936 (17)* | 27.85 | 7.10 |

Issued: #1920-1921, 1930, 6k, 7k, Jan. 30; #1922-1923, 1928-1929, 1932, 1936, Jan. 28, 1993; 1k, 3.20k, 3.85k, 7.70k, 1/2/96.

See Nos. 2207-2209, 2238.

### Olympic Champions Type of 1991

No. 1937, Gunde Svan, cross-country skiing, Sarajevo, 1984. No. 1938, Thomas Wassberg, cross-country skiing, Lake Placid, 1980. No. 1939, Tomas Gustafson, speed skating, Sarajevo, 1984. No. 1940, Ingemar Stenmark, slalom skiing, Lake Placid, 1980.

***Perf. 12x13 on 3 Sides***

**1992, Jan. 30 Litho. & Engr.**

| | | | |
|---|---|---|---|
| **1937** | A568 2.80k multicolored | 1.10 | .60 |
| **1938** | A568 2.80k multicolored | 1.10 | .60 |
| **1939** | A568 2.80k multicolored | 1.10 | .60 |
| **1940** | A568 2.80k multicolored | 1.10 | .60 |
| *a.* | Bklt. pane, 2 each #1937-1940 | 9.25 | |
| | *Nos. 1937-1940 (4)* | 4.40 | 2.40 |

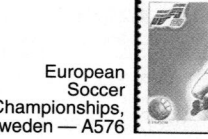

European Soccer Championships, Sweden — A576

**1992, Mar. 26 Engr. *Perf. 13 Vert.***

| | | | |
|---|---|---|---|
| **1941** | A576 2.80k shown | 1.00 | .35 |
| **1942** | A576 2.80k Two players | 1.00 | .35 |
| *a.* | Pair, #1941-1942 | 2.00 | 1.50 |

Sweden No. 1a A577

**Litho. & Engr.**

**1992, Mar. 26 *Perf. 13***

| | | | |
|---|---|---|---|
| **1943** | A577 2.80k No. 1 | 2.50 | 2.50 |
| **1944** | A577 4.50k No. 1 | 2.50 | 2.50 |
| **1945** | A577 5.50k shown | 2.00 | 1.60 |
| *a.* | Bklt. pane, #1943-1944, 2 #1945 | 7.50 | *8.50* |
| | *Nos. 1943-1945 (3)* | 7.00 | 6.60 |

No. 1945a sold for 25k. Surtax benefited stamp collecting.

Sailing Ships — A578

**1992, Mar. 26**

| | | | |
|---|---|---|---|
| **1946** | A578 4.50k Sprengtporten, 1785 | *2.10* | 1.50 |
| **1947** | A578 4.50k Superb, 1855 | *2.10* | 1.50 |
| **1948** | A578 4.50k Big T | *2.10* | 1.50 |
| *a.* | Bklt. pane of 3, #1946-1948 | *6.50* | *6.50* |

Europa. Discovery Race, Spain-Florida (No. 1948).

Children's Drawings A579

***Perf. 13x12½ on 3 Sides***

**1992, May 21 Litho.**

| | | | |
|---|---|---|---|
| **1949** | A579 2.50k Rabbit | .95 | .25 |
| **1950** | A579 2.50k Horses | .95 | .25 |
| **1951** | A579 2.50k Cat | .95 | .25 |
| **1952** | A579 2.50k Elephant | .95 | .25 |
| *a.* | Bklt. pane, 5 ea #1949-1952 | 19.00 | |
| | *Nos. 1949-1952 (4)* | 3.80 | 1.00 |

See note after No. 1277.

### Olympic Champions Type of 1991

Designs: No. 1953, Gunnar Larsson, swimming, 1972. No. 1954, Bernt Johansson, cycling, 1976. No. 1955, Anders Garderud, steeplechase, 1976. No. 1956, Gert Fredriksson, kayaking, 1948-1956.

***Perf. 12x13 on 3 Sides***

**1992, May 21 Litho. & Engr.**

| | | | |
|---|---|---|---|
| **1953** | A568 5.50k multicolored | 2.10 | 2.10 |
| **1954** | A568 5.50k multicolored | 2.10 | 2.10 |
| **1955** | A568 5.50k multicolored | 2.10 | 2.10 |
| **1956** | A568 5.50k multicolored | 2.10 | 2.10 |
| *a.* | Bklt. pane, 2 ea #1953-1956 | 17.00 | |
| | *Nos. 1953-1956 (4)* | 8.40 | 8.40 |

Greetings Stamps — A580

***Perf. 13x12 on 3 Sides***

**1992, Aug. 14 Litho.**

| | | | |
|---|---|---|---|
| **1957** | A580 2.80k Hand with flower | 1.10 | .85 |
| **1958** | A580 2.80k Cheese | 1.10 | .85 |
| **1959** | A580 2.80k Baby | 1.10 | .85 |
| **1960** | A580 2.80k Hand holding pen | 1.10 | .85 |
| *b.* | Bklt. pane, 2 each #1957-1960 | 9.00 | |
| | *Nos. 1957-1960 (4)* | 4.40 | 3.40 |

88th Inter-Parliamentary Union Conference, Stockholm — A581

Swedish Patent and Registration Office, Cent. — A582

#1961, Riksdag building. #1962, First automatic lighthouse, Gustaf Dalen's sun valve.

***Perf. 12½ Vert.***

**1992, Aug. 27 Engr.**

| | | | |
|---|---|---|---|
| **1961** | A581 2.80k violet, *tan* | 1.25 | .25 |

***Perf. 13 Horiz.***

| | | | |
|---|---|---|---|
| **1962** | A582 2.80k blue & black | 1.25 | .35 |

Kitchen Maid, by Rembrandt A583

The Triumph of Venus, by Francois Boucher A584

Paintings: No. 1965, Portrait of a Girl, by Albrecht Durer. No. 1966, Rorstrand Vase, by Erik Wahlberg. No. 1967, Motif from the Seine/The Tree and the River Bend III, by Carl Fredrik Hill. No. 1968, Sergel in his Studio, by Carl Larsson.

***Perf. 12½ on 3 Sides***

**1992, Aug. 27 Litho. & Engr.**

| | | | |
|---|---|---|---|
| **1963** | A583 5.50k multicolored | 2.25 | 1.75 |
| **1964** | A584 5.50k multicolored | 2.25 | 1.75 |
| **1965** | A583 5.50k multicolored | 2.25 | 1.75 |
| **1966** | A583 5.50k multicolored | 2.25 | 1.75 |
| **1967** | A584 5.50k multicolored | 2.25 | 1.75 |
| **1968** | A583 5.50k multicolored | 2.25 | 1.75 |
| *a.* | Bklt. pane of 6, #1963-1968 | 13.50 | *14.50* |

National Museum of Fine Arts, 200th anniv.

Prehistoric Animals — A585

***Perf. 13x12½ on 3 Sides***

**1992, Oct. 3 Litho. & Engr.**

| | | | |
|---|---|---|---|
| **1969** | A585 2.80k Plateosaurus | 1.25 | .90 |
| **1970** | A585 2.80k Thoracosaurus scanicus | 1.25 | .90 |
| **1971** | A585 2.80k Coelodonta antiquitatis | 1.25 | .90 |
| **1972** | A585 2.80k Mammuthus primigenius | 1.25 | .90 |
| *a.* | Bklt. pane, 2 ea #1969-1972 | 10.40 | |
| | *Nos. 1969-1972 (4)* | 5.00 | 3.60 |

No. 1972a sold for 27k to benefit stamp collecting.

1950 Automobiles A586

**1992, Oct. 3 Engr. *Perf. 12½ Vert.***

| | | | |
|---|---|---|---|
| **1973** | A586 4k Saab 92 | 1.50 | .75 |
| **1974** | A586 4k Volvo P 831 | 1.50 | .75 |
| *a.* | Pair, #1973-1974 | 3.00 | 3.00 |

Birds of the Baltic Shores — A587

**1992, Oct. 3 Litho. & Engr. *Perf. 13***

**1975** A587 4.50k Pandion haliaetus 1.75 1.25
**1976** A587 4.50k Limosa limosa 1.75 1.25
**1977** A587 4.50k Mergus merganser 1.75 1.25
**1978** A587 4.50k Tadorna tadorna 1.75 1.25
*a.* Bklt. pane of 4, #1975-1978 7.00 *7.50*

See Estonia Nos. 231-234, Latvis Nos. 332-335, and Lithuania Nos. 427-430.

A588 A589 A590 A591

Christmas

Icons: No. 1979, Joachim and Anna, 16th cent. No. 1980, Madonna and Child, 14th cent. No. 1981, Archangel Gabriel, 12th cent. No. 1982, St. Nicholas, 16th cent.

***Perf. 12½x13 on 3 Sides***

**1992, Nov. 27 Litho. & Engr.**

**1979** A588 2.30k multicolored .85 .50
**1980** A589 2.30k multicolored .85 .50
**1981** A590 2.30k multicolored .85 .50
**1982** A591 2.30k multicolored .85 .50
*a.* Bklt. pane, 3 ea #1979-1982 10.50
*Nos. 1979-1982 (4)* 3.40 2.00

See Russia Nos. 6103-6106.

Derek Walcott, Nobel Laureate in Literature, 1992 — A592

**1992, Nov. 27 Engr. *Perf. 12½ Vert.***

**1983** A592 5.50k Text 2.25 1.60
**1984** A592 5.50k Portrait 2.25 1.60
*a.* Pair, #1983-1984 5.00 5.00

1993 Sports Championships — A593

***Perf. 12½x13 on 3 Sides***

**1993, Jan. 28 Litho. & Engr.**

**1985** A593 6k Gliding 2.40 1.90
**1986** A593 6k Wrestling 2.40 1.90
**1987** A593 6k Table tennis 2.40 1.90
**1988** A593 6k Bowling 2.40 1.90
**1989** A593 6k Team handball 2.40 1.90
**1990** A593 6k Cross-country skiing 2.40 1.90
*a.* Booklet pane, #1985-1990 14.50 13.50

World Gliding Championships, Borlange (#1985). World Wrestling Championships, Stockholm (#1986). World Table Tennis Championships, Gothenburg (#1987). European Bowling Championships, Malmo (#1988). World Team Handball Championships, Gothenburg (#1989). World Cross-Country Skiing Championships, Falun (#1990).

Uppsala Convocation, 400th Anniversary A594

**Litho. & Engr.**

**1993, Mar. 25 *Perf. 13 Vert.***

**1991** A594 2.90k Stone carving 1.25 .45
**1992** A594 2.90k Uppsala Cathedral 1.25 .45
*a.* Pair, #1991-1992 2.50 2.00

A595

Tourist Attractions in Gothenburg: No. 1993, Roller coaster Liseberg Loop, Liseburg Amusement Park. No. 1994, Fountain of Poseidon, by Carl Milles.

**1993, Mar. 25**

**1993** A595 3.50k multicolored 1.25 *1.40*
**1994** A595 3.50k multicolored 1.25 *1.40*
*a.* Pair, #1993-1994 2.75 *3.25*

Fruit

A596 A596a

***Perf. 12½ on 3 Sides***

**1993-95 Engr.**

**1995** A596 2.40k Ribes uva crispa 1.10 .75
**1996** A596 2.40k Pyrus communis 1.10 .75
*b.* Bklt. pane, 5 ea #1996-1996 11.00
**1997** A596 2.80k Victoria plum 1.25 .60
**1998** A596 2.80k Opal plum .95 .60
*b.* Bklt. pane, 5 ea #1997-1998 12.50
**2001** A596a 3.35k Ribes nigrum 1.40 .60
**2002** A596a 3.35k Rubus idaeus 1.40 .60
*a.* Bklt. pane, 5 ea #2001-2002 13.50
Complete booklet, #2002a 13.50

***Perf. 12½ Vert.***

**2004** A596 2.40k Prunus avium 1.00 .75
**2005** A596 2.80k James Grieve apple 1.40 .50

***Perf. 12½ Horiz.***

**2008** A596a 3.35k Fragaria ananassa 1.40 .60
*Nos. 1995-2008 (9)* 11.00 5.75

Issued: #1995-1996, 2004, 3/25/93; #1997-1998, 2005, 1/17/94; 3.35k, 1/2/95.

This is an expanding set. Numbers may change.

Oxe-eye Daisy — A597

Poppy — A598

Buttercup A599

Bluebell A600

***Perf. 12½x13 on 3 Sides***

**1993, May 21 Litho.**

**2013** A597 2.60k multicolored .95 .35
**2014** A598 2.60k multicolored .95 .35
**2015** A599 2.60k multicolored .95 .35
**2016** A600 2.60k multicolored .95 .35
*b.* Bklt. pane, 5 ea #2013-2016 19.00
*Nos. 2013-2016 (4)* 3.80 1.40

See note after No. 1277.

Contemporary Art — A601

Europa: No. 2017, Oguasark, by Olle Baertling (1911-81). No. 2018, Ade-Lidic-Nander II, by Oyvind Fahlstrom (1928-76), horiz. No. 2019, The Cubist Chair, by Otto G. Carlsund (1897-1948).

**Litho. & Engr.**

**1993, May 21 *Perf. 13***

**2017** A601 5k multicolored 2.10 1.90
**2018** A601 5k multicolored 2.10 1.90
**2019** A601 5k multicolored 2.10 1.90
*a.* Booklet pane of 3, #2017-2019 6.50 *7.50*

Butterflies — A602

**1993, May 21 *Perf. 12½ Horiz.***

**2020** A602 6k Papilio machaon 2.25 2.10
**2021** A602 6k Nymphalis antiopa 2.25 2.10
**2022** A602 6k Colias palaeno 2.25 2.10
**2023** A602 6k Euphydryas maturna 2.25 2.10
*a.* Booklet pane, 2 each #2020-2023 with gutter between 19.00
*Nos. 2020-2023 (4)* 9.00 8.40

A603 A604

A605 A606

Greetings

***Perf. 13 on 3 Sides***

**1993, Aug. 6 Litho.**

**2024** A603 2.90k multicolored 1.00 .40
**2025** A604 2.90k multicolored 1.25 .75
**2026** A605 2.90k multicolored 1.00 .40
**2027** A606 2.90k multicolored 1.25 .75
*b.* Booklet pane, 3 each #2024, 2026, 2 each #2025, 2027 11.00
*Nos. 2024-2027 (4)* 4.50 2.30

Sea Birds A607

***Perf. 12½ Horiz.***

**1993, Aug. 26 Engr.**

**2028** A607 5k Mergus serrator 2.00 1.60
**2029** A607 5k Melanitta fusca 2.00 1.60
**2030** A607 5k Aythya fuligula 2.00 1.60
**2031** A607 5k Somateria mollissima 2.00 1.60
*a.* Booklet pane, 2 each #2028-2031 with gutter between 16.00
*Nos. 2028-2031 (4)* 8.00 6.40

A608

A609

**1993, Oct. 2 Engr. *Perf. 13 Vert.***

**2032** A608 2.90k Modern echo sounding 1.20 .35
**2033** A608 2.90k 1643 Method 1.20 .35
*a.* Pair, #2032-2033 2.90 1.75

Hydrographic survey.

**1993, Oct. 2 Engr. *Perf. 13***

**2034** A609 8k King holding flag 3.25 2.75
**2035** A609 10k King 3.75 3.50
**2036** A609 10k Queen Silvia 3.75 3.50

**Size: 75x43mm**

**2037** A609 12k Royal family 4.50 *5.25*
*a.* Booklet pane, #2034-2037 15.00 *15.50*
*Nos. 2034-2037 (4)* 15.25 15.00

Reign of King Carl XVI Gustaf, 20th anniv.

Christmas — A610

***Perf. 12½ on 3 Sides***

**1993, Nov. 25 Engr.**

**2038** A610 2.40k Plaited heart .95 .40
**2039** A610 2.40k Straw goat .95 .40
*b.* Bklt pane, 5 ea #2038-2039 9.50

Toni Morrison, Nobel laureate in Literature, 1993 — A611

#2041, Stockholm City Hall.

**1993, Nov. 25 Engr. *Perf. 12½ Vert.***

**2040** A611 6k red brown & brown 2.40 1.75
**2041** A611 6k multicolored 2.40 1.75
*a.* Pair, #2040-2041 5.00 4.25

European Economic Assoc. Agreement A612

**1994, Jan. 17 *Perf. 12½ Vert.***

**2042** A612 5k Mother Svea 2.25 .65

Domestic Animals — A613

No. 2047, North Sweden horse, vert. No. 2048, Two horses, vert. No. 2049, Red polled cattle, vert. No. 2050, Goat, vert. No. 2054, Swedish dwarf poultry. No. 2055, Gotland sheep. No. 2059, Mountain cow. No. 2060, Scanian goose. No. 2060A, Yellow duck.

**1994-95 Engr. *Perf. 13 on 3 Sides***

| | | | | |
|---|---|---|---|---|
| **2047** | A613 3.20k multicolored | | 1.25 | .25 |
| **2048** | A613 3.20k multicolored | | 1.25 | .25 |
| *a.* | Bklt. pane, 5 ea #2047-2048 | | 12.50 | |
| **2049** | A613 3.70k multicolored | | 1.40 | .30 |
| **2050** | A613 3.70k multicolored | | 1.40 | .30 |
| *a.* | Bklt. pane, 5 ea #2049-2050 | | 14.00 | |
| | Complete booklet, #2050a | | 14.00 | |

***Perf. 13 Vert.***

| | | | |
|---|---|---|---|
| **2054** | A613 3.10k multicolored | 1.40 | .45 |
| **2055** | A613 3.20k multicolored | 1.50 | .30 |
| **2059** | A613 6.40k multicolored | 3.00 | .60 |
| **2060** | A613 7.40k multicolored | 3.00 | .60 |
| **2060A** | A613 7.50k multicolored | 3.00 | 2.10 |
| | *Nos. 2047-2060A (9)* | 17.20 | 5.15 |

Issued: #2047-2048, 2055, 2059, 1/17/94; #2049-2050, 2054, 1/2/95; 2060-2060A, 3/17/95.

This is an expanding set. Numbers may change.

Cats — A614

**Litho. & Engr.**

**1994, Mar. 18** ***Perf. 13***

| | | | |
|---|---|---|---|
| **2061** | A614 4.50k Siamese | 1.75 | 1.60 |
| **2062** | A614 4.50k Persian | 1.75 | 1.60 |
| **2063** | A614 4.50k European | 1.75 | 1.60 |
| **2064** | A614 4.50k Abyssinian | 1.75 | 1.60 |
| *a.* | Booklet pane of 4, #2061-2064 | 7.00 | *8.50* |

Roman De La Rose — A615

Swedish, French Flags A616

Swedish-French cultural relations: No. 2067, House of the Nobility, designed by Simon and Jean de la Vallee. No. 2068, Household Chores, by Hillestrom. No. 2069, Banquet for Gustavus III at the Trianon, 1784, by Lafrensen. No. 2070, Charles XIV John, by Gerard.

**Litho. & Engr., Litho. (#2066)**

**1994, Mar. 18** ***Perf. 13 on 3 Sides***

| | | | |
|---|---|---|---|
| **2065** | A615 5k multicolored | 2.25 | 2.25 |
| **2066** | A616 5k multicolored | 2.25 | 2.25 |
| **2067** | A615 5k multicolored | 2.25 | 2.25 |
| **2068** | A615 5k multicolored | 2.25 | 2.25 |
| **2069** | A616 5k multicolored | 2.25 | 2.25 |
| **2070** | A615 5k multicolored | 2.25 | 2.25 |
| *a.* | Booklet pane of 6, #2065-2070 | 14.00 | *15.50* |

See France Nos. 2410-2415.

Roses — A617

Swedish Design — A618

***Perf. 12½x13 on 3 Sides***

**1994, May 11** **Litho.**

| | | | |
|---|---|---|---|
| **2071** | A617 3.20k Nyponros rosa dumalis | 1.10 | .45 |
| **2072** | A617 3.20k Rosa alba maxima | 1.10 | .45 |
| **2073** | A617 3.20k Tuscany superb | 1.10 | .45 |
| **2074** | A617 3.20k Peace | 1.10 | .45 |
| **2075** | A617 3.20k Quatre saisons | 1.10 | .45 |
| *a.* | Bklt. pane, 2 ea #2071-2075 | 11.00 | |
| | *Nos. 2071-2075 (5)* | 5.50 | 2.25 |

***Perf. 12½ on 3 Sides***

**1994, May 11** **Litho. & Engr.**

#2076, Vase with Irises, by Gunnar Wennerberg, 1897. #2077, Table and Chair, by Carl Malmsten; Wallpaper, by Uno Ahren, 1917. #2078, Cabinet, 1940s, and textile, 1920s, by Josef Franck. #2079, Fireworks Bowl, by Edward Hald, 1921. #2080, Silver water jug, by Wiwen Nilsson, 1941. #2081, Towel, by Astrid Sampe; Plate, by Stig Lindberg; Fork and Spoon, by Sigurd Persson, 1955.

| | | | |
|---|---|---|---|
| **2076** | A618 6.50k multicolored | 2.50 | 2.25 |
| **2077** | A618 6.50k multicolored | 2.50 | 2.25 |
| **2078** | A618 6.50k multicolored | 2.50 | 2.25 |
| **2079** | A618 6.50k multicolored | 2.50 | 2.25 |
| **2080** | A618 6.50k multicolored | 2.50 | 2.25 |
| **2081** | A618 6.50k multicolored | 2.50 | 2.25 |
| *a.* | Bklt. pane, #2076-2081 | 15.50 | *17.50* |

1994 World Cup Soccer Championships, US — A619

**1994, May 11 Engr. *Perf. 12½ Vert.***

| | | | |
|---|---|---|---|
| **2082** | A619 3.20k red & blue | 1.60 | .50 |

First Manned Moon Landing, 25th Anniv. A620

**1994, May 11**

| | | | |
|---|---|---|---|
| **2083** | A620 6.50k multicolored | 2.50 | 2.25 |

Greetings A621

***Perf. 12½ on 3 Sides***

**1994, Aug. 5** **Litho.**

| | | | |
|---|---|---|---|
| **2084** | A621 3.20k Cat | 1.10 | .40 |
| **2085** | A621 3.20k Snail | 1.10 | .40 |
| **2086** | A621 3.20k Frog | 1.20 | .70 |
| **2087** | A621 3.20k Dog | 1.20 | .70 |
| *a.* | Booklet pane, 3 each #2084-2085, 2 each #2086-2087 | 11.50 | |
| | *Nos. 2084-2087 (4)* | 4.60 | 2.20 |

Swedish Explorers A622

Europa: No. 2088, Erland Nordenskiold (1877-1932), explored South America. No. 2089, Eric Von Rosen (1879-1948), explored Africa. No. 2090, Sten Bergman (1895-1975), explored Asia and the Pacific.

**Litho. & Engr.**

**1994, Aug. 26** ***Perf. 12½***

| | | | |
|---|---|---|---|
| **2088** | A622 5.50k multicolored | 2.50 | 2.00 |
| **2089** | A622 5.50k multicolored | 2.50 | 2.00 |
| **2090** | A622 5.50k multicolored | 2.50 | 2.00 |
| *a.* | Booklet pane of 3, #2088-2090 | 7.50 | *8.75* |

Finland-Sweden Track and Field Meet — A623

#2091, Seppo Raty, Finland, javelin. #2092, Patrick Sjoberg, Sweden, high jump.

**1994, Aug. 26 *Perf. 12½ on 3 Sides***

| | | | |
|---|---|---|---|
| **2091** | A623 4.50k multicolored | 1.75 | 1.50 |
| **2092** | A623 4.50k multicolored | 1.75 | 1.50 |
| *a.* | Bklt. pane, 2 ea #2091-2092 | 7.50 | 7.50 |

See Finland Nos. 942-943.

Johan Helmich Roman (1694-1758), Composer A624

No. 2094, Opera House, Gothenburg.

***Perf. 12½ Vert.***

**1994, Aug. 26** **Engr.**

| | | | |
|---|---|---|---|
| **2093** | A624 3.20k multicolored | 1.25 | .25 |
| **2094** | A624 3.20k multicolored | 1.25 | .25 |

Yes & No Stamps — A625

**1994, Oct. 1 Litho. *Perf. 12½ Vert.***

| | | | |
|---|---|---|---|
| **2095** | A625 3.20k Ja | 1.25 | .60 |
| **2096** | A625 3.20k Nej | 1.25 | .60 |

See Nos. 2107-2108.

World Wildlife Fund — A626

#2097, Sterna caspia. #2098, Haliaeetus albicilla. #2099, Dendrocopos leucotos. #2100, Anser erythropus.

**Litho. & Engr.**

**1994, Oct. 1** ***Perf. 12½***

| | | | |
|---|---|---|---|
| **2097** | A626 5.50k multicolored | 2.25 | 1.75 |
| **2098** | A626 5.50k multicolored | 2.25 | 1.75 |
| **2099** | A626 5.50k multicolored | 2.25 | 1.75 |
| **2100** | A626 5.50k multicolored | 2.25 | 1.75 |
| *a.* | Booklet pane of 4, #2097-2100 | 9.00 | *10.00* |

Frans G. Bengtsson (1894-1954), Writer — A627

**1994, Oct. 1 Engr. *Perf. 12½ Vert.***

| | | | |
|---|---|---|---|
| **2101** | A627 6.40k multicolored | 2.75 | 2.00 |

Nobel Laureates in Literature A628

Christmas A629

Designs: 4.50k, Erik Axel Karlfeldt (1864-1931). 5.50k, Eyvind Johnson (1900-76). 6.50k, Harry Martinson (1904-78).

**1994, Nov. 11**

| | | | |
|---|---|---|---|
| **2102** | A628 4.50k multicolored | 1.90 | 1.00 |
| **2103** | A628 5.50k multicolored | 2.25 | 1.25 |
| **2104** | A628 6.50k multicolored | 2.75 | 1.40 |
| | *Nos. 2102-2104 (3)* | 6.90 | 3.65 |

***Perf. 12½x13 on 3 Sides***

**1994, Nov. 11** **Litho. & Engr.**

Scenes from medieval altar pieces: No. 2105, Annunciation. No. 2106, Flight to Egypt.

| | | | |
|---|---|---|---|
| **2105** | A629 2.80k multicolored | 1.25 | .40 |
| **2106** | A629 2.80k multicolored | 1.25 | .40 |
| *a.* | Bklt. pane, 5 ea #2105-2106 | 12.50 | |

**Yes & No Type of 1994**

**1995, Jan. 2 Litho. *Perf. 12½ Vert.***

| | | | |
|---|---|---|---|
| **2107** | A625 3.70k Ja | 1.10 | .40 |
| **2108** | A625 3.70k Nej | 1.10 | .40 |

Houses A630

Designs: No. 2109, Country cottage. No. 2110, Soldier's log house. No. 2111, Farmhouse courtyard. No. 2112, Timbered farmhouse. No. 2113, Manor house.

***Perf. 14 Horiz.***

**1995, Mar. 17** **Litho. & Engr.**

| | | | |
|---|---|---|---|
| **2109** | A630 3.70k multicolored | 1.60 | .65 |
| **2110** | A630 3.70k multicolored | 1.60 | .65 |
| **2111** | A630 3.70k multicolored | 1.60 | .65 |
| **2112** | A630 3.70k multicolored | 1.60 | .65 |
| **2113** | A630 3.70k multicolored | 1.60 | .65 |
| *a.* | Booklet pane of 5, #2109-2113 | 8.00 | 8.00 |
| | Complete booklet, #2113a | 8.50 | |

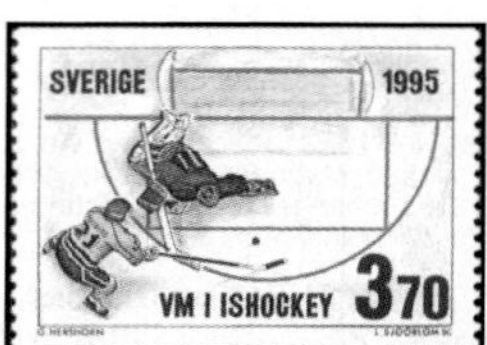


1995 Ice Hockey World Championships — A631

1995 World Track & Field Championships A632

**Litho. & Engr.**

**1995, Mar. 17** ***Perf. 13 Vert.***

| | | | |
|---|---|---|---|
| **2114** | A631 3.70k multicolored | 3.00 | 1.00 |

***Perf. 13 Horiz.***

| | | | |
|---|---|---|---|
| **2115** | A632 3.70k multicolored | 1.90 | .50 |

A633

Wood Sculptures, by Bror Hjorth — A634

Europa: Nos. 2116, 2118, Walt Whitman, Christ, Socrates. Nos. 2117, 2119, Patrice Lumumba, Albert Schweitzer, children dancing.

**1995, Mar. 17 Litho. *Perf. 13***

| | | | |
|---|---|---|---|
| **2116** | A633 5k multicolored | *2.25* | 1.75 |
| **2117** | A634 5k multicolored | *2.25* | 1.75 |
| **2118** | A633 6k multicolored | *2.50* | 2.00 |

2119 A634 6k multicolored 2.50 2.00
a. Bklt. pane of 4, #2116-2119 *9.50 10.00*
Complete booklet, 2 #2119a *19.00*

Swedish Membership in European Union — A635

**1995, Mar. 17** ***Perf. 13 Vert.***
2120 A635 6k multicolored 2.40 1.10

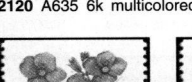

Rock Speedwell A636

Cloudberry A637

Mountain Heath — A638

Alpine Arnica — A639

***Perf. 13 on 3 Sides***
**1995, May 12** **Litho.**
2121 A636 3.70k multicolored 1.25 .45
2122 A637 3.70k multicolored 1.50 .60
2123 A638 3.70k multicolored 1.25 .45
2124 A639 3.70k multicolored 1.50 .60
a. Booklet pane, 3 each #2121, 2123, 2 each #2122, 2124 13.50
Complete booklet, #2124a 13.50
*Nos. 2121-2124 (4)* 5.50 2.10

Tourist Attractions — A640

#2125, Canal boat Wilhelm Tham on Gota Canal. #2126, Sail boat anchored on Lake Vattern.

**1995, May 12** **Engr.**
2125 A640 5k dark green 2.10 1.40
2126 A640 5k dark violet 2.10 1.40
a. Bklt. pane, 2 ea #2125-2126 8.50
Complete booklet, #2126a 8.50

Trams A641

#2127, Gothenburg, c. 1900. #2128, Norrkoping, 1905. #2129, Helsingborg, 1921. #2130, Kiruna, 1958. #2131, Stockholm, 1967.

**1995, May 12** ***Perf. 13 Horiz.***
2127 A641 7.50k rose claret 3.00 2.75
2128 A641 7.50k dp brown vio 3.00 2.75
2129 A641 7.50k dk green 3.00 2.75
2130 A641 7.50k dk gray violet 3.00 2.75
2131 A641 7.50k dk violet blue 3.00 2.75
a. Bklt. pane of 5, #2127-2131 15.00 *16.00*
Complete booklet, #2131a 15.00

UN, 50th Anniv. A642

**1995, Aug. 3** **Engr.** ***Perf. 13 Vert.***
2132 A642 3.70k multicolored 1.75 .35

Greetings A643

Children's drawings: No. 2133, "The Ball is Yours," by M. Angesjo. No. 2134, Happy man, by E. Sandstrom. No. 2135, Teddy Bear saying "I miss you," by L. Nordenhem. No. 2136, Mussel saying "Hello," by C. Stenbom.

**1995, Aug. 3** **Litho.** ***Perf. 13x12½***
2133 A643 3.70k multicolored 1.40 .55
2134 A643 3.70k multicolored 1.40 .55
2135 A643 3.70k multicolored 1.75 1.00
2136 A643 3.70k multicolored 1.75 1.00
a. Booklet pane, 3 each #2133-2134, 2 each #2135-2136 15.50
Complete booklet, #2136a 15.50
*Nos. 2133-2136 (4)* 6.30 3.10

1995 IAAF World Track & Field Championships, Gothenburg A644

***Perf. 13 Horiz.***
**1995, Aug. 3** **Litho. & Engr.**
2137 A644 7.50k Maria Akraka 3.00 2.25

Motion Picture, Cent. A645

Scenes from films: No. 2138, Soldier Bom, 1948. No. 2139, Sir Arne's Treasure, 1919. No. 2140, Wild Strawberries, 1957. No. 2141, House of Angels, 1992. No. 2142, One Summer of Happiness, 1951. No. 2143, The Apple War, 1971.

**Litho. & Engr.**
**1995, Oct. 7** ***Perf. 12½x13***
**Booklet Stamps**
2138 A645 6k multicolored 2.50 2.50
2139 A645 6k multicolored 2.50 2.50
2140 A645 6k multicolored 2.50 2.50
2141 A645 6k multicolored 2.50 2.50
2142 A645 6k multicolored 2.50 2.50
2143 A645 6k multicolored 2.50 2.50
a. Booklet pane, #2138-2143 15.00 *18.00*
Complete booklet, #2143a 15.00

Fritiof Nilsson (1895-1972), Writer — A646

**Litho. & Engr.**
**1995, Oct. 27** ***Perf. 13 Vert.***
2144 A646 3.70k blue & claret 1.75 .40

Ancient Artifacts — A647

Designs: No. 2145, Bronze cult figures of man with beak, nude woman, Bronze Age. No. 2146, Detail of gold collar, Great Migration period. No. 2147, Bracteate pendant picturing figure on horse, Great Migration period. No. 2148, Circular bronze cult object, Bronze Age.

**1995, Oct. 27** ***Perf. 13***
2145 A647 3.70k multicolored 1.50 1.25
2146 A647 3.70k multicolored 1.50 1.25
2147 A647 3.70k multicolored 1.50 1.25
2148 A647 3.70k multicolored 1.50 1.25
a. Booklet pane of 4, #2145-2148 6.00 *7.50*
Complete booklet, 2 #2148a 12.00

A648

A649

Tycho Brache (1546-1601), Astronomer: 5k, Uranienborg Observatory, Ven Island. 6k, Sextant.

**Litho. & Engr.**
**1995, Oct. 27** ***Perf. 13 Vert.***
2149 A648 5k multicolored 1.90 1.25
2150 A648 6k multicolored 2.50 2.00

See Denmark Nos. 1035-1036.

***Perf. 12½x13 on 3 Sides***
**1995, Nov. 9** **Litho.**

Christmas candlesticks.

2151 A649 3.35k Santa 1.10 .45
2152 A649 3.35k Apple 1.50 .80
2153 A649 3.35k Wrought iron 1.10 .45
2154 A649 3.35k Red wooden 1.50 .80
a. Booklet pane, 3 ea #2151, 2153, 2 ea #2152, 2154 12.50
Complete booklet, No. 2151a 12.50
*Nos. 2151-2154 (4)* 5.20 2.50

Nobel Prize Fund Established, Cent. — A650

Designs: No. 2155, Alfred Nobel, last will and testament. No. 2156, Nobel's home, 59 Avenue de Malakoff, Paris. No. 2157, Björkborn Laboratory, Karlkoga. No. 2158, Wilhelm Röntgen receiving the first physics prize, 1901.

**Photo. & Engr.**
**1995, Nov. 9** ***Perf. 13 Horiz.***
2155 A650 6k multicolored 2.40 2.25
2156 A650 6k multicolored 2.40 2.25
2157 A650 6k multicolored 2.40 2.25
2158 A650 6k multicolored 2.40 2.25
a. Booklet pane, #2155-2158 9.50 *11.00*
Complete booklet, No. 2158a 9.50

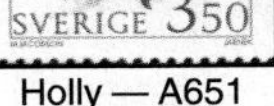

Holly — A651

Rowan Berries — A652

Rose Hips & Juniper — A653

Lingonberries & Sloe — A654

**1996, Jan. 2** **Litho.** ***Perf. 13 Horiz.***
2159 A651 3.50k multicolored 1.50 .75
2160 A652 7.50k multicolored 3.25 1.60

***Perf. 13 on 3 Sides***
2161 A653 3.50k multicolored 1.25 .55
2162 A654 3.50k multicolored 1.25 .55
a. Bklt. pane, 5 ea, #2161-2162 12.50
Complete booklet, #2162a 12.50
*Nos. 2159-2162 (4)* 7.25 3.45

End of Railway Mail Sorting — A655

**1996, Mar. 29** **Engr.** ***Perf. 13 Vert.***
2163 A655 6k multicolored 2.50 1.25

King Carl XVI Gustaf, 50th Birthday — A656

King Carl XVI Gustaf: No. 2164, In forest. No. 2165, In front of portrait of King Charles XIV John. No. 2166, In carriage with King Albert of Belgium, 1994. 20kr, With family.

**Litho. & Engr.**
**1996, Apr. 19** ***Perf. 13x12½***
2164 A656 10k multicolored 3.25 3.50
2165 A656 10k multicolored 3.25 3.50
2166 A656 10k multicolored 3.25 3.50

**Size: 80x48mm**
2167 A656 20k multicolored 6.75 6.50
a. Booklet pane, #2164-2167 16.50 *22.50*

Historic Buildings — A657

Designs: No. 2168, Railway station, Halsingland. No. 2169, Motala Assembly Hall, Ostergotland. No. 2170, Parish storehouse, Smaland. No. 2171, Half-timbered barn, Vasterbotten. No. 2172, Sheep shelter, Gotland. No. 2173, Old Town Hall, Lidkoping.

***Perf. 13 on 2 or 3 Sides***
**1996, Apr. 19**
2168 A657 3.85k multicolored 1.50 .60
2169 A657 3.85k multicolored 1.50 .60

**Size: 28x29mm**
2170 A657 3.85k multicolored 1.50 .85
2171 A657 3.85k multicolored 1.50 .85

**Size: 28x38mm**
2172 A657 3.85k multicolored 1.50 .85
2173 A657 3.85k multicolored 1.50 .85
a. Booklet pane of 6, #2168-2173 9.00 *10.00*

Famous Women — A658

Europa: No. 2174, Karin Kock (1891-1976), economist. No. 2175, Astrid Lindgren (b. 1907), creator of Pippi Longstocking.

***Perf. 13 on 3 Sides***
**1996, May 3** **Engr.**
2174 A658 6k multicolored *3.25* 2.25
2175 A658 6k multicolored *3.25* 2.25
a. Bklt. pane, 2 ea #2174-2175 *9.00*
Complete booklet, #2175a *9.00*

Summer Scenes A659

Paintings by: No. 2176, Sven X:Et Erixson (1899-1970). No. 2177, Roland Svensson (b. 1910). No. 2178, Eric Hallström (1893-1946),

No. 2179, Thage Nordholm (1927-90). No. 2180, Ragnar Sandberg (1902-72).

*Perf. 13 on 2 Sides*

**1996, May 24** **Litho.**
**2176** A659 3.85k multicolored 1.50 .40
**2177** A659 3.85k multicolored 1.50 .40
**2178** A659 3.85k multicolored 1.50 .40
**2179** A659 3.85k multicolored 1.50 .40
**2180** A659 3.85k multicolored 1.50 .40
*a.* Bklt. pane, 2 ea #2176-2180 15.00
Complete booklet, #2180a 15.00
*Nos. 2176-2180 (5)* 7.50 2.00

Golf — A660

**1996, Aug. 23** **Engr.** ***Perf. 13 Horiz.***
**2181** A660 3.50k dark green, *buff* 2.25 1.25

Greetings Stamps — A661

Designs: No. 2182, Masks of comedy, tragedy, "don't worry, be happy." No. 2183, Hearts, "Var Glad (Be happy)," vert. No. 2184, Posthorn. No. 2185, Hearts, person, "Minns du mig? (Do you remember me?)."

***Perf. 13x12½ on 3 Sides***

**1996, Aug. 23** **Litho.**
**2182** A661 3.85k multicolored 1.40 .40
**2183** A661 3.85k multicolored 1.40 .40
**2184** A661 3.85k multicolored 1.60 .75
**2185** A661 3.85k multicolored 1.60 .75
*a.* Booklet pane, 3 each #2182-2183, 2 each #2184-2185 15.00
Complete booklet, #2185a 15.00
*Nos. 2182-2185 (4)* 6.00 2.30

Mushrooms — A662

3.85k, Boletus edulis. #2187, Russula integra. #2188, Cantharellus cibarius. #2189, Craterellus cornucopioides. #2190, Coprinus comatus.

***Perf. 13 Horiz.***

**1996, Aug. 23** **Litho. & Engr.**
**2186** A662 3.85k multicolored 1.75 .45

***Perf. 12½x13 on 3 Sides***

**2187** A662 5k multicolored 1.75 1.25
**2188** A662 5k multicolored 1.75 1.25
**2189** A662 5k multicolored 1.75 1.25
**2190** A662 5k multicolored 1.75 1.25
*a.* Booklet pane of 4, #2187-2190 7.00 *8.50*
Complete booklet, #2190a 7.00
*Nos. 2186-2190 (5)* 8.75 5.45

Ecopark, Stockholm A663

Designs: No. 2191, Pelousen, grassy area, Haga Park. No. 2192, Copper tents, Haga Park. No. 2193, Rosendals Palace, roe deer. No. 2194, Isbladskarret, marsh birds.

**Litho. & Engr.**

**1996, Aug. 23** ***Perf. 12½Vert.***
**2191** A663 7.50k multicolored 2.50 2.50
**2192** A663 7.50k multicolored 2.50 2.50
**2193** A663 7.50k multicolored 2.50 2.50
**2194** A663 7.50k multicolored 2.50 2.50
*a.* Booklet pane of 4, #2191-2194 10.50 *12.50*
Complete booklet, #2194a 10.50

Four Decades A664

Designs: No. 2195, Errand boy, 1930's. No. 2196, Flower child, 1960's. No. 2197, Zootsuiter, 1940's. No. 2198, Biker, 1950's.

***Perf. 12½x13 on 3 Sides***

**1996, Oct. 5** **Litho. & Engr.**
**2195** A664 3.85k multicolored 1.75 .65
**2196** A664 3.85k multicolored 2.25 1.50
**2197** A664 3.85k multicolored 1.75 .65
**2198** A664 3.85k multicolored 2.25 1.50
*a.* Bklt. pane, 3 ea #2195, 2197, 2 ea #2196, 2198 17.50
Complete booklet, #2198a 17.50
*Nos. 2195-2198 (4)* 8.00 4.30

The Baroque Chair, by Endre Nemes — A665

**1996, Oct. 5** ***Perf. 12½ Horiz.***
**2199** A665 6k multicolored 2.25 1.60

See Czech Republic #2995, Slovakia #255.

Christmas A666

Illustrations from Book of Hours (15th cent.): No. 2200, The Annunciation. No. 2201, The Birth. No. 2202, Adoration of the Magi.

***Perf. 12½ Vert.***

**1996, Nov. 8** **Litho. & Engr.**
**2200** A666 3.50k multicolored 1.50 .90

***Perf. 12½x13 on 3 Sides***

**2201** A666 3.50k multicolored 1.10 .45
**2202** A666 3.50k multicolored 1.10 .45
*a.* Bklt. pane, 5 ea #2201-2202 11.00
Complete booklet, #2202a 11.00
*Nos. 2200-2202 (3)* 3.70 1.80

Nobel Laureates in Physiology or Medicine — A667

#2203, Sune Bergström (b. 1916), medical chemist. #2204, Bengt Samuelsson (b. 1934), medical chemist. #2205, Hugo Theorell (1903-82), biochemist. #2206, Ragnar Granit (1900-91), neurophysiologist.

***Perf. 13x12½ on 3 Sides***

**1996, Nov. 8** **Engr.**
**2203** A667 5k blue, grn & blk + label 2.00 1.50
**2204** A667 5k grn, blue & blk+ label 2.00 1.50
**2205** A667 5k blue, grn & blk+ label 2.75 2.25
**2206** A667 5k green & black+ label 2.75 2.25
*a.* Booklet pane, 3 each #2203-#2204, 2 each #2205-2206 23.00
Complete booklet, #2206a 23.00
*Nos. 2203-2206 (4)* 9.50 7.50

**Wild Animal Types of 1992**

**1997, Jan. 2** **Engr.** ***Perf. 13 Vert.***
**2207** A574 3.20k Gulo gulo 1.25 1.10
**2208** A574 3.50k Nyclea scandiaca 1.25 .70

***Perf. 13 Horiz.***

**2209** A575 7.70k Ciconia ciconia 3.25 2.75
*Nos. 2207-2209 (3)* 5.75 4.55

Churches — A668

Illustration reduced.

***Perf. 13 Horiz.***

**1997, Jan. 2** **Litho. & Engr.**
**2210** A668 3.85k Dalby 1.25 1.25
**2211** A668 3.85k Vendel 1.25 1.25

**Size: 27x23mm**

***Perf. 13x12½ on 2 or 3 Sides***

**2212** A668 3.85k Hagby 1.50 *1.60*
**2213** A668 3.85k Overtornea 1.50 *1.60*

**Size: 27x37mm**

**2214** A668 3.85k Varnhem 1.50 *1.60*
**2215** A668 3.85k Ostra Amtervik 1.50 *1.60*
*a.* Booklet pane of 6, #2210-2215 8.50 *11.50*
Complete booklet, #2215a 8.50

Kalmar Union, 600th Anniv. — A669

Design: Queen Margareta, Erik of Pomerania, coronation document. Illustration reduced.

**1997, Jan. 2** **Engr.** ***Perf. 12½ Vert.***
**2216** A669 3.85k dark blue 1.50 .50

Love Stamps — A670

***Perf. 13x12½ on 3 Sides***

**1997, Jan. 2** **Litho.**
**2217** A670 3.85k gray & multi 1.75 .75
**2218** A670 3.85k yellow & multi 1.75 .75
*a.* Bklt. pane, 5 ea #2217-2218 17.50
Complete booklet, #2218a 17.50

**Stamps that follow, with denominations in parenthesis, are inscribed "Brev," "Ekonomibrev," "Foreningsbrev," etc.**

Wild Animals — A671

***Perf. 13 on 2 Sides***

**1997, Feb. 28** **Engr.**
**2219** A671 (4.50k) Alopex lagopus 1.60 .55
**2220** A671 (5k) Equus przewalskii 2.25 .35

***Perf. 13 on 3 Sides***

**2221** A671 (5k) Panthera unica, adult 1.75 .35
**2222** A671 (5k) same, cubs 1.75 .35
*a.* Bklt. pane, 3 ea #2221-2222 11.00
Complete booklet, #2222a 11.00
Complete booklet, 1 ea #2221-2222 7.00
*Nos. 2219-2222 (4)* 7.35 1.60

No. 2220 is 28x21mm.

Easter Stamps — A672

***Perf. 13x12½ on 3 Sides***

**1997, Feb. 28** **Litho.**
**2223** A672 (5k) Rooster 2.10 .55
**2224** A672 (5k) Daffodils 2.10 .55
*a.* Bklt. pane, 3 ea #2223-2224 12.50
Complete booklet, #2224a 12.50

Pheasants A673

Designs: No. 2225, Phasianus colchicus. No. 2226, Chrysolophus amherstiae.

***Perf. 12½ Horiz.***

**1997, May 9** **Litho. & Engr.**
**2225** A673 2k multicolored .85 .60
**2226** A673 2k multicolored .85 .60
*a.* Pair, #2225-2226 1.75 *1.40*

See China (PRC) Nos. 2763-2764.

Garden Flowers — A674

#2227, Iris sibirica. #2228, Lonicera periclymenum. #2229, Aquilegia vulgaris. #2230, Hemerocallis flava. #2231, Viola x wittrokiana.

**1997, May 9** **Litho.** ***Perf. 12½x13***
**2227** A674 (5k) multicolored 2.10 .45
**2228** A674 (5k) multicolored 2.10 .45
**2229** A674 (5k) multicolored 2.10 .45
**2230** A674 (5k) multicolored 2.10 .45
**2231** A674 (5k) multicolored 2.10 .45
*a.* Bklt. pane, 2 ea #2227-2231 21.00
Complete booklet, #2231a 21.00
*Nos. 2227-2231 (5)* 10.50 2.25

A675 A676

6k, Ship's figurehead, 18th cent., Naval Museum, Karlskrona. 7k, Compass rose, 18th cent. atlas. 8k, Compass rose, 1568 atlas.

***Perf. 12½ Vert.***

**1997, May 9** **Litho. & Engr.**
**2232** A675 6k multicolored 2.10 1.20

**Litho.**

***Perf. 12½ Horiz.***

**2233** A676 7k multicolored 2.40 1.50
**2234** A676 8k multicolored 2.90 1.75
*Nos. 2232-2234 (3)* 7.40 4.45

18th Intl. Cartographic Conf. (#2233-2234).

Gnomes and Trolls — A677

Illustrations from "Among Trolls and Sprites," by John Bauer: No. 2235, Troll looking through treasure chest, gnome. No. 2236, Trolls looking at girl seated on rock. No. 2237, Troll talking with boy.

**Litho. & Engr.**

**1997, May 9** *Perf. 12x13*

**2235** A677 7k multicolored 2.75 2.00
**2236** A677 7k multicolored 2.75 2.00
**2237** A677 7k multicolored 2.75 2.00
*a.* Bklt. pane, 2 ea, #2235-2237 16.50
Complete booklet, #2237a 16.50
*Nos. 2235-2237 (3)*

Europa.

**Wild Animal Type of 1992**

*Perf. 12½ Horiz.*

**1997, Aug. 21** **Engr.**

**2238** A575 (3.50k) Ailurus fulgens, vert. 1.75 1.20

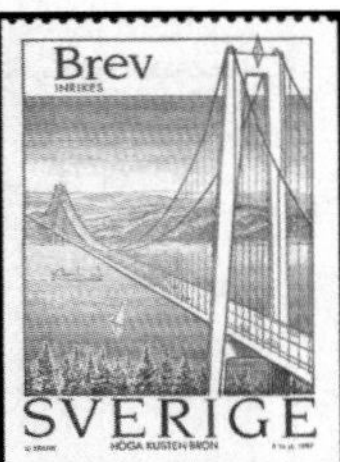


Construction of High Coast Bridge — A678

**1997, Aug. 21**

**2239** A678 (5k) multicolored 2.25 .55

Swedish Elk A679

Designs: No. 2240, Elk as fantasy character. No. 2241, Bar code elk. No. 2242, Swedish elk, yellow bars. No. 2243, Forest elk, green background. No. 2244, Road sign elk, black silhouette against yellow. No. 2245, Old Norse elks, adult & calf.

**1997, Aug. 21** **Litho.** *Perf. 13*

**2240** A679 (5k) multicolored 2.10 .85
**2241** A679 (5k) multicolored 2.10 .85
**2242** A679 (5k) multicolored 2.10 .85
**2243** A679 (5k) multicolored 2.10 .85
**2244** A679 (5k) multicolored 2.10 .85
**2245** A679 (5k) multicolored 2.10 .85
*a.* Booklet pane, #2240-2245 12.00 13.50
Complete booklet, #2245a 12.00

Perforations at each corner of Nos. 2240-2245 end in a large hole within the pane or semi-circles at the edges of the pane, giving the corners of each stamp a slightly concave appearance.

King Gustav III's Museum of Antiquities, Stockholm Palace — A680

*Perf. 13x12½ on 3 Sides*

**1997, Aug. 21** **Engr.**

**2246** A680 8k Muses Gallery 3.00 2.10
**2247** A680 8k Endymion 3.00 2.10
*a.* Booklet pane, 2 each #2246-2247 + 4 labels 12.00
Complete booklet, #2247a 12.00

Classic Cars A681

#2248, 1958 Volvo Duett. #2249, 1955 Chevrolet Bel-Air. #2250, 1959 Porsche 356A Coupé. #2251, 1952, Citroen B11. #2252, 1963 Saab 96. #2253, 1961 E-Type Jaguar.

*Perf. 12½x13 on 3 Sides*

**1997, Oct. 4** **Litho. & Engr.**

**Booklet Stamps**

**2248** A681 (5k) multicolored 2.25 2.25
**2249** A681 (5k) multicolored 2.25 2.25
**2250** A681 (5k) multicolored 2.25 2.25
**2251** A681 (5k) multicolored 2.25 2.25
**2252** A681 (5k) multicolored 2.25 2.25
**2253** A681 (5k) multicolored 2.25 2.25
*a.* Booklet pane, #2248-2253 13.50 15.00
Complete booklet, #2253a 13.50

Alfred Nobel (1833-1896), Founder of Nobel Prize — A682

Design: No. 2255, Paul Karrer (1889-1971), winner of Nobel prize for chemistry, 1937.

*Perf. 12½x13 on 3 Sides*

**1997, Nov. 13** **Litho. & Engr.**

**2254** A682 7k lt pink & black 3.00 2.50
**2255** A682 7k gray & black 3.00 2.50
*a.* Bklt. pane, 2 ea #2254-2255 12.00 14.50
Complete booklet, #2255a 9.00

See Switzerland Nos. 1004-1005.

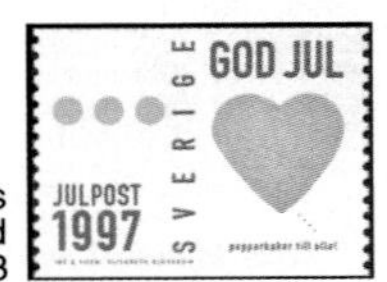


Christmas Gingerbread A683

*Perf. 12½ Vert.*

**1997, Nov. 20** **Litho.**

**2256** A683 (3.50k) Heart 1.75 1.50

*Perf. 12½ on 3 Sides*

**2257** A683 (3.50k) Animals 1.50 1.00
**2258** A683 (3.50k) People 1.50 1.00
*a.* Bklt. pane, 5 ea #2257-2258 15.00
Complete booklet, #2258a 15.00

Christmas Angels — A684

Angels from altarpiece, Litslena Church: No. 2259, Playing horn, mandolin. No. 2260, Playing pipes, harp.

**1997, Nov. 20** *Perf. 13x12½*

**2259** A684 6k multicolored 2.25 1.70
**2260** A684 6k multicolored 2.25 1.70
*a.* Booklet pane, 5 each #2259-2260 + 10 labels 22.50
Complete booklet, #2260a 22.50

Photographer Jan Lindblad (1932-87) and His Tigers — A685

*Perf. 12½ Horiz.*

**1998, Jan. 15** **Litho. & Engr.**

**2261** A685 (3.50k) shown 1.60 1.00
**2262** A685 (3.50k) Two tigers on rock 1.60 1.00
*a.* Pair, #2261-2262 3.25 2.50

New Modern Museum of Art, Stockholm A686

#2263, Fungus Sculpture, by Yves Klein. #2264, Skeppsholmen, by Göran Gidenstam. #2265, Monogram, by Robert Rauschenberg.

**1998, Jan. 15** *Perf. 12½ Vert.*

**2263** A686 (5k) multicolored 2.25 .65
**2264** A686 (5k) multicolored 2.25 .65
**2265** A686 (5k) multicolored 2.25 .65
*a.* Booklet pane of 3, #2263-2265 6.75 7.00
Complete booklet, 2 #2265a 13.50

Valentine's Day — A687

*Perf. 13 (on 3 Sides)*

**1998, Jan. 15** **Litho.**

**2266** A687 (5k) dp grn & org red 2.00 .50
**2267** A687 (5k) dp blue & rose red 2.00 .50
*a.* Bklt. pane, 3 ea #2266-2267 12.00
Complete booklet, #2267a 12.00

Swedish Confederation of Trade Unions, Cent. — A688

*Perf. 12½ Horiz.*

**1998, Mar. 19** **Engr.**

**2268** A688 (5k) multicolored 2.10 .50

Public Buildings A689

#2269, Fire station, Gävle. #2270, Shoe shop, Askersund. #2271, Fish halls, Gothenburg. #2272, Rödalvarm (Red Mill) Cinema, Halmstad. #2273, Town Hotel, Eksjö.

**1998, Mar. 19** *Perf. 12½ Horiz.*

**2269** A689 (5k) multicolored 2.00 .60
**2270** A689 (5k) multicolored 2.00 .60
**2271** A689 (5k) multicolored 2.00 .60
**2272** A689 (5k) multicolored 2.00 .60
**2273** A689 (5k) multicolored 2.00 .60
*a.* Booklet pane, #2269-2273 10.00
Complete booklet, #2273a 10.00

Queen Christina, Medallion Commemorating the Peace of Westphalia, 1648 — A690

**1998, Mar. 19** **Engr.** *Perf. 12½ Vert.*

**2274** A690 7k rose brn & dp grn 2.75 1.25

Handicrafts A691

Designs: (4.50k), Apron from costume, Dalecarlia. (5k), Wrought iron ornamental designs. No. 2277, Lovikka mitten. No. 2278, Boxes made from wood shavings.

**1998, Mar. 19** *Perf. 13 Vert.*

**2275** A691 (4.50k) multicolored 1.60 1.10
**2276** A691 (5k) multicolored 2.00 .40

*Perf. 12½ on 3 Sides*

**2277** A691 8k multicolored 2.75 2.75
**2278** A691 8k multicolored 2.75 2.75
*a.* Bklt. pane, 2 ea #2277-2278 11.00
Complete booklet, #2278a + 4 labels 11.00

Wetland Flowers
A692 A693

*Perf. 13 on 3 Sides*

**1998, May 14** **Litho.**

**2279** A692 (5k) Marsh violet 2.00 .35
**2280** A693 (5k) Great willow-herb 2.00 .35
*a.* Bklt pane, 5 ea #2279-2280 20.00
Complete booklet, #2280a 20.00

City of Stockholm — A694

Designs: Nos. 2281, 2287, Stockholm Palace. Nos. 2282, 2288, Skerry boats. No. 2283, Opera House, cent. No. 2284, Sail boats. No. 2285, Langholmen Beach, vert. No. 2286, Fireworks over City Hall, vert.

Illustration reduced.

*Perf. 13 on 2 or 3 Sides*

**1998, May 14** **Litho. & Engr.**

**2281** A694 (5k) multicolored 2.10 1.25
**2282** A694 (5k) multicolored 2.10 1.25

**Size: 27x22mm**

**2283** A694 (5k) multicolored 2.25 1.60
**2284** A694 (5k) multicolored 2.25 1.60

**Size: 27x36mm**

**2285** A694 (5k) multicolored 2.25 1.60
**2286** A694 (5k) multicolored 2.25 1.60
*a.* Booklet pane, #2281-2286 13.00 14.50
Complete booklet, #2286a 13.00 14.50

**Size: 58x23mm**

**2287** A694 7k multicolored 2.10 1.50
**2288** A694 7k multicolored 2.10 1.50
*a.* Bklt. pane, 2 ea #2287-2288 8.50
Complete booklet, #2288a 8.50

Cruise Ship Albatros in Stockholm Harbor — A695

**1998, May 14** *Perf. 13 Vert.*

**Coil Stamp**

**2289** A695 6k multicolored 2.25 2.25

Festivals and Holidays — A696

Europa: No. 2290, Crayfish party, paper moon. No. 2291, Dancing around maypole, Midsummer in June.

***Perf. 13 on 3 Sides***

**1998, May 14** **Litho.**

| | | |
|---|---|---|
| **2290** A696 7k multicolored | *2.75* | 2.75 |
| **2291** A696 7k multicolored | *2.75* | 2.75 |
| *a.* Bklt. pane, 2 ea #2289-2290 | *11.00* | *13.00* |
| Complete booklet, #2291a + 4 labels | *11.00* | *13.00* |

King Carl XVI Gustaf, 25th Anniv. of Accession to the Throne — A697

**1998, May 14** **Engr.** ***Perf. 13 Vert.***

| | | |
|---|---|---|
| **2292** A697 (5k) multicolored | 2.25 | .50 |

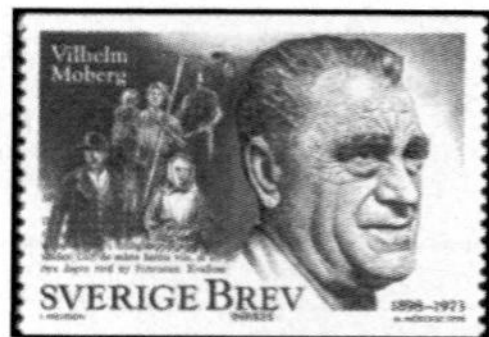


Vilhelm Moberg (1898-1973), Writer — A698

**Litho. & Engr.**

**1998, Aug. 20** ***Perf. 13 Vert.***

**Coil Stamp**

| | | |
|---|---|---|
| **2293** A698 (5k) multicolored | 2.25 | .65 |

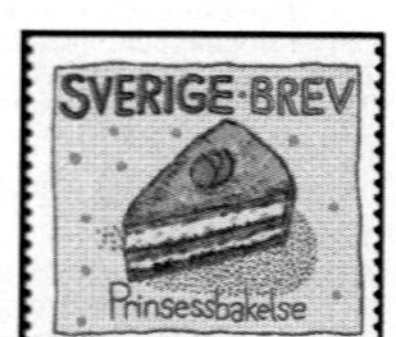


Pastries A699

Designs: No. 2294, Princess cake. No. 2295, Gustav Adolf pastry. No. 2296, Napoleon pastry. No. 2297, Mocha cake. No. 2298, National pastry. No. 2299, Lent bun (semla).

***Perf. 13 on 3 Sides***

**1998, Aug. 20** **Litho.**

| | | |
|---|---|---|
| **2294** A699 (5k) multicolored | 2.25 | 1.25 |
| **2295** A699 (5k) multicolored | 2.25 | 1.25 |
| **2296** A699 (5k) multicolored | 2.25 | 1.25 |
| **2297** A699 (5k) multicolored | 2.25 | 1.25 |
| **2298** A699 (5k) multicolored | 2.25 | 1.25 |
| **2299** A699 (5k) multicolored | 2.25 | 1.25 |
| *a.* Booklet pane, #2294-2299 | 13.50 | *14.50* |
| Complete booklet, #2299a | 13.50 | |

The Millennium — A700

Swedish developments during 1900's: No. 2300, Painting, "Flowers on the Window Sill," by Carl Larsson. No. 2301, Stockholm Stadium, poster for 1912 Olympic Games. No. 2302, Power plant, Porjus, Lapland. No. 2303, Inventions; zippers, ball bearings, vacuum cleaners, refrigerators. No. 2304, Johnson (shipping) Line. No. 2305, AB Radiotjänst, 1924. No. 2306, Jazz music, Charleston dance. No. 2307, Ellen Key, Kerstin Hesselgren, pioneers for women's rights. No. 2308, Arne Borg, swimmer, Gillis Grafström, figure skater, world champions. No. 2309, Ernst Rolf, entertainer, 1920's.

***Perf. 12½ Horiz.***

**1998, Oct. 3** **Litho. & Engr.**

| | | |
|---|---|---|
| **2300** A700 (5k) multicolored | 2.50 | 2.50 |
| **2301** A700 (5k) multicolored | 2.50 | 2.50 |
| **2302** A700 (5k) multicolored | 2.50 | 2.50 |
| **2303** A700 (5k) multicolored | 2.50 | 2.50 |
| **2304** A700 (5k) multicolored | 2.50 | 2.50 |
| **2305** A700 (5k) multicolored | 2.50 | 2.50 |
| **2306** A700 (5k) multicolored | 2.50 | 2.50 |
| **2307** A700 (5k) multicolored | 2.50 | 2.50 |
| **2308** A700 (5k) multicolored | 2.50 | 2.50 |
| **2309** A700 (5k) multicolored | 2.50 | 2.50 |
| *a.* Booklet pane, #2300-2309 | 25.00 | *30.00* |
| Complete booklet, #2309a | 25.00 | |

See Nos. 2327-2336, 2379-2388.

Nobel Laureates A701

***Perf. 13x12½ on 3 Sides***

**1998, Oct. 3** **Engr.**

| | | |
|---|---|---|
| **2310** A701 6k Nadine Gordimer, 1991 | 2.25 | 1.75 |
| **2311** A701 6k Sigrid Undset, 1928 | 2.25 | 1.75 |
| *a.* Bklt. pane, 2 ea #2310-2311 | 9.00 | |
| Complete booklet, #2311a + 4 labels | 9.00 | |

Sigismund (1566-1632), King of Sweden and Poland — A702

***Perf. 12½ Horiz.***

**1998, Oct. 3** **Litho. & Engr.**

| | | |
|---|---|---|
| **2312** A702 7k multicolored | 2.75 | 2.00 |

See Poland No. 3421.

A703

A704

***Perf. 12½ Horiz.***

**1998, Nov. 19** **Litho.**

| | | |
|---|---|---|
| **2313** A703 (4k) Hyacinth | 2.00 | 1.25 |

***Perf. 12½ on 3 Sides***

| | | |
|---|---|---|
| **2314** A703 (4k) Mistletoe | 1.60 | .50 |
| **2315** A703 (4k) Amaryllis | 1.60 | .50 |
| *a.* Bklt. pane, 5 ea #2314-2315 | 16.00 | |
| Complete booklet, #2315a | 16.00 | |
| **2316** A703 6k Wreath | 2.10 | 1.50 |
| **2317** A703 6k Azalea | 2.10 | 1.50 |
| *a.* Bklt. pane, 5 ea #2316--2317 | 21.00 | |
| Complete booklet, #2317a | 21.00 | |
| *Nos. 2313-2317 (5)* | 9.40 | 5.25 |

Christmas.

**1999, Jan. 14** **Litho.** ***Perf. 13 Vert.***

| | | |
|---|---|---|
| **2318** A704 (5k) multicolored | 2.10 | .40 |

Swedish Cooperative Union, cent.

A705

A706

Swedish Coins: No. 2319, Gustav Vasa daler. No. 2320, Carl XIV John riksdaler.

**1999, Jan. 14** **Engr.** ***Perf. 12½ Vert.***

| | | |
|---|---|---|
| **2319** A705 (4.50k) dark green | 1.60 | 1.00 |
| **2320** A705 (5k) dark blue | 2.00 | .40 |

***Perf. 12½ on 3 Sides***

**1999, Jan. 14** **Litho.**

Easter Eggs: No. 2321, Sugar egg. No. 2322, Egg filled with marzipan chicks.

**Panel Color**

| | | |
|---|---|---|
| **2321** A706 (5k) green | 2.25 | 1.00 |
| **2322** A706 (5k) red | 2.25 | 1.00 |
| *a.* Bklt. pane, 3 ea #2321-2322 | 13.50 | |
| Complete booklet, #2322a | 13.50 | |

"Little Sister Rabbit," by Ulf Nilsson — A707

Rabbits: No. 2323, Preparing meal over fireplace. No. 2324, Feeding Little Sister. No. 2325, Dancing to music. No. 2326, Hopping through thicket.

***Perf. 12½ Vert.***

**1999, Jan. 14** **Litho. & Engr.**

| | | |
|---|---|---|
| **2323** A707 (5k) multicolored | 2.00 | 1.00 |
| **2324** A707 (5k) multicolored | 2.00 | 1.00 |
| **2325** A707 (5k) multicolored | 2.00 | 1.00 |
| **2326** A707 (5k) multicolored | 2.00 | 1.00 |
| *a.* Booklet pane, #2323-2326 | 8.00 | 7.50 |
| Complete booklet, #2326a | 8.00 | |

**The Millennium Type of 1998**

Sweden in years 1939-1969: No. 2327, Scene from Bergman's film "Smiles of a Summer Night," 1955. No. 2328, Vällingby Centre. No. 2329, Silhouette of soldier, singer Ulla Bilquist. No. 2330, Cobra telephone, three-point seat belt, ASEA high voltage cables and breakers, Tetra Pak's milk carton. No. 2331, Scandinavian Airlines System formed, DC-4 over New York City, 1946. No. 2332, "Hyland's Corner," Carl-Gustaf Lindstedt, Prime Minister Tage Erlander on television. No. 2333, Protests of the 60's, Hep Stars band. No. 2334, Volvo Amazon car, family picnic. No. 2335, Ingemar Johansson, heavy-weight boxing champion, 1959, Mora-Nisse Karlsson, skiing champion, Gunder Hägg, running champion, 1941-45. No. 2336, Jazz singer Alice Babs, opera singer Jussi Björling.

***Perf. 12½ Horiz.***

**1999, Mar. 11** **Litho.**

| | | |
|---|---|---|
| **2327** A700 (5k) multicolored | 2.10 | 1.25 |
| **2328** A700 (5k) multicolored | 2.10 | 1.25 |
| **2329** A700 (5k) multicolored | 2.10 | 1.25 |
| **2330** A700 (5k) multicolored | 2.10 | 1.25 |
| **2331** A700 (5k) multicolored | 2.10 | 1.25 |
| **2332** A700 (5k) multicolored | 2.10 | 1.25 |
| **2333** A700 (5k) multicolored | 2.10 | 1.25 |
| **2334** A700 (5k) multicolored | 2.10 | 1.25 |
| **2335** A700 (5k) multicolored | 2.10 | 1.25 |
| **2336** A700 (5k) multicolored | 2.10 | 1.25 |
| *a.* Booklet pane, #2327-2336 | 21.00 | 21.00 |
| Complete booklet, #2336a | 21.00 | |

Construction of the Oresund Bridge — A708

(5k), Swan Pontoon Crane. 6k, Building bridge.

**1999, Mar. 11** ***Perf. 12½ Vert.***

| | | |
|---|---|---|
| **2337** A708 (5k) multicolored | 2.00 | .40 |
| **2338** A708 6k multicolored | 2.25 | 2.00 |

Swedish Ships A709

***Perf. 12½x13 on 3 Sides***

**1999, Mar. 11** **Litho. & Engr.**

| | | |
|---|---|---|
| **2339** A709 8k East Indiaman | 2.50 | 2.10 |
| **2340** A709 8k Mary Anne | 2.50 | 2.10 |
| **2341** A709 8k Beatrice | 2.50 | 2.10 |
| **2342** A709 8k SS Austalic | 2.50 | 2.10 |
| *a.* Booklet pane, #2339-2342 | 10.00 | *12.50* |
| Complete booklet, #2342a + 4 labels | 10.00 | |

Australia '99 World Stamp Expo.

Pyramid Orchid — A710

Lady's Slipper — A711

Marsh Helleborine A712

Green-Winged Ordhid A713

***Perf. 12½ on 3 Sides***

**1999, May 20** **Litho.**

| | | |
|---|---|---|
| **2343** A710 (5k) multicolored | 2.10 | .40 |
| **2344** A711 (5k) multicolored | 2.50 | .75 |
| **2345** A712 (5k) multicolored | 2.10 | .40 |
| **2346** A713 (5k) multicolored | 2.50 | .75 |
| *a.* Booklet pane, 3 each #2343, 2345, 2 each #2344, #2346 | 22.50 | |
| Complete booket, #2346a | 22.50 | |
| *Nos. 2343-2346 (4)* | 9.20 | 2.30 |

Council of Europe, 50th Anniv. — A714

**1999, May 20** ***Perf. 12½ Horiz.***

| | | |
|---|---|---|
| **2347** A714 7k multicolored | 2.75 | 1.75 |

Europa — A715

***Perf. 12½x13 on 3 Sides***

**1999, May 20**

| | | |
|---|---|---|
| **2348** A715 7k Tyresta Natl. Park | *2.50* | 2.00 |
| **2349** A715 7k Gotska Sandön Natl. Park | *2.50* | 2.00 |
| *a.* Bklt. pane, 2 ea #2348-2349 | *10.00* | *11.00* |
| Complete bklt., #2349a+4 labels | *10.00* | |

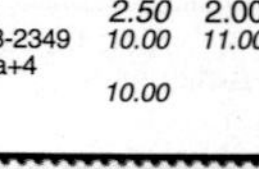

Post Bike — A716

Racing Bike — A717

Town Bike — A718

Messenger Bike — A719

**Engr., Litho. (#2351)**

**1999, May 20** ***Perf. 12½ Horiz.***

**2350** A716 (3.50k) multicolored 1.75 1.40

***Perf. 12½ Vert.***

**2351** A717 (5k) multicolored 2.00 .90
**2352** A718 6k multicolored 2.25 1.50
**2353** A719 8k multicolored 2.75 *2.25*
*Nos. 2350-2353 (4)* 8.75 6.05

Signs of the Zodiac A720

No. 2354: a, Aquarius. b, Pisces. c, Aries. d, Taurus. e, Gemini. f, Cancer.
No. 2355: a, Leo. b, Virgo. c, Libra. d, Scorpio. e, Sagittarius. f, Capricorn.

**Litho. & Engr.**

**1999, Aug. 12** ***Perf. 13***

**2354** Booklet pane of 6 15.00 10.00
***a.-f.*** A720 (5k) any single 2.50 1.60
**2355** Booklet pane of 6 15.00 10.00
***a.-f.*** A720 (5k) any single 2.50 1.60
Complete booklet, #2354-2355 30.00

Perforations at each corner of Nos. 2354a-2354f, 2355a-2355f end in a large hole within the pane or semi-circles at the edges of the pane, giving the corners of each stamp a slightly concave appearance.

Butterflies A721

a, Inachis io. b, Junonia orithya wallacei. c, Hypolimnas bolina. d, Vanessa atalanta.

**1999, Aug. 12** ***Perf. 12½x13***

**2356** Booklet pane of 4 9.00 *10.50*
***a.-d.*** A721 6k any single 2.25 1.75
Complete bklt., #2356 + 4 labels 9.00

See Singapore Nos. 903-907.

Nobel Laureates in Peace — A722

#2357, Auguste Beernaert (1829-1912). #2358, Henri La Fontaine (1854-1943).

***Perf. 13x12½ on 3 sides***

**1999, Sept. 30** **Litho. & Engr.**

**2357** A722 7k gold & blue 2.75 2.25
**2358** A722 7k gold & red 2.75 2.25
***a.*** Bklt. pane, 2 ea #2357-2358 11.00
Complete booklet, #2358a + 4 labels 11.00

See Belgium Nos. 1749-1750.

Dance Bands A723

Designs: a, Thorleifs. b, Arvingarna. c, Lotta Engbergs. d, Sten & Stanley.

**Litho. & Engr.**

**1999, Oct. 2** ***Perf. 12¾***

**2359** Booklet pane of 4 9.00 *9.50*
***a.-d.*** A723 (5k) any single 2.90 1.75
Complete booklet, 2 #2359 18.00

A724

Christmas A725

Stained glass: No. 2360, Nativity, Klinte Church. No. 2361, Nativity, Hablingbro Church. No. 2362, Three kings, Hablingbro Church.

Madonna and child icons from: No. 2363, Bälinge Church. No. 2364, Skänninge Church.

***Perf. 12½ Vert.***

**1999, Nov. 18** **Litho.**

**2360** A724 (4.50k) multicolored 1.75 1.25

***Perf. 12¾ on 3 sides***

**2361** A724 (4.50k) multicolored 1.50 .60
**2362** A724 (4.50k) multicolored 1.50 .60
***a.*** Bklt. pane, 5 ea #2361-2362 15.00
Complete booklet, # 2362a 15.00

**Litho. & Engr.**

**2363** A725 6k multicolored 2.25 1.60
**2364** A725 6k multicolored 2.25 1.60
***a.*** Booklet pane, 5 each #2363-2364 + 10 labels 22.50
Complete booklet, # 2364a 22.50
*Nos. 2360-2364 (5)* 9.25 5.65

Millennium — A726

Sun rays touching Heligholmen Island: No. 2365, Island rocks. No. 2366, Island map.

***Perf. 12¾ Horiz.***

**1999, Dec. 27** **Litho. & Engr.**

**2365** A726 5k multicolored 2.25 1.75
**2366** A726 5k multicolored 2.25 1.75
***a.*** Bklt. pane, 2 ea #2365-2366 9.00
Complete booklet, 2 #2366a 18.00

New Year 2000 (Year of the Dragon) A727

Dragon from children's book "The Dragon with Red Eyes," by Astrid Lindgren: No. 2367, In flight (shown). No. 2368, With basket. No. 2369, In flight, diff.

***Perf. 12¾ Horiz.***

**2000, Jan. 13** **Litho.**

**2367** A727 (5k) multi 2.25 1.10
**2368** A727 (5k) multi 2.25 1.10
**2369** A727 (5k) multi 2.25 1.10
***a.*** Bklt. pane, 2 ea #2367-2369 13.50
Complete booklet, #2369a 13.50

A728

A729

Love.

**2000, Jan. 13** ***Perf. 12¾ on 3 sides***

**2370** A728 (5k) shown 2.00 1.00
**2371** A728 (5k) Heart, diff. 2.00 1.00
***a.*** Bklt. pane, 3 ea #2370-2371 12.00
Complete booklet, #2371a 12.00

**2000, Jan. 13** **Engr.** ***Perf. 12½ Vert.***

Watch of King Karl XII, 1701: (4.50k), Works. (5k), Face.

**2372** A729 (4.50k) blue 1.60 1.00
**2373** A729 (5k) claret brown 2.25 .45

Souvenir Sheet

Detail of "Great Deeds by Swedish Kings," by David Ehrenstrahl — A730

**Litho. & Engr.**

**2000, Mar. 17** ***Perf. 12¾***

**2374** A730 50k multi 11.50 *14.50*

Czeslaw Slania's 1000th postage stamp.

Forests — A731

Designs: (3.80k), People in forest. No. 2376, Elk in forest. No. 2377, Bird in forest. 6k, Birch forest.

***Perf. 12¾ Vert.***

**2000, Mar. 17** **Litho.**

**2375** A731 (3.80k) multi 1.75 1.10
**2376** A731 (5k) multi 1.90 .55
**2377** A731 (5k) multi 1.90 .55
***a.*** Pair, #2376-2377 3.75 3.50
**2378** A731 6k multi 2.25 1.75
*Nos. 2375-2378 (4)* 7.80 3.95

**Millennium Type of 1998**

Sweden in the years 1970-99: No. 2379, Art in Stockholm subway stations. No. 2380, Swedish UN forces, postal clerk. No. 2381, Computer, mouse and mobile phone. No. 2382, Cullberg Ballet, Svenska Ord repertory company. No. 2383, Jönköping railway station. No. 2384, Youth with spiked hair, musical group ABBA. No. 2385, European Union flag, map of member countries. No. 2386, Scene from film, "The Apple War." No. 2387, Skiers Pernilla Wiberg, Ingemar Stenmark, tennis player Björn Borg. No. 2388, Photo of child in womb, taken by Lennart Nilsson.

***Perf. 12¾ Horiz.***

**2000, Mar. 17** **Litho.**

**2379** A700 (5k) multi 2.00 1.40
**2380** A700 (5k) multi 2.00 1.40
**2381** A700 (5k) multi 2.00 1.40
**2382** A700 (5k) multi 2.00 1.40
**2383** A700 (5k) multi 2.00 1.40
**2384** A700 (5k) multi 2.00 1.40
**2385** A700 (5k) multi 2.00 1.40
**2386** A700 (5k) multi 2.00 1.40
**2387** A700 (5k) multi 2.00 1.40
**2388** A700 (5k) multi 2.00 1.40
***a.*** Booklet pane, #2379-2388 20.00 *20.00*
Complete booklet, #2388a 20.00

Art by Philip von Schantz (1928-98) — A732

Designs: No. 2389, A Peck of Apples. No. 2390, A Bowl of Blueberries.

***Perf. 12¾ on 3 sides***

**2000, May 9** **Litho.**

**2389** A732 (5k) multi 1.75 .60
**2390** A732 (5k) multi 1.75 .60
***a.*** Bklt. pane, 5 ea #2389-2390 19.00
Complete booklet, #2390a 19.00

A733

Oresund Bridge, Sweden-Denmark — A734

Illustration A734 reduced.

**2000, May 9** **Engr.** ***Perf. 12½ Vert.***

**2391** A733 (5k) blue & ultra 2.25 .75

**Litho.**

***Perf. 12¾ Horiz.***

**2392** A734 6k shown 2.50 1.75
**2393** A734 6k Map 2.50 1.75
***a.*** Booklet pane, 2 each #2392-2393, + 4 etiquettes 10.00
Complete booklet, #2393a 10.00

See Denmark Nos. 1187-1188.

**Europa Issue**

Common Design Type

**2000, May 9** **Litho.** ***Perf. 12¾ Horiz.***

**2394** CD17 7k multi *2.25 2.25*

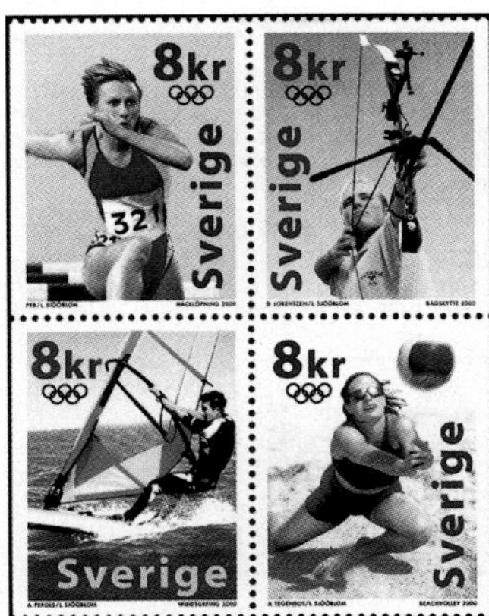


2000 Summer Olympics, Sydney — A735

No. 2395: a, Hurdler Ludmila Engquist. b, Archer Magnus Petersson. c, Windsurfer

Fredrik Palm. d, Beach volleyball player Lena Malm.

*Perf. 12¾x12½ on 3 sides*

**2000, Aug. 17 Litho.**

| | | | |
|---|---|---|---|
| **2395** | A735 Booklet pane of 4 | 11.00 | *12.50* |
| *a.-d.* | 8k Any single | 2.75 | 2.25 |
| | Booklet, #2395 + 4 etiquettes | 11.00 | |

Sky Conditions A736

No. 2396: a, Clouds and sun. b, Clouds and lightning. c, Clouds and rainstorm. d, Aurora borealis. e, Rainbow. f, Cumulus clouds.

**2000, Aug. 17 *Die Cut Perf. 9¾x10***

**Self-Adhesive**

| | | | |
|---|---|---|---|
| **2396** | Booklet of 6 | 12.00 | |
| *a.-f.* | A736 (5k) Any single | 2.00 | 1.25 |

King Carl XVI Gustaf — A737

Design: 8k, Queen Silvia.

*Perf. 12¾ Vert.*

**2000, Aug. 17 Engr.**

| | | | |
|---|---|---|---|
| **2397** | A737 (5k) blue | 2.25 | .50 |
| **2398** | A737 8k red | 2.75 | 2.00 |

Nobel Laureates for Literature — A738

a, Wislawa Szymborska. b, Nelly Sachs.
Illustration reduced.

*Perf. 12¾x12½ on 3 sides*

**2000, Oct. 7 Engr.**

| | | | |
|---|---|---|---|
| **2399** | A738 Pair | 5.00 | 5.00 |
| *a.-b.* | 7k Any single | 2.50 | 2.40 |
| *c.* | Booklet pane, 2 #2399 | 10.00 | |
| | Booklet, #2399c + 4 etiquettes | 10.00 | |

Toys — A739

No. 2400: a, Doll, tea set, teddy bear. b, Marbles, tin soldier, yo-yo, jump rope. c, Pine cone cow, doll, horse-drawn wagon. d, Cars and policeman. e, Model train, mechanical men. f, Lego car, robot, Furbee.

*Perf. 12¾ on 3 sides*

**2000, Oct. 7 Litho. & Engr.**

| | | | |
|---|---|---|---|
| **2400** | Booklet of 6 | 13.50 | *15.00* |
| *a.-f.* | A739 (5k) Any single | 2.25 | 2.25 |

Christmas Songs — A740

Christmas Snowflakes — A741

Designs: No. 2401, Hey, Santas.
No. 2402, vert.: a, It's Christmas Again (four children, tree). b, Three Gingerbread Men. c, The Fox Runs Over the Ice. d, Christmas Has Come to Our House (three children, candles).
No. 2403: a, White background. b, Blue background.
Illustration A741 reduced.

*Perf. 12¾ Vert.*

**2000, Nov. 16 Litho.**

| | | | |
|---|---|---|---|
| **2401** | A740 (4.30k) multi | 1.50 | 1.00 |

*Perf. 12¾ on 3 sides*

| | | | |
|---|---|---|---|
| **2402** | Block of 4 | 6.00 | 5.50 |
| *a.-d.* | A740 (4.30k) Any single | 1.50 | .70 |
| *e.* | Booklet pane, 3 ea #2402a, 2402c, 2 ea #2402b, 2402d | 15.00 | |
| | Booklet, #2402e | 15.00 | |
| **2403** | A741 Pair | 4.50 | *5.50* |
| *a.-b.* | 6k Any single | 2.25 | 2.25 |
| *c.* | Booklet pane, 5 #2403 + 10 etiquettes | 22.50 | |
| | Booklet, #2403c | 22.50 | |
| | *Nos. 2401-2403 (3)* | 12.00 | 12.00 |

Rock Carvings, Tanum World Heritage Site — A742

Swedish World Heritage Site A743

Designs: (4.50k), Rock carvings of animals and people. (5k), Rock carvings of ships.
No. 2406: a, Gammelstad Church Village. b, Karlskrona Naval Port. c, Theater, Drottningholm Palace. d, Engelsberg Ironworks.

**2001, Jan. 31 Engr. *Perf. 12½ Vert.***

| | | | |
|---|---|---|---|
| **2404** | A742 (4.50k) blue, *gray* | 1.75 | 1.25 |
| **2405** | A742 (5k) red, *gray* | 1.90 | .45 |

**Litho.**

*Perf. 12½x12¾ on 3 sides*

| | | | |
|---|---|---|---|
| **2406** | Booklet pane of 4 | 8.00 | *10.00* |
| *a.-d.* | A743 6k Any single | 2.00 | 2.00 |
| | Booklet, #2406 + 4 etiquettes | 8.00 | |

New Year 2001 (Year of the Snake) — A744

No. 2407: a, Snake with tongue extended. b, Snake curled up.
Illustration reduced.

*Perf. 12¾ on 3 sides*

**2001, Jan. 31 Litho.**

| | | | |
|---|---|---|---|
| **2407** | A744 Pair | 4.00 | 2.75 |
| *a.-b.* | (5k) Any single | 2.00 | 1.00 |
| *c.* | Booklet pane, 3 #2407 | 12.00 | |
| | Booklet, #2407c | 12.00 | |

Dogs — A745

No. 2408: a, Golden retriever. b, German shepherd. c, Labrador retriever. d, Dachshund.

**2001, Jan. 31 *Perf. 12¾ Vert.***

| | | | |
|---|---|---|---|
| **2408** | Booklet of 4 | 8.00 | 7.50 |
| *a.-d.* | A745 (5k) Any single | 2.00 | 1.00 |

Birds — A746

Designs: (3.80k), Vanellus vanellus. (5k), Pica pica. 6k, Larus argentatus. 7k, Aegithalos caudatus.

**2001, Mar. 22 Engr. *Perf. 12¾ Vert.***

| | | | |
|---|---|---|---|
| **2409** | A746 (3.80k) multi | 1.75 | 1.25 |
| **2410** | A746 (5k) multi | 1.90 | .50 |
| **2411** | A746 6k multi | 2.00 | 1.50 |
| **2412** | A746 7k multi | 2.25 | 1.75 |
| | *Nos. 2409-2412 (4)* | 7.90 | 5.00 |

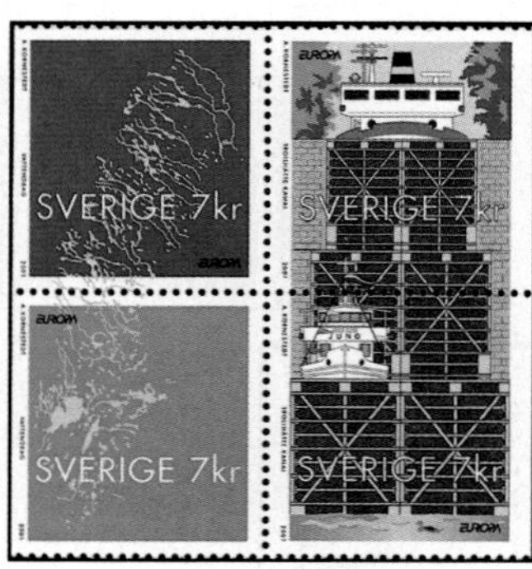


Europa — A747

No. 2413: a, Waterways of northern Sweden. b, Large ship in Trollhätte Canal, trees. c, Waterways of southern Sweden. d, Ship "Juno" in Trollhätte Canal, duck.
Illustration reduced.

*Perf. 12¾ on 3 Sides*

**2001, Mar. 22 Litho.**

| | | | |
|---|---|---|---|
| **2413** | A747 Booklet pane of 4 | *11.00* | *12.00* |
| *a.-d.* | 7k Any single | 2.75 | 2.25 |
| | Booklet, #2413 + 4 etiquettes | *11.00* | |

Easter A748

No. 2414: a, Orange egg. b, Purple egg. c, Chick.

**2001, Mar. 22 *Die Cut Perf. 9¾x10***

**Self-Adhesive**

| | | | |
|---|---|---|---|
| **2414** | A748 Booklet pane of 3 | 6.00 | 6.00 |
| *a.-c.* | (5k) Any single | 1.90 | 1.60 |
| | Booklet, 2 #2414 | 12.00 | |

Nobel Prize, Cent. A749

No. 2415: a, Alfred Nobel, Peace medal, obverse of Physics, Chemistry, Physiology or Medicine, Literature medal. b, Reverse of Physiology or Medicine medal. c, Reverse of medal for Physics or Chemistry. d, Reverse of Literature medal.

*Perf. 12¾x13½ on 3 Sides*

**2001, Mar. 22 Litho. & Engr.**

| | | | |
|---|---|---|---|
| **2415** | Vert. strip of 4 | 10.00 | 12.50 |
| *a.-d.* | A749 8k Any single | 2.50 | 2.50 |
| *e.* | Booklet pane, #2415 + 4 etiquettes + 4 blank labels | 10.00 | |
| | Booklet, #2415e | 10.00 | |

See United States No. 3504.

Ivar Lo-Johansson (1901-90), Writer — A750

No. 2416: a, Portrait. b, Lo-Johansson, truck.
Illustration reduced.

**2001, May 17 Engr. *Perf. 12¾ Vert.***

| | | | |
|---|---|---|---|
| **2416** | A750 Pair | 3.75 | 3.50 |
| *a.-b.* | (5k) Any single | 1.90 | .90 |

Peonies — A751

No. 2417: a, Fernleaf peony (two flowers, one bud). b, Chinese peony "Mons Jules Elie." c, Herbaceous peony (yellow). d, Common peony (flower and bud). e, Tree peony.

*Perf. 12¾ on 3 Sides*

**2001, May 17 Litho.**

| | | | |
|---|---|---|---|
| **2417** | Horiz. strip of 5 | 9.25 | 6.00 |
| *a.-e.* | A751 (5k) Any single | 1.90 | 1.10 |
| *f.* | Booklet pane, 2 #2417 | 19.00 | |
| | Booklet, #2417f | 19.00 | |

Nobel Prize, Cent. — A752

Past winners: a, Doctors Without Borders. b, Red Cross.
Illustration reduced.

*Perf. 12¾ Vert.*

**2001, Aug. 16 Litho.**

| | | | |
|---|---|---|---|
| **2418** | A752 Horiz. pair | 5.50 | 6.50 |
| *a.-b.* | 8k Any single | 2.75 | 2.75 |

Daniel Solander (1733-82), Botanist on Endeavour A753

No. 2419: a, Barringtonia calyptrata and Solander. b, Cochlospermum gillivraei and Endeavour.

*Perf. 12½x12¾ on 3 Sides*

**2001, Aug. 16 Litho. & Engr.**

**2419** A753 Vert. pair 5.00 *5.50*
*a.-b.* 8k Any single 2.50 2.25
*c.* Booklet pane, 2 #2419 10.00
Booklet, #2419c + 4 etiquettes 10.00

See Australia Nos. 1996-1997.

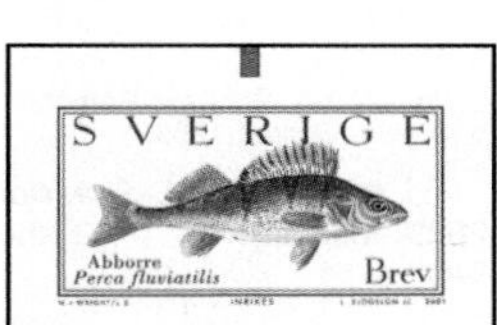

Fish A754

Designs: a, Perca fluviatilis. b, Abramis brama. c, Triglopsis quadricornis.

*Die Cut Perf. 13½ Horiz.*

**2001, Aug. 16 Litho. & Engr.**

**Self-Adhesive**

**2420** Booklet pane of 3 5.75 5.50
*a.-c.* A754 (5k) Any single 1.90 1.20
*d.* Booklet, 2 #2420 11.50

Souvenir Sheet

Aviation — A755

No. 2421: a, Lilienthal glider, 1895. b, Royal Swedish Aero Club. c, Saab J-29, 1962. d, Friedrichshafen FF49. e, Trike ultralight, 1999. f, Douglas DC-3, 1938.

*Perf. 12½x12¾*

**2001, Oct. 6 Litho. & Engr.**

**2421** A755 Sheet of 6 18.00 13.50
*a.-f.* 5k Any single 2.00 1.75

Stamp Design Contest Winners — A756

No. 2422: a, Rollerblader, by Emilie Kilström, Kikebo School, Oskarshamn. b, The Letter, by Thomas Fröhling.
Illustration reduced.

*Perf. 12¾ on 3 Sides*

**2001, Oct. 6 Litho.**

**2422** A756 Horiz. pair 4.00 *4.50*
*a.-b.* (5k) Any single 2.00 1.25
*c.* Booklet pane, 3 #2422 12.00
Booklet, #2422c 12.00

A757

Christmas — A758

Designs: No. 2423, Christmas tree.
No. 2424 — Tree ornaments (26x20mm): a, Star. b, Cracker. c, Angel. d, Heart e, Cone.
No. 2425 — Crumpled paper art by Yrjö Edelmann: a, Straw goat. b, Christmas tree.
Illustration A758 reduced.

*Perf. 12¾ Vert.*

**2001, Nov. 21 Litho.**

**2423** A757 (4.50k) multi 1.90 1.25

**Self-Adhesive**

*Die Cut Perf. 10¾x11¼*

**2424** Vert. strip of 5 8.25 8.25
*a.-e.* A757 (4.50k) Any single 1.60 .80
Booklet, 2 #2424 16.50

**Water-Activated Gum**

*Perf. 12¾ on 3 Sides*

**2425** A758 Horiz. pair 4.50 *5.25*
*a.-b.* 6k Any single 2.25 2.25
*c.* Booklet pane, 5 #2425 + 10 etiquettes 22.50
Booklet, #2425c 22.50
*Nos. 2423-2425 (3)* 14.65

World Ice Hockey Championships A759

**2002, Jan. 24 Litho. *Perf. 12¾ Vert.***

**2426** A759 (5k) multi 2.00 1.10

Pandion Haliaetus A760

**2002, Jan. 24 Engr.**

**2427** A760 10k multi 2.25 1.25

New Year 2002 (Year of the Horse) — A761

No. 2428 — The Stones Family, by Bertil Almqvist: a, Boy and girl on horse. b, Girl on, and boy leading horse, dog running.
Illustration reduced.

*Perf. 12¾ on 3 Sides*

**2002, Jan. 24 Litho.**

**2428** A761 Horiz. pair 4.00 2.50
*a.-b.* (5k) Any single 2.00 1.00
*c.* Booklet pane, 5 #2428 20.00 —
Booklet, #2428c 17.50

Love and Miss Terrified, by Joanna Rubin Dranger A762

No. 2429: a, "Det tror. . ." b, "Men jag. . ." c, "Anej!!!"

*Die Cut Perf. 13¾ Horiz.*

**2002, Jan. 24 Litho.**

**Self-Adhesive**

**2429** A762 Booklet pane of 3 6.00 5.00
*a.-c.* (5k) Any single 2.00 1.25
*d.* Booklet, 2 #2429 12.00

Antarctic Expedition of Otto Nordenskjöld, Cent. — A763

No. 2430: a, Scientists, ship, gull. b, Ship, penguin.

**Litho. & Engr., Litho. (#2430b)**

**2002, Jan. 24 *Perf. 12¾ Horiz.***

**2430** A763 Vert. pair 6.00 *6.25*
*a.-b.* 10k Any single 3.00 2.75
*c.* Booklet pane, 2 #2430 12.00 —
Booklet, #2430c + 4 etiquettes 12.00

Astrid Lindgren (1907-2002), Children's Book Writer — A764

Designs: a, Pippi Langstrump (Pippi Longstocking). b, Karlsson pa Taket. c, Bröderna Lejonhjärta, vert. d, Lindgren (24x29mm). e, Emil i Lönneberga, vert. f, Lotta pa Brakmakargatan. g, Madicken.

**2002, Mar. 5 Litho. *Perf. 13x13¼***

**2431** A764 Booklet pane of 7 14.00 *17.50*
*a.-g.* 5k Any single 2.00 *2.50*
Booklet, #2431 14.00

Stockholm, 750th Anniv. — A765

Painting of Stockholm, 1535: (5k), Town and Lake Mälaren. 10k, Close-up view of Cathedral and palace.

**2002, Mar. 21 Engr. *Perf. 12¾ Vert.***

**2432** A765 (5k) shown 1.75 1.10

**Size: 28x28mm**

**2433** A765 10k claret 3.00 2.25

A766

Swedish World Heritage Sites A767

Artifacts from Birka archaeological site: (3.80k), Cross. (4.50k), Runic stone. (5k), Man's face.
No. 2437 — Scenes from Visby: a, Town and ring wall. b, Wall towers. c, Burmeister building, flowers. d, Square, walls of St. Catherine's Church.

**2002, Mar. 21 Engr. *Perf. 12½ Vert.***

**2434** A766 (3.80k) purple 1.40 1.10
**2435** A766 (4.50k) blue 1.75 .75
**2436** A766 (5k) brn & claret 1.75 .75
*Nos. 2434-2436 (3)* 4.90 2.60

**Litho. & Engr.**

*Perf. 12½x12¾ on 3 Sides*

**2437** Booklet pane of 4 7.25 *8.00*
*a.-d.* A767 (5k) Any single 1.75 1.20
Booklet, #2437 7.25

Kristianstad Sculptures — A768

No. 2438: a, Structure by Takashi Naraha. b, Sprung From, by Pal Svensson.
Illustration reduced.

*Perf. 12¾ Vert.*

**2002, Mar. 23 Litho. & Engr.**

**2438** A768 Horiz. pair 5.50 5.50
*a.-b.* 8k Any single 2.75 2.50

Europa — A769

No. 2439: a, Charlie Rivel (1896-1983), clown. b, Clowns Without Borders (boy and clown). c, Cirkus Cirkör (performer with balloon). d, Cirkus Scott (woman on elephant).
Illustration reduced.

*Perf. 12¾ on 3 Sides*

**2002, May 2 Litho.**

**2439** A769 Booklet pane of 4 *11.00 12.50*
*a.-d.* 8k Any single *2.75 3.00*
Booklet, #2439 + 4 etiquettes *11.00*

Art From Sweden and New Zealand A770

No. 2440: a, Rain Forest, glass vase blown by Ola Höglund, Sweden. b, Maori basket, by Willa Rogers, New Zealand.

*Perf. 12½x12¾ on 3 Sides*

**2002, May 2 Litho. & Engr.**

**2440** A770 Vert. pair 10.00 *12.00*
*a.-b.* 10k Any single 5.00 4.50
*c.* Booklet pane, 2 #2440 20.00 —
Booklet, #2440c + 4 etiquettes 20.00

See New Zealand Nos. 1780, 1786.

A771

Summer in Bohuslän — A772

Designs: No. 2441, Waterfront building.
No. 2442: a, Lighthouse and gull. b, Lighthouse and three birds. c, Bridge, sailboat, waterfront buildings. d, Boat with outboard motor.
Illustration A772 reduced.

**2002, May 10 Engr. *Perf. 12¾ Vert.***
**2441** A771 (5k) multi 1.75 .85

**Litho.**
**Self-Adhesive**
***Serpentine Die Cut 6¾***

**2442** A772 Block of 4 7.00 7.50
*a.-d.* (5k) Any single 1.75 1.00
*e.* Booklet, #2442c-2442d, 2 #2442 17.50

Grönköpings Veckoblad Satirical Newspaper, Cent. — A773

No. 2443: a, Newspaper and fictitious Postmaster of Grönköping. b, Fictitious police chief and criminal.
Illustration reduced.

***Perf. 12¾ Vert.***
**2002, Aug. 29 Litho. & Engr.**
**2443** A773 Pair 4.00 3.75
*a.-b.* (5k) Either single 2.00 1.75

Chefs A774

No. 2444: a, Charles Emil Hagdahl (1809-97) and Cajsa Warg (1703-69). b, Marit "Hiram" Huldt, cook with cauldron and bird, flowers. c, Tore Wretman and medal. d, Leif Mannerström, fish and lobster. e, Gert Klötzke and Swedish Culinary Team. f, Christer Lingström, poultry, peas and apples.

***Perf. 12½x12¾ on 3 Sides***
**2002, Aug. 29 Litho.**
**2444** Booklet pane of 6 10.50 *10.50*
*a.-f.* A774 (5k) Any single 1.75 1.25
Booklet, #2444 10.50

Royal Palaces A775

No. 2445: a, Sweden. b, Thailand.

***Perf. 12½x13 on 3 Sides***
**2002, Oct. 5 Litho. & Engr.**
**2445** A775 Vert. pair 8.00 8.00
*a.-b.* 5k Either single 4.00 3.50
*c.* Booklet pane, 2 #2445 16.00 —
Booklet, #2445c 16.00

See Thailand Nos. 2040-2041.

Motorcycle Racers — A776

No. 2446: a, Hakan Carlqvist. b, Sten Lundin. c, Anders Eriksson. d, Ulf Karlsson.
No. 2447: a, Ove Fundin. b, Tony Rickardsson. c, Peter Linden. d, Varg-Olle Nygren.

**2002, Oct. 5 Litho. *Perf. 12¾***
**2446** A776 Booklet pane of 4 6.50 *9.00*
*a.-d.* 5k Any single 1.60 *2.00*

**Litho. & Engr.**

**2447** A776 Booklet pane of 4 6.50 *9.00*
*a.-d.* 5k Any single 1.60 *2.00*
Booklet, #2446-2447 13.00

Animated Film *Karl-Bertil Jonsson's Christmas* A777

Designs: No. 2448, Man with arm on Karl-Bertil's shoulder.
No. 2449: a, Karl-Bertil and mail sack of Christmas parcels. b, Karl-Bertil asleep with Robin Hood hat. c, Karl-Bertil giving parcel to poor man. d, Karl-Bertil with man, woman and child.

***Perf. 12¾ Vert.***
**2002, Nov. 21 Litho.**
**2448** A777 (4.50k) multi 1.50 1.50

**Self-Adhesive**
***Serpentine Die Cut 6½x6 on 3 Sides***

**2449** Block of 4 5.50 6.50
*a.-d.* A777 (4.50k) Any single 1.40 1.00
*e.* Booklet pane, 3 #2449a-2449b, 2 #2449c-2449d 14.00

Churches — A778

No. 2450: a, Kiruna Church. b, Habo Church. c, Sundborn Church. d, Tensta Bell Tower.
Illustration reduced.

**2002, Nov. 21 *Perf. 12¾ on 3 Sides***
**2450** A778 Block of 4 11.00 11.00
*a.-d.* 8k Any single 2.50 2.25
*e.* Booklet pane, 3 #2450a-2450b, 2 #2450c-2450d 27.50 —
Booklet, #2450e 27.50

St. Bridget (1303-73) — A779

**2003, Jan. 20 Engr. *Perf. 12¾ Vert.***
**2451** A779 (5.50k) red & brown 1.90 1.25

Swedish Sports Federation, Cent. — A780

No. 2452: a, Woman and child. b, Wheelchair racer. c, Snowboarder and sign language. d, Girl running.

***Serpentine Die Cut 8½***
**2003, Jan. 20 Litho.**
**Self-Adhesive**

**2452** Booklet pane, 3 each #2452a, 2452c, 2 each #2452b, 2452d 15.00
*a.-d.* A780 (5.50k) Any single 1.50 1.10

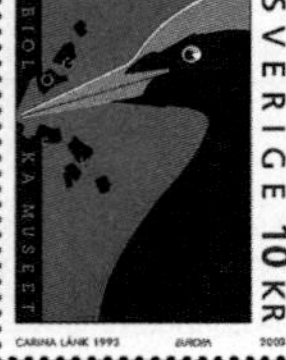

Europa — A781

Posters by: a, Anders Beckman, 1935. b, Georg Magnusson, 1930. c, Owe Gustafson, 1984. d, Carina Länk, 1993.
Illustration reduced.

***Perf. 12¾x12½ on 3 Sides***
**2003, Jan. 20**
**2453** A781 Booklet pane of 4 *11.00 12.50*
*a.-d.* 10k Any single *2.75* 2.50
Booklet, #2453 + 4 etiquettes *11.00*

Knots — A782

Various knots.

**2003, Jan. 20 Engr. *Perf. 12½ Vert.***
**2454** A782 (4.80k) green 1.40 1.75
**2455** A782 (5k) blue 1.50 1.00
**2456** A782 (5.50k) red 1.75 .65
*Nos. 2454-2456 (3)* 4.65 3.40

Regional Houses — A783

***Perf. 12¼ Vert. Syncopated***
**2003, Mar. 20 Engr.**
**2457** A783 2k Närke .75 .55
**2458** A783 4k Bohuslän 1.25 1.10
**2459** A783 5k Medelpad 1.50 1.40
*Nos. 2457-2459 (3)* 3.50 3.05

Nobel Prize Winners For Physiology or Medicine From Spain — A784

No. 2460: a, Santiago Ramón y Cajal, 1906. b, Severo Ochoa, 1959.

***Perf. 12 Vert. Syncopated***
**2003, Mar. 20 Litho. & Engr.**
**2460** A784 Horiz. pair 5.50 *6.00*
*a.-b.* 10k Either single 2.75 2.75

See Spain No. 3204.

Flowers — A785

No. 2461: a, Hepatica nobilis. b, Primula veris. c, Tussilago farfara.

***Die Cut Perf. 9¾x10***
**2003, Mar. 20 Litho.**
**Self-Adhesive**

**2461** Booklet pane of 3 4.50 *5.50*
*a.-c.* A785 (5.50k) Any single 1.50 1.25
Booklet, 2 #2461 9.00

Oland Moorland, UNESCO World Heritage Site A786

No. 2462: a, Windmills. b, Megaliths and windmill. c, Cow and linear village. d, Sheep and lighthouse.

***Perf. 12¾ Horiz.***
**2003, Mar. 20 Litho. & Engr.**
**2462** Booklet pane of 4 7.75 7.00
*a.-d.* A786 (5.50k) Any single 1.90 1.50
Booklet, #2462 7.75

A787

Garden Pavilions A788

Designs: No. 2463, 1820s pavilion, by Frederik Blom.
No. 2464: a, Pavilion of Emanuel Swedenborg. b, Pavilion of Ebba Brahe. c, Västana farm pavilion, Borensberg. d, Godegard pavilion.

***Perf. 12½ Vert. Syncopated***
**2003, May 16 Engr.**
**2463** A787 (5.50k) multi 1.75 1.40

**Litho.**
**Self-Adhesive**
***Serpentine Die Cut 6½ on 3 Sides***

**2464** Block of 4 7.00 *7.50*
*a.-d.* A788 (5.50k) Any single 1.75 1.25
*e.* Booklet pane, 3 #2464a-2464b, 2 #2464c-2464d 17.50

Souvenir Sheet

St. Bridget (1303-73) — A789

**Litho. & Engr.**

**2003, May 31** ***Perf. 13***
**2465** A789 40k multi 10.50 *12.50*

No. 2465 exists with and without numbers printed in LL and LR corners of the margin.

**Royalty Type of 2000**

Designs: (5.50k), King Carl XVI Gustaf. 10k, Queen Silvia.

***Perf. 13 Vert. Syncopated***

**2003, Aug. 21** **Engr.**
**2466** A737 (5.50k) red brown 1.50 .75
**2467** A737 10k purple 2.50 2.00

Harvest Time — A790

No. 2468: a, Tree, radicchio, parsnip, cucumber, beet, onion. b, Pitchfork, artichoke, pear, gourd, raspberries, apple, plum, pumpkin, eggplant. c, Trowel, garlic, peas, cabbage, tomato, potato, turnip, carrots. d, Strawberries, sunflower, cherries, plums, apple, pear.

***Serpentine Die Cut 6½ on 3 Sides***

**2003, Aug. 21** **Litho.**

**Self-Adhesive**

**2468** A790 Block of 4 6.50 *7.50*
*a.-d.* (5.50k) Any single 1.60 1.25
*e.* Booklet pane, 3 each #2468a-2468b, 2 each #2468c-2468d 16.00

Birds — A791

No. 2469: a, Recurvirostra avosetta. b, Podiceps auritus. c, Gavia arctica. d, Podiceps cristatus.
Illustration reduced.

***Perf. 12½x12¾ on 3 Sides***

**2003, Oct. 4** **Litho. & Engr.**
**2469** A791 Booklet pane of 4 12.00 *13.50*
*a.-d.* 10k Any single 3.00 2.75
Complete booklet, #2469 + 4 etiquettes 12.00

See Hong Kong Nos. 1052-1055.

Building of East Indiaman "Götheborg" — A792

No. 2470: a, Figurehead (19x23mm). b, Ship under construction (19x23mm). c, Side view of ship, horiz. (23x40mm). d, Ship at sea (39x50mm).
Illustration reduced.

**2003, Oct. 4** ***Perf. 12½x12¾***
**2470** A792 Booklet pane of 4 19.00 *25.00*
*a.-b.* 5.50k Either single 2.50 2.50
*c.* 10k multi 3.50 4.00
*d.* 30k multi 10.00 12.00
Complete booklet, #2470 + label 19.00

Christmas at Sundborn, by Carl Larsson — A793

No. 2471: a, Martina med Frukostbrickan. b, Kerstis Slädfärd.
Illustration reduced.

***Perf. 12¾ on 3 Sides***

**2003, Nov. 10** **Litho.**
**2471** A793 Horiz. pair 5.25 *6.00*
*a.-b.* 9k Either single 1.75 2.25
*c.* Booklet pane, 5 #2471 +10 etiquettes 26.50
Complete booklet, #2471c 26.50

Christmas Paintings by Carl Larsson — A794

Designs: No. 2472, Aftonvarden.
No. 2473, vert.: a, Esbjörn pa Skidor. b, Brita med Julljus. c, Farfar och Esbjörn. d, Garden och Brygghuset.

***Perf. 12¾ Vert. Syncopated***

**2003, Nov. 10**
**2472** A794 (5k) multi 1.50 1.40

**Self-Adhesive**

***Serpentine Die Cut 6½x6 on 3 Sides***

**2473** A794 Block of 4 6.50 7.50
*a.-d.* (5k) Any single 1.60 1.40
*e.* Booklet pane, #2473b, 2473d, 2 #2473 16.00

Anna Lindh (1957-2003), Murdered Minister of Foreign Affairs — A795

***Perf. 12¾ on 3 Sides***

**2003, Nov. 11** **Engr.**
**2474** A795 Pair 4.50 5.50
*a.* (5.50k) claret 1.60 1.60
*b.* 10k blue 2.75 2.75
*c.* Booklet pane, 2 each #2474a-2474b 9.00 —
Complete booklet, #2474c 9.00

No. 2474c sold for 35k, 4k of which went to the Anna Lindh Memorial Fund.

Woodworking Tools — A796

Designs: (4.80k), Brace and bit. (5k), Saw. (5.50k), Plane.

***Perf. 12 Vert. Syncopated***

**2004, Jan. 26** **Engr.**
**2475** A796 (4.80k) green 1.40 1.40
**2476** A796 (5k) blue 1.40 1.00
**2477** A796 (5.50k) claret 1.60 .60
*Nos. 2475-2477 (3)* 4.40 3.00

Flowers A797

No. 2478: a, Tulip. b, Lily. c, Hibiscus. d, Amaryllis. e, Calla lily.

***Perf. 12¾ Horiz.***

**2004, Jan. 26** **Litho.**
**2478** Vert. strip of 5 7.75 7.75
*a.-e.* A797 (5.50k) Any single 1.50 1.25
*f.* Booklet pane, 2 #2478 15.50 —
Complete booklet, #2478f 15.50

Europa A798

No. 2479 — Views of Lapland: a, Mountain with purple sky. b, Tents near lake.

***Perf. 12¾x13½ on 3 Sides***

**2004, Jan. 26**
**2479** A798 Pair 5.75 6.50
*a.-b.* 10k Either single 2.75 2.75
*c.* Booklet pane, 2 #2479 11.50 —
Complete booklet, #2479c + 4 etiquettes 11.50

Souvenir Sheet

Norse Mythology — A799

No. 2480 — Return to Valhalla: a, Return of a warrior (denomination at LR). b, Welcoming Valkyrie (denomination at UR).

**Litho. & Engr.**

**2004, Mar. 26** ***Perf. 12¾***
**2480** A799 Sheet of 2 5.75 7.00
*a.-b.* 10k Either single 2.75 3.00

Falun, UNESCO World Heritage Site — A800

No. 2481: a, Excavation pit, red mine shaft entrance building. b, Yellow green and green copper weighing building, red, white and purple mining operations building. c, Gray mine entrance building. d, Miners and houses.
Illustration reduced.

***Perf. 12½x12¾ on 3 Sides***

**2004, Mar. 26** **Litho.**
**2481** A800 Block of 4 9.50 8.50
*a.-d.* (5.50k) Any single 1.50 1.75
*e.* Booklet pane, #2481b, 2481d, 2 each #2481a, 2481c 9.00 —
Complete booklet, #2481e 9.00

Swedish Soccer Association, Cent. — A801

No. 2482: a, Nils Liedholm. b, Hanna Ljungberg. c, Fredrik Ljungberg. d, Henrik Larsson. e, Victoria Svensson. f, Thomas Ravelli.

***Serpentine Die Cut 7x6¼ on 3 Sides***

**2004, Mar. 26**

**Self-Adhesive**

**2482** Booklet pane of 6 10.50 *13.00*
*a.-f.* A801 (5.50k) Any single 1.75 1.75

Sunset Scenes — A802

No. 2483: a, Fisherman. b, Lighthouse.
Illustration reduced.

***Perf. 12½ Vert. Syncopated***

**2004, May 13** **Engr.**
**2483** A802 Horiz. pair 3.50 3.00
*a.-b.* (5.50k) Either single 1.75 1.25

Stockholm Archipelago A803

No. 2484: a, Sailboat, red house, Gillöga. b, Rowboat, houses, Langviksskär. c, Ferry, Stora Nassa. d, Sailboat, lighthouse, Nämdöfjärden.

***Serpentine Die Cut 6¾ on 3 Sides***

**2004, May 13** **Litho.**

**Self-Adhesive**

**2484** Block of 4 7.00 7.50
*a.-d.* A803 (5.50k) Any single 1.75 1.50
*e.* Booklet pane, 3 #2484a-2484b, 2 #2484c-2484d 15.00

Cottages A804

Designs: 3k, Blacksmith's cottage, Uppland. 6k, Dalsland cottage. 8k, Stone cottage, Gotland.

***Perf. 12¾ Vert. Syncopated***

**2004, Aug. 19 — Engr.**

**2485** A804 3k multi .80 .60
**2486** A804 6k multi 1.60 .90
**2487** A804 8k multi 2.10 1.50
*Nos. 2485-2487 (3)* 4.50 3.00

Birds — A805

Designs: (5k), Streptopelia decaocto. (5.50k), Swedish tumbler. 10k, Columba palumbus.

**2004, Aug. 19**

**2488** A805 (5k) multi 1.40 1.25
**2489** A805 (5.50k) multi 1.50 .60
**2490** A805 10k multi 2.75 2.50
*Nos. 2488-2490 (3)* 5.65 4.35

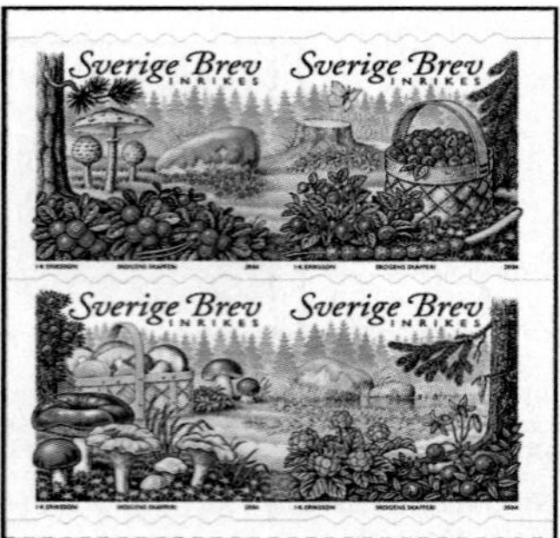


Forest Larder — A806

No. 2491: a, Mushrooms, lingonberries. b, Wild strawberries, butterfly, basket of blueberries. c, Juniper berries, basket of mushrooms. d, Cloudberries, cranberries.

***Serpentine Die Cut 6½ on 3 Sides***

**2004, Aug. 19 — Litho.**

**Self-Adhesive**

**2491** A806 Block of 4 7.25 6.00
*a.-d.* (5.50k) Any single 1.75 1.25
*e.* Booklet pane, 3 each #2491a-2491b, 2 each #2491c-2491d 15.00

Nobel Prize Winners for Literature from Ireland — A807

No. 2492: a, William Butler Yeats, 1923. b, George Bernard Shaw, 1925. c, Samuel Beckett, 1969. d, Seamus Heaney, 1995.
Illustration reduced.

***Perf. 12½x13½ on 3 Sides***

**2004, Oct. 1 — Litho. & Engr.**

**2492** A807 Booklet pane of 4 11.00 *12.50*
*a.-d.* 10k Any single 2.75 2.75
Complete booklet, #2492 + 4 etiquettes 11.00

See Ireland Nos. 1576-1579.

Rock Music, 50th Anniv. — A808

No. 2493: a, Jerry Williams (29x39mm). b, Elvis Presley (36x39mm). c, Eva Dahlgren (29x39mm). d, Ulf Lundell (36x39mm). e, Tomas Ledin (29x39mm). f, Pugh Rogefeldt (29x33mm). g, Sahara Hotnights (36x33mm). h, Louise Hoffsten (29x33mm).

**Litho., Litho. & Engr. (#2493b, 2493d)**

**2004, Oct. 2 — *Perf. 12x12¾***

**2493** Booklet pane of 8 + 2 labels 14.00 *16.50*
*a.-h.* A808 5.50k Any single 1.75 1.75
Complete booklet, #2493 14.00
*i.* Sheet of 9 #2493b 17.00 —

Labels and margins of Nos. 2493 and 2493i have perforations reading "Rock 54-04." No. 2493i sold for 55k.

**Regional Houses Type of 2003 and**

Log Cabin — A809

Scanian Farm House — A810

Designs: 1k, Miner's house. 9k, Blekinge cottage.

***Perf. 12 Vert. Syncopated***

**2004, Nov. 11 — Engr.**

**2494** A809 50o multi .30 .25

***Perf. 12¼ Vert. Syncopated***

**2495** A783 1k multi .35 .30
**2496** A810 7k multi 2.00 1.25
**2497** A810 9k multi 2.75 2.00
*Nos. 2494-2497 (4)* 5.40 3.80

Birds — A811

No. 2498: a, Parus major. b, Emberiza citrinella. c, Pinicola enucleator. d, Pyrrhula pyrrhula.
Illustration reduced.

***Perf. 12¾ on 3 Sides***

**2004, Nov. 11 — Litho.**

**2498** A811 Booklet pane of 4 12.00 *13.00*
*a.-d.* 10k Any single 3.00 2.75
Complete booklet, #2498 + 4 etiquettes 12.00

Christmas A812

Designs: No. 2499, Gnomes playing leap frog.
No. 2500: a, Three gnomes. b, Gnome with Christmas tree. c, Two gnomes with chair on skis. d, Gnome, birds at mail box.

***Perf. 12¼ Vert. Syncopated***

**2004, Nov. 11**

**2499** A812 (5k) multi 1.50 1.50

**Self-Adhesive**

***Serpentine Die Cut 6¼x6 on 3 Sides***

**2500** Block of 4 6.00 *6.75*
*a.-d.* A812 (5k) Any single 1.50 1.50
*e.* Booklet pane, 3 each #2500a-2500b, 2 each #2500c-2500d 15.00

King Carl XVI Gustaf — A813

Queen Silvia — A814

***Perf. 12½ Vert. Syncopated***

**2005, Jan. 27 — Engr.**

**2501** A813 (5.50k) multi 1.60 1.00
**2502** A814 10k multi 3.00 2.50

High Coast, UNESCO World Heritage Site — A815

No. 2503: a, Högbonden Lighthouse, birds on rocks. b, Cliffs and eagles, Storön Nature Reserve. c, Fishing boat at dock, Ulvön. d, Lakes near Häggvik.
Illustration reduced.

***Perf. 12¾x13½ on 3 Sides***

**2005, Jan. 27 — Litho. & Engr.**

**2503** A815 Booklet pane of 4 12.00 *14.00*
*a.-d.* 10k Any single 3.00 3.00
Complete booklet, #2503 + 4 etiquettes 12.00

Swedish Design A816

No. 2504: a, Glassware, by Ingegerd Raman. b, Turn-o-matic number ticket machine, by A/E Design. c, Speedway 9000 welding helmet, by Carl-Göran Crafoord and Hakan Bergkvist. d, Camilla chair and Pilaster shelving unit, by John Kandell. e, Women's watch, by Vivianna Torun Bülow-Hübe. f, Streamliner toy car, by Ulf Hanses.

***Die Cut Perf. 12½ Horiz.***

**2005, Jan. 27**

**Self-Adhesive**

**2504** Booklet pane of 6 9.75 10.00
*a.-f.* A816 (5.50k) Any single 1.60 1.25

Oriolus Oriolus A817

***Perf. 12½ Vert. Syncopated***

**2005, Mar. 10 — Litho. & Engr.**

**2505** A817 11k multi 3.25 2.50

Dag Hammarskjold (1905-61), UN Secretary General — A818

No. 2506: a, Hammarskjold. b, United Nations flag.
Illustration reduced.

**2005, Mar. 10 — Engr.**

**2506** A818 Horiz. pair 3.25 3.25
*a.-b.* (5.50k) Either single 1.60 1.60

Europa A819

No. 2507: a, Lemon, star anise, elderberry marmalade. b, Apples, rosemary, Jerusalem artichokes. c, Chives, goat cheese, beets.

**2005, Mar. 10 — Litho. — *Perf. 12¾***

**2507** A819 Vert. strip of 3 *5.00* 5.00
*a.-c.* (5.50k) Any single *1.60* 1.00
*d.* Booklet pane, 2 #2507 *10.00* —
Complete booklet, #2507d *10.00*

Spring Flowers A820

No. 2508: a, Convallaria majalis. b, Gagea lutea. c, Pulsatilla vulgaris. d, Anemone nemorosa.

***Serpentine Die Cut 10 on 3 Sides***

**2005, Mar. 10**

**Self-Adhesive**

**2508** Block of 4 6.50 6.50
*a.-d.* A820 (5.50k) Any single 1.60 1.10
*e.* Booklet pane, 3 each #2508a-2508b, 2 each #2508c-2508d 16.00
*f.* As "a," serpentine die cut 6¾ on 3 sides *17.50* —
*g.* As "b," serpentine die cut 6¾ on 3 sides *17.50* —
*h.* As "c," serpentine die cut 6¾ on 3 sides *17.50* —
*i.* As "d," serpentine die cut 6¾ on 3 sides *17.50* —
*j.* Booklet pane, 3 each #2508f-2508g, 2 each #2508h-2508i *70.00*

Nos. 2508f-2508i issued 9/6.

Mother Svea A821

***Perf. 12½ Vert. Syncopated***

**2005, May 26 — Litho. & Engr.**

**2509** A821 15k multi 4.00 4.00

Tumba Bruk, manufacturer of Swedish banknotes, 250th anniv.

A822

Allotment Gardens — A823

No. 2511: a, Girl near shrub, man tending vegetable garden. b, Woman at table. b, Man tending garden, woman with basket of vegetables. c, Man watering garden.

***Perf. 12¾ Vert. Syncopated***

**2005, May 26** **Litho.**

**2510** A822 (5.50k) multi 1.50 1.50

**Self-Adhesive**

***Serpentine Die Cut 10 on 3 Sides***

**2511** A823 Block of 4 6.00 *7.50*
*a.-d.* (5.50k) Any single 1.50 1.50
*e.* Complete booklet, 3 each #2511a, 2511c, 2 each #2511b, 2511d 15.00

A824

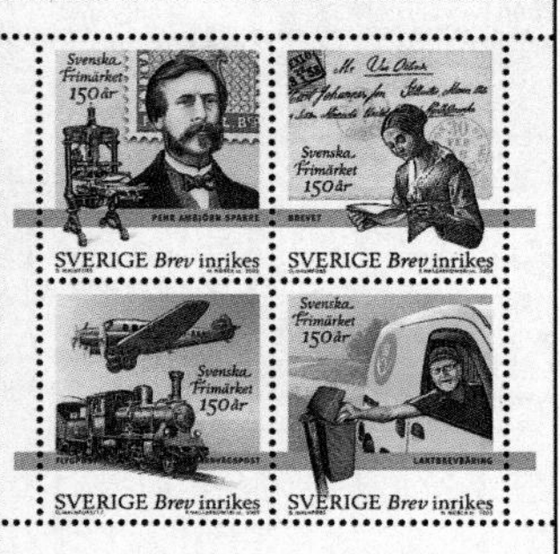


Swedish Postage Stamps, 150th Anniv. — A825

No. 2512 — Details from stamps: a, #944 (1972). b, #430 (1951). c, #250 (1936). d, #1490 (1984).

No. 2513: a, Count Pehr Ambjörn Sparre, #2, printing press. b, Woman reading letter, cover. c, Airplane, train. d, Mailman in van at mailbox.

Illustrations reduced.

**2005, May 26** **Litho.** ***Perf. 12¾***

**2512** A824 Booklet pane of 4 6.00 *8.50*
*a.-d.* (5.50k) Any single 1.50 1.50

**Litho. & Engr.**

**2513** A825 Booklet pane of 4 6.00 *8.50*
*a.-d.* (5.50k) Any single 1.50 1.50
*e.* Miniature sheet, 9 #2513a 15.00 —
Complete booklet, #2512-2513 12.00

No. 2513e sold for 55k.

Souvenir Sheet

Dissolution of Union of Sweden and Norway, Cent. — A826

No. 2514 — Svinesund Bridge: a, View of roadway with cars. b, View from valley.

***Perf. 12½x12¾***

**2005, May 27** **Litho. & Engr.**

**2514** A826 Sheet of 2 6.50 6.75
*a.-b.* 10k Either single 3.25 2.75

See Norway Nos. 1430-1431.

Varberg Radio Station World Heritage Site — A827

Skogskyrkogarden Cemetery World Heritage Site — A828

***Perf. 12½ Vert. Syncopated***

**2005, Sept. 23** **Engr.**

**2515** A827 (4.80k) grn & violet 1.40 1.40
**2516** A828 (5k) multi 1.60 .50

Greta Garbo (1905-90), Actress — A829

No. 2517: a, Portrait. b, Caricature and "Greta."

***Perf. 12¾x12½ on 3 Sides***

**2005, Sept. 23** **Litho. & Engr.**

**2517** A829 Pair 5.50 6.50
*a.-b.* 10k Either single 2.75 2.75
*c.* Booklet pane, 2 each #2517a-2517b 11.00 —
Complete booklet, #2517c + 4 etiquettes 11.00
*d.* Souvenir sheet of 4 #2517a, perf. 12¾x12½ *110.00* *125.00*

No. 2517d sold for 45k and has a lithographed sheet margin. Single stamps from #2517d are perforated on all four sides.

See United States No. 3943.

Juvenile Wild Animals — A830

No. 2518: a, Lynx. b, Bear. c, Wolf. d, Fox.

***Serpentine Die Cut 10 on 3 Sides***

**2005, Sept. 23** **Litho.**

**Self-Adhesive**

**2518** A830 Block of 4 6.00
*a.-d.* (5.50k) Any single 1.60 1.60
*e.* Complete booklet, 3 each #2518a-2518b, 2 each #2518c-2518d 16.00

A831

Mopeds — A832

No. 2519: a, Man, woman, Fram moped. b, Husqvarna moped. c, Kuli moped engine and wheel. d, Two men sitting on mopeds.

No. 2520: a, Man repairing hoisted moped. b, Three-wheeled platform scooter. c, Zundapp moped engine. d, Man riding moped.

**Litho., Litho. & Engr. (#2519b, 2519c, 2520b, 2520c)**

**2005, Sept. 24** ***Perf. 12¾***

**2519** A831 Booklet pane of 4 6.00 7.50
*a.-d.* 5.50k Any single 1.50 1.50
*e.* Sheet of 9 #2519d 14.50 14.50
**2520** A832 Booklet pane of 4 6.00 7.50
*a.-d.* 5.50k Any single 1.50 1.50
Complete booklet, #2519-2520 12.00

No. 2519e sold for 55k.

Christmas A833

Illustrations from Christmas in a Noisy Village, by Astrid Lindgren: No. 2521, Dog, child on skis.

No. 2522: a, Children near fence. b, Dog, children with sled. c, Girl wrapping gifts. d, Children looking at Christmas tree.

***Perf. 12¾ Vert. Syncopated***

**2005, Nov. 10** **Litho.**

**2521** A833 (5k) multi 1.25 1.25

**Self-Adhesive**

***Serpentine Die Cut 10 on 3 Sides***

**2522** Block of 4 6.50 6.50
*a.-d.* A833 (5k) Any single 1.50 1.25
*e.* Booklet pane, 3 each #2522a-2522b, 2 each #2522c-2522d 12.50

Angel Musicians, Sculptures by Carl Milles — A834

No. 2523: a, Angel with horn facing right. b, Angel with horn facing left. c, Angel with flute facing right. d, Angel with flute facing forward.

***Perf. 12¾ on 3 Sides***

**2005, Nov. 10** **Litho. & Engr.**

**2523** A834 Booklet pane of 4 10.00 13.00
*a.-d.* 10k Any single 2.50 2.50
Complete booklet, #2523 + 4 etiquettes 10.00

Swedish Railroads, 150th Anniv. — A835

Designs: 10k, X40 train.

No. 2525: a, Mallet steam locomotive (green). b, Gasoline-powered Rail bus (tan). c, SJ Class D electric locomotive (orange). d, R steam locomotive (black). e, RC electric locomotive (red).

***Perf. 12½ Vert. Syncopated***

**2006, Jan. 26** **Litho.**

**2524** A835 10k multi 2.60 1.90

**Litho. & Engr.**

**Booklet Stamps**

***Perf. 12½ Horiz.***

**2525** Vert. strip of 5 8.00 8.00
*a.-e.* A835 (5.50k) Any single 1.60 1.50
*f.* Booklet pane, 2 #2525 16.00 —
Complete booklet, #2525f 16.00

Hearts — A836

No. 2526: a, Tattooed heart. b, Red heart. c, Heart-shaped leaf. d, Heart carved in tree trunk.

***Serpentine Die Cut 10 on 3 Sides***

**2006, Jan. 26** **Litho.**

**Self-Adhesive**

**2526** A836 Block of 4, #a-d 6.00 5.00
*a.-d.* (5.50k) Any single 1.50 1.40
*e.* Booklet pane, 2 each #2526c-2526d, 3 each #2526a-2526b 15.00

### Souvenir Sheet

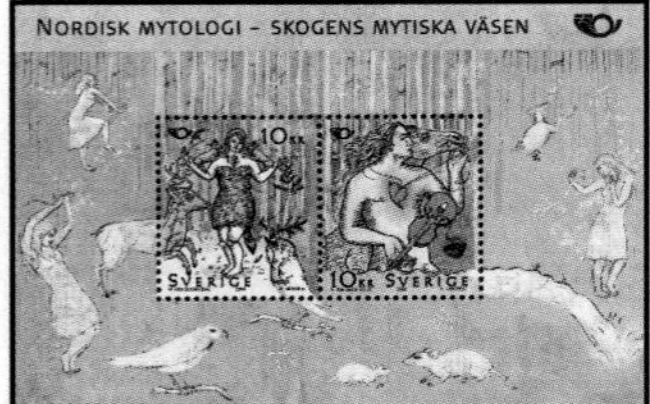


Norse Mythology — A837

No. 2527: a, Skogsraet, reindeer, goats and bird. b, Näcken, horse and violin.

**Litho. & Engr.**

**2006, Mar. 29** *Perf. 12¾*

**2527** A837 Sheet of 2 5.25 6.25
*a.-b.* 10k Either single 2.60 2.60

### Souvenir Sheet

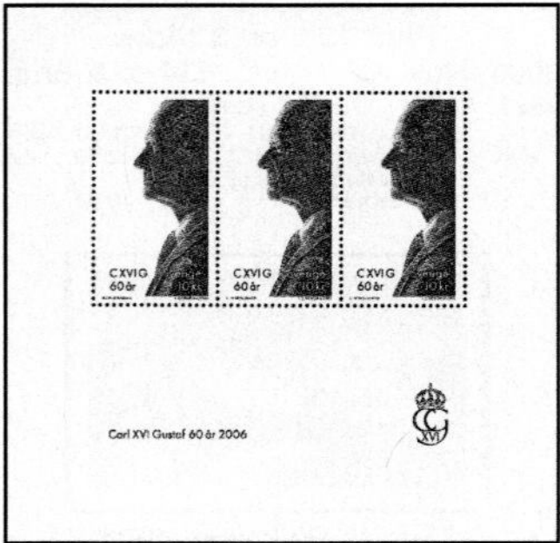


King Carl XVI Gustaf, 60th Birthday — A838

**2006, Mar. 29 Engr.** *Perf. 13x12¾*

**2528** A838 Sheet, #2528a, 2 #2528b 8.00 8.00
*a.* 10k blue 2.60 2.60
*b.* 10k black 2.60 2.60

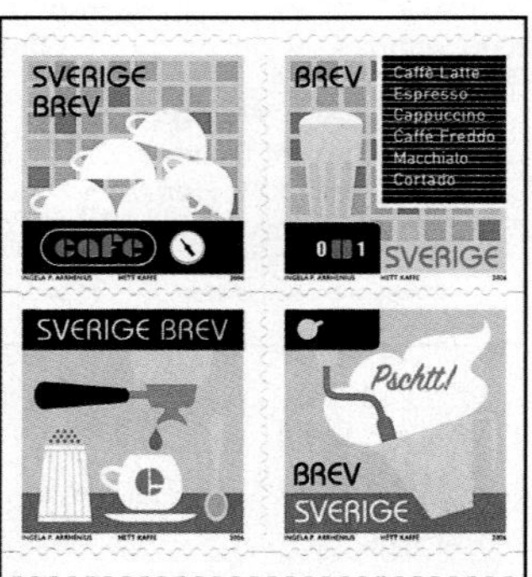


Coffee — A839

No. 2529: a, Coffee cups stacked on coffeemaker. b, Glass of cappucino. c, Espresso machine and cup, sugar dispenser and spoon. d, Steamed milk dispenser and measuring cup.

***Serpentine Die Cut 10 on 3 Sides***

**2006, Mar. 29** **Litho.**

**Self-Adhesive**

**2529** A839 Block of 4 6.25 7.00
*a.-d.* (5.50k) Any single 1.60 1.25
*e.* Booklet pane, 3 each #2529a-2529b, 2 each #2529c-2529d 15.50

Suomenlinna (Sveaborg) Fortress, Helsinki, Finland — A840

No. 2530: a, Ship without oars, flagpole at fortress. b, Ship with oars facing fortress. c, Ship with oars, windmill.

**Litho. & Engr.**

**2006, May 4** *Perf. 12¾*

**2530** A840 Booklet pane of 3 8.25 9.00
*a.-c.* 10k Any single 2.75 3.25
Complete booklet, #2530 8.25

See Finland No. 1266.

Track and Field Athletes — A841

Designs: (4.80k), Stefan Holm, high jump. 10k, Christian Olsson, triple jump.

No. 2533: a, Carolina Klüft, heptathlon. b, Kajsa Bergqvist, high jump.

***Perf. 13¼ Vert. Syncopated***

**2006, May 4** **Litho.**

**2531** A841 (4.80k) grn & multi 1.40 1.40
**2532** A841 10k gray & multi 3.00 2.75
**2533** Horiz. pair 3.00 3.00
*a.-b.* A841 (5.50k) Either single 1.50 1.00
*Nos. 2531-2533 (3)* 7.40 7.15

Europa A842

No. 2534 — Children's art by: a, Alexandros Terzis. b, Linda Wong.

***Perf. 12¾x12½ on 3 Sides***

**2006, May 4**

**2534** A842 Pair 5.50 *6.50*
*a.-b.* 10k Either single 2.75 2.75
*c.* Booklet pane, 2 each #2534a-2534b 11.00
Complete booklet, #2534c + 4 etiquettes 11.00

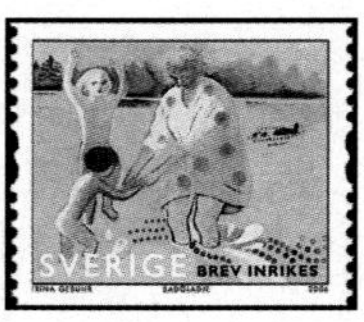


Summer by the Lake — A843

No. 2536: a, Elk and immigrant women's picnic. b, Father and daughter fishing. c, Dog watching swimmers. d, Frog and boaters.

***Perf. 12¼ Vert. Syncopated***

**2006, May 4**

**2535** A843 (5.50k) shown 1.50 1.50

**Self-Adhesive**

**Size: 34x24mm**

**2536** Block of 4 6.00 7.00
*a.-d.* A843 (5.50k) Any single 1.50 1.00
*e.* Booklet pane, 3 each #2536a-2536b, 2 each #2536c-2536d 15.00

Famous Men — A844

Designs: (4.80k,) Carl Michael Bellman (1740-95), poet. (5k), Joseph Martin Kraus (1756-92), composer. (5.50k), Wolfgang Amadeus Mozart (1756-91), composer.

**2006, Sept. 7 Engr.** *Perf. 12¾*

**2537** A844 (5.50k) multi 1.75 1.75

**Coil Stamps**

***Perf. 12½ Vert. Syncopated***

**2538** A844 (4.80k) multi 1.40 1.40
**2539** A844 (5k) multi 1.40 1.40
**2540** A844 (5.50k) multi 1.50 1.50
*Nos. 2537-2540 (4)* 6.05 6.05

No. 2537 was issued in a sheet of 6 stamps that sold for 38k.

Hanseatic League, 650th Anniv. — A845

Designs: No. 2541, Hanseatic cog, 1380. No. 2542, Building and ships, Visby. No. 2543, City seal, shopper and salesman, Stockholm.

***Perf. 12½x13½ on 3 Sides***

**2006, Sept. 7** **Litho. & Engr.**

**2541** A845 10k multi 2.75 2.75
**2542** A845 10k multi 2.75 2.75
**2543** A845 10k multi 2.75 2.75
*a.* Booklet pane, #2542-2543, 2 #2541 11.00 —
Complete booklet, #2543a 11.00

### Souvenir Sheets

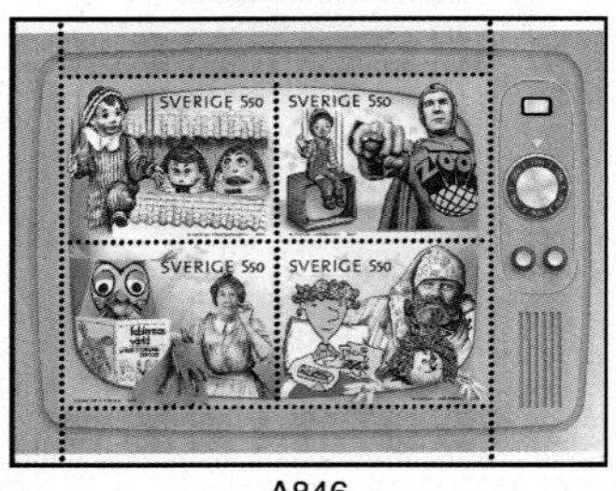


A846

Characters from Swedish Children's Television Shows — A847

No. 2544: a, Andy Pandy (marionette), Humle and Dumle (puppets). b, Anita on Television, Captain Zoom. c, Fablernas Värld (owl), Teskedsgumman (woman). d, Kalles Klätterträd (cartoon), Beppe Wolgers Godnattstunden (man in pajamas).

No. 2545: a, Trazan and Banarne, pink elephant. b, Pippi Longstockings, bear. c, Dinosaur, characters from Tjet och Allram Eest. d, Loophole, Bananas in Pajamas.

**Litho. & Engr.**

**2006, Sept. 30** *Perf. 12½x13*

**2544** A846 Sheet of 4 6.00 6.00
*a.-d.* 5.50k Any single 1.50 1.50
**2545** A847 Sheet of 4 6.00 6.00
*a.-d.* 5.50k Any single 1.50 1.50
*e.* Booklet pane, #2544-2545 12.00 —
Complete booklet, #2545e 12.00
*f.* Sheet of 9 #2545a 15.00 15.00

No. 2545e has a row of rouletting separating No. 2544 from No. 2545, and has a wider margin where the pane is attached to the booklet cover.

Winter Scenes in Art — A848

No. 2546: a, Bourdelle's Heracles in Snow, by Prince Eugen. b, Lelle-Kalle, by Sven Ljundberg. c, Modification of a Winter Landscape by W. O. Petersen, by Philip von Schantz. d, Rime Frost on Ice, by Gustaf Adolf Fjaestad.

Illustration reduced.

***Perf. 12¾ on 3 Sides***

**2006, Nov. 9** **Litho.**

**2546** A848 Booklet pane of 4 12.00 —
*a.-d.* 10k Any single 3.00 3.00
Complete booklet, #2546 + 4 etiquettes 12.00

Christmas A849

Designs: No. 2547, Santa Claus, New Year's ornament, candles.

No. 2548: a, Star ornament. b, Spherical and New Year's ornaments. c, Bird at feeder, poinsettia. d, Candles.

***Perf. 12½ Vert. Syncopated***

**2006, Nov. 9**

**2547** A849 (5k) multi 1.50 1.50

**Self-Adhesive**

**Size: 25x25mm**

***Serpentine Die Cut 10 on 3 Sides***

**2548** Block of 4 6.00
*a.-d.* A849 (5k) Any single 1.50 1.50
*e.* Booklet pane, 3 each #2548a-2548b, 2 each #2548c-2548d 15.00

Linnaea Borealis — A850

Enneandria and Carl von Linné (1707-78), Creator of Linnaean Taxonomic System — A851

***Perf. 12½ Vert. Syncopated***

**2007, Jan. 25** **Engr.**

**2549** A850 (5.50k) multi 1.60 1.60

**Litho. & Engr.**

**2550** A851 11k multi 3.25 3.25

Spring — A852

No. 2551: a, Birds, heart, musical notes. b, Sun, cloud, person. c, Flower, heart, person. d, Bird, sun, musical notes.

***Serpentine Die Cut 10 on 3 Sides***

**2007, Jan. 25 Litho.**

**2551** A852 Block of 4 6.25
*a.-d.* (5.50k) Any single 1.50 1.50
*e.* Booklet pane, 3 each #2551a-2551b, 2 each #2551c-2551d 15.50

Souvenir Sheet

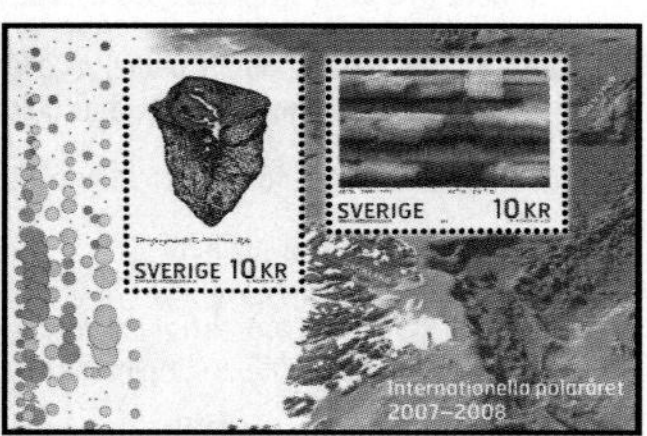
Intl. Polar Year — A853

No. 2552: a, Stenfragment I, etching by Svenerik Jakobsson. b, Arctic Ocean 2001 88 Degrees North, 145 Degrees East, by Johan Petterson.

***Perf. 13, 12¾x13¼ (#2552b)***

**2007, Jan. 25 Litho. & Engr.**

**2552** A853 Sheet of 2 5.75 5.75
*a.-b.* 10k Either single 2.75 2.75

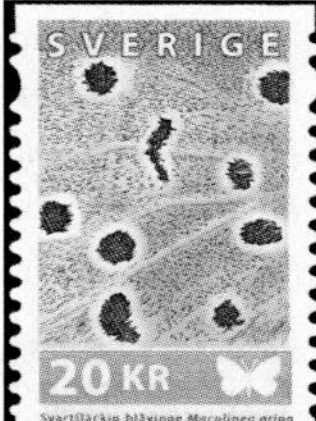
Wing of Maculinea Arion Butterfly — A854

***Serpentine Die Cut 9 Vert. Syncopated***

**2007, Mar. 22 Litho. & Engr.**

**Self-Adhesive**

**2553** A854 20k multi 5.75 5.75

Printed in sheets of 40.

Swedish Sea Rescue Society, Cent. — A855

Designs: (4.80k), Rowboat, rescuer on jet-ski. (5k), Helicopter rescue. (5.50k), Nautical chart, rescue boat.

**Litho. & Engr., Engr. (#2554, 2557)**

**2007, Mar. 22** ***Perf. 13x12¾***

**2554** A855 (5.50k) multi 1.90 1.90

***Perf. 12½ Vert. Syncopated***

**2555** A855 (4.80k) multi 1.40 1.40
**2556** A855 (5k) multi 1.40 1.40
**2557** A855 (5.50k) multi 1.60 1.60
*Nos. 2554-2557 (4)* 6.30 6.30

No. 2554 was printed in sheets of 6 that sold for 38k.

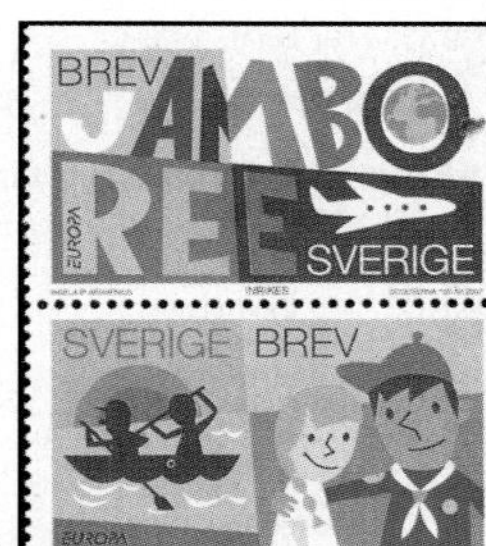
Europa A856

No. 2558: a, "Jamboree", globe and airplane. b, Scouts.

***Perf. 13½x12¾ on 3 Sides***

**2006, Mar. 22 Litho.**

**2558** A856 Horiz. or vert. pair 3.25 3.25
*a.-b.* (5.50k) Either single 1.60 1.60
*c.* Booklet pane, 2 each #2558a-2558b 6.50 —

Swedish Inventions — A857

No. 2559: a, Wall anchor for screws, by Oswald Thorsman. b, Allergy globe for flowers, by Elisabeth Gagnemyhr. c, Cooling food cover, by Birgitta Folcker-Sundell. d, Adjustable wrench, by Johan Petter Johansson.

***Serpentine Die Cut 9 Horiz.***

**2007, Mar. 22**

**2559** Horiz. strip or block of 4 5.75
*a.-d.* A857 (5k) Any single 1.40 1.40
*e.* Booklet paneof 20, 5 each #2559a-2559d 29.00

---

## SEMI-POSTAL STAMPS

Type of 1872-91 Issues Surcharged in Dark Blue

***Perf. 13x13½***

**1916, Dec. 21 Wmk. 181**

**B1** A5 5o + 5o on 2o org 5.50 *7.75*
**B2** A5 5o + 5o on 3o yel brn 5.50 *7.75*
**B3** A5 5o + 5o on 4o gray 5.50 *7.75*
**B4** A5 5o + 5o on 5o grn 5.50 *7.75*
**B5** A5 5o + 5o on 6o lilac 5.50 *7.75*
**B6** A5 10o + 10o on 12o pale bl 5.50 *7.75*
**B7** A5 10o + 10o on 20o red org 5.50 *7.75*
**B8** A5 10o + 10o on 24o yel 5.50 *7.75*
**B9** A5 10o + 10o on 30o brn 5.50 *7.75*
**B10** A5 10o + 10o on 50o rose red 5.50 *7.75*
*Nos. B1-B10 (10)* 55.00 *77.50*

The surtax on Nos. B1-B31 was for the militia. See note after No. B21.
For surcharges see Nos. B22-B31.

No. 66 Surcharged in Dark Blue

**1916, Dec. 21 Wmk. 180** ***Perf. 13***

**B11** A12 10o + 4.90k on 5k 150.00 *325.00*

Nos. J12-J22 Surcharged in Dark Blue

**1916, Dec. 21 Unwmk.** ***Perf. 13***

**B12** D1 5o + 5o on 1o 18.50 10.50
**B13** D1 5o + 5o on 3o 5.00 5.50
**B14** D1 5o + 5o on 5o 8.25 5.50
**B15** D1 5o + 10o on 6o 5.00 6.00
**B16** D1 5o + 15o on 12o 42.50 27.50
**B17** D1 10o + 20o on 20o 15.00 21.00
**B18** D1 10o + 40o on 24o 60.00 *82.50*
**B19** D1 10o + 20o on 30o 5.50 6.00
**B20** D1 10o + 40o on 50o 22.50 *37.50*
**B21** D1 10o + 90o on 1kr 140.00 *375.00*
*Nos. B12-B21 (10)* 322.25 *577.00*

The surtax on Nos. B12-B21 is indicated not in figures, but in words at bottom of surcharge: Fem, 5; Tio, 10; Femton, 15; Tjugo, 20; Fyrtio, 40; Nittio, 90.

Nos. B1-B10 Surcharged

**1918, Dec. 18 Wmk. 181**

**B22** A5 7o + 3o on #B1 8.75 8.25
**B23** A5 7o + 3o on #B2 2.75 1.25
**B24** A5 7o + 3o on #B3 2.75 1.25
**B25** A5 7o + 3o on #B4 2.75 1.25
**B26** A5 7o + 3o on #B5 2.75 1.25
**B27** A5 12o + 8o on #B6 2.75 1.25
**B28** A5 12o + 8o on #B7 2.75 1.25
**B29** A5 12o + 8o on #B8 2.75 1.25
**B30** A5 12o + 8o on #B9 2.75 1.25
**B31** A5 12o + 8o on #B10 2.75 1.25
*Nos. B22-B31 (10)* 33.50 19.50

The 12o+8o surcharge exists on Nos. B1-B5 and the 7o+3o surcharge exists on Nos. B6-B10. Value, each $72.50.
Nos. B24, B26, B28 and B30 exist with surcharge inverted. Value unused, each $140.

SP1

King Gustaf V — SP2

**Unwmk.**

**1928, June 16 Engr.** ***Perf. 10***

**B32** SP1 5o (+ 5o) yel grn 2.75 *6.00*
**B33** SP1 10o (+ 5o) dk vio 2.75 *6.00*
**B34** SP1 15o (+ 5o) car 2.75 *4.50*
Complete booklet, pane of 8 ea. #B32, B33, B34 275.00
**B35** SP1 20o (+ 5o) org 4.75 2.75
**B36** SP1 25o (+ 5o) dk bl 4.75 3.25
*Nos. B32-B36 (5)* 17.75 *22.50*
Set, never hinged 27.50

70th birthday of King Gustaf V. The surtax was used for anti-cancer work.

**Catalogue values for unused stamps in this section, from this point to the end of the section, are for Never Hinged items.**

**1948, June 16** ***Perf. 12½ Vertically***

**B37** SP2 10o + 10o green .55 .60
**B38** SP2 20o + 10o red .80 .75
**B39** SP2 30o + 10o ultra .55 .60

***Perf. 12½ on 3 Sides***

**B40** SP2 10o + 10o green .65 .70
*a.* Booklet pane of 20 10.00
**B41** SP2 20o + 10o red .80 .90
*a.* Booklet pane of 20 12.00
*Nos. B37-B41 (5)* 3.35 3.55

90th anniv. of the birth of King Gustaf V. The surtax provided aid for Swedish youth.

King Gustaf VI Adolf — SP3

Henri Dunant — SP4

**1952, Nov. 11** ***Perf. 12½ Horiz.***

**B42** SP3 10o + 10o green .35 *.40*
**B43** SP3 25o + 10o car rose .35 *.40*
**B44** SP3 40o + 10o ultra .65 *.60*

***Perf. 12½ on 3 Sides***

**B45** SP3 10o + 10o green .35 *.40*
*a.* Booklet pane of 20 6.50
**B46** SP3 25o + 10o car rose .35 *.40*
*a.* Booklet pane of 20 7.00
*Nos. B42-B46 (5)* 2.05 2.20

70th birthday of King Gustaf VI Adolf. The surtax was used to promote Swedish culture.

**1959, May 8** ***Perf. 12½ Horizontally***

**B47** SP4 30o + 10o red .50 *.75*

***Perf. 12½ on 3 Sides***

**B48** SP4 30o + 10o red 1.00 *1.25*
*a.* Booklet pane of 20 18.00

Centenary of the Red Cross idea. The surtax went to the Swedish Red Cross.

King Gustav VI Adolf — SP5

***Perf. 12½ Vertically***

**1962, Nov. 10 Engr. Unwmk.**

**Size: 58x24mm**

**B49** SP5 20o + 10o brown .30 .30
**B50** SP5 35o + 10o blue .30 .30

***Perf. 12½ Horizontally***

**B51** SP5 20o + 10o brown .30 .40
*a.* Booklet pane of 10 3.00
**B52** SP5 35o + 10o blue .30 .40
*a.* Booklet pane of 10 3.00
*Nos. B49-B52 (4)* 1.20 1.40

80th birthday of King Gustav VI Adolf. The surtax went to the King Gustav VI Adolf 80th anniv. Foundation for Swedish Cultural Activities.

**Ship Types of Regular Issues**

Imprint: "1966"

Designs (Ships): 10o, "The Lion of Smaland." 15o, "Kalmar Nyckel." 20o, Old Sailing Packet. 25o, Mail Paddle Steamship. 30o, "Kung Karl." 40o, Stern of "Amphion."

**1966, Nov. 15** ***Perf. 12½ on 3 Sides***

**B53** A76 10o vermilion .30 .45
**B54** A50 15o vermilion .30 .45
**B55** A38 20o slate grn .30 .45
**B56** A39 25o ultra .20 .20
**B57** A76 30o vermilion .30 .55
**B58** A76 40o vermilion .30 .55
*a.* Bklt. pane. #B53-B54, B57-B58, 2 #B55, 4 #B56 2.75
*Nos. B53-B58 (6)* 1.70 2.65

The booklet sold for 3.50k and the surtax of 1.15k went to the National Cancer Fund.

---

## AIR POST STAMPS

Official Stamps Surcharged in Dark Blue

**1920, Sept. 17 Wmk. 181** ***Perf. 13***

**C1** O3 10o on 3o brn 2.75 *7.75*
*a.* Inverted surcharge 275.00 *700.00*
**C2** O3 20o on 2o org 4.50 *11.00*
*a.* Inverted surcharge 275.00 *700.00*
**C3** O3 50o on 4o vio 20.00 25.00
*a.* Inverted surcharge 275.00 *700.00*
*Nos. C1-C3 (3)* 27.25 *43.75*
Set, never hinged 55.00

**Wmk. 180**
**C4** O3 20o on 2o org 2,250.
**C5** O3 50o on 4o vio 160.00 *350.00*

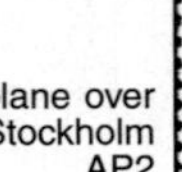
Airplane over Stockholm AP2

*Perf. 10 Vertically*
**1930, May 9 Engr. Unwmk.**
**C6** AP2 10o deep blue .20 .60
**C7** AP2 50o dark violet .65 1.75
Set, never hinged 1.50

Flying Swans — AP3

**1942-53** ***Perf. 12½ on 3 Sides***
**C8** AP3 20k brt ultra ('53) 4.50 .65
Never hinged 7.00
*a.* Bklt. pane of 20 ('53) 725.00
*b.* Bklt. pane of 10 ('68) 65.00
*c.* Perf. on 4 sides 75.00 13.50
Never hinged 140.00
*d.* As "c," bklt. pane of 10 1,350.

Issued: #C8c, May 4, 1942; #C8, July 7.

## POSTAGE DUE STAMPS

D1

**1874 Unwmk. Typo.** ***Perf. 14***
**J1** D1 1o black 50.00 40.00
**J2** D1 3o rose 50.00 40.00
**J3** D1 5o brown 50.00 35.00
**J4** D1 6o yellow 100.00 77.50
**J5** D1 12o pale red 7.75 5.25
**J6** D1 20o blue 62.50 40.00
**J7** D1 24o violet 450.00 260.00
**J8** D1 24o gray 55.00 52.50
**J9** D1 30o dk grn 52.50 40.00
**J10** D1 50o brown 175.00 57.50
**J11** D1 1k blue & bister 225.00 72.50
*Nos. J1-J11 (11)* 1,277. 720.25

**1877-86** ***Perf. 13***
**J12** D1 1o black ('80) 2.75 4.00
**J13** D1 3o rose 6.25 7.25
**J14** D1 5o brown 4.50 4.50
**J15** D1 6o yellow 4.50 4.50
*a.* Printed on both sides 1,000.
**J16** D1 12o pale red ('82) 14.50 17.00
**J17** D1 20o pale blue ('78) 5.25 4.50
**J18** D1 24o red lilac ('86) 26.00 29.00
*a.* 24o violet ('84) 26.00 29.00
**J19** D1 24o gray lil ('82) 125.00 150.00
**J20** D1 30o yellow green 6.50 4.50
**J21** D1 50o yellow brown 10.50 5.75
**J22** D1 1k blue & bister 30.00 17.50
*Nos. J12-J22 (11)* 235.75 248.50

Nos. J12-J17, J19-J22 exist imperf. Value, pairs, each $400.

For surcharges see Nos. B12-B21.

## STAMPS FOR CITY POSTAGE

S1

*Perf. 14x13½*
**1856-62 Typo. Unwmk.**
**LX1** S1 (1sk or 3o) blk 950.00 450.00
**LX2** S1 (3o) bis brn ('62) 600.00 475.00

From 1856 to 1858 No. LX1 was sold at 1sk, from 1858 to 1862 at 3o. The paper of the 1sk black is thin while the paper of the 3o black is medium thick.

*No. LX1 was reprinted three times with perf. 14, once with perf. 13. No. LX2 was reprinted once with each perforation. Value of lowest-cost Perf. 14 reprints, $250 each. Perf. 13, $175 each.*

## OFFICIAL STAMPS

O1

O3

**1874-77 Unwmk. Typo.** ***Perf. 14***
**O1** O1 3o bister 72.50 40.00
**O2** O1 4o gray ('77) 250.00 70.00
**O3** O1 5o yel green 140.00 52.50
**O4** O1 6o lilac 250.00 65.00
**O5** O1 6o gray 525.00 175.00
**O6** O1 12o blue 160.00 2.50
**O7** O1 20o pale red 950.00 90.00
**O8** O1 24o yellow 950.00 20.00
*a.* 24o orange 950.00 22.50
**O9** O1 30o pale brn 425.00 35.00
**O10** O1 50o rose 575.00 125.00
**O11** O1 1k bl & bis 1,650. 65.00
*Nos. O1-O11 (11)* 5,947. 740.00

**Imperf., Pairs**
*O1a* O1 3o 575.
*O2a* O1 4o 575.
*O3a* O1 5o 900.
*O4a* O1 6o 900.
*O6a* O1 12o 575.
*O7a* O1 20o 2,350.
*O8b* O1 24o 1,800.
*O9a* O1 30o 1,050.
*O10a* O1 50o 1,300.
*O11a* O1 1k 3,250.

**1881-95** ***Perf. 13***
**O12** O1 2o org ('91) 1.40 2.00
**O13** O1 3o bis brn 1.40 2.25
**O14** O1 4o gray blk ('93) 2.50 .70
*a.* 4o gray ('82) 16.00 2.25
**O15** O1 5o grn ('84) 5.25 .60
**O16** O1 6o red lil ('82) 40.00 *60.00*
*a.* 6o lilac ('81) 45.00 *65.00*
**O17** O1 10o car ('95) 3.00 .20
*b.* 10o rose ('85) 45.00 1.25
**O18** O1 12o blue 57.50 21.00
**O19** O1 20o ver ('82) 200.00 2.50
**O20** O1 20o dk bl ('91) 5.75 .60
**O21** O1 24o yellow 72.50 22.50
*a.* 24o orange 65.00 22.50
**O22** O1 30o brown 26.00 .70
**O23** O1 50o pale rose 140.00 22.50
**O24** O1 50o pale gray ('93) 18.00 1.90
**O25** O1 1k dk bl & yel brn 9.00 6.50
*Nos. O12-O25 (14)* 582.30 143.95

**Imperf., Pairs**
*O12a* O1 2o 250.00
*O17a* O1 10o No. O17 300.00
*c.* No. O17b 300.00
*O20a* O1 20o 45.00
*O24a* O1 50o 250.00

Surcharged in Dark Blue

**1889**
**O26** O1 10o on 12o blue 11.50 15.00
*a.* Inverted surcharge 1,000. *2,250.*
*b.* Perf. 14 — *3,500.*
**O27** O1 10o on 24o yel 15.00 22.00
*a.* Inverted surcharge *3,000.* *2,500.*
*b.* Perf. 14 *3,000.* *3,000.*

**1910-12 Wmk. 180 Typo.**
**O28** O3 1o black .20 .45
**O29** O3 2o orange 1.40 3.00
**O30** O3 4o pale violet 2.10 4.00
**O31** O3 5o green .65 1.10
**O32** O3 8o claret .65 1.10
**O33** O3 10o red 12.00 .70
**O34** O3 15o red brown 1.10 .85
**O35** O3 20o deep blue 8.25 1.60
**O36** O3 25o red orange 8.25 2.10
**O37** O3 30o chocolate 8.00 3.25
**O38** O3 50o gray 8.25 3.25
**O39** O3 1k black, *yellow* 7.75 7.75
**O40** O3 5k claret, *yellow* 11.00 4.00
*Nos. O28-O40 (13)* 69.60 33.15

**1910-19 Wmk. Wavy Lines (181)**
**O41** O3 1o black 3.00 *3.25*
**O42** O3 2o orange .30 *.40*
**O43** O3 3o pale brown .40 *1.00*
**O44** O3 4o pale violet .30 *.40*
**O45** O3 5o green .30 *.40*
**O46** O3 7o gray green .45 *1.25*
**O47** O3 8o rose 20.00 *27.50*
**O48** O3 10o red .30 .20
**O49** O3 12o rose red .30 .30
**O50** O3 15o org brown .30 .30
**O51** O3 20o deep blue .45 .30
**O52** O3 25o orange 1.00 .50
**O53** O3 30o chocolate .55 .55
**O54** O3 35o dark violet .85 *1.00*
**O55** O3 50o gray 3.25 2.10
*Nos. O41-O55 (15)* 31.75 39.45

For surcharges see Nos. C1-C5.

Use of official stamps ceased on 7/1/20.

## PARCEL POST STAMPS

Regular Issue of 1914 Surcharged

**1917 Wmk. 180** ***Perf. 13***
**Q1** A14 1.98k on 5k claret, *yel* 1.40 *5.25*
**Q2** A14 2.12k on 5k claret, *yel* 1.40 *5.25*

## SWITZERLAND

'swit-sər-lənd

### (Helvetia)

LOCATION — Central Europe, between France, Germany and Italy
GOVT. — Republic
AREA — 15,943 sq. mi.
POP. — 7,062,400 (1998 est.)
CAPITAL — Bern

100 Rappen or Centimes = 1 Franc

**Catalogue values for unused stamps in this country are for Never Hinged items, beginning with Scott 365 in the regular postage section, Scott B272 in the semi-postal section, Scott C46 in the airpost section, Scott CB1 in the airpost semi-postal section, and Scott 3O94, 4O40, 5O26, 7O31, 8O1, 9O1, 10O1, 11O1, 12O1 in the official sections.**

#### Watermarks

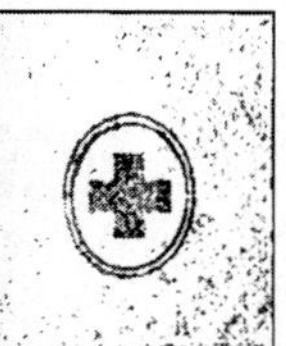

Wmk. 182 — Cross in Oval

Wmk. 183 — Swiss Cross

Watermark 182 is not a true watermark, having been impressed after the paper was manufactured. There are two types:
Type 1 — width just under 9mm.
Type 2 — width just under 8½mm.
There are many other differences of 1/10mm to 1/5mm.

### CANTONAL ADMINISTRATION

Unused values of Nos. 1L1-3L1 are for stamps without gum.
Counterfeit and repaired copies of Nos. 1L1-3L1 abound.

#### Zurich

A1

Numerals of Value — A2

**1843 Unwmk. Litho. *Imperf.***
**Red Vertical Lines**

**1L1** A1 4r black *20,000. 17,500.*
**1L2** A2 6r black *6,500. 1,750.*

**1846 Red Horizontal Lines**

**1L3** A1 4r black *17,500. 22,500.*
**1L4** A2 6r black 1,900. 1,600.

Five varieties of each value.

*Reprints of the Zurich stamps show signs of wear and lack the red lines. Values 4r, $5,500; 6r, $1,800.*

Coat of Arms — A3

**1850 Unwmk. *Imperf.***

**1L5** A3 2½r black & red *6,500. 4,000.*

No. 1L5 has separation designs in the margins between stamps as shown. Values are for stamps showing part of the separation design on all four sides.

#### Geneva

Coat of Arms — A4

**1843 Unwmk. Litho. *Imperf.***

**2L1** A4 10c blk, *yel grn* *60,000. 40,000.*
*a.* Either half *22,500. 9,000.*
*b.* Stamp composed of right half at left & left half at right *85,000. 62,500.*

A5

A6

**1845-48**

**2L2** A5 5c blk, *yel grn* 2,750. 1,750.
**2L3** A6 5c blk, *yel grn* ('46) 2,100. 1,750.
**2L4** A6 5c blk, *dk grn* ('48) 4,000. 3,000.

A7

Coat of Arms — A8

**1849-50**

**2L5** A7 4c black & red *35,000. 21,000.*
**2L6** A7 5c blk & red ('50) 2,500. 1,750.

**1851**

**2L7** A8 5c black & red *9,750. 4,000.*

### ENVELOPE STAMP USED AS ADHESIVE

E1

**1847 Unwmk. *Imperf.***

**2LU1** E1 5c yel grn, see footnote *21,000.*

Authorized for use from Feb. 19, 1847. Value is for cut-out stamp used on folded letters. Value of unused envelope (1846) or cut-out, from $400. Value of used cut-out off cover, $2,800.

#### Basel

Dove of Basel — A9

**Typo. & Embossed**
**1845 Unwmk. *Imperf.***

**3L1** A9 2½r blk, crim & bl *14,000. 12,500.*

Proofs are black, vermilion and green. Value, $3,600.

### FEDERAL ADMINISTRATION

Due to its tendency to damage the paper and/or the color of the stamps, the gum on Nos. 1-40 very often is removed. Unused values for Nos. 1-40 are for stamps without gum. Stamps with original gum sell for about the same prices.

A10

A11

**1850 Unwmk. Litho. *Imperf.***
**Full Black Frame Around Cross**

1 A10 2½r black & red 3,000. 1,600.
2 A11 2½r black & red 2,500. 1,500.

**Without Frame Around Cross**

3 A10 2½r black & red 5,750. 2,750.
4 A11 2½r blk & red *42,500. 25,000.*

Forty types of each.

A12

A13

**1850**
**Full Black Frame Around Cross**

5 A12 5r dk bl, blk & red 5,000. 1,250.
*a.* 5r dk grayish bl, blk & red 5,000. 1,250.
6 A13 10r yel, blk & red *110,000.*

No. 6 used, with only parts of frame around cross showing, value $175 to $900.
Beware of copies of Nos. 7-8 with faked frame added.

**Without Frame Around Cross**

7 A12 5r lt bl, blk & red 1,750. 500.00
*a.* 5r dp bl, blk & red 3,500. 1,000.
*b.* 5r pur bl, blk & red — *5,500.*
*c.* 5r grnsh bl, blk & red 2,000. 575.00
8 A13 10r yel, blk & red 925.00 125.00
*a.* 10r buff, blk & red 1,275. 225.00
*b.* 10r org yel, blk & red 1,250. 250.00
*c.* Half used as 5r on cover *12,500.*

**1851**
**Full Blue Frame Around Cross**

9 A12 5r light blue & red *140,000.*

No. 9 used, with only parts of frame around cross showing, value $180 to $3,750.
Beware of copies of No. 10 with faked frame added.

**Without Frame Around Cross**

10 A12 5r lt blue & red 575.00 125.00

Forty types of each.

A14

A15

A16

**1852**
**Vermilion Frame Around Cross**

11 A14 15r vermilion *15,000.* 700.00
12 A15 15r vermilion 2,500. 125.00
13 A16 15c vermilion *14,000.* 1,000.

Ten types of each.
On October 1st, 1854, all stamps of the preceding issues were declared obsolete.

Helvetia — A17

**1854 Embossed. Unwmk.**
**Thin Paper, Fine Impressions**
**Emerald Silk Threads**

14 A17 5r orange brn *8,000. 1,600.*
15 A17 5r red brown 550.00 140.00
16 A17 10r blue 775.00 80.00
17 A17 15r carmine rose 1,250. 175.00
*a.* 15r pale rose 1,250. 175.00
18 A17 40r pale yel grn *10,000.* 1,250.
19 A17 40r yellow grn 1,250. 275.00

**1854-55**
**Emerald Silk Threads**
**Medium Thick Paper**
**Fine Impressions**

20 A17 5r pale yel brn 650.00 150.00
21 A17 10r blue 1,600. 110.00
22 A17 15r rose 925.00 100.00
23 A17 20r pale orange 1,400. 175.00

**1855-57**

**Colored Silk Threads**
**Medium Thick Paper**
**Fine to Rough Impressions**

| No. | Description | Unused | Used |
|---|---|---|---|
| 24 | A17 5r yel brn (yel) | 575.00 | 100.00 |
| 25 | A17 5r dk brown (blk) | 325.00 | 35.00 |
| 26 | A17 10r mlky bl (red) | 925.00 | 175.00 |
| 27 | A17 10r blue (car) | 300.00 | 45.00 |
| *a.* | Thin paper | 5,000. | 425.00 |
| 28 | A17 15r rose (bl) | 550.00 | 65.00 |
| 29 | A17 40r yel grn (mar) | 1,000. | 100.00 |
| 30 | A17 1fr lav (blk) | 1,400. | 925.00 |
| 31 | A17 1fr lav (yel) | 1,400. | 925.00 |
| *a.* | Thin paper | *20,000.* | 7,250. |

**1857**

**Thin (Emergency) Paper**
**Rough Impressions**
**Green Silk Threads**

| No. | Description | Unused | Used |
|---|---|---|---|
| 32 | A17 5r pale gray brn | 4,500. | 1,000. |
| 32A | A17 10r blue | 6,500. | 925. |
| 33 | A17 15r pale dl rose | 3,250. | 325. |
| 34 | A17 20r pale dl org | 3,250. | 250. |

**1858-62**

**Thick Ordinary Paper**
**Rough Impressions**
**Green Silk Threads**

| No. | Description | Unused | Used |
|---|---|---|---|
| 35 | A17 2r gray | 250.00 | 550.00 |
| *a.* | One and one-half used as 3r on newspaper or wrapper | | *14,000.* |
| *c.* | Half used as 1r on cover | | |
| 36 | A17 5r brown | 225.00 | 20.00 |
| *a.* | 5r black brown | 275.00 | 40.00 |
| *b.* | Half used as 2r on cover | | *1,400.* |
| 37 | A17 10r dark blue | 240.00 | 20.00 |
| *a.* | Half used as 5r on cover | | *7,250.* |
| 38 | A17 15r dark rose | 375.00 | 65.00 |
| 39 | A17 20r dark orange | 475.00 | 70.00 |
| *a.* | Half used as 10r on cover | | *17,500.* |
| 40 | A17 40r dk yellow grn | 450.00 | 85.00 |
| *a.* | Half used as 20r on cover | | *27,500.* |
| | *Nos. 35-40 (6)* | 2,015. | 810.00 |

Helvetia — A18

Double embossing errors, Nos. 43c, 44a, 55b, 60a, 61a, 61b, 67b, have the design impressed twice. These do not refer to the "embossed" watermark.

**Embossed**

**1862-64 Wmk. 182 *Perf. 11½***

**White Wove Paper**

| No. | Description | Unused | Used |
|---|---|---|---|
| 41 | A18 2c gray | 140.00 | 4.25 |
| 42 | A18 3c black | 14.50 | *125.00* |
| 43 | A18 5c dark brown | 3.50 | .85 |
| *a.* | 5c bister brown | 110.00 | 6.75 |
| *b.* | 5c gray brown | 110.00 | 32.50 |
| *c.* | Dbl. embossing, one invtd. | 4,000. | 425.00 |
| *d.* | Double impression of lower left "5" | | 1,450. |
| 44 | A18 10c blue | 725.00 | .85 |
| *a.* | Dbl. embossing, one invtd. | | *8,000.* |
| 45 | A18 20c orange | 2.50 | 2.75 |
| *a.* | 20c yellow orange | 350.00 | 2.90 |
| 46 | A18 30c vermilion | 1,700. | 40.00 |
| 47 | A18 40c green | 1,600. | 65.00 |
| 48 | A18 60c bronze | 1,450. | 150.00 |
| 50 | A18 1fr gold | 20.00 | *120.00* |
| *a.* | 1fr yellowish bronze ('64) | 1,450. | 425.00 |

**1867-78**

| No. | Description | Unused | Used |
|---|---|---|---|
| 52 | A18 2c bister brown | 2.50 | 1.80 |
| *a.* | 2c red brown | 675.00 | 275.00 |
| 53 | A18 10c carmine | 3.50 | 1.00 |
| 54 | A18 15c lemon | 4.25 | *42.50* |
| 55 | A18 25c blue green | 1.80 | *4.25* |
| *a.* | 25c yellow green | 60.00 | 40.00 |
| *b.* | Dbl. embossing, one invtd. | | 575.00 |
| 56 | A18 30c ultra | 575.00 | 10.00 |
| *a.* | 30c blue | *2,000.* | 250.00 |
| 58 | A18 40c gray | 1.80 | *160.00* |
| 59 | A18 50c violet | 57.50 | 65.00 |
| | *Nos. 52-59 (7)* | 646.35 | *284.55* |

**1881**

**Granite Paper**

| No. | Description | Unused | Used |
|---|---|---|---|
| 60 | A18 2c bister | .55 | *25.00* |
| *a.* | Dbl. embossing, one invtd. | 350.00 | |
| 61 | A18 5c brown | .55 | *13.00* |
| *a.* | Dbl. embossing, one invtd. | 30.00 | *425.00* |
| *b.* | Double embossing of lower left "5" | | *1,150.* |
| 62 | A18 10c rose | 5.00 | *10.50* |
| 63 | A18 15c lemon | 10.50 | *475.00* |
| 64 | A18 20c orange | .55 | *160.00* |
| 65 | A18 25c green | .55 | *105.00* |
| 66 | A18 40c gray | 1.80 | *3,400.* |
| 67 | A18 50c deep violet | 18.00 | *575.00* |
| *b.* | Dbl. embossing, one invtd. | 250.00 | *4,500.* |
| 68 | A18 1fr gold | 21.50 | *1,300.* |

The granite paper contains fragments of blue and red silk threads.

Forged or backdated cancellations are found frequently on Nos. 42, 50, 54, 58 and 60-68.

All stamps of the preceding issues were declared obsolete on October 1st, 1883. Some of the remainders of Nos. 41-68 were overprinted "AUSSER KURS" (Obsolete) diagonally in black.

Numeral — A19

**1882-99 Typo. *Perf. 11½***

**Granite Paper**

| No. | Description | Unused | Used |
|---|---|---|---|
| 69 | A19 2c bister | 1.80 | .60 |
| 70 | A19 3c gray brown | 3.00 | *8.50* |
| *a.* | 3c gray | 47.50 | 45.00 |
| 71 | A19 5c maroon | 18.00 | .60 |
| *a.* | Tête bêche pair | | |
| 72 | A19 5c deep grn ('99) | 8.00 | .60 |
| 73 | A19 10c red | 7.25 | .60 |
| *a.* | 10c carmine | 55.00 | .90 |
| *b.* | 10c light rose | 250.00 | 5.00 |
| 74 | A19 12c ultra | 8.00 | .60 |
| *a.* | 12c chalky blue | 22.50 | 19.00 |
| *b.* | 12c greenish blue | *450.00* | |
| 75 | A19 15c yellow | 140.00 | 29.00 |
| *a.* | 15c orange | *14,500.* | *4,000.* |
| *b.* | Tête bêche pair | | |
| 76 | A19 15c violet ('89) | 45.00 | 2.25 |
| | *Nos. 69-76 (8)* | 231.05 | *42.75* |

Nos. 69-74, 76 are watermark type 1. Nos. 70a, 73a-73b, 75-75a are type 2.

**1882**

**White Paper**

| No. | Description | Unused | Used |
|---|---|---|---|
| 77 | A19 2c bister | 375.00 | 300.00 |
| 78 | A19 5c maroon | 825.00 | 100.00 |
| 79 | A19 10c rose | 2,100. | 70.00 |
| 80 | A19 12c chalky blue | 150.00 | 26.00 |
| 81 | A19 15c yellow | 225.00 | 250.00 |

Watermark type 1.

See Nos. 113-118.

Helvetia (Large numerals) A20

Helvetia (Small numerals) A21

**1882-1904 Engr. *Perf. 11½ - 11¾***

| No. | Description | Unused | Used |
|---|---|---|---|
| 82 | A20 20c orange | 150.00 | 5.50 |
| 83 | A20 25c green | 82.50 | 3.00 |
| *95b* | A20 30c brown | — | *16,750.* |
| 84 | A20 40c gray | 120.00 | 40.00 |
| 85 | A21 40c gray ('04) | 37.50 | 21.00 |
| 86 | A20 50c blue | 125.00 | 21.00 |
| 87 | A20 1fr claret | 210.00 | 6.00 |
| 88 | A20 3fr yel brn ('91) | 180.00 | 19.00 |

**1888 *Perf. 9½***

| No. | Description | Unused | Used |
|---|---|---|---|
| 89 | A20 20c orange | 800.00 | 100.00 |
| 90 | A20 25c yellow grn | 150.00 | 15.00 |
| 91 | A20 40c gray | 800.00 | 650.00 |
| 92 | A20 50c blue | 1,100. | 325.00 |
| 93 | A20 1fr claret | 850.00 | 87.50 |

Values for Nos. 89-93 are for well-centered stamps with slightly uneven perforations. Stamps missing perforations sell for much less.

**1891-99 *Perf. 11½x11***

| No. | Description | Unused | Used |
|---|---|---|---|
| *82a* | A20 20c orange | 47.50 | 1.75 |
| *83a* | A20 25c green | 10.00 | 1.75 |
| 94 | A20 25c blue ('99) | 11.00 | 1.75 |
| 95 | A20 30c red brn ('92) | 30.00 | 1.90 |
| *84a* | A20 40c gray | 67.50 | 4.75 |
| *86a* | A20 50c blue | 40.00 | 11.00 |
| 96 | A20 50c green ('99) | 42.50 | 21.00 |
| *87a* | A20 1fr claret | 37.50 | 4.00 |
| 97 | A20 1fr carmine | 80.00 | 8.00 |
| *88a* | A20 3fr yellow brown | 135.00 | 25.00 |

**1901-03 *Perf. 11½x12***

| No. | Description | Unused | Used |
|---|---|---|---|
| *82b* | A20 20c orange | 25.00 | 1.60 |
| *94a* | A20 25c blue | 12.00 | 1.10 |
| *95a* | A20 30c red brown | 35.00 | 1.90 |
| *84b* | A20 40c gray | 75.00 | 30.00 |
| *96a* | A20 50c green | 60.00 | 7.00 |
| *87b* | A20 1fr claret | *2,000.* | 250.00 |
| *97a* | A20 1fr carmine ('03) | 375.00 | 32.50 |
| *88b* | A20 3fr yellow brown | 180.00 | 19.00 |

Numerous retouches and plate flaws exist on all values of this issue.

Nos. 82-88 have wmk. type 1 and are ½mm taller (paper size) than Nos. 82b-88b, which have wmk. type 2.

See Nos. 105-112, 119-125.

UPU Allegory — A22

**1900 *Perf. 11½***

| No. | Description | Unused | Used |
|---|---|---|---|
| 98 | A22 5c gray green | 30.00 | 1.60 |
| 99 | A22 10c carmine rose | 10.00 | 1.60 |
| 100 | A22 25c blue | 25.00 | 30.00 |
| | *Nos. 98-100 (3)* | 65.00 | 33.20 |

**Re-engraved**

| No. | Description | Unused | Used |
|---|---|---|---|
| 101 | A22 5c gray green | 3.00 | 1.50 |
| 102 | A22 10c carmine rose | 45.00 | 35.00 |
| 103 | A22 25c blue | 700.00 | *10,000.* |

Universal Postal Union, 25th anniv.

The impression of the re-engraved stamps is much clearer, especially the horizontally lined background. The figures of value are lined instead of being solid.

**Helvetia Types of 1882-1904**

**1905 Wmk. 183 *Perf. 11½x11***

**White Paper**

| No. | Description | Unused | Used |
|---|---|---|---|
| 105 | A20 20c orange | 3.75 | 2.25 |
| 106 | A20 25c blue | 5.00 | *9.00* |
| 107 | A20 30c brown | 5.00 | 2.00 |
| *108a* | A21 40c gray | 90.00 | *140.00* |
| 109 | A20 50c green | 30.00 | 7.25 |
| 110 | A20 1fr carmine | 77.50 | 3.00 |
| 111 | A20 3fr yellow brn | 200.00 | 110.00 |

Some clichés in the plates of the 20c, 25c, 30c, 50c and 3fr have been retouched.

**1906 Re-engraved *Perf. 11½x11***

| No. | Description | Unused | Used |
|---|---|---|---|
| 112 | A20 25c pale blue | 6.00 | 2.25 |

In the re-engraved stamp the stars are larger and the background below "FRANCO" is of horiz. or horiz. and vert. crossed lines, instead of horiz. and curved lines.

**1906 *Perf. 11½***

| No. | Description | Unused | Used |
|---|---|---|---|
| *112a* | A20 25c pale blue | 85.00 | 7.50 |
| 108 | A21 40c gray | 27.50 | 11.00 |

**1907 *Perf. 11½x12***

| No. | Description | Unused | Used |
|---|---|---|---|
| *105a* | A20 20c orange | 6.00 | 6.00 |
| *109a* | A20 50c green | 37.50 | 12.00 |
| *110a* | A20 1fr carmine | 100.00 | 9.00 |
| *111a* | A20 3fr yellow brown | 240.00 | 190.00 |

**Numeral Type of 1882-99**

**1905 Typo. *Perf. 11½***

**Granite Paper**

| No. | Description | Unused | Used |
|---|---|---|---|
| 113 | A19 2c dull bister | 4.25 | 1.90 |
| 114 | A19 3c gray brown | 4.50 | *60.00* |
| 115 | A19 5c green | 4.25 | .50 |
| 116 | A19 10c scarlet | 4.25 | .50 |
| 117 | A19 12c ultra | 5.50 | 2.00 |
| 118 | A19 15c brown vio | 60.00 | 13.50 |
| | *Nos. 113-118 (6)* | 82.75 | *78.40* |

**Helvetia Types of 1882-1904**

**1907 Engr. *Perf. 11½x12***

**Granite Paper**

| No. | Description | Unused | Used |
|---|---|---|---|
| 119 | A20 20c orange | 2.25 | 3.75 |
| 120 | A20 25c blue | 7.75 | *10.00* |
| 121 | A20 30c red brown | 6.50 | *17.50* |
| 122 | A21 40c gray | 21.00 | *45.00* |
| *a.* | Helvetia without diadem | 300.00 | *1,050.* |
| 123 | A20 50c gray green | 5.50 | *17.50* |
| 124 | A20 1fr carmine | 19.00 | 9.25 |
| *125a* | A20 3fr yellow brown | | *10,500.* |

There are retouches and plate flaws on all values.

***Perf. 11½x11***

| No. | Description | Unused | Used |
|---|---|---|---|
| *120a* | A20 25c deep blue | 10.00 | 6.50 |
| *121a* | A20 30c red brown | 140.00 | *325.00* |
| *122b* | A21 40c gray | | *13,000.* |
| *124a* | A20 1fr carmine | | *10,000.* |
| 125 | A20 3fr yel brn | 100.00 | 65.00 |

William Tell's Son — A23

Helvetia
A24 A25

**1907-25 Typo. *Perf. 11½***

**Granite Paper**

| No. | Description | Unused | Used |
|---|---|---|---|
| 126 | A23 2c pale bister | .30 | .55 |
| 127 | A23 3c lilac brn | .25 | *10.00* |
| 128 | A23 5c yellow grn | 2.25 | .50 |
| 129 | A24 10c rose red | 1.50 | .50 |
| 130 | A24 12c ocher | .30 | *3.50* |
| 131 | A24 15c red vio | 3.00 | *13.00* |
| 132 | A25 20c red & yel ('08) | 2.25 | 1.00 |
| 133 | A25 25c dp blue ('08) | 1.90 | .65 |
| *a.* | Tête bêche pair | 17.00 | *55.00* |
| 134 | A25 30c yel brn & pale grn ('08) | 1.60 | .50 |
| 135 | A25 35c yel grn & yel ('08) | 1.90 | 1.40 |
| 136 | A25 40c red vio & yel ('08) | 12.50 | 1.00 |
| *a.* | Designer's name in full on the rock ('08) | 6.00 | *82.50* |
| 137 | A25 40c deep blue ('22) | 1.75 | .50 |
| *a.* | 40c light blue ('21) | 5.50 | 1.90 |
| 138 | A25 40c red vio & grn ('25) | 25.00 | .50 |
| 139 | A25 50c dp grn & pale grn ('08) | 11.00 | .50 |
| 140 | A25 60c brn org & buff ('18) | 9.25 | .65 |
| 141 | A25 70c dk brn & buff ('08) | 55.00 | 17.00 |
| 142 | A25 70c vio & buff ('24) | 14.50 | 2.25 |
| 143 | A25 80c slate & buff ('15) | 9.75 | 1.10 |
| 144 | A25 1fr dp cl & pale grn ('08) | 7.00 | .55 |
| 145 | A25 3fr bis & yel ('08) | 275.00 | 2.10 |
| | *Nos. 126-145 (20)* | 436.00 | *57.75* |

No. 136 has two leaves and "CL" below sword hilt. No. 136a has three leaves and designer's full name below hilt.

For surcharges and overprints see Nos. 189, 199, O10-O13, O15, 1O6-1O8, 1O14-1O16, 2O18-2O26, 3O14-3O22.

**1933**

**With Grilled Gum**

| No. | Description | Unused | Used |
|---|---|---|---|
| *135a* | A25 35c yel grn & yel | 1.40 | *12.50* |
| *138a* | A25 40c red vio & grn | 32.50 | 1.50 |
| *139a* | A25 50c dp grn & pale grn | 9.00 | 1.50 |
| *140a* | A25 60c brn org & buff | 12.00 | 1.50 |
| *142a* | A25 70c vio & buff | 17.50 | 3.75 |
| *143a* | A25 80c slate & buff | 13.00 | 4.25 |
| *144a* | A25 1fr dp cl & pale grn | 19.00 | 6.50 |
| | *Nos. 135a-144a (7)* | 104.40 | 31.50 |

"Grilled" Gum

In 1930-44 many Swiss stamps were treated with a light grilling process, applied with the gumming to counteract the tendency to curl. It resembles a faint grill of vertical and horizontal ribs covering the entire back of the stamp, and can be seen after the gum has been removed. Listings of the grilled gum varieties begin with No. 135a.

William Tell's Son — A26

Bow-string in front of stock

**1909 *Perf. 11½, 12***

**Granite Paper**

| No. | Description | Unused | Used |
|---|---|---|---|
| 146 | A26 2c bister | .25 | 1.40 |
| *a.* | Tête bêche pair | 3.25 | *17.50* |
| 147 | A26 3c dark violet | .25 | *14.00* |
| 148 | A26 5c green | 3.75 | .20 |
| *a.* | Tête bêche pair | 14.00 | *50.00* |
| | *Nos. 146-148 (3)* | 4.25 | *15.60* |

See Nos. 149-163. For surcharges and overprints see Nos. 186, 193-195, 207-208, 1O1-1O3, 1O9-1O11, 2O1-2O7, 3O1-3O5.

First Redrawing

Bow-string behind stock. Thin loop above crossbow. Letters of "HELVETIA" without serifs.

**1910-17**

**Granite Paper**

| No. | Type | Description | Unused | Used |
|---|---|---|---|---|
| **149** | A26 | 2c bister ('10) | 8.75 | 8.00 |
| **150** | A26 | 3c dk violet ('10) | .20 | .20 |
| *a.* | | Tête bêche pair | 2.75 | 2.75 |
| *b.* | | Booklet pane of 6 | 12.50 | |
| **151** | A26 | 3c brown org ('17) | .20 | .20 |
| *a.* | | Tête bêche pair | 8.25 | 11.00 |
| **152** | A26 | 5c green ('10) | 21.00 | 6.50 |
| *a.* | | Tête bêche pair | 92.50 | 175.00 |
| | | *Nos. 149-152 (4)* | 30.15 | 14.90 |

Second Redrawing

Bow-string behind stock. Thick loop above crossbow. Letters of "HELVETIA" have serifs.

7½ CENTIMES:

Type I — Top of "7" is ½mm thick. The "1" of "½" has only traces of serifs. The two base plates of the statue are of even thickness.

Type II — Top of "7" is 1mm thick. The "1" of "½" has distinct serifs. The upper base plate is thinner than the lower.

**1911-30**

**Granite Paper**

| No. | Type | Description | Unused | Used |
|---|---|---|---|---|
| **153** | A26 | 2c bister ('11) | .20 | .20 |
| *a.* | | Tête bêche pair | 3.25 | 1.60 |
| **154** | A26 | 2½c claret ('18) | .20 | *1.10* |
| **155** | A26 | 2½c ol, *buff* ('28) | .55 | *2.10* |
| **156** | A26 | 3c ultra, *buff* ('30) | 2.75 | *6.00* |
| **157** | A26 | 5c green ('11) | 1.75 | .20 |
| *a.* | | Tête bêche pair | 5.50 | *10.00* |
| **158** | A26 | 5c org, *buff* ('21) | .20 | .20 |
| *a.* | | Bklt. pane of 6 (5 #158, 168) | 14.00 | *47.50* |
| **159** | A26 | 5c gray vio, *buff* ('24) | .20 | .20 |
| *a.* | | Bklt. pane of 6 (5 #159, 168) | 6.50 | *19.00* |
| **160** | A26 | 5c red vio, *buff* ('27) | .20 | .20 |
| *a.* | | Bklt. pane 6 (5 #160, 168) | 30.00 | *65.00* |
| **161** | A26 | 5c dk grn, *buff* ('30) | .30 | .25 |
| *a.* | | Bklt. pane 6 (5 #161, 169) | 27.50 | *70.00* |
| **162** | A26 | 7½c gray (I) ('18) | 1.10 | .20 |
| *a.* | | Tête bêche pair | 13.00 | *45.00* |
| *c.* | | 7½c slate (II) | 4.50 | 2.75 |
| **163** | A26 | 7½c dp grn, *buff* (I) ('28) | .30 | *3.25* |
| | | *Nos. 153-163 (11)* | 7.75 | *13.90* |

**1933 — With Grilled Gum**

| No. | Type | Description | Unused | Used |
|---|---|---|---|---|
| *156a* | A26 | 3c ultra, *buff* | 4.75 | *17.50* |
| *161b* | A26 | 5c dark green, *buff* | .55 | *5.00* |

Helvetia A27

William Tell A28

**1909**

**Granite Paper**

| No. | Type | Description | Unused | Used |
|---|---|---|---|---|
| **164** | A27 | 10c carmine | .60 | .40 |
| *a.* | | Tête bêche pair | 2.25 | *6.00* |
| **165** | A27 | 12c bister brn | .85 | .40 |
| **166** | A27 | 15c red violet | 26.00 | 1.10 |
| | | *Nos. 164-166 (3)* | 27.45 | 1.90 |

For surcharge see No. 187.

**1914-30 Granite Paper *Perf. 11½***

TEN CENTIMES:

Type I — Bust 16½mm high. "HELVETIA" 15½mm wide. Cross bar of "H" at middle of the letter.

Type II — Bust 15mm high. "HELVETIA" 15mm wide. Cross bar of "H" above middle of the letter.

| No. | Type | Description | Unused | Used |
|---|---|---|---|---|
| **167** | A28 | 10c red, *buff* (type II) | .75 | .20 |
| *a.* | | 10c red, *buff* (type I) | 2.50 | *26.00* |
| *b.* | | Tête bêche pair (II) | 3.25 | 4.25 |
| *d.* | | Bklt. pane, #172, 167 | 50.00 | *160.00* |
| **168** | A28 | 10c grn, *buff* (type II) ('21) | .20 | .20 |
| *a.* | | Tête bêche pair | 1.10 | 1.40 |
| **168C** | A28 | 10c bl grn, *buff* (type II) ('28) | .20 | .20 |
| *d.* | | Tête bêche pair | 2.50 | 2.50 |
| **169** | A28 | 10c vio, *buff* (type II) ('30) | 2.25 | .20 |
| *a.* | | Tête bêche pair | 9.25 | 1.40 |
| **170** | A28 | 12c brn, *buff* | .20 | *3.25* |
| **171** | A28 | 13c ol grn, *buff* ('15) | 1.40 | .50 |
| **172** | A28 | 15c vio, *buff* | 3.50 | .20 |
| *b.* | | 15c dk vio, *buff* | 32.50 | 4.25 |
| *c.* | | Tête bêche pair | 87.50 | 125.00 |
| **173** | A28 | 15c brn red, *buff* ('28) | 2.50 | 2.75 |
| **174** | A28 | 20c red vio, *buff* ('21) | 3.25 | .20 |
| *a.* | | Tête bêche pair | 6.50 | 7.50 |
| **175** | A28 | 20c ver, *buff* ('24) | 1.00 | .50 |
| *a.* | | Tête bêche pair | 5.75 | 9.25 |
| **176** | A28 | 20c car, *buff* ('25) | .25 | .20 |
| *a.* | | Tête bêche pair | 2.50 | .55 |
| **177** | A28 | 25c ver, *buff* ('21) | 2.25 | 1.60 |
| **178** | A28 | 25c car, *buff* ('22) | 1.10 | .85 |
| **179** | A28 | 25c brn, *buff* ('25) | 3.25 | 1.25 |
| **180** | A28 | 30c dp bl, *buff* ('24) | 9.25 | .50 |
| | | *Nos. 167-180 (15)* | 31.35 | 12.60 |

**1932-33 — With Grilled Gum**

| No. | Type | Description | Unused | Used |
|---|---|---|---|---|
| *169c* | A28 | 10c violet, *buff* | 4.50 | 1.50 |
| *173a* | A28 | 15c brn red, *buff* ('33) | 50.00 | *52.50* |
| *176c* | A28 | 20c carmine, *buff* | 7.25 | 1.50 |
| *179a* | A28 | 25c brown, *buff* ('33) | 125.00 | 35.00 |
| *180a* | A28 | 30c deep blue, *buff* | 72.50 | 2.50 |
| | | *Nos. 169c-180a (5)* | 259.25 | 93.00 |

For surcharges and overprints see Nos. 188, 196-198, 1O4-1O5, 1O12-1O13, 2O8-2O17, 3O6-3O13.

The Mythen A29

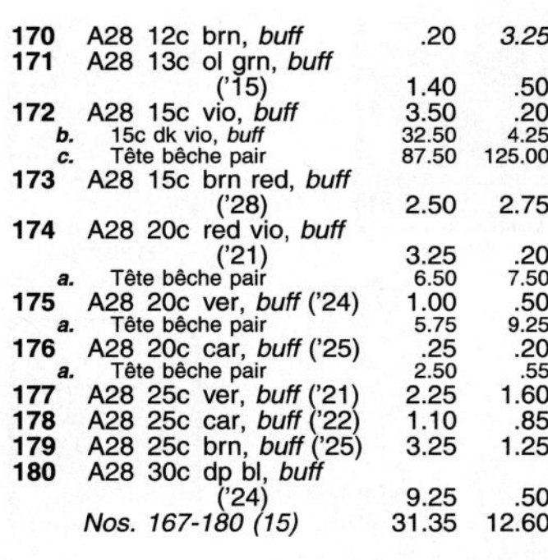

The Rütli — A30

The Jungfrau A31

**1914-30 Engr. Granite Paper**

| No. | Type | Description | Unused | Used |
|---|---|---|---|---|
| **181** | A29 | 3fr dk green | 650.00 | 6.50 |
| **182** | A29 | 3fr red ('18) | 87.50 | 1.40 |
| **183** | A30 | 5fr dp ultra | 35.00 | 3.00 |
| **184** | A31 | 10fr dull violet | 100.00 | 3.25 |
| **185** | A31 | 10fr gray grn ('30) | 225.00 | 37.50 |
| | | *Nos. 181-185 (5)* | 1,097. | 51.65 |

See No. 206. For overprints see Nos. 2O27-2O30, 3O23-3O26.

Stamps of 1909-14 Surcharged

a

b

c

**1915**

| No. | Type | Description | Unused | Used |
|---|---|---|---|---|
| **186** | A26(a) | 1c on 2c bister | .25 | 1.25 |
| **187** | A27(b) | 13c on 12c bis brn | .25 | *9.25* |
| **188** | A28(c) | 13c on 12c brn, *buff* | .30 | .90 |
| | | *Nos. 186-188 (3)* | .80 | *11.40* |

No. 141 Surcharged

| No. | Type | Description | Unused | Used |
|---|---|---|---|---|
| **189** | A25 | 80c on 70c | 25.00 | 17.50 |

Significant of Peace A32

"Peace" A33

"Dawn of Peace" A34

***Perf. 11½***

**1919, Aug. 1 Typo. Unwmk.**

| No. | Type | Description | Unused | Used |
|---|---|---|---|---|
| **190** | A32 | 7½c olive drab & blk | .80 | *2.25* |
| **191** | A33 | 10c red & yel | 1.10 | *8.75* |
| **192** | A34 | 15c violet & yel | 1.90 | 2.75 |
| | | *Nos. 190-192 (3)* | 3.80 | 13.75 |

Commemorating Peace after World War I.

Nos. 151, 149, 162, 171-172, 133 Surcharged in Black, Red or Dark Blue

a

b

c

**1921 Wmk. 183**

| No. | Type | Description | Unused | Used |
|---|---|---|---|---|
| **193** | A26(a) | 2½c on 3c (Bl) | .20 | 1.10 |
| *a.* | | Tête bêche pair | 1.10 | *3.25* |
| *b.* | | Inverted surcharge | 800.00 | *1,550.* |
| *c.* | | Double surcharge | *550.00* | *775.00* |
| **194** | A26(a) | 5c on 2c (R) | .20 | *4.50* |
| *a.* | | Double surcharge | *450.00* | *450.00* |
| **195** | A26(a) | 5c on 7½c (R) | .20 | .55 |
| *a.* | | Tête bêche pair | 6.50 | *55.00* |
| *b.* | | Double surcharge | *550.00* | *550.00* |
| *c.* | | 5c on 7½c slate (II) | *2,200.* | *4,500.* |
| **196** | A28(b) | 10c on 13c (R) | .20 | *2.25* |
| *a.* | | Double surcharge | *550.00* | *550.00* |
| **197** | A28(c) | 20c on 15c (Bk) | .55 | 2.75 |
| *a.* | | Tête bêche pair | 2.50 | *55.00* |
| *b.* | | Double surcharge | *875.00* | *875.00* |
| **198** | A28(c) | 20c on 15c (Bl) | 2.25 | 5.50 |
| *b.* | | Double surcharge | *875.00* | *875.00* |
| **199** | A25(c) | 20c on 25c dp bl (R) | .20 | .55 |
| *a.* | | Tête bêche pair | 1.50 | 4.50 |
| | | *Nos. 193-199 (7)* | 3.80 | *17.20* |

A36

**1924 Typo. *Perf. 11½***

**Granite Paper, Surface Colored**

| No. | Type | Description | Unused | Used |
|---|---|---|---|---|
| **200** | A36 | 90c grn & red, *grn* | 15.00 | 2.75 |
| **201** | A36 | 1.20fr brn rose & red, *rose* | 5.25 | 5.25 |
| **202** | A36 | 1.50fr bl & red, *bl* | 37.50 | 6.50 |
| **203** | A36 | 2fr gray blk & red, *gray* | 47.50 | 6.75 |
| | | *Nos. 200-203 (4)* | 105.25 | 21.25 |
| | | Set, never hinged | 325.00 | |

**1933 — With Grilled Gum**

| No. | Type | Description | Unused | Used |
|---|---|---|---|---|
| *200a* | A36 | 90c | 17.50 | 3.25 |
| *201a* | A36 | 1.20fr | 47.50 | 5.50 |
| *202a* | A36 | 1.50fr | 32.50 | 6.50 |
| *203a* | A36 | 2fr | 27.50 | 8.25 |
| | | *Nos. 200a-203a (4)* | 125.00 | 23.50 |
| | | Set, never hinged | 300.00 | |

For overprints see Nos. O16-O18, 2O31-2O34, 3O27-3O30.

Building in Bern, Location of 1st UPU Congress, 1874

A37 A38

**1924, Oct. 9 Engr. Wmk. 183**

**Granite Paper**

| No. | Type | Description | Unused | Used |
|---|---|---|---|---|
| **204** | A37 | 20c vermilion | .55 | 1.60 |
| **205** | A38 | 30c dull blue | 1.10 | 6.25 |
| | | Set, never hinged | 3.25 | |

50th anniv. of the UPU.

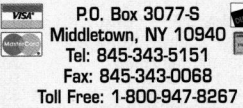

The Rütli — A39

Type of 1914 Issue

**1928 Re-engraved *Perf. 11½***

| | | | |
|---|---|---|---|
| **206** | A39 5fr blue | 110.00 | 9.75 |
| | Never hinged | 300.00 | |
| *a.* | Imperf., pair, never hinged | *10,000.* | |

In the re-engraved stamp the picture is clearer and lighter than on No. 183. "HELVETIA" is in smaller letters. The names at foot of the stamp are "Grasset-J. Sprenger" instead of "E. GRASSET-A. BURKHARD."

For overprints see Nos. 2O35, 3O31.

Nos. 155 and 163 Surcharged

**1930, June *Perf. 11½***

| | | | |
|---|---|---|---|
| **207** | A26 3c on 2½c ol grn, *buff* | .20 | *2.75* |
| **208** | A26 5c on 7½c dp grn, *buff* | .20 | *8.00* |
| | Set, never hinged | 1.10 | |

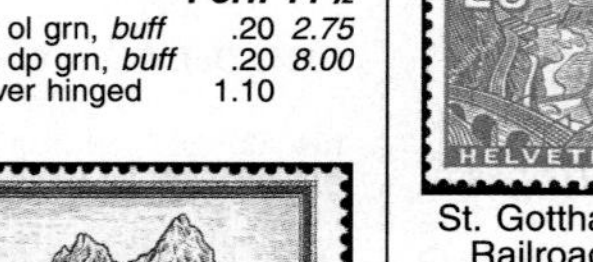

The Mythen A40

**1931 Engr. Granite Paper**

| | | | |
|---|---|---|---|
| **209** | A40 3fr orange brown | 65.00 | 5.25 |
| | Never hinged | 150.00 | |

For overprints see Nos. 2O56, 3O47.

Dove on Broken Sword — A41

"Peace" A42

**1932, Feb. 2 Typo. *Perf. 11½***

**Granite Paper**

| | | | |
|---|---|---|---|
| **210** | A41 5c peacock blue | .20 | .20 |
| **211** | A41 10c orange | .20 | .20 |
| **212** | A41 20c cerise | .25 | .20 |
| **213** | A41 30c ultra | 2.25 | 1.60 |
| **214** | A41 60c olive brown | 17.50 | 8.75 |

**Unwmk.**

**Photo.**

| | | | |
|---|---|---|---|
| **215** | A42 1fr olive gray & bl | 17.50 | 8.75 |
| | *Nos. 210-215 (6)* | 37.90 | 19.70 |
| | Set, never hinged | 95.00 | |

Intl. Disarmament Conf., Geneva, Feb. 1932.

For overprints see #2O36-2O41, 3O32-3O37.

Louis Favre — A43

Alfred Escher — A44

Design: 30c, Emil Welti.

**Wmk. 183**

**1932, May 31 Engr. *Perf. 11½***

**Granite Paper**

| | | | |
|---|---|---|---|
| **216** | A43 10c red brown | .20 | .20 |
| **217** | A44 20c vermilion | .25 | .20 |
| **218** | A44 30c deep ultra | .55 | *2.10* |
| | *Nos. 216-218 (3)* | 1.00 | *2.50* |
| | Set, never hinged | 3.00 | |

Completion of the St. Gotthard tunnel, 50th anniv.

Nos. 216-218 exist imperforate.

Staubbach Falls A46

Mt. Pilatus A47

Chillon Castle A48

Rhone Glacier A49

St. Gotthard Railroad A50

Via Mala Gorge A51

Rhine Falls — A52

**1934, July 2 Typo. *Perf. 11½***

**Granite Paper**

| | | | |
|---|---|---|---|
| **219** | A46 3c olive | .20 | *3.00* |
| **220** | A47 5c emerald | .20 | .20 |
| **221** | A48 10c brt violet | .40 | .20 |
| **222** | A49 15c orange | .50 | 3.25 |
| **223** | A50 20c red | .60 | .45 |
| **224** | A51 25c brown | 7.75 | 8.25 |
| **225** | A52 30c ultra | 25.00 | 2.10 |
| | *Nos. 219-225 (7)* | 34.65 | 17.45 |
| | Set, never hinged | 100.00 | |

**Tête bêche Pairs**

| | | | |
|---|---|---|---|
| *220a* | A47 5c | 1.60 | 1.60 |
| *221a* | A48 10c | 1.50 | .85 |
| *222a* | A49 15c | 1.75 | 3.00 |
| *223a* | A50 20c | 3.50 | 2.25 |

**Souvenir Sheet**

**1934, Sept. 29**

| | | | |
|---|---|---|---|
| **226** | Sheet of 4 | 500.00 | *550.00* |
| | Never hinged | 900.00 | |

No. 226 was issued in connection with the Swiss National Philatelic Exhibition at Zurich, Sept. 29 to Oct. 7, 1934. It contains one each of Nos. 220-223. Size: 62x72mm.

For overprints see Nos. 2O42-2O46, 3O48.

Staubbach Falls A53

Mt. Pilatus A54

Chillon Castle A55

Rhone Glacier A56

St. Gotthard Railroad A57

Via Mala Gorge A58

Rhine Falls — A59

Balsthal Pass — A60

Alpine Lake of Säntis — A61

Two types of 10c red violet:

I — Shading inside "0" of 10 has only vertical lines.

II — Shading in "0" includes two diagonal lines.

**1936-42 Unwmk. Engr. *Perf. 11½***

| | | | |
|---|---|---|---|
| **227** | A53 3c olive | .20 | .20 |
| **228** | A54 5c blue green | .20 | .20 |
| **229** | A55 10c red vio (II) | .85 | .20 |
| *b.* | Type I | .85 | .20 |
| **230** | A55 10c dk red brn ('39) | .20 | .20 |
| **230B** | A55 10c org brn ('42) | .20 | .20 |
| **231** | A56 15c orange | .40 | 1.10 |
| **232** | A57 20c carmine | 4.75 | .20 |
| **233** | A58 25c lt brown | .50 | 1.10 |
| **234** | A59 30c ultra | .90 | .20 |
| **235** | A60 35c yellow grn | 1.10 | 1.25 |
| **236** | A61 40c gray | 6.00 | .20 |
| | *Nos. 227-236 (11)* | 15.30 | 5.05 |
| | Set, never hinged | 37.50 | |

Two types of the 20c. See Nos. 316-321.

For overprints see Nos. O1-O4, O6-O9, O19-O19-O22, O24-O27, 2O47-2O55, 2O68-2O68A, 2O70-2O73, 2O75-2O78, 3O38-3O46, 3O60-3O60A, 3O62-3O65, 3O67-3O70, 4O1-4O4, 4O6-4O9, 4O23-4O24, 4O27-4O28, 5O1-5O2, 5O5.

**Tête bêche Pairs**

| | | | |
|---|---|---|---|
| *228a* | A54 5c blue green | .45 | .30 |
| *229a* | A55 10c red violet (II) | 4.50 | 5.50 |
| *230a* | A55 10c dark red brown | 1.75 | 1.10 |
| *230d* | A55 10c orange brown | .50 | .60 |
| *232a* | A57 20c carmine | 25.00 | 35.00 |

**1936-40 With Grilled Gum**

| | | | |
|---|---|---|---|
| *227a* | A53 3c olive | .65 | *6.25* |
| *228d* | A54 5c blue green | .30 | .25 |
| *229d* | A55 10c red violet (II) | .30 | .25 |
| *e.* | Type I | 1.00 | .25 |
| *230e* | A55 10c dark red brn ('40) | 1.90 | *25.00* |
| *231a* | A56 15c orange | .30 | 1.10 |
| *232c* | A57 20c carmine | 6.75 | .25 |
| *233a* | A58 25c light brown | 1.00 | *5.00* |
| *234a* | A59 30c ultra | .95 | .25 |
| *235a* | A60 35c yellow green | 1.40 | 3.25 |
| *236a* | A61 40c gray | 9.25 | .50 |
| | *Nos. 227a-236a (10)* | 22.80 | *42.10* |
| | Set, never hinged | 47.50 | |

Mobile Post Office A62

**1937, Sept. 5 Photo.**

**Granite Paper**

| | | | |
|---|---|---|---|
| **237** | A62 10c black & yellow | .25 | .50 |
| | Never hinged | .55 | |

No. 237 was sold exclusively by the traveling post office. It exists on two kinds of granite paper, black and red fibers or blue and red fibers. See No. 307 for type A62 redrawn.

View of Labor Building from Lake Geneva A63

Palace of League of Nations A64

Main Building, Palace of League of Nations A65

Labor Building and Albert Thomas Monument A66

**1938, May 2 *Perf. 11½***

**Granite Paper**

| | | | |
|---|---|---|---|
| **238** | A63 20c red & buff | .20 | .20 |
| **239** | A64 30c blue & lt blue | .45 | .20 |
| **240** | A65 60c brown & buff | 1.75 | *2.25* |
| **241** | A66 1fr black & buff | 7.50 | *17.00* |
| | *Nos. 238-241 (4)* | 9.90 | *19.65* |
| | Set, never hinged | 25.00 | |

Opening of Assembly Hall of the Palace of the League of Nations.

For overprints see #2O57-2O64, 3O49-3O56.

Souvenir Sheet

A67

**Engraved and Typographed**

**1938, Sept. 17 Unwmk. *Perf. 11½***

**Granite Paper**

| | | | |
|---|---|---|---|
| **242** | A67 Sheet of 3 | 37.50 | 32.50 |
| | Never hinged | 70.00 | |
| *a.* | 10c on 65c gray bl & dp bl | 19.00 | *25.00* |
| *b.* | A68 20c red | 1.10 | *2.50* |

Natl. Phil. Exhib. at Aarau, Sept. 17-25, and 25th anniv. of Swiss air mail. No. 242 contains 2 No. 243, but on granite paper, and a 10c on 65c similar to No. C22 but redrawn, with wing tips 1½mm from side frame lines; overall size 37x20½mm; no watermark.

On No. C22, wing tips touch frame lines; size is 36x21½mm; Wmk. 183.

Lake Lugano — A68

First Federal Pact, 1291 A69

Diet of Stans, 1481 A70

Citizens Voting A71

**1938, Sept. 17 Engr. *Perf. 11½***

243 A68 20c red .25 .25
a. Tête bêche pair .50 *.85*
c. Grilled gum .40 *.40*
d. As "c," tête bêche pair 1.40 *15.00*

**Granite Paper**

244 A69 3fr brn car, *grnsh* 11.00 8.75
245 A70 5fr slate bl, *grnsh* 7.50 6.00
246 A71 10fr grn, *grnsh* 47.50 35.00
*Nos. 243-246 (4)* 66.25 50.00
Set, never hinged 190.00

No. 243 is printed on ordinary paper. Nos. 244-246 are on granite surface-colored paper. The greenish surface coating has faded on most copies.

For type A68 in orange brown, see No. 318.

See Nos. 242b, 284-286. For overprints see Nos. O5, O23, 2O65-2O67, 2O69, 2O74, 2O88-2O90, 3O57-3O59, 3O61, 3O66, 3O80-3O82, 4O5, 4O19-4O21, O4O25, 5O3, 5O23-5O25, 7O18-7O20.

Deputation of Trades and Professions — A72

Swiss Family A73

Alpine Scenery A74

**Engr., Photo. (30c)**

**1939, Feb. 1 *Perf. 11½***

**Inscribed in French**

247 A72 10c dl pur & red .20 .20
248 A73 20c lake & red .50 .20
249 A74 30c dp blue & red 2.50 *3.00*

**Inscribed in German**

250 A72 10c dl pur & red .20 .20
251 A73 20c lake & red .40 .20
252 A74 30c dp blue & red 2.10 *8.25*

**Inscribed in Italian**

253 A72 10c dl pur & red .20 .20
254 A73 20c lake & red 1.90 .20
255 A74 30c dp blue & red 2.25 *9.25*
*Nos. 247-255 (9)* 10.25 *21.70*
Set, never hinged 27.50

National Exposition of 1939, Zurich.

Tree and Crossbow — A75

**1939, May 6 Photo. *Perf. 11½***

**Granite Paper**

**Inscribed in French**

256 A75 5c deep green .55 *1.60*
257 A75 10c gray brown .55 *1.90*
258 A75 20c brt carmine 1.10 *1.60*
259 A75 30c violet blue 3.00 *8.00*

**Inscribed in German**

260 A75 5c deep green .55 *2.50*
261 A75 10c gray brown .55 *2.50*
262 A75 20c brt carmine 1.10 *3.50*
263 A75 30c violet blue 8.75 *9.50*

**Inscribed in Italian**

264 A75 5c deep green .85 *4.50*
265 A75 10c gray brown .55 *3.50*
266 A75 20c brt carmine 1.10 *4.25*
267 A75 30c violet blue 3.25 *11.00*
*Nos. 256-267 (12)* 21.90 *54.35*
Set, never hinged 32.50

National Exposition of 1939.

The 5c, 10c and 20c stamps in the three languages exist se-tenant in coils.

**1939 With Grilled Gum**

256a A75 5c deep green .75 *2.25*
257a A75 10c gray brown .75 *2.25*
258a A75 20c bright carmine 1.90 *3.00*
260a A75 5c deep green .75 *1.60*
262a A75 20c bright carmine 1.90 1.60
264a A75 5c deep green 1.10 *3.75*
265a A75 10c gray brown 1.00 *3.00*
266a A75 20c bright carmine 1.90 *3.25*
*Nos. 256a-266a (8)* 10.05 *20.70*

View of Geneva A76

***Perf. 11½***

**1939, Aug. 22 Photo. Unwmk.**

**Granite Paper**

268 A76 20c red, car & buff .20 .20
269 A76 30c blue, car & gray .30 *2.75*
Set, never hinged 1.40

75th anniv. of the founding of the Intl. Red Cross Society.

"The Three Swiss" — A77

William Tell — A78

Fighting Soldier — A79

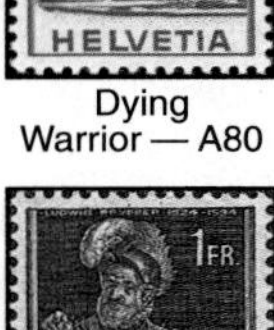

Dying Warrior — A80

Standard Bearer — A81

Ludwig Pfyffer — A82

Jürg Jenatsch — A83

Francois de Reynold — A84

Joachim Forrer — A85

**1941-59 Engr. *Perf. 11½***

**Granite Paper**

270 A77 50c dp pur, *grnsh* 4.25 .20
271 A78 60c red brn, *buff* 5.50 .20
272 A79 70c rose vio, *pale lil* 2.75 1.00
273 A80 80c blk, *pale gray* 1.10 .20
a. 80c black, *pale lilac* ('58) .80 .50
274 A81 90c dk red, *pale rose* 1.00 .20
a. 90c dark red, *buff* ('59) 1.00 *1.25*
275 A82 1fr dk grn, *grnsh* 1.00 .20
276 A83 1.20fr red vio, *pale gray* 1.10 .20
a. 1.20fr red vio, *pale lil* ('58) 1.90 .75
277 A84 1.50fr dk bl, *buff* 1.50 .25
278 A85 2fr mar, *pale rose* 2.25 .20
a. 2fr maroon, *buff* ('59) 2.25 .50
*Nos. 270-278 (9)* 20.45 2.65
Set, never hinged 47.50

For overprints see Nos. O28-O36, 2O79-2O87, 3O71-3O79, 4O10-4O18, 5O17-5O22, 6O6-6O8, 7O12-7O17.

Farmer Plowing A86

**1941, Mar. 21 Photo.**

**Granite Paper**

279 A86 10c brown & buff .20 *.50*
Never hinged .20

Natl. Agriculture Development Plan of 1941.

Masons, Knight and Bern Coat of Arms A87

**1941, Sept. 6**

**Granite Paper**

280 A87 10c multicolored .20 *.75*
Never hinged .20

750th anniversary of Bern.

"In order to Endure, Reclaim Used Materials" Inscribed in French A88

**1942, Mar. 21 Unwmk. *Perf. 11½***

281 A88 10c shown .35 *.50*
282 A88 10c German .40 *1.00*
283 A88 10c Italian 6.25 4.00
*Nos. 281-283 (3)* 7.00 5.50
Set, never hinged 14.00
Sheet of 25 90.00 *550.00*

Printed in sheets of 25, containing 8 No. 281, 12 No. 282 and 5 No. 283.

**Types of 1938**

**1955 Engr.**

**Cream-surfaced Granite Paper**

284 A69 3fr brown car 7.00 .75
285 A70 5fr slate blue 5.00 .80
286 A71 10fr green 7.00 3.00
*Nos. 284-286 (3)* 19.00 4.55
Set, never hinged 27.50

**1942 Cream paper**

284a A69 3fr 22.50 .50
285a A70 5fr 10.00 .50
286a A71 10fr 32.50 2.00
*Nos. 284a-286a (3)* 65.00 3.00
Set, never hinged 160.00

The 1955 set is on cream-surfaced granite paper with white back, and blue and red fibers. The 1942 set is on colored-through cream paper with black and red fibers.

Zurich Stamps of 1843 A91

**1943, Feb. 26**

287 A91 10c blk & salmon .20 .20
Never hinged .20

Centenary of postage stamps of Switzerland. See Nos. B130-B131.

Apollo Statue — A94

**1944, Mar. 21 Photo.**

**Granite Paper**

290 A94 10c org yel & gray blk .20 *1.00*
291 A94 20c cer & gray blk .30 *1.00*
292 A94 30c lt bl & gray blk .60 *6.00*
*Nos. 290-292 (3)* 1.10 *8.00*
Set, never hinged 2.50

Olympic Jubilee.

Numeral of Value — A95

Olive Branch A96

Designs: 60c, Keys of peace. 80c, Horn of plenty. 1fr, Dove of peace. 2fr, Plowing. 3fr, Field of crocus. 5fr, Clasped hands. 10fr, Aged couple.

**1945, May 9 Unwmk. *Perf. 12***

**Granite Paper**

293 A95 5c gray & green .20 *.50*
294 A95 10c gray & brown .25 .25
295 A95 20c gray & car rose .35 .25
296 A95 30c gray & ultra .70 *3.00*
297 A95 40c gray & orange 2.00 *10.00*
298 A96 50c dark red 2.75 *19.00*
299 A96 60c dull gray 2.75 *6.75*
300 A96 80c slate green 6.25 *85.00*
301 A96 1fr blue 8.75 *95.00*
302 A96 2fr red brown 22.50 *160.00*

**Engr.**

303 A96 3fr dk sl grn, *buff* 30.00 *65.00*
304 A96 5fr brn lake, *buff* 100.00 *325.00*
305 A96 10fr rose vio, *buff* 110.00 *125.00*
*Nos. 293-305,B145 (14)* 286.80 *895.50*
Set, never hinged 525.00

End of war in Europe.

Johann Heinrich Pestalozzi — A104

**1946, Jan. 12 Engr. *Perf. 11½***

306 A104 10c rose violet .20 .20
Never hinged .20

200th anniversary of the birth of J. H. Pestalozzi, educational reformer.

For overprint see No. 4O22.

**Mobile P.O. Type of 1937**

Redrawn

**1946, July 6 Photo.**

**Granite Paper**

307 A62 10c black & yellow 1.10 .20
Never hinged 3.00

The designer's and printer's names are larger on the redrawn stamp. There are many minor differences in the two designs. Sizes: 1937, 37½x21mm. 1946, 38x22½mm.

First Swiss Steam Locomotive — A105

Modern Steam Locomotive — A106

Electric Gotthard Express A107

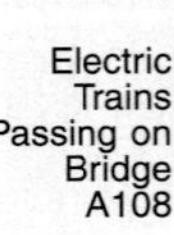

Electric Trains Passing on Bridge A108

**1947, Aug. 6 Photo. *Perf. 11½***

**Granite Paper**

| | | | | |
|---|---|---|---|---|
| **308** | A105 | 5c dk grn, blk & yel | .40 | *.50* |
| **309** | A106 | 10c dk brn, gray & blk | .40 | *.50* |
| **310** | A107 | 20c dk red & red | .35 | *.50* |
| **311** | A108 | 30c dk bl & bl gray | .90 | *1.75* |
| | | *Nos. 308-311 (4)* | 2.05 | *3.25* |
| | | Set, never hinged | 5.00 | |

Centenary of the opening of the first Swiss railroad, between Zurich and Baden.

Johann Rudolf Wettstein A109

Castle at Neuchatel A110

"Helvetia" A111

Symbol of Swiss Federal State A112

**1948, Feb. 27 Granite Paper**

| | | | | |
|---|---|---|---|---|
| **312** | A109 | 5c dp grn | .20 | *.50* |
| **313** | A110 | 10c gray blk | .20 | .20 |
| **314** | A111 | 20c dk red | .30 | .20 |
| **315** | A112 | 30c dk bl & red | .45 | *1.25* |
| | | *Nos. 312-315 (4)* | 1.15 | *2.15* |
| | | Set, never hinged | 2.00 | |

Tercentenary of the acknowledgment of independence of the Swiss Confederation, and the centenaries of the Neuchatel Revolution and the Swiss Federal State.

See Nos. B178a and B178b for 10c and 20c denominations, type A109.

**Types of 1936-42 and**

Grisons National Park — A113

**1948, Mar. 1 Engr.**

| | | | | |
|---|---|---|---|---|
| **316** | A54 | 5c chocolate | .20 | .20 |
| *a.* | | Tête bêche pair | 1.25 | 1.25 |
| **317** | A55 | 10c green | .20 | .20 |
| *a.* | | Tête bêche pair | 1.25 | 1.50 |
| **318** | A68 | 20c org brn | .30 | .20 |
| *a.* | | Tête bêche pair | 1.65 | 2.25 |
| **319** | A113 | 25c carmine | 1.50 | 1.50 |
| **320** | A59 | 30c grnsh bl | 6.25 | 4.00 |
| **321** | A61 | 40c ultra | 11.00 | .75 |
| | | *Nos. 316-321 (6)* | 19.45 | 6.85 |
| | | Set, never hinged | 42.50 | |

For overprints see Nos. 4O26, 5O4.

Figures Encircling Globe A114

Designs: 25c, Globe and inscribed ribbon. 40c, Globe and pigeons.

***Perf. 11½***

**1949, May 16 Photo. Unwmk.**

| | | | | |
|---|---|---|---|---|
| **322** | A114 | 10c green | .20 | .20 |
| **323** | A114 | 25c dark red | .40 | *6.25* |
| **324** | A114 | 40c brt blue | .60 | *4.00* |
| | | *Nos. 322-324 (3)* | 1.20 | *10.45* |
| | | Set, never hinged | 2.00 | |

75th anniv. of the UPU.

Post Horn A115

Horse Drawn Mail Coach A116

Design: 30c, Post bus with trailer.

**1949, May 16**

| | | | | |
|---|---|---|---|---|
| **325** | A115 | 5c gray, yel & pink | .20 | *.50* |
| **326** | A116 | 20c pur, gray & yel | .25 | *.30* |
| **327** | A116 | 30c dk org brn, gray & yel | .45 | *6.75* |
| | | *Nos. 325-327 (3)* | .90 | *7.55* |
| | | Set, never hinged | 1.50 | |

Centenary of the establishment of the Federal Post in Switzerland.

High Tension Conductors A117

Viaducts — A118

Mountain Railway — A119

Rotary Snow Plow — A120

Reservoir, Grimsel — A121

Lake Dam — A122

Dam and Power Station — A123

Alpine Postal Road — A124

Harbor of the Rhine — A125

Suspension Railway — A126

Railway Viaduct — A127

Triangulation Point — A128

Two types of 20c:
Type I — Three lines above curved rock.
Type II — Two lines above rock.

***Perf. 12x11½***

**1949, Aug. 1 Engr. Unwmk.**

| | | | | |
|---|---|---|---|---|
| **328** | A117 | 3c gray | 1.50 | *4.00* |
| **329** | A118 | 5c orange | .20 | .20 |
| *a.* | | Tête bêche pair | .90 | .20 |
| **330** | A119 | 10c yel grn | .20 | .20 |
| *a.* | | Tête bêche pair | .60 | .20 |
| **331** | A120 | 15c aqua | .20 | *.50* |
| **332** | A121 | 20c brown car (II) | .30 | .20 |
| *a.* | | Tête bêche pair | 1.75 | .75 |
| *c.* | | Type I | *2,000.* | *67.50* |
| | | Type I, never hinged | *3,750.* | |
| **333** | A122 | 25c red | .25 | .20 |
| **334** | A123 | 30c olive | .25 | .20 |
| **335** | A124 | 35c red brown | .45 | *.60* |
| **336** | A125 | 40c deep blue | 1.40 | .20 |
| **337** | A126 | 50c slate gray | 1.40 | .20 |
| **338** | A127 | 60c blue green | 4.00 | .50 |
| **339** | A128 | 70c purple | 1.10 | .30 |
| | | *Nos. 328-339 (12)* | 11.25 | 7.30 |
| | | Set, never hinged | 22.50 | |

For use in vending machines, some printings of the 5c, 10c, 20c (II), 25c, 30c and 40c carry a control number on the back of every fifth stamp. The number was applied on top of the gum.

For overprints see Nos. O37-O47, 3O83-3O93, 4O29-4O39, 5O6-5O16, 6O1-6O5, 7O1-7O11.

Symbolical of the Telegraph — A129

10c, Telephone. 20c, Radio. 40c, Television.

**1952, Feb. 1 Photo. *Perf. 11½***

| | | | | |
|---|---|---|---|---|
| **340** | A129 | 5c org & yel | .25 | .50 |
| **341** | A129 | 10c brt grn & pink | .30 | .20 |
| **342** | A129 | 20c dp red lil & gray bl | .45 | .20 |
| **343** | A129 | 40c dp bl & lt bl | 1.40 | *4.75* |
| | | *Nos. 340-343 (4)* | 2.40 | *5.65* |
| | | Set, never hinged | 5.25 | |

"A century of telecommunications."

Zurich Airport and Tail of Plane A130

**1953, Aug. 29**

| | | | | |
|---|---|---|---|---|
| **344** | A130 | 40c blue, red & gray | 3.25 | *10.50* |
| | | Never hinged | 5.50 | |

Opening of Zurich-Kloten airport.

Alpine Post Bus, Winter Background — A131

Design: 20c, Same, summer background.

**1953, Oct. 8**

| | | | | |
|---|---|---|---|---|
| **345** | A131 | 10c dk grn, grn & yel | .20 | .20 |
| **346** | A131 | 20c dk red, red brn & yel | .30 | .20 |
| | | Set, never hinged | 1.00 | |

Sold only on Swiss alpine post buses.

Symbols of Agriculture, Forestry and Horticulture — A132

Map and Nautical Emblems A133

Alphorn Blower A135

Lausanne Cathedral A134

20c, Winged spoon. 40c, Football and map.

**1954, Mar. 15 *Perf. 14***

| | | | | |
|---|---|---|---|---|
| **347** | A132 | 10c multicolored | .20 | .25 |
| **348** | A132 | 20c multicolored | .40 | .25 |
| **349** | A133 | 25c red, dk ol grn & gray | 1.00 | *3.00* |
| **350** | A132 | 40c bl, yel & brn | 1.60 | *3.50* |
| | | *Nos. 347-350 (4)* | 3.20 | *7.00* |
| | | Set, never hinged | 6.00 | |

Nos. 347-348 were issued to publicize exhibitions at Lucerne and Bern; No. 349, fifty years of navigation on the Rhine; No. 350, the 1954 World Soccer Championships in Switzerland.

**1955, Feb. 15** ***Perf. 11½***

Designs: 10c, Vaud costume hat. 40c, Automobile steering wheel.

**351** A134 5c multi .20 *.60*
**352** A134 10c grn, yel & red .25 *.50*
*a.* Souvenir sheet of 2 60.00 *80.00*
Never hinged 90.00
**353** A135 20c red & sepia .55 .50
**354** A134 40c bl, pink & gray 1.25 *2.10*
*Nos. 351-354 (4)* 2.25 *3.70*
Set, never hinged 5.50

No. 352a contains 10c and 20c multicolored, imperf. stamps of Cathedral type A134. Size: 104x52mm.

National Philatelic Exhibition (5c, #352a), Winegrowers' Festival (10c), Alpine Herdsman and Costume Festival (20c) and 25th Intl. Automobile Show (40c).

First Swiss Post Bus — A136

10c, North Gate of Simplon Tunnel and Stockalper Palace. 20c, Children crossing street and road signs. 40c, Planes and emblem of Swissair, vert.

**1956, Mar. 1** **Photo.**
**Granite Paper**

**355** A136 5c ol gray, blk & yel .20 *.50*
**356** A136 10c brt grn, gray & red .25 .20
**357** A136 20c multi .45 *.50*
**358** A136 40c blue & red 1.00 *1.40*
*Nos. 355-358 (4)* 1.90 *2.60*
Set, never hinged 4.50

50th anniv. of the Swiss Motor Coach Service (#355); 50th anniv. of the opening of Simplon Tunnel (#356); Accident prevention (#357); 25th anniv. of the founding of Swissair (#358).

Inking Device, Printing Machine A137

10c, Train on southern ramp of Gotthard Railroad. 20c, Shield of civil defense and coat of arms. 40c, Munatius Plancus and view of Basel.

Two types of 10c:
I — "Black" bottom line on train.
II — Brown bottom line.

**1957, Feb. 27** ***Perf. 11½***
**Granite Paper**

**359** A137 5c multicolored .20 .20
**360** A137 10c lt bl grn, dk grn & red brn (I) 1.10 .20
*a.* Type II 1.00 .50
Never hinged 2.75
**361** A137 20c red org & gray .25 *.50*
**362** A137 40c multicolored .75 *1.25*
*Nos. 359-362 (4)* 2.30 *2.15*
Set, never hinged 4.50

Intl. Exhibition for Graphic Arts, Lausanne, June 1-16, 1957 (#359). 75th anniv. of St. Gotthard railroad (#360). Civil defense (#361). 2000th anniv. of Basel (#362).

Rope and Symbol of European Unity — A138

**1957, July 15** **Engr.** ***Perf. 11½***

**363** A138 25c lt red .50 .35
**364** A138 40c blue .80 .35
Set, never hinged *4.50*

Issued to emphasize European unity.

**Catalogue values for unused stamps in this section, from this point to the end of the section, are for Never Hinged items.**

Nyon Castle and Corinthian Capital A139

Designs: 10c, Woman's head and ribbons in Swiss colors. 20c, Crossbow emblem. 40c, Salvation Army hat.

**1958, Mar. 5** **Photo.** **Unwmk.**
**Granite Paper**

**365** A139 5c ol bis & dl pur .20 .20
**366** A139 10c grn, dk grn & red .20 .20
**367** A139 20c ver, lil & car .50 .20
**368** A139 40c multicolored 1.40 1.25
*Nos. 365-368 (4)* 2.30 1.85

2000th anniv. of Nyon (#365). Saffa Exhibition, Zurich, July 17-Sept. 15 (#366). 25th anniv. of Swiss manufacturing emblem (#367). 75th anniv. of the Salvation Army in Switzerland (#368).

Symbol of Nuclear Fission A140

**1958, Aug. 25** ***Perf. 11½***
**Granite Paper**

**369** A140 40c blue, yel & red .60 .60

2nd UN Atomic Conf. for peaceful uses of atomic power, Geneva, Sept. 1958.

"Transportation" — A141

Designs: 10c, Fasces and post horn. 20c, Owl, rabbit and fish. 50c, Jean Calvin, Theodore de Beze and University of Geneva.

**1959, Mar. 9** **Photo.** **Unwmk.**
**Granite Paper**

**370** A141 5c multicolored .20 .20
**371** A141 10c emer, yel & lt gray .30 .20
*a.* Souvenir sheet of 2, imperf. 14.00 14.00
**372** A141 20c multicolored .60 .20
**373** A141 50c multicolored 1.25 .75
*Nos. 370-373 (4)* 2.35 1.35

Opening of the Swiss House of Transport and Communications (5c). Natl. Phil. Exhib., St. Gall, Aug. 21-30 (10c and #371a). Protection of animals (20c). 400th anniv. of the University of Geneva (50c).

No. 371a contains a 10c green, gold and light gray and a 20c deep carmine. Sold for 2fr; the money went for the St. Gall Phil. Exhib.

Chain Symbolizing European Unity — A142

**1959, June 22** **Engr.** ***Perf. 11½***

**374** A142 30c brick red *1.60* .30
**375** A142 50c lt ultra *2.75* .45

Issued to emphasize European Unity.

**Overprinted "REUNION DES PTT D'EUROPE 1959" in Ultramarine or Red**

**1959, June 22**

**376** A142 30c brick red *37.50 6.50*
**377** A142 50c lt ultra *37.50 6.50*

European Conference of PTT Administrations, Montreux, June 22-July 31. Nos. 376-377 were on sale only during the conference at a special P. O. in Montreux.

"Cancer Control" A143

Designs: 20c, Founding charter and scepter of University of Basel. 50c, Uprooted Oak Emblem. 75c, Swissair Jet DC-8.

**1960, Apr. 7** **Photo.** ***Perf. 11½***
**Granite Paper**

**378** A143 10c brt grn & red .55 .20
**379** A143 20c car rose, gray blk & yel .55 .20
**380** A143 50c ultra & yel .75 1.25
**381** A143 75c lt bl, gray & red 3.50 4.00
*Nos. 378-381 (4)* 5.35 5.65

50th anniv. of the Swiss League for Cancer Control (10c). 500th anniv. of the University of Basel (20c). World Refugee Year, July 1, 1959-June 30, 1960 (50c). Swissair's entry into the jet age (75c).

Messenger, Fribourg A144

Cathedral, Lausanne A145

Designs: 10c, Messenger, Schwyz. 15c, Messenger and pack animal. 20c, Postilion on horseback. 30c, Grossmünster (church), Zürich. 35c, 1.30fr, Woodcutters' Guildhall, Biel. 40c, Cathedral, Geneva. 50c, Spalen Gate, Basel. 60c, Clock Tower, Berne. 70c, 2.80fr, Sts. Peter and Stephen Church, Bellinzona (tower omitted on 2.80fr). 75c, Bridge and water tower, Lucerne. 80c, Cathedral, St. Gallen. 90c, Munot tower, Schaffhausen. 1fr, Townhall, Fribourg. 1.20fr, Basel gate, Solothurn. 1.50fr, Reding house, Schwyz. 1.70fr, 2fr, 2.20fr, Church, Einsiedeln.

Two types of 5c, 10c, 20c, 50c:
**5 Centimes:**
Type I — Four lines on pike at left of hand.
Type II — Three lines.
**10 Centimes:**
Type I — Dot on pike below head.
Type II — No dot.
**20 Centimes:**
Type I — Ten dots on horiz. harness strip.
Type II — Nine dots.
**50 Centimes:**
Type I — 3 shading lines at right above arch.
Type II — 2 shading lines.

**1960-63** **Engr.** ***Perf. 11½***
**1.30fr, 1.70fr, 2.20fr, 2.80fr on Granite Paper, Red and Blue Fibers**

**382** A144 5c lt ultra (I) .20 .20
*c.* Tête bêche pair .20 .20
**383** A144 10c blue grn (I) .20 .20
*c.* Tête bêche pair .40 .20
**384** A144 15c lt red brn .20 .20
**385** A144 20c rose pink (I) .30 .20
*c.* Tête bêche pair .90 .45
**386** A145 25c emerald .35 .20
**387** A145 30c vermilion .45 .20
**388** A145 35c orange red .50 .30
**389** A145 40c lilac .60 .20
**390** A145 50c lt vio bl (I) .75 .20
*c.* Tête bêche pair 2.75 2.75
**391** A145 60c rose red .90 .20
**392** A145 70c orange 1.10 .40
**393** A145 75c lt blue 1.20 .20
**394** A145 80c dp claret 1.25 .20
**395** A145 90c olive green 1.30 .20
**396** A144 1fr dull orange 1.50 .20
**397** A144 1.20fr dull red 1.75 .30
**397A** A145 1.30fr red brn, *pink* ('63) 1.90 .20
**398** A144 1.50fr brt green 2.25 .50
**398A** A144 1.70fr rose lil, *pink* ('63) 2.50 .20
**399** A144 2fr brt blue 3.25 .50
**399A** A144 2.20fr bl grn, *grn* ('63) 3.25 .50
**399B** A145 2.80fr org, *buff* ('63) 3.75 .40
*Nos. 382-399B (22)* 29.45 5.90

See Nos. 440-455.

**1963-76**
**Violet Fibers, Fluorescent Paper**

*382d* A144 5c lt ultra (I) .20 .20
*g.* Tête bêche pair ('68) .20 .20
*383d* A144 10c bl grn (I) .20 .20
*e.* Bklt. pane of 2 + 2 labels ('68) .65 .65
*g.* Tête bêche pair ('68) .35 .25
*384a* A144 15c lt red brn .55 .55
*385d* A144 20c rose pink (I) .30 .20
*g.* Tête bêche pair ('68) .70 .45
*386a* A145 25c emerald .35 .20
*387a* A145 30c vermilion .35 .20
*c.* Tête bêche pair ('68) 1.00 .75
*389a* A145 40c lilac ('67) .55 .35
*c.* Tête bêche pair ('76) 1.25 1.10
*390d* A145 50c lt vio bl (I) .75 .20
*391a* A145 60c rose red ('67) .80 .30
*393a* A145 75c lt blue ('68) 1.25 .45
*394a* A145 80c dp claret 1.00 .20
*395a* A145 90c olive grn ('67) 1.00 .20
*396a* A144 1fr dull org ('67) 2.00 .20
*397b* A144 1.20fr dl red ('68) 3.00 1.75
*398b* A144 1.50fr brt green ('68) 3.00 1.75
*Nos. 382d-398b (15)* 15.30 6.95

**Coil Stamps**

**1960** **White Paper**

*382b* A144 5c lt ultra (II) 1.40 1.40
*383b* A144 10c blue grn (II) .85 .85
*385b* A144 20c rose pink (II) .85 .85
*390b* A145 50c lt vio bl (II) 4.00 4.00
*Nos. 382b-390b (4)* 7.10 7.10

The coil stamps were printed in sheets (available to collectors) and pasted into coils. Every fifth stamp has a control number on the back.

Other denominations issued in coils on white paper are: 40c, 60c, 90c, 1fr, 1.30fr, 1.70fr, 2.20fr and 2.80fr.

Denominations issued in coils on granite paper (red & blue fibers) are: 1.30fr, 1.70fr, 2.20fr and 2.80fr.

**Coil Stamps**

**1965-68**
**Violet Fibers, Fluorescent Paper**

*382e* A144 5c lt ultra (II) 1.25 1.25
*383h* A144 10c blue grn (II) .60 .30
*385e* A144 20c rose pink (II) .60 .30
*390e* A145 50c lt vio bl (II) 4.00 4.00
*Nos. 382e-390e (4)* 6.45 5.85

Other denominations issued in coils on violet-fiber paper are: 40c, 60c, 90c and 1fr.

---

Common Design Types pictured following the introduction.

---

**Europa Issue, 1960**
Common Design Type

**1960, Sept. 19** **Unwmk.** ***Perf. 11½***
**Size: 33x23mm**

**400** CD3 30c vermilion .50 .25
**401** CD3 50c ultra .75 .40

Wall under Construction and Globe — A146

Designs: 10c, Symbolic sun (HYSPA Emblem). 20c, Ice hockey stick and puck. 50c, Wiring diagram on map of Switzerland.

**1961, Feb. 20** **Photo.** ***Perf. 11½***
**Granite Paper**

**402** A146 5c gray, brick red & grnsh bl .35 .20
**403** A146 10c aqua & yel .35 .20
**404** A146 20c multicolored 1.50 .60
**405** A146 50c ultra, gray & car rose 1.25 1.00
*Nos. 402-405 (4)* 3.45 2.00

Development aid to new nations (5c). HYSPA 1961, Health and Sports Exhibition, Bern, May 18-July 17 (10c). Intl. Ice Hockey Championships, Lausanne and Geneva, Mar. 2-12 (20c). Fully automatic Swiss telephone service (50c).

St. Matthew and Angel — A147

Evangelists: 5fr, St. Mark and winged lion. 10fr, St. Luke and winged ox. 20fr, St. John and eagle.

*Perf. 11½*

**1961, Sept. 18 Unwmk. Engr.**

**Granite Paper**

**406** A147 3fr rose carmine 4.00 .20
**407** A147 5fr dark blue 6.50 .20
**408** A147 10fr dark brown 8.25 .45
**409** A147 20fr red 20.00 3.00
*Nos. 406-409 (4)* 38.75 3.85

Designs are after 15th century wood carvings from St. Oswald's church, Zug.

**Europa Issue, 1961**

Common Design Type

**1961, Sept. 18**

**Size: 26x21mm**

**410** CD4 30c vermilion .50 .20
**411** CD4 50c blue .75 .35

Trans-Europe Express A148

10c, Rower. 20c, Jungfrau railroad station and Mönch. 50c, WHO Anti-malaria emblem.

**1962, Mar. 19 Photo. *Perf. 11½***

**412** A148 5c multicolored .50 .20
**413** A148 10c brt grn, lem & lil .45 .20
**414** A148 20c rose lil, pale bl & bis .90 .25
**415** A148 50c ultra, lt grn & rose lil .90 .60
*Nos. 412-415 (4)* 2.75 1.25

Introduction of Swiss electric TEE trains (5c). Rowing world championship, Lucerne, Sept. 6-9 (10c). 50th anniv. of the railroad station on the Jungfrau mountain (20c). WHO Anti-Malaria campaign (50c).

**Europa Issue, 1962**

Common Design Type

**1962, Sept. 17 Unwmk. *Perf. 11½***

**Size: 33x23mm**

**416** CD5 30c orange, yel & brn .65 .40
**417** CD5 50c ultra, lt grn & brn 1.00 .60

Boy Scout — A149

Designs: 10c, Swiss Alpine Club emblem. 20c, Luegelkinn viaduct. 30c, Wheat Emblem. No. 426, 428a, Red Cross Jubilee Emblem. No. 427, Post Office Building, Paris, 1863.

**1963, Mar. 21 Photo.**

**422** A149 5c gray, dk red & brn .55 .20
**423** A149 10c dk grn, gray & red .40 .20
**424** A149 20c dk car, brn & gray 1.10 .20
**425** A149 30c yel grn, yel & org 1.60 1.60
**426** A149 50c blue, sil & red .85 .80
**427** A149 50c ultra, pink, yel & gray .90 .75
*Nos. 422-427 (6)* 5.40 3.75

**Souvenir Sheet**

***Imperf***

**428** Sheet of 4 7.00 6.00
***a.*** A149 50c bl, lt bl, sil & red 1.75 1.25

50 years of Swiss Boy Scouts (5c). Cent. of Swiss Alpine Club (10c). 50 years Lötschberg Railroad (20c). FAO "Freedom from Hunger" campaign (30c). Red Cross Cent. (#426, 428). 1st Intl. Postal Conf., Paris 1863 (#427).
No. 428 sold for 3fr.

**Europa Issue, 1963**

Common Design Type

**1963, Sept. 16 Unwmk. *Perf. 11½***

**Granite Paper**

**Size: 26x21mm**

**429** CD6 50c ultra & ocher .90 .60

EXPO Emblem A150

50c, EXPO emblem on globe & moon ("Outlook"). 75c, EXPO emblem on globe ("Insight").

**1963, Sept. 16 Unwmk. *Perf. 11½***

**Granite Paper**

**430** A150 10c brt grn & dk grn .30 .20
**431** A150 20c red & maroon .35 .20
**432** A150 50c ultra & red .65 .40
**433** A150 75c purple & red 1.00 .45
*Nos. 430-433 (4)* 2.30 1.25

Issued to publicize the Swiss National Exhibition, Lausanne, Apr. 30-Oct. 25, 1964.

Road Tunnel Through Great St. Bernard A151

10c, Symbolic water god & waves. 20c, Soldiers of 1864 & 1964. 50c, Standards of Swiss Confederation & Geneva.

**1964, Mar. 9 Photo.**

**Granite Paper**

**434** A151 5c ol, ultra & red .20 .20
**435** A151 10c Prus bl & grn .20 .20
**436** A151 20c red, ultra, blk & sal .40 .20
**437** A151 50c ultra, red, yel & blk .95 .65
*Nos. 434-437 (4)* 1.75 1.25

1st Trans-Alpine Automobile route from Switzerland to Italy (5c). "Pro Aqua" water conservation campaign (10c). Centenary of the Swiss Noncommissioned Officers' Association (20c). Sesqui. of union of Geneva with Swiss Confederation (50c).

**Europa Issue, 1964**

Common Design Type

**1964, Sept. 14 Engr. *Perf. 11½***

**Size: 21x26mm**

**Violet Fibers, Fluorescent Paper**

**438** CD7 20c vermilion *.40* .20
**439** CD7 50c ultra *.85* .25

**Type of Regular Issue, 1960-63**

Designs: 5c, Lenzburg. 10c, Freuler Mansion, Näfels. 15c, St. Mauritius Church, Appenzell. 20c, Planta House, Samedan. 30c, Gabled houses, Gais. 50c, Castle and Abbey Church, Neuchâtel. 70c, Lussy House, Wolfenschiessen. 1fr, Santa Croce Church, Riva San Vitale. 1.20fr, Abbey Church, Payerne. 1.30fr, Church of St. Pierre de Clages. 1.50fr, La Porte de France, Porrentruy. 1.70fr, Frauenfeld Castle. 2fr, A Pro Castle, Seedorf. 2.20fr, Thomas Tower and Gate. Liestal. 2.50fr, St. Oswald's Church, Zug. 3.50fr, Benedictine Abbey, Engelberg.

**1964-68 Engr. *Perf. 11½***

**Violet Fibers, Fluorescent Paper**

**440** A144 5c car rose ('68) .20 .20
**441** A144 10c violet bl ('68) .20 .20
***b.*** Tête bêche pair .25 .20
***c.*** Booklet pane of 2 + 2 labels .70
**442** A144 15c brown red ('68) .20 .20
***b.*** Tête bêche pair .35 .35
**443** A144 20c blue grn ('68) .30 .20
***b.*** Tête bêche pair .65 .35
**444** A144 30c vermilion ('68) .45 .20
***b.*** Tête bêche pair 1.00 .80
**445** A144 50c ultra ('68) .75 .20
**446** A145 70c brown ('67) 1.00 .20
**447** A145 1fr dk green ('68) 1.50 .20
**448** A145 1.20fr brown red ('68) 1.75 .25
**449** A145 1.30fr violet bl ('66) 1.75 .75
**450** A145 1.50fr green ('68) 2.25 .40
**451** A145 1.70fr brown org ('66) 2.50 1.25
**452** A145 2fr orange ('67) 3.00 .40
**453** A145 2.20fr green 3.25 .80
**454** A145 2.50fr Prus grn ('67) 3.50 .55
**455** A145 3.50fr purple ('67) 4.25 .60
*Nos. 440-455 (16)* 26.85 6.60

The 15c was issued in coils in 1972 (?) with control number on the back of every fifth stamp.

Nurse and Patient A152

Seated Helvetia, 1854 — A153

Women's Army Auxiliary A154

Intercontinental Communications Map — A155

**1965, Mar. 8 Photo. *Perf. 11½***

**Violet Fibers, Fluorescent Paper**

**462** A152 5c lt ultra & red .20 .20
**463** A153 10c emer, brn & blk .20 .20
**464** A154 20c red & multi .30 .20

**Granite Paper, Red and Blue Fibers**

**465** A155 50c dl bl grn & mar .75 .50
*Nos. 462-465 (4)* 1.45 1.10

Nursing and auxiliary medical professions (5c). Natl. Postage Stamp Exhibition, NABRA, Bern, Aug. 27-Sept. 5, 1965 (10c). 20th anniv. of Women's Army Auxiliary Corps (20c). Cent. of ITU (50c).
See No. B344.

Swiss Arms, Cantonal Emblems of Valais, Neuchatel, Geneva A156

**1965, June 1 Unwmk. *Perf. 11½***

**Granite Paper, Red and Blue Fibers**

**466** A156 20c multicolored .30 .20

150th anniversary of the entry of the cantons of Valais, Neuchatel and Geneva in the Swiss Confederation.

Matterhorn A157

30c, like 10c but inscribed in French "Cervin."

**1965, June 1 Photo.**

**Granite Paper, Red and Blue Fibers**

**467** A157 10c grn, slate & dk red .20 .20

**Violet Fibers, Fluorescent Paper**

**468** A157 30c dk red, grn & slate .45 .40

Year of the Alps; the cent. of the 1st wintertime visitors to the Alps and cent. of the 1st ascent of the Matterhorn. Nos. 467-468 on sale only at Swiss Alpine post buses.

**Europa Issue, 1965**

Common Design Type

**1965, Sept. 14 Unwmk. *Perf. 11½***

**Violet Fibers, Fluorescent Paper**

**469** CD8 50c bl, dk bl & grn .75 .25

Figure Skating A159

**1965, Sept. 14 Photo.**

**Violet Fibers, Fluorescent Paper**

**470** A159 5c grn, dl bl & blk .20 .20

Issued to publicize the World Figure Skating Championships, Davos, Feb. 22-27, 1966.

ITU Emblem and Atom Diagram A160

Cent. of the ITU: 30c, Symbol of communications, waves.

**1965, Sept. 14**

**Violet Fibers, Fluorescent Paper**

**471** A160 10c ultra & multi .20 .20

**Granite Paper, Red and Blue Fibers**

**472** A160 30c org, red & gray .45 .40

Violet Fibers, Fluorescent Paper
Paper from No. 473 onward is fluorescent and has violet fibers, unless otherwise noted.

European Kingfisher A161

Mercury's Helmet and Laurel A162

Flags of 13 Member Nations and Nuclear Fission A163

**1966, Feb. 21 Photo.**

**473** A161 10c emer & multi .20 .20
**474** A162 20c dp mag, red & brt grn .30 .20
**475** A163 50c slate blue & multi .70 .40
*Nos. 473-475 (3)* 1.20 .80

Intl. Cong. for Conservation "Pro Natura," Lucerne (10c). 50th anniv. of Swiss Trade Fair, Basel, Apr. 16-26 (20c). European Organization for Nuclear Research, CERN (50c).

Emblem of Society of Swiss Abroad — A164

**1966, June 1 Photo. *Perf. 11½***

**476** A164 20c ultra & ver .30 .25

50th anniv. of the Society of Swiss Abroad.

**Europa Issue, 1966**

Common Design Type

**1966, Sept. 26 Engr. *Perf. 11½***

**Size: 21x26mm**

**477** CD9 20c vermilion .25 .20
**478** CD9 50c ultra .80 .35

Finsteraarhorn — A165

**1966, Sept. 26** **Photo.**
**479** A165 10c lt grnsh bl, dk bl & dk red .30 .25

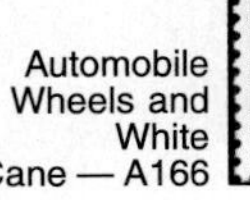

Automobile Wheels and White Cane — A166

Flags of EFTA Members A167

**1967, Mar. 13** **Photo.** ***Perf. 11½***
**480** A166 10c bl grn, blk & yel .20 .20
**481** A167 20c multicolored .30 .20

No. 480 issued to publicize the white cane as a distinguishing mark for blind pedestrians. No. 481 publicizes the European Free Trade Association, EFTA. See note after Norway No. 501.

**Europa Issue, 1967**
Common Design Type

**1967, Mar. 13**
**482** CD10 30c blue gray .60 .25

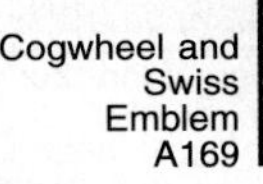
Cogwheel and Swiss Emblem A169

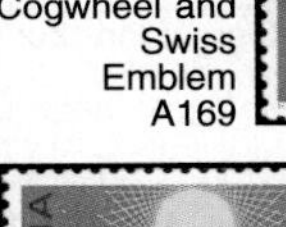

Hourglass and Sun — A170

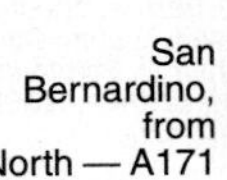

San Bernardino, from North — A171

Railroad Wheel A172

**1967, Sept. 18** **Photo.** ***Perf. 11½***
**483** A169 10c multicolored .20 .20
**484** A170 20c red, yel & blk .25 .20
**485** A171 30c multicolored .40 .25
**486** A172 50c multicolored .65 .50
*Nos. 483-486 (4)* 1.50 1.15

50th anniv. of Swiss Week (10c). 50th anniv. of the Foundation for the Aged (20c). Opening of the San Bernardino Road Tunnel (30c). 75th anniv. of the Central Office for Intl. Railroad Transportation (50c).

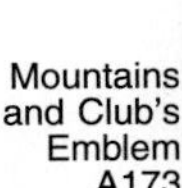

Mountains and Club's Emblem A173

Golden Key with CEPT Emblem A174

Rook and Chessboard A175

Aircraft Tail and Satellites A176

**1968, Mar. 14** **Photo.** ***Perf. 11½***
**487** A173 10c grn, lt ultra & red .20 .20
**488** A174 20c Prus bl, yel & brn .35 .20
**489** A175 30c dk ol bis & vio bl .45 .20
**490** A176 50c dk blue & red .70 .35
*Nos. 487-490 (4)* 1.70 .95

50th anniv. of the Swiss Women's Alpine Club (10c). A unified Europe through postal cooperation (20c). 18th Chess Olympics, Lugano, Oct. 17-Nov. 6 (30c). Inauguration of the new Geneva-Cointrin Air Terminal (50c).

Worker's Protective Helmet A177

Double Geneva and Zurich Stamps of 1843 — A178

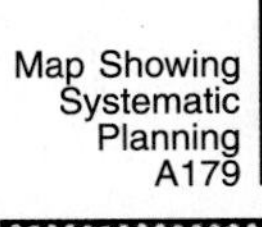
Map Showing Systematic Planning A179

Flag of Rhine Navigation Committee A180

**1968, Sept. 12** **Photo.** ***Perf. 11½***
**491** A177 10c bl grn & yel .20 .20
**492** A178 20c dp car, blk & yel grn .30 .20
**493** A179 30c multicolored .45 .20
**494** A180 50c bl, yel & blk .70 .50
*Nos. 491-494 (4)* 1.65 1.10

50th anniv. of the Swiss Accident Insurance comp., SUVA (10c). 125th anniv. of 1st Swiss postage stamps (20c). 25th anniv. of the Swiss Society for Territorial Planning (30c). Cent. of the Rhine Navigation Act (50c).

Swiss Girl Scouts' Emblem and Camp — A181

Pegasus Constellation A182

Comptoir Suisse Emblem and Beaulieu Building, Lausanne A183

Gymnaestrada Emblem (Man in Circle) — A184

Swissair DC-8 and DH-3 — A185

**1969, Feb. 12** **Photo.** ***Perf. 11½***
**495** A181 10c multicolored .20 .20
**496** A182 20c dark blue .30 .20
**497** A183 30c red, ocher, grn & gray .45 .20
**498** A184 50c vio bl, bl, red, grn & sil .70 .50
**499** A185 2fr bl, dk bl & red 2.50 2.00
*Nos. 495-499 (5)* 4.15 3.10

50th anniv. of Swiss Girl Scouts (10c). Opening of 1st Swiss Planetarium, Lucerne, July 1 (20c). 50th anniv. of the Comptoir Suisse (trade fair, 30c). 5th Gymnaestrada (gymnastic meet), Basel, July 1-5 (50c). 50th anniv. of Swiss airmail service (2fr).

**Europa Issue, 1969**
Common Design Type

**1969, Apr. 28**
**Size: 32½x23mm**
**500** CD12 30c brn org & multi .40 .25
**501** CD12 50c chlky bl & multi .60 .35

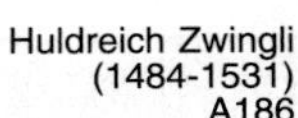

Huldreich Zwingli (1484-1531) A186

Famous Swiss: 20c, Gen. Henri Guisan (1874-1960). 30c, Francesco Borromini, architect (1599-1667). 50c, Othmar Schoeck, musician (1886-1957). 80c, Germaine de Stael, writer (1766-1817).

**1969, Sept. 18** **Engr.** ***Perf. 11½***
**502** A186 10c brt purple .20 .20
**503** A186 20c green .30 .20
**504** A186 30c deep carmine .45 .20
**505** A186 50c deep blue .90 .60
**506** A186 80c red brown 1.20 1.00
*Nos. 502-506 (5)* 3.05 2.20

Kreuzberge, Alpstein Mountains A187

Children Crossing Street — A188

Steelworker A189

**1969, Sept. 18** **Photo.**
**507** A187 20c blue & multi .40 .20
**508** A188 30c car & multi .40 .20
**509** A189 50c violet & multi .70 .45
*Nos. 507-509 (3)* 1.50 .85

No. 508 publicizes the traffic safety campaign; No. 509 for 50th anniv. of the ILO.

Telex Tape — A190

Fireman Rescuing Child — A191

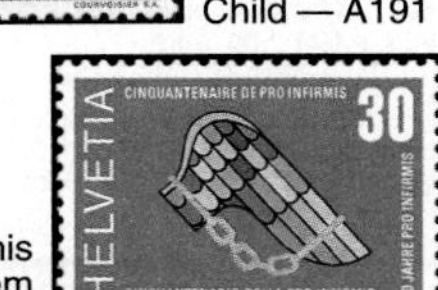
Pro Infirmis Emblem A192

United Nations Emblem A193

New UPU Headquarters A194

**1970, Feb. 26** **Photo.** ***Perf. 11½***
**510** A190 20c dk grn, yel & blk .25 .20
**511** A191 30c dk car & multi .45 .20
**512** A192 30c red & multi .45 .20
**513** A193 50c dk bl, lt grnsh bl & sil .65 .35
**514** A194 80c dk pur, sep & tan 1.10 .70
*Nos. 510-514 (5)* 2.90 1.65

75th anniv. of the Swiss Telegraph Agency (20c). Cent. of the Swiss Firemen's Assoc. (No. 511). 50th anniv. of the Pro Infirmis Foundation (No. 512). UN, 5th anniv. (50c). New Headquarters of the UPU in Bern (80c).

**Europa Issue, 1970**
Common Design Type

**1970, May 4** **Engr.** ***Perf. 11½***
**Size: 21x26mm**
**515** CD13 30c vermilion .45 .20
**516** CD13 50c brt blue .65 .35

Soccer A195

Census Form — A196

Piz Palu, Grisons A197

"Nature Conservation"
A198

Numeral
A199

**1970, Sept. 17 Photo. *Perf. 11½***

**517** A195 10c green & multi .40 .20
**518** A196 20c dk grn & multi .30 .20
**519** A197 30c slate bl & multi .50 .20
**520** A198 50c dk bl & multi .70 .65
*Nos. 517-520 (4)* 1.90 1.25

75th anniv. of Swiss Soccer Association (10c). Federal Census of 1970 (20c). Swiss Alps (30c). Nature Conservation Year (50c).

**Coil Stamps**

**1970, Sept. 17 Engr. *Perf. 11½***

**521** A199 10c brown lake .20 .20
**522** A199 20c olive grn .35 .20
**523** A199 50c ultra .70 .60
*Nos. 521-523 (3)* 1.25 1.00

Control number in stamp's color on back of every fifth stamp. Nos. 521-523 were regularly issued only in coils, but exist in sheets of 50.

Gymnastic Trio — A200

Rose — A201

Switzerland No. 8 — A202

Rising Spiral — A203

Intelsat 4 Satellite
A204

Adaptation of 1850 Design — A205

Design: No. 525, Runners (men).

**1971, Mar. 11 Photo. *Perf. 11½***

**524** A200 10c ol, brn & bl .25 .30
**525** A200 10c gray, brn & yel .25 .30
*a.* Pair, #524-525 .50 .30
**526** A201 20c dk grn & multi .30 .20
**527** A202 30c dp car & multi .45 .30
**528** A203 50c dk bl & bis .70 .60
**529** A204 80c multicolored 1.10 1.00
*Nos. 524-529 (6)* 3.05 2.70

**Souvenir Sheet**

**Typo.**

***Imperf***

**530** A205 2fr blue & multi 3.00 3.00

New article on gymnastics and sports in Swiss Constitution (10c); Intl. Child Welfare Org. (20c); NABA Natl. Postage Stamp Exhibition, Basel, June 4-13 (30c, 2fr); 2nd decade of development aid (50c); Intl. Space Communications Conf., Geneva, June-July, 1971 (80c).

#525a printed checkerwise. #530 sold for 3fr.

**Europa Issue, 1971**

Common Design Type

**1971, May 3 Engr. *Perf. 11½***

**Size: 26x21mm**

**531** CD14 30c rose car & org .45 .20
**532** CD14 50c blue & org .65 .40

Les Diablerets, Vaud — A206

Telecommunications Symbols — A207

**1971, Sept. 23 Photo. *Perf. 11½***

**533** A206 30c rose lil & bl gray .50 .30
**534** A207 40c ultra, yel & brt pink .65 .55

No. 534 for the 50th anniv. of Radio-Suisse, which is also in charge of air traffic control.

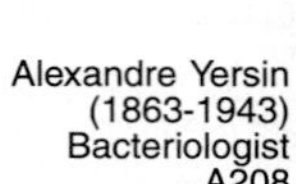

Alexandre Yersin (1863-1943) Bacteriologist
A208

Physicians: 20c, Auguste Forel (1848-1931), psychiatrist. 30c, Jules Gonin (1870-1935), ophthalmologist. 40c, Robert Koch (1843-1910), German bacteriologist. 80c, Frederick G. Banting (1891-1941), Canadian physiologist.

**1971, Sept. 23 Engr.**

**535** A208 10c gray olive .20 .20
**536** A208 20c bluish green .30 .20
**537** A208 30c carmine rose .40 .20
**538** A208 40c dark blue .60 .55
**539** A208 80c brt purple 1.10 .90
*Nos. 535-539 (5)* 2.60 2.05

Wrench, Road Sign, Club Emblems
A209

Electronic Switch Panel — A210

Boy's Head and Radio Waves
A211

Symbolic Tree — A212

**1972, Feb. 17 Photo. *Perf. 11½***

**540** A209 10c multicolored .20 .20
**541** A210 20c olive & multi .30 .20
**542** A211 30c orange & maroon .45 .30
**543** A212 40c blue, grn & pur .60 .60
*Nos. 540-543 (4)* 1.55 1.30

75th anniv. of the touring and automobile clubs of Switzerland (10c). 125th anniv. of Swiss railroads (20c). 50th anniv. of Swiss radio (30c). 50th annual congress of Swiss citizens living abroad, Bern, Aug. 25-27 (40c).

**Europa Issue 1972**

Common Design Type

**1972, May. 2**

**Size: 21x26mm**

**544** CD15 30c multicolored .45 .20
**545** CD15 40c multicolored .90 .35

Alberto Giacometti (1901-66), Painter and Sculptor — A213

Portraits and Signatures: 20c, Charles Ferdinand Ramuz (1878-1947), writer. 30c, Le Corbusier (Charles Edouard Jeanneret; 1887-1965) architect. 40c, Albert Einstein (1879-1955), physicist. 80c, Arthur Honegger (1892-1955), composer.

**Engraved & Photogravure**

**1972, Sept. 21 *Perf. 11½***

**546** A213 10c ocher & blk .20 .20
**547** A213 20c lt olive & blk .30 .20
**548** A213 30c pink & blk .45 .20
**549** A213 40c lt blue & blk .60 .60
**550** A213 80c lil rose & blk 1.10 .75
*Nos. 546-550 (5)* 2.65 1.95

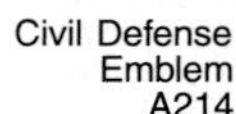

Civil Defense Emblem
A214

Spannörter, Swiss Alps — A215

Red Cross Rescue Helicopter
A216

Clean Air, Fire, Earth and Water — A217

**1972, Sept. 21 Photo.**

**551** A214 10c org, bl & yel .20 .20
**552** A215 20c bl grn & multi .40 .30
**553** A216 30c lilac, red & indigo .75 .20
**554** A217 40c lt blue & multi .70 .60
*Nos. 551-554 (4)* 2.05 1.30

Earth Satellite Station, Leuk, World Map — A218

Quill Pen and Arrows in Circle — A219

INTERPOL Emblem
A220

**1973, Feb. 15 Photo. *Perf. 11½***

**555** A218 15c gray, yel & bl .25 .25
**556** A219 30c multicolored .40 .20
**557** A220 40c dp bl, lt bl & gray .60 .50
*Nos. 555-557 (3)* 1.25 .95

Opening of the satellite station at Leuk; Swiss Association of Commercial Employees, cent. (30c); International Criminal Police Organization (INTERPOL), 59th anniv.

Sottoceneri
A221

Sign of Inn "Zur Sonne," Toggenburg
A222

Villages: 10c, Graubunden. 15c, Central Switzerland. 25c, Jura. 30c, Simme Valley. 35c, Central Switzerland (2 buildings). 40c, Vaud. 50c, Valais. 60c, Engadine. 70c, Sopraceneri. 80c, Eastern Switzerland.

Designs: 1fr, Rose window, Lausanne Cathedral. 1.10fr, Gallus Portal, Basel Cathedral. 1.20fr, Romanesque capital (eagle), St. Jean Baptiste Church, Grandson. 1.50fr, Ceiling medallion (bird feeding nestlings), Stein am Rhein Convent. 1.70fr, Romanesque capital (St. George and dragon), St. Jean Baptiste, Grandson. 1.80fr, Gargoyle, Bern Cathedral. 2fr, Bay window, Schaffhausen. 2.50fr, Cock weather vane, St. Ursus Cathedral, Solothurn. 3fr, Font, St. Maurice Church, Saanen. 3.50fr, Astronomical clock, Bern clock tower.

**1973-80 Engr. *Perf. 11½***

**Fluorescent, No Violet Fibers**

**558** A221 5c dl yel & dk bl .20 .20
**559** A221 10c rose lil & ol grn .20 .20
**560** A221 15c org & vio bl .20 .20
**561** A221 25c emer & vio bl .35 .20
**562** A221 30c brick red & dk bl .45 .20
**563** A221 35c red org & brt vio ('75) .45 .20
**564** A221 40c brt bl & blk .55 .20
**565** A221 50c ol grn & org .70 .25
**566** A221 60c yel brn & gray .85 .25
**567** A221 70c sep & dk grn 1.00 .25
**568** A221 80c brt grn & brick red 1.10 .25

**Violet Fibers, Fluorescent Paper**

**569** A222 1fr pur ('74) 1.40 .20
*a.* Without fibers, fluorescent paper ('78) 2.00 1.50
**570** A222 1.10fr Prus bl ('75) 1.50 .40
**571** A222 1.20fr rose red ('74) 1.60 1.25
**572** A222 1.30fr ocher 2.00 .90
**573** A222 1.50fr grn ('74) 2.00 1.25
**574** A222 1.70fr gray 2.25 .60
**575** A222 1.80fr dp org 2.50 .60
**576** A222 2fr ultra ('74) 2.75 .40
*a.* Without fibers, fluorescent paper ('78) 4.50 3.50

| | | | | |
|---|---|---|---|---|
| **577** | A222 | 2.50fr gldn brn ('75) | 3.25 | .60 |
| **578** | A222 | 3fr dk car ('79) | 4.00 | 1.00 |
| **579** | A222 | 3.50fr ol grn ('80) | 4.50 | 1.25 |
| | | *Nos. 558-579 (22)* | 33.80 | 10.85 |

No. 577 exists without tagging. Value, $60 unused, $30 used.

**Europa Issue 1973**

Common Design Type

**1973, Apr. 30 Engr. and Photo.**

**Size: 38x28mm**

| | | | | |
|---|---|---|---|---|
| **580** | CD16 | 25c brown & yel | .40 | .25 |
| **581** | CD16 | 40c ultra & yel | .70 | .35 |

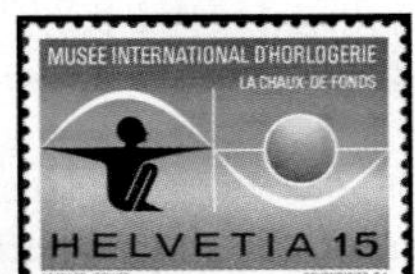

"Man and Time" — A223

Skier and Championship Emblem A224

Child — A225

**1973, Aug. 30 Photo. *Perf. 11½***

| | | | | |
|---|---|---|---|---|
| **582** | A223 | 15c multicolored | .25 | .20 |
| **583** | A224 | 30c pink & multi | .40 | .20 |
| **584** | A225 | 40c blue vio & blk | .60 | .50 |
| | | *Nos. 582-584 (3)* | 1.25 | .90 |

Opening of the Intl. Clock Museum, La Chaux-de-Fonds, 1974 (15c); Intl. Alpine Skiing Championships, St. Moritz, Feb. 2-10, 1974 (30c); "Terre des hommes" children's aid program (40c).

Souvenir Sheet

Medieval Postal Couriers — A226

**1974, Jan. 29 Photo. *Perf. 11½***

| | | | | |
|---|---|---|---|---|
| **585** | A226 | Sheet of 4 | 5.50 | 5.50 |
| *a.* | | 30c Basel (with staff) | 1.10 | 1.10 |
| *b.* | | 30c Zug (without staff) | 1.10 | 1.10 |
| *c.* | | 60c Uri | 1.10 | 1.10 |
| *d.* | | 80c Schwyz | 1.10 | 1.10 |

Cent. of UPU and for INTERNABA 74 Intl. Phil. Exhib., Basel, June 7-16. No. 585 sold for 3fr.

Pine and Cabin on Globe — A227

Gymnast and Hurdlers A228

Target and Pistol — A229

**1974, Jan. 29**

| | | | | |
|---|---|---|---|---|
| **586** | A227 | 15c lt green & multi | .20 | .20 |
| **587** | A228 | 30c red & multi | .40 | .20 |
| **588** | A229 | 40c blue & multi | .70 | .30 |
| | | *Nos. 586-588 (3)* | 1.30 | .70 |

50th anniv. of Swiss Youth Hostels (15c); Cent. of Swiss Workers' Gymnast and Sports Association (SATUS) (30c); World Marksmanship Championships, Thun and Bern, Sept. 1974 (40c).

Old Houses, Parliament RR Station, Bern — A230

Eugéne Borel — A231

Designs: No. 590, Castle, Town Hall, Chauderon Center, Lausanne. 40c, Heinrich von Stephan. 80c, Montgomery Blair.

**1974, Mar. 28 Photo. *Perf. 11½***

| | | | | |
|---|---|---|---|---|
| **589** | A230 | 30c orange & multi | .50 | .25 |
| **590** | A230 | 30c scarlet & multi | .50 | .25 |

**Engr.**

| | | | | |
|---|---|---|---|---|
| **591** | A231 | 30c rose & blk | .40 | .25 |
| **592** | A231 | 40c gray & blk | .60 | .50 |
| **593** | A231 | 80c lt yel grn & blk | 1.10 | .75 |
| | | *Nos. 589-593 (5)* | 3.10 | 2.00 |

Cent. of the UPU. Nos. 589-590 publicize the Cent. Cong., Lausanne, May 22-July 5; Nos. 591-593 honor the founders of the UPU.

"Continuity," by Max Bill — A232

Europa: 40c, "Amazon," bronze sculpture by Carl Burckhardt.

**1974, Mar. 28 Photo.**

| | | | | |
|---|---|---|---|---|
| **594** | A232 | 30c red & black | .45 | .20 |
| **595** | A232 | 40c ultra & sepia | .75 | .35 |

Oath of Allegiance, by Werner Witschi — A233

Sports Foundation Emblem A234

Conveyor Belts, Paths of Mail Transport and Delivery A235

**1974, Sept. 19 Photo. *Perf. 11½***

| | | | | |
|---|---|---|---|---|
| **596** | A233 | 15c lil, ol & dk ol | .20 | .20 |
| **597** | A234 | 30c silver & multi | .40 | .20 |
| **598** | A235 | 30c plum & multi | .40 | .20 |
| | | *Nos. 596-598 (3)* | 1.00 | .60 |

Centenary of Swiss Constitution (15c); Swiss Sports Foundation (No. 597); 125th anniversary of Swiss Federal Post (No. 598).

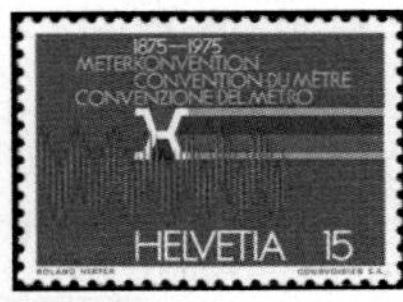

Standard Meter, Krypton Spectrum A236

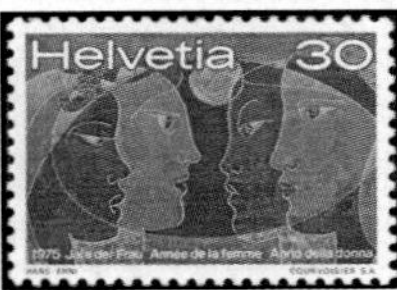

Women of Four Races A237

Red Cross Flag, Barbed Wire — A238

"Ville de Lucerne" Dirigible A239

**1975, Feb. 13 Photo. *Perf. 11½***

| | | | | |
|---|---|---|---|---|
| **599** | A236 | 15c grn, org & ultra | .25 | .25 |
| **600** | A237 | 30c brown & multi | .45 | .20 |
| **601** | A238 | 60c ultra, blk & red | .75 | .40 |
| **602** | A239 | 90c blue & multi | 1.20 | 1.00 |
| | | *Nos. 599-602 (4)* | 2.65 | 1.85 |

Cent. of Intl. Meter Convention, Paris, 1875 (15c); Intl. Women's Year 1975 (30c); 2nd Session of Diplomatic Conf. on Humanitarian Intl. Law, Geneva, Feb. 1975 (60c); Aviation and Space Travel exhibition in Museum of Transport and Communications, Lucerne (90c).

Mönch, by Ferdinand Hodler — A240

Vineyard Worker, by Maurice Barraud — A241

Europa: 50c, Still Life with Guitar, by René Auberjonois.

**1975, Apr. 28 Photo. *Perf. 12x11½***

| | | | | |
|---|---|---|---|---|
| **603** | A240 | 30c gray & multi | .45 | .20 |
| **604** | A241 | 50c multicolored | .75 | .50 |
| **605** | A241 | 60c bl gray & multi | .90 | .80 |
| | | *Nos. 603-605 (3)* | 2.10 | 1.50 |

Man Pulling Wheel Chair Upstairs A242

"The Helping Hand" A243

Architectural Heritage Year Emblem A244

Beat Fischer von Reichenbach A245

**1975, Sept. 11 Photo.**

| | | | | |
|---|---|---|---|---|
| **606** | A242 | 15c lilac, blk & grn | .25 | .20 |
| **607** | A243 | 30c red, blk & car | .40 | .20 |
| **608** | A244 | 50c yel brn & mar | .70 | .60 |
| **609** | A245 | 60c blue & multi | .80 | .75 |
| | | *Nos. 606-609 (4)* | 2.15 | 1.75 |

Special building features for the handicapped (15c); interdenominational telephone pastoral counseling (30c); European Architectural Heritage Year 1975 (50c); Fischer Post, Bern, tercentenary (60c).

Forest A246

Fruits and Vegetables A247

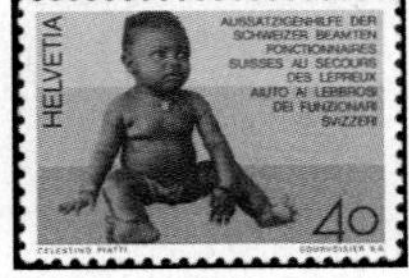

Black Infant — A248

Telephones of 1876 and 1976 — A249

**1976, Feb. 12 Photo. *Perf. 11½***

**Fluorescent, No Violet Fibers**

| | | | | |
|---|---|---|---|---|
| **610** | A246 | 20c green & multi | .50 | .25 |
| **611** | A247 | 40c car & multi | .60 | .20 |
| **612** | A248 | 40c lil rose & multi | .60 | .20 |

**Engr.**

**Violet Fibers, Fluorescent Paper**

| | | | | |
|---|---|---|---|---|
| **613** | A249 | 80c lt bl & dk bl | 1.10 | 1.00 |
| | | *Nos. 610-613 (4)* | 2.80 | 1.65 |

Centenary of Federal forest laws (20c); healthy nutrition to combat alcoholism (No. 611); fight against leprosy (No. 612); telephone centenary (80c).

Cotton and Gold Lace, St. Gall — A250

Pocket Watch, 18th Century — A251

**1976, May 3 Engr. *Perf. 11½***

**614** A250 40c red brn & multi .65 .25
**615** A251 80c black & multi 1.40 .90

Europa. Both 40c and 80c are on fluorescent paper, the 80c having violet fibers.

Fawn, Frog and Swallow A252

"Conserve Energy" A253

St. Gotthard Mountains A254

Skater A255

**1976, Sept. 16 Photo. *Perf. 11½***

**Fluorescent, No Violet Fibers**

**616** A252 20c multicolored .75 .30
**617** A253 40c multicolored .60 .20
**618** A254 40c multicolored .65 .30
**619** A255 80c multicolored 1.10 .90
*Nos. 616-619 (4)* 3.10 1.70

Wildlife protection (20c); energy conservation (No. 617); Pizzo Lucendro to Pizzo Rotondo, seen from Altanca (No. 618); World Men's Skating Championships, Davos, Feb. 5-6, 1977 (80c).

Oskar Bider, Bleriot Monoplane A256

Swiss Aviation Pioneers: 80c, Eduard Spelterini and balloon gondola. 100c, Armand Dufaux and Dufaux plane. 150c, Walter Mittelholzer and Dornier hydroplane.

**1977, Jan. 27 Engr. *Perf. 11½***

**620** A256 40c multicolored .65 .65
**621** A256 80c multicolored 1.50 1.25
**622** A256 100c multicolored 1.25 1.00
**623** A256 150c multicolored 2.00 1.75
*Nos. 620-623 (4)* 5.40 4.65

Blue Cross — A257

Festival Emblem A258

Balloons Carrying Letters A259

**1977, Jan. 27 Photo.**

**624** A257 20c gray, bl & blk .30 .25
**625** A258 40c red, gold & brn .50 .20
**626** A259 80c lt bl & multi 1.10 1.00
*Nos. 624-626 (3)* 1.90 1.45

Blue Cross Society (care of alcoholics and fight against alcoholism), centenary (20c); Vintage Festival, Vevey, July 30-Aug. 14 (40c); JUPHILEX 77 Youth Philatelic Exhibition, Bern, Apr. 7-11 (80c).

---

Fluorescent Paper

From No. 624 onward the paper lacks violet fibers but is fluorescent, unless otherwise noted.

---

St. Ursanne on Doubs River — A260

Europa: 80c, Sils-Baselgia on Inn River.

**1977, May 2 Engr. *Perf. 11½***

**627** A260 40c multicolored .65 .25
**628** A260 80c multicolored 1.40 .70

Worker and Factories A261

Ionic Column and Shield A262

Swiss Cross, Arrow and Butterfly A263

**1977, Aug. 25 Photo. *Perf. 11½***

**629** A261 20c multicolored .30 .25
**630** A262 40c multicolored .55 .40
**631** A263 80c multicolored 1.10 1.00
*Nos. 629-631 (3)* 1.95 1.65

Federal Factories Act, centenary (20c); protection of cultural monuments (40c); Swiss hiking trails (80c).

Star Singer, Bergün — A264

Folk Customs: 10c, Horse race, Zürich. 20c, New Year's Eve costumes, Herisau. 25c, Chesslete, Solothurn. 30c, Rollelibutzen, Altstatten. 35c, Cutting off the goose, Sursee. 40c, Herald reading proclamation and men scaling wall, Geneva. 45c, Klausjagen, Kussnacht. 50c, Masked men, Laupen. 60c, Schnabelgeissen, Ottenbach. 70c, Procession (horse and masked men), Mendrisio. 80c, Griffins, Basel. 90c, Masked men, Lotschental.

**1977-84 Engr. *Perf. 11½***

**632** A264 5c blue grn .20 .20
*a.* Bklt. pane of 4 ('84) .25
**633** A264 10c dark red .20 .20
*a.* Bklt. pane of 2 + 2 labels ('79) .45
*b.* Bklt. pane of 4 ('84) .50
**634** A264 20c orange .30 .20
*a.* Booklet pane of 4 ('79) 1.20
**635** A264 25c brown .35 .20
**636** A264 30c brt green .45 .20
**637** A264 35c olive .50 .20
*a.* Bklt. pane of 4 ('84) 2.00
**638** A264 40c brown lake .60 .20
*a.* Booklet pane of 4 ('79) 2.50
*b.* Violet fibers, flourescent paper ('78) .60 .20
**639** A264 45c gray blue .60 .30
**640** A264 50c red brown .75 .20
*a.* Bklt. pane of 2+2 labels ('84) 1.50
*b.* Bklt. pane of 4 ('84) 3.00

**641** A264 60c gray brown .90 .45
**642** A264 70c purple 1.00 .30
**643** A264 80c steel blue 1.10 .75
**644** A264 90c deep brown 1.25 .90
*Nos. 632-644 (13)* 8.20 4.30

Issue dates: 30c, Nov. 25, 1982; 25c, 40c, 60c, Sept. 11, 1984; others, Aug. 25, 1977.

Arms of Vaud Canton A265

Old Lucerne A266

Title Page of "Melusine" A267

Stylized Lens and Bellows A268

Steamers on Swiss Lakes — A269

**1978, Mar. 9 Photo. *Perf. 11½***

**652** A265 20c multicolored .30 .20
**653** A266 40c multicolored .75 .25
**654** A267 70c multicolored .90 .80
**655** A268 80c multicolored 1.10 1.00
*Nos. 652-655 (4)* 3.05 2.25

**Miniature Sheet**

**656** A269 Sheet of 8 7.00 7.00
*a.* 20c La Suisse, 1910 .30 .30
*b.* 20c Il Verbano, 1826 .30 .30
*c.* 40c MS Gotthard, 1970 .85 .85
*d.* 40c Ville de Neuchatel, 1972 .85 .85
*e.* 40c MS Romanshorn, 1958 .85 .85
*f.* 40c Le Winkelried, 1871 .85 .85
*g.* 70c DS Loetschberg, 1914 .90 .90
*h.* 80c DS Waedenswil, 1895 1.25 1.25

LEMANEX 78 Philatelic Exhibition, Lausanne, May 26-June 4 (#652); Founding of Lucerne, 800th anniv. (#653); printing in Geneva, 500th anniv. (#654); 2nd Intl. Triennial Photography Exhibition, Fribourg, June 17-Oct. 22 (#655).

Size of No. 656: 134x129mm. Sold for 5fr.

Stockalper Palace, Brig — A270

Europa: 80c, Diet Hall, Bern.

**1978, May 2 Engr. *Perf. 11½***

**657** A270 40c multicolored .75 .30
**658** A270 80c multicolored 1.50 .75

Machinist A271

Joseph Bovet (1879-1951), Composer — A272

#660, Chemical worker (French inscription). #661, Construction worker (Italian inscription).

**1978, Sept. 14 Photo. *Perf. 11½***

**659** A271 40c multicolored .65 .45
**660** A271 40c multicolored .65 .45
**661** A271 40c multicolored .65 .45
*a.* Strip of 3, #659-661 2.25 2.25

Industrial safety.

**1978, Sept. 14 Engr.**

Portraits: 40c, Henri Dunant (1828-1910), founder of Red Cross. 70c, Carl Gustave Jung (1875-1961), psychologist. 80c, Auguste Piccard (1884-1962), physicist and balloonist.

**662** A272 20c dull green .30 .20
**663** A272 40c rose lake .55 .20
**664** A272 70c gray 1.00 .75
**665** A272 80c blue gray 1.10 .90
*Nos. 662-665 (4)* 2.95 2.05

Arms of Switzerland and Jura — A273

**1978, Sept. 25 Photo. *Perf. 11½***

**666** A273 40c buff, red & blk .55 .35

Admission of Jura as 23rd Canton.

Rainer Maria Rilke (1875-1926), Poet, Muzot Castle — A274

Designs: 40c, Paul Klee (1879-1940), painter and "heroic roses." 70c, Hermann Hesse (1877-1962), writer, and vines. 80c, Thomas Mann (1875-1955), writer, and Lubeck buildings.

**1979, Feb. 21 Engr. *Perf. 11½***

**667** A274 20c gray green .30 .20
**668** A274 40c red .60 .30
**669** A274 70c brown .90 .70
**670** A274 80c gray blue 1.10 1.00
*Nos. 667-670 (4)* 2.90 2.20

O. H. Ammann, Verrazano-Narrows Bridge, NY — A275

Target Hit with Pole and Lucerne Flag — A276

Hot Air Balloon A277

Airport, Swissair and Air France Jets — A278

**1979, Feb. 21** **Photo.**

| | | | | |
|---|---|---|---|---|
| **671** | A275 | 20c multicolored | .30 | .20 |
| **672** | A276 | 40c multicolored | .60 | .25 |
| **673** | A277 | 70c multicolored | .90 | .70 |
| **674** | A278 | 80c multicolored | 1.10 | 1.00 |
| | | *Nos. 671-674 (4)* | 2.90 | 2.15 |

Othmar H. Ammann (1879-1965), engineer, bridge builder in US; 50th Federal Riflemen's Festival, Lucerne, July 7-22; World Esperanto Congress, Lucerne; new runway at Basel-Mulhouse Intl. Airport.

Letter Box, 1845, Spalentor, Basel — A279

Europa: 80c, Microwave radio relay station on Jungfraujoch.

**1979, Apr. 30** **Engr.** ***Perf. 11½***

| | | | | |
|---|---|---|---|---|
| **675** | A279 | 40c multicolored | .65 | .35 |
| **676** | A279 | 80c multicolored | 1.40 | .90 |

Helvetian Gold Quarter Stater, 2nd Century B.C. — A280

Three-stage Launcher Ariane — A283

Child and Dove — A281

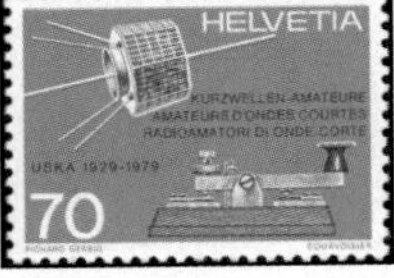


Morse Key and Satellite A282

**1979, Sept. 6** **Photo.**

| | | | | |
|---|---|---|---|---|
| **677** | A280 | 20c multicolored | .30 | .20 |
| **678** | A281 | 40c multicolored | .55 | .25 |
| **679** | A282 | 70c multicolored | .90 | .70 |
| **680** | A283 | 80c multicolored | 1.10 | .90 |
| | | *Nos. 677-680 (4)* | 2.85 | 2.05 |

Centenary of Swiss Numismatic Society; International Year of the Child; Union of Swiss Radio Amateurs, 50th anniv.; European Space Agency (ESA).

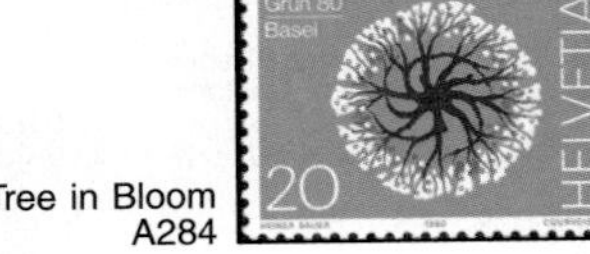


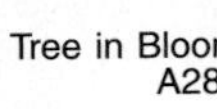

Tree in Bloom A284

Hand Carved Milk Bucket A285

Winterthur Town Hall — A286

"Pic-Pic," 1930 — A287

**1980, Feb. 21** **Photo.**

| | | | | |
|---|---|---|---|---|
| **681** | A284 | 20c multicolored | .30 | .20 |
| **682** | A285 | 40c multicolored | .55 | .25 |
| **683** | A286 | 70c multicolored | 1.00 | .80 |
| **684** | A287 | 80c multicolored | 1.10 | 1.00 |
| | | *Nos. 681-684 (4)* | 2.95 | 2.25 |

Green '80, Swiss Horticultural & Gardening Expo., Basel, 4/12-9/9/12; Swiss Arts Crafts Centers, 50th anniv.; Soc. for Swiss Art History, cent.; 50th Intl. Automobile Show, Geneva, 3/16.

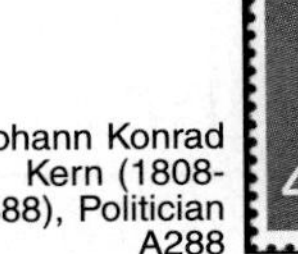

Johann Konrad Kern (1808-1888), Politician A288

Europa: 80c, Gustav Adolf Hasler (1830-1900), communications pioneer.

**1980, Apr. 28** **Lith. & Engr.**

**Granite Paper**

| | | | | |
|---|---|---|---|---|
| **685** | A288 | 40c multicolored | .50 | .20 |
| **686** | A288 | 80c multicolored | 1.00 | .90 |

Postal Giro System A289

Postal Bus System A290

Security Printing Plant, 50th Anniversary A291

Swiss Telephone Service Centenary A292

**Photo., Photo. & Engr. (70c)**

**1980, Sept. 5** ***Perf. 12***

| | | | | |
|---|---|---|---|---|
| **687** | A289 | 20c multicolored | .30 | .20 |
| **688** | A290 | 40c multicolored | .55 | .25 |
| **689** | A291 | 70c multicolored | 1.00 | .75 |
| **690** | A292 | 80c multicolored | 1.20 | 1.10 |
| | | *Nos. 687-690 (4)* | 3.05 | 2.30 |

Swiss Meteorological Office Centenary A293

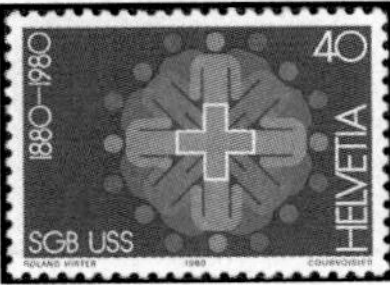


Swiss Trade Union Federation Centenary A294

Opening of St. Gotthard Tunnel for Year-round Traffic — A295

**1980, Sept. 5** **Photo.**

| | | | | |
|---|---|---|---|---|
| **691** | A293 | 20c multicolored | .35 | .20 |
| **692** | A294 | 40c multicolored | .55 | .20 |
| **693** | A295 | 80c multicolored | 1.25 | 1.00 |
| | | *Nos. 691-693 (3)* | 2.15 | 1.40 |

Granary, Kiesen, 17th Century A296

International Year of the Disabled A297

The Parish Clerk, by Albert Anker — A298

Theodolite and Rod — A299

DC-9 (50th Anniversary of Swissair) A300

**1981, Mar. 9** **Photo.** ***Perf. 11½***

| | | | | |
|---|---|---|---|---|
| **694** | A296 | 20c multicolored | .30 | .20 |
| **695** | A297 | 40c multicolored | .55 | .20 |
| **696** | A298 | 70c multicolored | 1.00 | .80 |
| **697** | A299 | 80c multicolored | 1.10 | .90 |
| **698** | A300 | 110c multicolored | 1.60 | 1.10 |
| | | *Nos. 694-698 (5)* | 4.55 | 3.20 |

Ballenberg Open-air Museum of Rural Architecture, Furnishing and Crafts; Albert Anker (1831-1910), artist (70c); 16th Congress of the International Federation of Surveyors, Montreux, Aug. (80c).

**Europa Issue 1981**

Couple Dancing in Native Costumes — A301

**1981, May 4** **Photo.** ***Perf. 11½***

| | | | | |
|---|---|---|---|---|
| **699** | A301 | 40c shown | .45 | .35 |
| **700** | A301 | 80c Stone putting | 1.25 | 1.00 |

Seal of Fribourg A302

**1981, Sept. 3** **Photo. & Engr.**

| | | | | |
|---|---|---|---|---|
| **701** | A302 | 40c shown | .55 | .25 |
| **702** | A302 | 40c Seal of Solothurn | .55 | .25 |
| **703** | A302 | 80c Old Town Hall, Stans | 1.25 | 1.00 |
| | | *Nos. 701-703 (3)* | 2.35 | 1.50 |

Diet of Stans, 50th anniv., and entry of Fribourg & Solothurn into the Swiss Confederation.

Voltage Regulator A303

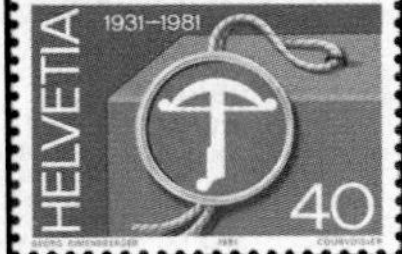


Crossbow Quality Emblem A304

Youths A305

Flower Mosaic, St. Peter's Cathedral, Geneva A306

**1981, Sept. 3** **Photo.**

| | | | | |
|---|---|---|---|---|
| **704** | A303 | 20c multi | .30 | .20 |
| **705** | A304 | 40c multi | .55 | .30 |
| **706** | A305 | 70c multi | .90 | .75 |
| **707** | A306 | 1.10fr multi | 1.40 | 1.25 |
| | | *Nos. 704-707 (4)* | 3.15 | 2.50 |

Technorama Industrial Fair, Winterthur; Crossbow Quality Emblem, 50th anniv.; Swiss Youth Assoc., 50th anniv.; restoration of St. Peter's Cathedral.

Gotthard Railway Centenary A307

Designs: Locomotives. Nos. 708-709 se-tenant with label showing workers' monument.

**1982, Feb. 18** **Photo.**

| | | | | |
|---|---|---|---|---|
| **708** | A307 | 40c Steam | .60 | .30 |
| **709** | A307 | 40c Electric | .60 | .30 |

Swiss Hoteliers' Assoc. Centenary A308

Federal Gymnastic Society Sesquicentennial — A309

Intl. Gas Union, 50th Anniv. Convention, Lausanne A310

Bern Museum of Natural History Sesquicentennial — A311

Society of Chemical Industries Centenary A312

**1982, Feb. 18**

| | | | | | |
|---|---|---|---|---|---|
| **710** | A308 | 20c | multicolored | .30 | .20 |
| **711** | A309 | 40c | multicolored | .60 | .30 |
| **712** | A310 | 70c | multicolored | .90 | .75 |
| **713** | A311 | 80c | multicolored | 1.10 | 1.00 |
| **714** | A312 | 110c | multicolored | 1.50 | 1.10 |
| | | | *Nos. 710-714 (5)* | 4.40 | 3.35 |

Europa 1982 — A313

**1982, May 3** **Photo.** ***Perf. 11½***

| | | | | | |
|---|---|---|---|---|---|
| **715** | A313 | 40c | Oath of Eternal Fealty | .75 | .30 |
| **716** | A313 | 80c | Pact of 1291 | 1.50 | 1.00 |

Virgo, Schwarzee above Zermatt — A314

Signs of the Zodiac and City Views.

**Photogravure and Engraved**

**1982-86** ***Perf. 11½***

| | | | | | |
|---|---|---|---|---|---|
| **717** | A314 | 1fr | Aquarius, Old Bern | 1.25 | .30 |
| **718** | A314 | 1.10fr | Pisces, Nax near Sion | 1.40 | .30 |
| **719** | A314 | 1.20fr | Aries, Graustock | 1.60 | .30 |
| **719A** | A314 | 1.40fr | Gemini, Bischofszell | 2.00 | 1.40 |
| **720** | A314 | 1.50fr | Taurus, Basel Cathedral | 2.10 | .30 |
| **721** | A314 | 1.60fr | Gemini, Schonengrund | 2.10 | 1.10 |
| **722** | A314 | 1.70fr | Cancer, Wetterhorn, Grindelwald | 2.25 | .30 |
| **723** | A314 | 1.80fr | Leo, Areuse Gorge, Neuchatel | 2.25 | 1.00 |
| **724** | A314 | 2fr | Virgo, Jungfrau Monch Eiger Mts. | 2.75 | 2.25 |
| **725** | A314 | 2fr | shown | 2.75 | .30 |
| **726** | A314 | 2.50fr | Libra, Fechy | 3.25 | .80 |
| **727** | A314 | 3fr | Scorpio, Corippo | 4.00 | 1.25 |
| **728** | A314 | 4fr | Sagittarius, Glarus | 5.50 | 1.50 |

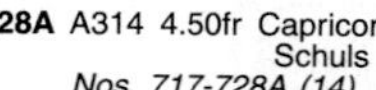

| | | | | | |
|---|---|---|---|---|---|
| **728A** | A314 | 4.50fr | Capricorn, Schuls | 5.75 | 2.00 |
| | | | *Nos. 717-728A (14)* | 38.95 | 13.10 |

Issued: #717-719, 720-721, 8/23/82; #719A, 2/11/86; #722-724, 2/17/83; #725, 11/24/83; #726-727, 2/19/85; #728-728A, 2/21/84.

Zurich Tram Centenary A315

Centenary of Salvation Army in Switzerland A316

World Dressage Championship, Lausanne, Aug. 25-29 — A317

Intl. Water Supply Assoc., 14th World Congress, Zurich, Sept. 6-10 — A318

**1982, Aug. 23** **Photo.**

| | | | | | |
|---|---|---|---|---|---|
| **729** | A315 | 20c | multicolored | .40 | .20 |
| **730** | A316 | 40c | multicolored | .55 | .25 |
| **731** | A317 | 70c | multicolored | 1.00 | .90 |
| **732** | A318 | 80c | multicolored | 1.10 | 1.00 |
| | | | *Nos. 729-732 (4)* | 3.05 | 2.35 |

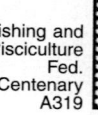

Fishing and Pisciculture Fed. Centenary A319

Zurich University Sesquicentennial — A320

Journalists' Fed. Centenary A321

Machine Manufacturers' Assoc. Centenary — A322

**1983, Feb. 17** **Photo.**

**Granite Paper**

| | | | | | |
|---|---|---|---|---|---|
| **733** | A319 | 20c | Perch | .45 | .20 |
| **734** | A320 | 40c | multicolored | .55 | .30 |
| **735** | A321 | 70c | Computer print outs | 1.00 | .90 |
| **736** | A322 | 80c | Micrometer, cycloidal computer pattern | 1.10 | 1.00 |
| | | | *Nos. 733-736 (4)* | 3.10 | 2.40 |

Europa 1983 A323

Basel Seal, 1832-1848 A324

**Photogravure and Engraved**

**1983, May 3** ***Perf. 11½***

| | | | | | |
|---|---|---|---|---|---|
| **737** | A323 | 40c | Celestial globe, 1594 | .50 | .25 |
| **738** | A323 | 80c | Cog railway, 1871 | 1.40 | 1.00 |

**1983, May 26** **Photo.**

| | | | | | |
|---|---|---|---|---|---|
| **739** | A324 | 40c | multicolored | .60 | .35 |

Basel Canton sesquicentennial (land division).

Octodurus Martigny Bimillenium A325

Swiss Kennel Club Centenary A326

Bicycle and Motorcycle Federation Centenary A327

World Communications Year — A328

**1983, Aug. 22** **Photo.**

| | | | | | |
|---|---|---|---|---|---|
| **740** | A325 | 20c | multicolored | .30 | .20 |
| **741** | A326 | 40c | multicolored | .65 | .25 |
| **742** | A327 | 70c | multicolored | 1.00 | .90 |
| **743** | A328 | 80c | multicolored | 1.10 | .90 |
| | | | *Nos. 740-743 (4)* | 3.05 | 2.25 |

NABA-ZURI'84 Natl. Stamp Show, Zurich, June 22-July 1 — A329

1100th Anniv. of Saint Imier — A330

Upper City, Lausanne A331

**1984, Feb. 21** **Photo.**

| | | | | | |
|---|---|---|---|---|---|
| **744** | A329 | 25c | multicolored | .40 | .25 |
| **745** | A330 | 50c | multicolored | .70 | .35 |
| **746** | A331 | 80c | multicolored | 1.40 | 1.10 |
| | | | *Nos. 744-746 (3)* | 2.50 | 1.70 |

Selection of Lausanne as permanent headquarters for the Intl. Olympic Committee (80c).

Europa (1959-1984) A332

**1984, May 2** **Photo.** ***Perf. 11½***

| | | | | | |
|---|---|---|---|---|---|
| **747** | A332 | 50c | lilac rose | .80 | .50 |
| **748** | A332 | 80c | ultra | 1.60 | 1.00 |

Souvenir Sheet

Panoramic View of Zurich — A333

**1984, May 24**

| | | | | | |
|---|---|---|---|---|---|
| **749** | A333 | | Sheet of 4 | 5.00 | 5.00 |
| *a.-d.* | | | 50c any single | 1.20 | 1.20 |

NABA-ZURI '84 Stamp Show. Sold for 3fr.

Fire Prevention A334

**1984, Sept. 11** **Photo.**

| | | | | | |
|---|---|---|---|---|---|
| **750** | A334 | 50c | Flames, match | .70 | .35 |

Railway Staff Association, Cent. — A335

Rheto-Roman Culture Bimillennium A336

Lake Geneva Rescue Soc., Cent. — A337

Intl. Congress on Large Dams, Lausanne A338

**1985, Feb. 19** **Photo.** ***Perf. 12x11½***

| | | | | | |
|---|---|---|---|---|---|
| **751** | A335 | 35c | Conductor's hat, paraphernalia | .50 | .25 |
| **752** | A336 | 50c | Engraved artifact, Chur | .65 | .25 |
| **753** | A337 | 70c | Rescuing drowning victim | 1.10 | .90 |
| **754** | A338 | 80c | Grande Dizence Dam, Canton Valais | 1.25 | 1.10 |
| | | | *Nos. 751-754 (4)* | 3.50 | 2.50 |

Europa 1985 — A339

Designs: 50c, Ernest Ansermet (1883-1969), composer, conductor. 80c, Frank Martin (1890-1974), composer.

**1985, May 7 Photo. *Perf. 11½x12***

**755** A339 50c multicolored .60 .20
**756** A339 80c multicolored 1.40 1.00

Swiss Master Bakers and Confectioners Federation, Bern, Cent. — A340

Swiss Radio Intl., 50th Anniv. A341

Postal, Telegraph & Telephone Intl. Congress, Sept. 16-21, Interlaken A342

**1985, Sept. 10 Photo. *Perf. 12x11½***

**757** A340 50c Baker .65 .20
**758** A341 70c multi 1.00 .75
**759** A342 80c PTTI 75th anniv. 1.20 .90
*Nos. 757-759 (3)* 2.85 1.85

Swiss Worker's Relief Org., 50th Anniv. A343

Battle of Sempach, 600th Anniv. A344

Roman Chur Bimillennium A345

Vindonissa Bimillennium A346

Zurich Bimillennium A347

**1986, Feb. 11 Photo. *Perf. 12***

**772** A343 35c Knot .50 .40
**773** A344 50c Military map, 1698 .65 .20
**774** A345 80c Mercury statue 1.10 .90
**775** A346 90c Gallic head 1.25 1.00
**776** A347 1.10fr Augustus coin 1.60 1.25
*Nos. 772-776 (5)* 5.10 3.75

Europa 1986 A348

Mail Handling A349

**1986, Apr. 22 Photo. *Perf. 13½***

**777** A348 50c Woman .65 .30
**778** A348 90c Man 1.60 1.25

**Photo. & Engr.**

**1986-89 *Perf. 13½x13***

**779** A349 5c Franz mail van, 1911 .20 .20
**780** A349 10c Parcel sorting .20 .20
**781** A349 20c Mule post .30 .20
**782** A349 25c Letter-facing, canceling .40 .20
**783** A349 30c Mail coach, 1735-1960 1.10 .90
**784** A349 35c Counter service .55 .40
**785** A349 45c Packet steamer, 1837-40 .65 .45
**786** A349 50c Postman, 1986 .75 .35
*a.* Bklt. pane of 10 ('88) 7.50
**787** A349 60c Loading airmail, 1986 .90 .45
**788** A349 75c 17th Cent. courier 1.10 .75
**789** A349 80c Postman, ca. 1900 1.25 .80
**790** A349 90c Railroad mail car 1.40 1.00
*Nos. 779-790 (12)* 8.80 5.90

Issued: 5c, 10c, 25c, 35c, 80c, 90c, 9/9/86; 20c, 30c, 45c, 50c, 60c, 3/10/87; 75c, 3/7/89.

For surcharge see No. B535.

Intl. Peace Year — A351

Swiss Winter Relief Fund, 50th Anniv. A352

Berne Convention for the Protection of Literary and Artistic Copyrights, Cent. — A353

25th Intl. Red Cross Conference, Geneva, Oct. 23-31 A354

**1986, Sept. 9 Photo. *Perf. 12x11½***

**799** A351 35c multicolored .50 .30
**800** A352 50c multicolored .70 .25
**801** A353 80c multicolored 1.25 1.00
**802** A354 90c multicolored 1.30 1.10
*Nos. 799-802 (4)* 3.75 2.65

Mobile P.O., 50th Anniv. A355

Lausanne University, 450th Anniv. A356

Swiss Engineers & Architects Assoc., Sesquicent. A357

Cointrin Airport-Geneva, Rail Link Opening, June 1, 1987 — A358

Baden Hot Springs, 2000th Anniv. A359

**1987, Mar. 10 Photo.**

**803** A355 35c multicolored .55 .35
**804** A356 50c multicolored .70 .20
**805** A357 80c multicolored 1.20 1.00
**806** A358 90c multicolored 1.40 1.25
**807** A359 1.10fr multicolored 1.60 1.50
*Nos. 803-807 (5)* 5.45 4.30

Europa 1987 — A360

Sculpture: 50fr, Scarabaeus, 1979, by Bernard Luginbuhl. 90fr, Carnival Fountain, 1977, by Jean Tinguely, Basel Theater.

**1987, May 26 Photo. *Perf. 11½***

**808** A360 50c multicolored .75 .30
**809** A360 90c multicolored 1.90 1.25

Swiss Master Butchers' Federation, Cent. — A361

Stamp Day, 50th Anniv. A362

Swiss Dairy Assoc., Cent. — A363

**1987, Sept. 4 Photo. *Perf. 12x11½***

**810** A361 35c multicolored .50 .40
**811** A362 50c multicolored .75 .40
**812** A363 90c Cheesemaker 1.50 1.00
*Nos. 810-812 (3)* 2.75 1.80

Tourism Industry, Bicent. — A364

Switzerland's four language regions: 50c, Clock Tower, Zug, German. 80c, Church of San Carlo, Blenio Valley, Italian. 90c, Witches' Tower, Sion Castle, French. 140c, Jorgenberg Castle ruins, Waltensburg/Vuorz, Surselva, Rhaeto-Romansh.

**1987, Sept. 4 *Perf. 11½***

**813** A364 50c multicolored .70 .40
**814** A364 80c multicolored 1.25 .75
**815** A364 90c multicolored 1.50 1.00
**816** A364 140c multicolored 2.00 1.50
*a.* Souvenir sheet of 4, #813-816 5.00
*Nos. 813-816 (4)* 5.45 3.65

Swiss Women's Benevolent Soc., Cent. — A365

Swiss Hairdressers Assoc., Cent. — A366

Battle of Naefels, 600th Anniv. A367

European Campaign to Protect Undeveloped and Developing Lands A368

Intl. Music Festival, Lucerne, 50th Anniv. A369

**1988, Mar. 8 Photo. *Perf. 12x11½***

**817** A365 25c multicolored .40 .25
**818** A366 35c multicolored .55 .40
**819** A367 50c Banner of St. Fridolin, medieval manuscript .80 .25
**820** A368 80c multicolored 1.25 .90
**821** A369 90c Girl playing a shawm 1.40 1.25
*Nos. 817-821 (5)* 4.40 3.05

Europa 1988 — A370

**1988, May 24 Photo. *Perf. 11½***

**822** A370 50c Arrows (transport) .65 .40
**823** A370 90c Circuitry (communication) 1.75 1.25

Swiss Accident Prevention Office, 50th Anniv. A371

Assoc. of Metalworkers and Watchmakers, Cent. — A372

Federal Topography Office, 150th Anniv. A373

Intl. Red Cross Museum, Geneva A374

**1988, Sept. 13 Photo. Perf. 12x11½**

**824** A371 35c multicolored .45 .40
**825** A372 50c multicolored .70 .25
**826** A373 80c Triangulation pyramid, theodolite, map 1.10 .90
**827** A374 90c multicolored 1.30 1.10
*Nos. 824-827 (4)* 3.55 2.65

*Metamecanique,* by Jean Tinguely — A375

**1988, Nov. 25 Photo. Perf. 13x12½**

**828** A375 90c multicolored 3.75 3.00

See France No. 2137.

Military Post, Cent. — A376

Delemont Municipal Charter, 700th Anniv. A377

Public Transport Assoc., Cent. — A378

Rhaetian Railway, Cent. — A379

Great St. Bernard Pass Bimillennium A380

25c, Army postman. 35c, Fontaine du Sauvage & the Porte au Loup, Delemont. 50c, Eye, modes of transportation. 80c, Train, viaduct. 90c, St. Bernard dog, statue of saint, hospice on summit.

**1989, Mar. 2 Photo. Perf. 12x11½**

**829** A376 25c multicolored .45 .25
**830** A377 35c multicolored .55 .40
**831** A378 50c multicolored .75 .25
**832** A379 80c multicolored 1.25 1.00
**833** A380 90c multicolored 1.50 1.10
*Nos. 829-833 (5)* 4.50 3.00

Europa — A381

Industry — A382

Children's games: 50c, Hopscotch. 90c, Blindman's buff.

**1989, May 23 Perf. 11½**

**834** A381 50c multicolored .60 .50
**835** A381 90c multicolored 1.50 1.25

**Engr., Litho. & Eng. (2.80, 3, 3.60, 4, 5fr)**

**1989-94 Perf. 13x13½**

**842** A382 2.75fr Bricklayer 3.50 2.25
**843** A382 2.80fr Cook 3.75 2.40
**844** A382 3fr Cabinet maker 3.75 1.75
**845** A382 3.60fr Pharmacist 4.75 3.00
**846** A382 3.75fr Fisherman 4.50 3.50
**847** A382 4fr Wine grower 5.25 3.00
**848** A382 5fr Cheesemaker 6.50 4.00
**849** A382 5.50fr Dressmaker 6.50 4.00
*Nos. 842-849 (8)* 38.50 23.90

Issued: 2.75fr, 5.50fr, 8/29/89; 3.75fr, 3/6/90; 2.80fr, 3.60fr, 1/24/92; 5fr, 9/7/93; 4fr, 3/15/94; 3fr, 7/5/94.

Swiss Electricians' Assoc., Cent. — A383

Swiss Travel Fund, 50th Anniv. A384

Fribourg University, Cent. — A385

Opening of the Natl. Sound-Recording Archives, 1st Anniv. — A386

Interparliamentary Union, Cent. — A387

**1989, Aug. 25 Photo. Perf. 11½**

**851** A383 35c multicolored .55 .45
**852** A384 50c multicolored .75 .25
**853** A385 80c "Wisdom" and "Science" 1.20 .80
**854** A386 90c multicolored 1.30 1.00
**855** A387 140c multicolored 1.75 1.25
*Nos. 851-855 (5)* 5.55 3.75

Union of Swiss Philatelic Societies, Cent. — A388

Urban Railway System, Zurich A389

Assistance for Mountain Communities, 50th Anniv. A390

1990 World Ice Hockey Championships — A391

**1990, Mar. 6**

**856** A388 25c 5c maroon type A19, 50c stamp type A20 .40 .20
**857** A389 35c Locomotives .75 .40
**858** A390 50c Mountain farmer .70 .30
**859** A391 90c Athletes 1.25 1.00
*Nos. 856-859 (4)* 3.10 1.90

Europa 1990 — A393

Post offices.

**Litho. & Engr.**

**1990, May 22 Perf. 13½**

**861** A393 50c Lucerne .75 .25
**862** A393 90c Geneva 1.90 1.25

Conrad Ferdinand Meyer (1825-1898), Writer — A394

Designs: 50c, Angelika Kaufmann (1741-1807), painter. 80c, Blaise Cendrars (1887-1961), journalist. 90c, Frank Buchser (1828-1890), artist.

**1990, Sept. 5 Litho.**

**863** A394 35c green & blk .55 .40
**864** A394 50c blue & blk .75 .30
**865** A394 80c yellow & blk 1.20 .80
**866** A394 90c vermilion & blk 1.50 1.10
*Nos. 863-866 (4)* 4.00 2.60

Swiss Confederation, 700th Anniv. in 1991 — A395

**1990, Sept. 5 Photo. Perf. 11½**

**867** A395 50c shown .75 .40
**868** A395 90c multi, diff. 1.60 1.25

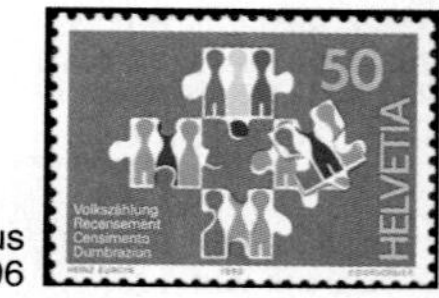
Natl. Census A396

**1990, Nov. 20**

**869** A396 50c multicolored .75 .40

Animals — A397

**1990-95 Litho. & Engr. Perf. 13**

**870** A397 10c Cow .30 .25
**871** A397 50c House cats .70 .30
**872** A397 70c Rabbit 1.00 .65
  *a.* Booklet pane of 10 12.00
  Complete booklet, #872a 12.00
**873** A397 80c Barn owls 1.10 .60
**874** A397 100c Horses 1.30 .80
**875** A397 110c Geese 1.60 .60
**876** A397 120c Dog 1.75 1.00
**877** A397 140c Sheep 2.00 .75
**878** A397 150c Goats 2.00 .75
**879** A397 160c Turkey 2.00 1.25
**880** A397 170c Donkey 2.50 .90
**881** A397 200c Chickens 3.00 1.75
*Nos. 870-881 (12)* 19.25 9.60

Issued: 50c, 3/6/90; 70c, 80c, 1/15/91; 10c, 160c, 1/24/92; 100c, 120c, 3/16/93; 150c, 200c, 7/5/94; #872a, 110c, 140c, 170c, 11/28/95.

This is an expanding set. Nos. 882-883 will be used for high values if necessary.

Swiss Confederation, 700th Anniv. — A398

Swiss Parliament, US Capitol A399

**1991, Feb. 22 Photo. Perf. 12**

**884** A398 50c "700 jahre" .80 .25
**885** A398 50c "700 onns" .80 .25
**886** A398 50c "700 ans" .80 .25
**887** A398 50c "700 anni" .80 .25
  *a.* Block of 4, #884-887 3.25 1.00
**888** A399 1.60fr multicolored 2.50 .80
*Nos. 884-888 (5)* 5.70 1.80

See US No. 2532.

Bern, 800th Anniv. — A400

**1991, Feb. 22** ***Perf. 11½***
**889** A400 80c multicolored 1.25 .60

Europa — A401

**1991, May 14 Litho.** ***Perf. 11½***
**890** A401 50c Ariane payload fairing 1.00 .25
**891** A401 90c Giotto probe 1.75 1.00

Union of Postal, Telephone and Telegraph Officials, Cent. — A402

**1991, Sept. 10 Photo.** ***Perf. 11½***
**892** A402 80c multicolored 1.20 .70

Bridges A403

Designs: 50c, Stone bridge near Lavertezzo. 70c, Wooden "New Bridge" near Bremgarten. 80c, Railway bridge between Koblenz and Felsenau. 90c, Ganter Bridge, Simplon Pass.

**1991, Sept. 10**
**893** A403 50c multicolored .75 .25
**894** A403 70c multicolored 1.10 .55
**895** A403 80c multicolored 1.30 .75
**896** A403 90c multicolored 1.50 .90
*Nos. 893-896 (4)* 4.65 2.45

Mountain Lakes — A404

A404a

A404b

Design: 60c, Lake de Tanay.

**Litho., Litho. & Engr. (60c, #908)**
**1991-95** ***Perf. 13½x13***
**904** A404 50c blue & multi .70 .20
**905** A404 60c blue & multi .90 .25
*a.* Booklet pane of 10 8.50
**907** A404 80c red & multi, diff. 1.10 .50
**908** A404a 80c multicolored 1.10 .40
**909** A404b 90c multicolored 1.50 .75
*a.* Booklet pane of 10 15.00
Complete booklet, #909a 15.00
*Nos. 904-909 (5)* 5.30 2.10

Issued: 50c, #907, 12/16/91; 60c, #908, 1/19/993; 90c, 11/28/95.
See No. 1102.

Bird Over Rhine River — A405

Faces of Parents, Child — A406

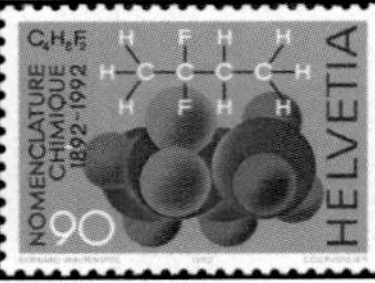


Molecular Formula, Structure and Model A407

**1992, Mar. 24 Photo.** ***Perf. 11½***
**911** A405 50c multicolored .70 .25
**912** A406 80c multicolored 1.20 .60
**913** A407 90c multicolored 1.20 1.00
*Nos. 911-913 (3)* 3.10 1.85

Intl. Rhine Regulation, cent. (No. 911), Pro Familia Switzerland, 50th anniv. (No. 912), Intl. Chemical Nomenclature Conf., Geneva, cent. (No. 913).

A408

A409

Europa: 90c, Columbus, map of voyage.

**1992, Mar. 24**
**914** A408 50c multicolored 1.00 .50
**915** A408 90c multicolored 2.00 1.10

Discovery of America, 500th anniv.

**1992, May 22 Photo.** ***Perf. 12***
**916** A409 90c multicolored 1.30 .90

Protect the Alps.
See Austria No. 1571.

Comic Strips A410

**1992, May 22** ***Perf. 11½***
**917** A410 50c Cosey .70 .30
**918** A410 80c Zep 1.20 .60
**919** A410 90c Aloys 1.40 1.00
*Nos. 917-919 (3)* 3.30 1.90

World of the Circus A411

50c, Clowns on trapeze. 70c, Sea lion, clown. 80c, Clown, elephant. 90c, Lipizzaner, harlequin.

**1992, Aug. 25 Photo.** ***Perf. 12x11½***
**920** A411 50c multicolored .75 .30
**921** A411 70c multicolored 1.10 .60
**922** A411 80c multicolored 1.20 .60
**923** A411 90c multicolored 1.40 1.00
*Nos. 920-923 (4)* 4.45 2.50

Central Office for Intl. Carriage by Rail, Cent. (in 1993) — A412

**1992, Nov. 24 Photo.** ***Perf. 11½***
**924** A412 90c multicolored 1.40 .75

First Swiss Postage Stamps, 150th Anniv. — A413

Designs: 60c, Zurich Types A1, A2, Geneva Type A1. 80c, Stylized canceled stamp. 100c, Stylized stamps on album page.

**1993, Mar. 16 Photo.** ***Perf. 11½***
**925** A413 60c multicolored 1.00 .50
**926** A413 80c multicolored 1.25 .60
**927** A413 100c multicolored 1.50 1.00
*Nos. 925-927 (3)* 3.75 2.10

Paracelsus (1493-1541), Physician A414

Opening of Olympic Museum, Lausanne A415

Intl. Metalworkers' Federation, Cent. — A416

**1993, Mar. 16 Photo.** ***Perf. 11½***
**928** A414 60c blue & sepia .90 .35
**929** A415 80c multicolored 1.20 .75
**930** A416 180c multicolored 2.60 1.75
*Nos. 928-930 (3)* 4.70 2.85

Lake Constance Steamer Hohentwiel A417

**1993, May 5 Photo.** ***Perf. 11½x12***
**931** A417 60c multicolored .95 .50

See Austria No. 1598, Germany No. 1786.

Contemporary Architecture A418

Europa: 60c, Media House, Villeurbanne, France. 80c, House, Breganzona, Switzerland.

**Litho. & Engr.**
**1993, May 5** ***Perf. 13½***
**932** A418 60c multicolored .90 .40
**933** A418 80c red & black 1.30 .90

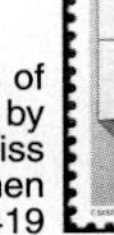

Works of Art by Swiss Women A419

Designs: 60c, Work No. 095, by Emma Kunz. 80c, Grande Cantatrice Lilas Goergens, by Aloise Corbaz. 100c, Under the Rain Cloud, by Meret Oppenheim. 120c, Four Spaces in Horizontal Bands, by Sophie Taeuber-Arp.

**1993, Sept. 7 Photo.** ***Perf. 11½***
**934** A419 60c multicolored .90 .40

**Size: 33x33½mm**
**935** A419 80c multicolored 1.20 .75
**936** A419 100c multicolored 1.50 1.00
**937** A419 120c multicolored 2.00 1.25
*Nos. 934-937 (4)* 5.60 3.40

Swiss Sports School, 50th Anniv. A420

Jakob Bernoulli (1654-1705), Mathematician A421

Swiss Telecom PTT Participation in Unisource A422

ICAO, 50th Anniv. A423

**1994, Mar. 15 Photo.** ***Perf. 11½***
**938** A420 60c multicolored .90 .40
**939** A421 80c multicolored 1.25 .45
**940** A422 100c multicolored 1.50 .85
**941** A423 180c multicolored 2.75 1.25
*Nos. 938-941 (4)* 6.40 2.95

Intl. Congress of Mathematicians, Zurich (#939).

"Books and the Press" Exhibition, Geneva A424

**1994, Mar. 15**
**942** A424 60c Early manuscripts .95 .40
**943** A424 80c Letterpress 1.25 .75
**944** A424 100c Electronic publishing 1.50 1.00
*Nos. 942-944 (3)* 3.70 2.15

1994 World Cup Soccer Championships, U.S. — A425

**1994, Mar. 15**
**945** A425 80c multicolored 1.20 .65

Research Vehicles of August & Jacques Piccard — A426

Europa: 60c, Bathyscaphe Trieste. 100c, Stratospheric balloon.

**1994, May 17 Photo. *Perf. 12***

| | | | | |
|---|---|---|---|---|
| **946** | A426 | 60c multicolored | 1.00 | .50 |
| **947** | A426 | 100c multicolored | 1.90 | 1.00 |

Georges Simenon (1903-89), Writer A427

**Litho. & Engr.**

**1994, Oct. 15 *Perf. 13***

| | | | | |
|---|---|---|---|---|
| **948** | A427 | 100c multicolored | 1.50 | .90 |

See Belgium No. 1567, France No. 2443.

A428

A429

**1994, Oct. 15 Photo. *Perf. 11½***

| | | | | |
|---|---|---|---|---|
| **949** | A428 | 60c multicolored | .95 | .35 |

Campaign to stop AIDS.

**1995, Mar. 7 Photo. *Perf. 11½***

Endangered species.

| | | | | |
|---|---|---|---|---|
| **950** | A429 | 60c European beaver | .90 | .30 |
| **951** | A429 | 80c Map butterfly | 1.25 | .50 |
| **952** | A429 | 100c Green tree frog | 1.50 | .75 |
| **953** | A429 | 120c Litte owl | 1.90 | .90 |
| | | *Nos. 950-953 (4)* | 5.55 | 2.45 |

Swiss Wrestling Assoc., Cent. — A430

Swiss Assoc. of Producers & Distributors of Electricity, Cent. — A431

Swiss News Agency, Cent. — A432

UN, 50th Anniv. A433

**1995, Mar. 7**

| | | | | |
|---|---|---|---|---|
| **954** | A430 | 60c blue & black | 1.00 | .55 |
| **955** | A431 | 60c multicolored | 1.00 | .55 |
| **956** | A432 | 80c multicolored | 1.25 | 1.50 |
| **957** | A433 | 180c multicolored | 2.50 | 1.75 |
| | | *Nos. 954-957 (4)* | 5.75 | 4.35 |

Peace & Freedom A434

Europa: 60c, Dove, faces. 100c, Zeus disguised as bull, abducting Europa, daughter of King of Phoenicia.

**Litho., Engr. & Embossed**

**1995, May 16 *Perf. 13***

| | | | | |
|---|---|---|---|---|
| **958** | A434 | 60c lt blue & dk blue | 1.00 | .40 |
| **959** | A434 | 100c orange & brown | 1.75 | .85 |

Switzerland-Liechtenstein Postal Relationship A435

**Litho. & Engr.**

**1995, Sept. 5 *Perf. 13½***

| | | | | |
|---|---|---|---|---|
| **960** | A435 | 60c multicolored | .90 | .50 |

See Liechtenstein No. 1055.

No. 960 and Liechtenstein No. 1055 are identical. This issue was valid for postage in both countries.

Motion Pictures, Cent. — A436

Scenes from motion pictures: 60c, La Vocation d'Andre Carrel. 80c, Anna Goldin-The Last Witch. 150c, Pipilotti's Mistakes-Absolution.

**1995, Sept. 5 Photo. *Perf. 11½***

| | | | | |
|---|---|---|---|---|
| **961** | A436 | 60c multicolored | .90 | .40 |
| **962** | A436 | 80c multicolored | 1.20 | .70 |
| **963** | A436 | 150c multicolored | 2.00 | 1.25 |
| | | *Nos. 961-963 (3)* | 4.10 | 2.35 |

Telecom '95, Geneva — A437

**1995, Sept. 5**

| | | | | |
|---|---|---|---|---|
| **964** | A437 | 180c multicolored | 3.00 | 1.00 |

Swiss Charities, Solidarity Chain, 50th Anniv. A438

Touring Club, Cent. — A439

Federal Music Festival, Interlaken A440

Swiss Natl. Assoc. Pro Filia, Cent. — A441

Jean Piaget (1896-1980), Psychologist A442

**1996, Mar. 12 Photo. *Perf. 11½***

| | | | | |
|---|---|---|---|---|
| **965** | A438 | 70c multicolored | 1.00 | .50 |
| **966** | A439 | 70c multicolored | 1.00 | .50 |
| **967** | A440 | 90c multicolored | 1.40 | .60 |
| **968** | A441 | 90c multicolored | 1.40 | .60 |
| **969** | A442 | 180c multicolored | 2.50 | 2.00 |
| | | *Nos. 965-969 (5)* | 7.30 | 4.20 |

Famous Women — A443

Europa: 70c, S. Corinna Bille (1912-79), author. 110c, Iris von Roten-Meyer (1917-90), writer, painter.

**Litho. & Engr.**

**1996, May 14 *Perf. 13½***

| | | | | |
|---|---|---|---|---|
| **970** | A443 | 70c multicolored | 1.00 | .50 |
| **971** | A443 | 110c multicolored | 1.60 | 1.10 |

Modern Olympic Games, Cent. — A444

**1996, May 14 Litho. *Perf. 13½***

| | | | | |
|---|---|---|---|---|
| **972** | A444 | 180c multicolored | 3.00 | 1.50 |

Guinness Record Stamp — A445

Design: Aerial view of 11,000 gymnasts arranged as No. 909, making record as world's largest living postage stamp.

**1996, June 27 Litho. *Perf. 13½x13***

| | | | | |
|---|---|---|---|---|
| **973** | A445 | 90c multicolored | 1.75 | .80 |

Greeting Stamps A446

Various ornate or floral patterns.

***Serpentine Die Cut 7 Vert.***

**1996, Sept. 10 Typo.**

**Self-Adhesive**

**Booklet Stamps**

| | | | | |
|---|---|---|---|---|
| **974** | A446 | 90c yellow & black | 1.50 | 1.00 |
| **975** | A446 | 90c blue & multi | 1.50 | 1.00 |
| **976** | A446 | 90c red & multi | 1.50 | 1.00 |
| **977** | A446 | 90c green & multi | 1.50 | 1.00 |
| *a.* | | Booklet pane of 4, #974-977 | 6.00 | |
| | | Complete booklet, 2 #977a | 12.00 | |

Music Boxes and Automata A447

Designs: 70c, Ring with mechanical figures, musical movement, by Isaac-Daniel Piguet. 90c, Basso-piccolo mandolin cylinder music box, by Eduard Jaccard. 110c, Station automaton, by Paillard and Co. 180c, Kalliope disk music box.

**1996, Sept. 10 Photo. *Perf. 11½***

| | | | | |
|---|---|---|---|---|
| **978** | A447 | 70c multicolored | 1.10 | .40 |
| **979** | A447 | 90c multicolored | 1.40 | .60 |
| **980** | A447 | 110c multicolored | 1.75 | 1.00 |
| **981** | A447 | 180c multicolored | 2.75 | 1.50 |
| | | *Nos. 978-981 (4)* | 7.00 | 3.50 |

Stamp Design Competition Winners — A448

Designs: 70c, Golden cow. 90c, Smiling creature. 110c, Leaves. 180c, Dove.

**1996, Nov. 26 Photo. *Perf. 11½***

| | | | | |
|---|---|---|---|---|
| **982** | A448 | 70c blue & bister | 1.10 | .55 |
| **983** | A448 | 90c multicolored | 1.40 | .80 |
| **984** | A448 | 110c multicolored | 1.75 | 1.00 |
| **985** | A448 | 180c multicolored | 2.75 | 1.75 |
| | | *Nos. 982-985 (4)* | 7.00 | 4.10 |

"Globi" as Postman A449

**1997, Mar. 11 Litho. *Perf. 13x13½***

| | | | | |
|---|---|---|---|---|
| **986** | A449 | 70c multicolored | 1.20 | .45 |

Swiss Railways, 150th Anniv. A450

Designs: 70c, Locomotive 2000, 1990's. 90c, Red Arrow, 1930's. 140c, Pullman coach, 1920's-30's. 170c, Limmat steam locomotive, 1800's.

**1997, Mar. 11 Photo. *Perf. 11½***

| | | | | |
|---|---|---|---|---|
| **987** | A450 | 70c multicolored | 1.10 | .40 |
| **988** | A450 | 90c multicolored | 1.40 | .55 |
| **989** | A450 | 140c multicolored | 2.25 | 1.25 |
| **990** | A450 | 170c multicolored | 2.50 | 1.75 |
| | | *Nos. 987-990 (4)* | 7.25 | 3.95 |

Gallo-Roman Art — A451

Archaeological finds: 70c, Venus of Octodurus. 90c, Bronze bust of Bacchus. 110c, Ceramic fragment depicting Victoria. 180c, Mosaic theatrical mask.

**1997, Mar. 11**

| | | | | |
|---|---|---|---|---|
| **991** | A451 | 70c multicolored | 1.10 | .40 |
| **992** | A451 | 90c multicolored | 1.40 | .50 |
| **993** | A451 | 110c multicolored | 1.60 | .80 |
| **994** | A451 | 180c multicolored | 2.50 | 1.25 |
| | | *Nos. 991-994 (4)* | 6.60 | 2.95 |

Swiss Air's North Atlantic Service, 50th Anniv. — A452

**1997, Mar. 11 Litho. *Perf. 13½***
**995** A452 180c multicolored 2.75 1.10

Swiss Farmers' Union, Cent. — A453

**1997, May 13 Litho. *Perf. 13½***
**996** A453 70c shown 1.10 .35
**997** A453 90c Street map 1.30 .65

Swiss Municipalities' Union, cent. (#997).

Stories and Legends — A454

Europa: Devil and Billy Goat from legend of the "Devil's Bridge."

**1997, May 13 Litho. & Engr.**
**998** A454 90c multicolored 1.40 1.10

King of Thailand's Visit to Switzerland, Cent. — A455

King Chulalongkorn (Rama V), Pres. Adolf Deucher.

**1997, Sept. 12 Litho. *Perf. 13½***
**999** A455 90c multicolored 1.25 .75

Energy 2000 — A456

**1997, Sept. 12 Photo. *Perf. 11½***
**1000** A456 70c Air (clouds) 1.00 .35
**1001** A456 90c Fire 1.40 .65
**1002** A456 110c Water 1.60 .95
**1003** A456 180c Earth 2.75 1.50
*Nos. 1000-1003 (4)* 6.75 3.45

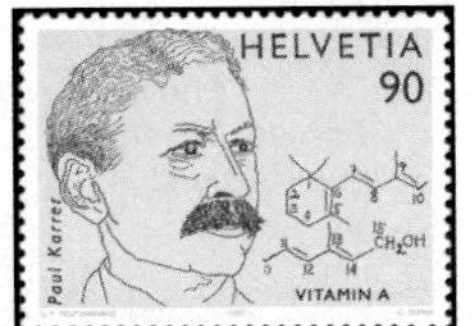

Paul Karrer (1889-1971), Winner of Nobel Prize for Chemistry, 1937 — A457

Design: 110c, Alfred Nobel (1833-96), founder of Nobel Prize.

**Litho. & Engr.**

**1997, Nov. 13 *Perf. 13***
**1004** A457 90c gray & blk 1.40 .50
**1005** A457 110c lt gray brn & blk 1.75 .75

Nos. 1004-1005 each issued in sheets of 8. See Sweden Nos. 2254-2255.

Swiss Postal Service A458

Various people from different generations, cultures. Each stamp inscribed in one of Switzerland's four national languages with message to keep in touch.

**1997, Nov. 20 Litho. *Perf. 13***
**Color of Denomination**
**1006** A458 70c blue 1.00 .40
**1007** A458 70c yellow 1.00 .40
**1008** A458 70c green 1.00 .40
**1009** A458 70c red 1.00 .40
*a.* Strip of 4, #1006-1009 3.25 1.40

Division of Swiss PTT — A459

**1998, Jan. 7 Litho. *Perf. 13½***
**1010** A459 90c Swisscom 1.10 .40
**1011** A459 90c Swiss Post 1.10 .40

Confederation, 150th Anniv. and Helvetic Republic, Bicent. — A460

Stylized design, proclamation in one of four languages, location of denomination: No. 1012, German, LL. No. 1013, Romansch, LR. No. 1014, French, UL. No. 1015, Italian, UR.

**1998, Mar. 10 Photo. *Perf. 11½***
**1012** A460 90c multicolored 1.40 1.00
**1013** A460 90c multicolored 1.40 1.00
**1014** A460 90c multicolored 1.40 1.00
**1015** A460 90c multicolored 1.40 1.00
*a.* Block of 4, #1012-1015 5.75 5.00

Printed in continuous design.

Swiss Old Age and Survivors' Insurance, 50th Anniv. A461

Opening of Natl. Museum, Prangins Castle A462

St. Gallen University, Cent. — A463

**1998, Mar. 10**
**1016** A461 70c multicolored 1.00 .40
**1017** A462 70c multicolored 1.00 .40
**1018** A463 90c multicolored 1.40 .80
*Nos. 1016-1018 (3)* 3.40 1.60

View of Switzerland A464

Designs: 10c, Simplon Pass. 20c, Snow-covered winter scene. 50c, Fence posts along country road. 70c, Hobbyhorses, posts. 90c, Stream, route marker. 110c, Lake, shoreline.

**1998, Mar. 10 Litho. *Perf. 13x13½***
**1019** A464 10c multicolored .20 .20
**1020** A464 20c multicolored .30 .20
**1021** A464 50c multicolored .70 .30
**1022** A464 70c multicolored 1.00 .30
**1023** A464 90c multicolored 1.40 .30
**1024** A464 110c multicolored 1.60 .75
*Nos. 1019-1024 (6)* 5.20 2.05

See Nos. 1027-1029.

Sion, Candidate for 2006 Winter Olympic Games — A465

**1998, Feb. 12 Litho. *Perf. 13½***
**1025** A465 90c multicolored 1.40 .75

National Day — A466

**1998, May 12**
**1026** A466 90c multicolored 1.25 1.10

Europa.

**View of Switzerland Type of 1998**

140c, City of Zug. 170c, Olive grove, Castagnola. 180c, Road, mountains outside Reutigen.

**1998, Sept. 8 Litho. *Perf. 13***
**1027** A464 140c multicolored 1.90 .50
**1028** A464 170c multicolored 2.50 .60
**1029** A464 180c multicolored 2.75 .75
*Nos. 1027-1029 (3)* 7.15 1.85

Youth Sports — A467

***Die Cut x Serpentine Die Cut***

**1998, Sept. 8 Photo.**
**Self-Adhesive**
**Booklet Stamps**
**1030** A467 70c Roller blading 1.10 .50
**1031** A467 70c Snow boarding 1.10 .50
**1032** A467 70c Mountain biking 1.10 .50
**1033** A467 70c Street basketball 1.10 .50
**1034** A467 70c Beach volleyball 1.10 .50
*a.* Booklet pane, #1030-1034 + label 5.50
Complete booklet, 2 #1034a 11.00

Universal Declaration of Human Rights, 50th Anniv. — A468

**1998, Nov. 25 Litho. *Perf. 13½***
**1035** A468 70c multicolored 1.10 .50

Christmas A469

**1998, Nov. 25**
**1036** A469 90c multicolored 1.40 .75

Bridge 24, Slender West Lake, Yangzhou A470

Chillon Castle, Lake Geneva A470A

**Photo. & Engr.**

**1998, Nov. 25 *Perf. 13½***
**1037** A470 20c multicolored .30 .20

**Photo.**
**1038** A470A 70c multicolored 1.00 .55
*a.* Sheet of 4 each, #1038-1039 5.25 5.00

**Souvenir Sheet**
***Perf. 11½***
**1039** A470A 90c Castle, Bridge 24 1.50 1.50

No. 1039 contains one 53x45mm stamp. See China (PRC) Nos. 2920-2921.

No. 1039 exists with China 1999 World Philatelic Exhibition emblem and a hologram in margin. These were sold for 3.50fr only canceled on cover.

Switzerland Post, 150th Anniv. A471

**1999, Jan. 21 Photo. *Perf. 12***
**1040** A471 90c multicolored 1.40 .75

Pingu the Penguin as Postman A472

**1999, Mar. 9 Litho. *Perf. 13½***
**1041** A472 70c Carrying package 1.00 .50
**1042** A472 90c In delivery cart 1.40 .65

See Nos. 1064-1065 for redrawn designs.

Comic Book, "Les Amours de Monsieur Vieux Bois," by Rodolphe Töpffer (1799-1846) A473

Vieux Bois: No. 1043, Waving out of window, lady walking away. No. 1044, Down on knees, lady. No. 1045, In air after knocking over furniture. No. 1046, Pulling lady up to lift her over wall. No. 1047, Standing with his lady to be married.

***Die Cut x Serpentine Die Cut***

**1999, Mar. 9**
**Self-Adhesive**
**Booklet Stamps**
**1043** A473 90c multicolored 1.40 .55
**1044** A473 90c multicolored 1.40 .55
**1045** A473 90c multicolored 1.40 .55
**1046** A473 90c multicolored 1.40 .55
**1047** A473 90c multicolored 1.40 .55
*a.* Booklet pane, #1043-1047 + label 7.00
Complete booklet, 2 #1047a 15.00

First Non-stop Balloon Flight Around World by Bertrand Piccard and Brian Jones — A473a

**1999, Mar. 24 Litho. *Perf. 13½***
**1047B** A473a 90c multicolored 1.40 .55

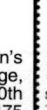

UPU, 125th Anniv. — A474

**1999, May 5 Photo. *Perf. 12***
**1048** A474 20c shown .35 .25
**1049** A474 70c UPU emblem 1.00 .65
*a.* Pair, #1048-1049 1.35 1.25

No. 1049 is 56x30mm. Issued in sheets of 8 stamps.

SOS Children's Village, Wabern, 50th Anniv. — A475

**1999, May 5 Litho. *Perf. 13½***
**1050** A475 70c multicolored 1.00 .45

Vintners Festival, Vevey — A476

**1999, May 5**
**1051** A476 90c multicolored 1.40 .55
Complete booklet, 10 #1051 14.00

Council of Europe, 50th Anniv. — A477

**1999, May 5 Photo. *Perf. 11½***
**1052** A477 90c multicolored 1.40 .55

Swiss National Park — A478

**1999, May 5 Litho. *Perf. 13½***
**1053** A478 90c Horns of an ibex 1.40 1.10

Europa.

Geneva Convention, 50th Anniv. — A479

**1999, May 5**
**1054** A479 110c multicolored 1.75 .85

Field Marshal Aleksandr Suvorov's Alpine Campaign, 200th Anniv. A481

Designs: 70c, Suvorov and soldiers, monument at Schöllenen Gorge. 110c, Suvorov's vanguard by Lake Klöntal.

**1999, Sept. 24 Photo. *Perf. 11¾***
**1056** A481 70c multicolored 1.10 .50
**1057** A481 110c multicolored 1.75 .70

Nos. 1056-1057 each issued in sheets of 8 stamps.
See Russia Nos. 6534-6535.

Rights of the Child — A482

**1999, Sept. 24 Litho. *Perf. 13½***
**1058** A482 70c multicolored 1.00 .45

Carl Lutz (1895-1975), Diplomat, Rescuer of Jews — A483

**1999, Sept. 24**
**1059** A483 90c multicolored 1.40 .55

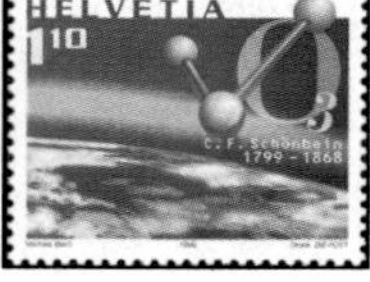

Christian Friedrich Schönbein (1799-1868), Discoverer of Ozone — A484

**1999, Sept. 24**
**1060** A484 1.10fr multicolored 1.60 .60

Midday in the Alps, by Giovanni Segantini (1858-99) A485

**1999, Sept. 24**
**1061** A485 180c multicolored 2.75 1.25

Christmas — A486

***Perf. 13½x13¼***
**1999, Nov. 23 Litho.**
**1062** A486 90c multicolored 1.40 .75

Millennium A487

***Perf. 11¾x11½***
**1999, Nov. 23 Photo.**
**1063** A487 90c multicolored 1.40 .55

No. 1063 was printed in sheets of 8 stamps and 8 se-tenant labels with text or blank. Swiss Post offered to print photos or artwork sent in by customers on the blank labels. Personalized sheets sold for 14fr per sheet.

**Pingu The Penguin Type of 1999**
Redrawn to Omit Strings on Packages

**1999, Dec. 6 Litho. *Perf. 13¼x13½***
**1064** A472 70c Like #1041 1.10 .55
**1065** A472 90c Like #1042 1.40 .70

Intl. Cycling Union, Cent. — A488

**2000, Mar. 7 Litho. *Perf. 13¼x13½***
**1066** A488 70c multicolored 1.00 .40

Swiss Souvenirs — A489

Souvenirs in snow domes: 10c, Alphorn. 20c, Fondue pot. 30c, Wine pitchers. 50c, Figurine of ibex. 60c, Neuchâtel "Pendule" wall clock. 70c, St. Bernard dog.

**2000, Mar. 7 Litho. *Perf. 13x13¼***
**1067** A489 10c multicolored .20 .20
**1068** A489 20c multicolored .30 .20
**1069** A489 30c multicolored .45 .35
**1070** A489 50c multicolored .75 .45
**1071** A489 60c multicolored .85 .50
**1072** A489 70c multicolored 1.10 .60
*Nos. 1067-1072 (6)* 3.65 2.30

See No. 1101.

National Council of Women, Cent. A490

**2000, May 10 Litho. *Perf. 13¼***
**1073** A490 70c multi 1.10 .55

**Europa, 2000**
Common Design Type

**2000, May 10**
**1074** CD17 90c multi 1.25 .75

Embroidery — A491

Illustration reduced.

**Embroidered**
**2000, June 21 *Imperf.***
**Self-Adhesive**
**1075** A491 5fr multi 12.00 12.00
*a.* Sheet of 4 175.00 175.00

A492

Designs: 120c, Payerne Church, violin. 130c, Church of St. Saphorin, waiter's tray. 180c, Vals hot springs, bather.

**2000, June 21 Litho. *Perf. 13x13¼***
**1076** A492 120c multi 1.75 .75
**1077** A492 130c multi 1.90 .80
**1078** A492 180c multi 2.50 1.00
*Nos. 1076-1078 (3)* 6.15 2.55

See Nos. 1089-1092.

2000 Census — A493

**2000, Sept. 15 *Perf. 13¼x13½***
**1079** A493 70c multi 1.00 .55

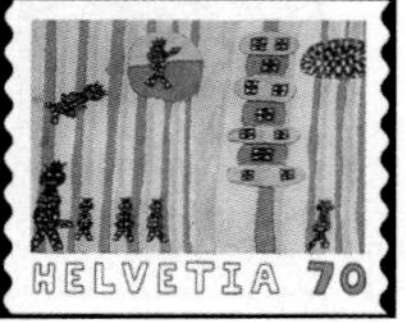

A Perfect World, by Sandra Dobler A494

My Town, by Stephanie Aerschmann A495

Stampin' the Future children's stamp design contest winners: No. 1080, Alien From Outer Space, by Yannik Kehrli. No. 1081, Looks Below the Sun, by Charlotte Bättig.

***Serpentine Die Cut 5¾ Vert.***
**2000, June 15**
**Booklet Stamps**
**Self-Adhesive**
**1080** A494 70c multi 1.20 .60
**1081** A494 70c multi 1.20 .60
**1082** A494 70c shown 1.20 .60
**1083** A495 70c shown 1.20 .60
*a.* Booklet pane, #1080-1083 4.75
Booklet, 2 #1083a 9.50

The booklet, which was sold unfolded, has rouletting between panes.

2000 Summer Olympics, Sydney A496

**2000, Sept. 15 Photo. *Die Cut***
**Booklet Stamps**
**Self-Adhesive**
**1084** A496 90c Swimmer 1.50 .60
**1085** A496 90c Cyclist 1.50 .60
**1086** A496 90c Runner 1.50 .60
*a.* Booklet pane, #1084-1086 4.50
Booklet, #1086a 4.50

No. 1086a is separated from booklet cover by rouletting. The booklet was sold folded.
See Nos. 1201-1202.

Stamp Day — A497

*Perf. 13¼x13½*

**2000, Nov. 21** **Litho.**
**1087** A497 70c multi 1.10 .40

Christmas — A498

**2000, Nov. 21 Photo.** ***Perf. 11½***
**Granite Paper**
**1088** A498 90c multi 1.60 .50

**Type of 2000**

Designs: 200c, Mountain, hiker. 300c, Cyclist, bridge and church, Biasca.

**2000-01 Litho.** ***Perf. 13x13¼***
**1089** A492 200c multi 3.00 2.00
**1090** A492 220c multi 3.25 2.25
**1091** A492 300c multi 4.50 3.00
**1092** A492 400c multi 6.00 3.75

Issued: 200c, 300c, 11/21/00. 220c, 400c, 3/13/01.

Alice Rivaz (1901-98), Writer — A499

*Perf. 13¼x13½*

**2001, Mar. 13** **Litho. & Engr.**
**1093** A499 70c multi 1.10 .40

Aero Club, Cent. A500

**2001, Mar. 13 Litho.** ***Perf. 13¼***
**1094** A500 90c multi 1.40 .55

Congratulations A501

**2001, Mar. 13** ***Perf. 13¼x13½***
**1095** A501 90c multi 1.50 .60

Caritas, Cent. — A502

**2001, Mar. 13**
**1096** A502 110c multi 1.60 .75

UN High Commissioner for Refugees, 50th Anniv. — A503

**2001, Mar. 13**
**1097** A503 130c multi 1.90 1.00

Vela Museum, Ligornetto A504

**2001, May 9**
**1098** A504 70c multi 1.10 .50

Europa — A505

**2001, May 9**
**1099** A505 90c multi 1.40 .60

Chocosuisse, Cent. — A506

**2001, May 9 Photo.** ***Perf. 11½***
**Granite Paper**
**1100** A506 90c multi 1.40 .50

No. 1100 has a scratch-and-sniff coating with a chocolate aroma.

**Swiss Souvenirs Type of 2000**
***Serpentine Die Cut 5¾ Horiz.***
**2001, May 9** **Litho.**
**Self-Adhesive**
**1101** A489 70c Like #1072 1.10 .40
*a.* Booklet of 12 13.00

**Type of 1995**
***Serpentine Die Cut 5¾ Vert.***
**2001, May 9** **Typo.**
**Self-Adhesive**
**1102** A404b 90c multi 1.40 .45
*a.* Booklet of 12 16.50

**Type of 2000**

Designs: 90c, Farm house, Willisau, people feeding horse. 100c, Boat on Lake Geneva, woman at water's edge. 110c, Kleine Matterhorn Glacier, skier.

**2001, Sept. 20 Litho.** ***Perf. 13x13¼***
**1103** A492 90c multi 1.40 .50
**1104** A492 100c multi 1.50 .50
**1105** A492 110c multi 1.60 .60
*Nos. 1103-1105 (3)* 4.50 1.60

The Birth of Venus, by Arnold Böcklin (1827-1901) A507

**2001, Sept. 20** ***Perf. 13½***
**1106** A507 180c multi 2.50 2.00

Souvenir Sheet

Flowers — A508

**2001, Sept. 20** ***Perf. 13¼x12¾***
**1107** A508 Sheet of 4 5.75 5.50
*a.* 70c Melastoma malabathricum 1.00 .80
*b.* 90c Saraca cauliflora 1.40 .90
*c.* 110c Leontopodium alpinum 1.60 1.25
*d.* 130c Gentiana clusii 1.75 1.50

See Singapore Nos. 984-988.

Illustrations from Children's Book, "The Rainbow Fish," by Marcus Pfister — A509

**2001, Sept. 20 Photo.** ***Perf. 12¾x14***
**1108** A509 70c Fish, coral 1.10 .40
**1109** A509 90c Fish, starfish 1.40 .50

Stamp Day Stamp Design Competition Winner — A510

*Perf. 13¼x13½*

**2001, Nov. 20** **Litho.**
**1110** A510 70c multi 1.10 .45

Christmas — A511

**2001, Nov. 20** ***Perf. 11½***
**Granite Paper**
**1111** A511 90c multi 1.50 .60

Geneva Escalade, 400th Anniv. — A512

*Perf. 13¼x13½*

**2002, Mar. 12** **Litho.**
**1112** A512 70c multi 1.10 .40

Federal Parliament Building, Cent. — A513

**2002, Mar. 12**
**1113** A513 90c multi 1.40 .50

Rega Air Rescue Foundation A514

**Litho. with Hologram Affixed**
**2002, Mar. 12** ***Perf. 13x13¾***
**1114** A514 180c multi 2.75 2.00

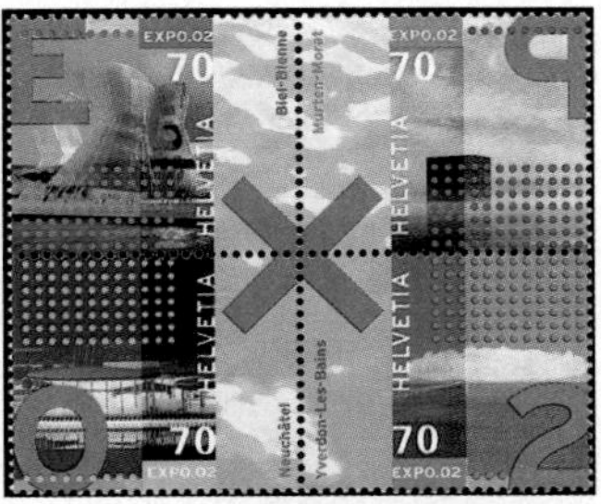

Expo.02, Switzerland — A515

No. 1115: a, "E." b, Backwards "P." c, "0." d, "2."

**2002, Mar. 12 Photo.** ***Perf. 14x13¼***
**Granite Paper**
**1115** A515 Block of 4 4.50 4.50
*a.-d.* 70c Any single 1.10 .80

Swiss Railways, Cent. — A516

Designs: 70c, RABDe 500 Inter-city tilting train. 90c, Inter-city 2000 double-deck train. 120c, Seetal line railcar. 130c, Re 460 locomotive.

**2002, Mar. 12** ***Perf. 12¾x14***
**1116** A516 70c multi 1.20 .40
**1117** A516 90c multi 1.60 .70
**1118** A516 120c multi 1.75 .75
**1119** A516 130c multi 2.00 1.00
*Nos. 1116-1119 (4)* 6.55 2.85

Souvenir Sheet

Arteplage Mobile du Jura — A517

**2002, May 15 Photo.** ***Perf. 14***
**1120** A517 90c multi 1.40 1.25

Expo.02, Switzerland.

Europa A518

**2002, May 15 Litho.** ***Perf. 13¼***
**1121** A518 70c Clown 1.10 .40
**1122** A518 90c Clown, diff. 1.40 .50

Teddy Bears, Cent. — A519

No. 1123 — Teddy bear from: a, France, 1925 (round, with tan frame, 26mm diameter).

b, Switzerland, 1950s (square with cut in corners, 25x25mm). c, Germany, 1904 (oval, 23x33mm). d, Switzerland, 2002 (rectangular, 26x23mm). e, England, c. 1920 (round, with blue and red frame, 26mm diameter).

**2002, May 15** ***Die Cut***
**Self-Adhesive**

**1123** A519 Booklet pane of 5 7.00
*a.-e.* 90c Any single 1.40 1.00
*f.* Booklet, 2 #1123 14.00

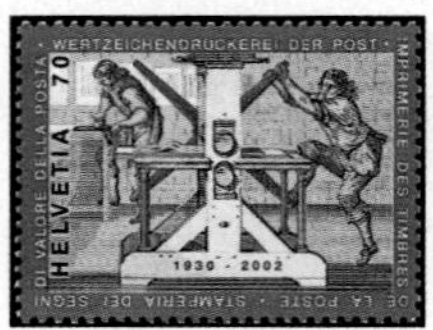


Cessation of Production at Swiss Post Stamp Printers A520

**Litho. & Engr.**
**2002, Sept. 17** ***Perf. 13¼***
**1124** A520 70c multi 1.10 .40

Ladybug — A521

Illustration reduced.

***Serpentine Die Cut 12¼ Vert.***
**2002, Sept. 17** **Litho.**
**Self-Adhesive**

**1125** A521 90c multi + label 1.40 .55
*a.* Booklet pane of 10 14.00

Insects — A522

Designs: 10c, Anax imperator. 20c, Mesoacidalia aglaja. 50c, Rosalia alpina. 100c, Graphosoma lineatum.

***Perf. 13¾x14¼***
**2002, Sept. 17** **Litho.**

**1126** A522 10c multi .20 .20
**1127** A522 20c multi .30 .20
**1128** A522 50c multi .75 .20
**1129** A522 100c multi 1.50 .30
*Nos. 1126-1129 (4)* 2.75 .90

Minerals — A523

Designs: 200c, Quartz crystal. 500c, Titanite.

**2002-05** **Litho.** ***Perf. 13¾***
**1130** A523 200c multi 3.00 1.50
**1131** A523 500c multi 7.50 2.75
*a.* Perf. 13¾x14¼ 8.00 2.75

Issued: Nos. 1130-1131, 9/17/02. No. 1131a, 5/10/05.

Switzerland's Entry Into United Nations — A524

***Perf. 13¾x14¼***
**2002, Sept. 10** **Litho.**
**1132** A524 90c multi 1.40 .50

Stamp Day — A525

**2002, Nov. 19** ***Perf. 13¾x14***
**1133** A525 70c multi 1.10 .45

World Alpine Skiing Championships, St. Moritz — A526

**2002, Nov. 19** ***Perf. 14x13¾***
**1134** A526 90c multi 1.40 .50

Emblem of Switzerland Tourism — A527

***Serpentine Die Cut 13¼ Vert.***
**2002, Nov. 19**
**Self-Adhesive**

**1135** A527 (1.30fr) blue & multi 2.00 .50
*a.* Booklet pane of 6 12.00
**1136** A527 (1.80fr) red & multi 2.75 .75
*a.* Booklet pane of 6 16.50

Nos. 1135-1136 were valid only on post cards sent to European (#1135) or non-European (#1136) addresses, and could not be used in combination with other stamps. No. 1135a sold for 7.20fr, and No. 1136a for 10fr.

Christmas — A528

**2002, Nov. 19** **Photo.** ***Perf. 11½***
**Granite Paper**
**1137** A528 90c multi 1.40 .50

Swiss Natl. Association of and for the Blind, Cent. — A529

**Litho. & Embossed**
**2003, Mar. 6** ***Perf. 14¾x14½***
**1138** A529 70c red & carmine 1.10 .45

100th Natl. Horse Market and Show, Saignelégier A530

**2003, Mar. 6** **Litho.** ***Perf. 13¼x13½***
**1139** A530 90c multi 1.40 .50

2003 World Orienteering Championships, Rapperswil and Jona — A531

**2003, Mar. 6**
**1140** A531 90c multi 1.40 .50

Intl. Year of Water A532

**2003, Mar. 6** ***Perf. 13x13¼***
**1141** A532 90c multi 1.40 .50

Medicinal Plants — A533

Designs: 70c, Hypericum perforatum. 90c, Vinca minor. 110c, Valeriana officinalis. 120c, Arnica montana. 130c, Centaurium minus. 180c, Malva sylvestris. 220c, Matricaria chamomilla.

**2003-05** ***Perf. 14x13¾***
**1142** A533 70c multi 1.10 .50
**1143** A533 90c multi 1.40 .50
**1144** A533 110c multi 1.60 .65
**1145** A533 120c multi 1.75 .75
*a.* Perf. 14x14½ 1.90 .40
**1146** A533 130c multi 1.90 .90
**1147** A533 180c multi 2.60 1.10
*a.* Perf. 14x14½ 3.00 .60
**1148** A533 220c multi 3.25 1.50
*a.* Perf. 14x14½ 3.50 .70
*Nos. 1142-1148 (7)* 13.60 5.90

Issued: Nos. 1142-1148, 3/6/03; Nos. 1145a, 1147a, 1148a, 2005.

Europa — A534

**2003, May 8** **Litho.** ***Perf. 13¼x13***
**1149** A534 90c multi 1.40 .50

Comic Strip Art — A535

No. 1150 — Envelope and: a, Woman, birthday cake. b, Man, heart. c, Man, thunder cloud. d, Woman, musical note.
90c, Envelope, woman, duck.

**2003, May 8** ***Perf. 14¾***
**1150** A535 Block of 4 4.75 4.00
*a.-d.* 70c Any single 1.10 .50

**Souvenir Sheet**
**1151** A535 90c multi 1.50 1.25

20th Intl. Comics Festival, Sierre.

Souvenir Sheet

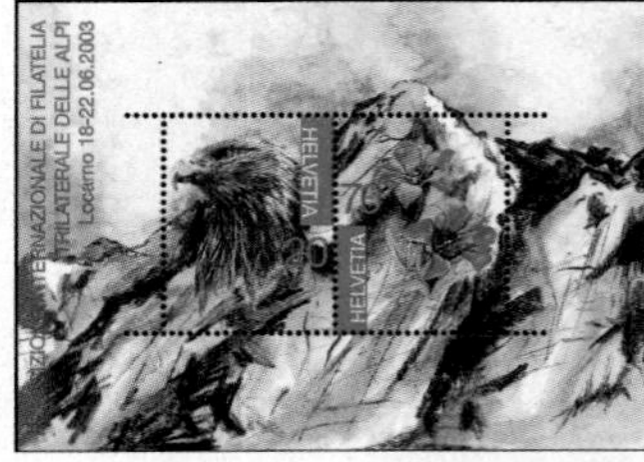


Trilateral Stamp Exhibition, Ticino — A536

**2003, May 8** ***Perf. 14¾***
**1152** A536 Sheet of 2 1.50 1.25
*a.* 20c Eagle .30 .20
*b.* 70c Gentian 1.20 .40

Switzerland's Victory in 2003 America's Cup Yacht Races — A537

**2003, Mar 7** **Litho.** ***Perf. 13x13¼***
**1153** A537 90c multi 1.40 .45

No. 1153 was not sent to standing order subscribers until September.

**Minerals Type of 2002**

Designs: 300c, Rutilated quartz. 400c, Green fluorite.

**2003, Sept. 9** ***Perf. 13¾x14¼***
**1154** A523 300c multi 4.50 2.00
**1155** A523 400c multi 5.75 3.00

Comic Strip "Diddl," by Thomas Goletz — A538

Designs: 70c, Mice reading love letters. 90c, Mouse chasing flying envelopes.

**2003, Sept. 9** ***Perf. 13¼x13½***
**1156** A538 70c multi 1.10 .45
**1157** A538 90c multi 1.40 .55

UNESCO World Heritage Sites — A539

Designs: No. 1158, Jungfrau-Aletsch-Bietschhorn. No. 1159, Three Castles, Bellinzona. No. 1160, Old City, Bern. No. 1161, Convent of St. Gall. No. 1162, Benedictine Convent of St. John, Müstair.

**2003, Sept. 9** ***Perf. 12¾***
**1158** A539 90c multi 1.40 .55
**1159** A539 90c multi 1.40 .55
**1160** A539 90c multi 1.40 .55
**1161** A539 90c multi 1.40 .55
**1162** A539 90c multi 1.40 .55
*Nos. 1158-1162 (5)* 7.00 2.75

Nos. 1158-1162 each issued in sheets of 6.

Stamp Day — A540

***Perf. 13¼x13½***
**2003, Nov. 19** **Litho.**
**1163** A540 70c multi 1.10 .45

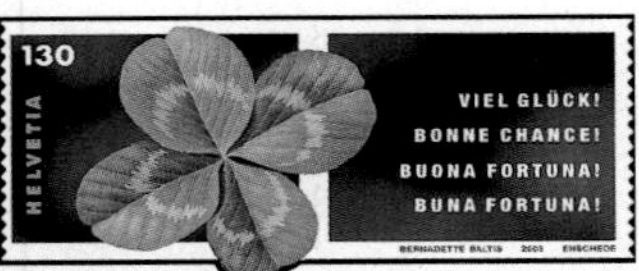

Four-leaf Clover — A541

Illustration reduced.

***Serpentine Die Cut 12¼ Vert.***

**2003, Nov. 19**

**Self-Adhesive**

**1164** A541 130c multi + label 1.90 .65
*a.* Booklet of 10 19.00

Christmas — A542

Ornaments: 70c, Horseman. 90c, Santa Claus.

**2003, Nov. 19 Photo. *Perf. 11½***

**1165** A542 70c multi 1.10 .45
**1166** A542 90c multi 1.40 .55

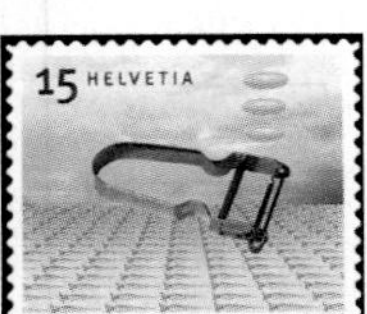

Swiss Design — A543

Designs: 15c, Rex potato peeler, 1947, designed by Alfred Neweczeral. 50c, Zipper, 1924, designed by M.O. Winterthaler. 85c, Station clock, 1944, designed by Hanls Hilfiker. No. 1169, Le Fauteuil Grand Confort (black armchair), 1928, designed by Le Corbusier. No. 1170, Landi chair (aluminum chair), 1938, designed by Hans Coray.

***Serpentine Die Cut 12***

**2003-04 Litho.**

**Self-Adhesive**

**1167** A543 15c multi .25 .20
*a.* Booklet pane of 10 2.50
**1168** A543 85c multi 1.40 .30
*a.* Booklet pane of 10 14.00
**1169** A543 100c multi + etiquette 1.60 .30
*a.* Booklet pane of 10 + 10 etiquettes 16.00
*b.* Nos. 1167-1169 on translucent paper 3.25
**1170** A543 100c multi + etiquette 1.60 .30
*a.* Booklet pane of 10 + 10 etiquettes 16.00

**Coil Stamp**

**1171** A543 50c multi .80 .20
*Nos. 1167-1171 (5)* 5.65 1.30

Issued: 15c, 85c, No. 1169, 12/30; No. 1170, 3/31/04; 50c, 9/7/04.

See No. 1206.

FIFA (Fédération Internationale de Football Association), Cent. — A544

**2004, Mar. 9 *Perf. 13¼***

**1172** A544 100c multi 1.60 .55

UEFA (European Football Union), 50th Anniv. — A545

**2004, Mar. 9 *Perf. 13¼x13½***

**1173** A545 130c multi 2.00 .65

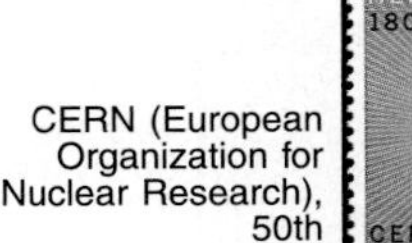

CERN (European Organization for Nuclear Research), 50th Anniv. — A546

**2004, Mar. 9 *Perf. 13½x13¼***

**1174** A546 180c multi 2.75 .90

Comic Strip "Titeuf," by Zep — A547

Titeuf: No. 1175, Giving spring flower to Nadia. No. 1176, Sitting in refrigerator. No. 1177, Running through raked leaves. No. 1178, Pointing at snowman.

**2004, Mar. 9 *Perf. 14x13½***

**1175** A547 85c multi 1.40 .45
**1176** A547 85c multi 1.40 .45
**1177** A547 85c multi 1.40 .45
**1178** A547 85c multi 1.40 .45
*Nos. 1175-1178 (4)* 5.60 1.80

**Souvenir Sheet**

Cycling — A548

No. 1179 — Cyclists and marker for: a, Route 5. b, Route 3.

**2004, Mar. 9 *Perf. 14x13½***

**1179** A548 Sheet of 2 3.25 1.10
*a.-b.* 100c Either single 1.60 .55

Doorbell Button — A549

**2004, May 6 *Perf. 14½x14¼***

**1180** A549 85c multi 1.40 .45

Europa A550

**2004, May 6 *Perf. 14¼x14½***

**1181** A550 100c multi 1.60 .55

2004 Summer Olympics, Athens A551

**2004, May 6 *Perf. 13x13¼***

**1182** A551 100c multi 1.60 .55

See No. 1203.

Zeppelin NT — A552

**2004, May 6 *Perf. 14x13½***

**1183** A552 180c multi 2.75 .90

**Diddl Type of 2003**

Designs: 85c, Diddl with teddy bear, Pimboli, and butterflies. 100c, Diddl with flower.

**2004, May 6 *Perf. 13¼x13½***

**1184** A538 85c multi 1.40 .45
**1185** A538 100c multi 1.60 .55

**UNESCO World Heritage Type of 2003**

Design: Monte San Giorgio.

**2004, Sept. 7 *Perf. 13¾x14¼***

**1186** A539 100c multi 1.60 .55

Issued in sheets of 6.

Suisse Balance Health Program A553

**2004, Sept. 7 *Perf. 13¼x13½***

**1187** A553 85c multi 1.40 .45

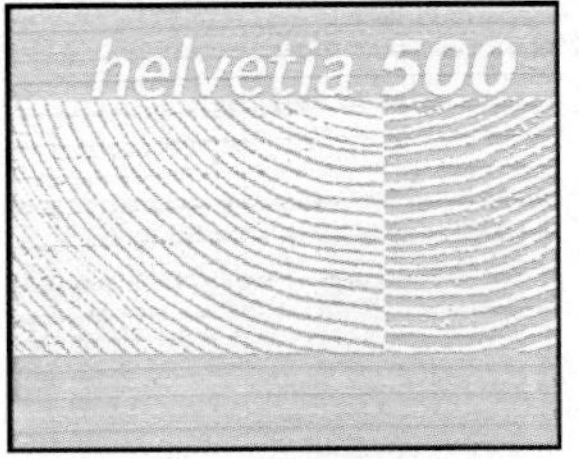

Wood — A554

**Silk-screened on Wood**

**2004, Sept. 7 *Imperf.***

**Self-Adhesive**

**1188** A554 500c white 8.00 2.75

Cheesemaking A555

Designs: 100c, Cheesemaker inspecting curds and whey. 130c, Cheeses, grapes and nuts.

**2004, Sept. 7 Litho. *Perf. 13¼x13½***

**1189** A555 100c multi 1.60 .55
**1190** A555 130c multi 2.10 .70

Animal Protection A556

**2004, Sept. 7 *Perf. 14x13½***

**1191** A556 85c Cat 1.40 .45
**1192** A556 100c Hedgehog 1.60 .55
**1193** A556 130c Pig 2.10 .70
*Nos. 1191-1193 (3)* 5.10 1.70

Nos. 1191-1193 each issued in sheets of 6.

**Souvenir Sheet**

Sitting Helvetia Stamps and Coins, 150th Anniv. — A557

No. 1194: a, Type A17. b, Coin.

**Litho. (#1194a), Litho. & Embossed (#1194b)**

***Perf. 14¼x13¾ on 3 Sides***

**2004, Sept. 7**

**1194** A557 Sheet of 2 2.80 .90
*a.-b.* 85c Either single 1.40 .45

Stamp Day — A558

***Perf. 13¼x13½***

**2004, Nov. 23 Litho.**

**1195** A558 85c multi 1.50 .50

Sports A559

**2004, Nov. 23 Litho. *Perf. 13x13½***

**1196** A559 180c multi 3.25 1.10

No. 1196 is identical to United Nations Offices in Geneva No. 433. The stamp, available for use throughout Switzerland, also served as an official stamp for the International Olympic Committee.

**Christmas Ornaments Types of 2000-2003**

**2004, Nov. 23 Photo. *Perf. 13x13½***

**1197** Sheet of 5 8.50 8.50
*a.* A511 85c Snowflake 1.50 .50
*b.* A528 85c Church 1.50 .50
*c.* A498 100c Angel 1.75 .60
*d.* A542 100c Horseman 1.75 .60
*e.* A542 100c Santa Claus 1.75 .60

Photographs by René Burri — A560

No. 1198: a, Children kissing, German inscription. b, Teenagers on bicycle, French inscription. c, Man and woman kissing, Italian inscription. d, Man and woman in bumper car, Romansch inscription.

***Serpentine Die Cut 12***

**2005, Jan. 3** **Litho.**

**Self-Adhesive**

**1198** Block of 4, #a-d + 4 etiquettes 6.75
*a.-d.* A560 100c Any single 1.60 .35
*e.* Booklet pane, 2 each #1198a-1198d + 8 etiquettes 13.50

No. 1198 lacks self-adhesive selvage, and is on a translucent paper that is rouletted on the left and right sides. No. 1198e has a white paper backing, has each stamp and its se-tenant etiquette surrounded by self-adhesive selvage, and is rouletted through the selvage and backing paper.

Swiss Federal Institute of Technology, Zurich, 150th Anniv. A561

**2005, Mar. 8** ***Perf. 13***
**1199** A561 85c multi 1.50 .50

Matterhorn Superimposed Over Inverted Map of Africa — A562

**2005, Mar. 8** ***Perf. 13x13¼***
**1200** A562 85c multi 1.50 .50

Discovery of rocks from Africa making up top of the Matterhorn.

Unspunnen Traditional Costume and Alpine Herdsman's Festival, Bicent. — A563

**2005, Mar. 8** ***Perf. 13¼x13***
**1201** A563 100c multi 1.75 .60

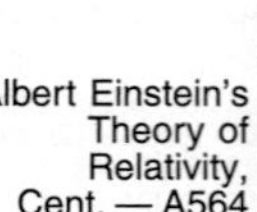

Albert Einstein's Theory of Relativity, Cent. — A564

**2005, Mar. 8** ***Perf. 13½x13¼***
**1202** A564 130c multi 2.25 .75

Cartoon Mouse, by Uli Stein — A565

Mouse with: 85c, Slice of Swiss cheese in typewriter. 100c, Golf club and letter on tee.

**2005, Mar. 8** ***Perf. 13¼x13½***
**1203** A565 85c multi 1.50 .50
**1204** A565 100c multi 1.75 .60

Souvenir Sheet

Geneva International Auto Show, Cent. — A566

**2005, Mar. 8** ***Perf. 13¾x14¼***
**1205** A566 Sheet of 2 4.00 4.00
*a.* 100c Front of car 1.75 .60
*b.* 130c Side of car 2.25 .75

**Swiss Design Type of 2003-04**

Design: Fixpencil, by Caran d'Ache.

**2005, May 10** ***Serpentine Die Cut 12***

**Self-Adhesive**

**1206** A543 220c multi + etiquette 3.75 .75
*a.* Serpentine die cut 12¼x12 + etiquette 3.75 .75
*b.* Booklet pane, 6 #1206, 4 #1206a + 10 etiquettes 37.50

Europa A567

**2005, May 10** ***Perf. 13x13¼***
**1207** A567 100c multi 1.75 .60

Soccer for the Visually Impaired A568

**2005, May 10** ***Perf. 13¾x14¼***
**1208** A568 100c multi 1.75 .60

Printed in sheets of 6.

Opening of Paul Klee Center, Bern — A569

**2005, May 10** ***Perf. 13¼x14***
**1209** A569 100c multi 1.75 .60

Printed in sheets of 6.

Stylized Butterflies A570

***Serpentine Die Cut 11¾***

**2005, May 10**

**Self-Adhesive**

**1210** A570 100c multi 1.75 .60
*a.* Booklet pane of 10 + 10 labels 17.50

Felix the Bunny, by Annette Langen A571

Felix and: 85c, Lambs, cows. 100c, Swans and Chillon Castle.

**2005, May 10** ***Perf. 13x13¼***
**1211** A571 85c multi 1.50 .50
**1212** A571 100c multi 1.75 .60

Subtractive Color Combinations — A572

Additive Color Combinations — A573

***Serpentine Die Cut 12½***

**2005, Sept. 6** **Litho.**

**Self-Adhesive**

**1213** A572 50c multi .80 .30
**1214** A573 100c multi 1.60 .55

Swiss Timepieces A574

Designs: 100c, Watchmaker, pocket watch and mechanism. 130c, Woman, wristwatches.

**2005, Sept. 6** ***Perf. 13¼x13½***
**1215** A574 100c multi 1.60 .55
**1216** A574 130c multi 2.10 .70

Cell Phone Pictures A575

Images: 85c, On Horseback, by Brigit Rohrbach. 100c, Mountain Hike, by Peter Schumacher. 130c, On Top of the World, by Rémy Sager. 180c, Tracks in the Snow, by Debora Ronchi.

**2005, Sept. 6** ***Perf. 14¼x14***
**1217** A575 85c multi 1.40 .45
**1218** A575 100c multi 1.60 .55
**1219** A575 130c multi 2.10 .70
**1220** A575 180c multi 3.00 1.00
*Nos. 1217-1220 (4)* 8.10 2.70

Souvenir Sheet

Friends of Nature Switzerland, Cent. — A576

**2005, Sept. 6** ***Perf. 13½***
**1221** A576 Sheet of 4 7.00 7.00
*a.* 85c Skiers 1.40 1.40
*b.* 100c Chalet, vert. 1.60 1.60
*c.* 110c People fording stream 1.75 1.75
*d.* 130c Mountain climber, vert. 2.10 2.10

Stamp Day — A577

***Perf. 13¼x13½***

**2005, Nov. 22** **Litho.**
**1222** A577 85c multi 1.40 .45

2006 Winter Olympics, Turin, Italy — A578

**2005, Nov. 22** ***Perf. 13¾***
**1223** A578 100c Curling 1.60 .55

Issued in sheets of 6. See No. 1204.

Swiss Papal Guards, 500th Anniv. A579

Designs: 85c, Guard and drummers. 100c, Guards and St. Peter's Basilica.

**2005, Nov. 22** ***Perf. 14x14¼***
**1224** A579 85c multi 1.40 .45
**1225** A579 100c multi 1.60 .55

Nos. 1224-1225 each issued in sheets of 6. See Vatican City Nos. 1315-1316.

Christmas — A580

Designs: 85c, Crozier and miter. 100c, Gingerbread man.

**2005, Nov. 22** ***Perf. 13½x13¼***
**1226** A580 85c multi 1.40 .45
**1227** A580 100c multi 1.60 .55

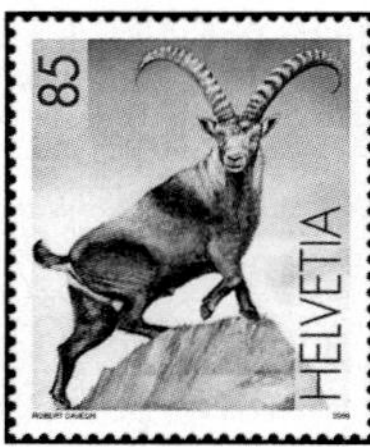

Reintroduction of Alpine Ibex in Switzerland, Cent. — A581

**2006, Mar. 7 Litho. *Perf. 13¼x13***

| | | | | |
|---|---|---|---|---|
| **1228** | A581 85c multi | | 1.40 | .45 |

Youth Soccer — A582

**2006, Mar. 7 *Perf. 13¼x13½***

| | | | | |
|---|---|---|---|---|
| **1229** | A582 85c multi | | 1.40 | .45 |

Cuculus Canorus A583

***Serpentine Die Cut 12***

**2006, Mar. 7 Photo.**

**Self-Adhesive**

| | | | | |
|---|---|---|---|---|
| **1230** | A583 240c multi + etiquette | | 3.75 | .75 |
| *a.* | Block of 10 + 10 etiquettes | | 37.50 | |

No. 1230a is on a backing paper with bar codes on the reverse.

Railroad Anniversaries A584

Designs: 85c, Simplon Tunnel, cent. 100c, Bern-Lötschberg-Simplon Railway, cent.

**2006, Mar. 7 Litho. *Perf. 14x13¾***

| | | | | |
|---|---|---|---|---|
| **1231** | A584 85c multi | | 1.40 | .45 |
| **1232** | A584 100c multi | | 1.60 | .55 |

Art Nouveau Exhibition, La Chaux-de-Fonds — A585

Designs: 100c, "Fir." 180c, "Petal."

**2006, Mar. 7**

| | | | | |
|---|---|---|---|---|
| **1233** | A585 100c multi | | 1.60 | .55 |
| **1234** | A585 180c multi | | 2.75 | .90 |

Post Buses, Cent. — A586

Various post buses and passengers.

***Serpentine Die Cut 10¾x11***

**2006, Mar. 7 Litho.**

**Self-Adhesive**

| | | | | |
|---|---|---|---|---|
| **1235** | A586 85c blue & multi | | 1.40 | .45 |
| *a.* | Block of 4 on backing paper | | 5.75 | |
| **1236** | A586 100c red & multi | | 1.60 | .55 |
| *a.* | Block of 4 on backing paper | | 6.50 | |
| **1237** | A586 130c grn & multi | | 2.00 | .65 |
| *a.* | Block of 4 on backing paper | | 8.00 | |
| *b.* | Block of 3, #1235-1237 on backing paper | | 5.00 | |
| | *Nos. 1235-1237 (3)* | | 5.00 | 1.65 |

Nos. 1235-1237 each were issued in sheets of 20. Stamps are adjacent on Nos. 1235a-1237a and on a shiny, but opaque backing paper.

Kasperli, Children's Theater Puppet — A587

**2006, May 9 Litho. *Perf. 14x13¾***

| | | | | |
|---|---|---|---|---|
| **1238** | A587 85c multi | | 1.40 | .45 |

Europa A588

**2006, May 9 *Perf. 13x13¼***

| | | | | |
|---|---|---|---|---|
| **1239** | A588 100c multi | | 1.75 | .60 |

Mountains — A589

No. 1240: a, Eiger (35x36mm). b, Monch (30x36mm). c, Jungfrau (39x36mm). Illustration reduced.

**2006, May 9 *Perf. 13¼x13½***

| | | | | |
|---|---|---|---|---|
| **1240** | A589 Horiz. strip of 3 | | 4.25 | 4.25 |
| *a.-c.* | 85c Any single | | 1.40 | .45 |

Caricatures of Cows by Patrice Killoffer A590

Cow: 85c, On back. 100c, In water. 130c, Seated. 180c, In snow.

**2006, May 9 *Perf. 14x14¼***

| | | | | |
|---|---|---|---|---|
| **1241** | A590 85c multi | | 1.40 | .45 |
| **1242** | A590 100c multi | | 1.75 | .60 |
| **1243** | A590 130c multi | | 2.25 | .75 |
| **1244** | A590 180c multi | | 3.00 | 1.00 |
| | *Nos. 1241-1244 (4)* | | 8.40 | 2.80 |

First Session of United Nations Human Rights Council A591

***Perf. 13¾x14¼***

**2006, June 19 Litho.**

| | | | | |
|---|---|---|---|---|
| **1245** | A591 100c multi | | 1.75 | .60 |

Dimitri the Clown — A592

**2006, Sept. 7 *Perf. 13¼x13***

| | | | | |
|---|---|---|---|---|
| **1246** | A592 100c multi | | 1.60 | .55 |

Victorinox Swiss Army Knives — A593

Designs: 100c, First model, 1897, khaki pants. 130c, Modern model, blue jeans.

**2006, Sept. 7 *Perf. 14x13¾***

| | | | | |
|---|---|---|---|---|
| **1247** | A593 100c multi | | 1.60 | .55 |
| **1248** | A593 130c multi | | 2.10 | .70 |

Cocolino the Cooking Cat, by Oskar Weiss — A594

***Serpentine Die Cut 10¾x11***

**2006, Sept. 7**

**Self-Adhesive**

| | | | | |
|---|---|---|---|---|
| **1249** | A594 85c multi | | 1.40 | .45 |
| *a.* | Booklet pane of 10 | | 14.00 | |

Fruit — A595

Designs: 200c, Gelterkinder cherries. 300c, Spätlauber apple. 400c, Hauszwetschge plums.

**2006 Photo. *Serpentine Die Cut 12***

**Self-Adhesive**

| | | | | |
|---|---|---|---|---|
| **1250** | A595 200c multi | | 3.25 | 1.10 |
| **1251** | A595 300c multi | | 5.00 | 1.60 |
| *a.* | Pair, #1250-1251 on backing paper | | 8.25 | |
| **1252** | A595 400c multi | | 6.75 | 2.25 |
| | *Nos. 1250-1252 (3)* | | 15.00 | 4.95 |

Issued: 200c, 300c, 9/7; 400c, 11/21.Nos. 1250-1252 each were printed in sheets of 50.

Town of Olten, Boy Wearing Train Conductor's Hat — A596

***Perf. 13½x13¼***

**2006, Nov. 21 Litho.**

| | | | | |
|---|---|---|---|---|
| **1253** | A596 85c multi | | 1.50 | .50 |

Stamp Day.

Christmas — A597

Designs: 85c, Star singers. 100c, Advent wreath.

**2006, Nov. 21**

| | | | | |
|---|---|---|---|---|
| **1254** | A597 85c multi | | 1.50 | .50 |
| **1255** | A597 100c multi | | 1.75 | .60 |

Women's Soccer — A598

**2007, Mar. 6 Litho. *Perf. 13¼x13½***

| | | | | |
|---|---|---|---|---|
| **1256** | A598 85c multi | | 1.40 | .45 |

Printed in sheets of 6.

Leonhard Euler (1707-83), Mathematician A599

**2007, Mar. 6**

| | | | | |
|---|---|---|---|---|
| **1257** | A599 130c multi | | 2.10 | .70 |

Stein am Rhein, 1000th Anniv. — A600

No. 1258: a, Town Hall (28x36mm). b, Houses on Town Hall Square (40x36mm). c, Municipal Fountain (34x36mm). Illustration reduced.

**2007, Mar. 6 *Perf. 13¾x13½***

| | | | | |
|---|---|---|---|---|
| **1258** | A600 Horiz. strip of 3 | | 4.25 | 3.50 |
| *a.-c.* | 85c Any single | | 1.40 | .45 |

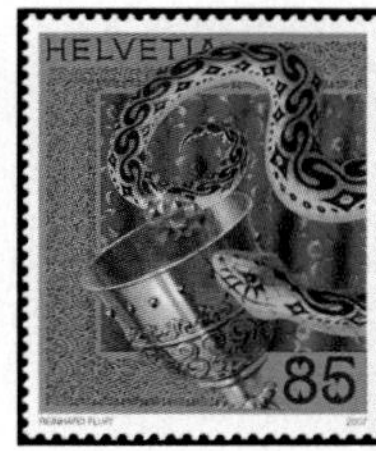

Legends A601

Designs: 85c, Charlemagne and the Snake. 100c, Fenetta, the Island Maiden. 130c, The Judge of Bellinzona. 180c, Margaretha.

**2007, Mar. 6 *Perf. 13½x14***

| | | | | |
|---|---|---|---|---|
| **1259** | A601 85c multi | | 1.40 | .45 |
| **1260** | A601 100c multi | | 1.60 | .55 |
| **1261** | A601 130c multi | | 2.10 | .70 |
| **1262** | A601 180c multi | | 3.00 | 1.00 |
| | *Nos. 1259-1262 (4)* | | 8.10 | 2.70 |

Swiss Club for Bernese Mountain Dogs, Cent. — A602

***Serpentine Die Cut 11x10¾***

**2007, Mar. 6**

**Self-Adhesive**

| | | | | |
|---|---|---|---|---|
| **1263** | A602 85c multi | | 1.40 | .45 |

Swiss National Bank, Cent. — A603

Designs: 85c, Banknote security devices. 100c, Artwork from 100-franc banknote.

**2007, Mar. 6** **Litho.**
**Self-Adhesive**

**1264** A603 85c multi 1.40 .45
**1265** A603 100c multi 1.60 .55
*a.* Horiz. pair, #1264-1265 3.00

Roger Federer, Tennis Player — A604

**2007, Apr. 10** ***Perf. 13¾x14¼***

**1266** A604 100c multi 1.75 .60

Swiss Assoc. of Day Care Centers, Cent. — A605

**2007, Apr. 27** ***Perf. 13½x13¾***

**1267** A605 85c multi 1.40 .45

Europa — A606

**2007, Apr. 27** ***Perf. 14***

**1268** A606 100c multi 1.75 .60

Scouting, cent. Printed in sheets of 18 + 12 labels.

Art Brut Movement — A607

Designs: 100c, Saint Adolf-Throne-Rock Face-Flower, by Adolf Wölfli. 180c, Untitled work by Carlo Zinelli.

**2007, Apr. 27** ***Perf. 14¼x14***

**1269** A607 100c multi 1.75 .60
**1270** A607 180c multi 3.00 1.00

Museum of Communications, Cent. — A608

People with: 85c, Lake in background. 100c, Building in background.

**Litho. With Three-Dimensional Plastic Affixed**
***Serpentine Die Cut 10½***

**2007, Apr. 27**
**Self-Adhesive**

**1271** A608 85c multi 1.40 .45
**1272** A608 100c multi 1.75 .60

---

## SEMI-POSTAL STAMPS

Nos. B1-B76, B81-B84 were sold at premiums of 2c for 3c stamps, 5c for 5c-20c stamps and 10c for 30c-40c stamps.

Helvetia and Matterhorn — SP2

***Perf. 11½, 12***

**1913, Dec. 1** **Typo.** **Wmk. 183**
**Granite Paper**

**B1** SP2 5c green 2.75 *8.25*
Never hinged 7.75

Boy (Appenzell) SP3

Girl (Lucerne) SP4

**1915, Dec. 1** ***Perf. 11½***

**B2** SP3 5c green, *buff* 3.25 *8.25*
*a.* Tête bêche pair 82.50 *875.00*
*l* Never hinged 160.00
**B3** SP4 10c red, *buff* 100.00 87.50
Set, never hinged 225.00

Girl (Fribourg) SP5

Dairy Boy (Bern) SP6

Girl (Vaud) — SP7

**1916, Dec. 1**

**B4** SP5 3c vio, *buff* 5.00 *37.50*
**B5** SP6 5c grn, *buff* 11.00 9.25
**B6** SP7 10c brn red, *buff* 47.50 *77.50*
*Nos. B4-B6 (3)* 63.50 *124.25*
Set, never hinged 175.00

Girl (Valais) SP8

Girl (Unterwalden) SP9

Girl (Ticino) — SP10

**1917, Dec. 1**

**B7** SP8 3c vio, *buff* 3.25 *50.00*
**B8** SP9 5c green, *buff* 7.75 5.50
**B9** SP10 10c red, *buff* 19.00 22.50
*Nos. B7-B9 (3)* 30.00 *78.00*
Set, never hinged 87.50

Uri SP11

Geneva SP12

**1918, Dec. 1**
**Straw-Surfaced Paper**

**B10** SP11 10c red, org & blk 7.75 *25.00*
**B11** SP12 15c vio, red, org & blk 9.25 *11.00*
Set, never hinged 52.50

Nidwalden SP13

Vaud SP14

Obwalden — SP15

**1919, Dec. 1**
**Cream-Surfaced Paper**

**B12** SP13 7½c gray, red & blk 2.50 *14.00*
**B13** SP14 10c lake, grn & blk 2.50 *14.00*
**B14** SP15 15c pur, red & blk 5.00 *7.25*
*Nos. B12-B14 (3)* 10.00 *35.25*
Set, never hinged 22.50

Schwyz SP16

Zürich SP17

Ticino — SP18

**1920, Dec. 1**
**Cream-Surfaced Paper**

**B15** SP16 7½c gray & red 2.75 *11.50*
**B16** SP17 10c red & lt bl 5.00 *12.50*
**B17** SP18 15c violet, red & bl 2.75 *6.00*
*Nos. B15-B17 (3)* 10.50 *30.00*
Set, never hinged 25.00

Valais SP19

Bern SP20

Switzerland — SP21

**1921, Dec. 1**
**Cream-Surfaced Paper**

**B18** SP19 10c grn, red & blk .65 *3.00*
**B19** SP20 20c vio, red, org & blk 1.90 *3.50*
**B20** SP21 40c blue & red 7.25 *47.50*
*Nos. B18-B20 (3)* 9.80 *54.00*
Set, never hinged 25.00

Zug SP22

Fribourg SP23

Lucerne SP24

Switzerland SP25

**1922, Dec. 1**
**Cream-Surfaced Paper**

**B21** SP22 5c org, pale bl & blk .50 *5.50*
**B22** SP23 10c ol grn & blk .60 *2.50*
**B23** SP24 20c vio, pale bl & blk 1.00 *2.50*
**B24** SP25 40c bl & red 8.75 *47.50*
*Nos. B21-B24 (4)* 10.85 *58.00*
Set, never hinged 26.00

Basel SP26

Glarus (St. Fridolin) SP27

Neuchâtel SP28

Switzerland SP29

**1923, Dec. 1**
**Cream-Surfaced Paper**

**B25** SP26 5c org & blk .40 *3.50*
**B26** SP27 10c multi .40 *1.90*
**B27** SP28 20c multi .45 *1.90*
**B28** SP29 40c dk bl & red 7.75 *37.50*
*Nos. B25-B28 (4)* 9.00 *44.80*
Set, never hinged 21.00

Appenzell SP30

Solothurn SP31

Schaffhausen SP32

Switzerland SP33

**1924, Dec. 1**
**Cream-Surfaced Paper**

**B29** SP30 5c dk vio & blk .25 *1.60*
**B30** SP31 10c grn, red & blk .40 *1.00*
**B31** SP32 20c car, yel & blk .65 *1.00*
**B32** SP33 30c bl, red & blk 1.40 *11.00*
*Nos. B29-B32 (4)* 2.70 *14.60*
Set, never hinged 6.50

St. Gallen (Canton)
SP34

Appenzell-Ausser-Rhoden
SP35

Grisons
SP36

Switzerland
SP37

**1925, Dec. 1**

**Cream-Surfaced Paper**

**B33** SP34 5c vio, grn & blk .25 *1.10*
**B34** SP35 10c grn & blk .25 *.85*
**B35** SP36 20c multi .25 *.85*
**B36** SP37 30c dk bl, red & blk 1.10 *8.25*
*Nos. B33-B36 (4)* 1.85 *11.05*
Set, never hinged 4.50

Thurgau
SP38

Basel
SP39

Aargau
SP40

Switzerland
SP41

**1926, Dec. 1**

**Cream-Surfaced Paper**

**B37** SP38 5c vio, bis & grn .25 *1.40*
**B38** SP39 10c gray grn, red & blk .25 *1.40*
**B39** SP40 20c red, blk & bl .25 *1.40*
**B40** SP41 30c dk bl & red 1.10 *12.50*
*Nos. B37-B40 (4)* 1.85 *16.70*
Set, never hinged 4.50

Orphan
SP42

Orphan at Pestalozzi School
SP43

SP44

J. H. Pestalozzi
SP45

**1927, Dec. 1 Typo. Wmk. 183**

**Granite Paper**

**B41** SP42 5c red vio & yel, *grysh* .20 *1.60*
**B42** SP43 10c grn & fawn, *grnsh* .20 *.60*

**Engr.**

**B43** SP44 20c red .20 *.60*

**Unwmk.**

**Photo.**

**B44** SP45 30c gray bl & blk 1.10 *6.50*
*Nos. B41-B44 (4)* 1.70 *9.30*
Set, never hinged 3.25

Nos. B43-B44 for the centenary of the death of Johann Heinrich Pestalozzi, the Swiss educational reformer.

Lausanne
SP46

Winterthur
SP47

St. Gallen (City) — SP48

J. H. Dunant
SP49

**1928, Dec. 1 Typo. Wmk. 183**

**Cream-Surfaced Paper.**

**B45** SP46 5c dk vio, red & blk .20 *1.60*
**B46** SP47 10c bl grn, org red & blk .20 *.90*
**B47** SP48 20c brn red, blk & yel .20 *.90*

**Unwmk.**

**Photo.**

**Thick White Paper**

**B48** SP49 30c dl bl & red 1.10 *7.00*
*Nos. B45-B48 (4)* 1.70 *10.40*
Set, never hinged 3.50

No. B48 for the centenary of the birth of Jean Henri Dunant, Swiss author, philanthropist and founder of the Red Cross Society.

Lake Lugano and Mt. Salvatore
SP50

Lake Engstlen and Mt. Titlis
SP51

Mt. Lyskamm
SP52

Nicholas von der Flüe
SP53

**1929, Dec. 1** ***Perf. 11x11½***

**B49** SP50 5c dk vio & red org .20 *1.40*
**B50** SP51 10c ol brn & gray bl .20 *1.10*
**B51** SP52 20c brn garnet & bl .25 *1.10*
**B52** SP53 30c dk blue 1.25 *12.50*
*Nos. B49-B52 (4)* 1.90 *16.10*
Set, never hinged 4.50

No. B52 for Nicholas von der Flüe, the Swiss patriot. By his advice the Swiss Confederation was continued and Swiss independence was saved.

Fribourg
SP54

Altdorf
SP55

Schaffhausen
SP56

Jeremias Gotthelf
SP57

**Wmk. 183**

**1930, Dec. 1 Typo.** ***Perf. 11½***

**Cream-Surfaced Paper**

**B53** SP54 5c dp grn, dl bl & blk .20 *1.40*
**B54** SP55 10c multicolored .20 *.90*
**B55** SP56 20c multicolored .30 *.90*

**Engr.**

**White Paper**

**B56** SP57 30c slate blue 1.25 *6.00*
*Nos. B53-B56 (4)* 1.95 *9.20*
Set, never hinged 4.00

No. B56 for Jeremias Gotthelf, pen name of Albrecht Bitzius, pastor and author.

Lakes Silvaplana and Sils
SP58

Wetterhorn
SP59

Lake Geneva
SP60

Alexandre Vinet
SP61

**1931, Dec. 1 Photo. Unwmk.**

**Granite Paper**

**B57** SP58 5c dp grn .45 *1.60*
**B58** SP59 10c dk vio .40 *.85*
**B59** SP60 20c brn red .55 *1.10*

**Wmk. 183**

**Engr.**

**B60** SP61 30c ultra 4.50 *19.00*
*Nos. B57-B60 (4)* 5.90 *22.55*
Set, never hinged 14.00

No. B60 for Alexandre Rudolph Vinet, critic and theologian.

Flag Swinger
SP62

Putting the Stone
SP63

Wrestling
SP64

Eugen Huber
SP65

**1932, Dec. 1 Typo. Unwmk.**

**Granite Paper**

**B61** SP62 5c dk grn & red .30 *1.90*
**B62** SP63 10c orange .45 *2.25*
**B63** SP64 20c scarlet .55 *1.90*

**Wmk. 183**

**Engr.**

**B64** SP65 30c ultra 2.25 *8.75*
*Nos. B61-B64 (4)* 3.55 *14.80*
Set, never hinged 9.50

No. B64 for Eugen Huber, jurist and author of the Swiss Civil Law Book.

Girl of Vaud — SP66

Girl of Bern — SP67

Girl of Ticino
SP68

Jean Baptiste Girard (Le Père Grégoire)
SP69

**1933, Dec. 1 Photo. Unwmk.**

**Granite Paper**

**B65** SP66 5c grn & buff .30 *1.50*
**B66** SP67 10c vio & buff .30 *1.10*
**B67** SP68 20c red & buff .45 *2.10*

**Wmk. 183**

**Engr.**

**B68** SP69 30c ultra 2.50 *8.50*
*Nos. B65-B68 (4)* 3.55 *13.20*
Set, never hinged 8.25

Girl of Appenzell
SP70

Girl of Valais
SP71

Girl of Grisons
SP72

Albrecht von Haller
SP73

**1934, Dec. 1 Photo. Unwmk.**

**B69** SP70 5c grn & buff .30 *1.60*
**B70** SP71 10c vio & buff .45 *1.10*
**B71** SP72 20c red & buff .45 *1.60*

**Wmk. 183**

**Engr.**

**B72** SP73 30c ultra 2.50 *8.75*
*Nos. B69-B72 (4)* 3.70 *13.05*
Set, never hinged 8.25

Girl of Basel
SP74

Girl of Lucerne
SP75

Girl of Geneva
SP76

Stefano Franscini
SP77

**1935, Dec. 1 Photo. Unwmk.**
**Granite Paper**

| | | | |
|---|---|---|---|
| **B73** SP74 | 5c grn & buff | .25 | *1.75* |
| **B74** SP75 | 10c vio & buff | .45 | *1.10* |
| **B75** SP76 | 20c red & buff | .45 | *2.75* |

**Wmk. 183**
**Engr.**

| | | | |
|---|---|---|---|
| **B76** SP77 | 30c ultra | 2.50 | *8.75* |
| | *Nos. B73-B76 (4)* | 3.65 | *14.35* |
| | Set, never hinged | 8.25 | |

No. B76 honors Stefano Franscini (1796-1857), political economist and educator.

Alpine Herdsman — SP78

***Perf. 11½***
**1936, Oct. 1 Photo. Unwmk.**
**Granite Paper**

| | | | |
|---|---|---|---|
| **B77** SP78 | 10c + 5c vio | .55 | *1.00* |
| **B78** SP78 | 20c + 10c dk red | .85 | *4.25* |
| **B79** SP78 | 30c + 10c ultra | 3.75 | *20.00* |
| | *Nos. B77-B79 (3)* | 5.15 | *25.25* |
| | Set, never hinged | 11.00 | |

**Souvenir Sheet**

| | | | |
|---|---|---|---|
| **B80** SP78 | Sheet of 3 | 35.00 | *125.00* |
| | Never hinged | 70.00 | |
| *a.* | Block of 4 sheets | 190.00 | *875.00* |
| | Never hinged | 300.00 | |

Swiss National Defense Fund Drive.

No. B80 contains stamps similar to Nos. B77-B79, but on grilled granite paper with blue and red fibers instead of black and red. Sold for 2fr. Size: 120x130mm.

Johann Georg Nägeli
SP79

Girl of Neuchâtel
SP80

Girl of Schwyz
SP81

Girl of Zurich
SP82

**Wmk. 183**
**1936, Dec. 1 Engr. *Perf. 11½***
**Granite Paper**

| | | | |
|---|---|---|---|
| **B81** SP79 | 5c green | .25 | *.70* |

**Unwmk.**
**Photo.**

| | | | |
|---|---|---|---|
| **B82** SP80 | 10c vio & buff | .55 | *.70* |
| **B83** SP81 | 20c red & buff | .25 | *1.90* |
| **B84** SP82 | 30c ultra & buff | 3.50 | *30.00* |
| | *Nos. B81-B84 (4)* | 4.55 | *33.30* |
| | Set, never hinged | 11.00 | |

Gen. Henri Dufour — SP83

Nicholas von der Flüe — SP84

Boy
SP85

Girl
SP86

***Perf. 11½***
**1937, Dec. 1 Unwmk. Engr.**

| | | | |
|---|---|---|---|
| **B85** SP83 | 5c + 5c bl grn | .20 | *.55* |
| **B86** SP84 | 10c + 5c red vio | .20 | *.55* |

**Photo.**
**Granite Paper**

| | | | |
|---|---|---|---|
| **B87** SP85 | 20c + 5c red & silver | .30 | *.55* |
| **B88** SP86 | 30c + 10c ultra & sil | 1.25 | *5.50* |
| | *Nos. B85-B88 (4)* | 1.95 | *7.15* |
| | Set, never hinged | 3.75 | |

25th anniv. of the Pro Juventute (child welfare) stamps.

**Souvenir Sheet**
**1937, Dec. 20 *Imperf.***

| | | | |
|---|---|---|---|
| **B89** | Sheet of 2 | 6.50 | *57.50* |
| *a.* | SP85 20c + 5c red & silver | 1.60 | *17.00* |
| *b.* | SP86 30c + 10c ultra & silver | 1.60 | *17.00* |
| | Never hinged | 7.50 | |

Simulated perforation in silver. Sheet sold for 1fr.

Tell Chapel, Lake Lucerne
SP87

**1938, June 15 *Perf. 11½***
**Granite Paper**

| | | | |
|---|---|---|---|
| **B90** SP87 | 10c + 10c brt vio & yel | .45 | *1.10* |
| | Never hinged | 1.10 | |
| *a.* | Grilled gum | 22.50 | *77.50* |
| | Never hinged | 32.50 | |

National Fête Day.

Salomon Gessner
SP88

Girl of St. Gallen
SP89

Girl of Uri — SP90

Girl of Aargau — SP91

**1938, Dec. 1 Engr. *Perf. 11½***

| | | | |
|---|---|---|---|
| **B91** SP88 | 5c + 5c dp bl grn | .20 | *.50* |

**Photo.**
**Granite Paper**

| | | | |
|---|---|---|---|
| **B92** SP89 | 10c + 5c pur & buff | .25 | *.55* |
| **B93** SP90 | 20c + 5c red & buff | .25 | *.55* |
| **B94** SP91 | 30c + 10c ultra | 1.60 | *6.50* |
| | *Nos. B91-B94 (4)* | 2.30 | *8.10* |
| | Set, never hinged | 4.50 | |

Castle at Laupen
SP92

**1939, June 15**

| | | | |
|---|---|---|---|
| **B95** SP92 | 10c + 10c brn, gray & red | .30 | *1.10* |
| | Never hinged | 1.10 | |

600th anniversary of the Battle of Laupen. The surtax was used to aid needy mothers.

Hans Herzog
SP93

Girl of Fribourg
SP94

Girl of Nidwalden
SP95

Girl of Basel
SP96

***Perf. 11½***
**1939, Dec. 1 Unwmk. Engr.**

| | | | |
|---|---|---|---|
| **B96** SP93 | 5c + 5c dk grn | .20 | *.45* |

**Photo.**
**Granite Paper**

| | | | |
|---|---|---|---|
| **B97** SP94 | 10c + 5c rose vio & buff | .20 | *.45* |
| **B98** SP95 | 20c + 5c org red | .30 | *1.40* |
| **B99** SP96 | 30c + 10c ultra & buff | 1.60 | *11.50* |
| | *Nos. B96-B99 (4)* | 2.30 | *13.80* |
| | Set, never hinged | 5.00 | |

Sempach, 1386 — SP97

Giornico, 1478 — SP98

Calven, 1499
SP99

WWI Ranger
SP100

**1940, Mar. 20 Photo.**
**Granite Paper**

| | | | |
|---|---|---|---|
| **B100** SP97 | 5c + 5c emer, blk & red | .30 | *1.25* |
| **B101** SP98 | 10c + 5c brn org, blk & car | .30 | *.55* |
| **B102** SP99 | 20c + 5c brn red, blk & car | 2.25 | *.95* |
| **B103** SP100 | 30c + 10c brt bl, brn blk & red | 1.60 | *8.25* |

National Fête Day. The surtax was for the National Fund and the Red Cross.

**Redrawn**

| | | | |
|---|---|---|---|
| **B104** SP99 | 20c + 5c brn red, blk & car | 9.75 | 6.50 |
| | *Nos. B100-B104 (5)* | 14.20 | *17.50* |
| | Set, never hinged | 26.00 | |

The base of statue has been heavily shaded "Calven 1499" moved nearer to bottom line of base. Top line of base removed.

**Souvenir Sheet**
**Unwmk.**
**1940, July 16 Photo. *Imperf.***
**Granite Paper**

| | | | |
|---|---|---|---|
| **B105** | Sheet of 4 | 250.00 | *575.00* |
| | Never hinged | 425.00 | |
| *a.* | SP97 5c+5c yel grn, blk & red | 11.00 | *26.00* |
| *b.* | SP98 10c+5c org yel, blk & red | 47.50 | *210.00* |
| *c.* | SP99 20c+5c brn red, blk & red (redrawn) | 47.50 | *210.00* |
| *d.* | SP100 30c+10c chlky bl, blk & red | 11.00 | *26.00* |

National Fete Day. Sheets measure 125x65mm and sold for 5fr.

Gottfried Keller
SP102

Girl of Thurgau
SP103

Girl of Solothurn
SP104

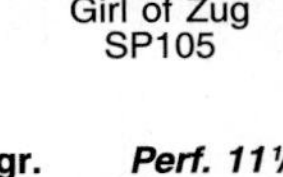
Girl of Zug
SP105

**1940, Dec. 1 Engr. *Perf. 11½***

| | | | |
|---|---|---|---|
| **B106** SP102 | 5c + 5c dk bl grn | .20 | *.40* |

**Photo.**

| | | | |
|---|---|---|---|
| **B107** SP103 | 10c + 5c brn & buff | .20 | *.30* |
| **B108** SP104 | 20c + 5c org red & buff | .20 | *.40* |
| **B109** SP105 | 30c + 10c dp ultra & buff | 1.40 | *9.50* |
| | *Nos. B106-B109 (4)* | 2.00 | *10.60* |
| | Set, never hinged | 4.00 | |

Lake Lucerne, Arms of Cantons
SP106

Tell Chapel at Chemin Creux SP107

**1941, June 15**

**B110** SP106 10c + 10c multi .30 *.75*
**B111** SP107 20c + 10c org, red & lt buff .30 *1.25*
Set, never hinged 2.00

Natl. Fête Day and 650th anniv. of Swiss Independence.

Johann Lavater SP108

Girl of Schaffhausen SP109

Girl of Obwalden SP110

Daniel Jean Richard SP111

**1941, Dec. 1** **Engr.**

**B112** SP108 5c + 5c dk grn .20 *.30*
**B113** SP111 30c + 10c dp ultra .25 *.40*

**Photo.**

**B114** SP109 10c + 5c chnt & buff .25 *.40*
**B115** SP110 20c + 5c ver & buff .80 *5.00*
*Nos. B112-B115 (4)* 1.50 *6.10*
Set, never hinged 3.50

**Souvenir Sheet**
***Imperf***

**B116** Sheet of 2 60.00 *350.00*
*a.* SP109 10c +5c chnt & buff 17.00 *125.00*
*b.* SP110 20c +5c ver & buff 17.00 *125.00*
Never hinged 100.00

Issued in sheets measuring 75x70mm and sold for 2fr. The surtax was used for charity.

Ancient Geneva SP113

Soldiers' Monument, Forch SP114

**1942, June 15** ***Perf. 11½***

**B117** SP113 10c + 10c gray blk, red & yel .25 *.50*
**B118** SP114 20c + 10c cop red, red & buff .25 *.85*
Set, never hinged 1.25

National Fête Day, 1942. No. B117 for the 2000th anniv. of the City of Geneva.

**Souvenir Sheet**
***Imperf***

**B119** Sheet of 2 50.00 *225.00*
*a.* SP113 10c +10c gray black, red & yellow 14.00 *80.00*
*b.* SP113 20c +10c copper red, red & buff 14.00 *80.00*
Never hinged 82.50

Issued in sheets measuring 105x63mm in commemoration of National Fete and the 2000th anniv. of the City of Geneva. Sold for 2fr. The surtax was divided between the Swiss Alliance of Samaritans and the National Community Chest.

Niklaus Riggenbach SP116

Girl of Appenzell SP117

Girl of Glarus SP118

Konrad Escher von der Linth SP119

**1942, Dec. 1** **Engr.** ***Perf. 11½***

**B120** SP116 5c + 5c deep grn .20 *.50*
**B121** SP119 30c + 10c royal bl 1.10 *4.50*

**Photo.**

**B122** SP117 10c + 5c dp brn & buff .25 *.50*
**B123** SP118 20c + 5c org red .20 *.50*
*Nos. B120-B123 (4)* 1.75 *6.00*
Set, never hinged 3.75

Intragna SP120

Parliament Buildings, Bern SP121

**1943, June 15** **Photo.** ***Perf. 11½***

**B124** SP120 10c + 10c blk brn, buff & dk red .25 *.75*
**B125** SP121 20c + 10c cop red, buff & dk red .30 *1.50*
Set, never hinged 1.25

National Fête Day, 1943.

Emanuel von Fellenberg SP122

Silver Thistle SP123

20c+5c, Lady slipper. 30c+10c, Gentian.

**1943, Dec. 1** **Engr.**

**B126** SP122 5c + 5c green .20 *.50*

**Photo.**

**B127** SP123 10c + 5c sl grn & ocher .20 *.50*
**B128** SP123 20c + 5c copper red & yel .25 *.50*
**B129** SP123 30c + 10c royal bl & lt bl 1.10 *8.50*
*Nos. B126-B129 (4)* 1.75 *10.00*
Set, never hinged 3.25

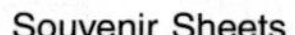
Souvenir Sheets

SP126

**1943** **Engr.** ***Imperf.***

**B130** SP126 Sheet of 12 37.50 *60.00*
*a.* 10c black, single stamp 1.10 *3.75*
Never hinged 77.50

Sold for 5fr. Size: 165x140mm.

SP127

**Red Horizontal Lines**

**B131** SP127 Sheet of 2 42.50 *52.50*
*a.* 4c black & red 13.00 *20.00*
*b.* 6c black & red 13.00 *20.00*
Never hinged 75.00

Sold for 3fr. Size: 70x75mm.

Arms of Geneva — SP128

**B132** SP128 Sheet of 2 40.00 *40.00*
*a.* 5c green & black 11.50 *15.00*
Never hinged 65.00

Sold for 3fr. Size: 72x72mm. Centenary of Swiss postage stamps. The surtax aided the Swiss Red Cross.

Heiden SP129

St. Jacob SP130

Mesocco SP131

Basel SP132

***Perf. 11½***
**1944, June 15** **Photo.** **Unwmk.**

**B133** SP129 5c + 5c dk bl grn, red & buff .20 *2.25*
**B134** SP130 10c + 10c gray blk, red & buff .20 *.50*
**B135** SP131 20c + 10c hn, red & buff .20 *1.00*
**B136** SP132 30c + 10c brt ultra & red 2.10 *17.50*
*Nos. B133-B136 (4)* 2.70 *21.25*
Set, never hinged 6.00

National Fete Day.

Numa Droz SP133

Edelweiss SP134

Designs: 20c+5c, Lilium martagon. 30c+10c, Aquilegia alpina.

**1944, Dec. 1** **Engr.**

**B137** SP133 5c + 5c green .20 *.35*

**Photo.**

**B138** SP134 10c + 5c dk sl grn, yel & gray .25 *.40*
**B139** SP134 20c + 5c red, yel & gray .35 *.40*
**B140** SP134 30c + 10c bl, gray & lt bl 1.10 *8.50*
*Nos. B137-B140 (4)* 1.90 *9.65*
Set, never hinged 4.00

Symbol of Faith, Hope and Love — SP137

Lifeboat Making a Rescue — SP138

**1945, Feb. 20** ***Perf. 11½***

**B141** SP137 10c + 10c multi .30 *.50*
**B142** SP137 20c + 60c multi .90 *5.75*
Set, never hinged 2.50

*Imperf*

**Souvenir Sheet**

**B143** SP138 3fr + 7fr bl gray 110.00 *225.00*
Never hinged 200.00

Issued in sheets measuring 70x110mm. Surtax for the benefit of war victims.

Souvenir Sheet

Dove of Basel — SP139

**1945, Apr. 14** **Typo.**

**B144** SP139 Sheet of 2 70.00 *95.00*
*a.* 10c gray, maroon & black 16.00 *26.00*
Never hinged 150.00

Cent. of the Basel Cantonal Stamp. The sheets measure 71x63mm and sold for 3fr. The surtax was for the Pro Juventute Foundation.

Numeral of Value and Red Cross — SP140

**1945** **Photo.** ***Perf. 12***

**B145** SP140 5c + 10c grn & red .30 *.75*
Never hinged .65

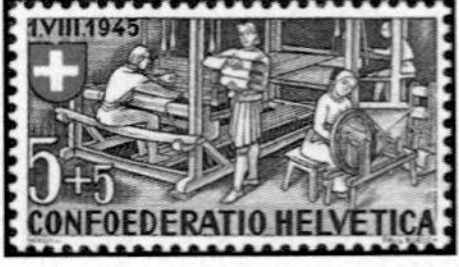


Weaver SP141

Farm of Jura SP142

Farm of Emmental SP143

Frame House, Eastern Switzerland — SP144

**1945, June 15** **Engr.** ***Perf. 11½***

**B146** SP141 5c + 5c bl grn & red .35 *2.00*

**Photo.**

**B147** SP142 10c + 10c brn, gray bl & red .35 *.75*
**B148** SP143 20c + 10c hn brn, buff & red .55 *.75*
**B149** SP144 30c + 10c saph & red 5.50 *35.00*
*Nos. B146-B149 (4)* 6.75 *38.50*
Set, never hinged 14.50

The surtax was for needy mothers.

Ludwig Forrer — SP145

Susanna Orelli — SP146

Alpine Dog-Rose SP147

Crocus SP148

**1945, Dec. 1** **Engr.**

**B150** SP145 5c + 5c dk grn .20 *.50*
**B151** SP146 10c + 10c dk red brn .20 *.50*

**Photo.**

**B152** SP147 20c + 10c rose brn, rose & yel org .30 *.50*
**B153** SP148 30c + 10c dk bl, gray & lil 1.50 *7.50*
*Nos. B150-B153 (4)* 2.20 *9.00*
Set, never hinged 4.50

Cheese Making SP149

Farm Buildings and Vineyards SP150

House in Appenzell SP151

House in Engadine SP152

**1946, June 15** **Engr.**

**B154** SP149 5c + 5c bl grn & red .35 *2.00*

**Photo.**

**B155** SP150 10c + 10c brn, buff & red .25 *.75*
**B156** SP151 20c + 10c henna, buff & red .35 *.75*
**B157** SP152 30c + 10c saph & red 3.00 *9.50*
*Nos. B154-B157 (4)* 3.95 *13.00*
Set, never hinged 9.50

Rodolphe Toepffer SP153

Narcissus SP154

20c+10c, Mountain sengreen. 30c+10c, Blue thistle.

**1946, Nov. 30** **Engr.**

**B158** SP153 5c + 5c green .20 *.50*

**Photo.**

**B159** SP154 10c + 10c dk sl grn, gray & red org .20 *.50*
**B160** SP154 20c + 10c brn car, gray & yel .30 *.75*
**B161** SP154 30c + 10c dk bl, gray & pink 1.40 *6.00*
*Nos. B158-B161 (4)* 2.10 *7.75*
Set, never hinged 3.75

Railroad Laborers SP157

Railroad Station, Rorschach SP158

Lüen-Castiel Station — SP159

Flüelen Station SP160

***Perf. 11½***

**1947, June 14** **Engr.** **Unwmk.**

**B162** SP157 5c + 5c dk grn & red .25 *2.10*

**Photo.**

**B163** SP158 10c + 10c gray blk, cream & red .30 *.75*
**B164** SP159 20c + 10c rose lil, cream & red .30 *1.00*
**B165** SP160 30c + 10c bl, gray & red 3.50 *9.00*
*Nos. B162-B165 (4)* 4.35 *12.85*
Set, never hinged 10.00

The surtax was for professional education of invalids and for the fight against cancer.

Jakob Burckhardt SP161

Alpine Primrose SP162

20c+10c, Red lily. 30c+10c, Cyclamen.

**1947, Dec. 1** **Engr.**

**B166** SP161 5c + 5c dk grn .20 *.45*

**Photo.**

**B167** SP162 10c + 10c sl blk, gray & yel .20 *.45*
**B168** SP162 20c + 10c red brn, gray & cop red .30 *.40*
**B169** SP162 30c + 10c dk bl, gray & pink 1.25 *5.75*
*Nos. B166-B169 (4)* 1.95 *7.05*
Set, never hinged 3.50

Sun and Olympic Emblem SP165

Icehockey Player SP167

10c+10c, Snowflake and Olympic Emblem. 30c+10c, Ski-runner.

**1948, Jan. 15**

**B170** SP165 5c + 5c dk bl grn & yel .25 *1.50*
**B171** SP165 10c + 10c choc & bl .30 *1.00*
**B172** SP167 20c + 10c dp mag, gray & org yel .40 *1.50*
**B173** SP167 30c + 10c dk bl, bl & gray blk 1.25 *5.50*
*Nos. B170-B173 (4)* 2.20 *9.50*
Set, never hinged 5.50

Issued to publicize the 5th Olympic Winter Games, St. Moritz, Jan. 30-Feb. 8, 1948.

Frontier Guard SP169

House of Fribourg SP170

House of Valais SP171

House of Ticino SP172

**1948, June 15** **Engr.**

**B174** SP169 5c + 5c dk grn & red .20 *1.25*

**Photo.**

**B175** SP170 10c + 10c sl & gray .20 *.75*
**B176** SP171 20c + 10c brn red & pink .30 *1.00*
**B177** SP172 30c + 10c bl & gray 2.25 *7.50*
*Nos. B174-B177 (4)* 2.95 *10.50*
Set, never hinged 6.00

Johann R. Wettstein — SP173

**1948, Aug. 21** ***Perf. 11x12½***

**B178** SP173 Sheet of 2 50.00 *65.00*
*a.* 10c rose lilac 14.00 *25.00*
*b.* 20c chalky blue 14.00 *25.00*
Never hinged 77.50

Intl. Phil. Expo., Basel, Aug. 21-29, 1948. Sheet, size 110x60mm, sold for 3fr, of which the surtax was used for the exhibition and charitable purposes.

Gen. Ulrich Wille SP174

Foxglove SP175

20c+10c, Alpine rose. 40c+10c, Lily of paradise.

**1948, Dec. 1** **Engr.** ***Perf. 11½***

**B179** SP174 5c + 5c dk vio brn .20 *.45*

**Photo.**

**B180** SP175 10c + 10c dk grn, yel grn & yel .25 *.45*
**B181** SP175 20c + 10c brn, crim & buff .30 *.45*
**B182** SP175 40c + 10c bl, gray & org 1.25 *5.50*
*Nos. B179-B182 (4)* 2.00 *6.85*
Set, never hinged 4.50

Postman
SP176

Mountain Farmhouse
SP177

House of Lucerne
SP178

House of Prattigau
SP179

**Engraved and Photogravure**

**1949, June 15**

**Shield in Carmine**

**B183** SP176 5c + 5c rose vio .30 *1.50*

**Photo.**

**B184** SP177 10c + 10c bl grn & car .30 *.75*
**B185** SP178 20c + 10c dk brn & cr .30 *.75*
**B186** SP179 40c + 10c bl & pale bl 2.50 *10.00*
*Nos. B183-B186 (4)* 3.40 *13.00*
Set, never hinged 7.25

The surtax was for professional education of Swiss youth.

Niklaus Wengi
SP180

Anemone Sulphureous
SP181

20c+10c, Alpine clematis. 40c+10c, Superb pink.

**1949, Dec. 1 Engr. *Perf. 11½***

**B187** SP180 5c + 5c vio brn .20 *.45*

**Photo.**

**B188** SP181 10c + 10c grn, gray & yel .20 *.45*
**B189** SP181 20c + 10c brn, bl & yel .25 *.45*
**B190** SP181 40c + 10c bl, lav & yel 1.40 *5.50*
*Nos. B187-B190 (4)* 2.05 *6.85*
Set, never hinged 4.00

Adaptation of 1850 Design
SP182

Putting the Stone
SP183

Designs: 20c+10c, Wrestlers. 30c+10c, Runners. 40c+10c, Target shooting.

**1950, June 1 Engr. & Photo.**

**Shield in Red**

**B191** SP182 5c + 5c black .20 *.75*

**Photo.**

**Inscribed: "I. VIII. 1950"**

**B192** SP183 10c + 10c green .50 *.80*
**B193** SP183 10c + 20c brown ol .50 *1.25*
**B194** SP183 30c + 10c rose lil 3.75 *17.00*
**B195** SP183 40c + 10c dull bl 4.75 *11.00*
*Nos. B191-B195 (5)* 9.70 *30.80*
Set, never hinged 20.00

The surtax was for the Red Cross and the Society of Swiss History of Art.

Theophil Sprecher von Bernegg
SP184

Admiral Butterfly
SP185

Designs: 20c+10c, Blue Underwing Butterfly. 30c+10c, Bee. 40c+10c, Sulphur Butterfly.

**1950, Dec. 1 Engr.**

**B196** SP184 5c + 5c sepia .20 *.30*

**Photo.**

**B197** SP185 10c + 10c multi .25 *.40*
**B198** SP185 20c + 10c multi .30 *.50*
**B199** SP185 30c + 10c rose lil, gray & dk brn 3.00 *13.50*
**B200** SP185 40c + 10c bl, dk brn & yel 3.00 *9.25*
*Nos. B196-B200 (5)* 6.75 *23.95*
Set, never hinged 13.50

Arms of Switzerland and Zurich — SP186

Valaisan Polka
SP187

20c+10c, Flag-swinging. 30c+10c, Hornussen (natl. game). 40c+10c, Blowing alphorn.

**1951, June 1 Engr.**

**Shield in Red**

**B201** SP186 5c + 5c gray .20 *.50*

**Photo.**

**Inscribed: "1. VIII. 1951"**

**Shield in Red, Figure Shaded in Gray**

**B202** SP187 10c + 10c green .40 *.50*
**B203** SP187 20c + 10c ol bis .60 *.85*
**B204** SP187 30c + 10c red vio 4.50 *11.50*
**B205** SP187 40c + 10c brt blue 4.50 *13.50*
*Nos. B201-B205 (5)* 10.20 *26.85*
Set, never hinged 20.00

The surtax was used primarily for needy mothers.

**Souvenir Sheet**

**1951, Sept. 29 *Imperf.***

**B206** SP187 40c brt bl, sheet 175.00 *190.00*
Never hinged 275.00

No. B206 sold for 3fr, size: 74x56mm. Natl. Phil. Exhib., LUNABA, Sept. 29-Oct. 7, 1951, Lucerne. The net proceeds were used for Swiss schools abroad.

Johanna Spyri
SP189

Dragonfly
SP190

Butterflies: 20c+10c, Black-Veined. 30c+10c Orange-Tip. 40c+10c, Saturnia pyri.

**1951, Dec. 1 Engr. *Perf. 11½***

**B207** SP189 5c + 5c red brn .20 *.30*

**Photo.**

**B208** SP190 10c + 10c grn & dk bl .20 *.30*
**B209** SP190 20c + 10c rose lil, cr & blk .30 *.50*
**B210** SP190 30c + 10c ol grn, gray & org 2.00 *8.50*
**B211** SP190 40c + 10c bl, dk brn & car 2.50 *8.50*
*Nos. B207-B211 (5)* 5.20 *18.10*
Set, never hinged 10.00

Arms of Switzerland, Glarus and Zug — SP191

Doubs River — SP192

Designs: 20c+10c, Lake of St. Gotthard. 30c+10c, Moesa River. 40c+10c, Lake of Marjelen.

**1952, May 31 Engr. & Typo.**

**B212** SP191 5c + 5c gray & red .25 *1.00*

**Photo.**

**B213** SP192 10c + 10c blue green .25 *.50*
**B214** SP192 20c + 10c brown car .30 *.50*
**B215** SP192 30c + 10c brown 2.50 *6.50*
**B216** SP192 40c + 10c blue 3.00 *8.75*
*Nos. B212-B216 (5)* 6.30 *17.25*
Set, never hinged 12.50

The surtax was used primarily for historical research and popular culture.

See Nos. B222-B226, B233-B236, B243-B246, B253-B256.

Portrait of a Boy, by Albert Anker
SP193

Ladybug
SP194

20c+10c, Barred-wing butterfly. 30c+10c, Argus butterfly. 40c+10c, Silkworm moth.

***Perf. 11½***

**1952, Dec. 1 Unwmk. Engr.**

**B217** SP193 5c + 5c brown car .20 *.35*

**Photo.**

**B218** SP194 10c + 10c bluish grn, blk & org red .20 *.35*
**B219** SP194 20c + 10c rose lil, cr & blk .30 *.50*
**B220** SP194 30c + 10c brn, blk & gray bl 2.00 *8.25*
**B221** SP194 40c + 10c pale vio, brn & buff 1.90 *8.75*
*Nos. B217-B221 (5)* 4.60 *18.20*
Set, never hinged 10.00

See Nos. B227-B231, B238-B241.

**Types Similar to 1952**

Designs: 5c+5c, Arms of Switzerland and Bern. 10c+10c, Reuss River. 20c+10c, Sihl Lake. 30c+10c, Bisse River. 40c+10c, Lake of Geneva.

**Engraved and Photogravure**

**1953, June 1**

**B222** SP191 5c + 5c gray & red .20 *.75*

**Photo.**

**B223** SP192 10c + 10c blue green .25 *.50*
**B224** SP192 20c + 10c brown car .30 *.75*
**B225** SP192 30c + 10c brown 2.50 *7.00*
**B226** SP192 40c + 10c blue 2.50 *6.50*
*Nos. B222-B226 (5)* 5.75 *15.50*
Set, never hinged 12.50

The surtax was used for Swiss nationals abroad and for disabled persons.

Booklet Panes

Panes consisting of blocks, strips or pairs removed from large sheets of regular issue and fastened or enclosed within a cover or folder, often by stapling or sewing in the sheet margin, are no longer being listed. Such panes contain no straight edges and can easily be made privately.

**Types Similar to 1952, Dated "1953"**

5c+5c, Portrait of a girl, by Albert Anker. 10c+10c, Nun moth. 20c+10c, Camberwell beauty butterfly. 30c+10c, Purple longicorn beetle. 40c+10c, Self-portrait, Ferdinand Hodler, facing left.

**1953, Dec. 1 Engr. *Perf. 11½***

**B227** SP193 5c + 5c rose brown .20 *.35*

**Photo.**

**B228** SP194 10c + 10c multi .25 *.30*
**B229** SP194 20c + 10c multi .30 *.50*
*a.* Sheet of 24 200.00
Never hinged 375.00
*b.* Bklt. pane, 4 #B229, 2 #B230 32.50
**B230** SP194 30c + 10c ol, blk & red 1.90 *8.25*

**Engr.**

**B231** SP193 40c + 10c blue 2.75 *7.00*
*Nos. B227-B231 (5)* 5.40 *16.40*
Set, never hinged 12.00

No. B229a consists of 16 No. B229 and 8 No. B230, arranged to include four se-tenant pairs and four pairs which are both se-tenant and tête bêche.

Opening Bars of "Swiss Hymn"
SP195

Jeremias Gotthelf
SP196

**Types Similar to 1952, Dated "1954"**

Views: 10c+10c, Neuchatel lake. 20c+10c, Maggia river. 30c+10c, Cascade, Taubenloch gorge. 40c+10c, Sils lake.

**1954, June 1 Engr. *Perf. 11½***

**B232** SP195 5c + 5c dk bl grn .25 *.75*

**Photo.**

**B233** SP192 10c + 10c blue grn .25 *.50*
**B234** SP192 20c + 10c deep plum .35 *.50*
**B235** SP192 30c + 10c dk brown 2.00 *6.75*

**B236** SP192 40c + 10c dp blue 2.25 *7.25*
*Nos. B232-B236 (5)* 5.10 *15.75*
Set, never hinged 12.00

The surtax was used to aid vocational training and home nursing.
No. B232 commemorates the centenary of the death of Alberik Zwyssig, composer of the "Swiss Hymn."

### Types Similar to 1952, Dated "1954"

Insects: 10c+10c, Garden tiger. 20c+10c, Bumble bee. 30c+10c, Ascalaphus. 40c+10c, Swallow-tail.

**1954, Dec. 1** **Engr.**
**B237** SP196 5c + 5c dk red brn .20 *.30*

**Photo.**

**B238** SP194 10c + 10c multi .20 *.30*
**B239** SP194 20c + 10c multi .35 *.50*
**B240** SP194 30c + 10c rose vio, brn & yel 2.00 *6.75*
**B241** SP194 40c + 10c multi 2.25 *7.25*
*Nos. B237-B241 (5)* 5.00 *15.10*
Set, never hinged 11.00

### Type Similar to 1952, Dated "1955," and

Federal Institute of Technology, Zurich — SP197

Views: 10c+10c, Saane river. 20c+10c, Lake of Aegeri. 30c+10c, Grappelen Lake. 40c+10c, Lake of Bienne.

**1955, June 1** **Engr.** ***Perf. 11½***
**B242** SP197 5c + 5c gray .20 *.75*

**Photo.**

**B243** SP192 10c + 10c dp green .25 *.50*
**B244** SP192 20c + 10c rose brn .35 *.50*
**B245** SP192 30c + 10c brown 2.00 *6.00*
**B246** SP192 40c + 10c dp blue 2.25 *7.50*
*Nos. B242-B246 (5)* 5.05 *15.25*
Set, never hinged 11.50

The surtax aided mountain dwellers.
No. B242 for the centenary of the Federal Institute of Technology in Zurich.

Charles Pictet de Rochemont SP198

Peacock Butterfly SP199

Insects: 20c+10c, Great Horntail. 30c+10c, Yellow Bear moth. 40c+10c, Apollo butterfly.

**1955, Dec. 1** **Engr.** **Unwmk.**
**B247** SP198 5c + 5c brn car .20 *.30*

**Photo.**

**Insects in Natural Colors**

**B248** SP199 10c + 10c yel grn .20 *.30*
**B249** SP199 20c + 10c red .30 *.50*
**B250** SP199 30c + 10c dk ocher 2.50 *4.75*
**B251** SP199 40c + 10c ultra 2.25 *5.75*
*Nos. B247-B251 (5)* 5.45 *11.60*
Set, never hinged 11.50

### Types Similar to 1952, Dated "1956", and

"Woman's Work" — SP200

Designs: 10c+10c, Rhone at St. Maurice. 20c+10c, Katzensee. 30c+10c, Rhine at Trin. 40c+10c, Lake Wallen.

**1956, June 1** **Engr.** ***Perf. 11½***
**B252** SP200 5c + 5c turq bl .20 *1.00*

**Photo.**

**B253** SP192 10c + 10c green .25 *.50*
**B254** SP192 20c + 10c brn car .30 *.75*
**B255** SP192 30c + 10c brown 2.00 *4.75*
**B256** SP192 40c + 10c ultra 1.75 *5.75*
*Nos. B252-B256 (5)* 4.50 *12.75*
Set, never hinged 10.00

The surtax was for the National Day Collection, the National Library and Academy of Arts and Letters. No. B252 was issued in honor of Swiss women.

Carlo Maderno SP201

Burnet Moth SP202

Insects: 20c+10c, Purple Emperor. 30c+10c, Blue ground beetle. 40c+10c, Cabbage butterfly.

**1956, Dec. 1** **Engr.** ***Perf. 11½***
**B257** SP201 5c + 5c brn car .20 *.30*

**Photo.**

**Granite Paper**

**B258** SP202 10c + 10c grn, dk grn & car rose .20 *.30*
**B259** SP202 20c + 10c multi .30 *.30*
**B260** SP202 30c + 10c yel & dp bl 1.40 *4.50*
**B261** SP202 40c + 10c lt ultra, pale yel & sep 1.40 *5.00*
*Nos. B257-B261 (5)* 3.50 *10.40*
Set, never hinged 7.50

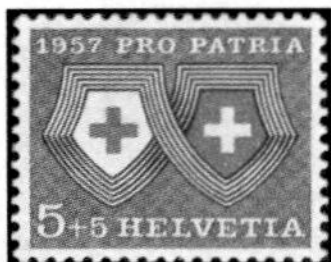

Red Cross and Swiss Emblems SP203

"Charity" — SP204

**Engraved and Photogravure**

**1957, June 1** **Unwmk.** ***Perf. 11½***
**B262** SP203 5c + 5c gray & red .20 *.55*

**Photo.**

**Granite Paper**

**Cross in Deep Carmine**

**B263** SP204 10c + 10c brt grn & gray .20 *.30*
**B264** SP204 20c + 10c red & bl gray .30 *.30*
**B265** SP204 30c + 10c brn & vio gray 1.75 *4.50*
**B266** SP204 40c + 10c brt bl & bis 1.90 *5.75*
*Nos. B262-B266 (5)* 4.35 *11.40*
Set, never hinged 10.00

The surtax went to the Red Cross for the needs of the sick and to combat cancer.

Leonhard Euler — SP205

Clouded Yellow — SP206

Insects: 20c+10c, Magpie moth. 30c+10c, Rose Chafer. 40c+10c, Red Underwing.

**1957, Nov. 30** **Engr.** ***Perf. 11½***
**B267** SP205 5c + 5c brn car .20 *.30*

**Photo.**

**Granite Paper**

**B268** SP206 10c + 10c multi .20 *.30*
**B269** SP206 20c + 10c lil rose, blk & yel .30 *.50*
**B270** SP206 30c + 10c rose brn, ind & brt grn 1.40 *4.50*
**B271** SP206 40c + 10c multi 1.40 *3.50*
*Nos. B267-B271 (5)* 3.50 *9.10*
Set, never hinged 7.50

**Catalogue values for unused stamps in this section, from this point to the end of the section, are for Never Hinged items.**

Mother and Child — SP207

Fluorite — SP208

Designs: 20c+10c, Ammonite. 30c+10c, Garnet. 40c+10c, Rock Crystal.

***Perf. 11½***

**1958, May 31** **Unwmk.** **Engr.**
**B272** SP207 5c + 5c brn car .40 *.40*

**Photo.**

**Granite Paper**

**B273** SP208 10c + 10c multi .55 *.55*
**B274** SP208 20c + 10c blk, red & ol bis .75 *.75*
**B275** SP208 30c + 10c blk, dl yel & mag 3.25 *5.25*
**B276** SP208 40c + 10c blk, chlky bl & sl bl 3.25 *5.00*
*Nos. B272-B276 (5)* 8.20 *11.95*

The surtax was for needy mothers.
See #B283-B286, B292-B295, B304-B307.

Albrecht von Haller — SP209

Pansy — SP210

Flowers: 20c+10c, China aster. 30c+10c, Morning glory. 40c+10c, Christmas rose.

**1958, Dec. 1** **Engr.** ***Perf. 11½***
**B277** SP209 5c + 5c brn car .25 *.30*

**Photo.**

**Granite Paper**

**B278** SP210 10c + 10c grn, yel & brn .25 *.30*
**B279** SP210 20c + 10c multi .55 .30
**B280** SP210 30c + 10c multi 2.00 *3.50*
**B281** SP210 40c + 10c dk bl, yel & grn 2.00 *3.50*
*Nos. B277-B281 (5)* 5.05 *7.90*

See Nos. B287-B291.

### Mineral Type of 1958 and

Globe and Swiss Flags — SP211

Designs: 10c+10c, Agate. 20c+10c, Tourmaline. 30c+10c, Amethyst. 40c+10c, Fossil salamander (andrias).

**1959, June 1** **Engr.** ***Perf. 11½***
**B282** SP211 5c + 5c dl grn & red .40 *.50*

**Photo.**

**Granite Paper**

**B283** SP208 10c + 10c gray, yel grn & ver .50 *.50*
**B284** SP208 20c + 10c blk, lil rose & bl grn .65 .50
**B285** SP208 30c + 10c blk, lt brn & vio 2.25 *3.00*
**B286** SP208 40c + 10c blk, bl & gray 2.50 *3.00*
*Nos. B282-B286 (5)* 6.30 *7.50*

### Types of 1958

Designs: 5c+5c, Karl Hilty. 10c+10c, Marigold. 20c+10c, Poppy. 30c+10c, Nasturtium. 50c+10c, Sweet pea.

**1959, Dec. 1** **Engr.** ***Perf. 11½***
**B287** SP209 5c +5c brn car .20 *.25*

**Photo.**

**Granite Paper**

**B288** SP210 10c + 10c dk grn, grn & yel .30 .25
**B289** SP210 20c + 10c mag, red & grn .50 .25
**B290** SP210 30c + 10c multi 2.25 *3.00*
**B291** SP210 50c + 10c multi 2.25 *3.00*
*Nos. B287-B291 (5)* 5.50 *6.75*

### Mineral Type of 1958 and

Owl, T-Square and Hammer — SP212

Designs: 5c+5c, Smoky quartz. 10c+10c, Feldspar. 20c+10c, Gryphaea, fossil. 30c+10c, Azurite.

**1960, June 1** **Photo.** ***Perf. 11½***

**Granite Paper**

**B292** SP208 5c + 5c blk, bl & ocher .55 *.75*
**B293** SP208 10c + 10c blk, yel grn & pink .60 .50
**B294** SP208 20c + 10c blk, lil rose & yel .85 .50
**B295** SP208 30c + 10c multi 4.00 3.75

**Engr.**

**B296** SP212 50c + 10c bl & gold 4.75 3.50
*Nos. B292-B296 (5)* 10.75 9.00

**Souvenir Sheet**

***Imperf***

**Typo.**

**B297** Sheet of 4 40.00 20.00

#B297 contains 4 50c+10c stamps of design SP212 in gold & blue. Size: 84x75mm. Sold for 3fr.

Alexandre Calame SP213

Dandelion SP214

Flowers: 20c+10c, Phlox. 30c+10c, Larkspur. 50c+10c, Thorn apple.

**1960, Dec. 1** **Engr.** **Unwmk.**
**B298** SP213 5c + 5c grnsh bl .25 .20

**Photo.**

**Granite Paper**

**B299** SP214 10c + 10c grn, yel & gray .30 .20
**B300** SP214 20c + 10c mag, grn & gray .45 .20
**B301** SP214 30c + 10c org brn, grn & bl 3.50 3.50
**B302** SP214 50c + 10c ultra & grn 3.50 3.50
*Nos. B298-B302 (5)* 8.00 7.60

See Nos. B308-B312, B329-B333, B339-B343.

### Mineral Type of 1958 and

Book of History with Symbols of Time and Eternity — SP215

Designs: 10c+10c, Fluorite. 20c+10c, Petrified fish. 30c+10c, Lazulite. 50c+10c, Petrified fern.

**1961, June 1 Engr. *Perf. 11½***
**B303** SP215 5c + 5c lt blue .35 *.50*

**Photo.**
**Granite Paper**

**B304** SP208 10c + 10c gray, grn & pink .50 .35
**B305** SP208 20c + 10c gray & car rose .60 .35
**B306** SP208 30c + 10c gray, org & grnsh bl 1.60 *2.50*
**B307** SP208 50c + 10c gray, bl & bis 2.25 *3.50*
*Nos. B303-B307 (5)* 5.30 *7.20*

### Types of 1960

Designs: 5c+5c, Jonas Furrer. 10c+10c, Sunflower. 20c+10c, Lily of the valley. 30c+10c, Iris. 50c+10c, Silverweed.

**1961, Dec. 1 Engr. *Perf. 11½***
**B308** SP213 5c + 5c dk blue .20 .20

**Photo.**
**Granite Paper**

**B309** SP214 10c + 10c grn, yel & org .20 .20
**B310** SP214 20c + 10c dk red, grn & gray .30 .20
**B311** SP214 30c + 10c multi 1.75 *2.00*
**B312** SP214 50c + 10c dk bl, yel & grn 2.00 *2.50*
*Nos. B308-B312 (5)* 4.45 *5.10*

Jean Jacques Rousseau SP216

Half-Thaler, Obwalden, 1732 SP217

Coins: 20c+10c, Ducat, Schwyz, ca. 1653. 30c+10c, "Steer Head" Batzen, Uri, 1659. 50c+10c, Nidwalden Batzen.

***Perf. 11½***

**1962, June 1 Unwmk. Engr.**
**B313** SP216 5c + 5c dk blue .20 .20

**Photo.**
**Granite Paper**

**B314** SP217 10c + 10c grn & stl bl .20 *.20*
**B315** SP217 20c + 10c car rose & yel .50 *.50*
**B316** SP217 30c + 10c org & sl bl 1.25 *1.65*
**B317** SP217 50c + 10c ultra & vio bl 1.25 *1.65*
*Nos. B313-B317 (5)* 3.40 *4.20*

Apple Blossoms SP218

Mother and Child SP219

Designs: 10c+10c, Boy chasing duck. 30c+10c, Girl and sunflowers. 50c+10c, Forsythia. 1fr+20c, Mother and child, facing right.

**1962, Dec. 1 *Perf. 11½***
**Granite Paper**

**B318** SP218 5c + 5c bl gray, pink, grn & yel .20 .20
**B319** SP218 10c + 10c grn, pink & dk grn .20 .20
**B320** SP219 20c + 10c org red, brn, grn & pink .60 .50
**B321** SP218 30c + 10c org, red & yel 1.10 *2.00*
**B322** SP218 50c + 10c dp bl, yel & brn 1.50 *2.50*
*Nos. B318-B322 (5)* 3.60 *5.40*

**Souvenir Sheet**
***Imperf***

**B323** SP219 1fr + 20c Sheet of 2 5.25 5.25

50th anniv. of the Pro Juventute (Youth Aid) Foundation. No. B323 sold for 3fr.

Anna Heer, M.D. — SP220

Bandage Roll — SP221

Designs: 20c+10c, Gift parcel. 30c+10c, Plasma bottles. 50c+10c, Red Cross armband.

**1963, June 1 Engr. *Perf. 11½***
**B324** SP220 5c + 5c dk blue .20 .20

**Photo.**
**Granite Paper**
**Cross in Red**

**B325** SP221 10c + 10c lt & dk grn & gray .20 .20
**B326** SP221 20c + 10c rose, gray & blk .50 .20
**B327** SP221 30c + 10c multicolored 1.10 *1.50*
**B328** SP221 50c + 10c bl, gray & blk 1.25 *1.50*
*Nos. B324-B328 (5)* 3.25 *3.60*

### Types of 1960

Designs: 5c+5c, Portrait of a Boy by Albert Anker. 10c+10c, Daisy. 20c+10c, Geranium. 30c+10c, Cornflower. 50c+10c, Carnation.

**1963, Nov. 30 Engr. *Perf. 11½***
**B329** SP213 5c + 5c blue .20 *.30*
*a.* Booklet pane of 4 3.00

**Photo.**

**B330** SP214 10c + 10c grn, gray & yel .30 *1.25*
*a.* Booklet pane of 4 4.00
**B331** SP214 20c + 10c multi 1.40 *2.50*
*a.* Booklet pane of 4 5.75
**B332** SP214 30c + 10c multi 1.40 *1.50*
**B333** SP214 50c + 10c ultra, lil rose & grn 1.75 1.50
*Nos. B329-B333 (5)* 5.05 *7.05*

Nos. B329-B331 were printed on two kinds of paper: I. Fluorescent, with violet fibers. II. Non-fluorescent, the 10c+10c and 20c+10c with mixed red and blue fibers. Nos. B332-B333 exist only on violet-fibered, fluorescent paper. The booklet panes, Nos. B329a, B330a and B331a, exist only on non-fluorescent paper.

Johann Georg Bodmer SP222

Copper Coin, Zurich SP223

Coins: 20c+10c, Doppeldicken, Basel. 30c+10c, Silver taler, Geneva. 50c+10c, Gold half florin, Bern.

**Violet Fibers, Fluorescent Paper**

**1964, June 1 Engr. *Perf. 11½***
**B334** SP222 5c + 5c blue .20 .20

**Photo.**

**B335** SP223 10c + 10c grn, bis & blk .20 .20
**B336** SP223 20c + 10c rose car, gray & blk .30 .25
**B337** SP223 30c + 10c org, gray & blk .55 .50

**Granite Paper, Red and Blue Fibers**

**B338** SP223 50c + 10c ultra, yel & brn .80 .65
*Nos. B334-B338 (5)* 2.05 1.80

Fluorescent Paper

Paper of Nos. B334-B425, B427 and B429 is fluorescent and has violet fibers.

Nos. B426, B428 and all semipostals from No. B430 onward are fluorescent but lack violet fibers, unless otherwise noted.

### Types of 1960

Designs: 5c+5c, Portrait of a Girl by Albert Anker. 10c+10c, Daffodil. 20c+10c, Rose. 30c+10c, Clover. 50c+10c, Water lily.

**1964, Dec. 1 Engr. *Perf. 11½***
**B339** SP213 5c + 5c grnsh bl .20 .20

**Photo.**

**B340** SP214 10c + 10c dp grn, yel & org .20 .20
**B341** SP214 20c + 10c dp car, rose & grn .30 .20
**B342** SP214 30c + 10c brn, lil & grn .55 .55
**B343** SP214 50c + 10c multi .75 .75
*Nos. B339-B343 (5)* 2.00 1.90

### Type of Regular Issue, 1965
**Souvenir Sheet**

10c, 20r Seated Helvetia. 20c, 40r Seated Helvetia.

**1965, Mar. 8 Photo. *Imperf.***
**Granite Paper, Nonfluorescent**

**B344** A153 Sheet of 2 1.50 1.00
*a.* 10c grn, pale orange & blk .75 .50
*b.* 20c dark red, yel grn & blk .75 .50

Natl. Postage Stamp Exhib., NABRA, Bern, Aug. 27-Sept. 5, 1965. Sold for 3fr, the net proceeds were used to cover expenses of the exhibition and to promote philately.

Father Theodosius Florentini SP224

The Temptation of Christ SP225

Ceiling Paintings from Church of St. Martin at Zillis, 12th century: 10c+10c, Symbol of evil (goose with fishtail). 20c+10c, Magi on horseback. 30c+10c, Fishermen on Sea of Galilee.

***Perf. 11½***

**1965, June 1 Unwmk. Engr.**
**B345** SP224 5c + 5c blue .20 .20

**Photo.**

**B346** SP225 10c + 10c ol grn, ocher & bl .20 .20
**B347** SP225 20c + 10c dk brn, red & buff .30 .20
**B348** SP225 30c + 10c dk brn, sep & bl .50 .30
**B349** SP225 50c + 10c vio bl, bl & brn .60 .30
*Nos. B345-B349 (5)* 1.80 1.20

See Nos. B355-B359, B365-B369.

Hedgehogs — SP226

Designs: 10c+10c, Alpine marmots. 20c+10c, Red deer. 30c+10c, European badgers. 50c+10c, Varying hares.

**1965, Dec. 1 Photo. *Perf. 11½***
**B350** SP226 5c + 5c multi .20 .20
**B351** SP226 10c + 10c multi .20 .20
**B352** SP226 20c + 10c multi .30 .20
**B353** SP226 30c + 10c multi .50 .20
**B354** SP226 50c + 10c multi .60 .30
*Nos. B350-B354 (5)* 1.80 1.10

See Nos. B360-B364.

### Types of 1965

5c+5c, Heinrich Federer (1866-1928), writer. 10c+10c, Joseph's dream. 20c+10c, Joseph on his way. 30c+10c, Virgin and Child fleeing to Egypt. 50c+10c, Angel leading the way. Nos. B356-B359 from ceiling paintings, Church of St. Martin at Zillis.

**1966, June 1 Engr. *Perf. 11½***
**B355** SP224 5c + 5c dp blue .20 .20

**Photo.**

**B356** SP225 10c + 10c multi .20 .20
**B357** SP225 20c + 10c multi .30 .20
**B358** SP225 30c + 10c multi .50 .25
**B359** SP225 50c + 10c multi .60 .35
*Nos. B355-B359 (5)* 1.80 1.20

Animal Type of 1965

5c+5c, Ermine. 10c+10c, Red squirrel. 20c+10c, Red fox. 30c+10c, Hares. 50c+10c, Two chamois.

**1966, Dec. 1 Photo. *Perf. 11½***
**Animals in Natural Colors**

**B360** SP226 5c + 5c grnsh bl .20 .20
**B361** SP226 10c + 10c emer .20 .20
**B362** SP226 20c + 10c ver .30 .20
**B363** SP226 30c + 10c brt lemon .50 .20
**B364** SP226 50c + 10c ultra .60 .35
*Nos. B360-B364 (5)* 1.80 1.15

Types of 1965

Designs: 5c+5c, Dr. Theodor Kocher. 10c+10c, Annunciation to the Shepherds. 20c+10c, Jesus and the Samaritan Woman at the Well. 30c+10c, Adoration of the Magi. 50c+10c St. Joseph. (Ceiling paintings, St. Martin at Zillis).

***Perf. 11½***

**1967, June 1 Unwmk. Engr.**
**B365** SP224 5c + 5c blue .20 .20

**Photo.**

**B366** SP225 10c + 10c multi .20 .20
**B367** SP225 20c + 10c multi .30 .20
**B368** SP225 30c + 10c multi .50 .20
**B369** SP225 50c + 10c multi .60 .35
*Nos. B365-B369 (5)* 1.80 1.15

Roe Deer — SP227

Hunter, Month of May — SP228

Designs: 20c+10c, Pine marten. 30c+10c, Alpine ibex. 50c+20c, Otter.

**1967, Dec. 1 Photo. *Perf. 11½***
**Animals in Natural Colors**

**B370** SP227 10c + 10c yel grn .20 .20
**B371** SP227 20c + 10c dp car .30 .20
**B372** SP227 30c + 10c ol bis .50 .25
**B373** SP227 50c + 20c ultra .75 .50
*Nos. B370-B373 (4)* 1.75 1.15

**1968, May 30 Photo. *Perf. 11½***

Designs from Rose Window, Lausanne Cathedral: 20c+10c, Leo. 30c+10c, Libra. 50c+20c, Pisces.

**B374** SP228 10c + 10c multi .20 .20
**B375** SP228 20c + 10c multi .30 .20
**B376** SP228 30c + 10c multi .50 .30
**B377** SP228 50c + 20c multi .70 .70
*Nos. B374-B377 (4)* 1.70 1.40

Capercaillie SP229

St. Francis SP230

Birds: 20c+10c, Bullfinch. 30c+10c, Woodchat shrike. 50c+20c, Firecrest.

**1968, Nov. 28 Photo. *Perf. 11½***
**Birds in Natural Colors**

**B378** SP229 10c + 10c dull yel .20 .20
**B379** SP229 20c + 10c olive grn .30 .20
**B380** SP229 30c + 10c lilac rose .40 .20
**B381** SP229 50c + 20c dp violet .70 .50
*Nos. B378-B381 (4)* 1.60 1.10

See Nos. B386-B389.

**1969, May 29 Photo. *Perf. 11½***

Designs: 10c+10c, St. Francis Preaching to the Birds, Königsfelden Convent Church. 20c+10c, Israelites Drinking from Spring of Moses, Berne Cathedral. 30c+10c, St. Christopher, Laufelfinger Church (now Basel Museum). 50c+20c, Virgin and Child, Chapel at Grapplang (now National Museum).

**B382** SP230 10c + 10c multi .20 .20
**B383** SP230 20c + 10c multi .30 .20
**B384** SP230 30c + 10c multi .50 .25
**B385** SP230 50c + 20c multi .70 .45
*Nos. B382-B385 (4)* 1.70 1.10

### Bird Type of 1968

Birds: 10c+10c, European goldfinch. 20c+10c, Golden oriole. 30c+10c, Wall creeper. 50c+20c, Eurasian jay.

**1969, Dec. 1 Photo. *Perf. 11½***

**Birds in Natural Colors**

| | | | | |
|---|---|---|---|---|
| **B386** | SP229 | 10c + 10c gray | .20 | .20 |
| **B387** | SP229 | 20c + 10c green | .30 | .20 |
| **B388** | SP229 | 30c + 10c plum | .40 | .25 |
| **B389** | SP229 | 50c + 20c ultra | .70 | .55 |
| | | *Nos. B386-B389 (4)* | 1.60 | 1.20 |

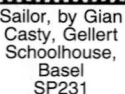

Sailor, by Gian Casty, Gellert Schoolhouse, Basel SP231

Blue Titmice SP232

Contemporary Stained Glass Windows: 20c+10c, Abstract composition, by Celestino Piatti. 30c+10c, Bull (Assyrian god Marduk), by Hans Stocker. 50c+20c, Man and Woman, by Max Hunziker and Karl Ganz.

**1970, May 29 Photo. *Perf. 11½***

| | | | | |
|---|---|---|---|---|
| **B390** | SP231 | 10c + 10c multi | .20 | .20 |
| **B391** | SP231 | 20c + 10c multi | .30 | .20 |
| **B392** | SP231 | 30c + 10c multi | .50 | .25 |
| **B393** | SP231 | 50c + 20c multi | .70 | .50 |
| | | *Nos. B390-B393 (4)* | 1.70 | 1.15 |

See Nos. B398-B401.

**1970, Dec. 1 Photo. *Perf. 11½***

Birds: 20c+10c, Hoopoe. 30c+10c, Greater spotted woodpecker. 50c+20c, Crested grebes.

**Birds in Natural Colors**

| | | | | |
|---|---|---|---|---|
| **B394** | SP232 | 10c + 10c orange | .20 | .20 |
| **B395** | SP232 | 20c + 10c emerald | .30 | .20 |
| **B396** | SP232 | 30c + 10c brt rose | .50 | .20 |
| **B397** | SP232 | 50c + 20c blue | .80 | .75 |
| | | *Nos. B394-B397 (4)* | 1.80 | 1.35 |

See Nos. B402-B405.

### Art Type of 1970

Contemporary Stained Glass Windows: 10c+10c, "Composition," by Jean-François Comment. 20c+10c, Cock, by Jean Prahin. 30c+10c, Fox, by Kurt Volk. 50c+20c, "Composition," by Bernard Schorderet.

**1971, May 27 Photo. *Perf. 11½***

| | | | | |
|---|---|---|---|---|
| **B398** | SP231 | 10c + 10c multi | .20 | .20 |
| **B399** | SP231 | 20c + 10c multi | .30 | .20 |
| **B400** | SP231 | 30c + 10c multi | .40 | .25 |
| **B401** | SP231 | 50c + 20c multi | .70 | .45 |
| | | *Nos. B398-B401 (4)* | 1.60 | 1.10 |

### Bird Type of 1970

Birds: 10c+10c, European redstarts. 20c+10c, White-spotted bluethroats. 30c+10c, Peregrine falcon. 40c+20c, Mallards.

**1971, Dec. 1**

| | | | | |
|---|---|---|---|---|
| **B402** | SP232 | 10c + 10c multi | .20 | .20 |
| **B403** | SP232 | 20c + 10c multi | .30 | .20 |
| **B404** | SP232 | 30c + 10c multi | .50 | .20 |
| **B405** | SP232 | 40c + 20c multi | .75 | .60 |
| | | *Nos. B402-B405 (4)* | 1.75 | 1.20 |

Harpoon Heads, Late Stone Age SP233

McGredy's Sunset SP234

Archaeological Treasures: 20c+10c, Bronze hydria, Hallstadt period. 30c+10c, Gold bust of Emperor Marcus Aurelius, Roman period. 40c+20c, Horseback rider (decorative disk), early Middle Ages.

**1972, June 1**

| | | | | |
|---|---|---|---|---|
| **B406** | SP233 | 10c + 10c multi | .20 | .20 |
| **B407** | SP233 | 20c + 10c multi | .35 | .20 |
| **B408** | SP233 | 30c + 10c multi | .50 | .20 |
| **B409** | SP233 | 40c + 20c multi | 1.25 | .70 |
| | | *Nos. B406-B409 (4)* | 2.30 | 1.30 |

**1972, Dec. 1 Photo. *Perf. 11½***

Famous Roses: 20c+10c, Miracle. 30c+10c, Papa Meilland. 40c+20c, Madame Dimitriu.

| | | | | |
|---|---|---|---|---|
| **B410** | SP234 | 10c + 10c multi | .25 | .20 |
| **B411** | SP234 | 20c + 10c multi | .30 | .20 |
| **B412** | SP234 | 30c + 10c multi | .50 | .20 |
| **B413** | SP234 | 40c + 20c multi | 1.25 | 1.10 |
| | | *Nos. B410-B413 (4)* | 2.30 | 1.70 |

Rauraric (Gallic) Jug — SP235

Chestnut — SP236

Archeologic Finds: 30c+10c, Bronze head of a Gaul. 40c+20c, Alemannic dress fasteners (fish), 6th century. 60c+20c, Gold bowl, 6th century B.C.

**1973, May 29 Photo. *Perf. 11½***

| | | | | |
|---|---|---|---|---|
| **B414** | SP235 | 15c + 5c multi | .20 | .20 |
| **B415** | SP235 | 30c + 10c multi | .50 | .20 |
| **B416** | SP235 | 40c + 20c multi | 1.00 | .60 |
| **B417** | SP235 | 60c + 20c multi | 1.25 | .85 |
| | | *Nos. B414-B417 (4)* | 2.95 | 1.85 |

See Nos. B422-B425.

**1973, Nov. 29 Photo. *Perf. 11½***

Fruits of the Forest: 30c+10c, Sweet cherries. 40c+20c, Blackberries. 60c+20c, Blueberries.

| | | | | |
|---|---|---|---|---|
| **B418** | SP236 | 15c + 5c multi | .20 | .20 |
| **B419** | SP236 | 30c + 10c multi | .30 | .20 |
| **B420** | SP236 | 40c + 20c multi | .75 | .60 |
| **B421** | SP236 | 60c + 20c multi | 1.25 | .70 |
| | | *Nos. B418-B421 (4)* | 2.50 | 1.70 |

### Archaeological Type of 1973

Archaeological Finds: 15c+5c, Polychrome glass bowl. 30c+10c, Bull's head. 40c+20c, Gold fibula. 60c+20c, Ceramic bird.

**1974, May 30 Photo. *Perf. 11½***

| | | | | |
|---|---|---|---|---|
| **B422** | SP235 | 15c + 5c multi | .20 | .20 |
| **B423** | SP235 | 30c + 10c multi | .50 | .30 |
| **B424** | SP235 | 40c + 20c multi | .90 | .55 |
| **B425** | SP235 | 60c + 20c multi | 1.25 | .70 |
| | | *Nos. B422-B425 (4)* | 2.85 | 1.75 |

Laurel — SP237

Gold Fibula, 6th Century — SP238

Designs: 30c+20c, Belladonna. 50c+20c, Laburnum. 60c+25c, Mistletoe.

**1974, Nov. 29 Photo. *Perf. 11½***

| | | | | |
|---|---|---|---|---|
| **B426** | SP237 | 15c + 10c multi | .20 | .20 |
| **B427** | SP237 | 30c + 20c multi | .50 | .20 |
| **B428** | SP237 | 50c + 20c multi | .80 | .60 |
| **B429** | SP237 | 60c + 25c multi | 1.10 | .80 |
| | | *Nos. B426-B429 (4)* | 2.60 | 1.80 |

**1975, May 30 Photo. *Perf. 11½***

Archaeological Treasures: 30c+20c, Bronze head of Bacchus, 2nd century. 50c+20c, Bronze daggers, 1800-1600 B.C. 60c+25c, Colored glass bottle, 1st century.

| | | | | |
|---|---|---|---|---|
| **B430** | SP238 | 15c + 10c multi | .35 | .20 |
| **B431** | SP238 | 30c + 20c multi | .60 | .25 |
| **B432** | SP238 | 50c + 20c multi | 1.00 | .70 |
| **B433** | SP238 | 60c + 25c multi | 1.10 | .75 |
| | | *Nos. B430-B433 (4)* | 3.05 | 1.90 |

Mail Bucket SP239

Hepatica SP240

Forest Plants: 30c+20c, Mountain ash berries. 50c+20c, Yellow nettle. 60c+25c, Sycamore maple.

**1975, Nov. 27 Photo. *Perf. 11½***

| | | | | |
|---|---|---|---|---|
| **B434** | SP239 | 10c + 5c multi | .20 | .20 |
| **B435** | SP240 | 15c + 10c multi | .20 | .20 |
| **B436** | SP240 | 30c + 20c multi | .50 | .30 |
| **B437** | SP240 | 50c + 20c multi | .80 | .65 |
| **B438** | SP240 | 60c + 25c multi | 1.00 | .75 |
| | | *Nos. B434-B438 (5)* | 2.70 | 2.10 |

See Nos. B443-B446.

Castles SP241

**1976, May 28 Photo. *Perf. 11½***

| | | | | |
|---|---|---|---|---|
| **B439** | SP241 | 20c + 10 Kyburg | .40 | .20 |
| **B440** | SP241 | 40c + 20 Grandson | .75 | .30 |
| **B441** | SP241 | 40c + 20 Murten | .75 | .30 |
| **B442** | SP241 | 80c + 40 Bellinzona | 2.25 | .85 |
| | | *Nos. B439-B442 (4)* | 4.15 | 1.65 |

See #B447-B450, B455-B458, B463-B466.

### Plant Type of 1975

Medicinal Forest Plants: 20c+10c, Barberry. No. B444, Black elder. No. B445, Linden. 80+40c, Pulmonaria.

**1976, Nov. 29 Photo. *Perf. 11½***

| | | | | |
|---|---|---|---|---|
| **B443** | SP240 | 20c + 10c multi | .30 | .20 |
| **B444** | SP240 | 40c + 20c lil & multi | .55 | .20 |
| **B445** | SP240 | 40c + 20c terra cotta & multi | .55 | .20 |
| **B446** | SP240 | 80c + 40c multi | 1.25 | .80 |
| | | *Nos. B443-B446 (4)* | 2.65 | 1.40 |

### Castle Type of 1976

**1977, May 26 Photo. *Perf. 11½***

| | | | | |
|---|---|---|---|---|
| **B447** | SP241 | 20c + 10c Aigle | .40 | .25 |
| **B448** | SP241 | 40c + 20c Pratteln | .60 | .35 |
| **B449** | SP241 | 70c + 30c Sargans | 1.25 | .90 |
| **B450** | SP241 | 80c + 40c Hallwil | 1.50 | 1.00 |
| | | *Nos. B447-B450 (4)* | 3.75 | 2.50 |

Wild Rose — SP242

Communal Arms — SP243

Designs: Roses.

**1977, Nov. 28 Photo. *Perf. 11½***

| | | | | |
|---|---|---|---|---|
| **B451** | SP242 | 20c + 10c multi | .30 | .20 |
| **B452** | SP242 | 40c + 20c multi | .60 | .20 |
| **B453** | SP242 | 70c + 30c multi | 1.00 | .80 |
| **B454** | SP242 | 80c + 40c multi | 1.25 | 1.00 |
| | | *Nos. B451-B454 (4)* | 3.15 | 2.20 |

See Nos. B492-B496.

### Castle Type of 1976

**1978, May 26 Photo. *Perf. 11½***

| | | | | |
|---|---|---|---|---|
| **B455** | SP241 | 20c + 10c Hagenwil | .30 | .30 |
| **B456** | SP241 | 40c + 20c Burgdorf | .60 | .60 |
| **B457** | SP241 | 70c + 30c Tarasp | 1.25 | 1.25 |
| **B458** | SP241 | 80c + 40c Chillon | 1.50 | 1.50 |
| | | *Nos. B455-B458 (4)* | 3.65 | 3.65 |

**1978, Nov. 28 Photo. *Perf. 11½***

| | | | | |
|---|---|---|---|---|
| **B459** | SP243 | 20c + 10c Aarburg | .30 | .20 |
| **B460** | SP243 | 40c + 20c Gruyeres | .60 | .25 |
| **B461** | SP243 | 70c + 30c Castasegna | 1.00 | 1.00 |
| **B462** | SP243 | 80c + 40c Wangen an der Aare | 1.50 | 1.25 |
| | | *Nos. B459-B462 (4)* | 3.40 | 2.70 |

See #B467-B470, B475-B478, B484-B487.

### Castle Type of 1976

**1979, May 25 Photo. *Perf. 11½***

| | | | | |
|---|---|---|---|---|
| **B463** | SP241 | 20c + 10c Oron | .30 | .30 |
| **B464** | SP241 | 40c + 20c Spiez | .60 | .45 |
| **B465** | SP241 | 70c + 30c Porrentruy | 1.10 | 1.00 |
| **B466** | SP241 | 80c + 40c Rapperswil | 1.50 | 1.50 |
| | | *Nos. B463-B466 (4)* | 3.50 | 3.25 |

### Arms Type of 1978

**1979, Nov. 28 Photo. *Perf. 11***

| | | | | |
|---|---|---|---|---|
| **B467** | SP243 | 20c + 10c Cadro | .30 | .20 |
| **B468** | SP243 | 40c + 20c Rute | .60 | .25 |
| **B469** | SP243 | 70c + 30c Schwamendingen | 1.00 | .85 |
| **B470** | SP243 | 80c + 40c Perroy | 1.50 | 1.10 |
| | | *Nos. B467-B470 (4)* | 3.40 | 2.40 |

Masons' and Carpenters' Sign — SP244

**1980, May 29 Photo. *Perf. 11½***

| | | | | |
|---|---|---|---|---|
| **B471** | SP244 | 20c + 10c shown | .30 | .30 |
| **B472** | SP244 | 40c + 20c Barber | .45 | .30 |
| **B473** | SP244 | 70c + 30c Hat maker | 1.00 | 1.00 |
| **B474** | SP244 | 80c + 40c Baker | 1.25 | 1.25 |
| | | *Nos. B471-B474 (4)* | 3.00 | 2.85 |

### Arms Type of 1978

**1980, Nov. 26 Photo. *Perf. 11½***

| | | | | |
|---|---|---|---|---|
| **B475** | SP243 | 20c + 10c Cortaillod | .30 | .20 |
| **B476** | SP243 | 40c + 20c Sierre | .55 | .25 |
| **B477** | SP243 | 70c + 30c Scuol | 1.00 | .90 |
| **B478** | SP243 | 80c + 40c Wolfenschiessen | 1.25 | .95 |
| | | *Nos. B475-B478 (4)* | 3.10 | 2.30 |

Icarus in Flight SP245

**1981, Mar. 9 Photo.**

| | | | | |
|---|---|---|---|---|
| **B479** | SP245 | 2fr + 1fr multi | 3.00 | 3.00 |

Swissair, 50th Anniversary. Surtax was for Pro Aero Foundation Issued in sheet of 8.

Post Office Sign, Aarburg, 1685 — SP246

Post Office Signs (c. 1849).

**1981, May 4 Photo.**

| | | | | |
|---|---|---|---|---|
| **B480** | SP246 | 20c + 10c shown | .30 | .30 |
| **B481** | SP246 | 40c + 20c Fribourg | .60 | .50 |
| **B482** | SP246 | 70c + 30c Gordola | 1.10 | 1.10 |
| **B483** | SP246 | 80c + 40c Splugen | 1.25 | 1.25 |
| | | *Nos. B480-B483 (4)* | 3.25 | 3.15 |

### Arms Type of 1978

**1981, Nov. 26 Photo. *Perf. 11½***

| | | | | |
|---|---|---|---|---|
| **B484** | SP243 | 20c + 10c Uffikon | .30 | .20 |
| **B485** | SP243 | 40c + 20c Torre | .60 | .30 |
| **B486** | SP243 | 70c + 30c Benken | 1.00 | .60 |
| **B487** | SP243 | 80c + 40c Preverenges | 1.10 | .75 |
| | | *Nos. B484-B487 (4)* | 3.00 | 1.85 |

Sonne Inn Sign, Willisau SP247

**1982, May 27 Photo. *Perf. 11½***

**B488** SP247 20c + 10c shown .30 .20
**B489** SP247 40c + 20c A L'Onde, St. Saphorin .55 .30
**B490** SP247 70c + 30c Three Kings, Rheinfelden .90 .55
**B491** SP247 80c + 40c Krone, Winterthur 1.25 .70
*Nos. B488-B491 (4)* 3.00 1.75

See Nos. B497-B500.

### Rose Type of 1977

Designs: 10c+10c, Letter balance. 20c+10c, La Belle Portugaise. 40c+20c, Hugh Dickson. 70c+30c, Mermaid. 80c+40c, Madame Caroline.

**1982, Nov. 25 Photo.**

**B492** SP242 10c + 10c multi .25 .20
**B493** SP242 20c + 10c multi .40 .20
**B494** SP242 40c + 20c multi .70 .30
**B495** SP242 70c + 30c multi 1.25 .80
**B496** SP242 80c + 40c multi 1.40 1.10
*Nos. B492-B496 (5)* 4.00 2.60

### Inn Sign Type of 1982

**1983, May 26 Photo.**

**B497** SP247 20c + 10c Lion Inn, Heimiswil, 1669 .40 .30
**B498** SP247 40c + 20c Cross Hotel, Sachseln, 1489 .75 .50
**B499** SP247 70c + 30c Tankard Inn, 1830 1.25 .80
**B500** SP247 80c + 40c Au Cavalier Inn, Vaud 1.40 1.00
*Nos. B497-B500 (4)* 3.80 2.60

Antique Toys — SP248

**1983, Nov. 24**

**B501** SP248 20c + 10c Kitchen stove, 1850 .35 .20
**B502** SP248 40c + 20c Rocking horse, 1826 .70 .35
**B503** SP248 70c + 30c Doll, 1870 1.10 .55
**B504** SP248 80c + 40c Steam locomotive, 1900 1.40 .70
*Nos. B501-B504 (4)* 3.55 1.80

Ceramic Tiled Stoves — SP249

**1984, May 24 Photo. *Perf. 11½***

**B505** SP249 35c + 15c 1566 .55 .40
**B506** SP249 50c + 20c 1646 .70 .50
**B507** SP249 70c + 30c 1768 1.00 .70
**B508** SP249 80c + 40c 18th cent. 1.25 .90
*Nos. B505-B508 (4)* 3.50 2.50

Children's Stories SP250

**1984, Nov. 26 Photo.**

**B509** SP250 35c + 15c Heidi .60 .40
**B510** SP250 50c + 20c Pinocchio .75 .50
**B511** SP250 70c + 30c Pippi Longstocking 1.10 .70
**B512** SP260 80c + 40c Max and Moritz 1.40 .90
*Nos. B509-B512 (4)* 3.85 2.50

Musical Museum Exhibits SP251

**1985, May 28 Photo. *Perf. 11½***

**B513** SP251 25c + 10c Music box, 1895 .30 .20
**B514** SP251 35c + 15c Rattle box, 18th cent. .50 .20
**B515** SP251 50c + 20c Emmenthal necked zither, 1828 .70 .20
**B516** SP251 70c + 30c Drum, 1571 1.00 .30
**B517** SP251 80c + 40c Diatonic accordion, 20th cent. 1.25 .35
*Nos. B513-B517 (5)* 3.75 1.25

Surtax for Swiss cultural programs.

Hansel and Gretel SP252

Fairy tales by Jakob (1785-1863) and Wilhelm (1786-1859) Grimm.

**1985, Nov. 26 Photo.**

**B518** SP252 35c + 15c shown .55 .20
**B519** SP252 50c + 20c Snow White .80 .20
**B520** SP252 80c + 40c Little Red Riding Hood 1.25 .35
**B521** SP252 90c + 40c Cinderella 1.40 .40
*Nos. B518-B521 (4)* 4.00 1.15

Surtax for Pro Juventute Foundation and youth welfare orgs.

Man, Vitality and Movement SP253

**1986, Feb. 11 Photo. *Perf. 12***

**B522** SP253 50c + 20c multi .90 .25

Surtax for Natl. Sports Federation and cultural programs.

Paintings in Natl. Museums SP254

Swiss art: 35c+15c, Bridge in the Sun, 1907, by Giovanni Giacometti (1868-1933). 50c+20c, The Violet Hat, 1907, by Cuno Amiet (1868-1961). 80c+40c, After the Funeral, 1905, by Max Buri (1868-1915). 90c+40c, Still Life, 1914, by Felix Valloton (1865-1925).

**1986, Apr. 22 Photo. *Perf. 11½***

**B523** SP254 35c + 15c multi .50 .20
**B524** SP254 50c + 20c multi .70 .25
**B525** SP254 80c + 40c multi 1.25 .40
**B526** SP254 90c + 40c multi 1.40 .45
*Nos. B523-B526 (4)* 3.85 1.30

Surtax for Natl. Day Collection &monuments preservation, social & cultural organizations.

Children's Toys — SP255

**1986, Nov. 25 Photo.**

**B527** SP255 35c + 15c Teddy bear .60 .20
**B528** SP255 50c + 20c Top .90 .30
**B529** SP255 80c + 40c Steamroller 1.50 .50
**B530** SP255 90c + 40c Doll 1.60 .55
*Nos. B527-B530 (4)* 4.60 1.55

Surtax was for youth welfare organizations and the Pro Juventute Foundation.

Antique Furniture SP256

Designs: 35c+15c, Saane Valley wall cabinet, 1764, Vieux Pays d'Enhaut Museum, Chateau d'Oex. 50c+20c, Raised chest, 16th cent., Rhaetian Museum, Chur. 80c+40c, Ticino canton cradle, 1782, Valmaggia Museum, Cevio. 90c+40c, Appenzell region wardrobe, 1698, St. Gallen Historical Museum.

**1987, May 26 Photo.**

**B531** SP256 35c + 15c multi .55 .25
**B532** SP256 50c + 20c multi .80 .35
**B533** SP256 80c + 40c multi 1.40 .60
**B534** SP256 90c + 40c multi 1.50 .60
*Nos. B531-B534 (4)* 4.25 1.80

Surtax for Red Cross and patriotic funds.

### No. 786 Surcharged with Clasped Hands and "7.9.87" in Red

**Photo. & Engr.**

**1987, Sept. 7 *Perf. 13½x13***

**B535** A349 50c + 50c multi 1.25 .45

Surtaxed to benefit flood victims.

Christmas SP257

Child Development SP258

**1987, Nov. 24 Photo. *Perf. 11½***

**B536** SP257 25c +10c shown .50 .20
**B537** SP258 35c +15c shown .70 .20
**B538** SP258 50c +20c Boy, building blocks .95 .30
**B539** SP258 80c +40c Boy, girl in sandbox 1.60 .55
**B540** SP258 90c +40c Father, child 1.75 .60
*Nos. B536-B540 (5)* 5.50 1.85

Surtax for national youth welfare projects and the Pro Juventute Foundation.
See Nos. B555-B558.

Junkers JU-52, 1939, and the Matterhorn SP259

**1988, Mar. 8 Photo.**

**B541** SP259 140c +60c multi 2.50 2.50

Pro Aero Foundation, Zurich, 50th Anniv. Issued in sheets of 8.

SP260

SP261

Minnesingers.

**1988, May 24 Photo.**

**B542** SP260 35c +15c Count Rudolf of Neuchatel .60 .25
**B543** SP260 50c +20c Rudolf von Rotenburg .85 .35
**B544** SP260 80c +40c Master Johannes Hadlaub 1.50 .60
**B545** SP260 90c +40c The Hardegger 1.60 .65
*Nos. B542-B545 (4)* 4.55 1.85

700 Years of art and culture.

**1988, Nov. 25 *Perf. 11½***

**B546** SP261 35c +15c Reading .65 .20
**B547** SP261 50c +20c Music .95 .30
**B548** SP261 80c +40c Math 1.65 .55
**B549** SP261 90c +40c Art 1.75 .60
*Nos. B546-B549 (4)* 5.00 1.65

Child development. Surtax for natl. youth welfare projects and the Pro Juventute Foundation.

700 Years of Art and Culture SP262

Illuminations in Zurich Central, Bern Burgher and Lucerne Central libraries: No. B550, King Friedrich II presenting Bern municipal charter, 1218, *Bendicht Tschachtlan Chronicle,* 1470. No. B551, Capt. Adrian von Bubenberg and troops passing through Murten town gate, 1476, *Bern Chronicle,* by Diebold Schilling, 1483. No. B552, Official messenger of Schwyz before the Council of Zurich, c. 1440, *Gerold Edlibach Chronicle,* 1485. No. B553, Schilling presenting manuscript to the mayor and councilmen in the council chamber, Lucerne, c. 1500, *Diebold Schilling's Lucerne Chronicle,* 1513.

**1989, May 23**

**B550** SP262 35c +15c multi .65 .20
**B551** SP262 50c +20c multi .90 .30
**B552** SP262 80c +40c multi 1.50 .50
**B553** SP262 90c +40c multi 1.75 .55
*Nos. B550-B553 (4)* 4.80 1.55

Surtax to benefit women's and cultural organizations.

Gymnastics SP263

**1989, Aug. 25 Photo. *Perf. 11½***

**B554** SP263 50c +20c multi .80 .30

Surtax to benefit Swiss Natl. Sports Federation, cultural and social work.

### Child Development Type of 1987

**1989, Nov. 24**

**B555** SP258 35c +15c Community work .60 .20
**B556** SP258 50c +20c Friendship .85 .25
**B557** SP258 80c +40c Vocational training 1.50 .50
**B558** SP258 90c +40c Higher education and research 1.60 .55
*Nos. B555-B558 (4)* 4.55 1.50

Surtax for natl. youth welfare projects and the Pro Juventute Foundation.

700 Years of Art and Culture — SP264

Street criers: No. B559, Fly swatter and starch-sprinkler vendor. No. B560, Clock vendor. No. B561, Knife grinder. No. B562, Pinewood sellers.

**1990, May 22** **Photo.**

| | | | | |
|---|---|---|---|---|
| **B559** | SP264 35c +15c multi | .70 | .25 |
| **B560** | SP264 50c +20c multi | .95 | .30 |
| **B561** | SP264 80c +40c multi | 1.60 | .55 |
| **B562** | SP264 90c +40c multi | 1.75 | .60 |
| | *Nos. B559-B562 (4)* | 5.00 | 1.70 |

Souvenir Sheet

Natl. Philatelic Exhibition, Geneva '90 — SP265

a, Brass badge worn by Geneva Cantonal post drivers before 1849. b, Place du Bourg-de-Four and entrance to Rue Etienne-Dumont. c, Ile Rousseau and Pont des Bergues. d, No. 2L1 on cover.

**1990, Sept. 5**

| | | | | |
|---|---|---|---|---|
| **B563** | SP265 Sheet of 4 | 4.00 | 1.40 |
| *a.-d.* | 50c +25c any single | 1.00 | .35 |

Child Development SP266

**1990, Nov. 20**

| | | | |
|---|---|---|---|
| **B564** | SP266 35c +15c Model making | .70 | .25 |
| **B565** | SP266 50c +20c Youth groups | 1.00 | .30 |
| **B566** | SP266 80c +40c Sports | 1.70 | .55 |
| **B567** | SP266 90c +40c Music | 1.85 | .60 |
| | *Nos. B564-B567 (4)* | 5.25 | 1.70 |

700 Years of Art and Culture SP267

Contemporary paintings by: 50c+20c, Wolf Barth. 70c+30c, Helmut Federle. 80c+40c, Matthias Bosshart. 90c+40c, Werner Otto Leuenberger.

**1991, May 14** **Photo.** ***Perf. 11½***

| | | | |
|---|---|---|---|
| **B568** | SP267 50c +20c multi | 1.00 | .30 |
| **B569** | SP267 70c +30c multi | 1.40 | .45 |
| **B570** | SP267 80c +40c multi | 1.75 | .55 |
| **B571** | SP267 90c +40c multi | 1.75 | .60 |
| | *Nos. B568-B571 (4)* | 5.90 | 1.90 |

Woodland Flowers SP268

50c+25c, Allium ursinum. 70c+30c, Geranium sylvaticum. 80c+40c, Campanula trachelium. 90c+40c, Hieracium murorum.

**1991, Nov. 26**

| | | | |
|---|---|---|---|
| **B572** | SP268 50c +25c multi | 1.00 | .40 |
| **B573** | SP268 70c +30c multi | 1.40 | .45 |
| **B574** | SP268 80c +40c multi | 1.60 | .55 |
| **B575** | SP268 90c +40c multi | 1.80 | .60 |
| | *Nos. B572-B575 (4)* | 5.80 | 2.00 |

Surtax for youth and family welfare projects and the Pro Juventute Foundation.

Swiss Folk Art — SP269

50c + 20c, Earthenware plate, Heimberg, 18th cent. 70c + 40c, Paper cutout by Johann Jakob Hauswirth (1809-1871). 80c + 40c, Cream spoon, Gruyeres. 90c + 40c, Embroidered silk carnation, Grisons.

**1992, May 22** **Photo.** ***Perf. 11½***

| | | | |
|---|---|---|---|
| **B576** | SP269 50c +20c multi | .95 | .30 |
| **B577** | SP269 70c +30c multi | 1.25 | .45 |
| **B578** | SP269 80c +40c multi | 1.60 | .50 |
| **B579** | SP269 90c +40c multi | 1.75 | .60 |
| | *Nos. B576-B579 (4)* | 5.55 | 1.85 |

Surtax for preservation of cultural heritage.

Unfinished Work, by Jean Tinguely SP270

**1992, Aug. 25** **Photo.** ***Perf. 12***

| | | | |
|---|---|---|---|
| **B580** | SP270 50c +20c blue & black | 1.10 | .40 |

Surtax for Natl. Sports Federation and sports-related social and cultural activities.

Wood Puppet of Melchior, 18th Cent. — SP271

Trees — SP272

**1992, Nov. 24** **Photo.** ***Perf. 11½***

| | | | |
|---|---|---|---|
| **B581** | SP271 50c +25c multi | 1.00 | .35 |
| **B582** | SP272 50c +25c Copper beech | 1.00 | .35 |
| **B583** | SP272 70c +30c Norway maple | 1.40 | .50 |
| **B584** | SP272 80c +40c Common oak | 1.60 | .55 |
| **B585** | SP272 90c +40c Spruce | 1.75 | .60 |
| | *Nos. B581-B585 (5)* | 6.75 | 2.35 |

Christmas. Surtax for youth and family welfare projects and the Pro Juventute Foundation.

Swiss Folk Art — SP273

Designs: No. B586, Appenzell dairyman's earring. No. B587, Fluhli glassware. 80c + 40c, Painting of cattle drive, by Sylvestre Pidoux. 100c + 40c, Straw hat ornament.

**1993, May 5** **Photo.** ***Perf. 11½***

| | | | |
|---|---|---|---|
| **B586** | SP273 60c +30c multi | 1.25 | .40 |
| **B587** | SP273 60c +30c multi | 1.25 | .40 |
| **B588** | SP273 80c +40c multi | 1.10 | .35 |
| **B589** | SP273 100c +40c multi | 2.00 | .70 |
| | *Nos. B586-B589 (4)* | 5.60 | 1.85 |

**Architectural Heritage Type of 1960**

Design: 80c+20c, Kapell Bridge and Water Tower, Lucerne.

**1993, Sept. 7** **Litho.** ***Perf. 13½x13***

| | | | |
|---|---|---|---|
| **B590** | A145 80c +20c orange & red | 1.40 | .45 |

Surtax for reconstruction of Kapell Bridge with any excess for preservation of architectural heritage.

SP274 SP275

Woodland plants.

**1993, Nov. 23** **Photo.** ***Perf. 11½***

| | | | |
|---|---|---|---|
| **B591** | SP274 60c +30c Christmas wreath | 1.25 | .40 |
| **B592** | SP274 60c +30c Male fern | 1.25 | .40 |
| **B593** | SP274 80c +40c Guelder rose | 1.60 | .55 |
| **B594** | SP274 100c +50c Mnium punctatum | 2.00 | .65 |
| | *Nos. B591-B594 (4)* | 6.10 | 2.00 |

Christmas. Surtax for youth and family welfare projects and the Pro Juventute Foundation.

**1994, May 17** **Photo.** ***Perf. 11½***

Swiss Folk Art: No. B595, Weight-driven Neuchatel clock. No. B598, Linen-embroidered pomegranate. 80c+40c, Biscuit mold for Krafli. 100c+40c, Paper bird mobile for child's cradle.

| | | | |
|---|---|---|---|
| **B595** | SP275 60c +30c multi | 1.25 | .40 |
| **B596** | SP275 60c +30c multi | 1.25 | .40 |
| **B597** | SP275 80c +40c multi | 1.60 | .55 |
| **B598** | SP275 100c +40c multi | 1.90 | .65 |
| | *Nos. B595-B598 (4)* | 6.00 | 2.00 |

Christmas SP276

Mushrooms SP277

Designs: No. B600, Wood blewit. 80c+40c, Red boletus. 100c+50c, Shaggy pholiota.

**1994, Nov. 28** **Litho.** ***Perf. 11½***

| | | | |
|---|---|---|---|
| **B599** | SP276 60c +30c multi | 1.10 | .45 |
| **B600** | SP277 60c +30c multi | 1.10 | .45 |
| **B601** | SP277 80c +40c multi | 1.40 | .60 |
| **B602** | SP277 100c +50c multi | 1.75 | .80 |
| | *Nos. B599-B602 (4)* | 5.35 | 2.30 |

Surtax for youth and family welfare projects and the Pro Juventute Foundation.

Swiss Folk Art — SP278

Designs: No. B603, Wooden cream pail. No. B604, Straw hat. 80c+40c, Chest lock, c. 1580. 100c+40c, Langnau pottery sugar bowl.

**1995, May 16** **Photo.** ***Perf. 11½***

| | | | |
|---|---|---|---|
| **B603** | SP278 60c +30c multi | 1.10 | .50 |
| **B604** | SP278 60c +30c multi | 1.10 | .50 |
| **B605** | SP278 80c +40c multi | 1.50 | .70 |
| | Complete booklet, 10 #B605 | 15.00 | |
| **B606** | SP278 100c +40c multi | 1.90 | .80 |
| | *Nos. B603-B606 (4)* | 5.60 | 2.50 |

Surtax for Swiss Pro Patria Foundation and special cultural, social projects.

Souvenir Sheet

Basler Taube '95 Philatelic Exhibition, Basel — SP279

Designs: a, 80c+30c, like Switzerland #3L1. Engraved panorama of Basel, by Matthaus Merian, 17th cent.: b, 60c+30c, Buildings, twin church steeples. c, 100c+50c, Buildings. d, 100c+50c, Buildings, bridge.

**1995, May 16** **Photo.** ***Perf. 13x14***

| | | | |
|---|---|---|---|
| **B607** | SP279 Sheet of 4 | 7.00 | 3.00 |
| *a.* | 80c +30c multi | 1.25 | .60 |
| *b.* | 60c +30c black & blue | 1.25 | .55 |
| *c.-d.* | 100c +50c any single | 2.50 | .90 |

Nos. B607b-B607d are a continuous design.

Christmas SP280

Life In and Around Water — SP281

#B608, Angel from "The Annunciation," by Bartolome. #B609, River trout. 80c+40c, Grey wagtail. 100c+50c, Spotted salamander.

**1995, Nov. 28** **Photo.** ***Perf. 11½***

| | | | |
|---|---|---|---|
| **B608** | SP280 60c +30c multi | 1.10 | .50 |
| | Complete booklet, 10 #B608 | 11.00 | |
| **B609** | SP281 60c +30c multi | 1.10 | .50 |
| **B610** | SP281 80c +40c multi | 1.40 | .65 |
| **B611** | SP281 100c +50c multi | 1.75 | .80 |
| | *Nos. B608-B611 (4)* | 5.35 | 2.45 |

Surtax for Pro Juventute Foundation.

For Sports SP282

**1996, Mar. 12** **Photo.** ***Perf. 11½***

| | | | |
|---|---|---|---|
| **B612** | SP282 70c +30c multi | 1.60 | .85 |
| | Complete booklet, 10 #B612 | 16.00 | |

SP283

Restorations, projects: No. B613, Magdalena Chapel, Wolfenschiessen. No. B614, Underground mills, Col-des-Roches. 90c+40c, Pfäfers Baroque spa complex. 110c+50c, Roman road over Great St. Bernhard.

**1996, May 14 Photo. *Perf. 11½***

**B613** SP283 70c +35c multi 1.25 .60
**B614** SP283 70c +35c multi 1.25 .60
**B615** SP283 90c +40c multi 1.75 .75
Complete booklet, 10 #B615 17.50
**B616** SP283 110c +50c multi 2.10 .90
*Nos. B613-B616 (4)* 6.35 2.85

Christmas SP284

Life In and Around Water — SP285

**1996, Nov. 26 Photo. *Perf. 11½***

**B617** SP284 70c +35c Star, constellations 1.25 .55
**B618** SP285 70c +35c Grayling 1.25 .55
Complete booklet, 10 #B618 12.50
**B619** SP285 90c +45c Crayfish 1.60 .70
**B620** SP285 110c +55c Otter 1.90 .80
*Nos. B617-B620 (4)* 6.00 2.60

SP286

Designs: No. B621, St. Valbert Church, Soubey. No. B622, Culture Mill, Lützelflüh. 90c+40c, Ittingen Charterhouse, Thurgau. 110c+50c, Municipal Building, Onsernone Valley.

**1997, May 13 Photo. *Perf. 11½***

**B621** SP286 70c +35c multi 1.25 1.25
**B622** SP286 70c +35c multi 1.25 1.25
**B623** SP286 90c +40c multi 1.60 1.60
Complete booklet, 10 #B623 16.00
**B624** SP286 110c +50c multi 2.00 2.00
*Nos. B621-B624 (4)* 6.10 6.10

Christmas SP287

Life In and Around Water — SP288

Designs: No. B625, Misteltoe twig. No. B626, Three-spined stickleback. 90c+45c, Yellow-bellied toad. 110c+55c, Ruff.

**1997, Nov. 20 Photo. *Perf. 11½***

**B625** SP287 70c +35c multi 1.25 1.25
**B626** SP288 70c +35c multi 1.25 1.25
Complete booklet, 10 #B626 12.50
**B627** SP288 90c +45c multi 1.60 1.60
**B628** SP288 110c +55c multi 1.90 1.90
*Nos. B625-B628 (4)* 6.00 6.00

Surtax for Pro Juventute Foundation.

Pro Patria Stamps, 60th Anniv. SP289

Heritage and landscapes: No. B629, St. Gall Rhine Valley. No. B630, Round Church, Saas Balen. No. B631, Natural forest preserves, Bödmeren. No. B632, St. Gotthard Refuge. 110c +50c, Blacksmiths, Corcelles.

**1998, May 12 Photo. *Perf. 11½***

**B629** SP289 70c + 35c multi 1.25 1.25
**B630** SP289 70c + 35c multi 1.25 1.25
**B631** SP289 90c + 40c multi 1.50 1.50
Complete booklet, 10 #B631 15.00
**B632** SP289 90c + 40c multi 1.50 1.50
**B633** SP289 110c + 50c multi 1.90 1.90
*Nos. B629-B633 (5)* 7.40 7.40

Christmas SP290

Life Near Water — SP291

No. B634, Bell, holly on ribbon. No. B635, Ramshorn snail. 90c+45c, Great crested grebe. 110c+55c, Pike.

**1998, Nov. 25 Photo. *Perf. 11½***

**B634** SP290 70c +35c multi 1.25 1.25
**B635** SP291 70c +35c multi 1.25 1.25
**B636** SP291 90c +45c multi 1.60 1.60
Complete booklet, 6 #B634, 4 #B636 16.00
**B637** SP291 110c +55c multi 1.90 1.90
*Nos. B634-B637 (4)* 6.00 6.00

Pro Patria — SP292

Heritage and landscapes: No. B638, Chestnut groves, Malcantone. No. B639, La Sarraz Castle. 90c+40c, Lake Lucerne steamship. 110c+50c, St. Paul's Chapel, Rhäzüns.

**1999, May 5 Litho. *Perf. 13½***

**B638** SP292 70c +35c multi 1.40 1.40
**B639** SP292 70c +35c multi 1.40 1.40
**B640** SP292 90c +40c multi 1.75 1.75
Complete booklet, 10 #B640 17.50
**B641** SP292 110c +50c multi 2.10 2.10
*Nos. B638-B641 (4)* 6.65 6.65

Souvenir Sheet

NABA 2000 Philatelic Exhibition, St. Gallen — SP293

a, 70c+30c, St. Laurenzen Church spire. b, 20c+10c, Top of town house. c, 90c+30c, Oriel window.
Illustration reduced.

**1999, Sept. 9 Photo. *Perf. 11¾***

**Sheet of 3**

**B642** SP293 #a.-c. + label 3.50 3.50
*a.* 70c+30c multicolored 1.25 1.25
*b.* 20c+10c multicolored .40 .40
*c.* 90c+30c multicolored 1.60 1.60

Christmas SP294

Nicolo the Clown From Children's Book by Verena Pavoni SP295

Designs: No. B643, Children, snowman. No. B644, Nicolo, circus tent. 90c+45c, Nicolo and his father. 110c+55c, Nicolo and donkey.

***Perf. 13½x13¼***

**1999, Nov. 23 Litho.**

**B643** SP294 70c +35c multi 1.40 1.40
**B644** SP295 70c +35c multi 1.40 1.40
**B645** SP295 90c +45c multi 1.75 1.75
Complete booklet, 6 #B644, 4 #B645 16.00
**B646** SP295 110c +55c multi 2.10 2.10
*Nos. B643-B646 (4)* 6.65 6.65

Surtax for Pro Juventute Foundation.

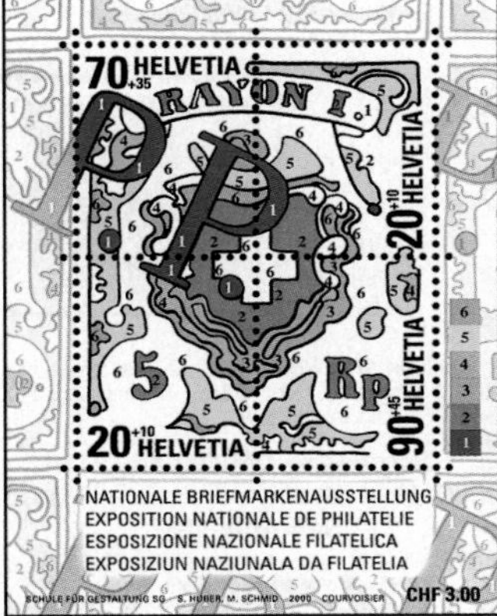
Cities With Pro Patria Foundation Renovation Projects SP296

***Perf. 13¼x13½***

**2000, May 10 Litho. & Engr.**

**B647** SP296 70c +35c Näfles 1.25 1.25
**B648** SP296 70c +35c Tengia 1.25 1.25
**B649** SP296 90c +40c Brugg 1.60 1.60
**B650** SP296 90c +40c Carouge 1.60 1.60
Booklet, 10 #B650 16.00
*Nos. B647-B650 (4)* 5.70 5.70

Souvenir Sheet

NABA 2000 Philatelic Exhibition, St. Gallen — SP297

Quadrants of stylized No. 5: a, UL. b, UR. c, LL. d, LR.
Illustration reduced.

**2000, May 10 Photo. *Perf. 11¾***

**B651** SP297 Sheet of 4 3.75 3.75
*a.* 70c+35c multicolored 1.25 1.25
*b.-c.* 20c+10c any single .35 .35
*d.* 90c+45c multicolored 1.75 1.75

Christmas SP298

Illustrations from Little Albert, by Albert Manser SP299

Designs: No. B652, St. Nicholas and Schmutzli in sleigh. No. B653, Children at fence. No. B654, Little Albert with umbrella. No. B655, Children on sleds.

***Perf. 13¼x13½***

**2000, Nov. 21 Litho.**

**B652** SP298 70c +35c multi 1.25 1.25
**B653** SP299 70c +35c multi 1.25 1.25
**B654** SP299 90c +45c multi 1.50 1.50
Booklet, 6 #B653, 4 #B654 13.50
**B655** SP299 90c +45c multi 1.50 1.50
*Nos. B652-B655 (4)* 5.50 5.50

Surtax for Pro Juventute Foundation.

Landmarks SP300

Designs: No. B656, Hauterive Abbey. No. B657, La Chaux-de-Fonds Theater. No. B658, Granary, Rorschach. No. B659, Bishop's Castle, Leuk.

**2001, May 9 Litho. *Perf. 13¼x13½***

**B656** SP300 70c +35c multi 1.25 1.25
**B657** SP300 70c +35c multi 1.25 1.25
**B658** SP300 90c +40c multi 1.50 1.50
**B659** SP300 90c +40c multi 1.50 1.50
Booklet, 10 #B659 15.00
*Nos. B656-B659 (4)* 5.50 5.50

Surtax for Pro Patria Foundation.

**Pro Juventute Types of 1999**

Art from children's books: No. B660, What's Santa Claus Doing?, by Karin von Oldershausen. No. B661, Leopold the Leopard, from Leopold and the Sun, by Stephan Brülhart. No. B662, Honeybear, from Leopold and the Sun. No. B663, Tom the Monkey, from Leopold and the Sun.

***Perf. 13½x13¼***

**2001, Nov. 20 Litho.**

**B660** SP294 70c +35c multi 1.25 1.25
**B661** SP295 70c +35c multi 1.25 1.25
**B662** SP295 90c +45c multi 1.60 1.60
Booklet, 6 #B661, 4 #B662 14.00
**B663** SP295 90c +45c multi 1.60 1.60
*Nos. B660-B663 (4)* 5.70 5.70

Surtax for Pro Juventute Foundation.

Mills — SP301

Location: No. B664, Bruzella. No. B665, Oberdorf. No. B666, Büren an der Aare. No. B667, Lussery-Villars.

**2002, May 15 Litho. *Perf. 13¼x13½***

**B664** SP301 70c +35c multi 1.40 1.40
**B665** SP301 70c +35c multi 1.40 1.40
**B666** SP301 90c +40c multi 1.60 1.60
Booklet, 10 #B666 16.00
**B667** SP301 90c +40c multi 1.60 1.60
*Nos. B664-B667 (4)* 6.00 6.00

Surtax for Pro Patria Foundation.

Roses — SP302

Designs: No. B668, Christmas rose (gold background). No. B669, Ingrid Bergman rose (white background). No. B670, Belle Vaudoise rose (orange petals). No. B671, Charmian rose (pink petals). 130c+65c, Frühlingsgold rose.

*Perf. 13¾x13¼*

**2002, Nov. 19** **Litho.**

**B668** SP302 70c +35c multi 1.40 1.40
**B669** SP302 70c +35c multi 1.40 1.40
**B670** SP302 90c +45c multi 1.90 1.90
Booklet, 6 #B669, 4 #B670 16.00
**B671** SP302 90c +45c multi 1.90 1.90
**B672** SP302 130c +65c multi 2.60 2.60
*Nos. B668-B672 (5)* 9.20 9.20

Surtax for Pro Juventute Foundation. No. B668 is impregnated with a pine needle, cinnamon and clove scent, and Nos. B669-B672 with a rose scent.

Bridges
SP303

Designs: No. B673, Wynigen Bridge, Burgdorf, 1776. No. B674, Salginatobel Bridge, Schiers, 1929. No. B675, Pont St. Jean, Saint Ursanne, 15th cent. No. B676, Reuss Bridge, Rottenschwil, 1907.

**2003, May 8** **Litho.** ***Perf. 13¼x13½***

**B673** SP303 70c +35c multi 1.60 1.60
**B674** SP303 70c +35c multi 1.60 1.60
**B675** SP303 90c +40c multi 2.00 2.00
Booklet, 10 #B675 20.00
**B676** SP303 90c +40c multi 2.00 2.00
*Nos. B673-B676 (4)* 7.20 7.20

Rights of the Child — SP304

Children: 70c+35c, Christmas tree, toy tractor, gift. 85c+35c, Playing as storekeeper and shopper. 90c+45c, Skateboarding with dog. 100c+45c, Playing guitar and drums.

***Serpentine Die Cut 10½x11***

**2003, Nov. 19** **Litho.**

**Self-Adhesive**

**B677** SP304 70c +35c multi 1.75 1.75
*a.* Block of 4 on translucent backing paper 7.00
**B678** SP304 85c +35c multi 1.90 1.90
*a.* Block of 4 on translucent backing paper 7.60
**B679** SP304 90c +45c multi 2.10 2.10
*a.* Block of 4 on translucent backing paper 8.40
**B680** SP304 100c +45c multi 2.25 2.25
*a.* Block of 4 on translucent backing paper 9.00
*b.* Nos. B677-B680 on translucent backing paper 8.00
*c.* Booklet, 6 each #B678, B680 22.50
*Nos. B677-B680 (4)* 8.00 8.00

Nos. B677-B680 each were printed in sheets of 20 stamps with a white paper backing.

Small Buildings
SP305

Designs: No. B681, Bathing pavilion, Gorgier. No. B682, Granary, Oberramsern. No. B683, Ossuary, Gentilino. No. B684, Dock house, Lucerne.

**2004, May 6** **Litho.** ***Perf. 13¾x14¼***

**B681** SP305 85c +40c multi 1.90 1.90
**B682** SP305 85c +40c multi 1.90 1.90
**B683** SP305 100c +50c multi 2.40 2.40
**B684** SP305 100c +50c multi 2.40 2.40
Complete booklet, 6 #B681, 4 #B684 22.50

Complete booklet sold for 14.50fr.

Rights of the Child — SP306

Designs: No. B685, Children playing card game. No. B686, Children, man, giraffe. No. B687, Children, teacher. No. B688, Child, elderly man and woman.

***Serpentine Die Cut 10½x11***

**2004, Nov. 23** **Litho.**

**Self-Adhesive**

**B685** SP306 85c +40c multi 2.25 2.25
*a.* Block of 4 on translucent paper 9.00
**B686** SP306 85c +40c multi 2.25 2.25
*a.* Block of 4 on translucent paper 9.00
**B687** SP306 100c +50c multi 2.75 2.75
*a.* Block of 4 on translucent paper 11.00
*b.* Booklet pane, 6 each #B685, B687 30.00
**B688** SP306 100c +50c multi 2.75 2.75
*a.* Block of 4 on translucent paper 11.00
*b.* Nos. B685-B688 on translucent paper 10.00
*Nos. B685-B688 (4)* 10.00 10.00

Nos. B685-B688 were each printed in sheets of 20 stamps. No. B687b sold for 17fr.

Historic Buildings
SP307

Designs: No. B689, Rotach Houses, Zurich. No. B690, Monte Carasso Abbey, Monte Carasso. No. B691, St. Katharinental Abbey, Diessenhofen. No. B692, Palais Wilson, Geneva.

**2005, May 10** **Litho.** ***Perf. 13¼x13½***

**B689** SP307 85c +40c multi 2.10 2.10
**B690** SP307 85c +40c multi 2.10 2.10
**B691** SP307 100c +50c multi 2.50 2.50
Complete booklet, 6 #B690, 4 #B691 23.00
**B692** SP307 100c +50c multi 2.50 2.50
*Nos. B689-B692 (4)* 9.20 9.20

Surtax for Pro Patria Foundation.

Children's Rights
SP308

Children and: No. B693, Life preserver. No. B694, Cherries. No. B695, Computer. No. B696 Candle in window.

***Serpentine Die Cut 10½x11***

**2005, Nov. 22** **Photo.**

**Self-Adhesive**

**B693** SP308 85c +40c multi 1.90 1.90
*a.* Block of 4 on translucent paper 7.75
**B694** SP308 85c +40c multi 1.90 1.90
*a.* Block of 4 on translucent paper 7.75
**B695** SP308 100c +50c multi 2.25 2.25
*a.* Block of 4 on translucent paper 9.00
*b.* Booklet pane, 2 each #B693, B695 8.50
Complete booklet, 3 #B695b 26.00
**B696** SP308 100c +50c multi 2.25 2.25
*a.* Block of 4 on translucent paper 9.00
*b.* Nos. B693-B696 on translucent paper 8.50
*Nos. B693-B696 (4)* 8.30 8.30

Nos. B693-B696 were each printed in sheets of 20. Complete booklet sold for €17.

Gardens and Parks — SP309

Designs: No. B697, Prangins Castle, Prangins. No. B698, Heidegg Castle, Gelfingen. No. B699, Birseck Castle, Arlesheim. No. B700, Villa Garbald, Castasegna.

**2006, May 9** **Litho.** ***Perf. 14x13¾***

**B697** SP309 85c +40c multi 2.10 2.10
**B698** SP309 85c +40c multi 2.10 2.10
**B699** SP309 100c +50c multi 2.50 2.50
**B700** SP309 100c +50c multi 2.50 2.50
Complete booklet, 6 #B698, 4 #B700 24.00
*Nos. B697-B700 (4)* 9.20 9.20

Complete booklet sold for €14.50.

Souvenir Sheet

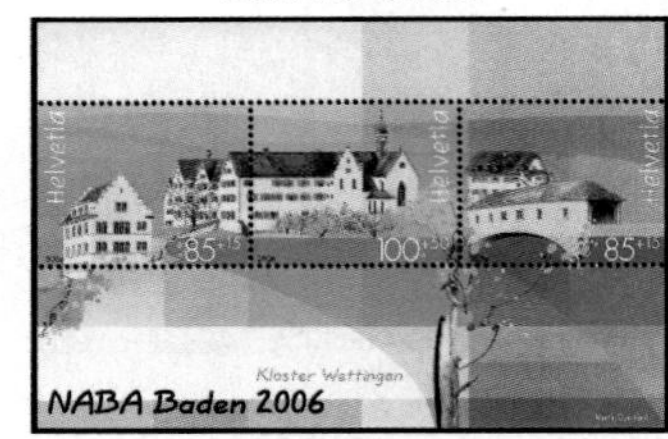


Wettingen Monastery — SP310

No. B701: a, Building, country name at left. b, Building and bridge, country name at right. c, Main building.

**2006, May 9** ***Perf. 13¾x14¼***

**B701** SP310 Sheet of 3 6.00 6.00
*a.-b.* 85c+15c Either single 1.75 1.75
*c.* 100c+50c multi 2.50 2.50

NABA Baden 2006.

Souvenir Sheet

NABA Baden 2006 Philatelic Exhibition — SP311

No. B702: a, Baden City Tower. b, Fountain.

***Perf. 14¼x13¾ on 3 Sides***

**2006, Sept. 7** **Litho.**

**B702** SP311 Sheet of 2 5.00 5.00
*a.-b.* 100c +50c Either single 2.50 2.50

Children's Art Competition
SP312

Designs: No. B703, Singer, by Veronica Jesus Garcia Pinto. No. B704, Car in garage, by Stephane Arada. No. B705, Bandaged dog, by Lea Mayer. No. B706, Angel, by Ted Scapa, judge of competition.

***Serpentine Die Cut 10¾x11***

**2006, Nov. 21**

**Self-Adhesive**

**B703** SP312 85c +40c multi 2.10 2.10
*a.* Block of 4, #B703 8.50
**B704** SP312 85c +40c multi 2.10 2.10
*a.* Block of 4, #B704 8.50
**B705** SP312 100c +50c multi 2.50 2.50
*a.* Booklet pane, 6 each #B704-B705 28.00
*b.* Block of 4, #B705 10.00
**B706** SP312 100c +50c multi 2.50 2.50
*a.* Block of 4, #B703-B706 9.25
*b.* Block of 4, #B706 10.00
*Nos. B703-B706 (4)* 9.20 9.20

Surtax for Pro Juventute Foundation.

Historic Roads
SP313

Designs: No. B707, Via Jura, Chateau de Vorbourg. No. B708, Via Jacobi, Chapel of St. Apollonia. No. B709, Via Cook, Grandhotel Giessbach. No. B710, Via Gottardo, Alte Sust.

**2007, Apr. 27** **Litho.** ***Perf. 13½x13¼***

**B707** SP313 85c +40c multi 2.10 2.10
**B708** SP313 85c +40c multi 2.10 2.10
**B709** SP313 100c +50c multi 2.50 2.50
Complete booklet, 6 #B708, 4 #B709 23.00
**B710** SP313 100c +50c multi 2.50 2.50
*Nos. B707-B710 (4)* 9.20 9.20

Surtax for Pro Patria Foundation.

---

## AIR POST STAMPS

Nos. 134 and 139 Overprinted in Carmine

**1919-20** **Wmk. 183** ***Perf. 11½***

**Granite Paper**

**C1** A25 30c yel brn & pale grn ('20) 110.00 *1,250.*
**C2** A25 50c dp & pale grn 32.50 *110.00*
Set, never hinged 350.00

Counterfeits of overprint and fraudulent cancellations exist.

Airplane
AP1

Pilot at Controls of Airplane
AP2

Biplane against Sky — AP3

Allegorical Figure of Flight
AP4

***Perf. 11½, 12 and Compound***

**1923-25** **Typo.**

**C3** AP1 15c brn red & ap grn 2.25 *8.25*
**C4** AP1 20c grn & lt grn ('25) .90 *6.00*
**C5** AP1 25c dk bl & bl 7.75 *22.50*
**C6** AP2 35c brn & buff 11.00 *42.50*
**C7** AP2 40c vio & gray vio 14.50 *45.00*
**C8** AP3 45c red & ind 1.60 *7.25*
**C9** AP3 50c blk & red 12.50 *17.00*

***Perf. 11½***

**C10** AP4 65c gray bl & dp bl ('24) 3.25 *16.00*
**C11** AP4 75c org & brn red ('24) 15.00 *55.00*
**C12** AP4 1fr vio & dp vio ('24) 42.50 32.50
*Nos. C3-C12 (10)* 111.25 *252.00*
Set, never hinged 275.00

For surcharges see Nos. C19, C22, C26.

**1933-37 With Grilled Gum**

*C4a* AP1 20c grn & lt grn ('37) .30 .40
*C5a* AP1 25c dk bl & bl ('34) 5.00 *50.00*
*C8a* AP3 45c red & indigo ('37) 2.50 *52.50*
*C9a* AP3 50c gray grn & scar ('35) 1.10 1.60
*C10a* AP4 65c gray bl & dp bl ('37) 2.75 *8.50*
*C11a* AP4 75c org & brn red ('36) 27.50 *175.00*
*C12a* AP4 1fr vio & deep vio 2.10 *3.25*
*Nos. C4a-C12a (7)* 41.25 *291.25*
Set, never hinged 65.00

See Grilled Gum note after No. 145.

Allegory of Air Mail — AP5

Bird Carrying Letter AP6

**1929-30 Granite Paper**

**C13** AP5 35c red brn, bis & claret 15.00 *42.50*
**C14** AP5 40c dl grn, yel grn & bl 57.50 *82.50*
**C15** AP6 2fr blk brn & red brn, *gray* ('30) 85.00 *85.00*
*Nos. C13-C15 (3)* 157.50 *210.00*
Set, never hinged 425.00

**1933-35 With Grilled Gum**

*C13a* AP5 35c red brn, bis & cl 5.00 *50.00*
*C14a* AP5 40c dk grn, yel grn & bl 37.50 *77.50*
*C15a* AP6 2fr blk brn & red brn ('35) 7.25 *12.00*
*Nos. C13a-C15a (3)* 49.75 *139.50*
Set, never hinged 140.00

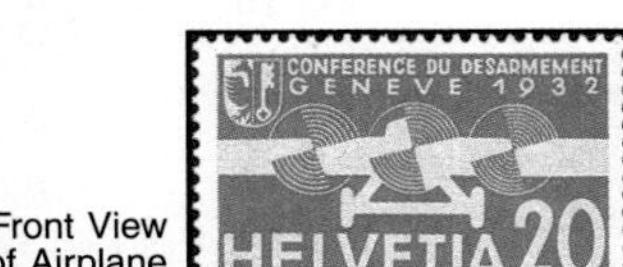


Front View of Airplane AP7

**1932, Feb. 2 Granite Paper**

**C16** AP7 15c dp grn & lt grn .55 *1.60*
**C17** AP7 20c dk red & buff 1.10 *2.50*
**C18** AP7 90c dp bl & gray 7.25 *30.00*
*Nos. C16-C18 (3)* 8.90 *34.10*
Set, never hinged 22.50

Intl. Disarmament Conf., Geneva, Feb. 1932.
For surcharges see Nos. C20-C21, C23-C25.

**Nos. C3, C10, C16-C18 Surcharged with New Values and Bars in Black or Red**

**1935-38**

**C19** AP1 10c on 15c 4.75 *32.50*
**C20** AP7 10c on 15c .40 *.55*
*a.* Inverted surcharge 6,500. *12,000.*
**C21** AP7 10c on 20c ('36) .45 *2.25*
**C22** AP4 10c on 65c ('38) .20 *.40*
**C23** AP7 30c on 90c ('36) 3.00 *14.00*
**C24** AP7 40c on 20c ('37) 3.75 *15.00*
**C25** AP7 40c on 90c ('36) (R) 3.25 *14.50*
*a.* Vermilion surcharge 92.50 *800.00*
Never hinged, #C25a 150.00
*Nos. C19-C25 (7)* 15.80 *79.20*
Set, never hinged 40.00

Stamp similar to No. C22, but from souvenir sheet, is listed as No. 242a.

Type of Air Post Stamp of 1923 Surcharged in Black

**1938, May 22 Wmk. 183 *Perf. 11½***

**C26** AP3 75c on 50c gray & scar 6.50

"Pro Aero" Meeting, May 21-22.
No. C26 was not sold to the public in the ordinary way, but affixed to air mail letters by postal officials. It was not regularly obtainable unused.

Jungfrau — AP8

Designs: 40c, View of Valais. 50c, Lake Geneva. 60c, Alpstein. 70c, View of Ticino. 1fr, Lake Lucerne. 2fr, The Engadine. 5fr, Churfirsten.

***Perf. 11½***

**1941, May 1 Unwmk. Engr.**

**Tinted Granite Paper**

**C27** AP8 30c ultra .55 .25
**C28** AP8 40c gray blk .55 .25
**C29** AP8 50c slate grn .55 .30
**C30** AP8 60c chestnut .85 .30
**C31** AP8 70c plum .90 .55
**C32** AP8 1fr Prus grn 1.75 .60
**C33** AP8 2fr car lake 5.75 3.50
**C34** AP8 5fr deep blue 19.00 15.00
*Nos. C27-C34 (8)* 29.90 20.75
Set, never hinged 80.00

See Nos. C43-C44.

Type of 1941 Overprinted in Red

**1941, May 12**

**C35** AP8 1fr blue green 5.50 *19.00*
Never hinged 10.00

Issued to commemorate special flights between Payerne and Buochs, May 28, 1941.

Parliament Buildings, Bern AP16

**1943, July 13 Photo.**

**C36** AP16 1fr cop red, buff & blk 1.60 *10.00*
Never hinged 3.75

30th anniv. of the 1st Alpine flight, by Oscar Bider, July 13, 1913.

DH-3 Haefeli AP17

Fokker AP18

Lockheed-Orion — AP19

**1944, Sept. 1**

**C37** AP17 10c gray brn & pale grn .20 *.50*
**C38** AP18 20c rose car & buff .30 *.50*
**C39** AP19 30c ultra & pale gray .35 *1.25*
*Nos. C37-C39 (3)* .85 *2.25*
Set, never hinged 1.50

25th anniv. of the 1st regular air route in Switzerland.

Douglas DC-3 AP20

**1944, Sept. 20 Granite Paper**

**C40** AP20 1.50fr multi 5.50 *17.50*
Never hinged 11.00

25th anniv. of the Zurich-Geneva air route.

Zoegling Training Glider AP21

**1946, May 1 Granite Paper**

**C41** AP21 1.50fr henna brn & gray 11.50 *27.50*
Never hinged 20.00

Valid for use only on two special flights.

Douglas DC-4 Linking Geneva and New York AP22

**1947, Mar. 17 Granite Paper**

**C42** AP22 2.50fr bl gray, dk bl & red 7.00 *20.00*
Never hinged 13.00

Valid only on the Geneva-New York flight of May 2, 1947.
Because of bad weather at NYC the flight ended at Washington.

**Types of 1941**

**1948, Oct. 1 Engr.**

**Tinted Granite Paper**

**C43** AP8 30c dk slate bl 4.50 *12.50*
**C44** AP8 40c deep ultra 21.00 2.75
Set, never hinged 57.50

Glider in Symbolized Aerodynamic Buoyancy — AP23

**1949, Apr. 11 Engr. & Typo.**

**C45** AP23 1.50fr dk vio & yel 16.00 *37.50*
Never hinged 30.00

Valid only on special flights, Apr. 27-29, 1949. Proceeds were for the advancement of national aviation.

**Catalogue values for unused stamps in this section, from this point to the end of the section, are for Never Hinged items.**

Glider and Jets AP24

**1963, June 1 Photo. *Perf. 11½***

**Granite Paper**

**C46** AP24 2fr multicolored 4.00 3.50

50th anniversary of the first Alpine flight by Oscar Bider, July 13, 1913. Valid for postage on July 13, 1963, on flights from Bern to Locarno and Langenbruck to Bern. Proceeds went to the Pro Aero Foundation.

## AIR POST SEMI-POSTAL STAMP

**Catalogue values for unused stamps in this section are for Never Hinged items.**

Boeing 747 — SPAP1

**1972, Feb. 17 Photo. *Perf. 12½***

**Violet Fibers, Fluorescent Paper**

**CB1** SPAP1 2fr + 1fr dp bl, red & gray 2.50 2.25

50th anniv. of 1st Swiss Intl. flight, Zurich to Nuremberg, and 25th anniv. of 1st Swissair trans-Atlantic flight, Zurich to NYC. Valid on all mail but obligatory on special flights from Geneva to NYC in May, and from Geneva to Nuremberg in June, 1972.
Surtax was for Pro Aero Foundation and the training of young airmen, and for the Swiss Air Rescue Service.

## POSTAGE DUE STAMPS

D1 D2

**Wmk. 182**

**1878-80 Typo. *Perf. 11½***

**J1** D1 1c ultra 1.90 1.60
**J2** D2 2c ultra 1.90 1.60
**J3** D2 3c ultra 17.00 16.00
**J4** D2 5c ultra 17.00 6.75
**J5** D2 10c ultra 180.00 6.00
**J6** D2 20c ultra 210.00 6.00
**J7** D2 50c ultra 400.00 20.00
**J8** D2 100c ultra 525.00 17.00
**J9** D2 500c ultra 475.00 27.50
*Nos. J1-J9 (9)* 1,827. 102.45

A 5c in design D1 exists.

**1882-83**

**Granite Paper**

**J10** D2 10c ultra 175.00 40.00
**J11** D2 20c ultra 400.00 52.50
**J12** D2 50c ultra 2,400. 525.00
**J13** D2 100c ultra 800.00 400.00
**J14** D2 500c ultra *13,750.* 210.00

**1883-84**

**Numerals in Red**

**J15** D2 5c blue green 42.50 30.00
**J16** D2 10c blue green 65.00 25.00
**J17** D2 20c blue green 120.00 22.50
**J18** D2 50c blue green 140.00 72.50
**J19** D2 100c blue green 350.00 350.00
**J20** D2 500c blue green 775.00 190.00
*Nos. J15-J20 (6)* 1,492. 690.00

**1884-97**

**Numerals in Red**

**J21** D2 1c olive green .65 .65
**J22** D2 3c olive green 5.75 6.50
**J23** D2 5c olive green 1.60 .65
*a.* 5c yellow green 25.00 12.50

**J24** D2 10c olive green 3.75 .85
*a.* 10c yellow green 110.00 16.00
**J25** D2 20c olive green 8.25 1.30
*a.* 20c yellow green 110.00 16.00
**J26** D2 50c olive green 12.00 2.50
*a.* 50c yellow green 100.00 32.50
**J27** D2 100c olive green 14.00 2.75
*a.* 100c yellow green 100.00 80.00
**J28** D2 500c olive green 150.00 160.00
*a.* 500c yellow green 125.00 60.00

**1908-09 Wmk. 183**

**Numerals in Red**

**J29** D2 1c olive green .30 *1.10*
**J30** D2 5c olive green .60 *.90*
**J31** D2 10c olive green 1.50 *2.25*
**J32** D2 20c olive green 3.00 *5.00*
**J33** D2 50c olive green 15.00 1.10
**J34** D2 100c olive green 30.00 2.25
*Nos. J29-J34 (6)* 50.40 *12.60*

D3

**1910 Perf. 11½, 12**

**Numerals in Red**

**J35** D3 1c blue green .20 .20
**J36** D3 3c blue green .20 .20
**J37** D3 5c blue green .20 .20
**J38** D3 10c blue green 11.00 .20
**J39** D3 15c blue green .65 *1.10*
**J40** D3 20c blue green 17.50 .20
**J41** D3 25c blue green 1.25 .65
**J42** D3 30c blue green 1.25 .55
**J43** D3 50c blue green 1.50 1.10
*Nos. J35-J43 (9)* 33.75 4.40

See Nos. S1-S12.

No. J36 Surcharged

**1916**

**J44** D3 5c on 3c bl grn & red .40 .25

Nos. J35-J36, J43 Surcharged

**1924**

**J45** D3 10c on 1c .25 *8.25*
**J46** D3 10c on 3c .25 *1.50*
**J47** D3 20c on 50c .95 *1.50*
*Nos. J45-J47 (3)* 1.45 *11.25*

D4

D5

**Wmk. 183**

**1924-26 Typo. Perf. 11½**

**Granite Paper**

**J48** D4 5c ol grn & red .65 .25
**J49** D4 10c ol grn & red 2.75 .20
**J50** D4 15c ol grn & red ('26) 2.50 .55
**J51** D4 20c ol grn & red 6.00 .20
**J52** D4 25c ol grn & red 2.75 .55
**J53** D4 30c ol grn & red 2.75 .85
**J54** D4 40c ol grn & red ('26) 3.75 .70
**J55** D4 50c ol grn & red 3.75 .70
*Nos. J48-J55 (8)* 24.90 4.00

**1924**

**With Grilled Gum**

*J48a* D4 5c olive green & red .65 .60
*J49a* D4 10c olive green & red 2.50 1.10
*J51a* D4 20c olive green & red 4.75 1.50
*J52a* D4 25c olive green & red 7.25 *65.00*
*Nos. J48a-J52a (4)* 15.15 *68.20*

See Grilled Gum note after No. 145.

**Nos. J50, J53 and J55 Surcharged with New Value in Black**

**1937**

**J56** D4 5c on 15c .90 *4.25*
**J57** D4 10c on 30c .90 *1.50*
**J58** D4 20c on 50c 1.50 *5.00*
**J59** D4 40c on 50c 2.50 *12.00*
*Nos. J56-J59 (4)* 5.80 *22.75*
Set, never hinged 10.50

**1938 Engr. Unwmk.**

**J60** D5 5c scarlet .40 .20
**J61** D5 10c scarlet .55 .20
**J62** D5 15c scarlet 1.25 *2.25*
**J63** D5 20c scarlet .95 .20
**J64** D5 25c scarlet 1.40 *1.90*
**J65** D5 30c scarlet 1.40 1.25
**J66** D5 40c scarlet 1.60 .45
**J67** D5 50c scarlet 1.90 *2.25*
*Nos. J60-J67 (8)* 9.45 *8.70*
Set, never hinged 19.00

**1938**

**With Grilled Gum**

*J60a* D5 5c scarlet .65 *1.60*
*J61a* D5 10c scarlet .65 *1.25*
*J62a* D5 15c scarlet 1.40 *2.50*
*J63a* D5 20c scarlet 1.25 .55
*J64a* D5 25c scarlet 1.40 *9.50*
*J65a* D5 30c scarlet 1.40 *2.25*
*J66a* D5 40c scarlet 2.10 2.10
*J67a* D5 50c scarlet 2.50 *3.50*
*Nos. J60a-J67a (8)* 11.35 *23.25*
Set, never hinged 29.00

See Grilled Gum note after No. 145.

---

## OFFICIAL STAMPS

### For General Use

With Perforated Cross

In 1935 the government authorized the use of regular postage issues perforated with a nine-hole cross for all government departments. Twenty-seven different stamps were so perforated. These were succeeded in 1938 by the cross overprints.

Values for canceled Official Stamps are for those canceled to order. Postally used stamps sell for considerably less. This note does not apply to Nos. 1O1-1O16, 2O27-2O30, 3O23-3O26.

Counterfeit overprints exist of most official stamps.

Official stamps without unused values were not made available to the public unused.

Regular Issues of 1908-36 Overprinted in Black

**1938 Unwmk. Perf. 11½**

**O1** A53 3c olive .20 .20
**O2** A54 5c blue green .20 .20
**O3** A55 10c red violet .95 .45
**O4** A56 15c orange .25 *1.60*
**O5** A68 20c red .45 .25
**O6** A58 25c brown .45 *1.40*
**O7** A59 30c ultra .60 *1.00*
**O8** A60 35c yellow green .60 *1.25*
**O9** A61 40c gray .60 *1.00*

**Wmk. 183**

**With Grilled Gum**

**O10** A25 50c dp grn & pale grn .60 *1.50*
**O11** A25 60c brn org & buff 1.25 *2.50*
**O12** A25 70c vio & buff 1.25 *4.25*
**O13** A25 80c sl & buff 1.25 *3.25*
**O14** A36 90c grn & red, *grn* 3.00 *3.25*
**O15** A25 1fr dp cl & pale grn 1.50 *3.25*
**O16** A36 1.20fr brn rose & red, *rose* 1.50 *4.50*
**O17** A36 1.50fr bl & red, *bl* 2.50 *6.00*
**O18** A36 2fr gray blk & red, *gray* 3.00 *7.00*
*Nos. O1-O18 (18)* 20.15 *42.85*
Set, never hinged 65.00

Nos. O14, O16, O17 and O18 are on surface-colored paper.

**1938 Unwmk. With Grilled Gum**

*O1a* A53 3c olive 4.50 .45
*O2a* A54 5c blue green 1.25 .25
*O3a* A55 10c red violet 1.50 .55
*O4a* A56 15c orange 2.75 1.25
*O5a* A68 20c red 1.50 .70
*O6a* A58 25c brown 75.00 7.75
*O7a* A59 30c ultra 2.50 1.10
*O8a* A60 35c yellow green 1.90 1.90
*O9a* A61 40c gray 2.50 1.00
*Nos. O1a-O9a (9)* 93.40 14.95
Set, never hinged 190.00

See Grilled Gum note after No. 145.

Postage Stamps of 1936-42 Overprinted in Black

**1942-45 Unwmk. Perf. 11½**

**O19** A53 3c olive .30 *2.10*
**O20** A54 5c blue green .30 .20
**O21** A55 10c dk red brn .55 .55
**O21A** A55 10c orange brn ('45) .20 *.45*
**O22** A56 15c orange .60 *1.90*
**O23** A68 20c red .60 .45
**O24** A58 25c lt brown .60 *2.25*
**O25** A59 30c ultra .95 .90
**O26** A60 35c yellow grn 1.25 *2.75*
**O27** A61 40c gray 1.25 .60
**O28** A77 50c dp pur, *grnsh* 3.75 *4.25*
**O29** A78 60c red brn, *buff* 4.50 4.25
**O30** A79 70c rose vio, *pale lil* 5.00 *8.25*
**O31** A80 80c blk, *pale gray* 1.40 *1.60*
**O32** A81 90c dk red, *pale rose* 1.60 *2.25*
**O33** A82 1fr dk grn, *grnsh* 1.60 1.60
**O34** A83 1.20fr red vio, *pale gray* 2.25 *2.75*
**O35** A84 1.50fr dk bl, *buff* 2.25 *3.25*
**O36** A85 2fr mar, *pale rose* 3.25 *4.00*
*Nos. O19-O36 (19)* 32.20 *44.35*
Set, never hinged 60.00

Same Overprint on Nos. 329-339

**1950 Unwmk. Perf. 12x11½**

**O37** A118 5c orange .40 *.55*
**O38** A119 10c yellow grn .65 .55
**O39** A120 15c aqua 5.50 *15.00*
**O40** A121 20c brown car 2.10 .65
**O41** A122 25c red 3.25 *8.25*
**O42** A123 30c olive 2.50 *3.25*
**O43** A124 35c red brown 3.50 *11.00*
**O44** A125 40c deep blue 2.75 *3.25*
**O45** A126 50c slate gray 4.50 *5.75*
**O46** A127 60c blue green 5.50 *7.75*
**O47** A128 70c purple 16.00 *22.50*
*Nos. O37-O47 (11)* 46.65 *78.50*
Set, never hinged 77.50

---

### FOR THE WAR BOARD OF TRADE

Regular Issues of 1908-18 Overprinted

**1918 Wmk. 183 Perf. 11½, 12**

**1O1** A26 3c brown org 110.00 *225.00*
**1O2** A26 5c green 10.00 *32.50*
**1O3** A26 7½c gray (I) 300.00 *450.00*
*a.* 7½c slate (II) 550.00 *950.00*
**1O4** A28 10c red, *buff* 15.00 *40.00*
**1O5** A28 15c vio, *buff* 12.50 *45.00*
**1O6** A25 20c red & yel 125.00 *500.00*
**1O7** A25 25c dp bl 125.00 *500.00*
**1O8** A25 30c yel brn & pale grn 125.00 *450.00*
*Nos. 1O1-1O8 (8)* 822.50 *2,242.*

*Most unused copies of Nos. 1O1-1O8 are reprints made using the original overprint forms.*

Counterfeits exist.

Overprinted

**1918**

**1O9** A26 3c brown orange 4.25 *35.00*
**1O10** A26 5c green 12.00 *52.50*
**1O11** A26 7½c gray 4.50 *22.50*
**1O12** A28 10c red, *buff* 45.00 *87.50*
**1O13** A28 15c vio, *buff* 87.50
**1O14** A25 20c red & yel 8.75 *52.50*
**1O15** A25 25c dp blue 8.75 *52.50*
**1O16** A25 30c yel brn & pale grn 14.50 *87.50*
*Nos. 1O9-1O16 (8)* 185.25

No. 1O13 was never placed in use.

Fraudulent cancellations are found on Nos. 1O1-1O16.

---

### FOR THE LEAGUE OF NATIONS

Regular Issues Overprinted

**On 1908-30 Issues**

**1922-31 Wmk. 183 Perf. 11½, 12**

**2O1** A26 2½c ol, *buff* ('28) .45
**2O2** A26 3c ultra, *buff* ('30) 8.25
**2O3** A26 5c orange, *buff* 5.50
**2O4** A26 5c gray vio, *buff* ('26) 2.75
**2O5** A26 5c red vio, *buff* ('27) 2.25
**2O6** A26 5c dk grn, *buff* ('31) 25.00
**2O7** A26 7½c dp grn, *buff* ('28) .55
**2O8** A28 10c green, *buff* .55
**2O9** A28 10c bl grn, *buff* ('28) 1.10
**2O10** A28 10c vio, *buff* ('31) 2.75
**2O11** A28 15c brn red, *buff* ('28) 1.10
**2O12** A28 20c red vio, *buff* 8.25
**2O13** A28 20c car, *buff* ('26) 2.25
**2O14** A28 25c ver, *buff* 8.25
**2O15** A28 25c car, *buff* 1.10
**2O16** A28 25c brn, *buff* ('27) 17.00
**2O17** A28 30c dp bl, *buff* ('25) 8.25
**2O18** A25 30c yel brn & pale grn 14.00
**2O19** A25 35c yel grn & yel 10.00
**2O20** A25 40c deep blue 1.40
**2O21** A25 40c red vio & grn ('28) 14.00
**2O22** A25 50c dp grn & pale grn 11.00
**2O23** A25 60c brn org & buff 30.00 1.60
**2O24** A25 70c vio & buff ('25) 26.00
**2O25** A25 80c slate & buff 2.75
**2O26** A25 1fr dp cl & pale grn 6.75
**2O27** A29 3fr red 32.50
**2O28** A30 5fr ultra 60.00
**2O29** A31 10fr dull violet 140.00
**2O30** A31 10fr gray grn ('30) 140.00
*Nos. 2O1-2O30 (30)* 555.35

**1930-44 With Grilled Gum**

*2O2a* A26 3c ultra, *buff* ('33) 10.00
*2O6a* A26 5c dk grn, *buff* ('33) 19.00
*2O17a* A28 30c dp bl, *buff* 425.00
*2O22a* A25 50c dp grn & pale grn ('35) .90 2.25
*2O23a* A25 60c brn org & buff ('44) 25.00 *225.00*
*2O24a* A25 70c violet & buff ('32) 1.60 2.25
*2O25a* A25 80c slate & buff ('42) 2.75 2.50
*2O26a* A25 1fr dp cl & pale grn ('42) 5.25

**1935-36**

**With Grilled Gum**

**2O31** A36 90c grn & red, *grn* ('36) 5.00
**2O32** A36 1.20fr brn rose & red, *rose* ('36) 2.75 *4.50*
*b.* Inverted overprint *4,250.*
**2O33** A36 1.50fr bl & red, *bl* 2.75 *4.50*
**2O34** A36 2fr gray blk & red, *gray* ('36) 2.75 *5.25*

**1922-25 Ordinary Gum**

*2O31a* A36 90c 14.00
*2O32a* A36 1.20fr ('25) 14.00
*2O33a* A36 1.50fr ('25) 13.00
*2O34a* A36 2fr ('25) 12.00

**1928**

**2O35** A39 5fr blue 87.50

### On 1932 Issue

**1932**

2O36 A41 5c peacock bl 19.00
2O37 A41 10c orange 1.60
2O38 A41 20c cerise 1.60
2O39 A41 30c ultra 55.00
2O40 A41 60c olive brn 15.00

**Unwmk.**

2O41 A42 1fr ol gray & bl 15.00
*Nos. 2O36-2O41 (6)* 107.20

### On 1934 Issue

**1934-35 Wmk. 183**

2O42 A46 3c olive .25
2O43 A47 5c emerald .65
2O44 A49 15c orange ('35) 1.50
2O45 A51 25c brown 19.00
2O46 A52 30c ultra 1.60
*Nos. 2O42-2O46 (5)* 23.00

### On 1936 Issue

**1937 Unwmk.**

2O47 A53 3c olive .20 .25
2O48 A54 5c blue green .25 .25
2O49 A55 10c red violet 1.10
2O50 A56 15c orange .45 .55
2O51 A57 20c carmine 1.90
2O52 A58 25c brown .65 1.10
2O53 A59 30c ultra .65 1.00
2O54 A60 35c yellow green .65 1.00
2O55 A61 40c gray .95 1.25
*Nos. 2O47-2O55 (9)* 8.40

**1937 With Grilled Gum**

*2O47a* A53 3c olive .30
*2O48a* A54 5c blue green .45
*2O49a* A55 10c red violet 6.25
*2O50a* A56 15c orange .70
*2O51a* A57 20c carmine 2.25
*2O52a* A58 25c brown 1.40
*2O53a* A59 30c ultra 1.10
*2O54a* A60 35c yellow green 4.25
*2O55a* A61 40c gray 4.25
*Nos. 2O47a-2O55a (9)* 20.95

### On 1931 Issue

**1937 Wmk. 183**

2O56 A40 3fr orange brown 190.00

### On 1938 Issue

**1938 Unwmk. Perf. 11½**

**Granite Paper**

2O57 A63 20c red & buff 1.90
2O58 A64 30c blue & lt blue 3.00
2O59 A65 60c brown & buff 5.75
2O60 A66 1fr black & buff 9.25
*Nos. 2O57-2O60 (4)* 19.90

Regular Issue of 1938 Overprinted in Black or Red

**Granite Paper**

2O61 A63 20c red & buff 2.25
2O62 A64 30c blue & lt blue 4.00
2O63 A65 60c brown & buff 7.25
2O64 A66 1fr black & buff (R) 12.50
*Nos. 2O61-2O64 (4)* 26.00

Regular Issue of 1938 Overprinted in Black

**1939**

2O65 A69 3fr brn car, *buff* 3.25 11.00
2O66 A70 5fr slate bl, *buff* 5.50 15.00
2O67 A71 10fr green, *buff* 11.00 32.50
*Nos. 2O65-2O67 (3)* 19.75 58.50

Same Overprint in Black on Regular Issues of 1939-42

**1942-43**

2O68 A55 10c dk red brown .85
2O68A A55 10c orange brn ('43) .40 .85
2O69 A68 20c red .50 1.00
*Nos. 2O68-2O69 (3)* 2.70

Stamps of 1936-42 Overprinted in Black

**1944**

2O70 A53 3c olive .20 .25
2O71 A54 5c blue green .20 .25
2O72 A55 10c orange brown .80 .40
2O73 A56 15c orange .20 .50
2O74 A68 20c red .40 .75
2O75 A58 25c lt brown .40 1.00
2O76 A59 30c ultra .50 1.00
2O77 A60 35c yellow green .50 1.00
2O78 A61 40c gray .55 1.25

Nos. 2O73-2O75 and 2O78 exist with grilled gum. Value each $2,000 unused, $2,250 used.

Stamps of 1941 Overprinted in Black

2O79 A77 50c dp pur, *grnsh* 1.00 1.75
2O80 A78 60c red brn, *buff* 1.25 2.50
2O81 A79 70c rose vio, *pale lil* 1.25 2.50
2O82 A80 80c blk, *pale gray* 1.10 2.00
2O83 A81 90c dk red, *pale rose* 1.10 2.00
2O84 A82 1fr dk grn, *grnsh* 1.10 2.25
2O85 A83 1.20fr red vio, *pale gray* 1.75 3.00
2O86 A84 1.50fr dk bl, *buff* 2.00 3.50
2O87 A85 2fr mar, *pale rose* 2.50 4.00

Stamps of 1942 Overprinted in Black

**Unwmk. Perf. 11½**

2O88 A69 3fr brn car, *cr* 4.50 9.00
2O89 A70 5fr slate bl, *cr* 7.00 12.50
2O90 A71 10fr green, *cr* 12.00 24.00
*Nos. 2O70-2O90 (21)* 40.30 75.40
Set, never hinged 65.00

---

## FOR THE INTERNATIONAL LABOR BUREAU

Regular Issues Overprinted

### On 1908-30 Issues

**1923-30 Wmk. 183 Perf. 11½, 12**

3O1 A26 2½c ol grn, *buff* ('28) .30
3O2 A26 3c ultra, *buff* ('30) 1.10
3O3 A26 5c org, *buff* .55
3O4 A26 5c red vio, *buff* ('28) .20
3O5 A26 7½c dp grn, *buff* ('28) .45
3O6 A28 10c grn, *buff* .55
3O7 A28 10c bl grn, *buff* ('28) 1.10
3O8 A28 15c brn red, *buff* ('28) 1.10
3O9 A28 20c red vio, *buff* 17.00
3O10 A28 20c car, *buff* ('27) 5.00
3O11 A28 25c car, *buff* 1.25
3O12 A28 25c brn, *buff* ('28) 3.00
3O13 A28 30c dp bl, *buff* ('25) 2.50
3O14 A25 30c yel brn & pale grn 65.00
3O15 A25 35c yel grn & yel 11.00
3O16 A25 40c deep blue 1.25
3O17 A25 40c red vio & grn ('28) 17.00
3O18 A25 50c dp grn & pale grn 5.00
3O19 A25 '60c brn org & buff 1.60 1.90
3O20 A25 70c vio & buff ('24) 26.00
3O21 A25 80c slate & buff 14.00 2.25
3O22 A25 1fr dp cl & pale grn 2.75
3O23 A29 3fr red 25.00
3O24 A30 5fr ultra 37.50
3O25 A31 10fr dull violet 150.00
3O26 A31 10fr gray grn ('30) 150.00
*Nos. 3O1-3O26 (26)* 528.75

**1937-44 With Grilled Gum**

*3O18a* A25 50c dp grn & pale grn ('42) 1.75 2.25
*3O20a* A25 70c vio & buff 1.75 2.25
*3O21a* A25 80c slate & buff ('44) 25.00 175.00
*3O22a* A25 1fr dp cl & pale grn ('42) 3.25

**1925-42 With Grilled Gum**

3O27 A36 90c grn & red, *grn* ('37) 9.75
*a.* Ordinary gum 5.00
3O28 A36 1.20fr brn rose & red, *rose* ('42) 14.00 4.00
*a.* Ordinary gum 4.50
3O29 A36 1.50fr bl & red, *bl* ('37) 2.75 3.00
*a.* Ordinary gum 14.00
3O30 A36 2fr gray blk & red, *gray* ('36) 3.25 6.25
*a.* Ordinary gum 32.50
*Nos. 3O27-3O30 (4)* 23.00

**1928**

3O31 A39 5fr blue 82.50

### On 1932 Issue

**1932**

3O32 A41 5c peacock blue 1.10
3O33 A41 10c orange .90
3O34 A41 20c cerise 1.25
3O35 A41 30c ultra 7.75
3O36 A41 60c olive brown 7.75

**Unwmk.**

3O37 A42 1fr ol gray & bl 10.00
*Nos. 3O32-3O37 (6)* 28.75

### On 1936 Issue

**1937**

3O38 A53 3c olive .20 .55
3O39 A54 5c blue green .20 .55
3O40 A55 10c red violet 2.75
3O41 A56 15c orange .45 1.10
3O42 A57 20c carmine 2.25
3O43 A58 25c brown .60 1.40
3O44 A59 30c ultra .60 1.10
3O45 A60 35c yellow green .60 1.60
3O46 A61 40c gray .95 1.90
*Nos. 3O38-3O46 (9)* 13.20

**1937 With Grilled Gum**

*3O38a* A53 3c olive 1.10
*3O39a* A54 5c blue green 1.10
*3O40a* A55 10c red violet 1.60
*3O41a* A56 15c orange 1.90
*3O42a* A57 20c carmine 1.60
*3O43a* A58 25c brown 2.25
*3O44a* A59 30c ultra 2.25
*3O45a* A60 35c yellow green 2.75
*3O46a* A61 40c gray 2.25
*Nos. 3O38a-3O46a (9)* 16.80

### On 1931 Issue

**1937 Wmk. 183**

3O47 A40 3fr orange brown 175.00

### On 1934 Issue

3O48 A46 3c olive 5.50

### On 1938 Issue

**1938 Unwmk. Perf. 11½**

**Granite Paper**

3O49 A63 20c red & buff 1.60
3O50 A64 30c blue & lt blue 3.25
3O51 A65 60c brown & buff 6.00
3O52 A66 1fr black & buff 8.75
*Nos. 3O49-3O52 (4)* 19.60

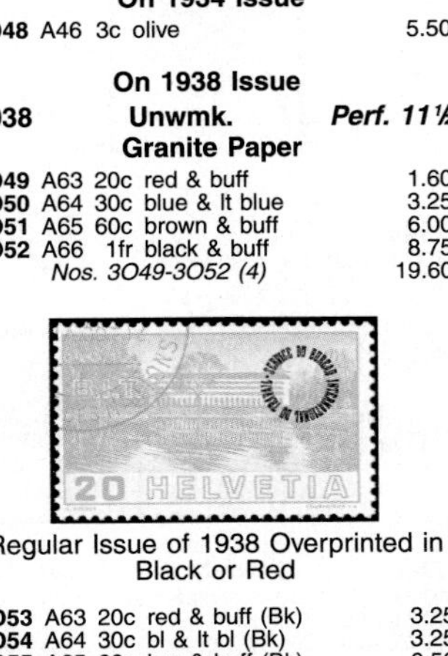

Regular Issue of 1938 Overprinted in Black or Red

3O53 A63 20c red & buff (Bk) 3.25
3O54 A64 30c bl & lt bl (Bk) 3.25
3O55 A65 60c brn & buff (Bk) 6.50
3O56 A66 1fr blk & buff (R) 7.00
*Nos. 3O53-3O56 (4)* 20.00

Regular Issue of 1938 Overprinted in Black

S.d.N.
Bureau
international
du Travail

**1939**

3O57 A69 3fr brn car, *buff* 4.50 8.25
3O58 A70 5fr slate bl, *buff* 5.50 17.00
3O59 A71 10fr green, *buff* 10.00 30.00
*Nos. 3O57-3O59 (3)* 20.00 55.25

Same Overprint in Black on Regular Issues of 1939-42

**1942-43**

3O60 A55 10c dark red brown .80
3O60A A55 10c orange brn ('43) .50 .80
3O61 A68 20c red .55 .80
*Nos. 3O60-3O61 (3)* 2.40

Stamps of 1936-42 Overprinted in Black

**1944**

3O62 A53 3c olive .20 .20
3O63 A54 5c blue green .20 .20
3O64 A55 10c orange brn .20 .25
3O65 A56 15c orange .50 .50
3O66 A68 20c red .35 .50
3O67 A58 25c lt brown .55 .70
3O68 A59 30c ultra .50 1.10
3O69 A60 35c yellow grn .70 1.25
3O70 A61 40c gray .75 1.40

Stamps of 1941 Overprinted

3O71 A77 50c dp pur, *grnsh* 1.50 8.00
3O72 A78 60c red brn, *buff* 1.50 8.00
3O73 A79 70c rose vio, *pale lil* 1.75 8.00
3O74 A80 80c blk, *pale gray* .45 1.40
3O75 A81 90c dk red, *pale rose* .45 1.40
3O76 A82 1fr dk grn, *grnsh* .45 1.40
3O77 A83 1.20fr red vio, *pale gray* .75 1.75
3O78 A84 1.50fr dull bl, *buff* 1.00 2.25
3O79 A85 2fr mar, *pale rose* 1.25 3.00

Stamps of 1942 Overprinted

3O80 A69 3fr brown car, *cr* 3.25 6.00
3O81 A70 5fr slate blue, *cr* 5.00 10.50
3O82 A71 10fr green, *cr* 10.00 20.00
*Nos. 3O62-3O82 (21)* 31.30 77.80
Set, never hinged 60.00

Nos. 329-339 Overprinted in Black

**1950 Unwmk. Perf. 12x11½**

3O83 A118 5c orange 4.00 4.75
3O84 A119 10c yellow green 4.00 5.25
3O85 A120 15c aqua 5.00 7.50
3O86 A121 20c brown carmine 5.00 7.50
3O87 A122 25c red 6.00 7.75
3O88 A123 30c olive 6.00 7.75
3O89 A124 35c red brown 6.00 7.75
3O90 A125 40c deep blue 6.00 7.75
3O91 A126 50c slate gray 7.50 8.25
3O92 A127 60c blue green 9.00 12.50
3O93 A128 70c purple 10.00 17.50
*Nos. 3O83-3O93 (11)* 68.50 94.25
Set, never hinged 110.00

**Catalogue values for unused stamps in this section, from this point to the end of the section, are for Never Hinged items.**

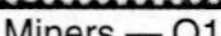

Miners — O1

Globe, Chimney and Wheel — O2

**1956-60 Unwmk. Engr. *Perf. 11½***

| No. | Type | Description | Unused | Used |
|---|---|---|---|---|
| 3O94 | O1 | 5c dark gray | .20 | .20 |
| 3O95 | O1 | 10c green | .20 | .20 |
| 3O96 | O2 | 20c vermilion | 1.25 | 2.25 |
| 3O97 | O2 | 20c car rose ('60) | .20 | .20 |
| 3O98 | O2 | 30c orange ver ('60) | .25 | .40 |
| 3O99 | O1 | 40c blue | 1.25 | 2.75 |
| 3O100 | O1 | 50c lt ultra ('60) | .25 | .50 |
| 3O101 | O2 | 60c reddish brown | .30 | .50 |
| 3O102 | O2 | 2fr rose violet | 1.10 | 1.50 |
| | | *Nos. 3O94-3O102 (9)* | 5.00 | 8.50 |

**Type of 1960 Overprinted: "Visite du / Pape Paul VI / Genève / 10 juin 1969"**

**1969, June 10**

**Violet Fibers, Fluorescent Paper**

| No. | Type | Description | Unused | Used |
|---|---|---|---|---|
| 3O103 | O2 | 30c orange vermilion | .30 | .30 |

Visit of Pope Paul VI to the Intl. Labor Bureau to celebrate its 50th anniv., Geneva, June 10.

ILO Headquarters, Geneva — O3

**1974, May 30 Photo. *Perf. 11½***

**Violet Fibers, Fluorescent Paper**

| No. | Type | Description | Unused | Used |
|---|---|---|---|---|
| 3O104 | O3 | 80c blue, yellow & gray | .85 | .80 |

Inauguration of the new International Labor Organization Building.

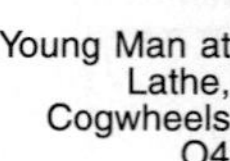

Young Man at Lathe, Cogwheels O4

Designs: 60c, Woman at drilling machine. 90c, Welder and lab assistant using protective devices and clothing. 100c, Surveyor with theodolite and topographical map. 120c, Professional education for youth.

**1975-88 Photo. *Perf. 11½***

| No. | Type | Description | Unused | Used |
|---|---|---|---|---|
| 3O105 | O4 | 30c red brn & dk brn | .30 | .30 |
| 3O106 | O4 | 60c ultra & blk | .60 | .60 |
| 3O107 | O4 | 100c dk green & blk | 1.00 | 1.00 |
| 3O108 | O4 | 120c multicolored | 1.25 | 1.25 |

***Perf. 12x11½***

| No. | Type | Description | Unused | Used |
|---|---|---|---|---|
| 3O109 | O4 | 90c multicolored | 1.00 | 1.00 |
| | | *Nos. 3O105-3O109 (5)* | 4.15 | 4.15 |

Issued: 30c-100c, 2/13; 120c, 8/22/83; 90c, 9/13/88.

ILO, 75th Anniv. — O5

**1994, May 17 Litho. *Perf. 13***

| No. | Type | Description | Unused | Used |
|---|---|---|---|---|
| 3O110 | O5 | 180c multicolored | 2.00 | 2.00 |

## FOR THE INTERNATIONAL BUREAU OF EDUCATION

Regular Issues of 1936-42, Overprinted in Black

**1944 Unwmk. *Perf. 11½***

| No. | Type | Description | Unused | Used |
|---|---|---|---|---|
| 4O1 | A53 | 3c olive | .40 | 1.00 |
| 4O2 | A54 | 5c blue grn | .55 | 1.25 |
| 4O3 | A55 | 10c orange brn | .55 | 1.50 |
| 4O4 | A56 | 15c orange | .55 | 1.50 |
| 4O5 | A68 | 20c red | .55 | 1.50 |
| 4O6 | A58 | 25c lt brown | .65 | 1.75 |
| 4O7 | A59 | 30c ultra | .85 | 2.25 |
| 4O8 | A60 | 35c yellow grn | .85 | 2.25 |
| 4O9 | A61 | 40c gray | 1.10 | 2.50 |

Regular Issue of 1941, Overprinted in Black

| No. | Type | Description | Unused | Used |
|---|---|---|---|---|
| 4O10 | A77 | 50c dp pur, *grnsh* | 5.00 | 13.00 |
| 4O11 | A78 | 60c red brn, *buff* | 5.00 | 13.00 |
| 4O12 | A79 | 70c rose vio, *pale lil* | 5.00 | 13.00 |
| 4O13 | A80 | 80c blk, *pale gray* | .60 | 1.50 |
| 4O14 | A81 | 90c dk red, *pale rose* | .70 | 1.75 |
| 4O15 | A82 | 1fr dk grn, *grnsh* | .85 | 2.25 |
| 4O16 | A83 | 1.20fr red vio, *pale gray* | 1.00 | 2.50 |
| 4O17 | A84 | 1.50fr dk bl, *buff* | 1.25 | 3.00 |
| 4O18 | A85 | 2fr mar, *pale rose* | 1.60 | 4.00 |

Regular Issue of 1942, Overprinted in Black

| No. | Type | Description | Unused | Used |
|---|---|---|---|---|
| 4O19 | A69 | 3fr brn car, *cr* | 7.00 | 17.00 |
| 4O20 | A70 | 5fr slate bl, *cr* | 10.00 | 25.00 |
| 4O21 | A71 | 10fr green, *cr* | 15.00 | 40.00 |
| | | *Nos. 4O1-4O21 (21)* | 59.05 | 151.50 |
| | | Set, never hinged | 110.00 | |

No. 306 Overprinted in Carmine

**1946**

| No. | Type | Description | Unused | Used |
|---|---|---|---|---|
| 4O22 | A104 | 10c rose violet | .20 | .50 |
| | | Never hinged | .50 | |

Nos. 316-321 Overprinted in Black

**1948 Unwmk. *Perf. 11½***

| No. | Type | Description | Unused | Used |
|---|---|---|---|---|
| 4O23 | A54 | 5c chocolate | 1.75 | 3.00 |
| 4O24 | A55 | 10c green | 1.75 | 3.00 |
| 4O25 | A68 | 20c orange brn | 1.75 | 3.00 |
| 4O26 | A113 | 25c carmine | 1.75 | 3.00 |
| 4O27 | A59 | 30c grnsh blue | 2.00 | 3.00 |
| 4O28 | A61 | 40c ultra | 2.00 | 3.00 |
| | | *Nos. 4O23-4O28 (6)* | 11.00 | 18.00 |
| | | Set, never hinged | 20.00 | |

Same Overprint on Nos. 329-339

**1950 *Perf. 12x11½***

**Overprint 18mm wide**

| No. | Type | Description | Unused | Used |
|---|---|---|---|---|
| 4O29 | A118 | 5c orange | .65 | 1.75 |
| 4O30 | A119 | 10c yellow grn | .65 | 2.10 |
| 4O31 | A120 | 15c aqua | .65 | 2.10 |
| 4O32 | A121 | 20c brown car | 2.00 | 5.75 |
| 4O33 | A122 | 25c red | 4.50 | 10.50 |
| 4O34 | A123 | 30c olive | 4.50 | 10.50 |
| 4O35 | A124 | 35c red brn | 3.50 | 8.75 |
| 4O36 | A125 | 40c deep blue | 3.50 | 8.75 |
| 4O37 | A126 | 50c slate gray | 4.00 | 9.75 |
| 4O38 | A127 | 60c blue green | 4.75 | 11.50 |
| 4O39 | A128 | 70c purple | 5.50 | 13.50 |
| | | *Nos. 4O29-4O39 (11)* | 34.20 | 84.95 |
| | | Set, never hinged | 60.00 | |

**Catalogue values for unused stamps in this section, from this point to the end of the section, are for Never Hinged items.**

Globe and Books — O1

Designs: 20c, 30c, 60c, 2fr, Pestalozzi Monument at Yverdon.

**1958-60 Engr. *Perf. 11½***

| No. | Type | Description | Unused | Used |
|---|---|---|---|---|
| 4O40 | O1 | 5c dark gray | .20 | .20 |
| 4O41 | O1 | 10c green | .20 | .20 |
| 4O42 | O1 | 20c vermilion | 2.25 | 2.25 |
| 4O43 | O1 | 20c car rose ('60) | .20 | .20 |
| 4O44 | O1 | 30c org ver ('60) | .20 | .35 |
| 4O45 | O1 | 40c blue | 2.75 | 2.75 |
| 4O46 | O1 | 50c lt ultra ('60) | .30 | .50 |
| 4O47 | O1 | 60c reddish brn | .30 | .50 |
| 4O48 | O1 | 2fr rose violet | 1.10 | 1.50 |
| | | *Nos. 4O40-4O48 (9)* | 7.50 | 8.45 |

## FOR THE WORLD HEALTH ORGANIZATION

No. 316-319, 321 Overprinted in Black

**1948 Unwmk. *Perf. 11½***

| No. | Type | Description | Unused | Used |
|---|---|---|---|---|
| 5O1 | A54 | 5c chocolate | 2.25 | 2.50 |
| 5O2 | A55 | 10c green | 2.25 | 3.50 |
| 5O3 | A68 | 20c orange brn | 2.25 | 3.50 |
| 5O4 | A113 | 25c carmine | 2.25 | 4.50 |
| 5O5 | A61 | 40c ultra | 2.50 | 5.00 |
| | | *Nos. 5O1-5O5 (5)* | 11.50 | 19.00 |
| | | Set, never hinged | 20.00 | |

Regular Issues of 1941, 1942 and 1949 Overprinted in Black

**1948-50**

| No. | Type | Description | Unused | Used |
|---|---|---|---|---|
| 5O6 | A118 | 5c orange | .50 | 1.00 |
| 5O7 | A119 | 10c yellow grn | .65 | 1.50 |
| 5O8 | A120 | 15c aqua | .90 | 2.00 |
| 5O9 | A121 | 20c brown car | 2.25 | 6.00 |
| 5O10 | A122 | 25c red | 2.25 | 6.00 |
| 5O11 | A123 | 30c olive | 1.50 | 5.00 |
| 5O12 | A124 | 35c red brown | 2.10 | 7.00 |
| 5O13 | A125 | 40c deep blue | 2.10 | 3.50 |
| 5O14 | A126 | 50c slate gray | 2.25 | 6.00 |
| 5O15 | A127 | 60c blue green | 2.50 | 7.00 |
| 5O16 | A128 | 70c purple | 3.00 | 7.00 |
| 5O17 | A80 | 80c blk, *pale gray* ('48) | 2.00 | 3.75 |
| 5O18 | A81 | 90c dk red, *pale rose* | 4.25 | 8.50 |
| 5O19 | A82 | 1fr dk grn, *grnsh* ('48) | 2.50 | 4.50 |
| 5O20 | A83 | 1.20fr red vio, *pale gray* | 5.50 | 12.00 |
| 5O21 | A84 | 1.50fr dk bl, *buff* | 11.00 | 12.00 |
| 5O22 | A85 | 2fr mar, *pale rose* ('48) | 3.50 | 6.50 |
| 5O23 | A69 | 3fr brn car, *cr* | 22.50 | 37.50 |
| 5O24 | A70 | 5fr sl bl, *cr* ('48) | 7.50 | 11.50 |
| 5O25 | A71 | 10fr grn, *cr* | 45.00 | 65.00 |
| | | *Nos. 5O6-5O25 (19)* | 121.25 | 208.75 |
| | | Set, never hinged | 250.00 | |

**Catalogue values for unused stamps in this section, from this point to the end of the section, are for Never Hinged items.**

WHO Emblem — O2

**1957-60 Unwmk. Engr. *Perf. 11½***

| No. | Type | Description | Unused | Used |
|---|---|---|---|---|
| 5O26 | O2 | 5c gray | .20 | .20 |
| 5O27 | O2 | 10c lt grn | .20 | .20 |
| 5O28 | O2 | 20c vermilion | 2.25 | 2.25 |
| 5O29 | O2 | 20c car rose ('60) | .25 | .25 |
| 5O30 | O2 | 30c org ver ('60) | .35 | .35 |
| 5O31 | O2 | 40c blue | 2.75 | 2.75 |
| 5O32 | O2 | 50c lt ultra ('60) | .50 | .50 |
| 5O33 | O2 | 60c red brn | .50 | .50 |
| 5O34 | O2 | 2fr rose lilac | 1.50 | 1.50 |
| | | *Nos. 5O26-5O34 (9)* | 8.50 | 8.50 |

**No. 5O32 Overprinted: "ERADICATION DU PALUDISME"**

**1962, Mar. 19**

| No. | Type | Description | Unused | Used |
|---|---|---|---|---|
| 5O35 | O2 | 50c lt ultra | .75 | .75 |

WHO drive to eradicate malaria.

World Health Organization Emblem — O3

**1975-95 Typo. *Perf. 11½***

| No. | Type | Description | Unused | Used |
|---|---|---|---|---|
| 5O36 | O3 | 30c multi | .30 | .30 |
| 5O37 | O3 | 60c lt bl & multi | .60 | .30 |
| 5O38 | O3 | 90c lilac & multi | .90 | .90 |
| 5O39 | O3 | 100c orange & multi | 1.00 | 1.00 |

**Litho.**

***Perf. 12***

| No. | Type | Description | Unused | Used |
|---|---|---|---|---|
| 5O40 | O3 | 140c lt grn, scar & grn | 1.50 | 1.50 |

***Perf. 13½x13***

| No. | Type | Description | Unused | Used |
|---|---|---|---|---|
| 5O41 | O3 | 180c multicolored | 2.10 | 2.10 |
| | | *Nos. 5O36-5O41 (6)* | 6.40 | 6.10 |

Issued: 140c, 5/27/86; 180c, 11/28/95; others, 2/13/75.

## FOR THE INTERNATIONAL ORGANIZATION FOR REFUGEES

Stamps of 1941 and 1949 Overprinted in Black

**1950 Unwmk. *Perf. 12x11½, 11½***

| No. | Type | Description | Unused | Used |
|---|---|---|---|---|
| 6O1 | A118 | 5c orange | 11.00 | 14.00 |
| 6O2 | A119 | 10c yellow green | 11.00 | 14.00 |
| 6O3 | A121 | 20c brown carmine | 11.00 | 14.00 |
| 6O4 | A122 | 25c red | 11.00 | 14.00 |
| 6O5 | A125 | 40c deep blue | 11.00 | 14.00 |
| 6O6 | A80 | 80c blk, *pale gray* | 11.00 | 14.00 |
| 6O7 | A82 | 1fr dk grn, *grnsh* | 11.00 | 14.00 |
| 6O8 | A85 | 2fr mar, *pale rose* | 11.00 | 14.00 |
| | | *Nos. 6O1-6O8 (8)* | 88.00 | 112.00 |
| | | Set, never hinged | 150.00 | |

## FOR THE UNITED NATIONS EUROPEAN OFFICE

See No. 513 for postage issue commemorating the United Nations.

Stamps of 1941-49 Overprinted in Black

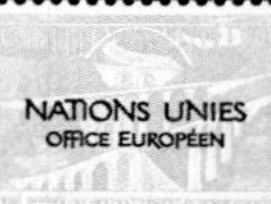

**1950 Unwmk. *Perf. 12x11½, 11½***

| No. | Type | Description | Unused | Used |
|---|---|---|---|---|
| **7O1** | A118 | 5c orange | .20 | *2.25* |
| **7O2** | A119 | 10c yellow grn | .35 | *2.25* |
| **7O3** | A120 | 15c aqua | .55 | *3.00* |
| **7O4** | A121 | 20c brown car | .85 | *4.25* |
| **7O5** | A122 | 25c red | 1.10 | *7.50* |
| **7O6** | A123 | 30c olive | 1.40 | *7.50* |
| **7O7** | A124 | 35c red brown | 1.40 | *7.50* |
| **7O8** | A125 | 40c deep blue | 2.10 | *8.75* |
| **7O9** | A126 | 50c slate gray | 2.50 | *10.50* |
| **7O10** | A127 | 60c blue green | 2.75 | *12.50* |
| **7O11** | A128 | 70c purple | 3.50 | *12.50* |
| **7O12** | A80 | 80c blk, *pale gray* | 5.50 | *10.00* |
| **7O13** | A81 | 90c dk red, *pale rose* | 5.50 | *10.00* |
| **7O14** | A82 | 1fr dk grn, *grnsh* | 5.50 | *10.00* |
| **7O15** | A83 | 1.20fr red vio, *pale gray* | 6.50 | *13.00* |
| **7O16** | A84 | 1.50fr dk bl, *buff* | 6.50 | *13.00* |
| **7O17** | A85 | 2fr mar, *pale rose* | 6.50 | *13.00* |
| **7O18** | A69 | 3fr brn car, *cr* | 65.00 | *125.00* |
| **7O19** | A70 | 5fr sl bl, *cr* | 67.50 | *125.00* |
| **7O20** | A71 | 10fr grn, *cr* | 90.00 | *160.00* |
| | | *Nos. 7O1-7O20 (20)* | 275.20 | *557.50* |
| | | Set, never hinged | 500.00 | |

UN Emblem — O1

Statue from UN Building, Geneva — O2

**1955-59 Engr. *Perf. 11½***

| No. | Type | Description | Unused | Used |
|---|---|---|---|---|
| **7O21** | O1 | 5c dk violet brn | .20 | .20 |
| **7O22** | O1 | 10c green | .20 | .20 |
| **7O23** | O2 | 20c vermilion | 2.00 | 4.00 |
| **7O24** | O2 | 20c car rose ('59) | .20 | .20 |
| **7O25** | O2 | 30c org ver ('59) | .20 | .30 |
| **7O26** | O1 | 40c ultra | 2.25 | 4.50 |
| **7O27** | O1 | 50c ultra ('59) | .20 | .40 |
| **7O28** | O2 | 60c red brown | .25 | .50 |
| **7O29** | O2 | 2fr lilac | .80 | 1.60 |
| | | *Nos. 7O21-7O29 (9)* | 6.30 | 11.90 |
| | | Set, never hinged | 12.50 | |

See Nos. 7O34-7O37. For overprints see Nos. 7O31-7O32.

United Nations Emblem — O3

**1955, Oct. 24 Photo.**

| No. | Type | Description | Unused | Used |
|---|---|---|---|---|
| **7O30** | O3 | 40c dark blue & bister | 1.60 | *3.75* |
| | | Never hinged | 3.00 | |

10th anniv. of the UN, Oct. 24, 1955.

**Catalogue values for unused stamps in this section, from this point to the end of the section, are for Never Hinged items.**

Nos. 7O24 and 7O27 Overprinted in Black or Red: "ANNÉE MONDIALE DU RÉFUGIÉ 1959 1960"

**1960**

| No. | Type | Description | Unused | Used |
|---|---|---|---|---|
| **7O31** | O2 | 20c carmine rose | .20 | .20 |
| **7O32** | O1 | 50c ultra (R) | .50 | .50 |

World Refugee Year, 7/1/59-6/30/60.

Palace of Nations, Geneva O4

**1960 Granite Paper *Perf. 11½***

| No. | Type | Description | Unused | Used |
|---|---|---|---|---|
| **7O33** | O4 | 5fr blue | 3.75 | *4.00* |

Types of 1955 Inscribed: "MUSÉE PHILATÉLIQUE" (O1) or "ONU MUSÉE PHILATÉLIQUE" (O2)

**Engraved; Inscription Typographed**

**1962, Oct. 24 Unwmk. *Perf. 11½***

| No. | Type | Description | Unused | Used |
|---|---|---|---|---|
| **7O34** | O1 | 10c green & red | .20 | .20 |
| **7O35** | O2 | 30c org ver & ultra | .30 | .30 |
| **7O36** | O1 | 50c ultra & org | .50 | .50 |
| **7O37** | O2 | 60c red brn & emer | .60 | .60 |
| | | *Nos. 7O34-7O37 (4)* | 1.60 | 1.60 |

Opening of the Philatelic Museum, UN European Office, Geneva.

O5 O6

UNCSAT Emblem

**1963, Feb. 4 Engr. *Perf. 11½***

| No. | Type | Description | Unused | Used |
|---|---|---|---|---|
| **7O38** | O5 | 50c ultra & car rose | .50 | .50 |
| **7O39** | O6 | 2fr lilac & emer | 2.00 | 2.00 |

UN Conf. on the Application of Science and Technology for the Benefit of the Less Developed Areas (UNCSAT), Geneva, Feb. 4-20.

Stamps issued, starting Oct. 4, 1969, by the UN in Swiss currency for use by UN staff members or the public are listed under "United Nations" in Vol. 1 of this catalogue and in Scott's U.S. Specialized Catalogue. These stamps are on sale in various UN post offices, but are valid only in the UN enclave in Geneva. They are not inscribed "Helvetia."

## FOR THE WORLD METEOROLOGICAL ORGANIZATION

**Catalogue values for unused stamps in this section are for Never Hinged items.**

Sun, Cloud, Rain and Snow — O1

Design: 20c, 30c, 60c, 2fr, Direction indicator and anemometer.

**1956-60 Unwmk. Engr. *Perf. 11½***

| No. | Type | Description | Unused | Used |
|---|---|---|---|---|
| **8O1** | O1 | 5c dark gray | .20 | .20 |
| **8O2** | O1 | 10c green | .20 | .20 |
| **8O3** | O1 | 20c vermilion | 2.25 | 2.25 |
| **8O4** | O1 | 20c car rose ('60) | .25 | .25 |
| **8O5** | O1 | 30c org ver ('60) | .35 | .35 |
| **8O6** | O1 | 40c blue | 2.75 | 2.75 |
| **8O7** | O1 | 50c lt ultra ('60) | .50 | .50 |
| **8O8** | O1 | 60c reddish brn | .60 | .60 |
| **8O9** | O1 | 2fr rose violet | 2.00 | 2.00 |
| | | *Nos. 8O1-8O9 (9)* | 9.10 | 9.10 |

WMO Emblem O2

**1973, Aug. 30 Engr. *Perf. 11½***

**Violet Fibers, Fluorescent Paper**

| No. | Type | Description | Unused | Used |
|---|---|---|---|---|
| **8O10** | O2 | 30c carmine | .20 | *.30* |
| **8O11** | O2 | 40c blue | .20 | *.30* |
| **8O12** | O2 | 1fr ocher | 1.00 | 1.00 |
| | | *Nos. 8O10-8O12 (3)* | 1.40 | 1.60 |

**Type O2 Inscribed: "OMI / OMM / 1873 / 1973"**

**1973, Aug. 30 Photo. *Perf. 11½***

**Violet Fibers, Fluorescent Paper**

| No. | Type | Description | Unused | Used |
|---|---|---|---|---|
| **8O13** | O2 | 80c deep violet & gold | .80 | .80 |

Intl. meteorological cooperation, cent.

## FOR THE INTERNATIONAL BUREAU OF THE UNIVERSAL POSTAL UNION

**Catalogue values for unused stamps in this section are for Never Hinged items.**

See Nos. 98-103, 204-205, 514, 589-590 for postage issues commemorating the UPU.

UPU Monument, Bern — O1

Design: 10c, 20c, 30c, 60c, Pegasus.

**1957-60 Unwmk. Engr. *Perf. 11½***

| No. | Type | Description | Unused | Used |
|---|---|---|---|---|
| **9O1** | O1 | 5c gray | .20 | .20 |
| **9O2** | O1 | 10c lt grn | .20 | .20 |
| **9O3** | O1 | 20c vermilion | 2.25 | 2.25 |
| **9O4** | O1 | 20c car rose ('60) | .20 | .20 |
| **9O5** | O1 | 30c org ver ('60) | .35 | .35 |
| **9O6** | O1 | 40c blue | 2.75 | 2.75 |
| **9O7** | O1 | 50c lt ultra ('60) | .50 | .50 |
| **9O8** | O1 | 60c red brn | .60 | .60 |
| **9O9** | O1 | 2fr rose lilac | 2.00 | 2.00 |
| | | *Nos. 9O1-9O9 (9)* | 9.05 | 9.05 |

First Class Mail — O2

Parcel Post — O3

Money Orders — O4

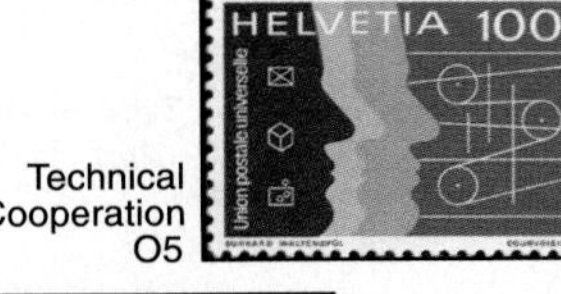


Technical Cooperation O5

Intl. Reply and Notication Service — O6

Express Mail Service — O7

Post NET System O8

**1976-95 Photo. *Perf. 11½***

**Fluorescent Paper**

| No. | Type | Description | Unused | Used |
|---|---|---|---|---|
| **9O10** | O2 | 40c multi | .40 | .40 |
| **9O11** | O3 | 80c multi | .80 | .80 |
| **9O12** | O4 | 90c multi | .90 | .90 |
| **9O13** | O5 | 100c multi | 1.00 | 1.00 |
| **9O14** | O6 | 120c multi | 1.25 | 1.25 |
| **9O15** | O7 | 140c multi | 1.50 | 1.50 |

***Perf. 13½x13***

| No. | Type | Description | Unused | Used |
|---|---|---|---|---|
| **9O16** | O8 | 180c multicolored | 2.10 | 2.10 |
| | | *Nos. 9O10-9O16 (7)* | 7.95 | 7.95 |

Issued: 120c, 8/22/83; 140c, 3/7/89; 180c, 11/28/95; others, 9/16/76.

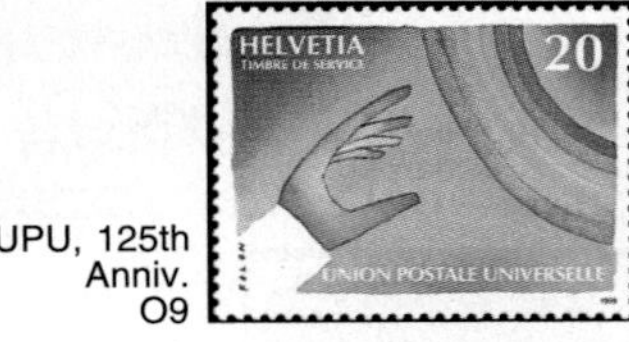


UPU, 125th Anniv. O9

**1999, Mar. 9 *Perf. 13***

| No. | Type | Description | Unused | Used |
|---|---|---|---|---|
| **9O17** | O9 | 20c shown | .30 | .20 |
| **9O18** | O9 | 70c Hand holding rainbow | .85 | .65 |

Service Quality Improvement O10

**2003, Sept. 9 Litho. *Perf. 13¾x14¼***

| No. | Type | Description | Unused | Used |
|---|---|---|---|---|
| **9O19** | O10 | 90c multi | 1.40 | .45 |

Methods of Mail Transport O11

**2005, Sept. 6 Litho. *Perf. 13½x14¼***

| No. | Type | Description | Unused | Used |
|---|---|---|---|---|
| **9O20** | O11 | 100c multi | 1.60 | 1.60 |

## FOR THE INTERNATIONAL TELECOMMUNICATION UNION

**Catalogue values for unused stamps in this section are for Never Hinged items.**

Transmitter — O1

ITU Headquarters, Geneva — O2

Designs: 20c, 30c, 60c, 2fr, Antenna.

**1958-60 Unwmk. Engr. *Perf. 11½***

| No. | Type | Description | Unused | Used |
|---|---|---|---|---|
| **10O1** | O1 | 5c dark gray | .20 | .20 |
| **10O2** | O1 | 10c green | .20 | .20 |
| **10O3** | O1 | 20c vermilion | 2.25 | 2.25 |
| **10O4** | O1 | 20c car rose ('60) | .20 | .20 |
| **10O5** | O1 | 30c org ver ('60) | .35 | .35 |
| **10O6** | O1 | 40c blue | 2.75 | 2.75 |
| **10O7** | O1 | 50c lt ultra ('60) | .50 | .50 |
| **10O8** | O1 | 60c redsh brn | .60 | .60 |
| **10O9** | O1 | 2fr rose vio | 2.00 | 2.00 |
| | | *Nos. 10O1-10O9 (9)* | 9.05 | 9.05 |

**1973, Aug. 30 Photo. *Perf. 11½***
**Violet Fibers, Fluorescent Paper**

**10O10** O2 80c blue & black .80 .80

Sound Waves, ITU Emblem O3

Airplane, Ocean Liner — O4

Radio Waves, Face on TV, Microphone O5

**Photogravure and Engraved**
**1976, Feb. 12 *Perf. 11½***
**Violet Fibers, Fluorescent Paper**

**10O11** O3 40c dp org & vio bl .40 .40
**10O12** O4 90c bl, vio bl & yel .90 .90
**10O13** O5 1fr grn & multi 1.00 1.00
*Nos. 10O11-10O13 (3)* 2.30 2.30

ITU activities: world telecommunications, mobile radio and mass media.

Fiber Optic Communication Links — O6

**1988, Sept. 13 Litho. *Perf. 12x11½***
**10O14** O6 1.40fr multi 1.40 1.40

Radio Waves, ITU Emblem — O7

**1994, May 17 Litho. *Perf. 13½***
**10O15** O7 1.80fr multicolored 2.10 2.10

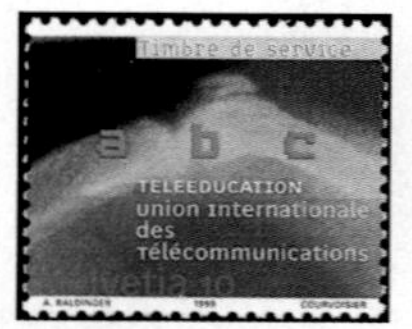


Telecommunications — O8

**1999, Mar. 9 Photo. *Perf. 11½***
**10O16** O8 10c Teleeducation .20 .20
**10O17** O8 100c Telemedicine 1.10 1.10

Stylized Face — O9

**2003, Sept. 9 Litho. *Perf. 13¾x14¼***
**10O18** O9 90c multi 1.40 .45

---

**FOR THE WORLD INTELLECTUAL PROPERTY ORGANIZATION**

**Catalogue values for unused stamps in this section are for Never Hinged items.**

WIPO Emblem O1

**1982, May 27 Photo. *Perf. 12x11½***
**11O1** O1 40c shown .40 .40
**11O2** O1 80c Headquarters, Geneva .80 .80
**11O3** O1 100c Industrial symbols 1.00 1.00
**11O4** O1 120c Educational and artistic symbols 1.25 1.25

**1985, Sept. 10 Photo. *Perf. 12x11½***
**11O5** O1 50c Mind in action .55 .55
*Nos. 11O1-11O5 (5)* 4.00 4.00

This is an expanding set. Numbers will change if necessary.

---

**FOR THE INTERNATIONAL OLYMPIC COMMITTEE**

**Catalogue values for unused stamps in this section are for Never Hinged items.**

**Olympics Type of Regular Issue**

Hand and plant with leaves of Olympic rings and: 20c, Orange frame. 70c, Green frame.

**2000, Sept. 15 Photo. *Die Cut***
**Booklet Stamps**
**Self-Adhesive**

**12O1** A496 20c multi .25 .25
**12O2** A496 70c multi .80 .80
*a.* Booklet pane, #12O1-12O2 1.10
Booklet, #12O2a 1.10

No. 12O2a is separated from booklet cover by rouletting. The booklet was sold folded.

**Olympics Type of Regular Issue, 2004**

Design: Runner, "40," Olympic rings, scene from 1896 Athens Olympics.

**2004, May 6 Litho. *Perf. 13x13¼***
**12O3** A551 100c multi 1.60 1.60

**2006 Winter Olympics Type of 2005**
**2005, Nov. 22 Litho. *Perf. 13½x13***
**12O4** A578 130c Ice hockey 2.00 2.00

Issued in sheets of 6.

---

**FRANCHISE STAMPS**

These stamps were distributed to many institutions and charitable societies for franking their correspondence.

F1

Control Figures Overprinted in Black

214

***Perf. 11½, 12***
**1911-21 Typo. Wmk. 183**
**Blue Granite Paper**

**S1** F1 2c ol grn & red .20 .25
**S2** F1 3c ol grn & red 2.50 .55
**S3** F1 5c ol grn & red 1.10 .20
**S4** F1 10c ol grn & red 1.40 .20
**S5** F1 15c ol grn & red 21.00 4.00
**S6** F1 20c ol grn & red 5.00 .60
*Nos. S1-S6 (6)* 31.20 5.80

**Without Control Figures**

*S1a* F1 2c olive green & red .55 *19.00*
*S2a* F1 3c olive green & red .55 *25.00*
*S3a* F1 5c olive green & red 4.75 *32.50*
*S4a* F1 10c olive green & red 8.25 *50.00*
*S5a* F1 15c olive green & red 5.25 *125.00*
*S6a* F1 20c olive green & red 9.50 *50.00*
*Nos. S1a-S6a (6)* 28.85 *301.50*

Control Figures Overprinted in Black

**1926**

**S7** F1 5c ol grn & red 12.50 4.50
**S8** F1 10c ol grn & red 7.75 3.25
**S9** F1 20c ol grn & red 10.00 3.75
*Nos. S7-S9 (3)* 30.25 11.50

Control Figures Overprinted in Black

**1927**
**White Granite Paper**

**S10** F1 5c green & red 5.00 .40
**S11** F1 10c green & red 2.50 .20
*b.* Grilled gum 325.00 *725.00*
**S12** F1 20c green & red 3.50 .30
*Nos. S10-S12 (3)* 11.00 .90

**Without Control Figures**

*S10a* F1 5c green & red 32.50 *140.00*
*S11a* F1 10c green & red 32.50 *140.00*
*c.* Grilled gum 150.00 *650.00*
*S12a* F1 20c green & red 32.50 *140.00*

Nurse — F2

Nun — F3

J. H. Dunant — F4

**Control Figures Overprinted in Black**

**1935 *Perf. 11½***
**S13** F2 5c turq green 2.25 *5.50*
*b.* Grilled gum 3.25 .40
**S14** F3 10c lt violet 2.25 *5.50*
*b.* Grilled gum 3.25 .20
**S15** F4 20c scarlet 2.25 *6.50*
*b.* Grilled gum 3.75 .45
*Nos. S13-S15 (3)* 6.75 *17.50*
*Nos. S13b-S15b (3)* 10.25 1.05

**Without Control Figures**

*S13a* F2 5c turquoise green 1.40 *3.75*
*c.* Grilled gum 15.00 1.40
*S14a* F3 10c light violet 1.40 *3.75*
*c.* Grilled gum 15.00 1.40
*S15a* F4 20c scarlet 1.40 *5.00*
*c.* Grilled gum 15.00 1.50
*Nos. S13a-S15a (3)* 4.20 *12.50*
*Nos. S13c-S15c (3)* 45.00 4.30

---

# SYRIA

ˈsir-ē-ə

LOCATION — Asia Minor, bordering on Turkey, Iraq, Lebanon, Israel and the Mediterranean Sea
GOVT. — Republic
AREA — 71,498 sq. mi.
POP. — 14,972,000 (1997 est.)
CAPITAL — Damascus

Syria was originally part of the Turkish province of Sourya conquered by British and Arab forces in late 1918 and later partitioned. The British assumed control of the Palestine and Transjordan regions; the French were permitted to occupy the sanjaks of Lebanon, Alaouites and Alexandretta; and the remaining territory, including the vilayets of Damascus and Aleppo, was established as an independent Arab kingdom, under which the first Syrian stamps were issued.

French forces from Beirut deposed King Faisal in July 1920, and two years of military occupation followed until Syria was mandated to France in July 1922. Syrian autonomy was substituted for the mandate in 1934, but full independence was not again achieved until 1946. In 1958, Syria and Egypt merged to form the United Arab Republic. Syria left this union in 1961, adopting the name Syrian Arab Republic. UAR issues for Syria are listed following Syria's 1919-20 Issues of the Arabian Government.

10 Milliemes = 1 Piaster
40 Paras = 1 Piaster (Arabian Govt.)
100 Centimes = 1 Piaster (1920)
100 Piasters = 1 Syrian Pound

**Catalogue values for unused stamps in this country are for Never Hinged items, beginning with Scott 314 in the regular postage section, Scott B13 in the semi-postal section, Scott C124 in the airpost section, Scott CB5 in the airpost semipostal section, Scott J40 in the postage due section, and all of the items in the UAR sections.**

**Watermarks**

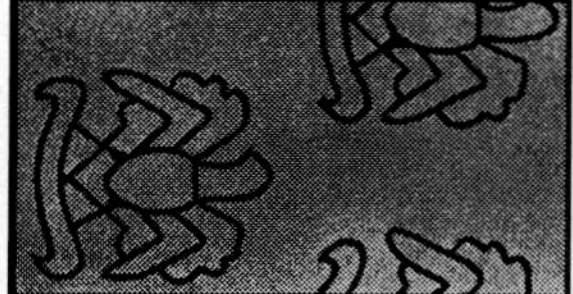

Wmk. 291 — National Emblem Multiple

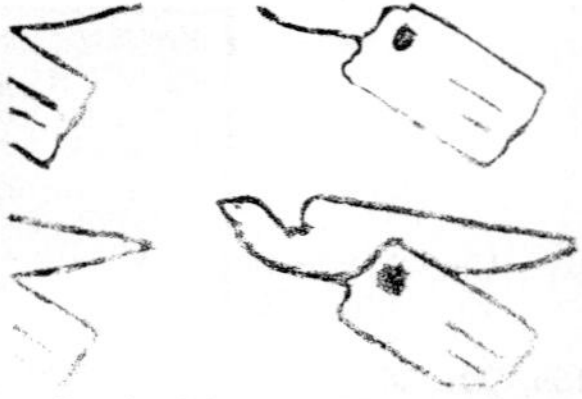

Carrier Pigeon — Wmk. 403

**Issued under French Occupation**

Stamps of France, 1900-07, Surcharged

***Perf. 14x13½***
**1919, Nov. 21 Unwmk.**

**1** A16 1m on 1c gray 200.00 200.00
**2** A16 2m on 2c vio brn 550.00 *550.00*
**3** A16 3m on 3c red org 240.00 240.00
**4** A20 4m on 15c gray grn 47.50 47.50
**5** A22 5m on 5c dp grn 25.00 22.50
**6** A22 1p on 10c red 37.50 32.50
**7** A22 2p on 25c blue 17.50 15.00
**8** A18 5p on 40c red & pale bl 25.00 22.50
**9** A18 9p on 50c bis brn & lav 55.00 50.00
**10** A18 10p on 1fr cl & ol grn 87.50 80.00
*Nos. 1-10 (10)* 1,285. 1,260.

The letters "T.E.O." are the initials of "Territoires Ennemis Occupés." There are two types of the numerals in the surcharges on Nos. 2, 3, 8 and 9.

Stamps of French Offices in Turkey, 1902-03, Surcharged

**1919**

| | | | | |
|---|---|---|---|---|
| **11** | A2 | 1m on 1c gray | 1.10 | .80 |
| **12** | A2 | 2m on 2c violet brn | 1.10 | .80 |
| **13** | A2 | 3m on 3c red orange | 2.50 | 1.40 |
| **14** | A3 | 4m on 15c pale red | 1.10 | .80 |
| **15** | A2 | 5m on 5c green | 1.10 | .80 |

Overprinted

| | | | | |
|---|---|---|---|---|
| **16** | A5 | 1p on 25c blue | 1.00 | .75 |
| **17** | A6 | 2p on 50c bis brn & lav | 1.90 | 1.25 |
| **18** | A6 | 4p on 1fr claret & ol grn | 3.25 | 2.50 |
| **19** | A6 | 8p on 2fr gray vio & yel | 10.00 | 8.00 |
| *a.* | | "T.E.O." double | 75.00 | 75.00 |
| **20** | A6 | 20p on 5fr dk bl & buff | 300.00 | 210.00 |
| | | *Nos. 11-20 (10)* | 323.05 | 227.10 |

On Nos. 17-20 "T.E.O." reads vertically up.

Nos. 1-20 were issued in Beirut and mainly used in Lebanon. Nos. 16-20 were also used in Cilicia.

Inverted surcharges exist on several values of this issue.

Stamps of France, 1900-07, Surcharged

**1920**

| | | | | |
|---|---|---|---|---|
| **21** | A16 | 1m on 1c gray | 5.00 | 4.50 |
| *a.* | | Inverted surcharge | 45.00 | 45.00 |
| *b.* | | Double surcharge | | |
| **22** | A16 | 2m on 2c vio brn | 6.00 | 4.75 |
| *a.* | | Double surcharge | 25.00 | |
| **23** | A22 | 3m on 5c green | 12.00 | 12.00 |
| *a.* | | Double surcharge | 40.00 | 40.00 |
| **24** | A18 | 20p on 5fr dk bl & buff | 450.00 | 450.00 |
| | | *Nos. 21-23 (3)* | 23.00 | 21.25 |

The letters "O.M.F." are the initials of "Occupation Militaire Francaise."

Stamps of France, 1900-07, Surcharged in Black or Red

**1920**

| | | | | |
|---|---|---|---|---|
| **25** | A16 | 1m on 1c gray | 1.10 | .95 |
| **26** | A16 | 2m on 2c violet brn | 1.25 | 1.00 |
| **27** | A22 | 3m on 5c green | 2.00 | 2.00 |
| **28** | A22 | 5m on 10c red | 2.25 | 2.25 |
| *a.* | | Inverted surcharge | | |
| **29** | A18 | 20p on 5fr dk bl & buff | 70.00 | 70.00 |
| **30** | A18 | 20p on 5fr dk bl & buff (R) | 275.00 | 250.00 |
| | | *Nos. 25-30 (6)* | 351.60 | 326.20 |

Stamps of France, 1900-21, Surcharged in Black or Red:

**1920-22**

| | | | | |
|---|---|---|---|---|
| **31** | A16 | 25c on 1c gray | 1.75 | 1.00 |
| **32** | A16 | 50c on 2c vio brn | 1.75 | 1.00 |
| **33** | A16 | 75c on 3c red org | 1.75 | 1.00 |
| **34** | A22 | 1p on 5c green (R) | 2.00 | 2.00 |
| **35** | A22 | 1p on 5c green | 1.00 | 1.00 |
| **36** | A22 | 1p on 20c red brn ('21) | .50 | .25 |
| **37** | A22 | 1.25p on 25c bl ('22) | 1.25 | .95 |
| **38** | A22 | 1.50p on 30c org ('22) | 1.40 | .80 |
| **39** | A22 | 2p on 10c red | 1.00 | 1.00 |
| **40** | A22 | 2p on 25c bl (R) | 1.00 | 1.00 |
| **41** | A18 | 2p on 40c red & pale bl ('21) | 1.40 | .75 |
| **42** | A20 | 2.50p on 50c dl bl ('22) | 1.10 | 1.10 |
| *a.* | | Final "S" of "Piastres" omitted | 10.00 | 10.00 |
| **43** | A22 | 3p on 25c bl (R) | 1.10 | 1.10 |
| **44** | A18 | 3p on 60c vio & ultra ('21) | 1.50 | 1.10 |
| **45** | A20 | 5p on 15c gray grn | 2.25 | 2.25 |
| **46** | A18 | 5p on 1fr cl & ol grn ('21) | 2.50 | 1.50 |
| **47** | A18 | 10p on 40c red & pale bl | 3.25 | 3.25 |
| **48** | A18 | 10p on 2fr org & pale bl ('21) | 5.00 | 3.00 |
| **49** | A18 | 25p on 50c bis brn & lav | 4.50 | 4.00 |
| **50** | A18 | 25p on 5fr dk bl & buff ('21) | 100.00 | 95.00 |
| **51** | A18 | 50p on 1fr cl & ol grn | 22.50 | 20.00 |
| *a.* | | "PIASRTES" | *1,650.* | *1,650.* |
| **52** | A18 | 100p on 5fr dk bl & buff (R) | 45.00 | 45.00 |
| **53** | A18 | 100p on 5fr dk bl & buff (Bk) | 240.00 | 225.00 |
| *a.* | | "PIASRTES" | *1,650.* | *1,650.* |
| | | *Nos. 31-53 (23)* | 443.50 | 413.05 |

In first printing, space between "Syrie" and numeral is 2mm, second printing, 1mm.

Surcharge is found inverted on Nos. 32, 35-38, 42, 44-45. Value, each $2-$3.

Surcharge is found double on Nos. 31, 37, 40, 42. Value, each $2.

For overprints see Nos. C1-C9.

Surcharged in Black or Red

**1920-23**

| | | | | |
|---|---|---|---|---|
| **54** | A16 | 10c on 2c violet ('23) | 1.10 | .90 |
| **55** | A22 | 10c on 5c org (R) ('23) | .80 | .65 |
| **56** | A16 | 25c on 1c dk gray | .90 | .90 |
| *a.* | | 50c on 1c dk gray (error) | 4.50 | 4.50 |
| **57** | A22 | 25c on 5c green ('21) | .90 | .60 |
| **58** | A22 | 25c on 5c orange ('22) | .80 | .80 |
| *a.* | | "CENTIEMES" omitted | 26.00 | 26.00 |
| **59** | A16 | 50c on 2c vio brn | .90 | .90 |
| **60** | A22 | 50c on 10c red ('21) | 1.00 | .55 |
| **61** | A22 | 50c on 10c green ('22) | 1.25 | 1.25 |
| **62** | A16 | 75c on 3c red orange | 2.50 | 2.00 |
| **63** | A20 | 75c on 15c sl grn ('21) | 1.10 | .90 |
| | | *Nos. 54-63 (10)* | 11.25 | 9.45 |

Surcharge is found inverted on Nos. 54-55, 58-59, 62-63; double on Nos. 60, 62. Value $1.50-$2.

Preceding Issues Overprinted

**1920**

**Black Overprint**

| | | | | |
|---|---|---|---|---|
| **64** | A16 | 25c on 1c sl gray | 11.00 | 10.00 |
| **65** | A16 | 50c on 2c vio brn | 12.00 | 11.00 |
| **66** | A22 | 1p on 5c green | 10.00 | 9.00 |
| **67** | A22 | 2p on 25c blue | 16.00 | 14.50 |
| **68** | A20 | 5p on 15c gray grn | 50.00 | 47.50 |
| **69** | A18 | 10p on 40c red & pale bl | 77.50 | 75.00 |
| **70** | A18 | 25p on 50c bis brn & lav | 200.00 | 190.00 |
| **71** | A18 | 50p on 1fr cl & ol grn | 650.00 | 625.00 |
| **72** | A18 | 100p on 5fr dk bl & buff | 2,000. | 1,900. |
| | | *Nos. 64-72 (9)* | 3,026. | 2,882. |

**Red Overprint**

| | | | | |
|---|---|---|---|---|
| **73** | A16 | 25c on 1c sl gray | 11.00 | 10.00 |
| **74** | A16 | 50c on 2c vio brn | 9.50 | 8.50 |
| **75** | A22 | 1p on 5c green | 9.50 | 8.50 |
| **76** | A22 | 2p on 25c blue | 7.50 | 6.50 |
| **77** | A20 | 5p on 15c gray grn | 50.00 | 47.50 |
| **78** | A18 | 10p on 40c red & pale bl | 77.50 | 75.00 |
| **79** | A18 | 25p on 50c bis brn & lav | 200.00 | 180.00 |
| **80** | A18 | 50p on 1fr cl & ol grn | 450.00 | 425.00 |
| **81** | A18 | 100p on 5fr dk bl & buff | 1,650. | 1,650. |
| | | *Nos. 73-81 (9)* | 2,465. | 2,411. |

Nos. 64-81 were used only in the vilayet of Aleppo where Egyptian gold currency was still in use.

A1

Black or Red Surcharge

**1921** *Perf. 11½*

| | | | | |
|---|---|---|---|---|
| **82** | A1 | 25c on ⅒p lt brn | 1.00 | .85 |
| *a.* | | "25 Centiemes" omitted | | |
| **83** | A1 | 50c on ²⁄₁₀p grn | 1.00 | .85 |
| **84** | A1 | 1p on ³⁄₁₀p yel | 1.40 | .85 |
| *a.* | | "²⁄₁₀" for "³⁄₁₀" | 12.50 | 12.50 |
| **85** | A1 | 1p on 5m rose | 1.75 | 1.10 |
| **86** | A1 | 2p on 5m rose | 2.25 | 1.25 |
| *a.* | | Tête bêche pair | 110.00 | 110.00 |
| **87** | A1 | 3p on 1p gray bl | 2.75 | 1.25 |
| **88** | A1 | 5p on 2p bl grn | 4.75 | 3.50 |
| **89** | A1 | 10p on 5p vio brn | 10.00 | 5.75 |
| **90** | A1 | 25p on 10p gray (R) | 12.00 | 8.00 |
| | | *Nos. 82-90 (9)* | 36.90 | 23.40 |

Nos. 82-90 are surcharged on stamps of the Arabian Government Nos. 85, 87-93 and have the designs and sizes of those stamps.

Surcharge is found inverted on Nos. 84-88, 90; double on No. 86.

**Kilis Issue**

A2

***Sewing Machine Perf. 9***

**1921** **Handstamped**

**Pelure Paper**

| | | | | |
|---|---|---|---|---|
| **91** | A2 | (1p) violet | *50.00* | *45.00* |

Issued at Kilis to meet a shortage of the regular issue, caused by the sudden influx of a large number of Armenian refugees from Turkey. The Kilis area was restored to Turkey in Oct. 1923.

Stamps of France, Surcharged

**1921-22** *Perf. 14x13½*

| | | | | |
|---|---|---|---|---|
| **92** | A18 | 2p on 40c red & pale bl | 1.00 | .90 |
| **93** | A18 | 2.50p on 50c bis brn & lav ('22) | 1.10 | 1.00 |
| *a.* | | 2p on 50c bister brown & lavender (error) | 60.00 | 47.50 |
| **94** | A18 | 3p on 60c vio & ultra | 1.00 | .90 |
| **95** | A18 | 5p on 1fr cl & ol grn | 6.50 | 6.00 |
| **96** | A18 | 10p on 2fr org & pale bl | 13.00 | 11.00 |
| **97** | A18 | 25p on 5fr dk bl & buff | 12.00 | 10.00 |
| | | *Nos. 92-97 (6)* | 34.60 | 29.80 |

On No. 93 the surcharge reads: "2 PIASTRES 50."

Surcharge is found inverted on Nos. 92-95; double on No. 94. Value $2-$3.

For overprints see Nos. C10-C17.

**French Mandate**

French Stamps of 1900-23 Surcharged

**1923**

| | | | | |
|---|---|---|---|---|
| **104** | A16 | 10c on 2c vio brn | .40 | .25 |
| **105** | A22 | 25c on 5c orange | .75 | .75 |
| **106** | A22 | 50c on 10c green | .90 | .85 |
| *a.* | | 25c on 10c green (error) | 170.00 | |
| **107** | A20 | 75c on 15c sl grn | 1.60 | 1.50 |
| **108** | A22 | 1p on 20c red brn | .75 | .70 |
| **109** | A22 | 1.25p on 25c blue | 1.40 | 1.25 |
| **110** | A22 | 1.50p on 30c orange | 1.10 | .90 |
| **111** | A22 | 1.50p on 30c red | 1.10 | .90 |
| **112** | A20 | 2.50p on 50c dl bl | .70 | .60 |

**On Pasteur Stamps of 1923**

| | | | | |
|---|---|---|---|---|
| **113** | A23 | 50c on 10c green | 2.00 | 1.75 |
| **114** | A23 | 1.50p on 30c red | 1.75 | 1.50 |
| **115** | A23 | 2.50p on 50c blue | 2.00 | 1.75 |

Surcharge is found inverted on #104-108, 110, 115; double on #104, 106. Value $1.50-$2.

Surcharged

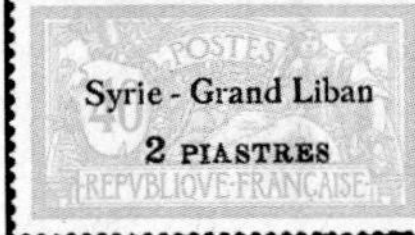


| | | | | |
|---|---|---|---|---|
| **116** | A18 | 2p on 40c red & pale bl | .75 | .70 |
| *a.* | | Inverted surcharge | 14.00 | |
| *b.* | | Double surcharge | 17.00 | |
| *c.* | | "Liabn" | *450.00* | *450.00* |
| **117** | A18 | 3p on 60c vio & ultra | 1.50 | 1.25 |
| *a.* | | "Liabn" | *450.00* | *450.00* |
| **118** | A18 | 5p on 1fr cl & ol grn | 2.00 | 1.50 |
| *a.* | | "Liabn" | *450.00* | *450.00* |
| **119** | A18 | 10p on 2fr org & pale bl | 7.50 | 7.00 |
| *a.* | | "Liabn" | *450.00* | *450.00* |
| **120** | A18 | 25p on 5fr dk bl & buff | 22.50 | 20.00 |
| *a.* | | Inverted surcharge | | |
| | | *Nos. 104-120 (17)* | 48.70 | 43.15 |

Stamps of France, 1900-21, Surcharged

**1924** *Perf. 14x13½*

| | | | | |
|---|---|---|---|---|
| **121** | A16 | 10c on 2c vio brn | .40 | .25 |
| *a.* | | Double surcharge | — | |
| **122** | A22 | 25c on 5c orange | .70 | .60 |
| *a.* | | "25" omitted | 16.50 | |
| **123** | A22 | 50c on 10c green | .70 | .60 |
| **124** | A20 | 75c on 15c sl grn | .70 | .60 |
| **125** | A22 | 1p on 20c red brn | .60 | .50 |
| *a.* | | "1 PIASTRES" | 15.00 | |
| **126** | A22 | 1.25p on 25c blue | 1.10 | .90 |
| **127** | A22 | 1.50p on 30c orange | 1.10 | .90 |
| **128** | A22 | 1.50p on 30c red | 1.00 | .85 |
| **129** | A20 | 2.50p on 50c dl bl | 1.00 | .85 |

Same on Pasteur Stamps of France, 1923

**1924**

| | | | | |
|---|---|---|---|---|
| **130** | A23 | 50c on 10c grn | .90 | .70 |
| **131** | A23 | 1.50p on 30c red | 1.40 | 1.10 |
| **132** | A23 | 2.50p on 50c blue | .75 | .70 |
| | | *Nos. 121-132 (12)* | 10.35 | 8.55 |

**Olympic Games Issue**

Stamps of France, 1924, Surcharged "SYRIE" and New Values

**1924**

| | | | | |
|---|---|---|---|---|
| **133** | A24 | 50c on 10c gray grn & yel grn | 30.00 | 27.50 |
| **134** | A25 | 1.25p on 25c rose & dk rose | 30.00 | 27.50 |
| **135** | A26 | 1.50p on 30c brn red & blk | 30.00 | 27.50 |
| **136** | A27 | 2.50p on 50c ultra & dk bl | 30.00 | 27.50 |
| | | *Nos. 133-136 (4)* | 120.00 | 110.00 |

See Nos. 166-169.

Stamps of France 1900-20 Surcharged

**137** A18 2p on 40c red & pale bl .90 .50
**138** A18 3p on 60c vio & ultra .70 .65
**139** A18 5p on 1fr claret & ol grn 3.50 3.25
**140** A18 10p on 2fr org & pale bl 3.50 3.00
**141** A18 25p on 5fr dk bl & buff 5.25 4.50
*Nos. 137-141 (5)* 13.85 11.90

For overprints see Nos. C18-C21.

Stamps of France 1900-21, Surcharged

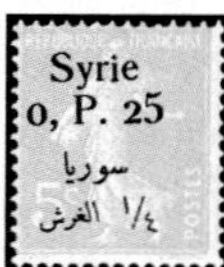


or

Syrie
2 Piastres

**1924-25**

**143** A16 10c on 2c vio brn .40 .25
*a.* Double surcharge 20.00
*b.* Inverted surcharge 22.50
**144** A22 25c on 5c orange .40 .25
*a.* Double surcharge 20.00
**145** A22 50c on 10c green .75 .50
*a.* Double surcharge 20.00
*b.* Inverted surcharge 22.50
**146** A20 75c on 15c gray grn .90 .70
*a.* Double surcharge 20.00
*b.* Inverted surcharge 22.50
**147** A22 1p on 20c red brn .60 .40
*a.* Inverted surcharge 22.50
**148** A22 1.25p on 25c blue .95 .75
*a.* Inverted surcharge 22.50
**149** A22 1.50p on 30c red .90 .70
*a.* Double surcharge 20.00
**150** A22 1.50p on 30c orange 26.00 25.00
**151** A22 2p on 35c violet ('25) 1.00 .80
**152** A18 2p on 40c red & pale bl .75 .50
*a.* Arabic "Piastre" in singular 1.75 1.75
**153** A18 2p on 45c grn & bl ('25) 5.00 4.00
**154** A18 3p on 60c vio & ultra 1.10 .75
**155** A20 3p on 60c lt vio ('25) 1.25 .75
**156** A20 4p on 85c ver .45 .25
**157** A18 5p on 1fr cl & ol grn 1.25 .75
**158** A18 10p on 2fr org & pale bl 2.00 1.50
**159** A18 25p on 5fr dk bl & buff 2.75 1.50
*Nos. 143-159 (17)* 46.45 39.35

On No. 152a, the surcharge is as illustrated. The correct fourth line ("2 Piastres" -plural), as it appears on Nos. 151, 152 and 153, has four characters, the third resembling "9."

For overprints see Nos. C22-C25.

Same Surcharge on Pasteur Stamps of France

**1924-25**

**160** A23 50c on 10c green 1.25 1.00
**161** A23 75c on 15c grn ('25) 1.25 1.00
**162** A23 1.50p on 30c red 1.25 1.00
**163** A23 2p on 45c red ('25) 1.25 1.00
**164** A23 2.50p on 50c blue 1.75 1.25
**165** A23 4p on 75c blue 1.75 1.25
*Nos. 160-165 (6)* 8.50 6.50

**Olympic Games Issue**

Stamps of France, 1924, Surcharged "Syrie" and New Values in French and Arabic

**1924**

**Same Colors as #133-136**

**166** A24 50c on 10c 29.00 29.00
**167** A25 1.25p on 25c 29.00 29.00
**168** A26 1.50p on 30c 29.00 29.00
**169** A27 2.50p on 50c 29.00 29.00
*Nos. 166-169 (4)* 116.00 116.00

**Ronsard Issue**

Same Surcharge on France No. 219

**1925**

**170** A28 4p on 75c bl, *bluish* 1.00 .75

Mosque at Hama
A3

Mosque at Damascus
A5

View of Merkab
A4

Designs: 50c, View of Alexandretta. 75c, View of Hama. 1p, Omayyad Mosque, Damascus. 1.25p, Latakia Harbor. 1.50p, View of Damascus. 2p, View of Palmyra. 2.50p, View of Kalat Yamoun. 3p, Bridge of Daphne. 5p, View of Aleppo. 10p, View of Aleppo. 25p, Columns at Palmyra.

***Perf. 12½, 13½***

**1925 Litho. Unwmk.**

**173** A3 10c dark violet .35 .20

**Photo.**

**174** A4 25c olive black .75 .55
**175** A4 50c yellow green .30 .25
**176** A4 75c brown orange .40 .20
**177** A5 1p magenta .40 .20
**178** A4 1.25p deep green 1.25 1.10
**179** A4 1.50p rose red .50 .20
**180** A4 2p dark brown 1.00 .20
**181** A4 2.50p peacock blue .90 .50
**182** A4 3p orange brn .90 .20
**183** A4 5p violet .80 .20
**184** A4 10p violet brown 1.75 .30
**185** A4 25p ultra 2.25 1.25
*Nos. 173-185 (13)* 11.55 5.35

For surcharges see Nos. 186-206, B1-B12, C26-C45, CB1-CB4.

Surcharged in Black or Red

**1926-30**

**186** A4 1p on 3pi org brn ('30) .90 .50
**187** A4 2p on 1p25 dp grn (R) ('28) .60 .40
*a.* Double surcharge 16.00 16.00
**188** A4 3.50p on 75c org brn .50 .35
*a.* Double surcharge 16.00 16.00
**189** A4 4p on 25c ol blk .85 .35
**190** A4 4p on 25c ol blk ('27) .75 .45
**191** A4 4p on 25c ol blk (R) ('28) .70 .35
**192** A4 4.50p on 75c brn org .75 .35
**193** A4 6p on 2p50 pck bl .55 .35
**194** A4 7.50p on 2p50 pck bl .60 .35
**195** A4 7.50p on 2p50 pck bl (R) ('28) 1.75 .90
*a.* Double surcharge 29.00
**196** A4 12p on 1p25 dp grn .75 .40
*a.* Surcharge on face and back 50.00 42.50
**197** A4 15p on 25p ultra 1.40 .90
**198** A4 20p on 1p25 dp grn 1.10 .70
*Nos. 186-198 (13)* 11.20 6.35

Size of numerals and arrangement of this surcharge varies on the different denominations.

No. 189 has slanting foot on "4."

No. 190, foot straight.

No. 173 Surcharged in Red

**1928**

**199** A3 05c on 10c dk vio .50 .20

Stamps of 1925 Issue Overprinted in Red or Blue

**1929** ***Perf. 13½***

**200** A4 50c yellow grn (R) 2.60 2.00
**201** A5 1p magenta (Bl) 2.60 2.00
**202** A4 1.50p rose red (Bl) 2.60 2.00
**203** A4 3p orange brn (Bl) 2.60 2.00
**204** A4 5p violet (R) 2.60 2.00
**205** A4 10p violet brn (Bl) 2.60 2.00
**206** A4 25p ultra (R) 2.60 2.00
*Nos. 200-206 (7)* 18.20 14.00

Industrial Exhibition, Damascus, Sept. 1929.

View of Hama — A6

View of Alexandretta — A9

Citadel at Aleppo
A10

Great Mosque of Damascus
A11

Ruins of Bosra
A13

Mosque at Homs
A15

View of Sednaya
A16

Citadel at Aleppo
A17

Ancient Bridge at Antioch
A18

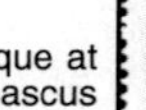

Mosque at Damascus
A22

Designs: 20c, Great Mosque, Aleppo. 25c, Minaret, Hama. 2p, View of Antioch. 4p, Square at Damascus. 15p, Mosque at Hama. 25p, Monastery of St. Simeon the Stylite (ruins). 50p, Sun Temple (ruins), Palmyra.

***Perf. 12x12½***

**1930-36 Litho. Unwmk.**

**208** A6 10c red violet .35 .20
**209** A6 10c vio brn ('33) .35 .35
**209A** A6 10c vio brn, redrawn ('35) .35 .20
**210** A6 20c dark blue .35 .20
**211** A6 20c brn org ('33) .35 .20
**212** A6 25c gray green .35 .20
**213** A6 25c dk bl gray ('33) .55 .45

**Photo.**

***Perf. 13***

**214** A9 50c violet .35 .20
**215** A15 75c org red ('32) .35 .20
**216** A10 1p green .40 .20
**217** A10 1p bis brn ('36) .90 .40
**218** A11 1.50p bister brown 4.25 3.00
**219** A11 1.50p dp grn ('33) .60 .50
**220** A9 2p dark violet .40 .25
**221** A13 3p yellow green 1.10 .70
**222** A10 4p yellow orange .40 .25
**223** A15 4.50p rose carmine 1.00 .55
**224** A16 6p grnsh black 1.40 .50
**225** A17 7.50p dull blue 1.40 .70
**226** A18 10p dark brown 1.10 .50
**227** A10 15p deep green 1.90 1.00
**228** A18 25p violet brown 1.75 1.10
**229** A15 50p olive brown 6.00 4.50
**230** A22 100p red orange 11.50 9.75
*Nos. 208-230 (24)* 37.45 26.10

On No. 209A Arabic inscriptions, upper right, are entirely redrawn with lighter lines. Hyphen added in "Helio-Vaugirard" imprint. Lines in buildings and background more distinct.

On No. 215 the letters of "VAUGIRARD" in the imprint are reversed as in a mirror.

For overprints and surcharges see Nos. 253-268, 346, M1-M2.

**Autonomous Republic**

Parliament Building
A23

abu-al-Ala al-Maarri — A24

President Ali Bek el Abed — A25

Saladin — A26

**1934, Aug. 2 Engr.** ***Perf. 12½***

**232** A23 10c olive green .90 *1.00*
**233** A23 20c black .90 *1.00*
**234** A23 25c red orange .95 *1.00*
**235** A23 50c ultra 1.00 *1.00*
**236** A23 75c plum 1.00 *1.00*
**237** A24 1p vermilion 3.00 3.00
**238** A24 1.50p green 3.50 3.50
**239** A24 2p red brown 3.50 3.50
**240** A24 3p Prus blue 3.50 3.50
**241** A24 4p brt violet 3.75 3.50
**242** A24 4.50p carmine 4.00 3.75
**243** A24 5p dark blue 4.00 3.75
**244** A24 6p dark brown 4.00 3.75

**245** A24 7.50p dark ultra 4.25 3.75
**246** A25 10p dark brown 6.25 6.00
**247** A25 15p dull blue 8.75 8.50
**248** A25 25p rose red 13.50 13.00
**249** A26 50p dark brown 20.00 20.00
**250** A26 100p lake 32.50 32.50
*Nos. 232-250 (19)* 119.25 117.00

Proclamation of the Republic. See Nos. C57-C66. For surcharge see No. M3.

Stamps of 1930-36 Overprinted in Red or Black

**1936, Apr. 15**

**253** A9 50c violet (R) 1.75 1.50
**254** A10 1p bister brn (Bk) 1.75 1.50
**255** A9 2p dk violet (R) 1.75 1.50
**256** A13 3p yellow grn (Bk) 2.00 1.50
**257** A10 4p yellow org (Bk) 2.00 1.50
**258** A15 4.50p rose car (Bk) 2.00 1.50
**259** A16 6p grnsh blk (R) 2.40 2.00
**260** A17 7.50p dull blue (R) 3.00 2.75
**261** A18 10p dk brown (Bk) 3.75 3.75
*Nos. 253-261 (9)* 20.40 17.50

Industrial Exhibition, Damascus, May 1936. See Nos. C67-C71.

Stamps of 1930 Surcharged in Black

**1937-38** ***Perf. 13½x13***

**262** A10 2.50p on 4p yel org ('38) .55 .40
**263** A22 10p on 100p red orange 1.00 .90

Stamps of 1930-33 Surcharged in Red or Black

**1938** ***Perf. 13½***

**264** A15 25c on 75c org red (Bk) .30 .20
**265** A11 50c on 1.50p dp grn (R) .40 .30
**266** A17 2p on 7.50p dl bl (R) .70 .60
**267** A17 5p on 7.50p dl bl (R) 1.10 .90
**268** A15 10p on 50p ol brn (Bk) 1.10 .95
*Nos. 264-268 (5)* 3.60 2.95

President Hashem Bek el Atassi — A27

**1938-43** **Photo.** **Unwmk.**

**268A** A27 10p dp blue ('43) .85 .85
**269** A27 12.50p on 10p dp bl (R) .90 .90
**270** A27 20p dark brown .85 .85
*Nos. 268A-270 (3)* 2.60 2.60

The 10pi and 20pi exist imperf.

Columns at Palmyra A28

**1940** **Litho.** ***Perf. 11½***

**271** A28 5p pale rose 1.00 .65

Exists imperf.

Museum at Damascus — A29

Hotel at Bloudan A30

Kasr-el-Heir A31

**1940** **Typo.** ***Perf. 13x14***

**272** A29 10c bright rose .25 .20
**273** A29 20c light blue .25 .20
**274** A29 25c fawn .30 .20
**275** A29 50c ultra .30 .20

**Engr.**

***Perf. 13***

**276** A30 1p peacock blue .35 .20
**277** A30 1.50p chocolate .70 .70
**278** A30 2.50p dark green .35 .30
**279** A31 5p violet .40 .40
**280** A31 7.50p vermilion .90 .40
**281** A31 50p sepia 1.50 1.25
*Nos. 272-281 (10)* 5.30 4.05

For overprints see Nos. 298-299.

President Taj Eddin Hassani A32

**1942, Apr. 6** **Litho.** ***Perf. 11½***

**282** A32 50c sage green 3.00 2.50
**283** A32 1.50p dull gray brn 3.25 2.50
**284** A32 6p fawn 3.50 2.50
**285** A32 15p light blue 3.75 2.50
*Nos. 282-285,C96-C97 (6)* 19.75 16.25

Proclamation of independence by the Allies, Sept. 27, 1941.

President Taj Eddin Hassani — A33

President Hassani and Map of Syria — A34

**1942** **Photo.** **Unwmk.**

**286** A33 6p rose lake & salmon rose 2.00 1.25
**287** A33 15p dull blue & blue 2.00 1.25
*Nos. 286-287,C98 (3)* 8.00 6.50

Nos. 286-287 exist imperf.

**1943** **Litho.**

**288** A34 1p light green 2.00 1.25
**289** A34 4p buff 2.00 1.25
**290** A34 8p pale violet 2.00 1.25
**291** A34 10p salmon 2.00 1.25
**292** A34 20p dull chalky blue 2.00 1.25
*Nos. 288-292,C99-C102 (9)* 19.00 15.25

Proclamation of a United Syria. Exist imperf.

Stamps of 1943 Overprinted with Border in Black

**1943**

**293** A34 1p light green 2.00 1.25
**294** A34 4p buff 2.00 1.25
**295** A34 8p pale violet 2.00 1.25
**296** A34 10p salmon 2.00 1.25
**297** A34 20p dl chalky bl 2.00 1.25
*Nos. 293-297,C103-C106 (9)* 19.00 15.25

Mourning for President Hassani. Exist imperf.

Nos. 278 and 280 Overprinted in Carmine or Black

**1944** **Unwmk.** ***Perf. 13***

**298** A30 2.50p dk green (C) 2.50 2.50
**299** A31 7.50p vermilion (Bk) 2.75 2.75
*Nos. 298-299,C114-C116 (5)* 33.75 33.75

1000th anniv. of the Arab poet and philosopher, abu-al-Ala al-Maarri.

President Shukri el Kouatly — A35

**1945, Mar. 15** **Litho.** ***Perf. 11½***

**300** A35 4p pale lilac .40 .35
**301** A35 6p dull blue .55 .40
**302** A35 10p salmon .55 .40
**303** A35 15p dark brown .90 .50
**304** A35 20p slate green .90 .50
**305** A35 40p orange 1.25 1.00
*Nos. 300-305,C117-C123 (13)* 20.65 10.25

Resumption of constitutional government.

A36

A37

A38

A39

Fiscal Stamps Overprinted or Surcharged in Black

**1945** **Typo.** ***Perf. 11, 11½x11***

**306** A36 12½p on 15p yel grn 2.00 1.25
**307** A37 25p buff 4.00 1.75
**307A** A38 25p on 25s lt vio brn 2.50 1.40
**308** A39 50p on 75p brn org 5.00 2.50
**309** A39 75p brown org 6.50 3.25
**310** A37 100p yellow grn 9.50 4.00
*Nos. 306-310 (6)* 29.50 14.15

Type of 1945 and Nos. 308 and 310 Overprinted in Black

a

b

**1945** **Unwmk.** ***Perf. 11***

**311** A37(b) 50p magenta 2.75 1.50
**312** A39(a) 50p on 75p brn org 2.00 .90
**313** A37(b) 100p yellow green 3.50 1.50
*Nos. 311-313 (3)* 8.25 3.90

**Catalogue values for unused stamps in this section, from this point to the end of the section, are for Never Hinged items.**

**Independent Republic**

A40

Fiscal Stamp Overprinted in Carmine

**1946**

**314** A40 200p light blue 20.00 7.50

Sun and Ears of Wheat — A41

President Shukri el Kouatly — A42

**1946** **Litho.** ***Perf. 13x13½***

**315** A41 50c brown orange .30 .20
**316** A41 1p violet .55 .20
**317** A41 2.50p blue gray .65 .30
**318** A41 5p lt blue green .95 .20

**Photo.**

***Perf. 13½x13, 13x13½***

**319** A42 7.50p dark brown .30 .20
**320** A42 10p Prussian green .40 .20
**321** A42 12.50p deep violet 1.10 .20
*Nos. 315-321 (7)* 4.25 1.50

For overprints see Nos. 328-329, 335-336.

Arab Horse A44

**1946-47** **Litho.**

**325** A44 50p olive brown 5.25 .90
**326** A44 100p dk blue grn ('47) 11.00 2.00
**327** A44 200p rose violet ('47) 60.00 5.50
*Nos. 325-327 (3)* 76.25 8.40

For overprints and surcharges see Nos. 330, 337, 356-357.

Nos. 320, 321 and 325 Overprinted in Black or Green

**1946, Apr. 17**

**328** A42 10p Prus green .60 .45
**329** A42 12.50p deep violet .80 .65
**330** A44 50p olive brown (G) 2.10 1.60
*Nos. 328-330,C135 (4)* 5.50 3.70

Evacuation of British and French troops from Syria. For surcharge see No. 347.

President Shukri el Kouatly — A45

**1946 Unwmk. Litho. *Perf. 13½x13***

| | | | | |
|---|---|---|---|---|
| **331** | A45 | 15p red | .50 | .20 |
| **332** | A45 | 20p violet | .70 | .25 |
| **333** | A45 | 25p ultra | 1.10 | .30 |
| | | *Nos. 331-333 (3)* | 2.30 | .75 |

No. 333 Overprinted in Magenta

**1946, Aug. 28**

| | | | | |
|---|---|---|---|---|
| **334** | A45 | 25p ultra | 1.60 | 1.10 |
| | | *Nos. 334,C136-C138 (4)* | 11.10 | 6.60 |

8th Arab Medical Cong., Aleppo, 8/28-9/4.

Nos. 328 to 330 With Additional Overprint in Black

e

f

***Perf. 13½x13, 13x13½***

**1947, June 10**

| | | | | |
|---|---|---|---|---|
| **335** | A42(e) | 10p Prus green | .70 | .20 |
| **336** | A42(e) | 12.50p deep violet | .80 | .25 |
| **337** | A44(f) | 50p olive brown | 2.10 | .75 |
| | | *Nos. 335-337,C139 (4)* | 5.60 | 2.45 |

Evacuation of British and French troops, 1st anniv.

Hercules and the Lion — A46

Mosaics from Omayyad Mosque, Damascus A47

**1947, Nov. 15 Litho. *Perf. 11½***

| | | | | |
|---|---|---|---|---|
| **338** | A46 | 12.50p slate green | 1.00 | .40 |
| **339** | A47 | 25p gray blue | 1.60 | .85 |
| | | *Nos. 338-339,C140-C141 (4)* | 8.10 | 3.50 |

1st Arab Archaeological Cong., Damascus, Nov.

See No. C141a.

Courtyard of Azem Palace A48

Telephone Building A49

**1947, Nov. 15**

| | | | | |
|---|---|---|---|---|
| **340** | A48 | 12.50p deep claret | 1.00 | .50 |
| **341** | A49 | 25p brt blue | 1.50 | .70 |
| | | *Nos. 340-341,C142-C143 (4)* | 7.00 | 3.45 |

3rd Congress of Arab Engineers, Damascus, Nov.

See No. C143a.

House of Parliament A50

Pres. Shukri el Kouatly — A51

**1948, June 23 Unwmk. *Perf. 10½***

| | | | | |
|---|---|---|---|---|
| **342** | A50 | 12.50p black & org | .50 | .20 |
| **343** | A51 | 25p deep rose | 1.00 | .45 |
| | | *Nos. 342-343,C144-C145 (4)* | 4.65 | 1.90 |

Reelection of Pres. Shukri el Kouatly. See No. C145a.

National Emblem — A52

Syrian Flag and Soldier — A53

**1948, June 23 Litho.**

| | | | | |
|---|---|---|---|---|
| **344** | A52 | 12.50p gray & choc | .75 | .25 |
| **345** | A53 | 25p multicolored | 1.00 | .45 |
| | | *Nos. 344-345,C146-C147 (4)* | 4.50 | 1.75 |

Inauguration of compulsory military training. See No. C147a.

Nos. 215 and 327 Surcharged with New Value and Bars in Black

**1948 *Perf. 13, 13x13½***

| | | | | |
|---|---|---|---|---|
| **346** | A15 | 50c on 75c org red | .40 | .20 |
| **347** | A44 | 25p on 200p rose vio | 2.50 | .30 |

Col. Husni Zayim — A54

Palmyra — A56

Ain el Arous A55

**1949, June 20 Litho. *Perf. 11½***

| | | | | |
|---|---|---|---|---|
| **348** | A54 | 25p blue | 1.00 | .40 |

Revolution of Mar. 30, 1949. See No. C153.

A souvenir sheet comprises Nos. 348 and C153, imperf. Value $80.

**1949, June 20**

| | | | | |
|---|---|---|---|---|
| **349** | A55 | 12.50p violet | 2.00 | 1.50 |
| **350** | A56 | 25p blue | 3.50 | 2.75 |
| | | *Nos. 349-350,C154-C155 (4)* | 32.00 | 22.75 |

UPU, 75th anniv. See note after #C155.

Pres. Husni Zayim and Map — A57

**Wmk. 291**

**1949, Aug. 6 Litho. *Perf. 11½***

| | | | | |
|---|---|---|---|---|
| **351** | A57 | 25p blue & brown | 3.00 | 1.25 |

Election of President Husni Zayim. See Nos. C156, C156a.

Tel-Chehab Waterfall — A58

Damascus Scene A59

**1949**

| | | | | |
|---|---|---|---|---|
| **352** | A58 | 5p gray | .40 | .20 |
| **353** | A58 | 7.50p olive gray | .55 | .20 |
| **354** | A59 | 12.50p violet brown | .70 | .20 |
| **355** | A59 | 25p blue | 1.25 | .40 |
| | | *Nos. 352-355 (4)* | 2.90 | 1.00 |

See No. 376.

Nos. 327 and 326 Surcharged with New Value and Bars in Black

**1950 Unwmk. *Perf. 13x13½***

| | | | | |
|---|---|---|---|---|
| **356** | A44 | 2.50p on 200p rose vio | .40 | .20 |
| **357** | A44 | 10p on 100p dk bl grn | .50 | .20 |

National Emblem — A60

Road to Damascus A61

Postal Administration Building, Damascus — A62

**1950-51 Litho. *Perf. 11½***

| | | | | |
|---|---|---|---|---|
| **358** | A60 | 50c orange brn | .30 | .20 |
| **359** | A60 | 2.50p pink | .40 | .20 |
| **360** | A61 | 10p purple ('51) | .50 | .20 |
| **361** | A61 | 12.50p sage grn ('51) | .75 | .40 |
| **362** | A62 | 25p blue ('51) | 1.25 | .20 |
| **363** | A62 | 50p black ('51) | 4.00 | .60 |
| | | *Nos. 358-363 (6)* | 7.20 | 1.80 |

Nos. 358 to 363 exist imperforate.

Parliament Building, Damascus A63

**1951, Apr. 14**

| | | | | |
|---|---|---|---|---|
| **364** | A63 | 12.50p gray blk | .40 | .20 |
| **365** | A63 | 25p blue | .75 | .35 |
| | | *Nos. 364-365,C162-C163 (4)* | 2.80 | 1.75 |

New constitution adopted Sept. 5, 1950.

Nos. 364-365 exist imperforate.

Water Wheel, Hama A64

Palace of Justice, Damascus A65

***Perf. 11½***

**1952, Apr. 22 Litho. Unwmk.**

| | | | | |
|---|---|---|---|---|
| **366** | A64 | 50c dark brown | .30 | .20 |
| **367** | A64 | 2.50p dark blue | .35 | .20 |
| **368** | A64 | 5p blue green | .40 | .20 |
| **369** | A64 | 10p red | .45 | .20 |
| **370** | A65 | 12.50p gray black | .75 | .20 |
| **371** | A65 | 15p lilac rose | 4.00 | .25 |
| **372** | A65 | 25p deep blue | 2.00 | .35 |
| **373** | A65 | 100p olive brown | 7.50 | 2.00 |
| | | *Nos. 366-373 (8)* | 15.75 | 3.60 |

Nos. 366-373 exist imperforate.

Type of 1949 and

Crusaders' Fort — A66

Crusaders' Fort — A67

**1953 Photo.**

| | | | | |
|---|---|---|---|---|
| **374** | A67 | 50c rose red | .40 | .20 |
| **375** | A66 | 2.50p dark brown | .40 | .20 |
| **376** | A58 | 7.50p green | .50 | .20 |
| **377** | A67 | 12.50p deep blue | 1.75 | .20 |
| | | *Nos. 374-377 (4)* | 3.05 | .80 |

Farm Workers — A68

Family Group A69

Designs: 1pi, 5pi, Farm workers. 10pi, 12½p, Family group. 20pi, 25pi, 50pi, Factory and construction workers.

**1954** *Perf. 11½*

| | | | | |
|---|---|---|---|---|
| **378** | A68 | 1p olive | .25 | .20 |
| **379** | A68 | 2½p brown red | .30 | .20 |
| **380** | A68 | 5p deep blue | .40 | .20 |
| **381** | A69 | 7½p brown red | .50 | .20 |
| **382** | A69 | 10p black | .60 | .20 |
| **383** | A69 | 12½p violet | .70 | .20 |
| **384** | A69 | 20p deep plum | .85 | .20 |
| **385** | A69 | 25p violet | 1.25 | .35 |
| **386** | A69 | 50p dark green | 3.00 | .75 |
| | | *Nos. 378-386 (9)* | 7.85 | 2.50 |

For overprints see #387-388, UAR 20, 34.

Nos. 382 and 385 Overprinted in Carmine

**1954, Oct. 9**

| | | | | |
|---|---|---|---|---|
| **387** | A69 | 10p black | 1.00 | .35 |
| **388** | A69 | 25p violet | 1.25 | .45 |
| | | *Nos. 387-388,C185-C186 (4)* | 5.35 | 3.40 |

Cotton Festival, Aleppo, October 1954.

Globe — A69a

Mother and Child — A70

**Arab Postal Union Issue**

**1955** **Photo.** *Perf. 13½x13*

| | | | | |
|---|---|---|---|---|
| **389** | A69a | 12½p green | .50 | .20 |
| **390** | A69a | 25p violet | .95 | .35 |
| | | *Nos. 389-390,C191 (3)* | 1.85 | .80 |

Founding of the APU, 7/1/54. Exist imperf. For overprints see #396-399, C203, C207.

**1955, May 13** **Litho.** *Perf. 11½*

| | | | | |
|---|---|---|---|---|
| **391** | A70 | 25p red | .60 | .25 |
| | | *Nos. 391,C194-C195 (3)* | 3.10 | 1.80 |

Mother's Day.

United Nations Emblem A71

**1955** **Photo.**

| | | | | |
|---|---|---|---|---|
| **392** | A71 | 7½p crimson | .50 | .25 |
| **393** | A71 | 12½p Prus green | 1.00 | .50 |
| | | *Nos. 392-393,C200-C201 (4)* | 3.75 | 1.75 |

UN, 10th anniv., Oct. 24. For overprints see Nos. 401-402.

Aqueduct at Aleppo A72

**1955** **Litho.** **Unwmk.**

| | | | | |
|---|---|---|---|---|
| **394** | A72 | 7.50p lilac | .55 | .25 |
| **395** | A72 | 12.50p carmine | 1.00 | .35 |
| | | *Nos. 394-395,C202 (3)* | 3.55 | 1.70 |

New aqueduct bringing water from the Euphrates to Northern Syria. Exist imperf.

Nos. 389-390 Overprinted in Ultramarine or Green

**1955** **Photo.** *Perf. 13½x13*

| | | | | |
|---|---|---|---|---|
| **396** | A69a | 12½p green | .40 | .20 |
| **397** | A69a | 25p vio (G) | 1.25 | .40 |
| | | *Nos. 396-397,C203 (3)* | 2.15 | .80 |

APU Congress held at Cairo, Mar. 15.

Nos. 389-390 Overprinted in Black

**1956**

| | | | | |
|---|---|---|---|---|
| **398** | A69a | 12½p green | .50 | .25 |
| **399** | A69a | 25p violet | 1.25 | .55 |
| | | *Nos. 398-399,C207 (3)* | 2.25 | 1.00 |

Visit of King Hussein of Jordan to Damascus, Apr. 1956.

Cotton — A73

**1956** **Unwmk.** **Litho.** *Perf. 11½*

| | | | | |
|---|---|---|---|---|
| **400** | A73 | 2½p bluish green | .50 | .25 |

Issued to publicize a Cotton Festival.

Nos. 392-393 Overprinted in Black

**1956** **Photo.** *Perf. 11½*

| | | | | |
|---|---|---|---|---|
| **401** | A71 | 7½p crimson | .50 | .20 |
| **402** | A71 | 12½p Prussian green | .75 | .35 |
| | | *Nos. 401-402,C221-C222 (4)* | 4.00 | 2.40 |

UN, 11th anniv.

People's Army A74

**1957** **Litho.** *Perf. 11½*

| | | | | |
|---|---|---|---|---|
| **403** | A74 | 5p lilac rose | .30 | .20 |
| **404** | A74 | 20p gray green | .50 | .25 |

Formation of the Popular Resistance Movement.
For overprints see Nos. 405-406, 413-414.

Nos. 403-404 Overprinted in Black or Red

**1957**

| | | | | |
|---|---|---|---|---|
| **405** | A74 | 5p lilac rose | .30 | .20 |
| **406** | A74 | 20p gray green (R) | .50 | .30 |

Evacuation of Port Said by British and French troops, Dec. 22, 1956.

Azem Palace, Damascus A75

**1957** **Litho.** *Perf. 11½*

| | | | | |
|---|---|---|---|---|
| **407** | A75 | 12½p lilac | .30 | .20 |
| **408** | A75 | 15p gray | .50 | .20 |

For overprint see UAR No. 33.

Map of Near East, Scales and Damascus Skyline — A76

Cotton, Bale and Ship — A77

**1957** **Wmk. 291** *Perf. 11½*

| | | | | |
|---|---|---|---|---|
| **409** | A76 | 12½p bright green | .40 | .20 |
| | | *Nos. 409,C240-C241 (3)* | 1.70 | 1.00 |

3rd Congress of the Union of Arab Lawyers, Damascus, Sept. 21-25.

**1957**

| | | | | |
|---|---|---|---|---|
| **410** | A77 | 12½p lt bl grn & blk | .50 | .20 |
| | | *Nos. 410,C242-C243 (3)* | 2.50 | 1.10 |

Cotton Festival, Aleppo, Oct. 3-5.

Children — A78

**1957, Oct. 7**

| | | | | |
|---|---|---|---|---|
| **411** | A78 | 12½p olive | .75 | .20 |
| | | *Nos. 411,C244-C245 (3)* | 3.50 | 1.20 |

Intl. Children's Day, Oct. 7.
For overprint see UAR Nos. 13A, C10-C11.

Mailing and Receiving Letter A79

**1957** **Unwmk.**

| | | | | |
|---|---|---|---|---|
| **412** | A79 | 5p magenta | .50 | .20 |

Intl. Letter Writing Week, Oct. 6-12. See No. C246.

Nos. 403-404 Overprinted in Black or Red

**1957** *Perf. 11½*

| | | | | |
|---|---|---|---|---|
| **413** | A74 | 5p lilac rose | .40 | .20 |
| **414** | A74 | 20p gray green (R) | .50 | .20 |

Digging of fortifications along the Syrian-Israeli frontier.

Scales, Torch and Map A80

**1957, Nov. 8** **Wmk. 291**

| | | | | |
|---|---|---|---|---|
| **415** | A80 | 20p olive gray | .55 | .20 |
| | | *Nos. 415,C247-C248 (3)* | 1.80 | 1.05 |

Congress of Afro-Asian Jurists, Damascus.

Glider A81

**1957, Nov. 8** **Litho.** *Perf. 11½*

| | | | | |
|---|---|---|---|---|
| **416** | A81 | 25p red brown | 1.10 | .30 |
| **417** | A81 | 35p green | 1.50 | .40 |
| **418** | A81 | 40p ultra | 3.00 | .70 |
| | | *Nos. 416-418 (3)* | 5.60 | 1.40 |

Issued to commemorate a glider festival.

Khaled ibn el Walid Mosque, Homs — A82

**1957** **Unwmk.** *Perf. 12*

| | | | | |
|---|---|---|---|---|
| **419** | A82 | 2½p dull brown | .40 | .20 |

Scroll, Communications Building and Telephone — A83

**1958** **Wmk. 291** *Perf. 11½*

| | | | | |
|---|---|---|---|---|
| **420** | A83 | 25p ultra | .30 | .20 |
| | | *Nos. 420,C249-C250 (3)* | 1.05 | .65 |

**Issues of 1958-61 released by the United Arab Republic are listed following the listings of Syria, Issues of the Arabian Government.**

**Syrian Arab Republic**

Hall of Parliament, Damascus A83a

**1961** **Unwmk.** **Litho.** *Perf. 12*

| | | | | |
|---|---|---|---|---|
| **420A** | A83a | 15p magenta | .40 | .25 |
| **420B** | A83a | 35p olive gray | .75 | .25 |

Establishment of Syrian Arab Republic.

Water Wheel, Hama — A84

Roman Arch of Triumph, Latakia — A85

Qalb Lozah Church, Aleppo A86

7½p, 10p, Khaled ibn el Walid Mosque, Homs.

*Perf. 11½x11*

**1961-62 Unwmk. Litho.**

**421** A84 2½p rose red .30 .20
**422** A84 5p blue .30 .20
**423** A84 7½p blue grn ('62) .30 .20
**424** A84 10p orange ('62) .35 .20

*Perf. 12x11½*

**425** A85 12½p gray brn .60 .20
**426** A86 17½p olive gray ('62) .50 .20
**427** A85 25p dull red brown .70 .20
**428** A86 35p dull green ('62) .65 .20
*Nos. 421-428 (8)* 3.70 1.60

Types of 1961, Regular and Air Post

Designs: 2½p, 5p, 7½p, 10p, Arch, Jupiter Temple. 12½p, 15p, 17½p, 22½p, "The Beauty of Palmyra."

**1962** *Perf. 11½x11*

**429** A84 2½p gray blue .30 .20
**430** A84 5p brown orange .30 .20
**431** A84 7½p olive bister .30 .20
**432** A84 10p claret .30 .20

*Perf. 12x11½*

**Size: 26x38mm**

**433** AP68 12½p gray olive .35 .20
**434** AP68 15p ultra .50 .20
**435** AP68 17½p brown .50 .20
**436** AP68 22½p grnsh blue .70 .20
*Nos. 429-436 (8)* 3.25 1.60

Martyrs' Memorial — A87

Pres. Nazem el-Kodsi — A88

**1962, June 11 Litho.**

**440** A87 12½p tan & sepia .30 .20
**441** A87 35p green & bl grn .35 .20

1925 Revolution.

**1962, Dec. 14** *Perf. 12x11½*

**442** A88 12½p sepia & lt bl .30 .20

1st anniv. of the election of Pres. Nazem el-Kodsi. See No. C278.

Queen Zenobia — A89

Central Bank of Syria A90

Designs: 2½p, 5p, "The Beauty of Palmyra." 17½p, Hejaz Railway Station, Damascus. 22½p, Mouassat Hospital, Damascus. 35p, P.T.T. Jalaa Avenue Office, Damascus.

**1963 Unwmk.** *Perf. 11½x11*

**443** A89 2½p dk bl gray .30 .20
**444** A89 5p rose lilac .30 .20
**445** A89 7½p dull blue .35 .20
**446** A89 10p olive gray .70 .20
**447** A89 12½p ultra 1.00 .20
**448** A89 15p violet brn 1.50 .20

*Perf. 11½x12*

**449** A90 17½p dull violet .60 .20
**450** A90 22½p brt violet .30 .20
**451** A90 25p bister brown .30 .20
**452** A90 35p bright pink .35 .20
*Nos. 443-452 (10)* 5.70 2.00

Wheat Emblem and Globe — A91

Boy Playing Ball and UN Emblem — A92

**1963, Mar. 21 Litho.** *Perf. 12x11½*

**453** A91 12½p ultra & blk .30 .20

FAO "Freedom from Hunger" Campaign. See No. C291 and souvenir sheet No. C291a.

Cotton Festival Type of Air Post Issue, 1962, Inscribed "1963"

**1963, Sept. 26** *Perf. 12x11½*

**455** AP75 17½p multi .30 .20
**456** AP75 22½p multi .35 .20

The 1963 Cotton Festival, Aleppo.

**1963, Oct. 24** *Perf. 12x11½*

**457** A92 12½p emer & sl grn .30 .20
**458** A92 22½p rose red & dk grn .30 .20

Issued for International Children's Day.

Ugharit Princess — A93

**1964 Litho.** *Perf. 11½x11*

**459** A93 2½p gray .30 .20
**460** A93 5p brown .30 .20
**461** A93 7½p rose claret .30 .20
**462** A93 10p emerald .30 .20
**463** A93 12½p light violet .30 .20
**464** A93 17½p ultra .30 .20
**465** A93 20p rose carmine .45 .20
**466** A93 25p orange .75 .20
*Nos. 459-466 (8)* 3.00 1.60

Map of North Africa and Middle East, Flag of Syria, and Crowd A94

**1965, Mar. 8 Litho.** *Perf. 11½x12*

**467** A94 12½p multicolored .30 .20
**468** A94 17½p multicolored .30 .20
**469** A94 20p multicolored .30 .20
*Nos. 467-469 (3)* .90 .60

Mar. 8 Revolution, 2nd anniv.

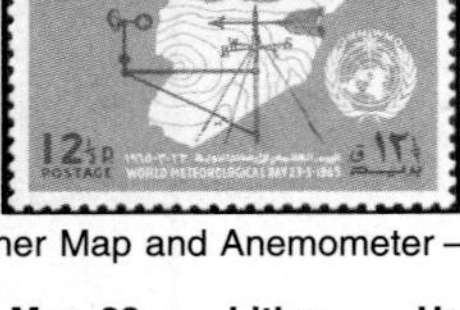


Weather Map and Anemometer — A95

**1965, Mar. 23 Litho. Unwmk.**

**470** A95 12½p dl lilac & blk .30 .20
**471** A95 27½p lt blue & blk .30 .20

Fifth World Meteorological Day.

"Evacuation of Apr. 17, 1946" — A96

Peasants' Union Emblem — A97

**1965, Apr. 17 Litho.** *Perf. 12x11½*

**472** A96 12½p bl & brt yel grn .30 .20
**473** A96 27½p rose red & lt lil .30 .20

19th anniv. of the evacuation of British and French troops from Syria.

**1965, Aug. Unwmk.** *Perf. 11½x11*

**474** A97 2½p blue green .30 .20
**475** A97 12½p purple .30 .20
**476** A97 15p maroon .30 .20
*Nos. 474-476 (3)* .90 .60

Issued to publicize the Peasants' Union.

Torch, Map of Arab Countries and Farmer, Soldier, Woman, Intellectual and Worker — A98

Workers, Factory and Emblem — A99

**1965, Nov. 23** *Perf. 12x11½*

**477** A98 12½p multicolored .30 .20
**478** A98 25p multicolored .30 .20

National Council of the Revolution, a legislative body working for a socialist and democratic society.

**1966, Jan. Litho.** *Perf. 11½x11*

**479** A99 12½p blue .30 .20
**480** A99 15p carmine .30 .20
**481** A99 20p dull violet .30 .20
**482** A99 25p olive gray .30 .20
*Nos. 479-482 (4)* 1.20 .80

Establishment of the General Union of Trade Unions.

Roman Lamp A100

Islamic Vessel, 12th Century A101

**1966 Litho.** *Perf. 11½x11*

**483** A100 2½p slate green .30 .20
**484** A100 5p magenta .30 .20
**485** A101 7½p brown .30 .20
**486** A101 10p brt rose lilac .30 .20
*Nos. 483-486 (4)* 1.20 .80

"Evacuation of Troops" — A102

Bust of Core, Terra Cotta Vase — A103

**1966, Apr. 17 Litho.** *Perf. 12x11½*

**487** A102 12½p multi .30 .20
**488** A102 27½p multi .30 .20

20th anniv. of the evacuation of British and French troops from Syria.

**1967** *Perf. 11½x11*

Design: 15p, 20p, 25p, 27½p, Bronze vase in form of seated African woman.

**489** A103 2½p brt green .30 .20
**490** A103 5p salmon pink .30 .20
**491** A103 10p grnsh blue .30 .20
**492** A103 12½p dull brown .30 .20
**493** A103 15p brt pink .30 .20
**494** A103 20p brt blue .30 .20
**495** A103 25p green .30 .20
**496** A103 27½p violet blue .30 .20
*Nos. 489-496 (8)* 2.40 1.60

Arab Revolution Monument, Damascus A104

**1968, Mar. 8 Litho.** *Perf. 12x12½*

**497** A104 12½p black, yel & brn .30 .20
**498** A104 25p blk, pink & car rose .30 .20
**499** A104 27½p blk, lt grn & grn .30 .20
*Nos. 497-499 (3)* .90 .60

Mar. 8 Revolution, 5th anniversary.

Map of Syria — A105

Hands Holding Wrench, Gun and Torch — A106

**1968, Apr. 4 Litho.** *Perf. 12x12½*

**500** A105 12½p pink & multi .30 .20
**501** A105 60p gray & multi .40 .20

Arab Baath Socialist Party, 21st anniv.

**1968, Apr. 13**

**502** A106 12½p tan & multi .30 .20
**503** A106 17½p rose & multi .30 .20
**504** A106 25p yellow & multi .30 .20
*Nos. 502-504 (3)* .90 .60

Issued to publicize the mobilization effort.

Rising Sun, Power Lines and Railroad Tracks A107

**1968, Apr. 17 Litho. *Perf. 12½x12***
**505** A107 12½p multicolored .30 .20
**506** A107 27½p violet & multi .30 .20

22nd anniv. of the evacuation of British and French troops from Syria.

Oil Wells and Oil Pipe Line on Map — A108

**1968, May 1**
**507** A108 12½p lt & dk grn & ultra .30 .20
**508** A108 17½p pink, brn & ultra .30 .20

Syrian oil exploitation; completion of the oil pipe line to Tartus.

Map of Palestine and Torch — A109

Citadel of Aleppo, Wheat and Cogwheel A110

**1968, May Litho. *Perf. 12x12½***
**509** A109 12½p ultra, blk & red .30 .20
**510** A109 25p ol bis, blk & red .35 .20
**511** A109 27½p gray, blk & red .40 .20
*Nos. 509-511 (3)* 1.05 .60

Issued for Palestine Day.

**1968, July 18 Litho. *Perf. 12x12½***
**512** A110 12½p multi .30 .20
**513** A110 27½p multi .30 .20

Industrial and Agricultural Fair, Aleppo.

Fair Emblem, Globe, Grain, Wheel and Horse — A111

Woman Carrying Cotton, and Castle of Aleppo — A112

Design: 27½p, Syrian flag, hand with torch, fair emblem, globe, grain and wheel.

***Perf. 12x12½, 12½x12***

**1968, Aug. 25 Litho.**
**514** A111 12½p dp brn, blk & emer .30 .20
**515** A111 27½p multicolored .30 .20
**516** A111 60p bl gray, blk & dp org .30 .20
*Nos. 514-516 (3)* .90 .60

15th Intl. Damascus Fair, Aug. 25-Sept. 20.

**1968, Oct. 3 Litho. *Perf. 12x12½***
**517** A112 12½p multi .30 .20
**518** A112 27½p multi .30 .20

13th Cotton Festival, Aleppo.

Al Jahez — A113

Oil Derrick and Pipe Line — A114

**1968, Nov. 9 Litho. *Perf. 12x12½***
**519** A113 12½p black & buff .30 .20
**520** A113 27½p black & gray .60 .20

9th Science Week; Al Jahez Abu Uthman Amr ben Bahr (776-868).

**1968 *Perf. 12x11***
**521** A114 2½p grnsh bl & dk grn .30 .20
**522** A114 5p grn & vio bl .30 .20
**523** A114 7½p lt yel grn & bl .30 .20
**524** A114 10p brt yel & grn .30 .20
**525** A114 12½p yellow & ver .30 .20
**526** A114 15p ol bis & dk brn .30 .20
**527** A114 27½p dl org & dk red brn .30 .20
*Nos. 521-527 (7)* 2.10 1.40

Broken Chains and Sun A115

**1969, Mar. 8 Litho. *Perf. 12½x12***
**Sun in Yellow and Red**
**528** A115 12½p vio bl & blk .30 .20
**529** A115 25p gray & blk .30 .20
**530** A115 27½p dull grn & blk .30 .20
*Nos. 528-530 (3)* .90 .60

March 8 Revolution, 6th anniversary.

"Sun of Freedom, Young Man and Woman" — A116

Liberation through Knowledge and Construction A117

**1969, Mar. 29 *Perf. 12x12½***
**531** A116 12½p multi .30 .20
**532** A116 25p multi .30 .20

Youth Week; 5th Youth Festival, Homs, 4/18-24.

**1969, Apr. 17 Litho. *Perf. 12x12½***
**533** A117 12½p yellow & multi .30 .20
**534** A117 27½p gray & multi .30 .20

23rd anniv. of the evacuation of British and French troops from Syria.

Mahatma Gandhi — A118

Cotton — A119

**1969, Oct. 7 Litho. *Perf. 12x12½***
**535** A118 12½p brown & dull yel .30 .20
**536** A118 27½p green & yellow .30 .20

Mohandas K. Gandhi (1869-1948), leader in India's fight for independence.

**1969, Oct. 10**
**537** A119 12½p multi .30 .20
**538** A119 17½p multi .30 .20
**539** A119 25p multi .30 .20
*Nos. 537-539 (3)* .90 .60

14th Cotton Festival, Aleppo.

Map of Arab Countries A120

Designs: 25p, Arab Academy. 27½p, Damascus University.

**1969, Nov. 2 Litho. *Perf. 12½x12***
**540** A120 12½p ultra & lt grn .30 .20
**541** A120 25p dk pur & dp pink .30 .20
**542** A120 27½p dp bis & yel grn .30 .20
*Nos. 540-542 (3)* .90 .60

10th Science Week, and 6th Arab Scientific Conf. No. 541 also for 50th anniv. of the Arab Academy and No. 542, the 50th anniv. of the Medical School of the Damascus University.

Symbols of Progress A121

**1970, Mar. 8 Litho. *Perf. 12½x12***
**543** A121 12½p brt bl, blk & bis brn .30 .20
**544** A121 25p red, blk & dp bl .30 .20
**545** A121 27½p lt grn, blk & tan .30 .20
*Nos. 543-545 (3)* .90 .60

March 8 Revolution, 7th anniversary.

Map of Arab League Countries, Flag and Emblem A122

**1970, Mar. 22**
**546** A122 12½p multi .30 .20
**547** A122 25p gray & multi .30 .20
**548** A122 27½p multi .35 .20
*Nos. 546-548 (3)* .95 .60

25th anniversary of the Arab League.

Sultan Saladin and Battle of Hattin, 1187, between Saracens and Crusaders — A123

**1970, Apr. 17 Litho. *Perf. 12½x12***
**549** A123 15p brn & buff .30 .20
**550** A123 35p lilac & buff .35 .20

24th anniv. of the evacuation of British and French troops from Syria.

Development of Agriculture and Industry — A124

**1970-71 Litho. *Perf. 11x11½***
**551** A124 2½p brn & red ('71) .30 .20
**552** A124 5p orange & bl .30 .20
**553** A124 7½p lil & gray ('71) .30 .20
**554** A124 10p lt & dk brn .30 .20
**555** A124 12½p blue & org ('71) .30 .20
**556** A124 15p grn & red lil .30 .20
**557** A124 20p vio & red brn .30 .20
**558** A124 22½p red brn & blk ('71) .30 .20
**559** A124 25p gray & vio bl ('71) .30 .20
**560** A124 27½p brt grn & dk brn ('71) .30 .20
**561** A124 35p rose red & emer ('71) .35 .20
*Nos. 551-561 (11)* 3.35 2.20

Young Man and Woman, Map of Arab Countries A125

**1970, May 7 Unwmk. *Perf. 12½x12***
**569** A125 15p green & ocher .30 .20
**570** A125 25p brown & ocher .30 .20

First Youth Week, Latakia, Apr. 23-29. Inscribed "Youth's First Weak" (sic.).

Refugee Family A126

**1970, May 15**
**571** A126 15p multicolored .30 .20
**572** A126 25p gray & multi .30 .20
**573** A126 35p green & multi .30 .20
*Nos. 571-573 (3)* .90 .60

Issued for Arab Refugee Week.

Cotton — A127

**1970, Aug. 18 Litho. *Perf. 12½***

**574** A127 5p shown .30 .20
**575** A127 10p Tomatoes .30 .20
**576** A127 15p Tobacco .30 .20
**577** A127 20p Beets .30 .20
**578** A127 35p Wheat .75 .25
*a.* Strip of 5, #574-578 2.00 2.00

Industrial and Agricultural Fair, Aleppo.

Boy Scout, Tent, Emblem and Map of Arab Countries A128

**1970, Aug. 25 *Perf. 12½x12***

**579** A128 15p gray green .40 .20

9th Pan-Arab Boy Scout Jamboree, Damascus.

Olive Tree and Emblem A129

**1970, Sept. 28 Litho. *Perf. 11½x12***

**580** A129 15p gray grn, yel & blk .30 .20
**581** A129 25p red brn, yel & blk .50 .20

Issued to publicize World Olive Year.

Protection of Industry, Agriculture, Arts and Commerce — A130

**1971, Mar. 8 Litho. *Perf. 12½x12***

**582** A130 15p olive, yel & bl .30 .20
**583** A130 22½p red brn, yel & ol .30 .20
**584** A130 27½p bl, yel & red brn .30 .20
*Nos. 582-584 (3)* .90 .60

March 8 Revolution, 8th anniversary.

Workers Memorial, Hands with Wrench and Olive Branch A131

**1971, May 1 Litho. *Perf. 12½x12***

**585** A131 15p brn vio, yel & bl .30 .20
**586** A131 25p dk bl, bl & yel .30 .20

Labor Day.

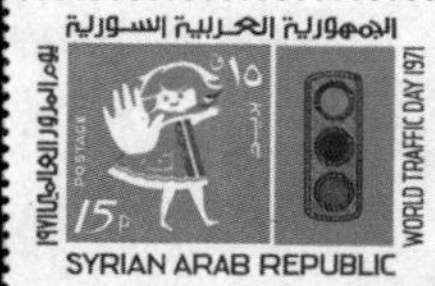


Child and Traffic Lights A132

World Traffic Day: 25p, Road signs, traffic lights, children, vert.

**1971, May 4 *Perf. 11½x12, 12x11½***

**587** A132 15p black, red & bl .30 .20
**588** A132 25p gray & multi .30 .20
**589** A132 45p black, red & yel .30 .20
*Nos. 587-589 (3)* .90 .60

Factories, Cogwheel and Cotton A133

**1971, July 15 Litho. *Perf. 12½x12***

**590** A133 15p lt grn, bl & blk .30 .20
**591** A133 30p red & black .30 .20

11th Industrial and Agricultural Fair, Aleppo.

Arab Postal Union Emblem — A134

Flag, Map of Syria, Egypt and Libya — A135

**1971, Sep. 1 *Perf. 12x12½***

**592** A134 15p claret & multi .30 .20
**593** A134 20p vio bl & multi .30 .20

25th anniv. of the Conference of Sofar, Lebanon, establishing the APU.

**1971, Aug. 13 *Perf. 12x11½***

**594** A135 15p car, dl grn & blk .30 .20

Confederation of the Arab states of Syria, Libya and Egypt.

Red Pepper and Chemical Factory (Fertilizer Industry) — A136

18th Intl. Damascus Fair: 15p, Electronics industry (TV, telephone, computer). 35p, Glass industry (old map and glass manufacture). 50p, Carpet industry (carpet and looms).

**1971, Aug. 25 *Perf. 12½***

**595** A136 5p violet & multi .30 .20
**596** A136 15p dull grn & multi .30 .20
**597** A136 35p multicolored .30 .20
**598** A136 50p yel grn & multi .50 .20
*Nos. 595-598 (4)* 1.40 .80

Pres. Hafez al Assad and Crowd — A137

UNESCO Emblem, Radar, Spacecraft, Telephone A138

**1971, Nov. Litho. *Perf. 12x12½***

**599** A137 15p vio bl, blk & car .30 .20
**600** A137 20p dk & lt grn, car & blk .30 .20

1st anniv. of Correctionist Movement of Nov. 16, 1970.

**1971, Dec. 8**

**601** A138 15p vio bl & multi .30 .20
**602** A138 50p green & multi .30 .20

25th anniv. of UNESCO.

UNICEF Emblem and Playing Children — A139

**1971, Dec. 21**

**603** A139 15p ultra, dk bl & dp car .30 .20
**604** A139 25p grnsh bl, ocher & dk bl .30 .20

UNICEF, 25th anniv.

Conference Emblem — A140

**1971, Dec. *Perf. 12½x12***

**605** A140 15p blk, grnsh bl & org .30 .20

Scholars' Conference.

Book Year Emblem A141

**1972, Jan. 2**

**606** A141 15p tan, lt bl & vio .30 .20
**607** A141 20p brn, lt grn & grn .30 .20

International Book Year.

Wheel, "8" and Scales of Justice — A142

Baath Party Emblem — A143

**1972, Mar. 8 Litho. *Perf. 12x12½***

**608** A142 15p blue grn & vio .30 .20
**609** A142 20p olive bis & car .30 .20

March 8 Revolution, 9th anniversary.

**1972, Mar. 7**

**610** A143 15p dk blue & multi .30 .20
**611** A143 20p violet & multi .30 .20

Arab Baath Socialist Party, 25th anniv.

Eagle, Chimneys, Grain and Oil Rigs — A144

**1972, Apr. 17 *Perf. 12½x12***

**612** A144 15p gold, blk & car .30 .20

Federation of Arab Republics, 1st anniv.

Symbolic Flower, Broken Chain — A145

Hand Holding Wrench and Spade — A146

**1972, Apr. 17 *Perf. 12x11½***

**613** A145 15p rose red & gray .30 .20
**614** A145 50p pale bl grn & gray .30 .20

26th anniv. of the evacuation of British and French troops from Syria.

**1972, May 1**

**615** A146 15p ol grn, bl & blk .30 .20
**616** A146 50p vio bl, brn & blk .30 .20

Labor Day.

Environment Emblem, Crystals, Microscope A147

Dove over Factory — A148

**1972, June 5**

**617** A147 15p multicolored .30 .20
**618** A147 50p blue & multi .35 .20

UN Conference on Human Environment, Stockholm, June 5-16.

**1972, July 17 Litho. *Perf. 12x11½***

**619** A148 15p yellow & multi .30 .20
**620** A148 20p yellow & multi .30 .20

Agricultural and Industrial Fair, Aleppo.

Folk Dance — A149

**1972, Aug. 25 Litho. *Perf. 12x12½***

**621** A149 15p shown .30 .20
**622** A149 20p Women and tambourine player .30 .20
**623** A149 50p Men and drummer .50 .20
*Nos. 621-623 (3)* 1.10 .60

19th International Damascus Fair.

Olympic Rings, Discus, Soccer, Swimming — A150

Warriors on Horseback, Olympic Emblems — A151

Design: 60p, Olympic rings, running, gymnastics, fencing.

**1972 Litho. *Perf. 12½x12***

**624** A150 15p ol bis, blk & vio .50 .20
**625** A150 60p dull bl, blk & org .60 .20

**Souvenir Sheet**

***Imperf***

**626** A151 75p lt grn, bl & blk 2.00 2.00

20th Olympic Games, Munich, Aug. 26-Sept. 11, 1972.

Emblem of Revolution and Prancing Horse A152

**1973, Mar. 8 Litho. *Perf. 11½x12***

**627** A152 15p brt grn, blk & red .30 .20
**628** A152 20p dull org, blk & red .30 .20
**629** A152 25p blue, blk & red .30 .20
*Nos. 627-629 (3)* .90 .60

March 8 Revolution, 10th anniversary.

Heart and WHO Emblem A153

**1973, Mar. 21**

**630** A153 15p gray & multi .30 .20
**631** A153 50p lt brown & multi .35 .20

WHO, 25th anniversary.

Cogwheel and Grain Emblem — A154

**1973, Apr. 17 *Perf. 12x12½***

**632** A154 15p blue & multi .30 .20
**633** A154 20p multicolored .30 .20

27th anniv. of the evacuation of British and French troops from Syria.

Workers and Globe A155

**1973, May 1 *Perf. 11½x12***

**634** A155 15p rose & multi .30 .20
**635** A155 50p blue & multi .35 .20

Labor Day.

UN, FAO Emblems, People and Symbols — A156

Stock — A157

**1973, May 7 *Perf. 12x11½***

**636** A156 15p lt grn & red brn .30 .20
**637** A156 50p lilac & blue .35 .20

World food program, 10th anniv.

**1973, May 15**

**638** A157 5p shown .30 .20
**639** A157 10p Gardenia .30 .20
**640** A157 15p Jasmine .30 .20
**641** A157 20p Rose .30 .20
**642** A157 25p Narcissus .30 .20
*a.* Strip of 5, #638-642 1.50 1.50

Intl. Flower Show, Damascus.

Children and Flame — A158

Children's Day: 3 children's heads and flame in different arrangements; 25p, 35p, 70p, vertical.

***Perf. 11½x12, 12x11½***

**1973-74 Litho.**

**643** A158 2½p lt olive grn .30 .20
**644** A158 5p orange .30 .20
**645** A158 7½p dk brown .30 .20
**646** A158 10p crimson .30 .20
**647** A158 15p ultra .30 .20
**648** A158 25p gray .30 .20
**649** A158 35p brt blue .30 .20
**650** A158 55p green .30 .20
**651** A158 70p rose lilac .35 .20
*Nos. 643-651 (9)* 2.75 1.80

Issued: 15p, 55p, 70p, 5/73; others, 3/74.

Fair Emblem A159

**1973, June 17 *Perf. 11½x12***

**652** A159 15p multicolored .30 .20

13th Agricultural and Industrial Fair, Aleppo.

Euphrates Dam and Power Plant — A160

**1973, July 5 *Perf. 12½x12***

**653** A160 15p green & multi .30 .20
**654** A160 50p brown & multi .30 .20

Euphrates River diversion and dam project.

Woman from Deir Ezzor — A161

Map of Palestine, Barbed Wire, Human Rights Emblem — A162

Women's Costumes from: 10p, Hassaké. 20p, As Sahel. 25p, Zakié. 50p, Sarakeb.

**1973, July 25 Litho. *Perf. 12***

**655** A161 5p multicolored .30 .20
**656** A161 10p multicolored .30 .20
**657** A161 20p multicolored .30 .20
**658** A161 25p multicolored .30 .20
**659** A161 50p multicolored .30 .20
*a.* Strip of 5, #655-659 1.50 1.50

20th International Damascus Fair.

**1973, Aug. 20 *Perf. 12x11½***

**660** A162 15p lt green & multi .30 .20
**661** A162 50p lt blue & multi .50 .20

25th anniversary of the Universal Declaration of Human Rights.

Citadel of Ja'abar A163

15p, Minaret of Meskeneh, vert. 25p, Statue of Psyche at Anab al Safinah, vert.

***Perf. 11½x12, 12x11½***

**1973, Sept. 5 Litho.**

**662** A163 10p black, org & blue .30 .20
**663** A163 15p black, org & blue .30 .20
**664** A163 25p black, org & blue .30 .20
*Nos. 662-664 (3)* .90 .60

Salvage of monuments threatened by Euphrates Dam.

WMO Emblem A164

**1973, Sept. 12 *Perf. 11½x12***

**665** A164 70p yellow & multi .50 .20

Intl. meteorological cooperation, cent.

Maalula A165

Design: 50p, Ruins of Afamia.

**1973, Oct. 22 Litho. *Perf. 11½x12***

**666** A165 15p gray blue & blk .30 .20
**667** A165 50p brown & blk .30 .20

Arab Emigrants' Congress, Buenos Aires.

Workers and Soldiers A166

**1973, Nov. 16 Litho. *Perf. 12½x12***

**668** A166 15p ultra & yellow .30 .20
**669** A166 25p purple & red brn .30 .20

3rd anniv. of Correctionist Movement of Nov. 16, 1970.

Nicolaus Copernicus A167

UPU Emblem — A169

Arms of Syria and Emblems A168

Design: 25p, Abu-al-Rayhan al-Biruni.

**1973, Dec. 15** ***Perf. 12x11½***
**670** A167 15p gold & black .30 .20
**671** A167 25p gold & black .30 .20

14th Science Week.

**1974, Mar. 8** ***Perf. 11x12***
**672** A168 20p gray & blue .30 .20
**673** A168 25p lt green & vio .30 .20

11th anniversary of March 8th Revolution.

**1974, Mar. 15** ***Perf. 12x11½, 11½x12***

20p, Air mail letter and UPU emblem, horiz.

**674** A169 15p gray & multi .30 .20
**675** A169 20p multicolored .30 .20
**676** A169 70p gray & multi .50 .20
*Nos. 674-676 (3)* 1.10 .60

Centenary of Universal Postal Union.

Arab Postal Institute A170

**1974, Apr. 10** ***Perf. 11½x12***
**677** A170 15p multicolored .30 .20

Inauguration of the Higher Arab Postal Institute, Damascus, Apr. 10.

Sun and Monument A171

**1974, Apr. 10**
**678** A171 15p emerald, blk & org .30 .20
**679** A171 20p dp org, blk & org .30 .20

28th anniversary of the evacuation of British and French troops from Syria.

Machine Shop Worker A172

Abulfeda A173

**1974, May 1** ***Perf. 12x12½***
**680** A172 15p black, yel & bl .30 .20
**681** A172 50p black, buff & bl .30 .20

Labor Day.

**1974** **Litho.** ***Perf. 11½x11***

Design: 200p, al-Farabi.

**682** A173 100p pale green .50 .20
**683** A173 200p lt brown 1.00 .45

Damascus Fair Emblem — A174

Figs — A175

Design: 25p, Cog wheel and sun.

**1974, July 25** ***Perf. 11½x11***
**684** A174 15p multicolored .30 .20
**685** A174 25p blue, blk & yel .30 .20

21st International Damascus Fair.

**1974, Aug. 21** ***Perf. 12x12½***

Fruits: 15p, Grapes. 20p, Pomegranates. 25p, Cherries. 35p, Rose hips.

**686** A175 5p gray & multi .30 .20
**687** A175 15p gray & multi .30 .20
**688** A175 20p gray & multi .30 .20
**689** A175 25p gray & multi .30 .20
**690** A175 35p gray & multi .30 .20
*a.* Strip of 5, #686-690 2.50 2.50

Agricultural and Industrial Fair, Aleppo.

Burning Fuse and Flowers — A176

Rook and Knight — A177

20p, Bomb and star-shaped holes in target.

**1974, Oct. 6** **Litho.** ***Perf. 12x12½***
**691** A176 15p multicolored .75 .20
**692** A176 20p multicolored 1.00 .20

First anniv. of October Liberation War (Yom Kippur War).

**1974, Nov. 23**

Design: 50p, Knight and chess board.

**693** A177 15p blue & black .50 .20
**694** A177 50p orange, blk & bl .75 .35

Chess Federation, 50th anniversary.

WPY Emblem — A178

Ishtup, Ilum — A179

**1974, Dec. 4** **Litho.** ***Perf. 12x12½***
**695** A178 50p black, slate & red .30 .20

World Population Year.

**1975** ***Perf. 12x11½***

Ancient Statuettes: 55p, Woman holding pitcher. 70p, Ur-Nina.

**696** A179 20p brt green .30 .20
**697** A179 55p brown .30 .20
**698** A179 70p gray blue .50 .20
*Nos. 696-698 (3)* 1.10 .60

"A," People and Sun — A180

Postal Savings Bank Emblem, Family — A181

**1975, Mar. 8** **Litho.** ***Perf. 12x11½***
**699** A180 15p gray & multi .30 .20

12th anniversary, March 8th Revolution.

**1975, Mar. 17**

Design: 20p, Family depositing money, and stamped envelope.

**700** A181 15p brt green & multi .30 .20
**701** A181 20p orange & black .30 .20

Publicity for Savings Certificates and Postal Savings Bank.

"Sun" and Dove — A182

**1975, Apr. 17** **Litho.** ***Perf. 12x11½***
**702** A182 15p bister, red & blk .30 .20
**703** A182 25p bister, grn & blk .30 .20

29th anniversary of the evacuation of British and French troops from Syria.

"Worker and Industry" — A183

Camomile A184

**1975, May 1** **Litho.** ***Perf. 12x11½***
**704** A183 15p blue grn & blk .30 .20
**705** A183 25p brown, yel & blk .30 .20

Labor Day.

**1975, May 17**

Flowers: 10p, Chincherinchi. 15p, Carnation. 20p, Poppy. 25p, Honeysuckle.

**706** A184 5p ultra & multi .30 .20
**707** A184 10p lilac & multi .30 .20
**708** A184 15p blue & multi .35 .20
**709** A184 20p gray grn & multi .40 .20
**710** A184 25p vio bl & multi .75 .25
*a.* Strip of 5, #706-710 2.10 2.10

International Flower Show, Damascus.

Kuneitra Destroyed and Rebuilt — A185

**1975, June 5** ***Perf. 12½***
**711** A185 50p black & multi .35 .20

Re-occupation of Kuneitra by Syria.

Apples A186

**1975, July 7**
**712** A186 5p shown .30 .20
**713** A186 10p Quince .30 .20
**714** A186 15p Apricots .35 .20
**715** A186 20p Grapes .40 .20
**716** A186 25p Figs .50 .20
*a.* Strip of 5, #712-716 1.90 1.90

Agricultural and Industrial Fair, Aleppo.

22nd Intl. Damascus Fair — A187

Farm Woman — A189

Pres. Hafez al Assad A188

**1975, July 25 Litho. *Perf. 12x11½***
**717** A187 15p olive grn & multi .30 .20
**718** A187 35p brown & multi .30 .20

**1975, Nov. 29 Litho. *Perf. 11½x12***
**719** A188 15p green & multi .30 .20
**720** A188 50p blue & multi .30 .20

5th anniv. of Correctionist Movement of Nov. 16, 1970.

**1975, Nov. 29 *Perf. 12x11½***

IWY Emblem and: 15p, Mother. 25p, Student. 50p, Laboratory technician.

**721** A189 10p buff & multi .30 .20
**722** A189 15p rose & black .30 .20
**723** A189 25p dull green & blk .35 .20
**724** A189 50p orange & blk .50 .20
*Nos. 721-724 (4)* 1.45 .80

International Women's Year.

Horse-shaped Bronze Lamp A190

Man's Head Inkstand A191

Designs: 10p, 25p, like 20p. 35p, like 30p. 50p, 60p, Nike. 75p, Hera. 100p, Imdugug-Mari (winged animal). 500p, Palmyrene coin of Vasalathus. 1000p, Abraxas coin.

**1976 *Perf. 11½x12, 12x11½***
**725** A190 10p brt bluish grn .30 .20
**726** A190 20p lilac rose .30 .20
**727** A190 25p violet blue .30 .20
**728** A191 30p brown .30 .20
**729** A191 35p olive .30 .20
**730** A191 50p brt blue .30 .20
**731** A191 60p violet .30 .20
**732** A191 75p orange .35 .20
**733** A191 100p lilac rose .50 .20
**734** A191 500p grnsh gray 2.00 1.75
**735** A191 1000p dk green 4.00 2.25
*Nos. 725-735 (11)* 8.95 5.80

See Nos. 798-803.

National Theater, Damascus and Pres. al Assad A192

**1976, Mar. 8 Litho. *Perf. 11½x12***
**736** A192 25p brt grn, sil & blk .30 .20
**737** A192 35p olive, sil & blk .30 .20

13th anniversary of March 8 Revolution.

Syria, Arabian Government #85 — A193

**1976, Apr. 12 *Perf. 12x12½***
**738** A193 25p brt green & multi .30 .20
**739** A193 35p blue & multi .30 .20

Post's Day.

Nurse and Emblem — A194

Eagle and Stars — A195

**1976, Apr. 8 *Perf. 12x11½***
**740** A194 25p blue, blk & red .30 .20
**741** A194 100p violet, blk & red .50 .30

Arab Red Cross and Red Crescent Societies, 8th Conference, Damascus.

**1976, Apr. 17**
**742** A195 25p blk, red & brt grn .30 .20
**743** A195 35p blk, red & brt grn .30 .20

30th anniversary of the evacuation of British and French troops from Syria.

Hand Holding Wrench — A196

Cotton and Factory — A197

May Day: 60p, Hand holding globe.

**1976, May 1**
**744** A196 25p blue & black .30 .20
**745** A196 60p citron & multi .40 .20

**1976, July 1**
**746** A197 25p vio & multi .30 .20
**747** A197 35p bl & multi .30 .20

Agricultural and Industrial Fair, Aleppo.

Tulips — A198

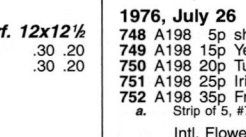

**1976, July 26**
**748** A198 5p shown .30 .20
**749** A198 15p Yellow daisies .30 .20
**750** A198 20p Turk's-cap lilies .30 .20
**751** A198 25p Irises .50 .20
**752** A198 35p Freesia .75 .20
*a.* Strip of 5, #748-752 2.25 2.25

Intl. Flower Show, Damascus.

People, Globe and Olive Branch A199

60p, Symbolic arrow piercing darkness.

**1976, Sept. 2 *Perf. 11½x12***
**753** A199 40p yel & multi .30 .20
**754** A199 60p multi .35 .20

5th Summit Conference of Non-aligned Countries, Colombo, Sri Lanka, Aug. 9-19.

Soccer, Pan Arab Games Emblem A200

**1976, Oct. 6 Litho. *Perf. 12½***
**755** A200 5p shown .30 .20
**756** A200 10p Swimming .30 .20
**757** A200 25p Running .30 .20
**758** A200 35p Basketball .30 .20
**759** A200 50p Javelin .30 .20
*a.* Strip of 5, #755-759 1.50 1.50

**Souvenir Sheet**

***Imperf***

**760** A200 100p Steeplechase 2.00 2.00

5th Pan Arab Sports Tournament. Size of stamp of No. 760: 55x35mm.

"Development" A201

The Fox and the Crow — A202

**1976, Nov. 16 *Perf. 12½x12½***
**761** A201 35p multi .30 .20

Correctionist Movement pof Nov. 16, 1970.

**1976, Dec. 7 *Perf. 12x12½, 12½x12***

Fairy Tales: 15p, The Hare and the Tortoise, horiz. 20p, Little Red Riding Hood. 25p, The Lamb and the Wolf, horiz. 35p, The Lamb and the Wolf.

**762** A202 10p multi .30 .20
**763** A202 15p multi .30 .20
**764** A202 20p multi .30 .20
**765** A202 25p multi .30 .20
**766** A202 35p multi .30 .20
*Nos. 762-766 (5)* 1.50 1.00

Children's literature.

Syrian Airlines Boeing 747 — A203

**1977, Feb. Litho. *Perf. 12½x12***
**767** A203 35p multi .30 .20

Civil Aviation Day.

Muhammad Kurd-Ali (1876-1953), Philosopher, Birth Cent. — A204

**1977, Feb. *Perf. 12x12½***
**768** A204 25p lt grn & multi .30 .20

Woman Holding Syrian Flag — A205

APU Emblem — A207

Warrior on Horseback — A206

**1977, Mar. 8 Litho. *Perf. 12x12½***
**769** A205 35p multi .30 .20

14th anniversary of March 8 Revolution.

**1977, Apr. 10 Litho. *Perf. 12½***
**770** A206 100p multi .30 .20

31st anniversary of the evacuation of British and French troops from Syria.

**1977, Apr. 12 Litho. *Perf. 12x12½***
**771** A207 35p silver & multi .30 .20

Arab Postal Union, 25th anniversary.

Tools and Factories A208

**1977, May 1** *Perf. 12½x12*
**772** A208 60p multi .35 .20

Labor Day.

ICAO Emblem, Plane and Globe A209

**1977, May 11**
**773** A209 100p multi .50 .25

Intl. Civil Aviation Org., 30th anniv.

Pioneers A210

Citrus Fruit A211

**1977, Aug. 15 Litho.** *Perf. 12x12½*
**774** A210 35p multi .30 .20

Al Baath Pioneer Organization.

**1977, Aug. 1**

| | | | | |
|---|---|---|---|---|
| **775** | A211 10p Lemon | | .30 | .20 |
| **776** | A211 20p Lime | | .30 | .20 |
| **777** | A211 25p Grapefruit | | .30 | .20 |
| **778** | A211 35p Oranges | | .30 | .20 |
| **779** | A211 60p Tangerines | | .40 | .20 |
| *a.* | Strip of 5, #775-779 | | 1.60 | 1.60 |

Agricultural and Industrial Fair, Aleppo.

Flowers A212

**1977, Aug. 6 Litho.** *Perf. 12½x12*

| | | | |
|---|---|---|---|
| **780** | A212 10p Mallow | .30 | .20 |
| **781** | A212 20p Coxcomb | .30 | .20 |
| **782** | A212 25p Morning glories | .30 | .20 |
| **783** | A212 35p Almond blossoms | .30 | .20 |
| **784** | A212 60p Lilacs | .30 | .20 |
| *a.* | Strip of 5, #780-784 | 1.50 | 1.50 |

Intl. Flower Show, Damascus.

Coffeepot and Ornament A213

**1977, Sept. 10** *Perf. 12x12½*
**785** A213 25p blk, bl & red .30 .20
**786** A213 60p blk, grn & brn .35 .20

24th Intl. Damascus Fair.

Blind Man, Globe and Eye — A214

Globe and Measures A215

**1977, Nov. 17 Litho.** *Perf. 12x12½*
**787** A214 55p multi .30 .20
**788** A214 70p multi .30 .20

World Blind Week.

**1977, Nov. 5**
**789** A215 15p grn & multi .30 .20

World Standards Day, Oct. 14.

Microscope, Book, Harp, UNESCO Emblem — A216

**1977, Nov. 5** *Perf. 12½x12*
**790** A216 25p multi .30 .20

30th anniversary of UNESCO.

Archbishop Capucci, Map of Palestine, Bars — A217

Fight Cancer Shield, Crab and Surgeon — A218

**1977, Nov. 17** *Perf. 12x12½*
**791** A217 60p multi .50 .20

Palestinian Archbishop Hilarion Capucci, jailed by Israel in 1974.

**1977, Nov. 17**
**792** A218 100p multi .50 .20

Fight Cancer Week.

Dome of the Rock, Jerusalem — A219

**1977, Dec. 6** *Perf. 12*
**793** A219 5p multi .50 .20
**794** A219 10p multi .75 .20

Palestinian fighters and their families.

Mural — A220

Pres. Hafez al Assad — A221

Designs: 10p, 15p, Murals from Dura-Europos, in National Museum, Damascus.

**1978, Jan. 22 Litho.** *Perf. 12x11½*

| | | | |
|---|---|---|---|
| **795** | A220 5p gray grn | .30 | .20 |
| **796** | A220 10p vio bl | .30 | .20 |
| **797** | A220 15p brown, horiz. | .30 | .20 |
| | *Nos. 795-797 (3)* | .90 | .60 |

Types of 1976

Designs: 40p, Man's head inkstand. 55p, Nike. 70p, 80p, Hera. 200p, Arab-Islamic astrolabe. 300p, Palmyrene (Herod) coin.

**1978 Litho.** *Perf. 12x11½, 11½x12*

| | | | |
|---|---|---|---|
| **798** | A191 40p pale org | .30 | .20 |
| **799** | A191 55p brt rose | .30 | .20 |
| **800** | A191 70p vermilion | .35 | .20 |
| **801** | A191 80p green | .35 | .20 |
| **802** | A191 200p lt ultra | 1.00 | .30 |
| **803** | A190 300p rose lil | 1.50 | .50 |
| | *Nos. 798-803 (6)* | 3.80 | 1.60 |

**1978** *Perf. 12x11½*
**805** A221 50p multi .40 .20

Anniversary of "Correction Movement."

Blood Circulation, WHO Emblem — A222

Factory — A223

**1978, Apr. 7 Litho.** *Perf. 12x11½*
**806** A222 100p multi .50 .20

World Health Day, fight against hypertension.

**1978, Apr. 17**
**807** A223 35p multi .30 .20

32nd anniversary of the evacuation of British and French troops from Syria.

Rosette — A224

Map of Arab Countries, Police, Flag and Eye — A225

**1978, Apr. 21**
**808** A224 25p blk & grn .30 .20

14th Arab Engineering Conference, Damascus, Apr. 21-26.

**1978, May**
**809** A225 35p multi .30 .20

6th Conf. of Arab Police Commanders.

European Goldfinch A226

Birds: 20p, Peregrine falcon. 25p, Rock dove. 35p, Eurasian hoopoe. 60p, Old World quail.

**1978** *Perf. 11½x12*

| | | | |
|---|---|---|---|
| **810** | A226 10p multi | .40 | .20 |
| **811** | A226 20p multi | .40 | .20 |
| **812** | A226 25p multi | .40 | .20 |
| **813** | A226 35p multi | .50 | .20 |
| **814** | A226 60p multi | .60 | .20 |
| *a.* | Strip of 5, #810-814 | 2.40 | 2.40 |

Trout A227

Designs: Various fish.

**1978, July Litho.** *Perf. 11½x12*

| | | | |
|---|---|---|---|
| **815** | A227 10p multi | .40 | .20 |
| **816** | A227 20p multi | .40 | .20 |
| **817** | A227 25p multi | .40 | .20 |
| **818** | A227 35p multi | .50 | .20 |
| **819** | A227 60p multi | .55 | .25 |
| *a.* | Strip of 5, #815-819 | 2.25 | 2.25 |

Pres. Assad Type of Air Post, 1978
Miniature Sheet

**1978, Sept. Litho.** *Imperf.*
**820** AP161 100p gold & multi 1.00 1.00

Reelection of President Assad. Size of stamp: 58x80mm.

Flowering Cactus A228

Fair Emblem — A229

Designs: Flowering cacti.

**1978 Litho. *Perf. 12½***

| | | | | |
|---|---|---|---|---|
| **821** | A228 25p multi | .50 | .20 |
| **822** | A228 30p multi | .50 | .20 |
| **823** | A228 35p multi | .50 | .20 |
| **824** | A228 50p multi | .50 | .20 |
| **825** | A228 60p multi | .50 | .20 |
| ***a.*** | Strip of 5, #821-825 | 2.50 | 2.50 |

International Flower Show, Damascus.

**1978 Litho. *Perf. 12x12½***

| | | | |
|---|---|---|---|
| **826** | A229 25p sil & multi | .30 | .20 |
| **827** | A229 35p sil & multi | .30 | .20 |

**Miniature Sheet**

***Imperf***

| | | | |
|---|---|---|---|
| **828** | A229 100p sil & multi | 1.00 | 1.00 |

25th Intl. Damascus Fair. No. 828 shows different ornament, size of stamp: 40x46mm.

Euphrates Dam and Pres. Assad — A230

**1978, Dec. Litho. *Perf. 12½x12***

| | | | |
|---|---|---|---|
| **829** | A230 60p multi | .50 | .20 |

Inauguration of Euphrates Dam.

Pres. Hafez al Assad — A231

**1978, Nov. 16 Litho. *Perf. 12x12½***

| | | | |
|---|---|---|---|
| **830** | A231 60p multi | .40 | .20 |

Nov. 16 Movement.

Racial Equality Emblem A232

**1978, Mar. Litho. *Perf. 12½***

| | | | |
|---|---|---|---|
| **831** | A232 35p multi | .40 | .20 |

International Year to Combat Racism.

Averroes — A233

Human Rights Flame and Globe — A234

**1979, Mar.**

| | | | |
|---|---|---|---|
| **832** | A233 100p multi | .75 | .25 |

Averroes (1126-1198), Spanish-Arabian philosopher and physician.

**1978, Dec. *Perf. 12x12½***

| | | | |
|---|---|---|---|
| **833** | A234 60p multi | .50 | .20 |

30th anniversary of Universal Declaration of Human Rights (in 1978).

Symbolic Design — A235

Princess, 2nd Century Shield — A236

**1979, Mar.**

| | | | |
|---|---|---|---|
| **834** | A235 100p multi | .50 | .20 |

16th anniversary of March 8 Revolution.

**1979 Litho. *Perf. 11½***

Designs: 20p, Helmet of Homs. 35p, Ishtar.

| | | | |
|---|---|---|---|
| **836** | A236 20p green | .30 | .20 |
| **837** | A236 25p rose car | .30 | .20 |
| **838** | A236 35p sepia | .30 | .20 |
| | *Nos. 836-838 (3)* | .90 | .60 |

Molar, Emblem with Mosque — A237

Flame Emblem — A238

**1979 Litho. *Perf. 12x11½***

| | | | |
|---|---|---|---|
| **846** | A237 35p multi | .30 | .20 |

Intl. Middle East Dental Congress.

**1979**

| | | | |
|---|---|---|---|
| **847** | A238 35p multi | .30 | .20 |

33rd anniversary of evacuation.

Ibn Assaker, 900th Anniv. A239

**1979 *Perf. 11½x12***

| | | | |
|---|---|---|---|
| **848** | A239 75p multi | .30 | .20 |

Telephone Lineman — A240

Girl with IYC Emblem — A242

Wright Brothers' Plane A241

**1979, May 1 Litho. *Perf. 12x11½***

| | | | |
|---|---|---|---|
| **849** | A240 50p multi | .30 | .20 |
| **850** | A240 75p multi | .30 | .20 |

May Day.

**1979 *Perf. 11½x12***

Designs: 75p, Bleriot's plane crossing English Channel. 100p, Spirit of St. Louis.

| | | | |
|---|---|---|---|
| **851** | A241 50p multi | .30 | .20 |
| **852** | A241 75p multi | .30 | .20 |
| **853** | A241 100p multi | .50 | .20 |
| | *Nos. 851-853 (3)* | 1.10 | .60 |

75th anniversary of 1st powered flight.

**1979 *Perf. 12x11½***

Design: 15p, Boy, globe, IYC emblem.

| | | | |
|---|---|---|---|
| **854** | A242 10p multi | .30 | .20 |
| **855** | A242 15p multi | .35 | .20 |

International Year of the Child.

Power Plant — A243

Flags and Pavilion — A244

**1979 *Perf. 11x11½***

| | | | |
|---|---|---|---|
| **856** | A243 5p blue | .30 | .20 |
| **857** | A243 10p lil rose | .30 | .20 |
| **858** | A243 15p gray grn | .30 | .20 |
| | *Nos. 856-858 (3)* | .90 | .60 |

**1979 Photo. *Perf. 12x11½***

Design: 75p, Lamppost and flags.

| | | | |
|---|---|---|---|
| **859** | A244 60p multi | .30 | .20 |
| **860** | A244 75p multi | .35 | .20 |

26th International Damascus Fair.

Correction Movement, 9th Anniversary — A245

**1979 Photo. *Perf. 11½x12***

| | | | |
|---|---|---|---|
| **861** | A245 100p multi | .50 | .20 |

Games Emblem, Running A246

**1979, Nov.**

| | | | |
|---|---|---|---|
| **862** | A246 25p shown | .30 | .20 |
| **863** | A246 35p Diving | .30 | .20 |
| **864** | A246 50p Soccer | .30 | .20 |
| | *Nos. 862-864 (3)* | .90 | .60 |

8th Mediterranean Games, Split, Yugoslavia, Sept. 15-29.

Butterfly — A247

Damascus Intl. Flower Show A248

Designs: Various butterflies.

**1979, Dec. Litho. *Perf. 12x11½***

| | | | |
|---|---|---|---|
| **865** | A247 20p multi | .50 | .20 |
| **866** | A247 25p multi | .50 | .20 |
| **867** | A247 30p multi | .50 | .20 |
| **868** | A247 35p multi | .50 | .20 |
| **869** | A247 50p multi | .50 | .20 |
| | *Nos. 865-869 (5)* | 2.50 | 1.00 |

**1980, Jan. 9 Litho. *Perf. 12½***

Design: Roses.

| | | | |
|---|---|---|---|
| **870** | A248 5p multi | .50 | .20 |
| **871** | A248 10p multi | .50 | .20 |
| **872** | A248 15p multi | .50 | .20 |
| **873** | A248 50p multi | .50 | .20 |
| **874** | A248 75p multi | .50 | .20 |
| **875** | A248 100p multi | .80 | .20 |
| | *Nos. 870-875 (6)* | 3.30 | 1.20 |

March 8 Revolution, 17th Anniv. — A249

Astrolabe A250

**1980, Mar. 25 Litho.** ***Perf. 12x11½***

**876** A249 40p multi .30 .20

**1980, May 2** ***Perf. 12½***

**877** A250 50p violet .30 .20
**878** A250 100p sepia .50 .20
**879** A250 1000p gray grn 4.00 1.25
*Nos. 877-879 (3)* 4.80 1.65

2nd International History of Arabic Sciences Symposium, Apr. 5.

Lit Cigarette, Skull — A251

Evacuation, 34th Anniversary A252

**1980, June 25 Photo.** ***Perf. 12x11½***

**880** A251 60p Smoker .60 .25
**881** A251 100p shown 1.00 .30

World Health Day; anti-smoking campaign.

**1980, June 25** **Litho.**

**882** A252 40p multi .30 .20
**883** A252 60p multi .35 .20

27th International Damascus Fair — A263

Moscow '80 Emblem and Wrestling A253

**1980, July Litho.** ***Perf. 11½x12***

**884** A253 15p shown .30 .20
**885** A253 25p Fencing .30 .20
**886** A253 35p Weight lifting .35 .20
**887** A253 50p Judo .50 .20
**888** A253 75p Boxing 1.00 .25
*a.* Strip of 5, #884-888 2.50 2.50

**Souvenir Sheet**

***Imperf***

**888B** A253 300p Discus, running 5.00 5.00

22nd Summer Olympic Games, Moscow, July 19-Aug. 3.

Sinbad the Sailor A254

**1980 Litho.** ***Perf. 11½x12***

**889** A254 15p shown .30 .20
**890** A254 25p Scheherezade and Shahrayar .30 .20
**891** A254 35p Ali Baba and the Forty Thieves .35 .20
**892** A254 50p Hassan the Clever .50 .20
**893** A254 100p Aladdin's Lamp 1.00 .30
*a.* Strip of 5, #889-893 2.50 2.50

Popular stories.

Savings Certificates — A255

**1980**

**894** A255 25p multi .30 .20

Hegira, 1500th Anniv. — A256

**1980** ***Perf. 12½x12***

**895** A256 35p multi .35 .20

Intl. Flower Show, Damascus A257

**1980** ***Perf. 12x11½***

**896** A257 20p Daffodils .50 .20
**897** A257 30p Chrysanthemums .50 .20
**898** A257 40p Clematis .55 .20
**899** A257 60p Yellow roses .60 .20
**900** A257 100p Chrysanthemums, diff. .75 .25
*a.* Strip of 5, #896-900 3.00 3.00

May Day — A258

Children's Day — A259

**1980, May**

**901** A258 35p multi .40 .20

**1980**

**902** A259 25p multi .40 .20

November 16th Movement, 10th Anniv. — A260

**1980** ***Perf. 11½x12***

**903** A260 100p multi 1.00 .25

Steam-powered Passenger Wagon — A261

**1980**

**904** A261 25p shown .35 .20
**905** A261 35p Benz, 1899 .40 .20
**906** A261 40p Rolls-Royce, 1903 .60 .20
**907** A261 50p Mercedes, 1906 .75 .25
**908** A261 60p Austin, 1915 1.00 .30
*a.* Strip of 5, #904-908 3.25 3.25

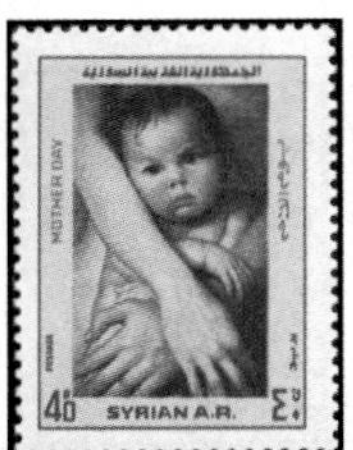


Mother's Day — A262

**1980** ***Perf. 12x11½***

**909** A262 40p shown .50 .20
**910** A262 100p Mother and child 1.00 .20

**1981, Jan. 24** ***Perf. 11½x12***

**911** A263 50p multi .45 .20
**912** A263 100p multi .80 .20

Army Day — A264

**1981, Jan. 24** ***Perf. 12½x12***

**913** A264 50p multi .45 .20

A265

A266

**1981, Mar. 8 Litho.** ***Perf. 12x11½***

**914** A265 50p multi .35 .20

18th anniv. of March 8th revolution.

**1981, Apr. 17 Litho.** ***Perf. 12x11½***

**915** A266 50p multi .35 .20

35th anniversary of evacuation.

World Conference on History of Arab and Islamic Civilization, Damascus — A267

**1981, May 30 Photo.** ***Perf. 12½x12***

**916** A267 100p multi .60 .20

Intl. Workers' Solidarity Day — A268

Housing and Population Census — A269

**1981, May 30 Litho.** ***Perf. 12x11½***

**917** A268 100p multi .60 .20

**1981, June 1**

**918** A269 50p multi .35 .20

Umayyad Window A270

Abdul Malik Gold Coin A270a

10p, figurine. 15p, Rakkla's cavalier, Abbcid ceramic. 160p, like 5p. 500p, Umar B. Abdul Aziz gold coin.

**1981** ***Perf. 12x11½, 11½x12***

**919** A270 5p crim rose .20 .20
**920** A270 10p brt grn .20 .20
**921** A270 15p dp rose lil .20 .20
**922** A270a 75p blue .35 .20
**923** A270 160p dk grn .70 .35
**924** A270a 500p dk brn 2.50 1.10
*Nos. 919-924 (6)* 4.15 2.25

Olives A270b

Harbor A270c

**1982** ***Perf. 12x11½***

**925** A270b 50p ol grn .40 .20
**926** A270b 60p bl gray .45 .20
**929** A270c 100p lilac .55 .25
**930** A270c 180p red 1.10 .55
*Nos. 925-930 (4)* 2.50 1.20

Saving Certificates Plan — A271

Avicenna (980-1037), Philosopher and Physician A272

**1981, June 22**

**931** A271 50p gldn brn & blk .35 .20

**1981, Aug.**

**932** A272 100p multi .60 .20

Syria-P.L.O. Solidarity, Intl. Conference A273

**1981, June 22**

**933** A273 160p multi 3.50 .90

Grand Mosque, Damascus — A274

**1981** ***Perf. 12½***

**934** A274 50p Glass lamp, 13th cent. .30 .20
**935** A274 180p shown 1.40 .40
**936** A274 180p Hunter 1.40 .40
*Nos. 934-936 (3)* 3.10 1.00

Youth Festival A275

**1981** ***Perf. 12½***

**937** A275 60p multi .40 .20

28th Intl. Damascus Fair — A276

Intl. Palestinian Solidarity Day — A277

**1981** ***Perf. 12x11½***

**938** A276 50p Ornament .30 .20
**939** A276 160p Emblem 1.00 .45

**1981**

**940** A277 100p multi .75 .20

1300th Anniv. of Bulgaria A278

**1981** ***Perf. 11½x12***

**941** A278 380p multi 2.25 1.00

Intl. Children's Day A279

**1981**

**942** A279 180p multi 1.10 .45

World Food Day, Oct. 16 A280

**1981**

**943** A280 180p multi 1.10 .45

9th Intl. Flower Show, Damascus A281

Designs: Flowers.

**1981** ***Perf. 12x11½***

**944** A281 25p multi .25 .20
**945** A281 40p multi .40 .25
**946** A281 50p multi .50 .30
**947** A281 60p multi .75 .35
**948** A281 100p multi 1.10 .50
*a.* Strip of 5, #944-948 3.00 2.00

Souvenir Sheet

Koran Competition — A282

**1981** **Litho.** ***Imperf.***

**949** A282 500p multi 5.00 5.00

11th Anniv. of Correction Movement A283

**1981, Nov.** ***Perf. 12x11½***

**950** A283 60p multi .45 .30

TB Bacillus Centenary A284

**1982** **Litho.** ***Perf. 11½x12***

**951** A284 180p multi 1.25 .65

Mothers' Day — A285

Mar. 8th Revolution, 19th Anniv. — A286

**1982** ***Perf. 11½***

**952** A285 40p green .25 .20
**953** A285 75p brown .50 .25

**1982, Mar.** ***Perf. 12x11½***

**954** A286 50p multi .35 .20

Intl. Year of the Disabled (1981) — A287

Pres. Hafez al Assad — A288

**1982** ***Perf. 12x11½***

**955** A287 90p multi .75 .30

**1982** ***Perf. 11½***

**956** A288 150p ultra .90 .50

36th Anniv. of Evacuation A289

World Traffic Day — A290

**1982** ***Perf. 12x11½***

**957** A289 70p multi .50 .25

**1982**

**958** A290 180p multi 1.25 .65

Intl. Workers' Solidarity Day — A291

**1982**

**959** A291 180p multi 1.25 .65

World Telecommunication Day, May 17 — A292

**1982**
**960** A292 180p multi 1.25 .65

Soldier Holding Rifles — A293

Arab Postal Union, 30th Anniv. — A294

**1982 Photo.** ***Perf. 12x11½***
**961** A293 50p multi .30 .20

**1982**
**962** A294 60p multi .45 .20

1982 World Cup — A295

Various soccer players. 300p, Ball.

**1982, July** ***Perf. 12½***
**963** A295 40p multi .25 .20
**964** A295 60p multi .40 .20
**965** A295 100p multi .65 .40
*Nos. 963-965 (3)* 1.30 .80

**Size: 75x55mm**
***Imperf***
**966** A295 300p multi *10.00 10.00*

10th Intl. Flower Show, Damascus A297

**1982** ***Perf. 12x11½***
**967** A297 50p Honeysuckle .45 .20
**968** A297 60p Geraniums .60 .30

Scouting Year A298

**1982, Nov. 4** ***Perf. 11½x12***
**969** A298 160p green 1.40 .75

Ladybug A299

**1982** ***Perf. 12x12½***
**970** Strip of 5 .75 .40
*a.* A299 5p Dragonfly .20 .20
*b.* A299 10p Stag Beetle .20 .20
*c.* A299 20p shown .20 .20
*d.* A299 40p Grasshopper .20 .20
*e.* A299 50p Honeybee .30 .20

ITU Plenipotentiaries Conference, Nairobi, Sept — A300

**1982** ***Perf. 11½x12***
**971** A300 50p Map .30 .25
**972** A300 180p Dish antenna 1.40 .75

12th Anniv. of Correction Movement A301

**1982, Nov.**
**973** A301 50p dk bl & sil .35 .20

A302

Factory — A302a

Walled Arch — A302b

Ruins — A302c

**1982-83 Litho.** ***Perf. 11½***
**974** A302 30p brown .20 .20
**975** A302a 50p dark green .25 .20
**976** A302b 70p green .35 .20
**977** A302c 200p red 1.00 .55
*Nos. 974-977 (4)* 1.80 1.15

Issued: 50p, 11/16/83; others, 11/4/82.

Dove and Satellite — A303

Intl. Palestinian Solidarity Day — A304

**1982 Litho.** ***Perf. 12x11½***
**978** A303 50p multi .50 .30

2nd UN Conference on Peaceful Uses of Outer Space, Vienna, Aug. 9-21.

**1982**
**979** A304 50p multi .90 .20

20th Anniv. of March 8th Revolution — A305

**1983** ***Perf. 12½x12***
**980** A305 60p multi 1.00 .50

World Communications Year — A305a

**1983**
**981** A305a 180p multi 1.25 .65

9th Anniv. of Liberation of Al-Kuneitra A306

25th Anniv. of Intl. Maritime Org. A308

Arab Pharmacists' Day, Apr. 2 — A307

**1983, June 26 Litho.** ***Perf. 11½***
**982** A306 50p View 1.50 .50
**983** A306 100p View, diff. 3.00 .65

**1983, Apr. 2** ***Perf. 11½x12***
**984** A307 100p multi .75 .30

**1983, June** ***Perf. 12x11½***
**985** A308 180p multi 1.40 .75

Namibia Day, Aug. 26 A309

**1983, Aug. 26** ***Perf. 11½x12***
**986** A309 180p multi 1.40 .75

Eibla Sculpture, 3rd Cent. BC A310

**1983**
**987** A310 380p ol & brn 2.50 1.40

World Standards Day — A311

11th Intl. Flower Show, Damascus A312

**1983, Oct. 14 Photo.** ***Perf. 11½***
**988** A311 50p Factory, emblem .40 .20
**989** A311 100p Measuring equipment .80 .40

**1983, Oct. 14 Litho.** ***Perf. 11½***
**990** A312 50p multi .40 .20
**991** A312 60p multi, diff. .50 .25

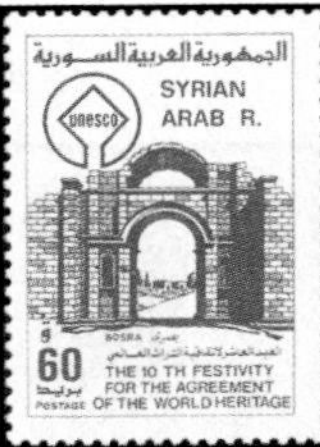
World Heritage Day — A313

**1983, Oct. 14 Photo.** ***Perf. 11½***
**992** A313 60p dk brn .50 .25

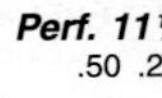

World Food Day A313a

**1983, Oct. 16 Litho.** ***Perf. 11½x12***
**992A** A313a 180p multi 1.50 .75

Waterwheels of Hama — A314

***Perf. 11x11½, 11½x11***

**1982-84 Litho.**

| | | | | | |
|---|---|---|---|---|---|
| **993** | A314 | 5p | sepia | .20 | .20 |
| **994** | A314 | 10p | violet | .20 | .20 |
| **995** | A314 | 20p | red | .25 | .20 |
| **997** | A314 | 50p | dk grn | .60 | .30 |
| | | | *Nos. 993-997 (4)* | 1.25 | .90 |

Issued: 50p, 11/25/82; others, 1/15/84.
On No. 997 "50" is in outlined numbers.

Statue — A316

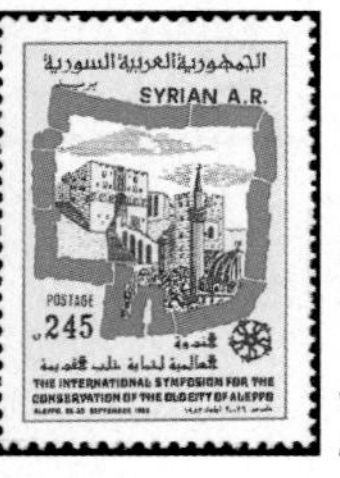

View of Aleppo — A317

**1983** ***Perf. 12***
**1003** A316 225p brown 2.00 1.00

Intl. Symposium on History and Archaeology of Deir Ez-zor.

**1983** ***Perf. 12x12½***
**1004** A317 245p multi 2.25 1.10

Intl. Symposium on Conservation of Old City of Aleppo, Sept. 26-30.

Mar. 8th Revolution, 21st Anniv. — A318

**1984, Mar. 8** ***Perf. 12½x12***
**1005** A318 60p Alassad Library .75 .35

Massacre at Sabra and Shatilla A319

**1983 Litho.** ***Perf. 11½x12***
**1006** A319 225p Victims, mother & child 2.00 .50

Mothers' Day — A320

12th Intl. Flower Show, Damascus A321

**1984, Mar. 21** ***Perf. 12x11½***
**1007** A320 245p Mother & child 2.50 1.25

**1984, May 25**

Various flowers.

**1008** A321 245p multi 2.50 1.25
**1009** A321 285p multi 2.75 1.40

1984 Summer Olympics — A322

Aleppo Agricultural & Industrial Fair — A324

9th Regional Pioneers' Festival A323

**1984 Litho.** ***Perf. 12x11½***

| | | | |
|---|---|---|---|
| **1010** | Strip of 5 | 3.00 | 2.40 |
| *a.* | A322 30p Swimming | .30 | .20 |
| *b.* | A322 50p Wrestling | .50 | .25 |
| *c.* | A322 60p Running | .60 | .30 |
| *d.* | A322 70p Boxing | .65 | .35 |
| *e.* | A322 90p Soccer | .90 | .45 |

**Souvenir Sheet**

***Imperf***

**1011** A322 200p Soccer, diff. 3.50 3.50

**1984** ***Perf. 11½x12***
**1012** A323 50p Pioneers .50 .25
**1013** A323 60p Pioneers, diff. .60 .30

**1984, June 12 Litho.** ***Perf. 12x12½***
**1014** A324 150p Peppers, Aleppo Castle 1.25 .50

Supreme Council of Science, 25th Anniv. A325

**1985, Feb. 23** ***Perf. 12½x12***
**1015** A325 65p multi .40 .20

Aleppo University, 25th Anniv. A326

**1985, Feb. 23**
**1016** A326 45p multi .25 .20

Syrian Arab Army, 39th Anniv. A327

**1985, Feb. 23**
**1017** A327 65p brn & gldn brn .40 .20

Pres. Assad, Soldier Saluting, Troops A328

**1984, Aug. 1** ***Perf. 11½x12***
**1018** A328 60p multi .60 .30

4th General Revolutionary Youth Conference.

ITU Emblem, Satellite Dish, Telephone A329

**1984, Oct. 2** ***Perf. 12½***
**1019** A329 245p multi 1.75 .90

Intl. Telecommunications Day.

APU Emblem and Administration Building, Damascus — A330

**1984, Oct. 9**
**1020** A330 60p multi .60 .30

Arab Postal Union Day.

Gearwheel, Arabesque Pattern — A331

Gold Necklace — A332

**1984, Oct. 27** ***Perf. 12x12½, 12x11½***
**1021** A331 45p multi .45 .20
**1022** A332 100p multi 1.00 .45

Intl. Fair, Damascus.

Intl. Civil Aviation Org., 40th Anniv. A333

**1984, Oct. 27** ***Perf. 11½x12***
**1023** A333 45p brt bl & lt bl .25 .20
**1024** A333 245p brt ultra, brt bl & lt bl 1.25 .60

14th Anniv. of 11-16-70 Movement A334

**1984, Dec. 3** ***Perf. 12½x12***
**1025** A334 65p red brn, blk & org .65 .35

Pres. Assad, Text on Scroll A335

**1984, Nov. 29** ***Perf. 12½***
**1026** A335 50p grn, brn org & sep .50 .25

Vow of Dedication taken by Youth of the Revolution.

Agricultural Exhibition — A336

**1984, June 12** ***Perf. 12½x12***
**1027** A336 65p multi .65 .35

Al-Kuneitra Memorial, Rose — A337

**1984**
**1028** A337 70p multi 1.25 .35

Roman Arch and Colonnades, Palmyra — A338

**1984, Dec. 3**
**1029** A338 100p multi 1.00 .50

Intl. Tourism Day.

Woodland Conservation — A339

**1984**
**1030** A339 45p multi .25 .20

March 8 Revolution, 22nd Anniv. — A340

UPU Emblem, Postal Headquarters, Damascus A341

**1985, Apr. 27**
**1031** A340 60p multi .40 .20

**1985, Apr. 27**
**1032** A341 285p multi 3.00 1.50

World Post Day.

APU Building, Damascus — A342

**1985, Apr. 27** ***Perf. 12½***
**1033** A342 245p multi 2.50 1.25

Arab Parliamentary Union, 10th Anniv.

Natl. Flag, Map of Arab Countries A343

**1985** ***Perf. 12½x12***
**1034** A343 50p multi .50 .25

Arab League.

Re-election of President Assad A344

**1985, Mar. 12** ***Perf. 12½***
**1035** A344 200p multi 1.25 .70
**1036** A344 300p multi 2.00 1.00
**1037** A344 500p multi 3.25 1.75
*a.* Souvenir sheet of 3, #1035-1037, imperf. 7.00 5.50
*Nos. 1035-1037 (3)* 6.50 3.45

Arab Postal Union, 12th Congress, Damascus A345

**1985, Aug. 12** ***Perf. 12x12½***
**1038** A345 60p multi .60 .30

Labor Day — A346

**1985, Aug. 12** ***Perf. 12½***
**1039** A346 60p Order of Labor .60 .30

32nd Intl. Fair, Damascus A347

**1986, Feb. 1** **Litho.** ***Perf. 12½***
**1040** A347 60p multi .50 .25

2nd Scientific Symposium — A348

**1985, Nov. 16** ***Perf. 12½***
**1041** A348 60p Locomotives .60 .30

UN Child Survival Campaign A349

**1985, Nov. 16** ***Perf. 12½x12***
**1042** A349 60p Malnourished child .50 .25

UN, 40th Anniv. — A350

**1985, Nov. 16** ***Perf. 12x12½***
**1043** A350 245p multi 2.25 1.10

November 16th Movement, 15th Anniv. — A351

**1985, Nov. 16** ***Perf. 12½***
**1044** A351 60p Pres. Assad, highway .50 .25

Abdul Rahman Dakhei in Andalusia, 1200th Anniv. A352

**1986, Feb. 1** ***Perf. 12½x12***
**1045** A352 60p beige & brn .60 .30

Tulips — A353

World Traffic Day — A355

Dental Congress, Damascus — A354

**1986, Feb. 1** ***Perf. 12½***
**1046** A353 30p multi .30 .20
**1047** A353 60p multi, diff. .60 .30

Intl. Flower Show, Damascus.

**1986** ***Perf. 12½x12***
**1048** A354 110p yel, grysh grn & bl 1.10 .55

**1986** ***Perf. 12x12½***
**1049** A355 330p multi 3.00 1.50

Syrian Investment Certificates, 15th Anniv. — A357

Day of Internal Security Forces — A359

Liberation of Al-Kuneitra, 12th Anniv. — A358

**1986** **Litho.** ***Perf. 12x11½***
**1055** A357 100p multi 1.00 .50

**1986** **Litho.** ***Perf. 11½x12***
**1056** A358 110p Government Building .75 .40

**1986** ***Perf. 12x11½***
**1057** A359 110p multi .75 .40

Labor Day — A360

1986 World Cup Soccer Championships, Mexico — A361

**1986, Aug. 12**

**1058** A360 330p multi 1.25 .60

**1986, July 7**

**1059** A361 330p multi 3.25 1.75
**1060** A361 370p multi 3.50 1.90

**Booklet Stamp**
**Size: 105x80mm**
***Imperf***

**1061** A361 500p Hemispheres, ball 5.00 2.50
*Nos. 1059-1061 (3)* 11.75 6.15

Pres. Hafez al Assad — A362

**1986-90 Litho. *Perf. 12x11½***

| No. | Type | Value | Color | Unused | Used |
|---|---|---|---|---|---|
| **1068** | A362 | 10p | rose | .20 | .20 |
| **1069** | A362 | 30p | dl ultra | .20 | .20 |
| **1070** | A362 | 50p | claret | .40 | .20 |
| **1071** | A362 | 100p | brt lt bl | .65 | .30 |
| **1072** | A362 | 150p | brn vio | 1.40 | .65 |
| **1073** | A362 | 175p | violet | 1.60 | .80 |
| **1074** | A362 | 200p | pale red brn | 1.40 | .65 |
| **1075** | A362 | 300p | brt rose lil | 2.00 | 1.00 |
| **1076** | A362 | 500p | orange | 3.25 | 1.60 |
| **1077** | A362 | 550p | pink | 5.00 | 2.50 |
| **1078** | A362 | 600p | dull grn | 5.25 | 2.75 |
| **1079** | A362 | 1000p | brt pink | 6.50 | 3.25 |
| **1080** | A362 | 2000p | pale grn | 13.00 | 6.50 |
| | *Nos. 1068-1080 (13)* | | | 40.85 | 20.60 |

Issued: 150p, 175p, 550p, 600p, 1988; 50p, 9/30/90.

Intl. Day for Solidarity with the Palestinian People — A363

Mothers' Day — A364

**1986, Aug. 7 Litho.**

**1081** A363 110p multi 1.10 .55

**1986, Aug. 7**

**1082** A364 100p multi 1.00 .50

March 8 Revolution, 23rd Anniv. — A365

**1986, Aug. 7 *Perf. 11½x12***

**1083** A365 110p multi 1.10 .55

Arab Post Day A366

**1986, Aug. 7**

**1084** A366 110p multi 1.10 .55

A367

33rd Intl. Damascus Fair A368

**1986, Dec. 9 Litho. *Perf. 11½x12***

**1085** A367 110p multi .90 .45
**1086** A368 330p multi 2.50 .60

14th Intl. Flower Show, Damascus — A369

Various flowers.

**1986, Oct. 11 *Perf. 12½***

**1087** Strip of 5 6.50 5.00
*a.* A369 10p multi .20 .20
*b.* A369 50p multi .50 .25
*c.* A369 100p multi 1.00 .50
*d.* A369 110p multi 1.10 .60
*e.* A369 330p multi 3.50 1.75

Syria-Soviet Joint Space Project — A370

World Children's Day — A371

**1986, Nov. 16 Litho. *Perf. 12½***

**1088** A370 330p multi 3.50 1.75

**1986 *Perf. 12x12½, 12½x12***

**1089** A371 330p shown 1.75 .90
**1090** A371 330p Youth art exhibition, horiz. 1.75 .90

World Post Day A372

**1986, Jan. 28 *Perf. 12½x12***

**1091** A372 330p multi 1.75 .90

Intl. Tourism Day A373

Women wearing folk costumes, landmarks.

**1986**

**1092** A373 330p multi 1.75 .90
**1093** A373 370p multi 2.00 1.00

Pres. Assad, Tishreen Palace — A374

**1986, Nov. 16 Litho. *Perf. 12½***

**1094** A374 110p multi 1.25 .60

Nov. 16 Corrective Movement.

March 8th Revolution, 24th Anniv. — A375

**1987, Mar. 6**

**1095** A375 100p multi .60 .30

Intl. Peace Year — A376

**1987, Mar. 8 *Perf. 12x11½***

**1096** A376 370p multi 2.25 1.25

Arab Baath Socialist Party, 40th Anniv. A377

**1987, Apr. 7 Litho. *Perf. 12½***

**1097** A377 100p multi .60 .30

Arab Post Day, 35th Anniv. A378

**1987, May 1 *Perf. 11½x12***

**1098** A378 110p multi .70 .35

Evacuation, Day, 41st Anniv. — A379

**1987, Apr. 17 *Perf. 12½x12***

**1099** A379 100p multi .60 .30

Labor Day — A380

Al-Kuneitra Monument A382

Hitteen's Battle, 800th Anniv. — A381

**1987, May 1 *Perf. 12x11½***

**1100** A380 330p multi 2.00 1.00

**1987, June 25 Litho. *Perf. 12½***

**1101** A381 110p multi 1.00 .45

**1987, June 25 *Perf. 12x11½***

**1102** A382 100p multi .65 .30

Child Vaccination Campaign — A383

**1987, June 25 *Perf. 11½x12***

**1103** A383 100p multi .50 .30
**1104** A383 330p multi 2.00 1.10

A384

A385

Syrian-Soviet Joint Space Flight, July 22-30 — A386

Designs: No. 1105, Launch, July 22. No. 1106, Docking at space station, July 24. No. 1107, Landing, July 30, vert. No. 1108a, Lift-off. No. 1108b, Parachute landing. No. 1108c, Docked at space station. No. 1108d, Cosmonauts.

***Perf. 12½, 11½x12, 12x11½***

**1987** **Litho.**

**1105** A384 330p multi 2.00 1.00
**1106** A385 330p multi 2.00 1.00
**1107** A385 330p multi 2.00 1.00
*Nos. 1105-1107 (3)* 6.00 3.00

**Souvenir Sheet**

***Imperf***

**1108** Sheet of 4 10.00 10.00
***a.-d.*** A386 300p, any single 2.25 2.25

6th Conference of Arab Ministers of Culture A387

**1987, Apr. 21** **Litho.** ***Perf. 12½***

**1109** A387 330p dull blue grn & blk 3.00 1.50

President Assad Conversing with Syrian Cosmonaut — A388

**1987, Aug. 12**

**1110** A388 500p multi 3.50 1.75

10th Mediterranean Games, Latakia — A389

Designs: 100p, Gymnastic rings, weight lifting, vert. 330p, Phoenician sailing ship. 370p, Flags spelling "SYRIA." No. 1115a, Emblem, gymnastics. No. 1115b, Emblem, weight lifting. No. 1115c, Emblem, tennis. No. 1115d, Emblem, soccer.

***Perf. 12x11½, 11½x12***

**1987, Sept. 10**

**1111** A389 100p brt rose lil & blk .70 .35
**1112** A389 110p shown .75 .40

**Size: 58x28mm**

***Perf. 12½***

**1113** A389 330p multi 2.25 1.10
**1114** A389 370p multi 2.50 1.25
*Nos. 1111-1114 (4)* 6.20 3.10

**Souvenir Sheet**

***Imperf***

**1115** Sheet of 4 7.75 7.75
***a.-d.*** A389 300p any single 1.90 1.90

34th Intl. Damascus Fair — A390

Arbor Day — A392

Intl. Flower Show, Damascus A391

**1987** ***Perf. 12x11½***

**1116** A390 330p multi 2.00 1.00

**1987, Oct. 20** ***Perf. 11½x12***

**1117** A391 330p Poppies 1.90 1.00
**1118** A391 370p Gentian 2.00 1.00

**1987, Oct. 20** ***Perf. 12x11½***

**1119** A392 330p multi 2.00 1.00

Army Day — A393

Intl. Palestine Day — A394

**1987, Oct. 20** **Litho.** ***Perf. 12x11½***

**1120** A393 100p multi .60 .30

**1987, Nov. 16**

**1121** A394 500p multi 3.50 1.75

Corrective Movement, 17th Anniv. — A395

**1987, Nov. 16** ***Perf. 12½***

**1122** A395 150p Assad waving to crowd 1.00 .50

World Post Day — A396

**1988, Mar. 8** **Litho.** ***Perf. 12½x12***

**1123** A396 500p multi 3.00 1.50

Intl. Tourism Day A397

Women wearing folk costumes and: No. 1124, Palmyra Ruins. No. 1125, Reconstructed Roman amphitheater, Busra.

**1988, Feb. 25** **Litho.** ***Perf. 11½x12***

**1124** A397 500p multi 3.00 1.50
**1125** A397 500p multi 3.00 1.50

See Nos. 1147-1148, 1178-1179.

Intl. Children's Day — A398

**1988, Feb. 27** ***Perf. 12½***

**1126** A398 500p multi 3.00 1.50

March 8th Revolution, 25th Anniv. — A399

Mothers' Day — A400

**1988, Mar. 15** **Litho.** ***Perf. 12x11½***

**1127** A399 150p multi 1.00 .50

**Size: 110x81mm**

***Imperf***

**1128** A399 500p multi, diff. 4.75 4.75

No. 1128 pictures vignette like 150p without denomination, in diff. colors, and Arab Revolt flag, text, outline map; denomination at LR in sheet.

**1988, Apr. 12** **Litho.** ***Perf. 12x12½***

**1129** A400 500p multi 3.00 1.50

Arab Post Day A401

**1988, Apr. 17** ***Perf. 12½x12***

**1130** A401 150p multi 1.00 .50

1946 Evacuation A402

Labor Day — A403

**1988, Apr. 17** ***Perf. 12x12½***

**1131** A402 150p multi 1.00 .50

**1988, May 1**

**1132** A403 550p multi 3.00 1.50

Intl. Flower Show, Damascus A404

Arab Engineers' Union — A405

**1988, May 25** ***Perf. 12x11½***

**1133** A404 550p Tiger Lily 3.25 1.60
**1134** A404 600p Carnations 3.75 1.90

**1988, May 25**

**1135** A405 150p multi 1.00 .50

A406

A407

**1988, Aug. 28 Litho. *Perf. 12x11½***
**1136** A406 600p blk, grn & olive 3.50 1.75
Intl. Children's Day.

**1988, Aug. 28 *Perf. 12½***
**1137** A407 550p multi 3.00 1.50
Restoration of San'a, Yemen Arab Republic.

Ebla Intl. Symposium on Archaeology of Idlib — A408

**1988, Aug. 28**
**1138** A408 175p Hieroglyphic tablet 1.00 .50
**1139** A408 550p Bas-relief (votive basin) 3.00 1.50
**1140** A408 600p Gold statue, 3000 B.C. 3.50 1.75
*Nos. 1138-1140 (3)* 7.50 3.75

1988 Summer Olympics, Seoul A409

**1988, Sept. 17 *Perf. 11½x12***
**1141** A409 550p Cycling 3.50 1.60
**1142** A409 600p Soccer 3.75 1.75

**Size: 81x61mm**

***Imperf***

**1143** A409 1200p Emblem, character trademark 12.50 12.50
*Nos. 1141-1143 (3)* 19.75 15.85

35th Intl. Fair, Damascus A410

WHO, 40th Anniv. — A411

**1988, Aug. 28 *Perf. 12x11½***
**1144** A410 600p multi 3.50 1.75

**1988, Aug. 28 Litho. *Perf. 12x11½***
**1145** A411 600p multi 3.25 1.60

Arab Scouting Movement, 50th Anniv. — A412

**1988, Sept. 17 *Perf. 12½x12***
**1146** A412 150p multi 1.50 .75

**Tourism Type of 1988**

Women wearing folk costumes and: 550p, Euphrates Bridge, Deir-ez-Zor. 600p, The Tetrapylon, Latakia.

**1988, Oct. 18**
**1147** A397 550p multi 3.25 1.60
**1148** A397 600p multi 3.50 1.75

World Post Day — A413

Arbor Day — A414

**1988, Dec. 7 Litho. *Perf. 12x12½***
**1149** A413 600p multi 3.50 1.75

**1988, Nov. 16**
**1150** A414 600p multi 3.50 1.75

Shelter for the Homeless — A415

**1988-89 *Perf. 12½x12***
**1151** A415 150p Arab Housing Day .65 .35
**1151A** A415 175p Intl. Year of Shelter for the Homeless 1.25 .60
**1152** A415 550p World Housing Day 2.50 1.25
**1153** A415 600p as No. 1151A 2.75 1.50
*Nos. 1151-1153 (4)* 7.15 3.70

The IYSH emblem is pictured on the 175p, 550p and 600p.
Issued: 175p, 2/6/89; others, 10/18/88.

Al-Assad University Hospital — A416

**1988, Nov. 16 Litho. *Perf. 12½***
**1154** A416 150p multi .90 .45
Corrective Movement, 18th anniv.

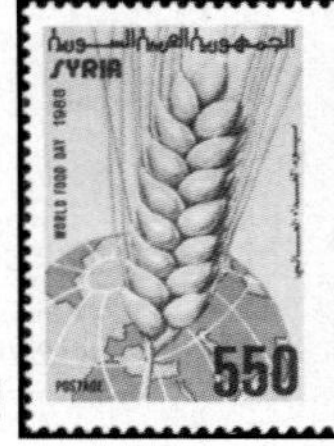
World Food Day — A417

**1988, Oct. 18 *Perf. 12x12½***
**1155** A417 550p multi 2.75 1.40

Birds A418

**1989, Mar. 21 Litho. *Perf. 11½x12***
**1156** A418 600p Goldfinch 1.50 .75
**1157** A418 600p Turtledove 1.50 .75
**1158** A418 600p Bee eater 1.50 .75
*Nos. 1156-1158 (3)* 4.50 2.25

Jawaharlal Nehru, 1st Prime Minister of Independent India — A419

**1989, Mar. 8 *Perf. 12½***
**1159** A419 550p brn & chest 1.10 .55

Mothers' Day — A420

**1989, Mar. 21**
**1160** A420 550p multi 1.10 .55

Teacher's Day A421

**1989, Mar. 8 Litho. *Perf. 11½x12***
**1161** A421 175p multi .70 .35

5th General Congress of the Union of Women A422

**1989, Mar. 8 *Perf. 12½***
**1162** A422 150p multi .30 .20

March 8th Revolution, 26th Anniv. — A423

**1989, Mar. 8 *Perf. 11½x12***
**1163** A423 150p multi .30 .20

Arab Board for Medical Specializations, 10th Anniv. — A424

**1989, Feb. 6 *Perf. 12½***
**1164** A424 175p multi .60 .30

1946 Evacuation of British and French Troops — A425

**1989, Apr. 17 Litho. *Perf. 11½x12***
**1165** A425 150p multi .40 .20

Intl. Flower Show, Damascus A426

**1989, June 3 *Perf. 12½***
**1166** Strip of 5 5.00 4.00
*a.* A426 150p Snapdragon .30 .20
*b.* A426 150p Canaria .30 .20
*c.* A426 450p Compositae .90 .45
*d.* A426 850p Clematis sackmani 1.75 .85
*e.* A426 900p Gesneriaceae 1.75 .90

A427

A428

**1989, May 1** ***Perf. 12x11½***
**1167** A427 850p blue grn & blk 1.75 .90

Labor Day.

**1989, June 6 Litho.** ***Perf. 12x11½***
**1168** A428 175p multi .50 .25

13th General Congress of the Arab Teachers' Union.

Arab Post Day — A429

Liberation of Al-Kuneitra, 15th Anniv. — A430

**1989, June 6**
**1169** A429 175p multi .50 .25

**1989, June 26**
**1170** A430 450p multi 1.25 .60

17th Congress of the Arab Advocates Union A431

**1989, June 19** ***Perf. 11½x12***
**1171** A431 175p multi .50 .25

World Post Day A432

**1989, June 26**
**1172** A432 550p multi 1.50 .75

World Telecommunications Day — A433

**1989, June 6**
**1173** A433 550p multi 1.50 .75

Interparliamentary Union, Cent. — A434

**1989. July 12** ***Perf. 12½***
**1174** A434 900p multi 2.50 1.25

Butterflies A435

**1989, June 6**
**1175** A435 550p Small white 1.50 .75
**1176** A435 550p Clouded yellow 1.50 .75
**1177** A435 550p Painted Lady 1.50 .75
*Nos. 1175-1177 (3)* 4.50 2.25

Intl. Tourism Day Type of 1988

Women wearing folk costumes and: 550p, Jaabar Castle, Rakka. 600p, Temple of the Bell, Palmyra.

**1989, Oct. 16 Litho.** ***Perf. 11½x12***
**1178** A397 550p multicolored 3.75 1.75
**1179** A397 600p multicolored 4.00 2.00

36th Intl. Fair, Damascus A436

**1989, Oct. 16** ***Perf. 12x11½***
**1180** A436 450p multicolored 3.00 1.50

Fish A437

**1989, Oct. 24** ***Perf. 11½x12***
**1181** A437 550p Carp 3.75 1.75
**1182** A437 600p Trout 4.00 2.00

2nd Anniv. of the Palestinian Uprising — A438

**1989, Oct. 24** ***Perf. 12x11½***
**1183** A438 550p Child's drawing 3.75 1.75

Corrective Movement, 19th Anniv. — A439

**1989, Nov. 16 Litho.** ***Perf. 12½x12***
**1184** A439 150p multicolored 1.00 .50

A440

A441

**1990, Feb. 13 Litho.** ***Perf. 12x11½***
**1185** A440 850p multicolored 1.00 .50

World Children's Day.

**1990**
**1186** A441 600p multicolored .70 .35

March 8th Revolution, 27th anniv.

Revolutionary Youth Union A442

**1990** ***Perf. 12½***
**1187** A442 150p multicolored .20 .20

World Food Day A443

**1990, Feb. 13 Litho.** ***Perf. 11½x12***
**1188** A443 850p multicolored 1.00 .50

Dated 1989.

Evacuation of British and French Troops, 1946 — A444

**1990, Apr. 17** ***Perf. 12x11½***
**1189** A444 175p multicolored .20 .20

Mother's Day — A445

**1990, Apr. 17** ***Perf. 12½***
**1190** A445 550p multicolored .65 .30

Labor Day — A446

**1990, May 1 Litho.** ***Perf. 12x12½***
**1191** A446 550p multicolored .75 .35

World Cup Soccer Championships, Italy — A447

***Perf. 11½x12, 12x11½***
**1990, June 8** **Litho.**
**1192** A447 550p shown .40 .20
**1193** A447 550p Denomination at right .40 .20
**1194** A447 600p Map, soccer ball, vert. .45 .25
*Nos. 1192-1194 (3)* 1.25 .65

**Miniature Sheet**

***Imperf***

**1195** A447 1300p Stadium 3.50 1.75

Intl. Flower Show, Damascus A448

**1990, May 27** ***Perf. 12x11½***
**1196** A448 600p Lily 1.10 .50
**1197** A448 600p Pastelkleurig 1.10 .50
**1198** A448 600p Marigold 1.10 .50
**1199** A448 600p Viburnum opulus 1.10 .50
**1200** A448 600p Swan river daisy 1.10 .50
*Nos. 1196-1200 (5)* 5.50 2.50

World Health Day — A449

**1990, May 1 Litho. *Perf. 12½***

**1201** A449 600p multicolored 2.50 1.25

Liberation of Al-Kuneitra, 16th Anniv. — A450

Intl. Literacy Year — A451

**1990, June 26 *Perf. 12x11½***

**1202** A450 550p multicolored 2.50 1.25

**1990, June 26**

**1203** A451 550p multicolored 2.25 1.10

UN Conference on Least Developed Countries — A452

**1990, July 10 *Perf. 11½x12***

**1204** A452 600p multicolored 2.40 1.25

37th Damascus Intl. Fair — A453

Arbor Day — A455

World Meteorology Day — A454

**1990, Aug. 28 *Perf. 12x11½***

**1205** A453 550p multicolored 2.25 1.10

**1990, Aug. 28 *Perf. 11½x12***

**1206** A454 450p multicolored 1.90 .95

**1990, Oct. 30 *Perf. 12x11½***

**1207** A455 550p multicolored 2.25 1.10

World Food Day — A456

**1990, Oct. 30 *Perf. 12½***

**1208** A456 850p multicolored 3.25 1.75

Al Maqdisi, Cartographer A457

**1990, Nov. 6 *Perf. 12x11½***

**1209** A457 550p multicolored 2.25 1.10

A458

A459

Pres. Hafez al Assad A460

**1990, Nov. 16 Litho. *Perf. 11½***

| | | | | | |
|---|---|---|---|---|---|
| **1210** | A458 | 50p | claret | .20 | .20 |
| **1211** | A458 | 70p | gray | .25 | .20 |
| **1212** | A458 | 100p | blue | .35 | .20 |
| **1213** | A458 | 150p | brown | .60 | .30 |

***Perf. 12x11½***

| | | | | | |
|---|---|---|---|---|---|
| **1214** | A459 | 175p | multicolored | .70 | .35 |
| **1215** | A459 | 300p | multicolored | 1.25 | .55 |
| **1216** | A459 | 550p | multicolored | 2.25 | 1.10 |
| **1217** | A459 | 600p | multicolored | 2.40 | 1.25 |

***Perf. 11½x12***

| | | | | | |
|---|---|---|---|---|---|
| **1219** | A460 | 1000p | multicolored | 4.00 | 2.00 |
| **1220** | A460 | 1500p | multicolored | 6.00 | 3.00 |
| **1222** | A460 | 2000p | multicolored | 8.00 | 4.00 |
| **1224** | A460 | 2500p | multicolored | 10.00 | 5.00 |
| | *Nos. 1210-1224 (12)* | | | 36.00 | 18.15 |

This may be an expanding set. Numbers will change if necessary.

**1992, May 19 Litho. *Perf. 11½***

**Without Date at Right**

| | | | | | |
|---|---|---|---|---|---|
| **1225** | A458 | 150p | brown | .60 | .30 |
| **1225A** | A458 | 300p | violet | 1.25 | .60 |
| **1225B** | A458 | 350p | gray | 1.40 | .70 |
| **1225C** | A458 | 400p | red | 1.60 | .80 |
| | *Nos. 1225-1225C (4)* | | | 4.85 | 2.40 |

Souvenir Sheet

Corrective Movement, 20th Anniv. — A461

a, Pres. Assad with children. b, Assad addressing crowd. c, Assad, memorial. d, Assad, dam.

**1990, Nov. 16 *Imperf.***

**1227** A461 550p Sheet of 4, #a.-d. 9.00 9.00

UN Development Program, 40th Anniv. — A462

**1990, Dec. 11 *Perf. 11½x12***

**1228** A462 550p multicolored 2.25 1.10

Arab Civil Aviation Day A463

**1990, Dec. 11**

**1229** A463 175p multicolored 1.00 .50

World Post Day — A464

Intl. Children's Day — A465

**1990, Dec. 11 *Perf. 12x11½***

**1230** A464 550p multicolored 2.25 1.10

**1990, Dec. 11**

**1231** A465 550p multicolored 2.25 1.10

Arab-Spanish Cultural Symposium A466

World AIDS Day — A467

**1990, Dec. 24**

**1232** A466 550p multicolored 2.25 1.10

**1990, Dec. 24**

**1233** A467 550p multicolored 2.25 1.10

March 8th Revolution, 28th Anniv. — A468

**1991, Mar. 8 Litho. *Perf. 11½x12***

**1234** A468 150p multicolored .60 .30

Butterflies A469

**1991, Mar. 17 *Perf. 12½***

| | | | | | |
|---|---|---|---|---|---|
| **1235** | A469 | 550p | Small tortoise-shell | 2.25 | 1.10 |
| **1236** | A469 | 550p | Changeful great mars | 2.25 | 1.10 |
| **1237** | A469 | 550p | Papillion machaon | 2.25 | 1.10 |
| | *Nos. 1235-1237 (3)* | | | 6.75 | 3.30 |

Birds — A470

Mother's Day — A471

**1991, Mar. 17** ***Perf. 12x11½***
**1238** A470 600p Golden oriole 2.40 1.25
**1239** A470 600p European roller 2.40 1.25
**1240** A470 600p House sparrow 2.40 1.25
*Nos. 1238-1240 (3)* 7.20 3.75

**1991, Mar. 21**
**1241** A471 550p multicolored 2.25 1.10

1946 Evacuation of British and French Troops — A472

**1991, Apr. 17** ***Perf. 11½x12***
**1242** A472 150p multicolored .60 .30

Labor Day A473

**1991, May 1**
**1243** A473 550p multicolored 2.25 1.10

Intl. Flower Show, Damascus — A474

**1991, July 8** ***Perf. 12x12½***
**1244** A474 550p Narcissus 2.25 1.10
**1245** A474 600p Monarda didyma 2.40 1.25

Liberation of Kuneitra, 17th Anniv. A475

**1991, July 22** ***Perf. 11½x12***
**1246** A475 550p multicolored 2.25 1.10

11th Mediterranean Games, Athens — A476

**1991, July 22**
**1247** A476 550p Running 2.25 1.10
**1248** A476 550p Soccer 2.25 1.10
**1249** A476 600p Equestrian 2.25 1.25

**Size: 80x64mm**

***Imperf***

**1250** A476 1300p Dolphins playing water polo 5.25 5.25
*Nos. 1247-1250 (4)* 12.00 8.70

38th Damascus Intl. Fair — A477

**1991, Aug. 28** ***Perf. 12x12½***
**1251** A477 550p multicolored 2.25 1.10

Intl. Tourism Day A478

Designs: 450p, Woman at Khan Asaad Pasha El Azem. 550p, Woman at Castle of Arwad Island.

**1991, Sept. 27** ***Perf. 11½x12***
**1252** A478 450p multicolored 1.90 .95
**1253** A478 550p multicolored 2.25 1.10

Housing Day — A479

Intl. Children's Day — A480

**1991, Oct. 7** ***Perf. 12x11½***
**1254** A479 175p multicolored 1.00 .50

**1991, Oct. 16**
**1255** A480 600p multicolored 2.40 1.25

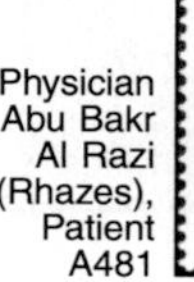
Physician Abu Bakr Al Razi (Rhazes), Patient A481

**1991, Nov. 2** **Litho.** ***Perf. 12½x12***
**1256** A481 550p multicolored 2.25 1.10

31st Science Week.

World Post Day A482

**1991, Nov. 12**
**1257** A482 550p multicolored 2.25 1.10

World Food Day A483

**1991, Nov. 12**
**1258** A483 550p multicolored 2.25 1.10

Tomb of Unknown Soldier, Damascus A484

**1991, Nov. 16** ***Perf. 12½***
**1259** A484 600p multicolored 2.40 1.25

**Size: 65x80mm**

***Imperf***

**1260** A484 1000p multicolored 4.00 2.00

Corrective Movement, 21st Anniv. — A485

Illustration reduced.

**1991, Nov. 16** ***Imperf.***
**1261** A485 2500p multicolored 10.00 5.00

Protect the Environment — A486

**1991, Nov. 20** ***Perf. 12½x12***
**1262** A486 175p multicolored .70 .35

World Telecommunications Fair — A487

**1991, Nov. 20** ***Perf. 12x12½***
**1263** A487 600p multicolored 2.40 1.25

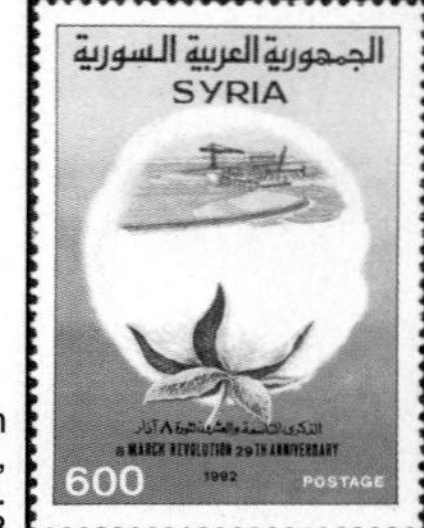
March 8th Revolution, 29th Anniv. A488

**1992, Mar. 8** **Litho.** ***Perf. 12½***
**1264** A488 600p multicolored 2.40 1.25

Re-election of Pres. Assad — A489

**1992, Mar. 12** **Litho.** ***Imperf.***
**1265** A489 5000p shown 20.00 10.00

**Size: 100x85mm**

**1266** A489 5000p inscription at right 20.00 10.00

Nos. 1265-1266 incorporate designs of #1036, C496 & C506.

Baath Party, 45th Anniv. A490

**1992, Apr. 7** ***Perf. 12½x12***
**1267** A490 850p multicolored 3.50 1.75

Labor Day — A491

Mother's Day — A492

**1992, May 1** ***Perf. 12x12½***
**1268** A491 900p multicolored 3.50 1.75

**1992, May 19**
**1269** A492 900p multicolored 3.50 1.75

Evacuation of British and French Troops, 46th Anniv. — A493

**1992, May 19** ***Perf. 12½x12***
**1270** A493 900p multicolored 3.50 1.75

Traffic Safety Day — A494

Intl. Flower Show, Damascus A495

**1992, May 19** ***Perf. 12x12½***
**1271** A494 850p multicolored 3.50 1.75

***Perf. 11½x12, 12x11½***
**1992, July 5** **Litho.**

Designs: 300p, Linum mucronatum, horiz. 800p, Yucca filamentosa. 900p, Zinnia elegans.

**1272** A495 300p multicolored 1.25 .65
**1273** A495 800p blue & multi 3.25 1.60
**1274** A495 900p multicolored 3.50 1.75
*Nos. 1272-1274 (3)* 8.00 4.00

1992 Summer Olympics, Barcelona A496

No. 1275: a, 150p, Team handball. b, 150p, Running. c, 450p, Swimming. d, 750p, Wrestling. 5000p, Incorporates designs of Nos. 1275a-1275d.

**1992, July 25** **Litho.** ***Perf. 12x11½***
**1275** A496 Strip of 4, #a.-d. 6.00 5.00

***Imperf***
**Size: 80x124mm**
**1276** A496 5000p multicolored 20.00 10.00

Anti-Smoking Campaign A497

39th Intl. Damascus Fair — A498

**1992, Aug. 28** ***Perf. 12x12½***
**1277** A497 750p multicolored 3.00 1.50

**1992, Aug. 28**
**1278** A498 900p multicolored 3.50 1.75

7th Arab Games, Damascus — A499

Designs: a, 750p, Soccer. b, 850p, Pommel horse. c, 900p, Pole vault.

**1992, Sept. 4** ***Perf. 12½***
**1279** A499 Strip of 3, #a.-c. 10.00 5.00

World Post Day — A500

World Children's Day — A501

**1992, Oct. 9** ***Perf. 12x12½***
**1280** A500 600p multicolored 2.40 1.25

**1992, Nov. 7** ***Perf. 12x11½***
**1281** A501 850p multicolored 3.50 1.75

Sebtt El Mardini (826-912) A502

**1992, Nov. 7** **Litho.** ***Perf. 12x11½***
**1282** A502 850p multicolored 3.50 1.75

1992 Special Olympics, Madrid A503

**1992, Nov. 7** ***Perf. 12½***
**1283** A503 850p multicolored 3.50 1.75

Corrective Movement, 22nd Anniv. — A504

**1992, Nov. 16** ***Perf. 11½x12***
**1284** A504 450p multicolored 1.75 .90

Arbor Day — A505

**1992, Dec. 31** ***Perf. 12x12½***
**1285** A505 600p multicolored 2.40 1.25

2nd Intl. Conference of PACO — A506

Design: 1150p, Eye surrounded by scenes of day and night, rainbow.

**1993, May 12** **Litho.** ***Perf. 12***
**1286** A506 1100p multicolored 1.00 .50

**Size: 35½x24mm**
***Perf. 11½x12***
**1287** A506 1150p multicolored 1.10 .55

Syrian Ophthamological Society, 25th anniv. (#1287).

March 8th Revolution, 30th Anniv. — A507

**1993, Mar. 8** **Litho.** ***Perf. 11½x12***
**1288** A507 1100p multicolored .80 .40

Butterflies A508

Designs: a, 1000p, Common blue. b, 1500p, Silver-washed fritillary. c, 2500p, Precis orithya.

**1993, Mar. 13**
**1289** A508 Strip of 3, #a.-c. 4.75 4.75

Mother's Day — A509

**1993, Apr. 17** ***Perf. 12x11½***
**1290** A509 1100p multicolored .80 .40

Evacuation of British and French Troops, 47th Anniv. — A510

**1993, Apr. 17** ***Perf. 11½x12***
**1291** A510 1100p multicolored .80 .40

A511

**1993, Apr. 17** **Litho.** ***Perf. 11½x12***
**1292** A511 2500p multicolored 1.75 .85

Agricultural Reform, 25th Anniv. — A512

**1993, Apr. 20** **Litho.** ***Perf. 11½x12***
**1293** A512 1150p multicolored .90 .45

A513

A514

**1993, May 1** ***Perf. 12x11½***
**1294** A513 1100p multicolored .80 .40

Labor day.

**1993, June 17 Litho. *Perf. 12x11½***

Intl. Flower Show, Damascus: a, 1000p, Alcea setosa. b, 1100p, Primulaceae. c, 1150p, Gesneriaceae.

**1295** A514 Strip of 3, #a.-c. 2.25 2.25

Tourism A515

**1993, Sept. 27 *Perf. 11½x12***

**1296** A515 1000p Woman, prism tomb 1.00 .50

World Post Day A516

**1993, Oct. 9 *Perf. 12½x12***

**1297** A516 1000p multicolored 1.00 .50

World Child Day A517

**1993, Nov. 6 *Perf. 11½x12***

**1298** A517 1150p multicolored 1.10 .55

Ibn El Bittar, Chemist — A518

**1993, Nov. 6 *Perf. 12x11½***

**1299** A518 1150p multicolored 1.10 .55

Corrective Movement, 23rd Anniv. — A519

Illustration reduced.

**1993, Nov. 16 Litho. *Imperf.***

**1300** A519 2500p multicolored 2.50 2.50

Arabian Horses A520

**1994, Jan. Litho. *Perf. 12½***

**1301** A520 1000p shown .60 .30
**1302** A520 1000p White horse .60 .30
**1303** A520 1500p Tan horse .90 .45
**1304** A520 1500p Black horse .90 .45
*a.* Strip of 4, #1301-1304 3.00 3.00

Arbor Day A521

**1994, Jan. Litho. *Perf. 12½x12***

**1305** A521 1100p multicolored 1.75 .85

40th Intl. Damascus Fair A522

**1994, Jan.**

**1306** A522 1100p multicolored 1.75 .85

Basel Al Assad (1962-94) — A523

**1994, Mar. 1 *Perf. 12x12½***

**1307** A523 2500p multicolored 4.00 2.00

March 8th Revolution, 31st Anniv. — A524

a, Oranges. b, Mandarin oranges. c, Lemons.

**1994, Mar. 8 *Perf. 12½x12***

**1308** A524 1500p Strip of 3, #a.-c. 7.50 7.50

Evacuation of British and French Troops, 48th Anniv. — A525

**1994, Apr. 17**

**1309** A525 1800p multicolored 2.75 1.40

Mother's Day A526

**1994, May 1 Litho. *Perf. 12½x12***

**1310** A526 1800p multicolored 2.75 1.40

Labor Day A527

**1994, May 1**

**1311** A527 1700p multicolored 2.75 1.40

ILO, 75th Anniv. A528

**1994, June 1**

**1312** A528 1700p multicolored 2.75 1.40

1994 World Cup Soccer Championships, U.S. — A529

Various soccer plays.

**1994, June 17 *Perf. 12½***

**1313** A529 1700p Pair, #a.-b. 5.75 2.75

**Size: 80x80mm**

***Imperf***

**1314** A529 4000p multicolored 6.75 6.75

41st Intl. Fair, Damascus A530

Intl. Flower Show, Damascus A531

**1994, Aug. 3 Litho. *Perf. 12x12½***

**1315** A530 1800p multicolored 1.60 .80

**1994, Aug. 3 *Perf. 12x11½***

a, Daisies. b, Red flowers. c. Yellow flowers.

**1316** A531 1800p Strip of 3, #a.-c. 4.50 4.50

Intl. Olympic Committee, Cent. — A532

**1994, Aug. 3 *Perf. 11½x12***

**1317** A532 1700p multicolored 1.50 .75

Butterflies A533

a, Apollo (shown). b, Purple emperor, value at right. c, Birdwing, value at left.

**1994, Aug. 9 Litho. *Perf. 11½x12***

**1318** A533 1700p Strip of 3, #a.-c. 8.25 8.25

4th Natl. Census A534

**1994, Aug. 15**

**1319** A534 1000p multicolored 1.50 .75

Science Week A535

Design: £10, Al Kindi, philosopher.

**1994, Nov. 5 *Perf. 12½***

**1320** A535 £10 multicolored 1.50 .75

Corrective Movement, 24th Anniv. — A536

Illustration reduced.

**1994, Nov. 16 *Imperf.***

**1321** A536 £25 multicolored 6.50 6.50

ICAO, 50th Anniv. — A537

**1994, Dec. 7 Litho. *Perf. 12½***
**1322** A537 17p multicolored 1.50 .75

Martyr's Square A538

**1994, Dec. 7 Litho. *Perf. 11½x12***
**1323** A538 £50 purple 7.25 3.75

See Nos. 1472-1474, 1518, 1538.

Intl. Children's Day — A539

World Post Day — A540

**1994, Dec. 19 *Perf. 12x11½***
**1324** A539 £10 multicolored 1.50 .75

**1994, Dec. 19**
**1325** A540 £10 multicolored 1.50 .75

Intl. Tourism Day — A541

**1994, Dec. 19**
**1326** A541 £17 multicolored 2.50 1.25

March 8 Revolution, 32nd Anniv. — A542

**1995, Mar. 8 Litho. *Perf. 11½x12***
**1327** A542 £18 multicolored 2.75 1.40

Arab League, 50th Anniv. A543

**1995, Mar. 22 *Perf. 12½***
**1328** A543 £17 multicolored 2.50 1.25

World Water Day — A544

**1995, Apr. 9 Litho. *Perf. 12x12½***
**1329** A544 £17 multicolored 1.25 .60

Mother's Day A545

**1995, Apr. 9 Litho. *Perf. 12½x12***
**1330** A545 £17 multicolored 2.00 1.00

Arbor Day — A546

**1995, Apr. 9 Litho. *Perf. 12x12½***
**1331** A546 1800p multicolored 1.50 .75

A547

A548

**1995, Aug. 13 Litho. *Perf. 12x11½***
**1332** A547 £18 multicolored 2.75 1.40

UN, 50th anniv.

**1995, Aug. 21**
**1333** A548 £18 multicolored 2.75 1.40

4th World Conference on Women, Beijing.

Desert Festival, Tourism Day A549

**1995, June 25 *Perf. 12½x12***
**1334** A549 £18 multicolored 1.25 .65

A550

A551

**1995, June 25 *Perf. 12x12½***
**1335** A550 £10 Labor Day .75 .40

**1995, Apr. 30 Litho. *Perf. 12x11½***
**1336** A551 £17 multicolored 1.25 .60

Evacuation of British & French Troops, 49th anniv.

A552

A553

**1995, Apr. 30 Litho. *Perf. 12x11½***
**1337** A542 £17 multicolored 1.40 .70

Intl. Year of the Family.

**1995, Apr. 30 Litho. *Perf. 12x12½***
**1338** A553 £17 multicolored 2.00 1.00

Arab Apiculture Union, 1st anniv.

FAO, 50th Anniv. A554

**1995, June 25 *Perf. 12½x12***
**1339** A554 £15 multicolored 1.75 .85

42nd Intl. Fair, Damascus A555

**1995, Aug. 28 Litho. *Perf. 11½x12***
**1340** A555 £15 multicolored 1.50 .75

Int'l Flower Show, Damascus A556

**1995, July 30 Litho. *Perf. 12½***
**1341** A556 £10 Astilbe .50 .25
**1342** A556 £10 Evening primrose .50 .25
**1343** A556 £10 Blue carpet .50 .25
*a.* Strip of 3, #1341-1343 1.50 1.50

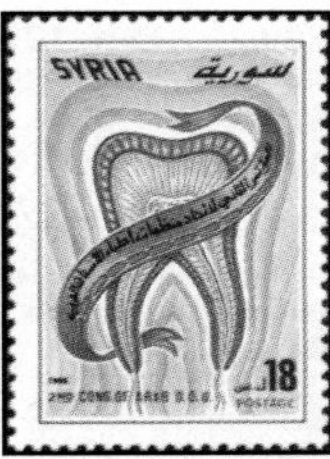
Second Congress of Arab Dentists' Assoc. — A557

**1995, Sept. 16 Litho. *Perf. 12x11½***
**1344** A557 £18 multicolored 1.50 .75

Syrian Army, 50th Anniv. A558

**1995, Oct. 2 Litho. *Perf. 11½x12***
**1345** A558 £18 multicolored 1.40 .70

World Post Day A559

**1995, Oct. 2 Litho. *Perf. 11½x12***
**1346** A559 £15 multicolored 1.60 .85

World Children's Day — A560

**1995, Oct. 2 *Perf. 12x11½***
**1347** A560 £18 multicolored 2.00 1.00

Ahmed ben Maged, Cartographer, 500th Death Anniv. — A561

**1995, Nov. 4 Litho. *Perf. 11½x12***
**1348** A561 £18 multicolored 2.00 1.00

Corrective Movement, 25th Anniv. A562

Design: £50, like #1349 with Nos. 1044, 720, 1227b, 903.

**1995, Nov. 11 Litho. *Perf. 12½***
**1349** A562 £10 multicolored 1.10 .55

***Imperf***
**Size: 100x64mm**
**1350** A562 £50 multicolored 5.50 2.75

Songbirds A563

Designs: a, Group on tree branch. b, One in snow, flower. c, One on fence rail.

**1995, Dec. 5 Litho. *Perf. 12½***
**1351** A563 £18 Strip of 3, #a.-c. 7.25 7.25

Louis Pasteur (1822-95) A564

**1995, Dec. 21 *Perf. 12½x12***
**1352** A564 £18 multicolored 2.00 1.00

March 8 Revolution, 33rd Anniv. — A565

**1996, Mar. 8 Litho. *Perf. 11½x12***
**1353** A565 £25 Hydro-electric plant 2.00 1.00

Evacuation Day, 50th Anniv. — A566

**1996, Apr. 17 *Perf. 12½***
**1354** A566 £10 black & multi .85 .40
**1355** A566 £25 bister & multi 2.00 1.00

**Size: 57x46mm**
***Imperf***
**1356** A566 £25 bis, blk, & multi *5.25 2.75*

Liberation of Kuneitra A567

**1996, June 26 Litho. *Perf. 11½x12***
**1357** A567 £10 multicolored .60 .30

1996 Summer Olympic Games, Atlanta A568

**1996, July 19 *Perf. 11½x12***
**1358** A568 £17 Wrestling 1.10 .55
**1359** A568 £17 Swimming 1.10 .55
**1360** A568 £17 Running 1.10 .55
*a.* Strip of 3, #1358-1360 3.25 3.25

**Size: 55x41mm**
***Imperf***
**1361** A568 £25 Soccer 1.60 .80
*Nos. 1358-1361 (4)* 4.90 2.45

Intl. Flower Show, Damascus A569

Cactus: No. 1362, Notocactus graessnerii. No. 1363, Mammilaria erythosperma.

**1996, July 1 Litho. *Perf. 12½***
**1362** A569 £18 multicolored 1.25 .65
**1363** A569 £18 multicolored 1.25 .65

Ba'ath Party, 50th Anniv. A570

**1996, July 1 *Perf. 11½x12***
**1364** A570 £18 multicolored 1.25 .65

Pres. Hafez al-Assad — A571

**1995 Litho. *Perf. 11½***
**1365** A571 100p bright blue .20 .20
**1366** A571 500p bright orange .55 .25
**1367** A571 £10 bright lilac 1.10 .55
**1368** A571 £17 rose lake 1.90 .95
**1369** A571 £18 slate green 2.00 1.00
*Nos. 1365-1369 (5)* 5.75 2.95

Issued: £10, 5/3; 100p, 500p, £17, £18, 12/31.

Arbor Day — A572

Mother's Day — A573

**1996, Mar. 8 Litho. *Perf. 12¼x12½***
**1370** A572 £17 multicolored .80 .40

**1996, May 1 *Perf. 12x11½***
**1370A** A573 £10 multicolored .50 .25

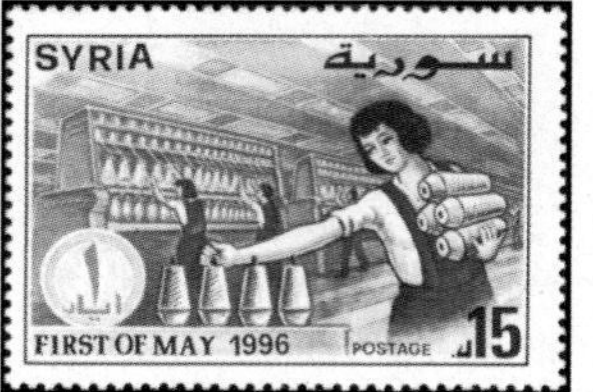
Labor Day — A574

**1996, May 1 *Perf. 12¼x12½***
**1371** A574 £15 multicolored .70 .35

Radio, Cent. — A575

**1996, Aug. 18 Litho. *Perf. 12½***
**1372** A575 £17 multicolored 1.10 .55

World AIDS Day — A576

43rd Intl. Fair, Damascus A577

**1996, Aug. 18 *Perf. 12x11½***
**1373** A576 £17 multicolored 1.10 .55

**1996, Aug. 28**
**1374** A577 £17 multicolored 1.10 .55

NICE, 5th Anniv. A578

**1996, Sept. 5 *Perf. 11½x12***
**1375** A578 £18 multicolored 1.10 .60

World Child Day — A579

World Post Day — A580

**1996, Oct. 9 *Perf. 12x11½***
**1376** A579 £10 multicolored .65 .30

**1996, Oct. 9**
**1377** A580 £17 multicolored 1.10 .55

UNICEF, 50th Anniv. — A581

**1996, Nov. 20**
**1378** A581 £17 multicolored 1.10 .55

36th Science Week — A582

Design: Musa Iben Shaker's sons.

**1996, Nov. 2 *Perf. 12½x12***
**1379** A582 £10 multicolored .65 .35

Corrective Movement, 26th Anniv. A583

**1996, Nov. 16** ***Perf. 12½***
**1380** A583 £10 multicolored .65 .35

**Size: 65x90mm**
***Imperf***

**1381** A583 £50 like No. 1380 3.25 1.60

Natl. Advance Party — A584

March 8 Revolution, 34th Anniv. — A585

**1997, Mar. 7** **Litho.** ***Perf. 12x11½***
**1382** A584 £3 multicolored .20 .20

**1997, Mar. 8**
**1383** A585 £15 multicolored 1.00 .50

Arbor Day — A586

**1996, Apr. 8** **Litho.** ***Perf. 12x12½***
**1384** A586 £10 multicolored .75 .40

Fish — A587

**1996, Apr. 8** ***Perf. 12½x12***
**1385** A587 £17 Two dorsal fins 1.00 .50
**1386** A587 £17 One dorsal fin 1.00 .50
*a.* Pair, #1385-1386 2.00 2.00

Mother's Day — A588

**1997, Apr. 8** ***Perf. 12x11½***
**1387** A588 £15 multicolored 1.00 .50

Baath Party Revolution, 50th Anniv. A589

**1997, Apr. 3** ***Perf. 12½***
**1388** A589 £25 multicolored 1.60 .80

**Size: 90x65mm**
***Imperf***

**1389** A589 £25 multicolored 1.60 .80

World Tourism Day — A590

**1997, Apr. 8** ***Perf. 12x11½***
**1390** A590 £17 multicolored 1.10 .60

Evacuation Day, 51st Anniv. — A591

**1997, Apr. 17** ***Perf. 11½x12***
**1391** A591 £15 multicolored 1.00 .50

Labor Day — A592

**1997, May 1** ***Perf. 12x11½***
**1392** A592 £15 multicolored 1.00 .50

World Book Day — A592a

**1997, June 16** **Litho.** ***Perf. 12½***
**1392A** A592a £10 multicolored .50 .25

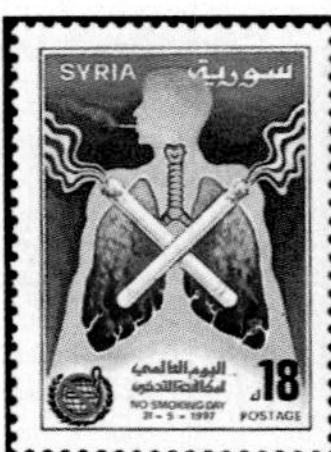
A592b

A593

**1997, June 16** ***Perf. 12x11½***
**1392B** A592b £18 multicolored .70 .35

No smoking day.

**1997, June 21** **Litho.** ***Perf. 12x11½***

No. 1393, Echino ereus. No. 1394, Iris.

**1393** A593 £18 multicolored 1.10 .60
**1394** A593 £18 multicolored 1.10 .60
*a.* Pair, #1393-1394 2.25 2.25

Intl. Flower Show, Damascus.
See Nos. 1412-1413.

4th Congress of Arab Denistry — A594

44th Intl. Fair, Damascus A595

**1997, Sept. 4**
**1395** A594 £10 multicolored .65 .35

**1997, Sept. 4**
**1396** A595 £17 multicolored 1.10 .55

World Post Day A596

**1997, Sept. 27** ***Perf. 11½x12***
**1397** A596 £17 multicolored 1.10 .55

World Children's Day A597

**1997, Sept. 27**
**1398** A597 £17 multicolored 1.10 .55

Intl. Tourism Day A598

**1997, Sept. 27**
**1399** A598 £17 multicolored 1.10 .55

37th Science Week — A599

**1997, Nov. 1** **Litho.** ***Perf. 12x11½***
**1400** A599 £17 multicolored 1.10 .55

Corrective Movement, 27th Anniv. A600

**1997, Nov. 16** ***Perf. 12½***
**1401** A600 £10 multicolored .70 .35

**Size: 92x67mm**
***Imperf***

**1402** A600 £50 like #1401 3.25 3.25

Islamic Conference, 30th Anniv. — A601

**1997, Dec. 9** **Litho.** ***Perf. 11½x12***
**1403** A601 £10 multicolored .70 .35

March 8 Revolution, 35th Anniv. — A602

**1998, Mar. 8** **Litho.** ***Perf. 12½x12***
**1404** A602 £17 multicolored 1.10 .55

Mother's Day A603

**1998, March 21** ***Perf. 11½x12***
**1405** A603 £10 multicolored .70 .35

Evacuation Day, 52nd Anniv. — A604

Labor Day — A605

**1998, Apr. 17** **Litho.** ***Perf. 12x11½***
**1406** A604 £10 multicolored .70 .35

**1998, May 1**
**1407** A605 £18 multicolored 1.10 .55

World Tourism Day — A606

Mother Teresa (1910-97) A607

**1998, July 22** **Litho.** ***Perf. 12x11½***
**1408** A606 £17 Princess of Banias 1.10 .55

**1998, July 22**
**1409** A607 £18 multicolored 1.10 .55

1998 World Cup Soccer Championships, France — A608

**1998, June 22** ***Perf. 12x12½***
**1410** A608 £10 shown .60 .30

**Size: 60x55mm**

***Imperf***

**1411** A608 £25 Soccer players, diff. 2.25 1.10

Intl. Flower Show Type of 1997

Flowers: No. 1412, Plum-colored with yellow centers. No. 1413, Red hibiscus.

**1998, June 22** ***Perf. 12x11½***
**1412** A593 £17 multicolored 1.10 1.10
**1413** A593 £17 multicolored 1.10 1.10
*a.* Pair, #1412-1413 2.25 2.25

45th Intl. Damascus Fair A609

**1998, Sept. 26** **Litho.** ***Perf. 11½x12***
**1414** A609 £18 multicolored 1.10 .55

World Children's Day — A610

**1998, Sept. 26** ***Perf. 12x11½***
**1415** A610 £18 multicolored 1.10 .55

World Post Day A611

**1998, Sept. 26** **Litho.** ***Perf. 11½x12***
**1416** A611 £18 multicolored 1.10 .55

Day to Stop Smoking — A612

**1998, Sept. 26** ***Perf. 12x11½***
**1417** A612 £15 multicolored .95 .50

Arab Post Day — A613

**1998, Sept. 26** ***Perf. 12½***
**1418** A613 £10 multicolored .60 .30

Arab-Israeli October War, 25th Anniv. — A614

Illustration reduced.

**1998, Oct. 6** ***Imperf.***
**1419** A614 £25 multicolored 1.60 .80

Science Week A615

**1998, Nov. 3** ***Perf. 11½x12***
**1420** A615 £10 multicolored .65 .35

Camels A616

**1998, Nov. 25** ***Perf. 12½***
**1421** A616 £17 multicolored 1.10 .55

Corrective Movement, 28th Anniv. A617

**1998, Nov. 16** **Litho.** ***Perf. 12½***
**1422** A617 £10 multicolored .65 .30

**Size: 99x65mm**

***Imperf***

**1423** A617 £25 multicolored .65 .30

Jerusalem — A618

**1998, Nov. 25** ***Perf. 12½***
**1424** A618 £10 multicolored .65 .30

Re-election of Pres. Assad A619

£50, Portrait with designs from Nos. 1036, C496, C506, & portrait from No. 1265.

**1999, Feb. 11** **Litho.** ***Perf. 12½***
**1425** A619 £10 red brn & multi .50 .25
**1426** A619 £17 pale yel & multi .90 .45
**1427** A619 £18 pale grn & multi .95 .45

**Size: 140x110mm**

***Imperf***

**1428** A619 £50 pale grn & multi 2.50 2.50
*Nos. 1425-1428 (4)* 4.85 3.65

Arbor Day — A620

**1999, Apr. 29** **Litho.** ***Perf. 12½***
**1429** A620 £17 multicolored 1.10 .55

Evacuation Day, 53rd. Anniv. — A621

Mother's Day — A622

**1999, Apr. 29** ***Perf. 12x11½***
**1430** A621 £18 multicolored 1.10 .55

**1999, Apr. 29**
**1431** A622 £17 multicolored 1.10 .55

Intl. Flower Show, Damascus A623

Designs: a, Jasminum. b, Acanthaceae.

**1999, June 20** **Litho.** ***Perf. 12x11½***
**1432** A623 £10 Pair, #a.-b. .85 .45

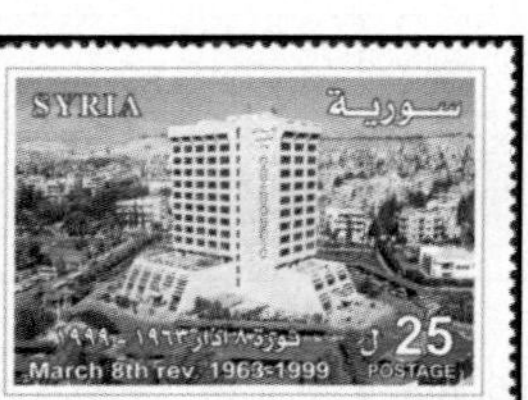


March 8 Revolution, 36th Anniv. — A624

**1999, Mar. 8** **Litho.** ***Perf. 12¼x12½***
**1433** A624 £25 shown 1.50 .75

**Size: 75x110mm**

***Imperf***

**1434** A624 £25 Building, monument 1.50 .75

Declaration of Human Rights, 50th Anniv. — A625

**1999, June 5** ***Perf. 11½x12***
**1435** A625 £18 multicolored .95 .45

Labor Day — A626

**1999, June 5 Litho.** ***Perf. 12x11½***
**1436** A626 £10 multicolored .55 .30

10th Amity Festival A627

**1999, Aug. 1 Litho.** ***Perf. 11½x12***
**1437** A627 £10 multicolored .65 .30

A628

A630

A629

**1999, Oct. 12 Litho.** ***Perf. 12x11½***
**1438** A628 £10 multi .65 .30

Arab Post Day.

**1999, Aug. 28** ***Perf. 11½x12***
**1439** A629 £15 multi .95 .45

46th Intl. Fair, Damascus.

**1999, Sept. 21** ***Perf. 12x11½***
**1440** A630 £17 multi 1.10 .55

Arab Dentists Assoc., 7th Congress.

A631

A632

**1999, Nov. 16**
**1441** A631 £18 multi 1.10 .55

World Children's Day.

**1999, Oct. 12**
**1442** A632 £17 multi 1.10 .55

UPU, 125th anniv.

Corrective Movement, 29th Anniv. — A633

#1443, Building, statue. #1444, Close-up of statue. £25, Building statue, fountain.

**1999, Nov. 16** ***Perf. 12½***
**1443** A633 £17 multi 1.10 .55
**1444** A633 £17 multi, vert. 1.10 .55

***Imperf***

**Size: 115x76mm**

**1445** A633 £25 multi 1.60 1.60
*Nos. 1443-1445 (3)* 3.80 2.70

Abu Hanifah al-Deilouri, Botanist — A634

**1999, Oct. 12** ***Perf. 11½x12***
**1446** A634 £17 multi 1.10 .55

Christianity, 2000th Anniv. — A635

**1999, Nov. 16** ***Perf. 12½***
**1447** A635 £17 multi 1.10 .55

March 8 Revolution, 37th Anniv. A636

**2000, Mar. 8 Litho.** ***Perf. 12½***
**1448** A636 £18 multi 1.10 .55

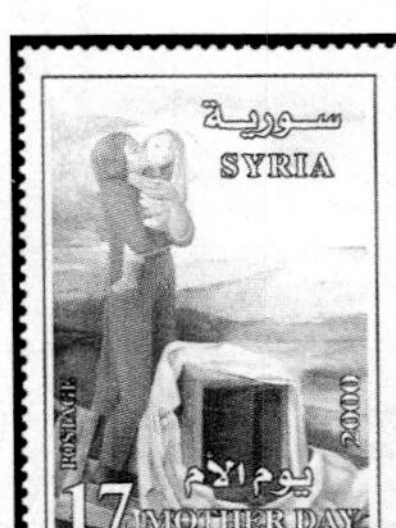

Mother's Day — A637

**2000, Mar. 21**
**1449** A637 £17 multi 1.00 .50

Evacuation Day, 54th Anniv. — A638

Illustration reduced.

**2000, Apr. 17** ***Imperf.***
**1450** A638 £25 multi 1.50 1.50

Labor Day — A639

**2000, May 1 Litho.** ***Perf. 12x11½***
**1451** A639 £10 multi .40 .20

Installation of Bashar al-Assad as President A640

**2000, July 17** ***Perf. 12¼***
**1452** Strip of 4 1.90 1.90
*a.* A640 £3 lt blue & multi .20 .20
*b.* A640 £10 tan & multi .40 .20
*c.* A640 £17 bl gray & multi .65 .30
*d.* A640 £18 gray & multi .65 .35

***Imperf***

**Size: 110x74mm**

**1453** A640 £50 multi 1.90 1.90

Arab Post Day A641

**2000, Aug. 20 Litho.** ***Perf. 11½x12***
**1454** A641 £18 multi 1.10 .55

47th Damascus Fair — A642

**2000, Aug. 20**
**1455** A642 £15 multi .90 .45

2000 Summer Olympics, Sydney — A643

No. 1456: a, £17, Weight lifting. b, £18, Women's shot put.
Illustration reduced.

**2000, Oct. 1 Litho.** ***Perf. 12x11½***
**1456** A643 Pair, #a-b 1.40 .70

***Imperf***

**Size: 80x77mm**

**1457** A643 £25 Javelin .95 .50

World Tourism Day — A644

Illustration reduced.

**2000, Dec. 6 Litho.** ***Imperf.***
**1458** A644 £50 Mosaic 3.00 3.00

World Post Day A645

**2000, Aug. 20** ***Perf. 11½x12***
**1459** A645 £18 multi 1.10 .55

Nasir ad-Din at-Tusi (1201-74), Scientist A646

**2000, Nov. 1 Litho.** ***Perf. 12½x12¼***
**1460** A646 £15 multi .60 .30

Science week.

Arbor Day — A647

**2000, May 15** ***Perf. 12x11½***
**1461** A647 £18 multi .65 .35

Butterflies — A648

a, £17, Charaxes jasius. b, £18, Apaturairis. Illustration reduced.

**2000, May 15** ***Perf. 12½***
**1462** A648 Pair, #a-b 1.40 .70

World Children's Day — A649

**2000, Aug. 20 Litho.** ***Perf. 12x11½***
**1463** A649 £10 multi .60 .30

World Meteorological Organization, 50th Anniv. — A650

**2000, Dec. 6**
**1464** A650 £10 multi .60 .30

March 8 Revolution, 38th Anniv. — A651

**2001 Litho.** ***Perf. 12x11½***
**1465** A651 £25 multi .95 .50

Mother's Day — A652

**2001**
**1466** A652 £10 multi .40 .20

Evacuation Day, 55th Anniv. — A653

**2001**
**1467** A653 £25 multi .95 .50

Book and Author's Rights — A654

**2001**
**1468** A654 £10 multi .40 .20

Intl. Flower Show, Damascus — A655

No. 1469: a, Weigela. b, Mertensia. Illustration reduced.

**2001**
**1469** A655 £10 Horiz. pair, #a-b .75 .40

Syrian Engineering Syndicate, 50th Anniv. A656

**2001, Feb. 1 Litho.** ***Perf. 12½***
**1470** A656 £17 multi .65 .35

**Size: 95x85mm**
***Imperf***
**1471** A656 £25 multi .95 .50

**Martyr's Square Type of 1994**

**2001** ***Perf. 11½x12***
**1472** A538 100p brt blue grn .20 .20
**1473** A538 £10 red .35 .20
**1474** A538 £50 blue 1.90 .95
*Nos. 1472-1474 (3)* 2.45 1.35

Labor Day — A657

**2001 Litho.** ***Perf. 12x11½***
**1475** A657 £18 multi .75 .40

48th Damascus Fair — A658

**2001 Litho.** ***Perf. 12x11½***
**1476** A658 £10 multi .40 .20

Re-occupation of Kuneitra by Syria, 27th Anniv. — A659

**2001** ***Perf. 11½x12***
**1477** A659 £17 multi .65 .35

Anti-Smoking Campaign — A660

**2001**
**1478** A660 £18 multi .70 .35

UN High Commissioner for Refugees, 50th Anniv. — A661

**2001**
**1479** A661 £17 multi .65 .35

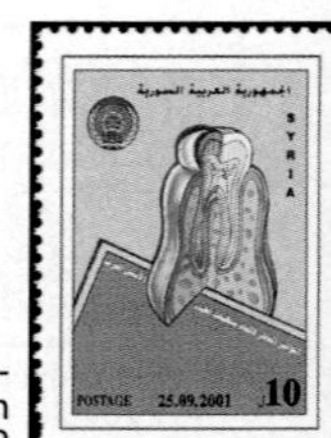


Tooth Cross-section A662

**2001** ***Perf. 12x11½***
**1480** A662 £10 multi .40 .20

World Children's Day — A663

**2001** ***Perf. 12x11½***
**1481** A663 £18 multi .70 .35

A664

**2001** ***Perf. 12x11½***
**1482** A664 £10 multi .40 .20

**Size: 84x111mm**
***Imperf***
**1483** A664 £25 multi 1.00 1.00

A665

Aga Khan Award for Architecture — A666

**2001** ***Perf. 11½x12***
**1484** A665 £10 multi .40 .20
**1485** A666 £17 multi .65 .35
**1486** A666 £18 multi .70 .35
*Nos. 1484-1486 (3)* 1.75 .90

Installation of Bashar al-Assad as President, 1st Anniv. — A667

Assad and: a, £10, Silver frame. b, £17, Gold frame.
Illustration reduced.

**2001 Litho.** ***Perf. 12½x12¼***
**1487** A667 Horiz. pair, #a-b 1.10 .55

Arab Post Day A668

**2001** *Perf. 11½x12*
**1488** A668 £18 multi .75 .35

World Post Day A669

**2001**
**1489** A669 £10 multi .40 .20

Arbor Day — A670

**2001** *Perf. 12x11½*
**1490** A670 £5 multi .20 .20

World Tourism Day — A671

**2001** *Perf. 12½*
**1491** A671 £17 multi .70 .35

Palestinian Intifada — A672

**2001** *Perf. 12x11½*
**1492** A672 £17 multi .70 .35

Pres. Hafez al-Assad (1930-2000) — A673

**2001** *Perf. 12¼x12½*
**1493** A673 £25 multi 1.00 .50

Correctionist Movement, 31st Anniv. — A674

Text color: £5, Black. £15, Red.

**2001** *Perf. 11½x12*
**1494-1495** A674 Set of 2 .80 .40

Evacuation Day, 56th Anniv. — A675

**2002, Apr. 7** **Litho.** *Perf. 12x11½*
**1496** A675 £15 multi .65 .30

Labor Day — A676

**2002, May 1** *Perf. 12x12½*
**1497** A676 £10 multi .45 .20

Intl. Flower Show, Damascus — A677

No. 1498: a, £15, Yellow flowers. b, £17, White lilies.

**2002, May 1** *Perf. 12x11½*
**1498** A677 Horiz. pair, #a-b 1.40 .70

March 8 Revolution, 39th Anniv. A678

**2002, Mar. 8** **Litho.** *Perf. 11½x12*
**1499** A678 £15 multi .65 .30

Mother's Day — A679

**2002, Mar. 21** *Perf. 12x11½*
**1500** A679 £25 multi 1.10 .55

Gazelle A680

**2002, Mar. 8** *Perf. 12½*
**1501** A680 £15 multi .65 .30

Baath Party, 55th Anniv. A681

**2002, Apr. 7** *Perf. 11½x12*
**1502** A681 £15 multi .65 .30

2002 World Cup Soccer Championships, Japan and Korea — A682

No. 1503 — Various players: a, £5. b, £10.
£25, Goalie making save, horiz.
Illustration reduced.

**2002, May 31** *Perf. 12½*
**1503** A682 Horiz. pair, #a-b .65 .30

**Size: 78x65mm**
***Imperf***
**1504** A682 £25 multi 1.10 .55

World Tourism Day — A683

**2002, Sep. 27** *Perf. 12½*
**1505** A683 £10 multi .40 .20

First Syrian Railroad, Cent. — A684

**2002, Nov. 9**
**1506** A684 £10 multi .40 .20

Abd al-Rahman al-Kawakibi (1849-1902), Arab Nationalist — A685

**2002, Aug. 13** *Perf. 12x11½*
**1507** A685 £10 multi .40 .20

Intifada — A686

Designs: £10, Flag bearer, four rock throwers, tank.
£25, Flag bearer, rock thrower, tank.

**2002, Sep. 28** *Perf. 12x11½*
**1508** A686 £10 multi .40 .20

**Size: 66x79mm**
***Imperf***
**1509** A686 £25 multi 1.10 .55

Birds A687

**2002, Sep. 27** *Perf. 11½x12*
**1510** Vert. strip of 4 1.40 .70
*a.* A687 £3 Sand grouse .20 .20
*b.* A687 £5 Francolin .20 .20
*c.* A687 £10 Duck .40 .20
*d.* A687 £15 Goose .65 .30

Arab Post Day A688

Frame color: £5, Blue. £10, Red violet.

**2002, Aug. 3** *Perf. 11½x12*
**1511-1512** A688 Set of 2 .65 .30

49th Intl. Damascus Fair — A689

Emblem and: a, £5, "X's." b, £10, Squares and diamonds.

**2002, Aug. 28** *Perf. 12x11½*
**1513** A689 Horiz. pair, #a-b .65 .30

World Post Day — A690

No. 1514: a, Dove, envelope, rainbow. b, Envelope, UPU emblem, horiz.

***Perf. 12x11½, 11½x12 (#1514b)***

**2002, Oct. 9**
**1514** A690 £10 Horiz. pair, #a-b .80 .40

Arbor Day — A691

**2002, Dec. 26** ***Perf. 12x11½***
**1515** A691 £10 multi .40 .20

Intl. Children's Day — A692

**2002, Oct. 16** ***Perf. 12½***
**1516** A692 £10 multi .40 .20

Corrective Movement, 32nd Anniv. A693

**2002, Oct. 16** ***Perf. 11½x12***
**1517** A693 £10 multi .40 .20

**Martyr's Square Type of 1994**

**2003, May 5 Litho.** ***Perf. 11½x12***
**1518** A538 300p brown .20 .20

March 8 Revolution, 40th Anniv. — A694

**2003, Mar. 8** ***Perf. 12¼x12½***
**1519** A694 £15 multi .65 .30

Teacher's Day — A695

**2003, Mar. 8** ***Perf. 12x11½***
**1520** A695 £17 multi .75 .40

Mother's Day — A696

**2003, Mar. 21**
**1521** A696 £32 multi 1.40 .70

Evacuation Day, 57th Anniv. — A697

**2003, Apr. 17**
**1522** A697 £15 multi .65 .30

Labor Day — A698

**2003, May 1**
**1523** A698 £25 multi 1.10 .55

Intl. Flower Show, Damascus A699

No. 1524: a, Damask roses and violets. b, Anemones. c, Daisies. d, Damask roses and gillyflowers. e, Sunflowers.

**2003, June 15** ***Perf. 12½x12¼***
**1524** Horiz. strip of 5 2.25 1.10
*a.-e.* A699 £10 Any single .45 .20

50th Intl. Damascus Fair — A700

Designs: £32, Flags, emblems. £50, Open orbs, horiz.

**2003, Sep. 3** ***Perf. 12x12½***
**1525** A700 £32 multi 1.40 .70

**Size: 89x66mm**

***Imperf***

**1526** A700 £50 multi 2.25 2.25

World Tourism Day — A701

**2003, Sep. 27** ***Perf. 12¼x12½***
**1527** A701 £32 multi 1.40 .70

Election of Pope John Paul II, 25th Anniv. — A702

**2003, Oct. 16** ***Perf. 12½x12¼***
**1528** A702 £32 multi 1.40 .70

World Post Day A703

**2003, Oct. 14 Litho.** ***Perf. 11½x12***
**1529** A703 £10 multi .45 .20

Corrective Movement, 33rd Anniv. — A704

**2003, Nov. 16** ***Perf. 12x11½***
**1530** A704 £15 multi .65 .30

Intl. Children's Day A705

**2003, Dec. 8** ***Perf. 11½x12***
**1531** A705 £15 multi .65 .30

Birds A706

**2003, Dec. 8** ***Perf. 12½x12¼***
**1532** Horiz. strip of 5 2.75 2.75
*a.* A706 £5 Woodcock .20 .20
*b.* A706 £10 Lapwing .45 .20
*c.* A706 £15 European roller .65 .30
*d.* A706 £17 Teal .70 .35
*e.* A706 £18 Bustard .75 .40

Pres. Bashar al-Assad — A707

***Perf. 11¾x11¼***

**2003, Dec. 8** **Unwmk.**
**1533** A707 £15 brt blue green .65 .30
**1534** A707 £25 blue 1.10 .55
**1535** A707 £50 lilac 2.10 1.10
*Nos. 1533-1535 (3)* 3.85 1.95

See Nos. 1585-1594.

World Summit on the Information Society, Geneva — A708

**2003, Dec. 10** ***Perf. 12x11½***
**1536** A708 £15 multi .65 .30

Arbor Day — A709

**2003, Dec. 25** **Litho.**
**1537** A709 £25 multi 1.10 .55

**Martyr's Square Type of 1994**

**2004** ***Perf. 11½x12***
**1538** A538 £5 blue .20 .20

March 8 Revolution, 41st Anniv. — A710

**2004, Mar 8** *Perf. 12½x12*

**1539** A710 £10 multi .40 .20

Teacher's Day — A711

**2004, Mar. 13** *Perf. 12x11½*

**1540** A711 £5 multi .20 .20

Mother's Day A712

**2004, Mar. 21** *Perf. 11½x12*

**1541** A712 £15 multi .65 .30

Evacuation Day, 58th Anniv. — A713

**2004, Apr. 17** **Litho.**

**1542** A713 £10 multi .40 .20

Labor Day A714

**2004, May 1**

**1543** A714 £10 multi .40 .20

A715

A716

A717

A718

FIFA (Fédération Internationale de Football Association), Cent. — A719

Illustration A719 reduced.

**2004, May 21** *Perf. 11½x12*

**1544** A715 £5 multi .20 .20

**1545** A716 £10 multi .40 .20

*Perf. 12½x12¼*

**1546** A717 £15 multi .60 .30

*Perf. 12¼x12½*

**1547** A718 £32 multi 1.25 .60

*Nos. 1544-1547 (4)* 2.45 1.30

*Imperf*

**1548** A719 £25 multi 1.00 1.00

Intl. Flower Show, Damascus A720

No. 1549: a, Gladiola lavender. b, Jasmine. c, Iris. d, Orange nesrien. e, Tulip.

**2004, June 15** *Perf. 12x11½*

**1549** Horiz. strip of 5 1.00 1.00

*a.-e.* A720 £5 Any single .20 .20

Children and War Campaign of Intl. Committee of the Red Cross — A721

**2004, June 17** *Perf. 12¼x12½*

**1550** A721 £32 red & black 1.25 .60

2004 Summer Olympics, Athens — A722

Designs: £5, Track. £10, Boxing, horiz. £25, Swimming, horiz.

*Perf. 12x11½, 11½x12*

**2004, Aug. 13**

**1551-1553** A722 Set of 3 1.60 .80

51st Intl. Damascus Fair — A723

**2004, Sept. 3** *Perf. 12x11½*

**1554** A723 £25 multi 1.00 .50

2004 Census A724

**2004, Sept. 14** *Perf. 12½*

**1555** A724 £10 multi .45 .20

World Tourism Day A725

Designs: £5, Locomotive. No. 1557, £10, Building. No. 1558, £10, Train.

*Perf. 11½x12*

**2004, Sept. 27** **Litho.** **Unwmk.**

**1556-1558** A725 Set of 3 1.00 .50

World Post Day — A726

**2004, Oct. 9** **Litho.** *Perf. 12x11½*

**1559** A726 £17 multi .70 .35

Intl. Children's Day A727

**2004, Oct. 16** *Perf. 11½x12*

**1560** A727 £18 multi .70 .35

Corrective Movement, 34th Anniv. — A728

**2004, Nov. 16** *Perf. 12½x12*

**1561** A728 £25 multi 1.00 .50

Arbor Day — A729

**2004, Dec. 30** *Perf. 12x11½*

**1562** A729 £10 multi .40 .20

Northern Bald Ibis — A730

*Perf. 12½x12¼*

**2004, Dec. 30** **Litho.** **Unwmk.**

**1563** A730 £10 multi .40 .20

Farm Animals A731

**2004, Dec. 30** *Perf. 11½x12*

**1564** Vert. strip of 4 2.10 1.10

*a.* A731 £5 Shami goat .20 .20

*b.* A731 £15 Awassi ewe .55 .25

*c.* A731 £17 Bull .65 .30

*d.* A731 £18 Shami cow .70 .35

March 8 Revolution, 42nd Anniv. — A732

*Perf. 12¼x12½*

**2005, Mar. 8** **Wmk. 403**

**1565** A732 £17 multi .65 .30

Teacher's Day A733

**2005, Mar. 13** *Perf. 11½x12*

**1566** A733 £25 multi 1.00 .50

Mother's Day — A734

**2005, Mar. 21** ***Perf. 12x11½***

**1567** A734 £18 multi .70 .35

Arab League, 60th Anniv. — A735

**2005, Mar. 22**

**1568** A735 £10 multi .40 .20

National Day — A736

**2005, Apr. 17**

**1569** A736 £17 multi .65 .30

Labor Day — A737

**2005, May 1** **Wmk. 403**

**1570** A737 £15 multi .60 .30

Intl. Flower Show, Damascus A738

**2005, June 15** **Litho.**

**1571** Horiz. strip of 5 2.50 1.25
- ***a.*** A738 £5 Hyacinth .20 .20
- ***b.*** A738 £10 Sternbergia clusiana .40 .20
- ***c.*** A738 £15 Primula obconica .55 .30
- ***d.*** A738 £17 Primula malacoides .65 .30
- ***e.*** A738 £18 Canaria .70 .35

Butterflies A739

No. 1572: a, Papilio ulysses. b, Monarch. c, Baeotus baeotus. d, Lacewing. e, Tiger swallowtail.

**2005, Aug. 7** ***Perf. 12½***

**1572** Horiz. strip of 5 2.00 1.00
- ***a.-e.*** A739 £10 Any single .40 .20

52nd Intl. Damascus Fair — A740

**2005, Sept. 3** ***Perf. 12x11½***

**1573** A740 £15 multi .60 .30

Mevlana Jalal ad-Din ar-Rumi (1207-73), Islamic Philosopher A741

**2005, Sept. 25** ***Perf. 12½x12¼***

**1574** A741 £25 multi 1.00 .50

See Afghanistan No. , Iran No. 2911, and Turkey No. 2971.

World Tourism Day A742

**2005, Sept. 27** ***Perf. 11½x12***

**1575** A742 £17 multi .65 .30

World Post Day — A743

**2005, Oct. 9** ***Perf. 12x11½***

**1576** A743 £18 multi .70 .35

Intl. Children's Day — A744

**2005, Oct. 16** ***Perf. 12¼x12½***

**1577** A744 £17 multi .65 .30

Corrective Movement, 35th Anniv. — A745

**2005, Nov. 16** ***Perf. 11½x12***

**1578** A745 £25 multi 1.00 .50

World Summit on the Information Society, Tunis — A746

**2005, Nov. 16** ***Perf. 12¼x12½***

**1579** A746 £17 multi .65 .30

Poets A747

No. 1580: a, Nizar Kabbani (1923-98). b, Sadalah Wannous (1941-97). c, Omar Abu Reisheh (1910-90).

**2005, Dec. 20** ***Perf. 12½x12¼***

**1580** Horiz. strip of 3 1.75 .85
- ***a.*** A747 £10 multi .40 .20
- ***b.*** A747 £17 multi .65 .30
- ***c.*** A747 £18 multi .70 .35

Arbor Day — A748

**2005, Dec. 25** **Wmk. 403**

**1581** A748 £17 multi .65 .30

March 8 Revolution, 43rd Anniv. — A749

***Perf. 12x11½***

**2006, Mar. 8** **Litho.** **Wmk. 403**

**1582** A749 £18 multi .70 .35

Aleppo, 2006 Capital of Islamic Culture A750

No. 1583: a, £17, Aleppo Castle. b, £18, Mosque, vert.
£25, Emblem and buildings.

**2006, Mar. 16** ***Perf. 11½x12, 12x11½***

**1583** A750 Pair, #a-b 1.40 .70

***Imperf***

**Size: 79x60mm**

**1584** A750 £25 multi .95 .50

**Pres. Bashir al-Assad Type of 2003**

**2006** **Wmk. 403** ***Perf. 11¾x11¼***

| | | | | |
|---|---|---|---|---|
| **1585** | A707 | £1 brt blue | .20 | .20 |
| **1586** | A707 | £3 lilac rose | .20 | .20 |
| **1587** | A707 | £5 brown | .20 | .20 |
| **1588** | A707 | £10 purple | .40 | .20 |
| **1589** | A707 | £15 brt blue grn | .60 | .30 |
| **1590** | A707 | £17 orange brn | .65 | .35 |
| **1591** | A707 | £18 dark blue | .70 | .35 |
| **1592** | A707 | £25 blue | .95 | .50 |
| **1593** | A707 | £50 lilac | 1.90 | .95 |
| **1594** | A707 | £100 green | 4.00 | 2.00 |
| | | *Nos. 1585-1594 (10)* | 9.80 | 5.25 |

Issued: £1, 9/7; £3, 8/24; £5, 8/1; £10, 6/2; £15, £25, £50, 3/19; £17, 5/11; £18, 6/8; £100, 9/27.

Mother's Day — A751

***Perf. 12x11½***

**2006, Mar. 21** **Wmk. 403**

**1595** A751 £17 multi .65 .35

National Day — A752

No. 1596: a, Sultan Pasha al-Atrach (1889-1982). b, Yousef al-Azmeh (1884-1920). c, Sheikh Saleh al-Ali (1885-1950). d, Ibrahim Hanano (1889-1935). e, Ahmad Moraiwed (1886-1926).

**2006, Apr. 17**

**1596** Horiz. strip of 5 1.90 .95
- ***a.-e.*** A752 £10 Any single .35 .20

Labor Day — A753

**2006, May 1**

**1597** A753 £17 multi .65 .35

Intl. Flower Show, Damascus — A754

No. 1598: a, £5,Hyoscyamus aureus. b, £10, Cistus salviaefolius.

**2006, May 15** ***Perf. 11½x12***

**1598** A754 Vert. pair, #a-b .60 .30

2006 World Cup Soccer Championships, Germany — A755

No. 1599: a, £17, Players, aerial view of stadium. b, £18, Players under stadium roof. £50, Players, vert.

**2006, June 25** ***Perf. 11½x12***

**1599** A755 Vert. pair, #a-b 1.40 .70

***Imperf***

**Size: 60x80mm**

**1600** A755 £50 multi 1.90 .95

Diplomatic Relations Between Syria and People's Republic of China, 50th Anniv. — A756

**2006, Aug. 1** ***Perf. 12½x12¼***

**1601** A756 £10 multi .40 .20

Intl. Year of Deserts and Desertification — A757

**2006, Aug. 13** **Wmk. 403**

**1602** A757 £10 multi .40 .20

53rd Intl. Damascus Fair — A758

**2006, Sept. 3** ***Perf. 12x11½***

**1603** A758 £10 multi .40 .20

A759

World Tourism Day — A760

**2006, Sept. 27** ***Perf. 11½x12***

**1604** A759 £10 multi .40 .20

***Perf. 12¼x12½***

**1605** A760 £10 multi .40 .20

World Post Day — A761

**2006, Oct. 19** ***Perf. 12x11½***

**1606** A761 £17 multi .65 .35

Artists — A762

No. 1607: a, Fateh Almudarres (1922-99). b, Adham Ismail (1922-63). c, Saeed Makhlouf (1925-2000). d, Burhan Karkutli (1932-2003). e, Michael Kirsheh (1900-73).

**2006, Nov. 12** **Litho.**

**1607** Horiz. strip of 5 1.90 .95

*a.-e.* A762 £10 Any single .35 .20

Corrective Movement, 36th Anniv. — A763

**2006, Nov. 16** ***Perf. 12½x12¼***

**1608** A763 £15 multi .60 .30

Arbor Day — A764

**2006, Dec. 28** ***Perf. 12¼x12½***

**1609** A764 £15 multi .60 .30

Fish A765

No. 1610: a, Light-colored fish, green and violet seaweed. b, Dark-colored fish, green and violet seaweed. c, Light-colored fish, green seaweed.

**2006, Dec. 28** ***Perf. 11½x12***

**1610** A765 £15 Vert. strip of 3, #a-c 1.75 .85

---

## SEMI-POSTAL STAMPS

Nos. 174-185 Surcharged in Red or Black

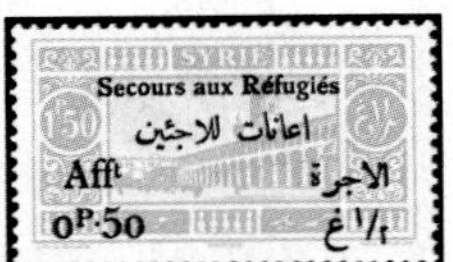


**1926** **Unwmk.** ***Perf. 12½, 13½***

| | | | | |
|---|---|---|---|---|
| **B1** | A4 | 25c + 25c ol blk (R) | 2.25 | 2.00 |
| **B2** | A4 | 50c + 25c yel grn | 2.25 | 2.00 |
| **B3** | A4 | 75c + 25c brown org | 2.25 | 2.00 |
| **B4** | A5 | 1p + 50c magenta | 2.25 | 2.00 |
| **B5** | A4 | 1.25p + 50c dp grn (R) | 2.25 | 2.00 |
| **B6** | A4 | 1.50p + 50c rose red | 2.25 | 2.00 |
| **B7** | A4 | 2p + 75c dk brn (R) | 2.25 | 2.00 |
| **B8** | A4 | 2.50p + 75c pck bl (R) | 2.25 | 2.00 |
| **B9** | A4 | 3p + 1p org brn (R) | 2.25 | 2.00 |
| **B10** | A4 | 5p + 1p violet | 2.25 | 2.00 |
| **B11** | A4 | 10p + 2p vio brn | 2.25 | 2.00 |
| **B12** | A4 | 25p + 5p ultra (R) | 2.25 | 2.00 |
| | | *Nos. B1-B12 (12)* | 27.00 | 24.00 |
| | | Set, never hinged | 36.00 | |

On No. B4 the surcharge is set in six lines to fit the shape of the stamp.

The surcharge was a contribution to the relief of refugees from the Djebel Druze War. See Nos. CB1-CB4.

**Catalogue values for unused stamps in this section, from this point to the end of the section, are for Never Hinged items.**

### Syrian Arab Republic

Jordanian Flags on Map of Israel, and Arabs — SP1

**1965, June 12** **Litho.** ***Perf. 12x11½***

**B13** SP1 12½p + 5p multi .20 .20

**B14** SP1 25p + 5p multi .20 .20

Issued for Palestine Week.

Father with Children and Red Crescent SP2

**1968, May** **Litho.** ***Perf. 12½x12***

**B15** SP2 12½p + 2½p multi .25 .25

**B16** SP2 27½p + 7½p multi .25 .25

The surtax was for refugees.

---

## AIR POST STAMPS

POSTE
PAR
AVION

a

AVION

b

Nos. 35, 45, 47 Handstamped Type "a" in Violet

**1920, Dec.** **Unwmk.** ***Perf. 13½***

| | | | | |
|---|---|---|---|---|
| **C1** | A22 | 1p on 5c | 160.00 | 40.00 |
| **C2** | A20 | 5p on 15c | 290.00 | 47.50 |
| **C3** | A18 | 10p on 40c | 425.00 | 77.50 |
| | | *Nos. C1-C3 (3)* | 875.00 | 165.00 |

Nos. 36, 46, 48 Overprinted Type "a" in Violet

**1921, June 12**

| | | | | |
|---|---|---|---|---|
| **C4** | A22 | 1p on 20c | 87.50 | 40.00 |
| **C5** | A18 | 5p on 1fr | 425.00 | 150.00 |
| **C6** | A18 | 10p on 2fr | 425.00 | 150.00 |
| | | *Nos. C4-C6 (3)* | 937.50 | 340.00 |

Excellent counterfeits exist of Nos. C1-C6.

Nos. 36, 46, 48 Overprinted Type "b"

**1921, Oct. 5**

**C7** A22 1p on 20c 60.00 18.50
**C8** A18 5p on 1fr 150.00 37.50
*a.* Inverted overprint 325.00 240.00
**C9** A18 10p on 2fr 200.00 47.50
*a.* Double overprint 475.00 400.00
*Nos. C7-C9 (3)* 410.00 103.50

Nos. 92, 94-96 Overprinted

c

**1922, May 28**

**C10** A18 2p on 40c 25.00 25.00
*a.* Inverted overprint
**C11** A18 3p on 60c 25.00 25.00
**C12** A18 5p on 1fr 25.00 25.00
**C13** A18 10p on 2fr 25.00 25.00
*Nos. C10-C13 (4)* 100.00 100.00

Nos. 116-119 Overprinted Type "c"

**1923, Nov. 22**

**C14** A18 2p on 40c 29.00 29.00
*b.* Inverted surcharge
**C15** A18 3p on 60c 29.00 29.00
**C16** A18 5p on 1fr 29.00 29.00
**C17** A18 10p on 2fr 29.00 29.00
*b.* Double overprint
*Nos. C14-C17 (4)* 116.00 116.00

**Overprinted "Liabn"**

*C14a* A18 2p on 40c 400.00 400.00
*C15a* A18 3p on 60c 400.00 400.00
*C16a* A18 5p on 1fr 400.00 400.00
*C17a* A18 10p on 2fr 400.00 400.00

Nos. 137-140 Overprinted Type "c"

**1924, Jan. 13**

**C18** A18 2p on 40c 3.50 3.50
*a.* Double overprint *27.50*
**C19** A18 3p on 60c 3.50 3.50
*a.* Inverted overprint *47.50*
**C20** A18 5p on 1fr 3.50 3.50
*a.* Double overprint *50.00 30.00*
**C21** A18 10p on 2fr 3.50 3.50
*Nos. C18-C21 (4)* 14.00 14.00

Nos. 152, 154, 157-158 Overprinted

**1924, July 17**

**C22** A18 2p on 40c 5.00 5.00
*a.* Inverted overprint 32.50
**C23** A18 3p on 60c 5.00 5.00
*a.* Inverted overprint 32.50
*b.* Double overprint 20.00
**C24** A18 5p on 1fr 5.00 5.00
**C25** A18 10p on 2fr 5.00 5.00
*a.* Inverted overprint 32.50
*Nos. C22-C25 (4)* 20.00 20.00

Regular Issue of 1925 Overprinted in Green

**1925, Mar. 1**

**C26** A4 2p dark brown 1.90 1.90
**C27** A4 3p orange brown 1.90 1.90
**C28** A4 5p violet 1.90 1.90
**C29** A4 10p violet brown 1.90 1.90
*Nos. C26-C29 (4)* 7.60 7.60

Regular Issue of 1925 Overprinted in Red

f

**1926**

**C30** A4 2p dark brown 1.50 1.50
*a.* Inverted overprint 32.50
**C31** A4 3p orange brown 1.60 1.60
*a.* Inverted overprint 32.50
**C32** A4 5p violet 1.75 1.75
*a.* Inverted overprint 32.50
*b.* Double overprint
**C33** A4 10p violet brown 1.75 1.75
*a.* Inverted overprint 32.50
*b.* Double overprint
*Nos. C30-C33 (4)* 6.60 6.60

Nos. C30-C33 received their first airmail use June 16, 1929, at the opening of the Beirut-Marseille line.

For surcharges see Nos. CB1-CB4.

Regular Issue of 1925 Overprinted Type "f" in Red or Black

**1929**

**C34** A4 50c yellow green (R) 1.00 1.00
*a.* Inverted overprint 40.00
*b.* Overprinted on face and back 22.50
*c.* Double overprint 40.00
*d.* Double overprint, one inverted 60.00
*e.* Pair, one without overprint
**C35** A5 1p magenta (Bk) 1.10 1.10
*a.* Reversed overprint
*b.* Red overprint
**C36** A4 25p ultra (R) 4.00 4.00
*a.* Inverted overprint 82.50
*b.* Pair, one without overprint
*Nos. C34-C36 (3)* 6.10 6.10

On No. C35, the overprint is vertical, with plane nose down.

No. 197 Overprinted Type "f" in Red

**1929, July 9**

**C37** A4 15p on 25p ultra 2.40 2.40
*a.* Inverted overprint

Air Post Stamps of 1926-29 Overprinted in Various Colors

**1929, Sept. 5**

**C38** A4 50c yellow grn (R) 2.25 2.25
**C39** A5 1p magenta (Bl) 2.25 2.25
**C40** A4 2p dk brown (V) 2.25 2.25
**C41** A4 3p orange brn (Bl) 2.25 2.25
*a.* Inverted overprint 70.00
**C42** A4 5p violet (R) 2.25 2.25
**C43** A4 10p violet brn (Bl) 2.25 2.25
**C44** A4 25p ultra (R) 2.25 2.25
*Nos. C38-C44 (7)* 15.75 15.75

Damascus Industrial Exhibition.

AP1

Red Surcharge

**1930, Jan. 30**

**C45** AP1 2p on 1.25p dp grn 2.25 2.25
*a.* Inverted surcharge
*b.* Double surcharge 60.00

Plane over Homs AP2

Designs: 1pi, City Wall, Damascus. 2pi, Euphrates River. 3pi, Temple Ruins, Palmyra. 5pi, Deir-el-Zor. 10pi, Damascus. 15pi, Aleppo, Citadel. 25pi, Hama. 50pi, Zebdani. 100pi, Telebisse.

**1931-33 Photo. Unwmk.**

**C46** AP2 50c ocher .60 .35
**C47** AP2 50c black brn ('33) 1.00 .85
**C48** AP2 1p chestnut brown .85 .50
**C49** AP2 2p Prus blue 1.75 1.50
**C50** AP2 3p blue grn 1.10 .80
**C51** AP2 5p red violet 1.10 .80
**C52** AP2 10p slate grn 1.10 .80
**C53** AP2 15p orange red 1.50 1.00
**C54** AP2 25p orange brn 1.75 1.50
**C55** AP2 50p black 2.25 2.00
**C56** AP2 100p magenta 2.50 2.00
*Nos. C46-C56 (11)* 15.50 12.10

Nos. C46 to C56 exist imperforate. Value, $425.

For overprints see Nos. C67-C71, C110-C112, C114-C115, MC1-MC4.

Village of Bloudan AP12

**1934, Aug. 2 Engr. *Perf. 12½***

**C57** AP12 50c yel brown 1.25 1.25
**C58** AP12 1p green 1.50 1.50
**C59** AP12 2p peacock bl 1.75 1.75
**C60** AP12 3p red 2.00 2.00
**C61** AP12 5p plum 2.25 2.25
**C62** AP12 10p brt violet 15.00 15.00
**C63** AP12 15p orange brn 18.50 18.50
**C64** AP12 25p dk ultra 23.00 23.00
**C65** AP12 50p black 42.50 42.50
**C66** AP12 100p red brown 77.50 77.50
*Nos. C57-C66 (10)* 185.25 185.25

Proclamation of the Republic. Exist imperf. Value, set $1,200.

Also exists without figures of value. Value, set $900.

Air Post Stamps of 1931-33 Overprinted in Red or Black

**1936, Apr. 15 *Perf. 13½x13, 13½***

**C67** AP2 50c black brown 3.75 3.75
**C68** AP2 1p chnt brown (Bk) 3.75 3.75
**C69** AP2 2p Prus blue 3.75 3.75
**C70** AP2 3p blue green 3.75 3.75
**C71** AP2 5p red violet (Bk) 3.75 3.75
*Nos. C67-C71 (5)* 18.75 18.75

Industrial Exhibition, Damascus, May 1936.

Syrian Pavilion at Paris Exposition AP13

**1937, July 1 Photo. *Perf. 13½***

**C72** AP13 ½p yellow green 1.75 1.75
**C73** AP13 1p green 1.75 1.75
**C74** AP13 2p lt brown 1.75 1.75
**C75** AP13 3p rose red 1.75 1.75
**C76** AP13 5p brown orange 1.75 1.75
**C77** AP13 10p grnsh black 3.25 3.25
**C78** AP13 15p blue 4.00 4.00
**C79** AP13 25p dark violet 4.50 4.50
*Nos. C72-C79 (8)* 20.50 20.50

Paris International Exposition. Exist imperf.

Ancient Citadel at Aleppo AP14

Omayyad Mosque and Minaret of Jesus at Damascus AP15

**1937 Engr. *Perf. 13***

**C80** AP14 ½ dark violet .50 .50
**C81** AP15 1p black .50 .50
**C82** AP14 2p deep green .50 .50
**C83** AP15 3p deep ultra .50 .50
**C84** AP14 5p rose lake 1.50 1.50
**C85** AP15 10p red brown .85 .85
**C86** AP14 15p lake brown 3.25 3.25
**C87** AP15 25p dark blue 4.00 4.00
*Nos. C80-C87 (8)* 11.60 11.60

No. C80 to C87 exist imperforate. Value, set $175.

For overprint see No. C109.

Maurice Noguès and Route of France-Syria Flight — AP16

**1938, July Photo. *Perf. 11***

**C88** AP16 10p dark green 2.25 2.25
*a.* Souv. sheet of 4, perf. 13½ 17.50 17.50
*b.* Perf. 13½ 4.00 4.00

10th anniversary of first Marseille-Beirut flight, by Maurice Noguès.

No. C88a exists imperf.; value $800.

Bridge at Deir-el-Zor AP17

**1940 Engr. *Perf. 13***

**C89** AP17 25c brown black .20 .20
**C90** AP17 50c peacock blue .20 .20
**C91** AP17 1p deep ultra .25 .20
**C92** AP17 2p dk orange brn .40 .30
**C93** AP17 5p green .65 .50
**C94** AP17 10p rose carmine 1.00 .90
**C95** AP17 50p dark violet 2.25 1.75
*Nos. C89-C95 (7)* 4.95 4.05

Exist imperf. Value, set $125.

President Taj Eddin Hassani AP18

**1942 Litho. *Perf. 11½***

**C96** AP18 10p blue gray 3.00 3.00
**C97** AP18 50p gray lilac 3.25 3.25

Proclamation of Independence by the Allies, Sept. 27, 1941.

President Taj Eddin Hassani AP19

President Hassani and Map of Syria AP20

**1942 Photo.**

**C98** AP19 10p sl grn & yel grn 4.00 4.00

Exists imperforate. Value, $30.

**1943 Litho.**

**C99** AP20 2p dull brown 2.25 2.25
**C100** AP20 10p red violet 2.25 2.25
**C101** AP20 20p aqua 2.25 2.25
**C102** AP20 50p rose pink 2.25 2.25
*Nos. C99-C102 (4)* 9.00 9.00

Proclamation of United Syria.

Same, Overprinted with Black Border

**1943, May 5**

**C103** AP20 2p dull brown 2.25 2.25
**C104** AP20 10p red violet 2.25 2.25
**C105** AP20 20p aqua 2.25 2.25
**C106** AP20 50p rose pink 2.25 2.25
*Nos. C103-C106 (4)* 9.00 9.00

Mourning for President Hassani. Exist imperf.

President Shukri el Kouatly — AP21

**1944**

**C107** AP21 200p sepia 9.00 7.00
**C108** AP21 500p dull blue 13.50 10.00

For overprints see Nos. C113, C116.

Stamps of 1931-44 Overprinted in Black, Blue or Carmine

**1944** *Perf. 13, 13½, 11½*

**C109** AP15 10p red brn (Bk) 2.50 2.50
**C110** AP2 15p orange red 2.75 2.75
**C111** AP2 25p org brown 2.75 2.75
**C112** AP2 100p magenta 6.75 6.75
**C113** AP21 200p sepia (C) 12.00 12.00
*Nos. C109-C113 (5)* 26.75 26.75
Set, never hinged 34.00

1st congress of Arab lawyers held in Damascus, Sept. 1944.

Nos. C53-C54, C108 Overprinted in Black or Orange

**1944**

**C114** AP2 15p orange red 3.00 3.00
**C115** AP2 25p org brown 3.00 3.00
**C116** AP21 500p dull blue (O) 22.50 22.50
*Nos. C114-C116 (3)* 28.50 28.50
Set, never hinged 35.00

See note after No. 299.

President Shukri el Kouatly AP22

**1945, Mar. 15** **Litho.** *Perf. 11½*

**C117** AP22 5p pale green .50 .20
**C118** AP22 10p dull red .50 .20
**C119** AP22 15p orange .60 .25
**C120** AP22 25p lt blue 1.25 .50
**C121** AP22 50p lt violet 1.75 .70
**C122** AP22 100p deep brown 3.50 1.25
**C123** AP22 200p fawn 8.00 4.00
*Nos. C117-C123 (7)* 16.10 7.10
Set, never hinged 22.50

Resumption of constitutional government.

**Catalogue values for unused stamps in this section, from this point to the end of the section, are for Never Hinged items.**

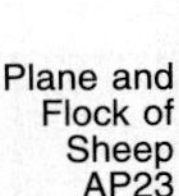

Plane and Flock of Sheep AP23

Kattineh Dam AP24

Kanawat, Djebel Druze AP25

Sultan Ibrahim Mosque AP26

**1946-47** *Perf. 13x13½*

**C124** AP23 3p rose brown .50 .20
**C125** AP23 5p lt bl grn ('47) .50 .20
**C126** AP23 6p dp org ('47) .50 .20
**C127** AP24 10p sl gray ('47) .35 .20
**C128** AP24 15p scarlet ('47) .35 .20
**C129** AP24 25p blue .45 .20
**C130** AP25 50p violet .75 .25
**C131** AP25 100p blue green 1.75 .40
**C132** AP25 200p brown ('47) 4.00 1.25
**C133** AP26 300p red brn ('47) 14.50 2.50
**C134** AP26 500p ol gray ('47) 16.00 3.50
*Nos. C124-C134 (11)* 39.65 9.10

For overprints and surcharges see Nos. C135-C139, C148-C152, C157, C172.

No. C129 Overprinted in Red

**1946, Apr. 17**

**C135** AP24 25p blue 2.00 1.00

Evacuation of British and French troops from Syria.

Nos. C129-C131 Overprinted in Magenta

**1946, Aug. 28**

**C136** AP24 25p blue 2.00 1.25
**C137** AP25 50p violet 2.50 1.50
**C138** AP25 100p blue green 5.00 2.75
*Nos. C136-C138 (3)* 9.50 5.50

See note after No. 334.

No. C135 with Additional Overprint in Black

**1947, June 10** *Perf. 13x13½*

**C139** AP24 25p blue 2.00 1.25

1st anniv. of the evacuation of British and French troops from Syria.

Window at Kasr El-Heir El-Gharbi AP27

Ram-headed Sphinxes Carved in Ivory, from King Hazael's Bed — AP28

**1947, Nov. 15** **Litho.** *Perf. 11½*

**C140** AP27 12.50p dark violet 1.50 .50
**C141** AP28 50p brown 4.00 1.75
*a.* Souv. sheet of 4, #338-339, C140-C141 60.00 60.00

1st Arab Archaeological Cong., Damascus, Nov.
No. C141a sold for 125 piasters.

Kasr El-Heir El-Charqui AP29

Congress Emblem — AP30

**1947, Nov. 15**

**C142** AP29 12.50p olive black 1.00 .50
**C143** AP30 50p dull violet 3.50 1.75
*a.* Souv. sheet of 4, #340, 341, C142, C143 50.00 50.00

3rd Cong. of Arab Engineers, Damascus, Nov.
No. C143a sold for 125 piasters.

Kouatly Types of Regular Issue

**1948, June 22** **Litho.** *Perf. 10½*

**C144** A50 12.50p dp bl & vio brn .65 .25
**C145** A51 50p violet brn & grn 2.50 1.00
*a.* Souv. sheet, #342, 343, C144, C145, imperf 150.00 150.00

Reelection of Pres. Shukri el Kouatly.

Military Training Types of Regular Issue

**1948, June 22**

**C146** A52 12.50p blue & dk bl .75 .25
**C147** A53 50p green, car & blk 2.00 .80
*a.* Souv. sheet of 4, #344, 345, C146, C147, imperf. 140.00 140.00

Inauguration of compulsory military training.

Nos. C124, C126 and C132 to C134 Surcharged with New Value and Bars in Black or Carmine

**1948, Oct. 18** *Perf. 13x13½*

**C148** AP23 2.50p on 3p .30 .20
**C149** AP23 2.50p on 6p .35 .20
**C150** AP25 25p on 200p (C) .80 .25
**C151** AP26 50p on 300p *10.00* .75
**C152** AP26 50p on 500p *10.00* .75
*Nos. C148-C152 (5)* 21.45 2.15

Husni Zayim Type of Regular Issue

**1949, June 20** **Litho.** *Perf. 11½*

**C153** A54 50p brown 3.75 2.50

Revolution of March 30, 1949.

Pigeons and Globe AP36

Husni Zayim and View of Damascus AP37

**1949, June 20** **Unwmk.**

**C154** AP36 12.50p claret 7.50 6.00
**C155** AP37 50p gray black 19.00 12.50

UPU, 75th anniv. A souvenir sheet of 4 contains #349, 350, C154, C155. Value $125.

Election Type of Regular Issue

**Wmk. 291**

**1949, Aug. 6** **Litho.** *Perf. 11½*

**C156** A57 50p car rose & dk grnsh bl 3.75 2.50
*a.* Souv. sheet of 2, #351, C156, imperf. 175.00 175.00

Election of Pres. Husni Zayim.

No. C131 Surcharged with New Value and Bars in Black

**1950** **Unwmk.** *Perf. 13x13½*

**C157** AP25 2.50p on 100p bl grn .40 .20

Port of Latakia AP38

**1950, Dec. 25** *Perf. 11½*

**C158** AP38 2.50p dull lilac .50 .20
**C159** AP38 10p grnsh blue 1.10 .20
**C160** AP38 15p orange brown 2.50 .40
**C161** AP38 25p bright blue 5.50 .35
*Nos. C158-C161 (4)* 9.60 1.15

Exist imperf. Value, $35. See No. C173. For overprint see No. C169.

Symbolical of Constitution AP39

**1951, Apr. 14** **Unwmk.**

**C162** AP39 12.50p crimson rose .40 .20
**C163** AP39 50p brown violet 1.25 1.00

New constitution adopted Sept. 5, 1950. Exist imperf.

Ruins, Palmyra AP40

Citadel at Aleppo AP41

**1952, Apr. 22** **Litho.** *Perf. 11½*

**C164** AP40 2.50p vermilion .30 .20
**C165** AP40 5p green .35 .20
**C166** AP40 15p violet .50 .20
**C167** AP41 25p deep blue .75 .35
**C168** AP41 100p lilac rose 5.50 1.00
*Nos. C164-C168 (5)* 7.40 1.95

Nos. C164-C168 exist imperforate.
For overprints see Nos. C170-C171, C186.

Stamps of 1946-52 Overprinted in Black

**1953, Feb. 16** *Perf. 13x13½, 11½*

**C169** AP38 10p grnsh blue 2.00 1.00
**C170** AP40 15p violet 2.25 1.10
**C171** AP41 25p deep blue 3.25 1.60
**C172** AP25 50p violet 8.00 2.25
*Nos. C169-C172 (4)* 15.50 5.95

UN Social Welfare Seminar, Damascus, Dec. 8-20, 1952.

Type of 1950 and

Post Office, Aleppo AP42

**1953, Oct.** **Photo.** *Perf. 11½*

**C173** AP38 10p violet blue .50 .20
**C174** AP42 50p red brown 1.60 .30

For overprint see No. C185.

Building at Hama and PTT Emblem — AP43

University of Syria, Damascus AP44

**1954**

**C175** AP43 5p violet .25 .20
**C176** AP43 10p brown .30 .20
**C177** AP43 15p dull green .35 .20
**C178** AP44 30p dark brown .45 .20
**C179** AP44 35p blue .80 .25
**C180** AP44 40p orange 1.75 .40
**C181** AP44 50p deep plum 1.25 .60
**C182** AP44 70p purple 3.25 .70
*Nos. C175-C182 (8)* 8.40 2.75

For overprints see UAR Nos. C27-C28.

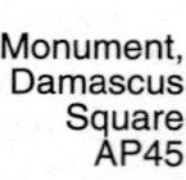

Monument, Damascus Square AP45

Mosque and Syrian Flag — AP46

**1954, Sept. 2**

**C183** AP45 40p carmine rose 1.00 .45
**C184** AP46 50p green 1.25 .55

Damascus Fair, Sept. 1954.
Nos. C183-C184 exist imperforate.

Nos. C174 and C168 Overprinted in Blue or Black

**1954, Oct. 9**

**C185** AP42 50p red brown (Bl) 1.10 1.00
**C186** AP41 100p lilac rose 2.00 1.60

Cotton Festival, Aleppo, October 1954.

Virgin of Sednaya Concent AP47

Omayyad Mosque AP48

**1955, Mar. 27** **Photo.** *Perf. 11½*

**C187** AP47 25p deep purple .60 .40
**C188** AP47 75p deep blue green 1.75 1.25

50th anniv. of the founding of Rotary Intl. Exist imperforate.

**1955, Mar. 26**

**C189** AP48 35p cerise .95 .60
**C190** AP48 65p deep green 1.75 1.10

1955 Regional Cong. of Rotary Intl., Damascus.

Arab Postal Union Type of Regular Issue

**1955, Jan. 1** *Perf. 13½x13*

**C191** A69a 5p yellow brown .40 .25

Founding of the APU, July 1, 1954.
For overprints see Nos. C203, C207.

Young Couple and View of Damascus AP49

60p, Tank and planes leading advancing troops.

**1955, Apr. 16** **Litho.** *Perf. 11½*

**C192** AP49 40p dark rose lake .60 .30
**C193** AP49 60p ultra 2.25 .35

9th anniv. of the evacuation of British and French troops from Syria.

Mother's Day Type of Regular Issue

**1955, May 13** **Unwmk.**

**C194** A70 35p violet 1.00 .60
**C195** A70 40p black 1.50 .95

Issued to publicize Mother's Day.

Emigrants under Syrian Flag — AP51

Mother and Child — AP52

15p, Airplane over globe and fountain.

**1955, July 26** *Perf. 11½*

**C196** AP51 5p magenta .55 .25
**C197** AP51 15p light blue .75 .40

Emigrants' Congress. Exist imperf.

**1955, Oct. 3** **Photo.**

**C198** AP52 25p deep blue .75 .50
**C199** AP52 50p plum 1.25 .90

International Children's Day.

Globe, Scales and Dove AP53

**1955, Oct. 30**

**C200** AP53 15p ultra .75 .40
**C201** AP53 35p brown black 1.50 .60

10th anniv. of the UN, Oct. 24, 1955.
For overprints see Nos. C221-C222.

Aqueduct Type of Regular Issue

**1955, Nov. 21** **Litho.** **Unwmk.**

**C202** A72 30p dark blue 2.00 1.10

No. C191 Overprinted in Ultramarine

**1955, Dec. 29** **Photo.** *Perf. 13½x13*

**C203** A69a 5p yellow brown .50 .20

APU Congress, Cairo, Mar. 15, 1955.

Liberation Monument — AP54

Designs: 65p, Winged figure with shield and sword. 75p, President Shukri el Kouatly.

**1956, Apr. 17** **Litho.** *Perf. 11½*

**C204** AP54 35p black brown .60 .40
**C205** AP54 65p rose red 1.00 .60
**C206** AP54 75p dk slate green 1.90 1.00
*Nos. C204-C206 (3)* 3.50 2.00

10th anniv. of the evacuation of British and French troops from Syria.

No. C191 Overprinted in Black

**1956, Apr. 11** **Photo.** *Perf. 13½x13*

**C207** A69a 5p yellow brown .50 .20

Visit of King Hussein of Jordan to Damascus, Apr. 1956.

President Shukri el Kouatly AP55

Gate of Kasr el Heir, Palmyra AP56

**1956, July 7** **Litho.** *Perf. 11½*

**C208** AP55 100p black 1.25 1.00
**C209** AP55 200p violet 2.50 1.25
**C210** AP55 300p dull rose 4.00 2.75
**C211** AP55 500p dk bl grn 7.50 5.00
*Nos. C208-C211 (4)* 15.25 10.00

Nos. CB5-CB8 Overprinted with 3 Bars Obliterating Surtax

**1956**

**C212** SPAP1 25p gray black .60 .20
**C213** SPAP2 35p ultra .75 .25
**C214** SPAP2 40p rose lilac 1.50 .60
**C215** SPAP1 70p Prus green 1.75 .90
*Nos. C212-C215 (4)* 4.60 1.95

**1956, Sept. 1** **Unwmk.**

Designs: 20p, Hand loom and modern mill. 30p, Ox-drawn plow and tractor. 35p, Cogwheels and galley. 50p, Textiles and vase.

**C216** AP56 15p gray .50 .50
**C217** AP56 20p brt ultra .75 .75
**C218** AP56 30p blue green 1.00 1.00
**C219** AP56 35p blue 1.25 1.25
**C220** AP56 50p rose lilac 1.50 1.50
*Nos. C216-C220 (5)* 5.00 5.00

3rd International Fair, Damascus.

#C200-C201 Overprinted in Red or Green

**1956, Oct. 30** **Photo.** *Perf. 11½*

**C221** AP53 15p ultra (R) 1.00 .60
**C222** AP53 35p brown blk (G) 1.75 1.25

United Nations, 11th anniversary.

Clay Tablet with First Alphabet AP57

Helmet of Syrian Legionary and Ornament — AP58

50p, Lintel from Temple of the Sun, Palmyra.

**1956, Oct. 8** **Typo.**

**C223** AP57 20p gray 1.00 .40
**C224** AP58 30p magenta 1.25 .50
**C225** AP57 50p gray brown 1.90 1.00
*Nos. C223-C225 (3)* 4.15 1.90

Intl. Museum Week (UNESCO), Oct. 8-14.

Trees and Mosque AP59

**1956, Dec. 27** **Litho.** *Perf. 11½*

**C226** AP59 10p olive bister .40 .25
**C227** AP59 40p slate green .90 .45

Day of the Tree, Dec. 27, 1956.
See UAR #36. For overprint see UAR #49.

Mother and Child AP60

Sword and Shields AP61

Design: 60p, Mother holding infant.

**1957, Mar. 21** **Unwmk.**

| | | | | |
|---|---|---|---|---|
| C228 | AP60 | 40p ultra | .75 | .60 |
| C229 | AP60 | 60p vermilion | 1.25 | .85 |

Mother's Day, 1957.

**1957, Apr. 20** **Wmk. 291**

Designs: 15p, 35p, Map and "Syria" holding torch. 25p, Pres. Kouatly.

| | | | | |
|---|---|---|---|---|
| C230 | AP61 | 10p redsh brn | .30 | .20 |
| C231 | AP61 | 15p bl grn | .40 | .25 |
| C232 | AP61 | 25p violet | .50 | .35 |
| C233 | AP61 | 35p cerise | .75 | .50 |
| C234 | AP61 | 40p gray | 1.10 | .60 |
| | | *Nos. C230-C234 (5)* | 3.05 | 1.90 |

British-French troop evacuation, 11th anniv.

Ship Loading — AP62

Sugar Production AP63

30p, 40p, Harvesting grain and cotton.

**1957, Sept. 1** **Unwmk.** ***Perf. 11½***

| | | | | |
|---|---|---|---|---|
| C235 | AP62 | 25p magenta | .50 | .30 |
| C236 | AP62 | 30p light red brown | .60 | .35 |
| C237 | AP63 | 35p light blue | .75 | .40 |
| C238 | AP62 | 40p blue green | 1.00 | .50 |
| C239 | AP62 | 70p olive bister | 1.25 | .90 |
| | | *Nos. C235-C239 (5)* | 4.10 | 2.45 |

4th International Fair, Damascus.

Arab Lawyers Type of Regular Issue

**1957, Sept. 21** **Litho.** **Wmk. 291**

| | | | | |
|---|---|---|---|---|
| C240 | A76 | 17½p red | .40 | .30 |
| C241 | A76 | 40p black | .90 | .50 |

Cotton Festival Type of Regular Issue

**1957, Oct. 17**

| | | | | |
|---|---|---|---|---|
| C242 | A77 | 17½p org & blk | .75 | .40 |
| C243 | A77 | 40p lt bl & blk | 1.25 | .50 |

Children's Day Type of Regular Issue

**1957, Oct. 3**

| | | | | |
|---|---|---|---|---|
| C244 | A78 | 17½p ultra | 1.25 | .50 |
| C245 | A78 | 20p red brn | 1.50 | .50 |

International Children's Day, Oct. 7.
For overprints see UAR Nos. C10-C11.

Family Writing and Reading Letters AP64

**1957, Oct. 18** **Litho.** **Unwmk.**

| | | | | |
|---|---|---|---|---|
| C246 | AP64 | 5p brt grn | .40 | .20 |

Intl. Letter Writing Week Oct. 6-12.
For overprint see No. C26.

Afro-Asian Jurists Type of Regular Issue

**1957, Nov.** **Wmk. 291** ***Perf. 11½***

| | | | | |
|---|---|---|---|---|
| C247 | A80 | 30p lt bl grn | .50 | .35 |
| C248 | A80 | 50p lt vio | .75 | .50 |

Type of Regular Issue and

Radio, Telegraph and Telephone — AP65

**1958, Feb. 12** ***Perf. 11½***

| | | | | |
|---|---|---|---|---|
| C249 | A83 | 10p brt grn | .35 | .20 |
| C250 | AP65 | 15p brown | .40 | .25 |

**Syrian Arab Republic**

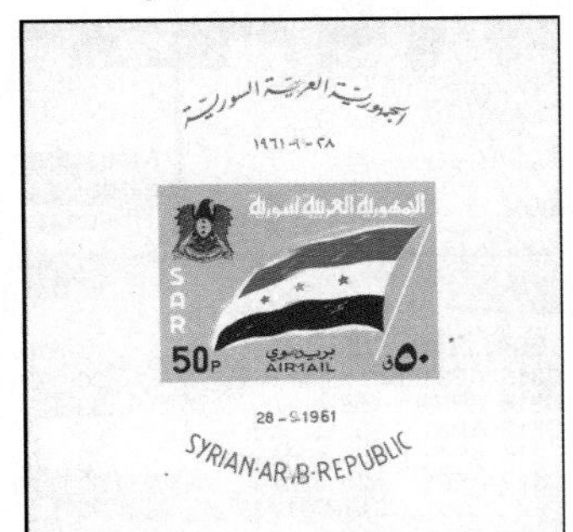


Syrian Flag — AP67

Souvenir Sheet

**1961** **Unwmk.** **Litho.** ***Imperf.***

| | | | | |
|---|---|---|---|---|
| C253 | AP67 | 50p multi | 2.75 | 2.75 |

Establishment of Syrian Arab Republic.

"The Beauty of Palmyra" — AP68

Archway, Palmyra — AP69

Design: 200p, 300p, 500p, 1000p, Niche, King Zahir Bibar's tomb.

**1961-63** **Litho.** ***Perf. 12x11½***

| | | | | |
|---|---|---|---|---|
| C255 | AP68 | 45p citron | .40 | .20 |
| C256 | AP68 | 50p red org | .50 | .25 |
| C257 | AP69 | 85p sepia | 1.00 | .30 |
| C258 | AP69 | 100p lilac | 1.25 | .35 |
| C259 | AP69 | 200p slate grn ('62) | 2.25 | .65 |
| C260 | AP69 | 300p dk bl ('62) | 2.75 | .75 |
| C261 | AP69 | 500p lilac ('63) | 4.00 | 1.50 |
| C262 | AP69 | 1000p dk gray ('63) | 8.25 | 2.75 |
| | | *Nos. C255-C262 (8)* | 20.40 | 6.75 |

See Nos. 433-436.

Arab League Building, Cairo, and Emblem — AP70

Malaria Eradication Emblem — AP71

**1962, Apr. 1** ***Perf. 12x11½***

| | | | | |
|---|---|---|---|---|
| C264 | AP70 | 17½p Prus grn & yel grn | .30 | .20 |
| C265 | AP70 | 22½p dk & lt bl | .30 | .20 |
| C266 | AP70 | 50p dk brn & dl org | .75 | .30 |
| | | *Nos. C264-C266 (3)* | 1.35 | .70 |

Arab League Week, Mar. 22-28.

**1962, Apr. 7**

| | | | | |
|---|---|---|---|---|
| C267 | AP71 | 12½p ol, lt bl & pur | .40 | .20 |
| C268 | AP71 | 50p brn, yel & grn | .75 | .40 |

WHO drive to eradicate malaria.

Rearing Horse — AP72

Gen. Yusef al-Azmeh AP73

**1962, Apr. 17**

| | | | | |
|---|---|---|---|---|
| C269 | AP72 | 45p vio & org | .55 | .20 |
| C270 | AP73 | 55p vio bl & lt bl | .75 | .20 |

Evacuation Day, 1962.

Martyrs' Square Memorial, Globe and Handshake AP74

Cotton and Cogwheel AP75

Design: 40p, 45p, Eastern Gate at Fair.

**1962, Aug. 25** **Litho.** ***Perf. 12x11½***

| | | | | |
|---|---|---|---|---|
| C271 | AP74 | 17½p rose cl & brn | .30 | .20 |
| C272 | AP74 | 22½p ver & magenta | .30 | .20 |
| C273 | AP74 | 40p vio brn & lt brn | .30 | .20 |
| C274 | AP74 | 45p grnsh bl & lt grn | .50 | .20 |
| | | *Nos. C271-C274 (4)* | 1.40 | .80 |

9th International Damascus Fair.

**1962, Sept. 20** ***Perf. 12x11½***

| | | | | |
|---|---|---|---|---|
| C275 | AP75 | 12½p multi | .35 | .20 |
| C276 | AP75 | 50p multi | .50 | .20 |

Cotton Festival, Aleppo. See Nos. 455-456.

President Type of Regular Issue

**1962, Dec. 14** **Unwmk.**

| | | | | |
|---|---|---|---|---|
| C278 | A88 | 50p bl gray & tan | .75 | .25 |

1st anniv. of the election of Pres. Nazem el-Kodsi.

Queen Zenobia of Palmyra — AP76

Saad Allah El Jabri — AP77

**1962, Dec. 28** ***Perf. 12x11½***

| | | | | |
|---|---|---|---|---|
| C279 | AP76 | 45p violet | 1.00 | .25 |
| C280 | AP76 | 50p rose red | 1.00 | .25 |
| C281 | AP76 | 85p blue green | 1.00 | .30 |
| C282 | AP76 | 100p rose claret | 1.25 | .55 |
| | | *Nos. C279-C282 (4)* | 4.25 | 1.35 |

**1962, Dec. 30** **Litho.**

| | | | | |
|---|---|---|---|---|
| C283 | AP77 | 50p dull blue | .50 | .20 |

Saad Allah El Jabri (1894-1947), a leader in Syria's struggle for independence.

Woman from Mohardé — AP78

Eagle in Flight — AP79

Regional Costumes: 40p, Marje Sultan. 45p, Kalamoun. 55p, Jabal-Al-Arab. 60p, Afrine. 65p, Hauran.

**1963** ***Perf. 12***

**Costumes in Original Colors**

| | | | | |
|---|---|---|---|---|
| C285 | AP78 | 40p pale lil & blk | .55 | .20 |
| C286 | AP78 | 45p pink & blk | .60 | .20 |
| C287 | AP78 | 50p lt grn & blk | .60 | .20 |
| C288 | AP78 | 55p lt bl & blk | .75 | .30 |
| C289 | AP78 | 60p tan & blk | .80 | .30 |
| C290 | AP78 | 65p pale grn & blk | 1.00 | .40 |
| | | *Nos. C285-C290 (6)* | 4.30 | 1.60 |

Hunger Type of Regular Issue

50p, Wheat emblem & bird feeding nestlings.

***Perf. 12x11½***

**1963, Mar. 21** **Unwmk.**

| | | | | |
|---|---|---|---|---|
| C291 | A91 | 50p ver & blk | .45 | .20 |
| *a.* | | Souv. sheet of 2, #453, C291, imperf. | 1.50 | 1.50 |

FAO "Freedom from Hunger" campaign.

**1963, Apr. 18** **Litho.**

**C292** AP79 12½p brt grn .30 .20
**C293** AP79 50p lilac rose .35 .20

Revolution of Mar. 8, 1963.

Faris el Khouri — AP80

Arms and Wreath — AP81

**1963, Apr. 27** ***Perf. 12x11½***

**C294** AP80 17½p gray .30 .20
**C295** AP81 22½p bl grn & blk .30 .20

Evacuation Day, 1963.

abu-al-Ala al-Maarri — AP82

Copper Pitcher, Arch and Fair — AP83

**1963, Aug. 19** ***Perf. 12x11½***

**C296** AP82 50p violet blue .40 .20

abu-al-Ala al-Maarri (973-1057), poet and philosopher.

**1963, Aug. 25**

**C297** AP83 37½p ultra, yel & brn .45 .20
**C298** AP83 50p brt bl, yel & brn .50 .20

10th International Damascus Fair.

Centenary Emblem — AP84

Abou Feras al Hamadani AP85

50p, Centenary emblem and globe.

**1963, Sept. 19** **Litho.**

**C299** AP84 15p chlky bl, red & blk .40 .20
**C300** AP84 50p yel grn, blk & red .50 .20

Centenary of the International Red Cross.

**1963, Nov. 13** ***Perf. 12x11½***

**C301** AP85 50p yel ol & dk brn .50 .20

Abou Feras (932-968), poet.

Heads of Three Races and Flame — AP86

**1964, Jan. 6** **Unwmk.**

**C302** AP86 17½p multi .30 .20
**C303** AP86 22½p grn, blk & red .30 .20
**C304** AP86 50p vio, blk & red .40 .20
*a.* Souv. sheet of 3 1.10 1.10
*Nos. C302-C304 (3)* 1.00 .60

Universal Declaration of Human Rights, 15th anniv. #C304a contains 3 imperf. stamps similar to #C302-C304 with simulated perforations.

Flag, Torch and Map of Arab Countries AP87

**1964, Mar. 8** **Unwmk.** ***Perf. 11½***

**C305** AP87 15p multi .30 .20
**C306** AP87 17½p multi .30 .20
**C307** AP87 22½p multi .30 .20
*Nos. C305-C307 (3)* .90 .60

Revolution of Mar. 8, 1963, 1st anniv.

Kaaba, Mecca, and Mosque, Damascus AP88

**1964, Mar. 14** **Litho.** ***Perf. 11½x12***

**C308** AP88 12½p bl & blk .30 .20
**C309** AP88 22½p rose lil & blk .30 .20
**C310** AP88 50p lt grn & blk .35 .20
*Nos. C308-C310 (3)* .95 .60

First Arab Conference of Moslem Wakf Ministers, Damascus.

Young Couple and View of Damascus AP89

**1964, Apr. 17** **Unwmk.**

**C311** AP89 20p blue .30 .20
**C312** AP89 25p rose car .30 .20
**C313** AP89 60p emerald .35 .20
*Nos. C311-C313 (3)* .95 .60

Evacuation Day, Apr. 17, 1964.

Abul Kasim (Albucasis) AP90

**1964, Apr. 21** ***Perf. 12x11½***

**C314** AP90 60p brown .40 .20

4th Arab Congress of Dental and Oral Surgery, Damascus.

Mosaic, Chahba, Thalassa AP91

***Perf. 11½x12***

**1964, June-July** **Litho.**

**C315** AP91 27½p car rose .30 .20
**C316** AP91 45p gray .30 .20
**C317** AP91 50p brt grn .40 .20
**C318** AP91 55p slate grn .40 .20
**C319** AP91 60p ultra .50 .20
*Nos. C315-C319 (5)* 1.90 1.00

Hanging Lamp, Fair Emblem — AP92

Globe and Fair Emblem — AP93

**1964, Aug. 28** ***Perf. 12x11½***

**C320** AP92 20p multi .30 .20
**C321** AP93 25p multi .30 .20

11th International Damascus Fair.

Industrial and Agricultural Symbols — AP94

**1964, Sept. 22** **Litho.** **Unwmk.**

**C322** AP94 25p multi .30 .20

**Same Overprinted with two Red Lines in Arabic**

**C323** AP94 25p multi .30 .20

Cotton Festival, Aleppo. Overprint on No. C323 translates: "Market for Industrial and Agricultural Products."

Arms of Syria and Aero Club Emblem AP95

**1964, Oct. 8** **Litho.** ***Perf. 11½x12***

**C324** AP95 12½p emer & blk .30 .20
**C325** AP95 17½p crim & blk .30 .20
**C326** AP95 20p brt bl & blk .40 .20
*Nos. C324-C326 (3)* 1.00 .60

10th anniversary of Syrian Aero Club.

Arab Postal Union Emblem — AP96

Grain and Hands Holding Book — AP97

**1964, Nov. 12** **Litho.** ***Perf. 12x11½***

**C327** AP96 12½p org & blk .30 .20
**C328** AP96 20p emer & blk .30 .20
**C329** AP96 25p dp lil rose & blk .30 .20
*Nos. C327-C329 (3)* .90 .60

10th anniv. of the permanent office of the APU.

**1964, Nov. 30** **Unwmk.**

**C330** AP97 12½p emer & blk .30 .20
**C331** AP97 17½p mar & blk .30 .20
**C332** AP97 20p dp bl & blk .30 .20
*Nos. C330-C332 (3)* .90 .60

Burning of the library of Algiers, 6/7/62.

Tennis Player — AP98

17½p, Wrestlers and drummer. 20p, Weight lifter. 100p, Wrestlers and drummer.

**1965, Feb. 7** ***Perf. 12x11½***

**C333** AP98 12½p multi .30 .20
**C334** AP98 17½p multi .30 .20
**C335** AP98 20p multi, horiz. .30 .20
*Nos. C333-C335 (3)* .90 .60

**Souvenir Sheet**

**C336** AP98 100p multi 1.25 1.25

18th Olympic Games, Tokyo, 10/10-25/64. #C336 contains one 45x33mm stamp.

Ramses Battling the Hittites AP99

Design: 50p, Two statues of Ramses II.

**1965, Mar. 21 Litho. *Perf. 11x12***
**C337** AP99 22½p emer, ultra & blk .30 .20
**C338** AP99 50p ultra, emer & blk .40 .20

UNESCO world campaign to save historic monuments in Nubia.

Al-Sharif Al-Radi — AP100

Dagger in Map of Palestine AP102

Hippocrates and Avicenna — AP101

**1965, Apr. 3 Litho. *Perf. 12x11½***
**C339** AP100 50p gray brn .50 .20

5th Poetry Festival held in Latakia; Al-Sharif Al-Radi (970-1015), poet.

**1965, Apr. 19 *Perf. 11½***
**C340** AP101 60p dl bl grn & blk .55 .30

"Medical Days of the Near and Middle East," a convention held at Damascus Apr. 19-25.

**1965, May 15**
**C341** AP102 12½p multi .30 .20
**C342** AP102 60p multi .35 .20

Deir Yassin massacre, Apr. 9, 1948.

ITU Emblem, Old and New Communication Equipment — AP103

***Perf. 11½x12***
**1965, May 24 Litho. Unwmk.**
**C343** AP103 12½p multi .30 .20
**C344** AP103 27½p multi .30 .20
**C345** AP103 60p multi .50 .25
*Nos. C343-C345 (3)* 1.10 .65

ITU, centenary.

Syrian Welcoming AP104

Bridge and Gate — AP105

**1965, Aug. Unwmk. *Perf. 12x11½***
**C346** AP104 25p pur & multi .30 .20
**C347** AP104 100p blk & multi .75 .25

Issued to welcome Arab immigrants.

**1965, Aug. 28 Litho.**

27½p, Fair emblem. 60p, Jug & ornaments.

**C348** AP105 12½p blk, brt ultra & brn .30 .20
**C349** AP105 27½p multi .30 .20
**C350** AP105 60p multi .40 .20
*Nos. C348-C350 (3)* 1.00 .60

12th International Damascus Fair.

Fair Emblem and Cotton Pickers — AP106

**1965, Sept. 30 *Perf. 12x11½***
**C351** AP106 25p olive & multi .30 .20

10th Cotton Festival, Aleppo.

Same with Red Overprint

**1965, Sept. 30**
**C352** AP106 25p olive & multi .30 .20

Industrial and Agricultural Fair, Aleppo.

View of Damascus and ICY Emblem AP107

**1965, Oct. 24 *Perf. 11½x12***
**C353** AP107 25p multi .30 .20

International Cooperation Year.

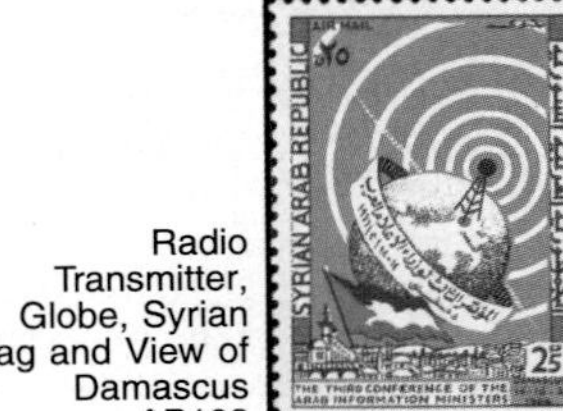

Radio Transmitter, Globe, Syrian Flag and View of Damascus AP108

Hand (shaped like a dove) Holding Flower — AP109

**1966, Feb. 16 Litho. *Perf. 12x11½***
**C354** AP108 25p multi .30 .20
**C355** AP108 60p multi .35 .20

3rd Conference of Arab Information Ministers, Damascus, Feb. 14-18.

**1966, Mar. 8 *Perf. 12x11½, 11½x12***

Design: 17½p, Stylized people, horiz.

**C356** AP109 12½p multi .30 .20
**C357** AP109 17½p multi .30 .20
**C358** AP109 50p multi .75 .25
*Nos. C356-C358 (3)* 1.35 .65

March 8 Revolution, 3rd anniversary.

Statues of Ramses II from Abu Simbel — AP110

**1966, Mar. 15 *Perf. 12x11½***
**C359** AP110 25p dark blue .30 .20
**C360** AP110 60p dark slate green .40 .20

Arab "Save the Nubian Monument Week."

UN Headquarters Building and Emblem — AP111

Design: 100p, UN Flag.

**1966, Apr. 11 Litho. *Perf. 11½x12***
**C361** AP111 25p blk & gray .30 .20
**C362** AP111 50p blk & pale grn .35 .20

**Souvenir Sheet**

***Imperf***

**C363** AP111 100p yel, brt bl & blk 1.25 1.25

20th anniv. (in 1965) of the UN. No. C363 contains one stamp 42x36mm.

Marching Workers AP112

**1966, May 1 Litho. *Perf. 11½x12***
**C364** AP112 60p multi .40 .20

Issued for May Day.

Inauguration of WHO Headquarters, Geneva — AP113

**1966, May 3**
**C365** AP113 60p blk, bl & yel .40 .20

Map of Arab Countries and Traffic Signals — AP114

Astarte & Tyche, 1st cent. Basrelief, Palmyra AP115

**1966, May 4 *Perf. 12x11½***
**C366** AP114 25p gray & multi .30 .20

Issued to publicize Traffic Day.

**1966, July 26 Litho. *Perf. 12x11½***
**C367** AP115 50p pale brn .35 .20
**C368** AP115 60p slate .50 .25

Symbolic Flag, Wheat, Globe and Fair Emblem AP116

Shuttle and Symbols of Agriculture, Industry and Cotton — AP117

**1966, Aug. 25 Litho. *Perf. 12x11½***
**C369** AP116 12½p multi .30 .20
**C370** AP116 60p multi .35 .20

13th Intl. Damascus Fair, Aug. 25-Sept. 20.

**1966, Sept. 9 Litho. *Perf. 12x11½***
**C371** AP117 50p sil, blk & plum .35 .20

11th Cotton Festival, Aleppo.

Symbolic Water Cycle — AP118

Abd-el Kader — AP119

**1966, Oct. 24 Litho. *Perf. 12x11½***

**C372** AP118 12½p emer, blk & org .30 .20
**C373** AP118 60p ultra, blk & org .35 .20

Hydrological Decade (UNESCO), 1965-74.

**1966, Nov. 7**

**C374** AP119 12½p brt grn & blk .30 .20
**C375** AP119 50p brt grn & red brn .35 .20

Transfer from Damascus to Algiers of the ashes of Abd-el Kader (1807?-1883), Emir of Mascara.

Clasped Hands over Map of South Arabia — AP120

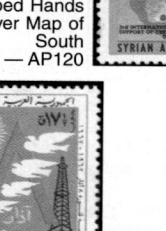

Pipelines and Pigeons AP121

**1967, Feb. 8 Litho. *Perf. 12x11½***

**C376** AP120 20p pink & multi .30 .20
**C377** AP120 25p multi .30 .20

3rd Congress of Solidarity with the Workers and People of Aden, Damascus, Jan. 15-18.

**1967, Mar. 8 Litho. *Perf. 12x11½***

**C378** AP121 17½p multi .30 .20
**C379** AP121 25p multi .30 .20
**C380** AP121 27½p multi .30 .20
*Nos. C378-C380 (3)* .90 .60

4th anniversary of March 8 Revolution.

Soldier, Woman and Man Holding Flag — AP122

Workers' Monument, Damascus AP123

**1967, Apr. 17 Litho. *Perf. 12x11½***

**C381** AP122 17½p green .30 .20
**C382** AP122 25p dp claret .30 .20
**C383** AP122 27½p vio blue .30 .20
*Nos. C381-C383 (3)* .90 .60

21st anniv. of the evacuation of British and French troops from Syria.

**1967, May 1**

**C384** AP123 12½p bl grn .30 .20
**C385** AP123 50p brt pink .35 .20

Issued for Labor Day, May 1.

Fair Emblem and Gate, Minaret, Omayyad Mosque — AP124

**1967, Aug. 25 Litho. *Perf. 12x12½***

**C386** AP124 12½p multi .30 .20
**C387** AP124 60p multi .35 .20

14th Intl. Damascus Fair, Aug. 25-Sept. 20.

Statue of Ur-Nina and ITY Emblem AP125

**1967, Sept. 2 *Perf. 12½x12***

**C388** AP125 12½p lt bl, brt rose lil & blk .30 .20
**C389** AP125 25p lt bl, ver & blk .30 .20
**C390** AP125 27½p lt bl, dk bl & blk .30 .20
*Nos. C388-C390 (3)* .90 .60

**Souvenir Sheet**

***Imperf***

**C391** AP125 60p lt bl & vio bl 1.00 1.00

Intl. Tourist Year.

Cotton Boll and Cogwheel Segment AP126

**1967, Sept. 28 Litho. *Perf. 12x12½***

**C392** AP126 12½p ocher, brn & blk .30 .20
**C393** AP126 60p ap grn, brn & blk .40 .20

12th Cotton Festival, Aleppo.

Same with Red Overprint

**1967, Sept. 28**

**C394** AP126 12½p multi .30 .20
**C395** AP126 60p multi .35 .20

Industrial and Agricultural Production Fair, Aleppo.

Head of Young Man, Amrith, 4th-5th Century B.C. — AP127

**1967, Oct. 7**

100p, 500p, Bronze bust of a Princess, 2nd cent.

**C396** AP127 45p orange .30 .20
**C397** AP127 50p brt pink .40 .20
**C398** AP127 60p grnsh bl .50 .20
**C399** AP127 100p green .60 .30
**C400** AP127 500p brn red 2.25 1.50
*Nos. C396-C400 (5)* 4.05 2.40

Ibn el-Naphis AP128

**1967, Dec. 28 Litho. *Perf. 12x12½***

**C401** AP128 12½p grn & org .30 .20
**C402** AP128 27½p dk bl & lil rose .30 .20

700th death anniv. of Ibn el-Naphis (1210-1288), Arab physician.

Human Rights Flame and People AP129

Design: 100p, Heads of various races and Human Rights flame.

**1968, Feb. 21 Litho. *Perf. 12½x12***

**C403** AP129 12½p lt grnsh bl, bl & blk .30 .20
**C404** AP129 60p pink, blk & dl red .40 .20

**Souvenir Sheet**

***Imperf***

**C405** AP129 100p multi 1.00 1.00

20th anniv. of the Declaration of Human Rights; Intl. Human Rights Year.

Old Man and Woman Reading AP130

Design: 17½p, 45p, Torch and book.

**1968, Mar. 3 *Perf. 12x12½***

**C406** AP130 12½p rose car, blk & org .30 .20
**C407** AP130 17½p multi .30 .20
**C408** AP130 25p grn, blk & org .30 .20
**C409** AP130 45p bl & multi .30 .20
*Nos. C406-C409 (4)* 1.20 .80

Issued to publicize the literacy campaign.

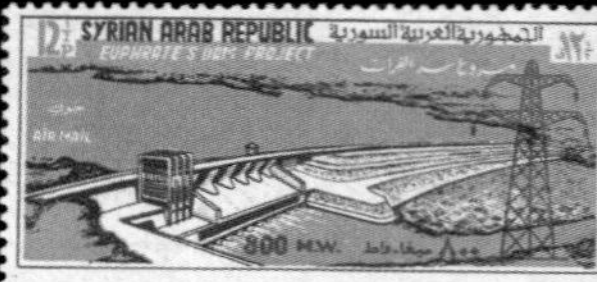

Euphrates Dam Project — AP131

**1968, Apr. 11 Litho. *Perf. 12½x12***

**C410** AP131 12½p multi .30 .20
**C411** AP131 17½p multi .30 .20
**C412** AP131 25p multi .30 .20
*Nos. C410-C412 (3)* .90 .60

Proposed dam across Euphrates River.

WHO Emblem and Avenzoar (1091-1162) — AP132

WHO Emblem and: 25p, Rhazes (Razi, 850-923). 60p, Geber (Jabir 721-776).

**1968, June 10 Litho. *Perf. 12½x12***

**C413** AP132 12½p brn, grn & sal .30 .20
**C414** AP132 25p brn, gray & sal .30 .20
**C415** AP132 60p brn, gray bl & sal .40 .20
*Nos. C413-C415 (3)* 1.00 .60

WHO, 20th anniv.

Monastery of St. Simeon the Stylite AP133

Designs: 17½p, El Tekkieh Mosque, Damascus, vert. 22½p, Columns, Palmyra, vert. 45p, Chapel of St. Paul, Bab Kisan. 50p, Theater of Bosra.

***Perf. 12½x12, 12x12½***

**1968, Oct. 10 Litho.**

**C416** AP133 15p pale grn & rose brn .30 .20
**C417** AP133 17½p redsh brn & dk red brn .30 .20
**C418** AP133 22½p grn gray & dk red brn .30 .20
**C419** AP133 45p yel & dk red brn .30 .20
**C420** AP133 50p lt bl & dk red brn .30 .20
*Nos. C416-C420 (5)* 1.50 1.00

Hammer Throw — AP134

Designs: 25p, Discus. 27½p, Running. 60p, Basketball. 50p, Polo, horiz.

**1968, Dec. 19 Litho. *Perf. 12x12½***

**C421** AP134 12½p brt pink, blk & grn .30 .20
**C422** AP134 25p red, grn & blk .30 .20
**C423** AP134 27½p blk, gray & grn .30 .20
**C424** AP134 60p multi .30 .20
*Nos. C421-C424 (4)* 1.20 .80

**Souvenir Sheet**

***Imperf***

**C425** AP134 50p multi 1.00 1.00

19th Olympic Games, Mexico City, Oct. 12-27. #C425 contains one 52x80mm horiz. stamp.

Construction of Damascus Intl. Airport — AP135

**1969, Jan. 20 Litho. *Perf. 12½x12***

**C426** AP135 12½p yel, brt bl & grn .30 .20
**C427** AP135 17½p org, pur & lt grn .30 .20
**C428** AP135 60p car, blk & yel .40 .20
*Nos. C426-C428 (3)* 1.00 .60

Baal Shamin Temple, Palmyra AP136

Designs: 45p, Interior of Omayyad Mosque, Damascus, vert. 50p, Amphitheater, Palmyra. 60p, Khaled ibn al-Walid Mosque, Homs, vert. 100p, Ruins of St. Simeon, Djebel Samaan.

**1969, Jan. 20 Photo. *Perf. 12x11½***

**C429** AP136 25p multi .30 .20
**C430** AP136 45p bl & multi .30 .20
**C431** AP136 50p multi .30 .20
**C432** AP136 60p multi .30 .20
**C433** AP136 100p vio & multi .60 .25
*Nos. C429-C433 (5)* 1.80 1.05

Workers, ILO Emblem, Cogwheel AP137

Design: 60p, ILO emblem.

**1969, May 1 Litho. *Perf. 12½x12***

**C434** AP137 12½p multi .30 .20
**C435** AP137 27½p multi .30 .20

**Miniature Sheet**

***Imperf***

**C436** AP137 60p multi .60 .60

ILO, 50th anniv. No. C436 contains one stamp 53½x47mm.

Ballet Dancers AP138

Designs: 12½p, Russian dancers. 45p, Lebanese singer and dancers. 55p, Egyptian dancer and musicians. 60p, Bulgarian dancers.

**1969, Aug. 25 Litho. *Perf. 12½x12***

**C437** AP138 12½p multi .30 .20
**C438** AP138 27½p bl & multi .30 .20
**C439** AP138 45p multi .30 .20
**C440** AP138 55p multi .30 .20
**C441** AP138 60p multi .40 .20
*a.* Strip of 5, #C437-C441 1.75 1.75

16th Intl. Fair, Damascus, Aug. 25-Sept. 20.

Children Playing — AP139

Fortuna — AP140

**1969, Oct. 6 Litho. *Perf. 12x12½***

**C442** AP139 12½p aqua, dk bl & emer .30 .20
**C443** AP139 25p brn red, dk bl & lt vio .30 .20
**C444** AP139 27½p ultra, dk bl & gray .30 .20
*Nos. C442-C444 (3)* .90 .60

Issued for Children's Day.

**1969, Oct. 10**

Designs: 25p, Seated woman from Palmyra. 60p, Motherhood. All sculptures from Greco-Roman period.

**C445** AP140 17½p blk, yel grn & grn .30 .20
**C446** AP140 25p dk brn, red brn & lt grn .30 .20
**C447** AP140 60p blk, lt gray & bl gray .40 .20
*Nos. C445-C447 (3)* 1.00 .60

9th Intl. Congress for Classical Archaeology, Oct. 11-20.

Damascus Agricultural Museum — AP141

**1969, Dec. 24 Litho. *Perf. 12½x12***

**C448** AP141 12p Cock .30 .20
**C449** AP141 17½p Cow .30 .20
**C450** AP141 20p Corn .30 .20
**C451** AP141 50p Olives .30 .20
*a.* Strip of 4, #C448-C451 + label 1.25 1.25

Weather Balloon Tracking and UN Emblem AP142

**1970, Mar. 23 Litho. *Perf. 12½x12***

**C452** AP142 25p blk, sl grn & yel .30 .20
**C453** AP142 60p blk, dk bl & yel .35 .20

10th World Meteorological Day.

Lenin (1870-1924) AP143

**1970, Apr. 15 Litho. *Perf. 12x12½***

**C454** AP143 15p red & dk brn .30 .20
**C455** AP143 60p red & grn .35 .20

Workers' Syndicate Emblem AP144

**1970, May 1 Litho. *Perf. 12½x12***

**C456** AP144 15p dk brn & brt grn .30 .20
**C457** AP144 60p dk brn & org .35 .20

Issued for Labor Day.

Radar and Open Book AP145

**1970, May 17**

**C458** AP145 15p brt pink & blk .30 .20
**C459** AP145 60p bl & blk .35 .20

International Telecommunications Day.

Opening of UPU Headquarters, Bern — AP146

**1970, May 30**

**C460** AP146 15p multi .30 .20
**C461** AP146 60p multi .35 .20

"Zahier Piebers and Maarouf" — AP147

Folk Tales: 10p, Two warriors on horseback. 15p, Two warriors on white horses. 20p, Lady and warrior on horseback. 60p, Warriors, woman and lion.

**1970, Aug. 12 Litho. *Perf. 12½***

**C462** AP147 5p lt bl & multi .30 .20
**C463** AP147 10p lt bl & multi .30 .20
**C464** AP147 15p lt bl & multi .30 .20
**C465** AP147 20p lt bl & multi .30 .20
**C466** AP147 60p lt bl & multi .50 .20
*a.* Strip of 5, #C462-C466 1.75 1.75

Al Aqsa Mosque on Fire AP148

**1970, Aug. 21 *Perf. 12½x12***

**C467** AP148 15p multi .30 .20
**C468** AP148 60p multi .35 .20

1st anniv. of the burning of Al Aqsa Mosque, Jerusalem.

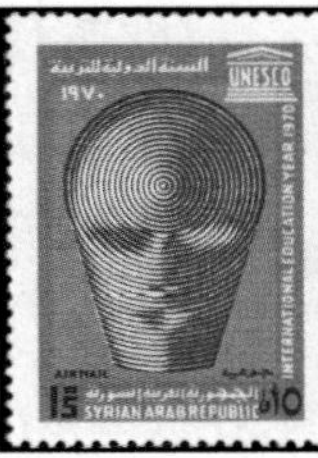

Wood Carving — AP149

Handicrafts: 20p, Jewelry. 25p, Glass making. 30p, Copper engraving. 60p, Shellwork.

**1970, Aug. 25 *Perf. 12½***

**C469** AP149 15p vio & multi .30 .20
**C470** AP149 20p ol & multi .30 .20
**C471** AP149 25p multi .30 .20
**C472** AP149 30p multi .30 .20
**C473** AP149 60p multi .50 .20
*a.* Strip of 5, #C469-C473 1.75 1.75

17th Intl. Fair, Damascus.

Education Year Emblem AP150

**1970, Nov. 2 Litho. *Perf. 12***

**C474** AP150 15p dl grn & dk brn .30 .20
**C475** AP150 60p vio bl & dk brn .35 .20

International Education Year.

UN Emblem, Symbols of Progress, Justice and Peace AP151

**1970, Nov. 3**

**C476** AP151 15p lt ultra, red & blk .30 .20
**C477** AP151 60p bl, yel & blk .35 .20

United Nations, 25th anniversary.

Khaled ibn-al-Walid AP152

Woman with Garland AP153

**1970-71 *Perf. 12x11½, 12½x12½***

**C478** AP152 45p brt pink .30 .20
**C479** AP152 50p green .35 .20
**C480** AP152 60p vio brn .50 .20
**C481** AP152 100p dk bl .60 .20
**C482** AP152 200p grnsh gray ('71) 1.10 .50
**C483** AP152 300p lil ('71) 1.50 .95
**C484** AP152 500p gray ('71) 3.00 1.60
*Nos. C478-C484 (7)* 7.35 3.85

**1971, Apr. 17 Litho. *Perf. 12***

**C485** AP153 15p dl red, blk & grn .30 .20
**C486** AP153 60p grn, blk & dk red .35 .20

25th anniv. of the evacuation of British and French troops from Syria.

People Dancing Around Globe AP154

**1971, Apr. 28 Litho. *Perf. 12½x12***

**C487** AP154 15p vio & multi .30 .20
**C488** AP154 60p grn & multi .30 .20

Intl. Year against Racial Discrimination.

Pres. Hafez al Assad and Council Chamber — AP155

**1971, Sept. 30 Litho. *Perf. 12½x12***

**C489** AP155 15p grn & multi .30 .20
**C490** AP155 65p bl & multi .60 .20

People's Council and presidential election.

Gamal Abdel Nasser (1918-1970), President of Egypt — AP156

**1971, Oct. 17 *Perf. 12x12½***

**C491** AP156 15p lt ol grn & brn .30 .20
**C492** AP156 20p gray & brn .30 .20

Globe and Arrows AP157

**1972, May 17 Litho. *Perf. 11½***

**C493** AP157 15p bl, vio bl & pink .30 .20
**C494** AP157 50p org, yel & sep .30 .20

4th World Telecommunications Day.

Pres. Hafez al Assad — AP158

Airline Emblem, Eastern Hemisphere AP159

**1972, July Litho. *Perf. 12x11½***

**C495** AP158 100p dk grn .60 .25
**C496** AP158 500p dk brn 3.00 1.10

**1972, Sept. 16 Litho. *Perf. 12x11½***

**C497** AP159 15p blk, lt bl & Prus bl .30 .20
**C498** AP159 50p blk, gray & Prus bl .30 .20

Syrianair, Syrian airline, 25th anniversary.

Pottery — AP160

Handicraft Industries: 25p, Rugs. 30p, Metal (weapons). 35p, Straw (baskets, mats). 100p, Wood carving.

**1976, July Litho. *Perf. 12x12½***

**C499** AP160 10p multi .30 .20
**C500** AP160 25p multi .30 .20
**C501** AP160 30p multi .30 .20
**C502** AP160 35p multi .30 .20
**C503** AP160 100p multi .50 .30
*a.* Strip of 5, #C499-C503 1.75 1.75

23rd Intl. Damascus Fair.

Pres. Hafez al Assad AP161

**1978, Sept. Litho. *Perf. 12½x12***

**C504** AP161 25p sil & multi .50 .20
**C505** AP161 35p grn & multi .50 .20
**C506** AP161 60p gold & multi .50 .20
*Nos. C504-C506 (3)* 1.50 .60

Reelection of Pres. Assad. See No. 820.

## AIR POST SEMI-POSTAL STAMPS

Nos. C30-C33 Surcharged Like Nos. B1-B12 in Black and Red

**1926, Apr. 1 Unwmk. *Perf. 13½***

**CB1** A4 2p + 1p dk brown 3.00 2.75
**CB2** A4 3p + 2p org brn 2.75 2.75
**CB3** A4 5p + 3p violet 2.75 2.75
**CB4** A4 10p + 5p vio brn 2.75 2.75
*Nos. CB1-CB4 (4)* 11.25 11.00

The new value is in red and rest of the surcharge in black on Nos. CB1-CB3. The entire surcharge is black on No. CB4.

See note following Nos. B1-B12.

**Catalogue values for unused stamps in this section, from this point to the end of the section, are for Never Hinged items.**

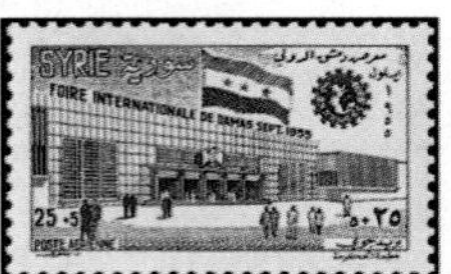

Fair Entrance SPAP1

Industry, Handicraft and Farming SPAP2

Design: 70p+10p, Fairgrounds.

***Perf. 11½, Imperf.***

**1955 Litho. Unwmk.**

**CB5** SPAP1 25p + 5p gray black .40 .40
**CB6** SPAP2 35p + 5p ultra .40 .40
**CB7** SPAP2 40p + 10p rose lilac .60 .60
**CB8** SPAP1 70p + 10p Prus grn 1.10 1.10
*Nos. CB5-CB8 (4)* 2.50 2.50

Intl. Fair, Damascus, Sept. 1955.

For overprint see Nos. C212-C215.

United Nations Refugee Emblem SPAP3

**1966, Dec. 12 Litho. *Perf. 11½x12***

**CB9** SPAP3 12½p + 2½p ultra & blk .25 .20
**CB10** SPAP3 50p + 5p grn & blk .50 .25

UN Day, 21st anniv.; Refugee Week, Oct. 24-31.

## POSTAGE DUE STAMPS

### Under French Occupation

Stamps of French Offices in the Turkish Empire, 1902-03, Surcharged

O. M. F
Syrie
Ch. taxe
1 PIASTRE

**1920 Unwmk. *Perf. 14x13½***

**J1** A3 1p on 10c rose red 160.00 160.00
**J2** A3 2p on 20c brn vio 160.00 160.00
**J3** A3 3p on 30c lil 160.00 160.00
**J4** A4 4p on 40c red & pale bl 160.00 160.00
*Nos. J1-J4 (4)* 640.00 640.00

Postage Due Stamps of France, 1893-1920, Surcharged in Black or Red

**1920**

**J5** D2 1p on 10c brown 3.25 3.25
**J6** D2 2p on 20c ol grn (R) 3.25 3.25
*a.* "PIASTRE" 900.00 900.00
**J7** D2 3p on 30c red 3.25 3.25
*a.* "PIASTRE"
**J8** D2 4p on 50c brn vio 4.75 4.75
*a.* 3p in setting of 4p 525.00 525.00
*Nos. J5-J8 (4)* 14.50 14.50

**1921-22**

**J9** D2 50c on 10c brown 1.40 1.40
*a.* "75" instead of "50" 90.00
*b.* "CENTI MES" instead of "CENTIEMES" 7.50
**J10** D2 1p on 20c ol grn 1.40 1.40
**J11** D2 2p on 30c red 3.25 3.25
**J12** D2 3p on 50c brn vio 3.50 3.50
**J13** D2 5p on 1fr red brn, *straw* 5.00 5.00
*Nos. J9-J13 (5)* 14.55 14.55

D3

D4

**1921 *Perf. 11½***

**Red Surcharge**

**J14** D3 50c on 1p black 3.75 3.75
**J15** D3 1p on 1p black 3.75 3.75

**1922**

**J16** D4 2p on 5m rose 10.00 6.50
*a.* "AX" of "TAXE" inverted 175.00 175.00
**J17** D4 3p on 1p gray bl 15.00 12.00

### French Mandate

Postage Due Stamps of France, 1893-1920, Surcharged

**1923**

**J18** D2 50c on 10c brown 1.50 1.50
**J19** D2 1p on 20c ol grn 2.25 2.25
**J20** D2 2p on 30c red 1.90 1.90
**J21** D2 3p on 50c vio brn 1.90 1.90
**J22** D2 5p on 1fr red brn, *straw* 3.75 3.75
*Nos. J18-J22 (5)* 11.30 11.30

Postage Due Stamps of France, 1893-1920, Surcharged

**1924**

**J23** D2 50c on 10c brown 1.00 1.00
**J24** D2 1p on 20c ol grn 1.00 1.00
**J25** D2 2p on 30c red 1.10 1.10
**J26** D2 3p on 50c vio brn 1.50 1.50
**J27** D2 5p on 1fr red brn, *straw* 1.50 1.50
*Nos. J23-J27 (5)* 6.10 6.10

Postage Due Stamps of France, 1893-1920, Surcharged

**1924**

**J28** D2 50c on 10c brown .75 .75
**J29** D2 1p on 20c ol grn .75 .75
**J30** D2 2p on 30c red 1.00 1.00
**J31** D2 3p on 50c vio brn 1.40 1.40
**J32** D2 5p on 1fr red brn, *straw* 1.75 1.75
*Nos. J28-J32 (5)* 5.65 5.65

Water Wheel at Hama D5

Bridge at Antioch — D6

Designs: 2p, The Tartous. 3p, View of Banias. 5p, Chevaliers' Castle.

**1925 Photo. *Perf. 13½***

**J33** D5 50c brown, *yel* .25 .25
**J34** D6 1p violet, *rose* .25 .25
**J35** D5 2p black, *blue* .55 .55
**J36** D5 3p black, *red org* 1.25 1.25
**J37** D5 5p black, *bl grn* 1.50 1.50
*Nos. J33-J37 (5)* 3.80 3.80

D7

Lion — D8

**1931**

**J38** D7 8p black, *gray blue* 3.50 3.50
**J39** D8 15p black, *dull rose* 6.00 6.00

**Catalogue values for unused stamps in this section, from this point to the end of the section, are for Never Hinged items.**

**Syrian Arab Republic**

D9

| **1965** | **Unwmk.** | **Litho.** | ***Perf. 11½x11*** | |
|---|---|---|---|---|
| **J40** D9 | 2½p violet blue | | .20 | .20 |
| **J41** D9 | 5p black brown | | .20 | .20 |
| **J42** D9 | 10p green | | .20 | .20 |
| **J43** D9 | 17½p carmine rose | | .20 | .20 |
| **J44** D9 | 25p blue | | .20 | .20 |
| | *Nos. J40-J44 (5)* | | 1.00 | 1.00 |

## MILITARY STAMPS

**Free French Administration**

Syria No. 222 Surcharged in Black

| **1942** | **Unwmk.** | ***Perf. 13*** | |
|---|---|---|---|
| **M1** A10 | 50c on 4p yel org | 5.75 | 5.75 |

Lebanon Nos. 155 and 142A Surcharged in Carmine

| | | | |
|---|---|---|---|
| **M2** A13 | 1fr on 5p grnsh bl | 4.25 | 4.25 |
| **M3** A25 | 2.50fr on 12½p dp ultra | 4.25 | 4.25 |

Camel Corps, Palmyra — M1

| **1942** | **Unwmk.** | **Litho.** | ***Perf. 11½*** | |
|---|---|---|---|---|
| **M4** M1 | 1fr deep rose | | .40 | .30 |
| **M5** M1 | 1.50fr bright violet | | .40 | .30 |
| **M6** M1 | 2fr orange | | .40 | .30 |
| **M7** M1 | 2.50fr brown gray | | .40 | .30 |
| **M8** M1 | 3fr Prussian blue | | .75 | .60 |
| **M9** M1 | 4fr deep green | | 1.10 | 1.10 |
| **M10** M1 | 5fr deep claret | | 1.25 | 1.25 |
| | *Nos. M4-M10 (7)* | | 4.70 | 4.15 |

Nos. M4 to M10 exist imperforate.
For surcharges see Nos. MB1-MB2, MC10.

## MILITARY SEMI-POSTAL STAMPS

**Free French Administration**

Military Stamps of 1942 Surcharged in Black

| **1943** | **Unwmk.** | ***Perf. 11½*** | |
|---|---|---|---|
| **MB1** M1 | 1fr + 9fr deep rose | 4.00 | 4.00 |
| **MB2** M1 | 5fr + 20fr deep claret | 4.00 | 4.00 |

## MILITARY AIR POST STAMPS

**Free French Administration**

Syria Nos. C55-C56 Surcharged in Black, Carmine or Orange

| **1942** | **Unwmk.** | ***Perf. 13*** | |
|---|---|---|---|
| **MC1** AP2 | 4fr on 50p blk (C) | 3.25 | 3.25 |
| **MC2** AP2 | 6.50fr on 50p blk (C) | 3.25 | 3.25 |
| **MC3** AP2 | 8fr on 50p blk (O) | 3.25 | 3.25 |
| **MC4** AP2 | 10fr on 100p mag | 3.25 | 3.25 |
| | *Nos. MC1-MC4 (4)* | 13.00 | 13.00 |

Winged Shields and Cross of Lorraine MAP1

| **1942** | **Litho.** | ***Perf. 11½*** | |
|---|---|---|---|
| **MC5** MAP1 | 6.50fr pale pink & rose car | .90 | .90 |
| **MC6** MAP1 | 10fr lt bl & dl vio | 1.00 | 1.00 |

Nos. MC5 and MC6 exist imperforate.
See Nos. MC7-MC8. For surcharges see Nos. MC9, MCB1-MCB2.

Souvenir Sheets

| **1942** | **Without Gum** | ***Perf. 11*** | |
|---|---|---|---|
| **MC7** | Sheet of 2 | 9.50 | 9.50 |
| *a.* | MAP1 6.50fr pale pink & rose carmine | 2.50 | 2.50 |
| *b.* | MAP1 10fr lt bl & dl violet | 2.50 | 2.50 |
| | ***Imperf*** | | |
| **MC8** | Sheet of 2 | 9.50 | 9.50 |
| *a.* | MAP1 6.50fr pale pink & rose carmine | 2.50 | 2.50 |
| *b.* | MAP1 10fr lt bl & dl violet | 2.50 | 2.50 |

No. MC5 Surcharged in Rose Carmine With New Value and Bars

| **1942** | ***Perf. 11½*** | |
|---|---|---|
| **MC9** MAP1 4fr on 6.50fr | 1.00 | 1.00 |

Military Stamp of 1942 Surcharged in Black

| **1943** | | |
|---|---|---|
| **MC10** M1 4fr on 3fr Prus blue | 1.00 | 1.00 |

## MILITARY AIR POST SEMI-POSTAL STAMPS

**Free French Administration**

Military Air Post Stamps of 1942 Surcharged in Black

| **1943** | **Unwmk.** | ***Perf. 11½*** | |
|---|---|---|---|
| **MCB1** MAP1 | 6.50fr + 48.50fr | 12.50 | 12.50 |
| **MCB2** MAP1 | 10fr + 100fr | 12.50 | 12.50 |

## POSTAL TAX STAMPS

Revenue Stamps Overprinted in Red or Black

R1

a

طابع الجيش السوري

b

| **1945** | **Unwmk.** | ***Perf. 10½x11½*** | |
|---|---|---|---|
| **RA1** R1(a) | 5p dark blue (R) | *90.00* | *22.50* |

On Stamps Overprinted

| | | | |
|---|---|---|---|
| **RA2** R1(a) | 5p dk bl (Bk+Bk) | *75.00* | *27.50* |
| **RA3** R1(a) | 5p dk bl (Bk+R) | *75.00* | *27.50* |
| **RA4** R1(a) | 5p dk bl (R+R) | *90.00* | *27.50* |
| **RA5** R1(b) | 5p dk bl (R+R) | *82.50* | *24.00* |

On Stamps Overprinted 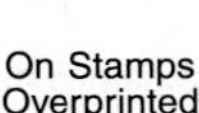

| | | | |
|---|---|---|---|
| **RA6** R1(a) | 5p dk bl (Bk+Bk) | *75.00* | *30.00* |
| **RA7** R1(a) | 5p dk bl (Bk+R) | *75.00* | *30.00* |
| **RA8** R1(a) | 5p dk bl (R+R) | *75.00* | *30.00* |
| **RA9** R1(b) | 5p dk bl (R+R) | *90.00* | *30.00* |
| | *Nos. RA1-RA9 (9)* | *727.50* | *249.00* |

The tax was for national defense.

R2

Revenue Stamp Surcharged in Black

| **1945** | **Unwmk.** | ***Perf. 11*** | |
|---|---|---|---|
| **RA10** R2 | 5p on 25c on 40c rose red | *75.00* | *32.50* |

The surcharge reads "Tax (postal) for Syrian Army."

Revenue Stamp Surcharged in Black

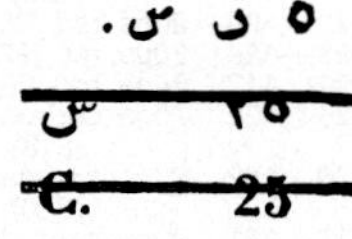

| **1945** | | |
|---|---|---|
| **RA11** R2 5p on 25c on 40c rose red | *75.00* | 32.50 |

No. RA11 Overprinted in Black

| | |
|---|---|
| **RA12** R2 5p on 25c on 40c | *67.50* |

The tax on #RA11-RA12 was for the army.
This overprint exists on No. RA10.

Revenue stamps without overprints occasionally were used as postage on covers through at least 1948.

## ISSUES OF THE ARABIAN GOVERNMENT

The following issues replaced the British Military Occupation (E.E.F.) stamps (Palestine Nos. 2-14) which were used in central and eastern Syria from Nov. 1918 until Jan. 1920.

Turkish Stamps of 1913-18 Handstamped in Various Colors

Also Handstamp Surcharged with New Values as:

1 millieme

1 Egyptian piaster

The Seal reads: "Hakuma al Arabie" (The Arabian Government)

***Perf. 11½, 12, 12½, 13½***

| **1919-20** | | | **Unwmk.** | |
|---|---|---|---|---|
| **1** | A24 | 1m on 2pa red lil (254) | .85 | .85 |
| **2** | A25 | 1m on 4pa dk brn (255) | .85 | .85 |
| **3** | A26 | 2m on 5pa vio brn (256) | 1.40 | 1.40 |
| **4** | A15 | 2m on 5pa on 10pa gray grn (291) | .95 | .95 |
| **5** | A18 | 2m on 5pa ocher (304) | 22.50 | 22.50 |
| **6** | A41 | 2m on 5pa grn (345) | *275.00* | *250.00* |
| **7** | A18 | 2m on 5pa ocher (378) | *47.50* | *47.50* |
| **8** | A28 | 4m on 10pa grn (258) | 6.50 | 6.50 |
| **9** | A28 | 4m on 10pa grn (271) | .85 | .85 |
| **10** | A22 | 4m on 10pa bl grn (329) | 1.75 | 1.75 |
| **11** | A41 | 4m on 10pa car (346) | 37.50 | 37.50 |
| **12** | A23 | 4m on 10pa grn (415) | 7.25 | 7.25 |
| **13** | A44 | 4m on 10pa grn (424) | 1.25 | 1.25 |
| **14** | A11 | 4m on 10pa on 20pa vio brn (B38) | 1.25 | 1.25 |
| **15** | A41 | 4m on 10pa car (B42) | .85 | .85 |

**16** SP1 4m on 10pa red vio (B46) 1.40 1.40
**17** SP1 4m on 10pa on 20pa car rose (B47) 1.40 1.40
**19** A21 5pa ocher (317)
**21** A21 20pa car rose (153) *92.50 110.00*
**22** A29 20pa red (259) 1.40 1.40
**23** A29 20pa red (272) *275.00 275.00*
**24** A17 20pa car (299) 2.75 2.75
**25** A21 20pa car rose (318) 2.75 2.75
**26** A22 20pa car rose (330) 11.00 11.00
**27** A21 20pa car rose (342) 5.00 5.00
**28** A41 20pa ultra (347) 2.75 2.75
**29** A16 20pa mag (363) 11.00 11.00
**30** A17 20pa car (371)
**31** A18 20pa car (379) 7.75 7.75
**32** A45 20pa dp rose (425) 3.75 3.75
**33** A21 20pa car rose (B8) 2.75 2.75
**34** A22 20pa car rose (B33) 2.75 2.75
**35** A22 20pa car rose (B36) 13.00 13.00
**36** A41 20pa ultra (B43) .55 .55
**37** A16 20pa mag (P140) 2.75 2.75
**38** A17 20pa car (P144) *250.00 250.00*
**39** A30 1pi bl (260) 2.75 2.75
**40** A31 1pi on 1½pi car & blk (261) *375.00 375.00*
**41** A30 1pi bl (273) 92.50 92.50
**42** A30 1pi on 1pi bl (273) 125.00 125.00
**43** A17 1pi blue (300) 4.75 4.75
**44** A18 1pi blue (307) 57.50 57.50
**45** A22 1pi ultra (331) 5.75 5.75
**46** A21 1pi ultra (343) 10.00 10.00
**47** A41 1pi vio & blk (348) 1.75 1.75
**48** A18 1pi brt bl (389) 5.75 5.75
**49** A46 1pi dl vio (426) 1.75 1.75
**50** A47 1pi on 50pa ultra (428) 1.10 1.10
**51** A21 1pi ultra (B9) 6.00 6.00
**52** A22 1pi ultra (B15) 10.00 10.00
**53** A18 1pi brt bl (B21) 6.00 6.00
**54** A18 1pi blue (B23) 15.00 15.00
**55** A22 1pi ultra (B34) 12.50 12.50
**56** A41 1pi vio & blk (B44) 2.75 2.75
**57** A33 2pi grn & blk (263) 72.50 72.50
**58** A13 2pi brn org (289) 2.00 2.00
**59** A18 2pi slate (308) 27.50 27.50
**60** A18 2pi slate (314) 27.50 27.50
**61** A21 2pi bl blk (320) 5.25 5.25
**62** A17 2pi org (373) 4.25 4.25
**63** A18 5pi brn (310) 12.00 12.00
**64** A22 5pi dl vio (333) 23.50 23.50
**65** A41 5pi yel brn & blk (349) 4.75 4.75
**66** A41 5pi yel brn & blk (418) 4.75 4.75
**67** A53 5pi on 2pa Prus bl (547) 7.75 7.75
**68** A21 5pi dk vio (B10) 275.00 275.00
**69** A17 5pi lil rose (B20) 47.50 47.50
**70** A41 5pi yel brn & blk (B45) 4.75 4.75
**72** A50 10pi dk grn (431) 130.00 130.00
**73** A50 10pi dk vio (432) 110.00 110.00
**74** A50 10pi dk brn (433) *375.00*
**75** A18 10pi org brn (B2) 350.00 350.00
**76** A37 25pi ol grn (267) *350.00 350.00*
**77** A40 25pi on 200pi grn & blk (287) *500.00 500.00*
**78** A17 25pi brn (303) 375.00 375.00
**79** A51 25pi car, *straw* (434) 92.50 92.50
**81** A52 50pi ind (438) 200.00 200.00

The variety "surcharge omitted" exists on Nos. 1-5, 12-13, 16, 32, 49-50, 67.

A few copies of No. 377 (50pi) and No. 269 (100pi) were overprinted but not regularly issued.

Overprinted

The Inscription reads "Hakum Soria Arabie" (Syrian-Arabian Government)

**On Stamp of 1913**

**83** A26 2m on 5pa vio brn (256) 5.00 5.00

**On Stamp of 1916-18**

**84** A45 20pa dp rose (425) .55 .55

A1

**Litho.** ***Perf. 11½***

**85** A1 5m rose .55 .55
*a.* Tête bêche pair 22.50 10.00
*b.* Imperf.

**Independence Issue**

Arabic Overprint in Green: "Souvenir of Syrian Independence March 8, 1920"

**86** A1 5m rose 250.00 150.00
*a.* Tête bêche pair
*b.* Inverted overprint 375.00 375.00

A2

**Litho.**

**Size: 22x18mm**

**87** A2 1/10pi lt brn .25 .20

**Size: 28x22mm**

**88** A2 2/10pi yel grn .30 .20
*a.* 2/10pi yellow (error) 10.00 10.00
**89** A2 3/10pi yellow .40 .30
**90** A2 1pi gray blue .35 .25
**91** A2 2pi blue grn 2.00 1.00

**Size: 31x25mm**

**92** A2 5pi vio brn 2.75 1.50
**93** A2 10pi gray 2.75 2.00
*Nos. 86-93 (8)* 258.80 155.45

Nos. 86-93 exist imperf.
For overprint see No. J5.

PF1

PF2

Revenue Stamps Surcharged as on Postage Stamps, for Postal Use

**1920** **Unwmk.** ***Perf. 11½***

**94** PF1 5m on 5pa red .50 .35
**95** PF2 1m on 5pa red .50 .20
**96** PF2 2m on 5pa red .40 .25
**97** PF2 1pi on 5pa red 1.00 .65

Surcharged in Syrian Piasters

**98** PF2 2pi on 5pa red .35 .20
**99** PF2 3pi on 5pa red .35 .20
*Nos. 94-99 (6)* 3.10 1.85

## ISSUES OF THE ARABIAN GOVERNMENT POSTAGE DUE STAMPS

Postage Due Stamps of Turkey, 1914, Handstamped and Surcharged with New Value

**1920** **Unwmk.** ***Perf. 12***

**J1** D1 2m on 5pa claret 6.75 6.75
**J2** D2 20pa red 6.75 6.75
**J3** D3 1pi dark blue 6.75 6.75
**J4** D4 2pi slate 6.75 6.75
*Nos. J1-J4 (4)* 27.00 27.00

**Type of Regular Issue**

***Perf. 11½***

**Litho.**

**5** A2 1pi black 1.25 1.25

## UNITED ARAB REPUBLIC

**Catalogue values for unused stamps in this section are for Never Hinged items.**

See Egypt for stamps of types A1, A4, A7, A8, A14, A17, A19, A20, A24 with denomination in "M" (milliemes).

**Issues for Syria**

Linked Maps of Egypt and Syria — A1

***Perf. 11½***

**1958, Feb. 1** **Unwmk.** **Litho.**

**1** A1 12½p yellow & green .20 .20

Establishment of UAR. See No. C1.
See also Egypt No. 436.

Freedom Monument A2

**1958, May**

**2** A2 5p yel & vio .40 .20
**3** A2 15p yel grn & brn red .65 .35
*Nos. 2-3,C2-C3 (4)* 3.00 1.30

British-French troop evacuation, 12th anniv.

Bronze Rattle — A3

Hand Holding Torch, Broken Chain and Flag — A4

Antique Art: 15p, Goddess. 20p, Lamgi Mari. 30p, Mithras fighting bull. 40p, Aspasia. 60p, Minerva. 75p, Flask. 100p, Enameled Vase. 150p, Mosaic from Omayyad Mosque, Damascus.

**1958, Sept. 14** **Litho.** ***Perf. 12***

**4** A3 10p lt ol grn .20 .20
**5** A3 15p brown org .20 .20
**6** A3 20p rose lilac .20 .20
**7** A3 30p lt brown .20 .20
**8** A3 40p gray .30 .20
**9** A3 60p green .50 .20
**10** A3 75p blue .80 .30
**11** A3 100p brown car 1.20 .40
**12** A3 150p dull purple 2.25 .60
*Nos. 4-12 (9)* 5.85 2.50

Archaeological collections and museums.

**1958, Oct. 14** ***Perf. 11½***

**13** A4 12.50p car rose .20 .20

Establishment of Republic of Iraq.
See Egypt No. 454.

Syria No. 411 Overprinted

RAU

**1958, Oct. 6** **Wmk. 291** ***Perf. 11½***

**13A** A78 12½p olive *37.50 35.00*
*Nos. 13A,C10-C11 (3)* *87.50 85.00*

Intl. Children's Day, 1958.

View of Damascus — A5

**1958, Dec. 10** **Unwmk.**

**14** A5 12½p green .20 .20

4th Near East Regional Conference, Damascus, Dec. 10-20. See No. C14.

Secondary School, Damascus — A6

**1959, Feb. 26** **Litho.** ***Perf. 12***

**15** A6 12½p dull green .20 .20

See No. 26.

Flags of UAR and Yemen A7

***Perf. 13x13½***

**1959, Mar. 8** **Photo.** **Wmk. 318**

**16** A7 12½p grn, red & blk .20 .20

1st anniversary of United Arab States.
See Egypt No. 465.

Arms of UAR — A8

Mother and Children — A9

***Perf. 12x11½***

**1959, Feb. 22** **Litho.** **Wmk. 291**

**17** A8 12½p grn, blk & red .20 .20

United Arab Republic, 1st anniv.
See Egypt No. 462.

**1959, Mar. 21** ***Perf. 11½***

**18** A9 15p carmine rose .20 .20
**19** A9 25p dk slate grn .30 .25

Arab Mother's Day, Mar. 21.
For overprints see Nos. 41-42.

Syria No. 378 Surcharged "U.A.R." in Arabic and English, and New Value in Red

**1959, Apr. 6 Photo. Unwmk.**

**20** A68 2½p on 1p olive .20 .20

Type of 1959 and

A10

Boys' School, Damascus — A11

Designs: 5p, 7½p, 10p, Various arabesques. 12½p, St. Simeon's Monastery. 17½p, Hittin school. 35p, Normal School for Girls, Damascus.

**1959-61 Unwmk. Litho. *Perf. 11½***

| | | | | |
|---|---|---|---|---|
| **21** | A10 | 2½p violet | .20 | .20 |
| **22** | A10 | 5p olive bister | .20 | .20 |
| **23** | A10 | 7½p ultra | .20 | .20 |
| **24** | A10 | 10p bl grn | .20 | .20 |
| **25** | A11 | 12½p lt bl ('61) | .20 | .20 |
| **26** | A6 | 17½p brt lilac ('60) | .20 | .20 |
| **27** | A11 | 25p brt grnsh bl | .30 | .20 |
| **28** | A11 | 35p brown ('60) | .40 | .20 |
| | | *Nos. 21-28 (8)* | 1.90 | 1.60 |

Male Profile and Fair Emblem — A12

Fair Emblem and Globe — A13

**1959, Aug. 30 Unwmk. *Perf. 11½***

**30** A12 35p gray, grn & vio .40 .20

**Souvenir Sheet**

***Imperf***

**31** A13 30p dl yel & grn 1.50 1.50

6th International Damascus Fair.

Shield and Cogwheel — A14

***Perf. 13½x13***

**1959, Oct. 20 Wmk. 328**

**32** A14 50p sepia .60 .35

Issued for Army Day, 1959.

See Egypt No. 491.

Syria Nos. 408 and 386 with Red Overprint Similar to

**1959 Unwmk. Litho. *Perf. 11½***

**33** A75 15p gray .20 .20

**Photo.**

**34** A69 50p dk grn .60 .40

The overprints differ in size and lettering: No. 33 is 28x8½mm; No. 34 is 21x6mm. A period follows "R" on Nos. 33-34. The Arabic overprint means "United Arab Republic."

Cogwheel, Wheat and Cotton — A15

A. R. Kawakbi — A16

**1959, Oct. 30 Litho.**

**35** A15 35p gray, bl & ocher .40 .20

Industrial and Agricultural Production Fair, Aleppo. For overprint see No. 46.

Type of Syria Air Post, 1956, Inscribed "U.A.R."

**1959, Dec. 31 Unwmk. *Perf. 13½***

**36** AP59 12½p gray ol & bister .20 .20

Day of the Tree. For overprint see No. 49.

**1960, Jan. 11 *Perf. 12x11½***

**37** A16 15p dark green .20 .20

Kawakbi, Arabic writer, 50th death anniv.

Arms and Flag — A17

***Perf. 13½x13***

**1960, Feb. 22 Photo. Wmk. 328**

**38** A17 12½p red & dk sl grn .20 .20

United Arab Republic, 2nd anniversary. See Egypt No. 499.

Diesel Train and Old Town — A18

***Perf. 11½x11***

**1960, Mar. 15 Litho. Unwmk.**

**39** A18 12½p brn & brt bl .35 .20

Construction of the Latakia-Aleppo railroad.

Arab League Center, Cairo, and Arms of UAR A19

***Perf. 13x13½***

**1960, Mar. 22 Photo. Wmk. 328**

**40** A19 12½p dl grn & blk .20 .20

Opening of the Arab League Center and the Arab Postal Museum in Cairo. See Egypt No. 502.

Nos. 18-19 Overprinted in Black or Magenta

**Wmk. 291**

**1960, Apr. 3 Litho. *Perf. 11½***

| | | | | |
|---|---|---|---|---|
| **41** | A9 | 15p car rose | .20 | .20 |
| **42** | A9 | 25p dk slate grn (M) | .35 | .20 |

Issued for Arab Mother's Day.

Refugees Pointing to Map of Palestine A20

***Perf. 13x13½***

**1960, Apr. 7 Photo. Wmk. 328**

| | | | | |
|---|---|---|---|---|
| **43** | A20 | 12½p car rose | .40 | .20 |
| **44** | A20 | 50p green | .70 | .30 |

World Refugee Year, 7/1/59-6/30/60. See Egypt Nos. 503-504.

A21

***Perf. 11½***

**1960, May 12 Unwmk. Litho.**

**45** A21 12½p vio, rose & pale grn .20 .20

Evacuation Day, 1960.

No. 35 Overprinted in Red

**1960**

**46** A15 35p gray, bl & ocher .30 .20

1960 Industrial and Agricultural Production Fair, Aleppo.

Souvenir Sheet

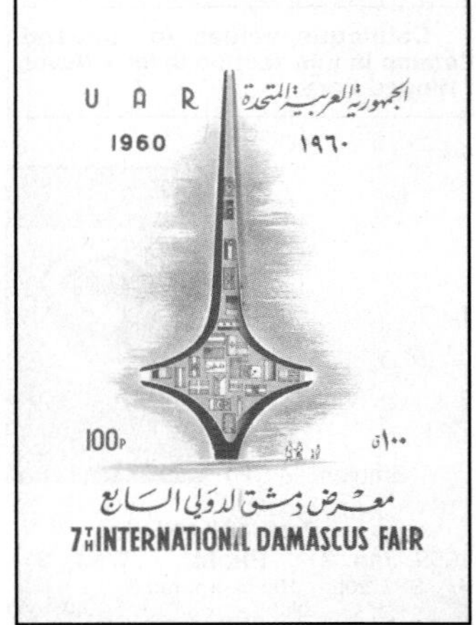


Flags in Symbolic Design — A22

**1960 Unwmk. *Imperf.***

**47** A22 100p gray, brn & lt bl 1.50 1.50

7th Intl. Damascus Fair.

Child — A23

**1960 Litho. *Perf. 11½***

**48** A23 35p dk grn & fawn .40 .20

Issued for Children's Day.

No. 36 Overprinted in Carmine

**1960 Unwmk. *Perf. 11½***

**49** AP59 12½p gray ol & bis .20 .20

Issued to publicize the Day of the Tree.

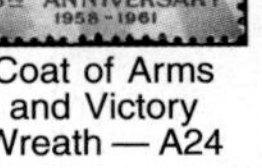

Coat of Arms and Victory Wreath — A24

Cogwheel, Retort and Ear of Wheat — A25

***Perf. 13½x13***

**1961, Feb. 22 Photo. Wmk. 328**

**50** A24 12½p lt vio .20 .20

United Arab Republic, 3rd anniversary. See Egypt No. 517.

***Perf. 11½***

**1961, June 8 Unwmk. Litho.**

**51** A25 12½p multi .20 .20

Industrial and Agricultural Fair, Aleppo.

## UAR SEMI-POSTAL STAMP

**Catalogue values for unused stamp in this section is for a Never Hinged item.**

Postal Emblem — SP1

***Perf. 13½x13***

**1959, Jan. 2 Photo. Wmk. 318**

**B1** SP1 20p + 10p bl grn, red & blk .40 .40

Issued for Post Day. The surtax went to the social fund for postal employees.

See Egypt No. B18 for similar stamp with denomination in "M" (milliemes).

---

## UAR AIR POST STAMPS

**Catalogue values for unused stamps in this section are for Never Hinged items.**

Map Type of Regular Issue

***Perf. 11½***

**1958, Apr. 3 Unwmk. Litho.**

**C1** A1 17½p ultra & brn .35 .20

Broken Chain, Dove and Olive Branch AP1

**1958, May 17**

**C2** AP1 35p rose & blk .70 .35
**C3** AP1 45p bl & brn 1.25 .40

British-French troop evacuation, 12th anniv.

Scout Putting up Tent AP2

**1958, Aug. 31** ***Perf. 12***

**C4** AP2 35p dk brn 1.50 1.50
**C5** AP2 40p ultra 2.00 2.00

3rd Pan-Arab Boy Scout Jamboree.

View of Damascus Fair — AP3

UAR Flag and Fair Emblem — AP4

Designs: 30p, Minaret, vase and emblem, vert. 45p, Mosque, chimneys and wheel, vert.

**1958, Sept. 1 Litho.** ***Perf. 11½***

**C6** AP3 25p vermilion .70 .60
**C7** AP3 30p brt bl grn 1.00 .60
**C8** AP3 45p violet .80 .55
*Nos. C6-C8 (3)* 2.50 1.75

**Souvenir Sheet**

***Imperf***

**C9** AP4 100p brt grn, car & blk 50.00 50.00

Fifth Damascus International Fair.

Syria Nos. C244-C245 Overprinted

RAU

**1958, Oct. 6 Wmk. 291** ***Perf. 11½***

**C10** A78 17½p ultra *25.00 25.00*
**C11** A78 20p red brn *25.00 25.00*

International Children's Day.

Cotton and Cotton Material — AP5

**1958, Oct. 10 Unwmk.** ***Perf. 12***

**C12** AP5 25p brn & yel .40 .40
**C13** AP5 35p brn & brick red .70 .50

Cotton Festival, Aleppo, Oct. 9-11.

Type of Regular Issue, 1958

**1958, Dec. 10**

**C14** A5 17½p brt vio .20 .20

Children and Glider — AP6

**1958, Dec. 1 Litho.** ***Perf. 12***

**C15** AP6 7½p gray green .50 .30
**C16** AP6 12½p olive 2.00 1.25

1958 glider festival.

UN Emblem — AP7

**1958, Dec. 10**

**C17** AP7 25p dl pur .20 .20
**C18** AP7 35p light blue .35 .25
**C19** AP7 40p brn red .45 .30
*Nos. C17-C19 (3)* 1.00 .75

10th anniv. of the signing of the Universal Declaration of Human Rights.

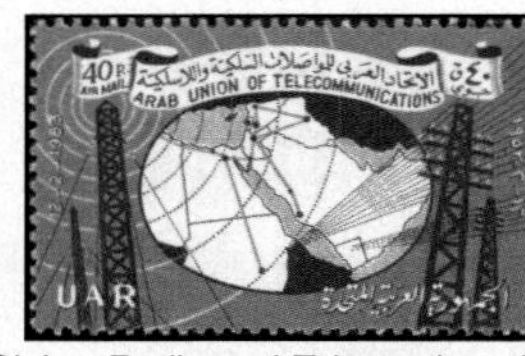

Globe, Radio and Telegraph — AP8

**1959, Mar. 1** ***Perf. 12***

**C20** AP8 40p grn & blk .50 .35

Arab Union of Telecommunications.

See Egypt No. 464 for similar stamp with denomination in "M" (milliemes).

Same Overprinted in Red

**1959, Mar. 1**

**C21** AP8 40p grn & blk .40 .20

2nd Conference of the Arab Union of Telecommunications, Damascus.

Laurel and Map of Syria — AP9

Design: 35p, Torch and broken chain.

**1959, Apr. 17** ***Perf. 12x11½***

**C22** AP9 15p ocher & green .20 .20
**C23** AP9 35p gray & carmine .40 .20

British-French troop evacuation, 13th anniv.

"Emigration" — AP10

**1959, Aug. 4 Unwmk.** ***Perf. 11½x12***

**C24** AP10 80p brt grn, blk & red .70 .40

Convention of the Assoc. of Arab Emigrants in the US.

Refinery AP11

**1959, Aug. 12 Litho.**

**C25** AP11 50p bl, blk & car .90 .40

Opening of first oil refinery in Syria.

Syria Nos. C246 and C181-C182 Overprinted like Nos. 33-34

**1959** ***Perf. 11½***

**C26** AP64 5p bright green .20 .20
**C27** AP44 50p deep plum .40 .20
**C28** AP44 70p purple .70 .30
*Nos. C26-C28 (3)* 1.30 .70

The overprints differ in size and lettering: #C26 is 25½x9½mm; #C27-C28 are 27x8mm. A period follows "R" on #C27-C28.

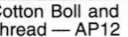

Cotton Boll and Thread — AP12

Boy and Building Blocks — AP13

**1959, Oct. 1 Litho.** ***Perf. 11½***

**C29** AP12 45p gray blue .40 .20
**C30** AP12 50p claret .40 .30

Cotton Festival, Aleppo.

For overprints see Nos. C33-C34.

**1959, Oct. 5**

**C31** AP13 25p dl lil, red & dk bl .20 .20

Issued for Children's Day.

Crane and Compass AP14

**1960 Unwmk.** ***Perf. 11½***

**C32** AP14 50p lt brn, crim & blk .40 .30

7th Damascus International Fair.

Nos. C29-C30 Overprinted in Claret or Gray Blue

**1960 Litho.** ***Perf. 11½***

**C33** AP12 45p gray blue (C) .40 .20
**C34** AP12 50p claret (GB) .45 .30

1960 Cotton Festival, Aleppo.

17th Olympic Games, Rome — AP15

Globe, Laurel and "UN" — AP16

**1960, Dec. 27 Unwmk. *Perf. 12***

| | | |
|---|---|---|
| **C35** AP15 15p Basketball | .20 | .20 |
| **C36** AP15 20p Swimmer | .35 | .20 |
| **C37** AP15 25p Fencing | .35 | .20 |
| **C38** AP15 40p Horsemanship | .60 | .30 |
| *Nos. C35-C38 (4)* | 1.50 | .90 |

**1960, Dec. 31**

| | | |
|---|---|---|
| **C39** AP16 35p multi | .35 | .20 |
| **C40** AP16 50p bl, red & yel | .40 | .20 |

United Nations, 15th anniversary.

Ibrahim Hanano — AP17

Soldier with Flag — AP18

**1961 Litho. *Perf. 12x11½***

| | | |
|---|---|---|
| **C41** AP17 50p buff & slate grn | .35 | .20 |

Hanano, leader of liberation movement.

**1961, Apr. 17 Wmk. 291 *Perf. 11½***

| | | |
|---|---|---|
| **C42** AP18 40p gray green | .35 | .20 |

Issued for Evacuation Day, 1961.

Arab and Map of Palestine — AP19

Abu-Tammam AP20

**1961, May 15 *Perf. 12***

| | | |
|---|---|---|
| **C43** AP19 50p ultra & blk | .50 | .25 |

Issued for Palestine Day.

**1961, July 20 Unwmk. *Perf. 11½***

| | | |
|---|---|---|
| **C44** AP20 50p brown | .40 | .20 |

Abu-Tammam (807-845?), Arabian poet.

Discus Thrower and Lyre AP21

**1961, Aug. 23 Litho. *Perf. 11½***

| | | |
|---|---|---|
| **C45** AP21 15p crimson & blk | .20 | .20 |
| **C46** AP21 35p bl grn & vio | .50 | .20 |

5th University Youth Festival.

A souvenir sheet contains one each of Nos. C45-C46 imperf.

Fair Emblem — AP22

UAR Pavilion — AP23

**1961, Aug. 25**

| | | |
|---|---|---|
| **C47** AP22 17½p vio & grn | .20 | .20 |
| **C48** AP23 50p brt lil & blk | .35 | .20 |
| *a.* Black omitted | | |

8th International Damascus Fair.

St. Simeon's Monastery AP24

**1961, Oct. Litho. *Perf. 12***

| | | |
|---|---|---|
| **C49** AP24 200p violet blue | 1.50 | .90 |

No. C49 was issued by the Syrian Arab Republic after dissolution of the UAR.

## UAR AIR POST SEMI-POSTAL STAMP

**Catalogue value for the unused stamp in this section is for a Never Hinged item.**

Eye, Hand and UN Emblem SPAP1

***Perf. 12x11½***

**1961, Apr. 29 Litho. Wmk. 291**

| | | |
|---|---|---|
| **CB1** SPAP1 40p + 10p sl grn & blk | .30 | .30 |

UN welfare program for the blind.

## TAHITI

tə-'hēt-ē

LOCATION — An island in the South Pacific Ocean, one of the Society group
GOVT. — A part of the French Oceania Colony
AREA — 600 sq. mi.
POP. — 19,029
CAPITAL — Papeete

The stamps of Tahiti were replaced by those of French Oceania (see French Polynesia in Vol. 2).

100 Centimes = 1 Franc

---

Counterfeits exist of surcharges and overprints on Nos. 1-31.

---

Stamps of French Colonies Surcharged in Black:

25c
a

TAHITI 25c
b

TAHITI 5c
c

TAHITI 10c
d

**1882 Unwmk. Imperf.**

| No. | Type | Description | Unused | Used |
|---|---|---|---|---|
| 1 | A8(a) | 25c on 35c dk vio, *org* | 325. | 275. |
| 1A | A8(b) | 25c on 35c dk vio, *org* | *3,500.* | *3,500.* |
| 1B | A8(a) | 25c on 40c ver, *straw* | *5,000.* | *5,750.* |

Nos. 1-1B exist with surcharges inverted. Values for Nos. 1 and 1A are approximately the same as for normal copies; No. 1B with surcharge inverted is worth about half the value of a normal copy.

Surcharge exists reading either up or down on Nos. 1 and 1A, and double, one inverted on No. 1B. See *Scott Classic Specialized Catalogue of Stamps and Covers* for detailed listings of these and later Tahiti issues.

**1884 Perf. 14x13½**

| No. | Type | Description | Unused | Used |
|---|---|---|---|---|
| 2 | A9(c) | 5c on 20c red, *grn* | 200.00 | 175.00 |
| 3 | A9(d) | 10c on 20c red, *grn* | 275.00 | 225.00 |
| | | ***Imperf*** | | |
| 4 | A8(b) | 25c on 1fr brnz grn, *straw* | 625.00 | 550.00 |

Inverted and vertical surcharges on Nos. 2-4 are same value as normally placed surcharges.

Handstamped in Black

**1893 Perf. 14x13½**

| No. | Type | Description | Unused | Used |
|---|---|---|---|---|
| 5 | A9 | 1c blk, *lil bl* | 800.00 | 725.00 |
| 6 | A9 | 2c brown, *buff* | *2,500.* | *1,900.* |
| 7 | A9 | 4c claret, *lav* | 1,175. | 875.00 |
| 8 | A9 | 5c green, *grnsh* | 40.00 | 35.00 |
| 9 | A9 | 10c black, *lav* | 40.00 | 35.00 |
| 10 | A9 | 15c blue | 40.00 | 35.00 |
| 11 | A9 | 20c red, *green* | 57.50 | 50.00 |
| 12 | A9 | 25c yel, *straw* | *6,500.* | *5,500.* |
| 13 | A9 | 25c blk, *rose* | 40.00 | 35.00 |
| 14 | A9 | 35c violet, *org* | *1,900.* | *1,700.* |
| 15 | A9 | 75c carmine, *rose* | 70.00 | 57.50 |
| 16 | A9 | 1fr brnz grn, *straw* | 80.00 | 65.00 |

Nearly all values of this set are known with overprint inverted, sloping up, sloping down and horizontal. Some occur double. Values the same as for the listed stamps.

Nos. 6, 12 and 14 are valued in the grade of Fine.

Overprinted in Black

**1893**

| No. | Type | Description | Unused | Used |
|---|---|---|---|---|
| 17 | A9 | 1c blk, *lil bl* | 725. | 650. |
| 18 | A9 | 2c brn, *buff* | *2,900.* | *2,300.* |
| 19 | A9 | 4c claret, *lav* | 1,450. | 1,250. |
| 20 | A9 | 5c grn, *grnsh* | 875. | 725. |
| 21 | A9 | 10c black, *lav* | 275. | 275. |
| 22 | A9 | 15c blue | 40. | 35. |
| 23 | A9 | 20c red, *grn* | 40. | 35. |
| 24 | A9 | 25c yel, *straw* | *40,000.* | *30,000.* |
| 25 | A9 | 25c black, *rose* | 40. | 35. |
| 26 | A9 | 35c violet, *org* | *1,900.* | *1,700.* |
| 27 | A9 | 75c carmine, *rose* | 40. | 35. |
| *b.* | | Double overprint | *275.* | |
| 28 | A9 | 1fr brnz grn, *straw* | 45. | 40. |

No. 18 is valued in the grade of Fine.

**Inverted Overprint**

| No. | Type | Description | Unused | Used |
|---|---|---|---|---|
| *17a* | A9 | 1c blk, *lil bl* | *1,000.* | 950. |
| *18a* | A9 | 2c brn, *buff* | *3,300.* | 3,100. |
| *19a* | A9 | 4c claret, *lav* | *1,600.* | 1,550. |
| *20a* | A9 | 5c grn, *grnsh* | *1,150.* | *1,150.* |
| *21a* | A9 | 10c black, *lav* | *725.* | *650.* |
| *22a* | A9 | 15c blue | *175.* | *160.* |
| *23a* | A9 | 20c red, *grn* | *175.* | *160.* |
| *25a* | A9 | 25c black, *rose* | *175.* | *160.* |
| *26a* | A9 | 35c violet, *org* | *2,350.* | 2,250. |
| *27a* | A9 | 75c carmine, *rose* | *175.* | *160.* |
| *28a* | A9 | 1fr brnz grn, *straw* | *190.* | *170.* |

Stamps of French Polynesia Surcharged in Black or Carmine:

g

TAHITI 10 centimes
h

**1903**

| No. | Type | Description | Unused | Used |
|---|---|---|---|---|
| 29 | A1 (g) | 10c on 15c bl (Bk) | 7.25 | 7.25 |
| *a.* | | Double surcharge | 42.50 | 42.50 |
| *b.* | | Inverted surcharge | 42.50 | 42.50 |
| 30 | A1 (h) | 10c on 25c blk, *rose* (C) | 7.25 | 7.25 |
| *a.* | | Double surcharge | 47.50 | 47.50 |
| *b.* | | Inverted surcharge | 72.50 | 72.50 |
| 31 | A1 (h) | 10c on 40c red, *straw* (Bk) | 8.75 | 8.75 |
| *a.* | | Double surcharge | 55.00 | 55.00 |
| *b.* | | Inverted surcharge | 52.50 | 52.50 |
| | | *Nos. 29-31 (3)* | 23.25 | 23.25 |

In the surcharges on Nos. 29-31 there are two varieties of the "1" in "10," i. e. with long and short serif.

---

### SEMI-POSTAL STAMPS

Stamps of French Polynesia Overprinted in Red

**1915 Unwmk. Perf. 14x13½**

| No. | Type | Description | Unused | Used |
|---|---|---|---|---|
| B1 | A1 | 15c blue | 225.00 | 225.00 |
| *a.* | | Inverted overprint | 800.00 | 800.00 |
| B2 | A1 | 15c gray | 25.00 | 25.00 |
| *a.* | | Inverted overprint | 325.00 | 325.00 |

Counterfeits exist.

---

### POSTAGE DUE STAMPS

---

Counterfeits exist of overprints on Nos. J1-J26.

Inverted overprints exist on most, and double overprints on many, Tahiti postage due stamps. See the *Scott Classic Specialized Catalogue of Stamps and Covers* for detailed listings.

---

Postage Due Stamps of French Colonies Handstamped in Black like Nos. 5-16

**1893 Unwmk. Imperf.**

| No. | Type | Description | Unused | Used |
|---|---|---|---|---|
| J1 | D1 | 1c black | *310.* | *310.* |
| J2 | D1 | 2c black | *330.* | *330.* |
| J3 | D1 | 3c black | *350.* | *350.* |
| J4 | D1 | 4c black | *350.* | *350.* |
| J5 | D1 | 5c black | *350.* | *350.* |
| J6 | D1 | 10c black | *350.* | *350.* |
| J7 | D1 | 15c black | *350.* | *350.* |
| J8 | D1 | 20c black | *290.* | *290.* |
| J9 | D1 | 30c black | *350.* | *350.* |
| J10 | D1 | 40c black | *350.* | *350.* |
| J11 | D1 | 60c black | *400.* | *400.* |
| J12 | D1 | 1fr brown | *800.* | *800.* |
| J13 | D1 | 2fr brown | *800.* | *800.* |
| | | *Nos. J1-J13 (13)* | *5,380.* | *5,380.* |

Overprinted in Black like Nos. 17-28

**1893**

| No. | Type | Description | Unused | Used |
|---|---|---|---|---|
| J14 | D1 | 1c black | *1,900.* | *1,900.* |
| *a.* | | Inverted overprint | *2,700.* | *2,700.* |
| J15 | D1 | 2c black | *450.* | *450.* |
| J16 | D1 | 3c black | *450.* | *450.* |
| J17 | D1 | 4c black | *450.* | *450.* |
| J18 | D1 | 5c black | *450.* | *450.* |
| J19 | D1 | 10c black | *450.* | *450.* |
| J20 | D1 | 15c black | *450.* | *450.* |
| J21 | D1 | 20c black | *450.* | *450.* |
| J22 | D1 | 30c black | *450.* | *450.* |
| J23 | D1 | 40c black | *450.* | *450.* |
| J24 | D1 | 60c black | *450.* | *450.* |
| J25 | D1 | 1fr brown | *450.* | *450.* |
| J26 | D1 | 2fr brown | *450.* | *450.* |
| | | *Nos. J14-J26 (13)* | *7,300.* | *7,300.* |

Nos. J15-J20, J22-J26 exist with overprint inverted, double or both. Value, each $600.

---

## TAJIKISTAN

tä-jik-i-'stan

### (Tadzhikistan)

LOCATION — Asia, bounded by Uzbekistan, Kyrgyzstan, People's Republic of China and Afghanistan
GOVT. — Republic
AREA — 55,240 sq. mi.
POP. — 6,102,854 (1999 est.)
CAPITAL — Dushanbe

With the breakup of the Soviet Union on Dec. 26, 1991, Tajikistan became independent.

100 Kopecks = 1 Ruble
100 Tanga = 1 Ruble
100 Dinars = 1 Somoni (2000)

**Catalogue values for all unused stamps in this country are for Never Hinged items.**

Gold Statue of Man on Horse — A1

**1992, May 20 Litho. Perf. 12x12½**

| No. | Type | Description | Unused | Used |
|---|---|---|---|---|
| 1 | A1 | 50k multicolored | .30 | .30 |

For surcharge see No. 12.

Sheik Muslihiddin Mosque — A2

**1992, May 25 Photo. Perf. 11½**

| No. | Type | Description | Unused | Used |
|---|---|---|---|---|
| 2 | A2 | 50k multicolored | .30 | .30 |

Musical Instruments of Tajikistan — A3

**Photo. & Engr.**

**1992, Aug. 15 Perf. 12x11½**

| No. | Type | Description | Unused | Used |
|---|---|---|---|---|
| 3 | A3 | 35k multicolored | .25 | .25 |

For surcharges see Nos. 5-7.

Ram — A4

**1992, Aug. 21 Photo. Perf. 12x12½**

| No. | Type | Description | Unused | Used |
|---|---|---|---|---|
| 4 | A4 | 30k multicolored | .25 | .25 |

No. 3 Surcharged in Black or Blue

**Photo. & Engr.**

**1992, Nov. 12 Perf. 12x11½**

| No. | Type | Description | Unused | Used |
|---|---|---|---|---|
| 5 | A3 | 15r on 35k | .75 | .75 |
| 6 | A3 | 15r on 35k (Bl) | 2.50 | 2.50 |
| 7 | A3 | 50r on 35k | .75 | .75 |
| | | *Nos. 5-7 (3)* | 4.00 | 4.00 |

Russia No. 5838 Surcharged

**1992, Jan. 4 Litho. Perf. 12x12½**

| No. | Type | Description | Unused | Used |
|---|---|---|---|---|
| 8 | A2765 | 3r on 1k | .35 | .35 |
| 9 | A2765 | 100r on 1k | 2.10 | 2.10 |

No. 1 Surcharged in Black and Russia No. 5984 Surcharged in Violet Blue or Green

**1992, May 7 Litho. Perf. 12x12½**

| No. | Type | Description | Unused | Used |
|---|---|---|---|---|
| 10 | A2765 | 10r on 2k (VB) | .60 | .20 |
| 11 | A2765 | 15r on 2k (Gr) | .60 | .20 |
| 12 | A1 | 60r on 50k | 1.00 | 1.00 |
| | | *Nos. 10-12 (3)* | 2.20 | 1.40 |

Location and size of lettering on Nos. 10-11 varies.

No. 2 Surcharged

**Methods and Perfs as Before**

**1992, Sept. 18**

| No. | Type | Description | Unused | Used |
|---|---|---|---|---|
| 13 | A2 | 5r on 50k multi | .40 | .40 |
| 14 | A2 | 25r on 50k multi | 1.00 | 1.00 |

Wild Animals A5

Designs: 3r, Ursus arctos. 10r, Cervas elaphus. 15r, Capra falconeri. 25r, Hystrix leucura. 100r, Uncia uncia.

**1993, June 8 Litho. *Perf. 13½***

**15** A5 3r multicolored .20 .20
**16** A5 10r multicolored .25 .20
**17** A5 15r multicolored .25 .20
**18** A5 25r multicolored .50 .25
**19** A5 100r multicolored 1.75 .35
*Nos. 15-19 (5)* 2.95 1.20

Fortress, 19th Cent. — A6

Academy — A6a

1r, Statue of Rudaki, poet, vert. 5r, Mountains, river. 10r, Statue with oriental inscription, vert. 15r, Mausoleum of Aini, poet, vert. 20r, Map, flag. 35r, Post office. 50r, Aini Opera House. #29, Theater. #30, Flag, map, diff. #31, Observatory. #32, Academy.

**1993-94**

**20** A6 1r multicolored .20 .20
**22** A6 5r multicolored .20 .20
**23** A6 10r multicolored .20 .20
**24** A6 15r multicolored .20 .20
**25** A6 20r green & multi .20 .20
**26** A6 25r multicolored .35 .35
**27** A6 35r multicolored .20 .20
**28** A6 50r multicolored .55 .55
**29** A6 100r multicolored .50 .50
**30** A6 100r blue & multi 1.00 1.00
**31** A6 160r multicolored .60 .60
**32** A6a 160r shown .60 .60
*Nos. 20-32 (12)* 4.80 4.80

Issued: 1r, 5r, 15r, 20r, 25r, 50r, No. 30, 6/8/93, others, 9/8/94.
This is an expanding set. Numbers will change if necessary.

Souvenir Sheet

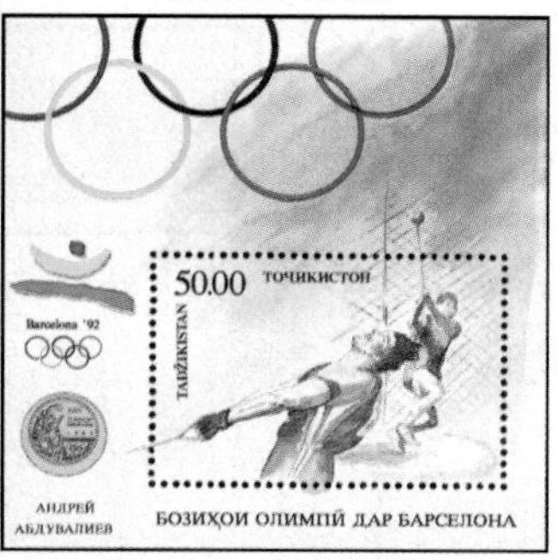


1992 Summer Olympics, Barcelona — A7

**1993, June 8**

**33** A7 50r multicolored 5.25 5.25

For surcharge see No. 52A.

Epic Poem "Book of Kings", by Ferdowsi, 1000th Anniv. A8

Designs: 5r, Combat with swords. 20r, Two men on horseback fighting with spears. 30r, Men in combat stopped by guide on giant bird, vert. 50r, Ferdowsi (c. 935-c. 1020), vert.

**1993, June 8 Litho. *Perf. 13½***

**34** A8 5r multicolored .25 .25
**35** A8 20r multicolored .75 .75
**36** A8 30r multicolored 1.00 1.00
*a.* Sheet, 2 each # 34-36, + 4 labels 12.00 —
*Nos. 34-36 (3)* 2.00 2.00

**Souvenir Sheet**

**37** A8 50r multicolored 2.00 2.00

No. 37 contains one 30x45mm stamp.

Traditional Art Pattern — A8a

**1993, July 1 Litho. *Perf. 12x11½***

**37A** A8a 1.50r multicolored *.45* .45

Dated 1992.
For surcharges see Nos. 62-65.

Ali Hamadani (1314-85), Persian Mystic — A9

**1994, Feb. 22 Litho. *Perf. 13½***

**38** A9 1000r multicolored 2.50 2.50
**39** A9 1000r multicolored 2.50 2.50

Name in latin letters on No. 38 and in cyrillic letters on No. 39.

Natl. Arms — A10

**1994, Feb. 22**

**40** A10 10r black brown & multi .20 .20
**41** A10 15r purple & multi .20 .20
**43** A10 35r olive & multi .20 .20
**44** A10 50r red & multi .20 .20
**46** A10 100r green & multi .20 .20
**47** A10 160r blue & multi .20 .20

**Size: 23x36mm**

**50** A10 500r blue & multi .45 .45
**52** A10 1000r brown & multi .95 .95
*Nos. 40-52 (8)* 2.60 2.60

This is an expanding set. Numbers will change if necessary.

No. 33 Ovptd.

**1994, Apr. 13 Litho. *Perf. 13½***

**52A** A7 50r multicolored *4.00* 4.00

Prehistoric Animals A11

Designs: No. 53, Diatryma. No. 54, Triceratops. No. 55, Anatosaurus. No. 56, Tyrannosaurus. No. 57, Parasaurolophus. No. 58, Incorrectly inscribed "Tyrannosaurus," with horns, resembling an Ankalysaurus. No. 59, Spinosaurus. No. 60, Stegosaurus.

**1994, Sept. 8 Litho. *Perf. 13½***

**53-60** A11 500r Set of 8 6.50 2.50

Issued both in separate sheetlets of nine and together in a collective sheetlet sheetlet of nine, containing Nos. 53-60 and one label.

No. 37A Surcharged in Green

**1995, Mar. 10 Litho. *Perf. 12x11½***

**62** A8a 100r on 1.50r multi .20 .20
**63** A8a 600r on 1.50r multi .40 .40
**64** A8a 1000r on 1.50r multi .75 .75
**65** A8a 5000r on 1.50r multi 3.00 3.00
*a.* Strip, #64-65, 2 ea #62-63 6.50 6.50
*Nos. 62-65 (4)* 4.35 4.35

Issued in sheets of 36 stamps. Each vertical and horizontal strip has stamps in different order.
For surcharges see Nos. 111-114.

Membership Admissions — A13

Designs: No. 66, Member of UN. No. 67, Member of UPU, vert. No. 68, Member of OSCE (Organization of Security & Cooperation in Europe), vert.

**1995, May 4 Litho. *Perf. 13½***

**66** A13 1000r multicolored .85 .75
**67** A13 1000r multicolored .85 .75
**68** A13 1000r multicolored .85 .75
*Nos. 66-68 (3)* 2.55 2.25

Lizards A14

#69, Alsophylax loricatus. #70, Varanus griseus. #71, Phrynocephalus mystaceus. #72, Phrynocephalus helioscopus. #73, Phrynocephalus sogdianus. #74, Teratoscincus scineus.
5000r, Eumeces schneideri.

**1995, May 4 Litho. *Perf. 13½***

**69** A14 500r multicolored .50 .50
**70** A14 500r multicolored .50 .50
**71** A14 500r multicolored .50 .50
**72** A14 500r multicolored .50 .50
**73** A14 500r multicolored .50 .50
**74** A14 500r multicolored .50 .50
*Nos. 69-74 (6)* 3.00 3.00

**Souvenir Sheet**

**75** A14 5000r multicolored 5.00 3.00

For overprints see Nos. 77-78.

Souvenir Sheet

End of World War II, 50th Anniv. — A15

Illustration reduced.

**1995, May 8 Litho. *Perf. 13½***

**76** A15 5000r multicolored 3.50 3.50
*a.* As #76, color diff. 2.50 2.50

On No. 76 emblem in margin is bister, black & red. No. 76a emblem is yellow, black & red with missing letter "E" from second line of text.

No. 70 Ovptd.

No. 71 Ovptd.

**1995, Dec. 1 Litho. *Perf. 13½***

**77** A14 500r on #70 2.40 2.40
**78** A14 500r on #71 2.40 2.40

Singapore '95 (#77), Beijing '95 (#78).

New Natl. Arms — A16

**1995, Dec. 20**

**79** A16 1r olive & multi .20 .20
**80** A16 2r brown & multi .20 .20
**81** A16 5r green & multi .20 .20
**82** A16 12r red & multi .25 .20
**83** A16 40r green blue & multi .60 .60
*Nos. 79-83 (5)* 1.45 1.40

Birds A17

Designs: No. 84, Syrrhaptes tibetana. No. 85, Perdix daurica turcomana. No. 86, Tetraogallus tibetanus. No. 87, Otis undulata macqueeni. No. 88, Larus brunnicephalus. No. 89, Anser indicus.
600r, Phasianus colchicus.

**1996, Feb. 1**

**84** A17 200r multicolored 1.25 1.25
**85** A17 200r multicolored 1.25 1.25
**86** A17 200r multicolored 1.25 1.25
**87** A17 200r multicolored 1.25 1.25
**88** A17 200r multicolored 1.25 1.25
**89** A17 200r multicolored 1.25 1.25
*Nos. 84-89 (6)* *7.50* 7.50

**Souvenir Sheet**

**90** A17 600r multicolored 6.00 6.00

Two each of Nos. 84-89 were issued in sheet of 12 + label.

UN, 50th Anniv. A18

Designs: 100r, UN headquarters, New York. 500r, Headquarters at night.

**1996**

**90A** A18 100r multicolored *1.00* 1.00

**Souvenir Sheet**

**90B** A14 500r multicolored *4.00* 4.00

Issued: 100r, 4/10; 500r, 2/1.

### Souvenir Sheet

Save the Aral Sea — A19

Designs: a, Felis caracal. b, Salmo trutta aralensis. c, Hyaena hyaena. d, Pseudoscaphirhynchus kaufmanni. e, Aspiolucius esocinus.

**1996, May 3 Litho. *Perf. 14***

**91** A19 100r Sheet of 5, #a.-e. *6.00* 6.00

See Kazakhstan No. 145, Kyrgyzstan No. 107, Turkmenistan No. 52, Uzbekistan No. 113.

Octocolobus Manul — A20

Designs: Nos. 92-95, 98, Octocolobus manul (different views). No. 96, Felis chaus oxiana. No. 97, Felix lynx isabellina.

**1996, June 28 Litho. *Perf. 13½***

**92** A20 100r brown & multi 2.00 2.00
**93** A20 100r yellow & multi 2.00 2.00
**94** A20 150r blue & multi 2.00 2.00
**95** A20 150r lilac & multi 2.00 2.00
**96** A20 200r multicolored 2.00 2.00
**97** A20 200r multicolored 2.00 2.00
*Nos. 92-97 (6)* 12.00 12.00

### Souvenir Sheet

**98** A20 500r multicolored 8.00 8.00

World Wildlife Fund (#92-95).

1996 Summer Olympic Games, Atlanta A21

**1996, July 12 Litho. *Perf. 13½***

**99** A21 200r Judo 1.50 1.50
**100** A21 200r Diving 1.50 1.50
**101** A21 200r Hammer throw 1.50 1.50
**102** A21 200r Soccer 1.50 1.50
**103** A21 200r Pierre de Coubertin 1.50 1.50
*Nos. 99-103 (5)* 7.50

Kamol Khujandi, Poet — A22

**1996, Sept. 7 Litho. *Perf. 13½***

**104** A22 500r Cyrillic name 14mm long 3.75 3.75
*a.* Cyrillic name 13mm long 7.00 7.00
**105** A22 500r English inscriptions 3.75 3.75

Central Asian Postal Union, 5th Anniv. A23

**1996, Dec. 25 *Perf. 12¾***

**106** A23 100r multicolored 4.00 4.00

Mountains A24

**1997, July 16 *Perf. 13x12¾***

**107** A24 100r Communism Peak 1.50 1.50
**108** A24 100r Peak Korzhenevskoj 1.50 1.50
**109** A24 100r Lenin Peak 1.50 1.50
*a.* Strip of 3, #107-109 6.00 6.00

### Souvenir Sheet

**110** A24 500r Mountain climber 6.00 6.00

Nos. 62-65 Surcharged

**1997, Oct. 27 Litho. *Perf. 12x11½***

**111** A8a (A) on 100r #62 .75 .75
**112** A8a (A) on 600r #63 .75 .75
**113** A8a (A) on 1000r #64 .75 .75
**114** A8a (A) on 5000r #65 .75 .75
*a.* Strip, #113-114, 2 ea #111-112 4.50 4.50
*Nos. 111-114 (4)* 3.00 3.00

A25

Traditional Costumes: #115, Woman with red shawl draped over head, carrying pitcher. #116, Woman in long formal dress, cape, tiara. #117, Man wearing long striped coat. #118, Man wearing long blue coat.

**1998, Feb. 20 Litho. *Perf. 12½x13***

**115** A25 100r multicolored *.90* .90
**116** A25 100r multicolored .90 .90
**117** A25 150r multicolored 1.40 1.40
*a.* Pair, #115, 117 2.30 2.30
**118** A25 150r multicolored 1.40 1.40
*a.* Pair, #116, 118 2.30 2.30
*Nos. 115-118 (4)* 4.60 4.60

Handicrafts — A26

**1998, Feb. 20 Litho. *Perf. 12¾***

**119** A26 30r Urn .40 .40
**119A** A26 100r Cradles 1.25 1.25

### Size: 64x64mm

***Imperf***

**120** A26 300r Ceramic tile 4.00 4.00
*Nos. 119-120 (3)* 5.65 5.65

A27

**1998, Apr. 3 Litho. *Perf. 12½x13***

Flowers: 12r, Tulipa greigii. 30r, Crocus korolkowii. 70r, Iris darwasica. 150r, Petilium eduardii. 300r, Juno nicolai.

**121** A27 12r multicolored .40 .40
**122** A27 30r multicolored .60 .60
**123** A27 70r multicolored 1.25 1.25
**124** A27 150r multicolored 2.75 2.75
*a.* Sheet of 4, #121-124 5.50 5.50
*Nos. 121-124 (4)* 5.00 5.00

### Souvenir Sheet

**125** A27 300r multicolored 5.00 5.00

Stamps in No. 124a have margins continuing the background design of the sheet.

Butterflies A28

12r, Catocala timur. 30r, Celerio chamyla apocyni. 70r, Colias sieversi. 150r, Papilio alexanor.
300r, Anthocharis tomyris.

**1998, Apr. 3 *Perf. 13x12½***

**126** A28 12r multicolored .75 .75
**127** A28 30r multicolored .90 .90
**128** A28 70r multicolored 1.25 1.25
**129** A28 150r multicolored 2.50 2.50
*a.* Sheet of 4, #126-129 7.00 7.00
*Nos. 126-129 (4)* 5.40 5.40

### Souvenir Sheet

**130** A28 300r multicolored 6.50 6.50

Stamps of No. 129a have margins continuing the background design of the sheet.

Gems A29

**1998, Aug. 21 Litho. *Perf. 13x12¾***

**131** A29 1r Sapphire .20 .20
**132** A29 1r Ruby .20 .20
**133** A29 12r Lapis lazuli .30 .30
**134** A29 12r Tourmaline .30 .30
**135** A29 150r Spinel 1.75 1.75
**136** A29 150r Amethyst 1.75 1.75
*a.* Sheet of 6, #131-136, + 2 labels 4.50 4.50
*Nos. 131-136 (6)* 4.50 4.50

### Souvenir Sheet

**137** A29 350r Agate 4.50 4.50

Bobojon Ghafurov, Academician (1908-98) — A30

**1998, Aug. 21 *Perf. 12¾x13***

**138** A30 12r blue & multi .25 .25
**139** A30 150r red & multi 2.00 2.00

Each printed in sheets of 10.

Aleksander Pushkin (1799-1837), Russian Poet — A31

**1999, June Litho. *Perf. 13¼x13½***

**140** A31 100r Self-portrait drawing .40 .40
**141** A31 270r Painting by Kiprensky 1.10 1.10
*a.* Pair, #140-141 1.50 1.50

### "ILLEGAL" STAMPS

Tajikistan postal officials have declared as "illegal" the following items.

Sheets of nine stamps of various denominations depicting:

Elvis Presley, Barry White, Michael Douglas, Robert DeNiro, Grace Kelly, the television show "Ally McBeal," Harry Potter, Batman, Superman (two different sheets), Warner Brothers cartoon characters, U.S. Political Cartoons concerning the 2000 Presidential election, Mushrooms, Mushrooms in Art, Major League Baseball players, Sydney 2002 Olympic Games (two different sheets), Various golfers, U.S. Open Golf Championship, Golfer Eduardo Romero, Tiger Woods (two different sheets), Pope John Paul II, and Masonic emblems.

Sheet of 3 stamps of various denominations depicting Marilyn Monroe.

A32

A32a

A32b

**1999, June 5 Litho. *Perf. 13½***

**142** A32 (40r) multi .20 .20
**143** A32a (100r) multi .55 .55
**144** A32b (270r) multi 1.40 1.40
*Nos. 142-144 (3)* 2.15 2.15

Samanid Dynasty — A33

**1999, Aug. Litho. *Perf. 12¾x13***

**145** A33 30r Lion figurine .20 .20
**146** A33 50r Round emblem .35 .35
**147** A33 100r Handled figurine .70 .70
**148** A33 270r Three figurines 1.90 1.90
*Nos. 145-148 (4)* 3.15 3.15

### Souvenir Sheet

**149** A33 500r King 3.50 3.50
*a.* Sheet, #149, 2 ea #145-148 10.00 10.00

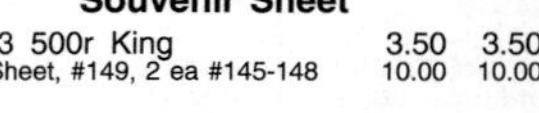

Samanid Dynasty, 1100th Anniv. — A34

Illustration reduced.

No. 150: a, 100r, King. b, 500r, Pres. Emomali Rakhmonov.

**1999, Oct. Litho.** ***Perf. 13½x13***
**150** A34 Sheet of 2, #a.-b. 8.00 8.00

Mushrooms A35

Designs: Nos. 151, 153a, 100r, Pleurotus eryngii. Nos. 152, 153b, 270r, Lepista nuda. 500r, Morchella steppicola.

**1999, Nov.** ***Perf. 13¼x13***
**151** A35 100r multi 1.00 1.00
**152** A35 270r multi 3.00 3.00

**Miniature Sheet**

**153** A35 Sheet, 2 ea #153a-153b 2.75 2.75

**Souvenir Sheet**

**154** A35 500r multi 2.25 2.25

Nos. 151-152 have white borders, while Nos. 153a-153b have borders which continue the sheet's central design.

Fish — A36

Designs: 40r, Ophiocephalus argus. 100r, Barbus brachycephalus. 230r, Schizopygopsis stoliczkai. 270r, Pseudoscaphihynchus fedtschenkoi.
500r, Pseudoscaphihynchus kaufmanni.
Illustration reduced.

**2000 Litho.** ***Perf. 13¼x13***
**155-158** A36 Set of 4 3.00 3.00
*158a* Souvenir sheet, #155-158 3.50 3.50

**Souvenir Sheet**

**159** A36 500r multi 3.50 3.50

UPU, 125th Anniv. (in 1999) — A37

**2000**
**160** A37 270r multi .75 .75

100 Dinars = 1 Somoni (2000)

Birds of Prey A38

Designs: 10d, Pandion haliaetus. 27d, Aquila chrysaetus, vert. 50d, Gyps himalayensis. 70d, Circaetus ferox, vert.
1s, Falco peregrinus, vert.

**2001, Jan. 23 Litho.** ***Perf. 14***
**161-164** A38 Set of 4 5.00 5.00

**Souvenir Sheet**

**165** A38 1s multi 3.00 3.00

No. 165 contains one 42x56mm stamp. Dated 2000.

Chess — A39

Designs: 15d, Mikhail Botvinnik. 41d, Bobby Fischer.
No. 168: a, 10d, Wilhelm Steinitz. b, 25d, Chess board, five people. c, 50d, José Raul Capablanca. d, 70d, Emanuel Lasker. e, 90d, Chess board, four people. f, 1s, Alexander Alekhine.

**2001, May 29** ***Perf. 14¼x14***
**166-167** A39 Set of 2 2.00 2.00

**Souvenir Sheet**

**168** A39 Sheet of 6, #a-f 8.00 8.00

No. 26 Surcharged in Green, Red or Black

a

b

c

**2001, June 4** ***Perf. 13½***
**169** A6(a) (6d) multi (G) .35 .35
**170** A6(b) (15d) multi (R) .65 .65
**171** A6(c) (41d) multi (Bk) 2.25 2.25
*Nos. 169-171 (3)* 3.25 3.25

Souvenir Sheet

Satellite Communications — A40

**2001, July 25** ***Perf. 13¼x13***
**172** A40 1.50s multi 3.50 3.50

Souvenir Sheets

Nurec Hydroelectric Station — A41

Pres. Emomali Rakhmonov — A42

Independence, 10th Anniv. — A43

No. 175: a, 41d, Map, flag and arms (29x29mm). b, 54d, Emblem (29x29mm). c, 95d, Ratification of constitution (49x29mm).

**2001, Sept. 7** ***Perf. 13¼x13¾***
**173** A41 2.50s multi 17.50 17.50

***Perf. 12¾x13¼***

**174** A42 3s multi 21.00 21.00

***Perf. 14x13¾***

**175** A43 Sheet of 3, #a-c 15.00 15.00
Independence, 10th anniv.

Tajikistan postal officials have declared as "illegal" the following items:
Sheets of nine stamps of various denominations depicting Bruce Lee, Michael Jordan, Osama bin Laden, Captain America, Fantastic Four, Queen Mother's 100th Birthday, Formula 1 Racing, Motor Sports and the Netherlands Royal Wedding.
Sheets of six stamps of various denominations depicting Pope John Paul II and Motorcycle racers.
Sheet of three stamps of various denominations depicting Pope John Paul II.

Transportation — A44

Designs: 1s, Tu-154M Airplane.
No. 177: a, 41d, Vehicles on road. b, 90d, Locomotive.

**2001, Dec. 12 Litho.** ***Perf. 14x13¼***
**176** A44 1s multi 2.50 2.50

**Souvenir Sheet**

**177** A44 Sheet of 3, #176, 177a, 177b 6.00 6.00

Commonwealth of Independent States, 10th Anniv. — A45

**2001, Dec. 17** ***Perf. 14¼x14***
**178** A45 50d multi 1.75 1.75

Souvenir Sheet

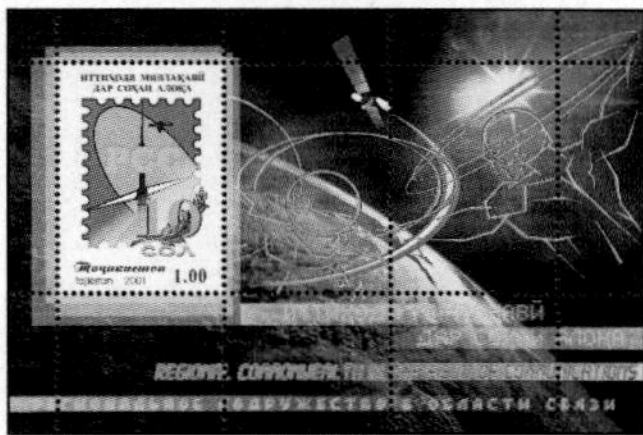
Regional Communications Accord — A46

**2001, Dec. 17**
**179** A46 1s multi + 2 labels 3.25 3.25

Avesta, 2700th Anniv. — A47

Zoroastrian: 2d, Goddess Anahita. 3d, Priest.
No. 182: a, 70d, Goddess Haoma. b, 90d, God Farroh. c, 1s, God Surush. d, 2s, Goddess Din.

**2002, Jan. 1 Litho.** ***Perf. 10***
**180-181** A47 Set of 2 1.50 1.50

**Souvenir Sheet**

**182** A47 Sheet of 4, #a-d 10.00 10.00

No. 182 contains four 27x44mm stamps. Dated 2001.

Miniature Sheet

UN High Commissioner for Refugees, 50th Anniv. (in 2001) — A48

No. 183: a, Mothers holding children, refugees. b, Military helicopter, sun, refugees. c, Cloud, rainbow, moon, soldier, child.

**2002, Jan. 1**
**183** A48 50d Sheet of 3, #a-c 3.50 3.50
Dated 2001.

Flora and Fauna of Central Asia — A49

No. 184: a, Bird facing right. b, Bird facing left. c, Mushrooms and snail. d, Rodent. e, Butterfly. f, Butterfly and tulip. g, Cat. h, Cat and tulip.

**2002, Apr. 12 Litho.** ***Perf. 13¾x13½***

| | | | |
|---|---|---|---|
| **184** | Miniature sheet of 8 | 7.00 | 7.00 |
| *a.* | A49 6d multi | .40 | .40 |
| *b.* | A49 15d multi | .40 | .40 |
| *c.* | A49 41d multi | .40 | .40 |
| *d.* | A49 50d multi | .50 | .50 |
| *e.* | A49 95d multi | .90 | .90 |
| *f.-h.* | A49 1.50s any single | 1.40 | 1.40 |

Worldwide Fund for Nature (WWF) — A50

Reed cats: a, 1s, Two cats. b, 1.50s, One cat walking. c, 2s, One cat resting. d, 2s, Three kittens.
Illustration reduced.

**2002, Apr. 12** ***Perf. 14x14¼***

| | | | |
|---|---|---|---|
| **185** A50 | Block of 4, #a-d | 6.50 | 6.50 |
| *e.* | Sheet, 2 #185 | 15.00 | 15.00 |

Dushanbe Zoo, 40th Anniv. — A51

Designs: 2d, Pan troglodytes. 3d, Cervus nippon hortulorum. 10d, Panthera tigris altaice. 41d, Diceros bicornis michaeli. 50d, Giraffa camelopardis reticulata. 1s, Panthera leo.

**2002, Aug. 29 Litho.** ***Perf. 14¼x14***

**186-191** A51 Set of 6 5.75 5.75

Souvenir Sheet

Navruz — A52

No. 192: a, 1s, Wheat bundle. b, 50d, Dancers in red costumes. c, 1s, Dancer in purple costume.

**2002, Aug. 29**

**192** A52 Sheet of 3, #a-c 5.00 5.00

A53 A54

Istravashan, 2500th Anniv.
A55 A56

**2002, Sept. 6**

| | | | | |
|---|---|---|---|---|
| **193** | A53 50d brown & multi | .90 | .90 |
| **194** | A54 50d green & multi | .90 | .90 |
| **195** | A55 50d brown & multi | .90 | .90 |
| **196** | A56 50d green & multi | .90 | .90 |
| | *Nos. 193-196 (4)* | 3.60 | 3.60 |

**No. 168 Overprinted "2002" on Stamps and With Text in Margin**

Souvenir Sheet

Designs as before.

**2002, Sept. 20 Litho.** ***Perf. 14¼x14***

**197** A39 Sheet of 6, #a-f 8.50 8.50

No. 197 is overprinted in bottom sheet margin "Chess Super Championship / between teams of the World and Russia / 08-11.09.2002. Moscow" and in left sheet margin with similar text in Cyrillic characters.

No. 197 exists imperf. Value $300.

No. 197 also exists with violet overprint. Value: perf, $30; imperf $350.

Tajikistan postal officials have declared as "illegal" the following items.

Sheets of nine stamps of various denominations depicting: 20th Century Dreams (6 different sheets), Elephants and Rotary Intl. emblem, Owls, mushrooms and Rotary International emblem, Pandas, Chess, The Beatles, Locomotives, Princess Diana, the movie The Blair Witch Project, Defenders of Peace and Freedom, 2002 Brazilian World Cup Soccer Team, Harry Potter, Cartoon characters from South Park (Christmas), Warner Brothers Cartoon Characters (Christmas).

Sheets of six stamps of various denominations depicting Pokemon characters (eight sheets), Pope John Paul II, Dinosaurs.

Sheet of three stamps of various denominations depicting Elvis Presley.

Souvenir sheets of one stamp with 25.00 denomination depicting Harry Potter (2 different sheets), Penguins,

Souvenir sheet of one stamp with 20.00 denomination depicting Pope John Paul and New York fireman.

New Year 2002 (Year Of the Horse) — A57

No. 198: a, 2d, Thoroughbread racing. b, 3d, Harness racing. c, 95d, Troika. d, 95d, Polo.

No. 199: a, 50d, Dressage. b, 50d, Fox hunting. c, 1s, Steeplechase. d, 1s, Show jumping.

1.50s, Horses in circus act, vert.

Illustration reduced.

**2002, Oct. 15 Litho.** ***Perf. 14x14¼***

**Blocks of 4, #a-d**

**198-199** A57 Set of 2 7.50 7.50

**Souvenir Sheet**

***Perf. 14¼x14***

**200** A57 1.50s multi + 2 labels 4.00 4.00

Oriental Bazaar — A58

No. 201: a, Man in donkey cart. b, Man on donkey. c, Melon vendor. d, Man cooking shashliks.

**2002, Dec. 25 Litho.** ***Perf. 14¼x14***

**201** A58 65d Block of 4, #a-d 4.00 4.00

Traditional Sports A59

Designs: 1d, Archery. 20d, Horse racing. 53d, Polo. 65d, Stone throwing. 1s, Buzkashi. 1.24s, Wrestling.

**2002, Dec. 25** ***Perf. 14x14¼***

**202-207** A59 Set of 6 6.00 6.00

Lunar Calendar — A60

Designs: 53d, Sun and zodiac animals. 65d, Zodiac animals and ram. 1s, Ram in circle.
1.50s, Ram.

**2003, Mar. 11** ***Perf. 14¼x14***

**208-210** A60 Set of 3 4.50 4.50

**Souvenir Sheet**

**211** A60 1.50s multi + 2 labels 3.50 3.50

Monument to Ismail Somoni — A61

**2003, Mar. 11** ***Perf. 13¼x14***

| | | | |
|---|---|---|---|
| **212** | A61 1d emerald | .40 | .40 |
| **213** | A61 2d red violet | .40 | .40 |
| **214** | A61 3d blue green | .40 | .40 |
| **215** | A61 4d purple | .40 | .40 |
| **216** | A61 12d brown | .40 | .40 |
| **217** | A61 20d blue | .40 | .40 |
| | *Nos. 212-217 (6)* | 2.40 | 2.40 |

Souvenir Sheet

No. 158 Surcharged in Purple

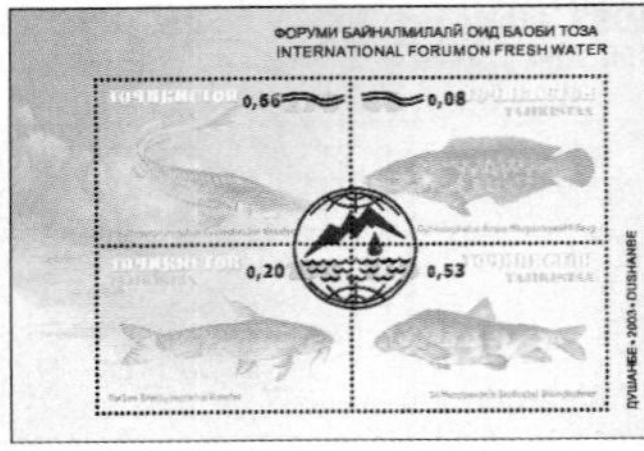

No. 218: a, 8d on 40r, Ophiocephalus argus. b, 20d on 100r, Barbus brachycephalus. c, 53d on 230r, Schizopygopsis stoliczkai. d, 66d on 270r, Pseudoscaphihynchus fedtschenkoi.

**2003, May 12 Litho.** ***Perf. 13¼x13***

**218** A36 Sheet of 4, #a-d 7.00 7.00

2004 Summer Olympics, Athens and 2008 Summer Olympics, Beijing — A62

No. 219: a, 53d, Archery. b, 1s, Track and field. c, 1.23s, Soccer. d, 2s, Gymnastics.

**2003, May 20** ***Perf. 14x13½***

**219** A62 Sheet of 4, #a-d, + 2 labels 9.00 9.00

Exists imperf. with additional designs in margin.

Philatelic Exhibitions and Fauna — A63

No. 220: a, 8d, 16th Asian Intl. Stamp Exhibition, China. b, 20d, Panthera tigris. c, 53d, Inachis io. d, 66d, Bangkok 2003 World Philatelic Exhibition. e, 1s, Rupicapra rupicapra. f, 1.50s, Ailuropoda melanoleuca. g, 1.50s, Leontopithecus rosalia. h, 2s, Elephas maximus.

**2003, May 20**

**220** A63 Sheet of 8, #a-h 12.00 12.00

Exists imperf.

Intl. Forum on Fresh Water — A64

Designs: No. 221, 1.50s, Peak of Moskvin. No. 222, 1.50s, Iskanderkul.

**2003, June 7** ***Perf. 13½***
**221-222** A64 Set of 2 6.00 6.00

Nos. 221-222 were printed setenant, both vertically and horiziontally, in one sheet.

Famous Men — A65

Designs: No. 223, 1.23s, Nosir Khusrav (1004-88), poet. No. 224, 1.23s, Sadridin Aini (1878-1954), writer.

**2003, Sept. 1**
**223-224** A65 Set of 2 4.75 4.75

Intl. Association of Academies of Science, 10th Anniv. — A66

No. 225: a, Head, satellite dish, airplane, chemicals. b, Association emblem, cosmonaut, robotic hand, computer.
Illustration reduced.

**2003, Sept. 1**
**225** A66 1.23s Horiz. pair, #a-b 5.25 5.25

Intl. Year of Fresh Water — A67

Children's art: a, Fish above lake. b, Sun, river, tree and hills. c, River, hills and trees. d, Waterfalls.
Illustration reduced.

**2003, Oct. 20** ***Perf. 14x14¼***
**226** A67 66d Block of 4, #a-d 5.00 5.00

Racing Airplanes — A68

No. 227: a, Aero L-29A Delfin Akrobat. b, Yak-55. c, Cessna 172. d, SIAI-Marchetti SF-260. e, Europa XS. f, MBB BO 209 Monsun. g, Mudry Cap 10. h, Soko 2.

**2003, Oct. 28** ***Perf. 14x13½***
**227** A68 1s Sheet of 8, #a-h 12.50 12.50

Exists imperf.

Fauna of Central Asia — A69

No. 228: a, 8d, Mimas tiliae. 20d, Mustela erminea. 53d, Testudo horsfieldii. 64d, Mantis religiosa. 1.23s, Lanius collurio. 1.27s, Canis aureus. 1.76s, Capra falconeri. 2.29s, Alcedo atthis.

**2003, Oct. 28**
**228** A69 Sheet of 8, #a-h 12.50 12.50

No. 153 Surcharged in Red

**2004, Jan. 4 Litho.** ***Perf. 13¼x13***
**229** A35 Miniature sheet, 2 each #a-b 6.50 6.50
*a.* 20d on 100r #153a 1.50 1.50
*b.* 66d on 270r #153b 3.00 3.00

National Dances — A70

No. 230 — Various dancers and frame color of: a, Brown. b, Purple. c, Green. d, Bright pink.

**2004, Jan. 19 Litho.** ***Perf. 14¼x14***
**230** A70 53d Block of 4, #a-d 4.75 4.75

Adjacent blocks in sheet are tete-beche. No. 230 exists with visible tagging that reads "Belarus."

No. 28 Surcharged in Black and Red

**2004, Apr. 26 Litho.** ***Perf. 13½***
**231** A6 A on 50r multi .90 .90

Sold for 8d on day of issue.

No. 31 Surcharged in Black

**2004, Apr. 26**
**232** A6 b on 160r multi .90 .90

Sold for 20d on day of issue.

Miniature Sheet

New Year 2004 (Year of the Monkey) — A71

No. 233: a, 1s, Monkey covering eyes. b, 1.20s, Monkey covering ears. c, 1.50s, Monkey covering mouth.

**2004, Aug. 13** ***Perf. 13¾x13½***
**233** A71 Sheet of 3, #a-c 6.00 6.00

Dushanbe Buildings — A72

Designs: 1d, National Circus. 2d, Ferdowsi National Library. 3d, National Bank. 8d, Finance Ministry. 20d, Communications Ministry. 50d, City Government Building.

**2004, Aug. 13** ***Perf. 13¾x13¼***
**234** A72 1d multi .60 .60
**235** A72 2d multi .60 .60
**236** A72 3d multi .60 .60
**237** A72 8d multi .60 .60
**238** A72 20d multi .60 .60
**239** A72 50d multi 1.00 1.00
*Nos. 234-239 (6)* 4.00 4.00

FIFA (Fédération Internationale de Football Association), Cent. — A73

Designs: 50d, Goalie, World Cup. 70d, FIFA General Secretariat Building, Zurich. 1s, Player with red shirt, vert. 2s, Player with yellow shirt, vert.

***Perf. 13½x13¾, 13¾x13½***
**2004, Aug. 30**
**240-243** A73 Set of 4 7.50 7.50

Nos. 240-243 exist imperf.

Miniature Sheet

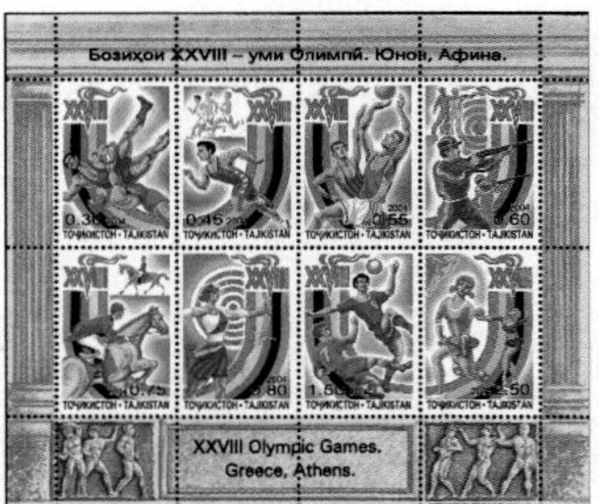


2004 Summer Olympics, Athens — A74

No. 244: a, 30d, Wrestling. b, 45d, Track. c, 55d, Basketball. d, 60d, Shooting. e, 75d, Equestrian. f, 80d, Women's archery. g, 1.50s, Soccer. h, 2.50s, Rhythmic gymnastics.

**2004, Sept. 6** ***Perf. 14x13½***
**244** A74 Sheet of 8, #a-h 12.00 12.00

Exists imperf.

Miniature Sheet

Dushanbe Circus — A75

No. 245: a, 20d, Circus building. b, 50d, Tightrope walkers. c, 1s, Elephant and trainer. d, 1.10s, Genie, lamp and cat. e, 1.50s, Man riding donkey, dog. f, 1.70s, Bareback rider.

**2004, Dec. 21** ***Perf. 14x13½***
**245** A75 Sheet of 6, #a-f 10.00 10.00

Exists imperf.

Miniature Sheet

Vehicles — A76

No. 246: a, Fire engine. b, Ambulance and helicopter. c, Police cars. d, Postal van and train. e, Wrecker and damaged car. f, School bus.

**2004, Dec. 21**
**246** A76 1s Sheet of 6, #a-f 10.00 10.00

Exists imperf.

Miniature Sheet

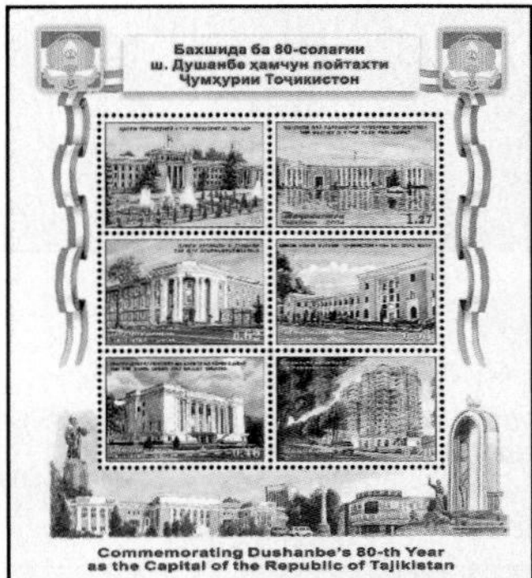


Dushanbe as Capital City, 80th Anniv. — A77

No. 247: a, 20d, New apartment buildings on Rudaki Ave. b, 46d, Aini State Opera and Ballet Theater. c, 53d, National Bank. d, 62d, City Government Building. e, 1.27s, Parliament Building. f, 1.76s, Presidential Palace.

**2004, Nov. 16 Litho.** ***Perf. 11½***
**247** A77 Sheet of 6, #a-f 10.00 10.00

Musical Instruments — A78

No. 248: a, Gejak and bow. b, Adirna. Illustration reduced.

**2004, Nov. 29** ***Perf. 11½x11¾***

**248** A78 2.50s Horiz. pair, #a-b 10.00 10.00

See Kazakhstan No. 470.

Fruit — A79

Designs: Nos. 249, 255, Apples. Nos. 250, 256, Apricots. Nos. 251, 257, Plums. Nos. 252, 258, Pears. Nos. 253, 259, Quince. Nos. 254, 260, Pomegranates.

**2005, Mar. 19** ***Perf. 14x14¼***

**Panel Color**

**White Background**

**249** A79 6d lilac .20 .20
**250** A79 7d blue .20 .20
**251** A79 8d brn orange .20 .20
**252** A79 10d rose .20 .20
**253** A79 11d green .20 .20
**254** A79 12d yel orange .20 .20

**Pale Yellow Background**

**255** A79 20d purple .35 .35
**256** A79 50d violet .75 .75
**257** A79 55d red .85 .85
**258** A79 75d red violet 1.00 1.00
**259** A79 2s dk olive 3.00 3.00
**260** A79 3s brown red 5.00 5.00
*Nos. 249-260 (12)* 12.15 12.15

Lake Sarez — A80

No. 261: a, Katta Nardjonoi Bay (denomination in white). b, Iriht Bay (denomination in black).
Illustration reduced.

**2005, Apr. 4** ***Perf. 13½***

**261** A80 2s Horiz. pair, #a-b 6.50 6.50

Souvenir Sheet

End of World War II, 60th Anniv. — A81

No. 262: a, 18d. b, 75d.

**2005, Apr. 15** ***Perf. 14¼x14***

**262** A81 Sheet of 2, #a-b, + central label 4.00 4.00

Souvenir Sheet

Hunting — A82

No. 263: a, 1s, Hunter facing left. b, 1.70s, Hunter facing right. c, 2.30s, Like 1s.

**2005, July 27** ***Perf. 13¾x13½***

**263** A82 Sheet of 3, #a-c 10.00 10.00

Compare with Type A89.

Airbus A-380 — A83

No. 264 — Inset of airplane and: a, 1.50s, Left wing. b, 1.50s, Nose. c, 1.80s, Tail. d, 1.80s, Right wing.
Illustration reduced.

**2005, July 27** ***Perf. 13½x14***

**264** A83 Block of 4, #a-d 12.00 12.00

Miniature Sheet

Mammals — A84

No. 265: a, 20d, Hyena on cliff. b, 20d, Turkestan lynx on tree branch. c, 75d, Badger. d, 75d, Fox. e, 80d, Snow leopard. f, 1s, Bear. g, 1.50s, Leopard. h, 1.80s, Tiger.

**2005, Aug. 10** ***Perf. 13½x14***

**265** A84 Sheet of 8, #a-h 12.00 12.00

Worldwide Fund for Nature (WWF) — A85

No. 266 — Various views of bharals: a, 1s. b, 1.45s. c, 1.70s. d, 2.25s.
Illustration reduced.

**2005, Aug. 26** ***Perf. 13½x14***

**266** A85 Block of 4, #a-d 7.50 7.50

Avicenna (980-1037), Scientist — A86

**2005, Oct. 3** ***Perf. 13¼x13¾***

**267** A86 6d Prus bl & blk .20 .20
**268** A86 8d brn & black .20 .20
**269** A86 10d purple & lilac .20 .20
**270** A86 12d blue .30 .30
**271** A86 50d blue green 1.00 1.00
**272** A86 1s orange 2.00 2.00
*Nos. 267-272 (6)* 3.90 3.90

World Post Day — A87

**2005, Oct. 3** ***Perf. 13¼x13¾***

**273** A87 5d blue & black .20 .20
**274** A87 7d brown .20 .20
**275** A87 11d green & lt grn .20 .20
**276** A87 20d purple .30 .30
**277** A87 55d gray blue 1.00 1.00
**278** A87 75d orange 2.00 2.00
*Nos. 273-278 (6)* 3.90 3.90

Mountains — A88

No. 279: a, 1s, Pendjikent. b, 1.50s, Muminabod. c, 2s, Pamir. d, 2.50s, Isfara.
Illustration reduced.

**2005, Dec. 6** ***Perf. 13½***

**279** A88 Block of 4, #a-d 12.00 12.00

Souvenir Sheet

Hunting — A89

No. 280: a, Hunter holding falcon. b, Hunter killing leopard.

**2005, Dec. 31** ***Perf. 13¾x13½***

**280** A89 2.50s Sheet of 2, #a-b, + central label 9.00 9.00

Compare with type A82.

Fairy Tales — A90

No. 281: a, 55d, The Peasant and the Bear. b, 75d, Three Brothers. c, 2s, Iradj-bogatyr. d, 3s, The Gold Fox.

**2006, Mar. 20** ***Perf. 14¼x14***

**281** A90 Block of 4, #a-d 9.00 9.00

Stamps in vertical columns are tete-beche.

Traditional Costumes — A91

No. 282: a, 75d, Man from Samarkand wearing red headdress. b, 75d, Man from Sugd wearing blue headdress. c, 1s, Woman from Bukhara with arms together. d, 1s, Woman from Kalayhum with arms apart.

**2006, June 20** **Litho.** ***Perf. 14¼x14***

**282** A91 Block or horiz. strip of 4, #a-d 6.00 6.00

Printed in sheets of eight containing two of each stamp.

Miniature Sheet

Fauna of Asia — A92

No. 283: a, 8d, Aquila chrysaetos. b, 20d, Panthera tigris longipilis. c, 55d, Hystrix hirsutirostris. d, 70d, Alluropoda melanoleuca. e, 75d, Meles meles. f, 1.60s, Ursus arctos. g, 1.92s, Mustela erminea. h, 2s, Bubo coromandus.

**2006, June 29** ***Perf. 13¾x13½***

**283** A92 Sheet of 8, #a-h 12.00 12.00

2006 World Cup Soccer Championships, Germany — A93

No. 284: a, 1.50s, Five players. b, 1.50s, Three players and goalie. c, 1.50s, Four players. d, 2s, Three players and goalie, diff.
Illustration reduced.

**2006, June 29** ***Perf. 13½x13¾***

**284** A93 Block of 4, #a-d 10.00 10.00
*e.* Miniature sheet, 2 each #284a-284d 20.00 20.00

Souvenir Sheet

Kulob, 2700th Anniv. — A94

No. 285: a, Anniversary emblem, flag of Tajikistan. b, Mausoleum of Mir Said Ali Hamadoni.

**2006, Aug. 30**

**285** A94 2s Sheet of 2, #a-b 6.75 6.75

Miniature Sheet

Independence, 15th Anniv. — A95

No. 286: a, 1.50s, Presidential Palace. b, 2.50s, Arms of Tajikistan. c, 3s, Flag of Tajikistan, Pres. Emomali Rakhmonov.

**2006, Aug. 30** ***Perf. 14x14¼***

**286** A95 Sheet of 3, #a-c, + 3 labels 12.00 12.00

Souvenir Sheet

Commonwealth of Independent States, 15th Anniv. — A96

No. 287: a, Emblem of Commonwealth of Independent States, flags of member nations. b, Emblem of Regional Communications Commonwealth.

**2006, Sept. 12** ***Perf. 14¼x14***

**287** A96 1.50s Sheet of 2, #a-b, + central label 6.25 6.25

Cotton — A97

**2006, Dec. 15** ***Perf. 13½x13¾***

**Background Color**

| No. | Type | Value | Color | Unused | Used |
|---|---|---|---|---|---|
| **288** | A97 | 5d | olive green | .30 | .30 |
| **289** | A97 | 6d | rose | .30 | .30 |
| **290** | A97 | 7d | lilac | .30 | .30 |
| **291** | A97 | 8d | light blue | .30 | .30 |
| **292** | A97 | 20d | green | .50 | .50 |
| **293** | A97 | 75d | blue | 1.40 | 1.40 |
| | | | *Nos. 288-293 (6)* | *3.10* | *3.10* |

Headdresses — A98

No. 294 — Various headdresses with gray geometrical design at: a, LR. b, LL. c, UR. d, UL.

**2006, Dec. 28** ***Perf. 14x14¼***

**294** A98 1.50s Block of 4, #a-d 8.50 8.50

Dogs — A99

Designs: 20d, West Siberian laika. 55d, Perdiguero de burgos. 75d, Afghan hound. 1s, Sredneasiatckaia ovtcharka. 2s, Saluki. 3s, Tosa.

**2006** ***Perf. 13¾x13½***

**295-300** A99 Set of 6 11.50 11.50

# TANGANYIKA

ˌtan-gə-ˈnyē-kə

LOCATION — Southeastern Africa bordering on the Indian Ocean
GOVT. — Republic within British Commonwealth
AREA — 362,688 sq. mi.
POP. — 9,404,000 (est. 1961)
CAPITAL — Dar es Salaam

Before World War I, this area formed part of German East Africa. It was mandated to Britain after World War I and (in 1946) became a trust territory under the United Nations. In 1935, stamps of the mandate were replaced by those used jointly by Kenya, Uganda and Tanganyika (see Kenya, Uganda and Tanzania). On Dec. 9, 1961, Tanganyika became independent. On Dec. 9, 1962, it became a republic. April 26, 1964, it joined Zanzibar to form the United Republic of Tanganyika and Zanzibar (later renamed Tanzania). See Tanzania.

100 Cents = 1 Rupee
100 Cents = 1 Shilling (1922)
20 Shillings = 1 Pound

**Catalogue values for unused stamps in this country are for Never Hinged items, beginning with Scott 45 in the regular postage section and Scott O1 in the officials section.**

Stamps of Kenya, Uganda & Tanganyika Overprinted

**1921** **Wmk. 4** ***Perf. 14***

| No. | Type | Value | Color | Unused | Used |
|---|---|---|---|---|---|
| **1** | A1 | 12c | gray | 7.50 | *110.00* |
| **2** | A1 | 15c | ultra | 3.75 | *6.25* |
| **3** | A1 | 50c | dull violet & blk | 11.50 | *97.50* |

Overprinted

| No. | Type | Value | Color | Unused | Used |
|---|---|---|---|---|---|
| **4** | A2 | 2r | black & red, *blue* | 37.50 | *140.00* |
| **5** | A2 | 3r | gray green & violet | 80.00 | *210.00* |
| **7** | A2 | 5r | dull violet & ultra | 110.00 | *290.00* |
| | | | *Nos. 1-7 (6)* | 250.25 | *853.75* |

Overprinted in Red or Black

**1922**

| No. | Type | Value | Color | Unused | Used |
|---|---|---|---|---|---|
| **8** | A1 | 1c | black (R) | .90 | *21.00* |
| **9** | A1 | 10c | orange (Bk) | .90 | *16.00* |

Giraffe
A3 A4

***Perf. 14½x14***

**1922-25** **Engr.** **Wmk. 4**

| No. | Type | Value | Color | Unused | Used |
|---|---|---|---|---|---|
| **10** | A3 | 5c | dk violet & blk | 2.75 | .20 |
| **11** | A3 | 5c | grn & blk ('25) | 3.75 | 1.75 |
| **12** | A3 | 10c | green & blk | 2.75 | .95 |
| **13** | A3 | 10c | yel & blk ('25) | 5.25 | 1.75 |
| **14** | A3 | 15c | carmine & blk | 2.25 | .20 |
| **15** | A3 | 20c | orange & blk | 2.00 | .20 |
| **16** | A3 | 25c | black | 6.25 | *7.50* |
| **17** | A3 | 25c | blue & blk ('25) | 4.50 | *20.00* |
| **18** | A3 | 30c | blue & blk | 5.75 | 5.75 |
| **19** | A3 | 30c | dull vio & blk ('25) | 4.75 | *16.00* |
| **20** | A3 | 40c | brown & black | 3.25 | 5.25 |
| **21** | A3 | 50c | gray black | 2.75 | 1.75 |
| **22** | A3 | 75c | bister & black | 3.75 | *21.00* |
| | | | ***Perf. 14*** | | |
| **23** | A4 | 1sh | green & black | 3.50 | *12.50* |
| *a.* | | | Wmk. sideways | 4.75 | *16.00* |
| **24** | A4 | 2sh | brn vio & blk | 5.25 | *29.00* |
| *a.* | | | Wmk. sideways | 6.25 | *17.50* |
| **25** | A4 | 3sh | blk, wmk. sideways | 21.00 | *32.50* |
| **26** | A4 | 5sh | red & black | 18.00 | *85.00* |
| *a.* | | | Wmk. sideways | 37.50 | *97.50* |
| **27** | A4 | 10sh | dp blue & blk | 62.50 | *125.00* |
| *a.* | | | Wmk. sideways | 140.00 | *250.00* |
| **28** | A4 | £1 | orange & black | 200.00 | *375.00* |
| *a.* | | | Wmk. sideways | 225.00 | *400.00* |
| | | | *Nos. 10-28 (19)* | 360.00 | *741.30* |

On No. 28 the words of value are in a curve between the circle and "POSTAGE & REVENUE."

King George V
A5 A6

**1927-31** **Typo.**

| No. | Type | Value | Color | Unused | Used |
|---|---|---|---|---|---|
| **29** | A5 | 5c | green & black | 2.00 | .20 |
| **30** | A5 | 10c | yellow & black | 2.25 | .20 |
| **31** | A5 | 15c | red & black | 2.00 | .20 |
| **32** | A5 | 20c | orange & black | 3.00 | .20 |
| **33** | A5 | 25c | ultra & black | 4.25 | 2.25 |
| **34** | A5 | 30c | dull violet & blk | 3.25 | 3.00 |
| **35** | A5 | 30c | ultra & blk ('31) | 29.00 | .35 |
| **36** | A5 | 40c | brown & black | 2.25 | 5.25 |
| **37** | A5 | 50c | gray & black | 2.90 | 1.10 |
| **38** | A5 | 75c | olive grn & blk | 2.25 | *17.50* |
| **39** | A6 | 1sh | green & black | 4.75 | 3.25 |
| **40** | A6 | 2sh | violet brn & blk | 22.50 | 5.25 |
| **41** | A6 | 3sh | black | 26.00 | *70.00* |
| **42** | A6 | 5sh | scarlet & blk | 22.50 | 21.00 |
| **43** | A6 | 10sh | ultra & black | 62.50 | *110.00* |
| **44** | A6 | £1 | brown org & blk | 175.00 | *350.00* |
| | | | *Nos. 29-44 (16)* | 366.40 | *589.75* |

**Catalogue values for unused stamps in this section, from this point to the end of the section, are for Never Hinged items.**

**Independent State**

Nurse and Infant — A7

Torch above Mt. Kilimanjaro — A8

5c, Teacher instructing villagers, horiz. 15c, Coffee picker. 20c, Harvesting corn. 30c, Flag, horiz. 50c, Serengeti lions. 1sh, Nurse showing infant to mother & hospital. 2sh, Dar es Salaam harbor. 5sh, Tractor & field workers. 10sh, Diamond mine & rose diamond. 1sh, 2sh, 5sh, 10sh, horiz.

***Perf. 14x14½, 14½x14***

**1961, Dec. 9** **Photo.** **Unwmk.**

| No. | Type | Value | Color | Unused | Used |
|---|---|---|---|---|---|
| **45** | A7 | 5c | sepia & yel grn | .30 | .30 |
| **46** | A7 | 10c | Prussian green | .30 | .30 |
| **47** | A7 | 15c | sepia & blue | .30 | .30 |
| *b.* | | | Blue omitted | *400.00* | |
| **48** | A7 | 20c | orange brown | .30 | .30 |
| **49** | A7 | 30c | dp green, blk & yel | .30 | .30 |
| **50** | A7 | 50c | sepia & yellow | .30 | .30 |
| | | | ***Perf. 14½*** | | |
| **51** | A8 | 1sh | cit brn & gray bl | .30 | .30 |
| **52** | A8 | 1sh30c | multicolored | 3.50 | .30 |
| **53** | A8 | 2sh | multicolored | 1.10 | .30 |
| **54** | A8 | 5sh | Prus grn & dp org | 1.10 | .30 |
| **55** | A8 | 10sh | blk, bl & rose | 17.50 | 5.25 |
| *a.* | | | Rose (diamond) omitted | 125.00 | |
| **56** | A8 | 20sh | multicolored | 4.50 | *10.00* |
| | | | *Nos. 45-56 (12)* | 29.80 | 18.25 |

Tanganyika's independence, Dec. 9, 1961.
For overprints see Nos. O21-O28.

Pres. Julius Nyerere with Pickax — A9

Designs: 50c, Flag hoisting on Mt. Kilimanjaro. 1sh30c, Presidential emblem. 2sh50c, Independence monument, Mnazi Moja.

**1962, Dec. 9** ***Perf. 14½x14***

| No. | Type | Value | Color | Unused | Used |
|---|---|---|---|---|---|
| **57** | A9 | 30c | bright green | .20 | .20 |
| **58** | A9 | 50c | multicolored | .20 | .20 |
| **59** | A9 | 1sh30c | multicolored | .20 | .20 |
| **60** | A9 | 2sh50c | dk blue, blk & red | .75 | .50 |
| | | | *Nos. 57-60 (4)* | 1.35 | 1.10 |

Issued to commemorate the establishment of the Republic of Tanganyika, Dec. 9, 1962.

## OFFICIAL STAMPS

**Catalogue values for unused stamps in this section are for Never Hinged items.**

**Issued for use by the Tanganyika Government**

Stamps of Kenya, Uganda & Tanganyika, 1954-59, Overprinted

***Perf. 12½x13, 13x12½***

**1959** **Engr.** **Wmk. 4**

| No. | Type | Value | Color | Unused | Used |
|---|---|---|---|---|---|
| **O1** | A18 | 5c | choc & blk | .20 | *1.25* |
| **O2** | A19 | 10c | carmine | .20 | *1.25* |
| **O3** | A20 | 15c | lt bl & blk (on #106) | .35 | *1.25* |
| **O4** | A19 | 20c | org & blk | .20 | .20 |
| *a.* | | | Double overprint | | *700.00* |
| **O5** | A18 | 30c | ultra & black | .20 | *.95* |
| **O6** | A19 | 50c | dp red lilac | .25 | .20 |
| **O7** | A19 | 1sh | dp mag & blk | .25 | *.85* |
| **O8** | A20 | 1sh30c | pur & red org | 3.75 | 2.25 |
| **O9** | A20 | 2sh | dp grn & gray | 1.40 | 1.10 |
| **O10** | A20 | 5sh | black & org | 4.00 | 3.50 |
| **O11** | A20 | 10sh | ultra & blk | 2.25 | *4.00* |
| **O12** | A21 | £1 | black & ver | 7.50 | *17.50* |
| | | | *Nos. O1-O12 (12)* | 20.55 | 34.30 |

Stamps of Kenya, Uganda & Tanganyika, 1960, Overprinted

*Perf. 14½x14*

**1960, Oct. 1 Photo. Wmk. 314**

| | | | | | |
|---|---|---|---|---|---|
| **O13** | A23 | 5c dull blue | .20 | *1.75* |
| **O14** | A23 | 10c lt olive green | .20 | *1.75* |
| **O15** | A23 | 15c dull purple | .20 | *1.75* |
| **O16** | A23 | 20c brt lilac rose | .20 | *.55* |
| **O17** | A23 | 30c brt vermilion | .20 | .20 |
| **O18** | A23 | 50c dull violet | .35 | *1.10* |

Overprinted

**Engr.** *Perf. 14*

| | | | | |
|---|---|---|---|---|
| **O19** | A24 | 1sh violet & lilac red | .45 | .30 |
| **O20** | A24 | 5sh rose red & lilac | 16.00 | 1.50 |
| | | *Nos. O13-O20 (8)* | 17.80 | 8.90 |

Nos. 45-51 and 54 Overprinted "OFFICIAL" in Sans-serif Type of Various Sizes

*Perf. 14x14½, 14½x14*

**1961, Dec. 9 Unwmk.**

| | | | | |
|---|---|---|---|---|
| **O21** | A7 | 5c sepia & yellow grn | .20 | .20 |
| **O22** | A7 | 10c Prussian green | .20 | .20 |
| **O23** | A7 | 15c sepia & blue | .20 | .20 |
| **O24** | A7 | 20c orange brown | .20 | .20 |
| **O25** | A7 | 30c dp grn blk & yel | .20 | .20 |
| **O26** | A7 | 50c sepia & yellow | .20 | .20 |
| **O27** | A8 | 1sh citron brn & gray bl | .20 | .20 |
| **O28** | A8 | 5sh Prus grn & dp org | 1.00 | 1.00 |
| | | *Nos. O21-O28 (8)* | 2.40 | 2.40 |

## TANNU TUVA

ˈtä-nə ˈtü-və

### (Tuva People's Republic)

LOCATION — Between Siberia and northwestern Mongolia at the sources of the Yenisei, in the basin formed by the Tannu-Ola and Sayan Mountains.
GOVT. — A former republic closely identified with Soviet Russia in Asia
AREA — 64,000 sq. mi. (approx.)
POP. — 95,000 (1941 est.)
CAPITAL — Kyzyl

This region, traditionally called Uriankhai, was ruled by the Mongols until the mid-18th century, when it became part of the Chinese Empire. Russia and China struggled for control of the country 1914-21, until it became independent as the Tannu Tuva People's Republic in 1921. In 1944 it was incorporated into the U.S.S.R. as an autonomous region of the Russian Soviet Federated Socialist Republic.

Russian, later Soviet, stamps were used in Tuva prior to 1926 and after 1944.

100 Mongo=1 Tugrik
100 Kopecks = 1 Ruble
100 Kopecks = 1 Tugrik (1934)
100 Kopecks = 1 Aksha (1936)

**Watermark**

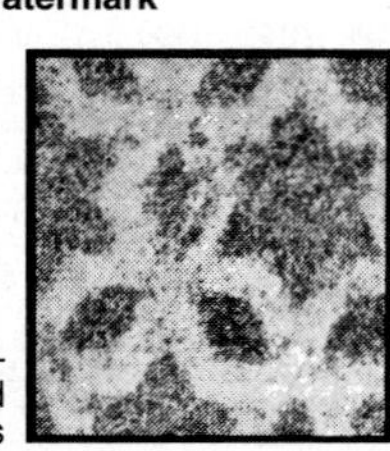

Wmk. 204 — Stars and Diamonds

Wmk. 170 — Greek Border and Rosettes

Most used examples of Nos. 1-38, 45-52a, 54-92 and C1-C18 on the market are cancelled to order, and the used values below are for such stamps.

Tuvan stamps, except for Nos. 117-123 and most of the overprints, were printed by the State Security Printers in Moscow.

Wheel of Truth — A1

**1926 Litho. Wmk. 204** *Perf. 13½*

**Size: 20x26mm**

| | | | | |
|---|---|---|---|---|
| **1** | A1 | 1k red | 1.25 | 1.00 |
| **2** | A1 | 2k light blue | 1.50 | 1.00 |
| **3** | A1 | 5k orange | 1.50 | 1.00 |
| **4** | A1 | 8k yel green | 1.75 | 1.00 |
| **5** | A1 | 10k violet | 2.00 | 1.00 |
| **6** | A1 | 30k dark brown | 1.75 | 1.00 |
| **7** | A1 | 50k gray black | 2.00 | 1.25 |

**Size: 22½x30mm**

*Perf. 10½*

| | | | | |
|---|---|---|---|---|
| **8** | A1 | 1r blue green | 5.50 | 2.50 |
| **9** | A1 | 3r red brown | 8.00 | 4.00 |
| **10** | A1 | 5r dark ultra | 13.50 | 6.00 |
| | | *Nos. 1-10 (10)* | 38.75 | 19.75 |

Nos. 1-10 have crackled white gum. Reprints can be distinguished by their smooth gum.

Nos. 1-10 in different colors are proofs.

Nos. 7-10 Surcharged in Red or Black

**1927** *Perf. 13½*

| | | | | |
|---|---|---|---|---|
| **11** | A1 | 8k on 50k | 25.00 | 12.50 |

*Perf. 10½*

| | | | | |
|---|---|---|---|---|
| **12** | A1 | 14k on 1r | 25.00 | 12.50 |
| **13** | A1 | 18k on 3r (Bk) | 25.00 | 12.50 |
| **14** | A1 | 28k on 5r (Bk) | 25.00 | 12.50 |
| | | *Nos. 11-14 (4)* | 100.00 | 50.00 |

Nos. 11-14 were surcharged with a shiny ink. Reprints are overprinted with a dull ink and are often smudged.

Nos. 11-14 exist with surcharge inverted and No. 14 with surcharge double. Value $35.00 each.

*Reprints exist of Nos. 1-14.*

Tuvan Woman — A3

Map of Tannu Tuva A8

Sheep Herding — A11

Fording a Stream — A13

Tuvans Riding Reindeer — A16

Designs: 2k, Stag. 3k, Mountain goat. 4k, Tuvan and tent. 5k, Tuvan man. 10k, Archery competition. 14k, Camel caravan. 28k, Landscape. 50k, Weaving. 70k, Tuvan on horseback.

**1927 Typo.** *Perf. 12½*

| | | | | |
|---|---|---|---|---|
| **15** | A3 | 1k blk, lt brn & red | 1.00 | .60 |
| **16** | A3 | 2k pur, dp brn & grn | 1.20 | .55 |
| **17** | A3 | 3k blk, bl grn & yel | 2.00 | .60 |
| **18** | A3 | 4k vio bl & choc | .90 | .60 |
| **19** | A3 | 5k org, blk & dk bl | .90 | .65 |

*Perf. , 12½x12*

| | | | | |
|---|---|---|---|---|
| **20** | A8 | 8k ol brn, pale bl & red brn | 1.00 | .65 |
| **21** | A8 | 10k blk, grn & brn red | 5.50 | 1.00 |
| **22** | A8 | 14k vio bl & red org | 10.00 | 3.50 |

*Perf. 10, 10½*

| | | | | |
|---|---|---|---|---|
| **23** | A11 | 18k dk bl & red brn | 10.00 | 5.00 |
| **24** | A11 | 28k emer & blk brn | 7.25 | 2.75 |
| **25** | A13 | 40k rose & bl grn | 5.00 | 2.50 |
| **26** | A13 | 50k blk, grn & red brn | 3.50 | 2.00 |
| **27** | A13 | 70k dl red & bis | 7.00 | 4.00 |
| **28** | A16 | 1r yel brn & vio | 16.00 | 6.75 |
| | | *Nos. 15-28 (14)* | 71.25 | 31.15 |

Nos. 15-28 were issued with a crackled white gum. Reprints of the 1k-5k values exist and can be distinguished by their smooth gum.

Nos. 15-28 in different colors are proofs.

Nos. 25-27, 20-22 Surcharged "Tuva", "Posta" and New Values in Various Colors

**1932**

| | | | | |
|---|---|---|---|---|
| **29** | A13 | 1k on 40k (Bk) | 9.00 | *10.00* |
| **30** | A13 | 2k on 50k (Br) | 10.00 | 10.00 |
| **31** | A13 | 3k on 70k (Bl) | 10.00 | 10.00 |
| *a.* | | Inverted surcharge | *300.00* | |
| **32** | A8 | 5k on 8k (Bk) | 10.00 | 10.00 |
| **33** | A8 | 10k (Bk) | 10.00 | 10.00 |
| **34** | A8 | 15k on 14k (Bk) | 15.00 | 15.00 |
| | | *Nos. 29-34 (6)* | 64.00 | 65.00 |

Issued in connection with the Romanization of the alphabet.

#23-24 Surcharged in Black

No. 37

No. 38

**1933 Wmk. 204**

| | | | | |
|---|---|---|---|---|
| **35** | A8 | 10k on 8k | 180.00 | 100.00 |
| **36** | A8 | 15k on 14k | 300.00 | 200.00 |
| **37** | A11 | 35k on 18k | 140.00 | 100.00 |
| **38** | A11 | 35k on 28k | 140.00 | 100.00 |
| | | *Nos. 35-38 (4)* | 760.00 | 500.00 |

A19

Revenue Stamps Surcharged "Posta" and New Values

Three types: type 1, figures of value 6.7mm high; type 2, figures of value 6.7mm high, letter "p" lengthened at bottom; type 3, figures of value 5.1mm high.

**1933** *Perf. 12x12½*

| | | | | |
|---|---|---|---|---|
| **39** | A19 | 15k on 6k org yel, type 1 | 300.00 | 150.00 |
| **40** | A19 | 15k on 6k org yel, type 2 | 300.00 | 150.00 |
| **41** | A19 | 15k on 6k org yel, type 3 | 500.00 | 300.00 |
| **42** | A19 | 35k on 15k red brn, type 1 | — | *4,000.* |
| **42** | A19 | 35k on 15k red brn, type 2 | — | *4,000.* |
| **44** | A19 | 35k on 15k red brn, type 3 | *1,500.* | 800.00 |

Mounted Hunter — A20

Tuvan Inside of Yurt — A21

Tuvan Milking Yak — A22

Designs: 2k, Hunter stalking game. 4k, Tractor. 10k, Camel caravan. 15k, Herdsman lassoing reindeer. 20k, Hunter shooting fox with arrow.

Two dies on 10k: Die I, Crown at center top is light and matches the shade of the sky below; Die II, Crown at center top is bold, consistent with rest of design and darker than the sky.

Printed by State Security Printers, Moscow.

**Wmk. 170**

**1934, Apr. Photo. *Perf. 12***

| | | | | |
|---|---|---|---|---|
| **45** | A20 | 1k red orange | 1.25 | 1.00 |
| **46** | A20 | 2k olive green | 1.25 | 1.00 |
| **47** | A21 | 3k rose red | 1.25 | 1.00 |
| **48** | A21 | 4k slate purple | 3.00 | 1.75 |
| **49** | A22 | 5k ultramarine | 3.00 | 1.75 |
| **50** | A22 | 10k brown, die II | 3.00 | 1.75 |
| *c.* | | 10k brown, die I | 8.00 | 2.00 |
| **51** | A22 | 15k dark lilac | 3.00 | 1.75 |
| **52** | A22 | 20k gray black | 4.00 | 2.75 |
| | | *Nos. 45-52 (8)* | 19.75 | 12.75 |
| | | Set, never hinged | 50.00 | |
| | | Set, Imperf | 50.00 | |
| | | Set, imperf, never hinged | 100.00 | |

Nos. 45-52 are inscribed "REGISTERED," but were used as regular postage stamps.

Nos. 46, 48 and 50 exist perf 11, and No. 50 also exists perf 11x10. No. 48 exists perf 11½, reportedly as a color trial proof.

### #51 Surcharged in Black

Surcharged by numbering machine in Kyzyl.

**1935**

| | | | | |
|---|---|---|---|---|
| **53** | A22 | 20k on 15k | *175.00* | *325.00* |
| *a.* | | Inverted surcharge | | *400.00* |

Map of Tuva — A23

Badger A25

Squirrel — A26

Fox — A27

Elk — A28

Yak — A29

Rocky Outcropping — A24

Designs: 3k, 5k, 10k, Different scenes of Yenisei River. 25k, Bei-kem rapids. 50k, Mounted hunters.

Printed by State Security Printers, Moscow.

**Wmk. 170**

**1935, Mar. Photo. *Perf. 14***

| | | | | |
|---|---|---|---|---|
| **54** | A23 | 1k yellow orange | 1.20 | .90 |
| **55** | A23 | 3k deep green | 1.20 | .90 |
| **56** | A23 | 5k carmine red | 1.50 | 1.00 |
| **57** | A23 | 10k violet | 1.60 | 1.00 |
| *b.* | | Pair, imperf between | | — |
| **58** | A24 | 15k olive green | 1.75 | 1.25 |
| **59** | A24 | 25k violet blue | 2.00 | 1.25 |
| **60** | A24 | 50k dark brown | 3.00 | 1.50 |
| | | *Nos. 54-60 (7)* | 12.25 | 7.80 |
| | | Set, never hinged | 25.00 | |

Nos. 54-60 in different colors, perf and imperf, are proofs.

Designs: 5k, Ermine. 25k, Otter. 50k, Lynx. 3t, Bactrian camels. 5t, Bear.

Printed by State Security Printers, Moscow.

**1935, Mar.**

| | | | | |
|---|---|---|---|---|
| **61** | A25 | 1k orange | 1.60 | 1.00 |
| **62** | A26 | 3k emerald green | 1.60 | 1.00 |
| *a.* | | Imperf, pair | *300.00* | |
| **63** | A25 | 5k rose red | 1.60 | 1.10 |
| **64** | A27 | 10k crimson red | 1.60 | 1.10 |
| **65** | A27 | 25k orange red | 2.50 | 1.20 |
| **66** | A27 | 50k deep blue | 2.50 | 1.20 |
| **67** | A28 | 1t violet | 2.50 | 1.20 |
| *a.* | | Pair, imperf between | — | |
| **68** | A29 | 2t royal blue | 3.50 | 1.20 |
| **69** | A29 | 3t red brown | 4.00 | 1.35 |
| **70** | A28 | 5t indigo | 5.00 | 1.75 |
| *a.* | | Imperf, pair | *300.00* | |
| *b.* | | Pair, imperf between | — | |
| | | *Nos. 61-70 (10)* | 26.40 | 12.10 |
| | | Set, never hinged | 50.00 | |

Nos. 61-70 in different colors are proofs.

Tuvan Arms — A30

Wrestlers — A31

Herdsman on Bull — A32

Athletic Competitions — A33

Soldiers A34

Designs: 2k, Pres. Ch(aumlaut char='u')rmit-Dazhy. 3k, Tuvan with Bactrian camel. 5k, 8k, Archer. 10k, 15k, Spearfishing. 12k, 20k, Bear-hunting. 30k, Camel and train. 40k, 50k, Horse race. 80k, Partisans. 3t, Partisans confiscating cattle. 5t, 1921 battle scene.

Printed by State Security Printers, Moscow.

**1936, July *Perf. 11, 14***

| | | | | |
|---|---|---|---|---|
| **71** | A30 | 1k bronze green | 1.50 | .70 |
| **72** | A30 | 2k dark brown | 2.00 | 1.50 |
| **73** | A30 | 3k indigo blue | 2.00 | .75 |
| **74a** | A31 | 4k orange red | 2.50 | .75 |
| **75** | A31 | 5k brown purple | 4.00 | .70 |
| **76** | A31 | 6k myrtle green | 3.75 | .70 |
| **77** | A31 | 8k plum | 3.75 | .70 |
| **78** | A31 | 10k rose red | 4.25 | 1.00 |
| **79** | A31 | 12k black brown | 5.00 | 1.25 |
| **80a** | A31 | 15k bronze green | 6.00 | 1.25 |
| **81** | A31 | 20k deep blue | 6.00 | 1.20 |
| **82a** | A32 | 25k orange red | 6.00 | .90 |
| **83** | A32 | 30k plum | 18.00 | 1.25 |
| **84a** | A32 | 35k rose red | 6.00 | 1.25 |
| **85** | A32 | 40k deep brown | 6.00 | 1.50 |
| **86a** | A32 | 50k indigo blue | 6.00 | 1.50 |
| **87** | A33 | 70k plum | 7.25 | 2.00 |
| **88** | A33 | 80k green | 7.00 | 2.00 |
| **89** | A34 | 1a orange red | 7.00 | 2.00 |
| *a.* | | 1a rose red (error) | — | — |
| **90** | A34 | 2a rose red | 7.00 | 3.00 |
| **91** | A33 | 3a indigo blue | 15.00 | 2.00 |
| **92** | A33 | 5a black brown | 7.25 | 2.50 |
| | | *Nos. 71-92 (22)* | 133.25 | 30.40 |
| | | Set, never hinged | 260.00 | |

15th anniversary of independence.

Values for Nos. 71-92 are for the most common varieties. For detailed listings, see the *Scott Classic Specialized Catalogue*.

Imperfs are remainders, later sold by the Soviet Postal Museum.

Values for Nos. 93-98 and 104-116 are for genuine examples. Expertization is essential for these issues.

### Issues of 1934-36 Handstamped with Large Numerals and Old Values Obliterated with Bars or Blocks

**1938, Aug.**

| | | | |
|---|---|---|---|
| **93** | A34 | 5k on 2a (#90a) | *300.00* |
| **94** | AP5 | 5k on 2a (#C17) | *225.00* |
| **95** | AP1 | 10k on 1t (#C8) | *200.00* |
| **96** | A24 | 20k on 50k (#60) | *200.00* |
| | | On cover | — |
| **97** | AP5 | 30k on 2a (#C17) | *200.00* |
| **98** | AP5 | 30k on 3a (#C18) | *175.00* |

### Types of 1935-36 with Modified Designs and New Colors

**1938, Dec. Unwmk. *Perf. 12½***

| | | | | |
|---|---|---|---|---|
| **99** | A25 | 5k deep green | 60.00 | — |
| **100** | A31 | 10k indigo (dates removed) | 60.00 | — |
| **101** | AP3 | 15k red brown ("AIR MAIL," dates removed) | 60.00 | — |
| **102** | A31 | 20k orange red (dates removed) | 85.00 | — |
| **103** | A33 | 30k maroon (dates removed) | 60.00 | — |
| | | *Nos. 99-103 (5)* | 325.00 | |
| | | Set, never hinged | 500.00 | |

Some experts believe that these stamps were issued in March 1941.

### Stamps of 1934-35 Handstamp Surcharged with New Values in Black or Violet at Kyzyl

**1939**

| | | | |
|---|---|---|---|
| **104** | AP1 | 10k on 1t (#C8) | 225.00 |
| **105** | AP1 | 10k on 1t (#C8) (V) | 225.00 |
| **106** | A24 | 20k on 50k (#60) (V) | 200.00 |

Old values obliterated on Nos. 104-106.

### Stamps of 1934-36 Handstamp Surcharged with New Values at Kyzyl

**1940, Oct.-1941**

| | | | | |
|---|---|---|---|---|
| **107** | AP1 | 10k on 1t (#C8) | — | 90.00 |
| *a.* | | Double surcharge | — | — |
| **108** | A24 | 20k on 50k (#60) | — | 100.00 |
| **109** | A27 | 20k on 50k (#66) | — | 300.00 |
| **110** | A32 | 20k on 50k (#86a) | — | 300.00 |
| **111** | AP4 | 20k on 50k (#C14) | — | 65.00 |
| **112** | A33 | 20k on 70k (#87a) | — | — |
| **113** | AP4 | 20k on 75k (#C15) | — | 75.00 |
| **114** | A33 | 20k on 80k (#88) | — | *500.00* |

The old values are not obliterated on Nos. 107 or 108.

### Nos. 91, 92 Handstamp Surcharged with New Values at Kyzyl

**1942**

| | | | | |
|---|---|---|---|---|
| **115** | A33 | 25k on 3a (#91) | 1,200. | — |
| **116** | A33 | 25k on 5a (#92) | — | — |

Government House — A35

Exhibition Hall — A36

Tuvan Woman — A37

**1942 Typo. Unwmk. *Imperf.***

| | | | | |
|---|---|---|---|---|
| **117** | A35 | 25k steel blue | 750.00 | 100.00 |
| **118** | A36 | 25k steel blue | 750.00 | 100.00 |
| **119** | A37 | 25k steel blue | 750.00 | 150.00 |
| | | *Nos. 117-119 (3)* | 2,250. | 350.00 |

21st anniversary of independence.

Nos. 117-119 were hand-printed together in small sheetlets of five (117+119+

118+117+119), so various se-tenant combinations are possible. Value, pane $2,000.

Two additional values, a 25k depicting a Tuvan man and a 50k depicting a soldier on a horse, were prepared, but not issued. A collective proof sheetlet of five, containing Nos. 117-119 and these two values, in the same color as the issued stamps, is also known.

Coat of Arms — A38

Government Building — A39

**1943** ***Perf. 11 (1 or 2 Sides)***

**Buff Paper**

| | | | | |
|---|---|---|---|---|
| **120** | A38 25k slate blue | | — | — |
| **121** | A38 25k black | | 100.00 | — |
| **122** | A38 25k blue green | | 90.00 | — |
| **123** | A39 50k blue green | | 90.00 | — |
| | *Nos. 120-123 (3)* | | 280.00 | |

**White Paper**

| | | | | |
|---|---|---|---|---|
| **120a** | A38 25k slate blue | | 90.00 | — |
| *b.* | Strip of 3, imperf between | | *250.00* | |
| **121a** | A38 25k black | | 125.00 | — |
| **122a** | A38 25k blue green | | 95.00 | — |
| **123a** | A39 50k blue green | | 95.00 | — |
| | With gum | | *175.00* | |
| | *Nos. 120a-123a (4)* | | 405.00 | |

22nd anniversary of independence.

Nos. 120 and 121 were each printed in vertical strips of five, perforated 11 between stamps and imperf on outside edges, so that these stamps may be perforated on top edge only, bottom edge only, or on both top and bottom edges. To make maximum use of limited wartime paper supplies, they were sometimes printed in strips of four. These smaller strips are rare.

Nos. 122 and 123 were printed together in blocks of four, containing a vertical pair of the 25k and a vertical pair of the 50k, perforated internally both vertically and horizontally and imperf on the outer edges. Setenant pairs, Value $225 (#122+123), $275 (#122a+123a).

Nos. 121 and 123a were issued with gum, No. 123a both with and without gum, and the balance of the set without gum.

Used examples and covers exist but are extremely rare.

## AIR POST STAMPS

Airplane and Yaks — AP1

Airplane and Capercaillie — AP2

Designs, airplane over: 5k, 15k, Camels. 25k, Argali (wild sheep). 75k, Ox and cart. 2t, Roe deer.

Printed by State Security Printers, Moscow.

**Wmk. 170**

**1934, Apr. 4** **Photo.** ***Perf. 14***

| | | | | | |
|---|---|---|---|---|---|
| **C1** | AP1 | 1k orange red | | 1.40 | 1.00 |
| **C2** | AP1 | 5k emer green | | 1.40 | 1.00 |
| **C3** | AP2 | 10k purple brown | | 4.50 | 3.00 |
| **C4** | AP1 | 15k rose red | | 2.75 | 1.00 |
| **C5** | AP2 | 25k slate purple | | 2.75 | 1.00 |
| **C6** | AP1 | 50k dp bl green | | 2.75 | 1.00 |
| **C7** | AP2 | 75k lake | | 2.75 | 1.75 |
| **C8** | AP1 | 1t royal blue | | 3.50 | 2.00 |
| **C9** | AP2 | 2t ultra, 61x31mm | | 20.00 | *25.00* |
| *a.* | | 54.5x29mm | | 40.00 | — |
| | | *Nos. C1-C9 (9)* | | 41.80 | 36.75 |
| | | Set, never hinged | | 55.00 | |

Nos. C1-C9 imperf or perf 11½ and stamps printed in different colors are proofs.

Tuvan Leading Laden Yak — AP3

Horseman and Zeppelin AP4

Seaplane Above Dragon — AP5

Designs: 10k, Tuvan plowing. 50k, Villagers with biplane overhead.

Printed by State Security Printers, Moscow.

**1936** **Unwmk.**

| | | | | |
|---|---|---|---|---|
| **C10** | AP3 | 5k indigo & beige | 2.00 | 1.50 |
| **C11** | AP3 | 10k purple & cinnamon | 3.00 | 1.50 |
| **C12** | AP3 | 15k black brown & pale gray | 3.00 | 1.50 |
| **C13** | AP4 | 25k plum & cream | 5.00 | 2.00 |
| *c.* | | Horiz. pair, perf 11, imperf between | — | — |
| **C14** | AP4 | 50k rose red & cream | 5.00 | 2.00 |
| **C15** | AP4 | 75k emer grn & pale yellow | 5.00 | 2.00 |
| **C16** | AP5 | 1a blue green & pale bl grn | 8.00 | 4.00 |
| **C17** | AP5 | 2a rose red & cream | 7.50 | 3.00 |
| **C18** | AP5 | 3a dark brown & beige | 8.00 | 3.00 |
| | | *Nos. C10-C18 (9)* | 46.50 | 20.50 |
| | | Set, never hinged | 93.00 | |

15th anniversary of independence.

Nos. C10-C18 exist imperf.

# TANZANIA

ˌtan-zə-ˈnē-ə

(Tanganyika and Zanzibar)

LOCATION — Southeastern Africa bordering on the Indian Ocean, and a group of islands about 20 miles off the coast

GOVT. — United republic in British Commonwealth

AREA — 364,886 sq. mi.

POP. — 31,270,820 (1999 est.)

CAPITAL — Dodoma

Tanganyika joined Zanzibar on April 26, 1964, to form the United Republic of Tanganyika and Zanzibar. In October 1965 the name was changed to United Republic of Tanzania.

Zanzibar stamps include two (Nos. 331, 334) inscribed "Tanzania."

100 Cents = 1 Shilling

**Catalogue values for all unused stamps in this country are for Never Hinged items.**

**Watermark**

Wmk. 387 — Squares and Rectangles

Map — A1

Design: 30c, 1sh30c, Emblem (hands holding torch and spear).

***Perf. 14x14½***

**1964, July 7** **Photo.** **Unwmk.**

| | | | | |
|---|---|---|---|---|
| **1** | A1 | 20c blue & emerald | .20 | .20 |
| **2** | A1 | 30c brn, dk & lt bl | .20 | .20 |
| **3** | A1 | 1.30sh ultra, blk & org | .30 | .30 |
| **4** | A1 | 2.50sh ultra & purple | .60 | .60 |
| | | *Nos. 1-4 (4)* | 1.30 | 1.30 |

Union of Tanganyika and Zanzibar. Not sold in Zanzibar, nor valid there.

Flag A2

Native Handicraft A3

Designs: 5c, Hale hydroelectric plant. 15c, Army squad. 20c, Road building. 40c, Giraffes. 50c, Zebras. 65c, Mt. Kilimanjaro. 1sh, Dar es Salaam harbor. 1.30sh, Zinjanthropus skull and Olduvai Gorge excavation. 2.50sh, Sailfish, dhow and map of Mafia Island. 5sh, Sisal industry. 10sh, State House, Dar es Salaam. 20sh, Tanzania coat of arms.

***Perf. 14x14½, 14½x14***

**1965, Dec. 9** **Photo.** **Unwmk.**

**Size: 21x17½mm, 17½x21mm**

| | | | | |
|---|---|---|---|---|
| **5** | A2 | 5c orange & ultra | .35 | .50 |
| **6** | A2 | 10c ultra, grn, yel & blk | .35 | .50 |
| **7** | A3 | 15c grn, bl, brn & buff | .35 | .50 |
| **8** | A2 | 20c blue & brown | .35 | .50 |
| **9** | A3 | 30c black & red brn | .35 | .50 |
| **10** | A3 | 40c blue, yel grn & brn | .35 | .50 |
| **11** | A2 | 50c yellow grn & blue | .35 | .50 |
| **12** | A2 | 65c ultra, grn & red brn | .45 | .60 |

***Perf. 14½***

**Size: 41½x25, 25x41½mm**

| | | | | |
|---|---|---|---|---|
| **13** | A2 | 1sh bl, grn, yel & brn | .55 | .50 |
| **14** | A2 | 1.30sh multicolored | .80 | .50 |
| **15** | A2 | 2.50sh blue & red brn | 1.25 | .75 |
| **16** | A2 | 5sh bl, brt grn & red brn | 2.40 | 1.10 |
| **17** | A2 | 10sh blue & yellow | 4.75 | 3.00 |
| **18** | A3 | 20sh gray & multi | 9.50 | 6.75 |
| | | *Nos. 5-18 (14)* | 22.15 | 16.70 |

For overprints see Nos. O1-O8.

Turkeyfish — A4

Fish: 5c, Cardinalfish. 10c, Mudskipper. 15c, Toby puffer. 20c, Two sea horses. 30c, Batfish. 40c, Sweetlips. 50c, Birdfish. 65c, Butterflyfish. 70c, Grouper. 1.30sh, Surgeonfish. 1.50sh, Caesio xanthonotus. 2.50sh, Emperor snapper. 5sh, Moorish idol. 10sh, Striped triggerfish. 20sh, Squirrelfish.

**1967-71** **Photo.** ***Perf. 14x14½***

**Size: 21x17½mm**

**Fish in Natural Colors**

| | | | | |
|---|---|---|---|---|
| **19** | A4 | 5c black & citron | .20 | .20 |
| **20** | A4 | 10c brown & olive | .20 | .20 |
| **21** | A4 | 15c brown & blue | .20 | .20 |
| **22** | A4 | 20c brn & dk bl grn | .20 | .20 |
| **23** | A4 | 30c black & yel grn | .20 | .20 |
| **24** | A4 | 40c brown & emerald | .20 | .20 |
| **25** | A4 | 50c blk & dull bl grn | .20 | .20 |
| **26** | A4 | 65c blk & gray grn | .60 | .60 |
| **27** | A4 | 70c blk & olive ('69) | .50 | .50 |

***Perf. 14½***

**Size: 41x25mm**

| | | | | |
|---|---|---|---|---|
| **28** | A4 | 1sh brown & multi | .40 | *.20* |
| **29** | A4 | 1.30sh black & olive | .60 | *.20* |
| **30** | A4 | 1.50sh black & ol ('69) | .70 | .20 |
| **31** | A4 | 2.50sh brn yel & grn | 1.25 | *.20* |
| **32** | A4 | 5sh black & bl grn | 2.00 | *.20* |
| **33** | A4 | 10sh brn & gray grn | 4.50 | *.60* |
| **34** | A4 | 20sh blk & gray olive | 10.00 | *1.40* |
| | | *Nos. 19-34 (16)* | 21.95 | *5.50* |

Issued: #27, 30, 9/15/69; others, 12/9/67.

Values of Nos. 28-34 are for canceled-to-order stamps with printed cancellations. Postally used copies sell for higher prices.

For overprints see Nos. O9-O16.

Papilio Hornimani A5

Euphaedra Neophron A6

Butterflies: 10c, Colotis ione. 15c, Amauris makuyuensis. 20c, Libythea laius. 30c, Danaus chrysippus. 40c, Sallya rosa. 50c, Axiocerses styx. 60c, Eurema hecabe. 70c, Acraea insignis. 1.50sh, Precis octavia. 2.50sh, Charaxes eupale. 5sh, Charaxes pollux. 10sh, Salamis parhassus. 20sh, Papilio ophidicephalus.

**1973, Dec. 3** **Photo.** ***Perf. 14½x14***

| | | | | |
|---|---|---|---|---|
| **35** | A5 | 5c yellow grn & multi | .35 | .35 |
| *a.* | | Booklet pane of 4 | .20 | |
| **36** | A5 | 10c lt brown & multi | .35 | .35 |
| *a.* | | Booklet pane of 4 | .20 | |
| **37** | A5 | 15c ultra & multi | .35 | .35 |
| **38** | A5 | 20c fawn & multi | .35 | .35 |
| *a.* | | Booklet pane of 4 | .20 | |
| **39** | A5 | 30c yellow & multi | .35 | .35 |
| *a.* | | Booklet pane of 4 | .30 | |
| **40** | A5 | 40c multicolored | .35 | .35 |
| *a.* | | Booklet pane of 4 | .40 | |
| **41** | A5 | 50c citron & multi | .35 | .35 |
| *a.* | | Booklet pane of 4 | .52 | |

**42** A5 60c multicolored .35 .35
**43** A5 70c brt green & multi .35 .35
*a.* Booklet pane of 4 .70

***Perf. 14½***

**44** A6 1sh green & multi .50 .50
**45** A6 1.50sh orange & multi .85 .85
**46** A6 2.50sh multicolored 1.60 1.60
**47** A6 5sh multicolored 3.50 3.50
**48** A6 10sh lt green & multi 6.50 6.50
**49** A6 20sh blue & multi 13.00 13.00
*Nos. 35-49 (15)* 29.10 29.10

For surcharges and overprints see Nos. 50-53, 135-136, O17-O26.

Nos. 42, 45-46, 49 Surcharged with New Value and 2 Bars

***Perf. 14½x14, 14½***

**1975, Nov. 17** **Photo.**

**50** A5 80c on 60c multi *2.75 2.75*
**51** A6 2sh on 1.50sh multi *5.00 5.00*
**52** A6 3sh on 2.50sh multi *18.00 18.00*
**53** A6 40sh on 20sh multi *8.50 8.50*
*Nos. 50-53 (4)* *34.25 34.25*

A6a

Designs: 50c, Microwave tower. 1sh, Cordless switchboard and operators, horiz. 2sh, Telephones of 1880, 1930 and 1976. 3sh, Message switching center, horiz.

**1976, Apr. 15** **Litho.** ***Perf. 14½***

**54** A6a 50c blue & multi .20 .20
**55** A6a 1sh red & multi .20 .20
**56** A6a 2sh yellow & multi .30 .25
**57** A6a 3sh multicolored .45 .35
*a.* Souvenir sheet of 4 1.75 1.75
*Nos. 54-57 (4)* 1.15 1.00

Telecommunications development in East Africa. No. 57a contains 4 stamps similar to Nos. 54-57 with simulated perforations.

Exist imperf. from Format International liquidation stock.

A6b

Designs: 50c, Akii Bua, Ugandan hurdler. 1sh, Filbert Bayi, Tanzanian runner. 2sh, Steve Muchoki, Kenyan boxer. 3sh, Olympic torch, flags of Kenya, Tanzania and Uganda.

**1976, July 5** **Litho.** ***Perf. 14½***

**58** A6b 50c blue & multi .20 .20
**59** A6b 1sh red & multi .20 .20
**60** A6b 2sh yellow & multi .30 .25
**61** A6b 3sh blue & multi .40 .35
*a.* Souv. sheet of 4, #58-61, perf. 13 *4.50 4.50*
*Nos. 58-61 (4)* 1.10 1.00

21st Olympic Games, Montreal, Canada, July 17-Aug. 1.

Exist imperf. from Format International liquidation stock.

A6c

Rail Transport in East Africa: 50c, Tanzania-Zambia Railway. 1sh, Nile Bridge, Uganda. 2sh, Nakuru Station, Kenya. 3sh, Class A locomotive, 1896.

**1976, Oct. 4** **Litho.** ***Perf. 14½***

**62** A6c 50c lilac & multi .20 .20
**63** A6c 1sh emerald & multi .30 .20
**64** A6c 2sh brt rose & multi .60 .35
**65** A6c 3sh yellow & multi .90 .60
*a.* Souv. sheet of 4, #62-65, perf. 13 8.50 8.50
*Nos. 62-65 (4)* 2.00 1.35

A6d

**1977, Jan. 10** **Litho.** ***Perf. 14½***

**66** A6d 50c Nile perch .20 .20
**67** A6d 1sh Tilapia .35 .30
**68** A6d 3sh Sailfish 1.00 .75
**69** A6d 5sh Black marlin 1.75 1.50
*a.* Souvenir sheet of 4, #66-69 4.25 3.25
*Nos. 66-69 (4)* 3.30 2.75

A6e

50c, Masai tribesmen bleeding cow. 1sh, Dancers from Uganda. 2sh, Makonde sculpture. 3sh, Tribesmen skinning hippopotamus.

**1977, Jan. 15** ***Perf. 13½x14***

**70** A6e 50c multicolored .20 .20
**71** A6e 1sh multicolored .25 .20
**72** A6e 2sh multicolored .45 .30
**73** A6e 3sh multicolored .75 .45
*a.* Souvenir sheet of 4, #70-73 2.75 2.75
*Nos. 70-73 (4)* 1.65 1.15

2nd World Black and African Festival, Lagos, Nigeria, Jan. 15-Feb. 12.

A6f

50c, Automobile passing through village. 1sh, Winner at finish line. 2sh, Car going through washout. 5sh, Car, elephants and Mt. Kenya.

**1977, Apr. 5** **Litho.** ***Perf. 14***

**74** A6f 50c multicolored .20 .20
**75** A6f 1sh multicolored .20 .20
**76** A6f 2sh multicolored .55 .30
**77** A6f 5sh multicolored 1.40 .85
*a.* Souvenir sheet of 4, #74-77 3.50 3.50
*Nos. 74-77 (4)* 2.35 1.55

25th Safari rally, Apr. 7-11.

A6g

Designs: 50c, Rev. Canon Apolo Kivebulaya. 1sh, Uganda Cathedral. 2sh, Early grass-topped Cathedral. 5sh, Early tent congregation, Kigezi.

**1977, June 20** **Litho.** ***Perf. 14***

**78** A6g 50c multicolored .20 .20
**79** A6g 1sh multicolored .20 .20
**80** A6g 2sh multicolored .25 .20
**81** A6g 5sh multicolored .75 .55
*a.* Souvenir sheet of 4, #78-81 3.00 3.00
*Nos. 78-81 (4)* 1.40 1.15

Church of Uganda, centenary.

A6h

Endangered species: 50c, Pancake tortoise. 1sh, Nile crocodile. 2sh, Hunter's hartebeest. 3sh, Red Colobus monkey. 5sh, Dugong.

**1977, Sept. 26** **Litho.** ***Perf. 14x13½***

**82** A6h 50c multicolored .60 .20
**83** A6h 1sh multicolored 1.75 .40
**84** A6h 2sh multicolored 4.25 1.50
**85** A6h 3sh multicolored 7.00 2.00
**86** A6h 5sh multicolored 8.00 4.00
*a.* Souvenir sheet of 4, #83-86 14.00 10.00
*Nos. 82-86 (5)* 21.60 8.10

Prince Philip and Julius Nyerere, 1961 — A7

5sh, Queen Elizabeth II, Prince Philip, Prime Minister Nyerere in London, 1975. 10sh, Royal crown, flags of Tanzania and Commonwealth nations. 20sh, Coronation.

**1977, Nov. 23** **Litho.** ***Perf. 14x13½***

**87** A7 50c multicolored .20 .20
**88** A7 5sh multicolored .20 .20
**89** A7 10sh multicolored .30 .30
**90** A7 20sh multicolored .55 .55
*a.* Souvenir sheet of 4, #87-90 1.25 1.25
*Nos. 87-90 (4)* 1.25 1.25

25th anniv. of reign of Elizabeth II.

For overprints see Nos. 99-102, 179-180.

Women Fetching Water from Stream and Tap — A8

1sh, Flag raising. 3sh, Health care, laboratory and hospital. 5sh, Pres. Julius Nyerere.

**1978, Feb. 5** **Litho.** ***Perf. 13½x14***

**91** A8 50c multicolored .20 .20
**92** A8 1sh multicolored .20 .20
**93** A8 3sh multicolored .35 .30
**94** A8 5sh multicolored .60 .50
*a.* Souvenir sheet of 4, #91-94 1.25 1.25
*Nos. 91-94 (4)* 1.35 1.20

First anniversary of the New Revolutionary Party (Chama cha Mapinduzi).

A8a

50c, Soccer scene and Joe Kadenge. 1sh, Mohammed Chuma receiving trophy, and his portrait. 2sh, Shot on goal and Omari S. Kidevu. 3sh, Backfield defense and Polly Ouma.

**1978, Apr. 17** **Litho.** ***Perf. 14x13½***

**95** A8a 50c green & multi .20 .20
**96** A8a 1sh lt brown & multi .20 .20
**97** A8a 2sh lilac & multi .35 .30
**98** A8a 3sh dk blue & multi .55 .40
*a.* Souvenir sheet of 4, #95-98 1.75 1.75
*Nos. 95-98 (4)* 1.30 1.10

World Soccer Cup Championships, Argentina '78, June 1-25.

Nos. 87-90a Overprinted in Large Serifed Letters: "25th ANNIVERSARY / CORONATION / 2nd JUNE 1953"

**1978, June 2**

**99** A7 50c multicolored .20 .20
**100** A7 5sh multicolored .20 .20
**101** A7 10sh multicolored .30 .30
**102** A7 20sh multicolored .55 .55
*a.* Souvenir sheet of 4, #99-102 1.00 1.00
*Nos. 99-102 (4)* 1.25 1.25

25th anniv. of coronation of Elizabeth II.

Nos. 99-102a also exist overprinted with smaller, sans serif letters, perf. 12. Same values or less. The perf. 12 set does not exist without overprint.

"Do not Drink when Driving" — A9

Designs: 1sh, "Courtesy to the young, old and handicapped." 3sh, "Observe highway code." 5sh, "Do not drive faulty vehicle."

**1978, July 1** **Litho.** ***Perf. 13½x13***

**103** A9 50c multicolored .20 .20
**104** A9 1sh multicolored .25 .25
**105** A9 3sh multicolored .60 .60
**106** A9 5sh multicolored 2.50 2.50
*a.* Souv. sheet, #103-106, perf. 14 3.00 3.00
*Nos. 103-106 (4)* 3.55 3.55

Road Safety Campaign.

Lake Manyara Hotel — A10

Designs: 1sh, Lobo Wildlife Lodge. 3sh, Ngorongoro Crater Lodge. 5sh, Ngorongoro Wildlife Lodge. 10sh, Mafia Island Lodge. 20sh, Mikumi Wildlife Lodge.

**1978, Sept. 11** **Litho.** ***Perf. 13½***

**107** A10 50c multicolored .20 .20
**108** A10 1sh multicolored .20 .20
**109** A10 3sh multicolored .30 .30
**110** A10 5sh multicolored .55 .55
**111** A10 10sh multicolored 1.10 1.10
**112** A10 20sh multicolored 2.25 2.25
*a.* Souvenir sheet of 6, #107-112 6.25 6.25
*Nos. 107-112 (6)* 4.60 4.60

Game Lodges of Tanzania.

Chained African — A11

1sh, Division of races (black and white heads). 2.50sh, Racial harmony (black and white handshake and heads). 5sh, End of suppression and rise of freedom (hands breaking loose from chains).

**1978, Oct. 24** **Litho.** ***Perf. 14½x14***

**113** A11 50c multicolored .20 .20
**114** A11 1sh multicolored .20 .20
**115** A11 2.50sh multicolored .45 .45
**116** A11 5sh multicolored .90 .90
*a.* Souvenir sheet of 4, #113-116 2.25 2.25
*Nos. 113-116 (4)* 1.75 1.75

Anti-Apartheid Year.

Fokker Friendship at Dar Es Salaam Airport — A12

Designs: 1sh, Single-engine Dragon, 1930, Zanzibar. 2sh, British Airways Concorde. 5sh, Wright Brothers' Flyer 1, 1903.

**1978, Dec. 28** **Litho.** ***Perf. 13½***

**117** A12 50c multicolored .30 .30
**118** A12 1sh multicolored .45 .45
**119** A12 2sh multicolored .85 .85

**120** A12 5sh multicolored 2.10 2.10
*a.* Souvenir sheet of 4, #117-120 4.00 4.00
*Nos. 117-120 (4)* 3.70 3.70

75th anniversary of 1st powered flight.

Emblem A13

Design: 5sh, Headquarters buildings.

**1979, Feb. 3 Litho. *Perf. 14½x14***

**121** A13 50c multicolored .20 .20
**122** A13 5sh multicolored .75 .75
*a.* Souvenir sheet of 2, #121-122 1.25 1.25

Tanzania Post and Telecommunications Corporation, 1st anniversary.

Pres. Nyerere and Children — A14

Designs (UNICEF and Tanzanian IYC Emblems and): 1sh, Kindergarten. 2sh, Vaccination of infant. 5sh, Emblems.

**1979, June 25 Litho. *Perf. 14½***

**123** A14 50c multicolored .20 .20
**124** A14 1sh multicolored .20 .20
**125** A14 2sh multicolored .25 .25
**126** A14 5sh multicolored .60 .60
*a.* Souvenir sheet of 4, #123-126 2.25 2.25
*Nos. 123-126 (4)* 1.25 1.25

International Year of the Child.

Tree Planting — A15

Forest Preservation and Expansion: 1sh, Seedling. 2sh, Rainfall. 5sh, Forest fire.

**1979, Sept. 29 Litho. *Perf. 14½***

**127** A15 50c multicolored .20 .20
**128** A15 1sh multicolored .25 .25
**129** A15 2sh multicolored .50 .50
**130** A15 5sh multicolored 1.25 1.25
*Nos. 127-130 (4)* 2.20 2.20

Mwenge Satellite Earth Station Opening A16

**1979, Dec. 3 Litho. *Perf. 13½***

**131** A16 10c multicolored .20 .20
**132** A16 40c multicolored .20 .20
**133** A16 50c multicolored .20 .20
**134** A16 1sh multicolored .25 .20
*Nos. 131-134 (4)* .85 .80

### Nos. 36, 43 Surcharged

**1979 Litho. *Perf. 14½x14***

**135** A5 40c (10 + 30) multi 1.90 1.90
**136** A5 50c on 70c multi 3.25 3.25

Tabata Dispensary, Dar-es-Salaam, Rotary Emblem — A17

**1980, Mar. 1 Litho. *Perf. 13x13½***

**137** A17 50c shown .20 .20
**138** A17 1sh Ngomvu water project .20 .20
**139** A17 5sh Flying doctor service .45 .45
**140** A17 20sh Torch, anniversary emblem 2.25 2.25
*a.* Souvenir sheet of 4, #137-140 3.25 3.25
*Nos. 137-140 (4)* 3.10 3.10

Rotary International, 75th anniversary. For overprints see Nos. 149-152.

Zanzibar Nos. 49 and 309, "Stamp History" Cancel A18

Cancel and: 50c, Tanganyika #58, postal worker, vert. 10sh, Tanganyika #16, 52. 20sh, Penny Black, Rowland Hill, vert.

**1980, Apr. *Perf. 14***

**141** A18 40c multicolored .20 .20
**142** A18 50c multicolored .20 .20
**143** A18 10sh multicolored .70 .70
**144** A18 20sh multicolored 1.40 1.40
*a.* Souvenir sheet of 4, #141-144 3.00 3.00
*Nos. 141-144 (4)* 2.50 2.50

Sir Rowland Hill (1795-1879), originator of penny postage; Tanzanian stamp history.

### Overprinted: "LONDON 1980" / PHILATELIC EXHIBITION

**1980, May 6 Litho. *Perf. 14***

**145** A18 40c multicolored .20 .20
**146** A18 50c multicolored .20 .20
**147** A18 10sh multicolored .70 .70
**148** A18 20sh multicolored 1.40 1.40
*a.* Souvenir sheet of 4, #145-148 3.25 3.25
*Nos. 145-148 (4)* 2.50 2.50

London 80 Intl. Stamp Exhib., May 6-14.

### Nos. 137-140a with Additional Inscription on 1 or 2 Lines: "District 920-55th Annual / Conference, Arusha, Tanzania"

**1980, June 23 Litho. *Perf. 13x13½***

**149** A17 50c multicolored .20 .20
**150** A17 1sh multicolored .20 .20
**151** A17 5sh multicolored .85 .85
**152** A17 20sh multicolored 3.50 3.50
*a.* Souvenir sheet of 4, #149-152 5.00 5.00
*Nos. 149-152 (4)* 4.75 4.75

District 920 Rotary Club, 55th Annual Conference, Arusha.

Pan African Postal Union and U.P.U. Emblems A19

**1980, July 1 *Perf. 13x13½***

**153** A19 50c purple & blk .20 .20
**154** A19 1sh ultra & blk .20 .20
**155** A19 5sh red orange & blk .75 .75
**156** A19 10sh green & blk 1.50 1.50
*Nos. 153-156 (4)* 2.65 2.65

Pan African Postal Union Plenipotentiary Conference, Arusha, Jan. 8-18.

Gidamis Shahanga, Marathon — A20

Tanzanian Olympic Team: 1sh, Nzael Kyomo and sprinters. 10sh, Zakayo Malekwa and javelin. 20sh, William Lyimo and boxers.

**1980, Aug. 18 Litho. *Perf. 13x13½***

**157** A20 50c multicolored .20 .20
**158** A20 1sh multicolored .20 .20
**159** A20 10sh multicolored 1.10 1.10
**160** A20 20sh multicolored 2.25 2.25
*a.* Souvenir sheet of 4, #157-160 4.00 4.00
*Nos. 157-160 (4)* 3.75 3.75

22nd Summer Olympic Games, Moscow, July 19-Aug. 3.
Issued also in sheets of 20 (5 of each value).

Spring Hare — A21

**1980, Oct. 1 Litho. *Perf. 14***

**161** A21 10c shown .20 .20
**162** A21 20c Genet .20 .20
**163** A21 40c Mongoose .20 .20
**164** A21 50c Ratel .20 .20
**165** A21 75c Rock hyrax .20 .20
**166** A21 80c Leopard .20 .20

***Perf. 14½***
**Size: 40x24mm**

**167** A21 1sh Impalas .20 .20
**168** A21 1.50sh Giraffes .20 .20
**169** A21 2sh Zebras .20 .20
**170** A21 3sh Buffalo .25 .25
**171** A21 5sh Lions .40 .40
**172** A21 10sh Rhinoceros .80 .80
**173** A21 20sh Elephants 1.60 1.60
**174** A21 40sh Cheetahs 3.25 3.25
*Nos. 161-174 (14)* 8.10 8.10

For overprints see Nos. O27-O36.

National Parks Emblem A22

**1981, Jan. 26 Litho. *Perf. 13x13½***

**175** A22 50c Ngorongoro Park .20 .20
**176** A22 1sh shown .20 .20
**177** A22 5sh Friends of Serengeti .70 .70
**178** A22 20sh Friends of Ngorongoro 3.00 3.00
*Nos. 175-178 (4)* 4.10 4.10

Ngorongoro & Serengeti Parks, 60th anniv. For overprints see Nos. 299-302.

### Nos. 89-90 Overprinted: "ROYAL WEDDING/ H.R.H. PRINCE CHARLES/ 29th JULY 1981"

**1981, July 29 Litho. *Perf. 14x13½***

**179** A7 10sh multicolored .35 .35
**180** A7 20sh multicolored .65 .65
*a.* Souvenir sheet of 2, #179-180 5.25 5.25

Mail Runner A23

**1981, Oct. 23 Litho. *Perf. 12½x12***

**181** A23 50c shown .20 .20
**182** A23 1sh Letter sorting .20 .20
**183** A23 5sh Post horn, carrier pigeon .70 .70
**184** A23 10sh Commonwealth members' flags 1.50 1.50
*a.* Souvenir sheet of 4, #181-184 3.00 3.00
*Nos. 181-184 (4)* 2.60 2.60

Commonwealth Postal Administrations Conference, Arusha, June 29-July 10.

Intl. Year of the Disabled A24

**1981, Nov. 30 Litho. *Perf. 14***

**185** A24 50c Morris Nyunyusa, blind drummer .25 .25
**186** A24 1sh Sewing .30 .30
**187** A24 5sh Prostheses 1.50 1.50
**188** A24 10sh Children 2.75 2.75
*Nos. 185-188 (4)* 4.80 4.80

20th Anniv. of Independence — A25

**1982, Jan. 13 Litho. *Perf. 13x13½***

**189** A25 50c Pres. Nyerere, flag .20 .20
**190** A25 1sh Zanzibar Electricity Plant .20 .20
**191** A25 3sh Sisal plant, weaver .50 .50
**192** A25 10sh Pupils 1.75 1.75
*a.* Souvenir sheet of 4, #189-192 3.25 3.25
*Nos. 189-192 (4)* 2.65 2.65

Ostrich — A26

**1982, Jan. 25 Litho. *Perf. 13½***

**193** A26 50c shown .55 .55
**194** A26 1sh Secretary bird .80 .80
**195** A26 5sh Kori bustard 4.00 4.00
**196** A26 10sh Saddle-bill stork 8.00 8.00
*Nos. 193-196 (4)* 13.35 13.35

1982 World Cup A27

**1982, June 2 Litho. *Perf. 14***

**197** A27 50c Jella Mtagwa .35 .35
**198** A27 1sh Stadium .35 .35
**199** A27 10sh Diego Armando Maradona 3.20 3.20
**200** A27 20sh Globe 7.00 7.00
*a.* Souvenir sheet of 4, #197-200 10.50 10.50
*Nos. 197-200 (4)* 10.90 10.90

Jade of Seronera and her Cubs A28

Animals Appearing in Movies or TV Shows: 1sh, Wild dog and puppies, Havoc. 5sh, Fifi and sons, Gombe. 10sh, Bahati and twins Rashidi and Ramadhani, Lake Manyara.

**1982, July 15 Litho. *Perf. 14***

**201** A28 50c multicolored .20 .20
**202** A28 1sh multicolored .25 .25
**203** A28 5sh multicolored 1.25 1.25
**204** A28 10sh multicolored 2.50 2.50
*a.* Souv. sheet, #201-204, perf. 14½ 5.50 5.50
*Nos. 201-204 (4)* 4.20 4.20

Scouting Year A29

**1982, Aug. 25**

**205** A29 50c Brick laying .20 .20
**206** A29 1sh Camping .20 .20
**207** A29 10sh Tracing marks 1.75 1.75

**208** A29 20sh Baden-Powell 3.50 3.50
*a.* Souvenir sheet of 4, #205-208 6.50 6.50
*Nos. 205-208 (4)* 5.65 5.65

For overprint see No. 303.

World Food Day — A30

**1982, Oct. 16** **Litho.** ***Perf. 14***
**209** A30 50c Plowing .20 .20
**210** A30 1sh Dairy cows .20 .20
**211** A30 5sh Corn harvest 1.00 1.00
**212** A30 10sh Grain storage 2.00 2.00
*a.* Souvenir sheet of 4, #209-212 3.50 3.50
*Nos. 209-212 (4)* 3.40 3.40

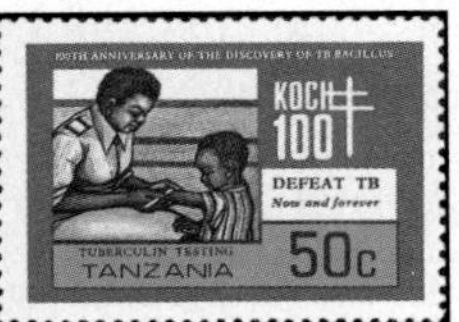

TB Bacillus Centenary A31

**1982, Dec. 5** ***Perf. 12½x12***
**213** A31 50c Child immunization .20 .20
**214** A31 1sh Koch .20 .20
**215** A31 5sh TB emblem 1.00 1.00
**216** A31 10sh WHO emblem 2.00 2.00
*Nos. 213-216 (4)* 3.40 3.40

A31a

**1983, Mar. 14** **Litho.** ***Perf. 14***
**217** A31a 50c Pres. Nyerere .20 .20
**218** A31a 1sh Running, boxing .20 .20
**219** A31a 5sh Flags 1.00 1.00
**220** A31a 10sh Pres. Nyerere, Royal Family 2.00 2.00
*a.* Souvenir sheet of 4, #217-220 3.50 3.50
*Nos. 217-220 (4)* 3.40 3.40

Commonwealth Day. For overprint see #407.

5th Anniv. of Posts and Telecommunications Dept. — A32

**1983, Feb. 3** **Litho.** ***Perf. 12½x12***
**221** A32 50c Letter post .20 .20
**222** A32 1sh Training Institute .20 .20
**223** A32 5sh Satellite communications 1.00 1.00
**224** A32 10sh Emblems 2.00 2.00
*a.* Souvenir sheet of 4, #221-224 3.50 3.50
*Nos. 221-224 (4)* 3.40 3.40

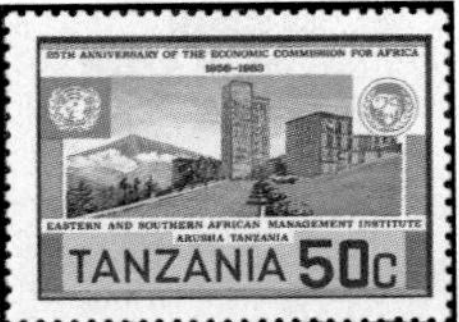

25th Anniv. of Economic Commission for Africa — A33

**1983, Sept. 12** **Litho.** ***Perf. 12½x12***
**225** A33 50c Eastern & Southern African Management Institute, Arusha .40 .40
**226** A33 1sh Emblems .50 .50
**227** A33 5sh Mineral collections 2.25 2.25
**228** A33 10sh Emblems, diff. 4.50 4.50
*a.* Souvenir sheet of 4, #225-228 7.50 7.50
*Nos. 225-228 (4)* 7.65 7.65

World Communications Year — A34

**1983, Oct. 17** **Litho.** ***Perf. 14***
**229** A34 50c Rural telephone service .20 .20
**230** A34 1sh Emblems .20 .20
**231** A34 5sh Post Office 1.00 1.00
**232** A34 10sh Microwave tower 2.00 2.00
*a.* Souvenir sheet of 4, #229-232 3.50 3.50
*Nos. 229-232 (4)* 3.40 3.40

Historical Buildings A35

**1983, Dec. 12** **Litho.** ***Perf. 12½x12***
**233** A35 1sh Bagamoyo Boma .20 .20
**234** A35 1.50sh Beit-El-Ajaib .30 .30
**235** A35 5sh Anglican Church .90 .90
**236** A35 10sh State House, old and new 1.75 1.75
*a.* Souvenir sheet of 4, #233-236 3.50 3.50
*Nos. 233-236 (4)* 3.15 3.15

20th Anniv. of Revolution A36

**1984, June 18** **Litho.** ***Perf. 14***
**237** A36 1sh Muasisi Kwanza .20 .20
**238** A36 1.50sh Clove farming .30 .30
**239** A36 5sh Industrial development 1.00 1.00
**240** A36 10sh Housing developments 2.00 2.00
*Nos. 237-240 (4)* 3.50 3.50

### Souvenir Sheet

**241** A36 15sh Map, ship 3.25 3.25

1984 Summer Olympics A37

**1984, Aug. 6** ***Perf. 12½x12***
**242** A37 1sh Boxing .20 .20
**243** A37 1.50sh Running .20 .20
**244** A37 5sh Basketball .75 .75
**245** A37 20sh Soccer 2.25 2.25
*a.* Souvenir sheet of 4, #242-245 3.50 3.50
*Nos. 242-245 (4)* 3.40 3.40

For overprints see Nos. 275-278.

Intl. Civil Aviation Org. 40th Anniv. A38

**1984, Nov. 15** **Litho.** ***Perf. 13***
**246** A38 1sh Icarus .20 .20
**247** A38 1.50sh Air Tanzania jets, traffic controller .20 .20
**248** A38 5sh Aircraft maintenance .75 .75
**249** A38 10sh ICAO emblem 1.25 1.25
*a.* Souvenir sheet of 4, #246-249 2.25 2.25
*Nos. 246-249 (4)* 2.40 2.40

Traditional Houses A39

**1984, Dec. 20** ***Perf. 12½x12***
**250** A39 1sh Sochi .20 .20
**251** A39 1.50sh Isyenga .20 .20
**252** A39 5sh Tembe .65 .65
**253** A39 10sh Banda 1.25 1.25
*a.* Souvenir sheet of 4, #250-253 2.75 2.75
*Nos. 250-253 (4)* 2.30 2.30

Textile Industry A40

5th anniversary of the Southern Africa Development Coordination Conference.

**1985, Apr. 1** ***Perf. 14***
**254** A40 1.50sh shown .50 .50
**255** A40 4sh Mining 1.25 1.25
**256** A40 5sh Transportation and communications 1.40 1.40
**257** A40 20sh Flags of member nations 5.75 5.75
*a.* Souvenir sheet of 4, #254-257 9.00 9.00
*Nos. 254-257 (4)* 8.90 8.90

Rare Species of Zanzibar A41

***Perf. 13½x13, 13x13½***
**1985, May 8** **Litho.**
**258** A41 1sh Tortoise .45 .45
**259** A41 4sh Leopard 1.40 1.40
**260** A41 10sh Civet cat 2.75 2.75
**261** A41 17.50sh Red colobus, vert. 4.50 4.50
*Nos. 258-261 (4)* 9.10 9.10

### Souvenir Sheet

**262** Sheet of 2 3.75 3.75
*a.* A41 15sh Black rhinoceros 1.50 1.50
*b.* A41 20sh Giant ground pangolin 2.25 2.25

For overprints see Nos. 408-409, 411.

Automobile Centenary — A42

Classic autos manufactured by Rolls-Royce.

**1985, May 14** ***Perf. 14½x14***
**263** A42 1.50sh 1936 20/25 .20 .20
**264** A42 5sh 1933 Phantom II .20 .20
**265** A42 10sh 1926 Phantom I .20 .20
**266** A42 30sh 1907 Silver Ghost .70 .70
*a.* Souvenir sheet of 4, #263-266 1.10 1.10
*Nos. 263-266 (4)* 1.30 1.30

Queen Mother, 85th Birthday — A43

**1985, Sept. 30**
**267** A43 20sh Waving .20 .20
**268** A43 20sh Facing left .20 .20
**269** A43 100sh Wearing green hat .20 .20
*a.* Souvenir sheet, #267, 269 .50 .50
**270** A43 100sh Facing right .20 .20
*a.* Souvenir sheet, #268, 270 .50 .50
*Nos. 267-270 (4)* .80 .80

For overprints see Nos. 295-298.

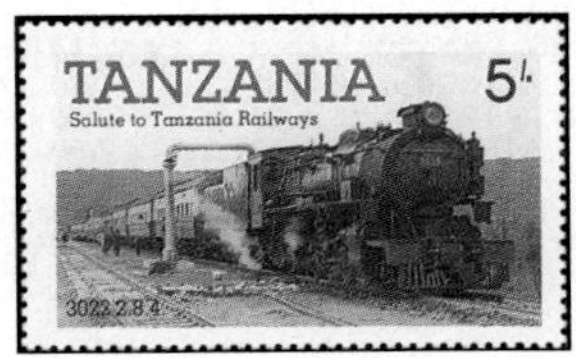

Tanzania Railways Locomotives — A44

**1985, Oct. 7** **Litho.** ***Perf. 14½x14***
**271** A44 5sh No. 3022 .20 .20
**272** A44 10sh No. 3107 .20 .20
**273** A44 20sh No. 6004 .30 .30
**274** A44 30sh No. 3129 .50 .50
*a.* Souvenir sheet of 4, #271-274 1.40 1.40
*Nos. 271-274 (4)* 1.20 1.20

Nos. 242-245 Ovptd. with Winners and "GOLD MEDAL" in 2 or 3 Lines

**1985, Oct. 22** ***Perf. 12½x12***
**275** A37 1sh Henry Tillman, USA .20 .20
**276** A37 1.50sh USA .20 .20
**277** A37 5sh USA .50 .50
**278** A37 20sh France 2.00 2.00
*a.* Souvenir sheet of 4, #275-278 8.00 8.00
*Nos. 275-278 (4)* 2.90 2.90

Pottery A45

**1985, Nov. 4**
**279** A45 1.50sh Water and cooking pots .20 .20
**280** A45 2sh Frying pot and caldron .20 .20
**281** A45 5sh Woman selling pots .50 .50
**282** A45 40sh Beer pot 3.75 3.75
*Nos. 279-282 (4)* 4.65 4.65

### Souvenir Sheet

**283** A45 30sh Water pot 4.00 4.00

Locomotives — A46

**1985, Nov. 25**
**284** A46 1.50sh Class 64 .20 .20
**285** A46 2sh Class 36 .20 .20
**286** A46 5sh Shunting DFH1013 .55 .55
**287** A46 10sh Diesel Electric DE1001 1.10 1.10
**288** A46 30sh Zanzibar, 1906 3.25 3.25
*Nos. 284-288 (5)* 5.30 5.30

### Souvenir Sheet

**289** Sheet of 2 5.50 5.50
*a.* A46 15sh Class 30 steam 2.50 2.50
*b.* A46 20sh Class 11 steam 3.00 3.00

For overprints see Nos. 381A-381E.

Intl. Youth Year — A47

**1986, Jan. 20** ***Perf. 14***

**290** A47 1.50sh Young Pioneers .20 .20
**291** A47 4sh Health care .50 .50
**292** A47 10sh Uhuru torch race 1.00 1.00
**293** A47 20sh World map 1.75 1.75
*Nos. 290-293 (4)* 3.45 3.45

**Souvenir Sheet**

**294** A47 30sh Agriculture 3.00 3.00

Nos. 267-270 Ovptd. "CARIBBEAN/ ROYAL VISIT/ 1985" in Silver or Gold

**1986, Feb. 10** ***Perf. 14½x14***

**295** A43 20sh on #267 *7.50 7.50*
**296** A43 20sh on #268 *7.50 7.50*
**297** A43 100sh on #269 *7.50 7.50*
*a.* Souvenir sheet, #295, 297 *20.00* —
**298** A43 100sh on #270 *7.50 7.50*
*a.* Souvenir sheet, #296, 298 *20.00* —
*Nos. 295-298 (4)* 30.00 30.00

See footnote following No. 303.

Nos. 175-178, 208a Ovptd. "75th ANNIVERSARY GIRL GUIDES/ 1910-1985" in Silver or Black

**1986, Feb. Litho.** ***Perf. 13x13½, 14***

**299** A22 50c multicolored (S) *15.00 15.00*
**300** A22 1sh multicolored *15.00 15.00*
**301** A22 5sh multicolored *15.00 15.00*
**302** A22 20sh multicolored *15.00 15.00*

**Souvenir Sheet**

**303** Sheet of 4 *45.00 45.00*
*a.* A29 50c multicolored — —
*b.* A29 1sh multicolored — —
*c.* A29 10sh multicolored — —
*d.* A29 20sh multicolored — —

The status of this set, the Caribbean Royal Visit set and at least 12 stamps overprinted congratulating the Duke and Duchess of York on their marriage are in question.

Rotary Intl., World Chess Championships — A48

**1986, Mar. 17** ***Perf. 14***

**304** A48 20sh shown .25 .25
**305** A48 100sh Chess board 1.25 1.25
*a.* Souvenir sheet of 2, #304-305 1.50 1.50

Audubon Birth Bicent. — A49

Illustrations of American bird species by Audubon.

**1986, May 22**

**306** A49 5sh Mallard .20 .20
**307** A49 10sh American eider .20 .20
**308** A49 20sh Scarlet ibis .35 .35
**309** A49 30sh Roseate spoonbill .55 .55
*a.* Souvenir sheet of 4, #306-309 1.50 1.50
*Nos. 306-309 (4)* 1.30 1.30

Gemstones A50

**1986, May 22**

**310** A50 1.50sh Pearls .55 .55
**311** A50 2sh Sapphires .70 .70
**312** A50 5sh Tanzanite 1.75 1.75
**313** A50 40sh Diamonds 11.50 11.50
*Nos. 310-313 (4)* 14.50 14.50

**Souvenir Sheet**

**314** A50 30sh Rubies 14.00 14.00

Indigenous Flowers — A51

Endangered Wildlife — A52

**1986, June 2**

**315** A51 1.50sh Hibiscus calyphyllus .20 .20
**316** A51 5sh Aloe graminicola .20 .20
**317** A51 10sh Nersium oleander .20 .20
**318** A51 30sh Nymphaea caerulea .50 .50
*a.* Souvenir Sheet of 4, #315-318 .90 .90
*Nos. 315-318 (4)* 1.10 1.10

**1986, June 30 Litho.** ***Perf. 14x14½***

**319** A52 5sh Oryx .20 .20
**320** A52 10sh Giraffe .20 .20
**321** A52 20sh Rhinoceros .25 .25
**322** A52 30sh Cheetah .35 .35
*a.* Miniature sheet of 4, #319-322 .80 .80
*Nos. 319-322 (4)* 1.00 1.00

UN Child Survival Campaign A53

**1986, July 29** ***Perf. 12½x12***

**323** A53 1.50sh Immunization .35 .35
**324** A53 2sh Growth monitoring .35 .35
**325** A53 5sh Oral rehydration therapy .35 .35
**326** A53 40sh Breast feeding 2.75 2.75
*Nos. 323-326 (4)* 3.80 3.80

**Souvenir Sheet**

**327** A53 30sh Healthy child 1.75 1.75

For overprints see Nos. 406, 410, 412.

Marine Life A54

**1986, Aug. 20**

**328** A54 1.50sh Butterflyfish .80 .80
**329** A54 4sh Parrotfish 1.75 1.75
**330** A54 10sh Sea turtle 3.00 3.00
**331** A54 20sh Octopus 4.50 4.50
*Nos. 328-331 (4)* 10.05 10.05

**Souvenir Sheet**

**332** A54 30sh Coral 3.25 3.25

Queen Elizabeth II, 60th Birthday — A55

Photographs: 5sh, Royal family, Buckingham Palace balcony. 10sh, With princes in open carriage. 40sh, Elizabeth II. 60sh, Greeting crowd.

**1987, Mar. 24 Litho.** ***Perf. 14***

**333** A55 5sh multicolored *.20*
**334** A55 10sh multicolored *.20*
**335** A55 40sh multicolored *.50*
**336** A55 60sh multicolored *.75*
*a.* Souvenir sheet of 4, #333-336 *1.50*
*Nos. 333-336 (4)* *1.65*

1986 World Cup Soccer Championships, Mexico — A57

Designs: 1.50sh, Map, team captains, officials. 2sh, Foul. 10sh, Goal. 20sh, Goalie save. 30sh, Argentine natl. team.

**1986, Oct. 30 Litho.** ***Perf. 14***

**341** A57 1.50sh multicolored .30 .30
**342** A57 2sh multicolored .30 .30
**343** A57 10sh multicolored .75 .75
**344** A57 20sh multicolored 1.40 1.40
*Nos. 341-344 (4)* 2.75 2.75

**Souvenir Sheet**

**345** A57 30sh multicolored 1.25 1.25

Hair Styles — A58

**1987, Mar. 16** ***Perf. 14½***

**346** A58 1.50sh Nungu Nungu .35 .35
**347** A58 2sh Upanga wa Jogoo .60 .60
**348** A58 10sh Morani 1.10 1.10
**349** A58 20sh Twende Kilioni 1.75 *1.75*
*Nos. 346-349 (4)* 3.80 *3.80*

**Souvenir Sheet**

**350** A58 30sh Kusuka Nywele 3.75 3.75

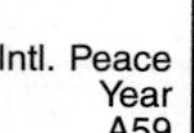

Intl. Peace Year A59

Designs: 1.50sh, Julius K. Nyerere, Beyond War Award winner. 2sh, Peace among nations. 10sh, Peaceful use of outer space. 20sh, Emblem, UN building. 30sh, Emblem, handshake.

**1986, Dec. 22 Litho.** ***Perf. 14½***

**351** A59 1.50sh multicolored .45 .45
**352** A59 2sh multicolored .75 .75
**353** A59 10sh multicolored 1.90 1.90
**354** A59 20sh multicolored 2.75 2.75
*Nos. 351-354 (4)* 5.85 5.85

**Souvenir Sheet**

**355** A59 30sh multicolored 2.50 2.50

Natl. Bank of Commerce, 20th Anniv. — A60

**1987, Feb. 6 Litho.** ***Perf. 14***

**356** A60 1.50sh Mobile bank .45 .45
**357** A60 2sh Headquarters .75 .75
**358** A60 5sh Pres. Mwinyi laying foundation stone 1.25 1.25
**359** A60 20sh Cotton harvest 3.25 3.25
*Nos. 356-359 (4)* 5.70 5.70

New Revolutionary Party (CCM), 10th Anniv. — A61

**1987, Apr. 10** ***Perf. 14½x14***

**360** A61 2sh Soldiers in formation .20 .20
**361** A61 3sh Woman picking coffee beans .20 .20
**362** A61 10sh Speaker at podium .45 .45
**363** A61 30sh Nyerere, Mwinyi 1.25 1.25
*Nos. 360-363 (4)* 2.10 2.10

Arush Declaration, 20th anniv.

Insects A62

**1987, Apr. 22** ***Perf. 12½x12***

**364** A62 1.50sh Bees .70 .70
**365** A62 2sh Greater grain borer .95 .95
**366** A62 10sh Tse-tse fly 2.10 2.10
**367** A62 20sh Wasp 3.50 3.50
*Nos. 364-367 (4)* 7.25 7.25

**Souvenir Sheet**

**368** A62 30sh Mosquito 5.75 5.75

Reptiles A63

**1987, July 2**

**369** A63 2sh Crocodiles .70 .70
**370** A63 3sh Black-striped grass snake .70 .70
**371** A63 10sh Adder 1.40 1.40
**372** A63 20sh Green mamba 2.75 2.75
*Nos. 369-372 (4)* 5.55 5.55

**Souvenir Sheet**

**373** A63 30sh Tortoise 1.75 1.75

Posts and Telecommunications, Railways Emblems — A64

**1987, July 27** ***Perf. 14***

**374** A64 2sh shown .60 .60
**375** A64 8sh Air Tanzania, Port Authority 1.25 1.25

**Souvenir Sheet**

**376** A64 20sh Modes of communication and transportation 4.75 4.75

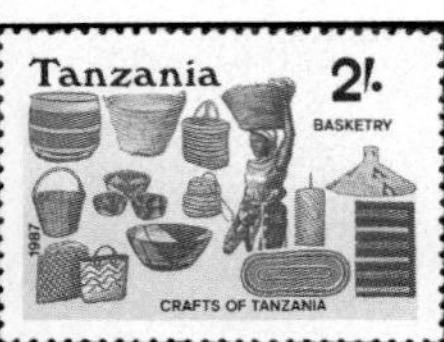


Traditional Crafts A65

**1987, Dec. 15 Litho.** ***Perf. 12½x12***

**377** A65 2sh Baskets .30 .30
**378** A65 3sh Gourds .30 .30
**379** A65 10sh Stools .45 .45
**380** A65 20sh Makonde carvings .85 .85
*Nos. 377-380 (4)* 1.90 1.90

**Souvenir Sheet**

**381** A65 40sh Makonde carver at work 1.75 1.75

Nos. 284-288 Ovptd.

**1987, Dec. 30 Litho.** ***Perf. 12½x12***

**381A** A46 1.50sh multicolored .60 .60
**381B** A46 2sh multicolored .60 .60
**381C** A46 5sh multicolored .75 .75
**381D** A46 10sh multicolored 1.50 1.50
**381E** A46 30sh multicolored 4.50 4.50
*Nos. 381A-381E (5)* 7.95 7.95

Plateosaurus — A66

**1988, Apr. 22** ***Perf. 12½***

**382** A66 2sh shown .50 .50
**383** A66 3sh Pteranodon .50 .50
**384** A66 5sh Brontosaurus .50 .50
**385** A66 7sh Lions .55 .55
**386** A66 8sh Tiger .55 .55
**387** A66 12sh Orangutans .60 .60
**388** A66 20sh Elephants .85 .85
**389** A66 100sh Stegosaurus 2.25 2.25
*Nos. 382-389 (8)* 6.30 6.30

Traditional Games A67

**1988, Feb. 15 Litho.** ***Perf. 12½x12***

**390** A67 2sh Mdako (marbles) .30 .30
**391** A67 3sh Mieleka (wrestling) .30 .30
**392** A67 8sh Bull fight .30 .30
**393** A67 20sh Bao (African chess) .50 .50
*Nos. 390-393 (4)* 1.40 1.40

**Souvenir Sheet**

**394** A67 30sh Kulenga shabaha (archery) 1.25 1.25

Dated 1987.

Miniature Sheets

Statue of Liberty, Cent. (in 1986) — A68

No. 395: 1sh, Re-opening gala (evening), 1986. 2sh, Musicians performing. 3sh, Cheerleaders. 15sh, Statue holding tablet. 30sh, Tablet inscription. 40sh, Liberty Island. 50sh, Re-opening gala (afternoon), 1986. 60sh, Blimps over Liberty Island.

No. 396: 4sh, Statue, blimp. 5sh, Torch. 6sh, Torch and crown observatories lit at night, scaffolding. 7sh, Worker gilding torch. 8sh, Statue shrouded in scaffolding. 10sh, Two workers, torch. 12sh, Head, scaffolding. 18sh, Celebrant at re-opening (evening). 20sh, Goodyear blimp, skirt of Statue. 25sh, Boys' choir, statue. 35sh, Torch held aloft, full moon. 45sh, Worker cleaning tablet.

**1988, June 15 Litho.** ***Perf. 14***

**395** Sheet of 8 + label 8.50 8.50
*a.* A68 1sh multicolored .25 .25
*b.* A68 2sh multicolored .25 .25
*c.* A68 3sh multicolored .25 .25
*d.* A68 15sh multicolored .60 .60
*e.* A68 30sh multicolored 1.25 1.25
*f.* A68 40sh multicolored 1.60 1.60
*g.* A68 50sh multicolored 2.00 2.00
*h.* A68 60sh multicolored 2.40 2.40
**396** Sheet of 12 8.50 8.50
*a.* A68 4sh multicolored .25 .25
*b.* A68 5sh multicolored .25 .25
*c.* A68 6sh multicolored .25 .25
*d.* A68 7sh multicolored .25 .25
*e.* A68 8sh multicolored .35 .35
*f.* A68 10sh multicolored .40 .40
*g.* A68 12sh multicolored .45 .45
*h.* A68 18sh multicolored .75 .75
*i.* A68 20sh multicolored .80 .80
*j.* A68 25sh multicolored 1.00 1.00
*k.* A68 35sh multicolored 1.40 1.40
*l.* A68 45sh multicolored 1.75 1.75

No. 395 contains a center label inscribed "THE STATUE / OF LIBERTY / 100th ANNIVERSARY."

Natl. Monuments — A69

**1988, June 15 Litho.**

**397** A69 5sh Independence Torch .25 .25
**398** A69 12sh Arusha Declaration .25 .25
**399** A69 30sh Askari .30 .30
**400** A69 60sh Independence .60 .60
*Nos. 397-400 (4)* 1.40 1.40

**Souvenir Sheet**

**401** A69 100sh Soldier (Askari detail) 2.50 2.50

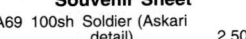

3rd Natl. Census, Aug. 28 — A70

**1988, Aug. 8**

**402** A70 2sh shown .20 .20
**403** A70 3sh Enumeration .20 .20
**404** A70 10sh Health care .30 .30
**405** A70 20sh Population figures .55 .55
*Nos. 402-405 (4)* 1.25 1.25

**Souvenir Sheet**

**405A** A70 40sh Segments of economy and society 1.25 1.25

Stamps of 1983-86 Ovptd:

*A53* "125TH ANNIVERSARY / INTERNATIONAL RED CROSS / AND RED CRESCENT"

*CD334* "40TH WEDDING ANNIVERSARY / H.M. QUEEN ELIZABETH II / H.R.H. THE DUKE OF EDINBURGH"

*A41* "63RD ANNIVERSARY / ROTARY INTERNATIONAL / IN AFRICA"

**1988, Aug. 15** ***Perfs. as Before***

**406** A53 5sh on #325 .80 .80
**407** A31a 10sh on #220 11.00 11.00
*a.* Souv. sheet of 4, #218-220, 407 2.50 2.50
**408** A41 10sh on #260 4.00 4.00
**409** A41 17.50sh on #261 7.50 7.50
**410** A53 40sh on #326 9.75 9.75
*Nos. 406-410 (5)* 33.05 33.05

**Souvenir Sheets**

**411** Sheet of 2 5.00 5.00
*a.* A41 15sh on #262a 1.25 1.25
*b.* A41 20sh on #262b 2.75 2.75
**412** A53 30sh on #327 5.00 5.00

1988 Olympics, Seoul and Calgary — A71

**1988, Aug. 29** ***Perf. 14***

**414** A71 5sh Biathlon .40 .40
**415** A71 10sh Soccer .20 .20
**416** A71 20sh Cycling .70 .70
**417** A71 25sh Pairs figuring skating .80 .80
**418** A71 50sh Fencing .75 .75
**419** A71 50sh Downhill skiing 1.40 1.40
**420** A71 70sh Volleyball .90 .90
**421** A71 75sh Bobsled 1.60 1.60
*Nos. 414-421 (8)* 6.75 6.75

**Souvenir Sheets**

**422** A71 100sh Flags, hockey sticks 2.50 2.50
**423** A71 100sh Gymnastics 2.50 2.50

For overprint see No. 534A-534J.

1988 Summer Olympics, Seoul A71a

**1988, Sept. 5 Litho.** ***Perf. 12½x12***

**423A** A71a 2sh Javelin .85 .85
**423B** A71a 3sh Hurdles .90 .90
**423C** A71a 7sh Long distance running 1.40 1.40
**423D** A71a 12sh Relay race 1.75 1.75
*Nos. 423A-423D (4)* 4.90 4.90

A souvenir sheet exists.

Disney Characters, Special Occasions — A72

**1988, Sept. 9** ***Perf. 14***

**424** A72 4sh Love You, Dad .30 .30
**425** A72 5sh Happy Birthday .30 .30
**426** A72 10sh Trick or Treat .45 .45
**427** A72 12sh Be Kind to Animals .45 .45
**428** A72 15sh Love .55 .55
**429** A72 20sh Let's Celebrate .80 .80
**430** A72 30sh Keep In Touch 1.75 1.75
**431** A72 50sh Love You, Mom 3.50 3.50
*Nos. 424-431 (8)* 8.10 8.10

**Souvenir Sheets**

**432** A72 150sh Let's Work Together 4.00 4.00
**433** A72 150sh Have a Super Sunday 4.00 4.00

Mickey Mouse, 60th anniv.

Domestic Animals A73

**1988, Sept. 9**

**434** A73 4sh Goat, vert. .50 .50
**435** A73 5sh Rabbit .50 .50
**436** A73 8sh Cows .70 .70
**437** A73 10sh Cat .95 .95
**438** A73 12sh Horse, vert. 1.25 1.25
**439** A73 20sh Dog, vert. 1.90 1.90
*Nos. 434-439 (6)* 5.80 5.80

**Souvenir Sheet**

**440** A73 100sh Chicken 4.00 4.00

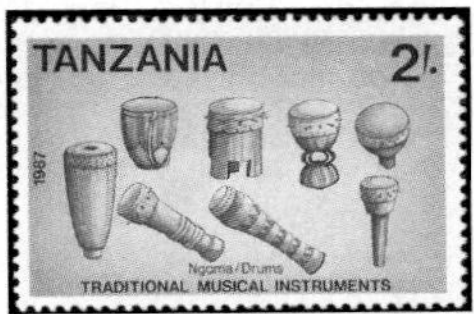


Traditional Musical Instruments — A74

**1988, Sept. 30 Litho.** ***Perf. 14***

**441** A74 2sh Drums .60 .60
**442** A74 3sh Xylophones .60 .60
**443** A74 10sh Thumb pianos 1.25 1.25
**444** A74 20sh Fiddles 1.90 1.90
*Nos. 441-444 (4)* 4.35 4.35

**Souvenir Sheet**

**445** A74 40sh Violins with calabash resonators 1.75 1.75

Dated 1987.

Butterflies A75

**1988, Oct. 17** ***Perf. 14½***

**446** A75 8sh Charaxes varanes .65 .65
**447** A75 30sh Neptis melicerta 1.10 1.10
**448** A75 40sh Mylothris chloris 1.10 1.10
**449** A75 50sh Charaxes bohemani 1.40 1.40
**450** A75 60sh Myrina ficedula 1.75 1.75
**451** A75 75sh Papilio phorcas 2.25 2.25
**452** A75 90sh Cyrestis camillus 2.75 2.75
**453** A75 100sh Salamis temora 2.75 2.75
*Nos. 446-453 (8)* 13.75 13.75

**Souvenir Sheets**

**454** A75 200sh Asterope rosa 6.00 6.00
**455** A75 250sh Kallima rumia 7.25 7.25

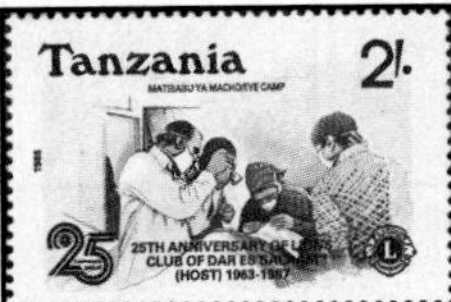


Intl. Lions Club at Dar es Salaam, 25th Anniv. A76

**1988, Nov, 30 Litho.** ***Perf. 14½***

**456** A76 2sh Eye operation .40 .40
**457** A76 3sh Shallow water well .40 .40
**458** A76 7sh Map, rhinoceros 1.25 1.25
**459** A76 12sh Donating school desks .50 .50
*Nos. 456-459 (4)* 2.55 2.55

**Souvenir Sheet**

**460** A76 40sh Emblem 1.75 1.75

Community services: Matibabu Ya Macho Eye Camp (2sh); sanitary water supply in Dar es Salaam (3sh); wildlife conservation (7sh); aid to local schools (12sh).

Intl. Red Cross and Red Crescent Organizations, 125th Annivs. — A77

Design: 2sh, Assisting the wounded and sick. 3sh, Postnatal care clinic. 7sh, Red Cross flag. 12sh, Jean-Henry Dunant, founder. 40sh, Dunant, Thomas Maunier, Louis Appia, Gustave Moynier and Gen. Guillaume Henri Dufour, members of intl. committee that sponsored the conference in 1863 where the Red Cross was founded.

**1988, Dec. 30 Litho.** ***Perf. 12½x12***

**461** A77 2sh multicolored .40 .40
**462** A77 3sh multicolored .40 .40
**463** A77 7sh multicolored .45 .45
**464** A77 12sh multicolored .65 .65
*Nos. 461-464 (4)* 1.90 1.90

**Souvenir Sheet**

**465** A77 40sh multicolored 1.75 1.75

Miniature Sheet

Paradise Whydah — A78

Birds: a, Paradise whydah. b, Black-collared barbet. c, Bataleur eagle. d, Openbill storks, lilac-breasted roller. e, Scarlet-tufted malachite sunbird. f, Dark chanting goshawk. g, White-fronted bee-eater, little bee-eater, carmine bee-eater. h, Marabou stork, Narina's trocon. i, African gray parrot. j, Hoopoe. k, Yellow-collared lovebird. l, Yellow-billed hornbill. m, Hammerkop. n, Flamingos, violet-crested turaco. o, Malachite kingfisher. p, Greater flamingo. q, Yellow-billed stork. r, Shoebill stork. s, Saddle-billed stork, blacksmith plover. t, Crowned crane.

**1989, Jan. 10** ***Perf. 14***

**466** Sheet of 20 27.00 27.00
***a.-t.*** A78 20sh any single .70 .70

**Souvenir Sheets**

**467** A78 350sh Helmeted guineafowl 7.50 7.50
**467A** A78 350sh Ostrich 7.50 7.50

No. 466 has a continuous design.

Endangered Species
A79 A80

World Wildlife Fund: Various bushbabies, *Galago zanzibaricus.* 350sh, African palm civet.

**1989, Jan. 24** ***Perf. 14***

**468** A79 5sh shown .70 .70
**469** A79 10sh multi, horiz. .75 .75
**470** A79 20sh multi, diff. 1.10 1.10
**471** A79 45sh multi, diff., horiz. 2.25 2.25
*Nos. 468-471 (4)* 4.80 4.80

**Souvenir Sheet**

**472** A79 350sh multi, horiz. 9.00 9.00

**1989, Jan. 24**

30sh, Black cobra, umbrella acacia. 70sh, Red-tailed tropic bird, tree fern. 100sh, African tree frog, cocoa tree. 150sh, African black-necked heron, Egyptian papyrus. 350sh, Pink-backed pelicans, baobab tree.

**473** A80 30sh shown .85 .85
**474** A80 70sh multicolored 4.25 4.25
**475** A80 100sh multicolored 4.25 4.25
**476** A80 150sh multicolored 7.75 7.75
*Nos. 473-476 (4)* 17.10 17.10

**Souvenir Sheet**

**477** A80 350sh multicolored 8.25 8.25

Steam Locomotives — A81

**1989, Jan. 31**

**478** A81 10sh Class P36, USSR .75 .75
**479** A81 25sh Class 12, Belgium .80 .80
**480** A81 60sh Class C62, Japan 1.25 1.25
**481** A81 75sh Class T1, Pennsylvania R.R. 1.40 1.40
**482** A81 80sh Class WP, India 1.50 1.50
**483** A81 90sh Class 59, East African Railways 1.75 1.75
**484** A81 150sh People Class 4-6-2, China 2.75 2.75
**485** A81 200sh Southern Pacific *Daylight Express,* US 2.75 2.75
*Nos. 478-485 (8)* 12.95 12.95

**Souvenir Sheets**

**486** A81 350sh Stephenson's *Planet,* Britain 6.00 6.00
**487** A81 350sh *Coronation Scot,* Britain 6.00 6.00

Nos. 486-487 vert.

World-Class Athletes — A82

Designs: 4sh, Juma Ikangaa, Tanzania, marathon. 8.50sh, Steffi Graf, West Germany, tennis. 12sh, Yannick Noah, France, tennis. 40sh, Pele, Brazil, soccer. 100sh, Erhard Keller, West Germany, speed skater. 125sh, Sadanoyama, Japan, Sumo wrestler. 200sh, Taino, Japan, Sumo wrestler. 250sh, I. Aoki, Japan, golfer. No. 496, Joe Louis, US, world heavyweight boxing champion, 1937-1949. No. 497, T. Nakajima, Japan, golfer.

**1989, Feb. 7**

**488** A82 4sh multicolored .40 .40
**489** A82 8.50sh multicolored .40 .40
**490** A82 12sh multicolored .40 .40
**491** A82 40sh multicolored 1.25 1.25
**492** A82 100sh multicolored 3.00 3.00
**493** A82 125sh multicolored 3.50 3.50
**494** A82 200sh multicolored 5.25 5.25
**495** A82 250sh multicolored 6.75 6.75
*Nos. 488-495 (8)* 20.95 20.95

**Souvenir Sheets**

**496** A82 350sh multicolored 7.25 7.25
**497** A82 350sh multicolored 7.25 7.25

History of Space Exploration and 20th Anniv. of the 1st Moon Landing — A83

**1989, July 20**

**498** A83 20sh Luna 3 .45 .45
**499** A83 30sh Rendezvous of Gemini 6&7 .55 .55
**500** A83 40sh 1st US space walk .60 .60
**501** A83 60sh First man on Moon .85 .85
**502** A83 70sh Experiments on Moon .90 .90
**503** A83 100sh Apollo 15 lunar rover 1.25 1.25
**504** A83 150sh Apollo-Soyuz 1.50 1.50
**505** A83 200sh Spacelab 1.90 1.90
*Nos. 498-505 (8)* 8.00 8.00

**Souvenir Sheets**

**506** A83 250sh Futuristic space station 3.00 3.00
**507** A83 250sh *Eagle* lunar module 3.00 3.00

History of space exploration (Nos. 498-500, 503-506); others 20th anniv. of 1st Moon Landing.

St. Mary Magdalene in Penitence A84

Details from paintings by Titian: 10sh, Averoldi Polyptych. 15sh, St. Margaret. 50sh, Venus and Adonis. 75sh, Venus and the Lutenist. 100sh, Tarquin and Lucretia. 125sh, St. Jerome. 150sh, Madonna and Child with Saints. No. 516, St. Catherine of Alexandria at Prayer. No. 517, Adoration of the Holy Trinity. No. 517A, The Supper at Emmaus.

**1989, Nov. 15 Litho.** ***Perf. 13½x14***

**508** A84 5sh multicolored .40 .40
**509** A84 10sh multicolored .40 .40
**510** A84 15sh multicolored .40 .40
**511** A84 50sh multicolored .90 .90
**512** A84 75sh multicolored 1.40 1.40
**513** A84 100sh multicolored 1.60 1.60
**514** A84 125sh multicolored 2.00 2.00
**515** A84 150sh multicolored 2.50 2.50
*Nos. 508-515 (8)* 9.60 9.60

**Souvenir Sheets**

**516** A84 300sh multicolored 4.00 4.00
**517** A84 300sh multicolored 4.00 4.00
**517A** A84 300sh multicolored 4.00 4.00

500th birth anniv. of Titian.
#517A was not available until Jan. 8, 1991.

World Cup Soccer Championships, Italy — A85

**1989, Nov. 15** ***Perf. 14***

**Uniform colors**

**518** A85 25sh green, red & yel .85 .85
**519** A85 60sh green, yel & blue 1.90 1.90
**520** A85 75sh orange & blue 2.40 2.40
**521** A85 200sh blue & white 6.50 6.50
*Nos. 518-521 (4)* 11.65 11.65

**Souvenir Sheets**

**522** A85 350sh orange & bl, diff. 5.25 5.25
**523** A85 350sh grn, yel & bl, diff. 5.25 5.25

Souvenir Sheet

Union Station, Washington, DC — A86

**1989, Nov. 17**

**524** A86 500sh multicolored 8.50 8.50

World Stamp Expo '89.

Fish A87

**1989, Dec. 14**

**525** A87 9sh Tiger tilapia .35 .35
**526** A87 13sh Picasso fish .35 .35
**527** A87 20sh Powder-blue surgeonfish .50 .50
**528** A87 40sh Butterflyfish .90 .90
**529** A87 70sh Guenther's notho 1.60 1.60
**530** A87 100sh Ansorge's noelebias 2.40 2.40
**531** A87 150sh Lyretail panchax 3.75 3.75
**532** A87 200sh Regal angelfish 5.00 5.00
*Nos. 525-532 (8)* 14.85 14.85

**Souvenir Sheets**

**533** A87 350sh Batfish 7.00 7.00
**534** A87 350sh Jewel cichlid 7.00 7.00

Nos. 533-534 each contain one 38x51mm stamp.

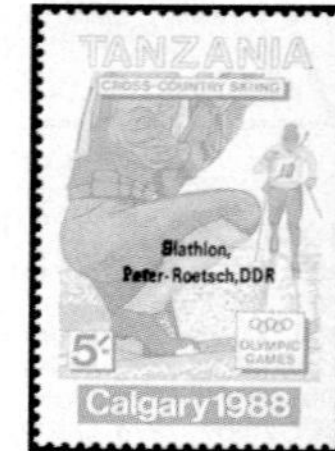


Nos. 414-423 Ovptd. and Similarly

***Perfs. as Before***

**1989, Dec. 19** **Litho.**

**534A** A71 5sh shown .35 .35
**534B** A71 10sh "Gold - USSR / Silver - Brazil / Branze - W. Germany" .50 .50
**534C** A71 20sh "Men's Match Sprint / Lutz Hesslich, DDR" 1.75 1.75
**534D** A71 25sh "Pairs, Gordeeva & Grinkov, USSR" .90 .90
**534E** A71 50sh "Epee, Schmitt, W. Germany" 1.40 1.40
**534F** A71 50sh "Zurbriggen, Switzerland" 1.40 1.40
**534G** A71 70sh "Men's Team, USA" 2.10 2.10
**534H** A71 75sh "Gold-USSR / Silver-DDR / Bronze-DDR" 1.75 1.75
*Nos. 534A-534H (8)* 10.15 10.15

**Souvenir Sheets**

**534I** A71 100sh "Ice Hockey: / Gold-USSR" 7.50 7.50
**534J** A71 100sh "Women's Team, / Gold-USSR" 2.50 2.50

Silver and Bronze medalists overprinted on margins of souvenir sheets.

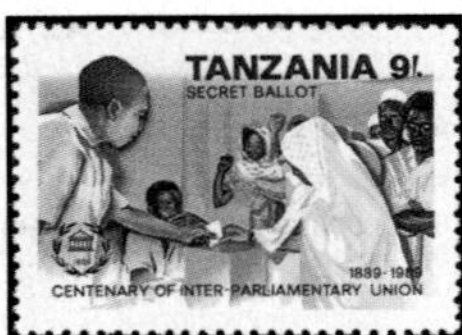


Inter-Parliamentary Union, Cent. — A88

Designs: 9sh, Secret ballot. 13sh, Parliament, Dar Es Salaam. 40sh, Sir William Randal Cremer, Frederic Passy. 80sh, Parliament in session. 100sh, IPU emblem.

**1989, Dec. 22** ***Perf. 12½x12***

**535** A88 9sh multicolored .20 .20
**536** A88 13sh multicolored .20 .20
**537** A88 80sh multicolored .85 .85
**538** A88 100sh lt bl, dp bl & blk 1.00 1.00
*Nos. 535-538 (4)* 2.25 2.25

**Souvenir Sheet**

**539** A88 40sh multicolored 1.25 1.25

Pan-African Postal Union, 10th Anniv. A89

**1990, Jan. 17** ***Perf. 13½***

**540** A89 9sh PAPU emblem .30 .30
**541** A89 13sh Post offices boxes .30 .30
**542** A89 70sh Mail early, prompt delivery 1.10 1.10
**543** A89 100sh Modes of mail delivery 2.10 2.10
*Nos. 540-543 (4)* 3.80 3.80

**Souvenir Sheet**

**544** A89 40sh Tanzania Post, PAPU, UPU emblems 1.50 1.50

Extinct Animals A90

**1990, Feb. 4** ***Perf. 14***

**545** A90 25sh Tecopa pupfish .60 .60
**546** A90 40sh Thylacine .90 .90
**547** A90 50sh Quagga 1.25 1.25
**548** A90 60sh Passenger pigeon 1.40 1.40
**549** A90 75sh Rodriguez saddleback tortoise 1.75 1.75
**550** A90 100sh Toolache wallaby 2.25 2.25
**551** A90 150sh Texas red wolf 3.50 3.50
**552** A90 200sh Utah lake sculpin 4.50 4.50
*Nos. 545-552 (8)* 16.15 16.15

**Souvenir Sheets**

**553** A90 350sh Hawaiian O-O, vert. 7.00 7.00
**554** A90 350sh South island whekau 7.00 7.00

Nina, Admiral's Flag A91

**1990, Feb. 20**

**555** A91 50sh shown 1.90 1.90
**556** A91 60sh Pinta, flag 2.25 2.25
**557** A91 75sh Santa Maria, flag 2.75 2.75
**558** A91 200sh Map of Columbus' first voyage 7.50 7.50
*Nos. 555-558 (4)* 14.40 14.40

**Souvenir Sheet**

**559** A91 350sh Ships, bird's head 8.50 8.50

Discovery of America, 500th anniv. (in 1992).

Modern Discoveries — A92

Designs: 9sh, Bell X-1 breaking the sound barrier. 13sh, Bathyscaph Trieste reaches the deepest ocean bottom. 150sh, Transistor and computer chips. 250sh, Discovery of DNA structure. 350sh, Voyager 2 visits Neptune.

**1990, Feb. 20**

**560** A92 9sh multicolored .55 .55
**561** A92 13sh multicolored .55 .55
**562** A92 150sh multicolored 1.25 1.25
**563** A92 250sh multicolored 2.10 2.10
*Nos. 560-563 (4)* 4.45 4.45

**Souvenir Sheet**

**564** A92 350sh multicolored 5.25 5.25

Girl Guides, 60th Anniv. A93

**1990, Feb. 22** ***Perf. 12½x12***

**565** A93 9sh Hiking .20 .20
**566** A93 13sh Planting trees .20 .20
**567** A93 50sh Teaching writing .60 .60
**568** A93 100sh Teaching health care 1.00 1.00
*Nos. 565-568 (4)* 2.00 2.00

**Souvenir Sheet**

***Perf. 12x12½***

**569** A93 40sh Nursing school, vert. 1.25 1.25

Disney Characters, Automobiles — A94

**1990, Mar. 20** ***Perf. 14x13½***

**570** A94 20sh Herbie, The Love Bug .45 .45
**571** A94 30sh The Absent-Minded Professor's car .50 .50
**572** A94 45sh Chitty-Chitty Bang-Bang .65 .65
**573** A94 60sh Mr. Toad's wild ride .90 .90
**574** A94 75sh Scrooge's limousine 1.10 1.10
**575** A94 100sh Shaggy dog's car 1.50 1.50
**576** A94 150sh Donald Duck's car 2.40 2.40
**577** A94 200sh Firetruck in "Dumbo" 2.50 2.50
*Nos. 570-577 (8)* 10.00 10.00

**Souvenir Sheets**

**578** A94 350sh Cruella de Vil 5.75 5.75
**579** A94 350sh Mickeymobile 5.75 5.75

Black Entertainers A95

**1990, Mar. 30** **Litho.** ***Perf. 14***

**580** A95 9sh Miriam Makeba .25 .25
**581** A95 13sh Manu Dibango .25 .25
**582** A95 25sh Fela .25 .25
**583** A95 70sh Smokey Robinson 1.00 1.00
**584** A95 100sh Gladys Knight 1.25 1.25
**585** A95 150sh Eddie Murphy 2.25 2.25
**586** A95 200sh Sammy Davis, Jr. 2.75 2.75
**587** A95 250sh Stevie Wonder 2.75 2.75
*Nos. 580-587 (8)* 10.75 10.75

**Souvenir Sheets**

***Perf. 14½***

**588** A95 350sh Bill Cosby 3.00 3.00
**589** A95 350sh Michael Jackson 3.00 3.00

Union of Tanganyika and Zanzibar, 25th Anniv. (in 1989) — A95a

Designs: 9sh, Fishing. 13sh, Grapes. 50sh, Cloves. 100sh, Presidents Nyerere and Karume exchanging Union instruments, vert. 40sh, Natl. arms, vert.

***Perf. 12½x12, 12x12½***

**1990, Apr. 25** **Litho.**

**589A** A95a 9sh multicolored .40 .40
**589B** A95a 13sh multicolored .40 .40
**589C** A95a 50sh multicolored 1.25 1.25
**589D** A95a 100sh multicolored 2.50 2.50
*Nos. 589A-589D (4)* 4.55 4.55

**Souvenir Sheet**

**589E** A95a 40sh multicolored 2.00 2.00

Southern Africa Development Coordinating Conf. (SADCC), 10th Anniv. — A96

**1990, Aug. 8** ***Perf. 13½***

**590** A96 8sh Railway transport .40 .40
**591** A96 11.50sh Paper industry .40 .40
**592** A96 25sh Tractor production .70 .70
**593** A96 100sh Flags, map 2.50 2.50
*Nos. 590-593 (4)* 4.00 4.00

**Souvenir Sheet**

***Perf. 12½***

**594** A96 50sh Map 2.50 2.50

A97

A98

Pope John Paul II's Visit to Tanzania: 15sh, Wearing red vestments. 20sh, Wearing miter. 100sh, Papal arms. No. 599: a, Pope with arms outstretched. b, St. Joseph's Cathedral, Dar Es Salaam. c, Christ the King Cathedral, Moshi. d, Saint Theresa's Cathedral, Tabora. e, Cathedral of the Epiphany, Bugando Mwanza. f, St. Mathias Mulumba Kalemba Cathedral, Songea.

**1990, Sept. 1** **Litho.** ***Perf. 14***

**595** A97 10sh shown .25 .25
**596** A97 15sh multicolored .35 .35
**597** A97 20sh multicolored .40 .40
**598** A97 100sh multicolored 1.00 1.00
*Nos. 595-598 (4)* 2.00 2.00

**Souvenir Sheet**

**599** Sheet of 6 6.00 6.00
*a.-f.* A97 50sh any single .50 .50

**1990, Sept. 28**

Players from participating countries.

**600** A98 10sh West Germany .75 .75
**601** A98 60sh Italy 1.25 1.25
**602** A98 100sh Scotland 2.25 2.25
**603** A98 300sh Yugoslavia 4.25 4.25
*Nos. 600-603 (4)* 8.50 8.50

**Souvenir Sheets**

**604** A98 400sh Costa Rica 5.75 5.75
**605** A98 400sh Belgium 5.75 5.75

World Cup Soccer Championships, Italy.

Birds — A99

**1990-91** **Litho.** ***Perf. 14***

**606** A99 5sh Masked weaver .35 .35
**607** A99 9sh Emerald cuckoo .35 .35
**608** A99 13sh Little bee-eater .60 .60
**609** A99 15sh Red bishop .60 .60
**610** A99 20sh Bateleur .80 .80
**611** A99 25sh Scarlet-chested sunbird .80 .80
*a.* Bklt. pane, 2 ea #606-611 2.00 2.00
**611B** A99 30sh Pigeons .80 .80

**Size: 42x28mm**

**612** A99 40sh Lesser flamingo .80 .80
**613** A99 70sh Helmeted guineafowl .85 .85
**614** A99 100sh White pelican 1.00 1.00
**615** A99 170sh Saddle-billed stork 1.40 1.40
**616** A99 200sh Crowned crane 1.60 1.60
**616A** A99 300sh Pied crow 1.75 1.75
**616B** A99 400sh White-headed vulture 2.10 2.10
**617** A99 500sh Ostrich 2.10 2.10
*Nos. 606-617 (15)* 15.90 15.90

**Souvenir Sheet**

**Stamp size: 42x28mm**

**617A** Sheet of 2 5.75 5.75
*b.* A99 40sh Superb starling 1.00 1.00
*c.* A99 60sh Lilac-breasted roller 1.50 1.50

Issued: 30sh, 300sh, 400sh, 1991; others, 10/1/90.

For surcharges, see Nos. 1723A, 1723B, 2157-2159C.

Boats A100

**1990, Oct. 10** **Litho.** ***Perf. 12½x12***

**618** A100 9sh Canoe .40 .40
**619** A100 13sh Outrigger canoe .40 .40
**620** A100 25sh Dhow .60 .60
**621** A100 100sh Freighter 2.75 2.75
*Nos. 618-621 (4)* 4.15 4.15

**Souvenir Sheet**

**622** A100 40sh Boat 2.75 2.75

Commonwealth Games, New Zealand — A101

**1990, Oct. 22** ***Perf. 14***

**623** A101 9sh Sprinting .35 .35
**624** A101 13sh Netball, vert. .65 .65
**625** A101 25sh Pole vault .90 .90
**626** A101 100sh Long jump, vert. 2.75 2.75
*Nos. 623-626 (4)* 4.65 4.65

**Souvenir Sheet**

**627** A101 40sh Boxing 2.25 2.25

Orchids — A102

**1990, Nov. 12**

**628** A102 10sh Phalaenopsis .30 .30
**629** A102 25sh Lycaste .30 .30
**630** A102 30sh Vuylstekeara, Cambria "Plush" .35 .35
**631** A102 50sh Vuylstekeara, Monica "Burnham" .55 .55
**632** A102 90sh Odontocidium 1.00 1.00
**633** A102 100sh Oncidioda 1.25 1.25
**634** A102 250sh Sophrolaelio-cattleya 3.00 3.00
**635** A102 300sh Laeliocattleya 3.50 3.50
*Nos. 628-635 (8)* 10.25 10.25

**Souvenir Sheets**

**636** A102 400sh Cymbidium, Baldoyle "Melbury" 5.25 5.25
**637** A102 400sh Cymbidium, Tapestry "Long Beach" 5.25 5.25

Expo '90, the Intl. Garden and Greenery Exposition, Osaka, Japan.

1990 World Cup Soccer Championships, Italy — A102a

**1990, Nov. 17 Litho. *Perf. 14***

**637A** A102a 9sh Long throw-in .60 .60
**637B** A102a 13sh Penalty kick .60 .60
**637C** A102a 25sh Dribbling .80 .80
**637D** A102a 100sh Corner kick 3.25 3.25
*Nos. 637A-637D (4)* 5.25 5.25

**Souvenir Sheet**

**637E** A102a 50sh Trophy, map 3.75 3.75

Racing A103

5sh, Olympic Soling Class Yacht racing. 20sh, Olympic downhill ski racing. 30sh, Tour de France bicycle race. 40sh, Le Mans 24 hour endurance auto race. 75sh, Olympic 2-man bobsled. 100sh, Belgian Grand Prix motorcycle race. 250sh, Indianapolis 500 auto race. 300sh, Power boat gold cup racing. #646, Colorado 500 enduro motorcycle race. #647, Schneider Trophy air races.

**1990, Nov. 19**

**638** A103 5sh multicolored .45 .45
**639** A103 20sh multicolored .85 .85
**640** A103 30sh multicolored 1.40 1.40
**641** A103 40sh multicolored 1.40 1.40
**642** A103 75sh multicolored 1.60 1.60
**643** A103 100sh multicolored 2.40 2.40
**644** A103 250sh multicolored 2.75 2.75
**645** A103 300sh multicolored 3.00 3.00
*Nos. 638-645 (8)* 13.85 13.85

**Souvenir Sheets**

**646** A103 400sh multicolored 6.50 6.50
**647** A103 400sh multicolored 6.50 6.50

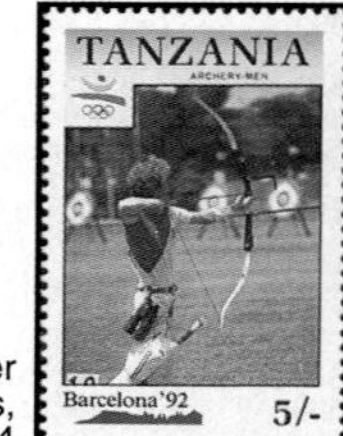

1992 Summer Olympics, Barcelona — A104

**1990, Nov. 30**

**648** A104 5sh Archery .30 .30
**649** A104 10sh Women's gymnastics .30 .30
**650** A104 25sh Boxing .30 .30
**651** A104 50sh Two-man kay-ak race .55 .55
**652** A104 100sh Men's volley-ball 1.10 1.10
**653** A104 150sh Mens' gym-nastics 1.75 1.75
**654** A104 200sh 4x100 meter relay 2.25 2.25
**655** A104 300sh Judo 3.50 3.50
*Nos. 648-655 (8)* 10.05 10.05

**Souvenir Sheets**

**656** A104 400sh Men's 400 meter hur-dles 5.50 5.50
**657** A104 400sh Men's cycling 5.50 5.50

Cog Railroads A105

Cog locomotives: 8sh, Petersberg Cog Railway, West Germany. 25sh, Engine *Waumbek* on Mt. Washington Cog Railway, US. 50sh, Doubleheaded cog engines on Dubrovnik-Sarajevo line, Yugoslavia. 100sh, Cog Railway, Budapest, Hungary 1874. 150sh, Vordenberg-Eisenerz line, Austria. 200sh, Rimutaka Incline, New Zealand, 1955. 250sh, John Stevens' cog engine, Hoboken, NJ, 1825. 300sh, Pilatusbahn Cog Railway, Switzerland, 1889. No. 666, Schneebergbahn of the OBB, Austria. No. 667, Sylvester Marsh, Mt. Washington Cog Railway, 1869.

**1990, Dec. 8**

**658** A105 8sh multicolored .30 .30
**659** A105 25sh multicolored .30 .30
**660** A105 50sh multicolored .60 .60
**661** A105 100sh multicolored 1.10 1.10
**662** A105 150sh multicolored 1.75 1.75
**663** A105 200sh multicolored 2.25 2.25
**664** A105 250sh multicolored 3.00 3.00
**665** A105 300sh multicolored 3.50 3.50
*Nos. 658-665 (8)* 12.80 12.80

**Souvenir Sheets**

**666** A105 400sh multicolored 6.25 6.25
**667** A105 400sh multicolored 6.25 6.25

First Postage Stamps, 150th Anniv. A106

Designs: No. 668, German Post Office at Dar Es Salaam, German East Africa No. 16. No. 669, Mailboat S.S. Reichstag, 1890, Germany No. 40 cancelled in Zanzibar. No. 670, Dhows used as mailboats, Zanzibar No. 1. No. 671, Mailplane Singapore I on Lake Victoria, 1928, Tanganyika No. 22. No. 672, Mailplane, Livingston's House, Zanzibar No. 316. No. 673, Passenger-mail train at Moshi Station, Tanganyika No. 52. No. 674, Royal mail coach, 1840. 150sh, Stephenson's *Rocket*, mail car, 1838. 200sh, Handley Page HP-42 mailplane. No. 677, Hand delivery of mail, Thurn & Taxis No. 44 on cover. No. 678, Sir Rowland Hill.

**1990, Dec. 12**

**668** A106 50sh multicolored 1.10 1.10
**669** A106 50sh multicolored 1.10 1.10
*a.* Pair, #668-669 1.10 1.10
**670** A106 75sh multicolored 1.40 1.40
**671** A106 75sh multicolored 1.40 1.40
*a.* Pair, #670-671 1.50 1.50
**672** A106 100sh multicolored 2.10 2.10
**673** A106 100sh multicolored 2.10 2.10
*a.* Pair, #672-673 2.25 2.25
**674** A106 100sh multicolored 2.10 2.10
**675** A106 150sh multicolored 3.00 3.00
**676** A106 200sh multicolored 3.00 3.00
*Nos. 668-676 (9)* 17.30 17.30

**Souvenir Sheets**

**677** A106 350sh multicolored 6.50 6.50
**678** A106 350sh multicolored 6.50 6.50

500th anniv. of Thurn and Taxis Post (No. 677).

For overprints see Nos. 928-934.

Intl. Literacy Year — A107

Nos. 679a-681i depict various Walt Disney characters and a letter of the alphabet.

No. 682, Mickey's train hauls Russian alphabet. No. 683, Children learning Hebrew.

**1990, Dec. 27 *Perf. 13½x14***

**Miniature Sheets**

**679** Sheet of 9 7.50 7.50
*a.* A107 1sh "ABC" .20 .20
*b.* A107 2sh "A" .20 .20
*c.* A107 3sh "B" .20 .20
*d.* A107 15sh "C" .20 .20
*e.* A107 55sh "D" .45 .45
*f.* A107 80sh "E" .65 .65
*g.* A107 120sh "F" .95 .95
*h.* A107 145sh "G" 1.10 1.10
*i.* A107 200sh "H" 1.60 1.60
**680** Sheet of 9 7.25 7.25
*a.* A107 10sh "I" .20 .20
*b.* A107 20sh "J" .20 .20
*c.* A107 30sh "K" .25 .25
*d.* A107 40sh "L" .30 .30
*e.* A107 50sh "M" .40 .40
*f.* A107 60sh "N" .50 .50
*g.* A107 100sh "O" .80 .80
*h.* A107 125sh "P" 1.00 1.00
*i.* A107 150sh "Q" 1.25 1.25
**681** Sheet of 9 7.50 7.50
*a.* A107 5sh "R" .20 .20
*b.* A107 18sh "S" .20 .20
*c.* A107 25sh "T" .20 .20
*d.* A107 35sh "U" .30 .30
*e.* A107 45sh "V" .35 .35
*f.* A107 75sh "W" .60 .60
*g.* A107 90sh "X" .70 .70
*h.* A107 160sh "Y" 1.25 1.25
*i.* A107 175sh "Z" 1.40 1.40

**Souvenir Sheets**

**682** A107 600sh multicolored 8.25 8.25
**683** A107 600sh multicolored 8.25 8.25

Intl. Literacy Year A108

**1991, Mar. 15 Litho. *Perf. 14***

**684** A108 9sh Learning to read .30 .30
**685** A108 13sh Learning to write .35 .35
**686** A108 25sh Blackboard, books .45 .45
**687** A108 100sh Reading news-papers 2.50 2.50
*Nos. 684-687 (4)* 3.60 3.60

**Souvenir Sheet**

**688** A108 50sh Adult education 2.00 2.00

For surcharge see No. 1431A.

Mickey Mouse — A109

Character roles: 5sh, Western cowboy. 10sh, Boxer. 15sh, Astronaut. 20sh, Romantic lead with Minnie. 100sh, Swashbuckling hero. 200sh, Detective with Donald Duck and Pistol Pete. 350sh, King with Donald as court jester. 450sh, Sailor with Donald and Goofy. No. 697, Minnie, Mickey as archaeologists in Egypt, Donald as a mummy. No. 698, Mickey as Canadian Mountie.

**1991, Feb. 11 Litho. *Perf. 14x13½***

**689** A109 5sh multicolored .45 .45
**690** A109 10sh multicolored .50 .50
**691** A109 15sh multicolored .50 .50
**692** A109 20sh multicolored .50 .50
**693** A109 100sh multicolored 2.00 2.00
**694** A109 200sh multicolored 4.00 4.00
**695** A109 350sh multicolored 4.50 4.50
**696** A109 450sh multicolored 4.50 4.50
*Nos. 689-696 (8)* 16.95 16.95

**Souvenir Sheets**

**697** A109 600sh multicolored 8.50 8.50
**698** A109 600sh multicolored 8.50 8.50

Craters and Caves — A109a

Designs: 3sh, Ngorongoro Crater. 5sh, Kondoa Caves, prehistoric rock paintings. 9sh, Mount Kilimanjaro's inner crater. 12sh, Olduvai Gorge.

Amboni Caves: No. 698f, Open area of cave. g, People viewing cave, large stalactite. h, Woman seated beside welcome sign. i, Man climbing up to view cave.

**1991, Mar. 28 Litho. *Perf. 14½***

**698A** A109a 3sh mul-ticolored 3.25 3.25
**698B** A109a 5sh mul-ticolored 3.25 3.25
**698C** A109a 9sh mul-ticolored 4.00 4.00
**698D** A109a 12sh mul-ticolored 5.75 5.75
*Nos. 698A-698D (4)* 16.25 16.25

**Souvenir Sheet**

**698E** A109a 10sh Sheet of 4, #f.-i. 7.00 7.00

Nos. 698A-698E were not available to the philatelic community until Mar. 1994.

Miniature Sheet

Peter Paul Rubens, 350th Death Anniv. — A110

Cycle of Decius Mus: No. 699a, Proclamation of the Vision. b, Divining of the Entrails. c, Dispatch of the Lictors. d, Dedication to Death. e, Victory and Death of Decius Mus. f, Funeral Rites. No. 700, Trophy of War, vert.

**1991, Apr. 10 Litho. *Perf. 14x13½***

**699** A110 85sh Sheet of 6, #a.-f. 13.50 13.50

**Souvenir Sheet**

***Perf. 13½x14***

**700** A110 500sh multicolored 11.50 11.50

Tanzania Investment Bank, 20th Anniv. — A111

Designs: 10sh, Dairy farming. 13sh, Industrial development. 25sh, Engineering. 100sh, Tea harvesting.

**1991, June 7 *Perf. 14***

**701** A111 10sh multicolored .50 .50
**702** A111 13sh multicolored .50 .50
**703** A111 25sh multicolored .50 .50
**704** A111 100sh multicolored 3.25 3.25
*a.* Souvenir sheet of 4, #701-704 3.25 3.25
*Nos. 701-704 (4)* 4.75 4.75

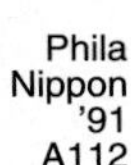

Phila Nippon '91 A112

Japanese locomotives: 10sh, First Japanese steam. 25sh, Series 4500 steam. 35sh, C 62 steam. 50sh, Mikado steam. 75sh, Series 6250 steam. 100sh, C 11 steam. 200sh, E 10 steam. 300sh, Series 8550 steam. No. 713, EF 58 electric. No. 714, DD 51 diesel. No. 715, Series 400 electric. No. 716, EH 10 electric.

**1991, Aug. 15 Litho. *Perf. 14***

**705** A112 10sh multicolored .85 .85
**706** A112 25sh multicolored 1.25 1.25
**707** A112 35sh multicolored 1.50 1.50
**708** A112 50sh multicolored 1.75 1.75
**709** A112 75sh multicolored 2.25 2.25
**710** A112 100sh multicolored 2.75 2.75
**711** A112 200sh multicolored 3.00 3.00
**712** A112 300sh multicolored 4.00 4.00
*Nos. 705-712 (8)* 17.35 17.35

**Souvenir Sheets**

**713** A112 400sh multicolored 4.50 4.50
**714** A112 400sh multicolored 4.50 4.50
**715** A112 400sh multicolored 4.50 4.50
**716** A112 400sh multicolored 4.50 4.50

Fauna in Natl. Game Parks A113

Species and park: 10sh, Common zebra, golden-winged sunbird, Ngorongoro Crater Conservation Area. 25sh, Greater kudu, African elephant, Ruaha. 30sh, Sable antelope, red and yellow barbet, Mikumi. 50sh, Wildebeest, leopard, Serengeti. 90sh, Giraffe, white-starred bush robin, Ngurdoto Crater. 100sh, Eland, Abbot's duiker, Kilimanjaro. 250sh, Lion, impala, Lake Manyara. 300sh, Black rhinoceros, ostrich, Tarangire. No. 725, Paradise whydah, oryx, Mkomazi Game Reserve. No. 726, Blue-breasted kingfisher, defassa waterbuck, Selous Game Reserve.

**1991, Aug. 22 Litho. *Perf. 14***

**717** A113 10sh multicolored .25 .25
**718** A113 25sh multicolored .55 .55
**719** A113 30sh multicolored .70 .70
**720** A113 50sh multicolored 1.10 1.10
**721** A113 90sh multicolored 1.90 1.90
**722** A113 100sh multicolored 2.25 2.25
**723** A113 250sh multicolored 5.25 5.25
**724** A113 300sh multicolored 6.50 6.50
*Nos. 717-724 (8)* 18.50 18.50

**Souvenir Sheets**

**725** A113 400sh multicolored 9.00 9.00
**726** A113 400sh multicolored 9.00 9.00

Butterflies — A114

Designs: 10sh, Vine leaf vagrant. 15sh, Blue spot commodore. 35sh, Orange admiral. 75sh, Wanderer. 100sh, Jackson's leaf. 150sh, Painted empress. 200sh, Double-banded orange. 300sh, Crawshay's sapphire blue. No. 735, Noble swallowtail. No. 736, Club-tailed charaxes. No. 737, Satyr charaxes. No. 738, Green patch swallowtail.

**1991, Aug. 28 Litho. *Perf. 14***

**727** A114 10sh multicolored .35 .35
**728** A114 15sh multicolored .35 .35
**729** A114 35sh multicolored .75 .75
**730** A114 75sh multicolored 1.60 1.60
**731** A114 100sh multicolored 2.00 2.00
**732** A114 150sh multicolored 3.00 3.00
**733** A114 200sh multicolored 4.00 4.00
**734** A114 300sh multicolored 6.00 6.00
*Nos. 727-734 (8)* 18.05 18.05

**Souvenir Sheets**

**735** A114 400sh multicolored 5.00 5.00
**736** A114 400sh multicolored 5.00 5.00
**737** A114 400sh multicolored 5.00 5.00
**738** A114 400sh multicolored 5.00 5.00

While Nos. 727-736 have the same issue date as Nos. 737-738, the dollar value of Nos. 737-738 was lower when they were released.

Intelsat, 25th Anniv. A115

Designs: 10sh, Microwave link. 25sh, Earth. 100sh, Mwenge standard "B" Earth station. 500sh, Mwenge standard "A" Earth station. 50sh, World map.

**1991, Sept. 5 Litho. *Perf. 14***

**739** A115 10sh multicolored .30 .30
**740** A115 25sh multicolored .45 .45
**741** A115 100sh multicolored 2.00 2.00
**742** A115 500sh multicolored 7.25 7.25
*Nos. 739-742 (4)* 10.00 10.00

**Souvenir Sheet**

**743** A115 50sh multicolored 3.25 3.25

UN Development Program, 40th Anniv. — A116

Designs: 10sh, Irrigated rice farming. 15sh, Vocational training. 100sh, Terrace farming. 500sh, Architectural renovations, vert. 40sh, Helping people to help themselves, vert.

**1991, Sept. 16 *Perf. 13½***

**744** A116 10sh multicolored .25 .25
**745** A116 15sh multicolored .25 .25
**746** A116 100sh multicolored 1.40 1.40
**747** A116 500sh multicolored 6.75 6.75
*Nos. 744-747 (4)* 8.65 8.65

**Souvenir Sheet**

***Perf. 13x12½***

**748** A116 40sh black & blue 1.75 1.75

All Africa Games, Cairo — A117

***Perf. 12x12½, 12½x12***

**1991, Sept. 20**

**749** A117 10sh Netball .35 .35
**750** A117 15sh Soccer, horiz. .35 .35
**751** A117 100sh Tennis 2.10 2.10
**752** A117 200sh Running 2.50 2.50
**753** A117 500sh Baseball, horiz. 6.00 6.00
*Nos. 749-753 (5)* 11.30 11.30

**Souvenir Sheet**

**754** A117 500sh Basketball 9.00 9.00

Telecom '91 — A118

**1991, Oct. 1 *Perf. 13½x14, 14x13½***

**755** A118 10sh shown .25 .25
**756** A118 15sh Telecom '91, horiz. .25 .25
**757** A118 35sh arrows .35 .35
**758** A118 100sh like #757, horiz. 1.00 1.00
*Nos. 755-758 (4)* 1.85 1.85

World Telecommunications Day (Nos. 757-758).

Dinosaurs A119

**1991, Oct. 28 *Perf. 12x12½***

**759** A119 10sh Stegosaurus .30 .30
**760** A119 15sh Triceratops .30 .30
**761** A119 25sh Edmontosaurus .45 .45
**762** A119 30sh Plateosaurus .55 .55
**763** A119 35sh Diplodocus .65 .65
**764** A119 100sh Iguanodon 1.75 1.75
**765** A119 200sh Silviasaurus 3.50 3.50
*Nos. 759-765 (7)* 7.50 7.50

**Souvenir Sheet**

**766** A119 150sh Rhamphorhynchus 3.50 3.50

Animals and Fish A120

No. 767 — Horses: a, Shire. b, Thoroughbred. c, Kladruber. d, Appaloosa. e, Hanoverian. f, Arab. g, Breton. h, Exmoor. i, Connemara. j, Lipizzaner. k, Shetland. l, Percheron. m, Pinto. n, Orlov. o, Palomino. p, Welsh cob.

No. 768 — Cats: a, Japanese bobtail. b, Cornish rex. c, Malayan. d, Tonkinese. e, Abyssinian. f, Russian blue. g, Cymric. h, Somali. i, Siamese. j, Himalayan. k, Singapura. l, Manx. m, Oriental shorthair. n, Maine coon. o, Persian. p, Birman.

No. 769, vert. — African elephants: a, One walking left. b, Two with tusks entangled. c, One facing forward. d, One under tree. e, Adult and calf in water, zebra. f, Adult and calf walking into water. g, Two adults and calf in water. h, Adult and calf standing in water. i, One walking right. j, Two, one raising trunk in air. k, One raising trunk in air. l, One facing forward, trunk down, zebra. m, Adult, calf at edge of water, antelope. n, Adult and calf, two more in background. o, One walking toward water. p, Adult with trunk on calf.

No. 770 — Aquarium fish: a, Jewel tetra. b, Five-banded barb. c, Simpson platy. d, Guppy, e, Zebra danio. f, Neon tetra. g, Siamese fighting fish. h, Tiger barb. i, Red lyretail. j, Goldfish. k, Pearl gourami. l, Angelfish. m, Clown loach. n, Red swordtail. o, Brown discus. p, Rosy barb.

No. 771 — Birds: a, Budgerigar. b, Rainbow bunting. c, Golden-fronted leafbird. d, Black-headed caique. e, Java sparrow. f, Diamond sparrow. g, Peach-faced lovebird. h, Golden conure. i, Military macaw. j, Celestial parrotlet. k, Sulphur-crested cockatoo. l, Spectacled Amazon parrot. m, Paradise tanager. n, Gouldian finch. o, Masked lovebird. p, Hill mynah.

**1991, Oct. 28 Litho. *Perf. 14***

**767** A120 50sh Sheet of 16, #a.-p. 16.00 16.00
**768** A120 50sh Sheet of 16, #a.-p. 16.00 16.00
**769** A120 75sh Sheet of 16, #a.-p. 19.00 19.00
**770** A120 75sh Sheet of 16, #a.-p. 16.00 16.00
**771** A120 75sh Sheet of 16, #a.-p. 16.00 16.00
*Nos. 767-771 (5)* 83.00 83.00

For overprints see Nos. 1529-1530.

Paintings by Vincent Van Gogh A121

Designs: 10sh, Peasant Woman Sewing. 15sh, Head of a Peasant Woman with Greenish Lace Cap. 35sh, Flowering Orchard. 75sh, Portrait of a Girl. 100sh, Portrait of a Woman with a Red Ribbon. 150sh, Vase with Flowers. 200sh, Houses in Antwerp. 400sh, Seated Peasant Woman with White Cap. No. 780, The Parsonage Garden at Nuenen in the Snow, horiz. No. 781, Bulb Fields, horiz.

**1991, Nov. 20 Litho. *Perf. 13½x14***

**772** A121 10sh multicolored .25 .25
**773** A121 15sh multicolored .25 .25
**774** A121 35sh multicolored .60 .60
**775** A121 75sh multicolored 1.25 1.25
**776** A121 100sh multicolored 1.50 1.50
**777** A121 150sh multicolored 2.40 2.40
**778** A121 200sh multicolored 3.00 3.00
**779** A121 400sh multicolored 6.00 6.00
*Nos. 772-779 (8)* 15.25 15.25

**Size: 127x102mm**

***Imperf***

**780** A121 400sh multicolored 7.50 7.50
**781** A121 400sh multicolored 7.50 7.50

Walt Disney Christmas Cards — A122

Design and date of card: 10sh, "Joy", 1968. 25sh, Mickey, Pluto and Goofy at fireplace, 1981. 35sh, Robin Hood and merry men celebrating, 1973. 75sh, Tree of greetings, Mickey, 1967. 100sh, Goofy, Mickey and Donald trying to catch Santa coming down chimney, 1969, vert. 150sh, Mickey on top of Christmas ornament, 1976, vert. 200sh, Clarabelle Cow with bells, 1935, vert. 300sh, Orphan mice reading book of tricks, 1935, vert. No. 790, Mickey wearing Santa hat and surrounded by Disney characters, 1968, vert. No. 791, Mickey with present for Donald, 1935, vert.

***Perf. 13½x14, 14x13½***

**1991, Dec. Litho.**

**782** A122 10sh multicolored .30 .30
**783** A122 25sh multicolored .55 .55
**784** A122 35sh multicolored .70 .70
**785** A122 75sh multicolored 1.40 1.40
**786** A122 100sh multicolored 2.00 2.00
**787** A122 150sh multicolored 2.50 2.50
**788** A122 200sh multicolored 3.00 3.00
**789** A122 300sh multicolored 4.00 4.00
*Nos. 782-789 (8)* 14.45 14.45

**Souvenir Sheets**

**790** A122 500sh multicolored 8.25 8.25
**791** A122 500sh multicolored 8.25 8.25

Elephants A123

Designs: 10sh, 15sh, 25sh, 100sh, Various pictures of elephas maximus. 30sh, 35sh, 200sh, Various pictures of loxodonta africana. 400sh, Mammut mammuthus.

***Perf. 12x12½, 12½x12***

**1991, Nov. 28 Litho.**

**792** A123 10sh multi, vert. .50 .50
**793** A123 15sh multi, vert. .50 .50
**794** A123 25sh multi, vert. .75 .75
**795** A123 30sh multi, vert. 1.00 1.00
**796** A123 35sh multicolored 1.25 1.25

**797** A123 100sh multicolored 3.25 3.25
**798** A123 200sh multicolored 6.25 6.25
*Nos. 792-798 (7)* 13.50 13.50

**Souvenir Sheet**

**799** A123 400sh multicolored 6.75 6.75

Locomotives — A124

**1991, Dec. 10** ***Perf. 12½x12, 12x12½***

**800** A124 10sh USSR 1930 .25 .25
**801** A124 15sh Japan 1964 .25 .25
**802** A124 25sh Russia 1834, vert. .40 .40
**803** A124 35sh France 1979 .65 .65
**804** A124 60sh France 1972 1.10 1.10
**805** A124 100sh United Kingdom 1972 1.60 1.60
**806** A124 300sh Russia 1837, vert. 5.25 5.25
*Nos. 800-806 (7)* 9.50 9.50

**Souvenir Sheet**

**807** A124 100sh France, 1952, vert. 2.50 2.50

Entertainers — A125

Nos. 808a-808i, 812, Various portraits of Elvis Presley.

Nos. 809a-809i, 813, Various portraits of Marilyn Monroe.

Nos. 810a-810i, 814, Various portraits of Bruce Lee.

Black entertainers: No. 811: a, Scott Joplin. b, Sammy Davis, Jr. c, Joan Armatrading. d, Louis Armstrong. e, Miriam Makeba. f, Lionel Ritchie. g, Whitney Houston, h, Bob Marley. i, Tina Turner. No. 815, Kouyate family.

**1992, Feb. 15** ***Perf. 14***

**808** A125 75sh Sheet of 9, #a.-i. 9.50 9.50
**809** A125 75sh Sheet of 9, #a.-i. 9.50 9.50
**810** A125 75sh Sheet of 9, #a.-i. 9.50 9.50
**811** A125 75sh Sheet of 9, #a.-i. 9.50 9.50
*Nos. 808-811 (4)* 38.00 38.00

**Souvenir Sheets**

**812** A125 500sh multicolored 8.75 8.75
**813** A125 500sh multicolored 8.75 8.75
**814** A125 500sh multicolored 8.75 8.75
**815** A125 500sh multicolored 8.75 8.75
*Nos. 812-815 (4)* 35.00 35.00

Nos. 812-815 each contain one 29x43mm stamp.

See #949 for #808 inscribed "15th Anniversary."

Fish of Tanzania A126

Designs: 10sh, Malacanthus latovittatus. 15sh, Lamprologus tretocephalus. 25sh, Lamprologus calvus. 35sh, Hemichromis bimaculatusl. 60sh, Aphyosemion bivittatum. No. 821, Synanceia verrucosa. 300sh, Aphyosemion ahli. No. 823, Regalecus glesne.

**1992, Mar. 8** ***Perf. 12½x12***

**816** A126 10sh multicolored .55 .55
**817** A126 15sh multicolored .70 .70
**818** A126 25sh multicolored .90 .90
**819** A126 35sh multicolored 1.10 1.10
**820** A126 60sh multicolored 1.40 1.40
**821** A126 100sh multicolored 1.90 1.90
**822** A126 300sh multicolored 5.00 5.00
*Nos. 816-822 (7)* 11.55 11.55

**Souvenir Sheet**

**823** A126 100sh multicolored 2.75 2.75

World War II in the Pacific A127

Designs: No. 824a, British-designed radar at Pearl Harbor. b, Churchill declares war on Japan. c, Repulse destroyed. d, Prince of Wales sunk. e, Singapore falls to Japanese. f, Hermes is sunk off Ceylon. g, Airfields in Malaya attacked. h, Hong Kong falls to Japanese. i, Japanese Daihatsu landing craft. j, Japanese cruiser Haguro in Java Sea.

**1992, Apr. 27** ***Perf. 14½x15***

**824** A127 75sh Sheet of 10, #a.-j. 21.00 21.00

Visits of Poe John Paul II — A128

No. 825, 100sh: a, Dominican Republic, 1979. b, Mexico, 1979. c, Poland, 1979. d, Ireland, 1979. e, UN, New York, 1979. f, US, 1979. g, Turkey, 1979. h, Zaire, 1980. i, Congo, 1980. j, Kenya, 1980. k, Ghana, 1980. l, Upper Volta, 1980.

No. 826, 100sh: a, Ivory Coast, 1980. b, France, 1980. c, Brazil, 1980. d, West Germany, 1980. e, Pakistan, 1981. f, Philippines, 1981. g, Guam, 1981. h, Japan, 1981. h, Alaska, 1981. i, Nigeria, 1982. j, Benin, 1982. l. Gabon, 1982.

No. 827, 100sh: a, Equatorial Guinea, 1982. b, Portugal, 1982. c, Great Britain, 1982. d, Argentina, 1982. e, UN, Geneva, 1982. f, San Marino, 1982. g, Spain, 1982. h, Costa Rica, 1983. i, Panama, 1983. j, El Salvador, 1983. k, Nicaragua, 1983. l, Guatemala, 1983.

No. 828, 100sh: a, Honduras, 1983. b, Belize, 1983. c, Haiti, 1983. d, Poland, 1983. e, France, 1983. f, Austria, 1983. g, Alaska, 1984. h, South Korea, 1984. i, Papua New Guinea, 1984. j, Solomon Islands, 1984. k, Thailand, 1984. l, Switzerland, 1984.

No. 829, 100sh: a, Canada, 1984. b, Dominican Republic, 1984. c, Puerto Rico, 1984. d, Venezuela, 1985. e, Ecuador, 1985. f, Peru, 1985. g, Trinidad & Tobago, 1985. h, Netherlands, 1985. i, Luxembourg, 1985. j, Belgium, 1985. k, Togo, 1985. l, Ivory Coast, 1985.

No. 830, 100sh: a, Cameroun, 1985. b, Central African Republic, 1985. c, Zaire, 1985. d, Kenya, 1985. e, Morocco, 1985. f, Liechtenstein, 1985. g, India, 1986. h, Colombia, 1986. i, St. Lucia, 1986. j, France, 1986. k, Bangladesh, 1986. l, Singapore, 1986.

No. 831, 100sh: a, Fiji, 1986. b, New Zealand, 1986. c, Australia, 1986. d, Seychelles, 1986. e, Uruguay, 1987. f, Chile, 1987. g, Argentina, 1987. h, West Germany, 1987. i, Poland, 1987. j, US, 1987. k, Canada, 1987. l, Uruguay, 1988.

No. 832, 100sh: a, Bolivia, 1988. b, Peru, 1988. c, Paraguay, 1988. d, Austria, 1988. e, Zimbabwe, 1988. f, Botswana, 1988. g, Lesotho, 1988. h, Swaziland, 1988. i, Mozambique, 1988. j, France, 1988. k, Madagascar, 1989. l, Reunion, 1989.

No. 833, 100sh: a, Zambia, 1989. b, Malawi, 1989. c, Norway, 1989. d, Iceland, 1989. e, Finland, 1989. f, Denmark, 1989. g, Sweden, 1989. h, Spain, 1989. i, South Korea, 1989. j, Indonesia, 1989. k, Mauritius, 1989. l, Cape Verde, 1990.

No. 834, 100sh: a, Mali, 1990. b, Guinea-Bissau, 1990. c, Burkina Faso, 1990. d, Chad, 1990. e, Czechoslovakia, 1990. f, Mexico, 1990. g, Curacao, 1990. h, Malta, 1990. i, Tanzania, 1990. j, Burundi, 1990. k, Rwanda, 1990. l, Ivory Coast, 1990.

**1992, Apr. 13** ***Perf. 14***

**Sheets of 12 + 4 Labels**

**825-834** A128 Set of 10 180.00 180.00

Zanzibar Stone Town A129

Designs: No. 839a, 150sh, Old fort. b, 300sh, Maruhubi ruins.

**1992, Apr. 15** ***Perf. 12x12½, 12½x12***

**835** A129 10sh Balcony .55 .55
**836** A129 20sh Bahlnara mosque 1.25 1.25
**837** A129 30sh High Court bldg. 1.75 1.75
**838** A129 200sh Natl. museum 8.00 8.00
*Nos. 835-838 (4)* 11.55 11.55

**Souvenir Sheet**

**839** A129 Sheet of 2, #a.-b. 9.50 9.50

Nos. 835-837 are vert.

Wolfgang Amadeus Mozart, Death Bicent. A130

Designs: 10sh, Marcella Sembrich as Zerlina in Don Giovanni. 50sh, Symphony Number 41, Jupiter. 300sh, Luciano Pavarotti as Idamente in Idomeneo. 500sn, Wolfgang Amadeus Mozart, vert.

**1992, Aug. 1** ***Perf. 14***

**840** A130 10sh violet & blk 1.10 1.10
**841** A130 50sh multicolored 2.75 2.75
**842** A130 300sh violet & blk 6.50 6.50
*Nos. 840-842 (3)* 10.35 10.35

**Souvenir Sheet**

**843** A130 500sh olive brn & blk 10.00 10.00

While No. 843 has the same issue date as Nos. 840-842, the dollar value was lower when it were released.

No. 843 contains one 38x50mm stamp.

**1992, Aug. 1**

Designs: 10sh, Insignia, giraffe and elephant. 15sh, Scouts in canoe. 400sh, John Glenn's Gemini space capsule orbiting Earth. 500sh, Boy scout, vert.

**844** A130 10sh multicolored .35 .35
**845** A130 15sh multicolored .35 .35
**846** A130 400sh multicolored 8.00 8.00
*Nos. 844-846 (3)* 8.70 8.70

**Souvenir Sheet**

**847** A130 500sh multicolored 7.50 7.50

Lord Robert Baden-Powell, Founder of Boy Scouts, 50th Death Anniv. (in 1991).

While No. 847 has the same issue date as Nos. 844-846, the dollar value was lower when it were released.

No. 847 contains one 38x50mm stamp.

**1992, Aug. 1**

Charles de Gaulle (1890-1970): 25sh, French Resistance Monument and medal. 30sh, First Free French tank at Omaha beach, Normandy. 150sh, Concorde at de Gaulle Airport. 500sh, France #439 with Cross of Lorraine overprint and Free French stamp, vert.

**848** A130 25sh multicolored .70 .70
**849** A130 30sh multicolored .80 .80
**850** A130 150sh multicolored 7.75 7.75
*Nos. 848-850 (3)* 9.25 9.25

**Souvenir Sheet**

**851** A130 500sh multicolored 10.50 10.50

While No. 851 has the same issue date as Nos. 848-850, the dollar value was lower when it was released.

No. 851 contains one 38x50mm stamp.

Common Chimpanzee A131

Various chimpanzees in natural habitat.

**1992**

**852** A131 10sh multicolored .30 .30
**853** A131 15sh multicolored .30 .30
**854** A131 35sh multicolored .70 .70
**855** A131 75sh multicolored 1.60 1.60
**856** A131 100sh multicolored 1.90 1.90
**857** A131 150sh multicolored 3.00 3.00
**858** A131 200sh multicolored 3.75 3.75
**859** A131 300sh multicolored 5.75 5.75
*Nos. 852-859 (8)* 17.30 17.30

**Souvenir Sheets**

**860** A131 400sh Swinging from tree 5.75 5.75
**861** A131 400sh Eating termites 5.75 5.75

Spanish Art — A132

Drawings by Goya: 25sh, A Picador mounted on the shoulders of a Chulo, spears a Bull. 100sh, The Dream of Reason brings forth Monsters, vert. 150sh, Another Madness (of Martincho) in the Plaza de Zaragoza. 200sh, Recklessness of Martincho in the Plaza de Zaragoza.

No. 866, Seascape, by Mariana Salvador Maella.

**1992** ***Perf. 13***

**862** A132 25sh blk & red brn .50 .50
**863** A132 100sh black & brn 1.75 1.75
**864** A132 150sh blk & red brn 2.75 2.75
**865** A132 200sh blk & red brn 3.00 3.00

**Size: 120x95mm**

***Imperf***

**866** A132 400sh multicolored 5.00 5.00
*Nos. 862-866 (5)* 13.00 13.00

Granada '92.

**1992** ***Perf. 13***

Drawings by Diego da Silva Velazquez: 35sh, Philip IV at Fraga. 50sh, The Head of the Stag. 75sh, The Cardinal Infante Don Fernando as a Hunter. 300sh, Pablo de Valladolid. No. 871, Two Men at Table.

**867** A132 35sh multicolored .75 .75
**868** A132 50sh multicolored .90 .90
**869** A132 75sh multicolored 1.40 1.40
**870** A132 300sh multicolored 4.00 4.00

**Size: 120x95mm**

***Imperf***

**871** A132 400sh multicolored 5.50 5.50
*Nos. 867-871 (5)* 12.55 12.55

Granada '92.

A133

Chimpanzees of Gombe — A134

Designs: No. 872, Melisa and Mike. No. 873, Leakey and David Greybeard. No. 874, Fifi eating termites. No. 875 Galahad.

No. 876a, 10sh, Leakey. b, 15sh, Fifi. c, 20sh, Faben. d, 30sh, David Greybeard. e, 35sh, Mike. f, 50sh, Galahad. g, 100sh, Melisa. h, 200sh, Flo.

No. 877, Fifi, Flo, and Faben.

**1992, May 29 Litho. *Perf. 14***

**872** A133 10sh multicolored .70 .70
**873** A133 15sh multicolored .85 .85
**874** A133 30sh multicolored 1.10 1.10
**875** A133 35sh multicolored 1.25 1.25
*Nos. 872-875 (4)* 3.90 3.90

**Miniature Sheet**

**876** A134 Sheet of 8, #a.-h. 10.50 10.50

**Souvenir Sheet**

**877** A133 100sh multicolored 4.25 4.25

Natl. Bank of Commerce, 25th Anniv. — A135

Designs: 10sh, Sorghum plants. 15sh, Samora Avenue branch, computer operator, vert. 30sh, Head office. 35sh, Bankers Training Center. 40sh, Batik tie dyeing.

**1992, June 22**

**878** A135 10sh multicolored .50 .50
**879** A135 15sh multicolored .55 .55
**880** A135 35sh multicolored .85 .85
**881** A135 40sh multicolored .90 .90
*Nos. 878-881 (4)* 2.80 2.80

**Souvenir Sheet**

**882** A135 30sh multicolored 2.25 2.25

Traditional Dress — A136

Designs: 3sh, Gogo, central area. 5sh, Swahili, coastal area. 9sh, Hehe, southern highlands and Makonde, southern area. 12sh, Maasai, northern area. 40sh, Mwarusha.

**1992, Apr. 30 Litho. *Perf. 14½***

**883** A136 3sh multicolored .55 .55
**884** A136 5sh multicolored .65 .65
**885** A136 9sh multicolored .70 .70
**886** A136 12sh multicolored .90 .90
*Nos. 883-886 (4)* 2.80 2.80

**Souvenir Sheet**

**887** A136 40sh multicolored 3.00 3.00

Dated 1989.

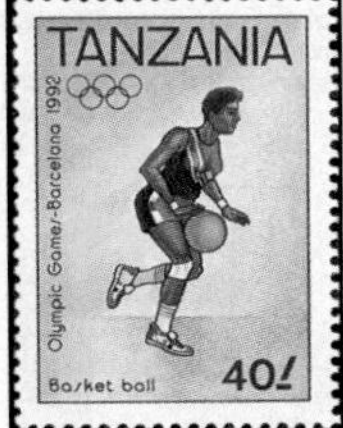
1992 Summer Olympics, Barcelona A137

**1992, July 23 *Perf. 12x12½***

**888** A137 40sh Basketball .80 .80
**889** A137 100sh Billiards 1.25 1.25
**890** A137 200sh Table tennis 2.00 2.00
**891** A137 400sh Darts 4.25 4.25
*Nos. 888-891 (4)* 8.30 8.30

**Souvenir Sheet**

**892** A137 500sh Weight lifting 5.50 5.50

Fish A138

No. 893: a, Tilapia mariae. b, Capoeta hulstaerti. c, Tropheus moorii. d, Synodontis angelicus. e, Julidochromis dickfeldi. f, Tilapia nilotica. g, Nothobranchius rachovii. h, Pseudotropheus crabro. i, Lamprologus leleupi. j, Pseudotropheus zebra. k, Julidochromis marlieri. l, Chalinochromis brichardi.

Designs: No. 894, Haplochromis "electric blue." No. 895, Lamprologus brevis. No. 896, Nothobranchius palmqvisti.

**1992, Oct. Litho. *Perf. 13½***

**893** A138 100sh Sheet of 12, #a.-l. 17.00 17.00

**Souvenir Sheets**

**894** A138 500sh multicolored 6.00 6.00
**895** A138 500sh multicolored 6.00 6.00
**896** A138 500sh multicolored 6.00 6.00

Discovery of America, 500th Anniv. A139

**1992, Oct. Litho. *Perf. 14***

**897** A139 70sh Sailing ship 1.40 1.40
**898** A139 300sh Columbus 5.50 5.50

**Souvenir Sheet**

**899** A139 500sh Columbus, diff. 4.50 4.50

Miniature Sheet

Flowers in Rio de Janeiro Botanical Garden — A140

No. 900: a, Couroupita guianensis. b, Jacaranda acutifolia. c, Psychopsis papilio. d, Nelumbo nucifera. e, Brownea grandiceps. f, Coffea arabica. g, Monodora myristica. h, Calaranthus rosea. i, Hibiscus schizopetalus. j, Carpobrotus edulis. k, Adenium obesum. l, Delonix regia. m, Agapanthus praecox. n, Zantedeschia aethiopica. o, Protea cynaroides. p, Cassia fistula. q, Aganisia cyanea. r, Heliconia rostrata. s, Cattelya luteola. t, Lagerstroemia speciosa.

500sh, Avenue of Royal Palms, Rio.

**1992, Nov. 5 Litho. *Perf. 14½***

**900** A140 70sh Sheet of 20, #a.-t. 22.00 22.00

**Souvenir Sheet**

**901** A140 500sh multicolored 7.00 7.00

Dinosaurs A141

No. 902: a, Iguanodon. b, Saltasaurus. c, Cetiosaurus. d, Camarasaurus. e, Spinosaurus. f, Stegosaurus. g, Allosaurus. h, Ceratosaurus. i, Lesothosaurus. j, Anchisaurus. k, Ornithomimus. l, Baronyx. m, Pachycephalosaurus. n, Heterodontosaurus. o, Dryosaurus. p, Coelophysis.

**1992, Nov. 5 Litho. *Perf. 14***

**902** A141 100sh Sheet of 16, #a.-p. 19.00 19.00

1992 Olympics, Albertville and Barcelona A142

Designs: 20sh, 4000-meter pursuit cycling, vert. 40sh, Double sculls. 50sh, Water polo. 70sh, Women's single luge. 100sh, Marathon. 150sh, Uneven parallel bars. 200sh, Ice hockey, vert, 400sh, Rings, vert.

No. 911, Tennis, vert. No. 912, Soccer, vert.

**1992, Nov. 16 Litho. *Perf. 14***

**903** A142 20sh multicolored .35 .35
**904** A142 40sh multicolored .55 .55
**905** A142 50sh multicolored .60 .60
**906** A142 70sh multicolored .85 .85
**907** A142 100sh multicolored 1.25 1.25
**908** A142 150sh multicolored 1.75 1.75
**909** A142 200sh multicolored 2.40 2.40
**910** A142 400sh multicolored 4.75 4.75
*Nos. 903-910 (8)* 12.50 12.50

**Souvenir Sheets**

**911** A142 500sh multicolored 7.25 7.25
**912** A142 500sh multicolored 7.25 7.25

Mickey's Portrait Gallery A142a

Donald Duck in scenes from Disney movies: No. 915, Sea Scouts, 1939. 35sh, Fire Chief, 1940. 50sh, Truant Officer Donald, 1941. 500sh, With Daisy in Mr. Duck Steps Out, 1940.

No. 925, Daisy in Don Donald, 1937.

Disney characters in scenes from Disney movies: No. 913, Hawaiian Holiday, 1937. No. 914, Society Dog Show, 1939. 75sh, Clock Cleaners, 1937. No. 919, Magician Mickey, 1937. No. 920, Goofy and Wilbur, 1939. 200sh, The Nifty Nineties, 1941. 300sh, Society Dog Show, 1939. 400sh, Pluto's Quin-Puplets, 1937. No. 926, Brave Little Tailor, 1938, horiz. No. 927, Forever Goofy.

**1992, Nov. 30 Litho. *Perf. 13½x14***

**913** A142a 25sh multicolored .50 .50
**914** A142a 25sh multicolored .50 .50
**915** A142a 25sh multicolored .50 .50
**916** A142a 35sh multicolored .65 .65
**917** A142a 50sh multicolored .90 .90
**918** A142a 75sh multicolored 1.10 1.10
**919** A142a 100sh multicolored 1.25 1.25
**920** A142a 100sh multicolored 1.25 1.25
**921** A142a 200sh multicolored 2.00 2.00
**922** A142a 300sh multicolored 2.75 2.75
**923** A142a 400sh multicolored 3.00 3.00
**924** A142a 500sh multicolored 3.00 3.00
*Nos. 913-924 (12)* 17.40 17.40

**Souvenir Sheets**

**925** A142a 600sh multicolored 5.00 5.00

***Perf. 14x13½***

**926** A142a 600sh multicolored 5.00 5.00

***Perf. 13½x14***

**927** A142a 600sh multicolored 5.00 5.00

Nos. 668-673 & 678 Ovptd. in Black or Red

**1992 Litho. *Perf. 14***

**928** A106 50sh on #668 .35 .35
**929** A106 50sh on #669 .35 .35
*a.* Pair, #928-929 .70 .70
**930** A106 75sh on #670 .55 .55
**931** A106 75sh on #671 .55 .55
*a.* Pair, #930-931 1.10 1.10
**932** A106 100sh on #672 .75 .75
**933** A106 100sh on #673 .75 .75
*a.* Pair, #932-933 1.50 1.50
*Nos. 928-933 (6)* 3.30 3.30

**Souvenir Sheet**

**934** A106 350sh on #678 (R) 2.50 2.50

Overprint appears on one line in sheet margin of No. 934.

Traditional Hunting A143

Designs: 20sh, Slingshots used on birds. 40sh, Various weapons. 70sh, Bow and arrow used on gazelles. 100sh, Long knife, wooden club used on gazelles. 150sh, Spear and shield used on lion.

**1992 Litho. *Perf. 13½***

**935** A143 20sh multicolored 1.25 1.25
**936** A143 70sh multicolored 1.60 1.60
**937** A143 100sh multicolored 2.75 2.75
**938** A143 150sh multicolored 4.00 4.00
*Nos. 935-938 (4)* 9.60 9.60

**Souvenir Sheet**

***Perf. 12½***

**939** A143 40sh multicolored 2.75 2.75

Shells — A144

Designs: 10sh, Lambis truncata Humphrey. 15sh, Cypraecassis rufa. 25sh, Vexillum rugosum. 30sh, Conus litteratus. 35sh, Corculum cardissa. 50sh, Murex ramosus. 250sh, Melo melo. 300sh, Tridacha gigas.

**1992, June 30 *Perf. 12x12½***

**940** A144 10sh multicolored .45 .45
**941** A144 15sh multicolored .55 .55
**942** A144 25sh multicolored .75 .75
**943** A144 30sh multicolored .75 .75
**944** A144 35sh multicolored .75 .75
**945** A144 50sh multicolored 1.10 1.10
**946** A144 250sh multicolored 4.50 4.50
*Nos. 940-946 (7)* 8.85 8.85

**Souvenir Sheet**

**947** A144 300sh multicolored 5.50 5.50

No. 808 Inscribed Vertically "15th Anniversary"

**1992 Litho. *Perf. 14***

**949** A125 75sh Sheet of 9, #a.-i. 11.50 11.50

Marine Life A145

**1992 Litho. *Perf. 14***

**950** A145 20sh Seal .60 .60
**951** A145 30sh Whale 1.50 1.50
**952** A145 70sh Shark .90 .90
**953** A145 100sh Walrus 1.50 1.50
*Nos. 950-953 (4)* 4.50 4.50

**Souvenir Sheet**

**954** A145 500sh Sea turtle 7.25 7.25

A146

Anniversaries and Events — A147

Designs: 30sh, Count Ferdinand von Zeppelin. 70sh, Apollo-Soyuz. No. 957, Child being offered apple. No. 958, African elephant. No. 959, Lions Intl. emblem, man being given glasses. No. 960, Zebra. 300sh, Graf Zeppelin. No. 962, Space shuttle in Earth orbit. No. 963, Wolfgang Amadeus Mozart.

No. 964, Voyager 2. No. 965, Unidentified zeppelin. No. 966, African elephant, diff. No. 967, Scene from "The Magic Flute."

**1992 Litho. *Perf. 14***

| | | | | | |
|---|---|---|---|---|---|
| **955** | A146 | 30sh multicolored | | 3.25 | 3.25 |
| **956** | A146 | 70sh multicolored | | 4.50 | 4.50 |
| **957** | A146 | 150sh multicolored | | 2.00 | 2.00 |
| **958** | A146 | 150sh multicolored | | 3.25 | 3.25 |
| **959** | A146 | 200sh multicolored | | 2.40 | 2.40 |
| **960** | A146 | 200sh multicolored | | 3.25 | 3.25 |
| **961** | A146 | 300sh multicolored | | 3.25 | 3.25 |
| **962** | A146 | 400sh multicolored | | 4.50 | 4.50 |
| **963** | A147 | 400sh multicolored | | 3.25 | 3.25 |
| | | *Nos. 955-963 (9)* | | 29.65 | 29.65 |

**Souvenir Sheets**

| | | | | |
|---|---|---|---|---|
| **964** | A146 | 500sh multicolored | 4.25 | 4.25 |
| **965** | A146 | 500sh multicolored | 4.00 | 4.00 |
| **966** | A146 | 500sh multicolored | 4.25 | 4.25 |
| **967** | A147 | 800sh multicolored | 6.00 | 6.00 |

Count Zeppelin, 75th death anniv. (#955, 961, 965). Intl. Space Year (#956, 962, 964). Intl. Conference on Nutrition (#957). Earth Summit, Rio de Janeiro (#958, 960, 966).Lions Intl., 75th anniv. (#959). Wolfgang Amadeus Mozart, bicent. of death (in 1991) (#963, 967).

Issued: Nos. 955-956, 961-962, 964-965, Nov.; Nos. 957-960, 966, Dec.

Cats — A147a

**1992, Dec. 3 Litho. *Perf. 12x12½***

| | | | | |
|---|---|---|---|---|
| **967A** | A147a | 20sh Abyssinian | .70 | .70 |
| **967B** | A147a | 30sh Havana | .70 | .70 |
| **967C** | A147a | 50sh Persian black | .85 | .85 |
| **967D** | A147a | 70sh Persian blue | 1.00 | 1.00 |
| **967E** | A147a | 100sh European silver tabby | 1.25 | 1.25 |
| **967F** | A147a | 150sh Persian silver tabby | 1.40 | 1.40 |
| **967G** | A147a | 200sh Maine | 1.90 | 1.90 |
| | | *Nos. 967A-967G (7)* | 7.80 | 7.80 |

**Souvenir Sheet**

| | | | | |
|---|---|---|---|---|
| **967H** | A147a | 300sh European | 4.50 | 4.50 |

Model Trains A148

Lionel models: 10sh, B & O Tunnel locomotive #5, 2⅞-inch gauge, 1904. 20sh, Liberty Bell #385E, standard gauge, 1930. 30sh, Armored motor car #203, standard gauge, 1917. 50sh, Open trolley #202, standard gauge, 1910-14. 70sh, Macy special #450, standrad gauge. 100sh, Milwaukee Road bipolar electric #381E, standard gauge, 1929. 200sh, New York Central "S" type, standard gauge, 1912. 300sh, 4-4-0 American #7 (thick rim), standard gauge, 1914.

No. 976, Wind-up hand car with Mickey and Minnie Mouse, O-27 gauge, 1936. No. 977, Clear plastic F-3 display model, O gauge, 1947.

**1992, Dec. 10 Litho. *Perf. 14***

| | | | | |
|---|---|---|---|---|
| **968** | A148 | 10sh multicolored | .65 | .65 |
| **969** | A148 | 20sh multicolored | .75 | .75 |
| **970** | A148 | 30sh multicolored | .80 | .80 |
| **971** | A148 | 50sh multicolored | 1.25 | 1.25 |
| **972** | A148 | 70sh multicolored | 1.50 | 1.50 |
| **973** | A148 | 100sh multicolored | 1.60 | 1.60 |
| **974** | A148 | 200sh multicolored | 2.25 | 2.25 |
| **975** | A148 | 300sh multicolored | 3.00 | 3.00 |
| | | *Nos. 968-975 (8)* | 11.80 | 11.80 |

**Souvenir Sheets**

| | | | | |
|---|---|---|---|---|
| **976** | A148 | 500sh multicolored | 5.00 | 5.00 |
| **977** | A148 | 500sh multicolored | 5.00 | 5.00 |

Genoa '92.

Birds — A149

**1992, Dec. 10 Litho. *Perf. 12x12½***

| | | | | |
|---|---|---|---|---|
| **978** | A149 | 5sh Superb starling | .60 | .60 |
| **979** | A149 | 10sh Canary | .75 | .75 |
| **980** | A149 | 15sh Four-colored bush shrike | .75 | .75 |
| **981** | A149 | 25sh Grey-headed kingfisher | .80 | .80 |
| **982** | A149 | 30sh Common king-fisher | .80 | .80 |
| **983** | A149 | 35sh Yellow-billed ox-pecker | .80 | .80 |
| **984** | A149 | 150sh Black throated honeyquide | 2.00 | 2.00 |
| | | *Nos. 978-984 (7)* | 6.50 | 6.50 |

**Souvenir Sheet**

***Perf. 12½x12***

| | | | | |
|---|---|---|---|---|
| **985** | A149 | 300sh European cuckoo, horiz. | 4.00 | 4.00 |

Makonde Art — A149a

Various carved faces.

**1992, Dec. 24 Litho. *Perf. 12x12½***

| | | | | |
|---|---|---|---|---|
| **985A** | A149a | 20sh multicolored | .25 | .25 |
| **985B** | A149a | 30sh multicolored | .25 | .25 |
| **985C** | A149a | 50sh multicolored | .45 | .45 |
| **985D** | A149a | 70sh multicolored | .65 | .65 |
| **985E** | A149a | 100sh multicolored | .90 | .90 |
| **985F** | A149a | 150sh multicolored | 1.40 | 1.40 |
| **985G** | A149a | 200sh multicolored | 1.90 | 1.90 |
| | | *Nos. 985A-985G (7)* | 5.80 | 5.80 |

**Souvenir Sheet**

| | | | | |
|---|---|---|---|---|
| **985H** | A149a | 350sh multicolored | 4.50 | 4.50 |

Bicycles A149b

**1992, Dec. 30 Litho. *Perf. 12½x12***

| | | | | |
|---|---|---|---|---|
| **985I** | A149b | 20sh Russia, 1813 | .40 | .40 |
| **985J** | A149b | 30sh Germany, 1840 | .40 | .40 |
| **985K** | A149b | 50sh Germany, 1818 | .60 | .60 |
| **985L** | A149b | 70sh Germany, 1850 | .60 | .60 |
| **985M** | A149b | 100sh Italy, 1988 | .65 | .65 |
| **985N** | A149b | 150sh Sweden, 1982 | 1.40 | 1.40 |
| **985O** | A149b | 300sh Italy, 1989 | 1.60 | 1.60 |
| | | *Nos. 985I-985O (7)* | 5.65 | 5.65 |

**Souvenir Sheet**

| | | | | |
|---|---|---|---|---|
| **985P** | A149b | 350sh Great Britain, 1887 | 4.50 | 4.50 |

Discovery of America, 500th Anniv. — A150

Designs: 10sh, Symbols of luck. 15sh, "Is this course right?," compass, chart. 25sh, "Earth!," first sight of land. 30sh, First meetings, horiz. 35sh, Nina, horiz. 75sh, Santa Maria, horiz. 250sh, Ship running aground, vert. 200sh, Columbus.

***Perf. 12x12½, 12½x12***

**1992, Sept. 30 Litho.**

| | | | | |
|---|---|---|---|---|
| **986** | A150 | 10sh multicolored | .30 | .30 |
| **987** | A150 | 15sh multicolored | .35 | .35 |
| **988** | A150 | 25sh multicolored | .50 | .50 |
| **989** | A150 | 30sh multicolored | .55 | .55 |
| **990** | A150 | 35sh multicolored | .65 | .65 |
| **991** | A150 | 75sh multicolored | 1.10 | 1.10 |
| **992** | A150 | 250sh multicolored | 2.25 | 2.25 |
| | | *Nos. 986-992 (7)* | 5.70 | 5.70 |

**Souvenir Sheet**

| | | | | |
|---|---|---|---|---|
| **993** | A150 | 200sh multicolored | 5.00 | 5.00 |

Louvre Museum, Bicent. A151

No. 994 — Paintings by Jean-Baptiste-Simeon Chardin (1699-1779): a, Young Artist. b, The Buffet. c, The Provider. d, A Mother Working. e, Grace. f, The Copper Fountain. g, House of Cards. h, Child with Teetotum. 500sh, The Ray, horiz.

**1993, Mar. 8 Litho. *Perf. 12***

| | | | | |
|---|---|---|---|---|
| **994** | A151 | 100sh Sheet of 8, #a.-h. + label | 9.50 | 9.50 |

**Souvenir Sheet**

***Perf. 14½***

| | | | | |
|---|---|---|---|---|
| **995** | A151 | 500sh multicolored | 4.50 | 4.50 |

No. 995 contains one 88x55mm stamp.

Coronation of Queen Elizabeth II, 40th Anniv. A152

No. 996: a, 100sh, Official coronation photograph. b, 150sh, Exeter salt. c, 200sh, Photograph of ceremony, 1953. d, 300sh, Queen, Prince Andrew.

500sh, Princess Elizabeth Opening the New Broadgate Coventry, by Dame Laura Knight, 1948.

**1993, June 2 Litho. *Perf. 13½x14***

| | | | | |
|---|---|---|---|---|
| **996** | A152 | Sheet, 2 ea #a.-d. | 12.50 | 12.50 |

**Souvenir Sheet**

***Perf. 14***

| | | | | |
|---|---|---|---|---|
| **997** | A152 | 500sh multicolored | 5.25 | 5.25 |

No. 997 contains one 28x43mm stamp.

Famous Women — A153

Designs: a, 20sh, Valentina Tereshkova. b, 40sh, Marie Curie. c, 50sh, Indira Gandhi. d, 70sh, Wilma Rudolph. e, 100sh, Margaret Mead. f, 150sh, Golda Meir. g, 200sh, Dr. Elizabeth Blackwell. h, 400sh, Margaret Thatcher.

No. 999, Mother Teresa.

**1993, July 15 *Perf. 14***

| | | | | |
|---|---|---|---|---|
| **998** | A153 | Sheet of 8, #a.-h. | 13.00 | 13.00 |

**Souvenir Sheet**

| | | | | |
|---|---|---|---|---|
| **999** | A153 | 500sh multicolored | 5.75 | 5.75 |

Wildlife — A154

No. 1000 — Wildlife at watering hole: No. 1000: a, Elephant. b, Gazelles. c, Hartebeest. d, Duiker. e, Genet. f, Civet. g, Pelicans. h, Waterbuck. i, Blacksmith plovers. j, Pied kingfisher. k, Black-winged stilts. l, Bush pig.

No. 1000M: n, Brown-hooded kingfisher. o, Sable antelope (n). p, Impala (q). q, Buffalo. r, Leopard. s, Aardvark (t). t, Hippopotamus. u, Spotted hyena. v, Crowned crane (w). w, Crocodile. x, Flamingo. y, Baboon.

No. 1001 — Wildlife on the plains: No. 1001: a, Potto. b, Flamingos. c, Grey-headed kingfisher. d, Red colobus monkey. e, Dik-dik. f, Aardwolf. g, Black-backed jackal. h, Tree pangolin. i, Serval. j, Yellow-billed hornbill. k, Pygmy mongoose. l, Bat-eared fox.

No. 1001M: n, Bushbaby. o, Egyptian vulture. p, Ostrich. q, Greater kudu. r, Diana monkey. s, Giraffe (w). t, Cheetah (s). u, Wildebeeest (t). v, Chimpanzee. w, Warthog. x, Zebra. y, Rhinoceros.

No. 1002, Lions, horiz. No. 1003, African elephants, horiz.

**1993, June 30**

| | | | | |
|---|---|---|---|---|
| **1000** | A154 | 100sh Sheet of 12, #a.-l. | 9.50 | 9.50 |
| **1000M** | A154 | 100sh Sheet of 12, #n.-y. | 9.50 | 9.50 |
| **1001** | A154 | 100sh Sheet of 12, #a.-l. | 9.50 | 9.50 |
| **1001M** | A154 | 100sh Sheet of 12, #n.-y. | 9.50 | 9.50 |
| | | *Nos. 1000-1001M (4)* | 38.00 | 38.00 |

**Souvenir Sheets**

| | | | | |
|---|---|---|---|---|
| **1002** | A154 | 500sh multi | 5.75 | 5.75 |
| **1003** | A154 | 500sh multi | 5.75 | 5.75 |

For overprints see Nos. 1531, 1534.

Pancake Tortoise A155

**1993, June 30**

| | | | | |
|---|---|---|---|---|
| **1004** | A155 | 20sh On rock | .60 | .60 |
| **1005** | A155 | 30sh Drinking | .80 | .80 |
| **1006** | A155 | 50sh Crawling from under rocks | 1.10 | 1.10 |
| **1007** | A155 | 70sh Hatchling | 1.40 | 1.40 |
| | | *Nos. 1004-1007 (4)* | 3.90 | 3.90 |

World Wildlife Federation.

Mushrooms
A156

Designs: 20sh, Macrolepiota rhacodes. 40sh, Mycena pura. 50sh, Chlorophyllum molybdites. 70sh, Agaricus campestris. 100sh, Volvariella volvacea. 150sh, Leucoagaricus naucinus. 200sh, Oudemansiella radicata. 300sh, Clitocybe nebularis.

No. 1016, Omphalotus olearius. No. 1017, Lepista nuda.

**1993, June 18 Litho. *Perf. 14***

**1008** A156 20sh multicolored .35 .35
**1009** A156 40sh multicolored .55 .55
**1010** A156 50sh multicolored .60 .60
**1011** A156 70sh multicolored .85 .85
**1012** A156 100sh multicolored 1.40 1.40
**1013** A156 150sh multicolored 1.75 1.75
**1014** A156 200sh multicolored 2.40 2.40
**1015** A156 300sh multicolored 4.00 4.00
*Nos. 1008-1015 (8)* 11.90 11.90

**Souvenir Sheets**

**1016** A156 500sh multicolored 4.75 4.75
**1017** A156 500sh multicolored 4.75 4.75

Sports — A157

**1992, May 28 Litho. *Perf. 12x12½***

**1018** A157 20sh Boxing .30 .30
**1019** A157 50sh Field hockey .70 .70
**1020** A157 70sh Horse racing .55 .55
**1021** A157 100sh Marathon .65 .65
**1022** A157 150sh Soccer .85 .85
**1023** A157 200sh Diving 1.10 1.10
**1024** A157 400sh Basketball 2.25 2.25
*Nos. 1018-1024 (7)* 6.40 6.40

**Souvenir Sheet**

***Perf. 12½x12***

**1025** A157 300sh High jump, horiz. 3.50 3.50

Animals
A158

No. 1026: a, Female Grant's zebra, running. b, Male Grant's zebra, standing. c, Female Grant's gazelle. d, Male Grant's gazelle. e, Thompson's gazelle. f, White-bearded gnu, calf.

No. 1027: a, Female cheetah, cubs. b, Young cheetah. c, Lioness carrying her cub. d, Two hunting dogs. e, Three hunting dogs. f, Hunting dogs before an attack.

No. 1028, African rhinoceros. No. 1029, African elephant.

**1993, June 30 Litho. *Perf. 14***

**1026** A158 100sh Sheet of 6, #a.-f. 7.50 7.50
**1027** A158 100sh Sheet of 6, #a.-f. 7.50 7.50

**Souvenir Sheets**

**1028** A158 500sh multicolored 8.00 8.00
**1029** A158 500sh multicolored 8.00 8.00

For overprints see Nos. 1532-1533, 1535.

A159

A160

1994 Winter Olympics, Lillehammer, Norway: 300sh, Matti Nykanen, ski jumping, 1988. 400sh, Stefan Krause, Jan Behrendt, double luge, 1992. 500sh, Downhill skiing, 1972.

**1993, June 10 Litho. *Perf. 14***

**1030** A159 300sh multicolored 2.25 2.25
**1031** A159 400sh multicolored 2.75 2.75

**Souvenir Sheet**

**1032** A159 500sh multicolored 3.50 3.50

**1993, June 10**

**1033** A160 100sh Telescope .70 .70
**1034** A160 300sh Radio telescope 2.25 2.25

**Souvenir Sheet**

**1035** A160 500sh Copernicus 3.50 3.50

Copernicus, 450th anniv. of death.

Picasso (1881-1973)
A160a

Various details of painting, Guernica, 1937.

**1993, June 10 Litho. *Perf. 14***

**1035A** A160a 30sh multi .20 .20
**1035B** A160a 200sh multi 1.40 1.40
**1035C** A160a 300sh multi 2.00 2.00
*Nos. 1035A-1035C (3)* 3.60 3.60

**Souvenir Sheet**

**1035D** A160a 500sh multi 3.50 3.50

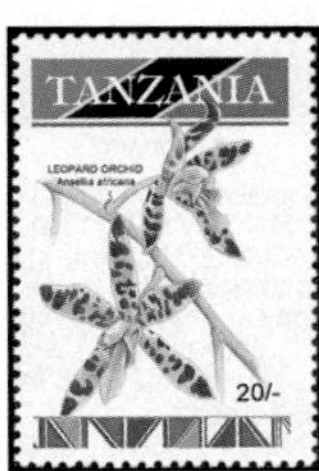


Flowers — A161

Polska '93 — A162

Designs: 20sh, Leopard orchid. 30sh, African violet. 40sh, Stapelia semota lutea. 50sh, Busy Lizzie. 60sh, Senecio petraeus. 70sh, Kalanchoe velutina. 100sh, Dwarf ginger lily. 150sh, Nymphaea colorata. 200sh, Thunbergia battiscombei. 250sh, Crossandra nilotica. 300sh, African tulip tree. 350sh, Ruttya fruticosa.

No. 1048, False African violet. No. 1049, Glory lily.

**1993, Nov. 8 Litho. *Perf. 13½***

**1036** A161 20sh multicolored .35 .35
**1037** A161 30sh multicolored .40 .40
**1038** A161 40sh multicolored .45 .45
**1039** A161 50sh multicolored .45 .45
**1040** A161 60sh multicolored .55 .55
**1041** A161 70sh multicolored .60 .60
**1042** A161 100sh multicolored .70 .70
**1043** A161 150sh multicolored 1.10 1.10
**1044** A161 200sh multicolored 1.25 1.25
**1045** A161 250sh multicolored 1.25 1.25
**1046** A161 300sh multicolored 1.50 1.50
**1047** A161 350sh multicolored 1.50 1.50
*Nos. 1036-1047 (12)* 10.10 10.10

**Souvenir Sheets**

***Perf. 13***

**1048** A161 500sh multicolored 4.00 4.00
**1049** A161 500sh multicolored 4.00 4.00

**1993 Litho. *Perf. 14***

Paintings: 200sh, Stone Masons, by Aleksander Kobzdej, 1952. 300sh, Child Wearing Plumed Helmut, by Z. Waliszewski, 1932.

500sh, In the Marketplace, by Stanislaw Osostowicz, 1939.

**1050** A162 200sh multicolored 1.40 1.40
**1051** A162 300sh multicolored 2.00 2.00

**Souvenir Sheet**

**1052** A162 500sh multicolored 3.50 3.50

Butterflies
A163

No. 1053: a, Gold-banded forester. b, Twin dotted border. c, Aphnaeus flavescens. d, Orange-and-lemon. e, Club-tailed charaxes. f, Broad blue-banded swallowtail. g, African map. h, Buxton's hairstreak. i, Bush charaxes. j, Lilac nymph. k, Large striped swordtail. l, Charaxes acuminatus. m, African leaf. n, African wood white. o, Trimen's false acraea. p, Red line sapphire. q, Mother-of-pearl. r, Flame-bordered charaxes. s, Large blue charaxes. t, Emperor swallowtail.

No. 1054: a, Angled grass yellow. b, Figtree blue. c, Iolaus ismenias. d, Green-veined charaxes. e, Commodore. f, African monarch. g, Bush scarlet. h, Eyed pansy. i, Zebra white. j, Azure hairstreak. k, Yellow pansy. l, Regal purple tip.

No. 1054M: n, Iolaus aphnaeoides. o, Green charaxes. p, Beautiful monarch. q, Short-tailed admiral. r, Dusky dotted border. s, Charaxes anticlea. t, Blue salamis. u, Nepheronia argia. v, Acraea pseudolycia. w, Blue-banded diadem. x, Golden tip. y, Acraea bonasia.

No. 1055, Blood-red cymothoe. No. 1056, Precis octavia. No. 1056A, Noble swallowtail. No. 1056B, Violet-spotted charaxes.

**1993, Nov. 8 Litho. *Perf. 13***

**1053** A163 100sh Sheet of 20, #a.-t. 30.00 30.00
**1054** A163 100sh Sheet of 12, #a.-l. 15.00 15.00
**1054M** A163 100sh Sheet of 12, #n.-y. 15.00 15.00

**Souvenir Sheets**

**1055** A163 500sh multi 6.25 6.25
**1056** A163 500sh multi 6.25 6.25
**1056A** A163 500sh multi 6.25 6.25
**1056B** A163 500sh multi 6.25 6.25

A164

A165

Players, country: 20sh, Gullit, Holland. 30sh, Sheedy, Ireland. 50sh, Giannini, Italy. 70sh, Cesar, Brazil. 250sh, Barnes, England; Grun, Belgium. 300sh, Chendo, Spain. 350sh, Rijkaard, Holland. 400sh, Matthaeus, Germany.

No. 1065, 500sh, Berti, Italy; Caligiuri, US. No. 1066, 500sh, Walker, England; Gilhaus, Holland.

**1993, Dec. *Perf. 14***

**1057-1064** A164 Set of 8 9.50 9.50

**Souvenir Sheets**

**1065-1066** A164 Set of 2 9.50 9.50

1994 World Cup Soccer Championships, US.

**1994, Feb. 10**

Hummel Figurines: 20sh, Boy with accordian. 40sh, Girl with guitar, boy with banjo. 50sh, Boy with tuba. 70sh, Boy with harmonica, bird. 100sh, Bird in tree, boy seated on fence. 150sh, Boy playing horn. 200sh, Boy with horn, bird. 300sh, Girl playing banjo. 350sh, Boy with cello on back. 400sh, Girls with banjo and sheet music.

No. 1077, 500sh, Four carolers. No. 1078, 500sh, Two figures in tower blowing horns at angel below.

**1067-1076** A165 Set of 10 10.50 10.50

**Souvenir Sheets**

**1077-1078** A165 Set of 2 10.50 10.50

Black Athletes — A166

No. 1079: a, 20sh, Arthur Ashe. b, 40sh, Michael Jordan. c, 50sh, Daley Thompson. d, 70sh, Jackie Robinson. e, 100sh, Kareem Abdul-Jabbar. f, 150sh, Florence Joyner. g, 200sh, Jesse Owens. h, 400sh, Jack Johnson.

500sh, Muhammad Ali, horiz.

**1993, July 15**

**1079** A166 Sheet of 8, #a.-h. 7.50 7.50

**Souvenir Sheet**

**1080** A166 500sh multicolored 4.25 4.25

First US Gas Balloon Flight, Bicent.
A167

Designs: 200sh, Balloons filling with hot air. 400sh, Jean-Pierre Blanchard (1753-1809), balloon. 500sh, Hot air balloons in flight, vert.

**1994, Apr. 25 Litho. *Perf. 14***

**1081** A167 200sh multicolored 2.00 2.00
**1082** A167 400sh multicolored 3.75 3.75

**Souvenir Sheet**

**1083** A167 500sh multicolored 5.75 5.75

Royal Air Force, 75th Anniv.
A168

Designs: 200sh, Sopwith Camel. 400sh, BAE Harrier. 500sh, Supermarine Spitfire.

**1993, Dec.**

**1084** A168 200sh multicolored 2.25 2.25
**1085** A168 400sh multicolored 4.50 4.50

**Souvenir Sheet**

**1086** A168 500sh multicolored 6.75 6.75

Automotive Anniversaries — A171

Designs: No. 1099, 200sh, 1893 Benz, 1993 500 SEL. No. 1100, 200sh, Henry Ford, 1922 Model T. No. 1101, 400sh, Karl Benz, emblem. No. 1102, 400sh, 1893 Ford, Mustang Cobra.

No. 1103, 500sh, Emblem, 1937 540 K. No. 1104, 500sh, Henry Ford, first Ford factory.

**1994, Apr. 25 Litho. *Perf. 14***

**1099-1102** A171 Set of 4 9.50 9.50

**Souvenir Sheets**

**1103-1104** A171 Set of 2 8.50 8.50

First Benz 4-wheel motor car, cent. (#1099, 1101, 1103). First Ford motor, cent. (#1100, 1102, 1104).

Birds A172

No. 1105, vert. : a, 20sh, African hawk eagle. b, 30sh, Shoe-bill stork. c, 50sh, Harrier eagle. d, 70sh, Casqued hornbill. e, 100sh, Crowned crane. f, 150sh, Greater flamingo.
No. 1106: a, 200sh, Pelican. b, 250sh, Jacana, black crake. c, 300sh, Ostrich. d, 350sh, Helmeted guinea fowl. e, 400sh, Malachite kingfisher. f, 500sh, Saddle-billed stork.

**1994, May 11**

**1105** A172 Sheet of 6, #a.-f. 9.00 9.00
**1106** A172 Sheet of 6, #a.-f. 11.00 11.00

Hong Kong '94 A173

Red-cap white pearl-scale goldfish and: No. 1107, Scarus ghobban. No. 1108, Regal angelfish.

**1994, Feb. 18**

**1107** A173 350sh multicolored 2.00 2.00
**1108** A173 350sh multicolored 2.00 2.00
*a.* Pair, #1107-1108 4.00 4.00

Nos. 1107-1108 issued in sheets of 5 pairs. No. 1108a is a continuous design.

Mickey Mouse, 65th Anniv. — A176

Disney characters on tour: 10sh, Boarding plane. 20sh, Dancing, Tonga. 30sh, Lawn bowling, Australia. 40sh, Building igloo, Arctic region. 50sh, Royal Palace Guard, London. 60sh, Esna bazaar, Egypt. 70sh, Zsambox cowboys, Hungary, vert. 100sh, Grand Canal, Venice, vert. 150sh, Dancing, Bali, Indonesia, vert. 200sh, Monks studying text, Bangkok, Thailand, vert. 300sh, Water skiing, Taj Mahal, India, vert. 400sh, Himalayas, Nepal.
No. 1125, Kilimanjaro Uhuru Peak, Kibo, Tanzania, vert. No. 1126, Kigoma railway station, Dar es Salaam, Tanzania, vert. No. 1127, Memorial to Dr. Livingstone, shores of Lake Tanganyika, Tanzania.

**1994, Apr. 6** ***Perf. 14x13½, 13½x14***

**1113** A176 10sh multicolored .30 .30
**1114** A176 20sh multicolored .30 .30
**1115** A176 30sh multicolored .30 .30
**1116** A176 40sh multicolored .45 .45
**1117** A177 50sh multicolored .50 .50
**1118** A176 60sh multicolored .55 .55
**1119** A176 70sh multicolored .70 .70
**1120** A176 100sh multicolored 1.10 1.10
**1121** A176 150sh multicolored 1.50 1.50
**1122** A176 200sh multicolored 2.10 2.10
**1123** A176 300sh multicolored 3.00 3.00
**1124** A176 400sh multicolored 4.00 4.00
*Nos. 1113-1124 (12)* 14.80 14.80

**Souvenir Sheets**

**1125** A176 500sh multicolored 4.50 4.50
**1126** A176 500sh multicolored 4.50 4.50
**1127** A176 500sh multicolored 4.50 4.50

Reptiles A177

Designs: 20sh, Geochelone elephantopus, vert. 50sh, Iguana iguana, vert. 70sh, Varanus salvator. 100sh, Naja oxiana, vert. 150sh, Chamaeleo jacksonii. 200sh, Eunectes murinus. 250sh, Alligator mississippensis.
500sh, Vipera berus, vert.

***Perf. 12x12½, 12½x12***

**1993, June 28** **Litho.**

**1128-1134** A177 Set of 7 6.00 6.00

**Souvenir Sheet**

**1135** A177 500sh multicolored 4.75 4.75

Nos. 1128-1135 were were not available until July 1994.

Sharks A178

Designs: 20sh, Isurus oxyrinchus. 30sh, Etmopterus hillianus. 50sh, Galeocerdo cuvier. 70sh, Sguatina afrikana. 100sh, Pristiophorus cirratus. 150sh, Triaenodon obesus. 200sh, Sphyrna lewini.
350sh, Hexanchus grisens, vert.

**1993, July 27** ***Perf. 12½x12***

**1136-1142** A178 Set of 7 4.50 4.50

**Souvenir Sheet**

***Perf. 12x12½***

**1143** A178 350sh multicolored 3.00 3.00

Nos. 1136-1143 were not available until July 1994.

Dogs — A179

Designs: 20sh, Gordon setter. 30sh, Zwergschnauzer. 50sh, Labrador retriever. 70sh, Wire fox terrier. 100sh, English springer spaniel. 150sh, Newfoundlander. 200sh, Moscow toy terrier.
350sh, Doberman pinscher.

**1993, Sept. 27** ***Perf. 12x12½***

**1144-1150** A179 Set of 7 5.25 5.25

**Souvenir Sheet**

**1151** A179 350sh multicolored 2.50 2.50

Nos. 1144-1151 were not available until July 1994.

Horses A180

Designs: 20sh, Norman-Arab. 40sh, Nonius. 50sh, Boulonnais. 70sh, Arab. 100sh, Anglo-Arab. 150sh, Tarpan. 200sh, Thorougbred.
No. 1159, Anglo-Norman.

**1993, Nov. 30** ***Perf. 12½x12***

**1152-1158** A180 Set of 7 5.50 5.50

**Souvenir Sheet**

***Perf. 12x12½***

**1159** A180 400sh multicolored 2.75 2.75

Nos. 1152-1159 were not available until July 1994.

Military Aircraft A181

Designs: 20sh, ALFA jet. 30sh, Northrup F-5E. 50sh, Mirage 3NG. 70sh, MB-339C. 100sh, MIG-31. 150sh, C-101 AVIOJET. 200sh, F-16B.
500sh, EAP fighter, vert.

**1994, Apr. 25** **Litho.** ***Perf. 12½x12***

**1160-1166** A181 Set of 7 5.75 5.75

**Souvenir Sheet**

***Perf. 12x12½***

**1167** A181 500sh multicolored 3.25 3.25

A182

Customs Co-operation Council Meeting, Arusha — A183

Designs: 20sh, Trans-border trade. 50sh, Customs-international trade by ship. 100sh, Customs-air transportation. 150sh, Postal service-customs co-operation, Customs and UPU emblems.
500sh, Emblem.

**1994, Aug. 23** **Litho.** ***Perf. 13½***

**1168-1171** A182 Set of 4 2.25 2.25

**Souvenir Sheet**

***Perf. 12½***

**1172** A183 500sh multicolored 3.00 3.00

1994 World Cup Soccer Championships, US — A184

No. 1173: a, Giuseppe Signori. b, Ruud Gullit. c, Roberto Mancini. d, Marco Van Bastien. e, Dennis Bergkamp. f, Oscar Ruggeri. g, Frank Rijkaard. h, Peter Schmeichel.
1000sh, World Cup trophy.

**1994, Sept. 26** ***Perf. 14***

**1173** A184 300sh Sheet of 8, #a.-h. 10.50 10.50

**Souvenir Sheet**

**1174** A184 1000sh multicolored 5.75 5.75

1994 World Cup Soccer Championships, US — A184a

Letter in soccer ball: 40sh, B. 50sh, C. 70sh, D. 100sh, E. 170sh, A. 200sh, none. 250sh, F.
500sh, Two players and goalie.

**1994, Sept. 30** **Litho.** ***Perf. 12½x12***

**1174A-1174G** A184a Set of 7 7.50 7.50
*i.* Souv. sheet of 6, #1174A-1174E, 1174G + 3 labels 4.00 4.00

**Souvenir Sheet**

**1174H** A184a 500sh multi 5.50 5.50

Dogs — A185

No. 1175, 120sh: a, Alsatian (German Shepherd). b, Japanese chin. c, Shetland sheepdog. d, Italian spinone. e, Great dane. f, English setter. g, Pembroke (welsh corgi). h, St. Bernard. i, Irish wolfhound.
No. 1176, 120sh: a, Afghan hound. b, Basenji (Congo dog). c, Siberian husky. d, Irish setter. e, Norwegian elkhound. f, Bracco Italiano (Italian hound). g, Australian cattle dog. h, German short haired pointer. i, Rhodesian ridgeback.
No. 1177, 120sh: a, Alaskan malamute. b, Scottish cairn terrier. c, American foxhound. d, British bulldog. e, Boston terrier. f, Borzoi (Russian wolfhound). g, Shar pei (Chinese fighting dog). h, Saluki (Persian greyhound). i, Bernese mountain dog.
No. 1178, 120sh: a, Doberman pinscher. b, Chihuahua. c, Bloodhound. d, Keeshond (Dutch barge dog). e, Tibetan spaniel. f, Japanese akita. g, Tervueren (Belgian shepherd dog). h, Chow chow (Chinese Spitz). i, Pharaoh hound.
No. 1179, 1000sh, Like #1175e. No. 1180, 1000sh, Like #1176b.

**1994, Sept. 30**

**Sheets of 9, #a-i**

**1175-1178** A185 Set of 4 19.00 19.00

**Souvenir Sheets**

**1179-1180** A185 Set of 2 11.50 11.50

Miniature Sheets of 8

Orchids — A186

No. 1181, 200sh: a, Rangaeris amaniensis. b, Eulophia macowanii. c, Cyrtorchis arcuata. d, Centrostigma occultans. e, Cirrhopetalum umbellatum. f, Ansellia gigantea. g, Angraecum ramosum. h, Disa englerana.
No. 1182, 200sh: a, Nervilia stolziana. b, Satyrium orbiculare. c, Schzochilus sulphureus. d, Disa stolzii. e, Platycoryne mediocris. f, Satyrium breve. g, Eulophia nuttii. h, Disa ornithantha.
No. 1183, 1000sh, Eulophia thomsonii, horiz. No. 1184, 1000sh, Phaius P. tankervilliae, horiz.

**1994, Oct. 7**

**Sheets of 8, #a-h**

**1181-1182** A186 Set of 2 15.00 15.00

**Souvenir Sheets**

**1183-1184** A186 Set of 2 11.50 11.50

Natl. Parks A187

Designs: 20sh, Ngorongoro Crater. 50sh, Ngurdoto Crater. 70sh, Kilimanjaro Natl. Park. 100sh, Gombe Natl. Park. 150sh, Selous Natl. Park. 200sh, Mikumi Natl. Park. 250sh, Serengeti Natl. Park.
500sh, Lake Manyara Natl. Park, vert.

**1993, Oct. 29** **Litho.** ***Perf. 12***

**1185-1191** A187 Set of 7 3.75 3.75

**Souvenir Sheet**

**1192** A187 500sh multicolored 2.50 2.50

Nos. 1185-1192 are dated 1993 but were not available until Oct. 1994.

Historical African Costumes
A188

Designs: 20sh, Berts style. 40sh, Galla style. 50sh, Guinean warrior. 70sh, Goloff style. 100sh, Peul style. 150sh, Abyssinian warrior. 200sh, Pahuin style.
350sh, Zulu style.

**1993, Dec. 30**

**1193-1199** A188 Set of 7 2.75 2.75

**Souvenir Sheet**

**1200** A189 350sh multicolored 1.50 1.50

Nos. 1193-1200 are dated 1993 but were not available until Oct. 1994.

1994 Winter Olympics, Lillehammer
A189

Designs: 40sh, Downhill skiing. 50sh, Ice hockey. 70sh, Speed skating. 100sh, Bobsled. 120sh, Figure skating. 170sh, Free style skiing. 250sh, Biathlon.
500sh, Slalom skiing.

**1994, Feb. 12**

**1201-1207** A189 Set of 7 4.25 4.25

**Souvenir Sheet**

**1208** A189 500sh multicolored 2.25 2.25

Sailing Ships — A190

Designs: 40sh, Jahazi. 50sh, Caravel. 70sh, Carrack. 100sh, Galeas. 170sh, Line of battle ship. 200sh, Frigate. 250sh, Brig.
No. 1210, Bark.

**1994, Apr. 20**

**1209-1215** A190 Set of 7 3.75 3.75

**Souvenir Sheet**

**1216** A190 500sh multicolored 2.25 2.25

Prehistoric Animals — A191

Designs: 40sh, Diatruma. 50sh, Tyranosaurus. 100sh, Uintaterius. 120sh, Stiracosaurus. 170sh, Diplodocus. 250sh, Archaeopteryx. 300sh, Sordes.
500sh, Dimetrodon, vert.

**1994, June 30**

**1217-1223** A191 Set of 7 7.50 7.50

**Souvenir Sheet**

**1224** A191 500sh multicolored 2.25 2.25

Intl. Year of the Family — A192

Designs: 40sh, Family. 120sh, Father playing ball with children. 170sh, People at clinic, horiz. 250sh, Woman harvesting in field.
300sh, Emblem.

***Perf. 12x12½, 12½x12***

**1994, Aug. 30** **Litho.**

**1225-1228** A192 Set of 4 3.75 3.75

**Souvenir Sheet**

**1229** A192 300sh multicolored 3.50 3.50

Zanzibar Revolution, 30th Anniv. — A193

Designs: 40sh, Pres. Salmin Amour. 70sh, Abeid Amani Karume, first president. 120sh, Processing cloves, horiz. 250sh, Zanzibar door.
500sh, Hands clasped over map.

**1994, Aug. 1**

**1230-1233** A193 Set of 4 3.75 3.75

**Souvenir Sheet**

**1234** A193 500sh multicolored 3.25 3.25

Arachnids
A194

Designs: 40sh, Trombidium. 50sh, Eurypelma. 100sh, Salticus. 120sh, Micrommata rosea, vert. 170sh, Araneus, vert. 250sh, Micrathena, vert. 300sh, Araneus diadematus, vert.
500sh, Hadogenes, vert.

***Perf. 12½x12, 12x12½***

**1994, Aug. 31**

**1235-1241** A194 Set of 7 4.75 4.75

**Souvenir Sheet**

**1242** A194 500sh multicolored 2.25 2.25

Butterflies and Flowers
A195

No. 1243, 120sh: a, Lunaria biennis, papilio glaucus. b, Phlox paniculata, danaus plexippus. c, Rudbeckia gloriosa, papilio troilus. d, Tithonia rotundifolia, hypolimnas antevorta. e, Osteospermum, cirrochroa imperatrix. f, Ursinia anethoides, vanessa atalanta. g, Wahlenbergia gloriosa, limenitis archippus. h, Mentzelia lindleyi, hypolimnas pandarus. i, Paeonia suffruticosa, anthocharis belia.

No. 1244, 120sh: a, Coreopsis laneolata, limenitis sydyi. b, Lantana camara, agraulis vanillae. c, Asclepias tuberosa, danaus chrysippus. d, Verbena canadensis, eurytides marcellus. e, Lonicera japonica, artopoetes pryeri. f, Pentas bussei, heliconius charitonius. g, Echinacea purpurea, limenitis weidemeyerii. h, Myosotis alpestris, phoebis sennae. i, Aster amellus, timelaea albescens.

No. 1245, 1000sh, Buddleia davidii, papilio polyxenes. No. 1246, 1000sh, Helianthus annuus, vanessa cardui.

**1994, Nov. 19** ***Perf. 14***

**Sheets of 9, #a-i**

**1243-1244** A195 Set of 2 15.00 15.00

**Souvenir Sheets**

**1245-1246** A195 Set of 2 12.50 12.50

First Manned Moon Landing, 25th Anniv.
A196

No. 1247, 150sh: a, Map of landing site. b, Location of Sea of Tranquility shown on Moon. c, Craters. d, Launch. e, Second stage separation. f, Separation of lunar modules. g, Command module, "Columbia," landing module, "Eagle." h, "Eagle" descending. i, Inside module.

No. 1248, 150sh: a, Michael Collins, Neil Armstrong, Edwin "Buzz" Aldrin. b, "Eagle" on lunar surface. c, Stepping foot on moon. d, Erecting solar wind devices. e, Gathering soil samples. f, Reflection in helmet. g, Astronaut, US flag. h, Carrying equipment. i, "Eagle" ascending from lunar surface.

No. 1249, 150sh: a, "Columbia" above lunar surface, Earth on horizon. b, "Eagle" above lunar surface. c, Release of S-4B rocket. d, Heading toward Earth. e, Re-entering atmosphere. f, Splashdown. g, Pickup at sea. h, Helicopter lifting men on board. i, Astronauts in quarantine.

**1994, Nov. 30**

**Sheets of 9, #a-i**

**1247-1249** A196 150sh Set of 3 26.00 26.00

A197

Dinosaurs — A198

No. 1250: a, Brontosaurus (e). b, Albertosaurus. c, Parasaurolophus. d, Pteranodon. e, Stegosaurus. f, Tyrannosaurus. g, Triceratops. h, Ornitholestes. i, Camarasaurus. j, Ankylosaurus. k, Trachodon. l, Allosaurus. m, Corythosaurus. n, Struthiomimus. o, Camptosaurus. p, Heterodontosaurus.

No. 1251: a, Deinonychus. b, Styracosaurus. c, Anatosaurus. d, Plateosaurus. e, Iguanodon. f, Oviraptor. g, Dimorphodon. h, Ornithomimus. i, Lambeosaurus. j, Megalosaurus. k, Cetiosaurus. l, Hypsilophodon. m, Rhamphorhynchus. n, Scelidosaurus. o, Antrodemus. p, Dimetrodon.

1000sh, Brachiosaurus, vert.

**1994, Dec. 26**

**1250** A197 120sh Sheet of 16, #a.-p. 13.50 13.50

**1251** A198 120sh Sheet of 16, #a.-p. 13.50 13.50

**Souvenir Sheet**

**1252** A197 1000sh multi 7.00 7.00

No. 1250 is a continuous design.

Mickey Mouse, Safari Club — A199

Designs: No. 1253, 70sh, Donald, Mickey, lion cubs. No. 1254, 70sh, Goofy leaning on Donald. No, 1255, 100sh, Donald wearing tree disguise. No. 1256, 100sh, Donald under elephant. No. 1257, 120sh, Donald, hippopotamus. No. 1258, 120sh, Mickey writing in diary. No. 1259, 150sh, Goofy carrying gear, Donald, Mickey. No. 1260, 150sh, Mickey, elephant, Donald, Goofy in rain. No. 1261, 200sh, Donald, Goofy, Mickey reading book, lion. No. 1262, 200sh, Goofy, zebras. No. 1263, 250sh, Mickey, giraffe. No. 1264, 250sh, Donald filming picture.

No. 1265, 1000sh, Goofy hanging from tree, vert. No. 1266, 1000sh, Goofy holding camera, Donald, vert. No. 1267, 1000sh, Mickey holding camera, vert.

**1994, Dec. 26** ***Perf. 14x13½***

**1253-1264** A199 Set of 12 12.50 12.50

**Souvenir Sheets**

***Perf. 13½x14***

**1265-1267** A199 Set of 3 15.00 15.00

A200

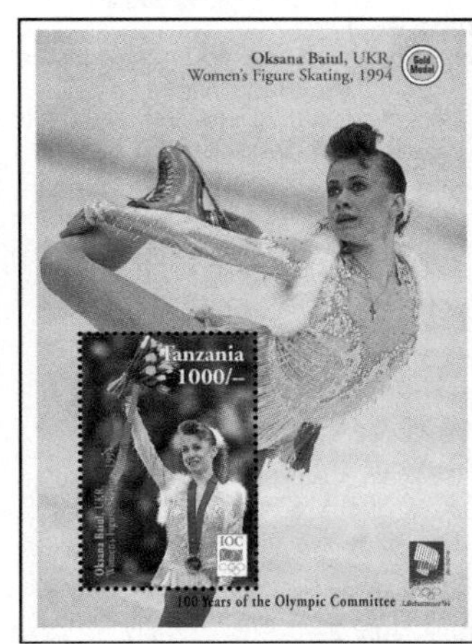


Olympic Gold Medalists — A201

Designs: 350sh, Kristin Otto, Germany, 50m free-style swimming, 1988. 500sh, Carl Lewis, US, track & field, 1984, 1988.
1000sh, Oksana Baiul, Ukraine, women's figure skating, 1994.

**1994, Dec. 12** **Litho.** ***Perf. 14***

**1268** A200 350sh multicolored 1.60 1.60

**1269** A200 500sh multicolored 2.25 2.25

**Souvenir Sheet**

**1270** A201 1000sh multicolored 4.50 4.50

Intl. Olympic Committee, cent. (#1270).

D-Day, 50th Anniv.
A202

350sh, Combined forces attack Atlantic wall. 600sh, Waterproofed tanks support Marines at Omaha Beach.

No. 1273, 200sh: a, Gen. Eisenhower, US forces, Omaha Beach. b, P-51 Mustang, D-Day armada. c, US Coast Guard cutter, landing craft. d, US troops approaching Omaha Beach. e, US troops landing on Omaha Beach. f, US forces on Omaha Beach.

No. 1274, 200sh: a, Gen. Montgomery, White Ensign flies over Normandy beach. b, British forces with Churchill Avre tank, Gold Beach. c, USS Thompson refueled en route to Omaha Beach. d, HMS Warspite fires on German positions, Sword Beach. e, Royal Marine commandoes landing, Juno Beach. f, Sherman Crab flail tank landing on Normandy beach.

No. 1275, 200sh: a, Supermarine Spitfire over Normandy beaches. b, Bren gun carriers, Gold Beach. c, Le Regiment de la Chaudiere, Juno Beach. d, Canadian forces land on Juno Beach. e, Sherman tank on Normandy beach. f, German artillery fires on D-Day Armada.

No. 1276, 1000sh, US forces prepare to embark from England to Normandy beaches. No. 1277, 1000sh, US forces on Utah Beach. No. 1278, 1000sh, Beach obstacles.

**1994, Dec. 12 Litho. *Perf. 14***

| | | | |
|---|---|---|---|
| **1271** A202 350sh multicolored | 1.75 | 1.75 |
| **1272** A202 600sh multicolored | 3.25 | 3.25 |

**Sheets of 6, #a-f**

| | | |
|---|---|---|
| **1273-1275** A202 Set of 3 | 18.00 | 18.00 |

**Souvenir Sheets**

| | | |
|---|---|---|
| **1276-1278** A202 Set of 3 | 15.00 | 15.00 |

Raptors A203

Designs: 40sh, Terathopius ecaudatus, vert. 50sh, Spizaetus ornatus, vert. 100sh, Pandion haliaetus, vert. 120sh, Vultur gryphus, vert. 170sh, Haliaetus vocifer. 250sh, Sarcoramphus papa, vert. 400sh, Falco peregrinus.

500sh, Pseudogyps africanus, vert.

***Perf. 12x12½, 12½x12***

**1994, Sept. 30**

| | | |
|---|---|---|
| **1279-1285** A203 Set of 7 | 7.50 | 7.50 |

**Souvenir Sheet**

| | | |
|---|---|---|
| **1286** A203 500sh multicolored | 3.00 | 3.00 |

Endangered Species — A204

Designs: 40sh, Phascolasctos cinereus. 70sh, Ailurus fulgens. 100sh, Aguila. 120sh, Loxodonta africana. 250sh, Monachus tropicalis. 400sh, Eschrichtius gibbosus. 500sh, Cetacea.

500sh, Panthera tigris, vert.

**1994, July 29 *Perf. 12½x12***

| | | |
|---|---|---|
| **1287-1293** A204 Set of 7 | 7.25 | 7.25 |

**Souvenir Sheet**

***Perf. 12x12½***

| | | |
|---|---|---|
| **1294** A204 500sh multicolored | 2.75 | 2.75 |

No. 1288 shows a Giant Panda, and is incorrectly inscribed with the scientific name of the Lesser Panda.

Crabs — A205

Designs: 40sh, Astacus leptodactytus, horiz. 100sh, Eriocheir sinensis. 120sh, Caneer opillo. 170sh, Cardisoma quanhumi, horiz. 250sh, Birgus latro. 300sh, Menippe mercenaria, horiz. 400sh, Dromia vulgaris.

No. 1302, Callinectes sapidus, horiz.

***Perf. 12½x12, 12x12½***

**1994, Nov. 30 Litho.**

| | | |
|---|---|---|
| **1295-1301** A205 Set of 7 | 4.50 | 4.50 |

**Souvenir Sheet**

| | | |
|---|---|---|
| **1302** A205 500sh multicolored | 2.25 | 2.25 |

Flowers — A206

Designs: 40sh, Dicentra spectabilis. 100sh, Thunbergia alata. 120sh, Cyrtanthus minimiflorus. 170sh, Nepenthes hybrida. 250sh, Allamanda cathartica. 300sh, Encyclia pentotis. 400sh, Protea lacticolor.

500sh, Tradescantia.

**1995, Oct. 31 *Perf. 12x12½***

| | | |
|---|---|---|
| **1303-1309** A206 Set of 7 | 6.00 | 6.00 |

**Souvenir Sheet**

| | | |
|---|---|---|
| **1310** A206 500sh multicolored | 2.25 | 2.25 |

Dated 1994.

Woodstock Music Festival, 25th Anniv. — A207

Illustration reduced.

**1995 Litho. *Imperf.***

**Size: 124x84mm**

| | | |
|---|---|---|
| **1311** A207 2000sh Jimi Hendrix | 9.00 | 9.00 |

**Souvenir Sheet**

**Self-Adhesive**

| | | |
|---|---|---|
| **1312** A207 2000sh Carlos Santana | 9.00 | 9.00 |

**Size: 115x122mm**

***Imperf***

**Self-Adhesive**

| | | |
|---|---|---|
| **1313** A207 2000sh John Lee Hooker | 9.00 | 9.00 |

Issued: #1311, 2/27; #1312, 5/15; #1313, 8/22.

Space Probes and Satellites A208

Designs: 40sh, Hubble telescope. 100sh, Mariner. 120sh, Voyager 2. 170sh, Work Package 03. 250sh, Orbiting solar observatory (OSO). 300sh, Magellan. 400sh, Galileo.

500sh, FOBOS.

**1994, Dec. 30 Litho. *Perf. 12½x12***

| | | |
|---|---|---|
| **1319-1325** A208 Set of 7 | 6.25 | 6.25 |

**Souvenir Sheet**

| | | |
|---|---|---|
| **1326** A208 500sh multicolored | 3.00 | 3.00 |

Sierra Club, Cent. A209

No. 1327, 150sh, vert: a, Black rhinoceros. b, Aye-aye. c, Aye-aye, holding claw at mouth. d, Giraffes, Masai Mara Reserve. e, Red lechwe, group. f, Red lechwe running. g, White-handed gibbon, white coat. h, White-handed gibbon, dark coat. i, White-handed gibbon, ready to climb tree.

No. 1328, 150sh: a, Aye-aye. b, Black rhinoceros facing each other. c, Black rhinoceros. d, Red lechwe. e, Lions fighting, Masai Mara Reserve. f, Hyena, Masai Mara Reserve. g, Nile crocodile in water. h, Nile crocodile, mouth open. i, Nile crocodile in grass.

**1995, July 6 Litho. *Perf. 14***

**Sheets of 9, #a-i**

| | | |
|---|---|---|
| **1327-1328** A209 Set of 2 | 17.00 | 17.00 |

Fruit A210

Designs: 70sh, Coconuts. 100sh, Pineapple. 150sh, Pawpaw. 200sh, Tomato.

500sh, Coconuts.

**1995, June 30**

| | | |
|---|---|---|
| **1329-1332** A210 Set of 4 | 4.75 | 4.75 |

**Souvenir Sheet**

| | | |
|---|---|---|
| **1333** A210 500sh multicolored | 4.75 | 4.75 |

Miniature Sheets of 9

The Beatles — A211

No. 1334, 100sh: a, George Harrison. b, d, e, f, h, Various group portraits. c, Ringo Starr. g, Paul McCartney. i, John Lennon.

No. 1335, 100sh, vert.: a-i, Various portraits of John Lennon.

No. 1336, 500sh, John Lennon, vert. No. 1337, 500sh, Paul McCartney.

**1995 *Perf. 12½***

**Sheets of 9, #a-i**

| | | |
|---|---|---|
| **1334-1335** A211 100sh Set of 2 | 6.25 | 6.25 |

**Souvenir Sheets**

| | | |
|---|---|---|
| **1336-1337** A211 500sh Set of 2 | 5.25 | 5.25 |

No. 1336 contains one 51x76mm stamp. No. 1337 contains one 57x51mm stamp.

Trains A212

No. 1338, 200sh: a, 0-6-0 Italy. b, 0-4-4-OT Mallet, Germany. c, 4-8-0 Tender Engine, Ghana. d, Mallet Tanks, Germany. e, 0-6-2T on the Zillertalbahn, Switzerland. f, Rack Lines, Austria. g, Sweden Jodemans Railway, Norway. h, 4-6-0 Portugal. i, 60CM gauge, Mine Railway, Spain.

No. 1339, 200sh: a, 640 Class 2-6-0s, Italy. b, Norway electric. c, Gordon Highlander 4-40s. d, High Line 9600 class 2-8-0 Japan. e, 4-6-0 Henschel, Portugal. f, Federal German State Railway 220 hydraulic. g, Caledonian 4-2-2, Scotland. h, M2 Locomotive, Denmark. i, Denver & Rio Grande, Western US.

No. 1340, 1000sh, Karl Golsdorf 2-6-0 tank engine, "Germany." No. 1341, 1000sh, High speed ET 403, Germany. No. 1342, 1000sh, AKO 1920, US. No. 1343 1000sh, Porter 2-4-OS, Hawaii.

**1995, July 5 Litho. *Perf. 14***

**Sheets of 9, #a-i**

| | | |
|---|---|---|
| **1338-1339** A212 Set of 2 | 17.00 | 17.00 |

**Souvenir Sheets**

| | | |
|---|---|---|
| **1340-1343** A212 Set of 4 | 19.00 | 19.00 |

Singapore '95.

FAO, 50th Anniv: — A213

No. 1344: a, Boy eating. b, Baby, mother eating. c, Two young people eating.

1000sh, Woman picking fruit, horiz.

**1995, Aug. 14**

| | | |
|---|---|---|
| **1344** A213 250sh Strip of 3, #a.-c. | 4.75 | 4.75 |

**Souvenir Sheet**

| | | |
|---|---|---|
| **1345** A213 1000sh multicolored | 5.00 | 5.00 |

No. 1344 is a continuous design.

Rotary International, 90th Anniv. — A214

Designs: 600sh, Paul Harris, Rotary emblem. 1000sh, Natl. flag, Rotary emblem.

**1995, Aug. 14**

| | | |
|---|---|---|
| **1346** A214 600sh multicolored | 3.25 | 3.25 |

**Souvenir Sheet**

| | | |
|---|---|---|
| **1347** A214 1000sh multicolored | 5.00 | 5.00 |

Queen Mother, 95th Birthday A215

No. 1348: a, Drawing. b, With Queen Elizabeth II. c, Formal portrait. d, In black outfit.

1000sh, Blue dress with pearls.

**1995, Aug. 14 *Perf. 13½x14***

| | | |
|---|---|---|
| **1348** A215 250sh Block or strip of 4, #a.-d. | 4.75 | 4.75 |

**Souvenir Sheet**

| | | |
|---|---|---|
| **1349** A215 1000sh multicolored | 5.00 | 5.00 |

No. 1348 was issued in sheets of 8 stamps.

Sheets of Nos. 1348-1349 exist with black borders overprinted in sheet margins and text "In Memoriam 1900-2002."

End of World War II, 50th Anniv. A216

No. 1350 - Flags of countries shaped as "VJ:" a, Singapore. b, Fiji. c, Malaysia. d, Marshall Islands. e, Philippines. f, Solomon Islands.

No. 1351: a, Pearl Harbor. b, North Africa. c, Battle of Atlantic. d, War in Soviet Union. e, "D" Day, June 6, 1944. f, Holocaust. g, War in Pacific. h, Hiroshima, Enola Gay, mushroom cloud.

No. 1352, 1000sh, Battle of Britain. No. 1353, 1000sh, British soldier, donkey with backpack.

**1995, Aug. 14 Litho. *Perf. 14***

| | | |
|---|---|---|
| **1350** A216 250sh Sheet of 6, #a.-f. + label | 7.50 | 6.00 |

**1351** A216 250sh Sheet of 8, #a.-h. + label 8.00 8.00

**Souvenir Sheets**

**1352-1353** A216 Set of 2 13.00 4.00

Reptiles A217

No. 1354: a, African rock python. b, Bell's hinged tortoise. c, Gaboon viper. d, Royal python. e, Savannah monitor. f, Nile monitor. g, Three-horned chameleon. h, Nile crocodile. i, Rough-scaled bush viper. j, Puff adder. k, Rhinocerous viper. l, Leopard tortoise.

No. 1355, 1000sh, Bush viper. No. 1356, 1000sh, Spitting cobra.

**1995, Sept. 5**

**1354** A217 200sh Sheet of 12, #a.-l. 11.00 11.00

**Souvenir Sheets**

**1355-1356** A217 Set of 2 9.00 9.00

UN, 50th Anniv. — A218

No. 1357 - Various races of people, within group: a, Woman holding baby on shoulders. b, Man holding child in arms. c, One child standing.

1000sh, UN soldier using binoculars.

**1995, Aug. 14 Litho. *Perf. 14***

**1357** A218 250sh Strip of 3, #a.-c. 4.75 4.75

**Souvenir Sheet**

**1358** A218 1000sh multicolored 4.75 4.75

No. 1357 is a continuous design.

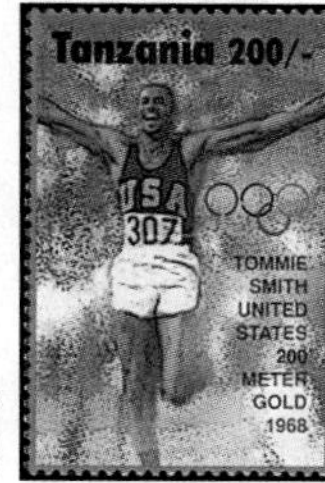


Summer Olympics Gold Medal Winners — A219

No. 1359, 200sh, : a, Tommie Smith, US, 1968. b, Jack Lovelock, New Zealand, 1936. c, Al Oerter, US, 1956-68. d, Daley Thompson, Great Britain, 1980. e, Greg Louganis, US, 1984-88. f, Sammy Lee, US, 1948. g, Dan Gable, US, 1972. h, Helen Meany, US, 1928. i, Sugar Ray Leonard, US, 1976.

No. 1360, 200sh: a, Robert Mathias, US, 1948-52 . b, Larissa Latynina, USSR, 1956. c, Martin Sheridan, US, 1904-08. d, Vera Caslavska, Czechoslovakia, 1968. e, Edwin Moses, US, 1984. f, Jesse Owens, US, 1936. g, Mary Lou Retton, US, 1984. h, Bobby Morrow, US, 1956. i, Joan Benoit, US, 1984.

No. 1361, 1000sh, Florence Griffith Joyner, Jackie Joyner-Kersee, US, 1988. No. 1362, 1000sh, Vasily Alexeyev USSR, 1972-76.

**1995, Sept. 18**

**Sheets of 9, #a-i**

**1359-1360** A219 Set of 2 14.50 14.50

**Souvenir Sheets**

**1361-1362** A219 Set of 2 8.50 8.50

Wild Animals A220

No. 1363: a, Snake, vulture. b, Vulture. c, Giraffe (d, g, h, k, l). d, African bateleur. e, Elephants (f). f, Kob, rhino (b, e, i, j, n). g, Rhinos. h, Baboon. i, Kob (m, n). j, Saddle billed stork, warthog (n). k, Cheetahs (g, j, n). l, African lion (h, k, o, p). m, Vulture. n, Dik-diks. o, Lion cubs. p, Lions (o).

No. 1364: a, Elands. b, Zebras. c, Lions. d, Baboons.

No. 1365, 1000sh, Rhinoceros. No. 1366, 1000sh, Leopard.

**1995, Sept. 15**

**1363** A220 100sh Sheet of 16, #a.-p. 7.75 7.75

**1364** A220 250sh Sheet of 4, #a.-d. 4.75 4.75

**Souvenir Sheets**

**1365-1366** A220 Set of 2 8.50 8.50

UN, 50th Anniv. A221

Designs: 70sh, Corn farming, vert. 100sh, Cultivating land. 150sh, Women spinning cotton in factory. 200sh, Boy drawing at desk, vert.

500sh, UN emblem, "50."

**Wmk. 387**

**1995, Oct. 24 Litho. *Perf. 14***

**1367-1371** A221 Set of 4 4.25 4.25

**Souvenir Sheet**

**1372** A221 500sh multicolored 4.75 4.75

East African Treaty, 2nd Anniv. A222

Designs: 100sh, Heads of State. 150sh, Map, flags, vert. 180sh, Map, cotton, vert. 200sh, Fishing on Lake Victoria.

500sh, Heads of State.

**1995, Oct. 24**

**1373-1376** A222 Set of 4 4.75 4.75

**Souvenir Sheet**

**1377** A222 500sh multicolored 4.75 4.75

Hoofed Animals — A224

Designs: 70sh, Hippopotamus amphibius, horiz. 100sh, Litocranius walleri. 150sh, Sincerus caffer, horiz. 180sh, Antilocapridae, horiz. 200sh, Alcelphus buselaphus. 260sh, Taurotragus oryx. 380sh, Strepsiceros.

500sh, Giraffa camelopardalis.

***Perf. 12½x12, 12x12½***

**1995, May 31 Litho.**

**1380-1386** A224 Set of 7 6.00 6.00

**Souvenir Sheet**

**1387** A224 500sh multicolored 5.75 5.75

Cactus Flowers — A225

Designs: 70sh, Weingartia fidaiana. 100sh, Rebutia spegazziniana. 150sh, Caralluma lugarii. 180sh, Cerochlamys pachyphylla. 200sh, Schlumbergera orssighiana. 260sh, Epiphyllum darrahii. 380sh, Ceropegia nilotica.

500sh, Neoporteria nigrihorrida.

**1995, Aug. 31 *Perf. 12x12½***

**1388-1394** A225 Set of 7 6.00 6.00

**Souvenir Sheet**

**1395** A225 500sh multicolored 5.75 5.75

Bats A226

Designs: 70sh, Cheiromeles torquatus, vert. 100sh, Hypsignatus monstrosus, vert. 150sh, Rhinolophus, ferrum-equinum, vert. 180sh, Plecotus auritus. 200sh, Syconycteris australis, vert. 260sh, Plecotus auritus, vert. 380sh, Otomops martiensseni.

500sh, Pteropus.

**1995, July 31 *Perf. 12x12½, 12½x12***

**1396-1402** A226 Set of 7 6.25 6.25

**Souvenir Sheet**

**1403** A226 500sh multicolored 5.75 5.75

Marine Life of Coral Reefs A227

Designs: 70sh, Medusa. 100sh, Surgeonfish. 150sh, Angelfish. 180sh, Octopus. 200sh, Zebra fish. 260sh, Shark. 380sh, Ray.

500sh, Turtle.

**1995, June 15 *Perf. 12½x12***

**1404-1410** A227 Set of 7 6.00 6.00

**Souvenir Sheet**

**1411** A227 500sh multicolored 5.75 5.75

Jerry Garcia (d. 1995), Musician A228

Scenes of Grateful Dead performing on stage and: No. 1413A, Bears. No. 1413B, Skeletons.

**1995 Litho. *Perf. 12½***

**1412** A228 200sh multicolored 1.00 1.00

**Souvenir Sheet**

**1413** A228 1000sh multicolored 8.50 8.50

**Size: 140x92mm**

***Imperf***

**Self-Adhesive**

**1413A** A228 2000sh multicolored 7.50 7.50

**1413B** A228 2000sh multicolored 7.50 7.50

No. 1412 was issued in sheets of 9. No. 1413 contains one 51x57mm stamp.

Issued: #1412-1413, 11/15/95; #1413A-1413B, 12/21/95.

Rock and Roll Stars A229

No. 1414: a, Chuck Berry. b, Bob Dylan. c, Aretha Franklin. d, The Supremes. e, Buddy Holly. f, Bruce Springsteen. g, Elton John. h, The Rolling Stones. i, Michael Jackson.

1000sh, The Beach Boys (Al Jardin, Mike Love, Brian Wilson, Carl Wilson, Dennis Wilson), horiz.

**1995, Dec. 1 *Perf. 13½x14***

**1414** A229 250sh Sheet of 9, #a.-i. 13.50 13.50

**Souvenir Sheet**

***Perf. 14x13½***

**1415** A229 1000sh multi 7.50 7.50

Motion Pictures, Cent. A230

No. 1416: a, Noah's Ark, Dolores Costello. b, Ben-Hur, 1926, Ramon Novarro. c, Ben-Hur, 1926, Francis X. Bushman. d, Ben-Hur, 1959, Charlton Heston. e, Ben-Hur, 1959, Haya Harareet. f, Ben-Hur, 1959, Sam Jaffe. g, The Ten Commandments, 1923, Theodore Roberts. h, Samson and Delilah, Victor Mature. i, Samson and Delilah, Hedy Lamarr.

No. 1417, The Ten Commandments, Theodore Roberts.

**1995, Dec. 1 *Perf. 13½x14***

**1416** A230 250sh Sheet of 9, #a.-i. 17.00 17.00

**Souvenir Sheet**

**1417** A230 1000sh multi 7.50 7.50

World Tourism Organization, 20th Anniv. — A231

Designs: 100sh, Olduvai Gorge, "Cradle of Mankind." 300sh, First State House, Bagamoyo. 400sh, Mount Kilimanjaro.

500sh, Rhinoceroses, Ngorongoro Crater.

**1995, Dec. 18 Litho. *Perf. 14***

**1418-1420** A231 Set of 3 5.75 5.75

**Souvenir Sheet**

**1421** A231 500sh multicolored 5.50 5.50

Predatory Animals A232

Designs: 70sh, Acinonyx jubatus. 100sh, Felus serval. 150sh, Huaena buana. 200sh, Otocyon megalotis. 250sh, Lucaon pictus. 280sh, Pantera pardus. 300sh, Pantera leo.

500sh, Alligator.

**1995, Sept. 30 Litho.** ***Perf. 12½x12***
**1422-1428** A232 Set of 7 9.50 9.50

**Souvenir Sheet**

**1429** A232 500sh multicolored 4.75 4.75

Horses — A233

No. 1430: a, True black Freisian. b, Appaloosa. c, Arab. d, Paint. e, Chestnut saddlebred. f, Standard thoroughbred. g, Belgian. h, Liver chestnut quarter. i, Hackney.
1000sh, Clydesdale.

**1995** ***Perf. 14***
**1430** A233 250sh Sheet of 9, #a.-i. 17.00 17.00

**Souvenir Sheet**

**1431** A233 1000sh multi 9.50 9.50

No. 685 Surcharged

**70/-**

**1995, May 30 Litho.** ***Perf. 14***
**1431A** A108 70sh on 13sh #685

Paintings from the Metropolitan Museum of Art — A234

No. 1432, 200sh: a, La Orana Maria, by Gauguin. b, Young Herdsman with Cows, by Cuyp. c, Moses and the Burning Bush by, Domenichino. d, Path in the Île Saint-Martin, Vétheuil, by Monet. e, Dances, Pink and Green, by Degas. f, Terrace at Sainte-Adresse, by Monet. g, The Rehearsal Onstage, by Degas. h, Study for "A Sunday on La Grande Jatte," by Seurat.
No. 1433, 200sh: a, Madame Marsollier and Daughter, by Nattier. b, Christ and the Woman of Samaria, by Rembrandt. c, Rubens and His Wife and Son, by Rubens. d, Portrait of a Young Woman, by Vermeer. e, Portrait of a Man, by Van Dyck. f, Young Woman with a Water Jug, by Vermeer. g, Self Portrait, by Rembrandt. h, Young Man and Woman in an Inn, by Hals.
No. 1434, 1000sh, On the Beach at Trouville, by Boudin. No. 1435, 1000sh, A Dance in the Country, by G.D. Tiepolo.

**1996, Mar. 7** ***Perf. 13½x14***

**Sheets of 8, #a-h, + Label**

**1432-1433** A234 Set of 2 19.00 19.00

**Souvenir Sheets**

***Perf. 14***

**1434-1435** A234 Set of 2 15.00 15.00

Nos. 1434-1435 each contain one 81x53mm stamp.

Miniature Sheet

Cats and Dogs — A235

No. 1436 — Cats: a, Siberian. b, Classic silver tabby Persian. c, Brown Burmese. d, Norwegian forest. e, Tabby. f, Blue & white maine coon. g, Brown California spangled cat. h, Black & white bicolor Persian. i, Shaded silver American shorthair.
No. 1437 — Dogs: a, Red labrador. b, St. Bernard. c, Cocker spaniel. d, Black labrador. e, Bernese mountain dog. f, Beagle. g, Miniature pincher. h, Basset hound. i, German shepherd.
No. 1438, Silver tabby British shorthair. No. 1439, Alaskan malamute.

**1996, Mar. 4 Litho.** ***Perf. 14***
**1436** A235 250sh Sheet of 9, #a.-i. 13.50 13.50
**1437** A235 250sh Sheet of 9, #a.-i. 13.50 13.50

**Souvenir Sheets**

**1438** A235 1000sh multi 7.50 7.50
**1439** A235 1000sh multi 7.50 7.50

Souvenir Sheets

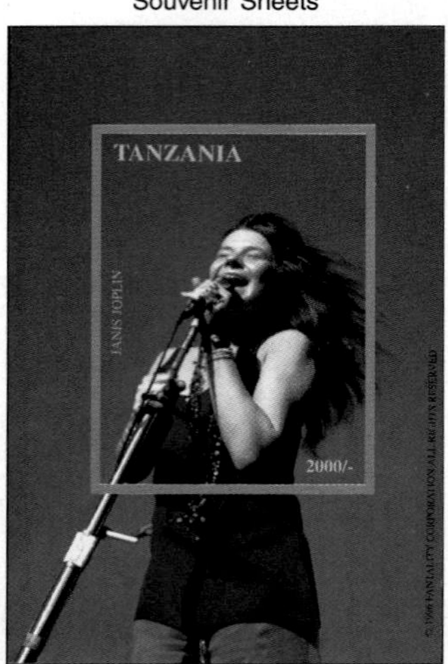


Janis Joplin (1943-70), Rock Musician — A235a

Design: No. 1439B, Joplin seated atop a psychedelically-painted Porsche, horiz. Illustration reduced.

**1996, Apr. 10 Litho.** ***Imperf.***

**Self-Adhesive**

**1439A** A235a 2000sh shown *11.00 11.00*
**1439B** A235a 2000sh multi *11.00 11.00*

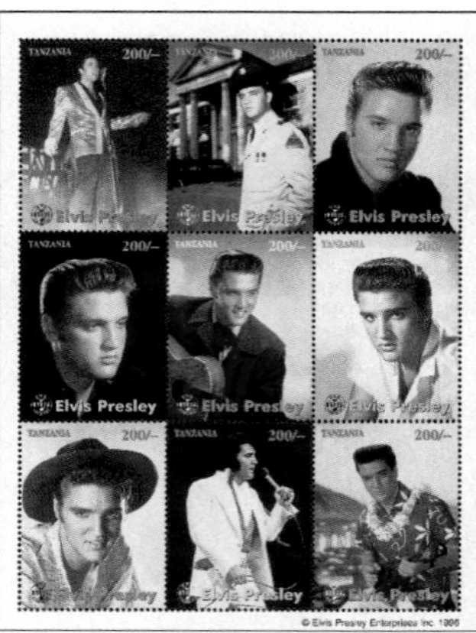


Elvis Presley (1935-77) — A235b

Various photographs with EPE (Elvis Presley Enterprises) official product emblem.

**1996, Mar. 13 Litho.** ***Perf. 12½***
**1439C** A235b 200sh Sheet of 9, #d.-l. 11.50 11.50

New Year 1996 (Year of the Rat) A236

No. 1440: a, Arvicola oryzivora. b, Meriones hudsonicus. c, Mus missouriensis. d, Mus aureolus.
500sh, Fiber zibethicus.

**1996, Apr. 12**
**1440** A236 200sh Block of 4, #a.-d. 4.25 4.25
*e.* Souvenir sheet of 1 #1440 4.25 4.25

**Souvenir Sheet**

**1442** A236 500sh multicolored 4.25 4.25

No. 1440 was issued in sheets of 16 stamps.

Deng Xiaoping, Chinese Communist Leader A237

Various portraits.

**1996, May 6 Litho.** ***Perf. 13***
**1443** A237 250sh Sheet of 6, #a.-f. 11.25 11.25

**Souvenir Sheet**

**1444** A237 500sh multicolored 4.75 4.75

CHINA '96, 9th Asian Intl. Philatelic Exhibition (#1443).

Butterflies A238

Designs: 70sh, Dirphia multicolor. 100sh, Inachis io, vert. 150sh, Automerisio. 200sh, Saturnia pyri. 250sh, Arctia villica. 260sh, Arctia caja. 300sh, Celerio euforbiae, vert.
500sh, Zygaena laeta.

***Perf. 12½x12, 12x12½***

**1996, Jan. Litho.**
**1445-1451** A238 Set of 7 9.50 9.50

**Souvenir Sheet**

**1452** A238 500sh multicolored 4.75 4.75

Frogs A239

Designs: 100sh, Bufo bufo laur. 140sh, Pyxicephalus adspersus. 180sh, Megalixalus laevis. 200sh, Xenopus laevis. 210sh, Hemisus marmoratus. 260sh, Rana beccarii. 300sh, Hyperolius cinctiventrus.
500sh, Rana goliaph.

**1996, Jan. 31** ***Perf. 12½x12***
**1453-1459** A239 Set of 7 7.50 7.50

**Souvenir Sheet**

**1460** A239 500sh multicolored 6.00 6.00

Souvenir Sheet

China 1996 Intl. Philatelic Exhibition — A239a

**1996, June 5 Litho.** ***Perf. 12½***
**1460A** A239a 300sh multi 1.00 1.00

Souvenir Sheet

Shanghai Intl. Tea Culture Festival — A239b

**1996** **Litho.** ***Perf. 12½***
**1460B** A239b 300sh multi 1.00 1.00

Queen Elizabeth II, 70th Birthday — A240

No. 1461: a, Portrait. b, As young woman in evening dress. c, Wearing tiara, jewels.
1000sh, Portrait as young woman.

**1996, July 3 Litho.** ***Perf. 13½x14***
**1461** A240 300sh Strip of 3, #a.-c. 6.00 6.00

**Souvenir Sheet**

**1462** A240 1000sh multicolored 7.00 7.00

No. 1461 was issued in sheets of 9 stamps.

Crocodiles, Alligators — A241

Designs: 100sh, Melanosuchus niger. 150sh, Caiman latirostris. 200sh, Alligator mississipiensis. 250sh, Gavialis gangeticus. 260sh, Crocodylus niloticus. 300sh, Crocodylus cataphractus. 380sh, Crocodylus rhombifer.
500sh, Crocodile.

**1996** ***Perf. 12½x12***
**1463-1469** A241 Set of 7 8.50 8.50

**Souvenir Sheet**

**1470** A241 500sh multicolored 6.75 6.75

Snakes A242

Designs: 100sh, Naja pallida. 140sh, Agkistrodon contortrix. 180sh, Bungarus fasciatus. 200sh, Micrurus frontalis, vert. 260sh, Bitis gabonica, vert. 300sh, Elaphe moellendorffi, vert. 400sh, Vipera ursini, vert.
700sh, Corallus caninus, vert.

**1996** ***Perf. 12½x12, 12x12½***
**1471-1477** A242 Set of 7 8.50 8.50

**Souvenir Sheet**

**1478** A242 700sh multicolored 6.75 6.75

Famous People, Events — A243

No. 1479, 250sh: a, Gandhi. b, Mao Tse-tung. c, Jonas Salk. d, John F. Kennedy. e, Neil Armstrong. f, Mikhail Gorbachev. g, Nelson Mandela. h, Gen. Colin Powell.
No. 1480, 250sh: a, Orville, Wilbur Wright. b, Battle of Verdun, 1916. c, Charles Lindbergh. d, Al Jolson. e, Alexander Fleming. f, Amelia Earhart. g, Franklin Roosevelt, Joseph Stalin, Winston Churchill, Yalta Conference, 1945. h, Atomic bomb blast, 1945, Enrico Fermi.
1000sh, Deng Xiaoping.

**1996, July 15** **Litho.** ***Perf. 14***

**Sheets of 8, #a-h**

**1479-1480** A243 250sh Set of 2 16.00 16.00

**Souvenir Sheet**

**1481** A243 1000sh multicolored 7.50 7.50

A244

Birds — A245

Fruits of East Africa: 140sh, Pineapple. 180sh, Orange, lime. 200sh, Pear, apple. 300sh, Bananas.

**1996, Sept. 4** **Litho.** ***Perf. 13***
**1482-1485** A244 Set of 4 6.00 6.00
*1485a* Souv. sheet of 1 #1485 3.75 3.75

**1996, Sept. 16** ***Perf. 14***

No. 1486, 300sh: a, Vidua macroura. b, Tockus erythrorynchus. c, Trachyphonus erythrocephalus. d, Bubo capensis. e, Gyps ruppellii. f, Sarkidiornis melanotus. g, Dendrocygna bicolor. h, Struthio camelus.
No. 1487, 300sh: a, Gypohierax angolensis. b, Aquila chrysaetos. c, Spilornis rufipectus. d, Eutriorchis astur. e, Haliaeetus albicilla. f, Ichthyophaga ichthyaetus. g, Spilornis holospilus. h, Dryotriorchis spectabilis.
No. 1488, African paradise flycatcher. No. 1489, Haliaeetus leucocephala, horiz.

**Sheets of 8, #a-h**

**1486-1487** A245 300sh Set of 2 22.50 22.50

**Souvenir Sheets**

**1488** A245 1000sh multicolored 7.50 7.50
**1489** A245 1000sh multicolored 7.50 7.50

Reef Fish A246

Designs: 100sh, Yellowtail wrasse. 150sh, Jewel grouper. 250sh, Barred thick-lipped wrasse. 500sh, Bullethead parrotfish.
No. 1494: a, Golden cardinal fish. b, Yellowhead butterfly fish. c, Common banner fish (diver). d, Zanzibar butterfly fish. e, Lemon damsel. f, Blue and gold fusilier. g, Red firegoby. h, Threadfin fairy basslet. i, Rein rock basslet.
No. 1495, 1000sh, African pygmy angelfish. No. 1496, 1000sh, Blue green chromis.

**1996, Sept. 23**
**1490-1493** A246 Set of 4 7.50 7.50
**1494** A246 200sh Sheet of 9, #a.-i. 11.50 11.50

**Souvenir Sheets**

**1495-1496** A246 Set of 2 8.00 8.00

Ferrari Cars A247

No. 1497: a, 1964 250LM. b, 1992 456 GT. c, 1995 F50. d, 1995 F512 M "Testarossa." e, 1984 BB 512. f, 1955 410 S coupe.
1000sh, 1964 250 GTO.

**1996, Sept. 27** **Litho.** ***Perf. 14***
**1497** A247 250sh Sheet of 6, #a.-f. 11.50 11.50

**Souvenir Sheet**

**1498** A247 1000sh multi 7.50 7.50

No. 1498 contains one 85x28mm stamp.

Radio, Cent. A248

Designs: 70sh, Franklin D. Roosevelt, 1st fireside chat, 1933. 100sh, Harry S. Truman announces US use of atomic bomb, 1945. 150sh, Orson Welles, "Alien Invasion" broadcast, 1938. 200sh, Fiorello La Guardia reads newspaper comics via radio.
1000sh, Robin Williams as Adrian Cronauer, "Good Morning Viet Nam."

**1996, July 15** **Litho.** ***Perf. 13½x14***
**1499-1502** A248 Set of 4 3.75 3.75

**Souvenir Sheet**

**1503** A248 1000sh multicolored 7.50 7.50

Mercedes-Benz Automobiles — A249

No. 1504: a, 1952 300SL Coupè 1. b, 1932 680S. c, 1934 500K. d, 1934 Type 150. e, 1934 Type 150 Sport Roadster "Heck." f, 1937 W125.
1000sh, 1936 540K Roadster Class A.

**1996, Sept. 27** ***Perf. 14***
**1504** A249 250sh Sheet of 6, #a.-f. 10.50 10.50

**Souvenir Sheet**

**1505** A249 1000sh multi 7.50 7.50

UNICEF, 50th Anniv. — A250

Designs: 200sh, Child holding bowl. 250sh, Mother breastfeeding infant. 500sh, Tetsuko Kuroyanaga holding child.
1000sh, Girl.

**1996, Oct. 4**
**1506-1508** A250 Set of 3 6.75 6.75

**Souvenir Sheet**

**1509** A250 1000sh multicolored 7.00 7.00

UNESCO, 50th Anniv. — A251

Designs: 200sh, Ngorongoro Conservation Area, Tanzania. 250sh, Los Katios Natl. Park, Colombia. 600sh, Kilwa Kisiwani Makutani Complex, Tanzania.
1000sh, Kilimanjaro Natl. Park, Tanzania.

**1996, Oct. 4**
**1510-1512** A251 Set of 3 7.50 7.50

**Souvenir Sheet**

**1513** A251 1000sh multicolored 7.50 7.50

Flowers — A252

No. 1514, 300sh: a, Lily of the valley. b, Spanish iris. c, Spiderwort. d, Morning glory. e, Gazania. f, Pansy. g, Begonia. h, Madonna lily.
No. 1515, 300sh: a, Snowdrop. b, Treesia. c, Cosmos. d, Daffodil. e, Blue himalayan poppy. f, Blue daisy. g, Zinnia flore-pleno. h, Oriental poppy.
No. 1516, 1000sh, Fuchsia. No. 1517, 1000sh, Hanson's lily.

**1996, Oct. 25**

**Sheets of 8, #1-h + Label**

**1514-1515** A252 Set of 2 24.00 24.00

**Souvenir Sheets**

**1516-1517** A252 Set of 2 13.50 13.50

Domestic Cats A253

Designs: 100sh, Lilac point Siamese. 150sh, Somali. 200sh, British blue shorthair.
No. 1521: a, American shorthair silver tabby. b, Scottish fold. c, Persian blue. d, Ocicat.
1000sh, Ragdoll.

**1996, Dec. 10** **Litho.** ***Perf. 14***
**1518-1520** A253 Set of 3 2.75 2.75
**1521** A253 300sh Sheet of 4, #a.-d. 7.00 7.00

**Souvenir Sheet**

**1522** A253 1000sh multicolored 7.50 7.50

Dogs A254

Designs: 70sh, Shar-pei. 250sh, Beagle. 600sh, Keeshond.
No. 1527: a, St. Bernard. b, Shetland sheepdog. c, Samoyed. d, Australian cattle dog.
1000sh, Collie.

**1996, Dec. 10** **Litho.** ***Perf. 14***
**1524-1526** A254 Set of 3 5.75 5.75
**1527** A254 300sh Sheet of 4, #a.-d. 8.50 8.50

**Souvenir Sheet**

**1528** A254 1000sh multicolored 7.50 7.50

Nos. 767-768, 1001-1002, 1026-1028 Ovptd.

a

b

c

**1996, Dec. 16**
**1529** A120(a-b) 50sh Sheet of 16, #a.-p. (#767) 3.25 3.25
**1530** A120(c) 50sh Sheet of 16, #a.-p. (#768) 3.25 3.25
**1531** A154(a-b) 100sh Sheet of 12, #a.-l. (#1001) 4.75 4.75
**1532** A158(c) 100sh Sheet of 6, #a.-f. (#1026) 2.40 2.40
**1533** A158(c) 100sh Sheet of 6, #a.-f. (#1027) 2.40 2.40

**Souvenir Sheets**

**1534** A154(c) 500sh on #1002 2.00 2.00
**1535** A158(a) 500sh on #1028 2.00 2.00

Size and location of overprint varies.
Overprints types a-b appear on alternating stamps of Nos. 1529, 1531.
Nos. 1529-1533 have additional overprints in sheet margin.

Mushrooms A255

No. 1536, 300sh: a, Amanita phalloides. b, Amanita muscaria. c, Morchella vulgaris. d, Tricholoma aurantium. e, Amanita caesarea. f, Psalliota haemorrhoidaria. g, Russula virescens. h, Boletus crocipodius.

No. 1537, 300sh: a, Coprinus comatus. b, Amanitopsis vaginata. c, Clitocybe geotropa. d, Cortinarius violaceus. e, Russula sardonia. f, Cortinarius collinitus. g, Boletus aereus. h, Lepiota procera.

No. 1538, 1000sh, Ganoderma lucidum. No. 1539, 1000sh, Collybia distorta.

**1996, Dec. 17**

**Sheets of 8, #a-h**

**1536-1537** A255 Set of 2 26.00 26.00

**Souvenir Sheets**

**1538-1539** A255 Set of 2 13.00 13.00

Souvenir Sheet

Watercolor Painting — A256

Illustration reduced.

**1996, May 6 Litho. *Perf. 13***

**1540** A256 500sh multicolored 4.25 4.25

China '96. No. 1540 was not available until March 1997.

Sun Yat-Sen (1866-1925) A257

Various portraits.

**1997 *Perf. 14***

**1541** A257 300sh Sheet of 6, #a.-f. 11.50 11.50

**Souvenir Sheet**

**1542** A257 1000sh multi 7.50 7.50

Hong Kong '97.

Horses A258

No. 1543: a, Blue Arabian horse. b, English thoroughbred. c, Tennessee walking horse. d, Anglo-Arab horse.

No. 1544: a, Trakehner. b, American saddlebred. c, Morgan. d, Frederiksborg. e, Mirror of #d. f, Mirror of #c. g, Mirror of #b. h, Mirror of #a.

No. 1545, 1000sh, Wielkopolski. No. 1546, 1000sh, Thiawari, vert.

**1997, Mar. 20 Litho. *Perf. 14***

**1543** A258 250sh Strip of 4, #a.-d. 7.50 7.50

**1544** A258 250sh Sheet of 8, #a.-h. 13.50 13.50

**Souvenir Sheets**

**1545-1546** A258 Set of 2 13.00 13.00

No. 1543 was issued in sheets of 8 stamps with second strip in reverse order.

COMESA A259

Designs140sh, Tourism. 180sh, Fishing. 200sh, Dar es Salaam Port. 300sh, TAZARA Railway.

**1997 *Perf. 13***

**1547-1550** A259 Set of 4 6.25 6.25

**Souvenir Sheet**

**1551** A259 500sh Cotton 4.50 4.50

UN Volunteers, 25th Anniv. A260

Designs: 140sh, Health of mother and child. 200sh, Food distribution. 260sh, Clean water distribution. 300sh, Public education.

500sh, Refugee camp.

**1997**

**1552-1555** A260 Set of 4 6.75 6.75

**Souvenir Sheet**

**1556** A260 500sh multicolored 4.75 4.75

Birds A261

Designs: 150sh, Mockingbird. 200sh, House finch. 410sh, Bridled titmouse. 500sh, Cactus wren.

No. 1561: a, Sooty tern. b, Nunbird. c, Mottled wood owl. d, Turquoise-browed mot mot. e, Emerald toucanet. f, Dusky-headed conure.

No. 1562: a, Maguari stork. b, Spoonbills. c, Flamingo. d, Hammerkop. e, Limpkin. f, Pink-backed pelican.

No. 1563, 1000sh, Masked booby. No. 1564, 1000sh, Brown pelican.

**1997, May 5 Litho. *Perf. 14***

**1557-1560** A261 Set of 4 7.50 7.50

**1561** A261 140sh Sheet of 6, #a.-f. 4.50 4.50

**1562** A261 370sh Sheet of 6, #a.-f. 12.00 12.00

**Souvenir Sheets**

**1563-1564** A261 Set of 2 11.00 11.00

Flowers

A262 A263

Designs: 100sh, Plumeria rubra acutifolia. 140sh, 150sh, Liliaceae. 180sh, Alamanda. 200sh, Lilaceae, diff. 210sh, Zinnia. 260sh, Malvaviscus penduliflorus. 300sh, Carna. 380sh, Nerium oleander carneum. 400sh, Hibiscus rosa sinensis. 500sh, Catharanthus roseus. 600sh, Cartharanthus roseus. 700sh, Bougainvillea formosa. 750sh, Acalypha.

No. 1577: a, like #1571. b, like #1569. c, like #1572. d, like #1575.

**1997-2004(?) *Perf. 14½x15***

| | | | | |
|---|---|---|---|---|
| **1565** | A262 100sh multi | .40 | .40 |
| **1566** | A262 140sh multi | .60 | .60 |
| **1566A** | A262 150sh multi | | |
| **1567** | A262 180sh multi | .75 | .75 |
| **1568** | A262 200sh multi | .80 | .80 |
| **1569** | A262 210sh multi | .85 | .85 |
| **1570** | A262 260sh multi | 1.00 | 1.00 |
| **1571** | A262 300sh multi | 1.25 | 1.25 |
| **1572** | A262 380sh multi | 1.50 | 1.50 |
| **1573** | A262 400sh multi | 1.60 | 1.60 |
| **1573A** | A262 500sh multi | 1.00 | 1.00 |
| **1574** | A262 600sh multi | 2.40 | 2.40 |
| **1575** | A262 700sh multi | 2.75 | 2.75 |
| **1576** | A262 750sh multi | 3.00 | 3.00 |
| | *Nos. 1565-1566,1567-1576 (13)* | 17.90 | 17.90 |

**Souvenir Sheet**

***Perf. 14½x14***

**1577** A263 125sh Sheet of 4, #a.-d. 2.00 2.00

Issued: #1566A, 1997; #1573A, 2004(?); others, 5/19.

For overprint see No. O49.

Modern Olympic Games, Cent., 1996 Summer Olympic Games, Atlanta, — A264

**1996 Litho. *Perf. 11½***

| | | | |
|---|---|---|---|
| **1578** | A264 100sh Tennis | .80 | .80 |
| **1579** | A264 150sh Baseball | 1.25 | 1.25 |
| **1580** | A264 200sh Soccer | 1.50 | 1.50 |
| **1581** | A264 300sh Boxing | 2.50 | 2.50 |
| | *Nos. 1578-1581 (4)* | 6.05 | 6.05 |

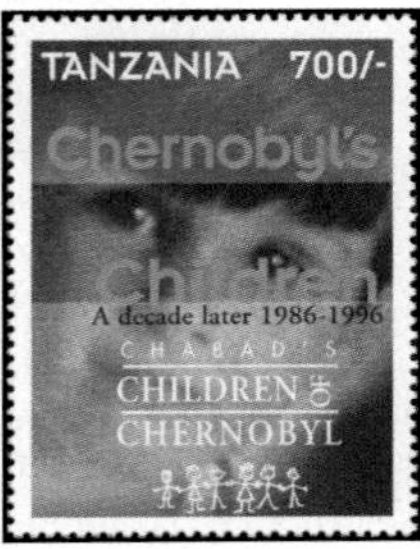


Chernobyl Disaster, 10th Anniv. A265

Designs: No. 1582, Chabad's Children of Chernobyl. No. 1583, UNESCO.

**1997, Apr. 25 Litho. *Perf. 13½x14***

**1582** A265 700sh multicolored 4.75 4.75

**1583** A265 700sh multicolored 4.75 4.75

Flowers A266

No. 1583A: b, Prunus dulcis. c, Spassky Clock tower. d, Crataegus monogyna. e, Amica montana. f, Campanula patula. g, Papaver orientalis.

No. 1584: a, Malus niedzwetzkayana. b, Golden domes of the Cathedral of the Annunciation, Moscow. c, Polygonatum multiflorum. d, Leucanthemum vulgare, e, Hypencum perforatum. f, Pulsatilla vulgaris.

No. 1585, 1000sh, Laburnum anagyroides, St. Basil's Cathedral, vert. No. 1585A, 1000sh, Rosa canina, Church of Christ Resurrection, Moscow.

**1997 *Perf. 14x14½***

**1583A** A266 200sh Sheet of 6, #b.-g. 9.00 9.00

**1584** A266 300sh Sheet of 6, #a.-f. 13.50 13.50

**Souvenir Sheets**

**1585-1585A** A266 Set of 2 13.00 13.00

No. 1585 contains one 30x38mm stamp.

World AIDS Day A267

Designs: 140sh, Condom protects against AIDS, vert. 310sh, Caution, you may contract AIDS. 370sh, Control of AIDS is our responsibility. 410sh, Care and support AIDS orphans.

500sh, Like #1586.

**1997 Litho. *Perf. 13***

**1586-1589** A267 Set of 4 8.50 8.50

**Souvenir Sheet**

**1590** A267 500sh multicolored 4.25 4.25

Paintings by Hiroshige (1797-1858) A268

No. 1591: a, Aoi Slope, Outside Toranomon Gate. b, Bikuni Bridge in Snow. c, Mount Atago, Shiba. d, Akasaka Kiribatake. e, Zojoji Pagoda & Akabane. f, Hibiya & Soto-Sakurada from Yamashita-cho.

No. 1592, 1000sh, Shiba Shinmei Shrine. No. 1593, 1000sh, Kanasugibashi Shibaura.

**1997, July 21 Litho. *Perf. 13½x14***

**1591** A268 250sh Sheet of 6, #a.-f. 9.50 9.50

**Souvenir Sheets**

**1592-1593** A268 Set of 2 6.50 6.50

Queen Elizabeth II and Prince Philip, 50th Anniv. A269

No. 1594: a, Engagement picture of Queen. b, Royal arms. c, Queen, Prince in casual attire. d, Prince, Queen. e, Balmoral Castle. f, Prince Philip.

1500sh, Formal portrait.

**1997, July 21 Litho. *Perf. 14***

**1594** A269 370sh Sheet of 6, #a.-f. 9.50 9.50

**Souvenir Sheet**

**1595** A269 1500sh multicolored 9.50 9.50

Return of Hong Kong to China — A270

No. 1596 — Split design comparing modern and early photographs of: a, Clock Tower, Tsim Sha Tsu, former terminal of Kowloon-Canton Railways. b, Legislative Council Building, previously Supreme Court.

No. 1597: a, Signing of Sino-British Joint Declaration on Question of Hong Kong, 1984. b, Deng Xiaoping, Chinese leaders, c, C.F. Tung, first Chinese chief executive of Hong Kong, 1996.

Illustration reduced.

**1997, July 21** *Perf. 14½*

**1596** A270 1000sh Sheet of 2, #a.-b. 6.75 6.75
**1597** A270 1000sh Sheet of 3, #a.-c. 10.00 10.00

No. 1597 contains 3 59x28mm stamps.

Grimm's Fairy Tales A271

Mother Goose — A272

No. 1598 — Rumpelstiltskin: a, Woman at spinning wheel, Prince. b, Woman, Rumpelstiltskin at spinning wheel. c, Prince, woman playing mandolin.
No. 1599, Girl whistling. No. 1600, Rumpelstiltskin.

**1997** *Perf. 13½x14*

**1598** A271 400sh Sheet of 3, #a.-c. 4.00 4.00

**Souvenir Sheets**

*Perf. 14*

**1599** A272 1000sh multicolored 3.25 3.25

*Perf. 13½x14*

**1600** A271 1500sh multicolored 5.00 5.00

1998 Winter Olympic Games, Nagano — A273

Designs: 100sh, Torvill & Dean, ice dancing. 200sh, Katarina Witt, figure skating. 500sh, First Olympic winter games, 1924, curling introduced. 600sh, Pirmin Zurbriggen, downhill skiing.
No. 1605: a, Dan Jansen, 1000m speed skating. b, Alberto Tomba, slalom & giant slalom skiing. c, Herma Plank-Szabo, figure skating. d, Donna Weinbrecht, mogul skiing.
No. 1606, 1000sh, Yukio Kasaya, ski jump. No. 1607, 1000sh, Barbara Ann Scott, figure skating.

**1997, Oct. 6** **Litho.** *Perf. 14*

**1601-1604** A273 Set of 4 8.00 8.00
**1605** A273 250sh Block or strip of 4, #a.-d. 5.50 5.50

**Souvenir Sheets**

**1606-1607** A273 Set of 2 11.50 11.50

Sinking of MV Bukoba A274

Designs: 140sh, Ship sinking. 350sh, Removing bodies. 370sh, Identification of the dead. 410sh, Mass funeral.
500sh, MV Bukoba.

**1997, May 21** **Litho.** *Perf. 14*

**1608-1611** A274 Set of 4 7.50 7.50

**Souvenir Sheet**

*Perf. 14½*

**1612** A274 500sh multicolored 3.75 3.75

Tourist Attractions of East Africa — A275

Designs: 140sh, Mount Kilimanjaro. 310sh, Masai. 370sh, Zanzibar old stonetown. 410sh, Buffalo, plains of Ruaha.
500sh, Mount Kilimanjaro Kibo Peak.

**1997, Oct. 9** *Perf. 13½*

**1613-1616** A275 Set of 4 7.50 7.50

**Souvenir Sheet**

**1617** A275 500sh multicolored 3.75 3.75

1998 World Cup Soccer Championships, France — A276

Teams: 100sh, Italy, 1938. 150sh, Brazil, 1970. 200sh, Uruguay, 1930. 250sh, W. Germany, 1954. 500sh, Argentina, 1978. 600sh, England, 1966.
No. 1624, 250sh, vert. — Players: a, Muller, W. Germany. b, Kocsis, Hungary. c, Pele, Brazil. d, Schillaci, Italy. e, Fontaine, France. f, Nejedly, Czechoslovakia. g, Rahn, W. Germany. h, Lineker, England.
No. 1625, 250sh — Stadiums: a, The Rose Bowl, US, 1994. b, Torino Stadium, Italy, 1934. c, Olympia Stadium, Germany, 1974. d, Azteca Satdium, Mexico, 1970, 1986. e, Wembley, England, 1966. f, Maracana, Brazil, 1950. g, Centenary Stadium, Uruguay, 1930. h, Bernabeu Stadium, Spain, 1982.
No. 1626, 1000sh, Pele, Brazil. No. 1627, 1000sh, Eusebio, Portugal.

**1997, Oct. 20** *Perf. 14x13½, 13½x14*

**1618-1623** A276 Set of 6 6.00 6.00

**Sheets of 8, #a-h, + Label**

**1624-1625** A276 Set of 2 13.50 13.50

**Souvenir Sheet**

**1626-1627** A276 Set of 2 8.00 8.00

Endangered Species A277

Fauna A278

No. 1628, 250sh — Animals of Asia: a, Tiger. b, Japanese macaque. c, Slender loris. d, Musk deer. e, Przewalski's horse. f, Red panda.
No. 1629, 250sh — Animals of Latin America: a, Night monkey. b, Woolly opossum. c, Jaguar. d, Red uakaris. e, Ringtailed coati. f, Cotton-top tamarin.
No. 1630, 250sh — Animals of North America: a, Bobcat. b, Moose. c, American bison. d, Mountain goat. e, Walrus. f, Common racoon.
No. 1630G — Animals of Africa: h, Cheetah. i, Zebra. j, Gorilla. k, Brown lesser mouse lemur. l, Rhinoceros. m. Chimpanzee.
No. 1631, 250sh — Northern wilderness animals: a, Great horned owl. b, Bald eagle. c, Coyotes. d, Grizzly bear. e, Caribou (d). f, Walrus. g, Hooded seal. h, Humpback whale (g). i, Harp seal.
No. 1632, 250sh — African safari animals a, Barbary macaque. b, Turaco. c, Giraffe (f). d, Mountain gorilla, African elephant (a, b, e, g, h). e, Zebra. f, Grant's gazelle. g, Monarch butterfly, meerkat. h, African lion. i, Rhinoceros (f).
No. 1633, 1500sh, Maned wolf. No. 1634, 1500sh, Giant panda. No. 1635, 1500sh, Gray wolf. No. 1636, 1500sh, African elephant, diff.

**1997, Oct. 30** *Perf. 14*

**Sheets of 6, #a-f**

**1628-1630** A277 Set of 3 35.00 35.00
**1630G** A277 250sh Sheet of 6, #h.-m. 11.50 11.50

**Sheets of 9, #a-i**

**1631-1632** A278 250sh Set of 2 30.00 30.00

**Souvenir Sheets**

**1633-1636** A277 1500sh Set of 4 40.00 40.00

A279

A280

No. 1637 — Modern architecture: a, Sydney Opera House, Australia. b, Brasilia Cathedral, Brazil. c, Metropolitan Cathedral of Christ the King, Liverpool, England. d, Einstein Tower, Potsdam, Berlin, Germany. e, Solomon Guggenheim Museum, New York City, US. f, Palace of the Natl. Congress, Brasilia.
No. 1638 — Ancient wonders of the world, vert.: a, Temple of Artemis at Ephesus. b, Great Pyramid of Cheops. c, Mausoleum at Halicarnassus. d, Statue of Zeus at Olympia. e, Hanging Gardens of Babylon. f, Colossus of Rhodes.
No. 1639, 1000sh, Notre Dame Du Haut Chapel, Ronchamp, France. No. 1640, 1000sh, Lighthouse of Alexandria.

**1997, Nov. 5** *Perf. 14*

**1637** A279 140sh Sheet of 6, #a.-f. 5.00 5.00
**1638** A279 370sh Sheet of 6, #a.-f. 14.00 14.00

**Souvenir Sheets**

**1639-1640** A279 Set of 2 13.50 13.50

Nos. 1639-1640 contain one 42x57mm or 57x42mm stamp, respectively.

**1997, Nov. 28** **Wmk. 233**

Coastal Birds: 140sh, Red hornbill. 350sh, Sacred ibis, horiz. 370sh, Sea gulls, horiz. 410sh, Ring-necked dove, horiz.
500sh, Hornbill, ibis, gulls, doves, horiz.

**1641-1644** A280 Set of 4 8.00 8.00

**Souvenir Sheet**

**1645** A280 500sh multicolored 3.25 3.25

Aircraft A281

Fighter Planes: 100sh, P-51D. 200sh, Lockheed P-38J Lightning. 300sh, B-29 Superfortress. 400sh, Lockheed P-80 Shooting Star P-80 A1. 500sh, Curtiss P-36A.
No. 1651, 150sh — Spitfires: a, MK IX providing altitude cover for bomber formations. b, MK Vc dog fighting. c, PRMK XIX, Photographic Reconnaissance Development Unit, RAF. d, MK Vb over North Africa. e, FR XIVE firing rockets. f, MK VIII (ZPZ), Japanese bomber. g, Supermarine Seafire being catapulted from HMS Indomitable. h, MK IX during D-Day landings. i, MK XII attacking V1 Flying Bomb.
No. 1652, 150sh — Spitfires: a, MK IXc, excorting crippled Lancaster Bomber. b, MK 1a dog fighting. c, PR MK XI, 14th Photo Sqdn., US 8th Air Force. d, MK Vb, North Africa. e, MK VIII with lightning bolt on nose. f, MK Vc with RAF, Yugoslav, American markings. g, Supermarine Seafire landing on British carrier. h, MK IXc D-Day. i, MK XII destroying V-1 Flying Bomb.
No. 1653: a, MKII in desert. b, Hurribomber dog fighting. c, MK 24, photo reconnaissance. d, Canadian MK 1 foreign squadron. e, Mark IXC convoy protection. f, Spitfire with clipped wings flanked by MK 22. g, Hurricanes MKII in desert. h, Hurribomber.
No. 1654, 1000sh, Boeing P-26. No. 1655, 1000sh, SR-71A. No. 1656, 1000sh, MK Vb. No. 1657, 1000sh,MK V Float plane. No. 1658, 1000sh, MK 1.

**1997, Dec. 23** **Litho.** *Perf. 14*

**1646-1650** A281 Set of 5 10.00 10.00

**Sheets of 9, #a-i**

**1651-1652** A281 Set of 2 13.00 13.00
**1653** A281 250sh Sheet of 8, #a.-h. 20.00 20.00

**Souvenir Sheets**

**1654-1658** A281 Set of 5 32.50 32.50

No. 1656 contains one 85x28mm stamp. Nos. 1657-1658 each contain one 57x42mm stamp.

Jackie Chan, Movie Star A282

Various portraits.

**1997, Dec. 30**

**1659** A282 370sh Sheet of 6, #a.-f. 13.50 13.50

PAPU (Pan African Postal Union), 18th Anniv. A283

Designs: 150sh, Natl. flag of Tanzania, flag of PAPU. 250sh, PAPU emblem. 400sh, Delivery by EMS motorcycles. 500sh, Giraffes.

**1998, Jan. 18** *Perf. 13½*

**1660-1663** A283 Set of 4 8.50 8.50

A284

A285

**1998** **Litho.** *Perf. 14*

**1664** A284 410sh Mt. Kilimanjaro 2.75 2.75

**1998, Jan. 23**

Diana, Princess of Wales (1961-97): 150sh, In red jacket. 250sh, In lilac dress.
1000sh, In teal suit with Prince Harry (in sheet margin).

**1665** A285 150sh multicolored 1.00 1.00
**1666** A285 250sh multicolored 1.75 1.75

**Souvenir Sheet**

**1667** A285 1000sh multicolored 6.25 6.25

Nos. 1665-1666 were each issued in sheets of 9.

Marine Life and Sea Birds A286

No. 1668: a, Black-browed albatross. b, Unidentified bird. c, Xantusi murrelet. d, Empress angelfish. e, Bottle nosed dolphins. f, Queen angelfish. g, Red sponge. h, Unidentified red and tan fish. i, Reef shark. j, Sea star. k, Unidentified white and black fish. l, Stingray.
No. 1669, 250sh: a, Black-saddled pufferfish. b, Harlequin tuskfish. c, Emperor angelfish. d, Foxface. e, Yellow tang. f, Catalina goby. g, Fifteen-spined stickleback. h, Banded pipefish. i, Weather loach.
No. 1670, 250sh, vert.: a, Octopus. b, Pantherfish. c, Hawksbill turtle. d, Skate. e, Jellyfish. f, White tip shark. g, Blue starfish. h, Brain coral. i, Anemone.
No. 1671, 1000sh, Clown fish. No. 1672, 1000sh, Shark. No. 1673, 1000sh, Yellow seahorse, vert.

**1998, Jan. 30**

**1668** A286 200sh Sheet of 12, #a.-l. 15.00 15.00

**Sheets of 9, #a-i**

**1669-1670** A286 Set of 2 29.50 29.50

**Souvenir Sheets**

**1671-1673** A286 Set of 3 17.50 17.50

For overprints see #1697-1702, 1750-1751.

Traditional Weapons — A287

Designs: 150sh, Slingshot. 250sh, Cutlass and club. 400sh, Gun. 500sh, Bow, arrows.

**1998, Mar. 16 Litho. *Perf. 14***

**1674-1677** A287 Set of 4 8.25 8.25

New Year 1998 (Year of the Tiger) — A288

No. 1678 — Stylized tiger: a, Walking right. b, Walking left. c, Lying down. d, Seated.
1500sh, Tiger standing.

**1998, Mar. 30 Litho. *Perf. 13½***

**1678** A288 370sh Sheet of 4, #a.-d. 9.00 9.00

**Souvenir Sheet**

**1679** A288 1500sh multicolored 9.00 9.00

John Denver (1943-97), Rock Musician — A288a

No. 1679A: c, Wearing green sweater. d, Wearing brown sweater (shoulders in middle of stamp). e, Wearing brown sweater (shoulder near corner of stamp). f, Wearing green sweater, hand at face.
1500sh, Wearing blue shirt.

**1998, Apr. 30 Litho. *Perf. 14***

**1679A** A288a 370sh Sheet of 4, #c-f 3.00 3.00

**Souvenir Sheet**

**1679B** A288a 1500sh multi 3.00 3.00

Most examples of Nos. 1679A-1679B were not available in the philatelic marketplace until Dec. 2002.

Antique Automobiles — A289

No. 1680, 370sh: a, 1901 Mercedes 35hp. b, 1903 Ford Model A. c, 1908 Legnano Type A. d, 1908-09 Rolls Royce 40-50hp Silver Ghost. e, 1910 Renault Petit Duc. f, 1913 Fischer Torpedo.
No. 1681, 370sh: a, 1923-24 Peugeot 18cv. b, 1926 Daimler 25-85hp. c, 1932 Bugatti Type 50T. d, 1933 Pierce-Arrow V12 "Silver Arrow." e, 1934 Tatra V8. f, 1937 Grosser Mercedes Benz.
No. 1682, 1000sh, 1900 Benz. No. 1683, 1000sh, 1893 Duryea.

**1998, Aug. 4 Litho. *Perf. 14***

**Sheets of 6, #a-f**

**1680-1681** A289 Set of 2 28.00 28.00

**Souvenir Sheets**

**1682-1683** A289 Set of 2 13.00 13.00

Nos. 1682-1683 each contain one 64x48mm stamp.

Flowers and Insects A290

No. 1684, vert: a, Euanthe sanderiana, teiratenia surinama. b, "Clown Mixed." c, Pansies, caterpillar of papilio polyxenes. d, "Prelude." e, Dendrobium primulinum, wasp beetle. f, Carrion beetle, clematis "Lasurstern." g, Sunflowers, "Autumn Beauty" & "Italian White," elder borer, painted daisy. h, Grape hyacinth.
No. 1685, 250sh: a, Platinum sun. b, Vespid wasp, oriental poppy. c, Anemone. d, Ipomoea alba, king's bee hawkmoth. e, Aussie delight, potter wasp. f, Colorado potato beetle, Japanese iris. g, Bomarea caldasii, azure damselfly. h, Hybrid macranthe, queen bumblebee. i, Love with lace iris, click beetle.
No. 1686, 250sh: a, Golden ray lily, South African longhorn beetle. b, Oncidium macianthum. c, Agelia petali, dendrobium. c, Cobaea scandens. d, Goldsmith beetle, paphiopedilum gilda. e, Iceland poppies, potter wasp. f, Pink beauty. g, Annual chrysanthemums. h, Little mal, m. femurrubrum.
No. 1687, 1500sh, Carolina Queen. No. 1688, 1500sh, Robert E. Lee daffodils. No. 1689, 1500sh, Orange scarlet hybrid "Tempo." No. 1690, 1500sh, Pansies.

**1998, Aug. 18 Litho. *Perf. 14***

**1684** A290 250sh Sheet of 8, #a.-h. 17.00 17.00

**Sheets of 9, #a-i**

**1685-1686** A290 Set of 2 19.00 19.00

**Souvenir Sheets**

**1687-1690** A290 Set of 2 34.00 34.00

A291

TANZANIA 370/- GIANT SABLE ANTELOPE

Endangered Species — A292

No. 1691: a, Hyacinth macaw. b, Gibbon. c, Bosman's potto. d, Scarlet crowned barbets. e, Giant anteater. f, Cacomistle. g, Tiger. h, Mara. i, Mandrill. j, Crocodile. k, Wood turtle. l, Baribusa.
No. 1692: a, Giant sable antelope. b, Cheetah. c, Giraffe. d, Black bear. e, African elephant. f, Giant panda.
No. 1693: a, Tiger. b, Bald eagle (a, c). c, Mountain gorilla. d, Sea lion. e, Green sea turtle. f, Hippopotamus.
No. 1694, Emerald tanager.
No. 1695, 1500sh, Florida manatee. No. 1696, 1500sh, Orangutan.

**1998, Aug. 31 Litho. *Perf. 14***

**1691** A291 200sh Sheet of 12, #a.-l. 14.00 14.00
**1692** A292 370sh Sheet of 6, #a.-f. 13.00 13.00
**1693** A292 370sh Sheet of 6, #a.-f. 13.00 13.00

**Souvenir Sheets**

**1694** A291 1500sh multi 13.50 13.50
**1695-1696** A292 Set of 2 27.00 27.00

Nos. 1692, 1695 each contain 51x38mm stamps. No. 1696 contains 43x28mm stamps.

Nos. 1668-1673 Ovptd.

**1998, Sept. 2 Litho. *Perf. 14***

**1697** A286 200sh Sheet of 12, #a.-l. (#1668) 21.00 21.00
**1698** A286 250sh Sheet of 9 #a.-i. (#1669) 9.50 9.50
**1699** A286 250sh Sheet of 9 #a.-i. (#1670) 9.50 9.50

**Souvenir Sheets**

**1700** A286 1000shmulti (#1671) 5.75 5.75
**1701** A286 1000shmulti (#1672) 5.75 5.75
**1702** A286 1000shmulti (#1673) 5.75 5.75

The stamps of Nos. 1697-1699, 1701-1702 were ovptd. with Intl. Year of the Ocean emblem and the sheet margins contain one or two emblems with words "INTERNATIONAL YEAR OF THE OCEAN." No. 1700 has overprint only on sheet margin.

Aircraft A293

No. 1703, 300sh: a, Antoinette IV, 1908. b, Deperdussin Racer, 1912. c, Demoiselle, 1909. d, Bleriot XI, 1909. e, Avro FAV Roe, 1912. f, Breguet IV, 1910.
No. 1704, 300sh: a, Deperdussin. b, Ultralight, 1979-86. c, Amphibian, 1929-30. d, Pitts Special, 1930. e, BAC-221, 1960. f, Avro Tutor, 1931.
No. 1705, 300sh: a, KI-44 Tojo. b, Hawker Fury. c, Mustang. d, Zero. e, Travel Air Mystery Ship. f, F8F Bearcat.
No. 1706, 1000sh, USAAF Curtiss P-40M. No. 1707, 1000sh, Biplane. No. 1708, 1000sh, Balloon.

**1998, Aug. 4 Litho. *Perf. 14***

**Sheets of 6, #a-f**

**1703-1705** A293 Set of 3 27.00 27.00

**Souvenir Sheets**

**1706-1708** A293 Set of 3 17.50 17.50

No. 1704a incorrectly inscribed 1900.

Eagles A294

No. 1709: a, Pallas's fish. b, Bateleur. c, Martial. d, Golden. e, Wedge-tailed. f, Java hawk.
1500sh, Wedge-tailed, diff.

**1998, Aug. 31**

**1709** A294 370sh Sheet of 6, #a.-f. 13.00 13.00

**Souvenir Sheet**

**1710** A294 1500sh multicolored 9.50 9.50

Fauna and Flora A295

Designs: 250sh, Takahe. 410sh, Lear's macaw. 500sh, Ring-tailed lemur. 600sh, Arabian oryx.
No. 1715, 370sh, : a, Japanese crested ibis. b, Kuai O'o. c, Bourke's hairstreak. d, Quokka. e, Tahitian lorikeet. f, Black-faced tamarin.
No. 1716, 370sh: a, Loggerhead turtle. b, Snow leopard. c, Gurney's pitta. d, Lowland gorilla. e, Echo parakeet. f, Orangutan.
No. 1717, 1500sh, Giant panda. No. 1718, 1500sh, Bengal tiger.

**1998, Aug. 31 *Perf. 14x14½***

**1711-1714** A295 Set of 4 11.50 11.50

**Sheets of 6, #a-f**

**1715-1716** A295 Set of 2 17.00 17.00

**Souvenir Sheets**

**1717-1718** A295 Set of 2 10.00 10.00

Children's Rights A296

Designs: 150sh, Equal rights for boys and girls. 250sh, Right to education. 400sh, Right not to be beaten, vert. No. 1722, 500sh, Right to be loved, vert.
No. 1723, Right to education.

**1998 *Perf. 13***

**1719-1722** A296 Set of 4 7.00 7.00

**Souvenir Sheet**

**1723** A296 500sh multicolored 2.75 2.75

Nos. 608, 610 Surcharged

**1998 Method and Perf. as Before**

**1723A** A99 150sh on 13sh #608 — —
**1723B** A99 150sh on 20sh #610 — —

Issued: No. 723A, 1/26; No. 1723B, 3/16.

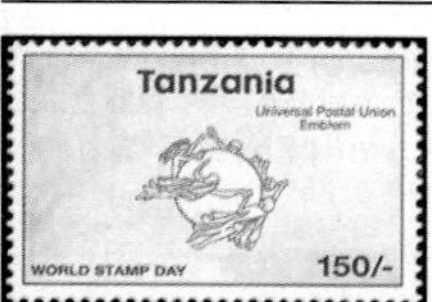


World Stamp Day — A297

Designs: 150sh, UPU Emblem. 250sh, Letter facing and date stamping. 400sh, Trusted messenger. 500sh, Letter posting.

No. 1728, Trusted messenger, letter posting, UPU emblem.

**1998, Oct. 9 Wmk. 387 *Perf. 14***

**1724-1727** A297 Set of 4 7.00 7.00

**Souvenir Sheet**

**1728** A297 500sh multicolored 2.75 2.75

A298

Marine Life, Sea Birds A299

Designs: 150sh, Equal sea star. 250sh, Mountain crab. 400sh, Wolffish. 500sh, Purple sea urchin.

No. 1733: a, Barred antshrike. b, Yellow-nosed albatross, common tern. c, Common tern, killer whale. d, Crimson-rumped toucanet. e, French angelfish. f, Grey shark (e). g, Manta ray (f, h). h, Yellow-backed damselfish. i, Green parrot wrasse. j, Silver badgerfish, pyjama wrasse. k, Skate, red-knobbed starfish (h). l, Striped snapper.

No. 1734: a, Common dolphin. b, Blue marlin. c, Arctic tern. d, Blackedge moray. e, Loggerhead turtle. f, Blacktip shark. g, Two-spotted octopus. h, Manta ray. i, Sailfin tang.

No. 1735, 1000sh, Aequipecten opercularis. No. 1736, 1000sh, Chrysaora quinquecirrha. 1500sh, Skate.

**1998, Oct. 12**

**1729-1732** A298 Set of 4 7.75 7.75

**1733** A299 200sh Sheet of 12, #a.-l. 13.50 13.50

**1734** A298 300sh Sheet of 9, #a.-i. 16.00 16.00

**Souvenir Sheets**

**1735-1736** A298 Set of 2 12.00 12.00

**1737** A299 1500sh multi 9.00 9.00

Intl. Year of the Ocean (#1733-1737).

Mushrooms and Insects — A300

Designs: 140sh, Cardinal beetle, tricholoma batschii. 150sh, Tricholoma catigatum, painted lady. 200sh, Lyophylum decastes, speckled wood butterfly. 250sh, Tricholoma flavovfrens, speckled bush cricket. 370sh, Boletus chrysenteron, shieldbug. 410sh, Boletus zelleri, darter dragonfly. 500sh, Gyroporus castaneus, tortoise beetle. 600sh, Hissing cockroach, boletus satanas.

No. 1746, 250sh: a, Hygrocybe miniata, shieldbug. b, Peacock butterfly, cystolepiata adulterina. c, Collybia dryophila, bush cricket. d, Omphalotus olearius, halloween pennant butterfly. e, Macrolepiota rhacodes, helicon butterfly. f, Macrole piota puellaris, hornet. g, Carpenter bee. h, Mycena epipteryia, South African longhorn beetle. i, Amanita muscaria, skipper butterfly.

No. 1747 250sh, vert.: a, Leaf hopper cicadia, pleurotus ostreatus. b, Amanita muscaria, froghopper beetle. c, Wasp, amanita umbrinolutea. d, Butterfly, onnia tomentosa. e, Monarch butterfly, ganoderma lucidum. f, Broad-bodied libellua, macrolepiota procera. g, Butterfly anthocharis, suillus granulatus. h, Egyptian grasshopper, cortinarius praestans. i, Flying bush cricket, marasmius ramealis.

No. 1748, 1500sh, Coprinus silvaticus, thornbug. No. 1749, 1500sh, Black swallowtail, chroogomphus rutilus.

**1998, Nov. 27**

**1738-1745** A300 Set of 8 15.00 15.00

**Sheets of 9, #a-i**

**1746-1747** A300 Set of 2 27.00 27.00

**Souvenir Sheets**

**1748-1749** A300 Set of 2 17.00 17.00

Rudolph the Red-Nosed Reindeer A301

No. 1752, 200sh: a, Milo. b, Rudolph (face). c, Leonard. d, Stormella. e, Ridley. f. Boone.

No. 1753, 200sh: a, Santa. b, Rudolph. c, Doggle. d, Edgar. e, Baby Rudolph. f, Toys.

No. 1754, 1000sh, Leonard, horiz. No. 1755, 1000sh, Rudolph. No. 1756, 1000sh, Baby Rudolph with ball on nose, diff. No. 1757, 1000sh, Santa with Rudolph.

***Perf. 13½x14, 14x13½***

**1998, Dec. 15 Litho.**

**Sheets of 6, #a-f**

**1752-1753** A301 Set of 2 8.00 8.00

**Souvenir Sheets**

**1754-1757** A301 Set of 4 14.00 14.00

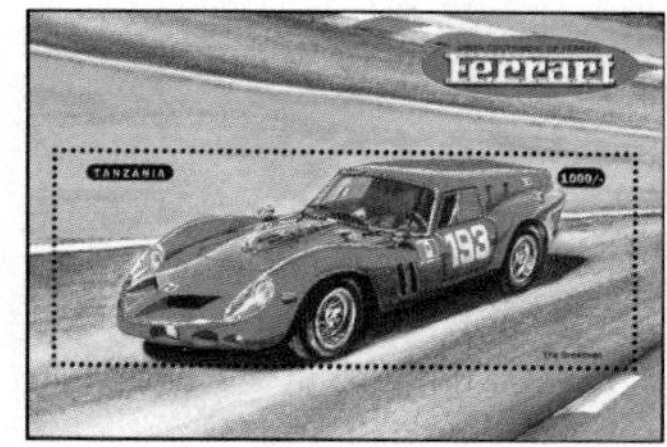


Ferrari Automobiles — A301a

No. 1757A: c, GTO. d, F40. e, 512S. 100sh, Breadvan.

Illustration reduced.

**1998, Dec. 16 Litho. *Perf. 14***

**1757A** A301a 500sh Sheet of 3, #c-e 4.50 4.50

**Souvenir Sheet**

***Perf. 13¾x14¼***

**1757B** A301a 1000sh multi 3.00 3.00

No. 1757A contains three 39x25mm stamps.

Diana, Princess of Wales (1961-97) A302

**1998, Dec. 16 *Perf. 14***

**1758** A302 600sh multicolored 2.00 2.00

No. 1758 was issued in sheets of 6.

Picasso — A303

Paintings: No. 1759, 400sh, Jacquelin with Crossedhand, 1954. No. 1760, 400sh, Straw Hat with Blue Foilage, 1936. 500sh, Reading the Letter, 1921.

1500sh, Woman Writing, 1934.

**1998, Dec. 16 *Perf. 14½***

**1759-1761** A303 Set of 3 4.50 4.50

**Souvenir Sheet**

**1762** A303 1500sh multicolored 5.00 5.00

Mohandas Gandhi — A304

**1998, Dec. 16 *Perf. 14***

**1763** A304 370sh Portrait 1.25 1.25

**Souvenir Sheet**

**1764** A304 1500sh Jawaharlal Nehru 5.00 5.00

No. 1763 was issued in sheets of 4.

1998 World Scout Jamboree, Chile A305

No. 1765: a, US Pres. William Howard Taft greets scouts during early years, 1908. b, Early Cub Scout pack enjoys musical camp break, 1930's. c, Dan Beard demonstrates tomahawk throw at Silver Bay, 1912.

1500sh, Ernest Thompson Seton (1860-1946), first Chief Scout.

**1998, Dec. 16 Litho. *Perf. 14***

**1765** A305 600sh Sheet of 3, #a.-c. 6.00 6.00

**Souvenir Sheet**

**1766** A305 1500sh multicolored 5.00 5.00

Royal Air Force, 80th Anniv. A306

No. 1767: a, Panavia Tornado F3. b, Sepecat Jaguar GR1A. c, Jaguar GR1A. d, Jaguar GR1A, diff.

No. 1768, 1000sh, Harrier, Eurofighter. No. 1769, 1000sh, Biplane, hawk.

**1998, Dec. 16 *Perf. 14***

**1767** A306 500sh Sheet of 4, #a.-d. 6.75 6.75

**Souvenir Sheets**

**1768-1769** A306 Set of 2 7.00 7.00

New Year 1999 (Year of the Rabbit) A307

No. 1770 - Color of rabbit : a, Red brown. b, Spotted. c, Yellow. d, Brown.

1500sh, White.

**1999, Jan. 18 *Perf. 14***

**1770** A307 250sh Sheet of 4, #a.-d. 3.50 3.50

**Souvenir Sheet**

**1771** A307 1500sh multicolored 5.00 5.00

Tourism in Zanzibar A308

Designs: 100sh, Dhow Harbor, vert. 150sh, Girl on giant tortoise, vert. 250sh, Children with giant tortoise. 300sh, Street in Stone Town, vert. 400sh, Old fort. 500sh, Red colobus monkeys.

600sh, Girl on tortoise, street in Stone Town.

**1998, Nov. 10 Litho. *Perf. 14***

**1772-1777** A308 Set of 6 5.75 5.75

**Souvenir Sheet**

**1778** A308 600sh multicolored 2.00 2.00

Tanzanian Posts Corp., 5th Anniv. A309

Designs: 150sh, Rural post office. 250sh, Overnight mail service. 350sh, Money fax service. 400sh, Post shop business.

500sh, Exterior view of high rise building, vert.

**1999, Jan. 1**

**1779-1782** A309 Set of 4 3.75 3.75

**Souvenir Sheet**

**1783** A309 500sh multicolored 1.60 1.60

Butterflies A310

200sh, Calycopis cecrops. 250sh, Heliconis melpomena, vert. 370sh, Citherias menander, vert. 410sh, Heliconis antiochus, vert.

No. 1788, 200sh: a, Acraea cerasa. b, Acraea semivitrea. c, Euchrysops scintilla. d, Papilio phorcas. e, Euphaedra eusemoides. f, Acraea masamba. g, Phyciodes emerantia. h, Hypothiris tricolor. i, Orimba jansoni.

No. 1789, 200sh: a, Papilio zagreus. b, Chlosyne narva. c, Phyciodes alsina. d, Pyronia bathseba. e, Eurema daira. f, Eurytides xanticles. g, Clossiana titania. h, Euphydryas cynthia. i, Polygonia c-album.

No. 1790, 1500sh, Ornithoptera priamus, vert. No. 1791, 1500sh, Phyciodes, vert.

**1999, Feb. 18**

**1784-1787** A310 Set of 4 3.75 3.75

**Sheets of 9, #a-i**

**1788-1789** A310 Set of 2 12.00 12.00

**Souvenir Sheets**

**1790-1791** A310 Set of 2 10.00 10.00

Birds A311

No. 1792, 370sh: a, Yellow billed stork. b, Black egret. c, Crowned lapwing. d, Snowy plover. e, Crowned crane. f, Saddlebilled stork.

No. 1793, 370sh: a, Great blue heron. b, Chinese egret. c, Horned puffins. d, White faced ibis. e, Greater flamingo. f, Blue footed boobie.

No. 1794, 370sh: a, Blacksmith plover. b, Brolga crane. c, Green-backed heron. d, Straw-necked ibis. e, Little bittern. f, Marabou stork.

No. 1795, 370sh, vert.: a, Sandhill crane. b, Great egret. c, Spoonbill. d, Yellow-crowned night heron. e, Glossy ibis. f, Willet.

No. 1796, 1500sh, Purple heron. No. 1797, 1500sh, Kittliz's sandplover, vert. No. 1798, 1500sh, Black-crowned night heron. No. 1799, 1500sh, Black-headed heron.

**1999, Feb. 18**

**Sheets of 6, #a-f**

**1792-1795** A311 Set of 4 27.00 27.00

**Souvenir sheets**

**1796-1799** A311 Set of 4 18.00 18.00

A312

A313

Cats A314

Designs: No. 1800, 200sh, Bengal, horiz. No. 1801, 250sh, Seal lynx point birman. No. 1802, 370sh, Calico British shorthair, horiz. No. 1803, 420sh, Blue & white cornish rex.

Nos. 1804, 100sh, Burmese. No. 1805, 140sh, Burmilla. No. 1806, 150sh, Turkish van. No. 1807, 200sh, Snowshoe. No. 1808, 250sh, Bombay. No. 1809, 370sh, Seychellois longhair.

No. 1810: a, Silver classic tabby. b, Auburn Turkish van. c, Seal bicolor ragdoll. d, European shorthair. e, Black & white British shorthair. f, Gold California spangled. g, Chocolate tipped Burmilla. h, Red classic tabby manx.

No. 1811, 370sh: a, Pekeface Persian. b, American curl shorthair. c, Korat. d, Himalayan Persian. e, Exotic shorthair. f, Scottish fold.

No. 1812, 370sh: a, European shorthair. b, Chartreux. c, British shorthair. d, Maine coon. e, Japanese bobtail. f, Birman.

No. 1813 - Kittens chasing butterflies: a, Black & white kitten, butterfly UL. b, Black & white kitten, butterfly UR. c, Black & yellow kitten, butterfly UR. d, Yellow kitten, butterfly UL.

No. 1814, 1500sh, Black & white Persian, horiz. No. 1815, 1500sh, Cream tabby European shorthair.

No. 1816, 1500sh, American shorthair. No. 1817, 1500sh, American wirehair. No. 1818, Kitten, butterfly, vert.

**1999, Feb. 23**

**1800-1803** A312 Set of 4 4.00 4.00
**1804-1809** A313 Set of 6 4.00 4.00
**1810** A312 250sh Sheet of 8, #a.-h. 6.25 6.25

**Sheets of 6, #a-f**

**1811-1812** A313 Set of 2 14.50 14.50
**1813** A314 500sh Sheet of 4, #a.-d. 6.25 6.25

**Souvenir Sheets**

**1814-1815** A312 Set of 2 10.00 10.00
**1816-1817** A313 Set of 2 10.00 10.00
**1818** A314 1500sh multi 5.00 5.00

19th Century Ships A315

No. 1819, 370sh: a, Prince Consort (1). b, USS Kearsage (2). c, HMS Victoria (3). d, USS Brooklyn (4). e, Mount Stewart (5). f, Hougomont (6).

No. 1820, 370sh: a, Charles W. Morgan (1). b, RMS Britannia (2). c, Great Britain (3). d, Flying Cloud (4). e, HMS Warrior (5). f, Lightning (6).

No. 1821, 1500sh, Cutty Sark. No. 1822, 1500sh, Great Eastern.

**1999, Feb. 9 Litho. *Perf. 14***

**Sheets of 6, #a-f**

**1819-1820** A315 Set of 2 15.00 15.00

**Souvenir Sheets**

**1821-1822** A315 Set of 2 10.00 10.00

Nos. 1821-1822 each contain one 57x43mm stamp.

Military Helicopters — A316

No. 1823: a, Germany DF 4. b, Germany. c, France. d, US, with rocket pods. e, US, with suspended lift sling. f, France, red on tail boom & stabilizers.

**1999**

**1823** A316 370sh Sheet of 6, #a.-f. 7.50 7.50

Unidentified Flying Objects (UFOs) — A317

No. 1824, 370sh: a, US, 1968. b, Trinidad, 1958. c, Belgium, 1990. d, Finland, 1970. e, New Zealand, 1951. f, Australia, 1954.

No. 1825, 370sh: a, McMinnville, 1950. b, Albuquerque, 1963. c, Gulf Breeze, 1988. d, Madre de Dios, 1952. e, Merlin, 1964. f, Mexico City, 1991.

No. 1826, 1500sh, The Arnold Sighting, 1947. No. 1827, 1500sh, The Mantell case, 1948.

**1999**

**Sheets of 6, #a-f**

**1824-1825** A317 Set of 2 15.00 15.00

**Souvenir Sheets**

**1826-1827** A317 Set of 2 10.00 10.00

Dogs A318

No. 1828: a, Boston terrier. b, Tyrolean hound. c, Rottweiler. d, Golden retriever. e, English bulldog. f, Spanish greyhound. g, Long-haired dachshund. h, Scottish terrier. i, Pekingese.

1500sh, English cocker spaniel.

**1999**

**1828** A318 200sh Sheet of 9, #a.-i. 5.50 5.50

**Souvenir Sheet**

**1829** A318 1500sh multicolored 5.00 5.00

Dinosaurs — A319

Designs: 200sh, Stegosaurus (inscribed Edmontonia). 250sh, Archaeopteryx. 370sh, Stegosaurus. 410sh, Lagosuchus.

No. 1834, 370sh: a, Dromiceiomimus. b, Saurolophus. c, Camarosaurus. d, Protoceratops. e, Psittacosaurus. f, Stegoceras.

No. 1835, 370sh: a, Gallimimus. b, Peteinosaurus. c, Lambeosaurus. d, Coelophysis. e, Parasaurolophus. f, Tyrannosaurus rex.

No. 1836, 1500sh, Quetzalcoatlus. No. 1837, 1500sh, Rhomaleosaurus.

**1999, Apr. 30 Litho. *Perf. 14***

**1830-1833** A319 Set of 4 4.00 4.00

**Sheets of 6, #a-f**

**1834-1835** A319 Set of 2 15.00 15.00

**Souvenir Sheets**

**1836-1837** A319 Set of 2 10.00 10.00

Tourism A320

No. 1838: a, Hoofed animals. b, Mount Kilimanjaro, crater. c, Animal life. d, Sacred ibis. e, Ngorongoro crater. f, Giraffe. g, Lions. h, Dik diks. i, Vulture. j, Lion cubs. k, Elephants. l, African lion. m, Stone Town, Zanzibar. n, National Museum. o, Carved door, Zanzibar. p, Map showing Zanzibar, Pemba, Indian Ocean. q, Herding animals. r, Fishing. s, Lion cub. t, Buildings, boats along shore. u, Masai. v, Birds wading in water. w, Buffalo stampede. x, Like #1838b, closer view.

**1999 *Perf. 14½x14***

**Booklet Stamps**

**1838** A320 Souvenir Booklet 11.00
*a.-x.* 150sh any single .45 .45
*y.* Booklet pane, #1838a-1838f 2.75
*z.* Booklet pane, #1838g-1838l 2.75
*aa.* Bklt. pane, #1838m-1838r 2.75
*ab.* Bklt. pane, #1838s-1838x 2.75

Space Exploration — A321

Designs: 70sh, Edward White. 100sh, Gemini 7. 150sh, Mir, Russian space station, vert. 200sh, Laika, Russian space dog. 250sh, Apollo Command & Service Modules. 370sh, Apollo Lunar Module.

1500sh, Saturn V Moon Rocket, vert.

**1999 *Perf. 14***

**1839-1844** A321 Set of 6 3.75 3.75

**Souvenir Sheet**

**1845** A321 1500sh multicolored 5.00 5.00

Airships, Balloons — A322

No. 1846: a, Graf Zeppelin, 1935 (b). b, Knabenshue Airship, 1905. c, British R-100, 1931. d, Hindenburg, 1937 (c). e, French Balloon, 1783. f, French Balloon, 1912.

1500sh, Sport ballooning.

**1999**

**1846** A322 370sh Sheet of 6, #a.-f. 7.00 7.00

**Souvenir Sheet**

**1847** A322 1500sh multicolored 4.50 4.50

Marine Life A323

Designs: 200sh, Powder blue surgeon. 250sh, Frilled anemone. 310sh, Red-finned batfish. 410sh, Red beard sponge.

No. 1852, 250sh: a, Right whale. b, Fin whale. c, Humpback whale. d. Tucuxi. e, Gray's beaked whale. f, Sperm whale. g, Bottlenose dolphin. h, Hector's dolphin. i, Hourglass dolphin.

No. 1853, 250sh: a, Horn shark. b, Nurse shark. c, Bonnethead. d, Tiger shark. e, Bull shark. f, Leopard shark. g, Blue shark. h, Zebra shark. i, Oceanic whitetip.

No. 1854, 1500sh, Pacific Electric ray, vert. No. 1855, 1500sh, Loggerhead turtle, vert.

**1999, Feb. 9 Litho. *Perf. 14***

**1848-1851** A323 Set of 4 3.00 3.00

**Sheets of 9, #a.-i.**

**1852-1853** A323 Set of 2 14.00 14.00

**Souvenir Sheets**

**1854-1855** A323 Set of 2 9.00 9.00

Airplanes A324

Designs: 20sh, Oiseau Bleu, 1929. 100sh, Beechcraft Model 17, 1934. No. 1858, 140sh, US Army Air Corps Beechcraft YC-43. No. 1859, 140sh, Deperdussin, 1913. 150sh, Beechcraft E17B, 1937. 200sh, Beechcraft B17L, 1936. 250sh, Beechcraft Model-G175, 1946. 370sh, Beechcraft Staggerwing Model-C17L.

No. 1864: a, Bird of Passage, Voisin Brothers, 1909. b, BS1, Geoffrey de Havilland, 1913. c, Taube-IGO Etrich, 1910. d, Curtiss Rheims Flyer, Glenn Curtiss, 1909. e, Wright Flyer III, Wright Brothers, 1905. f, Russky Vitvas, Igor Sikorsky, 1913.

No. 1865: a, Sikorsky S-38. b, EFA Eurofighter. c, F-16. d, Hawker Hurricane. e, Artiplast. f, Islander.

No. 1866, 1500sh, Piper Cherokee. No. 1867, 1500sh, MiG.

**1999, Feb. 14**

**1856-1863** A324 Set of 8 4.25 4.25

**Sheets of 6**

**1864** A324 370sh Sheet of 6, #a.-f. 6.75 6.75
**1865** A324 370sh Sheet of 6, #a.-f. 5.50 5.50

**Souvenir Sheets**

**1866-1867** A324 Set of 2 9.00 9.00

Nos. 1866-1867 contain one 56x42mm stamp.

Stamp inscriptions are incorrect on Nos. 1865b, 1865c, and perhaps others.

African Wildlife A325

Designs: 100sh, Black rhinoceros. 140sh, Zebra, vert. 150sh, Hippopotomus. 200sh, Nile crocodile. 250sh, African elephant, vert. 370sh, Cape buffalo.

No. 1874, 1500sh, Royal python. No. 1875, 1500sh, Giraffe.

**1999, Feb. 18**

**1868-1873** A325 Set of 6 3.75 3.75

**Souvenir Sheets**

**1874-1875** A325 Set of 2 9.00 9.00

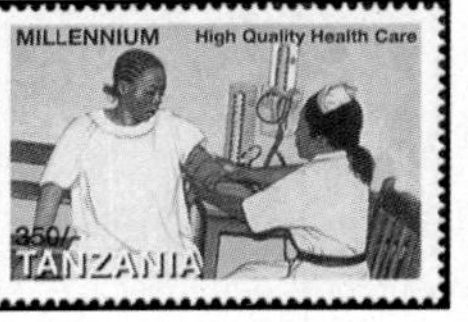

Millennium — A326

Designs: 350sh, High quality health care. 400sh, Good upbringing. 700sh, An abundance of food. 750sh, Clean water for all.

1500sh, Ostrich, "Enhancement of tourism promotion," vert.

**1999, Mar. 29**

**1876-1879** A326 Set of 4 6.75 6.75

**Souvenir Sheet**

**1880** A326 1500sh multicolored 4.50 4.50

Sharks A327

Designs: 200sh, Sand tiger. 250sh, Mako. 370sh, Great white. 410sh, Bull.
No. 1885: a, Basking. b, Whale. c, Tiger. d, Thresher. e, Caribbean reef. f, Nurse.
No. 1886, 1500sh, Scalloped hammerhead. No. 1887, 1500sh, Blue.

**1999 Litho. *Perf. 14***
**1881-1884** A327 Set of 4 3.00 3.00
**1885** A327 370sh Sheet of 6, #a.-f. 6.75 6.75

**Souvenir Sheets**
**1886-1887** A327 Set of 2 9.00 9.00

Rotary Club of Dar Es Salaam, 50th Anniv. A328

Designs: 150sh, Emblem. 250sh, Polio plus immunization, vert. 350sh, Paul P. Harris, founder of Rotary, Intl., vert. 400sh, Water supply.
500sh, Emblem, vert.

**1999, June 30**
**1888-1891** A328 Set of 4 3.50 3.50

**Souvenir Sheet**
**1892** A328 500sh multicolored 1.50 1.50

Endangered or Extinct Species — A330

No. 1898: a, Atitlan grebe. b, Cabot's tragopan. c, Spider monkey. d, Dibatag. e, Right whale. f, Imperial parrot. g, Cheetah. h, Brown-eared pheasant. i, Leatherback turtle. j, Imperial woodpecker. k, Andean condor. l, Barbary deer. m, Gray gentle lemur. n, Cuban parrot. o, Numbat. p, Short-tailed albatross. q, Green turtle. r, White rhinoceros. s, Diademed sifaka. t, Galapagos penguin.
No. 1899 — Tigers, horiz.: a, Caspian. b, Bengal. c, Javan. d, Indochinese. e, In white phase. f, Sumatran. g, Chinese. h, Bali. i, Siberian.
No. 1900, 1500sh, Rabbit-eared bandicoot. No. 1901, 1500sh, Grenada dove.

**1999, Feb. 18**
**1898** A330 100sh Sheet of 20, #a.-t. 5.00 5.00
**1899** A330 250sh Sheet of 9, #a.-i. 5.75 5.75

**Souvenir Sheets**
**1900-1901** A330 Set of 2 7.50 7.50

Queen Mother (b. 1900) — A331

No. 1902: a, In Kenya, 1959. b, In 1980. c, With Prince Charles, 1950. d, Iin 1990.
1500sh, In Kenya, 1959, diff.

**1999, Aug. 4 Litho. *Perf. 14***
**1902** A331 600sh Sheet of 4, #a.-d. + label 6.00 6.00

**Souvenir Sheet**
***Perf. 13¾***
**1903** A331 1500sh black 3.75 3.75

No. 1903 contains one 38x51mm stamp.

UPU, 125th Anniv. A332

Designs: 150sh, Mail conveyance. 300sh, Letter writing competition. 350sh, UPU committee meeting. 400sh, EMS Post net track and trace.
500sh, UPU emblem.

**Wmk. 387**
**1999, Aug. 10 Litho. *Perf. 14***
**1904-1907** A332 Set of 4 3.00 3.00

**Souvenir Sheet**
**1908** A332 500sh multicolored 1.25 1.25

Souvenir Sheets

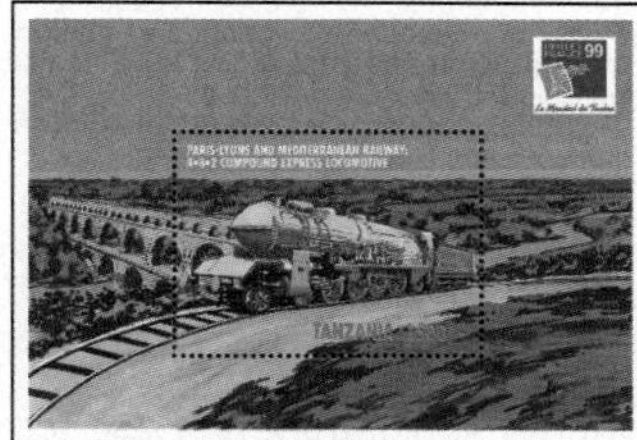
Philex France 99 — A333

Illustration reduced.
Trains: No. 1909, 1500sh, 4-8-2 compound express locomotive. No. 1910, 1500sh, TGV.

**1999, Aug. 20 Litho. *Perf. 13¾***
**1909-1910** A333 Set of 2 7.50 7.50

Inscriptions are misspelled on Nos. 1909-1910.

Birds of Japan A334

No. 1911, 250sh: a, Steller's sea eagle. b, Japanese blue flycatcher. c, Great gray shrike. d, Kingfisher. e, Hen harrier. f, Siberian meadow bunting. g, Mandarin duck. h, Red-necked grebe. i, Fairy pitta.
No. 1912, 250sh: a, Black paradise flycatcher. b, Laysan albatross. c, Collared Scops owl. d, Ryukyu robin. e, Japanese green woodpecker. f, Lidth's jay. g, White-naped crane. h, Copper pheasant. i, Okinawa rail.
No. 1913, 1500sh, Gyrfalcon. No. 1914, 1500sh, Japanese yellow bunting.

**1999, Aug. 20**
**Sheets of 9, #a.-i.**
**1911-1912** A334 Set of 2 11.50 11.50

**Souvenir Sheets**
**1913-1914** A334 Set of 2 7.50 7.50

Inscription on No. 1912b, and perhaps others, is misspelled.
APS StampShow '99 (#1911-1912).

Hokusai Paintings — A335

No. 1915: a, A Ferry Boat at Onmayagashi. b, A Drum Bridge at Kameido. c, Sea Life (fish). d, Sea Life (Octopus). e, Measuring a Pine Tree at Mishima Pass. f, Mount Fuji Seen From the Banks of Minobu River.
1500sh, Mount Fuji and Edo Castle Seen From Nihonbashi, vert.

**1999, Aug. 20**
**1915** A335 400sh Sheet of 6, #a.-f. 6.00 6.00

**Souvenir Sheet**
**1916** A335 1500sh multicolored 3.75 3.75

Masks — A336

Military Scenes — A337

Various masks: 150sh, 250sh, 300sh, 350sh.

**1999, Aug. 20 *Perf. 14***
**1917-1920** A336 Set of 4 2.60 2.60

**Souvenir Sheet**
**1921** A336 1500sh multicolored 3.75 3.75

**1999, Sept. 30**

150sh, British defeat Spanish Armada, 1588, horiz. No. 1923, 250sh, Battle of Waterloo. No. 1924, 250sh, Rorke's Drift, 24th Regiment, South Wales Borderers. No. 1925, 250sh, Special Air Services, Desert Storm. No. 1926, 300sh, Soldier on horseback. No. 1927, 300sh, World War I, horiz. No. 1928, 300sh, Bland's Dragoons, Battle of Dettingen. No. 1929, 350sh, Battle of Trafalgar, horiz. No. 1930, 350sh, Light Brigade. No. 1931, 350sh, Squadron 617, the "Dam Busters." No. 1932, 400sh, World War I tank, horiz. No. 1933, 400sh, Battle of Inkerman. No. 1934, 400sh, Battle of Salamanca, horiz. No. 1935, 500sh, Gen. James Wolfe, Battle of Quebec. No. 1936, 500sh, Parachute Regiment, Battle of Arnhem. No. 1937, 500sh, Battle of the Bulge.
No. 1938, 1500sh, Battle of the Nile. No. 1939, 1500sh, Battle of Albuhera.

**1922-1937** A337 Set of 16 14.00 14.00

**Souvenir Sheets**
**1938-1939** A337 Set of 2 7.50 7.50

Ships A338

No. 1940, 400sh: a, Bayan. b, Flying Cloud. c, Mayflower. d, Santa Maria. e, Morning Star. f, Ben Venue.
No. 1941, 400sh: a, Georg Stag. b, E. Starr Jones. c, Indiana. d, Brazilian coasting vessel. e, Nova Queen. f, Rainbow.
No. 1942, 1500sh, Dutch East Indiaman. No. 1943, 1500sh, Junk.

**1999, Sept. 30**
**Sheets of 6, #a.-f.**
**1940-1941** A338 Set of 2 12.00 12.00

**Souvenir Sheets**
**1942-1943** A338 Set of 2 7.50 7.50

Trains A339

No. 1944, 400sh: a, Adler 2-2-2, 1835. b, Beuth 2-2-2, 1843. c, Class 500 4-6-0, 1900. d, Northumbrian 0-2-2, 1830. e, Class 4-6-2, 1901. f, Claud Hamilton class 4-4-0.
No. 1945, 400sh: a, Firefly class 2-2-2, 1840. b, Single, 1854. c, 4-4-0, 1891. d, Medoc class 2-4-0, 1857. e, 4-4-0, 1893. f, Numar, 1846.
No. 1946, 1500sh, Planet class 2-2-0, 1830. No. 1947, 1500sh, Vauxhall 2-2-0, 1834. No. 1948, 1500sh, Class PB 4-6-0, 1906. No. 1949, 1500sh, 4-4-0, 1855.

**1999, Sept. 30**
**Sheets of 6, #a.-f.**
**1944-1945** A339 Set of 2 12.00 12.00

**Souvenir Sheets**
**1946-1949** A339 Set of 4 15.00 15.00

Airplanes A340

Designs: 200sh, Amref. No. 1951, 250sh, Westwind 2. 300sh, Morning Star. 400sh, Piper Warrior III.
No. 1954: a, Glasair Super II. b, Glastar. c, Cessna 120. d, Europa XS. e, Beechcraft Bonanza. f, Comache GTO. g, Lancir IV. h, Comanche 400.
No. 1955, 1500sh, Glastar, diff. No. 1956, 1500sh, Piper Archer III.

**1999, Sept. 30 Litho. *Perf. 14***
**1950-1953** A340 Set of 4 3.00 3.00
**1954** A340 250sh Sheet of 8, #a.-h. 5.00 5.00

**Souvenir Sheets**
**1955-1956** A340 Set of 2 7.50 7.50

Automobiles — A341

No. 1957, 400sh: a, Audi TT Coupe. b, Mitsubishi SST Spyder. c, Honda Dream. d, Renault 20. e, Renault Spider. f, Hyundai Euro I.
No. 1958, 400sh: a, Pininfarina Ethos. b, Jaguar XK120. c, Pininfarina Ethos II. d, Rinspeed E-GO Rocket. e, Volkswagen W12 Roadster. f, Chrysler Pronto Cruiser.
No. 1959, 1500sh, Ferrari Mythos. No. 1960, 1500sh, Hyundai Euro I, diff.

**1999, Sept. 30**
**Sheets of 6, #a.-f.**
**1957-1958** A341 Set of 2 12.00 12.00

**Souvenir Sheets**
**1959-1960** A341 Set of 2 7.50 7.50

Flowers A342

Designs; 150sh, Lilium longiflorum. 250sh, Strelitzia reginae. 400sh, Zantedeschia anim lily. 500sh, Iris.
600sh, Like 400sh.

**1999, Oct. 6 Litho. *Perf. 14***
**1961-1964** A342 Set of 4 3.25 3.25

**Souvenir Sheet**
**1965** A342 600sh multicolored 1.50 1.50

Butterflies — A343

No. 1966: a, Basilarchia archippus. b, Eueides isabella. c, Colobura dirce. d, Papilio cresphontes. e, Agrias claudia. f, Callicore maimuna.
No. 1967, 1500sh, Anteos clorinade, horiz. No. 1968, 1500sh, Tithorea harmonia, horiz.

**1999, Nov. 15**

**1966** A343 400sh Sheet of 6, #a.-f. 6.00 6.00

**Souvenir Sheets**

**1967-1968** A343 Set of 2 7.50 7.50

Sea Birds A344

Designs: 150sh, Rockhopper penguin, vert. No. 1970, 250sh, Jackass penguin, vert. 300sh, Adelie penguin, vert. 350sh, White tern. 400sh, Great frigatebird. 500sh, Brown pelican.

No. 1975, 250sh: a, Manx shearwater. b, Ring-billed gull. c, Herring gull. d, Red-tailed tropic bird. e, Laysan albatross. f, Black-headed gull. g, Blue-footed booby. h, Parakeet auklet. i, Red-legged cormorant.

No. 1976, 250sh: a, Razorbill. b, Southern giant petrel. c, Atlantic puffin. d, Great cormorant. e, Northern gannet. f, Masked booby. g, Tufted puffin. h, Galapagos penguin. i, Macaroni penguin.

No. 1977, 1500sh, King penguin, vert. No. 1978, 1500sh, Emperor penguin, vert.

**1999, Nov. 15**

**1969-1974** A344 Set of 6 5.00 5.00

**Sheets of 9, #a.-i.**

**1975-1976** A344 Set of 2 11.50 11.50

**Souvenir Sheets**

**1977-1978** A344 Set of 2 7.50 7.50

Dogs A345

No. 1979: a, Boxer. b, Mixed breed. c, Afghan hound. d, Chihuahua. e, Basset hound. f, Cavalier King Charles.

1500sh, Cocker spaniel.

**1999, Nov. 15**

**1979** A345 400sh Sheet of 6, #a.-f. 6.00 6.00

**Souvenir Sheet**

**1980** A345 1500sh multicolored 3.75 3.75

Paintings by Xu Beihong (1895-1953) A346

No. 1981: a, Chang K'uei. b, Fisherman. c, Orchid. d, Cock and Sunflower. e, Eagle. f, Sprite of the Mountain. g, Horse. h, Geese. i, Pigeon and Bamboo. j, Cat and Bamboo.

No. 1982: a, Spring Rain of Li River, horiz. b, The Himalayas, horiz.

**1999** ***Perf. 12½***

**1981** A346 150sh Sheet of 10, #a.-j. 3.75 3.75

***Perf. 13***

**1982** A346 600sh Sheet of 2, #a.-b. 3.00 3.00

China 1999 World Philatelic Exhibition.

Return of Macao to People's Republic of China — A347

No. 1983 — Nam Van: a, In 1850s. b, In 1930s. c, At present. d, View of lakes project.

**1999 Litho. *Perf. 13¾***

**1983** A347 300sh Sheet of 4, #a.-d. 3.00 3.00

China 1999 World Philatelic Exhibition.

Animals of the Central American Rain Forest — A348

No. 1984: a, Red howler monkey. b, Scarlet macaw. c, Rainbow boa, tree sloth. d, Iguana. e, Fruit bat. f, Rainbow boa. g, Crocodile. h, Manatee. i, Jaguar.

1500sh, Jaguar, diff.

**1999, Nov. 15 Litho. *Perf. 14***

**1984** A348 350sh Sheet of 9, #a.-i. 8.00 8.00

**Souvenir Sheet**

**1985** A348 1500sh multi 3.75 3.75

Dinosaurs — A349

No. 1986: a, Tyrannosaurus. b, Coelurus. c, Stegosaurus. d, Corythosaurus. e, Thadeosaurus. f, Brachiosaurus.

1500sh, Ceratosaurus.

**1999, Nov. 15**

**1986** A349 400sh Sheet of 6, #a.-f. 6.00 6.00

**Souvenir Sheet**

**1987** A349 1500sh multi 3.75 3.75

Nos. 1986-1987 dated 1998. Inscription on No. 1986f is misspelled.

Cats A350

No. 1988: a, Si-Rex. b, Spotted Mist. c, Angora. d, Persian. e, Sphynx. f, Alaskan Snow.

1500sh, Ragdoll.

**1999, Nov. 15**

**1988** A350 400sh Sheet of 6, #a.-f. 6.00 6.00

**Souvenir Sheet**

**1989** A350 1500sh multi 3.75 3.75

Mushrooms A351

150sh, Tricholoma portentosum. 250sh, Tricholomopsis rutilans. 300sh, Russula foetens. 350sh, Russula aeruginea. #1994, 400sh, Cortinarius varius. 500sh, Hygrocybe coccineocrenata.

No. 1996, 400sh: a, Agaricus abruptibulbus. b, Anellaria semiovata. c, Cystoderma carcharias. d, Amanita rubescens. e, Amanita fulva. f, Tricholoma sulphureum.

No. 1997, 400sh: a, Xerocomus rubellus. b, Geastrum rufescens. c, Lactarius salmonicolor. d, Gomphus clavatus. e, Russula rhodopoda. f, Russula paludosa.

No. 1998, 1500sh, Owl. No. 1999, 1500sh, Chipmunk and Stropharia hornemanii, horiz.

**1999, Nov. 15**

**1990-1995** A351 Set of 6 5.00 5.00

**Sheets of 6, #a.-f.**

**1996-1997** A351 Set of 2 12.00 12.00

**Souvenir Sheets**

**1998-1999** A351 Set of 2 7.50 7.50

Flora and Fauna A352

Designs: No. 2000, 150sh, Lion, vert. No. 2001, 150sh, Mountain gorilla, vert. No. 2002, 250sh, Pygmy hippopotamus, vert. No. 2003, 250sh, Japanese macaque, vert. No. 2004, 300sh, Cheetah. No. 2005, 300sh, Desert hare, vert. No. 2006, 350sh, Horned puffin. No. 2007, 350sh, Salvin's Amazon parrot. No. 2008, 400sh, Blueberries. No. 2009, 400sh, Bird's foot violet. No. 2010, 500sh, Orange groundsel. No. 2011, 500sh, Iguana.

No. 2012, 400sh: a, Polar bear. b, Woodland caribou. c, Snowy owl. d, Arctic fox. e, Willow ptarmigan. f, Arctic hare.

No. 2013, 400sh: a, White-tailed deer. b, Monarch butterfly. c, Yellow trumpet pitcher plants. d, Great blue heron. e, Yellow mud turtle. f, American alligator.

No. 2014, 400sh: a, Three-toed sloth. b, Emerald toucan. c, Praying mantis. d, Mouse opossum. e, Green palm viper. f, Phyllomedusa lemur.

No. 2015, 400sh: a, Ficus stupenda. b, Slow loris. c, Sambar deer. d, Thick-billed green pigeon. e, Bush cricket. f, Monitor lizard.

No. 2016, 1500sh, Three-toed jacamar. No. 2017, 1500sh, Chuckwallas. No. 2018, 1500sh, Swallowtail butterfly. No. 2019, 1500sh, Otter, vert.

**1999, Nov. 15**

**2000-2011** A352 Set of 12 9.75 9.75

**Sheets of 6, #a.-f.**

**2012-2015** A352 Set of 4 24.00 24.00

**Souvenir Sheets**

**2016-2019** A352 Set of 4 15.00 15.00

Flowers — A353

Designs: 150sh, Foxglove. 250sh, Chrysanthemum. 400sh, Amaryllis. 500sh, Hidden lilies.

No. 2024, 350sh, horiz.: a, Gerbara daisies. b, Begonias. c, Clematis. d, Violas. e, Southern magnolia. f, Dwarf balloon flowers. g, Camellias. h, Day lilies. i, Roses.

No. 2025, 350sh, horiz.: a, Daffodils. b, Columbines. c, Nasturtiums. d, Gazanias. e, Rose. f, Crocuses. g, Trumpet vine. h, Dahlia. i, Oriental poppies.

No. 2026, 1500sh, Siberian iris. No. 2027, 1500sh, Water lily, horiz.

**1999, Nov. 15 Litho. *Perf. 14***

**2020-2023** A353 Set of 4 3.25 3.25

**Sheets of 9, #a.-i.**

**2024-2025** A353 Set of 2 16.00 16.00

**Souvenir Sheets**

**2026-2027** A353 Set of 2 7.50 7.50

Military Vehicles — A354

Illustration reduced.

No. 2028, 400sh: a, French Hotchkiss H35 tank. b, German Panzer IV tank. c, US M4 tank. d, German Tiger tank. e, US Half track. f, British Cromwell tank.

No. 2029, 400sh: a, British MK IV tank. b, Japanese Type 95 tank. c, German Hunting Panther tank. d, French AMX30 tank. e, Israeli Merkava tank. f, US M1 tank.

No. 2030, 1500sh, AH-64A Apache helicopter. No. 2031, 1500sh, Austin armored car, vert.

**1999, Sept. 30 Litho. *Perf. 14***

**Sheets of 6, #a.-f.**

**2028-2029** A354 Set of 2 12.00 12.00

**Souvenir Sheets**

**2030-2031** A354 Set of 2 7.50 7.50

African Flowers — A355

Designs: 150sh, Canarina abyssinica. 250sh, Diaphananthe kamerunensis. 350sh, Protea barbigera. 500sh, Angraecum scottianum.

No. 2036, 400sh: a, Bolusanthus speciosus. b, Cassia abbreviata. c, Erythrina lysistemon. d, Leucodendron discolor. e, Romulea fischeri. f, Lupinus princei.

No. 2037, 400sh: a, Ansellia africana. b, Kigelia africana. c, Aerangis brachycarpa. d, Brachcorythis kalbreyeri. e, Begonia meyerii-johannis. f, Saintpaulia ionantha.

No. 2038, 1500sh, Nymphaea caerulea. No. 2039, 1500sh, Aloe petricola.

**1999, Nov. 15**

**2032-2035** A355 Set of 4 3.25 3.25

**Sheets of 6, #a.-f.**

**2036-2037** A355 Set of 2 12.00 12.00

**Souvenir Sheets**

**2038-2039** A355 Set of 2 7.50 7.50

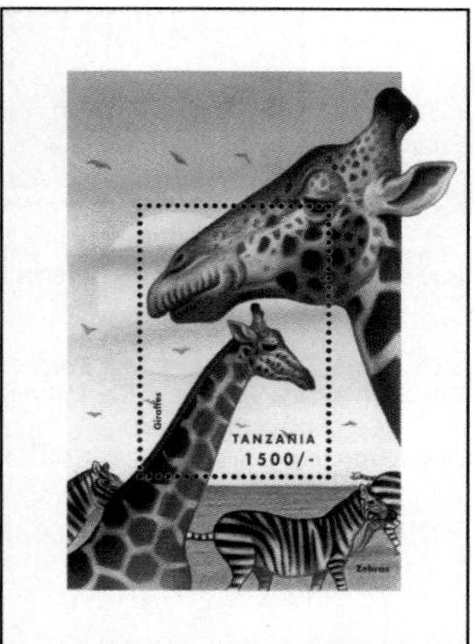


African Wildlife — A356

Illustration reduced.

No. 2040, horiz.: a, Mountain gorilla. b, Zebras. c, East African elephant. d, Crowned cranes. e, Cheetah. f, Tiger. g, Pygmy chimpanzee. h, Hippopotamus.

No. 2041, 1500sh, Giraffes. No. 2042, 1500sh, Rhinoceros.

**1999, Nov. 15**

**2040** A356 300sh Sheet of 8, #a.-h. 6.00 6.00

**Souvenir Sheets**

**2041-2042** A356 Set of 2 7.50 7.50

Marine Life A357

Designs: 350sh, Beluga whale. 400sh, Ghost crab. 500sh, Emperor penguin, vert.

No. 2046: a, Herring gulls. b, Dusky dolphin. c, Sandwich tern. d, Humpback whale. e, Right whale. f, Dusky dolphin, sergeant major. g, White-tipped shark. h, Manta ray, trunkfish. i, Purple moon angel. j, Scalloped hammerhead shark. k, Manatee. l, Striped fingerfish.

No. 2047, 1500sh, Humpback whales. No. 2048, 1500sh, Tiger shark.

**1999, Nov. 15**

**2043-2045** A357 Set of 3 3.25 3.25

**2046** A357 250sh Sheet of 12, #a.-l. 7.50 7.50

**Souvenir Sheets**

**2047-2048** A357 Set of 2 7.50 7.50

Ballet A358

Designs: 300sh, Romeo and Juliet. 350sh, The Dying Swan. 400sh, Giselle, vert. 500sh, Spartacus, vert.

No. 2053, 1500sh, The Firebird, vert. No. 2054, 1500sh, Swan Lake, vert.

**1999, Aug. 20 Litho. *Perf. 14***

**2049-2052** A358 Set of 4 4.00 4.00

**Souvenir Sheets**

**2053-2054** A358 Set of 2 7.50 7.50

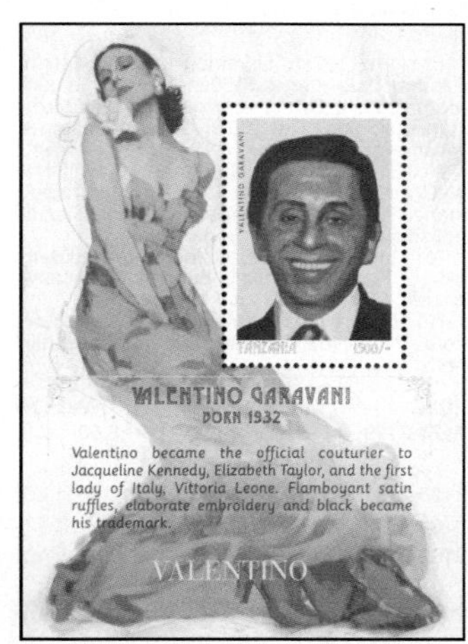

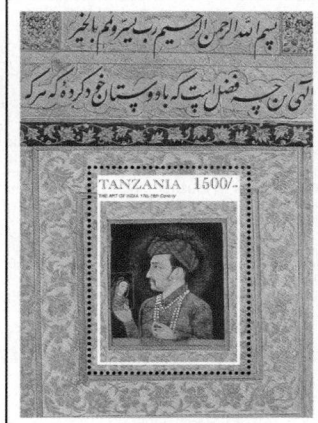


17th and 18th Century Indian Art — A359

No. 2055, 500sh: a, Krishna and the Gopis (large tree). b, Krishna Painting the Feet of Radha. c, Krishna Yearning for the Moon (woman with fan). d, Games of Krishna and Radha (boat).

No. 2056, 500sh: a, Balwant Singh Having His Beard Cut. b, Festival of Hou (women at right). c, Ragini Bialvali (woman with fan, woman on seat). d, Krishna Holding a Ball of Butter.

No. 2057, 1500sh, Portrait of Emperor Jahanoir (man with necklace), vert. No. 2058, 1500sh, Krishna and the Gopis, diff., vert.

Illustration reduced.

**1999, Aug. 20 *Perf. 13¾***

**Sheets of 4, #a-d**

**2055-2056** A359 Set of 2 10.00 10.00

**Souvenir Sheets**

**2057-2058** A359 Set of 2 7.50 7.50

Fashion Designers — A360

No. 2059: a, Christian Dior. b, Model wearing Dior fashions. c, Bottle of Chanel No. 5, model wearing Chanel Fashions. d, Gabrielle "Coco" Chanel. e, Gianni Versace. f, Model wearing Versace fashions. g, Model wearing Yves Saint Laurent fashions. h, Yves Saint Laurent.

1500sh, Valentino Garavani.

**1999, Aug. 20 *Perf. 14***

**2059** A360 300sh Sheet of 8, #a-h 6.00 6.00

**Souvenir Sheet**

**2060** A360 1500sh multi 3.75 3.75

Nos. 2059b-2059c, 2059f-2059g are 53x39mm.

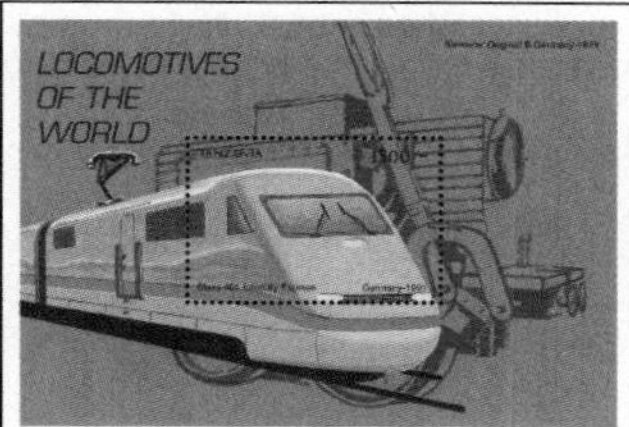


Locomotives — A361

No. 2061: a, Class EF 81 Bo-Bo, Japan. b, Class 120 Bo-Bo, West Germany. c, Shao Shan I Co-Co, China. d, TGV, France. e, F40 PH Bo-Bo, US. f, LRC Bo-Bo, Canada.

1500sh, Class 401 Intercity Express, Germany.

Illustration reduced.

**1999, Sept. 30**

**2061** A361 400sh Sheet of 6, #a-f 6.00 6.00

**Souvenir Sheet**

**2062** A361 1500sh multi 3.75 3.75

Marine Life A362

Designs: 150sh, Great barracuda. 250sh, Common squid. No. 2065, 300sh, Atlantic salmon. 350sh, Ocean sunfish. 400sh, Lobster. 500sh, Yellowfin tuna.

No. 2069, 300sh: a, Flying fish. b, Sailfish. c, Common dolphin. d, Sperm whale. e, Spinner dolphin. f, Manta ray. g, Green turtle. h, Hammerhead shark. i, Marlin.

No. 2070, 300sh: a, Walrus. b, Killer whale. c, Arctic tern. d, White shark. e, Narwhal. f, Blue whale. g, Giant clam. h, Octopus. i, Conger eel.

No. 2071, 1500sh, Whale shark. No. 2072, 1500sh, Beluga, vert.

**1999, Nov. 15**

**2063-2068** A362 Set of 6 5.00 5.00

**Sheets of 9, #a-i**

**2069-2070** A362 Set of 2 13.50 13.50

**Souvenir Sheets**

**2071-2072** A362 Set of 2 7.50 7.50

Pres. Julius K. Nyerere (1922-99) A363

Nyerere: 200sh, As young man and old man. 500sh, With Edward Moringe Sokonie. 600sh, The Compassionate leader, vert. 800sh, During the early days of independence, vert.

1000sh, Mausoleum.

**2000, Apr. 13 *Perf. 13***

**2073-2076** A363 Set of 4 5.25 5.25

**Souvenir Sheet**

***Perf. 13x13½***

**2077** A363 1000sh multi 2.50 2.50

No. 2077 contains one 35x28mm stamp.

Tourism A364

Designs: 400sh, Lion, Seronera Wildlife Lodge. No. 2079, 800sh, Hippopotami and hyenas, Selous Game Reserve. No. 2080, 800sh, Fish, Mafia Island. No. 2081, 800sh, Giraffes, Lobo Wildlife Lodge. No. 2082, 800sh, Rhinoceros, Ngorongoro Crater Wildlife Lodge. No. 2083, 800sh, Elephant, Mikumi Natl. Park. No. 2084, 800sh, Elephant, Lake Manyara Natl. Park. No. 2085, 800sh, Elephants, rhinoceros, Kibo Peak, Mt. Kilimanjaro.

1000sh, Lion, giraffes, elephant, rhinoceros, Lake Manyara Natl. Park, vert.

***Perf. 13x13½, 13½x13***

**2000, June 10 Litho.**

**2078-2085** A364 Set of 8 15.00 15.00

**Souvenir Sheet**

**2086** A364 1000sh multi 2.50 2.50

See Nos. 2102-2125.

Activities of World Vision A365

Designs: 200sh, Children with water pots on heads. 600sh, Family preparing food. 800sh, Nurse, family. 1000sh, Education of children.

**2000, July 20 Litho. *Perf. 13x13¼***

**2087-2090** A365 Set of 4 6.50 6.50

**Souvenir Sheet**

**2091** A365 500sh Two children 1.25 1.25

2000 Summer Olympics, Sydney A366

Designs: 150sh, Soccer. 350sh, Basketball, vert. 400sh, Women's 1500-meter race, vert. 800sh, Boxing.

500sh, Medal ceremony, vert.

**2000, Sept. 15 *Perf. 13¾***

**2092-2095** A366 Set of 4 4.25 4.25

**Souvenir Sheet**

**2096** A366 500sh multi 1.25 1.25

Universities of East Africa A367

Designs: 150sh, Medical students, Muhimbili University College of Health Sciences. 200sh, Zanzibar University. 600sh, Makerere University, Uganda, vert. 800sh, Egerton University, Kenya.

500sh, Emblem of Inter-university Council for East Africa.

**2000 *Perf. 13x13¼, 13¼x13***

**2097-2100** A367 Set of 4 4.50 4.50

***Perf. 14½***

**Size: 84x83mm**

**2101** A367 500sh multi 1.25 1.25

**Tourism Type of 2000**

No. 2102, 400sh, No. 2110, 500sh, No. 2118, 600sh, Like #2079. No. 2103, 400sh, No. 2111, 500sh, No. 2119, 600sh, Like #2080. No. 2104, 400sh, No. 2112, 500sh, No. 2120, 600sh, Like #2081. No. 2105, 400sh, No. 2113, 500sh, No. 2121, 600sh, Like #2082. No. 2106, 400sh, No. 2114, 500sh, No. 2122, 600sh, Like #2083. No. 2107, 400sh, No. 2115, 500sh, No. 2123, 600sh, Like #2084. No. 2108, 400sh, No. 2116, 500sh, No. 2124, 600sh, Like #2085. No. 2109, 500sh, No. 2117, 600sh, No. 2125, 800sh, Like #2078.

**2000, June 1 Litho. *Perf. 13x13½***

**2102-2125** A364 Set of 24 35.00 35.00

Flowers A368

150sh, Bacciflava. 250sh, Hybridus pendulus. #2128, 300sh, Rhaphiolepis umbellata. 350sh, Magnoliaeflora. 400sh, Magnolia, vert. 500sh, Margot Koster, vert.

No. 2132, 300sh: a, Viola pedata. b, Magnolia. c, Felicia amelloides. d, Lythrum. e, Hemerocallis. f, Tithonia rotundifolia. g, Lilium. h, Iris. i, Stokesia laevis.
No. 2133, 300sh, vert.: a, Prunus subhirtella. b, Sanguinaria canadensis. c, Rosa palustris. d, Gordonia lasianthius. e, Aquilegia caerulea. f, Fremontodendron. g, Hypericum calycinum. h, Anemone vitifolia. i, Clematis.
No. 2134, Iris cristata, vert. No. 2134A, Aster prikartil.

**2000** ***Perf. 14***
**2126-2131** A368 Set of 6 5.00 5.00

**Sheets of 9, #a-i**
**2132-2133** A368 Set of 2 13.50 13.50

**Souvenir Sheet**
**2134-2134A** A368 Set of 2 7.50 7.50

Social Security Fund A369

Designs: 200sh, Retirement. 350sh, Employment injury. 600sh, Invalidity. 800sh, Health insurance.

**2000** **Wmk. 387** ***Perf. 13¾***
**2135-2138** A369 Set of 4 5.00 5.00

**Souvenir Sheet**
**2139** A369 500sh Maternity 1.25 1.25

Environmental Care — A370

Designs: 200sh, Tree planting campaign. 400sh, Water sources protection. 600sh, Cleaning sewage. 800sh, Protecting forests.

**2000** **Wmk. 387** ***Perf. 13x13¼***
**2140-2143** A370 Set of 4 5.00 5.00

**Souvenir Sheet**
**2144** A370 1000sh Mountain 2.50 2.50

Zanzibar Millennium A371

Designs: 150sh, Fishing industry. 200sh, Trade and tourism. 400sh, Child and emblem, vert. 800sh, Right to higher learning, vert.
500sh, Peace and tranquility, vert.

**2000** **Wmk. 387** ***Perf. 13¾***
**2145-2148** A371 Set of 4 4.00 4.00

**Souvenir Sheet**
**2149** A371 500sh multi 1.25 1.25

Orchids A372

Designs: 200sh, Vanilla planifolia. 250sh, Pleurothallus tuerckheimii. No. 2152, 370sh, Trichopilia fragrans.
No. 2153, 370sh: a, Cyrtopodium andersonii. b, Cochleanthes discolor. c, Catasetum barbatum. d, Caularthron bicornutum. e, Broughtonia sanguinea. f, Brassavola nodosa.
No. 2154, 370sh: a, Oeceoclades maculata. b, Isochilus linearis. c, Eulophia alta. d, Ionopsis utricularioides. e, Epidendrum ciliare. f, Dimerandra emarginata.
No. 2155, 1500sh, Brassavola cucullata. No. 2156, 1500sh, Epidendrum nocturnum.

**2000** **Litho.** ***Perf. 14***
**2150-2152** A372 Set of 3 2.00 2.00

**Sheets of 6, #a-f**
**2153-2154** A372 Set of 2 11.00 11.00

**Souvenir Sheets**
**2155-2156** A372 Set of 2 7.25 7.25

Nos. 607, 610, 612, 615, 617 Surcharged

**Methods and perfs as before**

**1998-2001**
**2157** A99 100sh on 40sh multi
**2158** A99 150sh on 9sh multi
**2159** A99 200sh on 170sh multi
**2159A** A99 230sh on 20sh multi — —
**2159B** A99 230sh on 170sh multi
**2159C** A99 800sh on 500sh multi 2.00 2.00

Issued: No. 2158, 1/26/98; No. 2157, 8/6/98; No. 2159, 6/4/00; No. 2159C, 4/6/00; No. 2159B, 11/20/00; No. 2159A, 11/20/01.

Rare Birds A373

Designs: 150sh, Taita falcon. 300sh, Banded green. 400sh, Spotted ground thrush. 500sh, Fischer's turaco. 600sh, Blue swallow.

**2000** **Litho.** ***Perf. 14***
**2160** A373 150sh multi
**2161** A373 300sh multi
**2162** A373 400sh multi
**2163** A373 500sh multi

**Souvenir Sheet**
**2164** A373 600sh multi

Architecture — A374

Designs: 150sh, Ruins of Great Mosque, Kilwa Kisiwani. 200sh, German Boma, Mikindani. 250sh, German Boma, Bagamoyo. 300sh, Butiama Museum, Mara. 350sh, Chief Government Chemist Office. 400sh, Old Post Office, Dar es Salaam. 500sh, Dr. David Livingstone Lodge, Kwihara Tabora. 600sh, Original and present State Houses, vert. 700sh, Ngoni-Nyamwezi traditional houses. 800sh, The People's Palace Beit Elajaib, Zanzibar. 900sh, Tongoni Ruins, Tanga. 1000sh, Karimjee Hall, Dar es Salaam.
1500sh, Old Boma, Mikindani.

**2000 (?)** **Litho.** ***Perf. 13***
**2165** A374 150sh multi
**2166** A374 200sh multi
**2166A** A374 250sh multi
**2167** A374 300sh multi
**2167A** A374 350sh multi
**2168** A374 400sh multi
**2168A** A374 500sh multi
**2169** A374 600sh multi
**2169A** A374 700sh multi
**2170** A374 800sh multi
**2170A** A374 900sh multi
**2171** A374 1000sh multi

**Souvenir Sheet**
**2172** A374 1500sh multi

Flora and Fauna — A375

Designs: 100sh, Common babbler. 140sh, Eastern blue darner. 150sh, Cavalier mushroom. 200sh, Orange-barred sulphur. 250sh, Harlequin bug. No. 2179, 370sh, Brassolae liocattleya.
No. 2180, 370sh: a, Common yellowthroat. b, Great orange tip. c, Tiger lily. d, Shaggy mane. e, Sri Lanka grasshopper. f, Woodhouse's toad.
No. 2181, 370sh: a, Golden-crowned warbler. b, Fuchsia. c, Alfalfa butterfly. d, Lycaste aquila. e, Snail. f, Ground beetle.
No. 2182, 1500sh, Rufous-collared sparrow, horiz. No. 2183, 1500sh, Monarch butterfly, horiz.

**2000** **Litho.** ***Perf. 14***
**2174-2179** A375 Set of 6 3.00 3.00

**Sheets of 6, #a-f**
**2180-2181** A375 Set of 2 11.00 11.00

**Souvenir Sheets**
**2182-2183** A375 Set of 2 7.50 7.50

Activities of World Vision — A375a

Design: 200sh, Children have a right to education, horiz. 600sh, Children have a right to happiness, horiz. 800sh, Children have a right not to be exploited. 1000sh, Children have a right to be heard.

**2001, Apr. 30** **Litho.** ***Perf. 13***
**2183A** A375a 200sh multi — —
**2183B** A375a 600sh multi — —
**2183C** A375a 800sh multi — —
**2183D** A375a 1000sh multi — —

**Souvenir Sheet**
**2183E** A375a 500sh multi — —

Endangered Animals A376

Designs: 200sh, Leopard. 400sh, Rhinoceros. No. 2186, 600sh, Crocodile. 800sh, Hunting wild dogs.
No. 2188, 600sh, Cheetah.

**2001, June 15** **Litho.** ***Perf. 13***
**2184-2187** A376 Set of 4 4.50 4.50

**Souvenir Sheet**
**2188** A376 600sh multi 1.40 1.40

UN High Commissioner for Refugees, 50th Anniv. — A377

Designs: 200sh, Refugee child being vaccinated. 400sh, Refugees crossing Lake Tanganyika. 600sh, Refugee woman, vert. 800sh, Fleeing refugees, vert.

**2001, July 31**
**2189-2192** A377 Set of 4 4.50 4.50
*2191a* Souvenir sheet of 1 1.40 1.40

Landscapes A378

Designs: 200sh, Rufiji River, Selous Game Reserve. 400sh, Mangapwani Beach, Zanzibar. 600sh, Mountains, Mikumi Natl. Park. 800sh, Balancing Stones, Shore of Lake Victoria, Mwanza, vert.
700sh, Ruaha Natl. Park, vert.

**2001, Nov. 30** **Litho.** ***Perf. 13***
**2193-2196** A378 Set of 4 4.50 4.50

**Souvenir Sheet**
**2197** A378 700sh multi 1.50 1.50

Year of Dialogue Among Civilizations A379

Designs: 200sh, Talking with children. 400sh, Formal dress. 600sh, Exchanging ideas. 800sh, Letter writing.
700sh, Communication linkages, vert.

**2001, Oct. 9** **Litho.**
**2198-2201** A379 Set of 4 4.50 4.50

**Souvenir Sheet**
**2202** A379 700sh multi 1.50 1.50

Conservation of Zanzibar Rare Species — A380

Designs: 250sh, Dolphins. 300sh, Coral reefs. 450sh, Coral reefs, diff. 800sh, Zanzibar red colobus, vert.
700sh, Zanzibar red colobus, diff.

**2002, Aug. 30** **Litho.** ***Perf. 13***
**2203-2206** A380 Set of 4 4.00 4.00

**Souvenir Sheet**
**2207** A380 700sh multi 1.60 1.60

Historic Sites of East Africa A381

Designs: 250sh, Fort Kilwa. 300sh, Maruhubi Palace ruins, Zanzibar. 400sh, Old Provincial Office, Nairobi, 1913. 800sh, Mparu Tombs, Hoima, Uganda.
700sh, Map of East Africa, ship.

**2001, Oct. 19**
**2208-2211** A381 Set of 4 3.75 3.75

**Souvenir Sheet**

**2212** A381 700sh multi 1.50 1.50

Independence, 40th Anniv. — A382

Designs: 180sh, Tea estates. 230sh, Regional integration with Uganda and Kenya, vert. 350sh, University graduates, vert. 450sh, 1000sh, Lion, elephant, buffalo, cheetah, rhinoceros, Mt. Kilimanjaro. 650sh, Referral hospitals. 950sh, Mining industry.

**2001, Dec. 30 Litho. *Perf. 14***
**2213-2218** A382 Set of 6 6.00 6.00

**Souvenir Sheet**

**2219** A382 1000sh multi 2.10 2.10

Ceremonial Costumes — A383

Designs: 250sh, Makonde mask dance. 350sh, Zanzibar Mwaka koga festival. 400sh, Lizombe dancer. 450sh, Zaramo bride's celebration.
500sh, Like 400sh.

**Wmk. 387**
**2002, Mar. 30 Litho. *Perf. 13¾***
**2220-2223** A383 Set of 4 3.00 3.00

**Souvenir Sheet**

**2224** A383 500sh multi 1.00 1.00

Mountains A384

Designs: 250sh, Mt. Kilimanjaro. 350sh, Usambara Mountains. 400sh, Uluguru Mountains. 450sh, Mwanihana Peak, Udzungwa Mountains.
500sh, Like 250sh.

**2002, June 30 Wmk. 387**
**2225-2228** A384 Set of 4 3.00 3.00

**Souvenir Sheet**

**2229** A384 500sh multi 1.10 1.10

National Census A385

Census emblem and: 200sh, School children, vert. 250sh, Group of people. 350sh, Family. 600sh, Boy, census figures.
800sh, Group of people, vert.

***Perf. 13x13¼ Sync., 13¼x13 Sync.***
**2002, Aug. 13 Unwmk.**
**2230-2233** A385 Set of 4 3.00 3.00

**Souvenir Sheet**
***Perf. 13x13¼***

**2234** A385 800sh multi 1.60 1.60

Arts of Zanzibar A386

Designs: 200sh, Mat making. 250sh, Handsewn hats. 350sh, Chair making. 600sh, Hina painting.
800sh, Zanzibar door.

**2002, Sept. 13 Unwmk. *Perf. 13¼***
**2235-2238** A386 Set of 4 3.00 3.00

**Souvenir Sheet**
***Perf. 13***

**2239** A386 800sh multi 1.60 1.60

Souvenir Sheet

Wildlife — A387

No. 2240: a, Leopard. b, Elephant. c, Rhinoceros. d, Lion. e, Buffalo.

***Perf. 13x14***
**2002, Apr. 30 Wmk. 387**
**2240** A387 250sh Sheet of 5, #a-e 2.60 2.60

Compare No. 2240 with No. 2251.

Archaeology A388

Designs: 250sh, Ancient city of Kisimkazi, Zanzibar, vert. 400sh, Ruins of Kaole town, Bagamoyo. 450sh, Kondoa Irangi rock paintings, vert. 600sh, Great Mosque, Kilwa Kisiwani.
1000sh, Like 450sh.

***Perf. 13¼***
**2002, Sept. 30 Unwmk. Litho.**
**2241-2244** A388 Set of 4 3.50 3.50

**Souvenir Sheet**
***Perf. 13***

**2245** A388 1000sh multi 2.10 2.10

Wildlife A389

Designs: 400sh, Rhinoceroses. 500sh, Elephant. 600sh, Lion. 800sh, Leopard, vert. 1000sh, Buffalo.
1500sh, Rhinoceros, elephant, lion, leopard, buffalo, vert.

***Perf. 13¼x12¾, 12¾x13¼***
**2003, Apr. 22 Litho. Wmk. 387**
**2246-2250** A389 Set of 5 6.50 6.50

**Size: 85x115mm**
***Imperf***

**2251** A389 1500sh multi 3.00 3.00

Compare No. 2251 with No. 2240.

Cash Crops — A390

Designs: 250sh, Cotton. 300sh, Cashews. 600sh, Sisal. 800sh, Cloves.
1000sh, Tea, horiz.

***Perf. 13x13¼ Syncopated***
**2003, June 10 Unwmk.**
**2252-2255** A390 Set of 4 3.75 3.75

**Souvenir Sheet**
***Perf. 13¼x13 Syncopated***

**2256** A390 1000sh multi 1.90 1.90

Activities of World Vision A391

Designs: 300sh, Better nutrition with vitamin A. 600sh, Education opportunity for all children. 800sh, Clean and safe water for all, vert. 1000sh, Malaria prevention with treated mosquito nets.
500sh, Children have a right to be heard.

**2003, July 3 *Perf. 13***
**2257-2260** A391 Set of 4 5.25 5.25

**Souvenir Sheet**

**2261** A391 500sh multi .95 .95

Traditional Dances A392

Dances: 300sh, Nyamwezi. 500sh, Luo. 600sh, Pemba. 800sh, Baganda.
1000sh, Masai.

***Perf. 13¼x13 Syncopated***
**2003, July 25**
**2262-2265** A392 Set of 4 4.25 4.25

**Souvenir Sheet**

**2266** A392 1000sh multi 1.90 1.90

Nos. 612 and 1567 Surcharged

**Methods and Perfs As Before**
**2002**
**2267** A99 250sh on 40sh #612 .50 .50
**2268** A262 250sh on 180sh #1567 .50 .50

Issued: No. 2267, 7/23/02; No. 2268, 8/30/02.

Northern Circuit Tourist Attractions A393

Designs: 300sh, Lion, lioness, Mt. Kilimanjaro. 350sh, Kibo Peak, Mt. Kilimanjaro. 400sh, Zebras, Serengeti Natl. Park. 500sh, Elephants, Kilimanjaro Natl. Park. 600sh, Leopards, Serengeti Natl. Park. 800sh, Rhinoceros, Ngorongoro Crater.
1000sh, Buffalo, Arusha Natl. Park.

**2003, Apr. 30 Litho. *Perf. 13¼x13***
**2269-2274** A393 Set of 6 5.75 5.75

**Souvenir Sheet**

**2275** A393 1000sh multi 2.00 2.00

Landscapes A394

Designs: 300sh, Rufiji Delta. 400sh, Zanzibar shore. 500sh, Lake Manyara, Rift Valley. 800sh, Kalambo Falls, vert.
1000sh, Coastal mangroves.

**2003, July 22 Litho. *Perf. 13¼x13***
**2276-2279** A394 Set of 4 4.00 4.00

**Souvenir Sheet**

**2280** A394 1000sh multi 1.90 1.90

Zanzibar Tourist Attractions A395

Designs: 300sh, Old Fort. 500sh, Door, Beit al Ajaib, vert. 600sh, Coconut palm tree, Michamvi Beach, vert. 800sh, Dhow, Beit al Ajaib.

***Perf. 13¼x13, 13x13¼***
**2003, Sept. 30 Litho.**
**2281-2284** A395 Set of 4 4.25 4.25
*2284a* Souvenir sheet, #2281, 2283, 2284 3.25 3.25

Marine Mammals A396

Designs: 300sh, Common dolphin. 350sh, Sperm whale. 400sh, Southern right whale. 600sh, Dugong.
500sh, Bottlenose dolphin.

**2003, Oct. 11 Litho. *Perf. 13¼x13***
**2285-2288** A396 Set of 4 3.25 3.25

**Souvenir Sheet**

**2289** A396 500sh multi .95 .95

Religious Festivals — A396a

Designs: 300sh, Muslims on pilgrimage to Mecca. 500sh, Choir at Christmas. 600sh, Prophet Mohammed's Birthday. 800sh, Church at Christmas.
1000sh, Crucifixion of Jesus.

**Wmk. 387**

**2003, Nov. 4 Litho. *Perf. 14***

**2289A-2289D** A396a Set of 4 4.25 4.25

**Souvenir Sheet**

**2289E** A396a 1000sh multi 1.90 1.90

Tanzania Posts Corporation, 10th Anniv. — A397

Designs: 350sh, Counter automation. 400sh, Overnight mail delivery services. 600sh, Workers' participation. 800sh, Expedited mail services.
1000sh, Post Cargo.

**Unwmk.**

**2004, Jan. 19 Litho. *Perf. 13***

**2290-2293** A397 Set of 4 4.00 4.00
*2293a* Souvenir sheet, #2290-2293 4.00 4.00

**Souvenir Sheet**

**2294** A397 1000sh multi 1.90 1.90

Western Union Money Transfer A398

Designs: 300sh, Exchange of American and Tanzanian currency. 400sh, Busalanga Primary School. 500sh, Woman, child, Tanzanian currency, vert. 600sh, World map.
800sh, Like 300sh, without Western Union emblem.

***Perf. 13¼x13, 13x13¼***

**2004, Feb. 3 Litho.**

**2295-2298** A398 Set of 4 3.25 3.25

**Souvenir Sheet**

**2299** A398 800sh multi 1.50 1.50

Girl Guides in Tanzania, 75th Anniv. A399

Designs: 300sh, Guides demonstrating solar cookers. 400sh, Camp training. 600sh, Bravery training. 800sh, Guides assisting at a mother and child clinic session.
1000sh, Like 800sh.

**2004, May 15 *Perf. 13¼x13***

**2300-2303** A399 Set of 4 3.75 3.75

**Souvenir Sheet**

**2304** A399 1000sh multi 1.90 1.90

Tanganyika Christian Refugee Service, 40th Anniv. A400

Designs: 350sh, Truck carrying refugees and bicycles. 600sh, Public water source. 800sh, Students in classroom. 1000sh, Afforestation campaign.
1200sh, Four vignettes combined.

**Unwmk.**

**2004, May 24 Litho. *Perf. 14***

**2305-2308** A400 Set of 4 5.00 5.00

**Souvenir Sheet**

***Perf. 14¼***

**2309** A400 1200sh multi 2.25 2.25

No. 2309 contains one 44x34mm stamp.

Zanzibar Watercraft Races A401

Designs: 350sh, Crowd cheering race winners. 400sh, Punt race. 600sh, Dhow race. 800sh, Sailboat race.
1000sh, Dhow, vert.

**2004, June 25 *Perf. 13***

**2310-2313** A401 Set of 4 4.00 4.00
*2313a* Souvenir sheet, #2310-2313 4.00 4.00

**Souvenir Sheet**

**2314** A401 1000sh multi 1.90 1.90

Flora, Fauna and Mushrooms — A402

No. 2315, 550sh, horiz. — Animals: a, Red colobus monkey. b, Leopard. c, Giraffe. d, Eland. e, Zebra. f, African elephant.
No. 2316, 550sh, horiz. — Birds: a, European roller. b, Little swift. c, African gray parrot. d, Bateleur. e, European bee-eater. f, Hoopoe.
No. 2317, 550sh, horiz. — Butterflies: a, Gold-banded forester. b, Two-tailed pasha. c, Plain tiger. d, Common dotted border. e, African migrant. f, Forest queen.
No. 2318, 550sh, horiz. — Orchids: a, Cynorkis kassnerana. b, Habenaria rhodocheila. c, Vanilla planifola. d, Ansellia africana. e, Disa uniflora. f, Calathe rosea.
No. 2319, 550sh, horiz. — Mushrooms: a, Fly mushroom. b, Rosy-gill fairy helmet. c, Purple coincap. d, Velvet shank. e, Thick-footed morel. f, King bolete.
No. 2320, 2000sh, Olive baboon. No. 2321, 2000sh, Gray crowned crane. No. 2322, 2000sh, Blue diadem butterfly. No. 2323, 2000sh, Disa uniflora, diff. No. 2324, 2000sh, Sharp-scaled parasol mushroom.

**2004, July 19 *Perf. 14***

**Sheets of 6, #a-f**

**2315-2319** A402 Set of 5 30.00 30.00

**Souvenir Sheets**

**2320-2324** A402 Set of 5 18.50 18.50

Mining A403

Designs: 350sh, Diamond mining at Williamson Diamond Mwadui. 500sh, Semi-processed jewels. No. 2327, 600sh, Drillers in deep mine. 800sh, Gold miners.
No. 2329, Unprocessed gemstones.

**2004, July 30 *Perf. 13¼x12¾***

**2325-2328** A403 Set of 4 4.25 4.25
*2328a* Souvenir sheet, #2325-2328 4.25 4.25

**Souvenir Sheet**

**2329** A403 600sh multi 1.10 1.10

Southern African Development Community, 24th Anniv. A404

Designs: 350sh, Removal of water hyacinths from beach. 500sh, Irrigation ditch in corn field. 600sh, irrigation ditch at rice paddy. 800sh, Workers installing pipe in borehole, vert.
1000sh, Farm workers hoeing corn field irrigation ditches.

**2004, Aug. 17 *Perf. 14x13, 13x14***

**2330-2333** A404 Set of 4 4.25 4.25
*2333a* Souvenir sheet, #2330-2333, perf. 13½x13, 13x13½ 4.25 4.25

**Souvenir Sheet**

**2334** A404 1000sh multi 1.90 1.90

Nos. 1565, 1569 and 2166 Surcharged

#2335

#2336

**Methods and Perfs As Before**

**2004, Nov. 13**

**2335** A262 350sh on 100sh #1565 — —
**2336** A374 350sh on 200sh #2166 — —
**2337** A262 350sh on 210sh #1569 — —

Children's Rights A405

Inscriptions: No. 2338, 350sh, Involve children in school development. No. 2339, 350sh, Let's equip children with life skills. 400sh, Children need education before employment. 500sh, 1000sh, Disabled children need to be educated.

**2004, Nov. 4 Litho. *Perf. 13¼x12¾***

**2338-2341** A405 Set of 4 3.00 3.00

**Souvenir Sheet**

**2342** A405 1000sh multi 1.90 1.90

Law and Peace in the Great Lakes Zone — A405a

Designs: 350sh, Julius K. Nyerere acting as facilitator in Burundi peace negotiations. 500sh, Burundi refugees at border. No. 2342C, 600sh, Nelson Mandela and Tanzania Pres. Banjamin W. Mkapa at Arusha peace talks. 800sh, Pres. Mkapa with Uganda Pres. Yoweri Musaveni and Burundi Pres. Domitien Ndayizeye at Dar es Salaam peace talks.
No. 2342E, 600sh, Arusha Intl. Conference Center.

**2004, Oct. 15 Litho. *Perf. 14x13***

**2342A-2342D** A405a Set of 4 4.25 4.25
*2342Df* Souvenir sheet, #2342A-2342D 4.25 4.25

**Souvenir Sheet**

**2342E** A405a 600sh multi 1.10 1.10

Rotary International, Cent. — A406

Designs: 350sh, Rotary officials honor Tanzania Pres. Julius Nyerere. 500sh, Emblem of Dar es Salaam North Tanzania Club, vert. No. 2345 600sh, Eradication of polio. 800sh, Map and flags of District 9200 countries, Eritrea, Ethiopia, Uganda, Kenya and Tanzania, vert.
No. 2347: a, Environmental project. b, Self-reliance to the handicapped. c, Basic health care project, vert. d, Jaipur foot project. e, Malaria project. f, Eradication of river blindness project.
1000sh, Centenary emblem, vert.

**2005, Feb. 23 Litho. *Perf. 13***

**2343-2346** A406 Set of 4 4.25 4.25

**2347** A406 600sh Sheet of 6, #a-f 6.50 6.50

**Souvenir Sheet**

**2348** A406 1000sh multi 1.90 1.90

Safari Circuit Animals — A407

Designs: 350sh, Lionesses. 500sh, Cheetahs, horiz. No. 2351, 600sh, Red colobus monkey. 800sh, Zebras, horiz.
No. 2353, horiz.: a, Elephants. b, Rhinoceroses. c, Giraffes. d, Crocodile. e, Chimpanzees. f, Buffaloes.
No. 2354, horiz.: a, Leopard. b, Wild hunting dogs.

***Perf. 12¾x13¼, 13¼x12¾***

**2005, Apr. 30**

**2349-2352** A407 Set of 4 4.25 4.25
**2353** A407 600sh Sheet of 6, #a-f 6.50 6.50
**2354** A407 1000sh Sheet of 2, #a-b 3.75 3.75

Zanzibar Heritage and Culture A408

Designs: 350sh, Bull fighting. 400sh, Narrow street in Stone Town, vert. No. 2357, 600sh, Women's traditional dress, vert. 800sh, Clove harvesting, vert.
No. 2359, 600sh: a, House of Wonders. b, Local Taarabu musicians. c, Man holding fish. d, Coconut palm. e, Women's indoor traditional dress. f, Old museum building.
500sh, Pemba-Zanzibar ferry boat.

***Perf. 13½x13, 13x13½***

**2005, June 30 Litho.**

**2355-2358** A408 Set of 4 4.00 4.00
**2359** A408 600sh Sheet of 6, #a-f 6.50 6.50

**Souvenir Sheet**

**2360** A408 500sh multi .90 .90

2004 Summer Olympics, Athens — A409

Designs: No. 2361, 350sh, Greco-Roman wrestlers. No. 2362, 350sh, Baron Godefroy de Blonay, vert. 500sh, Commemorative medal for 1928 Amsterdam Summer Olympics, vert. 1000sh, Greek javelin thrower sculpture, vert.

**2005, May 2 Litho. *Perf. 13¼***

**2361-2364** A409 Set of 4 4.00 4.00

Souvenir Sheet

Reign of Pope John Paul, 25th Anniv. (in 2003) — A410

No. 2365: a, Pope as boy, with mother, 1921. b, Visit to Poland, 1979. c, Meeting with Pres. George W. Bush, 2001. d, In Armenia, 2001.

**2005, May 2** ***Perf. 13½***
**2365** A410 1000sh Sheet of 4, #a-d 7.25 7.25

Locomotives, Bicent. — A411

No. 2366: a, West Side Lumber 3-truck shay, Georgetown Loop Railroad. b, LK&P 0-4-0 Saddletanker. c, Double-headed C&T steam locomotive. d, Baldwin 4-6-0, Huckleberry Railroad.
2500sh, Heber Valley Railroad 2-8-0.

**2005, May 2**
**2366** A411 1000sh Sheet of 4, #a-d 7.25 7.25

**Souvenir Sheet**

**2367** A411 2500sh multi 4.50 4.50

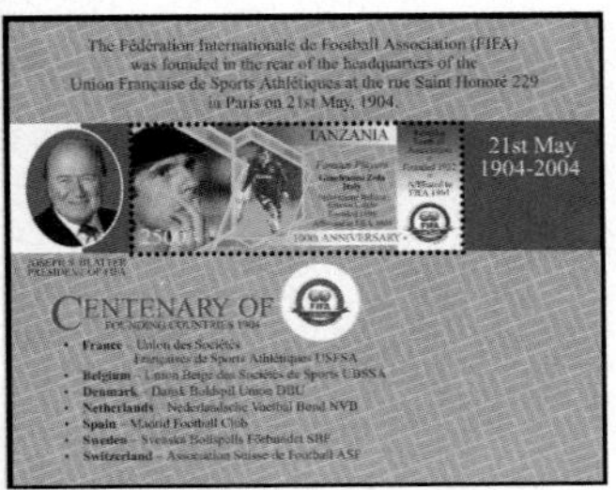


FIFA (Fédération Internationale de Football Association) Cent. (in 2004) — A412

No. 2368: a, Franco Baresi. b, Daniel Passarella. c, Miroslav Klose. d, Michel Platini.
2500sh, Gianfranco Zola.

**2005, May 2** **Litho.** ***Perf. 13½***
**2368** A412 1000sh Sheet of 4, #a-d 7.25 7.25

**Souvenir Sheet**

**2369** A412 2500sh multi 4.50 4.50

D-Day, 60th Anniv. (in 2004) — A413

No. 2370, vert.: a, Map of invasion. b, Gen. Dwight D. Eisenhower. c, American troops landing at Omaha Beach. d, British Mosquitos. e, Fleet Admiral Ernest J. King. f, Gen. George C. Marshall.
2500sh, Battle for Fox Green Beach.

**2006, May 2**
**2370** A413 600sh Sheet of 6, #a-f 6.50 6.50

**Souvenir Sheet**

**2371** A413 2500sh multi 4.50 4.50

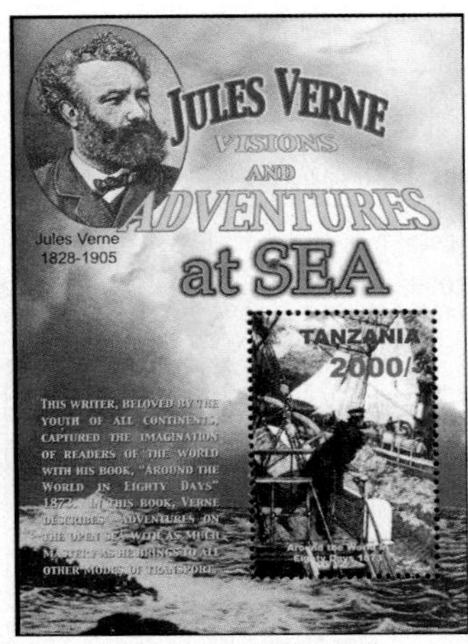


Jules Verne (1828-1905), Writer — A414

No. 2372, 800sh: a, Voyages Extraordinaires. b, Twenty Thousand Leagues Under the Sea. c, A Floating City (book cover). d, Adventures of Three Englishmen and Three Russians in South Africa.
No. 2373, 800sh: a, Mathias Sandorf. b, The Steam House, The Demon of Cawnpore. c, Hector Servadec on the Career of a Comet. d, An Antarctic Mystery.
No. 2374, 800sh: a, Around the World in Eighty Days. b, Dr. Ox's Experiment. c, The Purchase of the North Pole. d, Adrift in the Pacific.
No. 2375, 800sh: a, The Archipelago on Fire. b, The Vanished Diamond. c, Mistress Branican. d, The Castle of the Carpathians.
No. 2376, 800sh: a, The Invasion of the Sea. b, The Floating Island. c, A Floating City (men near ship railing). d, Dick Sands, Boy Captain.
No. 2377, 2000sh, Around the World in Eighty Days, diff. No. 2378, 2000sh, Five Weeks in a Balloon. No. 2379, 2000sh, The Mysterious Island. No. 2380, 2000sh, The Adventures of a Chinaman. No. 2381, 2000sh, The Invasion of the Sea, diff.

**2005, May 16** ***Perf. 13½***

**Sheets of 4, #a-d**

**2372-2376** A414 Set of 5 29.00 29.00

**Souvenir Sheets**

**2377-2381** A414 Set of 5 18.00 18.00

Fish of Lake Victoria A415

Designs: No. 2382, 350sh, Labeo victorianus. 400sh, Lates niloticus. 600sh, Pundamilia nyererei. 800sh, Brycinus sadleri.
No. 2386, 350sh: a, Haplochromis sharpsnout. b, Haplochromis chilotes. c, Mormyrus kannume. d, Clarias gariepinus. e, Synodontis afrofischeri. f, Protopterus aethiopicus.
500sh, Oreochromis niloticus.

**2005, Aug. 30** ***Perf. 13¼x13¾***
**2382-2385** A415 Set of 4 3.75 3.75
**2386** A415 350sh Sheet of 6, #a-f 3.75 3.75

**Souvenir Sheet**

**2387** A415 500sh multi .90 .90

Pope John Paul II (1920-2005), and Pres. Bill Clinton — A416

**2005, Sept. 22** ***Perf. 12¾***
**2388** A416 1500sh multi 2.75 2.75

Printed in sheets of 4, with each stamp having a slightly different background.

Rotary International, Cent. — A417

No. 2389: a, Child receiving polio vaccine. b, Dr. Jonas E. Salk, polio researcher. c, Hands, test tube.
2500sh, Salk and Rotary International centenary emblem.

**2005, Sept. 22**
**2389** A417 1200sh Sheet of 3, #a-c 6.50 6.50

**Souvenir Sheet**

**2390** A417 2500sh multi 4.50 4.50

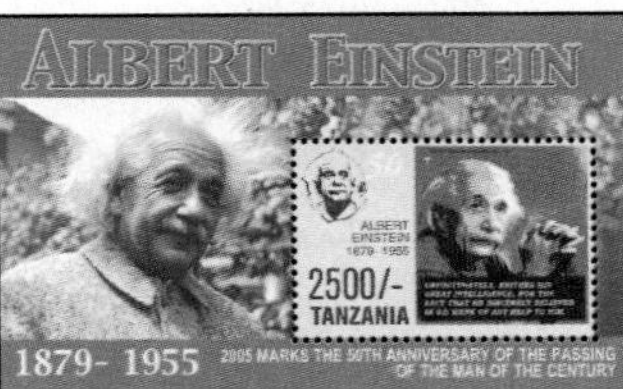


Albert Einstein (1879-1955), Physicist — A418

No. 2391 — Sketch of Einstein and: a, 1979 Swiss 5-franc coin. b, Time Magazine cover. c, Israel #117.
2500sh, Portrait of Einstein.

**2005, Sept. 22**
**2391** A418 1300sh Sheet of 3, #a-c 7.00 7.00

**Souvenir Sheet**

**2392** A418 2500sh multi 4.50 4.50

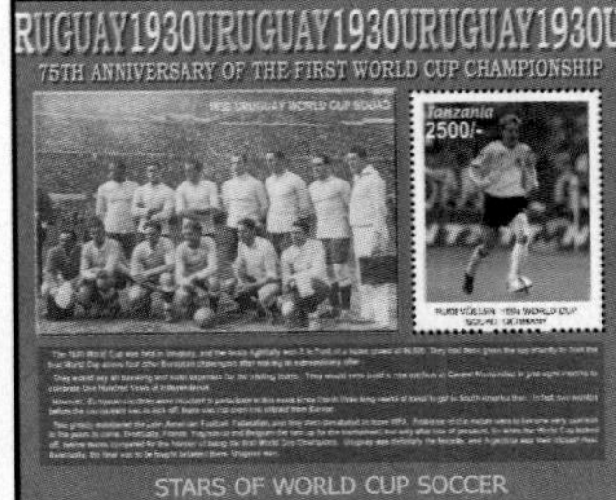


First World Cup Soccer Championships, 75th Anniv. — A419

No. 2393: a, Christian Ziege. b, Marko Rehmer. c, Jens Nowotny.
2500sh, Rudi Völler.

**2005, Sept. 22** ***Perf. 13¼***
**2393** A419 1200sh Sheet of 3, #a-c 6.50 6.50

**Souvenir Sheet**

**2394** A419 2500sh multi 4.50 4.50

Butterflies A420

Designs: 350sh, Papilio ufipa. No. 2396, 500sh, Mylothris sagala mahale. No. 2397, 600sh, Amauris tartarea tukuyuensis. 800sh, Charaxes lucyae gabriellae.
No. 2399, 600sh: a, Like 350sh. b, Euphaedra neophron kiellandi. c, Like 800sh. d, Abisara zanzibarica. e, Acrae utengulensis.
No. 2400, 500sh, Charaxes usambarae maridadi.

**2005, Oct. 27** ***Perf. 13¾x13½***
**2395-2398** A420 Set of 4 4.00 4.00
**2399** A420 600sh Sheet of 6, #2397, 2399a-2399e 6.50 6.50

**Souvenir Sheet**

**2400** A420 500sh multi .90 .90

Anniversaries and Events A421

Designs: 350sh, Person with amputated leg. No. 2402, 500sh, Line of people at polling station. No. 2403, 600sh, Pope John Paul II, kneeling at airport. 800sh, Laurean Cardinal Rugambwa, Pope John Paul II and Pres. Alis Hassan Mwinyi.
No. 2405, 600sh: a, Pres. Julius Nyerere and Abeid Aman Karume signing Union Treaty. b, Woman holding child, casting ballot. c, Pope John Paul II, Pres. Mwinyi and Julius and Maria Nyerere. d, Pope John Paul II and Cardinal Rugambwa and car roof. e, Majimaji Museum, Songea. f, President B. W. Mkapa at fire.
No. 2406, 500sh, Majimaji Monument, vert.

**2005, Dec. 9** ***Perf. 13¼x12¾***
**2401-2404** A421 Set of 4 4.00 4.00
**2405** A421 600sh Sheet of 6, #a-f 6.25 6.25

**Souvenir Sheet**

***Perf. 12¾x13¼***

**2406** A421 500sh multi .90 .90

World Diabetes Day (350sh); 2005 general elections (#2402, 2405b), Visit of Pope John Paul II, 15th anniv. (800sh, #2405c, 2405d).

Birds A422

Designs: 350sh, Rufous-winged sunbird. No. 2408, 500sh, Pemba white-eye. No. 2409, 600sh, Kilombero weaver. 800sh, Usambara eagle owl.
No. 2411, 600sh: a, Pemba scops owl. b, Spike-heeled lark. c, Pemba green pigeon. d, Uluguru bush shrike. e, Yellow-collared love birds. f, Usambara nightjar.
No. 2412, 500sh, Moreau's sunbird, vert.

**2006, Mar. 25** ***Perf. 13***
**2407-2410** A422 Set of 4 3.75 3.75
**2411** A422 600sh Sheet of 6, #a-f 6.00 6.00

**Souvenir Sheet**

**2412** A422 500sh multi .85 .85

No. 2412 contains one 39x49mm stamp.

2006 World Cup Soccer Championships, Germany — A423

Designs: 350sh, New National Stadium, Dar es Salaam. 500sh, Map of Africa and flags of participating countries, vert. No. 2415, 600sh, Pres. Jakaya Kikwete holding World Cup trophy. 800sh, Mascot for 2006 World Cup, vert.
No. 2417, 600sh, World Cup Trophy and 2006 World Cup emblem.

***Perf. 13¼x12¾, 12¾x13¼***

**2006, Mar. 25**

**2413-2416** A423 Set of 4 3.75 3.75
*2416a* Miniature sheet, #2413-2416 3.75 3.75

**Souvenir Sheet**

**2417** A423 600sh multi 1.00 1.00

Miniature Sheet

Wolfgang Amadeus Mozart (1756-91), Composer — A424

No. 2418: a, Portrait of Mozart (blue panel). b, Mozart's birthplace, Salzburg. c, Poster for Don Giovanni. d, Portrait of Mozart (purple panel).

**2006, June 13** ***Perf. 12¾***

**2418** A424 1200sh Sheet of 4, #a-d 7.75 7.75

Release of Elvis Presley Movie, *Jailhouse Rock,* 50th Anniv. — A425

No. 2419 — Presley with: a, Both arms at side. b, Arm raised above head. c, Arms outstretched and jacket pulled up behind head. d, Hand in front of chest.

**2006, June 13** ***Perf. 13½***

**2419** A425 1200sh Sheet of 4, #a-d 7.75 7.75

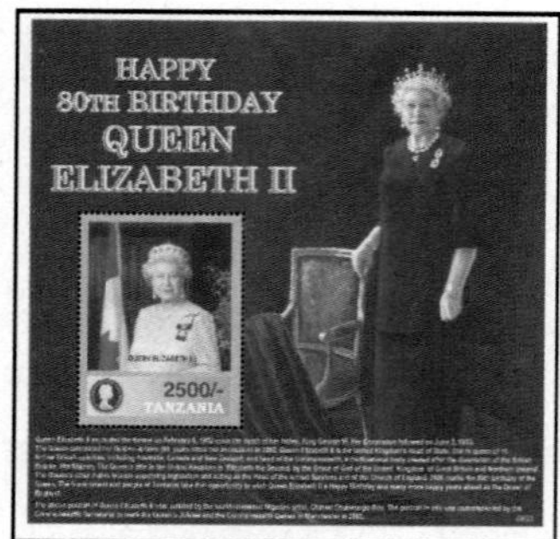


Queen Elizabeth II, 80th Birthday — A426

No. 2420 — Queen: a, Wearing blue robe. b, On reviewing stand. c, On horse. d, Wearing feathered hat.
2500sh, Wearing tiara.

**2006, June 13** ***Perf. 14¼***

**2420** A426 1200sh Sheet of 4, #a-d 7.75 7.75

**Souvenir Sheet**

**2421** A426 2500sh multi 4.00 4.00

Rembrandt (1606-69), Painter — A427

No. 2422 — Painting details: a, Jan Pellicorne and His Son Caspar (Jan Pellicorne). b, Jan Pellicorne and His Son Caspar (Caspar). c, Susanna Van Collen, Wife of Jan Pellicorne, and Her Daughter, Eva Susanna (Susanna). d, Susanna Van Collen, Wife of Jan Pellicorne, and Her Daughter, Eva Susanna (Eva Susanna).
3000sh, A Turk.

**2006, June 13** ***Perf. 13¼***

**2422** A427 1000sh Sheet of 4, #a-d 6.50 6.50

***Imperf***

**Size: 70x100mm**

**2423** A427 3000sh multi 4.75 4.75

Beauty of Zanzibar A428

Designs: 350sh, Man and woman in traditional Zanzibar dress. No. 2425, 500sh, Zanzibar Museum. No. 2426, 600sh, Maruhubi Palace ruins. 800sh, Man climbing coconut tree.
No. 2428, 600sh: a, Green turtle at Mnemba Island. b, Red colobus monkey. c, Giant tortoise at Changuu Island. d, Dhow, Zanzibar sunset. e, Dhow sailing near Matemwe. f, Coconut crab, Chumbe Island.
No. 2429, 500sh, vert.: a, Clove foliage and enlargement of flower buds. b, Light Signal Tower.

**2006, June 30** ***Perf. 13½x13***

**2424-2427** A428 Set of 4 3.75 3.75
**2428** A428 600sh Sheet of 6, #a-f 5.75 5.75

**Souvenir Sheet**

***Perf. 13x13½***

**2429** A428 500sh Sheet of 2, #a-b 1.60 1.60

Mountains — A429

Designs: 350sh, Mt. Kenya. 400sh, Udzungwa Mountain Range. 600sh, Sanje Falls, vert. 800sh, Ruwenzori Range.
No. 2434, 1000sh: a, Kiko Summit and Mawenzi, Mt. Kilimanjaro. b, Giraffe and Mt. Kilimanjaro.
No. 2435, 1000sh: a, Cattle, herder and Ol Doinyo Lengai. b, Ol Doinyo Lengai summit and crater, vert.

***Perf. 13½x13¾, 13¾x13½***

**2006, Aug. 24**

**2430-2433** A429 Set of 4 3.25 3.25

**Sheets of 2, #a-b**

**2434-2435** A429 Set of 2 6.00 6.00

Miniature Sheet

Tazara Railway, 30th Anniv. — A430

No. 2436: a, 350sh, Map of Tanzania and Zambia, waterfall, mountain, people waving, and men signing agreement. b, 350sh, Men and train, elephant and antelope. c, 600sh, Dar es Salaam Station, sign and wreaths with Chinese inscriptions. d, 600sh, New Kapiri Mposhi Station, people near train. e, 800sh, Train, bridge and tunnel, zebra and giraffe. f, 800sh, Train on bridge, lion and lioness.

**2006, Oct. 25** ***Perf. 12***

**2436** A430 Sheet of 6, #a-f 5.50 5.50

Worldwide Fund for Nature (WWF) — A431

No. 2437 — Damaliscus lunatus jimela: a, Males butting heads. b, Close-up view of head. c, Adult and juvenile. d, Adult on mound.

**2006, Nov. 24** ***Perf. 13¼***

**2437** Horiz. or vert. strip 3.75 3.75
*a.-d.* A431 600sh Any single .90 .90
*e.* Miniature sheet, 2 each #2437a-2437d 7.50 7.50

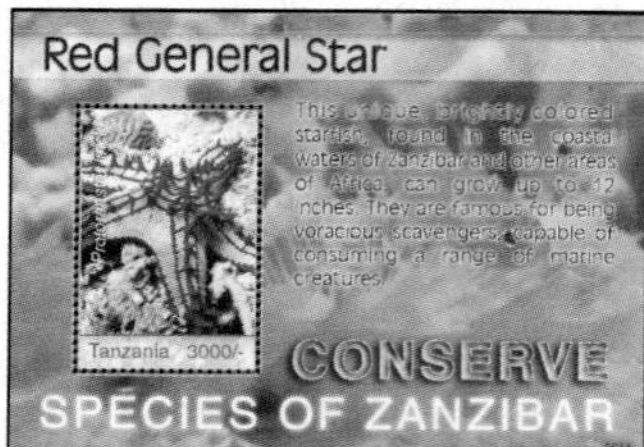


Zanzibar Flora and Fauna — A432

No. 2438, 1000sh: a, Coconut crab. b, Frangipane. c, Sykes monkey. d, Green sea turtle.
No. 2439, 1000sh: a, African civet. b, Four-toed elephant shrew. c, Lesser bushbaby. d, Pemba sunbird.
No. 2440, 3000sh, Protoreaster linckii. No. 2441, 3000sh, Tauraco fischeri.

**2006, Nov. 24** ***Perf. 13¼***

**Sheets of 4, #a-d**

**2438-2439** A432 Set of 2 12.50 12.50

**Souvenir Sheets**

**2440-2441** A432 Set of 2 9.50 9.50

## SEMI-POSTAL STAMPS

Natl. Solidarity Walk — SP1

**1988, July 1** **Litho.** ***Perf. 14½***

**B1** SP1 2sh +1sh Flag, crowd .50 .50
**B2** SP1 3sh +1sh Map, Pres. Mwinyi .50 .50

**Souvenir Sheet**

**B3** SP1 50sh +1sh Flag, Pres. Mwinyi 1.25 1.25

Surtax for Chama Cha Mapinduzi party activities.

Natl. Solidarity Walk — SP2

**1989, July 1** **Litho.** ***Perf. 14½***

**B4** SP2 5sh +1sh Party flag .35 .35
**B5** SP2 10sh +1sh Pres. Mwinyi, walk .35 .35

**Souvenir Sheet**

**B6** SP2 50sh +1sh Pres. Mwinyi 1.00 1.00

Natl. Solidarity Walk SP3

Designs: 4sh + 1sh, Pres. Mwinyi marching with crowd. 9sh + 1sh, Crowd around party flag. 13sh + 1sh, Pres. Mwinyi. 30sh + 1sh, Pres. Mwinyi planting tree. No. B11, Pres. Mwinyi sorting cloves. No. B12, Handshake across map, vert.

**1991-92** **Litho.** ***Perf. 13½***

**B7** SP3 4sh +1sh multicolored ('92) .50 .50
**B8** SP3 9sh +1sh multicolored .70 .70
**B9** SP3 13sh +1sh multicolored .70 .70
**B10** SP3 30sh +1sh multicolored ('92) 1.25 1.25
*Nos. B7-B10 (4)* 3.15 3.15

**Souvenir Sheets**

***Perf. 12½***

**B11** SP3 50sh +1sh multicolored 2.25 2.25
**B12** SP3 50sh +1sh multicolored 1.75 1.75

Issued: Nos. B8-B9, 7/6/90. Nos. B7, B10, 7/5/91.

## POSTAGE DUE STAMPS

D1

D2

***Perf. 14x14½***

**1978, July 31** **Litho.** **Unwmk.**

**J1** D1 5c red .20 *.70*
**J2** D1 10c green .20 *.70*
**J3** D1 20c dark blue .20 *.70*
**J4** D1 30c reddish brown .20 *.70*
**J5** D1 40c bright rose lilac .20 *.70*
**J6** D1 1sh orange .30 *1.75*
*Nos. J1-J6 (6)* 1.30 5.25

**1967, Jan. 3** ***Perf. 14x13½***

*J1a* D1 5c red .20 *1.00*
*J2a* D1 10c green .20 *1.00*
*J3a* D1 20c dark blue .30 *1.75*
*J4a* D1 30c reddish brown .50 *2.50*

| | | | | | |
|---|---|---|---|---|---|
| *J5a* | D1 | 40c | bright rose lilac | .65 | *3.50* |
| *J6a* | D1 | 1sh | orange | 1.75 | *7.50* |
| | | | *Nos. J1a-J6a (6)* | 3.60 | 17.25 |

**1969-71** ***Perf. 14x15***

| | | | | | |
|---|---|---|---|---|---|
| *J1b* | D1 | 5c | red | .20 | *1.00* |
| *J2b* | D1 | 10c | green | .20 | *1.00* |
| *J3b* | D1 | 20c | dark blue | .40 | *1.75* |
| *J4b* | D1 | 30c | reddish brown | .60 | *2.50* |
| *J5b* | D1 | 40c | bright rose lilac | .80 | *3.50* |
| *J6b* | D1 | 1sh | orange ('71) | 2.00 | *7.50* |
| | | | *Nos. J1b-J6b (6)* | 4.20 | 17.25 |

**1973, Dec. 12** ***Perf. 15***

| | | | | | |
|---|---|---|---|---|---|
| *J1c* | D1 | 5c | red | .20 | *1.00* |
| *J2c* | D1 | 10c | green | .20 | *1.00* |
| *J3c* | D1 | 20c | dark blue | .30 | *2.00* |
| *J4c* | D1 | 30c | reddish brown | .45 | *3.00* |
| *J5c* | D1 | 40c | bright rose lilac | .60 | *4.00* |
| *J6c* | D1 | 1sh | orange | 1.50 | *10.00* |
| | | | *Nos. J1c-J6c (6)* | 3.25 | 21.00 |

**1984?** ***Perf. 14¾x14***

*J4d* D1 30c reddish brown

Additional stamps of this type with this perforation have been reported. The editors would like to examine any examples.

**1990** **Litho.** ***Perf. 15x14***

| | | | | | |
|---|---|---|---|---|---|
| **J7** | D2 | 50c | dark green | .20 | .20 |
| **J8** | D2 | 80c | bright blue | .20 | .20 |
| **J9** | D2 | 1sh | orange brown | .20 | .20 |
| **J10** | D2 | 2sh | light olive green | .20 | .20 |
| **J11** | D2 | 3sh | purple | .20 | .20 |
| **J12** | D2 | 5sh | gray | .20 | .20 |
| **J13** | D2 | 10sh | brown | .20 | .20 |
| **J14** | D2 | 20sh | bister | .20 | .20 |
| | | | *Nos. J7-J14 (8)* | 1.60 | 1.60 |

### OFFICIAL STAMPS

Nos. 5-9, 11, 13 and 16 Overprinted: "OFFICIAL"

***Perf. 14x14½, 14½x14***

**1965, Dec. 9** **Photo.** **Unwmk.**

**Size: 21x17½mm, 17½x21mm**

| | | | | | |
|---|---|---|---|---|---|
| **O1** | A2 | 5c | orange & ultra | .20 | .20 |
| **O2** | A2 | 10c | multicolored | .20 | .20 |
| **O3** | A3 | 15c | grn bl, brn & buff | .20 | .20 |
| **O4** | A2 | 20c | blue & brown | .20 | .20 |
| **O5** | A3 | 30c | black & red brn | .20 | .20 |
| **O6** | A2 | 50c | yellow grn & blk | .20 | .20 |

***Perf. 14½***

**Size: 41½x25**

| | | | | | |
|---|---|---|---|---|---|
| **O7** | A2 | 1sh | multicolored | .30 | .20 |
| **O8** | A2 | 5sh | bl, brt grn & red brn | 1.50 | 1.00 |
| | | | *Nos. O1-O8 (8)* | 3.00 | 2.40 |

Overprint size: 17mm on 5c, 10c, 20c, 50c. 14mm on 15c, 30c. 29x3½mm on 1sh, 5sh.

The overprint was also applied in 1967 in Dar es Salaam to 50c, 1sh and 5sh. Size: 29x3mm.

Nos. 19-23, 25, 27 and 30 Overprinted: "OFFICIAL"

**1967, Dec. 9** **Photo.** ***Perf. 14x14½***

**Fish in Natural Colors**

**Size: 21x17½mm**

**Overprint Litho., 17mm Wide**

| | | | | | |
|---|---|---|---|---|---|
| **O9** | A4 | 5c | black & citron | .20 | .60 |
| **O10** | A4 | 10c | brown & olive | .20 | .30 |
| **O11** | A4 | 15c | brown & blue | .20 | .20 |
| **O12** | A4 | 20c | brown & dk blue grn | .20 | .20 |
| **O13** | A4 | 30c | black & yel grn | .20 | .20 |
| **O14** | A4 | 50c | black & dull bl grn | .20 | .50 |

***Perf. 14½***

**Size: 41x25mm**

**Overprint 29mm Wide**

| | | | | | |
|---|---|---|---|---|---|
| **O15** | A4 | 1sh | brown & multi | .40 | *1.00* |
| **O16** | A4 | 5sh | black & blue grn | 1.75 | *4.00* |
| | | | *Nos. O9-O16 (8)* | 3.35 | 7.00 |

**1970-73**

**Overprint Typo., 17½mm Wide**

| | | | | | |
|---|---|---|---|---|---|
| *O9a* | A4 | 5c | black & citron | .20 | .20 |
| *O10a* | A4 | 10c | brown & olive | .20 | .20 |
| *O12a* | A4 | 20c | brn & dk bl grn | .20 | .20 |
| *O13a* | A4 | 30c | blk & yel grn | .30 | .20 |
| **O13B** | A4 | 40c | multicolored ('73) | | |
| | | | *Nos. O9a-O13a (4)* | .90 | .80 |

The overprint was also applied in 1973 to 15c, 50c, 1sh (28mm wide), and 5sh.

Nos. 35-36, 38, 40-41, 43-47 Overprinted

a b

**1973, Dec. 10** **Photo.** ***Perf. 14½x14***

| | | | | | |
|---|---|---|---|---|---|
| **O17** | A5(a) | 5c | multicolored | .50 | *2.00* |
| **O18** | A5(a) | 10c | multicolored | .60 | .35 |
| **O19** | A5(a) | 20c | multicolored | .70 | .35 |
| **O20** | A5(a) | 40c | multicolored | 1.00 | .35 |
| **O21** | A5(a) | 50c | multicolored | 1.00 | .35 |
| **O22** | A5(a) | 70c | multicolored | 1.00 | .35 |

***Perf. 14½***

| | | | | | |
|---|---|---|---|---|---|
| **O23** | A6(b) | 1sh | multicolored | 1.50 | .40 |
| **O24** | A6(b) | 1.50sh | multicolored | 1.75 | *2.00* |
| **O25** | A6(b) | 2.50sh | multicolored | 2.50 | *3.00* |
| **O26** | A6(b) | 5sh | multicolored | 3.50 | *5.00* |
| | | | *Nos. O17-O26 (10)* | 14.05 | 14.15 |

A larger overprint (17½mm wide instead of 14½mm) was applied locally to 10c, 20c, 40c, and 50c.

Provisional use of some values for regular postage is known.

Nos. 161-171 Overprinted: OFFICIAL

**1980, Oct. 1** ***Perf. 14***

| | | | | | |
|---|---|---|---|---|---|
| **O27** | A21 | 10c | multicolored | .20 | .20 |
| **O28** | A21 | 20c | multicolored | .20 | .20 |
| **O29** | A21 | 40c | multicolored | .20 | .20 |
| **O30** | A21 | 50c | multicolored | .20 | .20 |
| **O31** | A21 | 75c | multicolored | .20 | .20 |
| **O32** | A21 | 80c | multicolored | .20 | .20 |

***Perf. 14½***

| | | | | | |
|---|---|---|---|---|---|
| **O33** | A21 | 1sh | multicolored | .20 | .20 |
| **O33A** | A21 | 1.50sh | multicolored | | |
| **O34** | A21 | 2sh | multicolored | .40 | .40 |
| **O35** | A21 | 3sh | multicolored | .60 | .60 |
| **O36** | A21 | 5sh | multicolored | 1.00 | 1.00 |
| | | | *Nos. O27-O33,O34-O36 (10)* | 3.40 | 3.40 |

Overprint measures 13mm on Nos. O33-O36; reads up or down.

Nos. 606-614 Inscribed "OFFICIAL"

**1990-91** **Litho.** ***Perf. 14***

| | | | | | |
|---|---|---|---|---|---|
| **O37** | A99 | 5sh | multi | .20 | .20 |
| **O38** | A99 | 9sh | multi | .20 | .20 |
| **O39** | A99 | 13sh | multi | .20 | .20 |
| **O40** | A99 | 15sh | multi | .20 | .20 |
| **O41** | A99 | 20sh | multi | .30 | .30 |
| **O42** | A99 | 25sh | multi | .35 | .35 |
| **O42A** | A99 | 30sh | multi ('91) | .45 | .45 |
| **O43** | A99 | 40sh | multi | .60 | .60 |
| **O44** | A99 | 70sh | multi | 1.00 | 1.00 |
| **O45** | A99 | 100sh | multi | 1.50 | 1.50 |
| | | | *Nos. O37-O45 (10)* | 5.00 | 5.00 |

Inscription on Nos. O37-O42A is 15½mm long. Insription on Nos. O43-O45 is 19mm long.

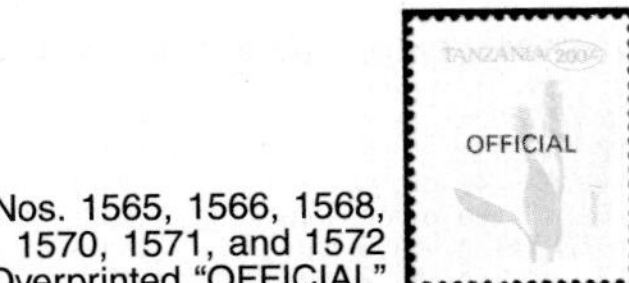

Nos. 1565, 1566, 1568, 1570, 1571, and 1572 Overprinted "OFFICIAL"

**1997 (?)** **Litho.** ***Perf. 14½x15***

| | | | | | |
|---|---|---|---|---|---|
| **O47** | A262 | 100sh | multi | — | — |
| **O48** | A262 | 140sh | multi | — | — |
| **O49** | A262 | 200sh | multi | — | — |
| **O50** | A262 | 260sh | multi | — | — |
| **O51** | A262 | 300sh | multi | — | — |
| **O52** | A262 | 380sh | multi | — | — |

The editors suspect there are additional stamps in this set, and would like to examine any examples.

## TETE

'tāt-ə

LOCATION — In southeastern Africa between Nyasaland and Southern Rhodesia

GOVT. — A district of the Portuguese East Africa Colony

AREA — 46,600 sq. mi. (approx.)

POP. — 367,000 (approx.)

CAPITAL — Tete

This district was formerly a part of Zambezia. Stamps of Mozambique replaced those of Tete. See Mozambique.

100 Centavos = 1 Escudo

Vasco da Gama Issue of Various Portuguese Colonies Surcharged as

**1913** **Unwmk.** ***Perf. 12½, 16***

**On Stamps of Macao**

| | | | | | |
|---|---|---|---|---|---|
| **1** | CD20 | ¼c | on ½a bl grn | 5.00 | *5.00* |
| **2** | CD21 | ½c | on 1a red | 1.75 | *3.00* |
| **3** | CD22 | 1c | on 2a red vio | 1.75 | *3.00* |
| **4** | CD23 | 2½c | on 4a yel grn | 1.75 | *3.00* |
| **5** | CD24 | 5c | on 8a dk blue | 1.75 | *2.10* |
| **6** | CD25 | 7½c | on 12a vio brn | 2.40 | *3.00* |
| **7** | CD26 | 10c | on 16a bis brn | 1.75 | *2.10* |
| **8** | CD27 | 15c | on 24a bister | 1.75 | *2.10* |
| | | | *Nos. 1-8 (8)* | 17.90 | *23.30* |

**On Stamps of Portuguese Africa**

| | | | | | |
|---|---|---|---|---|---|
| **9** | CD20 | ¼c | on 2½r bl grn | 1.75 | *2.10* |
| **10** | CD21 | ½c | on 5r red | 1.75 | *2.10* |
| **11** | CD22 | 1c | on 10r red vio | 1.75 | *2.10* |
| **12** | CD23 | 2½c | on 25r yel grn | 1.75 | *2.10* |
| **13** | CD24 | 5c | on 50r dk blue | 1.75 | *2.10* |
| **14** | CD25 | 7½c | on 75r vio brn | 2.40 | *3.00* |
| **15** | CD26 | 10c | on 100r bis brn | 1.75 | *2.10* |
| **16** | CD27 | 15c | on 150r bister | 1.75 | *2.10* |
| | | | *Nos. 9-16 (8)* | 14.65 | *17.70* |

**On Stamps of Timor**

| | | | | | |
|---|---|---|---|---|---|
| **17** | CD20 | ¼c | on ½a bl grn | 1.75 | *2.10* |
| **18** | CD21 | ½c | on 1a red | 1.75 | *2.10* |
| **19** | CD22 | 1c | on 2a red vio | 1.75 | *2.10* |
| *a.* | | | Inverted overprint | 30.00 | 30.00 |
| **20** | CD23 | 2½c | on 4a yel grn | 1.75 | *2.10* |
| **21** | CD24 | 5c | on 8a dk blue | 1.75 | *2.10* |
| **22** | CD25 | 7½c | on 12a vio brn | 2.40 | *3.00* |
| **23** | CD26 | 10c | on 16a bis brn | 1.75 | *2.10* |
| **24** | CD27 | 15c | on 24a bister | 1.75 | *2.10* |
| | | | *Nos. 17-24 (8)* | 14.65 | *17.70* |
| | | | *Nos. 1-24 (24)* | 47.20 | *58.70* |

Common Design Types pictured following the introduction.

Ceres — A1

**1914** **Typo.** ***Perf. 15x14***

**Name and Value in Black**

| | | | | | |
|---|---|---|---|---|---|
| **25** | A1 | ¼c | olive brn | 1.40 | *2.25* |
| **26** | A1 | ½c | black | 1.40 | *2.25* |
| **27** | A1 | 1c | blue grn | 1.40 | *2.25* |
| **28** | A1 | 1½c | lilac brn | 1.40 | *2.25* |
| **29** | A1 | 2c | carmine | 1.40 | *2.25* |
| **30** | A1 | 2½c | light vio | 1.40 | *2.25* |
| **31** | A1 | 5c | deep blue | 1.40 | *2.25* |
| **32** | A1 | 7½c | yel brn | 2.25 | *3.25* |
| **33** | A1 | 8c | slate | 2.25 | *3.25* |
| **34** | A1 | 10c | org brn | 2.75 | *4.00* |
| **35** | A1 | 15c | plum | 3.25 | *4.50* |
| **36** | A1 | 20c | yel green | 3.25 | *4.50* |
| **37** | A1 | 30c | brn, *green* | 3.25 | *4.50* |
| **38** | A1 | 40c | brn, *pink* | 4.00 | *7.00* |
| **39** | A1 | 50c | org, *salmon* | 7.00 | *9.00* |
| **40** | A1 | 1e | grn, *blue* | 10.00 | *10.00* |
| | | | *Nos. 25-40 (16)* | 47.80 | *65.75* |

## THAILAND

'tī-ˌland

(Siam)

LOCATION — Western part of the Malay peninsula in southeastern Asia

GOVT. — Republic

AREA — 198,250 sq. mi.

POP. — 60,609,046 (1999 est.)

CAPITAL — Bangkok

32 Solot = 16 Atts = 8 Sio = 4 Sik = 2 Fuang = 1 Salung

4 Salungs = 1 Tical

100 Satangs (1909) = 1 Tical = 1 Baht (1912)

**Catalogue values for unused stamps in this country are for Never Hinged items, beginning with Scott 264 in the regular postage section, Scott B34 in the semi-postal section, Scott C20 in the airpost section, and Scott O1 in the official section.**

**Watermarks**

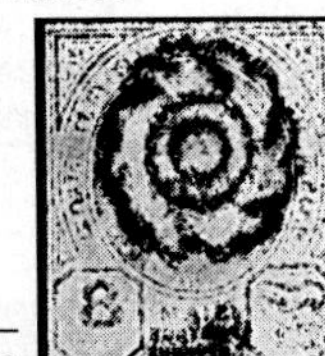

Wmk. 176 — Chakra

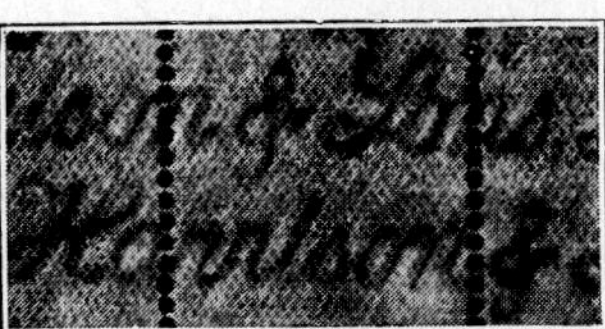

Wmk. 233 — Harrison & Sons, London in Script Letters

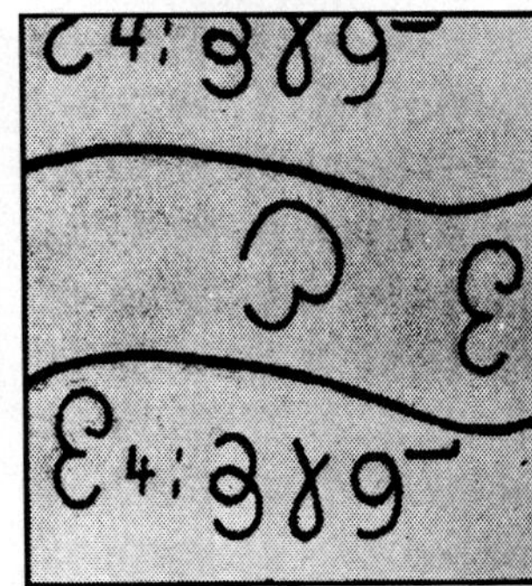

Wmk. 299 — Thai Characters and Wavy Lines

Wmk. 329 — Zigzag Lines

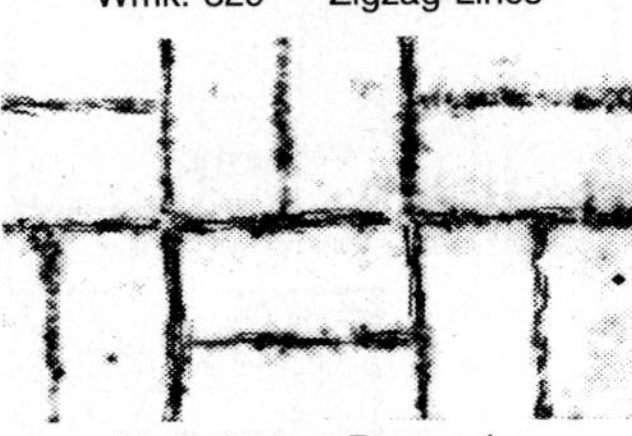

Wmk. 334 — Rectangles

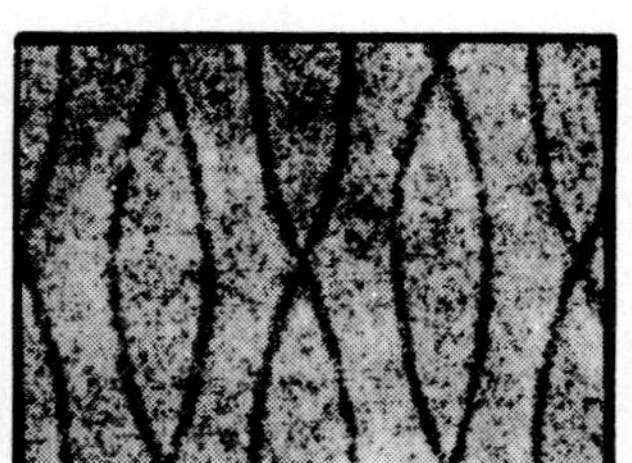

Wmk. 340 — Alternating Interlaced Wavy Lines

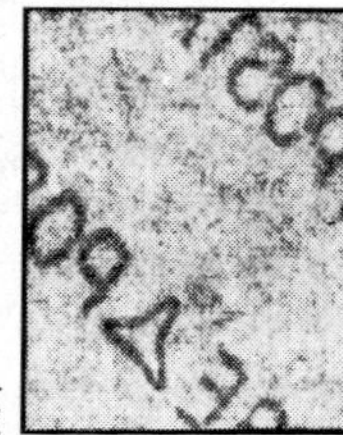

Wmk. 356 — POSTAGE

Wmk. 368 — JEZ Multiple

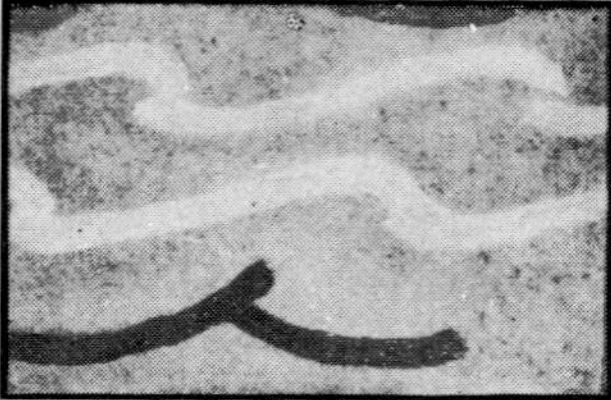

Wmk. 371 — Wavy Lines

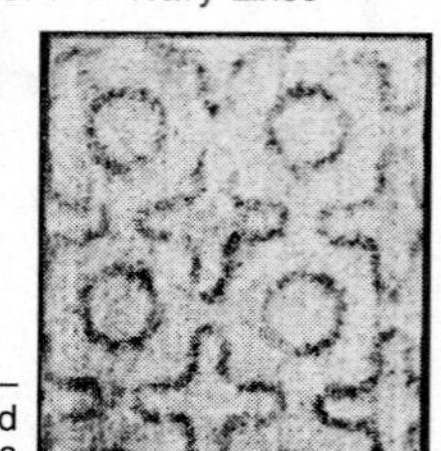

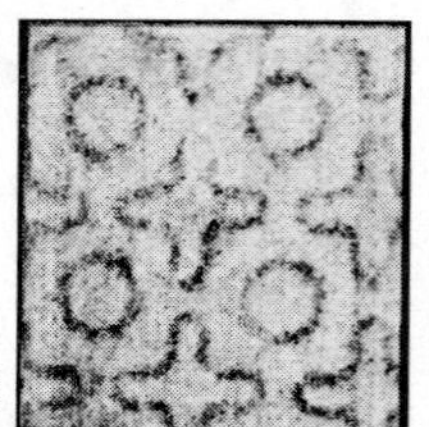

Wmk. 374 — Circles and Crosses

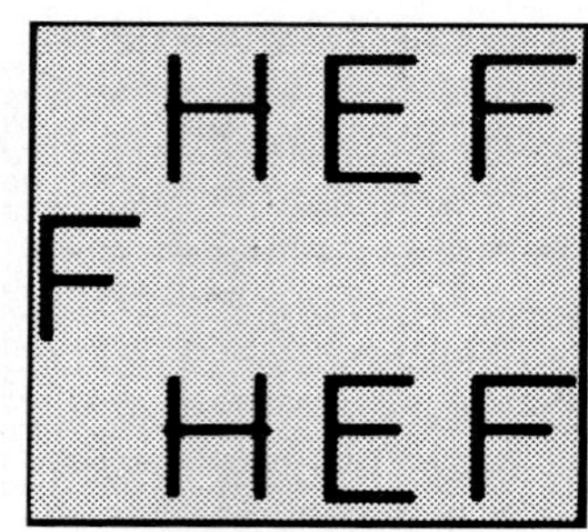

Wmk. 375 — Letters

Wmk. 377 — Interlocking Circles

Wmk. 385 — CARTOR

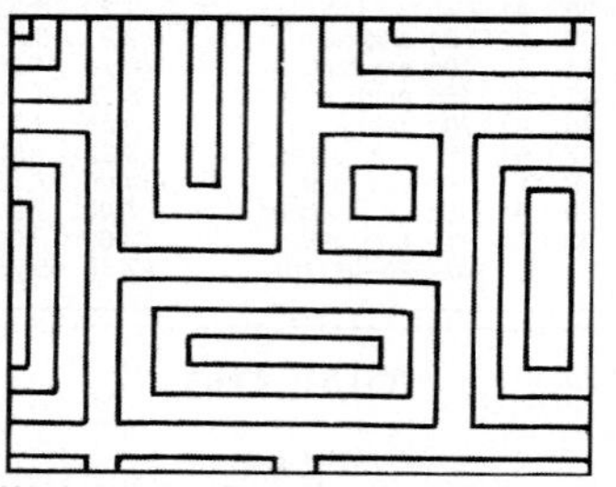

Wmk. 387 — Squares and Rectangles

King Chulalongkorn
A1 A2

A4

***Perf. 14½, 15***

**1883, Aug. 4 Unwmk. Engr.**

| | | | | |
|---|---|---|---|---|
| 1 | A1 1sol blue | | 9.00 | 9.00 |
| *b.* | Imperf., pair | | | *4,500.* |
| 2 | A1 1att carmine | | 9.00 | 9.00 |
| 3 | A1 1sio vermilion | | 20.00 | 18.00 |
| 4 | A2 1sik yellow | | 12.00 | 15.00 |
| 5 | A4 1sa orange | | 45.00 | 45.00 |
| *a.* | 1sa ocher | | 50.00 | 50.00 |
| | *Nos. 1-5 (5)* | | 95.00 | 96.00 |

There are three types of No. 1, differing mainly in the background of the small oval at the top.

A 1 fuang red, of similar design to the foregoing, was prepared but not placed in use. Value, $900.

For surcharges see Nos. 6-8, 19.

No. 1 Handstamp Surcharged in Red:

1 TICAL
*a*

1 Tical *b* 1 Tical *c*

1 Tical *d* 1 Tical *e*

**1885, July 1**

| | | | |
|---|---|---|---|
| 6 | A1 (a) 1t on 1sol blue | *425.* | *425.* |
| 7 | A1 (b) 1t on 1sol blue | *350.* | *350.* |
| *c.* | "1" inverted | *1,100.* | *1,100.* |
| 8 | A1 (c) 1t on 1sol blue | *450.* | *450.* |

Surcharges of Nos. 6-8 have been counterfeited.

Types "d" and "e" are typeset *official reprints.*

As is usual with handstamps, double impressions, etc., exist.

King Chulalongkorn — A7

**1887-91 Typo. Wmk. 176 *Perf. 14***

| | | | | |
|---|---|---|---|---|
| 11 | A7 | 1a green ('91) | 3.00 | 1.00 |
| 12 | A7 | 2a green & car | 4.50 | 1.00 |
| 13 | A7 | 3a grn & blue | 11.00 | 4.00 |
| 14 | A7 | 4a grn & org brn | 9.00 | 3.00 |
| 15 | A7 | 8a green & yel | 9.00 | 7.00 |
| 16 | A7 | 12a lilac & car | 15.00 | 1.50 |
| 17 | A7 | 24a lilac & blue | 21.00 | 1.75 |
| 18 | A7 | 64a lil & org brn | 80.00 | 25.00 |
| | | *Nos. 11-18 (8)* | 152.50 | 44.25 |

The design of No. 11 has been redrawn and differs from the illustration in many minor details.

Issue dates: #12-18, Apr. 1; #11, Feb.

For surcharges see Nos. 20-69, 109, 111, 126.

No. 3 Handstamp Surcharged

**1889, Aug. Unwmk. *Perf. 15***

| | | | |
|---|---|---|---|
| 19 | A1 1a on 1sio | 18.00 | 18.00 |

Three different handstamps were used. Doubles, etc. exist.

Nos. 12 and 13 Handstamp Surcharged ๑ อัฐ 1

**1889-90 Wmk. 176 *Perf. 14***

| | | | |
|---|---|---|---|
| 20 | A7 1a on 2a | 4.00 | 3.00 |
| *a.* | "1" omitted | *250.00* | *250.00* |
| *c.* | 1st Siamese character invtd. | | |
| *d.* | First Siamese character omitted | *300.00* | *300.00* |
| 21 | A7 1a on 3a ('90) | 9.00 | 9.00 |
| *a.* | Inverted "1" | *150.00* | *150.00* |

For surcharge see No. 29.

๑ อัฐ 1

| | | | |
|---|---|---|---|
| 22 | A7 1a on 2a grn & car | *450.00* | *450.00* |

๑ อัฐ 1

| | | | |
|---|---|---|---|
| 24 | A7 1a on 2a grn & car | *175.00* | *175.00* |

๑ อัฐ 1

| | | | |
|---|---|---|---|
| 25 | A7 1a on 2a grn & car | *1,000.* | *1,000.* |

| | | | |
|---|---|---|---|
| 26 | A7 1a on 3a grn & bl | | |

Some authorities consider No. 26 a forgery. Doubles, etc., exist in this issue.

Issue dates: Nov. 1889. Sept. 1890.

No. 13 Handstamp Surcharged ๒ อัฐ 2

**1891**

| | | | |
|---|---|---|---|
| 27 | A7 2a on 3a grn & bl | 55.00 | 55.00 |

๒ อัฐ 2

| | | | |
|---|---|---|---|
| 28 | A7 2a on 3a grn & bl | 50.00 | 50.00 |
| *a.* | Double surcharge | *250.00* | *250.00* |
| *b.* | "2" omitted | *250.00* | |

No. 21 with Additional 2 Att Surcharge

๒ อัฐ 2

| | | | |
|---|---|---|---|
| 29 | A7 2a on 1a on 3a grn & bl | *1,500.* | *1,500.* |

On No. 29 the 2a surcharge consists of Siamese numeral like No. 27 and English numeral like No. 28.

Most examples of No. 29 show attempts to remove the "1" of the first surcharge.

๒ อัฐ 2

**Typeset Surcharge**

| | | | |
|---|---|---|---|
| 30 | A7 2a on 3a grn & bl | 40.00 | 40.00 |

There are 7 types of this surcharge in the setting.

Issued: #27-28, Jan.; #29, Feb.; #30, Mar.

No. 17 Handstamp Surcharged:

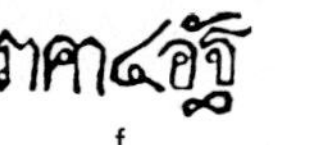

f g

**1892, Oct.**

**33** A7 (f) 4a on 24a lil & bl 50.00 50.00
**34** A7 (g) 4a on 24a lil & bl 35.00 35.00

Surcharges exist double on Nos. 33-34 and inverted on No. 33.

Nos. 33-34 Handstamp Surcharged in English

4 atts

**1892, Nov.**

**35** A7 4a on 24a lil & bl 8.00 8.00
*c.* Inverted "s" 45.00 45.00

**36** A7 4a on 24a lil & bl 13.00 9.00
*a.* Inverted "s" 40.00 40.00

**37** A7 4a on 24a lil & bl 12.00 12.00

4 atts.

**38** A7 4a on 24a lil & bl 13.00 15.00

Numerous inverts., doubles, etc., exist.

Nos. 18 and 17 Typeset Surcharged in English (Shown) and Siamese

1 Atts

**1894**

**39** A7 1a on 64a lil & org brn 3.50 3.50
*a.* Inverted "s" 42.50 42.50
*b.* Inverted surcharge 900.00 900.00
*d.* Italic "s" 55.00 55.00
*e.* Italic "1" 55.00 55.00

1 Att.

**40** A7 1a on 64a lil & org brn 2.00 2.00
*a.* Inverted capital "S" added to the surcharge 175.00 200.00

2 Atts. *h* 2 Atts. *i*

2 Atts. *j* 2 Atts. *k*

2. Atts. *l* 2 Atts. *m*

**41** A7 (h) 2a on 64a 24.00 24.00
*a.* Inverted "s" 42.50 42.50
*b.* Double surcharge 100.00 100.00
**42** A7 (i) 2a on 64a 3,000. 3,000.
**43** A7 (j) 2a on 64a 60.00 60.00
**44** A7 (k) 2a on 64a 35.00 35.00
**45** A7 (l) 2a on 64a 55.00 55.00
**46** A7 (m) 2a on 64a 2.00 2.00
*a.* "Att.s" 42.50 42.50

Nos. 41-46 were in one plate of 120 subjects. The quanrtities were: h, 38; i, 1; j, 8; k, 18; l, 11 and m, 44.

1 Att.

**1894, Oct. 12**

**47** A7 1a on 64a 2.50 2.50
*a.* Surcharged on face and back 150.00
*b.* Surcharge on back inverted 200.00
*c.* Double surcharge 475.00
*d.* Inverted surcharge 500.00
*e.* Siamese surcharge omitted 400.00

2 Atts.

**48** A7 2a on 64a 3.00 3.00
*a.* "Att" 35.00 35.00
*b.* Inverted surcharge 300.00 300.00
*c.* Surch. on face and back 400.00 400.00
*d.* Surcharge on back inverted 400.00 400.00
*e.* Double surcharge 300.00 300.00
*f.* Double surch., one inverted 1,100. 1,100.
*g.* Inverted "s" 42.50 42.50

10 Atts.

**1895, July 23**

**49** A7 10a on 24a lil & bl 7.00 2.00
*a.* Inverted "s" 42.50 42.50
*b.* Surch. on face and back 175.00 175.00
*c.* Surcharge on back inverted 175.00 175.00

No. 16 Surcharged in English (Shown) and Siamese

4 Atts.

**1896**

**50** A7 4a on 12a lil & car 15.00 7.00
*a.* Inverted "s" 50.00 50.00
*b.* Surch. on face and back 175.00 175.00
*c.* Double surcharge on back 175.00 175.00

Two types of surcharge.

Nos. 16-18 Surcharged in English (Shown) and Siamese Antique Surcharges:

1 Atts. *a* 1 Att. *b* 2 Atts. *c*

3 Atts. *d* 4 Atts. *e* 10 Atts. *f*

Atts.

Antique Letters

Atts.

Roman Letters

**1898-99**

**51** A7 (a) 1a on 12a 350.00 350.00
**52** A7 (b) 1a on 12a 17.50 7.00
**53** A7 (c) 2a on 64a ('99) 30.00 9.00
**54** A7 (d) 3a on 12a 12.00 4.00
*a.* Double surcharge 350.00 350.00
**55** A7 (e) 4a on 12a 12.00 5.00
*a.* Double surcharge 350.00 350.00
**56** A7 (e) 4a on 24a ('99) 35.00 12.00
**57** A7 (f) 10a on 24a ('99) 775.00 775.00

Roman Surcharges:

1 Atts. *g* 1 Att. *h* 2 Atts. *i*

3 Atts. *j* 4 Atts. *k* 10 Atts. *l*

**58** A7 (g) 1a on 12a 425.00 425.00
**59** A7 (h) 1a on 12a 42.50 20.00
**60** A7 (i) 2a on 64a ('99) 35.00 10.00
**61** A7 (j) 3a on 12a 85.00 19.00
**62** A7 (k) 4a on 12a 40.00 14.00
*a.* Double surcharge 175.00 175.00
*b.* No period after "Atts." 35.00 35.00
**63** A7 (k) 4a on 24a ('99) 60.00 25.00
**64** A7 (l) 10a on 24a ('99) 725.00 725.00
*Nos. 58-64 (7)* 1,412. 1,238.

In making the settings to surcharge Nos. 51 to 64 two fonts were mixed. Antique and Roman letters are frequently found on the same stamp.

Issued: #54-55, 61-62, Feb. 22; #51-52, 58-59, June 4; #56-57, 63-64, Oct. 3.

Nos. 16 and 18 Surcharged in English (Shown) and Siamese Surcharged:

1 Att. *m* 1 Att. *n*

1 Att. *o*

2 Atts. *p* 2 Atts. *r*

**1894-99**

**65** A7 (m) 1a on 12a 20.00 4.00
**66** A7 (n) 1a on 12a 18.00 8.00
*a.* Inverted "1" 150.00 150.00
*b.* Inverted 1st "t" 150.00 150.00
**67** A7 (o) 1a on 64a 5.00 5.00
**68** A7 (p) 2a on 64a 9.00 9.00
*a.* "1 Atts." 500.00 500.00
**69** A7 (r) 2a on 64a 24.00 5.00
*Nos. 65-69 (5)* 76.00 31.00

Issued: #67, 10/12/94; others, 2/14/99.

A13

A14

**1899, Oct.** **Typo.** **Unwmk.**

**70** A13 1a dull green 130. 80.
**71** A13 2a dl grn & rose 225. 120.
**72** A13 3a carmine & blue 325. 175.
**73** A13 4a black & grn 2,000. 625.
**74** A13 10a carmine & grn 2,300. 900.
*Nos. 70-74 (5)* 4,980. 1,900.

The King rejected Nos. 70-74 in 1897, but some were released by mistake to three post offices in Oct. 1899. Used values are for copies canceled to order at Korat in Dec. 1899. Postally used examples sell for more.

**1899-1904**

**75** A14 1a gray green 2.00 1.00
**76** A14 2a yellow green 2.25 1.25
**77** A14 2a scarlet & bl 3.75 1.75
**78** A14 3a red & blue 7.00 2.00
**79** A14 3a green 20.00 12.00
**80** A14 4a dark rose 4.00 1.50
**81** A14 4a vio brn & rose 8.00 2.00
**82** A14 6a dk rose 35.00 14.00
**83** A14 8a dk grn & org 9.00 1.50
**84** A14 10a ultra 9.00 3.00
**85** A14 12a brn vio & rose 40.00 2.00
**86** A14 14a ultra 22.50 18.00
**87** A14 24a brn vio & bl 325.00 26.00
**88** A14 28a vio brn & bl 25.00 25.00
**89** A14 64a brn vio & org brn 70.00 11.00
*Nos. 75-89 (15)* 582.50 122.00

Two types of 1a differ in size and shape of Thai "1" are in drawing of spandrel ornaments.

Issue dates: 6a, 14a, 28a, Nos. 77, 79, 81, Jan. 1, 1904; others, Sept. 1899.

For surcharges see Nos. 90-91, 112, 125, 127.

Nos. 78 and 85 With Typewritten Surcharge of 6 or 7 Siamese Characters (1 line) in Violet

**1902**

*78a* A14 2a on 3a 4,000. 4,500.
*85a* A14 10a on 12a 4,000. 4,500.

Nos. 78a and 85a were authorized provisionals, surcharged and issued by the Battambang postmaster.

Nos. 86 and 88 Surcharged in Black

**1905, Feb.**

**90** A14 1a on 14a 10.00 8.00
*a.* No period after "Att" 35.00 35.00
**91** A14 2a on 28a 12.00 12.00
*a.* Double surcharge 125.00 125.00

King Chulalongkorn — A15

King Chulalongkorn — A16

**1905-08** **Engr.**

**92** A15 1a orange & green 2.00 1.00
**93** A15 2a violet & slate 3.00 1.00
**94** A15 2a green ('08) 11.00 4.00
**95** A15 3a green 3.00 2.00
**96** A15 3a vio & sl ('08) 10.00 5.00
**97** A15 4a gray & red 4.00 1.00
**98** A15 4a car & rose ('08) 6.00 1.50
**99** A15 5a carmine & rose 8.00 3.00
**100** A15 8a blk & ol bis 8.00 1.50
**101** A15 9a blue ('08) 22.50 9.00
**102** A15 12a blue 18.00 4.00
**103** A15 18a red brn ('08) 55.00 16.00
**104** A15 24a red brown 32.50 7.00
**105** A15 1t dp bl & brn org 45.00 10.00
*Nos. 92-105 (14)* 228.00 66.00

Issue dates: Dec. 1905, Apr. 1, 1908.

For surcharges and overprints see Nos. 110, 113-117, 128-138, 161-162, B15, B21.

**1907, Apr. 24**

**Black Surcharge**

**106** A16 10t gray green 325. 100.
**107** A16 20t gray green 3,300. 290.
**108** A16 40t gray green 2,400. 450.
*Nos. 106-108 (3)* 6,025. 840.00

Counterfeits of Nos. 106-108 exist. In the genuine, the surcharged figures correspond to the Siamese value inscriptions on the basic revenue stamps.

No. 17 Surcharged

**1907, Dec. 16**

**109** A7 1a on 24a lil & bl 2.00 1.00
*a.* Double surcharge 400.00

No. 99 Surcharged

**1908, Sept.**

**110** A15 4a on 5a car & rose 11.00 4.00

The No. 110 surcharge is found in two spacings of the numerals: normally 15mm apart, and a narrow, scarcer spacing of 13½mm.

Nos. 17 and 84 Surcharged in Black:

**111** A7 2a on 24a lil & bl 2.00 1.00
*a.* Inverted surcharge 325.00 325.00
**112** A14 9a on 10a ultra 12.00 5.00
*a.* Inverted surcharge 325.00 325.00

## Jubilee Issue

Nos. 92, 95, 110, 100 and 103 Overprinted in Black or Red

**1908, Nov. 11**

113 A15 1a 2.00 1.00
a. Siamese date "137" instead of "127" *900.00 900.00*
b. Pair, one without ovpt.
114 A15 3a 3.00 2.00
115 A15 4a on 5a 4.50 3.00
a. Horiz. pair, imperf. btwn. *500.00*
116 A15 8a (R) 21.00 21.00
117 A15 18a 30.00 18.00
*Nos. 113-117 (5)* 60.50 45.00

40th year of the reign of King Chulalongkorn.
Nos. 113 to 117 exist with a small "i" in "Jubilee."

Statue of King Chulalongkorn
A19

**1908, Nov. 11 Engr. *Perf. 13½***

118 A19 1t green & vio 29.00 3.00
119 A19 2t red vio & org 57.50 11.00
120 A19 3t pale ol & bl 85.00 14.00
121 A19 5t dl vio & dk grn 120.00 25.00
122 A19 10t bister & car *1,250.* 87.50
123 A19 20t gray & red brn 300.00 85.00
124 A19 40t sl bl & blk brn 475.00 290.00
*Nos. 118-124 (7)* *2,316.* 515.50

The inscription at the foot of the stamps reads: "Coronation Commemoration-Forty-first year of the reign-1908."

Stamps of 1887-1904 Surcharged

**1909 *Perf. 14***

125 A14 6s on 6a dk rose 2.00 2.00
126 A7 14s on 12a lil & car 100.00 100.00
127 A14 14s on 14a ultra 18.00 18.00
*Nos. 125-127 (3)* 120.00 120.00

Nos. 92-102 Surcharged with Bar and

**1909, Aug. 15**

128 A15 2s on 1a #92 2.00 1.00
129 A15 2s on 2a #93 57.50 57.50
130 A15 2s on 2a #94 2.00 1.00
a. "2" omitted *85.00*
131 A15 3s on 3a #95 3.00 1.00
132 A15 3s on 3a #96 3.00 1.00
133 A15 6s on 4a #97 60.00 60.00
134 A15 6s on 4a #98 4.00 1.00
135 A15 6s on 5a #99 3.00 3.00
136 A15 12s on 8a #100 7.00 1.00
137 A15 14s on 9a #101 11.00 2.00
138 A15 14s on 12a #102 21.00 21.00
*Nos. 128-138 (11)* 173.50 149.50

King Chulalongkorn — A20

**1910 Engr. *Perf. 14x14½***

139 A20 2s org & green 1.50 .50
140 A20 3s green 2.00 .50
141 A20 6s carmine 3.00 .50
142 A20 12s blk & ol brn 6.00 1.00
143 A20 14s blue 19.00 2.00
144 A20 28s red brown 45.00 9.00
*Nos. 139-144 (6)* 76.50 13.50

Issue dates: 12s, June 5. Others, May 5.
For surcharges see Nos. 163, 223-224.

A21 King Vajiravudh — A22

Printed at the Imperial Printing Works, Vienna

**1912 *Perf. 14½***

145 A21 2s brown orange 1.25 .20
a. Vert. pair, imperf. btwn. *500.00 500.00*
b. Horiz. pair, imperf. btwn. *500.00 500.00*
146 A21 3s yellow green 1.25 .20
a. Horiz. pair, imperf. btwn. *500.00 500.00*
147 A21 6s carmine rose 2.25 .55
148 A21 12s gray blk & brn 3.25 .60
149 A21 14s ultramarine 5.25 .80
150 A21 28s chocolate 20.00 8.00
151 A22 1b blue & blk 20.00 2.00
a. Pair, imperf. btwn. *1,250. 1,250.*
152 A22 2b car rose & ol brn 24.00 3.00
153 A22 3b yel grn & bl blk 32.50 6.00
154 A22 5b vio & blk 50.00 7.00
155 A22 10b ol grn & vio brn 250.00 85.00
156 A22 20b sl bl & red brn 410.00 85.00
*Nos. 145-156 (12)* 819.75 198.35

See Nos. 164-175.
For surcharges and overprints see Nos. 157-160, 176-186, 206, B1-B14, B16-B20, B22, B31-B33.

Nos. 147-150 Surcharged in Red or Blue

**1914-15**

157 A21 2s on 14s (R) ('15) 1.75 .35
a. Vert. pair, imperf. btwn. *900.00 900.00*
b. Double surcharge 62.50 40.00
158 A21 5s on 6s (Bl) 3.25 .35
a. Horiz. pair, imperf. btwn. *900.00 900.00*
b. Double surcharge 67.50 67.50
159 A21 10s on 12s (R) 4.00 .45
a. Double surcharge 67.50 67.50
160 A21 15s on 28s (Bl) 5.00 .60
*Nos. 157-160 (4)* 14.00 1.75

The several settings of the surcharges on Nos. 157 to 160 show variations in the figures and letters.

Nos. 92-93 Surcharged

**1915, Apr. 3**

161 A15 2s on 1a org & grn 5.00 3.00
a. Pair, one without surcharge *350.00 350.00*
162 A15 2s on 2a vio & slate 5.00 3.00

No. 143 Surcharged in Red

**1916, Oct.**

163 A20 2s on 14s blue 2.50 1.10

Printed by Waterlow & Sons, London
Types of 1912 Re-engraved

**1917, Jan. 1 *Perf. 14***

164 A21 2s orange brown .65 .25
165 A21 3s emerald .95 .35
166 A21 5s rose red 2.50 .25
167 A21 10s black & olive 2.00 .25
168 A21 15s blue 4.00 .50
170 A22 1b bl & gray blk 17.50 2.00
171 A22 2b car rose & brn 70.00 26.00
172 A22 3b yel grn & blk 500.00 250.00
173 A22 5b dp violet & blk 125.00 85.00
174 A22 10b ol gray & vio brn 400.00 10.00
a. Perf. 12½ 500.00 37.50
175 A22 20b sea grn & brn 500.00 50.00
a. Perf. 12½ 600.00 85.00
*Nos. 164-175 (11)* 1,622. 424.60

The re-engraved design of the satang stamps varies in numerous minute details from the 1912 issue. Four lines of the background appear between the vertical strokes of the "M" of "SIAM" in the 1912 issue and only three lines in the 1917 stamps.

The 1912 stamps with value in bahts are 37½mm high; those of 1917 are 39mm. In the latter the king's features, especially the eyes and mouth, are more distinct and the uniform and decorations are more sharply defined.

The 1912 stamps have seven pearls between the earpieces of the crown. On the 1917 stamps there are nine pearls in the same place. Nos. 174 and 175 exist imperforate.

Nos. 164-173 Overprinted in Red

**1918, Dec. 2**

176 A21 2s orange brown .55 .45
a. Double overprint 110.00 110.00
177 A21 3s emerald .85 .75
178 A21 5s rose red 1.40 1.25
a. Double overprint 150.00 150.00
179 A21 10s black & olive 1.40 1.25
180 A21 15s blue 2.75 2.50
181 A22 1b bl & gray blk 22.50 17.00
182 A22 2b car rose & brn 45.00 35.00
183 A22 3b yel grn & blk 110.00 65.00
184 A22 5b dp vio & blk 375.00 275.00
*Nos. 176-184 (9)* 559.45 398.20

Counterfeits of this overprint exist.

Nos. 147-148 Surcharged in Green or Red

**1919-20**

185 A21 5s on 6s (G) 1.75 .30
186 A21 10s on 12s (R) ('20) 6.00 1.00

Issue dates: 5s, Nov. 11. 10s, Jan. 1.

King Vajiravudh
A23

Throne Room
A24

**1920-26 Engr. *Perf. 14-15, 12½***

187 A23 2s brn, *yel* ('21) 2.00 .40
188 A23 3s grn, *grn* ('21) 3.25 .55
189 A23 3s chocolate ('24) 3.25 .40
190 A23 5s rose, *pale rose* 3.75 .40
191 A23 5s green ('22) 30.00 5.00
192 A23 5s dk vio, *lil* ('26) 7.50 .40
193 A23 10s blk & org ('21) 5.75 .40
194 A23 15s bl, *bluish* ('21) 8.50 .40
195 A23 15s carmine ('22) 40.00 5.00
196 A23 25s chocolate ('21) 24.00 2.00
197 A23 25s dk blue ('22) 27.50 1.00
198 A23 50s och & blk ('21) 25.00 2.00
*Nos. 187-198 (12)* 180.50 17.95

For overprints see Nos. 205, B23-B30.

**1926, Mar. 5 *Perf. 12½***

199 A24 1t gray vio & grn 12.00 2.00
200 A24 2t car & org red 27.50 6.00
201 A24 3t ol grn & bl 45.00 25.00
202 A24 5t dl vio & ol grn 65.00 19.00
203 A24 10t red & ol bis 300.00 22.50
204 A24 20t gray bl & brn 325.00 67.50
*Nos. 199-204 (6)* 774.50 142.00

This issue was intended to commemorate the fifteenth year of the reign of King Vajiravudh. Because of the King's death the stamps were issued as ordinary postage stamps.

Nos. 195 and 150 with Surcharge similar to 1914-15 Issue in Black or Red

**1928, Jan.**

205 A23 5s on 15s car 4.00 2.00
206 A21 10s on 28s choc (R) 9.00 1.00

King Prajadhipok
A25 A26

**1928 Engr. *Perf. 12½***

207 A25 2s deep red brown .60 .20
208 A25 3s deep green .75 .20
209 A25 5s dark violet .60 .20
210 A25 10s deep rose .75 .20
211 A25 15s dark blue .90 .40
212 A25 25s black & org 3.50 .60
213 A25 50s brn org & blk 1.75 1.25
214 A25 80s blue & black 3.00 .80
216 A26 1b dk blue & blk 6.00 1.25
217 A26 2b car rose & blk brn 12.00 3.00
218 A26 3b yellow grn & blk 9.00 3.00
219 A26 5b dp vio & gray blk 20.00 5.00
220 A26 10b ol grn & red vio 37.50 10.00
221 A26 20b Prus grn & brn 80.00 17.50
222 A26 40b dk grn & ol brn 160.00 47.50
*Nos. 207-222 (15)* 336.35 91.10
Set, never hinged 450.00

On the single colored stamps, type A25, the lines in the background are uniform; those of the bicolored values are shaded and do not extend to the frame.

Issue dates: 5s, 10s, 2b-40b, Apr. 15; 2s, 3s, 15s, 25s, 50s, May 1; 1b, June 1; 80s, Nov. 15.

For overprints & surcharge see #300-301, B34.

Nos. 142, 144 Surcharged in Red or Blue

**1930 *Perf. 14***

223 A20 10s on 12s 6.00 1.00
224 A20 25s on 28s (Bl) 30.00 2.00
Set, never hinged 37.50

King Prajadhipok and Chao P'ya Chakri
A27 A28

Statue of Chao P'ya Chakri — A29

**1932, Apr. 1 Engr. *Perf. 12½***

225 A27 2s dark brown 1.00 .25
226 A27 3s deep green 2.00 .40
227 A27 5s dull violet 1.25 .25
228 A28 10s red brn & blk 2.00 .25
229 A28 15s dull blue & blk 7.75 .95
230 A28 25s violet & black 11.00 1.40
231 A28 50s claret & black 50.00 5.00
232 A29 1b blue black 75.00 12.50
*Nos. 225-232 (8)* 150.00 21.00
Set, never hinged 225.00

150th anniv. of the Chakri dynasty, the founding of Bangkok in 1782, and the opening of the memorial bridge across the Chao Phraya River.

Assembly Hall, Bangkok A30

**1939, June 24 Litho. *Perf. 11, 12***

233 A30 2s dull red brown 3.25 1.00
234 A30 3s green 6.75 2.25
235 A30 5s dark violet 3.25 .20
236 A30 10s carmine 13.50 .20
237 A30 15s dark blue 32.50 2.00
*Nos. 233-237 (5)* 59.25 5.65
Set, never hinged 70.00

7th anniv. of the Siamese Constitution.

Chakri Palace, Bangkok — A31

**1940 Typo. *Perf. 12½***

238 A31 2s dull brown 3.25 1.00
239 A31 3s dp yellow grn 6.25 2.25
a. Cliché of 5s in plate of 3s 900.00 725.00
240 A31 5s dark violet 4.75 .20
241 A31 10s carmine 17.50 .20
242 A31 15s dark blue 37.50 1.00
*Nos. 238-242 (5)* 69.25 4.65
Set, never hinged 90.00

Issued: 2s, 3s, 5/13; 5s, 5/24; 15s, 5/28; 10s, 5/30.

King Ananda Mahidol — A32

Plowing Rice Field — A33

Royal Pavilion at Bang-pa-in A34

King Ananda Mahidol A35

**1941, Apr. 17 Engr.**

243 A32 2s brown .40 .25
244 A32 3s deep green .40 .40
245 A32 5s violet .40 .25
246 A32 10s dark red .40 .25
247 A33 15s dp bl & gray blk .55 .25
248 A33 25s slate & org .70 .40
249 A33 50s red org & gray .80 .40
250 A34 1b brt ultra & gray 7.75 .90
251 A34 2b dk car rose & gray 14.00 2.00
252 A34 3b dp grn & gray 17.50 4.25
253 A34 5b blk & rose red 45.00 19.00
a. Horiz. pair, imperf. btwn.
254 A34 10b ol blk & yel 67.50 45.00
*Nos. 243-254 (12)* 155.40 73.35
Set, never hinged 250.00

**1943, May 1 Unwmk. *Perf. 11***

255 A35 1b dark blue 19.00 2.00
a. Horiz. pair, imperf. btwn. 85.00 85.00
b. Vert. pair, imperf. btwn. 85.00 85.00

See No. 274.

Indo-China War Monument A36

Bangkhaen Monument A37

**1943 Engr. *Perf. 11, 12½***

256 A36 3s dark green 17.50 17.50

**Litho.**

***Perf. 12½x11***

257 A36 3s dull green 3.00 1.00

Issue dates: #256, June 1. #257, Nov. 2.

**1943, Nov. 25 *Perf. 12½, 12½x11***

Two types of 10s:
I — Size 19½x24mm.
II — Size 20¾x25¼mm.

258 A37 2s brown orange 2.50 1.75
259 A37 10s car rose (I) 4.00 .60
a. Type II 8.00 5.00

10th anniv. of the quelling of a counter-revolution led by a member of the royal family on Oct. 11, 1933.

Stamps of similar design, but with values in "cents," are listed under Malaya, Occupation Stamps. See Nos. 2N1-2N6.

King Bhumibol Adulyadej A38 A39

**1947, Dec. 5 *Pin-perf. 12½x11***

260 A38 5s orange 1.75 1.25
261 A38 10s olive ('48) 1.75 1.25
a. 10s light brown 75.00 75.00
262 A38 20s blue 7.00 1.25
263 A38 50s blue green 14.00 2.50
*Nos. 260-263 (4)* 24.50 6.25

Coming of age of King Bhumibol Adulyadej. Issued with and without gum.

**Catalogue values for unused stamps in this section, from this point to the end of the section, are for Never Hinged items.**

**1947-49 Unwmk. Engr. *Perf. 12½***

**Size: 20x25mm**

264 A39 5s violet .60 .20
265 A39 10s red 1.50 .20
266 A39 20s chocolate .90 .20
267 A39 50s olive 1.50 .20

**Size: 22x27mm**

268 A39 1b vio & dp bl 9.25 .30
269 A39 2b ultra & green 20.00 1.10
270 A39 3b brn red & blk 30.00 2.25
271 A39 5b bl grn & brn red 72.50 6.00
272 A39 10b dk brn & pur 260.00 3.00
273 A39 20b blk & rose brn 300.00 9.00
*Nos. 264-273 (10)* 696.25 22.45

Issued: 5s, 20s, 11/15/47; 10s, 50s, 1/3/49; 1b-20b, 11/1/48.

For surcharges see Nos. 302-303.

Type of 1943

***Perf. 11½, 12½x11½***

**1948, Jan. Litho.**

274 A35 1b chalky blue 50.00 8.00
a. Horiz. pair, imperf. btwn. 150.00 150.00
b. Vert. pair, imperf. btwn. 150.00 150.00

King Bhumibol Adulyadej and Palace

A40 A41

***Perf. 12½***

**1950, May 5 Unwmk. Engr.**

275 A40 5s red violet .65 .20
276 A40 10s red .65 .25
277 A40 15s purple 3.25 2.75
278 A40 20s chocolate 1.25 .20
279 A40 80s green 9.00 3.75
280 A40 1b deep blue 3.00 .25
281 A40 2b orange yellow 18.00 2.00
282 A40 3b gray 90.00 11.00
*Nos. 275-282 (8)* 125.80 20.40

Coronation of Bhumibol Adulyadej as Rama IX, May 5, 1950.

**1951-60 *Perf. 12½, 13x12½***

283 A41 5s rose lilac .30 .20
284 A41 10s deep green .30 .20
285 A41 15s red brown .90 .20
285A A41 20s chocolate .90 .20
286 A41 25s carmine .30 .20
287 A41 50s gray olive .90 .20
288 A41 1b deep blue 1.25 .20
289 A41 1.15b deep blue .30 .50
290 A41 1.25b orange brn 4.50 .35
291 A41 2b dull blue grn 5.50 .35
292 A41 3b gray 9.00 .50
293 A41 5b aqua & red 40.00 .75
294 A41 10b black brn & vio 310.00 4.00
295 A41 20b gray & olive 275.00 17.50
*Nos. 283-295 (14)* 649.15 25.35

Issued: 25s, 2/15; 5s, 10s, 1b, 6/4; 2b, 3b, 12/1; 15s, 2/15/52; 1.15b, 9/1/53; 1.25b, 10/1/54; 5b, 10b, 20b, 2/1/55; 50s, 10/15/56; 20s, 1960.

United Nations Day — A42

**1951, Oct. 24**

296 A42 25s ultramarine 3.75 2.50

Overprinted "1952" in Carmine

**1952, Oct.**

297 A42 25s ultramarine 2.75 2.00

Overprinted "1953" in Carmine

**1953, Oct.**

298 A42 25s ultramarine 1.75 1.10

Overprinted "1954" in Carmine

**1954, Oct. 24**

299 A42 25s ultramarine 4.75 3.50
*Nos. 296-299 (4)* 13.00 9.10

For more overprints see Nos. 315, 320.

Nos. 209 and 210 Overprinted in Black

**1955, Jan. 4 *Perf. 12½***

300 A25 5s dark violet 8.50 7.50
301 A25 10s deep rose 8.50 7.50

**No. 266 Surcharged with New Value in Black or Carmine**

302 A39 5s on 20s choc 2.00 .75
303 A39 10s on 20s choc (C) 3.00 .75
*Nos. 300-303 (4)* 22.00 16.50

King Naresuan (1555-1605), on War Elephant — A43

Tao Suranari — A44

***Perf. 13½***

**1955, Feb. 15 Unwmk. Engr.**

304 A43 25s brt carmine 1.75 .20
305 A43 80s rose violet 20.00 5.00
306 A43 1.25b dark olive grn 50.00 3.00
307 A43 2b deep blue 12.50 1.25
308 A43 3b henna brown 35.00 2.00
*Nos. 304-308 (5)* 119.25 11.45

**1955, Apr. 15 *Perf. 12x13½***

309 A44 10s purple 2.50 .40
310 A44 25s emerald 1.75 .20
311 A44 1b brown 40.00 2.40
*Nos. 309-311 (3)* 44.25 3.00

Lady Mo, called Tao Suranari (Brave Woman) for her role in stopping an 1826 rebellion.

King Taksin Statue at Thonburi A45

Don Jedi Monument A46

**1955, May 1 *Perf. 12½x12***

312 A45 5s violet blue 1.50 .30
313 A45 25s Prus green 11.00 .20
314 A45 1.25b red 37.50 2.50
*Nos. 312-314 (3)* 50.00 3.00

King Somdech P'ya Chao Taksin (1734-1782).

No. 296 Overprinted "1955" in Red

**1955, Oct. 24 *Perf. 12½***

315 A42 25s ultramarine 4.75 3.00

United Nations Day, Oct. 24, 1955.

**1956, Feb. 1 *Perf. 13½x13***

316 A46 10s emerald 3.50 2.50
317 A46 50s reddish brown 22.50 2.00
318 A46 75s violet 7.00 .75
319 A46 1.50b brown orange 19.00 1.25
*Nos. 316-319 (4)* 52.00 6.50

No. 296 Overprinted "1956" in Red Violet

**1956, Oct. 24**

320 A42 25s ultramarine 2.00 1.60

United Nations Day, Oct. 24, 1956.

Dharmachakra and Deer — A47

20s, 25s, 50s, Hand of peace and Dharmachakra. 1b, 1.25b, 2b, Pagoda of Nakon Phatom.

**Wmk. 329**

**1957, May 13 Photo. *Perf. 13½***

321 A47 5s dark brown 1.00 .40
322 A47 10s rose lake 1.00 .40
323 A47 15s brt green 2.00 1.50
324 A47 20s orange 2.00 1.75
325 A47 25s reddish brown .75 .40
326 A47 50s magenta 2.00 .60
327 A47 1b olive brown 2.25 .70

**328** A47 1.25b slate blue 32.50 6.00
**329** A47 2b deep claret 7.50 .90
*Nos. 321-329 (9)* 51.00 12.65

2500th anniversary of birth of Buddha.

UN Day — A48

Thai Archway — A49

**1957, Oct. 24** ***Perf. 13½***

**330** A48 25s olive 1.00 .30
**331** A48 25s bright ocher ('58) 1.00 .30
**332** A48 25s indigo ('59) 1.40 .30
*Nos. 330-332 (3)* 3.40 .90

Issued: Oct. 24.

**1959, Oct. 15** **Photo.** ***Perf. 13½***

Designs (inscribed "SEAP Games 1959"): 25s, Royal tiered umbrellas. 1.25b, Thai archer, ancient costume. 2b, Wat Arun pagoda and prow of royal barge.

**333** A49 10s orange .80 .20
**334** A49 25s dk carmine rose 1.00 .20
**335** A49 1.25b bright green 5.00 1.25
**336** A49 2b light blue 4.50 .80
*Nos. 333-336 (4)* 11.30 2.45

Issued to publicize the South-East Asia Peninsula Games, Bangkok, Dec. 12-17.

Wat Arun, WRY Emblem — A50

Wat Arun, Bangkok — A51

**1960, Apr. 7**

**337** A50 50s chocolate .60 .20
**338** A50 2b yellow green 2.00 .50

WRY, July 1, 1959-June 30, 1960.

**1960, Aug.** **Wmk. 329** ***Perf. 13½***

**339** A51 50s carmine rose .50 .20
**340** A51 2b ultramarine 4.00 1.00

Anti-leprosy campaign.

Elephants in Teak Forest — A52

Globe and SEATO Emblem — A53

**1960, Aug. 29** **Photo.** ***Perf. 13½***

**341** A52 25s emerald 1.25 .20

5th World Forestry Cong., Seattle, WA, Aug. 29-Sept. 10.

**1960, Sept. 8**

**342** A53 50s chocolate 1.40 .20

SEATO Day, Sept. 8.

Siamese Child — A54

Hand with Pen and Globe — A55

**1960, Oct. 3** **Wmk. 329**

**343** A54 50s magenta .60 .20
**344** A54 1b orange 5.00 .75

Children's Day, 1960.

**1960, Oct. 3**

**345** A55 50s carmine rose .75 .20
**346** A55 2b blue 5.50 .90

Intl. Letter Writing Week, Oct. 3-9.

UN Emblem and Globe A56

King Bhumibol Adulyadej A57

**1960, Oct. 24** ***Perf. 13½***

**347** A56 50s purple 1.75 .25

15th anniversary of the United Nations. See Nos. 369, 390.

***Perf. 13½x13***

| **1961-68** | | **Engr.** | **Wmk. 334** | |
|---|---|---|---|---|
| **348** | A57 | 5s rose cl ('62) | .30 | .20 |
| **349** | A57 | 10s green ('62) | .30 | .20 |
| **350** | A57 | 15s red brn ('62) | .55 | .20 |
| **351** | A57 | 20s brown ('62) | .30 | .20 |
| **352** | A57 | 25s carmine ('63) | .55 | .20 |
| **353** | A57 | 50s olive ('62) | .60 | .20 |
| **354** | A57 | 80s orange ('62) | 2.25 | 1.00 |
| **355** | A57 | 1b vio bl & brn | 2.00 | .20 |
| **355A** | A57 | 1.25b red & citron ('65) | 7.25 | 1.25 |
| **356** | A57 | 1.50b dk vio & yel green | 2.00 | .35 |
| **357** | A57 | 2b red & violet | 2.25 | .20 |
| **358** | A57 | 3b brn & bl | 6.00 | .35 |
| **358A** | A57 | 4b olive bis & blk ('68) | 9.00 | 1.40 |
| **359** | A57 | 5b blue & green | 29.00 | 1.00 |
| **360** | A57 | 10b red org & blk | 87.50 | 2.00 |
| **361** | A57 | 20b emer & ultra | 75.00 | 5.00 |
| **362** | A57 | 25b green & blue | 42.50 | 4.00 |
| **362A** | A57 | 40b yellow & blk ('65) | 80.00 | 7.00 |
| | | *Nos. 348-362A (18)* | 347.35 | 24.95 |

For overprint see No. 588.

Children in Garden — A58

Pen and Envelope with Map — A59

**Wmk. 329**

**1961, Oct. 2** **Photo.** ***Perf. 13½***

**363** A58 20s indigo .75 .25
**364** A58 2b purple 4.25 .70

Issued for Children's Day.

**1961, Oct. 9**

1b, 2b, Pen and letters circling globe.

**365** A59 25s gray green .55 .20
**366** A59 50s rose lilac .30 .20
**367** A59 1b bright rose 1.75 .40
**368** A59 2b ultramarine 2.25 .55
*Nos. 365-368 (4)* 4.85 1.35

Intl. Letter Writing Week, Oct. 2-8.

**UN Type of 1960**

**1961, Oct. 24** **Wmk. 329** ***Perf. 13½***

**369** A56 50s maroon 1.00 .25

Issued for United Nations Day, Oct. 24.

Scout Emblem — A60

Scouts Saluting and Tents — A61

Design: 2b, King Vajiravudh and Scouts.

**1961, Nov. 1** **Photo.**

**370** A60 50s carmine rose .60 .30
**371** A61 1b bright green 1.75 .50
**372** A61 2b bright blue 2.00 .65
*Nos. 370-372 (3)* 4.35 1.45

Thai Boy Scouts, 50th anniversary.

Malaria Eradication Emblem and Siamese Designs
A62 A63

**1962, Apr. 7** **Wmk. 329** ***Perf. 13***

**373** A62 5s orange brown .30 .20
**374** A62 10s sepia .30 .20
**375** A62 20s blue .50 .20
**376** A62 50s carmine rose .30 .20
**377** A63 1b green 1.25 .25
**378** A63 1.50b dk car rose 3.50 .55
**379** A63 2d dark blue 1.75 .35
**380** A63 3b violet 5.00 2.50
*Nos. 373-380 (8)* 12.90 4.45

WHO drive to eradicate malaria.

View of Bangkok and Seattle Fair Emblem A64

**1962, Apr. 21** **Wmk. 329** ***Perf. 13***

**381** A64 50s red lilac .75 .20
**382** A64 2b deep blue 7.00 .75

"Century 21" Intl. Expo., Seattle, WA, Apr. 21-Oct. 12.

Mother and Child A65

Globe, Letters, Carrier Pigeons A66

**Wmk. 329**

**1962, Oct. 1** **Photo.** ***Perf. 13***

**383** A65 25s lt blue green 1.00 .30
**384** A65 50s bister brown 1.25 .20
**385** A65 2b bright pink 6.25 .75
*Nos. 383-385 (3)* 8.50 1.25

Issued for Children's Day.

**1962, Oct. 8**

Design: 1b, 2b, Quill pen and scroll.

**386** A66 25s violet .65 .30
**387** A66 50s red .35 .20
**388** A66 1b lemon 3.25 .60
**389** A66 2b lt bluish green 5.50 .65
*Nos. 386-389 (4)* 9.75 1.75

Intl. Letter Writing Week, Oct. 7-13.

UN Type of 1960

**1962, Oct. 24** ***Perf. 13½***

**390** A56 50s carmine rose 1.00 .25

United Nations Day, Oct. 24.

Exhibition Emblem — A67

Temple Lion — A69

Woman Harvesting Rice — A68

**1962, Nov. 1** **Unwmk.**

**391** A67 50s olive bister 1.75 .20

Students' Exhibition, Bangkok.

**Wmk. 334**

**1963, Mar. 21** **Engr.** ***Perf. 14***

**392** A68 20s green 2.00 .45
**393** A68 50s ocher 1.50 .25

FAO "Freedom from Hunger" campaign.

**1963, Apr. 1** **Wmk. 329** ***Perf. 13½***

**394** A69 50s green & bister 1.25 .20

1st anniv. of the formation of the Asian-Oceanic Postal Union, AOPU.

New and Old Post and Telegraph Buildings — A70

**Wmk. 334**

**1963, Aug. 4** **Engr.** ***Perf. 14***

**395** A70 50s org, bluish blk & grn .85 .25
**396** A70 3b grn, dk red & brn 6.50 1.50

80th anniv. of the Post and Telegraph Dept.

King Bhumibol Adulyadej A71

Child with Dolls A72

***Perf. 13x13½***

| **1963-71** | | **Wmk. 329** | **Photo.** | |
|---|---|---|---|---|
| **397** | A71 | 5s dk car rose | .30 | .20 |
| **398** | A71 | 10s dark green | .30 | .20 |
| **399** | A71 | 15s red brown | .30 | .20 |
| **400** | A71 | 20s black brown | .30 | .20 |
| **401** | A71 | 25s carmine | .35 | .20 |
| **402** | A71 | 50s olive gray | .40 | .20 |
| **402A** | A71 | 75s brt vio ('71) | .50 | .20 |
| **403** | A71 | 80s dull orange | 2.00 | .45 |
| **404** | A71 | 1b dk bl & dk brn | 1.75 | .20 |
| **404A** | A71 | 1.25b org brn & ol ('65) | 6.25 | 1.00 |
| **405** | A71 | 1.50b vio bl & grn | 1.75 | .50 |
| **406** | A71 | 2b dk red & vio | 1.00 | .20 |
| **407** | A71 | 3b brn & dk bl | 2.00 | .25 |
| **407A** | A71 | 4b dp bis & blk ('68) | 2.75 | .25 |
| **408** | A71 | 5b blue & green | 13.00 | .25 |
| **409** | A71 | 10b orange & blk | 22.50 | 1.00 |
| **410** | A71 | 20b brt grn & ind | 160.00 | 5.00 |
| **411** | A71 | 25b dk grn & bl | 6.00 | .50 |
| **411A** | A71 | 40b yel & blk ('65) | 150.00 | 8.00 |
| | | *Nos. 397-411A (19)* | 371.45 | 19.00 |

Nos. 397-403 were issued in 1963; Nos. 404, 405-407, 408-411 in 1964.
For overprint see No. 589.

**1963, Oct. 7 Litho. *Perf. 13½***

**412** A72 50s rose red 1.75 .20
**413** A72 2b dull blue 5.75 .75

Issued for Children's Day.

Garuda Carrying Letter — A73

Design: 2b, 3b, Thai women writing letters.

**1963, Oct. 7 Wmk. 329**

**414** A73 50s lt blue & claret 1.50 .20
**415** A73 1b lt grn & vio brn 4.75 .80
**416** A73 2b yel brn & turq bl 32.50 2.00
**417** A73 3b org brn & yel grn 17.00 3.00
*Nos. 414-417 (4)* 55.75 6.00

Intl. Letter Writing Week, Oct. 6-12.

UN Emblem — A74

UNICEF Emblem — A76

King Bhumibol Adulyadej — A75

**1963, Oct. 24 Wmk. 329 *Perf. 13½***

**418** A74 50s bright blue 1.00 .20

United Nations Day, Oct. 24.

**1963, Dec. 5 Photo. *Perf. 13½***

**419** A75 1.50b blue, org & ind 4.00 .50
**420** A75 5b brt lil rose, org & blk 23.00 3.00

King Bhumibol's 36th birthday.

**1964, Jan. 13 Litho.**

**421** A76 50s blue .75 .20
**422** A76 2b olive green 4.25 .45

17th anniv. of UNICEF.

Hand (flags), Pigeon and Globe — A77

Designs: 1b, Girls and world map. 2b, Pen, pencil and unfolded world map. 3b, Globe and hand holding quill.

**1964, Oct. 5 Wmk. 329 *Perf. 13½***

**423** A77 50s lilac & lt grn .25 .20
**424** A77 1b red brown & grn 4.50 .80
**425** A77 2b yellow & vio bl 11.50 1.00
**426** A77 3b blue & dk brown 6.25 2.50
*Nos. 423-426 (4)* 22.50 4.50

Intl. Letter Writing Week, Oct. 5-11.

UN Emblem and Globe — A78

King and Queen — A79

**1964, Oct. 24 Photo. *Perf. 13½***

**427** A78 50s gray 1.25 .20

United Nations Day, Oct. 24.

**1965, Apr. 28 Wmk. 329 *Perf. 13½***

**428** A79 2b brown & multi 14.00 .40
**429** A79 5b violet & multi 21.00 2.00

15th wedding anniversary of King Bhumibol Adulyadej and Queen Sirikit.

ITU Emblem, Old and New Communications Equipment — A80

**1965, May 17 Photo.**

**430** A80 1b bright green 4.50 .50

Cent. of the ITU.

World Map, Letters and Goddess — A81

2b, 3b, World map, letters and handshake.

**1965, Oct. 3 Wmk. 329 *Perf. 13½***

**431** A81 50s dp plum, gray & sal .25 .25
**432** A81 1b dk vio bl, lt vio & yel 2.75 .60
**433** A81 2b dk gray, bis & dp org 11.00 .60
**434** A81 3b multicolored 16.00 2.75
*Nos. 431-434 (4)* 30.00 4.20

Intl. Letter Writing Week, Oct. 3-9.

A82

A83

Gates of Royal Chapel of Emerald Buddha.

**Engr. & Litho.**
***Perf. 13½x14***

**1965, Oct. 24 Wmk. 356**

**435** A82 50s slate grn, bl & ocher 1.50 .20

International Cooperation Year, 1965.

**Wmk. 329**

**1965, Nov. 1 Litho. *Perf. 13½***

Map of Thailand and UPU monument, Bern.

**436** A83 20s dk blue & lilac .50 .20
**437** A83 50s gray & blue 1.75 .20
**438** A83 1b orange brn & vio bl 4.25 .35
**439** A83 3b green & bister 11.50 2.25
*Nos. 436-439 (4)* 18.00 3.00

80th anniv. of Thailand's admission to the UPU.

Lotus Blossom and Child — A84

Design: 1b, Boy with book walking up steps.

**1966, Jan. 8 Wmk. 334 *Perf. 13½***

**440** A84 50s henna brn & blk .30 .20
**441** A84 1b green & black 3.25 .60

Issued for Children's Day, 1966.

Bicycling — A85

**1966, Aug. 4 Photo. Wmk. 329**

**442** A85 20s shown .60 .20
**443** A85 25s Tennis .90 .30
**444** A85 50s Running .60 .20
**445** A85 1b Weight lifting 2.50 .60
**446** A85 1.25b Boxing 3.75 2.50
**447** A85 2b Swimming 7.00 .45
**448** A85 3b Netball 17.50 4.00
**449** A85 5b Soccer 50.00 14.00
*Nos. 442-449 (8)* 82.85 22.25

5th Asian Games, Bangkok.

Trade Fair Emblem and Temple of Dawn — A86

**1966, Sept. 1 Litho. *Perf. 13½***

**450** A86 50s lilac 1.10 .40
**451** A86 1b brown red 2.40 .75

1st Intl. Asian Trade Fair, Bangkok.

Letter Writer A87

Design: 50s, 1b, Letters, maps and pen.

**1966, Oct. 3 Photo. Wmk. 329**

**452** A87 50s scarlet .30 .20
**453** A87 1b orange brown 1.90 .60
**454** A87 2b brt violet 9.50 .60
**455** A87 3b brt blue grn 6.00 2.25
*Nos. 452-455 (4)* 17.70 3.65

Intl. Letter Writing Week, Oct. 6-12.

UN Emblem — A88

Pra Buddha Bata Monastery, UNESCO Emblem — A90

Rice Field A89

**Wmk. 334**

**1966, Oct. 24 Litho. *Perf. 13½***

**456** A88 50s ultramarine 1.00 .20

United Nations Day, Oct. 24.

**1966, Nov. 1 Engr. Wmk. 329**

**457** A89 50s dp bl & grnsh bl 1.50 .60
**458** A89 3b plum & pink 13.50 4.00

Intl. Rice Year under sponsorship of the FAO.

**1966, Nov. 4 Photo. Wmk. 329**

**459** A90 50s black & yel grn .70 .20

20th anniv. of UNESCO.

Thai Boxing A91

Designs: 1b, Takraw (three men playing ball). 2b, Kite fighting. 3b, Cudgel play.

**1966, Dec. 9 Wmk. 329 *Perf. 13½***

**460** A91 50s black, brn & red 1.25 .25
**461** A91 1b black, brn & red 4.50 2.00
**462** A91 2b black, brn & red 27.50 4.00
**463** A91 3b black, brn & red 25.00 12.00
*Nos. 460-463 (4)* 58.25 18.25

5th Asian Games.

Snakehead — A92

Pigmy Mackerel — A93

Fish: 3b, Barb. 5b, Siamese fighting fish.

**1967, Jan. 1 Photo.**

**464** A92 1b brt blue & multi 6.00 1.50
**465** A93 2b multicolored 26.00 3.00
**466** A93 3b yel grn & multi 15.00 7.00
**467** A92 5b pale grn & multi 18.00 8.00
*Nos. 464-467 (4)* 65.00 19.50

Dharmachakra, Globe and Temples — A94

**Wmk. 329**

**1967, Jan. 15 Litho. *Perf. 13½***

**468** A94 2b black & yellow 4.00 .70

Establishment of the headquarters of the World Fellowship of Buddhists in Thailand.

Great Hornbill A95

Ascocentrum Curvifolium A96

Birds: 25s, Hill myna. 50s, White-rumped shama. 1b, Diard's fireback pheasant. 1.50b,

Spotted dove. 2b, Sarus crane. 3b, White-breasted kingfisher. 5b, Asiatic open-bill (stork).

**1967, Feb. 1** **Photo.**

| | | | | | |
|---|---|---|---|---|---|
| **469** | A95 | 20s | tan & multi | .70 | .60 |
| **470** | A95 | 25s | lt gray & multi | 1.00 | .90 |
| **471** | A95 | 50s | yel grn & multi | 1.75 | .30 |
| **472** | A95 | 1b | olive & multi | 4.25 | 1.25 |
| **473** | A95 | 1.50b | dull yel & multi | 4.25 | 1.50 |
| **474** | A95 | 2b | pale sal & multi | 25.00 | 2.00 |
| **475** | A95 | 3b | gray & multi | 15.00 | 7.75 |
| **476** | A95 | 5b | multicolored | 25.00 | 8.00 |
| | | | *Nos. 469-476 (8)* | 76.95 | 22.30 |

**1967, Apr. 1** **Wmk. 329** ***Perf. 13½***

Orchids: 20s, Vandopsis parishii. 80s, Rhynchostylis retusa. 1b, Rhynchostylus gigantea. 1.50b, Dendrobium falconerii. 2b, Paphiopedilum callosum. 3b, Dendrobium formosum. 5b, Dendrobium primulinum.

| | | | | | |
|---|---|---|---|---|---|
| **477** | A96 | 20s | black & multi | .50 | .45 |
| **478** | A96 | 50s | brt blue & multi | 1.00 | .30 |
| **479** | A96 | 80s | black & multi | 1.75 | 1.40 |
| **480** | A96 | 1b | blue & multi | 5.25 | 1.25 |
| **481** | A96 | 1.50b | black & multi | 3.50 | 1.25 |
| **482** | A96 | 2b | ver & multi | 22.50 | 2.00 |
| **483** | A96 | 3b | brown & multi | 15.00 | 7.75 |
| **484** | A96 | 5b | multicolored | 25.00 | 6.25 |
| | | | *Nos. 477-484 (8)* | 74.50 | 20.65 |

Thai Architecture — A97

**1967, Apr. 6** **Engr.**

| | | | | | |
|---|---|---|---|---|---|
| **485** | A97 | 50s | Mansion | 1.40 | .40 |
| **486** | A97 | 1.50b | Pagodas | 4.00 | 1.50 |
| **487** | A97 | 2b | Bell tower | 22.50 | 2.00 |
| **488** | A97 | 3b | Temple | 14.00 | 5.00 |
| | | | *Nos. 485-488 (4)* | 41.90 | 8.90 |

Grand Palace and Royal Barge on Chao Phraya River — A98

**1967, Sept. 15** **Wmk. 329** ***Perf. 13½***

**489** A98 2b ultra & sepia 5.25 1.00

International Tourist Year, 1967.

Globe, Dove, People and Letters A99

2b, 3b, Clasped hands, globe and doves.

**1967, Oct. 8** **Photo.**

| | | | | | |
|---|---|---|---|---|---|
| **490** | A99 | 50s | dk blue & multi | .85 | .20 |
| **491** | A99 | 1b | multicolored | 2.00 | .60 |
| **492** | A99 | 2b | brt yel grn & blk | 5.00 | .75 |
| **493** | A99 | 3b | brown & blk | 8.00 | 3.00 |
| | | | *Nos. 490-493 (4)* | 15.85 | 4.55 |

Intl. Letter Writing Week, Oct. 6-12.

UN Emblem — A100

**1967, Oct. 24** **Wmk. 329** ***Perf. 13½***

**494** A100 50s multicolored .70 .20

Issued for United Nations Day, Oct. 24.

Flag and Map of Thailand — A101

**1967, Dec. 5** **Photo.** ***Perf. 13½***

| | | | | | |
|---|---|---|---|---|---|
| **495** | A101 | 50s | greenish blue, red & vio bl | .75 | .20 |
| **496** | A101 | 2b | ol gray, red & vio bl | 5.75 | 1.25 |

50th anniversary of the flag.

Elephant Carrying Teakwood — A102

**1968, Mar. 1** **Engr.** **Wmk. 329**

**497** A102 2b rose claret & gray ol 3.75 .75

See Nos. 537, 566.

Syncom Satellite over Thai Tracking Station — A103

**1968, Apr. 1** **Photo.** ***Perf. 13***

| | | | | | |
|---|---|---|---|---|---|
| **498** | A103 | 50s | multicolored | .50 | .20 |
| **499** | A103 | 3b | multicolored | 3.00 | 1.25 |

Earth Goddess — A104

**1968, May 1** **Wmk. 329** ***Perf. 13***

**500** A104 50s blk, gold, red & bl grn .70 .20

Hydrological Decade (UNESCO), 1965-74.

Snake-skinned Gourami — A105

Fish: 20s, Red-tailed black "shark." 25s, Tor tambroides. 50s, Pangasius sanitwongsei. 80s, Bagrid catfish. 1.25b, Vaimosa rambaiae. 1.50b, Catlocarpio siamensis. 4b, Featherback.

**1968, June 1** **Photo.** ***Perf. 13***

| | | | | | |
|---|---|---|---|---|---|
| **501** | A105 | 10s | multicolored | .55 | .20 |
| **502** | A105 | 20s | multicolored | .55 | .20 |
| **503** | A105 | 25s | multicolored | .75 | .35 |
| **504** | A105 | 50s | multicolored | .95 | .20 |
| **505** | A105 | 80s | multicolored | 2.50 | 1.50 |
| **506** | A105 | 1.25b | multicolored | 4.75 | 3.25 |
| **507** | A105 | 1.50b | multicolored | 24.00 | 4.00 |
| **508** | A105 | 4b | multicolored | 50.00 | 17.50 |
| | | | *Nos. 501-508 (8)* | 84.05 | 27.20 |

Arcturus Butterfly — A106

Various butterflies.

**1968, July 1** **Wmk. 329** ***Perf. 13***

| | | | | | |
|---|---|---|---|---|---|
| **509** | A106 | 50s | lt blue & multi | 5.00 | .30 |
| **510** | A106 | 1b | multicolored | 7.75 | 1.25 |
| **511** | A106 | 3b | multicolored | 17.50 | 6.25 |
| **512** | A106 | 4b | buff & multi | 29.00 | 11.00 |
| | | | *Nos. 509-512 (4)* | 59.25 | 18.80 |

Queen Sirikit — A107

Designs: Various portraits of Queen Sirikit.

**Photogravure and Engraved**
***Perf. 13½x14***

**1968, Aug. 12** **Wmk. 334**

| | | | | | |
|---|---|---|---|---|---|
| **513** | A107 | 50s | gold & multi | .55 | .20 |
| **514** | A107 | 2b | gold & multi | 2.10 | .85 |
| **515** | A107 | 3b | gold & multi | 5.50 | 2.50 |
| **516** | A107 | 5b | gold & multi | 11.00 | 2.75 |
| | | | *Nos. 513-516 (4)* | 19.15 | 6.30 |

Queen Sirikit's 36th birthday, or third 12-year "cycle."

WHO Emblem and Medical Apparatus — A108

**1968, Sept. 1** **Photo.** ***Perf. 12½***

**517** A108 50s olive, blk & gray .70 .20

20th anniv. of the WHO.

Globe, Pen and Envelope — A109

1b, 3b, Pen nib, envelope and globe.

**1968, Oct. 6** **Wmk. 329** ***Perf. 13½***

| | | | | | |
|---|---|---|---|---|---|
| **518** | A109 | 50s | brown & multi | .25 | .20 |
| **519** | A109 | 1b | pale brown & multi | 1.25 | .25 |
| **520** | A109 | 2b | multicolored | 2.75 | .40 |
| **521** | A109 | 3b | violet & multi | 5.75 | 1.60 |
| | | | *Nos. 518-521 (4)* | 10.00 | 2.45 |

Intl. Letter Writing Week, Oct. 7-13.

UN Emblem and Flags — A110

King Rama II — A112

Human Rights Flame and Bas-relief — A111

**1968, Oct. 24**

**522** A110 50s multicolored .70 .20

Issued for United Nations Day.

**1968, Dec. 10** **Photo.** ***Perf. 13½***

**523** A111 50s sl grn, red & vio .85 .20

International Human Rights Year.

**1968, Dec. 30** **Engr.** **Wmk. 329**

**524** A112 50s sepia & bister .70 .20

Rama II (1768-1824), who reigned 1809-24.

National Assembly Building — A113

**Photogravure and Engraved**

**1969, Feb. 10** **Wmk. 329** ***Perf. 13½***

| | | | | | |
|---|---|---|---|---|---|
| **525** | A113 | 50s | multicolored | .80 | .20 |
| **526** | A113 | 2b | multicolored | 3.00 | .60 |

First constitutional election day.

ILO Emblem and Cogwheels — A114

**1969, May 1** **Photo.** ***Perf. 13½***

**527** A114 50s rose vio & dk bl .50 .20

50th anniv. of the ILO.

Ramwong Dance — A115

Designs: 1b, Candle dance. 2b, Krathop Mai dance. 3b, Nohra dance.

**1969, July 15** **Wmk. 329** ***Perf. 13***

| | | | | | |
|---|---|---|---|---|---|
| **528** | A115 | 50s | multicolored | .30 | .20 |
| **529** | A115 | 1b | multicolored | 1.10 | .50 |
| **530** | A115 | 2b | multicolored | 2.50 | .35 |
| **531** | A115 | 3b | multicolored | 4.50 | 1.50 |
| | | | *Nos. 528-531 (4)* | 8.40 | 2.55 |

Posting and Receiving Letters — A116

Design: 2b, 3b, Writing and posting letters.

**1969, Oct. 5** **Photo.** **Wmk. 334**

| | | | | | |
|---|---|---|---|---|---|
| **532** | A116 | 50s | multicolored | .25 | .20 |
| **533** | A116 | 1b | multicolored | .80 | .35 |
| **534** | A116 | 2b | multicolored | 1.60 | .50 |
| **535** | A116 | 3b | multicolored | 2.75 | 1.25 |
| | | | *Nos. 532-535 (4)* | 5.40 | 2.30 |

International Letter Writing Week.

Hand Holding Globe — A117

**1969, Oct. 24 Wmk. 329 *Perf. 13***
**536** A117 50s multicolored .60 .20

Issued for United Nations Day.

Teakwood Type of 1968

**1969, Nov. 18 Engr. *Perf. 13½***
**537** A102 2b Tin mine 3.75 .40

Issued to publicize tin export, and the 2nd Technical Conf. of the Intl. Tin Council, Bangkok.

Loy Krathong Festival — A118

Designs: 1b, Marriage ceremony. 2b, Khwan ceremony. 5b, Songkran festival.

**1969, Nov. 23 Photo. Wmk. 329**
**538** A118 50s gray & multi .30 .20
**539** A118 1b multicolored .85 .30
**540** A118 2b multicolored 1.10 .40
**541** A118 5b multicolored 4.00 1.40
*Nos. 538-541 (4)* 6.25 2.30

Biplane, Mailmen and Map of First Thai Airmail Flight, 1919 — A119

**1969, Dec. 10 Engr. *Perf. 13½***
**542** A119 1b multicolored 1.10 .25

50th anniversary of Thai airmail service.

Shadow Play — A120

**Photogravure and Engraved**

**1969, Dec. 18 Wmk. 329**
**543** A120 50s Phra Rama .25 .20
**544** A120 2b Ramasura 3.25 .30
**545** A120 3b Mekhala 2.75 1.10
**546** A120 5b Ongkhot 3.75 1.40
*Nos. 543-546 (4)* 10.00 3.00

Symbols of Agriculture, Industry and Shipping — A121

**1970, Jan. 1 Photo.**
**547** A121 50s multicolored .60 .20

Productivity Year 1970.

World Map, Thai Temples and Emblem — A122

**1970, Jan. 31 Litho.**
**548** A122 50s brt blue & blk .70 .20

19th triennial meeting of the Intl. Council of Women, Bangkok.

Earth Station Radar and Satellite — A123

***Perf. 14½x15***

**1970, Apr. 1 Litho. Wmk. 356**
**549** A123 50s multicolored .55 .20

Communication by satellite.

Household and Population Statistics — A124

***Perf. 13x13½***

**1970, Apr. 1 Photo. Wmk. 329**
**550** A124 1b multicolored .65 .20

Issued to publicize the 1970 census.

Inauguration of New UPU Headquarters, Bern — A125

**Lithographed and Engraved**

**1970, June 15 Wmk. 334 *Perf. 13½***
**551** A125 50s lt bl, lt grn & grn .55 .20

Khun Ram Kamhang Teaching (Mural) — A126

**1970, July 1 Litho.**
**552** A126 50s black & multi .60 .20

Issued for International Education Year.

Swimming Stadium — A127

1.50b, Velodrome. 3b, Subhajalasaya Stadium. 5b, Kittikachorn Indoor Stadium.

**Lithographed and Engraved**

**1970, Sept. 1 Wmk. 329 *Perf. 13½***
**553** A127 50s yellow, red & pur .40 .20
**554** A127 1.50b ultra, grn & dk red .90 .40
**555** A127 3b gold, black & dk red 1.25 .55
**556** A127 5b brt grn, ultra & dk red 2.75 .85
*Nos. 553-556 (4)* 5.30 2.00

6th Asian Games, Bangkok.

Children Writing Letters — A128

Designs: 1b, Woman writing letter. 2b, Two women reading letters. 3b, Man reading letter.

**1970, Oct. 4 Photo. *Perf. 13½***
**557** A128 50s black & multi .35 .20
**558** A128 1b black & multi .90 .35
**559** A128 2b black & multi 2.00 .35
**560** A128 3b black & multi 2.75 1.10
*Nos. 557-560 (4)* 6.00 2.00

Intl. Letter Writing Week, Oct. 6-12.

Royal Palace, Bangkok, and UN Emblem — A129

**1970, Oct. 24 Photo. *Perf. 13½***
**561** A129 50s multicolored .90 .20

25th anniversary of the United Nations.

Heroes of Bangrachan — A130

1b, Monument to Thao Thepkrasatri & Thao Srisunthorn. 2b, Queen Suriyothai riding elephant. 3b, Phraya Phichaidaphak and battle scene.

**1970, Oct. 25 Engr. *Perf. 13½***
**562** A130 50s pink & violet .30 .20
**563** A130 1b violet & maroon .90 .60
**564** A130 2b rose & brown 3.00 .75
**565** A130 3b blue & green 2.50 .90
*Nos. 562-565 (4)* 6.70 2.45

Heroes from Thai history.

Teakwood Type of 1968

**1970, Nov. 1 Engr.**
**566** A102 2b Rubber plantation 2.50 .30

Issued to publicize rubber export.

King Bhumibol Lighting Flame — A131

**1970, Dec. 9 Photo. Wmk. 329**
**567** A131 1b multicolored 1.00 .20

Opening of 6th Asian Games, Bangkok.

Woman Playing So Sam Sai — A132

Women Playing Classical Thai Musical Instruments: 2b, Khlui Phiang-O. 3b, Krachappi. 5b, Thon Rammana.

**1970, Dec. 20**
**568** A132 50s multicolored .40 .20
**569** A132 2b multicolored .95 .30
**570** A132 3b multicolored 2.25 .65
**571** A132 5b multicolored 4.25 1.10
*Nos. 568-571 (4)* 7.85 2.25

Chocolate Point Siamese Cats — A133

Siamese Cats: 1b, Blue point. 2b, Seal point. 3b, Pure white cat and kittens.

***Perf. 13½x14***

**1971, Mar. 15 Litho. Wmk. 356**
**572** A133 50s multicolored .40 .20
**573** A133 1b multicolored 4.50 .50
**574** A133 2b multicolored 6.00 .55
**575** A133 3b multicolored 8.50 1.75
*Nos. 572-575 (4)* 19.40 3.00

Muang Nakhon Temple — A134

Temples: 1b, Phanom. 3b, Pathom Chedi. 4b, Doi Suthep.

**Lithographed and Engraved**

**1971, Mar. 30 Wmk. 329 *Perf. 13½***
**576** A134 50s rose, black & brn .45 .20
**577** A134 1b emerald, bis & pur .75 .30
**578** A134 3b org, brn & dk brn 1.75 .40
**579** A134 4b ultra, ocher & brn 3.50 2.10
*Nos. 576-579 (4)* 6.45 3.00

Corn and Tractor in Field
A135

**1971, Apr. 20 Engr. Wmk. 329**

**580** A135 2b multicolored 1.75 .30

Export promotion.

Buddha's Birthplace, Lumbini, Nepal — A136

Buddha's: 1b, Place of Enlightenment, Bihar. 2b, Place of first sermon, Benares. 3b, Place of death, Kusinara.

**1971, May 9 Engr. *Perf. 13½***

**581** A136 50s violet blue & blk .35 .20
**582** A136 1b green & black 1.00 .30
**583** A136 2b dull yellow & blk 2.40 .50
**584** A136 3b red & black 2.40 1.00
*Nos. 581-584 (4)* 6.15 2.00

20th anniv. of World Fellowship of Buddhists.

King Bhumibol and Subjects — A137

Floating Market — A138

***Perf. 13½***

**1971, June 9 Unwmk. Litho.**

**585** A137 50s silver & multi 1.25 .20

King Bhumibol's Silver Jubilee.

**1971, June 20 Photo. Wmk. 329**

**586** A138 4b gold & multi 2.00 .50

Visit Asia Year.

Boy Scouts Saluting — A139

**1971, July 1 Litho.**

**587** A139 50s orange & multi .95 .20

60th anniversary of Thai Boy Scouts.

Blocks of four of Nos. 354 and 403 Overprinted in Dark Blue

a

b

***Perf. 13½x13***

**1971, Aug. Wmk. 334 Engr.**

**588** A57 (a) Block of 4 3.00 3.00
*a.* 80s orange, single stamp .55 .55

***Perf. 13x13½***

**Photo. Wmk. 329**

**589** A71 (b) Block of 4 3.00 3.00
*a.* 80s dull orange, single stamp .55 .55

THAILANDPEX '71, Philatelic Exhib., Aug. 4-8.

Woman Writing Letter — A140

Designs: 1b, Women reading mail. 2b, Woman sitting on porch. 3b, Man handing letter to woman.

**Wmk. 334**

**1971, Oct. 3 Litho. *Perf. 13½***

**590** A140 50s gray & multi .60 .20
**591** A140 1b red brown & multi .80 .25
**592** A140 2b ultra & multi 1.60 .50
**593** A140 3b lt gray & multi 2.50 1.25
*Nos. 590-593 (4)* 5.50 2.20

Intl. Letter Writing Week, Oct. 6-12.

Wat Benchamabopit (Marble Temple), Bangkok — A141

***Perf. 13½x14***

**1971, Oct. 24 Litho. Unwmk.**

**594** A141 50s multicolored .50 .20

United Nations Day, Oct. 24.

Duck Raising — A142

Rural occupations: 1b, Raising tobacco. 2b, Fishermen. 3b, Rice winnowing.

**Wmk. 329**

**1971, Nov. 15 Photo. *Perf. 12½***

**595** A142 50s lt blue & multi .45 .20
**596** A142 1b multicolored .65 .30
**597** A142 2b blue & multi 1.40 .40
**598** A142 3b buff & multi 2.00 1.10
*Nos. 595-598 (4)* 4.50 2.00

UNICEF Emblem, Mother and Child — A143

**1971, Dec. 11 Wmk. 334 *Perf. 13½***

**599** A143 50s blue & multi .50 .20

25th anniv. of UNICEF.

Thai Costumes, 17th Century — A144

Thai Costumes: 1b, 13th-14th cent. 1.50b, 14th-17th cent. 2b, 18th-19th cent.

***Perf. 13½x14***

**1972, Jan. 12 Litho. Unwmk.**

**600** A144 50s multicolored .45 .20
**601** A144 1b multicolored .90 .25
**602** A144 1.50b multicolored 1.75 .45
**603** A144 2b blue & multi 2.25 .70
*Nos. 600-603 (4)* 5.35 1.60

Globe A145

***Perf. 13x13½***

**1972, Apr. 1 Photo. Wmk. 334**

**604** A145 75s violet blue .50 .20

Asian-Oceanic Postal Union, 10th anniv.

King Bhumibol Adulyadej — A146

***Perf. 13½x13***

**1972-77 Litho. Wmk. 329**

**Size: 21x26mm**

**605** A146 10s yellow green .30 .20
**606** A146 20s blue .30 .20
**607** A146 25s rose red .30 .20
**608** A146 75s lilac .30 .20

**Engr.**

**609** A146 1.25b yel grn & pink 1.25 .20
**610** A146 2.75b red brn & blue grn .55 .20
**611** A146 3b brn & dk blue ('74) 2.50 .25
**612** A146 4b blue & org red ('73) 1.25 .20
**613** A146 5b dk vio & red brown 1.25 .35
**614** A146 6b green & vio 2.50 .45
**615** A146 10b ver & black 2.00 .65
**616** A146 20b org & yel grn 4.00 1.10
**617** A146 40b dp bis & lilac ('74) 55.00 3.25
**618** A146 50b pur & brt grn ('77) 30.00 2.75
**619** A146 100b dp org & dk bl ('77) 52.50 5.25
*Nos. 605-619 (15)* 154.00 15.45

See Nos. 835-838, 907-908.

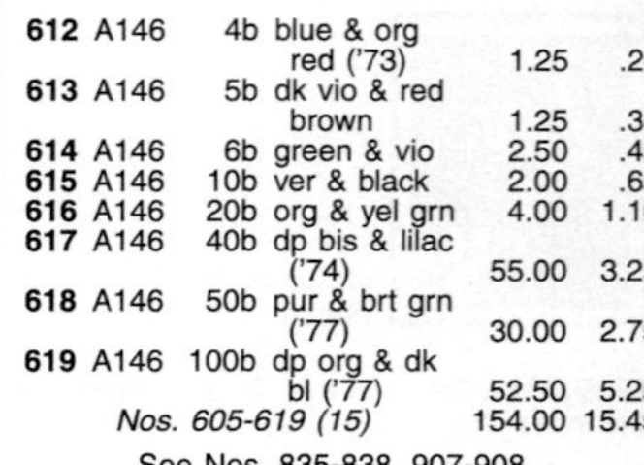
Iko Women — A147

Hill Tribes: 2b, Musoe musician. 4b, Yao weaver. 5b, Maeo farm woman.

**Wmk. 334**

**1972, May 11 Photo. *Perf. 13½***

**620** A147 50s multicolored .65 .20
**621** A147 2b dark gray & multi 2.25 .30
**622** A147 4b multicolored 6.50 3.50
**623** A147 5b multicolored 7.50 1.00
*Nos. 620-623 (4)* 16.90 5.00

Ruby A148

Precious Stones: 2b, Yellow sapphire. 4b, Zircon. 6b, Star sapphire.

**1972, June 7 Litho.**

**624** A148 75s gray & multi 1.00 .25
**625** A148 2b multicolored 6.00 .55
**626** A148 4b multicolored 10.00 4.50
**627** A148 6b crimson & multi 15.00 5.00
*Nos. 624-627 (4)* 32.00 10.30

Prince Vajiralongkorn A149

Thai Costume A150

***Perf. 13½x13***

**1972, July 28 Photo. Wmk. 329**

**628** A149 75s tan & multi .60 .20

20th birthday of Prince Vajiralongkorn, heir apparent.

***Perf. 14x13½***

**1972, Aug. 12 Litho. Wmk. 356**

Designs: Costumes of Thai women.

**629** A150 75s tan & multi .40 .20
**630** A150 2b multicolored 1.60 .20
**631** A150 4b yellow & multi 2.50 2.25

632 A150 5b gray & multi 4.50 1.10
a. Souvenir sheet of 4, #629-632 37.50 9.00
*Nos. 629-632 (4)* 9.00 3.75

Rambutan — A151

Fruits: 1b, Mangosteen. 3b, Durian. 5b, Mango.

**1972, Sept. 7 Wmk. 334 *Perf. 13½***
633 A151 75s multicolored .80 .20
634 A151 1b multicolored 1.75 .40
635 A151 3b pink & multi 5.50 .75
636 A151 5b lt ultra & multi 11.00 2.25
*Nos. 633-636 (4)* 19.05 3.60

Lod Cave, Phangnga — A152

1.25b, Kang Krachara Reservoir. 2.75b, Erawan Waterfalls, Kanchanaburi. 3b, Nok-Kaw Cliff, Loei.

**1972, Nov. 15 Litho. Wmk. 334**
637 A152 75s multicolored .65 .20
638 A152 1.25b multicolored 1.10 .20
639 A152 2.75b multicolored 2.75 .50
640 A152 3b multicolored 3.50 1.50
*Nos. 637-640 (4)* 8.00 2.40

Intl. Letter Writing Week, Oct. 9-15.

Princess Mother Visiting Old People — A153

**1972, Oct. 21 Photo. Wmk. 329**
641 A153 75s dk green & ocher .75 .20

Princess Mother Sisangwan, 72nd birthday.

UN Emblem and Globe — A154

**Wmk. 334**
**1972, Nov. 15 Litho. *Perf. 14***
642 A154 75s blue & multi .50 .20

25th anniversary of the Economic Commission for Asia and the Far East (ECAFE).

Educational Center and Book Year Emblem — A155

**1972, Dec. 8 *Perf. 13½***
643 A155 75s multicolored .50 .20

International Book Year 1972.

Crown Prince Vajiralongkorn A156

**1972, Dec. 28 Photo. Wmk. 329**
644 A156 2b brt blue & multi .95 .20

Investiture of Prince Vajiralongkorn Salayacheevin as Crown Prince.

Flag, Soldiers and Civilians — A157

**1973, Feb. 3 Wmk. 334 *Perf. 13½***
645 A157 75s multicolored .50 .20

25th anniversary of Veterans Day.

Savings Bank, Emblem and Coin — A158

**1973, Apr. 1 Wmk. 329**
646 A158 75s emerald & multi .50 .20

60th anniv. of Government Savings Bank.

WHO Emblem and Deity — A159

**1973, Apr. 1 Wmk. 329**
647 A159 75s brt green & multi .50 .20

25th World Health Organization Day.

Water Lily A160

Designs: Various water lilies (Thai lotus).

***Perf. 11x13***
**1973, May 15 Litho. Wmk. 356**
648 A160 75s violet & multi 1.00 .25
649 A160 1.50b brown & multi 2.00 .35
650 A160 2b dull grn & multi 2.75 .75
651 A160 4b black & multi 9.00 2.50
*Nos. 648-651 (4)* 14.75 3.85

King Bhumibol Adulyadej — A161

***Perf. 14x13½***
**1973-81 Photo. Wmk. 334**
652 A161 5s purple .50 .20
653 A161 20s blue .55 .20
a. Perf. 14½, wmk. 233 .55 .20
654 A161 25s rose carmine .65 .20

**Wmk. 233 *Perf. 14½***
655 A161 25s brown red ('81) .65 .25
656 A161 50s dk olive grn ('79) 1.25 .20
657 A161 75s violet 1.25 .20
a. Perf. 14x13½, wmk. 334 1.25 .20

**Wmk. 334**
**Engr. *Perf. 13***
658 A161 5b violet & brown 5.50 .65
659 A161 6b green & violet 3.50 1.00
660 A161 10b red & black 11.00 1.10
661 A161 20b org & yel grn ('75) 125.00 6.00
*Nos. 652-661 (10)* 149.85 10.00

For surcharges see Nos. 1168A, 1548.

Silversmiths — A162

**1973, June 15 Litho. *Perf. 13½***
662 A162 75s shown .50 .20
663 A162 2.75b Lacquerware 2.00 .55
664 A162 4b Pottery 3.50 3.00
665 A162 5b Paper umbrellas 5.00 1.00
*Nos. 662-665 (4)* 11.00 4.75

Thai handicrafts.

Fresco from Temple of the Emerald Buddha — A163

Designs: Frescoes illustrating Ramayana in Temple of the Emerald Buddha.

**1973, July 17 Photo. Wmk. 329**
666 A163 25s multicolored .20 .20
667 A163 75s multicolored .35 .20
668 A163 1.50b multicolored 1.75 .20
669 A163 2b multicolored 2.50 .85
670 A163 2.75b multicolored 2.25 .30
671 A163 3b multicolored 7.75 1.25
672 A163 5b multicolored 11.00 3.00
673 A163 6b multicolored 4.00 1.25
*Nos. 666-673 (8)* 29.80 7.25

Development of Postal Service — A164

2b, Telecommunications development.

**1973, Aug. 4 *Perf. 13½***
674 A164 75s multicolored .55 .20
675 A164 2b multicolored 1.10 .65

90th anniv. of Post and Telegraph Dept.

No. 1 and Other Stamps — A165

Various Stamps and: 1.25b, No. 147. 1.50b, No. 209. 2b, No. 244.

**1973, Aug. 4 Photo. & Engr.**
676 A165 75s dp rose & dk bl .90 .20
677 A165 1.25b blue & dp rose 1.25 .30
678 A165 1.50b olive & vio blk 1.50 .55
679 A165 2b orange & sl grn 2.75 1.10
a. Souvenir sheet of 4 16.00 2.50
*Nos. 676-679 (4)* 6.40 2.15

2nd Natl. Phil. Exhib., THAIPEX '73, Aug. 4-8. No. 679a contains 4 stamps with simulated perforations similar to Nos. 676-679.

INTERPOL Emblem — A166

**1973, Sept. 3 Photo.**
680 A166 75s gray & multi .50 .20

Intl. Criminal Police Organization, 50th anniv.

"Lilid Pralaw" — A167

Designs: Scenes from Thai literature.

***Perf. 11x13***
**1973, Oct. 7 Litho. Wmk. 368**
681 A167 75s green & multi .65 .30
682 A167 1.50b blue & multi 1.40 .60
683 A167 2b multicolored 2.50 1.10
684 A167 5b blue & multi 5.25 2.00
a. Souvenir sheet of 4, #681-684, perf. 13x14 30.00 10.00
*Nos. 681-684 (4)* 9.80 4.00

Intl. Letter Writing Week, Oct. 7-13.

Wat Suan Dok, Chiangmai; UN Emblem — A168

**1973, Oct. 24 *Perf. 13x11***
685 A168 75s blue & multi .50 .35

United Nations Day.

Schomburgk's Deer — A169

**Wmk. 329**
**1973, Nov. 14 Photo. *Perf. 13½***
686 A169 20s shown .30 .20
687 A169 25s Kouprey .40 .20
688 A169 75s Gorals .65 .20
689 A169 1.25b Water buffalos 1.90 .30
690 A169 1.50b Javan rhinoceros 7.00 1.50
691 A169 2b Eld's deer 7.00 1.50
692 A169 2.75b Asiatic 2-horned rhinoceros 8.00 .50
693 A169 4b Serows 12.00 3.00
*Nos. 686-693 (8)* 37.25 7.40

Protected animals.

Human Rights Flame — A170

**Wmk. 371**

**1973, Dec. 10 Litho. *Perf. 12½***
**694** A170 75s multicolored .85 .20

25th anniversary of the Universal Declaration of Human Rights.

Children and Flowers — A171

**1974, Jan. 12 Litho. *Perf. 13***
**695** A171 75s multicolored .70 .20

Children's Day.

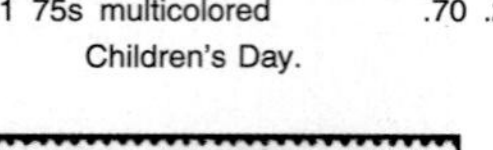

Siriraj Hospital and Statue of Prince Nakarin — A172

***Perf. 13x13½***

**1974, Mar. 17 Photo. Wmk. 368**
**696** A172 75s multicolored .50 .20

84th anniversary of Siriraj Hospital, oldest medical school in Thailand.

Phala Piang Lai — A173

Classical Thai Dances: 2.75b, Phra Lux Phlaeng Rit. 4b, Chin Sao Sai. 5b, Charot Phra Sumen.

**Wmk. 334**

**1974, June 25 Litho. *Perf. 14***
**697** A173 75s pink & multi .70 .20
**698** A173 2.75b gray bl & multi 1.90 .25
**699** A173 4b gray & multi 3.00 2.00
**700** A173 5b yellow & multi 3.50 .80
*Nos. 697-700 (4)* 9.10 3.25

Large Teak Tree in Uttaradit Province — A174

**1974, July 5 Wmk. 329 *Perf. 12½***
**701** A174 75s multicolored .50 .20

15th Arbor Day.

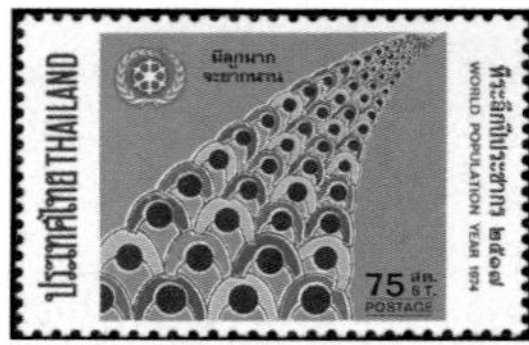

People and WPY Emblem — A175

***Perf. 10½x13***

**1974, Aug. 19 Litho. Wmk. 368**
**702** A175 75s multicolored .45 .20

World Population Year, 1974.

Ban Chiang Painted Vase — A176

75s, Royal chariot. 2.75b, Avalokitesavara Bodhisattva. 3b, King Mongkut, Rama IV.

**1974, Sept. 19 Wmk. 262 *Perf. 12½***
**703** A176 75s blue & multi .50 .20
**704** A176 2b black, brn & bis 1.25 .50
**705** A176 2.75b black, brn & tan 1.50 .40
**706** A176 3b black & multi 2.25 .80
*Nos. 703-706 (4)* 5.50 1.90

Centenary of National Museum. Inscribed "BATH" in error.

Purging Cassia — A177

**1974, Oct. 6 Wmk. 368 *Perf. 11x13***
**707** A177 75s shown .45 .20
**708** A177 2.75b Butea 2.00 .25
**709** A177 3b Jasmine 2.25 .30
**710** A177 4b Lagerstroemia 2.50 .75
*a.* Souvenir sheet of 4, #707-710, perf. 13½x14 *30.00* 10.00
*Nos. 707-710 (4)* 7.20 1.50

Intl. Letter Writing Week, Oct. 6-12.

"UPU" and UPU Emblem — A178

**1974, Oct. 9 Wmk. 371 *Perf. 12½***
**711** A178 75s dk green & multi .50 .20

Centenary of Universal Postal Union.

Wat Suthat Thepvararam — A179

**Wmk. 329**

**1974, Oct. 24 Photo. *Perf. 13***
**712** A179 75s multicolored .50 .20

United Nations Day.

Elephant Roundup — A180

**Wmk. 371**

**1974, Nov. 16 Engr. *Perf. 12½***
**713** A180 4b multicolored 2.50 1.40

Tourist publicity.

Vanda Coerulea — A181

Orchids: 2.75b, Dendrobium aggregatum. 3b, Dendrobium scabrilingue. 4b, Aerides falcata.

***Perf. 11x13***

**1974, Dec. 5 Photo. Wmk. 368**
**714** A181 75s red & multi .75 .20
**715** A181 2.75b multicolored 1.60 .25
**716** A181 3b olive & multi 2.50 .65
**717** A181 4b green & multi 3.00 1.50
*a.* Souvenir sheet of 4, #714-717, perf. 13½x14 *37.50* 11.00
*Nos. 714-717 (4)* 7.85 2.60

See Nos. 745-748.

Boy — A182

***Perf. 14x13½***

**1975, Jan. 11 Litho. Wmk. 374**
**718** A182 75s vermilion & multi .75 .20

Children's Day.

Democracy Monument — A183

Designs: 2b, Mother with children and animals, bas-relief from Democracy Monument. 2.75b, Workers, bas-relief from Democracy Monument. 5b, Top of Democracy Monument and quotation from speech of King Rama VII.

***Perf. 14x14½***

**1975, Jan. 26 Wmk. 233**
**719** A183 75s dull grn & multi .35 .20
**720** A183 2b multicolored 1.00 .20
**721** A183 2.75b blue & multi 1.40 .25
**722** A183 5b multicolored 2.75 1.00
*Nos. 719-722 (4)* 5.50 1.65

Movement of Oct. 14, 1973, to re-establish democratic institutions.

Marbled Tiger Cat — A184

**1975, Mar. 5 Wmk. 334 *Perf. 13½***
**723** A184 20s shown .45 .20
**724** A184 75s Gaurs 1.75 .20
**725** A184 2.75b Asiatic elephant 5.00 .55
**726** A184 3b Clouded leopard 6.25 1.50
*Nos. 723-726 (4)* 13.45 2.45

Protected animals.

White-eyed River Martin — A185

Birds: 2b, Paradise flycatchers. 2.75b, Long-tailed broadbills. 5b, Sultan tit.

**Wmk. 371**

**1975, Apr. 2 Litho. *Perf. 12½***
**727** A185 75s ocher & multi .75 .20
**728** A185 2b lt blue & multi 1.90 .20
**729** A185 2.75b lt violet & multi 3.00 .35
**730** A185 5b rose & multi 5.75 1.25
*Nos. 727-730 (4)* 11.40 2.00

King Bhumibol Adulyadej and Queen Sirikit — A186

3b, King, Queen, different background design.

***Perf. 10½x13***

**1975, Apr. 28 Photo. Wmk. 368**
**731** A186 75s violet bl & multi .25 .20
**732** A186 3b multicolored 1.10 .40

25th wedding anniversary of King Bhumibol Adulyadej and Queen Sirikit.

Round-house Kick — A187

Thai Boxing: 2.75b, Reverse elbow. 3b, Flying knee. 5b, Ritual homage.

**Wmk. 371**

**1975, May 20 Litho. *Perf. 12½***
**733** A187 75s green & multi .75 .20
**734** A187 2.75b blue & multi 2.75 .30
**735** A187 3b orange & multi 4.00 1.00
**736** A187 5b orange & multi 5.75 2.00
*Nos. 733-736 (4)* 13.25 3.50

Tosakanth Mask — A188

Masks: 2b, Kumbhakarn. 3b, Rama. 4b, Hanuman.

**1975, June 10 Litho. Wmk. 371**
**737** A188 75s dark gray & multi .80 .20
**738** A188 2b dull vio & multi 2.25 .30
**739** A188 3b purple & multi 4.25 .75
**740** A188 4b multicolored 8.50 3.75
*Nos. 737-740 (4)* 15.80 5.00

Thai art and literature.

THAIPEX 75 Emblem — A189

THAIPEX 75 Emblem and: 2.75b, Stamp designer. 4b, Stamp printing plant. 5b, Stamp collector.

**1975, Aug. 4 Wmk. 371 *Perf. 12½***

| | | | | | |
|---|---|---|---|---|---|
| **741** | A189 | 75s | yellow & multi | .35 | .20 |
| **742** | A189 | 2.75b | orange & multi | 1.40 | .30 |
| **743** | A189 | 4b | lt blue & multi | 2.00 | 1.00 |
| **744** | A189 | 5b | carmine & multi | 2.50 | .60 |
| | | | *Nos. 741-744 (4)* | 6.25 | 2.10 |

THAIPEX 75, Third National Philatelic Exhibition, Aug. 4-10.

Orchid Type of 1974

Orchids: 75s, Dendrobium cruentum. 2b, Dendrobium parishii. 2.75b, Vanda teres. 5b, Vanda denisoniana.

***Perf. 11x13***

**1975, Aug. 12 Photo. Wmk. 368**

| | | | | | |
|---|---|---|---|---|---|
| **745** | A181 | 75s | olive & multi | .75 | .20 |
| **746** | A181 | 2b | multicolored | 1.75 | .40 |
| **747** | A181 | 2.75b | scarlet & multi | 2.75 | .40 |
| **748** | A181 | 5b | ultra & multi | 4.25 | 1.25 |
| *a.* | | | Souv. sheet, #745-748, perf 13½ | *35.00* | *9.00* |
| | | | *Nos. 745-748 (4)* | 9.50 | 2.25 |

Mytilus Smaragdinus — A190

Sea Shells: 1b, Turbo marmoratus. 2.75b, Oliva mustelina. 5b, Cypraea moneta.

***Perf. 14x14½***

**1975, Sept. 5 Litho. Wmk. 375**

| | | | | | |
|---|---|---|---|---|---|
| **749** | A190 | 75s | yellow & multi | .85 | .40 |
| **750** | A190 | 1b | ver & multi | 1.40 | .20 |
| **751** | A190 | 2.75b | blue & multi | 4.00 | .30 |
| **752** | A190 | 5b | green & multi | 11.00 | 3.00 |
| | | | *Nos. 749-752 (4)* | 17.25 | 3.90 |

Yachting and Games Emblem — A191

Designs: 1.25b, Badminton. 1.50b, Volleyball. 2b, Target shooting.

***Perf. 11x13***

**1975, Sept. 20 Litho. Wmk. 368**

| | | | | | |
|---|---|---|---|---|---|
| **753** | A191 | 75s | ultra & black | .30 | .20 |
| **754** | A191 | 1.25b | brt rose & blk | .80 | .25 |
| **755** | A191 | 1.50b | red & black | 1.40 | .65 |
| **756** | A191 | 2b | apple grn & blk | 2.00 | .60 |
| *a.* | | | Souv. sheet, #753-756, perf 13½ | 30.00 | 8.00 |
| | | | *Nos. 753-756 (4)* | 4.50 | 1.70 |

8th SEAP Games, Bangkok, Sept. 1975.

Pataya Beach A192

Views: 2b, Samila Beach. 3b, Prachuap Bay. 5b, Laem Singha Bay.

**1975, Oct. 5 Wmk. 371 *Perf. 12½***

| | | | | | |
|---|---|---|---|---|---|
| **757** | A192 | 75s | orange & multi | .65 | .20 |
| **758** | A192 | 2b | orange & multi | 1.25 | .30 |
| **759** | A192 | 3b | orange & multi | 1.50 | .40 |
| **760** | A192 | 5b | orange & multi | 4.50 | 1.25 |
| | | | *Nos. 757-760 (4)* | 7.90 | 2.15 |

Intl. Letter Writing Week, Oct. 6-12.

"u n," UN Emblem, Food and Education for Children — A193

**1975, Oct. 24 Litho. Wmk. 371**

| | | | | | |
|---|---|---|---|---|---|
| **761** | A193 | 75s | ultra & multi | .50 | .20 |

United Nations Day.

Morse Telegraph — A194

Design: 2.75b, Teleprinter and radar.

***Perf. 14x14½***

**1975, Nov. 4 Litho. Wmk. 334**

| | | | | | |
|---|---|---|---|---|---|
| **762** | A194 | 75s | multicolored | .60 | .20 |
| **763** | A194 | 2.75b | blue & multi | 1.75 | .30 |

Centenary of telegraph system.

Sukhrip Khrong Mueang Barge — A195

Thai ceremonial barges: 1b, Royal escort barge Anekchat Phuchong. 2b, Royal barge Anantanakarat. 2.75b, Krabi Ran Ron Rap barge. 3b, Asura Wayuphak barge. 4b, Asura paksi barge. 5b, Royal barge Sri Suphanahong, 6b, Phali Rang Thawip barge.

**Wmk. 371**

**1975, Nov. 18 Litho. *Perf. 12½***

| | | | | | |
|---|---|---|---|---|---|
| **764** | A195 | 75s | multicolored | .55 | .20 |
| **765** | A195 | 1b | multicolored | .65 | .30 |
| **766** | A195 | 2b | lilac & multi | 2.75 | .40 |
| **767** | A195 | 2.75b | multicolored | 4.00 | .45 |
| **768** | A195 | 3b | yellow & multi | 5.00 | .45 |
| **769** | A195 | 4b | multicolored | 6.25 | 1.25 |
| **770** | A195 | 5b | gray & multi | 11.00 | 4.00 |
| **771** | A195 | 6b | blue & multi | 10.00 | 2.50 |
| | | | *Nos. 764-771 (8)* | 40.20 | 9.55 |

Thai Flag, Arms of Chakri Royal Family — A196

King Bhumibol Adulyadej — A197

***Perf. 15x14***

**1975, Dec. 5 Litho. Wmk. 375**

| | | | | | |
|---|---|---|---|---|---|
| **772** | A196 | 75s | multicolored | .30 | .20 |
| **773** | A197 | 5b | multicolored | 1.50 | .50 |

King Bhumibol's 48th birthday.

Shot Put and SEAP Emblem — A198

2b, Table tennis. 3b, Bicycling. 4b, Relay race.

**1975, Dec. 9 Wmk. 368 *Perf. 11x13***

| | | | | | |
|---|---|---|---|---|---|
| **774** | A198 | 1b | orange & black | .50 | .20 |
| **775** | A198 | 2b | brt green & blk | 1.10 | .85 |
| **776** | A198 | 3b | ocher & blk | 1.75 | .40 |
| **777** | A198 | 4b | violet & blk | 2.00 | .85 |
| *a.* | | | Souvenir sheet of 4, #774-777, perf. 13½ | *27.50* | *8.00* |
| | | | *Nos. 774-777 (4)* | 5.35 | 2.30 |

8th SEAP Games, Bangkok, Dec. 9-20.

IWY Emblem and Globe — A199

***Perf. 14x14½***

**1975, Dec. 20 Wmk. 375**

| | | | | | |
|---|---|---|---|---|---|
| **778** | A199 | 75s | blk, org & vio bl | .50 | .20 |

International Women's Year.

Children Writing on Slate — A200

***Perf. 13x14***

**1976, Jan. 10 Litho. Wmk. 368**

| | | | | | |
|---|---|---|---|---|---|
| **779** | A200 | 75s | lt green & multi | .60 | .20 |

Children's Day.

Macrobrachium Rosenbergii — A201

Designs: 2b, Penaeus merguiensis. 2.75b, Panulirus ornatus. 5b, Penaeus monodon.

**1976, Feb. 18 *Perf. 11x13***

| | | | | | |
|---|---|---|---|---|---|
| **780** | A201 | 75s | multicolored | 2.25 | .20 |
| **781** | A201 | 2b | multicolored | 3.75 | .85 |
| **782** | A201 | 2.75b | multicolored | 4.75 | .20 |
| **783** | A201 | 5b | multicolored | 9.00 | 1.75 |
| | | | *Nos. 780-783 (4)* | 19.75 | 3.00 |

Shrimp and lobster exports.

Golden-backed Three-toed Woodpecker A202

Ban Chiang Vase — A203

Birds: 1.50b, Greater green-billed malcoha. 3b, Pomatorhinus hypoleucos. 4b, Green magpie.

**Wmk. 371**

**1976, Apr. 2 Litho. *Perf. 12½***

| | | | | | |
|---|---|---|---|---|---|
| **784** | A202 | 1b | multicolored | .70 | .20 |
| **785** | A202 | 1.50b | multicolored | 1.25 | .20 |
| **786** | A202 | 3b | yellow & multi | 2.50 | .65 |
| **787** | A202 | 4b | rose & multi | 2.75 | .65 |
| | | | *Nos. 784-787 (4)* | 7.20 | 1.70 |

***Perf. 14½x14***

**1976, May 5 Litho. Wmk. 375**

Designs: Ban Chiang painted pottery, various vessels, Bronze Age.

| | | | | | |
|---|---|---|---|---|---|
| **788** | A203 | 1b | olive & multi | .90 | .20 |
| **789** | A203 | 2b | dp blue & multi | 2.00 | .20 |
| **790** | A203 | 3b | green & multi | 3.75 | .35 |
| **791** | A203 | 4b | org red & multi | 5.00 | 1.75 |
| | | | *Nos. 788-791 (4)* | 11.65 | 2.50 |

Mailman, 1883 — A204

Designs: 3b, Mailman, 1935. 4b, Mailman, 1950. 5b, Mailman, 1974.

**Wmk. 377**

**1976, Aug. 4 Litho. *Perf. 12½***

| | | | | | |
|---|---|---|---|---|---|
| **792** | A204 | 1b | multicolored | *.55* | .20 |
| **793** | A204 | 3b | multicolored | *2.00* | .50 |
| **794** | A204 | 4b | multicolored | *3.25* | .80 |
| **795** | A204 | 5b | multicolored | *3.50* | 1.00 |
| | | | *Nos. 792-795 (4)* | *9.30* | 2.50 |

Development of mailmen's uniforms.

Kinnari — A205

Thai Mythology: 2b, Suphan-mat-cha. 4b, Garuda. 5b, Naga.

**1976, Oct. 3 Wmk. 368 *Perf. 11x13***

| | | | | | |
|---|---|---|---|---|---|
| **796** | A205 | 1b | green & multi | .50 | .20 |
| **797** | A205 | 2b | ultra & multi | 1.10 | .20 |
| **798** | A205 | 4b | gray & multi | 3.75 | .45 |
| **799** | A205 | 5b | slate & multi | 4.50 | .50 |
| | | | *Nos. 796-799 (4)* | 9.85 | 1.35 |

International Letter Writing Week.

UN Emblem, Drug Addicts, Alcohol, Cigarettes, Drugs — A206

**Wmk. 329**

**1976, Oct. 24 Photo.** ***Perf. 13½***

| | | | | |
|---|---|---|---|---|
| **800** | A206 1b ultra & multi | .50 | .20 |

United Nations Day.

Old and New Telephones — A207

***Perf. 14x14½***

**1976, Nov. 10 Litho. Wmk. 375**

| | | | |
|---|---|---|---|
| **801** | A207 1b multicolored | .50 | .20 |

Centenary of first telephone call by Alexander Graham Bell, Mar. 10, 1876.

Sivalaya-Mahaprasad Hall — A208

Royal Houses: 2b, Cakri-Mahaprasad. 4b, Mahisra-Prasad. 5b, Dusit-Mahaprasad.

***Perf. 14x15***

**1976, Dec. 5 Wmk. 375 Litho.**

| | | | |
|---|---|---|---|
| **802** | A208 1b multicolored | *1.00* | .20 |
| **803** | A208 2b multicolored | *1.50* | .50 |
| **804** | A208 4b multicolored | *5.00* | .75 |
| **805** | A208 5b multicolored | *5.50* | .80 |
| | *Nos. 802-805 (4)* | *13.00* | 2.25 |

Banteng — A209

Protected animals: 2b, Tapir and young. 4b, Sambar deer and fawn. 5b, Hog deer family.

**Wmk. 334**

**1976, Dec. 26 Litho.** ***Perf. 11***

| | | | |
|---|---|---|---|
| **806** | A209 1b multicolored | *1.00* | .20 |
| **807** | A209 2b multicolored | *1.25* | .30 |

**Wmk. 368**

| | | | |
|---|---|---|---|
| **808** | A209 4b multicolored | *3.50* | .60 |
| **809** | A209 5b multicolored | *4.25* | 1.00 |
| | *Nos. 806-809 (4)* | *10.00* | 2.10 |

Child Casting Shadow of Man — A210

**Wmk. 329**

**1977, Jan. 8 Photo.** ***Perf. 13½***

| | | | |
|---|---|---|---|
| **810** | A210 1b multicolored | .50 | .20 |

National Children's Day.

Alsthom's Electric Engine — A211

Locomotives: 2b, Davenport's electric engine. 4b, Pacific's steam engine. 5b, George Egestoff's steam engine.

***Perf. 11x13***

**1977, Mar. 26 Litho. Wmk. 368**

| | | | |
|---|---|---|---|
| **811** | A211 1b multicolored | 1.90 | .20 |
| **812** | A211 2b multicolored | 4.75 | .35 |
| **813** | A211 4b multicolored | 13.50 | 2.00 |
| **814** | A211 5b multicolored | 19.00 | .80 |
| | *Nos. 811-814 (4)* | 39.15 | 3.35 |

80th anniv. of State Railroad of Thailand.

Chulalongkorn University Auditorium — A212

**1977, Mar. 26 Photo.**

| | | | |
|---|---|---|---|
| **815** | A212 1b multicolored | .70 | .20 |

Chulalongkorn University, 60th anniversary.

Flags of AOPU Members — A213

**Wmk. 371**

**1977, Apr. 1 Litho.** ***Perf. 12½***

| | | | |
|---|---|---|---|
| **816** | A213 1b multicolored | .70 | .20 |

Asian-Oceanic Postal Union (AOPU), 15th anniv.

Invalid in Wheelchair and Soldiers — A214

**Wmk. 329**

**1977, Apr. 2 Photo.** ***Perf. 13½***

| | | | |
|---|---|---|---|
| **817** | A214 5b multicolored | 1.40 | .45 |

Sai-Jai-Thai Day, to publicize Sai-Jai-Thai Foundation which helps wounded soldiers.

Phra Aphai Mani and Phisua Samut A215

Puppets: 3b, Rusi and Sutsakhon. 4b, Nang Vali and Usren. 5b, Phra Aphai Mani and Nang Laweng's portrait.

***Perf. 11x13***

**1977, June 16 Wmk. 368**

| | | | |
|---|---|---|---|
| **818** | A215 2b multicolored | .55 | .20 |
| **819** | A215 3b multicolored | .75 | .25 |
| **820** | A215 4b multicolored | 1.50 | .45 |
| **821** | A215 5b multicolored | 2.00 | .55 |
| | *Nos. 818-821 (4)* | 4.80 | 1.45 |

Thai plays and literature.

Drum Dance — A216

Designs: 3b, Dance of dip nets. 4b, Harvest dance. 5b, Kan dance.

**1977, July 14 Photo.** ***Perf. 13x11***

| | | | |
|---|---|---|---|
| **822** | A216 2b rose & multi | .65 | .20 |
| **823** | A216 3b lt green & multi | .75 | .20 |
| **824** | A216 4b yellow & multi | 1.25 | .40 |
| **825** | A216 5b lt violet & multi | 1.50 | .40 |
| | *Nos. 822-825 (4)* | 4.15 | 1.20 |

Thailand No. 609, Various Stamps and Thaipex Emblem — A217

**Wmk. 377**

**1977, Aug. 4 Litho.** ***Perf. 12½***

| | | | |
|---|---|---|---|
| **826** | A217 75s multicolored | .70 | .20 |

THAIPEX 77, 4th National Philatelic Exhibition, Aug. 4-12.

Scenes from Thai Literature — A218

***Perf. 11x13***

**1977, Oct. 5 Photo. Wmk. 368**

| | | | |
|---|---|---|---|
| **827** | A218 75s multicolored | .70 | .20 |
| **828** | A218 2b multi, diff. | 1.10 | .20 |
| **829** | A218 5b multi, diff. | 3.00 | .40 |
| **830** | A218 6b multi, diff. | 4.00 | .65 |
| | *Nos. 827-830 (4)* | 8.80 | 1.45 |

Intl. Letter Writing Week, Oct. 6-12.

Old and New Buildings, UN Emblem — A219

**1977, Oct. 5 Litho.** ***Perf. 11x13***

| | | | |
|---|---|---|---|
| **831** | A219 75s multicolored | .85 | .20 |

United Nations Day.

King Bhumibol as Scout Leader, Camp and Emblem — A220

**1977, Nov. 21 Photo. Wmk. 368**

| | | | |
|---|---|---|---|
| **832** | A220 75s multicolored | 1.50 | .20 |

9th National Jamboree, Nov. 21-27.

Diseased Hand and Elbow — A221

**1977, Dec. 20** ***Perf. 11x13***

| | | | |
|---|---|---|---|
| **833** | A221 75s multicolored | .70 | .20 |

World Rheumatism Year.

Map of South East Asia and ASEAN Emblem — A222

**Wmk. 377**

**1977, Dec. 1 Litho.** ***Perf. 12½***

| | | | |
|---|---|---|---|
| **834** | A222 5b multicolored | 1.75 | .35 |

ASEAN, 10th anniv.

King Type of 1972-74 Redrawn

**1976** ***Perf. 12½x13***

**Size: 21x27mm**

| | | | |
|---|---|---|---|
| **835** | A146 20s blue | *2.50* | .20 |
| **836** | A146 75s lilac | *2.50* | .20 |

**Engr.**

| | | | |
|---|---|---|---|
| **837** | A146 10b vermilion & blk | *25.00* | 1.00 |
| **838** | A146 40b bister & lilac | *20.00* | 2.25 |
| | *Nos. 835-838 (4)* | *50.00* | 3.65 |

Numerals are taller and thinner and leaves in background have been redrawn.

Children Carrying Flag of Thailand — A223

**Wmk. 329**

**1978, Jan. 9 Photo.** ***Perf. 13½***

| | | | |
|---|---|---|---|
| **839** | A223 75s multicolored | .75 | .20 |

Children's Day.

Dendrobium Heterocarpum — A224

Orchids: 1b, Dendrobium pulchellum. 1.50b, Doritis pulcherrima. 2b, Dendrobium hercoglossum. 2.75b, Aerides odorata. 3b, Trichoglottis fasciata. 5b, Dendrobium wardianum. 6b, Dendrobium senile.

***Perf. 11x14***

**1978, Jan. 18 Wmk. 368**

| | | | |
|---|---|---|---|
| **840** | A224 75s multicolored | .20 | .20 |
| **841** | A224 1b multicolored | .25 | .20 |
| **842** | A224 1.50b multicolored | .40 | .20 |
| **843** | A224 2b multicolored | .70 | .60 |
| **844** | A224 2.75b multicolored | 2.75 | .20 |
| **845** | A224 3b multicolored | 1.00 | .30 |
| **846** | A224 5b multicolored | 1.50 | .50 |
| **847** | A224 6b multicolored | 4.00 | .60 |
| | *Nos. 840-847 (8)* | 10.80 | 2.80 |

9th World Orchid Conference.

Census Chart, Symbols of Agriculture — A225

**Wmk. 377**

**1978, Mar. 1 Litho. *Perf. 12½***
**848** A225 75s multicolored .40 .20

Agricultural census, Apr. 1978.

Anabas Testudineus — A226

Fish: 2b, Datnioides microlepis. 3b, Kryptopterus apogon. 4b, Probarbus Jullieni.

***Perf. 11x13***

**1978, Apr. 13 Photo. Wmk. 368**
**849** A226 1b multicolored .30 .20
**850** A226 2b multicolored .70 .20
**851** A226 3b multicolored 1.25 .35
**852** A226 4b multicolored 1.75 .55
*Nos. 849-852 (4)* 4.00 1.30

Birth of Prince Siddhartha — A227

Murals: 3b, Prince Siddhartha cuts his hair. 5b, Buddha descending from Tavatimsa Heaven. 6b, Buddha entering Nirvana.

**Wmk. 329**

**1978, June 15 Photo. *Perf. 13½***
**853** A227 2b multicolored *1.40* .25
**854** A227 3b multicolored *2.00* .50
**855** A227 5b multicolored *6.00* .80
**856** A227 6b multicolored *4.50* 1.10
*Nos. 853-856 (4)* *13.90* 2.65

Story of Gautama Buddha, murals in Puthi Savan Hall, National Museum, Bangkok.

Bhumibol Dam — A228

Dams and Reservoirs: 2b, Sirikit dam. 2.75b, Vajiralongkorn dam. 6b, Ubol Ratana dam.

***Perf. 14x14½***

**1978, July 28 Litho. Wmk. 233**
**857** A228 75s multicolored .95 .20
**858** A228 2b multicolored 1.25 .20
**859** A228 2.75b multicolored 1.75 .20
**860** A228 6b multicolored 3.25 .90
*Nos. 857-860 (4)* 7.20 1.50

Idea Lynceus — A229

Butterflies: 3b, Sephisa chandra. 5b, Charaxes durnfordi. 6b, Cethosia penthesilea methypsia.

***Perf. 11x13***

**1978, Aug. 25 Litho. Wmk. 368**
**861** A229 2b lilac, blk & red 1.60 .20
**862** A229 3b multicolored 2.00 .30
**863** A229 5b multicolored 3.25 .50
**864** A229 6b multicolored 5.25 1.00
*Nos. 861-864 (4)* 12.10 2.00

Chedi Chai Mongkhon Temple — A230

Mother and Children, UN Emblem — A231

Temples: 2b, That Hariphunchai. 2.75b, Borom That Chaiya. 5b, That Choeng Chum.

**1978, Oct. 8 *Perf. 13x11***
**865** A230 75s multicolored *.90* .20
**866** A230 2b multicolored *1.25* .20
**867** A230 2.75b multicolored *1.75* .20
**868** A230 5b multicolored *2.75* .80
*Nos. 865-868 (4)* *6.65* 1.40

Intl. Letter Writing Week, Oct. 6-12.

***Perf. 14½x14***

**1978, Oct. 24 Litho. Wmk. 375**
**869** A231 75s multicolored .50 .20

United Nations Day.

Boxing, Soccer, Pole Vault — A232

Designs: 2b, Javelin, weight lifting, running. 3b, Ball games and sailing. 5b, Basketball, hockey stick and boxing gloves.

***Perf. 14x14½***

**1978, Oct. Wmk. 233 Litho.**
**870** A232 75s multicolored *.40* .20
**871** A232 2b multicolored *1.00* .20
**872** A232 3b multicolored *1.40* .25
**873** A232 5b multicolored *2.00* .80
*Nos. 870-873 (4)* *4.80* 1.45

8th Asian Games, Bangkok.

Five Races and World Map A233

**1978, Nov.**
**874** A233 75s multicolored .45 .20

Anti-Apartheid Year.

Children Painting Thai Flag — A234

Children and Children's SOS Village, Tambol Bangpu — A235

**1979, Jan. 17 *Perf. 14x14½***
**875** A234 75s multicolored .70 .20
**876** A235 75s multicolored .70 .20

International Year of the Child.

Matuta Lunaris — A236

Crabs: 2.75b, Matuta planipes fabricius. 3b, Portunus pelagicus. 5b, Scylla serrata.

**Wmk. 377**

**1979, Mar. 22 Litho. *Perf. 12½***
**877** A236 2b multicolored *1.50* .20
**878** A236 2.75b multicolored *4.75* .20
**879** A236 3b multicolored *3.00* .25
**880** A236 5b multicolored *5.25* .70
*Nos. 877-880 (4)* *14.50* 1.35

A237

A238

**1979, June 25**
**881** A237 1b Sweetsop *1.25* .20
**882** A237 2b Pineapple *1.00* .20
**883** A237 5b Bananas *4.00* .45
**884** A237 6b Longans (litchi) *3.75* 1.25
*Nos. 881-884 (4)* *10.00* 2.10

See Nos. 1145-1148.

***Perf. 13x11***

**1979, July 10 Litho. Wmk. 368**

Young man and woman planting tree.

**885** A238 75s multicolored .50 .20

20th Arbor Day.

Pencil, Pen, Thaipex '79 Emblem — A239

Thaipex '79 Emblem and: 2b, Envelopes. 2.75b, Stamp album. 5b, Magnifying glass and tongs.

**1979, Aug. 4 *Perf. 11x13***
**886** A239 75s multicolored .30 .20
**887** A239 2b multicolored .80 .20
**888** A239 2.75b multicolored 1.25 .20
**889** A239 5b multicolored 2.00 .30
*Nos. 886-889 (4)* 4.35 .90

Thaipex '79, 5th National Philatelic Exhibition, Bangkok, Aug. 4-12.

Floral Arrangement A240

UN Day — A241

Designs: Decorative arrangements.

***Perf. 14½x14***

**1979, Oct. 7 Litho. Wmk. 233**
**890** A240 75s multicolored .45 .20
**891** A240 2b multicolored .80 .20
**892** A240 2.75b multicolored 1.25 .20
**893** A240 5b multicolored 1.90 .60
*Nos. 890-893 (4)* 4.40 1.20

Intl. Letter Writing Week, Oct. 8-14.

**1979, Oct. 24 Litho. *Perf. 14½x14***
**894** A241 75s multicolored .50 .20

Frigate Makut Rajakumarn — A242

Thai Naval Ships: 3b, Frigate Tapi. 5b, Fast strike craft, Prabparapak. 6b, Patrol boat T-91.

**Wmk. 329**

**1979, Nov. 20 Photo. *Perf. 13½***
**895** A242 2b multicolored *.70* .20
**896** A242 3b multicolored *1.10* .25
**897** A242 5b multicolored *5.25* .70
**898** A242 6b multicolored *6.50* 1.00
*Nos. 895-898 (4)* *13.55* 2.15

Thai Royal Orders (Medallions and Ribbons) — A243

Designs: #900a, Rajamitrabhorn Order. #902a, House of Chakri. #904a, The nine gems. #906a, Chula Chom Klao. Pairs have continuous design.

*Perf. 13x11*

**1979, Dec. 5 Litho. Wmk. 368**

**899** 1b multicolored *.40* .25
**900** 1b multicolored *.40* .25
***a.*** A243 Pair, #899-900 *.80* .50
**901** 2b multicolored *.85* .20
**902** 2b multicolored *.85* .20
***a.*** A243 Pair, #901-902 *1.75* .40
**903** 5b multicolored *2.00* .40
**904** 5b multicolored *2.00* .40
***a.*** A243 Pair, #903-904 *4.00* .80
**905** 6b multicolored *2.75* .60
**906** 6b multicolored *2.75* .60
***a.*** A243 Pair, #905-906 *5.50* 1.25
*Nos. 899-906 (8)* *12.00* 2.90

See Nos. 1278-1285.

King Type of 1972-77

*Perf. 13½x13*

**1979, Dec. 23 Litho. Wmk. 329**

**Size: 21x26mm**

**907** A146 50s olive green .50 .20

**Engr.**

**908** A146 2b org red & lilac .65 .20

Rice Planting — A245

Children's Day: No. 910, Family in rice field.

*Perf. 13x11*

**1980, Jan. 12 Litho. Wmk. 368**

**909** A245 75s multicolored .55 .20
**910** A245 75s multicolored .55 .20

Family, House, Map of Thailand — A246

Gold-fronted Leafbird — A247

*Perf. 15x14*

**1980, Feb. 1 Litho. Wmk. 233**

**911** A246 75s multicolored .65 .30

Natl. Population & Housing Census, Apr.

*Perf. 13x11*

**1980, Feb. 26 Wmk. 368**

**912** A247 75s shown .40 .20
**913** A247 2b Yellow-cheeked tit .60 .25
**914** A247 3b Chestnut-tailed siva 1.40 .40
**915** A247 5b Scarlet minivet 2.40 1.10
*Nos. 912-915 (4)* 4.80 1.95

Intl. Commission for Bird Preservation, 9th Conf. of Asian Section, Chieng-mai, 2/26-29.

Smokers and Lungs, WHO Emblem — A248

**1980, Apr. 7 Wmk. 329** ***Perf. 13½***

**916** A248 75s multicolored .60 .25

World Health Day; fight against cigarette smoking.

Garuda and Rotary Emblem — A249

**1980, May 6 Wmk. 368** ***Perf. 13x11***

**917** A249 5b multicolored 1.50 .25

Rotary International, 75th anniversary.

Sai Yok Falls, Kanchanaburi — A250

*Perf. 14x15*

**1980, July 1 Litho. Wmk. 233**

**918** A250 1b shown .40 .20
**919** A250 2b Punyaban Falls, Ranong .60 .25
**920** A250 5b Heo Suwat Falls, Nakhon Ratchasima 2.10 .85
**921** A250 6b Siriphum Falls, Chiang Mai 1.90 1.25
*Nos. 918-921 (4)* 5.00 2.55

Queen Sirikit — A251

Family with Cattle, Ceres Medal (Reverse) — A252

No. 524, Ceres medal (obverse), potters.

***Perf. 13½, 11x13 (5b)***

**Wmk. 329, 368 (5b)**

**1980, Aug. 12 Litho.**

**922** A251 75s multicolored .40 .20
**923** A252 5b multicolored 1.60 .80
**924** A252 5b multicolored 1.60 .80
*Nos. 922-924 (3)* 3.60 1.80

Queen Sirikit's 48th birthday.

Khao Phanomrung Temple, Buri Ram — A253

Intl. Letter Writing Week, Oct. 6-12 (Temples): 2b, Prang Ku, Chailyaphum. 2.75b, Phimai, Nakhon Ratchasima. 5b, Sikhoraphum, Surin.

*Perf. 11x13*

**1980, Oct. 5 Litho. Wmk. 368**

**925** A253 75s multicolored .25 .20
**926** A253 2b multicolored .60 .25
**927** A253 2.75b multicolored .80 .30
**928** A253 5b multicolored 1.90 1.00
*Nos. 925-928 (4)* 3.55 1.75

Princess Mother — A254

Golden Mount, Bangkok — A255

*Perf. 15x14*

**1980, Oct. 21 Litho. Wmk. 233**

**929** A254 75s multicolored 1.75 .45

Princess Mother, 80th birthday.

**1980, Oct. 24**

**930** A255 75s multicolored .60 .25

United Nations Day.

King Bhumibol Adulyadej — A256

*Perf. 11x13*

**1980-84(?) Litho. Wmk. 368**

**932** A256 25s salmon 2.00 .20
**933** A256 50s olive green .20 .20
***b.*** Wmk. 233, perf. 14x15 *5.00* .20
***c.*** Wmk. 387, perf. 11x13 1.00 .20
**934** A256 75s lilac .50 .20
**935** A256 1.25b yellow green .50 .20
***a.*** Wmk. 387, perf. 11x13 2.00 .20
***b.*** Wmk. 233, perf. 14x15 6.00 .20

*Perf. 13½x13*

**Engr. Wmk. 329**

**936** A256 3b brown & dk bl *4.75* .20
**937** A256 5b purple & brn *7.25* .30
**938** A256 6b dk green & pur *9.50* .35
**939** A256 8.50b grn & brn org 2.00 .50
**940** A256 9.50b olive & dk grn 2.50 .55
*Nos. 932-940 (9)* *29.20* 2.70

Issued: 50s, 1.25b, 1981. 3b-9.50b, 1983.

See Nos. 1080-1093. For surcharges see Nos. 1226-1226A.

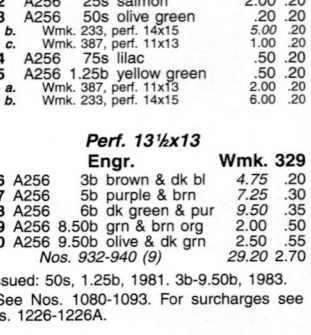

King Rama VII Monument Inauguration A257

*Perf. 15x14*

**1980, Dec. 10 Wmk. 233**

**946** A257 75s multicolored .75 .25

Bencharongware Bowl — A258

*Perf. 11x13*

**1980, Dec. 15 Wmk. 368**

**947** A258 2b shown .80 .40
**948** A258 2.75b Covered bowls .80 .40
**949** A258 3b Covered jar 1.60 .60
**950** A258 5b Stem plates 1.60 1.00
*Nos. 947-950 (4)* 4.80 2.40

King Vajiravudh Birth Centenary A259

Children's Day — A260

**1981, Jan. 1 Wmk. 233** ***Perf. 15x14***

**951** A259 75s multicolored .85 .25

*Perf. 13x11*

**1981, Jan. 16 Wmk. 368**

**952** A260 75s multicolored .60 .20

Hegira, 1500th Anniv. — A261

**Wmk. 377**

**1981, Jan. 18 Litho. *Perf. 12½***

**953** A261 5b multicolored 2.40 .75

Dolls in Native Costumes — A262

**Wmk. 368**

**1981, Feb. 6 Litho. *Perf. 13½***

**954** A262 75s Palm-leaf fish mobile .45 .20
**955** A262 75s Teak elephants .45 .20
**956** A262 2.75b shown 1.25 .60
**957** A262 2.75b Baskets 1.25 .60
*Nos. 954-957 (4)* 3.40 1.60

CONEX '81 International Crafts Exhibition.

Scout Leader and Boy on Crutches — A263

**1981, Feb. 28 *Perf. 13x11***

**958** A263 75s shown .40 .20
**959** A263 5b Diamond cutter in wheelchair 1.60 .60

International Year of the Disabled.

Dindaeng-Tarua Expressway Opening — A264

**1981, Oct. 29 *Perf. 13½***

**960** A264 1b Klongtoey .25 .20
**961** A264 5b Vipavadee Rangsit Highway 2.00 .65

Ongkhot, Khon Mask — A265

Designs: Various Khon masks.

**1981, July 1 Litho. *Perf. 13x11***

**962** A265 75s shown .45 .25
**963** A265 2b Maiyarab .70 .30
**964** A265 3b Sukrip 1.60 .50
**965** A265 5b Indrajit 1.75 1.10
*Nos. 962-965 (4)* 4.50 2.15

Exhibition Emblem, No. 83 — A266

**Wmk. 370**

**1981, Aug. 4 Litho. *Perf. 12***

**966** A266 75s shown .35 .20
**967** A266 75s No. 144 .35 .20
**968** A266 2.75b No. 198 1.00 .60
**969** A266 2.75b No. 226 1.00 .60
*Nos. 966-969 (4)* 2.70 1.60

A267

A268

***Perf. 15x14***

**1981, Aug. 26 Wmk. 233**

**970** A267 1.25b multicolored .65 .25

Luang Praditphairo, court Musician, birth centenary. THAIPEX '81 Intl. Stamp Exhibition.

**1981, Oct. 4 Wmk. 329**

Designs: Dwarfed trees.

**971** A268 75s Mai hok-hian *.40* .20
**972** A268 2b Mai kam-ma-lo *.65* .40
**973** A268 2.75b Mai khen *1.00* .25
**974** A268 5b Mai khabuan *2.50* 1.25
*Nos. 971-974 (4)* *4.55* 2.10

25th Intl. Letter Writing Week, Oct. 6-12.

World Food Day A269

**Wmk. 370**

**1981, Oct. 16 Litho. *Perf. 12***

**975** A269 75s multicolored .60 .25

United Nations Day — A270

**1981, Oct. 24 Wmk. 368 *Perf. 13½***

**976** A270 1.25b Samran Mukhamat Pavilion .60 .25

King Cobra A271

**1981, Dec. 1 Wmk. 329 *Perf. 13½***

**977** A271 75s shown .25 .20
**978** A271 2b Banded krait 1.25 .55
**979** A271 2.75b Thai cobra 1.25 .25
**980** A271 5b Malayan pit viper 2.25 1.00
*Nos. 977-980 (4)* 5.00 2.00

Children's Day — A272

Scouting Year — A273

**1982, Jan. 9 Wmk. 370 *Perf. 12***

**981** A272 1.25b multicolored .75 .25

**1982, Feb. 22**

**982** A273 1.25b multicolored .60 .25

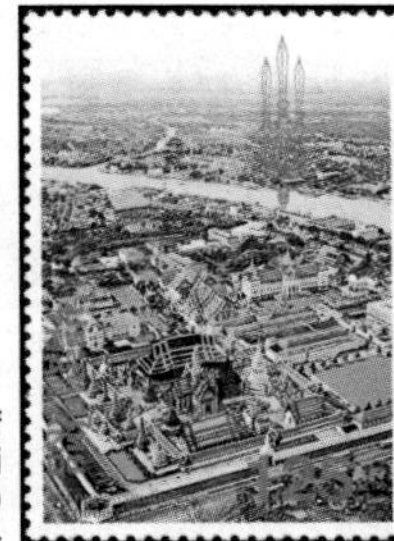

Bicentenary of Bangkok (Thai Capital) A274

Chakri Dynasty kings. (Rama I-Rama IX).

**1982, Apr. 4 Litho. *Perf. 12***

**983** A274 1b Buddha Yod-Fa (1736-1809) *.45* .25
**984** A274 1.25b shown *.60* .30
**985** A274 2b Buddha Lert La Naphalai (1767-1824) *.90* .25
**986** A274 3b Nang Klao (1787-1851) *1.60* .35
**987** A274 4b Mongkut (1804-1868) *1.25* .50
**988** A274 5b Chulalongkorn (1853-1910) *2.00* .75
**989** A274 6b Vajiravudh (1880-1925) *2.50* .75
**990** A274 7b Prachathipok (1893-1941) *5.25* 2.50
**991** A274 8b Ananda Mahidol (1925-1946) *2.75* 1.50
**992** A274 9b Bhumibol Adulyadej (b. 1927) *2.75* 1.00
*a.* Souv. sheet of 10, 205x142mm *42.50* 32.50
*b.* Souv. sheet of 1, 195x180mm *42.50* 32.50
*Nos. 983-992 (10)* *20.05* 8.15

Nos. 992a-992b each contain Nos. 983-992. No. 992a sold for 60b, No. 992b for 70b.

Values for #992a-992b include folder.

TB Bacillus Centenary — A275

**Wmk. 368**

**1982, Apr. 7 Litho. *Perf. 13½***

**993** A275 1.25b multicolored .60 .25

Local Flowers — A276

***Perf. 14x14½***

**1982, June 30 Wmk. 233**

**994** A276 1.25b Quisqualis indica .35 .20
**995** A276 1.50b Murraya anicu-lata .55 .30
**996** A276 6.50b Mesua ferrea 2.00 .80
**997** A276 7b Desmos chinen-sis 1.60 .50
*Nos. 994-997 (4)* 4.50 1.80

Buddhist Temples in Bangkok — A277

**1982, Aug. 4 Wmk. 368 *Perf. 13½***

**998** A277 1.25b shown .40 .20
**999** A277 4.25b Wat Pho 1.00 .40
**1000** A277 6.50b Mahathat Yuwarat Rangsarit 1.25 .75
**1001** A277 7b Phra Sri Rat-tana Sat-sadaram 2.10 .55
*a.* Souv. sheet of 4, #998-1001, perf. 12½ 70.00 55.00
*Nos. 998-1001 (4)* 4.75 1.90

BANGKOK '83 Intl. Stamp Exhibition, Aug. 4-13, 1983. No. 1001a sold for 30b.

See Nos. 1025-1026.

A278

A279

**1982, Aug. 9 Wmk. 370 *Perf. 12***

**1002** A278 1.25b LANDSAT Satel-lite .60 .25

2nd UN Conference on Peaceful Uses of Outer Space, Vienna, Aug. 9-21.

**1982, Sept. 14 Wmk. 233 *Perf. 14***

Prince Purachatra of Kambaengbejra (1882-1936).

**1003** A279 1.25b multicolored .60 .25

26th Intl. Letter Writing Week, Oct. 6-12 — A280

Sangalok Pottery.

**1982, Oct. 3 Wmk. 329 *Perf. 13½***

**1004** A280 1.25b Covered glazed jar .45 .25
**1005** A280 3b Painted jar 1.25 .50
**1006** A280 4.25b Glazed plate .90 .65
**1007** A280 7b Painted plate 1.75 1.00
*Nos. 1004-1007 (4)* 4.35 2.40

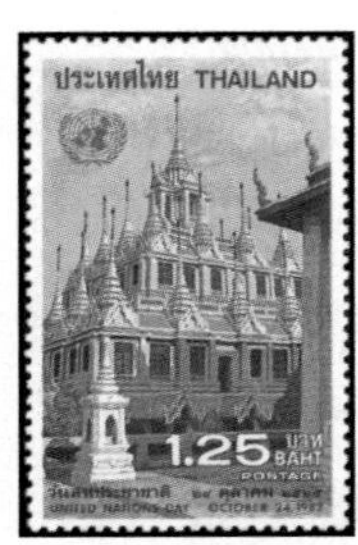


UN Day — A281

**1982, Oct. 24**

**1008** A281 1.25b Loha Prasat Tower .60 .25

Musical Instruments — A282

**1982, Nov. 30 Wmk. 370 *Perf. 12***

**1009** A282 50s Chap, ching *.20* .20
**1010** A282 1b Pi nai, pi nok *.60* .25
**1011** A282 1.25b Klong that, taphon *.40* .20
**1012** A282 1.50b Khong mong, krap *.40* .30
**1013** A282 6b Khong wong yai *4.00* 1.40
**1014** A282 7b Khong wong lek *1.60* .50
**1015** A282 8b Ranat ek *1.40* .50
**1016** A282 9b Ranat thum *1.40* .50
*Nos. 1009-1016 (8)* *10.00* 3.85

Pileated Gibbon — A283

ASEAN Members' Flags — A284

**1982, Dec. 26**

**1017** A283 1.25b shown *.60* .25
**1018** A283 3b Pig-tailed macaque *2.90* .45
**1019** A283 5b Slow loris *1.75* 1.00
**1020** A283 7b Silvered leaf monkey *2.25* 1.10
*Nos. 1017-1020 (4)* *7.50* 2.80

**1982, Dec. 26 Wmk. 233**

**1021** A284 6.50b multicolored 1.60 .40

15th Anniv. of Assoc. of Southeast Asian Nations.

Children's Day — A285

***Perf. 14½x14***

**1983, Jan. 8 Litho. Wmk. 233**

**1022** A285 1.25b multicolored .60 .25

First Anniv. of Postal Code A286

**1983, Feb. 25 Wmk. 329 *Perf. 13½***

**1023** A286 1.25b Codes .60 .25
**1024** A286 1.25b Code on envelope .60 .25

BANGKOK '83 Type of 1982

Design: Old General Post Office.

**1983, Feb. 25 Wmk. 368 Photo.**

**1025** A277 7b multicolored 1.60 .30
**1026** A277 10b multicolored 2.40 .50
*a.* Souv. sheet of 2, #1025-1026, perf. 12½ 25.00 22.50

25th Anniv. of Intl. Maritime Org. — A287

***Perf. 14x14½***

**1983, Mar. 17 Litho. Wmk. 233**

**1029** A287 1.25b Chinese junks .60 .25

Civil Servants' Day — A288

Prince Sithiporn Kridakara (1883-1971) A289

**1983, Apr. 1 Wmk. 370 *Perf. 12***

**1030** A288 1.25b multicolored .60 .25

***Perf. 14½x14***

**1983, Apr. 11 Wmk. 233**

**1031** A289 1.25b multicolored .60 .25

Domestic Satellite Communications System Inauguration — A290

**Wmk. 368**

**1983, Aug. 4 Litho. *Perf. 13½***

**1032** A290 2b Map, dish antenna, satellite .60 .25

BANGKOK '83 Intl. Stamp Show, Aug. 4-13 — A291

**1983, Aug. 4 Wmk. 370 *Perf. 12***

**1033** A291 1.25b Mail collection .25 .20
**1034** A291 7.50b Posting letters 1.75 .60
**1035** A291 8.50b Mail transport 1.25 .75
**1036** A291 9.50b Mail delivery 1.25 .75
*a.* Souv. sheet of 4, #1033-1036 32.50 29.00
*Nos. 1033-1036 (4)* 4.50 2.30

No. 1036a exist imperf, sold for 50b. Value, $140.

A292

A293

Prince Bhanurangsi memorial statue.

***Perf. 15x14***

**1983, Aug. 4 Litho. Wmk. 233**

**1037** A292 1.25b multicolored .60 .25

**Wmk. 370**

**1983, Sept. 27 Litho. *Perf. 12***

**1038** A293 1.25b multicolored .25 .20
**1039** A293 7b multicolored 1.50 .75

Malaysia/ Thailand/ Singapore submarine cable inauguration.

Intl. Letter Writing Week — A294

**1983, Oct. 6 Wmk. 329 *Perf. 13½***

**1040** A294 2b Acropora asper .70 .25
**1041** A294 3b Platygyra lamellina 1.60 .25
**1042** A294 4b Fungia .70 .70
**1043** A294 7b Pectinia lactuca 2.00 1.10
*Nos. 1040-1043 (4)* 5.00 2.30

Prince Mahidol of Songkhla — A295

**Wmk. 370**

**1983, Oct. 10 Litho. *Perf. 12***

**1044** A295 9.50b multicolored 1.50 .75

Siriraj Hospital Faculty of Medicine and Rockefeller Foundation, 60th Anniv. of cooperation.

World Communications Year — A296

3b, Telecommunications equipment, diff.

***Perf. 14x14½***

**1983, Oct. 24 Litho. Wmk. 233**

**1045** A296 2b multicolored .60 .25
**1046** A296 3b multicolored .60 .25

United Nations Day — A297

**1983, Oct. 24**

**1047** A297 1.25b multicolored .60 .25

Thai Alphabet, 700th Anniv. — A298

Designs: 3b, Painted pottery, Sukothai period. 7b, Thai characters, reign of King Ramkamhaeng. 8b, Buddha, Sukothai period. 9b, Mahathat Temple, Sukothai province.

**1983, Nov. 17 Wmk. 370 *Perf. 12***

1048 A298 3b multicolored 1.00 .25
1049 A298 7b multicolored 1.90 .45
1050 A298 8b multi, vert. 1.00 .50
1051 A298 9b multi, vert. 1.00 .50
*Nos. 1048-1051 (4)* 4.90 1.70

National Development Program — A299

#1052, King and Queen initiating Royal Projects. #1053, Technical aid. #1054, Terrace farming, Irrigation dam. #1055, Gathering grain. #1056, Receiving the peoples' gratitude.

**1984, May 5**

1052 A299 1.25b multicolored .60 .25
1053 A299 1.25b multicolored .60 .25
1054 A299 1.25b multicolored .60 .25
1055 A299 1.25b multicolored .60 .25
1056 A299 1.25b multicolored .60 .25
*a.* Strip of 5, #1052-1056 3.00 1.50

Children's Day — A300

**1984, Jan. 14 Wmk. 329 *Perf. 13½***

1057 A300 1.25b multicolored .60 .25

17th Natl. Games, Jan. 22-28 — A301

**1984, Jan. 22**

1058 A301 1.25b Running .65 .20
1059 A301 3b Soccer .45 .25

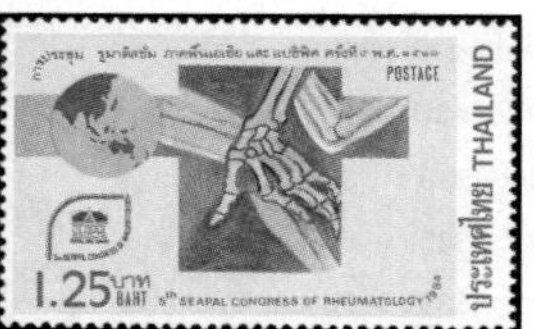

5th Rheumatology Congress, Jan. 22-27 — A302

***Perf. 14x15***

**1984, Jan. 22 Wmk. 233**

1060 A302 1.25b Rheumatic joints .75 .25

Armed Forces Day — A303

50th Anniv. of Royal Institute — A304

**1984, Jan. 25 *Perf. 15x14***

1061 A303 1.25b King Naresuan, tanks, jet, ship .60 .25

**1984, Mar. 31**

1062 A304 1.25b multicolored .60 .25

Thammasat University, 50th Anniv. — A305

**1984, June 27 *Perf. 14x15***

1063 A305 1.25b Dome Building .60 .25

Asia-Pacific Broadcasting Union, 20th Anniv. — A306

**1984, July 1 Wmk. 387 *Perf. 12***

1064 A306 4b Map, emblem 1.00 .35

Seated Buddha, Chiang Saen Style — A307

Intl. Letter Writing Week — A308

Seated Buddhas in various styles.

***Perf. 14½x14***

**1984, July 12 Wmk. 233**

1065 A307 1.25b shown .25 .20
1066 A307 7b Sukhothai 2.10 .80
1067 A307 8.50b U-Thong 1.00 1.00
1068 A307 9.50b Ayutthaya 1.00 1.00
*Nos. 1065-1068 (4)* 4.35 3.00

**Wmk. 385**

**1984, Oct. 7 Litho. *Perf. 13½***

Medicinal Succulents: 1.50b, Alocasia indica. 2b, Aloe barbadensis. 4b, Gynura pseudochina DC. 10b, Rhoeo spathacea.

1069 A308 1.50b multicolored .35 .25
1070 A308 2b multicolored .55 .25
1071 A308 4b multicolored .90 .45
1072 A308 10b multicolored 2.75 1.25
*Nos. 1069-1072 (4)* 4.55 2.20

Princess Mother (b. 1900) — A309

UN Day — A310

***Perf. 15x14***

**1984, Oct. 21 Wmk. 233**

1073 A309 1.50b Portrait .60 .25

**1984, Oct. 24 Wmk. 233**

1074 A310 1.50b Woman threshing rice .60 .25

Local Butterflies — A311

**Wmk. 329**

**1984, Nov. 27 Photo. *Perf. 13½***

1075 A311 2b Bhutanitis lidderdalei .65 .30
1076 A311 3b Stichophthalma louisa .65 .30
1077 A311 5b Parthenos sylvia 1.40 .90
1078 A311 7b Stichophthalma godfreyi 2.40 .90
*Nos. 1075-1078 (4)* 5.10 2.40

King Type of 1980

***Perf. 13½x13, 14x15 (1.50b, 2b)***

**Wmk. 329, 233 (1.50b, 2b)**

**1984-87 Litho.**

1080 A256 1b Prus blue .25 .20
1081 A256 1.50b brt yel org ('85) .35 .20
1082 A256 2b dk car ('85) .45 .20
*a.* Wmk. 387, perf. 11x13½ ('86?) 4.00 .50
*b.* Wmk. 387, perf. 14½x14 ('87) 1.50 .30

**Engr.**

1083 A256 2b hn brn & gray vio 5.00 .20
1084 A256 4b turq bl & hn brn .75 .25
1085 A256 6.50b dk yel grn & ol brn 1.00 .35
1086 A256 7b dl red brn & sep 1.25 .40
1087 A256 7.50b dk org & saph ('85) 1.25 .50
1088 A256 8b brn vio & ol grn ('85) 1.40 .50
1089 A256 9b int bl & dk ol bis ('85) 1.75 .60
1090 A256 10b hn brn & sl grn 2.00 .65
1091 A256 20b dk org & grn 7.00 1.25
1092 A256 50b dp vit & grn 8.50 3.00
1093 A256 100b dp org & dk bl 17.00 6.00
*Nos. 1080-1093 (14)* 47.95 14.30

For surcharge see No. 1212.

Children's Day — A313

Children's drawings.

**Wmk. 385**

**1985, Jan. 12 Litho. *Perf. 13½***

1101 A313 1.50b Pedestrians, overpass .40 .20
1102 A313 1.50b Climbing overpass, vert. .40 .20

Bangkok Mail Center Opening — A314

**1985, Feb. 25**

1103 A314 1.50b multicolored .60 .25

Phuket Province Heroes Bicent. — A315

***Perf. 15x14***

**1985, Mar. 13 Litho. Wmk. 233**

1104 A315 2b multicolored .35 .25

Tao-Thep-Krasattri, Tao-Sri-Sundhorn Monument.

Government Savings Bank, 72nd Anniv. — A316

**1985, Apr. 1 *Perf. 14x15***

1105 A316 1.50b King Rama VI, headquarters .60 .25

Intl. Telecommunications Satellite Org., 20th Anniv. — A317

**1985, Apr. 6 Wmk. 387 *Perf. 12***

1106 A317 2b multicolored .60 .25

Thai Airways Intl., 25th Anniv. — A318

**Wmk. 385**

**1985, May 1 Litho. *Perf. 13***

**1107** A318 2b DC-6 .30 .20
**1108** A318 7.50b DC-10 1.40 .65
**1109** A318 8.50b Airbus A-300 1.60 .90
**1110** A318 9.50b Boeing 747 1.60 1.00
*Nos. 1107-1110 (4)* 4.90 2.75

Natl. Flag and UPU Emblem — A319

**1985, July 1 Wmk. 387 *Perf. 12***

**1111** A319 2b shown .25 .20

***Perf. 13½***

**Wmk. 385**

**1112** A319 10b Flag and ITU emblem 1.25 .90

Thai membership to UPU and Intl. Telecommunications Union, cent.

Natl. Communications Day, Aug. 5 — A320

**1985, Aug. 4 Wmk. 329 *Perf. 13½***

**1113** A320 2b multicolored .60 .25

THAIPEX '85, Aug. 4-13 — A321

**1985, Aug. 4 Wmk. 385**

**1114** A321 2b Aisvarya Pavilion, vert. .50 .20
**1115** A321 3b Varopas Piman Pavilion .75 .25
**1116** A321 7b Vehas Camrun Pavilion 1.25 .60
**1117** A321 10b Vitoon Tassana Tower, vert. 1.50 .95
*a.* Souv. sheet of 4, #1114-1117 57.50
*Nos. 1114-1117 (4)* 4.00 2.00

No. 1117a exists imperf, sold for 40b.

Natl. Science Day, Aug. 18 — A322

**1985, Aug. 18 Wmk. 387 *Perf. 12***

**1118** A322 2b King Rama IV, solar eclipse .60 .60

1885 Seal, Modern Map and Crest — A323

***Perf. 14½x15***

**1985, Sept. 3 Wmk. 233**

**1119** A323 2b multicolored .60 .25

Royal Thai Survey Department, Cent.

13th SEA Games, Bangkok, Dec. 8-17 — A324

Designs: a, Boxing. b, Shot put. c, Badminton. d, Javelin. e, Weight lifting.

**1985, Oct. 1 Wmk. 387 *Perf. 12***

**1120** Strip of 5 2.75 2.50
*a.-e.* A324 2b, any single .50 .20
*f.* Souv. sheet of 5, #a.-e. + label 27.50 22.50

No. 1120f sold for 20b.

Climbing Plants — A325

UN Child Survival Campaign A326

**1985, Oct. 6 Wmk. 385 *Perf. 13½***

**1121** A325 2b Allemanda cathartica .65 .25
**1122** A325 3b Jasminum auriculatum .90 .25
**1123** A325 7b Passiflora laurifolia 1.40 .70
**1124** A325 10b Antigonon leptopus 1.60 .80
*Nos. 1121-1124 (4)* 4.55 2.00

International Letter Writing Week.

**1985, Oct. 24**

**1125** A326 2b multicolored .60 .25

UN Day.

Prince Kromamun Bidyalabh Bridhyakorn (1885-1974), Govt. Minister — A327

Rangsit (1885-1951), Prince of Jainad — A328

**1985, Nov. 7**

**1126** A327 2b multi 5.75 1.25
**1126A** A327 2b multi, diff. .75 .25
*b.* Pair, #1126-1126A 35.00 29.00

No. 1126A has flower design framing portrait reversed.

***Perf. 15x14½***

**1985, Nov. 12 Wmk. 233**

**1127** A328 1.50b multicolored .60 .25

Asian-Pacific Postal Union, 5th Congress, Nov. 25-Dec. 4 — A329

**1985, Nov. 25 Wmk. 385 *Perf. 13½***

**1128** A329 2b multicolored .20 .20
**1129** A329 10b multicolored 1.00 .50

Intl. Youth Year A330

***Perf. 14x15***

**1985, Nov. 26 Wmk. 233**

**1130** A330 2b multicolored .60 .25

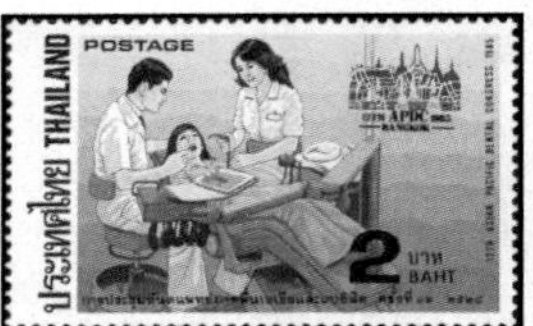

12th Asian-Pacific Dental Congress, Bangkok, Dec. 5-10 — A331

**1985, Dec. 5**

**1131** A331 2b multicolored .60 .25

13th SEA Games — A332

French Envoys — A333

**1985, Dec. 8 Wmk. 387 *Perf. 12***

**1132** A332 1b Volleyball .60 .30
**1133** A332 2b Sepak-takraw .60 .30
**1134** A332 3b Women's gymnastics .60 .30
**1135** A332 4b Bowling 1.00 .60
*a.* Souv. sheet, #1132-1135 + label 25.00 21.00
*Nos. 1132-1135 (4)* 2.80 1.50

No. 1135a sold for 20b.

**1985, Dec. 12 Wmk. 385 *Perf. 13½***

**1136** A333 2b shown .25 .20
**1137** A333 8.50b Thai envoys 1.25 .70

Diplomatic relations with France, 300th anniv.

Domestic Express Mail Service Inauguration — A334

**1986, Jan. 1**

**1138** A334 2b multicolored .60 .25

Intl. Express Mail Service, EMS, 3rd anniv.

Wildlife Conservation — A335

Marine turtles.

**1986, Jan. 8 Wmk. 329**

**1139** A335 1.50b Chelonia mydas .45 .25
**1140** A335 3b Eretmochelys imbricata .85 .25
**1141** A335 5b Dermochelys coriacea 2.50 .45
**1142** A335 10b Lepidochelys olivacea 2.10 .65
*Nos. 1139-1142 (4)* 5.90 1.60

Natl. Children's Day — A336

Statue of Sunthon Phu, Poet — A337

Design: Children picking lotus, by Areeya Makarabhundhu, age 12.

**1986, Jan. 11** **Wmk. 385**
**1143** A336 2b multicolored .60 .25

**1986, June 26**
**1144** A337 2b multicolored .60 .25

Fruit Type of 1979

**1986, June 26** **Wmk. 385**
**1145** A237 2b Watermelon *1.00* .25
**1146** A237 2b Malay apple *1.00* .25
**1147** A237 6b Pomelo *1.50* .65
**1148** A237 6b Papaya *1.50* .65
*Nos. 1145-1148 (4)* *5.00* 1.80

Nos. 1145-1148 horiz.

Natl. Year of the Trees A338

**1986, July 21**
**1149** A338 2b multicolored .60 .25

Communications Day — A339

**1986, Aug. 4**
**1150** A339 2b multicolored .60 .25

Bamboo Baskets — A340

**1986, Oct. 5**
**1151** A340 2b Chalom .50 .20
**1152** A340 2b Krabung .50 .20
**1153** A340 6b Kratib 1.00 .45
**1154** A340 6b Kaleb 1.00 .45
*Nos. 1151-1154 (4)* 3.00 1.30

Intl. Letter Writing Week.

Intl. Peace Year A341

**1986, Oct. 24**
**1155** A341 2b multicolored .60 .25

Productivity Year — A342

**1986, Oct. 24** **Wmk. 329**
**1156** A342 2b multicolored .60 .25

6th ASEAN Orchid Congress — A343

**1986, Nov. 7** **Wmk. 385**
**1157** A343 2b Vanda varavuth, vert. .60 .25
**1158** A343 3b Ascocenda emma, vert. .60 .30
**1159** A343 4b Dendrobium srisiam 1.10 .85
**1160** A343 5b Dendrobium ekapol panda 1.10 .60
*a.* Souv. sheet of 4, #1157-1160 85.00 67.50
*Nos. 1157-1160 (4)* 3.40 2.00

No. 1160a sold for 25b.

Fungi A344

***Perf. 13x13½***
**1986, Nov. 26** **Wmk. 329** **Photo.**
**1161** A344 2b Volvariella volvacea .55 .20
**1162** A344 2b Pleurotus ostreatus .55 .20
**1163** A344 6b Auricularia polytricha 1.40 .65
**1164** A344 6b Pleurotus cystidiosus 1.40 .65
*Nos. 1161-1164 (4)* 3.90 1.70

Fisheries Dept., 60th Anniv. — A345

**Wmk. 385**
**1986, Dec. 16** **Litho.** ***Perf. 13½***
**1165** A345 2b Morulius chrysophekadion .60 .25
**1166** A345 2b Notopterus blanci .60 .25
**1167** A345 7b Scleropages formosus 1.10 .65
**1168** A345 7b Pangasianodon gigas 1.10 .65
*Nos. 1165-1168 (4)* 3.40 1.80

No. 653 Surcharged in Dark Olive Green

***Perf. 14x13½***
**1986, Dec.** **Photo.** **Wmk. 233**
**1168A** A161 1b on 20s blue .60 .25

Children's Day — A346

Child's drawing.

***Perf. 14½x15***
**1987, Jan. 10** **Litho.** **Wmk. 387**
**1169** 2b School, playground .60 .25
**1170** 2b Pool .60 .25
*a.* A346 Pair, #1169-1170 1.25 1.00

No. 1170a has continuous design.

F-16 & F-5 Fighter Planes, Pilot — A347

**1987, Mar. 27** **Wmk. 385** ***Perf. 13½***
**1171** A347 2b multicolored .60 .25

Royal Thai Air Force, 72nd anniv.

King Rama III (Nang Klao, 1787-1851) — A348

***Perf. 15x14½***
**1987, Mar. 31** **Wmk. 387**
**1172** A348 2b multicolored .60 .25

Ministry of Communications, 75th Anniv. — A349

**1987, Apr. 1**
**1173** A349 2b multicolored .60 .25

Forestry Year — A350

**1987, July 11** **Wmk. 385** ***Perf. 13½***
**1174** A350 2b multicolored .60 .25

THAIPEX '87 — A351

Gold artifacts.

**1987, Aug. 4** **Wmk. 385**
**1175** A351 2b Peacock, vert. .40 .20
**1176** A351 2b Hand mirrors, vert. .40 .20
**1177** A351 6b Water urn, finger bowls 1.10 .55
**1178** A351 6b Dragon vase 1.10 .55
*a.* Souv. sheet of 4, #1175-1178 57.50 47.50
*Nos. 1175-1178 (4)* 3.00 1.50

No. 1178a exists imperf.

ASEAN, 20th Anniv. — A352

**1987, Aug. 20**
**1179** A352 2b multicolored .30 .20
**1180** A352 3b multicolored .60 .30
**1181** A352 4b multicolored .60 .40
**1182** A352 5b multicolored .90 .45
*Nos. 1179-1182 (4)* 2.40 1.35

Natl. Communications Day — A353

**1987, Aug. 4**
**1183** A353 2b multicolored .60 .25

Chulachamklao Royal Military Academy, Cent. — A354

Design: School crest, King Rama V, and King Rama IX conferring sword on graduating officer.

**1987, Aug. 5**
**1184** A354 2b multicolored 1.00 .25

Intl. Literacy Day — A355

Tourism Year — A356

**1987, Sept. 8**
**1185** A355 2b multicolored .60 .25

**1987, Sept. 18**

2b, Flower-offering ceremony, Saraburi province. 3b, Duan Sib Festival, Nakhon Si Thammarat province. 5b, Bang Fai Festival, Yasothon province. 7b, Loi Krathong Festival, Sukhothai province.

**1186** A356 2b multicolored .25 .20
**1187** A356 3b multicolored .60 .30
**1188** A356 5b multicolored .90 .40
**1189** A356 7b multicolored 1.25 .60
*Nos. 1186-1189 (4)* 3.00 1.50

Auditor General's Office, 72nd Anniv. — A357

**1987, Sept. 18**
**1190** A357 2b multicolored .60 .25

Diplomatic Relations Between Thailand and Japan, Cent. — A358

**1987, Sept. 26** **Wmk. 329**
**1191** A358 2b multicolored .60 .25

Intl. Letter Writing Week — A359

Floral garlands.

**1987, Oct. 4** **Wmk. 385**
**1192** A359 2b Floral tassel .35 .20
**1193** A359 3b Tasselled garland .65 .30
**1194** A359 5b Wrist garland .75 .40
**1195** A359 7b Double-ended garland 1.25 .65
*Nos. 1192-1195 (4)* 3.00 1.55

Thai Pavilion — A360

**1987, Oct. 9** **Wmk. 387** ***Perf. 15***
**1196** A360 2b multicolored .60 .25

Social Education and Cultural Center inauguration.

A361

A362

King Bhumibol Adulyadej, 60th Birthday — A363

Royal ciphers and: #1197, Adulyadej as a child. #1198, King and Queen, wedding portrait, 1950. #1199, King taking the Oath of Accession, 1950. #1200, King dressed as a monk, collecting alms. #1201, Greeting 100 year-old woman. #1202, In military uniform holding pen and with hill tribes. #1203, Royal couple visiting wounded servicemen. #1204, Visiting farm. #1205, Royal family. #1206, King, Queen Sirikit. #1207, Princess Mother Somdej Phra Sri Nakarindra Boromrajjonnani, emblem of Medical Volunteer Assoc. #1208, Crown Prince Maha Vajiralongkorn, crown prince's royal standard. #1209, Princess Maha Chakri Sirindhorn, emblem of Sai Jai Thai Foundation. #1210, Princess Chulabhorn, Albert Einstein gold medal awarded by UNESCO.

**Wmk. 329**

**1987, Dec. 5** **Photo.** ***Perf. 13½***
**1197** A361 2b shown .55 .25
**1198** A361 2b multicolored .55 .25
**1199** A361 2b multicolored .55 .25
**1200** A361 2b multicolored .55 .25
**1201** A361 2b multicolored .55 .25
**1202** A361 2b multicolored .55 .25
**1203** A361 2b multicolored .55 .25
**1204** A361 2b multicolored .55 .25
*a.* Souv. sheet, #1197-1204 35.00 30.00

**Litho.**

**Wmk. 385**

**1205** A362 2b multicolored 1.10 .30
**1206** A362 2b multicolored 1.10 .30
**1207** A362 2b multicolored 1.10 .30
**1208** A362 2b multicolored 1.10 .30
**1209** A362 2b multicolored 1.10 .30
**1210** A362 2b multicolored 1.10 .30

**Litho. & Embossed**

**1211** A363 100b vio blue & gold 65.00 65.00
*Nos. 1197-1211 (15)* 76.00 68.80

Size of Nos. 1206-1210: 45x27mm. No. 1211 printed in sheets of 10. No. 1204a sold for 40b.

No. 1081 Surcharged

**1987** **Litho.** **Wmk. 233** ***Perf. 14x15***
**1212** A256 2b on 1.50b brt yel org .60 .25

Children's Day — A364

Thai Agricultural Cooperatives, 72nd Anniv. — A365

***Perf. 14x14½***

**1988, Jan. 9** **Litho.** **Wmk. 387**
**1213** A364 2b multicolored .60 .25

**1988, Feb. 26** **Wmk. 387**
**1214** A365 2b Prince Bridhyalongkorn, founder .60 .25

Royal Siam Soc., 84th Anniv. A366

**1988, Mar. 10** ***Perf. 14½x14***
**1215** A366 2b multicolored .60 .25

Cultural Heritage Preservation — A367

Ruins in Sukhothai Historic Park.

**1988, Apr. 2** ***Perf. 14½x14***
**1216** A367 2b Wat Phra Phai Luang .25 .20
**1217** A367 3b Wat Traphang Thonglang .60 .30
**1218** A367 4b Wat Maha That .90 .60
**1219** A367 6b Thewalai Maha Kaset 1.25 .70
*Nos. 1216-1219 (4)* 3.00 1.80

Red Cross Fair A368

**1988, Apr.** **Wmk. 387** ***Perf. 14***
**1220** A368 2b Prevention of rabies .60 .25

King Rama V, Founder — A369

Intl. Council of Women, Cent. — A371

Pheasants — A370

***Perf. 14x14½***

**1988, Apr. 26** **Wmk. 387**
**1221** A369 5b multicolored 2.10 .70

Siriraj Hospital, cent.

**Wmk. 329**

**1988, June 15** **Photo.** ***Perf. 13½***
**1222** A370 2b Crested fireback .30 .20
**1223** A370 3b Kalij .60 .25
**1224** A370 6b Silver pheasant 1.25 .60
**1225** A370 7b Hume's pheasant 1.50 .75
*Nos. 1222-1225 (4)* 3.65 1.80

Nos. 935a, 935 Surcharged

a

b

***Perf. 11x13***

**1988-92** **Litho.** **Wmk. 387**
**1226** A256(a) 1b on 1.25b .60 .25
**1226A** A256(b) 1b on 1.25b .75 .25
*b.* Wmk. 368 1.40 1.10

Issued: #1226, 1988; #1226A, Dec. 5, 1992.

**1988, June 26** **Wmk. 385** ***Perf. 13½***
**1227** A371 2b multicolored .60 .25

King Bhumibol Adulyadej
A372 A372a

***Perf. 13½x13***

**1988-95** **Litho.** **Wmk. 387**
**1228** A372 25s brown .20 .20

***Perf. 14x14½***

**1229** A372 50s olive .20 .20
*a.* Wmk. 329 .60 .20
**1230** A372 1b brt blue .20 .20
Complete booklet, 5 #1230 1.25
*a.* Photo, wmk. 233 1.00 .20
*b.* Photo., wmk. 340, perf. 13½x13¾ .20 .20
**1233** A372 2b scarlet .75 .20
Complete booklet, 5 #1233 1.25
*a.* Wmk. 329 .75 .20
*b.* Photo., wmk. 340, perf. 13½x13¾ .25 .25
Complete booklet, 5 #1233b 1.25

**Photo.**

**Wmk. 233**

***Perf. 14½***

**1236** A372 1b bright blue .20 .20
*Nos. 1228-1236 (5)* 1.55 1.00

No. 1236 has blue background without halo effect around head. See #1230.

Issued: 25s, 8/12/92; 1b-2b, 7/2/88; 50s, 7/28/93; #1230a, 1236, 1990; #1233a, 1992; #1230b, 1233b, 12/5/94; #1229a, 1995.

***Perf. 13½x13***

**1988-90** **Engr.** **Wmk. 329**
**1241** A372a 3b brn & bluish gray .35 .25
**1242** A372a 4b brt bl & red brn .45 .30
**1243** A372a 5b violet & brn .40 .30
**1244** A372a 6b green & vio .45 .35
**1245** A372a 7b red brn & dk brn .80 .55
**1246** A372a 8b red brn & gray ol .65 .40
**1247** A372a 9b dk blue & brn .70 .40
**1248** A372a 10b henna brn & blk 1.00 .25
**1249** A372a 20b brn org & sage grn 2.00 .65
**1250** A372a 25b olive grn & dark blue 2.50 .90
**1251** A372a 50b violet & grn 5.00 1.00
**1252** A372a 100b brn org & bluish blk 10.00 2.00
*Nos. 1241-1252 (12)* 24.30 7.35

Issued:3b, 10b, 50b, 100b, 12/5; 5b, 6b, 8b, 9b, 7/1/89; 4b, 7b, 20b, 12/5/89; 25b, 1/9/90.

A373

A375

King Bhumibol's Reign (since 1950) — A374

Designs: No. 1253, King Bhumibol.

Regalia: No. 1254, Great Crown of Victory. No. 1255, Sword of Victory and matching scabbard. No. 1256, Scepter. No. 1257, Fan and feather fly swatter. No. 1258, Royal slippers.

Canopied thrones in the Grand Palace: No. 1259, Queen's round ottoman on 1-tier dais in front of decorative screen. No. 1260, King's throne on 1-tier dais in front of decorative screen. No. 1261, 3-Tier throne with 3 gilded trees. No. 1262, 3-Canopy throne on high gold dais. No. 1263, 3-Tier throne with 4 gilded trees, altar in background. No. 1264, 3-Canopy throne on 5-stair dais, in front of arch flanked by columns.

**Wmk. 385**

**1988, July 2 Litho. *Perf. 13½***

| | | | | | |
|---|---|---|---|---|---|
| **1253** | A373 | 2b | shown | 2.00 | .25 |

**Photo.**

**Wmk. 329**

| | | | | | |
|---|---|---|---|---|---|
| **1254** | A374 | 2b | multi, vert. | .60 | .30 |
| **1255** | A374 | 2b | multicolored | .60 | .30 |
| **1256** | A374 | 2b | multicolored | .60 | .30 |
| **1257** | A374 | 2b | multicolored | .60 | .30 |
| **1258** | A374 | 2b | multicolored | .60 | .30 |

**Litho.**

***Perf. 14x14½***

**Wmk. 387**

| | | | | | |
|---|---|---|---|---|---|
| **1259** | A375 | 2b | multicolored | .60 | .30 |
| **1260** | A375 | 2b | multicolored | .60 | .30 |
| **1261** | A375 | 2b | multicolored | .60 | .30 |
| **1262** | A375 | 2b | multicolored | .60 | .30 |
| **1263** | A375 | 2b | multicolored | .60 | .30 |
| **1264** | A375 | 2b | multicolored | .60 | .30 |
| *a.* | | | Souv. sheet of 6, #1259-1264 | 57.50 | 47.50 |
| | | | *Nos. 1253-1264 (12)* | 8.60 | 3.55 |

No. 1264a sold for 25b.

Arbor Year A376

***Perf. 14½x14***

**1988, July 29 Litho. Wmk. 387**

| | | | | | |
|---|---|---|---|---|---|
| **1265** | A376 | 2b | multicolored | .60 | .25 |

Natl. Communications Day — A377

**Wmk. Alternating Interlaced Wavy Lines (340)**

**1988, Aug. 4 *Perf. 13½***

| | | | | | |
|---|---|---|---|---|---|
| **1266** | A377 | 2b | multicolored | .60 | .25 |

Intl. Letter Writing Week — A378

Designs: Coconut leaf sculptures.

***Perf. 14½x14***

**1988, Oct. 9 Wmk. 387**

| | | | | | |
|---|---|---|---|---|---|
| **1267** | A378 | 2b | Grasshopper | .40 | .20 |
| **1268** | A378 | 2b | Fish | .40 | .20 |
| **1269** | A378 | 6b | Bird | 1.10 | .50 |
| **1270** | A378 | 6b | Takro (box) | 1.10 | .50 |
| | | | *Nos. 1267-1270 (4)* | 3.00 | 1.40 |

Housing Development — A379

**Wmk. 233**

**1988, Oct. 24 Litho. *Perf. 14***

| | | | | | |
|---|---|---|---|---|---|
| **1271** | A379 | 2b | multicolored | .60 | .25 |

Traffic Safety — A380

King's Bodyguard, 120th Anniv. — A381

**1988, Nov. 11 Wmk. 329 *Perf. 13½***

| | | | | | |
|---|---|---|---|---|---|
| **1272** | A380 | 2b | multicolored | .60 | .25 |

**1988, Nov. 11 Wmk. 385**

| | | | | | |
|---|---|---|---|---|---|
| **1273** | A381 | 2b | Chulalongkorn | 3.00 | .40 |

New Year — A382

Flowers.

**1988, Dec. 1 Wmk. 387**

| | | | | | |
|---|---|---|---|---|---|
| **1274** | A382 | 1b | Crotalaria sessiliflora | .45 | .30 |
| **1275** | A382 | 1b | Uvaria grandiflora | .45 | .30 |
| **1276** | A382 | 1b | Reinwardtia trigyna | .45 | .30 |
| **1277** | A382 | 1b | Impatiens griffithii | .45 | .30 |
| | | | *Nos. 1274-1277 (4)* | 1.80 | 1.20 |

Thai Royal Orders Type of 1979

Floral background: Nos. 1278-1279, Knight Grand Commander, Order of Rama, 1918. Nos. 1280-1281, Knight Grand Cordon, Order of the White Elephant, 1861. Nos. 1282-1283, Knight Grand Cordon, Order of the Crown of Thailand, 1869. Nos. 1284-1285, Ratana Varabhorn Order of Merit, 1911. Pairs have continuous designs.

**1988, Dec. 5 Wmk. 385**

| | | | | | |
|---|---|---|---|---|---|
| **1278** | A243 | 2b | multicolored | .25 | .20 |
| **1279** | A244 | 2b | multicolored | .25 | .20 |
| *a.* | | | Pair, #1278-1279 | .50 | .40 |
| **1280** | A243 | 3b | multicolored | .50 | .25 |
| **1281** | A244 | 3b | multicolored | .50 | .25 |
| *a.* | | | Pair, #1280-1281 | .50 | .50 |
| **1282** | A243 | 5b | multicolored | 1.00 | .75 |
| **1283** | A244 | 5b | multicolored | .75 | .30 |
| *a.* | | | Pair, #1282-1283 | 1.50 | 1.10 |
| **1284** | A243 | 7b | multicolored | 1.00 | .40 |
| **1285** | A244 | 7b | multicolored | 1.00 | .40 |
| *a.* | | | Pair, #1284-1285 | 2.00 | 1.50 |
| | | | *Nos. 1278-1285 (8)* | 5.25 | 2.75 |

A383

Buddha Monthon Celebrations, Tambol Salaya — A384

***Perf. 14x15, 15x14***

**1988, Dec. 5 Wmk. 233**

| | | | | | |
|---|---|---|---|---|---|
| **1286** | A383 | 2b | Birthplace | .35 | .20 |
| **1287** | A383 | 3b | Enlightenment place | .45 | .25 |
| **1288** | A383 | 4b | Location of 1st sermon | .65 | .45 |
| **1289** | A383 | 5b | Place Buddha achieved nirvana | .85 | .40 |
| **1290** | A384 | 6b | Statue | 1.00 | .50 |
| | | | *Nos. 1286-1290 (5)* | 3.30 | 1.80 |

**Souvenir Sheet**

***Perf. 14½x14***

| | | | | | |
|---|---|---|---|---|---|
| **1291** | A384 | 6b | like No. 1290 | 24.00 | 20.00 |

No. 1291 sold for 15b.

Children's Day — A385

"Touch" paintings by blind youth: No. 1292, *Floating Market,* by Thongbai Siyam. No. 1293, *Flying Bird,* by Kwanchai Kerd-Daeng. No. 1294, *Little Mermaid,* by Chalermpol Jiengmai. No. 1295, *Golden Fish,* by Natetip Korsantirak.

**Wmk. 387**

**1989, Jan. 14 Litho. *Perf. 13½***

| | | | | | |
|---|---|---|---|---|---|
| **1292** | A385 | 2b | multicolored | .45 | .25 |
| **1293** | A385 | 2b | multicolored | .45 | .25 |
| **1294** | A385 | 2b | multicolored | .45 | .25 |
| **1295** | A385 | 2b | multicolored | .45 | .25 |
| | | | *Nos. 1292-1295 (4)* | 1.80 | 1.00 |

Communications Authority of Thailand, 12th Anniv. — A386

**1989, Feb. 25 *Perf. 14½x14***

| | | | | | |
|---|---|---|---|---|---|
| **1296** | A386 | 2b | multicolored | .60 | .25 |

Chulalongkorn University, 72nd Anniv. — A387

Design: 2b, Statue of Chulalongkorn and King Vajiravudh in front of university auditorium.

**1989, Mar. 26**

| | | | | | |
|---|---|---|---|---|---|
| **1297** | A387 | 2b | multicolored | .60 | .25 |

A388

A389

***Perf. 15x14***

**1989, Mar. 31 Litho. Wmk. 233**

| | | | | | |
|---|---|---|---|---|---|
| **1298** | A388 | 2b | shown | .60 | .30 |

**Wmk. 387**

***Perf. 13½***

| | | | | | |
|---|---|---|---|---|---|
| **1299** | A388 | 10b | Emblem | 1.50 | .60 |

Thai Red Cross Society, 96th anniv. (2b); Intl. Red Cross and Red Crescent organizations, 125th annivs. (10b).

***Perf. 14x14½***

**1989, Apr. 2 Wmk. 387**

Phra Nakhon Khiri Historical Park: 2b, Wat Phra Kaeo. 3b, Chatchawan Wiangchai Observatory. 5b, Phra That Chom Phet Stupa. 6b, Wetchayan Wichian Phrasat Throne Hall.

| | | | | | |
|---|---|---|---|---|---|
| **1300** | A389 | 2b | multicolored | .30 | .20 |
| **1301** | A389 | 3b | multicolored | .90 | .40 |
| **1302** | A389 | 5b | multicolored | 1.25 | .90 |
| **1303** | A389 | 6b | multicolored | 1.25 | .90 |
| | | | *Nos. 1300-1303 (4)* | 3.70 | 2.40 |

Natl. Lottery Office, 50th Anniv. — A390

**1989, Apr. 5** *Perf. 13½*
**1304** A390 2b multicolored .50 .25

Seashells — A391

**1989, June 28 Wmk. 329** *Perf. 13½*
**1305** A391 2b Conus thailandis .30 .20
**1306** A391 3b Spondylus princeps .60 .30
**1307** A391 6b Cyprea guttata .95 .75
**1308** A391 10b Nautilus pompilius 3.00 1.50
*Nos. 1305-1308 (4)* 4.85 2.75

Arts and Crafts Year A392

**Wmk. 387**
**1989, June 28 Litho.** *Perf. 13½*
**1309** A392 2b Ceramic figurines .40 .20
**1310** A392 2b Gold niello ginger jar, chicken .40 .20
**1311** A392 6b Textiles 1.10 .50
**1312** A392 6b Gemstone flower ornament 1.10 .50
*Nos. 1309-1312 (4)* 3.00 1.40

Asia-Pacific Telecommunications Organization, 10th Anniv. — A393

APT emblem, map of submarine cable network and satellites of member nations.

**1989, July 1 Wmk. 329** *Perf. 13½*
**1313** A393 9b multicolored 1.00 .50

Phya Anuman Rajadhon (1888-1969), Ethnologist A394

9th Natl. Phil. Exhib., Aug. 4-13 — A395

**1989, July 1 Wmk. 387** *Perf. 13½*
**1314** A394 2b multicolored .50 .20

**1989, Aug. 4 Wmk. 233** *Perf. 15x14*

Various mailboxes.

**1315** A395 2b multicolored .30 .20
**1316** A395 3b multi, diff. .45 .25
**1317** A395 4b multi, diff. .60 .35
**1318** A395 5b multi, diff. .75 .40
**1319** A395 6b multi, diff. .90 .50
*a.* Souv. sheet, #1315-1319, perf 14 35.00 29.00
*Nos. 1315-1319 (5)* 3.00 1.70

No. 1319a sold for 30b.

A396

A398

A397

**Wmk. 387**
**1989, June 26 Litho.** *Perf. 13½*
**1320** A396 2b multicolored .50 .20

Intl. Anti-drug Day.

**1989, Aug. 4 Wmk. 233** *Perf. 14x15*
**1321** A397 2b multicolored .50 .20

Post and Telecommunications School, cent.

**1989, Aug. 4 Wmk. 387** *Perf. 13½*
**1322** A398 2b multicolored .50 .20

Natl. Communications Day.

Dragonflies — A399

**Wmk. 329**
**1989, Oct. 8 Photo.** *Perf. 13½*
**1323** A399 2b shown .40 .20
**1324** A399 5b multi, diff. .75 .50
**1325** A399 6b multi, diff. 1.25 .60
**1326** A399 10b Damselfly 1.60 1.50
*a.* Souv. sheet of 4, #1323-1326 30.00 30.00
*Nos. 1323-1326 (4)* 4.00 2.80

Intl. Letter Writing Week. #1326a sold for 40b.

Transport and Communications Decade for Asia and the Pacific — A400

*Perf. 14½x14*
**1989, Oct. 24 Litho. Wmk. 387**
**1327** A400 2b multicolored .50 .20

Mental Health Care, Cent. — A401

New Year 1990 — A402

**1989, Nov. 1 Wmk. 233** *Perf. 15x14*
**1328** A401 2b multicolored .50 .20

*Perf. 14x14½*
**1989, Nov. 15 Wmk. 387**

Flowering plants.

**1329** A402 1b Hypericum uralum .30 .25
**1330** A402 1b Uraria rufescens .30 .25
**1331** A402 1b Manglietia garrettii .30 .25
**1332** A402 1b Aeschynanthus macranthus .30 .25
*a.* Souv. sheet of 4, #1329-1332 6.00 6.00
*Nos. 1329-1332 (4)* 1.20 1.00

No. 1332a sold for 14b.

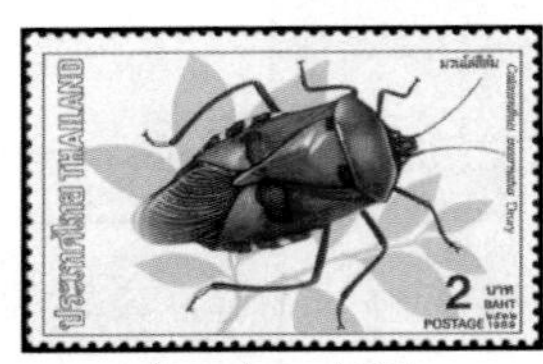

Insects — A403

**Wmk. 329**
**1989, Nov. 15 Photo.** *Perf. 13½*
**1333** A403 2b Catacanthus incarnatus .40 .20
**1334** A403 3b Aristobia approximator .60 .30
**1335** A403 6b Chrysochroa chinensis .90 .50
**1336** A403 10b Enoplotrupes sharpi 1.60 1.25
*Nos. 1333-1336 (4)* 3.50 2.25

Population and Housing Census of 1990 — A404

**Wmk. 387**
**1990, Jan. 1 Litho.** *Perf. 13½*
**1337** A404 2b multicolored .50 .20

Children's Day A405

Emblems A406

*Perf. 15x14*
**1990, Jan. 13 Wmk. 233**
**1338** A405 2b Jumping rope, horiz. .45 .20
**1339** A405 2b Sports .45 .20

**1990, Mar. 29 Wmk. 387** *Perf. 13½*
**1340** A406 2b multicolored .50 .20

WHO Fight AIDS Worldwide campaign and the Natl. Red Cross Soc.

Thai Heritage Conservation Day — A407

Prize-winning inlaid mother-of-pearl containers: No. 1341, Tiap (footed bowl with lid), vert. No. 1342, Phan waenfa (two-tiered vessel), vert. No. 1343, Lung (lidded bowl). No. 1344, Chiat klom (spade-shaped lidded container signifying noble rank).

**1990, Apr. 2 Photo. Wmk. 329**
**1341** A407 2b multicolored .40 .20
**1342** A407 2b multicolored .40 .20
**1343** A407 8b multicolored 1.10 .90
**1344** A407 8b multicolored 1.10 .90
*Nos. 1341-1344 (4)* 3.00 2.20

A408

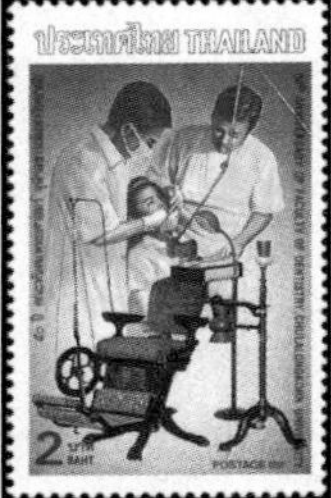

A409

Minerals.

*Perf. 14x14½*
**1990, June 29 Litho. Wmk. 387**
**1345** A408 2b Tin .45 .25
**1346** A408 3b Zinc .70 .40
**1347** A408 5b Lead .85 .60
**1348** A408 6b Fluorite 1.00 .80
*a.* Souv. sheet of 4, #1345-1348 6.25 6.25
*Nos. 1345-1348 (4)* 3.00 2.05

No. 1348a sold for 30b, exists imperf.

**1990, May 16**
**1349** A409 2b multicolored .50 .20

Faculty of Dentistry, Chulalongkorn Univ., 50th anniv.

Communications Day — A410

**1990, Aug. 4** ***Perf. 14½x14***
**1350** A410 2b multicolored .50 .20

Asian-Pacific Postal Training Center, 20th Anniv. — A411

**1990, Sept. 10**
**1351** A411 2b multicolored .35 .20
**1352** A411 8b multicolored .90 .65

Rotary Intl. in Thailand, 60th Anniv. — A412

**1990, Sept. 16** ***Perf. 13½***
**1353** A412 2b Health care .45 .25
**1354** A412 3b Immunizations .60 .30
**1355** A412 6b Literacy project .90 .55
**1356** A412 8b Thai museum project 1.50 1.00
*Nos. 1353-1356 (4)* 3.45 2.10

Intl. Letter Writing Week, 1990 — A413

Illustration reduced.

**1990, Oct. 7** ***Perf. 14***
**1357** A413 2b multicolored .45 .25
**1358** A413 3b multi, diff. .70 .40
**1359** A413 5b multi, diff. .85 .60
**1360** A413 6b multi, diff. 1.00 .80
*a.* Souv. sheet of 4, #1357-1360 6.25 6.25
*Nos. 1357-1360 (4)* 3.00 2.05

No. 1360a sold for 30b. Exists imperf, value same as perf.

Dept. of Comptroller-General, Cent. — A414

**1990, Oct. 7** ***Perf. 14½x14***
**1361** A414 2b multicolored .50 .20

A415 A416

**1990, Oct. 21** ***Perf. 14x14½***
**1362** A415 2b multicolored 1.75 .25

Princess Mother, 90th birthday.

**1990, Nov. 15 Wmk. 233** ***Perf. 14½***

Flowers: No. 1363, Cyrtandromoea grandiflora. No. 1364, Rhododendron arboreum. No. 1365, Merremia vitifolia. No. 1366, Afgekia mahidolae.

**1363** A416 1b multicolored .30 .25
**1364** A416 1b multicolored .30 .25
**1365** A416 1b multicolored .30 .25
**1366** A416 1b multicolored .30 .25
*a.* Sheet of 4, #1363-1366 3.75 3.75
*Nos. 1363-1366 (4)* 1.20 1.00

New Year 1991. No. 1366a sold for 10b. Exists imperf, value same as perf.
See Nos. 1417-1420.

Wiman Mek Royal Hall — A417

Royal Throne Rooms in the Dusit Palace: 3b, Ratcharit Rungrot Royal House. 4b, Aphisek Dusit Royal Hall. 5b, Amphon Sathan Palace. 6b, Udon Phak Royal Hall. 8b, Anantasamakhom Throne Hall.

**Wmk. 329**
**1990, Dec. 5 Photo.** ***Perf. 13½***
**1367** A417 2b multicolored .30 .20
**1368** A417 3b multicolored .65 .25
**1369** A417 4b multicolored .65 .40
**1370** A417 5b multicolored .75 .50
**1371** A417 6b multicolored .95 .50
**1372** A417 8b multicolored 1.10 .75
*Nos. 1367-1372 (6)* 4.40 2.60

Somdet Phra Maha Samanachao Kromphra Paramanuchitchinorot (1790-1853), Supreme Patriarch — A418

**1990, Dec. 11 Wmk. 387** ***Perf. 13½***
**1373** A418 2b multicolored .50 .20

Petroleum Authority, 12th Anniv. — A419

***Perf. 14½x14***
**1990, Dec. 29 Litho. Wmk. 387**
**1374** A419 2b multicolored .50 .20

Locomotives — A420

Designs: 2b, No. 6, Krauss & Co., Germany, 1908. 3b, No. 32, Kyosan Kogyo, Japan, 1949. 5b, No. 715, C56, Japan, 1946. 6b, No. 953, Mikado, Japan, 1949-1951.

***Perf. 14½x14***
**1990, Dec. 29 Litho. Wmk. 387**
**1375** A420 2b multicolored .35 .25
**1376** A420 3b multicolored .70 .35
**1377** A420 5b multicolored 1.00 1.00
**1378** A420 6b multicolored 1.40 1.10
*a.* Souv. sheet of 4, #1375-1378 7.50 7.50
*Nos. 1375-1378 (4)* 3.45 2.70

No. 1378a sold for 25b. Exists imperf, value same as perf.

Children's Day — A421

Children's games: 2b, Tops. 5b, Race. 6b, Blind-man's buff.

**1991, Jan. 12**
**1379** A421 2b multicolored .35 .25
**1380** A421 3b shown .35 .30
**1381** A421 5b multicolored .70 .40
**1382** A421 6b multicolored 1.10 .50
*Nos. 1379-1382 (4)* 2.50 1.45

A422

A423

**1991, Feb. 17** ***Perf. 14x14½***
**1383** A422 2b multicolored .50 .20

Land titling project.

***Perf. 14x14½***
**1991, Mar. 30 Litho. Wmk. 387**
**1384** A423 2b Princess Maha 1.00 .20
*a.* Souvenir sheet of 1 5.00 5.00

Red Cross. No. 1384a sold for 8b. Exists imperf, value same as perf.

Cultural Heritage A424

Floral decorations: 2b, Indra's heavenly abode. 3b, Celestial couch. 4b, Crystal ladder. 5b, Crocodile.

**Wmk. 329**
**1991, Apr. 2 Photo.** ***Perf. 13½***
**1385** A424 2b multicolored .40 .25
**1386** A424 3b multicolored .50 .30
**1387** A424 4b multicolored .75 .50
**1388** A424 5b multicolored .85 .60
*a.* Souv. sheet of 4, #1385-1388 6.25 6.25
*Nos. 1385-1388 (4)* 2.50 1.65

No. 1388a sold for 30b. Exists imperf, value same as perf.

Songkran Day — A425

***Perf. 14x14½***
**1991, Apr. 13 Wmk. 387 Litho.**
**1389** A425 2b Demon on sheep 2.50 1.00
*a.* Souvenir sheet of 1 10.00 10.00

No. 1389a sold for 8b. Exists imperf, value same as perf.
See #1467, 1530, 1566, 1606, 1662, 1724, 1801, 1869, 1940.

Prince Narisranuvattivongs (1863-1947) — A426

**1991, Apr. 28** ***Perf. 14½x14***
**1390** A426 2b brown & yellow .50 .25

Mosaics — A427

Various lotus flowers.

**1991, May 28** ***Perf. 13½***
**1391** A427 2b multi, vert. .30 .20
**1392** A427 3b multi, vert. .40 .25
**1393** A427 5b multi .65 .45
**1394** A427 6b multi .80 .55
*Nos. 1391-1394 (4)* 2.15 1.45

Natl. Communications Day — A428

**Wmk. 387**
**1991, Aug. 4 Litho.** ***Perf. 13½***
**1395** A428 2b multicolored .60 .25

Thaipex '91, Natl. Philatelic Exhibition A429

Various fabric designs.

**1991, Aug. 4** *Perf. 14x14½*

**1396** A429 2b multicolored .45 .25
**1397** A429 4b multicolored .70 .35
**1398** A429 6b multicolored .85 .50
**1399** A429 8b multicolored 1.00 .90
*a.* Souv. sheet of 4, #1396-1399 6.00 6.00
*Nos. 1396-1399 (4)* 3.00 2.00

No. 1399a sold for 30b. Exists imperf, value $24. No. 1399a overprinted with Philanippon emblem in lower left corner of margin sold for 200b. Value, $190.

Intl. Productivity Congress — A430

*Perf. 14½x14*

**1991, Sept. 3** **Litho.** **Wmk. 387**

**1400** A430 2b multicolored .50 .25

26th Intl. Council of Women Triennial — A431

**Wmk. 387**

**1991, Sept. 23** **Litho.** *Perf. 13½*

**1401** A431 2b multicolored .50 .25

Bantam Chickens — A432

**Wmk. 329**

**1991, Oct. 6** **Photo.** *Perf. 13½*

**1402** A432 2b Black bantams .35 .25
**1403** A432 3b Black-tailed buff bantams .65 .30
**1404** A432 6b Fancy bantams 1.00 .45
**1405** A432 8b White bantams 1.25 1.00
*a.* Souv. sheet of 4, #1402-1405 7.50 7.50
*Nos. 1402-1405 (4)* 3.25 2.00

No. 1405a sold for 35b. Exists imperf, value same as perf.

Intl. Letter Writing Week.

World Bank/Intl. Monetary Fund Annual Meetings — A433

Temples, meeting emblem and: 2b, Silver coin of King Rama IV. 4b, Pod Duang money. 8b, Chieng and Hoi money. 10b, Funan, Dvaravati and Srivijaya money.

*Perf. 14½x14*

**1991, Oct. 15** **Litho.** **Wmk. 387**

**1406** A433 2b multicolored .20 .20
**1407** A433 4b multicolored .45 .30
**1408** A433 8b multicolored .90 .60
**1409** A433 10b multicolored 1.10 .75
*a.* Souv. sheet of 4, #1406-1409 6.25 6.25
*Nos. 1406-1409 (4)* 2.65 1.85

No. 1409a sold for 35b. Exists imperf, value same as perf.

1993 World Philatelic Exhibition, Bangkok — A434

**1991, Oct. 23** *Perf. 14x14½*

**1410** A434 2b No. 118 .20 .20
**1411** A434 3b No. 119 .30 .20
**1412** A434 4b No. 120 .40 .30
**1413** A434 5b No. 121 .55 .40
**1414** A434 6b No. 122 .65 .45
**1415** A434 7b No. 123 .75 .50
**1416** A434 8b No. 124 .85 .60
*a.* Souvenir sheet of 1 5.00 5.00
*Nos. 1410-1416 (7)* 3.70 2.65

No. 1416a sold for 15b. Exists imperf, value same as perf.

Flower Type of 1990

**1991, Nov. 5** *Perf. 13½*

**1417** A416 1b Dillenia obovata .20 .20
**1418** A416 1b Melastoma sanguineum .20 .20
**1419** A416 1b Commelina diffusa .20 .20
**1420** A416 1b Plumbago indica .20 .20
*a.* Souv. sheet of 4, #1417-1420 3.00 3.00
*Nos. 1417-1420 (4)* .80 .80

No. 1420a sold for 10b. Exists imperf, value same as perf.

Asian Elephants — A435

**Wmk. 329**

**1991, Nov. 5** **Photo.** *Perf. 13½*

**1421** A435 2b shown .30 .20
**1422** A435 4b Pulling logs .55 .30
**1423** A435 6b Lying down .80 .45
**1424** A435 8b In river 1.10 .60
*a.* Souvenir sheet of 1, litho. 7.50 7.50
*Nos. 1421-1424 (4)* 2.75 1.55

No. 1424a sold for 22b and stamp does not have border. No. 1424a exists imperf, value same as perf.

Wild Animals — A436

*Perf. 14½x14*

**1991, Dec. 26** **Wmk. 387** **Litho.**

**1425** A436 2b Viverra zibetha .25 .20
**1426** A436 3b Prionodon linsang .40 .25
**1427** A436 6b Felis temmincki .80 .50
**1428** A436 8b Ratufa bicolor 1.10 .65
*a.* Sheet of 4, #1425-1428 6.25 6.25
*Nos. 1425-1428 (4)* 2.55 1.60

No. 1428a sold for 30b. Exists imperf, value same as perf.

Prince Mahidol of Songkla (1891-1929), Medical Pioneer — A437

**1992, Jan. 1** *Perf. 14x14½*

**1429** A437 2b multicolored .35 .25

Department of Mineral Resources, Cent. — A438

No. 1430, Locating fossils. No. 1431, Mining excavation. No. 1432, Drilling for natural gas and petroleum. No. 1433, Digging artesian wells.

*Perf. 14½x14*

**1992, Jan. 1** **Litho.** **Wmk. 387**

**1430** A438 2b multicolored .35 .20
**1431** A438 2b multicolored .35 .20
**1432** A438 2b multicolored .35 .20
**1433** A438 2b multicolored .35 .20
*Nos. 1430-1433 (4)* 1.40 .80

Children's Day — A439

Children's drawings on "World Under the Sea": 2b, Divers, fish. 3b, Fish, sea grass. 5b, Mermaid.

**1992, Jan. 11** **Wmk. 329** *Perf. 13½*

**1434** A439 2b multicolored .30 .20
**1435** A439 3b multicolored .40 .30
**1436** A439 5b multicolored, vert. .65 .50
*Nos. 1434-1436 (3)* 1.35 1.00

Duel on Elephants, 400th Anniv. — A440

*Perf. 14½x14*

**1992, Jan. 18** **Litho.** **Wmk. 387**

**1437** A440 2b multicolored .50 .20

Orchids (Paphiopedilum) — A441

**1992, Jan. 20**

**1438** A441 2b Bellatulum .25 .20
**1439** A441 2b Exul .25 .20
**1440** A441 3b Concolor .35 .30
**1441** A441 3b Godefroyae .35 .30
**1442** A441 6b Niveum .70 .55
**1443** A441 6b Villosum .70 .55
**1444** A441 10b Parishii 1.25 .90
*a.* Souv. sheet of 4, #1438, 1440, 1442, 1444 5.00 5.00
**1445** A441 10b Sukhakulii 1.25 .90
*a.* Souv. sheet of 4, #1439, 1441, 1443, 1445 5.00 5.00
*Nos. 1438-1445 (8)* 5.10 3.90

Fourth Asia Pacific Orchid Conference.

Nos. 1444a-1445a each sold for 30b. Each exists imperf, value same as perf.

21st Intl. Society of Sugar Cane Technologists Conf. — A442

**1992, Mar. 5** *Perf. 14x14½*

**1446** A442 2b multicolored .50 .25

Intl. Red Cross A443

*Perf. 14½x14*

**1992, Mar.** **Litho.** **Wmk. 387**

**1447** A443 2b multicolored .50 .20

Ministry of Justice, Cent. — A444

Designs: 3b, Prince Rabi Badhanasakdi of Ratchaburi, founder of Thailand's School of Law. 5b, King Rama V, reformer of court system.

**1992, Mar. 25** *Perf. 13½*

**1448** A444 3b multicolored .40 .30
**1449** A444 5b multicolored .60 .40

Ministry of Agriculture and Cooperatives, Cent. — A445

**1992, Apr. 1** *Perf. 14½x14*

**1450** A445 2b gray & multi .25 .20
**1451** A445 3b lil & multi .40 .30
**1452** A445 4b pink & multi .45 .35
**1453** A445 5b gray bl & multi .60 .40
*Nos. 1450-1453 (4)* 1.70 1.25

A446

A447

Ministry of Interior, Cent.: No. 1454, Prince Damrong Rajanubharb, first Minister of the Interior. No. 1455, People voting. No. 1456, Police and fire protection. No. 1457, Water and electricity provided to remote areas.

**1992, Apr. 1** *Perf. 14x14½*

**1454** A446 2b multicolored .35 .20
**1455** A446 2b multicolored .35 .20
**1456** A446 2b multicolored .35 .20
**1457** A446 2b multicolored .35 .20
*Nos. 1454-1457 (4)* 1.40 .80

**1992, Apr. 1**

**1458** A447 2b Ships, truck .25 .20
**1459** A447 3b Truck, bus, train .40 .30
**1460** A447 5b Airplanes .60 .40
**1461** A447 6b Truck, satellites .75 .50
*Nos. 1458-1461 (4)* 2.00 1.40

Ministry of Transport and Communications, 80th anniv.

Ministry of Education, Cent. — A448

*Perf. 14x14½*

**1992, Apr. 1 Litho. Wmk. 387**

**1462** A448 2b multicolored .30 .20

Carts A449

**1992, Apr. 2** *Perf. 14½x14*

**1463** A449 2b West .25 .20
**1464** A449 3b North .35 .25
**1465** A449 5b Northeast .55 .40
**1466** A449 10b East 1.10 .90
*a.* Souv. sheet of 4, #1463-1466 4.50
*Nos. 1463-1466 (4)* 2.25 1.75

Heritage Conservation Day. No. 1466a sold for 30b and exists imperf without sheet price in margin.

Songkran Day Type of 1991

**1992, Apr. 13** *Perf. 14x14½*

**1467** A425 2b Demon on monkey, zodiac .60 .25
*a.* Souvenir sheet of 1 3.75

No. 1467a sold for 8b and exists imperf. with sale price in different colors.

Department of Livestock Development, 50th Anniv. — A451

*Perf. 14½x14*

**1992, May 5 Litho. Wmk. 387**

**1468** A451 2b multicolored .30 .20

Wisakhabucha Day — A452

Scenes from Buddha's life: 2b, Birth. 3b, Enlightenment. 5b, Death.

**Wmk. 387**

**1992, May 16 Litho.** *Perf. 14½*

**1469** A452 2b multicolored .30 .20
**1470** A452 3b multicolored .35 .25
**1471** A452 5b multicolored .60 .40
*Nos. 1469-1471 (3)* 1.25 .85

Meteorological Department, 50th Anniv. — A453

**1992, June 23** *Perf. 14x14½*

**1472** A453 2b multicolored .30 .20

1993 World Philatelic Exhibition, Bangkok — A454

Visit ASEAN Year — A455

*Perf. 14x14½*

**1992, July 1 Litho. Wmk. 387**

**1473** A454 2b No. 18 .25 .20
**1474** A454 3b No. 156 .35 .25
**1475** A454 5b No. 222 .55 .40
**1476** A454 7b No. 255 .85 .50
**1477** A454 8b No. 273 1.00 .65
*a.* Souv. sheet of 5, #1473-1477 + label 6.00 6.00
*Nos. 1473-1477 (5)* 3.00 2.00

No. 1477a sold for 35b. Exists imperf. with sheet price in blue, value same as #1477a.

**1992, July 1**

Designs: 2b, Bua Tong field, Mae Hong Son Province. 3b, Klong Larn Waterfall, Kamphaeng Phet Province. 4b, Coral, Chumphon Province. 5b, Khao Ta-Poo, Phangnga Province.

**1478** A455 2b multicolored .30 .20
**1479** A455 3b multicolored .40 .25
**1480** A455 4b multicolored .50 .35
**1481** A455 5b multicolored .60 .40
*Nos. 1478-1481 (4)* 1.80 1.20

Prince Chudadhuj Dharadilok of Bejraburna (1892-1923) A456

**Wmk. 368**

**1992, July 5 Litho.** *Perf. 13½*

**1482** A456 2b multicolored .30 .20

Natl. Communications Day — A457

*Perf. 14½x14*

**1992, Aug. 4 Litho. Wmk. 387**

**1483** A457 2b multicolored .30 .20

ASEAN, 25th Anniv. — A458

Flags and: 2b, Cultures and sports. 3b, Tourist attractions. 5b, Transportation, communications. 7b, Agriculture.

**1992, Aug. 8 Wmk. 368** *Perf. 13½*

**1484** A458 2b multicolored .25 .20
**1485** A458 3b multicolored .35 .25
**1486** A458 5b multicolored .55 .40
**1487** A458 7b multicolored .85 .55
*Nos. 1484-1487 (4)* 2.00 1.40

Queen Sirikit, 60th Birthday — A459

#1488, Wedding, with King, Queen being anointed. #1489, Coronation, King and Queen on throne. #1490, Being crowned, Queen with crown, being anointed. #1491, Formal portrait, Queen seated. #1492, Visiting wounded. #1493, Visiting public.

**Wmk. 329**

**1992, Aug. 12 Photo.** *Perf. 13½*

**1488** A459 2b multicolored .30 .20
**1489** A459 2b multicolored .30 .20
**1490** A459 2b multicolored .30 .20
**1491** A459 2b multicolored .30 .20
**1492** A459 2b multicolored .30 .20
**1493** A459 2b multicolored .30 .20
*a.* Souv. sheet of 6, #1488-1493 3.75
*Nos. 1488-1493 (6)* 1.80 1.20

No. 1493a sold for 30b and exists imperf. with sale price in different colors.

Royal Regalia of Queen Sirikit — A460

No. 1494, Tray. No. 1495, Kettle. No. 1496, Bowl. No. 1497, Box. No. 1498, Covered dish.

**1992, Aug. 12**

**Background Colors**

**1494** A460 2b dark blue .25 .20
**1495** A460 2b violet .25 .20
**1496** A460 2b yellow green .25 .20
**1497** A460 2b Prussian blue .25 .20
**1498** A460 2b dark green .25 .20
*Nos. 1494-1498 (5)* 1.25 1.00

Opening of Sirikit Medical Center — A461

*Perf. 14½x14*

**1992, Aug. 12 Litho. Wmk. 387**

**1499** A461 2b multicolored .30 .20

Queen Sirikit, 60th Birthday — A462

**Litho. & Embossed**

**1992, Aug. 12** *Perf. 13½*

**1500** A462 100b blue & gold 10.00 10.00

No. 1500 printed in sheets of 10.

A463

A464

**Wmk. 387**

**1992, Aug. 25 Litho.** ***Perf. 13½***
**1501** A463 2b multicolored .25 .20

Prince Wan Waithayakon Krommun Naradhip Bongsprabandh (1891-1976).

**1992, Sept. 15** ***Perf. 14x14½***
**1502** A464 2b multicolored .30 .20

Professor Silpa Bhirasri, Sculptor, cent. of birth.

Coral A465

***Perf. 14½x14***

**1992, Oct. 4 Litho. Wmk. 387**
**1503** A465 2b Cataláphyllia jardinei .25 .20
**1504** A465 3b Porites lutea .30 .25
**1505** A465 6b Tubastraea coccinea .65 .50
**1506** A465 8b Favia pallida .90 .70
*a.* Souv. sheet of 4, #1503-1506 5.25
*Nos. 1503-1506 (4)* 2.10 1.65

Intl. Letter Writing Week. No. 1506a sold for for 30b.

New Year 1993 — A466

Flowers: No. 1507, Rhododendron simsii. No. 1508, Cynoglossum lanceolatum. No. 1509, Tithonia diversifolia. No. 1510, Agapetes parishii.

***Perf. 14x13½***

**1992, Nov. 15 Wmk. 368 Litho.**
**1507** A466 1b multicolored .20 .20
**1508** A466 1b multicolored .20 .20
**1509** A466 1b multicolored .20 .20
**1510** A466 1b multicolored .20 .20
*a.* Souv. sheet of 4, #1507-1510 3.00
*Nos. 1507-1510 (4)* .80 .80

Nos. 1510a sold for 10b. Exists imperf. with sheet price in green.

1st Asian Congress of Allergies and Immunology A467

**1992, Nov. 22** ***Perf. 13½***
**1511** A467 2b black, red & yellow .30 .20

Natl. Assembly, 60th Anniv. — A468

**Wmk. 387**

**1992, Dec. 10 Litho.** ***Perf. 13½***
**1512** A468 2b multicolored .30 .20

Bank of Thailand, 50th Anniv. — A469

**1992, Dec. 10** ***Perf. 14½x14***
**1513** A469 2b multicolored .30 .20

Children's Day — A470

Children's drawings: No. 1514, River scene. No. 1515, Wild animals, forest. No. 1516, Trains, planes, monorail.

**1993, Jan. 9 Wmk. 368** ***Perf. 13½***
**1514** A470 2b multicolored .25 .20
**1515** A470 2b multicolored .25 .20
**1516** A470 2b multicolored .25 .20
*Nos. 1514-1516 (3)* .75 .60

Pottery — A471

Designs: 3b, Jug with bird's neck spout, two bottles. 6b, Pear-shaped vase, two jars. 7b, Three bowls. 8b, Three jars.

**1993, Jan. 9 Photo. Wmk. 329**
**1517** A471 3b multicolored .35 .25
**1518** A471 6b multicolored .70 .50
**1519** A471 7b multicolored .80 .55
**1520** A471 8b multicolored .95 .70
*a.* Souv. sheet of 4, #1517-1520 4.00
*Nos. 1517-1520 (4)* 2.80 2.00

1993 World Philatelic Exhibition, Bangkok. No. 1520a sold for 35b.

Thai Teachers' Training Institute, Cent. — A472

***Perf. 13½x14***

**1993, Jan. 16 Litho. Wmk. 368**
**1521** A472 2b multicolored .30 .25

Kasetsart University, 50th Anniv. — A473

**1993, Feb. 2 Wmk. 329** ***Perf. 13½***
**1522** A473 2b multicolored .30 .25

Maghapuja Day — A474

**Wmk. 387**

**1993, Mar. 7 Litho.** ***Perf. 14½***
**1523** A474 2b multicolored .30 .20

Queen Sri Bajarindra A475

**1993, Mar. 27** ***Perf. 14x14½***
**1524** A475 2b multicolored .30 .20

Thai Red Cross, cent.

Office of Attorney General, Cent. — A476

**1993, Apr. 1 Wmk. 368** ***Perf. 12½***
**1525** A476 2b multicolored .30 .20

Heritage Conservation Day — A477

Historical landmarks, Si Satchanalai Park: 3b, Wat Chedi Chet Thaeo. 4b, Wat Chang Lom. 6b, Wat Phra Si Rattanamahathat (Chaliang). 7b, Wat Suan Kaeo Utthayan Noi.

**Wmk. 368**

**1993, Apr. 2 Litho.** ***Perf. 13½***
**1526** A477 3b multicolored .30 .25
**1527** A477 4b multicolored .45 .30
**1528** A477 6b multicolored .65 .50
**1529** A477 7b multicolored .75 .55
*a.* Souv. sheet of 4, #1526-1529 4.00
*Nos. 1526-1529 (4)* 2.15 1.60

No. 1529a sold for 25b.

See Nos. 1561-1564, 1650-1653, 1797-1800.

Songkran Day Type of 1991

***Perf. 14x14½***

**1993 Litho. Wmk. 387**
**1530** A425 2b Demon on rooster's back, zodiac .40 .20
*a.* Souvenir sheet of 1 2.50
*b.* #1530a ovptd. in gold 7.75

No. 1530b overprinted on sheet margin in both Thai and Chinese for Chinpex '93.

Nos. 1530a-1530b sold for 8b and exist imperf. with sale price in different colors.

Issued: #1530, 1530a, Apr. 13.

Mushrooms — A478

**Wmk. 368**

**1993, July 1 Litho.** ***Perf. 13½***
**1531** A478 2b Marasmius .25 .20
**1532** A478 4b Coprinus .50 .30
**1533** A478 6b Mycena .70 .45
**1534** A478 8b Cyathus .90 .60
*a.* Souv. sheet of 4, #1531-1534 4.25
*Nos. 1531-1534 (4)* 2.35 1.55

No. 1534a sold for 30b.

Natl. Communications Day — A479

**1993, Aug. 4 Wmk. 387** ***Perf. 13½***
**1535** A479 2b multicolored .30 .20

Post and Telegraph Department, 110th Anniv. — A480

**Wmk. 387**

**1993, Aug. 4 Litho.** ***Perf. 13½***
**1536** A480 2b multicolored .30 .20

Queen Suriyothai's Monument — A481

**1993, Aug. 12**
**1537** A481 2b multicolored .30 .25

Fruit — A482

**Wmk. 368**

**1993, Oct. 1 Photo.** ***Perf. 13½***
**1538** A482 2b Citrus reticulata .25 .20
**1539** A482 3b Musa sp. .40 .25
**1540** A482 6b Phyllanthus distichus .75 .45
**1541** A482 8b Bouea burmanica 1.00 .60
*Nos. 1538-1541 (4)* 2.40 1.50

Thai Ridgeback Dogs — A483

Various dogs.

**1993, Oct. 1**

**1542** A483 2b multicolored .20 .20
**1543** A483 3b multicolored .30 .20
**1544** A483 5b multicolored .50 .40
**1545** A483 10b multicolored 1.00 .75
*a.* Souv. sheet of 4, #1542-1545 3.75
*Nos. 1542-1545 (4)* 2.00 1.55

Intl. Letter Writing Week. No. 1545a sold for 30b.

5th Conference & Exhibition of ASEAN Council on Petroleum (ASCOPE) — A484

**Wmk. 387**

**1993, Nov. 2 Litho.** ***Perf. 13½***

**1546** A484 2b multicolored .30 .20

King Rama VII (1893-1941) A485

**1993, Nov. 8** ***Perf. 14x14½***

**1547** A485 2b multicolored .30 .20

No. 655 Surcharged

**1993 Photo. Wmk. 233** ***Perf. 14½***

**1548** A161 1b on 25s brown red *.50* .20

Bencharong and Lai Nam Thong Wares — A486

Designs: 3b, Bencharong cosmetic jar, divinity design. 5b, Bencharong cosmetic jar, gold knob. 6b, Lai Nam Thong cosmetic jar, floral design. 7b, Lai Nam Thong cosmetic jar, floral design, diff.

**Wmk. 368**

**1993, Oct. 1 Photo.** ***Perf. 13½***

**1549** A486 3b multicolored .30 .20
**1550** A486 5b multicolored .55 .40
**1551** A486 6b multicolored .65 .45
**1552** A486 7b multicolored .75 .55
*a.* Souv. sheet of 4, #1549-1552 4.00
*Nos. 1549-1552 (4)* 2.25 1.60

Bangkok '93. No. 1552a sold for 30b.
No. 1552a exists imperf.

New Year 1994 — A487

***Perf. 14½x14***

**1993, Nov. 15 Litho. Wmk. 387**

**1553** A487 1b Ipomoea cairica .20 .20
**1554** A487 1b Decaschistia parviflora .20 .20
**1555** A487 1b Hibiscus tiliaceus .20 .20
**1556** A487 1b Passiflora foetida .20 .20
*a.* Souv. sheet of 4, #1553-1556 1.25
*Nos. 1553-1556 (4)* .80 .80

No. 1556a sold for 10b.

THAICOM, Natl. Satellite Project — A488

**1993, Dec. 1** ***Perf. 14x14½***

**1557** A488 2b multicolored .30 .20

Children's Day — A489

**1994, Jan. 8** ***Perf. 14½x14***

**1558** A489 2b Play land .25 .20

Administrative Building, Chulalongkorn Hospital, 80th Anniv. — A490

***Perf. 14½x14***

**1994, Mar. 30 Litho. Wmk. 387**

**1559** A490 2b multicolored .25 .20

Thai Red Cross.

Royal Institute, 60th Anniv. — A491

**1994, Mar. 31** ***Perf. 14x14½***

**1560** A491 2b multicolored .25 .20

Heritage Conservation Day Type of 1993

Historical landmarks, Phra Nakhon Si Ayutthaya Park: 2b, Wat Ratchaburana. 3b, Wat Maha That. 6b, Wat Maheyong. 9b, Wat Phra Si Samphet.

**1994, Apr. 2** ***Perf. 14½x14***

**1561** A477 2b multicolored .20 .20
**1562** A477 3b multicolored .35 .25
**1563** A477 6b multicolored .65 .50
**1564** A477 9b multicolored 1.25 .95
*a.* Souv. sheet of 4, #1561-1564 2.50
*Nos. 1561-1564 (4)* 2.45 1.90

No. 1564a sold for 25b.

Opening of Friendship Bridge, Thailand-Laos — A492

**1994, Apr. 8**

**1565** A492 9b multicolored 1.00 .75

Songkran Day Type of 1991

**1994, Apr. 13 Litho.**

**1566** A425 2b Demon on dog's back, zodiac .25 .20
*a.* Souvenir sheet of 1 1.00
*b.* As "a," inscribed in margin .25

No. 1566a sold for 8b and exists imperf with frame around stamp and sale price in different color.

Sheet margin of No. 1566b has no value inscription and is overprinted in violet with Thai and Chinese inscriptions for Beijing Stamp Exhibition. Issued: May 1994. No. 1566b also exists imperf.

Intl. Olympic Committee, Cent. — A493

**Wmk. 387**

**1994, June 23 Litho.** ***Perf. 14***

**1567** A493 2b Soccer .20 .20
**1568** A493 3b Running .30 .20
**1569** A493 5b Swimming .50 .40
**1570** A493 6b Weight lifting .60 .45
**1571** A493 9b Boxing .90 .75
*Nos. 1567-1571 (5)* 2.50 2.00

Thammasat University, 60th Anniv. — A494

**Wmk. 387**

**1994, June 27 Litho.** ***Perf. 14***

**1572** A494 2b multicolored .20 .20

Asalhapuja Day — A495

**1994, July 22 Wmk. 329** ***Perf. 13½***

**1573** A495 2b multicolored .20 .20

Natl. Communications Day — A496

**1994, Aug. 4 Wmk. 368**

**1574** A496 2b multicolored .20 .20

Crabs A497

3b, Phricotelphusa limula. 5b, Thaipotamon chulabhorn. 6b, Phricotelphusa sirindhorn. 10b, Thaiphusa sirikit.

**Wmk. 340 (340)**

**1994, Aug. 12 Photo.** ***Perf. 13½x13***

**1575** A497 3b multicolored .30 .20
**1576** A497 5b multicolored .50 .40
**1577** A497 6b multicolored .60 .45
**1578** A497 10b multicolored 1.00 .75
*a.* Souv. sheet of 4, #1575-1578 3.00
*b.* As "a," inscribed in margin 3.00
*Nos. 1575-1578 (4)* 2.40 1.80

No. 1578b has PHILAKOREA '94 Exhibition emblem added to sheet margin.

Intl. Letter Writing Week — A498

Winning paintings in design contest: 2b, Gold niello bowls, octagonal footed tray. 6b, Pumpkin shaped bowls. 8b, Silver niello betel-nut set. 9b, Covered square bowl with gold finial, small lotus-shaped footed tray.

**Wmk. 368**

**1994, Oct. 9 Photo.** ***Perf. 13½***

**1579** A498 2b multicolored .20 .20
Complete booklet, 5 #1579 .80
**1580** A498 6b multicolored .50 .35
**1581** A498 8b multicolored .60 .50
**1582** A498 9b multicolored .70 .55
*a.* Souv. sheet of 4, #1579-1582 2.50
*Nos. 1579-1582 (4)* 2.00 1.60

No. 1582a sold for 30b.

ILO, 75th Anniv. A499

***Perf. 15x14***

**1994, Oct. 29 Litho. Wmk. 387**

**1583** A499 2b multicolored .20 .20
Complete booklet, 5 #1583 1.25

New Year 1995 — A500

Herbs: No. 1584, Utricularia delphinioides. No. 1585, Utricularia minutissima. No. 1586, Eriocaulon odoratum. No. 1587, Utricularia bifida.

**1994, Nov. 15** ***Perf. 14x14½***

**1584** A500 1b multicolored .20 .20
**1585** A500 1b multicolored .20 .20
**1586** A500 1b multicolored .20 .20
**1587** A500 1b multicolored .20 .20
*a.* Souv. sheet of 4, #1584-1587 1.00
*Nos. 1584-1587 (4)* .80 .80

No. 1587a sold for 10b.

Suan Dusit Teachers College, 60th Anniv. — A501

*Perf. 14½x14*

**1994, Dec. 4 Litho. Wmk. 387**

**1588** A501 2b multicolored .20 .20
Complete booklet, 5 #1588 1.25

Council of State, 120th Anniv. — A502

**1994, Dec. 5 Wmk. 368 *Perf. 13½***

**1589** A502 2b multicolored .20 .20
Complete booklet, 5 #1589 1.25

ICAO, 50th Anniv. A503

*Perf. 14½x14*

**1994, Dec. 7 Wmk. 387**

**1590** A503 2b multicolored .20 .20
Complete booklet, 5 #1590 1.25

Pharmacy in Thailand, 80th Anniv. — A504

Grinding stones: 2b, Dvaravati, 7th-11th cent. 6b, Lopburi Period, 11th-13th cent. 9b, Bangkok Period, 18th-20th cent.

**1994, Dec. 13**

**1591** A504 2b multicolored .20 .20
Complete booklet, 5 #1591 1.25
**1592** A504 6b multicolored .45 .35
**1593** A504 9b multicolored .70 .55
*Nos. 1591-1593 (3)* 1.35 1.10

Bar Assoc., 80th Anniv. — A505

Design: 2b, First Bar Assoc. headquarters, King Vajiravudh, King Bhumibol.

**1995, Jan. 1 Wmk. 368 *Perf. 13½***

**1594** A505 2b multicolored .20 .20
Complete booklet, 5 #1594 1.10

A506

A507

Children's drawings: No. 1595, Kites Decorate the Summer Sky. No. 1596, Trees and Streams, horiz. No. 1597, Youths and Religion, horiz.

**1995, Jan. 14 Wmk. 387 *Perf. 14***

**1595** A506 2b multicolored .20 .20
Complete booklet, 5 #1595 1.10
**1596** A506 2b multicolored .20 .20
Complete booklet, 5 #1596 1.10
**1597** A506 2b multicolored .20 .20
Complete booklet, 5 #1597 1.10
*Nos. 1595-1597 (3)* .60 .60

Children's Day.

**1995, Mar. 4**

**1598** A507 2b multicolored .20 .20
Complete booklet, 5 #1598 1.10

First Thai newspaper, Bangkok Recorder, 150th anniv.

Royal Thai Air Force, 80th Anniv. A508

**1995, Mar. 27 Wmk. 368 *Perf. 13½***

**1599** A508 2b multicolored .20 .20
Complete booklet, 5 #1599 1.10

Red Cross Floating Clinic, Wetchapha — A509

**1995, Mar. 30**

**1600** A509 2b multicolored .20 .20
Complete booklet, 5 #1600 1.10

Phimai Historical Park — A510

Paintings: 3b, Naga Bridge. 5b, Brahmin Hall. 6b, Gateway of the Inner Wall. 9b, Main Pagoda.

*Perf. 14½x14*

**1995, Apr. 2 Wmk. 387**

**1601** A510 3b multicolored .25 .20
**1602** A510 5b multicolored .40 .30
**1603** A510 6b multicolored .50 .35
**1604** A510 9b multicolored .75 .55
*a.* Souv. sheet of 4, #1601-1604 2.50
*Nos. 1601-1604 (4)* 1.90 1.40

Heritage Conservation Day.
No. 1604a sold for 30b.

Ministry of Defense, 108th Anniv. — A511

Design: 2b, Admin. building, King Rama V.

**1995, Apr. 8 Wmk. 387 *Perf. 14***

**1605** A511 2b multicolored .20 .20
Complete booklet, 5 #1605 1.10

Songkran Day Type of 1991

**1995, Apr. 13 *Perf. 11x13***

**1606** A425 2b Demon on boar's back, zodiac .20 .20
*a.* Souvenir sheet of 1 .60
Complete booklet, 5 #1606 1.10

No. 1606a sold for 8b and exists imperf with sale price in different color. No. 1606a and the similar imperf sheet exist with a red marginal inscription in Thai and Chinese (without sale price).

Ministry of Foreign Affairs, 120th Anniv. — A512

2b, Saranrom Palace, King Rama V.

**1995, Apr. 14 *Perf. 14***

**1607** A512 2b multicolored .20 .20
Complete booklet, 5 #1607 1.10

Visakhapuja Day — A513

Sculptures of Buddha: 2b, Emerald Buddha, temple of Wat Phra Si Rattana Satsadaram, Bangkok. 6b, Phra Phuttha Chinnarat, Wat Phra Si Rattana Maha That, Phitsanulok Province. 8b, Phra Phuttha Sihing, Wat Phra Sing, Chiang Mai Province. 9b, Phra Sukhothai Traimit, Wat Traimit Witthayaram, Bangkok.

**Wmk. 340**

**1995, May 13 Photo. *Perf. 13½***

**1608** A513 2b multicolored .20 .20
**1609** A513 6b multicolored .45 .35
**1610** A513 8b multicolored .60 .50
**1611** A513 9b multicolored .75 .55
*a.* Souv. sheet of 4, #1608-1611 2.75
*Nos. 1608-1611 (4)* 2.00 1.60

No. 1611a sold for 35b.

ASEAN Environment Year — A514

**1995, June 5 Litho. Wmk. 368**

**1612** A514 2b multicolored .20 .20
Complete booklet, 5 #1612 1.10

Information Technology Year — A515

**1995, June 9 Wmk. 340**

**1613** A515 2b multicolored .20 .20
Complete booklet, 5 #1613 1.10

Thailand-People's Republic of China Diplomatic Relations, 20th Anniv. — A516

#1614, Elephants walking right into water. #1615, Elephants walking left into water.

**Wmk. 340**

**1995, July 1 Photo. *Perf. 13½***

**1614** A516 2b multicolored .20 .20
**1615** A516 2b multicolored .20 .20
*a.* Pair, Nos. 1614-1615 .30 .20
*b.* Souv. sheet, #1614-1615 .65
*c.* As "b," diff. inscriptions in sheet margin 18.00

No. 1615c contains Jakarta '95 exhibition emblem and does not have sheet value in margin.

#1615b sold for 8b. #1615c sold for 28b.

No. 1615b exists with serial number in sheet margin, The same number is on China (PRC) No. 2462a. These two souvenir sheets were sold as a set. Value, set $26.50.

See People's Republic of China Nos. 2579-2580.

Natl. Communications Day — A517

**1995, Aug. 4 Litho. *Perf. 14½x14***

**1616** A517 2b multicolored .20 .20
Complete booklet, 5 #1616 1.10

A518

A519

Domestic cats: 3b, Khoa Manee. 6b, Korat or Si-Sawat. 7b, Seal point Siamese. 9b, Burmese.

**1995, Aug. 4 Photo. *Perf. 13½***

**1617** A518 3b multicolored .25 .20
**1618** A518 6b multicolored .50 .40
**1619** A518 7b multicolored .55 .45
**1620** A518 9b multicolored .70 .55
*a.* Souv. sheet, Nos. 1617-1620 2.00
*b.* As "a," diff. inscriptions in margin *10.00*
*Nos. 1617-1620 (4)* 2.00 1.60

Thaipex '95.

No. 1620b contains Singapore '95 exhibition emblem added to sheet margin and does not have value inscription.

No. 1620a sold for 35b. No. 1620b sold for 46b.

**1995, Sept. 2 Litho. *Perf. 14x14½***

**1621** A519 2b multicolored .20 .20
Complete booklet, 5 #1621 1.10

Revenue Department, 80th anniv.

Natl. Auditing & Office of Auditor General, 120th Anniv. — A520

**1995, Sept. 18 *Perf. 14½x14***

**1622** A520 2b multicolored .20 .20
Complete booklet, 5 #1622 1.10

Intl. Letter Writing Week — A521

Wicker: No. 1623, Vase with handles, legs. No. 1624, Oval-shaped container. No. 1625, Lamp shade. No. 1626, Vase.

**Wmk. 340**

**1995, Oct. 8 Photo. *Perf. 13½***

**1623** A521 2b multicolored .20 .20
Complete booklet, 5 #1623 1.10
**1624** A521 2b multicolored .20 .20
Complete booklet, 5 #1624 1.10
**1625** A521 9b multicolored .75 .55
**1626** A521 9b multicolored .75 .55
*a.* Souv. sheet, #1623-1626 1.75
*Nos. 1623-1626 (4)* 1.90 1.50

FAO, 50th Anniv. A522

**1995, Oct. 16 Litho. *Perf. 14½x14***

**1627** A522 2b multicolored .20 .20
Complete booklet, 5 #1627 1.10

Total Solar Eclipse in Thailand — A523

**1995, Oct. 24 *Perf. 13½***

**1628** A523 2b multicolored .20 .20
Complete booklet, 5 #1628 1.10

UN, 50th Anniv. A524

***Perf. 13½x14***

**1995, Oct. 24 Wmk. 387**

**1629** A524 2b multicolored .20 .20
Complete booklet, 5 #1629 1.10

World Agricultural and Industrial Exhibition, Nkhon Ratchasima Province — A525

2b, Worldtech '95 Thailand Symbol Tower, vert. 5b, Farming equipment, food products, vert. 6b, Computers, equipment. 9b, Factory, beach.

***Perf. 14x14½, 14½x14***

**1995, Nov. 4 Wmk. 340**

**1630** A525 2b multicolored .20 .20
Complete booklet, 5 #1630 1.10
**1631** A525 5b multicolored .40 .30
**1632** A525 6b multicolored .50 .40
**1633** A525 9b multicolored .75 .55
*Nos. 1630-1633 (4)* 1.85 1.45

New Year 1996 — A526

#1634, Adenium obesum. #1635, Bauhinia acuminata. #1636, Cananga odorata. #1637, Thumbergia erecta.

**1995, Dec. 9 *Perf. 13½***

**1634** A526 2b multicolored .20 .20
**1635** A526 2b multicolored .20 .20
*a.* Souvenir sheet, #1634-1635 4.50
**1636** A526 2b multicolored .20 .20
**1637** A526 2b multicolored .20 .20
*a.* Souvenir sheet, #1634-1637 1.25
*b.* As "a," inscribed in margin 5.00
*c.* Souvenir sheet, #1636-1637 4.50
*Nos. 1634-1637 (4)* .80 .80

No. 1637a sold for 15b.

Nos. 1635a, 1637c have "CHINA '96" emblem inscribed in sheet margin and sold for 22b each. No. 1637b is inscribed in sheet margin with "Indonesia '96" emblem and has the gold 15b value removed. No. 1637b sold for 14b.

Issued: #1635a, 1637b-1637c, 5/18/96.

Veterinary Science in Thailand, 60th Anniv. — A527

**1995, Dec. 9 *Perf. 14½x14***

**1638** A527 2b multicolored .20 .20
Complete booklet, 5 #1638 1.10

A528

A529

***Perf. 14x14½***

**1996, Jan. 12 Litho. Wmk. 340**

**1639** A528 2b multicolored .20 .20
Complete booklet, 5 #1639 1.10

Siriraj School of Nursing and Midwifery, cent.

**1996, Jan. 13 Wmk. 387 *Perf. 13½***

Paintings of Buddha instructing people with: No. 1640, Bright light, deer. No. 1641, Children, animal, person reclined, horiz. No. 1642, Followers, large tree, river.

**1640** A529 2b multicolored .20 .20
Complete booklet, 5 #1640 1.10
**1641** A529 2b multicolored .20 .20
Complete booklet, 5 #1641 1.10
**1642** A529 2b multicolored .20 .20
Complete booklet, 5 #1642 1.10
*Nos. 1640-1642 (3)* .60 .60

Natl. Children's Day.

Natl. Aviation Day — A530

***Perf. 14½x14***

**1996, Jan. 13 Wmk. 340**

**1643** A530 2b multicolored .20 .20
Complete booklet, 5 #1643 1.10

Asia-Europe Economic Meeting — A531

***Perf. 14x14½***

**1996, Mar. 1 Litho. Wmk. 340**

**1644** A531 2b multicolored .20 .20
Complete booklet, 5 #1644 1.10

Maghapuja Day — A532

Scenes from the Ten Jataka stories: 2b, Man on knee, another holding chariot. 6b, Two people flying over sea. 8b, Archer approaching man with arrow in side. 9b, Charioteer pointing.

**Wmk. 340**

**1996, Mar. 3 Photo. *Perf. 13½***

**1645** A532 2b multicolored .20 .20
**1646** A532 6b multicolored .50 .35
**1647** A532 8b multicolored .60 .50
**1648** A532 9b multicolored .70 .50
*a.* Souvenir Sheet, #1645-1548 2.75
*Nos. 1645-1648 (4)* 2.00 1.55

No. 1648a sold for 36b.

Cremation of Princess Mother Somdej Phra Sri Nakharindra Barommarajjonnani — A533

**Litho. & Embossed**

***Perf. 14½x14***

**1996, Mar. 10 Wmk. 340**

**1649** A533 2b gold & multi .20 .20
Complete booklet, 5 #1649 1.75

Heritage Conservation Day Type of 1993

Historical landmarks, Kamphaeng Phet Park: 2b, Wat Phra Kaeo. 3b, Wat Phra Non. 6b, Wat Chang Rop. 9b, Wat Phra Si Iriyabot.

**Wmk. 387**

**1996, Apr. 2 Litho. *Perf. 13½***

**1650** A477 2b multicolored .20 .20
Complete booklet, 5 No. 1650 1.10
**1651** A477 3b multicolored .25 .20
**1652** A477 6b multicolored .50 .35
**1653** A477 9b multicolored .70 .50
*a.* Souvenir sheet, #1650-1653 2.25
*Nos. 1650-1653 (4)* 1.65 1.25

No. 1653a sold for 28b.

Chiang Mai, 700th Anniv. — A534

Anniv. logo of Chiang Mai and: 2b, Buddhist Pagoda of Wat Chiang Man. 6b, Sculpted angel on wall, Wat Chet Yot's Pagoda. 8b, Insignia of Wat Phan Tao's Vihara. 9b, Sattaphanta.

**Wmk. 340**

**1996, Apr. 12 Photo. *Perf. 13½***

**1654** A534 2b multicolored .20 .20
Complete booklet, 5 #1654 1.10
**1655** A534 6b multicolored .50 .35
**1656** A534 8b multicolored .60 .45
**1657** A534 9b multicolored .70 .50
*a.* Souvenir sheet, #1654-1657 2.90
*Nos. 1654-1657 (4)* 2.00 1.50

No. 1657a sold for 37b.

Second Intl. Asian Hornbill Workshop A535

#1658, White-crowned. #1659, Rufous-necked. #1660, Plain-pouched. #1661, Rhinoceros.

**1996, Apr. 12**

**1658** A535 3b multicolored .25 .20
**1659** A535 3b multicolored .25 .20
**1660** A535 9b multicolored .70 .50
**1661** A535 9b multicolored .70 .50
*a.* Souvenir sheet, #1658-1661 2.75
*b.* As "a," inscribed in margin 3.75
*Nos. 1658-1661 (4)* 1.90 1.40

No. 1661a sold for 35b. No. 1661b was issued 6/8/96, contains CAPEX '96 exhibition emblem in sheet margin, no value inscription, and sold for 47b.

Songkran Day Type of 1991

***Perf. 13½x14***

**1996, Apr. 13 Litho. Wmk. 387**

**1662** A425 2b Demon on rat's back, zodiac .20 .20
Complete booklet, 5 #1662 1.10
*a.* Souvenir sheet of 1 .65

*b.* Souv. sheet, #1389, 1467, 1530, 1566, 1606, 1662 — 1.60
*c.* As "a," inscribed in margin — 4.00
*d.* As "b," inscribed in margin — 10.00

No. 1662c contains CHINA '96 exhibition emblem and "CHINA '96-9th Asian International Philatelic Exhibition" in Chinese and English and no value inscription in sheet margin. No. 1662d contains CHINA '96 and Hong Kong '96 exhibition emblems in margin and no value inscription.

#1662a sold for 8b. #1662b sold for 20b. #1662c, issued 5/15/96, sold for 14b. #1662d, issued 5/10/96, sold for 25b. #1662a-1662d exist imperf.

A536

King Bhumibol Adulyadej, 50th Anniv. of Assession to the Throne A537

Designs: No. 1663, Royal Ablutions Ceremony. No. 1664, Pouring of the Libation. No. 1665, Grand Audience. No. 1666, Royal Progress by Land. No. 1667, Audience from Balcony.

**1996, June 9 Photo. *Perf. 11½***
**Granite Paper**

**1663** A536 3b multicolored .25 .20
*a.* Souvenir sheet .65
**1664** A536 3b multicolored .25 .20
*a.* Souvenir sheet .65
**1665** A536 3b multicolored .25 .20
*a.* Souvenir sheet .65
**1666** A536 3b multicolored .25 .20
*a.* Souvenir sheet .65
**1667** A536 3b multicolored .25 .20
*a.* Souvenir sheet .65

**Litho. & Typo.**
**Wmk. 387**
***Perf. 13½***

**1668** A537 100b gold & multi 8.00 6.00
*Nos. 1663-1668 (6)* 9.25 7.00

Nos. 1663a 1664a, 1665a, 1666a, 1667a have a continuous design and each sold for 8b.

Development Programs of King Bhumibol Adulyadej — A538

#1669, Using Vetiver grass to prevent soil erosion. #1670, Chai pattana aerator to improve water quality. #1671, Rain making project to counter droughts. #1672, Dam, natural water resource development. #1673, Reforestation.

**Wmk. 340**
**1996, June 9 Litho. *Perf. 13½***

**1669** A538 3b multicolored .25 .20
**1670** A538 3b multicolored .25 .20
**1671** A538 3b multicolored .25 .20
**1672** A538 3b multicolored .25 .20
**1673** A538 3b multicolored .25 .20
*a.* Souv. sheet, #1669-1673+label 2.00
*Nos. 1669-1673 (5)* 1.25 1.00

No. 1671 has a holographic image. Soaking in water may affect the hologram. No. 1673a sold for 25b.

Royal Utensils — A539

#1674, Gold-enameled cuspidor, golden spittoon. #1675, Royal betel, areca-nut set, vert. #1676, Royal water urn, vert.

**Wmk. 329**
**1996, June 9 Photo. *Perf. 13½***

**1674** A539 3b green & multi .25 .20
**1675** A539 3b blue & multi .25 .20
**1676** A539 3b purple & multi .25 .20
*a.* Souvenir sheet, #1674-1676 1.30
*Nos. 1674-1676 (3)* .75 .60

No. 1676a sold for 17b.

Modern Olympic Games, Cent. — A540

2b, Pierre de Coubertin, grave site. 3b, 1st lighting of Olympic torch, Olympia, Greece. 5b, Olympic Stadium, Athens, Olympic flag. 9b, Discus thrower, medal from 1896 games.

***Perf. 14x14½***
**1996, June 23 Litho. Wmk. 340**

**1677** A540 2b multicolored .20 .20
Complete booklet, 5 #1677 1.25
**1678** A540 3b multicolored .25 .20
**1679** A540 5b multicolored .40 .30
**1680** A540 9b multicolored .75 .55
*Nos. 1677-1680 (4)* 1.60 1.25

Nat. Communications Day — A541

**1996, Aug. 4 Wmk. 340**

**1681** A541 2b King using radio .20 .20
Complete booklet, 5 #1681 1.25

Royal Forest Department, Cent. — A542

***Perf. 14½x14***
**1996, Sept. 18 Litho. Wmk. 340**
**Type of Forest**

**1682** A542 3b Tropical rain .25 .20
**1683** A542 6b Hill evergreen .50 .40
**1684** A542 7b Swamp .55 .30
**1685** A542 9b Mangrove .70 .55
*a.* Souvenir sheet, #1682-1685 2.75
*Nos. 1682-1685 (4)* 2.00 1.45

No. 1685a sold for 35b.

Intl. Letter Writing Week — A543

Classical Thai novels, characters: No. 1686, "Ramayana," King Rama following deer. No. 1687, "Inao," Inao kidnapping Budsaba, taking her to cave. No. 1688, "Ngao Pa," Lumhap touring forest. No. 1689, "Mathanapatha," Nang Mathana being cursed.

**Wmk. 340**
**1996, Oct. 6 Photo. *Perf. 13½***

**1686** A543 3b multicolored .25 .20
**1687** A543 3b multicolored .25 .20
**1688** A543 9b multicolored .70 .55
**1689** A543 9b multicolored .70 .55
*a.* Souvenir sheet, #1686-1689 3.00
*Nos. 1686-1689 (4)* 1.90 1.50

No. 1689a sold for 36b.

Rotary Intl. 1996 Asia Regional Conference A544

***Perf. 14x14½***
**1996, Oct. 25 Litho. Wmk. 340**

**1690** A544 2b multicolored .20 .20
Complete booklet, 5 #1609 1.10

UNESCO, 50th Anniv. — A545

**1996, Nov. 4 *Perf. 14½x14***

**1691** A545 2b multicolored .20 .20
Complete booklet, 5 #1691 1.10

Royal Barge — A546

Illustration reduced.

**1996, Nov. 7 Unwmk. *Perf. 11½***
**Granite Paper**

**1692** A546 9b multicolored .70 .55
*a.* Souvenir sheet of 1 1.25 .95

No. 1692a sold for 16b.

New Year 1997 — A547

Designs: No. 1693, Limnocharis flava. No. 1694, Crinum thaianum, vert. No. 1695, Monochoria hastata, vert. No. 1696, Nymphoides indicum.

***Perf. 14x14½, 14½x14***
**1996, Nov. 15 Litho. Wmk. 387**

**1693** A547 2b multicolored .20 .20
**1694** A547 2b multicolored .20 .20
**1695** A547 2b multicolored .20 .20
**1696** A547 2b multicolored .20 .20
*a.* Souvenir sheet, #1693-1696 1.20
*b.* As "a," inscribed in margin .60
*Nos. 1693-1696 (4)* .80 .80

No. 1696a sold for 15b. No. 1696b inscribed in sheet margin with Hong Kong '97 emblem and vertical Chinese inscription.
No. 1696b issued 2/12/97.

Ducks A548

#1697, Sarkidiornis melanotos. #1698, Dendrocygna javanica, vert. #1699, Cairina scutulata, vert. #1700, Nettapus coromandelianus.

**Wmk. 340**
**1996, Dec. 1 Photo. *Perf. 13½***

**1697** A548 3b multicolored .25 .20
**1698** A548 3b multicolored .25 .20
**1699** A548 7b multicolored .55 .40
**1700** A548 7b multicolored .55 .40
*a.* Souvenir sheet, #1697-1700 2.50
*Nos. 1697-1700 (4)* 1.60 1.20

No. 1700a sold for 33b.

UNICEF, 50th Anniv. — A549

***Perf. 14½x14***
**1996, Dec. 11 Litho. Wmk. 340**

**1701** A549 2b multicolored .20 .20
Complete booklet, 5 #1701 1.10

King Bhumibol Adulyadej — A550

***Perf. 14x14½***
**1996, Dec. 5 Litho. Wmk. 340**

**1702** A550 2b carmine .20 .20
Complete booklet, 5 #1702 1.10
*a.* Unwmkd., granite paper .20 .20

No. 1702a issued 9/1/98.
See Nos. 1725-1729, 1743-1745, 1756-1757, 1794-1795, 1819-1820, 1876-1879, 2067.

Thailand's 1st Olympic Gold Medal, 1996 — A552

**Litho. & Embossed**
***Perf. 14½x14***
**1996, Dec. 16 Wmk. 340**

**1704** A552 6b multicolored .45 .35

Mahavajiravudh School, Songkhla, Cent. — A553

*Perf. 14x14½*

**1997, Jan. 1** **Wmk. 387**

**1705** A553 2b multicolored .20 .20
Complete booklet, 5 #1705 1.00

Children's Day — A554

Children' paintings: No. 1706, Children processing fish. No. 1707, Monument, children in praise.

**1997, Jan. 11** **Wmk. 340**

**1706** A554 2b multicolored .20 .20
Complete booklet, 5 #1706 1.00
**1707** A554 2b multicolored .20 .20
Complete booklet, 5 #1707 1.00

Communications Authority of Thailand, 20th Anniv. — A555

*Perf. 14½x14*

**1997, Feb. 25** **Litho.** **Wmk. 340**

**1708** A555 2b multicolored .20 .20
Complete booklet, 5 #1708 1.00

Statue of Prince Bhanurangsi A556

**1997, Feb. 25** ***Perf. 14x14½***

**1709** A556 2b multicolored .20 .20
Complete booklet, 5 #1709 1.00

Laksi Mail Center A557

#1710, Outside view of building. #1711, Computerized mail sorting machine.

**1997, Feb. 25** ***Perf. 14½x14***

**1710** A557 2b multicolored .20 .20
**1711** A557 2b multicolored .20 .20
*a.* Pair, #1710-1711 .30 .25

State Railway, Cent. — A558

3b, 0-6-0 Type. 4b, Garratt. 6b, Sulzer diesel. 7b, Hitachi diesel leaving tunnel.

**Wmk. 387**

**1997, Mar. 26** **Litho.** ***Perf. 13***

**1712** A558 3b multicolored .25 .20
*a.* Souvenir sheet of 1 1.50 1.50
**1713** A558 4b multicolored .30 .25
**1714** A558 6b multicolored .45 .35
**1715** A558 7b multicolored .55 .40
*a.* Souv. sheet of 4, #1712-1715 2.25
*Nos. 1712-1715 (4)* 1.55 1.20

No. 1712a sold for 20b, No. 1715a sold for 30b.

Chulalongkorn University, 80th Anniv. — A559

Designs: No. 1716, Palace of Prince Maha Vajirunhis. No. 1717, Faculty of Arts building.

*Perf. 14½x14*

**1997, Mar. 26** **Wmk. 340**

**1716** A559 2b yellow & multi .20 .20
Complete booklet, 5 #1716 1.00
**1717** A559 2b rose & multi .20 .20
Complete booklet, 5 #1717 1.00

Thai Red Cross A560

**1997, Mar. 28**

**1718** A560 3b Rajakarun building .25 .20

Govt. Savings Bank, 84th Anniv. — A561

**1997, Apr. 1**

**1719** A561 2b multicolored .20 .20
Complete booklet, 5 #1719 1.00

Heritage Conservation Day — A562

Phanomrung historical Park: No. 1720, Outer stairway. No. 1721, Pavilion. No. 1722, Passage, stairway to sanctuary. No. 1723, Naga balustrade, Central Gate of Eastern Gallery.

**1997, Apr. 2**

**1720** A562 3b multicolored .25 .20
**1721** A562 3b multicolored .25 .20
**1722** A562 7b multicolored .55 .40
**1723** A562 7b multicolored .55 .40
*a.* Souvenir sheet, #1720-1723 2.25
*Nos. 1720-1723 (4)* 1.60 1.20

No. 1723a sold for 30b.

Songkran Day Type of 1991

**1997-2002** **Wmk. 340** ***Perf. 14x14½***

**1724** A425 2b Demon on ox's back, zodiac .20 .20
Complete booklet, 5 #1724 1.00 .75
*a.* Souvenir sheet of 1 .65
*b.* Unwmkd., granite paper .20 .20

Issued: Nos. 1724, 1724a, 4/13/97; No. 1724b, 4/13/02. No. 1724b issued only in No. 2017b.

No. 1724a sold for 8b and exists imperf.

King Bhumibol Adulyadej Type of 1996

**Litho, Litho & Engraved (#1728-1729)**

*Perf. 14x14½*

**1997, May 5** **Wmk. 340**

**1725** A550 4b blue & red brown .30 .25
*a.* Perf. 13¼, unwmkd. .30 .25
*b.* Unwmkd., granite paper .20 .20
**1726** A550 5b pur & org brn .40 .30
*a.* Perf. 13½, unwmk., granite paper .25 .20
*b.* Unwmkd., granite paper .20 .20
**1727** A550 7b pink & green .55 .40

**Wmk. 329**

*Perf. 13½x13*

**1728** A550 10b orange & brown .80 .60
**1729** A550 20b violet & maroon 1.60 1.25
*Nos. 1725-1729 (5)* 3.65 2.80

Issued: No. 1726a, 12/28/98; No. 1725a, 10/8/99. 1725b, 1726b, 12/1/00.

Waterfowl — A563

Designs: No. 1730, Pheasant-tailed jacana. No. 1731, Bronze-winged jacana. No. 1732, Painted stork. No. 1733, Black-winged stilt.

*Perf. 11½x12*

**1997, May 15** **Photo.** **Unwmk.**

**Granite Paper**

**1730** A563 3b multicolored .25 .20
**1731** A563 3b multicolored .25 .20
**1732** A563 7b multicolored .55 .40
**1733** A563 7b multicolored .55 .40
*a.* Souvenir sheet, #1730-1733 2.25
*b.* As "a," with added inscription 2.25
*Nos. 1730-1733 (4)* 1.60 1.20

No. 1733a sold for 30b. No. 1733b has PACIFIC 97 emblem in sheet margin, while sales price has been removed from sheet margin. No. 1728b sold for 42b.

King Bhumibol Adulyadej, National Telecommunications — A564

2b, King using hand-held radio, "Suthee" aerial. 3b, King using hand-held radio for communication in local areas. 6b, King using computer. 9b, King, classroom using satellite information.

*Perf. 14½x14*

**1997, June 9** **Litho.** **Wmk. 340**

**1734** A564 2b multicolored .20 .20
Complete booklet, 5 #1734 1.00
**1735** A564 3b multicolored .25 .20
**1736** A564 6b multicolored .50 .40
**1737** A564 9b multicolored .70 .50
*a.* Souvenir sheet, #1734-1737 2.40
*Nos. 1734-1737 (4)* 1.65 1.30

No. 1737a sold for 30b.

Motion Pictures in Thailand, Cent. — A565

Designs: No. 1738, King Rama VII filming movie, film showing King Chulalongkorn's state visit to Europe. No. 1739, Early motion picture equipment, advertisement, Prince Sanbassatra, founder of Thai motion picures. No. 1740, Poster from "Double Luck," band playing in front of movie theater. No. 1741, Open air theater, poster from "Going Astray."

**1997, June 10**

**1738** A565 3b multicolored .25 .20
**1739** A565 3b multicolored .25 .20
**1740** A565 7b multicolored .55 .40
**1741** A565 7b multicolored .55 .40
*Nos. 1738-1741 (4)* 1.60 1.20

Faculty of Medicine, Chulalongkorn University, 50th Anniv. — A566

King Rama VIII, building, operating room.

**1997, June 11**

**1742** A566 2b multicolored .20 .20
Complete booklet, 5 #1742 1.00

King Bhumibol Adulyadej Type of 1996

*Perf. 14x14½*

**1997, July 19** **Litho.** **Wmk. 340**

**1743** A550 6b grn & gray vio .40 .30
**1744** A550 9b dk bl & brn org .60 .45

*Litho. & Engr.* **Wmk. 329** ***Perf. 13½x13***

**1745** A550 100b lem & dk bl grn 6.25 4.75
*Nos. 1743-1745 (3)* 7.25 5.50

Thai-Russian Diplomatic Relations, Cent. — A567

Design: Peterhof Palace, King Chulalongkorn (King Rama V).

**1997, July 3** **Litho.** ***Perf. 14½x14***

**1746** A567 2b multicolored .20 .20
Complete booklet, 5 #1746 .65

Asalhapuja Day — A568

3b, Mahosathajataka (scene with man on elephant). 4b, Bhuridattajataka (scene with two men, large snake). 6b, Candakumarajataka (scene with pot of fire, three men on knees, man in sky, Buddha). 7b, Naradajataka (scene with people praising human figure with four arms hovering above roof).

***Perf. 11½ Syncopated***

**1997, July 19** **Photo.** **Unwmk.**

**Granite Paper**

**1747** A568 3b multicolored .20 .20
*a.* Souvenir sheet of 1 .40
*b* As "a," inscribed in margin .20
**1748** A568 4b multicolored .25 .20
*a.* Souvenir sheet of 1 .50
*b* As "a," inscribed in margin .25
**1749** A568 6b multicolored .40 .25
*a.* Souvenir sheet of 1 .65
*b* As "a," inscribed in margin .40
**1750** A568 7b multicolored .45 .35
*a.* Souvenir sheet of 1 .75
*b.* Souvenir sheet, #1747-1750 1.90
*c* As "a," inscribed in margin .45 .35
*Nos. 1747-1750 (4)* 1.30 1.00

#1747a sold for 6b; #1748a for 8b; #1749a for 10b; #1750a for 12b; #1750b for 30b.

Sheet margins of lack value inscriptions, but contain Shanghai '97 exhibition emblem (#1747b, 1748b), Chinese insription; Bangkok '97 exhibition emblem (#1749b, 1750c).

1997 Thailand Philatelic Exhibition — A569

Houses from: 2b, Northern region. 5b, Central region. 6b, Northeastern region. 9b, Southern region.

**Wmk. 329**

**1997, Aug. 2 Litho. *Perf. 13½***

**1751** A569 2b multicolored .20 .20
Complete booklet, 5 #1751 1.00
**1752** A569 5b multicolored .30 .25
**1753** A569 6b multicolored .40 .30
**1754** A569 9b multicolored .55 .45
*a.* Souvenir sheet, #1751-1754 2.00
*Nos. 1751-1754 (4)* 1.45 1.20

No. 1754a sold for 32b.

No. 1754a exists imperf, sold with an exhibition book.

Natl. Communications Day — A570

***Perf. 14x14½***

**1997, Aug. 4 Wmk. 340**

**1755** A570 2b multicolored .20 .20
Complete booklet, 5 #1755 1.00

Greeting Stamps — A570a

Lotus flowers: No. 1755A, Nymphaea capensis. No. 1755B, Nymphaea stellata.

***Perf. 14x14½***

**1997, Aug. 4 Litho. Wmk. 387**

**Booklet Stamps**

**1755A** A570a (2b) multicolored .30 .30
**1755B** A570a (2b) multicolored .30 .30
*c.* Bklt. pane, 5 ea #1755A-1755B + 4 labels 3.00
Complete bklt., #1755Bc 3.00

Nos. 1755A-1755B were sold only at 7-11 stores, not at post offices or philatelic agencies.

King Bhumibol Adulyadej Type of 1996

**Litho. & Engr.**

***Perf. 13½x13***

**1997, Aug. 8 Wmk. 329**

**1756** A550 25b bl grn & ol blk 1.60 1.25
**1757** A550 200b lil rose & vio blk 12.50 6.25

ASEAN, 30th Anniv. — A571

Designs: No. 1758, Thi Lo Su Falls, Tak. No. 1759, Luang Chiang Dao Mountain, Chiang Mai. No. 1760, Phromthep Cape, Phuket. No. 1761, Thalu Island, Chumphon.

***Perf. 14½x14***

**1997, Aug. 8 Wmk. 340**

**1758** A571 2b multicolored .20 .20
Complete booklet, 5 #1758 1.00
**1759** A571 2b multicolored .20 .20
Complete booklet, 5 #1759 1.00
**1760** A571 9b multicolored .60 .45
**1761** A571 9b multicolored .60 .45
*Nos. 1758-1761 (4)* 1.60 1.30

Dinosaurs — A572

Designs: 2b, Phuwiangosaurus sirindhornae. 3b, Siamotyrannus isanensis. 6b, Siamosaurus suteethorni. 9b, Psittacosaurus sattayaraki.

***Perf. 13½x13 Syncopated***

**1997, Aug. 28 Photo. Unwmk.**

**1762** A572 2b multicolored .20 .20
Complete booklet, 5 #1762 1.00
**1763** A572 3b multicolored .20 .20
**1764** A572 6b multicolored .35 .25
**1765** A572 9b multicolored .50 .35
*a.* Souvenir sheet, #1762-1765 1.75
*Nos. 1762-1765 (4)* 1.25 1.00

No. 1765a sold for 30b.

King Chulalongkorn's Visit to Switzerland, Cent. — A573

***Perf. 14x14½***

**1997, Sept. 12 Litho. Wmk. 340**

**1766** A573 2b multicolored .20 .20
Complete booklet, 5 #1766 .65

Intl. Letter Writing Week — A574

Winning drawings: No. 1767, Tricycle, combining rickshaw and tricycle. No. 1768, Tricycle with side seat. No. 1769, Motor tricycle. No. 1770. Motor tricycle with light on roof.

***Perf. 11½x12***

**1997, Oct. 5 Photo. Unwmk.**

**Granite Paper**

**1767** A574 3b multicolored .20 .20
**1768** A574 3b multicolored .20 .20
**1769** A574 9b multicolored .40 .30
**1770** A574 9b multicolored .40 .30
*a.* Souvenir sheet, #1767-1770 1.25
*Nos. 1767-1770 (4)* 1.20 1.00

No. 1770a sold for 30b.

Shells of Thailand and Singapore A575

Designs: No. 1771, Drupa morum. No. 1772, Nerita chamaelon. No. 1773, Littoraria melanostoma. No. 1774, Cryptospira elgans.

**1997, Oct. 9 Litho. *Perf. 11½***

**Granite Paper**

**1771** A575 2b multicolored .20 .20
Complete booklet, 5 #1771 1.00
**1772** A575 2b multicolored .20 .20
Complete booklet, 5 #1772 1.00
**1773** A575 9b multicolored .40 .30
**1774** A575 9b multicolored .40 .30
*a.* Souvenir sheet, #1771-7774 1.25
*Nos. 1771-1774 (4)* 1.20 1.00

No. 1774a sold for 30b. See Singapore Nos. 825-828A.

Chalerm Prakiat Energy Conserving Building — A576

***Perf. 14½x14***

**1997, Nov. 10 Litho. Wmk. 340**

**1775** A576 2b multicolored .20 .20
Complete booklet, 5 #1775 1.00

Christening of Suphannahong Royal Barge, 86th Anniv. — A577

Illustration reduced.

***Perf. 11½***

**1997, Nov. 13 Photo. Unwmk.**

**Granite Paper**

**1776** A577 9b multicolored .40 .30
*a.* Souvenir sheet of 1 .90
*b.* As "a," ovptd. in margin 1.10
*c.* As "a," ovptd. in margin .90

#1776a, 1776b, 1776c sold for 20b.

The sheet margin of #1776b is ovptd in gold with Thai and Chinese inscriptions for Bangkok/China 98. Issued 10/16/98.

No. 1776c overprinted in margin with World Stamp Expo 2000 emblem in gold. Issued 7/7/00.

New Year 1998 — A578

Flowers: No. 1777, Cassia alata. No. 1778, Strophanthus caudatus. No. 1779, Clinacanthus nutans. No. 1780, Acanthus ilicifolius.

**1997, Nov. 15 Litho. *Perf. 13½x13***

**Granite Paper**

**1777** A578 2b multicolored .20 .20
**1778** A578 2b multicolored .20 .20
**1779** A578 2b multicolored .20 .20
**1780** A578 2b multicolored .20 .20
*a.* Souvenir sheet, #1777-1780 .70
*b.* As "a," with added inscription .35
*Nos. 1777-1780 (4)* .80 .80

No. 1780a sold for 15b. No. 1780b contains Indepex '97 exhibition emblem, but no value inscription in sheet margin.

King Bhumibol Adulyadej's 70th Birthday — A579

#1781, Playing saxophone. #1782, Painting picture. #1783, Building sailboat. #1784, Wearing gold medal, sailboats. 6b, Taking photograph. 7b, Writing book. 9b, Working at computer.

**1997, Dec. 5 Photo. *Perf. 11½***

**Granite Paper**

**1781** A579 2b multicolored .20 .20
**1782** A579 2b multicolored .20 .20
**1783** A579 2b multicolored .20 .20
**1784** A579 2b multicolored .20 .20
**1785** A579 6b multicolored .25 .20
**1786** A579 7b multicolored .30 .25
**1787** A579 9b multicolored .40 .30
*Nos. 1781-1787 (7)* 1.75 1.55

A580

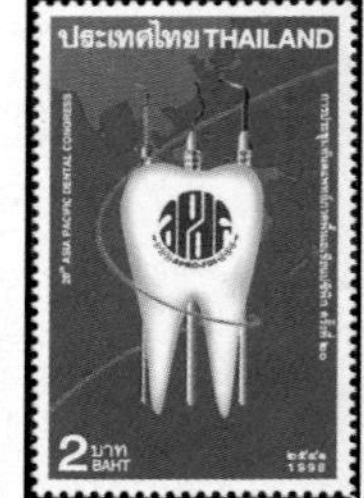

A581

Winners in Yuvabadhana Foundation, "Sports Develop Mind and Body" drawing competition: No. 1788, Children in wheelchair race. No. 1789, Flying kites. No. 1790, Gymnastics. No. 1791, Windsurfing.

***Perf. 14x14½***

**1998, Jan. 10 Litho. Wmk. 340**

**1788** A580 2b multicolored .20 .20
Complete booklet, 5 #1788 .45
**1789** A580 2b multicolored .20 .20
Complete booklet, 5 #1789 .45
**1790** A580 2b multicolored .20 .20
Complete booklet, 5 #1790 .45
**1791** A580 2b multicolored .20 .20
*a.* Complete booklet, 5 #1791 .45
*Nos. 1788-1791 (4)* .80 .80

Natl. Childrens' Day.

**1998, Jan. 17 Unwmk.**

**Granite Paper**

**1792** A581 2b multicolored .20 .20
Complete booklet, 5 #1792 .45

20th Asia Pacific Dental Congress.

A582

A583

**1998, Feb. 3 Wmk. 340**

**1793** A582 2b multicolored .20 .20

Veteran's Day, 50th anniv.

King Bhumibol Adulyadej Type of 1996

**1998, Feb. 25 Photo. *Perf. 11½x12***

**Granite Paper**

**1794** A550 50s dk ol & lt ol .20 .20

**Litho. & Engr.**

**Wmk. 329**

***Perf. 13½x13***

**1795** A550 50b dp vio & dk grn 2.50 1.90

*Perf. 14x14½*

**1998, Mar. 27 Litho. Wmk. 340**

**1796** A583 2b Queen Sirikit .20 .20
Complete booklet, 5 #1796 .50

1998 Thai Red Cross Fair.

Heritage Conservation Day Type of 1993

Paintings of Phanomrung Historical Park: 3b, Main Tower. 4b, Minor Tower. 6b, Scripture Repository. 7b, Lintel depicting Vishnu sleeping in ocean, doorway of Main Tower.

*Perf. 14½x14*

**1998, Apr. 2 Litho. Wmk. 340**

**1797** A477 3b multicolored .20 .20
**1798** A477 4b multicolored .20 .20
**1799** A477 6b multicolored .30 .25
**1800** A477 7b multicolored .35 .30
*a.* Souvenir sheet, #1797-1800 1.40

No. 1800a sold for 27b.

Songkran Day Type of 1991

**1998-2002** ***Perf. 14x14½***

**1801** A425 2b Demon on tiger's back, zodiac .20 .20
Complete booklet, 5 #1801 .50
*a.* Souvenir sheet of 1 .40
*b.* As "a," inscribed in margin .40
*c.* Unwmkd., granite paper .20 .20

Issued: Nos. 1801-1801b, 4/13/98. No. 1801c, 4/13/02. No. 1801c issued only in No. 2017b.

No. 1801a sold for 8b and exists imperf.

Sheet margin of No. 1801b contains flags of Thailand and China (PRC), Thai and Chinese inscriptions, no value inscription, and exists imperf.

No. 1801b sold for 8b and was issued 10/16/98.

Wild Cats A584

Paintings: 2b, Felis viverrina. 4b, Panthera tigris. 6b, Panthera pardus. 8b, Felis chaus.

**1998, Apr. 13** ***Perf. 14½x14***

**1802** A584 2b multicolored .20 .20
Complete booklet, 5 #1802 .50
**1803** A584 4b multicolored .20 .20
**1804** A584 6b multicolored .30 .25
**1805** A584 8b multicolored .40 .35
*a.* Souvenir sheet, #1802-1805 1.50
*Nos. 1802-1805 (4)* 1.10 1.00

No. 1805a sold for 30b.

AEROTHAI (Aeronautical Radio of Thailand, Ltd.), 50th Anniv. — A585

**1998, Apr. 15**

**1806** A585 2b multicolored .20 .20
Complete booklet, 5 #1806 .50

Visakhapuja Day — A586

Paintings of the "Ten Jataka Stories:" 3b, Riding horse above buildings, Vidhurajataka. 4b, In chariot, Vessantarajataka. 6b, Two figures seated before larger figure, Vessantarajataka. 7b, Figures in front of building, Vessantarajataka.

**1998, May 10** ***Perf. 13½***

**1807** A586 3b multicolored .20 .20
**1808** A586 4b multicolored .20 .20
**1809** A586 6b multicolored .30 .25
**1810** A586 7b multicolored .30 .25
*a.* Souvenir sheet, #1807-1810 1.00
*Nos. 1807-1810 (4)* 1.00 .90

No. 1810a sold for 30b.

Adm. Abhakara Kiartiwongse (1880-1923), Father of Royal Thai Navy — A587

**1998, May 19** ***Perf. 14½x14***

**1811** A587 2b multicolored .20 .20
Complete booklet, 5 #1811 .50

Educational Development — A588

*Perf. 14½x14*

**1998, June 15 Litho. Wmk. 340**

**1812** A588 2b multicolored .20 .20
Complete booklet, 5 #1812 .50

King Chulalongkorn's 1st State Visit to Europe, Cent. — A589

Illustration reduced.

**Unwmk.**

**1998, July 1 Litho.** ***Perf. 13***

**Granite Paper**

**1813** A589 6b multicolored .30 .25

**Litho. & Embossed**

**1814** A589 20b multicolored 1.00 .75

Intl. Year of the Ocean A590

2b, Orchaella brevirostris. 3b, Tursiops truncatus. 6b, Physeter catodon. 9b, Dugong dugon.

**1998, July 19 Litho.** ***Perf. 14½x14***

**Granite Paper**

**1815** A590 2b multicolored .20 .20
Complete booklet, 5 #1815 .50
**1816** A590 3b multicolored .20 .20
**1817** A590 6b multicolored .30 .30
**1818** A590 9b multicolored .45 .45
*a.* Souvenir sheet, #1815-1818 1.50
*Nos. 1815-1818 (4)* 1.15 1.15

No. 1818a sold for 30b.

King Bhumibol Adulyadej Type of 1996

**1998 Photo. Unwmk.** ***Perf. 11½x12***

**Granite Paper**

**1819** A550 2b carmine .20 .20
**1820** A550 9b dark bl & brn org .60 .45

Irrigation Engineering in Thailand, 60th Anniv. — A591

*Perf. 14½x14*

**1998, Aug. 1 Litho. Unwmk.**

**Granite Paper**

**1821** A591 2b multicolored .20 .20
Complete booklet, 5 #1821 .50

Natl. Communications Day — A592

**1998, Aug. 4**

**Granite Paper**

**1822** A592 2b multicolored .20 .20
Complete booklet, 5 #1822 .50

School of Political Science, Chulalongkorn University, 50th Anniv. — A593

**1998, Aug. 19**

**Granite Paper**

**1823** A593 2b multicolored .20 .20
Complete booklet, 5 #1823 .50

Sukhothai Thammathirat Open University, Award for Excellence — A594

**1998, Sept. 5 Litho.** ***Perf. 14½x14***

**Granite Paper**

**1824** A594 2b multicolored .20 .20
Complete booklet, 5 #1824 .50

Amazing Thailand, 1998-99, Thai Arts and Culture A595

**1998, Sept. 15** ***Perf. 13½***

**Granite Paper**

**1825** A595 3b With bow & arrow .20 .20
**1826** A595 3b Combat .20 .20
**1827** A595 7b Seizing opponent .35 .25
**1828** A595 7b Sky hovering .35 .25
*Nos. 1825-1828 (4)* 1.10 .90

Chinese Stone Statues — A596

Warriors holding: No. 1829, Staff with loop. No. 1830, Spear with slightly curved blade. No. 1831, Mace. No. 1832, Spear with jagged blade.

**1998, Sept. 15** ***Perf. 14x14½***

**Granite Paper**

**1829** A596 2b multicolored .20 .20
Complete booklet, 5 #1829 .50
**1830** A596 2b multicolored .20 .20
Complete booklet, 5 #1830 .50
**1831** A596 10b multicolored .50 .40
**1832** A596 10b multicolored .50 .40
*a.* Souvenir sheet, #1829-1832, perf 13¼ 1.75
*b.* As "a," with added marginal inscription 1.90
*Nos. 1829-1832 (4)* 1.40 1.20

China 1999 World Philatelic Exhibition (#1832b). #1832a-1832b sold for 35b.

#1832 is perf 13¼ and was issued 8/21/99.

Intl. Letter Writing Week — A597

Himavanta mythical animals created by ancient Thai artists: #1836, Kraisara Rajasiha, 3 king lions, white body, golden collars. #1837, Gajasiha, 2 tusked lions. #1838, Kesara Singha, 2 hoofed lions. #1839, Singha, 3 gray lions.

*Perf. 11½*

**1998, Oct. 3 Photo. Unwmk.**

**Granite Paper**

**1836** A597 2b multicolored .20 .20
Complete booklet, 5 #1836 .55
**1837** A597 2b multicolored .20 .20
Complete booklet, 5 #1837 .55
**1838** A597 12b multicolored .65 .50
**1839** A597 12b multicolored .65 .50
*a.* Souvenir sheet, #1836-1839 2.25
*Nos. 1836-1839 (4)* 1.70 1.40

No. 1839a sold for 40b.

Thai Presidency of the Intl. Assoc. of Lions Clubs — A598

**1998, Oct. 8 Litho.** ***Perf. 14½x14***

**Granite Paper**

**1840** A598 2b multicolored .20 .20
Complete booklet, 5 #1840 .55

New Year 1999 — A599

Flowers: No. 1841, Barleria lupulina. No. 1842, Gloriosa superba. No. 1843, Asclepias curassavica. No. 1844, Sesamum indicum.

*Perf. 14½x14*

**1998, Nov. 15 Photo. Unwmk.**

**Granite Paper**

**1841** A599 2b multicolored .20 .20
**1842** A599 2b multicolored .20 .20
**1843** A599 2b multicolored .20 .20

**1844** A599 2b multicolored .20 .20
*a.* Souvenir sheet, #1841-1844 .85
*Nos. 1841-1844 (4)* .80 .80

No. 1844a sold for 15b.

Knight Grand Cross, Most Admirable Order of the Direkgunabhorn — A600

***Perf. 14x14½***
**1998, Dec. 5 Litho. Unwmk.**
**Granite Paper**

**1845** 15b shown .80 .60
**1846** 15b Decoration .80 .60
*a.* A600 Pair, #1845-1846 1.60 1.40

Children's Day — A601

Paintings from competition, "Sports develop body and mind:" No. 1847, Sepak Takraw (game of kicking ball over net). No. 1848, Swimming. No. 1849, Volleyball. No. 1850, Equestrian sports.

***Perf. 14½x14***
**1999, Jan. 9 Litho. Unwmk.**
**Granite Paper**

**1847** A601 2b multicolored .20 .20
Complete booklet, 5 #1847 .55
**1848** A601 2b multicolored .20 .20
Complete booklet, 5 #1848 .55
**1849** A601 2b multicolored .20 .20
Complete booklet, 5 #1849 .55
**1850** A601 2b multicolored .20 .20
Complete booklet, 5 #1850 .55
*Nos. 1847-1850 (4)* .80 .80

Asian and Pacific Decade of Disabled Persons — A602

**1999, Jan. 10**
**Granite Paper**

**1851** A602 2b multicolored .20 .20
*a.* Complete booklet, 5 #1851 .55

Thai Rice Production — A603

#1852, Planting rice. #1853, Harvesting rice by hand. #1854, Harvesting rice with machinery. #1855, Rice in field, bowl of rice.

**1999, Feb. 25 Litho. *Perf. 14½x14***
**Granite Paper**

**1852** A603 6b multicolored .35 .25
**1853** A603 6b multicolored .35 .25
**1854** A603 12b multicolored .65 .50
**1855** A603 12b multicolored .65 .50
*a.* Souvenir sheet, #1852-1855 2.50
*Nos. 1852-1855 (4)* 2.00 1.50

No. 1855a sold for 45b.

Maghapuja Day (Buddhist Holiday) — A604

Designs: 3b, Birth of Mahajanaka. 6b, Mani Mekkhala carrying Mahajanaka to Mithila City. 9b, Two mango trees. 15b, Mahajanaka founding an educational institution.

**1999, Mar. 1 Litho. *Perf. 13½***
**Granite Paper**

**1856** A604 3b multicolored .30 .25
**1857** A604 6b multicolored .35 .25
**1858** A604 9b multicolored .55 .40
**1859** A604 15b multicolored .80 .60
*a.* Souvenir sheet, #1856-1859 2.40
*Nos. 1856-1859 (4)* 2.00 1.50

No. 1859a sold for 45b.

Somdetch Phra Sri Savarindira Baromma Raja Devi Phra Phan Vassa Ayika Chao, Queen Grandmother — A605

***Perf. 14x14½***
**1999, Mar. 30 Litho. Wmk. 340**

**1860** A605 2b multicolored .20 .20
Complete booklet, 5 #1860 .55

1999 Red Cross Fair.

Bangkok 2000 World Youth Stamp Expo, 13th Asian Intl. Stamp Expo — A606

Thai children's games: No. 1861, Kite flying. No. 1862, Wheel rolling. No. 1863, Catching last one in line (children going under arms). No. 1864, Snatching baby from mother snake.

***Perf. 14½x14***
**1999, Mar. 30 Unwmk.**
**Granite Paper**

**1861** A606 2b multicolored .20 .20
**1862** A606 2b multicolored .20 .20
**1863** A606 15b multicolored .80 .60
**1864** A606 15b multicolored .80 .60
*a.* Souvenir sheet, #1861-1864, perf. 13½ 2.40
*Nos. 1861-1864 (4)* 2.00 1.60

No. 1864a sold for 45b.

Heritage Conservation Day — A607

Various Thai silk designs for "Mudmee" textiles.

**1999, Apr. 2 *Perf. 14x14½***
**Granite Paper**

**1865** A607 2b bl grn & multi .20 .20
Complete booklet, 5 #1865 .55
**1866** A607 4b red & multi .20 .20
**1867** A607 12b vermilion & multi .65 .50
**1868** A607 15b black & multi .80 .60
*a.* Souvenir sheet, #1865-1868 2.40
*Nos. 1865-1868 (4)* 1.85 1.50

No. 1868a sold for 45b.

Songkran Day Type of 1991

**1999, Apr. 13**
**Granite Paper**

**1869** A425 2b Woman on rabbit's back, zodiac .20 .20
Complete booklet, 5 #1869 .55
*a.* Souvenir sheet of 1 .45
*b.* As "a," with added marginal inscription .45

China 1999 World Philatelic Exhibition (#1869b). #1869a-1869b sold for 8b and exist imperf.

Issued: #1869b, 8/21.

Consumer Protection Years, 1998-99 — A608

**1999, Apr. 30 *Perf. 14½x14***
**Granite Paper**

**1870** A608 2b multicolored .20 .20
Complete booklet, 5 #1870 .55

King Bhumibol Adulyadej's 72nd Birthday — A609

Royal palaces: No. 1871, Chitralada Villa, Dusit Palace, Bangkok, tree branch at UL. No. 1872, Phu Phing Ratchaniwet Palace, circular drive, white fence. No. 1873, Phu Phan Ratchaniwet Palace, adjoining buildings, light posts. No. 1874, Thaksin Ratchaniwet Palace, four trees reaching to second story windows.

Illustration reduced.

**1999, May 5 Photo. *Perf. 11½***
**Granite Paper**

**1871** A609 6b multicolored .35 .25
**1872** A609 6b multicolored .35 .25
**1873** A609 6b multicolored .35 .25
**1874** A609 6b multicolored .35 .25
*a.* Souvenir sheet, #1871-1874 2.25
*Nos. 1871-1874 (4)* 1.40 1.00

No. 1874a sold for 40b.

Political Science Dept., Thammasat University, 50th Anniv. — A610

**1999, June 14 Litho. *Perf. 14x14½***

**1875** A610 3b multicolored .20 .20

**King Bhumibol Adulyadej Type of 1996**

**Litho. & Engr.**
**1999 Wmk. 329 *Perf. 13***

**1876** A550 12b bl grn & bl .60 .40
**1877** A550 15b yel brn & grn .80 .60
**1878** A550 30b pink & brown 1.60 1.40

**Size: 25x30mm**
***Perf. 12¾x13¼***

**1879** A550 500b org & claret 30.00 19.00
*Nos. 1876-1879 (4)* 33.00 21.40

Issued: 12b, 15b, 30b, 7/1; 500b, 9/10.

UPU, 125th Anniv. A611

Designs: 2b, Floating Vessel of Light Festival. 15b, Buddhist Candle Festival, Ubon Ratchathani.

**1999, July 1 Litho. *Perf. 14½x14***
**Granite Paper**

**1880** A611 2b multicolored .20 .20
Complete booklet, 5 #1880 .55
**1881** A611 15b multicolored .80 .60

Customs Dept., 125th Anniv. — A612

**1999, July 3**

**1882** A612 6b multicolored .30 .20

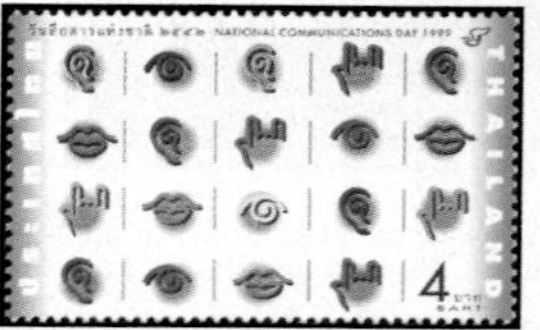

Natl. Communications Day — A613

**1999, Aug. 4 Litho. *Perf. 14½x14***
**Granite Paper**

**1883** A613 4b multicolored .20 .20

Thaipex '99 — A614

**1999, Aug. 4 Granite Paper**
**Color of Rabbits**

**1884** A614 6b black & white .30 .20
**1885** A614 6b golden brown, brown .30 .20
**1886** A614 12b white .60 .40
**1887** A614 12b gray .60 .40
*a.* Souvenir sheet, #1884-1887, perf. 13½ 2.50
*Nos. 1884-1887 (4)* 1.80 1.20

No. 1887a sold for 50b and exists imperf.

Bangkok 2000 Stamp Exhibition — A615

Scenes from Thai folk tales and literature: No. 1888, Boy on dragon-like horse. No. 1889, Rishi transforming tiger cub and calf into humans. No. 1890, Boy exiting conch shell. No. 1891, Children playing with kitchenware.

**1999, Aug. 4** ***Perf. 14½x14***

**Granite Paper**

**1888** A615 2b multicolored .20 .20
**1889** A615 2b multicolored .20 .20
**1890** A615 15b multicolored .80 .55
**1891** A615 15b multicolored .80 .55
*a.* Souvenir sheet, #1888-1891, perf. 13½ 2.40
*Nos. 1888-1891 (4)* 2.00 1.50

No. 1891a sold for 45b.

King Bhumibol Adulyadej's 72nd Birthday A616

King: No. 1892, On father's knee. No. 1893, With mother, sister and brother. No. 1894, With brother, in suits. No. 1895, With brother, in military uniforms. No. 1896, With wife on wedding day. No. 1897, At coronation ceremony. No. 1898, As Buddhist monk. No. 1899, With Queen, Prince and Princesses. No. 1900, Wearing royal robe.

**1999, Sept. 10** **Photo.** ***Perf. 11¾***

**Granite Paper**

**1892** A616 3b multicolored .20 .20
**1893** A616 3b multicolored .20 .20
**1894** A616 3b multicolored .20 .20
**1895** A616 6b multicolored .30 .20
**1896** A616 6b multicolored .30 .20
**1897** A616 6b multicolored .30 .20
**1898** A616 12b multicolored .60 .40
**1899** A616 12b multicolored .60 .40
**1900** A616 12b multicolored .60 .40
*a.* Souvenir sheet, #1892-1900 4.75
*Nos. 1892-1900 (9)* 3.30 2.40

No. 1900a sold for 90b.

Intl. Year of Older Persons — A617

**1999, Oct. 1** **Litho.** ***Perf. 14½x14***

**Granite Paper**

**1901** A617 2b multi .20 .20
Complete booklet, 5 #1901 1.00

Bauhinia Variegata — A618

Intl. Letter Writing Week: No. 1903, Bombax ceiba. No. 1904, Radermachera ignea (orange flowers). No. 1905, Bretschneidera sinensis (pink flowers).

**1999, Oct. 2** ***Perf. 14x14½***

**Granite Paper**

**1902** A618 2b shown .20 .20
Complete booklet, 5 #1902 .55
**1903** A618 2b multi .20 .20
Complete booklet, 5 #1903 .55
**1904** A618 12b multi .65 .45
**1905** A618 12b multi .65 .45
*a.* Souvenir sheet, #1902-1905, perf. 13¼ 1.90
*Nos. 1902-1905 (4)* 1.70 1.30

No. 1905a sold for 35b.

King Bhumibol Adulyadej's 72nd Birthday — A619

King: #1906, And vehicle. #1907, And Buddhist monks. #1908, And Queen. #1909, And soldiers. #1910, And crowd. #1911, And disabled boy. #1912, Wearing green army uniform. #1913, In white suit with camera. #1914, With crowd waving flags.

**1999, Oct. 21** **Photo.** ***Perf. 14½***

**Granite Paper**

**1906** A619 3b multi .20 .20
**1907** A619 3b multi .20 .20
**1908** A619 3b multi .20 .20
**1909** A619 6b multi .30 .20
**1910** A619 6b multi .30 .20
**1911** A619 6b multi .30 .20
**1912** A619 12b multi .65 .45
**1913** A619 12b multi .65 .45
**1914** A619 12b multi .65 .45
*a.* Souvenir sheet, #1906-1914 4.75
*Nos. 1906-1914 (9)* 3.45 2.55

No. 1914a sold for 90b. Numbers have been reserved for additional stamps in this set.

Design A39 — A620

**Litho. & Embossed with Foil Application**

**1999, Dec. 5** **Wmk. 387** ***Perf. 13¼***

**1915** A620 100b blue & bronze 7.00 3.50
**1916** A620 100b blue & silver 7.00 3.50
**1917** A620 100b blue & gold 7.00 3.50
*a.* Souvenir sheet, #1915-1917 25.00
*Nos. 1915-1917 (3)* 21.00 10.50

King Bhumibol Adulyadej's 72nd birthday. No. 1917a sold for 350b.

New Year 2000 — A621

Medicinal plants: No. 1918, Thunbergia laurifolia. No. 1919, Gmelina arborea. No. 1920, Prunus cerasoides. No. 1921, Fagraea fragrans.

***Perf. 14½x14¼***

**1999, Nov. 15** **Litho.**

**Granite Paper**

**1918** A621 2b multi .20 .20
**1919** A621 2b multi .20 .20
**1920** A621 2b multi .20 .20
*a.* Souv. sheet, 5 ea #1918-1920 + 10 labels 4.00
**1921** A621 2b multi .20 .20
*a.* Souvenir sheet, #1918-1921 .80 .60
*Nos. 1918-1921 (4)* .80 .80

No. 1921a sold for 15b.

No. 1920a was issued 3/25/00 and sold for 60b. For an additional fee the blank labels could be personalized with photos taken at a booth not operated by the Thailand postal authorities at the Bangkok 2000 Stamp Exhibition.

Investiture of Crown Prince Vajiralongkorn, 27th Anniv. — A622

**1999, Dec. 28** ***Perf. 14x14½***

**Granite Paper**

**1922** A622 3b multi .20 .20

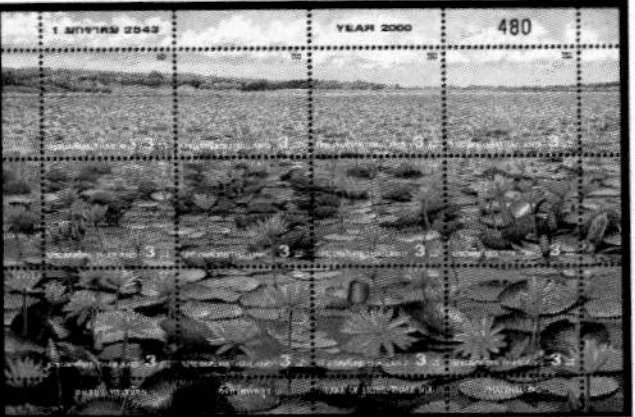

Lake of Lilies, Thale Noi — A623

Kulap Khao Flowers, Doi Chang Dao — A624

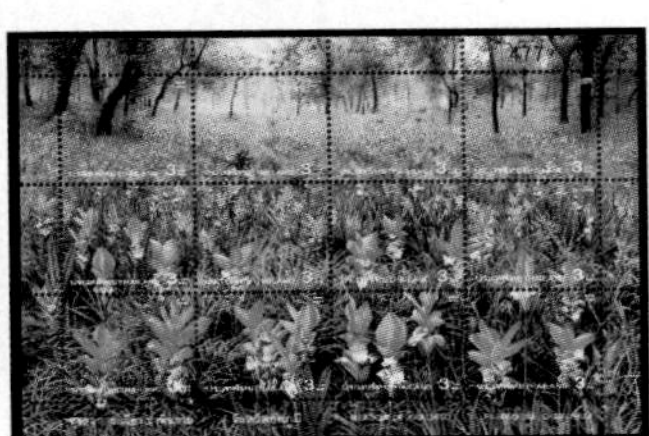

Krachieo Flowers, Pa Hin Ngam — A625

Bua Tong Flowers, Doi Mae Ukor — A626

Illustrations reduced.

***Perf. 14½x14¼***

**2000** **Litho.** **Unwmk.**

**Granite Paper**

**1923** A623 Sheet of 12, #a-l 1.75 1.75
*a.-l.* 3b Any single .20 .20
**1924** A624 Sheet of 12, #a-l 1.75 1.75
*a.-l.* 3b Any single .20 .20
**1925** A625 Sheet of 12, #a-l 1.75 1.75
*a.-l.* 3b Any single .20 .20
**1926** A625 Sheet of 12, #a-l 1.60 1.60
*a.-l.* 3b Any single .20 .20
*Nos. 1923-1926 (4)* 6.85 6.85

Issued: #1923, 1/1; #1924, 2/25; #1925, 7/16. #1926, 11/15.

Bees — A627

#1927, Apis andreniformis. #1928, Apis florea. #1929, Apis cerana. #1930, Apis dorsata.

**2000, Mar. 19** **Photo.** ***Perf. 11¾***

**Granite Paper**

**1927-1930** A627 3b Set of 4 .55 .40

**Souvenir Sheets of 1**

*1927a-1930a* Set of 4 1.50

Nos. 1927a-1930a do not have white margin on stamps and sold for 8b each.

Bangkok 2000 Stamp Exhibition — A628

Ceremonies: #1931, 2b, 1st month blessing (family & baby). #1932, 2b, Tonsure. #1933, 15b, Teacher respect (teacher, 3 children). #1934, 15b, Novice ordination.

**2000, Mar. 25** **Litho.** ***Perf. 14½x14***

**Granite Paper**

**1931-1934** A628 Set of 4 1.60 1.25
*1934a* Souvenir sheet, #1931-1934, perf. 13½x14 2.10

No. 1934a sold for 45b. It exists imperf.

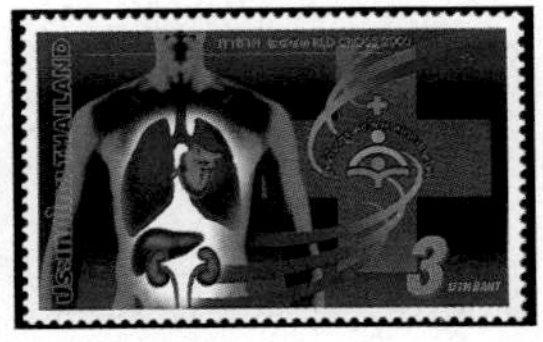

Thai Red Cross Fair A629

**2000, Mar. 30** ***Perf. 14½x14***

**Granite Paper**

**1935** A629 3b multi .20 .20

Thai Heritage Conservation — A630

Chok cloths from: 3b, Hat Seio. 6b, Mae Chaem. 8b, Ban Rai. 12b, Khu Bua.

**2000, Apr. 2** **Wmk. 387** ***Perf. 13¼***

**1936-1939** A630 Set of 4 1.40 1.00
*1939a* Souvenir sheet, #1936-1939 1.90

No. 1939a sold for 40b.

**Songkran Day Type of 1991**

***Perf. 14x14½***

**2000, Apr. 13** **Litho.** **Unwmk.**

**Granite Paper**

**1940** A425 2b Angel on serpent .20 .20
Booklet, 5 #1940 .50
*a.* Souvenir sheet of 1 .40

No. 1940a sold for 8b and exists imperf.

50th Wedding Anniv. of King and Queen — A631

No. 1941 — King Bhumibol Adulyadej and Queen Sirikit: a, Sitting on grass. b, Standing. c, Sitting on thrones. d, With family. e, Standing, wearing regalia.
Illustration reduced.

**2000, Apr. 28** **Photo.** ***Perf. 11¾***

**Granite Paper**

**1941** Vert. strip of 5 2.25 1.75
*a.-e.* A631 10b Any single .45 .35

Asalhapuja Day — A632

**2000, July 16 Litho. *Perf. 14x14½***
**Granite Paper**

1942 A632 3b multi .20 .20

Crown Prince Maha Vajiralongkorn, 48th Birthday — A633

**2000, July 28 *Perf. 14½x14***
**Granite Paper**

1943 A633 2b multi .20 .20
Booklet, 5 #1943 .50
a. Souvenir sheet of 1, perf. 13¼ .40

No. 1943a sold for 8b.

Natl. Communications Day — A634

**2000, Aug. 4**
**Granite Paper**

1944 A634 3b multi .20 .20

A635

A636
Intl. Letter Writing Week — A636

Various tea sets.

***Perf. 14½x14***
**2000, Oct. 7 Litho. Unwmk.**
**Granite Paper**

1945 A635 6b shown .25 .20
1946 A635 6b multi, diff. .25 .20
1947 A636 12b shown .55 .40
1948 A636 12b multi, diff. .55 .40
a. Souvenir sheet, #1945-1948, perf. 13¼ 2.00
*Nos. 1945-1948 (4)* 1.60 1.20

No. 1948a sold for 45b.

Princess Srinagarindra, Birth Cent. — A637

**2000, Oct. 21 Granite Paper**

1949 A637 2b multi .20 .20
Booklet, 5 #1949 .45
a. Souvenir sheet of 1, perf. 13¼ .35

No. 1949a sold for 8b.

Royal Barge Anantanakkharat — A638

Illustration reduced.

***Perf. 13¼x14***
**2000, Nov. 15 Photo. Wmk. 340**

1950 A638 9b multi .40 .30
a. Souvenir sheet of 1 .65

No. 1950a sold for 15b.

New Year 2001 — A639

Flowers: No. 1951, 2b, Clerodendrum philippinum. No. 1952, 2b, Capparis micracantha. No. 1953, 2b, Belamcanda chinensis. No. 1954, 2b, Memecylon caeruleum.

***Perf. 14½x14¼***
**2000, Nov. 15 Litho. Unwmk.**
**Granite Paper**

1951-1954 A639 Set of 4 .35 .25
*1954a* Souvenir sheet, #1951-1954 .65

No. 1954a sold for 15b.

Parrots — A640

Designs: 2b, Psittacula alexandri. 5b, Psittacula eupatria. 8b, Psittinus cyanurus. 10b, Psittacula roseata.

**2001, Jan. 13 *Perf. 14x14½***
**Granite Paper**

1955-1958 A640 Set of 4 1.10 .85
Booklet, 5 #1955 .45
a. Souvenir sheet, #1955-1958, perf. 13¼ 1.50
b. As "a," without price and with show emblem in margin 2.25

No. 1955a sold for 35b. No. 1955b, Hong Kong 2001 Stamp Exhibition, sold for 50b.

King Chulalongkorn and Land Deed — A641

**2001, Feb. 17 Granite Paper**

1959 A641 5b multi .20 .20

Dept. of Lands, cent.

Marine Life — A642

Designs: a, Ray. b, Turtle. c, Jellyfish, fish. d, Lionfish. e, Black, yellow fish, coral. f, Eel. g, School of striped fish, angelfish, coral, vert. h, Pufferfish, blue fish, vert. i, Shark, fish.

Stamp sizes: Nos. 1960a-1960f, 29x24mm, Nos. 1960g-1960h, 29x48mm. No. 1960i, 58x42mm.

***Perf. 13¾x14¼***
**2001, Mar. 15 Photo.**
**Granite Paper**

1960 A642 Sheet of 9 1.60 1.60
a.-f. 3b Any single .20 .20
g.-i. 6b Any single .25 .20

Gems A643

Designs: 3b, Diamond. 4b, Green sapphire. 6b, Pearl. 12b, Blue sapphire.

**2001 Litho. *Perf. 14½x14***
**Granite Paper**

1961-1964 A643 Set of 4 1.10 .85
a. Souvenir sheet, #1961-1964, perf. 13½x14 1.50
b. As "a," ovptd. in margin in gold 1.50

Issued, Nos. 1961-1964a, 3/30; No. 1964b, 6/9.

No. 1964a sold for 35b.

No. 1964b has Belgica 2001 emblem overprint.

Red Cross A644

***Perf. 14½x14***
**2001, Apr. 1 Litho. Unwmk.**
**Granite Paper**

1965 A644 4b multi .20 .20

Ancient Brocades From Nakhon Si Thammarat National Museum — A645

Colors of brocade: 2b, Orange red, lilac, and gold. 3b, Green and gold. No. 1968, 10b, Orange and gold. No. 1969, 10b, Bright pink and gold.

**2001, Apr. 2 *Perf. 14x14½***
**Granite Paper**

1966-1969 A645 Set of 4 1.10 .85
Booklet, 5 #1966 .45
a. Souvenir sheet, #1966-1969, perf. 13¼ 1.60

Heritage Conservation Day.
No. 1969a sold for 35b.

**Songkran Day Type of 1991**
***Perf. 13½x13¾***
**2001-2002 Wmk. 387**

1970 A425 2b Man on snake, zodiac .20 .20
Booklet, 5 #1970 .45
a. Souvenir sheet of 1 .35 .35
b. Unwmkd., granite paper, perf. 14x14½ .20 .20

Issued: Nos. 1970-1970a, 4/13/01. No. 1970b, 4/13/02. No. 1970b issued only in No. 2017b.

No. 1970a sold for 8b and exists imperf.

Visakhapuja Day — A646

**2001, May 7 Unwmk. *Perf. 14x14½***
**Granite Paper**

1971 A646 3b multi .20 .20

Demon Statues — A647

Designs: 2b, Maiyarap. 5b, Wirunchambang. 10b, Thotsakan. 12b, Sahatsadecha.

***Perf. 14x14½***
**2001, June 13 Litho. Unwmk.**
**Granite Paper**

1972-1975 A647 Set of 4 1.40 1.10
Booklet, 5 #1972 .45
*1975a* Souvenir sheet, #1972-1975, perf. 13½ 1.50

No. 1975a sold for 33b.

Prince Purachartra Jayakara and Rotary Intl. Emblem — A648

**2001, July 1 Granite Paper**

1976 A648 3b multi .20 .20

Rotary Intl. in Thailand, 66th anniv.

Mushrooms — A649

Designs: 2b, Schizophyllum commune. 3b, Lentinus giganteus. 5b, Pleurotus citrinopileatus. 10b, Pleurotus flabellatus.

**2001, July 4 Photo. *Perf. 13¾x14***
**Granite Paper**

**1977-1980** A649 Set of 4 .90 .70
Booklet, 5 # 1977 .45
*1980a* Souvenir sheet, #1977-1980, perf. 13½ 1.25

No. 1980 sold for 26b.

Insects A650

Designs: 2b, Cheirotonus parryi. 5b, Mouhotia batesi. 6b, Cladognathus giraffa. 12b, Mormolyce phyllodes.

**2001, July 4 Wmk. 329 *Perf. 13½***

**1981-1984** A650 Set of 4 1.10 .85
Booklet, 5 #1981 .45
*a.* Souvenir sheet, #1981-1984 1.50
*b.* As "a," with Phila Nippon '01 emblem in margin 1.50 —

No. 1984a sold for 34b.
No. 1984b sold for 34b, and was issued 8/1.

Natl. Communications Day — A651

***Perf. 14½x14***
**2001, Aug. 4 Litho. Unwmk.**
**Granite Paper**

**1985** A651 4b multi .20 .20

Thaipex '01 — A652

Various domesticated fowl: 3b, 4b, 6b, 12b.

**2001, Aug. 4 Photo. *Perf. 13¼***
**Granite Paper**

**1986-1989** A652 Set of 4 1.10 .85
*1989a* Souvenir sheet, #1986-1989 1.50 —

No. 1989 sold for 33b, also exists imperf.

Queen Suriyothai, Heroine of Thailand — A653

**2001, Aug. 12 Litho. *Perf. 14x14¾***
**Granite Paper**

**1990** A653 3b multi .20 .20
*a.* Souvenir sheet of 1, perf. 13¼ .45 —

No. 1990a sold for 10b.

Queen Sirikit's Visit to the People's Republic of China — A654

**2001, Aug. 12 *Perf. 14¾x14***
**Granite Paper**

**1991** A654 5b multi .25 .20

Butterflies — A655

Designs: 2b, Pachliopta aristolochiae goniopeltis. 4b, Rhinopalpa polynice. 10b, Poritia erycinoides. 12b, Spindasis lohita.

***Perf. 13½ Syncopated***
**2001, Sept. 10 Photo.**

**1992-1995** A655 Set of 4 1.25 .95
Booklet, 5 #1992 .45
*1995a* Souvenir sheet, #1992-1995 1.90 —
*1995b* As "a," with Hafnia '01 emblem in margin 2.00 2.00

No. 1995a sold for 40b.
No. 1995b issued 11/16. No. 1995b sold for 43b.

Intl. Letter Writing Week — A656

Medicinal herbs: 2b, Piper nigrum. 3b, Solanum trilobatum. 5b, Boesenbergia rotunda. 10b, Ocimum tenuiflorum.

***Perf. 14x14½***
**2001, Oct. 6 Litho. Unwmk.**
**Granite Paper**

**1996-1999** A656 Set of 4 .90 .70
Booklet, 5 #1996 .45
*1999a* Souvenir sheet, #1996-1999, perf. 13½x13¼ 1.10 —

No. 1999a sold for 25b.

Police Cadet Academy, Cent. — A657

**2001, Oct. 13 Litho. *Perf. 14½x14***
**Granite Paper**

**2000** A657 5b multi .25 .20

Royal Barge Anekkachat Puchong — A658

Illustration reduced.

**2001, Nov. 15 Photo. *Perf. 14¼***
**Granite Paper**

**2001** A658 9b multi .40 .30
*a.* Souvenir sheet of 1 .75 —

No. 2001a sold for 17b.

New Year 2002 — A659

Flowers: No. 2002, 2b, Pedicularis siamensis. No. 2003, 2b, Schoutenia glomerata. No. 2004, 2b, Gentiana crassa. No. 2005, 2b, Colquhounia coccinea.

**2001, Nov. 15 Litho. *Perf. 14x14½***
**Granite Paper**

**2002-2005** A659 Set of 4 .35 .25
*2005a* Souvenir sheet, #2002-2005 .50 —

No. 2005a sold for 11b.

Laying of Foundation Stone for Suvarnabhumi Airport Passenger Terminal — A660

**2002, Jan. 19 Litho. *Perf. 14½x14***
**Granite Paper**

**2006** A660 3b multi .20 .20

Rose — A661

**2002, Feb. 1 *Perf. 13¾***
**Granite Paper**

**2007** A661 4b multi .20 .20

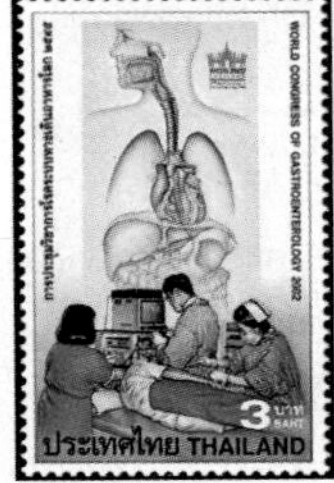
12th World Congress of Gastroenterology A662

**2002, Feb. 24 *Perf. 14x14½***
**Granite Paper**

**2008** A662 3b multi .20 .20

Communications Authority of Thailand, 25th Anniv. — A663

No. 2009: a, Satellite dish, CAT Telecom Co. emblem. b, Envelope, mailbox, Thailand Post emblem.
Illustration reduced.

**2002, Feb. 25 *Perf. 14½x14***
**Granite Paper**

**2009** A663 3b Horiz. pair, #a-b .30 .20
*c.* Souvenir sheet, #2009, perf. 13¼x13½ .45 —

No. 2009c sold for 10b.

Maghapuja Day — A664

**2002, Feb. 26 *Perf. 14½x14***
**Granite Paper**

**2010** A664 3b multi .20 .20

2002 Red Cross Fair A665

**2002, Mar. 30 Granite Paper**

**2011** A665 4b multi .20 .20

Ministry of Transport and Communications, 90th Anniv. — A666

**2002, Apr. 1 Litho. *Perf. 14½x14***
**Granite Paper**

**2012** A666 3b multi .20 .20

Heritage Conservation Day — A667

String puppets: No. 2013, 3b, Man. No. 2014, 3b, Woman. 4d, Demon. 15b, Monkey.

**2002, Apr. 2 *Perf. 14x14½***
**Granite Paper**

**2013-2016** A667 Set of 4 1.25 .90
*2016a* Souvenir sheet, #2013-2016, perf. 13¼ 1.40 —

No. 2016a sold for 30b.

**Songkran Day Type of 1991**

**2002, Apr. 13 *Perf. 14x14½***
**Granite Paper**

**2017** A425 2b Angel on horse, zodiac .20 .20
*a.* Souvenir sheet of 1 .35 .35
*b.* Souvenir sheet, #1724b, 1801c, 1869, 1940, 1970b, 2017 .65 .65
*c.* As "b," with Beijing 2002 emblem in margin and selling price removed 1.40 1.40

Nos. 2017a and 2017b sold for 8b and 14b respectively. Both exist imperf.
Issued: No. 2017c, 9/29. No. 2017c sold for 30b.

Fighting Fish A668

Designs: No. 2018, 3b, Betta imbellis. No. 2019, 3b, Betta splendens. 4b, Betta splendens, diff. 15b, Betta splendens, diff.

**2002, May 15 Litho. *Perf. 14½x14***
**Granite Paper**

**2018-2021** A668 Set of 4 1.25 .90
*2021a* Souvenir sheet, #2018-2021, perf. 13½ 1.40 1.40
*2021b* As "a," with Amphilex 2002 emblem and selling price removed 1.50 1.50

Issued: No. 2021b, 8/30. No. 2021a sold for 30b; No. 2021b sold for 31b.

Temples — A669

Designs: No. 2022, 3b, Wat Phra Si Rattanasatsadaram. No. 2023, 3b, Wat Phra Chetuphon Wimon Mangkhalaram. 4b, Wat Arun Ratchawararam. 12b, Wat Benchamabophit Dusit Wanaram.

**2002, June 17** ***Perf. 14½x14***

**Granite Paper**

**2022-2025** A669 Set of 4 1.10 .85
*2025a* Souvenir sheet, #2022-2025, perf. 13½ 1.25 1.25
*2025b* As "a," with Philakorea 2002 emblem and selling price removed 1.25 1.25

Issued: No. 2025b, 8/2. Nos. 2025a and 2025b each sold for 27b.

Crown Prince Maha Vajiralongkorn, 50th Birthday — A670

**2002, July 28** ***Perf. 14x14½***

**Granite Paper**

**2026** A670 3b multi .20 .20

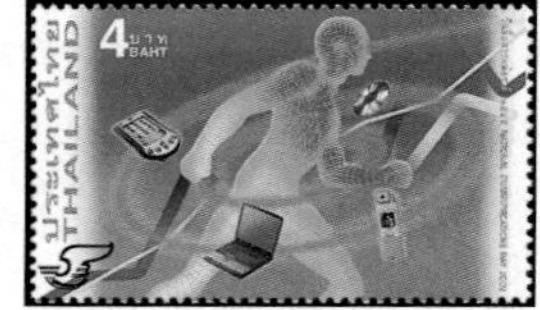

Natl. Communications Day — A671

**2002, Aug. 4** **Granite Paper**

**2027** A671 4b multi .20 .20

Thailand — Australia Diplomatic Relations, 50th Anniv. — A672

Designs: No. 2028, 3b, Nelumbo nucifera (pink flower). No. 2029, 3b, Nymphaea immutabilis (purple flower).

**2002, Aug. 6** ***Perf. 14½x14***

**Granite Paper**

**2028-2029** A672 Set of 2 .30 .25
*2029a* Souvenir sheet, #2028-2029, perf. 13½ .45 .45

See Australia Nos. 2072-2073. No. 2029a sold for 9b.

Queen Sirikit, 70th Birthday — A673

Designs: No. 2030, 3b, Queen and roses. No. 2031, 3b, Queen Sirikit rose. 4b, Queen Sirikit orchid. 15b, Queen Sirikit dona shrub.

**2002, Aug. 12** ***Perf. 14½x14***

**Granite Paper**

**2030-2033** A673 Set of 4 1.25 .90
*2033a* Souvenir sheet, #2030-2033, perf. 13½ 1.50 1.50

No. 2033a sold for 31b.

National Archives, 50th Anniv. — A674

**2002, Aug. 18** ***Perf. 14½x14***

**2034** A674 3b multi .20 .20

Thai Bank Notes, Cent. A675

**2002, Sept. 7** **Engr.** ***Perf. 13½***

**Granite Paper**

**2035** A675 5b org & brown .25 .20
*a.* Souvenir sheet of 1 .50 .50

No. 2035a sold for 11b.

Vimanmek Mansion Art Objects — A676

Designs: No. 2036, 3b, Round, lidded betel nut box. No. 2037, 3b, Bowl. 4b, Bowl, diff. 12b, Rectangular betel nut box.

**2002, Sept. 7** **Litho.** ***Perf. 14½x14***

**Granite Paper**

**2036-2039** A676 Set of 4 1.00 .75
*2039a* Souvenir sheet, #2036-2039, perf. 13½ 1.25 1.25

No. 2039a sold for 26b.

Royal Palaces A677

Designs: No. 2040, 4b, Thailand. No. 2041, 4b, Sweden.

***Perf. 12½x13½ Syncopated***

**2002, Oct. 5** **Litho. & Engr.**

**2040-2041** A677 Set of 2 .40 .30

See Sweden No. 2445.

Intl. Letter Writing Day A678

Designs: No. 2042, 3b, Animal-shaped coconut grater. No. 2043, 3b, Strainer. 4b, Coconut shell ladle. 15b, Earthenware stove and pot.

**2002, Oct. 5** **Litho.** ***Perf. 14½x14***

**Granite Paper**

**2042-2045** A678 Set of 4 1.25 .90
*2045a* Souvenir sheet, #2042-2045, perf. 13½ 1.40 1.40

No. 2045a sold for 31b.

Bangkok 2003 World Philatelic Exhibition — A679

Foods from: No. 2046, 3b, Central Thailand (red tablecloth). No. 2047, 3b, Southern Thailand (brown and yellow tablecloth). 4b, Northeastern Thailand. 15b, Northern Thailand.

**2002, Oct. 5** ***Perf. 14½x14***

**2046-2049** A679 Set of 4 1.25 .90
*2049a* Souvenir sheet, #2046-2049, perf. 13½ 1.40 1.40

No. 2049a sold for 30b.

New Year 2003 — A680

Flowers: No. 2050, 3b, Guaiacum officinale. No. 2051, 3b, Nyctanthes arbor-tristis. No. 2052, 3b, Barleria cristata. No. 2053, 3b, Thevetia peruviana.

***Perf. 14½x14¼***

**2002, Nov. 15** **Litho.**

**Granite Paper**

**2050-2053** A680 Set of 4 .55 .40
*2053a* Souvenir sheet, #2050-2053 .75 .55

No. 2053a sold for 16b.

20th World Scout Jamboree — A681

Designs: 3b, Scouts. 12b, Jamboree site.

**2002, Dec. 28** ***Perf. 14½x14***

**Granite Paper**

**2054-2055** A681 Set of 2 .70 .55

New Year 2003 (Year of the Goat) — A682

**2003, Jan. 1** ***Perf. 13***

**Granite Paper**

**2056** A682 3b multi .20 .20

National Children's Day — A683

Pangpond and his: a, Dog, Big (blue background). b, Friend, Hanuman (orange background). c, Girlfriend, Namo (green background). d, Teacher (red background).

Illustration reduced.

**2003, Jan. 11** ***Perf. 14½x14***

**Granite Paper**

**2057** A683 3b Block of 4, #a-d .55 .40

Rose — A684

**2003, Feb. 1** ***Perf. 13***

**Granite Paper**

**2058** A684 4b multi .20 .20

No. 2058 is impregnated with rose scent. Compare with Type A716.

Blue Green, by Fua Haribhitak A685

Portrait of Chira Chongkon, by Chamras Kietkong A686

Moonlight, by Prasong Padmanuja A687

Lotus Flowers, by Thawee Nandakwang — A688

**2003, Feb. 24** ***Perf. 13¼***

**Granite Paper**

**2059** A685 3b multi .20 .20
**2060** A686 3b multi .20 .20
**2061** A687 3b multi .20 .20
**2062** A688 15b multi .70 .55
*Nos. 2059-2062 (4)* 1.30 1.15

Bangkok 2003 World Philatelic Exhibition — A689

Tourist attractions: No. 2063, 3b, Doi Inthanon Temple, Chiang Mai. No. 2064, 3b, River Kwai Bridge, Kanchanaburi. No. 2065, 3b, Phu Kradung (cliff), Loei. 15b, Maya Bay, Krabi.

**2003, Mar. 3** ***Perf. 14½x14***

**Granite Paper**

**2063-2066** A689 Set of 4 1.10 .85
*2066a* Souvenir sheet, #2063-2066, perf. 13¼ 1.40 1.10

No. 2066a sold for 29b.

**King Bhumibol Adulyadej Type of 1996**

***Perf. 14x14½***

**2003, Mar. 14 Litho. Unwmk.**

**Granite Paper**

**2067** A550 1b blue .20 .20

2003 Red Cross Fair — A690

**2003, Mar. 28** ***Perf. 14x14½***

**Granite Paper**

**2068** A690 3b multi .20 .20

Kick Boxing — A691

Designs: No. 2069, 3b, Boxers punching. No. 2070, 3b, Boxer in black trunks with knee raised. No. 2071, 3b, Boxer in red trunks kicking. 15b, Boxer in red trunks kicking, diff.

**2003, Apr. 2 Litho.** ***Perf. 13¼***

**Granite Paper**

**2069-2072** A691 Set of 4 1.10 .85
*2072a* Souvenir sheet, #2069-2072 1.40 1.10
*2072b* As "a," with China 2003 Philatelic Exhibition emblem in margin 1.50 1.10

No. 2072a sold for 29b.
Issued: No. 2072b, 11/20. No. 2072b sold for 29b.

Princess Maha Chakri Sirindhorn, 48th Birthday — A692

**2003, Apr. 2** ***Perf. 14x14½***

**Granite Paper**

**2073** A692 3b multi .20 .20

Princess Galyani Vadhana, 80th Birthday — A693

**2003, May 6 Granite Paper**

**2074** A693 3b multi .20 .20

Kings Chulalongkorn and Vajiravudh A694

**2003, May 6 Granite Paper**

**2075** A694 3b multi .20 .20

Inspector General Dept., cent.

King Prajadhipok Day — A695

**2003, May 30** ***Perf. 14½x14***

**Granite Paper**

**2076** A695 3b multi .20 .20

Bantam Chickens — A696

Designs: No. 2077, 3b, White ears jungle fowl. No. 2078, 3b, Sugarcane husk colored. No. 2079, 3b, Black-tailed white. 15b, Dark gray.

**2003 Litho.** ***Perf. 13***

**Granite Paper**

**2077-2080** A696 Set of 4 1.25 .95
*2080a* Souvenir sheet, #2077-2080 1.40 1.10
*2080b* As "a," with Lanka Philex 2003 emblem in margin 1.40 1.10

Issued: Nos. 2077-2080, 2080a, 6/10; No. 2080b, 7/31. Nos. 2080a and 2080b each sold for 29b.

Asalhapuja Day — A697

**2003, July 13** ***Perf. 14x14½***

**Granite Paper**

**2081** A697 3b multi .20 .20

National Communications Day — A698

**2003, Aug. 4** ***Perf. 14½x14***

**Granite Paper**

**2082** A698 3b multi .20 .20

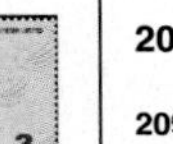

Communications Organization Emblems — A699

No. 2083: a, Thailand Post Company Limited. b, Communications Authority of Thailand (23x27mm). c, CAT Telecom Public Company Limited.
Illustration reduced.

***Perf. 14¼x14½***

**2003, Aug. 14 Litho. Wmk. 340**

**2083** A699 3b Horiz. strip of 3, #a-c .45 .35

King Chulalongkorn (1853-1910) A700

**Litho. & Embossed**

**2003, Sept. 20 Unwmk.** ***Perf. 13¼***

**2084** A700 100b gold & multi 5.25 4.00
*a.* Souvenir sheet of 4 21.00 16.00

No. 2084a issued 9/30.
No. 2084a exists imperf. with Bangkok 2003 emblem at lower left.

Government Housing Bank, 50th Anniv. — A701

**2003, Sept. 24 Litho.** ***Perf. 14½x14***

**Granite Paper**

**2085** A701 3b multi .20 .20

Bangkok 2003 World Philatelic Exhibition — A702

Handicrafts: No. 2086, 3b, Basketry. No. 2087, 3b, Pottery. No. 2088, 3b, Leatherwork. 15b, Wood carving.

**2003, Oct. 4**

**Granite Paper**

**2086-2089** A702 Set of 4 1.25 .95
*2089a* Souvenir sheet, #2086-2089, perf. 13¼ 1.50 1.10

A varnish with a rough surface was applied to portions of the designs. No. 2089a sold for 29b, and exists imperf.

Trees of Thailand and Canada — A703

No. 2090: a, Cassia fistula (Thailand). b, Maple leaves (Canada).

**2003, Oct. 4** ***Perf. 14x14½***

**Granite Paper**

**2090** A703 3b Horiz. pair, #a-b .30 .25
*c.* Souvenir sheet, #2090, perf. 13¼ .45 .35

No. 2090c sold for 9b.

Lychees — A704

Rose Apples — A705

Fruit: No. 2093, Coconuts. 15b, Jackfruit.

**2003, Oct. 4**

**Granite Paper**

**2091** A704 3b shown .20 .20
**2092** A705 3b shown .20 .20
**2093** A704 3b multi .20 .20
**2094** A704 15b multi .75 .55
*a.* Souvenir sheet, #2091-2094, perf. 13¼ 1.50 1.10

International Letter Writing Week. No. 2094a sold for 29b.

Oct. 14, 1973 Student Uprisings, 30th Anniv. — A706

**2003, Oct. 14** ***Perf. 14½x14***

**Granite Paper**

**2095** A706 3b multi .20 .20

Asia-Pacific Economic Cooperation Meeting — A707

**2003, Oct. 20 Granite Paper**

**2096** A707 3b multi .20 .20

New Year 2004 — A708

Flowers: No. 2097, 3b, Bougainvillea spectabilis. No. 2098, 3b, Eucrosia bicolor. No. 2099, 3b, Canna x generalis. No. 2100, 3b, Zinnia violacea.

**2003, Nov. 15** ***Perf. 14½x14¼***

**Granite Paper**

**2097-2100** A708 Set of 4 .60 .45
*2100a* Souvenir sheet, #2097-2100 .80 .60

| | | | |
|---|---|---|---|
| *2100b* | As "a," with 2004 Hong Kong Stamp Expo emblem in margin | .85 | .60 |

No. 2100a sold for 16b.
Issued: No. 2100b, 1/30/04. No. 2100b sold for 16b.

Thailand Flag A709

Thai Pavilion A710

Elephants A711

Cassia Fistula A712

**2003, Dec. 1** ***Perf. 14¼x14½***
**Granite Paper**

| | | | |
|---|---|---|---|
| **2101** | A709 3b multi | .20 | .20 |
| **2102** | A710 3b multi | .20 | .20 |
| **2103** | A711 3b multi | .20 | .20 |
| **2104** | A712 3b multi | .20 | .20 |
| | *Nos. 2101-2104 (4)* | .80 | .80 |

Elephants — A713

No. 2105: a, Asian elephant. b, African elephants.
Illustration reduced.

**2003, Dec. 9** ***Perf. 14½x14***
**Granite Paper**

| | | | |
|---|---|---|---|
| **2105** | A713 3b Horiz. pair, #a-b | .30 | .25 |
| ***c.*** | Souvenir sheet, #2105a, perf. 13¼ | .45 | .35 |

No. 2105c sold for 9b.
Thailand-South Africa diplomatic relations, 10th anniv. See South Africa No. 1330.

**King Bhumibol Adulyadej Type of 1996**

**2003-04** **Litho.** ***Perf. 14x14½***
**Granite Paper**

| | | | |
|---|---|---|---|
| **2106** | A550 50s olive brown | .20 | .20 |

Issued: 50s, 12/3. 1b, 1/22/04.

**Zodiac Animal Type of 2003**

**2004, Jan. 1** **Litho.** ***Perf. 13***
**Granite Paper**

| | | | |
|---|---|---|---|
| **2108** | A682 3b Monkey | .20 | .20 |

Children's Day — A714

**2004, Jan. 10** ***Perf. 14½x14***
**Granite Paper**

| | | | |
|---|---|---|---|
| **2109** | A714 3b multi | .20 | .20 |

Paintings of Hem Vejakorn A715

Designs: No. 2110, 3b, A Scene in Thai History (dancers). No. 2111, 3b, Maha Bharatayudh (charioteer). No. 2112, 3b, Khun Chang — Khun Phaen (women with horse). No. 2113, 3b, Phra Lor (woman and rooster).

**2004, Jan. 17** ***Perf. 13¼***
**Granite Paper**

| | | | |
|---|---|---|---|
| **2110-2113** | A715 Set of 4 | .65 | .50 |
| *2113a* | Souvenir sheet, #2110-2113 | .85 | .60 |

No. 2113a sold for 16b.

Rose — A716

**2004, Feb. 1** ***Perf. 13***
**Granite Paper**

| | | | |
|---|---|---|---|
| **2114** | A716 4b multi | .20 | .20 |

Compare with type A684. No. 2114 is impregnated with rose scent.

Turtles — A717

Designs: No. 2115, 3b, Cuora amboinensis. No. 2116, 3b, Platysternon megacephalum. No. 2117, 3b, Indotestudo elongata. No. 2118, 3b, Heosemys spinosa.

**2004, Mar. 1** ***Perf. 14½x14***
**Granite Paper**

| | | | |
|---|---|---|---|
| **2115-2118** | A717 Set of 4 | .65 | .50 |
| *2118a* | Souvenir sheet, #2115-2118, perf. 13¼ | .85 | .60 |
| *2118b* | Similar to "a," with 2004 Singapore World Stamp Championship emblem in margin | .80 | .60 |

Issued: No. 2118b, 8/28.
Nos. 2118a and 2118b sold for 16b.

Siam Society, Cent. — A718

**2004, Mar. 10** ***Perf. 14½x14***

| | | | |
|---|---|---|---|
| **2119** | A718 3b multi | .20 | .20 |

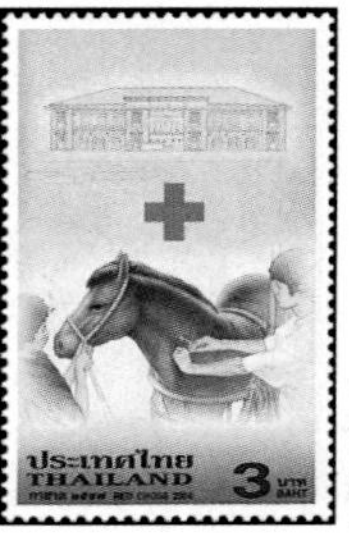
2004 Red Cross Fair — A719

**2004, Mar. 29** ***Perf. 14x14½***
**Granite Paper**

| | | | |
|---|---|---|---|
| **2120** | A719 3b multi | .20 | .20 |

Heritage Conservation Day — A720

Fringe colors of hand woven clothes: No. 2121, 3b, Rose red. No. 2122, 3b, Blue. No. 2123, 3b, Green. No. 2124, 3b, Orange red. Denomination is at LL on Nos. 2122, 2124.

**2004, Apr. 2** **Litho.** ***Perf. 14x14½***
**Granite Paper**

| | | | |
|---|---|---|---|
| **2121-2124** | A720 Set of 4 | .65 | .50 |
| *2124a* | Souvenir sheet, #2121-2124, perf. 13¼ | .85 | .60 |
| *2124b* | As "a," with España 2004 emblem in margin, perf. 13¼ | .95 | .65 |

Issued: No. 2124b, 5/22. No. 2124a sold for 16b; No. 2124b for 18b.

Architecture in Thailand and Italy — A721

No. 2125: a, Golden Mountain Temple, Bangkok. b, Colosseum, Rome.
Illustration reduced.

**2004, Apr. 21** ***Perf. 14½x14***
**Granite Paper**

| | | | |
|---|---|---|---|
| **2125** | A721 3b Horiz. pair, #a-b | .30 | .20 |
| *2125c* | Souvenir sheet, #2125, perf. 13¼ | .50 | .35 |

No. 2125c sold for 10b.
See Italy No. 2602.

Sculpture A722

Designs: No. 2126, 3b, One-sided Drum, by Chit Rienpracha (yellow green background). No. 2127, 3b, Dance Drama, by Sitthidet Saenghiran (rose red background). No. 2128, 3b, Heavenly Flute, by Khien Yimsiri (Prussian blue background). No. 2129, 3b, The Calf, by Paitun Muangsomboom, horiz.

**2004, May 3** ***Perf. 13¼***

| | | | |
|---|---|---|---|
| **2126-2129** | A722 Set of 4 | .60 | .40 |

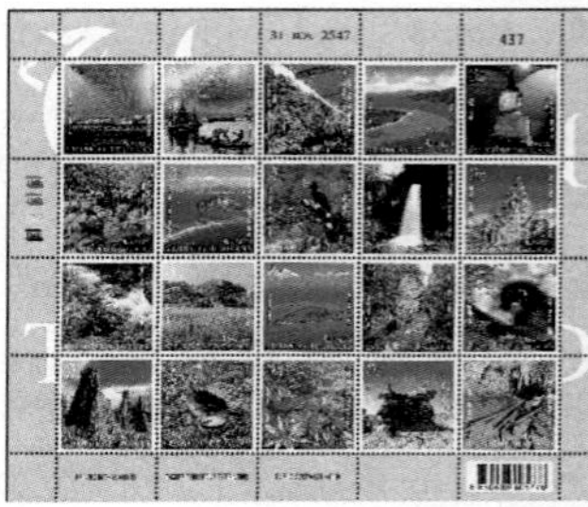
Unseen Tourist Attractions — A723

No. 2130: a, Non Ngai Buddha, Suphan Buri. b, Khao Laem Dam, Kanchanaburi. c, Mural, Temple fo the Emerald Buddha, Bangkok. d, Ko Li-Pe, Satun. e, Buddha, Wat Phra Thong, Phuket. f, Khao Luang National Park, Nakhon Si Thammarat. g, Miracle Beach, Ko Damikhwan, Krabi. h, Hornbill, Hala-Bala Forest, Narathiwat. i, Long Ru Waterfall, Ubon Ratchathani. j, Prasat Hin Phanom Rung, Buri Ram. k, Red maple leaves, Phu Kradueng National Park, Loei. l, Phukhao Ya, Ranong. m, Ko Kradat, Trat. n, Op Luang National Park, Chiang Mai. o, Dusky leaf monkey, Phetchaburi. p, Lalu, Sra Kaeo. q, Pu Kai, Mu Ko Similan, Phang-Nga. r, Tha Le Noi Waterfowl Park. Phatthalung. s, Phu Pha Thoep, Mukdahan National Park. t, Phi Maen Cave, Mae Hong Son.

**2004, May 31** ***Perf. 13***
**Granite Paper**

| | | | |
|---|---|---|---|
| **2130** | A723 3b Sheet of 20, #a-t | 3.00 | 2.10 |

See Nos. 2137, 2147, 2158.

Buddha Sculptures A724

No. 2131: a, Phra Nangpaya. b, Phra Kampaeng Soumkhor. c, Phra Somdej Wat Rakangkhositaram. d, Phar Rod. e, Phra Phongsuphan.

**Litho. & Embossed**

**2004, June 1** ***Perf. 13¼***
**Granite Paper**

| | | | |
|---|---|---|---|
| **2131** | Horiz. strip of 5 | 2.25 | 1.60 |
| ***a.-e.*** | A724 9b Any single | .45 | .30 |
| ***f.*** | Souvenir sheet, #2131a-2131e | 2.60 | 1.90 |

No. 2131f sold for 53b.

Visakhapuja Day — A725

**2004, June 2** **Litho.** ***Perf. 14x14½***
**Granite Paper**

| | | | |
|---|---|---|---|
| **2132** | A725 3b multi | .20 | .20 |

Bridges — A726

Designs: No. 2133, 5b, Phra Buddha Yodfa Bridge. No. 2134, 5b, Rama VI Bridge. No.

2135, 5b, Rama VIII Bridge. No. 2136, 5b, Rama IX Bridge.
Illustration reduced.

**2004, July 1 Litho. *Perf. 14¼x14½***
**Granite Paper**

**2133-2136** A726 Set of 4 1.00 .65

On Nos. 2135 and 2136 portions of the design were produced by a thermographic process which produces a shiny, raised effect.

**Unseen Tourist Attractions Type of 2004**

No. 2137: a, Wat Pho Prathap Chang, Phichit. b, Phra Prathan Chaturathit, Wat Phumin, Nan. c, Thalenai, Angthong Archipelago, Surat Thani. d, Wat Na Phra Men, Phra Nakhon Si Ayutthaya. e, Sanam Chan Palace, Nakhon Pathom. f, Piyamitr Tunnel, Yala. g, Ban Khamchanot, Udon Thani. h, Rail line along Pasak Cholasit Dam, Lop Buri. i, Khlong Lan Waterfall, Khlong Lan National Park, Kamphaeng Phet. j, Mo-I-Daeng Cliff, Khao Phra Wihan National Park, Si Sa Ket. k, Changkra Wild Orchid Park, Khon Kaen. l, Canoeists at Ti Lo Re, Tak. m, Khao Ta Mong Lai, Prachuap Khiri Khan. n, Suriya Patithin solar calendar, Prasat Phu Phek, Sakon Nakhon. o, Traditional boat racing, Chumphon. p, Mokochu Range Mae Wong National Park, Nakhon Sawan. q, Ordination by elephant in the sixth month, Surin. r, Rock climbing, Tan Rattana Waterfall, Khao Yai National Park, Prachin Buri. s, Monks collecting alms on horseback, Chiang Rai. t, Cycling in Thung Salaeng Luang, Phitsanulok.

**2004, July 28 *Perf. 13***
**Granite Paper**

**2137** A723 3b Sheet of 20, #a-t 3.00 2.10

Jasmine Flower — A727

**Litho. & Embossed**
**2004, Aug. 2 *Perf. 13***
**Granite Paper**

**2138** A727 5b multi .25 .20

No. 2138 is impregnated with a jasmine scent.

Princess Maha Chakri Sirindhorn Information Technology Program — A728

**2004, Aug. 4 Litho. *Perf. 14x14½***
**Granite Paper**

**2139** A728 3b multi .20 .20

National Communications Day — A729

**2004, Aug. 4 *Perf. 14½x14***
**Granite Paper**

**2140** A729 3b multi .20 .20

Opening of First Subway Line — A730

**2004, Aug. 12 Litho. *Perf. 14½x14***
**Granite Paper**

**2141** A730 3b multi .20 .20

Queen Sirikit, 72nd Birthday A731

**Litho. & Embossed**
**2004, Aug. 12 *Perf. 13¼***

**2142** A731 100b multi 5.00 3.25

Boats A732

Designs: No. 2143, 3b, Thai junk. No. 2144, 3b, Sampan boat. No. 2145, 3b, Krachaeng boat. 15b, Packet boat.

**2004-05 Litho. *Perf. 14½x14***
**Granite Paper**

**2143-2146** A732 Set of 4 1.25 .85
*2146a* Souvenir sheet, #2143-2146, perf. 13¼ 1.40 .95
*b.* As "a," with Pacific Explorer 2005 emblem in margin 1.50 1.50

No. 2146a sold for 29b. No. 2146b sold for 30b.
Issued: Nos. 2143-2146a, 9/1/04; No. 2146b, 4/21/05.

**Unseen Tourist Attractions Type of 2004**

No. 2147: a, Phra Nang Din, Phayad. b, Phra That Kong Khao Noi, Yasothon. c, Phra Atchana, Wat Sri Chum, Sukothai. d, Wat Bang Kung, Samut Songkhram. e, Ku Kut, Wat Phrathat Chamthewi, Lamphun. f, Dolphin watching, Chachoengsao. g, Tak Bat Dok Mai tradition, Saraburi. h, Hat Chao Lao, Chanthaburi. i, Phu Kum Khao dinosaur fossils, Kalasin. j, Reversed stupa, Wat Phra That Lampang Luang, Lampang. k, Khu Khut Waterfowl Park, Songkhla. l, Plant Market Khlong 15, Nakhon Nayok. m, Huppatad, Uthai Thani. n, Thai Muang Beach, Nakhon Phanom. o, Wild gaur, Khao Yai National Park, Nakhon Ratchasima. p, Canoeing, Le Khao Kop Cave, Trang. q, Sea of flowers, Pru Soi Dao, Uttaradit. r, Kolae boat, Ban Paseyawo, Pattani. s, Sea of Mist, Thap Boek, Phu Hin Rongkla National Park, Phetchabun. t, Bats, Khao Chung Phran, Ratchaburi.

**2004, Sept. 28 *Perf. 13***
**Granite Paper**

**2147** A723 3b Sheet of 20, #a-t 3.00 2.10

Intl. Letter Writing Week — A733

Kites: No. 2148, 3b, Snake. No. 2149, 3b, Star-shaped. No. 2150, 3b, Diamond-shaped with tail. 15b, Buffalo.

**2004, Oct. 9 Litho. *Perf. 14x14½***
**Granite Paper**

**2148-2151** A733 Set of 4 1.25 .85
*2151a* Souvenir sheet, #2148-2151, perf. 13¼ 1.40 1.40
*2151b* Similar to "a," with Beijing 2004 emblem in margin 1.50 1.50

Issued: No. 2151b, 10/28. No. 2151a sold for 29b; No. 2151b for 30b.

King Mongkut (1804-68) A734

**2004, Oct. 18 *Perf. 14x14½***
**Granite Paper**

**2152** A734 4b multi .20 .20

E-customs System — A735

**2004, Nov. 15 *Perf. 14½x14***
**Granite Paper**

**2153** A735 3b multi .20 .20

New Year 2005 — A736

Flowers: No. 2154, 3b, Wrightia sirikitiae. No. 2155, 3b, Eria amica. No. 2156, 3b, Burmannia coelestris. No. 2157, 3b, Utricularia bifida.

**2004, Nov. 15 *Perf. 14¼x14½***
**Granite Paper**

**2154-2157** A736 Set of 4 .65 .45
*2157a* Souvenir sheet, #2154-2157, perf. 14¼x14½ .85 .85

No. 2157a sold for 16b.

**Unseen Tourist Attractions Type of 2004**

No. 2158: a, Phra That Cho Hae, Phrae. b, Wat Karuna, Chai Nat. c, Wat Nang Sao, Samut Sakhon. d, Phra Mutao Pagoda, Nonthaburi. e, Phu Kao Phu Phan Kham National Park, Nong Bua Lam Phu. f, Airvata (three-headed elephant), Erawan Museum, Samut Prakan. g, Wat Chedi Hoi, Pathum Thani. h, White krajiaw field, Chaiyaphum. i, Chet Si Waterfall, Nong Khai. j, Summer Palace, Ko Si Chang, Choi Buri. k, Traditional Drum-making village (Ban Bang Phae), Ang Thong. l, Ko Thalu, Rayong. m, Kosamphi Forest Park, Maha Sarakham. n, Cannonball tree, Wat Phra Non Chaksi, Sing Buri. o, Tung Kula Rong Hai, Roi Et. p, Phu Sra Dok Bua, Amnat Charoen.

**2004, Nov. 26 *Perf. 13***
**Granite Paper**

**2158** A723 3b Sheet of 16, #a-p, + 4 labels 2.50 2.50

Bangkok Fashion City Initiative — A737

No. 2159: a, 3b, Man and woman. b, 3b, Woman in pink dress. c, 3b, Woman with green shirt. d, 15b, Woman with brown eyeshade.
Illustration reduced.

**2004, Dec. 5 *Perf. 14x14½***
**Granite Paper**

**2159** A737 Horiz. strip of 4, #a-d 1.25 1.25
*e.* Souvenir sheet, #2159a-2159d, perf. 13½ 1.50 1.50

No. 2159e sold for 30b.

Queen Rambhai Bharni (1904-84) A738

**2004, Dec. 20 *Perf. 14x14½***
**Granite Paper**

**2160** A738 3b multi .20 .20

**Zodiac Animal Type of 2003**

**2005, Jan. 1 *Perf. 13***
**Granite Paper**

**2161** A682 3b Cock .20 .20

Children's Day — A739

**2005, Jan. 8 *Perf. 14½x14***
**Granite Paper**

**2162** A739 3b multi .20 .20

Thailand - Argentina Diplomatic Relations, 50th Anniv. — A740

No. 2163: a, Tango dancers, Argentina. b, Tom-tom dancers, Thailand.
Illustration reduced.

**2005, Feb. 2 *Perf. 13¼***
**Granite Paper**

**2163** A740 3b Horiz. pair, #a-b .35 .35

See Argentina Nos. 2312-2313.

Rose — A741

**2005, Feb. 10** *Perf. 12½*
**Flocked Paper**

**2164** A741 10b multi .55 .40

No. 2164 is impregnated with rose scent.

Maghapuja Day — A742

**2005, Feb. 23** *Perf. 14x14½*
**Granite Paper**

**2165** A742 3b multi .20 .20

Rotary International, Cent. — A743

**2005, Feb. 23** *Perf. 14½x14*
**Granite Paper**

**2166** A743 3b multi .20 .20

Red Cross A744

**2005, Mar. 30** **Litho.**
**Granite Paper**

**2167** A744 3b multi .20 .20

Princess Maha Chakri Sirindhorn, 50th Birthday — A774a

**2005, Apr. 2** **Litho.** *Perf. 13¼*
**Granite Paper**

**2167A** A774a 3b multi .20 .20

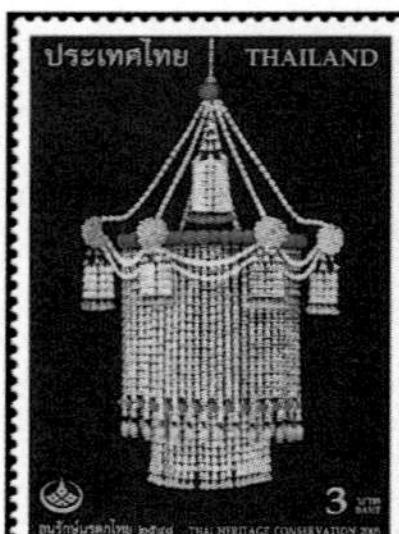
A745

Hanging Art — A746

**2005, Apr. 2** **Litho.** *Perf. 13¼*
**Granite Paper**

**2168** A745 3b shown .20 .20
**2169** A746 3b shown .20 .20
**2170** A746 3b multi, diff. .20 .20
**2171** A745 15b multi, diff. .75 .55
*a.* Souvenir sheet, #2168-2171 1.50 1.50
*Nos. 2168-2171 (4)* 1.35 1.15

Heritage Conservation Day. No. 2171 sold for 30b.

Authors Born in 1905 — A747

Designs: No. 2172, 3b, Dokmaisod (olive green background). No. 2173, 3b, Sri Burapha (Prussian blue background). No. 2174, 3b, Maimuangderm (dark blue background). No. 2175, 3b, Arkatdumkeung Rabibhadana (rose pink background).

**2005, May 5** *Perf. 14½x14*
**Granite Paper**

**2172-2175** A747 Set of 4 .65 .45
*2175a* Souvenir sheet, #2172-2175, perf. 13¼ .90 .90

No. 2175a sold for 17b.

Insects — A748

Designs: No. 2176: a, Coccinella transversalis. b, Chrysochroa buqueti rugicollis (47x28mm). c, Sagra femorata. d, Chrysochroa maruyamai (47x28mm).

**Litho. & Embossed**
**2005, May 31** *Perf. 14¼x14½*
**Granite Paper**

**2176** Horiz. strip or block of 4 1.00 .65
*a.-d.* A748 5b Any single .25 .20
*e.* Sheet, 2 each #2176a-2176d 3.00 3.00

Embossed portions of stamps are covered with a glossy varnish.

No. 2176e issued May 2006, Washington 2006 World Philatelic Exhibition. No. 2176e sold for 54b.

Heart Balloons and Mail Truck — A749

Balloons — A749a

**2005** **Litho.** *Perf. 13*
**Granite Paper**

**2177** A749 3b multi .20 .20
**2177A** A749a 3b multi .20 .20

Issued: No. 2177, June; No. 2177A, 7/15. Nos. 2177 and 2177A were issued in sheets of 12 + 12 personalizable labels the same size as the stamp.

Buddha Amulets A750

No. 2178: a, Phra Ruang Lang Rang Puen. b, Phra Hu Yan. c, Phra Chinnarat Bai Sema. d, Phra Mahesuan. e, Phra Tha Kradan.

**Litho. & Embossed**
**2005, June 19** *Perf. 13¼*
**Granite Paper**

**2178** Horiz. strip of 5 2.25 1.50
*a.-e.* A750 9b Any single .45 .30
*f.* Souvenir sheet, #2178a-2178e 2.75 2.75
*g.* As "f," with Taipei 2005 emblem in margin 4.25 4.25

No. 2178f sold for 55b.

No. 2178g issued 8/19/05. No. 2178g sold for 85b.

Thailand - People's Republic of China Diplomatic Relations, 30th Anniv. — A751

Panda: a, Showing tongue. b, Feeding on bamboo.

Illustration reduced.

**2005, July 1** **Litho.** *Perf.*
**Granite Paper**

**2179** A751 Horiz. pair .30 .20
*a.-b.* 3b Either single .20 .20
*c.* Souvenir sheet, #2179a-2179b .75 .75

No. 2179 has perf. 13¼ line of perforations between the two stamps, and the surrounding selvage is rouletted 11¾. No. 2179c, which sold for 15b, lacks the perforations between the stamps and has no rouletting.

Thaipex 2005 — A752

Dancers in play "Chuck Nark": No. 2180, 3b, Pra Rama and Princess Srida. No. 2181, 3b, Hanuman (white mask). No. 2182, 3b, Thotsakan (green mask). 15b, Pra Rama and Thotsakan.

**Litho. with Foil Application**
**2005, Aug. 3** *Perf. 13¼*
**Granite Paper**

**2180-2183** A752 Set of 4 1.25 .85
*2183a* Souvenir sheet, #2180-2183 1.50 1.50

No. 2183a sold for 30b.

Natl. Communications Day — A753

**2005, Aug. 4** **Litho.** *Perf. 14½x14*
**Granite Paper**

**2184** A753 3b multi .20 .20

Building Gables — A754

No. 2185: a, Prasat Phanom Rung. b, Phra Prang at Wat Phra Phai Luang. c, Uposatha Hall at Wat Khao Bandai It. d, Scripture Library at Wat Phra Sing Woramahawihan.

*Perf. 13¼x13½*
**2005, Aug. 4** **Photo.** **Wmk. 340**

**2185** Horiz. strip of 4 + central label 1.00 .65
*a.-d.* A754 5b Any single .25 .20

Orchids — A755

Designs: No. 2189, 3b, Rhynchostylis gigantea Alba (white flowers). No. 2190, 3b, Rhynchostylis gigantea (pink and red flowers). No. 2191, 3b, Dendrobium gratiosissimum. 15b, Dendrobium thyrsiflorum.

*Perf. 14½*
**2005, Sept. 1** **Litho.** **Unwmk.**
**Granite Paper**

**2189-2192** A755 Set of 4 1.25 .85
*2192a* Souvenir sheet, #2189-2192, perf. 13¼ 1.50 1.50

No. 2192a sold for 30b.

Intl. Day of Peace — A756

**2005, Sept. 21** ***Perf. 13***
**Granite Paper**

**2193** A756 3b multi .20 .20

Intl. Letter Writing Week — A757

Water buffalo: No. 2194, 3b, Head. No. 2195, 3b, Standing in field. No. 2196, 3b, In mud. 15b, Attached to plow.

***Perf. 14½x14***
**2005, Oct. 8 Litho. Unwmk.**
**Granite Paper**

**2194-2197** A757 Set of 4 1.25 .85
*2197a* Souvenir sheet, #2194-2197, perf. 13¼ 1.50 1.50

National Library, Cent. — A758

**2005, Oct. 12** ***Perf. 14½x14***
**Granite Paper**

**2198** A758 3b multi .20 .20

Abolition of Slavery, Cent. — A759

**2005, Oct. 23 Litho.**
**Granite Paper**

**2199** A759 3b multi .20 .20

New Year 2006 — A760

Flowers: No. 2200, 3b, Beaumontia murtonii. No. 2201, 3b, Hibiscus mutabilis. No. 2202, 3b, Hibiscus rosa-sinensis. No. 2203, 3b, Cochlospermum religiosum.

**2005, Nov. 15** ***Perf. 14x14½***
**Granite Paper**

**2200-2203** A760 Set of 4 .60 .40
*2203a* Souvenir sheet, #2200-2203 .85 .85

No. 2203a sold for 17b.

Princess Bejaratana, 80th Birthday — A761

**2005, Nov. 24** ***Perf. 14x14½***
**Granite Paper**

**2204** A761 3b multi .20 .20

Siamese Roosters — A762

Designs: No. 2205, 3b, Golden Rooster, by Pichai Nirand (olive green panel). No. 2206, 3b, Rooster at Dawn, by Prayat Pongdam (black panel). No. 2207, 3b, Legendary Rooster, by Chakrabhand Posayakrit (dancing woman, brown panel). No. 2208, 3b, Divine Rooster, by Chalermchai Kositpipat (blue panel), horiz.

***Perf. 14x14½, 14½x14***
**2005, Nov. 24**

**2205-2208** A762 Set of 4 .60 .40

King Bhumibol Adulyadej's "New Theory" Agriculture — A763

No. 2209: a, King, easel, farmers, animals. b, King and farmers.

**2005, Dec. 5** ***Perf. 14¼x14½***
**Granite Paper**

**2209** Horiz. pair, #a-b, + central label .30 .20
***a.-b.*** A763 3b Either single .20 .20

Buddhist Monks A764

No. 2210: a, Somdet Phra Phutthachan (1788-1872). b, Phra Ratchamuni Samiram Khunupamachan (1582-1682). c, Phra Achan Man Bhuridatto (1870-1949). d, Khruba Si wichai (1877-1938).

**Litho. & Engr.**
**2005, Dec. 5** ***Perf. 13½***
**Granite Paper**

**2210** Horiz. strip of 4 1.00 .65
***a.-d.*** A764 5b Any single .25 .20
***e.*** Souvenir sheet, #2210a-2210d 1.50 1.50

No. 2210e sold for 30b.

Dec. 26, 2004 Tsunami, 1st Anniv. — A765

No. 2211: a, Wave. b, Undivided Kindness of Thai People, by Chanipa Temprom. Illustration reduced.

**2005, Dec. 26 Litho.** ***Perf. 14½x14***
**Granite Paper**

**2211** A765 3b Horiz. pair, #a-b .30 .20

**King Bhumibol Adulyadej Type of 1996**

**2006 Litho.** ***Perf. 14x14½***
**Granite Paper**

**2212** A550 10b orange & brown .50 .35
**2213** A550 15b yel brn & green .75 .50

New Year 2006 (Year of the Dog) — A766

**2006, Jan. 1 Litho.** ***Perf. 13***
**Granite Paper**

**2214** A766 3b multi .20 .20

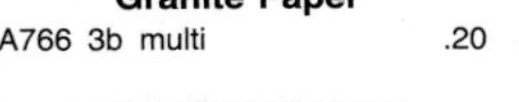

Prince Chaturantarasmi Krom Phra Chakrabardibongse (1856-1900), Finance Minister — A767

**2006, Jan. 13** ***Perf. 14x14½***
**Granite Paper**

**2215** A767 3b multi .20 .20

Natl. Children's Day — A768

Winning designs in children's stamp design competition with panel colors of: No. 2216, 3b, Orange brown. No. 2217, 3b, Blue. No. 2218, 3b, Red violet. No. 2219, 3b, Green.

**2006, Jan. 14** ***Perf. 14½x14***
**Granite Paper**

**2216-2219** A768 Set of 4 .60 .40

Rose — A769

**Litho. & Embossed**
**2006, Feb. 7** ***Perf. 13***
**Granite Paper**

**2220** A769 5b multi .25 .20

Diplomatic Relations Between Thailand and Iran, 50th Anniv. — A770

**2006, Feb. 11 Litho.** ***Perf. 14½x14***
**Granite Paper**

**2221** A770 3b multi .20 .20

Queen Sirikit Center for Breast Cancer — A771

**2006, Mar. 29** ***Perf. 14½x14***
**Granite Paper**

**2222** A771 3b multi .20 .20

Heritage Conservation Day — A772

Sites in Phu Phrabat Historical Park: No. 2223, 3b, Buddha's Footprint (monument). No. 2224, 3b, Upright rocks and trees, horiz. No. 2225, 3b, Thao Barot horse stable (rock overhang), horiz. 15b, Nang Usa rock pillar.

**2006, Apr. 2** ***Perf. 14x14½, 14½x14***
**Granite Paper**

**2223-2226** A772 Set of 4 1.25 .85
*2226a* Souvenir sheet, #2223-2226, perf. 13¼ 1.90 1.90

No. 2226a sold for 36b.

Thon Buri Palace — A773

No. 2227: a, Throne Hall. b, King Taksin's Shrine. c, Two Chinese-style residences. d, King Pinklao's residence.

**2006, Apr. 2** ***Perf. 14½x14***
**Granite Paper**

**2227** A773 3b Block of 4, #a-d .60 .40
***e.*** Souvenir sheet, #2227, perf. 13¼ .90 .90

No. 2227e sold for 17b.

A774

King Bhumibol Adulyadej, 60th Anniv. of Accession — A775

King Bhumibol Adulyadej: No. 2228, 3b, Wearing tie, red brown background (shown). No. 2229, 3b, Wearing tie, blue background. No. 2230, 3b, Wearing tie, olive brown background. No. 2231, 3b, Without tie, blue violet background. No. 2232, Without tie, green background. No. 2233, 3b, Without tie, brown background.

**2006 Photo. *Perf. 13¼***
**Granite Paper**

**2228-2233** A774 Set of 6 .95 .65
*2233a* Miniature sheet, #2228-2233 1.60 1.60

**Litho. & Embossed With Foil Application**

**2234** A775 100b gold & multi 5.25 3.50

Issued: Nos. 2228-2233, 2233a, 5/5; No. 2234, 6/9. No. 2233a sold for 30b.

Visakhapuja Day — A776

**2006, May 12 Litho. *Perf. 14x14½***
**Granite Paper**

**2235** A776 3b multi .20 .20

Buddhadasa Bhikkhu (1906-93), Buddhist Philosopher A777

No. 2236: a, Buddhadasa seated between trees. b, Profile of Buddhadasa. c, Gathering of monks. d, Stone fence.

**2006, May 27 *Perf. 13***
**Granite Paper**

**2236** Horiz. strip of 4 .65 .45
*a.-d.* A777 3b Any single .20 .20
*e.* Miniature sheet, #2236a-2236d .90 .90

No. 2236e sold for 17b.

Anemonefish — A778

Designs: No. 2237, 3b, Amphiprion clarkii. No. 2238, 3b, Amphiprion perideraion. No. 2239, 3b, Amphiprion ocellaris. No. 2240, 3b, Amphiprion polymnus.

**2006 *Perf. 14½x14***
**Granite Paper**

**2237-2240** A778 Set of 4 .65 .45
*2240a* Miniature sheet, #2237-2240, perf. 13½ 1.10 1.10
*2240b* As "a," with Belgica '06 emblem in margin 1.75 1.75

Issued: Nos. 2237-2240, 2240a, 6/24; No. 2240b, Dec. No. 2240a sold for 20b; No. 2240b, for 30b.

Natl. Communications Day — A779

**2006, Aug. 4 Litho.**
**Granite Paper**

**2241** A779 3b multi .20 .20

Mitrephora Sirikitiae — A780

**Litho. & Embossed**
**2006, Aug. 12 *Perf. 13***
**Granite Paper**

**2242** A780 5b multi .30 .20

Royal Dog Tongdaeng A781

Dog: No. 2243, 3b, Sitting. No. 2244, 3b, Standing. No. 2245, 3b, Laying down. No. 2246, 3b, With puppies.

**2006 Litho. *Perf. 13½***
**Granite Paper**

**2243-2246** A781 Set of 4 .65 .45
*2246a* Miniature sheet, #2243-2246 .90 .90
*2246b* As "a," with MonacoPhil 2006 emblem in margin 1.50 1.50

Issued: Nos. 2243-2246, 2246a, 9/1; No. 2246b, Dec. No. 2246a sold for 17b; No. 2246b, for 26b.

Suvarnabhumi Airport — A782

**2006, Sept. 28 *Perf. 14½x14***
**Granite Paper**

**2247** A782 3b multi .20 .20

Nos, 606, 653a, 934 and 1081 Surcharged

**Methods, Perfs and Watermarks As Before**

**2006, Sept. ?**

**2248** A146 2b on 20s #606 .20 .20
**2249** A161 2b on 20s #653a .20 .20
**2250** A256 2b on 75s #934 .20 .20
**2251** A256 2b on 1.50b #1081 .20 .20
*Nos. 2248-2251 (4)* .80 .80

Location and size of surcharges differs.

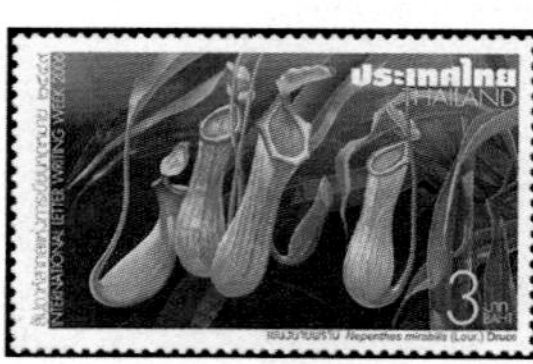
Intl. Letter Writing Week — A784

Carnivorous plants: No. 2253, 3b, Nepenthes mirabilis. No. 2254, 3b, Rafflesia kerrii. No. 2255, 3b, Sapria poilanei. 15b, Drosera burmannii.

**2006 Litho. Unwmk. *Perf. 14½x14***
**Granite Paper**

**2253-2256** A784 Set of 4 1.40 .95
*2256a* Miniature sheet, #2253-2256, perf. 13½ 1.60 1.60
*2256b* As "a," with Beijing 2006 emblem in margin 2.40 2.40

Issued: Nos. 2253-2256, 2256a, 10/9; No. 2256b, Dec. No. 2256a sold for 29b; No. 2256b, for 44b.

New Year 2007 — A785

Flowers: No. 2257, 3b, Hypoxis aurea. No. 2258, 3b, Murdannia gigantea. No. 2259, 3b, Impatiens phuluangensis. No. 2260, 3b, Caulokaempferia alba.

**2006, Nov. 15 *Perf. 14½x14***
**Granite Paper**

**2257-2260** A785 Set of 4 .70 .45
*2260a* Miniature sheet, #2257-2260 .90 .90

No. 2260a sold for 16b.

Royal Thai Naval Academy, Cent. — A786

**2006, Nov. 20**
**Granite Paper**

**2261** A786 3b multi .20 .20

King Bhumibol Adulyadej, 60th Anniv. of Accession A787

King Bhumibol Adulyadej: No. 2262, 5b, Standing in forest. No. 2263, 5b, Seated on walkway, taking notes. No. 2264, 5b, Standing on wooden plank over water. No. 2265, 5b, Pointing to ground. No. 2266, 5b, Riding cow. No. 2267, 5b, Walking up hill.

**2006, Dec. 5 Photo. *Perf. 13½***
**Granite Paper**

**2262-2267** A787 Set of 6 1.75 1.25
*2267a* Miniature sheet, #2262-2267 2.50 2.50

No. 2267a sold for 44b.

Opening of Second Thai-Lao Friendship Bridge — A788

No. 2268 — Bridge and flag of: a, Thailand (denomination at LL). b, Laos (denomination at LR).
Illustration reduced.

**2006, Dec. 20 Litho. *Perf. 14½x14***
**Granite Paper**

**2268** A788 3b Horiz. pair, #a-b .35 .25

New Year 2007 (Year of the Pig) — A789

**2007, Jan. 1 *Perf. 13***
**Granite Paper**

**2269** A789 3b multi .20 .20

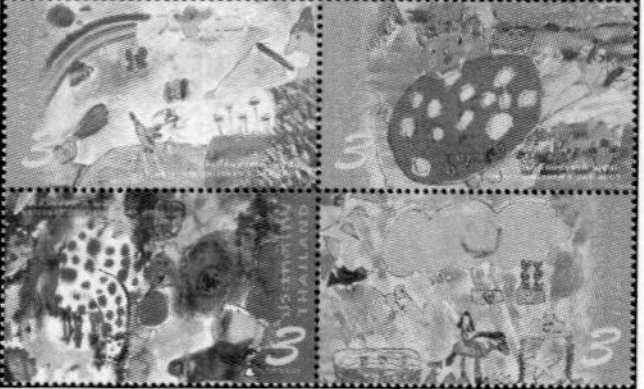
Natl. Children's Day — A790

No. 2270 — Children's drawings: a, Rainbow, birds and butterflies. b, Cat with green face and butterflies. c, Spotted animals. d, Birds, cloud, sun and girl riding horse.
Illustration reduced.

**2007, Jan. 13 *Perf. 14½x14***
**Granite Paper**

**2270** A790 3b Block of 4, #a-d .75 .50

Siam Commercial Bank Public Company, Cent. — A791

**2007, Jan. 30 *Perf. 14x14½***
**Granite Paper**

**2271** A791 3b multi .20 .20

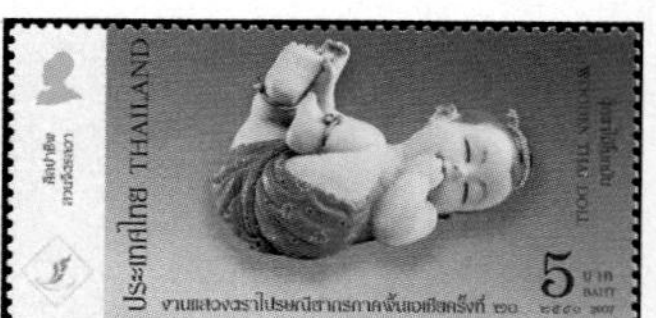
Bangkok 2007 Intl. Stamp Exhibition — A792

Various carved wooden dolls depicting Thai children with background colors of: No. 2272, 5b, Blue. No. 2273, 5b, Olive green. No. 2274, 5b, Brown olive. No. 2275, 5b, Rose.
Illustration reduced.

**Litho. With Foil Application**

**2007, Feb. 1** ***Perf. 13***

**Granite Paper**

**2272-2275** A792 Set of 4 1.25 .80
*2275a* Miniature sheet, #2272-2275 1.90 1.90

No. 2275a sold for 33b.

Yellow Rose — A793

**2007, Feb. 7** **Litho.** ***Perf. 13***

**Granite Paper**

**2276** A793 5b multi .30 .20

No. 2276 is impregnated with a rose scent.

---

## SEMI-POSTAL STAMPS

Nos. 164-175 Overprinted in Red

**1918, Jan. 11** **Unwmk.** ***Perf. 14***

**B1** A21 2s orange brown 2.00 1.00
**B2** A21 3s emerald 2.00 1.00
**B3** A21 5s rose red 4.50 2.00
**B4** A21 10s black & olive 7.00 3.00
**B5** A21 15s blue 7.00 3.00
**B6** A22 1b bl & gray blk 35.00 15.00
**B7** A22 2b car rose & brn 60.00 25.00
**B8** A22 3b yel grn & blk 90.00 40.00
**B9** A22 5b dp vio & blk 225.00 65.00
*a.* Double overprint 775.00 400.00
**B10** A22 10b ol grn & vio brn 575.00 175.00
**B11** A22 20b sea grn & brn 2,100. 600.00
*Nos. B1-B11 (11)* 3,107. 930.00

Excellent counterfeit overprints are known.
These stamps were sold at an advance over face value, the excess being given to the Siamese Red Cross Society.

Stamps of 1905-19 Handstamp Overprinted

**1920, Feb.**

**On Nos. 164, 146, 168**

**B12** A21 2s (+ 3s) org brn 37.50 37.50
**B13** A21 3s (+ 2s) green 40.00 40.00
**B14** A21 15s (+ 5s) blue 90.00 90.00

**On No. 105**

**B15** A15 1t (+ 25s) 325.00 290.00

**On Nos. 185-186**

**B16** A21 5s (+ 5s) on 6s 55.00 55.00
*a.* Overprint inverted
**B17** A21 10s (+ 5s) on 12s 60.00 60.00
*Nos. B12-B17 (6)* 607.50 572.50
Set, never hinged 850.00

Sold at an advance over face value, the excess being for the benefit of the Wild Tiger Corps. Counterfeits exist.

Stamps of 1905-20 Handstamp Overprinted

**On Nos. 164, 146, 168**

**B18** A21 2s (+ 3s) org brn 35.00 35.00
**B19** A21 3s (+ 2s) green 35.00 35.00
*a.* Pair, one without ovpt.
**B20** A21 15s (+ 5s) blue 52.50 52.50

**On No. 105**

**B21** A15 1t (+ 25s) 260.00 260.00

**On No. 186**

**B22** A21 10s on 12s (+ 5s) 55.00 55.00

**On No. 190**

**B23** A23 5s (+ 5s) 85.00 85.00
*Nos. B18-B23 (6)* 522.50 522.50
Set, never hinged 800.00

Sold at an advance over face value, the excess being for the benefit of the Wild Tiger Corps. Counterfeits exist.

Nos. 187-188, 190, 193-194, 196, 198 Overprinted in Blue or Red

**1920, Dec. 21**

**B24** A23 2s brown, *yel* 13.00 13.00
**B25** A23 3s grn, *grn* (R) 13.00 13.00
**B26** A23 5s rose, *pale rose* 13.00 13.00
**B27** A23 10s blk & org (R) 13.00 13.00
**B28** A23 15s bl, *bluish* (R) 25.00 25.00
**B29** A23 25s chocolate 85.00 85.00
**B30** A23 50s ocher & blk (R) 190.00 190.00
*Nos. B24-B30 (7)* 352.00 352.00
Set, never hinged 550.00

Sold at an advance over face value, the excess being for the benefit of the Wild Tiger Corps. Counterfeits exist.

Nos. 170-172 Surcharged in Red

**1939, Apr. 6** **Unwmk.** ***Perf. 14***

**B31** A22 5s + 5s on 1b 20.00 20.00
**B32** A22 10s + 5s on 2b 26.00 26.00
**B33** A22 15s + 5s on 3b 26.00 26.00
*Nos. B31-B33 (3)* 72.00 72.00
Set, never hinged 110.00

Founding of the Intl. Red Cross Soc., 75th anniv.
Bottom line of overprint is different on Nos. B32-B33.

**Catalogue values for unused stamps in this section, from this point to the end of the section, are for Never Hinged items.**

No. 214 Surcharged in Carmine

**1952** **Unwmk.** ***Perf. 12½***

**B34** A25 80s + 20s blue & blk 21.00 12.00

New constitution.

Red Cross and Dancer — SP1

**Lithographed, Cross Typographed**

**1953, Apr. 6** **Wmk. 299** ***Perf. 11***

**Cross in Red, Dancer Dark Blue**

**B35** SP1 25s + 25s yellow grn 11.00 4.00
**B36** SP1 50s + 50s brt rose 22.50 7.00
**B37** SP1 1b + 1b lt blue 29.00 8.00
*Nos. B35-B37 (3)* 62.50 19.00

60th anniv. of the founding of the Siamese Red Cross Society.

Nos. B35-B37 Overprinted with Year Date "24 98," in Black

**1955, Apr. 3**

**Cross in Red, Dancer Dark Blue**

**B38** SP1 25s + 25s yel grn 55.00 15.00
**B39** SP1 50s + 50s brt rose 120.00 25.00
**B40** SP1 1b + 1b lt blue 140.00 35.00
*Nos. B38-B40 (3)* 315.00 75.00

Counterfeits exist.

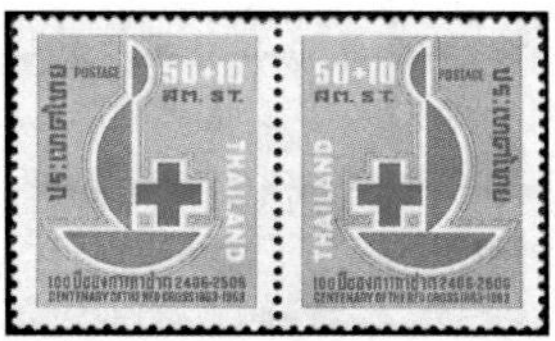

Red Cross Cent. Emblem — SP2

**1963** **Wmk. 334** **Litho.** ***Perf. 13½***

**B41** 50s + 10s cross at right .30 .20
**B42** 50s + 10s cross at left .30 .20
*a.* SP2 Pair, #B41-B42 .60

Cent. of the Intl. Red Cross.

Nos. B41-B42 Surcharged

**1973, Feb. 15**

**B43** SP2 75s + 25s on 50s + 10s .75 .75
**B44** SP3 75s + 25s on 50s + 10s .75 .75
*a.* Pair, #B43-B44 2.00

Red Cross Fair, Feb. 15-19.

Nos. B41-B42 Surcharged

**1974, Feb. 2**

**B45** SP2 75s + 25s on 50s + 10s .40 .30
**B46** SP3 75s + 25s on 50s + 10s .40 .30
*a.* Pair, #B45-B46 1.50

Red Cross Fair, Feb. 1974. Position of surcharge reversed on No. B46.

Nos. B41-B42 Surcharged

**1975, Feb 11 52**

**B47** SP2 75s + 25s on 50s + 10s .50 .30
**B48** SP3 75s + 25s on 50s + 10s .50 .30
*a.* Pair, #B47-B48 1.50

Red Cross Fair, Feb. 1975. Position of surcharge reversed on No. B48.

Nos. B41-B42 Surcharged

**1976, Feb. 26**

**B49** SP2 75s + 25s on 50s + 10s .40 .40
**B50** SP3 75s + 25s on 50s + 10s .40 .40
*a.* Pair, #B49-B50 1.50

Red Cross Fair, Feb. 16-Mar. 1. Position of surcharge reversed on #B50.

Nos. B41-B42 Surcharged

**1977, Apr. 6** **Wmk. 334** ***Perf. 13½***

**B51** SP2 75s + 25s on 50s + 10s .45 .30
**B52** SP3 75s + 25s on 50s + 10s .45 .30
*a.* Pair, #B51-B52 1.50

Red Cross Fair 1977.

Red Cross Blood Collection SP4

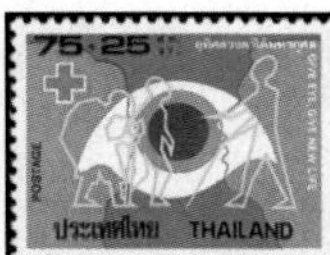

Eye and Blind People SP5

**Wmk. 329**

**1978, Apr. 6** **Photo.** ***Perf. 13***

**B53** SP4 2.75b + 25s multi 1.00 .25

"Give blood, save life."
For surcharge see No. B58.

***Perf. 14x13½***

**1979, Apr. 6** **Litho.** **Wmk. 368**

**B54** SP5 75s + 25s multi .55 .20

"Give an eye, save new life." Red Cross Fair. Surtax was for Thai Red Cross.
For surcharge see No. B59.

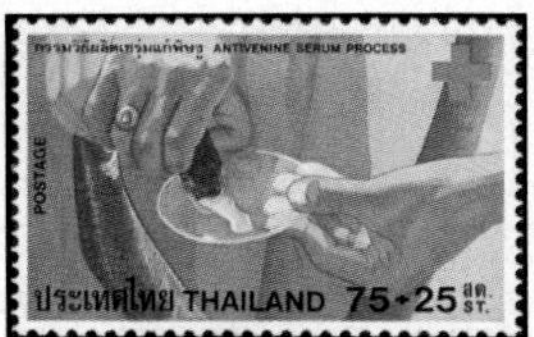

Extracting Snake Venom, Red Cross — SP6

**1980, Apr.** ***Perf. 11x13***

**B55** SP6 75s + 25s multi .90 .90

Red Cross Fair. Surtax was for Thai Red Cross.
For surcharge see No. B60.

Nurse Helping Victim — SP7

**1981, Apr. 6 Wmk. 377 *Perf. 12½***
**B56** SP7 75 + 25s red & gray grn 1.25 1.25

Red Cross Fair (canceled). Surtax was for Thai Red Cross.
For surcharge see No. B65.

Red Cross Fair SP8

***Perf. 13x13½***
**1983, Apr. 6 Litho. Wmk. 329**
**B57** SP8 1.25b + 25s multi .75 .75

Surtax was for Thai Red Cross.

No. B53 Surcharged

**1984, Apr. Photo. *Perf. 13***
**B58** SP4 3.25b + 25s on 2.75b + 25s 2.00 2.00

Red Cross Fair. Surtax was for Thai Red Cross. Overprint translates: Red Cross Donation.

No. B54 Surcharged

**Wmk. 368**
**1985, Mar. 30 Litho. *Perf. 13***
**B59** SP5 2b + 25c on 75s + 25s 1.50 1.50

Surtax for the Thai Red Cross.

No. B55 Overprinted and Surcharged

**1986, Apr. 6 Wmk. 368 *Perf. 11x13***
**B60** SP6 2b + 25s on 75s + 25s 1.50 1.50

Natl. Children's Day. Surtax for Natl. Red Cross Society. Overprint translates "Red Cross Donation."

Natl. Scouting Movement, 75th Anniv., 15th Asia-Pacific Conference, Thailand — SP9

#B61, Scouts, saluting, community service. #B62, Scout activities. #B63, King & queen at ceremony. #B64, 15th Asia-Pacific conf.

**1986, Nov. 7 Wmk. 385 *Perf. 13½***
**B61** SP9 2b + 50s multi .35 .35
**B62** SP9 2b + 50s multi .35 .35
**B63** SP9 2b + 50s multi .35 .35
**B64** SP9 2b + 50s multi .35 .35
*Nos. B61-B64 (4)* 1.40 1.40

Surtax for the Natl. Scouting Fund.

No. B56 Surcharged

**1987, Apr. Wmk. 377 *Perf. 12½***
**B65** SP7 2b + 50s on 75s + 25s .95 .20

Sports
SP10 SP11

Designs: No. B66, Hurdles, medal winners. No. B67, Race, nurse treating injured cyclist. No. B68, Boxers training. No. B69, Soccer.

**1989, Dec. 16 Wmk. 387 *Perf. 13½***
**B66** SP10 2b +1b multi .40 .25
**B67** SP10 2b +1b multi .40 .25
**B68** SP10 2b +1b multi .40 .25
**B69** SP10 2b +1b multi .40 .25
*Nos. B66-B69 (4)* 1.60 1.00

Surtax for sports welfare organizations.

**1990, Dec. 16**
**B70** SP11 2b +1b Judo .40 .25
**B71** SP11 2b +1b Archery .40 .25
**B72** SP11 2b +1b High jump .40 .25
**B73** SP11 2b +1b Windsurfing .40 .25
*Nos. B70-B73 (4)* 1.60 1.00

Surtax for sports welfare organization.

Sports — SP12

**Wmk. 387**
**1991, Dec. 16 Litho. *Perf. 13½***
**B74** SP12 2b +1b Jogging .30 .20
**B75** SP12 2b +1b Cycling .30 .20
**B76** SP12 2b +1b Soccer, jump-ing rope .30 .20
**B77** SP12 2b +1b Swimming .30 .20
*Nos. B74-B77 (4)* 1.20 .80

Surtax for sports welfare organizations.

18th South East Asian Games, Chiang Mai — SP13

No. B78: a, Water polo. b, Tennis. c, Hurdles. d, Gymnastics.
No. B79: a, Fencing. b, Pool. c, Diving. d, Pole vault.

**1994, Dec. 16 Wmk. 340**
**B78** SP13 2b +1b Strip of 4, #a.-d. 1.00 .75
*e.* Souvenir sheet, #B78 1.25 1.00

**Wmk. 387**
**B79** SP13 2b +1b Strip of 4, #a.-d. 1.00 .75
*e.* Souvenir sheet, #B79 1.25 1.25

Nos. B78e, B79e sold for 15b.
Issued: #B78, 12/16/94; #B79, 12/9/95.

SP14

13th Asian Games, Bangkok — SP15

**1998, Mar. 27 *Perf. 14½x14***
**B80** SP14 2b +1b Shooting .20 .20
**B81** SP14 3b +1b Rhythmic gymnastics .20 .20
**B82** SP14 4b +1b Swimming .25 .20
**B83** SP14 7b +1b Wind-surfing .35 .30
*Nos. B80-B83 (4)* 1.00 .90

***Perf. 14½x14***
**1998, Dec. 6 Litho. Unwmk.**
**Granite Paper**
**B84** SP15 2b +1b Field hockey .20 .20
**B85** SP15 3b +1b Wrestling .20 .20
**B86** SP15 4b +1b Rowing .25 .20
**B87** SP15 7b +1b Equestrian .35 .30
*Nos. B84-B87 (4)* 1.00 .90

## AIR POST STAMPS

Garuda — AP1

**1925 Unwmk. Engr. *Perf. 14, 14½***
**C1** AP1 2s brown, *yel* 2.00 .50
**C2** AP1 3s dark brown 2.00 .50
**C3** AP1 5s green 6.00 .50
**C4** AP1 10s black & org 17.50 1.00
**C5** AP1 15s carmine 5.00 1.50
**C6** AP1 25s dark blue 5.00 1.50
**C7** AP1 50s brown org & blk 35.00 9.00
**C8** AP1 1b blue & brown 32.50 11.00
*Nos. C1-C8 (8)* 105.00 25.50
Set, never hinged 165.00

Issued: 2s, 50s, 4/21; others, 1/3.

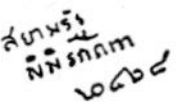

Nos. C1-C8 received this overprint ("Government Museum 2468") in 1925, but were never issued. The death of King Vajiravudh caused cancellation of the fair at which this set was to have been released.

They were used during 1928 only in the interdepartmental service for accounting purposes of the money-order sections of various Bangkok post offices, and were never sold to the public. Value for canceled set, $25.

**1930-37 *Perf. 12½***
**C9** AP1 2s brown, *yel* 5.00 1.00
**C10** AP1 5s green 1.25 .20
**C11** AP1 10s black & org 2.50 .20
**C12** AP1 15s carmine 25.00 6.00
**C13** AP1 25s dark blue ('37) 1.50 1.00
*a.* Vert. pair, imperf. btwn. 450.00
**C14** AP1 50s brn org & blk ('37) 3.00 1.50
*Nos. C9-C14 (6)* 38.25 9.90
Set, never hinged 62.50

Monument of Democracy, Bangkok AP2

**1942-43 Engr. *Perf. 11***
**C15** AP2 2s dk org brn ('43) 1.75 .80
**C16** AP2 3s dk grn ('43) 32.50 19.00
*a.* Vert. pair, imperf. btwn. 100.00 100.00
**C17** AP2 5s deep claret 2.00 .25
*a.* Horiz. pair, imperf. btwn. 75.00 75.00
*b.* Vert. pair, imperf. btwn. 75.00 75.00
**C18** AP2 10s carmine ('43) 15.00 .60
*a.* Vert. pair, imperf. btwn. 100.00 100.00
**C19** AP2 15s dark blue 3.00 2.00
*a.* Vert. pair, imperf. btwn. 100.00 100.00
*Nos. C15-C19 (5)* 54.25 22.65
Set, never hinged 80.00

**Catalogue values for unused stamps in this section, from this point to the end of the section, are for Never Hinged items.**

Garuda and Bangkok Skyline — AP3

**1952-53 *Perf. 13x12½***
**C20** AP3 1.50b red violet ('53) 4.75 .25
**C21** AP3 2b dark blue 11.00 2.50
**C22** AP3 3b gray ('53) 16.00 1.10
*Nos. C20-C22 (3)* 31.75 3.85

Issue dates: June 15, 1952. Sept. 15, 1953.

## OFFICIAL STAMPS

**Catalogue values for unused stamps in this section are for Never Hinged items.**

O1

O2

***Perf. 10½ Rough***
**1963, Oct. 1 Typo. Unwmk.**
**Without Gum**
**O1** O1 10s pink & dp car .20 .20
**O2** O1 20s brt grn & car rose .20 .20
**O3** O1 25s blue & dp car .30 *.35*
**O4** O1 50s deep carmine 1.00 *2.00*
**O5** O2 1b silver & car rose 1.00 *3.00*
**O6** O2 2b bronze & car rose 2.00 1.50
*Nos. O1-O6 (6)* 4.70 7.25

Issued as an official test from Oct. 1, 1963, to Jan. 31, 1964, to determine the amount of mail sent out by various government departments.
Nos. O5, O9, O10 exist with oval frame of type O1.

**1964 Without Gum**
**O7** O1 20s green .50 .50
**O8** O1 25s blue .50 .50
**O9** O2 1b silver 1.00 1.00
**O10** O2 2b bister 2.50 2.50
*Nos. O7-O10 (4)* 4.50 4.50

Others values exist printed in one color.

# THRACE

'thrās

LOCATION — In southeastern Europe between the Black and Aegean Seas
GOVT. — Former Turkish Province
AREA — 89,361 sq. mi. (approx.)

Thrace underwent many political changes during the Balkan Wars and World War I. It was finally divided among Turkey, Greece and Bulgaria.

100 Lepta = 1 Drachma
40 Paras = 1 Piaster
100 Stotinki = 1 Leva (1919)

### Giumulzina District Issue

Turkish Stamps of 1909 Surcharged in Blue or Red

**1913** **Unwmk.** ***Perf. 12, 13½***

| No. | Type | Description | Unused | Used |
|---|---|---|---|---|
| 1 | A21 | 10 l on 20pa rose (Bl) | 20.00 | *30.00* |
| 2 | A21 | 25 l on 10pa bl grn | 47.50 | *47.50* |
| 3 | A21 | 25 l on 20pa rose (Bl) | 60.00 | 60.00 |
| 4 | A21 | 25 l on 1pi ultra | 80.00 | *92.50* |
| | | *Nos. 1-4 (4)* | 207.50 | 230.00 |

Counterfeits exist of Nos. 1-4.

Turkish Inscriptions
A1 A2

**1913** **Litho.** ***Imperf.***
**Laid Paper**
**Control Mark in Rose**
**Without Gum**

| No. | Type | Description | Unused | Used |
|---|---|---|---|---|
| 5 | A1 | 1pi blue | 17.00 | 17.00 |
| 6 | A1 | 2pi violet | 20.00 | 20.00 |

**Wove Paper**

| No. | Type | Description | Unused | Used |
|---|---|---|---|---|
| 7 | A2 | 10pa vermilion | 35.00 | 32.50 |
| 8 | A2 | 20pa blue | 35.00 | 32.50 |
| 9 | A2 | 1pi violet | 37.50 | 32.50 |
| | | *Nos. 5-9 (5)* | 144.50 | 134.50 |

Turkish Stamps of 1908-13 Surcharged in Red or Black

P. ١ بر غروش

**1913** ***Perf. 12***

| No. | Type | Description | Unused | Used |
|---|---|---|---|---|
| 10 | A22 | 1pi on 2pa ol grn (R) | 12.00 | 12.00 |
| 10A | A22 | 1pi on 2pa ol grn | 12.00 | 12.00 |
| 11 | A22 | 1pi on 5pa ocher | 16.00 | 14.50 |
| 11A | A22 | 1pi on 5pa ocher (R) | 17.50 | 17.00 |
| 12 | A22 | 1pi on 20pa rose | 26.00 | 25.00 |
| 13 | A21 | 1pi on 5pi dk vio (R) | 60.00 | 60.00 |
| 13A | A21 | 1pi on 5pi dk vio | 55.00 | 55.00 |
| 14 | A21 | 1pi on 10pi dl red | 90.00 | 90.00 |
| 15 | A19 | 1pi on 25pi dk grn | 425.00 | 425.00 |
| | | *Nos. 10-15 (9)* | 713.50 | 710.50 |

On Nos. 13-15 the surcharge is vertical, reading up. No. 15 exists with double surcharge, one black, one red.
Nos. 10-15 exist with forged surcharges.

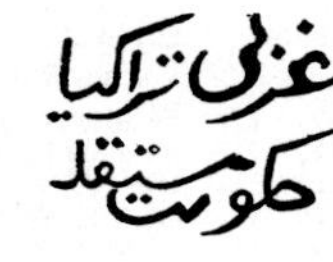


Bulgarian Stamps of 1911 Handstamp Surcharged in Red or Blue

١ غروش

**1913**

| No. | Type | Description | Unused | Used |
|---|---|---|---|---|
| 16 | A20 | 10pa on 1s myr grn (R) | 20.00 | 20.00 |
| 17 | A21 | 20pa on 2s car & blk | 20.00 | 20.00 |
| 18 | A23 | 1pi on 5s grn & blk (R) | 20.00 | 20.00 |
| 19 | A22 | 2pi on 3s lake & blk | 26.00 | 26.00 |
| 20 | A24 | 2½pi on 10s dp red & blk | 40.00 | 40.00 |
| 21 | A25 | 5pi on 15s brn bis | 62.50 | 62.50 |
| | | *Nos. 16-21 (6)* | 188.50 | 188.50 |

Same Surcharges on Greek Stamps
**On Issue of 1911**

**1913** ***Serrate Roulette 13½***

| No. | Type | Description | Unused | Used |
|---|---|---|---|---|
| 22 | A24 | 10pa on 1 l grn (R) | 21.00 | 21.00 |
| 23 | A24 | 10pa on 1 l grn | 22.50 | 22.50 |
| 25 | A25 | 10pa on 25 l ultra (R) | 30.00 | 30.00 |
| 26 | A25 | 20pa on 2 l car rose | 20.00 | 20.00 |
| 27 | A24 | 1pi on 3 l ver | 20.00 | 20.00 |
| 28 | A26 | 2pi on 5 l grn (R) | 47.50 | 47.50 |
| 29 | A24 | 2½pi on 10 l car rose | 47.50 | 47.50 |
| 30 | A25 | 5pi on 40 l dp bl (R) | 82.50 | 82.50 |
| | | *Nos. 22-30 (8)* | 291.00 | 291.00 |

**On Occupation Stamps of 1912**

| No. | Type | Description | Unused | Used |
|---|---|---|---|---|
| 31 | O1 | 10pa on 1 l brn | 14.00 | 14.00 |
| 32 | O1 | 20pa on 1 l brn | 14.00 | 14.00 |
| 33 | O1 | 1pi on 1 l brn | 14.00 | 14.00 |
| | | *Nos. 31-33 (3)* | 42.00 | 42.00 |

These surcharges were made with handstamps, two of which were required for each surcharge. One or both parts may be found inverted, double or omitted.
Nos. 16-33 exist with forged surcharges.

## OCCUPATION STAMPS

### Issued under Allied Occupation

Bulgarian Stamps of 1915-19 Handstamped in Violet Blue

***Perf. 11½, 11½x12, 14***
**1919** **Unwmk.**

| No. | Type | Description | Unused | Used |
|---|---|---|---|---|
| N1 | A43 | 1s black | 2.00 | 2.00 |
| N2 | A43 | 2s olive green | 2.00 | 2.00 |
| N3 | A44 | 5s green | .75 | .75 |
| N4 | A44 | 10s rose | .75 | .75 |
| N5 | A44 | 15s violet | .85 | .85 |
| N6 | A26 | 25s indigo & black | .85 | .85 |
| | | *Nos. N1-N6 (6)* | 7.20 | 7.20 |

The overprint on Nos. N1-N6 is frequently inverted and known in other positions.

Bulgarian Stamps of 1911-19 Overprinted in Red or Black

**1919**

| No. | Type | Description | Unused | Used |
|---|---|---|---|---|
| N7 | A43 | 1s black (R) | .20 | .20 |
| N8 | A43 | 2s olive green | .20 | .20 |
| N9 | A44 | 5s green | .20 | .20 |
| N10 | A44 | 10s rose | .20 | .20 |
| N11 | A44 | 15s violet | .20 | .20 |
| N12 | A26 | 25s indigo & black | .25 | .25 |
| N13 | A29 | 1 l chocolate | 4.00 | 4.00 |
| N14 | A37a | 2 l brown orange | 6.00 | 6.00 |
| N15 | A38 | 3 l claret | 10.00 | 10.00 |
| | | *Nos. N7-N15 (9)* | 21.25 | 21.25 |

Overprint is vertical, reading up, on Nos. N9-N13.

The following varieties are found in the setting of "INTERALLIEE": Inverted "V" for "A," second "L" inverted, "F" instead of final "E."

Bulgarian Stamps of 1919 Overprinted

**1920**

| No. | Type | Description | Unused | Used |
|---|---|---|---|---|
| N16 | A44 | 5s green | .25 | .25 |
| N17 | A44 | 10s rose | .25 | .25 |
| N18 | A44 | 15s violet | .25 | .25 |
| N19 | A44 | 50s yellow brown | .70 | .70 |
| | | *Nos. N16-N19 (4)* | 1.45 | 1.45 |

The varieties: "Irteraliiee" and final "e" inverted are found on all values.

Bulgarian Stamps of 1919 Overprinted

**1920** ***Perf. 12x11½***

| No. | Type | Description | Unused | Used |
|---|---|---|---|---|
| N20 | A44 | 5s green | .25 | .25 |
| a. | | Inverted overprint | 19.00 | |
| N21 | A44 | 10s rose | .25 | .25 |
| a. | | Inverted overprint | 19.00 | |
| N22 | A44 | 15s violet | .25 | .25 |
| N23 | A44 | 25s deep blue | .25 | .25 |
| N24 | A44 | 50s ocher | .25 | .25 |

***Imperf***

| No. | Type | Description | Unused | Used |
|---|---|---|---|---|
| N25 | A44 | 30s chocolate | .75 | .75 |
| | | *Nos. N20-N25 (6)* | 2.00 | 2.00 |

No. N25 is not known without overprint.

## ISSUED UNDER GREEK OCCUPATION

### For Use in Western Thrace

Greek Stamps of 1911-19 Overprinted

***Serrate Roulette 13½***
**1920** **Litho.** **Unwmk.**

| No. | Type | Description | Unused | Used |
|---|---|---|---|---|
| N26 | A24 | 1 l green | .20 | *.35* |
| a. | | Inverted overprint | 15.00 | |
| N27 | A25 | 2 l rose | .20 | *.35* |
| N28 | A24 | 3 l vermilion | .20 | *.35* |
| N29 | A26 | 5 l green | .20 | *.35* |
| N30 | A24 | 10 l rose | .30 | *.50* |
| N31 | A25 | 15 l dull blue | .35 | *.65* |
| a. | | Inverted overprint | 16.00 | |
| b. | | Dbl. ovpt., one inverted | 24.00 | |
| N32 | A25 | 25 l blue | .40 | *.75* |
| N33 | A26 | 30 l rose | 29.00 | *50.00* |
| N34 | A25 | 40 l indigo | 1.90 | *4.00* |
| N35 | A26 | 50 l violet brn | 1.90 | *5.00* |
| N36 | A27 | 1d ultra | 6.50 | *14.00* |
| N37 | A27 | 2d vermilion | 17.50 | *32.50* |

**Engr.**

| No. | Type | Description | Unused | Used |
|---|---|---|---|---|
| N38 | A25 | 2 l car rose | .60 | .60 |
| N39 | A24 | 3 l vermilion | .60 | .60 |
| N40 | A27 | 1d ultra | 25.00 | *52.50* |
| N41 | A27 | 2d vermilion | 25.00 | *55.00* |
| N42 | A27 | 3d car rose | 37.50 | *70.00* |
| N43 | A27 | 5d ultra | 14.50 | *22.50* |
| N44 | A27 | 10d deep blue | 14.00 | *20.00* |
| | | *Nos. N26-N44 (19)* | 175.85 | *330.00* |

Nos. N42-N44 are overprinted on the reissues of Greece Nos. 210-212. See footnote below Greece No. 213. Counterfeits exist of Nos. N26-N84.

Overprinted **ΔΙΟΙΚΗΣΙΣ ΔΥΤΙΚΗΣ ΘΡΑΚΗΣ**

| No. | Type | Description | Unused | Used |
|---|---|---|---|---|
| N45 | A28 | 25d deep blue | 40.00 | *65.00* |

This overprint reads: "Administration Western Thrace."

With Additional Overprint

**Litho.**

| No. | Type | Description | Unused | Used |
|---|---|---|---|---|
| N46 | A24 | 1 l green | .55 | *1.10* |
| N47 | A25 | 2 l rose | .20 | *.40* |
| a. | | Inverted overprint | 77.50 | |
| N48 | A24 | 10 l rose | .55 | *.65* |
| N49 | A25 | 20 l slate | .55 | *.65* |
| N50 | A26 | 30 l rose | .65 | *1.00* |

**Engr.**

| No. | Type | Description | Unused | Used |
|---|---|---|---|---|
| N51 | A27 | 2d vermilion | 19.00 | *32.50* |
| N52 | A27 | 3d car rose | 8.50 | *22.50* |
| N53 | A27 | 5d ultra | 25.00 | *42.50* |
| N54 | A27 | 10d deep blue | 19.00 | *32.50* |
| a. | | Double overprint | 45.00 | |
| | | *Nos. N46-N54 (9)* | 74.00 | *133.80* |

### For Use in Eastern and Western Thrace

Greek Stamps of 1911-19 Overprinted

**1920** **Litho.**

| No. | Type | Description | Unused | Used |
|---|---|---|---|---|
| N55 | A24 | 1 l green | .20 | *.30* |
| a. | | Pair, one without ovpt. | 22.50 | |
| N56 | A25 | 2 l rose | .20 | *.30* |
| N57 | A24 | 3 l vermilion | .20 | *.30* |
| a. | | Double overprint | 11.50 | |
| N58 | A26 | 5 l green | .25 | *.45* |
| a. | | Pair, one without ovpt. | 24.00 | |
| N59 | A24 | 10 l rose | .40 | *.70* |
| a. | | Double overprint | 27.50 | |
| N60 | A25 | 20 l slate | .65 | *1.25* |
| a. | | Inverted overprint | 15.00 | |
| N61 | A25 | 25 l blue | 1.25 | *2.00* |
| N62 | A25 | 40 l indigo | 2.40 | *6.50* |
| N63 | A26 | 50 l violet brn | 3.00 | *8.50* |
| N64 | A27 | 1d ultra | 12.00 | *20.00* |
| N65 | A27 | 2d vermilion | 22.50 | *35.00* |

**Engr.**

| No. | Type | Description | Unused | Used |
|---|---|---|---|---|
| N66 | A24 | 3 l vermilion | 2.75 | *4.75* |
| N67 | A25 | 20 l gray lilac | 9.50 | *22.50* |
| N68 | A28 | 25d deep blue | 47.50 | *90.00* |
| | | *Nos. N55-N68 (14)* | 102.80 | *192.55* |

This overprint reads "Administration Thrace."

With Additional Overprint as Nos. N46-N54

**Litho.**

| No. | Type | Description | Unused | Used |
|---|---|---|---|---|
| N69 | A25 | 2 l car rose | .25 | *.50* |
| N70 | A26 | 5 l green | 1.50 | *3.00* |
| N71 | A25 | 20 l slate | .25 | *.50* |
| N72 | A26 | 30 l rose | .25 | *.50* |

**Engr.**

| No. | Type | Description | Unused | Used |
|---|---|---|---|---|
| N73 | A27 | 3d car rose | 7.50 | *14.00* |
| N74 | A27 | 5d ultra | 18.00 | *30.00* |
| N75 | A27 | 10d deep blue | 32.50 | *60.00* |
| | | *Nos. N69-N75 (7)* | 60.25 | *108.50* |

Turkish Stamps of 1916-20 Surcharged in Blue, Black or Red

**1920** ***Perf. 11½, 12½***

| No. | Type | Description | Unused | Used |
|---|---|---|---|---|
| N76 | A43 | 1 l on 5pa org (Bl) | .40 | *.50* |
| N77 | A32 | 5 l on 3pi blue | .40 | *.50* |
| N78 | A30 | 20 l on 1pi bl grn | .50 | *.70* |
| N79 | A53 | 25 l on 5pi on 2pa Prus bl (R) | .60 | *.75* |
| N80 | A49 | 50 l on 5pi bl & blk (R) | 4.75 | *4.75* |
| N81 | A45 | 1d on 20pa dp rose (Bl) | 1.60 | 1.40 |
| N82 | A22 | 2d on 10pa on 2pa ol grn (R) | 2.50 | *2.50* |
| N83 | A57 | 3d on 1pi dp bl (R) | 9.50 | *9.50* |
| N84 | A23 | 5d on 20pa rose | 9.00 | *9.00* |
| | | *Nos. N76-N84 (9)* | 29.25 | 29.60 |

Nos. N77, N78 and N84 are on the 1920 issue with designs modified. Nos. N81, N82 and N83 are on stamps with the 1919 overprints.

Varieties found on some values of this issue include: inverted surcharge, double surcharge with one inverted, and surcharge on both face and back.

## POSTAGE DUE STAMPS

**Issued under Allied Occupation**
Bulgarian Postage Due Stamps of 1919 Overprinted like Nos. N7-N15 Reading Vertically Up

**1919 Unwmk. *Perf. 12x11½***

| | | | | |
|---|---|---|---|---|
| **NJ1** | D6 | 5s emerald | .30 | .30 |
| **NJ2** | D6 | 10s purple | .70 | .70 |
| **NJ3** | D6 | 50s blue | .70 | .60 |
| | | *Nos. NJ1-NJ3 (3)* | 1.70 | 1.60 |

Type of Bulgarian Postage Due Stamps of 1919-22 Overprinted

**1920 *Imperf.***

| | | | | |
|---|---|---|---|---|
| **NJ4** | D6 | 5s emerald | .20 | .20 |
| **NJ5** | D6 | 10s deep violet | 1.40 | 1.40 |
| **NJ6** | D6 | 20s salmon | .25 | .25 |
| **NJ7** | D6 | 50s blue | 1.25 | 1.10 |
| | | ***Perf. 12x11½*** | | |
| **NJ8** | D6 | 10s deep violet | 1.00 | .80 |
| | | *Nos. NJ4-NJ8 (5)* | 4.10 | 3.75 |

## TIBET

tə-'bet

LOCATION — A high tableland in Central Asia
GOVT. — A semi-independent state, nominally under control of China (under Communist China since 1950-51). In 1965 Tibet became a nominally autonomous region of the People's Republic of China.
AREA — 463,200 sq. mi.
POP. — 1,500,000 (approx.)
CAPITAL — Lhasa

Tibet's postage stamps were valid only within its borders.

6 ⅔ Trangka = 1 Sang

"Stamps" produced by the "Tibetan Government in Exile" have no postal value. These include four-value sets for Himalayan animals and the UPU that were put on sale in the early 1970s.

Excellent counterfeits of Nos. 1-18 exist. Numerous shades of all values.
All stamps issued without gum
Small bits of foreign matter (inclusions) are to be expected in Native Paper. These do not reduce the value of the stamp unless they have caused serious damage to the design or paper.

A1

Lion

A2

**1912-50 Unwmk. Typo. *Imperf.***
**Native Paper**

| | | | | |
|---|---|---|---|---|
| **1** | A1 | ⅙t green | 35.00 | *40.00* |
| **2** | A1 | ⅓t blue | 40.00 | *45.00* |
| ***a.*** | | ⅓t ultramarine | 45.00 | *55.00* |
| **3** | A1 | ½t violet | 40.00 | *45.00* |
| **4** | A1 | ⅔t carmine | 45.00 | *50.00* |
| ***a.*** | | "POTSAGE" | 140.00 | *150.00* |
| **5** | A1 | 1t vermilion | 50.00 | *60.00* |
| **6** | A1 | 1s sage green ('50) | 90.00 | *100.00* |
| | | *Nos. 1-6 (6)* | 300.00 | *340.00* |

The "POTSAGE" error is found on all shades of the ⅔t (positions 6 and 7).
Pin-perf. copies of Nos. 1 and 3 exist.
Issued in sheets of 12.
**Beware of private reproductions of #1-5 that were printed in the US around 1986. Sheets of 12 bear "J. Crow Co." imprint. The set of 5 sheets was sold for $5.**

Printed Using Shiny Enamel Paint

**1920**

| | | | | |
|---|---|---|---|---|
| *1a* | A1 | ⅙t green | 50.00 | 30.00 |
| *2b* | A1 | ⅓t blue | 450.00 | 450.00 |
| *3d* | A1 | ½t purple | 90.00 | *100.00* |
| *4h* | A1 | ⅔t carmine | 90.00 | *100.00* |
| *i.* | | "POTSAGE" | *200.00* | *225.00* |
| *5c* | A1 | 1t carmine | 300.00 | 300.00 |

In some 1920-30 printings, European enamel paint was used instead of ink. It has a glossy surface.

**1914**

| | | | | |
|---|---|---|---|---|
| **7** | A2 | 4t milky blue | 675. | *725.* |
| ***a.*** | | 4t dark blue | 1,000. | 1,000. |
| **8** | A2 | 8t carmine rose | 160. | 160. |
| ***a.*** | | 8t carmine | 1,000. | *1,100.* |

Issued in sheets of 6.

Printed Using Shiny Enamel Paint

**1920**

| | | | | |
|---|---|---|---|---|
| *7b* | A2 | 4t blue | 1,200. | *1,250.* |
| *8b* | A2 | 8t carmine | 1,200. | *1,250.* |

See note following No. 5c.

A3

Thin White Native Paper

**1933 *Pin-perf.***

| | | | | |
|---|---|---|---|---|
| **9** | A3 | ½t orange | 82.50 | *95.00* |
| **10** | A3 | ⅔t dark blue | 82.50 | *110.00* |
| **11** | A3 | 1t rose carmine | 82.50 | *110.00* |
| **12** | A3 | 2t scarlet | 82.50 | *110.00* |
| **13** | A3 | 4t emerald | 82.50 | *110.00* |
| | | *Nos. 9-13 (5)* | 412.50 | *535.00* |

Issued in sheets of 12.
Exist imperf.

Heavy Toned Native Paper

**1934 *Imperf.***

| | | | | |
|---|---|---|---|---|
| **14** | A3 | ½t yellow | 13.00 | *16.00* |
| **15** | A3 | ⅔t blue | 10.00 | *11.00* |
| **16** | A3 | 1t orange ver | 8.75 | *10.00* |
| ***a.*** | | 1t carmine | 11.00 | 11.00 |
| **17** | A3 | 2t red | 10.00 | 10.00 |
| ***a.*** | | 2t orange vermilion | 7.75 | 7.75 |
| **18** | A3 | 4t green | 7.75 | 7.75 |
| ***a.*** | | 25x25mm instead of 24x24mm | 50.00 | *60.00* |
| | | *Nos. 14-18 (5)* | 49.50 | *54.75* |

Nos. 14-18 are also known with a private pin-perf.
The ½t and 1t exist printed on both sides.
Issued in sheets of 12.

## OFFICIAL STAMPS

O1

O2

Various Designs and Sizes Inscribed "STAMP"

Sizes: No. O1, 32½x32½mm. No. O2, 38x28½mm. No. O3, 34x33mm. No. O4, 44x44mm. No. O5, 66x66mm.

**1945 Unwmk. Typo. *Imperf.***
**Native Paper**

| | | |
|---|---|---|
| **O1** | O1 | ⅙t bronze green |
| **O2** | O2 | ⅓t slate black |
| **O3** | O1 | ⅔t reddish brown |
| **O4** | O1 | 1⅓t olive green |
| **O5** | O1 | 1s dark gray blue |

The status of Nos. O1-O5 is in question. Other values exist.

## TIMOR

'tē-ˌmor

LOCATION — The eastern part of Timor island, Malay archipelago
GOVT. — Former Portuguese Overseas Territory
AREA — 7,330 sq. mi.
POP. — 660,000 (est. 1974)
CAPITAL — Dili

The Portuguese territory of Timor was annexed by Indonesia May 3, 1976. Timor-Leste achieved independent statehood status on May 20, 2002.

1000 Reis = 1 Milreis
78 Avos = 1 Rupee (1895)
100 Avos = 1 Pataca
100 Centavos = 1 Escudo (1960)
100Cents = 1 Dollar (2000)

**Catalogue values for unused stamps in this country are for Never Hinged items, beginning with Scott 256 in the regular postage section, Scott J31 in the postage due section, and Scott RA11 in the postal tax section.**

**Watermark**

Wmk. 232 — Maltese Cross

Stamps of Macao Overprinted in Black or Carmine **TIMOR**

**1885 Unwmk. *Perf. 12½, 13½***

| | | | | |
|---|---|---|---|---|
| **1** | A1 | 5r black (C) | 5.50 | 1.60 |
| ***a.*** | | Double overprint | 37.50 | 37.50 |
| ***b.*** | | Triple overprint | 115.00 | |
| **2** | A1 | 10r green | 8.00 | 3.50 |
| ***a.*** | | Overprint on Mozambique stamp | *22.50* | *14.00* |
| ***b.*** | | Overprinted on Portuguese India stamp | *210.00* | *150.00* |
| **3** | A1 | 20r rose, perf. 13½ | 9.00 | 4.50 |
| ***a.*** | | Double overprint | 22.50 | |
| ***b.*** | | Perf. 12½ | 9.50 | 5.00 |
| **4** | A1 | 25r violet | 2.25 | 1.10 |
| ***a.*** | | Perf. 13½ | 22.00 | 11.00 |
| **5** | A1 | 40r yellow | 5.50 | 3.00 |
| ***a.*** | | Double overprint | 17.50 | |
| ***b.*** | | Inverted overprint | *21.00* | *21.00* |
| ***c.*** | | Perf. 13½ | 14.00 | 11.00 |
| **6** | A1 | 50r blue | 4.50 | 1.50 |
| ***a.*** | | Perf. 13½ | 12.00 | 9.50 |
| **7** | A1 | 80r slate | 11.00 | 3.00 |
| **8** | A1 | 100r lilac | 5.50 | 1.50 |
| ***a.*** | | Double overprint | 22.50 | |
| ***b.*** | | Perf. 13½ | 9.00 | 3.50 |
| **9** | A1 | 200r org, perf. 13½ | 9.00 | 3.50 |
| ***a.*** | | Perf. 12½ | 11.00 | 3.50 |
| **10** | A1 | 300r brown | 8.00 | 3.00 |
| | | *Nos. 1-10 (10)* | 68.25 | 26.20 |

The 20r brown, 25r rose and 50r green were prepared for use but not issued.
*The reprints are printed on a smooth white chalky paper, ungummed, with rough perforation 13½, and on thin white paper with shiny white gum and clean-cut perforation 13½.*

King Luiz — A2

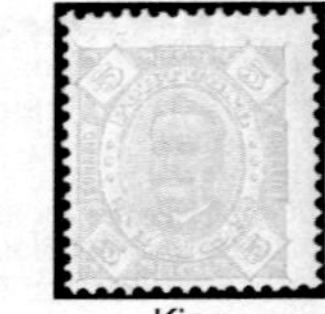

King Carlos — A3

**1887 Embossed *Perf. 12½***

| | | | | |
|---|---|---|---|---|
| **11** | A2 | 5r black | 2.00 | 1.75 |
| **12** | A2 | 10r green | 3.50 | 3.00 |
| **13** | A2 | 20r bright rose | 3.50 | 3.00 |
| **14** | A2 | 25r violet | 6.75 | 3.50 |
| **15** | A2 | 40r chocolate | 11.50 | 4.50 |
| **16** | A2 | 50r blue | 14.00 | 5.50 |
| **17** | A2 | 80r gray | 14.00 | 7.50 |
| **18** | A2 | 100r yellow brown | 20.00 | 9.00 |
| **19** | A2 | 200r gray lilac | 25.00 | 16.00 |
| **20** | A2 | 300r orange | 25.00 | 16.00 |
| | | *Nos. 11-20 (10)* | 125.25 | 69.75 |

*Reprints of Nos. 11, 16, 18 and 19 have clean-cut perforation 13½.*
For surcharges see Nos. 34-43, 83-91.

Macao No. 44 Surcharged in Black

**1892 Without Gum *Perf. 12½, 13***

| | | | | |
|---|---|---|---|---|
| **21** | A7 | 30r on 300r orange | 8.25 | 5.50 |

For surcharge see No. 44.

**1894 Typo. *Perf. 11½***

| | | | | |
|---|---|---|---|---|
| **22** | A3 | 5r yellow | 1.10 | .65 |
| **23** | A3 | 10r red violet | 1.50 | .65 |
| **24** | A3 | 15r chocolate | 2.75 | .95 |
| **25** | A3 | 20r lavender | 3.50 | 1.10 |
| **26** | A3 | 25r green | 4.25 | .80 |
| **27** | A3 | 50r light blue | 5.50 | 3.50 |
| ***a.*** | | Perf. 13½ | *150.00* | *125.00* |
| **28** | A3 | 75r rose | 6.75 | 2.75 |
| **29** | A3 | 80r light green | 7.25 | 4.25 |
| **30** | A3 | 100r brown, *buff* | 5.50 | 2.75 |
| **31** | A3 | 150r car, *rose* | 12.00 | 6.75 |
| **32** | A3 | 200r dk bl, *lt bl* | 12.50 | 8.00 |
| **33** | A3 | 300r dk bl, *salmon* | 14.00 | 9.50 |
| | | *Nos. 22-33 (12)* | 76.60 | 41.65 |

For surcharges and overprints see Nos. 92-102, 120-122, 124-128, 131-133, 183-193, 199.

Stamps of 1887 Surcharged in Red, Green or Black

**1895 Without Gum *Perf. 12½***

| | | | | |
|---|---|---|---|---|
| **34** | A2 | 1a on 5r black (R) | 1.00 | .85 |
| **35** | A2 | 2a on 10r green | 1.25 | .85 |
| ***a.*** | | Double surcharge | 17.50 | |
| **36** | A2 | 3a on 20r brt rose (G) | 2.75 | 1.75 |
| **37** | A2 | 4a on 25r violet | 2.75 | 1.10 |
| **38** | A2 | 6a on 40r choc | 4.50 | 2.50 |
| **39** | A2 | 8a on 50r blue (R) | 4.00 | 2.25 |
| **40** | A2 | 13a on 80r gray | 14.00 | 9.00 |
| **41** | A2 | 16a on 100r yellow brn | 15.00 | 6.75 |
| **42** | A2 | 31a on 200r gray lilac | 27.50 | 17.50 |
| **43** | A2 | 47a on 300r org (G) | 27.50 | 20.00 |
| | | *Nos. 34-43 (10)* | 100.25 | 62.55 |

No. 21 Surcharged 5 avos PROVISORIO 仙伍

**1895 Without Gum *Perf. 12½, 13***

| | | | | |
|---|---|---|---|---|
| **44** | A7 | 5a on 30r on 300r org | 8.50 | 5.00 |

Common Design Types pictured following the introduction.

### Vasco da Gama Issue
Common Design Types

**1898** **Engr.** ***Perf. 14 to 15***

**45** CD20 ½a blue green 1.50 .85
**46** CD21 1a red 1.50 .85
**47** CD22 2a red violet 1.50 .85
**48** CD23 4a yellow green 1.50 .85
**49** CD24 8a dark blue 3.00 1.25
**50** CD25 12a violet brown 3.50 1.40
**51** CD26 16a bister brown 4.00 1.90
**52** CD27 24a bister 5.00 2.50
*Nos. 45-52 (8)* 21.50 10.45

400th anniversary of Vasco da Gama's discovery of the route to India.

For overprints and surcharge see Nos. 148-155.

King Carlos
A5 A6

**1898-1903** **Typo.** ***Perf. 11½***
**Name & Value in Black Except #79**

**53** A5 ½a gray .35 .25
*a.* Perf. 12½ 2.50 1.75
**54** A5 1a orange .35 .30
*a.* Perf. 12½ 2.50 1.75
**55** A5 2a light green .35 .30
**56** A5 2½a brown 1.25 1.10
**57** A5 3a gray violet 1.25 1.10
**58** A5 3a gray green ('03) 1.50 1.00
**59** A5 4a sea green 1.60 1.00
**60** A5 5a rose ('03) 1.50 1.00
**61** A5 6a pale yel brn ('03) 1.50 1.00
**62** A5 8a blue 2.00 1.10
**63** A5 9a red brown ('03) 1.50 1.25
**64** A5 10a slate blue ('00) 2.00 1.10
**65** A5 10a gray brown ('03) 1.50 1.00
**66** A5 12a rose 4.25 3.00
**67** A5 12a dull blue ('03) 15.00 8.50
**68** A5 13a violet 4.50 3.75
**69** A5 13a red lilac ('03) 3.50 1.75
**70** A5 15a gray lilac ('03) 5.50 3.75
**71** A5 16a dark bl, *bl* 4.50 3.75
**72** A5 20a brn, *yelsh* ('00) 5.25 3.75
**73** A5 22a brn org, *pink* ('03) 5.25 3.50
**74** A5 24a brown, *buff* 5.50 3.75
**75** A5 31a red lil, *pinkish* 5.50 3.75
**76** A5 31a brn, *straw* ('03) 5.75 3.50
**77** A5 47a dk blue, *rose* 9.00 4.25
**78** A5 47a red vio, *pink* ('03) 6.50 3.50
**79** A5 78a blk & red, *bl* ('00) 11.00 6.00
**80** A5 78a dl bl, *straw* ('03) 14.00 8.00
*Nos. 53-80 (28)* 121.65 76.00

Most of Nos. 53-80 were issued without gum.

For surcharges & overprints see #81-82, 104-119, 129-130, 134-147, 195-196.

**1899**

**Black Surcharge**

**81** A6 10a on 16a dk bl, *bl* 3.00 2.50
**82** A6 20a on 31a red lil, *pnksh* 3.00 2.50

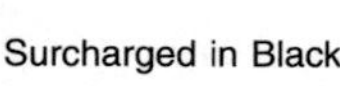

Surcharged in Black

**1902**

**On Issue of 1887**

**83** A2 5a on 25r violet 2.50 1.75
**84** A2 5a on 200r gray lil 4.00 2.50
**85** A2 6a on 10r blue grn 75.00 40.00
**86** A2 6a on 300r orange 3.75 3.50
**87** A2 9a on 40r choc 4.50 3.50
**88** A2 9a on 100r yel brn 4.50 3.50
**89** A2 15a on 20r rose 4.50 3.50
**90** A2 15a on 50r blue 75.00 40.00
**91** A2 22a on 80r gray 7.50 5.00
*Nos. 83-91 (9)* 181.25 103.25

*Reprints of Nos. 83-88, 90-91, 104A have clean-cut perf. 13½.*

**On Issue of 1894**

**92** A3 5a on 5r yellow 1.90 1.10
*a.* Inverted surcharge 40.00 30.00
**93** A3 5a on 25r green 2.25 1.10
**94** A3 5a on 50r lt blue 2.25 1.40
**95** A3 6a on 20r lavender 2.25 1.40
**96** A3 9a on 15r choc 2.25 1.40
**97** A3 9a on 75r rose 2.25 1.40
**98** A3 15a on 10r red vio 4.00 2.25
**99** A3 15a on 100r brn, *buff* 4.00 2.25
**100** A3 15a on 300r bl, *sal* 4.00 2.25
**101** A3 22a on 80r lt green 6.00 4.00
**102** A3 22a on 200r bl, *blue* 8.00 4.00

**On Newspaper Stamp of 1893**

**103** N2 6a on 2½r brn 1.00 .85
*a.* Inverted surcharge 27.50 27.50
*Nos. 92-103 (12)* 40.15 23.40

Nos. 93-97, 99-102 issued without gum.

Stamps of 1898 Overprinted in Black

**104** A5 3a gray violet 3.00 1.40
**104A** A5 12a rose 6.00 3.75

Reprint noted after No. 91.

No. 67 Surcharged in Black

**1905**

**105** A5 10a on 12a dull blue 3.50 2.50

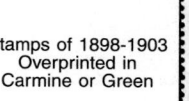

Stamps of 1898-1903 Overprinted in Carmine or Green

**1911**

**106** A5 ½a gray .30 .30
*a.* Inverted overprint 20.00 20.00
**107** A5 1a orange .30 .30
*a.* Perf. 12½ 16.00 16.00
**108** A5 2a light green .40 .35
**109** A5 3a gray green .50 .35
**110** A5 5a rose (G) .50 .35
**111** A5 6a yel brown .50 .35
**112** A5 9a red brown .75 .45
**113** A5 10a gray brown .75 .45
**114** A5 13a red lilac .80 .50
**115** A5 15a gray lilac 1.60 1.25
**116** A5 22a brn org, *pink* 1.60 1.25
**117** A5 31a brown, *straw* 1.60 1.25
**118** A5 47a red vio, *pink* 3.00 2.50
**119** A5 78a dl bl, *straw* 4.75 3.50
*Nos. 106-119 (14)* 17.35 13.15

Preceding Issues Overprinted in Red

**1913**

**Without Gum**

**On Provisional Issue of 1902**

**120** A3 5a on 5r yellow 4.00 4.00
**121** A3 5a on 25r green 4.00 4.00
**122** A3 5a on 50r lt bl 6.00 7.00
**123** N2 6a on 2½r brn 6.00 7.00
**124** A3 6a on 20r lavender 4.00 4.00
**125** A3 9a on 15r choc 4.00 4.00
**126** A3 15a on 100r brn, *buff* 6.00 5.50
**127** A3 22a on 80r lt grn 9.00 8.00
**128** A3 22a on 200r bl, *bl* 8.00 7.50

**On Issue of 1903**

**129** A5 3a gray green 5.00 *7.50*

**On Issue of 1905**

**130** A5 10a on 12a dull bl 4.50 *4.00*
*Nos. 120-130 (11)* 60.50 *62.50*

Overprinted in Green or Red

**1913**

**On Provisional Issue of 1902**

**131** A3 9a on 75r rose (G) 4.50 4.50
**132** A3 15a on 10r red vio (G) 3.75 3.75
*a.* Inverted overprint *35.00* *35.00*
**133** A3 15a on 300r bl, *sal* (R) 6.50 6.50
*a.* "REUBPLICA" 19.00 19.00
*b.* "REPBLICAU" 19.00 19.00

**On Issue of 1903**

**134** A5 5a rose (G) 3.00 3.00
*Nos. 131-134 (4)* 17.75 17.75

Stamps of 1898-1903 Overprinted in Red

**1913**

**135** A5 6a yellow brown 4.00 1.75
**136** A5 9a red brown 4.00 1.75
**137** A5 10a gray brown 4.00 1.75
**138** A5 13a violet 6.00 2.50
*a.* Inverted overprint 40.00 40.00
**139** A5 13a red lilac 5.00 2.50
**140** A5 15a gray lilac 6.00 3.25
**141** A5 22a brn org, *pnksh* 7.00 3.50
**142** A5 31a red lil, *pnksh* 7.00 3.50
**143** A5 31a brown, *straw* 9.00 5.50
**144** A5 47a blue, *pink* 10.00 5.50
**145** A5 47a red vio, *pink* 12.00 8.00
**146** A5 78a dl bl, *straw* 12.00 6.50

No. 79 Overprinted in Red

**147** A5 78a blk & red, *bl* 12.00 8.00
*Nos. 135-147 (13)* 98.00 54.00

Vasco da Gama Issue of 1898 Overprinted or Surcharged in Black:

**1913**

**148** CD20 ½a blue green .65 .60
**149** CD21 1a red .65 .60
**150** CD22 2a red violet .65 .60
**151** CD23 4a yellow green .65 .60
**152** CD24 8a dark blue 1.40 1.10
**153** CD25 10a on 12a vio brn 2.50 2.00
**154** CD26 16a bister brown 2.00 1.75
**155** CD27 24a bister 2.75 2.25
*Nos. 148-155 (8)* 11.25 9.50

Ceres — A7

**1914-23** **Typo.** ***Perf. 15x14, 12x11½***
**Name and Value in Black**

**156** A7 ½a olive brown .20 .20
**157** A7 1a black .20 .20
**158** A7 1½a yel grn ('23) .60 *1.10*
**159** A7 2a blue green .25 .25
**160** A7 3a lilac brown 1.00 .75
**161** A7 4a carmine 1.00 .75
**162** A7 6a light violet 1.00 .75
**163** A7 7a lt green ('23) 1.75 *1.75*
**164** A7 7½a ultra ('23) 3.25 *3.50*
**165** A7 9a blue ('23) 4.00 *6.75*
**166** A7 10a deep blue 1.25 .75
**167** A7 11a gray ('23) 4.00 *6.75*
**168** A7 12a yellow brown 1.50 1.25
**169** A7 15a lilac ('23) 8.00 *7.25*
**170** A7 16a slate 2.00 3.75
**171** A7 18a dp blue ('23) 10.00 6.25
**172** A7 19a gray grn ('23) 10.00 5.50
**173** A7 20a org brown 15.00 6.00
**174** A7 36a turq blue ('23) 9.00 4.25
**175** A7 40a plum 9.00 4.50
**176** A7 54a choc ('23) 10.00 6.25
**177** A7 58a brown, *grn* 10.00 5.00
**178** A7 72a brt rose ('23) 16.00 16.00
**179** A7 76a brown, *rose* 11.50 6.50
**180** A7 1p org, *salmon* 20.00 11.00
**181** A7 3p green, *blue* 35.00 25.00
**182** A7 5p car rose ('23) 70.00 52.50
*Nos. 156-182 (27)* 255.50 184.50

For surcharges see Nos. 200-201, MR1.

Preceding Issues Overprinted in Carmine

**1915** ***Perf. 11½***

**On Provisional Issue of 1902**

**183** A3 5a on 5r yellow 1.00 .55
**184** A3 5a on 25r green 1.00 .55
**185** A3 5a on 50r lt blue 1.00 .55
**186** A3 6a on 20r lavender 1.00 .55
**187** A3 9a on 15r chocolate 1.00 .55
**188** A3 9a on 75r rose 1.50 .55
**189** A3 15a on 10r red vio 1.50 1.50
**190** A3 15a on 100r brn, *buff* 2.00 1.50
**191** A3 15a on 300r bl, *sal* 2.00 3.00
**192** A3 22a on 80r lt grn 3.25 2.75
**193** A3 22a on 200r bl, *bl* 5.00 5.00

**On No. 103**

**194** N2 6a on 2½r, perf. 13½ 1.00 .55
*a.* Perf. 12½ 2.00 1.25
*b.* Perf. 11½ 4.00 1.75

**On No. 104**

**195** A5 3a gray violet 1.00 .60

**On No. 105**

**196** A5 10a on 12a dull bl 1.10 .60
*Nos. 183-196 (14)* 23.35 18.80

Type of 1915 with Additional Surcharge in Black

***Perf. 11½***

**199** A3 ½a on 5a on 50r lt bl 12.50 7.00
*a.* Perf. 13½ 35.00 12.50

Nos. 178 and 169 Surcharged

**1932** ***Perf. 12x11½***

**200** A7 6a on 72a brt rose 1.50 1.25
**201** A7 12a on 15a lilac 1.50 1.25

"Portugal" and Vasco da Gama's Flagship "San Gabriel" — A8

***Perf. 11½x12***

**1935** **Typo.** **Wmk. 232**

**202** A8 ½a bister .20 .20
**203** A8 1a olive brown .20 .20
**204** A8 2a blue green .20 .20
**205** A8 3a red violet .60 .60
**206** A8 4a black .60 .60
**207** A8 5a gray .70 .65
**208** A8 6a brown .85 .65
**209** A8 7a bright rose 1.00 1.00
**210** A8 8a bright blue 1.10 1.10
**211** A8 10a red orange 1.60 1.20
**212** A8 12a dark blue 2.75 2.10
**213** A8 14a olive green 3.25 2.10
**214** A8 15a maroon 3.00 2.75
**215** A8 20a orange 3.50 2.75
**216** A8 30a apple green 4.00 2.75
**217** A8 40a violet 7.50 4.50

**218** A8 50a olive bister 8.75 4.50
**219** A8 1p light blue 21.00 12.00
**220** A8 2p brn orange 42.50 22.50
**221** A8 3p emerald 52.50 32.50
**222** A8 5p dark violet 82.50 45.00
*Nos. 202-222 (21)* 238.30 139.85

Common Design Types

**1938 Unwmk. Engr. *Perf. 13½x13***
**Name and Value in Black**

**223** CD34 1a gray green .20 .20
**224** CD34 2a orange brown .20 .30
**225** CD34 3a dk violet brn .20 .30
**226** CD34 4a brt green .20 .65
**227** CD35 5a dk carmine .20 1.75
**228** CD35 6a slate .45 .20
**229** CD35 8a rose violet .65 1.10
**230** CD37 10a brt red violet .65 1.75
**231** CD37 12a red 1.10 2.50
**232** CD37 15a orange 1.75 2.50
**233** CD36 20a blue 1.75 .80
**234** CD36 40a gray black 3.75 1.25
**235** CD36 50a brown 3.75 1.25
**236** CD38 1p brown carmine 7.00 4.50
**237** CD38 2p olive green 14.00 3.50
**238** CD38 3p blue violet 17.50 8.00
**239** CD38 5p red brown 35.00 11.50
*Nos. 223-239 (17)* 88.35 42.05

For overprints see Nos. 245A-245K.

Mozambique Nos. 273, 276, 278, 280, 282 and 283 Surcharged in Black

**1946 *Perf. 13½x13***

**240** CD34 1a on 15c dk vio brn 6.75 5.00
**241** CD35 4a on 35c brt grn 6.75 5.00
**242** CD35 8a on 50c brt red vio 6.75 5.00
**243** CD36 10a on 70c brn vio 6.75 5.00
**244** CD36 12a on 1e red 6.75 5.00
**245** CD37 20a on 1.75e blue 6.75 5.00
*Nos. 240-245 (6)* 40.50 30.00

Nos. 223-227 and 229-234 Overprinted "Libertacao"

**1947**

**245A** CD34 1a gray green 18.00 12.50
**245B** CD34 2a org brown 28.00 11.50
**245C** CD34 3a dk vio brn 11.50 6.75
**245D** CD34 4a brt green 11.50 9.00
**245E** CD35 5a dark car 5.00 2.40
**245F** CD35 8a rose violet 2.50 1.75
**245G** CD37 10a brt red vio 7.00 3.75
**245H** CD37 12a red 7.25 3.00
**245I** CD37 15a orange 5.75 3.00
**245J** CD36 20a blue 62.50 40.00
*m.* Inverted overprint *90.00 77.50*
**245K** CD36 40a gray black 17.50 9.25
*Nos. 245A-245K (11)* 176.50 102.90

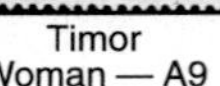

Timor Woman — A9

UPU Symbols — A10

Designs: 3a, Gong ringer. 4a, Girl with basket. 8a, Aleixo de Ainaro. 10a, 1p, 3p, Heads of various chieftains. 20a, Warrior and horse.

**1948 Litho. *Perf. 14***

**246** A9 1a aqua & dk brn .50 .50
**247** A9 3a gray & dk brn 1.10 .60
**248** A9 4a pink & dk grn 1.40 .60
**249** A9 8a red & blue blk .80 .35
**250** A9 10a blue grn & org .80 .50
**251** A9 20a ultra, aqua & bl .85 .45
**252** A9 1p org, bl & ultra 16.00 3.00
**253** A9 3p vio & dk brn 16.00 5.00
*a.* Sheet of 8, #246-253 55.00 55.00
*Nos. 246-253 (8)* 37.45 11.00

No. 253a sold for 5p.

**Lady of Fatima Issue**

Common Design Type

**1948, Oct.**

**254** CD40 8a slate gray 3.00 3.00

**UPU Issue**

**1949 Unwmk. *Perf. 14.***

**255** A10 16a brown & buff 4.00 *5.00*

UPU, 75th anniversary.

**Catalogue values for unused stamps in this section, from this point to the end of the section, are for Never Hinged items.**

Craftsman A11

Timor Woman A12

**1950 *Perf. 14½***

**256** A11 20a dull vio blue 1.10 .70
**257** A12 50a dull brown 4.50 1.40

**Holy Year Issue**

Common Design Types

**1950, May *Perf. 13x13½***

**258** CD41 40a green 1.50 1.25
**259** CD42 70a black brown 2.25 2.00

Blackberry Lily — A13

Designs: Various flowers.

**1950 Unwmk. Litho. *Perf. 14½***

**260** A13 1a multicolored .35 .30
**261** A13 3a multicolored 1.40 1.00
**262** A13 10a multicolored 1.75 1.00
**263** A13 16a multicolored 3.50 1.25
**264** A13 20a multicolored 1.40 1.00
**265** A13 30a multicolored 1.75 1.10
**266** A13 70a multicolored 2.25 1.25
**267** A13 1p multicolored 3.75 2.00
**268** A13 2p multicolored 6.00 3.50
**269** A13 5p multicolored 9.50 4.50
*Nos. 260-269 (10)* 31.65 16.90

**Holy Year Extension Issue**

Common Design Type

**1951 *Perf. 14***

**270** CD43 86a bl & pale bl + label 2.00 1.75

Stamp without label attached sells for much less.

**Medical Congress Issue**

Common Design Type

Design: Weighing baby.

**1952 Litho. *Perf. 13½***

**271** CD44 10a ol blk & brn .90 .85

**St. Francis Xavier Issue**

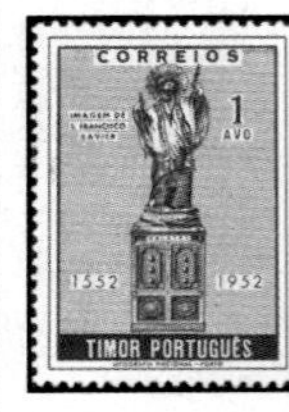

Statue of St. Francis Xavier — A14

Designs: 16a, Miraculous Arm of St. Francis. 1p, Tomb of St. Francis.

**1952, Oct. 25 *Perf. 14***

**272** A14 1a black .25 .20
**273** A14 16a blk brn & brn 1.00 .80
**274** A14 1p dk car & gray 5.00 2.00
*Nos. 272-274 (3)* 6.25 3.00

400th death anniv. of St. Francis Xavier.

Madonna and Child — A15

Stamp of Portugal and Arms of Colonies — A16

**1953 *Perf. 13x13½***

**275** A15 3a dk brn & dull gray .25 .20
**276** A15 16a dk brown & cream 1.00 .60
**277** A15 50a dk bl & dull gray 3.00 1.40
*Nos. 275-277 (3)* 4.25 2.20

Exhibition of Sacred Missionary Art, Lisbon, 1951.

**Stamp Centenary Issue**

**1953 Photo. *Perf. 13***

**278** A16 10a multicolored 1.10 1.00

**Sao Paulo Issue**

Common Design Type

**1954 Litho. *Perf. 13½***

**279** CD46 16a dk brn red, bl & blk .85 .70

Map of Timor — A17

**1956 Unwmk. *Perf. 14x12½***
**Inscription and design in brown, red, green, ultramarine & yellow**

**280** A17 1a pale salmon .20 .20
**281** A17 3a pale gray blue .25 .20
**282** A17 8a buff .30 .20
**283** A17 24a pale green .40 .20
**284** A17 32a lemon .50 .20
**285** A17 40a pale gray .75 .30
**286** A17 1p yellow 1.75 1.10
**287** A17 3p pale blue 4.25 1.50
*Nos. 280-287 (8)* 8.40 3.90

For surcharges see Nos. 291-300.

**Brussels Fair Issue**

Exhibition Emblems and View — A18

**1958 *Perf. 14½***

**288** A18 40a multicolored .50 .40

**Tropical Medicine Congress Issue**

Common Design Type

Design: Calophyllum inophyllum.

**1958 *Perf. 13½***

**289** CD47 32a multicolored 3.00 2.75

Symbolical Globe — A19

Carved Elephant Jar — A20

**1960 Unwmk. Litho. *Perf. 13½***

**290** A19 4.50e multicolored .50 .35

500th death anniv. of Prince Henry the Navigator.

Nos. 280-287 Surcharged with New Value and Bars

**1960 Unwmk. *Perf. 14x12½***
**Inscription and design in brown, red, green, ultramarine & yellow**

**291** A17 5c on 1a pale salmon .20 .20
**292** A17 10c on 3a pale gray bl .20 .20
**293** A17 20c on 8a buff .25 .20
**294** A17 30c on 24a pale grn .30 .20
**295** A17 50c on 32a lemon .40 .20
**296** A17 1e on 40a pale gray .50 .20
**297** A17 2e on 40a pale gray .60 .20
**298** A17 5e on 1p yellow .75 1.00
**299** A17 10e on 3p pale blue 1.75 2.50
**300** A17 15e on 3p pale blue 2.50 2.00
*Nos. 291-300 (10)* 7.45 6.90

**1961 Litho. *Perf. 11½x12***

Native Art: 10c, House on stilts. 20c, Madonna and Child. 30c, Silver rosary. 50c, Two men in boat, horiz. 1e, Silver box in shape of temple. 2.50e, Archer. 4.50e, Elephant. 5e, Man climbing tree. 10e, Woman carrying pot on head. 20e, Cockfight. 50e, House on stilts and animals.

**Multicolored Designs**

**301** A20 5c pale violet .20 .30
**302** A20 10c pale green .20 .30
*a.* Value & legend inverted *72.50 72.50*
**303** A20 20c pale blue .20 .30
**304** A20 30c rose .25 .20
**305** A20 50c pale grnsh bl .20 .20
**306** A20 1e bister .70 .20
**307** A20 2.50e pale ol bis .50 .20
**308** A20 4.50e lt salmon .50 .20
**309** A20 5e lt gray .60 .20
**310** A20 10e gray 1.40 .30
**311** A20 20e yellow 2.75 1.00
**312** A20 50e lt bluish gray 9.25 2.50
*Nos. 301-312 (12)* 16.75 5.90

**Sports Issue**

Common Design Type

Sports: 50c, Duck hunting. 1e, Horseback riding. 1.50e, Swimming. 2e, Gymnastics. 2.50e, Soccer. 15e, Big game hunting.

**1962, Mar. 22 Unwmk. *Perf. 13½***
**Multicolored Designs**

**313** CD48 50c gray & bis .25 .20
**314** CD48 1e olive bister .60 .30
**315** CD48 1.50e gray & bl grn .70 .40
**316** CD48 2e buff .85 .35
**317** CD48 2.50e gray 1.00 .50
**318** CD48 15e salmon 3.00 1.90
*Nos. 313-318 (6)* 6.40 3.65

**Anti-Malaria Issue**

Common Design Type

Design: Anopheles sundaicus.

**1962 Litho. *Perf. 13½***

**319** CD49 2.50e multicolored .75 .60

**National Overseas Bank Issue**

Common Design Type

Design: 2.50e, Manuel Pinheiro Chagas.

**1964, May 16 Unwmk. *Perf. 13½***

**320** CD51 2.50e grn, gray, yel, lt bl & blk .75 .60

**ITU Issue**

Common Design Type

**1965, May 17 Litho. *Perf. 14½***

**321** CD52 1.50e multicolored 1.50 .90

**National Revolution Issue**

Common Design Type

Design: 4.50e, Dr. Vieira Machado Academy and Dili Health Center.

**1966, May 28 Litho. *Perf. 11½***

**322** CD53 4.50e multicolored 1.50 .90

### Navy Club Issue
Common Design Type

10c, Capt. Gago Coutinho and gunboat Patria. 4.50e, Capt. Sacadura Cabral and seaplane Lusitania.

**1967, Jan. 31 Litho. *Perf. 13***
**323** CD54 10c multicolored 2.00 1.00
**324** CD54 4.50e multicolored 2.00 1.00

Sepoy Officer, 1792 — A21

Our Lady of Fatima — A22

Designs: 1e, Officer, 1815. 1.50e, Infantry soldier, 1879. 2e, Infantry soldier, 1890. 2.50e, Infantry officer, 1903. 3e, Sapper, 1918. 4.50e, Special forces soldier, 1964. 10e, Paratrooper, 1964.

**1967, Feb. 12 Photo. *Perf. 13½***
**325** A21 35c multicolored .25 .30
**326** A21 1e multicolored 1.50 1.00
**327** A21 1.50e multicolored .60 .30
**328** A21 2e multicolored .60 .20
**329** A21 2.50e multicolored .60 .25
**330** A21 3e multicolored .75 .35
**331** A21 4.50e multicolored 1.10 .45
**332** A21 10e multicolored 2.25 .65
*Nos. 325-332 (8)* 7.65 3.50

**1967, May 13 Litho. *Perf. 12½x13***
**333** A22 3e multicolored .60 .30

Apparition of the Virgin Mary to three shepherd children at Fatima, Portugal, 50th anniv.

### Cabral Issue

Map of Brazil, by Lopo Homem-Reinéis, 1519 — A23

**1968, Apr. 22 Litho. *Perf. 14***
**334** A23 4.50e multicolored .80 .50

See note after Macao No. 416.

### Admiral Coutinho Issue
Common Design Type

Design: 4.50e, Adm. Coutinho and frigate Adm. Gago Coutinho.

**1969, Feb. 17 Litho. *Perf. 14***
**335** CD55 4.50e multicolored 1.10 .85

View of Dili, 1834 — A24

**1969, July 25 Litho. *Perf. 14***
**336** A24 1e multicolored .30 .20

Bicentenary of Dili as capital of Timor.

da Gama Medal in St. Jerome's Convent — A25

Emblem of King Manuel, St. Jerome's Convent — A26

### Vasco da Gama Issue

**1969, Aug. 29 Litho. *Perf. 14***
**337** A25 5e multicolored .40 .30

Vasco da Gama (1469-1524), navigator.

### Administration Reform Issue
Common Design Type

**1969, Sept. 25 Litho. *Perf. 14***
**338** CD56 5e multicolored .40 .25

### King Manuel I Issue

**1969, Dec. 1 Litho. *Perf. 14***
**339** A26 4e multicolored .40 .25

King Manuel I, 500th birth anniv.

Capt. Ross Smith, Arms of Great Britain, Portugal and Australia, and Map of Timor
A27

**1969, Dec. 9**
**340** A27 2e multicolored .50 .40

50th anniv. of the first England to Australia flight of Capt. Ross Smith and Lt. Keith Smith.

### Marshal Carmona Issue
Common Design Type

Antonio Oscar Carmona in civilian clothes.

**1970, Nov. 15 Litho. *Perf. 14***
**341** CD57 1.50e multicolored .20 .20

### Lusiads Issue

Sailing Ship and Monks Preaching to Islanders — A28

**1972, May 25 Litho. *Perf. 13***
**342** A28 1e brown & multi .20 *.35*

4th centenary of publication of The Lusiads by Luiz Camoens.

### Olympic Games Issue
Common Design Type

Design: 4.50e, Soccer, Olympic emblem.

**1972, June 20 *Perf. 14x13½***
**343** CD59 4.50e multicolored .50 .50

### Lisbon-Rio de Janeiro Flight Issue
Common Design Type

Design: 1e, Sacadura Cabral and Gago Coutinho in cockpit of "Lusitania."

**1972, Sept. 20 Litho. *Perf. 13½***
**344** CD60 1e multicolored .25 *.40*

### WMO Centenary Issue
Common Design Type

**1973, Dec. 15 Litho. *Perf. 13***
**345** CD61 20e multicolored 1.75 *2.00*

### United Nations Transitional Authority in East Timor

A30

**2000, Apr. 29 Litho. *Perf. 12x11¾***
**350** A30 Dom. red & multi .25 .25
**351** A30 Int. blue & multi 1.25 1.25

No. 350 sold for 10c and No. 351 sold for 50c on day of issue.

### INDEPENDENT STATE OF TIMOR-LESTE

Independence — A31

Designs: 25c, Crocodile. 50c, Palm fronds. $1, Coffee beans and picker. $2, Flag.

**2002, May 20 Litho. *Perf. 14½x14***
**352-355** A31 Set of 4 7.50 7.50

A32

Flag and: 10c, Pres. Xanana Gusmao. 50c, Map of country.

**2002 Litho. *Perf. 13x13¼***
**356-357** A32 Set of 2 1.25 1.25

## AIR POST STAMPS

Common Design Type

**1938 Unwmk. Engr. *Perf. 13½x13***
**Name and Value in Black**
**C1** CD39 1a red orange .85 .45
**C2** CD39 2a purple .90 .55
**C3** CD39 3a orange .90 .60
**C4** CD39 5a ultra 1.00 .65
**C5** CD39 10a lilac brown 1.60 1.10
**C6** CD39 20a dark green 3.00 1.40
**C7** CD39 50a red brown 6.00 4.00
**C8** CD39 70a rose carmine 7.00 5.25
**C9** CD39 1p magenta 13.00 6.00
*Nos. C1-C9 (9)* 34.25 20.00

No. C7 exists with overprint "Exposicao Internacional de Nova York, 1939-1940" and Trylon and Perisphere. Counterfeits exist.

For overprints see Nos. C15-C23.

Mozambique Nos. C3, C4, C6, C7 and C9 Surcharged in Black

**1946 Unwmk. *Perf. 13½x13***
**C10** CD39 8a on 50c orange 6.25 4.00
**C11** CD39 12a on 1e ultra 6.25 4.00
**C12** CD39 40a on 3e dk green 6.25 4.00
**C13** CD39 50a on 5e red brn 6.25 4.00
**C14** CD39 1p on 10e mag 6.25 4.00
*Nos. C10-C14 (5)* 31.25 20.00

Nos. C1-C9 Overprinted "Libertacao"

**1947**
**C15** CD39 1a scarlet 20.00 15.00
**C16** CD39 2a purple 20.00 15.00
**C17** CD39 3a orange 20.00 15.00
**C18** CD39 5a ultra 20.00 15.00
**C19** CD39 10a lilac brown 6.50 3.75
**C20** CD39 20a dark green 6.50 4.25
**C21** CD39 50a red brown 6.75 3.75
**C22** CD39 70a rose carmine 27.50 9.00
**C23** CD39 1p magenta 10.50 3.75
*Nos. C15-C23 (9)* 137.75 84.50

## POSTAGE DUE STAMPS

D1

**1904 Unwmk. Typo. *Perf. 12***
**Without Gum**
**Name and Value in Black**
**J1** D1 1a yellow green .50 .50
**J2** D1 2a slate .50 .50
**J3** D1 5a yellow brown 2.25 1.50
**J4** D1 6a red orange 2.25 2.25
**J5** D1 10a gray brown 2.50 2.00
**J6** D1 15a red brown 3.75 2.75
**J7** D1 24a dull blue 6.25 5.50
**J8** D1 40a carmine 7.50 5.50
**J9** D1 50a orange 10.50 7.50
**J10** D1 1p dull violet 17.00 13.00
*Nos. J1-J10 (10)* 53.00 41.00

Overprinted in Carmine or Green

**1911 Without Gum**
**J11** D1 1a yellow green .25 .25
**J12** D1 2a slate .30 .25
*a.* Inverted overprint
**J13** D1 5a yellow brown .60 .40
**J14** D1 6a deep orange .80 .50
**J15** D1 10a gray brown 1.50 .70
**J16** D1 15a brown 1.75 1.10
**J17** D1 24a dull blue 2.50 2.00
**J18** D1 40a carmine (G) 3.25 2.50
**J19** D1 50a orange 3.75 2.50
**J20** D1 1p dull violet 7.50 7.00
*Nos. J11-J20 (10)* 22.20 17.20

Nos. J1-J10 Overprinted in Red or Green

**1913 Without Gum**
**J21** D1 1a yellow green 8.00 *9.00*
**J22** D1 2a slate 8.00 *9.00*
**J23** D1 5a yellow brown 4.50 *4.50*
**J24** D1 6a deep orange 4.50 *4.50*
*a.* Inverted surcharge 30.00
**J25** D1 10a gray brown 4.50 *6.00*
**J26** D1 15a red brown 4.50 *6.00*
**J27** D1 24a dull blue 6.00 *6.00*
**J28** D1 40a carmine (G) 6.00 *6.00*
**J29** D1 50a orange 10.00 *12.00*
**J30** D1 1p gray violet 10.00 *12.00*
*Nos. J21-J30 (10)* 66.00 75.00

**Catalogue values for unused stamps in this section, from this point to the end of the section, are for Never Hinged items.**

Common Design Type

**1952 Photo. & Typo. *Perf. 14***
**Numeral in Red, Frame Multicolored**
**J31** CD45 1a chocolate .40 .40
**J32** CD45 3a brown .40 .40
**J33** CD45 5a dark green .40 .40
**J34** CD45 10a green .40 .40
**J35** CD45 30a purple .65 .65
**J36** CD45 1p brown carmine 1.25 1.25
*Nos. J31-J36 (6)* 3.50 3.50

## WAR TAX STAMP

Regular Issue of 1914 Surcharged in Red

**1919** **Unwmk.** ***Perf. 15x14***
**Without Gum**
**MR1** A7 2a on ½a ol brn 22.50 20.00

See note after Macao No. MR2.

### NEWSPAPER STAMPS

King Luiz — N1

Stamps of Macao Surcharged in Black

**1892** **Unwmk.** ***Perf. 12½***
**Without Gum**
**P1** N1 2½r on 20r brt rose 2.00 .75
*a.* "TIMOR" inverted
**P2** N1 2½r on 40r chocolate 2.00 .75
*a.* "TIMOR" inverted
*b.* Perf. 13½ 4.50 3.00
*c.* As "a," perf. 13½
**P3** N1 2½r on 80r gray 2.00 .75
*a.* "TIMOR" inverted
*b.* Perf. 13½ 12.50 8.00
*Nos. P1-P3 (3)* 6.00 2.25

N2

N3

**1893-95** **Typo.** ***Perf. 11½, 13½***
**P4** N2 2½r brown .40 .35
*a.* Perf. 12½ 2.00 1.50
**P5** N3 ½a on 2½r brn ('95) .45 .30

For surcharges see Nos. 103, 123, 194.

### POSTAL TAX STAMPS

**Pombal Issue**
Common Design Types

**1925** **Unwmk.** ***Perf. 12½***
**RA1** CD28 2a lake & black .30 .30
**RA2** CD29 2a lake & black .30 .30
**RA3** CD30 2a lake & black .30 .30
*Nos. RA1-RA3 (3)* .90 .90

Type of War Tax Stamp of Portuguese India Overprinted in Red

**1934-35** ***Perf. 12***
**RA4** WT1 2a green & blk 6.50 *8.00*
**RA5** WT1 5a green & blk 8.00 8.00

**Surcharged in Black**
**RA6** WT1 7a on ½a rose & blk ('35) 9.00 7.50
*Nos. RA4-RA6 (3)* 23.50 *23.50*

The tax was for local education.

Type of War Tax Stamp of Portuguese India Overprinted in Black

**1936** ***Perf. 12x11½***
**RA7** WT1 10a rose & black 7.00 *9.00*

**1937** ***Perf. 11½***
**RA8** WT1 10a green & blk 5.50 *8.25*

PT1

PT2

**1948** **Unwmk.** **Typo.** ***Perf. 11½***
**Without Gum**
**RA9** PT1 10a dark blue 3.00 2.00
**RA10** PT1 20a green 3.50 3.00

The 20a bears a different emblem.

**Catalogue values for unused stamps in this section, from this point to the end of the section, are for Never Hinged items.**

**1960** **Without Gum** ***Perf. 11½***
**RA11** PT2 70c dark blue 1.50 1.25
**RA12** PT2 1.30e green 2.25 2.25

See Nos. RA13-RA16. For surcharges see Nos. RA20-RA25.

Type of 1960 Redrawn

**1967** **Typo.** ***Perf. 10½***
**Without Gum**
**RA13** PT2 70c deep blue 12.00 12.00
**RA14** PT2 1.30e emerald 3.00 2.50

The denominations of Nos. RA13-RA14 are 2mm high. They are 2½mm high on Nos. RA11-RA12. Other differences exist. The printed area of No. RA13 measures 18x31mm; "Republica" 16mm.

Type of 1960
Serif Type Face

**1967**
**RA14A** PT2 70c deep blue 12.00 10.00

Type of 1960, 2nd Redrawing

**1967-68** **Typo.** ***Perf. 10½***
**Without Gum**
**RA15** PT2 70c violet blue .60 .60
**RA16** PT2 1.30e bluish grn ('68) 1.25 1.25

The printed area measures 13x30mm on Nos. RA15-RA16; "Republica" measures 10½mm.

Woman and Star — PT3

**1969-70** **Litho.** ***Perf. 13½***
**RA17** PT3 30c vio bl & lt bl ('70) .20 .20
**RA18** PT3 50c dl org & maroon .20 .20
**RA19** PT3 1e yellow & brown .20 .20
*Nos. RA17-RA19 (3)* .60 .60

The 2.50e and 10e in design PT3 were revenue stamps. Value $1.50 each.

Nos. RA15-RA16 Surcharged in Red or Carmine

**1970** **Typo.** ***Perf. 10½***
**Without Gum**
**RA20** PT2 30c on 70c 7.00 6.00
**RA21** PT2 30c on 1.30e 6.00 6.00
**RA22** PT2 50c on 70c *225.00* *175.00*
**RA23** PT2 50c on 1.30e 6.00 6.00
**RA24** PT2 1e on 70c (C) *225.00* *175.00*
**RA25** PT2 1e on 1.30e 8.00 7.25
*Nos. RA20-RA25 (6)* *477.00* *375.25*

### POSTAL TAX DUE STAMPS

**Pombal Issue**
Common Design Types

**1925** **Unwmk.** ***Perf. 12½***
**RAJ1** CD28 4a lake & black .40 *1.00*
**RAJ2** CD29 4a lake & black .40 *1.00*
**RAJ3** CD30 4a lake & black .40 *1.00*
*Nos. RAJ1-RAJ3 (3)* 1.20 *3.00*

## TOBAGO

tə-ˈbā-ˌgō

LOCATION — An island in the West Indies lying off the Venezuelan coast north of Trinidad
GOVT. — British Colony
AREA — 116 sq. mi.
POP. — 25,358
CAPITAL — Scarborough (Port Louis)

In 1889 Tobago, then an independent colony, was united with Trinidad under the name of Colony of Trinidad and Tobago. It became a ward of that colony January 1, 1899.

12 Pence = 1 Shilling
20 Shillings = 1 Pound

Queen Victoria
A1 A2

**Wmk. Crown and C C (1)**
**1879** **Typo.** ***Perf. 14***
**1** A1 1p rose 97.50 77.50
**2** A1 3p blue 97.50 62.50
**3** A1 6p orange 47.50 *67.50*
**4** A1 1sh green 425.00 75.00
*a.* Half used as 6p on cover
**5** A1 5sh slate 775.00 700.00
**6** A1 £1 violet *4,500.*

Stamps of the above set with revenue cancellations sell for a small fraction of the price of postally used copies.

Stamps of Type A1, watermarked Crown and C A, are revenue stamps.

**1880**
**Manuscript Surcharge**
**7** A1 1p on half of 6p org *5,250.* *875.*

**1880**
**8** A2 ½p brown violet 47.50 *72.50*
**9** A2 1p red brown 125.00 62.50
*a.* Half used as ½p on cover *2,250.*
**10** A2 4p yellow green 290.00 30.00
*a.* Half used as 2p on cover *2,250.*
**11** A2 6p bister brown 400.00 125.00
**12** A2 1sh bister 77.50 *87.50*
*a.* Imperf.
*Nos. 8-12 (5)* 940.00 377.50

No. 11 Surcharged in Black

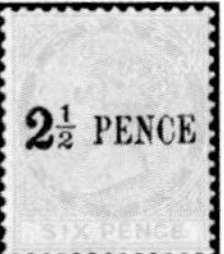


**1883**
**13** A2 2½p on 6p bister brn 62.50 62.50
*a.* Double surcharge 3,250. 1,500.

**1882-96** **Wmk. Crown and C A (2)**
**14** A2 ½p brown vio ('82) 2.25 *14.50*
**15** A2 ½p dull green ('86) 2.75 1.40
**16** A2 1p red brown ('82) 4.75 2.50
*a.* Diagonal half used as ½p on cover —
**17** A2 1p rose ('89) 3.50 1.40
**18** A2 2½p ultra ('83) 8.50 1.10
*a.* 2½p dull blue ('83) 40.00 2.25
*b.* 2½p bright blue 8.50 1.10
**19** A2 4p yel grn ('82) 210.00 100.00
**20** A2 4p gray ('85) 3.25 2.25
*a.* Imperf., pair 2,000.
**21** A2 6p bis brn ('84) 625.00 550.00
*a.* Imperf.
**22** A2 6p brn org ('86) 2.75 *5.75*
**23** A2 1sh olive bis ('94) 3.25 *19.00*
**24** A2 1sh brn org ('96) 11.00 *77.50*

Stamps of 1882-96 Surcharged in Black:

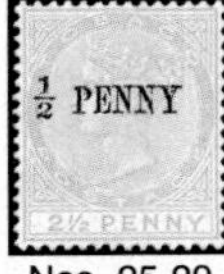

Nos. 25-29

No. 30

**1886-92**
**25** A2 ½p on 2½p ultra 6.50 *16.00*
*a.* Inverted surcharge
*b.* Pair, one without surcharge 11,000.
*c.* Space between "½" and "PENNY" 3mm 30.00 *67.50*
*d.* Double surcharge 2,400. 1,900.
**26** A2 ½p on 4p gray 22.50 *62.50*
*a.* Space between "½" and "PENNY" 3mm
*b.* Double surcharge 2,250.
**27** A2 ½p on 6p bis brn 3.50 *22.50*
*a.* Inverted surcharge 1,600.
*b.* Space between "½" and "PENNY" 3mm 30.00 *125.00*
*c.* Double surcharge 1,900.
**28** A2 ½p on 6p brn org 110.00 150.00
*a.* Space between "½" and "PENNY" 3mm 350.00 *375.00*
*b.* Double surcharge 1,400.
**29** A2 1p on 2½ ultra 70.00 19.00
*a.* Space between "1" and "PENNY" 4mm 175.00 *85.00*
*b.* Half used as ½p on cover *1,650.*
**30** A2 2½p on 4p gray 10.00 *9.00*
*a.* Double surcharge 2,250. 2,250.
*Nos. 25-30 (6)* 222.50 *279.00*

Revenue Stamp Type A1 Surcharged in Black

**1896**
**31** A1 ½p on 4p lilac & rose 72.50 40.00
*a.* Space between "½" and "d" 1½ to 2½mm 140.00 80.00

Tobago stamps were replaced by those of Trinidad or Trinidad and Tobago.

## TOGO

'tō-ˌgō

LOCATION — Western Africa, bordering on the Gulf of Guinea
GOVT. — Republic
AREA — 20,400 sq. mi.
POP. — 4,320,000 (1997 est.)
CAPITAL — Lome

The German Protectorate of Togo was occupied by Great Britain and France in World War I, and later mandated to them. The British area became part of Ghana. The French area was granted internal autonomy in 1956 and achieved independence in 1958.

100 Pfennig = 1 Mark
12 Pence = 1 Shilling
100 Centimes = 1 Franc

**Catalogue values for unused stamps in this country are for Never Hinged items, beginning with Scott 309 in the regular postage section, Scott B11 in the semi-postal section, Scott C14 in the airpost section, Scott J32 in the postage due section, and Scott O1 in the official section.**

**Watermark**

Wmk. 125 — Lozenges

**German Protectorate**

AREA — 34,934 sq. mi.
POP. — 1,000,368 (1913)

Stamps of Germany Overprinted in Black

**1897 Unwmk. *Perf. 13½x14½***

| | | | | |
|---|---|---|---|---|
| 1 | A9 | 3pf dark brown | 4.75 | *6.25* |
| *a.* | | 3pf yellow brown | 8.25 | *22.50* |
| *b.* | | 3pf reddish brown | 32.50 | *95.00* |
| 2 | A9 | 5pf green | 4.50 | *2.50* |
| 3 | A10 | 10pf carmine | 5.25 | *2.75* |
| 4 | A10 | 20pf ultra | 5.25 | *12.00* |
| 5 | A10 | 25pf orange | 30.00 | *52.50* |
| 6 | A10 | 50pf red brown | 30.00 | *52.50* |
| | | *Nos. 1-6 (6)* | 79.75 | *128.50* |

A3

Kaiser's Yacht, the "Hohenzollern" — A4

**1900 Typo. *Perf. 14***

| | | | | |
|---|---|---|---|---|
| 7 | A3 | 3pf brown | .90 | *1.10* |
| 8 | A3 | 5pf green | 10.50 | 1.75 |
| 9 | A3 | 10pf carmine | 19.00 | 1.50 |
| 10 | A3 | 20pf ultra | .90 | *1.25* |
| 11 | A3 | 25pf org & blk, *yel* | .90 | *9.00* |
| 12 | A3 | 30pf org & blk, *sal* | 1.10 | *9.00* |
| 13 | A3 | 40pf lake & blk | .90 | *9.00* |
| 14 | A3 | 50pf pur & blk, *sal* | 1.10 | *6.75* |
| 15 | A3 | 80pf lake & blk, *rose* | 2.25 | *15.00* |

**Engr.**
***Perf. 14½x14***

| | | | | |
|---|---|---|---|---|
| 16 | A4 | 1m carmine | 3.00 | *47.50* |
| 17 | A4 | 2m blue | 4.75 | *82.50* |
| 18 | A4 | 3m black vio | 6.25 | *125.00* |
| 19 | A4 | 5m slate & car | 95.00 | *450.00* |
| | | *Nos. 7-19 (13)* | 146.55 | *759.35* |

Counterfeit cancellations are found on Nos. 10-19 and 22.

**1909-19 Wmk. 125 Typo. *Perf. 14***

| | | | | |
|---|---|---|---|---|
| 20 | A3 | 3pf brown ('19) | .75 | |
| 21 | A3 | 5pf green | 1.10 | *2.00* |
| 22 | A3 | 10pf carmine ('14) | 1.50 | *95.00* |

**Engr.**
***Perf. 14½x14***

| | | | | |
|---|---|---|---|---|
| 23 | A4 | 5m slate & car ('19) | 21.00 | |
| | | *Nos. 20-23 (4)* | 24.35 | |

Nos. 20 and 23 were never placed in use.

**British Protectorate**

Nos. 7, 10-19, 21-22 Overprinted or Surcharged

First (Wide) Setting
3mm between Lines
2mm between "Anglo" & "French"

**Wmk. 125 (5pf, 10pf); Unwmkd.**

**1914, Oct. 1 *Perf. 14, 14½***

| | | | | |
|---|---|---|---|---|
| 33 | A3 | ½p on 3pf brown | 225.00 | 175.00 |
| *a.* | | Thin "y" in "penny" | 500.00 | 450.00 |
| 34 | A3 | 1p on 5pf green | 225.00 | 175.00 |
| *a.* | | Thin "y" in "penny" | 500.00 | 500.00 |
| 35 | A3 | 3pf brown | 130.00 | 100.00 |
| 36 | A3 | 5pf green | 125.00 | 100.00 |
| 37 | A3 | 10pf carmine | 150.00 | 110.00 |
| *a.* | | Inverted overprint | 8,500. | 4,000. |
| *b.* | | Unwmk. | | 6,250. |
| 38 | A3 | 20pf ultra | 30.00 | 37.50 |
| 39 | A3 | 25pf org & blk, *yel* | 30.00 | 30.00 |
| 40 | A3 | 30pf org & blk, *sal* | 32.50 | 47.50 |
| 41 | A3 | 40pf lake & blk | 275.00 | 275.00 |
| 42 | A3 | 50pf pur & blk, *sal* | 10,000. | 8,500. |
| 43 | A3 | 80pf lake & blk, *rose* | 275.00 | 300.00 |
| 44 | A4 | 1m carmine | 5,750. | 2,800. |
| 45 | A4 | 2m blue | 9,000. | 10,000. |
| *a.* | | Inverted overprint | — | |
| *b.* | | "Occupation" double | — | — |

On Nos. 33-34, the surcharge line ("Half penny" or "One penny") was printed separately and its position varies in relation to the 3-line overprint. On Nos. 46-47, the surcharge and overprint lines were printed simultaneously.

Second (Narrow) Setting
2mm between Lines
2mm between "Anglo" & "French"

**1914, Oct.**

| | | | | |
|---|---|---|---|---|
| 46 | A3 | ½p on 3pf brown | *40.00* | *30.00* |
| *a.* | | Thin "y" in "penny" | *70.00* | *70.00* |
| *b.* | | "TOG" | *475.00* | *350.00* |
| 47 | A3 | 1p on 5pf green | *5.00* | *5.00* |
| *a.* | | Thin "y" in "penny" | *15.00* | *17.50* |
| *b.* | | "TOG" | *150.00* | 125.00 |
| 48 | A3 | 3pf brown | *5,250.* | *1,000.* |
| *a.* | | "Occupation" omitted | | |
| 49 | A3 | 5pf green | *1,400.* | *800.00* |
| 50 | A3 | 10pf carmine | | *3,100.* |
| 51 | A3 | 20pf ultra | *20.00* | *14.00* |
| *a.* | | "TOG" | *4,750.* | *4,750.* |
| *b.* | | Vert. pair, #51 & #38 | *7,250.* | |
| 52 | A3 | 25pf org & blk, *yel* | *27.50* | *35.00* |
| *a.* | | "TOG" | *13,750.* | |
| 53 | A3 | 30pf org & blk, *sal* | 22.50 | *32.50* |
| 54 | A3 | 40pf lake & blk | *5,250.* | *1,750.* |
| 55 | A3 | 50pf pur & blk, *sal* | | *6,750.* |
| 56 | A3 | 80pf lake & blk, *rose* | *2,100.* | *2,100.* |
| 57 | A4 | 1m carmine | *8,500.* | *4,500.* |
| 58 | A4 | 2m blue | | *10,000.* |
| 59 | A4 | 3m black violet | | 45,000. |
| 60 | A4 | 5m slate & car | | 45,000. |

Third Setting
1¼mm btwn. "Anglo" & "French"
2mm between Lines
"Anglo-French" 15mm Wide

**1915, Jan. 7**

| | | | | |
|---|---|---|---|---|
| 61 | A3 | 3pf brown | *8,500.* | *3,250.* |
| 62 | A3 | 5pf green | *225.* | *150.* |
| 63 | A3 | 10pf carmine | *225.* | *150.* |
| 64 | A3 | 20pf ultra | *1,600.* | *600.* |
| 64A | A3 | 40pf lake & blk | | *8,500.* |
| 65 | A3 | 50pf pur & blk, *sal* | *14,000.* | *11,000.* |

Stamps of Gold Coast Overprinted Locally

**1915, May Wmk. 3 *Perf. 14***

| | | | | |
|---|---|---|---|---|
| 66 | A7 | ½p green | .35 | *1.90* |
| *a.* | | Double overprint | *525.00* | *550.00* |
| 67 | A8 | 1p scarlet | .35 | .55 |
| *a.* | | Double ovpt. | *375.00* | *500.00* |
| *b.* | | Inverted ovpt. | *200.00* | *275.00* |
| *c.* | | As "b," "Togo" omitted | | |
| 68 | A7 | 2p gray | .35 | 1.40 |
| 69 | A7 | 2½p ultra | 2.25 | *4.00* |

**Chalky Paper**

| | | | | |
|---|---|---|---|---|
| 70 | A7 | 3p violet, *yel* | 2.25 | *3.00* |
| 71 | A7 | 6p dl vio & red vio | 1.60 | *2.00* |
| 72 | A7 | 1sh black, *grn* | 2.50 | *6.00* |
| *a.* | | Double overprint | *1,300.* | |
| 73 | A7 | 2sh vio & bl, *bl* | 11.00 | *16.00* |
| 74 | A7 | 2sh6p blk & red, *bl* | 5.25 | *25.00* |
| 75 | A7 | 10sh grn & red, *grn* | 42.50 | *70.00* |
| 76 | A7 | 20sh vio & blk, *red* | 150.00 | *175.00* |

**Surfaced-Colored Paper**

| | | | | |
|---|---|---|---|---|
| 77 | A7 | 3p violet, *yel* | 4.50 | *20.00* |
| 78 | A7 | 5sh grn & red, *yel* | 9.25 | *17.50* |
| | | *Nos. 66-78 (13)* | 232.15 | *342.35* |

Nos. 66-78 exist with small "F" in "French" and thin "G" in "Togo." Several values are known without the hyphen between "Anglo-French" and all but No. 77 without the first "O" in "Occupation."

Stamps of Gold Coast Overprinted in London

**1916, Apr.**

**Ordinary Paper**

| | | | | |
|---|---|---|---|---|
| 80 | A7 | ½p green | .35 | *2.90* |
| 81 | A8 | 1p scarlet | .35 | *1.00* |
| *a.* | | Inverted overprint | | |
| 82 | A7 | 2p gray | .60 | *.90* |
| 83 | A7 | 2½p ultra | .65 | *1.75* |

**Chalky Paper**

| | | | | |
|---|---|---|---|---|
| 84 | A7 | 3p violet, *yel* | 3.00 | .80 |
| 85 | A7 | 6p dl vio & red vio | 2.25 | 1.10 |
| 86 | A7 | 1sh black, *grn* | 4.00 | *7.50* |
| *a.* | | 1sh black, *emerald* | 350.00 | *750.00* |
| *b.* | | 1sh black, *bl grn, ol back* | 7.50 | *17.50* |
| 87 | A7 | 2sh vio & ultra, *bl* | 5.25 | 9.75 |
| 88 | A7 | 2sh6p blk & red, *bl* | 5.25 | *8.00* |
| 89 | A7 | 5sh grn & red, *yel* | 21.00 | *30.00* |
| 90 | A7 | 10sh grn & red, *grn, ol back* | 20.00 | *80.00* |
| *a.* | | 10sh green & red, *grn* | 27.50 | *75.00* |
| 91 | A7 | 20sh vio & blk, *red* | 150.00 | *180.00* |
| | | *Nos. 80-91 (12)* | 212.70 | *323.70* |

The overprint on Nos. 80-91 is in heavier letters than on Nos. 66-78 and the 2nd and 3rd lines are each ½mm longer. The letter "O" on Nos. 80-91 is narrower and more oval.

**Issued under French Occupation**

Stamps of German Togo Surcharged:

c

d

e

f

g

h

i

**Wmk. Lozenges (5pf and 10pf) (125), Unwmk. (other values)**

**1914 *Perf. 14, 14½***

| | | | | |
|---|---|---|---|---|
| 151 | A3(c+d) | 5c on 3pf brn | 57.50 | 57.50 |
| 152 | A3(c+e) | 5c on 3pf brn | 57.50 | 57.50 |
| 153 | A3(c+f) | 5c on 3pf brn | 60.00 | 60.00 |
| 154 | A3(c+g) | 10c on 5pf grn | 19.00 | 19.00 |
| *a.* | | Double surcharge | 1,050. | 1,050. |
| 155 | A3(c+h) | 10c on 5pf grn | 19.00 | 19.00 |
| 156 | A3(c+i) | 10c on 5pf grn | 26.00 | 26.00 |
| 158 | A3(c) | 20pf ultra | 45.00 | 45.00 |
| *a.* | | 3½mm between "TOGO" and "Occupation" | 750.00 | 700.00 |
| 159 | A3(c) | 25pf org & blk, *yel* | 52.50 | 52.50 |
| 160 | A3(c) | 30pf org & blk, *sal* | 95.00 | 95.00 |
| 161 | A3(c) | 40pf lake & blk | 575.00 | 525.00 |
| 162 | A3(c) | 80pf lake & blk, *rose* | 575.00 | 525.00 |
| | | *Nos. 151-162 (11)* | 1,581. | 1,481. |

Surcharged or Overprinted in Sans-Serif Type:

TOGO
Occupation
franco anglaise
**05**

**1915**

| | | | | |
|---|---|---|---|---|
| 164 | A3 | 5c on 3pf brown | *14,000.* | *4,400.* |
| 165 | A3 | 5pf green | 900. | 425. |
| 166 | A3 | 10pf carmine | 1,050. | 425. |
| *a.* | | Inverted overprint | *27,000.* | *15,000.* |
| 167 | A3 | 20pf ultra | *1,300.* | 900. |
| 168 | A3 | 25pf org & blk, *yel* | *14,000.* | *7,000.* |
| 169 | A3 | 30pf org & blk, *sal* | *14,000.* | *7,000.* |
| 170 | A3 | 40pf lake & blk | *14,000.* | *7,000.* |
| 171 | A3 | 50pf pur & blk, *sal* | *20,000.* | *12,000.* |
| 172 | A4 | 1m carmine | | *75,000.* |
| 173 | A4 | 2m blue | | *21,000.* |
| 174 | A4 | 3m black vio | | *29,000.* |
| 175 | A4 | 5m slate & car | 27,000. | *29,000.* |

Stamps of Dahomey, 1913-17, Overprinted

**1916-17 Unwmk. *Perf. 13½x14***

**176** A5 1c violet & blk .25 .25
**177** A5 2c choc & rose .25 .25
**178** A5 4c black & brn .35 .35
*a.* Double overprint 425.00 425.00
**179** A5 5c yel grn & bl grn .60 .60
**180** A5 10c org red & rose .55 .55
**181** A5 15c brn org & dk vio 1.50 1.50
**182** A5 20c gray & choc .60 .60
**183** A5 25c ultra & dp bl .90 .90
**184** A5 30c choc & vio .90 .90
**185** A5 35c brown & blk 1.50 1.50
**186** A5 40c blk & red org 1.25 1.25
**187** A5 45c gray & ultra 1.40 1.40
**188** A5 50c choc & brn 1.40 1.40
**189** A5 75c blue & vio 6.00 6.00
**190** A5 1fr bl grn & blk 7.50 7.50
**191** A5 2fr buff & choc 11.00 11.00
**192** A5 5fr vio & do bl 13.00 13.00
*Nos. 176-192 (17)* 48.95 48.95

All values of the 1916-17 issue exist on chalky paper and all but the 15c, 25c and 35c on ordinary paper.

**French Mandate**

AREA — 21,893 sq. mi.
POP. — 780,497 (1938)

Type of Dahomey, 1913-39, Overprinted

**1921**

**193** A5 1c gray & yel grn .20 .20
*a.* Overprint omitted 100.00
**194** A5 2c blue & org .20 .20
**195** A5 4c ol grn & org .25 .25
**196** A5 5c dull red & blk .25 .25
*a.* Overprint omitted 325.00
**197** A5 10c bl grn & yel grn .55 .55
**198** A5 15c brown & car .60 .60
**199** A5 20c bl grn & org 1.00 1.00
**200** A5 25c slate & org 1.00 1.00
**201** A5 30c dp rose & ver 1.10 1.10
**202** A5 35c red brn & yel grn 1.00 1.00
**203** A5 40c bl grn & ol 1.40 1.40
**204** A5 45c red brn & ol 1.25 1.25
**205** A5 50c deep blue 1.25 1.25
**206** A5 75c dl red & ultra 1.40 1.40
**207** A5 1fr gray & ultra 1.60 1.60
**208** A5 2fr ol grn & rose 5.00 5.00
**209** A5 5fr orange & blk 9.00 9.00
*Nos. 193-209 (17)* 27.05 27.05

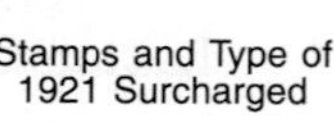

Stamps and Type of 1921 Surcharged

**1922-25**

**210** A5 25c on 15c ol brn & rose red .30 .30
**211** A5 25c on 2fr ol grn & rose .45 .45
**212** A5 25c on 5fr org & blk .45 .45
**213** A5 60c on 75c vio, *pnksh* .75 .75
*a.* "60" omitted 175.00 175.00
**214** A5 65c on 45c red brn & ol 1.25 1.25
*a.* "TOGO" omitted 150.00
**215** A5 85c on 75c dull red & ultra 2.00 2.00
*Nos. 210-215 (6)* 5.20 5.20

Issue years: #213, 1922; #211-212, 1924; others, 1925.

Coconut Grove A6

Cacao Trees — A7

Oil Palms A8

**1924-38 Typo.**

**216** A6 1c yellow & blk .20 .20
**217** A6 2c dp rose & blk .20 .20
**218** A6 4c dk blue & blk .20 .20
**219** A6 5c dp org & blk .20 .20
**220** A6 10c red vio & blk .20 .20
**221** A6 15c green & blk .20 .20
**222** A7 20c gray & blk .25 .25
**223** A7 25c grn & blk, *yel* .55 .55
**224** A7 30c gray grn & blk .25 .25
**225** A7 30c dl grn & lt grn ('27) .40 .40
**226** A7 35c lt brown & blk .60 .60
**227** A7 35c dp bl grn & grn ('38) .55 .45
**228** A7 40c red org & blk .25 .25
**229** A7 45c carmine & blk .25 .25
**230** A7 50c ocher & blk, *bluish* .40 .40
**231** A7 55c vio bl & car rose ('38) .75 .60
**232** A7 60c vio brn & blk, *pnksh* .25 .25
**233** A7 60c dp red ('26) .40 .40
**234** A7 65c gray lil & brn .55 .55
**235** A7 75c blue & black .55 .55
**236** A7 80c ind & dl vio ('38) 1.60 1.50
**237** A7 85c brn org & brn 1.00 1.00
**238** A7 90c brn red & cer ('27) .75 .75
**239** A8 1fr red brn & blk, *bluish* .70 .70
**240** A8 1fr blue ('26) .60 .60
**241** A8 1fr gray lil & grn ('28) 2.25 1.90
**242** A8 1fr dk red & red org ('38) .75 .55
**243** A8 1.10fr vio & dk brn ('28) 3.50 3.50
**244** A8 1.25fr mag & rose ('33) 1.25 1.25
**245** A8 1.50fr bl & lt bl ('27) .60 .60
**246** A8 1.75fr bis & pink ('33) 7.50 4.25
**247** A8 1.75fr vio bl & ultra ('38) 1.25 1.00
**248** A8 2fr bl blk & blk, *bluish* 1.00 1.00
**249** A8 3fr bl grn & red org ('27) 1.25 1.25
**250** A8 5fr red org & blk, *bluish* 1.75 1.75
**251** A8 10fr ol brn & rose ('26) 2.25 2.25
**252** A8 20fr brn red & blk, *yel* ('26) 2.50 2.50
*Nos. 216-252 (37)* 37.70 33.30

For surcharges see #253, 301-302, B8-B9.

No. 240 Surcharged with New Value and Bars in Red

**1926**

**253** A8 1.25fr on 1fr lt bl .60 .60

Common Design Types pictured following the introduction.

**Colonial Exposition Issue**
Common Design Types
**Engr., "TOGO" Typo. in Black**

**1931, Apr. 13 *Perf. 12½***

**254** CD70 40c deep green 5.00 5.00
**255** CD71 50c violet 5.00 5.00
**256** CD72 90c red orange 5.00 5.00
**257** CD73 1.50fr dull blue 5.00 5.00
*Nos. 254-257 (4)* 20.00 20.00

**Paris International Exposition Issue**
Common Design Types

**1937 *Perf. 13***

**258** CD74 20c deep violet 1.50 1.50
**259** CD75 30c dark green 1.50 1.50
**260** CD76 40c carmine rose 1.50 1.50
**261** CD77 50c dark brown 1.50 1.50
**262** CD78 90c red 1.50 1.50
**263** CD79 1.50fr ultra 1.50 1.50
*Nos. 258-263 (6)* 9.00 9.00

**Colonial Arts Exhibition Issue**
Souvenir Sheet
Common Design Type

**1937 *Imperf.***

**264** CD77 3fr Prus bl & blk 6.00 *7.50*

**Caillié Issue**
Common Design Type

**1939, Apr. 5 *Perf. 12½x12***

**265** CD81 90c org brn & org .75 .75
**266** CD81 2fr brt violet .75 .75
**267** CD81 2.25fr ultra & dk bl .75 .75
*Nos. 265-267 (3)* 2.25 2.25

**New York World's Fair Issue**
Common Design Type

**1939, May 10**

**268** CD82 1.25fr carmine lake .90 .90
**269** CD82 2.25fr ultra .90 .90

Togolese Women
A9 A12

Mono River Bank A10

Hunters A11

**1941 Engr. *Perf. 12½***

**270** A9 2c brown vio .20 .20
**271** A9 3c yellow grn .20 .20
**272** A9 4c brown blk .20 .20
**273** A9 5c lilac rose .20 .20
**274** A9 10c light blue .20 .20
**275** A9 15c chestnut .20 .20
**276** A10 20c plum .20 .20
**277** A10 25c violet blue .20 .20
**278** A10 30c brown blk .20 .20
**279** A10 40c dk carmine .25 .25
**280** A10 45c dk green .25 .25
**281** A10 50c chestnut .25 .25
**282** A10 60c red violet .55 .55
**283** A11 70c black .75 .75
**284** A11 90c lt violet 1.10 1.10
**285** A11 1fr yellow grn .40 .40
**286** A11 1.25fr cerise 1.00 1.00
**287** A11 1.40fr orange brn .60 .60
**288** A11 1.60fr orange .60 .60
**289** A11 2fr lt ultra .75 .75
**290** A12 2.25fr ultra 1.10 1.10
**291** A12 2.50fr lilac rose .75 .75
**292** A12 3fr brown vio .90 .90
**293** A12 5fr vermilion .90 .90
**294** A12 10fr rose violet 1.50 1.50
**295** A12 20fr brown blk 2.00 2.00
*Nos. 270-295 (26)* 15.45 15.45

For surcharges see Nos. 303-308, B7, B10.

Mono River Bank and Marshal Pétain A12a

**1941 Engr. *Perf. 12½x12***

**296** A12a 1fr green .55
**297** A12a 2.50fr blue .55

Nos. 296-297 were issued by the Vichy government in France, but were not placed on sale in Togo.

For surcharges, see Nos. B10D-B10E.

Types of 1941 Without "RF"

**1942-44 *Perf. 12½***

**298** A9 10c blue green .25
**299** A9 15c yel brn & black .60
**300** A10 20c lilac brn & black .75
**300A** A11 1fr yellow grn .85
**300B** A11 1.50fr lilac & green .60
**300C** A12 3fr brown violet .85
**300D** A12 5fr red brown .85
**300E** A12 10fr rose violet 1.40
**300F** A12 20fr black 1.50
*Nos. 298-300F (9)* 7.65

Nos. 298-300F were issued by the Vichy government in France, but were not placed on sale in Togo.

Nos. 231, 238, 284 Surcharged with New Values in Various Colors

a

b

**1943-44 *Perf. 14x13½, 12½* Unwmk.**

**301** A7(a) 1.50fr on 55c (Bk) .85 .85
**302** A7(a) 1.50fr on 90c (Bk) .85 .85
**303** A11(b) 3.50fr on 90c (Bk) .70 .70
**304** A11(b) 4fr on 90c (R) .85 .85
**305** A11(b) 5fr on 90c (Bl) 1.50 1.50
**306** A11(b) 5.50fr on 90c (Br) 1.50 1.50
**307** A11(b) 10fr on 90c (G) ('44) 1.50 1.50
**308** A11(b) 20fr on 90c (R) 2.00 2.00
*Nos. 301-308 (8)* 9.75 9.75

**Catalogue values for unused stamps in this section, from this point to the end of the section, are for Never Hinged items.**

Extracting Palm Oil — A13

Hunter — A14

Cotton Spinners — A15

Village of Atakpamé A16

Red-fronted Gazelles — A17

Houses of the Cabrais
A18

**1947, Oct. 6** **Engr.** ***Perf. 12½***

**309** A13 10c dark red .40 .20
**310** A13 30c brt ultra .40 .20
**311** A13 50c bluish green .40 .20
**312** A14 60c lilac rose .40 .20
**313** A14 1fr chocolate .70 .35
**314** A14 1.20fr yellow grn .90 .40
**315** A15 1.50fr brown org .90 .45
**316** A15 2fr olive .90 .45
**317** A15 2.50fr gray blk 2.10 .90
**318** A16 3fr slate 1.00 .45
**319** A16 3.60fr rose car 1.50 .75
**320** A16 4fr Prus green 1.10 .35
**321** A17 5fr black brn 2.50 .35
**322** A17 6fr ultra 2.50 1.00
**323** A17 10fr orange red 3.50 .35
**324** A18 15fr dp yel grn 3.25 .50
**325** A18 20fr grnsh black 3.25 .75
**326** A18 25fr lilac rose 3.50 .75
*Nos. 309-326 (18)* 29.20 8.60

**Military Medal Issue**
Common Design Type
**Engr. & Typo.**

**1952, Dec. 1** ***Perf. 13***

**327** CD101 15fr multicolored 4.50 4.00

Gathering Palm Nuts
A19

**1954, Nov. 29** **Engr.**

**328** A19 8fr vio & vio brn 1.00 .60
**329** A19 15fr indigo & dk brn 1.25 .60

Goliath Beetle — A20

**1955, May 2**

**330** A20 8fr black & green 2.25 1.75

Intl. Exhibition for Wildlife Protection, Paris, May 1955.

**FIDES Issue**
Common Design Type

Design: 15fr, Teacher and children planting tree.

**1956** **Unwmk.** ***Perf. 13x12½***

**331** CD103 15fr dk vio brn & org brn 4.50 2.25

**Republic**

Woman Holding Flag — A21

**1957, June 8** **Engr.** ***Perf. 13***

**332** A21 15fr dk bl grn, sepia & red .65 .20

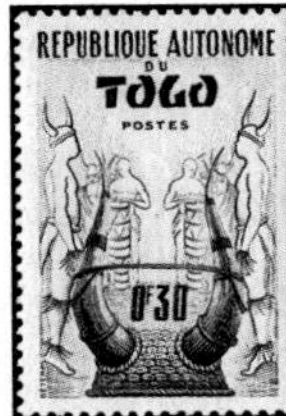


Konkomba Helmet — A22

Teak Forest
A23

Design: 4fr, 5fr, 6fr, 8fr, 10fr, Buffon's kob.

**1957, Oct.** **Unwmk.**

**333** A22 30c violet & claret .30 .20
**334** A22 50c indigo & blue .30 .20
**335** A22 1fr pur & lil rose .30 .20
**336** A22 2fr dk brn & olive .30 .20
**337** A22 3fr black & green .30 .20
**338** A22 4fr blue & gray .60 .20
**339** A22 5fr bluish gray & mag .60 .20
**340** A22 6fr crim rose & bl gray .65 .20
**341** A22 8fr bluish gray & vio .65 .25
**342** A22 10fr grn & red brn .65 .25
**343** A23 15fr multicolored .45 .20
**344** A23 20fr violet, mar & org .50 .20
**345** A23 25fr indigo & bis brn .65 .25
**346** A23 40fr dk brn, ol & dk grn 1.10 .35
*Nos. 333-346 (14)* 7.35 3.10

See Nos. 350-363.

Flags, Dove and UN Emblem — A24

**1958, Dec. 10** **Engr.** ***Perf. 13***

**347** A24 20fr dk grn & rose red .65 .20

Universal Declaration of Human Rights, 10th anniversary.

**Flower Issue**
Common Design Type

Designs: 5fr, Flower of Bombax tree (kapok). 20fr, Tectona grandis (teakwood) flower, horiz.

***Perf. 12x12½, 12½x12***

**1959, Jan. 15** **Photo.** **Unwmk.**

**348** CD104 5fr dp bl, rose & grn .50 .20
**349** CD104 20fr black, yel & grn .50 .20

Types of 1957 Inscribed: "Republique du Togo"

**1959, Jan. 15** **Engr.** ***Perf. 13***
**Designs as Before**

**350** A22 30c ultra & gray .35 .20
**351** A22 50c org & brt grn .35 .20
**352** A22 1fr red lil & lt ol grn .35 .20
**353** A22 2fr olive & bl grn .35 .20
**354** A22 3fr vio & rose car .35 .20
**355** A22 4fr lil rose & pale pur .35 .20
**356** A22 5fr green & brown .35 .20
**357** A22 6fr ultra & gray bl .35 .20
**358** A22 8fr sl grn & bis .35 .20
**359** A22 10fr vio & lt brn .35 .20
**360** A23 15fr dk brn, bis & cl .35 .20
**361** A23 20fr blk, bl grn & brn .35 .20
**362** A23 25fr sep, red brn, ol & vio .45 .20
**363** A23 40fr dk grn, org brn & bl .45 .20
*Nos. 350-363 (14)* 5.10 2.80

"Five Continents," Ceiling Painting, Palais des Nations, Geneva — A25

**1959, Oct. 24** **Engr.** ***Perf. 12½***
**Centers in Dark Ultramarine**

**364** A25 15fr brown .35 .20
**365** A25 20fr purple .35 .20
**366** A25 25fr dark orange .35 .20
**367** A25 40fr dark green .55 .25
**368** A25 60fr carmine rose .60 .30
*Nos. 364-368 (5)* 2.20 1.15

Issued for United Nations Day, Oct. 24.

Skier
A26

Bicyclist
A27

Sports: 50c, Ice Hockey. 1fr, Tobogganing. 15fr, Discus thrower, vert. 20fr, Boxing, vert. 25fr, Runner.

**1960** **Unwmk.** ***Perf. 13***

**369** A26 30c sl grn, car & bl grn .45 .20
**370** A26 50c red & black .45 .20
**371** A26 1fr red, blk & emer .45 .20
**372** A27 10fr brown, ultra & sl .45 .20
**373** A27 15fr dk red brn & grn .45 .20
**374** A27 20fr dk grn, gldn brn & brn .55 .20
**375** A27 25fr orange, mag & brn .65 .20
*Nos. 369-375 (7)* 3.45 1.40

8th Winter Olympic Games, Squaw Valley, Calif. (Nos. 369-371); 17th Olympic Games, Rome (Nos. 372-375).

Prime Minister Sylvanus Olympio and Togo Flag — A28

**1960, Apr. 27** **Litho.**
**Center in Green, Red, Yellow & Brown**

**376** A28 30c black & buff .20 .20
**377** A28 50c brown & buff .20 .20
**378** A28 1fr lilac & buff .20 .20
**379** A28 10fr blue & buff .20 .20
**380** A28 20fr red & buff .20 .20
**381** A28 25fr green & buff .20 .20
*Nos. 376-381 (6)* 1.20 1.20

Proclamation of Togo's full independence, Apr. 27, 1960.
See Nos. C31-C33.

Flags of "Big Four," and British Flag — A29

**1960, May 21** ***Perf. 14x14½***

**382** A29 50c shown .35 .20
**383** A29 1fr USSR .35 .20
**384** A29 20fr France .35 .20
**385** A29 25fr US .35 .20
*Nos. 382-385 (4)* 1.40 .80

Summit Conference of France, Great Britain, United States and USSR, Paris, May 16.

Flag of Togo and UN Emblem A30

**1961, Jan. 6** ***Perf. 14½x15***
**Flag in red, olive green & yellow**

**386** A30 30c red .30 .20
**387** A30 50c brown .30 .20
**388** A30 1fr ultramarine .30 .20
**389** A30 10fr maroon .30 .20
**390** A30 25fr black .30 .20
**391** A30 30fr violet .30 .20
*Nos. 386-391 (6)* 1.80 1.20

Togo's admission to United Nations.

Crowned Cranes over Map — A31

Augustino de Souza — A32

**1961, Apr. 1** ***Perf. 14½x15***

**392** A31 1fr multicolored .40 .20
**393** A31 10fr multicolored .40 .20
**394** A31 25fr multicolored .50 .20
**395** A31 30fr multicolored .70 .20
*Nos. 392-395 (4)* 2.00 .80

**1961, Apr. 27** **Litho.** ***Perf. 15***

**396** A32 50c yellow, red & blk .35 .20
**397** A32 1fr emerald, brn & blk .35 .20
**398** A32 10fr grnsh bl, vio & blk .35 .20
**399** A32 25fr salmon, grn & blk .35 .20
**400** A32 30fr rose lil, bl & blk .35 .20
*Nos. 396-400 (5)* 1.75 1.00

1st anniv. of independence; "Papa" Augustino de Souza, leader of the independence movement.

Daniel C. Beard A33

Designs: 1fr, Lord Baden-Powell. 10fr, Togolese Scout and emblems. 25fr, Togolese Scout and flag, vert. 30fr, Symbolic tents and fire, vert. 100fr, Three hands of different races giving Scout sign.

**1961, Oct. 7** **Photo.** ***Perf. 13***

**401** A33 50c brt rose & grn .45 .20
**402** A33 1fr dp violet & car .45 .20
**403** A33 10fr dk gray & brn .45 .20
**404** A33 25fr multicolored .45 .20
**405** A33 30fr grn, red & org brn .55 .20
**406** A33 100fr rose car & bl 1.25 .25
*Nos. 401-406 (6)* 3.60 1.25

Togolese Boy Scouts; 20th anniv. of the deaths of Daniel C. Beard and Lord Baden-Powell.

Four imperf. souvenir sheets each contain the six stamps, Nos. 401-406. Two sheets have a solid background of bright yellow, two a background of pale grayish brown. One yellow and one brown sheet have simulated perforations around the stamps. Size: 120x145mm. "REPUBLIQUE DU TOGO" is inscribed in white on bottom sheet margin. Value, each $4.

Plane, Ship and Part of Map of Africa — A34

Part of Map of Africa and: 25fr, Electric train and power mast. 30fr, Tractor and oil derricks. 85fr, Microscope and atomic symbol.

**1961, Oct. 24** **Litho.**
**Black Inscriptions; Map in Ocher**

**407** A34 20fr vio bl, org & yel .45 .20
**408** A34 25fr gray, org & yel .45 .20
**409** A34 30fr dk red, yel & org .55 .20
**410** A34 85fr blue, yel & org 1.00 .20
*a.* Souvenir sheet of 4 3.50 2.50
*Nos. 407-410 (4)* 2.45 .80

UN Economic Commission for Africa. No. 410a contains one each of Nos. 407-410, imperf., printed without separating margin between the individual stamps to show a complete map of Africa.

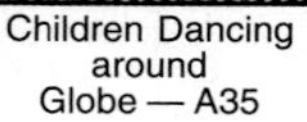

Children Dancing around Globe — A35

Cmdr. Alan B. Shepard — A36

UNICEF Emblem, children and globe.

**1961, Dec. 9 Unwmk. *Perf. 13½***
**Black Inscription; Multicolored Design**

**411** A35 1fr ultra .40 .20
**412** A35 10fr red brown .40 .20
**413** A35 20fr lilac .40 .20
**414** A35 25fr gray .40 .20
**415** A35 30fr bright blue .45 .20
**416** A35 85fr deep lilac .85 .25
*Nos. 411-416 (6)* 2.90 1.25

UNICEF, 15th anniv.
Nos. 411-416 assembled in two rows show the globe and children of various races dancing around it.

**1962, Feb. 24 *Perf. 15x14***

Design: 1fr, 30fr, Yuri A. Gagarin.

**417** A36 50c green .40 .20
**418** A36 1fr carmine rose .40 .20
**419** A36 25fr blue .40 .20
**420** A36 30fr purple .40 .20
*Nos. 417-420 (4)* 1.60 .80

Astronauts of 1961.
Issued in sheets of 50 and in miniature sheets of 12 stamps plus four central labels showing photographs of Alan B. Shepard (US), Virgil I. Grissom (US), Yuri A. Gagarin (USSR), Gherman S. Titov (USSR).

No. 417 Surcharged: "100F COL. JOHN H. GLENN USA VOL ORBITAL 20 FEVRIER 1962" and Bars in Black

**1962, Apr. 7**

**421** A36 100fr on 50c green 2.40 .50
*a.* Carmine surcharge 2.40 .50

Orbital flight of Lt. Col. John H. Glenn, Jr., US, Feb. 20, 1962.

Independence Monument, Lomé — A37

Woman Carrying Fruit Basket — A38

**1962, Apr. 27 Litho. *Perf. 13½x14***

**422** A37 50c multicolored .30 .20
**423** A38 1fr green & pink .30 .20
**424** A37 5fr multicolored .30 .20
**425** A38 20fr purple & yel .30 .20
**426** A37 25fr multicolored .30 .20
**427** A38 30fr red & yellow .30 .20
*a.* Souv. sheet of 3, #424-425, 427, imperf. 2.00 1.50
*Nos. 422-427 (6)* 1.80 1.20

2nd anniversary of Togo's independence.

Malaria Eradication Emblem A39

**1962, June 2 *Perf. 13½x13***
**Multicolored Design**

**428** A39 10fr yellow green .55 .20
**429** A39 25fr pale lilac .55 .20
**430** A39 30fr ocher .55 .20
**431** A39 85fr light blue 1.10 .20
*Nos. 428-431 (4)* 2.75 .80

WHO drive to eradicate malaria.

Capitol, Pres. John F. Kennedy and Pres. Sylvanus Olympio — A40

**1962, July 4 Unwmk. *Perf. 13***
**Inscription and Portraits in Slate Green**

**432** A40 50c yellow .20 .20
**433** A40 1fr blue .20 .20
**434** A40 2fr vermilion .20 .20
**435** A40 5fr lilac .20 .20
**436** A40 25fr pale violet .45 .20
**437** A40 100fr brt green 1.75 .80
*a.* Souvenir sheet, imperf. 6.00 5.75
*Nos. 432-437 (6)* 3.00 1.80

Visit of Pres. Sylvanus Olympio of Togo to the US, Mar. 1962.

Mail Coach and Stamps of 1897 — A41

50c, Mail ship, stamps of 1900. 1fr, Mail train, stamps of 1915. 10fr, Motorcycle truck, stamp of 1924. 25fr, Mail truck, stamp of 1941. 30fr, DC-3, stamp of 1947.

**1963, Jan. 12 Photo. *Perf. 13***

**438** A41 30c multicolored .50 .20
**439** A41 50c multicolored .50 .20
**440** A41 1fr multicolored .50 .20
**441** A41 10fr vio, dp org & blk .50 .20
**442** A41 25fr dk red brn, blk & yel grn .50 .20
**443** A41 30fr ol brn & lil rose .50 .20
*Nos. 438-443,C34 (7)* 4.40 1.50

65th anniv. of Togolese mail service.
For souvenir sheet see No. C34a.

Hands Reaching for FAO Emblem A42

**1963, Mar. 21 *Perf. 14***

**444** A42 50c bl, org & dk brn .60 .20
**445** A42 1fr ol grn, org & dk brn .60 .20
**446** A42 25fr brn, dk brn & org .60 .20
**447** A42 30fr vio, dk brn & org .80 .20
*Nos. 444-447 (4)* 2.60 .80

FAO "Freedom from Hunger" campaign.

Togolese Flag and Lomé Harbor — A43

**1963, Apr. 27 Litho. *Perf. 13x12½***
**Flag in Red, Green and Yellow**

**448** A43 50c red brn & blk .30 .20
**449** A43 1fr dk car rose & blk .30 .20
**450** A43 25fr dull bl & blk .30 .20
**451** A43 50fr bister & blk .40 .20
*Nos. 448-451 (4)* 1.30 .80

3rd anniversary of independence.

Centenary Emblem — A44

**1963, June 1 Photo. *Perf. 14***
**Flag in Red, Olive Green, Yellow**

**452** A44 25fr blue, blk & red 1.10 .20
**453** A44 30fr dull grn, blk & red 1.50 .20

International Red Cross centenary.

Lincoln, Broken Fetters, Maps of Africa and US. — A45

**1963, Oct. Unwmk. *Perf. 13x14***

**454** A45 50c multicolored .35 .20
**455** A45 1fr multicolored .35 .20
**456** A45 25fr multicolored .35 .20
*Nos. 454-456,C35 (4)* 2.30 .90

Centenary of the emancipation of the American slaves. See souvenir sheet No. C35a.
For overprints see Nos. 473-475, C41.

UN Emblem and "15" — A46

Hibiscus — A47

**1963, Dec. 10 Photo. *Perf. 14x13***

**457** A46 50c ultra, dk bl & rose red .30 .20
**458** A46 1fr yel grn, dk bl & rose red .30 .20
**459** A46 25fr lil, dk bl & rose red .30 .20
**460** A46 85fr gold, dk bl & rose red 1.10 .25
*Nos. 457-460 (4)* 2.00 .85

15th anniv. of the Universal Declaration of Human Rights.

**1964 *Perf. 14***

Designs: 50c, Orchid. 2fr, Butterfly. 5fr, Hinged tortoise. 8fr, Ball python. 10fr, Bunea alcinoe (moth). 20fr, Octopus. 25fr, John Dory (fish). 30fr, French angelfish. 40fr, Hippopotamus. 60fr, Bohor reedbuck. 85fr, Anubius baboon.

**Size: 22½x31mm**

**461** A47 50c multicolored 1.25 .20
**462** A47 1fr yellow, car & grn 1.25 .20
**463** A47 2fr lilac, yel & blk 1.25 .20
**464** A47 5fr gray & multi 1.25 .20
**465** A47 8fr cit, red brn & blk 1.25 .20
**466** A47 10fr multicolored 1.25 .20
**467** A47 20fr dl bl, yel & brn 1.25 .20
**468** A47 25fr dl bl, grn & yel 1.25 .20
**469** A47 30fr multicolored 1.55 .20
**470** A47 40fr grn, red brn & blk 1.90 .20
**471** A47 60fr grnsh bl & red brn 2.75 .20
**472** A47 85fr lt grn, brn & org 4.00 .25
*Nos. 461-472 (12)* 20.20 2.45

See Nos. 511-515, C36-C40, J56-J63.

Nos. 454-456 Overprinted Diagonally: "En Mémoire de / JOHN F. KENNEDY / 1917-1963"

**1964, Mar. 7 *Perf. 13x14***

**473** A45 50c multicolored .35 .20
**474** A45 1fr multicolored .35 .20
**475** A45 25fr multicolored .35 .20
*Nos. 473-475 (3)* 1.05 .60

Issued in memory of John F. Kennedy.
See No. C41 and note on souvenir sheets following it.

Isis of Kalabsha A48

Designs: 25fr, Head of Ramses II. 30fr, Colonnade of Birth House at Philae.

**1964, Mar. 8 Litho. *Perf. 14***

**476** A48 20fr blk, pale grn & red .45 .20
**477** A48 25fr black & lil rose .45 .20
**478** A48 30fr black & citron .55 .20
*a.* Souvenir sheet of 3 2.40 2.00
*Nos. 476-478 (3)* 1.45 .60

UNESCO world campaign to save historic monuments in Nubia. No. 478a contains three imperf. stamps similar to Nos. 476-478 with simulated perforations.

Phosphate Mine, Kpeme A49

25fr, Phosphate plant, Kpeme. 60fr, Phosphate train. 85fr, Loading ship with phosphate.

**1964, Apr. 27 Unwmk. *Perf. 14***

**479** A49 5fr brown & bis brn .30 .20
**480** A49 25fr dk pur & brn car .30 .20
**481** A49 60fr dk green & olive .70 .20
**482** A49 85fr vio blk & Prus bl 1.00 .25
*Nos. 479-482 (4)* 2.30 .85

Fourth anniversary of independence.

African Breaking Slavery Chain, and Map — A50

**1964, May 25 Photo. *Perf. 14x13***

**483** A50 5fr dp orange & brn .40 .20
**484** A50 25fr olive grn & brn .40 .20
**485** A50 85fr rose car & brn 1.00 .20
*Nos. 483-485,C42 (4)* 3.30 .90

1st anniv. of the meeting of African heads of state at Addis Ababa.

Pres. Nicolas Grunitzky and Butterfly A51

**1964, Aug. 18 Litho. *Perf. 14***

**486** A51 1fr shown .55 .20
**487** A51 5fr Dove .55 .20
**488** A51 25fr Flower .55 .20
**489** A51 45fr as 1fr .90 .20
**490** A51 85fr Flower 1.75 .25
*Nos. 486-490 (5)* 4.30 1.05

National Union and Reconciliation.

Soccer A52

**1964, Oct. Photo. *Perf. 14***

**491** A52 1fr shown .50 .20
**492** A52 5fr Runner .50 .20
**493** A52 25fr Discus .50 .20
**494** A52 45fr as 1fr .65 .20
*Nos. 491-494,C43 (5)* 4.05 1.10

18th Olympic Games, Tokyo, Oct. 10-25.
For souvenir sheet see No. C43a.

**Cooperation Issue**
Common Design Type

**1964, Nov. 7 Engr. *Perf. 13***

**495** CD119 25fr mag, dk brn & ol bis .80 .20

Dirigible and Balloons — A53

25fr, 45fr, Otto Lilienthal's glider, 1894; Wright Brothers' plane, 1903; Boeing 707.

**1964, Dec. 5 Photo. *Perf. 14x13***

**496** A53 5fr org lil & grn .55 .20
**497** A53 10fr brt grn, dl bl & dk red .55 .20
**498** A53 25fr bl, vio bl & org .55 .20
**499** A53 45fr brt pink, vio bl & grn .70 .20
*a.* Souv. sheet of 4 5.50 4.50
*Nos. 496-499,C44 (5)* 3.15 1.10

Inauguration of the national airline, Air Togo. #499a contains 4 imperf. stamps similar to #497-499 and #C44 with simulated perfs.

Orbiting Geophysical Observatory and Mariner — A54

Space Satellites: 15fr, 25fr, Tiros, Telstar and Orbiting Solar Observatory. 20fr, 50fr, Nimbus, Syncom and Relay.

**1964, Dec. 12 Litho. *Perf. 14***

**500** A54 10fr dp rose, bl & yel .40 .20
**501** A54 15fr multi .40 .20
**502** A54 20fr yel, grn & vio .40 .20
**503** A54 25fr multi .40 .20
**504** A54 45fr brt grn, dk bl & yel .55 .20
**505** A54 50fr yel, grn & org .75 .20
*a.* Souv. sheet, #502-505, imperf. 3.00 2.50
*Nos. 500-505 (6)* 2.90 1.20

Intl. Quiet Sun Year.

Togo Olympic Stamps Printed in Israel — A55

Arms of Israel and Togo — A56

Pres. Nicolas Grunitzky of Togo and: 20fr, Church of the Mount of Beatitudes. 45fr, Ruins of Synagogue at Capernaum.

***Perf. 13½x14½, 14x13½***

**1964, Dec. 26 Photo.**

**506** A55 5fr rose violet .40 .20
**507** A56 20fr grnsh bl, grn & dl pur .40 .20
**508** A56 25fr red & bluish grn .40 .20
**509** A56 45fr dl yel, ol & dl pur .85 .25
**510** A56 85fr mag & bluish grn .65 .20
*a.* Souv. sheet of 4, imperf. 4.50 3.50
*Nos. 506-510 (5)* 2.70 1.05

Israel-Togo friendship.

Type of Regular Issue, 1964

**1965, June Unwmk. *Perf. 14***

Designs: 3fr, Morpho aega butterfly. 4fr, Scorpion. 6fr, Bird-of-paradise flower. 15fr, Flap-necked chameleon. 45fr, Ring-tailed palm civet.

**Size: 23x31mm**

**511** A47 3fr bister & multi 1.40 .20
**512** A47 4fr org & bluish blk 1.40 .20
**513** A47 6fr multi 1.40 .20
**514** A47 15fr brt pink, yel & brn 1.40 .20
**515** A47 45fr dl grn, org & brn 2.00 .20
*Nos. 511-515 (5)* 7.60 1.00

Syncom Satellite, Radar Station and ITU Emblem — A57

**1965, June *Perf. 13x14***

**516** A57 10fr Prus blue .45 .20
**517** A57 20fr olive bister .45 .20
**518** A57 25fr bright blue .45 .20
**519** A57 45fr crimson .65 .20
**520** A57 50fr green .75 .20
*Nos. 516-520 (5)* 2.75 1.00

ITU, centenary.

Abraham Lincoln — A58

Discus Thrower, Flags of Togo and Congo — A59

**1965, June 26 Photo. *Perf. 13x14***

**521** A58 1fr magenta .40 .20
**522** A58 5fr dull green .40 .20
**523** A58 20fr brown .40 .20
**524** A58 25fr slate .40 .20
*Nos. 521-524,C45 (5)* 3.50 1.10

Death cent. of Abraham Lincoln. For souvenir sheet see No. C45a.

**1965, July Unwmk. *Perf. 14x13***

Flags and: 10fr, Javelin thrower. 15fr, Handball player. 25fr, Runner.

**Flags in Red, Yellow and Green**

**525** A59 5fr deep magenta .40 .20
**526** A59 10fr dark blue .40 .20
**527** A59 15fr brown .40 .20
**528** A59 25fr dark purple .40 .20
*Nos. 525-528,C46 (5)* 3.20 1.10

1st African Games, Brazzaville, July 18-25.

Winston Churchill and "V" — A60

Stalin, Roosevelt and Churchill at Yalta — A61

***Perf. 13½x14, 14x13½***

**1965, Aug. 7 Photo.**

**529** A60 5fr dull green .40 .20
**530** A61 10fr brt vio & gray .40 .20
**531** A60 20fr brown .40 .20
**532** A61 45fr Prus bl & gray .70 .20
*Nos. 529-532,C47 (5)* 3.50 1.10

Sir Winston Spencer Churchill (1874-1965), British statesman and World War II leader.

Unisphere and New York Skyline — A62

10fr, Togolese dancers & drummer, Unisphere. 50fr, Michelangelo's Pieta & Unisphere.

**1965, Aug. 28 Photo. *Perf. 14***

**533** A62 5fr grnsh bl & vio blk .35 .20
**534** A62 10fr yel grn & dk brn .35 .20
**535** A62 25fr brn org & dk grn .35 .20
**536** A62 50fr vio & sl grn .50 .20
**537** A62 85fr rose red & brn 1.10 .30
*a.* Souvenir sheet of 2 2.75 1.75
*Nos. 533-537 (5)* 2.65 1.10

New York World's Fair, 1964-65. No. 537a contains two imperf. stamps similar to Nos. 536-537 with simulated perforations.

"Constructive Cooperation" and Olive Branch — A63

Designs: 25fr, 40fr, Hands of various races holding globe and olive branch. 85fr, Handclasp, olive branch and globe.

**1965, Sept. 25 Unwmk. *Perf. 14***

**538** A63 5fr violet, lt bl & org .35 .20
**539** A63 15fr brn, org & gray .35 .20
**540** A63 25fr blue & orange .35 .20
**541** A63 40fr dp car, gray & org .55 .20
**542** A63 85fr green & org 1.00 .30
*Nos. 538-542 (5)* 2.60 1.10

International Cooperation Year.

Major White and Gemini 4 — A64

25fr, Lt. Col. Alexei Leonov and Voskhod 2.

**1965, Nov. 25 Photo. *Perf. 13½x14***

**543** A64 25fr dp bl & brt car rose .60 .20
**544** A64 50fr green & brown 1.00 .20

"Walks in Space" of Lt. Col. Alexei Leonov (USSR), and Major Edward H. White (US). Printed in sheets of 12 with ornamental borders.

For overprints and surcharges see Nos. 563-566.

Adlai E. Stevenson and UN Headquarters — A65

5fr, "ONU" and doves. 10fr, UN emblem and headquarters. 20fr, "ONU" and orchids.

**1965, Dec. 15 *Perf. 14x13½***

**545** A65 5fr dk brn, yel & lt bl .40 .20
**546** A65 10fr org, dk bl & grn .40 .20
**547** A65 20fr dk grn, yel grn & org brn .40 .20
**548** A65 25fr brt yel, dk bl & bluish grn .40 .20
*Nos. 545-548,C48 (5)* 3.35 1.20

UN, 20th anniv.; Adlai E. Stevenson (1900-1965), US ambassador to the UN.

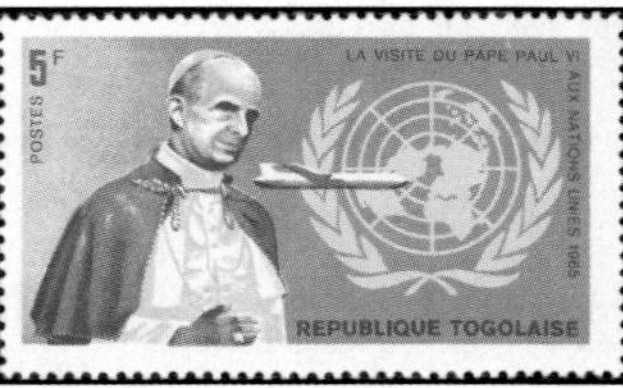


Pope Paul VI, Plane and UN Emblem — A66

15fr, 30fr, Pope addressing UN General Assembly & UN emblem, vert. 20fr, Pope, NYC skyline with UN Headquarters.

**1966, Mar. 5 Litho. *Perf. 12***

**549** A66 5fr blue & multi .40 .20
**550** A66 15fr lt violet & multi .40 .20
**551** A66 20fr bister & multi .40 .20
**552** A66 30fr lt ultra & multi .40 .20
*Nos. 549-552,C49-C50 (6)* 3.60 1.20

Visit of Pope Paul VI to the UN, New York City, Oct. 4, 1965.

Surgical Operation and Togolese Flag — A67

Togolese Flag and: 10fr, 30fr, Blood transfusion. 45fr, Profiles of African man and woman.

**1966, May 7 Litho. *Perf. 12***

**553** A67 5fr multicolored .40 .20
**554** A67 10fr multicolored .40 .20
**555** A67 15fr multicolored .40 .20
**556** A67 30fr multicolored .40 .20
**557** A67 45fr multicolored .60 .20
*Nos. 553-557,C51 (6)* 4.10 1.30

Togolese Red Cross, 7th anniversary.

Talisman Roses and WHO Headquarters, Geneva — A68

Various flowers & WHO Headquarters.

**1966, May Litho. *Perf. 12***

**558** A68 5fr lt yel grn & multi .45 .20
**559** A68 10fr pale pink & multi .45 .20
**560** A68 15fr dull yel & multi .45 .20
**561** A68 20fr pale gray & multi .45 .20
**562** A68 30fr tan & multi .45 .20
*Nos. 558-562,C52-C53 (7)* 4.65 1.40

Inauguration of WHO Headquarters, Geneva.

Nos. 543-544 Overprinted or Surcharged in Red

**1966, July 11 Photo. *Perf. 13½x14***

**563** A64 50fr Envolée Surveyor 1 .55 .20
**564** A64 50fr Envolée Gemini 9 .55 .20
*a.* Pair, #563-564 1.25 .50
**565** A64 100fr on 25fr Envolée Luna 9 1.25 .20
**566** A64 100fr on 25fr Envolée Venus 3 1.25 .20
*a.* Pair, #565-566 3.00 .75
*Nos. 563-566 (4)* 3.60 .80

US and USSR achievements in Space.

Wood Carver — A69

Togolese Dancer — A70

Arts and Crafts: 10fr, Basket maker. 15fr, Woman weaver. 30fr, Woman potter.

**1966, Sept. Photo. *Perf. 13x14***

**567** A69 5fr blue, yel & dk brn .40 .20
**568** A69 10fr emer, org & dk brn .40 .20
**569** A69 15fr ver, yel & dk brn .40 .20
**570** A69 30fr lilac, dk brn & yel .40 .20
*Nos. 567-570,C55-C56 (6)* 4.00 1.20

**1966, Nov. Photo. *Perf. 13x14***

Designs: 5fr, Togolese man. 20fr, Woman dancer from North Togo holding branches. 25fr, Male dancer. 30fr, Male dancer from North Togo with horned helmet. 45fr, Drummer.

**571** A70 5fr emerald & multi .40 .20
**572** A70 10fr dl yel & multi .40 .20
**573** A70 20fr lt ultra & multi .40 .20
**574** A70 25fr dp orange & multi .40 .20
**575** A70 30fr red violet & multi .40 .20
**576** A70 45fr blue & multi .50 .20
*Nos. 571-576,C57-C58 (8)* 4.30 1.60

Soccer Players and Jules Rimet Cup — A71

Various Soccer Scenes.

**1966, Dec. 14 Photo. *Perf. 14x13***

**577** A71 5fr blue, brn & red .50 .20
**578** A71 10fr brick red & multi .50 .20
**579** A71 20fr ol, brn & dk grn .50 .20
**580** A71 25fr vio, brn & org .50 .20
**581** A71 30fr ocher & multi .50 .20
**582** A71 45fr emerald, brn & mag .60 .20
*Nos. 577-582,C59-C60 (8)* 5.20 1.60

England's victory in the World Soccer Cup Championship, Wembley, July 30. For souvenir sheet see No. C60a.

African Mouthbreeder and Sailboat — A72

Designs: 10fr, Yellow jack and trawler. 15fr, Banded distichodus and seiner. 25fr, Jewelfish and galley. 30fr, like 5fr.

**1967, Jan. 14 Photo. *Perf. 14***

**Fish in Natural Colors**

**583** A72 5fr lt ultra & blk .45 .20
**584** A72 10fr brn org & brn .45 .20
**585** A72 15fr brt rose & dk bl .45 .20
**586** A72 25fr olive & blk .45 .20
**587** A72 30fr grnsh bl & blk .60 .20
*Nos. 583-587,C61-C62 (7)* 5.40 1.50

African Boy and Greyhound — A73

UNICEF Emblem and: 10fr, Boy and Irish setter. 20fr, Girl and doberman.

**1967, Feb. 11 Photo. *Perf. 14x13½***

**588** A73 5fr orange, plum & blk .45 .20
**589** A73 10fr yel grn, red brn & dk grn .45 .20
**590** A73 15fr brt rose, brn & blk .45 .20
**591** A73 20fr bl, vio bl & blk .45 .20
**592** A73 30fr ol, sl grn & blk .45 .20
*Nos. 588-592,C63-C64 (7)* 4.75 1.45

UNICEF, 20th anniv. (in 1966).

French A-1 Satellite — A74

5fr, Diamant rocket, vert. 15fr, Fr-1 satellite, vert. 20fr, 40fr, D-1 satellite. 25fr, A-1 satellite.

***Perf. 14x13½, 13½x14***

**1967, Mar. 18 Photo.**

**593** A74 5fr multi .40 .20
**594** A74 10fr multi .40 .20
**595** A74 15fr multi .40 .20
**596** A74 20fr multi .40 .20
**597** A74 25fr multi .40 .20
**598** A74 40fr multi .50 .20
*Nos. 593-598,C65-C66 (8)* 5.00 1.65

French achievements in space.

Johann Sebastian Bach and Organ — A75

UNESCO Emblem and: 10fr, Ludwig van Beethoven, violin and oboe. 15f, Duke Ellington, saxophone, trumpet, drums. 20fr, Claude A. Debussy, piano and harp. 30fr, like 15fr.

**1967, Apr. 15 Photo. *Perf. 14x13½***

**599** A75 5fr org & multi .50 .20
**600** A75 10fr multi .50 .20
**601** A75 15fr multi .50 .20
**602** A75 20fr lt bl & multi .50 .20
**603** A75 30fr lil & multi .50 .20
*Nos. 599-603,C67-C68 (7)* 5.40 1.40

20th anniv. (in 1966) of UNESCO.

EXPO Emblem, British Pavilion and Day Lilies — A76

10fr, French pavilion, roses. 30fr, African village, bird-of-paradise flower.

**1967, May 30 Photo. *Perf. 14***

**604** A76 5fr brt pink & multi .45 .20
**605** A76 10fr dull org & multi .45 .20
**606** A76 30fr blue & multi .45 .20
*Nos. 604-606,C69-C72 (7)* 6.00 1.55

EXPO '67 Intl. Exhibition, Montreal, Apr. 28-Oct. 27.

For overprints see Nos. 628-630, C86-C89.

Lions Emblem — A77

20fr, 45fr, Lions emblem and flowers.

**1967, July 29 Photo. *Perf. 13x14***

**607** A77 10fr yellow & multi .45 .20
**608** A77 20fr multicolored .45 .20
**609** A77 30fr green & multi .55 .20
**610** A77 45fr blue & multi .80 .20
*Nos. 607-610 (4)* 2.25 .80

50th anniversary of Lions International.

Montagu's Harriers — A78

5fr, Bohor reedbucks. 15fr, Zebras. 20fr, 30fr, Marsh harriers. 25fr, Leopard.

**1967, Aug. 19 Photo. *Perf. 14x13½***

**611** A78 5fr lilac & org brn .55 .20
**612** A78 10fr dk red, yel & dl bl .55 .20
**613** A78 15fr grn, blk & lil .55 .20
**614** A78 20fr dk brn, yel & dl bl .55 .20
**615** A78 25fr brn, ol & yel .55 .20
**616** A78 30fr vio, yel & dl bl .65 .20
*Nos. 611-616,C79-C80 (8)* 6.10 1.60

Stamp Auction and Togo Nos. 16 and C42 — A79

10fr, 45fr, Exhibition, #67 (British) & 520. 15fr, 30fr, Stamp store, #230. 20fr, Stamp packet vending machine, #545.

**1967, Oct. 14 Photo. *Perf. 14x13***

**Stamps on Stamps in Original Colors**

**617** A79 5fr purple .30 .20
**618** A79 10fr dk brown .30 .20
**619** A79 15fr deep blue .30 .20
**620** A79 20fr slate green .35 .20
**621** A79 30fr red brown .50 .20
**622** A79 45fr Prus blue .80 .20
*Nos. 617-622,C82-C83 (8)* 5.80 1.85

70th anniv. of the 1st Togolese stamps. For souvenir sheet see No. C82a.

See Nos. 853-855, C205.

**Monetary Union Issue**

Common Design Type

**1967, Nov. 4 Engr. *Perf. 13***

**623** CD125 30fr dk bl, vio bl & brt grn .60 .20

Broad Jump, Summer Olympics Emblem and View of Mexico City — A80

15fr, Ski jump, Winter Olympics emblem, ski lift. 30fr, Runners, Summer Olympics emblem, view of Mexico City. 45fr, Bobsledding, Winter Olympics emblem, ski lift.

**1967, Dec. 2 Photo. *Perf. 13x14***

**624** A80 5fr orange & multi .45 .20
**625** A80 15fr multicolored .45 .20
**626** A80 30fr multicolored .45 .20
**627** A80 45fr multicolored .55 .20
*Nos. 624-627,C84-C85 (6)* 4.35 1.60

1968 Olympic Games. For souvenir sheet see No. C85a.

Nos. 604-606 Overprinted: "JOURNÉE NATIONALE / DU TOGO / 29 SEPTEMBRE 1967"

**1967, Dec. *Perf. 14***

**628** A76 5fr multicolored .30 .20
**629** A76 10fr multicolored .30 .20
**630** A76 30fr blue & multi .40 .20
*Nos. 628-630,C86-C89 (7)* 5.40 1.60

National Day, Sept. 29, 1967.

The Gleaners, by François Millet and Phosphate Works, Benin — A81

Industrialization of Togo: 20fr, 45fr, 90fr, The Weaver at the Loom, by Vincent van Gogh, and textile plant, Dadia.

**1968, Jan. Photo. *Perf. 14***

**631** A81 10fr olive & multi .35 .20
**632** A81 20fr multicolored .35 .20
**633** A81 30fr brown & multi .45 .20
**634** A81 45fr multicolored .50 .20

**635** A81 60fr dk blue & multi .75 .20
**636** A81 90fr multicolored 1.25 .25
*Nos. 631-636 (6)* 3.65 1.25

Togolese Women Brewing Beer — A82

The Beer Drinkers, by Edouard Manet — A83

Design: 45fr, Modern beer bottling plant.

**1968, Mar. 26 Litho. *Perf. 14***
**637** A82 20fr emerald & multi .55 .20
**638** A83 30fr dk car & multi .70 .20
**639** A82 45fr orange & multi .85 .20
*Nos. 637-639 (3)* 2.10 .60

Publicity for local beer industry.

Symbolic Water Cycle, Flower and Cogwheels A84

**1968, Apr. 6**
**640** A84 30fr multicolored .65 .20

Hydrological Decade (UNESCO), 1965-74. See No. C90.

Viking Ship and Portuguese Brigantine — A85

10fr, Fulton's steamship and modern steamship. 20fr, Harbor activities and map of Africa.

**1968, Apr. 26 Photo. *Perf. 14x13½***
**641** A85 5fr brt green & multi .40 .20
**642** A85 10fr dp orange & multi .40 .20
**643** A85 20fr green & multi .40 .20
**644** A85 30fr yel grn & multi .40 .20
*Nos. 641-644,C91-C92 (6)* 4.00 1.20

Inauguration of Lomé Harbor.

Adenauer and 1968 Europa Emblem — A86

**1968, May 25 Photo. *Perf. 14***
**645** A86 90fr olive grn & brn org 1.90 .20

Konrad Adenauer (1876-1967), chancellor of West Germany (1949-63).

Adam and Eve Expelled from Paradise, by Michelangelo — A87

Paintings: 20fr, The Anatomy Lesson of Dr. Tulp, by Rembrandt. 30fr, The Anatomy Lesson, by Rembrandt (detail). 45fr, Jesus Healing the Sick, by Raphael.

**1968, June 22 Photo. *Perf. 14***
**646** A87 15fr crimson & multi .45 .20
**647** A87 20fr multicolored .45 .20
**648** A87 30fr green & multi .45 .20
**649** A87 45fr multicolored .55 .20
*Nos. 646-649,C93-C94 (6)* 4.60 1.20

WHO, 20th anniv.

Olympic Monument, San Salvador Island, Bahamas — A88

**1968, July 27 *Perf. 14x13½***
**650** A88 15fr Wrestling .40 .20
**651** A88 20fr Boxing .40 .20
**652** A88 30fr Judo .40 .20
**653** A88 45fr Running .50 .20
*Nos. 650-653,C95-C96 (6)* 4.05 1.20

19th Olympic Games, Mexico City, 10/12-27.

Chick Holding Lottery Ticket — A89

Scout Before Tent — A90

45fr, Lottery ticket, horseshoe & 4-leaf clover.

**1968, Oct. 5 Litho. *Perf. 14***
**654** A89 30fr dk green & multi .65 .20
**655** A89 45fr multicolored .75 .20

2nd anniversary of National Lottery.

**1968, Nov. 23**

10fr, 45fr, Scout leader training cub scouts, horiz. 20fr, First aid practice, horiz. 30fr, Scout game.

**656** A90 5fr dp org & multi .30 .20
**657** A90 10fr emerald & multi .30 .20
**658** A90 20fr multicolored .30 .20
**659** A90 30fr multicolored .40 .20
**660** A90 45fr blue & multi .50 .20
*Nos. 656-660,C97-C98 (7)* 4.20 1.60

Issued to honor the Togolese Boy Scouts.

Adoration of the Shepherds, by Giorgione — A91

Paintings: 20f, Adoration of the Magi, by Pieter Brueghel. 30fr, Adoration of the Magi, by Botticelli. 45fr, Adoration of the Magi, by Durer.

**1968, Dec. 28 Litho. *Perf. 14***
**661** A91 15fr green & multi .40 .20
**662** A91 20fr multicolored .40 .20
**663** A91 30fr multicolored .50 .20
**664** A91 45fr multicolored .60 .20
*Nos. 661-664,C100-C101 (6)* 5.05 1.30

Christmas.

Martin Luther King, Jr. — A92

Portraits and Human Rights Flame: 20fr, Professor René Cassin (author of Declaration of Human Rights). 45fr, Pope John XXIII.

**1969, Feb. 1 Photo. *Perf. 13½x14***
**665** A92 15fr brn org & sl grn .45 .20
**666** A92 20fr grnsh bl & vio .45 .20
**667** A92 30fr ver & slate bl .45 .20
**668** A92 45fr olive & car rose .60 .20
*Nos. 665-668,C102-C103 (6)* 4.20 1.30

International Human Rights Year.
For overprints see Nos. 683-686, C110-C111.

Omnisport Stadium and Soccer — A93

Stadium and: 15fr, Handball. 20fr, Volleyball. 30fr, Basketball. 45fr, Tennis.

**1969, Apr. 26 Photo. *Perf. 14x13½***
**669** A93 10fr emer, dp car & dk brn .45 .20
**670** A93 15fr org, ultra & dk brn .45 .20
**671** A93 20fr yel, ol & dk brn .45 .20
**672** A93 30fr dl grn, bl & dk brn .45 .20
**673** A93 45fr org, lil & dk brn .55 .20
*Nos. 669-673,C105-C106 (7)* 4.70 1.45

Opening of Omnisport Stadium, Lomé.

Astronaut and Eagle on Moon, Earth and Stars in Sky — A94

Designs: 1f, 30f, Lunar Module Eagle Landing on Moon. 45fr, Astronaut and Eagle on moon, earth and stars in sky.

**1969, July 21 Litho. *Perf. 14***
**674** A94 1fr green & multi .40 .20
**675** A94 20fr brown & multi .40 .20
**676** A94 30fr scarlet & multi .40 .20
**677** A94 45fr ultra & multi .70 .20
*Nos. 674-677,C107-C108 (6)* 4.10 1.40

Man's 1st landing on the moon, 7/20/69. US astronauts Neil A. Armstrong & Col. Edwin E. Aldrin, Jr., with Lieut. Col. Michael Collins piloting Apollo 11.
For overprints see #710-712, C120-C121.

Christ at Emmaus, by Velazquez A95

Paintings: 5fr, The Last Supper, by Tintoretto. 20fr, Pentecost, by El Greco. 30fr, The Annunciation, by Botticelli. 45fr, Like 10fr.

**1969, Aug. 16 Litho. *Perf. 14***
**678** A95 5fr red, gold & multi .50 .20
**679** A95 10fr multicolored .50 .20
**680** A95 20fr grn, gold & multi .50 .20
**681** A95 30fr multicolored .50 .20
**682** A95 45fr pur, gold & multi .70 .20
*Nos. 678-682,C109 (6)* 5.10 1.40

Nos. 665-668 Overprinted

**1969, Sept. 1 Photo. *Perf. 13½x14***
**683** A92 15fr brn org & sl grn .50 .20
**684** A92 20fr grnsh bl & vio .50 .20
**685** A92 30fr ver & slate bl .50 .20
**686** A92 45fr olive & car rose .60 .20
*Nos. 683-686,C110-C111 (6)* 4.60 1.25

Gen. Dwight D. Eisenhower (1890-1969), 34th President of the US.

African Development Bank and Emblem — A96

Designs: 45fr, Bank emblem and hand holding railroad bridge and engine.

**1969, Sept. 10 Photo. *Perf. 13x14***
**687** A96 30fr ultra, blk gold & grn 1.00 .20
**688** A96 45fr grn, dk bl, gold & dk red 1.40 .20

5th anniv. of the African Development Bank. See No. C112.

Louis Pasteur and Help for 1968 Flood Victims — A97

Designs: 15fr, Henri Dunant and Red Cross workers meeting Biafra refugees at airport. 30fr, Alexander Fleming and help for flood victims. 45fr, Wilhelm C. Roentgen and Red Cross workers with children in front of Headquarters.

**1969, Sept. 27 Litho. *Perf. 14***

**689** A97 15fr red & multi .50 .20
**690** A97 20fr emerald & multi .50 .20
**691** A97 30fr purple & multi .50 .20
**692** A97 45fr brt blue & multi .70 .20
*Nos. 689-692,C113-C114 (6)* 4.90 1.40

League of Red Cross Societies, 50th anniv.

Glidji Agricultural Center A98

Designs (Emblem of Young Pioneer and Agricultural Organization and): 1fr, Corn harvest. 3fr, Founding meeting of Agricultural Pioneer Youths, Mar. 7, 1967. 4fr, Class at Glidji Agricultural School. 5fr, Boys forming human pyramid. 7fr, Farm students threshing. 8fr, Instruction in gardening. 10fr, 50fr, Cooperative village. 15fr, Gardening School. 20fr, Cattle breeding. 25fr, Chicken farm. 30fr, Independence parade. 40fr, Boys riding high wire. 45fr, Tractor and trailer. 60fr, Instruction in tractor driving.

**1969-70 Litho. *Perf. 14***

**693** A98 1fr multi ('70) .45 .20
**694** A98 2fr multi .45 .20
**695** A98 3fr multi ('70) .45 .20
**696** A98 4fr multi ('70) .45 .20
**697** A98 5fr ultra & multi .45 .20
**698** A98 7fr multi ('70) .45 .20
**699** A98 8fr red & multi .45 .20
**700** A98 10fr bl & multi ('70) .45 .20
**701** A98 15fr red & multi ('70) .45 .20
**702** A98 20fr lilac & multi .45 .20
**703** A98 25fr multi ('70) .45 .20
**704** A98 30fr brt bl & multi .45 .20
**705** A98 40fr brt yel & multi .45 .20
**706** A98 45fr rose lil & multi .60 .20
**707** A98 50fr blue & multi .60 .20
**708** A98 60fr orange & multi .60 .20
*Nos. 693-708,C115-C119 (21)* 24.30 5.35

Books and Map of Africa A99

**1969, Nov. 27 Litho. *Perf. 14***

**709** A99 30fr lt blue & multi .60 .20

12th anniv. of the Intl. Assoc. for the Development of Libraries in Africa.

**Christmas Issue**

Nos. 674-675, 677 Overprinted "JOYEUX NOEL"

**1969, Dec. Litho. *Perf. 14***

**710** A94 1fr green & multi .55 .20
**711** A94 20fr brown & multi 1.90 .35
**712** A94 45fr ultra & multi 3.50 .65
*Nos. 710-712,C120-C121 (5)* 14.70 2.20

George Washington — A100

Portraits: 20fr, Albert Luthuli. 30fr, Mahatma Gandhi. 45fr, Simon Bolivar.

**1969, Dec. 27 Photo. *Perf. 14x13½***

**713** A100 15fr dk brn, emer & buff .50 .20
**714** A100 20fr dk brn, org & buff .50 .20
**715** A100 30fr dk brn, grnsh bl & ocher .50 .20
**716** A100 45fr dk brn, sl grn & dl yel .50 .20
*Nos. 713-716,C122-C123 (6)* 4.60 1.30

Issued to honor leaders for world peace.

For overprint & surcharges see #764-766, C143.

Plower, by M.K. Klodt and ILO Emblem A101

Paintings and ILO Emblem: 10fr, Gardening, by Camille Pissarro. 20fr, Fruit Harvest, by Diego Rivera. 30fr, Spring Sowing, by Vincent van Gogh. 45fr, Workers, by Rivera.

**1970, Jan. 24 Litho. *Perf. 12½x13***

**717** A101 5fr gold & multi .80 .20
**718** A101 10fr gold & multi .80 .20
**719** A101 20fr gold & multi .80 .20
**720** A101 30fr gold & multi 1.00 .20
**721** A101 45fr gold & multi 1.40 .20
*Nos. 717-721,C124-C125 (7)* 8.70 1.40

ILO, 50th anniversary.

Togolese Hair Styles — A102

Various hair styles. 20fr, 30fr, vertical.

**1970, Feb. 21 *Perf. 13x12½, 12½x13***

**722** A102 5fr multicolored .60 .20
**723** A102 10fr ver & multi .60 .20
**724** A102 20fr purple & multi .60 .20
**725** A102 30fr yellow grn & multi .80 .20
*Nos. 722-725,C126-C127 (6)* 5.00 1.30

Togo No. C127 and Independence Monument, Lomé — A103

30fr, Pres. Etienne G. Eyadéma, Presidential Palace and Independence Monument. 50fr, Map of Togo, dove and Independence Monument, vert.

***Perf. 13x12½, 12½x13***

**1970, Apr. 27 Litho.**

**726** A103 20fr multicolored .65 .20
**727** A103 30fr multicolored .65 .20
**728** A103 50fr multicolored .95 .20
*Nos. 726-728,C128 (4)* 3.20 .80

10th anniv. of independence.

Inauguration of UPU Headquarters, Bern — A104

**1970, May 30 Photo. *Perf. 14x13½***

**729** A104 30fr orange & pur 1.25 .20

See No. C129.

Soccer, Jules Rimet Cup and Flags of Italy and Uruguay — A105

Designs (Various Scenes from Soccer, Rimet Cup and Flags of): 10fr, Great Britain and Brazil. 15fr, USSR and Mexico. 20fr, Germany and Morocco. 30fr, Romania and Czechoslovakia.

**1970, June 27 Litho. *Perf. 13x14***

**730** A105 5fr olive & multi .55 .20
**731** A105 10fr pink & multi .55 .20
**732** A105 15fr yellow & multi .55 .20
**733** A105 20fr multicolored .55 .20
**734** A105 30fr emerald .80 .20
*Nos. 730-734,C130-C132 (8)* 6.40 1.70

Soccer Championships for the Jules Rimet Cup, Mexico City, May 30-June 21, 1970.

Lenin and UNESCO Emblem A106

**1970, July 25 Litho. *Perf. 12½***

**735** A106 30fr fawn & multi 1.90 .20

Lenin (1870-1924), Russian communist leader. See No. C133.
For surcharge see No. C179.

EXPO '70 Emblem and View of US Pavilion — A107

Designs: 2fr, Paper carp flying over Sanyo pavilion. 30fr, Russian pavilion. 50fr, Tower of the Sun pavilion. 60fr, French and Japanese pavilions.

**1970, Aug. 8 Litho. *Perf. 13***

**Size: 56½x35mm**

**736** A107 2fr gray & multi .45 .20

**Size: 50x33mm**

**737** A107 20fr blue & multi .45 .20
**738** A107 30fr blue & multi .45 .20
**739** A107 50fr blue & multi .55 .20
**740** A107 60fr blue & multi .65 .20
*a.* Strip of 4, #737-740 2.25 1.25
*Nos. 736-740 (5)* 2.55 1.00

EXPO '70 Intl. Exhibition, Osaka, Japan, Mar. 15-Sept. 13. No. 740a has continuous view of EXPO. See No. C134.

Neil A. Armstrong, Michael Collins and Edwin E. Aldrin, Jr. — A108

Designs: 2fr, US flag, moon rocks and Apollo 11 emblem. 20fr, Astronaut checking Surveyor 3 on moon, and Apollo 12 emblem. 30fr, Charles Conrad, Jr., Richard F. Gordon, Jr., Alan L. Bean and Apollo 12 emblem. 50fr, US flag, moon rocks and Apollo 12 emblem.

**1970, Sept. 26**

**741** A108 1fr multi .50 .20
**742** A108 2fr multi .50 .20
**743** A108 20fr multi .50 .20
**744** A108 30fr multi .65 .20
**745** A108 50fr multi 1.25 .20
*Nos. 741-745,C135 (6)* 5.90 1.55

Moon landings of Apollo 11 and 12.
For overprints see Nos. 746-750, C136.

Nos. 741-745 Inscribed: "FELICITATIONS / BON RETOUR APOLLO XIII"

**1970, Sept. 26**

**746** A108 1fr multi .50 .20
**747** A108 2fr multi .50 .20
**748** A108 20fr multi .50 .20
**749** A108 30fr multi .65 .20
**750** A108 50fr multi 1.10 .20
*Nos. 746-750,C136 (6)* 5.75 1.55

Safe return of the crew of Apollo 13.

Forge of Vulcan, by Velazquez, and ILO Emblem — A109

Paintings and Emblems of UN Agencies: 15fr, Still Life, by Delacroix, and FAO emblem. 20fr, Portrait of Nicholas Kratzer, by Holbein, and UNESCO emblem. 30fr, UN Headquarters, New York, and UN emblem. 50fr, Portrait of a Little Girl, by Renoir, and UNICEF emblem.

**1970, Oct. 24 Litho. *Perf. 13x12½***

**751** A109 1fr car, gold & dk brn .65 .20
**752** A109 15fr ultra, gold & blk .65 .20
**753** A109 20fr grnsh bl, gold & dk grn .65 .20
**754** A109 30fr lil & multi .80 .20
**755** A109 50fr org brn, gold & sepia 1.25 .20
*Nos. 751-755,C137-C138 (7)* 6.85 1.50

United Nations, 25th anniversary.

Euchloron Megaera — A110

Butterflies and Moths: 2fr, Cymothoe chrysippus. 30fr, Danaus chrysippus. 50fr, Morpho.

**1970, Nov. 21 Litho. *Perf. 13x14***

**756** A110 1fr yellow & multi 2.00 .20
**757** A110 2fr lt vio & multi 2.00 .20
**758** A110 30fr multicolored 2.00 .20
**759** A110 50fr orange & multi 3.75 .20
*Nos. 756-759,C139-C140 (6)* 20.25 1.20

For surcharge see No. 859.

Nativity, by Botticelli — A111

Paintings: 20fr, Adoration of the Shepherds, by Veronese. 30fr, Adoration of the Shepherds, by El Greco. 50fr, Adoration of the Kings, by Fra Angelico.

**1970, Dec. 26 Litho. *Perf. 12½x13***
**760** A111 15fr gold & multi .65 .20
**761** A111 20fr gold & multi .65 .20
**762** A111 30fr gold & multi .65 .20
**763** A111 50fr gold & multi 1.10 .20
*Nos. 760-763,C141-C142 (6)* 6.80 1.30

Christmas.

### Nos. 715, C123, 714 Surcharged and Overprinted: "EN MEMOIRE / Charles De Gaulle / 1890-1970"

**1971, Jan. 9 Photo. *Perf. 14x13½***
**764** A100 30fr multicolored 2.00 .20
**765** A100 30fr on 90fr multi 2.00 .20
**766** A100 150fr on 20fr multi 8.50 .35
*Nos. 764-766,C143 (4)* 24.00 1.35

"Aerienne" obliterated with heavy bar on No. 765.

De Gaulle and Churchill A112

De Gaulle and: 30fr, Dwight D. Eisenhower. 40fr, John F. Kennedy. 50fr, Konrad Adenauer.

**1971, Feb. 20 Photo. *Perf. 13x14***
**767** A112 20fr blk & brt blue .90 .20
**768** A112 30fr blk & crimson .90 .20
**769** A112 40fr blk & dp green 1.40 .20
**770** A112 50fr blk & brown 1.60 .20
*Nos. 767-770,C144-C145 (6)* 10.00 1.25

Nos. 764-770 issued in memory of Charles de Gaulle (1890-1970), President of France.

Resurrection, by Raphael — A113

Easter: 30fr, Resurrection, by Master of Trebon. 40fr, like 1fr.

**1971, Apr. 10 Litho. *Perf. 10½x11½***
**771** A113 1fr gold & multi .50 .20
**772** A113 30fr gold & multi .50 .20
**773** A113 40fr gold & multi .50 .20
*Nos. 771-773,C146-C148 (6)* 5.20 1.30

Cmdr. Alan B. Shepard, Jr. — A114

Designs: 10fr, Edgar D. Mitchell and astronaut on moon. 30fr, Stuart A. Roosa, module on moon. 40fr, Take-off from moon, and spaceship.

**1971, May Litho. *Perf. 12½***
**774** A114 1fr blue & multi .30 .20
**775** A114 10fr green & multi .30 .20
**776** A114 30fr dull red & multi .30 .20
**777** A114 40fr dk green & multi .35 .20
*Nos. 774-777,C149-C151 (7)* 4.65 2.00

Apollo 14 moon landing, Jan. 31-Feb. 9. For overprints see Nos. 788, C162-C164.

Cacao Tree and Pods — A115

Designs: 40fr, Sorting and separating beans and pods. 50fr, Drying cacao beans.

**1971, June 6 Litho. *Perf. 14***
**778** A115 30fr multicolored .60 .20
**779** A115 40fr ultra & multi .65 .20
**780** A115 50fr multicolored .65 .20
*Nos. 778-780,C152-C154 (6)* 5.15 1.45

International Cacao Day, June 6.

Napoleon, Death Sesquicentennial — A115a

***Die Cut Perf. 12***

**1971, June 11 Embossed**
**780A** A115a 1000fr gold 40.00 40.00
*b.* Sheet of 1, imperf. 26.00 26.00

No. 780Ab contains one 48x69mm stamp.

Control Tower and Plane — A116

**1971, June 26 Litho. *Perf. 14***
**781** A116 30fr multicolored 1.00 .20

10th anniv. of the Agency for the Security of Aerial Navigation in Africa and Madagascar (ASECNA). See No. C155.

Great Market, Lomé — A117

Tourist publicity: 30fr, Bird-of-paradise flower and sculpture of a man. 40fr, Aledjo Gorge and anubius baboon.

**1971, July 17**
**782** A117 20fr multicolored .45 .20
**783** A117 30fr multicolored .45 .20
**784** A117 40fr multicolored .55 .20
*Nos. 782-784,C156-C158 (6)* 4.50 1.35

For surcharge and overprint see Nos. 804, C172.

Great Fetish of Gbatchoume — A118

Religions of Togo: 30fr, Chief Priest in front of Atta Sakuma Temple. 40fr, Annual ceremony of the sacred stone.

**1971, July 31 Litho. *Perf. 14½***
**785** A118 20fr multicolored .40 .20
**786** A118 30fr multicolored .40 .20
**787** A118 40fr multicolored .50 .20
*Nos. 785-787,C159-C161 (6)* 3.65 1.25

### No. 777 Overprinted in Silver: "EN MEMOIRE / DOBROVOLSKY — VOLKOV — PATSAYEV / SOYUZ 11"

**1971, Aug. *Perf. 12½***
**788** A114 40fr multicolored .40 .20
*Nos. 788,C162-C164 (4)* 4.60 1.25

Russian astronauts Lt. Col. Georgi T. Dobrovolsky, Vladislav N. Volkov and Victor I. Patsayev, who died during the Soyuz 11 space mission, June 6-30, 1971.

Sapporo '72 Emblem and Speed Skating — A119

Sapporo '72 Emblem and: 10fr, Slalom skiing. 20fr, Figure skating, pairs. 30fr, Bobsledding. 50fr, Ice hockey.

**1971, Oct. 30 *Perf. 14***
**789** A119 1fr multicolored .30 .20
**790** A119 10fr multicolored .30 .20
**791** A119 20fr multicolored .30 .20
**792** A119 30fr multicolored .30 .20
**793** A119 50fr multicolored .55 .20
*Nos. 789-793,C165 (6)* 4.00 1.50

11th Winter Olympic Games, Sapporo, Japan, Feb. 3-13, 1972.

Toy Crocodile and UNICEF Emblem — A120

Toys and UNICEF Emblem: 30fr, Fawn and butterfly. 40fr, Monkey. 50fr, Elephants.

**1971, Nov. 27**
**794** A120 20fr multicolored .35 .20
**795** A120 30fr violet & multi .35 .20
**796** A120 40fr green & multi .45 .20
**797** A120 50fr bister & multi .65 .20
*Nos. 794-797,C167-C168 (6)* 3.60 1.25

UNICEF, 25th anniv.
For overprints see Nos. 918, C263-C264.

Virgin and Child, by Botticelli A121

Virgin and Child by: 30fr, Master of the Life of Mary. 40fr, Dürer. 50fr, Veronese.

**1971, Dec. 24 *Perf. 14x13***
**798** A121 10fr purple & multi .50 .20
**799** A121 30fr green & multi .50 .20
**800** A121 40fr brown & multi .75 .20
**801** A121 50fr dk blue & multi 1.00 .20
*Nos. 798-801,C169-C170 (6)* 5.50 1.45

Christmas.

St. Mark's Basilica — A122

Design: 40fr, Rialto Bridge.

**1972, Feb. 26 Litho. *Perf. 14***
**802** A122 30fr multicolored .55 .20
**803** A122 40fr multicolored .70 .20
*Nos. 802-803,C171 (3)* 3.25 .80

UNESCO campaign to save Venice.

### No. 784 Surcharged with New Value, Two Bars and "VISITE DU PRESIDENT / NIXON EN CHINE / FEVRIER 1972"

**1972, Mar. Litho. *Perf. 14***
**804** A117 300fr on 40fr multi 3.50 1.25

Visit of Pres. Richard M. Nixon to the People's Republic of China, Feb. 20-27. See No. C172.

Crucifixion, by Master MS — A123

Easter (Paintings): 30fr, Pietà, by Botticelli.

**1972, Mar. 31**
**805** A123 25fr gold & multi .80 .20
**806** A123 30fr gold & multi .80 .20
**807** A123 40fr gold & multi 1.00 .20
*Nos. 805-807,C173-C174 (5)* 7.25 1.05

Heart, Smith, WHO Emblem A124

Video Telephone A125

Org. of African and Malagasy Union Conf. — A124a

Heart, WHO Emblem and: 40fr, Typist. 60fr, Athlete with javelin.

**1972, Apr. 4**

| No. | Type | Description | Unused | Used |
|---|---|---|---|---|
| **808** | A124 | 30fr multicolored | .40 | .20 |
| **809** | A124 | 40fr multicolored | .55 | .20 |
| **810** | A124 | 60fr multicolored | .85 | .20 |
| | | *Nos. 808-810,C175 (4)* | 3.20 | 1.00 |

"Your heart is your health," World Health Day.

### *Die Cut Perf. 12x12½*

**1972, Apr. 24 Litho. & Embossed**
**Self-adhesive**

| No. | Type | Description | Unused | Used |
|---|---|---|---|---|
| **810A** | A124a | 1000fr gold, red & grn | 8.00 | 8.00 |

On No. 810A embossing may cut through stamp and embossed backing paper may not adhere well to the unused stamps.
For overprint see No. 893A.

**1972, June 24 Litho. *Perf. 14***

| No. | Type | Description | Unused | Used |
|---|---|---|---|---|
| **811** | A125 | 40fr violet & multi | 1.00 | .25 |

4th World Telecommunications Day. See No. C176.
For overprints see Nos. 880, C229.

Grating Cassava A126

Basketball A127

25fr, Cassava collection by truck, horiz.

**1972, June 30**

| No. | Type | Description | Unused | Used |
|---|---|---|---|---|
| **812** | A126 | 25fr yellow & multi | .45 | .20 |
| **813** | A126 | 40fr multicolored | .60 | .20 |
| | | *Nos. 812-813,C177-C178 (4)* | 3.40 | .90 |

Cassava production.
For overprint & surcharge see #866-867.

**1972, Aug. 26 Litho. *Perf. 14***

| No. | Type | Description | Unused | Used |
|---|---|---|---|---|
| **814** | A127 | 30fr shown | .35 | .20 |
| **815** | A127 | 40fr Running | .40 | .20 |
| **816** | A127 | 50fr Discus | .55 | .20 |
| | | *Nos. 814-816,C180-C181 (5)* | 4.70 | 1.60 |

20th Olympic Games, Munich, 8/26-9/11.
For overprints see Nos. C234-C235.

Pin-tailed Whydah — A128

Paul P. Harris, Rotary Emblem — A129

Birds: 30fr, Broad-tailed widowbird. 40fr, Yellow-shouldered widowbird. 60fr, Yellow-tailed widowbird.

**1972, Sept. 9**

| No. | Type | Description | Unused | Used |
|---|---|---|---|---|
| **817** | A128 | 25fr citron & multi | .80 | .20 |
| **818** | A128 | 30fr lt blue & multi | 1.00 | .20 |
| **819** | A128 | 40fr multicolored | 1.00 | .20 |
| **820** | A128 | 60fr lt green & multi | 1.60 | .20 |
| | | *Nos. 817-820,C182 (5)* | 6.90 | 1.15 |

**1972, Oct. 7 Litho. *Perf. 14***

50fr, Flags of Togo and Rotary Club.

| No. | Type | Description | Unused | Used |
|---|---|---|---|---|
| **821** | A129 | 40fr green & multi | .30 | .20 |
| **822** | A129 | 50fr multicolored | .55 | .20 |
| ***a.*** | | Souvenir sheet of 2 | 2.00 | 1.25 |
| | | *Nos. 821-822,C183-C185 (5)* | 3.20 | 1.35 |

Rotary International, Lomé. No. 822a contains 2 stamps with simulated perforations similar to Nos. 821-822.
For overprints see Nos. 862, 898, C212-C213, C244-C235.

Mona Lisa, by Leonardo da Vinci A130

40fr, Virgin and Child, by Giovanni Bellini.

**1972, Oct. 21**

| No. | Type | Description | Unused | Used |
|---|---|---|---|---|
| **823** | A130 | 25fr gold & multi | .90 | .20 |
| **824** | A130 | 40fr gold & multi | 1.10 | .20 |
| | | *Nos. 823-824,C186-C188 (5)* | 9.50 | 1.25 |

### West African Monetary Union Issue
Common Design Type

Design: 40fr, African couple, city, village and commemorative coin.

**1972, Nov. 2 Engr. *Perf. 13***

| No. | Type | Description | Unused | Used |
|---|---|---|---|---|
| **825** | CD136 | 40fr red brn, rose red & gray | .60 | .20 |

Presidents Pompidou and Eyadema, Party Headquarters — A131

**1972, Nov. 23 Litho. *Perf. 14***

| No. | Type | Description | Unused | Used |
|---|---|---|---|---|
| **826** | A131 | 40fr purple & multi | 1.90 | .20 |

Visit of Pres. Georges Pompidou of France to Togo, Nov. 1972. See No. C189.

Christmas A132

Paintings: 25fr, Anunciation, Painter Unknown. 30fr, Nativity, Master of Vyshchibrod. 40fr, Like 25fr.

**1972, Dec. 23**

| No. | Type | Description | Unused | Used |
|---|---|---|---|---|
| **827** | A132 | 25fr gold & multi | .50 | .20 |
| **828** | A132 | 30fr gold & multi | .50 | .20 |
| **829** | A132 | 40fr gold & multi | .60 | .20 |
| | | *Nos. 827-829,C191-C193 (6)* | 6.00 | 1.50 |

Raoul Follereau and Lepers — A133

**1973, Jan. 23 Photo. *Perf. 14x13½***

| No. | Type | Description | Unused | Used |
|---|---|---|---|---|
| **830** | A133 | 40fr violet & green | 2.00 | .20 |

World Leprosy Day and 20th anniv. of the Raoul Follereau Foundation. See No. C194.

WHO Emblem — A134

Christ on the Cross — A135

**1973, Apr. 7 Photo. *Perf. 14x13***

| No. | Type | Description | Unused | Used |
|---|---|---|---|---|
| **831** | A134 | 30fr blue & multi | .50 | .20 |
| **832** | A134 | 40fr dp yellow & multi | .65 | .20 |

WHO, 25th anniv.

**1973, Apr. 21 Litho. *Perf. 14***

| No. | Type | Description | Unused | Used |
|---|---|---|---|---|
| **833** | A135 | 25fr shown | .50 | .20 |
| **834** | A135 | 30fr Pietá | .50 | .20 |
| **835** | A135 | 40fr Ascension | .60 | .20 |
| | | *Nos. 833-835,C195 (4)* | 3.00 | 1.00 |

Easter.

Eugene Cernan, Ronald Evans, Harrison Schmitt, Apollo 17 Badge — A136

Design: 40fr, Lunar rover on moon.

**1973, June 2 Litho. *Perf. 14***

| No. | Type | Description | Unused | Used |
|---|---|---|---|---|
| **836** | A136 | 30fr multicolored | .45 | .20 |
| **837** | A136 | 40fr multicolored | .55 | .20 |
| | | *Nos. 836-837,C196-C197 (4)* | 5.40 | 1.40 |

Apollo 17 moon mission, Dec. 7-19, 1972.

Scouts Pitching Tent — A137

Nicolaus Copernicus A138

20fr, Campfire, horiz. 30fr, Rope climbing.

**1973, June 30**

| No. | Type | Description | Unused | Used |
|---|---|---|---|---|
| **838** | A137 | 10fr multicolored | .40 | .20 |
| **839** | A137 | 20fr multicolored | .40 | .20 |
| **840** | A137 | 30fr violet & multi | .40 | .20 |
| **841** | A137 | 40fr ocher & multi | .55 | .20 |
| | | *Nos. 838-841,C198-C199 (6)* | 6.40 | 1.85 |

24th Boy Scout World Conference (1st in Africa), Nairobi, Kenya, July 16-21.
For overprints see Nos. C265-C266.

**1973, July 18**

Designs: 10fr, Heliocentric system. 30fr, Seated figure of Astronomy and spacecrafts around earth and moon. 40fr, Astrolabe.

| No. | Type | Description | Unused | Used |
|---|---|---|---|---|
| **842** | A138 | 10fr multicolored | .60 | .20 |
| **843** | A138 | 20fr multicolored | .60 | .20 |
| **844** | A138 | 30fr multicolored | .60 | .20 |
| **845** | A138 | 40fr lilac & multi | .75 | .20 |
| | | *Nos. 842-845,C200-C201 (6)* | 6.40 | 1.50 |

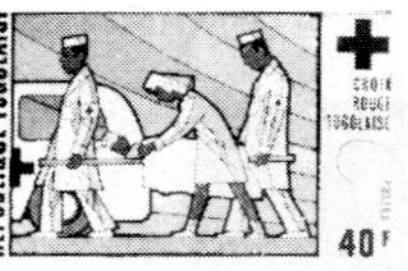

Red Cross Ambulance Crew A139

**1973, Aug. 4**

| No. | Type | Description | Unused | Used |
|---|---|---|---|---|
| **846** | A139 | 40fr multicolored | 1.60 | .20 |

Togolese Red Cross. See No. C202.
For overprints see Nos. 846, C294.

Teacher and Students — A140

40fr, Hut and man reading under tree, vert.

**1973, Aug. 18 Litho. *Perf. 14***

| No. | Type | Description | Unused | Used |
|---|---|---|---|---|
| **847** | A140 | 30fr multicolored | .50 | .20 |
| **848** | A140 | 40fr multicolored | .65 | .20 |
| | | *Nos. 847-848,C203 (3)* | 2.65 | .75 |

Literacy campaign.

### African Postal Union Issue
Common Design Type

**1973, Sept. 12 Engr. *Perf. 13***

| No. | Type | Description | Unused | Used |
|---|---|---|---|---|
| **849** | CD137 | 100fr yel, red & claret | 1.25 | .35 |

INTERPOL Emblem and Headquarters A141

Weather Vane and WMO Emblem A142

**1973, Sept. 29 Photo. *Perf. 13½x14***

| No. | Type | Description | Unused | Used |
|---|---|---|---|---|
| **850** | A141 | 30fr yel, brn & gray grn | .55 | .20 |
| **851** | A141 | 40fr yel grn, bl & mag | .65 | .20 |

50th anniv. of Intl. Criminal Police Org.

**1973, Oct. 4 *Perf. 14x13***

| No. | Type | Description | Unused | Used |
|---|---|---|---|---|
| **852** | A142 | 40fr yel, dp brn & grn | 1.00 | .20 |

Intl. meteorological cooperation, cent. See No. C204.

### Type of 1967

Designs: 25fr, Old and new locomotives, No. 795. 30fr, Mail coach and bus, No. 613. 90fr, Mail boat and ship, Nos. C61 and 469.

**1973, Oct. 20 Photo. *Perf. 14x13***
**853** A79 25fr multicolored .55 .20
**854** A79 30fr purple & green .70 .20
**855** A79 90fr dk blue & multi 1.90 .30
*Nos. 853-855,C205 (4)* 5.40 1.00

Togolese postal service, 75th anniv.

John F. Kennedy and Adolf Schaerf — A143

Virgin and Child, Italy, 15th Century — A144

Designs: 30fr, Kennedy and Harold MacMillan. 40fr, Kennedy and Konrad Adenauer.

**1973, Nov. 22 Litho. *Perf. 14***
**856** A143 20fr blk, gray & vio .40 .20
**857** A143 30fr blk, rose & brn .40 .20
**858** A143 40fr blk, lt grn & grn .50 .20
*Nos. 856-858,C206-C208 (6)* 6.95 2.00

John F. Kennedy (1917-1963).

No. 758 Surcharged with New Value, 2 Bars and Overprinted in Ultramarine: "SECHERESSE SOLIDARITE AFRICAINE"

**1973, Dec. Photo. *Perf. 13x14***
**859** A110 100fr on 30fr multi 1.40 .50

African solidarity in drought emergency.

**1973, Dec. 22 Litho. *Perf. 14***

30fr, Adoration of the Kings, Italy, 15th cent.

**860** A144 25fr gold & multi .40 .20
**861** A144 30fr gold & multi .50 .20
*Nos. 860-861,C210-C211 (4)* 3.40 1.00

Christmas.

No. 821 Overprinted: "PREMIERE CONVENTION / 210eme DISTRICT / FEVRIER 1974 / LOME"

**1974, Feb. 21 Litho. *Perf. 14***
**862** A129 40fr green & multi .40 .20
*Nos. 862,C212-C213 (3)* 2.05 .75

First convention of Rotary Intl., District 210, Lomé, Feb. 22-24.

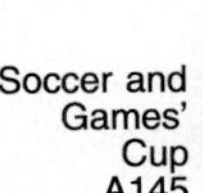

Soccer and Games' Cup A145

Various soccer scenes and games' cup.

**1974, Mar. 2 Litho. *Perf. 14***
**863** A145 20fr lt blue & multi .25 .20
**864** A145 30fr yellow & multi .30 .20
**865** A145 40fr lilac & multi .35 .20
*Nos. 863-865,C214-C216 (6)* 4.65 2.10

World Soccer Championships, Munich, Germany, June 13-July 7.

Nos. 812-813 Overprinted and Surcharged: "10e ANNIVERSAIRE DU P.A.M."

**1974, Mar. 25 Litho. *Perf. 14***
**866** A126 40fr multicolored .65 .20
**867** A126 100fr on 25fr multi 1.40 .50

10th anniv. of World Food Program. Overprint on No. 866 is in one line; 2 lines on No. 867 and 2 bars through old denomination.

Girl Before Mirror, by Picasso — A146

Mailman, UPU Emblem — A148

Kpeme Village and Wharf A147

Paintings by Picasso: 30fr, The Turkish Shawl. 40fr, Mandolin and Guitar.

**1974, Apr. 6**
**868** A146 20fr vio blue & multi .40 .20
**869** A146 30fr maroon & multi .55 .20
**870** A146 40fr multicolored .65 .20
*Nos. 868-870,C217-C219 (6)* 7.35 1.90

Pablo Picasso (1881-1973), Spanish painter.

**1974, Apr. 20**

Design: 40fr, Tropicana tourist village.

**871** A147 30fr multicolored .45 .20
**872** A147 40fr multicolored .45 .20
*Nos. 871-872,C220-C221 (4)* 3.25 1.00

**1974, May 10 Litho. *Perf. 14***

Design: 40fr, Mailman, different uniform.

**873** A148 30fr salmon & multi .45 .20
**874** A148 40fr multicolored .50 .20
*Nos. 873-874,C222-C223 (4)* 2.90 .95

UPU, centenary.

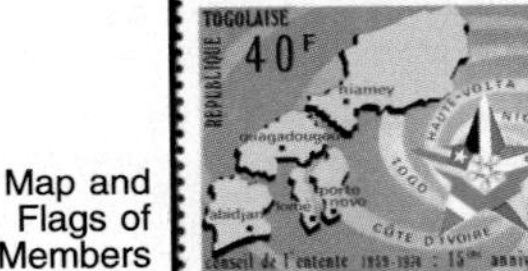


Map and Flags of Members — A148a

**1974, May 29 Litho. *Perf. 13x12½***
**875** A148a 40fr blue & multi .60 .25

15th anniversary of the Council of Accord.

Fisherman with Net A149

40fr, Fisherman casting net from canoe.

**1974, June 22 Litho. *Perf. 14***
**876** A149 30fr multicolored .55 .20
**877** A149 40fr multicolored .65 .20
*Nos. 876-877,C224-C226 (5)* 5.70 1.55

Lagoon fishing.

Pioneer Communicating with Earth — A150

30fr, Radar station and satellite, vert.

**1974, July 6 *Perf. 14***
**878** A150 30fr multicolored .35 .20
**879** A150 40fr multicolored .40 .20
*Nos. 878-879,C227-C228 (4)* 3.65 1.40

US Jupiter space probe.

No. 811 Overprinted with INTERNABA Emblem in Silver Similar to No. C229

**1974, July**
**880** A125 40fr multicolored 3.00 .55

INTERNABA 1974 Intl. Philatelic Exhibition, Basel, June 7-16. See No. C229.
No. 880 exists overprint in black. Value, unused $10.

Tympanotomus Radula — A151

Designs: Seashells.

**1974, July 13 Litho. *Perf. 14***
**881** A151 10fr shown .75 .20
**882** A151 20fr Tonna galea .75 .20
**883** A151 30fr Conus mercator .90 .20
**884** A151 40fr Cardium costatum 1.25 .20
*Nos. 881-884,C230-C231 (6)* 7.25 1.40

Groom with Horses A152

Design: 40fr, Trotting horses.

**1974, Aug. 3 Litho. *Perf. 14***
**885** A152 30fr multicolored .80 .20
**886** A152 40fr multicolored .95 .20
*Nos. 885-886,C232-C233 (4)* 5.90 1.00

Horse racing.

Leopard A153

**1974, Sept. 7 Litho. *Perf. 14***
**887** A153 20fr shown .65 .20
**888** A153 30fr Giraffes .65 .20
**889** A153 40fr Elephants .85 .20
*Nos. 887-889,C236-C237 (5)* 6.05 1.25

Wild animals of West Africa.

**1974, Oct. 14**
**890** A153 30fr Herding cattle .40 .20
**891** A153 40fr Milking cow .55 .20
*Nos. 890-891,C238-C239 (4)* 3.30 1.00

Domestic animals.

Churchill and Frigate F390 A154

Design: 40fr, Churchill and fighter planes.

**1974, Nov. 1 Photo. *Perf. 13x13½***
**892** A154 30fr multicolored .50 .20
**893** A154 40fr multicolored .60 .20
*Nos. 892-893,C240-C241 (4)* 4.60 1.30

Winston Churchill (1874-1965).

No. 810A Ovptd. "Inauguration de l'hotel de la Paix 9-1-75"

**Litho. & Embossed**
**1975, Jan. 9 *Perf. 12½***
**Self-adhesive**
**893A** A124a 1000fr gold, red & grn 8.00 8.00

On No. 893A embossing may cut through stamp and embossed backing paper may not adhere well to the unused stamps.

Chlamydocarya Macrocarpa — A155

Flowers of Togo: 25fr, Strelitzia reginae, vert. 30fr, Storphanthus sarmentosus, vert. 60fr, Clerodendrum scandens.

**1975, Feb. 15 Litho. *Perf. 14***
**894** A155 25fr multicolored .55 .20
**895** A155 30fr multicolored .55 .20
**896** A155 40fr multicolored .70 .20
**897** A155 60fr multicolored .95 .20
*Nos. 894-897,C242-C243 (6)* 7.25 1.55

No. 821 Overprinted: "70e ANNIVERSAIRE / 23 FEVRIER 1975"

**1975, Feb. 23 Litho. *Perf. 14***
**898** A129 40fr green & multi .55 .20
*Nos. 898,C244-C245 (3)* 2.45 .80

Rotary Intl., 70th anniv.

Radio Station, Kamina A156

30fr, Benedictine Monastery, Zogbegan. 40fr, Causeway, Atchinedji. 60fr, Ayome Waterfalls.

**1975, Mar. 1 Photo. *Perf. 13x14***
**899** A156 25fr multicolored .36 .20
**900** A156 30fr multicolored .36 .20
**901** A156 40fr multicolored .45 .20
**902** A156 60fr multicolored .65 .25
*Nos. 899-902 (4)* 1.82 .85

Jesus Mocked, by El Greco — A157

Paintings: 30fr, Crucifixion, by Master Janoslet. 40fr, Descent from the Cross, by Bellini. 90fr, Pietà, painter unknown.

**1975, Apr. 19 Litho. *Perf. 14***
**903** A157 25fr black & multi .35 .20
**904** A157 30fr black & multi .45 .20
**905** A157 40fr black & multi .55 .20
**906** A157 90fr black & multi 1.10 .30
*Nos. 903-906,C246-C247 (6)* 5.45 1.70

Easter.

Stilt Walking, Togolese Flag A158

Design: 30fr, Flag and dancers.

**1975, Apr. 26 Litho. *Perf. 14***

**907** A158 25fr multicolored .40 .20
**908** A158 30fr multicolored .40 .20
*Nos. 907-908,C248-C249 (4)* 2.00 .80

15th anniv. of independence.

Rabbit Hunter with Club
A159

40fr, Beaver hunter with bow and arrow.

**1975, May 24 Photo. *Perf. 13x13½***

**909** A159 30fr multicolored .65 .20
**910** A159 40fr multicolored .85 .20
*Nos. 909-910,C250-C251 (4)* 5.00 .90

Pounding Palm Nuts
A160

Design: 40fr, Man extracting palm oil, vert.

**1975, June 28 Litho. *Perf. 14***

**911** A160 30fr multicolored .45 .20
**912** A160 40fr multicolored .45 .20
*Nos. 911-912,C252-C253 (4)* 2.65 .90

Palm oil production.

Apollo-Soyuz Link-up — A161

**1975, July 15**

**913** A161 30fr multicolored .40 .20
*Nos. 913,C254-C258 (6)* 5.80 1.70

Apollo Soyuz space test project (Russo-American cooperation), launching July 15; link-up July 17.

Women's Heads, IWY Emblem — A162

**1975, July 26 Litho. *Perf. 12½***

**914** A162 30fr blue & multi .50 .20
**915** A162 40fr multicolored .60 .20

International Women's Year.

Dr. Schweitzer and Children — A163

**1975, Aug. 23 Litho. *Perf. 14x13½***

**916** A163 40fr multicolored .65 .20
*Nos. 916,C259-C261 (4)* 4.00 1.10

Dr. Albert Schweitzer (1875-1965), medical missionary and musician.

Merchant Writing Letter, by Vittore Carpaccio
A164

Virgin and Child, by Mantegna
A165

**1975, Oct. 9 Litho. *Perf. 14***

**917** A164 40fr multicolored .60 .20

Intl. Letter Writing Week. See No. C262.

No. 797 Overprinted: "30ème Anniversaire / des Nations-Unies"

**1975, Oct. 24 Litho. *Perf. 14***

**918** A120 50fr multi .50 .25
*Nos. 918,C263-C264 (3)* 1.85 .70

UN, 30th anniv.

**1975, Dec. 20 Litho. *Perf. 14***

Paintings of the Virgin and Child: 30fr, El Greco. 40fr, Barend van Orley.

**919** A165 20fr red & multi .35 .20
**920** A165 30fr bl & multi .40 .20
**921** A165 40fr red & multi .50 .20
*Nos. 919-921,C267-C269 (6)* 4.70 1.60

Christmas.

Crashed Plane and Pres. Eyadema
A166

**1976, Jan. 24 Photo. *Perf. 13***

**922** A166 50fr multi 10.00 .40
**923** A166 60fr multi 14.00 .45

Airplane crash at Sara-kawa, Jan. 24, 1974, in which Pres. Eyadema escaped injury.

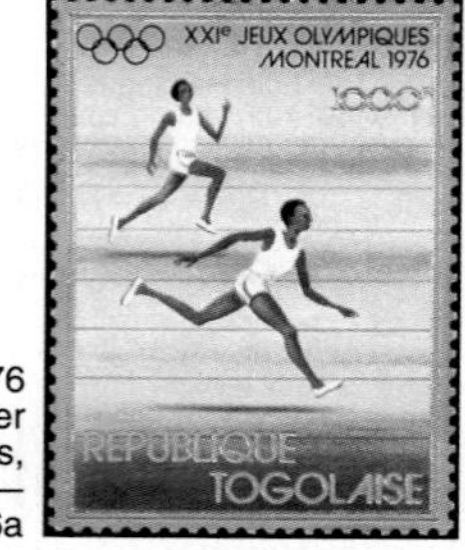


1976 Summer Olympics, Montreal — A166a

**Litho. & Embossed**

**1976, Feb. 24 *Perf. 11***

**923A** A166a 1000fr Diving 15.00 —
**923B** A166a 1000fr Track 15.00 —
**923C** A166a 1000fr Pole vault 15.00 —
**923D** A166a 1000fr Equestrian 15.00 —
**923E** A166a 1000fr Cycling 15.00 —
*Nos. 923A-923E (5)* 75.00

Exist imperf.

Frigates on the Hudson — A167

American Bicentennial: 50fr, George Washington, by Gilbert Stuart, and Bicentennial emblem, vert.

**1976, Mar. 3 Litho. *Perf. 14***

**924** A167 35fr multicolored .45 .20
**925** A167 50fr multicolored .65 .25
*Nos. 924-925,C270-C273 (6)* 5.50 1.65

For overprints see Nos. C280-C283.

ACP and CEE Emblems
A168

50fr, Map of Africa, Europe and Asia.

**1976, Apr. 24 Photo. *Perf. 13x14***

**926** A168 10fr orange & multi .25 .20
**927** A168 50fr pink & multi .40 .25
*Nos. 926-927,C274-C275 (4)* 1.65 .85

First anniv. of signing of treaty between Togo and European Common Market, Lomé, Feb. 28, 1975.

Cable-laying Ship — A169

30fr, Telephone, tape recorder, speaker.

**1976, Mar. 10 Photo. *Perf. 13x14***

**928** A169 25fr ultra & multi .25 .20
**929** A169 30fr pink & multi .25 .20
*Nos. 928-929,C276-C277 (4)* 1.80 1.00

Centenary of first telephone call by Alexander Graham Bell, Mar. 10, 1876.

Blind Man and Insect — A170

Marine Exhibition Hall — A171

**1976, Apr. 8 *Perf. 14x13***

**930** A170 50fr brt grn & multi .60 .20

World Health Day: "Foresight prevents blindness." See No. C278.

Air Post Type, 1976, and Type A171

10fr, Pylon, flags of Ghana, Togo and Dahomey.

**1976 Litho. *Perf. 14***

**931** A171 5fr multicolored .30 .20
**932** AP19 10fr multicolored .30 .20
**933** A171 50fr multicolored .45 .25
*Nos. 931-933,C279 (4)* 1.60 .85

Marine Exhibition, 10th anniv. (5fr, 50fr). Ghana-Togo-Dahomey electric power grid, 1st anniversary (10fr).

Issue dates: 50fr, May 8; 5fr, 10fr, August.

Running — A172

Montreal Olympic Emblem and: 30fr, Kayak. 50fr, High jump.

**1976, June 15 Photo. *Perf. 14x13***

**934** A172 25fr multicolored .30 .20
**935** A172 30fr multicolored .30 .20
**936** A172 50fr multicolored .45 .20
*Nos. 934-936,C284-C286 (6)* 4.10 1.90

21st Olympic Games, Montreal, Canada, July 17-Aug. 1.

For overprints see Nos. 947, C298-C299.

Titan 3 and Viking Emblem — A173

50fr, Viking trajectory, Earth to Mars.

**1976, July 15 Litho. *Perf. 14***

**937** A173 30fr blue & multi .30 .20
**938** A173 50fr rose & multi .45 .20
*Nos. 937-938,C287-C290 (6)* 4.25 1.70

US Viking Mars missions.

Young Routy at Celeyran, by Toulouse-Lautrec
A174

Mohammed Ali Jinnah, Flags of Togo and Pakistan — A176

Adoration of the Shepherds, by Pontormo — A175

Paintings by Toulouse-Lautrec: 20fr, Model in Studio. 35fr, Louis Pascal, portrait.

**1976, Aug. 7 Litho. *Perf. 14***

**939** A174 10fr black & multi .45 .20
**940** A174 20fr black & multi .45 .20
**941** A174 35fr black & multi .60 .20
*Nos. 939-941,C291-C293 (6)* 5.70 1.60

Henri Toulouse-Lautrec (1864-1901), French painter, 75th death anniversary.

No. 846 Overprinted: "Journée / Internationale / de l'Enfance"

**1976, Nov. 27** **Litho.** ***Perf. 14***
**942** A139 40fr multi .40 .20

Intl. Children's Day. See No. C294.

**1976, Dec. 18**

Paintings: 30fr, Nativity, by Carlo Crivelli. 50fr, Virgin and Child, by Jacopo da Pontormo.

**943** A175 25fr multi .35 .20
**944** A175 30fr multi .35 .20
**945** A175 50fr multi .50 .20
*Nos. 943-945,C295-C297 (6)* 4.45 1.70

Christmas.

**1976, Dec. 24** **Litho.** ***Perf. 13***
**946** A176 50fr multi .60 .20

Jinnah (1876-1948), first Governor General of Pakistan.

No. 936 Overprinted: "CHAMPIONS OLYMPIQUES / SAUT EN HAUTEUR / POLOGNE"

**1976, Dec.** **Photo.** ***Perf. 14x13***
**947** A172 50fr multi .50 .20
*Nos. 947,C298-C299 (3)* 2.70 1.00

Olympic winners.

Queen Elizabeth II, Silver Jubilee — A176a

Designs: No. 947A, Portrait. No. 947B, Wearing coronation regalia.

**Litho. & Embossed**

**1977, Jan. 10** ***Perf. 11***
**947A** A176a 1000fr silver & multi 6.50

**Souvenir Sheet**

**947B** A176a 1000fr silver & multi 9.00

Exist imperf.

Kpeme Phosphate Mine, Sarakawa Crash A177

**1977, Jan. 13** **Photo.** ***Perf. 13x14***
**948** A177 50fr multi .45 .20
*Nos. 948,C300-C301 (3)* 1.85 .70

Presidency of Etienne Eyadema, 10th anniv.

Musical Instruments A178

**1977, Feb. 7** **Litho.** ***Perf. 14***
**949** A178 5fr Gongophone .45 .20
**950** A178 10fr Tamtam, vert. .45 .20
**951** A178 25fr Dondon .45 .20
*Nos. 949-951,C302-C304 (6)* 4.30 1.25

Victor Hugo and his Home A179

**1977, Feb. 26** ***Perf. 13x14***
**952** A179 50fr multi .65 .20

Victor Hugo (1802-1885), French writer, 175th birth anniversary. See No. C305.

For overprints see Nos. 959, C316.

Beethoven and Birthplace, Bonn A180

50fr, Bronze bust, 1812, & Heiligenstadt home.

**1977, Mar. 7** ***Perf. 14***
**953** A180 30fr multi .40 .20
**954** A180 50fr multi .60 .20
*Nos. 953-954,C306-C307 (4)* 4.20 3.75

Benz, 1894, Germany — A181

Early Automobiles: 50fr, De Dion Bouton, 1903, France.

**1977, Apr. 11** **Litho.** ***Perf. 14***
**955** A181 35fr multi .50 .20
**956** A181 50fr multi .70 .20
*Nos. 955-956,C308-C311 (6)* 6.05 1.75

Lindbergh, Ground Crew and Spirit of St. Louis — A182

50fr, Lindbergh and Spirit of St. Louis.

**1977, May 9**
**957** A182 25fr multi .30 .20
**958** A182 50fr multi .55 .20
*Nos. 957-958,C312-C315 (6)* 4.20 1.25

Charles A. Lindbergh's solo transatlantic flight from New York to Paris, 50th anniv.

No. 952 Overprinted: "10ème ANNIVERSAIRE DU / CONSEIL INTERNATIONAL / DE LA LANGUE FRANCAISE"

**1977, May 17** **Litho.** ***Perf. 14***
**959** A179 50fr multi .60 .20

Intl. French Language Council, 10th anniv. See No. C316.

African Slender-snouted Crocodile — A183

Endangered wildlife: 15fr, Nile crocodile.

**1977, June 13**
**960** A183 5fr multi .35 .20
**961** A183 15fr multi .35 .20
*Nos. 960-961,C317-C320 (6)* 5.90 1.35

Agriculture School, Tove A184

**1977, July 11** **Litho.** ***Perf. 14***
**962** A184 50fr multi .45 .20
*Nos. 962,C321-C323 (4)* 3.25 1.00

Agricultural development.

Landscape with Cart, by Peter Paul Rubens (1577-1640) — A185

Rubens Painting: 35fr, Exchange of the Princesses at Hendaye, 1623.

**1977, Aug. 8**
**963** A185 15fr multi .35 .20
**964** A185 35fr multi .45 .20
*Nos. 963-964,C324-C325 (4)* 2.60 .80

Orbiter 101 on Ground — A186

Designs: 30fr, Launching of Orbiter, vert. 50fr, Ejection of propellant tanks at take-off.

**1977, Oct. 4** **Litho.** ***Perf. 14***
**965** A186 20fr multi .30 .20
**966** A186 30fr multi .40 .20
**967** A186 50fr multi .50 .20
*Nos. 965-967,C326-C328 (6)* 4.50 1.35

Space shuttle trials in the US.

Lafayette Arriving in Montpelier, Vt. — A187

Design: 25fr, Lafayette, age 19, vert.

**1977, Nov. 7** ***Perf. 14x13, 13x14***
**968** A187 25fr multi .25 .20
**969** A187 50fr multi .45 .20
*Nos. 968-969,C329-C330 (4)* 2.05 .80

Arrival of the Marquis de Lafayette in North America, 200th anniv.

Lenin, Cruiser Aurora, Red Flag A188

**1977, Nov. 7** **Litho.** ***Perf. 12***
**970** A188 50fr multi 1.20 .20

Russian October Revolution, 60th anniv.

Virgin and Child, by Lorenzo Lotto — A189

Edward Jenner — A190

Virgin and Child by: 30fr, Carlo Bellini. 50fr, Cosimo Tura.

**1977, Dec. 19** ***Perf. 14***
**971** A189 20fr multi .25 .20
**972** A189 30fr multi .30 .20
**973** A189 50fr multi .45 .20
*Nos. 971-973,C331-C333 (6)* 4.30 1.35

Christmas.

***Perf. 14x13, 13x14***

**1978, Jan. 9** **Litho.**

Design: 20fr, Vaccination clinic, horiz.

**974** A190 5fr multi .20 .20
**975** A190 20fr multi .20 .20
*Nos. 974-975,C334-C335 (4)* 1.15 .80

Worldwide eradication of smallpox.

Orville and Wilbur Wright — A191

Design: 50fr, Wilbur Wright flying at Kill Devil Hill, 1902.

**1978, Feb. 6** **Litho.** ***Perf. 14***
**976** A191 35fr multi .35 .20
**977** A191 50fr multi .50 .20
*Nos. 976-977,C336-C339 (6)* 7.10 1.75

75th anniversary of first motorized flight.

Anniversaries and Events — A192

Designs: No. 978, High jump. No. 979, Westminster Abbey. No. 980, Soccer players, World Cup. No. 981, Apollo 8. No. 982, Duke of Wellington, by Goya. No. 983, Hurdles. No. 984, Coronation coach. No. 985, Soccer players. No. 986, Apollo launch. No. 987, Dona Isabel Cobos de Porcel, by Goya.

**1978, Mar. 13** **Litho.** ***Perf. 11***
**978** A192 1000fr gold & multi *8.00*
**979** A192 1000fr gold & multi *8.00*
**980** A192 1000fr gold & multi *8.00*
**981** A192 1000fr gold & multi *8.00*
**982** A192 1000fr gold & multi *8.00*

**Souvenir Sheets**

**983** A192 1000fr gold & multi *8.00*
**984** A192 1000fr gold & multi *8.00*
**985** A192 1000fr gold & multi *8.00*
**986** A192 1000fr gold & multi *8.00*
**987** A192 1000fr gold & multi *8.00*

Nos. 978, 983, 1980 Summer Olympics, Moscow. Nos. 979, 984, Coronation of Queen Elizabeth II, 25th anniv. Nos. 980, 985, 1978 World Cup Soccer Championships, Argentina. Nos. 981, 986, 1st manned lunar orbit, 10th anniv. Nos. 982, 987, Death sesquicent. of Francisco Goya.

For overprints see Nos. 1056A-1056B, 1094A-1094B.

Exist imperf.

John, the Evangelist and Eagle — A197

Evangelists: 10fr, Luke and ox. 25fr, Mark and lion. 30fr, Matthew and angel.

**1978, Mar. 20** **Litho.** ***Perf. 13½x14***
**988** A197 5fr multi .20 .20
**989** A197 10fr multi .20 .20
**990** A197 25fr multi .20 .20
**991** A197 30fr multi .25 .20
*a.* Souvenir sheet of 4 .90 .60
*Nos. 988-991 (4)* .85 .80

No. 991a contains one each of Nos. 988-991 with simulated perforations.

Anchor, Fishing Harbor, Lomé A199

**1978, Apr. 26 Photo. *Perf. 13***
**997** A199 25fr multi .25 .20
*Nos. 997,C340-C342 (4)* 3.05 1.00

Venera I, USSR — A200

Soccer — A201

Designs: 30fr, Pioneer, US, horiz. 50fr, Venera, fuel base and antenna.

**1978, May 8 Litho. *Perf. 14***
**998** A200 20fr multi .25 .20
**999** A200 30fr multi .30 .20
**1000** A200 50fr multi .40 .20
*Nos. 998-1000,C343-C345 (6)* 3.90 1.35

US Pioneer and USSR Venera space missions.

**1978, June 5 *Perf. 14***

50fr, Soccer players and Argentina '78 emblem.

**1001** A201 30fr multi .30 .20
**1002** A201 50fr multi .45 .20
*Nos. 1001-1002,C346-C349 (6)* 5.55 1.65

11th World Cup Soccer Championship, Argentina, June 1-25.

Celerifère, 1818 A202

History of the Bicycle: 50fr, First bicycle sidecar, c. 1870, vert.

***Perf. 13x14, 14x13***
**1978, July 10 Photo.**
**1003** A202 25fr multi .25 .20
**1004** A202 50fr multi .45 .20
*Nos. 1003-1004,C350-C353 (6)* 3.65 1.30

Thomas A. Edison, Sound Waves — A203

Dunant's Birthplace, Geneva — A204

Design: 50fr, Victor's His Master's Voice phonograph, 1905, and dancing couple.

**1978, July 8 Photo. *Perf. 14x13***
**1005** A203 30fr multicolored .30 .20
**1006** A203 50fr multicolored .40 .20
*Nos. 1005-1006,C354-C357 (6)* 5.35 1.65

Centenary of the phonograph, invented by Thomas Alva Edison.

**1978, Sept. 4 Photo. *Perf. 14x13***

Designs: 10fr, Henri Dunant and red cross. 25fr, Help on battlefield, 1864, and red cross.

**1007** A204 5fr Prus bl & red .25 .20
**1008** A204 10fr red brn & red .25 .20
**1009** A204 25fr grn & red .25 .20
*Nos. 1007-1009,C358 (4)* 1.20 .80

Dunant (1828-1910), founder of Red Cross.

Threshing, by Raoul Dufy — A205

50fr, Horsemen on Seashore, by Paul Gauguin.

**1978, Nov. 6 Litho. *Perf. 14***
**1010** A205 25fr multi .25 .20
**1011** A205 50fr multi .45 .20
*Nos. 1010-1011,C359-C362 (6)* 4.25 1.85

Eiffel Tower, Paris — A206

Virgin and Child, by Antonello da Messina — A207

**1978, Nov. 27 Photo. *Perf. 14x13***
**1012** A206 50fr multi .40 .20
*Nos. 1012,C365-C367 (4)* 3.25 1.40

Centenary of the Congress of Paris.

**1978, Dec. 18 Litho. *Perf. 14***

Paintings (Virgin and Child): 30fr, by Cario Crivelli. 50fr, by Francesco del Cossa.

**1013** A207 20fr multi .25 .20
**1014** A207 30fr multi .35 .20
**1015** A207 50fr multi .45 .20
*Nos. 1013-1015,C368-C370 (6)* 4.20 1.90

Christmas.

Capt. Cook's Ship off New Zealand — A208

Entry into Jerusalem A209

Design: 50fr, Endeavour in drydock, N.E. Coast of Australia, horiz.

**1979, Feb. 12 Litho. *Perf. 14***
**1016** A208 25fr multi .25 .20
**1017** A208 50fr multi .45 .20
*Nos. 1016-1017,C371-C374 (6)* 4.25 2.40

200th death anniv. of Capt. James Cook.

**1979, Apr. 9**

Easter: 40fr, The Last Supper, horiz. 50fr, Descent from the Cross, horiz.

**1018** A209 30fr multi .25 .20
**1019** A209 40fr multi .30 .20
**1020** A209 50fr multi .35 .20
*Nos. 1018-1020,C375-C377 (6)* 3.35 1.80

Einstein Observatory, Potsdam — A210

Design: 50fr, Einstein and James Ramsay MacDonald, Berlin, 1931.

**1979, July 2 Photo. *Perf. 14x13***
**1021** A210 35fr multi .25 .20
**1022** A210 50fr multi .35 .20
*Nos. 1021-1022,C380-C383 (6)* 3.65 1.90

Albert Einstein (1879-1955), theoretical physicist.

Children and Children's Village Emblem — A211

Man Planting Tree — A212

IYC: 10fr, Mother and children. 15fr, Map of Africa, Children's Village emblem, horiz. 20fr, Woman and children walking to Children's Village, horiz. 25fr, Children sitting under African fan palm. 30fr, Map of Togo with location of Children's Villages.

**1979, July 30 Photo. *Perf. 14x13***
**1023** A211 5fr multi .20 .20
**1024** A211 10fr multi .20 .20
**1025** A211 15fr multi .20 .20
**1026** A211 20fr multi .20 .20
**1027** A211 25fr multi .20 .20
**1028** A211 30fr multi .25 .20
*a.* Souv. sheet of 2, #1027-1028 .75 .45
*Nos. 1023-1028 (6)* 1.25 1.20

**1979, Aug. 13 *Perf. 14x13***
**1029** A212 50fr lilac & green .60 .20

Second Arbor Day. See No. C384.

Sir Rowland Hill (1795-1879), Originator of Penny Postage — A213

Olympic Flame, Lake Placid 80 Emblem, Slalom — A215

Norris Locomotive, 1843 — A214

30fr, French mail-sorting office, 18th cent., horiz. 50fr, Mailbox, Paris, 1850.

**1979, Aug. 27**
**1030** A213 20fr multi .25 .20
**1031** A213 30fr multi .30 .20
**1032** A213 50fr multi .40 .20
*Nos. 1030-1032,C385-C387 (6)* 3.80 1.90

**1979, Oct. 1 Litho. *Perf. 14***

35fr, Stephenson's "Rocket," 1829, vert.

**1033** A214 35fr multi .35 .20
**1034** A214 50fr multi .50 .20
*Nos. 1033-1034,C388-C391 (6)* 4.10 1.90

**1979, Oct. 18 Litho. *Perf. 13½***

1980 Olympic Emblems, Olympic Flame and: 30fr, Yachting 50fr, Discus.

**1035** A215 20fr multi .25 .20
**1036** A215 30fr multi .30 .20
**1037** A215 50fr multi .40 .20
*Nos. 1035-1037,C392-C394 (6)* 3.90 1.90

13th Winter Olympic Games, Lake Placid, NY, 2/12-24/80 (90fr); 22nd Summer Olympic Games, Moscow, 7/19-8/3/80.

Catholic Priests A216

Design: 30fr, Native praying, vert.

**1979, Oct. 29 *Perf. 13x14***
**1038** A216 30fr multi .30 .20
**1039** A216 50fr multi .40 .20
*Nos. 1038-1039,C396-C397 (4)* 1.65 .85

Religions in Togo.

Astronaut Walking on Moon — A217

Design: 50fr, Space capsule orbiting moon.

**1979, Nov. 5**

**1040** A217 35fr multi .30 .20
**1041** A217 50fr multi .40 .20
*Nos. 1040-1041,C398-C401 (6)* 5.25 2.50

Apollo 11 moon landing, 10th anniversary.

Telecom 79 — A218

**1979, Nov. 26 Photo. *Perf. 13x14***

**1042** A218 50fr multi .40 .20

3rd World Telecommunications Exhibition, Geneva, Sept. 20-26. See No. C402.

Holy Family — A219

Rotary Emblem — A220

Christmas: 30fr, Virgin and Child. 50fr, Adoration of the Kings.

**1979, Dec. 17 Litho. *Perf. 14***

**1043** A219 20fr multi .25 .20
**1044** A219 30fr multi .30 .20
**1045** A219 50fr multi .45 .20
*Nos. 1043-1045,C403-C405 (6)* 4.05 1.90

**1980, Jan. 14**

Rotary Emblem and: 30fr, Anniversary emblem. 40fr, Paul P. Harris, Rotary founder.

**1046** A220 25fr multi .20 .20
**1047** A220 30fr multi .25 .20
**1048** A220 40fr multi .30 .20
*Nos. 1046-1048,C406-C408 (6)* 3.25 1.90

Rotary International, 75th anniversary.

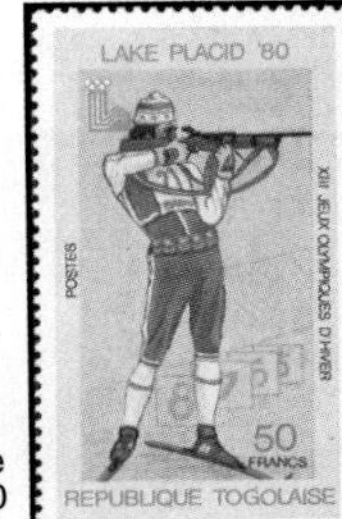


Biathlon, Lake Placid '80 Emblem — A221

**1980, Jan. 31 Litho. *Perf. 13½***

**1049** A221 50fr multi .40 .20
*Nos. 1049,C409-C411 (4)* 3.00 1.40

13th Winter Olympic Games, Lake Placid, NY, Feb. 12-24. See No. C412.

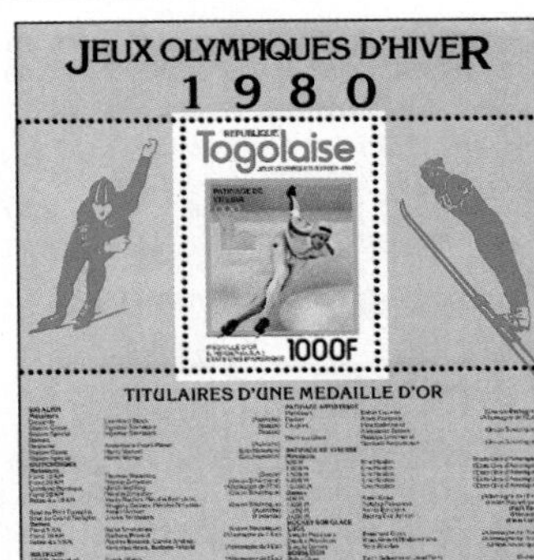


1980 Winter Olympics, Lake Placid — A221a

Gold medalist: No. 1049F, Hanni Wenzel, Liechtenstein, women's slalom. No. 1049G, Eric Heiden, US, men's speed skating. No. 1049H, Jouko Tormanen, Finland, 90-meter ski jumping. No. 1049I, Erich Schaerer, Josef Benz, Switzerland, 2-man bobsled. No. 1049J, US, ice hockey.

**1980 Litho. *Perf. 11***

**Souvenir Sheets**

**1049F** A221a 1000fr gold & multi —
**1049G** A221a 1000fr gold & multi —
**1049H** A221a 1000fr gold & multi —
**1049I** A221a 1000fr gold & multi —
**1049J** A221a 1000fr gold & multi —

Exist imperf.

Swimming, Moscow '80 Emblem — A222

**1980, Feb. 29 Litho. *Perf. 13½***

**1050** A222 20fr shown .20 .20
**1051** A222 30fr Gymnastics .25 .20
**1052** A222 50fr Running .45 .25
*Nos. 1050-1052,C413-C415 (6)* 5.90 3.15

22nd Summer Olympic Games, Moscow, July 19-Aug. 3.

Christ and the Angels, by Andrea Mantegna A223

Easter 1980 (Paintings by): 40fr, Carlo Crivelli. 50fr, Jacopo Pontormo.

**1980, Mar. 31 *Perf. 14***

**1053** A223 30fr multi .35 .20
**1054** A223 40fr multi .40 .20
**1055** A223 50fr multi .45 .20
*Nos. 1053-1055,C416-C418 (6)* 3.90 1.80

Jet over Map of Africa A224

**1980, Mar. 24 Litho. *Perf. 12½***

**1056** A224 50fr multi .60 .20

ASECNA (Air Safety Board), 20th anniv. See No. C419.

Nos. 979, 984 Ovptd. "Londres / 1980"

**Litho. & Embossed**

**1980, May 6 *Perf. 11***

**1056A** A192 1000fr gold & multi 6.50 —

**Souvenir Sheet**

**1056B** A192 1000fr gold & multi 7.25 —

12th World Telecommunications Day — A225

**1980, May 17 Photo. *Perf. 14x13½***

**1057** A225 50fr multi .50 .20

See No. C420.

Red Cross over Globe Showing Lomé, Togo — A226

**1980, June 16 Photo. *Perf. 14x13***

**1058** A226 50fr multi .60 .20

Togolese Red Cross. See No. C421.

Jules Verne (1828-1905), French Science Fiction Writer — A227

Baroness James de Rothschild, by Ingres — A228

50fr, Shark (20,000 Leagues Under the Sea).

**1980, July 14 Litho. *Perf. 14***

**1059** A227 30fr multi .30 .20
**1060** A227 50fr multi .45 .20
*Nos. 1059-1060,C422-C425 (6)* 4.20 1.85

**1980, Aug. 29 Litho. *Perf. 14***

Paintings by Jean Auguste Dominique Ingres (1780-1867): 30fr, Napoleon I on Imperial Throne. 40fr, Don Pedro of Toledo and Henri IV.

**1061** A228 25fr multi .25 .20
**1062** A228 30fr multi .35 .20
**1063** A228 40fr multi .40 .20
*Nos. 1061-1063,C426-C428 (6)* 4.25 1.90

Minnie Holding Mirror for Leopard A229

Disney Characters and Animals from Fazao Reserve: 2fr, Goofy (Dingo) cleaning teethof hippopotamus. 3fr, Donald holding snout of crocodile. 4fr, Donald dangling over clifffrom horn of rhinoceros. 5fr, Goofy riding water buffalo. 10fr, Monkey taking picture of Mickey. 100fr, Mickey as doctor examining giraffe with sore throat. 200fr, Pluto in party hat. No. 1071, Elephant giving shower to Goofy. No. 1072, Lion carrying Goofy by seat of his pants. No. 1072A, Pluto.

**1980, Sept. 15 *Perf. 11***

**1064** A229 1fr multi .20 .20
**1065** A229 2fr multi .20 .20
**1066** A229 3fr multi .20 .20
**1067** A229 4fr multi .20 .20
**1068** A229 5fr multi .20 .20
**1069** A229 10fr multi .20 .20
**1070** A229 100fr multi .75 .35
**1070A** A229 200fr multi 1.50 .75
**1071** A229 300fr multi 2.25 1.10
*Nos. 1064-1071 (9)* 5.70 3.40

**Souvenir Sheets**

**1072** A229 300fr multi 3.00 1.10
**1072A** A229 300fr multi 3.00 1.10

50th anniv. of the Disney character Pluto.

Market Activities, Women Preparing Meat A230

**1980-81 *Perf. 14***

**1073** A230 1fr Grinding savo .20 .20
**1074** A230 2fr shown .20 .20
**1075** A230 3fr Truck going to market .20 .20
**1076** A230 4fr Unloading produce .20 .20
**1077** A230 5fr Sugar cane vendor .20 .20
**1078** A230 6fr Barber curling child's hair, vert. .20 .20
**1079** A230 7fr Vegetable vendor .20 .20
**1080** A230 8fr Sampling mangos, vert. .20 .20
**1081** A230 9fr Grain vendor .20 .20
**1082** A230 10fr Spiced fish vendor .20 .20
**1083** A230 15fr Clay pot vendor .20 .20
**1084** A230 20fr Straw baskets .20 .20
**1085** A230 25fr Selling lemons and onions, vert. .20 .20
**1086** A230 30fr Straw baskets, diff. .25 .20
**1087** A230 40fr Shore market .30 .20
**1087A** A230 45fr Vegatable stall .30 .20
**1088** A230 50fr Women carrying produce, vert. .40 .20
**1088A** A230 60fr Rice wine .40 .20
*Nos. 1073-1088A (18)* 4.25 3.60

Issued: 45fr, 60fr, 3/8/81; others, 3/17/80.
Nos. 1087A, 1088A dated 1980.
See Nos. C440-C445, J68-J71. For overprints see Nos. C486-C487.

Commemorative Wreath — A231

Famous Men of the Decade: 40fr, Mao Tse-tung, vert.

**1980, Feb. 11** ***Perf. 14x13***
**1089** A231 25fr multi .40 .20
**1090** A231 40fr emer grn & dk grn .60 .20
*Nos. 1089-1090,C429-C431 (5)* 5.10 1.70

World Tourism Conference, Manila, Sept. 27 — A232

**1980, Sept. 15** **Litho.** ***Perf. 14***
**1091** A232 50fr Hotel tourism emblem, vert. .50 .25
**1092** A232 150fr shown 1.50 .75

Map of Australia and Human Rights Flame A233

**1980, Oct. 13** **Photo.** ***Perf. 13x14***
**1093** A233 30fr shown .30 .20
**1094** A233 50fr Europe and Asia map .50 .25
*Nos. 1093-1094,C432-C433 (4)* 2.20 1.15

Declaration of Human Rights, 30th anniv.

#980, 985 Ovptd. in Gold & Black

**Litho. & Embossed**

**1980, Nov. 24** ***Perf. 11***
**1094A** A192 1000fr gold & multi 8.00 —

**Souvenir Sheet**

**1094B** A192 1000fr gold & multi 7.25 —

No. 1094B ovptd. with additional text and black bars in sheet margin.

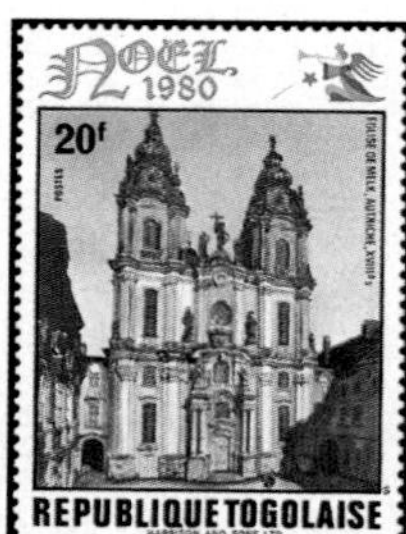

Melk Monastery, Austria, 18th Century A234

***Perf. 14½x13½***

**1980, Dec. 22** **Litho.**
**1095** A234 20fr shown .25 .20
**1096** A234 30fr Tarragon Cathedral, Spain, 12th cent. .35 .20
**1097** A234 50fr St. John the Baptist, Florence, 1964 .55 .25
*Nos. 1095-1097,C435-C437 (6)* 4.35 2.15

Christmas.

African Postal Union, 5th Anniversary A235

**1980, Dec. 24** **Photo.** ***Perf. 13½***
**1098** A235 100fr multi .75 .35

February 2nd Hotel Opening A236

**1981, Feb. 2** **Litho.** ***Perf. 12½x13***
**1099** A236 50fr multi .60 .25

See No. C437B.

A236a

A237

**1981, Dec. 21** **Litho.** ***Perf. 12½***
**1100** A236a 70fr lt grn & multi .70 .35

West African Rice Development Assoc. See No. C461.

**1981, Apr. 13** ***Perf. 14½x13½***

Easter (Rembrandt Paintings): 30fr, Rembrandt's Father. 40fr, Self-portrait. 50fr, Artist's father as an old man. 60fr, Rider on Horseback.

**1101** A237 30fr multi .30 .20
**1102** A237 40fr multi .35 .20
**1103** A237 50fr multi .45 .20
**1104** A237 60fr multi .55 .25
*Nos. 1101-1104,C438-C439 (6)* 4.05 1.85

Wedding of Prince Charles and Lady Diana Spencer — A237a

**1981, July 29** **Litho.** ***Perf. 11***
**1105** A237a 1000fr gold & multi 5.75 3.00

**Souvenir Sheet**

**Litho. & Embossed**

**1106** A237a 1000fr Charles & Diana, diff. 7.25 3.50

No. 1105 printed with embossed se-tenant label.
For overprints see Nos. 1143A-1143B.

Red-headed Rock Fowl — A238

**1981, Aug. 10** ***Perf. 13½x14½***
**1107** A238 30fr shown .45 .20
**1108** A238 40fr Splendid sunbird .55 .20
**1109** A238 60fr Violet-backed starling .90 .20
**1110** A238 90fr Red-collared widowbird 1.40 .30
*Nos. 1107-1110,C446-C447 (6)* 5.60 1.45

1982 World Soccer Championships, Spain — A238a

Flags (Nos. 1110A-1110E) or Players (Nos. 1110F-1110J) and stadiums: Nos. 1110A, 1110F, Athletico de Madrid. Nos. 1110B, 1110G, Real Madrid C.F. Nos. 1110C, 1110H, R.C.D. Espanol. Nos. 1110D, 1110I, Real Zaragoza. Nos. 1110E, 1110J, Valencia.

**Litho. & Embossed**

**1981, Aug. 17** ***Perf. 11***
**1110A-1110E** A238a 1000fr Set of 5 37.50 9.00

**Souvenir Sheets**

**1110F-1110J** A238a 1000fr Set of 5 30.00 9.00

African Postal Union Ministers, 6th Council Meeting, July 28-20 A239

**1981, Aug. 31** **Litho.** ***Perf. 12½***
**1111** A239 70fr Dish antenna .50 .25
**1112** A239 90fr Computer operator, vert. .70 .35
**1113** A239 105fr Map .80 .40
*Nos. 1111-1113 (3)* 2.00 1.00

Intl. Year of the Disabled A240

**1981, Aug. 31** ***Perf. 14***
**1114** A240 70fr Blind man .75 .35
*Nos. 1114,C448-C449 (3)* 2.80 1.30

See No. C449A.

Woman with Hat, by Picasso, 1961 — A241

Picasso Birth Centenary: Sculptures.

**1981, Sept. 14** ***Perf. 14½x13½***
**1116** A241 25fr shown .25 .20
**1117** A241 50fr She-goat .45 .20
**1118** A241 60fr Violin, 1915 .50 .20
*Nos. 1116-1118,C450-C452 (6)* 4.45 1.90

Aix-la-Chapelle Cathedral, Germany — A242

World Heritage Year: 40fr, Geyser, Yellowstone Natl. Park. 50fr, Nahanni Natl. Park, Canada. 60fr, Stone churches, Ethiopia.

**1981, Sept. 28** ***Perf. 13½x14½***
**1119** A242 30fr multi .25 .20
**1120** A242 40fr multi .30 .20
**1121** A242 50fr multi .35 .20
**1122** A242 60fr multi .45 .30
*Nos. 1119-1122,C453-C454 (6)* 3.60 2.00

Yuri Gagarin's Vostok I, 20th. — A243

Space Anniversaries: 50fr, 20th Anniv. of Alan Shepard's Flight. 60fr, Lunar Orbiter I, 15th.

**1981, Nov.** ***Perf. 14***
**1123** A243 25fr multi .20 .20
**1124** A243 50fr multi .35 .20
**1125** A243 60fr multi .45 .25
*Nos. 1123-1125,C455-C456 (5)* 2.45 1.40

Christmas A244

Rubens Paintings: 20fr, Adoration of the Kings. 30fr, Adoration of the Shepherds. 50fr, St. Catherine.

*Perf. 14½x13½*

**1981, Dec. 10** **Litho.**
**1126** A244 20fr multi .25 .20
**1127** A244 30fr multi .25 .20
**1128** A244 50fr multi .40 .20
*Nos. 1126-1128,C457-C459 (6)* 5.20 2.60

15th Anniv. of Natl. Liberation — A245

**1982, Jan. 13** **Litho.** ***Perf. 12½***
**1129** A245 70fr Dove, flag .70 .35
**1130** A245 90fr Citizens, Pres. Eyadema, vert. .90 .45
*Nos. 1129-1130,C462-C463 (4)* 3.20 1.55

Scouting Year A246

**1982, Feb. 25** **Litho.** ***Perf. 14***
**1131** A246 70fr Pitching tent .55 .25
*Nos. 1131,C464-C467 (5)* 4.50 1.80

Easter — A247

Designs: The Ten Commandments.

**1982, Mar. 15** ***Perf. 14x14½***
**1132** A247 10fr multi .20 .20
**1133** A247 25fr multi .20 .20
**1134** A247 30fr multi .20 .20
**1135** A247 45fr multi .30 .20
**1136** A247 50fr multi .35 .20
**1137** A247 70fr multi .45 .25
**1138** A247 90fr multi .60 .30
*Nos. 1132-1138,C469-C470 (9)* 3.80 2.30

Papilio Dardanus A248

**1982, July 15** **Litho.** ***Perf. 14½x14***
**1139** A248 15fr shown .45 .20
**1140** A248 20fr Belenois calypso .45 .20
**1141** A248 25fr Palla decius .45 .20
*Nos. 1139-1141,C474-C475 (5)* 4.35 1.25

1982 World Cup — A249

Designs: Various soccer players.

**1982, July 26** ***Perf. 14x14½***
**1142** A249 25fr multi .25 .20
**1143** A249 45fr multi .35 .20
*Nos. 1142-1143,C477-C479 (5)* 4.90 2.40

For overprints see Nos. 1150-1155.

Nos. 1105-1106 Ovptd. "BEBE ROYALE 21 JUIN 1982" on one or two lines

**1982, Oct. 28** **Litho.** ***Perf. 11***
**1143A** A237a 1000fr gold & multi 7.25 3.50

**Souvenir Sheet**
**Litho. & Embossed**

**1143B** A237a 1000fr gold & multi 9.25 3.50

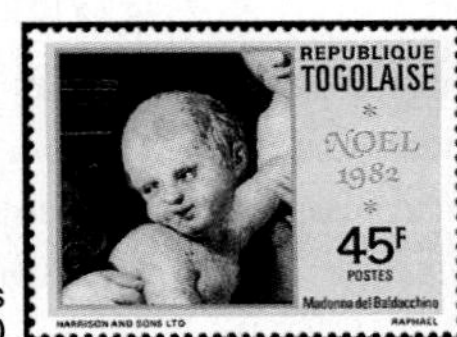


Christmas A250

Madonna of Baldacchino, by Raphael. #1144-1148 show details; #1149 entire painting.

**1982, Dec. 24** **Litho.** ***Perf. 14½x14***
**1144** A250 45fr multi .35 .20
**1145** A250 70fr multi .55 .25
**1146** A250 105fr multi .85 .35
**1147** A250 130fr multi 1.10 .40
**1148** A250 150fr multi 1.20 .50
*Nos. 1144-1148 (5)* 4.05 1.70

**Souvenir Sheet**
***Perf. 14x14½***

**1149** A250 500fr multi, vert. 4.00 1.60

Nos. 1142-1143, C477-C480 Overprinted: VAINQUER / COUPE DU MONDE / FOOTBALL 82 / "ITALIE"

**1983, Jan. 31** **Litho.** ***Perf. 14x14½***
**1150** A249 25fr multi .20 .20
**1151** A249 45fr multi .30 .20
**1152** A249 105fr multi .70 .35
**1153** A249 200fr multi 1.40 .65
**1154** A249 300fr multi 2.00 1.00
*Nos. 1150-1154 (5)* 4.60 2.40

**Souvenir Sheet**

**1155** A249 500fr multi 4.25 2.50

Italy's victory in 1982 World Cup. Nos. 1152-1155 airmail.

20th Anniv. of West African Monetary Union (1982) — A251

**1983, May** **Litho.** ***Perf. 12½x12***
**1156** A251 70fr Map .60 .25
**1157** A251 90fr Emblem .80 .30

Visit of Pres. Mitterand of France, Jan. 13-15 — A252

**1983, Jan. 13** **Litho.** ***Perf. 13***
**1158** A252 35fr Sokode Regional Hospital .30 .20
*a.* Souvenir sheet, imperf. .85 .45
**1159** A252 45fr Citizens joining hands .35 .20
*a.* Souvenir sheet, imperf. .85 .45
**1160** A252 70fr Soldiers, vert. .50 .25
*a.* Souvenir sheet, imperf. .85 .45
**1161** A252 90fr Pres. Mitterand, vert. .70 .30
*a.* Souvenir sheet, imperf. .85 .45
**1162** A252 105fr Pres. Eyadema, Mitterand, vert. .80 .35
*a.* Souvenir sheet, imperf. .85 .45
**1163** A252 130fr Greeting crowd 1.00 .40
*a.* Souvenir sheet, imperf. .85 .45
*Nos. 1158-1163 (6)* 3.65 1.70

Nos. 1161-1163 airmail.

Easter — A253

Paintings: 35fr, Mourners at the Death of Christ, by Bellini. 70fr, Crucifixion, by Raphael. 90fr, Descent from the Cross, by Carracci. 500fr Christ, by Reni.

**1983** **Litho.** ***Perf. 13½x14½***
**1164** A253 35fr multi .25 .20
**1165** A253 70fr multi, vert. .50 .20
**1166** A253 90fr multi .75 .20
*Nos. 1164-1166 (3)* 1.50 .60

**Souvenir Sheet**
***Perf. 14½x13½***

**1167** A253 500fr multi 4.00 1.50

90fr, 500fr airmail.

Folkdances — A254

**1983, Dec. 1** ***Perf. 14½x14***
**1168** A254 70fr Kondona .55 .20
**1169** A254 90fr Kondona, diff. .65 .20
**1170** A254 105fr Toubole .80 .20
**1171** A254 130fr Adjogbo .90 .20
*Nos. 1168-1171 (4)* 2.90 .80

90fr, 105fr, 130fr airmail.

World Communications Year — A255

**1983, June 20** **Litho.** ***Perf. 14x14½***
**1172** A255 70fr Drummer .60 .20
**1173** A255 90fr Modern communication .70 .20

90fr airmail.

Christmas — A256

**1983, Dec.** ***Perf. 13½x14½***
**1174** A256 70fr Catholic Church, Kante .25 .20
**1175** A256 90fr Altar, Dapaong Cathedral .30 .20
**1176** A256 105fr Protestant Church, Dapaong .35 .20
*Nos. 1174-1176 (3)* .90 .60

**Souvenir Sheet**

**1177** A256 500fr Ecumenical Church, Pya 4.00 1.50

90fr, 105fr, 500fr airmail.

Sarakawa Presidential Assassination Attempt, 10th Anniv. — A257

**1984, Jan. 24** **Litho.** ***Perf. 13***
**1178** A257 70fr Wrecked plane .55 .20
**1179** A257 90fr Plane, diff. .65 .20
**1180** A257 120fr Memorial Hall .90 .20
**1181** A257 270fr Pres. Eyadema statue, vert. 2.00 .40
*Nos. 1178-1181 (4)* 4.10 1.00

120fr, 270fr airmail.

20th Anniv. of World Food Program (1983) A258

**1984, May 2** **Litho.** ***Perf. 13***
**1182** A258 35fr Orchard .20 .20
**1183** A258 70fr Fruit tree .25 .20
**1184** A258 90fr Rice paddy .30 .20
*Nos. 1182-1184 (3)* .75 .60

**Souvenir Sheet**

**1185** A258 300fr Village, horiz. 2.25 1.50

25th Anniv. of Council of Unity — A259

Easter 1984 — A260

**1984, May 29** ***Perf. 12***
**1186** A259 70fr multi .50 .20
**1187** A259 90fr multi .65 .20

**1984** **Litho.** ***Perf. 14x14½***

Various stained-glass windows.

**1188** A260 70fr multi .50 .20
**1189** A260 90fr multi .60 .20
**1190** A260 120fr multi .75 .20
**1191** A260 270fr multi 1.75 .45
**1192** A260 300fr multi 1.90 .50
*Nos. 1188-1192 (5)* 5.50 1.55

**Souvenir Sheet**

**1193** A260 500fr multi 4.00 3.00

Nos. 1189-1193 airmail.

Centenary of German-Togolese Friendship — A261

#1194, Degbenou Catholic Mission, 1893. #1195, Kara Bridge, 1911. #1196, Treaty Site, Baguida, 1884. #1197, Degbenou Students, 1893. #1198, Sansane Administrative Post, 1908. #1199, Adjido Official School.

#1200, Sokode Cotton Market, 1910. #1201, William Fountain, Atakpame, 1906. #1202, Lome Main Street, 1895, No. 19. #1203, Police, 1905. #1204, Lome Railroad Construction. #1205, Governor's Palace, Lome, 1905. #1206, No. 9, Commerce Street, Lome.

#1207, Nos. 10, 17. #1208, Lome Wharf, 1903. #1209, G. Nachtigal. #1210, Wilhelm II. #1211, O.F. de Bismark. #1212, J. de Puttkamer. #1213, A. Koehler. #1214, W. Horn. #1215, J.G. de Zech. #1216, E. Bruckner. #1217, A.F. de Mecklenburg. #1218, H.G. de Doering. #1219, Land Development, 1908.

#1220, Postal Courier, No. 8. #1221, Treaty Signers, 1885. 150fr, German & Togolese Children, Flags. #1223, Aneho Line Locomotive, 1905. #1224, Mallet Locomotive, 1907. #1225, German Ship "Mowe," 1884. #1226, "La Sophie," 1884. 300fr, Pres. Eyadema, Helmut Kohl.

**1984, July 5 Litho. *Perf. 13***

| | | | | | |
|---|---|---|---|---|---|
| **1194** | A261 | 35fr | multi | .50 | .20 |
| **1195** | A261 | 35fr | multi | .50 | .20 |
| **1196** | A261 | 35fr | multi, vert. | .50 | .20 |
| **1197** | A261 | 35fr | multi | .50 | .20 |
| **1198** | A261 | 35fr | multi | .50 | .20 |
| **1199** | A261 | 35fr | multi | .50 | .20 |
| **1200** | A261 | 35fr | multi | .50 | .20 |
| **1201** | A261 | 45fr | multi, vert. | .50 | .20 |
| **1202** | A261 | 45fr | multi | .50 | .20 |
| **1203** | A261 | 45fr | multi | .50 | .20 |
| **1204** | A261 | 45fr | multi | .50 | .20 |
| **1205** | A261 | 45fr | multi | .50 | .20 |
| **1206** | A261 | 45fr | multi | .50 | .20 |
| **1207** | A261 | 70fr | multi | .60 | .20 |
| **1208** | A261 | 70fr | multi | .60 | .20 |
| **1209** | A261 | 90fr | multi, vert. | .75 | .20 |
| **1210** | A261 | 90fr | multi, vert. | .75 | .20 |
| **1211** | A261 | 90fr | multi, vert. | .75 | .20 |
| **1212** | A261 | 90fr | multi, vert. | .75 | .20 |
| **1213** | A261 | 90fr | multi, vert. | .75 | .20 |
| **1214** | A261 | 90fr | multi, vert. | .75 | .20 |
| **1215** | A261 | 90fr | multi, vert. | .75 | .20 |
| **1216** | A261 | 90fr | multi, vert. | .75 | .20 |
| **1217** | A261 | 90fr | multi, vert. | .75 | .20 |
| **1218** | A261 | 90fr | multi, vert. | .75 | .20 |
| **1219** | A261 | 90fr | multi | .75 | .20 |
| **1220** | A261 | 120fr | multi, vert. | 1.00 | .20 |
| **1221** | A261 | 120fr | multi | 1.00 | .20 |
| **1222** | A261 | 150fr | multi, vert. | 1.25 | .25 |
| **1223** | A261 | 270fr | multi | 2.25 | .45 |
| **1224** | A261 | 270fr | multi | 2.25 | .45 |
| **1225** | A261 | 270fr | multi | 2.25 | .45 |
| **1226** | A261 | 270fr | multi | 2.25 | .45 |
| **1227** | A261 | 300fr | multi | 2.40 | .50 |
| | | | *Nos. 1194-1227 (34)* | 30.60 | 8.15 |

Souvenir sheets of one exist for each design. Stamp size: 65x80mm. Value, set of 34, $35.

Donald Duck, 50th Anniv. A262

**1984, Sept. 21 Litho. *Perf. 11***

| | | | | | |
|---|---|---|---|---|---|
| **1230** | A262 | 1fr | Donald, Chip | .55 | .20 |
| **1231** | A262 | 2fr | Donald, Chip and Dale | .55 | .20 |
| **1232** | A262 | 3fr | Louie, Chip and Dale | .55 | .20 |
| **1233** | A262 | 5fr | Donald, Chip | .55 | .20 |
| **1234** | A262 | 10fr | Daisy Duck, Donald | .55 | .20 |
| **1235** | A262 | 15fr | Goofy, Donald | .55 | .20 |
| **1236** | A262 | 105fr | Huey, Dewey and Louie | .80 | .20 |
| **1237** | A262 | 500fr | Nephews, Donald | 3.75 | .70 |
| **1238** | A262 | 1000fr | Nephews, Donald | 8.25 | 1.40 |
| | | | *Nos. 1230-1238 (9)* | 16.10 | 3.50 |

**Souvenir Sheets**

***Perf. 14***

| | | | | | |
|---|---|---|---|---|---|
| **1239** | A262 | 1000fr | Surprised Donald | 7.50 | 7.50 |
| **1240** | A262 | 1000fr | Perplexed Donald | 7.50 | 7.50 |

Nos. 1236-1240 airmail.
For overprints see Nos. C551-C554.

Endangered Mammals — A263

**1984, Oct. 1 Litho. *Perf. 15x14½***

| | | | | | |
|---|---|---|---|---|---|
| **1241** | A263 | 45fr | Manatee swimming | .95 | .30 |
| **1242** | A263 | 70fr | Manatee eating | 1.25 | .30 |
| **1243** | A263 | 90fr | Manatees floating | 2.40 | .50 |
| **1244** | A263 | 105fr | Young manatee, mother | 3.00 | .50 |
| | | | *Nos. 1241-1244 (4)* | 7.60 | 1.60 |

**Souvenir Sheets**

***Perf. 14x15, 15x14***

| | | | | | |
|---|---|---|---|---|---|
| **1245** | A263 | 1000fr | Olive Colobus monkey, vert. | 10.00 | 6.00 |
| **1246** | A263 | 1000fr | Galago (Bushbaby) | 10.00 | 6.00 |

Nos. 1243-1246 airmail. See #1444-1447.

Birth Centenary of Eleanor Roosevelt A264

**1984, Oct. 10 Litho. *Perf. 13½***

| | | | | | |
|---|---|---|---|---|---|
| **1247** | A264 | 70fr | shown | .55 | .20 |
| **1248** | A264 | 90fr | Mrs. Roosevelt, Statue of Liberty | .70 | .20 |

No. 1248 airmail.

Classic Automobiles — A265

**1984, Nov. 15 Litho. *Perf. 15***

| | | | | | |
|---|---|---|---|---|---|
| **1249** | A265 | 1fr | 1947 Bristol | .85 | .20 |
| **1250** | A265 | 2fr | 1925 Frazer Nash | .85 | .20 |
| **1251** | A265 | 3fr | 1950 Healey | .85 | .20 |
| **1252** | A265 | 4fr | 1925 Kissell | .85 | .20 |
| **1253** | A265 | 50fr | 1927 La Salle | .85 | .20 |
| **1254** | A265 | 90fr | 1921 Minerva | 1.00 | .20 |
| **1255** | A265 | 500fr | 1950 Morgan | 5.75 | .70 |
| **1256** | A265 | 1000fr | 1921 Napier | 12.00 | 1.40 |
| | | | *Nos. 1249-1256 (8)* | 23.00 | 3.30 |

**Souvenir Sheets**

| | | | | | |
|---|---|---|---|---|---|
| **1257** | A265 | 1000fr | 1941 Nash | 9.00 | 2.00 |
| **1258** | A265 | 1000fr | 1903 Peugeot | 9.00 | 2.00 |

Nos. 1254-1258 airmail.
For overprints see Nos. 1328-1331, C542-C544, C564-C565.

Christmas A266

***Perf. 14½x13½***

**1984, Nov. 23 Litho.**

| | | | | | |
|---|---|---|---|---|---|
| **1259** | A266 | 70fr | Connestable Madonna | .50 | .20 |
| **1260** | A266 | 290fr | Cowper Madonna | 1.90 | .40 |
| **1261** | A266 | 300fr | Alba Madonna | 1.90 | .45 |
| **1262** | A266 | 500fr | Madonna of the Curtain | 3.25 | .70 |
| | | | *Nos. 1259-1262 (4)* | 7.55 | 1.75 |

**Souvenir Sheet**

| | | | | | |
|---|---|---|---|---|---|
| **1263** | A266 | 1000fr | Madonna with Child | 7.25 | 6.00 |

Nos. 1260-1263 airmail.

African Locomotives — A267

**1984, Nov. 30 Litho. *Perf. 15***

| | | | | | |
|---|---|---|---|---|---|
| **1264** | A267 | 1fr | Decapod, Madeira | .45 | .20 |
| **1265** | A267 | 2fr | 2-6-0, Egypt | .45 | .20 |
| **1266** | A267 | 3fr | 4-8-2+2-8-4, Algeria | .45 | .20 |
| **1267** | A267 | 4fr | Congo-Ocean diesel | .45 | .20 |
| **1268** | A267 | 50fr | 0-4-0+0-4-0, Libya | .45 | .20 |
| **1269** | A267 | 90fr | #49, Malawi | .55 | .20 |
| **1270** | A267 | 105fr | 1907 Mallet, Togo | .65 | .20 |
| **1271** | A267 | 500fr | 4-8-2, Rhodesia | 3.00 | .70 |
| **1272** | A267 | 1000fr | Beyer-Garratt, East Africa | 5.75 | 1.40 |
| | | | *Nos. 1264-1272 (9)* | 12.20 | 3.50 |

**Souvenir Sheets**

| | | | | | |
|---|---|---|---|---|---|
| **1273** | A267 | 1000fr | 2-8-2, Ghana | 9.00 | 6.00 |
| **1274** | A267 | 1000fr | Locomotive, Senegal | 9.00 | 6.00 |

Nos. 1269-1274 airmail.
For overprints see Nos. 1343-1346, 1356-1360, C541, C566.

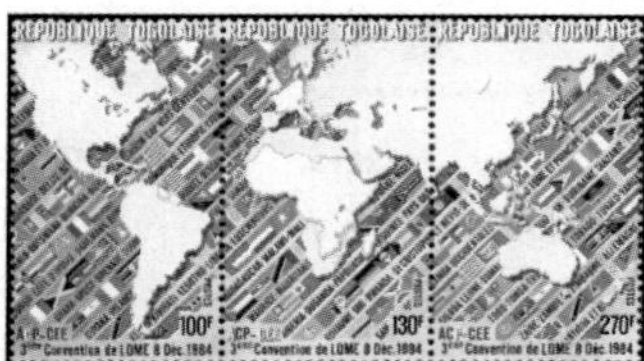
Economic Convention, Lome — A268

**1984, Dec. 8 Litho. *Perf. 12½***

| | | | | |
|---|---|---|---|---|
| **1275** | 100fr | Map of the Americas | .65 | .20 |
| **1276** | 130fr | Map of Eurasia, Africa | .95 | .20 |
| **1277** | 270fr | Map of Asia, Australia | 1.60 | .40 |
| ***a.*** | A268 | Strip of 3, #1275-1277 | 3.50 | 3.50 |

**Souvenir Sheet**

| | | | | | |
|---|---|---|---|---|---|
| **1278** | A268 | 500fr | President Eyadema | 4.00 | 3.50 |

No. 1277a has continuous design.

Intl. Civil Aviation Org., 40th Anniv. A269

Map of Togo, ICAO emblem and: 70fr, Lockheed Constellation, 1944. 105fr, Boeing 707, 1954. 200fr, Doublas DC-8-61, 1966. 500fr, Bac/Sud Concorde, 1966. 1000fr, Icarus, by Hans Erni.

**1984, Oct. 15 Litho. *Perf. 15x14***

| | | | | | |
|---|---|---|---|---|---|
| **1279** | A269 | 70fr | multi | .55 | .20 |
| **1280** | A269 | 105fr | multi | .70 | .20 |
| **1281** | A269 | 200fr | multi | 1.10 | .20 |
| **1282** | A269 | 500fr | multi | 2.75 | .50 |
| | | | *Nos. 1279-1282 (4)* | 5.10 | 1.10 |

**Souvenir Sheet**

| | | | | | |
|---|---|---|---|---|---|
| **1283** | A269 | 1000fr | multi | 6.50 | 6.00 |

Nos. 1280-1283 airmail.

Fresco of the 12 Apostles, Baptistry of the Aryans, Ravenna, Italy, — A270

Designs: 1fr, St. Paul. 2fr, St. Thomas. 3fr, St. Matthew. 4fr, St. James the Younger. 5fr, St. Simon. 70fr, St. Thaddeaus Judas. 90fr, St. Bartholomew. 105fr, St. Philip. 200fr, St. John. 270fr, St. James the Greater. 400fr, St. Andrew. 500fr, St. Peter. No. 1296, The Last Supper, by Andrea del Castagno, c. 1421-1457, horiz. No, 1297, Coronation of the Virgin, by Raphael, 1483-1520, horiz.

**1984, Dec. 14 *Perf. 15***

| | | | | | |
|---|---|---|---|---|---|
| **1284** | A270 | 1fr | multi | 1.00 | .20 |
| **1285** | A270 | 2fr | multi | 1.00 | .20 |
| **1286** | A270 | 3fr | multi | 1.00 | .20 |
| **1287** | A270 | 4fr | multi | 1.00 | .20 |
| **1288** | A270 | 5fr | multi | 1.00 | .20 |
| **1289** | A270 | 70fr | multi | 1.00 | .20 |
| **1290** | A270 | 90fr | multi | 1.00 | .20 |
| **1291** | A270 | 105fr | multi | 1.00 | .20 |
| **1292** | A270 | 200fr | multi | 2.25 | .20 |
| **1293** | A270 | 270fr | multi | 3.00 | .30 |
| **1294** | A270 | 400fr | multi | 4.25 | .40 |
| **1295** | A270 | 500fr | multi | 5.25 | .50 |
| | | | *Nos. 1284-1295 (12)* | 22.75 | 3.00 |

**Souvenir Sheets**

| | | | | |
|---|---|---|---|---|
| **1296-1297** | A270 | 1000fr each | 14.00 | 4.00 |

Nos. 1290-1297 airmail.
For overprints see Nos. C545-C547.

Race Horses A271

**1985, Jan. 10**

| | | | | | |
|---|---|---|---|---|---|
| **1298** | A271 | 1fr | Allez France | .70 | .20 |
| **1299** | A271 | 2fr | Arkle, vert. | .70 | .20 |
| **1300** | A271 | 3fr | Tingle Creek, vert. | .70 | .20 |
| **1301** | A271 | 4fr | Interco | .70 | .20 |
| **1302** | A271 | 50fr | Dawn Run | .70 | .20 |
| **1303** | A271 | 90fr | Seattle Slew, vert. | .70 | .20 |
| **1304** | A271 | 500fr | Nijinsky | 3.25 | .50 |
| **1305** | A271 | 1000fr | Politician | 6.50 | 1.00 |
| | | | *Nos. 1298-1305 (8)* | 13.95 | 2.70 |

**Souvenir Sheets**

| | | | | | |
|---|---|---|---|---|---|
| **1306** | A271 | 1000fr | Shergar | 9.00 | 6.50 |
| **1307** | A271 | 1000fr | Red Rum | 9.00 | 6.50 |

Nos. 1303-1307 airmail.
For overprints see Nos. 1353-1355A.

Easter — A272

Paintings by Raphael (1483-1520).

*Perf. 13½x14½, 14½x13½*

**1985, Mar. 7**

**1308** A272 70fr Christ and His Flock .70 .20
**1309** A272 90fr Christ and the Fishermen .70 .20
**1310** A272 135fr The Blessed Christ, vert. .85 .20
**1311** A272 150fr The Entombment, vert. 1.00 .20
**1312** A272 250fr The Resurrection, vert. 1.75 .25
*Nos. 1308-1312 (5)* 5.00 1.05

**Souvenir Sheet**

**1313** A272 1000fr The Resurrection, diff. 7.50 6.00

Nos. 1309-1313 airmail.

Technical & Cultural Cooperation Agency, 15th Anniv. — A273

**1985, Mar. 20** *Perf. 12½*

**1314** A273 70fr multi .60 .20
**1315** A273 90fr multi .60 .20

Philexafrica '85, Lome — A274

**1985, May 9** *Perf. 13*

**1316** A274 200fr Woman carrying fruit basket 1.90 .20
**1317** A274 200fr Man plowing field 1.90 .20
*a.* Pair, #1316-1317 + label 4.00 3.50

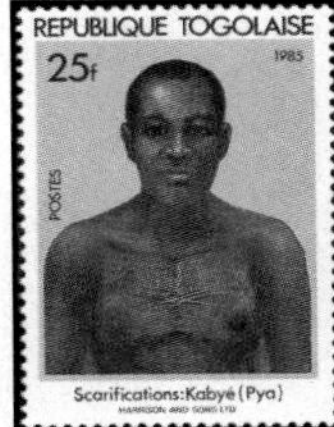


Scarification Ritual — A275

**1985, May 14** *Perf. 14x15*

**1318** A275 25fr Kabye (Pya) .60 .20
**1319** A275 70fr Mollah (Kotokoli) .60 .20
**1320** A275 90fr Maba (Dapaong) .60 .20
**1321** A275 105fr Kabye (Pagouda) .75 .20
**1322** A275 270fr Peda 1.75 .30
*Nos. 1318-1322 (5)* 4.30 1.10

Nos. 1320-1322 airmail.

Seashells A276

70fr, Clavatula muricata. 90fr, Marginella desjardini. 120fr, Clavatula nifat. 135fr, Cypraea stercoraria. 270fr, Conus genuanus. 1000fr, Dancers wearing traditional shell decorations.

**1985, June 1** *Perf. 15x14*

**1323** A276 70fr multi 1.00 .20
**1324** A276 90fr multi 1.00 .20
**1325** A276 120fr multi 1.25 .20
**1326** A276 135fr multi 1.25 .20
**1327** A276 270fr multi 2.75 .30
*Nos. 1323-1327 (5)* 7.25 1.10

**Souvenir Sheet**

**1327A** A276 1000fr multi 7.50 6.00

Nos. 1324-1327A airmail.

Nos. 1253, 1256-1258 Overprinted "Exposition Mondiale 1985 / Tsukuba, Japon"

**1985, June** *Perf. 15*

**1328** A265 50fr #1253 1.10 .20
**1329** A265 1000fr #1256 10.50 3.00

**Souvenir Sheets**

**1330** A265 1000fr #1257 9.00 3.50
**1331** A265 1000fr #1258 9.00 3.50

EXPO '85.

Audubon Birth Bicent. — A277

Illustrations by artist-naturalist J.J. Audubon (1785-1851).

**1985, Aug. 13** *Perf. 13*

**1332** A277 90fr Larus bonapartii .85 .20
**1333** A277 120fr Pelecanus occidentalis 1.10 .20
**1334** A277 135fr Cassidix mexicanus 1.10 .20
**1335** A277 270fr Aquila chrysaetos 2.40 .30
**1336** A277 500fr Picus erythrocephalus 4.25 .50
*Nos. 1332-1336 (5)* 9.70 1.40

**Souvenir Sheet**

**1337** A277 1000fr Dendroica petechia 7.50 6.00

Nos. 1332, 1334 and 1336-1337 airmail.

Dove, UN Emblem — A278

Kara Port Construction — A279

Designs: 115fr, Hands, UN emblem. 250fr, Millet crop, Atalote Research Facility. 500fr, UN, Togo flags, statesmen.

**1985, Oct. 24** **Litho.** *Perf. 13*

**1338** A278 90fr multi .60 .20
**1339** A278 115fr multi .75 .20
**1340** A279 150fr multi .90 .20
**1341** A279 250fr multi 1.50 .25
**1342** A279 500fr multi 3.00 .50
*Nos. 1338-1342 (5)* 6.75 1.35

UN, 40th anniv. Nos. 1340-1342 are airmail.

Nos. 1267, 1270, 1272, 1273 Ovptd. with Rotary Emblem and "80e ANNIVERSAIRE DU / ROTARY INTERNATIONAL"

**1985** **Litho.** *Perf. 15*

**1343** A267 4fr multi .65 .40
**1344** A267 105fr multi 1.25 1.10
**1345** A267 1000fr multi 12.50 6.50
*Nos. 1343-1345 (3)* 14.40 8.00

**Souvenir Sheet**

**1346** A267 1000fr multi 12.50 6.50

Nos. 1344-1346 are airmail.

Christmas A280

Religious paintings and statuary: 90fr, The Garden of Roses Madonna. 115fr, Madonna and Child, Byzantine, 11th cent. 150fr, Rest During the Flight to Egypt, by Gerard David (1450-1523). 160fr, African Madonna, 16th cent. 250fr, African Madonna, c. 1900. 500fr, Mystic Madonna, by Sandro Botticelli (1444-1510).

*Perf. 14½x13½*

**1985, Dec. 10** **Litho.**

**1347** A280 90fr multi .75 .20
**1348** A280 115fr multi .90 .20
**1349** A280 150fr multi 1.25 .20
**1350** A280 160fr multi 1.25 .20
**1351** A280 250fr multi 1.90 .35
*Nos. 1347-1351 (5)* 6.05 1.15

**Souvenir Sheet**

**1352** A280 500fr multi 4.00 3.00

Nos. 1348-1352 air airmail. No. 1352 contains one stamp 36x51mm.

Nos. 1302, 1305-1307 Ovptd. "75e Anniversaire / du Scoutisme Feminin"

**1986, Jan.** *Perf. 15*

**1353** A271 50fr multi 1.40 .25
**1354** A271 1000fr multi 13.00 3.00

**Souvenir Sheet**

**1355** A271 1000fr multi 7.50 6.00
**1355A** A271 1000fr multi 7.50 6.00

Nos. 1354-1355A airmail.

Nos. 1268-1269, 1271, 1273-1274 Ovptd. "150e ANNIVERSAIRE / DE CHEMIN FER 'LUDWIG'"

**1985, Dec. 27** **Litho.** *Perf. 15*

**1356** A267 50fr multi 1.25 .35
**1357** A267 90fr multi 1.25 .60
**1358** A267 500fr multi 8.00 3.50
*Nos. 1356-1358 (3)* 10.50 4.45

**Souvenir Sheets**

**1359** A267 1000fr No. 1273 9.00 6.50
**1360** A267 1000fr No. 1274 9.00 6.50

Halley's Comet A281

Designs: 70fr, Suisei space probe, comets. 90fr, Vega-1 probe. 150fr, Space telescope. 200fr, Giotto probe, comet over Togo. 1000fr, Edmond Halley, Sir Isaac Newton.

**1986, Mar. 27** *Perf. 13*

**1361** A281 70fr multi .60 .20
**1362** A281 90fr multi .75 .25
**1363** A281 150fr multi 1.25 .40
**1364** A281 200fr multi 1.75 .55
*Nos. 1361-1364 (4)* 4.35 1.40

**Souvenir Sheet**

**1365** A281 1000fr multi 7.50 6.00

Nos. 1362-1365 are airmail.
For overprints see Nos. 1405-1409.

Flowering and Fruit-bearing Plants A282

**1986, June** *Perf. 14*

**1366** A282 70fr Anacardium occidentale .60 .20
**1367** A282 90fr Ananas comosus .75 .25
**1368** A282 120fr Persea americana 1.00 .35
**1369** A282 135fr Carica papaya 1.10 .40
**1370** A282 290fr Mangifera indica, vert. 2.40 .80
*Nos. 1366-1370 (5)* 5.85 2.00

Nos. 1368-1370 airmail.

1986 World Cup Soccer Championships, Mexico — A283

Various soccer plays.

**1986, May 5** **Litho.** *Perf. 15x14*

**1371** A283 70fr multi .55 .20
**1372** A283 90fr multi .60 .25
**1373** A283 130fr multi .90 .35
**1374** A283 300fr multi 2.10 .80
*Nos. 1371-1374 (4)* 4.15 1.60

**Souvenir Sheet**

**1375** A283 1000fr multi 7.50 6.00

Nos. 1372-1375 are airmail.
For overprints see Nos. 1394-1397.

Mushrooms — A284

**1986, June 9** *Perf. 13x12½*

**1376** A284 70fr Ramaria moelleriana 1.00 .20
**1377** A284 90fr Hygrocybe firma 1.25 .25
**1378** A284 150fr Kalchbrennera corallocephala 2.00 .40
**1379** A284 200fr Cookeina tricholoma 2.75 .55
*Nos. 1376-1379 (4)* 7.00 1.40

Intl. Youth Year — A285

**1986, June** *Perf. 13½x14½*

**1380** A285 25fr shown .75 .20
**1381** A285 90fr Youths, doves 1.90 .25

Dated 1985.

Wrestling — A286

Wedding of Prince Andrew and Sarah Ferguson — A287

**1986, July 16** ***Perf. 14x15, 15x14***

**1382** A286 15fr Single-leg take-down move .30 .20
**1383** A286 20fr Completing take-down .30 .20
**1384** A286 70fr Pinning combination .50 .20
**1385** A286 90fr Riding .70 .25
*Nos. 1382-1385 (4)* 1.80 .85

Nos. 1384-1385 horiz. No. 1385 is airmail.

**1986, July 23** ***Perf. 14***

**1386** A287 10fr Sarah Ferguson .45 .20
**1387** A287 1000fr Prince Andrew 11.50 2.75

**Souvenir Sheet**

**1388** A287 1000fr Couple 7.50 6.00

Nos. 1387-1388 are airmail.

Easter A288

Paintings (details): 25fr, 1000fr, The Resurrection, by Andrea Mantegna (1431-1506), vert. 70fr, The Calvary, by Paolo Veronese (1528-1588), vert. 90fr, The Last Supper, by Jacopo Tintoretto (1518-1594). 200fr, Christ at the Tomb, by Alonso Berruguette (1486-1561).

***Perf. 14x15, 15x14***

**1986, Mar. 24** **Litho.**

**1389** A288 25fr multi .40 .20
**1390** A288 70fr multi .55 .20
**1391** A288 90fr multi .65 .25
**1392** A288 200fr multi 1.50 .55
*Nos. 1389-1392 (4)* 3.10 1.20

**Souvenir Sheet**

**1393** A288 1000fr multi 7.50 5.00

Nos. 1391-1393 are airmail.

Nos. 1371-1374 Ovptd. or Inscribed "DEMI-FINALE / ARGENTINE 2 / BELGIQUE 0," "DEMI-FINALE / ALLEMAGNE / DE L'OUEST 2 / FRANCE 0," "3 eme et 4 eme PLACE / FRANCE 4 / BELGIQUE 2," & "FINALE / ARGENTINE 3 / ALLEMAGNE / DE L'OUEST 2"

**1986, Aug. 4** **Litho.** ***Perf. 15x14***

**1394** A283 70fr multi .55 .20
**1395** A283 90fr multi .65 .25
**1396** A283 130fr multi .90 .35
**1397** A283 300fr multi 2.10 .80
*Nos. 1394-1397 (4)* 4.20 1.60

Nos. 1395-1397 are airmail.

Hotels — A289

**1986, Aug. 18** ***Perf. 12½***

**1398** A289 70fr Fazao .50 .20
**1399** A289 90fr Sarakawa .60 .25
**1400** A289 120fr Le Lac .80 .30
*Nos. 1398-1400 (3)* 1.90 .75

Nos. 1399-1400 are airmail.

Keran Natl. Park A290

**1986, Sept. 15** **Litho.** ***Perf. 14½***

**1401** A290 70fr Wild ducks .95 .20
**1402** A290 90fr Antelope 1.10 .25
**1403** A290 100fr Elephant 1.25 .30
**1404** A290 130fr Waterbuck 1.75 .35
*Nos. 1401-1404 (4)* 5.05 1.10

Nos. 1402-1404 are airmail.

Nos. 1361-1365 Ovptd. with Halley's Comet Emblem in Silver

**1986, Oct. 9** ***Perf. 13***

**1405** A281 70fr multi 1.50 .20
**1406** A281 90fr multi 1.75 .25
**1407** A281 150fr multi 3.00 .40
**1408** A281 200fr multi 4.00 .55
*Nos. 1405-1408 (4)* 10.25 1.40

**Souvenir Sheet**

**1409** A281 1000fr multi 18.00 6.00

Nos. 1406-1409 are airmail.

Frescoes from Togoville Church — A291

Togoville Church — A292

**1986, Dec. 22** **Litho.** ***Perf. 14½x15***

**1410** A291 45fr Annunciation .40 .20
**1411** A291 120fr Nativity 1.00 .30
**1412** A291 130fr Adoration of the Magi 1.10 .35
**1413** A291 200fr Flight into Egypt 1.75 .55
*Nos. 1410-1413 (4)* 4.25 1.40

**Souvenir Sheet**

**1414** A292 1000fr multi 7.50 6.00

Christmas. Nos. 1411-1414 are airmail.

Phosphate Mining — A293

Natl. Liberation, 20th Anniv. — A294

**1987, Jan. 13** **Litho.** ***Perf. 12½***

**1415** A293 35fr shown .25 .20
**1416** A293 50fr Sugar refinery, Anie .30 .20
**1417** A293 70fr Nangbeto Dam .40 .20
**1418** A293 90fr Hotel, post office in Lome .55 .30
**1419** A293 100fr Post office, Kara .60 .30
**1420** A293 120fr Peace monument .70 .35
**1421** A293 130fr Youth vaccination campaign .80 .45
*Nos. 1415-1421 (7)* 3.60 2.00

**Souvenir Sheet**

***Perf. 13***

**1422** A294 500fr shown 3.25 3.00

Nos. 1419-1422 are airmail.

Easter — A295

Paintings in Nadoba Church, Keran: 90fr, The Last Supper. 130fr, Christ on the Cross. 300fr, The Resurrection. 500fr, Evangelization in Tamberma, fresco, horiz.

**1987, Apr. 13** **Litho.** ***Perf. 14½x15***

**1423** A295 90fr multi .60 .30
**1424** A295 130fr multi .85 .40
**1425** A295 300fr multi 1.90 .90
*Nos. 1423-1425 (3)* 3.35 1.60

**Souvenir Sheet**

***Perf. 15x14½***

**1426** A295 500fr multi 3.25 3.00

Nos. 1424-1426 are airmail.

World Rugby Cup A296

**1987, May 11** ***Perf. 15x14½***

**1427** A296 70fr Dive .60 .20
**1428** A296 130fr Running with the ball 1.25 .40
**1429** A296 300fr Scrimmage 2.50 .90
*Nos. 1427-1429 (3)* 4.35 1.50

**Souvenir Sheet**

***Perf. 14½x15***

**1430** A296 1000fr Stands, goal, vert. 7.50 7.50

Nos. 1427-1429 are horiz. Nos. 1428-1430 are airmail.

Indigenous Flowers A297

**1987, June 22** **Litho.** ***Perf. 13***

**1431** A297 70fr Adenium obesum .70 .20
**1432** A297 90fr Amorphophallus abyssinicus, vert. .85 .25
**1433** A297 100fr Ipomoea mauritana .95 .30
**1434** A297 120fr Salacia togoica, vert. 1.25 .35
*Nos. 1431-1434 (4)* 3.75 1.10

Nos. 1432-1434 are airmail.

Fish A298

**1987, Sept. 8** **Litho.** ***Perf. 13***

**1435** A298 70fr Chaetodon hoefleri .60 .25
**1436** A298 90fr Tetraodon lineatus .70 .30
**1437** A298 120fr Chaetodipterus goreensis .90 .40
**1438** A298 130fr Labeo parvus 1.00 .45
*Nos. 1435-1438 (4)* 3.20 1.40

1988 Summer Olympics, Seoul — A299

Buddha and athletes

**1987, Sept. 14** ***Perf. 12½***

**1439** A299 70fr Long jump .55 .25
**1440** A299 90fr Relay .65 .30
**1441** A299 200fr Cycling 1.50 .70
**1442** A299 250fr Javelin 2.00 .85
*Nos. 1439-1442 (4)* 4.70 2.10

**Souvenir Sheet**

**1443** A299 1000fr Tennis 7.50 5.50

Nos. 1440-1443 are airmail.

World Wildlife Fund Type of 1984

**1987, Dec. 15** **Litho.** ***Perf. 14***

**Size: 32x24mm**

**1444** A263 60fr like 45fr 1.25 .20
**1445** A263 75fr like 70fr 1.40 .25
**1446** A263 80fr like 90fr 1.40 .30
**1447** A263 100fr like 105fr 1.90 .35
*Nos. 1444-1447 (4)* 5.95 1.10

No. 1447 is airmail.

Christmas A300

Eradication of Tuberculosis A301

Paintings: 40fr, Springtime in Paradise, horiz.. 45fr, Creation of Man, Sistine Chapel, by Michelangelo, horiz.. 105fr, Presentation in the Temple. 270fr, Original Sin. 500fr, Nativity, horiz.

***Perf. 15x14, 14x15***

**1987, Dec. 15** **Litho.**

**1448** A300 40fr multi .35 .20
**1449** A300 45fr multi .40 .20
**1450** A300 105fr multi 1.00 .40
**1451** A300 270fr multi 2.50 .95
*Nos. 1448-1451 (4)* 4.25 1.75

**Souvenir Sheet**

**1452** A300 500fr multi 4.50 4.00

Nos. 1450-1452 are airmail.

**1987, Dec. 28** ***Perf. 12½x13, 13x12½***

**1453** A301 80fr Inoculation, horiz. .55 .30
**1454** A301 90fr Family under umbrella .65 .30
**1455** A301 115fr Hospital, horiz. .80 .40
*Nos. 1453-1455 (3)* 2.00 1.00

Health for all by the year 2000. Nos. 1454-1455 are airmail.

Intl. Fund for Agricultural Development (IFAD), 10th Anniv. — A302

**1988, Feb. 25** **Litho.** ***Perf. 13½***

**1456** A302 90fr multi .75 .30

Easter 1988 — A303

Stained-glass windows: 70fr, Jesus and the Disciples at Emmaus. 90fr, Mary at the Foot of the Cross. 120fr, The Crucifixion. 200fr, St. Thomas Touching the Resurrected Christ. 500fr, The Agony of Jesus on the Mount of Olives.

**1988, June 6** **Litho.** ***Perf. 14x15***

**1457** A303 70fr multi .45 .20
**1458** A303 90fr multi .70 .30
**1459** A303 120fr multi .90 .40
**1460** A303 200fr multi 1.60 .70
*Nos. 1457-1460 (4)* 3.65 1.60

**Souvenir Sheet**

**1461** A303 500fr multi 3.75 3.00

Nos. 1459-1461 are airmail.

Paintings by Picasso (1881-1973) — A304

Designs: 45fr, The Dance. 160fr, Portrait of a Young Girl. No. 1464, Gueridon. No. 1465, Mandolin and Guitar.

**1988, Apr. 25** **Litho.** ***Perf. 12½x13***

**1462** A304 45fr multi .35 .20
**1463** A304 160fr multi 1.10 .50
**1464** A304 300fr multi 2.25 1.00
*Nos. 1462-1464 (3)* 3.70 1.70

**Souvenir Sheet**

**1465** A304 300fr multi 2.25 1.90

Nos. 1464-1465 are airmail.

A305

A306

**1988, Aug. 30** ***Perf. 14x15***

**1466** A305 70fr Basketball .50 .25
**1467** A305 90fr Tennis .65 .30
**1468** A305 120fr Archery .85 .40
**1469** A305 200fr Discus 1.40 .65
*Nos. 1466-1469 (4)* 3.40 1.60

**Souvenir Sheet**

**1470** A305 500fr Marathon 3.50 2.75

1988 Summer Olympics, Seoul. Nos. 1468-1470 are airmail.

**1988, Oct. 28** **Litho.** ***Perf. 13***

**1471** A306 80fr shown .55 .30
**1472** A306 125fr Emblems .85 .40

WHO, 40th anniv.

Traditional Costumes A307

**1988, July 25** **Litho.** ***Perf. 13½***

**1473** A307 80fr Watchi chief .55 .20
**1474** A307 125fr Watchi woman .85 .40
**1475** A307 165fr Kotokoli 1.10 .50
**1476** A307 175fr Ewe 1.25 .60
*Nos. 1473-1476 (4)* 3.75 1.70

**Souvenir Sheet**

**1477** A307 500fr Moba 3.50 2.75

PHILTOGO 3, Aug. 11-12 — A308

Children's drawings by: 10fr, B. Gossner. 35fr, K. Ekoue-Kouvahey. 70fr, A. Abbey. 90fr, T.D. Lawson. 120fr, A. Tazzar.

**1988, Dec. 3**

**1478** A308 10fr multi .25 .20
**1479** A308 35fr multi .35 .20
**1480** A308 70fr multi .60 .25
**1481** A308 90fr multi .65 .30
**1482** A308 120fr multi .90 .40
*Nos. 1478-1482 (5)* 2.75 1.35

Christmas — A309

Paintings: 80fr, Adoration of the Magi, by Brueghel. 150fr, The Virgin, Infant Jesus, Sts. Jerome and Dominic, by Lippi. 175fr, Madonna, Infant Jesus, St. Joseph and Infant John the Baptist, by Barocci. 195fr, Virgin and Child, by Bellini. 750fr, The Holy Family and a Shepherd, by Titian.

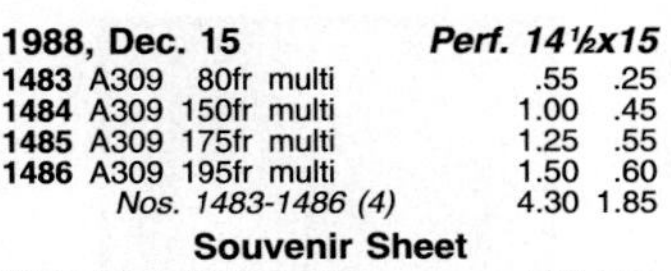

**1988, Dec. 15** ***Perf. 14½x15***

**1483** A309 80fr multi .55 .25
**1484** A309 150fr multi 1.00 .45
**1485** A309 175fr multi 1.25 .55
**1486** A309 195fr multi 1.50 .60
*Nos. 1483-1486 (4)* 4.30 1.85

**Souvenir Sheet**

**1487** A309 750fr multi 4.75 3.50

Nos. 1484-1487 are airmail.

Natl. Industries A310

**1988, May 28** **Litho.** ***Perf. 13***

**1488** A310 125fr Cement factory .80 .40
**1489** A310 165fr Bottling plant 1.25 .55
**1490** A310 195fr Phosphate mine 1.25 .65
**1491** A310 200fr Plastics factory 1.50 .70
**1492** A310 300fr Manufacturing plant 2.00 1.00
*Nos. 1488-1492 (5)* 6.80 3.30

John F. Kennedy A311

Designs: 125fr, Arrival in Paris, 1961. 155fr, At Hotel de Ville, vert. 165fr, With De Gaulle at Elysee Palace, vert. 180fr, Boarding Air Force One with Jackie at Orly, France. 750fr, Kennedy and De Gaulle, natl. colors, vert.

**1988, July 30** **Litho.** ***Perf. 14***

**1493** A311 125fr multi .85 .35
**1494** A311 155fr multi 1.10 .50
**1495** A311 165fr multi 1.25 .55
**1496** A311 180fr multi 1.50 .60
*Nos. 1493-1496 (4)* 4.70 2.00

**Souvenir Sheet**

***Perf. 13½x13***

**1497** A311 750fr multi 5.00 4.00

Hairstyles A312

**1988, Nov. 20** ***Perf. 13***

**1498** A312 80fr shown .55 .25
**1499** A312 125fr multi, diff. .85 .40
**1500** A312 170fr multi, diff. 1.25 .55
**1501** A312 180fr multi, diff., vert. 1.50 .60
*Nos. 1498-1501 (4)* 4.15 1.80

**Souvenir Sheet**

***Perf. 14***

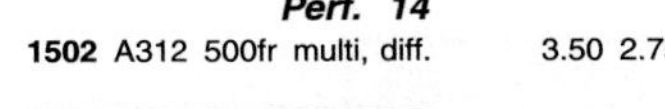

**1502** A312 500fr multi, diff. 3.50 2.75

Sarakawa Plane Crash, 15th Anniv. A313

Portrait and various views of the wreckage.

**1989, Jan. 24** ***Perf. 13½***

**1503** A313 10fr multi .20 .20
**1504** A313 80fr multi, vert. .50 .25
**1505** A313 125fr multi .80 .40
*Nos. 1503-1505 (3)* 1.50 .85

1990 World Cup Soccer Championships, Italy — A314

ITALIA '90 emblem, flag of Togo, athletes and architecture: 80fr, Cathedral of St. Januarius, Naples. 125fr, Milan Cathedral. 165fr, Bevilacqua Palace, Verona. 175fr, Baptistery of San Giovanni, Florence. 380fr, Madama Palace, Turin. 425fr, Cathedral of San Lorenzo, Genoa. 650fr, The Colosseum, Rome.

**1989, Jan. 10** **Litho.** ***Perf. 13½***

**1506** A314 80fr multi .55 .25
**1507** A314 125fr multi .85 .40
**1508** A314 165fr multi 1.10 .50
**1509** A314 175fr multi 1.25 .55
**1510** A314 380fr multi 2.50 1.25
**1511** A314 425fr multi 3.00 1.25
*Nos. 1506-1511 (6)* 9.25 4.20

**Souvenir Sheet**

**1512** A314 650fr multi 4.00 4.00

Nos. 1510-1512 are airmail.

A316

Prince Emanuel of Liechtenstein Foundation — A316a

1988 Summer Olympics, Seoul: Flags of Liechtenstein, Togo, athletes, Pres. Eyadema. No. 1522A, Olympic rings. No. 1522B, Tennis players Miroslav Mecir, Steffi Graf, vert.

**1989, May 25** **Litho.** ***Perf. 13½***

**1520** A316 80fr Boxing 1.10 .25
**1521** A316 125fr Long jump .90 .40
**1522** A316 165fr Running 2.25 .50
*Nos. 1520-1522 (3)* 4.25 1.15

**Litho. & Embossed**

**1522A** A316a 1500fr gold & multi 10.00
**1522B** A316a 1500fr gold & multi 10.00

Nos. 1522A-1522B are airmail and exist imperf. and in souvenir sheets of 1 both perf. and imperf.

Federal Republic of Germany, 40th Anniv. A317

**1989, June 1**

**1523** A317 90fr Palace .60 .25
**1524** A317 125fr Statesmen, vert. .80 .40
**1525** A317 180fr Natl. flag, crest 1.00 .50
*Nos. 1523-1525 (3)* 2.40 1.15

Council for Rural Development, 30th Anniv. — A318

**1989, June 19** ***Perf. 15x14***

**1526** A318 75fr Flags, well, tractor, field .50 .25

See Ivory Coast No. 874.

Intl. Red Cross, 125th Anniv. A319

**1989, June 30** ***Perf. 13½***

**1527** A319 90fr shown .60 .30
**1528** A319 125fr Geneva Convention, 1864 .80 .40

French Revolution, Bicent. A320

Designs: 90fr, Storming of the Bastille, vert. 125fr, Tennis Court Oath. 180fr, Abolition of privileges. 1000fr, Declaration of Human Rights and Citizenship, vert.

**1989, July 15**

**1529** A320 90fr multi .65 .30
**1530** A320 125fr multi .85 .40
**1531** A320 180fr multi 1.25 .55
*Nos. 1529-1531 (3)* 2.75 1.25

**Souvenir Sheet**

**1532** A320 1000fr multi 7.50 2.50

Electric Corp. of Benin, 20th Anniv. A321

**1989, July 15**

**1533** A321 80fr multi .60 .25
**1534** A321 125fr multi 1.00 .40

A322

PHILEXFRANCE '89, French Revolution, Bicent. — A322a

Figures and scenes from the revolution: 90fr, Jacques Necker (1732-1804), financier, statesman, and The Three Estates. 190fr, Guy Le Chapelier (1754-1794), politician, and abolition of feudalism (seigniorial privileges), Aug. 4, 1789. 425fr, Talleyrand-Perigord (1754-1838), statesman, and Lafayette's Oath at the Festival of Federation, July 14, 1790. 480fr, Paul Barras (1755-1829), revolutionary, and overthrowing of Robespierre during the Revolution of 9th Thermidor, July 27, 1794. 750fr, Georges Jacques Danton (1759-1794), revolutionary leader, and arrest of Louis XVI at Varennes, June 21, 1791, horiz. Nos. 1537-1539 are airmail.

No. 1539A, Assassination of Jean-Paul Marat (1743-93). No. 1539B, Fabré d'Eglantine (1750-94), making of the calendar of the republic.

**1989** **Litho.** ***Perf. 13½***

**1535** A322 90fr multi .65 .30
**1536** A322 190fr multi 1.25 .65
**1537** A322 425fr multi 3.00 1.50
**1538** A322 480fr multi 3.50 1.75
*Nos. 1535-1538 (4)* 8.40 4.20

**Souvenir Sheet**

**1539** A322 750fr multi 6.00 1.50

**Litho. & Embossed**

**1539A** A322a 1500fr gold & multi 15.00

**Souvenir Sheet**

**1539B** A322a 1500fr gold & multi 8.00

#1539A-1539B are airmail and exist imperf.

Nos. 1535-1538 exist in souvenir sheets of 1, No. 1539A in souvenir sheets of 1, perf. and imperf.

Issued: 90fr-750fr, 6/12; 1500fr, 7/15.

Gen. Kpalime's Role in Natl. Unity and Peace Struggle, 20th Anniv. A323

**1989, Aug. 21**

**1540** A323 90fr shown .65 .30
**1541** A323 125fr Giving speech .90 .45

A324

A325

Butterflies.

**1990, Apr. 30** **Litho.** ***Perf. 13½***

**1542** A324 5fr Danaus chrysippus .40 .20
**1543** A324 10fr Morpho aega .40 .20
**1544** A324 15fr Papilio demodocus .40 .20
**1545** A324 90fr Papilio dardanus 1.40 .40
*Nos. 1542-1545 (4)* 2.60 1.00

**Souvenir Sheet**

**1545A** A324 500fr Papilio zalmoxis 3.75 1.90

No. 1545A is airmail.

**1989, Dec. 1** **Litho.** ***Perf. 13½***

**1546** A325 40fr Apollo 11 liftoff .45 .20
**1547** A325 90fr Module transposition .90 .30
**1548** A325 150fr *Eagle* 1.40 .50
**1549** A325 250fr Splashdown 2.50 .90
*Nos. 1546-1549 (4)* 5.25 1.90

**Souvenir Sheet**

**1550** A325 500fr Astronaut on Moon 3.50 2.50

1st Moon Landing, 20th anniv.

Lome IV Conference, Dec. 1989 — A326

**1989, Dec. 15** **Litho.** ***Perf. 13***

**1551** A326 100fr "Dec. 89" .70 .35
**1552** A326 100fr "15 Dec. 89" .70 .35

A327

Boy Scouts, Flora and Fauna A327a

#1559A, *Kalchbrennera corallocephala.* #1559B, *Spindasis mozambica.*

**1990, Jan. 8** **Litho.** ***Perf. 13½***

**1553** A327 80fr *Myrina silenus* .60 .30
**1554** A327 90fr *Phlebobus silvaticus* .65 .35
**1555** A327 125fr *Volvariella esculenta* .90 .45
**1556** A327 165fr *Hypolicaena antifaunus* 1.10 .65
**1557** A327 380fr *Termitomyces striatus* 2.75 1.25
**1558** A327 425fr *Axiocerces harpax* 3.00 1.50
*Nos. 1553-1558 (6)* 9.00 4.50

**Souvenir Sheet**

**1559** A327 750fr *Cupidopsis jobates* 5.50 1.00

**Litho. & Embossed**

**1559A** A327a 1500fr gold & multi 10.00

**Souvenir Sheet**

**1559B** A327a 1500fr gold & multi 10.00

Nos. 1557-1559B are airmail. Nos. 1559A-1559B exist imperf. No. 1559A exists in souvenir sheet of 1 both perf. and imperf.

People's Republic of Togo, 20th Anniv. — A328

**1990, Jan. 8**

**1560** A328 45fr Government House, Kara .35 .20
**1561** A328 90fr Pres. Eyadema, House .65 .30

Pan-African Postal Union, 10th Anniv. — A329

**1990, Jan. 1** ***Perf. 13½***

**1562** A329 125fr bronze, blk & bl 1.00 .45

US-Togo Relations A330

180fr, Pres. Bush, Pres. Eyadema, horiz.

**1990, July 20** **Litho.** ***Perf. 13½***

**1563** A330 125fr multicolored .95 .50
**1564** A330 180fr multicolored 1.40 .70

**Size: 90 x 75mm**

**1565** A330 125fr multicolored 1.00 .50
**1566** A330 180fr multicolored 1.40 .70
*Nos. 1563-1566 (4)* 4.75 2.40

Nos. 1565-1566 printed in sheets of 1.

Reptiles A331

**1990, May 22**

**1567** A331 1fr Varanus niloticus .20 .20
**1568** A331 25fr Vipere bitis arietans .20 .20
**1569** A331 60fr Naja melaneuloca .50 .25
**1570** A331 90fr Python de sebae .70 .35
*Nos. 1567-1570 (4)* 1.60 1.00

Cowrie Shell Ornaments A332

**1990, July, 20** **Litho.** ***Perf. 13½***

**1571** A332 90fr shown .70 .35
**1572** A332 125fr Shell necklace 1.00 .50
**1573** A332 180fr Shells on horned helmet 1.40 .70
*Nos. 1571-1573 (3)* 3.10 1.55

Stamp Day A333

**1990, Aug. 23**
**1574** A333 90fr multicolored .75 .35

Traditional Homes A334

**1990, Sept. 9**
**1575** A334 90fr shown .70 .35
**1576** A334 125fr multi, diff. 1.00 .50
**1577** A334 190fr multi, diff. 1.50 .75
*Nos. 1575-1577 (3)* 3.20 1.60

Charles de Gaulle (1890-1970), Speech at Brazzaville, 1944 — A335

**1990, Aug. 30** **Litho.** ***Perf. 14***
**1578** A335 125fr multicolored 1.00 .50

New Lome Airport A336

**1990, Sept. 17** ***Perf. 13½***
**1579** A336 90fr multicolored .75 .35

Children's Art — A337

**1990, Sept. 28** **Litho.** ***Perf. 13½***
**1580** A337 90fr multicolored .75 .35

Forest Wildlife — A342

**1991, June 5** **Litho.** ***Perf. 13½x14***
**1593** A342 90fr Chimpanzee .70 .30
**1594** A342 170fr Green parrot 1.25 .60
**1595** A342 185fr White parrot 1.25 .65
*Nos. 1593-1595 (3)* 3.20 1.55

Python Regius A343

Various snakes emerging from eggs.

**1992, Aug. 24** **Litho.** ***Perf. 13½***
**1596** A343 90fr multicolored .70 .35
**1597** A343 125fr multicolored 1.00 .50
**1598** A343 190fr multicolored 1.50 .75
**1599** A343 300fr multicolored 2.25 1.10
*Nos. 1596-1599 (4)* 5.45 2.70

Dated 1991.

Voodoo Dances A344

Various women dancing.

**1992, Aug. 24**
**1600** A344 90fr multicolored .70 .35
**1601** A344 125fr multicolored 1.00 .50
**1602** A344 190fr multicolored 1.50 .75
*Nos. 1600-1602 (3)* 3.20 1.60

Dated 1991.

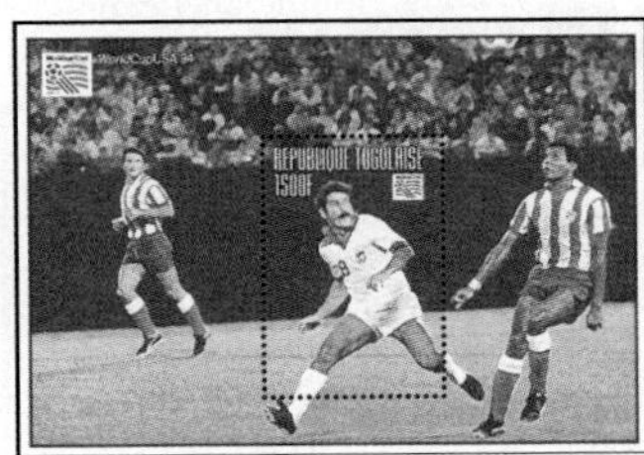

A345

1994 World Cup Soccer Championships, US — A346

Various soccer players in action: 5fr, 10fr, 25fr, 60fr, 90fr, 100fr, 200fr, 1000fr.
1500fr, Player in white & green uniform. 3000fr, Two players in air, horiz.

**1994, Nov. 15** **Litho.** ***Perf. 14***
**1603-1610** A345 Set of 8 5.75 3.00

**Souvenir Sheets**

**1611** A346 1500fr multicolored 5.75 3.00
**1612** A346 3000fr multicolored 11.50 5.75

UPU, 120th Anniv. — A347

Stamp Day — A348

**1994, July 29** ***Perf. 13½***
**1613** A347 180fr multicolored .70 .35

A miniature sheet may exist.

**1994, Oct. 9**
**1614** A348 90fr pale bl & multi .35 .20
**1615** A348 125fr pale yel & multi .50 .25

Intl. Olympic Committee, Cent. — A348a

Designs, each 300fr: b, Pierre de Coubertin, Olympic Hymn. c, Original members of IOC. d, Olympic flame.
900fr, Pierre de Coubertin holding document.

**1994, Oct.** **Litho.** ***Perf. 13½***
**1615A** A348a Strip of 3, #b.-d. 3.50 3.50

**Souvenir Sheet**

**1615E** A348a 900fr multicolored 3.50 1.75

Nos. 1615A, 1615E exist imperf. No. 1615c is 60x51mm. No. 1615E is airmail and contains one 36x51mm stamp.

Birds A349

Designs: #1616, 5fr, Secretary bird, vert. #1617, 10fr, Paradise flycather, vert. #1618, 25fr, African spoonbill. #1619, 60fr, Cordon bleu waxbill. #1620, 90fr, Orange-breasted sunbird, vert. #1621, 100fr, Yellow-billed hornbill, vert. #1621A, 180fr, Barn owl. #1622, 200fr, African hoopoe. #1622A, 300fr, Fire-crowned bishop, vert. #1623, 1000fr, Red-throated bee eater, vert.

**1995** **Litho.** ***Perf. 14***
**1616-1623** A349 Set of 10 7.75 3.75

**Souvenir Sheet**

**1624** A349 1500fr Vulture 5.75 2.75

Issued: 180fr, 300fr, 8/7; others, 1/23.

A350 A351

Motion Picture, Alien: a, Alien creature. b, Humans in combat with creature. c, Sigourney Weaver.

**1994** **Litho.** ***Perf. 13½***
**1625** A350 600fr Strip of 3, #a.-c. 7.50 3.75

No. 1625b is 60x48mm. No. 1625 is a continuous design and exists in souvenir sheets of 1.

**1994**

No. 1626, each 600fr: a, Edwin "Buzz" Aldrin. b, Eagle, olive branch, Neil Armstrong. c, Michael Collins.
No. 1627, each 600fr: a, Apollo emblem, footprint. b, Crew of Apollo 11. c, Moon rock, NASA emblem.

**Strips of 3, #a.-c.**

**1626-1627** A351 Set of 2 15.00 7.50

First manned Moon landing, 25th anniv.
Nos. 1626b, 1627b are each 60x47mm. Nos. 1626-1627 are continuous designs and exist in souvenir sheets of 1.

Dinosaurs — A352

125fr, Polacanthus. 180fr, Pachycephalosaurus. 425fr, Coelophysis. 480fr, Brachiosaurus. 500fr, Dilophosaurus. 1500fr, Scutellosaurus.
No. 1634, Velociraptor, vert.

**1994**
**1628-1633** A352 Set of 6 13.00 6.50

**Souvenir Sheet**

**1634** A352 1500fr multicolored 6.25 3.00

No. 1634 is airmail.

Flowers — A353

Easter — A354

Designs: 15fr, Belvache de Madagascar. 90fr, Oeuillets. 125fr, Agave, horiz.

**1995, May 12**
**1635-1637** A353 Set of 3 .90 .45

**1995, May 12**

Details or entire paintings: 90fr, The Resurrection, by A. Mantegna. 180fr, Calvary, by Veronese. 190fr, The Last Supper, by Tintoretto, horiz.

**1638-1640** A354 Set of 3 1.75 .90

Fish A355

10fr, Pike. 90fr, Capitaine. 180fr, Carp.

**1995, May 12**
**1641-1643** A355 Set of 3 1.10 .55

Miniature Sheets of 6 and 8

VJ Day, 50th Anniv. A356

Japanese leaders: No. 1644a, Adm. Isoroko Yamamoto. b, Gen. Hideki Tojo. c, Vice Adm. Shigeru Fukudome. d, Adm. Shigetaro Shimada. e, Contre-Adm. Chuichi Nagumo. f, Gen. Shizu Ichi Tanaka.

No. 1646, Japanese signing peace agreement.

VE Day: No. 1645a, 200fr, German fighter planes making final attacks. b. 200fr, Allies win Battle of the Atlantic. c, 200fr, Ludendorf Bridge at Remagen is taken intact. d, 200fr, Russian rockets fired at Berlin. e, 45fr, Hostilities suspended in Italy. f, 90fr, Russians capture devastated Warsaw. g, 125fr, Russian tanks enter Berlin. h, 500fr, UN flag.

No. 1647, German U-236 surrenders.

**1995, July 20 Litho. *Perf. 14***

**1644** A356 200fr #a.-f. 4.75 2.50
**1645** A356 #a.-h. 6.25 3.25

**Souvenir Sheets**

**1646** A356 1500fr multicolored 6.00 3.00
**1647** A356 1500fr multicolored 6.00 3.00

UN, 50th Anniv. — A357

No. 1648: a, 25fr, Doves, earth from space. b, 90fr, Doves, UN headquarters. c, 400fr, Doves, earth from space.

1000fr, Earth, dove.

**1995, June 26**

**1648** A357 Strip of 3, #a.-c. 1.25 .65

**Souvenir Sheet**

**1649** A357 1000fr multicolored 4.00 2.00

1995 Boy Scout Jamboree, Holland — A358

Designs: 90fr, Nat. flag. 190fr, Scout oath. 300fr, Lord Baden-Powell.

1500fr, Scout salute.

**1995, July 20**

**1650-1652** A358 Set of 3 1.60 .80

**Souvenir Sheet**

**1653** A358 1500fr multicolored 6.00 3.00

Queen Mother, 95th Birthday A359

No. 1654: a, Formal portrait. b, Cutting cake. c, As younger woman wearing jewels, waving. d, Drawing.

No. 1654E, Holding umbrella. No. 1654F, Formal portrait as young woman.

No. 1655, Royal attire, pearls.

No. 1655A, Early picture of King George VI, Queen Mother.

**1995, July 20 *Perf. 13½x14***

**1654** A359 250fr Strip of 4, #a.-d. 5.00 2.50
**1654E** A359 250fr multicolored 1.25 .65
**1654F** A359 250fr multicolored 1.25 .65
*g.* Block or strip of 4, #1654a, 1654d, 1654E, 1654F 5.00 2.50
*Nos. 1654-1654F (3)* 7.50 3.80

**Souvenir Sheets**

**1655** A359 1000fr multicolored 4.00 2.00
**1655A** A359 1000fr multicolored 4.00 2.00

Nos. 1654, 1654Fg were issued in sheets of 8 stamps.

Issued: #1654, 1655, 7/20; # 1654E, 1654F, 1655A, 11/22.

FAO, 50th Anniv. — A360

No. 1656: a, 45fr, Cattle. b, 125fr, Water buffalo. c, 200fr, Boy, man with water buffaloes.

1000fr, Woman milking cow.

**1995, Mar. 3 Litho. *Perf. 14***

**1656** A360 Strip of 3, #a.-c. 1.50 .75

**Souvenir Sheet**

**1657** A360 1000fr multicolored 4.25 2.00

No. 1656 is a continuous design.

A361

A362

No. 1658, each 200fr: a, Elihu Root, peace, 1912. b, Alfred Fried, peace, 1911. c, Henri Moissan, chemistry, 1906. d, Charles Barkla, physics, 1917. e, Rudolf Eucken, literature, 1908. f, Carl von Ossietzky, peace, 1935. g, Sir Edward Appleton, physics. 1947. h, Camillo Golgi, physiology, 1906. i, Wilhelm Roentgen, physics, 1901.

No. 1659, each 200fr: a, Manfred Eigen, chemistry, 1967. b, Donald J. Cram, chemistry, 1987. c, Paul J. Flory, chemistry, 1974. d, Johann Deisenhofer, chemistry, 1988. e, P.W. Bridgman, physics, 1946. f, Otto Stern, physics, 1943. g, Arne Tiselis, chemistry, 1948. h, J. Georg Bednorz, physics, 1987. i, Albert Claude, medicine, 1974.

Each 1500fr: No. 1660, Albert Einstein, physics, 1921. No. 1661, Woodrow Wilson, peace, 1919.

**1995, Aug. 21**

**Miniature Sheets of 9, a-i**

**1658-1659** A361 Set of 2 14.50 7.00

**Souvenir Sheets**

**1660-1661** A361 Set of 2 12.00 6.00

Nobel Prize winners.

**1995, July 20**

**1662** A362 1000fr shown 4.25 2.00

**Souvenir Sheet**

**1663** A362 1000fr Natl. flag, Rotary emblem 4.25 2.00

Rotary Intl., 90th anniv.

Miniature Sheets

Fauna A363

Primates, each 200fr, vert: No. 1664a, Black-faced monkey in tree. b, Brown monkey in tree. c, Black monkey. d, Baboon.

Wild animals, each 200fr: No. 1665a, Hyena. b, Hyrax. c, Mongoose. d, Elephant. e, Mandrill. f, Okapi. g, Hippopotamus. h, Flamingo. i, Wild boar.

1500fr, Potto.

**1995, Oct. 2 Litho. *Perf. 14***

**1664** A363 Sheet of 4, #a.-d. 3.25 1.60
**1665** A363 Sheet of 9, #a.-i. 7.25 3.50

**Souvenir Sheet**

**1666** A363 1500fr multicolored 6.00 3.00

FAO, 50th Anniv. A364

**1995, Mar. 3 Litho. *Perf. 14***

**1667** A364 125fr shown .50 .25

**Souvenir Sheet**

**1668** A364 300fr like No. 1667 1.25 .60

Sir Rowland Hill (1795-1879) A365

UN, 50th Anniv. — A366

**1995, June 3 *Perf. 13½***

**1669** A365 125fr multicolored .50 .25

**1995, June 26**

**1670** A366 180fr multicolored .75 .40

Miniature Sheets of 8

Mushrooms A367

No. 1671: a, Cortinarius violaceus. b, Hygrocybe flavescens. c, Mycena haematopus. d, Coprinus micaceus. e, Helvella lacunosa. f, Flammulina velutipes. g, Aleuria aurantia. h, Geastrum triplex.

No. 1672: a, Russula laurocerasi. b, Phyllotopsis nidulans. c, Xeromphalina campanella. d, Psathyrella hydrophila. e, Entoloma murraii. f, Hygrophorus speciosus. g, Mycena leaiana. h, Cystoderma amianthinum.

No. 1673, each 200fr: a, Amanita muscaria. b, Amanita virosa. c, Galerina autumnalis. d, Omphalotus illudens. e, Naematoloma fasciculare. f, Paxillus involutus. g, Russula emetica. h, Scleroderma citrinum.

No. 1674, each 200fr: a, Armillaria ponderosa. b, Agaricus augustus. c, Gomphidius subroseus. d, Morchella esculenta. e, Stropharia rugoso. f, Boletus edulis. g, Clitocybe nuda. h, Lactarius deliciosus.

Each 1500fr: No. 1675, Trametes versicolor. No. 1676, Collybia iocephala.

**1995, Nov. 1 *Perf. 14***

**1671** A367 180fr #a.-h. 5.75 2.75
**1672** A367 195fr #a.-h. 6.25 3.00
**1673-1674** A367 Set of 2, #a.-h. 13.00 6.50

**Souvenir Sheets**

**1675-1676** A367 Set of 2 12.00 6.00

Miniature Sheets

History of Transportation — A368

Steam locomotives: No. 1677, each 200fr: a, SNCF Class 231 D Le Havre-Paris Express. b, Princess Royal Class Pacific, England. c, Class 52 2-10-0, German Railroad. d, Class "15A" 4-6-4+4-6-4 Beyer-Garratt, Rhodesia. e, Japanese 2-8-0. f, Class 940, 2-8-2 engine, Italy.

Various vehicles: No. 1678, each 200fr: a, Semi truck. b, Roman chariot. c, Motorcycle. d, Hummer 4-wheel drive. e, Bicycle. f, London autobus. g, Lunar rover. h, 1954 Jaguar XK 140. i, Ski-doo.

No. 1679, First land vehicle to break sound barrier.

**1995, Dec. 1 Litho. *Perf. 14***

**1677** A368 Sheet of 6, #a.-f. 4.75 2.50
**1678** A368 Sheet of 9, #a.-i. 7.25 3.50

**Souvenir Sheet**

**1679** A368 1500fr multicolored 6.00 3.00

No. 1679 contains one 85x28mm stamp.

World Post Day A369

Designs: 220fr, Selling stamps. 315fr, Sorting stamps. 335fr, Post office workers handling large sacks of mail.

**1995 Litho. *Perf. 13½***

**1680-1682** A369 Set of 3 4.50 2.25

Christmas A370

Paintings: 90fr, Nativity scene, vert. 325fr, Adoration of the Magi, vert. 340fr, 500fr, Adoration of the shepherds.

**1995, Sept. 13 Litho. *Perf. 13½***

**1683-1685** A370 Set of 3 3.00 1.50

**Souvenir Sheet**

***Perf. 12½***

**1686** A370 500fr multi, vert. 2.00 1.00

Sheets of 6

Wildlife of Africa A371

No. 1687: a, Gorilla. b, Uroota suraka. c, Pan troglodytes. d, Panthera pardus. e, Crocodylus niloticus. f, Leptailurus serval.

No. 1688a, Papilio tynderaeus. b, Bongo taurotragus. c, Epiphora aldiba. d, Cephalophus zebra. e, Cercopithecus cephus. f, Arctocebus calabarensis.

**1996, May 10 Litho. *Perf. 14***
**1687** A371 150fr #a.-f. 3.50 1.75
**1688** A371 180fr #a.-f. 4.25 2.25

China '96, 9th Asian Intl. Philatelic Exhibition.

A372

1996 Summer Olympics, Atlanta — A373

Designs: 50fr, Olympic Stadium, Mexico, 1968, horiz. 90fr, Yevgeny Petrov, skeet shooter, Mexico, 1968, horiz. 220fr, Lia Manoliu, women's discus, Mexico, 1968, horiz. 325fr, Dumb-bell lifting, discontinued sport.

Medal winners from past games: No. 1693, each 200fr: a, China, Women's Volleyball, 1984. b, Wayne Wells, wrestling, 1972. c, Bob Beaman, long jump, 1968. d, Victor Kurentsov, weight lifting, 1968. e, Shirley Strong, 100m hurdles, 1984. f, Nadia Comaneci, balance beam, 1976. g, Giovanni Parisi, boxing, 1988. h, Emil Zatopek, 10,000m, 1948. i, USSR, Brazil, Germany, soccer, 1988.

1000fr, Helen Mayer, fencing, 1936.

**1996, July 8 Litho. *Perf. 14***
**1689-1692** A372 Set of 4 2.75 1.40
**1693** A372 Sheet of 9, #a.-i. 7.25 3.50

**Souvenir Sheet**

**1694** A372 1000fr multicolored 4.00 2.00

**1996, Mar. 25 *Perf. 12½***

100fr, Women's gymnastics. 150fr, Women's tennis. 200fr, Javelin. 300fr, Men's field hockey. 400fr, Weight lifting. 500fr, Men's soccer.

1000fr, Synchronized swimming.

**1695-1700** A373 Set of 6 7.50 3.75

**Souvenir Sheet**

**1701** A373 1000fr multicolored 5.50 2.75

Butterflies A374

Designs: 40fr, Euphaedra eleus, vert. 90fr, Papilio dardanus, vert. 220fr, Iolaus timon. 315fr, Charaxes cynthia.

**1996, June 17 Litho. *Perf. 13***
**1702-1705** A374 Set of 4 2.75 1.50

Beetles — A375

Designs: 100fr, Purpuricenus kaehleri. 150fr, Carabus auronitens. 200fr, Semanotus rassicus. 300fr, Rosalia alpina. 400fr, Mylabris variabilis. 500fr, Odontolabis cuvera.

1000fr, Psalidognathus atys.

**1996, May 5**
**1706-1711** A375 Set of 6 7.75 3.75

**Souvenir Sheet**
***Perf. 12½***

**1712** A375 1000fr multicolored 5.50 2.75

No. 1712 contains one 40x32mm stamp.

1998 World Cup Soccer Championships, France — A376

French flag, various action scenes: 100fr, 150fr, 200fr, 300fr, 400fr, 500fr.

**1996, Apr. 10 *Perf. 12½***
**1713-1718** A376 Set of 6 7.75 3.75

**Souvenir Sheet**

**1719** A376 1000fr multicolored 5.50 2.75

World Wildlife Fund — A377

Designs: a, 325fr, Cephalophus drosalis. b, 220fr, Cephalophus maxwelli. c, 180fr, Cephalophus rufilatus. d, 370fr, Cephalophus syvicultor.

1500fr, Cephalophus drosalis, diff.

**1996, July 30 *Perf. 14***
**1720** A377 Block of 4, #a.-d. 4.00 2.00

**Souvenir Sheet**

**1721** A377 1500fr multicolored 6.25 3.00

No. 1720 was issued in sheets of 16 stamps.

Endangered Species — A378

Designs, vert: 220fr, Zebra. 315fr, Leopard. 325fr, Antelope. 335fr, Madoqua Kirki.

No. 1726, each 200fr: a, African elephants. b, Toucan (c, d, e, f.) c, Mamba (f). d, Lionesses. e, Impala. f, Nyala. g, Hippoppotamus. h, Crocodile. i, Kingfisher.

Each 1500 fr: No. 1727, Buphagus erythyrorhynchus, vert. No. 1728, Leopard, vert.

**1996, July 30**
**1722-1725** A378 Set of 4 6.25 3.00
**1726** A378 Sheet of 9, #a.-i. 7.50 3.75

**Souvenir Sheets**

**1727-1728** A378 Set of 2 12.50 6.00

Endangered Species A379

75fr, Elephant. 90fr, Crocodile. 315fr, Deer.

**1996, July 30 Litho. *Perf. 13***
**1729-1731** A379 Set of 3 1.90 .95

Traditional Musical Instruments A380

90fr, Gongs. 220fr, Cymbals (balafon). 325fr, String instrument. 500fr, Drums.

**1996, July 15**
**1732-1735** A380 Set of 4 4.50 2.25

Traditional Dances A381

Designs: 10fr, Kamou dance, Kabyes. 90fr, Kondona dance, Kabyes. 220fr, Bassar. 315fr, Kloto. 335fr, Voudoussis.

**1996, June 30**
**1736-1740** A381 Set of 5 4.00 2.00

New Year 1997 (Year of the Ox) — A382

Paintings, by Ren Bonian (1840-95): No. 1741: a, Herdboy on Buffalo. b, Return from the Pasture. c, Grazing by the Pond.

500fr, Reading Beside an Ox.

**1997, Jan. 2 Litho. *Perf. 14***
**1741** A382 180fr Strip of 3, #a.-c. 2.25 2.25
*d.* Souvenir sheet of 6, 2x #a-c 4.50 4.50

**Souvenir Sheet**
***Perf. 13½x14***

**1742** A382 500fr multicolored 2.00 2.00

No. 1741 was issued in sheets of 6 stamps. No. 1742 contains one 34x46mm stamp.

Fruits A383

100fr, Mango. 150fr, Bananas. 200fr, Peaches. 300fr, Papaya. 400fr, Lemon. 500fr, Coconuts.

1000fr, Various fruits.

**1996, June 2 Litho. *Perf. 12½***
**1743-1748** A383 Set of 6 7.25 7.25

**Souvenir Sheet**
***Perf. 13***

**1749** A383 1000fr multicolored 5.25 5.25

No. 1749 contains one 40x32mm stamp.

Souvenir Sheet

Chinese Stone Carving — A384

Illustration reduced.

**1996, May 10 Litho. *Perf. 12***
**1750** A384 370fr multicolored 1.50 1.50

China '96. No. 1750 was not available until March 1997.

Jaffar Ballogou, Boxer — A384a

**1996 Litho. *Perf. 13***
**1750C** A384a 315fr multi

Two additional stamps were issued in this set. The editors would like to examine them. World Telecommunications Day.

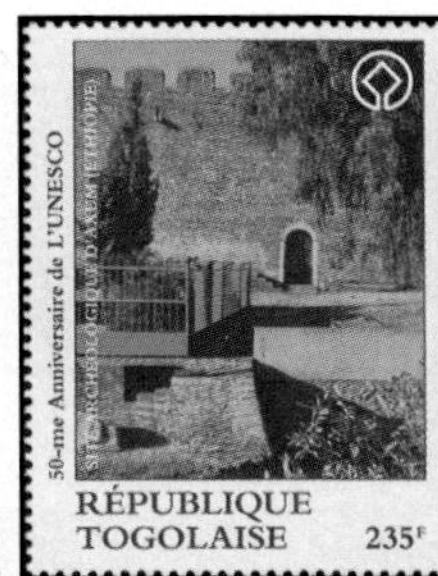

UNESCO, 50th Anniv. A385

World Heritage Sites: No. 1751, each 235fr: a, Axum archaeological site, Ethiopia. b, Victoria Falls, Zambia. c, Archaeological site, Zimbabwe. d, Nature reserve, Niger. e, Arguin Natl. Park, Mauritania. f, Goree Island, Senegal. g, Timgad Ruins, Algeria. h, Ait Ben-Haddou, Morocco.

No. 1752, each 235fr: a, Kyoto, Japan. b, Waterfalls, Colombia. c, Necropolis, Egypt. d, Old Rama Church, Finland. e, Palladian villa, Vicenza, Italy. f, Rock paintings, China. g, Church, Ouro Preto, Brazil. h, Rhodes, Greece.

No. 1753, each 235fr: a, Exterior of Cistercian Abbey, Fontenay, France. b, Dubrovnik Village, Croatia. c, Interior of Cistercian Abbey, Fontenay. d, e, Quedlinberg, Germany. f, Ironbridge Gorge, England. g, Grand Canyon, US. h, Village, Ironbridge Gorge, England.

Each 1000fr: No. 1754, Kyoto, Japan, horiz. No. 1755, Mt. Huangshan, China, horiz. No. 1756, Village, Ironbridge, England, horiz.

**1997, Mar. 24 Litho. *Perf. 14***
**Sheets of 8, a-h, + Label**

**1751-1753** A385 Set of 3 22.50 22.50

**Souvenir Sheets**

**1754-1756** A385 Set of 3 12.00 12.00

Cats A386

150fr, American shorthair. 200fr, Siamese, vert. 300fr, Java. 400fr, "Ocicat," vert. 500fr, Scottish fold. No. 1762, 1000fr, Persian, vert. No. 1763, Colorpoint shorthair, vert.

**1997 Litho. *Perf. 12½***
**1757-1762** A386 Set of 6 8.50 8.50

**Souvenir Sheet**

**1763** A386 1000fr multicolored 3.50 3.50

No. 1763 contains one 32x40mm stamp.

Military Uniforms — A387

Designs: 150fr, Officer of cuirassiers. 200fr, Norman regiment officer. 300fr, Volunteer battalion foot soldier. 400fr, Berlin Campaign Militiaman. 500fr, Foot soldier. No. 1769, 1000fr, Musketeer.

No. 1770, Belling Regiment Hussar.

**1997** ***Perf. 13x12½***

**1764-1769** A387 Set of 6 8.50 8.50

**Souvenir Sheet**

**1770** A387 1000fr multicolored 3.50 3.50

No. 1770 contains one 40x32mm stamp.

Return of Hong Kong to China — A388

Deng Xiaoping (1904-97) — A388a

Views of city: 220fr, Chinese flag as inscription, skyscraper. 315fr, Chinese flag as inscription, night scene. 325fr, Circular stair railing, skyscraper at night. 340fr, Chinese flag, view of city through inscription. 370fr, Deng Xiaoping (1904-97), fireworks over city.

#1775A: a, shown. b, Looking left.

Illustration reduced.

**1997, June 2** ***Perf. 14***

**1771-1775** A388 Set of 5 6.50 6.50

**Sheet of 2**

***Perf. 13½***

**1775A** A388a 500fr #a.-b. 3.75 3.75

Nos. 1771-1773 are 28x44mm and were each issued in sheets of 4. Nos. 1774-1775 were each issued in sheets of 3.

Queen Elizabeth II and Prince Philip, 50th Wedding Anniv. A389

No. 1776: a, Queen. b, Royal arms. c, Queen in yellow hat, Prince in military uniform. d, Queen in white hat, Prince. e, Windsor Castle. f, Prince.

1000fr, Portrait of Queen, Prince.

**1997, June 25**

**1776** A389 315fr Sheet of 6, #a.-f. 6.50 6.50

**Souvenir Sheet**

**1777** A389 1000fr multicolored 3.50 3.50

Locomotives — A390

150fr, Light locomotive, Adams Bridges. 200fr, Norris Type, England 1866. 300fr, Jones and Ports locomotive with long boiler, 1848. 400fr, Cargo and passenger locomotive, Ansaldo, 1850. 500fr, Birkenhead, Italy, 1863. #1783, 1000fr, Quarter locomotive, New York, 1890.

#1783A, Six-wheeled locomotive, Robert Stephenson, 1830, vert.

**1996, Dec. 5** **Litho.** ***Perf. 12½x12***

**1778-1783** A390 Set of 6 8.75 8.75

**Souvenir Sheet**

***Perf. 12½***

**1783A** A390 1000fr multi 3.50 3.50

Birds — A391

150fr, Poephila guttata. 200fr, Lonchura malacca. 300fr, Acanthis cannabina. 400fr, Fringilla coelebs. 500fr, Emblema guttata. #1789, 1000fr, Passerina amoena.

#1789A, Chloebia gouldiae.

**1996, Nov. 27** ***Perf. 13***

**1784-1789** A391 Set of 6 8.75 8.75

**Souvenir Sheet**

**1789A** A391 1000fr multicolored 3.50 3.50

Nos. 1784-1789 are dated 1996.
No. 1789A contains one 32x40mm stamp.

Turtles A392

Designs: 150fr, Asterochelys yniphora. 200fr, Staurotypus triporcatus. 300fr, Puxidea mouhoti. 400fr, Geomyda spengleri. 500fr, Cuora galbinifrons. #1795, 1000fr, Malaclemys terrapin.

#1795A, Asterochelys radiata.

**1996, Nov. 30**

**1790-1795** A392 Set of 6 6.50 6.50

**Souvenir Sheet**

**1795A** A392 1000fr multicolored 3.50 3.50

Nos. 1790-1795 are dated 1996.
No. 1795A contains one 40x32mm stamp.

Natl. Liberation, 30th Anniv. — A393

**1997** **Litho.** ***Perf. 13½***

**1796** A393 90fr yellow & multi .30 .30

**1797** A393 220fr green & multi .75 .75

Diana, Princess of Wales (1961-97) A394

Nos. 1798a-1798i: Various portraits of Princess Diana in designer gowns, each 180fr.

Views up close, each 180fr: No. 1799, like #1798a. No. 1800, like #1798c. No. 1801, like #1798d. No. 1802, like #1798e. No. 1803, like #1798h. No. 1804, like #1798i.

**1997**

**1798** A394 Sheet of 9, #a.-i. 7.50 7.50

**Souvenir Sheets**

**1799-1804** A394 Set of 6 32.50 32.50

Diana, Princess of Wales (1961-97) — A395

Nos. 1805-1807, Various pictures of Diana during her lifetime as Princess of Wales.

Each 1000fr: Pictures of Diana with (in margin): No. 1808, French Pres. Giscard d'Estaing. No. 1809, Mother Teresa. No. 1810, US First Lady Hillary Clinton.

**1998, Jan. 2** ***Perf. 14***

**Sheets of 6**

**1805** A395 240fr #a.-f. 5.00 5.00

**1806** A395 315fr #a.-f. 6.50 6.50

**1807** A395 340fr #a.-f. 7.25 7.25

**Souvenir Sheets**

**1808-1810** A395 Set of 3 10.50 10.50

Souvenir Sheet

Marilyn Monroe (1926-62) — A396

Illustration reduced.

**1997** **Litho.** ***Perf. 13½***

**1811** A396 2000fr multicolored 7.25 7.25

New Year 1998 (Year of the Tiger) — A397

Various paintings of tigers, by Liu Jiyou (1918-83): No. 1812: a, 180fr. b, 200fr. No. 1813: a, 90fr. b, 100fr, c, 180fr. d, 200fr.

**1998, Jan. 5** **Litho.** ***Perf. 14***

**1812** A397 Sheet of 2, #a.-b. 1.25 1.25

**1813** A397 Sheet of 4, #a.-d. 2.00 2.00

No. 1812 contains two 26x65mm stamps.

Hiroshige (1797-1858), Painter — A398

Paintings: No. 1814: a, Sixty-Nine Stations of the Kisokaido Road: Mochizuki. b, Eight Views of Lake Biwa Evening Snow at Mt. Hira. c, Kinkizan Temple on Enoshima Island, Sagami Provence. d, Cherry Blossoms. e, Evening Snow at Asakusa. f, Myhankoshi.

No. 1815: a, Two Terrapins (Fan print). b, Swimming Carp. c, Takanawa by Moonlight. d, Night Rain at Karasaki. e, Chiryu: The Summer Horse Fair. f, Shower over the Nihonbashi.

No. 1816, vert: a, Takata Riding Grounds. b, Sugatami & Omokage Bridges & Jariba at Takata. c, Dam on the Otonashi River at Oji. d, Basho's Hermitage and Camellia Hill. e, Fudo Falls, Oji. f, Takinogawa Oji.

Each 1000fr: No. 1817, Bird in a Tree. No. 1818, Title Page for Hiroshige's One Hundred Views of Edo, by Baisotei. No. 1819, Memorial Portrait of Hiroshige, by Utagawa. No. 1820, Street Stalls and Tradesmen in Jouricho. No. 1821, Cherry Blossom, Morning Glory, Cranes and Rabbits. No. 1822, Three Wild Geese Flying Across the Moon. No. 1823, Suwa Bluff, Nippori. Nos. 1817-1823 are vert.

***Perf. 14x13½, 13½x14***

**1998, Mar. 2** **Litho.**

**Sheets of 6**

**1814** A398 220fr #a.-f. 4.50 4.50

**1815** A398 315fr #a.-f. 6.50 6.50

**1816** A398 370fr #a.-f. 7.50 7.50

**Souvenir Sheets**

***Perf. 13½x14***

**1817-1823** A398 Set of 7 25.00 25.00

Nos. 1817-1823 each contain one 26x72mm stamp.

Fauna, Flora, Minerals — A399

Dolphins and whales: No. 1824: a, Souffleur nesarnack. b, Lagenorhynque. c, Sotalie du cameroun. d, Petit rorqual. e, Rorqual commun. f, Faux orque.

Insects and spiders: No. 1825: a, Lasius niger. b, Sceliphron spirifex. c, Peucetia. d, Mygale. e, Theraphoside. f, Dynaste hercule.

Precious stones, minerals: No. 1826: a, Ruby. b, Diamond in kimberlite. c, Cut diamond. d, Rock salt. e, Tiger's eye. f, Uraninite.

Moths and butterflies: No. 1827: a, Pirate. b, Euchromie des liserons. c, Asterope. d, Psalis de kiriakoff. e, Sphinx de fabricius. f, Pensee bleue.

Mushrooms: No. 1828: a, Lepiote. b, Hypholome. c, Lactaire. d, Russule fetide. e, Russule doree. f, Strophaire.

Each 2000fr: No. 1829, Tricholome a odeur de savon. No. 1830, Potto.

**1998(?)** **Litho.** ***Perf. 13½***

**Sheets of 6**

**1824** A399 180fr #a.-f. 4.00 4.00

**1825** A399 250fr #a.-f. 5.75 5.75

**1826** A399 300fr #a.-f. 6.75 6.75

**1827** A399 400fr #a.-f. 9.00 9.00

**1828** A399 450fr #a.-f. 10.25 10.25

**Souvenir Sheets**

**1829-1830** A399 Set of 2 15.50 15.50

Intl. Scouting, 90th Anniv. (#1825, 1827-1830). Nos. 1829-1830 each contain one 41x60mm stamp.

Jerry Garcia (1942-95) — A400

Various portraits.

**1998 Litho. *Perf. 13½***

**1831** A400 250fr Sheet of 9, #a.-i. 7.75 7.75

**Souvenir Sheet**

**1832** A400 2000fr multicolored 7.00 7.00

No. 1832 contains one 42x51mm stamp.

Dinosaurs — A401

Various unidentified dinosaurs.

**1998**

**1833** A401 290fr Sheet of 9, #a.-i. 10.00 10.00

**Souvenir Sheet**

**1834** A401 2000fr multicolored 7.50 7.50

No. 1834 contains one 42x51mm stamp.

1998 Winter Olympic Games, Nagano — A402

No. 1835: a, Hockey. b, Speed skating. c, Pairs figure skating. d, Luge. e, Curling. f, Bobsledding.

No. 1836: a, Downhill skiing. b, Freestyle ski jumping (blue skis). c, Ski jumping. d, Downhill skier in tuck. e, Snow boarding. f, Freestyle skiing (red skis).

**1998**

**Sheets of 6**

**1835** A402 250fr #a.-f. 5.75 5.75
**1836** A402 300fr #a.-f. 6.75 6.75

Nos. 1835-1836 each have 3 labels.

1998 World Cup Soccer Championships, France — A403

Player, country, vert: No. 1837, Kluivert, Netherlands. No. 1838, Asprilla, Colombia. No. 1839, Bergkamp, Netherlands. No. 1840, Gascoigne, England. No. 1841, Ravanelli, Italy. No. 1842, Sheringham, England.

No. 1843: a, Paul Gascoigne, England, diff. b, Ryan Giggs, Wales. c, Roy Keane, Ireland. d, Stuart Pearce, England. e, Tony Adams, England. f, Teddy Sheringham, England, diff. g, Paul Ince, England. h, Steve McManaman, England.

No. 1844: a, Rossi, Italy. b, Lineker, England. c, Lato, Poland. d, Futre, Poland. e, Klinsmann, Germany. f, Hurst, England. g, Kempes, Argentina. h, McCoist, Scotland.

World Cup Champions, year, vert. — #1845: a, Argentina, 1978. b, Italy, 1982. c, England, 1966. d, Uruguay, 1930. e, Germany, 1954. f, Argentina, 1986. g, Brazil, 1994.

Each 1500fr: No. 1846, Ronaldo, Brazil, vert. No. 1847, Gary Lineker, England, vert. No. 1848, Shearer, England, vert.

***Perf. 13½x14, 14x13½***

**1998, July 10 Litho.**

**1837-1842** A403 370fr Set of 6 7.50 7.50

**Sheets of 8 + Label**

**1843** A403 220fr #a.-h. 5.00 6.00
**1844** A403 315fr #a.-h. 8.50 8.50

**Sheet of 7 + 2 Labels**

**1845** A403 325fr #a.-g. 7.75 7.75

**Souvenir Sheets**

**1846-1848** A403 Set of 3 15.00 15.00

Bella Bellow (d. 1973), Singer — A403a

**1998-2002 Litho. *Perf. 13½***

| | | | | | |
|---|---|---|---|---|---|
| **1848A** | A403a | 5fr | yel orange | | |
| **1848B** | A403a | 10fr | olive green | | |
| **1848C** | A403a | 25fr | emerald | | |
| **1848D** | A403a | 40fr | violet | | |
| **1848E** | A403a | 50fr | black | | |
| **1848F** | A403a | 75fr | yel orange | | |
| **1848G** | A403a | 100fr | orange | | |
| **1848H** | A403a | 125fr | blue | | |
| **1848I** | A403a | 200fr | brt purple | | |
| **1848J** | A403a | 240fr | red violet | | |
| **1848K** | A403a | 280fr | green | | |
| **1848L** | A403a | 300fr | Prus blue | | |
| **1848M** | A403a | 320fr | red orange | | |
| **1848N** | A403a | 340fr | car lake | | |
| **1848O** | A403a | 390fr | car rose | | |
| **1848P** | A403a | 450fr | brt blue ('02) | — | — |
| **1848R** | A403a | 500fr | gray olive ('02) | — | — |

At least four additional values were issued in this set. The editors would like to examine any examples.

Star Wars Movies — A404

Return of the Jedi — #1849: a, Princess Leia. b, Darth Vader. c, Han Solo. d, R2-D2, C-3PO. e, Emperor Palpatine. f, Chewbacca. g, Leia on speeder. h, Luke Skywalker. i, Storm trooper on speeder.

Empire Strikes Back — #1850: a, Lando Calrissian. b, Yoda. c, Chewbacca. d, C-3PO, R2-D2. e, Luke Skywalker. f, Darth Vader. g, Battle on snow planet. h, Leia. i, Rider on snow planet.

2000fr, Han Solo, Luke Skywalker, Princess Leia, R2-D2.

**1997 Litho. *Perf. 13½***

**Sheets of 9**

**1849** A404 190fr #a.-i. 5.75 5.75
**1850** A404 350fr #a.-i. 10.50 10.50

**Souvenir Sheet**

**1851** A404 2000fr multicolored 7.00 7.00

No. 1851 contains one 42x60mm.

Jacqueline Kennedy Onassis (1929-94) — A405

No. 1852: Various portraits.

No. 1853: Various portraits of John F. Kennedy (1917-63).

**1997**

**Sheets of 9**

**1852** A405 250fr #a.-i. 7.50 7.50
**1853** A405 400fr #a.-i. 12.00 12.00

Diana, Princess of Wales (1961-97) — A406

No. 1854: Various portraits.

2000fr, Diana in black (Mother Teresa in sheet margin).

**1997**

**Sheet of 8 + Label**

**1854** A406 500fr #a.-h. 15.00 15.00

**Souvenir Sheet**

**1854I** A406 2000fr multicolored 8.25 8.25

Marilyn Monroe (1926-62) — A407

Various portraits, each 300fr.

**1997 Litho. *Perf. 13½***

**1855** A407 Sheet of 9, #a.-i. 9.00 9.00

Minerals A408

Designs: 100fr, Calcite. 150fr, Turquoise, vert. 200fr, Pyrite, vert. 300fr, Tourmaline, vert. 400fr, Pyrargirite, vert. 500fr, Malachite. 1000fr, Beryl, vert.

**1999 Litho. *Perf. 12¾***

**1856-1861** A408 Set of 6 5.00 5.00

**Souvenir Sheet**

***Perf. 13***

**1861A** A408 1000fr multicolored 3.00 3.00

No. 1861A contains one 32x40mm stamp.

Flowers — A409

Designs: No. 1862, Caralluma burchardii. No. 1863, Dimorphotheca barberiae. No. 1864, Hoya carnosa. No. 1865, Amaryllis belladonna. No. 1866, Watsonia beatricis. No. 1867, Anthurium schezerianum. No. 1868, Thumbergia alata. No. 1869, Arctotis breviscapa. No. 1870, Glauciun flavum. No. 1871, Impatiens petersiana. No. 1872, Chrysanthemum segetum. No. 1873, Zantedeschia aethiopica, horiz.

**1999** ***Perf. 12¼***

**1862** A409 100fr brown .30 .30
**1863** A409 100fr violet .30 .30
**1864** A409 100fr pale red .30 .30
**1865** A409 150fr dark grn bl .45 .45
**1866** A409 150fr red brown .45 .45
**1867** A409 150fr violet blue .45 .45
**1868** A409 200fr orange .60 .60
**1869** A409 200fr bright grn bl .60 .60
**1870** A409 300fr olive .90 .90
**1871** A409 300fr blue .90 .90
**1872** A409 500fr brown 1.50 1.50
**1873** A409 1000fr bright pink 3.00 3.00
*Nos. 1862-1873 (12)* 9.75 9.75

1998 World Cup Soccer Championship, France — A410

Predominant colors of player's shirts. No. 1874: a, Yellow. b, White. c, Blue. d, Red.
No. 1875: a, White. b, Blue. c, Red. d, Green.
No. 1876: a, White, with black shorts. b, Yellow, with blue shorts. c, Yellow, with yellow shorts. d, White, with white shorts.
No. 1877: a, Red. b, Green. c, White. d, Red & white striped.
No. 1878: a, Blue. b, Yellow. c, Red. d, White.
No. 1879: a, Orange. b, White. c, Red. d, Multicolored diamonds.
No. 1880: a, White, with black shorts. b, White, with blue and red chest stripes. c, White, with green trim. d, White, with red and blue arm stripes.
No. 1881: a, Blue & white stripes. b, Red & white checks. c, Yellow & green, d, Blue.
2000fr, Player, map of France.

**1998** **Litho.** ***Perf. 13¼***

**Sheets of 4**

**1874** A410 180fr #a.-d. 2.40 2.40
**1875** A410 200fr #a.-d. 2.60 2.60
**1876** A410 250fr #a.-d. 3.25 3.25
**1877** A410 290fr #a.-d. 3.75 3.75
**1878** A410 300fr #a.-d. 4.00 4.00
**1879** A410 350fr #a.-d. 4.75 4.75
**1880** A410 400fr #a.-d. 5.25 5.25
**1881** A410 425fr #a.-d. 5.50 5.50
*Nos. 1874-1881 (8)* 31.50 31.50

**Souvenir Sheet**

**1882** A410 2000fr multicolored 6.50 6.50

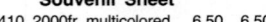

Birds A410a

Designs: 100fr, Luscinia svecica. 150fr, Oriolus oriolus. 200fr, Carduelis carduelis. 300fr, Parus caeruleus. 400fr, Fringilla coelebs. 500fr, Parus montanus.
1000fr, Regulus ignicapillus.

**1999** **Litho.** ***Perf. 12¾***

**1882A-1882F** A410a Set of 6 4.00 4.00

**Souvenir Sheet**

***Perf. 13x13¼***

**1882G** A410a 1000fr multi 2.40 2.40

No. 1882G contains one 40x32mm stamp.

Antique Automobiles — A410b

Designs: 100fr, 1913 Peugeot Bebe. 150fr, 1950 Rolls-Royce. 200fr, 1921 Stutz Bearcat. 300fr, 1923 Ford Model T. 400fr, 1907 Packard. 500fr, 1950 Citroen II Legere sedan.
1000fr, 1929 Ford Model A Tudor sedan.

**1999** ***Perf. 12¾***

**1882H-1882M** A410b Set of 6 4.00 4.00

**Souvenir Sheet**

***Perf. 13***

**1882N** A410b 1000fr multi 2.40 2.40

No. 1882N contains one 40x32mm stamp.

Cats — A411

No. 1883: a, 100fr, Colorpoint. b, 150fr, British shorthair.
No. 1884: a, 200fr, Ocicat. b, 300fr, Ragdoll.
No. 1885: a, 400fr, Balinese. b, 500fr, California Spangled.
1000fr, Somali.

**1999** **Litho.** ***Perf. 12½***

**1883** A411 Pair, #a.-b. .75 .75
**1884** A411 Pair, #a.-b. 1.50 1.50
**1885** A411 Pair, #a.-b. 2.75 2.75
*Nos. 1883-1885 (3)* 5.00 5.00

**Souvenir Sheet**

**1886** A411 1000fr multicolored 3.00 3.00

Millennium A412

No. 1886A, Invention of Paper by Chinese (with millennium emblem).
No. 1887 — Chinese Science & Technology: a, Lacquerware. b, Counting rods. c, Sericulture. d, Acupuncture. e, "Tuned chime bell." f, Piston bellows. g, Compass. h, Manufacture of steel. i. Crossbow. j, Spinning wheel. k, Water conservancy. l, Pulse taking. m, Multi-tube seed drill. n, Rotary winnowing fan. o, Like #1886A (no millennium emblem). p, Silk loom (60x40mm). q, Wheelbarrow.
No. 1888 — Highlights of the 11th Century: a, Chinese invent gunpowder. b, Islamic bronze griffin. c, Battle of Clontarf. d, William becomes Duke of Normandy. e, Norman knight. f, Spinning wheels in use in China. g, Yaroslav becomes Grand Prince of Kiev. h, Polyphonic singing introduced. i, Macbeth becomes King of Scotland. j, Edward the Confessor becomes King of England. k, Astrolabe. l, Harp introduced in Europe. m, Trier Cathedral. n, Mandingo Empire founded in Africa. o, Toltecs invade Yucatan. p, Vikings reach North Americam (60x40mm). q, Movable type used in China.
No. 1889 — Western Paintings of the 20th century by: a, Henri Matisse. b, Pablo Picasso. c, Marc Chagall. d, Wassily Kandinsky. e, Fernand Léger. f, Piet Mondrian. g, George Bellows. h, Georgia O'Keeffe. i, Salvador Dali. j, Francis Bacon. k, Edward Hopper. l, Andy Warhol. m, Helen Frankenthaler. n, Richard Anuszkiewicz. o, Audrey Flack. p, Jackson Pollack, Lee Krasner (60x40mm). q, Jean-Michel Basquiat.

**1999** **Litho.** ***Perf. 13¼x13***

**1886A** A412 120fr multi .35 .35

**Sheets of 17**

***Perf. 12½***

**1887** A412 120fr #a.-q. + label 6.75 6.75
**1888** A412 130fr #a.-q. + label 7.00 7.00
**1889** A412 140fr #a.-q. + label 7.75 7.75

Inscriptions on Nos. 1887b, 1887e, 1888i, and perhaps others, are incorrect or misspelled.
Issued: 130fr, 7/20.

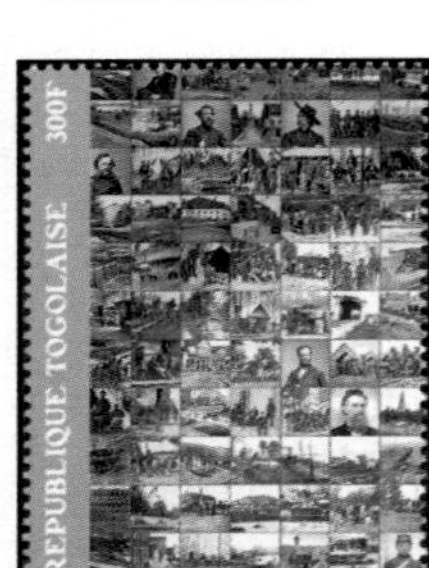


US Civil War Photographs A413

Various Civil War photographs making up a photomosaic of Abraham Lincoln, each 300fr.

**1999, July 20** **Litho.** ***Perf. 13½***

**1890** A413 Sheet of 8, #a.-h. 7.50 7.50

See Nos. 1939-1940.

Free Trade Zone, 10th Anniv. — A414

Symbol and: 125fr, Map. 240fr, Clouds. 340fr, Wall.

**1999** **Litho.** ***Perf. 12¾***

**1891** A414 125fr multi .35 .35
**1892** A414 240fr multi .65 .65
**1893** A414 340fr multi .90 .90
*Nos. 1891-1893 (3)* 1.90 1.90

Rural Development Council, 40th Anniv. — A414a

**1999** **Litho.** ***Perf. 13x13¼***

**1893A** A414a 240fr red & multi
**1893B** A414a 380fr vio & multi
**1893C** A414a 390fr blk & multi

Other stamps for this subject may exist. The editors would like to examine any examples. Numbers may change.

Goldfish A415

Various depictions of Carassius auratus auratus: 100fr, 150fr, 200fr, 300fr, 400fr, 500fr.

**1999**

**1894-1899** A415 Set of 6 4.75 4.75

**Souvenir Sheet**

***Perf. 13***

**1899A** A415 1000fr multi 3.00 3.00

No. 1899A contains one 40x31mm stamp.

SOS Children's Villages, 50th Anniv. — A416

**1999** **Litho.** ***Perf. 13¼x13***

**1900** A416 125fr multi ('01) .35 .35
**1901** A416 240fr multi
**1902** A416 340fr multi

Additional stamps may have been issued in this set. The editors would like to examine any examples.

Sailing Vessels — A417

Designs: 100fr, Phoenician boat. 150fr Roman cargo boat. 200fr, New Guinea fishing boat. 300fr, Caravel, vert. 400fr, 16th cent. English ship, vert. 500fr, 17th cent. English ship, vert.
1000fr, Steamship with sails.

**1999** **Litho.** ***Perf. 12½***

**1905-1910** A417 Set of 6 4.50 4.50

**Souvenir Sheet**

***Perf. 12¼x12***

**1911** A417 1000fr multi 2.75 2.75

No. 1911 contains one 42x30mm stamp.

Dogs — A417a

Designs: 100fr, St. Bernard. 150fr, Teckel. 200fr, German shepherd. 300fr, Italian hound. 400fr, Yorkshire terrier. 500fr, Schnauzer.

**1999** **Litho.** ***Perf. 12¾***

**1911A-1911F** A417a Set of 6 4.00 4.00

**Souvenir Sheet**

***Perf. 12½***

**1911G** A417a 1000fr Afghan hound 2.40 2.40

No. 1911G contains one 40x31mm stamp.

Trains A417b

Designs: 100fr, Baldwin 0-4-0. 150fr, Baldwin 2-6-2. 200fr, Baldwin gasoline locomotive. 300fr, H.K. Porter 0-4-0. 400fr, H.K. Porter 2-6-2. 500fr, Vulcan 0-4-0.

**1999** **Litho.** ***Perf. 12¾***

**1911H-1911M** A417b Set of 6 4.00 4.00

**Souvenir Sheet**

**1911N** A417b 1000fr Jordanian locomotive 2.40 2.40

No. 1911N contains one 40x31mm stamp.

Orchids
A417c

Designs: 100fr, Gramangis ellisii. 150fr, Habenaria columbae. 200fr, Epidendrum atropurpureum. 300fr, Odontoglossum majale. 400fr, Oncidium splendidum. 500fr, Zygopetalum mackai.
1000fr, Paphiopedilum pairieanum.

**1999, Nov. 8 Litho. *Perf. 12x12¼***
**1911O-1911T** A417c Set of 6 5.25 5.25

**Souvenir Sheet**
***Perf. 12½***

**1911U** A417c 1000fr multi 3.25 3.25

No. 1911U contains one 31x39mm stamp.

New Year 2000 (Year of the Dragon) — A418

Various views of dragon: 100fr, 150fr, 200fr, 300fr, 400fr, 500fr.
1000fr, Head of dragon, horiz.

**2000 *Perf. 12¾x12***
**1912-1917** A418 Set of 6 4.50 4.50

**Souvenir Sheet**
***Perf. 13¼***

**1918** A418 1000fr multi 2.75 2.75

No. 1918 contains one 40x32mm stamp.

Wild Cats
A419

Designs: 100fr, Panthera tigris. 150fr, Acinonyx jubatus. 200fr, Felis concolor. 300fr, Panthera leo, female. 400fr, Felis pardalis. 500fr, Panthera leo, male.
1000fr, Panthera tigris, diff.

**2000 *Perf. 13***
**1919-1924** A419 Set of 6 4.50 4.50

**Souvenir Sheet**

**1925** A419 1000fr multi 2.75 2.75

No. 1925 contains one 40x32mm stamp.

Flowers — A420

No. 1926, 290fr: a, Cyrtanthus contractus. b, Sandersonia aurantiaca. c, Anomateca grandiflora. d, Helichrysum ecklonis. e, Striga elegans. f, Nymphaea odorata.
No. 1927, 290fr: a, Leomotis leonii. b, Strelitzia reginae. c, Freesia refracta. d, Garzania nivea. e, Dimophotheca sinuata. f, Pelargonium domesticum.
No. 1928, 290fr: a, Gloriosa rothchiliana. b, Clematis vitalba. c, Rochea falcato. d, Plumbago capensis. e, Thunbergia alata. f, Lampranthus coccineus.
No. 1929, 1500fr, Epiphyllum hybrid. No. 1930, 1500fr, Agapanthus africanus.
Illustration reduced.

**2000, July 28 Litho. *Perf. 14***
**Sheets of 6, #a-f**

**1926-1928** A420 Set of 3 13.50 13.50

**Souvenir Sheets**

**1929-1930** A420 Set of 2 7.75 7.75

Wildlife
A421

Designs: 200fr, Thompson's gazelle. 300fr, Felis margarita. 400fr, Blesbok. 500fr, Kob.
No. 1935, 290fr, vert.: a, Hoopoe. b, Harpactira spider. c, Marabou. d, Bee-eater. e, Oryx. f, Okapi. g, Wart hog. h, Baboon.
No. 1936, 290fr, vert.: a, Hornbill. b, Pygmy kingfisher. c, Vulture. d, Bataleur eagle. e, Kudu. f, Hyena. g, Gorilla. h, Lizard.
No. 1937, 1500fr, Eland, vert. No. 1938, 1500fr, Mongoose, vert.

**2000, July 28**
**1931-1934** A421 Set of 4 3.75 3.75

**Sheets of 8, #a-h**

**1935-1936** A421 Set of 2 12.00 12.00

**Souvenir Sheets**

**1937-1938** A421 Set of 2 7.75 7.75

Mushrooms
A421a

Designs: 100fr, Hebeloma crustuliniforme. 150fr, Polyporellus squamosus, horiz. 200fr, Morchella deliciosa. 300fr, Disciotis venosa, horiz. 400fr, Cantharellus tubiformis. 500fr, Otidea onotica, horiz.
1000fr, Ixocomus granulatus, horiz.

**2000, July 30 Litho. *Perf. 12¾***
**1938A-1938F** A421a Set of 6 4.75 4.75

**Souvenir Sheet**
***Perf. 13***

**1938G** A421a 1000fr multi 2.75 2.75

No. 1938G contains one 39x31mm stamp.

**Civil War Photographs Type of 1999**

No. 1939, 290fr: Various photographs with a science theme making up a photomosaic of Albert Einstein.
No. 1940, 290fr: Various photographs with an Oriental theme making up a photomosaic of Mao Zedong.

**2000, Sept. 5 *Perf. 13¾***
**Sheets of 8, #a-h**

**1939-1940** A413 Set of 2 12.00 12.00

Queen Mother, 100th Birthday — A422

No. 1941: a, With Princesses Elizabeth and Margaret, 1931. b, With daughter, 1940. c, Black and white photo. d, In 1990.
1500fr, With Princess Margaret, 1939.
Illustration reduced.

**2000, Sept. 5 *Perf. 14***
**1941** A422 650fr Sheet of 4, #a-d, + label 6.75 6.75

**Souvenir Sheet**
***Perf. 13¾***

**1942** A422 1500fr With Princess Margaret, 1939 4.00 4.00

No. 1942 contains one 38x51mm stamp.

Popes — A423

No. 1943, 400fr: a, Anastasius I, 399-401. b, Boniface I, 418-22. c, Gaius, 283-96. d, Hilarius, 461-68. e, Hyginus, 136-40. f, Innocent I, 402-17.
No. 1944, 400fr: a, Martin I, 649-55. b, Nicholas I, 858-67. c, Paschal I, 817-24. d, Paul I, 757-67. e, Pelagius, 556-61. f, Pelagius II, 579-90.
No. 1945, 400fr: a, Sergius, 687-701. b, Sergius II, 844-47. c, Severinus, 640. d, Sisinnius, 708. e, Stephen II, 752-57. f, Stephen IV, 816-17.
No. 1946, 1500fr, Pontian, 230-35. No. 1947, 1500fr, Pelagius II, diff. No. 1948, 1500fr, Stephen V, 885-91.
Illustration reduced.

**2000, Sept. 5 *Perf. 12x12¼***
**Sheets of 6, #a-f**

**1943-1945** A423 Set of 3 19.00 19.00

**Souvenir Sheets**

**1946-1948** A423 Set of 3 11.50 11.50

British Monarchs — A424

No. 1949, 400fr: a, Charles II, 1660-85. b, Anne, 1702-14. c, George I, 1714-27. d, George IV, 1820-30. e, James II, 1685-88. f, George II, 1727-60.
No. 1950, 400fr: a, Elizabeth II, 1952-present. b, Edward VIII, 1936. c, George VI, 1936-52. d, George V, 1910-36. e, Edward VII, 1901-10. f, William IV, 1830-37.
No. 1951, 1500fr, William III and Mary, 1689-1702. No. 1952, 1500fr, Victoria, 1837-1901.
Illustration reduced.

**2000, Sept. 5**
**Sheets of 6, #a-f**

**1949-1950** A424 Set of 2 12.50 12.50

**Souvenir Sheets**

**1951-1952** A424 Set of 2 7.75 7.75

**Millennium Type of 1999**

Highlights of 1950-59: a, US sends troops to defend South Korea. b, Rock and roll hits the air waves. c, Death of Eva Peron. d, Structure of DNA revealed by Watson and Crick. e, Sir Edmund Hillary and Tenzing Norgay reach peak of Mt. Everest. f, John F. Kennedy marries Jacqueline Bouvier. g, Coronation of Queen Elizabeth II. h, Millionth Volkswagen produced. i, German soccer team wins World Cup. j, Roger Bannister runs 1st 4-minute mile. k, Dr. Jonas Salk develops polio vaccine. l, 1st McDonald's franchise. m, New phone lines cross Atlantic. n, Soviet Union launches Sputnik. o, Jack Kerouac writes "On the Road." p, China begins "Great Leap Forward." q, Communist revolution in Cuba. r, Computer chip patented.

**2000 *Perf. 12¾x12½***
**1953** A412 200fr Sheet of 18, #a-r, + label 9.25 9.25

36th Organization of African Unity Summit, Lomé — A425

OAU emblem, map of Africa, doves and panel color of: 10fr, Bright yellow. 25fr, Green. 100fr, Dull yellow. 125fr, Blue violet. 250fr, Red violet. 375fr, Red. 400fr, Brown. 425fr, Orange.
No. 1954: a, Peace dove statue. b, Hotel du 2 Février. c, Congress building, Lomé. d, Alédjo Fault. e, Temberma hut. f, Cacao plantation.
No. 1955: a, Pres. Gnassingbé Eyadema, map of Europe and Africa, handshakes. b, Algerian Pres. Abdelazir Bouteflika, Pres. Eyadema, and map of Africa. c, Pres. Eyadema and OAU emblem. d, Map of Africa, doves, OAU emblem.
Illustration reduced.

**2000 Litho. *Perf. 14x13¾***
**1953S-1953Z** A425 Set of 8 5.00 5.00

**Sheets of 6 and 4**

**1954** A425 350fr #a-f 5.50 5.50
**1955** A425 550fr #a-d 6.00 6.00

Trains — A426

No. 1956, 425fr: a, Richard Trevethick's engine. b, Stephenson's Adler. c, Crampton Continent. d, Atlantic Coastlines 4-4-2. e, Great Northern Railway Ivatt Atlantic. f, Great Western Railway City of Truro 4-4-0.
No. 1957, 425fr: a, Paris-Lyon-Mediterranean Railway, compound 4-8-2. b, Canadian Pacific Railway Royal Hudson 4-6-4. c, London-Midland Railway Duchess. d, New York Central Twentieth Century Limited. e, New Zealand Government Railway J class 4-8-4. f, British Railways Evening Star 5-10-0.

No. 1958, 1800fr, Eurostar. No. 1959, 1800fr, TGV Atlantique.
Illustration reduced.

**2000, Sept. 8 Litho. *Perf. 14***

**Sheets of 6, #a-f**

**1956-1957** A426 Set of 2 14.50 14.50

**Souvenir Sheets**

**1958-1959** A426 Set of 2 10.50 10.50

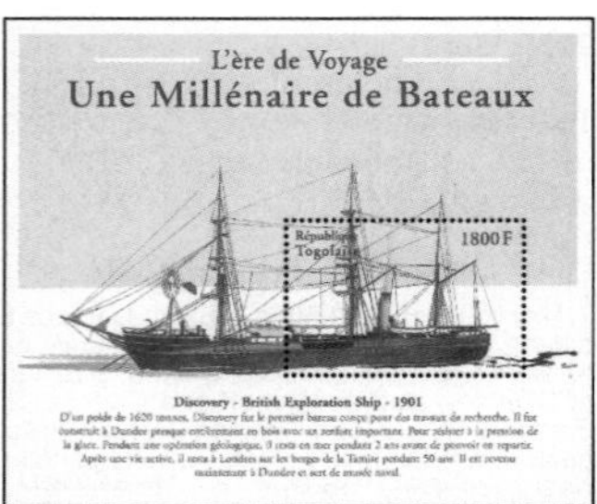


Ships — A427

No. 1960, 425fr: a, Norse knaar. b, Hanseatic cog. c, Iberian caravel. d, Henri Grace à Dieu. e, Ark Royal. f, Dutch Hooker.
No. 1961, 425fr: a, HMS Victory. b, HMS Warrior. c, Cutty Sark. d, USS Olympia. e, Empress of Canada. f, James Clark Ross.
No. 1962, 1800fr, Discovery. No. 1963, 1800fr, Sea Cat ferry.
Illustration reduced.

**2000, Sept. 8 Litho. *Perf. 14***

**Sheets of 6, #a-f**

**1960-1961** A427 Set of 2 14.50 14.50

**Souvenir Sheets**

**1962-1963** A427 Set of 2 10.50 10.50

Dogs and Cats — A428

Designs: 275fr, Bloodhound. 300fr, Sphinx cat. 325fr, Basset hound. 350fr, Cocker spaniel. No. 1968, 375fr, American curl cat. 400fr, Scottish fold cat.
No. 1970, 375fr, horiz. — Dogs: a, Bearded collie. b, Chow chow. c, Boxer. d, Irish setter. e, Bracco Italiano. f, Pointer.
No. 1971, 375fr, horiz. — Cats: a, Devon Rex. b, Cornish Rex. c, Siamese. d, Balinese. e, Birman. f, Korat.
No. 1972, 1500fr, Yorkshire terrier. No. 1973, 1500fr, Chinchilla cat.

***Perf. 13½x13¼, 13¼x13½***

**2001, Dec. 17 Litho.**

**1964-1969** A428 Set of 6 5.50 5.50

**Sheets of 6, #a-f**

**1970-1971** A428 Set of 2 12.50 12.50

**Souvenir Sheets**

**1972-1973** A428 Set of 2 8.25 8.25

Marine Life — A429

No. 1974, 200fr (31x31mm): a, Priacanthus arenatus. b, Diplodus annularis. c, Lithognathus mormgrus. d, Selene nomer. e, Perraeus duorarum. f, Arbacia lixula. g, Serranus scriba. h, Trachurus trachurus. i, Lepas amatifera. j, Octopus vulgaris. k, Scorpaena scrofa. l, Dardenus arroser.
No. 1975, 250fr (31x31mm): a, Porcupine fish. b, Blue shark. c, Sting ray. d, Physalia physalis. e, Turtles. f, Coryphaena hippurus. g, Carranx hippos. h, Sawfish. i, Todarupsis eblanae. j, Pompano. k, Diplodus cervinus. l, Barracuda.

No. 1976, 1500fr, Octopus vulgaris, diff. No. 1977, 1500fr, Blue shark, diff.

**2001, Dec. 17 *Perf. 12½***

**Sheets of 12, #a-l**

**1974-1975** A429 Set of 2 15.00 15.00

**Souvenir Sheets**

***Perf. 13¼x13½***

**1976-1977** A429 Set of 2 8.25 8.25

African Wildlife A430

Designs: 150fr, Okapia johnstoni, vert. 200fr, Sagittarius serpentarius. 250fr, Lemur catta, vert. 300fr, Gorilla gorilla. 350fr, Genetta genetta, vert. 400fr, Fennecus zerda.
No. 1984, 380fr: a, Papio hamadryas. b, Felis serval. c, Suricata suricatta. d, Orycteropus afer. e, Connochataetes taurinus. f, Tragelaphus strepsiceros.
No. 1985, 380fr: a, Panthera pardus. b, Loxodonta africana. c, Cercopithecus hamlyni. d, Ephippiorhynchuus senegalensis. e, Hippopotamus amphibius. f, Hippotragus niger.
No. 1986, 415fr: a, Equus burchelli boehmi. b, Ceratotherium simum. c, Achionyx jubatus. d, Gazella dama. e, Crocuta crocuta. f, Lyacon pictus.
No. 1987, 1500fr, Crocodylus niloticus. No. 1988, 1500fr, Panthera leo, vert. No. 1989, 1500fr, Giraffa camelopardalis.

***Perf. 13½x13¼, 13¼x13½***

**2001, Dec. 17**

**1978-1983** A430 Set of 6 4.50 4.50

**Sheets of 6, #a-f**

**1984-1986** A430 Set of 3 19.00 19.00

**Souvenir Sheets**

**1987-1989** A430 Set of 3 12.50 12.50

United We Stand A431

**2002, Mar. 18 Litho. *Perf. 14***

**1990** A431 400fr multi 1.10 1.10

**Bella Bellow Type of 1998-2002**

**2002 Litho. *Perf. 13½***

| | | | | |
|---|---|---|---|---|
| **1990A** | A403a | 20fr yel green | — | — |
| **1990B** | A403a | 30fr brown | — | — |
| **1990C** | A403a | 110fr blue green | — | — |

Numbers may change.

2004 Summer Olympics, Athens — A432

Designs: 150fr, Chariot rider and horses. 300fr, Pin from 1960 Rome Olympics, vert. 450fr, Emblem of 1960 Squaw Valley Winter Olympics, vert. 500fr, Diver, vert.

**2004, Aug. 25 Litho. *Perf. 13¼***

**1991-1994** A432 Set of 4 5.25 5.25

Pres. Gnassingbé Eyadema (1935-2005) A433

**2004 *Perf. 13½x13¼***

**Panel Color**

| | | | | | |
|---|---|---|---|---|---|
| **1995** | A433 | 25fr | dark blue | .20 | .20 |
| **1996** | A433 | 50fr | yel green | .20 | .20 |
| **1997** | A433 | 150fr | olive green | .60 | .60 |
| **1998** | A433 | 400fr | dull brown | 1.60 | 1.60 |
| **1999** | A433 | 550fr | green | 2.25 | 2.25 |
| **2000** | A433 | 650fr | brt blue | 2.75 | 2.75 |
| **2001** | A433 | 1000fr | lilac | 4.25 | 4.25 |
| **2002** | A433 | 2000fr | salmon pink | 8.25 | 8.25 |
| **2003** | A433 | 3000fr | blue green | 12.50 | 12.50 |
| | *Nos. 1995-2003 (9)* | | | 32.60 | 32.60 |

Pope John Paul II (1920-2005) A435

**2006, Jan. 24 Litho. *Perf. 13½***

**2007** A435 550fr multi 2.00 2.00

Printed in sheets of 4.

Jules Verne (1828-1905), Writer — A436

No. 2008:, a, Home of Verne from 1882-1900. b, Monument to Verne, Amiens, France. c, Sculpture of Verne, Amiens. d, Mysterious Island.

**2006, Jan. 24 Litho. *Perf. 13½***

**2008** A436 550fr Sheet of 4, #a-d 8.25 8.25

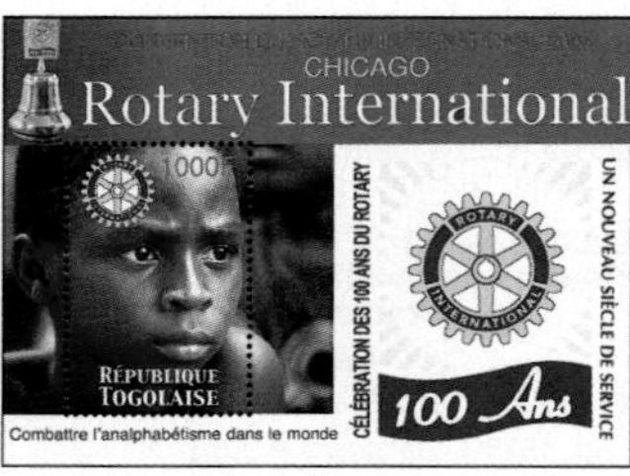


Rotary International, Cent. (in 2005) — A437

No. 2009 — Children and denomination in: a, Yellow in upper right. b, Red. c, Yellow in upper left.
1000fr, Child.

**2006, Jan. 24**

**2009** A437 700fr Sheet of 3, #a-c 7.75 7.75

**Souvenir Sheet**

**2010** A437 1000fr multi 3.75 3.75

Friedrich von Schiller (1759-1805), Writer — A438

No. 2011, vert. — Schiller: a, Monument. b, Bust. c, Portrait.
1000fr, Birthplace of Schiller.

**2006, Jan. 24**

**2011** A438 700fr Sheet of 3, #a-c 7.75 7.75

**Souvenir Sheet**

**2012** A438 1000fr multi 3.75 3.75

World Cup Soccer Championships, 75th Anniv. (in 2005) — A439

No. 2013: a, David Beckham. b, Ronaldo Nazario. c, Fernando Hierro.
1000fr, Eusebio.

**2006, Jan. 24**

**2013** A439 700fr Sheet of 3, #a-c 7.75 7.75

**Souvenir Sheet**

**2014** A439 1000fr multi 3.75 3.75

JOUR DE LA VICTOIRE EN EUROPE
8 MAI 1945
RÉPUBLIQUE TOGOLAISE
1000F
NAVIRE

V-E Day, 50th Anniv. (in 2005) — A440

No. 2015, vert.: a, Monument to victory. b, New York Times front page with war reports. c, Soldiers at Battle of the Bulge, 1944. d, Airplanes. e, Sculpture of Holocaust victim.
1000fr, DUKW.

**2006, Jan. 24 Litho. *Perf. 13¼***

**2015** A440 400fr Sheet of 5, #a-e 7.50 7.50

**Souvenir Sheet**

**2016** A440 1000fr multi 3.75 3.75

V-J Day, 50th Anniv. (in 2005) — A441

No. 2017: a, USS Charles Carroll. b, BB-35. c, LCT-515. d, LST-388. e, Destroyer Thompson DD-627. f, USS Thomas Jefferson.
1000fr, Battle of Iwo Jima.

**2006, Jan. 24**
**2017** A441 350fr Sheet of 6, #a-f 7.75 7.75

**Souvenir Sheet**
**2018** A441 1000fr multi 3.75 3.75

Railroads, Bicent. — A442

No. 2019: a, DX5287. b, W192. c, Central Pacific Jupiter. d, LWDHAM.
No. 2020, 1000fr, Rovos Ralf Class 25NC. No. 2021, 1000fr, Class 242 streamlined tank locomotive.

**2006, Jan. 24**
**2019** A442 550fr Sheet of 4, #a-d 8.25 8.25

**Souvenir Sheets**
**2020-2021** A442 Set of 2 7.50 7.50

Léopold Sédar Senghor Year — A443

**2006, July 28**

| | | | | |
|---|---|---|---|---|
| **2022** | A443 | 150fr multi | .60 | .60 |
| **2023** | A443 | 550fr multi | 2.25 | 2.25 |
| **2024** | A443 | 650fr multi | 2.60 | 2.60 |
| **2025** | A443 | 1000fr multi | 4.00 | 4.00 |
| **2026** | A443 | 2000fr multi, horiz. | 8.00 | 8.00 |
| **2027** | A443 | 3000fr multi, horiz. | 12.00 | 12.00 |
| **2028** | A443 | 5000fr multi, horiz. | 20.00 | 20.00 |
| **2029** | A443 | 10,000fr multi, horiz. | 40.00 | 40.00 |
| | | *Nos. 2022-2029 (8)* | 89.45 | 89.45 |

**Souvenir Sheet**

Wolfgang Amadeus Mozart (1756-91), Composer — A444

**2006, Dec. 21** ***Perf. 14***
**2030** A444 1500fr multi 6.00 6.00

Space Achievements — A445

Designs: 150fr, Luna 9. 300fr, Hayabusa probe. 450fr, Venus Express. 500fr, Space Shuttle Discovery, vert.
No. 2035: a, Intl. Space Station. b, Deep Impact probe. c, Muse Asteroid. d, Artist's view of L1 spacecraft. e, Odyssey. f, Calipso.
No. 2036: a, Viking 1 in oribit around Mars. b, Viking 1. c, Phobos. d, Viking Lander 1.
No. 2037, 1500fr, Mars Reconnaissance Orbiter. No. 2038, 1500fr, Apollo 11, vert.

**2006, Dec. 21** ***Perf. 13¼***

| | | | | |
|---|---|---|---|---|
| **2031-2034** | A445 | Set of 4 | 5.75 | 5.75 |
| **2035** | A445 | 400fr Sheet of 6, #a-f | 9.50 | 9.50 |
| **2036** | A445 | 550fr Sheet of 4, #a-d | 8.75 | 8.75 |

**Souvenir Sheets**
**2037-2038** A445 Set of 2 12.00 12.00

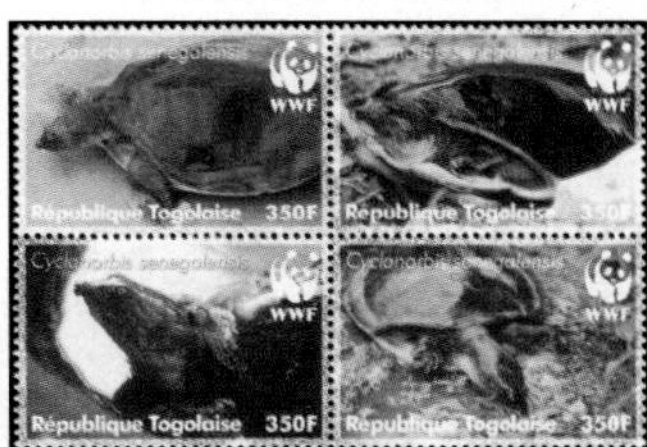


Worldwide Fund for Nature (WWF) — A446

No. 2039 — Cyclanorbis senegalensis: a, On sand, facing left. b, With foliage, facing left. c, Head. d, With foliage, facing right.
Illustration reduced.

**2006, Dec. 28**
**2039** A446 350fr Block or strip of 4, #a-d 5.75 5.75
*e.* Minature sheet, 2 each #a-d 11.50 11.50

Birds — A447

No. 2040: a, Platnea alba. b, Ceryle rudis. c, Ardea alba. d, Ephipphorhynchus senegalensis.
1500fr, Ephipphorhynchus senegalensis, diff.

**2006,Dec. 28** ***Perf. 14***
**2040** A447 450fr Sheet of 4, #a-d 7.25 7.25

**Souvenir Sheet**
**2041** A447 1500fr multi 6.00 6.00

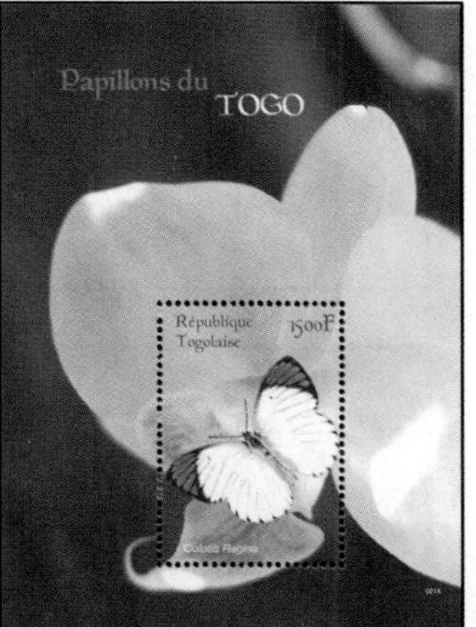

Mushrooms — A448

No. 2042: a, Coprinus micaceus. b, Cookeina sulcipes. c, Hygrocybe firma. d, Chlorophyllum molybdites.
1500fr, Volvariella esculenta.

**2006,Dec. 28**
**2042** A448 450fr Sheet of 4, #a-d 7.25 7.25

**Souvenir Sheet**
**2043** A448 1500fr multi 6.00 6.00

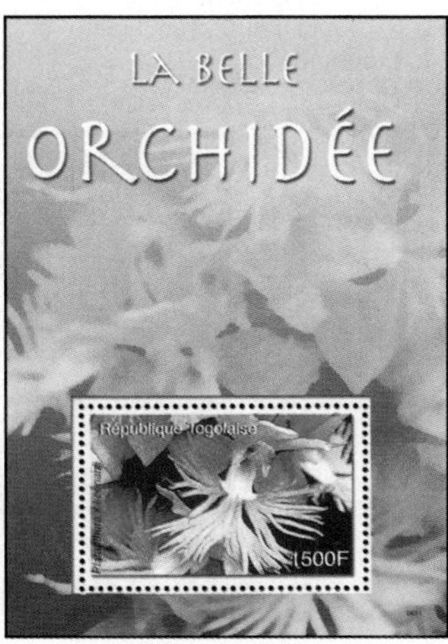


Butterflies — A449

No. 2044, horiz.: a, Papilio nobilis. b, Colotis celimene. c, Salamis anacardii. d, Eronia cleodora.
1500fr, Colotis regina.

**2006,Dec. 28** ***Perf. 14***
**2044** A449 450fr Sheet of 4, #a-d 7.25 7.25

**Souvenir Sheet**
**2045** A449 1500fr multi 6.00 6.00



Orchids — A450

No. 2046, vert.: a, Triphora trianthophora. b, Amerorchis rotundifolia. c, Cypripedium x andrewsii. d, Pogonia ophioglossoides.
1500fr, Platanthera x keenanii.

**2006,Dec. 28** ***Perf. 14***
**2046** A450 450fr Sheet of 4, #a-d 7.25 7.25

**Souvenir Sheet**
**2047** A450 1500fr multi 6.00 6.00

Rembrandt (1606-69), Painter A451

Designs: 50fr, Three Oriental Figures (Jacob and Laban). 100fr, The Pancake Woman. 150fr, The Goldsmith. 250fr, The Golf Player. 325fr, The Persian. 350fr, Jacob and Rachel Listening to an Account of Joseph's Dreams.
1250fr, The Conspiracy of Julius Civilis, horiz.

**2006** ***Perf. 14¼***
**2048-2053** A451 Set of 6 5.00 5.00

***Imperf***
**SizeL 106x76mm**
**2054** A451 1250fr multi 5.00 5.00

## SEMI-POSTAL STAMPS

**Curie Issue**
Common Design Type

**1938** **Unwmk.** **Engr.** ***Perf. 13***
**B1** CD80 1.75fr + 50c brt ultra 16.00 16.00

**French Revolution Issue**
Common Design Type

**Photo., Name and Value Typo. in Black**

**1939**

| | | | | |
|---|---|---|---|---|
| **B2** | CD83 | 45c + 25c green | 8.00 | 8.00 |
| **B3** | CD83 | 70c + 30c brown | 8.00 | 8.00 |
| **B4** | CD83 | 90c + 35c red org | 8.00 | 8.00 |
| **B5** | CD83 | 1.25fr + 1fr rose pink | 8.00 | 8.00 |
| **B6** | CD83 | 2.25fr + 2fr blue | 8.00 | 8.00 |
| | | *Nos. B2-B6 (5)* | 40.00 | 40.00 |

French Revolution, 150th anniv. Surtax for defense of the colonies.

Nos. 281, 236, 245, 289 Surcharged in Red or Black

**SECOURS**
**+ 1 fr.**
**NATIONAL**

**1941** ***Perf. 14 x 13½, 12½***

| | | | | |
|---|---|---|---|---|
| **B7** | A10 | 50c + 1fr | 1.50 | 1.50 |
| **B8** | A7 | 80c + 2fr | 4.50 | 4.50 |
| **B9** | A8 | 1.50fr + 2fr | 4.50 | 4.50 |
| **B10** | A11 | 2fr + 3fr (R) | 4.50 | 4.50 |
| | | *Nos. B7-B10 (4)* | 15.00 | 15.00 |

**Catalogue values for unused stamps in this section, from this point to the end of the section, are for Never Hinged items.**

Common Design Type and

Togolese Militiaman SP1

Military Infirmary SP2

**1941 Photo. *Perf. 13½***

**B10A** SP1 1fr + 1fr red .75
**B10B** CD86 1.50fr + 3fr maroon .75
**B10C** SP2 2.50fr + 1fr blue .75
*Nos. B10A-B10C (3)* 2.25

Nos. B10A-B10C were issued by the Vichy government in France, but were not placed on sale in Togo.

Nos. 296-297
Surcharged in Black or Red

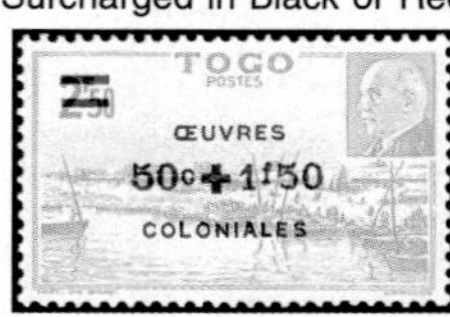


**1944 Engr. *Perf. 12x12½***

**B10D** 50c + 1.50fr on 2.50fr deep blue (R) .55
**B10E** + 2.50fr on 1fr green .55

Colonial Development Fund.
Nos. B10D-B10E were issued by the Vichy government in France, but were not placed on sale in Togo.

### Tropical Medicine Issue
Common Design Type

**1950 Engr. *Perf. 13***

**B11** CD100 10fr + 2fr indigo & dk bl 3.00 3.00

The surtax was for charitable work.

### Republic

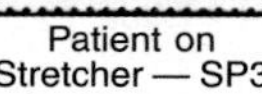


Patient on Stretcher — SP3

Uprooted Oak Emblem — SP4

Designs: 30fr+5fr, Feeding infant. 50fr+10fr, Blood transfusion.

**1959 Engr. *Perf. 13***

**B12** SP3 20fr + 5fr multicolored .75 .75
*a.* Souvenir sheet of 4 5.00 5.00
**B13** SP3 30fr + 5fr bl, car & brn .75 .75
*a.* Souvenir sheet of 4 5.00 5.00
**B14** SP3 50fr + 10fr emer, brn & car .75 .75
*a.* Souvenir sheet of 4 5.00 5.00
*Nos. B12-B14 (3)* 2.25 2.25

Issued for the Red Cross.
Nos. B12a, B13a, B14a exist imperf.; same values.

**1960 Unwmk. *Perf. 13***

#B16 similar to #B15, with emblem on top.

**B15** SP4 25fr + 5fr dk bl, brn & yel grn .45 .45
**B16** SP4 45fr + 5fr dk bl, brn & ol .80 .80

World Refugee Year, July 1, 1959-June 30, 1960. The surtax was for aid to refugees.

---

## AIR POST STAMPS

### Common Design Type

**1940 Unwmk. Engr. *Perf. 12½x12***

**C1** CD85 1.90fr ultra .25 .25
**C2** CD85 2.90fr dark red .45 .25
**C3** CD85 4.50fr dk gray grn .60 .40
**C4** CD85 4.90fr yellow bister .60 .60
**C5** CD85 6.90fr deep orange 1.00 1.00
*Nos. C1-C5 (5)* 2.90 2.50

### Common Design Type
Inscribed "Togo" across top

**1942**

**C6** CD88 50c car & bl .20
**C7** CD88 1fr brn & blk .25
**C8** CD88 2fr grn & red brn .30
**C9** CD88 3fr dk bl & scar .45
**C10** CD88 5fr vio & brn red .60

**Frame Engraved, Center Typographed**

**C11** CD89 10fr ultra, ind & org .75
**C12** CD89 20fr rose car, mag & gray blk .75
**C13** CD89 50fr yel grn, dl grn & lt vio 1.25 *2.25*
*Nos. C6-C13 (8)* 4.55

There is doubt whether Nos. C6-C12 were officially placed in use.

**Catalogue values for unused stamps in this section, from this point to the end of the section, are for Never Hinged items.**

Elephants — AP1

Plane — AP2

Plane — AP3

Post Runner and Plane — AP4

**1947, Oct. 6 Engr. *Perf. 12½***

**C14** AP1 40fr blue 6.00 3.00
**C15** AP2 50fr lt ultra, & red vio 3.50 1.25
**C16** AP3 100fr emer & dk brn 5.00 1.75
**C17** AP4 200fr lilac rose 8.50 3.00
*Nos. C14-C17 (4)* 23.00 9.00

### UPU Issue
Common Design Type

**1949, July 4 *Perf. 13***

**C18** CD99 25fr multi 6.00 6.00

### Liberation Issue
Common Design Type

**1954, June 6**

**C19** CD102 15fr indigo & pur 4.50 4.50

Freight Highway — AP5

**1954, Nov. 29**

**C20** AP5 500fr indigo & dk grn 42.50 37.50

### Republic

Independence Allegory — AP6

**Unwmk.**

**1957, Oct. 29 Engr. *Perf. 13***

**C21** AP6 25fr bl, olive bister & ver .60 .30

1st anniv. of Togo's autonomy.

Flag and Torch — AP7

Great White Egret — AP8

**1957, Oct. 29**

**C22** AP7 50fr multi .65 .35
**C23** AP7 100fr multi 1.10 .60
**C24** AP7 200fr multi 2.25 1.00
**C25** AP8 500fr ind, lt bl & grn 18.00 6.75
*Nos. C22-C25 (4)* 22.00 8.70

### Types of 1957 inscribed: "Republique du Togo" and

Flag, Plane and Map — AP9

**1959, Jan. 15 Engr. *Perf. 13***

**C26** AP9 25fr ultra, emer & vio brn .35 .20
**C27** AP7 50fr dk bl, dl grn & red .55 .30
**C28** AP7 100fr multi 1.20 .55
**C29** AP7 200fr dk grn, red & ultra 3.00 1.10
**C30** AP8 500fr blk brn, rose lil & grn 13.00 3.00
*Nos. C26-C30 (5)* 18.10 5.15

Hotel Le Benin AP10

Eagle and Map of Togo — AP11

***Perf. 14½x15, 15x14½***

**1960, Apr. 27 Litho. Unwmk.**

**C31** AP10 100fr crim, emer & yel 1.75 .25
**C32** AP10 200fr multi 4.00 .40
**C33** AP11 500fr grn & gldn brn 8.50 1.00
*Nos. C31-C33 (3)* 14.25 1.65

Proclamation of Togo's full independence, Apr. 27, 1960.

### Mail Service Type

100fr, Boeing 707 and stamps of 1960.

**1963, Jan. 12 Photo. *Perf. 13***

**C34** A41 100fr multi 1.40 .30
*a.* Souvenir sheet of 4 4.25 3.50

No. C34a contains 4 stamps similar to Nos. 441-443 and C34, with simulated perforations.

### Emancipation Type

**1963, Oct. Unwmk. *Perf. 13x14***

**C35** A45 100fr multi 1.25 .30
*a.* Souv. sheet of 4, #454-456, C35, imperf. 2.40 2.10

For overprint see No. C41.

### Type of 1964 Regular Issue

50fr, Black-bellied seed-cracker. 100fr, Blue-billed mannikin. 200fr, Redheaded lovebird. 250fr, African gray parrot. 500fr, Yellow-breasted barbet.

**1964-65 Photo. *Perf. 14***
**Size: 22½x31mm**
**Birds in Natural Colors**

**C36** A47 50fr yel grn 2.75 .25
**C37** A47 100fr ocher 5.50 .30
**C38** A47 200fr dl bl grn 10.50 .80
**C39** A47 250fr dl rose ('65) 14.00 1.00
**C40** A47 500fr violet 27.50 1.50
*Nos. C36-C40 (5)* 60.25 3.85

No. C35 Overprinted Diagonally: "En Mémoire de / JOHN F. KENNEDY / 1917-1963"

**1964, Feb. *Perf. 13x14***

**C41** A45 100fr multi 2.25 .30

Issued in memory of John F. Kennedy.
Same overprint was applied to stamps of No. C35a, with black border and commemorative inscription added. Two sheets exist: with and without gray silhouetted head of Kennedy covering all four stamps. Value: without silhouette, $17.50; with silhouette, $25.

### Liberation Type

**1964, May 25 *Perf. 14x13***

**C42** A50 100fr dl bl grn & dk brn 1.50 .30

### Olympic Games Type

**1964, Oct. Photo. *Perf. 14***

**C43** A52 100fr Tennis 1.90 .30
*a.* Souv. sheet of 3, #493-494, C43, imperf. 3.25 2.50

Flag of Togo and Jet — AP12

**1964, Dec. 5 Unwmk. *Perf. 14x13***

**C44** AP12 100fr multi .80 .30

Inauguration of the national airline "Air Togo." For souvenir sheet see No. 499a.

### Lincoln Type

**1965, June Photo. *Perf. 13½x14***

**C45** A58 100fr ol gray 1.90 .30
*a.* Souv. sheet, #545, C45, imperf 2.75 2.00

### Sports Type

100fr, Soccer player, flags of Togo and Congo.

**1965, July Unwmk. *Perf. 14x13***

**C46** A59 100fr multi 1.60 .30

### Churchill Type

**1965, Aug. 7 Photo. *Perf. 13½x14***

**C47** A60 85fr car rose 1.60 .30
*a.* Souv. sheet, #532, C47, imperf 2.50 2.00

### UN Type

100fr, Apple, grapes, wheat and "ONU."

**1965, Dec. 15** ***Perf. 14x13½***
**C48** A65 100fr dk bl & bis 1.75 .40
*a.* Souvenir sheet of 2 2.40 1.75

No. C48a contains two imperf. stamps similar to Nos. 548 and C48 with simulated perforations.

### Pope Type

Designs: 45fr, Pope speaking at UN rostrum, world map and UN emblem. 90fr, Pope, plane and UN emblem.

**1966, Mar. 5 Litho.** ***Perf. 12***
**C49** A66 45fr emer & multi .60 .20
**C50** A66 90fr gray & multi 1.40 .20
*a.* Souvenir sheet of 2, #C49-C50 3.00 1.75

### Red Cross Type

Jean Henri Dunant and Togolese Flag.

**1966, May 7 Litho.** ***Perf. 12***
**C51** A67 100fr multi 1.90 .30

### WHO Type

Flowers: 50fr, Daisies and WHO Headquarters. 90fr, Talisman roses and WHO Headquarters.

**1966, May Litho.** ***Perf. 12***
**C52** A68 50fr lt bl & multi .90 .20
**C53** A68 90fr gray & multi 1.50 .20
*a.* Souvenir sheet of 2, #C52-C53 3.00 2.00

### Air Afrique Issue
Common Design Type

**1966, Aug. 31 Photo.** ***Perf. 13***
**C54** CD123 30fr brt grn, blk & lem .65 .20

### Arts and Crafts Type

60fr, Basket maker. 90fr, Wood carver.

**1966, Sept.** ***Perf. 13x14***
**C55** A69 60fr ultra, org & blk .90 .20
**C56** A69 90fr brt rose, yel & blk 1.50 .20

### Dancer Type

50fr, Woman from North Togo holding branches. 60fr, Man from North Togo with horned helmet.

**1966, Nov. Photo.** ***Perf. 13x14***
**C57** A70 50fr multi .80 .20
**C58** A70 60fr olive & multi 1.00 .20

### Soccer Type

Designs: Different Soccer Scenes.

**1966, Dec. 14 Photo.** ***Perf. 14x13***
**C59** A71 50fr org, brn & pur 1.00 .20
**C60** A71 60fr ultra, brn & org 1.10 .20
*a.* Souv. sheet of 3, #582, C59-C60, imperf. 3.00 2.25

### Fish Type

Designs: 45fr, Yellow jack and trawler. 90fr, Banded distichodus and seiner.

**1967, Jan. 14 Photo.** ***Perf. 14***
**Fish in Natural Colors**
**C61** A72 45fr org & brn .90 .20
**C62** A72 90fr emer & dk bl 2.10 .30

### UNICEF Type

UNICEF Emblem and: 45fr, Girl and miniature poodle. 90fr, African boy and greyhound.

**1967, Feb. 11 Photo.** ***Perf. 14x13½***
**C63** A73 45fr yel, red brn & blk 1.00 .20
**C64** A73 90fr ultra, dk grn & blk 1.50 .25
*a.* Souvenir sheet of 2 3.00 1.75

No. C64a contains 2 imperf., lithographed stamps with simulated perforations similar to Nos. C63-C64.

### Satellite Type

50fr, Diamant rocket. 90fr, Fr-1 satellite.

**1967, Mar. 18 Photo.** ***Perf. 13½x14***
**C65** A74 50fr multi, vert. .90 .20
**C66** A74 90fr multi, vert. 1.60 .25
*a.* Souvenir sheet of 2 2.50 1.75

No. C66a contains 2 imperf. stamps similar to Nos. C65-C66 with simulated perforations.

### Musician Type

UNESCO Emblem and: 45fr, Johann Sebastian Bach and organ. 90fr, Ludwig van Beethoven, violin and oboe.

**1967, Apr. 15 Photo.** ***Perf. 14x13½***
**C67** A75 45fr multi .90 .20
**C68** A75 90fr pink & multi 2.00 .20
*a.* Souvenir sheet of 2 3.50 2.00

No. C68a contains 2 imperf. stamps similar to Nos. C67-C68 with simulated perforations.

### EXPO '67 Type

EXPO '67 Emblem and: 45fr, French pavilion, roses. 60fr, British pavilion, day lilies. 90fr, African village, bird-of-paradise flower. 105fr, US pavilion, daisies.

**1967, May 30 Photo.** ***Perf. 14***
**C69** A76 45fr multi .65 .20
**C70** A76 60fr multi 1.00 .20
**C71** A76 90fr yel & multi 1.25 .25
*a.* Souv. sheet, #C69-C71, imperf 3.50 2.50
**C72** A76 105fr multi 1.75 .30
*Nos. C69-C72 (4)* 4.65 .95

For overprints see Nos. C86-C89.

Mural by José Vela Zanetti — AP13

The designs are from a mural in the lobby of the UN Conf. Building, NYC. The mural depicting mankind's struggle for a lasting peace is shown across 3 stamps twice in the set: on the 5fr, 15fr, 30fr and 45fr, 60fr, 90fr.

**1967, July 15 Litho.** ***Perf. 14***
**C73** AP13 5fr multi .35 .20
**C74** AP13 15fr org & multi .35 .20
**C75** AP13 30fr multi .40 .20
**C76** AP13 45fr multi .65 .20
**C77** AP13 60fr car & multi 1.00 .20
**C78** AP13 90fr ind & multi 1.50 .25
*a.* Souvenir sheet of 3, #C76-C78 3.50 2.50
*Nos. C73-C78 (6)* 4.25 1.25

Issued to publicize general disarmament.

### Animal Type

**1967, Aug. 19 Photo.** ***Perf. 14x13½***
**C79** A78 45fr Lion 1.10 .20
**C80** A78 60fr Elephant 1.60 .20

### African Postal Union Issue, 1967
Common Design Type

**1967, Sept. 9 Engr.** ***Perf. 13***
**C81** CD124 100fr bl, brt grn & ol brn 1.90 .30

### Stamp Anniversary Type

Designs: 90fr, Stamp auction and Togo Nos. 16 and C42. 105fr, Father and son with stamp album and No. 474.

**1967, Oct. 14 Photo.** ***Perf. 14x13***
**Stamps on Stamps in Original Colors**
**C82** A79 90fr olive 1.25 .25
*a.* Souvenir sheet of 3 3.00 2.50
**C83** A79 105fr dk car rose 2.00 .40

No. C82a contains 3 imperf. stamps similar to Nos. 621-622 and C82 with simulated perforations.

### Pre-Olympics Type

View of Mexico City, Summer Olympics emblem and: 60fr, Runners. 90fr, Broad jump.

**1967, Dec. 2** ***Perf. 13x14***
**C84** A80 60fr pink & multi 1.25 .35
**C85** A80 90fr multi 1.20 .45
*a.* Souv. sheet of 3, #627, C84-C85, imperf. 4.25 2.50

Nos. C69-C72 Overprinted: "JOURNÉE NATIONALE / DU TOGO / 29 SEPTEMBRE 1967"

**1967, Dec. Photo.** ***Perf. 14***
**C86** A76 45fr multi .60 .20
**C87** A76 60fr multi .90 .20
**C88** A76 90fr yel & multi 1.40 .25
**C89** A76 105fr multi 1.50 .35
*Nos. C86-C89 (4)* 4.40 1.00

Issued for National Day, Sept. 29, 1967.

### Hydrological Decade Type

**1968, Apr. 6 Litho.** ***Perf. 14***
**C90** A84 60fr multi 1.00 .20

### Ship Type

Designs: 45fr, Fulton's and modern steamships. 90fr, US atomic ship Savannah and atom symbol.

**1968, Apr. 26 Photo.** ***Perf. 14x14½***
**C91** A85 45fr yel & multi .80 .20
**C92** A85 90fr bl & multi 1.60 .20
*a.* Souvenir sheet of 2 3.50 1.75

No. C92a contains 2 imperf. stamps similar to Nos. C91-C92 with simulated perforations.

### WHO Type

Paintings: 60fr, The Anatomy Lesson, by Rembrandt (detail). 90fr, Jesus Healing the Sick, by Raphael.

**1968, June 22 Photo.** ***Perf. 14***
**C93** A87 60fr multi 1.10 .20
**C94** A87 90fr pur & multi 1.60 .20
*a.* Souvenir sheet of 2 3.00 2.50

No. C94a contains 2 imperf. stamps similar to Nos. C93-C94 with simulated perforations.

### Olympic Games Type

**1968, July 27** ***Perf. 14x13½***
**C95** A88 60fr Wrestling .95 .20
**C96** A88 90fr Running 1.40 .20
*a.* Souvenir sheet of 2 2.50 2.00

No. C96a contains 2 imperf. stamps similar to Nos. C95-C96 with simulated perforations.

### Boy Scout Type

60fr, First aid practice, horiz. 90fr, Scout game.

**1968, Nov. 23 Litho.** ***Perf. 14***
**C97** A90 60fr ol & multi 1.00 .25
**C98** A90 90fr org & multi 1.40 .35
*a.* Souvenir sheet of 2 3.00 1.75

No. C98a contains 2 imperf. stamps with simulated perforations similar to Nos. C97-C98.

### PHILEXAFRIQUE Issue

The Letter, by Jean Auguste Franquelin AP14

**1968, Nov. 9 Photo.** ***Perf. 12½x12***
**C99** AP14 100fr multi 2.75 1.75

PHILEXAFRIQUE Philatelic Exhibition in Abidjan, Feb. 14-23. Printed with alternating light ultramarine label.

### Christmas Type

Paintings: 60fr, Adoration of the Magi, by Pieter Brueghel. 90fr, Adoration of the Magi, by Dürer.

**1968, Dec. 28 Litho.** ***Perf. 14***
**C100** A91 60fr red & multi 1.25 .20
**C101** A91 90fr multi 1.90 .30
*a.* Souvenir sheet 3.50 1.75

No. C101a contains 2 imperf. stamps similar to Nos. C100-C101 with simulated perforations.

### Human Rights Type

Human Rights Flame and: 60fr, Robert F. Kennedy. 90fr, Martin Luther King, Jr.

**1969, Feb. 1 Photo.** ***Perf. 13½x14***
**C102** A92 60fr brt rose lil & vio bl 1.00 .20
**C103** A92 90fr emer & brn 1.25 .30
*a.* Souvenir sheet 2.50 1.75

No. C103a contains 2 imperf. stamps similar to Nos. C102-C103 with simulated perforations.

For overprints see Nos. C110-C111.

### 2nd PHILEXAFRIQUE Issue
Common Design Type

Design: 50fr, Togo #16 and Aledjo Fault.

**1969, Feb. 14 Engr.** ***Perf. 13***
**C104** CD128 50fr red brn, grn & car rose 2.00 .40

### Sports Type

Stadium and: 60fr, Boxing. 90fr, Bicycling.

**1969, Apr. 26 Photo.** ***Perf. 14x13½***
**C105** A93 60fr bl, red & dk brn .85 .20
**C106** A93 90fr ultra, brt pink & dk brn 1.50 .25
*a.* Souvenir sheet 2.50 1.75

No. C106a contains 2 imperf. stamps similar to Nos. C105-C106 with simulated perforations.

### Lunar Type

Designs: 60fr, Astronaut exploring moon surface. 100fr, Astronaut gathering rocks.

**1969, July 21 Litho.** ***Perf. 14***
**C107** A94 60fr dk bl & multi .80 .20
**C108** A94 100fr multi 1.40 .40
*a.* Souvenir sheet 12.00 6.00

No. C108a contains 4 imperf. stamps with simulated perforations similar to Nos. 676-677 and C107-C108, magenta margin. No. C108a also exists with colors of 30fr and 100fr stamps changed, and margin in orange. Value, unused $6, used $2.

For overprints see Nos. C120-C121.

### Painting Type

Painting: 90fr, Pentecost, by El Greco.

**1969, Aug. 16 Litho.** ***Perf. 14***
**C109** A95 90fr multi 2.40 .40
*a.* Souvenir sheet 2.75 1.50

No. C109a contains two imperf. stamps with simulated perforations similar to Nos. 682 and C109.

Nos. C102-C103 Overprinted Like Nos. 683-686

**1969, Sept. 1 Photo.** ***Perf. 13½x14***
**C110** A92 60fr brt rose lil & vio bl 1.00 .20
**C111** A92 90fr emer & brn 1.50 .25
*a.* Souv. sheet of 2 3.00 2.00

#C111a is #C103a with Eisenhower overprint.

### Bank Type

Design: 100fr, Bank emblem and hand holding cattle and farmer.

**1969, Sept. 10 Photo.** ***Perf. 13x14***
**C112** A96 100fr multi 1.25 .40

### Red Cross Type

60fr, Wilhelm C. Roentgen & Red Cross workers with children in front of Togo Headquarters. 90fr, Henri Dunant & Red Cross workers meeting Biafra refugees at airport.

**1969, Sept. 27 Litho.** ***Perf. 14***
**C113** A97 60fr brn & multi 1.10 .25
**C114** A97 90fr ol & multi 1.60 .35
*a.* Souv. sheet of 2 2.75 2.00

No. C114a contains 2 imperf. stamps with simulated perforations similar to Nos. C113-C114.

### Agricultural Center Type

Emblem of Young Pioneer and Agricultural Organization and: 90fr, Manioc harvest. 100fr, Instruction in gardening. 200fr, Corn harvest. 250fr, Marching drum corps. 500fr, Parade of Young Pioneers.

**1969-70 Litho.** ***Perf. 14***
**C115** A98 90fr multi 1.25 .20
**C116** A98 100fr org & multi 1.40 .25
**C117** A98 200fr multi ('70) 3.00 .35
**C118** A98 250fr ol & multi 3.50 .60
**C119** A98 500fr multi ('70) 7.50 .75
*Nos. C115-C119 (5)* 16.65 2.15

### Christmas Issue
Nos. C107-C108, C108a Overprinted: "JOYEUX NOEL"

**1969, Dec. Litho.** ***Perf. 14***
**C120** A94 60fr multi 3.50 .40
**C121** A94 100fr multi 5.25 .60
*a.* Souvenir sheet of 4 55.00 55.00

### Peace Leaders Type

60fr, Friedrich Ebert. 90fr, Mahatma Gandhi.

**1969, Dec. 27 Litho.** ***Perf. 14x13½***
**C122** A100 60fr dk brn, dk red & yel 1.00 .20
**C123** A100 90fr dk brn, vio bl & ocher 1.60 .30

For surcharges see Nos. 765, C143.

### ILO Type

Paintings and ILO Emblem: 60fr, Spring Sowing, by Vincent van Gogh. 90fr, Workers, by Diego de Rivera.

**1970, Jan. 24 Litho. *Perf. 12½x13***
**C124** A101 60fr gold & multi 1.40 .20
**C125** A101 90fr gold & multi 2.50 .20
*a.* Souvenir sheet of 2 3.00 1.25

No. C125a contains two stamps similar to Nos. C124-C125, with simulated perforations.

### Hair Styles Type

Various hair styles. 45fr, vert. 90fr, horiz.

**1970, Feb. 21 *Perf. 12½x13, 13x12½***
**C126** A102 45fr car & multi .80 .20
**C127** A102 90fr multi 1.60 .30

### Independence Type

Design: 60fr, Togo No. C33 and Independence Monument, Lomé.

**1970, Apr. 27 Litho. *Perf. 13x12½***
**C128** A103 60fr yel & multi .95 .20

### UPU Type

**1970, May 30 Photo. *Perf. 14x13½***
**C129** A104 50fr grnsh bl & dk car .90 .20

### Soccer Type

Various Scenes from Soccer, Rimet Cup and Flags of: 50fr, Sweden and Israel. 60fr, Bulgaria and Peru. 90fr, Belgium and Salvador.

**1970, June 27 Litho. *Perf. 13x14***
**C130** A105 50fr multi .80 .20
**C131** A105 60fr lil & multi 1.10 .20
**C132** A105 90fr multi 1.50 .30
*a.* Souvenir sheet of 4 3.50 3.50
*Nos. C130-C132 (3)* 3.40 .70

No. C132a contains 4 stamps similar to Nos. 734, C130-C132, but imperf. with simulated perforations.

### Lenin Type

Design: 50fr, Lenin Meeting Peasant Delegation, by V. A. Serov, and UNESCO emblem.

**1970, July 25 Litho. *Perf. 12½***
**C133** A106 50fr multi 2.00 .20

For overprint see No. C179.

### EXPO '70 Type
Souvenir Sheet

150fr, Mitsubishi pavilion, EXPO '70 emblem.

**1970, Aug. 8 Litho. *Perf. 13***
**C134** A107 150fr yel & multi 3.50 2.25
*a.* Inscribed "AERINNE"

No. C134 contains one stamp 86x33mm.

### Astronaut Type

Design: 200fr, James A. Lovell, Fred W. Haise, Jr. and Tom Mattingly (replaced by John L. Swigert, Jr.) and Apollo 13 emblem.

**1970, Sept. 26**
**C135** A108 200fr multi 2.50 .55
*a.* Souv. sheet of 3 3.50 2.50

Space flight of Apollo 13. No. C135a contains 3 stamps similar to Nos. 741, 744 and C135, with simulated perforations.
For overprint see No. C136.

Nos. C135, C135a Inscribed: "FELICITATIONS / BON RETOUR APOLLO XIII"

**1970, Sept. 26**
**C136** A108 200fr multi 2.50 .55
*a.* Souvenir sheet of 3 3.50 2.50

Safe return of the crew of Apollo 13.

### UN Type

Paintings and Emblems of UN Agencies: 60fr, The Mailman Roulin, by van Gogh, and UPU emblem. 90fr, The Birth of the Virgin, by Vittore Carpaccio, and WHO emblem.

**1970, Oct. 24 Litho. *Perf. 13x12½***
**C137** A109 60fr grn, gold & blk 1.10 .20
**C138** A109 90fr red org, gold & brn 1.75 .30
*a.* Souvenir sheet of 4 3.50 2.50

No. C138a contains one each of Nos. 754-755 and C137-C138 with simulated perforations.

### Moth Type

Moths: 60fr, Euchloron megaera. 90fr, Pseudacraea boisduvali.

**1970, Nov. 21 Photo. *Perf. 13x14***
**C139** A110 60fr multi 5.25 .20
**C140** A110 90fr multi 5.25 .20

### Christmas Type

Paintings: 60fr, Adoration of the Shepherds, by Botticelli. 90fr, Adoration of the Kings, by Tiepolo.

**1970, Dec. 26 Litho. *Perf. 12½x13***
**C141** A111 60fr gold & multi 1.50 .20
**C142** A111 90fr gold & multi 2.25 .30
*a.* Souv. sheet of 2, #C141-C142 3.50 1.75

No. C122 Surcharged and Overprinted: "EN MEMOIRE / Charles De Gaulle / 1890-1970"

**1971, Jan. 9 Photo. *Perf. 14x13½***
**C143** A100 200fr on 60fr 11.50 .60

### De Gaulle Type

Designs: 60fr, De Gaulle and Pope Paul VI. 90fr, De Gaulle and satellite.

**1971, Feb. 20 Photo. *Perf. 13x14***
**C144** A112 60fr blk & dp vio 2.20 .20
**C145** A112 90fr blk & bl grn 3.00 .25
*a.* Souvenir sheet of 4 8.50 3.00

Nos. C143-C145 issued in memory of Charles De Gaulle (1890-1970), President of France. No. C145a contains 4 imperf. stamps similar to Nos. 769-770, C144-C145.

### Easter Type

Paintings: 50fr, Resurrection, by Matthias Grunewald. 60fr, Resurrection, by Master of Trebon. 90fr, Resurrection, by El Greco.

**1971, Apr. 10 Litho. *Perf. 10½x11½***
**C146** A113 50fr gold & multi .85 .20
**C147** A113 60fr gold & multi 1.25 .20
**C148** A113 90fr gold & multi 1.60 .30
*a.* Souvenir sheet of 4, #773, C146-C148 4.50 2.50
*Nos. C146-C148 (3)* 3.70 .70

### Apollo 14 Type

Designs: 50fr, 200f, Apollo 14 badge 100fr, Take-off from moon, and spaceship.

**1971, May Litho. *Perf. 12½***
**C149** A114 50fr grn & multi .50 .20
**C150** A114 100fr multi .90 .35
**C151** A114 200fr org & multi 2.00 .65
*a.* Souv. sheet of 4 4.50 4.25
*Nos. C149-C151 (3)* 3.40 1.20

No. C151a contains 4 stamps similar to Nos. 777 and C149-C151 with simulated perforations.
For surcharge and overprints see Nos. C162-C164.

### Cacao Type

60fr, Ministry of Agriculture. 90fr, Cacao tree and & pods. 100fr, Sorting & separating beans from pods.

**1971, June 6 Litho. *Perf. 14***
**C152** A115 60fr multi .75 .20
**C153** A115 90fr multi 1.10 .30
**C154** A115 100fr multi 1.40 .35
*Nos. C152-C154 (3)* 3.25 .85

### ASECNA Type

**1971, June 26**
**C155** A116 100fr multi 1.60 .35

### Tourist Type

Designs: 50fr, Château Viale and antelope. 60fr, Lake Togo and crocodile. 100fr, Old lime furnace, Tokpli, and hippopotamus.

**1971, July 17**
**C156** A117 50fr multi .75 .20
**C157** A117 60fr multi .90 .20
**C158** A117 100fr multi 1.40 .35
*Nos. C156-C158 (3)* 3.05 .75

For overprint see No. C172.

### Religions Type

Designs: 50fr, Mohammedans praying in front of Lomé Mosque. 60fr, Protestant service. 90fr, Catholic bishop and priests.

**1971, July 31 Litho. *Perf. 14½***
**C159** A118 50fr multi .60 .20
**C160** A118 60fr multi .65 .20
**C161** A118 90fr multi 1.10 .25
*a.* Souvenir sheet of 4, #787, C159-C161 4.25 2.50
*Nos. C159-C161 (3)* 2.35 .65

Nos. C149-C151 Overprinted and Surcharged in Black or Silver: "EN MEMOIRE / DOBROVOLSKY — VOLKOV — PATSAYEV / SOYUZ 11"

**C162** A114 90fr on 50fr multi .95 .25
**C163** A114 100fr multi (S) 1.00 .30
**C164** A114 200fr multi 2.25 .50
*a.* Souvenir sheet of 4, #788, C162-C164 5.50 5.50
*Nos. C162-C164 (3)* 4.20 1.05

See note after No. 788.

### Olympic Type

200fr, Sapporo '72 emblem and Ski jump.

**1971, Oct. 30 Litho. *Perf. 14***
**C165** A119 200fr multi 2.25 .50
*a.* Souvenir sheet of 4 4.25 3.50

No. C165 contains 4 stamps with simulated perforations similar to Nos. 791-793 and C165 printed on glazed paper.

### African Postal Union Issue, 1971
Common Design Type

Design: 100fr, Adjogbo dancers and UAMPT Building, Brazzaville, Congo.

**1971, Nov. 13 Photo. *Perf. 13x13½***
**C166** CD135 100fr bl & multi 1.25 .40

Intl. Organization for the Protection of Children (U.I.P.E.) — AP14a

***Die Cut Perf. 10½***

**1971, Nov. 13 Embossed**
**C166A** AP14a 1500fr gold 20.00

### UNICEF Type

Toys: 60fr, Turtle. 90fr, Parrot.

**1971, Nov. 27 Litho. *Perf. 14***
**C167** A120 60fr lt bl & multi .70 .20
**C168** A120 90fr multi 1.10 .25
*a.* Souvenir sheet of 4 2.75 2.50

No. C168a contains 4 stamps with simulated perforations similar to Nos. 796-797 and C167-C168.
For overprints see Nos. C263-C264.

### Christmas Type

Virgin and Child by: 60fr, Giorgione. 100fr, Raphael.

**1971, Dec. 24 *Perf. 14x13***
**C169** A121 60fr olive & multi 1.00 .25
**C170** A121 100fr multi 1.75 .40
*a.* Souvenir sheet of 4 5.25 2.25

No. C170a contains 4 stamps with simulated perforations similar to Nos. 800-801, C169-C170.

### Venice Type

Design: 100fr, Ca' d'Oro, Venice.

**1972, Feb. 26 Litho. *Perf. 14***
**C171** A122 100fr multi 2.00 .40
*a.* Souvenir sheet of 3 5.25 2.50

No. C171a contains 3 stamps similar to Nos. 802-803, C171 with simulated perforations.

No. C156 Overprinted "VISITE DU PRESIDENT / NIXON EN CHINE / FEVRIER 1972"

**1972, Mar. Litho. *Perf. 14***
**C172** A117 50fr multi .80 .20

Visit of Pres. Richard M. Nixon to the People's Republic of China, Feb. 20-27.

### Easter Type

Paintings: 50fr, Resurrection, by Thomas de Coloswa. 100fr, Ascension by Andrea Mantegna.

**1972, Mar. 31**
**C173** A123 50fr gold & multi 1.90 .20
**C174** A123 100fr gold & multi 2.75 .25
*a.* Souvenir sheet of 4 3.50 1.90

No. C174a contains 4 stamps similar to Nos. 806-807, C173-C174 with simulated perforations.

### Heart Type

100fr, Heart, WHO emblem and smith.

**1972, Apr. 4**
**C175** A124 100fr multi 1.40 .40
*a.* Souvenir sheet of 2 3.00 1.25

No. C175a contains 2 stamps similar to Nos. 810 and C175 with simulated perforations.

### Telecommunications Type

Design: 100fr, Intelsat 4 over Africa.

**1972, June 24 *Perf. 14***
**C176** A125 100fr multi 1.60 .30

For overprint see No. C229.

### Cassava Type

60fr, Truck and cassava processing factory, horiz. 80fr, Children, mother holding tapioca cake.

**1972, June 30**
**C177** A126 60fr multi 1.10 .25
**C178** A126 80fr multi 1.25 .25

No. C133 Surcharged in Deep Carmine: "VISITE DU PRESIDENT / NIXON EN RUSSIE / MAI 1972"

**1972, July 15 Litho. *Perf. 12½***
**C179** A106 300fr on 50fr multi 4.75 1.40

President Nixon's visit to the USSR, May 1972. Old denomination obliterated with 6x5mm rectangle.

### Olympic Type

**1972, Aug. 26 Litho. *Perf. 14***
**C180** A127 90fr Gymnastics 1.00 .35
*a.* Souv. sheet of 2 3.50 1.75
**C181** A127 200fr Basketball 2.40 .65

No. C180a contains 2 stamps with simulated perforations similar to Nos. 816 and C180.
For overprints see Nos. C234-C235.

### Bird Type

Bird: 90fr, Rose-ringed parakeet.

**1972, Sept. 9**
**C182** A128 90fr multi 2.50 .35
*a.* Souvenir sheet of 4 12.00 2.25

No. C182a contains 4 stamps similar to Nos. 818-820, C182 with simulated perforations.

### Rotary Type

Rotary Emblem and: 60fr, Map of Togo, olive branch. 90fr, Flags of Togo and Rotary Club. 100fr, Paul P. Harris.

**1972, Oct. 7 Litho. *Perf. 14***
**C183** A129 60fr brn & multi .55 .20
**C184** A129 90fr multi .80 .35
**C185** A129 100fr multi 1.00 .40
*Nos. C183-C185 (3)* 2.35 .95

For overprints see Nos. C212-C213, C244-C245.

### Painting Type, 1972

Designs: 60fr, Mystical Marriage of St. Catherine, by Assistant to the P. M. Master. 80fr, Self-portrait, by Leonardo da Vinci. 100fr, Sts. Mary and Agnes by Botticelli.

**1972, Oct. 21**
**C186** A130 60fr gold & multi 1.75 .20
**C187** A130 80fr gold & multi 2.00 .25
**C188** A130 100fr gold & multi 3.75 .40
*a.* Souvenir sheet of 4 4.50 2.00
*Nos. C186-C188 (3)* 7.50 .85

No. C188a contains 4 stamps with simulated perforations similar to Nos. 824, C186-188.

### Presidential Visit Type

Design: 100fr, Pres. Pompidou and Col. Etienne Eyadema, front view of party headquarters.

**1972, Nov. 23 Litho. *Perf. 14***
**C189** A131 100fr multi 2.40 .40

Johann Wolfgang von Goethe (1749-1832), German Poet and Dramatist
AP15

**1972, Dec. 2 Photo. *Perf. 13x14***
**C190** AP15 100fr grn & multi 1.60 .40

### Christmas Type

Paintings: 60fr, Nativity, by Master Vyshchibrod. 80fr, Adoration of the Kings, anonymous. 100fr, Flight into Egypt, by Giotto.

**1972, Dec. 23 Litho. *Perf. 14***
**C191** A132 60fr gold & multi 1.10 .20
**C192** A132 80fr gold & multi 1.40 .30
**C193** A132 100fr gold & multi 1.90 .40
*a.* Souvenir sheet of 4 4.50 2.50
*Nos. C191-C193 (3)* 4.40 .90

No. C193a contains 4 stamps with simulated perforations similar to Nos. 829, C191-C193.

### Leprosy Day Type

Design: 100fr, Dr. Armauer G. Hansen, apparatus, microscope and Petri dish.

**1973, Jan. 23 Photo. *Perf. 14x13½***
**C194** A133 100fr rose car & bl 3.00 .40

World Leprosy Day and centenary of the discovery of the Hansen bacillus, the cause of leprosy.

Miniature Sheets

1972 Summer Olympics, Munich — AP15a

Medalists: #C194A, Mark Spitz, US, swimming. #C194B, L. Linsenhoff, West Germany, equestrian. #C194C, D. Morelon, France, cycling.

### Litho. & Embossed

**1973, Jan. *Perf. 13½***
**C194A-C194C** AP15a 1500fr multi 375.00

Exist imperf.

Miniature Sheet

Apollo 17 Moon Landing — APb15

**1973, Jan.**
**C194D** AP15b 1500fr gold & multi 55.00

Exists imperf.

### Easter Type

**1973, Apr. 21 Litho. *Perf. 14***
**C195** A135 90fr Christ in Glory 1.40 .40
*a.* Souvenir sheet of 2 2.75 1.75

No. C195a contains one each of Nos. 835 and C195 with simulated perforations.

### Apollo 17 Type

Designs: 100fr, Astronauts on moon and orange rock. 200fr, Rocket lift-off at Cape Kennedy and John F. Kennedy.

**1973, June 2 Litho. *Perf. 14***
**C196** A136 100fr multi 1.40 .40
**C197** A136 200fr multi 3.00 .60
*a.* Souvenir sheet of 2 4.25 3.00

No. C197a contains 2 stamps similar to Nos. C196-C197 with simulated perforations.

### Boy Scout Type

100fr, Canoeing, horiz. 200fr, Campfire, horiz.

**1973, June 30 Litho. *Perf. 14***
**C198** A137 100fr bl & multi 1.40 .40
**C199** A137 200fr bl & multi 3.25 .65
*a.* Souvenir sheet of 2 4.00 2.25

No. C199a contains 2 stamps similar to Nos. C198-C199 with simulated perforations.
For overprints see Nos. C265-C266.

### Copernicus Type

Designs: 90fr, Heliocentric system. 100fr, Nicolaus Copernicus.

**1973, July 18**
**C200** A138 90fr multi 1.75 .30
**C201** A138 100fr bis & multi 2.10 .40
*a.* Souv. sheet of 2, #C200-C201 3.50 1.75

### Red Cross Type

Design: 100fr, Dove carrying Red Cross letter, sun, map of Togo.

**1973, Aug. 4**
**C202** A139 100fr multi 3.25 .35

For overprint see No. C294.

### Literacy Type

Design: 90fr, Woman teacher in classroom.

**1973, Aug. 18 Litho. *Perf. 14***
**C203** A140 90fr multi 1.50 .35

### WMO Type

**1973, Oct. 4 Photo. *Perf. 14x13***
**C204** A142 200fr dl bl, pur & brn 2.00 .60

### Type 1967

Early & contemporary planes, #758, C36.

**1973, Oct. 20 Photo. *Perf. 14x13***
**C205** A79 100fr multi 2.25 .30
*a.* Souvenir sheet of 2 2.75 1.50

75th anniversary of Togolese postal service. No. C205a contains 2 stamps similar to Nos. 855 and C205 with simulated perforations.

### Kennedy Type

Designs: 90fr, Kennedy and Charles De Gaulle. 100fr, Kennedy and Nikita Krushchev. 200fr, Kennedy and model of Apollo spacecraft.

**1973, Nov. 22 Litho. *Perf. 14***
**C206** A143 90fr blk & pink 1.25 .35
**C207** A143 100fr blk, lt bl & bl 1.40 .45
**C208** A143 200fr blk, buff & brn 3.00 .60
*a.* Souvenir sheet of 2 4.00 2.00
*Nos. C206-C208 (3)* 5.65 1.40

No. C208a contains 2 stamps similar to Nos. C207-208 with simulated perforations.

Human Rights Flame and People — AP16

**1973, Dec. 8 Photo. *Perf. 13x14***
**C209** AP16 250fr lt bl & multi 2.40 .80

25th anniversary of the Universal Declaration of Human Rights.

### Christmas Type

Paintings: 90fr, Virgin and Child. 100fr, Adoration of the Kings. Both after 15th century Italian paintings.

**1973, Dec. 22 Litho. *Perf. 14***
**C210** A144 90fr gold & multi 1.10 .25
**C211** A144 100fr gold & multi 1.40 .35
*a.* Souvenir sheet of 2 2.75 1.50

No. C211a contains 2 stamps with simulated perforations similar to Nos. C210-C211.

### Nos. C183 and C185 Overprinted: "PREMIERE CONVENTION / 210eme DISTRICT / FEVRIER 1974 / LOME"

**1974, Feb. 21 Litho. *Perf. 14***
**C212** A129 60fr brn & multi .65 .20
**C213** A129 100fr multi 1.00 .35

First convention of Rotary International, District 210, Lomé, Feb. 22-24.

### Soccer Type

Various soccer scenes and games' cup.

**1974, Mar. 2 Litho. *Perf. 14***
**C214** A145 90fr multi .85 .35
**C215** A145 100fr multi 1.00 .40
**C216** A145 200fr multi 1.90 .75
*a.* Souvenir sheet of 2 4.00 2.50
*Nos. C214-C216 (3)* 3.75 1.50

No. C216a contains 2 stamps with simulated perforations similar to Nos. C215-C216.

### Picasso Type

Paintings: 90fr, The Muse. 100fr, Les Demoiselles d'Avignon. 200fr, Sitting Nude.

**1974, Apr. 6 Litho. *Perf. 14***
**C217** A146 90fr brn & multi 1.25 .30
**C218** A146 100fr pur & multi 1.50 .35
**C219** A146 200fr multi 3.00 .65
*a.* Souvenir sheet of 3 5.50 3.00
*Nos. C217-C219 (3)* 5.75 1.30

No. C219a contains 3 stamps similar to Nos. C217-C219 with simulated perforations.

### Coastal Views Type

Designs: 90fr, Fishermen on Lake Togo. 100fr, Mouth of Anecho River.

**1974, Apr. 20**
**C220** A147 90fr multi 1.10 .25
**C221** A147 100fr multi 1.25 .35
*a.* Souvenir sheet of 2 2.50 1.25

No. C221a contains 2 stamps similar to Nos. C220-C221 with simulated perforations.

### UPU Type

Designs: Old mailmen's uniforms.

**1974, May 10 Litho. *Perf. 14***
**C222** A148 50fr multi .70 .20
**C223** A148 100fr multi 1.25 .35
*a.* Souvenir sheet of 2 40.00 17.00

No. C223a contains 2 stamps similar to Nos. C222-C223, rouletted.

### Fishing Type

Designs: 90fr, Fishermen bringing in net with catch. 100fr, Fishing with rod and line. 200fr, Fishing with basket, vert.

**1974, June 22 Litho. *Perf. 14***
**C224** A149 90fr multi 1.00 .25
**C225** A149 100fr multi 1.10 .25
**C226** A149 200fr multi 2.40 .65
*a.* Souvenir sheet of 3 5.25 2.50
*Nos. C224-C226 (3)* 4.50 1.15

No. C226a contains 3 stamps with simulated perforations similar to Nos. C224-C226.

### Jupiter Probe Type

Designs: 100fr, Rocket take-off, vert. 200fr, Satellite in space.

**1974, July 6 *Perf. 14***
**C227** A150 100fr multi .90 .35
**C228** A150 200fr multi 2.00 .65
*a.* Souvenir sheet of 2 5.50 4.00

No. C228a contains 2 stamps similar to Nos. C227-C228 with simulated perforations; imperf. or rouletted.

No. C176 Overprinted in Black

**1974, July *Perf. 14***
**C229** A125 100fr multi 3.50 1.20

INTERNABA 1974 Intl. Philatelic Exhibition, Basel, June 7-16.
No. C229 exists overprinted in silver. Value, unused $11.

### Seashell Type

**1974, July 13 Litho. *Perf. 14***
**C230** A151 90fr Alcithoe ponsonbyi 1.60 .25
**C231** A151 100fr Casmaria iredalei 2.00 .35
*a.* Souvenir sheet of 2 4.00 1.25

No. C231a contains 2 stamps similar to Nos. C230-C231 with simulated perforations.

### Horse Racing Type

90fr, Steeplechase. 100fr, Galloping horses.

**1974, Aug. 3 Litho. *Perf. 14***
**C232** A152 90fr multi 1.90 .25
**C233** A152 100fr multi 2.25 .35
*a.* Souvenir sheet of 2 6.00 2.00

No. C233a contains one each of Nos. C232-C233 with simulated perforations.

### Nos. C180, C180a and C181 Overprinted: "COUPE DU MONDE / DE FOOTBALL / VAINQUEURS / REPUBLIQUE FEDERALE / d'ALLEMAGNE"

**1974, Aug. 19**
**C234** A127 90fr multi .75 .25
*a.* Souvenir sheet of 2 18.00 —
**C235** A127 200fr multi 1.50 .65

World Cup Soccer Championship, Munich, 1974, victory of German Federal Republic. For description of No. C234a see note after No. C181.

### Animal Type

**1974, Sept. 7 Litho. *Perf. 14***
**C236** A153 90fr Lions 1.90 .30
**C237** A153 100fr Rhinoceroses 2.00 .35
*a.* Souvenir sheet of 3 3.50 1.75

Wild animals of West Africa. No. C237a contains 3 stamps similar to Nos. 889, C236-C237 with simulated perforations.

**1974, Oct. 14**
**C238** A153 90fr Herd at waterhole 1.10 .25
**C239** A153 100fr Village and cows 1.25 .35
*a.* Souvenir sheet of 2 2.50 1.25

Domestic animals. No. C239a contains 2 stamps with simulated perforations similar to Nos. C238-C239.

### Churchill Type

Designs: 100fr, Churchill and frigate. 200fr, Churchill and fighter planes.

**1974, Nov. 1 Photo. *Perf. 13x13½***
**C240** A154 100fr multi 1.10 .30
**C241** A154 200fr org & multi 2.40 .60
*a.* Souvenir sheet of 2 4.00 1.90

No. C241a contains 2 stamps similar to Nos. C240-C241; perf. or imperf.

### Flower Type

Flowers of Togo: 100fr, Clerodendrum thosonae. 200fr, Gloriosa superba.

**1975, Feb. 15 Litho. *Perf. 14***
**C242** A155 100fr multi 1.50 .25
**C243** A155 200fr multi 3.00 .50
*a.* Souvenir sheet of 2 7.50 2.50

No. C243a contains one each of Nos. C242-C243, perf. 13x14 or imperf.

Nos. C184-C185 Overprinted: "70e ANNIVERSAIRE / 23 FEVRIER 1975"

**1975, Feb. 23 Litho. *Perf. 14***
**C244** A129 90fr multi .90 .25
**C245** A129 100fr multi 1.00 .35

Rotary International, 70th anniversary.

### Easter Type

Paintings: 100fr, Christ Rising from the Tomb, by Master MS. 200fr, Holy Trinity (detail), by Dürer.

**1975, Apr. 19 Litho. *Perf. 14***
**C246** A157 100fr multi 1.00 .25
**C247** A157 200fr multi 2.00 .55
*a.* Souvenir sheet of 2 3.50 2.00

No. C247a contains 2 stamps similar to Nos. C246-C247 with simulated perforations.

### Independence Type

50fr, National Day parade, flag and map of Togo. 60fr, Warriors' dance and flag of Togo.

**1975, Apr. 26 Litho. *Perf. 14***
**C248** A158 50fr multi, vert. .50 .20
**C249** A158 60fr multi .70 .20
*a.* Souvenir sheet of 2 1.50 .75

No. C249a contains 2 stamps similar to Nos. C248-C249 with simulated perforations.

### Hunt Type

Designs: 90fr, Running deer. 100fr, Wild boar hunter with shotgun.

**1975, May 24 Photo. *Perf. 13x13½***
**C250** A159 90fr multi 1.60 .25
**C251** A159 100fr multi 1.90 .25

### Palm Oil Type

Designs: 85fr, Selling palm oil in market, vert. 100fr, Oil processing plant, Alokoegbe.

**1975, June 28 Litho. *Perf. 14***
**C252** A160 85fr multi .80 .25
**C253** A160 100fr multi .95 .25

### Apollo-Soyuz Type and

Soyuz Spacecraft
AP17

Designs: 60fr, Donald K. Slayton, Vance D. Brand and Thomas P. Stafford. 90fr, Aleksei A. Leonov and Valery N. Kubasov. 100fr, Apollo-Soyuz link-up, American and Russian flags. 200fr, Apollo-Soyuz emblem and globe.

**1975, July 15**
**C254** AP17 50fr yel & multi .50 .20
**C255** A161 60fr lil & multi .70 .20
**C256** A161 90fr bl & multi .85 .25
**C257** A161 100fr grn & multi 1.25 .40
**C258** A161 200fr yel & multi 2.10 .45
*a.* Souv. sheet of 4, #C255-C258 6.00 3.50
*Nos. C254-C258 (5)* 5.40 1.50

See note after No. 913.

### Schweitzer Type

Dr. Schweitzer: 80fr, playing organ, vert. 90fr, with pelican, vert. 100fr, and Lambarene Hospital.

**1975, Aug. 23 Litho. *Perf. 14x13½***
**C259** A163 80fr multi 1.00 .25
**C260** A163 90fr multi 1.10 .30
**C261** A163 100fr multi 1.25 .35
*Nos. C259-C261 (3)* 3.35 .90

### Letter Writing Type

80fr, Erasmus Writing Letter, by Hans Holbein.

**1975, Oct. 9 Litho. *Perf. 14***
**C262** A164 80fr multi 1.00 .25

Nos. C167-C168a Overprinted: "30ème Anniversaire / des Nations-Unies"

**1975, Oct. 24 Litho. *Perf. 14***
**C263** A120 60fr multi .60 .20
**C264** A120 90fr multi .75 .25
*a.* Souvenir sheet of 4 3.00 1.90

UN, 30th anniv. #C264a contains Nos. 796 (with overprint), 918, C263-C264.

Nos. C198-C199 Overprinted: "14ème JAMBOREE / MONDIAL / DES ECLAIREURS"

**1975, Nov. 7**
**C265** A137 100fr multi .55 .25
**C266** A137 200fr multi 1.10 .50
*a.* Souvenir sheet of 2 3.25 2.00

14th World Boy Scout Jamboree, Lillehammer, Norway, July 29-Aug. 7. No. C266a contains one each of Nos. C265-C266 with simulated perforations.

### Christmas Type

Paintings of the Virgin and Child: 90fr, Nativity, by Federico Barocci. 100fr, Bellini. 200fr, Correggio.

**1975, Dec. 20 Litho. *Perf. 14***
**C267** A165 90fr bl & multi .80 .25
**C268** A165 100fr red & multi .90 .25
**C269** A165 200fr bl & multi 1.75 .50
*a.* Souv. sheet of 2, #C268-C269 3.50 2.00
*Nos. C267-C269 (3)* 3.45 1.00

### Bicentennial Type

Paintings (and Bicentennial Emblem): 60fr, Surrender of Gen. Burgoyne, by John Trumbull. 70fr, Surrender at Trenton, by Trumbull, vert. 100fr, Signing of Declaration of Independence, by Trumbull. 200fr, Washington Crossing the Delaware, by Emanuel Leutze.

**1976, Mar. 3 Litho. *Perf. 14***
**C270** A167 60fr multi .65 .20
**C271** A167 70fr multi .75 .20
**C272** A167 100fr multi 1.00 .25
**C273** A167 200fr multi 2.00 .55
*a.* Souv. sheet of 2, #C272-C273 4.00 2.00
*Nos. C270-C273 (4)* 4.40 1.20

No. C273a also exists imperf. Value $22.50.
For overprints see Nos. C280-C283.

### Common Market Type

Designs: 60fr, ACP and CEE emblems. 70fr, Map of Africa, Europe and Asia.

**1976, Apr. 24 Photo. *Perf. 13x14***
**C274** A168 60fr lt bl & multi .45 .20
**C275** A168 70fr yel & multi .55 .20

### Telephone Type

Designs: 70fr, Thomas A. Edison, old and new communications equipment. 105fr, Alexander Graham Bell, old and new telephones.

**1976, Mar. 10 Photo. *Perf. 13x14***
**C276** A169 70fr multi .55 .20
**C277** A169 105fr multi .75 .40
*a.* Souv. sheet of 2, #C276-C277 1.75 1.10

No. C277a exists imperf. Value $10.00.

Eye Examination
AP18

Pylon, Flags of Ghana, Togo, Dahomey
AP19

**1976, Apr. 8 *Perf. 14x13***
**C278** AP18 60fr dk red & multi .60 .20

World Health Day: "Foresight prevents blindness."

**1976, May 8 Litho. *Perf. 14***
**C279** AP19 60fr multi .55 .20

Ghana-Togo-Dahomey electric power grid, 1st anniv. See No. 932.

Nos. C270-C273, C273a, Overprinted: "INTERPHIL / MAI 29-JUIN 6, 1976"

**1976, May 29**
**C280** A167 60fr multi .50 .20
**C281** A167 70fr multi .55 .20
**C282** A167 100fr multi .80 .25
**C283** A167 200fr multi 1.60 .55
*a.* Souvenir sheet of 2 3.00 3.00
*Nos. C280-C283 (4)* 3.45 1.20

Interphil 76 Intl. Philatelic Exhibition, Philadelphia, Pa., May 29-June 6. Overprint on No. C281 in 3 lines; overprint on No. C283a applied to each stamp.

### Olympic Games Type

Montreal Olympic Emblem and: 70fr, Yachting. 105fr, Motorcycling. 200fr, Fencing.

**1976, June 15 Photo. *Perf. 14x13***
**C284** A172 70fr multi .60 .25
**C285** A172 105fr multi .85 .40
**C286** A172 200fr multi 1.60 .65
*a.* Souvenir sheet of 2, #C285-C286, perf. 14 3.00 2.25
*Nos. C284-C286 (3)* 3.05 1.30

For overprints see Nos. C298-C299.

### Viking Type

60fr, Viking landing on Mars. 70fr, Nodus Gordii (view on Mars). 105fr, Lander over Mare Tyrrhenum. 200fr, Landing on Mars.

**1976, July 15 Litho. *Perf. 14***
**C287** A173 60fr bis & multi .50 .20
**C288** A173 70fr multi .60 .20
**C289** A173 105fr bl & multi .80 .35
**C290** A173 200fr multi 1.60 .55
*a.* Souv. sheet of 2, #C289-C290, perf. 14x13½ 3.00 2.00
*Nos. C287-C290 (4)* 3.50 1.30

### Toulouse-Lautrec Type, 1976

Paintings: 60fr, Carmen, portrait. 70fr, Maurice at the Somme. 200fr, "Messalina."

**1976, Aug. 7 Litho. *Perf. 14***
**C291** A174 60fr blk & multi .80 .20
**C292** A174 70fr blk & multi .90 .25
**C293** A174 200fr blk & multi 2.50 .55
*a.* Souv. sheet of 2, #C292-C293, perf. 13½x14 4.50 2.00
*Nos. C291-C293 (3)* 4.20 1.00

No. C202 Overprinted: "Journeé / Internationale / de l'Enfance"

**1976, Nov. 27 Litho. *Perf. 14***
**C294** A139 100fr multi .55 .35

International Children's Day.

### Christmas Type

Paintings: 70fr, Holy Family, by Lorenzo Lotto. 105fr, Virgin and Child with Saints, by Jacopo da Pontormo. 200fr, Virgin and Child with Saints, by Lotto.

**1976, Dec. 18**
**C295** A175 70fr multi .60 .20
**C296** A175 105fr multi .90 .35
**C297** A175 200fr multi 1.75 .55
*a.* Souv. sheet of 2, #C296-C297 3.50 2.00
*Nos. C295-C297 (3)* 3.25 1.10

No. C284 Overprinted: "CHAMPIONS OLYMPIQUES / YACHTING — FLYING DUTCHMAN / REPUBLIQUE FEDERALE ALLEMAGNE"
No. C286 Overprinted: "CHAMPIONS OLYMPIQUES / ESCRIME FLEURET PAR EQUIPES / REPUBLIQUE FEDERALE ALLEMAGNE"

**1976, Dec. Photo. *Perf. 14x13***
**C298** A172 70fr multi .60 .20
**C299** A172 200fr multi 1.60 .60
*a.* Souvenir sheet of 2 3.25 2.25

Olympic winners. No. C299a (on No. C286a) contains Nos. C285 and C299.

### Eyadema Anniversary Type

60fr, National Assembly Building. 100fr, Pres. Eyadema greeting people at Aug. 30th meeting.

**1977, Jan. 13 Photo. *Perf. 13x14***
**C300** A177 60fr multi .55 .20
**C301** A177 100fr multi .85 .30
*a.* Souv. sheet of 2, #C300-C301 1.75 1.10

### Musical Instrument Type

Musical Instruments: 60fr, Atopani. 80fr, African violin, vert. 105fr, African flutes, vert.

**1977, Feb. 7 Litho. *Perf. 14***
**C302** A178 60fr multi .80 .20
**C303** A178 80fr multi .90 .20
**C304** A178 105fr multi 1.25 .25
*a.* Souv. sheet of 2, #C303-C304 2.50 1.40
*Nos. C302-C304 (3)* 2.95 .65

### Victor Hugo Type

Victor Hugo in exile on Guernsey Island.

**1977, Feb. 26 *Perf. 13x14***
**C305** A179 60fr multi .80 .20
*a.* Souvenir sheet of 2, #952, C305 1.25 .75

For overprint see No. C316.

### Beethoven Type

Designs: 100fr, Beethoven's piano and 1818 portrait. 200fr, Beethoven on his deathbed and Holy Trinity Church, Vienna.

**1977, Mar. 7 *Perf. 14***
**C306** A180 100fr multi 1.10 .35
**C307** A180 200fr multi 2.10 3.00
*a.* Souv. sheet of 2, #C306-C307 3.00 1.60

### Automobile Type

Early Automobiles: 60fr, Cannstatt-Daimler, 1899, Germany. 70fr, Sunbeam, 1904, England. 100fr, Renault, 1908, France. 200fr, Rolls Royce, 1909, England.

**1977, Apr. 11 Litho. *Perf. 14***
**C308** A181 60fr multi .70 .20
**C309** A181 70fr multi .80 .20
**C310** A181 100fr multi 1.10 .30
**C311** A181 200fr multi 2.25 .65
*a.* Souv. sheet of 2, #C310-C311 4.50 1.75
*Nos. C308-C311 (4)* 4.85 1.35

### Lindbergh Type

Designs: 60fr, Lindbergh and son Jon, birds in flight. 85fr, Lindbergh home in Kent, England. 90fr, Spirit of St. Louis over Atlantic Ocean. 100fr, Concorde over NYC.

**1977, May 9**
**C312** A182 60fr multi .60 .20
**C313** A182 85fr multi .85 .20
**C314** A182 90fr multi .90 .20
**C315** A182 100fr multi 1.00 .25
*a.* Souv. sheet of 2, #C314-C315 2.25 1.25
*Nos. C312-C315 (4)* 3.35 .85

No. C305 Overprinted: "10ème ANNIVERSAIRE DU / CONSEIL INTERNATIONAL / DE LA LANGUE FRANCAISE"

**1977, May 17 Litho. *Perf. 14***
**C316** A179 60fr multi .70 .20

10th anniv. of the French Language Council.

### Wildlife Type

60fr, Colobus monkeys. 90fr, Chimpanzee, vert. 100fr, Leopard. 200fr, West African manatee.

**1977, June 13**
**C317** A183 60fr multi .70 .20
**C318** A183 90fr multi 1.00 .20
**C319** A183 100fr multi 1.10 .20
**C320** A183 200fr multi 2.40 .35
*a.* Souv. sheet of 2, #C319-C320 4.00 1.75
*Nos. C317-C320 (4)* 5.20 .95

### Agriculture Type

Designs: 60fr, Corn silo. 100fr, Hoeing and planting by hand. 200fr, Tractor on field.

**1977, July 11 Litho. *Perf. 14***
**C321** A184 60fr multi .45 .20
**C322** A184 100fr multi .75 .20
**C323** A184 200fr multi 1.60 .40
*a.* Souv. sheet of 2, #C322-C323, perf. 13x14 3.00 1.50
*Nos. C321-C323 (3)* 2.80 .80

### Rubens Type

Paintings: 60fr, Heads of Black Men, 1620. 100fr, Anne of Austria, 1624.

**1977, Aug. 8**
**C324** A185 60fr multi .70 .20
**C325** A185 100fr multi 1.10 .20
*a.* Souv. sheet of 2, #C324-C325, perf. 14x13 2.10 1.25

### Orbiter Type

90fr, Retrieval of unmanned satellite in space. 100fr, Satellite's return to space after repairs. 200fr, Manned landing of Orbiter.

**1977, Oct. 4 Litho. *Perf. 14***
**C326** A186 90fr multi, vert. .75 .20
**C327** A186 100fr multi .80 .20
**C328** A186 200fr multi 1.75 .35
*a.* Souv. sheet of 2, #C327-C328 3.00 1.50
*Nos. C326-C328 (3)* 3.30 .75

**Lafayette Type**

60fr, Lafayette landing in New York, 1824. 105fr, Lafayette and Washington at Valley Forge.

**1977, Nov. 7** *Perf. 13x14*
C329 A187 60fr multi .50 .20
C330 A187 105fr multi .85 .20
a. Souv. sheet of 2, #C329-C330 1.75 1.00

**Christmas Type**

Virgin & Child by: 90fr, 200fr, Carlo Crivelli, diff. 1 00fr, Bellini.

**1977, Dec. 19** *Perf. 14*
C331 A189 90fr multi .75 .20
C332 A189 100fr multi .80 .20
C333 A189 200fr multi 1.75 .35
a. Souv. sheet of 2, #C332-C333 3.25 1.50
*Nos. C331-C333 (3)* 3.30 .75

**Jenner Type**

Designs: 50fr, Edward Jenner. 60fr, Smallpox vaccination clinic, horiz.

**1978, Jan. 9** *Perf. 14x13, 13x14*
C334 A190 50fr multi .35 .20
C335 A190 60fr multi .40 .20
a. Souvenir sheet of 2 1.40 .65

No. C335a contains 2 stamps with simulated perforations similar to Nos. C334-C335.

**Wright Brothers Type**

Designs: 60fr, Orville Wright's 7½-minute flight. 70fr, Orville Wright injured in first aircraft accident, 1908. 200fr, Wrights' bicycle shop, Dearborn, Mich. 300fr, First flight, 1903.

**1978, Feb. 6 Litho.** *Perf. 14*
C336 A191 60fr multi .60 .20
C337 A191 70fr multi .65 .20
C338 A191 200fr multi 2.00 .35
C339 A191 300fr multi 3.00 .60
a. Souvenir sheet of 2 9.25 5.25
*Nos. C336-C339 (4)* 6.25 1.35

No. C339a contains one each of Nos. C338-C339 with simulated perforations.

**Port of Lomé Type, 1978**

Anchor and: 60fr, Industrial harbor. 100fr, Merchant marine harbor. 200fr, Bird's-eye view of entire harbor.

**1978, Apr. 26 Photo.** *Perf. 13*
C340 A199 60fr multi .45 .20
C341 A199 100fr multi .75 .20
C342 A199 200fr multi 1.60 .40
a. Souv. sheet of 2, #C341-C342 3.00 1.50
*Nos. C340-C342 (3)* 2.80 .80

**Space Type**

Designs: 90fr, Module camera, horiz. 100fr, Module antenna. 200fr, Pioneer, US, in orbit.

**1978, May 8 Litho.** *Perf. 14*
C343 A200 90fr multi .70 .20
C344 A200 100fr multi .75 .20
C345 A200 200fr multi 1.50 .35
a. Souv. sheet of 2, #C344-C345, perf. 13½x14 2.50 1.50
*Nos. C343-C345 (3)* 2.95 .75

**Soccer Type**

Various soccer scenes & Argentina '78 emblem.

**1978, June 5** *Perf. 14*
C346 A201 60fr multi .45 .20
C347 A201 80fr multi .60 .20
C348 A201 200fr multi 1.50 .35
C349 A201 300fr multi 2.25 .50
a. Souvenir sheet of 2, #C348-C349, perf. 13½x14 3.75 2.25
*Nos. C346-C349 (4)* 4.80 1.25

**Bicycle Type**

History of Bicycle: 60fr, Bantam, 1896, vert. 85fr, Fold-up bicycle for military use, 1897. 90fr, Draisienne, 1816, vert. 100fr, Penny-farthing, 1884, vert.

*Perf. 14x13, 13x14*

**1978, July 10 Photo.**
C350 A202 60fr multi .55 .20
C351 A202 85fr multi .75 .20
C352 A202 90fr multi .80 .25
C353 A202 100fr multi .85 .25
a. Souv. sheet of 2, #C352-C353 2.00 1.10
*Nos. C350-C353 (4)* 2.95 .90

**Phonograph Type**

60fr, Edison's original phonograph, horiz. 80fr, Emile Berliner's phonograph, 1888. 200fr, Berliner's improved phonograph, 1894, horiz. 300fr, His Master's Voice phonograph, 1900, horiz.

*Perf. 13x14, 14x13*

**1978, July 8 Photo.**
C354 A203 60fr multi .45 .20
C355 A203 80fr multi .60 .20
C356 A203 200fr multi 1.40 .35
C357 A203 300fr multi 2.20 .50
a. Souv. sheet of 2, #C356-C357 3.50 2.00
*Nos. C354-C357 (4)* 4.65 1.25

**Red Cross Type**

Design: 60fr, Red Cross and other pavilions at Paris Exhibition, 1867.

**1978, Sept. 4 Photo.** *Perf. 14x13*
C358 A204 60fr pur & red .45 .20
a. Souv. sheet, #1009, C358 1.10 .55

**Paintings Type**

60fr, Langlois Bridge, by Vincent van Gogh. 70fr, Witches' Sabbath, by Francisco Goya. 90fr, Jesus among the Doctors, by Albrecht Dürer. 200fr, View of Arco, by Dürer.

**1978, Nov. 6 Litho.** *Perf. 14*
C359 A205 60fr multi .55 .20
C360 A205 70fr multi .60 .25
C361 A205 90fr multi .80 .35
C362 A205 200fr multi 1.60 .65
a. Souv. sheet of 2, #C361-C362 3.00 1.25
*Nos. C359-C362 (4)* 3.55 1.45

Birth and death anniversaries of famous painters.

**Philexafrique II — Essen Issue**
Common Design Types

#C363, Warthog and Togo No. C36. #C364, Firecrest and Thurn and Taxis No. 1.

**1978, Nov. 1 Litho.** *Perf. 13x12½*
C363 CD138 100fr multi 2.50 2.00
C364 CD139 100fr multi 2.50 2.00
a. Pair, #C363-C364 + label 5.00 5.00

**Congress of Paris Type**

60fr, Mail ship "Slieve Roe" 1877, post horn. 105fr, Congress of Paris medal. 200fr, Locomotive, 1870. All horizontal.

**1978, Nov. 27 Photo.** *Perf. 14x13*
C365 A206 60fr multi .45 .20
C366 A206 105fr multi .80 .35
C367 A206 200fr multi 1.60 .65
a. Souv. sheet of 2, #C366-C367 2.50 1.25
*Nos. C365-C367 (3)* 2.85 1.20

**Christmas Type**

Paintings (Virgin and Child): 90fr, 200fr, by Carlo Crivelli, diff. 100fr, by Cosimo Tura.

**1978, Dec. 18**
C368 A207 90fr multi .70 .30
C369 A207 100fr multi .85 .35
C370 A207 200fr multi 1.60 .65
a. Souv. sheet of 2, #C369-C370 3.00 1.25
*Nos. C368-C370 (3)* 3.15 1.30

**Capt. Cook Type**

Designs: 60fr, "Freelove," Whitby Harbor, horiz. 70fr, Trip to Antarctica, 1773, horiz. 90fr, Capt. Cook. 200fr, Sails of Endeavour.

**1979, Feb. 12 Litho.** *Perf. 14*
C371 A208 60fr multi .50 .20
C372 A208 70fr multi .55 .25
C373 A208 90fr multi .75 .30
C374 A208 200fr multi 1.75 1.25
a. Souv. sheet of 2, #C373-C374 3.00 1.75
*Nos. C371-C374 (4)* 3.55 2.00

**Easter Type**

60fr, Resurrection. 100fr, Ascension. 200fr, Jesus appearing to Mary Magdalene.

**1979, Apr. 9**
C375 A209 60fr multi .40 .20
C376 A209 100fr multi .65 .35
C377 A209 200fr multi 1.40 .65
a. Souv. sheet of 2, #C376-C377 2.50 1.25
*Nos. C375-C377 (3)* 2.45 1.20

UPU Emblem, Drummer — AP20

Design: 100fr, UPU emblem, hands passing letter, satellites.

**1979, June 8 Engr.** *Perf. 13*
C378 AP20 60fr multi 1.40 .50
C379 AP20 100fr multi 1.20 1.00

Philexafrique II, Libreville, Gabon, June 8-17.

**Einstein Type**

Designs: 60fr, Sights and actuality diagram. 85fr, Einstein playing violin, vert. 100fr, Atom symbol and formula of relativity, vert. 200fr, Einstein portrait, vert.

*Perf. 14x13, 13x14*

**1979, July 2 Photo.**
C380 A210 60fr multi .40 .20
C381 A210 85fr multi .60 .30
C382 A210 100fr multi .65 .35
C383 A210 200fr multi 1.40 .65
a. Souv. sheet of 2, #C382-C383 2.50 1.25
*Nos. C380-C383 (4)* 3.05 1.50

**Tree Type**

Design: 60fr, Man watering tree.

**1979, Aug. 13** *Perf. 14x13*
C384 A212 60fr blk & brn .40 .20

**Rowland Hill Type**

Designs: 90fr, Bellman, England, 1820. 100fr, "Centercycles" used for parcel delivery, 1883, horiz. 200fr, French P.O. railroad car, 1848, horiz.

**1979, Aug. 27 Photo.**
C385 A213 90fr multi .65 .30
C386 A213 100fr multi .70 .35
C387 A213 200fr multi 1.50 .65
a. Souv. sheet of 2, #C386-C387 2.50 1.25
*Nos. C385-C387 (3)* 2.85 1.30

**Train Type**

Historic Locomotives: 60fr, "Le General," 1862. 85fr, Stephenson's, 1843. 100fr, "De Witt Clinton," 1831. 200fr, Joy's "Jenny Lind," 1847.

**1979, Oct. 1 Litho.** *Perf. 14*
C388 A214 60fr multi .55 .20
C389 A214 85fr multi .80 .30
C390 A214 100fr multi .90 .35
C391 A214 200fr multi 1.00 .65
a. Souv. sheet of 2, #C390-C391 4.25 2.25
*Nos. C388-C391 (4)* 3.25 1.50

**Olympic Type**

1980 Olympic Emblems and: 90fr, Ski jump. No. C393, Doubles canoeing, Olympic flame. No. C394, Rings. No. C395a, Bobsledding, horiz. No. C395b, Gymnast, horiz.

**1979, Oct. 18 Litho.** *Perf. 13½*
C392 A215 90fr multi .65 .30
C393 A215 100fr multi .70 .35
C394 A215 200fr multi 1.60 .65
*Nos. C392-C394 (3)* 2.95 1.30

**Souvenir Sheet**

C395 Sheet of 2 2.50 1.25
a. A215 100fr multi .65 .35
b. A215 200fr multi 1.40 .65

**Religion Type**

Designs: 60fr, Moslems praying. 70fr, Protestant ministers.

**1979, Oct. 29** *Perf. 13x14*
C396 A216 60fr multi .45 .20
C397 A216 70fr multi .50 .25
a. Souv. sheet, #C396-C397 1.40 .55

**Apollo 11 Type**

60fr, Astronaut leaving Apollo 11. 70fr, US flag. 200fr, Sun shield. 300fr, Lunar take-off.

**1979, Nov. 5**
C398 A217 60fr multi .45 .20
C399 A217 70fr multi .50 .25
C400 A217 200fr multi 1.50 .65
C401 A217 300fr multi 2.10 1.00
a. Souv. sheet of 2, #C400-C401 4.00 1.75
*Nos. C398-C401 (4)* 4.55 2.10

**Telecom Type**

Design: 60fr, Telecom 79, dish antenna.

**1979, Nov. 26 Photo.** *Perf. 14x13*
C402 A218 60fr multi .70 .20

**Miniature Sheets**

President Eyadema, 10th Anniv. of the People's Republic — AP21

Illustration reduced.

**Litho. & Embossed**

**1979, Nov. 30** *Perf. 13½*
C402A AP21 1000fr In uniform 6.00 —

*Imperf*

C402B AP21 1000fr In suit, vert. 6.00 —

Exist imperf.

**Christmas Type**

90fr, Adoration of the Kings. 100fr, Presentation of Infant Jesus. 200fr, Flight into Egypt.

**1979, Dec. 17 Litho.** *Perf. 14*
C403 A219 90fr multi .75 .30
C404 A219 100fr multi .80 .35
C405 A219 200fr multi 1.50 .65
a. Souv. sheet of 2, #C404-C405 3.00 1.25
*Nos. C403-C405 (3)* 3.05 1.30

**Rotary Type**

3-H Emblem and: 90fr, Man reaching for sun. 100fr, Fish, grain. 200fr, Family, globe.

**1980, Jan. 14**
C406 A220 90fr multi .60 .30
C407 A220 100fr multi .65 .35
C408 A220 200fr multi 1.25 .65
a. Souv. sheet of 2, C407-C408 2.50 1.25
*Nos. C406-C408 (3)* 2.50 1.30

Rotary Intl., 75th anniv.; 3-H program (health, hunger, humanity).

**Winter Olympic Type, 1980**

**1980, Jan. 31 Litho.** *Perf. 13½*
C409 A221 60fr Downhill skiing .45 .20
C410 A221 100fr Speed skating .75 .35
C411 A221 200fr Cross-country skiing 1.40 .65
*Nos. C409-C411 (3)* 2.60 1.20

**Souvenir Sheet**

C412 Sheet of 2 2.50 1.25
a. A221 100fr Ski jump, horiz. .65 .35
b. A221 200fr Hockey, horiz. 1.25 .65

**Olympic Type**

**1980, Feb. 29 Litho.** *Perf. 13½*
C413 A222 100fr Fencing .90 .45
C414 A222 200fr Pole vault 1.60 .80
C415 A222 300fr Hurdles 2.50 1.25
a. Souv. sheet of 2, #C414-C415 4.75 2.50
*Nos. C413-C415 (3)* 5.00 2.50

**Easter Type**

Easter 1980 (Paintings by): 60fr, Lorenzo Lotto. 100fr, El Greco. 200fr, Carlo Crivelli.

**1980, Mar. 31** *Perf. 14*
C416 A223 60fr multi .50 .20
C417 A223 100fr multi .70 .35
C418 A223 200fr multi 1.50 .65
a. Souv. sheet of 2, #C417-C418 2.50 1.25
*Nos. C416-C418 (3)* 2.70 1.20

**ASECNA Type**

**1980, Mar. 24 Litho.** *Perf. 12½*
C419 A224 60fr multi .60 .20

**Telecommunications Type**

**1980, May 17 Photo.** *Perf. 13½x14*
C420 A225 60fr "17 MAI", vert. .60 .20

**Red Cross Type**

**1980, June 16 Photo.** *Perf. 14x13*
C421 A226 60fr Nurses, patient .60 .20

**Jules Verne Type**

Designs: 60fr, Rocket (From Earth to Moon). 80fr, Around the World in 80 Days. 100fr, Rocket and moon (From Earth to Moon). 200fr, Octopus (20,000 Leagues Under the Sea).

**1980, July 14 Litho.** *Perf. 14*
C422 A227 60fr multi .50 .20
C423 A227 80fr multi .65 .25
C424 A227 100fr multi .80 .35

**C425** A227 200fr multi 1.50 .65
a. Souv. sheet of 2, #C424-C425, perf. 13½x14 2.50 1.25
*Nos. C422-C425 (4)* 3.45 1.45

### Ingres Type

Ingres Paintings: 90fr, Jupiter and Thetis. 100fr, Countess d'Hassonville. 200fr, "Tu Marcellus Eris."

**1980, Aug. 29 Litho. *Perf. 14***
**C426** A228 90fr multi .80 .30
**C427** A228 100fr multi .85 .35
**C428** A228 200fr multi 1.60 .65
a. Souv. sheet of 2, #C427-C428 3.00 1.25
*Nos. C426-C428 (3)* 3.25 1.30

### Famous Men Type

90fr, Salvador Allende, vert. 100fr, Pope Paul VI, vert. 200fr, Jomo Kenyatta, vert.

**1980, Feb. 11 Litho. *Perf. 14x13***
**C429** A231 90fr ultra & lt bl grn 1.00 .30
**C430** A231 100fr pur & pink 1.10 .35
**C431** A231 200fr brn & yel bis 2.00 .65
a. Souv. sheet of 2, #C430-C431 2.50 1.25
*Nos. C429-C431 (3)* 4.10 1.30

### Human Rights Type

**1980, Oct. 13 *Perf. 13x14***
**C432** A233 60fr Map of Americas .40 .20
**C433** A233 150fr Map of Africa 1.00 .50
a. Souv. sheet of 2, #C432-C433 1.75 1.25

American Order of Rosicrucians Emblem — AP22

**1980, Nov. 17 Litho. *Perf. 13***
**C434** AP22 60fr multi .60 .20

General Conclave of the American Order of Rosicrucians, meeting of French-speaking countries, Lome, Aug.

### Christmas Type

Designs: 100fr, Cologne Cathedral, Germany, 13th cent. 150fr, Notre Dame, Paris, 12th cent. 200fr, Canterbury Cathedral, England, 11th cent.

**1980, Dec. 22 *Perf. 14½x13½***
**C435** A234 100fr multi .70 .35
**C436** A234 150fr multi 1.10 .50
**C437** A234 200fr multi 1.40 .65
a. Souv. sheet of 2, #C436-C437 3.00 1.40
*Nos. C435-C437 (3)* 3.20 1.50

### Hotel Type of 1981

**1981, Feb. 2 Litho. *Perf. 12½x13***
**C437B** A236 60fr multi .60 .20

### Easter Type of 1981

Rembrandt Paintings: 100fr, Artist's Mother. 200fr, Man in a Ruff.

**1981, Apr. 13 Litho. *Perf. 14½x13½***
**C438** A237 100fr multi .80 .35
**C439** A237 200fr multi 1.60 .65
a. Souv. sheet of 2, #C438-C439 3.00 1.25

### Market Type

**1981, Mar. 8 Litho. *Perf. 14***
**C440** A230 90fr Fabric dealer .60 .30
**C441** A230 100fr Bananas .65 .35
**C442** A230 200fr Clay pottery 1.40 .65
**C443** A230 250fr Setting up 1.60 .80
**C444** A230 500fr Selling 3.50 1.60
**C445** A230 1000fr Measuring grain 6.50 3.50
*Nos. C440-C445 (6)* 14.25 7.20

For overprints see Nos. C486-C487.

### Bird Type

***Perf. 13½x14½***
**1981, Aug. 10 Litho.**
**C446** A238 50fr Violet-backed sunbird .80 .20
**C447** A238 100fr Red bishop 1.50 .35
a. Souv. sheet, #C446-C447 5.50 2.50

### IYD Type

**1981, Aug. 31 *Perf. 14***
**C448** A240 90fr Carpenter .65 .30
**C449** A240 200fr Basketball players 1.40 .65

### Souvenir Sheet

**C449A** A240 300fr Weaver 2.25 1.25

### Picasso Type

**1981, Sept. 14 *Perf. 14½x13½***
**C450** A241 90fr Violin and Bottle on Table, 1916 .75 .30
**C451** A241 100fr Baboon and Young .75 .35
**C452** A241 200fr Mandolin and Clarinet, 1914 1.75 .65
a. Souv. sheet of 2, #C451-C452 3.00 1.25
*Nos. C450-C452 (3)* 3.25 1.30

### World Heritage Year Type

**1981, Sept. 28 *Perf. 13½x14½***
**C453** A242 100fr Cracow Museum, Poland .75 .35
**C454** A242 200fr Goree Isld., Senegal 1.50 .75
a. Souv. sheet of 2, #C453-C454 2.50 1.25

### Space Type

**1981, Nov. *Perf. 14***
**C455** A243 90fr multi .70 .35
**C456** A243 100fr multi .75 .40

### Souvenir Sheet

***Perf. 13x14***
**C456A** A243 300fr multi, vert. 2.25 1.25

10th anniv. of Soyuz 10 (90fr) and Apollo 14 (100fr).

### Christmas Type

Rubens Paintings: 100fr, Adoration of the Kings. 200fr, Virgin and Child. 300fr, Virgin giving Chasuble to St. Idefonse.

***Perf. 14½x13½***
**1981, Dec. 10 Litho.**
**C457** A244 100fr multi .70 .35
**C458** A244 200fr multi 1.50 .65
**C459** A244 300fr multi 2.10 1.00
a. Souv. sheet of 2, #C458-C459 4.00 1.90
*Nos. C457-C459 (3)* 4.30 2.00

### West African Rice Development Assoc. Type

**1981, Dec. 21 Litho. *Perf. 12½***
**C461** A236a 105fr yel & multi .70 .35

### Liberation Type

Designs: 105fr, Citizens holding hands, Pres. Eyadema, vert. 130fr, Hotel.

**1982, Jan. 13 Litho. *Perf. 12½***
**C462** A245 105fr multi .70 .35
**C463** A245 130fr multi .90 .40

### Scouting Year Type

**1982, Feb. 25 Litho. *Perf. 14***
**C464** A246 90fr Semaphore .75 .30
**C465** A246 120fr Tower 1.00 .40
**C466** A246 130fr Scouts, canoe 1.10 .40
**C467** A246 135fr Scouts, tent 1.10 .45
*Nos. C464-C467 (4)* 3.95 1.55

### Souvenir Sheet

***Perf. 13x14***
**C468** A246 500fr Baden-Powell 4.25 1.60

### Easter Type

**1982, Apr. *Perf. 14x14½***
**C469** A247 105fr multi .70 .35
**C470** A247 120fr multi .80 .40

### Souvenir Sheet

**C471** A247 500fr multi 4.00 1.60

PHILEXFRANCE '82 Intl. Stamp Exhibition, Paris, June 11-21 — AP23

**1982 Litho. *Perf. 13***
**C472** AP23 90fr shown .70 .30
**C473** AP23 105fr ROMOLYMPHIL '82, vert. .90 .35

Issue dates: 90fr, June 11; 105fr, May 19.

### Butterfly Type

**1982, July 15 *Perf. 14½x14***
**C474** A248 90fr Euxanthe eurinome 1.40 .30
**C475** A248 105fr Mylothris rhodope 1.60 .35

### Souvenir Sheet

**C476** A248 500fr Papilio zalmoxis 4.25 1.60

### World Cup Type

**1982, July 26 *Perf. 14x14½***
**C477** A249 105fr multi .80 .35
**C478** A249 200fr multi 1.40 .65
**C479** A249 300fr multi 2.10 1.00
*Nos. C477-C479 (3)* 4.30 2.00

### Souvenir Sheet

**C480** A249 500fr multi 4.00 1.65

For overprints see Nos. 1152-1155.

Pre-Olympics, 1984 Los Angeles — AP24

**1983, Oct. 3 Photo. *Perf. 12½***
**C481** AP24 70fr Boxing .55 .20
**C482** AP24 90fr Hurdles .70 .20
**C483** AP24 105fr Pole vault .80 .20
**C484** AP24 130fr Runner .90 .20
*Nos. C481-C484 (4)* 2.95 .80

### Souvenir Sheet

**C485** AP24 500fr Runner, diff. 4.00 1.50

Nos. C443-C444 Overprinted: "19E CONGRES UPU HAMBOURG 1984"

**1984, June Litho. *Perf. 14***
**C486** A230 250fr multi 1.75 1.00
**C487** A230 500fr multi 3.75 2.00

1984 Summer Olympics — AP25

**1984, July 27 *Perf. 13***
**C488** AP25 70fr Pole vault .45 .20
**C489** AP25 90fr Bicycling .45 .20
**C490** AP25 120fr Soccer .75 .20
**C491** AP25 250fr Boxing 1.50 .40
**C492** AP25 400fr Running 2.25 .65
*Nos. C488-C492 (5)* 5.40 1.65

### Souvenir Sheet

**C493** AP25 1000fr like 120fr, without flag 7.50 6.50

Nos. C488-C490, C493 vert.

Olympic Champions AP26

Peace and Human Rights — AP28

**1984, Nov. 15 Litho. *Perf. 15***
**C494** AP26 500fr Jim Thorpe, US 7.25 3.25
**C495** AP26 500fr Jesse Owens, US 7.25 3.25
**C496** AP26 500fr Muhammad Ali, US 40.00 3.25
**C497** AP26 500fr Bob Beamon, US 7.25 3.25
*Nos. C494-C497 (4)* 61.75 13.00

### Souvenir Sheets

**C498** AP26 500fr Bill Steinkraus, US 7.25 3.25
**C499** AP26 500fr New Zealand rowing team 7.25 3.25
**C500** AP26 500fr Pakistani hockey team 7.25 3.25
**C501** AP26 500fr Yukio Endo, Japan 7.25 3.25

### West German Olympians

**1984, Nov. 15**
**C502** AP26 500fr Dietmar Mogenburg 7.25 3.25
**C503** AP26 500fr Fredy Schmidtke 7.25 3.25
**C504** AP26 500fr Matthias Behr 7.25 3.25
**C505** AP26 500fr Sabine Everts 7.25 3.25
*Nos. C502-C505 (4)* 29.00 13.00

### Souvenir Sheets

**C506** AP26 500fr Karl-Heinz Radschinsky 7.25 3.25
**C507** AP26 500fr Pasquale Passarelli 7.25 3.25
**C508** AP26 500fr Michale Gross 7.25 3.25
**C509** AP26 500fr Jurgen Hingsen 7.25 3.25

For overprints see Nos. C521-C536, C563.

**1985, Jan. 14 Litho. *Perf. 13½x14***

230fr, Map of Togo, globe, doves. 270fr, Palm tree, emblem. 500fr, Opencast mining operation. 1000fr, Human Rights Monument, UN, NYC.

**C510** AP28 230fr multi 1.50 .20
**C511** AP28 270fr multi 1.90 .30
**C512** AP28 500fr multi 3.50 .50
**C513** AP28 1000fr multi 7.00 1.00
*Nos. C510-C513 (4)* 13.90 2.00

Tribal Dances AP29

**1985, July *Perf. 15x14***
**C514** AP29 120fr Adifo, Adangbe .85 .20
**C515** AP29 135fr Fouet (whip), Kente .85 .20
**C516** AP29 290fr Idjombi, Pagouda 2.00 .30
**C517** AP29 500fr Moba, Dapaong 3.50 .50
*Nos. C514-C517 (4)* 7.20 1.20

Visit of Pope John Paul II — AP30

90fr, The Pope outside Lome Cathedral. 130fr, Blessing crowd in St. Peter's Square. 500fr, Greeting Pres. Eyadema.

**1985, Aug. 9** *Perf. 13*
C518 AP30 90fr multi .75 .20
C519 AP30 130fr multi, vert. 1.25 .25
C520 AP30 500fr multi 3.50 .50
*Nos. C518-C520 (3)* 5.50 .95

Nos. C495, C497, C499, C502, C505-508 Overprinted with Winners Names, Country and Type of Olympic Medal

**1985, Aug.** *Perf. 15*
C521 AP26 500fr Kirk Baptiste, US 6.50 1.50
C522 AP26 500fr Carl Lewis, US 6.50 1.50
C523 AP26 500fr Patrik Sjoborg, Sweden 6.50 1.50
C524 AP26 500fr Glynis Nunn, Australia 6.50 1.50
*Nos. C521-C524 (4)* 26.00 6.00

**Souvenir Sheets**
C525 AP26 500fr Rowing eights, Canada 3.50 3.00
C526 AP26 500fr Rolf Milser, W. Germany 3.50 3.00
C527 AP26 500fr Takashi Irie, Japan 3.50 3.00
C528 AP26 500fr Frederic Delcourt, France 3.50 3.00

Nos. C494, C496, C503-C504, C498, C500, C501, C509 Ovptd. with Winners Names, Country and Type of Olympic Medal

**1985, Sept. 19** **Litho.** *Perf. 15*
C529 AP26 500fr Italy 6.50 1.50
C530 AP26 500fr Kevin Barry 6.50 1.50
C531 AP26 500fr Rolf Golz 6.50 1.50
C532 AP26 500fr Philippe Boisse 6.50 1.50
*Nos. C529-C532 (4)* 26.00 6.00

**Souvenir Sheets**
C533 AP26 500fr Karen Stives 3.50 3.00
C534 AP26 500fr R.F.A. (West Germany) 3.50 3.00
C535 AP26 500fr Koji Gushiken 3.50 3.00
C536 AP26 500fr Daley Thompson 3.50 3.00

Traditional Instruments — AP31

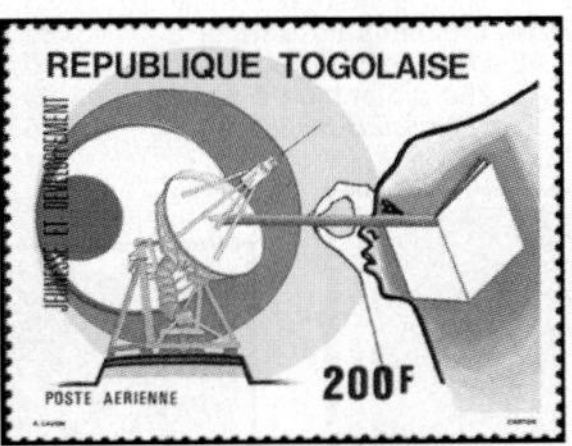

Youth and Development — AP32

Designs: No. C537, Xylophone, Kante horn, tambour. No. C538, Bongo drums, castanets, bassar horn. No. C539, Communications. No. C540, Agriculture and industry.

**1985** **Litho.** *Perf. 13*
C537 AP31 100fr multi .90 .60
C538 AP31 100fr multi .90 .60
a. Pair, #C537-C538 3.00 3.00
C539 AP32 200fr multi 1.75 1.25
C540 AP32 200fr multi 1.75 1.25
a. Pair, #C539-C540 7.50 7.50
*Nos. C537-C540 (4)* 5.30 3.70

PHILEXAFRICA '85, Lome, Togo, 11/16-24. Issued: 100fr, Nov. 4; 200fr, Nov. 16.

No. 1274 Ovptd. with Organization Emblem and "80e Anniversaire du Rotary International."

**1985, Nov. 15** **Litho.** *Perf. 15*
**Souvenir Sheet**
C541 A267 1000fr multi 20.00 6.50

Nos. 1254-1255, 1258 Ovptd. "10e ANNIVERSAIRE DE APOLLO-SOYUZ" in 1 or 2 lines

**1985, Dec. 27** **Litho.** *Perf. 15*
C542 A265 90fr multi 1.25 .40
C543 A265 500fr multi 6.75 2.00

**Souvenir Sheet**
C544 A265 1000fr multi 8.50 2.90

Nos. 1294-1295, 1297 Ovptd. "75e ANNIVERSAIRE DE LA MORT DE HENRI DUNANT FONDATEUR DE LA CROIX ROUGE" in 2 or 4 lines

**1985, Dec. 27**
C545 A270 400fr multi 4.75 1.50
C546 A270 500fr multi 6.25 2.00

**Souvenir Sheet**
C547 A270 1000fr multi 7.50 6.00

Statue of Liberty, Cent. — AP33

**1986, Apr. 10** *Perf. 13*
C548 AP33 70fr Eiffel Tower .55 .20
C549 AP33 90fr Statue of Liberty .65 .25
C550 AP33 500fr Empire State Building 3.75 1.40
*Nos. C548-C550 (3)* 4.95 1.85

Nos. 1237-1240 Ovptd. with AMERIPEX '86 Emblem

**1986, May 22** *Perf. 11*
C551 A262 500fr multi 6.50 1.40
C552 A262 1000fr multi 12.50 2.75

**Souvenir Sheets**
*Perf. 14*
C553 A262 1000fr No. 1239 8.50 3.50
C554 A262 1000fr No. 1240 8.50 3.50

Air Africa, 25th Anniv. AP34

**1986, Dec. 29** **Litho.** *Perf. 12½x13*
C555 AP34 90fr multi .75 .25

Konrad Adenauer (1876-1967) West German Chancellor — AP35

**1987, July 15** **Litho.** *Perf. 12½x13*
C556 AP35 120fr At podium .90 .60
C557 AP35 500fr With Pres. Kennedy, 1962 3.50 3.00

**Souvenir Sheet**
*Perf. 13x12½*
C558 AP35 500fr Portrait, vert. 3.50 3.00

Berlin, 750th Anniv. AP36

Designs: 90fr, Wilhelm I (1781-1864) coin, Victory statue. 150fr, Frederick III (1831-1888) coin, Brandenburg Gate. 300fr, Wilhelm II (1882-1951) coin, Reichstag building. 750fr, Otto Leopold von Bismarck (1815-1898), first chancellor of the German empire, and Charlottenburg Palace.

**1987, Aug. 31** **Litho.** *Perf. 13½*
C559 AP36 90fr multi .60 .30
C560 AP36 150fr multi 1.00 .50
C561 AP36 300fr multi 2.00 1.00
*Nos. C559-C561 (3)* 3.60 1.80

**Souvenir Sheet**
C562 AP36 750fr multi 5.50 4.25

Nos. C506, 1258, 1273 and 1274 Overprinted in Black for Philatelic Exhibitions

a

b

c

d

Additional overprints appear on souvenir sheets away from stamps.

**1988, Apr. 25** **Litho.** *Perf. 15*
**Souvenir Sheets**
C563 AP26 (a) 500fr #C506 9.50 3.00
C564 A265 (b) 1000fr #1258 10.00 5.50
C565 A265 (c) 1000fr #1273 10.00 5.50
C566 A267 (d) 1000fr #1274 10.00 5.50
*Nos. C563-C566 (4)* 39.50 19.50

## AIR POST SEMI-POSTAL STAMPS

Nursery — SPAP1

*Perf. 13½x12½*
**1942, June 22** **Unwmk.** **Photo.**
CB1 SPAP1 1.50fr + 3.50fr green .60
CB2 SPAP1 2fr + 6fr brown .60

Native children's welfare fund.

Nos. CB1-CB2 were issued by the Vichy government in France, but were not placed on sale in Togo

**Colonial Education Fund**
Common Design Type

**1942, June 22** **Engr.**
CB3 CD86a 1.20fr + 1.80fr blue & red .60

No. CB3 was issued by the Vichy government in France, but was not placed on sale in Togo.

## POSTAGE DUE STAMPS

Postage Due Stamps of Dahomey, 1914 Overprinted

**1921** **Unwmk.** *Perf. 14x13½*
J1 D2 5c green .60 .60
J2 D2 10c rose .60 .60
J3 D2 15c gray 1.25 1.25
J4 D2 20c brown 2.25 2.25
J5 D2 30c blue 2.50 2.50
J6 D2 50c black 2.00 2.00
J7 D2 60c orange 2.00 2.00
J8 D2 1fr violet 3.75 3.75
*Nos. J1-J8 (8)* 14.95 14.95

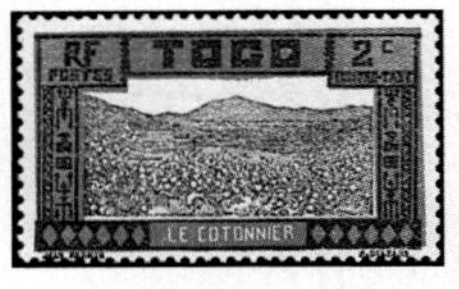

Cotton Field — D3

**1925** **Typo.** **Unwmk.**
J9 D3 2c blue & blk .20 .20
J10 D3 4c dl red & blk .20 .20
J11 D3 5c ol grn & blk .20 .20
J12 D3 10c cerise & blk .25 .25
J13 D3 15c orange & blk .60 .60
J14 D3 20c red vio & blk .40 .40
J15 D3 25c gray & blk .75 .75
J16 D3 30c ocher & blk .40 .40
J17 D3 50c brown & blk .85 .85
J18 D3 60c green & blk .85 .85
J19 D3 1fr dk vio & blk .85 .85
*Nos. J9-J19 (11)* 5.55 5.55

Type of 1925 Issue Surcharged

**1927**
J20 D3 2fr on 1fr rose red & vio 5.00 5.00
J21 D3 3fr on 1fr org brn, blk & ultra 5.00 5.00

Mask — D4

Carved Figures — D5

**1941** **Engr.** *Perf. 13*
J22 D4 5c brown black .20 .20
J23 D4 10c yellow green .20 .20
J24 D4 15c carmine .20 .20
J25 D4 20c ultra .25 .25
J26 D4 30c chestnut .55 .55
J27 D4 50c olive green 1.40 1.40
J28 D4 60c violet .55 .55
J29 D4 1fr light blue .85 .85
J30 D4 2fr orange vermilion .75 .75
J31 D4 3fr rose violet .90 .90
*Nos. J22-J31 (10)* 5.85 5.85

For type D4 without "RF," see Nos. J31A-J31F.

Type of 1941 Without "RF"

**1942-44**
J31A D4 5c brown black .20
J31B D4 10c green & violet .20
J31C D4 15c car rose & brn .25
J31D D4 30c brown & black .45

**J31E** D4 2fr brn org & brn vio .55
**J31F** D4 3fr violet & green .55
*Nos. J31A-J31F (6)* 2.20

Nos. J31A-J31F were issued by the Vichy government in France, but were not placed on sale in Togo.

**Catalogue values for unused stamps in this section, from this point to the end of the section, are for Never Hinged items.**

**1947**

| | | | | |
|---|---|---|---|---|
| **J32** D5 | 10c brt ultra | .20 | .20 |
| **J33** D5 | 30c red | .20 | .20 |
| **J34** D5 | 50c dp yellow grn | .20 | .20 |
| **J35** D5 | 1fr chocolate | .40 | .40 |
| **J36** D5 | 2fr carmine | .40 | .40 |
| **J37** D5 | 3fr gray blk | .40 | .40 |
| **J38** D5 | 4fr ultra | .70 | .70 |
| **J39** D5 | 5fr sepia | .85 | .85 |
| **J40** D5 | 10fr dp orange | .90 | .90 |
| **J41** D5 | 20fr dk blue vio | 1.25 | 1.25 |
| | *Nos. J32-J41 (10)* | 5.50 | 5.50 |

**Republic**

Konkomba Helmet
D6 D7

**1957 Engr. *Perf. 14x13***

| | | | |
|---|---|---|---|
| **J42** D6 | 1fr brt violet | .25 | .25 |
| **J43** D6 | 2fr brt orange | .25 | .25 |
| **J44** D6 | 3fr dk gray | .25 | .25 |
| **J45** D6 | 4fr brt red | .25 | .25 |
| **J46** D6 | 5fr ultra | .25 | .25 |
| **J47** D6 | 10fr dp green | .35 | .35 |
| **J48** D6 | 20fr dp claret | .50 | .50 |
| | *Nos. J42-J48 (7)* | 2.10 | 2.10 |

**1959 *Perf. 14x13***

| | | | |
|---|---|---|---|
| **J49** D7 | 1fr orange brn | .20 | .35 |
| **J50** D7 | 2fr lt blue grn | .20 | .35 |
| **J51** D7 | 3fr orange | .20 | .35 |
| **J52** D7 | 4fr blue | .20 | .45 |
| **J53** D7 | 5fr lilac rose | .20 | .45 |
| **J54** D7 | 10fr violet blue | .45 | .65 |
| **J55** D7 | 20fr black | .80 | .85 |
| | *Nos. J49-J55 (7)* | 2.25 | 3.45 |

**Type of Regular Issue**

Shells: 1fr, Conus papilionaceus. 2fr, Marginella faba. 3fr, Cypraea stercoraria. 4fr, Strombus latus. 5fr, Costate cockle (sea shell). 10fr, Cancellaria cancellata. 15fr, Cymbium pepo. 20fr, Tympanotomus radula.

**1964-65 Unwmk. Photo. *Perf. 14***
**Size: 20x25½mm**

| | | | |
|---|---|---|---|
| **J56** A47 | 1fr gray grn & red brn ('65) | .40 | .20 |
| **J57** A47 | 2fr tan & ol grn ('65) | .40 | .20 |
| **J58** A47 | 3fr gray, brn & yel ('65) | .40 | .20 |
| **J59** A47 | 4fr tan & multi ('65) | .40 | .20 |
| **J60** A47 | 5fr sep, org & grn | .60 | .30 |
| **J61** A47 | 10fr sl bl, brn & bis | .80 | .40 |
| **J62** A47 | 15fr grn & brn | 1.90 | 1.00 |
| **J63** A47 | 20fr sl, dk brn & yel | 2.40 | 1.25 |
| | *Nos. J56-J63 (8)* | 7.30 | 3.75 |

Tomatoes — D8

**1969-70 Litho. *Perf. 14***

| | | | |
|---|---|---|---|
| **J64** D8 | 5fr yellow & multi | .45 | .20 |
| **J65** D8 | 10fr blue & multi | .45 | .20 |
| **J66** D8 | 15fr multi ('70) | .65 | .30 |
| **J67** D8 | 20fr multi ('70) | .90 | .40 |
| | *Nos. J64-J67 (4)* | 2.45 | 1.10 |

**Market Type**

**1981, Mar. 8 Litho. *Perf. 14***
**Size: 23x32mm, 32x23mm**

| | | | |
|---|---|---|---|
| **J68** A230 | 5fr Millet, vert. | .25 | .20 |
| **J69** A230 | 10fr Packaged goods | .25 | .20 |
| **J70** A230 | 25fr Chickens | .25 | .20 |
| **J71** A230 | 50fr Ivory vendor | .30 | .20 |
| | *Nos. J68-J71 (4)* | 1.05 | .80 |

## OFFICIAL STAMPS

**Catalogue values for unused stamps in this section are for never hinged items.**

O1

**1991? Litho. *Perf. 13½***

| | | | |
|---|---|---|---|
| **O1** O1 | 15fr multicolored | .20 | — |
| **O2** O1 | 100fr multicolored | .35 | — |
| **O3** O1 | 125fr multicolored | .40 | — |
| **O4** O1 | 500fr multicolored | 1.40 | — |

**1991?**

| | | | |
|---|---|---|---|
| **O5** O1 | 10fr multicolored | — | — |
| **O6** O1 | 90fr yellow & multi | .30 | — |

**1991?**

| | | | |
|---|---|---|---|
| **O7** O1 | 180fr ap grn & multi | .50 | — |

**1991**

| | | | |
|---|---|---|---|
| **O8** O1 | 50fr yellow & multi | .20 | .20 |
| **O9** O1 | 300fr ap grn & multi | 1.00 | 1.00 |

The editors would like information on dates of issue and stamps of other denominations. The catalogue numbers will change.

# TOKELAU

'tō-kə-ˌlau

(Union Islands)

LOCATION — Pacific Ocean 300 miles north of Apia, Western Samoa
GOVT. — A dependency of New Zealand
AREA — 4 sq. mi.
POP. — 1,487 (1996)

The Tokelau islands consist of three atolls: Atafu, Nukunono and Fakaofo, which span 100 miles of ocean.

12 Pence = 1 Shilling
100 Cents = 1 Dollar (1967)

**Catalogue values for all unused stamps in this country are for Never Hinged items.**

Map and Scene on Atafu — A1

Nukunono Dwelling and Map — A2

Fakaofo Shore Line and Map — A3

***Perf. 13½x13***

**1948, June 22 Wmk. 253 Engr.**

| | | | |
|---|---|---|---|
| **1** A1 | ½p red brown & rose lilac | .20 | .40 |
| **2** A2 | 1p dp green & orange brn | .25 | .30 |
| **3** A3 | 2p deep ultra & green | .30 | .30 |
| | *Nos. 1-3 (3)* | .75 | 1.00 |

For surcharges see Nos. 5, 9-11.

**Coronation Issue**

Queen Elizabeth II — A3a

**1953, May 25 Photo. *Perf. 14x14½***

| | | | |
|---|---|---|---|
| **4** A3a | 3p brown | 3.50 | 2.50 |

No. 1 Surcharged in Black:

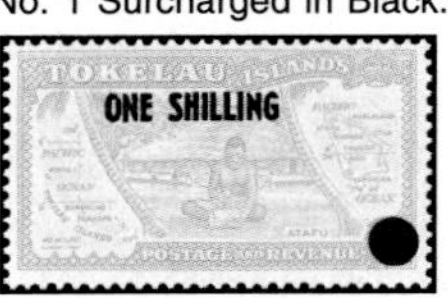


***Perf. 13½x13***

**1956, Mar. 27 Engr. Wmk. 253**

| | | | |
|---|---|---|---|
| **5** A1 | 1sh on ½p | 4.25 | 4.25 |

Postal-Fiscal Type of New Zealand, 1950, Surcharged

**Wmk. 253**

**1966, Nov. Typo. *Perf. 14***

| | | | |
|---|---|---|---|
| **6** A109 | 6p light blue | .75 | .35 |
| **7** A109 | 8p light green | 1.40 | .75 |
| **8** A109 | 2sh pink | 2.50 | 1.90 |
| | *Nos. 6-8 (3)* | 4.65 | 3.00 |

Nos. 1-3 Surcharged with New Value and Dots Obliterating Old Denomination

**1967, July 10 Engr. *Perf. 13½x13***

| | | | |
|---|---|---|---|
| **9** A2 | 1c on 1p | .60 | .60 |
| **10** A3 | 2c on 2p | 1.40 | 1.40 |
| **11** A1 | 10c on ½p | 4.75 | 4.75 |
| | *Nos. 9-11 (3)* | 6.75 | 6.75 |

The 1c and 2c surcharges include two dots, the 10c surcharge has only one.

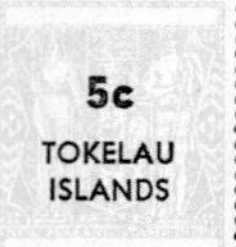


Postal Fiscal Type of New Zealand, 1950, Surcharged

**1967, July 10 Typo. *Perf. 14***

| | | | |
|---|---|---|---|
| **12** A109 | 3c light lilac | .35 | .35 |
| **13** A109 | 5c light blue | .70 | .70 |
| **14** A109 | 7c light green | 1.10 | 1.10 |
| **15** A109 | 20c pink | 2.50 | 2.50 |
| | *Nos. 12-15 (4)* | 4.65 | 4.65 |

1877, British Protectorate — A4

History of Tokelau: 10c, 1916, part of Gilbert and Ellice Islands Colony. 15c, 1925, administration transferred to New Zealand. 20c, 1948, New Zealand Territory.

***Perf. 13x12½***

**1969, Aug. 8 Litho. Wmk. 253**

| | | | |
|---|---|---|---|
| **16** A4 | 5c ultra, yellow & blk | .80 | .45 |
| **17** A4 | 10c rose red, yel & blk | 1.00 | .85 |
| **18** A4 | 15c dull grn, yel & blk | 1.10 | 1.40 |
| **19** A4 | 20c brown, yel & blk | 1.75 | 1.75 |
| | *Nos. 16-19 (4)* | 4.65 | 4.45 |

Nativity, by Federico Fiori — A4a

Adoration, by Correggio — A4b

**1969, Oct. 1 Photo. *Perf. 13½x14***

| | | | |
|---|---|---|---|
| **20** A4a | 2c multicolored | .40 | .40 |

Christmas.

***Perf. 12½***

**1970, Oct. 1 Unwmk. Litho.**

| | | | |
|---|---|---|---|
| **21** A4b | 2c multicolored | .40 | .40 |

Christmas.

"Dolphin," 1765, Map of Atafu — A5

Fan — A6

Designs: 10c, "Pandora," 1791, and map of Nukunono. 25c, "General Jackson," 1835, and map of Fakaofo, horiz.

**1970, Dec. 9 Unwmk. *Perf. 13½***

| | | | |
|---|---|---|---|
| **22** A5 | 5c yellow & multi | 1.00 | .90 |
| **23** A5 | 10c multicolored | 2.40 | 1.60 |
| **24** A5 | 25c pink & multi | 5.75 | 4.75 |
| | *Nos. 22-24 (3)* | 9.15 | 7.25 |

Discovery of Tokelau Islands.

**1971, Oct. 20 Litho. *Perf. 14***

Native Handicrafts: 2c, Round vessel. 3c, Hexagonal box. 5c, Shoulder bag. 10c, Handbag. 15c, Jewelry box with beads. 20c, Outrigger canoe model. 25c, Fish hooks.

| | | | |
|---|---|---|---|
| **25** A6 | 1c olive & multi | .20 | .20 |
| **26** A6 | 2c red & multi | .20 | .20 |
| **27** A6 | 3c dk violet & multi | .20 | .20 |
| **28** A6 | 5c dull blue & multi | .20 | .20 |
| **29** A6 | 10c dp orange & multi | .55 | .30 |
| **30** A6 | 15c emerald & multi | .85 | .55 |
| **31** A6 | 20c multicolored | 1.10 | .70 |
| **32** A6 | 25c violet blue & multi | 1.25 | .90 |
| | *Nos. 25-32 (8)* | 4.55 | 3.25 |

Windmill Pump, Map of Atafu — A7

Horny Coral — A8

South Pacific Commission Emblem and: 10c, Community well, map of Fakaofo. 15c, Eradication of rhinoceros beetle, map of Nukunono. 20c, members.

**1972, Sept. 6 Litho. *Perf. 14x13½***

| | | | |
|---|---|---|---|
| **33** A7 | 5c lt blue grn & multi | .35 | .25 |
| **34** A7 | 10c grnsh blue & multi | .75 | .45 |
| **35** A7 | 15c lilac & multi | 1.10 | .60 |
| **36** A7 | 20c violet bl & multi | 1.50 | .95 |
| | *Nos. 33-36 (4)* | 3.70 | 2.25 |

South Pacific Commission, 25th anniversary. On 15c, "PACIFIC" reads "PACFIC."

**1973, Sept. 12 Litho. *Perf. 13x13½***

**37** A8 3c shown 1.25 1.10
**38** A8 5c Soft coral 1.25 1.25
**39** A8 15c Mushroom coral 2.00 2.10
**40** A8 25c Staghorn coral 2.50 2.50
*Nos. 37-40 (4)* 7.00 6.95

Cowrie (Cypraea Mauritiana) A9

Cowrie shells: 5c, Cypraea tigris. 15c, Cypraea talpa. 25c, Cypraea argus.

**1974, Nov. 13 Litho. *Perf. 14***

**41** A9 3c apple grn & multi 1.25 1.10
**42** A9 5c dk blue & multi 1.50 1.10
**43** A9 15c blue & multi 2.00 2.25
**44** A9 25c green & multi 2.25 2.50
*Nos. 41-44 (4)* 7.00 6.95

Moorish Idol — A10

Fish: 10c, Long-nosed butterflyfish. 15c, Lined butterflyfish. 25c, Red firefish.

**1975, Nov. 19 Litho. *Perf. 14***

**45** A10 5c blue & multi .50 .30
**46** A10 10c brown & multi 1.10 .65
**47** A10 15c lilac & multi 1.90 1.10
**48** A10 25c multicolored 3.25 2.10
*Nos. 45-48 (4)* 6.75 4.15

Canoe Making A11

Designs: 2c, Reef fishing. 3c, Woman preparing pandanus leaves for weaving. 5c, Communal kitchen (umu). 9c, Wood carving. 20c, Husking coconuts. 50c, Wash day. $1, Meal time. 9c, 20c, 50c, $1, vertical.

**1976, Oct. 27 Litho. *Perf. 14***

**49** A11 1c pink & multi .55 *1.10*
**50** A11 2c multicolored .40 *1.40*
**51** A11 3c lt blue & multi .35 *.70*
**52** A11 5c yellow & multi .40 *.70*
**53** A11 9c bister & multi .25 *.85*
**54** A11 20c multicolored .25 *.70*
**55** A11 50c tan & multi .35 *.85*
**56** A11 $1 multicolored .70 *2.10*
*Nos. 49-56 (8)* 3.25 *8.40*

**1981, July 17 *Perf. 15***

*49a* A11 1c .40 .65
*51a* A11 3c .40 .65
*52a* A11 5c .40 .65
*53a* A11 9c .65 .65
*54a* A11 20c .65 .65
*55a* A11 50c .85 .90
*56a* A11 $1 1.25 1.25
*Nos. 49a-56a (7)* 4.60 5.40

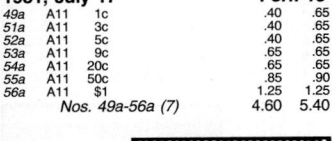

White Tern — A12

Birds of Tokelau: 10c, Turnstone. 15c, White-capped noddy. 30c, Brown noddy.

**1977, Nov. 16 Litho. *Perf. 14½x15***

**57** A12 8c multicolored .50 .35
**58** A12 10c multicolored .65 .40
**59** A12 15c multicolored .80 .65
**60** A12 30c multicolored 1.75 1.40
*Nos. 57-60 (4)* 3.70 2.80

Westminster Abbey — A13

10c, King Edward's Chair. 15c, Scepter, Crown, Orb, Bible and Staff of State. 30c, Elizabeth II.

**1978, June 28 Litho. *Perf. 14***

**61** A13 8c multicolored .25 .25
**62** A13 10c multicolored .35 .35
**63** A13 15c multicolored .55 .55
**64** A13 30c multicolored 1.00 1.00
*Nos. 61-64 (4)* 2.15 2.15

25th anniv. of coronation of Elizabeth II.

Canoe Racing A14

Designs: Various canoe races.

**1978, Nov. 8 Litho. *Perf. 13½x14***

**65** A14 8c multicolored .40 .40
**66** A14 12c multicolored .55 .55
**67** A14 15c multicolored .65 .65
**68** A14 30c multicolored 1.10 1.10
*Nos. 65-68 (4)* 2.70 2.70

**1979, Nov. 7 Photo. *Perf. 14***

**69** A14 10c Rugby .35 .35
**70** A14 15c Cricket .70 .70
**71** A14 20c Rugby, diff. .70 .70
**72** A14 30c Cricket, diff. .85 .85
*Nos. 69-72 (4)* 2.60 2.60

**1980, Nov. 5 Litho. *Perf. 13½***

**73** A14 10c Surfing .25 .25
**74** A14 20c Surfing, diff. .30 .25
**75** A14 30c Swimming .45 .40
**76** A14 50c Swimming, diff. .60 .55
*Nos. 73-76 (4)* 1.60 1.45

**1981, Nov. 4 Photo. *Perf. 14***

**77** A14 10c Pole vaulting, vert. .35 .35
**78** A14 20c Volleyball, vert. .40 .35
**79** A14 30c Running, vert. .50 .40
**80** A14 50c Volleyball, vert., diff. .60 .60
*Nos. 77-80 (4)* 1.85 1.70

Wood Carving — A15

Octopus Lure Fishing — A16

**1982, May 5 Litho. *Perf. 13½x13***

**81** A15 10s shown .35 .35
**82** A15 22s Bow-drilling sea shells .35 .35
**83** A15 34s Bowl finishing .50 .50
**84** A15 60s Basket weaving 1.00 1.00
*Nos. 81-84 (4)* 2.20 2.20

**1982, Nov. 3 Litho. *Perf. 14***

Designs: Fishing Methods.

**85** A16 5s shown .20 .20
**86** A16 18s Multiple-hook .20 .20
**87** A16 23s Ruvettus .25 .25
**88** A16 34s Netting flying fish .40 .40
**89** A16 63s Noose .70 .70
**90** A16 75s Bonito .85 .85
*Nos. 85-90 (6)* 2.60 2.60

Outrigger Canoe A17

**1983, May 4 Litho. *Perf. 13½x14***

**91** A17 5s shown .25 .25
**92** A17 18s Whale boat .25 .25
**93** A17 23s Aluminium whale boat .25 .25
**94** A17 34s Alia fishing boat .30 .30
**95** A17 63s Cargo ship .65 .65
**96** A17 75s Seaplane .90 .90
*Nos. 91-96 (6)* 2.60 2.60

Traditional Games A18

**1983, Nov. 2 Litho. *Perf. 14***

**97** A18 5s Javelin throwing .25 .25
**98** A18 18s Tifaga string game .25 .25
**99** A18 23s Fire making .25 .25
**100** A18 34s Shell throwing .30 .30
**101** A18 63s Handball .65 .65
**102** A18 75s Mass wrestling .90 .90
*Nos. 97-102 (6)* 2.60 2.60

Planting, Harvesting Copra — A19

Local Fish — A20

Copra Industry: b, Husking, splitting. c, Drying, cutting. d, Bagging, weighing. e, Shipping. Continuous design.

**1984, May 2 Litho. *Perf. 13½x13***

**103** Strip of 5 3.00 3.00
***a.-e.*** A19 48s any single .45 .45

**1984, Dec. 5 Litho. *Perf. 14½x14***

**104** A20 1c Manini .25 .25
**105** A20 2c Hahave .25 .25
**106** A20 5c Uloulo .25 .25
**107** A20 9c Ume Ihu .25 .25
**108** A20 23c Lifilafi .35 .35
**109** A20 34c Fagamea .50 .50
**110** A20 50c Kakahi .65 .65
**111** A20 75c Palu Po 1.00 1.00
**112** A20 $1 Mokoha 1.40 1.40
**113** A20 $2 Hakula 2.50 2.50
*Nos. 104-113 (10)* 7.40 7.40

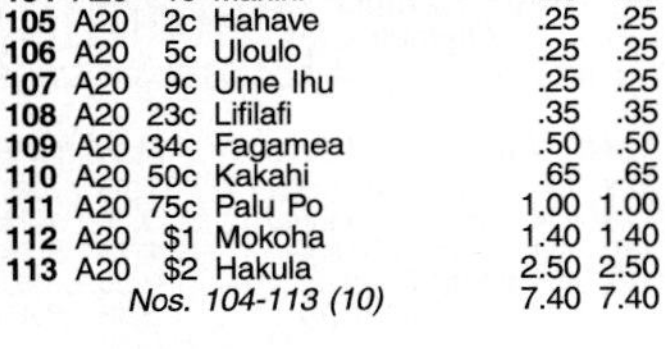


Trees, Fruits and Herbs — A21

**1985, June 26 Litho. *Perf. 13½***

**114** A21 5c Mati .20 .20
**115** A21 18c Nonu .20 .20
**116** A21 32c Ulu .45 .45
**117** A21 48c Fala .65 .65
**118** A21 60c Kanava .85 .85
**119** A21 75c Niu 1.00 1.00
*Nos. 114-119 (6)* 3.35 3.35

Public Buildings and Churches A22

Designs: 5c, Administration Center, Atafu. 18c, Administration Center, Nukunonu. 32c, Administration Center, Fakaofo. 48c, Congregational Church, Atafu. 60c, Catholic Church, Nukunonu. 75c, Congregational Church, Fakaofo.

**1985, Dec. 4**

**120** A22 5c multicolored .20 .20
**121** A22 18c multicolored .20 .20
**122** A22 32c multicolored .45 .45
**123** A22 48c multicolored .65 .65
**124** A22 60c multicolored .85 .85
**125** A22 75c multicolored 1.00 1.00
*Nos. 120-125 (6)* 3.35 3.35

Hospitals and Schools A23

Designs: 5c, Atafu Hospital. 18c, St. Joseph's Hospital, Nukunonu. 32c, Fenuafala Hospital, Fakaofo. 48c, Matauala School, Atafu. 60c, Matiti School, Nukunonu. 75c, Fenuafala School, Fakaofo.

**1986, May 7 *Perf. 13½***

**126** A23 5c multicolored .20 .20
**127** A23 18c multicolored .20 .20
**128** A23 32c multicolored .45 .45
**129** A23 48c multicolored .65 .65
**130** A23 60c multicolored .85 .85
**131** A23 75c multicolored 1.00 1.00
*Nos. 126-131 (6)* 3.35 3.35

Fauna A24

**1986, Dec. 3 Litho. *Perf. 14***

**132** A24 5c Coconut crab .20 .20
**133** A24 18c Pigs .20 .20
**134** A24 32c Chickens .50 .50
**135** A24 48c Turtles .75 .75
**136** A24 60c Goats .90 .90
**137** A24 75c Ducks 1.10 1.10
*Nos. 132-137 (6)* 3.65 3.65

Flora A25

**1987, May 6**

**138** A25 5c Gahu .60 .60
**139** A25 18c Puka .85 .85
**140** A25 32c Higano 1.10 1.10
**141** A25 48c Tialetiale 1.50 1.50
**142** A25 60c Gagie 1.75 1.75
**143** A25 75c Puapua 1.90 1.90
*Nos. 138-143 (6)* 7.70 7.70

Olympic Sports A26

**1987, Dec. 2 Litho. *Perf. 14x14½***

**144** A26 5c Javelin .40 .40
**145** A26 18c Shot put .70 .70
**146** A26 32c Long jump .90 .90
**147** A26 48c Hurdles 1.00 1.00
**148** A26 60c Running 1.25 1.25
**149** A26 75c Wrestling 1.75 1.75
*Nos. 144-149 (6)* 6.00 6.00

Australia Bicentennial, SYDPEX '88 — A27

Re-enactment of the arrival of the First Fleet in Sydney Harbor, Jan. 26, 1988 (in a continuous design): a, Ships in harbor, building (LL). b, Ships in harbor, tall ship (LR). c, Ships in harbor, Sydney Opera House. d, Bridge. e, North Sydney.

**1988, July 30 Litho. *Perf. 13½x13***
**150** Strip of 5 13.00 13.00
***a.-e.*** A27 50c any single 2.25 2.25

Political Development A28

Designs: 5c, Transfer of administration from the New Zealand Department of Maori and Island Affairs to the Ministry of Foreign Affairs, 1975. 18c, The General Fono empowered as the decision-making body of Tokelau, 1977. 32c, 1st Visit of New Zealand's prime minister, 1985. 48c, 1st Visit of UN representatives, 1976. 60c, 1st Tokelau delegation to go to the UN, 1987. 75c, 1st Tokelau appointed to the office of Official Secretary, 1987.

**1988, Aug. 10 *Perf. 14½***
**151** A28 5c multicolored .20 .20
**152** A28 18c multicolored .30 .30
**153** A28 32c multicolored .60 .60
**154** A28 48c multicolored .90 .90
**155** A28 60c multicolored 1.10 1.10
**156** A28 75c multicolored 1.40 1.40
*Nos. 151-156 (6)* 4.50 4.50

Island Christmas A29

Designs: 5c, Three Wise Men *(Na Makoi)*. 20c, Holy family *(He Tala)*. 40c, Escape into Egypt *(Fakagagalo ki Aikupito)*. 60c, Christmas presents *(Meaalofa Kilihimahi)*. 70c, Christ child *(Pepe ko Iesu)*. $1, Christmas parade *(Holo Tamilo)*.

**1988, Dec. 7 Litho. *Perf. 13½***
**157** A29 5c multicolored .25 .25
**158** A29 20c multicolored .25 .25
**159** A29 40c multicolored .60 .60
**160** A29 60c multicolored .90 .90
**161** A29 70c multicolored 1.00 1.00
**162** A29 $1 multicolored 1.50 1.50
*Nos. 157-162 (6)* 4.50 4.50

Food Gathering A30

Fishing and gathering coconuts. Printed se-tenant in continuous designs.

No. 163: a, Launching outrigger canoe. b, Outrigger canoe and sailboat starboard side. c, Outrigger canoe and sailboat stern.

No. 164: a, Outrigger and sailboat port side. b, Islander carrying baskets of coconuts. c, Gathering coconuts from palm trees.

**1989, June 28 Litho. *Perf. 14x14½***
**163** Strip of 3 4.75 4.75
***a.-c.*** A30 50c any single 1.50 1.50
**164** Strip of 3 4.75 4.75
***a.-c.*** A30 50c any single 1.50 1.50

Women's Work and Leisure — A31

**1990, May 2 Litho. *Perf. 14½***
**165** A31 5c Weavers .70 .55
**166** A31 20c Washing clothes 1.10 1.00
**167** A31 40c Resting among palm trees 1.75 1.50
**168** A31 60c Weaving mat 2.10 2.25
**169** A31 80c Weaving, diff. 3.00 3.25
**170** A31 $1 Basket weaver 3.25 3.50
*Nos. 165-170 (6)* 11.90 12.05

Souvenir Sheet

Penny Black, 150th Anniv. — A32

**1990, May 3 Litho. *Perf. 11½***
**171** A32 $3 multicolored 16.00 16.00

Men's Handicrafts — A33

**1990, Aug. 1 Photo. *Perf. 13***
**172** A33 50c shown 1.75 1.50
**173** A33 50c Carving pots 1.75 1.50
**174** A33 50c Tying rope on pot 1.75 1.50
***a.*** Strip of 3, #172-174 5.25 5.25
**175** A33 50c Finishing pots 1.75 1.50
**176** A33 50c Shaping a canoe 1.75 1.50
**177** A33 50c Three men working 1.75 1.50
***a.*** Strip of 3, #175-177 5.25 5.25

1992 Summer Olympics, Barcelona — A34

**1992, July 8 Litho. *Perf. 13½***
**178** A34 40c Swimming .95 .95
**179** A34 60c Long jump 1.25 1.25
**180** A34 $1 Volleyball 2.75 2.75
**181** A34 $1.80 Running 3.50 3.50
*Nos. 178-181 (4)* 8.45 8.45

Discovery of America, 500th Anniv. A35

**1992, Dec. 18**
**182** A35 40c Santa Maria 1.00 1.00
**183** A35 60c Columbus 1.25 1.25
**184** A35 $1.20 Columbus' fleet 3.00 3.00
**185** A35 $1.80 Landfall 4.00 4.00
*Nos. 182-185 (4)* 9.25 9.25

Coronation of Queen Elizabeth II, 40th Anniv. A36

**1993, July 8 Litho. *Perf. 13½***
**186** A36 25c Queen, early portrait .80 .80
**187** A36 40c Prince Philip 1.10 1.10
**188** A36 $1 Queen, recent portrait 1.90 1.90
**189** A36 $2 Queen & Prince Philip 3.25 3.25
*Nos. 186-189 (4)* 7.05 7.05

Birds A37

25c, Numenius tahitiensis. 40c, Phaethon rubricauda. $1, Egretta sacra. $2, Pluvialis fulva.

**1993-94 Litho. *Perf. 13½***
**190** A37 25c multicolored 1.00 1.00
**191** A37 40c multicolored 1.50 1.50
**192** A37 $1 multicolored 2.50 2.50
**193** A37 $2 multicolored 3.25 3.25
***a.*** Souvenir sheet of 4, #190-193, perf. 14x14½ 8.25 8.25
*Nos. 190-193 (4)* 8.25 8.25

No. 193a contains Hong Kong '94 emblem, inscription in Chinese and English in sheet margin and sold for $20 HK at the show.

Issued: #190-193, 12/15/93; #193a, 2/1/94.

PHILAKOREA '94 — A38

**1994, Aug. 16 Litho. *Perf. 12***
**194** A38 $2 White heron 4.00 4.00
***a.*** Souvenir sheet of 1 5.25 5.25

No. 194a has a continuous design.

Handicrafts A39

**1995 Litho. *Perf. 13½***
**195** A39 5c Outrigger canoe .25 .25
**196** A39 25c Plaited fan .35 .35
**197** A39 40c Plaited baskets .55 .55
**198** A39 50c Fishing box .75 .75
**199** A39 80c Water bottle 1.10 1.10
**200** A39 $1 Fishing hook 1.40 1.40
**201** A39 $2 Coconut gourds 2.75 2.75
**202** A39 $5 Shell necklace 7.25 7.25
*Nos. 195-202 (8)* 14.40 14.40

Souvenir Sheet

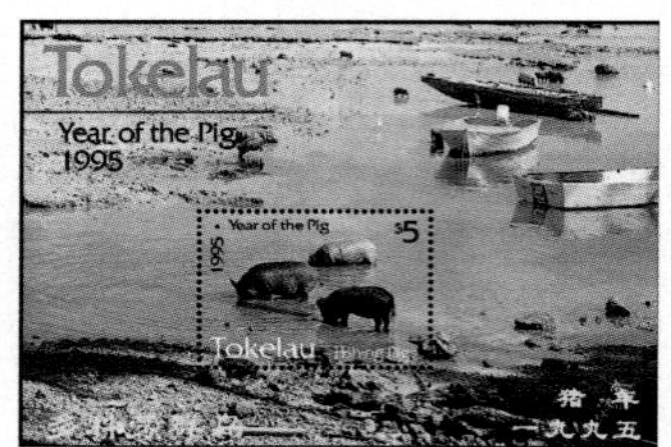

New Year 1995 (Year of the Boar) — A40

Illustration reduced.

**1995, Feb. 3 Litho. *Perf. 14***
**203** A40 $5 multicolored 9.50 9.50
***a.*** Ovptd. in sheet margin 13.00 13.00
***b.*** Ovptd. in sheet margin 8.75 8.75

No. 203a ovptd. in red in sheet margin "POST'X 95 / 3-6 February / 1995 / AUCKLAND" surrounded by simulated perforations.

No. 203b ovptd. in red in sheet margin with Singapore '95 exhibition emblem.

Pacific Imperial Pigeon A41

**1995, Apr. 27 Litho. *Perf. 13½***
**204** A41 25c shown .80 .80
**205** A41 40c Full view 1.25 1.25
**206** A41 $1 In tree, red berries 2.00 2.00
**207** A41 $2 Nesting 3.75 3.75
*Nos. 204-207 (4)* 7.80 7.80

World Wildlife Fund.

Reef Fish — A42

Designs: 25c, Long nosed butterfly fish. 40c, Emperor angelfish. $1, Moorish idol. $2, Lined butterfly fish.

$3, Red fire fish.

**1995, Sept. 1 Litho. *Perf. 12***
**208** A42 25c multicolored .50 .50
**209** A42 40c multicolored .75 .75
**210** A42 $1 multicolored 1.90 1.90
**211** A42 $2 multicolored 4.00 4.00
*Nos. 208-211 (4)* 7.15 7.15

**Souvenir Sheet**

**212** A42 $3 multicolored 5.25 5.25

No. 212 contains one 40x35mm stamp and is inscribed in sheet margin for Singapore '95.

Butterflies — A43

Designs: 25c, Danaus plexippus. 40c, Precis villida samoensis. $1, Hypolimnas bolina. $2, Euploea lewenii.

**1995, Oct. 16 Litho. *Perf. 12***
**213** A43 25c multicolored .75 .75
**214** A43 40c multicolored .95 .95
**215** A43 $1 multicolored 2.40 2.40
**216** A43 $2 multicolored 3.50 3.50
*Nos. 213-216 (4)* 7.60 7.60

Sea Turtles A44

**1995, Nov. 27 Litho. *Perf. 12***
**217** A44 25c Hawksbill .85 .85
**218** A44 40c Leatherback 1.10 1.10
**219** A44 $1 Green 2.75 2.75
**220** A44 $2 Loggerhead 4.00 4.00
*Nos. 217-220 (4)* 8.70 8.70

**Souvenir Sheet**

**221** A44 $3 like #220 5.75 5.75

No. 221 contains one 50x40mm stamp and is a continuous design.

Souvenir Sheet

New Year 1996 (Year of the Rat) — A45

Illustration reduced.

**1996, Feb. 19** **Litho.** ***Perf. 12***

**222** A45 $3 Pacific rat 5.25 5.25
*a.* Ovptd. in sheet margin 5.25 5.25
*b.* Ovptd. in sheet margin 5.25 5.25

Overprinted in sheet margin with red exhibition emblem: No. 222a, CHINA '96; No. 222b, TAIPEI '96.

---

Common Design Types pictured following the introduction.

---

### Queen Elizabeth II, 70th Birthday
Common Design Type

Various portraits of Queen, scenes of Tokelau: 40c, Nukunonu. $1, Atafu, silhouette of island, boat. $1.25, Atafu, building on island, boat. $2, Atafu, huts.
$3, Queen wearing tiara, formal dress.

**1996, Apr. 22** **Litho.** ***Perf. 13½***

**223** CD354 40c multicolored .60 .60
**224** CD354 $1 multicolored 1.90 1.90
**225** CD354 $1.25 multicolored 2.10 2.10
**226** CD354 $2 multicolored 3.00 3.00
*Nos. 223-226 (4)* 7.60 7.60

**Souvenir Sheet**

**227** CD354 $3 multicolored 5.25 5.25

Dolphins — A46

**1996, July 15** **Litho.** ***Perf. 14***

**228** A46 40c Fraser's 1.25 1.25
**229** A46 $1 Common 3.00 3.00
**230** A46 $1.25 Striped 3.00 3.00
**231** A46 $2 Spotted 4.25 4.25
*Nos. 228-231 (4)* 11.50 11.50

Shells A47

Designs: 40c, Cypraea talpa. $1, Cypraea mauritiana. $1.25, Cypraea argus. $2, Cypraea tigris.
$3, Cypraea mauritana, diff.

**1996, Oct. 16** **Litho.** ***Perf. 12***

**232** A47 40c multicolored .75 .75
**233** A47 $1 multicolored 1.75 1.75
**234** A47 $1.25 multicolored 2.25 2.25
**235** A47 $2 multicolored 3.50 3.50
*Nos. 232-235 (4)* 8.25 8.25

**Souvenir Sheet**

**236** A47 $3 multicolored 5.25 5.25

No. 236 contains one 50x40mm stamp with a continuous design.

Souvenir Sheet

New Year 1997 (Year of the Ox) — A48

Illustration reduced.

**1997, Feb. 12** **Litho.** ***Perf. 15x14***

**237** A48 $2 multicolored 4.25 4.25
*a.* Overprinted in gold 4.00 4.00
*b.* Overprinted in red 2.75 2.75

No. 237a ovptd. in sheet margin HONG KONG '97 / STAMP EXHIBITION" in English and Chinese.
No. 237b overprinted in sheet margin with Pacific 97 emblem. Issued 5/29.

Humpback Whale A49

Designs: 40c, With school of fish. $1, Calf, adult, young adult. $1.25, With mouth open, school of fish. $2, Adult, calf.
$3, Mouth, head of whale.

**1997, May 29** **Litho.** ***Perf. 12***

**238** A49 40c multicolored .65 .65
**239** A49 $1 multicolored 1.50 1.50
**240** A49 $1.25 multicolored 2.00 2.00
**241** A49 $2 multicolored 3.00 3.00
*Nos. 238-241 (4)* 7.15 7.15

**Souvenir Sheet**

**242** A49 $3 multicolored 4.25 4.25
*a.* Ovptd. in sheet margin 4.25 4.25

No. 242a ovptd. in sheet margin, "AUPEX '97 / 13-16 NOVEMBER / NZ NATIONAL / STAMP EXHIBITION." Issued: 11/13.

South Pacific Commission, 50th Anniv. — A50

**1997, Sept. 17** **Litho.** ***Perf. 14***

**243** A50 40c Church, waterfront .70 .70
**244** A50 $1 Beach, child 1.75 1.75
**245** A50 $1.25 Island 2.25 2.25
**246** A50 $2 Atoll 3.50 3.50
*Nos. 243-246 (4)* 8.20 8.20

Year of the Coral Reef — A51

Designs: No. 247, Gorgonian coral, emperor angelfish. No. 248, Soft coral. No. 249, Mushroom coral. No. 250, Staghorn coral. No. 251, Staghorn coral, Moorish idol.

**1997, Oct. 20** **Litho.** ***Perf. 13½***

**247** A51 $1 multicolored 1.40 1.40
**248** A51 $1 multicolored 1.40 1.40
**249** A51 $1 multicolored 1.40 1.40
**250** A51 $1 multicolored 1.40 1.40
**251** A51 $1 multicolored 1.40 1.40
*a.* Strip of 5, #247-251 7.00 7.00

Souvenir Sheet

New Year 1998 (Year of the Tiger) — A52

Illustration reduced.

**1998, Jan. 28** **Litho.** ***Perf. 14x14½***

**252** A52 $2 multicolored 2.75 2.75
*a.* Ovptd. in sheet margin 2.25 2.25

No. 252a overprinted in sheet margin with emblem of Singpex '98 Stamp Exhibition, Singapore.

### Diana, Princess of Wales (1961-97)
Common Design Type

Designs: No. 252B, Holding yellow flowers.
No. 253: a, Wearing high-collared ruffled blouse. b, Wearing red beret. c, Wearing pink and yellow jacket.

**1998, May 15** **Litho.** ***Perf. 14½x14***

**252B** CD355 $1 multi 1.25 1.25

**Souvenir Sheet**

**253** CD355 $1 Sheet of 4, #252B, 253a-253c 5.00 5.00

No. 253 sold for $4 + 50c, with surtax from international sales being donated to the Princess Diana Memorial Fund and surtax from national sales being donated to designated local charity.

Souvenir Sheet

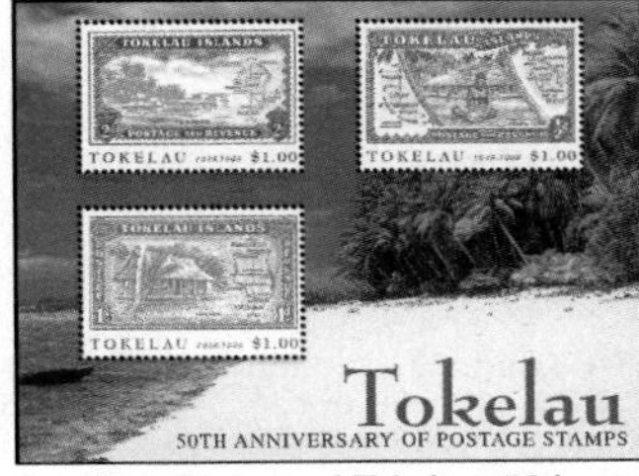


First Stamps of Tokelau, 50th Anniv. — A53

Designs: a, #3. b. #1. c, #2.

**1998, June 22** **Litho.** ***Perf. 14½***

**254** A53 $1 Sheet of 3, #a.-c. 3.75 3.75

Beetles A54

Designs: 40c, Oryctes rhinoceros. $1, Tribolium castaneum. $1.25, Coccinella repanda. $2, Amarygmus hyorophiloides.
$3, Coccinella repanda, diff.

**1998, Aug. 24** **Litho.** ***Perf. 14***

**255** A54 40c multicolored .55 .55
**256** A54 $1 multicolored 1.40 1.40
**257** A54 $1.25 multicolored 1.75 1.75
**258** A54 $2 multicolored 2.75 2.75
*Nos. 255-258 (4)* 6.45 6.45

**Souvenir Sheet**

**259** A54 $3 multicolored 4.25 4.25

Tropical Flowers A55

40c, Ipomoea pes-caprae. $1, Ipomoea littoralis. $1.25, Scaevola taccada. $2, Thespesia populnea.

**1998, Nov. 19** **Litho.** ***Perf. 14***

**260** A55 40c multicolored .55 .55
**261** A55 $1 multicolored 1.40 1.40
**262** A55 $1.25 multicolored 1.75 1.75
**263** A55 $2 multicolored 2.75 2.75
*Nos. 260-263 (4)* 6.45 6.45

Souvenir Sheet

New Year 1999 (Year of the Rabbit) — A56

Illustration reduced.

**1999, Feb. 16** **Litho.** ***Perf. 14***

**264** A56 $3 multicolored 4.25 4.25
*a.* Ovptd. in sheet margin 4.25 4.25

No. 264a overprinted in sheet margin with emblem of IBRA '99 Intl. Stamp Exhibtion, Nuremburg. Issued: 4/27.

Souvenir Sheet

Australia '99, World Stamp Exhibition — A57

Illustration reduced.

**1999, Mar. 19**

**265** A57 $3 HMS Pandora 4.25 4.25

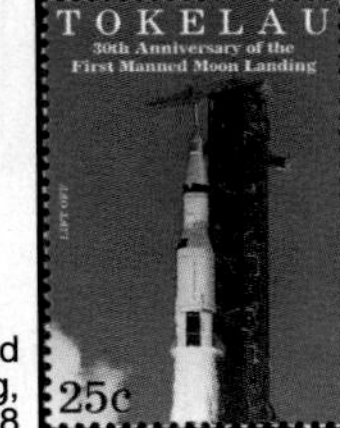


First Manned Moon Landing, 30th Anniv. — A58

Designs: 25c, Lift-off. 50c, Separation of stages. 75c, Aldrin deploying instruments on moon. $1, Planting flag. $1.25, Returning to Earth. $2, Splashdown.
$3, Apollo 11, Moon, Earth.

***Perf. 13½x13¼***

**1999, Aug. 31** **Litho.**

**266** A58 25c multicolored .35 .35
**267** A58 50c multicolored .70 .70
**268** A58 75c multicolored 1.00 1.00
**269** A58 $1 multicolored 1.40 1.40
**270** A58 $1.25 multicolored 1.75 1.75
**271** A58 $2 multicolored 2.75 2.75
*Nos. 266-271 (6)* 7.95 7.95

**Souvenir Sheet**

**272** A58 $3 multicolored 4.25 4.25

Crabs A59

**1999 Litho. *Perf. 14¼x14½***

**273** A59 40c Coconut .55 .55
**274** A59 $1 Ghost 1.40 1.40
**275** A59 $1.25 Land hermit 1.75 1.75
**276** A59 $2 Purple hermit 2.75 2.75
*Nos. 273-276 (4)* 6.45 6.45

**Souvenir Sheet**

**277** A59 $3 Ghost, diff. 4.25 4.25

Black-naped Tern — A60

Designs: 40c, Chick and egg. $1, On nest. $1.25, Pair near water. $2, Pair in flight.

***Perf. 13½x14***

**1999, Dec. 31 Litho. Unwmk.**

**278-281** A60 Set of 4 6.50 6.50

**Souvenir Sheet**

New Year 2000 (Year of the Dragon) — A61

Illustration reduced.

**2000 Litho. *Perf. 14x14¼***

**282** A61 $3 multi 4.50 4.50
*a.* Overprinted in sheet margin 4.00 4.00

No. 282a overprinted in sheet margin with emblem "Bangkok 2000," "World Youth Stamp Exhibition" and Thai text.

**Souvenir Sheet**

The Stamp Show 2000, London — A62

Illustration reduced.

**Unwmk.**

**2000, May 22 Litho. *Perf. 14***

**283** A62 $6 multi 8.50 8.50

Queen Mother, 100th Birthday — A63

Various photos. Denominations 40c, $1.20, $1.80, $3.

***Perf. 14½x14¼***

**2000, Aug. 4 Wmk. 373**

**284-287** A63 Set of 4 9.00 9.00

Lizards A64

Designs: 40c, Gehyra oceanica. $1, Lepidodactylus lugubris. $1.25, Gehyra mutilata. $2, Emoia cyanura.

**2001, Feb. 1 Litho. *Perf. 14***

**288-291** A64 Set of 4 6.75 6.75

**Souvenir Sheet**

New Year 2001 (Year of the Snake) — A65

**2001, Feb. 1**

**292** A65 $3 multi 4.25 4.25
*a.* With gold ovpt. in margin 4.25 4.25

Overprint in margin on No. 292a is for Hong Kong 2001 Stamp Exhibition.

Hippocampus Histrix — A66

Various views of seahorses. Denominations: 40c, $1, $1.25, $2.

**2001, Aug. 23 Litho. *Perf. 14***

**293-296** A66 Set of 4 6.75 6.75

**Souvenir Sheet**

**297** A66 $3 multi 4.25 4.25

Island Scenery A67

Designs: 40c, Sky over Atafu. $1, Waters of Fakaofo. $2, Sunrise over Nukunonu village. $2.50, Ocean, Nukunonu.

**Unwmk.**

**2001, Dec. 17 Litho. *Perf. 14***

**298-301** A67 Set of 4 8.25 8.25
*a.* Souvenir sheet, #298-301 7.50 7.50

Issued: No. 301a issued 5/27/06 for Washington 2006 World Philatelic Exhibition.

**Reign Of Queen Elizabeth II, 50th Anniv. Issue**

Common Design Type

Designs: Nos. 302, 306a, 40c, Princess Elizabeth, Prince Philip on honeymoon, 1947. Nos. 303, 306b, $1, Wearing purple hat. Nos. 304, 306c, $1.25, Holding Prince Charles, 1948. Nos. 305, 306d, $2, In 1996. No. 306e, $3, 1955 portrait by Annigoni (38x50mm).

***Perf. 14¼x14½, 13¾ (#306e)***

**2002, Feb. 6 Litho. Wmk. 373**

**With Gold Frames**

**302-305** CD360 Set of 4 6.50 6.50

**Souvenir Sheet**

**Without Gold Frames**

**306** CD360 Sheet of 5, #a-e 10.50 10.50

**Souvenir Sheet**

New Year 2002 (Year of the Horse) — A68

**2002, Feb. 12 Litho. *Perf. 14***

**307** A68 $4 multi 5.50 5.50
*a.* As #307, with gold ovpt. in margin 5.00 5.00

No. 307a was issued 2/22 and has overprint reading "STAMPEX 2002 / HONG KONG / 22-24 FEBRUARY 2002."

Worldwide Fund for Nature (WWF) — A69

Various views of Pelagic thresher shark: 40c, $1, $2, $2.50.

**2002, July 2 Litho. *Perf. 14¼***

**308-311** A69 Set of 4 8.75 8.75

**Queen Mother Elizabeth (1900-2002)**

Common Design Type

Designs: 40c, Wearing broad-brimmed hat (black and white photograph). $2, Wearing blue hat.

No. 314: a, $2.50, Wearing hat (black and white photograph). b, $4, Wearing purple hat.

**Wmk. 373**

**2002, Aug. 5 Litho. *Perf. 14¼***

**With Purple Frames**

**312-313** CD361 Set of 2 4.75 4.75

**Souvenir Sheet**

**Without Purple Frames**

***Perf. 14½x14¼***

**314** CD361 Sheet of 2, #a-b 10.50 10.50

New Zealand Navy Ships That Have Stopped at Tokelau A70

Designs: 40c, HMNZS Kaniere. $1, HMNZS Endeavour. $2, HMNZS Wellington. $2.50, HMNZS Monowai.

**2002, Dec. Litho. Unwmk. *Perf. 14***

**315-318** A70 Set of 4 8.25 8.25

**Souvenir Sheet**

New Year 2003 (Year of the Ram) — A71

**2003, Feb. 3**

**319** A71 $4 multi 5.50 5.50
*a.* With Bangkok 2003 overprint in gold in margin 4.75 4.75

Issued: No. 319a, 10/13.

**Coronation of Queen Elizabeth II, 50th Anniv.**

Common Design Type

Designs: Nos. 320, 322a, $2.50, Queen with maids of honor. Nos. 321, 322b, $4, Queen with Prince Philip.

***Perf. 14¼x14½***

**2003, June 2 Litho. Wmk. 373**

**Vignettes Framed, Red Background**

**320-321** CD363 Set of 2 10.00 10.00

**Souvenir Sheet**

**Vignettes Without Frame, Purple Panel**

**322** CD363 Sheet of 2, #a-b 10.00 10.00

**Prince William, 21st Birthday**

Common Design Type

No. 323: a, Color photograph at right. b, Color photograph at left.

**Wmk. 373**

**2003, June 21 Litho. *Perf. 14¼***

**323** Horiz. pair 6.25 6.25
*a.* CD364 $1.50 multi 2.00 2.00
*b.* CD364 $3 multi 4.25 4.25

**Souvenir Sheet**

Welpex 2003 Stamp Show, Wellington, New Zealand — A72

**Unwmk.**

**2003, Nov. 7 Litho. *Perf. 14***

**324** A72 $4 multi 5.50 5.50

**Souvenir Sheet**

New Year 2004 (Year of the Monkey) — A73

**2004 Litho. with Foil Application**

**325** A73 $4 multi 5.50 5.50
*a.* With 2004 Hong Kong Stamp Expo emblem in gold in margin 5.50 5.50

Issued: No. 325, 1/22; No. 325a, 1/28.

Island Scenes A74

Designs: 40c, Atafu dawn. $1, Return of the fishermen, Nukunonu. $2, A Fakaofo calm evening glow. $2.50, Solitude in Atafu.

**2004, June 30 Litho. *Perf. 14¼x14***

**326-329** A74 Set of 4 7.75 7.75

**No. 324 Overprinted in Silver**

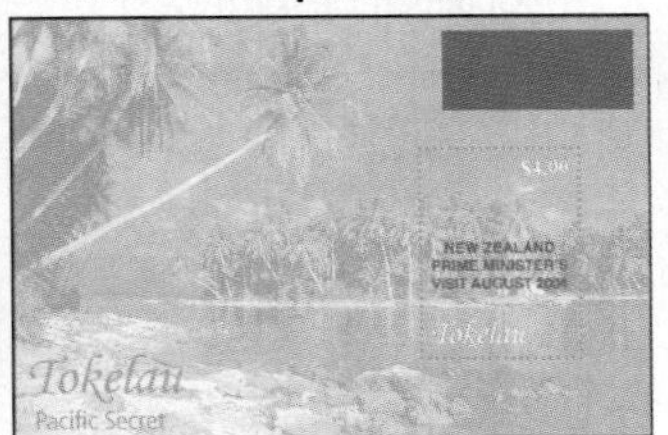


**2004, Aug. 8 Litho. *Perf. 14***
**330** A72 $4 multi 5.25 5.25

Fregata Ariel A75

Designs: 40c, Bird on nest. $1, Birds in flight. $2, Birds on nest and in flight. $2.50, Bird on nest, diff.

**2004, Dec. 20 Litho. *Perf. 14***
**331-334** A75 Set of 4 8.50 8.50

Souvenir Sheet

New Year 2005 (Year of the Rooster) — A76

**2005, Feb. 9**
**335** A76 $4 multi 6.00 6.00
***a.*** Ovptd. in gold in margin with Pacific Explorer 2005 emblem 6.00 6.00

No. 335a issued 4/21/05.

Pope John Paul II (1920-2005) A77

**2005, Aug. 18 Litho. *Perf. 14***
**336** A77 $1 multi 1.50 1.50

Visit of HMNZS Te Kaha A78

Various views of ship: 40c, $1, $2, $2.50.

**2005, Dec. 15 Litho. *Perf. 14***
**337-340** A78 Set of 4 8.25 8.25

Souvenir Sheet

New Year 2006 (Year of the Dog) — A79

**2006, Jan. 29**
**341** A79 $4 multi 5.50 5.50

Queen Elizabeth II, 80th Birthday A80

Queen: 40c, With head on hands. $1, In wedding gown. No. 344, $2, Wearing tiara. No. 345, $2.50, Wearing blue hat.

No. 346: a, $2, Like $1. b, $2.50, Like #344.

No. 347: a, #346a overprinted "KIWIPEX." b, #346b overprinted "2006"

**2006 Litho. *Perf. 14***
**With White Frames**
**342-345** A80 Set of 4 7.75 7.75

**Souvenir Sheets**
**Without White Frames**
**346** A80 Sheet of 2, #a-b 5.75 5.75

**Overprinted in Metallic Blue**
**347** A80 Sheet of 2, #a-b 6.00 6.00

Issued: Nos. 342-346, 4/21; No. 347, 11/2. No. 347 is also overprinted in sheet margin "National Stamp Exhibition, Christchurch, New Zealand."

Souvenir Sheet

New Year 2007 (Year of the Pig) — A81

**2007, Feb. 18 Litho. *Perf. 14***
**348** A81 $4 multi 5.50 5.50

## TONGA

'täŋ-gə

LOCATION — A group of islands in the south Pacific Ocean, south of Samoa
GOVT. — Kingdom in British Commonwealth
AREA — 289 sq. mi.
POP. — 109,082 (1999 est.)
CAPITAL — Nuku'alofa

This group, also known as the Friendly Islands, became a British Protectorate in 1900 under the Anglo-German Agreement of 1899. On June 4, 1970, the United Kingdom ceased to have any responsibility for the external relations of Tonga.

12 Pence = 1 Shilling
20 Shillings = 1 Pound
100 Seniti = 1 Pa'anga (1967)

**Catalogue values for unused stamps in this country are for Never Hinged items, beginning with Scott 87 in the regular postage section, Scott B1 in the semi-postal section, Scott C1 in the air post section Scott CE1 in the air post special delivery section, Scott CO1 in the air post official section, and Scott O11 in the officials section.**

**Watermarks**

Wmk. 62 — NZ and Small Star Wide Apart

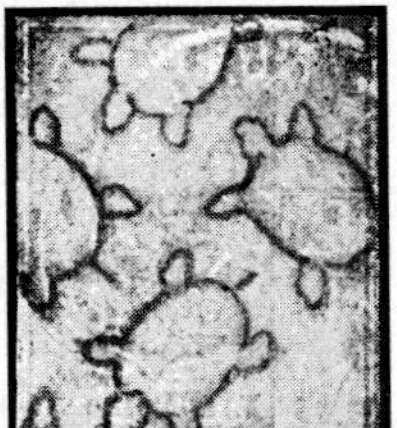
Wmk. 79 — Turtles

King George I — A1

***Perf. 12x11½***
**1886-92 Typo. Wmk. 62**
**1** A1 1p car rose ('87) 11.50 4.00
***a.*** Perf. 12½ 450.00 7.00
***b.*** Perf. 12½x10
**2** A1 2p violet ('87) 32.50 3.50
***a.*** Perf. 12½ 57.50 14.00
**3** A1 6p ultra ('88) 57.50 2.75
***a.*** Perf. 12½ 67.50 4.00
**4** A1 6p org yel ('92) 18.00 *30.00*
**5** A1 1sh blue grn ('88) 62.50 7.25
***a.*** Perf. 12½ 110.00 4.50
***b.*** Half used as 6p on cover
*Nos. 1-5 (5)* 182.00 *47.50*

For surcharges and overprints see #6-9, 24.

Nos. 1 and 2 Surcharged or Overprinted in Black:

a

b

**1891, Nov. 10 *Perf. 12x11½***
**6** A1(a) 4p on 1p car rose 3.50 *12.50*
***a.*** No period after "PENCE" 57.50 *125.00*
**7** A1(a) 8p on 2p violet 40.00 100.00

**1891, Nov. 23 *Perf. 12½***

Two types of overprint:
I — Solid stars, rays pointed and short.
II — Open-center stars, rays blunt and long.

**8** A1(b) 1p car rose (I) 5.00 *57.50*
***a.*** Overprinted with 3 stars (I) 375.00
***b.*** Overprinted with 4 stars (I) 475.00
***c.*** Overprinted with 5 stars (I) 750.00
***d.*** Type II 50.00 *57.50*
***e.*** Perf. 12x11½ (I or II) 350.00
**9** A1(b) 2p violet (I) 80.00 *42.50*
***a.*** Type II 80.00 *42.50*
***b.*** Perf. 12x11½ (I or II) 425.00

Coat of Arms A4

George I A5

**1892, Nov. 10 Typo. *Perf. 12x11½***
**10** A4 1p rose 14.00 *19.00*
***a.*** Diagonal half used as ½p on cover 975.00
**11** A5 2p olive gray 18.00 *18.00*
**12** A4 4p red brown 55.00 *80.00*
**13** A5 8p violet 62.50 *200.00*
**14** A5 1sh brown 90.00 *125.00*
*Nos. 10-14 (5)* 239.50 442.00

For surcharges and overprints see Nos. 15-23, 25-28, 36-37, O1-O10.

Types A4 and A5 Surcharged in Carmine or Black:

c

d

f

FIVE
PENCE.

**1893**
**15** A4 ½p on 1p ultra (C) 26.00 *30.00*
***a.*** Surcharge omitted
**16** A4 ½p on 1p ultra 50.00 *55.00*
**17** A5 2½p on 2p blue grn (C) 16.00 13.50
**18** A5 2½p on 2p blue grn 19.00 19.00
***a.*** Double surcharge 2,000.
**19** A4 5p on 4p org yel (C) 4.50 *7.50*
**20** A5 7½p on 8p rose (C) 27.50 *85.00*
*Nos. 15-20 (6)* 143.00 210.00

Stamps of 1886-92 Surcharged in Blue or Black:

g

h

**1894**
**21** A4 ½p on 4p red brn (Bl) 2.25 *8.00*
***a.*** "SURCHARCE" 10.00 *22.50*
***b.*** Pair, one without surcharge
***c.*** "HALF PENNY" omitted
**22** A5 ½p on 1sh brn (Bk) 2.75 *12.50*
***a.*** Double surcharge 310.00
***b.*** "SURCHARCE" 11.50 45.00
***c.*** As "b," double surcharge 1,000.
**23** A5 2½p on 8p vio (Bk) 5.75 *9.25*
***a.*** No period after "SURCHARGE" 35.00 *62.50*
**24** A1 2½p on 1sh blue grn (Bk) 62.50 27.50
***a.*** No period after "SURCHARGE" 200.00
***b.*** Perf. 12x11½ 17.50 47.50
*Nos. 21-24 (4)* 73.25 *57.25*

Type A5 with Same Surcharges in Carmine

**1895 Unwmk.**
**25** A5(g) 1p on 2p lt blue 50.00 25.00
**26** A5(h) 1½p on 2p lt bl, perf. 12x11 55.00 32.50
***a.*** Perf. 12 70.00 32.50
**27** A5(h) 2½p on 2p lt blue 45.00 50.00
***b.*** Without period 250.00 250.00

**28** A5(h) 7½p on 2p lt bl, perf. 12x11 70.00 50.00
*a.* Perf. 12 450.00
*Nos. 25-28 (4)* 220.00 157.50

King George II — A13

**1895, Aug. 16** ***Perf. 12***
**29** A13 1p gray green 22.50 *30.00*
*a.* Diagonal half used as ½p on cover — *850.00*
*b.* Horiz. pair, imperf. btwn. — *6,900.*
**30** A13 2½p dull rose 22.50 15.00
**31** A13 5p brt blue, perf. 12x11 26.00 *57.50*
*a.* Perf. 12 25.00 *57.50*
*b.* Perf. 11 400.00
**32** A13 7½p yellow 35.00 *55.00*
*Nos. 29-32 (4)* 106.00 *157.50*

### Type A13 Redrawn and Surcharged "g" or "h" in Black

**33** A13(g) ½p on 2½p red 35.00 *37.50*
*a.* "SURCHARCE" 80.00
*b.* Period after "Postage" 85.00
**34** A13(g) 1p on 2½p red 70.00 *45.00*
*a.* Period after "Postage" 125.00
**35** A13(h) 7½p on 2½p red 62.50 *70.00*
*a.* Period after "Postage" 110.00
*Nos. 33-35 (3)* 167.50 *152.50*

Nos. 26 and 28 with Additional Surcharge in Violet and Black

Half Penny-
VAEUA-OE-PENI

**1896, May** ***Perf. 12x11***
**36** A5 ½p on 1½p on 2p 500.00
*a.* Tongan surch. reading up 475.00 475.00
*b.* Perf. 12 475.00 *475.00*
*c.* As "a," perf. 12 500.00 *500.00*
*d.* "Haalf" 2,100.
**37** A5 ½p on 7½p on 2p 97.50 *125.00*
*a.* "Half penny" inverted 2,100.
*b.* "Half penny" double
*c.* Tongan surch. reading up 97.50 *125.00*
*d.* Tongan surcharge as "c" and double
*e.* "Hafl Penny" 1,750. *1,800.*
*f.* "Hafl" only 3,750.
*g.* "Hwlf"
*h.* Periods instead of hyphens after words 1,000.
*j.* Perf. 12 925.00

Coat of Arms — A17

Ovava Tree — A18

George II — A19

Prehistoric Trilithon, Tongatabu — A20

Breadfruit A21

Coral Formations A22

View of Haabai A23

Red-breasted Musk Parrot — A24

View of Vavau — A25

Two types of 2p:
I — Top of sword hilt shows above "2."
II — No hilt shows.

### Wmk. 79 Sideways

**1897-1934** **Engr.** ***Perf. 14***
**38** A17 ½p dark blue 4.75 3.00
**39** A17 ½p green ('34) 1.10 *1.40*
**40** A18 1p dp red & blk .90 .90
**41** A19 2p bis & sep (I) 18.00 6.25
*a.* bister & gray, type II 35.00 3.75
**42** A19 2½p lt blue & blk 7.00 1.60
*a.* "½" without fraction bar 110.00 75.00
**43** A20 3p ol grn & blk 4.00 *9.75*
**44** A21 4p dull vio & grn 4.25 *4.50*
**45** A19 5p orange & blk 35.00 16.00
**46** A22 6p red 15.00 7.00
**47** A19 7½p green & blk 18.00 *26.00*
*a.* Center inverted 5,500.
**48** A19 10p carmine & blk 50.00 *55.00*
**49** A19 1sh red brn & blk 16.00 8.50
**50** A23 2sh dk ultra & blk 70.00 *75.00*
**51** A24 2sh6p dk violet 57.50 35.00
**52** A25 5sh dull red & blk 55.00 55.00
*Nos. 38-52 (15)* 356.50 304.90

See Nos. 73-74, 77-78, 80-81. For surcharges see Nos. 63-69.

Stamp of 1897 Overprinted in Black

**1899, June 1**
**53** A18 1p red & black 35.00 *72.50*
*a.* "1889" instead of "1899" 225.00 *400.00*
*b.* Comma omitted after June
*c.* Double overprint

Marriage of George II to Lavinia, June 1, 1899. The letters "T L" are the initials of Taufa'ahau, the King's family name, and Lavinia.

Queen Salote — A26

Dies of 2p:
Die I — Ball of "2" smaller.
Die II — Ball of "2" larger. "U" has spur at left.

**1920-35** **Engr.** **Wmk. 79**
**54** A26 1½p gray blk ('35) .55 *3.50*
**55** A26 2p violet & sepia 9.75 *15.00*
**56** A26 2p dl vio & blk (I) ('24) 9.75 2.75
*a.* Die II 5.00 *7.50*
**57** A26 2½p blue & black 5.50 *45.00*
**58** A26 2½p ultra ('34) 2.25 1.10
**59** A26 5p red org & blk 3.75 *5.50*
**60** A26 7½p green & blk 2.00 2.00
**61** A26 10p carmine & blk 2.90 *5.50*
**62** A26 1sh red brown & blk 1.40 *2.90*
*Nos. 54-62 (9)* 37.85 83.25

See Nos. 75-76, 79.

Stamps of 1897 Surcharged in Dark Blue or Red

**1923**
**63** A19 2p on 5p org & blk 1.10 1.00
**64** A19 2p on 7½p grn & blk 20.00 32.50
**65** A19 2p on 10p car & blk 12.50 *57.50*
**66** A19 2p on 1sh red brn & blk 55.00 25.00
**67** A23 2p on 2sh ultra & blk (R) 22.50 *22.50*
**68** A24 2p on 2sh6p dk vio (R) 35.00 7.50
**69** A25 2p on 5sh dull red & blk (R) 16.00 16.00
*Nos. 63-69 (7)* 162.10 162.00

Queen Salote — A27

Inscribed "1918-1938"

**1938, Oct. 12** ***Perf. 14***
**70** A27 1p carmine & blk .50 *4.00*
**71** A27 2p violet & blk 4.50 3.00
**72** A27 2½p ultra & blk 4.50 3.75
*Nos. 70-72 (3)* 9.50 10.75
Set, never hinged 18.00

Accession of Queen Salote Tupou, 20th anniv.
See Nos. 82-86.

Types of 1897-1920

**1942** **Engr.** **Wmk. 4**

Die III of 2p:
Foot of "2" longer than in Die II, extending beyond curve of loop.

**73** A17 ½p green .30 *2.75*
**74** A18 1p scarlet & blk 1.25 *2.75*
**75** A26 2p dull vio & blk (II) 2.25 *3.00*
*a.* Die III 4.25 *8.25*
**76** A26 2½p ultra .90 *2.00*
**77** A20 3p green & black .30 *3.75*
**78** A22 6p orange red 1.50 *2.25*
**79** A26 1sh red brown & gray blk 1.40 *3.50*
**80** A24 2sh6p dk violet 22.50 *24.00*
**81** A25 5sh dull red & brn blk 14.00 *50.00*
*Nos. 73-81 (9)* 44.40 94.00
Set, never hinged 62.50

Type of 1938, Inscribed "1918-1943"

**1944, Jan. 25**
**82** A27 1p rose car & blk .20 *1.10*
**83** A27 2p purple & blk .20 *1.10*
**84** A27 3p dk yel grn & blk .20 *1.10*
**85** A27 6p red orange & blk .25 *2.00*
**86** A27 1sh dk red brn & blk .25 *2.00*
*Nos. 82-86 (5)* 1.10 7.30
Set, never hinged 2.00

25th anniv. of the accession of Queen Salote.

**Catalogue values for unused stamps in this section, from this point to the end of the section, are for Never Hinged items.**

### UPU Issue
Common Design Types

**Engr.; Name Typo. on 3p, 6p**
***Perf. 13½, 11x11½***

**1949, Oct. 10** **Wmk. 4**
**87** CD306 2½p ultra .40 *.90*
**88** CD307 3p deep olive 1.75 *3.25*
**89** CD308 6p deep carmine .55 .55
**90** CD309 1sh red brown .55 .55
*Nos. 87-90 (4)* 3.25 5.25

Common Design Types pictured following the introduction.

A28

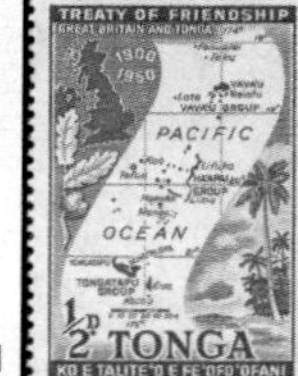
A29

Queen Salote — A30

**1950, Nov. 1** **Photo.** ***Perf. 12½***
**91** A28 1p cerise 1.00 *2.25*
**92** A29 5p green 1.00 *2.50*
**93** A30 1sh violet 1.00 *3.00*
*Nos. 91-93 (3)* 3.00 *7.75*

50th anniv. of the birth of Queen Salote.

Map and Island Scene — A31

Badges and Royal Palace A32

2½p, Queen Salote & coastal scene. 3p, Queen Salote & ship "Bellona." 5p, Flag of Tonga, island view. 1sh, Arms of Tonga & Great Britain.

***Perf. 13x13½ (1p), 13½x13, 12½ (3p)***
**1951, July 2** **Engr.** **Wmk. 4**
**94** A31 ½p deep green .30 *3.00*
**95** A32 1p carmine & black .30 3.00
**96** A32 2½p choc & dp grn .60 *3.00*
**97** A31 3p ultra & org yel 2.25 *3.00*
**98** A32 5p dp green & car 1.75 1.10
**99** A32 1sh purple & orange 2.50 1.10
*Nos. 94-99 (6)* 7.70 14.20

50th anniv. of the treaty of friendship between Tonga and Great Britain.

Royal Palace, Nukualofa A33

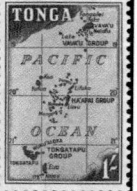

Map of Tonga Islands — A34

Designs: 1½p, Fisherman. 2p, Canoe and schooners. 3p, Swallows' Cave, Vavau. 3½p, Map of Tongatabu. 4p, Vavau harbor. 5p, Post Office, Nukualofa. 6p, Fuaamotu airport. 8p, Wharf, Nukualofa. 2sh, Beach at Lifuka, Haapai. 5sh, Mutiny on the Bounty. 10sh, Queen Salote. £1, Arms of Tonga.

***Perf. 11½x11, 11x11½***

**1953, July 1** **Wmk. 79**

**100** A33 1p chocolate & blk .30 .20
**101** A33 1½p emerald & ultra .30 .20
**102** A33 2p black & aqua .30 .20
**103** A34 3p dk grn & ultra .30 .20
**104** A33 3½p carmine & yel .30 .20
**105** A33 4p rose car & yel .30 .20
**106** A33 5p choc & ultra .30 .20
**107** A33 6p black & dp ultra .40 .20
**108** A33 8p purple & emer .45 .25
**109** A34 1sh black & ultra .75 .40
**110** A33 2sh choc & ol grn 5.00 .90
**111** A33 5sh purple & yel 15.00 5.00
**112** A34 10sh black & yellow 9.00 6.00
**113** A34 £1 ultra, car & yel 11.00 10.50
*Nos. 100-113 (14)* 43.70 24.65

For surcharges and overprints see Nos. 119-126, 158-174, 182-202, 210-215, 218-221, 237, 269-273, C34-C39, C47-C54, C87-C91, CO4-CO6, CO11-CO20, CO27-CO43.

Whaling Ship and Longboat A35

1p, Stamp of 1886. 4p, Post Office, Customs & Treasury Building & Queen Salote. 5p, Diesel-driven ship Aoniu. 1sh, Plane over Tongatabu.

**1961, Dec. 1** **Photo.** ***Perf. 14½x13½***

**114** A35 1p brn org & car rose .30 .20
**115** A35 2p ultra .90 .30
**116** A35 4p bright green .30 .30
**117** A35 5p purple .90 .30
**118** A35 1sh red brown 1.00 .60
*Nos. 114-118 (5)* 3.40 1.70

75th anniversary of postal service.

For surcharges & overprints see #146-151, 216-221, C16-C21, C55-C57, CO1-CO3, CO9-CO10.

### Stamps of 1953 and 1961 Overprinted in Red: "1862 / TAU'ATAINA / EMANCIPATION / 1962"

***Perf. 11½x11, 11x11½, 14½x13***

**Engr.; Photo. (4p)**

**1962, Feb. 7** **Wmk. 79**

**119** A33 1p choc & blk .20 *.60*
**120** A35 4p brt green .20 *.65*
**121** A33 5p choc & ultra .20 *.65*
**122** A33 6p black & dp ultra .20 *1.10*
**123** A33 8p purple & emer .50 *1.60*
**124** A34 1sh black & ultra .35 *.80*
**125** A34 2sh on 3p dk grn & ultra .60 *3.75*
**126** A33 5sh purple & yellow 6.25 3.75
*Nos. 119-126 (8)* 8.50 12.90

Cent. of emancipation. See Nos. CO1-CO6.

### Freedom from Hunger Issue

Common Design Type with Portrait of Queen Salote

***Perf. 14x14½***

**1963, June 4** **Wmk. 79** **Photo.**

**127** CD314 11p ultra .70 .35

Coat of Arms, ¼ Koula Coin, Reverse A36

Designs: 2p, 9p, 2sh, Queen Salote (head), ¼-koula coin, obverse.

**Litho.; Embossed on Gilt Foil**

**1963, July 15** **Unwmk.** ***Die Cut***

**Diameter: 40mm**

**128** A36 1p dp carmine .20 .20
**129** A36 2p violet blue .20 .20
**130** A36 6p dp green .30 .30
**131** A36 9p magenta .35 .35
**132** A36 1sh6p violet .70 .70
**133** A36 2sh emerald .75 .75
*Nos. 128-133,C1-C6,CO7 (13)* 13.45 13.50

1st gold coinage of Polynesia. Backed with paper inscribed in salmon-colored alternating rows: "TONGA" and "THE FRIENDLY ISLANDS" in multiple.

For surcharges see #140-145, C11-C15, CO8.

### Red Cross Centenary Issue

Common Design Type with Portrait of Queen Salote

**Wmk. 79**

**1963, Sept. 2** **Litho.** ***Perf. 13***

**134** CD315 2p black & red .25 .20
**135** CD315 11p ultra & red .75 1.00

Queen Salote on ¼-Koula Coin A37

**Litho.; Embossed on Gilt Foil**

**1964, Oct. 19** **Unwmk.** ***Die Cut***

**136** A37 3p pink .20 .20
**137** A37 9p light blue .20 .20
**138** A37 2sh yellow green .50 .50
**139** A37 5sh pale lilac 1.50 1.50
*Nos. 136-139,C7-C10 (8)* 5.50 5.50

Pan-Pacific and Southeast Asia Women's Association Conf., Nukualofa, Aug. 1964. See note on paper backing after No. 133.

For surcharges & overprints see #152-157, 263-268.

### Nos. 128-133 Surcharged in Red, White or Black

**1965, Mar. 18**

**140** A36 1sh3p on 1sh6p (R) .20 .20
**141** A36 1sh9p on 9p (W) .20 .20
**142** A36 2sh6p on 6p (R) .25 .25
**143** A36 5sh on 1p 22.50 22.50
**144** A36 5sh on 2p 4.00 4.00
**145** A36 5sh on 2sh .90 .90
*Nos. 140-145,C11-C15,CO8 (12)* 82.00 82.00

### Nos. 114-115 Overprinted and Surcharged in Purple or Red

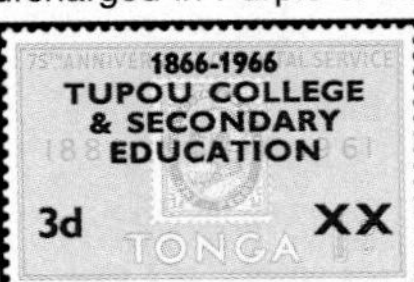


***Perf. 14½x13½***

**1966, June 18** **Photo.** **Wmk. 79**

**146** A35 1p (P) .20 .20
**147** A35 3p on 1p (P) .20 .20
**148** A35 6p on 2p (R) .20 .20
**149** A35 1sh2p on 2p (R) .20 .20
**150** A35 2sh on 2p (R) .35 .20
**151** A35 3sh on 2p (R) .35 .20
*Nos. 146-151,C16-C21,CO9-CO10 (14)* 5.55 3.10

Centenary of Tupou College and of secondary eucation.

### Nos. 136-137 Overprinted and Surcharged in Silver on Black or Ultramarine

Illustration reduced.

**Litho.; Embossed on Gilt Foil**

**1966, Dec. 16** **Unwmk.** ***Die Cut***

**152** A37 3p pink (U) .20 .20
**153** A37 5p on 9p lt blue .20 .20
**154** A37 9p lt bl .20 .20
**155** A37 1sh7p on 3p pink (U) .55 .55
**156** A37 3sh6p on 9p lt blue .95 .95
**157** A37 6sh6p on 3p pink (U) 1.75 1.75
*Nos. 152-157,C22-C26 (11)* 9.25 9.25

### Nos. 100-110, 147 and 151 Surcharged in Black or Red

***Perf. 11½x11, 11x11½, 14½x13½***

**1967, Mar. 25** **Wmk. 79**

**158** A33 1s on 1p .20 .20
**159** A33 2s on 4p .20 .20
**160** A33 3s on 5p .20 .20
**161** A33 4s on 5p .20 .20
**162** A33 5s on 3½p .20 .20
**163** A33 6s on 8p .20 .20
**164** A33 7s on 1½p .20 .20
**165** A33 8s on 6p .20 .20
**166** A34 9s on 3p .20 .20
**167** A34 10s on 1sh .25 .25
**168** A35 11s on 3p on 1p .35 .35
**169** A35 21s on 3sh on 2p .55 .55
**170** A33 23s on 1p .60 .60
**171** A33 30s on 2sh (R) (1-line surcharge 1.25 1.25
**172** A33 30s on 2sh (R) (3-line surcharge 1.40 1.40
**173** A33 50s on 6p (R) 1.60 1.60
**174** A33 60s on 2p (R) 2.00 2.00
*Nos. 158-174 (17)* 9.80 9.80

The size, typeface and arrangement of surcharge vary on the different denominations.

King Taufa'ahau IV — A38

Designs: 1s, 4s, 28s, 1pa, Coat of Arms, reverse of new palladium coins.

**Litho.; Embossed on Palladium Foil**

**1967, July 4** **Unwmk.** ***Die Cut***

Diameter: 1s, 44mm; 2s, 50s, 52mm; 4s, 59mm; 15s, 68mm; 28s, 40mm; 1pa, 74mm

**175** A38 1s orange & brt bl .20 .20
**176** A38 2s brt bl & dp mag .20 .20
**177** A38 4s emerald & mag .20 .20
**178** A38 15s blue grn & vio .35 .35
**179** A38 28s blk & brt red lil .60 .60
**180** A38 50s red & vio bl 1.10 1.10
**181** A38 1pa ultra & brt rose 2.75 2.75
*Nos. 175-181,C27-C33 (14)* 13.00 13.00

Coronation of King Taufa'ahau IV, July 4, 1967. Backed with paper inscribed in yellow alternating rows: "Tonga The Friendly Islands" and "Historically The First Palladium Coinage."

For surcharges and overprints see Nos. 203-209, C40-C46, CO21-CO24,

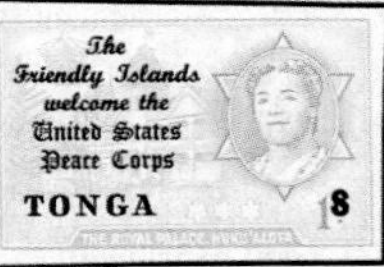


Types of Regular Issue, 1953, Surcharged

**Wmk. 79**

**1967, Dec. 15** **Engr.** ***Die Cut***

**182** A33 1s on 1p yellow & blk .20 .20
**183** A33 2s on 2p carmine & ultra .20 .20
**184** A34 3s on 3p brown org & yel .20 .20
**185** A33 4s on 4p purple & yel .20 .20
**186** A33 5s on 5p green & yel .20 .20
**187** A34 10s on 10p rose red & yel .20 .20
**188** A33 20s on 2sh carmine & ultra .25 .25
**189** A33 50s on 5sh sepia & yel 2.00 2.00
**190** A34 1pa on 10sh orange yel .75 .75
*Nos. 182-190,C34-C36,CO12-CO14 (15)* 7.70 7.70

Arrival of US Peace Corps.

### Nos. 100-111 Surcharged in Red, Black or Ultramarine

***Perf. 11½x11, 11x11½***

**1968, Apr. 6** **Engr.** **Wmk. 79**

**191** A33 1s on 1p (R) .20 .20
**192** A33 2s on 4p .20 .20
**193** A34 3s on 3p (U) .20 .20
**194** A33 4s on 5p (R) .20 .20
**195** A33 5s on 2p (R) .20 .20
**196** A33 6s on 6p (R) .20 .20
**197** A33 7s on 1½p (R) .20 .20
**198** A33 8s on 8p (R) .20 .20
**199** A33 9s on 3½p .30 .30
**200** A34 10s on 1sh (R) .30 .30
**201** A33 20s on 5sh (R) 1.25 1.25
**202** A33 2pa on 2sh (R) 2.75 2.75
*Nos. 191-202,C37-C39,CO15-CO18 (19)* 13.10 13.10

Surcharge on 3s and 10s is vertical.

### Nos. 175-181 Overprinted: "H.M'S BIRTHDAY / 4 July 1968" in Gold on Red Panel on 1s, 4s, 28s and 1pa. "HIS MAJESTY'S 50th BIRTHDAY" in Silver on Blue Panel on 2s, 15s and 50s

**Litho.; Embossed on Palladium Foil**

**1968, July 4** **Unwmk.** ***Die Cut***

**203** A38 1s orange & brt bl .20 .20
**204** A38 2s brt bl & dp mag .20 .20
**205** A38 4s emerald & mag .20 .20
**206** A38 15s blue grn & vio .55 .55
**207** A38 28s blk & brt red lil 1.10 1.10
**208** A38 50s red & vio bl 1.90 1.90
**209** A38 1pa ultra & brt rose 4.00 4.00
*Nos. 203-209,C40-C46,CO21-CO24 (18)* 31.25 27.75

### Types of 1953 Surcharged in Red, Black or Green: "Friendly Islands / Field & Track Trials / South Pacific Games / Port Moresby 1969"

Designs as before.

**Wmk. 79**

**1968, Dec. 19** **Engr.** ***Die Cut***

**210** A33 5s on 5p green & yel (R) .20 .20
**211** A34 10s on 1sh cer & buff .20 .20
**212** A33 15s on 2sh rose car & bl .20 .20
**213** A33 25s on 2p rose car & bl .30 .20
**214** A33 50s on 1p yel & blk .50 .30
**215** A34 75s on 10sh org (G) .85 .45
*Nos. 210-215,C47-C54,CO19-CO20 (16)* 8.00 4.75

Issued to publicize the field and track trials for the third South Pacific Games, Port Moresby, 1969. The overprint is in 5 lines on the horizontal stamps, in 7 lines on vertical stamps. On the vertical stamps "Trial" is printed on the line ahead of "Field & Track." On #215 the denomination is spelled out.

Nos. 149-150 and Types of 1953 Surcharged

*Perf. 14½x13½*

| 1968 | Photo. | Wmk. 79 | |
|---|---|---|---|
| 216 A35 | 1s on 1sh2p on 2p | 1.60 | 1.60 |
| 217 A35 | 1s on 2sh on 2p | 1.60 | 1.60 |

| | Engr. | Die Cut | |
|---|---|---|---|
| 218 A33 | 1s on 6p yellow & blk | .90 | .90 |
| 219 A33 | 2s on 3½p dk blue | 1.00 | 1.00 |
| 220 A33 | 3s on 1½p lt green | 1.00 | 1.00 |
| 221 A33 | 4s on 8p black & pale grn | 1.10 | 1.10 |
| | *Nos. 216-221,C55-C57 (9)* | 12.00 | 10.20 |

Banana — A39

**Unwmk.**

| 1969, Apr. 21 | Typo. Self-adhesive | Die Cut | |
|---|---|---|---|
| 222 A39 | 1s yellow, black & red | 1.00 | .85 |
| 223 A39 | 2s yel, black & emer | 1.10 | 1.00 |
| 224 A39 | 3s yellow, black & lil | 1.25 | 1.10 |
| 225 A39 | 4s yellow, black & ultra | 1.40 | 1.10 |
| 226 A39 | 5s yel, blk & ol grn | 1.75 | 1.75 |
| | *Nos. 222-226 (5)* | 6.50 | 5.80 |

Packed in boxes of 200. See Nos. 248-252, 297-301, O11-O15, design A75.

**Peelable Backing Inscribed**

Starting in 1969, self-adhesive stamps are attached to peelable paper backing printed with "TONGA where time begins" in multiple rows and various colors, unless otherwise stated.

Shot-putter — A40

| 1969, Aug. 13 | Litho. Self-adhesive | Die Cut | |
|---|---|---|---|
| 227 A40 | 1s bister, red & blk | .20 | .20 |
| 228 A40 | 3s bis, red & emer | .20 | .20 |
| 229 A40 | 6s bister, red & bl | .20 | .20 |
| 230 A40 | 10s bister, red & pur | .20 | .20 |
| 231 A40 | 30s bister, red & bl | .30 | .30 |
| | *Nos. 227-231,C58-C62,CO25-CO26 (12)* | 5.50 | 5.50 |

3rd Pacific Games, Port Moresby, Papua and New Guinea, Aug. 13-23.

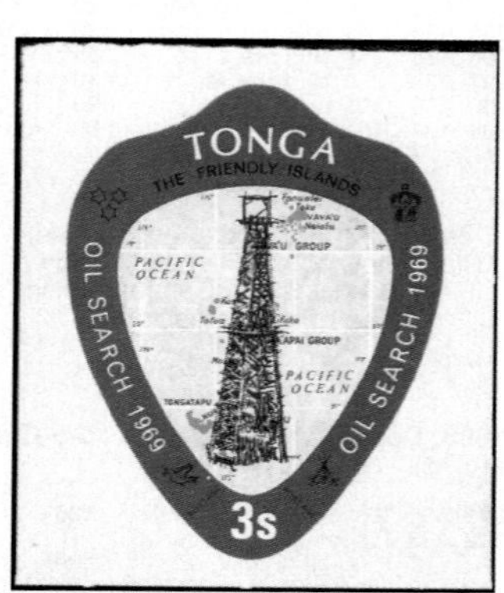

Oil Derrick and Map of Tonga Islands — A41

| 1969, Dec. 23 | Litho. Self-adhesive | Die Cut | |
|---|---|---|---|
| 232 A41 | 3s brown & multi | .20 | .20 |
| 233 A41 | 7s brt blue & multi | .20 | .20 |
| 234 A41 | 20s multicolored | .55 | .55 |
| 235 A41 | 25s orange & multi | .80 | .80 |
| 236 A41 | 35s henna brn & multi | 1.10 | 1.10 |

Type of Regular Issue, 1953, Surcharged in Red: "1969 / OIL / SEARCH / T$1.10" and Oil Derrick Obliterating Old Denomination

| | Wmk. 79 | Die Cut | |
|---|---|---|---|
| 237 A34 | 1.10pa on £1 green & multi | 3.50 | 3.50 |
| | *Nos. 232-237,C63-C67,CO27 (12)* | 12.70 | 12.70 |

First scientific search for oil in Tonga.

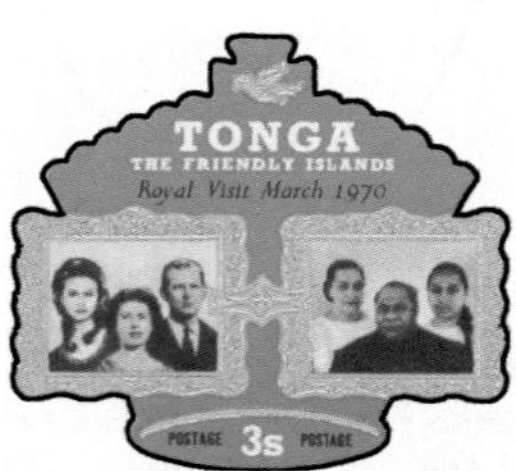

British and Tongan Royal Families — A42

| 1970, Mar. 7 | Litho.; Gold Embossed Self-adhesive | Die Cut | |
|---|---|---|---|
| 238 A42 | 3s multicolored | .20 | .20 |
| 239 A42 | 5s multicolored | .20 | .20 |
| 240 A42 | 10s multicolored | .55 | .40 |
| 241 A42 | 25s multicolored | 1.25 | .90 |
| 242 A42 | 50s multicolored | 2.75 | 2.00 |
| | *Nos. 238-242,C68-C72,CO28-CO30 (13)* | 27.45 | 18.75 |

Visit of Elizabeth II, Prince Philip and Princess Anne, Mar. 1970.

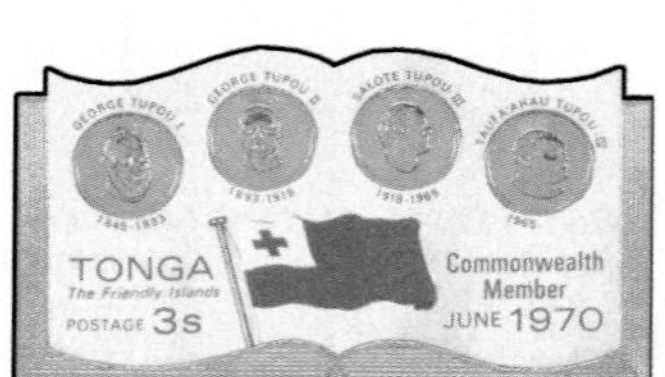

Open Book, George Tupou I and II, Salote Tupou III, Taufa'ahau Tupou IV and Tonga Flag — A43

| 1970, June 4 | Litho.; Gold Embossed Self-adhesive | Die Cut | |
|---|---|---|---|
| 243 A43 | 3s multicolored | .20 | .20 |
| 244 A43 | 7s multicolored | .25 | .25 |
| 245 A43 | 15s multicolored | .60 | .60 |
| 246 A43 | 25s multicolored | .70 | .70 |
| 247 A43 | 50s multicolored | 1.25 | 1.25 |
| | *Nos. 243-247,C73-C77,CO31-CO33 (13)* | 13.25 | 13.25 |

Tonga's independence and entry into the British Commonwealth of Nations.

For surcharges see Nos. CO49-CO51, CO71.

Banana Type of 1969 redrawn and

Coconut — A44

| 1970, June 9 | Self-adhesive | Typo. | |
|---|---|---|---|
| 248 A39 | 1s yellow, blk & mag | .40 | .40 |
| 249 A39 | 2s yellow, blk & bl | .50 | .50 |
| 250 A39 | 3s yellow, blk & brn | .50 | .50 |
| 251 A39 | 4s yellow, blk & grn | .50 | .50 |
| 252 A39 | 5s yellow, blk & org | .55 | .55 |

**Typo.; Embossed on Gilt Foil**

**Coconut Brown**

| | | | |
|---|---|---|---|
| 253 A44 | 6s blue, grn & mag | .65 | .65 |
| 254 A44 | 7s purple & green | .70 | .70 |
| 255 A44 | 8s gold, grn & vio bl | .75 | .75 |
| 256 A44 | 9s carmine & green | .85 | .85 |
| 257 A44 | 10s gold, grn & org | .85 | .85 |
| | *Nos. 248-257,O11-O20 (20)* | 16.00 | 16.00 |

Nos. 248-252 have no white shading in upper part of the banana, Nos. 222-226 have white shading. Nos. 253-256 have self-adhesive control numbers in lower left corner of paper backing. Paper backing is green on Nos. 253-257.

See Nos. 302-306, O26-O30.

Red Cross and Arms of Tonga A45

| 1970, Oct. 17 | Litho. Self-adhesive | Die Cut | |
|---|---|---|---|
| 258 A45 | 3s red, black & grn | .20 | .20 |
| 259 A45 | 7s red, blk & vio bl | .20 | .20 |
| 260 A45 | 15s red, blk & red lil | .55 | .55 |
| 261 A45 | 25s red, black & brt grn | .90 | .90 |
| 262 A45 | 75s red, black & brn | 4.50 | 4.50 |
| | *Nos. 258-262,C78-C82,CO34-CO36 (13)* | 28.25 | 28.25 |

Centenary of the British Red Cross.

Nos. 153, 152 Surcharged

| 1971, Jan. 31 | Litho.; Embossed on Gilt Foil | Die Cut | |
|---|---|---|---|
| 263 A37 | 2s on 9p lt blue | .20 | .20 |
| 264 A37 | 3s on 9p lt blue | .20 | .20 |
| 265 A37 | 5s on 3p pink | .35 | .20 |
| 266 A37 | 15s on 9p lt blue | 1.10 | .65 |
| 267 A37 | 25s on 3p pink | 1.50 | 1.00 |
| 268 A37 | 50s on 3p pink | 3.50 | 2.10 |
| | *Nos. 263-268,C83-C86,CO37-CO40 (14)* | 35.00 | 24.35 |

In memory of Queen Salote (1900-65). The "In Memoriam" inscription is in silver on black panel on the 2s, 3s and 15s; in silver on ultramarine panel on the 5s, 25s and 50s. The dates and denominations are all on black panels in silver and metallic red, green, bronze, magenta or gold respectively.

Type of Regular Issue, 1953, Surcharged in Red and Black

| 1971 | Engr. Wmk. 79 | Imperf | |
|---|---|---|---|
| 269 A33 | 3s on 8p black & pale grn | .20 | .20 |
| 270 A33 | 7s on 4p pur & yel | .25 | .20 |
| 271 A33 | 25s on 1p yel & blk | .55 | .40 |
| 272 A33 | 75s on 2sh car & ultra | 3.25 | 2.10 |
| | *Nos. 269-272,C87-C89,CO41-CO43 (10)* | 14.00 | 9.20 |

Philatokyo 71, Philatelic Exposition, Tokyo, Apr. 19-29.

Type of Regular Issue, 1971, Surcharged

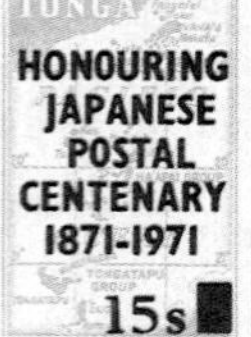

| 1971 | | | |
|---|---|---|---|
| 273 A34 | 15s on 1sh car & buff | .50 | .50 |
| | *Nos. 273,C90-C91 (3)* | 4.00 | 4.00 |

Centenary of Japanese postal service.

**Self-adhesive & Imperf.**

Starting with Nos. 274-278, all issues are self-adhesive and imperforate, unless otherwise stated.

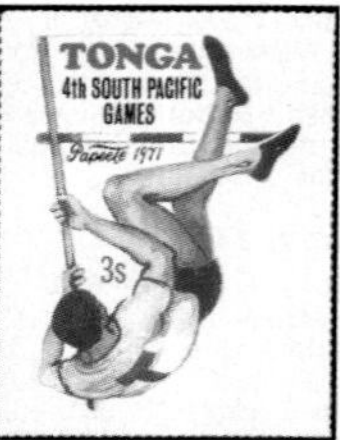

Pole Vault — A46 Gold Medal of Merit — A47

| 1971, July | Litho. | Unwmk. | |
|---|---|---|---|
| 274 A46 | 3s green, blk & brn | .20 | .20 |
| 275 A46 | 7s red, blk & brn | .20 | .20 |
| 276 A46 | 15s green, blk & brn | .35 | .35 |
| 277 A46 | 25s rose lil, blk & brn | .45 | .45 |
| 278 A46 | 50s dk bl, blk & brn | .95 | .95 |
| | *Nos. 274-278,C92-C96,CO44-CO46 (13)* | 8.50 | 8.50 |

4th South Pacific Games, Papeete, French Polynesia, Sept. 8-19.

For surcharges see Nos. 332, C140.

**1971, Oct. 30 Litho; Embossed**

24s, Silver Medal of Merit. 38s, Bronze Medal of Merit, obverse (King Taufa'ahau IV).

| | | | |
|---|---|---|---|
| 279 A47 | 3s gold & multi | .20 | .20 |
| 280 A47 | 24s silver & multi | .35 | .35 |
| 281 A47 | 38s bronze & multi | .75 | .75 |
| | *Nos. 279-281,C99-C101,CO49-CO51 (9)* | 8.70 | 8.70 |

First investiture of Tongan Medal of Merit.

For surcharges see Nos. 333-336.

Juggler, UNICEF Emblem A48

| 1971, Dec. | | Litho. | |
|---|---|---|---|
| 282 A48 | 2s violet & multi | .20 | .20 |
| 283 A48 | 4s multicolored | .20 | .20 |
| 284 A48 | 8s blue & multi | .20 | .20 |
| 285 A48 | 16s emerald & multi | .35 | .35 |
| 286 A48 | 30s lil rose & multi | .65 | .65 |
| | *Nos. 282-286,C102-C106,CO52-CO54 (13)* | 13.00 | 13.00 |

25th anniv. of UNICEF.

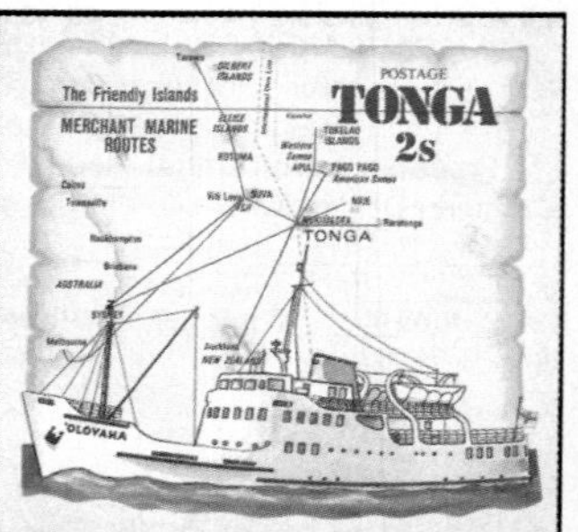

Merchant Marine Routes from Tonga and "Olovaha" — A49

| 1972, Apr. 14 | | | |
|---|---|---|---|
| 287 A49 | 2s blue & multi | .35 | .35 |
| 288 A49 | 10s magenta & multi | .85 | .35 |
| 289 A49 | 17s brown & multi | 1.25 | .35 |
| 290 A49 | 21s dk green & multi | 1.40 | .50 |
| 291 A49 | 60s multicolored | 6.50 | 4.00 |
| | *Nos. 287-291,C107-C111,CO55-CO57 (13)* | 41.95 | 28.75 |

Togan Merchant Marine publicity

For surcharges see Nos. C124, CO66-CO69.

King Taufa'ahau IV Coronation Coin, ¼ Hau — A50

**Litho.; Embossed on Metallic Foil**

**1972, July 15**

| | | | | |
|---|---|---|---|---|
| **292** | A50 | 5s silver & multi | .20 | .20 |
| **293** | A50 | 7s silver & multi | .20 | .20 |
| **294** | A50 | 10s silver & multi | .20 | .20 |
| **295** | A50 | 17s silver & multi | .40 | .40 |
| **296** | A50 | 60s silver & multi | 1.40 | 1.40 |
| | | *Nos. 292-296,C112-C116,CO58-CO60 (13)* | 12.75 | 12.75 |

Coronation of King Taufa'ahau IV, 5th anniv.

Coconut Type of 1970 and

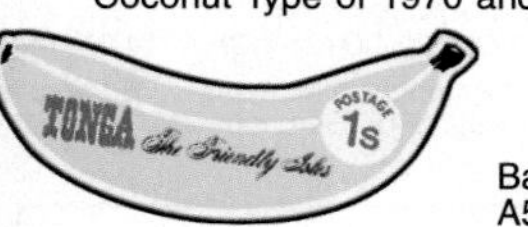


Banana A51

Watermelon — A52

**1972, Sept. 30** **Typo.**

| | | | | |
|---|---|---|---|---|
| **297** | A51 | 1s brt yel, red & blk | .35 | .20 |
| **298** | A51 | 2s brt yel, bl & blk | .40 | .20 |
| **299** | A51 | 3s brt yel, emer & blk | .45 | .20 |
| **300** | A51 | 4s brt yel & blk | .45 | .25 |
| **301** | A51 | 5s brt yel & brn blk | .45 | .25 |
| **302** | A44 | 6s brn, org & grn | .50 | .25 |
| **303** | A44 | 7s brn, ultra & grn | .55 | .30 |
| **304** | A44 | 8s brn, mag & grn | .55 | .30 |
| **305** | A44 | 9s brn, red & grn | .55 | .30 |
| **306** | A44 | 10s brn, bl & grn | .65 | .35 |
| **307** | A52 | 15s green, org brn & ultra | 1.40 | .50 |
| **308** | A52 | 20s grn, bl & red | 1.50 | .70 |
| **309** | A52 | 25s grn, red & brn | 1.75 | .80 |
| **310** | A52 | 40s grn, bl & org | 3.00 | 1.75 |
| **311** | A52 | 50s grn, dk bl & yel | 3.00 | 2.00 |
| | | *Nos. 297-311,O21-O35 (30)* | 27.85 | 16.70 |

Paper backing is brown on Nos. 302-311. Nos. 302-306 have self-adhesive control number in lower left corner of paper backing.

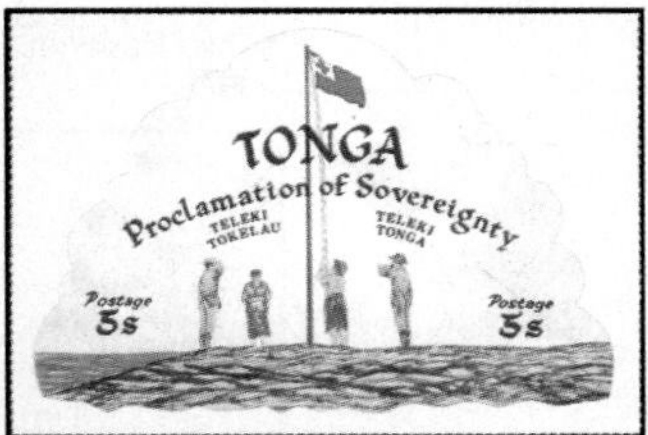


Flag Raising, Minerva Reef — A53

**1972, Dec. 9** **Litho.**

| | | | | |
|---|---|---|---|---|
| **312** | A53 | 5s black & multi | .20 | .20 |
| **313** | A53 | 7s green & multi | .20 | .20 |
| **314** | A53 | 10s purple & multi | .20 | .20 |
| **315** | A53 | 15s orange & multi | .35 | .35 |
| **316** | A53 | 40s ultra & multi | 1.40 | 1.40 |
| | | *Nos. 312-316,C119-C123,CO63-CO65 (13)* | 12.00 | 12.00 |

Tonga's proclamation of sovereignty over the Minerva Reefs, June 1972.

Tongan Coins and Bank Building — A54

**1973, Mar. 30** **Litho.**

| | | | | |
|---|---|---|---|---|
| **317** | A54 | 5s silver & multi | .20 | .20 |
| **318** | A54 | 7s silver & multi | .20 | .20 |
| **319** | A54 | 10s silver & multi | .20 | .20 |
| **320** | A54 | 20s silver & multi | .45 | .20 |
| **321** | A54 | 30s silver & multi | .60 | .35 |
| | | *Nos. 317-321,C125-C129,CO66-CO68 (13)* | 15.30 | 14.00 |

Establishment of Bank of Tonga.

Handshake, Outrigger Canoe — A55

**1973, June 29**

| | | | | |
|---|---|---|---|---|
| **322** | A55 | 5s silver & multi | .30 | .20 |
| **323** | A55 | 7s silver & multi | .45 | .20 |
| **324** | A55 | 15s silver & multi | 1.40 | .55 |
| **325** | A55 | 21s silver & multi | 1.90 | .70 |
| **326** | A55 | 50s silver & multi | 6.75 | 3.25 |
| | | *Nos. 322-326,C130-C134,CO69-CO71 (13)* | 135.00 | 70.00 |

Tongan Boy Scout Movement, 25th anniv.

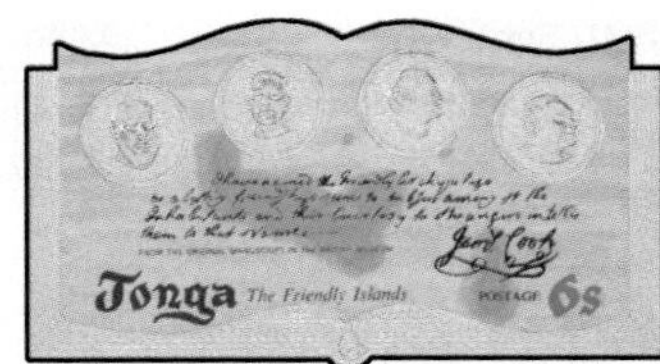


Capt. Cook's Report and Tongan Rulers — A56

**Litho.; Embossed on Gilt Foil**

**1973, Oct. 2**

| | | | | |
|---|---|---|---|---|
| **327** | A56 | 6s multicolored | .50 | .45 |
| **328** | A56 | 8s multicolored | .50 | .45 |
| **329** | A56 | 11s multicolored | .70 | .55 |
| **330** | A56 | 35s multicolored | 4.75 | 1.90 |
| **331** | A56 | 40s multicolored | 4.75 | 2.25 |
| | | *Nos. 327-331,C135-C139,CO72-CO74 (13)* | 60.00 | 31.45 |

Bicentenary of Capt. Cook's arrival. Design is from the manuscript in British Museum.

Nos. 278, 281, C100-C101 and 280 Surcharged and Overprinted in Silver or Gold on Red (12s, 14s) or Black Panels (5s, 20s, 50s): "Commonwealth Games Christchurch 1974"

**1973, Dec. 19** **Litho.**

| | | | | |
|---|---|---|---|---|
| **332** | A46 | 5s on 50s (G) | .20 | .20 |

**Litho.; Embossed**

| | | | | |
|---|---|---|---|---|
| **333** | A47 | 12s on 38s (S) | .45 | .20 |
| **334** | A47 | 14s on 75s (G) | .45 | .20 |
| **335** | A47 | 20s on 1pa (G) | .80 | .35 |
| **336** | A47 | 50s on 24s (S) | 1.60 | 1.25 |
| | | *Nos. 332-336,C140-C144,CO75-CO77 (13)* | 13.95 | 10.45 |

10th British Commonwealth Games, Christchurch, N.Z., Jan. 24-Feb. 2, 1974.

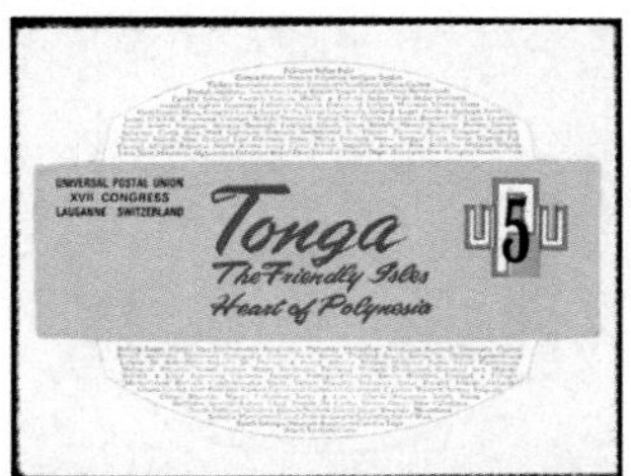


Letter Addressed to Tonga, Names of UPU Members — A57

**1974, June 20** **Typo.**

| | | | | |
|---|---|---|---|---|
| **337** | A57 | 5s tan & multi | .20 | .20 |
| **338** | A57 | 10s tan & multi | .20 | .20 |
| **339** | A57 | 15s tan & multi | .45 | .45 |
| **340** | A57 | 20s tan & multi | .50 | .50 |
| **341** | A57 | 50s tan & multi | 1.60 | 1.60 |
| | | *Nos. 337-341,C154-C158,CO87-CO89 (13)* | 13.80 | 13.80 |

Centenary of Universal Postal Union.

Girl Guide Badges — A58

**1974, Sept. 11** **Litho.**

| | | | | |
|---|---|---|---|---|
| **342** | A58 | 5s multicolored | .45 | .30 |
| **343** | A58 | 10s multicolored | .85 | .50 |
| **344** | A58 | 20s multicolored | 2.00 | 1.25 |
| **345** | A58 | 40s multicolored | 4.00 | 2.40 |
| **346** | A58 | 60s multicolored | 5.50 | 3.25 |
| | | *Nos. 342-346,C159-C163,CO90-CO92 (13)* | 49.00 | 29.20 |

Girl Guides of Tonga.

For surcharges see Nos. C189, C192.

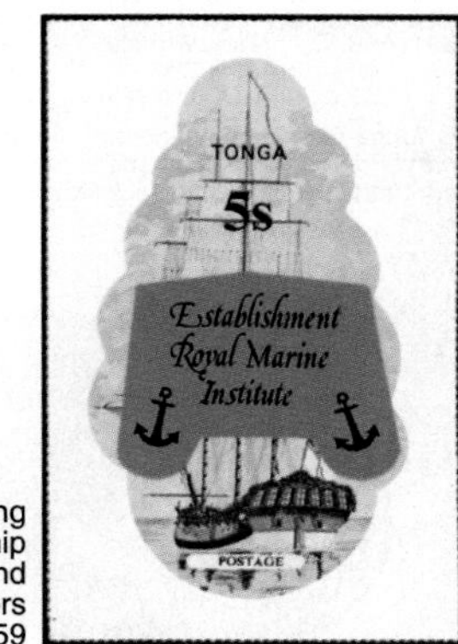


Sailing Ship and Anchors A59

**1974, Dec. 11**

| | | | | |
|---|---|---|---|---|
| **347** | A59 | 5s blue & multi | .40 | .35 |
| **348** | A59 | 10s blue & multi | .90 | .45 |
| **349** | A59 | 25s blue & multi | 2.00 | .80 |
| **350** | A59 | 50s blue & multi | 4.00 | 2.75 |
| **351** | A59 | 75s blue & multi | 6.00 | 4.50 |
| | | *Nos. 347-351,C164-C168,CO93-CO95 (13)* | 47.00 | 27.00 |

Establishment of Royal Marine Institute.

Dateline Hotel, Nukualofa — A60

**1975, Mar. 11**

| | | | | |
|---|---|---|---|---|
| **352** | A60 | 5s blue & multi | .20 | .20 |
| **353** | A60 | 10s green & multi | .20 | .20 |
| **354** | A60 | 15s scarlet & multi | .35 | .35 |
| **355** | A60 | 30s purple & multi | .75 | .75 |
| **356** | A60 | 1pa orange & multi | 2.75 | 2.75 |
| | | *Nos. 352-356,C169-C173,CO96-CO98 (13)* | 15.00 | 15.00 |

First meeting of South Pacific area Prime Ministers. See note after No. 226.

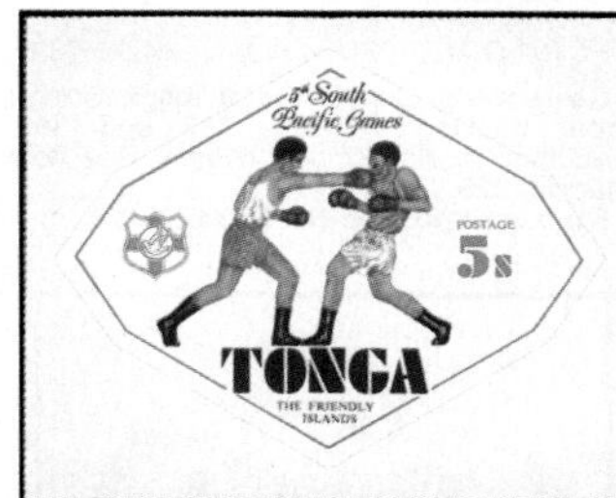


Boxing and Games' Emblem — A61

**1975, June 11** **Litho.**

| | | | | |
|---|---|---|---|---|
| **357** | A61 | 5s black & multi | .25 | .25 |
| **358** | A61 | 10s green & multi | .35 | .35 |
| **359** | A61 | 20s brown & multi | .55 | .55 |
| **360** | A61 | 25s orange & multi | .65 | .65 |
| **361** | A61 | 65s violet & multi | 1.40 | 1.40 |
| | | *Nos. 357-361,C174-C178,CO99-CO101 (13)* | 12.50 | 12.50 |

5th South Pacific Games, Guam, Aug. 1-10. See note after No. 226.

For surcharges see Nos. 412, 482.

King Taufa'ahau IV Coin — A62

Designs (FAO Coins): 5s, Chicken. 20s, like 1pa, (small coin, 27mm). 50s, School of fish. 2pa, Animals and plants on reverse, King on obverse (large coin, 42mm.).

**1975, Sept. 3**

| | | | | |
|---|---|---|---|---|
| **362** | A62 | 5s red, sil & blk | .25 | .25 |
| **363** | A62 | 20s ultra, grn, sil & blk | .55 | .55 |
| **364** | A62 | 50s blue, sil & blk | 1.10 | 1.10 |
| **365** | A62 | 1pa silver & black | 2.25 | 2.25 |
| **366** | A62 | 2pa silver & black | 3.75 | 3.75 |
| | | *Nos. 362-366,C179-C183 (10)* | 13.00 | 13.00 |

Coinage issued for the benefit of the FAO. Size of paper backing of 2pa: 82x50mm; others 45x45mm. See note after No. 226.

For surcharge see Nos. 413.

Coat of Arms, 5pa Coin, Reverse — A63

George Tupou I Coin, Reverse and Obverse — A64

Coins: 20s, King Taufa'ahau IV. 50s, King George Tupou II, 50pa obverse and reverse. 75s, 20pa reverse.

**Litho.; Embossed on Gilt Foil**
**1975, Nov. 4**
**Pink Background**

**367** A63 5s black, sil & vio bl .20 .20
**368** A64 10s gold, blk & red .35 .20
**369** A63 20s black, sil & grn .60 .35
**370** A64 50s gold, blk & vio 1.25 1.25
**371** A63 75s black, sil & red lil 2.25 2.25
*Nos. 367-371,C184-C188,CO102-CO104 (13)* 14.90 13.25

Centenary of Constitution of Tonga. Size of paper backing of Nos. 367 and 369: 65x60mm; of No. 371, 87x78mm. See note after No. 226.
For surcharges see Nos. C232, C296.

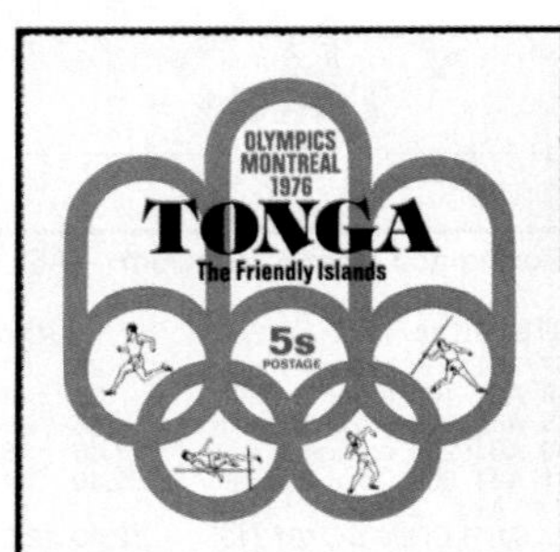


Montreal Olympic Games Emblem — A65

**1976, Feb. 24** **Litho.**

**372** A65 5s red, ultra & blk .40 .35
**373** A65 10s red, green & blk .60 .35
**374** A65 25s red, lt brown & blk 1.40 .80
**375** A65 35s red, lilac & blk 1.75 1.10
**376** A65 70s red, bister & blk 3.50 2.75
*Nos. 372-376,C189-C193,CO105-CO107 (13)* 31.00 20.05

21st Olympic Games, Montreal, Canada, July 17-Aug. 1. See note after No. 226.
For surcharges see Nos. 414, 478.

William Hooper, William Floyd, John Penn, Francis Lightfoot Lee — A66

Signers of Declaration of Independence, Flags of US and Tonga: 10s, Benjamin Franklin, Thomas Nelson, Jr., Benjamin Harrison, William Ellery. 15s, Oliver Wolcott, Lyman Hall, William Whipple, Carter Braxton. 25s, George Taylor, Thomas Stone, Arthur Middleton, Richard Stockton. 75s, Stephen Hopkins, Eldridge Gerry, James Wilson, Francis Hopkinson.

**1976, May 26** **Litho.**

**377** A66 9s buff & multi .45 .20
**378** A66 10s buff & multi .45 .20
**379** A66 15s buff & multi .65 .50
**380** A66 25s buff & multi 1.00 1.00
**381** A66 75s buff & multi 5.75 4.50
*Nos. 377-381,C194-C198,CO108-CO110 (13)* 31.00 20.50

American Bicentennial. Printed on peelable buff paper backing, inscribed in carmine with facsimile of Declaration of Independence.
For surcharges see #481, C233, C236-C237, C297.

Nathaniel Turner and John Thomas — A67

**1976, Aug. 25**

**382** A67 5s yellow & multi .25 .25
**383** A67 10s multicolored .40 .25
**384** A67 20s multicolored .90 .50
**385** A67 25s multicolored 1.00 .55
**386** A67 85s multicolored 2.75 2.75
*Nos. 382-386,C199-C203,CO111-CO113 (13)* 18.75 16.65

Sesquicentennial of the arrival of Methodist missionaries and establishment of Christianity in Tonga. Printed on peelable paper backing inscribed in manuscript with segments of John Thomas's Tonga diary.
For surcharges see Nos. 415-416, 479-480.

Wilhelm I and George Tupou I — A68

**1976, Nov. 1**

**387** A68 9s yellow & multi .35 .30
**388** A68 15s yellow & multi .55 .50
**389** A68 22s yellow & multi .80 .70
**390** A68 50s yellow & multi 1.40 1.25
**391** A68 73s yellow & multi 1.90 1.75
*Nos. 387-391,C204-C208,CO114-CO116 (13)* 14.85 13.50

Tonga-Germany Friendship Treaty, centenary. Printed on peelable paper backing showing reproduction of original treaty.

Queen Salote in Coronation Procession, 1953 — A69

**1977, Feb. 7** **Litho.**

**392** A69 11s blue & multi .40 .40
**393** A69 20s green & multi .50 .50
**394** A69 30s vio blue & multi .30 .30
**395** A69 50s lt green & multi .45 .45
**396** A69 75s violet & multi .80 .80
*Nos. 392-396,C209-C213,CO117-CO119 (13)* 20.00 15.50

25th anniv. of the reign of Elizabeth II. Printed on peelable paper backing showing replica of handwritten Proclamation of Accession.
For surcharge see No. 417.

Various Coins — A70

**1977, July 4**

**397** A70 10s multicolored .20 .20
**398** A70 15s multicolored .30 .30
**399** A70 25s multicolored .40 .40
**400** A70 50s multicolored .85 .85
**401** A70 75s multicolored 1.50 1.50
*Nos. 397-401,C214-C218,CO120-CO122 (13)* 10.75 10.75

10th anniversary of coronation of King Taufa'ahau IV. Printed on peelable paper backing showing multicolored replicas of Tongan stamps.

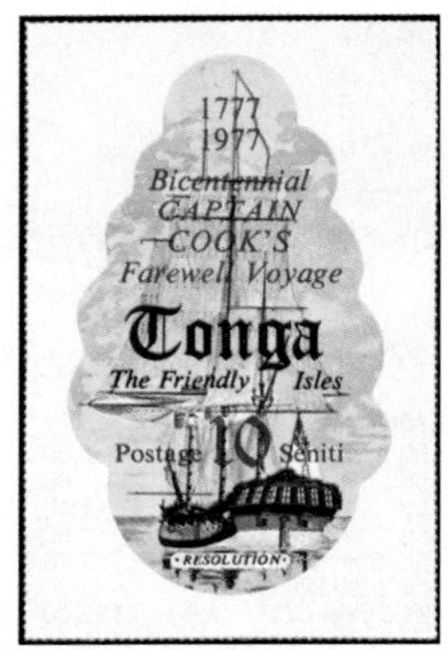


Capt. Cook's Resolution — A71

**1977, Sept. 27** **Litho.**

**402** A71 10s multicolored 1.00 .75
**403** A71 17s multicolored 2.25 1.25
**404** A71 25s multicolored 2.50 2.50
**405** A71 30s multicolored 3.50 3.00
**406** A71 40s multicolored 3.50 3.00
*Nos. 402-406,C219-C223,CO123-CO125 (13)* 81.95 61.90

Bicentenary of Capt. Cook's farewell voyage.

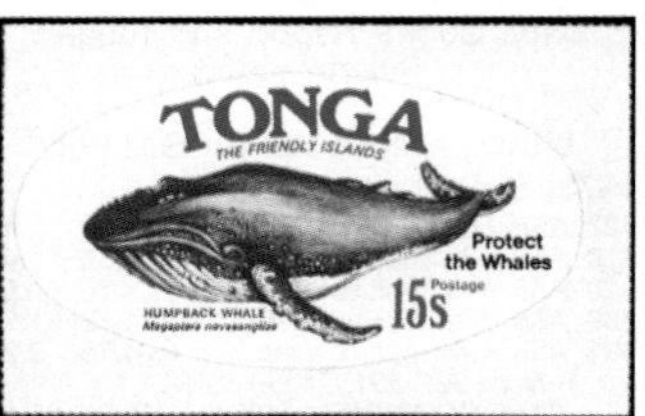


Humpback Whale — A72

**1977, Dec. 16**

**407** A72 15s ultra & black 4.25 .85
**408** A72 22s green & black 4.50 1.50
**409** A72 31s orange & black 5.25 2.00
**410** A72 38s lilac & black 5.50 5.25
**411** A72 64s red & black 9.25 5.50
*Nos. 407-411,C224-C228,CO126-CO128 (13)* 87.25 38.15

Whale protection.

Stamps of 1975-77 Surcharged in Black, Green, Brown or Black on Silver

**1978, Feb. 17**

**412** A61 15s on 20s (#359;B) 2.00 1.75
**413** A62 15s on 5s (#362;B) 2.00 1.75
**414** A65 15s on 10s (#373;G) 2.00 1.75
**415** A67 15s on 5s (#382;Br) 2.00 1.75
**416** A67 15s on 10s (#383;B) 2.00 1.75
**417** A69 15s on 11s (#392;B on S) *2.00 3.00*
**418** OA11 15s on 38s (#CO99;B) 2.00 1.75
*Nos. 412-418,C229-C238 (17)* *79.75 70.50*

The surcharge on No. 413 is only the "1," and on No. 418 includes "postage."

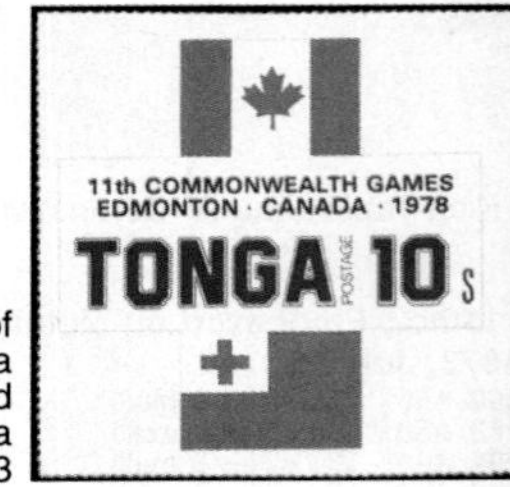


Flags of Canada and Tonga A73

**1978, May 5** **Litho.**

**419** A73 10s red & multi .20 .20
**420** A73 15s red & multi .35 .35
**421** A73 20s red & multi .45 .45
**422** A73 25s red & multi .60 .60
**423** A73 45s red & multi 2.00 2.00
*Nos. 419-423,C239-C243,CO129-CO131 (13)* 14.00 14.00

11th Commonwealth Games, Edmonton, Canada, Aug. 3-12. See note after No. 226.

King Taufa'ahau IV — A74

**1978, July 4**

**424** A74 2s multicolored .20 .20
**425** A74 5s multicolored .20 .20
**426** A74 10s multicolored .25 .25
**427** A74 25s multicolored .65 .65
**428** A74 75s multicolored 2.00 2.00
*Nos. 424-428,C244-C248,CO132-CO134 (13)* 13.00 13.00

60th birthday of King Taufa'ahau IV. See note after No. 226.

Two Bananas A75

Coconut — A76

Designs: 1s to 5s, Bananas. 6s to 10s, Coconuts. 15s to 1pa, Pineapples.

**1978, Sept. 29** **Typo.**

**429** A75 1s yellow & black .25 .25
**430** A75 2s yellow & dk blue .25 .25
**431** A75 3s multicolored .35 .35
**432** A75 4s multicolored .35 .35
**433** A75 5s multicolored .35 .35
**434** A76 6s multicolored .50 .50
**435** A76 7s multicolored .50 .50
**436** A76 8s multicolored .50 .50
**437** A76 9s multicolored .50 .50
**438** A76 10s brown & green .50 .50
**439** A76 15s green & lt brown 1.50 1.50
**440** A76 20s multicolored 1.75 1.75
**441** A76 30s multicolored 2.00 2.00
**442** A76 50s multicolored 2.50 2.50
**443** A76 1pa multicolored 3.00 3.00
*Nos. 429-443,O36-O50 (30)* 28.00 28.00

Nos. 429-443 issued in coils; self-adhesive control numbers on paper backing, except on 1s and 5s. See note after No. 226.

See No. 529.

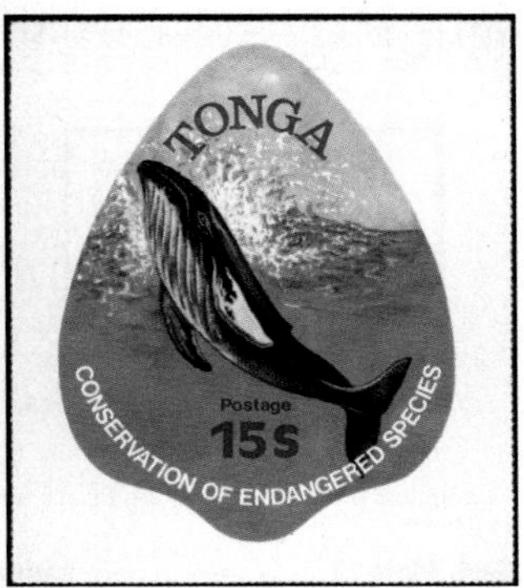


Whale — A77

**1978, Dec. 15** **Litho. & Typo.**

**444** A77 15s shown 3.50 1.75
**445** A77 18s Bat 3.50 1.75
**446** A77 25s Turtle 3.50 1.75
**447** A77 28s Parrot 5.50 2.50
**448** A77 60s like 15s 9.00 6.00
*Nos. 444-448,C249-C253,CO150-CO152 (13)* 73.25 40.25

Wildlife conservation. See note after No. 226.

Introduction of Metric System — A78

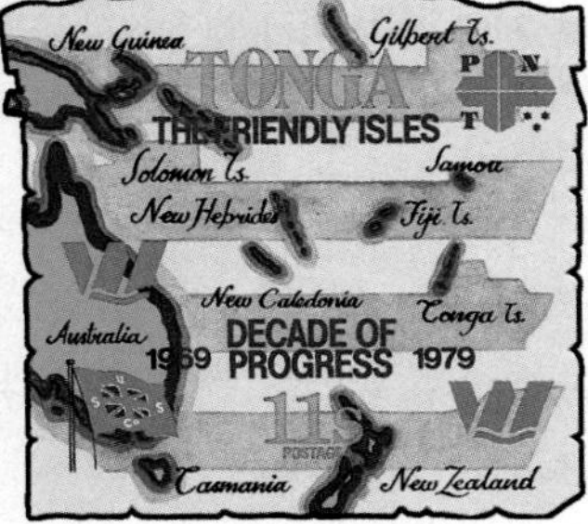


Shipping Routes, South Pacific Map — A79

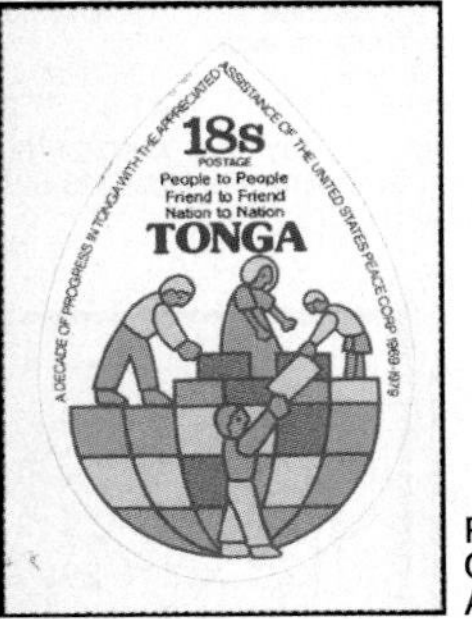


Peace Corps A80

22s, New church buildings. 50s, Air routes to Auckland, Suva, Apia & Pago Pago.

**1979, Feb. 16** **Litho.**

**449** A78 5s multicolored .20 .20
**450** A79 11s multicolored .35 .20
**451** A80 18s multicolored .50 .40
**452** A79 22s multicolored .60 .50
**453** A79 50s multicolored 1.50 .80
*Nos. 449-453,C254-C258,CO153-CO155 (13)* 14.25 9.15

Decade of Progress. Paper backing shows map of Tonga.

Tongan First Day Covers — A81

**1979, June 1**

**454** A81 5s multicolored .20 .20
**455** A81 10s multicolored .25 .25
**456** A81 25s multicolored .60 .60
**457** A81 50s multicolored 1.25 1.25
**458** A81 1pa multicolored 1.75 1.75
*Nos. 454-458,C259-C263,CO156-CO158 (13)* 11.55 11.55

10th anniversary of introduction of self-adhesive stamps and for Bernard Mechanick, inventor of self-adhesive, free-form stamps; death centenary of Sir Rowland Hill.

Printed on peelable paper backing showing advertisement.

For surcharges and overprints see Nos. 469-473.

Eua Island through Camera Lens — A82

**1979, Nov. 23** **Litho.**

**459** A82 10s multicolored .20 .20
**460** A82 18s multicolored .45 .45
**461** A82 31s multicolored .75 .75
**462** A82 50s multicolored 1.10 1.10
**463** A82 60s multicolored 1.40 1.40
*Nos. 459-463,C275-C279,CO170-CO172 (13)* 11.80 11.80

Printed on peelable paper backing showing film and camera.

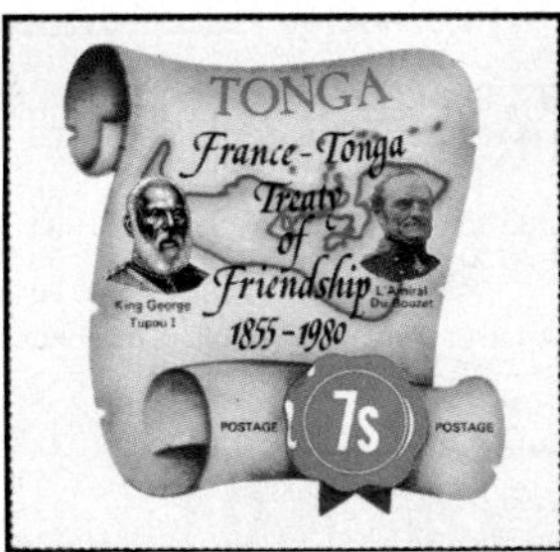


King George Tupou I, Admiral du Bouzet, Map of Tonga — A83

**1980, Jan. 9** **Litho.**

**464** A83 7s multicolored .20 .20
**465** A83 10s multicolored .35 .35
**466** A83 14s multicolored .45 .45
**467** A83 50s multicolored 1.40 1.40
**468** A83 75s multicolored 1.90 1.90
*Nos. 464-468,C280-C284,CO173-CO175 (13)* 13.50 13.50

Tongan-French Friendship Treaty, 125th anniversary. Printed on peelable paper; multicolored backing shows map of Tonga.

Nos. 454-458 Surcharged and Overprinted in Black on Silver: "1980 OLYMPIC GAMES," Moscow '80 and Bear Emblems

**1980, Apr. 30** **Litho.**

**469** A81 13s on 5s multi .50 .50
**470** A81 20s on 10s multi .75 .75
**471** A81 25s multicolored .90 .90
**472** A81 33s on 50s multi 1.10 1.10
**473** A81 1pa multicolored 3.50 3.50
*Nos. 469-473,C285-C289,CO176-CO178 (13)* 17.50 17.50

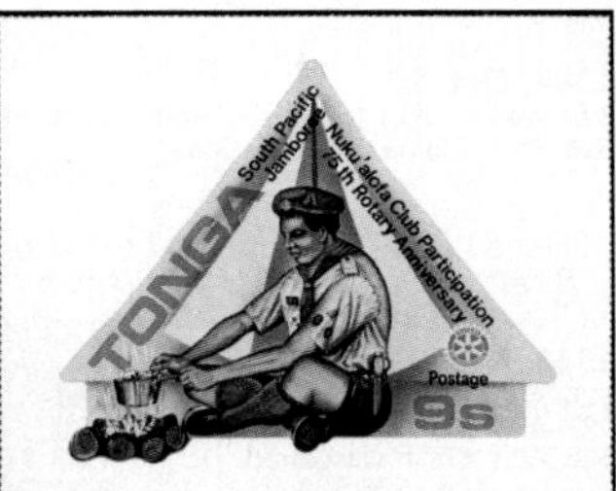


Boy Scout Cooking over Campfire — A84

**1980, Sept. 30** **Litho.**

**474** A84 9s multicolored .25 .25
**475** A84 13s multicolored .40 .40
**476** A84 15s multicolored .45 .45
**477** A84 30s multicolored .90 .90
*Nos. 474-477,C290-C293,CO179-CO180 (10)* 14.75 14.75

Boy Scout Jamboree; Rotary Intl., 75th anniv. Peelable backing shows map of Tonga.

Nos. 361, 375, 380, 384-385 Surcharged

**1980, Dec. 3** **Litho.**

**478** A65 9s on 35s multi .20 .20
**479** A67 13s on 20s multi .30 .30
**480** A67 13s on 25s multi .30 .30
**481** A66 19s on 25s multi .45 .45
**482** A61 1pa on 65s multi 2.50 2.50
*Nos. 478-482,C294-C299,CO181 (12)* 13.70 13.70

Intl. Year of the Disabled — A85

**1981, Sept. 9** **Litho.**

**483** A85 2pa multicolored 3.25 3.25
**484** A85 3pa multicolored 5.00 5.00
*Nos. 483-484,C300-C302 (5)* 10.05 10.05

Prince Charles and Lady Diana — A86

Designs: 13s, Charles, King Taufa'ahau. 47s, 1.50pa, Couple, diff.

**1981, Oct. 21** **Litho.**

**485** A86 13s multicolored .20 .20
**486** A86 47s multicolored .50 .50
**487** A86 1.50pa multicolored 1.75 1.75
**488** A86 3pa multicolored 3.50 3.50
*Nos. 485-488 (4)* 5.95 5.95

Royal Wedding and Gt. Britain-Tonga Friendship Treaty centenary. Issued in sheets of 20 (2x10) and 5 labels in vert. center row.

For surcharge see No. B1

Bicentenary of Discovery of Vavau by Francisco Maurelle A87

18th century Spanish engravings and maps.

**1981, Nov. 25** **Litho.**

**489** A87 9s multicolored .60 .50
**490** A87 13s multicolored .90 .60
**491** A87 47s multicolored 2.75 1.40
**492** A87 1pa multicolored 6.75 6.75
*a.* Souvenir sheet, imperf. 13.00 13.00
*Nos. 489-492 (4)* 11.00 9.25

No. 492a contains one No. 492 (32x25mm).

Bible Class, 1830 Print — A88

**1981, Nov. 25**

**493** A88 9s Open book .30 .30
**494** A88 13s Book, diff. .50 .40
**495** A88 32s Type 1.10 1.10
**496** A88 47s shown 1.60 1.60
*Nos. 493-496 (4)* 3.50 3.40

Christmas 1981 and sesquicentennial of books printed in Tonga.

175th Anniv. of Capture of The Port-au-Prince — A89

**1981, Dec. 16** **Litho.**

**497** A89 29s Battle 1.00 .75
**498** A89 32s Battle, diff. 1.25 .90
**499** A89 47s Map 1.60 1.50
**500** A89 47s Sinking ship 1.60 1.50
*a.* Pair, #499-500 3.25
**501** A89 1pa Ship 3.50 3.50
*Nos. 497-501 (5)* 8.95 8.15

Nos. CO179-CO180 Surcharged

**1982, Jan. 4** **Litho.**

**502** OA19 5pa on 25s multi 10.00 10.00
**503** OA19 5pa on 2pa multi 10.00 10.00

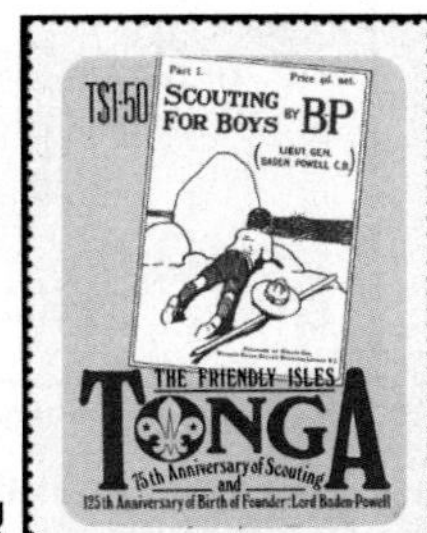


Scouting Year — A90

**1982, Feb. 22** **Litho.**

**504** A90 29s Brownsea Isld. Camp, 1907 1.00 .60
**505** A90 32s Baden-Powell, horse 1.00 .65
**506** A90 47s Imperial Jamboree, 1924 1.50 1.00
**507** A90 1.50pa "Scouting for Boys" 4.50 3.00
**508** A90 2.50pa Mafeking stamp 8.00 5.00
*Nos. 504-508 (5)* 16.00 10.25

1982 World Cup — A91

Designs: Various soccer players, map showing match sites.

**1982, July 7** **Litho.**

**509** A91 32s multicolored .85 .60
**510** A91 47s multicolored 1.25 .85
**511** A91 75s multicolored 1.90 1.40
**512** A91 1.50pa multicolored 3.50 2.50
*Nos. 509-512 (4)* 7.50 5.35

Inter-island Transport A92

9s, 13s, Ferry Olovaha. 47s, 1pa SPIA Twin Otter (Niuatoputapu Airport opening).

**1982, Aug. 11**

**513** A92 9s multicolored .40 .20
**514** A92 13s multicolored .50 .25
**515** A92 47s multicolored 1.75 .90
**516** A92 1pa multicolored 3.50 2.50
*Nos. 513-516 (4)* 6.15 3.85

Tin Can Mail Centenary A93

13s, 32s, 47s, Collecting mail. 2pa, Map. Nos. 517-519 form continuous design.

**1982, Sept. 29** **Litho.**

**517** A93 13s multicolored .20 .20
**518** A93 32s multicolored .45 .45
**519** A93 47s multicolored .75 .75
*a.* Souv. sheet of 3 (13s, 32s, 47s) 1.50 1.50
**520** A93 2pa multicolored 3.25 3.25
*a.* Souvenir sheet of 1 3.25 3.25
*Nos. 517-520 (4)* 4.65 4.65

No. 520 comes with different labels. For surcharges see Nos. 526-528.

Tonga College Centenary — A94

**1982, Oct. 25** **Size: 42x30mm (5s)**

**521** A94 5s Students .35 .35
**522** A94 29s King George Tupou I 2.25 2.25
**523** A94 29s Monument 2.25 2.25
*a.* Pair, #522-523 5.00
*Nos. 521-523 (3)* 4.85 4.85

Nos. 521-523 inscribed in English or Tongan.

12th Commonwealth Games, Brisbane, Australia, Sept. 30-Oct. 9 — A95

**1982, Oct. 25**

**524** A95 32s Decathlon, vert. 1.25 .60
**525** A95 1.50pa Opening ceremony 6.50 6.50

Nos. 517-519 Overprinted in Red or Silver in 1 or 2 Lines: "Christmas / Greetings / 1982"

**1982, Nov. 17**

**526** A93 13s multicolored .30 .30
**527** A93 32s multicolored .70 .70
**528** A93 47s multicolored 1.00 1.00
*Nos. 526-528 (3)* 2.00 2.00

Pineapple Type of 1978 and

Fruit — A96

**1982, Nov. 17**

**529** A76 13s multicolored .35 .25
**530** A96 2pa multicolored 5.75 4.00
**531** A96 3pa multicolored 8.75 6.00
*Nos. 529-531 (3)* 14.85 10.25

Capt. Cook's Resolution, 1777 and Canberra, 1983 — A96a

32s, like 29s. 47s, 1.50pa, Montgolfier Bros. balloon, 1783, Concorde. 2.50pa, Concorde, Canberra. 29s se-tenant with label showing Resolution.

**1983, Feb. 22** **Litho.**

**532** A96a 29s multicolored 2.25 1.50
**533** A96a 32s multicolored 3.00 1.50
**534** A96a 47s multicolored 4.25 2.50
**535** A96a 1.50pa multicolored 11.00 11.00
*Nos. 532-535 (4)* 20.50 16.50

**Souvenir Sheet**

**536** A96a 2.50pa multicolored 6.50 6.50

Pacific Forum of Sea and Air Transport (29s, 32s, 2.50pa); manned flight bicentenary (47s, 1.50pa).

For overprints see Nos. O68-O70.

A96b

**1983, Mar. 14**

**537** A96b 29s Map 1.40 1.40
**538** A96b 32s Dancers 1.60 1.60
**539** A96b 47s Fishermen 2.25 2.25
**540** A96b 1.50pa King Taufa'ahau IV, flag 7.00 7.00
*Nos. 537-540 (4)* 12.25 12.25

Commonwealth Day.

Niuafo'ou Airport Opening A97

**1983, May 11** **Litho.**

**541** A97 32s De Havilland Otter .90 .50
**542** A97 47s like 32s 1.25 .50
**543** A97 1pa Boeing 707 2.10 1.40
**544** A97 1.50pa like 1pa 3.75 2.10
*Nos. 541-544 (4)* 8.00 4.50

World Communications Year — A98

**1983, June 22** **Litho.**

**545** A98 29s Intelsat IV .40 .40
**546** A98 32s Intelsat IV-A .50 .50
**547** A98 75s Intelsat V 1.25 1.25

**Size: 45x32mm**

**548** A98 2pa Apollo 15 Moon post cover 3.25 3.25
*Nos. 545-548 (4)* 5.40 5.40

10th Anniv. of Bank of Tonga A99

Various banknotes.

**1983, Aug. 3** **Litho.**

**549** A99 1pa multicolored 2.25 2.25
**550** A99 2pa multicolored 4.25 4.25

Printing Press, 1830 — A100

**1983, Sept. 22** **Litho.**

**551** A100 13s shown .25 .25
**552** A100 32s Woon's arrival, 1831 .65 .65
**553** A100 1pa Print 1.60 1.60
**554** A100 2pa Tonga Chronicle 3.50 3.50
*Nos. 551-554 (4)* 6.00 6.00

Sesquicentennial of printing in Tonga (by missionary William Woon).

Christmas 1983 A101

Designs: Various sailboats off Vava'u.

**1983, Nov. 17** **Litho.**

**555** A101 29s multicolored .50 .40
**556** A101 32s multicolored .60 .50
**557** A101 1.50pa multicolored 2.40 2.40
**558** A101 2.50pa multicolored 4.25 4.25
*Nos. 555-558 (4)* 7.75 7.55

Abel Tasman, Discoverer of Tonga, and his Zeehan — A102

Navigators and Explorers of the Pacific and their Ships.

**1984, Mar. 12** **Litho.**

**559** A102 32s shown 2.00 2.00
**560** A102 47s Samuel Wallis, Dolphin 2.75 2.75
**561** A102 90s William Bligh, Bounty 5.00 5.00
**562** A102 1.50pa James Cook, Resolution 9.00 9.00
*Nos. 559-562 (4)* 18.75 18.75

See Nos. 593-596.

Swainsonia Casta — A103

Shells, fish.

**1984-85** **Litho.**

**563** A103 1s shown .45 *1.75*
**564** A103 2s Porites (coral) 1.10 *1.75*
**565** A103 3s Holocentrus ruber 1.40 *2.00*
**566** A103 5s Cypraea mappa viridis .55 *1.75*
**567** A103 6s Dardanus megistos (crab) 1.40 *2.00*
**568** A103 9s Stegostoma fasciatum 1.40 .80
*a.* Perf. 14½ ('85) 1.40 .80
**569** A103 10s Conus bullatus 1.10 *1.75*
**570** A103 13s Pterois volitans 1.75 .85
**571** A103 15s Conus textile 1.10 *2.00*
**572** A103 20s Dascyllus aruanus 2.60 2.60
**573** A103 29s Conus aulicus 2.00 1.10
**574** A103 32s Acanthurus leucosternon 3.50 1.10
**575** A103 47s Lambis truncata 3.50 1.75

**Size: 39x25mm**

**576** A103 1pa Millepora dichotama (coral) 11.00 11.00
**577** A103 2pa Birgus latro (crab) 16.00 *17.50*
**578** A103 3pa Chicoreus palma-rosae 10.00 *17.50*
**579** A103 5pa Thunnus albacares 12.50 *20.00*
*Nos. 563-579 (17)* 71.35 *87.20*

See Nos. 682-692, 701-709, 756-759. For surcharges and overprints see Nos. 618-625, 808-810, O52-O67, O71-O77.

Tonga Chronicle, 20th Anniv. A104

1984 Summer Olympics A105

**1984, June 26**

**580** A104 3s multicolored .20 .20
*a.* Sheet of 12 .75
**581** A104 32s multicolored .50 .50
*a.* Sheet of 12 7.00

Nos. 580-581 issued in sheets of 12; sheet backgrounds show pages of Chronicle, giving each stamp different background.

**1984, July 23**

**582** A105 29s Running .40 .40
**583** A105 47s Javelin .65 .65
**584** A105 1.50pa Shot put 2.00 2.00
**585** A105 3pa Torch 4.25 4.25
*Nos. 582-585 (4)* 7.30 7.30

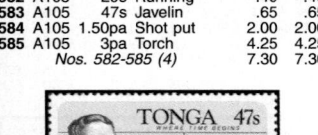

Intl. Dateline Centenary — A106

**1984, Aug. 20**

**586** A106 47s George Airy, Greenwich Meridian pioneer 1.75 1.25
**587** A106 2pa Sandford Fleming, time zone pioneer 8.00 5.50

Ausipex '84 — A107

**1984, Sept. 17**

**588** A107 32s Australia #18 1.00 .75
**589** A107 1.50pa Tonga #51 5.00 3.50

**Souvenir Sheet**

**589A** Sheet of 2, #588-589 5.00 5.00

Nos. 588-589 each printed se-tenant with label showing exhibition emblem.

No. 589A contains two imperf. stamps similar to Nos. 588-589, but with denomination replacing logo. No. 589A without denominations was not valid for postage.

Christmas 1984 — A108

**1984, Nov. 12** **Litho.**

Christmas Carols in local settings.

**590** A108 32s Silent Night .90 .50
**591** A108 47s Away in a Manger 1.60 .80
**592** A108 1pa I Saw Three Ships 3.25 3.25
*Nos. 590-592 (3)* 5.75 4.55

Famous Mariners

Designs: 32s, Willem Schouten (c. 1580-1625), The Eendracht, 1616. 47s, Jakob Le Maire (1585-1616), The Hoorn, 1615. 90s, Lt. Fletcher Christian, The Bounty, 1789. 1.50pa, Francisco Maurelle, La Princessa, 1781.

**1985, Feb. 27** **Litho.** ***Die Cut***

**593** A102 32s multicolored 2.50 1.50
*a.* Perf. 14 *50.00*
**594** A102 47s multicolored 3.75 1.75
**595** A102 90s multicolored 6.75 5.00
**596** A102 1.50pa multicolored 12.00 7.75
*Nos. 593-596 (4)* 25.00 16.00

Nos. 593-596 each printed se-tenant with self-adhesive label picturing anchor.

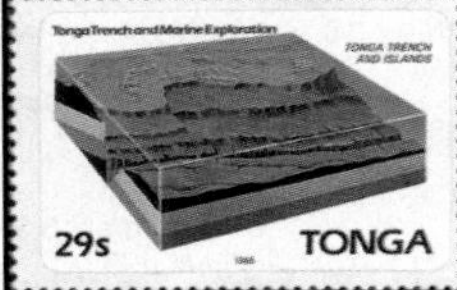


Geological Survey of Tonga Trench for Oil — A110

Designs: 29s, Tonga Trench and islands. 32s, Marine exploration, seismic surveying. 47s, Search for oil off Tongatapu, vert. No. 600, Exploration of sea bed, vert. No. 601, Angler fish.

**1985, Apr. 10**

**597** A110 29s multicolored 1.50 1.10
**598** A110 32s multicolored 1.60 1.10
**599** A110 47s multicolored 2.50 1.60
**600** A110 1.50pa multicolored 8.25 8.25
*Nos. 597-600 (4)* 13.85 12.05

**Souvenir Sheet**

**601** A110 1.50pa multicolored 13.00 7.75
*a.* Perf. 14 13.00 7.75

Nos. 597-600 printed in sheets of 40, 2 panes of 20 separated by labels inscribed "Proof 1," etc.

Adventures of Will Mariner — A111

29s, Readying Port au Prince for sail, Gravesend, 1805. 32s, Captured & set afire, 1806. 47s, Mariner taken prisoner by Chief Finow, Tonga. 1.50pa, Passage to China aboard brig Favourite. 2.50pa, Returning to England aboard East Indiaman Cuffnells, 1810.

**1985, June 18** ***Die Cut***

**602** A111 29s multicolored .60 .50
*a.* Perf. 14 .60 .50
**603** A111 32s multicolored .65 .55
*a.* Perf. 14 .65 .55
**604** A111 47s multicolored 1.00 .80
*a.* Perf. 14 1.00 .80
**605** A111 1.50pa multicolored 3.75 3.75
*a.* Perf. 14 3.75 3.75
**606** A111 2.50pa multicolored 6.00 6.00
*a.* Perf. 14 6.00 6.00
*Nos. 602-606 (5)* 12.00 11.60
*Nos. 602a-606a (5)* 12.00 11.60

Mutiny on the Bounty, Film 50th Anniv. A112

Designs: a, Byron Russell (Quintal), Stanley Fields (Muspratt) and Charles Laughton (Capt. Bligh). b, Laughton, Donald Crisp (Burkitt), Eddie Quillon (Ellison) and David Thursby (Maxwell). c, Clark Gable (Fletcher Christian). d, Russell, Alec Craig (McCoy), Laughton and Fields. e, Laughton and Franchot Tone (Roger Byam).

**1985, July 16** ***Perf. 14***

**607** Strip of 5 62.50 62.50
*a.-e.* A112 47s, any single 10.00 5.00

Sheets consist of four strips of 5 and a central strip of labels showing film credits.

Queen Mother, 85th Birthday A113

Designs: 32s, Age 10. 47s, At Hadfield Girl Guides rally, 1931. 1.50pa, In Guide uniform. 2.50pa, Portrait by Norman Parkinson, 1985.

**1985, Aug. 20** ***Imperf.***

**608** A113 32s multicolored 1.25 .90
*a.* Perf. 14 2.00 1.50
**609** A113 47s multicolored 2.00 1.50
*a.* Perf. 14 3.25 2.40
**610** A113 1.50pa multicolored 6.00 6.00
*a.* Perf. 14 9.25 9.25
**611** A113 2.50pa multicolored 9.75 9.75
*a.* Perf. 14 15.00 15.00
*Nos. 608-611 (4)* 19.00 18.15
*Nos. 608a-611a (4)* 29.50 28.15

Girl Guides movement, 75th anniv.

Christmas — A114

**1985, Nov. 12**

**612** A114 32s No room at the inn .50 .35
**613** A114 42s Shepherds follow star .75 .50
**614** A114 1.50pa The three kings 2.75 2.75
**615** A114 2.50pa Holy family 4.25 4.25
*Nos. 612-615 (4)* 8.25 7.85

Self-adhesive Discontinued

In 1986, imperforate self-adhesive stamps attached to peelable paper backing were no longer issued, unless otherwise stated.

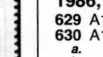

Halley's Comet A115

Designs: Nos. 616a, 617a, Comet. Nos. 616b, 617b, Edmond Halley. Nos. 616c, 617c, Solar system. Nos. 616d, 617d, Telescope. Nos. 616e, 617e, Giotto space probe.

**1986, Mar. 26** ***Perf. 14***

**616** Strip of 5 19.00 19.00
*a.-e.* A115 42s, any single 3.00 3.00
**617** Strip of 5 19.00 19.00
*a.-e.* A115 57s, any single 3.00 3.00

Nos. 564, 570, 565, 568, 567, 572, 577 and 579 Surcharged

**1986, Apr. 16** **Litho.** ***Imperf.***

**Self-adhesive**

**618** A103 4s on 2s, #564 1.10 *2.25*
**619** A103 4s on 13s, #570 1.10 *2.25*
**620** A103 42s on 3s, #565 2.90 1.75
**621** A103 42s on 9s, #568 2.90 1.75
**622** A103 57s on 6s, #567 3.50 2.50
**623** A103 57s on 20s, #572 3.50 2.50
**624** A103 2.50pa on 2pa, #577 11.00 11.00
**625** A103 2.50pa on 5pa, #579 11.00 11.00
*Nos. 618-625 (8)* 37.00 35.00

Royal Links with the United Kingdom A116

**1986, May 22** ***Perf. 14***

**626** A116 57s Taufa'ahau IV 1.25 1.25
**627** A116 57s Elizabeth II 1.25 1.25
*a.* Pair, #626-627 3.00 3.00

**Size: 40x40mm**

**628** A116 2.50pa King and queen 5.50 5.50
*Nos. 626-628 (3)* 8.00 8.00

Queen Elizabeth II, 60th birthday. No. 628 printed in sheets of 5 plus one label.

AMERIPEX '86, Chicago, May 22-June 1 — A117

Peace Corps activities: No. 629, Health care. No. 630, Education.

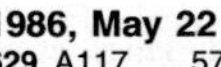

**1986, May 22**

**629** A117 57s multicolored 1.00 1.00
**630** A117 1.50pa multicolored 2.75 2.75
*a.* Souv. sheet, #629, 630, imperf 4.50 4.50
*b.* Pair, #629-630 5.50 5.50

Peace Corps in Tonga, 20th anniv.

Intl. Sporting Events — A118

Designs: 42s, 1986 Field Hockey World Cup, London. 57s, Women's basketball, 13th Commonwealth Games, Scotland. 1pa, Boxing, Commonwealth Games. 2.50pa, 1986 World Cup Soccer Championships, Mexico.

**1986, July 23** **Litho.** ***Perf. 14***

**631** A118 42s multicolored 1.25 1.25
**632** A118 57s multicolored 2.00 2.00
**633** A118 1pa multicolored 3.25 3.25
**634** A118 2.50pa multicolored 8.00 8.00
*Nos. 631-634 (4)* 14.50 14.50

Postage Stamp Cent. A119

Stamps on stamps: No. 635, #1. No. 636, #47a. No. 637, #91. No. 638, #628. No. 639a, #40, UL portion of #C29. No. 639b, UR portion of #C29, left side #245. No. 639c, Center of #245, Type AP10. No. 639d, Left side #245, #C148. No. 639e, LL portion of #C29, #429, #440. No. 639f, LR portion of #C29, #C135. No. 639g, #507. No. 639h, #514. Nos. 639a-639h, vert.

**1986, Aug. 27**

**635** A119 32s multi 2.50 1.75
**636** A119 42s multi 2.75 2.00
**637** A119 57s multi 3.50 2.00
**638** A119 2.50pa multi 5.75 5.75
*Nos. 635-638 (4)* 14.50 11.50

**Souvenir Sheet**

**639** Sheet of 8 15.00 15.00
*a.-h.* A119 50s, any single 1.50 1.50

Christmas — A120

Designs: 32s, Girls wearing shell jewelry. 42s, Boy, totem poles, vert. 57s, Folk dancers, vert. 2pa, outrigger canoe.

**1986, Nov. 12** **Litho.** ***Perf. 14***

**640** A120 32s multicolored 2.50 .75
**641** A120 42s multicolored 2.75 1.00
**642** A120 57s multicolored 3.00 1.50
**643** A120 2pa multicolored 6.25 6.25
*Nos. 640-643 (4)* 14.50 9.50

Nos. 641-642 Ovptd. with Jamboree Emblem and "BOY SCOUT / JAMBOREE / 5th-10th DEC '86" in Silver

**1986, Dec. 2** **Litho.** ***Perf. 14***

**644** A120 42s multicolored 3.50 3.50
**645** A120 57s multicolored 3.75 3.75

Dumont d'Urville's Second Voyage A121

Designs: 32s, D'Urville and ship Astrolabe. 42s, Four Tongan girls, detail fron D'Urville's engraving, Voyage au Pole et dans l'Oceanie. 1pa, Map of voyage. 2.50pa, Wreck of the Astrolabe.

**1987, Feb. 24**
**646** A121 32s multicolored 4.25 2.00
**647** A121 42s multicolored 4.25 2.00
**648** A121 1pa multicolored 10.00 6.00
**649** A121 2.50pa multicolored 16.00 16.00
*Nos. 646-649 (4)* 34.50 26.00

Dumont d'Urville (1790-1842), explorer and admiral.

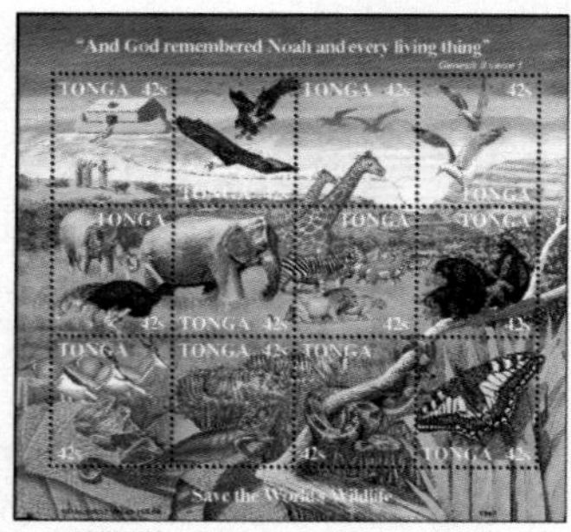

Wildlife Conservation — A122

Fauna: a, Noah's Ark. b, Eagles. c, Giraffes, birds. d, Seagulls. e, Elephants, ostriches. f, Elephant. g, Lions, zebras, antelopes. h, Chimpanzees. i, Antelope, frogs. j, Tigers, lizard. k, Tiger, snake. l, Butterfly.

**1987, May 6** ***Perf. 13½***
**650** Sheet of 12 62.50 62.50
***a.-l.*** A122 42s any single 4.00 4.00

1st Inter-island Canoe Race, Tonga to Samoa — A123

**1987, July 1** ***Perf. 14***
**651** A123 32s Two paddlers .55 .45
**652** A123 42s Five paddlers .85 .70
**653** A123 57s Three paddlers 1.10 .90
**654** A123 1.50pa Two, diff. 3.00 3.00
***a.*** Souvenir sheet of 4, #651-654 9.50 9.50
*Nos. 651-654 (4)* 5.50 5.05

Coronation of King Taufa'ahau IV, 20th Anniv. — A124

**Booklet Stamps**

**1987-88** ***Imperf.***

**Self-Adhesive**

**655** A124 1s green & yel grn .30 *.75*
**655A** A124 2s blk & pale yel org 3.50 3.50
**656** A124 5s black & brt pink .30 *.75*
***a.*** Bklt. pane of 12 (6 5s plus 1 5s, 2 10s, 3 15s with gutter between) 4.50
**657** A124 10s black & bluish lil .40 *.85*
**658** A124 15s brn blk & org ver .55 *.85*
***a.*** Bklt. pane of 12 (1s, 2 2s, 3 10s, plus 2 5s, 10s, 3 15s with gutter between) ('88) 12.50
**659** A124 32s Prus bl & aqua .65 *.90*
***a.*** Bklt. pane, 4 32s, 2 15s + 4 10s, 2 1s with gutter between) 6.25
***b.*** Bklt. pane, 6 32s + 2 2s, 4 1s with gutter btwn. ('88) 12.50
*Nos. 655-659 (6)* 5.70 7.60

Issued: 2s, 7/4/88; others, 7/1/87.

Parliament, 125th Anniv. — A125

**1987, Sept. 2 Litho.** ***Perf. 14½***
**660** A125 32s multicolored .50 .50
**661** A125 42s multicolored .75 .75
**662** A125 75s multicolored 1.50 1.50
**663** A125 2pa multicolored 3.00 3.00
*Nos. 660-663 (4)* 5.75 5.75

Christmas 1987 — A126

Cartoons featuring Octopus as Santa Claus and mouse as his helper.

**1987, Nov. 18 Litho.** ***Perf. 14***
**664** A126 42s Sack of gifts 1.50 .80
**665** A126 57s Delivering them by canoe 1.75 1.75
**666** A126 1pa By automobile 3.25 3.25
**667** A126 3pa Sipping tropical drinks 8.00 8.00
*Nos. 664-667 (4)* 14.50 13.80

King Taufa'ahau Tupou IV, 70th Birthday — A127

Portrait and: 32s, M.V. *Olovaha* inter-island ship, athlete pole vaulting and offshore oil derrick. 42s, Banknote and coins, Ha'Amonga Trilithon and traditional craftsman. 57s, Rowing, Red Cross nurse and communications satellite. 2.50pa, Tonga Scouts emblem, No. 506 and Friendly Islands Airways passenger plane.

**1988, July 4 Litho.** ***Perf. 11½***
**668** A127 32s multicolored 2.00 .90
**669** A127 42s multicolored 1.40 1.00
**670** A127 57s multicolored 1.50 1.00
**671** A127 2.50pa multicolored 7.50 7.50
*Nos. 668-671 (4)* 12.40 10.40

See Nos. 744-747 for stamps inscribed for the silver jubilee.

Souvenir Sheet

Australia Bicentennial — A128

Designs: a, Cook and his journal. b, List of stores shipped aboard the *Lady Juliana,* the ship, Arthur Philip, 1st gov. of New South Wales, 1788, and left half of the list of sentences of all the prisoners tried at Glo'ster Assizes. c, Right half of list of sentences, Australia Type A59 redrawn and aerial view of an early settlement. d, Robert O'Hara Burke (1820-61) and W.J. Wills (1834-61), the 1st explorers to cross Australia from south to north. e, Emu pictured on a Player's cigarette card, U.R. Stuart's (gold) prospecting license and opals. f, Australian Commonwealth Military Forces emblem, WW I recruit on cigarette card, and war poster. g, Souv. card commemorating 1st overland mail delivery by transcontinental railway, and Australia Type A4 on cover. h, Hand-canceled cover commemorating the 1st England-Australia transcontinental airmail flight, Nov. 12-Dec.10, 1919, aviator Capt. Ross Smith (1892-1922) and Great Britain #588. i, Don Bradman and Harold Larwood, cricket champions of the 1930s, on cigarette cards, and era newspaper frontispiece. j, Frontispiece of Hulton's natl. weekly *Picture Post* Victory Special issue, and WW II campaign medals. k, Australia #676 and a sheep station. l, Sydney Harbor Bridge, Opera House and theater tickets to *The Bartered Bride.*

**1988, July 11 Litho.** ***Perf. 13½***
**672** A128 Sheet of 12 45.00 45.00
***a.-l.*** 42s any single 3.00 3.00

1988 Summer Olympics, Seoul — A129

**1988, Aug. 11** ***Perf. 14***
**673** A129 57s Running .90 .90
**674** A129 75s Yachting 1.10 1.10
**675** A129 2pa Cycling 5.50 5.50
**676** A129 3pa Women's tennis 6.50 6.50
*Nos. 673-676 (4)* 14.00 14.00

Music of Tonga A130

**1988, Sept. 9 Litho.** ***Perf. 14***
**677** A130 32s shown .55 .45
**678** A130 42s Choir .75 .60
**679** A130 57s Tonga Police Band .95 .80
**680** A130 2.50pa The Jets 4.25 4.25
*Nos. 677-680 (4)* 6.50 6.10

**Souvenir Sheet**

**681** Sheet of 2 3.00 3.00
***a.*** A130 57s like 2.50pa 1.00 1.00
***b.*** A130 57s Olympic eternal flame 1.00 1.00

SPORT AID '88.

Marine Type of 1984

Two types of background shading on No. 690:
Type I: Shading at top and sides extends to vert. & horiz. edges of design.
Type II: Shading is oval shaped.

**1988 Litho.** ***Perf. 14½***

**Size: 27x34mm**

**682** A103 1s like No. 563 .25 .25
**683** A103 2s like No. 564 .35 .35
**684** A103 5s like No. 566 .45 .45
**685** A103 6s like No. 567 .90 .90
**686** A103 10s like No. 569 .55 .55
**687** A103 15s like No. 571 .55 .55
**688** A103 20s like No. 572 .80 .80
**689** A103 32s like No. 574 .90 .90
**690** A103 42s Fregata ariel, type I 3.25 .80
***a.*** Type II 30.00
**691** A103 57s Sula leucogaster 4.00 1.00

**Size: 41x27mm**

***Perf. 14***

**692** A103 3pa Like No. 578 2.50 *7.50*
*Nos. 682-692 (11)* 14.50 14.05

Issued: 1s, 5s, 10s, 20s, 32s, Oct. 4; 2s, 6s, 15s, 42s, 57s, 3pa, Oct. 18.

Nos. 683-684, 686, 689 exist inscribed "1990."

See #701-709. For surcharge see #808.

Tonga-US Treaty, Cent. A131

**1988, Oct. 20** ***Perf. 14***
**693** A131 42s *Resolution* 1.00 .75
**694** A131 57s *Santa Maria* 1.50 1.10
**695** A131 2pa Capt. Cook, Columbus 5.50 5.50
***a.*** Souvenir sheet of 3, #693-695 6.75 6.75
*Nos. 693-695 (3)* 8.00 7.35

Christmas — A132

Designs (a, Intl. Red Cross, b, Natl. Red Cross): 15s, Girl, teddy bear. 32s, Nurse reading to child. 42s, Checking pulse. 57s, Tucking child into bed. 1.50pa, Boy in wheelchair.

**1988, Nov. 17 Litho.** ***Perf. 14½***
**696** A132 15s Pair, #a.-b. .50 .50
**697** A132 32s Pair, #a.-b. 1.00 1.00
**698** A132 42s Pair, #a.-b. 1.10 1.10
**699** A132 57s Pair, #a.-b. 1.90 1.90
**700** A132 1.50pa Pair, #a.-b. 4.75 4.75
*Nos. 696-700 (5)* 9.25 9.25

Intl. Red Cross 125th anniv. and 25th anniv. of the natl. Red Cross.

Marine Type of 1984

**1989, Mar. 2 Litho.**

**Size: 27x34mm**

**701** A103 4s like No. 570 1.60 1.60
**702** A103 7s Diomedea exulans 3.75 2.50
**703** A103 35s Hippocampus 3.25 2.75
**704** A103 50s like No. 573 3.75 2.00

**Size: 41x27mm**

***Perf. 14***

**705** A103 1pa Chelonia mydas 6.00 4.50
**706** A103 1.50pa Megaptera novaeangliae 12.00 7.50
**707** A103 2pa like No. 577 8.75 8.75
**709** A103 5pa like No. 579 14.00 *17.00*
*Nos. 701-709 (8)* 53.10 46.60

Mutiny on the *Bounty,* Bicent. — A133

32s, Map of Tofua & Kao Isls., breadfruit. 42s, *Bounty,* chronometer. 57s, William Bligh & castaways in longboat. 2pa, Mutineers on the *Bounty,* vert. 3pa, Castaways.

***Perf. 13½x14, 14x13½***

**1989, Apr. 28 Photo.**
**710** A133 32s multicolored 4.50 2.50
**711** A133 42s multicolored 7.50 3.25
**712** A133 57s multicolored 10.00 4.75
*Nos. 710-712 (3)* 22.00 10.50

**Souvenir Sheet**

**713** Sheet of 2 17.00 17.00
***a.*** A133 2pa multicolored 5.00 5.00
***b.*** A133 3pa multicolored 7.50 7.50

Butterflies A134

**1989, May 15 Litho.** ***Perf. 14½***
**714** A134 42s *Hypolimnas bolina* 1.10 .75
**715** A134 57s *Jamides bochus* 1.40 1.00
**716** A134 1.20pa *Melanitis leda solandra* 3.25 2.50
**717** A134 2.50pa *Danaus plexippus* 6.25 6.25
*Nos. 714-717 (4)* 12.00 10.50

Opening of the Natl. Sports Stadium and the South Pacific Mini Games, Aug. 22
A135

Rugby (No. 718): a, Rugby Public School, 1870. b, Dave Gallaher and the Springboks vs. East Midlands, 1906. c, King George V inspecting Cambridge team of 1922 and Wavell Wakefield, captain of England. d, Ernie Crawford, captain of Ireland, Danie Craven demonstrating the dive pass and cigarette cards from the 1930's. e, Sioni Mafi, captain of Tonga, and match scene.

Tennis (No. 719): a, Royal tennis, 1659. b, Walter Clopton Wingfield and game of lawn tennis, 1873. c, Oxford and Cambridge teams of 1884. d, Bunny Ryan in 1910 and cigarette cards. e, Tennis players, 1980's.

Cricket (No. 720): a, Match in 1743 and bronze memorial to Fuller Pilch. b, W.G. Grace, 19th cent. c, *The Boys Own Paper,* 1909. d, Australian team of 1909 and cigarette cards. e, The Ashes trophy and modern match scene.

**1989, Aug. 22 Litho. *Perf. 14***

**718** Strip of 5 6.25 6.25
***a.-e.*** A135 32s any single 1.00 1.00
**719** Strip of 5 9.50 9.50
***a.-e.*** A135 42s any single 1.50 1.50
**720** Strip of 5 14.50 14.50
***a.-e.*** A135 57s any single 2.50 2.50
*Nos. 718-720 (3)* 30.25 30.25

Printed in sheets of 10 containing descriptions and emblem.

Natl. Aviation History — A136

Designs: 42s, Short S30. 57s, Vought F4U Corsair. 90s, Boeing 737. 3pa, Montgolfier brothers' hot-air balloon, the Wright Flyer, Concorde jet and space shuttle.

**1989, Oct. 23 Litho. *Perf. 14½x14***

**721** A136 42s multicolored 3.25 1.60
**722** A136 57s multicolored 3.75 2.00
**723** A136 90s multicolored 6.50 6.00

**Size: 97x126½mm**

**724** A136 3pa multicolored 16.00 16.00
*Nos. 721-724 (4)* 29.50 25.60

1st Flight to Tonga, 1939 (42s); military base on the island, 1943 (57s); civil aviation, Fua'amotu Airport (90s); aviation through the ages (3pa).

Flying Home for Christmas
A137

**1989, Nov. 9 *Perf. 14x13½***

**725** A137 32s Aircraft landing 2.00 .90
**726** A137 42s Islanders waving, aircraft 2.25 .90
**727** A137 57s Tongan in outrigger canoe, aircraft 2.50 1.25
**728** A137 3pa Islanders waving, aircraft, diff. 6.75 6.75
*Nos. 725-728 (4)* 13.50 9.80

World Stamp Expo '89
A138

20th UPU Congress, Washington, DC — A139

Postal history and communications (No. 730): a, Sir Rowland Hill, penny blacks on Mulready envelope. b, Clipper ship, early train. c, Pony Express advertisement, stagecoach, post rider. d, Hot-air balloon and flight cover. e, Samuel Morse, miniature, telegraph key. f, Early Royal Mail truck, mailbox. g, Biplane and early aviators. h, Zeppelin flight cover, HMS *Queen Mary.* i, Helicopter, truck. j, Computer operator, facsimile machine. k, Apollo 11 mission emblem, flight cover, planetary bodies. l, American space shuttle, UPU monument.

**1989, Nov. 17 Litho. *Perf. 14***

**729** A138 57s Pair, #730k-730 l 3.50 3.50

**Souvenir Sheet**

***Perf. 13½***

**730** A139 Sheet of 12 42.50 42.50
***a.-l.*** A139 57s any single 2.50 2.50

A140

A141

**1990, Feb. 14 Litho. *Perf. 14***

**731** A140 42s Boxing 1.25 .75
**732** A140 57s Archery 2.25 1.50
**733** A140 1pa Bowls 3.00 3.00
**734** A140 2pa Swimming 5.00 5.00
*Nos. 731-734 (4)* 11.50 10.25

1990 Commonwealth Games.

**1990, Apr. 11 Litho. *Perf. 14***

Protect the Environment: 32s, Wave power, ocean pollution. 57s, Wind power, acid rain. $1.20, Solar power, ozone layer. $2.50, Green earth, rain forests.

**735** A141 32s multicolored 2.50 .90
**736** A141 57s multicolored 3.50 1.50
**737** A141 1.20pa multicolored 7.00 7.00
*Nos. 735-737 (3)* 13.00 9.40

**Souvenir Sheet**

**738** A141 2.50pa multicolored 13.00 13.00

First Postage Stamps, 150th Anniv.
A142

**1990 Litho. *Perf. 14***

**739** A142 42s G. B. #1 2.10 1.50
**740** A142 42s G. B. #2 2.10 1.50
***a.*** Pair, #739-740 3.75 3.75
**741** A142 57s Tonga #1 2.50 1.50
**742** A142 1.50pa Tonga #CO180 6.00 6.00
**743** A142 2.50pa Tonga #736 9.00 9.00
*Nos. 739-743 (5)* 21.70 19.50

King's Birthday Type of 1988 Inscribed "Silver Jubilee of His Majesty King Taufa'ahau Tupou IV 1965-1990"

**1990, July 4 Litho. *Perf. 11½***

**744** A127 32s like No. 668 1.50 1.00
**745** A127 42s like No. 669 1.50 1.00
**746** A127 57s like No. 670 2.25 1.25
**747** A127 2.50pa like No. 671 7.75 7.75
*Nos. 744-747 (4)* 13.00 11.00

Native Catamaran — A143

**1990, June 6 *Perf. 14½***

**748** A143 32s buff & green 1.60 .75
**749** A143 42s buff & bl, diff. 1.60 .85
**750** A143 1.20pa buff & brn, diff. 4.25 4.25
**751** A143 3pa buff & vio, diff. 8.50 8.50
*Nos. 748-751 (4)* 15.95 14.35

Banded Iguana
A144

**1990, Sept. 12 Litho. *Perf. 14***

**752** A144 32s multicolored 2.00 1.25
**753** A144 42s multi, diff. 2.50 1.75
**754** A144 57s multi, diff. 3.25 2.25
**755** A144 1.20pa multi, diff. 8.25 4.75
*Nos. 752-755 (4)* 16.00 10.00

Marine Type of 1984

**1990, July 6 Litho. *Perf. 14***

**Size: 20x22mm**

**756** A103 2s like No. 564 1.10 .75
***a.*** Booklet pane of 10 11.00 11.00
**757** A103 5s like No. 566 1.10 .75
***a.*** Booklet pane of 10 11.00 11.00
**758** A103 10s like No. 569 1.10 .75
***a.*** Booklet pane of 10 11.00 11.00
**759** A103 32s like No. 574 2.00 2.00
***a.*** Booklet pane of 10 20.00 20.00
*Nos. 756-759 (4)* 5.30 4.25

Nos. 756-758 exist inscribed "1992."
For surcharge see No. 810.
Issue date: #756a-759a, Sept. 4.

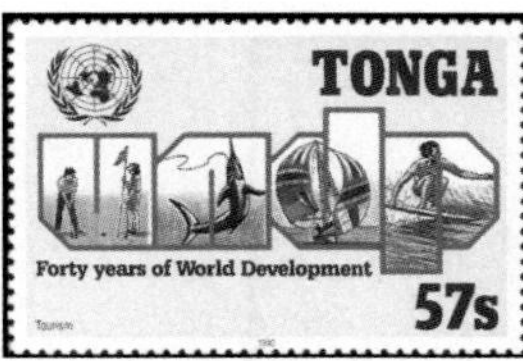


UN Development Program, 40th Anniv. — A145

**1990, Oct. 25 Litho. *Perf. 14***

**760** A145 57s Tourism 2.00 2.00
**761** A145 57s Agriculture, fisheries 2.00 2.00
***a.*** Pair, #760-761 4.50 4.50
**762** A145 3pa Education 10.00 10.00
**763** A145 3pa Healthcare 10.00 10.00
***a.*** Pair, #762-763 22.50 22.50
*Nos. 760-763 (4)* 24.00 24.00

Rotary Intl. — A146

Accident Prevention
A147

**1990, Nov. 28**

**764** A146 32s shown 1.00 .55
**765** A146 42s Two boys 1.50 .80
**766** A146 2pa Three children 5.00 5.00
**767** A146 3pa Two girls 6.50 6.50
*Nos. 764-767 (4)* 14.00 12.85

**1991, Apr. 10 Litho. *Perf. 14½***

No. 768: a, d, Care at work; hard hats save lives. b, c, Keep matches and medicines out of children's reach. e, as "d," corrected inscription

No. 769: a, d, Don't drink and drive. b, c, Crash helmets save lives; mind cyclists and children.

No. 770: a, d, Listen to forecasts; learn to swim. b, c, Swim from safe beaches; beware of broken glass.

"a" and "b" have English inscriptions, denominations at top; "c" and "d" have Tongan inscriptions, denominations at bottom.

**Strips of 4 + Label**

**768** A147 32s #a.-d. 5.25 5.25
***f.*** Strip of 4, #a.-c., e. 32.50
**769** A147 42s #a.-d. 7.50 7.50
**770** A147 57s #a.-d. 9.25 9.25
*Nos. 768-770 (3)* 22.00 22.00

Center label is a progressive proof.

No. 768d was incorrectly inscribed, "Ngauo tokanga." No. 768e was issued 8/11/91 with correct inscription, "Ngaue tokanga."

For surcharges see No. 811, 1124.

A148

A149

**1991, July 2 Litho. *Perf. 14½***

**771** A148 42s Fish .80 .70
**772** A148 57s Island, boat .95 .85
**773** A148 2pa Fruit, island 3.50 3.50
**774** A148 3pa Turtle, beach 6.25 6.25
*Nos. 771-774 (4)* 11.50 11.30

Heilala week.

**1991, July 2**

Racing yachts: a, Red spinnaker. b, Yellow spinnaker. c, Green striped spinnaker. d, Yacht at sunset. e, Yacht, moon.

**Miniature Sheet of 5 + Label**

**775** A149 1pa #775a-775e 13.00 13.00

Around the world yacht race.

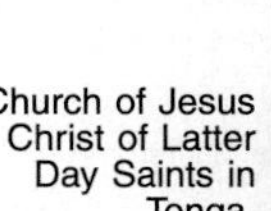

Church of Jesus Christ of Latter Day Saints in Tonga, Cent. — A150

**1991, Aug. 19**

**776** A150 42s Tonga Temple 1.75 1.75
**777** A150 57s Temple at night 2.75 2.75

Rowing Festival A151

**1991, Oct. 29 Litho. *Perf. 14***

**778** A151 42s Women's coxed eight 1.00 1.00
**779** A151 57s Men's longboat 1.50 1.50
**780** A151 1pa Outrigger 2.75 2.75
**781** A151 2pa Bow of large canoe 5.25 5.25
**782** A151 2pa Stern of large canoe 5.25 5.25
*a.* Pair, #781-782 11.00 11.00
*Nos. 778-782 (5)* 15.75 15.75

For surcharges see Nos. 898-899C.

Telecommunications — A152

No. 783: a, Recording television program. b, Communications Satellite. c, Watching television program.

No. 784: a, Man on telephone, woman at computer. b, Communications satellite, diff. c, Man in city on telephone.

No. 785: a, Seaman on sinking ship broadcasting SOS. b, Man on telephone, satellite relay station. c, Rescue missions.

No. 786: a, Weather satelite. b, Men at computers. c, Television weather report, storm.

**1991, Oct. 15 Litho. *Perf. 14½***

**783** A152 15s Strip of 3, #a.-c. 1.50 1.50
**784** A152 32s Strip of 3, #a.-c. 3.00 3.00
**785** A152 42s Strip of 3, #a.-c. 4.25 4.25
**786** A152 57s Strip of 3, #a.-c. 6.00 6.00
*Nos. 783-786 (4)* 14.75 14.75

For surcharges, see 1095-1097.

Christmas — A153

Designs: 32s, Turtles pulling Santa's sleigh. 42s, Santa on roof. 57s, Family with presents. 3.50pa, Waving goodbye to Santa.

**1991, Nov. 11 *Perf. 14***

**787** A153 32s multicolored 1.00 .70
**788** A153 42s multicolored 1.25 .90
**789** A153 57s multicolored 1.75 1.75
**790** A153 3.50pa multicolored 10.00 10.00
*Nos. 787-790 (4)* 14.00 13.35

For surcharges, see 1120-1122.

Armed Forces — A154

**1991, Dec. 15**

**791** 42s Royal Tonga Marine 1.00 1.00
**792** 42s Patrol boat Pangai 1.00 1.00
*a.* A154 Pair, #791-792 2.50 2.50
**793** 57s Patrol boat Neiafu 1.50 1.50
**794** 57s Tonga Royal Guards 1.50 1.50
*a.* A154 Pair, #793-794 3.50 3.50
**795** 2pa King Tupou IV, military parade 5.25 5.25
**796** 2pa Patrol boat Savea 5.25 5.25
*a.* A154 Pair, #795-796 11.00 11.00
*Nos. 791-796 (6)* 15.50 15.50

Miniature Sheet

Discovery of America, 500th Anniv. — A155

Designs: a, Columbus. b, Monastery of Santa Maria de la Chevas. c, Obverse and reverse of coin of Ferdinand and Isabella. d, Spain #C48, #426. e, Compass, astrolabe. f, Santa Maria. g, Map, Columbus' signature. h, Columbus arriving in New World. i, Lucayan artifacts, parrot. j, Pineapple, artifacts. k, Columbus announcing his discovery. l, Medal of Columbus, signature.

**1992, Apr. 28 Litho. *Perf. 13½***

**797** A155 57s Sheet of 12, #a.-l. 40.00 40.00

Marine Type of 1984 and

A155a

***Perf. 13x13½, 14 (15s, 20s, 10pa)***

**1992-93 Litho.**

**798** A155a 1s Swainsonia casta .20 .20
**799** A155a 3s Holocentrus ruber .20 .20
**800** A155a 5s Cypraea mappa viridis .20 .20
**801** A155a 10s Conus bullatus .20 .20
**802** A103 15s like #567 .25 .25
**803** A155a 20s Dascyllus aruanus .30 .30
**804** A155a 45s Lambis truncata .70 .70
**805** A155a 60s Conus aulicus .90 .90
**806** A155a 80s Pterois volitans 1.25 1.25

**Size: 27x41mm**

**807** A103 10pa like #568 18.00 18.00
*Nos. 798-807 (10)* 22.20 22.20

Issued: 1s, 3s, 5s, 10s, 20s, 45s, 60s, 80s, May 12, 1993. 15s, 10pa, May 5, 1992.

See Nos. 874-884. Area covered by background colors on Nos. 874, 876-879 has been reduced in size. See Nos. 920-924.

For inscribed stamps see Nos. O78-O87.

**Surcharges**

On #688

*xx*

*10s*

On #756 in Blue

On #759

On #769 in Red and Black

**1992-93 Litho. *Perf. 14½, 14***

**808** A103 1s on 20s #688 .20 .20
**809** A103 10s on 2s #756
**810** A103 45s on 32s #759 4.00 4.00
**811** A147 60s on 42s Strip of 4, #a.-d. + label 16.00 16.00

Issued: 1s, 5/19; 45s, 60s, 8/11; 10s, 1993.

Miniature Sheet

World War II in Pacific, 50th Anniv. A156

Designs: a, Newspaper headline, Japanese attack on Pearl Harbor. b, Map of Bataan, Corregidor, and Manila, pilot's wings, airplanes. c, Newspaper headline, troops landing in Gilbert Islands, Marine Corps emblem, dogtags. d, Uniform patch, B-29 "Enola Gay," troops landing on Iwo Jima. e, Map of Battle of Midway, Admiral Nimitz. f, Southwest Pacific campaign map, Gen. MacArthur. g, Map of Saipan and Tinian, Lt. Gen. Holland Smith. h, Map outling bombing of Japan, Maj. Gen. Curtis Lemay. i, Mitsubishi A6M Zero. j, Douglas SBD Dauntless. k, Grumman F4F Wildcat. l, Supermarine Seafire.

**1992, May 26 Litho. *Perf. 14***

**814** A156 42s Sheet of 12, #a.-l. 30.00 30.00

1992 Summer Olympics, Barcelona — A157

**1992, June 16**

**815** A157 42s Boxing 1.25 .85
**816** A157 57s Diving 1.75 1.10
**817** A157 1.50pa Tennis 4.50 4.50
**818** A157 3pa Cycling 9.50 9.50
*Nos. 815-818 (4)* 17.00 15.95

For surcharges, see 1123, 1125.

King Taufa'ahau IV, 25th Anniv. of Coronation A158

Designs: 45s, 2pa, King, Queen Halaevalu. No. 820a, King, crown. b, Extract from investiture ceremony. c, King, #C33.

**1992, July 4 *Perf. 13½x13***

**819** A158 45s multicolored 1.25 .90

**Size: 51x38mm**

***Perf. 12½x12***

**820** A158 80s Strip of 3, #a.-c. 6.50 6.50
**821** A158 2pa multicolored 5.25 5.25
*Nos. 819-821 (3)* 13.00 12.65

Sacred Bats of Kolovai — A159

Designs: No. 822a, Bats in flight. b, Close-up of flying bat. c, Flying bats, tree. d, Bats hanging in tree. e, Bat hanging from tree limb.

Origin of sacred bats: No. 823a, 45s, Kula leaving for Upolu to be tattooed as Tongan chief. b, 45s, Kula looking through path of fires. c, 2pa, Kula walking down path, Hina. d, 2pa, Hina waving, Kula leaving with pet fruit bats.

Nos. 823a-823d are horiz.

**1992, Oct. 20 Litho. *Perf. 14***

**822** A159 60s Strip of 5, #a.-e. 13.00 13.00

**Souvenir Sheet**

***Perf. 14½***

**823** A159 Sheet of 4, #a.-d. 14.00 14.00

Christmas A160

**1992, Nov. 10 *Perf. 14***

**824** A160 60s Pearls 1.50 1.10
**825** A160 80s Reef fish 2.00 1.40
**826** A160 2pa Pacific orchids 4.75 4.75
**827** A160 3pa Eua parrots 7.25 7.25
*Nos. 824-827 (4)* 15.50 14.50

For surcharges see Nos. 894-897.

Anniversaries and Events — A161

Designs: 60s, Tonga flag, Rotary emblem. 80sh, John F. Kennedy, Peace Corps emblem. 1.50pa, FAO, WHO emblems. 3.50pa, Globe, Rotary Foundation emblem.

**1992, Dec. 15 *Perf. 14½***

**828** A161 60s multicolored 1.40 1.00
**829** A161 80s multicolored 1.90 1.40
**830** A161 1.50pa multicolored 3.50 3.50
**831** A161 3.50pa multicolored 8.50 8.50
*Nos. 828-831 (4)* 15.30 14.40

Rotary Intl. in Tonga, 25th anniv. (#828). Peace Corps in Tonga, 25th anniv. (#829). Intl. Conference of FAO and WHO (#830). Rotary Foundation of Rotary Intl., 75th anniv. (#831).

For overprint see No. 868.

Family Planning — A163

Outdoor silhouette scenes: No. 832, Mother, girl, butterflies. No. 833, Child on tricycle pulling kite. No. 834, Girl, kittens. No. 835, Adult, child playing chess.

**1993, Jan. 26 *Perf. 14x13½***

**832** A163 15s Pair, #a.-b. 2.50 2.50
**833** A163 45s Pair, #a.-b. 3.50 3.50
**834** A163 60s Pair, #a.-b. 5.00 5.00
**835** A163 2pa Pair, #a.-b. 15.00 15.00
*Nos. 832-835 (4)* 26.00 26.00

Nos. 832a-835a have Tongan inscriptions. Nos. 832b-835b have English inscriptions and are mirror images of Nos. 832a-835a.

Health and Fitness — A164

Designs: 60s, Fresh fruit, fish, anti-smoking and anti-drug symbols. 80s, Anti-smoking symbol, weight training. 1.50pa, Anti-drug symbol, water sports. 2.50pa, Fresh fruit, fish, cyclist, jogger. Illustration reduced.

**1993, Mar. 16 Litho. *Perf. 14***

**836** A164 60s multicolored 2.00 2.00
**837** A164 80s multicolored 2.75 2.75
**838** A164 1.50pa multicolored 5.25 5.25
**839** A164 2.50pa multicolored 8.50 8.50
*Nos. 836-839 (4)* 18.50 18.50

Tonga Fire Service, 25th Anniv. A165

**1993, May 18 Litho. *Perf. 14***

840 A165 45s Fireman's badge 2.00 2.00
841 A165 45s Police van, badge 2.00 2.00
*a.* Pair, #840-841 3.50 3.50
842 A165 60s Police band 2.50 2.50
843 A165 60s Putting out fire 2.50 2.50
*a.* Pair, #842-843 4.50 4.50
844 A165 2pa Fire truck at station 9.00 9.00
845 A165 2pa Policeman, police dog 9.00 9.00
*a.* Pair, #844-845 15.00 15.00
*Nos. 840-845 (6)* 27.00 27.00

Tonga Police Training College, 25th anniv. (#841-842, 845).
For surcharges see Nos. 943-948.

A166

A167

Abel Tasman's Voyage to Eua, 350th Anniv.: 30s, Map of islands. 60s, Sailing ships, Heemskirk and Zeehaen. 80s, Sailing ships, natives in canoes. 3.50pa, Landing on Eua.

**1993, June 21**

846 A166 30s multicolored .80 .50
847 A166 60s multicolored 1.75 1.10
848 A166 80s multicolored 2.25 2.25
849 A166 3.50pa multicolored 10.00 10.00
*Nos. 846-849 (4)* 14.80 13.85

**1993, July 1 Litho. *Perf. 13x13½***

King Taufa'ahau IV, 75th Birthday: 45s, 2pa, Musical instruments.
No. 851a, Sporting events. b, Ancient landmarks. c, Royal Palace.

850 A167 45s multicolored .65 .65

***Perf. 12x12½***

**Size: 37x48mm**

851 A167 80s Strip of 3, #a.-c. 5.00 5.00
852 A167 2pa multicolored 3.00 3.00
*Nos. 850-852 (3)* 8.65 8.65

A168

A168a

Children's Stamp Designs: Nos. 853a, 854a, Beach scene. Nos. 853b, 854b, "Maui-The Fisher of the Islands." Nos. 853c, 854c, Raft on ocean. Nos. 853d, 854d, Woman with hands in mixing bowl. Nos. 853e, 854e, "Maui and his Hook." Nos. 853f, 854f, "Communication in the South Pacific."

**1993, Dec. 1 Litho. *Perf. 14***

853 A168 10s Strip of 6, #a.-f. 3.00 3.00
854 A168 80s Strip of 6, #a.-f. 14.00 14.00

**1993, Nov. 10 Litho. *Perf. 14***

Christmas traditions: 60s, Festive dinner. 80s, Shooting cannon. 1.50pa, Musicians. 3pa, Going to church.

855 A168a 60s multicolored 1.50 1.25
856 A168a 80s multicolored 2.00 1.50
857 A168a 1.50pa multicolored 3.75 3.75
858 A168a 3pa multicolored 7.75 7.75
*Nos. 855-858 (4)* 15.00 14.25

Miniature Sheet

Kindness to Animals — A169

Designs: a, 80s, Boy holding puppy. b, 80s, Girl holding kitten. c, 60s, Boy holding rooster (b). d, 60s, Girl with butterfly. e, 60s, Three dogs. f, 60s, Boy, puppy.

**1994, Jan. 14 *Perf. 14½***

859 A169 Sheet of 6, #a.-f. 17.50 17.50

For overprint see No. 868.

Game Fishing — A170

**1994, Feb. 28 Litho. *Perf. 12***

860 A170 60s Tiger shark 1.50 1.00
861 A170 80s Dolphin fish 2.00 1.40
862 A170 1.50pa Yellow fin tuna 4.00 4.00
863 A170 2.50pa Pacific blue marlin 6.50 6.50
*Nos. 860-863 (4)* 14.00 12.90

1994 World Cup Soccer Championships, US — A171

Designs: No. 864a, Player's legs. No. 864b, World Cup trophy. No. 865a, American player in red, white, & blue. No. 865b, German player in black shorts, white shirt.

**1994, June 1 *Perf. 14x14½***

864 A171 80s Pair, #a.-b. 4.00 4.00
865 A171 2pa Pair, #a.-b. 10.00 10.00

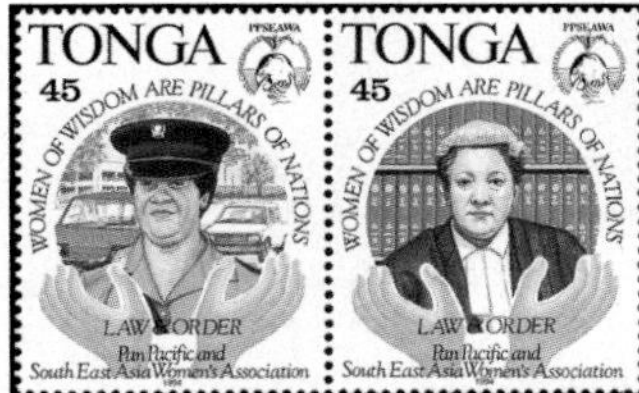

Pan Pacific & South East Asia Women's Assoc. Conference — A172

Career women: No. 866a, Lawyer. No. 866b, Policewoman. No. 867a, Doctor. No. 867b. Nurse.

**1994, Aug. 18 Litho. *Perf. 14***

866 A172 45s Pair, #a.-b. 3.50 3.50
867 A172 2.50pa Pair, #a.-b. 10.50 10.50

Nos. 859a, 859c-859f Ovptd. "MERRY / CHRISTMAS"
No. 859b Ovptd. "KILISIMASI FIEFIA"

**1994, Nov. 10 Litho. *Perf. 14½***

868 A169 Sheet of 6, #a.-f. 8.50 8.50

No. 831 Ovptd. in Dark Blue

**1994, Nov. 17 Litho. *Perf. 14½***

869 A161 60s on 3.50pa multi 4.00 4.00

Types of 1969-85 and

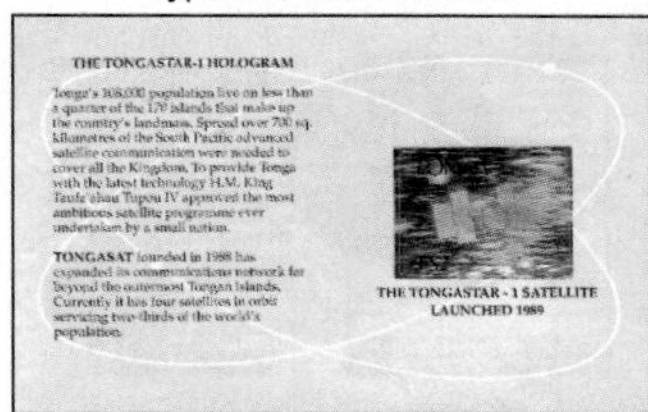

Tongastar 1 Satellite — A173

Design: a, 10s, Type A39 banana, size 22x11mm. b, 25s, Type AP12. c, Booklet pane, 12 #870a, 3 #870b. d, 45s, like #608. e, 45s, like #609. f, 45s, like #610. g, 45s, like #611. h, Booklet pane of 3 each #870d-870e, 2 #870f, 1 #870g. i, 60s, Type A72. j, 60s, Type OA19. k, 80s, Type OA17. l, Booklet pane, #870i-870k. m, 2pa, Tongastar 1. n, Booklet pane of 1 #870m.

**Unwmk.**

**1994, Dec. 14 Litho. *Die Cut***

**Self-adhesive**

870 A173 Souvenir booklet 26.50

First full-scale production of self-adhesive stamps by Tonga, 25th anniv. (#870). Satellite communications network for Tongan Islands (#870m).
No. 870b is airmail. Nos. 870j-870k are air post official stamps.
No. 870m contains a holographic image. Soaking in water may affect the hologram.

Marine Type of 1992-93 Redrawn

**1994-95 Litho. *Perf. 14***

874 A155a 10s like #799A .20 .20
876 A155a 20s like #801 .30 .30
877 A155a 45s like #803 .70 .70
878 A155a 60s like #804 .95 .95
879 A155a 80s like #806 1.25 1.25

**Size: 41x27mm, 41x27mm**

880 A155a 1pa like #705, horiz. 1.90 1.90
881 A155a 2pa like #577, horiz. 3.75 3.75
882 A155a 3pa like #578, horiz. 5.75 5.75
883 A155a 5pa like #706 9.50 9.50
884 A155a 10pa like #568 20.00 20.00
*Nos. 874-884 (10)* 44.30 44.30

Area covered by background colors on Nos. 874, 876-879 has been reduced in size.
Issued: 1pa, 2pa, 3pa, 6/21/94; 5pa, 9/21/94; 10pa, 1/18/95; 10s, 20s, 45s, 60s, 80s, 9/25/95.
This is an expanding set. Numbers may change.

FAO, 50th Anniv. A174

**1995, May 16 Litho. *Perf. 14***

886 A174 5pa multicolored 17.00 17.00

Tonga's Entry into British Commonwealth, 25th Anniv. — A175

Children with bicycles from parts of Commonwealth.

**1995, June 6**

887 A175 45s Polynesia 1.10 .90
888 A175 60s Asia 1.50 1.25
889 A175 80s Africa 1.75 1.75
890 A175 2pa India 4.50 4.50
891 A175 2.50pa Europe 6.00 6.00
*Nos. 887-891 (5)* 14.85 14.40

1995 Rugby World Cup, South Africa — A176

Designs: No. 892a, Player running right with ball, two others. b, Two players. No. 893a, Three players. b, Player ready to catch ball.

**1995, June 20 *Perf. 14½***

892 A176 80s Pair, #a.-b. 6.00 6.00
893 A176 2pa Pair, #a.-b. 13.50 13.50

Nos. 892-893 were each issued in sheets of 4 stamps.
For surcharges see Nos. 954A, 956A.

Nos. 824-827 Surcharged

i

j

**1995, June 30 Litho. *Perf. 14***

894 60s Pair 4.00 4.00
*a.* A160(i) on #824 1.75 1.75
*b.* A160(j) on #824 1.75 1.75
895 60s Pair 4.00 4.00
*a.* A160(i) on 80s #825 1.75 1.75
*b.* A160(j) on 80s #825 1.75 1.75
896 60s Pair 4.00 4.00
*a.* A160(i) on 2pa #826 1.75 1.75
*b.* A160(j) on 2pa #826 1.75 1.75
897 60s Pair 4.00 4.00
*a.* A160(i) on 3pa #827 1.75 1.75
*b.* A160(j) on 3pa #827 1.75 1.75
*Nos. 894-897 (4)* 16.00 16.00

Nos. 779-782 Surcharged

**1995, June 30 Litho. *Perf. 14***

898 A151 60s on 57s #779 1.40 1.40
899 A151 80s on 2pa #781 1.75 1.75
899A A151 80s on 2pa #782 1.75 1.75
*b.* Pair, #899-899A 3.50 3.50
899C A151 1pa on #780 2.25 2.25
*Nos. 898-899C (4)* 7.15 7.15

Victory in the Pacific, 50th Anniv. — A177

Nos. 900, 901: a, Soldier climbing from rope ladder. b, Ship, soldiers. c, Ship, landing craft with troops, soldiers up close. d, Ship, landing craft with troops. e, Map.

**1995, Aug. 1 Litho. *Perf. 14x14½***

**900** A177 60s Strip of 5, #a.-e. 10.00 10.00
**901** A177 80s Strip of 5, #a.-e. 12.00 12.00

Nos. 900-901 are continuous designs and were issued together in sheet containing ten stamps.

Singapore '95 — A178

Designs: No. 902a, 45s, #887. b, 60s, #888. 2pa, Boy cycling in Singapore.

**1995, Sept. 1 Litho. *Perf. 12***

**902** A178 Pair, #a.-b. 3.75 3.75

**Souvenir Sheet**

**903** A178 2pa multicolored 5.25 5.25

Souvenir Sheet

Beijing Intl. Coin & Stamp Show '95 — A179

Design: 1.40pa, Mount Song, Henan Province, China. Illustration reduced.

**1995, Sept. 14 *Perf. 14½***

**904** A179 1.40pa multicolored 5.00 5.00

End of World War II, UN, 50th Anniv. — A180

No. 905a, Holocaust survivors. b, UN emblem, "50." c, Children of Holocaust survivors in celebration.
No. 906a, Mushroom cloud from atom bomb explosion. b, Like #905b. c, Space shuttle.

**1995, Oct. 20 Litho. *Perf. 13***

**905** A180 60s Strip of 3, #a.-c. 4.00 4.00
**906** A180 80s Strip of 3, #a.-c. 7.50 7.50

Nos. 905b, 906b are 23x31mm.

Christmas and New Year — A181

Orchids: 20s, Calanthe triplicata. Nos. 908, Spathoglottis plicata, inscribed "MERRY CHRISTMAS." No. 909, like #908, inscribed "A HAPPY 1996." No. 910, Dendrobium platygastrium, inscribed "MERRY CHRISTMAS". No. 911, like #910, inscribed "A HAPPY 1996." 80s, Goodyera rubicunda. 2pa, Dendrobium toki. 2.50pa, Phaius tankervilliae.

**1995, Nov. 15 Litho. *Perf. 14x14½***

**907** A181 20s multicolored .75 .75
**908** A181 45s multicolored 1.00 1.00
**909** A181 45s multicolored 1.00 1.00
**910** A181 60s multicolored 1.25 1.25
**911** A181 60s multicolored 1.25 1.25
**912** A181 80s multicolored 1.75 1.75
**913** A181 2pa multicolored 5.00 5.00
**914** A181 2.50pa multicolored 6.00 6.00
*Nos. 907-914 (8)* 18.00 18.00

Humpback Whale — A182

**1996, Jan. 7 *Perf. 14***

**915** A182 45s In water 2.10 2.10
**916** A182 60s With calf 3.25 3.25
**917** A182 1.50pa Sounding 6.50 6.50
**918** A182 2.50pa Breaching 9.25 9.75
*Nos. 915-918 (4)* 21.10 21.60

World Wildlife Fund.

Miniature Sheet

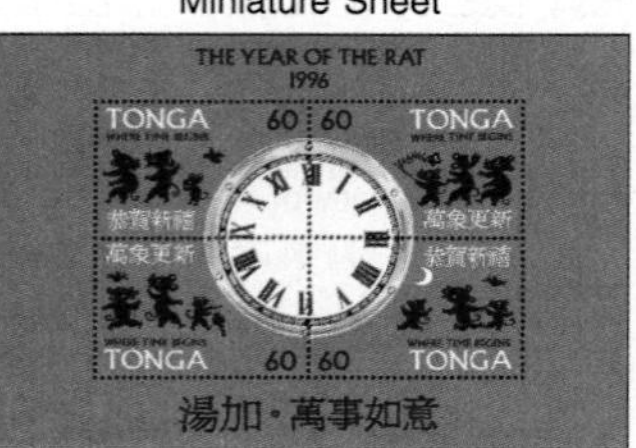
New Year 1996 (Year of the Rat) — A183

Denomination: a, UR. b, UL. c, LR. d, LL.

**1996, Feb. 23**

**919** A183 60s Sheet of 4, #a.-d. 7.50 7.50

No. 919 is a continuous design.
See Nos. 930-932, 932E, 942, 986.

Marine Type of 1992-93 Redrawn

**1996, May 31 Litho. *Perf. 14***

**Size: 40x26mm**

**920** A155a 1pa like #880 2.10 2.10
**921** A155a 2pa like #881 4.25 4.25
**922** A155a 3pa like #882 6.75 6.75
**923** A155a 5pa like #883 11.00 11.00
**924** A155a 10pa like #884 22.50 22.50
*Nos. 920-924 (5)* 46.60 46.60

Size of "TONGA" on Nos. 920-923 is smaller than on Nos. 880-883. Name of species appears at top instead of bottom on Nos. 920-924. Background colors vary. Inscribed "1996."

1996 Summer Olympic Games, Atlanta — A184

Statues of classical Greek figures, modern athletes: 45s, Zeus, runner. 80s, The Discus Thrower. 2pa, The Javelin Thrower. 3pa, The Horseman, dressage competitor.

**1996, July 2 Litho. *Perf. 14***

**925** A184 45s multicolored 1.25 .80
**926** A184 80s multicolored 2.00 1.90
**927** A184 2pa multicolored 5.75 5.75
**928** A184 3pa multicolored 9.00 9.00
*Nos. 925-928 (4)* 18.00 17.45

For surcharges & overprint see Nos. 949-952.

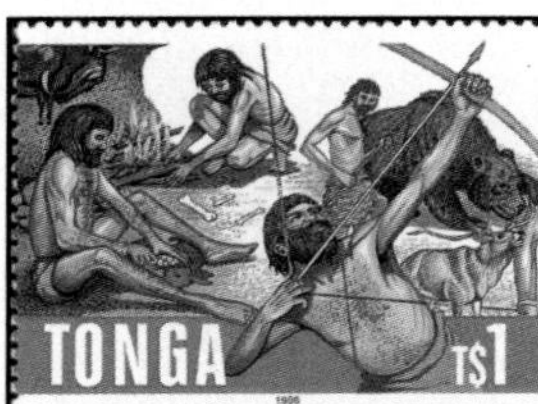
13th Congress of Intl. Union of Preshistoric and Protohistoric Sciences — A185

a, Prehistoric man using fire, knife, bow & arrow, animals. b, Ancient Egyptians, Greeks, Romans.

**1996, Sept. 5 Litho. *Perf. 12***

**929** A185 1pa Pair, #a.-b. 7.50 7.50

No. 929 was issued in sheets of 6 stamps.

New Year 1996 (Year of the Rat) Type

Denomination: a, UR. b, UL. c, LR. d, LL.

**1996, June 27 Litho. *Perf. 14***

**Sheets of 4**

**930** A183 10s #a.-d. 1.40 1.40
**931** A183 20s #a.-d. 2.75 2.75
**932** A183 45s #a.-d. 6.75 6.75
**932E** A183 60s #a.-d. 10.00 10.00

The denominations are larger on No. 932E than those on No. 919.

Christmas A186

Paintings: 20s, Virgin and Child, by Sassoferrato. 60s, Adoration of the Shepherds, by Murillo. 80s, Virgin and Child, by Delaroche. 1pa, Adoration of the Shepherds, by Champaigne.

**1996, Oct. 29 Litho. *Perf. 14***

**933** A186 20s multicolored .75 .50
**934** A186 60s multicolored 2.50 1.50
**935** A186 80s multicolored 2.75 2.50
**936** A186 1pa multicolored 8.50 8.50
*Nos. 933-936 (4)* 14.50 13.00

UNICEF, 50th Anniv. — A187

Children in sports activities: a, Running, playing rugby. b, Tennis. c, Cycling.

**1996, Oct. 29**

**937** A187 80s Strip of 3, #a.-c. 9.00 9.00

No. 937 is a continuous design.

Queen Halaevalu Mata'aho, 70th Birthday — A188

Designs: 60s, Queen, natl. flag. No. 939a, Queen, coin with portrait. No. 939b, Coin with natl. arms, Queen.

**1996, Nov. 27 Litho. *Perf. 12***

**938** A188 60s multicolored 3.50 3.50
**939** A188 2pa Pair, #a.-b. 10.50 10.50

Towards the Year 2000 — A189

Year "2000" rising out of Pacific, Tonga landmarks: Nos. 940a, 941a, The Ha'amonga stone monument, globe, Kao Island. Nos. 941b, 941b, Mount Talau overlooking Port of Reguge, Royal Palance, Tongatapu, communication satellite.

**1996, Dec. 9**

**940** A189 80s Pair, #a.-b. 4.00 4.00
**941** A189 2pa Pair, #a.-b. 9.50 9.50

New Year Type of 1996 Redrawn with Ox

Denomination located: a, 60s, UR. b, 60s, UL. c, 80s, LR. d, 2pa, LL.

**1997, Jan. 24 Litho. *Perf. 14***

**942** A183 Sheet of 4, #a.-d. 11.00 11.00

New Year 1997 (Year of the Ox).

Nos. 840-845 Surcharged

**1997, Mar. 3 Litho. *Perf. 14***

**943** A165 10s on 45s #840 3.50 3.25
**944** A165 10s on 45s #841 3.50 3.25
*a.* Pair, #943-944 6.00 6.00
**945** A165 10s on 60s #842 3.50 3.25
**946** A165 10s on 60s #843 3.50 3.25
*a.* Pair, #945-946 6.00 6.00
**947** A165 20s on 2pa #844 4.00 3.75
**948** A165 20s on 2pa #845 4.00 3.75
*a.* Pair, #947-948 7.00 7.00
*Nos. 943-948 (6)* 22.00 20.50

Nos. 925-928 Surcharged, Ovptd.

**1997, Mar. 24 Litho. *Perf. 14***

**949** A184 10s on 45s #925 .90 .90
**950** A184 10s on 80s #926 .90 .90
**951** A184 10s on 2pa #927 .90 .90
**952** A184 3pa #928 9.25 9.25
*Nos. 949-952 (4)* 11.95 11.95

Size and location of surcharge varies.

Nos. 892-893 Surcharged

a

b

**1997, Mar. 24** ***Perf. 14½***

**Sheets of 4**

| | | | | |
|---|---|---|---|---|
| **954A** | A176 | 10s on 80s | 2.00 | 2.00 |
| **956A** | A176 | 1pa on 2pa | 15.00 | 15.00 |

#954A contains #892a (a), #892b (a), #892b (b), #892a (b). #956A contains #893a (a), #893b ((a), #893b (b), #893a (b).

Christianity in Tonga, Birth of King George Tupou I, Bicent. — A190

#957, 961a, 962a, Arrival of missionary ship, Duff, Captain James Wilson. #958, King George Tupou I, village. #959, 961b, 962b, People in water, rowboats coming ashore from Duff. #960, 961c, 962c, Natives, missionaries, Duff.

**1997, Apr. 28** ***Perf. 14***

| | | | | |
|---|---|---|---|---|
| **957** | A190 10s multicolored | | .20 | .20 |
| **958** | A190 10s multicolored | | .20 | .20 |
| **959** | A190 10s multicolored | | .20 | .20 |
| **960** | A190 10s multicolored | | .20 | .20 |
| *a.* | Sheet of 6, #957, 959-960, 3 #958 | | 3.75 | 3.75 |
| **961** | A190 60s Strip of 3, #a.-c. | | 4.50 | 4.50 |
| **962** | A190 80s Strip of 3, #a.-c. | | 6.50 | 6.50 |

Nos. 961-962 were each issued in sheets of 9 stamps.

See Nos. 972-975.

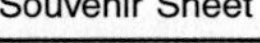
Souvenir Sheet

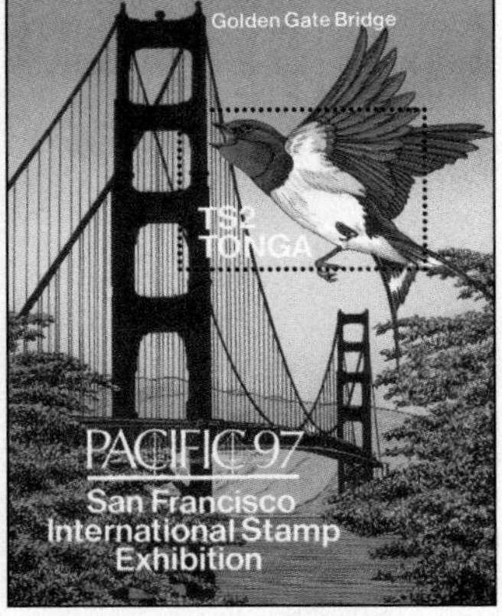

Pacific Swallow, Golden Gate Bridge — A191

Illustration reduced.

**1997, May 30**

| | | | |
|---|---|---|---|
| **963** | A191 2pa multicolored | 7.50 | 7.50 |

Pacific '97.

Tonga High School, 50th Anniv. A192

Designs: 20s, Students in uniforms outside of school. 60s, Dressed for sports. 80s, Brass band. 3.50pa, Running competition.

**1997, June 4**

| | | | |
|---|---|---|---|
| **964** | A192 20s multicolored | .75 | .40 |
| **965** | A192 60s multicolored | 1.75 | 1.10 |
| **966** | A192 80s multicolored | 2.25 | 1.50 |
| **967** | A192 3.50pa multicolored | 9.25 | 9.25 |
| | *Nos. 964-967 (4)* | 14.00 | 12.25 |

A193

A194

Nos. 968, 970: a, Queen, King with bowed heads, royal escorts. b, Coronation ceremony. c, Queen, King. 45s, 2pa, King's crown.

**1997, June 30** **Litho.** ***Perf. 13x13½***

| | | | |
|---|---|---|---|
| **968** | A193 10s Strip of 3, #a.-c. | 1.25 | 1.25 |
| **969** | A193 45s multicolored | 1.75 | 1.75 |

**Size: 34x47mm**

***Perf. 12***

| | | | |
|---|---|---|---|
| **970** | A193 60s Strip of 3, #a.-c. | 7.00 | 7.00 |
| **971** | A193 2pa multicolored | 8.50 | 8.50 |

King Taufa'ahau IV, Queen Halaevalu Mata'aho, 50th wedding anniv., coronation, 30th anniv.

Christianity in Tonga Type of 1997

**1997, Aug. 27** ***Perf. 14***

**Size: 27x18mm**

| | | | |
|---|---|---|---|
| **972** | A190 10s like #957 | .20 | .20 |
| **973** | A190 10s like #958 | .20 | .20 |
| **974** | A190 10s like #959 | .20 | .20 |
| **975** | A190 10s like #960 | .20 | .20 |
| *a.* | Sheet of 12, 6 #973, 2 each #972, #974-975 | 6.00 | 6.00 |

**1997, Oct. 1** **Litho.** ***Perf. 14***

Mushrooms: Nos. 976a, 977a, Lenzites elegans. Nos. 976b, 977b, Marasmiellus semiustus. No. 976c, 978a, Aseroe rubra. Nos. 976d, 978b, Podoscypha involuta. Nos. 976e, 979a, Microporus xanthopus. Nos. 976f, 979b, Lentinus tuberregium.

| | | | |
|---|---|---|---|
| **976** | A194 10s Strip of 6, #a.-f. | 2.25 | 2.25 |

**Size: 26x40mm**

| | | | |
|---|---|---|---|
| **977** | A194 20s Pair, #a.-b. | 2.00 | 2.00 |
| **978** | A194 60s Pair, #a.-b. | 6.00 | 6.00 |
| **979** | A194 2pa Pair, #a.-b. | 19.00 | 19.00 |
| *c.* | Sheet of 6, #977-979 | 26.50 | 26.50 |

No. 976 is a continuous design.

**Diana, Princess of Wales (1961-97)**

Common Design Type

Various portraits: a, 10s. b, 80s, c, 1pa. d, 2.50pa.

***Perf. 13½x14***

**1998, May 29** **Litho.** **Unwmk.**

| | | | |
|---|---|---|---|
| **980** | CD355 Strip of 4, #a.-d, | 6.75 | 6.75 |

No. 980 sold for 4.40pa + 50s with surtax from international sales going to the Princess Diana Memorial Fund and surtax from local sales going to designated local charity.

Flying Home for Christmas A195

Designs: 60s, Airplane on ground, people waving. 80s, People waving, house, plane overhead. 1.50pa, Man in outrigger canoe waving to airplane. 3.50pa, Man, woman, people in boat on lake waving, airplane overhead.

**1997, Oct. 20** **Litho.** ***Perf. 14x13½***

| | | | |
|---|---|---|---|
| **981** | A195 60s bister & red | .90 | .90 |
| **982** | A195 80s bister & red | 1.20 | 1.20 |
| **983** | A195 1.50pa bister & red | 2.20 | 2.20 |
| **984** | A195 3.50pa bister & red | 5.20 | 5.20 |
| | *Nos. 981-984 (4)* | 9.50 | 9.50 |

King Taufa'ahau Tupou IV, 80th Birthday — A196

**1998, July 4** **Litho.** ***Perf. 14***

| | | | |
|---|---|---|---|
| **985** | A196 2.70pa multicolored | 7.00 | 7.00 |
| *a.* | Souv. sheet, #985, Niuafo'ou #207 | 10.00 | 10.00 |

New Year 1998 (Year of the Tiger)

Tiger: a, 55s, Leaping down. b, 80s, Lying down. c, 1pa, Leaping upward. d, 1pa, Stalking.

**1998, July 23**

| | | | |
|---|---|---|---|
| **986** | A183 Sheet of 4, #a.-d. | 6.00 | 6.00 |

No. 986 is a continuous design. Singpex '98.

For surcharges, see No. 1098.

Birds A197

5s, Fairy tern, vert. 10s, Tongan whistler, vert. 15s, Common barn owl, vert. 20s, Purple swamp hen, vert. 30s, Red-footed booby, vert. 40s, Banded rail. 50s, Swamp harrier. 55s, Blue-crowned lorikeet, vert. 60s, Great frigate bird, vert. 70s, Friendly ground dove. 80s, Red-tailed tropic bird, vert. 1pa, Red shining parrot, vert. 2pa, Pacific pigeon, vert. 3pa, Pacific golden plover. 5pa, Tongan megapode.

***Perf. 14x14½, 14½x14***

**1998, Aug. 26** **Litho.**

| | | | |
|---|---|---|---|
| **992** | A197 5s multicolored | .20 | .20 |
| **993** | A197 10s multicolored | .20 | .20 |
| **994** | A197 15s multicolored | .20 | .20 |
| **995** | A197 20s multicolored | .25 | .25 |
| **996** | A197 30s multicolored | .45 | .45 |
| **997** | A197 40s multicolored | .60 | .60 |
| **998** | A197 50s multicolored | .70 | .70 |
| **999** | A197 55s multicolored | .80 | .80 |
| **1000** | A197 60s multicolored | .85 | .85 |
| **1001** | A197 70s multicolored | 1.00 | 1.00 |
| **1002** | A197 80s multicolored | 1.10 | 1.10 |
| **1003** | A197 1pa multicolored | 1.40 | 1.40 |
| **1004** | A197 2pa multicolored | 2.75 | 2.75 |
| **1005** | A197 3pa multicolored | 4.25 | 4.25 |
| **1006** | A197 5pa multicolored | 7.25 | 7.25 |
| | *Nos. 992-1006 (15)* | 22.00 | 22.00 |

For surcharges, see Nos. 1077A, 1077B, 1099-1114, 1126.

Fish A198

Designs: a, 10s, Chaetodon pelewensis. b, 55s, Chaetodon lunula. c, 1pa, Chaetodon ephippium.

**1998, Sept. 23** **Litho.** ***Perf. 14***

| | | | |
|---|---|---|---|
| **1008** | A198 Strip of 3, #a.-c. | 4.00 | 4.00 |

Intl. Year of the Ocean. No. 1008 was issued in sheets of 9 stamps.

Christmas A199

Designs: 10s, Angel, "Kilisimasi Fiefia." 80s, Angel, "Merry Christmas." 1pa, Children, candle, "Ta'u Fo'ou Monu'ia." 1.60pa, Children, candle, "Happy New Year."

**1998, Nov. 12** **Litho.** ***Perf. 14x14½***

| | | | |
|---|---|---|---|
| **1009** | A199 10s multicolored | .60 | .40 |
| **1010** | A199 80s multicolored | 2.50 | 1.25 |
| **1011** | A199 1pa multicolored | 2.75 | 2.25 |
| **1012** | A199 1.60pa multicolored | 3.50 | 3.50 |
| | *Nos. 1009-1012 (4)* | 9.35 | 7.40 |

New Year 1999 (Year of the Rabbit) A200

a, 10s, Three rabbits. b, 55s, Rabbit eating. c, 80s, Rabbit looking upward. d, 1pa, Rabbit hopping.

**1999, Feb. 16** ***Perf. 14***

| | | | |
|---|---|---|---|
| **1013** | A200 Sheet of 4, #a.-d. | 4.50 | 4.50 |

Explorers — A201

Explorer, ship: 55s, Tasman, Heemskerck, 1643. 80s, La Perouse, Astrolabe, 1788. 1pa, William Bligh, Bounty, 1789. 2.50pa, James Cook, Resolution, 1777.

**1999, Mar. 19** **Litho.** ***Perf. 14***

| | | | |
|---|---|---|---|
| **1014** | A201 55s multicolored | 1.00 | .60 |
| **1015** | A201 80s multicolored | 1.50 | 1.00 |
| **1016** | A201 1pa multicolored | 2.00 | 1.75 |
| **1017** | A201 2.50pa multicolored | 4.75 | 4.75 |
| *a.* | Souvenir sheet of 1 | 5.00 | 5.00 |
| | *Nos. 1014-1017 (4)* | 9.25 | 8.10 |

Australia '99 World Stamp Expo (#1017a).

Scenic Views, Vava'u A202

Designs: 10s, Neiafu. 55s, Boats on water, Port of Refuge. 80s, Aerial view, Port of Refuge. 1pa, Sunset, Neiafu. 2.50pa, Mounu Island.

**1999, May 19** ***Perf. 14½***

| | | | |
|---|---|---|---|
| **1018** | A202 10s multicolored | .50 | .40 |
| **1019** | A202 55s multicolored | 1.00 | .60 |
| **1020** | A202 80s multicolored | 1.60 | .80 |
| **1021** | A202 1pa multicolored | 1.75 | 1.40 |
| **1022** | A202 2.50pa multicolored | 3.50 | 3.50 |
| | *Nos. 1018-1022 (5)* | 8.35 | 6.70 |

Flowers A203

Designs: 10s, Fagraea berteroana. 80s, Garcinia pseudoguttifera. 1pa, Phlaeria disperma, vert. 2.50pa, Gardenia taitensis, vert.

*Perf. 13¼x13, 13x13¼*

**1999, Sept. 29** **Litho.**

**1023** A203 10s multicolored .25 .25
**1024** A203 80s multicolored 1.25 1.25
**1025** A203 1pa multicolored 1.60 1.60
**1026** A203 2.50pa multicolored 4.00 4.00
*Nos. 1023-1026 (4)* 7.10 7.10

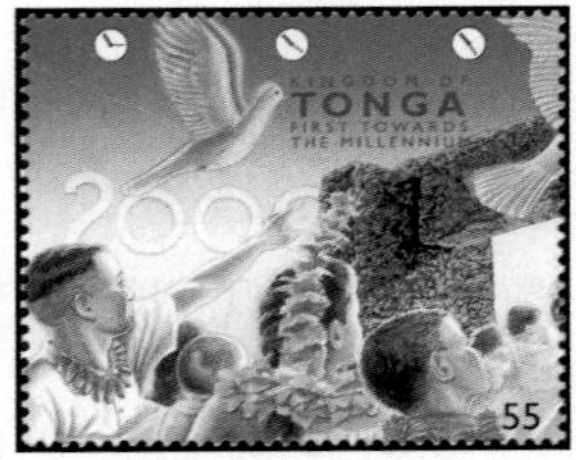


Millennium — A204

Designs: a, 55s, Ha'amonga monument, people, clocks at 11:15 to 11:25. b, 80s, Monument, people, clocks at 11:30 to 11:40. c, 1pa, People, clocks at 11:45 to 11:55. d, 2.50pa, King Taufa'ahau IV, clocks at 12:00, 12:05.

**1999, Dec. 1**

**1027** A204 Strip of 4, #a.-d. 7.00 7.00

Millennium — A205

Clock, dove and: 10s, Flowers. 1pa, Ha'amonga Monument. 2.50pa, Native boat. 2.70pa, Crown.

### Litho. & Embossed

**2000, Jan. 1** ***Perf. and Die Cut***

**1028** A205 10s multi .25 .25
**1029** A205 1pa multi 1.50 1.50
**1030** A205 2.50pa multi 3.50 3.50
**1031** A205 2.70pa multi 4.00 4.00
***a.*** Souv. sheet, #1030-1031 7.50 7.50
*Nos. 1028-1031 (4)* 9.25 9.25

Values are for stamps with attached selvage.

Souvenir Sheet

New Year 2000 (Year of the Dragon) — A206

Illustration reduced.

Various dragons; a, 10s. b, 55s, c, 80s. d, 1pa.

### Litho. with Foil Application

**2000, Feb. 4** ***Perf. 14½***

**1032** A206 Sheet of 4, #a.-d. 4.75 4.75

Souvenir Sheet

The Stamp Show 2000, London — A207

Illustration reduced.

### Litho. with Foil Application

**2000, May 22** ***Perf. 13x13¼***

**1033** A207 Sheet of 2 5.50 5.50
***a.*** 1pa Queen Mother 1.50 1.50
***b.*** 2.50pa Queen Salote Tupou III 3.50 3.50

Geostationary Orbital Slot Program — A208

Designs: 10s, Proton RU500 lauch vehicle, vert. 1pa, LM3 launch vehicle. 2.50pa, Apstar 1. 2.70pa, Gorizont.

### Litho. with Foil Application

**2000, July 5** ***Perf. 14½x15, 15x14½***

**1034-1037** A208 Set of 4 9.00 9.00
*1037a* Souvenir sheet, #1036-1037 8.25 8.25

World Stamp Expo 2000, Anaheim.

2000 Summer Olympics, Sydney — A209

No. 1038: a, Runner, koalas, sailboats. b, Boxers, kangaroos, Ayers Rock. c, Torchbearers, Ayers Rock, Sydney Opera House (60x45mm). d, Discus thrower, Sydney Harbour Bridge, flower. e, Weight lifter, kookaburra, fish.

**2000, Sept. 15** **Litho.** ***Perf. 14***

**1038** Horiz. strip of 5 5.50 5.50
***a.-e.*** A209 80s Any single 1.00 1.00

Commonwealth Membership, 30th Anniv. — A210

Designs: 10s, Education. 55s, Arts. 80s, Health. 2.70pa, Agriculture.

**2000, Oct. 25**

**1039-1042** A210 Set of 4 5.50 5.50

Souvenir Sheet

New Year 2001 (Year of the Snake) — A211

No. 1043 — Various snakes: a, 10s. b, 55s, c, 80s, d, 1pa.

### Litho. with Foil Application

**2001, Feb. 1** ***Perf. 14¼***

**1043** A211 Sheet of 4, #a-d 4.50 4.50

Hong Kong 2001 Stamp Exhibition.

Dance — A212

Designs: 10s, Ma'ulu'ulu. 55s, Me'etupaki. 80s, Tau'olunga. 2.70pa, Faha'iula.

**2001, Apr. 4** **Litho.** ***Perf. 13¼***

**1044-1047** A212 Set of 4 5.50 5.50

Year of the Mangrove A213

Designs: 10s, Fiddler crab. 55s, Black duck, gray mullet, vert. 80s, Red mangrove, emperor fish, vert. 1pa, Reef heron, mangrove. 2.70pa, Mangrove crab.

**2001, May 5** **Litho.** ***Perf. 13¾***

**1048-1052** A213 Set of 5 6.50 6.50
*1052a* Souvenir sheet, #1048-1052, perf. 13½ 7.00 7.00

Sport Fishing — A214

**2001, July 31** ***Perf. 14¾x14***

**1053** Horiz. strip of 4 with central label 8.25 8.25
***a.*** A214 45s Sailfish .50 .50
***b.*** A214 80s Blue marlin 1.00 1.00
***c.*** A214 2.40pa Wahoo 3.00 3.00
***d.*** A214 2.60pa Dorado 3.25 3.25

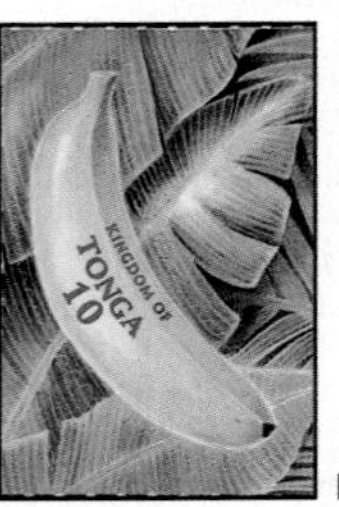


Fruit — A215

**2001, Sept. 19** ***Serpentine Die Cut***

**Self-Adhesive**

**1054** Horiz. strip of 5 6.00
***a.*** A215 10s Banana .25 .25
***b.*** A215 45s Coconut .50 .50
***c.*** A215 60s Pineapple .75 .75
***d.*** A215 80s Watermelon .85 .85
***e.*** A215 2.40pa Passion fruit 2.40 2.40

Shells A216

Designs: 10s, Haliotis ovina. 80s, Turbo petholatus. 1pa, Trochus niloticus. 2.70pa, Turbo marmoratus.

*Perf. 12¾*

**2001, Dec. 13** **Litho.** **Unwmk.**

**1055-1058** A216 Set of 4 6.25 6.25

Values are for copies with surrounding selvage.

### Reign Of Queen Elizabeth II, 50th Anniv. Issue

Common Design Type

Souvenir Sheet

No. 1059: a, 15s, Princess Elizabeth as child. b, 90s, Wearing yellow hat. c, 1.20pa, With Princess Anne and Prince Charles. d, 1.40pa, Wearing crown. e, 2.25pa, 1955 portrait by Annigoni (38x50mm).

***Perf. 14¼x14½, 13¾ (2.25pa)***

**2002, Feb. 6** **Litho.** **Wmk. 373**

**1059** CD360 Sheet of 5, #a-e 8.00 8.00

Souvenir Sheet

New Year 2002 (Year of the Horse) — A217

Various horses: a, 65s. b, 80s. c, 1pa. d, 2.50pa.

### Litho. With Foil Application

**2002, Feb. 12** **Unwmk.** ***Perf. 14***

**1060** A217 Sheet of 4, #a-d 6.75 6.75

Intl. Year of Ecotourism — A218

Designs: 5s, Whale, surfer. 15s, Woman, shoreline. 70s, Beach, fish. 1.40pa, Arch, man. 2.25pa, Boats, man.

**2002, Apr. 9** **Litho.** ***Perf. 13¼x13¾***

**1061-1065** A218 Set of 5 6.50 6.50

Pearls A219

Pearls and: 90s, Workers preparing oysters for pearl cultivation. 1pa, Diver checking strung oysters. 1.20pa, Woman, pearl on necklace. 2.50pa, Islands.

**2002, June 12** **Litho.** ***Perf. 13½***

**1066-1069** A219 Set of 4 7.50 7.50
*1069a* Souvenir sheet, #1068-1069 5.00 5.00

Values are for copies with surrounding selvage.

Participation of Tongan Team in Rugby Sevens Tournament — A220

Designs: 15s, Player leaping for ball. 30s, Players ready for scrum. 90s, Player attempting tackle. 4pa, Players on ground.

**2002, July 27**

**1070-1073** A220 Set of 4 7.25 7.25

Values are for copies with surrounding selvage.

Weaving — A221

Designs: 30s, Woman and young girl. 90s, Woman with work hanging on line, boy with baskets. 1.40pa, Women weaving baskets. 2.50pa, Woman weaving basket lid.

**2002, Sept. 17** ***Perf. 12¼***

**1074-1077** A221 Set of 4 7.00 7.00

Nos. 999, 1003 Surcharged

Type 1 — Slash Over First "5"

**Methods and Perfs As Before**

**2002, Sept.**

**1077A** A197 5s on 55s #999, Type 1 — —

**1077B** A197 15(s) on $1 #1003 — —

See Nos. 1099-1114 for additional surcharges on No. 999.

'Eua National Park, 10th Anniv. — A222

Various depictions of red shining parrots 45s, 1pa, 1.50pa, 2.50pa.

**2002, Nov. 27** **Litho.** ***Perf. 12¼***

**1078-1081** A222 Set of 4 7.50 7.50

New Year 2003 (Year of the Ram) — A223

No. 1082: a, 65s, One ram. 80s, Three sheep. 1pa, Three sheep, diff. 2.50pa, Two sheep.

**2003, Apr. 14** **Litho.** ***Perf. 13¼***

**1082** A223 Sheet of 4, #a-d 4.75 4.75

Coronation of Queen Elizabeth II, 50th Anniv. — A224

Designs: 90s, Queen Elizabeth II in coach. 1.20pa, Queen Salote of Tonga. 1.40pa, Queen Salote in coach. 2.50pa, Queen Elizabeth II.

**Litho. With Foil Application**

**2003, June 2**

**1083-1086** A224 Set of 4 10.00 10.00

Boats of Abel Tasman — A225

Various boats: 15s, 75s, 90s, 2.50pa.

**2003, Aug. 7** **Litho.** ***Perf. 13¼***

**1087-1090** A225 Set of 4 7.75 7.75

*1090a* Souvenir sheet, #1087-1090 8.00 8.00

Beaches — A226

Flower and: 15s, Euakafa Beach. 90s, Pangaimotu Beach. 1.40pa, Fafa Beach. 2.25pa, Nuku Beach.

**2003, Sept. 11**

**1091-1094** A226 Set of 4 8.50 8.50

Nos. 784, 785a, 785b, 786 Surcharged

**Methods and Perfs As Before**

**2003, Sept.**

**1095** A152 10s on 32s Horiz. strip of 3, #784a-784c — —

**1096** A152 10s on 42s #785a —

**1097** A152 10s on 42s #785b —

**1098** A152 10s on 57s Horiz. strip of 3, #786a-786c — —

A 10s surcharge on No. 785c has not yet been seen, though it is likely to have been printed.

No. 999 Surcharged

Type 2 — Small numerals and cent sign

Type 3 — Small numerals and "s"

Type 4 — Thin numerals and "s"

Type 5 — Large numerals and "s"

Type 6 — Medium-sized numerals and "s"

Type 7 — Very large, bold numerals and "c"

**Methods and Perfs As Before**

**2003-04**

**1099** A197 05s on 55s, Type 3 — —

*a.* Obliterators 2x1 ½mm —

**1100** A197 05s on 55s, Type 4 — —

**1101** A197 5s on 55s, Type 5 — —

**1102** A197 5c on 55s, Type 7 — —

**1103** A197 10s on 55s, Type 4 — —

**1104** A197 10s on 55s, Type 5 — —

**1105** A197 10c on 55s, Type 7 — —

**1106** A197 15c on 55s, Type 2 — —

**1107** A197 15s on 55s, Type 4 — —

**1108** A197 15s on 55s, Type 5 — —

**1109** A197 15c on 55s, Type 7 — —

**1110** A197 20c on 55s, Type 2 — —

**1111** A197 20s on 55s, Type 4 — —

**1112** A197 20s on 55s, Type 5 — —

**1113** A197 45c on 55s, Type 2 — —

**1114** A197 45s on 55s, Type 6 — —

Earliest known uses: Nos. 1099, 1106, 1110, 10/03; Nos. 1100, 1103, 1107, 1111, 12/03; Nos. 1101, 1108, 2/04; Nos. 1113, 4/04; Nos. 1104, 1112, 1114, 6/04; Nos. 1105, 1109, 8/04; No. 1102, 9/04;

Churches A227

Designs: 15s, Catholic Church, Neiafu, Vava'u. 90s, Wesleyan Church, Uiha, Ha'apai. 1.40pa, Cathedral of the Immaculate Conception of Mary. 2.25pa, Free Wesleyan Church, Nuku'alofa.

**2003, Nov. 10**

**1115-1118** A227 Set of 4 8.50 8.50

Christmas.

New Year 2004 (Year of the Monkey) — A228

No. 1119: a, 60s, Spider monkey. b, 80s, Ring-tailed lemur. c, 1pa, Cotton-top tamarin. d, 2.50pa, White-cheeked gibbon.

**2004, Feb. 12** **Litho.** ***Perf. 13¼***

**1119** A228 Sheet of 4, #a-d 5.75 5.75

Nos. 770, 787, 788, 815, 816, 1001, Niuafo'ou Nos. 140, 141 and 145 Surcharged

Type 1 — Small denomination and obliterator

Type 2 — Large denomination and obliterator

**Methods and Perfs As Before**

**2004**

**1120** A153 10s on 32s #787 — —

**1121** A153 10s on 42s #788, Type 1 — —

**1122** A153 10s on 42s #788, Type 2 — —
**1123** A157 10s on 42s #815 — —
**1124** A147 10s on 57s Horiz. strip of 4, + central label, #770a-770d — —
**1125** A157 10s on 57s #816 — —
**1126** A197 60s on 70s #1001 — —

### On Stamps of Niuafo'ou

**1127** A25 10s on 42s #140 — —
**1128** A26 10s on 42s #145 — —
**1129** A25 10s on 57s #141 — —

Size and location of obliterators and new denominations varies. Earliest known use: No. 1126, 3/04; Nos. 1120, 1121, 4/04; Nos. 1122, 1123, 1124, 1125, 1127, 1128, 1129, 6/04. The surcharged Niuafo'ou stamps were not necessarily sent only to Niuafo'ou for sale there.

Fruit Plants — A229

Designs: 45s, Mango. 60s, Pineapple. 80s, Coconut. 1.80pa, Banana.

**2004, Sept. 21 Litho. *Perf. 14¼x14***
**1130-1133** A229 Set of 4 3.75 3.75

Christmas A230

Designs: 65s, Madonna and Child. 80s, Journey to Bethlehem. 1.20pa, Annunciation to the Shepherds. 2.50pa, Magi.

**2004, Dec. *Perf. 14***
**1134-1137** A230 Set of 4 5.50 5.50

Royalty — A231

Designs: 65s, King George Tupou I. 90s, King George Tupou II. 1.40pa, Queen Salote Tupou III. 3.05pa, King Taufa'ahau Tupou IV.

**2004, July 7 Litho. *Perf. 14***
**1138-1141** A231 Set of 4 6.25 6.25

Souvenir Sheet

New Year 2005 (Year of the Rooster) — A232

No. 1142 — Various roosters with panel color of: a, 65s, Yellow orange. b, 80s, Light green. c, 1pa, Tan. d, 2.50pa, Gray blue.

**2005, Feb. 12**
**1142** A232 Sheet of 4, #a-d 5.25 5.25

Souvenir Sheet

Whales — A233

No. 1143 — Various whales with denominations in: a, 65s, Purple. b, 80s, Yellow. c, 1pa, Green. d, 2.50pa, Pink.

**2005, May 4 *Perf. 13¼***
**1143** A233 Sheet of 4, #a-d 5.25 5.25

### SEMI-POSTAL STAMP

**Catalogue values for unused stamps in this section are for Never Hinged items.**

No. 488 Surcharged in Silver for Cyclone Relief

**1982, Apr. 14 Litho.**
**B1** A86 3pa + 50s multi 3.00 3.00

### AIR POST STAMPS

**Catalogue values for unused stamps in this section are for Never Hinged items.**

Type of Regular Gold Coin Issue

Designs: 10p, 1sh1p, Queen Salote standing, ½-koula coin, obverse. 11p, Coat of arms, ½-koula coin, reverse. 2sh1p, 2sh9p, Queen Salote standing, 1-koula coin, obverse. 2sh4p, Coat of arms, 1-koula coin, reverse.

**Litho.; Embossed on Gilt Foil**
**1963, July 15 Unwmk. *Die Cut***
**Diameter: 54mm**

**C1** A36 10p dp carmine .45 .45
**C2** A36 11p green .55 .55
**C3** A36 1sh6p violet blue .50 .55

**Diameter: 80mm**

**C4** A36 2sh1p magenta 1.10 1.10
**C5** A36 2sh4p emerald 1.10 1.10
**C6** A36 2sh9p violet 1.50 1.50
*Nos. C1-C6 (6)* 5.20 5.25

See note after No. 133.

Map of Tongatabu and ¼-Koula Coin — AP1

**Litho.; Embossed on Gilt Foil**
**1964, Oct. 19**
**C7** AP1 10p deep green .20 .20
**C8** AP1 1sh2p black .20 .20
**C9** AP1 3sh6p carmine .95 .95
**C10** AP1 6sh6p purple 1.75 1.75
*Nos. C7-C10 (4)* 3.10 3.10

Pan-Pacific and Southeast Asia Women's Association Conf., Nukualofa, Aug. 1964. See note after No. 133.

Nos. C1-C2, C4-C6 Surcharged like Regular Issue, 1965, in Black, White or Red

**1965, Mar. 18**
**C11** A36 2sh3p on 10p (B) .20 .20
**C12** A36 2sh9p on 11p (W) .25 .25
**C13** A36 4sh6p on 2sh1p 18.00 18.00
**C14** A36 4sh6p on 2sh4p 18.00 18.00
**C15** A36 4sh6p on 2sh9p 11.00 11.00
*Nos. C11-C15 (5)* 47.45 47.45

Nos. 114-115, 117-118 Overprinted or Surcharged

***Perf. 14½x13½***
**1966, June 18 Wmk. 79**
**C16** A35 5p purple .25 .20
**C17** A35 10p on 1p brn org & car rose .25 .20
**C18** A35 1sh red brown .30 .20
**C19** A35 2sh9p on 2p ultra .35 .20
**C20** A35 3sh6p on 5p purple .35 .20
**C21** A35 4sh6p on 1sh red brn .75 .20
*Nos. C16-C21 (6)* 2.25 1.20

Centenary of Tupou College and secondary education. The overprint or surcharge is spaced differently on other values.

Nos. C7-C8 Overprinted and Surcharged in Silver or Gold on Black, or in Black on Gold

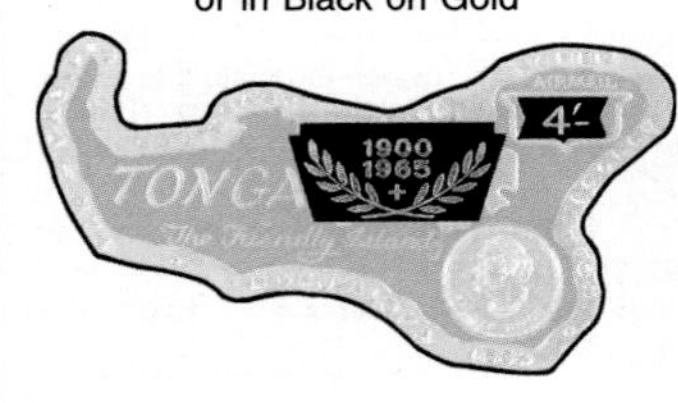


**Litho.; Embossed on Gilt Foil**
**1966, Dec. 16 Unwmk. *Die Cut***
**C22** AP1 10p (S on B) .20 .20
**C23** AP1 1sh2p (B on G) .20 .20
**C24** AP1 4sh on 10p (S on B) 1.00 1.00
**C25** AP1 5sh6p on 1sh2p (B on G) 1.50 1.50
**C26** AP1 10sh6p on 1sh2p (G on B) 2.50 2.50
*Nos. C22-C26 (5)* 5.40 5.40

In memory of Queen Salote (1900-65).

King Taufa'ahau Type of Regular Issue, 1967

Designs: 7s, 11s, 23s, 2pa, Taufa'ahau IV, obverse of new palladium coins. 9s, 21s, 29s, Coat of Arms, reverse.

**Litho.; Embossed on Palladium Foil**
**1967, July 4**

Diameter: 7s, 44mm; 9s, 29s, 52mm; 11s, 59mm; 21s, 68mm; 23s, 40mm; 2pa, 74mm.

**C27** A38 7s red & black .20 .20
**C28** A38 9s maroon & emer .25 .25
**C29** A38 11s brt blue & org .30 .30
**C30** A38 21s black & emer .55 .55
**C31** A38 23s magenta & emer .60 .60
**C32** A38 29s vio blue & emer .70 .70
**C33** A38 2pa magenta & orange 5.00 5.00
*Nos. C27-C33 (7)* 7.60 7.60

See note after No. 181.

Type of Regular Issue, 1953 Surcharged in Red or Black

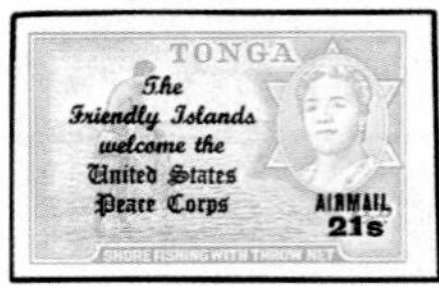


**Wmk. 79**
**1967, Dec. 15 Engr. *Die Cut***
**C34** A33 11s on 3½p ultra (R) .30 .30
**C35** A33 21s on 1½p emerald .30 .30
**C36** A33 23s on 3½p ultra (R) .30 .30
*Nos. C34-C36 (3)* .90 .90

Arrival of the United States Peace Corps.

No. 112 Surcharged in Red

**1968, Apr. 6 Engr. *Perf. 11x11½***
**C37** A34 11s on 10sh blk & yel .45 .45
**C38** A34 21s on 10sh blk & yel .60 .60
**C39** A34 23s on 10sh blk & yel .60 .60
*Nos. C37-C39 (3)* 1.65 1.65

Nos. C27-C33 Overprinted: "HIS MAJESTY'S 50th BIRTHDAY" in Silver on Blue Panel on 7s, 11s, 23s and 2pa. "H.M.'s BIRTHDAY / 4 . JULY . 1968" in Gold on Red Panel on 9s, 21s and 29s

**Litho.; Embossed on Palladium Foil**
**1968, July 4 Unwmk. *Die Cut***
**C40** A38 7s red & black .20 .20
**C41** A38 9s maroon & emer .20 .20
**C42** A38 11s brt blue & org .25 .20
**C43** A38 21s black & emerald .75 .35
**C44** A38 23s mag & emerald .75 .35
**C45** A38 29s vio blue & emer 1.00 .40
**C46** A38 2pa magenta & org 6.75 6.00
*Nos. C40-C46 (7)* 9.90 7.70

50th birthday of King Taufa'ahau IV.

Types of 1953 Surcharged: "Friendly Islands / Field & Track Trials / South Pacific Games / Port Moresby 1969 / AIRMAIL"

Designs as before.

**1968, Dec. 19 Engr. Wmk. 79**
**C47** A33 6s on 6p yel& blk .20 .20
**C48** A33 7s on 4p purple & yel .20 .20
**C49** A33 8s on 8p blk & lt grn .20 .20
**C50** A33 9s on 1½p emerald .20 .20
**C51** A34 11s on 3p brn org & yel .20 .20
**C52** A33 21s on 3½p dk blue .30 .30
**C53** A33 38s on 5sh sepia & yel 2.10 .50
**C54** A34 1pa on 10sh orange yel 1.00 .60
*Nos. C47-C54 (8)* 4.40 2.40

Issued to publicize the field and track trials for the third South Pacific Games, Port Moresby, 1969. The overprint is in 5 lines on the horizontal stamps, in 7 lines on the vertical stamps. On the vertical stamps "Trial" is printed on the line ahead of "Field & Track." On No. C54 the denomination is spelled out.

Nos. C19-C21 Surcharged

***Perf. 14½x13½***
**1968 Photo. Wmk. 79**
**C55** A35 1s on 2sh9p on 2p ultra 1.60 1.00
**C56** A35 1s on 3sh6p on 5p pur 1.60 1.00
**C57** A35 1s on 4sh6p on 1sh red brown 1.60 1.00
*Nos. C55-C57 (3)* 4.80 3.00

Pacific Games Type of Regular Issue

Design: Boxer.

**1969, Aug. 13 Litho. *Die Cut***
**Self-adhesive**
**C58** A40 9s orange, blk & pur .20 .20
**C59** A40 11s orange, blk & dk bl .20 .20
**C60** A40 20s org, blk & yel grn .25 .25
**C61** A40 60s orange, blk & scar .75 .75
**C62** A40 1pa orange, blk & grn 1.25 1.25
*Nos. C58-C62 (5)* 2.65 2.65

See note after No. 231.

Oil Derrick on Map of Tongatabu and King Taufa'ahau IV — AP2

**Litho.; Gold Embossed**

**1969, Dec. 23 Self-adhesive**

**C63** AP2 9s multicolored .25 .25
**C64** AP2 10s multicolored .25 .25
**C65** AP2 24s multicolored .70 .70
**C66** AP2 29s multicolored .80 .80
**C67** AP2 38s multicolored 1.10 1.10
*Nos. C63-C67 (5)* 3.10 3.10

1st scientific search for oil in Tonga.

King Taufa'ahau IV and Queen Elizabeth II — AP3

**Litho.; Gold Embossed**

**1970, Mar. 7 Self-adhesive**

**C68** AP3 7s multicolored .40 .30
**C69** AP3 9s multicolored .50 .35
**C70** AP3 24s multicolored 1.25 .65
**C71** AP3 29s multicolored 1.50 .75
**C72** AP3 38s multicolored 2.10 1.00
*Nos. C68-C72 (5)* 5.75 3.05

See note after No. 242.

King Taufa'ahau Tupou IV Medal — AP4

**Litho.; Gold Embossed**

**1970, June 4 Self-adhesive**

**C73** AP4 9s grnsh bl, ver & gold .25 .25
**C74** AP4 10s lilac, bl & gold .25 .25
**C75** AP4 24s yel, grn & gold .70 .70
**C76** AP4 29s ultra, org & gold .80 .80
**C77** AP4 38s ocher, emer & gold 1.00 1.00
*Nos. C73-C77 (5)* 3.00 3.00

See note after No. 247.

Red Cross Type of Regular Issue Without Coat of Arms

**1970, Oct. 17 Litho. *Die Cut***

**Self-adhesive**

**C78** A45 9s red & silver .25 .25
**C79** A45 10s red & magenta .25 .25
**C80** A45 18s red & brt green .75 .75
**C81** A45 38s red & brt blue 2.25 2.25
**C82** A45 1pa red & green 5.50 5.50
*Nos. C78-C82 (5)* 9.00 9.00

Centenary of the British Red Cross.

Nos. C22-C24 Surcharged

**Lithographed; Embossed on Gilt Foil**

**1971, Jan. 31 *Die Cut***

**C83** AP1 9s on #C22 (S on B) .70 .20
**C84** AP1 24s on #C24 (G on B) 1.50 1.00
**C85** AP1 29s on #C23 (R on B) 2.10 1.25
**C86** AP1 38s on #C23 (G on B) 3.25 1.60
*Nos. C83-C86 (4)* 7.55 4.05

In memory of Queen Salote (1900-1965).

Type of Regular Issue, 1953, Surcharged in Red and Black

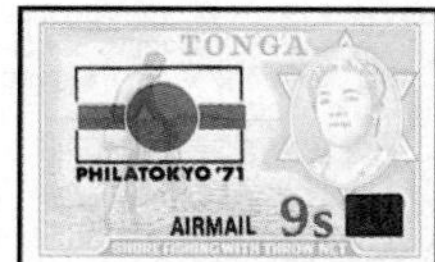


**1971 Engr. Wmk. 79 *Imperf***

**C87** A33 9s on 1½p green .25 .20
**C88** A33 10s on 4p purple & yel .25 .20
**C89** A33 38s on 1p yellow & blk 1.10 .60
*Nos. C87-C89 (3)* 1.60 1.00

See note after No. 272.

Types of Regular Issue Surcharged in Purple or Black: "AIRMAIL," New Denomination and "HONOURING JAPANESE POSTAL CENTENARY 1871-1971"

**1971**

**C90** A34 18s on 1sh car & buff (P) .50 .50
**C91** A33 1pa on 2sh car & ultra 3.00 3.00

Surcharge on #C90 in 6 lines, on #C91 in 4.

Self-adhesive & Imperf.

Starting with Nos. C92-C96, all airmail issues are self-adhesive and imperforate, unless otherwise stated.

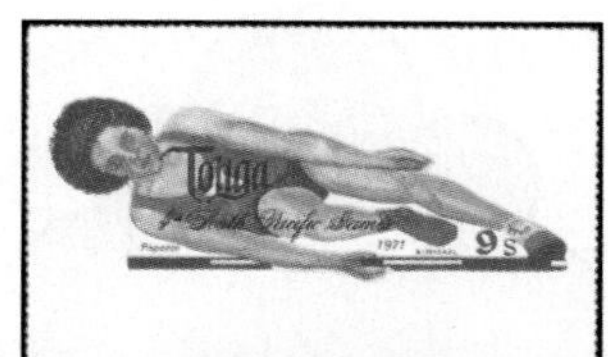


High Jump — AP5

**1971, July Litho. Unwmk.**

**C92** AP5 9s brown, mag & blk .20 .20
**C93** AP5 10s brown, blue & blk .20 .20
**C94** AP5 24s brn, dk grn & blk .45 .45
**C95** AP5 29s brown, vio & blk .60 .60
**C96** AP5 38s brown, red & blk .80 .80
*Nos. C92-C96 (5)* 2.25 2.25

4th South Pacific Games, Papeete, French Polynesia, Sept. 8-19.
For surcharges see Nos. C141-C142.

Prehistoric Trilithon, King's Watch and Portrait AP6

**Litho. and Embossed**

**1971, July 20**

**C97** AP6 14s dk brown & multi .65 .65
**C98** AP6 21s ocher & multi .90 .90

2nd anniversary of man's first landing on the moon and the placement of a Bulova Accutron there. See Nos. C117-118, CO47-CO48, CO61-CO62. Advertisement on peelable paper backing.

Medal Type of Regular Issue

Designs: 10s, Gold Medal of Merit, obverse (King Taufa'ahau IV). 75s, Silver Medal of Merit, obverse (King Taufa'ahau IV). 1pa, Bronze Medal of Merit, reverse.

**1971, Oct. 30 Litho. & Embossed**

**C99** A47 10s gold & multi .20 .20
**C100** A47 75s silver & multi 1.50 1.50
**C101** A47 1pa bronze & multi 1.60 1.60
*Nos. C99-C101 (3)* 3.30 3.30

Girl with Blocks and UNICEF Emblem — AP7

**1971, Dec. Litho.**

**C102** AP7 10s multicolored .20 .20
**C103** AP7 15s multicolored .35 .35
**C104** AP7 25s multicolored .60 .60
**C105** AP7 50s multicolored 1.25 1.25
**C106** AP7 1pa multicolored 2.50 2.50
*Nos. C102-C106 (5)* 4.90 4.90

25th anniversary of UNICEF.

Ship Type of Regular Issue

Design: Map of Merchant Marine routes from Tonga and cargo ship "Niuvakai."

**1972, Apr. 14**

**C107** A49 9s ver & multi .85 .35
**C108** A49 12s multicolored 1.10 .35
**C109** A49 14s dk purple & multi 1.25 .35
**C110** A49 75s olive & multi 6.75 5.00
**C111** A49 90s black & multi 7.00 6.50
*Nos. C107-C111 (5)* 16.95 12.55

For surcharge and overprint see No. C124.

Coin Type of Regular Issue

Design: Coins on top; panel at bottom inscribed "5th anniversary world's first palladium coinage."

**Litho.; Embossed on Metallic Foil**

**1972, July 15**

**C112** A50 9s silver & multi .20 .20
**C113** A50 12s silver & multi .30 .30
**C114** A50 14s silver & multi .35 .35
**C115** A50 21s silver & multi .50 .50
**C116** A50 75s silver & multi 1.75 1.75
*Nos. C112-C116 (5)* 3.10 3.10

Watch Type of 1971

**Litho. and Embossed**

**1972, July 20**

**C117** AP6 17s multicolored .75 .75
**C118** AP6 38s multicolored 1.50 1.50

Advertisement on peelable paper backing.

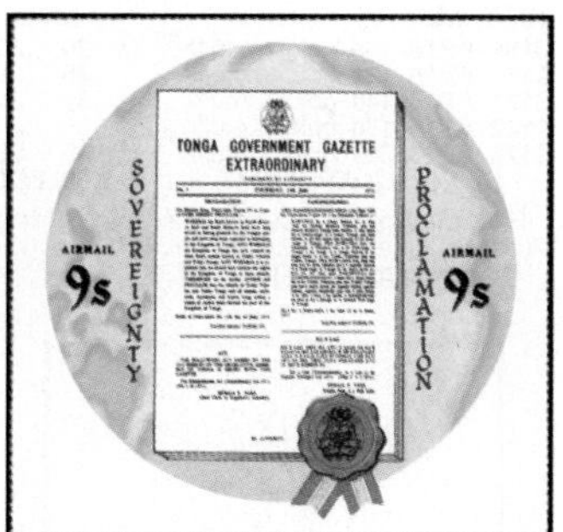


Proclamation of Sovereignty — AP8

**1972, Dec. 9 Litho.**

**C119** AP8 9s ultra & multi .20 .20
**C120** AP8 12s red brown & multi .25 .25
**C121** AP8 14s magenta & multi .35 .35
**C122** AP8 38s brn org & multi .95 .95
**C123** AP8 1pa olive & multi 2.50 2.50
*Nos. C119-C123 (5)* 4.25 4.25

Tonga's proclamation of sovereignty over the Minerva Reefs, June 1972.

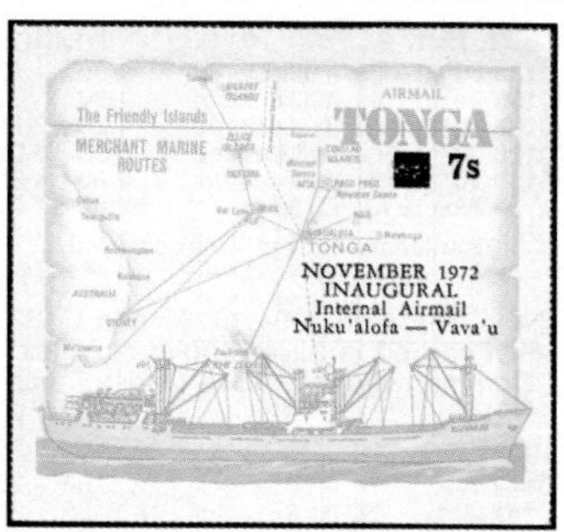


No. C107 Surcharged

**1972, Nov. Litho.**

**C124** A49 7s on 9s multicolored 1.50 1.50

Inauguration of internal airmail service Nukualofa-Vavau, Nov. 1972.

Tongan Bank Notes and Bank Building — AP9

**1973, Mar. 30 Litho.**

**C125** AP9 9s multicolored .25 .20
**C126** AP9 12s ultra & multi .25 .20
**C127** AP9 17s dp car & multi .40 .20
**C128** AP9 50s lt blue & multi 1.50 1.25
**C129** AP9 90s multicolored 2.75 2.75
*Nos. C125-C129 (5)* 5.15 4.60

Establishment of Bank of Tonga.

Boy Scout Emblem — AP10

**1973, June 29 Litho.**

**C130** AP10 9s silver & multi .70 .35
**C131** AP10 12s silver & multi .85 .45
**C132** AP10 14s silver & multi 1.25 .70
**C133** AP10 17s silver & multi 1.40 .85
**C134** AP10 1pa silver & multi 15.00 9.25
*Nos. C130-C134 (5)* 19.20 11.60

See note after No. 326.
For surcharges see Nos. C143-C144.

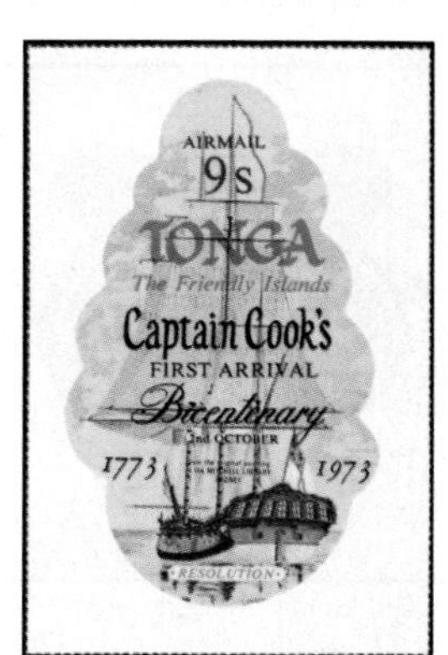


"Resolution" — AP11

**1973, Oct. 2** **Litho.**

| | | | | |
|---|---|---|---|---|
| **C135** | AP11 | 9s multicolored | .80 | .40 |
| **C136** | AP11 | 14s multicolored | 1.50 | .60 |
| **C137** | AP11 | 29s multicolored | 4.50 | 2.75 |
| **C138** | AP11 | 38s multicolored | 5.50 | 3.00 |
| **C139** | AP11 | 75s multicolored | 10.50 | 4.25 |
| | | *Nos. C135-C139 (5)* | 22.80 | 11.00 |

Bicentenary of Capt. Cook's arrival.

Nos. 277, C96, C94, C130 and C132 Surcharged in Silver, Violet or Black: "Commonwealth Games Christchurch 1974"

**1973, Dec. 19**

| | | | | |
|---|---|---|---|---|
| **C140** | A46 | 7s on 25s multi (S) | .20 | .20 |
| **C141** | AP5 | 9s on 38s multi (V) | .25 | .20 |
| **C142** | AP5 | 24s multicolored (B) | .95 | .35 |
| **C143** | AP10 | 29s on 9s multi (V) | 1.10 | .50 |
| **C144** | AP10 | 40s on 14s multi (B) | 1.60 | 1.10 |
| | | *Nos. C140-C144 (5)* | 4.10 | 2.35 |

10th British Commonwealth Games, Christchurch, New Zealand, Jan. 24-Feb. 2, 1974. No. C140 is overprinted "AIRMAIL" in black; the silver surcharge and overprint are on black panels.

Parrot of Eua — AP12

**1974, Mar. 20** **Litho.**

| | | | | |
|---|---|---|---|---|
| **C145** | AP12 | 7s multicolored | .50 | .25 |
| **C146** | AP12 | 9s multicolored | .60 | .30 |
| **C147** | AP12 | 12s multicolored | .60 | .30 |
| **C148** | AP12 | 14s multicolored | .90 | .45 |
| **C149** | AP12 | 17s multicolored | 1.00 | .50 |
| **C150** | AP12 | 29s multicolored | 1.75 | .90 |
| **C151** | AP12 | 38s multicolored | 2.50 | 1.25 |
| **C152** | AP12 | 50s multicolored | 3.00 | 1.50 |
| **C153** | AP12 | 75s multicolored | 4.50 | 2.25 |
| | | *Nos. C145-C153 (9)* | 15.35 | 7.70 |

Printed in rolls of 500. Self-adhesive rose red control number in upper left corner.

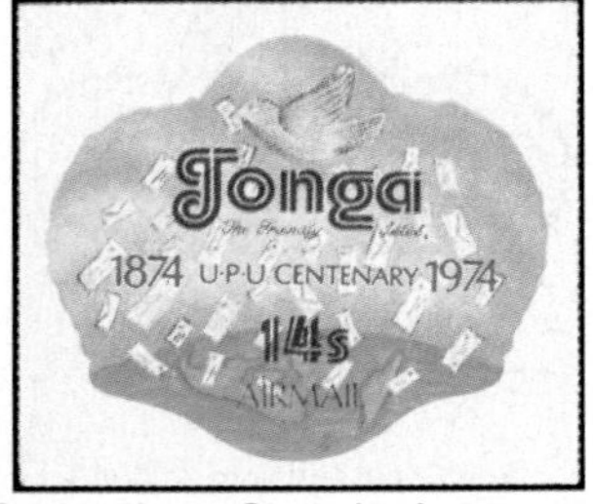


Carrier Pigeon Scattering Letters over Tonga — AP13

**1974, June 20** **Typo.**

| | | | | |
|---|---|---|---|---|
| **C154** | AP13 | 14s lt blue & multi | .45 | .45 |
| **C155** | AP13 | 21s lt blue & multi | .55 | .55 |
| **C156** | AP13 | 60s lt blue & multi | 1.75 | 1.75 |
| **C157** | AP13 | 75s lt blue & multi | 1.90 | 1.90 |
| **C158** | AP13 | 1pa lt blue & multi | 2.50 | 2.50 |
| | | *Nos. C154-C158 (5)* | 7.15 | 7.15 |

Centenary of Universal Postal Union.

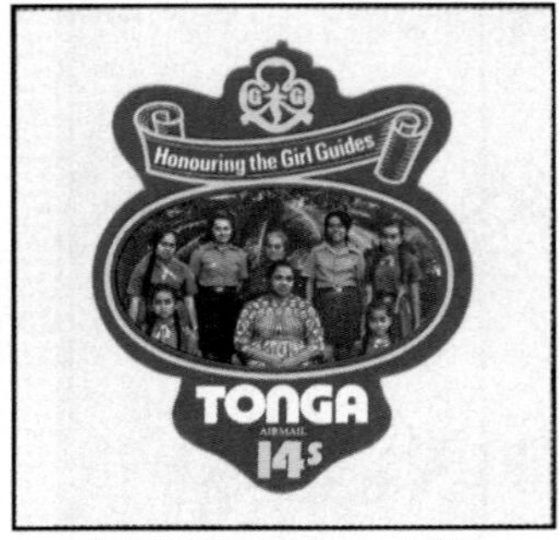


Girl Guide Leaders — AP14

**1974, Sept. 11** **Litho.**

| | | | | |
|---|---|---|---|---|
| **C159** | AP14 | 14s blue & multi | .80 | .50 |
| **C160** | AP14 | 16s blue & multi | 1.40 | .80 |
| **C161** | AP14 | 29s blue & multi | 2.75 | 1.60 |
| **C162** | AP14 | 31s blue & multi | 3.50 | 2.10 |
| **C163** | AP14 | 75s blue & multi | 7.50 | 4.50 |
| | | *Nos. C159-C163 (5)* | 15.95 | 9.50 |

Girl Guides of Tonga.

For surcharges and overprints see Nos. C190-C191, C193.

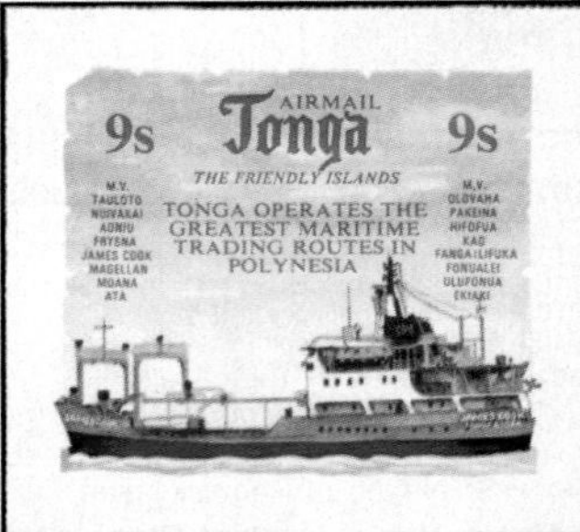


Freighter "James Cook" and List of Tongan Merchantmen — AP15

**1974, Dec. 11**

| | | | | |
|---|---|---|---|---|
| **C164** | AP15 | 9s blue & multi | .80 | .30 |
| **C165** | AP15 | 14s blue & multi | 1.40 | .55 |
| **C166** | AP15 | 17s blue & multi | 1.50 | .60 |
| **C167** | AP15 | 60s blue & multi | 5.50 | 3.75 |
| **C168** | AP15 | 90s blue & multi | 8.75 | 4.75 |
| | | *Nos. C164-C168 (5)* | 17.95 | 9.95 |

Establishment of Royal Marine Institute.

Beach AP16

Designs: 12s, 14s, like 9s. 17s, 38s, Surf.

**1975, Mar. 11** **Litho.**

| | | | | |
|---|---|---|---|---|
| **C169** | AP16 | 9s gold & multi | .20 | .20 |
| **C170** | AP16 | 12s gold & multi | .25 | .25 |
| **C171** | AP16 | 14s gold & multi | .30 | .30 |
| **C172** | AP16 | 17s gold & multi | .30 | .30 |
| **C173** | AP16 | 38s gold & multi | .95 | .95 |
| | | *Nos. C169-C173 (5)* | 2.00 | 2.00 |

First meeting of South Pacific area Prime Ministers. See note after No. 226.

For surcharges see Nos. C229, C298.

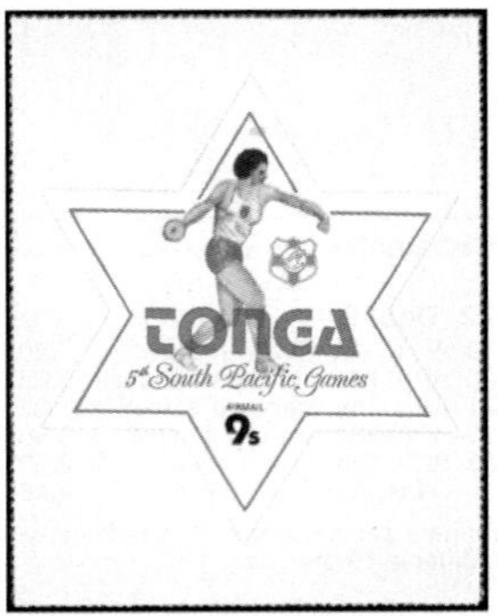


Women's Discus and Games' Emblem — AP17

**1975, June 11**

| | | | | |
|---|---|---|---|---|
| **C174** | AP17 | 9s multicolored | .35 | .35 |
| **C175** | AP17 | 12s multicolored | .45 | .45 |
| **C176** | AP17 | 14s multicolored | .45 | .45 |
| **C177** | AP17 | 17s black & multi | .55 | .55 |
| **C178** | AP17 | 90s olive & multi | 2.00 | 2.00 |
| | | *Nos. C174-C178 (5)* | 3.80 | 3.80 |

5th South Pacific Games, Guam, Aug. 1-10. See note after No. 226.

For surcharges see Nos. C230-C231.

FAO Type of 1975

Designs (FAO Coins): 12s, Coins showing cattle, corn and pig. 14s, Cornucopias; coins showing king, family planning emblem and melons. 25s, Bananas and treasure chest. 50s, King Taufa'ahau. 1pa, Palms.

**1975, Sept. 3**

| | | | | |
|---|---|---|---|---|
| **C179** | A62 | 12s multicolored | .45 | .45 |
| **C180** | A62 | 14s blue & multi | .45 | .45 |
| **C181** | A62 | 25s silver, blk & org | .70 | .70 |
| **C182** | A62 | 50s car, sil & blk | 1.25 | 1.25 |
| **C183** | A62 | 1pa silver & black | 2.25 | 2.25 |
| | | *Nos. C179-C183 (5)* | 5.10 | 5.10 |

Size of paper backing of 14s: 82x50mm; others 45x45mm. See note after No. 226.

Coin Type of 1975

Coins: 9s, King Taufa'ahau IV, obverse. 12s, Queen Salote III, 75pa reverse and obverse. 14s, 10pa reverse. 38s, King Taufa'ahau IV, 10pa reverse and observe. 1pa, Heads of four constitutional monarchs.

**1975, Nov. 4**

**Light Blue Background**

| | | | | |
|---|---|---|---|---|
| **C184** | A63 | 9s black, sil & red | .35 | .20 |
| **C185** | A63 | 12s gold, blk & grn | .45 | .35 |
| **C186** | A63 | 14s black, sil & ol | .45 | .35 |
| **C187** | A63 | 38s gold, blk & org | 1.00 | .50 |
| **C188** | A63 | 1pa black, sil & blue | 2.60 | 2.60 |
| | | *Nos. C184-C188 (5)* | 4.85 | 4.00 |

Size of paper backing of 1pa: 87x78mm, others 65x60mm. See note after No. 226.

Nos. 344-345, C160, C163 Surcharged and Overprinted in Carmine on Silver, Green or Gold

a

b

**1976, Feb. 24** **Litho.**

| | | | | |
|---|---|---|---|---|
| **C189** | A58 (a) | 12s on 20s (S) | .80 | .50 |
| **C190** | AP14 (b) | 14s on 16s (Gr) | .80 | .50 |
| **C191** | AP14 (b) | 16s (G) | 1.00 | .50 |
| **C192** | A58 (a) | 38s on 40s (G) | 2.50 | .70 |
| **C193** | AP14 (b) | 75s (S) | 4.50 | 2.75 |
| | | *Nos. C189-193 (5)* | 9.60 | 4.95 |

21st Olympic Games, Montreal, Canada, July 17-Aug. 1. See note after No. 226.

Bicentennial Type of 1976

Signers of Declaration of Independence, Flags of US and Tonga: 12s, Abraham Clark, George Ross, Thomas Lynch, Jr., Charles Carroll, Roger Sherman (no flags). 14s, Robert Treat Paine, Thomas Jefferson, Thomas McKean, John Adams. 17s, Button Gwinnett, Lewis Morris, Caesar Rodney, Richard Henry Lee. 38s, John Hart, Samuel Huntington, Philip Livingstone, John Morton. 1pa, John Hancock, Joseph Hewes, Josiah Bartlett, John Witherspoon.

**1976, May 26**

| | | | | |
|---|---|---|---|---|
| **C194** | A66 | 12s buff & multi | .65 | .20 |
| **C195** | A66 | 14s buff & multi | .75 | .20 |
| **C196** | A66 | 17s buff & multi | .80 | .45 |
| **C197** | A66 | 38s buff & multi | 3.50 | 1.00 |
| **C198** | A66 | 1pa buff & multi | 6.00 | 3.75 |
| | | *Nos. C194-C198 (5)* | 11.70 | 5.60 |

See note after No. 381.

Missionary Ship "Triton" — AP18

**1976, Aug. 25** **Litho.**

| | | | | |
|---|---|---|---|---|
| **C199** | AP18 | 9s pink & multi | .35 | .30 |
| **C200** | AP18 | 12s multicolored | .55 | .40 |
| **C201** | AP18 | 14s multicolored | .60 | .45 |
| **C202** | AP18 | 17s buff & multi | .80 | .55 |
| **C203** | AP18 | 38s multicolored | 1.40 | .90 |
| | | *Nos. C199-C203 (5)* | 3.70 | 2.60 |

See note after No. 386.

For surcharges see Nos. C234, C294, C299.

Treaty Signing Ceremony, Nukualofa — AP19

**1976, Nov. 1**

| | | | | |
|---|---|---|---|---|
| **C204** | AP19 | 11s multicolored | .45 | .40 |
| **C205** | AP19 | 17s multicolored | .60 | .55 |
| **C206** | AP19 | 18s multicolored | .65 | .60 |
| **C207** | AP19 | 31s multicolored | 1.10 | 1.00 |
| **C208** | AP19 | 39s multicolored | 1.40 | 1.25 |
| | | *Nos. C204-C208 (5)* | 4.20 | 3.80 |

See note after No. 391.

For surcharges see Nos. C235, C295.

Elizabeth II and Taufa'ahau IV — AP20

**1977, Feb. 7**

| | | | | |
|---|---|---|---|---|
| **C209** | AP20 | 15s gray & multi | .20 | .20 |
| **C210** | AP20 | 17s gray & multi | .35 | .35 |
| **C211** | AP20 | 22s gray & multi | *10.00* | *6.50* |
| **C212** | AP20 | 31s gray & multi | .50 | .50 |
| **C213** | AP20 | 39s gray & multi | .50 | .50 |
| | | *Nos. C209-C213 (5)* | *11.55* | *8.05* |

See note after No. 396.

Coronation Coin — AP21

**1977, July 4** **Litho.**

| | | | | |
|---|---|---|---|---|
| **C214** | AP21 11s multicolored | .30 | .30 |
| **C215** | AP21 17s multicolored | .40 | .40 |
| **C216** | AP21 18s multicolored | .40 | .40 |
| **C217** | AP21 39s multicolored | .65 | .65 |
| **C218** | AP21 1pa multicolored | 2.00 | 2.00 |
| | *Nos. C214-C218 (5)* | 3.75 | 3.75 |

See note after No. 401.
See Nos. CO120-CO122.

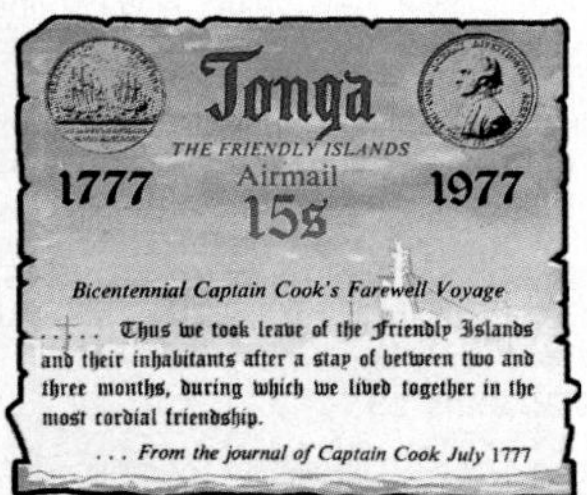


Capt. Cook Medal and Journal Quotation — AP22

**1977, Sept. 27**

| | | | |
|---|---|---|---|
| **C219** | AP22 15s multicolored | .90 | .75 |
| **C220** | AP22 22s multicolored | 1.40 | 1.25 |
| **C221** | AP22 31s multicolored | 3.50 | 3.00 |
| **C222** | AP22 50s multicolored | 10.00 | 5.00 |
| **C223** | AP22 1pa multicolored | 21.00 | 9.00 |
| | *Nos. C219-C223 (5)* | 36.80 | 19.00 |

Bicentenary of Capt. Cook's farewell voyage.
See Nos. CO123-CO125.

Sei and Fin Whales — AP23

**1977, Dec. 16**

| | | | |
|---|---|---|---|
| **C224** | AP23 11s blk, vio & bl | 4.25 | .80 |
| **C225** | AP23 17s blk, red & bl | 4.75 | .90 |
| **C226** | AP23 18s blk, grn & bl | 4.75 | 1.10 |
| **C227** | AP23 39s blk, brn & bl | 5.75 | 2.25 |
| **C228** | AP23 50s blk, mag & bl | 7.25 | 3.50 |
| | *Nos. C224-C228 (5)* | 26.75 | 8.55 |

Whale protection.
See Nos. CO126-CO128.

Stamps of 1975-77 Surcharged in Various Colors

**1978**

| | | | |
|---|---|---|---|
| **C229** | AP16 17s on 38s (#C173;Gr) | 2.25 | 1.50 |
| **C230** | AP17 17s on 9s (#C174;B) | 2.25 | 1.50 |
| **C231** | AP17 17s on 12s (#C175;DBl) | 2.25 | 1.50 |
| **C232** | A63 17s on 38s (#C187;B) | 2.25 | 1.50 |
| **C233** | A66 17s on 12s (#C194; R on G) | 2.25 | 1.50 |
| **C234** | AP18 17s on 9s (#C199; B) | 2.25 | 1.50 |
| **C235** | AP19 17s on 18s (#C206; G on Brn) | 2.25 | 1.50 |
| **C236** | A66 1pa on 75s (#381; Gr on S) | *11.75* | *9.50* |
| **C237** | A66 1pa on 38s (#C197; DBl on G) | *11.75* | *9.50* |
| **C238** | OA15 1pa on 1.10pa (#CO119; S on DBl) | *26.50* | *27.50* |

Edmonton Games Type of 1978

Canadian Maple leaf and Tongan coat of arms.

**1978, May 5** **Litho.**

| | | | |
|---|---|---|---|
| **C239** | A73 17s red & multi | .45 | .45 |
| **C240** | A73 35s red & multi | .90 | .90 |
| **C241** | A73 38s red & multi | .95 | .95 |
| **C242** | A73 40s red & multi | 2.00 | 2.00 |
| **C243** | A73 65s red & multi | 1.50 | 1.50 |
| | *Nos. C239-C243 (5)* | 5.80 | 5.80 |

See note after No. 423.

King Type of 1978

Design: Head of King Taufa'ahau IV within 6-pointed star.

**1978, July 4**

| | | | |
|---|---|---|---|
| **C244** | A74 11s multicolored | .25 | .25 |
| **C245** | A74 15s multicolored | .35 | .35 |
| **C246** | A74 17s multicolored | .45 | .45 |
| **C247** | A74 39s multicolored | 1.00 | 1.00 |
| **C248** | A74 1pa multicolored | 2.50 | 2.50 |
| | *Nos. C244-C248 (5)* | 4.55 | 4.55 |

See note after No. 226.

Wildlife Type of 1978

**1978, Dec. 15** **Litho. & Typo.**

| | | | |
|---|---|---|---|
| **C249** | A77 17s Whale | 3.50 | 1.75 |
| **C250** | A77 22s Bat | 3.50 | 1.75 |
| **C251** | A77 31s Turtle | 3.50 | 1.75 |
| **C252** | A77 39s Parrot | 7.00 | 3.00 |
| **C253** | A77 45s like 17s | 7.50 | 3.50 |
| | *Nos. C249-C253 (5)* | 25.00 | *11.75* |

Wildlife conservation. See note after No. 226.

Types of 1979

Designs: 15s, like No. 453. 17s, like No. 450. 31s, Rotary emblem. 39s, Ministry and tourism buildings, Bank of Tonga, GPO. 1pa, Dish antenna and map of Tonga.

**1979, Feb. 16** **Litho.**

| | | | |
|---|---|---|---|
| **C254** | A79 15s multicolored | .40 | .30 |
| **C255** | A79 17s multicolored | .50 | .35 |
| **C256** | A78 31s vio blue & gold | .75 | .45 |
| **C257** | A79 39s multicolored | 1.10 | .65 |
| **C258** | A79 1pa multicolored | 2.75 | 1.60 |
| | *Nos. C254-C258 (5)* | 5.50 | 3.35 |

Decade of Progress. Paper backing shows map of Tonga.

Type of 1979

Tongan self-adhesive, free-form stamps.

**1979, June 1**

| | | | |
|---|---|---|---|
| **C259** | A81 15s multicolored | .35 | .35 |
| **C260** | A81 17s multicolored | .45 | .45 |
| **C261** | A81 18s multicolored | .50 | .50 |
| **C262** | A81 31s multicolored | .75 | .75 |
| **C263** | A81 39s multicolored | .95 | .95 |
| | *Nos. C259-C263 (5)* | 3.00 | 3.00 |

See note after No. 458.

Jet — AP24

**1979, Aug. 17**

| | | | |
|---|---|---|---|
| **C264** | AP24 5s multicolored | .20 | .20 |
| **C265** | AP24 11s multicolored | .35 | .25 |
| **C266** | AP24 14s multicolored | .50 | .35 |
| **C267** | AP24 15s multicolored | .50 | .35 |
| **C268** | AP24 17s multicolored | .65 | .45 |
| **C269** | AP24 18s multicolored | .70 | .50 |
| **C270** | AP24 22s multicolored | .75 | .55 |
| **C271** | AP24 31s multicolored | 1.10 | .75 |
| **C272** | AP24 39s multicolored | 1.40 | .95 |
| **C273** | AP24 75s multicolored | 2.50 | 1.75 |
| **C274** | AP24 1pa multicolored | 3.50 | 2.50 |
| | *Nos. C264-C274 (11)* | 12.15 | 8.60 |

Nos. C264-C274 issued in coils; self-adhesive control number in lower left corner of paper backing except on 14s, 18s, 22s, 75s. See note after No. 226.
See Nos. C303-C305.

View Type of 1979

Design: Kao Island. See note after No. 463.

**1979, Nov. 23**

| | | | |
|---|---|---|---|
| **C275** | A82 5s multicolored | .20 | .20 |
| **C276** | A82 15s multicolored | .35 | .35 |
| **C277** | A82 17s multicolored | .45 | .45 |
| **C278** | A82 39s multicolored | .95 | .95 |
| **C279** | A82 75s multicolored | 1.75 | 1.75 |
| | *Nos. C275-C279 (5)* | 3.70 | 3.70 |

Friendship Treaty Type of 1980

George Tupou I, Admiral du Bouzet, Adventure. See notes over #464 & after #468.

**1980, Jan. 9** **Litho.**

| | | | |
|---|---|---|---|
| **C280** | A83 15s multicolored | .45 | .45 |
| **C281** | A83 17s multicolored | .55 | .55 |
| **C282** | A83 22s multicolored | .60 | .60 |
| **C283** | A83 31s multicolored | .85 | .85 |
| **C284** | A83 39s multicolored | 1.00 | 1.00 |
| | *Nos. C280-C284 (5)* | 3.45 | 3.45 |

Nos. C259-C263 Surcharged and Overprinted in Black on Silver: "1980 OLYMPIC GAMES," Moscow '80 and Bear Emblems

**1980, Apr. 30** **Litho.**

| | | | |
|---|---|---|---|
| **C285** | A81 9s on 15s multi | .30 | .30 |
| **C286** | A81 16s on 17s multi | .65 | .65 |
| **C287** | A81 29s on 18s multi | 1.00 | 1.00 |
| **C288** | A81 32s on 31s multi | 1.10 | 1.10 |
| **C289** | A81 47s on 39s multi | 1.60 | 1.60 |
| | *Nos. C285-C289 (5)* | 4.65 | 4.65 |

22nd Summer Olympic Games, Moscow, July 19-Aug. 3.

Scouting Activities in Rotary Emblem — AP25

**1980, Sept. 30** **Litho.**

| | | | |
|---|---|---|---|
| **C290** | AP25 29s multicolored | .90 | .90 |
| **C291** | AP25 32s multicolored | 1.00 | 1.00 |
| **C292** | AP25 47s multicolored | 1.40 | 1.40 |
| **C293** | AP25 1pa multicolored | 3.00 | 3.00 |
| | *Nos. C290-C293 (4)* | 6.30 | 6.30 |

Boy Scout Jamboree; Rotary International, 75th anniversary. Peelable backing shows map of Tonga.

Nos. C170, C185, C195, C200-C201, C208 Surcharged

**1980, Dec. 3** **Litho.**

| | | | |
|---|---|---|---|
| **C294** | AP18 29s on 14s multi | .70 | .70 |
| **C295** | AP19 29s on 39s multi | .70 | .70 |
| **C296** | A63 32s on 12s multi | .80 | .80 |
| **C297** | A66 32s on 14s multi | .80 | .80 |
| **C298** | AP16 47s on 12s multi | 1.10 | 1.10 |
| **C299** | AP18 47s on 12s multi | 1.10 | 1.10 |
| | *Nos. C294-C299 (6)* | 5.20 | 5.20 |

IYD Type of 1981

**1981, Sept. 9** **Litho.**

**Size: 25x32mm**

| | | | |
|---|---|---|---|
| **C300** | A85 29s multicolored | .45 | .45 |
| **C301** | A85 32s multicolored | .55 | .55 |
| **C302** | A85 47s multicolored | .80 | .80 |
| | *Nos. C300-C302 (3)* | 1.80 | 1.80 |

Jet Type of 1979

**1982, Nov. 17** **Litho.**

| | | | |
|---|---|---|---|
| **C303** | AP24 29s pink & black | 1.25 | .85 |
| **C304** | AP24 32s pale yel & blk | 1.40 | 1.00 |
| **C305** | AP24 47s lt brown & blk | 2.25 | 1.50 |
| | *Nos. C303-C305 (3)* | 4.90 | 3.35 |

## AIR POST SPECIAL DELIVERY

**Catalogue values for unused stamps in this section are for Never Hinged items.**

Owl — APSD1

**1990, Feb. 21** **Litho.** ***Perf. 11½***

| | | | |
|---|---|---|---|
| **CE1** | APSD1 10pa multi | 15.00 | 15.00 |

## AIR POST OFFICIAL STAMPS

**Catalogue values for unused stamps in this section are for Never Hinged items.**

Nos. 115, 117-118, 111-113 Overprinted "OFFICIAL AIR MAIL / 1862 / TAU'ATAINA / EMANCIPATION / 1962" in Red

**Engr.; Photo. (A35)**

**1962, Feb. 7** **Wmk. 79**

| | | | |
|---|---|---|---|
| **CO1** | A35 2p ultra | 10.00 | 7.50 |
| **CO2** | A35 5p purple | 11.00 | 8.00 |
| **CO3** | A35 1sh red brown | 8.00 | 4.00 |
| **CO4** | A33 5sh pur & yel | 85.00 | 50.00 |
| **CO5** | A34 10sh black & yel | 40.00 | 20.00 |
| **CO6** | A34 £1 ultra, car & yel | 65.00 | 30.00 |
| | *Nos. CO1-CO6 (6)* | 219.00 | 119.50 |

Centenary of emancipation.

Type of Regular Gold Coin Issue

Design: 15sh, Queen Salote standing, 1-koula coin, obverse.

**Litho.; Embossed on Gilt Foil**

**1963, July 15** **Unwmk.** ***Die Cut***

**Diameter: 80mm**

| | | | |
|---|---|---|---|
| **CO7** | A36 15sh black | 5.75 | 5.75 |

Note after No. 133 also applies to No. CO7.

No. CO7 Surcharged like Regular Issue of 1965 in Black

**1965, Mar. 18**

| | | | |
|---|---|---|---|
| **CO8** | A36 30sh on 15sh black | 6.50 | 6.50 |

No. 116 Surcharged in Italic Letters Similarly to Nos. C16-C21

***Perf. 14½x13½***

**1966, June 18** **Wmk. 79**

| | | | |
|---|---|---|---|
| **CO9** | A35 10sh on 4p brt green | .80 | .30 |
| **CO10** | A35 20sh on 4p brt green | 1.00 | .40 |

Centenary of Tupou College and secondary education.

No. 111 Surcharged in Red: "OFFICIAL / AIRMAIL / ONE PA'ANGA"

**1967, Mar. 25** **Engr.** ***Perf. 11½x11***

| | | | |
|---|---|---|---|
| **CO11** | A33 1p on 5sh pur & yel | 3.00 | 3.00 |

Type of Regular Issue Surcharged

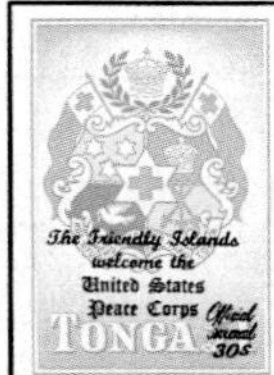


**1967, Dec. 15** **Wmk. 79** ***Die Cut***

| | | | |
|---|---|---|---|
| **CO12** | A34 30s on £1 multi | .55 | .55 |
| **CO13** | A34 70s on £1 multi | .80 | .80 |
| **CO14** | A34 1.50pa on £1 multi | 1.25 | 1.25 |
| | *Nos. CO12-CO14 (3)* | 2.60 | 2.60 |

Arrival of US Peace Corps.

No. 113 Surcharged with New Value and "OFFICIAL/AIRMAIL"

**1968, Apr. 6 Engr. *Perf. 11x11½***

| | | | | |
|---|---|---|---|---|
| **CO15** | A34 | 40s on £1 multi | .75 | .75 |
| **CO16** | A34 | 60s on £1 multi | 1.00 | 1.00 |
| **CO17** | A34 | 1pa on £1 multi | 1.25 | 1.25 |
| **CO18** | A34 | 2pa on £1 multi | 2.25 | 2.25 |
| | | *Nos. CO15-CO18 (4)* | 5.25 | 5.25 |

Type of 1953 Surcharged: "Friendly Islands / Trials / Field & Track / South Pacific / Games / Port Moresby / 1969 / OFFICIAL AIRMAIL"

**Wmk. 79**

**1968, Dec. 19 Engr. *Die Cut***

| | | | | |
|---|---|---|---|---|
| **CO19** | A34 | 20s on £1 grn & multi | .35 | .20 |
| **CO20** | A34 | 1pa on £1 grn & multi | 1.00 | .60 |

No. 176 Overprinted and Surcharged in Gold on Colored Panels (Green, Emerald, Violet or Lilac) like Nos. 203-209.

**Litho.; Embossed on Palladium Foil**

**1968 Unwmk.**

| | | | | |
|---|---|---|---|---|
| **CO21** | A38 | 40s on 2s (G) | 1.60 | .80 |
| **CO22** | A38 | 60s on 2s (E) | 2.10 | 1.60 |
| **CO23** | A38 | 1pa on 2s (V) | 3.50 | 3.50 |
| **CO24** | A38 | 2pa on 2s (L) | 6.00 | 6.00 |
| | | *Nos. CO21-CO24 (4)* | 13.20 | 11.90 |

50th birthday of King Taufa'ahau IV.

Pacific Games Type of Regular Issue

Design: Boxer.

**1969, Aug. 13 Litho. *Die Cut***

**Self-adhesive**

| | | | | |
|---|---|---|---|---|
| **CO25** | A40 | 70s gray, red & grn | .80 | .80 |
| **CO26** | A40 | 80s gray, red & org | .95 | .95 |

See note after No. 231.

Type of Regular Issue, 1953, Surcharged: "OFFICIAL AIRMAIL / 1969 OIL / SEARCH / 90s" and Oil Derrick Obliterating Old Denomination

**1969, Dec. 23 *Die Cut Wmk. 79***

| | | | | |
|---|---|---|---|---|
| **CO27** | A34 | 90s on £1 grn & multi | 3.25 | 3.25 |

First scientific search for oil in Tonga.

Type of Regular Issue, 1953, Surcharged: "Royal Visit / MARCH / 1970 / OFFICIAL / AIRMAIL" in Black, Violet Blue or Emerald

**1970, Mar. 7 Engr. Wmk. 79**

| | | | | |
|---|---|---|---|---|
| **CO28** | A34 | 75s on 1sh | 4.25 | 3.00 |
| **CO29** | A34 | 1pa on 1sh (VBl) | 5.50 | 4.00 |
| **CO30** | A34 | 1.25pa on 1sh (E) | 7.00 | 5.00 |
| | | *Nos. CO28-CO30 (3)* | 16.75 | 12.00 |

See note after No. 242.

Type of Regular Issue Surcharged in Black, Red or Emerald

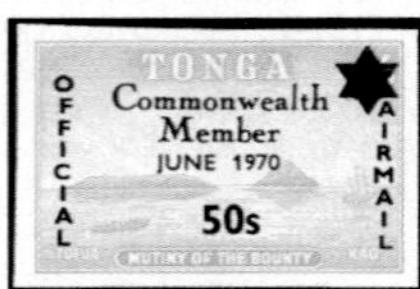


**1970, June 4 Wmk. 79 *Die Cut***

| | | | | |
|---|---|---|---|---|
| **CO31** | A33 | 50s on 5sh (B) | 1.50 | 1.50 |
| **CO32** | A33 | 90s on 5sh (R) | 2.25 | 2.25 |
| **CO33** | A33 | 1.50pa on 5sh (E) | 3.50 | 3.50 |
| | | *Nos. CO31-CO33 (3)* | 7.25 | 7.25 |

See note after No. 247.

Type of Regular Issue, 1953, Surcharged in Red and Purple or Black:

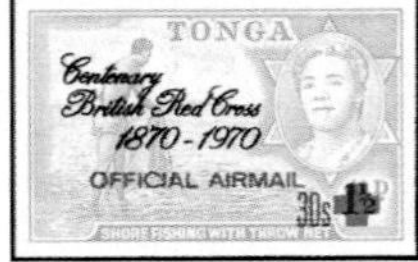


**1970, Oct. 17 Engr. *Die Cut***

| | | | | |
|---|---|---|---|---|
| **CO34** | A33 | 30s on 1½p (B & R) | 1.90 | 1.90 |
| **CO35** | A33 | 80s on 5sh (P & R) | 5.00 | 5.00 |
| **CO36** | A33 | 90s on 5sh (P & R) | 6.00 | 6.00 |
| | | *Nos. CO34-CO36 (3)* | 12.90 | 12.90 |

Centenary of the British Red Cross.

Type of Regular Issue, 1953, Surcharged in Black, Purple, Blue or Green

**1971, Jan. 31 Engr. *Die Cut***

| | | | | |
|---|---|---|---|---|
| **CO37** | A34 | 20s on 10sh (Bk) | 1.25 | .85 |
| **CO38** | A34 | 30s on 10sh (P) | 2.10 | 1.25 |
| **CO39** | A34 | 50s on 10sh (Bl) | 3.50 | 2.10 |
| **CO40** | A34 | 2pa on 10sh (G) | 13.75 | 11.75 |
| | | *Nos. CO37-CO40 (4)* | 20.60 | 15.95 |

In memory of Queen Salote (1900-1965).

Type of Regular Issue, 1953, Surcharged in Red and Blue, Black or Purple

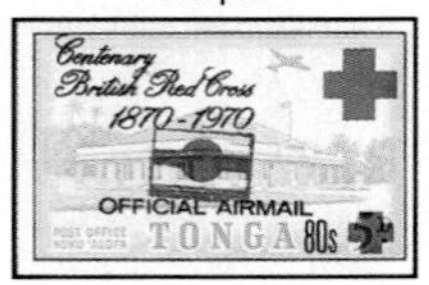


**1971 Engr. Wmk. 79 *Imperf***

**Colors: Green & Yellow**

| | | | | |
|---|---|---|---|---|
| **CO41** | A33 | 30s on 5p (R & Bl) | 1.40 | .80 |
| **CO42** | A33 | 80s on 5p (R & Bk) | 3.25 | 2.10 |
| **CO43** | A33 | 90s on 5p (R & P) | 3.50 | 2.40 |
| | | *Nos. CO41-CO43 (3)* | 8.15 | 5.30 |

See note after No. 272.

Self-adhesive & Imperf.

Starting with Nos. CO44-CO46, all airmail official issues are self-adhesive and imperforate, unless otherwise stated.

Soccer Ball — OA1

**1971, July Litho. Unwmk.**

| | | | | |
|---|---|---|---|---|
| **CO44** | OA1 | 50s multi | .95 | .95 |
| **CO45** | OA1 | 90s multi | 1.25 | 1.25 |
| **CO46** | OA1 | 1.50pa multi | 1.90 | 1.90 |
| | | *Nos. CO44-CO46 (3)* | 4.10 | 4.10 |

4th South Pacific Games, Papeete, French Polynesia, Sept. 8-19.

For overprints see Nos. CO75-CO77.

Watch Type of Air Post Issues

**Litho. and Embossed**

**1971, July 20**

| | | | | |
|---|---|---|---|---|
| **CO47** | AP6 | 14s brown & multi | .65 | .65 |
| **CO48** | AP6 | 21s brn red & multi | .90 | .90 |

Advertisement on peelable paper backing.

Nos. 243-244, 246 Surcharged

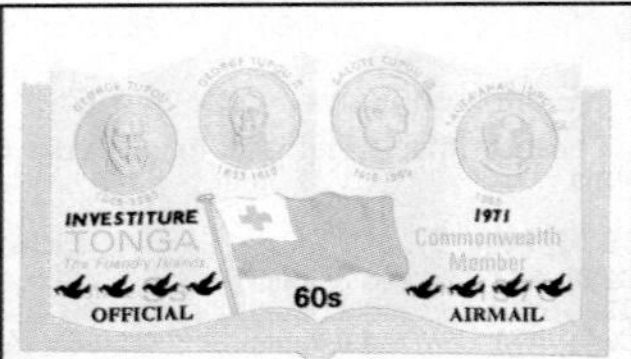

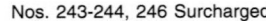

Reduced illustration.

**Litho.; Gold Embossed**

**1971, Oct. 30**

| | | | | |
|---|---|---|---|---|
| **CO49** | A43 | 60s on 3s multi | 1.10 | 1.10 |
| **CO50** | A43 | 80s on 25s multi | 1.40 | 1.40 |
| **CO51** | A43 | 1.10pa on 7s multi | 1.60 | 1.60 |
| | | *Nos. CO49-CO51 (3)* | 4.10 | 4.10 |

First investiture of Tongan Medal of Honor.

"UNICEF" — OA2

**1971, Dec. Litho.**

| | | | | |
|---|---|---|---|---|
| **CO52** | OA2 | 70s black & multi | 2.00 | 2.00 |
| **CO53** | OA2 | 80s multicolored | 2.25 | 2.25 |
| **CO54** | OA2 | 90s multicolored | 2.25 | 2.25 |
| | | *Nos. CO52-CO54 (3)* | 6.50 | 6.50 |

25th anniversary of UNICEF.

For overprint see No. CO70.

Ship Type of Regular Issue

Design: Map of Merchant Marine routes from Tonga and tanker "Aoniu."

**1972, Apr. 14**

| | | | | |
|---|---|---|---|---|
| **CO55** | A49 | 20s multi | 1.90 | .90 |
| **CO56** | A49 | 50s multi | 4.00 | 2.75 |
| **CO57** | A49 | 1.20pa multi | 8.75 | 7.00 |
| | | *Nos. CO55-CO57 (3)* | 14.65 | 10.65 |

Coin Type of Regular Issue

Design: Coins in center, inscription panel above, date below coins.

**Litho.; Embossed on Metallic Foil**

**1972, July 15**

| | | | | |
|---|---|---|---|---|
| **CO58** | A50 | 50s silver & multi | 1.50 | 1.50 |
| **CO59** | A50 | 70s silver & multi | 2.00 | 2.00 |
| **CO60** | A50 | 1.50pa silver & multi | 3.75 | 3.75 |
| | | *Nos. CO58-CO60 (3)* | 7.25 | 7.25 |

Watch Type of Air Post Issue

**1972, July 20 Litho.; Embossed**

| | | | | |
|---|---|---|---|---|
| **CO61** | AP6 | 17s multicolored | .60 | .60 |
| **CO62** | AP6 | 38s ocher & multi | 1.25 | 1.25 |

Advertisement on peelable paper backing.

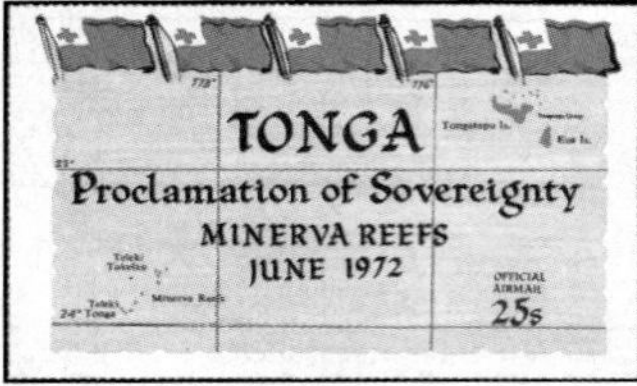


Flags and Map of Tonga Islands — OA3

**1972, Dec. 9 Litho.**

| | | | | |
|---|---|---|---|---|
| **CO63** | OA3 | 25s black & multi | .55 | .55 |
| **CO64** | OA3 | 75s multicolored | 1.60 | 1.60 |
| **CO65** | OA3 | 1.50pa multicolored | 3.25 | 3.25 |
| | | *Nos. CO63-CO65 (3)* | 5.40 | 5.40 |

Tonga's proclamation of sovereignty over the Minerva Reefs, June 1972.

No. 290 Surcharged in Black, Ultramarine or Green

1973
ESTABLISHMENT
BANK OF TONGA
40s
OFFICIAL AIRMAIL

**1973, Mar. 30 Litho.**

| | | | | |
|---|---|---|---|---|
| **CO66** | A49 | 40s on 21s (B) | 1.50 | 1.25 |
| **CO67** | A49 | 85s on 21s (U) | 3.25 | 3.25 |
| **CO68** | A49 | 1.25pa on 21s (G) | 3.75 | 3.75 |
| | | *Nos. CO66-CO68 (3)* | 8.50 | 8.25 |

Establishment of Bank of Tonga.

Nos. CO55, CO53 and 247 Overprinted or Surcharged in Silver:

No. CO69: New value, 4 wavy lines, fleur-de-lis and "SILVER JUBILEE / TONGAN SCOUTING / 1948-1973"

No. CO70: "SILVER / JUBILEE" (vertically), fleur-de-lis and "1948 1973"

No. CO71: Silver surcharge and overprint on dark blue panels "OFFICIAL AIRMAIL / T$1.40," "1948-1973" "SILVER / JUBILEE/ TONGAN / SCOUTING," "1948-1973" in dark blue

**1973, June 29**

| | | | | |
|---|---|---|---|---|
| **CO69** | A49 | 30s on 20s | 15.00 | 4.00 |
| **CO70** | OA2 | 80s multi | 37.50 | 14.50 |
| **CO71** | A43 | 1.40pa on 50s | 52.50 | 35.00 |
| | | *Nos. CO69-CO71 (3)* | 105.00 | 53.50 |

25th anniv. of Tongan Boy Scout movement.

Tanker James Cook and Cook Medal — OA4

**1973, Oct. 2 Litho.**

| | | | | |
|---|---|---|---|---|
| **CO72** | OA4 | 25s multi | 4.00 | 1.60 |
| **CO73** | OA4 | 80s multi | 10.00 | 5.00 |
| **CO74** | OA4 | 1.30pa multi | 12.00 | 8.25 |
| | | *Nos. CO72-CO74 (3)* | 26.00 | 14.85 |

Bicentenary of Capt. Cook's arrival.

Nos. CO44-CO46 Overprinted in Dark Blue, Black or Green with Games' Emblems and: "1974 / Commonwealth / Games / Christchurch"

**1973, Dec. 19**

| | | | | |
|---|---|---|---|---|
| **CO75** | OA1 | 50s multi (DBl) | 1.25 | 1.25 |
| **CO76** | OA1 | 90s multi (B) | 2.10 | 1.90 |
| **CO77** | OA1 | 1.50pa multi (G) | 3.00 | 2.75 |
| | | *Nos. CO75-CO77 (3)* | 6.35 | 5.90 |

10th British Commonwealth Games, Christchurch, N.Z., Jan. 24-Feb. 2, 1974.

Peace Dove OA5

**1974, Mar. 20 Litho.**

| | | | | |
|---|---|---|---|---|
| **CO78** | OA5 | 7s multicolored | .40 | .25 |
| **CO79** | OA5 | 9s multicolored | .50 | .30 |
| **CO80** | OA5 | 12s multicolored | .50 | .30 |
| **CO81** | OA5 | 14s multicolored | .75 | .45 |
| **CO82** | OA5 | 17s multicolored | .80 | .50 |
| **CO83** | OA5 | 29s multicolored | 1.50 | .90 |
| **CO84** | OA5 | 38s multicolored | 2.00 | 1.25 |

**CO85** OA5 50s multicolored 2.50 1.50
**CO86** OA5 75s multicolored 3.75 2.25
*Nos. CO78-CO86 (9)* 12.70 7.70

Printed in rolls of 500. Self-adhesive lilac control number in upper left corner.

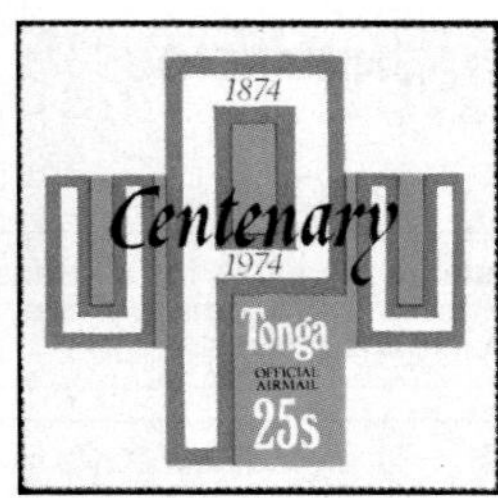


"UPU Centenary" — OA6

**1974, June 20** **Typo.**
**CO87** OA6 25s red, green & blk .85 .85
**CO88** OA6 35s yel, red lil & blk .95 .95
**CO89** OA6 70s dp org, bl & blk 1.90 1.90
*Nos. CO87-CO89 (3)* 3.70 3.70

Centenary of Universal Postal Union.

Lady Baden-Powell — OA7

**1974, Sept. 11** **Litho.**
**CO90** OA7 45s emer & multi 4.50 2.75
**CO91** OA7 55s emer & multi 6.50 3.75
**CO92** OA7 1pa emer & multi 9.25 5.50
*Nos. CO90-CO92 (3)* 20.25 12.00

Girl Guides of Tonga.
For overprints see Nos. CO105-CO107.

Handshake and Institute's Emblem — OA8

Institute's Emblem and Banknotes — OA9

**1974, Dec. 11**
**CO93** OA8 30s multicolored 3.25 1.60
**CO94** OA8 35s multicolored 3.75 2.10
**CO95** OA9 80s red & multi 8.75 4.50
*Nos. CO93-CO95 (3)* 15.75 8.20

Establishment of Royal Marine Institute.

Arch and Palms — OA10

Designs: 75s, 1.25pa, Dawn over lagoon.

**1975, Mar. 11** **Litho.**
**CO96** OA10 50s multi 1.75 1.75
**CO97** OA10 75s multi 3.00 3.00
**CO98** OA10 1.25pa multi 4.00 4.00
*Nos. CO96-CO98 (3)* 8.75 8.75

First meeting of South Pacific area Prime Ministers. See note after No. 226.

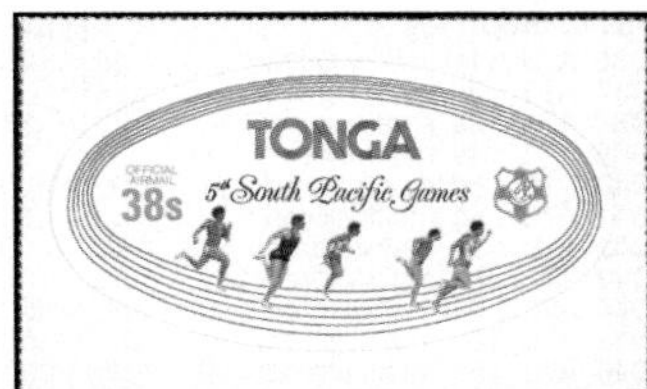


Track and Games' Emblem — OA11

**1975, June 11**
**CO99** OA11 38s multi 1.00 1.00
**CO100** OA11 75s multi 1.75 1.75
**CO101** OA11 1.20pa multi 2.75 2.75
*Nos. CO99-CO101 (3)* 5.50 5.50

5th South Pacific Games, Guam, Aug. 1-10. See note after No. 226.

For surcharge see No. 418.

Four Constitutional Monarchs — OA12

**Litho.; Embossed on Gilt Foil**

**1975, Nov. 4**
**CO102** OA12 17s multicolored .80 .65
**CO103** OA12 60s multicolored 2.00 1.75
**CO104** OA12 90s multicolored 2.60 2.60
*Nos. CO102-CO104 (3)* 5.40 5.00

No. CO90-CO92 Overprinted in Carmine on Blue, Silver or Gold

**1976, Feb. 24** **Litho.**
**CO105** OA7 45s multicolored (B) 3.50 1.40
**CO106** OA7 55s multicolored (S) 3.50 1.60
**CO107** OA7 1pa multicolored (G) 6.75 6.75
*Nos. CO105-CO107 (3)* 13.75 9.75

21st Olympic Games, Montreal, Canada, July 17-Aug. 1. See note after No. 226.

Bicentennial Type of 1976

Signers of Declaration of Independence: 20s, William Paca, Francis Lewis, George Read, Edward Rutledge, Thomas Heyward, Jr. 50s, George Walton, Matthew Thornton, Robert Morris, William Williams, James Smith. 1.15pa, Benjamin Rush, Samuel Adams, Samuel Chase, George Wythe, George Clymer.

**1976, May 26**
**CO108** A66 20s buff & multi 1.00 .75
**CO109** A66 50s buff & multi 3.25 2.50
**CO110** A66 1.15pa buff & multi 6.75 5.25
*Nos. CO108-CO110 (3)* 11.00 8.50

See note after No. 381.

Inside View of Lifuka Chapel — OA13

**1976, Aug. 25** **Litho.**
**CO111** OA13 65s multicolored 2.75 2.75
**CO112** OA13 85s multicolored 3.00 3.00
**CO113** OA13 1.15pa multicolored 4.00 4.00
*Nos. CO111-CO113 (3)* 9.75 9.75

See note after No. 386.
For surcharge see No. CO181.

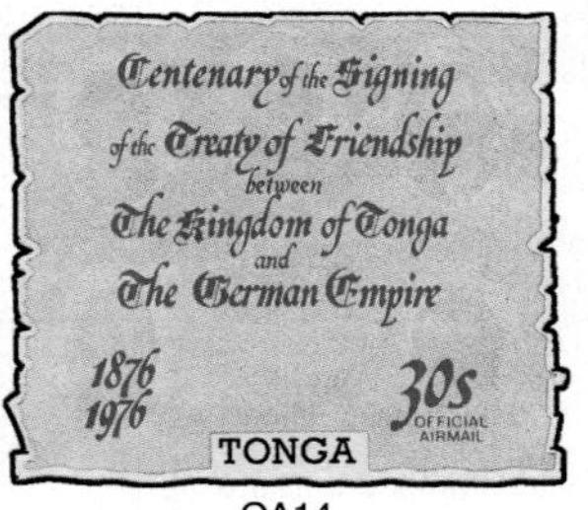


OA14

**1976, Nov. 1**
**CO114** OA14 30s silver & multi .80 .70
**CO115** OA14 60s silver & multi 1.60 1.50
**CO116** OA14 1.25pa silver & multi 3.25 3.00
*Nos. CO114-CO116 (3)* 5.65 5.20

See note after No. 391.

Flags and Arms of Great Britain and Tonga — OA15

**1977, Feb. 7** **Litho.**
**CO117** OA15 35s multi 4.00 3.25
**CO118** OA15 45s multi .50 .50
**CO119** OA15 1.10pa multi 1.50 1.25
*Nos. CO117-CO119 (3)* 6.00 5.00

See note after No. 396.
For surcharge see No. C238.

Coin Type of Air Post Stamps 1977

Design: Coronation coin, inscriptions in round upper panel.

**1977, July 4**
**CO120** AP21 20s multicolored .55 .55
**CO121** AP21 40s multicolored 1.10 1.10
**CO122** AP21 80s multicolored 2.10 2.10
*Nos. CO120-CO122 (3)* 3.75 3.75

See note after No. 401.

Capt. Cook Type of Air Post Stamps 1977

Design: Inscription and flying dove.

**1977, Sept. 27**
**CO123** AP22 20s gold & multi 1.40 1.40
**CO124** AP22 55s on 20s multi 10.00 10.00
**CO125** AP22 85s on 20s multi 21.00 21.00
*Nos. CO123-CO125 (3)* 32.40 32.40

Printed on peelable paper backing showing dark brown replica of entry in Capt. Cook's diary.

Whale Type of Air Post Stamps 1977

Design: Blue whale.

**1977, Dec. 16**
**CO126** AP23 45s multicolored 7.75 3.50
**CO127** AP23 65s multicolored 11.00 5.00
**CO128** AP23 85s multicolored 13.00 6.00
*Nos. CO126-CO128 (3)* 31.75 *14.50*

Whale protection.

Games' Emblem and Athletes OA16

**1978, May 5** **Litho.**
**CO129** OA16 30s red & multi .70 .70
**CO130** OA16 60s red & multi 1.40 1.40
**CO131** OA16 1pa red & multi 2.50 2.50
*Nos. CO129-CO131 (3)* 4.60 4.60

See note after No. 423.

King Type of 1978

Head of King Taufa'ahau IV on medal.

**1978, July 4**
**CO132** A74 26s multicolored .65 .65
**CO133** A74 85s multicolored 2.00 2.00
**CO134** A74 90s multicolored 2.50 2.50
*Nos. CO132-CO134 (3)* 5.15 5.15

See note after No. 226.

Wildlife Type of 1978

**1978, Dec. 15** **Litho. & Typo.**
**CO150** A77 40s Whale 7.00 3.50
**CO151** A77 50s Bat 7.00 3.50
**CO152** A77 1.10pa Turtle 9.25 7.75
*Nos. CO150-CO152 (3)* 23.25 14.75

Wildlife conservation. See note after No. 226.

Types of 1979

Designs: 38s, Red Cross and star. 74s, like No. 451. 80s, like No. 450.

**1979, Feb. 16** **Litho.**
**CO153** A78 38s multicolored 1.10 .70
**CO154** A80 74s multicolored 2.00 1.40
**CO155** A79 80s multicolored 2.50 1.60
*Nos. CO153-CO155 (3)* 5.60 3.70

Decade of Progress. Paper backing shows map of Tonga.

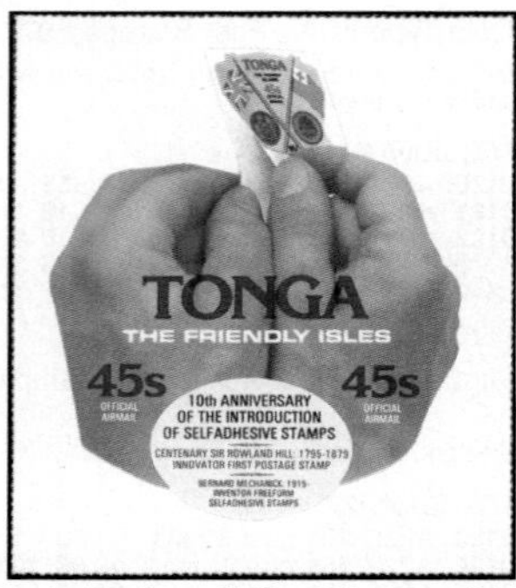

Hands Peeling off No. CO118 — OA17

**1979, June 1**

| | | | |
|---|---|---|---|
| **CO156** | OA17 45s multicolored | 1.10 | 1.10 |
| **CO157** | OA17 65s multicolored | 1.50 | 1.50 |
| **CO158** | OA17 80s multicolored | 1.90 | 1.90 |
| | *Nos. CO156-CO158 (3)* | 4.50 | 4.50 |

See note after No. 458.
For surcharges see Nos. CO176-CO178.

Parrot — OA18

**1979, Aug. 1**

| | | | |
|---|---|---|---|
| **CO159** | OA18 5s multicolored | .20 | .20 |
| **CO160** | OA18 11s multicolored | .25 | .25 |
| **CO161** | OA18 14s multicolored | .35 | .35 |
| **CO162** | OA18 15s multicolored | .35 | .35 |
| **CO163** | OA18 17s multicolored | .45 | .45 |
| **CO164** | OA18 18s multicolored | .50 | .50 |
| **CO165** | OA18 22s multicolored | .55 | .55 |
| **CO166** | OA18 31s multicolored | .75 | .75 |
| **CO167** | OA18 39s multicolored | .95 | .95 |
| **CO168** | OA18 75s multicolored | 1.75 | 1.75 |
| **CO169** | OA18 1pa multicolored | 2.25 | 2.25 |
| | *Nos. CO159-CO169 (11)* | 8.35 | 8.35 |

Nos. CO159-CO169 issued in coils. See note after No. 226.

The 5s exists with denomination in magenta and the leaves behind the bird missing. This seems to be a special printing that was not available for postal purposes.

View Type of 1979

Design: Niuatoputapu and Tafahi Islands. See note after No. 463.

**1979, Nov. 23** **Litho.**

| | | | |
|---|---|---|---|
| **CO170** | A82 35s multicolored | .85 | .85 |
| **CO171** | A82 45s multicolored | 1.10 | 1.10 |
| **CO172** | A82 1pa multicolored | 2.25 | 2.25 |
| | *Nos. CO170-CO172 (3)* | 4.20 | 4.20 |

Friendship Treaty Type of 1980

Design: Church. See note after No. 468.

**1980, Jan. 9** **Litho.**

| | | | |
|---|---|---|---|
| **CO173** | A83 40s multicolored | 1.10 | 1.10 |
| **CO174** | A83 55s multicolored | 1.40 | 1.40 |
| **CO175** | A83 1.25pa multicolored | 3.25 | 3.25 |
| | *Nos. CO173-CO175 (3)* | 5.75 | 5.75 |

Nos. CO156-CO158 Surcharged and Overprinted in Black on Silver: "1980 OLYMPIC GAMES," Moscow '80 and Bear Emblems

**1980, Apr. 30** **Litho.**

| | | | |
|---|---|---|---|
| **CO176** | OA17 26s on 45s | .95 | .95 |
| **CO177** | OA17 40s on 65s | 1.40 | 1.40 |
| **CO178** | OA17 1.10pa on 80s | 3.75 | 3.75 |
| | *Nos. CO176-CO178 (3)* | 6.10 | 6.10 |

22nd Summer Olympic Games, Moscow, July 19-Aug. 3.

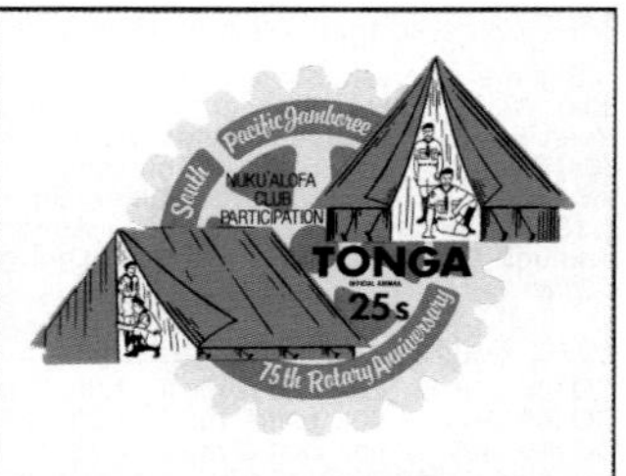

Tents and Rotary Emblem — OA19

**1980, Sept. 30** **Litho.**

| | | | |
|---|---|---|---|
| **CO179** | OA19 25s multicolored | .70 | .70 |
| **CO180** | OA19 2pa multicolored | 5.75 | 5.75 |

Boy Scout Jamboree; Rotary Intl., 75th anniv. Peelable backing shows map of Tonga.
For surcharges see Nos. 502-503.

No. CO111 Surcharged

**1980, Dec. 3** **Litho.**

| | | | |
|---|---|---|---|
| **CO181** | OA13 2pa on 65s multi | 4.75 | 4.75 |

**OFFICIAL STAMPS**

Types of Postage Issue of 1892 Overprinted in Carmine

*Perf. 12x11½*

**1893, Feb. 13** **Wmk. 62**

| | | | |
|---|---|---|---|
| **O1** | A4 1p ultra | 11.50 | *55.00* |
| *a.* | Half used as ½p on cover | | |
| **O2** | A5 2p ultra | 30.00 | *62.50* |
| **O3** | A4 4p ultra | 55.00 | *110.00* |
| **O4** | A5 8p ultra | 100.00 | *200.00* |
| **O5** | A5 1sh ultra | 110.00 | *210.00* |
| | *Nos. O1-O5 (5)* | 306.50 | *637.50* |

Values are for copies of good color. Faded and discolored copies sell for much less.

The overprinted initials stand for "Gaue Faka Buleaga" (On Government Service).

Nos. O1-O5 with Additional Surcharge Handstamped in Black

**1893**

| | | | |
|---|---|---|---|
| **O6** | A4 ½p on 1p ultra | 20.00 | *57.50* |
| **O7** | A5 2½p on 2p ultra | 27.50 | *50.00* |
| **O8** | A4 5p on 4p ultra | 27.50 | *50.00* |
| **O9** | A5 7½p on 8p ultra | 27.50 | *92.50* |
| **O10** | A5 10p on 1sh ultra | 32.50 | *95.00* |
| | *Nos. O6-O10 (5)* | 135.00 | *345.00* |

**Catalogue values for unused stamps in this section, from this point to the end of the section, are for Never Hinged items.**

Redrawn Banana and Coconut Types of Regular Issue, 1970, Inscribed "Official Post"

**1970, June 9** **Typo.** ***Die Cut***

**Self-adhesive**

| | | | |
|---|---|---|---|
| **O11** | A39 1s yel, blk & dp car | .55 | .55 |
| **O12** | A39 2s yel, blk & blue | .70 | .70 |
| **O13** | A39 3s yel, blk & brn | .70 | .70 |
| **O14** | A39 4s yel, blk & emer | .70 | .70 |
| **O15** | A39 5s yel, blk & org | .80 | .80 |

**Litho.; Embossed on Gilt Foil**

| | | | |
|---|---|---|---|
| **O16** | A44 6s brown & multi | .95 | .95 |
| **O17** | A44 7s brown & multi | 1.00 | 1.00 |
| **O18** | A44 8s brown & multi | 1.10 | 1.10 |
| **O19** | A44 9s brown & multi | 1.50 | 1.50 |
| **O20** | A44 10s brown & multi | 1.75 | 1.75 |
| | *Nos. O11-O20 (10)* | 9.75 | 9.75 |

Nos. O13, O17-O18 and O20 have self-adhesive control numbers in lower left corner of paper backing.

Types of Regular Issue 1970-72

**1972, Sept. 30** **Typo.**

**Self-adhesive**

| | | | |
|---|---|---|---|
| **O21** | A51 1s yel, red & brn | .20 | .20 |
| **O22** | A51 2s yel, grn & brn | .25 | .20 |
| **O23** | A51 3s yel, emer & brn | .35 | .20 |
| **O24** | A51 4s yel, blk & brn | .35 | .25 |
| **O25** | A51 5s yellow & brn | .35 | .25 |
| **O26** | A44 6s brown & green | .40 | .25 |
| **O27** | A44 7s brown & green | .45 | .30 |
| **O28** | A44 8s brown & green | .45 | .30 |
| **O29** | A44 9s brown & green | .45 | .30 |
| **O30** | A44 10s brown & green | .55 | .35 |
| **O31** | A52 15s green & ultra | .90 | .50 |
| **O32** | A52 20s green & ver | 1.10 | .70 |
| **O33** | A52 25s green & dk brn | 1.25 | .80 |
| **O34** | A52 40s green & org | 2.50 | 1.75 |
| **O35** | A52 50s green & vio bl | 2.75 | 2.00 |
| | *Nos. O21-O35 (15)* | 12.30 | 8.35 |

Paper backing is brown on Nos. O26-O35. Nos. O30-O35 have self-adhesive control number in lower left corner, Nos. O21-O29 lower right corner.

Types of Regular Issue 1978

Designs: 1s-5s, Bananas (similar to type A75). 6s-10s, Coconuts. 15s-1pa, Pineapples.

**1978, Sept. 29** **Typo.**

| | | | |
|---|---|---|---|
| **O36** | A75 1s yellow & lilac | .25 | .25 |
| **O37** | A75 2s yellow & brown | .25 | .25 |
| **O38** | A75 3s multicolored | .35 | .35 |
| **O39** | A75 4s multicolored | .35 | .35 |
| **O40** | A75 5s multicolored | .35 | .35 |
| **O41** | A76 6s multicolored | .50 | .50 |
| **O42** | A76 7s multicolored | .50 | .50 |
| **O43** | A76 8s multicolored | .50 | .50 |
| **O44** | A76 9s multicolored | .50 | .50 |
| **O45** | A76 10s multicolored | .50 | .50 |
| **O46** | A76 15s multicolored | 1.25 | 1.25 |
| **O47** | A76 20s multicolored | 1.40 | 1.40 |
| **O48** | A76 30s multicolored | 1.50 | 1.50 |
| **O49** | A76 50s multicolored | 2.00 | 2.00 |
| **O50** | A76 1pa multicolored | 3.00 | 3.00 |
| | *Nos. O36-O50 (15)* | 13.20 | 13.20 |

Nos. O36-O50 issued in coils; self-adhesive control numbers on paper backing except on 1s. See note after No. 226.

Type of 1984 Overprinted "OFFICIAL"

**1984-85** **Litho.** ***Die Cut***

| | | | |
|---|---|---|---|
| **O52** | A103 1s multicolored | .50 | .50 |
| **O53** | A103 2s multicolored | .50 | .50 |
| **O54** | A103 3s multicolored | .50 | .50 |
| **O55** | A103 5s multicolored | .50 | .50 |
| **O56** | A103 6s multicolored | .50 | .50 |
| **O57** | A103 9s multicolored | .75 | .75 |
| *a.* | Perf. 14½ ('85) | .75 | .75 |
| **O58** | A103 10s multicolored | .75 | .75 |
| **O59** | A103 13s multicolored | 1.25 | 1.25 |
| **O60** | A103 15s multicolored | 1.25 | 1.25 |
| **O61** | A103 20s multicolored | 1.50 | 1.50 |
| **O62** | A103 29s multicolored | 1.75 | 1.75 |
| **O63** | A103 32s multicolored | 1.75 | 1.75 |
| **O64** | A103 47s multicolored | 2.00 | 2.00 |
| **O65** | A103 1pa multicolored | 4.00 | 4.00 |
| **O66** | A103 2pa multicolored | 7.00 | 7.00 |
| **O67** | A103 5pa multicolored ('85) | 12.00 | 12.00 |
| | *Nos. O52-O67 (16)* | 36.50 | 36.50 |

Nos. 532-534 Ovptd. "OFFICIAL"

**1983, Feb. 22** **Litho.** ***Die Cut***

| | | | |
|---|---|---|---|
| **O68** | A96a 29s multicolored | 4.75 | 4.75 |
| **O69** | A96a 32s multicolored | 4.75 | 4.75 |
| **O70** | A96a 47s multicolored | 10.00 | 10.00 |
| | *Nos. O68-O70 (3)* | 19.50 | 19.50 |

O68-O70 handstamped.

Nos. 564-565, 567-568, 570, 572 and 577 Surcharged "OFFICIAL"

**1986, Apr. 16** **Litho.** ***Die Cut***

**Self-adhesive**

| | | | |
|---|---|---|---|
| **O71** | A103 4s on 2s, #564 | 1.00 | 1.00 |
| **O72** | A103 4s on 13s, #570 | 1.00 | 1.00 |
| **O73** | A103 42s on 3s, #565 | 3.25 | 3.25 |
| **O74** | A103 42s on 9s, #568 | 3.25 | 3.25 |
| **O75** | A103 57s on 6s, #567 | 3.50 | 3.50 |
| **O76** | A103 57s on 20s, #572 | 3.50 | 3.50 |
| **O77** | A103 2.50pa on 2pa, #577 | 12.00 | 12.00 |
| | *Nos. O71-O77 (7)* | 27.50 | 27.50 |

Marine Type Inscribed "POSTAGE & REVENUE" and "OFFICIAL"

**1995-96** **Litho.** ***Perf. 14***

| | | | |
|---|---|---|---|
| **O78** | A155a 10s multicolored | .60 | .60 |
| **O79** | A155a 20s multicolored | .90 | .40 |
| **O80** | A155a 45s multicolored | 1.10 | .70 |
| **O81** | A155a 60s multicolored | 1.40 | .95 |
| **O82** | A155a 80s multicolored | 1.75 | 1.25 |
| **O83** | A155a 1pa multicolored | 2.25 | 1.75 |
| **O84** | A155a 2pa multicolored | 4.00 | 4.00 |
| **O85** | A155a 3pa multicolored | 5.00 | 5.00 |
| **O86** | A155a 5pa multicolored | 9.75 | 9.75 |
| **O87** | A155a 10pa multicolored | 14.00 | 14.00 |
| | *Nos. O78-O87 (10)* | 40.75 | 38.40 |

Issued: 10s-80s, 9/25/95; 1pa-10pa, 5/31/96.

## NIUAFO'OU

### Tin Can Island

**Catalogue values for all unused stamps in this country are for Never Hinged items.**

Nos. 1-63 are self-adhesive stamps on peelable inscribed backing paper and imperforate.

Niuafo'ou Airport Type of Tonga

**1983, May 11** **Litho.** ***Die Cut***

| | | | |
|---|---|---|---|
| **1** | A97 29s multicolored | 1.75 | 1.75 |
| **2** | A97 1pa multicolored | 4.75 | 4.75 |

Map of Niuafo'ou — A1

**1983, May 11**

| | | | |
|---|---|---|---|
| **3** | A1 1s buff, blk & red | .35 | .35 |
| **4** | A1 2s buff, blk & brt green | .35 | .35 |
| **5** | A1 3s buff, blk & brt blue | .35 | .35 |
| **6** | A1 3s buff, blk & brn org | .35 | .35 |
| **7** | A1 5s buff, blk & deep rose lil | .35 | .35 |
| **8** | A1 6s buff, blk & grnsh blue | .35 | .35 |
| **9** | A1 9s buff, blk & lt ol grn | .35 | .35 |
| **10** | A1 10s buff, blk & brt bl | .35 | .35 |
| **11** | A1 13s buff, blk & brt grn | .40 | .40 |
| **12** | A1 15s buff, blk & brn org | .50 | .50 |
| **13** | A1 20s buff, blk & grnsh blue | .65 | .65 |
| **14** | A1 29s buff, blk & deep rose lil | 1.00 | 1.00 |
| **15** | A1 32s buff, blk & lt ol grn | 1.10 | 1.10 |
| **16** | A1 47s buff, blk & red | 1.60 | 1.60 |
| | *Nos. 3-16 (14)* | 8.05 | 8.05 |

See Nos. 19-22.

Tonga No. 520 Surcharged or Ovptd. in Purple or Gold "NIUAFO'OU / Kingdom of Tonga"

**1983, May 11**

| | | | |
|---|---|---|---|
| **17** | A93 1pa on 2pa multi (P) | 3.25 | 3.25 |
| **18** | A93 2pa multicolored (G) | 6.75 | 6.75 |

Nos. 17-18 each exist se-tenant with label.

Map Type of 1983

**Value Typo. in Violet Blue**

**1983, May 30**

| | | | |
|---|---|---|---|
| **19** | A1 3s buff & black | .30 | .30 |
| **20** | A1 5s buff & black | .30 | .30 |
| **21** | A1 32s buff & black | 1.50 | 1.50 |
| **22** | A1 2pa buff & black | 8.00 | 8.00 |
| | *Nos. 19-22 (4)* | 10.10 | 10.10 |

The denomination on Nos. 19-22 added like a surcharge and is larger than on Nos. 5-7, 15, covering part of the design.

Nos. 19-22 each exist se-tenant with label.

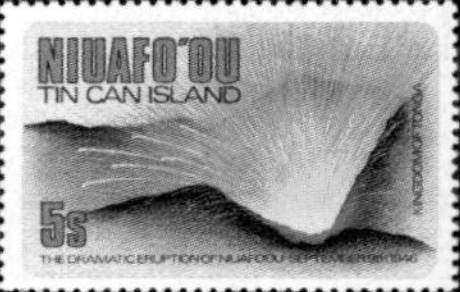

Eruption of Niuafo'ou, Sept. 9, 1946 — A2

**1983, Sept. 29**

| | | | |
|---|---|---|---|
| **23** | A2 5s shown | .50 | .35 |
| **24** | A2 29s Lava flow | 1.90 | 1.25 |
| **25** | A2 32s Moving to high ground | 2.10 | 1.25 |
| **26** | A2 1.50pa Evacuation to Eua | 6.50 | 6.50 |
| | *Nos. 23-26 (4)* | 11.00 | 9.35 |

Birds — A3

**1983, Nov. 15**

27 A3 1s Purple swamphen 1.00 1.00
28 A3 2s White-collared kingfisher 1.00 1.00
29 A3 3s Red-headed parrotfinch 1.00 1.00
30 A3 5s Banded rail 1.25 1.25
31 A3 6s Niuafo'ou megapode 1.60 1.60
32 A3 9s Giant forest honey-eater 2.50 2.50
33 A3 10s Purple swamphen, drinking 2.50 2.50
34 A3 13s Banded rail, diff. 2.75 2.75
35 A3 15s Niuafo'ou megapode, diff. 2.75 2.75

**Size: 25x39mm**

36 A3 20s like #34 3.25 3.25
37 A3 29s Red-headed parrotfinch, diff. 3.50 3.50
38 A3 32s White-collared kingfisher, diff. 3.50 3.50
39 A3 47s like #35 4.25 4.25

**Size: 32x42mm**

40 A3 1pa like #33 8.00 *9.75*
41 A3 2pa like #35 11.00 *14.00*
*Nos. 27-41 (15)* 49.85 *54.60*

Nos. 34-36, 39 and 41 horiz.
For surcharges see Nos. 66-73.

Wildlife A4

**1984, Mar. 7**

42 A4 29s Green turtle .90 .90
43 A4 32s Flying fox, vert. .90 .90
44 A4 47s Humpback whale 3.25 2.10
45 A4 1.50pa Niuafo'ou megapode, vert. 6.00 *8.25*
*Nos. 42-45 (4)* 11.05 *12.15*

Map A5

**1984, Aug. 20**

46 A5 47s Intl. Date Line, Cent. 1.00 1.00
47 A5 2pa shown 3.50 3.50

AUSIPEX '84 — A6

A7

**1984, Sept. 17**

48 A6 32s Australia No. 15 .90 .90
49 A6 1.50pa No. 10 4.50 4.50

**Souvenir Sheet**

50 Sheet of 2 4.50 4.50

No. 50 contains two imperf. stamps similar to Nos. 48-49, but with denomination replacing logo. No. 50 without denominations was not valid for postage.

**1985, Feb. 20**

Jacob Le Maire, 400th Birth Anniv.: 13s, Dutch band entertaining natives. 32s, Natives preparing kava. 47s, Native outrigger canoes. 1.50pa, Le Maire's ship at anchor.

51 A7 13s multicolored .50 .50
52 A7 32s multicolored 1.10 1.10
53 A7 47s multicolored 1.50 1.50
54 A7 1.50pa multicolor 4.50 *5.50*
*Nos. 51-54 (4)* 7.60 8.60

**Souvenir Sheet**

55 A7 1.50pa multicolored 4.00 4.00

Mail Ships A8

**1985, May 22** *Die Cut*

56 A8 9s Ysabel, 1902 .60 .60
a. Perf. 14 .90 .90
57 A8 13s Tofua I, 1908 1.25 1.25
a. Perf. 14 1.90 1.90
58 A8 47s Mariposa, 1934 1.90 1.90
a. Perf. 14 2.75 2.75
59 A8 1.50pa Matua, 1936 4.25 *6.00*
a. Perf. 14 6.50 *9.00*
*Nos. 56-59 (4)* 8.00 9.75
*Nos. 56a-59a (4)* 12.05 *14.55*

Rocket Mail — A9

Designs: 32s, Preparing to fire rocket. 42s, Rocket airborne. 57s, Captain watching rocket's progress. 1.50pa, Islanders reading mail.

**1985, Nov. 5**

60 A9 32s multicolored 1.50 .90
61 A9 42s multicolored 2.00 1.10
62 A9 57s multicolored 2.75 1.60
63 A9 1.50pa multicolored 5.75 *6.50*
*Nos. 60-63 (4)* 12.00 10.10

Self-adhesive stamps discontinued.

Halley's Comet — A10

Nos. 64, 65: a, Drawing of Comet in 684. b, Comet shown in Bayeux Tapestry, 1066. c, Edmond Halley. d, Comet, 1910. e, Infrared photography, 1986.

**1986, Mar. 26** *Perf. 14*

64 A10 42s Strip of #a.-e. 36.00 32.50
65 A10 57s Strip of #a.-e. 36.00 32.50

Nos. 32-39 Surcharged in Blue

**1986, Apr. 16** *Die Cut*

**Self-Adhesive**

66 A3 4s on 9s #32 1.50 *2.75*
67 A3 4s on 10s #33 1.50 *2.75*
68 A3 42s on 13s #34 3.75 2.75
69 A3 42s on 15s #35 3.75 2.75
70 A3 57s on 29s #37 4.75 3.25
71 A3 57s on 32s #38 4.75 3.25
72 A3 2.50pa on 20s #36 13.00 *14.00*
73 A3 2.50pa on 47s #39 13.00 *14.00*
*Nos. 66-73 (8)* 46.00 *45.50*

Placement of surcharge varies.

AMERIPEX '86 Type of Tonga

**1986, May 22** *Perf. 14*

74 A117 57s Surveying 3.00 3.00
75 A117 1.50pa Agriculture 5.50 5.50
a. Souv. sheet of 2, #74-75, imperf. 10.00 10.00

Peace Corps in Tonga, 25th anniv.

First Tongan Postage Stamps, Cent. A11

**1986, Aug. 27**

76 A11 42s Swimmers with mail 1.60 1.60
77 A11 57s Loading tin can mail into canoe 2.10 2.10
78 A11 1pa Rocket mail 3.75 3.75
79 A11 2.50pa Outrigger canoe 6.50 6.50
*Nos. 76-79 (4)* 13.95 13.95

**Souvenir Sheet**

80 A11 2.50pa Outrigger canoe, diff. 14.00 14.00

Red Cross — A12

**1987, Mar. 11** *Perf. 14x14½*

81 A12 15s Balanced diet 1.25 1.25
82 A12 42s Post-natal care 3.25 3.25
83 A12 1pa Insects spread disease 4.75 4.75
84 A12 2.50pa Fight against drugs, alcohol, smoking 7.50 7.50
*Nos. 81-84 (4)* 16.75 16.75

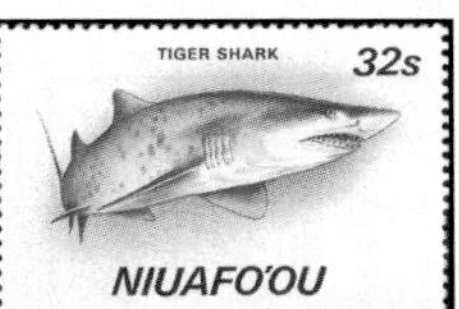

Sharks A13

**1987, Apr. 29** *Perf. 14*

85 A13 29s Hammerhead 3.00 2.75
86 A13 32s Tiger 3.00 2.75
87 A13 47s Gray nurse 3.50 3.00
88 A13 1pa Great white 6.00 *8.25*
*Nos. 85-88 (4)* 15.50 *16.75*

**Souvenir Sheet**

89 A13 2pa Shark attack 18.00 18.00

Aviators and Aircraft A14

Designs: 42s, Capt. E. C. Musick and Sikorsky S-42. 57s, Capt. J.W. Burgess and Shorts S-30. 1.50pa, Sir Charles Kingsford Smith and Fokker F.VIIb-3m. 2pa, Amelia Earhart and Lockheed Electra 10A.

**1987, Sept. 2**

90 A14 42s multicolored 2.50 1.75
91 A14 57s multicolored 3.00 2.00
92 A14 1.50pa multicolored 4.50 4.50
93 A14 2pa multicolored 5.25 5.25
*Nos. 90-93 (4)* 15.25 13.50

First Niuafo'ou Postage Stamps, 5th Anniv. A15

Designs: 42s, 57s, Niuafo'ou megapode, No. 15. 1pa, 2pa, Concorde, No. 1.

**1988, May 18**

94 A15 42s multicolored 1.50 1.00
95 A15 57s multicolored 1.50 1.10
96 A15 1pa multicolored 5.00 3.75
97 A15 2pa multicolored 6.00 4.75
*Nos. 94-97 (4)* 14.00 10.60

#96-97, Niuafo'ou Airport Inauguration, 5th anniv.

Settlement of Australia, Bicent. Type of Tonga Miniature Sheet

Designs: a, Arrival of First Fleet, Sydney Cove, Jan. 1788. b, Aborigines. c, Early settlement. d, Soldier on guard. e, Herd of sheep. f, Horseman. g, Locomotive, kangaroos. h, Train, kangaroos. i, Flying doctor service. j, Cricket players. k, Stadium, batsman guarding wicket. l, Sydney Harbor Bridge, Opera House.

**1988, July 11** *Perf. 13½*

98 A128 42s Sheet of 12, #98a-98 l 50.00 50.00

Polynesian Islands — A16

Birds and landmarks: 42s, Audubon's shearwater, blowholes at Houma, Tonga. 57s, Kiwi, Akaroa Harbor, New Zealand. 90s, Red-tailed tropicbird, Rainmaker Mountain, Samoa. 2.50pa, Laysan albatross, Kapoho Volcano, Hawaii.

**1988, Aug. 18** *Perf. 14*

99 A16 42s multicolored 1.50 1.00
100 A16 57s multicolored 2.50 1.60
101 A16 90s multicolored 2.75 2.75
102 A16 2.50pa multicolored 5.25 5.25
*Nos. 99-102 (4)* 12.00 10.60

Miniature Sheet

Mutiny on the Bounty, Bicent. — A17

Designs: a, Sextant. b, William Bligh. c, Royal Navy lieutenant. d, Midshipman. e, Contemporary newspaper, Tahitian girl. f, Breadfruit. g, *Mutiny on the Bounty* excerpt, pistol grip. h, Pistol barrel, illustration of Bounty castaways. i, Tahitian girl, newsprint. j, Bligh's and Fletcher Christian's signatures. k, Christian, Pitcairn Island. l, Tombstone of John Adams.

**1989, Apr. 28** *Perf. 13½*

103 A17 42s Sheet of 12, #a.-l. 30.00 30.00

Marine Conservation — A18

**1989, June 2** *Perf. 14*

104 A18 32s Hatchet fish 1.40 1.40
105 A18 42s Snipe eel 1.60 1.60
106 A18 57s Viper fish 2.00 2.00
107 A18 1.50pa Angler fish 5.00 5.00
*Nos. 104-107 (4)* 10.00 10.00

Evolution of the Earth — A19

A20

Designs: 1s, Formation of the crust. 2s, Cross-section of crust. 5s, Volcanism. 10s, Surface cools. 13s, Gem stones. 15s, Oceans form. 20s, Mountains develop. 32s, River valley. 42s, Silurian Era plant life. 45s, Early marine life. 50s, Trilobites, Cambrian Era marine life. 57s, Carboniferous Era forest, coal seams. 60s, Dinosaurs feeding. 80s, Dinosaurs fighting. 1pa, Carboniferous Era insect, amphibians. 1.50pa, Stegosaurus, Jurassic Era. 2pa, Birds and mammals, Jurassic Era. 5pa, Hominid family, Pleistocene Era. 10pa, Mammoth, saber tooth tiger.

**1989-93** ***Perf. 14½***

| No. | Description | Unused | Used |
|---|---|---|---|
| **108** | A19 1s multicolored | .70 | .70 |
| **109** | A19 2s multicolored | .70 | .70 |
| **110** | A19 5s multicolored | .90 | .90 |
| **111** | A19 10s multicolored | .90 | .90 |
| **111A** | A19 13s multicolored | 1.10 | 1.10 |
| **112** | A19 15s multicolored | .90 | .90 |
| **113** | A19 20s multicolored | .90 | .90 |
| **114** | A19 32s multicolored | 1.10 | 1.10 |
| **115** | A19 42s multicolored | 1.50 | 1.50 |
| **115A** | A19 45s multicolored | 1.50 | 1.50 |
| **116** | A19 50s multicolored | 1.60 | 1.60 |
| **117** | A19 57s multicolored | 1.60 | 1.60 |
| **117A** | A19 60s multicolored | 1.75 | 1.75 |
| **117B** | A19 80s multicolored | 2.10 | 2.10 |

**Size: 26x40mm**

***Perf. 14***

| No. | Description | Unused | Used |
|---|---|---|---|
| **118** | A19 1pa multicolored | 3.00 | 3.00 |
| **119** | A19 1.50pa multicolored | 4.75 | 4.75 |
| **120** | A19 2pa multicolored | 4.75 | 4.75 |
| **121** | A19 5pa multicolored | 9.25 | 9.25 |

***Perf. 14***

| No. | Description | Unused | Used |
|---|---|---|---|
| **121A** | A19 10pa multicolored | 16.00 | 16.00 |
| | *Nos. 108-121A (19)* | 55.00 | 55.00 |

Issued: 1s-10s, 15s-42s, 50s-57s, 6/6/89; 13s, 45s, 60s, 80s, 5/3/93; 10pa, 9/14/93; others, 8/1/89.

**1989, Nov. 17** ***Perf. 14***

| No. | Description | Unused | Used |
|---|---|---|---|
| **122** | A20 57s multicolored | 1.90 | 1.90 |

Miniature Sheet

Nos. 108-121 with UPU emblem: Nos. 123a-123e, #108-112, Nos. 123f-123j, #113-117, Nos. 123k-123n, #118-121.

| No. | Description | Unused | Used |
|---|---|---|---|
| **123** | Sheet of 15, #a.-n., 122 | 27.50 | 27.50 |
| ***a.-e.*** | A19 32s any single, perf. 14½ | 1.00 | 1.00 |
| ***f.-j.*** | A19 42s any single, perf. 14½ | 1.50 | 1.50 |
| ***k.-n.*** | A19 57s any single, perf. 14 | 2.00 | 2.00 |

Miniature Sheet

Lake Vai Lahi, Niuafo'ou A21

a, d, Left part of lake. b, e, Small islands in center of lake. c, f, Small islet in right side of lake.

**1990, Apr. 4** ***Perf. 14***

| No. | Description | Unused | Used |
|---|---|---|---|
| **124** | Sheet of 6 | 11.00 | 11.00 |
| ***a.-c.*** | A21 42s any single | 1.00 | 1.00 |
| ***d.-f.*** | A21 1pa any single | 2.25 | 2.25 |

Nos. 124a-124c and 124d-124f printed in continuous designs.

Penny Black, 150th Anniv. A22

Tin Can Mail and: 42s, Penny Black. 57s, US #2. 75s, Western Australia #1. 2.50pa, Cape of Good Hope #178.

**1990, May 1**

| No. | Description | Unused | Used |
|---|---|---|---|
| **125** | A22 42s multicolored | 1.75 | 1.40 |
| **126** | A22 57s multicolored | 1.90 | 1.60 |
| **127** | A22 75s multicolored | 2.10 | 2.10 |
| **128** | A22 2.50pa multicolored | 7.25 | 7.00 |
| | *Nos. 125-128 (4)* | 13.00 | 12.10 |

Polynesian Whaling — A23

Designs: 15s, Whale surfacing. 42s, Whale diving beneath outrigger canoe. 57s, Tail flukes. 1pa, 2pa, Old man, two whales.

**1990** ***Perf. 11½***

| No. | Description | Unused | Used |
|---|---|---|---|
| **129** | A23 15s multicolored | 2.50 | 2.50 |
| **130** | A23 42s multicolored | 3.50 | 3.50 |
| **131** | A23 57s multicolored | 3.75 | 3.75 |
| **132** | A23 2pa multicolored | 9.75 | 9.75 |
| | *Nos. 129-132 (4)* | 19.50 | 19.50 |

**Souvenir Sheet**

***Perf. 14x14½***

| No. | Description | Unused | Used |
|---|---|---|---|
| **133** | A23 1pa multicolored | 20.00 | 20.00 |

Issue dates: #133, Sept. 4, others, June 6.

The entire souvenir sheet, No. 133, shows a modified No. 132. The 37½x30½mm stamp shows the two whales.

For surcharges see Nos. 139, 174-178.

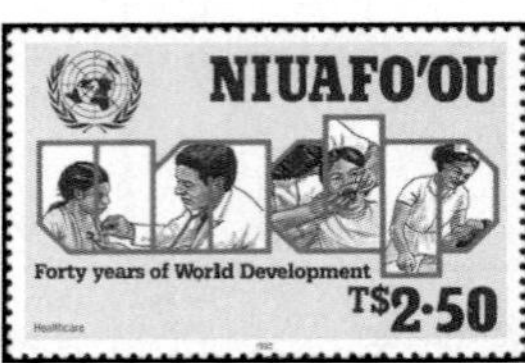

UN Development Program, 40th Anniv. — A24

Designs: No. 134a, Agriculture and fisheries. No. 134b, Education. No. 135a, Health care. No. 135b, Communications.

**1990, Oct. 25** ***Perf. 14***

| No. | Description | Unused | Used |
|---|---|---|---|
| **134** | A24 57s Pair, #a.-b. | 3.00 | 3.00 |
| **135** | A24 2.50pa Pair, #a.-b. | 12.00 | 12.00 |

Charting of Niuafo'ou, Bicent. — A24a

Designs: No. 136a, 32s, The Bounty. b, 42s, Chart showing location of Niuafo'ou and Tonga. c, 57s, The Pandora.

No. 137a, 2pa, Capt. Edwards of the Pandora. b, 3pa, Capt. Bligh of the Bounty.

**1991, July 25** **Litho.** ***Perf. 14½***

| No. | Description | Unused | Used |
|---|---|---|---|
| **136** | A24a Strip of 3, #a.-c. | 6.00 | 6.00 |

**Souvenir Sheet**

| No. | Description | Unused | Used |
|---|---|---|---|
| **137** | A24a Sheet of 2, #a.-b. | 18.00 | 18.00 |

No. 133 Surcharged in Dark Blue Violet

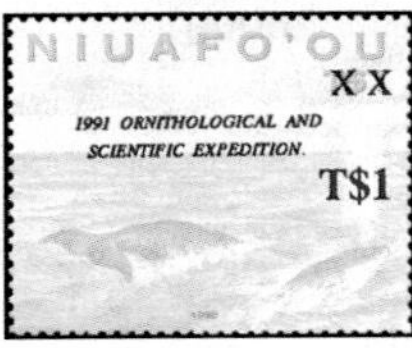


**1991, July 31** **Litho.** ***Perf. 14x14½***

| No. | Description | Unused | Used |
|---|---|---|---|
| **139** | A23 1pa on 1pa #133 | 13.00 | 13.00 |

"1991 Ornithological and Scientic Expedition" overprint appears on souvenir sheet at top center.

Ceresium Unicolor — A25

**1991, Sept. 11** ***Perf. 14½x14***

| No. | Description | Unused | Used |
|---|---|---|---|
| **140** | A25 42s Larva stage | 1.25 | 1.25 |
| **141** | A25 57s Mature beetle | 1.50 | 1.50 |
| **142** | A25 1.50pa Larva stage, diff. | 3.75 | 3.75 |
| **143** | A25 2.50pa Mature beetle on tree limb | 6.50 | 6.50 |
| | *Nos. 140-143 (4)* | 13.00 | 13.00 |

For surcharges, see Tonga Nos. 1127, 1129.

Christmas A26

Legend of the origin of the coconut tree: 15s, No. 146a, Heina bathing in lake being watched by eel. 42s, No. 146b, Heina weeping over plant growing from eel's grave. No. 146c, 1.50pa, Heina's boy climbing coconut tree. No. 146d, 3pa, "Eel's face" on coconut.

**1991, Nov. 12** **Litho.** ***Perf. 14½***

| No. | Description | Unused | Used |
|---|---|---|---|
| **144** | A26 15s multicolored | .75 | .75 |
| **145** | A26 42s multicolored | 2.00 | 2.00 |
| **146** | A26 Sheet of 4, #a.-d. | 17.50 | 17.50 |
| | *Nos. 144-146 (3)* | 20.25 | 20.25 |

For surcharge, see Tonga No. 1128.

Nos. 144-145 inscribed "Christmas Greetings 1991." No. 146 contains Nos. 144-145, 146a-146d inscribed "A Love Story."

Miniature Sheet

Discovery of America, 500th Anniv. — A27

Designs: a, Columbus. b, Queen Isabella, King Ferdinand. c, Columbus being blessed by Abbot of Palos. d, Men in boat, 15th century compass. e, Wooden traverse, wind rose, Nina. f, Bow of Santa Maria. g, Stern of Santa Maria. h, Pinta. i, Two men raising cross. j, Explorers, natives. k, Columbus kneeling before King and Queen. l, Columbus' second coat of arms.

**1992, Apr. 28** **Litho.** ***Perf. 13½***

| No. | Description | Unused | Used |
|---|---|---|---|
| **147** | A27 57s Sheet of 12, #a.-l. | 35.00 | 35.00 |

Miniature Sheet

World War II in Pacific, 50th Anniv. A28

Newspaper headline and: a, Battleship ablaze at Pearl Harbor. b, Destroyed aircraft. c, Japanese A6M Zero fighter. d, Declaration of war, Pres. Franklin D. Roosevelt. e, Japanese T95 tank, Gen. MacArthur, Japanese naval ensign. f, Douglas SBD Dauntless dive bomber, Admiral Nimitz. g, Bren gun, Gen. Sir Thomas Blamey. h, Australian mortar crew, Kokoda Trail. i, US battleship, Maj. Gen. Julian C. Smith. j, Aircraft carrier USS Enterprise. k, American soldier, flag, Maj. Gen. Curtis Lemay. l, B-29 bomber, surrender ceremony on USS Missouri in Tokyo bay.

**1992, May 12** **Litho.** ***Perf. 14***

| No. | Description | Unused | Used |
|---|---|---|---|
| **148** | A28 42s Sheet of 12, #a.-l. | 27.50 | 27.50 |

King Taufa'ahau IV, 25th Anniv. of Coronation A29

45s, 2pa, King, Queen Halaevalu during coronation. No. 150a, King, Tongan national anthem. b, Extract from investiture ceremony. c, Tongan national anthem, singers.

**1992, July 4** ***Perf. 13½x13***

| No. | Description | Unused | Used |
|---|---|---|---|
| **149** | A29 45s multicolored | 1.10 | 1.10 |

**Size: 51x38mm**

***Perf. 12½x12***

| No. | Description | Unused | Used |
|---|---|---|---|
| **150** | A29 80s Strip of 3, #a.-c. | 6.00 | 6.00 |
| **151** | A29 2pa multicolored | 5.00 | 5.00 |
| | *Nos. 149-151 (3)* | 12.10 | 12.10 |

Megapodius Pritchardii — A30

**1992, Sept. 15** **Litho.** ***Perf. 14***

| No. | Description | Unused | Used |
|---|---|---|---|
| **152** | A30 45s Female & male | 2.00 | 2.00 |
| **153** | A30 60s Female with egg | 2.50 | 2.50 |
| **154** | A30 80s Chick | 3.50 | 3.50 |
| **155** | A30 1.50pa Head of male | 6.00 | 6.00 |
| | *Nos. 152-155 (4)* | 14.00 | 14.00 |

World Wildlife Fund.

First Niuafo'ou Postage Stamps, 10th Anniv. A31

**1993, May 3** **Litho.** ***Perf. 14x14½***

| No. | Description | Unused | Used |
|---|---|---|---|
| **156** | A31 60s Nos. 4, 117A | 1.75 | 1.75 |
| **157** | A31 80s Nos. 7, 117B | 2.25 | 2.25 |

Aviation in Niuafo'ou, 10th Anniv. — A32

Airplanes of: 1pa, South Pacific Island Airways. 2.50pa, Friendly Islands Airways.

**1993, May 3**

| No. | Description | Unused | Used |
|---|---|---|---|
| **158** | A32 1pa multicolored | 3.50 | 3.50 |
| **159** | A32 2.50pa multicolored | 7.50 | 7.50 |

King's 75th Birthday Type of Tonga

King and: 45s, 2pa, Patrol boat Pangai.

No. 161a, Sporting events. b, Aircraft and communications. c, Musical instruments.

**1993, July 1** *Perf. 13x13½*
**160** A167 45s multicolored 1.00 1.00

*Perf. 12x12½*
**Size: 37x48mm**

**161** A167 80s Strip of 3, #a.-c. 5.50 5.50
**162** A167 2pa multicolored 4.25 4.25
*Nos. 160-162 (3)* 10.75 10.75

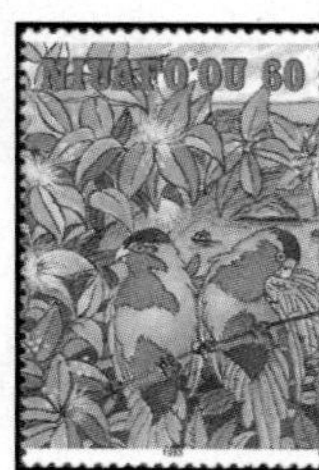

Wildlife — A33

Designs: a, Two parrots. b, Bird with fish. c, Butterfly, beetle. d, Birds, dragonfly, butterfly. e, Bird in flight, two on ground.

**1993, Aug. 10** **Litho.** *Perf. 14*
**163** A33 60s Strip of 5, #a.-e. 7.50 7.50

No. 163 is a continuous design.

Winners of Children's Painting Competition — A34

Designs: Nos. 164a, 165a, Ofato Beetle Grubbs of Niuafo'ou, by Peni Finau. Nos. 164b, 165b, Crater Lake Megapode, Volcano, by Paea Puletau.

**1993, Dec. 1** **Litho.** *Perf. 14*
**164** A34 10s Pair, #a.-b. 1.00 1.00
**165** A34 1pa Pair, #a.-b. 7.50 7.50

Beetles A35

**1994, Mar. 15** **Litho.** *Perf. 14*
**168** A35 60s Scarabaeidea 1.75 1.75
**169** A35 80s Coccinellidea 2.10 2.10
**170** A35 1.50pa Cerambycidea 3.75 3.75
**171** A35 2.50pa Pentatomidae 6.75 6.75
*Nos. 168-171 (4)* 14.35 14.35

A36

A37

Sailing Ships: a, Stern of HMS Bounty. b, Bow of HMS Bounty. c, HMS Pandora. d, Whaling ship. e, Trading schooner.

**1994, June 21** **Litho.** *Perf. 14*
**172** A36 80s Strip of 5, #a.-e. 17.50 17.50

No. 172 is a continuous design.

**1994, Sept. 21** **Litho.** *Perf. 14½*

1946 Volcanic Eruption: a, Blue-crowned lorikeet, lava flow. b, Black Pacific ducks, lava flow. c, Megapodes, palm trees (b). d, White-tailed tropic birds, people evacuating island (c). e, People wading out to sailboats, Pacific reef heron.

**173** A37 80s Strip of 5, #a.-e. 9.50 9.50

No. 173 is a continuous design.

Nos. 129-133 Surcharged in Blue

**1995, June 30** **Litho.** *Perf. 11½*
**174** A23 60s on 42s #130 2.50 2.50
**175** A23 80s on 15s #129 3.25 3.25
**176** A23 80s on 57s #131 3.50 3.50
**177** A23 2pa on #132 8.75 8.75
*Nos. 174-177 (4)* 18.00 18.00

**Souvenir Sheet**

**178** A23 1.50pa on 1pa #133 9.00 9.00

Size and location of surcharge varies. Surcharge on No. 178 includes "COME WHALE WATCHING / IN THE SOUTH PACIFIC."

**Victory in the Pacific Type of Tonga**

Nos. 179, 180: a, Soldier holding rifle. b, Soldier aiming rifle, tank. c, Front of tank. d, Troops coming off boat, firing weapons. e, Troops on beach.

**1995, Aug. 1** **Litho.** *Perf. 14x14½*
**179** A177 60s Strip of 5, #a.-e. 13.00 13.00
**180** A177 80s Strip of 5, #a.-e. 17.00 17.00

Nos. 179-180 are continuous designs and were issued together in sheets containing 10 stamps.

**Singapore '95 Type of Tonga**

Designs, vert: No. 181a, 45s, like #117A. b, 60s, like #117B.
2pa, Plesiosaurus.

**1995, Sept. 1** **Litho.** *Perf. 12*
**181** A178 Pair, #a.-b. 4.00 4.00

**Souvenir Sheet**

**182** A178 2pa multicolored 5.50 5.50

**Beijing Intl. Coin & Stamp Show '95 Type of Tonga**
Souvenir Sheet

Design: 1.40pa, The Great Wall of China.

**1995, Sept. 14** *Perf. 14½*
**183** A179 1.40pa multicolored 5.50 5.50

**End of World War II, UN, 50th Anniv. Type of Tonga**

No. 184: a, London blitz. b, UN emblem, "50." c, Concorde.
No. 185: a, Building of Siam-Burma Railway by Allied prisoners of war. b, Like #184b. c, Japanese bullet train.

**1995, Oct. 20** **Litho.** *Perf. 14*
**184** A180 60s Strip of 3, #a.-c. 5.50 5.50
**185** A180 80s Strip of 3, #a.-c. 7.50 7.50

Nos. 184b, 185b are 23x31mm.

Mailmen of Niuafo'ou A38

Portrait, illustration of postal history: 45s, Charles Stuart Ramsey, companions, floating with poles. 60s, Ramsey with can of mail encountering shark. 1pa, Walter George Quensell, mail being lowered from ship to canoes. 3pa, Quensell, original "tin can" mail cancels.

**1996, Aug. 21** **Litho.** *Perf. 14*
**186** A38 45s multicolored 1.25 1.25
**187** A38 60s multicolored 1.75 1.75
**188** A38 1pa multicolored 3.00 3.00
**189** A38 3pa multicolored 9.00 9.00
*Nos. 186-189 (4)* 15.00 15.00

**Congress of Preshistoric and Protohistoric Sciences Type of Tonga**

a, Prehistoric man making drawings, fire, living in huts, animals. b, Ancient Egyptians, Romans.

**1996, Sept. 5** *Perf. 12*
**190** A185 1pa Pair, #a.-b. 7.00 7.00

Evacuation of Niuafo'ou, 50th Anniv. — A39

a, Island, two canoes. b, Volcano, four canoes. c, Edge of island, canoe. d, Canoe. e, People boarding MV Matua.

**1996, Dec. 2** *Perf. 14*
**191** A39 45s Strip of 5, #a.-e. 6.00 6.00
**192** A39 60s Strip of 5, #a.-e. 9.00 9.00

Nos. 191-192 are continuous designs and were issued together in sheet containing 10 stamps.

**UNICEF, 50th Anniv. Type of Tonga**

Children's toys on checkerboard: a, Dolls, truck, balls on pegs. b, Tricycle, car, balls on pegs, teddy bear, train. c, Car, helicopter, ice skates, books, blocks.

**1996, Oct. 29** **Litho.** *Perf. 14*
**193** A187 80s Strip of 3, #a.-c. 6.50 6.50

No. 193 is a continuous design.

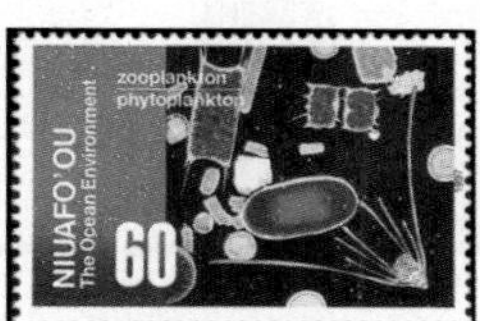

Ocean Environment — A40

Various zooplankton and phytoplankton.

**1997, May 19** **Litho.** *Perf. 14*
**194** A40 60s red & multi 1.50 1.50
**195** A40 80s brown & multi 2.00 2.00
**196** A40 1.50pa blue & multi 4.00 4.00
**197** A40 2.50pa green & multi 7.00 7.00
*Nos. 194-197 (4)* 14.50 14.50

**Pacific '97 Type of Tonga**
Souvenir Sheet

Design: Oakland Bay Bridge, back-naped tern.

**1997, May 30**
**198** A191 2pa multicolored 7.00 7.00

**1997 Wedding Anniv., Coronation Anniv. Type of Tonga**

No. 199: a, King Taufa'ahau, Queen Halaevalu Mata'aho on wedding day. b, King in coronation regalia.
5pa, King in coronation procession, horiz.

**1997, June 30** **Litho.** *Perf. 12*
**Size: 34x47mm**

**199** A193 80s vert. pair, #a.-b. 5.00 5.00

**Souvenir Sheet**

**200** A193 5pa multicolored 13.00 13.00

No. 199 was issued in sheets of 6 stamps.

**Diana, Princess of Wales (1961-97)**
Common Design Type

Various portraits: a, 10s. b, 80s, c, 1pa. d, 2.50pa.

*Perf. 13½x14*

**1998, May 29** **Litho.** **Unwmk.**
**201** CD355 Sheet of 4, #a.-d. 7.75 7.75

No. 201 sold for 4.40pa + 50s with surtax from international sales going to the Princess Diana Memorial Fund and surtax from local sales going to designated local charity.

Blue Crowned Lorikeet — A41

World Wildlife Fund: 10s, Young birds in nest. 55s, Adult on branch of flower. 80s, Adult on branch of bush. 3pa, Two adults on tree branch.

**1998, May 15** **Litho.** *Perf. 14½x15*
**202** A41 10s multicolored 1.00 1.00
**203** A41 55s multicolored 2.00 2.00
**204** A41 80s multicolored 2.50 2.50
**205** A41 3pa multicolored 7.75 7.75
*a.* Sheet, 2 each #202-205 *26.50 26.50*
*Nos. 202-205 (4)* 13.25 13.25

**King Taufa'ahau Tupou IV Type of Tonga**

**1998, July 4** **Litho.** *Perf. 14*
**207** A196 2.70pa multicolored 4.50 4.50

See Tonga #985a for souvenir sheet containing one #207.

Fish A43

a, 10s, Amphipiron melanopus. b, 55s, Amphipiron perideraion. c, 80s, Amphipiron chrysopterus.

**1998, Sept. 23** **Litho.** *Perf. 14*
**208** A43 Strip of 3, #a.-c. 2.50 2.50

Intl. Year of the Ocean. No. 208 was issued in sheets of 9 stamps.

**Year of the Tiger Type of Tonga**

Designs: a, 55s, Head of tiger with mouth open. b, 80s, Two tigers standing. c, 1pa, Two tigers lying down. 1pa, Head of tiger.

**1998, July 23** **Litho.** *Perf. 14*
**209** A183 Sheet of 4, #a.-d. 5.00 5.00

No. 209 is a continuous design. Singpex '98.

Christmas A44

Designs: 20s, Angel playing mandolin. 55s, Angel playing violin. 1pa, Children singing, bells. 1.60pa, Children singing, candles.

**1998, Nov. 12** *Perf. 14x14½*
**210** A44 20s multicolored .40 .40
**211** A44 55s multicolored 1.10 1.10
**212** A44 1pa multicolored 2.00 2.00
**213** A44 1.60pa multicolored 3.00 3.00
*Nos. 210-213 (4)* 6.50 6.50

New Year 1999 (Year of the Rabbit) A45

Stylized rabbits: a, 10s. b, 55s. c, 80s. d, 1pa.

**1999, Feb. 16** *Perf. 14*
**214** A45 Sheet of 4, #a.-d. 4.25 4.25

Jakob le Maire (1585-1616), Explorer — A46

**1999, Mar. 19 Litho.** *Perf. 14*
**215** A46 80s shown 1.25 1.25
**216** A46 2.70pa Tongiaki canoe 4.00 4.00
*a.* Souvenir sheet, #215-216 5.25 5.25

Australia '99 World Stamp Expo (#216a).

Flowers A47

55s, Cananga odorata. 80s, Gardenia tannaensis, vert. 1pa, Coleus amboinicus, vert. 2.50pa, Hernandia moerenhoutiana.

*Perf. 13x13¼, 13¼x13*

**1999, Sept. 29 Litho.**
**217** A47 55s multicolored .75 .75
**218** A47 80s multicolored 1.25 1.25
**219** A47 1pa multicolored 1.50 1.50
**220** A47 2.50pa multicolored 4.00 4.00
*Nos. 217-220 (4)* 7.50 7.50

Souvenir Sheet

Millennium — A48

a, 1pa, Dove. b, 2.50pa, Native boat.

**2000, Jan. 1 Litho.** *Perf. 14½x15*
**221** A48 Sheet of 2, #a.-b. 5.00 5.00

Souvenir Sheet

New Year 2000 (Year of the Dragon) — A49

Illustration reduced.
Various dragons; a, 10s. b, 55s, c, 80s. d, 1pa.

**Litho. with Foil Application**

**2000, Feb. 4** *Perf. 14½*
**222** A49 Sheet of 4, #a.-d. 4.50 4.50

Souvenir Sheet

The Stamp Show 2000, London — A50

Illustration reduced.

**Litho. with Foil Application**

**2000, May 22** *Perf. 13x13¼*
**223** A50 Sheet of 2 6.25 6.25
*a.* $1.50 Queen Mother 2.00 2.00
*b.* $2.50 Queen Salote Tupou III 3.25 3.25

Souvenir Sheet

World Stamp Expo 2001, Anaheim — A51

No. 224: a, 10s, Man and woman. b, 2.50pa, Satellite dish. c, 2.70pa, Intelsat.

**2000, July 7 Litho.** *Perf. 13x13¼*
**224** A51 Sheet of 3, #a-c 8.25 8.25

Butterflies — A52

Designs: 55s, Jamides bochus. 80s, Blue moon. 1pa, Eurema hecabe aprica. 2.70pa, Monarch.

**2000, Oct. 25** *Perf. 14*
**225-228** A52 Set of 4 8.00 8.00

Souvenir Sheet

New Year 2001 (Year of the Snake) — A53

No. 229 — Various snakes: a, 10s. b, 55s, c, 80s, d, 1pa.

**Litho. with Foil Application**

**2001, Feb. 1** *Perf. 14¼*
**229** A53 Sheet of 4, #a-d 4.25 4.25

Hong Kong 2001 Stamp Exhibition.

Fish — A54

Designs: 80s, Prognichthys sealei. 1pa, Xiphias gladius. 2.50pa, Katsuwonus pelamis.

**2001, June 5 Litho.** *Perf. 13¾*
**230-232** A54 Set of 3 7.00 7.00
*232a* Souvenir sheet, #230-232 7.00 7.00

Souvenir Sheet

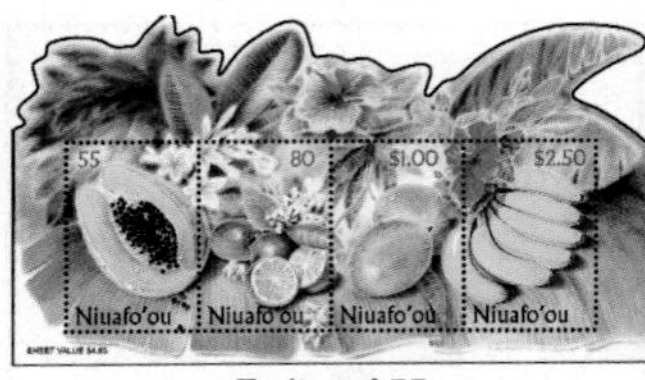
Fruit — A55

No. 233: a, 55s, Papaya. b, 80s, Limes. c, 1pa, Mangos. d, 2.50pa, Bananas.

*Perf. 14¼x14*

**2001, Sept. 19 Litho. Unwmk.**
**233** A55 Sheet of 4, #a-d 8.50 8.50

Barn Owl A56

Designs: Nos. 234, 238a, 10s, Owl in flight. Nos. 235, 238b, 55s, Adult feeding young. Nos. 236, 238c, 2.50pa, Four owls. Nos. 237, 238d, 2.70pa, Owl's head.

**2001, Nov. 21** *Perf. 12¾x13¼*

**Without Vertical Bister Line Separating Panels**

**234-237** A56 Set of 4 10.00 10.00

**Souvenir Sheet**

**With Vertical Bister Line Separating Panels**

**238** A56 Sheet of 4, #a-d 10.00 10.00

**Reign Of Queen Elizabeth II, 50th Anniv. Issue**

Common Design Type

Souvenir Sheet

No. 239: a, 15s, Princess Elizabeth with Queen Mother. b, 90s, Wearing purple hat. c, 1.20pa, As young woman. d, 1.40pa, Wearing red hat. e, 2.25pa, 1955 portrait by Annigoni (38x50mm).

*Perf. 14¼x14½, 13¾ (2.25pa)*

**2002, Feb. 6 Litho. Wmk. 373**
**239** CD360 Sheet of 5, #a-e 7.00 7.00

Souvenir Sheet

New Year 2002 (Year of the Horse) — A517

Various horses: a, 65s. b, 80s. c, 1pa. d, 2.50pa.

**Litho. With Foil Application**

**2002, Feb. 12 Unwmk.** *Perf. 14*
**240** A57 Sheet of 4, #a-d 8.00 8.00

Megapodius Pritchardii A58

Designs: 15s, Bird, eggs. 70s, Two birds. 90s, Bird, vert. 2.50pa, Two birds, vert.

*Perf. 14x13½, 13½x14*

**2002, Apr. 9 Litho.**
**241-244** A58 Set of 4 6.00 6.00
*244a* Souvenir sheet, #243-244 5.00 5.00

Nos. 243-244 lack white frame around stamp.

Cephalopods A59

Designs: 80s, Octopus vulgaris. 1pa, Sepioteuthis lessoniana. 2.50pa, Nautilus belauensis.

**2002, July 25 Litho.** *Perf. 13¾*
**245-247** A59 Set of 3 6.50 6.50
*247a* Souvenir sheet, #245-247 6.50 6.50

Souvenir Sheet

Mail Planes — A60

No. 248: a, 80c, Casa C-212 Aviocar. b, 1.40pa, Britten-Norman Islander. c, 2.50pa, DHC 6-300 Twin Otter.

**2002, Nov. 27 Litho.** *Perf. 12¾*
**248** A60 Sheet of 3, #a-c 7.00 7.00

**New Year 2003 (Year of the Ram) Type of Tonga**

No. 249: a, 65s, One ram. 80s, Three sheep. 1pa, Three sheep, diff. 2.50pa, Two sheep.

**2003, Apr. 14 Litho.** *Perf. 13¼*
**249** A223 Sheet of 4, #a-d 4.75 4.75

**Coronation of Queen Elizabeth II, 50th Anniv. Type of Tonga**

Designs: 90s, Queen Elizabeth II. 1.20pa, Queen Elizabeth II seated. 1.40pa, Queen Salote of Tonga in coach. 2.50pa, Queen Salote.

**2003, June 2 Litho.**
**250-253** A224 Set of 4 10.00 10.00

**New Year (Year of the Monkey) Type of Tonga**

No. 254: a, 60s, Spider monkey. b, 80s, Ring-tailed lemur. c, 1pa, Cotton-top tamarin. d, 2.50pa, White-cheeked gibbon.

**2004, Feb. 12 Litho.** *Perf. 13¼*
**254** A228 Sheet of 4, #a-d 5.75 5.75

**Trees Type of Tonga**

Designs: 45s, Pawpaw (papaya). 60s, Banana. 80s, Coconut. 1.80pa, Lime.

**2004 Litho.** *Perf. 14¼x14*
**255-258** A229 Set of 4 3.75 3.75

**Christmas Type of Tonga**

Designs: 15s, Madonna and Child. 90s, Journey to Bethlehem. 1.20pa, Annunciation to the Shepherds. 2.60pa, Magi.

**2004, Dec.** *Perf. 14*
**259-262** A230 Set of 4 5.25 5.25

**Royalty Type of Tonga**

Designs: 30s, King George Tupou I. 65s, King George Tupou II. 80s, Queen Salote Tupou III. 3.05pa, King Taufa'ahau Tupou IV.

**2004, July 7 Litho.** *Perf. 14*
**263-266** A231 Set of 4 5.75 5.75
*266a* Souvenir sheet, #263-266 5.75 5.75

**New Year 2005 (Year of the Rooster)**
**Type of Tonga**
Souvenir Sheet

No. 267 — Various roosters with panel color of: a, 65s, Gray. b, 80s, Grayish tan. c, 1pa, Gray. d, 2.50pa, Yellow green.

**2005, Feb. 12**
**267** A232 Sheet of 4, #a-d 5.25 5.25

# TRANSCAUCASIAN FEDERATED REPUBLICS

ˌtranˌtˌs-ko-ˈkā-zhən ˈfe-də-rāted ri-ˈpə-bliks

LOCATION — In southeastern Europe, south of the Caucasus Mountains between the Black and Caspian Seas
GOVT. — Former republic
AREA — 71,255 sq. mi.
POP. — 5,851,000 (approx.)
CAPITAL — Tiflis

The Transcaucasian Federation was made up of the former autonomies of Armenia, Georgia and Azerbaijan. Its stamps were replaced by those of Russia.

100 Kopecks = 1 Ruble

Russian Stamps of 1909-17 Overprinted in Black or Red

**1923 Unwmk. *Perf. 14½x15***
**1** A15 10k dark blue 3.00 *5.00*
**2** A14 10k on 7k lt bl 3.00 *5.00*
**3** A11 25k grn & gray vio 3.00 *5.00*
**4** A11 35k red brn & grn (R) 3.00 *5.00*
*a.* Double overprint 40.00 40.00
**5** A8 50k brn red & grn 3.00 *5.00*
**6** A9 1r pale brn, brn & org 8.25 *10.00*
**7** A12 3½r mar & lt grn 35.00

***Imperf***

**8** A9 1r pale brn, brn & red org 3.50 *6.00*
*Nos. 1-8 (8)* 61.75
*Nos. 1-6,8 (7)* *41.00*

No. 7 was prepared but not issued.

Overprinted on Stamps of Armenia Previously Handstamped:

a

c

***Perf. 14½x15***

**9** A11(c) 25k grn & gray vio *240.00 225.00*
**10** A8(c) 50k vio & grn *175.00 150.00*

***Perf. 13½***

**11** A9(a) 1r pale brn, brn & org *75.00 50.00*
**12** A9(c) 1r pale, brn, brn & org *75.00 50.00*

***Imperf***

**13** A9(c) 1r pale brn, brn & red org *35.00 35.00*
*Nos. 9-13 (5)* *600.00 510.00*

Counterfeit overprints exist.

Oil Fields — A1

Soviet Symbols — A2

**1923 *Perf. 11½***
**14** A1 40,000r red violet 1.50 *4.00*
**15** A1 75,000r dark grn 1.50 *4.00*
**16** A1 100,000r blk vio 1.50 *4.00*
**17** A1 150,000r red 1.50 *4.00*
**18** A2 200,000r dull grn 1.50 *4.00*
**19** A2 300,000r blue 1.50 *4.00*
**20** A2 350,000r dark brn 1.50 *4.00*
**21** A2 500,000r rose 1.50 *4.00*
*Nos. 14-21 (8)* 12.00 *32.00*

Nos. 14-15 Surcharged in Brown

**1923**
**22** A1 700,000r on 40,000r 3.00 *5.00*
*a.* Imperf., pair 13.00
**23** A1 700,000r on 75,000r 3.00 *5.00*
*a.* Imperf., pair 13.00

Types of Preceding Issue with Values in Gold Kopecks

**1923, Oct. 24**
**25** A2 1k orange 1.75 *5.00*
**26** A2 2k blue green 1.75 *5.00*
**27** A2 3k rose 2.50 *5.00*
**28** A2 4k gray brown 1.50 *5.00*
**29** A1 5k dark violet 1.50 *5.00*
**30** A1 9k deep blue 1.50 *5.00*
**31** A1 18k slate 1.50 *5.00*
*Nos. 25-31 (7)* 12.00 *35.00*

Nos. 14-21, 25-31 exist imperf. but are not known to have been issued in that condition. Value, $12 each.

# TRANSVAAL

tranˌtˌs-ˈväl

## (South African Republic)

LOCATION — Southern Africa
GOVT. — A former British Colony
AREA — 110,450 sq. mi.
POP. — 1,261,736 (1904)
CAPITAL — Pretoria

Transvaal was known as the South African Republic until 1877 when it was occupied by the British. The republic was restored in 1884 and continued until 1900 when it was annexed to Great Britain and named "The Transvaal."

12 Pence = 1 Shilling
20 Shillings = 1 Pound

Most unused stamps between Nos. 1-96, 119-122 and 136-137 were issued with gum, but do not expect gum on scarcer stamps as few examples retain their original gum. In many cases removal of the remaining gum may enhance the preservation of the stamps. Otherwise, values for unused stamps are for examples with original gum as defined in the catalogue introduction.

Very fine imperforate stamps will have adequate to large margins. However, rouletted stamps are valued as partly rouletted, with straight edges, and rouletted just into the design, as the rouletting methods were quite inaccurate.

**First Republic**

Coat of Arms
A1 A2

**Mecklenburg Printings**
By Adolph Otto, Gustrow
Fine Impressions
Thin Paper

A1 has spread wings on eagle.

**1869 Unwmk. *Imperf.***
**1** A1 1p brown lake 475.00
*a.* 1p red 625.00 625.00
**2** A1 6p ultra 200.00 200.00
**3** A1 1sh dark green 750.00 750.00
*a.* Tete beche pair

***Rouletted 15½, 16***

**4** A1 1p red 110.00
*a.* 1p brown lake 150.00
**5** A1 6p ultra 100.00 100.00
**6** A1 1sh blue green 125.00 125.00
*a.* 1sh yellow green 175.00 160.00
*b.* 1sh deep green 210.00 225.00

Nos. 1-6 were printed from 2 sets of plates, differing in the spacing between the stamps.

The only known example of No. 3a is in a museum.

See Nos. 9-24, 26-33, 35-36, 38-39, 41-42, 43-49, 119, 122. For overprints see Nos. 53-61, 63-66, 68-72, 75-78, 81-83, 86-87, 90-91, 94.

**1871-74**
**7** A2 3p lilac 90.00 *100.00*
*a.* 3p violet 100.00 110.00
**8** A2 6p brt ultra ('74) 67.50 27.50
*a.* Half used as 3p on cover *1,600.*

Many forgeries exist in colors duller or lighter than the genuine stamps.

In forgeries of type A1, all values, the "D" of "EENDRAGT" is not noticeably larger than the other letters and does not touch the top of the ribbon. In type A1 genuine stamps, the "D" is large and touches the ribbon top. The eagle's eye is a dot and its face white on the genuine stamps; the eye is a loop or blob attached to the beak, and the beak is strongly hooked, on the forgeries. Many forgeries of the 1sh have the top line of the ribbon broken above "EENDRAGT."

Forgeries of type A2 usually can be detected only by color.

A sharply struck cancellation of a numeral in three rings is found on many of these forgeries. The similar genuine cancellation is always roughly or heavily struck.

See Nos. 25, 34, 437, 40, 42B, 120-121. For overprints see Nos. 50-52, 62, 67, 73-74, 79-80, 84-85, 88-89, 92-93, 95-96.

**Local Printings**
(A) By M. J. Viljoen, Pretoria
Poor Impressions,
Overinked and Spotted
Thin Soft Paper

**1870 *Imperf.***
**9** A1 1p pink 100.00
*a.* 1p rose red 77.50
*b.* 1p carmine 80.00 72.50
**10** A1 6p dull ultra 350.00 80.00
*a.* Tete beche pair

The only known examples of No. 10a are in museums.

***Rouletted 15½, 16***

**11** A1 1p carmine 775.00 300.00
*a.* Rouletted 6½ 1,100.
**12** A1 6p dull ultra 225.00 110.00

**Hard Paper, Thick to Medium**
***Imperf***

**13** A1 1p carmine 80.00 90.00
**14** A1 6p ultra
**15** A1 1sh gray green 125.00 110.00
*a.* 1sh dark green *650.00 300.00*
*b.* Tete beche pair *23,000.*
*c.* Half used as 6p on cover 2,000.

The existence of No. 14 is questionable.

***Rouletted 15½, 16***

**16** A1 1p light carmine 80.00 97.50
*a.* 1p carmine 57.50 62.50
**17** A1 6p ultra 100.00 95.00
*a.* Tete beche pair *20,000. 15,000.*
**18** A1 1sh dark green 140.00 85.00
*a.* 1sh gray green 575.00 175.00

Copies of Nos. 16 to 18 are sometimes so heavily inked as to be little more than blots of color.

(B) By J. P. Borrius, Potchefstroom
Clearer Impressions Though Often Overinked
Thick Porous Paper

**1870 *Imperf.***
**19** A1 1p black 150.00 125.00
**20** A1 6p indigo 250.00

***Rouletted 15½, 16***

**21** A1 1p black 20.00 30.00
**22** A1 6p gray blue 160.00 70.00
*a.* 6p indigo 100.00 90.00
*b.* 6p bright ultra

**Thin Transparent Paper**

**23** A1 1p black 225.00 *750.00*
**24** A1 1p brt carmine 175.00 62.50
*a.* 1p deep carmine 75.00 45.00
**25** A2 3p gray lilac 110.00 57.50
**26** A1 6p ultra 75.00 35.00
**27** A1 1sh yellow green 92.50 47.50
*a.* 1sh deep green 92.50 47.50
*b.* Half used as 6p on cover —

**Thick Soft Paper**

**28** A1 1p dull rose 450.00 85.00
*a.* 1p brown rose 575.00 140.00
*b.* Printed on both sides
**29** A1 6p dull blue 100.00 50.00
*a.* 6p bright blue 225.00 75.00
*b.* 6p ultramarine 210.00 75.00
*c.* Rouletted 6½
**30** A1 1sh yellow green 950.00 750.00

The paper of Nos. 28 to 30 varies considerably in thickness.

(C) By P. Davis & Son, Natal
Thin to Medium Paper

**1874 *Perf. 12½***
**31** A1 1p red 110.00 45.00
*a.* 1p brownish red 110.00 45.00
**32** A1 6p deep blue 160.00 70.00
*a.* 6p blue 150.00 62.50
*b.* Horiz. pair, imperf. between

(D) By the Stamp Commission, Pretoria
Pelure Paper

**1875-76 *Imperf.***
**33** A1 1p pale red 57.50 57.50
*a.* 1p orange red 50.00 27.50
*b.* 1p brown red 62.50 35.00
*c.* Pin perf. — 400.00
**34** A2 3p gray lilac 57.50 47.50
*a.* 3p dull violet 60.00 45.00
*b.* Pin perf. 70.00 47.50
**35** A1 6p blue 57.50 47.50
*a.* 6p pale blue 57.50 57.50
*b.* 6p dark blue 62.50 50.00
*c.* Tete beche pair
*d.* Pin perf. — 400.00

The only known examples of No. 35c are in museums.

***Rouletted 15½, 16***

**36** A1 1p orange red 400.00 140.00
*a.* Rouletted 6½ 1,100. 225.00
**37** A2 3p dull violet 450.00 150.00
*a.* Rouletted 6½ *1,000.* 275.00
**38** A1 6p blue 175.00 110.00
*a.* Rouletted 6½ 1,100. 125.00

The paper of this group varies slightly in thickness and is sometimes divided into pelure and semipelure. We believe there was only one lot of the paper and that the separation is not warranted.

**Thick Hard Paper**
***Imperf***

**39** A1 1p orange red ('76) 27.50 20.00
**40** A2 3p lilac 425.00 125.00
**41** A1 6p deep blue 70.00 22.50
*a.* 6p blue 110.00 27.50
*b.* Tete beche pair *19,000.*

***Rouletted 15½, 16***

**42** A1 1p orange red ('76) 450.00 175.00
*a.* Rouletted 6½ ('75) 700.00 175.00
**42B** A2 3p lilac 400.00
**43** A1 6p deep blue *675.00* 300.00
*a.* 6p blue *850.00* 125.00
*b.* Rouletted 6½ ('75) *750.00* 275.00

**Soft Porous Paper**
***Imperf***

**44** A1 1p orange red 150.00 62.50
**45** A1 6p deep blue 225.00 60.00
*a.* 6p dull blue 400.00 100.00
**46** A1 1sh yellow green 400.00 125.00
*a.* Half used as 6p on cover 1,800.

***Rouletted 15½, 16***

**47** A1 1p orange red 425.00
*a.* Rouletted 6½ 500.00
**48** A1 6p deep blue 175.00
*a.* Rouletted 6½ 1,250.
**49** A1 1sh yellow grn 800.00 400.00
*a.* Rouletted 6½ 1,400.
*b.* Rouletted 15½-16x16½ 500.00 325.00

## First British Occupation

Stamps and Types of 1875 Overprinted

Red Overprint
Pelure Paper

**1877 Unwmk. *Imperf.***
**50** A2 3p lilac 1,500. 210.00
*a.* Overprinted on back 3,750. *3,750*
*b.* Double ovpt., red and black *7,000.*

***Rouletted 15½, 16***
**51** A2 3p lilac 1,800.
*a.* Rouletted 6½ 1,500.

**Thin Hard Paper**
***Imperf***
**52** A2 3p lilac 1,500. 350.00

**Soft Porous Paper**
**53** A1 6p blue 1,800. 200.00
*a.* 6p deep blue 275.00
*b.* Inverted overprint *6,250.*
*c.* Double overprint *5,100.* 1,100.
**54** A1 1sh yellow grn 700.00 210.00
*a.* Inverted overprint *5,100.*
*b.* Half used as 6p on cover *2,000.*

***Rouletted 15½, 16***
**55** A1 6p blue 1,900.
*a.* Rouletted 6½ 1,400.
**56** A1 1sh yellow grn 1,800. 850.00
*a.* Rouletted 6½ 3,500. 1,200.

**Black Overprint**
**Pelure Paper**
***Imperf***
**57** A1 1p red 300.00 110.00

***Rouletted 15½, 16***
**58** A1 1p red 1,200.

**Thick Hard Paper**
***Imperf***
**59** A1 1p red 27.50 25.00
*a.* Inverted overprint 625.00 575.00

***Rouletted 15½, 16***
**60** A1 1p red 175.00 57.50
*a.* Rouletted 6½ 750.00 225.00
*b.* Inverted overprint
*c.* Double overprint — 1,250.

**Soft Porous Paper**
***Imperf***
**61** A1 1p red 29.00 25.00
*a.* Double overprint 1,300.
**62** A2 3p lilac 92.50 47.50
*a.* 3p deep lilac 200.00 97.50
*b.* Inverted overprint —
**63** A1 6p dull blue 100.00 35.00
*a.* 6p bright blue 175.00 35.00
*b.* 6p dark blue 175.00 35.00
*d.* Inverted overprint — 850.00
*e.* Double overprint *4,000.*
**64** A1 6p blue, *rose* 92.50 55.00
*a.* Tete beche pair
*b.* Inverted overprint 110.00 55.00
*c.* Overprint omitted 4,000. 2,900.
*d.* Half used as 3p on cover
**65** A1 1sh yellow grn 110.00 57.50
*a.* Tete beche pair *22,500.* *22,500.*
*b.* Inverted overprint 1,250. 500.00
*c.* Half used as 6p on cover 1,250.

The only known examples of No. 64a are in museums.

***Rouletted 15½, 16***
**66** A1 1p red 85.00 85.00
*a.* Rouletted 6½ 750.00 175.00
**67** A2 3p lilac 200.00 75.00
*a.* Rouletted 6½ 850.00
**68** A1 6p dull blue 225.00 62.50
*a.* Inverted overprint — 850.00
*b.* Rouletted 6½ — 1,350
*c.* As "a," rouletted 6½ *4,500.*
**69** A1 6p blue, *rose* 200.00 80.00
*a.* Inverted overprint 625.00 80.00
*b.* Rouletted 6½
*c.* Tete beche pair
*d.* Overprint omitted
*e.* As "a," rouletted 6½ 750.00
*f.* As "d," rouletted 6½
**70** A1 1sh yellow grn 225.00 100.00
*a.* Inverted overprint 1,250. 575.00
*b.* Rouletted 6½ 525.00 150.00
*c.* As "a," rouletted 6½ 1,750. 700.00

In this issue the space between "V. R." and "TRANSVAAL" is normally 8½mm but in position 11 it is 12mm. In this and the following issues there are numerous minor varieties of the overprint, missing periods, etc.

The only known examples of No. 69c are in museums.

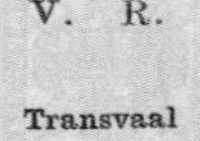


Types A1 and A2 Overprinted

**1877-79 *Imperf.***
**71** A1 1p red, *blue* 62.50 35.00
*a.* "Transvral" *6,250.* *2,900.*
*b.* Inverted overprint *900.00* 450.00
*c.* Double overprint *4,500.*
*d.* Overprint omitted
**72** A1 1p red, *org* ('78) 22.50 22.50
*a.* Printed on both sides
*b.* Pin perf.
**73** A2 3p lilac, *buff* 57.50 30.00
*a.* Inverted overprint 850.00
*b.* Pin perf.
**74** A2 3p lilac, *grn* ('79) 175.00 50.00
*a.* Inverted overprint 2,250.
*b.* Double overprint
*c.* Pin perf.
**75** A1 6p blue, *grn* 97.50 42.50
*a.* Tete beche pair *20,000.*
*b.* Inverted overprint 1,250.
*c.* Half used as 3p on cover
*d.* Pin perf.
**76** A1 6p blue, *bl* ('78) 62.50 30.00
*a.* Tete beche pair
*b.* Overprint omitted 2,500.
*c.* Inverted overprint 1,100.
*d.* Half used as 3p on cover 900.00
*e.* Double overprint 3,750.
*f.* Pin perf.
*Nos. 71-76 (6)* 477.50 210.00

The only known examples of No. 76a are in museums.

***Rouletted 15½, 16***
**77** A1 1p red, *blue* 100.00 42.50
*a.* "Transvral" 3,500.
*b.* Inverted overprint
*c.* Double overprint
**78** A1 1p red, *org* ('78) 35.00 30.00
*a.* Horiz. pair, imperf. vert. 700.00
*b.* Rouletted 6½ 275.00 125.00
**79** A2 3p lilac, *buff* 110.00 30.00
*a.* Inverted overprint 3,500.
*b.* Vert. pair, imperf. horiz.
*c.* Rouletted 6½ 125.00
**80** A2 3p lilac, *grn* ('79) 700.00 175.00
*a.* Inverted overprint
*b.* Rouletted 6½ 750.00 300.00
**81** A1 6p blue, *green* 97.50 32.50
*a.* Inverted overprint 75.00
*b.* Overprint omitted 4,500.
*c.* Tete beche pair
*d.* Half used at 3p on cover 800.00
*e.* Rouletted 6½ — 1,100.
**82** A1 6p blue, *bl* ('78) 250.00 62.50
*a.* Inverted overprint — 1,000.
*b.* Overprint omitted — 4,000.
*c.* Tete beche pair
*d.* Horiz. pair, imperf. vert.
*e.* Half used as 3p on cover 850.00
*f.* Double overprint
*g.* Rouletted 6½ 350.00
*h.* As "a," rouletted 6½
*Nos. 77-82 (6)* 1,292. 372.50

The only known examples of No. 81c are in museums. The existence of No. 82c is questioned.

Types A1 and A2 Overprinted

***Imperf***
**83** A1 1p red, *org* ('78) 62.50 50.00
**84** A2 3p lilac, *buff* ('78) 75.00 40.00
*a.* Pin perf. 850.00 850.00
**85** A2 3p lilac, *grn* ('79) 125.00 40.00
*a.* Inverted overprint 2,250.
*b.* Overprint omitted 4,000.
*c.* Printed on both sides 1,100.
**86** A1 6p blue, *bl* ('78) 125.00 35.00
*a.* Tete beche pair *17,500.*
*b.* Inverted overprint 700.00
*Nos. 83-86 (4)* 387.50 165.00

***Rouletted 15½, 16***
**87** A1 1p red, *org* ('78) 160.00 140.00
*a.* Rouletted 6½ 350.00
**88** A2 3p lilac, *buff* ('78) 175.00 125.00
*a.* Vert. pair, imperf. horiz.
*b.* Rouletted 6½ 400.00
**89** A2 3p lilac, *grn* ('79) 700.00 175.00
*a.* Inverted overprint
*b.* Overprint omitted
*c.* Rouletted 6½ ('97) 350.00
**90** A1 6p blue, *bl* ('78) 425.00 125.00
*a.* Tete beche pair
*b.* Inverted overprint — 1,250.
*c.* Rouletted 6½ 400.00
*e.* As "b," rouletted 6½

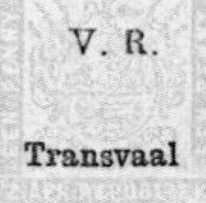


Types A1 and A2 Overprinted

**1879 *Imperf.***
**91** A1 1p red, *orange* 45.00 35.00
*a.* 1p red, *yellow* 50.00 42.50
*b.* Small capital "T" 350.00 225.00
**92** A2 3p lilac, *green* 45.00 29.00
*a.* Small capital "T" 250.00 125.00
**93** A2 3p lilac, *blue* 50.00 35.00
*a.* Small capital "T" 275.00 100.00
*Nos. 91-93 (3)* 140.00 99.00

***Rouletted 15½, 16***
**94** A1 1p red, *yellow* 400.00 225.00
*a.* 1p red, *orange* 850.00 425.00
*b.* Small capital "T" 1,100. 750.00
*c.* Rouletted 6½ 750.00 750.00
*d.* Pin perf. 850.00
**95** A2 3p lilac, *green* 850.00 275.00
*a.* Small capital "T"
*b.* Rouletted 6½
**96** A2 3p lilac, *blue* 200.00
*a.* Small capital "T" 800.00
*b.* Rouletted 6½ 950.00
*c.* Pin perf.

Queen Victoria — A3

**1878-80 Engr. *Perf. 14, 14½***
**97** A3 ½p vermilion ('80) 25.00 *90.00*
**98** A3 1p red brown 14.00 4.50
**99** A3 3p claret 17.50 5.00
**100** A3 4p olive green 24.00 6.25
**101** A3 6p slate 12.50 4.50
*a.* Half used as 3p on cover
**102** A3 1sh green 140.00 42.50
**103** A3 2sh blue 175.00 85.00
*Nos. 97-103 (7)* 408.00 237.75

For surcharges see Nos. 104-118, 138-139.

No. 101 Surcharged in Red or Black:

(a) Surcharged

**1879**
**104** A3 1p on 6p slate (R) 82.50 65.00
**105** A3 1p on 6p slate (Bk) 35.00 24.00

(b) Surcharged **1 Penny**

**106** A3 1p on 6p slate (R) 350.00 275.00
**107** A3 1p on 6p slate (Bk) 160.00 85.00

(c) Surcharged **1 Penny**

**108** A3 1p on 6p slate (R) 200.00 115.00
**109** A3 1p on 6p slate (Bk) 65.00 32.50

(d) Surcharged

**110** A3 1p on 6p slate (R) 210.00 125.00
**111** A3 1p on 6p slate (Bk) 55.00 50.00
*a.* Pair, one without surcharge

(e) Surcharged ***1 Penny***

**112** A3 1p on 6p slate (R) 350.00 225.00
**113** A3 1p on 6p slate (Bk) 150.00 75.00

(f) Surcharged **1 Penny**

**114** A3 1p on 6p slate (R) 325.00 150.00
**115** A3 1p on 6p slate (Bk) 90.00 55.00

(g) Surcharged **1 Penny**

**116** A3 1p on 6p slate (R) *1,500.*
**117** A3 1p on 6p slate (Bk) 500.00 150.00

Surcharge distinctions: a, "PENNY" in gothic capitals. b, "1" has heavy serif at base; "P," thin serif at base. c, No serif at base of "1." d, Heavy serifs at base of "1" and "p." e, Italics. f, "1" has long, sloping serif at top, thin serif at base. g, Tail of "y" missing.

## Second Republic

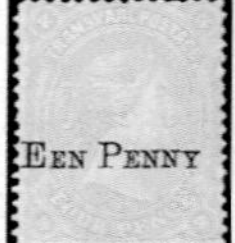


No. 100 Surcharged

**1882 Unwmk. *Perf. 14, 14½***
**118** A3 1p on 4p olive grn 15.00 5.00
*a.* Inverted surcharge 350.00 250.00

**1883 *Perf. 12***
**119** A1 1p black 5.75 2.00
*a.* Imperf.
*b.* Vert. pair, imperf. horiz. 625.00 400.00
*c.* Horiz. pair, imperf. vert. 275.00
**120** A2 3p red 11.00 2.50
*a.* Horiz. pair, imperf. vert.
*b.* Half used as 1p on cover 700.00
**121** A2 3p black, *rose* 26.00 5.75
*a.* Half used as 1p on cover 750.00
**122** A1 1sh green 62.50 4.50
*a.* Tete beche pair 950.00 175.00
*b.* Half used as 6p on cover 500.00
*Nos. 119-122 (4)* 105.25 14.75

The so-called reprints of this issue are forgeries. They were made from the counterfeit plates described in the note following No. 8, plus a new false plate for the 3p. The false 3p plate has many small flaws and defects.

Forgeries of No. 120 are in dull orange red, clearly printed on whitish paper, and those of No. 121 in brownish or grayish black on bright rose. Genuine copies of No. 120 lack the orange tint and the paper is yellowish; genuine copies of No. 121 are in black without gray or brown shade, on dull lilac rose paper.

A 6p in slate on white, apparently of this issue, is a late print from the counterfeit plate.

A4

***Perf. 13½, 11½x12, 12½, 12½x12***
**1885-93 Typo.**
**123** A4 ½p gray .80 .20
**124** A4 1p rose .80 .20
**125** A4 2p brown 2.00 *2.75*
**126** A4 2p olive bis ('87) 1.40 .20
**127** A4 2½p purple ('93) 2.50 .55
**128** A4 3p violet 2.75 1.40
**129** A4 4p bronze green 4.25 .90
**130** A4 6p blue 4.25 2.25
*a.* Imperf.
**131** A4 1sh green 2.75 .70
**132** A4 2sh6p yellow 9.00 2.50
**133** A4 5sh steel blue 9.00 4.50
**134** A4 10sh pale brown 35.00 9.00
**135** A4 £5 dark green ('92) 3,750. 210.00
*Nos. 123-134 (12)* 74.50 25.15

*Reprints of Nos. 123-137, 140-163, 166-174 closely resemble the originals. Paper is whiter; perf. 12½, large holes.*

Excellent counterfeits of No. 135 exist.

For overprint and surcharges see Nos. 140-147, 163, 213.

Nos. 120, 122 Surcharged

**1885 *Perf. 12***
**136** A2 ½p on 3p red 5.75 *11.00*
*a.* Surcharge reading down 5.75 *11.00*
**137** A1 ½p on 1sh green 25.00 57.50
*a.* Surcharge reading down 25.00 57.50
*b.* Tete beche pair 850.00 400.00

Almost all copies of No. 137b have telegraph cancellations. Postally used examples are rare.

Nos. 101, 128 Surcharged in Red or Black

***Perf. 14***

| | | | | |
|---|---|---|---|---|
| **138** | A3 | ½p on 6p slate | 62.50 | *97.50* |
| **139** | A3 | 2p on 6p slate | 6.25 | *12.50* |
| *a.* | | Horiz. pair, imperf. vert. | | |

***Perf. 11½x12, 12½x12***

| | | | | |
|---|---|---|---|---|
| **140** | A4 | ½p on 3p vio (Bk) | 4.50 | 4.50 |
| *a.* | | "PRNNY" | 45.00 | *70.00* |
| *b.* | | 2nd "N" of "PENNY" invtd. | 97.50 | *110.00* |

No. 128 Surcharged

No. 141

No. 142

**1887**

| | | | | |
|---|---|---|---|---|
| **141** | A4 | 2p on 3p violet | 1.75 | 3.75 |
| *a.* | | Double surcharge | 200.00 | 200.00 |
| **142** | A4 | 2p on 3p violet | 8.50 | 8.50 |
| *a.* | | Double surcharge | | 300.00 |

Nos. 126, 130, 131 Surcharged

Nos. 143-144

Nos. 145-146

No. 147

Red Surcharge

**1893**

| | | | | |
|---|---|---|---|---|
| **143** | A4 | ½p on 2p olive bis | .90 | 2.00 |
| *a.* | | Inverted surcharge | 2.75 | 2.75 |
| *b.* | | Bars 14mm apart | 1.75 | 2.75 |
| *c.* | | As "b," inverted | 5.75 | 11.00 |

**Black Surcharge**

| | | | | |
|---|---|---|---|---|
| **144** | A4 | ½p on 2p olive bis | .95 | 2.00 |
| *a.* | | Inverted surcharge | 5.00 | 5.75 |
| *b.* | | Bars 14mm apart | 1.25 | 2.25 |
| *c.* | | As "b," inverted | 22.50 | 17.50 |
| **145** | A4 | 1p on 6p blue | .80 | .85 |
| *a.* | | Inverted surcharge | 1.75 | 2.25 |
| *b.* | | Double surcharge | 62.50 | 50.00 |
| *c.* | | Pair, one without surcharge | 250.00 | |
| *d.* | | Bars 14mm apart | 1.10 | 1.10 |
| *e.* | | As "d," inverted | 5.75 | 4.50 |
| *f.* | | As "d," double | | 90.00 |
| **146** | A4 | 2½p on 1sh green | 1.40 | *4.25* |
| *a.* | | Inverted surcharge | 7.50 | *8.50* |
| *b.* | | Fraction line misplaced "2/12" | 35.00 | 70.00 |
| *c.* | | As "b," inverted | 400.00 | 350.00 |
| *d.* | | Bars 14mm apart | 1.75 | 4.25 |
| *e.* | | As "d," inverted | 8.50 | *18.00* |
| **147** | A4 | 2½p on 1sh green | 5.50 | 4.75 |
| *a.* | | Inverted surcharge | 8.50 | 8.50 |
| *b.* | | Bars 14mm apart | 9.00 | 9.50 |
| *c.* | | As "b," inverted | 22.50 | 22.50 |
| *d.* | | Double surcharge | 85.00 | *95.00* |
| | | *Nos. 143-147 (5)* | 9.55 | 13.85 |

A13

Wagon with Two Shafts

**1894** **Typo.** ***Perf. 12½***

| | | | | |
|---|---|---|---|---|
| **148** | A13 | ½p gray | .50 | .40 |
| **149** | A13 | 1p rose | 1.00 | .20 |
| **150** | A13 | 2p olive bister | 1.00 | .20 |
| **151** | A13 | 6p blue | 1.75 | .40 |
| **152** | A13 | 1sh yellow grn | 10.00 | *12.00* |
| | | *Nos. 148-152 (5)* | 14.25 | 13.20 |

Counterfeits of #148-152 are plentiful.
*See note following No. 135 for reprints.*

**1895-96** **Wagon with Pole**

| | | | | |
|---|---|---|---|---|
| **153** | A13 | ½p gray | .75 | .20 |
| **154** | A13 | 1p rose | .75 | .20 |
| **155** | A13 | 2p olive bister | .80 | .20 |
| **156** | A13 | 3p violet | 1.50 | .20 |
| **157** | A13 | 4p slate | 2.00 | .45 |
| **158** | A13 | 6p blue | 2.00 | .30 |
| **159** | A13 | 1sh green | 3.00 | .90 |
| **160** | A13 | 5sh slate blue ('96) | 13.00 | *20.00* |
| **161** | A13 | 10sh red brown ('96) | 13.00 | 3.50 |
| | | *Nos. 153-161 (9)* | 36.80 | 25.95 |

Most of the unused specimens of Nos. 153-161 now on the market are reprints.

See Nos. 166-174. For surcharge and overprints see Nos. 162, 214-220, 232-235.

*See note following No. 135 for reprints.*

Nos. 159, 127 Surcharged in Red or Green

**1895**

| | | | | |
|---|---|---|---|---|
| **162** | A13 | ½p on 1sh green (R) | .30 | .20 |
| *a.* | | Inverted surcharge | 5.25 | 5.25 |
| *b.* | | "Pennij" instead of "Penny" | 60.00 | 60.00 |
| *c.* | | Double surcharge | 60.00 | 60.00 |
| **163** | A4 | 1p on 2½p pur (G) | .60 | .20 |
| *a.* | | Inverted surcharge | 20.00 | 20.00 |
| *b.* | | Surcharge sideways | | |
| *c.* | | Surcharge on back | | |
| *d.* | | Space between "1" and "d" | 1.25 | 1.25 |

A16

**1895** ***Perf. 11½***

| | | | | |
|---|---|---|---|---|
| **164** | A16 | 6p rose (G) | .80 | .80 |
| *a.* | | Vertical pair, imperf. between | | |

Counterfeits of No. 164 are on the 6p dark red revenue stamp of 1898, and have a shiny green ink for the overprint. The false overprint is also found on other revenue denominations, though only the 6p rose was converted to postal use.

Coat of Arms, Wheat Field and Railroad Train — A17

**1895, Sept. 6** **Litho.**

| | | | | |
|---|---|---|---|---|
| **165** | A17 | 1p red | 1.00 | 1.00 |
| *a.* | | Imperf. | | |
| *b.* | | Vertical pair, imperf. between | 80.00 | 85.00 |

Penny Postage in Transvaal. Horiz. pair, imperf. between also exists.

For overprint see No. 245.

**With Pole**

**1896** **Typo.** ***Perf. 12½***

| | | | | |
|---|---|---|---|---|
| **166** | A13 | ½p green | .25 | .20 |
| **167** | A13 | 1p rose & grn | .25 | .20 |
| **168** | A13 | 2p brown & grn | .25 | .20 |
| **169** | A13 | 2½p ultra & grn | .40 | .20 |
| **170** | A13 | 3p red vio & grn | 1.00 | .75 |
| **171** | A13 | 4p olive & grn | 1.00 | .75 |
| **172** | A13 | 6p violet & grn | .50 | .40 |
| **173** | A13 | 1sh bister & grn | .75 | .20 |
| **174** | A13 | 2sh6p lilac & grn | 1.10 | 1.00 |
| | | *Nos. 166-174 (9)* | 5.50 | 3.90 |

*See note following No. 135 for reprints.*

For overprints and surcharges see Nos. 202-212, 214-235, 237-244, 246-251, Cape of Good Hope Nos. N5-N8.

**Pietersburg Issue**

Date large; "P" in Postzegel large — A18

Date small; "P" in Postzegel large — A19

Date small; "P" in Postzegel small — A20

**1901** **Typeset** ***Imperf.***

**Initials in Red**

| | | | |
|---|---|---|---|
| **175** | A18 | ½p black, *green* | 37.50 |
| *a.* | | Initials omitted | 125.00 |
| *b.* | | Initials in black | 45.00 |
| **176** | A19 | ½p black, *green* | 50.00 |
| *a.* | | Initials omitted | 125.00 |
| *b.* | | Initials in black | 45.00 |
| **177** | A20 | ½p black, *green* | 50.00 |
| *a.* | | Initials omitted | 125.00 |
| *b.* | | Initials in black | 45.00 |

**Initials in Black**

| | | | |
|---|---|---|---|
| **178** | A18 | 1p black, *rose* | 10.00 |
| **179** | A19 | 1p black, *rose* | 13.00 |
| **180** | A20 | 1p black, *rose* | 16.00 |
| **181** | A18 | 2p black, *orange* | 15.00 |
| **182** | A19 | 2p black, *orange* | 20.00 |
| **183** | A20 | 2p black, *orange* | 22.50 |
| **184** | A18 | 4p black, *dull blue* | 25.00 |
| **185** | A19 | 4p black, *dull blue* | 30.00 |
| **186** | A20 | 4p black, *dull blue* | 40.00 |
| **187** | A18 | 6p black, *green* | 32.50 |
| **188** | A19 | 6p black, *green* | 47.50 |
| **189** | A20 | 6p black, *green* | 65.00 |
| **190** | A18 | 1sh black, *yellow* | 75.00 |
| **191** | A19 | 1sh black, *yellow* | 55.00 |
| **192** | A20 | 1sh black, *yellow* | 140.00 |

***Perf. 11½***

**Initials in Red**

| | | | |
|---|---|---|---|
| **193** | A18 | ½p black, *green* | 13.00 |
| **194** | A19 | ½p black, *green* | 15.00 |
| **195** | A20 | ½p black, *green* | 20.00 |

**Initials in Black**

| | | | |
|---|---|---|---|
| **196** | A18 | 1p black, *rose* | 10.00 |
| *a.* | | Horiz. pair, imperf. vert. | 125.00 |
| **197** | A19 | 1p black, *rose* | 13.00 |
| *a.* | | Horiz. pair, imperf. vert. | 150.00 |
| **198** | A20 | 1p black, *rose* | 13.00 |
| *a.* | | Horiz. pair, imperf. vert. | 150.00 |
| **199** | A18 | 2p black, *orange* | 15.00 |
| **200** | A19 | 2p black, *orange* | 17.00 |
| **201** | A20 | 2p black, *orange* | 17.00 |

Nos. 193 to 201 inclusive are always imperforate on one side.

The setting consisted of 12 stamps of type A18, 6 of type A19, and 6 of type A20. Numerous type-setting varieties exist. The perforated stamps are from the first printing and were put into use first. Used copies are not valued as all seen show evidence of having been canceled to order.

**Second British Occupation Issued under Military Authority**

Nos. 166-174, 160-161, 135 Overprinted

**1900** **Unwmk.** ***Perf. 12½***

| | | | | |
|---|---|---|---|---|
| **202** | A13 | ½p green | .20 | .20 |
| *a.* | | "V.I.R." | 650.00 | |
| **203** | A13 | 1p rose & grn | .20 | .20 |
| **204** | A13 | 2p brown & grn | 1.40 | .40 |
| *a.* | | "V.I.R." | 650.00 | |
| **205** | A13 | 2½p ultra & grn | .50 | .40 |
| **206** | A13 | 3p red vio & grn | .50 | .20 |
| **207** | A13 | 4p olive & grn | 1.10 | .20 |
| *a.* | | "V.I.R." | 650.00 | |
| **208** | A13 | 6p violet & grn | 1.10 | .40 |
| **209** | A13 | 1sh bister & grn | 1.10 | .80 |
| **210** | A13 | 2sh6p hel & grn | 1.75 | 2.25 |
| **211** | A13 | 5sh slate blue | 3.50 | 4.00 |
| **212** | A13 | 10sh red brown | 5.25 | 4.50 |
| **213** | A4 | £5 dark green | | |
| | | *Nos. 202-212 (11)* | 16.60 | 13.55 |

Nos. 202 to 213 have been extensively counterfeited. The overprint on the forgeries is clear and clean, with small periods and letters showing completely. In the genuine, letters are worn and lack many or all serifs; the periods are large and oval.

The genuine overprint exists inverted; double; with period missing after "V," after "R," after "I," etc.

**Issued in Lydenburg**

Overprinted in Black

**1900**

| | | | | |
|---|---|---|---|---|
| **214** | A13 | ½p green | 110.00 | 110.00 |
| **215** | A13 | 1p rose & grn | 100.00 | 80.00 |
| **216** | A13 | 2p brown & grn | 800.00 | 700.00 |
| **217** | A13 | 2½p ultra & grn | | 800.00 |
| **218** | A13 | 4p olive & grn | 2,250. | 650.00 |
| **219** | A13 | 6p violet & grn | 2,250. | 575.00 |
| **220** | A13 | 1sh bister & grn | 2,500. | |

Beware of counterfeits.

No. 167 Surcharged

| | | | | |
|---|---|---|---|---|
| **221** | A13 | 3p on 1p rose & green | 80.00 | 70.00 |

**Issued in Rustenburg**

Nos. 166-170, 172-174 Handstamped in Violet

**1900** ***Perf. 12½***

| | | | | |
|---|---|---|---|---|
| **223** | A13 | ½p green | 100.00 | 100.00 |
| **224** | A13 | 1p rose & grn | 95.00 | 60.00 |
| **225** | A13 | 2p brown & grn | 200.00 | 190.00 |
| **226** | A13 | 2½p ultra & grn | 120.00 | 80.00 |
| **227** | A13 | 3p red vio & grn | 190.00 | 110.00 |
| **229** | A13 | 6p violet & grn | 650.00 | 500.00 |
| **230** | A13 | 1sh bister & grn | 1,300. | 650.00 |
| **231** | A13 | 2sh6p hel & grn | | *4,250.* |

**Issued in Schweizer Reneke**

Nos. 166-168 and 172 Handstamped "BESIEGED" in Black

**1900** **Typo.** ***Perf. 12½***

| | | | |
|---|---|---|---|
| **232** | A13 | ½p green | 250.00 |
| **233** | A13 | 1p rose & green | 275.00 |
| **234** | A13 | 2p brown & green | 450.00 |
| **235** | A13 | 6p violet & green | 900.00 |
| | | *Nos. 232-235 (4)* | 1,875. |

**Same Overprint on Cape of Good Hope No. 59 and Type of 1893**

***Perf. 14***

| | | | |
|---|---|---|---|
| **236** | A15 | ½p green | 650.00 |
| **236A** | A15 | 1p carmine | 650.00 |

In 1902 five revenue stamps overprinted "V.R.I." are said to have been used postally in Volksrust. There seems to be some doubt that this issue was properly authorized for postal use.

**Issued in Wolmaransstad**

Nos. 166-173 Handstamped in Blue or Red

**1900**

| | | | | |
|---|---|---|---|---|
| **237** | A13 | ½p green | 175.00 | |
| **238** | A13 | 1p rose & grn | 160.00 | *175.00* |
| **239** | A13 | 2p brown & grn | 1,400. | *1,400.* |
| **240** | A13 | 2½p ultra & grn (R) | 2,000. | *2,000.* |

| | | | | |
|---|---|---|---|---|
| **241** A13 | 3p red vio & grn | 2,500. | |
| **242** A13 | 4p olive & grn | 3,000. | *3,750.* |
| **243** A13 | 6p violet & grn | 2,750. | *4,250.* |
| **244** A13 | 1sh bister & grn | | |

No. 165 Overprinted in Blue

| | | | |
|---|---|---|---|
| **245** A17 1p red | 160.00 | *150.00* |

**Regular Issues**
No. 166-168, 170-171, 174 Surcharged or Overprinted

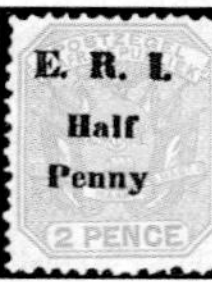


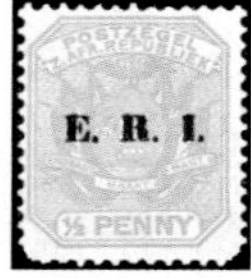


**1901-02**

| | | | |
|---|---|---|---|
| **246** A13 | ½p on 2p brn & grn | .80 | .65 |
| **247** A13 | ½p green | .40 | *.80* |
| **248** A13 | 1p rose & grn | .40 | .20 |
| *a.* | Overprint "E" omitted | 65.00 | |
| **249** A13 | 3p red vio & grn | 2.00 | 1.50 |
| **250** A13 | 4p olive & grn | 2.25 | 1.50 |
| **251** A13 | 2sh6p hel & grn | 7.75 | *10.00* |
| | *Nos. 246-251 (6)* | 13.60 | 14.65 |

Excellent counterfeits of Nos. 246 to 251 are plentiful. See note after No. 213 for the recognition marks of the counterfeits.

Edward VII — A27

Nos. 260, 262 to 267 and 275 to 280 have "POSTAGE" at each side; the other stamps of type A27 have "REVENUE" at the right.

**Wmk. Crown and C A (2)**

**1902-03 Typo. *Perf. 14***

| | | | |
|---|---|---|---|
| **252** A27 | ½p gray grn & blk | 1.40 | .20 |
| **253** A27 | 1p rose & blk | 1.25 | .20 |
| **254** A27 | 2p violet & blk | 3.25 | .30 |
| **255** A27 | 2½p ultra & blk | 5.75 | .80 |
| **256** A27 | 3p ol grn & blk | 6.00 | .30 |
| **257** A27 | 4p choc & blk | 4.75 | .35 |
| **258** A27 | 6p brn org & blk | 3.50 | .50 |
| **259** A27 | 1sh ol grn & blk | 12.00 | 6.00 |
| **260** A27 | 1sh red brn & blk | 11.00 | 1.25 |
| **261** A27 | 2sh brown & blk | 37.50 | 37.50 |
| **262** A27 | 2sh yel & blk | 15.00 | *9.00* |
| **263** A27 | 2sh6p black & vio | 13.00 | 10.00 |
| **264** A27 | 5sh vio & blk, *yel* | 20.00 | 20.00 |
| **265** A27 | 10sh vio & blk, *red* | 47.50 | 22.50 |
| **266** A27 | £1 violet & grn | 175.00 | 100.00 |
| **267** A27 | £5 violet & org | 1,300. | 575.00 |
| | *Nos. 252-266 (15)* | 356.90 | 208.90 |

Issue dates: 3p, 4p, Nos. 260, 262, £1, £5, 1903. Others, Apr. 1, 1902.

**1904-09 Wmk. 3**

| | | | |
|---|---|---|---|
| **268** A27 | ½p gray grn & blk | 4.00 | 1.75 |
| **269** A27 | 1p rose & blk | 2.75 | .20 |
| **270** A27 | 2p violet & blk | 5.50 | .50 |
| **271** A27 | 2½p ultra & blk | 7.50 | 2.25 |
| **272** A27 | 3p ol grn & blk | 2.50 | .20 |
| **273** A27 | 4p choc & blk | 3.00 | .50 |
| **274** A27 | 6p brn org & blk | 2.25 | .30 |
| **275** A27 | 1sh red brn & blk | 4.50 | .30 |
| **276** A27 | 2sh yellow & blk | 15.00 | 4.00 |
| **277** A27 | 2sh6p blk & red vio | 35.00 | 3.00 |
| **278** A27 | 5sh vio & blk, *yel* | 16.00 | 1.25 |
| **279** A27 | 10sh vio & blk, *red* | 37.50 | 2.00 |
| **280** A27 | £1 violet & grn | 160.00 | 17.50 |
| | *Nos. 268-280 (13)* | 295.50 | 33.75 |

The 2p and 3p are on chalky paper, the 2½p, 4p, 6p and £1 on both chalky and ordinary, and the other values on ordinary paper only.

Issue years: ½p, 1p, 5sh, 1904. 2½p, 6p, 1sh, 1905. 2p, 3p, 4p, 2sh, 1906. 10sh, 1907. £1, 1908. 2sh6p, 1909.

**1905-10**

| | | | |
|---|---|---|---|
| **281** A27 | ½p green | 1.50 | .20 |
| *a.* | Booklet pane of 6 | | |
| **282** A27 | 1p carmine | 1.00 | .20 |
| *a.* | Wmk. 16 (anchor) ('07) | | 275.00 |
| *b.* | Booklet pane of 6 | | |
| **283** A27 | 2p dull vio ('10) | 3.00 | .40 |
| **284** A27 | 2½p ultra ('10) | 11.00 | 4.00 |
| | *Nos. 281-284 (4)* | 16.50 | 4.80 |

Wmk. 16 is illustrated in the Cape of Good Hope.

Some of the above stamps are found with the overprint "C. S. A. R." for use by the Central South African Railway, the control mark being applied after the stamps had left the post office.

## POSTAGE DUE STAMPS

D1

**Wmk. Multiple Crown and C A (3)**

**1907 Typo. *Perf. 14***

| | | | |
|---|---|---|---|
| **J1** D1 | ½p green & blk | 3.50 | 1.10 |
| **J2** D1 | 1p carmine & blk | 4.25 | .65 |
| **J3** D1 | 2p brown & org | 4.25 | 1.00 |
| **J4** D1 | 3p blue & blk | 7.50 | 2.75 |
| **J5** D1 | 5p violet & blk | 2.25 | 10.00 |
| **J6** D1 | 6p red brown & blk | 4.50 | 11.00 |
| **J7** D1 | 1sh black & car | 10.00 | 7.00 |
| | *Nos. J1-J7 (7)* | 36.25 | 33.50 |

Most canceled copies of #J1-J7 were used outside the Transvaal under the Union of South Africa administration in 1910-16.

The stamps of Transvaal were replaced by those of South Africa.

## TRINIDAD

'tri-nə-,dad

LOCATION — West Indies, off the Venezuelan coast
GOVT. — British Colony which became part of the Colony of Trinidad and Tobago in 1889
AREA — 1,864 sq. mi.
POP. — 387,000
CAPITAL — Port of Spain

12 Pence = 1 Shilling
20 Shillings = 1 Pound

In 1847 David Bryce, owner of the "Lady McLeod," issued a blue, lithographed, imperf. stamp to prepay his 5-cent rate for carrying letters on his sail-equipped steamer between Port of Spain and San Fernando, another Trinidad port. The stamp pictures the "Lady McLeod" above the monogram "LMcL," expressing no denomination. Value, unused, $50,000, used (pen canceled), $12,500. Used stamps canceled by having a corner skinned off are worth less.

Values for unused stamps are for examples with original gum as defined in the catalogue introduction. However, Nos. 9-12 are seldom found with gum, and these are valued without gum.

Values for Nos. 18-26 are for stamps with pin perforations on two or three sides. Stamps with pin perforations on all four sides are not often seen and command large premiums.

Very fine examples of Nos. 27-47 will have perforations touching the design on one or more sides due to the narrow spacing of the stamps on the plates and imperfect perforating methods. These stamps with perfs clear of the design on all four sides are scarce and command substantially higher prices.

"Britannia"
A1 A2

**1851-53 Unwmk. Engr. *Imperf.***

**Blued Paper**

1 A1 (1p) brick red ('56) 200.00 85.00
a. (1p) brown red ('53) 360.00 77.50
2 A1 (1p) purple brown 18.00 *90.00*
3 A1 (1p) blue 18.00 *72.50*
a. (1p) deep blue, deeply blued paper 175.00 95.00
4 A1 (1p) gray brn ('53) 57.50 *90.00*
a. (1p) gray ('52) 90.00 77.50
*Nos. 1-4 (4)* 293.50 *337.50*

**1854-57**

**White Paper**

6 A1 (1p) brown red ('57) 3,250. 77.50
7 A1 (1p) gray 50.00 *95.00*
8 A1 (1p) black violet 30.00 *100.00*

See Nos. 14, 18, 22, 27, 33, 39, 43, 45, 48, 58. For surcharges see Nos. 62-64.

**1852 Litho.**

**Fine Impressions**

**Yellowish Paper**

9 A2 (1p) blue *11,500.* 1,950.
a. (1p) deep blue *11,500.* 1,950.
b. White paper 1,950.

**1853**

**Bluish Paper**

10 A2 (1p) blue *10,000.* 2,400.

Same, Lines of Background More or Less Worn

**1855-60**

**Thin Paper**

11 A2 (1p) slate blue *5,500.* 800.00
12 A2 (1p) blue *5,000.* 500.00
a. (1p) greenish blue 800.00
13 A2 (1p) rose 17.50 *750.00*
a. (1p) dull red 17.50 *725.00*

A3

**1859 Engr. *Imperf.***

**White Paper**

14 A1 (1p) dull rose — —
15 A3 4p gray lilac 125.00 *400.00*
a. 4p dull lilac —
16 A3 6p green *15,000.* 525.00
17 A3 1sh slate blue 125.00 *425.00*

***Pin-perf. 12½***

18 A1 (1p) dull rose red *2,000.* 70.00
a. (1p) lake *2,250.* 70.00
19 A3 4p brown lilac — 1,250.
a. 4p dull purple 7,500. 1,250.
20 A3 6p deep green *3,500.* 250.00
a. 6p yellow green 3,500. 250.00
21 A3 1sh black violet *9,000.* 1,750.

***Pin-perf. 14***

22 A1 (1p) rose red 275.00 35.00
a. (1p) carmine 2,500. 37.50
23 A3 4p brown lilac 250.00 *150.00*
a. 4p violet 600.00 160.00
b. 4p dull violet 1,650. 125.00
24 A3 6p deep green 800.00 100.00
25 A3 6p yellow green 200.00 160.00
a. Vert. pair, imperf. between *8,000.*
26 A3 1sh black violet *9,000.* *1,150.*

**1860 *Clean-cut Perf. 14 to 15½***

27 A1 (1p) dull rose 175.00 67.50
a. (1p) lake 100.00 40.00
b. Horiz. pair, imperf. vert. *3,000.*
29 A3 4p violet brown 200.00 95.00
a. 4p dull violet 375.00
30 A3 6p deep green 300.00 175.00
31 A3 6p yellow green 475.00 100.00
32 A3 1sh black violet

**1861 *Rough Perf. 14 to 16½***

33 A1 (1p) dull rose 160.00 32.50
34 A3 4p gray lilac 750.00 100.00
35 A3 4p brown lilac 325.00 85.00
a. 4p dull violet 750.00 115.00
36 A3 6p green 475.00 85.00
a. 6p blue green 325.00 95.00
37 A3 1sh indigo 1,000. 350.00
a. 1sh purplish blue 1,675. 550.00

**1863 *Perf. 11½ to 12***

**Thick Paper**

39 A1 (1p) carmine 160.00 24.00
a. Perf. 11½-12x11 2,000. *600.00*
40 A3 4p dull violet 225.00 72.50
41 A3 6p dp blue green *1,350.* 100.00
a. Perf. 11½-12x11 *8,000.*
42 A3 1sh indigo 2,750. 110.00

***Perf. 12½***

43 A1 (1p) lake 57.50 24.00

***Perf. 13***

45 A1 (1p) lake 27.50 15.00
46 A3 6p emerald 300.00 42.50
47 A3 1sh brt violet 4,000. 225.00

**1864-72 Wmk. 1 *Perf. 12½***

48 A1 (1p) red 65.00 3.00
a. (1p) lake 65.00 7.25
b. (1p) rose 65.00 3.00
c. (1p) carmine 65.00 3.25
d. Imperf., pair *800.00* *800.00*
49 A3 4p brt violet 140.00 14.50
a. 4p pale violet 250.00 20.00
b. Imperf. *600.00*
50 A3 4p lilac 200.00 20.00
a. 4p gray lilac
51 A3 4p gray ('72) 160.00 6.75
52 A3 6p blue green 160.00 9.00
a. 6p emerald 110.00 17.50
53 A3 6p yellow grn 100.00 5.50
a. 6p dp grn 500.00 9.00
b. Imperf., pair *800.00*
54 A3 1sh purple 200.00 10.00
a. 1sh lilac 150.00 10.00
b. 1sh violet 150.00 10.00
c. 1sh red lilac 160.00 10.00
d. Imperf. *750.00*
55 A3 1sh orange yel ('72) 175.00 1.75
*Nos. 48-55 (8)* 1,200. 70.50

See Nos. 59-61A, 65. For surcharge see No. 67.

Queen Victoria — A4

**1869-94 Typo. *Perf. 12½***

56 A4 5sh dull lake 200.00 90.00
a. Imperf., pair *1,250.*

***Perf. 14***

57 A4 5sh claret ('94) 67.50 *100.00*

For overprint see No. O7.

**1876 Engr. *Perf. 14***

58 A1 (1p) carmine 32.50 1.75
a. (1p) red 57.50 1.75
b. (1p) lake 32.50 1.75
c. Half used as ½p on cover 750.00
59 A3 4p gray 140.00 .85
60 A3 6p yellow green 115.00 2.25
a. 6p deep green 150.00 2.10
61 A3 1sh orange yellow 150.00 4.00
*Nos. 58-61 (4)* 437.50 8.85

***Perf. 14x12½***

61A A3 6p yellow green *6,750.*

Value for No. 61A is for stamp with perfs barely touching the design.

Type A1 Surcharged in Black

**1879 Wmk. 1 *Perf. 14***

62 A1 ½p lilac 14.50 10.00

Same Surcharge

**1882 Wmk. Crown and C A (2)**

63 A1 ½p lilac *250.00* 90.00
64 A1 1p carmine 42.50 1.75
a. Half used as ½p on cover 675.00

Type of 1859

**1882 Wmk. 2**

65 A3 4p gray 215.00 10.00

No. 60 Surcharged by pen and ink in Black or Red

**1882 Wmk. 1**

67 A3 1p on 6p green (R) 11.00 6.75
a. Half used as ½p on cover 400.00
b. Black surcharge *1,900.*

Counterfeits of No. 67b are plentiful. Various handwriting exists on both 60 and 60a.

A7 A8

A9

**1883-84 Typo. Wmk. 2**

68 A7 ½p green 6.00 1.50
69 A7 1p rose 12.00 .60
a. Half used as ½p on cover 950.00
70 A7 2½p ultra 15.00 .70
a. 2½p blue 15.00 .75
71 A7 4p slate 3.00 .70
72 A7 6p olive brn ('84) 4.75 *5.50*
73 A7 1sh orange brn ('84) 5.75 3.50
*Nos. 68-73 (6)* 46.50 12.50

For overprints see Nos. O1-O6.

**1896-1904 *Perf. 14***

ONE PENNY:
Type I — Round "O" in "ONE."
Type II — Oval "O" in "ONE."

74 A8 ½p lilac & green 4.00 .35
75 A8 ½p gray grn ('02) .75 *2.40*
76 A8 1p lil & car, type I 4.25 .20
77 A8 1p lil & car, type II ('00) 400.00 4.75
78 A8 1p blk, *red*, type II ('01) 1.50 .20
a. Value omitted *36,000.*
79 A8 2½p lilac & ultra 7.25 .25
80 A8 2½p vio & bl, *bl* ('02) 20.00 .75
81 A8 4p lilac & orange 7.75 *21.00*
82 A8 4p grn & ultra, *buff* ('02) 2.00 *20.00*
83 A8 5p lilac & violet 9.50 *16.00*
84 A8 6p lilac & black 9.00 6.50
85 A8 1sh grn & org brn 8.25 7.75
86 A8 1sh blk & bl, *yel* ('04) 22.50 6.50

**Wmk. C A over Crown (46)**

87 A9 5sh green & org 55.00 90.00
88 A9 5sh lil & red vio ('02) 60.00 77.50
89 A9 10sh grn & ultra 210.00 400.00
Revenue cancel 25.00
90 A9 £1 grn & car 175.00 240.00
*Nos. 74-90 (17)* 996.75 894.15

No. 82 also exists on chalky paper. Nos. 88 and 90 exist on both ordinary and chalky paper.

Circular "Registrar General" cancels are revenue usage and of minimal value.

See Nos. 92-104.

Landing of Columbus — A10

**1898 Engr. Wmk. 1**

**91** A10 2p gray vio & yel brn 2.50 1.25

400th anniv. of the discovery of the island of Trinidad by Columbus, July 31, 1498.

**1904-09 Wmk. 3**

**Chalky Paper**

**92** A8 ½p gray green 4.25 2.75
**93** A8 1p blk, *red*, type II 6.00 .20
**94** A8 2½p vio & bl, *bl* 27.50 1.10
**95** A8 4p blk & car, *yel* ('06) 2.00 10.00
**96** A8 6p lilac & blk ('05) 19.00 18.00
**97** A8 6p vio & dp vio ('06) 8.50 *12.00*
**98** A8 1sh blk & bl, *yel* 24.00 9.50
**99** A8 1sh vio & bl, *yel* 13.00 19.00
**100** A8 1sh blk, *grn* ('06) 2.00 1.50
**101** A9 5sh lil & red vio ('07) 55.00 110.00
**102** A9 £1 grn & car ('07) 175.00 300.00
*Nos. 92-102 (11)* 336.25 484.05

The ½p and 1p also exist on ordinary paper.
For overprints see Nos. O8-O9.

**1906-07**

**103** A8 1p carmine ('07) 1.75 .20
**104** A8 2½p ultramarine 4.50 .20

A11

A12

**1909**

**Ordinary Paper**

**105** A11 ½p gray green 5.00 .20
**106** A12 1p carmine 5.00 .20
**107** A11 2½p ultramarine 16.00 3.75
*Nos. 105-107 (3)* 26.00 4.15

For overprint see No. O10.

## POSTAGE DUE STAMPS

D1

**Wmk. Crown and C A (2)**

**1885, Jan. 1 Typo. *Perf. 14***

**J1** D1 ½p black 22.50 55.00
**J2** D1 1p black 7.75 .25
**J3** D1 2p black 35.00 .25
**J4** D1 3p black 60.00 .50
**J5** D1 4p black 42.50 4.75
**J6** D1 5p black 27.50 .70
**J7** D1 6p black 45.00 6.50
**J8** D1 8p black 65.00 4.00
**J9** D1 1sh black 77.50 9.00
*Nos. J1-J9 (9)* 382.75 80.95

**1906-07 Wmk. 3**

**J10** D1 1p black 5.50 .25
**J11** D1 2p black 32.50 .25
**J12** D1 3p black 15.00 3.25
**J13** D1 4p black 15.00 16.00
**J14** D1 5p black 15.00 16.00
**J15** D1 6p black 7.25 *12.00*
**J16** D1 8p black 14.50 *16.00*
**J17** D1 1sh black 15.00 *42.50*
*Nos. J10-J17 (8)* 119.75 106.25

See Trinidad and Tobago Nos. J1-J16.

## OFFICIAL STAMPS

Postage Stamps of 1869-84 Overprinted in Black

**1893-94 Wmk. 2 *Perf. 14***

**O1** A7 ½p green 42.50 *65.00*
**O2** A7 1p rose 45.00 *72.50*
**O3** A7 2½p ultra 55.00 *110.00*
**O4** A7 4p slate 57.50 *115.00*
**O5** A7 6p olive brown 57.50 *115.00*
**O6** A7 1sh orange brown 77.50 *150.00*

**Wmk. Crown and C C (1)**

***Perf. 12½***

**O7** A4 5sh dull lake 190.00 *575.00*
*Nos. O1-O7 (7)* 525.00 *1,202.*

Nos. 92 and 103 Overprinted

**1909-10 Wmk. 3 *Perf. 14***

**O8** A8 ½p gray green 1.25 9.00
**O9** A8 1p carmine 1.25 9.00
*a.* Double overprint 375.00
*b.* Inverted overprint 900.00 275.00
*c.* Vertical overprint 125.00 150.00

Same Overprint on No. 105

**1910**

**O10** A11 ½p gray green 6.50 9.00

Stamps of Trinidad have been superseded by those inscribed "Trinidad and Tobago."

# TRINIDAD AND TOBAGO

ˈtri-nə-ˌdad and tə-ˈbā-ˌgō

LOCATION — West Indies off the coast of Venezuela
GOVT. — Republic
AREA — 1,980 sq. mi.
POP. — 1,102,096 (1999 est.)
CAPITAL — Port-of-Spain

The two British colonies of Trinidad and Tobago were united from 1889 until 1899, when Tobago became a ward of the united colony. From 1899 until 1913 postage stamps of Trinidad were used. The two islands became a state in August 1962, and the independent Republic of Trinidad and Tobago on August 1, 1976.

12 Pence = 1 Shilling
20 Shillings = 1 Pound
100 Cents = 1 Dollar (1935)

**Catalogue values for unused stamps in this country are for Never Hinged items, beginning with Scott 62 in the regular postage section and Scott J9 in the postage due section.**

A1

"Britannia" — A2

**1913 Typo. Wmk. 3 *Perf. 14***

**Ordinary Paper**

**1** A1 ½p green 3.50 .20
**2** A1 1p scarlet 1.75 .20
*a.* 1p carmine 2.75 .20
**4** A1 2½p ultra 8.00 .50

**Chalky Paper**

**5** A1 4p scar & blk, *yel* .80 *7.00*
**6** A1 6p red vio & dull vio 11.00 5.00
**7** A1 1sh black, *emerald* 1.75 *3.50*
*a.* 1sh black, *green* 2.00 *5.00*
*b.* 1sh black, *bl grn*, ol back 9.50 *10.00*
*Nos. 1-2,4-7 (6)* 26.80 16.40

**1914**

**Surface-colored Paper**

**8** A1 4p scar & blk, *yel* 2.00 *11.00*
**9** A1 1sh black, *green* 1.60 *3.50*

**Chalky Paper**

**10** A2 5sh dull vio & red vio 70.00 *110.00*
**11** A2 £1 green & car 160.00 *210.00*
*Nos. 8-11 (4)* 233.60 *334.50*

**1921-22 Wmk. 4**

**Ordinary Paper**

**12** A1 ½p green 3.00 2.50
**13** A1 1p scarlet .70 .35
**14** A1 1p brown ('22) .70 *1.75*
**15** A1 2p gray ('22) 1.10 *1.40*
**16** A1 2½p ultra .90 *17.50*
**17** A1 3p ultra ('22) 4.00 *3.50*

**Chalky Paper**

**18** A1 6p red vio & dull vio 2.25 *17.50*
**19** A2 5sh dull vio & red vio 57.50 *175.00*
**20** A2 £1 green & car 110.00 *290.00*
*Nos. 12-20 (9)* 180.15 *509.50*

For overprints see #B2-B3, MR1-MR13, O1-O5.

"Britannia" and King George V — A3

**1922-28**

**Ordinary Paper**

**21** A3 ½p green .55 .20
**22** A3 1p brown .55 .20
**23** A3 1½p rose red 2.50 2.00
**24** A3 2p gray .55 *1.40*
**25** A3 3p ultra .55 *1.40*

**Chalky Paper**

**26** A3 4p red & blk, *yel* ('28) 3.75 3.75
**27** A3 6p red vio & dl vio 2.50 *29.00*
**28** A3 6p red & grn, *emer* ('24) 1.40 .70
**29** A3 1sh blk, *emer* ('25) 6.25 2.00
**30** A3 5sh vio & dull vio 25.00 *42.50*
**31** A3 £1 rose & green 125.00 *225.00*

**Wmk. Multiple Crown and C A (3)**

**Chalky Paper**

**32** A3 4p red & blk, *yel* 3.75 *11.00*
**33** A3 1sh blk, *emerald* 4.00 *11.00*
*Nos. 21-33 (13)* 176.35 *330.15*

First Boca — A4

Designs: 2c, Agricultural College. 3c, Mt. Irvine Bay, Tobago. 6c, Discovery of Lake Asphalt. 8c, Queen's Park, Savannah. 12c, Town Hall, San Fernando. 24c, Government House. 48c, Memorial Park. 72c, Blue Basin.

**1935-37 Engr. Wmk. 4 *Perf. 12***

**34** A4 1c emer & bl, perf. 12½ ('36) .35 .20
*a.* Perf. 12 .45 *1.00*
**35** A4 2c lt brn & ultra, perf. 12 .85 *1.10*
*a.* Perf. 12½ ('36) 1.10 .20
**36** A4 3c red & black, perf. 12½ ('36) 3.00 .35
*a.* Perf. 12 1.50 .35
**37** A4 6c bl & brn, perf. 12 4.75 2.75
*a.* Perf. 12½ ('37) 9.00 5.00
**38** A4 8c red org & yel grn 4.25 4.00
**39** A4 12c dk violet & blk 3.75 2.00
*a.* Perf. 12½ ('37) 9.00 7.00
**40** A4 24c ol grn & blk 3.75 1.75
*a.* Perf. 12½ ('37) 15.00 11.00
**41** A4 48c slate green 10.00 *17.00*
**42** A4 72c mag & sl grn 32.50 *35.00*
*Nos. 34-42 (9)* 63.20 64.15

Common Design Types pictured following the introduction.

**Silver Jubilee Issue**

Common Design Type

**1935, May 6 *Perf. 11x12***

**43** CD301 2c black & ultra .35 *.85*
**44** CD301 3c car & blue .35 *1.60*
**45** CD301 6c ultra & brn 1.75 *2.75*
**46** CD301 24c brn vio & ind 7.00 *17.50*
*Nos. 43-46 (4)* 9.45 22.70
Set, never hinged 20.00

**Coronation Issue**

Common Design Type

**1937, May 12 *Perf. 13½x14***

**47** CD302 1c deep green .20 .20
**48** CD302 2c yellow brown .20 .20
**49** CD302 8c deep orange .50 .50
*Nos. 47-49 (3)* .90 .90
Set, never hinged 1.50

First Boca — A13

George VI — A14

Various Frames and: 2c, Agricultural College. 3c, Mt. Irvine Bay, Tobago. 4c, Memorial Park. 5c, General Post Office and Treasury. 6c, Discovery of Lake Asphalt. 8c, Queen's Park, Savannah. 12c, Town Hall, San Fernando. 24c, Government House. 60c, Blue Basin.

***Perf. 11½x11***

**1938-41 Wmk. 4 Engr.**

**50** A13 1c emer & blue .25 .20
**51** A13 2c lt brn & ultra .25 .20
**52** A13 3c dk car & blk 7.75 1.10
**52A** A13 3c vio brn & bl grn ('41) .20 .20
**53** A13 4c brown 20.00 1.10
**53A** A13 4c red ('41) .25 .25
**54** A13 5c mag ('41) .20 .20
**55** A13 6c brt bl & sep 1.00 .65
**56** A13 8c red org & yel grn .95 .85
**57** A13 12c dk vio & blk 1.75 .20
**58** A13 24c dk ol grn & blk .50 .20
**59** A13 60c mag & sl grn 6.00 1.50

***Perf. 12***

**60** A14 $1.20 dk grn ('40) 7.00 1.00
**61** A14 $4.80 rose pink ('40) 14.00 25.00
*Nos. 50-61 (14)* 60.10 32.65
Set, never hinged 95.00

Watermark sideways on Nos. 50-59.

**Catalogue values for unused stamps in this section, from this point to the end of the section, are for Never Hinged items.**

**Peace Issue**

Common Design Type

***Perf. 13½x14***

**1946, Oct. 1 Engr. Wmk. 4**

**62** CD303 3c brown .20 .20
**63** CD303 6c deep blue .25 .25

**Silver Wedding Issue**
Common Design Types

**1948, Nov. 22 Photo. *Perf. 14x14½***
64 CD304 3c red brown .20 .20

**Engr. *Perf. 11½x11***
65 CD305 $4.80 rose car 22.50 *32.50*

**UPU Issue**
Common Design Types
**Engr.; Name Typo. on 6c, 12c**
***Perf. 13½, 11x11½***

**1949, Oct. 10 Wmk. 4**
66 CD306 5c red violet .40 .40
67 CD307 6c indigo 2.00 2.00
68 CD308 12c rose violet .50 .50
69 CD309 24c olive .50 .50
*Nos. 66-69 (4)* 3.40 3.40

**University Issue**
Common Design Types
Inscribed: "Trinidad"

**1951, Feb. 16 Engr. *Perf. 14x14½***
70 CD310 3c chocolate & grn .25 .20
71 CD311 12c purple & blk .60 .50

Types of 1938 with Portrait of Queen Elizabeth II

**1953, Apr. 20 *Perf. 11½x11***
72 A13 1c yel grn & dp blue .20 .20
73 A13 2c org brn & sl blue .20 .20
74 A13 3c vio brn & blue grn .20 .20
75 A13 4c red .20 .20
76 A13 5c magenta .20 .20
77 A13 6c blue & brown .55 .35
78 A13 8c red org & dp grn 2.50 .35
79 A13 12c dk violet & blk .35 .20
80 A13 24c dk ol grn & blk 2.50 .35
81 A13 60c rose car & grnsh blk 25.00 1.25

***Perf. 11½***
82 A14 $1.20 dark green 1.40 .65
a. Perf. 12 3.50 2.00
83 A14 $4.80 rose pink 10.00 *16.00*
a. Perf. 12 15.00 *17.50*
*Nos. 72-83 (12)* 43.30 20.15

For surcharge see No. 85.

**Coronation Issue**
Common Design Type

**1953, June 3 *Perf. 13½x13***
84 CD312 3c dark green & blk .20 .20

No. 73 Surcharged "ONE CENT"
***Perf. 11½x11***

**1956, Dec. 20 Wmk. 4**
85 A13 1c on 2c org brn & sl blue 1.40 *1.40*

**West Indies Federation**
Common Design Type
***Perf. 11½x11***

**1958, Apr. 22 Engr. Wmk. 314**
86 CD313 5c green .20 .20
87 CD313 6c blue .20 *.40*
88 CD313 12c carmine rose .30 .25
*Nos. 86-88 (3)* .70 .85

Cipriani Memorial, Port-of-Spain
A27

Queen's Hall, Port-of-Spain
A28

Designs: 5c, Whitehall. 6c, Treasury Building. 8c, Governor General's House. 10c, General Hospital, San Fernando. 12c, Oil refinery. 15c, Crest of colony. 25c, Scarlet ibis. 35c, Lake Asphalt (Pitch). 50c, Jinnah Memorial Mosque. 60c, Anthurium lilies. $1.20, Copper-rumped hummingbird and hibiscus. $4.80, Map.

***Perf. 13½x14, 14x13½***
**1960, Sept. 24 Photo. Wmk. 314**
**Size: 22½x25mm, 25x22½mm**
89 A27 1c dark gray & buff .20 .20
a. Wmkd. sideways ('66) .50 .50
90 A28 2c ultra .20 .20
91 A28 5c dark blue .20 .20
92 A28 6c lt red brown .20 .20
93 A28 8c yellow green .20 *.35*
94 A28 10c light purple .20 .20
95 A28 12c bright red .20 .20
96 A28 15c orange 1.10 .55
97 A28 25c dk blue & crim .90 .20
98 A28 35c green & black 4.00 .20
99 A28 50c blue, yel & olive .40 *.45*
100 A27 60c multicolored .60 .20
a. Perf. 14 ('65) 160.00 24.00

**Size: 48x25mm**
101 A28 $1.20 multicolored 16.00 3.00
102 A28 $4.80 lt bl & lt yel grn 25.00 *15.00*
*Nos. 89-102 (14)* 49.40 21.15

See #116. For overprints see #123-124, 126.

Scouts and Map of Trinidad and Tobago — A29

**1961, Apr. 4 *Perf. 13½x14***
103 A29 8c multicolored .20 .20
104 A29 25c multicolored .35 .35

2nd Caribbean Scout Jamboree, Valsayn Park, Trinidad, Apr. 4-14.

**Independent State**

Underwater Scene from Painting by Carlisle Chang — A30

Designs: 8c, Elizabeth II and new Terminal Building, Piarco Airport. 25c, Elizabeth II and Hilton Hotel. 35c, Map and greater bird of paradise. 60c, Map and scarlet ibis.

**1962, Aug. 31 Photo. *Perf. 14½***
105 A30 5c blue green .25 .20
106 A30 8c slate .40 .20
107 A30 25c purple .25 .20
108 A30 35c emer, yel, brn & blk 2.25 .20
109 A30 60c ultra, black & ver 2.75 *2.50*
*Nos. 105-109 (5)* 5.90 3.30

Issued to mark Trinidad and Tobago's independence, Aug. 31, 1962.

**Freedom from Hunger Issue**

Protein Food — A31

**1963, June 1 *Perf. 14x13½***
110 A31 5c henna brown .20 .20
111 A31 8c citron .20 .20
112 A31 25c violet blue .30 .30
*Nos. 110-112 (3)* .70 .70

See note in Common Design section.

Girl Guide Emblem
A32

***Perf. 14½x14***
**1964, Sept. 15 Wmk. 314**
113 A32 6c red, dk blue & yel .20 .20
114 A32 25c brt blue, dk bl & yel .20 .20
115 A32 35c lt green, dk bl & yel .30 .30
*Nos. 113-115 (3)* .70 .70

50th anniv. of the Trinidad and Tobago Girl Guide Association.

Arms of Independent State — A33

**1964, Sept. 15 *Perf. 14x13½***
116 A33 15c orange .40 .40

For overprint see No. 125.

ICY Emblem
A34

**Unwmk.**
**1965, Nov. 15 Litho. *Perf. 12***
**Granite Paper**
117 A34 35c dull yel, red brn & grn .35 .35

International Cooperation Year, 1965.

Eleanor Roosevelt — A35

***Perf. 13½x14***
**1965, Dec. 10 Wmk. 314**
118 A35 25c vio blue, red & blk .25 .25

Issued to honor Eleanor Roosevelt and to publicize the Eleanor Roosevelt Memorial Foundation.

"Redhouse," Parliament Building — A36

8c, Map of Trinidad & Tobago, royal yacht "Britannia," arms of State. 25c, Flag, map. 35c, Flag, Trinity Hills, General Post Office, sugar cane, coconut palms, derricks.

**1966, Feb. 8 Photo. Wmk. 314**
119 A36 5c ultra, red, blk & grn .45 .20
120 A36 8c ultra, sil, blk & yel brn 2.25 .25
121 A36 25c red, blk & emerald 2.25 1.25
122 A36 35c ultra, red, blk & grn 2.25 1.75
*Nos. 119-122 (4)* 7.20 3.45

Visit of Elizabeth II and Prince Philip.

Nos. 93, 94, 116 and 100 Overprinted: "FIFTH YEAR OF / INDEPENDENCE / 31st AUGUST 1967"
***Perf. 14x13½, 13½x14***

**1967, Aug. 31 Photo. Wmk. 314**
123 A28 8c yellow green .20 .20
124 A28 10c lt purple .20 .20
125 A33 15c orange .20 .20
126 A27 60c multicolored .30 .30
*Nos. 123-126 (4)* .90 .90

On 60c, the overprint is arranged in 5 lines.

Carnival Symbols
A37

Designs: 10c, Calypso King, vert. 15c, Steel band. 25c, Chinese masks. 35c, Carnival King, vert. 60c, Carnival Queen, vert.

**Unwmk.**
**1968, Feb. 16 Litho. *Perf. 12***
127 A37 5c pink & multi .25 .25
128 A37 10c vio blue & multi .25 .25
129 A37 15c multicolored .25 .25
130 A37 25c multicolored .25 .25
131 A37 35c dk purple & multi .25 .25
132 A37 60c brown ol & multi .45 .45
*Nos. 127-132 (6)* 1.70 1.70

Issued to publicize the Trinidad Carnival.

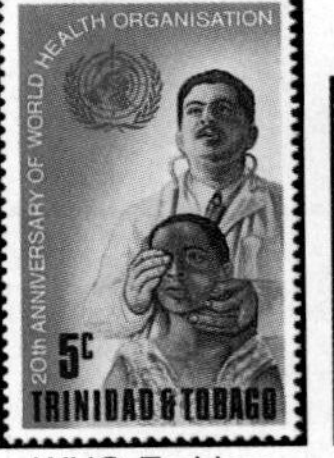

WHO Emblem and Eye Examination
A38

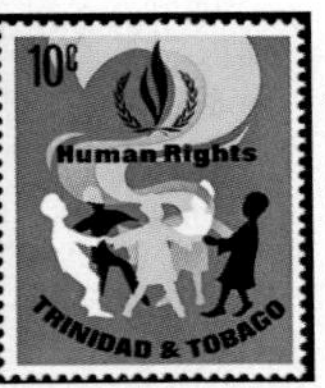

Dancing Children and Human Rights Flame
A39

**Wmk. 314**
**1968, May 7 Photo. *Perf. 14***
133 A38 5c rose red, gold & blk .20 .20
134 A38 25c orange, gold & blk .30 .30
135 A38 35c brt blue, gold & blk .40 .40
*Nos. 133-135 (3)* .90 .90

**1968, Aug. 5 *Perf. 14***
136 A39 5c carmine, yel & blk .20 .20
137 A39 10c brt blue, yel, & blk .20 .20
138 A39 25c yel grn, yel, & blk .25 .25
*Nos. 136-138 (3)* .65 .65

International Human Rights Year.

Bicycling and Map
A40

Designs (Olympic Rings, Map of Trinidad and Tobago and): 15c, Weight lifting. 25c, Relay race. 35c, Running. $1.20, Map of Mexico and flags of Mexico and Trinidad and Tobago.

**Photo.; Gold Impressed (except $1.20)**

**1968, Oct. 12 *Perf. 14***
139 A40 5c vio, gold & multi .20 .20
140 A40 15c red, gold & multi .20 .20
141 A40 25c org, gold & multi .20 .20
142 A40 35c brt grn, gold & multi .25 .20
143 A40 $1.20 blue, gold & multi 1.00 .70
*Nos. 139-143 (5)* 1.85 1.50

19th Olympic Games, Mexico City, 10/12-27.

Cacao
A41

Designs: 3c, Sugar refinery. 5c, Redtailed chachalaca. 6c, Oil refinery. 8c, Fertilizer plant. 10c, Green hermit (hummingbird) vert. 12c, Citrus fruit, vert. 15c, Coat of arms, vert. 20c, 25c, Flag and map of islands, vert. 30c, Wild poinsettia, vert. 40c, Scarlet ibis. 50c, Maracas Bay. $1, Blooming tabebuia (tree) vert. $2.50, Fishermen hauling in net. $5, Red House, Port-of-Spain.

**Photo.; Silver or Gold Impressed**
**1969, Apr. 1 Wmk. 314 *Perf. 14***
144 A41 1c silver & multi .20 .25
145 A41 3c gold & multi .20 .25
a. Wmk. upright ('74) .50 .50
146 A41 5c gold & multi .20 .25
a. Wmk. upright ('73) 7.50 4.00
147 A41 6c gold & multi .20 .25
a. Wmk. upright ('74) .30 .25
148 A41 8c silver & multi .20 .25
149 A41 10c gold & multi .20 .25
b. Wmk. 373 ('76) .30 .25
150 A41 12c silver & multi .20 .25
151 A41 15c silver & multi .20 .25
152 A41 20c gold & multi .20 .25

153 A41 25c silver & multi .25 .25
154 A41 30c silver & multi .30 .25
155 A41 40c gold & multi .45 .30
156 A41 50c silver & multi .55 .40
157 A41 $1 gold & multi 1.10 .95
158 A41 $2.50 gold & multi 3.25 3.75
159 A41 $5 gold & multi 6.75 7.00
*Nos. 144-159 (16)* 14.45 15.15

For overprint see No. 187.

Capt. A. A. Cipriani, ILO Emblem and Gate A42

ILO, 50th Anniv.: 15c, Industrial Court's & ILO emblems, & Woodford Square gate.

**Unwmk.**

**1969, May 1 Photo. *Perf. 12***
160 A42 6c dp car, gold & blk .20 .20
161 A42 15c brt blue, gold & blk .20 .20

Union Jack and Flags of CARIFTA Members A43

Designs: 6c, Cornucopia, vert. 30c, Map of Caribbean, vert. 40c, Jet plane and "Strength through Unity" emblem.

**1969, Aug. 1 *Perf. 14x13½, 13½x14***
162 A43 6c lilac, gold & multi .20 .20
163 A43 10c multicolored .20 .20
164 A43 30c red, emer, blk & gold .25 .25
165 A43 40c blue, blk, grn & gold .35 .35
*Nos. 162-165 (4)* 1.00 1.00

Caribbean Free Trade Area (CARIFTA).

Moon Landing and Earth — A44

40c, Lunar landing module & astronauts on moon. $1, Astronauts Aldrin at control panel, Armstrong collecting rocks.

**1969, Sept. 1 Litho. *Perf. 14***
166 A44 6c multi .20 .20
167 A44 40c multi, vert. .30 .30
168 A44 $1 multi .75 .75
*Nos. 166-168 (3)* 1.25 1.25

See note after US No. C76.

Maces of Senate and House of Representatives — A45

10c, Chamber of Parliament. 15c, View of Kennedy Complex, University of the West Indies at St. Augustine. 40c, Cannon & view of Scarborough from Fort King George.

***Perf. 14x13½***

**1969, Oct. 23 Photo. Wmk. 314**
169 A45 10c multicolored .20 .20
170 A45 15c multicolored .20 .20
171 A45 30c lt blue & multi .25 .25
172 A45 40c multicolored .25 .25
*Nos. 169-172 (4)* .90 .90

15th Conf. of the Commonwealth Parliamentary Assoc., Port-of-Spain, Oct. 4-19.

Congress Emblem and Landscape A46

Carnival King as "Man in the Moon" A47

6c, Congress emblem (steel drum and bird). 30c, Palms, landscape and emblem, horiz.

***Perf. 14x13½, 13½x14***

**1969, Nov. 2 Litho. Unwmk.**
173 A46 6c red, black & gold .20 .20
174 A46 30c lt blue, plum & gold .25 .25
175 A46 40c ultra, black & gold .25 .25
*Nos. 173-175 (3)* .70 .70

24th Cong. of the Intl. Junior Chamber of Commerce.

**1970, Feb. 2 Wmk. 314 *Perf. 14***

Designs: 5c, Carnival Queen as "City Beneath the Sea." 15c, Bambara god (antelope) from the Band of the Year. 30c, Pheasant Queen (Chanticleer) of Malaya. 40c, Steel Band of the Year with 1969 Calypso and Road March Kings, horiz.

176 A47 5c dk brown & multi .20 .20
177 A47 6c dk blue & multi .20 .20
178 A47 15c violet bl & multi .20 .20
179 A47 30c dk green & multi .25 .25
180 A47 40c green & multi .25 .25
*Nos. 176-180 (5)* 1.10 1.10

Issued to publicize the Trinidad Carnival.

Mahatma Gandhi and Indian Flag — A48

Design: 10c, Gandhi monument, vert.

**Unwmk.**

**1970, Mar. 2 Photo. *Perf. 12***
181 A48 10c ultra & multi .35 .25
182 A48 30c crimson & multi .90 .70

Mohandas K. Gandhi (1869-1948), leader in India's fight for independence.

"Culture, Science, Arts and Technology" A49

UN, 25th Anniv.: 10c, Children of various races, map of Trinidad and Tobago and "UNICEF." 20c, Noah's ark, rainbow, dove and UN emblem.

**1970, June 26 Photo. *Perf. 13½***
183 A49 5c multicolored .20 .20
184 A49 10c multicolored .25 .25
185 A49 20c multicolored .30 .30
*Nos. 183-185 (3)* .75 .75

UPU Headquarters, Bern — A50

**1970, June 26 Unwmk. *Perf. 12***
186 A50 30c ultra & multi .50 .50

Opening of new UPU Headquarters in Bern.

No. 146 Overprinted: "NATIONAL / COMMERCIAL / BANK / ESTABLISHED / 1.7.70"

**Photo.; Gold Embossed**

**1970, July 1 Wmk. 314 *Perf. 14***
187 A41 5c gold & multi .30 .20

San Fernando Town Hall — A51

Designs: 3c, East Indian Immigrants, 1820, after painting by Cazabon, vert. 40c, Ships in San Fernando Harbor, 1860, after painting by Michel J. Cazabon.

***Perf. 14x13½, 13½x14***

**1970, Nov. Litho. Wmk. 314**
188 A51 3c bister & multi .20 .20
189 A51 5c lemon & multi .20 .20
190 A51 40c lemon & multi .50 .50
*Nos. 188-190 (3)* .90 .90

Municipality of San Fernando, 125th anniv.

Madonna and Child, by Titian — A52

Paintings: 3c, Adoration of the Shepherds, School of Saville. 30c, Adoration of the Shepherds, by Louis Le Nain. 40c, Virgin and Child with St. John and Angel, by Morando. $1, Adoration of the Magi, by Paolo Veronese.

***Perf. 13½***

**1970, Dec. 8 Unwmk. Litho.**
191 A52 3c dull org & multi .20 .20
a. Booklet pane of 2 .20
192 A52 5c brt pink & multi .20 .20
a. Booklet pane of 2 .25
193 A52 30c lt utra & multi .25 .25
a. Booklet pane of 2 .60
194 A52 40c yellow grn & multi .25 .25
a. Booklet pane of 2 .75
b. Souvenir sheet of 4, #191-194 2.25 2.25
195 A52 $1 pale lilac & multi .60 .60
*Nos. 191-195 (5)* 1.50 1.50

Brocket Deer — A53

***Perf. 14x13½***

**1971, Aug. 9 Litho. Wmk. 314**
196 A53 3c shown .40 .25
197 A53 5c Collared peccary .50 .20
198 A53 6c Paca .60 .40
199 A53 30c Agouti 1.75 3.25
200 A53 40c Ocelot 1.75 2.40
*Nos. 196-200 (5)* 5.00 6.50

Capt. A. A. Cipriani A54

Virgin and Child with St. John, by Bartolommeo A55

Design: 30c, Chaconia medal (for distinction in social field).

**1971, Aug. 31 *Perf. 14***
201 A54 5c multicolored .20 .20
202 A54 30c multicolored .30 .30

9th anniversary of independence. Capt. Arthur Andrew Cipriani (died 1945) was mayor of Port of Spain and member of First Executive Council.

**1971, Oct. 25 Litho. *Perf. 14x14½***

Christmas: 5c, Local creche. 10c, Virgin and Child with Sts. Jerome and Dominic, by Filippino Lippi. 15c, Virgin and Child with St. Anne, by Gerolamo dai Libri.

203 A55 3c yellow & multi .20 .20
204 A55 5c dull blue & multi .20 .20
205 A55 10c red & multi .25 .25
206 A55 15c orange & multi .35 .35
*Nos. 203-206 (4)* 1.00 1.00

Satellite Earth Station, Matura A56

Dish Antenna A57

Design: 40c, Satellite over earth (Africa).

**1971, Nov. 18 *Perf. 14***
207 A56 10c ultra & multi .20 .20
208 A57 30c green & multi .25 .25
209 A57 40c black & multi .35 .35
a. Souvenir sheet of 3 1.40 1.40
*Nos. 207-209 (3)* .80 .80

Opening of Satellite Earth Station at Matura. No. 209a contains 3 imperf. stamps with simulated perforations similar to Nos. 207-209.

Morpho Hybrid A58

Butterflies: 5c, Purple mort bleu. 6c, Jaune d'abricot. 10c, Purple king shoemaker. 20c, Southern white pape. 30c, Little jaune.

**1972, Feb. 18 Photo. Wmk. 314**
210 A58 3c olive & multi 1.00 .80
211 A58 5c ocher & multi 1.50 .20
212 A58 6c yellow & multi 1.75 .80
213 A58 10c yel grn & multi 2.00 .30
214 A58 20c lilac & multi 3.00 2.40
215 A58 30c dull grn & multi 4.50 3.00
*Nos. 210-215 (6)* 13.75 7.50

S.S. Lady McLeod and Stamp A59

10c, Map of Trinidad and Tobago. 30c, Commemorative inscription.

**1972, Apr. 12 Litho. *Perf. 14½x14***

| | | | | |
|---|---|---|---|---|
| **216** | A59 | 5c blue & multi | .20 | .20 |
| **217** | A59 | 10c blue & multi | .25 | .25 |
| **218** | A59 | 30c blue & multi | .65 | .65 |
| *a.* | | Souvenir sheet of 3, #216-218 | 1.25 | 1.25 |
| | | *Nos. 216-218 (3)* | 1.10 | 1.10 |

125th anniv. of the Lady McLeod stamp.

Trinity Cross — A60

Medals: 10c, Chaconia medal. 20c, Hummingbird medal. 30c, Medal of Merit.

**1972, Aug. 28 Photo. *Perf. 13½x13***

| | | | | |
|---|---|---|---|---|
| **219** | A60 | 5c blue & multi | .20 | .20 |
| **220** | A60 | 10c multicolored | .20 | .20 |
| **221** | A60 | 20c yellow grn & multi | .25 | .30 |
| **222** | A60 | 30c brt rose & multi | .25 | .40 |
| *a.* | | Souvenir sheet of 4, #219-222 | 1.00 | 1.00 |
| | | *Nos. 219-222 (4)* | .90 | 1.10 |

10th anniversary of independence.
See Nos. 235-238.

Olympic Rings, Relay Race Medal, 1964 A61

Olympic Rings and: 20c, Bronze medal, 200-meters, 1964. 30c, Bronze medals, weight lifting, 1952. 40c, Silver medal, 400-meters, 1964. 50c, Silver medal, weight lifting, 1948.

**1972, Sept. 7 Litho. *Perf. 14***

| | | | | |
|---|---|---|---|---|
| **223** | A61 | 10c yellow & multi | .20 | .20 |
| **224** | A61 | 20c multicolored | .30 | .30 |
| **225** | A61 | 30c lilac & multi | .40 | .40 |
| **226** | A61 | 40c lt blue & multi | .50 | .50 |
| **227** | A61 | 50c orange & multi | .60 | .60 |
| *a.* | | Souv. sheet, #223-227 + label | 2.00 | 2.00 |
| | | *Nos. 223-227 (5)* | 2.00 | 2.00 |

20th Olympic Games, Munich, 8/26-9/11.

Holy Family, by Titian A62

Christmas: 3c, Adoration of the Kings, by Dosso Dossi. 30c, Like 5c.

**1972, Nov. 9 Photo. Wmk. 314**

| | | | | |
|---|---|---|---|---|
| **228** | A62 | 3c blue & multi | .20 | .20 |
| **229** | A62 | 5c rose lilac & multi | .20 | .20 |
| **230** | A62 | 30c lt green & multi | .50 | .50 |
| *a.* | | Souvenir sheet of 3, #228-230 | 1.50 | 1.50 |
| | | *Nos. 228-230 (3)* | .90 | .90 |

ECLA Headquarters, Santiago, Chile — A63

Designs: 20c, INTERPOL emblem. 30c, WHO emblem. 40c, University of West Indies Administration Building.

**1973, Aug. 15 Litho. Wmk. 314**

| | | | | |
|---|---|---|---|---|
| **231** | A63 | 10c orange & multi | .20 | .20 |
| **232** | A63 | 20c multicolored | .25 | .25 |
| **233** | A63 | 30c ultra & multi | .35 | .35 |
| **234** | A63 | 40c lilac & multi | .45 | .45 |
| *a.* | | Souvenir sheet of 4, #231-234 | 1.25 | 1.25 |
| | | *Nos. 231-234 (4)* | 1.25 | 1.25 |

Economic Commission for Latin America, 25th anniv. (10c); Intl. Criminal Police Organization, 50th anniv. (20c); Intl. Meteorological cooperation, cent. (30c); Admission of 1st students to the University of West Indies, 25th anniv. (40c).

### Medal Type of 1972 Redrawn

Medals: 10c, Trinity Cross. 20c, Medal of Merit. 30c, Chaconia medal. 40c, Hummingbird medal.

**1973, Aug. 30 Photo. *Perf. 14½x14***

| | | | | |
|---|---|---|---|---|
| **235** | A60 | 10c dark green & multi | .20 | .20 |
| **236** | A60 | 20c dark brown & multi | .20 | .20 |
| **237** | A60 | 30c dark blue & multi | .20 | .20 |
| **238** | A60 | 40c deep violet & multi | .40 | .40 |
| *a.* | | Souv. sheet, #235-238, perf. 14 | 1.25 | 1.25 |
| | | *Nos. 235-238 (4)* | 1.00 | 1.00 |

11th anniv. of independence. "Trinidad and Tobago" in one line on #235-238.

General Post Office, Port of Spain A64

40c, Conference Hall & flags, Chagaramas.

**1973, Oct. 8 Photo. *Perf. 14***

| | | | | |
|---|---|---|---|---|
| **239** | A64 | 30c multicolored | .25 | .25 |
| **240** | A64 | 40c multicolored | .40 | .40 |
| *a.* | | Souvenir sheet of 2, #239-240 | 1.00 | 1.00 |

2nd Commonwealth Conf. of Postal Administrations, Trinidad, Oct. 8-20. On #240a the perforations extend through margin and divide map.

Virgin and Child, by Murillo — A65

**1973, Oct. 22 *Perf. 14½x14***

| | | | | |
|---|---|---|---|---|
| **241** | A65 | 5c pink & multi | .20 | .20 |
| **242** | A65 | $1 lt blue & multi | .80 | .80 |
| *a.* | | Souv. sheet, #241-242, perf. 14 | 1.10 | 1.10 |

Christmas 1973.

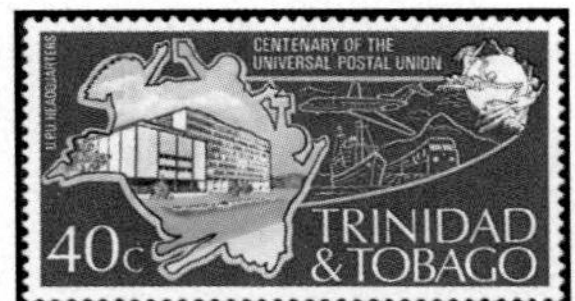


Post Office and UPU Emblem — A66

UPU, Cent.: 50c, Map of Islands, UPU emblem, means of transportation.

**1974, Nov. 18 Photo. *Perf. 13½x14***

| | | | | |
|---|---|---|---|---|
| **243** | A66 | 40c brt purple & multi | .40 | .40 |
| **244** | A66 | 50c blue gray & multi | .60 | .60 |
| *a.* | | Souvenir sheet of 2, #243-244 | 24.00 | *27.50* |

Humming Bird I, Transatlantic Crossing, 1960 — A67

Design: 50c, Globe, Humming Bird II, Harold and Kwailan La Borde.

**1974, Dec. 2 *Perf. 14½***

| | | | | |
|---|---|---|---|---|
| **245** | A67 | 40c multicolored | .50 | .50 |
| **246** | A67 | 50c multicolored | .70 | .70 |
| *a.* | | Souvenir sheet of 2, #245-246 | 2.50 | 2.50 |

First anniversary of the voyage around the world by Harold and Kwailan La Borde aboard Humming Bird II, 1969-1973.

"Equality" and IWY Emblem A68

**1975, June 23 Litho. Wmk. 314**

| | | | | |
|---|---|---|---|---|
| **247** | A68 | 15c multicolored | .20 | .20 |
| **248** | A68 | 30c multicolored | .40 | .40 |

International Women's Year 1975.

Dr. Pawan and Laboratory Equipment — A69

25c, Vampire bat, microscope, syringe, bat's head.

***Perf. 14x14½***

**1975, Sept. 23 Photo. Wmk. 373**

| | | | | |
|---|---|---|---|---|
| **249** | A69 | 25c yellow & multi | .45 | .45 |
| **250** | A69 | 30c lt blue & multi | .55 | .55 |

Isolation of rabies virus by Dr. Joseph Lennox Pawan (1887-1957).

Boeing 707, BWIA Emblem, Air Routes A70

Designs: 30c, Boeing 707 on ground. 40c, Boeing 707 in the air.

**Wmk. 373**

**1975, Nov. 27 Litho. *Perf. 14½***

| | | | | |
|---|---|---|---|---|
| **251** | A70 | 20c dark blue & multi | .40 | .40 |
| **252** | A70 | 30c deep ultra & multi | .60 | .60 |
| **253** | A70 | 40c dull green & multi | .75 | .75 |
| *a.* | | Souvenir sheet of 3, #251-253 | 1.75 | 1.75 |
| | | *Nos. 251-253 (3)* | 1.75 | 1.75 |

British West Indian Airways, 35th anniv.

Land of the Hummingbird Costume — A71

Carnival 1976: $1, Carib Prince riding pink ibis. Designs show prize-winning costumes from 1974 carnival.

**1976, Jan. 12 Photo. *Perf. 14½***

| | | | | |
|---|---|---|---|---|
| **254** | A71 | 30c multicolored | .20 | .20 |
| **255** | A71 | $1 multicolored | .70 | .70 |
| *a.* | | Souvenir sheet of 2, #254-255 | 1.10 | 1.10 |

Angostura Building, Port of Spain A72

Designs (Exposition Medals, obverse and reverse): 35c, New Orleans, 1885-86. 45c, Sydney, 1879. 50c, Brussels, 1897.

**1976, July 14 Litho. *Perf. 13***

| | | | | |
|---|---|---|---|---|
| **256** | A72 | 5c bister & multi | .20 | .20 |
| **257** | A72 | 35c yellow grn & multi | .20 | .20 |
| **258** | A72 | 45c blue & multi | .30 | .30 |
| **259** | A72 | 50c violet & multi | .30 | .30 |
| *a.* | | Souv. sheet, #256-259, perf. 14 | 1.10 | 1.10 |
| | | *Nos. 256-259 (4)* | 1.00 | 1.00 |

Sesquicentennial of the manufacture of Angostura Bitters.

Map of West Indies, Bats, Wicket and Ball A72a

Prudential Cup — A72b

**1976, Oct. 4 Unwmk. *Perf. 14***

| | | | | |
|---|---|---|---|---|
| **260** | A72a | 35c lt blue & multi | .55 | .55 |
| **261** | A72b | 45c lilac rose & blk | .75 | .75 |
| *a.* | | Souvenir sheet of 2, #260-261 | 2.00 | 2.00 |

World Cricket Cup, won by West Indies Team, 1975.

Columbus Sailing through the Bocas, by A. Camps-Campins — A73

Paintings: 10c, View, by Jean Michael Cazabon. 20c, Landscape, by Cazabon. 35c, Los Gallos Point, by Cazabon. 45c, Corbeaux Town, by Cazabon.

**1976, Nov. 1 Litho. Wmk. 373**

| | | | | |
|---|---|---|---|---|
| **262** | A73 | 5c ocher & multi | .55 | .55 |
| **263** | A73 | 10c lilac & multi | .55 | .55 |
| **264** | A73 | 20c green & multi | .55 | .55 |
| **265** | A73 | 35c red orange & multi | .55 | .55 |
| **266** | A73 | 45c blue & multi | .65 | .65 |
| *a.* | | Souvenir sheet of 5, #262-266 | 3.00 | 3.00 |
| | | *Nos. 262-266 (5)* | 2.85 | 2.85 |

For overprints see Nos. 325, 327.

Hasely Crawford and Gold Medal A74

**1977, Jan. 4 Litho. *Perf. 12½***

| | | | | |
|---|---|---|---|---|
| **267** | A74 | 25c multicolored | .50 | .45 |
| *a.* | | Souvenir sheet of 1 | .60 | .50 |

Hasely Crawford, winner of 100-meter dash at Montreal Olympic Games.

Sikorsky S-38 (Lindbergh's Plane) — A75

Designs: 35c, Charles Lindbergh delivering first airmail to Port of Spain, 1927. 45c, Boeing 707, British West Indies Airways. 50c, Boeing 747, British Airways.

**1977, Apr. Wmk. 373 *Perf. 13***

**268** A75 20c lt blue & multi .30 .30
**269** A75 35c lt blue & multi .50 .50
**270** A75 45c lt blue & multi .60 .60
**271** A75 50c lt blue & multi 1.10 .75
*a.* Souv. sheet, #268-271, perf. 14 4.75 4.75
*Nos. 268-271 (4)* 2.50 2.15

Airmail to Trinidad & Tobago, 50th anniv.

Trinidad and Tobago Flag — A76

White Poinsettia — A77

35c, Coat of arms. 45c, Government House.

**1977, July 26 Litho. *Perf. 13½x13***

**272** A76 20c yellow & multi .35 .35
**273** A76 35c red & multi .65 .65
**274** A76 45c lt blue & multi .85 .85
*a.* Souv. sheet, #272-274, perf. 14 1.90 1.90
*Nos. 272-274 (3)* 1.85 1.85

Inauguration of the Republic, Aug. 1, 1976.

**1977, Oct. 11 Litho. *Perf. 14½***

Christmas: 45c, 50c, Red poinsettia.

**275** A77 10c multicolored .20 .20
**276** A77 35c multicolored .35 .35
**277** A77 45c multicolored .50 .50
**278** A77 50c multicolored .55 .55
*a.* Souvenir sheet of 4, #275-278 1.60 1.60
*Nos. 275-278 (4)* 1.60 1.60

Robinson Crusoe Hotel, Tobago A78

15c, Turtle Beach Hotel, Tobago. 25c, Mount Irvine Hotel, Tobago. 70c, Mount Irvine beach, Tobago. $5, Holiday Inn, Trinidad.

**Wmk. 373**

**1978, Jan. 17 Litho. *Perf. 14***

**279** A78 6c multicolored .20 .20
**280** A78 15c multicolored .20 .20
**281** A78 25c multicolored .20 .20
**282** A78 70c multicolored .45 .45
**283** A78 $5 multicolored 3.25 3.25
*a.* Souvenir sheet of 5, #279-283 4.50 4.50
*Nos. 279-283 (5)* 4.30 4.30

For overprint see No. 326.

Paphinia Cristata A79

Orchids: 30c, Caularthron bicornutum. 40c, Miltassia. 50c, Oncidium ampliatum. $2.50, Oncidium papilio.

**1978, June 7 Wmk. 373 *Perf. 14***

**284** A79 12c multicolored .35 .35
**285** A79 30c multicolored .40 .40
**286** A79 40c multicolored .50 .50
**287** A79 50c multicolored .65 .65
**288** A79 $2.50 multicolored 3.25 3.25
*a.* Souvenir sheet of 5, #284-288 5.75 5.75
*Nos. 284-288 (5)* 5.15 5.15

Miss Universe and Trophy — A80

Designs: 35c, Portrait with crown. 45c, Miss Universe in evening dress.

**1978, Aug. 2 Litho. *Perf. 14½***

**289** A80 10c multicolored .45 .45
**290** A80 35c multicolored .65 .65
**291** A80 45c multicolored .80 .80
*a.* Souvenir sheet of 3, #289-291 1.90 1.90
*Nos. 289-291 (3)* 1.90 1.90

Janelle (Penny) Commissiong, Miss Universe, 1977.

Tayra A81

**1978, Nov. 7 *Perf. 13½x14***

**292** A81 15c shown .20 .20
**293** A81 25c Ocelot .30 .25
**294** A81 40c Porcupine .45 .40
**295** A81 70c Yellow anteater .95 .65
*a.* Souvenir sheet of 4, #292-295 2.40 2.40
*Nos. 292-295 (4)* 1.90 1.50

"Burst of Beauty" — A82

Day Care Center — A83

Costumes: 10c, Rain worshipper. 35c, Zodiac. 45c, Praying mantis. 50c, Eye of the hurricane. $1, Steel orchestra.

**1979, Feb. 1 Litho. *Perf. 13½***

**296** A82 5c multicolored .20 .20
**297** A82 10c multicolored .20 .20
**298** A82 35c multicolored .25 .25
**299** A82 45c multicolored .30 .30
**300** A82 50c multicolored .35 .35
**301** A82 $1 multicolored .70 .70
*Nos. 296-301 (6)* 2.00 2.00

**Unwmk.**

**1979, June 5 Litho. *Perf. 13***

IYC Emblem and: 10c, School lunch program. 35c, Dental care. 45c, Nursery school. 50c, Free school bus. $1, Medical care.

**302** A83 5c multicolored .20 .20
**303** A83 10c multicolored .20 .20
**304** A83 35c multicolored .25 .25
**305** A83 45c multicolored .30 .30
**306** A83 50c multicolored .30 .30
**307** A83 $1 multicolored .65 .65
*a.* Souvenir sheet of 6, #302-307 1.90 1.90
*Nos. 302-307 (6)* 1.90 1.90

International Year of the Child.

Geothermal Exploration A84

Designs: 35c, Hydrogeology. 45c, Petroleum exploration. 70c, Preservation of the environment.

**1979, July 3 Wmk. 373**

**308** A84 10c multicolored .20 .20
**309** A84 35c multicolored .30 .30
**310** A84 45c multicolored .35 .35
**311** A84 70c multicolored .55 .55
*a.* Souvenir sheet of 4, #308-311 2.10 2.10
*Nos. 308-311 (4)* 1.40 1.40

4th Latin American Geological Cong., July 7-15.

Map of Tobago and Tobago No. 1 — A85

15c, Tobago #2, 7. 35c, Tobago #28, 11. 45c, Tobago #25, 4. 70c, Great Britain #28 used in Scarborough and Tobago #5. $1, General Post Office, Scarborough and Tobago #6.

***Perf. 13½x14***

**1979, Aug. 1 Litho. Wmk. 373**

**312** A85 10c multicolored .20 .20
**313** A85 15c multicolored .20 .20
**314** A85 35c multicolored .25 .25
**315** A85 45c multicolored .30 .30
**316** A85 70c multicolored .45 .45
**317** A85 $1 multicolored .65 .65
*a.* Souvenir sheet of 6, #312-317 2.10 2.10
*Nos. 312-317 (6)* 2.05 2.05

Centenary of Tobago's postage stamps.

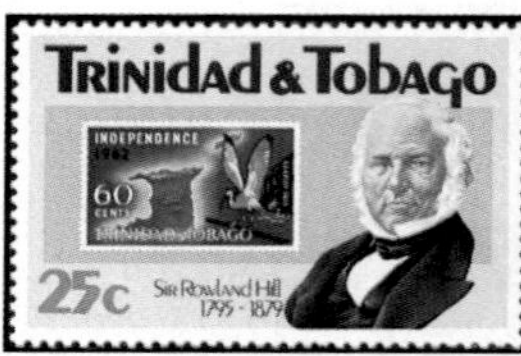


Rowland Hill, Trinidad and Tobago No. 109 — A86

Hill and: 45c, Trinidad and Tobago #273. $1, Trinidad #62, Tobago #10.

**1979, Oct. 4 *Perf. 13***

**318** A86 25c multicolored .25 .25
**319** A86 45c multicolored .40 .40
**320** A86 $1 multicolored .80 .80
*a.* Souvenir sheet of 3, #318-320 1.90 1.90
*Nos. 318-320 (3)* 1.45 1.45

Sir Rowland Hill (1795-1879), originator of penny postage.

Poui Tree A87

Designs: 10c, Court House. 50c, Royal Train locomotive. $1.50, Bacchante freighter.

**Wmk. 373**

**1980, Jan. 21 Litho. *Perf. 14½***

**321** A87 5c multicolored .20 .20
**322** A87 10c multicolored .20 .20
**323** A87 50c multicolored .45 .45
**324** A87 $1.50 multicolored 1.40 1.40
*a.* Souvenir sheet of 4, #321-324 2.40 2.40
*Nos. 321-324 (4)* 2.25 2.25

Princes Town centenary.

Nos. 262, 279, 263 Overprinted in 3 or 5 Lines: "1844-1980 POPULATION CENSUS 12th MAY 1980"

**1980, Apr. 8 Litho. *Perf. 14***

**325** A73 5c multicolored .20 .20
**326** A78 6c multicolored .20 .20
**327** A73 10c multicolored .20 .20
*Nos. 325-327 (3)* .60 .60

Scarlet Ibis Hen and Nest — A88

Scarlet Ibis: b, Nest and eggs. c, Chick in nest. d, Male. e, Male and female.

**Wmk. 373**

**1980, May 6 Litho. *Perf. 14½***

**328** Strip of 5, multi 5.75 5.75
*a.-e.* A88 single stamp .90 .90

Bronze and Silver Medals, 1948, 1952 A89

**Wmk. 373**

**1980, July 22 Litho. *Perf. 14***

**329** A89 10c shown .20 .20
**330** A89 15c Hasely Crawford, 1976 gold medal .20 .20
**331** A89 70c 1964 silver, bronze medals .65 .65
*Nos. 329-331 (3)* 1.05 1.05

**Souvenir Sheet**

**332** A89 $2.50 Moscow '80 emblem, vert. 1.60 1.60

22nd Summer Olympic Games, Moscow, July 19-Aug. 3.

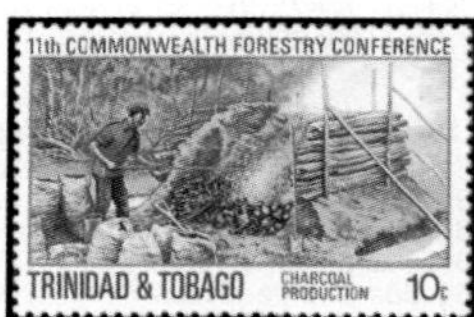


Charcoal Production — A90

**Wmk. 373**

**1980, Sept. 8 Litho. *Perf. 14***

**333** A90 10c shown .20 .20
**334** A90 55c Logging .30 .30
**335** A90 70c Teak plantation .40 .40
**336** A90 $2.50 Watershed management 1.50 1.50
*a.* Souvenir sheet of 4, #333-336 3.00 3.00
*Nos. 333-336 (4)* 2.40 2.40

11th Commonwealth Forestry Conference.

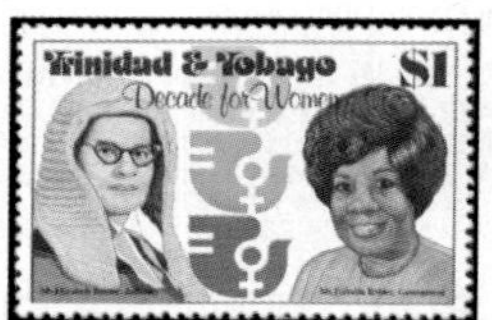


Elizabeth Bourne, Judiciary and Isabella Tesbier, Government — A91

Decade for Women: No. 338, Beryl McBurnie, dance and culture; Audrey Jeffers, social work. No. 339, Dr. Stella Abidh, public health; Louise Horne, nutrition.

**1980, Sept. 29**

**337** A91 $1 multicolored .70 .70
**338** A91 $1 multicolored .70 .70
**339** A91 $1 multicolored .70 .70
*Nos. 337-339 (3)* 2.10 2.10

Stadium and Netball League Emblem — A92

**1980, Oct. 21**
**340** A92 70c multicolored .55 .55

1979 World Netball Tournament, Port-of-Spain.

Athlete, Man in Wheelchair, IYD Emblem — A93

**Wmk. 373**
**1981, Apr. 6 Litho. *Perf. 14½***
**341** A93 10c shown .20 .20
**342** A93 70c Amputee with crutch .35 .35
**343** A93 $1.50 Blind people .85 .85
**344** A93 $2 IYD emblem 1.10 1.10
*Nos. 341-344 (4)* 2.50 2.50

International Year of the Disabled.

Marine Preservation — A94

**1981, July 7 Litho. *Perf. 13x13½***
**345** A94 10c Land .20 .20
**346** A94 55c shown .40 .40
**347** A94 $3 Sky 2.50 2.50
*a.* Souvenir sheet of 3, #345-347 4.00 4.00
*Nos. 345-347 (3)* 3.10 3.10

World Food Day — A95

**1981, Oct. 16 Litho. *Perf. 14½x14***
**348** A95 10c Produce .20 .20
**349** A95 15c Rice threshing, mill .20 .20
**350** A95 45c Bigeye .30 .30
**351** A95 55c Cow, pig, goats .40 .40
**352** A95 $1.50 Poultry 1.00 1.00
**353** A95 $2 Smallmouth grunt 1.40 1.40
*a.* Souvenir sheet of 6, #348-353 4.00 4.00
*Nos. 348-353 (6)* 3.50 3.50

President Awards — A96

**1981, Nov. 30 *Perf. 14***
**354** A96 10c First aid .20 .20
**355** A96 70c Motor mechanics .50 .50
**356** A96 $1 Hiking .70 .70
**357** A96 $2 President giving award 1.40 1.40
*Nos. 354-357 (4)* 2.80 2.80

Commonwealth Pharmaceutical Conference A97

**1982, Feb. 12 Litho. *Perf. 14½x14***
**358** A97 10c Pharmacist .65 .65
**359** A97 $1 Pluchea symphitfolia 2.75 2.75
**360** A97 $2 Nopalea cochenilifera 5.00 5.00
*Nos. 358-360 (3)* 8.40 8.40

Scouting Year — A98

25th Anniv. of Tourist Board — A99

**1982, June 28 Litho. *Perf. 14***
**361** A98 15c Production .20 .20
**362** A98 55c Tolerance .45 .45
**363** A98 $5 Discipline 4.00 4.00
*Nos. 361-363 (3)* 4.65 4.65

***Perf. 13½x14***
**1982, Oct. 18 Litho. Wmk. 373**
**364** A99 55c Charlotteville .45 .45
**365** A99 $1 Boating .85 .85
**366** A99 $3 Fort George 2.50 2.50
*Nos. 364-366 (3)* 3.80 3.80

Pa Pa Bois — A100

Designs: Various folklore characters.

**1982, Nov. 8**
**367** A100 10c multicolored .20 .20
**368** A100 15c multicolored .20 .20
**369** A100 65c multicolored .55 .55
**370** A100 $5 multicolored 4.25 4.25
*a.* Souvenir sheet of 4, #367-370 6.25 6.25
*Nos. 367-370 (4)* 5.20 5.20

Canefarmers' Centenary — A101

**1982, Dec. 13 Litho. *Perf. 14***
**371** A101 30c Harvest .40 .40
**372** A101 70c Loading bullock cart .95 .95
**373** A101 $1.50 Field 2.00 2.00
*a.* Souvenir sheet of 3, #371-373, perf. 14½ 5.50 5.50
*Nos. 371-373 (3)* 3.35 3.35

20th Anniv. of Independence — A102

**1982, Dec. 28 *Perf. 13½x14***
**374** A102 10c Natl. Stadium .20 .20
**375** A102 35c Caroni Arena Water Treatment Plant .25 .25
**376** A102 50c Mount Hope Maternity Hospital .40 .40
**377** A102 $2 Natl. Insurance Board Mall, Tobago 1.50 1.50
*Nos. 374-377 (4)* 2.35 2.35

Commonwealth Day — A103

**1983, Mar. 14 *Perf. 14***
**378** A103 10c Flags .20 .20
**379** A103 55c Satellite view .40 .40
**380** A103 $1 Oil industry, vert. .75 .75
**381** A103 $2 Maps, vert. 1.50 1.50
*Nos. 378-381 (4)* 2.85 2.85

10th Anniv. of CARICOM — A104

**1983, July 11 Litho. *Perf. 14***
**382** A104 35c Jet, map .65 .65

World Communications Year — A105

**1983, Aug. 5 *Perf. 14½***
**383** A105 15c Operator .20 .20
**384** A105 55c Scarborough PO, Tobago .45 .45
**385** A105 $1 Textel Building .85 .85
**386** A105 $3 Morne Bleu Receiving Station 2.50 2.50
*Nos. 383-386 (4)* 4.00 4.00

Commonwealth Finance Ministers Conference — A106

**Wmk. 373**
**1983, Sept. 19 Litho. *Perf. 14***
**387** A106 $2 multicolored 1.50 1.50

World Food Day — A107

**1983, Oct. 17 *Perf. 14x13½***
**388** A107 10c Kingfish .45 .45
**389** A107 55c Flying fish .95 .95
**390** A107 70c Queen conch 1.10 1.10
**391** A107 $4 Red shrimp 7.00 7.00
*Nos. 388-391 (4)* 9.50 9.50

Flowers — A108

**1983, Dec. 14 Wmk. 373 *Perf. 14***
**392** A108 5c Bois pois .20 .20
**393** A108 10c Maraval Lily .20 .20
**394** A108 15c Star grass .20 .20
**395** A108 20c Bois caco .20 .20
**396** A108 25c Strangling fig .20 .20
**397** A108 30c Cassia moschata .20 .20
**398** A108 50c Chalice flower .45 .50
**399** A108 65c Black stick .55 .65
**400** A108 80c Columnea scandens .70 .80
**401** A108 95c Cats Claws .80 .95
**402** A108 $1 Bois l'agli .90 1.00
**403** A108 $1.50 Eustoma exeltatum 1.25 1.50

**Size: 38½x26mm**
**404** A108 $2 Chaconia, horiz. 1.75 2.00
**405** A108 $2.50 Chysothemis pulchella, horiz. 2.25 2.50
**406** A108 $5 Centratherum punctatum, horiz. 4.50 5.25
**407** A108 $10 Savanna flower, horiz. 8.75 10.00
*Nos. 392-407 (16)* 23.10 26.35

"1984" imprint: #392, 393, 394, 396. Value $10.50.
"1986:" #393.
"1989:" #392.

**1985-89 Wmk. 384**
*392a* A108 5c .45 .45
*393a* A108 10c .45 .45
*395a* A108 20c ('89) .45 .45
*396a* A108 25c ('89) .45 .45
*397a* A108 30c ('87) .45 .45
*399a* A108 65c ('87) .90 .90
*400a* A108 80c ('87) 1.10 1.10
*401a* A108 95c 1.60 1.60
*402a* A108 $1 1.75 1.75
*403a* A108 $1.50 ('87) 2.00 2.00
*404a* A108 $2 ('87) 2.75 2.75
*405a* A108 $2.50 ('89) 3.50 3.50
*406a* A108 $5 8.25 8.25
*407a* A108 $10 17.50 17.50
*Nos. 392a-407a (14)* 41.60 41.60

"1985" imprint: #392a, 393a, 401a, 402a, 406a, 407a.
"1987:" #393a, 397a, 399a, 400a-404a, 406a-407a.
"1988:" #393a, 395a-397a, 399a-402a, 406a-407a.
"1989:" #393a, 395a-397a, 399a, 402a-407a.

Castles on Chess Board A109

1984 Summer Olympics A110

World Chess Federationn, 60th Anniv.: Various chess pieces.

**Wmk. 373**
**1984, Sept. 12 Litho. *Perf. 14***
**408** A109 50c multicolored 1.75 1.75
**409** A109 70c multicolored 2.50 2.50
**410** A109 $1.50 multicolored 5.25 5.25
**411** A109 $2 multicolored 7.25 7.25
*Nos. 408-411 (4)* 16.75 16.75

**1984, Sept. 21 *Perf. 14x14½***
**412** A110 15c Swimming .25 .25
**413** A110 55c Running .65 .65
**414** A110 $1.50 Yachting 1.60 1.60

**415** A110 $4 Bicycling 4.25 4.25
*a.* Souvenir sheet of 4, #412-415 7.25 7.25
*Nos. 412-415 (4)* 6.75 6.75

St. Mary's Children's Home, 125th Anniv. — A111

**1984, Nov. 13 Litho. *Perf. 13½***
**416** A111 10c Children's band .20 .20
**417** A111 70c St. Mary's Home .75 .75
**418** A111 $3 Group scene 3.25 3.25
*Nos. 416-418 (3)* 4.20 4.20

Christmas 1984 A112

**1984, Nov. Litho. *Perf. 14***
**419** A112 10c Parang Band .35 .35
**420** A112 30c Musical notes, Poinsettia .40 .40
**421** A112 $1 Bandola, Cuatro, Bandolin 1.50 1.50
**422** A112 $3 Fiddle, Guitar, Double Bass 4.50 4.50
*Nos. 419-422 (4)* 6.75 6.75

Emancipation, 150th Anniv. — A113

**1984, Oct. 22 Litho. *Perf. 13½x13***
**423** A113 35c Slave ship .75 .75
**424** A113 55c Map, Slave Triangle 1.25 1.25
**425** A113 $1 Book by Eric Williams 2.25 2.25
**426** A113 $2 Toussaint L'Ouverture 4.75 4.75
*a.* Souvenir sheet of 4, #423-426 9.75 9.75
*Nos. 423-426 (4)* 9.00 9.00

Labor Day — A114

Labor leaders: No. 427, A.A. Cipriani and T.U.B. Butler. No. 428, A. Cola Rienzi and C.T.W.E. Worrell. No. 429, C.P. Alexander and Q. O'Connor.

**Wmk. 373**
**1985, June 17 Litho. *Perf. 14***
**427** A114 55c dull rose & blk 1.10 1.10
**428** A114 55c brt green & blk 1.10 1.10
**429** A114 55c lt orange & blk 1.10 1.10
*Nos. 427-429 (3)* 3.30 3.30

Ships A115

**Wmk. 373**
**1985, Aug 20 Litho. *Perf. 14½***
**430** A115 30c Lady Nelson .60 .60
**431** A115 95c Lady Drake 1.75 1.75
**432** A115 $1.50 Federal Palm 2.75 2.75
**433** A115 $2 Federal Maple 3.50 3.50
*Nos. 430-433 (4)* 8.60 8.60

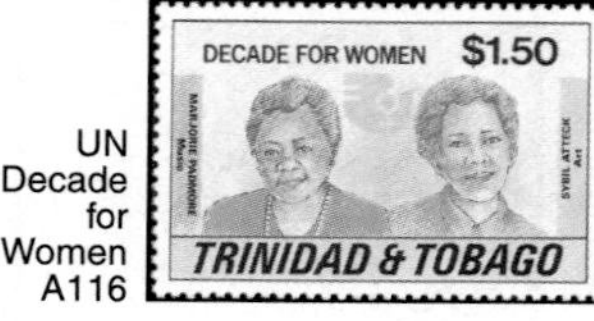


UN Decade for Women A116

Women in the arts, public service and education: No. 434, Sybill Atteck, Marjorie Padmore. No. 435, May Cherrie, Evelyn Tracey. No. 436, Jessica Smith-Phillips, Irene Omilta McShine.

**1985, Oct. 30 Wmk. 384 *Perf. 14***
**434** A116 $1.50 multicolored 1.75 1.75
**435** A116 $1.50 multicolored 1.75 1.75
**436** A116 $1.50 multicolored 1.75 1.75
*Nos. 434-436 (3)* 5.25 5.25

Intl. Youth Year — A117

Anniversaries and events: 10c, Natl. Cadet Force, 75th anniv. 65c, Girl Guides, 75th anniv.

**1985, Nov. 27 *Perf. 14x14½***
**437** A117 10c Cadet emblem 1.00 1.00
**438** A117 65c Badges, anniv. emblem 2.40 2.40
**439** A117 95c shown 3.25 3.25
*Nos. 437-439 (3)* 6.65 6.65

A118 A119

Sisters of St. Joseph de Cluny in Trinidad, 150th Anniv.: 10c, Sister Anne-Marie Javouhey, founder. 65c, St. Joseph's Convent, Port-of-Spain. 95c, Statue of Sr. Anne-Marie.

***Perf. 14x14½***
**1986, Mar. 19 Litho. Wmk. 384**
**440** A118 10c multicolored .20 .20
**441** A118 65c multicolored .55 .55
**442** A118 95c multicolored .90 .90
*Nos. 440-442 (3)* 1.65 1.65

**Wmk. 384**
**1986, Apr. 21 Litho. *Perf. 14½***
**443** A119 10c At the Cenotaph .30 .30
**444** A119 15c Aboard HMY Britannia .30 .30
**445** A119 30c With Pres. Clarke .30 .30
**446** A119 $5 Receiving bouquet 4.25 4.25
*Nos. 443-446 (4)* 5.15 5.15

Queen Elizabeth II, 60th birthday.

Locomotives, AMERIPEX '86 — A120

***Perf. 14½x14***
**1986, May 26 Wmk. 373**
**447** A120 65c Arma tank locomotive .30 .30
**448** A120 95c Canadian-built No. 22 .55 .55
**449** A120 $1.10 Tender engine .60 .60
**450** A120 $1.50 Saddle tank .85 .85
*a.* Souvenir sheet of 4, #447-450 2.50 2.50
*Nos. 447-450 (4)* 2.30 2.30

Boy Scouts, 75th Anniv. A121

**1986, July 21 Wmk. 384 *Perf. 14***
**451** A121 $1.70 Campsite 1.50 1.50
**452** A121 $2 Uniforms, 1911, 1986 2.00 2.00

Dr. Eric Williams (1911-1981), First Prime Minister — A122

**Wmk. 373**
**1986, Sept. 25 Litho. *Perf. 14***
**453** A122 10c Graduating college, 1935 .35 .35
**454** A122 30c Wearing red tie .35 .35
*a.* Black tie .45 .45
**455** A122 95c Pro-Chancellor of UWI 1.00 1.00
**456** A122 $5 Williams, prime minister's residence 5.25 5.25
*a.* Souvenir sheet of 4, #453-456 7.75 7.75
*Nos. 453-456 (4)* 6.95 6.95

Nos. 453-454 vert.

Intl. Peace Year A123

**1986, Oct. 30 Wmk. 384**
**457** A123 95c shown .60 .60
**458** A123 $3 Dove 2.40 2.40

Giselle LaRonde, Miss World 1986 — A124

**Wmk. 384**
**1987, July 27 Litho. *Perf. 14***
**459** A124 10c Wearing folk costume .70 .70
**460** A124 30c Bathing suit 1.50 1.50
**461** A124 95c Crown 3.25 3.25
**462** A124 $1.65 Crown and sash 5.25 5.25
*Nos. 459-462 (4)* 10.70 10.70

Republic Bank, 150th Anniv. A125

Designs: 10c, Colonial Bank, Port of Spain. 65c, Cocoa plantation. 95c, Oil fields. $1.10, Tramcar, Belmont Tramway Co.

**Wmk. 373**
**1987, Dec. 21 Litho. *Perf. 14***
**463** A125 10c buff, red brn & blk .55 .55
**464** A125 65c buff, red brn & blk .80 .80
**465** A125 95c buff, red brn & blk 1.40 1.40
**466** A125 $1.10 buff, red brn & blk 1.60 1.60
*Nos. 463-466 (4)* 4.35 4.35

Defense Force, 25th Anniv. — A126

Various army, coast guard and navy uniforms.

**Wmk. 384**
**1988, Feb. 29 Litho. *Perf. 14***
**467** A126 10c Army .75 .35
**468** A126 30c Army (women) 2.00 .45
**469** A126 $1.10 Navy, army, coast guard 3.75 3.25
**470** A126 $1.50 Navy 4.75 4.75
*Nos. 467-470 (4)* 11.25 8.80

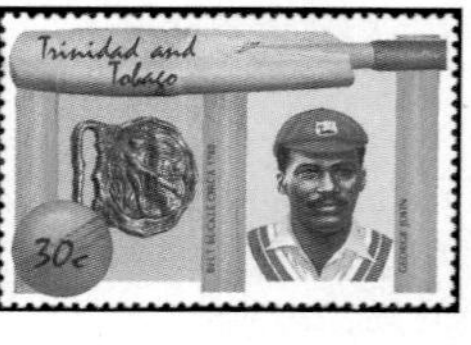


Cricket A127

Bat, wicket posts, ball, 18th cent. belt buckle and batters: 30c, George John. 65c, Learie Constantine. 95c, Sonny Ramadhin. $1.50, Gerry Gomez. $2.50, Jeffrey Stollmeyer.

**Wmk. 373**
**1988, June 6 Litho. *Perf. 14***
**471** A127 30c multicolored 1.60 .55
**472** A127 65c multicolored 3.00 1.40
**473** A127 95c multicolored 3.25 2.25
**474** A127 $1.50 multicolored 4.00 4.00
**475** A127 $2.50 multicolored 5.25 5.75
*Nos. 471-475 (5)* 17.10 13.95

Oilfield Workers' Trade Union, 50th Anniv. — A128

50, Star, oil well and: 10c, Uriah Buzz Butler, labor leader. 30c, Adrian C. Rienzi, pres. from 1937-42. 65c, John Rojas, pres. from 1943-62. $5, George Weekes, pres. from 1962-87.

**Wmk. 384**
**1988, July 11 Litho. *Perf. 14½***
**476** A128 10c multicolored .20 .20
**477** A128 30c multicolored .20 .20
**478** A128 65c multicolored .45 .45
**479** A128 $5 multicolored 2.25 2.25
*Nos. 476-479 (4)* 3.10 3.10

Borough of Arima, Cent. A129

20c, Mary Werges, Santa Rosa Church. 30c, Gov. W. Robinson, royal charter. $1.10, Mayor C.P. Lopez greeting Gov. Robinson at train station. $1.50, Mayor J.F. Wallen, centennial emblem.

**Wmk. 384**
**1988, Aug. 22 Litho. *Perf. 14½***
**480** A129 20c multicolored .25 .25
**481** A129 30c multicolored .25 .25
**482** A129 $1.10 multicolored .80 .80
**483** A129 $1.50 multicolored 1.10 1.10
*Nos. 480-483 (4)* 2.40 2.40

**Lloyds of London, 300th Anniv.**
Common Design Type

Designs: 30c, Queen Mother at the "Topping Out" ceremony of new Lloyds's building, 1984. $1.10, BWIA Tristar 500, horiz. $1.55, ISCOTT iron and steel mill, horiz. $2, *Atlantic Empress* on fire off Tobago.

**1988, Nov. 21 Litho. *Perf. 14***

**484** CD341 30c multicolored .75 .30
**485** CD341 $1.10 multicolored 2.75 1.50
**486** CD341 $1.55 multicolored 2.50 2.10
**487** CD341 $2 multicolored 4.75 3.00
*Nos. 484-487 (4)* 10.75 6.90

Unification of the Islands, Cent. — A130

Torch and: 40c, Natl. arms, 1889, and 1p Type A1. $1, Badge from Tobago flag and Tobago No. 31. $1.50, Badge from Trinidad flag and Trinidad No. 71. $2.25, Natl. arms, 1989, and No. 274.

**Wmk. 384**

**1989, Mar. 20 Litho. *Perf. 14½***

**488** A130 40c multicolored .70 .30
**489** A130 $1 multicolored 1.90 1.00
**490** A130 $1.50 multicolored 2.50 2.50
**491** A130 $2.25 multicolored 3.25 3.50
*Nos. 488-491 (4)* 8.35 7.30

Rare Species A131

Designs: a, *Pipile pipile.* b, *Phyllodytes auratus.* c, *Cebus albifrons trinitatis.* d, *Tamandua tetradactyla.* e, *Lutra longicaudis.* Printed in a continuous design.

***Perf. 14x14½***

**1989, July 31 Wmk. 373**

**492** Strip of 5 19.00 19.00
*a.-e.* A131 $1 any single 2.00 2.00

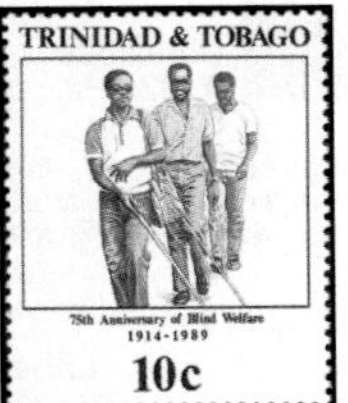


A132

A133

**1989, Oct. 2 *Perf. 14½***

**493** A132 10c Men using walking sticks .80 .45
**494** A132 40c City Hall .70 .45
**495** A132 $1 Guides and leader 2.25 1.10
**496** A132 $2.25 Volunteers, an-niv. emblem 3.50 3.50
*Nos. 493-496 (4)* 7.25 5.50

Blind Welfare, 75th anniv. (10c), Port-of-Spain City Hall, 75th anniv. (40c), Girl Guides, 75th anniv. ($1), and Red Cross, 50th anniv. ($2.25).

***Perf. 14½x14***

**1989, Nov. 30 Wmk. 384**

Drum instruments played in a steel band.

**497** A133 10c Tenor .30 .30
**498** A133 40c Guitar .30 .30
**499** A133 $1 Cello .60 .70
**500** A133 $2.25 Bass 1.50 1.75
*Nos. 497-500 (4)* 2.70 3.05

Mushrooms A134

**1990, May 3 *Perf. 14x13½***

**501** A134 10c *Xeromphalina tenuipes* .40 .40
**502** A134 40c *Dictyophora in-dusiata* .65 .65
**503** A134 $1 *Leucocoprinus birnbaumii* 1.60 1.60
**504** A134 $2.25 *Crinipellis perniciosa* 3.50 3.50
*Nos. 501-504 (4)* 6.15 6.15

Stamp World London '90.

Scarlet Ibis A135

**1990, Sept. 7 *Perf. 14***

**505** A135 40c Immature bird *2.50 .50*
**506** A135 80c Mating display *2.75 2.00*
**507** A135 $1 Adult male *3.25 2.00*
**508** A135 $2.25 Adult, egg & young *5.50 5.00*
*Nos. 505-508 (4)* *14.00 9.50*

World Wildlife Fund.

Yellow Oriole — A136

**1990, Dec. 17 Litho. Wmk. 384**

**509** A136 20c shown .25 .25
**510** A136 25c Green rumped parrotlet .55 .35
**511** A136 40c Fork-tailed fly-catcher .25 .25
**512** A136 50c Copper rumped hum-mingbird .60 .45
**513** A136 $1 Bananaquit .70 .45
**514** A136 $2 Semp 1.10 1.00
**515** A136 $2.25 Channel-billed toucan .55 .55
**516** A136 $2.50 Bay headed tanager .60 .60
**517** A136 $5 Green honey-creeper 3.75 3.75
*a.* Souvenir sheet of 1, wmk. 373 3.75 3.75
**518** A136 $10 Cattle egret 2.75 2.75
**519** A136 $20 Golden olive woodpecker 8.00 8.00
**520** A136 $50 Peregrine fal-con 20.00 20.00
*Nos. 509-520 (12)* 39.10 38.40

No. 517a issued 2/3/97 for Hong Kong '97.
For overprints & surcharge see #565-568, 597A.

**1994-98 Wmk. 373**

*510a* A136 25c .30 .30
*512a* A136 50c .20 .20
*513a* A136 $1 .30 .30
*514a* A136 $2 .65 .65
*516a* A136 $2.50 .80 .80
*517b* A136 $5 1.60 1.60
*518a* A136 $10 3.25 3.25
*519a* A136 $20 6.50 6.50
*Nos. 510a-519a (8)* 13.60 13.60

Issued: #510a, 8/94; #512a, 4/95; #510a, 8/94; #513a, 3/3/97; #516a, 518a, 519a, 10/14/98; #517b, 6/1996.
#510a, 513a, 514a, 517b dated 1990; #517a dated 1997.

University of the West Indies A137

Chancellors and Campus Buildings: 40c, HRH Princess Alice, Administration Building. 80c, Sir Hugh Wooding, Main Library. $1, Sir Allen Lewis, Faculty of Engineering. $2.25, Sir Shridath Ramphal, Faculty of Medical Studies.

***Perf. 13½x14***

**1990, Oct. 15 Litho. Wmk. 373**

**521** A137 40c multicolored .50 .50
**522** A137 80c multicolored 1.00 1.00
**523** A137 $1 multicolored 1.25 1.25
**524** A137 $2.25 multicolored 3.00 3.00
*Nos. 521-524 (4)* 5.75 5.75

Britsh West Indies Airways, 50th Anniv. A138

Airplanes: 40c, Lockheed Lodestar. 80c, Vickers Viking 1A. $1, Vickers Viscount 702. $2.25, Boeing 707. $5, Lockheed TriStar 500.

**1990, Nov. 27 *Perf. 14***

**525** A138 40c multicolored 1.60 .55
**526** A138 80c multicolored 2.25 1.60
**527** A138 $1 multicolored 2.50 1.60
**528** A138 $2.25 multicolored 4.50 5.75
*Nos. 525-528 (4)* 10.85 9.50

**Souvenir Sheet**

**529** A138 $5 multicolored 6.75 6.75

Ferns A139

**1991, July 1 *Perf. 13½***

**530** A139 40c Lygodium volubile .50 .50
**531** A139 80c Blechnum oc-cidentale 1.00 1.00
**532** A139 $1 Gleichenia bifida 1.25 1.25
**533** A139 $2.25 Polypodium lyco-podiodes 2.75 2.75
*Nos. 530-533 (4)* 5.50 5.50

Trinidad & Tobago in World War II — A140

Designs: 40c, Firing practice by Trinidad & Tobago regiment. 80c, Fairey Barracuda surprises U-boat. $1, Avro Lancaster returns from bombing raid. $2.25, River class frigate on convoy duty. No. 538a, Supermarine Spitfire. b, Vickers Wellington.

***Perf. 13½x14***

**1991, Dec. 7 Litho. Wmk. 384**

**534** A140 40c multicolored 1.00 1.00
**535** A140 80c multicolored 2.00 2.00
**536** A140 $1 multicolored 2.50 2.50
**537** A140 $2.25 multicolored 5.25 5.25
*Nos. 534-537 (4)* 10.75 10.75

**Souvenir Sheet of 2**

**538** A140 $2.50 #a.-b. 14.50 14.50

H. E. Rapsey — A141

Inca Clathrata Quesneli — A142

Holy Name Convent — A143

Religions of Trinidad and Tobago — A145

**1992, Mar. 30 Wmk. 373 *Perf. 14***

**539** A141 40c multicolored .60 .60
**540** A142 80c multicolored 1.25 1.25
**541** A143 $1 multicolored 1.60 1.60
*Nos. 539-541 (3)* 3.45 3.45

#539, Building and Loan Assoc., cent. #540, Trinidad & Tobago Field Naturalists' Club. #541, Holy Name Convent, cent.

**1992, Apr. 21 Litho. *Perf. 14***

#544, Baptist, baptism by immersion. #545, Muslim, minaret. #546, Hindu, Brahman..the source of all. #547, Christianity, cross. #548, Baha'i, slogan.

**544** A145 40c multicolored .80 .80
**545** A145 40c multicolored .80 .80
**546** A145 40c multicolored .80 .80
**547** A145 40c multicolored .80 .80
**548** A145 40c multicolored .80 .80
*Nos. 544-548 (5)* 4.00 4.00

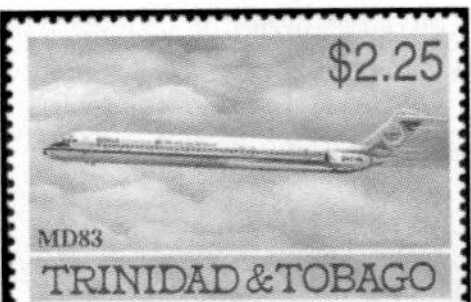


BWIA Aircraft A146

**Wmk. 373**

**1992, Aug. 6 Litho. *Perf. 14***

**549** A146 $2.25 MD83 3.25 3.25
**550** A146 $2.25 L1011 3.25 3.25

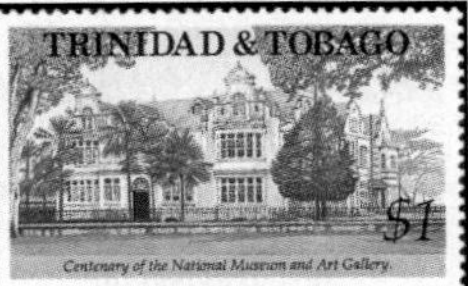


Natl. Museum and Art Gallery, Cent. A147

**Wmk. 384**

**1992, Dec. 7 Litho. *Perf. 14½***

**551** A147 $1 multicolored .50 .50

Christmas — A148

**1992, Dec. 21**

**552** A148 40c multicolored .20 .20

Trinidad Guardian, 75th Anniv. — A149

**1992, Dec. 23**

**553** A149 40c multicolored .20 .20

Philatelic Society of Trinidad & Tobago, 50th Anniv. A150

**1992, Dec. 30**

**554** A150 $2.25 multicolored 1.10 1.10

CARICOM (Caribbean Economic Community), 20th Anniv. — A151

Map of CARICOM nations, portraits of West Indian men: 50c, $1.50, $2.75, $3, Derek Walcott, Sir Shridath Ramphal, William Demas.

$6, Order of the Caribbean Community.

Illustration reduced.

***Perf. 13x13½***

**1994, Jan. 31 Litho. Wmk. 373**

**555** A151 50c pink & multi .25 .25
**556** A151 $1.50 green & multi .75 .75
**557** A151 $2.75 gray & multi 1.50 1.50
**558** A151 $3 violet & multi 1.50 1.50
*Nos. 555-558 (4)* 4.00 4.00

**Souvenir Sheet**

***Perf. 13½x13***

**559** A151 $6 multicolored 2.00 2.00

No. 559 contains one 34x56mm stamp.

Drum Instruments Played in a Steel Band — A152

**1994, Feb. 11 *Perf. 14x15***

**560** A152 50c Quadrophonic pan .25 .25
**561** A152 $1 Tenor base pan .50 .50
**562** A152 $2.25 Six pan 1.10 1.10
**563** A152 $2.50 Rocket pan 1.25 1.25
*Nos. 560-563 (4)* 3.10 3.10

Alwyn Roberts Kitchener, Calypso Singer — A153

**1994, Feb. 11 *Perf. 14***

**564** A153 50c multicolored 1.10 1.10

Nos. 510-511, 514, 518 Ovptd. with Hong Kong '94 Exhibition Emblem

**Wmk. 384**

**1994, Feb. 18 Litho. *Perf. 14***

**565** A136 25c multicolored .30 .30
**566** A136 40c multicolored .30 .30
**567** A136 $2 multicolored 1.10 1.10
**568** A136 $10 multicolored 5.50 5.50
*Nos. 565-568 (4)* 7.20 7.20

Hotels & Lodges A154

#569, Trinidad Hilton. #570, Sandy Point Village, Tobago. #571, Asa Wright Nature Center and Lodge. #572, ML's Bed and Breakfast.

**Wmk. 373**

**1994, Aug. 10 Litho. *Perf. 14***

**569** A154 $3 multicolored 1.40 1.40
**570** A154 $3 multicolored 1.40 1.40
**571** A154 $3 multicolored 1.40 1.40
**572** A154 $3 multicolored 1.40 1.40
*Nos. 569-572 (4)* 5.60 5.60

Snakes A155

50c, Boa constrictor. $1.25, Horse whip or vine snake. $2.50, Bushmaster. $3, Large coral snake.

**Wmk. 373**

**1994, Sept. 19 Litho. *Perf. 14***

**573** A155 50c multicolored .30 .30
**574** A155 $1.25 multicolored .75 .75
**575** A155 $2.50 multicolored 1.50 1.50
**576** A155 $3 multicolored 1.75 1.75
*Nos. 573-576 (4)* 4.30 4.30

Trinidad Art Society, 50th Anniv. — A156

Artworks: No. 577, Copper sculpture, by Ken Morris. No. 578, Fisherman, by Sybil Atteck. No. 579, Snowballman, by Mahmoud P. Alladin.

**1995, Mar. 6 Wmk. 384**

**577** A156 50c multicolored .80 .80
**578** A156 50c multicolored .80 .80
**579** A156 50c multicolored .80 .80
*Nos. 577-579 (3)* 2.40 2.40

Conservation — A157

Designs: $1.25, Leatherback turtle. $2.50, POS Lighthouse, vert. $3, "Knowsley" Ministry of Foreign Affairs.

**1995, Aug. 7**

**580** A157 $1.25 multicolored .70 .70
**581** A157 $2.50 multicolored 1.40 1.40
**582** A157 $3 multicolored 1.75 1.75
*Nos. 580-582 (3)* 3.85 3.85

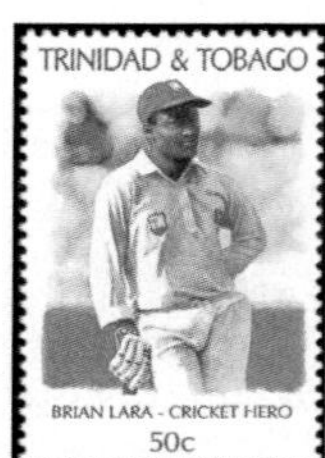

Brian Lara, Cricket Hero — A158

Designs: $1.25, Batting. $2.50, In batting stance. $3, Batting, diff.

No. 587: a, $3.75, With arms raised at crowd. b, $5.01, Down on one knee with bat.

***Perf. 13x13½***

**1996, May 15 Litho. Wmk. 373**

**583** A158 50c multicolored .25 .25
**584** A158 $1.25 multicolored .60 .60
**585** A158 $2.50 multicolored 1.10 1.10
**586** A158 $3 multicolored 1.40 1.40
*Nos. 583-586 (4)* 3.35 3.35

**Souvenir Sheet**

**587** A158 Sheet of 2, #a.-b. 3.50 3.50

Trinidad & Tobago Remembers World War II — A159

50c, Red Cross Economy Label. $1.25, Battleship USS Missouri. $2.50, US servicemen playing baseball, Queen's Park, Savannah, 1942. $3, Fulmar 1, Royal Naval Air Station.

No. 592: a, Grumman Goose seaplane. b, US Navy Airship.

**Wmk. 373**

**1996, June 7 Litho. *Perf. 14***

**588** A159 50c multicolored .35 .35
**589** A159 $1.25 multicolored .80 .80
**590** A159 $2.50 multicolored 1.60 1.60
**591** A159 $3 multicolored 1.90 1.90
*Nos. 588-591 (4)* 4.65 4.65

**Souvenir Sheet of 2**

**592** A159 $3 #a.-b. 6.75 6.75

A160

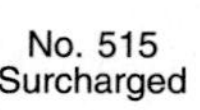

A161

Wendy Fitzwilliam, 1998 Miss Universe: $1.25, Lying on beach. $2.50, In traditional costume. $3, Wearing evening gown.

$5, After coronation.

**1999, May 3 Litho. *Perf. 14***

**593** A160 50c multicolored .35 .35
**594** A160 $1.25 multicolored .75 .75
**595** A160 $2.50 multicolored 1.50 1.50
**596** A160 $3 multicolored 1.75 1.75
*Nos. 593-596 (4)* 4.35 4.35

**Souvenir Sheet**

**597** A160 $5 multicolored 3.75 3.75

No. 511 Surcharged

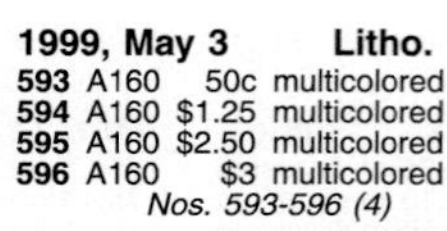

**1999 Method and Perf. as Before**

**597A** A136 75c on 40c multi

***Serpentine Die Cut***

**2000, Jan. 27 Litho.**

Angostura Bitters, 175th Anniv.: 75c, Angostura Bitters bottle. $3, Distillery. $4.50, Bitters bottle, cocktails.

**Self-Adhesive**

**598** A161 75c multi .35 .35
**599** A161 $3 multi 1.40 1.40
**600** A161 $4.50 multi 1.90 1.90
*a.* Souvenir sheet, #598-600 4.75 4.75

Tourism A162

Shoreline scenes: 75c, Maracas Bay. $1, Pirates Bay. $3.75, Pigeon Point. $5, Toco, North Coast.

**2000, July 25 Litho. *Perf. 14¼x14½***

**601** A162 75c multi .25 .25
**602** A162 $1 multi .40 .40
**603** A162 $3.75 multi 1.75 1.75
**604** A162 $5 multi 2.10 2.10

Christmas A163

Design: 75c, Caroni landscape. $3.75, Pastelles, sorrel and ginger beer. $4.50, Musicians under palm trees. $5.25, Angels with steel drums.

***Perf. 14¼x14½***

**2000, Nov. 14 Litho.**

**605** A163 75c multi .25 .25
**606** A163 $3.75 multi 1.75 1.75
**607** A163 $4.50 multi 2.00 2.00
**608** A163 $5.25 multi 2.40 2.40

No. 515 Surcharged

**Method and Perf. as Before**

**2001?**

**609** A136 75c on $2.25 multi

National Mail Center A164

Designs: $3, Building entrance. $10, Side of building.

*Perf. 14¼x14½*

**2000, Nov. 20** **Litho.**

**610-611** A164 Set of 2 4.25 4.25

Endangered Fauna A165

Designs: 25c, Pacca, 50c, Prehensile-tailed porcupine. 75c, Iguana. $1, Leatherback turtle. $2, Golden tegu. $2, Red howler monkey. $4, Weeping capuchin monkey, vert. $5, River otter. $10, Ocelot. $20, Trinidad piping guan, vert.

*Perf. 14¼x14½, 14½x14¼*

**2001, Feb. 6** **Litho.**

| | | | |
|---|---|---|---|
| **612** A165 25c multi | .20 | .20 |
| **613** A165 50c multi | .20 | .20 |
| **614** A165 75c multi | .30 | .30 |
| **615** A165 $1 multi | .40 | .40 |
| **616** A165 $2 multi | .90 | .90 |
| **617** A165 $3 multi | 1.25 | 1.25 |
| **618** A165 $4 multi | 1.75 | 1.75 |
| **619** A165 $5 multi | 2.25 | 2.25 |
| **620** A165 $10 multi | 4.75 | 4.75 |
| **621** A165 $20 multi | 9.50 | 9.50 |
| *Nos. 612-621 (10)* | 21.50 | 21.50 |

Salvation Army in Trinidad & Tobago, Cent. — A166

Designs: 75c, Emblem. $2, William Booth Memorial Hall.

**2001, Aug. 9** *Perf. 14½x14¼*

**622-623** A166 Set of 2 .90 .90

*623a* Souvenir sheet, #622-623, perf. 13¾x14¼ .90 .90

Natl. Library, 150th Anniv. A167

Designs: 75c, Port of Spain Public Library, Carnegie Free Library. $3.25, New National Library building.

**2001, Aug. 9** *Perf. 14¼x14½*

**624-625** A167 Set of 2 1.40 1.40

*625a* Souvenir sheet, #624-625 1.40 1.40

Under 17 World Soccer Championships — A168

Designs: $2, Emblem of Soca Warriors. $3.25, National flag. $4.50, Lion holding flag. $5.25, Stadiums.

**2001, Sept. 6** *Perf. 14½x14*

**626-629** A168 Set of 4 7.75 7.75

*629a* Souvenir sheet, #626-629 7.75 7.75

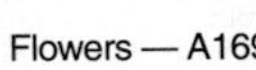

Flowers — A169

Designs: $1, Pachystachys coccinea. $2.50, Heliconia psittacorum. $3.25, Brownea latifolia, horiz. $3.75, Oncidium papilio.

**2001** *Perf. 14½x14¼, 14¼x14½*

**630-633** A169 Set of 4 5.75 5.75

Christmas — A170

People and: $1, Boats, church. $3.75, Flowers. $4.50, House, flowers. $5.25, Church, post office.

**2001** *Perf. 14½x14¼*

**634-637** A170 Set of 4 6.75 6.75

*637a* Souvenir sheet, #634-637 6.75 6.75

Butterflies A171

Designs: $1, Cracker. $3.75, Tiger . $4.50, Four continent. $5.25, "89."

**2002, June 19** **Litho.** *Perf. 13¼x13*

**638-641** A171 Set of 4 7.25 7.25

Hummingbirds A172

Designs: $1, Rufous-breasted hermit. $2.50, Black-throated mango. $3.25, Tufted coquette. $3.75, White-chested emerald.

**2002 ?** *Perf. 13x13¼*

**642-645** A172 Set of 4 4.75 4.75

Historic Forts — A173

Designs: $1, Fort Picton. $3.75, Fort George. $4.50, Fort King George. $5.25, Fort James.

**2002 ?** *Perf. 13¼x13*

**646-649** A173 Set of 4 6.50 6.50

*649a* Souvenir sheet, #646-649 6.50 6.50

Reign of Queen Elizabeth II, 50th Anniv. A174

Queen: $3.75, At Governor General's House. $4.50, With Mayor E. Taylor of Port of Spain. $5.25, At Red House, addressing Parliament, #119, and former personal flag of the Queen.

$10, In limousine, waving to crowd.

**2002** **Litho.** *Perf. 13¾*

**650-652** A174 Set of 3 4.50 4.50

**Souvenir Sheet**

**653** A174 $10 multi 3.25 3.25

Independence, 40th Anniv. — A175

**2002**

**654** A175 $1 multi .35 .35

Christmas A176

Designs: $1, Child opening gift of steel drum, vert. $2.50, People, musicians, house. $3.75, Houses. $5.25, Santa Claus on horse-drawn cart, vert.

*Perf. 14½x14¼, 14¼x14½*

**2002, Nov. 20** **Litho.**

**655-658** A176 Set of 4 4.25 4.25

Pan-American Health Organization, Cent. — A177

Designs: $1, Emblem. $2.50, National headquarters, Port of Spain. $3.25, Steel drum with symbols. $4.50, Joseph L. Pawan (1887-1957), discoverer of vampire bat rabies.

**2002, Dec. 2** *Perf. 14½x14¼*

**659-662** A177 Set of 4 3.75 3.75

Cricket Players — A178

Designs: $1, Ian Raphael Bishop. $2.50, Deryck Lance Murray. $4.50, Augustine Lawrence Logie. $5.25, Ann Browne John.

**2003, Feb. 7** *Perf. 13*

**663-666** A178 Set of 4 4.50 4.50

Carnival A179

Various costumed participants: $1, $2.50, $3.75, vert., $4.50, vert., $5.25, vert.

*Perf. 14¼x14½, 14½x14¼*

**2003, Feb. 25** **Litho.**

**667-671** A179 Set of 5 5.75 5.75

*671a* Souvenir sheet of 1 1.75 1.75

Inauguration of Intl. Criminal Court — A180

Designs: $1, Trinidad & Tobago Pres. Arthur N. R. Robinson and UN Secretary General Kofi Annan. $2.50, Robinson, Prof. Benjamin Ferencz, Prof. Cherif Bassiouni, Philippe Kirsch, UN Undersecretary for Legal Affairs Hans Corell. $3.75, Robinson and Corell. $4.50, Robinson, Emma Bonino, and Italian Pres. Carlo Ciampi.

$6, Robinson, vert.

*Perf. 14¾x14½, 14½x14¾*

**2003, Feb. 25**

**672-675** A180 Set of 4 4.00 4.00

**Souvenir Sheet**

**676** A180 $6 multi 2.00 2.00

Rainforest Flora & Fauna — A181

No. 677: a, Mountain immortelle. b, Blue-crowned motmot. c, Red howler monkey. d, Butterfly orchid. e, Channel-billed toucan. f, Ocelot. g, Bromeliads. h, Lineated woodpecker. i, Tamandua. j, Emperor butterfly.

*Serpentine Die Cut 12½*

**2003, Feb. 24** **Litho.**

**Self-Adhesive**

**677** Booklet pane of 10 3.25

*a.-j.* A181 $1 Any single .30 .30

Lighthouses A182

Designs: $1, Port-of-Spain. $3.75, Chacachacare. $4.50, Port-of-Spain, diff. $5.25, Chacachacare, diff.

No. 681B, Like No. 679, spelled "Chacacharie." No. 681C, Like No. 681, spelled "Chacacharie."

**2002-03** *Perf. 14½x14¼*

| | | | |
|---|---|---|---|
| **678-681** A182 Set of 4 | 4.75 | 4.75 |
| *681a* Souvenir sheet, #678-681 | 4.75 | 4.75 |
| **681B** A182 $3.75 multi | — | — |
| **681C** A182 $5.25 multi | — | — |

Nos. 678, 680, 681B and 681C were issued on 11/6/02 and all were withdrawn from sale later that day when the incorrect spelling of the lighthouse was discovered. Nos. 678 and 680 were put back on sale, along with new stamps with the corrected spelling of the lighthouse, Nos. 679 and 681, and the souvenir sheet with the stamps with the corrected spelling, No. 681a, on 5/26/03. The editors would like to examine any examples of the souvenir sheet with stamps with the incorrect spelling.

Scenes of Village Life — A183

Designs: $1, Dancing the cocoa. $2.50, Dirt oven. $3.75, River washing. $4.50, Box cart racing. $5.25, Pitching marbles.

**2003, Oct. 28**

**682-686** A183 Set of 5 5.50 5.50

Marine Life — A184

Designs: $1, Boulder brain coral. $2.50, Hawksbill turtle. $3.75, Green moray eel. $4.50, Creole wrasse. $5.25, Black-spotted sea goddess.
$10, Queen angelfish.

**2003, Oct. 28** *Perf. 14¼x14½*
**687-691** A184 Set of 5 5.50 5.50

**Souvenir Sheet**

**692** A184 $10 multi 3.25 3.25

Christmas — A185

Paintings by Jean Michel Cazabon (1813-88): $1, View of Port-of-Spain from Laventille Hill. $2.50, View of Diego Martin from Fort George. $3.75, Corbeaux Town, Trinidad. $4.50, Rain Clouds over Cedros. $5.25, Los Galos, Icacos Bay.
No. 698: a, $5, River at St. Ann's. b, $6.50, House in Trinidad.

**2003, Nov. 17** *Perf. 13¾*
**693-697** A185 Set of 5 5.50 5.50

**Souvenir Sheet**

**698** A185 Sheet of 2, #a-b 3.75 3.75

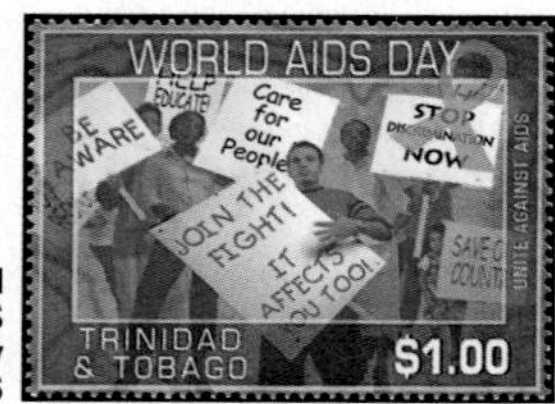

World AIDS Day A186

Designs: $1, Unite against AIDS. $2.50, Stigma isolates. $3.75, Care stops AIDS, vert. $4.50, Family protects, vert.
$10, People and AIDS ribbon.

**2003, Nov. 21**
**699-702** A186 Set of 4 4.00 4.00

**Souvenir Sheet**

**703** A186 $10 multi 3.25 3.25

2004 Carnival — A187

Calypso musicians: $1, Aldric Farrel, "The Lord Pretender." $2.50, Roy Lewis, "The Mystic Prowler." $3.75, Lord Kitchener, The Mighty Sparrow and The Roaring Lion. $4.50, McArthur Linda Sandy-Rose, "Calypso Rose." $5.25, Nap Hepburne, Lord Brynner and The Mighty Sparrow.
$10, McArthur Linda Sandy-Rose, diff.

**2004, Feb. 18**
**704-708** A187 Set of 5 5.50 5.50

**Souvenir Sheet**

**709** A187 $10 multi 3.25 3.25

2004 Summer Olympics, Athens — A188

Designs: $1, Track and field. $2.50, Boxing. $3.75, Taekwondo. $4.50, Swimming.

**2004, July 19** **Litho.** *Perf. 13*
**710-713** A188 Set of 4 3.75 3.75

Intl. Year Commemorating the Struggle Against Slavery and Its Abolition — A189

Designs: $1, Slave ship. $2.50, Rada community, Belmont. $3.75, Daaga, Prince of Popo. $4.50, Slaves singing freedom songs, horiz. $5.25, Providence Estate Aqueduct, Tobago, horiz.
$15, Sandy's escape, horiz.

**2004, Sept. 23** **Litho.** *Perf. 13*
**714-718** A189 Set of 5 5.50 5.50

**Souvenir Sheet**

**719** A189 $15 multi 5.00 5.00

Christmas A190

Paintings by Arthur Aldwin "Boscoe" Holder: $1, Lady with Ginger Lilies. $2.50, View from Maracas Lookout. $3.75, Lady in Peacock Chair. $4.50, Caribbean Beauty in White, horiz. $5.25, Teteron Bay, Chaguaramas, horiz.
$10, Creole Ladies in Straw Hats, horiz.

**2004, Nov. 22**
**720-724** A190 Set of 5 5.50 5.50

**Souvenir Sheet**

**725** A190 $10 multi 3.25 3.25

Fruits — A191

Designs: $1, Mango. $2.50, Lime. $3.75, Pineapple. $4.50, Coconut, horiz. $5.25, Orange, horiz.
$10, Guava, horiz.

**2004, June 7**
**726-730** A191 Set of 5 5.50 5.50

**Souvenir Sheet**

**731** A191 $10 multi 3.25 3.25

Carnival — A192

Designs: $1, Dame Lorraine. $2.50, Jab Jab. $3.25, Burrokeet, horiz. $3.75, Midnight Robber. $4.50, Fancy Indian.
$15, Fancy Sailor.

**2005, Jan. 18** **Litho.** *Perf. 13*
**732-736** A192 Set of 5 5.00 5.00

**Souvenir Sheet**

**737** A192 $15 multi 5.00 5.00

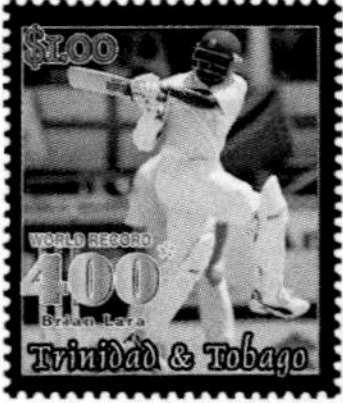

Brian Lara, Cricket Player — A193

Various photos of Lara in action: $1, $2.50, $3.75, $4.50, $5.25.
$15, Lara walking under raised cricket bats.

**2005, Apr. 12** **Litho.** *Perf. 13*
**738-742** A193 Set of 5 5.50 5.50

**Souvenir Sheet**

**743** A193 $15 multi 5.00 5.00

Tobago Heritage Festival — A194

Designs: $1, Belé. $2.50, Dancing the jig. $3.75, Goat race, horiz. $4.50, Harvest Festival, horiz. $5.25, Drumming Festival, horiz.
$15, Traditional Tobago wedding.

*Perf. 13½x13¼, 13¼x13½*

**2005, Aug. 15**
**744-748** A194 Set of 5 5.50 5.50

**Souvenir Sheet**

*Perf. 13¼*

**749** A194 $15 multi 5.00 5.00

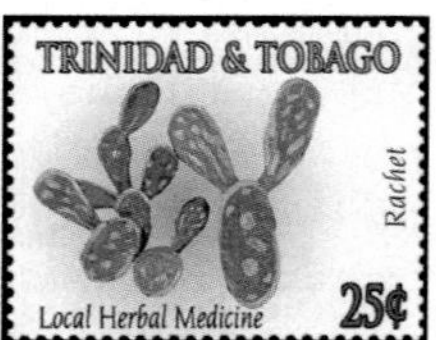

Medicinal Herbs A195

Designs: 25c, Rachet. 50c, Chandelier. 75c, Worm grass. $1, Black sage. $3, Wonder of the world. $3.25, Vervine. $4, Aloe vera. $5, Senna. $10, Bois bande. $20, Herbal garden.

**2005, May 18** *Perf. 13¼x13*

| | | | | | |
|---|---|---|---|---|---|
| **750** | A195 | 25c | multi | .20 | .20 |
| **751** | A195 | 50c | multi | .20 | .20 |
| **752** | A195 | 75c | multi | .25 | .25 |
| **753** | A195 | $1 | multi | .30 | .30 |
| **754** | A195 | $3 | multi | .95 | .95 |
| **755** | A195 | $3.25 | multi | 1.00 | 1.00 |
| **756** | A195 | $4 | multi | 1.25 | 1.25 |
| **757** | A195 | $5 | multi | 1.60 | 1.60 |
| **758** | A195 | $10 | multi | 3.25 | 3.25 |
| **759** | A195 | $20 | multi | 6.50 | 6.50 |
| | *Nos. 750-759 (10)* | | | 15.50 | 15.50 |

Fish and Marine Life — A196

No. 760: a, Foureye butterfly fish. b, Caribbean reef squid. c, Hawksbill turtle. d, Southern sting ray. e, Queen angelfish. f, Giant anemone. g, Peppermint shrimp. h, Rough file clam. i, White-speckled hermit crab. j, Christmas tree worm.

*Serpentine Die Cut 12½*

**2005, May 1** **Litho.**

**Self-Adhesive**

**760** Booklet of 10 3.25
*a.-j.* A196 $1 Any single .30 .30

Sir Solomon Hochoy (1905-83), First Governor-General — A197

Hochoy and: $1, Prime Minister Dr. Eric E. Williams. $2.50, Haile Selassie. $3.75, His wife, Thelma. $4.50, Queen Elizabeth II. $5.25, Honor Guard.
$15, Hochoy in uniform.

**2005, Aug. 22** *Perf. 13½x13*
**761-765** A197 Set of 5 5.50 5.50

**Souvenir Sheet**

*Perf. 13½x13¼*

**766** A197 $15 multi 4.75 4.75

Introduction of Women Police, 50th Anniv. — A198

**2005, Sept. 30** *Perf. 12¾*
**767** A198 $15 black 4.75 4.75

Souvenir Sheet

Children Against Cancer — A199

**2005, Nov. 7** *Perf. 13½x13¼*
**768** A199 $15 multi 6.50 6.50

No. 768 sold for $20.

Anansi and the Cricket Match — A200

Anansi: $1, And friends reading cricket brochure. $2.50, And friends hiding in bathroom. $3.75, And friends under umbrella. $4.50, Holding bag, talking to woman. $5.25, Laughing at friends paying woman.
$15, Anansi rubbing stomach.

**2005, Dec. 12** ***Perf. 13½x13***

**769-773** A200 Set of 5 5.50 5.50

**Souvenir Sheet**

**774** A200 $15 multi 4.75 4.75

Pope John Paul II (1920-2005) A201

Scenes from Pope's 1985 visit to Trinidad & Tobago: $1, Leaving airplane. $2.50, Kissing ground. $3.75, Shaking hands with priest. $4.50, With bishop, waving. $5.25, Celebrating mass.

$15, Waving to crowd from police vehicle.

**2006, Apr. 10** **Litho.** ***Perf. 13½x13¼***

**775-779** A201 Set of 5 5.50 5.50

**Souvenir Sheet**

**780** A201 $15 multi 4.75 4.75

2006 World Cup Soccer Championships, Germany — A202

Various images of Trinidad & Tobago soccer players in action: $1, $2.50, $3.75, $4.50.

***Perf. 13¼x13½***

**2006, June 28** **Litho.**

**781-784** A202 Set of 4 *3.75 3.75*

Initial reports said this set was available only with the purchase of a first day cover for $50, but the stamps have been made available individually at face value.

CARICOM Single Market and Economy A203

Designs: $1, Cables, palm tree. $2.50, Lighthouse, check. $3.75, Cell phone, diver. $4.50, Sprinter's hands, beach, horiz. $5.25, Hands on computer keyboard, globe, horiz.

$15, Map of Caribbean, horiz.

***Perf. 13½x13¼, 13¼x13½***

**2006, July 3**

**785-789** A203 Set of 5 5.50 5.50

**Souvenir Sheet**

**790** A203 $15 multi 4.75 4.75

Souvenir Sheet

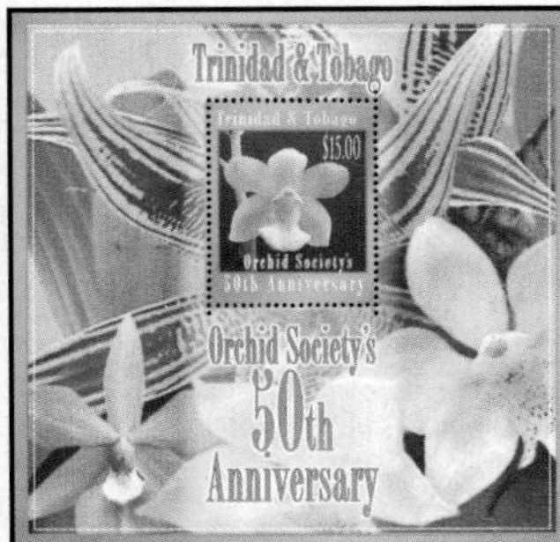


Orchid Society, 50th Anniv. — A204

**2006, Sept. 5** ***Perf. 13½x13¼***

**791** A204 $15 multi 5.00 5.00

Arrival of Chinese to Trinidad and Tobago, Bicent. A205

Art: $1, Guayaguayare Beach, by Ou Hing Wan. $2.50, Hosay, by Carlisle Chang. $3.75, Saddle Road, by Amy Leong Pang, vert. $4.50, Mother & Child, sculpture by Patrick Chu Foon, vert. $5.25, Still Life, by Sybil Atteck, vert.

$15, Inherent Nobility of Man, by Chang, vert.

***Perf. 14¼x14½, 14½x14¼***

**2006, Oct. 11**

**792-796** A205 Set of 5 5.50 5.50

**Souvenir Sheet**

***Perf. 13x13¼***

**797** A205 $15 multi 4.75 4.75

Children's Games — A206

Designs: $1, Rim driving. $2.50, Top spinning. $3.75, Playing 3A. $4.50, Farmer in the Den.

$15, Tire swing.

**2006, Nov. 29** ***Perf. 13¼***

**798-801** A206 Set of 4 3.75 3.75

**Souvenir Sheet**

**802** A206 $15 multi 4.75 4.75

## SEMI-POSTAL STAMPS

Emblem of Red Cross SP1

***Perf. 11, 12***

**1914, Sept. 18** **Typo.** **Unwmk.**

**B1** SP1 (½p) red (on cover) 210.00

This stamp was allowed to pay ½p postage on one day, Sept. 18, 1914, on circulars distributed by the Red Cross. Value on cover is for proper Red Cross usage. Value unused, $12.50.

No. 2 Overprinted in Red (Cross) and Black (Date):

a

b

**1915, Oct. 21** **Wmk. 3** ***Perf. 14***

**B2** A1 (a) 1p scarlet 1.50 1.50

**1916, Oct. 19**

**B3** A1 (b) 1p scarlet .50 *2.00*

*a.* Date omitted

## POSTAGE DUE STAMPS

D1

D2

**1923-45** **Typo.** **Wmk. 4** ***Perf. 14***

| | | | | |
|---|---|---|---|---|
| **J1** | D1 | 1p black | .75 | *1.50* |
| **J2** | D1 | 2p black | 1.50 | 1.50 |
| **J3** | D1 | 3p black ('25) | 1.50 | *2.25* |
| **J4** | D1 | 4p black ('29) | 2.75 | *20.00* |
| **J5** | D1 | 5p black ('45) | 35.00 | *92.50* |
| **J6** | D1 | 6p black ('45) | 55.00 | 35.00 |
| **J7** | D1 | 8p black ('45) | 42.50 | *160.00* |
| **J8** | D1 | 1sh black ('45) | 72.50 | *110.00* |
| | | *Nos. J1-J8 (8)* | 211.50 | 422.75 |

**Catalogue values for unused stamps in this section, from this point to the end of the section, are for Never Hinged items.**

Denominations in Cents

**1947, Sept. 1**

| | | | | |
|---|---|---|---|---|
| **J9** | D1 | 2c black | 1.40 | .75 |
| **J10** | D1 | 4c black | .80 | 1.00 |
| **J11** | D1 | 6c black | 1.00 | 2.00 |
| **J12** | D1 | 8c black | 1.00 | *6.00* |
| **J13** | D1 | 10c black | 1.00 | *.90* |
| **J14** | D1 | 12c black | 1.00 | *5.00* |
| **J15** | D1 | 16c black | 1.90 | *11.50* |
| **J16** | D1 | 24c black | 6.75 | *2.50* |
| | | *Nos. J9-J16 (8)* | 14.85 | *29.65* |

Nos. J9-J16 also exist on chalky paper.

**Wmk. 4a (error)**

| | | | |
|---|---|---|---|
| *J9a* | D1 | 2c | 50.00 |
| *J11a* | D1 | 6c | 100.00 |
| *J14a* | D1 | 12c | 125.00 |

**1970** **Unwmk.** **Litho.** ***Perf. 14x13½***

**Size: 18x23mm**

| | | | | |
|---|---|---|---|---|
| **J17** | D2 | 2c green | .20 | .55 |
| **J18** | D2 | 4c carmine rose | .20 | .85 |
| **J19** | D2 | 6c brown | .40 | 1.10 |
| **J20** | D2 | 8c lt violet | .50 | 1.25 |
| **J21** | D2 | 10c brick red | .50 | 1.25 |
| **J22** | D2 | 12c dull orange | .65 | 1.25 |
| **J23** | D2 | 16c brt yellow grn | .65 | .85 |
| **J24** | D2 | 24c gray | .65 | .90 |
| **J25** | D2 | 50c blue | .65 | 1.00 |
| **J26** | D2 | 60c olive green | .65 | 1.00 |
| | | *Nos. J17-J26 (10)* | 5.05 | 10.00 |

***Perf. 13½x14***

**1976-77** **Litho.** **Unwmk.**

**Size: 17x21mm**

| | | | | |
|---|---|---|---|---|
| **J27** | D2 | 2c green | .20 | .45 |
| **J28** | D2 | 4c carmine rose | .25 | .45 |
| **J29** | D2 | 6c brown | .25 | .60 |
| **J30** | D2 | 8c lt violet | .30 | .60 |
| **J31** | D2 | 10c brick red | .30 | .60 |
| **J32** | D2 | 12c dull orange | .45 | .80 |
| | | *Nos. J27-J32 (6)* | 1.75 | 3.50 |

Issued: 4c, 12c, 4/1/76; 2c, 6c, 8c, 10, 1977.

The letters in the top label on Nos. J27-J32 are larger with D's and O's more squarish than the oval letters on Nos. J17-J26. "Postage Due" is 13mm long and is composed of finer letters than on Nos. J17-J26, which have a 14mm inscription.

## WAR TAX STAMPS

Nos. 1-2 Overprinted

**1917** **Wmk. 3** ***Perf. 14***

**MR1** A1 1p scarlet 2.00 *2.75*

*a.* Invtd. overprint 175.00 *225.00*

Overprinted

**MR2** A1 ½p green .20 .20

*a.* Overprinted on face and back 400.00

*b.* Pair, one without overprint 250.00

**MR3** A1 1p scarlet .60 *1.75*

*a.* Pair, one without overprint 400.00 750.00

*b.* Double overprint 110.00

Overprinted

**MR4** A1 ½p green .20 *5.00*

**MR5** A1 1p scarlet .20 *.75*

Overprinted

**MR6** A1 ½p green .20 *2.50*

**MR7** A1 1p scarlet 2.75 1.00

Overprinted

**MR8** A1 ½p green .20 *2.50*

**MR9** A1 1p scarlet 27.50 22.50

Overprinted

**MR10** A1 1p scarlet .60 *1.00*

*a.* Inverted overprint 92.50 *92.50*

Overprinted

**MR11** A1 1p scarlet 1.25 .20

*a.* Double overprint 175.00 *175.00*

*b.* Inverted overprint 100.00 100.00

Overprinted

**1918**

**MR12** A1 ½p green .20 1.60

**MR13** A1 1p scarlet .75 1.25

*a.* Double overprint 110.00

The War Tax Stamps show considerable variations in the colors, thickness of the paper, distinctness of the watermark, and the gum. Counterfeits exist of the errors of Nos. MR1-MR13.

### OFFICIAL STAMPS

Regular Issue of 1913 Overprinted

**1913 Wmk. 3 *Perf. 14***

**O1** A1 ½p green .80 5.50

Same Overprinted

**1914**

**O2** A1 ½p green 1.50 10.00

Same Overprinted

**1916**

**O3** A1 ½p green 1.00 2.50
*a.* Double overprint 22.50

Same Overprint without Period

**1917**

**O4** A1 ½p green .50 5.50

Same Overprinted

**1917, Aug. 22**

**O5** A1 ½p green 1.00 14.00

The official stamps are found in several shades of green and on paper of varying thickness.

## TRIPOLITANIA

tri-ˌpä-lə-ˈtā-nyə

LOCATION — In northern Africa, bordering on Mediterranean Sea
GOVT. — A former Italian Colony
AREA — 350,000 sq. mi. (approx.)
POP. — 570,716 (1921)
CAPITAL — Tripoli

Formerly a Turkish province, Tripolitania became part of Italian Libya. See Libya.

100 Centesimi = 1 Lira

**Used values in italics are for postaly used stamps. CTO's or stamps with fake cancels sell for about the same as unused, hinged stamps.**

**Watermark**

Wmk. 140 — Crowns

**Propaganda of the Faith Issue**

Italian Stamps Overprinted

**1923, Oct. 24 Wmk. 140 *Perf. 14***

**1** A68 20c ol grn & brn org 7.50 *37.50*
**2** A68 30c claret & brn org 7.50 *37.50*
**3** A68 50c vio & brn org 4.50 *45.00*
**4** A68 1 l blue & brn org 4.50 *55.00*
*Nos. 1-4 (4)* 24.00 *175.00*
Set, never hinged 57.50

**Fascisti Issue**

Italian Stamps Overprinted in Red or Black

**1923, Oct. 29 Unwmk.**

**5** A69 10c dk green (R) 9.00 *13.50*
**6** A69 30c dk violet (R) 9.00 *13.50*
**7** A69 50c brown car 9.00 *15.00*

**Wmk. 140**

**8** A70 1 l blue 9.00 *37.50*
**9** A70 2 l brown 9.00 *45.00*
**10** A71 5 l blk & bl (R) 9.00 *60.00*
*Nos. 5-10 (6)* 54.00 *184.50*
Set, never hinged 125.00

**Manzoni Issue**

Stamps of Italy, 1923, Overprinted in Red

**1924, Apr. 1 Wmk. 140 *Perf. 14***

**11** A72 10c brown red & blk 12.00 *37.50*
**12** A72 15c blue grn & blk 12.00 *37.50*
**13** A72 30c black & slate 12.00 *37.50*
**14** A72 50c org brn & blk 12.00 *37.50*
**15** A72 1 l blue & blk 75.00 *275.00*
**16** A72 5 l violet & blk 500.00 *2,000.*
*Nos. 11-16 (6)* 623.00 *2,425.*
Set, never hinged 1,530.

On Nos. 15 and 16 the overprint is placed vertically at the left side.

**Victor Emmanuel Issue**

Italy Nos. 175-177 Overprinted

**1925-26 Unwmk. *Perf. 11***

**17** A78 60c brown car .75 *6.75*
**18** A78 1 l dark blue 1.50 *6.75*
*a.* Perf. 13½ 4.50 *22.50*

***Perf. 13½***

**19** A78 1.25 l dk blue ('26) 2.25 *21.00*
*a.* Perf. 11 1,050. *1,350.*
*Nos. 17-19 (3)* 4.50 *34.50*
Set, #17-19, 18a, 19a, never hinged 2,115.

**Saint Francis of Assisi Issue**

Italy Nos. 178-180 Overprinted

**1926, Apr. 12 Wmk. 140 *Perf. 14***

**20** A79 20c gray green 2.25 *10.50*
**21** A80 40c dark violet 2.25 *10.50*
**22** A81 60c red brown 2.25 *18.00*

Italy No. 182 and Type of A83 Overprinted in Red

**Unwmk.**

**23** A82 1.25 l dark blue 2.25 *26.00*
**24** A83 5 l + 2.50 l ol grn 6.00 *52.50*
*Nos. 20-24 (5)* 15.00 *117.50*
Set, never hinged 35.00

**Volta Issue**

Type of Italy Overprinted

**1927, Oct. 10 Wmk. 140 *Perf. 14***

**25** A84 20c purple 4.50 *30.00*
**26** A84 50c deep orange 7.50 *18.00*
*a.* Double overprint 165.00
**27** A84 1.25 l brt blue 10.50 *50.00*
*Nos. 25-27 (3)* 22.50 *98.00*
Set, never hinged 42.50

**Monte Cassino Issue**

Types of Italy Overprinted in Red or Blue

**1929, Oct. 14**

**28** A96 20c dk green (R) 4.50 *16.00*
**29** A96 25c red org (Bl) 4.50 *16.00*
**30** A98 50c + 10c crim (Bl) 4.50 *18.00*
**31** A98 75c + 15c ol brn (R) 4.50 *18.00*
**32** A96 1.25 l + 25c dk vio (R) 10.50 *32.50*
**33** A98 5 l + 1 l saph (R) 10.50 *37.50*

Overprinted in Red

**Unwmk.**

**34** A100 10 l + 2 l gray brn 10.50 *52.50*
*Nos. 28-34 (7)* 49.50 *190.50*
Set, never hinged 115.00

**Royal Wedding Issue**

Type of Italy Overprinted

**1930, Mar. 17 Wmk. 140**

**35** A101 20c yellow green 1.50 *4.50*
**36** A101 50c + 10c dp org 1.10 *7.50*
**37** A101 1.25 l + 25c rose red 1.10 *15.00*
*Nos. 35-37 (3)* 3.70 *27.00*
Set, never hinged 9.25

**Ferrucci Issue**

Types of Italy Overprinted in Red or Blue

**1930, July 26**

**38** A102 20c violet (R) 3.00 *3.75*
**39** A103 25c dk green (R) 3.00 *3.75*
**40** A103 50c black (R) 3.00 *7.50*
**41** A103 1.25 l deep blue (R) 3.00 *15.00*
**42** A104 5 l + 2 l dp car (Bl) 7.50 *26.00*
*Nos. 38-42,C1-C3 (8)* 42.00 *124.50*
Set, never hinged 100.00

**Virgil Issue**

Types of Italy Overprinted in Red or Blue

**1930, Dec. 4 Photo.**

**43** A106 15c violet black 1.10 *7.50*
**44** A106 20c orange brown 1.10 *3.00*
**45** A106 25c dark green 1.10 *3.00*
**46** A106 30c lt brown 1.10 *3.00*
**47** A106 50c dull violet 1.10 *3.00*
**48** A106 75c rose red 1.10 *6.00*
**49** A106 1.25 l gray blue 1.10 *7.50*

**Unwmk.**
**Engr.**

**50** A106 5 l + 1.50 l dk vio 3.25 *37.50*
**51** A106 10 l + 2.50 l ol brn 3.25 *55.00*
*Nos. 43-51,C4-C7 (13)* 30.70 *233.50*
Set, never hinged 77.50

**Saint Anthony of Padua Issue**

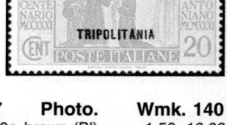

Types of Italy Overprinted in Blue or Red

**1931, May 7 Photo. Wmk. 140**

**52** A116 20c brown (Bl) 1.50 *16.00*
**53** A116 25c green (R) 1.50 *6.00*
**54** A118 30c gray brn (Bl) 1.50 *6.00*
**55** A118 50c dull vio (Bl) 1.50 *6.00*
**56** A120 1.25 l slate bl (R) 1.50 *30.00*

Overprinted in Red or Black

**Unwmk. Engr.**

**57** A121 75c black (R) 1.50 *16.00*
**58** A122 5 l + 2.50 l dk brn (Bk) 6.00 *65.00*
*Nos. 52-58 (7)* 15.00 *145.00*
Set, never hinged 37.50

Native Village Scene
A14

**1934, Oct. 16 Wmk. 140**

**73** A14 5c ol grn & brn 3.75 *18.00*
**74** A14 10c brown & black 3.75 *18.00*
**75** A14 20c scar & indigo 3.75 *15.00*
**76** A14 50c purple & brown 3.75 *15.00*
**77** A14 60c org brn & ind 3.75 *22.50*
**78** A14 1.25 l dk bl & grn 3.75 *37.50*
*Nos. 73-78,C43-C48 (12)* 45.00 252.00
Set, never hinged 110.00

2nd Colonial Arts Exhibition, Naples.

---

## SEMI-POSTAL STAMPS

Many issues of Italy and Italian Colonies include one or more semipostal denominations. To avoid splitting sets, these issues are generally listed as regular postage, airmail, etc., unless all values carry a surtax.

### Holy Year Issue

Italian Stamps of 1924 Overprinted in Black or Red

**1925 Wmk. 140 *Perf. 12***

**B1** SP4 20c + 10c dk grn & brn 3.00 *18.00*
**B2** SP4 30c + 15c dk brn & brn 3.00 *21.00*
**B3** SP4 50c + 25c vio & brn 3.00 *18.00*
**B4** SP4 60c + 30c dp rose & brn 3.00 *24.00*
**B5** SP8 1 l + 50c dp bl & vio (R) 3.00 *30.00*
**B6** SP8 5 l + 2.50 l org brn & vio (R) 3.00 *45.00*
*Nos. B1-B6 (6)* 18.00 *156.00*
Set, never hinged 42.50

### Colonial Institute Issue

Peace Substituting Spade for Sword — SP1

**1926, June 1 Typo. *Perf. 14***

**B7** SP1 5c + 5c brown .90 *7.50*
**B8** SP1 10c + 5c ol brn .90 *7.50*
**B9** SP1 20c + 5c bl grn .90 *7.50*
**B10** SP1 40c + 5c brn red .90 *7.50*
**B11** SP1 60c + 5c orange .90 *7.50*
**B12** SP1 1 l + 5c blue .90 *16.00*
*Nos. B7-B12 (6)* 5.40 *53.50*
Set, never hinged 13.50

The surtax was for the Italian Colonial Institute.

> Fiera Campionaria Tripoli
> See Libya for stamps with this inscription.

Types of Italian Semi-Postal Stamps of 1926 Overprinted like Nos. 17-19

**1927, Apr. 21 Unwmk. *Perf. 11***

**B19** SP10 40c + 20c dk brn & blk 2.25 *30.00*
**B20** SP10 60c + 30c brn red & ol brn 2.25 *30.00*
**B21** SP10 1.25 l + 60c dp bl & blk 2.25 *47.50*
**B22** SP10 5 l + 2.50 l dk grn & blk 3.75 *67.50*
*Nos. B19-B22 (4)* 10.50 *175.00*
Set, never hinged 25.00

The surtax was for the charitable work of the Voluntary Militia for Italian National Defense.

Allegory of Fascism and Victory — SP2

**1928, Oct. 15 Wmk. 140**

**B29** SP2 20c + 5c bl grn 2.25 *11.00*
**B30** SP2 30c + 5c red 2.25 *11.00*
**B31** SP2 50c + 10c pur 2.25 *18.00*
**B32** SP2 1.25 l + 20c dk bl 3.00 *22.50*
*Nos. B29-B32 (4)* 9.75 *62.50*
Set, never hinged 24.00

46th anniv. of the Societa Africana d'Italia. The surtax aided that society.

Types of Italian Semi-Postal Stamps of 1928 Overprinted

**1929, Mar. 4 Unwmk. *Perf. 11***

**B33** SP10 30c + 10c red & blk 3.75 *18.00*
**B34** SP10 50c + 20c vio & blk 3.75 *22.50*
**B35** SP10 1.25 l + 50c brn & bl 4.50 *37.50*
**B36** SP10 5 l + 2 l ol grn & blk 4.50 *67.50*
*Nos. B33-B36 (4)* 16.50 *145.50*
Set, never hinged 40.00

The surtax on these stamps was for the charitable work of the Voluntary Militia for Italian National Defense.

Types of Italian Semi-Postal Stamps of 1926, Overprinted in Black or Red Like Nos. B33-B36

**1930, Oct. 20**

**B50** SP10 30c + 10c dp grn & bl grn (Bk) 19.00 *30.00*
**B51** SP10 50c + 10c dk grn & vio (R) 19.00 *40.00*
**B52** SP10 1.25 l + 30c blk brn & red brn (R) 19.00 *52.50*
**B53** SP10 5 l + 1.50 l ind & grn (R) 60.00 *150.00*
*Nos. B50-B53 (4)* 117.00 *272.50*
Set, never hinged 290.00

Ancient Arch — SP3

**1930, Nov. 27 Photo. Wmk. 140**

**B54** SP3 50c + 20c ol brn 3.75 *18.00*
**B55** SP3 1.25 l + 20c dp bl 3.75 *18.00*
**B56** SP3 1.75 l + 20c green 3.75 *21.00*
**B57** SP3 2.55 l + 50c purple 6.00 *32.50*
**B58** SP3 5 l + 1 l deep car 6.00 *47.50*
*Nos. B54-B58 (5)* 23.25 *137.00*
Set, never hinged 57.50

25th anniv. of the Italian Colonial Agricultural Institute. The surtax was for the benefit of that institution.

---

## AIR POST STAMPS

### Ferrucci Issue

Type of Italian Air Post Stamps Overprinted in Blue or Red like #38-42

**1930, July 26 Wmk. 140 *Perf. 14***

**C1** AP7 50c brown vio (Bl) 3.75 *7.50*
**C2** AP7 1 l dk blue (R) 3.75 *13.50*
**C3** AP7 5 l + 2 l dp car (Bl) 15.00 *47.50*
*Nos. C1-C3 (3)* 22.50 *68.50*
Set, never hinged 55.00

### Virgil Issue

Types of Italian Air Post Stamps Overprinted in Red or Blue like #43-51

**1930, Dec. 4 Photo.**

**C4** AP8 50c deep green 2.25 *9.00*
**C5** AP8 1 l rose red 2.25 *9.00*

**Unwmk.**

**Engr.**

**C6** AP8 7.70 l + 1.30 l dk brn 6.00 *45.00*
**C7** AP8 9 l + 2 l gray 6.00 *45.00*
*Nos. C4-C7 (4)* 16.50 *108.00*
Set, never hinged 40.00

Airplane over Columns of the Basilica, Leptis — AP1

Arab Horseman Pointing at Airplane
AP2

**1931-32 Photo. Wmk. 140**

**C8** AP1 50c rose car .75 .20
**C9** AP1 60c red org 2.25 *7.50*
**C10** AP1 75c dp bl ('32) 2.25 *6.00*
**C11** AP1 80c dull violet 6.00 *11.00*
**C12** AP2 1 l deep blue 1.50 .20
**C13** AP2 1.20 l dk brown 18.00 *15.00*
**C14** AP2 1.50 l org red 7.50 *15.00*
**C15** AP2 5 l green 22.50 *22.50*
*Nos. C8-C15 (8)* 60.75 *77.40*
Set, never hinged 150.00

For surcharges and overprint see Nos. C29-C32.

Agricultural Institute, 25th Anniv.
AP3

**1931, Dec. 7**

**C16** AP3 50c dp blue 3.00 *18.00*
**C17** AP3 80c violet 3.00 *18.00*
**C18** AP3 1 l gray black 3.00 *26.00*
**C19** AP3 2 l deep green 6.00 *37.50*
**C20** AP3 5 l + 2 l rose red 9.00 *67.50*
*Nos. C16-C20 (5)* 24.00 *167.00*
Set, never hinged 60.00

### Graf Zeppelin Issue

Mercury, by Giovanni da Bologna, and Zeppelin
AP4

Designs: 3 l, 12 l, Mercury. 10 l, 20 l, Guido Reni's "Aurora." 5 l, 15 l, Arch of Marcus Aurelius.

**1933, May 5**

**C21** AP4 3 l dark brown 7.50 *95.00*
**C22** AP4 5 l purple 7.50 *95.00*
**C23** AP4 10 l deep green 7.50 *175.00*
**C24** AP4 12 l deep blue 7.50 *200.00*
**C25** AP4 15 l carmine 7.50 *200.00*
**C26** AP4 20 l gray black 45.00 *260.00*
*Nos. C21-C26 (6)* 45.00 *1,025.*
Set, never hinged 110.00

For overprints and surcharges see Nos. C38-C42.

### North Atlantic Flight Issue

Airplane, Lion of St. Mark
AP7

**1933, June 1**

**C27** AP7 19.75 l blk & ol brn 15.00 *500.00*
**C28** AP7 44.75 l dk bl & lt grn 15.00 *500.00*
Set, never hinged 75.00

Type of 1931 Overprinted or Surcharged

**1934, Jan. 20**

**C29** AP2 2 l on 5 l org brn 3.00 *60.00*
**C30** AP2 3 l on 5 l grn 3.00 *60.00*
**C31** AP2 5 l ocher 3.00 *67.50*
**C32** AP2 10 l on 5 l rose 4.50 *67.50*
*Nos. C29-C32 (4)* 13.50 *255.00*
Set, never hinged 25.00

For use on mail to be carried on a special flight from Rome to Buenos Aires.

Types of Libya Airmail Issue Overprinted in Black or Red

Plane Shadow on Desert
AP11

**1934, May 1 Wmk. 140**

**C38** AP4 50c rose red 9.00 *92.50*
**C39** AP4 75c lemon 9.00 *92.50*
**C40** AP4 5 l + 1 l brn 9.00 *92.50*
**C41** AP4 10 l + 2 l dk bl 175.00 *525.00*
**C42** AP5 25 l + 3 l pur 175.00 *525.00*
*Nos. C38-C42,CE1-CE2 (7)* 395.00 1,512.
Set, never hinged 1,030.

"Circuit of the Oases."

Designs: 25c, 50c, 75c, Plane shadow on desert. 80c, 1 l, 2 l, Camel corps.

**1934, Oct. 16 Photo.**

**C43** AP11 25c sl bl & org red 3.75 *18.00*
**C44** AP11 50c dk grn & ind 3.75 *15.00*
**C45** AP11 75c dk brn & org red 3.75 *15.00*

**C46** AP11 80c org brn & ol grn 3.75 *18.00*
**C47** AP11 1 l scar & ol grn 3.75 *22.50*
**C48** AP11 2 l dk bl & brn 3.75 *37.50*
*Nos. C43-C48 (6)* 22.50 *126.00*
Set, never hinged 55.00

Second Colonial Arts Exhibition, Naples.

---

### AIR POST SEMI-POSTAL STAMPS

King Victor Emmanuel III SPAP1

**1934, Nov. 5 Wmk. 140 *Perf. 14***

**CB1** SPAP1 25c + 10c gray grn 6.00 *13.50*
**CB2** SPAP1 50c + 10c brn 6.00 *13.50*
**CB3** SPAP1 75c + 15c rose red 6.00 *13.50*
**CB4** SPAP1 80c + 15c blk brn 6.00 *13.50*
**CB5** SPAP1 1 l + 20c red brn 6.00 *13.50*
**CB6** SPAP1 2 l + 20c brt bl 6.00 *13.50*
**CB7** SPAP1 3 l + 25c pur 21.00 *67.50*
**CB8** SPAP1 5 l + 25c org 21.00 *67.50*
**CB9** SPAP1 10 l + 30c rose vio 21.00 *67.50*
**CB10** SPAP1 25 l + 2 l dp grn 21.00 *67.50*
*Nos. CB1-CB10 (10)* 120.00 *351.00*
Set, never hinged 210.00

65th birthday of King Victor Emmanuel III; non-stop flight from Rome to Mogadiscio.

For overprint see No. CBO1.

---

### AIR POST SEMI-POSTAL OFFICIAL STAMP

Type of Air Post Semi-Postal Stamps Overprinted Crown and "SERVIZIO DI STATO" in Black

**1934 Wmk. 140 *Perf. 14***

**CBO1** SPAP1 25 l + 2 l cop red 2,450. *3,750.*
Never hinged 3,000.

---

### AIR POST SPECIAL DELIVERY STAMPS

Type of Libya Overprinted in Black Like Nos. C38-c42

**1934, May 1 Wmk. 140 *Perf. 14***

**CE1** APSD1 2.25 l red orange 9.00 *92.50*
**CE2** APSD1 4.50 l + 1 l dp rose 9.00 *92.50*
Set, never hinged 45.00

---

### AUTHORIZED DELIVERY STAMP

Authorized Delivery Stamp of Italy 1930, Overprinted like Nos. 38-42

**1931, Mar. Wmk. 140 *Perf. 14***

**EY1** AD2 10c dark brown 9.00 18.00
Never hinged 22.50

---

## TRISTAN DA CUNHA

ˌtris-tən-də-ˈkü-nə

LOCATION — Group of islands in the south Atlantic Ocean midway between the Cape of Good Hope and South America
GOVT. — A dependency of St. Helena
AREA — 40 sq. mi.
POP. — 313 (1988)

12 Pence = 1 Shilling
100 Cents = 1 Rand (1961)
12 Pence = 1 Shilling (1963)
20 Shillings = 1 Pound
100 Pence = 1 Pound (1971)

**Catalogue values for all unused stamps in this country are for Never Hinged items.**

Stamps of St. Helena, 1938-49, Overprinted in Black

**1952, Jan. 1 Wmk. 4 *Perf. 12½***

**1** A24 ½p purple .20 *2.10*
**2** A24 1p blue grn & blk .80 *1.90*
**3** A24 1½p car rose & blk .80 *1.90*
**4** A24 2p carmine & blk .80 *1.90*
**5** A24 3p gray 1.10 *1.90*
**6** A24 4p ultra 4.25 3.00
**7** A24 6p gray blue 5.00 3.00
**8** A24 8p olive 4.50 *6.50*
**9** A24 1sh sepia 5.00 *2.50*
**10** A24 2sh6p deep claret 22.50 *16.00*
**11** A24 5sh brown 24.00 *25.00*
**12** A24 10sh violet 45.00 *35.00*
*Nos. 1-12 (12)* 113.95 *100.70*
Set, hinged 70.00

---

Common Design Types pictured following the introduction.

---

### Coronation Issue
Common Design Type

**1953, June 2 Engr. *Perf. 13½x13***

**13** CD312 3p dk green & black .85 1.40

Tristan Crayfish — A1

Carting Flax — A2

Designs: 1½p, Rockhopper penguin. 2p, Factory. 2½p, Mollymauk. 3p, Island boat. 4p, View of Tristan. 5p, Potato patches. 6p, Inaccessible Island. 9p, Nightingale Island. 1sh, St. Mary's Church. 2sh 6p, Elephant seal. 5sh, Flightless rail. 10sh, Island spinning wheel.

**1954-58 *Perf. 12½***

**14** A1 ½p choc & red .20 .20
*a.* Bklt. pane of 4 ('58) 2.50
**15** A2 1p green & choc .20 *.60*
*a.* Bklt. pane of 4 ('58) 4.00
**16** A1 1½p dp plum & blk 2.00 1.40
*a.* Bklt. pane of 4 ('58) 7.00
**17** A2 2p org & vio blue .35 .20
**18** A2 2½p carmine & blk 1.75 .70
**19** A1 3p ol grn & ultra .80 1.40
*a.* Bklt. pane of 4 ('58) 10.50
**20** A2 4p dp bl & aqua .80 .75
*a.* Bklt. pane of 4 ('58) 13.00
**21** A2 5p gray & bl grn .80 .75
**22** A2 6p vio & dk ol grn .80 .75
**23** A2 9p henna brn & rose lil .80 .55
**24** A2 1sh choc & ol grn .80 .55
**25** A2 2sh6p blue & choc 25.00 11.50
**26** A2 5sh red org & blk 55.00 15.00
**27** A2 10sh red vio & org 26.00 17.50
*Nos. 14-27 (14)* 115.30 51.85
Set, hinged 60.00

Starfish — A3

Fish: 1p, Concha. 1½p, Klipfish. 2p, Heron fish (saury). 2½p, Snipefish ("swordfish"). 3d, Tristan crawfish. 4p, Soldier fish. 5p, Five finger fish. 6p, Mackeral scad. 9p, Stumpnose. 1sh, Bluefish. 2sh6p, Snoek (snake mackerel). 5sh, Shark. 10sh, Atlantic right whale.

***Perf. 12½x13***

**1960, Feb. 1 Engr. Wmk. 314**

**28** A3 ½p orange & black .20 .20
*a.* Booklet pane of 4 1.50
**29** A3 1p rose lilac & blk .25 .20
*a.* Booklet pane of 4 2.50
**30** A3 1½p grnsh bl & blk .35 .25
*a.* Booklet pane of 4 2.75
**31** A3 2p green & black .45 .35
**32** A3 2½p brown & black .50 .35
**33** A3 3p rose red & blk 1.40 1.40
*a.* Booklet pane of 4 8.00
**34** A3 4p gray ol & blk 1.25 .65
*a.* Booklet pane of 4 7.00
**35** A3 5p org yel & blk 1.60 .70
**36** A3 6p blue & black 1.60 .80
**37** A3 9p rose car & blk 1.90 .70
**38** A3 1sh brn org & blk 2.75 .60
**39** A3 2sh6p vio blue & blk 12.50 12.50
**40** A3 5sh emerald & blk 15.00 16.00
**41** A3 10sh violet & blk 50.00 50.00
*Nos. 28-41 (14)* 89.75 84.70

**1961, Apr. 15 *Perf. 12½x13***

**42** A3 ½c like No. 28 .20 .20
**43** A3 1c like No. 29 .20 .20
**44** A3 1½c like No. 30 .40 .40
**45** A3 2c like No. 32 .75 .75
**46** A3 2½c like No. 33 1.10 1.10
**47** A3 3c like No. 34 1.10 1.10
**48** A3 4c like No. 35 1.40 1.40
**49** A3 5c like No. 36 1.40 1.40
**50** A3 7½c like No. 37 1.40 1.40
**51** A3 10c like No. 38 2.25 1.60
**52** A3 25c like No. 39 9.00 9.00
**53** A3 50c like No. 40 22.50 17.50
**54** A3 1r like No. 41 45.00 40.00
*Nos. 42-54 (13)* 86.70 76.05

Nos. 46, 49-51 surcharged for "Tristan Relief" are listed as St. Helena Nos. B1-B4.

Types of St. Helena, 1961 Overprinted

***Perf. 11½x12, 12x11½***

**1963, Apr. 12 Photo. Wmk. 4**

**55** A29 1p rose, ultra, yel & grn .20 1.00
**56** A29 1½p bis, sep, yel & grn .20 .40
**57** A29 2p gray & red .25 1.00
**58** A30 3p dk bl, rose & grnsh bl .30 1.00
*a.* Double overprint
**59** A29 4½p slate, brn & grn .55 .70
**60** A29 6p cit, brn & dp car .80 .40
**61** A29 7p vio, blk & red brn .55 .40
**62** A29 10p bl & dp claret .55 .40
**63** A29 1sh red brn, grn & yel .55 .40
**64** A29 1sh6p gray bl & blk 5.50 1.10
**65** A29 2sh6p grnsh bl, yel & red 1.75 .75
**66** A29 5sh grn, brn & yel 7.00 1.75
**67** A29 10sh gray bl, blk & sal 7.00 1.75
*Nos. 55-67 (13)* 25.20 11.05

### Freedom from Hunger Issue
Common Design Type

***Perf. 14x14½***

**1963, Oct. 2 Photo. Wmk. 314**

**68** CD314 1sh6p rose carmine 1.00 .40

### Red Cross Centenary Issue
Common Design Type

**1964, Jan. 2 Litho. *Perf. 13***

**69** CD315 3p black & red .75 .40
**70** CD315 1sh6p ultra & red 1.25 .60

Flagship of Tristáo da Cunha, 1506 — A4

Queen Elizabeth II — A5

½p, Map of South Atlantic Ocean. 1½p, Dutch ship Heemstede, first landing, 1643. 2p, New England whaler. 3p, Confederate ship Shenandoah. 4½p, H.M.S. Galatea, 1867. 6p, H.M.S. Cilicia, 1942. 7p, H.M. Royal Yacht Britannia, 1957. 10p, H.M.S. Leopard, Evacuation, 1961. 1sh, Dutch ship Tjisadane, 1961. 1sh6p, M.V. Tristania. 2sh6p, M.V. Boissevain, returning islanders, 1963. 5sh, M.S. Bornholm, returning islanders, 1963.

***Perf. 11x11½***

**1965, Feb. 17 Engr. Wmk. 314**

**71** A4 ½p black & dk blue .20 .20
*a.* Booklet pane of 4 .25
**72** A4 1p black & emerald .85 .20
*a.* Booklet pane of 4 4.25
**73** A4 1½p black & ultra .85 .20
*a.* Booklet pane of 4 4.25
**74** A4 2p black & lilac .85 .20
**75** A4 3p blk & grnsh bl .85 .20
*a.* Booklet pane of 4 4.25
**76** A4 4½p black & brown .85 .20
**77** A4 6p black & green .70 .30
*a.* Booklet pane of 4 4.25
**78** A4 7p black & ver .85 .40
**79** A4 10p black & dk brn .85 .40
**80** A4 1sh black & lil rose .85 .50
**81** A4 1sh6p black & olive 4.50 2.75
**82** A4 2sh6p black & brn org 3.00 3.00
**83** A4 5sh black & violet 6.00 4.00

***Perf. 11½x11***

**84** A5 10sh lil rose & dk bl 2.00 1.50
*Nos. 71-84 (14)* 23.20 14.05

See Nos. 113-115. For surcharges see Nos. 108, 141-152. For overprints see Nos. 132.

### ITU Issue
Common Design Type

**1965, May 11 Litho. *Perf. 11x11½***

**85** CD317 3p vermilion & gray .55 .25
**86** CD317 6p purple & orange .85 .40

### Intl. Cooperation Year Issue
Common Design Type

**1965, Oct. 25 Wmk. 314 *Perf. 14½***

**87** CD318 1p blue grn & claret .20 .30
**88** CD318 6p lt violet & green 1.25 .45

### Churchill Memorial Issue
Common Design Type
**Wmk. 314**

**1966, Jan. 24 Photo. *Perf. 14***

**Design in Black, Gold and Carmine Rose**

**89** CD319 1p bright blue .20 .20
**90** CD319 3p green .30 .20
**91** CD319 6p brown 1.40 .70
**92** CD319 1sh6p violet 4.25 1.50
*Nos. 89-92 (4)* 6.15 2.60

### World Cup Soccer Issue
Common Design Type

**1966 Litho. *Perf. 14***

**93** CD320 3p multicolored .25 .20
**94** CD321 2sh6p multicolored 1.25 .55

Nos. 93-94 were issued Oct. 1 in Tristan da Cunha, but on July 1 in St. Helena.

Light Dragoon of 19th Century and Sailing Ship — A6

**Wmk. 314**

**1966, Aug. 15 Litho. *Perf. 14½***

**95** A6 3p pale green & multi .20 .20
**96** A6 6p tan & multi .20 .20
**97** A6 1sh6p gray & multi .50 .30
**98** A6 2sh6p multicolored .85 .45
*Nos. 95-98 (4)* 1.75 1.15

150th anniv. of the establishment of a garrison on Tristan da Cunha.

**WHO Headquarters Issue**
Common Design Type

**1966, Oct. 1 Litho. *Perf. 14***

**99** CD322 6p multicolored .35 .25
**100** CD322 5sh multicolored 1.90 1.00

**UNESCO Anniversary Issue**
Common Design Type

**1966, Dec. 1 Litho. *Perf. 14***

**101** CD323 10p "Education" .35 .20
**102** CD323 1sh6p "Science" .75 .40
**103** CD323 2sh6p "Culture" 1.40 .75
*Nos. 101-103 (3)* 2.50 1.35

Calshot Harbor A7

***Perf. 14x14½***

**1967, Jan. 2 Litho. Unwmk.**

**104** A7 6p dull green & multi .20 .20
**105** A7 10p brown & multi .20 .20
**106** A7 1sh6p dull blue & multi .20 .20
**107** A7 2sh6p orange brn & multi .25 .30
*Nos. 104-107 (4)* .85 .90

Opening of the artificial Calshot Harbor.

No. 76 Surcharged with New Value and Three Bars

***Perf. 11x11½***

**1967, May 10 Engr. Wmk. 314**

**108** A4 4p on 4½p blk & brn .30 .30

Tristan da Cunha, Prince Alfred, Queen Elizabeth II and Prince Philip — A8

**1967, July 10 Litho. *Perf. 14x14½***

**109** A8 3p blue grn, dk grn & blk .20 .20
**110** A8 6p dk carmine & blk .20 .20
**111** A8 1sh6p brt grn, gray grn & blk .20 .20
**112** A8 2sh6p dull ultra, sep & blk .25 .30
*Nos. 109-112 (4)* .85 .90

Cent. of the visit of Prince Alfred, First Duke of Edinburgh, to Tristan da Cunha.

Types of 1965

Designs: 4p, H.M.S. Challenger, 1870. 10sh, South African research vessel, R.S.A. £1, Queen Elizabeth II.

***Perf. 11x11½***

**1967, Sept. 1 Engr. Wmk. 314**

**113** A4 4p black & orange 5.25 3.75
**114** A4 10sh black & dull grn 16.00 14.00

***Perf. 11½x11***

**115** A5 £1 brn org & dk blue 16.00 *17.50*
*Nos. 113-115 (3)* 37.25 35.25

Wandering Albatross Nest — A9

Birds: 1sh, Big-billed buntings. 1sh6p, Tristan thrushes. 2sh6p, Great shearwaters.

***Perf. 14x14½***

**1968, May 15 Photo. Wmk. 314**

**116** A9 4p multicolored .20 .20
**117** A9 1sh multicolored .50 .30
**118** A9 1sh6p multicolored .85 .50
**119** A9 2sh6p multicolored 1.25 .85
*Nos. 116-119 (4)* 2.80 1.85

Union Jack and St. Helena Flag — A10

Design: 9p, 2sh6p, Map showing locations of St. Helena and Tristan da Cunha.

**1968, Nov. 1 Litho. Wmk. 314**

**120** A10 6p violet & multi .20 .20
**121** A10 9p brn, bl grn & vio bl .20 .20
**122** A10 1sh6p green & multi .25 .25
**123** A10 2sh6p dp car, bl grn & vio bl .35 .35
*Nos. 120-123 (4)* 1.00 1.00

30th anniv. of Tristan da Cunha as a Dependency of St. Helena.

Frigate A11

Designs: 1sh, Cape Horner. 1sh6p, Barque. 2sh6p, Tea Clipper.

***Perf. 11x11½***

**1969, June 1 Engr. Wmk. 314**

**124** A11 4p brt blue .20 .20
**125** A11 1sh rose carmine .45 .40
**126** A11 1sh6p green .65 .50
**127** A11 2sh6p sepia 1.10 .90
*Nos. 124-127 (4)* 2.40 2.00

Islanders Going to First Religious Service, 1851 — A12

Designs: 4p, Tristan da Cunha, birds and ship. 1sh6p, Landing at the beach. 2sh6p, St. Mary's Church, 1969, and procession.

***Perf. 14½x14***

**1969, Nov. 1 Litho. Wmk. 314**

**128** A12 4p multicolored .20 *.40*
**129** A12 9p multicolored .20 *.40*
**130** A12 1sh6p multicolored .35 *.55*
**131** A12 2sh6p multicolored .50 *.55*
*Nos. 128-131 (4)* 1.25 1.90

Issued to honor the work of the United Society for the Propagation of the Faith.

No. 77 Overprinted in Deep Orange: "NATIONAL / SAVINGS"

***Perf. 11x11½***

**1970, May 15 Engr. Wmk. 314**

**132** A4 6p black & green .30 .25

Issued to promote national savings. No. 132 also used as savings stamp.

In 1971, No. 132 was locally surcharged "2½p" and 3 short bars by means of a rubber handstamp.

Globe and Red Cross A13

1sh9p, 2sh6p, British & Red Cross flags, vert.

***Perf. 13½x13, 13x13½***

**1970, June 1 Litho.**

**133** A13 4p emer, red & grnsh bl .30 .20
**134** A13 9p bister, red & grnsh bl .45 .20
**135** A13 1sh9p gray, vio bl & red .75 .35
**136** A13 2sh6p rose cl, vio bl & red 1.00 .60
*Nos. 133-136 (4)* 2.50 1.35

Centenary of the British Red Cross Society.

Rock Lobster and Lobster Men Placing Trap — A14

10p, 2sh6p, Workers in processing plant and side view of rock lobster (jasus tristani).

***Perf. 12½x13***

**1970, Nov. 1 Litho. Wmk. 314**

**137** A14 4p lilac rose & multi .20 *.30*
**138** A14 10p dull yel & multi .25 *.35*
**139** A14 1sh6p brown org & multi .75 .60
**140** A14 2sh6p olive & multi 1.10 .75
*Nos. 137-140 (4)* 2.30 2.00

Tristan da Cunha rock lobster (crawfish) industry.

Nos. 72-74, 77-83, 113-114 Surcharged with New Value and Three Bars

***Perf. 11x11½***

**1971, Feb. 15 Engr. Wmk. 314**

**141** A4 ½p on 1p .20 .20
**142** A4 1p on 2p .20 .20
**143** A4 1½p on 4p .35 .20
**144** A4 2½p on 6p .35 .20
**145** A4 3p on 7p .35 .20
**146** A4 4p on 10p .35 .20
**147** A4 5p on 1sh .35 .20
**148** A4 7½p on 1sh6p 2.10 2.10
**149** A4 12½p on 2sh6p 3.00 3.00
**150** A4 15p on 1½p 3.00 3.50
**151** A4 25p on 5sh 3.00 *6.25*
**152** A4 50p on 10sh 4.25 *12.50*
*Nos. 141-152 (12)* 17.50 28.75

"Quest" — A15

4p, Presentation of Scout Troop flag in front of Tristan school. 7½p, Great Britain #167a with Tristan da Cunha cancellation. 12½p, Sir Ernest Henry Shackleton, boat & expedition cancellations.

***Perf. 13½x14***

**1971, June 1 Litho. Wmk. 314**

**153** A15 1½p lt blue & multi 1.10 .20
**154** A15 4p buff, yel grn & blk 1.10 .45
**155** A15 7½p pale grn, rose lil & blk 1.10 1.00
**156** A15 12½p buff & multi 1.50 1.75
*Nos. 153-156 (4)* 4.80 3.40

50th anniversary of the Shackleton-Rowett South Atlantic expedition.

"Victory" at Trafalgar and Thomas Swain Catching Nelson — A16

Ships and Island Families: 2½p, "Emily of Stonington" and inscribed P. W. Green, 1836. 4p, "Italia" and inscribed Gaetano Lavarello, 1892, and Andrea Repetto. 7½p, "Falmouth" and Corp. William Glass, 1816. 12½p, American Whaler and inscribed 1836 Joshua Rogers, 1849, Capt. Andrew Hangan.

**1971, Nov. 1**

**157** A16 1½p bister & multi .20 .20
**158** A16 2½p multicolored .25 .25
**159** A16 4p gray & multi .50 .55
**160** A16 7½p multicolored .80 .85
**161** A16 12½p blue & multi 1.25 1.40
*Nos. 157-161 (5)* 3.00 3.25

Cow Pudding — A17 Coxswain — A18

Native Flora: 1p, Peak berry and crater lake. 1½p, Sand flower, horiz. 2½p, New Zealand flax, horiz. 3p, Island tree. 4p, Bog fern and snow-capped mountain. 5p, Dog catcher and albatrosses. 7½p, Celery and terns. 12½p, Pepper tree and waterfall. 25p, Foul berry, horiz. 50p, Tussock and penguins. £1, Tussac and islands, horiz.

***Perf. 13½x13, 13x13½***

**1972, Feb. 26 Wmk. 314**

**162** A17 ½p gray & multi .20 .20
**163** A17 1p salmon & multi .20 .20
**164** A17 1½p green & multi .25 .25
**165** A17 2½p multicolored .25 .25
**166** A17 3p multicolored .25 .25
**167** A17 4p lemon & multi .35 .30
**168** A17 5p yel grn & multi .50 .30
**169** A17 7½p dull yel & multi 1.60 1.40
**170** A17 12½p multicolored 1.10 .80
**171** A17 25p gray & multi 2.10 1.90

**Litho. and Engr.**

**172** A17 50p multicolored 5.25 3.50
**173** A17 £1 lt blue & multi 9.25 3.50
*Nos. 162-173 (12)* 21.30 12.85

**1972, June 1 Litho. *Perf. 14***

2½p, Launching longboat. 4p, Men rowing longboat. 12½p, Longboat under sail.

**174** A18 2½p multi, horiz. .20 .20
**175** A18 4p multi, horiz. .20 .20
**176** A18 7½p multi .45 .30
**177** A18 12½p multi .75 .40
*Nos. 174-177 (4)* 1.60 1.10

**Silver Wedding Issue, 1972**
Common Design Type

Design: Queen Elizabeth II, Prince Philip, thrush and wandering albatrosses.

***Perf. 14x14½***

**1972, Nov. 20 Photo. Wmk. 314**

**178** CD324 2½p multicolored .20 .20
**179** CD324 7½p ultra & multi .50 .45

Altar, St. Mary's Church — A19

**1973, July 8 Litho. *Perf. 13½***

**180** A19 25p dk blue & multi 1.40 1.40

St. Mary's Church, Tristan da Cunha, 50th anniv.

"Challenger" off Tristan, Steil's Sounding Instrument — A20

Designs: 4p, Challenger's laboratory. 7½p, Challenger off Nightingale Island. 12½p, Map of Challenger's voyage. Each stamp shows an instrument for deep sea soundings.

***Perf. 13½x14***

**1973, Oct. 15 Wmk. 314**

**181** A20 4p multicolored .20 .20
**182** A20 5p multicolored .30 .30
**183** A20 7½p multicolored .50 .50
**184** A20 12½p multicolored 1.00 1.00
*a.* Souv. sheet, #181-184, perf. 13½ 2.25 2.25
*Nos. 181-184 (4)* 2.00 2.00

Centenary of "Challenger's" visit to Tristan da Cunha during oceanographic exploration world trip, 1872-76.

View of English Port from Shipboard — A21

5p, Inspectors at volcano rim. 7½p, Islanders disembarking from "Bornholm." 12½p, Islanders on board ship approaching Tristan da Cunha.

**1973, Nov. 10 *Perf. 14½***

**185** A21 4p yellow, blk & gold .20 .20
**186** A21 5p multicolored .25 .20
**187** A21 7½p multicolored .40 .30
**188** A21 12½p multicolored .55 .40
*Nos. 185-188 (4)* 1.40 1.10

10th anniversary of return of islanders to Tristan da Cunha.

**Princess Anne's Wedding Issue**

Common Design Type

**1973, Nov. 14 Wmk. 314 *Perf. 14***

**189** CD325 7½p multicolored .20 .20
**190** CD325 12½p bl grn & multi .25 .20

Rockhopper Penguin — A22

Designs: Rockhopper penguins.

**1974, May 1 Litho.**

**191** A22 2½p shown 2.50 1.25
**192** A22 5p Colony 2.75 1.65
**193** A22 7½p Penguins fishing 3.25 2.00
**194** A22 25p Penguin and fledgling 7.50 5.00
*Nos. 191-194 (4)* 16.00 9.90

Souvenir Sheet

Map of Tristan da Cunha, Penguin and Sea Gull — A23

**1974, Oct. 1 Wmk. 314 *Perf. 13½***

**195** A23 35p multicolored 4.25 3.75

Blenheim Palace A24

25p, Churchill and Queen Elizabeth II.

**Wmk. 373**

**1974, Nov. 30 Litho. *Perf. 14***

**196** A24 7½p black & yellow .20 .20
**197** A24 25p black & brown .50 .40
*a.* Souvenir sheet of 2, #196-197 1.10 1.10

Sir Winston Churchill (1874-1965).

Plocamium Fuscorubrum — A25

Aquatic Plants: 5p, Ulva lactuca. 10p, Epymenia flabellata. 20p, Macrocystis pyrifera.

***Perf. 13x14***

**1975, Apr. 16 Wmk. 314**

**198** A25 4p lilac & multi .20 .20
**199** A25 5p ultra & multi .20 .20
**200** A25 10p yellow & multi .40 .30
**201** A25 20p lt green & multi .75 .65
*Nos. 198-201 (4)* 1.55 1.35

Killer Whales — A26

**Wmk. 314**

**1975, Nov. 1 Litho. *Perf. 13½***

**202** A26 2p shown .30 .20
**203** A26 3p Rough-toothed dolphins .45 .20
**204** A26 5p Atlantic right whale 1.25 .60
**205** A26 20p Finback whales 3.00 1.40
*Nos. 202-205 (4)* 5.00 2.40

Tristan da Cunha No. 1 A27

Designs: 9p, Tristan da Cunha #13, vert. 25p, Freighter Tristania II.

***Perf. 13½x14, 14x13½***

**1976, May 6 Litho. Wmk. 373**

**206** A27 5p lilac, vio & blk .20 .20
**207** A27 9p bluish gray, grn & blk .25 .25
**208** A27 25p multicolored .85 .85
*a.* Souvenir sheet of 3 3.00 3.00
*Nos. 206-208 (3)* 1.30 1.30

Festival of Stamps 1976. #208a contains one each of Ascension #214, St. Helena #297 and Tristan da Cunha #208.

The Patches A28

Views, by Roland Svensson: 3p, Tristan house, vert. 10p, Tristan Settlement and Cliffs. 20p, Huts at Nightingale, vert.

**1976, Oct. 4 Litho. *Perf. 14***

**209** A28 3p multicolored .20 .20
**210** A28 5p multicolored .20 .20
**211** A28 10p multicolored .25 .25
**212** A28 20p multicolored .45 .45
*a.* Souvenir sheet of 4, #209-211 1.25 1.10
*Nos. 209-212 (4)* 1.10 1.10

An artist's view of Tristan da Cunha. See Nos. 234-237, 268-271.

Royal Yacht Britannia — A29

15p, Royal standard. 25p, Royal family.

**1977, Feb. 7 Wmk. 373 *Perf. 13***

**213** A29 10p multicolored .20 .20
**214** A29 15p multicolored .20 .20
**215** A29 25p multicolored .25 .25
*Nos. 213-215 (3)* .65 .65

25th anniv. of the reign of Elizabeth II. For surcharges see Nos. 220-221.

H.M.S. Eskimo, Sept. 1970 A30

Royal Naval Ships and Arms: 10p, Naiad, Nov. 1968. 15p, Jaguar, Mar. 1964. 20p, London, Dec. 1964. Dates of visits to island.

**1977, Oct. 1 Litho. *Perf. 14½***

**216** A30 5p multicolored .20 .20
**217** A30 10p multicolored .20 .20
**218** A30 15p multicolored .25 .25
**219** A30 20p multicolored .35 .35
*a.* Souvenir sheet of 4, #216-219 1.75 1.75
*Nos. 216-219 (4)* 1.00 1.00

Nos. 214-215 Surcharged with New Value and Bar

**1977, Oct. 13 Wmk. 373 *Perf. 13***

**220** A29 4p on 15p multi 2.25 *4.50*
**221** A29 7½p on 25p multi 2.25 *4.50*

Giant Fulmars — A31

***Perf. 13½x14, 14x13½***

**1977, Dec. 1 Litho.**

**222** A31 1p Pterodroma macroptera, horiz. .20 *.45*
**223** A31 2p Fregetta marina, horiz. .20 *.75*
**224** A31 3p Macronectes giganteus .20 *.75*
**225** A31 4p Pterodroma mollis .20 *.85*
**226** A31 5p Diomedea exulans .20 *.85*
**227** A31 10p Pterodroma brevirostris .30 *.85*
**228** A31 15p Sterna vittata .50 *1.10*
**229** A31 20p Puffinus gravis .65 *1.10*
**230** A31 25p Pachyptila vittata .80 *1.10*
**231** A31 50p Catharacta skua 1.75 1.10
**232** A31 £1 Pelecanoides urinatrix 2.50 2.00
**233** A31 £2 Diomedea chlororynchos 5.50 2.75
*Nos. 222-233 (12)* 13.00 13.65

Nos. 224-233 are vertical. For overprints see Nos. 318-319.

Painting Type of 1976

Views by Roland Svensson: 5p, St. Mary's Church. 10p, Longboats. 15p, A Tristan home. 20p, Harbor, 1970.

**Wmk. 373**

**1978, Mar. 1 Litho. *Perf. 14½***

**234** A28 5p multicolored .20 .20
**235** A28 10p multicolored .20 .20
**236** A28 15p multicolored .25 .25
**237** A28 20p multicolored .35 .35
*a.* Souvenir sheet of 4, #234-237 1.50 1.50
*Nos. 234-237 (4)* 1.00 1.00

An artist's view of Tristan da Cunha.

**Elizabeth II Coronation Anniversary**

Common Design Types

Souvenir Sheet

**1978, Apr. 21 Unwmk. *Perf. 15***

**238** Sheet of 6 1.40 1.40
*a.* CD326 25p King's Bull .25 .25
*b.* CD327 25p Elizabeth II .25 .25
*c.* CD328 25p Tristan crawfish .25 .25

No. 238 contains 2 se-tenant strips of Nos. 238a-238c, separated by horizontal gutter with commemorative and descriptive inscriptions and showing central part of coronation procession with coach.

Sodalite — A32

Local Minerals: 5p, Aragonite. 10p, Sulphur. 20p, Lava containing pyroxene crystal.

***Perf. 13½x14***

**1978, June 9 Litho. Wmk. 373**

**239** A32 3p multicolored .40 .40
**240** A32 5p multicolored .45 .45
**241** A32 10p multicolored .70 .70
**242** A32 20p multicolored 1.00 1.00
*Nos. 239-242 (4)* 2.55 2.55

Fish A33

**1978, Sept. 29 Litho. *Perf. 14***

**243** A33 5p Klipfish .20 .20
**244** A33 10p Fivefinger .20 .20
**245** A33 15p Concha .30 .30
**246** A33 20p Soldier .40 .40
*Nos. 243-246 (4)* 1.10 1.10

Orangeleaf and Navy Flag — A34

Royal Fleet Auxiliary Vessels: 10p, Tarbatness. 20p, Tidereach. 25p, Reliant.

**1978, Nov. 24 Litho. *Perf. 12½***

**247** A34 5p multicolored .25 .25
**248** A34 10p multicolored .25 .25
**249** A34 20p multicolored .35 .35

**250** A34 25p multicolored .40 .40
*a.* Souvenir sheet of 4, #247-250 1.50 *2.75*
*Nos. 247-250 (4)* 1.25 1.25

Fur Seals — A35

Wildlife conservation: 5p, Elephant seal. 15p, Tristan thrush. 20p, Tristan buntings.

**Wmk. 373**

**1979, Jan. 3 Litho. *Perf. 14***
**251** A35 5p multicolored .20 .20
**252** A35 10p multicolored .20 .20
**253** A35 15p multicolored .25 .25
**254** A35 20p multicolored .35 .35
*Nos. 251-254 (4)* 1.00 1.00

Tristan Longboat — A36

Ships: 10p, Queen Mary. 15p, Queen Elizabeth. 20p, QE II. 25p, QE II, longboat, view of Tristan.

**1979, Feb. 8 *Perf. 14½***
**255** A36 5p multicolored .20 .20
**256** A36 10p multicolored .20 .20
**257** A36 15p multicolored .25 .25
**258** A36 20p multicolored .35 .35
*Nos. 255-258 (4)* 1.00 1.00

**Souvenir Sheet**

**259** A36 25p multicolored *1.00 1.50*

Visit of cruise ship QE II, Feb. 8.

Tristan da Cunha No. 12 A37

Tristan da Cunha Stamps: 10p, No. 26. 25p, No. 58, vert. 50p, 1p-local "potatoe" stamp.

***Perf. 14½x14, 14x14½***

**1979, Aug. 27 Litho. Wmk. 373**
**260** A37 5p multicolored .20 .20
**261** A37 10p multicolored .20 .20
**262** A37 25p multicolored .40 .40
*Nos. 260-262 (3)* .80 .80

**Souvenir Sheet**

**263** A37 50p multicolored .75 .75

Sir Rowland Hill (1795-1879), originator of penny postage.

The Padre's House, IYC Emblem A38

IYC Emblem, Children's Drawings: 10p, "Houses in the Village." 15p, "St. Mary's Church." 20p, "Rockhopper Penguins."

**1979, Nov. 26 Litho. *Perf. 14***
**264** A38 5p multicolored .20 .20
**265** A38 10p multicolored .20 .20
**266** A38 15p multicolored .20 .20
**267** A38 20p multicolored .25 .25
*Nos. 264-267 (4)* .85 .85

International Year of the Child.

Painting Type of 1976

Views (Sketches by Roland Svensson):5p, Stoltenhoff Island. 10p, Nightingale from the East. 15p, The Administrator's abode, vert. 20p, "Ridge where the goat jumped off," vert.

**1980, Feb. Litho. *Perf. 14***
**268** A28 5p multicolored .20 .20
**269** A28 10p multicolored .20 .20
**270** A28 15p multicolored .20 .20
**271** A28 20p multicolored .25 .25
*a.* Souvenir sheet of 4, #268-271 .90 .90
*Nos. 268-271 (4)* .85 .85

Mail Pickup Boat — A40

Golden Hinde — A41

**1980, May 6 Litho. *Perf. 14***
**272** A40 5p shown .20 .20
**273** A40 10p Unloading mail .20 .20
**274** A40 15p Truck transport .20 .20
**275** A40 20p Delivery bell .20 .20
**276** A40 25p Distribution .30 .30
*Nos. 272-276 (5)* 1.10 1.10

London 80 Intl. Stamp Exhib., May 6-14.

**Queen Mother Elizabeth Birthday**

Common Design Type

**1980, Aug. 11 Litho. *Perf. 14***
**277** CD330 14p multicolored .30 .30

**1980, Sept. 6 *Perf. 14½***
**278** A41 5p shown .20 .20
**279** A41 10p Drake's route .20 .20
**280** A41 20p Sir Francis Drake .25 .25
**281** A41 25p Queen Elizabeth I .35 .35
*Nos. 278-281 (4)* 1.00 1.00

Sir Francis Drake's circumnavigation, 400th anniversary.

Humpty Dumpty A42

**Wmk. 373**

**1980, Oct. 31 Litho. *Perf. 13½***
**282** Sheet of 9 2.10 2.10
*a.* A42 15p shown .20 .20
*b.* A42 15p Mary had a Little Lamb .20 .20
*c.* A42 15p Little Jack Horner .20 .20
*d.* A42 15p Hey Diddle Diddle .20 .20
*e.* A42 15p London Bridge .20 .20
*f.* A42 15p Old King Cole .20 .20
*g.* A42 15p Sing a Song of Sixpence .20 .20
*h.* A42 15p Tom Tom the Piper's Son .20 .20
*i.* A42 25p Owl and the Pussy Cat .20 .20

Christmas 1980.

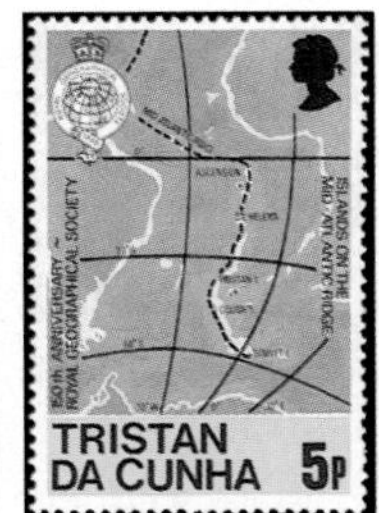


Islands on Mid-Atlantic Ridge, Society Emblem — A43

Royal Geographical Soc., 150th Anniv. (Maps and Expeditions): 10p, Tristan da Cunha, Francis Beaufort, 1806. 15p, Tristan Island, Norwegian expedition, 1937-1938. 20p, Gough Island, scientific survey, 1955-1956.

**1980, Dec. 15**
**283** A43 5p multicolored .20 .20
**284** A43 10p multicolored .20 .20
**285** A43 15p multicolored .25 .25
**286** A43 20p multicolored .35 .35
*Nos. 283-286 (4)* 1.00 1.00

Rev. Edwin Dodgson A44

**Wmk. 373**

**1981, Mar. 23 Litho. *Perf. 14***
**287** A44 10p portrait, vert. .20 .20
**288** A44 20p shown .35 .35
**289** A44 30p Dodgson preaching, vert. .45 .45
*a.* Souvenir sheet of 3, #287-289 1.00 1.00
*Nos. 287-289 (3)* 1.00 1.00

Centenary of arrival of Rev. Edwin H. Dodgson, who saved population from starvation.

Map of Tristan da Cunha showing L'heure du Berger Route, 1767 (Dalrymple's Map, 1781) — A45

Early Maps and Charts By: 5p, 21p, Capt. Denham, 1853 (diff.). 35p, Ivan Keulen, 1700.

**1981, May 22**
**290** A45 5p multicolored .20 .20
**291** A45 14p multicolored .40 .30
**292** A45 21p multicolored .50 .50
*Nos. 290-292 (3)* 1.10 1.00

**Souvenir Sheet**

**293** A45 35p multicolored .60 *.75*

**Royal Wedding Issue**

Common Design Type

**Wmk. 373**

**1981, July 22 Litho. *Perf. 14***
**294** CD331 5p Bouquet .20 .20
**295** CD331 20p Charles .20 .20
**296** CD331 50p Couple .35 .35
*Nos. 294-296 (3)* .75 .75

Hiking — A46

**1981, Sept. 14**
**297** A46 5p shown .20 .20
**298** A46 10p Camping .20 .20
**299** A46 20p Map reading .25 .25
**300** A46 25p Prince Philip .35 .25
*Nos. 297-300 (4)* 1.00 .90

Duke of Edinburgh's Awards, 25th anniv.

Inaccessible Island Rail — A47

**1981, Nov. 1 Litho. *Perf. 13½x14***
**301** Strip of 4 1.40 1.40
*a.* A47 10p Nest .30 .30
*b.* A47 10p Eggs .30 .30
*c.* A47 10p Chicks .30 .30
*d.* A47 10p Adult rail .30 .30

Six-gilled Shark A48

**1982, Feb. 8 Litho. *Perf. 13½x14***
**302** A48 5p shown .20 .20
**303** A48 14p Porbeagle shark .40 .25
**304** A48 21p Blue shark .65 .50
**305** A48 35p Hammerhead shark .95 .75
*Nos. 302-305 (4)* 2.20 1.70

Marcella — A49

**1982, Apr. 5 Litho. *Perf. 14***
**306** A49 5p shown .35 .35
**307** A49 15p Eliza Adams .35 .55
**308** A49 30p Corinthian .50 .75
**309** A49 50p Samuel & Thomas .80 1.00
*Nos. 306-309 (4)* 2.00 2.65

See Nos. 324-327.

**Princess Diana Issue**

Common Design Type

***Perf. 14½x14***

**1982, July 1 Litho. Wmk. 373**
**310** CD333 5p Arms .25 .20
**311** CD333 15p Diana .75 .20
**312** CD333 30p Wedding 1.50 .35
**313** CD333 50p Portrait 2.25 .60
*Nos. 310-313 (4)* 4.75 1.35

Scouting Year — A50

***Perf. 13½x13, 13x13½***

**1982, Aug. 23 Litho.**
**314** A50 5p Baden-Powell, vert. .20 .20
**315** A50 20p Brownsea Isld. camp, 1907, vert. .35 .35
**316** A50 50p Saluting .95 .95
*Nos. 314-316 (3)* 1.50 1.50

**Souvenir Sheet**

***Perf. 14***

**317** A50 50p Tree illustration, vert. 1.25 1.10

Nos. 226, 230 Overprinted: "1st PARTICIPATION / COMMONWEALTH / GAMES 1982"

***Perf. 13½x14***

**1982, Sept. 28 Litho. Wmk. 373**
**318** A31 5p multicolored .20 .20
**319** A31 25p multicolored .40 .40

12th Commonwealth Games, Brisbane, Australia, Sept. 30-Oct. 9.

Formation of Volcanic Island A51

**1982, Nov. 1 *Perf. 14x14½***
**320** A51 5p shown .25 .25
**321** A51 15p Surface cinder cones .40 .40
**322** A51 25p Eruption .50 .50
**323** A51 35p 1961 eruption .60 .60
*Nos. 320-323 (4)* 1.75 1.75

Ship Type of 1982

**1983, Feb. 1 Litho. *Perf. 14***

**324** A49 5p Islander, vert. .20 .20
**325** A49 20p Roscoe .50 .50
**326** A49 35p Columbia .90 .75
**327** A49 50p Emeline, vert. 1.25 1.10
*Nos. 324-327 (4)* 2.85 2.55

Tractor Pulling Trailer A52

**1983, May 2 Litho. *Perf. 14***

**328** A52 5p shown .20 .20
**329** A52 15p Pack mules .25 .20
**330** A52 30p Oxen pulling cart .50 .40
**331** A52 50p Jeep .80 .60
*Nos. 328-331 (4)* 1.75 1.40

Map of South Atlantic A53

Island History.

**Wmk. 373**

**1983, Aug. 1 Litho. *Perf. 14***

**332** A53 1p shown .20 .20
**333** A53 3p Tristao d'Acunha's flag-ship .20 .20
**334** A53 4p Landing, 1643 .20 .20
**335** A53 5p 17th cent. views .20 .20
**336** A53 10p Landing party, 1815 .25 .20
**337** A53 15p Settlement .35 .45
**338** A53 18p Governor Glass's house .45 .50
**339** A53 20p Rev. W.F. Taylor, Peter Green .50 .60
**340** A53 25p Three-master John and Elizabeth .60 .75
**341** A53 50p Dependency declaration of St. Helena, 1938 1.25 1.50
**342** A53 £1 Commissioning ceremony 2.50 3.00
**343** A53 £2 Evacuation, 1961 5.25 6.00
*Nos. 332-343 (12)* 11.95 13.80

Raphael, 500th Birth Anniv. — A54

**1983, Oct. 27 Litho. *Perf. 14½***

**344** A54 10p multicolored .25 .20
**345** A54 25p multicolored .65 .50
**346** A54 40p multicolored 1.10 .90
*Nos. 344-346 (3)* 2.00 1.60

**Souvenir Sheet**

**347** A54 50p multi, horiz. 1.50 1.25

Details from Christ's Charge to St. Peter.

St. Helena Colony Sesquicentenary — A55

**1984, Jan. 3 Litho. *Perf. 14***

**348** A55 10p No. 7 .20 .20
**349** A55 15p No. 9 .30 .25
**350** A55 25p No. 10 .50 .40
**351** A55 60p No. 12 1.25 1.00
*Nos. 348-351 (4)* 2.25 1.85

Local Fungi A56

**1984, Mar. 26**

**352** A56 10p Agrocybe praecox, vert. .65 *.75*
**353** A56 20p Laccaria tetraspora, vert. 1.00 1.00
**354** A56 30p Agrocybe cylindracea 1.50 1.50
**355** A56 50p Sarcoscypha coccinea 2.25 2.25
*Nos. 352-355 (4)* 5.40 5.50

Constellations A57

Sheep Shearing — A58

**1984, July 30 *Perf. 14½***

**356** A57 10p Orion .25 .20
**357** A57 20p Scorpius .55 .45
**358** A57 25p Canis Major .65 .55
**359** A57 50p Crux 1.40 1.10
*Nos. 356-359 (4)* 2.85 2.30

**1984, Oct. 1**

**360** A58 9p shown .25 .20
**361** A58 17p Carding wool .40 .35
**362** A58 29p Spinning .70 .60
**363** A58 45p Knitting 1.10 1.00
*a.* Souvenir sheet of 4, #360-363 2.60 2.25
*Nos. 360-363 (4)* 2.45 2.15

Stamps from No. 363a do not have white border around the design.

Christmas 1984 A59

**1984, Dec. 3 *Perf. 14***

**364** A59 10p Three angels, Christmas dinner .25 .20
**365** A59 20p Two angels, cart .50 .45
**366** A59 30p Candles, sailboat .80 .70
**367** A59 50p Trees, Nativity 1.25 1.10
*Nos. 364-367 (4)* 2.80 2.45

Shipwrecks — A60

**1985, Feb. 4 *Perf. 14x13½, 13½x14***

**368** A60 10p HMS Julia, 1817, vert. .90 .45
**369** A60 25p Bell from Mabel Clark, 1878, vert. 1.40 1.10
**370** A60 35p Barque Glenhuntley, 1898 2.00 1.50
*Nos. 368-370 (3)* 4.30 3.05

**Souvenir Sheet**

**371** A60 60p Map of shipwreck sites 2.40 1.90

No. 371 contains one 48x32mm stamp. See Nos. 393-396, 412-415.

**Queen Mother 85th Birthday**
Common Design Type
***Perf. 14½x14***

**1985, June 7 Litho. Wmk. 384**

**372** CD336 10p With Prince Charles, 1954 .30 .30
**373** CD336 20p With Margaret at Ascot .55 .55
**374** CD336 30p Queen Mother .80 .80
**375** CD336 50p Holding Prince Henry 1.00 1.00
*Nos. 372-375 (4)* 2.65 2.65

**Souvenir Sheet**

**376** CD336 80p With Anne 2.50 2.50

Flags A61

10p, Jonathan Lambert & flag of 1811, Isles of Refreshment. 15p, Cannon & flag of 21st Light Dragoons, 1816-17, Fort Malcolm. 25p, HMS Falmouth, 1816, & flag of HMS Atlantic Isle, HMS JOB 9, 1942-46. 60p, View of Tristan & Union Jack, 1816 to date.

**1985, Sept. 30 Wmk. 373 *Perf. 14***

**377** A61 10p multicolored .50 .40
**378** A61 15p multicolored .65 .55
**379** A61 25p multicolored 1.10 1.00
**380** A61 60p multicolored 3.00 2.25
*Nos. 377-380 (4)* 5.25 4.20

Nos. 378-380 vert.

Loss of The Lifeboat, Cent. — A62

**1985, Nov. 28**

**381** A62 10p Lifeboat, barque West Riding .30 .30
**382** A62 30p Map .90 .90
**383** A62 50p Death toll 1.50 1.50
*Nos. 381-383 (3)* 2.70 2.70

Halley's Comet A63

**1986, Mar. 3 Wmk. 384**

**384** A63 10p Bayeux Tapestry, c. 1092 .50 .50
**385** A63 20p Trajectory around Earth .90 .90
**386** A63 30p Comet over Inaccessible Is. 1.25 1.25
**387** A63 50p Ship Paramour 2.00 2.00
*Nos. 384-387 (4)* 4.65 4.65

**Queen Elizabeth II 60th Birthday**
Common Design Type

Designs: 10p, With Prince Charles, 1950. 15p, Birthday Parade, wearing uniform of Scots Guards, 1976. 25p, At Westminster Abbey, London, 1972, wearing mantle and robes of the Most Noble Order of Bath. 45p, Silver Jubilee Tour, Canada, 1977. 65p, Visiting Crown Agents' offices, 1983.

**1986, Apr. 21 *Perf. 14½***

**388** CD337 10p scarlet, blk & sil .25 .25
**389** CD337 15p ultra & multi .35 .35
**390** CD337 25p green & multi .60 .60
**391** CD337 45p violet & multi 1.00 1.00
**392** CD337 65p rose vio & multi 1.40 1.40
*Nos. 388-392 (5)* 3.60 3.60

For overprints see Nos. 429-433.

**Shipwrecks Type of 1985**

**1986, June 2 *Perf. 13½***

**393** A60 9p SV Allanshaw, 1893 .35 .35
**394** A60 20p Church font from Edward Vittery, 1881 .80 .75
**395** A60 40p Figurehead, 1940 1.75 1.60
*Nos. 393-395 (3)* 2.90 2.70

**Souvenir Sheet**
***Perf. 13½x13***

**396** A60 65p Barque Italia, 1892 2.75 2.75

Nos. 394-395 vert.

**Royal Wedding Issue, 1986**
Common Design Type

Designs: 10p, Informal portrait. 40p, Andrew operating helicopter.

**1986, July 23 *Perf. 14***

**397** CD338 10p multicolored .25 .25
**398** CD338 40p multicolored 1.25 1.25

A64

A65

**1986, Sept. 30**

**399** A64 5p Wandering albatross .20 .20
**400** A64 10p Daisy .40 .35
**401** A64 20p Vanessa butterfly .75 .70
**402** A64 25p Wilkins's bunting .95 .85
**403** A64 50p Ring-eye 1.90 1.75
*Nos. 399-403 (5)* 4.20 3.85

Flora & fauna of Inaccessible Island.

**1987, Jan. 23 *Perf. 14½***

Indigenous Flightless Species and Habitats: 10p, Flightless moth, Edinburgh Settlement. 25p, Strap-winged fly, Crater Lake. 35p, Flightless rail, Inaccessible Island. 50p, Gough Island moorhen, Gough Island.

**404** A65 10p multicolored .30 .30
**405** A65 25p multicolored .80 .80
**406** A65 35p multicolored 1.10 1.10
**407** A65 50p multicolored 1.60 1.60
*Nos. 404-407 (4)* 3.80 3.80

Rockhopper Penguins A66

**1987, June 22**

**408** A66 10p Swimming .60 .60
**409** A66 20p Nesting 1.25 1.25
**410** A66 30p Adult and young 1.90 1.90
**411** A66 50p Adult's head 3.50 3.50
*Nos. 408-411 (4)* 7.25 7.25

**Shipwrecks Type of 1985**

Designs: 11p, Castaways attacking sea elephant, vert. 17p, Henry A. Paull, 1879, Sandy Point. 45p, Gustav Stoltenhoff, Stoltenhoff Is., vert. 70p, Map of wrecks off Inaccessible Is.

**1987, Apr. 2 *Perf. 14***

**412** A60 11p olive gray & blk .60 .60
**413** A60 17p dark violet & blk 1.00 1.00
**414** A60 45p myrtle green & blk 3.00 3.00
*Nos. 412-414 (3)* 4.60 4.60

**Souvenir Sheet**

**415** A60 70p light blue, royal blue & apple grn 2.10 2.10

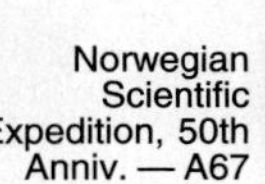

Norwegian Scientific Expedition, 50th Anniv. — A67

10p, Microscope and textbooks symbolic of expedition results. 20p, Scientists tagging a mollymawk. 30p, Expedition headquarters on the island. 50p, S.S. Thorshammer.

**Wmk. 384**

**1987, Dec. 7 Litho. *Perf. 14***

**416** A67 10p multicolored .85 .70
**417** A67 20p multicolored 1.75 1.25

**Wmk. 373**

**418** A67 30p multicolored 2.75 1.90
**419** A67 50p multicolored 4.25 3.25
*Nos. 416-419 (4)* 9.60 7.10

Fauna of Nightingale Island — A68

**1988, Mar. 21 Wmk. 384 *Perf. 14***

**420** A68 5p Tristan bunting .25 .25
**421** A68 10p Tristan thrush .50 .50
**422** A68 20p Yellow-nosed albatross .95 .95
**423** A68 25p Great shearwater 1.10 1.10
**424** A68 50p Elephant seal 2.50 2.50
*Nos. 420-424 (5)* 5.30 5.30

Handicrafts A69

**1988, May 30 *Perf. 14½***

**425** A69 10p Painted penguin eggs .35 .35
**426** A69 15p Moccasins .50 .50
**427** A69 35p Woolen clothing 1.25 1.25
**428** A69 50p Model canvas boats 1.75 1.75
*Nos. 425-428 (4)* 3.85 3.85

Nos. 388-392 Ovptd. "40TH WEDDING ANNIVERSARY" in Silver

**1988, Mar. 9**

**429** CD337 10p scar, blk & sil .25 .25
**430** CD337 15p ultra & multi .40 .40
**431** CD337 25p green & multi .65 .65
**432** CD337 45p violet & multi 1.10 1.10
**433** CD337 65p rose vio & multi 1.60 1.60
*Nos. 429-433 (5)* 4.00 4.00

19th Cent. Whaling A70

**1988, Oct. 6 *Perf. 14x14½***

**434** A70 10p "Trying out" blubber .70 .70
**435** A70 20p Harpoon guns 1.25 1.25
**436** A70 30p Scrimshaw 1.90 1.90
**437** A70 50p Ships 3.25 3.25
*Nos. 434-437 (4)* 7.10 7.10

**Souvenir Sheet**

**438** A70 £1 Right whale 4.50 4.50

**Lloyds of London, 300th Anniv.**

Common Design Type

10p, Lloyds's new building, 1988. 25p, Cargo ship *Tristania II*, horiz. 35p, Supply ship *St. Helena*, horiz. 50p, Square-rigger *Kobenhavn*, lost at sea.

**1988, Nov. 7 *Perf. 14***

**439** CD341 10p multicolored .45 .45
**440** CD341 25p multicolored 1.25 1.25
**441** CD341 35p multicolored 1.90 1.90
**442** CD341 50p multicolored 2.40 2.40
*Nos. 439-442 (4)* 6.00 6.00

Paintings of the Island, 1824, by Augustus Earle (1793-1838) — A71

Designs: 1p, Government House. 3p, Squall off Tristan. 4p, Rafting Blubber. 5p, Tristan. 10p, Man Killing an Albatross. 15p, View on the Summit. 20p, Nightingale Island. 25p, Tristan, diff. 35p, "Solitude," Watching the Horizon. 50p, North Eastern. £1, Tristan, diff. £2, Governor Glass and His Companions.

**1988, Dec. 10**

**443** A71 1p multicolored .20 .20
**444** A71 3p multicolored .20 .20
**445** A71 4p multicolored .20 .20
**446** A71 5p multicolored .20 .20
**447** A71 10p multicolored .30 .30
**448** A71 15p multicolored .45 .45
**449** A71 20p multicolored .60 .60
**450** A71 25p multicolored .75 .75
**451** A71 35p multicolored 1.10 1.10
**452** A71 50p multicolored 1.50 1.50
**453** A71 £1 multicolored 3.00 3.00
**454** A71 £2 multicolored 6.00 6.00
*Nos. 443-454 (12)* 14.50 14.50

Gough Is. Fauna — A72

Ferns — A73

**1989, Feb. 6 Litho. Wmk. 384**

**455** A72 5p Giant petrel .40 .40
**456** A72 10p Gough moorhen .75 .75
**457** A72 20p Gough bunting 1.40 1.40
**458** A72 25p Sooty albatross 1.60 1.60
**459** A72 50p Amsterdam fur seal 3.25 3.25
*Nos. 455-459 (5)* 7.40 7.40

**1989, May 22 Wmk. 373 *Perf. 14***

**460** A73 10p Eriosorus cheilanthoides .55 .55
**461** A73 25p Asplenium alvarezense 1.40 1.40
**462** A73 35p Elaphoglossum hybridum 2.00 2.00
**463** A73 50p Ophioglossum opacum 2.75 2.75
*Nos. 460-463 (4)* 6.70 6.70

A74

**1989, Nov. 20 Wmk. 384**

**464** A74 10p Cattle egret 1.10 .85
**465** A74 25p Spotted sandpiper 2.40 1.90
**466** A74 35p Purple gallinule 3.50 2.75
**467** A74 50p Barn swallow 4.50 3.75
*Nos. 464-467 (4)* 11.50 9.25

Artifacts on Exhibit in the Nautical Museum A75

**1989, Sept. 25**

**468** A75 10p Surgeon's mortar .60 .60
**469** A75 20p Parts of a harpoon 1.10 1.10
**470** A75 30p Compass with binnacle hood 1.75 1.75
**471** A75 60p Rope-twisting device 3.50 3.50
*Nos. 468-471 (4)* 6.95 6.95

Moths A76

**1990, Feb. 1 *Perf. 14***

**472** A76 10p Peridroma saucia .65 .65
**473** A76 15p Ascalapha odorata 1.00 1.00
**474** A76 35p Agrius cingulata 2.40 2.40
**475** A76 60p Eumorpha labruscae 4.25 4.25
*Nos. 472-475 (4)* 8.30 8.30

Starfish (Echinoderms) A77

**1990, June 12 *Perf. 14x13½***

**476** A77 10p shown .70 .70
**477** A77 20p multi, diff. 1.40 1.25
**478** A77 30p multi, diff. 2.25 1.90
**479** A77 60p multi, diff. 4.00 3.75
*Nos. 476-479 (4)* 8.35 7.60

**Queen Mother, 90th Birthday**

Common Design Types

**1990, Aug. 4 Wmk. 384 *Perf. 14x15***

**480** CD343 25p Queen Mother at the Coliseum 1.10 1.00

***Perf. 14½***

**481** CD344 £1 Broadcasting to women of the empire, 1939 4.75 4.25

Dunnottar Castle, 1942 — A78

Designs: 15p, RMS St. Helena, 1977-1990. 35p, Launching new RMS St. Helena, 1989. 60p, Duke of York launching new RMS St. Helena. £1, New RMS St. Helena.

**1990, Sept. 13 Wmk. 373 *Perf. 14½***

**482** A78 10p multicolored .80 .80
**483** A78 15p multicolored 1.25 1.25
**484** A78 35p multicolored 3.25 2.75
**485** A78 60p multicolored 5.25 4.50
*Nos. 482-485 (4)* 10.55 9.30

**Souvenir Sheet**

**486** A78 £1 multicolored 7.50 7.50

See Ascension Nos. 493-497, St. Helena Nos. 535-539.

Royal Navy Warships A79

***Perf. 14½x14***

**1990, Nov. 30 Litho. Wmk. 373**

**487** A79 10p Pyramus, 1829 1.10 1.00
**488** A79 25p Penguin, 1815 2.75 2.50
**489** A79 35p Thalia, 1886 3.75 3.50
**490** A79 50p Sidon, 1858 5.50 5.00
*Nos. 487-490 (4)* 13.10 12.00

See Nos. 547-550.

**1991, Feb. 4**

**491** A79 10p Milford, 1938 1.75 1.25
**492** A79 25p Dublin, 1923 2.75 2.25
**493** A79 35p Yarmouth, 1919 3.75 3.25
**494** A79 50p Carlisle, 1938 4.00 *4.75*
*Nos. 491-494 (4)* 12.25 11.50

**Souvenir Sheet**

Royal Viking Sun — A80

**Wmk. 384**

**1991, Apr. 1 Litho. *Perf. 14***

**495** A80 £1 multicolored 9.25 9.25

Prince Philip, 70th Birthday A81

Designs: 10p, HMS Galatea, Prince Alfred. 25p, Royal Visit, 1957. 30p, HMY Britannia, Prince Philip. 50p, Settlement of Edinburgh, Prince Philip.

**1991, June 10 Wmk. 373**

**496** A81 10p multicolored 1.10 1.00
**497** A81 25p multicolored 2.75 2.50
**498** A81 30p multicolored 3.50 3.00
**499** A81 50p multicolored 5.50 5.00
*Nos. 496-499 (4)* 12.85 11.50

Birds A82

**1991, Oct. 1**

**500** A82 8p Gough moorhens *2.50* 1.50
**501** A82 10p Gough bunting *2.50* 1.75
**502** A82 12p Gough moorhen in nest *2.75* 1.75
**503** A82 15p Gough bunting with chicks *3.00* 2.00
*Nos. 500-503 (4)* *10.75* 7.00

World Wildlife Fund.

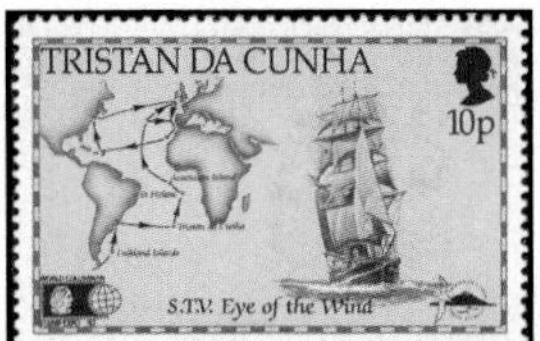

Discovery of America, 500th Anniv. — A83

**1992, Jan. 23**

**504** A83 10p STV Eye of the Wind .80 .65
**505** A83 15p STV Soren Larsen 1.10 .95
**506** A83 35p STV Pinta, Nina, Santa Maria 2.50 2.25
**507** A83 60p Columbus, Santa Maria 4.75 4.00
*Nos. 504-507 (4)* 9.15 7.85

World Columbian Stamp Expo '92, Chicago and Genoa '92 Intl. Philatelic Exhibitions.

### Queen Elizabeth II's Accession to the Throne, 40th Anniv.

Common Design Type

**1992, Feb. 6**

**508** CD349 10p multicolored .50 .45
**509** CD349 20p multicolored 1.00 .90
**510** CD349 25p multicolored 1.25 1.10
**511** CD349 35p multicolored 1.75 1.60
**512** CD349 65p multicolored 3.25 3.00
*Nos. 508-512 (5)* 7.75 7.05

Fish — A84

Designs: 10p, Caesioperca coatsii. 15p, Mendosoma lineatum. 35p, Physiculus karrerae. 60p, Decapterus longimanus.

**1992, June 1**

**513** A84 10p multicolored .80 .55
**514** A84 15p multicolored 1.25 .90
**515** A84 35p multicolored 2.50 2.00
**516** A84 60p multicolored 4.75 3.50
*Nos. 513-516 (4)* 9.30 6.95

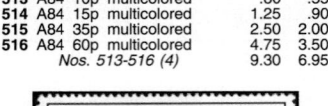

Wreck of the Italia, Cent. — A85

Designs: 10p, Italia leaving Greenock. 45p, In mid-Atlantic. 65p, Driving ashore on Stony Beach. £1, Italia in peaceful waters.

**1992, Sept. 18** ***Perf. 13½x14***

**517** A85 10p multicolored .85 .75
**518** A85 45p multicolored 3.50 3.25
**519** A85 65p multicolored 5.25 4.75
*Nos. 517-519 (3)* 9.60 8.75

**Souvenir Sheet**

**520** A85 £1 multicolored 9.75 9.75

Genoa '92 Intl. Philatelic Exhibition (#520).

Insects — A86

15p, Stenoscelis hylastoides. 45p, Trogloscaptomyza brevilamellata. 60p, Senilites tristanicola.

***Perf. 14x13½***

**1993, Feb. 2** **Litho.** **Wmk. 384**

**521** A86 15p multicolored 1.00 1.00
**522** A86 45p multicolored 3.25 3.25
**523** A86 60p multicolored 4.25 3.75
*Nos. 521-523 (3)* 8.50 8.00

Coronation of Queen Elizabeth II, 40th Anniv. — A87

Designs: 10p, Ampulla, spoon. 15p, Orb. 35p, Imperial State Crown. 60p, St. Edward's Crown.

**1993, June 14** ***Perf. 14½***

**524** A87 10p green & black .70 .60
**525** A87 15p red vio & black 1.00 .90
**526** A87 35p purple & black 2.25 2.00
**527** A87 60p blue & black 3.75 3.50
*Nos. 524-527 (4)* 7.70 7.00

Resettlement to Tristan, 30th Anniv. — A88

Ships: No. 528, Tristania, Frances Repetto. No. 529, Boissevain. 50p, Bornholm.

**1993, Nov. 10** ***Perf. 13½x14***

**528** A88 35p multicolored 2.75 2.50
**529** A88 35p multicolored 2.75 2.50
*a.* Pair, #528-529 5.50 5.00
**530** A88 50p multicolored 3.75 3.50
*Nos. 528-530 (3)* 9.25 8.50

Christmas — A89

Entire paintings or details: 5p, Madonna with Child, School of Botticelli. 15p, The Holy Family, by Daniel Gran. 35p, The Holy Virgin and Child, by Rubens. 65p, The Mystical Marriage of St. Catherine with the Holy Child, by Jan Van Balen.

**1993, Nov. 30** **Wmk. 373** ***Perf. 13***

**531** A89 5p multicolored .55 .55
**532** A89 15p multicolored 1.50 1.25
**533** A89 35p multicolored 3.50 2.75
**534** A89 65p multicolored 5.75 5.00
*Nos. 531-534 (4)* 11.30 9.55

Ships — A90

Designs: 1p, Duchess of Atholl, 1929. 3p, Empress of Australia, 1935. 5p, Anatolia, 1937. 8p, Viceroy of India, 1939. 10p, Rangitata, 1943. 15p, Caronia, 1950. 20p, Rotterdam, 1960. 25p, Leonardo da Vinci, 1972. 35p, Vistafjord, 1974. £1, World Discoverer, 1984. £2, Astor, 1984. £5, RMS St. Helena, 1992.

**1994, Feb. 3** **Wmk. 384** ***Perf. 14***

**535** A90 1p multicolored .25 .25
**536** A90 3p multicolored .25 .25
**537** A90 5p multicolored .25 .25
**538** A90 8p multicolored .25 .25
**539** A90 10p multicolored .35 .35
**540** A90 15p multicolored .50 .50
**541** A90 20p multicolored .65 .65
**542** A90 25p multicolored .85 .85
**543** A90 35p multicolored 1.25 1.25
**544** A90 £1 multicolored 3.25 3.25
**545** A90 £2 multicolored 6.50 6.50
**546** A90 £5 multicolored 17.00 17.00
*Nos. 535-546 (12)* 31.35 31.35

### Royal Navy Warships Type of 1990

**1994, May 2** **Wmk. 373**

**547** A79 10p HMS Nigeria, 1948 .90 .90
**548** A79 25p HMS Phoebe, 1949 2.25 2.25
**549** A79 35p HMS Liverpool, 1949 3.00 3.00
**550** A79 50p HMS Magpie, 1955 4.50 4.50
*Nos. 547-550 (4)* 10.65 10.65

Sharks — A91

**1994, Aug.** **Wmk. 384**

**551** A91 10p Blue shark .95 .95
**552** A91 45p Seven-gill shark 4.00 4.00
**553** A91 65p Mako shark 5.25 5.25
*Nos. 551-553 (3)* 10.20 10.20

Farm Animals — A92

**1994, Nov.** **Wmk. 373**

**554** A92 10p Donkeys .85 .85
**555** A92 20p Cattle 1.60 1.60
**556** A92 35p Ducks, geese 3.00 3.00
**557** A92 60p Girl feeding lamb 5.25 5.25
*Nos. 554-557 (4)* 10.70 10.70

Local Transport — A93

Designs: 15p, Pick-up truck. 20p, Leyland Daf Sherpa van. 45p, Yamaha motorcycle, scooter. 60p, Administrator's Landrover.

**Wmk. 384**

**1995, Feb. 27** **Litho.** ***Perf. 14***

**558** A93 15p multicolored 1.10 1.10
**559** A93 20p multicolored 1.40 1.40
**560** A93 45p multicolored 3.00 3.00
**561** A93 60p multicolored 4.25 4.25
*Nos. 558-561 (4)* 9.75 9.75

### End of World War II, 50th Anniv.

Common Design Types

Designs: 15p, Lewis gun instruction, 1943. 20p, Tristan defense volunteers, 1943-46. 45p, Radio, weather stations. 60p, HNS Birmingham, 1942.

£1, Reverse of War Medal, 1939-45.

***Perf. 13x13½***

**1995, June 19** **Litho.** **Wmk. 373**

**562** CD351 15p multicolored 1.25 1.25
**563** CD351 20p multicolored 1.75 1.75
**564** CD351 45p multicolored 3.50 3.50
**565** CD351 60p multicolored 5.00 5.00
*Nos. 562-565 (4)* 11.50 11.50

**Souvenir Sheet**

***Perf. 14***

**566** CD352 £1 multicolored 5.00 5.00

Souvenir Sheet

Queen Mother, 95th Birthday — A94

**1995, Aug. 4** **Litho.** ***Perf. 14½x14***

**567** A94 £1.50 multicolored 7.00 7.00

### UN, 50th Anniv.

Common Design Type

20p, Bedford 4-ton truck. 30p, Saxon armored personnel carrier. 45p, Mi26 heavy lift helicopter. 50p, RFA Sir Tristram transporting UN vehicles.

**1995, Oct. 24** ***Perf. 13½x13***

**568** CD353 20p multicolored 1.60 1.60
**569** CD353 30p multicolored 2.50 2.50
**570** CD353 45p multicolored 3.50 3.50
**571** CD353 50p multicolored 4.00 4.00
*Nos. 568-571 (4)* 11.60 11.60

Seals — A95

Sub Antarctic fur seal: 10p, On rock. 35p, Coming out of water with young.

Southern elephant seal: 45p, On beach with young. 50p, In water.

**1995, Nov. 3** ***Perf. 13½***

**572** A95 10p multicolored .75 .75
**573** A95 35p multicolored 2.75 2.75
**574** A95 45p multicolored 3.75 3.75
**575** A95 50p multicolored 4.00 4.00
*Nos. 572-575 (4)* 11.25 11.25

### Queen Elizabeth II, 70th Birthday

Common Design Type

Various portraits of Queen, island scenes: 15p, Tristan from sea. 20p, Traditional cottage. 45p, The Residency. 60p, With Prince Philip.

**1996, Apr. 22** **Litho.** ***Perf. 13½***

**576** CD354 15p multicolored .85 .85
**577** CD354 20p multicolored 1.10 1.10
**578** CD354 45p multicolored 2.50 2.50
**579** CD354 60p multicolored 3.25 3.25
*Nos. 576-579 (4)* 7.70 7.70

New Harbor — A96

15p, View of Old Harbor. 20p, Earthmoving, New Harbor construction. 45p, Crane, new construction. 60p, View of New Harbor. Nos. 581-582 are 45x28mm.

**1996, July 5** **Wmk. 373** ***Perf. 13***

**580** A96 15p multicolored 1.75 1.75
**581** A96 20p multicolored 2.75 2.75
**582** A96 45p multicolored 3.75 3.75
**583** A96 60p multicolored 4.50 4.50
*Nos. 580-583 (4)* 12.75 12.75

Nos. 581-582 are 45x28mm.

A97

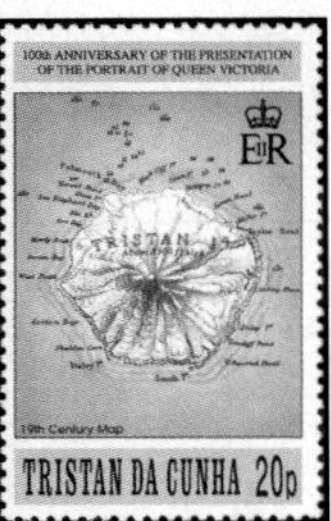

A98

Gough Island Birds: 15p, Gough moorhen. 20p, Wandering albatross. 45p, Sooty albatross. 60p, Gough bunting.

**1996, Oct. 1** ***Perf. 14***

**584** A97 15p multicolored .90 .90
**585** A97 20p multicolored 1.10 1.10
**586** A97 45p multicolored 2.50 2.50
**587** A97 60p multicolored 3.50 3.50
*a.* Souvenir sheet of 1 3.50 3.50
*Nos. 584-587 (4)* 8.00 8.00

No. 587a for return of Hong Kong to China, July 1, 1997. Issued 6/20/97.

**1996, Dec. 18** ***Perf. 13½***

Presentation of Portrait of Queen Victoria, Cent.: 20p, 19th cent. map of Trista da Cunha. 30p, HMS Magpie. 45p, Peter Green, former governor. 50p, Detail of portrait of Queen Victoria, by Heinrich Von Angell.

**588** A98 20p multicolored 1.25 1.25
**589** A98 30p multicolored 1.90 1.90
**590** A98 45p multicolored 2.75 2.75
**591** A98 50p multicolored 3.00 3.00
*Nos. 588-591 (4)* 8.90 8.90

Atlantic Marine Fauna of the Cretaceous — A99

Designs: a, Archelon. b, Trinacromerum. c, Platecarpus. d, Clidastes.

**1997, Feb. 10** **Wmk. 384** ***Perf. 14***

**592** A99 35p Sheet of 4, #a.-d. 8.75 8.75

See No. 619.

Visual Communications — A100

Designs: No. 593, Smoke signals. No. 594, HMS Eurydice. No. 595, HMS Challenger. No. 596, Flag hoists. No. 597, Semaphore. No. 598, HMS Carlisle. No. 599, Light signals. No. 600, HMS Cilicia.

**1997** **Litho.** **Wmk. 384** ***Perf. 14½***

**593** 10p multicolored .50 .50
**594** 10p multicolored .50 .50
*a.* A100 Pair, #593-594 1.00 1.00
**595** 15p multicolored .70 .70
**596** 15p multicolored .70 .70
*a.* A100 Pair, #595-596 1.40 1.40
**597** 20p multicolored .85 .85
**598** 20p multicolored .85 .85
*a.* A100 Pair, #597-598 1.75 1.75
**599** 35p multicolored 1.50 1.50
**600** 35p multicolored 1.50 1.50
*a.* Pair, #599-600 3.00 3.00
*Nos. 593-600 (8)* 7.10 7.10

### Farm Animals Type of 1994

**1997, Aug. 26** **Litho.** ***Perf. 14***

**601** A92 20p Chickens 1.00 1.00
**602** A92 30p Cattle 1.60 1.60
**603** A92 45p Sheep 2.40 2.40
**604** A92 50p Dogs 2.50 2.50
*Nos. 601-604 (4)* 7.50 7.50

Queen Elizabeth II and Prince Philip, 50th Wedding Anniv. — A101

Designs: No. 605, Queen up close. No. 606, Prince riding polo pony. No. 607, Queen with horse. No. 608, Prince up close. No. 609, Prince in military attire, Queen in green coat. No. 610, Princess Anne riding horse.

£1.50, Queen, Prince riding in open carriage, horiz.

**1997, Nov. 20** **Wmk. 373** ***Perf. 14***

**605** 15p multicolored .70 .70
**606** 15p multicolored .70 .70
*a.* A101 Pair, #605-606 1.40 1.40
**607** 20p multicolored 1.00 1.00
**608** 20p multicolored 1.00 1.00
*a.* A101 Pair, #607-608 2.00 2.00
**609** 45p multicolored 2.10 2.10
**610** 45p multicolored 2.10 2.10
*a.* A101 Pair, #609-610 4.25 4.25
*Nos. 605-610 (6)* 7.60 7.60

### Souvenir Sheet

**611** A101 £1.50 multicolored 8.00 8.00

First Lobster Survey, 50th Anniv. — A102

Ships: 15p, Hilary, Melodie. 20p, Tristania II, Hekla. 30p, Pequena, Frances Repetto. 45p, Tristania, Gillian Gaggins. 50p, MFV. Kelso, MV. Edinburgh.

£1.20, Fr. C.P. Lawrence, lobster.

**1998, Feb. 6** ***Perf. 14½***

**612** A102 15p multicolored .65 .65
**613** A102 20p multicolored .85 .85
**614** A102 30p multicolored 1.25 1.25
**615** A102 45p multicolored 2.00 2.00
**616** A102 50p multicolored 2.10 2.10
*Nos. 612-616 (5)* 6.85 6.85

### Souvenir Sheet

**617** A102 £1.20 multicolored 7.00 7.00

### Diana, Princess of Wales (1961-97)

Common Design Type

a, In beige dress. b, In white top with black collar. c, In striped top. d, In lilac & white print dress.

**1998, May 15** ***Perf. 14½x14***

**618** CD355 35p Strip of 4, #a.-d. 5.50 5.50

No. 618 sold for £1.40 + 20p with surtax from international sales going to the Princess Diana Memorial Fund and surtax from local sales going to a designated local charity.

### Atlantic Marine Fauna Type of 1997

Fauna of the Miocene Epoch: a, Carcharodon. b, Orycterocetus. c, Eurhinodelphis. d, Hexanchus (six gilled shark), myliobatis.

**1998, July 8** ***Perf. 14***

**619** A99 45p Sheet of 4, #a.-d. 8.75 8.75

Visiting Cruise Ships A103

**1998, Sept. 15** ***Perf. 14***

**620** A103 15p Livonia .95 .95
**621** A103 20p Professor Molchanov 1.25 1.25
**622** A103 45p Explorer 2.75 2.75
**623** A103 60p Hanseatic 3.75 3.75
*Nos. 620-623 (4)* 8.70 8.70

Sailing Ships A104

**1998, Nov. 23** **Wmk. 373** ***Perf. 14½***

**624** A104 15p H.G. Johnson, 1892 1.50 1.50
**625** A104 35p Theodore, 1893 2.75 2.75
**626** A104 45p Hesperides, 1893 3.75 3.75
**627** A104 50p Bessfield, 1894 4.00 4.00
*Nos. 624-627 (4)* 12.00 12.00

**1999, Mar. 19**

**628** A104 20p Derwent, 1895 2.00 2.00
**629** A104 30p Strathgryffe, 1898 2.75 2.75
**630** A104 50p Celestial Empire, 1898 4.00 4.00
**631** A104 60p Lamorna, 1902 4.25 4.25
*Nos. 628-631 (4)* 13.00 13.00
*Nos. 624-631 (8)* 25.00 25.00

Wandering Albatross — A105

World Wildlife Fund: 5p, Two adults. 8p, Adult, juvenile in nest. 12p, Adult spreading wings. 15p, Two in flight.

**1999, Apr. 27** **Wmk. 373** ***Perf. 14***

**632** A105 5p multicolored .65 .65
**633** A105 8p multicolored .70 .70
**634** A105 12p multicolored .75 .75
**635** A105 15p multicolored .85 .85
*a.* Strip of 4, #632-635 3.25 3.25
*Nos. 632-635 (4)* 2.95 2.95

Issued in sheets of 16.

### Wedding of Prince Edward and Sophie Rhys-Jones

Common Design Type

***Perf. 13¾x14***

**1999, June 18** **Litho.** **Wmk. 384**

**636** CD356 45c Separate portraits 1.75 1.75
**637** CD356 £1.20 Couple 4.50 4.50

### Queen Mother's Century

Common Design Type

Queen Mother: 20p, With Princess Elizabeth on her 18th birthday. 30p, With King George VI at Balmoral. 50p, With Royal Family, 94th birthday. 60p, As colonel-in-chief of Black Watch.

£1.50, Age 5 photo, airplanes from Battle of Britain, 1940.

**1999, Aug. 18** **Wmk. 384** ***Perf. 13½***

**638** CD358 20p multicolored .85 .85
**639** CD358 30p multicolored 1.25 1.25
**640** CD358 50p multicolored 2.10 2.10
**641** CD358 60p multicolored 2.50 2.50
*Nos. 638-641 (4)* 6.70 6.70

### Souvenir Sheet

**642** CD358 £1.50 black 6.25 6.25

Millennium — A106

Various birds.

**2000, Jan. 1** **Wmk. 373** ***Perf. 14***

**Color of Queen's Head**

**643** A106 20p bister .75 .75
**644** A106 30p green 1.10 1.10
**645** A106 50p blue 2.00 2.00
**646** A106 60p brown 2.50 2.50
*Nos. 643-646 (4)* 6.35 6.35

Royalty — A107

British monarchs on 8p-£5: 1p, King Manuel I of Portugal. 3p, Frederick Henry, Prince of Orange. 5p, Empress Maria Theresa of Austria. 8p, King George III. 10p, King George IV. 15p, King Willian IV. 20p, Queen Victoria. 25p, Edward VII. 35p, George V. £1, Edward VIII. £2, George VI. £5, Elizabeth II.

**2000, Feb. 1** **Wmk. 384** ***Perf. 14***

**647** A107 1p multi .20 .20
**648** A107 3p multi .20 .20
**649** A107 5p multi .20 .20
**650** A107 8p multi .25 .25
**651** A107 10p multi .35 .30
**652** A107 15p multi .55 .60
**653** A107 20p multi .70 .75
**654** A107 25p multi .90 .95
**655** A107 35p multi 1.25 1.40
**656** A107 £1 multi 3.50 4.00
**657** A107 £2 multi 7.50 8.00
**658** A107 £5 multi 18.00 19.00
*Nos. 647-658 (12)* 33.60 35.85

The Stamp Show 2000, London A108

Designs: 15p, Longboat under oars. 45p, Longboat under sail. 50p, Cutty Sark, 1876. 60p, Cutty Sark, 2000.

£1.50, Cutty Sark visiting Tristan da Cunha, 1876.

**Wmk. 373**

**2000, May 22** **Litho.** ***Perf. 14***

**659** A108 15p multi .60 .60
**660** A108 45p multi 1.75 1.75
**661** A108 50p multi 1.90 1.90
**662** A108 60p multi 2.25 2.25
*Nos. 659-662 (4)* 6.50 6.50

### Souvenir Sheet

**663** A108 £1.50 multi 7.00 7.00

### Prince William, 18th Birthday

Common Design Type

William: Nos. 664, 668a, As toddler, with Princes Charles and Harry, vert. Nos. 665, 668b, Holding paper, vert. Nos. 666, 668c, Wearing scarf. Nos. 667, 668d, Wearing suit and wearing sweater. No. 668e, As child, with Shetland pony.

***Perf. 13¾x14¼, 14¼x13¾***

**2000, June 21** **Litho.** **Wmk. 373**

**Stamps With White Border**

**664** CD359 45p multi 1.75 1.75
**665** CD359 45p multi 1.75 1.75
**666** CD359 45p multi 1.75 1.75
**667** CD359 45p multi 1.75 1.75
*Nos. 664-667 (4)* 7.00 7.00

### Souvenir Sheet

**Stamps Without White Border**

***Perf. 14¼***

**668** CD359 45p Sheet of 5, #a-e 8.50 8.50

Ships and Helicopters — A109

No. 669, 10p: a, SA Agulhas. b, SA 330J Puma, 1999.
No. 670, 15p: a, HMS London. b, Westland Wessex HAS 1, 1964.
No. 671, 20p: a, HMS Endurance. b, Westland Lynx HAS 3, 1996.
No. 672, 50p: a, USS Spiegel Grove. b, Sikorsky UH-19F, 1963.
Illustration reduced.

**Wmk. 373**
**2000, Sept. 4 Litho. *Perf. 14***
**Pairs, #a-b**
**669-672** A109 Set of 4 10.50 10.50

First Election of Winston Churchill to Parliament, Cent. — A110

Designs: 20p, During siege of Sidney Street, 1911. 30p, With Franklin D. Roosevelt, 1941. 50p, VE Day broadcast, 1945. 60p, Greeting Queen Elizabeth, 1955.

***Perf. 13¾x14***
**2000, Oct. 2 Wmk. 373**
**673-676** A110 Set of 4 6.25 6.25

Souvenir Sheet

New Year 2001 (Year of the Snake) — A111

No. 677: a, 30p, Inaccessible Island rail. b, 45p, Black-faced spoonbill.
Illustration reduced.

**Wmk. 373**
**2001, Feb. 1 Litho. *Perf. 14½***
**677** A111 Sheet of 2, #a-b 6.50 6.50

Hong Kong 2001 Stamp Exhibition.

Age of Victoria A112

Designs: 15p, Letter, 1846. 20p, Prince Alfred, Duke of Edinburgh, vert. 30p, HMS Galatea. 35p, Queen Victoria, vert. 50p, Charles Dickens, vert. 60p, Resupplying ships.
£1.50, Jubilee celebrations.

**Wmk. 373**
**2001, May 24 Litho. *Perf. 14***
**678-683** A112 Set of 6 8.50 8.50

**Souvenir Sheet**
**684** A112 £1.50 multi 6.75 6.75

Longboats — A113

No. 685: a, Boat with dark and light blue striped sails, island in distance. b, Boat with red and blue striped and white sails, boat with blue, red and yellow striped and blue and white striped sails. c, Prow and sail of boat, two boats in distance. d, Boat with blue red and yellow striped and blue and white striped sails. e, Boat with dark and light blue sails near shore. f, Boat with red and blue striped and white sails. g, Boat with gray, red and white sails. h, Boat with sails down.

**2001, July 12**
**685** A113 30p Sheet of 8, #a-h 6.75 6.75

Nos. 669-672 Overprinted in Blue Violet

Illustration reduced.

**Wmk. 373**
**2001, Sept. 17 Litho. *Perf. 14***

| | | | |
|---|---|---|---|
| **686** A109 10p Pair, #a-b | 1.00 | 1.00 |
| **687** A109 15p Pair, #a-b | 1.40 | 1.40 |
| **688** A109 20p Pair, #a-b | 1.90 | 1.90 |
| **689** A109 50p Pair, #a-b | 5.00 | 5.00 |
| *Nos. 686-689 (4)* | 9.30 | 9.30 |

Souvenir Sheet

Birdlife International World Bird Festival — A114

Spectacled petrel: a, Head. b, Diving (island in background). c, In flight with legs extended. d, Diving (sea in background). e, Chick.

**Wmk. 373**
**2001, Oct. 1 Litho. *Perf. 14½***
**690** A114 35p Sheet of 5, #a-e 5.25 5.25

Royal Navy Ships A115

Designs: No. 691, 20p, HMS Penguin, 1815. No. 692, 20p, HMS Julia, 1817. No. 693, 35p, HMS Beagle, 1901. No. 694, 35p, HMS Puma, 1962. No. 695, 60p, HMS Monmouth, 1997. No. 696, 60p, HMS Somerset, 1999.

**Wmk. 373**
**2001, Oct. 31 Litho. *Perf. 14***
**691-696** A115 Set of 6 7.50 7.50

Churches A116

Designs: No. 697, 35p, Exterior, St. Joseph's Catholic Church. No. 698, 35p, Exterior, St. Mary's Anglican Church. No. 699, 60p, Stained glass window, St. Joseph's. No. 700, 60p, Altar, St. Mary's.

***Perf. 13¼x13½, 13½x13¼***
**2001, Nov. 27**
**697-700** A116 Set of 4 7.50 7.50

Christmas, Arrival of first USPG missionary, 150th anniv.

Tristan da Cunha Postage Stamps, 50th Anniv. A117

Designs: Nos. 701, 45p, 705a, 45p, #5, 6, 9, 10 canceled. Nos. 702, 20p, 705, 45p, #7, 8, 11, 12 canceled. Nos. 703, 50p, 705c, 45p, #1-4 canceled. Nos. 704, 60p, 705d, 45p, Men at post office, 1952.

**2002, Jan. 1 *Perf. 13½***
**Without "Tristan da Cunha" in Script**
**701-704** A117 Set of 4 5.75 5.75

**Souvenir Sheet**
**With "Tristan da Cunha" in Script at Top or Bottom of Stamps**
**705** A117 45p Sheet of 4, #a-d 6.75 6.75

**Reign Of Queen Elizabeth II, 50th Anniv. Issue**
Common Design Type

Designs: Nos. 706, 710a, 15p, Princess Elizabeth, 1947. Nos. 707, 710b, 30p, Wearing tiara, 1991. Nos. 708, 710c, 45p, Wearing red coat. Nos. 709, 710d, 50p, Wearing purple hat, 1997. No. 710e, 60p, 1955 portrait by Annigoni (38x50mm).

***Perf. 14¼x14½, 13¾ (#710e)***
**2002, Feb. 6 Litho. Wmk. 373**
**With Gold Frames**
**706-709** CD360 Set of 4 4.00 4.00

**Souvenir Sheet**
**Without Gold Frames**
**710** CD360 Sheet of 5, #a-e 5.75 5.75

Fishing Industry A118

Designs: 20p, Pelagic armorhead. 35p, Yellowtail. 50p, Splendid alfonsino. 60p, Ship San Liberatore.

**Wmk. 373**
**2002, May Litho. *Perf. 14***

| | | |
|---|---|---|
| **711-713** A118 Set of 3 | 4.25 | 4.25 |
| **714** Souvenir sheet, #711-713, 714a | 5.00 | 5.00 |
| *a.* A118 60p multi | 1.75 | 1.75 |

**Queen Mother Elizabeth (1900-2002)**
Common Design Type

Designs: 20p, Wearing hat (black and white photograph). £1.50, Wearing blue green hat.
No. 717: a, 75p, Holding baby (black and white photograph). b, 75p, Wearing dark blue hat.

**Wmk. 373**
**2002, Aug. 5 Litho. *Perf. 14¼***
**With Purple Frames**
**715-716** CD361 Set of 2 6.50 6.50

**Souvenir Sheet**
**Without Purple Frames**
***Perf. 14½x14¼***
**717** CD361 Sheet of 2, #a-b 5.75 5.75

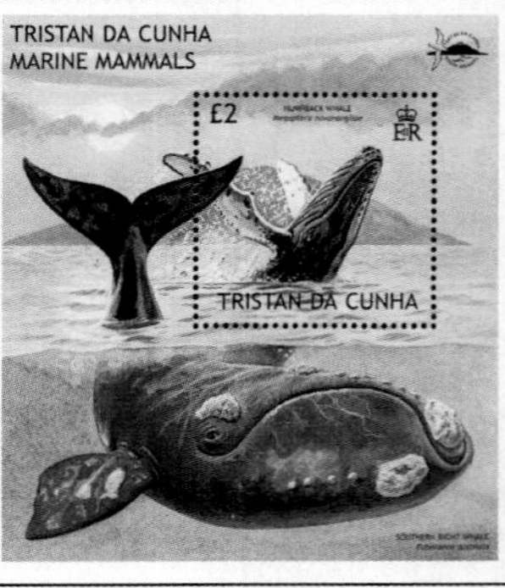


Marine Mammals — A119

No. 718: a, Gray's beaked whale. b, Dusky dolphin. c, False killer whale. d, Long-finned pilot whale. e, Sperm whale. f, Shepherd's beaked whale.
£2, Humpback whale.

**Wmk. 373**
**2002, Sept. 24 Litho. *Perf. 13¼***
**718** A119 30p Sheet of 6, #a-f 5.75 5.75

**Souvenir Sheet**
**719** A119 £2 multi 6.25 6.25

HMS Herald Survey, 150th Anniv. — A120

Designs: 20p, Captain Denham and officers. 35p, HMS Herald in Bay of Biscay. 50p, Surveying, Oct. 30, 1852. 60p, HMS Herald and Torch at sunset, 1852.

**2002, Nov. 11 *Perf. 14x14¾***
**720-723** A120 Set of 4 5.25 5.25

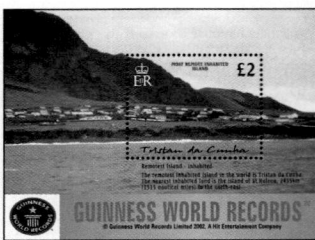

Guinness Book of World Records — A121

No. 724: a, Great Barrier Reef (longest reef). b, Greenland (biggest island). c, Sahara Desert (biggest desert). d, Amazon and Nile Rivers (longest rivers). e, Mt. Everest (biggest mountain). f, Tristan da Cunha (most remote inhabited island).
£2, Like No. 724f.

**Wmk. 373**
**2003, Jan. 10 Litho. *Perf. 13¾***
**724** A121 30p Sheet of 6, #a-f 6.75 6.75

**Souvenir Sheet**
**725** A121 £2 multi 7.50 7.50

Atlantic Yellow-nosed Albatross A122

Designs: Nos. 726, 730a, 15p, Heads of two birds. Nos. 727, 730b, 30p, Bird on nest, vert. Nos. 728, 730c, 45p, Bird in flight, vert. Nos. 729, 730d, Two birds in flight. No. 730e, £1, Two birds in flight, diff.

***Perf. 14¼x13¾, 13¾x14¼***

**2003, May 7 Litho.**

**Stamps With White Frames**

**726-729** A122 Set of 4 4.75 4.75

**Souvenir Sheet**

**Stamps Without Frames**

***Perf. 14¼x14½***

**730** A122 Sheet of 5, #a-e 9.00 9.00

Birdlife International.

**Head of Queen Elizabeth II**

Common Design Type

**Wmk. 373**

**2003, June 2 Litho.** ***Perf. 13¾***

**731** CD362 £2.80 multi 10.50 10.50

**Coronation of Queen Elizabeth II, 50th Anniv.**

Common Design Type

Designs: Nos. 732, 20p, 734a, Queen and extended family. Nos. 733, £1.50, 734b, Bishops paying homage to Queen at coronation.

***Perf. 14¼x14½***

**2003, June 2 Litho. Wmk. 373**

**Vignettes Framed, Red Background**

**732-733** CD363 Set of 2 6.50 6.50

**Souvenir Sheet**

**Vignettes Without Frame, Purple Panel**

**734** CD363 75p Sheet of 2, #a-b 5.75 5.75

**Prince William, 21st Birthday**

Common Design Type

No. 735: a, William in polo uniform at right. b, In sweater at left.

**Wmk. 373**

**2003, June 21 Litho.** ***Perf. 14¼***

**735** Horiz. pair 3.75 3.75

***a.-b.*** CD364 50p Either single 1.60 1.60

William Glass (1787-1853), Governor — A123

No. 736: a, Arrival of Glass on HMS Falmouth, 1816. b, As corporal, stationed on Tristan da Cunha. c, Glass and family onshore, 1817. d, Glass family with dog. e, Gov. Glass conducting daughter's marriage ceremony, 1833. f, Glass as old man.

***Perf. 14¼x14½***

**2003, Nov. 24 Litho. Wmk. 373**

**736** A123 30p Sheet of 6, #a-f, + 6 labels 6.00 6.00

Royal Navy Ships — A124

No. 737, 20p: a, RFA Tideflow. b, RFA Tidespring.

No. 738, 35p: a, RFA Gold Rover. b, RFA Diligence.

No. 739, 60p: a, RFA Wave Chief. b, HMY Britannia.

Illustration reduced.

**Wmk. 373**

**2003, Dec. 8 Litho.** ***Perf. 14***

**Horiz. pairs, #a-b**

**737-739** A124 Set of 3 8.00 8.00

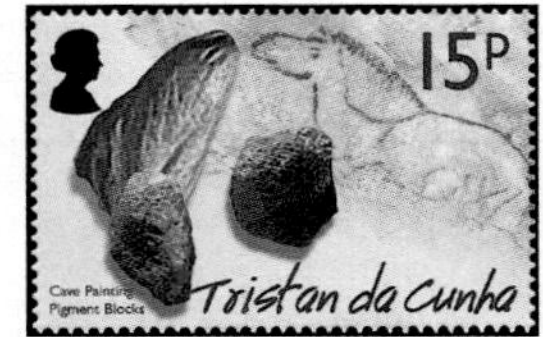


History of Writing Implements — A125

Designs: 15p, Cave paintings and pigment blocks. 20p, Clay tablet. 35p, Egyptian writing palette. 45p, Goose quill pen. 50p, Fountain pen. 60p, Ballpoint pen.

£1.50, Word processing.

**2004, Jan. 8** ***Perf. 13¾***

**740-745** A125 Set of 6 8.50 8.50

**Souvenir Sheet**

**Litho. with Margin Embossed**

**746** A125 £1.50 multi 5.75 5.75

Worldwide Fund for Nature (WWF) — A126

Subantarctic fur seal: No. 747, 35p, Underwater. No. 748, 35p, Pair on rocks. No. 749, 35p, Seal on rock. No. 750, 35p, Head.

**Wmk. 373**

**2004, July 12 Litho.** ***Perf. 14***

**747-750** A126 Set of 4 5.25 5.25

*750a* Sheet, 4 each #747-750 21.00 21.00

New Flag — A127

**2004, July 27 Unwmk.** ***Die Cut***

**Self-Adhesive**

**Booklet Stamp**

**751** A127 30p multi 1.10 1.10

***a.*** Booklet pane of 6 6.75

Complete booklet, 2 #751a 13.50

Merchant Ships A128

Designs: No. 752, 20p, RMS Dunnottar Castle. No. 753, 20p, RMS Caronia. No. 754, 35p, SA Agulhas. No. 755, 35p, MV Edinburgh. No. 756, 60p, MV Explorer. No. 757, 60p, MV Hanseatic.

**Wmk. 373**

**2004, Nov. 9 Litho.** ***Perf. 13¼***

**752-757** A128 Set of 6 8.50 8.50

Battle of Trafalgar, Bicent. — A129

Designs: 15p, Admiral Horatio Nelson's quadrant. 20p, HMS Royal Sovereign breaks the line, horiz. 25p, Thomas Swain aids the wounded Nelson, horiz. 35p, HMS Victory breaks the line, horiz. 50p, Nelson. 60p, HMS Victory, horiz.

No. 764: a, Capt. Thomas Masterman Hardy. b, HMS Victory.

***Perf. 13¼***

**2005, Jan. 20 Litho. Unwmk.**

**758-763** A129 Set of 6 7.75 7.75

**Souvenir Sheet**

**764** A129 75p Sheet of 2, #a-b 5.75 5.75

No. 763 has particles of wood from the HMS Victory embedded in the areas covered by a thermographic process that produces a shiny, raised effect.

Island Flora, Fauna and Scenes A130

No. 765 — Tristan da Cunha: a, Rockhopper penguins. b, Southern elephant seals. c, Tristan rock lobster. d, Crowberry. e, Tristan da Cunha island settlement and volcano.

No. 766 — Gough Island: a, Gough moorhen. b, Subantarctic fur seal. c, Bluefish. d, Gough tree fern. e, South African Weather Station.

No. 767 — Inaccessible Island: a, Inaccessible rail. b, Dusky dolphins. c, Sebastes capensis. d, Pepper tree. e, Inaccessible Island Waterfall.

No. 768 — Nightingale Island: a, Tristan thrush. b, Southern right whale. c, Fivefinger fish. d, Tussock grass. e, Nightingale Island.

No. 769 — Middle Island: a, Broad-billed prion. b, False killer whale. c, Wreckfih. d, Fern. e, Middle Island.

No. 770 - Stoltenhoff Island: a, Brown skua. b, Shepherd's beaked whales. c, Snoeks. d, Sea bind weed. e, Stoltenhoff Island.

**2005 Wmk. 373** ***Perf. 13¾***

**765** Horiz. strip of 5 10.00 10.00

***a.-e.*** A130 50p Any single 2.00 2.00

**766** Horiz. strip of 5 9.50 9.50

***a.-e.*** A130 50p Any single 1.90 1.90

**767** Horiz. strip of 5 9.50 9.50

***a.-e.*** A130 50p Any single 1.90 1.90

**768** Horiz. strip of 5 8.75 8.75

***a.-e.*** A130 50p Any single 1.75 1.75

**769** Horiz. strip of 5 8.75 8.75

***a.-e.*** A130 50p Any single 1.75 1.75

**770** Horiz. strip of 5 9.50 9.50

***a.-e.*** A130 50p Any single 1.90 1.90

Issued: No. 765, 2/21; No. 766, 3/28; No. 767, 4/18; No. 768, 2/7/06; No. 769, 3/30/06; No. 770, 9/27/06.

See No. 796.

Birds A131

Designs: 1p, Kerguelen petrel. 3p, Sooty albatross. 5p, Antarctic tern. 8p, Tristan bunting. 10p, Cape petrel. 15p, Tristan moorhen. 20p, Giant fulmar. 25p, Brown skua. 35p, Great-winged petrel. £1, Broad-billed prion. £2, Soft-plumaged petrel. £5, Rockhopper penguin.

***Perf. 14¼x14¾***

**2005, June 1 Litho. Wmk. 373**

| | | | | |
|---|---|---|---|---|
| **771** | A131 | 1p multi | .20 | .20 |
| **772** | A131 | 3p multi | .20 | .20 |
| **773** | A131 | 5p multi | .20 | .20 |
| **774** | A131 | 8p multi | .30 | .30 |
| **775** | A131 | 10p multi | .35 | .35 |
| **776** | A131 | 15p multi | .55 | .55 |
| **777** | A131 | 20p multi | .75 | .75 |
| **778** | A131 | 25p multi | .90 | .90 |
| **779** | A131 | 35p multi | 1.25 | 1.25 |
| **780** | A131 | £1 multi | 3.75 | 3.75 |
| **781** | A131 | £2 multi | 7.25 | 7.25 |
| **782** | A131 | £5 multi | 18.00 | 18.00 |
| | | *Nos. 771-782 (12)* | 33.70 | 33.70 |

Pope John Paul II (1920-2005) A132

**Wmk. 373**

**2005, Aug. 18 Litho.** ***Perf. 14***

**783** A132 50p multi 1.90 1.90

Battle of Trafalgar, Bicent. — A133

Designs: 20p, HMS Victory. 70p, Ships in battle, horiz. £1, Admiral Horatio Nelson.

***Perf. 13¼***

**2005, Oct. 18 Litho. Unwmk.**

**784-786** A133 Set of 3 6.75 6.75

Discovery of Tristan da Cunha, 500th Anniv. — A134

No. 787: a, 30p, Discovery by Tristao d'Acunha, 1506. b, 30p, First survey, 1767. c, 30p, Jonathan Lambert of Salem, 1810. d, 50p, William Glass, 1816. e, 50p, Duke of Gloucester (ship), 1824. f, 80p, Wreck of the Emily, 1836.

No. 788: a, 30p, Thomas Swain (1774-1862). b, 30p, HMS Challenger, 1873. c, 30p, Rev. Edwin Dodgson arrives, 1881. d, 50p, Wreck of the Italia, 1892. e, 50p, HMS Milford, 1938. f, 80p, Norwegian Expedition, 1937-38.

***Perf. 14¼x14½***

**2006 Litho. Wmk. 373**

**787** A134 Sheet of 6, #a-f 9.50 9.50

**788** A134 Sheet of 6, #a-f 9.50 9.50

Issued: Nos. 787-788, 2/2.

**Discovery of Tristan da Cunha, 500th Anniv. Type of 2006**

No. 789: a, 30p, World War II TDV training. b, 30p, HMS Atlantic Isle, 1944. c, 30p, Hands holding potatoes, 1946 potato stamp. d, 50p, Tristan da Cunha #5. e, 50p, Volcano eruption and evacuation, 1961. f, 80p, Gough Island Scientific Expedition, 1955.

No. 790: a, 30p, Royal Society Expedition, 1962. b, 30p, Resettlement, 1963. c, 30p, Denstone Expedition to Inaccessible Island, 1982. d, 50p, RMS St. Helena, 1992. e, 50p, New coat of arms, 2002. f, 80p, Hurricane disaster, 2001.

***Perf. 14¼x14¾***

**2006 Litho. Wmk. 373**

**789** A134 Sheet of 6, #a-f 10.50 10.50

**790** A134 Sheet of 6, #a-f 10.50 10.50

Issued: Nos. 789-790, 6/1.

Queen Elizabeth II, 80th Birthday A135

Queen: No. 791, 60p, As child. No. 792, 60p, Wearing feathered hat. No. 793, 60p, Wearing red hat. No. 794, 60p, Wearing sunglasses.

No. 795: a, 50p, Like No. 792. b, 50p, Like No. 793.

**2006, Apr. 21** ***Perf. 14***

**791-794** A135 Set of 4 9.00 9.00

**Souvenir Sheet**

**795** A135 50p Sheet of 2, #a-b 3.75 3.75

**Island Flora, Fauna and Scenes Type of 2005-06**
Miniature Sheet

No. 796: a, Map of Tristan da Cunha, flag. b, Map of Inaccessible Island, wandering albatross. c, Map of Nightingale Island, humpback whale. d, Map of Middle Island, traditional longboats. e, Map of Stoltenhoff Island, mackerel. f, Map of Gough Island, sub-antarctic fur seal.

**Wmk. 373**
**2007, Jan. 22 Litho. *Perf. 13¾***

| | | | |
|---|---|---|---|
| **796** | Sheet of 6 | 12.00 | 12.00 |
| *a.-f.* | A130 50p Any single | 2.00 | 2.00 |

### POSTAGE DUE STAMPS

**Type of Barbados 1934-47**
***Perf. 14***
**1957, Feb. 1 Wmk. 4 Typo.**
**Chalky Paper**

| | | | | |
|---|---|---|---|---|
| **J1** | D1 | 1p rose red | 3.00 | *7.00* |
| **J2** | D1 | 2p orange yellow | 3.75 | *9.25* |
| **J3** | D1 | 3p green | 4.00 | *11.50* |
| **J4** | D1 | 4p ultramarine | 4.75 | *13.50* |
| **J5** | D1 | 5p deep claret | 6.00 | *16.00* |
| | | *Nos. J1-J5 (5)* | 21.50 | *57.25* |

Numeral — D2

***Perf. 13½x14***
**1976, Sept. 3 Litho. Wmk. 373**

| | | | | |
|---|---|---|---|---|
| **J6** | D2 | 1p lilac rose | .20 | .20 |
| **J7** | D2 | 2p grayish green | .20 | .20 |
| **J8** | D2 | 4p violet | .20 | .20 |
| **J9** | D2 | 5p light blue | .25 | .40 |
| **J10** | D2 | 10p brown | .65 | .85 |
| | | *Nos. J6-J10 (5)* | 1.50 | 1.85 |

**1976, May 31 Wmk. 314**

| | | | | |
|---|---|---|---|---|
| *J6a* | D2 | 1p lilac rose | .20 | .20 |
| *J7a* | D2 | 2p grayish green | .20 | .20 |
| *J8a* | D2 | 4p violet | .20 | .20 |
| *J9a* | D2 | 5p light blue | .30 | .30 |
| *J10a* | D2 | 10p brown | .70 | .70 |
| | | *Nos. J6a-J10a (5)* | 1.60 | 1.60 |

Outline Map of Tristan da Cunha — D3

***Perf. 15x14***
**1986, Nov. 20 Litho. Wmk. 384**

| | | | | |
|---|---|---|---|---|
| **J11** | D3 | 1p pale yel brn & brn | .20 | .25 |
| **J12** | D3 | 2p orange & brown | .20 | .25 |
| **J13** | D3 | 5p crimson rose & brn | .20 | .25 |
| **J14** | D3 | 7p lt lilac & black | .20 | .25 |
| **J15** | D3 | 10p pale ultra & blk | .25 | .30 |
| **J16** | D3 | 25p lt green & blk | .70 | .90 |
| | | *Nos. J11-J16 (6)* | 1.75 | 2.20 |

## TRUCIAL STATES

'trü-shəl 'stāts

LOCATION — Qatar Peninsula, Persian Gulf
GOVT. — Sheikdoms under British Protection
AREA — 32,300 sq. mi.
POP. — 86,000
CAPITAL — Dubai

The Trucial States are: Abu Dhabi, Ajman, Dubai, Fujeira, Ras al Khaima, Sharjah and Kalba, and Umm al Qiwain.

Stamps inscribed "Trucial States" were issued and used only in Dubai. Beginning Aug. 1972 all Trucial States used the stamps of United Arab Emirates.

100 Naye Paise = 1 Rupee

**Catalogue values for all unused stamps in this country are for Never Hinged items.**

7 Palm Trees — A1

Dhow — A2

***Perf. 14½x14***
**1961, Jan. 7 Photo. Unwmk.**

| | | | | |
|---|---|---|---|---|
| **1** | A1 | 5np emerald | 1.50 | .20 |
| **2** | A1 | 15np red brown | .55 | .30 |
| **3** | A1 | 20np ultra | 1.50 | .20 |
| **4** | A1 | 30np orange | .55 | .20 |
| **5** | A1 | 40np purple | .55 | .20 |
| **6** | A1 | 50np brown olive | .55 | .20 |
| **7** | A1 | 75np gray | .75 | .20 |

**Engr. *Perf. 13x12½***

| | | | | |
|---|---|---|---|---|
| **8** | A2 | 1r emerald | 6.00 | 3.25 |
| **9** | A2 | 2r black | 6.50 | *19.00* |
| **10** | A2 | 5r rose red | 8.25 | *21.00* |
| **11** | A2 | 10r violet blue | 14.50 | *23.00* |
| | | *Nos. 1-11 (11)* | 41.20 | *67.75* |

Stamps inscribed "Trucial States" were withdrawn in June, 1963, when the individual states began issuing their own stamps.

## TUNISIA

tü-'nē-zhₑēₑə

LOCATION — Northern Africa, bordering on the Mediterranean Sea
GOVT. — Republic
AREA — 63,362 sq. mi.
POP. — 9,513,603 (1999 est.)
CAPITAL — Tunis

The former French protectorate became a sovereign state in 1956 and a republic in 1957.

100 Centimes = 1 Franc
1000 Millimes = 1 Dinar (1959)

**Catalogue values for unused stamps in this country are for Never Hinged items, beginning with Scott 163 in the regular postage section, Scott B78 in the semi-postal section, Scott C13 in the airpost section, Scott CB1 in the airpost semi-postal section, and Scott J33 in the postage due section.**

Coat of Arms — A1

***Perf. 14x13½***
**1888, July 1 Typo. Unwmk.**

| | | | | |
|---|---|---|---|---|
| **1** | A1 | 1c black, *blue* | 3.00 | 2.25 |
| **2** | A1 | 2c pur brn, *buff* | 3.00 | 2.25 |
| **3** | A1 | 5c green, *grnsh* | 22.50 | 9.25 |
| **4** | A1 | 15c blue, *grysh* | 45.00 | 17.50 |
| **5** | A1 | 25c black, *rose* | 92.50 | 52.50 |
| **6** | A1 | 40c red, *straw* | 92.50 | 60.00 |
| **7** | A1 | 75c car, *rose* | 85.00 | 65.00 |
| **8** | A1 | 5fr gray vio, *grysh* | 425.00 | 300.00 |
| | | *Nos. 1-8 (8)* | 768.50 | 508.75 |

All values exist imperforate.

*Reprints were made in 1893 and some values have been reprinted twice since then. The shades usually differ from those of the originals and some reprints have white gum instead of grayish. All values except the 15c and 40c have been reprinted from retouched designs, having a background of horizontal ruled lines.*

A2

A3

**1888-1902**

| | | | | |
|---|---|---|---|---|
| **9** | A2 | 1c blk, *lil bl* | 1.50 | .85 |
| **10** | A2 | 2c pur brn, *buff* | 1.50 | .85 |
| **11** | A2 | 5c grn, *grnsh* | 6.50 | .85 |
| **12** | A2 | 5c yellow grn ('99) | 5.75 | .85 |
| **13** | A2 | 10c blk, *lav* ('93) | 9.25 | 1.00 |
| **14** | A2 | 10c red ('01) | 5.75 | .85 |
| **15** | A2 | 15c blue, *grysh* | 45.00 | .85 |
| **16** | A2 | 15c gray ('01) | 9.25 | 1.25 |
| **17** | A2 | 20c red, *grn* ('99) | 17.00 | 1.50 |
| **18** | A2 | 25c blk, *rose* | 22.50 | 1.90 |
| **19** | A2 | 25c blue ('01) | 17.00 | 1.90 |
| **20** | A2 | 35c brown ('02) | 45.00 | 1.90 |
| **21** | A2 | 40c red, *straw* | 19.00 | 1.50 |
| **22** | A2 | 75c car, *rose* | 160.00 | 75.00 |
| **23** | A2 | 75c dp vio, *org* ('93) | 25.00 | 7.25 |
| **24** | A3 | 1fr olive, *olive* | 30.00 | 8.50 |
| **25** | A3 | 2fr dull violet ('02) | 160.00 | 140.00 |
| **26** | A3 | 5fr red lil, *lav* | 190.00 | 75.00 |
| | | Bar cancellation | | .50 |

**Quadrille Paper**

| | | | | |
|---|---|---|---|---|
| **27** | A2 | 15c bl, *grysh* ('93) | 45.00 | .75 |
| | | *Nos. 9-27 (19)* | 815.00 | 322.55 |

For surcharges see Nos. 28, 58-61.

No. 27 Surcharged in Red

**1902**

| | | | | |
|---|---|---|---|---|
| **28** | A2 | 25c on 15c blue | 3.00 | 3.00 |

Mosque at Kairouan A4

Plowing A5

Ruins of Hadrian's Aqueduct A6

Carthaginian Galley — A7

**1906-26 Typo.**

| | | | | |
|---|---|---|---|---|
| **29** | A4 | 1c blk, *yel* | .20 | .20 |
| **30** | A4 | 2c red brn, *straw* | .20 | .20 |
| **31** | A4 | 3c lt red ('19) | .20 | .20 |
| **32** | A4 | 5c grn, *grnsh* | .30 | .20 |
| **33** | A4 | 5c orange ('21) | .20 | .20 |
| **34** | A5 | 10c red | .30 | .20 |
| **35** | A5 | 10c green ('21) | .35 | .25 |
| **36** | A5 | 15c vio, *pnksh* | 1.10 | .25 |
| *a.* | | Imperf., pair | | |
| **37** | A5 | 15c brn, *org* ('23) | .25 | .25 |
| **38** | A5 | 20c brn, *pnksh* | .25 | .25 |
| **39** | A5 | 25c deep blue | 1.60 | .60 |
| *a.* | | Imperf., pair | | |
| **40** | A5 | 25c violet ('21) | .35 | .25 |
| **41** | A6 | 30c red brn & vio ('19) | .70 | .60 |
| **42** | A5 | 30c pale red ('21) | .90 | .60 |
| **43** | A6 | 35c ol grn & brn | 8.75 | 1.75 |
| **44** | A6 | 40c blk brn & red brn | 4.25 | .60 |
| **45** | A5 | 40c blk, *pnksh* ('23) | 1.10 | .60 |
| **46** | A5 | 40c gray grn ('26) | .20 | .20 |
| **47** | A5 | 50c blue ('21) | .60 | .60 |
| **48** | A6 | 60c ol grn & vio ('21) | .60 | .60 |
| **49** | A6 | 60c ver & rose ('25) | .60 | .35 |
| **50** | A6 | 75c red brn & red | .75 | .60 |
| **51** | A6 | 75c ver & dl red ('26) | .35 | .35 |
| **52** | A7 | 1fr red & dk brn | .90 | .60 |
| **53** | A7 | 1fr ind & ultra ('25) | .35 | .35 |
| **54** | A7 | 2fr brn & ol grn | 5.25 | 1.50 |
| **55** | A7 | 2fr grn & red, *pink* ('25) | .75 | .35 |
| **56** | A7 | 5fr violet & blue | 9.50 | 4.50 |
| **57** | A7 | 5fr gray vio & grn ('25) | .75 | .60 |
| | | *Nos. 29-57 (29)* | 41.60 | 17.80 |

For surcharges and overprints see Nos. 62-64, 70-73115-116, B1-B23, B25-B27, B29-B30, B32-B36, C1-C6.

Stamps and Type of 1888-1902 Surcharged

**1908, Sept.**

| | | | | |
|---|---|---|---|---|
| **58** | A2 | 10c on 15c gray, *lt gray* (R) | 1.40 | 1.40 |
| **59** | A3 | 35c on 1fr ol, *ol* (R) | 3.25 | 3.25 |
| **60** | A3 | 40c on 2fr dl vio (Bl) | 6.00 | 6.00 |
| **61** | A3 | 75c on 5fr red lil, *lav* (Bl) | 4.50 | 4.50 |
| | | *Nos. 58-61 (4)* | 15.15 | 15.15 |

No. 36 Surcharged

**1911**

| | | | | |
|---|---|---|---|---|
| **62** | A5 | 10c on 15c vio, *pinkish* | 1.50 | .60 |

No. 34 Surcharged

**1917, Mar. 16**

| | | | | |
|---|---|---|---|---|
| **63** | A5 | 15c on 10c red | .75 | .20 |
| *a.* | | "15c" omitted | 37.50 | |
| *b.* | | Double surcharge | 75.00 | |

No. 36 Surcharged

**1921**

| | | | | |
|---|---|---|---|---|
| **64** | A5 | 20c on 15c vio, *pinkish* | .90 | .25 |

Arab and Ruins of Dougga — A9

**1922-26 Typo. *Perf. 13½x14***

| | | | | |
|---|---|---|---|---|
| **65** | A9 | 10c green | .20 | .20 |
| **66** | A9 | 10c rose ('26) | .25 | .25 |
| **67** | A9 | 30c rose | 1.10 | 1.10 |
| **68** | A9 | 30c lilac ('26) | .40 | .40 |
| **69** | A9 | 50c blue | .65 | .65 |
| | | *Nos. 65-69 (5)* | 2.60 | 2.60 |

For surcharges see #117, B24, B28, B31.

Stamps and Type of 1906 Surcharged in Red or Black

a

b

**1923-25**

| | | | | |
|---|---|---|---|---|
| **70** | A4(a) | 10c on 5c grn, *grnsh* (R) | .35 | .35 |
| *a.* | | Double surcharge | 57.50 | |
| **71** | A5(b) | 20c on 15c vio (Bk) | .85 | .25 |
| **72** | A5(b) | 30c on 20c yel brn (Bk) ('25) | .35 | .35 |
| **73** | A5(b) | 50c on 25c blue (R) | .85 | .25 |
| | | *Nos. 70-73 (4)* | 2.40 | 1.20 |

Arab Woman Carrying Water — A10

Grand Mosque at Tunis — A11

Mosque, Tunis — A12

Roman Amphitheater, El Djem (Thysdrus) — A13

**1926-46 Typo. *Perf. 14x13½***

| No. | Type | Description | Unused | Used |
|---|---|---|---|---|
| 74 | A10 | 1c lt red | .20 | .20 |
| 75 | A10 | 2c olive grn | .20 | .20 |
| 76 | A10 | 3c slate blue | .20 | .20 |
| 77 | A10 | 5c yellow grn | .20 | .20 |
| 78 | A10 | 10c rose | .20 | .20 |
| 78A | A12 | 10c brown ('46) | .20 | .20 |
| 79 | A11 | 15c gray lilac | .20 | .20 |
| 80 | A11 | 20c deep red | .25 | .20 |
| 81 | A11 | 25c gray green | .35 | .25 |
| 82 | A11 | 25c lt violet ('28) | .60 | .25 |
| 83 | A11 | 30c lt violet | .35 | .35 |
| 84 | A11 | 30c blue grn ('28) | .35 | .25 |
| 84A | A12 | 30c dk ol grn ('46) | .20 | .20 |
| 85 | A11 | 40c deep brown | .25 | .20 |
| 85A | A12 | 40c lil rose ('46) | .25 | .25 |
| 86 | A11 | 45c emerald ('40) | .85 | .85 |
| 87 | A12 | 50c black | .25 | .20 |
| 88 | A12 | 50c ultra ('34) | .70 | .25 |
| 88B | A12 | 50c emerald ('40) | .20 | .20 |
| 88C | A12 | 50c lt blue ('46) | .25 | .25 |
| 89 | A12 | 60c red org ('40) | .20 | .20 |
| 89A | A12 | 60c ultra ('45) | .20 | .20 |
| 90 | A12 | 65c ultra ('38) | .55 | .25 |
| 91 | A12 | 70c dark red ('40) | .20 | .20 |
| 92 | A12 | 75c vermilion | .35 | .35 |
| 93 | A12 | 75c lil rose ('28) | 1.00 | .25 |
| 94 | A12 | 80c blue green | 1.00 | .35 |
| 94A | A12 | 80c blk brn ('40) | .25 | .25 |
| 94B | A12 | 80c emerald ('45) | .35 | .35 |
| 95 | A12 | 90c org red ('28) | .25 | .20 |
| 96 | A12 | 90c ultra ('39) | 8.50 | 8.50 |
| 97 | A12 | 1fr brown violet | .70 | .35 |
| 97A | A12 | 1fr rose ('40) | .20 | .20 |
| 98 | A13 | 1.05fr dl bl & mag | .60 | .45 |
| 98A | A12 | 1.20fr blk brn ('45) | .35 | .25 |
| 99 | A13 | 1.25fr gray bl & dk bl | .60 | .35 |
| 100 | A13 | 1.25fr car rose ('40) | 1.00 | 1.00 |
| 100A | A13 | 1.30fr bl & vio bl ('42) | .25 | .25 |
| 101 | A13 | 1.40fr brt red vio ('40) | 1.10 | 1.10 |
| 102 | A13 | 1.50fr bl & dp bl ('28) | 1.00 | .35 |
| 102A | A13 | 1.50fr rose red & red org ('42) | .45 | .45 |
| 102B | A12 | 1.50fr rose lil ('46) | .20 | .20 |
| 103 | A13 | 2fr rose & ol brn | 1.40 | .25 |
| 104 | A13 | 2fr red org ('39) | .30 | .30 |
| 104A | A12 | 2fr Prus grn ('45) | .25 | .20 |
| 105 | A13 | 2.25fr ultra ('39) | .90 | .90 |
| 105A | A13 | 2.40fr red ('46) | .55 | .35 |
| 106 | A13 | 2.50fr green ('40) | .85 | .85 |
| 107 | A13 | 3fr dl bl & org | 1.60 | .60 |
| 108 | A13 | 3fr violet ('39) | .25 | .25 |
| 108A | A13 | 3fr blk brn ('46) | .20 | .20 |
| 108B | A13 | 4fr ultra ('45) | .90 | .55 |
| 109 | A13 | 5fr red & grn, *grnsh* | 2.75 | .80 |
| 110 | A13 | 5fr dp red brn ('40) | 1.10 | 1.10 |
| 110A | A13 | 5fr dk green ('46) | .85 | .20 |
| 110B | A13 | 6fr dp ultra ('45) | .60 | .35 |
| 111 | A13 | 10fr brn red & blk, *bluish* | 9.50 | 2.75 |
| 112 | A13 | 10fr rose pink ('40) | .60 | .60 |
| 112A | A13 | 10fr ver ('46) | .55 | .35 |
| 112B | A13 | 10fr ultra ('46) | .55 | .25 |
| 112C | A13 | 15fr rose lil ('45) | .35 | .20 |
| 113 | A13 | 20fr lil & red, *pnksh* ('28) | 1.75 | .85 |
| 113A | A13 | 20fr dk green ('45) | .70 | .35 |
| 113B | A13 | 25fr violet ('45) | .70 | .55 |
| 113C | A13 | 50fr carmine ('45) | 1.25 | .70 |
| 113D | A13 | 100fr car rose ('45) | 1.50 | .90 |
| | | *Nos. 74-113D (66)* | 55.50 | 35.55 |

See Nos. 152A-162, 185-189, 199-206.

For surcharges and overprints see Nos. 114, 118-121, 143-152, B74-B77, B87-B88, B91-B95, B98, C7-C12.

No. 99 Surcharged with New Value and Bars in Red

**1927, Mar. 24**

| No. | Type | Description | Unused | Used |
|---|---|---|---|---|
| 114 | A13 | 1.50fr on 1.25fr | .55 | .25 |

Stamps of 1921-26 Surcharged

**1928, May 1**

| No. | Type | Description | Unused | Used |
|---|---|---|---|---|
| 115 | A4 | 3c on 5c orange | .25 | .20 |
| 116 | A5 | 10c on 15c brn, *org* | .60 | .25 |
| 117 | A9 | 25c on 30c lilac | .55 | .35 |
| 118 | A12 | 40c on 80c bl grn | .55 | .35 |
| 119 | A12 | 50c on 75c ver | .75 | .55 |
| | | *Nos. 115-119 (5)* | 2.70 | 1.70 |

No. 83 Surcharged

**1929**

| No. | Type | Description | Unused | Used |
|---|---|---|---|---|
| 120 | A11 | 10c on 30c lt violet | 3.50 | 2.00 |

No. 120 exists precanceled only. The value in first column is for a stamp which has not been through the post and has original gum. The value in the second column is for a postally used, gumless stamp. See No. 199a.

No. 85 Surcharged with New Value and Bars

**1930**

| No. | Type | Description | Unused | Used |
|---|---|---|---|---|
| 121 | A11 | 50c on 40c dp brn | 5.00 | .85 |

A14

A15

A16

A17

***Perf. 11, 12½, 12½x13***

**1931-34 Engr.**

| No. | Type | Description | Unused | Used |
|---|---|---|---|---|
| 122 | A14 | 1c deep blue | .20 | .20 |
| 123 | A14 | 2c yellow brn | .20 | .20 |
| 124 | A14 | 3c black | .35 | .35 |
| 125 | A14 | 5c yellow grn | .20 | .20 |
| 126 | A14 | 10c red | .20 | .20 |
| 127 | A15 | 15c dull violet | .60 | .55 |
| 128 | A15 | 20c dull brown | .20 | .20 |
| 129 | A15 | 25c rose red | .25 | .20 |
| 130 | A15 | 30c deep green | .55 | .45 |
| 131 | A15 | 40c red orange | .25 | .25 |
| 132 | A16 | 50c ultra | .25 | .25 |
| 133 | A16 | 75c yellow | 2.10 | 1.90 |
| 134 | A16 | 90c red | .60 | .60 |
| 135 | A16 | 1fr olive black | .45 | .35 |
| 136 | A16 | 1fr dk brown ('34) | .45 | .35 |
| 137 | A17 | 1.50fr brt ultra | .75 | .55 |
| 138 | A17 | 2fr deep brown | .70 | .70 |
| 139 | A17 | 3fr blue green | 8.50 | 8.50 |
| 140 | A17 | 5fr car rose | 22.50 | 18.00 |
| *a.* | | Perf. 12½ | 35.00 | 30.00 |
| 141 | A17 | 10fr black | 40.00 | 30.00 |
| 142 | A17 | 20fr dark brown | 52.50 | 42.50 |
| | | *Nos. 122-142 (21)* | 131.80 | 106.50 |

For surcharges see Nos. B54-B73.

Nos. 88, 102 Surcharged in Red or Black:

**1937 *Perf. 14x13½***

| No. | Type | Description | Unused | Used |
|---|---|---|---|---|
| 143 | A12 | 65c on 50c (R) | .55 | .20 |
| *b.* | | Double surcharge | 75.00 | 65.00 |
| 144 | A13 | 1.75fr on 1.50fr (R) | 5.00 | 1.25 |
| *a.* | | Double surcharge | 70.00 | 70.00 |

**1938**

| No. | Type | Description | Unused | Used |
|---|---|---|---|---|
| 145 | A12 | 65c on 50c (Bk) | .75 | .25 |
| 146 | A13 | 1.75fr on 1.50fr (R) | 7.75 | 6.50 |

Stamps of 1938-39 Surcharged in Red or Carmine:

**1940**

| No. | Type | Description | Unused | Used |
|---|---|---|---|---|
| 147 | A12 | 25c on 65c ultra (C) | .20 | .20 |
| 148 | A12 | 1fr on 90c ultra (R) | .35 | .35 |

Stamps of 1938-40 Surcharged in Red or Black:

**1941**

| No. | Type | Description | Unused | Used |
|---|---|---|---|---|
| 149 | A12 | 25c on 65c ultra (R) | .25 | .25 |
| 150 | A13 | 1fr on 1.25fr car rose | .55 | .55 |
| 151 | A13 | 1fr on 1.40fr brt red vio | .55 | .55 |
| 152 | A13 | 1fr on 2.25fr ultra (R) | .55 | .55 |
| | | *Nos. 149-152 (4)* | 1.90 | 1.90 |

Types of 1926 Without RF

**1941-45 Typo. *Perf. 14x13½***

| No. | Type | Description | Unused | Used |
|---|---|---|---|---|
| 152A | A11 | 30c carmine ('45) | .20 | .20 |
| 152B | A12 | 1.20fr int blue ('45) | .20 | .20 |
| 153 | A12 | 1.50fr brn red ('42) | .40 | .40 |
| 154 | A13 | 2.40fr car & brt pink ('42) | .40 | .40 |
| 155 | A13 | 2.50fr dk bl & lt bl | .40 | .40 |
| 156 | A13 | 3fr lt violet ('42) | .25 | .25 |
| 157 | A13 | 4fr blk & bl vio ('42) | .40 | .40 |
| 158 | A13 | 4.50fr ol grn & brn ('42) | .55 | .40 |
| 159 | A13 | 5fr brown blk ('42) | .45 | .45 |
| 160 | A13 | 10fr lil & dull vio | .55 | .40 |
| 161 | A13 | 15fr henna brn ('42) | 4.25 | 3.75 |
| 162 | A13 | 20fr lt vio & car | 2.50 | 1.40 |
| | | *Nos. 152A-162 (12)* | 10.55 | 8.65 |

**Catalogue values for unused stamps in this section, from this point to the end of the section, are for Never Hinged items.**

One Aim Alone - Victory A18

Mosque and Olive Tree A19

**1943 Litho. *Perf. 12***

| No. | Type | Description | Unused | Used |
|---|---|---|---|---|
| 163 | A18 | 1.50fr rose | .20 | .20 |

**1944-45 Unwmk. *Perf. 11½***

**Size: 15½x19mm**

| No. | Type | Description | Unused | Used |
|---|---|---|---|---|
| 165 | A19 | 30c yellow ('45) | .20 | .20 |
| 166 | A19 | 40c org brn ('45) | .20 | .20 |
| 168 | A19 | 60c red org ('45) | .45 | .45 |
| 169 | A19 | 70c rose pink ('45) | .20 | .20 |
| 170 | A19 | 80c Prus grn ('45) | .30 | .30 |
| 171 | A19 | 90c violet ('45) | .30 | .30 |
| 172 | A19 | 1fr red ('45) | .30 | .30 |
| 173 | A19 | 1.50fr dp bl ('45) | .30 | .30 |

**Size: 21¼x26½mm**

| No. | Type | Description | Unused | Used |
|---|---|---|---|---|
| 175 | A19 | 2.40fr red | .40 | .40 |
| 176 | A19 | 2.50fr red brn | .45 | .45 |
| 177 | A19 | 3fr lt vio | .65 | .65 |
| 178 | A19 | 4fr brt bl vio | .45 | .45 |
| 179 | A19 | 4.50fr apple grn | .45 | .45 |
| 180 | A19 | 5fr gray | .65 | .65 |
| 181 | A19 | 6fr choc ('45) | .50 | .50 |
| 182 | A19 | 10fr brn lake ('45) | .70 | .70 |
| 183 | A19 | 15fr copper brn | .75 | .75 |
| 184 | A19 | 20fr lilac | 1.00 | 1.00 |
| | | *Nos. 165-184 (18)* | 8.25 | 8.25 |

For surcharge see No. B79.

Types of 1926

**1946-47 Typo. *Perf. 14x13½***

| No. | Type | Description | Unused | Used |
|---|---|---|---|---|
| 185 | A12 | 2fr emerald ('47) | .60 | .60 |
| 186 | A12 | 3fr rose pink | .25 | .20 |
| 187 | A12 | 4fr violet ('47) | .60 | .60 |
| 188 | A13 | 4fr violet ('47) | .60 | .60 |
| 189 | A12 | 6fr carmine ('47) | .20 | .20 |
| | | *Nos. 185-189 (5)* | 2.25 | 2.20 |

Neptune, Bardo Museum A20

**1947-49 Engr. *Perf. 13***

| No. | Type | Description | Unused | Used |
|---|---|---|---|---|
| 190 | A20 | 5fr dk grn & bluish blk | .85 | .85 |
| 191 | A20 | 10fr blk brn & bluish blk | .40 | .25 |
| 192 | A20 | 18fr dk bl gray & Prus bl ('48) | 1.10 | .85 |
| 193 | A20 | 25fr dk bl & bl grn ('49) | 1.50 | .85 |
| | | *Nos. 190-193 (4)* | 3.85 | 2.80 |

For surcharge see No. B108.

Detail from Great Mosque at Kairouan A21

**1948-49**

| No. | Type | Description | Unused | Used |
|---|---|---|---|---|
| 194 | A21 | 3fr dk bl grn & bl grn | .80 | .55 |
| 195 | A21 | 4fr dk red vio & red vio | .55 | .40 |
| 196 | A21 | 6fr red brn & red | .20 | .20 |
| 197 | A21 | 10fr purple ('49) | .35 | .25 |
| 198 | A21 | 12fr henna brn | .80 | .55 |
| 198A | A21 | 12fr dk brn & org brn ('49) | .60 | .35 |
| 198B | A21 | 15fr dk red ('49) | .55 | .35 |
| | | *Nos. 194-198B (7)* | 3.85 | 2.65 |

See No. 225. For surcharge see No. B103.

Types of 1926

**1947-49 Typo. *Perf. 14x13½***

| No. | Type | Description | Unused | Used |
|---|---|---|---|---|
| 199 | A12 | 2.50fr brown orange | .55 | .35 |
| *a.* | | 2.50fr brown | 1.50 | .80 |
| 200 | A12 | 4fr brown org ('49) | .85 | .35 |
| 201 | A12 | 4.50fr lt ultra | .60 | .35 |
| 202 | A12 | 5fr blue ('48) | .55 | .55 |
| 203 | A12 | 5fr lt bl grn ('49) | .50 | .40 |
| 204 | A13 | 6fr rose red | .20 | .20 |
| 205 | A12 | 15fr rose red | .60 | .55 |
| 206 | A13 | 25fr red orange | 1.10 | .85 |
| | | *Nos. 199-206 (8)* | 4.95 | 3.60 |

No. 199a is known only precanceled. See note after No. 120.

Dam on the Oued Mellegue A22

**1949, Sept. 1 Engr. *Perf. 13***

| No. | Type | Description | Unused | Used |
|---|---|---|---|---|
| 207 | A22 | 15fr grnsh black | 2.50 | .75 |

UPU Symbols and Tunisian Post Rider — A23

Berber Hermes at Carthage — A24

**1949, Oct. 28**

**Bluish Paper**

| No. | Type | Description | Unused | Used |
|---|---|---|---|---|
| 208 | A23 | 5fr dark green | 1.25 | 1.25 |
| 209 | A23 | 15fr red brown | 1.25 | 1.25 |
| | | *Nos. 208-209,C13 (3)* | 4.25 | 4.25 |

UPU, 75th anniversary.
Nos. 208-209 exist imperf.

**1950-51**

| No. | Type | Description | Unused | Used |
|---|---|---|---|---|
| 210 | A24 | 15fr red brown | .60 | .55 |
| 211 | A24 | 25fr indigo ('51) | .60 | .55 |
| 212 | A24 | 50fr dark green ('51) | 1.90 | .55 |
| | | *Nos. 210-212 (3)* | 3.10 | 1.65 |

Horse, Carthage Museum — A25

**1950, Dec. 26 Typo. *Perf. 13½x14***

**Size: 21½x17½mm**

| No. | Type | Description | Unused | Used |
|---|---|---|---|---|
| 213 | A25 | 10c aquamarine | .20 | .25 |
| 214 | A25 | 50c brown | .20 | .20 |
| 215 | A25 | 1fr rose lilac | .25 | .20 |
| 216 | A25 | 2fr gray | .30 | .20 |
| 217 | A25 | 4fr vermilion | .50 | .50 |
| 218 | A25 | 5fr blue green | .30 | .20 |
| 219 | A25 | 8fr deep blue | .50 | .20 |
| 220 | A25 | 12fr red | 1.25 | .40 |
| 221 | A25 | 15fr carmine rose ('50) | .50 | .25 |
| | | *Nos. 213-221 (9)* | 4.00 | 2.40 |

See Nos. 222-224, 226-228.

**1951-53 Engr. *Perf. 13x14***

**Size: 22x18mm**

| No. | Type | Description | Unused | Used |
|---|---|---|---|---|
| 222 | A25 | 15fr carmine rose | .85 | .55 |
| 223 | A25 | 15fr ultra ('53) | 1.00 | .55 |
| 224 | A25 | 30fr deep ultra | 1.75 | .60 |
| | | *Nos. 222-224 (3)* | 3.60 | 1.70 |

Type of 1948-49

**1951, Aug. 1 *Perf. 13***

| No. | Type | Description | Unused | Used |
|---|---|---|---|---|
| 225 | A21 | 30fr dark blue | 1.50 | .55 |

Horse Type of 1950

**1952 Typo. *Perf. 13½x14***

| No. | Type | Description | Unused | Used |
|---|---|---|---|---|
| 226 | A25 | 3fr brown orange | .55 | .35 |
| 227 | A25 | 12fr carmine rose | 1.10 | .55 |
| 228 | A25 | 15fr ultra | .55 | .20 |
| | | *Nos. 226-228 (3)* | 2.20 | 1.10 |

Charles Nicolle — A26

Flags, Pennants and Minaret — A27

**1952, Aug. 4 Engr. *Perf. 13***

| No. | Type | Description | Unused | Used |
|---|---|---|---|---|
| 229 | A26 | 15fr black brown | 1.40 | .75 |
| 230 | A26 | 30fr deep blue | 1.40 | .75 |

Founding of the Society of Medical Sciences of Tunisia, 50th anniv.

**1953, Oct. 18**

| No. | Type | Description | Unused | Used |
|---|---|---|---|---|
| 231 | A27 | 8fr black brn & choc | 1.00 | 1.00 |
| 232 | A27 | 12fr dk green & emer | 1.00 | 1.00 |
| 233 | A27 | 15fr indigo & ultra | 1.00 | 1.00 |
| 234 | A27 | 18fr dk pur & pur | 1.00 | 1.00 |
| 235 | A27 | 30fr dk car & car | 1.00 | 1.00 |
| | | *Nos. 231-235 (5)* | 5.00 | 5.00 |

First International Fair of Tunis.

Courtyard at Sousse — A28

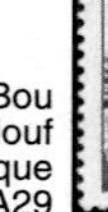

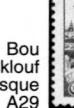

Sidi Bou Maklouf Mosque A29

Designs: 1fr, Courtyard at Sousse. 2fr, 4fr, Citadel, Takrouna. 5fr, 8fr, View of Tatahouine. 10fr, 12fr, Ruins at Matmata. 15fr, Street Corner, Sidi Bou Said. 20fr, 25fr, Genoese fort, Tabarka. 30fr, 40fr, Bab-El-Khadra gate. 50fr, 75fr, Four-story building, Medenine.

***Perf. 13½x13 (A28), 13***

**1954, May 29**

| No. | Type | Description | Unused | Used |
|---|---|---|---|---|
| 236 | A28 | 50c emerald | .20 | .20 |
| 237 | A28 | 1fr carmine rose | .20 | .20 |
| 238 | A28 | 2fr violet brown | .25 | .25 |
| 239 | A28 | 4fr turq blue | .35 | .20 |
| 240 | A28 | 5fr violet | .35 | .20 |
| 241 | A28 | 8fr black brown | .35 | .25 |
| 242 | A28 | 10fr dk blue grn | .35 | .20 |
| 243 | A28 | 12fr rose brown | .35 | .25 |
| 244 | A28 | 15fr dp ultra | 1.75 | .20 |
| 245 | A29 | 18fr chocolate | 1.50 | .60 |
| 246 | A29 | 20fr dp ultra | 1.00 | .25 |
| 247 | A29 | 25fr indigo | 1.00 | .25 |
| 248 | A29 | 30fr dp claret | 1.00 | .25 |
| 249 | A29 | 40fr dk Prus grn | 1.10 | .55 |
| 250 | A29 | 50fr dk violet | 1.90 | .20 |
| 251 | A29 | 75fr carmine rose | 4.25 | 2.00 |

**Typo.**

***Perf. 14x13½***

| No. | Type | Description | Unused | Used |
|---|---|---|---|---|
| 252 | A28 | 15fr ultra | .60 | .20 |
| | | *Nos. 236-252 (17)* | 16.50 | 6.25 |

Imperforates exist. Value $50. See Nos. 271-287. For surcharge see No. B125.

Mohammed al-Amin, Bey of Tunis — A30

**1954, Oct. *Perf. 13***

| No. | Type | Description | Unused | Used |
|---|---|---|---|---|
| 253 | A30 | 8fr bl & dk bl | 1.00 | 1.00 |
| 254 | A30 | 12fr lil gray & indigo | 1.00 | 1.00 |
| 255 | A30 | 15fr dp car & brn lake | 1.00 | 1.00 |
| 256 | A30 | 18fr red brn & blk brn | 1.00 | 1.00 |
| 257 | A30 | 30fr bl grn & dk bl grn | 1.25 | 1.25 |
| | | *Nos. 253-257 (5)* | 5.25 | 5.25 |

Theater Drapes, Dove and Sun — A31

**1955**

| No. | Type | Description | Unused | Used |
|---|---|---|---|---|
| 258 | A31 | 15fr dk red brn, bl & org | 1.00 | 1.00 |

Essor, Tunisian amateur theatrical society.

Rotary Emblem, Map and Symbols of Punic, Roman, Arab and French Civilizations A32

**1955, May 14 Unwmk.**

| No. | Type | Description | Unused | Used |
|---|---|---|---|---|
| 259 | A32 | 12fr vio brn & blk brn | .75 | .75 |
| 260 | A32 | 15fr vio gray & dk brn | .75 | .75 |
| 261 | A32 | 18fr rose vio & dk pur | .75 | .75 |
| 262 | A32 | 25fr blue & dp ultra | .75 | .75 |
| 263 | A32 | 30fr dk Prus grn & ind | 1.10 | 1.10 |
| | | *Nos. 259-263 (5)* | 4.10 | 4.10 |

Rotary International, 50th anniv.

Bey of Tunis A33

Embroiderers A34

**1955 Engr. *Perf. 13½x13***

| No. | Type | Description | Unused | Used |
|---|---|---|---|---|
| 264 | A33 | 15fr dark blue | .85 | .20 |

**1955, July 25 *Perf. 13***

15fr, 18fr, Potters. 20fr, 30fr, Florists.

| No. | Type | Description | Unused | Used |
|---|---|---|---|---|
| 265 | A34 | 5fr rose brown | .65 | .65 |
| 266 | A34 | 12fr ultra | .65 | .65 |
| 267 | A34 | 15fr Prussian green | .65 | .65 |
| 268 | A34 | 18fr red | .65 | .65 |
| 269 | A34 | 20fr dark violet | .95 | .95 |
| 270 | A34 | 30fr violet brown | .95 | .95 |
| | | *Nos. 265-270 (6)* | 4.50 | 4.50 |

For surcharge see No. B126.

**Independent Kingdom**

Types of 1954 Redrawn with "RF" Omitted

**1956, Mar. 1 *Perf. 13½x13, 13 (A29)***

| No. | Type | Description | Unused | Used |
|---|---|---|---|---|
| 271 | A28 | 50c emerald | .20 | .20 |
| 272 | A28 | 1fr carmine rose | .20 | .20 |
| 273 | A28 | 2fr violet brown | .20 | .20 |
| 274 | A28 | 4fr turquoise blue | .20 | .20 |
| 275 | A28 | 5fr violet | .20 | .20 |
| 276 | A28 | 8fr black brown | .20 | .20 |
| 277 | A28 | 10fr dk blue grn | .20 | .20 |
| 278 | A28 | 12fr rose brown | .20 | .20 |
| 279 | A28 | 15fr deep ultra | 1.25 | .20 |
| 280 | A29 | 18fr chocolate | .35 | .25 |
| 281 | A29 | 20fr deep ultra | .25 | .20 |
| 282 | A29 | 25fr indigo | .20 | .20 |
| 283 | A29 | 30fr deep claret | 1.10 | .20 |
| 284 | A29 | 40fr dk Prus grn | 1.10 | .20 |
| 285 | A29 | 50fr dark violet | .85 | .20 |
| 286 | A29 | 75fr carmine rose | 1.60 | 1.10 |

***Perf. 14x13***

**Typo.**

| No. | Type | Description | Unused | Used |
|---|---|---|---|---|
| 287 | A28 | 15fr ultra | .20 | .20 |
| | | *Nos. 271-287 (17)* | 8.50 | 4.35 |

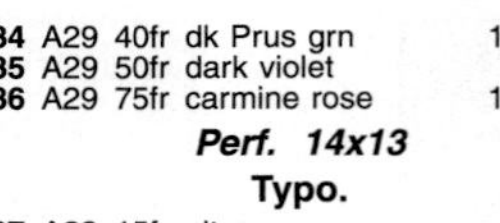

Mohammed al-Amin Bey of Tunis — A35

Farhat Hached — A36

Designs: 12fr, 18fr, 30fr, Woman and Dove. 5fr, 20fr, Bey of Tunis.

**1956 Unwmk. Engr. *Perf. 13***

| No. | Type | Description | Unused | Used |
|---|---|---|---|---|
| 288 | A35 | 5fr deep blue | .25 | .25 |
| 289 | A35 | 12fr brown violet | .35 | .35 |
| 290 | A35 | 15fr red | .35 | .35 |
| 291 | A35 | 18fr dk blue gray | .50 | .40 |
| 292 | A35 | 20fr dark green | .50 | .40 |
| 293 | A35 | 30fr copper brown | 1.00 | .50 |
| | | *Nos. 288-293 (6)* | 2.95 | 2.25 |

Issued to commemorate Tunisian autonomy.

**1956, May 1**

| No. | Type | Description | Unused | Used |
|---|---|---|---|---|
| 294 | A36 | 15fr rose brown | .35 | .35 |
| 295 | A36 | 30fr indigo | .40 | .40 |

Farhat Hached (1914-1952), nationalist leader.

Grapes — A37

Fruit Market A38

Designs: 15fr, Hand holding olive branch. 18fr, Wheat harvest. 20fr, Man carrying food basket ("Gifts for the wedding").

**1956-57 Unwmk. Engr. *Perf. 13***

| No. | Type | Description | Unused | Used |
|---|---|---|---|---|
| 296 | A37 | 12fr lil, vio & vio brn | .65 | .25 |
| 297 | A37 | 15fr ind, dk ol grn & red brn | .75 | .25 |
| 298 | A37 | 18fr brt violet blue | 1.10 | .40 |
| 299 | A37 | 20fr brown orange | 1.10 | .40 |
| 300 | A38 | 25fr chocolate | 1.50 | 1.00 |
| 301 | A38 | 30fr deep ultra | 1.60 | .65 |
| | | *Nos. 296-301 (6)* | 6.70 | 2.95 |

Habib Bourguiba — A39

Farmers and Workers A40

*Perf. 14 (A39), 11½x11 (A40)*

**1957, Mar. 20**

**302** A39 5fr dark blue .20 .20
**303** A40 12fr magenta .20 .20
**304** A39 20fr ultra .35 .35
**305** A40 25fr green .40 .25
**306** A39 30fr chocolate .50 .40
**307** A40 50fr crimson rose .90 .60
*Nos. 302-307 (6)* 2.55 2.00

First anniversary of independence.

Dove and Handclasp A41

Labor Bourse, Tunis — A42

**1957, July 5 Engr. *Perf. 13***

**308** A41 18fr dk red violet .35 .35
**309** A42 20fr crimson .40 .40
**310** A41 25fr green .40 .40
**311** A42 30fr dark blue .50 .50
*Nos. 308-311 (4)* 1.65 1.65

5th World Congress of the Intl. Federation of Trade Unions, Tunis, July 5-13.

### Republic

Officer and Soldier — A43

**1957, Aug. 8 Typo. *Perf. 11***

**312** A43 20fr rose pink 16.00 16.00
**313** A43 25fr light violet 16.00 16.00
**314** A43 30fr brown orange 16.00 16.00
*Nos. 312-314 (3)* 48.00 48.00

Proclamation of the Republic.

Bourguiba in Exile, Ile de la Galité A44

**1958, Jan. 18 Engr. *Perf. 13***

**315** A44 20fr blue & dk brn .50 .40
**316** A44 25fr lt blue & vio .50 .40

6th anniv. of Bourguiba's deportation.

Map of Tunisia — A45

25fr, Woman & child. 30fr, Hand holding flag.

**1958, Mar. 20 *Perf. 13***

**317** A45 20fr dk brown & emer .35 .20
**318** A45 25fr blue & sepia .35 .20
**319** A45 30fr red brown & red .50 .20
*Nos. 317-319 (3)* 1.20 .60

2nd anniv. of independence. See No. 321.

Andreas Vesalius and Abderrahman ibn Khaldoun — A46

**1958, Apr. 17 Unwmk.**

**320** A46 30fr bister & slate grn .50 .25

World's Fair, Brussels, Apr. 17-Oct. 19.

### Redrawn Type of 1958

**1958, June 1 Engr. *Perf. 13***

**321** A45 20fr brt bl & ocher .50 .50

Date has been changed to "1 Juin 1955-1958."

3rd anniv. of the return of Pres. Habib Bourguiba.

Gardener — A47

A48

**1958, May 1**

**322** A47 20fr multicolored .50 .30

Labor Day, May 1.

**1958, July 25 Unwmk. *Perf. 13***

**Blue Paper**

**323** A48 5fr dk vio brn & ol .50 .25
**324** A48 10fr dk grn & yel grn .50 .25
**325** A48 15fr org red & brn lake .50 .25
**326** A48 20fr vio, ol grn & yel .50 .25
**327** A48 25fr red lilac .50 .25
*Nos. 323-327 (5)* 2.50 1.25

First anniversary of the Republic.

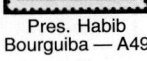

Pres. Habib Bourguiba — A49

Fishermen Casting Net — A50

**1958, Aug. 3 Unwmk. *Perf. 13***

**328** A49 20fr vio & brn lake .35 .25

Pres. Bourguiba's 55th birthday.

**1958, Oct. 18 Engr. *Perf. 13***

**329** A50 25fr dk brn, grn & red .65 .35

6th International Fair, Tunis.

UNESCO Building, Paris A51

**1958, Nov. 3**

**330** A51 25fr grnsh black .60 .35

Opening of UNESCO Headquarters, Nov. 3.

Woman Opening Veil — A52

Hand Planting Symbolic Tree — A53

Habib Bourguiba at Borj le Boeuf A54

**1959, Jan. 1 Engr. *Perf. 13***

**331** A52 20m greenish blue .40 .25

Emancipation of Tunisian women.

**1959, Mar. 2 Unwmk. *Perf. 13***

10m, Shield with flag and people holding torch. 20m, Habib Bourguiba at Borj le Boeuf, Sahara.

**332** A53 5m vio brn, car & sal .25 .20
**333** A53 10m multicolored .35 .20
**334** A53 20m blue .40 .25
**335** A54 30m grnsh bl, ind & org brn .75 .50
*Nos. 332-335 (4)* 1.75 1.15

25th anniv. of the founding of the Neo-Destour Party at Kasr Helal, Mar. 2, 1934.

"Independence" — A55

**1959, Mar. 20**

**336** A55 50m olive, blk & red .80 .40

3rd anniversary of independence.

Map of Africa and Drawings — A56

**1959, Apr. 15 Litho. *Perf. 13***

**337** A56 40m lt bl & red brn .65 .40

Africa Freedom Day, Apr. 15.

Camel Camp and Mosque, Kairouan A57

Horseback Rider — A58

Olive Picker — A59

Open Window A58a

Designs: ½m, Woodcock in Ain-Draham forest. 2m, Camel rider. 3m, Saddler's shop. 4m, Old houses of Medenine, gazelle and youth. 6m, Weavers. 8m, Woman of Gafsa. 10m, Unveiled woman holding fruit. 12m, Ivory craftsman. 15m, Skanes Beach, Monastir, and mermaid. 16m, Minaret of Ez-Zitouna University, Tunis. 20m, Oasis of Gabès. 25m, Oil, flowers and fish of Sfax. 30m, Modern and Roman aqueducts. 40m, Festival at Kairouan (drummer and camel). 45m, Octagonal minaret, Bizerte (boatman). 50m, Three women of Djerba island. 60m, Date palms, Djerid. 70m, Tapestry weaver. 75m, Pottery of Nabeul. 90m, Le Kef (man on horse). 100m, Road to Sidi-bou-Said. 200m, Old port of Sfax. ½d, Roman temple, Sbeitla. 1d, Farmer plowing with oxen, Beja.

**1959-61 Unwmk. Engr. *Perf. 13***

**338** A58 ½m emer, brn & bl grn ('60) .20 .20
**339** A57 1m lt bl & ocher .20 .20
**340** A58 2m multicolored .20 .20
**341** A58 3m slate green .20 .20
**342** A57 4m red brn ('60) .25 .20
**343** A58 5m gray green .20 .20
**344** A58 6m rose violet .25 .20
**345** A58 8m vio brn ('60) .85 .35
**346** A58 10m ol, dk grn & car .20 .20
**347** A58 12m vio bl & ol bis ('61) .65 .25
**348** A57 15m brt blue ('60) .35 .20
**349** A57 16m grnsh blk ('60) .35 .25
**350** A58a 20m grnsh blue 1.25 .35
**351** A58 20m grnsh blk, ol & mar ('60) 2.10 .25
**352** A57 25m multi ('60) .35 .25
**353** A58a 30m brn, grnsh bl & ol .50 .20
**354** A59 40m dp grn ('60) 1.90 .25
**355** A58a 45m brt grn ('60) .75 .35
**356** A58a 50m Prus grn, dk bl & rose ('60) 1.10 .25
**357** A58a 60m grn & red brn ('60) 1.10 .40
**358** A59 70m multi ('60) 1.60 .60
**359** A59 75m ol gray ('60) 1.50 .65
**360** A58a 90m brt grn, ultra & choc ('60) 1.50 .65
**361** A59 95m multicolored 2.10 1.25
**362** A58a 100m dk bl, ol & brn 2.10 1.10
**363** A58a 200m brt bl, bis & car 5.50 2.75
**363A** A59 ½d lt brn ('60) 13.50 7.50
**363B** A58a 1d sl grn & bis ('60) 25.00 15.00
*Nos. 338-363B (28)* 65.75 34.45

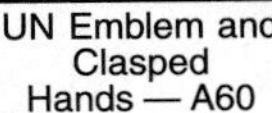

UN Emblem and Clasped Hands — A60

Dancer and Coin — A61

**1959, Oct. 24**

**364** A60 80m org brn, brn & ultra .85 .60

UN Day, Oct. 24.

**1959, Nov. 4**

**365** A61 50m grnsh bl & blk .65 .65

Central Bank of Tunisia, first anniversary.

Uprooted Oak Emblem — A62

Doves and WRY Emblem A63

**1960, Apr. 7 Engr. *Perf. 13***
**366** A62 20m blue black .50 .35
**367** A63 40m red lil & dk grn .65 .50

World Refugee Year, 7/1/59-6/30/60.

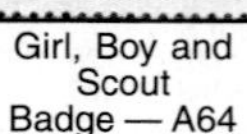


Girl, Boy and Scout Badge — A64

Cyclist — A65

Designs: 25m, Hand giving Scout sign. 30m, Bugler and tent. 40m, Peacock and Scout emblem. 60m, Scout and campfire.

**1960, Aug. 9**
**368** A64 10m lt blue green .35 .35
**369** A64 25m green, red & brn .50 .40
**370** A64 30m vio bl, grn & mar .60 .40
**371** A64 40m black, car & bl .65 .50
**372** A64 60m dk brn, vio blk & lake 1.40 .65
*Nos. 368-372 (5)* 3.50 2.30

4th Arab Boy Scout Jamboree, Tunis, Aug.

**1960, Aug. 25**

Designs: 10m, Olympic rings forming flower. 15m, Girl tennis player and minaret. 25m, Runner and minaret. 50m, Handball player and minaret.

**373** A65 5m dk brown & olive .35 .35
**374** A65 10m sl, red vio & emer .35 .35
**375** A65 15m rose red & rose car .35 .35
**376** A65 25m grnsh bl & gray bl .50 .50
**377** A65 50m brt green & ultra .90 .90
*Nos. 373-377 (5)* 2.45 2.45

17th Olympic Games, Rome, 8/25-9/11.

Symbolic Forest Design — A66

National Fair Emblems — A67

Designs: 15m, Man working in forest. 25m, Tree superimposed on leaf. 50m, Symbolic tree and bird.

**1960, Aug. 29**
**378** A66 8m multicolored .35 .25
**379** A66 15m dark green .50 .25
**380** A66 25m dk pur, crim & brt grn .65 .35
**381** A66 50m Prus grn, yel grn & rose lake 1.25 .60
*Nos. 378-381 (4)* 2.75 1.45

5th World Forestry Congress, Seattle, Wash., Aug. 29-Sept. 10.

**1960, June 1**
**382** A67 100m black & green .85 .60

5th Natl. Fair, Sousse, May 27-June 12.

Pres. Bourguiba Signing Constitution A68

Pres. Bourguiba A69

**1960, June 1**
**383** A68 20m choc, red & emer .50 .40
**384** A69 20m grayish blk .25 .20
**385** A69 30m blue, dl red & blk .35 .20
**386** A69 40m grn, dl red & blk .50 .25
*Nos. 383-386 (4)* 1.60 1.05

Promulgation of the Constitution (No. 383).

UN Emblem and Arms — A70

Dove and "Liberated Tunisia" — A71

**1960, Oct. 24 Engr. *Perf. 13***
**387** A70 40m mag, ultra & gray grn .65 .60

15th anniversary of the United Nations.

**1961, Mar. 20 *Perf. 13***

Design: 75m, Globe and arms.

**388** A71 20m maroon, bis & bl .25 .25
**389** A71 30m blue, vio & brn .35 .25
**390** A71 40m yel grn & ultra .65 .50
**391** A71 75m bis, red lil & Prus bl .85 .60
*Nos. 388-391 (4)* 2.10 1.60

5th anniversary of independence.

Map of Africa, Woman and Animals — A72

Mother and Child with Flags — A73

Map of Africa: 60m, Negro woman and Arab. 100m, Arabic inscription and Guinea masque. 200m, Hands of Negro and Arab.

**1961, Apr. 15 Engr. Unwmk.**
**392** A72 40m bis brn, red brn & dk grn .35 .25
**393** A72 60m sl grn, blk & org brn .40 .35
**394** A72 100m sl grn, emer & vio .85 .50
**395** A72 200m dk brn & org brn 1.50 1.25
*Nos. 392-395 (4)* 3.10 2.35

Africa Freedom Day, Apr. 15.

**1961, June 1 Unwmk. *Perf. 13***

Designs: 50m, Tunisians. 95m, Girl with wings and half-moon.

**396** A73 25m pale vio, red & brn .35 .20
**397** A73 50m bl grn, sep & brn .50 .25
**398** A73 95m pale vio, rose lil & ocher .75 .40
*Nos. 396-398 (3)* 1.60 .85

National Feast Day, June 1.

Dag Hammarskjold A74

Arms of Tunisia A75

**1961, Oct. 24 Photo. *Perf. 14***
**399** A74 40m ultramarine .65 .35

UN Day; Dag Hammarskjold (1905-1961), Secretary General of the UN, 1953-61.

**1962, Jan. 18 *Perf. 11½***
**Arms in Original Colors**
**400** A75 1m black & yellow .20 .20
**401** A75 2m black & pink .20 .20
**402** A75 3m black & lt blue .20 .20
**403** A75 6m black & gray .25 .25
*Nos. 400-403 (4)* .85 .85

Tunisia's campaign for independence, 10th anniv.

Mosquito in Spider Web and WHO Emblem — A76

Designs: 30m, Symbolic horseback rider spearing mosquito. 40m, Hands crushing mosquito, horiz.

**1962, Apr. 7 Engr. *Perf. 13***
**404** A76 20m chocolate .50 .35
**405** A76 30m red brn & slate grn .40 .35
**406** A76 40m dk brn, mar & grn .90 .40
*Nos. 404-406 (3)* 1.80 1.10

WHO drive to eradicate malaria.

Boy and Map of Africa — A77

African Holding "Africa" — A78

**1962, Apr. 15 Photo. *Perf. 14***
**407** A77 50m brown & orange .60 .40
**408** A78 100m blue, blk & org .85 .60

Africa Freedom Day, Apr. 15.

Farm Worker — A79

Industrial Worker — A80

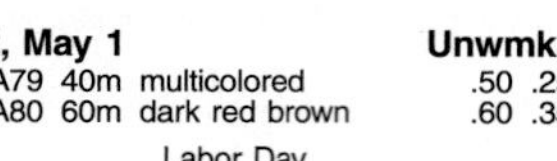

**1962, May 1 Unwmk.**
**409** A79 40m multicolored .50 .25
**410** A80 60m dark red brown .60 .35

Labor Day.

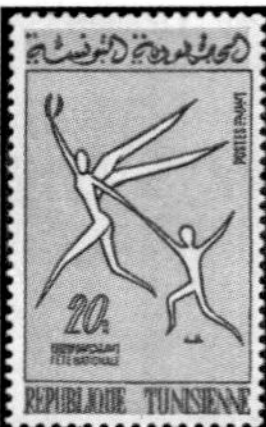


"Liberated Tunisia" — A81

Woman of Gabès — A82

**1962, June 1 Typo. *Perf. 13½x14***
**411** A81 20m salmon & blk .60 .35

National Feast Day, June 1.

**1962-63 Photo. *Perf. 11½***

Women in costume of various localities: 10m, 30m, Mahdia. 15m, Kairouan. 20m, 40m, Hammamet. 25m, Djerba. 55m, Ksar Hellal. 60m, Tunis.

**412** A82 5m multi .65 .25
**413** A82 10m multi .85 .40
**414** A82 15m multi ('63) 1.25 .60
**415** A82 20m multi 1.25 .65
**416** A82 25m multi ('63) 1.25 .65
**417** A82 30m multi 1.50 .85
**418** A82 40m multi 1.60 .85
**419** A82 50m multi 1.60 1.00
**420** A82 55m multi ('63) 2.50 1.25
**421** A82 60m multi ('63) 3.25 1.60
*Nos. 412-421 (10)* 15.70 8.10

6 stamps issued July 25, 1962 (July 25) for the 6th anniv. of Tunisia's independence. 4 issued June 1, 1963 for Natl. Feast Day. See Nos. 470-471.

UN Emblem, Flag and Dove — A83

Aboul-Qasim Chabbi — A84

30m, Leaves, globe, horiz. 40m, Dove, globe.

**1962, Oct. 24 Unwmk.**
**422** A83 20m gray, blk & scar .35 .20
**423** A83 30m multicolored .50 .25
**424** A83 40m claret brn, blk & bl .75 .40
*Nos. 422-424 (3)* 1.60 .85

Issued for United Nations Day, Oct. 24.

**1962, Nov. 20 Engr. *Perf. 13***
**425** A84 15m purple .40 .25

Aboul-Qasim Chabbi (1904-34), Arab poet.

Pres. Habib Bourguiba A85

Hached Telephone Exchange A86

**1962, Dec. 7 Photo. *Perf. 12½x13½***
**426** A85 20m bright blue .20 .20
**427** A85 30m rose claret .25 .20
**428** A85 40m green .25 .20
*Nos. 426-428 (3)* .70 .60

**1962, Dec. 7 Litho.**

Designs: 10m, Carthage Exchange. 15m, Sfax telecommunications center. 50m, Telephone operators. 100m, Symbol of automatization. 200m, Belvedere Central Exchange.

**429** A86 5m multicolored .35 .25
**430** A86 10m multicolored .85 .40
**431** A86 15m multicolored 1.40 .70
**432** A86 50m multicolored 1.50 .85

433 A86 100m multicolored 2.10 1.20
434 A86 200m multicolored 3.00 1.90
*Nos. 429-434 (6)* 9.20 5.30

1st Afro-Asian Philatelic Exhibition; automation of the telephone system.

Dove over Globe — A87

"Hunger" — A88

**1963, Mar. 21 Engr. *Perf. 13***
435 A87 20m brt bl & brn .35 .25
436 A88 40m bis brn & dk brn .50 .25

FAO "Freedom from Hunger" campaign.

Runner and Walker — A89

Centenary Emblem — A90

**1963, Feb. 17 Litho. *Perf. 13***
437 A89 30m brn, blk & grn .65 .50

Army Sports Day; 13th C.I.S.M. cross country championships.

**1963, May 8 Engr. *Perf. 13***
438 A90 20m brn, gray & red .60 .35

Centenary of International Red Cross.

"Human Rights" — A91

Hand Raising Gateway of Great Temple of Philae — A92

**1963, Dec. 10 Unwmk. *Perf. 13***
439 A91 30m grn & dk brn .50 .35

15th anniv. of the Universal Declaration of Human Rights.

**1964, Mar. 8 Engr.**
440 A92 50m red brn, bis & bluish blk .50 .35

UNESCO world campaign to save historic monuments in Nubia.

Sunshine, Rain and Barometer — A93

Mohammed Ali — A94

**1964, Mar. 8 Unwmk. *Perf. 13***
441 A93 40m brn, red lil & slate .50 .25

4th World Meteorological Day, Mar. 23.

**1964, May 15 Engr.**
442 A94 50m sepia .50 .40

Mohammed Ali (1894-1928), labor leader.

Map of Africa and Symbolic Flower — A95

Pres. Habib Bourguiba — A96

**1964, May 25 Photo. *Perf. 13x14***
443 A95 60m multicolored .60 .35

Addis Ababa charter on African Unity, 1st anniv.

**1964, June 1 Engr. *Perf. 12½x13½***
444 A96 20m vio bl .20 .20
445 A96 30m black .25 .20

"Ship and Torch" — A97

**1964, Oct. 19 Photo. *Perf. 11½x11***
446 A97 50m blk & grn .50 .35

Neo-Destour Congress, Bizerte. "Bizerte" in Arabic forms the ship and "Neo-Destour Congress 1964" the torch of the design.

Communication Equipment and ITU Emblem — A98

**1965, May 17 Engr. *Perf. 13***
447 A98 55m gray & blue .60 .35

ITU, centenary.

Carthaginian Coin — A99

Girl with Book — A100

***Perf. 12½x14***
**1965, July 9 Photo. Unwmk.**
448 A99 5m grn & blk brn .20 .20
449 A99 10m bis & blk brn .35 .25
450 A99 75m bl & blk brn .85 .25
*Nos. 448-450 (3)* 1.40 .70

Festival of Popular Arts, Carthage.

**1965, Oct. 1 Engr. *Perf. 13***
451 A100 25m brt bl, blk & red .35 .25
452 A100 40m blk, bl & red .40 .25
453 A100 50m red, bl & blk .50 .35
*a.* Souvenir sheet of 3, #451-453 5.50 5.50
*Nos. 451-453 (3)* 1.25 .85

Girl Students' Center; education for women. No. 453a sold for 200m. Issued perf. and imperf.; same value.

Links and ICY Emblem — A101

Man Pouring Water — A102

**1965, Oct. 24**
454 A101 40m blk, brt bl & rose lil .50 .25

International Cooperation Year.

**1966, Jan. 18 Photo. *Perf. 13x14***

Symbolic Designs: 10m, Woman and pool. 30m, Woman pouring water. 100m, Mountain and branches.

**Inscribed "Eaux Minerales"**
455 A102 10m gray, ocher & dk red .35 .25
456 A102 20m multicolored .50 .40
457 A102 30m yel, bl & red .50 .40
458 A102 100m ol, bl & yel 1.40 .75
*Nos. 455-458 (4)* 2.75 1.80

Mineral waters of Tunisia.

President Bourguiba and Hands A103

"Promotion of Culture" — A104

25m, "Independence" (arms raised), flag and doves. 40m, "Development."

**1966, June 1 Engr. *Perf. 13***
459 A103 5m dl pur & vio .20 .20
460 A103 10m gray grn & sl grn .25 .20

***Perf. 11½***
**Photo.**
461 A104 25m multi .25 .20
462 A104 40m multi, horiz. .65 .25
463 A104 60m multi 1.00 .40
*Nos. 459-463 (5)* 2.35 1.25

10th anniversary of independence.

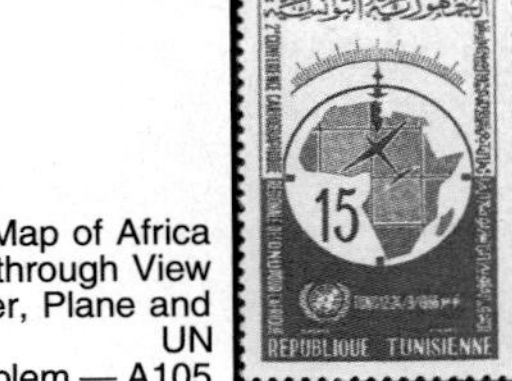
Map of Africa through View Finder, Plane and UN Emblem — A105

**1966, Sept. 12 Engr. *Perf. 13***
464 A105 15m lilac & multicolored .35 .25
465 A105 35m blue & multi .40 .25
466 A105 40m multicolored .60 .40
*a.* Souvenir sheet, #464-466 11.00 11.00
*Nos. 464-466 (3)* 1.35 .90

2nd UN Regional Cartographic Conference for Africa, held in Tunisia, Sept. 12-24.
No. 466a sold for 150m. Issued perf. and imperf.; same value.

UNESCO Emblem and Nine Muses A106

**1966, Oct. 24 *Perf. 13***
467 A106 100m blk & brn 1.10 .40

UNESCO, 20th anniv.

Runners and Mediterranean Map — A107

**1967, Mar. 20 Engr. *Perf. 13***
468 A107 20m dk red, brn ol & bl .25 .25
469 A107 30m brt bl & blk .50 .35

Mediterranean Games, Sept. 8-17.

Types of 1962-63 and 1965-66 with EXPO '67 Emblem and Inscription and

Symbols of Various Activities — A108

Designs: 50m, Woman of Djerba. 75m, Woman of Gabes. 155m, Pink flamingoes.

**Photo.; Engr. (A108)**
**1967, Apr. 28 *Perf. 11½, 13 (A108)***
470 A82 50m multicolored .50 .25
471 A82 75m multicolored .75 .35
472 A108 100m dk grn, sl bl & blk 1.25 .35
473 A108 110m dk brn, ultra & red 1.60 .65
474 AP6 155m multicolored 2.40 .85
*Nos. 470-474 (5)* 6.50 2.45

EXPO '67, Intl. Exhibition, Montreal, Apr. 28-Oct. 27.

Tunisian Pavilion, Pres. Bourguiba and Map of Tunisia — A109

Designs: 105m, 200m, Tunisian Pavilion and bust of Pres. Bourguiba.

**1967, June 13 Engr. *Perf. 13***
475 A109 65m red lil & dp org .50 .40
476 A109 105m multicolored .60 .40
477 A109 120m brt bl .75 .40
478 A109 200m red, lil & blk 1.25 .60
*Nos. 475-478 (4)* 3.10 1.80

Tunisia Day at EXPO '67.

"Tunisia" Holding 4-leaf Clovers A110

Woman Freeing Doves — A111

**1967, July 25 Litho. *Perf. 13½***

**479** A110 25m multicolored .25 .20
**480** A111 40m multicolored .40 .20

10th anniversary of the Republic.

Tennis Courts, Players and Games' Emblem — A112

10m, Games' emblem & sports emblems, vert. 15m, Swimming pool & swimmers. 35m, Sports Palace & athletes. 75m, Stadium & athletes.

**1967, Sept. 8 Engr. *Perf. 13***

**481** A112 5m sl grn & hn brn .25 .25
**482** A112 10m brn red & multi .25 .25
**483** A112 15m black .35 .25
**484** A112 35m dk brn & Prus bl .50 .25
**485** A112 75m dk car rose, vio & bl grn .95 .50
*Nos. 481-485 (5)* 2.30 1.50

Mediterranean Games, Tunis, Sept. 8-17.

Bird, Punic Period — A113

"Mankind" and Human Rights Flame — A114

History of Tunisia: 20m, Sea horse, medallion from Kerkouane. 25m, Hannibal, bronze bust, Volubilis. 30m, Stele, Carthage. 40m, Hamilcar, coin. 60m, Mask, funereal pendant.

**1967, Dec. 1 Litho. *Perf. 13½***

**486** A113 15m gray grn, pink & blk .35 .25
**487** A113 20m dp bl, red & blk .35 .25
**488** A113 25m dk grn & org brn .50 .25
**489** A113 30m grnsh gray, pink & blk .50 .25
**490** A113 40m red brn, yel & blk .65 .25
**491** A113 60m multicolored .75 .35
*Nos. 486-491 (6)* 3.10 1.60

**1968, Jan. 18 Engr. *Perf. 13***

**492** A114 25m brick red .50 .40
**493** A114 60m deep blue .50 .25

International Human Rights Year.

Computer Fantasy A115

**1968, Mar. 20 Engr. *Perf. 13***

**494** A115 25m mag, bl vio & ol .40 .35
**495** A115 40m ol grn, red brn & brn .40 .35
**496** A115 60m ultra, slate & brn .50 .40
*Nos. 494-496 (3)* 1.30 1.10

Introduction of electronic equipment for postal service.

Physician and Patient — A116

Arabian Jasmine — A117

**1968, Apr. 7 Engr. *Perf. 13***

**497** A116 25m dp grn & brt grn .50 .40
**498** A116 60m magenta & carmine .50 .40

WHO, 20th anniversary.

**1968-69 Photo. *Perf. 11½***

Flowers: 5m, Flax. 6m, Canna indica. 10m, Pomegranate. 15m, Rhaponticum acaule. 20m, Geranium. 25m, Madonna lily. 40m, Peach blossoms. 50m, Caper. 60m, Ariana rose. 100m, Jasmine.

**Granite Paper**

**499** A117 5m multicolored .25 .20
**500** A117 6m multicolored .25 .20
**501** A117 10m multicolored .35 .20
**502** A117 12m multicolored .35 .20
**503** A117 15m multicolored .40 .20
**504** A117 20m multicolored .50 .25
**505** A117 25m multicolored .65 .30
**506** A117 40m multicolored .75 .40
**507** A117 50m multicolored 1.00 .40
**508** A117 60m multicolored 1.40 .65
**509** A117 100m multicolored 1.90 .90
*Nos. 499-509 (11)* 7.80 3.90

Issued: 12, 50, 60, 100m, 4/9/68; others, 3/20/69.

Flower with Red Crescent and Globe — A118

Flutist — A119

25m, Dove with Red Crescent and globe.

**1968, May 8 Engr. *Perf. 13***

**510** A118 15m Prus bl, grn & red .40 .35
**511** A118 25m brt rose lil & red .50 .35

Red Crescent Society.

**1968, June 1 Litho. *Perf. 13***

**512** A119 20m vio & multi .40 .25
**513** A119 50m multicolored .50 .40

Stamp Day.

Jackal A120

Animals: 8m, Porcupine. 10m, Dromedary. 15m, Dorcas gazelle. 20m, Desert fox (fennec). 25m, Desert hedgehog. 40m, Arabian horse. 60m, Boar.

**1968-69 Photo. *Perf. 11½***

**514** A120 5m dk brn, lt bl & bis .35 .25
**515** A120 8m dk vio brn & yel grn .50 .25
**516** A120 10m dk brn, lt bl & ocher .65 .25
**517** A120 15m dk brn, ocher & yel grn .75 .25
**518** A120 20m dl yel & dk brn 1.25 .50
**519** A120 25m blk, tan & brt grn 1.60 .65
**520** A120 40m blk, lil & pale grn 2.00 1.00
**521** A120 60m dk brn, buff & yel grn 3.00 1.40
*Nos. 514-521 (8)* 10.10 4.55

Issued: 5, 8, 20, 60m, 9/15/68; others, 1/18/69.

Worker and ILO Emblem — A121

60m, Young man & woman holding banner.

**1969, May 1 Engr. *Perf. 13***

**522** A121 25m Prus bl, blk & bis .40 .35
**523** A121 60m rose car, bl & yel .60 .40

ILO, 50th anniversary.

Veiled Women and Musicians with Flute and Drum A122

**1969, June 20 Litho. *Perf. 14x13½***

**524** A122 100m dp yel grn & multi .95 .40

Stamp Day.

Tunisian Coat of Arms — A123

Lute — A125

Nurse and Maghrib Flags — A126

Symbols of Industry — A124

**1969, July 25 Photo. *Perf. 11½***

**525** A123 15m yel & multi .25 .25
**526** A123 25m pink & multi .35 .25
**527** A123 40m gray & multi .40 .25
**528** A123 60m lt bl & multi .50 .25
*Nos. 525-528 (4)* 1.50 1.00

**1969, Sept. 10 *Perf. 13x12***

**529** A124 60m blk, red & yel .50 .30

African Development Bank, 5th anniv.

Musical Instruments: 50m, Zither, horiz. 70m, Rebab (2-strings). 90m, Drums and flute, horiz.

**1970, Mar. 20 Photo. *Perf. 11½***

**Granite Paper**

**530** A125 25m multicolored .50 .40
**531** A125 50m multicolored .65 .40
**532** A125 70m multicolored .95 .40
**533** A125 90m multicolored 1.25 .40
*Nos. 530-533 (4)* 3.35 1.60

**1970, May 4 Photo. *Perf. 11½***

**534** A126 25m lilac & multi .20 .20

6th Medical Seminar of Maghrib Countries (Morocco, Algeria, Tunisia and Libya), Tunis, May 4-10.

Common Design Types pictured following the introduction.

**UPU Headquarters Issue**

Common Design Type

**1970, May 20 Engr. *Perf. 13***

**535** CD133 25m dl red & dk ol bis .50 .25

Mail Service Symbol A127

35m, Mailmen of yesterday and today, vert.

**1970, Oct. 15 Litho. *Perf. 12½x13***

**Size: 37x31½mm**

**536** A127 25m pink & multi .30 .25

**Size: 22x37½mm**

***Perf. 13x12½***

**537** A127 35m blk & multi .40 .25

United Nations, 25th anniversary.

Dove, Laurel and UN Emblem A128

**1970, Oct. 24 Photo. *Perf. 13x12½***

**538** A128 40m multicolored .50 .25

United Nations, 25th anniversary.

Jasmine Vendor and Veiled Woman — A129

Lenin, after N.N. Joukov — A130

Scenes from Tunisian Life: 25m, "The 3rd Day of the Wedding." 35m, Perfume vendor. 40m, Fish vendor. 85m, Waiter in coffeehouse.

**1970, Nov. 9 Photo. *Perf. 14***

**539** A129 20m dk grn & multi .25 .20
**540** A129 25m multicolored .30 .25
**541** A129 35m multicolored .50 .40
**542** A129 40m dp car & multi .60 .40
**543** A129 85m brt bl & multi .95 .40
*a.* Souvenir sheet of 5, #539-543 7.50 7.50
*Nos. 539-543 (5)* 2.60 1.65

No. 543a sold for 500m. Issued perf. and imperf.; same value.

**1970, Dec. 28 Engr. *Perf. 13***

**544** A130 60m dk car rose 1.25 .30

Lenin (1870-1924), Russian communist leader.

Radar, Flags and Carrier Pigeon — A131

UN Headquarters, Symbolic Flower — A132

**1971, May 17 Litho. *Perf. 13x12½***
**545** A131 25m lt bl & multi .50 .40

Coordinating Committee for Post and Telecommunications Administrations of Maghrib Countries.

**1971, May 10 Photo. *Perf. 12½x13***
**546** A132 80m brt rose lil, blk & yel .50 .30

Intl. year against racial discrimination.

"Telecommunications" — A133

**1971, May 17 *Perf. 13x12½***
**547** A133 70m sil, blk & lt grn .50 .25

3rd World Telecommunications Day.

Earth, Moon, Satellites A134

Design: 90m, Abstract composition.

**1971, June 21 Photo. *Perf. 13x12½***
**548** A134 15m brt bl & blk .40 .25
**549** A134 90m scar & blk .75 .30

Conquest of space.

"Pottery Merchant" A135

Life in Tunisia (stylized drawings): 30m, Esparto weaver selling hats and mats. 40m, Poultry man. 50m, Dyer.

**1971, July 24 Photo. *Perf. 14x13½***
**550** A135 25m gold & multi .40 .25
**551** A135 30m gold & multi .40 .25
**552** A135 40m gold & multi .50 .25
**553** A135 50m gold & multi .65 .25
*a.* Sheet of 4, #550-553, perf. 13½ 7.50 7.50
*Nos. 550-553 (4)* 1.95 1.00

No. 553a sold for 500m. Issued perf. and imperf.; same value.

Pres. Bourguiba Sick in 1938 A136

Designs: 25m, Bourguiba and "8," vert. 50m, Bourguiba carried in triumph, vert. 80m, Bourguiba and irrigation dam.

**1971, Oct. 11 *Perf. 13½x13, 13x13½***
**554** A136 25m multicolored .25 .25
**555** A136 30m multicolored .25 .25
**556** A136 50m multicolored .40 .35
**557** A136 80m blk, ultra & grn .60 .35
*Nos. 554-557 (4)* 1.50 1.20

8th Congress of the Neo-Destour Party.

Shah Mohammed Riza Pahlavi and Stone Head 6th Century B.C. — A137

50m, King Bahram-Gur hunting, 4th cent. 100m, Coronation, from Persian miniature, 1614.

**1971, Oct. 17 *Perf. 11½***
**Granite Paper**
**558** A137 25m multicolored .35 .35
**559** A137 50m multicolored .40 .25
**560** A137 100m multicolored .75 .30
*a.* Souvenir sheet of 3, #558-560 4.50 4.50
*Nos. 558-560 (3)* 1.50 .90

2500th anniv. of the founding of the Persian empire by Cyrus the Great. No. 560a sold for 500m. Issued perf. and imperf.; same value.

Pimento and Warrior A138

2m, Mint & farmer. 5m, Pear & 2 men under pear tree. 25m, Oleander & girl. 60m, Pear & sheep. 100m, Grapefruit & fruit vendor.

**1971, Nov. 15 Litho. *Perf. 13***
**561** A138 1m lt bl & multi .25 .20
**562** A138 2m gray & multi .30 .30
**563** A138 5m citron & multi .40 .30
**564** A138 25m lilac & multi .65 .40
**565** A138 60m multicolored 1.25 .30
**566** A138 100m buff & multi 1.90 .50
*a.* Souvenir sheet of 6, #561-566 8.50 8.50
*Nos. 561-566 (6)* 4.75 2.00

Fruit, flowers and folklore. No. 566a sold for 500m. Exists imperf.; same value.

Dancer and Musician — A139

**1971, Nov. 22 Photo. *Perf. 11½***
**567** A139 50m blue & multi .50 .25

Stamp Day.

Map of Africa, Communica-tion Symbols A139a

UNICEF Emblem, Mother and Child A140

***Perf. 13½x12½***
**1971, Nov. 30 Litho.**
**568** A139a 95m multicolored .60 .50

Pan-African telecommunications system.

**1971, Dec. 6 Photo. *Perf. 11½***
**569** A140 110m multicolored .60 .40

UNICEF, 25th anniv.

Symbolic Olive Tree and Oil Vat — A141

Gondolier in Flood Waters — A142

**1972, Jan. 9 Litho. *Perf. 13½***
**570** A141 60m multicolored .50 .25

International Olive Year.

**1972, Feb. 7 Photo. *Perf. 11½***

Designs: 30m, Young man and Doge's Palace. 50m, Gondola's prow and flood. 80m, Rialto Bridge and hand holding gondolier's hat, horiz.

**571** A142 25m lt bl & multi .30 .25
**572** A142 30m blk & multi .50 .25
**573** A142 50m yel grn, gray & blk .50 .40
**574** A142 80m bl & multi .95 .40
*Nos. 571-574 (4)* 2.25 1.30

UNESCO campaign to save Venice.

Man Reading and Book Year Emblem — A143

"Your Heart is Your Health" — A144

**1972, Mar. 27 Photo. *Perf. 11½***
**Granite Paper**
**575** A143 90m brn & multi .60 .50

International Book Year.

**1972, Apr. 7 *Perf. 13x13½***

World Health Day: 60m, Smiling man pointing to heart.

**576** A144 25m grn & multi .40 .25
**577** A144 60m red & multi .65 .40

"Only one Earth" Environment Emblem — A145

**1972, June 5 Engr. *Perf. 13***
**578** A145 60m lemon & slate green .60 .25

UN Conference on Human Environment, Stockholm, June 5-16.

Hurdler, Olympic Emblems A146

**1972, Aug. 26 Photo. *Perf. 11½***
**579** A146 5m Volleyball .25 .20
**580** A146 15m shown .30 .20
**581** A146 20m Athletes .30 .20
**582** A146 25m Soccer .30 .25
**583** A146 60m Swimming, women's .50 .25
**584** A146 80m Running .65 .30
*a.* Souv. sheet of 6 4.50 4.50
*Nos. 579-584 (6)* 2.30 1.40

20th Olympic Games, Munich, Aug. 26-Sept. 11. No. 584a contains 6 imperf. stamps similar to Nos. 579-584. Sold for 500m.

Chessboard and Pieces — A147

Fisherman A148

**1972, Sept. 25 Photo. *Perf. 11½***
**585** A147 60m grn & multi 2.25 1.00

20th Men's Chess Olympiad, Skopje, Yugoslavia, Sept.-Oct.

**1972, Oct. 23 Litho. *Perf. 13½***
**586** A148 5m shown .25 .20
**587** A148 10m Basket maker .25 .25
**588** A148 25m Musician .35 .25
**589** A148 50m Married Berber woman .85 .25
**590** A148 60m Flower merchant 1.10 .35
**591** A148 80m Festival 1.40 .50
*a.* Souvenir sheet of 6, #586-591 5.00 5.00
*Nos. 586-591 (6)* 4.20 1.80

Life in Tunisia. No. 591a sold for 500m; exists imperf.

Post Office, Tunis A149

**Litho. & Engr.**
**1972, Dec. 8 *Perf. 13***
**592** A149 25m ver, org & blk .30 .25

Stamp Day.

Dome of the Rock, Jerusalem A150

**1973, Jan. 22 Photo. *Perf. 13½***
**593** A150 25m multicolored .65 .35

Globe, Pen and Quill — A151

Family — A152

Design: 60m, Lyre and minaret.

**1973, Mar. 19 Photo. *Perf. 14x13½***
**594** A151 25m gold, brt mag & brn .25 .25
**595** A151 60m bl & multi .40 .25

9th Congress of Arab Writers.

**1973, Apr. 2 *Perf. 11½***

Family Planning: 25m, profiles and dove.

**596** A152 20m grn & multi .25 .25
**597** A152 25m lil & multi .40 .35

"10" and Bird Feeding Young A153

Design: 60m, "10" made of grain and bread, and hand holding spoon.

**1973, Apr. 26 Photo. *Perf. 11½***
**598** A153 25m multicolored .65 .25
**599** A153 60m multicolored .65 .25

World Food Program, 10th anniversary.

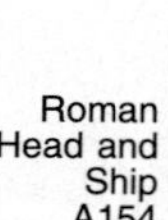

Roman Head and Ship A154

Drawings of Tools and: 25m, Mosaic with ostriches and camel. 30m, Mosaic with 4 heads and 4 emblems. 40m, Punic stele to the sun, vert. 60m, Outstretched hand & arm of Christian preacher; symbols of 4 Evangelists. 75m, 17th cent. potsherd with Arabic inscription, vert.

**1973, May 6**
**600** A154 5m multicolored .35 .25
**601** A154 25m multicolored .50 .40
**602** A154 30m multicolored .50 .40
**603** A154 40m multicolored .75 .40
**604** A154 60m multicolored .95 .40
**605** A154 75m multicolored 1.00 .50
*a.* Souvenir sheet of 6 9.25 9.25
*Nos. 600-605 (6)* 4.05 2.35

UNESCO campaign to save Carthage. No. 605a contains 6 imperf. stamps similar to Nos. 600-605. Sold for 500m.

Overlapping Circles — A155

Map of Africa as Festival Emblem — A156

Design: 75m, Printed circuit board.

**1973, May 17 Photo. *Perf. 14x13½***
**606** A155 60m yel & multi .40 .25
**607** A155 75m vio & multi .50 .25

5th Intl. Telecommunications Day.

**1973, July 15 Photo. *Perf. 13½x13***

40m, African heads, festival emblem in eye.

**608** A156 25m multicolored .40 .35
**609** A156 40m multicolored .50 .35

Pan-African Youth Festival, Tunis.

Scout Emblem and Pennants — A157

**1973, July 23 Litho. *Perf. 13½x13***
**610** A157 25m multicolored .40 .35

International Boy Scout Organization.

Crescent-shaped Racing Cars — A158

**1973, July 30 *Perf. 13x13½***
**611** A158 60m multicolored .50 .40

2nd Pan-Arab auto race.

Highway Cloverleaf A159

Traffic Lights and Signs — A160

Stylized Camel — A161

***Perf. 12½x13, 13x12½***
**1973, Sept. 28 Litho.**
**612** A159 25m lt bl & multi .65 .40
**613** A160 30m multicolored .75 .35

Highway safety campaign.

**1973, Oct. 8 Photo. *Perf. 13½***

Stamp Day: 10m, Stylized bird and philatelic symbols, horiz.

**614** A161 10m multicolored .40 .25
**615** A161 65m multicolored .50 .40

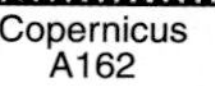

Copernicus A162

African Unity A163

**Lithographed and Engraved**
**1973, Oct. 16 *Perf. 13x12½***
**616** A162 60m blk & multi 1.25 .30

**1973, Nov. 4 Photo. *Perf. 14x13½***
**617** A163 25m blk & multi .50 .25

10th anniv. of the OAU.

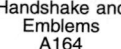

Handshake and Emblems A164

Globe, Hand Holding Carnation A165

**1973, Nov. 15 Litho. *Perf. 14½x14***
**618** A164 65m yel & multi .50 .40

25th anniv. of Intl. Criminal Police Org.

**1973, Dec. 10 Photo. *Perf. 11½***
**619** A165 60m blk & multi .65 .35

25th anniv. of Universal Declaration of Human Rights.

WMO Headquarters and Emblem — A166

Design: 60m, Globe and emblem.

**1973, Dec. 24 Litho. *Perf. 14x14½***
**620** A166 25m multicolored .50 .25
**621** A166 60m multicolored .65 .30

Intl. meteorological cooperation, cent.

Bourguiba in the Desert, 1945 — A167

Scientist with Microscope A168

Portraits of Pres. Habib Bourguiba: 25m, Exile transfer from Galite Island to Ile de la Groix, France, 1954. 60m, Addressing crowd, 1974. 75m, In Victory Parade, 1955. 100m, In 1934.

**1974, Mar. 2 Photo. *Perf. 11½***
**622** A167 15m plum & multi .25 .25
**623** A167 25m multicolored .25 .25
**624** A167 60m multicolored .30 .25
**625** A167 75m multicolored .40 .25
**626** A167 100m multicolored .50 .40
*a.* Souvenir sheet of 5, #622-626 2.75 2.75
*Nos. 622-626 (5)* 1.70 1.40

40th anniv. of the Neo-Destour Party. No. 626a sold for 500m. Issued perf. and imperf.; same value.

**1974, Mar. 21 *Perf. 14***
**627** A168 60m multicolored 1.00 .50

6th African Congress of Micropaleontology, Mar. 21-Apr. 3.

Woman with Telephones and Globe — A169

Pres. Bourguiba and Sun Flower Emblem — A171

WPY Emblem and Symbolic Design A170

60m, Telephone dial, telephones, wires.

**1974, July 1 Photo. *Perf. 11½***
**628** A169 15m multicolored .40 .40
**629** A169 60m multicolored .50 .50

Introduction of international automatic telephone dialing system.

**1974, Aug. 19 Photo. *Perf. 11½***
**630** A170 110m multicolored .65 .40

World Population Year.

**1974, Sept. 12 Photo. *Perf. 11½***

60m, Bourguiba and cactus flower, horiz. 200m, Bourguiba and verbena, horiz.

**631** A171 25m blk, ultra & grnsh bl .25 .25
**632** A171 60m red, car & yel .30 .25
**633** A171 200m blk, brt lil & grn 1.10 .60
*a.* Souv. sheet, #631-633, imperf. 3.25 3.25
*Nos. 631-633 (3)* 1.65 1.10

Congress of the Socialist Destour Party.

Jets Flying over Old World Map A172

**1974, Sept. 23 Litho. *Perf. 12½***
**634** A172 60m brn & multi .60 .40

25th anniversary of Tunisian aviation.

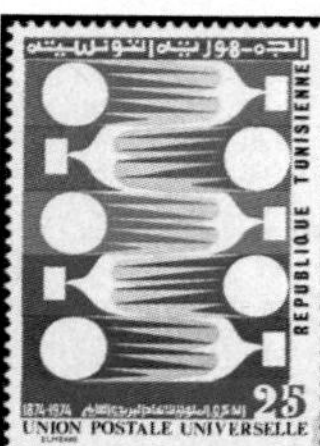

Symbolic Carrier Pigeons — A173

Handshake, Letter, UPU Emblem — A174

**1974, Oct. 9 Photo. *Perf. 13***

**635** A173 25m multicolored .40 .25
**636** A174 60m multicolored .50 .35

Centenary of Universal Postal Union.

Le Bardo, National Assembly — A175

Pres. Bourguiba Ballot — A176

**1974, Nov. 3 Photo. *Perf. 11½***

**637** A175 25m grn, bl & blk .40 .30
**638** A176 100m org & blk .60 .40

Legislative (25m) and presidential elections (100m), Nov. 1974.

Mailman with Letters and Bird — A177

Water Carrier — A178

**1974, Dec. 5 Litho. *Perf. 14½x14***

**639** A177 75m lt vio & multi .50 .25

Stamp Day.

**1975, Feb. 17 Photo. *Perf. 13½***

**640** A178 5m shown .25 .20
**641** A178 15m Perfume vendor .25 .25
**642** A178 25m Laundresses .25 .25
**643** A178 60m Potter .50 .25
**644** A178 110m Fruit vendor 1.00 .65
*a.* Souvenir sheet of 5, #640-644 5.00 5.00
*Nos. 640-644 (5)* 2.25 1.60

Life in Tunisia. No. 644a sold for 500m. Issued perf. and imperf.; same value.

Steel Tower, Skyscraper — A179

Geometric Designs and Arrow A180

***Perf. 14x13½, 13½x14***

**1975, Mar. 17 Photo.**

**645** A179 25m yel, org & blk .25 .25
**646** A180 65m ultra & multi .75 .35

Union of Arab Engineers, 13th Conference, Tunis, Mar. 17-21.

Brass Coffeepot and Plate — A181

15m, Horse and rider. 25m, Still life. 30m, Bird cage. 40m, Woman with earrings. 60m, Design patterns.

**1975, Apr. 14 *Perf. 13x14, 14x13***

**647** A181 10m blk & multi .25 .25
**648** A181 15m blk & multi .25 .25
**649** A181 25m blk & multi .35 .25
**650** A181 30m blk & multi, vert. .40 .25
**651** A181 40m blk & multi, vert. .40 .25
**652** A181 60m blk & multi .65 .30
*Nos. 647-652 (6)* 2.30 1.55

Artisans and their works.

Communications and Weather Symbols — A182

**1975, May 17 Photo. *Perf. 11½***

**653** A182 50m lt bl & multi .30 .25

World Telecommunications Day (communications serving meteorology).

Youth and Hope — A183

Tunisian Woman, IWY Emblem — A184

65m, Bourguiba arriving at La Goulette, Tunis.

**1975, June 1 Photo. *Perf. 11½***

**654** A183 25m multi .25 .25
**655** A183 65m multi, horiz. .40 .25

Victory (independence), 20th anniversary.

**1975, June 19 Litho. *Perf. 14x13½***

**656** A184 110m multicolored .75 .35

International Women's Year.

Children Crossing Street A185

**1975, July 5 Photo. *Perf. 13½x14***

**657** A185 25m multicolored .25 .25

Highway safety campaign, July 1-Sept. 30.

Djerbian Minaret, Hotel and Marina, Jerba A186

Old & new Tunisia: 15m, 17th cent. minaret & modern hotel, Tunis. 20m, Fortress, earring & hotel, Monastir. 65m, View of Sousse, hotel & pendant. 500m, Town wall, mosque & palms, Tozeur. 1d, Mosques & Arab ornaments, Kairouan.

**1975, July 12 Litho. *Perf. 14x14½***

**658** A186 10m multicolored .25 .25
**659** A186 15m multicolored .25 .25
**660** A186 20m multicolored .25 .25
**661** A186 65m multicolored .60 .40
**662** A186 500m multicolored 4.00 1.75
**663** A186 1d multicolored 6.50 2.50
*Nos. 658-663 (6)* 11.85 5.40

Victors — A187

Symbolic Ship A188

**1975, Aug. 23 Photo. *Perf. 13½***

**664** A187 25m olive & multi .25 .25
**665** A188 50m blue & multi .40 .25

7th Mediterranean Games, Algiers, 8/23-9/6.

Flowers in Vase, Birds Holding Letters — A189

**1975, Sept. 29 Litho. *Perf. 13½x13***

**666** A189 100m blue & multi .50 .25

Stamp Day.

Sadiki College, Young Bourguiba — A190

**Engr. & Litho.**

**1975, Nov. 17 *Perf. 13***

**667** A190 25m sepia, orange & olive .30 .25

Sadiki College, centenary.

Duck — A191

Vergil — A192

Mosaics: 10m, Fish. 25m, Lioness, horiz. 60m, Head of Medusa, horiz. 75m, Circus spectators.

**1976, Feb. 16 Photo. *Perf. 13***

**668** A191 5m multicolored .30 .25
**669** A191 10m multicolored .30 .25
**670** A192 25m multicolored .75 .50
**671** A192 60m multicolored .75 .50
**672** A192 75m multicolored .90 .50
**673** A192 100m multicolored 1.40 .50
*a.* Souvenir sheet of 6, #668-673 7.00 7.00
*Nos. 668-673 (6)* 4.40 2.50

Tunisian mosaics, 2nd-5th centuries.

No. 673a sold for 500m. Issued perf. and imperf.; same value.

Telephone A193

**1976, Mar. 10 Litho. *Perf. 14x13½***

**674** A193 150m blue & multi .65 .35

Centenary of first telephone call by Alexander Graham Bell, Mar. 10, 1876.

Pres. Bourguiba and "20" — A194

Pres. Bourguiba and: 100m, "20" and symbolic Tunisian flag. 150m, "Tunisia" rising from darkness, and 20 flowers.

**1976, Mar. 20 Photo. *Perf. 11½***

**675** A194 40m multicolored .25 .25
**676** A194 100m multicolored .50 .25
**677** A194 150m multicolored .75 .35
*Nos. 675-677 (3)* 1.50 .85

**Souvenir Sheets**

***Perf. 11½, Imperf.***

**678** Sheet of 3 3.50 3.50
*a.* A194 50m like 40m .50 .50
*b.* A194 200m like 100m 1.00 1.00
*c.* A194 250m like 150m 1.50 1.50

20th anniversary of independence.

Blind Man with Cane A195

Procession and Buildings A196

**1976, Apr. 7** **Engr.** ***Perf. 13***
**679** A195 100m black & red .50 .25

World Health Day: "Foresight prevents blindness."

**1976, May 31** **Photo.** ***Perf. 12x11½***
**680** A196 40m multicolored .40 .25

Habitat, UN Conf. on Human Settlements, Vancouver, Canada, May 31-June 11.

Face and Hands Decorated with Henna — A197

Old and new Tunisia: 50m, Sponge fishing at Jerba. 65m, Textile industry. 110m, Pottery of Guellala.

**1976, June 15** **Photo.** ***Perf. 13x13½***
**681** A197 40m multicolored .25 .25
**682** A197 50m multicolored .50 .25
**683** A197 65m multicolored .50 .25
**684** A197 110m multicolored .65 .50
*Nos. 681-684 (4)* 1.90 1.25

The Spirit of '76, by Archibald M. Willard A198

**1976, July 4** ***Perf. 13x14***
**685** A198 200m multicolored 1.75 .85

**Souvenir Sheets**

***Perf. 13x14, Imperf.***

**686** A198 500m multicolored 5.00 5.00

American Bicentennial.

Running A199

Montreal Olympic Games Emblem and: 75m, Bicycling. 120m, Peace dove.

**1976, July 17** **Photo.** ***Perf. 11½***
**687** A199 50m gray, red & blk .25 .25
**688** A199 75m red, yel & blk .40 .25
**689** A199 120m orange & multi .65 .35
*Nos. 687-689 (3)* 1.30 .85

21st Olympic Games, Montreal, Canada, July 17-Aug. 1.

Child Reading — A200

Heads and Bird — A201

**1976, Aug. 23** **Litho.** ***Perf. 13***
**690** A200 100m brown & multi .50 .25

Books for children.

**1976, Sept. 30** **Litho.** ***Perf. 13***
**691** A201 150m orange & multi .75 .25

Non-aligned Countries, 15th anniv. of 1st Conference.

Mouradite Mausoleum, 17th Century — A202

Electronic Tree and ITU Emblem — A204

Globe and Emblem A203

Cultural Heritage: 100m, Minaret, Kairawan Great Mosque and psalmodist. 150m, Monastir Ribat monastery and Alboracq (sphinx). 200m, Barber's Mosque, Kairawan andman's bust.

**1976, Oct. 25** **Photo.** ***Perf. 14***
**692** A202 85m multicolored .40 .25
**693** A202 100m multicolored .50 .25
**694** A202 150m multicolored .75 .25
**695** A202 200m multicolored 1.10 .40
*Nos. 692-695 (4)* 2.75 1.15

**1976, Dec. 24** **Photo.** ***Perf. 13x14***
**696** A203 150m multicolored .85 .35

25th anniv. of UN Postal Administration.

**1977, May 17** **Photo.** ***Perf. 14x13½***
**697** A204 150m multicolored .85 .50

9th World Telecommunications Day.

"Communication," Sassenage Castle, Grenoble — A205

**1977, May 19** **Litho.** ***Perf. 13½x13***
**698** A205 100m multicolored .90 .40

10th anniv. of Intl. French Language Council.

Soccer A206

**1977, June 27** **Photo.** ***Perf. 13½***
**699** A206 150m multicolored 1.00 .50

Junior World Soccer Tournament, Tunisia, June 27-July 10.

Gold Coin, 10th Century — A207

Cultural Heritage: 15m, Stele, Gorjani Cemetery, Tunis, 13th century. 20m, Floral design, 17th century illumination. 30m, Bird and flowers, glass painting, 1922. 40m, Antelope, from 11th century clay pot. 50m, Gate, Sidi Bou Said, 20th century.

**1977, July 9** **Photo.** ***Perf. 13***
**700** A207 10m multicolored .20 .20
**701** A207 15m multicolored .20 .20
**702** A207 20m multicolored .25 .20
**703** A207 30m multicolored .40 .25
**704** A207 40m multicolored .50 .25
**705** A207 50m multicolored .50 .25
*a.* Miniature sheet of 6, #700-705 3.75 3.75
*Nos. 700-705 (6)* 2.05 1.35

"The Young Republic" and Bourguiba — A208

Diseased Knee, Gears and Globe — A210

Symbolic Cancellation, APU Emblem — A209

Habib Bourguiba and: 100m, "The Confident Republic" and 20 doves. 150m, "The Determined Republic" and 20 roses.

**1977, July 25** **Photo.** ***Perf. 13x13½***
**706** A208 40m multicolored .40 .25
**707** A208 100m multicolored .50 .25
**708** A208 150m multicolored .85 .35
*a.* Souvenir sheet of 3, #706-708 2.75 2.75
*Nos. 706-708 (3)* 1.75 .85

20th anniv. of the Republic. No. 708a sold for 500m. Exists imperf., same value.

**1977, Aug. 16** **Litho.** ***Perf. 13x12½***
**709** A209 40m multicolored .25 .25

Arab Postal Union, 25th anniversary.

**1977, Sept. 26** **Photo.** ***Perf. 14x13½***
**710** A210 120m multicolored .75 .35

World Rheumatism Year.

Farmer, Road, Water and Electricity — A211

**1977, Dec. 15** **Photo.** ***Perf. 13½***
**711** A211 40m multicolored .20 .20

Rural development.

Factory Workers — A212

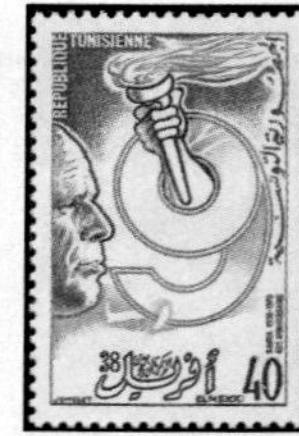

Pres. Bourguiba, Torch and "9" — A213

Designs: 20m, Bus driver and trains, horiz. 40m, Farmer driving tractor, horiz.

**1978, Mar. 6** ***Perf. 13x14, 14x13***
**712** A212 20m rose red & multi .25 .20
**713** A212 40m black & green .25 .25
**714** A212 100m multicolored .50 .35
*Nos. 712-714 (3)* 1.00 .80

5th development plan, creation of new jobs.

**1978, Apr. 9** **Engr.** ***Perf. 13***
**715** A213 40m shown .25 .25
**716** A213 60m Bourguiba and "9" .25 .25

40th anniv. of 1st fight for independence, 4/9/38.

A214

**1978, May 2** **Photo.** ***Perf. 13x13½***
**717** A214 150m Policeman .90 .35

6th Regional African Interpol Conference, Tunis, May 2-5.

A215

**1978, June 1** **Photo.** ***Perf. 13x14***

Designs: 40m, Tunisian Goalkeeper. 150m., Soccer player, maps of South America and Africa, flags.

**718** A215 40m multicolored .35 .25
**719** A215 150m multicolored 1.00 .40

11th World Cup Soccer Championship, Argentina, June 1-25.

Destruction of Apartheid, Map of South Africa — A216

Fight Against Apartheid: 100m, White and black doves flying in unison.

**1978, Aug. 30 Litho. *Perf. 13½x14***

**720** A216 50m multicolored .25 .25
**721** A216 100m multicolored .50 .35

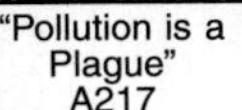

"Pollution is a Plague" A217

"Eradication of Smallpox" A218

Designs: 50m, "The Sea, mankind's patrimony." 120m, "Greening of the desert."

**1978, Sept. 11 Photo. *Perf. 14x13***

**722** A217 10m multicolored .25 .25
**723** A217 50m multicolored .50 .25
**724** A217 120m multicolored 1.20 .35
*Nos. 722-724 (3)* 1.95 .85

Protection of the environment.

**1978, Oct. 16 Litho. *Perf. 12½***

**725** A218 150m multicolored .75 .40

Global eradication of smallpox.

Jerba Wedding A219

5m, Horseman from Zlass. 75m, Women potters from the Mogods. 100m, Dove over Marabout Sidi Mahrez cupolas, Tunis. 500m, Plowing in Jenduba. 1d, Spring Festival in Tozeur (man on swing).

**1978, Nov. 1 Photo. *Perf. 13***

**726** A219 5m multi, vert. .20 .20
**727** A219 60m multi .35 .20
**728** A219 75m multi .50 .20
**729** A219 100m multi .50 .25
**730** A219 500m multi 3.75 1.25
**731** A219 1d multi 6.00 2.50
*Nos. 726-731 (6)* 11.30 4.60

Traditional Arab calligraphy.

Lenin and Red Banner over Kremlin — A220

Farhat Hached, Union Emblem — A221

**1978, Nov. 7 *Perf. 13½***

**732** A220 150m multicolored 1.20 .50

Russian October Revolution, 60th anniv.

**1978, Dec. 5 Photo. *Perf. 14***

**733** A221 50m multicolored .40 .20

Farhat Hached (1914-1952), founder of General Union of Tunisian Workers.

Family — A222

Sun with Man's Face — A223

**1978, Dec. 15 Photo. *Perf. 13½***

**734** A222 50m multicolored .50 .25

Tunisian Family Planning Assoc., 10th anniv.

**1978, Dec. 25 *Perf. 14***

**735** A223 100m multicolored .75 .25

Sun as a source of light and energy.

Plane, Weather Map and Instruments — A224

**1978, Dec. 29**

**736** A224 50m multicolored .40 .25

Tunisian civil aviation and meteorology, 20th anniv.

Habib Bourguiba and Constitution — A225

**1979, May 31 Photo. *Perf. 14x13½***

**737** A225 50m multicolored .50 .35

20th anniversary of Constitution.

El Kantaoui Port A226

**1979, June 3 *Perf. 13½x14***

**738** A226 150m multicolored .75 .35

Development of El Kantaoui as a resort area.

Landscapes — A227

**1979, July 14 *Perf. 12½x13½***

**739** A227 50m Korbous .25 .20
**740** A227 100m Mides .40 .20

Bow Net Weaving — A228

Pres. Bourguiba, "10" and Hands — A229

**1979, Aug. 15 Photo. *Perf. 11½***

**741** A228 10m shown .35 .20
**742** A228 50m Beekeeping .85 .25

**1979, Sept. 5**

**743** A229 50m multicolored .35 .20

Socialist Destour Party, 10th Congress.

Modes of Communication, ITU Emblem — A230

**1979, Sept. 20 Litho. *Perf. 11½***

**744** A230 150m multicolored .90 .50

3rd World Telecommunications Exhibition, Geneva, Sept. 20-26.

Arab Achievements — A231

**1979, Oct. 1 *Perf. 14½***

**745** A231 50m multicolored .25 .20

Children Crossing Street, IYC Emblem — A232

**1979, Oct. 16 *Perf. 14x13½***

**746** A232 50m shown .25 .20
**747** A232 100m Child and birds .60 .25

International Year of the Child.

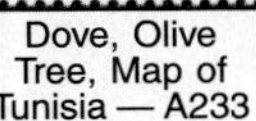

Dove, Olive Tree, Map of Tunisia — A233

Woman Wearing Crown — A234

**1979, Nov. 1 Litho. *Perf. 12***

**748** A233 150m multicolored .90 .40

2nd International Olive Oil Year.

**1979, Nov. 3 *Perf. 14½***

**749** A234 50m multicolored .25 .20

Central Bank of Tunisia, 20th anniversary.

Children and Jujube Tree — A235

**1979, Dec. 25 Litho. *Perf. 15x14½***

**750** A235 20m shown .30 .20
**751** A235 30m Peacocks .60 .25
**752** A235 70m Goats 1.10 .35
**753** A235 85m Girl, date palm 1.10 .40
*Nos. 750-753 (4)* 3.10 1.20

Postal Code Introduction — A236

**1980, Mar. 20 Photo. *Perf. 14***

**754** A236 50m multicolored .40 .25

Fight Against Cigarette Smoking A237

**1980, Apr. 7**

**755** A237 150m multicolored .75 .25

Pres. Bourguiba in Flower, Open Book — A238

**1980, June 1 Photo. *Perf. 11½***

**756** A238 50m shown .25 .25
**757** A238 100m Dove, Bourguiba, mosque .90 .40

Victory (independence), 25th anniversary.

Butterfly and Gymnast A239

**1980, June 3 Photo.** ***Perf. 12x11½***
**Granite Paper**

**758** A239 100m multicolored .50 .25

Turin Gymnastic Games, June 1-7.

Artisans
A240 A241

**1980, July 21 Photo.** ***Perf. 13½***

**759** A240 30m multicolored .30 .25
**760** A241 75m multicolored .50 .25

ibn-Khaldun (1332-1406), Historian — A242

Avicenna (Arab Physician), Birth Millenium — A243

**1980, July 28** ***Perf. 14***

**761** A242 50m multicolored .25 .25

**1980, Aug. 18 Engr.** ***Perf. 12½x13***

**762** A243 100m redsh brn & sepia .90 .35

Arab Achievements — A244

**1980, Aug. 25 Photo.** ***Perf. 13½x14***

**763** A244 50m multicolored .40 .25

Port Sidi bou Said A245

**1980, Sept. 4** ***Perf. 14***

**764** A245 100m multicolored .75 .35

World Tourism Conference, Manila, Sept. 27 — A246

**1980, Sept. 27 Photo.** ***Perf. 14***

**765** A246 150m multicolored .65 .25

Wedding in Jerba, by Yahia (1903-1969) — A247

**1980, Oct. 1** ***Perf. 12***

**766** A247 50m multicolored .60 .40

Tozeur-Nefta International Airport Opening — A248

**1980, Oct. 13 Photo.** ***Perf. 13x13½***

**767** A248 85m multicolored .40 .25

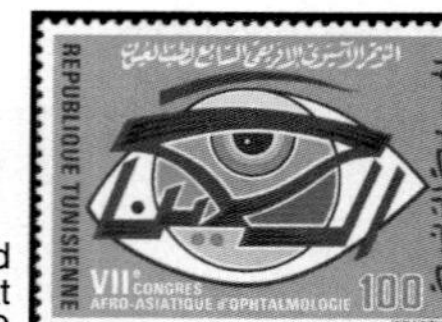

Eye and Text A249

**1980, Oct. 26 Litho.** ***Perf. 13½x14***

**768** A249 100m multicolored 1.10 .50

7th Afro-Asian Ophthalmologic Congress.

Hegira, 1500th Anniv. A250

**1980, Nov. 9**

**769** A250 50m Spiderweb .25 .25
**770** A250 80m City skyline .40 .25

Film Strip and Woman's Head — A251

**1980, Nov. 15 Photo.** ***Perf. 14x13½***

**771** A251 100m multicolored .50 .35

Carthage Film Festival.

Orchid A252

**1980, Nov. 17** ***Perf. 13½x14***

**772** A252 20m shown .65 .35
**773** A252 25m Wild cyclamen .85 .35

**Size: 39x27mm**

***Perf. 14***

**774** A252 50m Mouflon 1.60 .35
**775** A252 100m Golden eagle 3.50 .40
*Nos. 772-775 (4)* 6.60 1.45

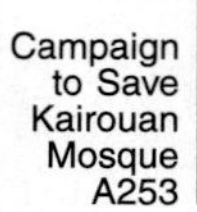

Campaign to Save Kairouan Mosque A253

**1980, Dec. 29 Photo.** ***Perf. 12***
**Granite Paper**

**776** A253 85m multicolored .40 .25

Heinrich von Stephan (1831-1897), Founder of UPU — A254

Blood Donors' Assoc., 20th Anniv. — A255

**1981, Jan. 7**

**777** A254 150m multicolored .75 .40

**1981, Mar. 5 Litho.** ***Perf. 14x13½***

**778** A255 75m multicolored .75 .50

Pres. Bourguiba and Flag — A256

**1981, Mar. 20 Photo.** ***Perf. 12x11½***
**Granite Paper**

**779** A256 50m shown .25 .25
**780** A256 60m Dove, "25" .40 .25
**781** A256 85m Doves .65 .40
**782** A256 120m Victory on winged horse .65 .40
*a.* Souvenir sheet of 4, #779-782 3.25 3.25
*Nos. 779-782 (4)* 1.95 1.30

25th anniversary of independence. No. 782 sold for 500m. Exists imperf., same value.

Pres. Bourguiba and Flower A257

**1981, Apr. 10 Photo.** ***Perf. 12x11½***

**783** A257 50m shown .25 .20
**784** A257 75m Bourguiba, flower, diff. .40 .25

Destourien Socialist Party Congress.

Mosque Entrance, Mahdia A258

**1981, Apr. 20** ***Perf. 13½***

**785** A258 50m shown .40 .25
**786** A258 85m Tozeur Great Mosque, vert. .40 .35
**787** A258 100m Needle Rocks, Tabarka .55 .25
*Nos. 785-787 (3)* 1.35 .85

A259

Youth Festival — A260

**1981, May 17 Litho.** ***Perf. 14x15***

**788** A259 150m multicolored .40 .35

13th World Telecommunications Day.

**1981, June 2 Photo.** ***Perf. 11½***
**Granite Paper**

**789** A260 100m multicolored .50 .25

A261 A262

**1981, June 15 Photo.** ***Perf. 14***

**790** A261 150m multicolored .85 .35

Kemal Ataturk (1881-1938), 1st president of Turkey.

**1981, July 15 Photo.** ***Perf. 11½x12***

**791** A262 150m Skifa, Mahdia .85 .40

Mohammed Tahar Ben Achour (1879-1973), Scholar — A263

**1981, Aug. 6** ***Perf. 13***

**792** A263 200m multicolored 1.10 .50

25th Anniv. of Personal Status Code (Women's Liberation) — A264

**1981, Aug. 13**

**793** A264 50m Woman .25 .25
**794** A264 100m shown .50 .35

Intl. Year of the Disabled — A265

**1981, Sept. 21 Photo.** ***Perf. 13½***

**795** A265 250m multicolored 1.25 .65

Pilgrimage to Mecca — A266

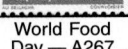

World Food Day — A267

**1981, Oct. 7 Photo. *Perf. 13½***
**796** A266 50m multicolored .40 .25

**1981, Oct. 16 Litho. *Perf. 12***
**Granite Paper**
**797** A267 200m multicolored 1.10 .65

Traditional Jewelry A268

150m, Mneguech silver earrings. 180m Mahfdha (silver medallion worn by married women). 200m, Essalta gold headdress.

**1981, Dec. 7 Photo. *Perf. 14***
**798** A268 150m multi, vert. .75 .35
**799** A268 180m multi .90 .40
**800** A268 200m multi, vert. 1.10 .50
*Nos. 798-800 (3)* 2.75 1.25

Bizerta Bridge A269

**1981, Dec. 14 Litho. *Perf. 12x11½***
**Granite Paper**
**801** A269 230m multicolored 1.00 .50

A270

A271

Chemist compounding honey mixture, manuscript miniature, 1224.

**1982, Apr. 3 Photo. *Perf. 13***
**802** A270 80m multicolored .65 .35

Arab Chemists' Union, 16th anniv.

**1982, May 12 Photo. *Perf. 13½***
**803** A271 150m multicolored 1.00 .60

Oceanic Enterprise Symposium, Tunis, 5/12-14.

A272

A273

**1982, June 26 *Perf. 12½***
**Granite Paper**
**804** A272 80m multicolored .40 .25

The Productive Family Employment campaign.

**1982, July 25 Litho. *Perf. 14x13½***

25th Anniv. of Republic: Pres. Bourguiba and Various Women.

**805** A273 80m multicolored .35 .25
**806** A273 100m multicolored .50 .35
**807** A273 200m multicolored .85 .40
*Nos. 805-807 (3)* 1.70 1.00

Scouting Year — A274

Tunisian Fossils — A274a

***Perf. 14½x14, 14x14½***
**1982, Aug. 23**
**808** A274 80m multicolored .40 .25
**809** A274 200m multicolored .85 .25

75th anniv. of scouting and 50th anniv. of scouting in Tunisia (80m, horiz.).

**1982, Sept. 20 Photo. *Perf. 11½x12***

Designs: 80m, Pseudophillipsia azzouzi, vert. 200m, Mediterraneotrigonia cherahilensis, vert. 280m, Numidiopleura enigmatica. 300m, Micreschara tunisiensis, vert. 500m, Mantelliceras pervinquieri, vert. 1000m, Elephas africanavus.

**809A** A274a 80m multi 1.00 .40
**809B** A274a 200m multi 2.00 .60
**809C** A274a 280m multi 2.40 .75
**809D** A274a 300m multi 3.00 1.00
**809E** A274a 500m multi 6.00 1.60
**809F** A274a 1000m multi 12.00 3.00
*Nos. 809A-809F (6)* 26.40 7.35

A275

A276

**1982, Sept. 29 *Perf. 14x13½***
**810** A275 80m shown .50 .25
**Size: 23x40mm**
**811** A275 200m Woman, buildings .85 .50

30th Anniv. of Arab Postal Union.

**1982, Oct. 1 Photo. *Perf. 12***
**Granite Paper**
**812** A276 200m multicolored .85 .25

ITU Plenipotentiaries Conf., Nairobi

World Food Day A277

Tahar Haddad (1899-1935), Social Reformer A278

**1982, Oct. 16 Litho. *Perf. 13***
**813** A277 200m multicolored .90 .35

**1982, Oct. 25 Engr.**
**814** A278 200m dark brown .75 .25

TB Bacillus Centenary A279

Folk Songs and Stories — A280

**1982, Nov. 16 Litho. *Perf. 13½***
**815** A279 100m multicolored .75 .25

**1982, Nov. 22 Photo. *Perf. 14***
**816** A280 20m Dancing in the Rain .25 .25
**817** A280 30m Woman Sweeping .25 .25
**818** A280 70m Fisherman and the Child .25 .25
**819** A280 80m Rooster and the Oranges, horiz. .30 .25
**820** A280 100m Woman and the Mirror, horiz. .50 .25
**821** A280 120m The Two Girls, horiz. .65 .30
*Nos. 816-821 (6)* 2.20 1.55

Intl. Palestinian Solidarity Day — A281

**1982, Nov. 30 Litho. *Perf. 13x12***
**822** A281 80m multicolored .40 .25

Farhat Hached (1914-1952) A282

Bourguiba Dam Opening A283

**1982, Dec. 6 Engr. *Perf. 13***
**823** A282 80m brown red .40 .25

**1982, Dec. 20 Litho. *Perf. 13½***
**824** A283 80m multicolored .50 .25

Environmental Training College Opening — A284

**1982, Dec. 29 Photo. *Perf. 11½***
**Granite Paper**
**825** A284 80m multicolored .40 .20

World Communications Year — A285

**1983, May 17 Litho. *Perf. 13½x14***
**826** A285 200m multicolored .60 .35

20th Anniv. of Org. of African Unity — A286

Aly Ben Ayed (1930-1972), Actor — A288

30th Anniv. of Customs Cooperation Council — A287

**1983, May 25 Photo. *Perf. 12***
**Granite Paper**
**827** A286 230m ultra & grnsh bl .85 .50

**1983, May 30 Litho. *Perf. 13½***
**828** A287 100m multicolored .40 .25

**1983, Aug. 15 Engr. *Perf. 13***
**829** A288 80m dk car, dl red & gray .35 .35

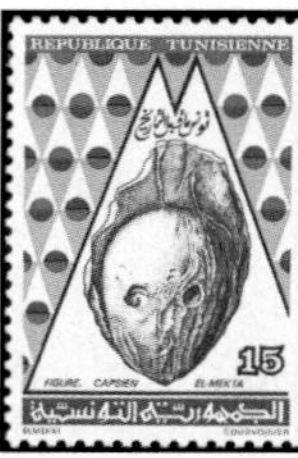

Stone-carved Face, El-Mekta — A289

Pre-historic artifacts: 20m, Neolithic necklace, Kel el-Agab. 30m, Mill and grindstone, Redeyef. 40m, Orynx head rock carving, Gafsa. 80m, Dolmen Mactar. 100m, Acheulian Bi-face flint, El-Mekta.

**1983, Aug. 20 Photo. *Perf. 11½x12***

| | | | | |
|---|---|---|---|---|
| **830** | A289 | 15m multicolored | .25 | .25 |
| **831** | A289 | 20m multicolored | .40 | .25 |
| **832** | A289 | 30m multicolored | .40 | .25 |
| **833** | A289 | 40m multicolored | .40 | .25 |
| **834** | A289 | 80m multicolored | .50 | .40 |
| **835** | A289 | 100m multicolored | .65 | .40 |
| | | *Nos. 830-835 (6)* | 2.60 | 1.80 |

Sports for All A290

**1983, Sept. 27 Litho. *Perf. 12½***

**836** A290 40m multicolored .25 .20

World Fishing Day A291

**1983, Oct. 17 *Perf. 14½***

**837** A291 200m multicolored 1.00 .25

Evacuation of French Troops, 20th Anniv. — A292

**1983, Oct. 17 Litho. *Perf. 14x13½***

**838** A292 80m multicolored .40 .25

Tapestry Weaver, by Hedi Khayachi (1882-1948) — A293

**1983, Nov. 22 Photo. *Perf. 11½***

**Granite Paper**

**839** A293 80m multicolored .65 .40

Natl. Allegiance A294

Jet, Woman's Head, Emblem A295

**1983, Nov. 30 Litho. *Perf. 14½***

**840** A294 100m Children, flag .40 .25

**1983, Dec. 21 *Perf. 13½***

**841** A295 150m multicolored .65 .25

Pres. Bourguiba A296

4th Molecular Biology Symposium A297

Destourien Socialist Party, 50th Anniv.: Portraits of Bourguiba. 200m, 230m horiz.

***Perf. 12½x12, 12x12½***

**1984, Mar. 2 Photo.**

**Granite Paper**

| | | | | |
|---|---|---|---|---|
| **842** | A296 | 40m multicolored | .25 | .20 |
| **843** | A296 | 70m multicolored | .25 | .20 |
| **844** | A296 | 80m multicolored | .40 | .25 |
| *a.* | | Pair, #843-844 | .75 | .75 |
| **845** | A296 | 150m multicolored | .65 | .40 |
| *a.* | | Pair, #842, 845 | 1.00 | 1.00 |
| **846** | A296 | 200m multicolored | .85 | .40 |
| **847** | A296 | 230m multicolored | .90 | .60 |
| *a.* | | Pair, #846-847 | 2.00 | 2.00 |
| | | *Nos. 842-847 (6)* | 3.30 | 2.05 |

Nos. 844a, 845a and 847a were printed checkerwise in sheets of ten.

**1984, Apr. 3 *Perf. 13½x13***

**848** A297 100m Map, diagram .60 .35

Ibn El Jazzar, Physician — A298

Economic Development Program, 20th Anniv. — A299

**1984, May 15 Photo. *Perf. 14x13***

**849** A298 80m multicolored .50 .40

**1984, June 15 *Perf. 11½***

**Granite Paper**

**850** A299 230m Merchant, worker .90 .40

Coquette, The Sorceress and the Fairy Carabosse A300

***Perf. 13½x14, 14x13½***

**1984, Aug. 27 Photo.**

| | | | | |
|---|---|---|---|---|
| **851** | A300 | 20m shown | .20 | .20 |
| **852** | A300 | 80m Counting with fingers | .40 | .25 |
| **853** | A300 | 100m Boy riding horse, vert. | .50 | .25 |
| | | *Nos. 851-853 (3)* | 1.10 | .70 |

Legends and folk tales.

Family and Education Org., 20th Anniv. — A301

**1984, Sept. 4 *Perf. 13x14***

**854** A301 80m Family looking into future .40 .25

Natl. Heritage Protection A302

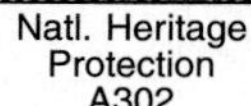

Aboul-Qasim Chabbi, Poet (1909-1934) A303

**1984, Sept. 13 *Perf. 14***

**855** A302 100m Medina Mosque Minaret, hand .50 .35

**1984, Oct. 9 Engr. *Perf. 12½x13***

**856** A303 100m multicolored .40 .25

40th Anniv., ICAO A304

**1984, Oct. 25 Photo. *Perf. 13***

**857** A304 200m Aircraft tail, bird .90 .60

Sahara Festival A305

**1984, Dec. 3 Litho. *Perf. 14½***

**858** A305 20m Musicians .65 .25

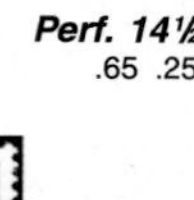

20th Anniv., Intelsat A306

***Perf. 13½x14½***

**1984, Dec. 25 Photo.**

**859** A306 100m Tunisian Earth Station .40 .25

Mediterranean Landscape, by Jilani Abdelwaheb (Abdul) — A307

**1984, Dec. 31 Photo. *Perf. 14½***

**860** A307 100m multicolored .65 .40

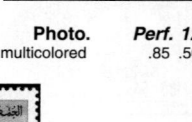

EXPO '85, Tsukuba, Japan A308

**1985, Mar. 20 Photo. *Perf. 12***

**861** A308 200m multicolored .85 .50

Civil Protection Week — A309

**1985, May 13 Litho. *Perf. 14***

**862** A309 100m Hands, water and fire .50 .40

Pres. Habib Bourguiba, Crowded Pier — A310

Pres. Bourguiba: 75m, On horseback, vert. 200m, Wearing hat, vert. 230m, Waving to crowd.

**1985, June 1 *Perf. 12½***

| | | | | |
|---|---|---|---|---|
| **863** | A310 | 75m multicolored | .25 | .20 |
| **864** | A310 | 100m multicolored | .40 | .25 |
| **865** | A310 | 200m multicolored | .85 | .50 |
| **866** | A310 | 230m multicolored | .90 | .65 |
| | | *Nos. 863-866 (4)* | 2.40 | 1.60 |

Natl. independence, 30th anniv.

Head of a Statue, Carthage and Pres. Bourguiba A311

**1985, June 4 *Perf. 14***

**867** A311 250m multicolored 1.00 .65

EXPO '85.

Intl. Amateur Film Festival, Kelibia — A312

Natl. Folk Tales — A313

**1985, July 20** *Perf. 14½x13*
**868** A312 250m multicolored 1.20 .65

**1985, July 29** *Perf. 14*
**869** A313 25m Sun, Sun Shine Again, horiz. .20 .20
**870** A313 50m I Met a Man With Seven Wives .25 .20
**871** A313 100m Uncle Shisbene .40 .25
*Nos. 869-871 (3)* .85 .65

Intl. Youth Year — A314

**1985, Sept. 30** *Perf. 14½x13½*
**872** A314 250m multicolored .90 .60

The Perfumers' Courtyard, 1912, by Hedi Larnaout — A315

**1985, Oct. 4** *Perf. 14*
**873** A315 100m multicolored .50 .25

Regional Bridal Costumes A316

UN, 40th Anniv. A317

**1985, Oct. 22** *Perf. 12*
**874** A316 20m Matmata .20 .20
**875** A316 50m Moknine .25 .20
**876** A316 100m Tunis .40 .25
*Nos. 874-876 (3)* .85 .65

**1985, Oct. 24** *Perf. 14x13½*
**877** A317 250m multicolored .90 .60

Self-Sufficiency in Food Production — A318

*Perf. 13½x14½*
**1985, Nov. 26** **Photo.**
**878** A318 100m Makhtar stele of feast .40 .25

League of Arab States, 40th Anniv. A319

**1985, Nov. 29** **Litho.** *Perf. 13½x14*
**879** A319 100m multicolored .50 .25

Aziza Othmana (d. 1669) — A320

Land Law, Cent. — A321

**1985, Dec. 16** **Engr.** *Perf. 12½x13*
**880** A320 100m dk grn, hn brn & brn .50 .25

**1985, Dec. 25** **Litho.** *Perf. 13½*
**881** A321 100m multicolored .40 .20

Natl. Independence, 30th Anniv. — A322

*Perf. 13x13½, 13½x13*
**1986, Mar. 20** **Photo.**
**882** A322 100m Dove, vert. .35 .25
**883** A322 120m Rocket .40 .25
**884** A322 280m Horse and rider 1.10 .65
**885** A322 300m Balloons, vert. 1.20 .75
*a.* Souvenir sheet of 4, #882-885 3.50 3.50
*Nos. 882-885 (4)* 3.05 1.90

No. 885a exists imperf. Same value.

A323

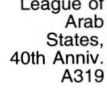

A324

**1986, Apr. 30** **Litho.** *Perf. 14x13½*
**886** A323 300m multicolored 1.50 .40
**887** A324 380m multicolored 1.90 .50

Prof. Hulusi Behcet (1889-1948), discovered virus causing Behcet's Disease affecting eyes and joints. 3rd Mediterranean Rheumatology Day (#886). Intl. Geographical Ophtalmological Soc. Cong. (#887).

12th Destourian Socialist Party Congress A325

**1986, June 19** **Photo.** *Perf. 12*
**888** A325 120m shown .40 .25
**889** A325 300m Torchbearer 1.10 .75

A326

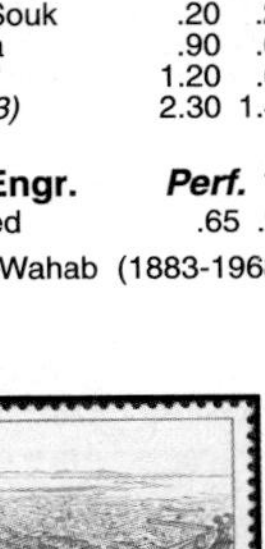

A327

Regional bridal costumes.

**1986, Aug. 25** **Litho.** *Perf. 14*
**890** A326 40m Homi-Souk .20 .20
**891** A326 280m Mahdia .90 .60
**892** A326 300m Nabeul 1.20 .65
*Nos. 890-892 (3)* 2.30 1.45

**1986, Sept. 20** **Engr.** *Perf. 13*
**893** A327 160m dark red .65 .25

Hassen Husni Abdul-Wahab (1883-1968), historian, archaeologist

Founding of Carthage, 2800th Anniv. — A328

**1986, Oct. 18** **Engr.** *Perf. 13*
**894** A328 2d dark violet 8.00 4.00

Protohistoric Artifacts — A329

Bedouins, by Ammar Farhat — A330

Design: 10m, Flint arrowhead, El Borma, c. 3000 B.C. 20m, Rock cut-out dwelling, Sejnane, c. 1000 B.C. 50m, Lintel bas-relief from a cult site in Tunis, c. 1000 B.C., horiz. 120m, Base of a Neolithic vase, Kesra. 160m, Phoenician trireme, petroglyph, c. 800 B.C., horiz. 250m, Ceramic pot, c. 700 B.C., found at Sejnane, vert.

**1986, Oct. 30** **Litho.** *Perf. 13½*
**895** A329 10m multicolored .25 .25
**896** A329 20m multicolored .25 .25
**897** A329 50m multicolored .40 .25
**898** A329 120m multicolored .65 .25

**899** A329 160m multicolored .85 .40
**900** A329 250m multicolored 1.60 .60
*Nos. 895-900 (6)* 4.00 2.00

**1986, Nov. 20** **Photo.** *Perf. 13½*
**901** A330 250m multicolored 1.40 .40

Intl. Peace Year A331

**1986, Nov. 24** *Perf. 13½x13*
**902** A331 300m multicolored 1.10 .40

FAO, 40th Anniv. — A332

Computer Education Inauguration A333

**1986, Nov. 27** *Perf. 13x13½*
**903** A332 280m multicolored .90 .60

**1986, Dec. 8** *Perf. 13½*
**904** A333 2d multicolored 7.50 2.75

Breast-feeding for Child Survival — A334

Wildlife, Natl. Parks — A335

**1986, Dec. 22** **Photo.** *Perf. 14*
**905** A334 120m multicolored .50 .25

**1986, Dec. 29** *Perf. 12*

Designs: 60m, Mountain gazelle, Chambi Natl. Park. 120m, Addax, Bou. Hedma. 350m, Seal, Zembretta. 380m, Greylag goose, Ichkeul.

**Granite Paper**
**906** A335 60m multicolored .25 .20
**907** A335 120m multicolored .50 .35
**908** A335 350m multicolored 1.40 1.00
**909** A335 380m multicolored 1.75 1.10
*Nos. 906-909 (4)* 3.90 2.65

City of Monastir, Cent. — A336

**1987, Jan. 24** **Litho.** *Perf. 12x11½*
**Granite Paper**
**910** A336 120m Pres. Bourguiba, city arms .40 .25

Invention of the Telegraph by Samuel F.B. Morse, 150th Anniv. A337

**1987, June 15 Litho.** ***Perf. 13½x14***
**911** A337 500m multicolored 1.75 1.00

30th Anniv. of the Republic A338

Pres. Bourguiba and women of various sects.

**1987, July 25 Photo.** ***Perf. 13½***
**912** A338 150m multi .60 .30
**913** A338 250m multi 1.00 .50
**914** A338 350m multi, diff. 1.40 .70
**915** A338 500m multi, diff. 2.00 1.00
*a.* Souvenir sheet of 4, #912-915 6.00 3.00
*Nos. 912-915 (4)* 5.00 2.50

No. 915a sold for 1.50d. Exists imperf.

UN Universal Vaccination by 1990 Campaign — A339

**1987, Sept. 14** ***Perf. 12***
**Granite Paper**
**916** A339 250m multicolored 1.00 .50

The Street, by Azouz ben Raiz (1902-1962) A340

**1987, Sept. 22 Granite Paper**
**917** A340 250m multicolored 1.00 .50

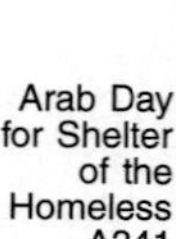

Arab Day for Shelter of the Homeless A341

**1987, Oct. 5 Photo.** ***Perf. 12x11½***
**Granite Paper**
**918** A341 150m multicolored .50 .25

Advisory Council for Postal Research, 30th Anniv. A342

**1987, Oct. 9** ***Perf. 14***
**919** A342 150m Express mail .50 .25
**920** A342 350m Use postal code 1.10 .60

The Arabs, by Ibn-Mandhour (1233-1312), Lexicographer A343

**1987, Oct. 26 Engr.** ***Perf. 13***
**921** A343 250m plum 1.00 .50

Pasteur Institute, Tunis A344

**1987, Nov. 21** ***Perf. 13x12½***
**922** A344 250m blk, grn & rose lake 1.00 .50

Pasteur Institute, Paris, cent.

Intl. Year of the Vine (Wine) — A345

6th Volleyball Championships of African Nations — A346

**1987, Nov. 27 Photo.** ***Perf. 14***
**923** A345 250m multicolored 1.00 .50

**1987, Dec. 2 Litho.** ***Perf. 14x13½***
**924** A346 350m multicolored 1.40 .70

African Basketball Championships A347

Folk Costumes A348

**1987, Dec. 15**
**925** A347 350m multicolored 1.50 .70

**1987, Dec. 25 Photo.**
**926** A348 20m Midoun .25 .20
**927** A348 30m Tozeur .25 .20
**928** A348 150m Sfax .85 .40
*Nos. 926-928 (3)* 1.35 .80

Flowering Plants — A349

**1987, Dec. 29** ***Perf. 14½***
**929** A349 30m Narcissus tazetta .20 .20
**930** A349 150m Gladiolus communis .60 .30
**931** A349 400m Iris xiphium 1.60 .80
**932** A349 500m Tulipa sylvestris 2.10 1.00
*Nos. 929-932 (4)* 4.50 2.30

Declaration of Nov. 7, 1987 A350

Cameo portrait of Pres. Zine el Abidine Ben Ali and: 150m, Scales of Justice. 200m, Girl with flowers (party badges) in her hair, vert. 350m, Mermaid, doves, natl. coat of arms. 370m, "CMA," emblem of the Maghreb states (Tunisia, Mauritania, Morocco, Algeria and Libya), vert.

**1988, Mar. 21 Photo.** ***Perf. 12***
**Granite Paper**
**933** A350 150m multicolored .50 .25
**934** A350 200m multicolored .60 .30
**935** A350 350m multicolored 1.10 .55
**936** A350 370m multicolored 1.10 .60
*Nos. 933-936 (4)* 3.30 1.70

Youth and Change A351

**1988, Mar. 22 Litho.** ***Perf. 14x14½***
**937** A351 75m shown .25 .20
**938** A351 150m Happy family .50 .25

Martyr's Day, 50th Anniv. A352

***Perf. 13x13½, 13½x13***
**1988, Apr. 9 Photo.**
**939** A352 150m shown .45 .25
**940** A352 500m Monument, vert. 1.50 .75

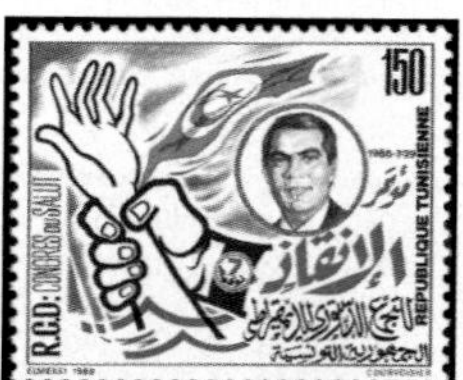

Opening Conference of the Constitutional Democratic Assembly — A353

**1988, July 30** ***Perf. 12x11½***
**Granite Paper**
**941** A353 150m Flag, Pres. Ben Ali .50 .25

1988 Summer Olympics, Seoul A354

**1988, Sept. 20 Photo.** ***Perf. 13½***
**942** A354 150m shown .50 .25
**943** A354 430m Running, boxing, weight lifting, wrestling 1.40 1.00

A355

A356

**1988, Sept. 21**
**944** A355 200m multicolored .60 .35

Restoration of the City of San'a, Yemen.

**1988, Nov. 7 Photo.** ***Perf. 14***
**945** A356 150m multicolored .70 .35

Appointment of Pres. Zine El Abidine Ben Ali, 1st anniv.

*Amilcar Beach,* 1942, by A. Debbeche — A357

**1988, Nov. 21 Photo.** ***Perf. 13½x13***
**946** A357 100m multicolored .50 .25

Tunis Air, 40th Anniv. A358

**1988, Nov. 28 Photo.** ***Perf. 12x11½***
**Granite Paper**
**947** A358 500m multicolored 1.60 .80

UN Declaration of Human Rights, 40th Anniv. — A359

**1988, Dec. 10** ***Perf. 12***
**Granite Paper**
**948** A359 370m black 1.25 .65

Tunisian Postage Stamp Cent. — A360

**1988, Dec. 16** ***Perf. 12½***
**Granite Paper**
**949** A360 150m multicolored .65 .40

A361

A362

Decorative doorways.

**1988, Dec. 26** *Perf. 14x13½*
**950** A361 50m multi .20 .20
**951** A361 70m multi, diff. .25 .20
**952** A361 100m multi, diff. .25 .20
**953** A361 150m multi, diff. .40 .25
**954** A361 370m multi, diff. .90 .40
**955** A361 400m multi, diff. 1.10 .40
*Nos. 950-955 (6)* 3.10 1.65

**1989, Mar. 7 Engr.** *Perf. 13½x13*
**956** A362 1000m dark blue 2.75 1.60

Ali Douagi (1909-49).

Natl. Day for the Handicapped A363

**1989, May 30 Photo.** *Perf. 13½*
**957** A363 150m multicolored .50 .25

Education A364

**1989, July 10** *Perf. 14*
**958** A364 180m multicolored .50 .25

Family Planning Assoc., 20th Anniv. — A365

**1989, Aug. 14 Litho.** *Perf. 14*
**959** A365 150m multicolored .40 .25

Family Care A366

**1989, Aug. 14 Litho.** *Perf. 14*
**960** A366 150m multicolored .40 .25

Fauna A367

**1989, Aug. 28 Photo.** *Perf. 13½x14*
**961** A367 250m Tortoise 1.00 .50
**962** A367 350m Oryx 1.40 .65

Intl. Fair, Tunis A368

Mohamed Beyram V (1840-1889) A369

**1989, Oct. 16 Photo.** *Perf. 14*
**963** A368 150m shown .40 .20
**964** A368 370m Pavilion, horiz. .90 .60

**1989, Oct. 28 Engr.** *Perf. 13*
**965** A369 150m blk & dp rose lil .40 .20

Theater, Carthage A370

Monument A371

**1989, Nov. 3 Photo.** *Perf. 14*
**966** A370 300m multicolored .85 .40

**1989, Nov. 7** *Perf. 11½x12*
**Granite Paper**
**967** A371 150m multicolored .40 .20

Appointment of Pres. Zine El Abidine Ben Ali, 2nd Anniv.

Nehru — A372

Flags — A373

**1989, Nov. 29 Engr.** *Perf. 13*
**968** A372 300m dark brown .90 .35

Jawaharlal Nehru, 1st prime minister of independent India.

**1990, Jan. 15 Photo.** *Perf. 12x11½*
**Granite Paper**
**969** A373 200m multicolored .60 .35

Maghreb Union summit, Tunis.

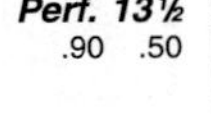
Museum of Bardo, Cent. A374

**1990, Feb. 20 Litho.** *Perf. 13½*
**970** A374 300m multicolored .90 .50

Pottery A375

**1990, Mar. 22** *Perf. 14*
**971** A375 75m multicolored .35 .20
**972** A375 100m multi, diff. .50 .35

Sheep Museum — A376

**1990, Apr. 13 Litho.** *Perf. 13½*
**973** A376 400m Sheep 1.25 .75
**974** A376 450m Ram's head 1.60 .85
*a.* Souvenir sheet of 2, #973-974 3.75 3.75

No. 974a sold for 1000m, exists imperf. Nos. 973-974 inscribed 1989.

Tunisian Olympic Movement — A377

**1990, May 27**
**975** A377 150m multicolored .40 .25

Child's Drawing A378

**1990, June 5** *Perf. 14*
**976** A378 150m multicolored .40 .25

A379

A380

Traditional costumes.

**1990, July 13 Photo.** *Perf. 14x14½*
**977** A379 150m Sbiba .50 .35
**978** A379 500m Bou Omrane 1.60 .85

**1990, Aug. 1 Litho.** *Perf. 14*

Relic from Punic city of Dougga.

**979** A380 300m multicolored .85 .50

Intl. Literacy Year A381

**1990, Sept. 8 Photo.** *Perf. 12x11½*
**Granite Paper**
**980** A381 120m multicolored .40 .25

A382

A383

**1990, Oct. 15** *Perf. 11½x12*
**Granite Paper**
**981** A382 150m multicolored .50 .25

Importance of water.

**1990, Nov. 7**
**Granite Paper**
**982** A383 150m shown .40 .25
**983** A383 150m Clock tower .40 .25

Appointment of Pres. Zine El Abidine Ben Ali, 3rd anniv.

A384

A385

**1990, Nov. 16 Engr.** *Perf. 13½x13*
**984** A384 150m green .50 .25

Kheireddine Et-Tounsi (1822-1889), politician.

**1990, Dec. 17 Photo.** *Perf. 13½*

Fauna and flora.

**985** A385 150m Cervus elaphus barbarus .40 .20
**986** A385 200m Cynara cardenculus .65 .35
**987** A385 300m Bubalus bubalis 1.00 .40
**988** A385 600m Ophris lutea 2.10 .85
*Nos. 985-988 (4)* 4.15 1.80

Maghreb Arab Union, 2nd Anniv. — A386

Harbor of Tabarka — A387

**1991, Jan. 21 Photo. *Perf. 13½***
**989** A386 180m multicolored .50 .25

**1991, Mar. 17**
**990** A387 450m multicolored 1.25 .50

Fish — A388

**1991, Sept. 10 Photo. *Perf. 14x13***
**991** A388 180m Pagre .60 .25
**992** A388 350m Rouget de roche 1.25 .40
**993** A388 450m Maquereau 1.25 .60
**994** A388 550m Pageot commun 2.10 .90
*Nos. 991-994 (4)* 5.20 2.15

Child Welfare — A389

**1991, Sept. 29 *Perf. 14***
**995** A389 450m multicolored 1.60 .85

A390

**1991, Oct. 9 *Perf. 13½x14***
**996** A390 400m multicolored 1.25 .50

A391

A392

Jewelry.

***Perf. 14x13, 13x14***
**1991, Oct. 22 Litho.**
**997** A391 120m Ring, bracelets, horiz. .40 .25
**998** A391 180m Necklace .50 .25
**999** A391 220m Earrings .65 .35
**1000** A391 730m shown 2.50 1.10
*Nos. 997-1000 (4)* 4.05 1.95

**1991, Nov. 7 *Perf. 11½***
**1001** A392 180m multicolored

Appointment of Pres. Zine El Abidine Ben Ali, 4th anniv.

Tunis-Carthage Center — A393

**1991, Nov. 22 Engr. *Perf. 13***
**1002** A393 80m red, blue & green 7.00 2.50

A394

A395

**1991, Dec. 12 Photo. *Perf. 14***
**1003** A394 450m bright blue 1.40 .55

World Day of the Rights of Man.

**1991, Dec. 26 Engr. *Perf. 12½x13***
**1004** A395 200m blue .50 .35

Mahmoud Bayram Et Tounsi (1893-1960), poet.

Expo '92, Seville — A396

General Post Office, Tunis, Cent. — A397

**1992, Apr. 20 Photo. *Perf. 13½***
**1005** A396 180m multicolored .50 .25

***Perf. 13x12½, 12½x13***
**1992, June 15 Engr.**
**1006** A397 180m red brn, horiz. .50 .25
**1007** A397 450m dark brown 1.40 .45

"When the Subconscious Awakes," by Moncef ben Amor — A398

**1992, July 21 Litho. *Perf. 13½***
**1008** A398 500m multicolored 1.50 .50

1992 Summer Olympics, Barcelona A399

**1992, Aug. 4**
**1009** A399 180m Running .85 .40
**1010** A399 450m Judo, vert. 1.90 .65

Birds — A400

A401

**1992, Sept. 22 Photo. *Perf. 11½***
**Granite Paper**
**1011** A400 100m Merops apiaster .60 .25
**1012** A400 180m Carduelis carduelis 1.10 .40
**1013** A400 200m Serinus serinus 1.25 .50
**1014** A400 500m Carduelis chloris 2.50 1.00
*Nos. 1011-1014 (4)* 5.45

**1992, Oct. 21 *Perf. 11½x12***
**Granite Paper**
**1015** A401 180m multicolored .65 .40

UN Conference on Rights of the Child.

African Human Rights Conference, Tunis — A402

**1992, Nov. 2 Photo. *Perf. 11½***
**Granite Paper**
**1016** A402 480m multicolored 1.60 .85

A403

A404

**1992, Nov. 7**
**Granite Paper**
**1017** A403 180m multicolored .65 .40
**1018** A404 730m multicolored 2.10 1.10

Appointment of Pres. Zine El Abidine Ben Ali, 5th anniv.

Arbor Day A405

**1992, Nov. 8 *Perf. 11½x12***
**Granite Paper**
**1019** A405 180m Acacia tortilis .75 .50

Intl. Conference on Nutrition, Rome — A406

**1992, Dec. 15 Litho. *Perf. 13½***
**1020** A406 450m multicolored 1.60 .65

Traditional Costumes — A407

**1992, Dec. 23**
**1021** A407 100m Chemesse .40 .25
**1022** A407 350m Hanifites 1.10 .50

Mosaics A408

**1992, Dec. 29**
**1023** A408 100m Goat .40 .25
**1024** A408 180m Duck .85 .35
**1025** A408 350m Horse 1.40 .50
**1026** A408 450m Gazelle 1.50 .90
*Nos. 1023-1026 (4)* 4.15 2.00

Arab-African Fair of Tunisia — A410

**1993, July 10 Litho. *Perf. 13½x14***
**1028** A410 450m multicolored 1.40 .50

Relaxation in the Patio, by Ali Guermassi A411

Reassembly of the Democratic Congress A412

**1993, July 20 Litho. *Perf. 13½***
**1029** A411 450m multicolored 1.40 .50

**1993, July 29 *Perf. 13½***
**1030** A412 180m multicolored .50 .25

A413

A414

**1993 *Perf. 13***
**1031** A413 20m Wolf .90 .25
**1032** A414 60m Hoya carnosa .60 .25

Appointment of Pres. Zine El Abidine, 6th Anniv.
A414A A415

**1993, Nov. 7 *Perf. 13½***
**1033** A414A 180m multicolored .50 .25
**1034** A415 450m multicolored 1.40 .50

Kairouan Tapestries — A416

Designs: Various ornate patterns.

**1993, Dec. 13 *Perf. 13½***
**1035** A416 100m multicolored .25 .20
**1036** A416 120m multicolored .35 .25
**1037** A416 180m multicolored .60 .35
**1038** A416 350m multicolored 1.40 .75
*Nos. 1035-1038 (4)* 2.60 1.55

Pasteur Institute of Tunis, Cent. A417

Design: 450m, Charles Nicolle (1866-1936), bacteriologist, 1928 Nobel medal.

**1993, Oct. 12 Litho. *Perf. 13½***
**1039** A417 450m multicolored 1.40 .65

A418

School Activities A419

**1993, Dec. 30 Litho. *Perf. 13½***
**1040** A418 180m Music .50 .25
**1041** A419 180m Art, reading .50 .25

19th African Cup of Nations Soccer Tournament — A420

**1994, Mar. 26**
**1042** A420 180m shown .50 .25
**1043** A420 350m Two players, diff. 1.00 .35
**1044** A420 450m Map, player 1.40 .65
*Nos. 1042-1044 (3)* 2.90 1.25

Presidential and Legislative Elections — A421

**1994, Mar. 20**
**1045** A421 180m multicolored .50 .25

Election of Pres. Zine El Abidine ben Ali — A422

**1994, May 15 Photo. *Perf. 11½***
**Granite Paper**
**1046** A422 180m multicolored .50 .35
**1047** A422 350m multicolored 1.00 .75
*a.* Souvenir sheet, #1046-1047 2.50 2.50

No. 1047a exists imperf.

ILO, 75th Anniv. — A423

**1994, May 12 *Perf. 13½x14***
**1048** A423 350m multicolored 1.20 .35

Intl. Year of the Family — A424

Plants — A425

**1994, May 15 Litho. *Perf. 14x13½***
**1049** A424 180m multicolored .85 .50

**1994, June 2**
**1050** A425 50m Prunus spinosa .20 .20
**1051** A425 100m Xeranthemum inapertum .25 .20
**1052** A425 200m Orchis simia .65 .30
**1053** A425 1d Scilla peruviana 3.00 1.50
*Nos. 1050-1053 (4)* 4.10 2.20

Organization of African Unity Summit Meeting, Tunis — A426

**1994, June 3 *Perf. 13½***
**1054** A426 480m multicolored 1.50 .75

Intl. Olympic Committee, Cent. A427

**1994, July 7 Litho. *Perf. 13½***
**1055** A427 450m multicolored 1.50 .65

Philakorea '94 — A428

**1994, Aug 18 Litho. *Perf. 13¼x13½***
**1056** A428 450m multi 1.50 .65

A429 A430

Butterflies: 100m, Colias croceus, horiz. 180m, Vanessa atalanta, horiz. 300m, Papilio podalirius. 350m, Danaus chrysippus, horiz. 450m, Vanessa cardui. 500m, Papilio machaon.

***Perf. 13½x14, 14x13½***
**1994, Oct. 13 Litho.**
**1057** A429 100m multicolored .40 .25
**1058** A429 180m multicolored .65 .35
**1059** A429 300m multicolored .90 .50
**1060** A429 350m multicolored 1.25 .65
**1061** A429 450m multicolored 1.60 .85
**1062** A429 500m multicolored 1.90 .90
*Nos. 1057-1062 (6)* 6.70 3.50

**1994, Nov. 16 *Perf. 13½***
**1063** A430 350m Pres. Ali, "7," horiz. 1.00 .50
**1064** A430 730m "7," Emblem 2.00 1.00

Pres. Zine El Abdine, 7th anniv. of taking office.

41st Military Boxing World Championships A431

**1994, Nov. 18 Litho. *Perf. 13½x14***
**1065** A431 450m multicolored 1.40 .70

Intl. Civil Aviation Organization, 50th Anniv. — A432

**1994, Dec. 7 Litho. *Perf. 13¾x14***
**1066** A432 450m multi 1.00 .50

Wildlife — A433

**1994, Dec. 27 Litho. *Perf. 13½***
**1067** A433 180m Anser anser .65 .40
**1068** A433 350m Aythya ferina, Aythya fuligula 1.10 .85
**1069** A433 500m Bubalus bubalis 1.60 1.25
**1070** A433 1d Lutra lutra, horiz. 3.00 2.75
*Nos. 1067-1070 (4)* 6.35 5.25

"Composition," by Ridha Bettaieb — A434

**1994, Dec. 29 Litho. *Perf. 13***
**1071** A434 500m multicolored 1.40 .85

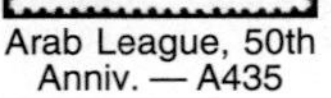
Arab League, 50th Anniv. — A435

Art of Glass Blowing — A436

**1995, May 29 Litho. *Perf. 13½***
**1072** A435 180m multicolored .55 .40

**1995, June 29**
**1073** A436 450m Water bottle 1.40 1.00
**1074** A436 730m Incense burner 2.25 1.60

Aboulkacem Chebbi (1909-34), Poet — A437

**1995, Aug. 12 Litho. *Perf. 13½***
**1075** A437 180m multicolored .55 .40

4th World Conference on Women, Beijing A438

**1995. Sept. 6 Litho. *Perf. 13½***
**1076** A438 180m multicolored .55 .40

FAO, 50th Anniv. A439

**1995, Oct. 2 Litho. *Perf. 13½x13***
**1077** A439 350m multicolored .90 .65

Hannibal (247-183BC), Carthaginian General — A440

**1995, Nov. 14 Engr. *Perf. 14x13½***
**1078** A440 180m maroon .65 .40
*a.* Souvenir sheet of 1 2.50 2.50

No. 1078a sold for 1d and exists imperf.

United Nations, 50th Anniv. A441

**1995, Oct. 24 Litho. *Perf. 14x13½***
**1079** A441 350m multicolored .90 .65

A442 A443

**1995, Nov. 7 Litho. *Perf. 13x13½***
**1080** A442 180m multicolored .50 .35
**1081** A443 350m multicolored .95 .65

Appointment of Pres. Zine El Abidine ben Ali, 8th anniv.

Campaign Against Desertification — A444

**1995, Oct. 31 Litho. *Perf. 13¼***
**1082** A444 180m multi .35 .35

Human Rights Day — A445

**1995, Dec. 10 Litho. *Perf. 13x13½***
**1083** A445 350m multicolored .95 .65

Pedestrian Security A446

**1995, Dec. 19 *Perf. 13½x13***
**1084** A446 350m multicolored .95 .65

Flora and Fauna A447

Traditional Costumes A448

Designs: 50m, Ophrys lapethica. 180m, Gazella dorcas. 300m, Scupellaria cypria. 350m, Chlamydotis undulata.

**1995, Dec. 28 *Perf. 13½***
**1085** A447 50m multicolored .20 .20
**1086** A447 180m multicolored .50 .25
**1087** A447 300m multicolored .80 .55
**1088** A447 350m multicolored .95 .75
*Nos. 1085-1088 (4)* 2.45 1.75

**1996, Mar.16 *Perf. 14x13½***
**1089** A448 170m Jebra, Khamri .50 .40
**1090** A448 200m Kaftan brode, Hammamet .50 .40

A449 A450

Independence, 40th Anniv.: 390m, Dove, rainbow, "20, 40."

**1996, Mar. 20 *Perf. 13x13½***
**1091** A449 200m multicolored .55 .30
**1092** A449 390m multicolored 1.00 .75

**1996, Jan. 20 Litho. *Perf. 13x13½***
**1093** A450 440m multicolored 1.50 .85

Natl. Trade Union, 50th anniv.

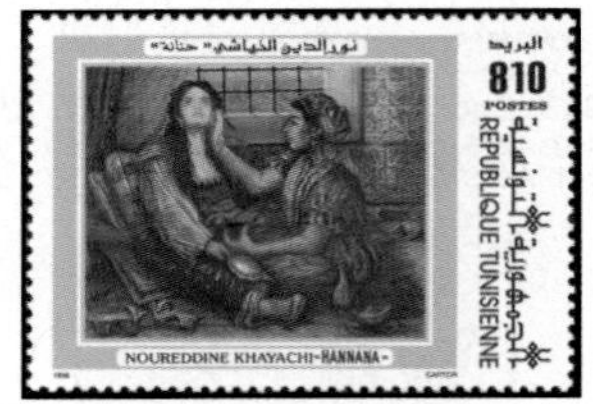
Painting, "Hannana," by Noureddine Khayachi (1917-87) — A451

**1996, Apr. 25 Litho. *Perf. 13½***
**1094** A451 810m multicolored 1.90 1.60

A451a A452

**1996, June 5 Litho. *Perf. 13x13½***
**1094A** A451a 390m multicolored .90 .75

Environment Day.

**1996, June 8 Litho. *Perf. 13x13½***
**1095** A452 200m multicolored .65 .35

CAPEX '96.

Insects A453

**1996, May 23 Litho. *Perf. 14x13½***
**1096** A453 200m Coccinella septempunctata .60 .40
**1097** A453 810m Apis mellifica 2.75 2.00

1996 Summer Olympic Games, Atlanta A455

Olympic emblem, and: 20m, Flags, Olympic rings, athletic field. 200m, Torch bearer, fireworks, "100," globe, vert. 390m, Early Olympic wrestlers.

**1996, July 19 Litho. *Perf. 13***
**1099** A455 20m multicolored .20 .20
**1100** A455 200m multicolored .50 .35
**1101** A455 390m multicolored 1.00 .85
*Nos. 1099-1101 (3)* 1.70 1.40

Code of Personal Status (Women's Liberation), 40th Anniv. — A456

**1996, Aug. 13 *Perf. 14***
**1102** A456 200m multicolored .50 .35

Landmarks A457

Intl. Year to Fight Poverty A458

Designs: 20m, Ramparts of Sousse, horiz. 200m, Numidian Mausoleum, Dougga. 390m, Arch of Trajan, Makthar, horiz.

**1996, Sept. 16 Photo. *Perf. 11½***
**Granite Paper**
**1103** A457 20m multicolored .20 .20
**1104** A457 200m multicolored .45 .35
**1105** A457 390m multicolored 1.00 .85
*Nos. 1103-1105 (3)* 1.65 1.40

**1996, Oct. 17 Litho. *Perf. 13x13½***
**1106** A458 390m multicolored .85 .65

Appointment of Pres. Zine El Abidine, 9th Anniv.
A459 A460

**1996, Nov. 7**
**1107** A459 200m multicolored .45 .35
**1108** A460 390m multicolored .75 .75

National Day of Saharan Tourism — A461

Designs: No. 1109, Camels, oasis, balloon. No. 1110, Decorative designs.
Illustration reduced.

**1996, Nov. 12 Litho. *Perf. 13¼x13***
**1109** 200m multi .40 .35
**1110** 200m multi .40 .35
*a.* A461 Horiz. pair, #1109-1110 1.00 1.00

Ezzitouna Mosque, 1300th Anniv. — A462

**1996, Nov. 25 Litho. *Perf. 14x13½***
**1111** A462 250m multicolored .55 .40

Natl. Solidarity Day
A463 A464

**1996, Dec. 8** ***Perf. 13x13½***

| | | | | |
|---|---|---|---|---|
| **1112** | A463 500m multicolored | .95 | .95 |
| **1113** | A464 500m multicolored | .95 | .95 |

World Human Rights Day — A465

UNICEF, 50th Anniv. — A466

**1996, Dec. 10**

**1114** A465 500m multicolored 1.10 .90

**1996, Dec. 11**

**1115** A466 810m multicolored 1.75 1.50

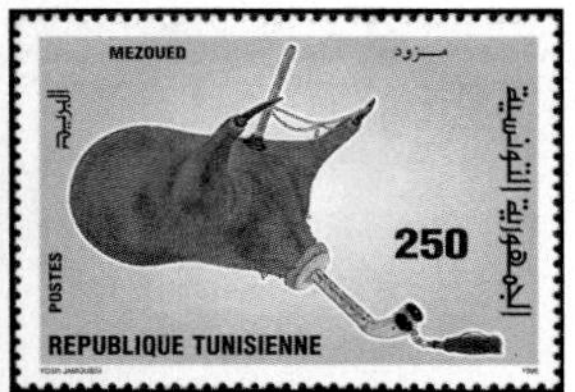

Musical Instruments — A467

**1996, Dec. 26** **Litho.** ***Perf. 13½***

| | | | |
|---|---|---|---|
| **1116** | A467 250m Mezoued | .60 | .50 |
| **1117** | A467 300m Gombri | .75 | .60 |
| **1118** | A467 360m Tabla | .85 | .65 |
| **1119** | A467 500m Tar Tounsi (Riq) | 1.25 | .90 |
| | *Nos. 1116-1119 (4)* | 3.45 | 2.65 |

World Book and Copyright Day A468

**1997, Apr. 23** **Litho.** ***Perf. 13½***

**1120** A468 1d multicolored 2.40 1.75

Marine Life A469

Designs: 50m, Mytilus galloprovincialis. 70m, Tapes decussatus. 350m, Octopus vulgaris. 500m, Sepia officinalis.

**1997, May 13**

| | | | |
|---|---|---|---|
| **1121** | A469 50m multicolored | .20 | .20 |
| **1122** | A469 70m multicolored | .20 | .20 |
| **1123** | A469 350m multicolored | .85 | .65 |
| **1124** | A469 500m multicolored | 1.40 | 1.25 |
| | *Nos. 1121-1124 (4)* | 2.65 | 2.30 |

PACIFIC 97, Intl. Stamp Exhibition, San Francisco — A470

**1997, May 29** **Photo.** ***Perf. 11½x12***
**Granite Paper**

**1125** A470 250m multicolored .70 .40

A471 A472

**1997, June 16** **Litho.** ***Perf. 13½***

**1126** A471 350m multicolored 1.10 .65

Mediterranean Games, Bari.

**1997, July 15**

**1127** A472 250m multicolored .70 .40

Tunis, 1997 Cultural Capital.

A473

Republic, 40th Anniv. A474

**1997, July 25**

| | | | |
|---|---|---|---|
| **1128** | A473 130m multicolored | .35 | .25 |
| **1129** | A474 500m multicolored | 1.25 | 1.00 |

Reptiles A475

100m, Uromastix acanthinurus. 350m, Chamaeleo chamaeleon, vert. 500m, Varanus griseus.

**1997, Sept. 9** **Litho.** ***Perf. 13½***

| | | | |
|---|---|---|---|
| **1130** | A475 100m multicolored | .25 | .20 |
| **1131** | A475 350m multicolored | 1.00 | .65 |
| **1132** | A475 500m multicolored | 1.25 | 1.10 |
| | *Nos. 1130-1132 (3)* | 2.50 | 1.95 |

Rosa Gallica Flore Pleno — A476

**1997, Sept. 23** **Litho.** ***Perf. 13½***

**1134** A476 350m multicolored .90 .85

Intl. Day for Protection of the Elderly A477

**1997, Oct. 1** **Litho.** ***Perf. 13½***

**1135** A477 250m multicolored .60 .40

Tunisian Works of Art — A478

#1136, "L'Automne," by Ammar Farhat. #1137, Sculpture, "Pecheur D'Hommes," by Hedi Selmi. #1138, "Au Cafe-Maure," by Farhat. #1139, "Le Viellard au Kanoun," by Farhat. #1140, "Cafe Des Nattes-Sidi Bou Said," by Hedi Khayachi. #1141, "Le Kouttab," by Yahia Turki. 1000d, "La Fileuse," by Farhat.

**1997, Nov. 5**

| | | | |
|---|---|---|---|
| **1136** | A478 250m multi, vert. | .55 | .55 |
| **1137** | A478 250m multi, vert. | .55 | .55 |
| **1138** | A478 250m multi, vert. | .55 | .55 |
| **1139** | A478 250m multi, vert. | .55 | .55 |
| **1140** | A478 500m multi | 1.10 | 1.10 |
| **1141** | A478 500m multi | 1.10 | 1.10 |
| **1142** | A478 1000m multi, vert. | 2.25 | 2.25 |
| *a.* | Sheet of 7, #1136-1142, + 3 labels | 7.25 | 7.25 |
| | *Nos. 1136-1142 (7)* | 6.65 | 6.65 |

No. 1142a issued 11/7.

A479

A480

**1997, Nov. 7**

| | | | |
|---|---|---|---|
| **1143** | A479 250m multicolored | .60 | .40 |
| **1144** | A480 500m multicolored | 1.10 | 1.10 |

Pres. Zine El Abdine, 10th anniv. of taking office.

Desert Rose — A481

**1997, Nov. 29**

**1145** A481 250m multicolored .60 .40

Intl. Human Rights Day — A482

**1997, Dec. 10** **Litho.** ***Perf. 13½***

**1146** A482 500m multicolored .90 .90

Horses A483

Designs: 50m, Arabian. 70m, Barb. 250m, Arabian barb, vert. 500m, Arabian, vert.

**1997, Dec. 18** ***Perf. 12½x13***

| | | | |
|---|---|---|---|
| **1147** | A483 50m multicolored | .20 | .20 |
| **1148** | A483 70m multicolored | .20 | .20 |
| **1149** | A483 250m multicolored | .75 | .40 |
| **1150** | A483 500m multicolored | 1.50 | .75 |
| | *Nos. 1147-1150 (4)* | 2.65 | 1.55 |

Bombing of Sakiet Sidi Yoncef, 40th Anniv. A484

**1998, Feb. 8**

**1151** A484 250m multicolored .60 .30

School Health Week A485

**1998, Feb. 16** **Litho.** ***Perf. 12½x13***

**1152** A485 250m multicolored .60 .30

Bar Assoc. of Tunisia, Cent. — A486

**1998, Mar. 27** ***Perf. 13x12½***

**1153** A486 250m multicolored .60 .30

Martyr's Day, 60th Anniv.
A487 A488

**1998, Apr. 9**

| | | | | |
|---|---|---|---|---|
| **1154** | A487 250m multicolored | .60 | .30 |
| **1155** | A488 520m multicolored | 1.25 | .60 |

Okba Ibn Nafaa Mosque, Kairouan — A489

**1998, May 28 Litho. *Perf. 13***

**1156** A489 500m multicolored 1.40 .70

1998 World Cup Soccer Championships, France — A490

250m, Tunisian team. 500m Player, trophy.

**1998, June 10 Litho. *Perf. 13***

| | | | |
|---|---|---|---|
| **1157** | A490 250m multi | .60 | .30 |
| **1158** | A490 500m multi, vert. | 1.25 | .60 |

Crustaceans — A491

**1998, July 8 *Perf. 12½x13***

| | | | |
|---|---|---|---|
| **1159** | A491 110m Crab | .25 | .20 |
| **1160** | A491 250m Shrimp | .60 | .30 |
| **1161** | A491 1000m Lobster | 2.25 | 1.10 |
| | *Nos. 1159-1161 (3)* | 3.10 | 1.60 |

21st Reassembly of the Democratic Congress (RCD) — A492

#1162, Pres. Zine El Abidine ben Ali, flag, emblems. #1163, People holding torches, flag, dove.

**1998, July 30 *Perf. 13***

| | | | |
|---|---|---|---|
| **1162** | A492 250m multi | .60 | .30 |
| **1163** | A492 250m multi, vert. | .60 | .30 |

36th Intl. Congress on the History of Medicine — A493

**1998, Sept. 6 Litho. *Perf. 13***

**1164** A493 500m multicolored 1.25 .60

Paintings — A494

#1165, "The Weaver," by Ali Guermassi (1923-92). #1166, "Woman Musician," by Noureddine Khayachi (1917-87). 500m, Still life by Ali Khouja (1947-91).

**1998, Oct. 8**

| | | | |
|---|---|---|---|
| **1165** | A494 250m multi | .60 | .30 |
| **1166** | A494 250m multi, vert. | .60 | .30 |
| **1167** | A494 500m multi, vert. | 1.25 | .60 |
| | *Nos. 1165-1167 (3)* | 2.45 | 1.20 |

Central Bank of Tunisia, 40th Anniv. A495

**1998, Nov. 10 Litho. *Perf. 13***

**1168** A495 250m multicolored .60 .30

A496

**1998, Nov. 7**

**1169** A496 250m multicolored .60 .30

Appointment of Pres. Zine El Abidine ben Ali, 11th anniv.

Universal Declaration of Human Rights, 50th Anniv. A497

**1998, Dec. 10 Litho. *Perf. 12½x13***

**1170** A497 250m multicolored .65 .35

Averroes (Ibn Rushd) (1126-1198), Philosopher — A498

**1998, Dec. 12**

**1171** A498 500m multicolored 1.25 .60

Musicians A499

**1998, Dec. 21 *Perf. 12½x13, 13x12½***

| | | | |
|---|---|---|---|
| **1172** | A499 250m Kaddour Srarfi | .60 | .30 |
| **1173** | A499 250m Saliha, vert. | .60 | .30 |
| **1174** | A499 500m Ali Riahi, vert. | 1.25 | .60 |
| | *Nos. 1172-1174 (3)* | 2.45 | 1.20 |

Boukornine Natl. Park — A500

**1998, Dec. 29 Litho. *Perf. 13***

| | | | |
|---|---|---|---|
| **1175** | A500 70m Gazelles | .20 | .20 |
| **1176** | A500 110m Rabbit | .25 | .20 |
| **1177** | A500 250m Eagles | .60 | .30 |
| **1178** | A500 500m Cyclamens | 1.25 | .60 |
| | *Nos. 1175-1178 (4)* | 2.30 | 1.30 |

Fruit Trees A501

**1999, Feb. 27 Litho. *Perf. 13***

| | | | |
|---|---|---|---|
| **1179** | A501 250m Orange | .65 | .30 |
| **1180** | A501 250m Date, vert. | .65 | .30 |
| **1181** | A501 500m Olive | 1.25 | .60 |
| | *Nos. 1179-1181 (3)* | 2.55 | 1.20 |

Archaeological Sites — A502

50m, Gate, Thuburbo Majus. 250m, Thermal baths, Bulla Regia. 500m, Zaghouan Aqueduct.

**1999, Mar. 31 Litho. *Perf. 13***

| | | | |
|---|---|---|---|
| **1182** | A502 50m multi, vert. | .20 | .20 |
| **1183** | A502 250m multi | .55 | .30 |
| **1184** | A502 500m multi | 1.25 | .60 |
| | *Nos. 1182-1184 (3)* | 2.00 | 1.10 |

Paintings by Tunisian Artists A503

Designs: No. 1185, "L'Intemporel," by Moncef Ben Amor. No. 1186, "Fiancailles," by Ali Guermassi. No. 1187, "La Poterie," by Ammar Farhat. No. 1188, "Vendeur d'ombrelles et d'eventails," by Yahia Turki.

**1999, May 6 Litho. *Perf. 13***

| | | | |
|---|---|---|---|
| **1185** | A503 250m multicolored | .55 | .30 |
| **1186** | A503 250m multicolored | .55 | .30 |
| **1187** | A503 500m multicolored | 1.10 | .55 |
| **1188** | A503 500m multicolored | 1.10 | .55 |
| | *Nos. 1185-1188 (4)* | 3.30 | 1.70 |

Constitution, 40th Anniv. — A504

**1999, June 1 Litho. *Perf. 13***

**1189** A504 250m multicolored .85 .40

Flowers — A505

70m, Acacia cyanophilla. #1191, Bouganvillea spectabilis. #1192, Papaver rhoeas. 500m, Dianthus caryophylius.

**1999, June 25 Litho. *Perf. 12¾***

| | | | |
|---|---|---|---|
| **1190** | A505 70m multicolored | .20 | .20 |
| **1191** | A505 250m multicolored | .55 | .25 |
| **1192** | A505 250m multicolored | .55 | .25 |
| **1193** | A505 500m multicolored | 1.10 | .55 |
| *a.* | Souvenir sheet, #1190-1193, imperf. | 4.00 | 4.00 |
| | *Nos. 1190-1193 (4)* | 2.40 | 1.25 |

No. 1193a sold for 1.50d.

Philex France 99 — A506

**1999, July 2 *Perf. 13x12¾***

**1194** A506 500m multicolored 1.10 .55

Tahar Haddad (b. 1899), Women's Rights Advocate — A507

**1999, Aug. 13 Litho.**

**1195** A507 500m multicolored 1.10 .50

Marine Life A508

**1999, Sept. 22 *Perf. 12¾***

| | | | |
|---|---|---|---|
| **1196** | A508 250m Caretta caretta | .55 | .25 |
| **1197** | A508 500m Epinephelus marginatus | 1.10 | .55 |

National Organ Donation Day — A509

**1999, Oct. 2** ***Perf. 13x12¾***

**1198** A509 250m multicolored .55 .25

UPU, 125th Anniv. — A510

Elections — A511

**1999, Oct. 9** ***Perf. 12¾***

**1199** A510 500m multicolored 1.10 .55

**1999, Oct. 10** **Litho.**

**1200** A511 500m multicolored 1.10 .55

Tamarisk A512

**1999, Oct. 28** **Litho.** ***Perf. 12¾x13***

**1201** A512 250m shown .55 .25

**1202** A512 500m Dromedary 1.10 .55

Appointment of Pres. Zine El Abidine Ben Ali, 12th Anniv. — A513

**1999, Nov. 7** ***Perf. 13x12¾***

**1203** A513 250m multi .60 .30

Human Rights Day — A514

Famous Tunisians — A515

**1999, Dec. 10** **Litho.** ***Perf. 13x12¾***

**1204** A514 250m multi .60 .30

**1999, Dec. 28** ***Perf. 13x12¾, 12¾x13***

#1205, Ahmed Ibn Abi Dhiaf (1802-74), historian. #1206, Abdelaziz Thaalbi (1876-1944), anti-colonial leader. 500m, Khemaies Tarnane (1894-1964), musician.

**1205** A515 250m multi .60 .30

**1206** A515 250m multi .60 .30

**1207** A515 500m multi, horiz. 1.25 .60

*Nos. 1205-1207 (3)* 2.45 1.20

Millennium — A516

**1999, Dec. 31** ***Perf. 13***

**1208** A516 250m multi .60 .30

A517

A518

Archaeology A519

Design: 100m, Methred cup. 110m, Aghlabide plate. 250m, Zaghouan water temple. 500m, Ulysses and the Sirens mosaic.

Illustration A517 reduced.

**2000, Apr. 22** **Litho.** ***Perf. 13x13¼***

**1209** A517 100m multi .20 .20

**1210** A517 110m multi .20 .20

***Perf. 13¼***

**1211** A518 250m multi .45 .25

**1212** A519 500m multi .90 .45

*Nos. 1209-1212 (4)* 1.75 1.10

Ferry Carthage — A520

**2000, Apr. 29** ***Perf. 13¼x13***

**1213** A520 500m multi .90 .45

*a.* Souvenir sheet, imperf. 3.75 1.90

No. 1213a sold for 2d.

Expo 2000, Hanover — A521

**2000, June 1** ***Perf. 13¼x13***

**1214** A521 1d multi 2.10 1.10

Trees A522

Designs: 50m, Carob. 100m, Apricot. 250m, Avocado, vert. 400m, Apple.

**2000, July 5** **Litho.** ***Perf. 12¾***

**1215-1218** A522 Set of 4 1.60 .80

2001 Mediterranean Games, Tunis — A523

**2000, Sept. 2** **Litho.** ***Perf. 13***

**1219** A523 500m multi .90 .45

*a.* Souvenir sheet of 1, imperf. 2.60 1.40

No. 1219a sold for 1500m.

2000 Summer Olympics, Sydney — A524

**2000, Sept. 22** ***Perf. 12¾***

**1220** A524 500m multi .90 .45

**Souvenir Sheet**

***Imperf***

**1221** A524 1500m multi 2.60 1.40

Flowers — A525

Designs: 110m, Freesias. 200m, Chrysanthemums. No. 1224, 250m, "Golden Times" roses. No. 1225, 250m, Vase with flowers (33x49mm). 500m, "Calibra" roses.

**2000, Oct. 21** ***Perf. 12¾, 13 (#1225)***

**1222-1226** A525 Set of 5 2.25 1.10

Appointment of Pres. Zine El Abidine Ben Ali, 13th Anniv. A526

**2000, Nov. 7** ***Perf. 13***

**1227** A526 250m multi .60 .30

Art — A527

Designs: 100m, Still Life, by Hédi Khayachi. No. 1229, 250m, Landscape, by Abdelaziz Berraies. No. 1230, 250m, The Knife Sharpener, by Ali Guermassi. 400m, Date and Milk Seller, by Yahia Turki, vert.

**2000, Nov. 18**

**1228-1231** A527 Set of 4 2.00 1.00

Intl. Human Rights Day — A528

**2000, Dec. 10**

**1232** A528 500m multi .90 .45

Shells — A529

Designs: 50m, Neverita josephinia. No. 1234, 250m, Phyllonotus trunculus. No. 1235, 250m, Columbella rustica. 1d, Arca noe.

Illustration reduced.

**2000, Dec. 29** ***Perf. 13x13¼***

**1233-1236** A529 Set of 4 3.00 1.50

A530

Famous Tunisians A531

Designs: No. 1237, 250m, Imam Sahnoun. No. 1238, 250m, Imam Ibn Arafa. No. 1239, 250m, Ali Belhaouane (1909-58), vert. 1d, Mohamed Jamoussi (1910-82), musician.

**2000, Dec. 30** ***Perf. 12¾***

**1237** A530 250m shown .45 .25

**1238** A530 250m multi .45 .25

**1239** A531 250m multi .45 .25

**1240** A531 1d shown 1.90 .95

*Nos. 1237-1240 (4)* 3.25 1.70

Tunisian Presidency of UN Security Council — A532

**2001, Feb. 19** **Litho.** ***Perf. 13***
**1241** A532 250m multi .45 .25

World Fund of Solidarity A533

**2001, Mar. 29**
**1242** A533 500m multi .90 .45

Year of Digital Culture — A534

**2001, May 17** ***Perf. 12¾***
**1243** A534 250m multi .45 .25

Mohamed Dorra, Child Killed in Israeli-Palestinian Violence — A535

**2001, May 30**
**1244** A535 600m multi 1.10 .55

A536

A537

Designs: No. 1245, 19th cent. ceramic tile, Qallaline. No. 1246, Gigthis, horiz. No. 1247, Tunis City Hall, horiz. 500m, Needles of Tabarka.

**2001, Aug. 24**
**1245** A536 250m multi .45 .25
**1246** A537 250m multi .45 .25
**1247** A537 250m multi .45 .25
**1248** A537 500m multi .90 .45
*Nos. 1245-1248 (4)* 2.25 1.20

2001 Mediterranean Games, Tunis — A538

Desings: No. 1249, 250m, No. 1251b, Track, stadium. No. 1250, 500m, No. 1251a, Runners, medal.

**2001, Sept. 2** ***Perf. 12¾***
**1249-1250** A538 Set of 2 1.40 .70

**Souvenir Sheet**

***Imperf***

**1251** A538 750m Sheet of 2, #a-b 2.75 1.40

Paintings — A539

Designs: No. 1252, 250m, Sidi Bou Said, by Pierre Boucherle. No. 1253, 250m, Still Life, by Boucherle. No. 1254, 250m, Dream in Traditional Space, by Aly Ben Salem, vert. 500m, Traditional Open-air Marriage, by Ben Salem.

**2001, Sept. 29** **Litho.** ***Perf. 13***
**1252-1255** A539 Set of 4 2.25 1.20

Year of Dialogue Among Civilizations A540

**2001, Oct. 9** ***Perf. 12¾x13***
**1256** A540 500m multi .90 .45

National Employment Fund — A541

**2001, Oct. 10**
**1257** A541 250m multi .45 .25

Appointment of Pres. Zine El Abidine Ben Ali, 14th Anniv. — A542

**2001, Nov. 7** ***Perf. 13x12¾***
**1258** A542 250m multi .45 .25

Butterflies — A543

Designs: Nos. 1259, 1263a, 250m, Ariane. No. 1260, 250m, No. 1263c, 500m, Pacha à deux queues. Nos. 1261, 1263b, 250m, Demi-deuil. Nos. 1262, 1263d, 500m, Grand paon de nuit.
Illustration reduced.

**2001, Nov. 15** ***Perf. 13x13¼***
**1259-1262** A543 Set of 4 2.25 1.10

**Souvenir Sheet**

***Imperf***

**1263** A543 Sheet of 4, #a-d 2.75 1.40

Birds — A544

Designs: No. 1264, 250m, No. 1268a, 300m, Bec-croise des sapins. 500m, Mesange charbonnière. No. 1266, 600m, Cigogne blanche. No. 1267, 600m, Geai des chenes.

**2001, Nov. 22** ***Perf. 13***
**1264-1267** A544 Set of 4 3.25 1.75

**Souvenir Sheet**

**1268** A544 Sheet, #1265-1267, 1268a 3.50 1.75

Intl. Human Rights Day — A545

**2001, Dec. 10** ***Perf. 13x12¾***
**1269** A545 250m multi .45 .25

Famous Men A546

Designs: No. 1270, 250m, Ibrahim ibn al-Aghlab (757-812), founder of Aghlabid dynasty. No. 1271, 250m, Ibn Rachiq al Kairaouani (1000-71). 350m, Abdelaziz Laroui (1898-1971). 650m, Assad ibn al-Fourat (759-828).

**2001, Dec. 29** ***Perf. 12¾x13***
**1270-1273** A546 Set of 4 2.75 1.40

Arabic Calligraphy A547

Designs: No. 1274, 350m, Shown. No. 1275, 350m, Calligraphy, vert.

**2001, Dec. 31** ***Perf. 12¾x13, 13x12¾***
**1274-1275** A547 Set of 2 1.25 .65

Archaeology
A548 A549

Designs: 250m, Kef casbah. 390m, Amphitheater, Oudhna, horiz. No. 1278, Baron of Erlanger Palace. No. 1279, Mosaic of Virgil.

***Perf. 13x12¾, 12¾x13***

**2002, Mar. 26** **Litho.**
**1276** A548 250m multi .35 .20
**1277** A548 390m multi .55 .25
**1278** A549 600m multi .80 .40
**1279** A549 600m multi .80 .40
*Nos. 1276-1279 (4)* 2.50 1.25

Animals of Zembra and Zembretta Natl. Park — A550

Designs: No. 1280, 250m, No. 1284a, 400m, Ovis musimon. No. 1281, 250m, No. 1284b, Oryctolagus cuniculus. No. 1282, 600m, Falco peregrinus brookei. No. 1283, 600m, Larus audouinii.

**2002, Apr. 10** ***Perf. 13***
**1280-1283** A550 Set of 4 2.25 1.10

**Souvenir Sheet**

**1284** A550 Sheet, #1282-1283, 1284a-1284b 2.75 1.40

Sahara Desert Tourism A551

Designs: No. 1285, 250m, No. 1289a, 400m, Gazella leptoceros. No. 1286, 390m, No. 1289b, 400m, Sahara village. No. 1287, 600m, Horseman. No. 1288, 600m, Tamaghza.

**2002, May 22** ***Perf. 13¼***
**1285-1288** A551 Set of 4 2.60 1.25

**Souvenir Sheet**

**1289** A551 Sheet, #1287-1288, 1289a-1289b, imperf. 2.75 1.40

2002 World Cup Soccer Championships, Japan and Korea — A552

World Cup, Emblem of Tunisia and World Cup tournament and: No. 1290, 390m, No. 1292a, 500m, Player, map of Japan and Korea. No. 1291, 600m, 1292b, 1000m, Ball in goal net.

**2002, May 29** ***Perf. 13***
**1290-1291** A552 Set of 2 1.40 .70

**Souvenir Sheet**

**1292** A552 Sheet of 2, #a-b 2.10 1.10

Famous Men — A553

Designs: 100m, Sheikh Mohamed Senoussi (1851-1900). No. 1294, 250m, Mosbah Jarbou (1914-58). No. 1295, 250m, Mohamed Daghbaji (1885-1924). 1.10d, Abou al-Hassen al-Housri (1029-95).

**2002, July 18** ***Perf. 12¾***
**1293-1296** A553 Set of 4 2.50 1.25

World Handicapped Games — A554

Tunisian flag and: 100m, Wheelchair racer. 700m, Discus thrower, vert.

**2002, July 20**
**1297-1298** A554 Set of 2 1.25 .60

27th World Veterinary Congress, Tunis A555

**2002, Sept. 25 Litho. *Perf. 12¾***
**1299** A555 600m multi .90 .45

Travel International Club, 20th Anniv. — A556

**2002, Oct. 25 Litho. *Perf. 13x13¼***
**1300** A556 600m multi .90 .45

Appointment of Pres. Zine El Abidine Ben Ali, 15th Anniv. — A557

**2002, Nov. 7 *Perf. 13x12¾***
**1301** A557 390m multi .60 .30

Assassination of Farhat Hached (1914-52) — A558

**2002, Dec. 3 Litho. *Perf. 13x12¾***
**1302** A558 390m multi .60 .30

Intl. Human Rights Day — A559

**2002, Dec. 10**
**1303** A559 700m multi 1.00 .50

### Art Type of 2001

Designs: No. 1304, 250m, Space for Gazelles, by Aly Ben Salem. No. 1305, 250m, Popular Arts, by Ammar Farhat, vert. No. 1306, 250m, Marriage, by Habib Bouabana, vert. 900m, Still Life, by Pierre Boucherle, vert.

**2002, Dec. 28 *Perf. 13***
**1304-1307** A539 Set of 4 2.50 1.25

Mosaics A560

Designs: 390m, Spinner. 600m, Africa.

**2003, Feb. 28**
**1308-1309** A560 Set of 2 1.50 .75

Scouting in Tunisia, 70th Anniv. — A561

"70" and scouts: 250m, Reading map, at computer, planting tree. 600m, Saluting flag, at computer, vert.

**2003, Mar. 29 Litho. *Perf. 13***
**1310-1311** A561 Set of 2 1.25 .60

National Book Year — A562

**2003, Apr. 23**
**1312** A562 390m multi .65 .30

The Washerwoman, by Yahia Turki — A563

**2003, June 13**
**1313** A563 1d multi 1.60 .80

National Tourism Day — A564

**2003, June 28 *Perf. 13¼***
**1314** A564 600m multi .95 .45

Parks — A565

Designs: 200m, Farhat Hached Park, Rades. 250m, Friguia Animal Park. 390m, La Marsa Park. 1d, Ennahli Park.

**2003, June 28 *Perf. 13***
**1315-1318** A565 Set of 4 3.00 1.50

A566

A567

**2003, July 28 Litho. *Perf. 13x12¾***
**1319** A566 250m multi .45 .25

Congress of Ambition.

**2003, Aug. 3**
**1320** A567 390m multi .65 .30

Pres. Habib Bourguiba (1903-2000).

A568

Flora and Fauna — A569

Designs: Nos. 1321a, 50m, 1326, 600m, Oryx dammah. Nos. 1321b, 50m, 1324, 250m, Nyctanthes sambac. Nos. 1321c, 100m, 1323, 250m, Aries. Nos. 1321d, 100m, 1327, 1d, Myrtus communis. Nos. 1321e, 200m, 1325, 390m, Struthio camelus. Nos. 1321f, 200m, 1322, 100m, Rosa canina.

**2003, Sept. 25 *Perf. 12¾***
**1321** Strip of 6 1.25 .65
*a.-b.* A568 50m Either single .20 .20
*c.-d.* A568 100m Either single .20 .20
*e.-f.* A568 200m Either single .35 .20
**1322-1327** A569 Set of 6 4.50 2.25

No. 1321 was issued in a sheet of 6 strips that sold for 4500m.

Appointment of Pres. Zine El Abidine Ben Ali, 16th Anniv. — A570

**2003, Nov. 7 Litho. *Perf. 13x12¾***
**1328** A570 250m multi .40 .20

First 5+5 Dialogue Summit, Tunis — A571

**2003, Dec. 5 *Perf. 13¼***
**1329** A571 600m multi 1.00 .50

Universal Declaration of Human Rights — A572

**2003, Dec. 10 *Perf. 13x12¾***
**1330** A572 350m multi .60 .30

Silver Items A573

Designs: No. 1331, 600m, Machmoum. No. 1332, 600m, Jewelry.

**2003, Dec. 18 *Perf. 12¾x13***
**1331-1332** A573 Set of 2 2.00 1.00
*1332a* Souvenir sheet, #1331-1332 2.50 2.50

No. 1332a sold for 1.50d.

African Soccer Championships — A574

Designs: 250m, Stylized soccer players, African cup, map. 600m, Map of Africa as soccer player.

**2004, Jan. 24 *Perf. 13***
**1333-1334** A574 Set of 2 1.40 .70

Values are for stamps with surrounding selvage.

Ksar Helal Congress, 70th Anniv. — A575

**2004, Mar. 2 Litho. *Perf. 13x12¾***
**1335** A575 250m multi .40 .20

Arab League Conference, Tunis
A576

**2004, May 22** ***Perf. 13***
**1336** A576 600m multi .95 .50

Copper Handicrafts — A577

Designs: 100m, Water jar, 18th cent. 200m, Ewer, 18th cent. 250m, Bucket, 19th cent. 600m, Brazier, 18th cent. 700m, Amphora, 18th cent. 1000m, Ewer, 19th cent.
Illustration reduced.

**2004, June 5** ***Perf. 13x13¼***
**1337-1342** A577 Set of 6 4.50 2.25
**1343** Sheet, 3 each #1337, 1338, 1343a-1343d 5.50 2.75
*a.* A577 50m Like #1340 .20 .20
*b.* A577 150m Like #1342 .25 .20
*c.* A577 250m Like #1341 .40 .20
*d.* A577 300m Like #1339 .50 .25

No. 1343 sold for 3500m.

Coins and Banknotes
A578

Designs: No. 1344, 250m, Gold coin, 706. No. 1345, 250m, Gold coin, 1767. No. 1346, 600m, Punic silver coin, 300 B.C. No. 1347, 600m, Punic gold coin, 310-290 B.C. 1000m, Banknote, 1847 (65x30mm).

**2004, July 23** ***Perf. 13¼***
**1344-1348** A578 Set of 5 4.25 2.10
*1348a* Souvenir sheet, #1344-1348 + label 4.75 2.40

No. 1348a sold for 3000m.

African Development Bank, 40th Anniv.
A579

**2004, Sept. 10** **Litho.** ***Perf. 13***
**1349** A579 700m multi 1.10 .55

Children's Art — A580

**2004, Oct. 20**
**1350** A580 250m multi .40 .20

Presidential and Legislative Elections
A581

**2004, Oct. 24**
**1351** A581 250m multi .40 .20

Appointment of Pres. Zine El Abidine Ben Ali, 17th Anniv.
A582

**2004, Nov. 7**
**1352** A582 250m multi .40 .20

El Abidine Mosque, Carthage — A583

**2004, Nov. 11**
**1353** A583 250m multi .40 .40

Birds — A584

Designs: 100m, Oxyura leucocephala. No. 1355, 600m, Phoenicurus moussieri. No. 1356, 600m, Aythya nyroca. 1000m, Marmaronetta angustirostris.

**2004, Nov. 20** ***Perf. 13¼***
**1354-1357** A584 Set of 4 4.00 2.00

Universal Declaration of Human Rights — A585

**2004, Dec. 10** ***Perf. 13x12¾***
**1358** A585 350m multi .60 .30

Famous People
A586

Designs: 250m, Ibn Chabbat (1221-85), writer. 500m, Ibn Charaf (1000-67), writer. No. 1361, 600m, Princess Elyssa. No. 1362, 600m, Hatem El Mekki (1918-2003), stamp designer, and #580, 619. No. 1363, 600m, Dr. Mongi Ben Hmida (1928-2002), neurologist.

**2004, Dec. 18** ***Perf. 12¾x13***
**1359-1363** A586 Set of 5 4.25 2.10

World Handball Championships — A587

**2005, Jan. 23** ***Perf. 13***
**1364** A587 600m multi 1.00 .50

Native Costumes — A588

Designs: 250m, Takhlila, Hammam Sousse. No. 1366, 390m, Tarf-Ras ceremonial costume, Kerkennah. No. 1367, 390m, Karmassoud jebba. 600m, Traditional bridal costume, Matmata.

**2005, Mar. 16** ***Perf. 13x12¾***
**1365-1368** A588 Set of 4 2.60 1.25

World Summit on the Information Society, Tunis
A589

**2005, Apr. 7** **Litho.** ***Perf. 13***
**1369** A589 600m multi 1.00 .50

Sculptures of the Punic and Roman Eras — A590

Designs: No. 1370, 250m, Victory, 2nd cent. No. 1371, 250m, Aesculapius, 2nd-3rd cent. 600m, Pottery mask of a woman's face, 4th-5th cent. B.C. 1000m, Baal Ammon, 1st cent.

**2005, May 18** ***Perf. 13¼***
**1370-1373** A590 Set of 4 3.25 1.60

World No Tobacco Day — A591

**2005, May 31** ***Perf. 13¼x13***
**1374** A591 250m multi .40 .20

Rotary International, Cent. — A592

**2005, June 22** ***Perf. 13x12¾***
**1375** A592 600m multi .90 .45

Intl. Year of Sport and Physical Education — A593

**2005, July 1**
**1376** A593 600m multi .90 .45

World Scout Conference
A594

**2005, Sept. 5**
**1377** A594 600m multi .95 .45

Intl. Year of Physics A595

**2005, Oct. 15** **Litho.** ***Perf. 13***
**1378** A595 2d multi 3.00 1.50

Appointment of Pres. Zine El Abidine Ben Ali, 18th Anniv. A596

**2005, Nov. 8**
**1379** A596 250m multi .40 .20

Universal Declaration of the Rights of Man, 57th Anniv. A598

**2005, Dec. 10** **Litho.** ***Perf. 13***
**1381** A598 350m multi .55 .25

Medicinal Plants — A599

Designs: 250m, Foeniculum. No. 1383, 600m, Mentha aquatica. No. 1384, 600m, Lavandula angustifloia. 1000m, Origanum majorana.

**2005, Dec. 22**

| | | | |
|---|---|---|---|
| **1382-1385** | A599 Set of 4 | 3.75 | 1.90 |
| **1386** | Booklet pane, 2 each #1383-1384, 1386a, 1386b | 7.25 | — |
| ***a.*** | A599 600m Like #1382 | .90 | .45 |
| ***b.*** | A599 600m Like #1385 | .90 | .45 |
| | Complete booklet, #1386 | 7.25 | |

Ibn Khaldun (1332-1406), Philosopher A600

**2006, Mar. 15** **Litho.** ***Perf. 13x12¾***
**1387** A600 390m multi .60 .30

A601

Independence, 50th Anniv. — A602

Designs: No. 1390, Stylized map and flag, doctor examining child. No. 1391, Bridge and ship. No. 1392, Stylized woman holding torch. No. 1393, Woman and book. No. 1394, Computer, man, woman, "@," and stylized dove.

**2006, Mar. 18** ***Perf. 13x12¾, 12¾x13***

| | | | |
|---|---|---|---|
| **1388** | A601 250m shown | .40 | .20 |
| **1389** | A602 250m shown | .40 | .20 |
| **1390** | A601 250m multi | .40 | .20 |
| **1391** | A601 250m multi | .40 | .20 |
| **1392** | A601 390m multi | .60 | .30 |
| **1393** | A601 390m multi | .60 | .30 |
| **1394** | A601 390m multi | .60 | .30 |
| ***a.*** | Souvenir sheet, #1388-1394, + 2 labels | 3.75 | 3.75 |
| | *Nos. 1388-1394 (7)* | 3.40 | 1.70 |

No. 1394a sold for 2.50d.

Punic and Roman Era Jewelry A604

Designs: No. 1396, 250m, Gold and garnet vestment clasps. No. 1397, 250m, Gold-plated bronze earrings. No. 1398, 600m, Ring depicting god Baal Hammon. No. 1399, 600m, Gold and amethyst pendants.

**2006, May 18** **Litho.** ***Perf. 13¼***
**1396-1399** A604 Set of 4 2.60 1.40

Special Handicapped Employment Program — A605

**2006, May 29** ***Perf. 13***
**1400** A605 2.35d multi 3.75 1.90

National Cleanliness and Environmental Protection Program — A606

**2006, June 11**
**1401** A606 250m multi .40 .20

2006 World Cup Soccer Championships, Germany — A607

Map, flags of Germany and Tunisia and: 250m, Feet of soccer players. 600m, Soccer player.

**2006, June 14**
**1402-1403** A607 Set of 2 1.40 .70

Tunisian Army, 50th Anniv. A608

**2006, June 24**
**1404** A608 250m multi .40 .20

Diplomatic Relations Between Tunisia and Japan, 50th Anniv. A609

**2006, July 7**
**1405** A609 700m multi 1.10 .55

Vacation Safety Program — A610

**2006, July 31**
**1406** A610 250m multi .40 .20

Personal Status Code, 50th Anniv. A611

**2006, Aug. 8**
**1407** A611 2.35d multi 3.75 1.90

Appointment of Pres. Zine El Abidine Ben Ali, 19th Anniv. A612

**2006, Nov. 7**
**1408** A612 250m multi .40 .20

Universal Declaration of Human Rights — A613

**2006, Dec. 10**
**1409** A613 700m multi 1.10 .55

## SEMI-POSTAL STAMPS

No. 36 Overprinted in Red

**1915, Feb.** **Unwmk.** ***Perf. 14x13½***
**B1** A5 15c vio, *pnksh* 1.00 1.00

No. 32 Overprinted in Red

**1916, Feb. 15**
**B2** A4 5c grn, *grnsh* 1.25 1.25

Types of Regular Issue of 1906 in New Colors and Surcharged

**1916, Aug.**

| | | | |
|---|---|---|---|
| **B3** | A5 10c on 15c brn vio, *bl* | 1.00 | 1.00 |
| **B4** | A5 10c on 20c brn, *org* | 1.00 | 1.00 |
| **B5** | A5 10c on 25c bl, *grn* | 3.25 | 3.25 |
| **B6** | A6 10c on 35c ol grn & vio | 6.50 | 6.50 |
| **B7** | A6 10c on 40c bis & blk | 3.00 | 3.00 |
| **B8** | A6 10c on 75c vio brn & grn | 8.50 | 8.50 |
| **B9** | A7 10c on 1fr red & grn | 3.50 | 3.50 |
| **B10** | A7 10c on 2fr bis & bl | 75.00 | 75.00 |
| **B11** | A7 10c on 5fr vio & red | 100.00 | 100.00 |
| | *Nos. B3-B11 (9)* | 201.75 | 201.75 |

Nos. B3 to B11 were sold at their face value but had a postal value of 10c only. The excess was applied to the relief of prisoners of war in Germany.

Types of Regular Issue of 1906 in New Colors and Surcharged in Carmine

**1918**

| | | | |
|---|---|---|---|
| **B12** | A5 15c on 20c blk, *grn* | 1.90 | 1.90 |
| **B13** | A5 15c on 25c dk bl, *buff* | 1.90 | 1.90 |

**B14** A6 15c on 35c gray grn & red 1.90 1.90
**B15** A6 15c on 40c brn & lt bl 4.25 4.25
**B16** A6 15c on 75c red brn & blk 7.50 7.50
**B17** A7 15c on 1fr red & vio 22.50 22.50
**B18** A7 15c on 2fr bis brn & red 70.00 70.00
**B19** A7 15c on 5fr vio & blk 125.00 125.00
*Nos. B12-B19 (8)* 234.95 234.95

The different parts of the surcharge are more widely spaced on the stamps of types A6 and A7. These stamps were sold at their face value but had a postal value of 15c only. The excess was intended for the relief of prisoners of war in Germany.

Types of 1906-22 Surcharged

**1923**

**B20** A4 0c on 1c blue .75 .75
**B21** A4 0c on 2c ol brn .75 .75
**B22** A4 1c on 3c green .75 .75
**B23** A4 2c on 5c red vio .75 .75
**B24** A9 3c on 10c vio, *bluish* .75 .75
**B25** A5 5c on 15c ol grn .75 .75
**B26** A5 5c on 20c bl, *pink* 1.50 1.50
**B27** A5 5c on 25c vio, *bluish* 1.50 1.50
**B28** A9 5c on 30c orange 1.60 1.60
**B29** A6 5c on 35c bl & vio 2.25 2.25
**B30** A6 5c on 40c bl & brn 2.25 2.25
**B31** A9 10c on 50c blk, *bluish* 3.00 3.00
**B32** A6 10c on 60c ol brn & bl 3.00 3.00
**B33** A6 10c on 75c vio & lt grn 5.00 5.00
**B34** A7 25c on 1fr mar & vio 5.00 5.00
**B35** A7 25c on 2fr bl & rose 16.00 16.00
**B36** A7 25c on 5fr grn & ol brn 57.50 57.50
*Nos. B20-B36 (17)* 103.10 103.10

These stamps were sold at their original values but had postal franking values only to the amounts surcharged on them. The difference was intended to be used for the benefit of wounded soldiers.

This issue was entirely speculative. Before the announced date of sale most of the stamps were taken by postal employees and practically none of them were offered to the public.

Mail Delivery — SP1

Type of Parcel Post Stamps, 1906, with Surcharge in Black

**1925, June 7** *Perf. 13½x14*

**B37** SP1 1c on 5c brn & red, *pink* .55 .55
*a.* Surcharge omitted 110.00 *110.00*
**B38** SP1 2c on 10c brn & bl, *yel* .55 .55
**B39** SP1 3c on 20c red vio & rose, *lav* 1.00 1.00
**B40** SP1 5c on 25c sl grn & rose, *bluish* 1.00 1.00
**B41** SP1 5c on 40c rose & grn, *yel* 1.00 1.00
**B42** SP1 10c on 50c vio & bl, *lav* 2.00 2.00
**B43** SP1 10c on 75c grn & ol, *grnsh* 1.50 1.50
**B44** SP1 25c on 1fr bl & grn, *bluish* 1.50 1.50
**B45** SP1 25c on 2fr rose & vio, *pnksh* 7.50 7.50
**B46** SP1 25c on 5fr red & brn, *lem* 35.00 35.00
*Nos. B37-B46 (10)* 51.60 51.60

These stamps were sold at their original values but paid postage only to the amount of the surcharged values. The difference was given to Child Welfare societies.

Tunis-Chad Motor Caravan SP2

**1928, Feb.** **Engr.** *Perf. 13½*

**B47** SP2 40c + 40c org brn 1.00 1.00
**B48** SP2 50c + 50c dp vio 1.40 1.40
**B49** SP2 75c + 75c dk bl 1.40 1.40
**B50** SP2 1fr + 1fr carmine 1.40 1.40
**B51** SP2 1.50fr + 1.50fr brt bl 1.40 1.40
**B52** SP2 2fr + 2fr dk grn 1.50 1.50
**B53** SP2 5fr + 5fr red brn 1.90 1.90
*Nos. B47-B53 (7)* 10.00 10.00

The surtax on these stamps was for the benefit of Child Welfare societies.

Nos. 122-135, 137-142 Surcharged in Black

a

b

**1938** *Perf. 11, 12½, 12½x13*

**B54** A14(a) 1c + 1c 1.50 1.50
**B55** A14(a) 2c + 2c 1.50 1.50
**B56** A14(a) 3c + 3c 1.50 1.50
**B57** A14(a) 5c + 5c 1.50 1.50
**B58** A14(a) 10c + 10c 1.50 1.50
**B59** A15(a) 15c + 15c 1.50 1.50
**B60** A15(a) 20c + 20c 1.50 1.50
**B61** A15(a) 25c + 25c 1.50 1.50
**B62** A15(a) 30c + 30c 1.50 1.50
**B63** A15(a) 40c + 40c 1.50 1.50
**B64** A16(a) 50c + 50c 1.50 1.50
**B65** A16(a) 75c + 75c 1.50 1.50
**B66** A16(a) 90c + 90c 1.50 1.50
**B67** A16(a) 1fr + 1fr 1.50 1.50
**B68** A17(b) 1.50fr + 1fr 1.50 1.50
**B69** A17(b) 2fr + 1.50fr 3.00 3.00
**B70** A17(b) 3fr + 2fr 3.75 3.75
**B71** A17(b) 5fr + 3fr 18.00 18.00
*a.* Perf. 12½ 92.50 92.50
**B72** A17(b) 10fr + 5fr 35.00 35.00
**B73** A17(b) 20fr + 10fr 60.00 60.00
*Nos. B54-B73 (20)* 142.25 142.25

50th anniversary of the post office.

Nos. 86, 100-101, 105 Surcharged in Black, Blue or Red

**1941** *Perf. 14x13½*

**B74** A11 1fr on 45c (Bk) .55 .55
**B75** A13 1.30fr on 1.25fr (Bl) .55 .55
**B76** A13 1.50fr on 1.40fr (Bk) .55 .55
**B77** A13 2fr on 2.25fr (R) .60 .60
*Nos. B74-B77 (4)* 2.25 2.25

The surcharge measures 11x14mm on #B74.

**Catalogue values for unused stamps in this section, from this point to the end of the section, are for Never Hinged items.**

British, French and American Soldiers SP3

**1943** **Litho.** *Perf. 12*

**B78** SP3 1.50fr + 8.50fr crimson .40 .20

Liberation of Tunisia.

Children — SP3a

**1944** **Engr.** *Perf. 13½*

**B78A** SP3a 1.20fr + 1.30fr brown .60
**B78B** SP3a 1.50fr + 2fr black brown .60
**B78C** SP3a 2fr + 3fr dark green .60
**B78D** SP3a 3fr + 4fr red orange .60
*Nos. B78A-B78D (4)* 2.40

National welfare fund.

Nos. B78A-B78D were issued by the Vichy government in France, but were not issued in Tunisia.

Native Scene — SP4

Surcharged in Black: "+ 48frcs / pour nos / Combattants"

**1944** *Perf. 11½*

**B79** SP4 2fr + 48fr red .90 .90

The surtax was for soldiers.

Sidi Mahrez Mosque — SP5

Ramparts of Sfax — SP6

Fort Saint — SP7

Sidi-bou-Said — SP8

**1945** **Unwmk.** **Litho.** *Perf. 11½*

**B80** SP5 1.50fr + 8.50fr choc & red .85 .85
**B81** SP6 3fr + 12fr dk bl grn & red .85 .85
**B82** SP7 4fr + 21fr brn org & red .90 .90
**B83** SP8 10fr + 40fr red & blk .90 .90
*Nos. B80-B83 (4)* 3.50 3.50

The surtax was for soldiers.

France No. B193 Overprinted in Black

c **TUNISIE**

**1945** *Perf. 14x13½*

**B84** SP147 2fr + 1fr red org .40 .40

The surtax was for the aid of tuberculosis victims.

Same Overprint on Type of France, 1945

**1945** **Engr.** *Perf. 13*

**B85** SP150 2fr + 3fr dk grn .55 .40

Stamp Day.

Same Overprint on France No. B192

**1945**

**B86** SP146 4fr + 6fr dk vio brn .40 .40

The surtax was for war victims of the P.T.T.

Types of 1926 Surcharged in Carmine

**1945** **Typo.** *Perf. 14x13½*

**B87** A10 4fr + 6fr on 10c ultra .40 .40
**B88** A12 10fr + 30fr on 80c dk grn .40 .40

The design of type A12 is redrawn, omitting "RF." The surtax was for war veterans.

Tunisian Soldier — SP9

**1946** **Unwmk.** **Engr.** *Perf. 13*

**B89** SP9 20fr + 30fr grn, red & blk 1.25 1.25

The surtax aided Tunisian soldiers in Indo-China.

Type of France Overprinted Type "c" in Carmine

**1946**

**B90** SP160 3fr + 2fr dk bl .90 .90

Stamp Day.

Stamps and Types of 1926-46 Surcharged in Carmine and Black

**1946** *Perf. 14x13½*

**B91** A12 80c + 50c emerald .90 .90
**B92** A12 1.50fr + 1.50fr rose lil .90 .90
**B93** A12 2fr + 2fr Prus grn .90 .90
**B94** A13 2.40fr + 2fr sal pink .90 .90
**B95** A13 4fr + 4fr ultra .90 .90
*Nos. B91-B95 (5)* 4.50 4.50

The two parts of the surcharge are more widely spaced on stamps of type A13.

Type of France Overprinted Type "c" in Carmine

**1947** *Perf. 13*

**B96** SP172 4.50fr + 5.50fr sepia .90 .90

**On Type of France Surcharged in Carmine with New Value and Bars**

**B97** SP158 10fr + 15fr on 2fr + 3fr brt ultra 1.00 1.00

Type of 1926 Surcharged in Carmine

**1947 Typo. *Perf. 14x13½***
**B98** A13 10fr + 40fr black 1.00 1.00

Feeding Young Bird — SP10

**1947 Engr. *Perf. 13***
**B99** SP10 4.50fr + 5.50fr dk bl grn 1.25 1.25
**B100** SP10 6fr + 9fr brt ultra 1.25 1.25
**B101** SP10 8fr + 17fr dp car 1.25 1.25
**B102** SP10 10fr + 40fr dk pur 1.25 1.25
*Nos. B99-B102 (4)* 5.00 5.00

The surtax was for child welfare.

Type of Regular Issue of 1948 Surcharged in Blue

**1948**
**B103** A21 4fr + 10fr ol grn & org .85 .85

The surtax was for anti-tuberculosis work.

Arch of Triumph, Sbeitla SP11

**1948**
**B104** SP11 10fr + 40fr ol grn & olive 1.25 1.25
**B105** SP11 18fr + 42fr dk bl & indigo 1.25 1.25

Surtax for charitable works of the army.

Arago Type of France Overprinted in Carmine

TUNISIE

**1948**
**B106** SP176 6fr + 4fr brt car 1.00 1.00

Stamp Day, Mar. 6-7.

Sleeping Child SP12

**1949, June 1**
**B107** SP12 25fr + 50fr dk grn 1.90 1.90

The surtax was for child welfare.

Neptune Type of 1947 Surcharged in Black with Lorraine Cross and "FFL+15F"

**1949, Dec. 8**
**B108** A20 10fr + 15fr dp ultra & car 1.25 1.25

The surtax was for the Tunisian section of the Association of Free French.

Type of France Overprinted in Carmine

e

**1949, Mar. 26**
**B109** SP180 15fr + 5fr indigo 1.25 1.25

Stamp Days, Mar. 26-27.

Type of France, 1950, Ovptd. Like No. B106 in Ultramarine

**1950, Mar. 11 Unwmk. *Perf. 13***
**B110** SP183 12fr + 3fr dk grn 1.75 1.75

Stamp Days, Mar. 11-12.

Tunisian and French Woman Shaking Hands SP13

**1950, June 5**
**B111** SP13 15fr + 35fr red 1.40 1.40
**B112** SP13 25fr + 45fr dp ultra 1.40 1.40

The surtax was for Franco-Tunisian Mutual Assistance.

Arab Soldier — SP14

**1950, Aug. 21 Engr.**
**B113** SP14 25fr + 25fr dp bl 2.00 2.00

The surtax was for old soldiers.

Type of France Overprinted Type "c" in Black

**1951, Mar. 10**
**B114** SP186 12fr + 3fr brnsh gray 1.50 1.40

Stamp Days, Mar. 10-11.

Mother Carrying Child SP15

**1951, June 19 Engr. *Perf. 13***
**B115** SP15 30fr + 15fr dp ultra 2.40 2.40

The surtax was for child welfare.

National Cemetery of Gammarth SP16

**1952, June 15**
**B116** SP16 30fr + 10fr blue 1.90 1.90

Surtax aided orphans of the military services.

**Type of France Overprinted Type "e" in Lilac**

**1952, Mar. 8 Unwmk.**
**B117** SP190 12fr + 3fr purple 1.40 1.40

Stamp Day, Mar. 8.

Stucco Work, Bardo SP17

Boy Campers SP18

**1952, May 5 Engr. *Perf. 13***
**B118** SP17 15fr + 1fr ultra & indigo 1.00 1.00

Surtax for charitable works of the army.

**1952, June 15**
**B119** SP18 30fr + 10fr dk grn 2.00 2.00

The surtax was for the Educational League vacation camps.

**Type of France Surcharged Type "c" and Surtax**

**1952, Oct. 15**
**B120** A226 15fr + 5fr bl grn 2.00 2.00

Creation of the French Military Medal, cent.

Type of France Overprinted Type "c"

**1953, Mar. 14**
**B121** SP193 12fr + 3fr vermilion 1.60 1.60

"Day of the Stamp."

**Type of France Overprinted Type "c"**

**1954, Mar. 20**
**B122** SP196 12fr + 3fr indigo 1.60 1.60

Stamp Day.

Balloon Post, 1870 SP19

**1955, Mar. 19**
**B123** SP19 12fr + 3fr red brown 1.60 1.60

Stamp Days, Mar. 19-20.

**Independent Kingdom**

Franz von Taxis SP20

**1956, Mar. 17**
**B124** SP20 12fr + 3fr dark green 1.25 1.25

Stamp Days, Mar. 17-18

**Republic**

No. 246 Surcharged in Red

**1957, Aug. 8 Engr.**
**B125** A29 20fr + 10fr dp ultra .75 .75

15th anniversary of the army.

**Florist Type of 1955 with Added Inscriptions, Surcharged in Red**

**1957, Oct. 19 *Perf. 13***
**B126** A34 20fr + 10fr dk vio .60 .60

No. B126 is inscribed "5e. Foire Internationale" at bottom and lines of Arabic at either side.

Mailman Delivering Mail — SP21

Ornamental Cock — SP22

**1959, May 1 Engr. *Perf. 13***
**B127** SP21 20fr + 5fr dk brn & org brn .50 .50

Day of the Stamp. The surtax was for the Post Office Mutual Fund.

**1959, Oct. 24 Litho. *Perf. 13***
**B128** SP22 10m + 5m yel, lt bl & red .35 .35

Surtax for the Red Crescent Society.

Mailman on Camel Phoning — SP23

Dancer of Kerkennah Holding Stamp — SP24

**1960, Apr. 16 Engr. *Perf. 13***
**B129** SP23 60m + 5m ol, org & ultra .75 .75

Day of the Stamp.

**1961, May 6 Unwmk. *Perf. 13***

Stamp Day: 15m+5m, Mail truck, horiz. 20m+6m, Hand holding magnifying glass and stamps. 50m+5m, Running boy, symbols of mail.

**B130** SP24 12m + 4m multi .60 .60
**B131** SP24 15m + 5m multi .75 .75
**B132** SP24 20m + 6m multi .85 .85
**B133** SP24 50m + 5m multi .95 .95
*Nos. B130-B133 (4)* 3.15 3.15

Nos. B130-B133 Overprinted

**1963, Oct. 24**

**B134** SP24 12m + 4m cl, vio & ol .35 .35
**B135** SP24 15m + 5m ol, cl & vio bl .40 .40
**B136** SP24 20m + 6m multi .50 .50
**B137** SP24 50m + 5m multi .85 .85
*Nos. B134-B137 (4)* 2.10 2.10

United Nations Day.

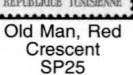

Old Man, Red Crescent SP25 — Nurse Holding Bottle of Blood SP26

Tunisian Red Crescent: 75m+10m, Mother, child and Red Crescent.

**1972, May 8 Engr. *Perf. 13***

**B138** SP25 10m + 10m pur & dk red .40 .35
**B139** SP25 75m + 10m bis brn & dl red .60 .40

**1973, May 10 Engr. *Perf. 13***

Design: 60m+10m, Red Crescent and blood donors' arms, horiz.

**B140** SP26 25m + 10m multi .50 .40
**B141** SP26 60m + 10m gray & car .85 .40

Red Crescent appeal for blood donors.

Blood Donors — SP27

Man Holding Scales with Balanced Diet — SP28

Red Crescent Society: 75m+10m, Blood transfusion, symbolic design.

**1974, May 8 Photo. *Perf. 14x13***

**B142** SP27 25m + 10m multi .40 .40
**B143** SP27 75m + 10m multi .50 .50

**1975, May 8 Photo. *Perf. 11½***

**B144** SP28 50m + 10m multi .50 .40

Tunisian Red Crescent fighting malnutrition.

Blood Donation, Woman and Man — SP29

**1976, May 8 Photo. *Perf. 11½***

**B145** SP29 40m + 10m multi .50 .35

Tunisian Red Crescent Society.

Litter Bearers and Red Crescent SP30

**1977, May 8 Photo. *Perf. 13½x14***

**B146** SP30 50m + 10m multi .50 .40

Tunisian Red Crescent Society.

Blood Donors SP31 — Hand and Red Crescent SP32

**1978, May 8 Photo. *Perf. 13x14***

**B147** SP31 50m + 10m multi .50 .40

Blood drive of Tunisian Red Crescent Society.

**1979, May 8 Photo. *Perf. 13½***

**B148** SP32 50m + 10m multi .50 .40

Tunisian Red Crescent Society.

Red Crescent Society SP33 — SP34

**1980, May 8 Photo. *Perf. 13½***

**B149** SP33 50m + 10m multi .50 .40

**1981, May 8 *Perf. 14½x13½***

**B150** SP34 50m + 10m multi .40 .35

Dome of the Rock, Jerusalem SP35

**1981, Nov. 29 Photo. *Perf. 13½***

**B151** SP35 50m + 5m multi .55 .35
**B152** SP35 150m + 5m multi 1.00 .60
**B153** SP35 200m + 5m multi 1.60 .70
*Nos. B151-B153 (3)* 3.15 1.65

Intl. Palestinian Solidarity Day.

Red Crescent Society SP36

**1982, May 8 Photo. *Perf. 13½***

**B154** SP36 80m + 10m multi .50 .40

Red Crescent Society — SP37

**1983, May 8 Litho. *Perf. 14x13½***

**B155** SP37 80m + 10m multi .60 .35

Sabra and Chatilla Massacre — SP38

**1983, Sept. 20 Photo. *Perf. 13***

**B156** SP38 80m + 5m multi .50 .50

Red Crescent Society — SP39

**1984, May 8 Litho. *Perf. 12½***

**B157** SP39 80m + 10m First aid .50 .40

Red Crescent Society SP40 — SP41

**1985, May 8 Litho. *Perf. 14***

**B158** SP40 100m + 10m multi .40 .25

**1986, May 9 Litho. *Perf. 14½x13½***

**B159** SP41 120m + 10m Map of Tunisia .50 .40

Red Crescent Society SP42

**1987, May 8 Litho. *Perf. 13x13½***

**B160** SP42 150m + 10m multi .60 .45

Intl. Red Cross and Red Crescent Organizations, 125th Annivs. — SP43

**1988, May 9 Photo. *Perf. 14***

**B161** SP43 150m + 10m multi .60 .40

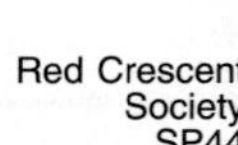

Red Crescent Society SP44

**1989, May 8 Photo. *Perf. 11½***
**Granite Paper**

**B162** SP44 150m +10m multi .45 .30

Red Crescent Society SP45 — SP46

**1990, May 8 Litho. *Perf. 14x13½***

**B163** SP45 150m +10m multi .45 .25

**1991, May 8 Litho. *Perf. 13½***

**B164** SP46 180m +10m multi .60 .45

Red Crescent Society — SP47

**1993, Aug. 17 Litho. *Perf. 14x13½***

**B165** SP47 120m +30m multi .60 .30

---

## AIR POST STAMPS

No. 43 Surcharged in Red

**1919, Apr. Unwmk. *Perf. 14x13½***

**C1** A6 30c on 35c ol grn & brn 1.25 1.25
- *a.* Inverted surcharge 130.00 130.00
- *b.* Double surcharge 130.00 130.00
- *c.* Double inverted surcharge 150.00 150.00
- *d.* Double surcharge, one inverted 130.00 130.00

Type A6, Overprinted in Rose

**1920, Apr.**

**C2** A6 30c ol grn, bl & rose .40 .40

Nos. 53 and 55 Overprinted in Red

**1927, Mar. 24**

**C3** A7 1fr indigo & ultra .90 .65
**C4** A7 2fr grn & red, *pink* 3.00 1.90

Nos. 51 and 57 Surcharged in Black or Red

**C5** A6 1.75fr on 75c (Bk) 1.00 .55
**C6** A7 1.75fr on 5fr (R) 3.00 2.00

Type A13 Ovptd. like #C3-C4 in Blue

**1928, Feb.**

**C7** A13 1.30fr org & lt vio 3.50 1.40
**C8** A13 1.80fr gray grn & red 4.25 .85
**C9** A13 2.55fr lil & ol brn 1.90 .95
*Nos. C7-C9 (3)* 9.65 3.20

Type A13 Surcharged like #C5-C6 in Blue

**1930, Aug.**

**C10** A13 1.50fr on 1.30fr org & lt vio 2.40 .75
**C11** A13 1.50fr on 1.80fr gray grn & red 4.25 .60
**C12** A13 1.50fr on 2.55fr lil & ol brn 7.75 1.75
*Nos. C10-C12 (3)* 14.40 3.10

**Catalogue values for unused stamps in this section, from this point to the end of the section, are for Never Hinged items.**

UPU Type of Regular Issue

**1949, Oct. 28 Engr. *Perf. 13***

**C13** A23 25fr dk bl, *bluish* 1.75 1.75

UPU, 75th anniv. Exists imperf.; value $35.

Bird from Antique Mosaic, Museum of Sousse AP2

(Arabic on one line) — AP3

**1949 Unwmk.**

**C14** AP2 200fr dk bl & indigo 5.50 1.90

**1950-51**

**C15** AP3 100fr bl grn & brn 3.00 1.40
**C16** AP3 200fr dk bl & ind ('51) 6.00 3.00

Monastir AP4

Coast at Korbous AP5

Design: 1000fr, Air view of Tozeur mosque.

**1953-54**

**C17** AP4 100fr dk bl, ind & dk grn ('54) 3.50 .75
**C18** AP4 200fr cl, blk brn & red brn ('54) 4.75 1.75
**C19** AP5 500fr dk brn & ultra 25.00 12.50
**C20** AP5 1000fr dk green 42.50 25.00
*Nos. C17-C20 (4)* 75.75 40.00

Imperforates exist.

**Independent Kingdom**

Types of 1953-54 Redrawn with "RF" Omitted

**1956, Mar. 1**

**C21** AP4 100fr slate bl, indigo & dk grn 1.75 .75
**C22** AP4 200fr multi 3.25 1.50
**C23** AP5 500fr dk brn & ultra 6.75 6.00
**C24** AP5 1000fr dk green 13.50 11.00
*Nos. C21-C24 (4)* 25.25 19.25

**Republic**

Desert Swallows — AP6

Birds: #C26, Butcherbird. #C27, Cream-colored courser. 100m, European chaffinch. 150m, Pink flamingoes. 200m, Barbary partridges. 300m, European roller. 500m, Bustard.

**1965-66 Photo. *Perf. 12½***

**Size: 23x31mm**

**C25** AP6 25m multi .85 .35
**C26** AP6 55m blk & lt bl 1.25 .85
**C27** AP6 55m multi ('66) 1.25 .65

**Size: 22½x33mm**

***Perf. 11½***

**C28** AP6 100m multi 1.75 1.00
**C29** AP6 150m multi ('66) 5.75 2.50
**C30** AP6 200m multi ('66) 6.25 2.75
**C31** AP6 300m multi ('66) 9.00 5.50
**C32** AP6 500m multi 13.00 6.75
*Nos. C25-C32 (8)* 39.10 20.35

See No. 474.

**AIR POST SEMI-POSTAL STAMP**

**Catalogue value for the unused stamp in this section is for a Never Hinged item.**

Window, Great Mosque of Kairouan — SPAP1

**Unwmk.**

**1952, May 5 Engr. *Perf. 13***

**CB1** SPAP1 50fr + 10fr blk & gray grn 3.25 3.25

Surtax for charitable works of the army.

**POSTAGE DUE STAMPS**

Regular postage stamps perforated with holes in the form of a "T," the holes varying in size and number, were used as postage due stamps from 1888 to 1901.

D1

D2

***Perf. 14x13½***

**1901-03 Unwmk. Typo.**

**J1** D1 1c black .40 .40
**J2** D1 2c orange .85 .55
**J3** D1 5c blue .60 .40
**J4** D1 10c brown .60 .55
**J5** D1 20c blue green 3.50 .75
**J6** D1 30c carmine 3.00 .75
**J7** D1 50c brown violet 1.75 .85
**J8** D1 1fr olive green 1.25 .85
**J9** D1 2fr carmine, *grn* 3.50 1.50
**J10** D1 5fr blk, *yellow* 45.00 35.00
*Nos. J1-J10 (10)* 60.45 41.60

No. J10 Surcharged in Blue

**1914, Nov.**

**J11** D1 2fr on 5fr blk, *yellow* 1.00 1.00

In Jan. 1917 regular 5c postage stamps were overprinted "T" in an inverted triangle and used as postage due stamps.

**1922-49**

**J12** D2 1c black .25 .25
**J13** D2 2c black, *yellow* .25 .25
**J14** D2 5c violet brown .55 .25
**J15** D2 10c blue .40 .25
**J16** D2 10c yel green ('45) .20 .20
**J17** D2 20c orange, *yel* .40 .40
**J18** D2 30c brown ('23) .40 .25
**J19** D2 50c rose red .75 .40
**J20** D2 50c blue vio ('45) .20 .20
**J21** D2 60c violet ('28) .75 .40
**J22** D2 80c bister ('28) .60 .30
**J23** D2 90c orange red ('28) .85 .55
**J24** D2 1fr green .55 .25
**J25** D2 2fr olive grn, *straw* 1.00 .40
**J26** D2 2fr car rose ('45) .25 .25
**J27** D2 3fr vio, *pink* ('29) .40 .25
**J28** D2 4fr grnsh bl ('45) .40 .40
**J29** D2 5fr violet .60 .40
**J30** D2 10fr cerise ('49) .40 .40
**J31** D2 20fr olive gray ('49) 1.10 .90
*Nos. J12-J31 (20)* 10.30 6.95

Inscribed: "Timbre Taxe"

**1950 Unwmk. *Perf. 14x13½***

**J32** D2 30fr blue 1.40 1.25

**Catalogue values for unused stamps in this section, from this point to the end of the section, are for Never Hinged items.**

**Independent Kingdom**

Grain and Fruit — D3

**1957, Apr. 1 Engr. *Perf. 14x13***

**J33** D3 1fr bright green .25 .25
**J34** D3 2fr orange brown .25 .25
**J35** D3 3fr bluish green .50 .50
**J36** D3 4fr indigo .50 .50
**J37** D3 5fr lilac .50 .50
**J38** D3 10fr carmine .50 .50
**J39** D3 20fr chocolate 1.60 1.60
**J40** D3 30fr blue 2.10 2.10
*Nos. J33-J40 (8)* 6.20 6.20

**Republic**

Inscribed "Republique Tunisienne"

**1960-77**

**J41** D3 1m emerald .20 .20
**J42** D3 2m red brown .20 .20
**J43** D3 3m bluish green .20 .20
**J44** D3 4m indigo .20 .20
**J45** D3 5m lilac .25 .25
**J46** D3 10m carmine rose .50 .50
**J47** D3 20m violet brown .75 .75
**J48** D3 30m blue .90 .90
**J49** D3 40m lake ('77) .25 .25
**J50** D3 100m blue green ('77) .50 .50
*Nos. J41-J50 (10)* 3.95 3.95

**PARCEL POST STAMPS**

Mail Delivery — PP1

Gathering Dates — PP2

**1906 Unwmk. Typo. *Perf. 13½x14***

**Q1** PP1 5c grn & vio brn .60 .40
**Q2** PP1 10c org & red .75 .40
**Q3** PP1 20c dk brn & org 1.10 .40
**Q4** PP1 25c blue & brn 1.90 .40
**Q5** PP1 40c gray & rose 2.40 .40
**Q6** PP1 50c vio brn & vio 1.90 .40
**Q7** PP1 75c bis brn & bl 3.00 .40
**Q8** PP1 1fr red brn & red 2.90 .25
**Q9** PP1 2fr carmine & bl 6.75 .60
**Q10** PP1 5fr vio & vio brn 20.00 1.25
*Nos. Q1-Q10 (10)* 41.30 4.90

**1926**

**Q11** PP2 5c pale brn & dk bl .40 .40
**Q12** PP2 10c rose & vio .40 .40
**Q13** PP2 20c yel grn & blk .40 .40
**Q14** PP2 25c org brn & blk .40 .40
**Q15** PP2 40c dp rose & dp grn 1.50 .65
**Q16** PP2 50c lt vio & blk 1.50 .65
**Q17** PP2 60c ol & brn red 1.50 .65
**Q18** PP2 75c gray vio & bl grn 1.50 .65
**Q19** PP2 80c ver & ol brn 1.50 .65
**Q20** PP2 1fr Prus bl & dp rose 1.50 .65
**Q21** PP2 2fr vio & mag 3.75 .65
**Q22** PP2 4fr red & blk 4.50 .65
**Q23** PP2 5fr red brn & dp vio 6.00 .65
**Q24** PP2 10fr dl red & grn, *grnsh* 12.50 .65
**Q25** PP2 20fr yel grn & dp vio, *lav* 24.00 1.25
*Nos. Q11-Q25 (15)* 61.35 9.35

Parcel post stamps were discontinued July 1, 1940.

# TURKEY

'tər-kē

LOCATION — Southeastern Europe and Asia Minor, between the Mediterranean and Black Seas
GOVT. — Republic
AREA — 300,947 sq. mi.
POP. — 65,599,206 (1999 est.)
CAPITAL — Ankara

The Ottoman Empire ceased to exist in 1922, and the Republic of Turkey was inaugurated in 1923.

40 Paras = 1 Piaster
40 Paras = 1 Ghurush (1926)
40 Paras = 1 Kurush (1926)
100 Kurush = 1 Lira

**Catalogue values for unused stamps in this country are for Never Hinged items, beginning with Scott 817 in the regular postage section, Scott B69 in the semi-postal section, Scott C1 in the airpost section, Scott J97 in the postage due section, Scott O1 in the official section, Scott P175 in the newspaper section, and Scott RA139 in the postal tax section.**

**Watermark**

Wmk. 394 — "PTT," Crescent and Star

Turkish (Arabic) Numerals

"Tughra," Monogram of Sultan Abdul-Aziz
A1 A2

A3

A4

**1863 Unwmk. Litho. *Imperf.***
**Red Band: 20pa, 1pi, 2pi**
**Blue Band: 5pi**
**Thin Paper**

1 A1 20pa blk, *yellow* 75.00 20.00
*a.* Tête bêche pair 250.00 200.00
*b.* Without band 100.00
*c.* Green band
2 A2 1pi blk, *dl vio* 125.00 20.00
*a.* 1pi black, *gray* 125.00 20.00
*b.* Tête bêche pair 400.00 300.00
*c.* Without band 140.00
*d.* Design reversed *175.00*
*e.* 1pi blk, *yel* (error) 250.00 150.00
4 A3 2pi blk, *grnsh bl* 110.00 20.00
*a.* 2pi black, *ind* 110.00 20.00
*b.* Tête bêche pair 400.00 300.00
*c.* Without band 140.00
5 A4 5pi blk, *rose* 225.00 45.00
*a.* Tête bêche pair 500.00 400.00
*b.* Without band 250.00
*c.* Green band *275.00*
*d.* Red band *275.00*

**Thick, Surface Colored Paper**

6 A1 20pa blk, *yellow* 250.00 37.50
*a.* Tête bêche pair 450.00 450.00
*b.* Design reversed 325.00 325.00
*c.* Without band 225.00 225.00
*d.* Paper colored through 225.00 225.00
7 A2 1pi blk, *gray* 275.00 35.00
*a.* Tête bêche pair 900.00 900.00
*b.* Design reversed
*c.* Without band
*d.* Paper colored through 300.00 225.00
*Nos. 1-7 (6)* 1,060. 177.50

The 2pi and 5pi had two printings. In the common printing, the stamps are more widely spaced and alternate horizontal rows of 12 are inverted. In the first and rare printing, the stamps are more closely spaced and no rows are tête bêche.
See Nos. J1-J4.

Crescent and Star, Symbols of Turkish Caliphate — A5

Surcharged

The bottom characters of this and the following surcharges denote the denomination. The characters at top and sides translate, "Ottoman Empire Posts."

**1865 Typo. *Perf. 12½***

8 A5 10pa deep green 8.50 *35.00*
*c.* "1" instead of "10" in each corner *300.00 300.00*
9 A5 20pa yellow 4.00 3.00
*a.* Star without rays 4.00 *3.00*
10 A5 1pi lilac 12.50 4.00
*a.* Star without rays 17.50 3.00
11 A5 2pi blue 5.50 4.00
12 A5 5pi carmine 4.00 4.50
*d.* Inverted surcharge
13 A5 25pi red orange 325.00 *250.00*

**Imperf., Pairs**

*8b* A5 10pa 125.00 125.00
*9b* A5 20pa 125.00 125.00
*10b* A5 1pi *100.00 90.00*
*11a* A5 2pi *100.00 90.00*
*12b* A5 5pi *110.00 110.00*
*13a* A5 25pi *750.00 750.00*

See Nos. J6-J35. For overprints and surcharges see Nos. 14-52, 64-65, 446-461, 467-468, J71-J77, Eastern Rumelia 1.

Surcharged

**1867**

14 A5 10pa gray green 7.50
*a.* Imperf., pair 55.00
15 A5 20pa yellow 12.50
*a.* Imperf., pair 75.00
16 A5 1pi lilac 20.00
*a.* Imperf., pair 110.00
*b.* Imperf., with surcharge of 5pi 25.00
17 A5 2pi blue 4.50 *40.00*
*a.* Imperf.
18 A5 5pi rose 3.50 *40.00*
*a.* Imperf.
19 A5 25pi orange 3,500.
*Nos. 14-18 (5)* 48.00

Nos. 14, 15, 16 and 19 were never placed in use.

Surcharged

**1869 *Perf. 13½***

20 A5 10pa dull violet 100.00 7.00
*a.* Printed on both sides
*b.* Imperf., pair *90.00 80.00*
*c.* Inverted surcharge *90.00*
*d.* Double surcharge
*e.* 10pa yellow (error) *300.00*
21 A5 20pa pale green 400.00 3.00
*a.* Printed on both sides *450.00 275.00*
22 A5 1pi yellow 10.00 2.50
*c.* Inverted surcharge *100.00*
*d.* Double surcharge
*e.* Surcharged on both sides
*f.* Printed on both sides
23 A5 2pi orange red 200.00 6.50
*b.* Imperf., pair 125.00 125.00
*c.* Printed on both sides 125.00
*d.* Inverted surcharge 70.00 70.00
*e.* Surcharged on both sides 140.00
24 A5 5pi blue 2.50 *10.00*
25 A5 5pi gray 25.00 37.50
26 A5 25pi dull rose 37.50 125.00
*Nos. 20-26 (7)* 775.00 *191.50*

***Pin-perf., Perf. 5 to 11 and Compound***

**1870-71**

27 A5 10pa lilac *550.00 25.00*
28 A5 10pa brown *500.00 8.00*
29 A5 20pa gray green 75.00 *2.50*
*a.* Printed on both sides
30 A5 1pi yellow *550.00 2.50*
*a.* Inverted surcharge *500.00 80.00*
*b.* Without surcharge
31 A5 2pi red 5.00 5.00
*a.* Imperf. 20.00 20.00
*b.* Printed on both sides *40.00*
*c.* Surcharged on both sides
32 A5 5pi blue 2.50 *12.50*
*a.* 5pi greenish blue 2.75 *8.00*
33 A5 5pi slate 40.00 50.00
*a.* Printed on both sides
*b.* Surcharged on both sides *40.00*
34 A5 25pi dull rose 40.00 *75.00*
*Nos. 27-34 (8)* 1,762. *180.50*

**1873 *Perf. 12, 12½***

35 A5 10pa dark lilac 90.00 25.00
*a.* Inverted surcharge 90.00
36 A5 10pa olive brown 110.00 17.50
*a.* 10pa bister 110.00 11.00
37 A5 2pi vermilion 2.50 *3.50*
*a.* Surcharged on both sides 22.50 22.50
*Nos. 35-37 (3)* 202.50 46.00

Surcharged

**1874-75 *Perf. 13½***

38 A5 10pa red violet 35.00 7.50
*a.* Imperf., pair 70.00 50.00
39 A5 20pa yellow green 15.00 4.00
*b.* Inverted surcharge 30.00 13.00
*c.* Double surcharge
40 A5 1pi yellow 45.00 15.00
*a.* Imperf., pair 100.00 80.00

***Perf. 12, 12½***

41 A5 10pa red violet 25.00 10.00
*a.* Inverted surcharge 45.00 60.00
*Nos. 38-41 (4)* 120.00 36.50

Surcharged

**1876, Apr. *Perf. 13½***

42 A5 10pa red lilac 1.50 .50
*a.* Inverted surcharge 70.00
*b.* Imperf., pair 15.00 15.00
43 A5 20pa pale green 1.50 .50
*b.* Inverted surcharge 70.00
*c.* Imperf., pair 15.00 15.00
44 A5 1pi yellow 1.50 .50
*a.* Imperf., pair 27.50 27.50
46 A5 5pi gray blue *1,000.*
47 A5 25pi dull rose *1,000.*
*Nos. 42-44 (3)* 4.50

Nos. 46 and 47 were never placed in use.
See Nos. 64-65.

Surcharged

**1876, Jan.**

48 A5 ¼pi on 10pa violet 2.50 2.50
49 A5 ½pi on 20pa yel grn 6.25 2.50
50 A5 1¼pi on 50pa rose 1.50 2.50
*a.* Imperf., pair 60.00
51 A5 2pi on 2pi redsh brn 40.00 7.50
52 A5 5pi on 5pi gray blue *3.00 50.00*
*Nos. 48-52 (5)* 53.25 *65.00*

The surcharge on Nos. 48-52 restates in French the value originally expressed in Turkish characters.

A7

**1876, Sept. Typo. *Perf. 13½***

53 A7 10pa black & rose lil 2.00 *6.00*
54 A7 20pa red vio & grn 62.50 5.00
55 A7 50pa blue & yellow .75 *10.00*
56 A7 2pi black & redsh brn 1.25 *5.00*
57 A7 5pi red & blue 3.00 *10.00*
*b.* Cliché of 25pi in plate of 5pi 400.00 375.00
58 A7 25pi claret & rose 15.00 *75.00*
*a.* Imperf. 160.00
*Nos. 53-58 (6)* 84.50 *111.00*

Nos. 56-58 exist perf. 11½, but were not regularly issued.
See Nos. 59-63, 66-91, J36-J38. For overprints see Nos. 462-466, 469-476, J78-J79, P10-P14, Eastern Rumelia 2-40.

**1880-84 *Perf. 13½***

59 A7 5pa black & ol ('81) 2.50 6.50
*a.* Imperf. 30.00
60 A7 10pa black & grn ('84) 2.00 3.50
61 A7 20pa black & rose 55.00 1.00
62 A7 1pi blk & bl *(piastres)* 75.00 2.00
*a.* 1pi black & gray blue 75.00
*b.* Imperf. 40.00
63 A7 1pi blk & bl *(piastre)* ('81) 110.00 3.00
*Nos. 59-63 (5)* 244.50 16.00

A cliché of No. 63 was inserted in a plate of the Eastern Rumelia 1pi (No. 13). This was found in the remainder stock.
Nos. 60-61 and 63 exist perf. 11½, but were not regularly issued.

**1881-82**
**Surcharged like Apr., 1876 Issue**

64 A5 20pa gray 3.00 .50
*a.* Inverted surcharge 13.50
*b.* Imperf., pair 25.00
65 A5 2pi pale salmon 2.00 .50
*a.* Inverted surcharge 22.50

**1884-86 *Perf. 11½, 13½***

66 A7 5pa lil & pale lil ('86) 200.00 *150.00*
67 A7 10pa grn & pale grn 1.25 1.25
68 A7 20pa rose & pale rose 1.25 1.25
69 A7 1pi blue & lt blue 1.25 1.25

***Perf. 11½***

70 A7 2pi och & pale och 2.00 1.25
71 A7 5pi red brn & pale brn 20.00 9.00
*c.* 5pi och & pale och (error) 12.00 12.00

***Perf. 11½, 13½***

73 A7 25pi blk & pale gray ('86) 300.00 *425.00*
*Nos. 66-73 (7)* 525.75 *589.00*

***Imperf***

*66a* A7 5pa 60.00
*67a* A7 10pa 20.00
*68b* A7 20pa 20.00
*69b* A7 1pi 20.00
*73a* A7 25pi 150.00

**1886 *Perf. 13½***

74 A7 5pa black & pale gray 1.25 2.50
75 A7 2pi orange & lt bl 1.25 2.00
76 A7 5pi grn & pale grn 3.00 25.00
77 A7 25pi bis & pale bis 30.00 *150.00*
*Nos. 74-77 (4)* 35.50 *179.50*

***Imperf***

*74a* A7 5pa 20.00
*75b* A7 2pi 20.00
*76b* A7 5pi 20.00
*77a* A7 25pi 35.00

Stamps of 1884-86, bisected and surcharged as above, 10pa, 20pa, 1pi and 2pi or surcharged "2" in red are stated to have been made privately and without authority. With the aid of employees of the post office, copies were passed through the mails.

**1888** *Perf. 13½*

| | | | | |
|---|---|---|---|---|
| **83** | A7 | 5pa green & yellow | 2.50 | 5.00 |
| **84** | A7 | 2pi red lilac & bl | 1.50 | 1.50 |
| **85** | A7 | 5pi dk brown & gray | 5.00 | *20.00* |
| **86** | A7 | 25pi red & yellow | 30.00 | *150.00* |
| | | *Nos. 83-86 (4)* | 39.00 | *176.50* |

***Imperf***

| | | | |
|---|---|---|---|
| *83a* | A7 | 5pa | 20.00 |
| *84a* | A7 | 2pi | 20.00 |
| *85a* | A7 | 5pi | 20.00 |
| *86a* | A7 | 25pi | 25.00 |

Nos. 74-86 exist perf. 11½, but were not regularly issued.

**1890** *Perf. 11½, 13½*

| | | | | |
|---|---|---|---|---|
| **87** | A7 | 10pa green & gray | 5.00 | 1.00 |
| **88** | A7 | 20pa rose & gray | 1.25 | 1.00 |
| **89** | A7 | 1pi blue & gray | 75.00 | 1.00 |
| **90** | A7 | 2pi yellow & gray | 70.00 | 7.50 |
| **91** | A7 | 5pi buff & gray | 5.00 | 22.50 |
| | | *Nos. 87-91 (5)* | 156.25 | *33.00* |

***Imperf***

| | | | |
|---|---|---|---|
| *87a* | A7 | 10pa | 20.00 |
| *88a* | A7 | 20pa | 20.00 |
| *89a* | A7 | 1pi | 20.00 |
| *90b* | A7 | 2pi | 25.00 |
| *91a* | A7 | 5pi | 25.00 |

Arms and Tughra of "El Gazi" (The Conqueror) Sultan Abdul Hamid

A10 A11

A12

A13

A14

No. 100

**1892-98** **Typo.** *Perf. 13½*

| | | | | |
|---|---|---|---|---|
| **95** | A10 | 10pa gray green | 1.50 | .50 |
| **96** | A11 | 20pa violet brn ('98) | 1.25 | .50 |
| *a.* | | 20pa dark pink | 7.50 | .30 |
| *b.* | | 20pa pink | 10.00 | .30 |
| **97** | A12 | 1pi pale blue | 110.00 | .50 |
| **98** | A13 | 2pi brown org | 2.00 | .50 |
| *a.* | | Tête bêche pair | *30.00* | *30.00* |
| **99** | A14 | 5pi dull violet | 3.00 | *15.00* |
| *a.* | | Turkish numeral in upper right corner reads "50" instead of "5" | 30.00 | 15.00 |
| | | *Nos. 95-99 (5)* | 117.75 | *17.00* |

See Nos. J39-J42. For surcharges and overprints see Nos. 100, 288-291, 350, 355-359, 477-478, B38, B41, J80-J82, P25-P34, P36, P121-P122, P134-P137, P153-P154.

Red Surcharge

**1897**

| | | | | |
|---|---|---|---|---|
| **100** | A10 | 5pa on 10pa gray grn | 3.00 | 1.25 |
| *a.* | | "Cniq" instead of "Cinq" | 10.00 | 10.00 |

Turkish stamps of types A11, A17-A18, A21-A24, A26, A28-A39, A41 with or without Turkish overprints and English surcharges with "Baghdad" or "Iraq" are listed under Mesopotamia in Vol. 4.

Turkish stamps of types A19 and A21 with Double-headed Eagle and "Shqipenia" handstamp are listed under Albania in Vol. 1.

A16

A17

**1901** **Typo.** *Perf. 13½*

**For Foreign Postage**

| | | | | |
|---|---|---|---|---|
| **102** | A16 | 5pa bister | 1.25 | .60 |
| **103** | A16 | 10pa yellow green | 1.25 | .60 |
| **104** | A16 | 20pa magenta | 1.25 | .60 |
| *a.* | | Perf. 12 | 1.25 | .60 |
| **105** | A16 | 1pi violet blue | 1.50 | 1.00 |
| **106** | A16 | 2pi gray blue | 2.50 | 1.00 |
| **107** | A16 | 5pi ocher | 7.50 | 3.00 |
| **108** | A16 | 25pi dark green | 100.00 | 30.00 |
| **109** | A16 | 50pi yellow | 250.00 | 100.00 |
| | | *Nos. 102-109 (8)* | 365.25 | 136.80 |

**For Domestic Postage**

***Perf. 12, 13½***

| | | | | |
|---|---|---|---|---|
| **110** | A17 | 5pa purple | 1.25 | .50 |
| **111** | A17 | 10pa green | 1.25 | .50 |
| **112** | A17 | 20pa carmine | 1.25 | .50 |
| **113** | A17 | 1pi blue | 1.25 | .50 |
| *a.* | | Imperf. | 20.00 | |
| **114** | A17 | 2pi orange | 2.00 | .50 |
| **115** | A17 | 5pi lilac rose | 5.75 | 1.00 |

***Perf. 13½***

| | | | | |
|---|---|---|---|---|
| **116** | A17 | 25pi brown | 10.00 | 2.00 |
| *a.* | | Perf. 12 | 12.50 | 5.25 |
| **117** | A17 | 50pi yellow brown | 32.50 | 3.50 |
| *a.* | | Perf. 12 | 45.00 | 15.00 |
| | | *Nos. 110-117 (8)* | 55.25 | 9.00 |

Nos. 110-113 exist perf. 12x13½.

See Nos. J43-J46.

For overprints and surcharges see Nos. 165-180, 292-303, 340-341, 361-377, 479-493, B19-B20, B37, P37-P48, P69-P80, P123-P126, P138-P146, P155-P164.

A18

A19

**1905** *Perf. 12, 13½ and Compound*

| | | | | |
|---|---|---|---|---|
| **118** | A18 | 5pa ocher | 1.00 | .50 |
| **119** | A18 | 10pa dull green | 1.00 | .50 |
| *a.* | | Imperf. | 4.00 | 3.50 |
| **120** | A18 | 20pa carmine | 1.00 | .50 |
| *a.* | | Imperf. | 4.00 | 3.50 |
| **121** | A18 | 1pi blue | 1.00 | .50 |
| **122** | A18 | 2pi slate | 1.50 | .50 |
| **123** | A18 | 2½pi red violet | 1.50 | .50 |
| *a.* | | Imperf. | 11.00 | 9.00 |
| **124** | A18 | 5pi brown | 2.00 | .50 |
| **125** | A18 | 10pi orange brn | 3.75 | .50 |
| **126** | A18 | 25pi olive green | 12.50 | 15.00 |
| **127** | A18 | 50pi deep violet | 50.00 | 30.00 |

See Nos. J47-J48. For overprints and surcharges see Nos. 128-131, 181-182, 304-314, 351-354, 378-389, 494-508, B1-B3, B21-B23, B39-B40, P49-P54, P127-P129, P147-P150, P165-P171.

Overprinted in Carmine or Blue

**1906**

| | | | | |
|---|---|---|---|---|
| **128** | A18 | 10pa dull green (C) | 3.00 | 1.00 |
| **129** | A18 | 20pa carmine (Bl) | 3.00 | 1.00 |
| **130** | A18 | 1pi blue (C) | 3.00 | 1.00 |
| **131** | A18 | 2pi slate (C) | 17.50 | 5.00 |
| | | *Nos. 118-131 (14)* | 101.75 | 57.00 |

Stamps bearing this overprint were sold to merchants at a discount from face value to encourage the use of Turkish stamps on foreign correspondence, instead of those of the various European powers which maintained post offices in Turkey. The overprint is the Arab "B," for "Béhié," meaning "discount."

**1908**

| | | | | |
|---|---|---|---|---|
| **132** | A19 | 5pa ocher | 1.25 | .50 |
| **133** | A19 | 10pa blue green | 1.75 | .50 |
| **134** | A19 | 20pa carmine | 40.00 | .50 |
| **135** | A19 | 1pi bright blue | 15.00 | .50 |
| *a.* | | 1pi ultramarine | 50.00 | 10.00 |
| **136** | A19 | 2pi blue black | 10.00 | .50 |
| **137** | A19 | 2½pi violet brown | 3.00 | .50 |
| **138** | A19 | 5pi dark violet | 80.00 | .50 |
| **139** | A19 | 10pi red | 70.00 | 2.50 |
| **140** | A19 | 25pi dark green | 10.00 | 5.00 |
| **141** | A19 | 50pi red brown | 50.00 | 35.00 |

See Nos. J49-J50. For overprints and surcharges see Nos. 142-145, 314B-316B, 390-396, 509-516A, B4-B6, B17, B24-B27, P55-P60, P130-P131, P151, P172, Thrace 15.

Overprinted in Carmine or Blue

| | | | | |
|---|---|---|---|---|
| **142** | A19 | 10pa blue green (C) | 7.50 | 2.50 |
| **143** | A19 | 20pa carmine (Bl) | 7.50 | 2.50 |
| **144** | A19 | 1pi brt blue (C) | 15.00 | 2.50 |
| **145** | A19 | 2pi blue black (C) | 25.00 | 12.50 |
| | | *Nos. 132-145 (14)* | 336.00 | 66.00 |

A20

***Perf. 12, 13½ & Compound***

**1908, Dec. 17**

| | | | | |
|---|---|---|---|---|
| **146** | A20 | 5pa ocher | .75 | .50 |
| **147** | A20 | 10pa blue green | 1.50 | .50 |
| **148** | A20 | 20pa carmine | 2.00 | 1.00 |
| **149** | A20 | 1pi ultra | 3.00 | 1.00 |
| **150** | A20 | 2pi gray black | 12.50 | 15.00 |
| | | *Nos. 146-150 (5)* | 19.75 | 18.00 |

***Imperf***

| | | | | |
|---|---|---|---|---|
| *146a* | A20 | 5pa | 3.00 | 3.00 |
| *147a* | A20 | 10pa | 4.00 | 4.00 |
| *148a* | A20 | 20pa | 5.50 | 5.50 |
| *149a* | A20 | 1pi | 3.00 | 3.00 |

Granting of a Constitution, the date of which is inscribed on the banderol: "324 Temuz 10" (July 24, 1908).

For overprints see Nos. 397, 517.

Tughra and "Reshad" of Sultan Mohammed V — A21

**1909, Dec.**

| | | | | |
|---|---|---|---|---|
| **151** | A21 | 5pa ocher | 1.00 | .50 |
| **152** | A21 | 10pa blue green | 1.00 | .50 |
| *a.* | | Imperf. | 3.00 | 3.00 |
| **153** | A21 | 20pa carmine rose | 1.00 | .50 |
| **154** | A21 | 1pi ultra | 3.00 | .50 |
| *a.* | | 1pi bright blue | 12.50 | .50 |
| **155** | A21 | 2pi blue black | 3.00 | .50 |
| **156** | A21 | 2½pi dark brown | 90.00 | 20.00 |
| **157** | A21 | 5pi dark violet | 3.00 | 1.00 |
| **158** | A21 | 10pi dull red | 37.50 | 1.00 |
| **159** | A21 | 25pi dark green | 350.00 | 100.00 |
| **160** | A21 | 50pi red brown | 125.00 | 80.00 |

The 2pa olive green, type A21, is a newspaper stamp, No. P68.

Two types exist for the 10pa, 20pa and 1pi. In the second type, the damaged crescent is restored.

See Nos. J51-J52. For overprints and surcharges see Nos. 161-164, 317-327, 342-343, 398-406, 518-528, 567, B7-B14, B18, B28-B32, P61-P68, P81, P132-P133, P152, P173, Turkey in Asia 67, 72, Thrace 1-4, 13, 13A, 14.

Overprinted in Carmine or Blue

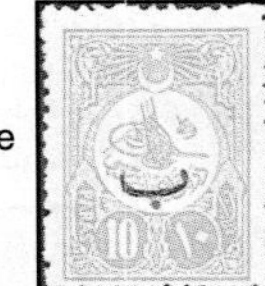

| | | | | |
|---|---|---|---|---|
| **161** | A21 | 10pa blue grn (C) | 1.75 | .75 |
| *a.* | | Imperf. | | |
| **162** | A21 | 20pa car rose (Bl) | 1.75 | .75 |
| *a.* | | Imperf. | | |
| **163** | A21 | 1pi ultra (C) | 3.50 | 2.00 |
| *a.* | | Imperf. | 4.00 | |
| *b.* | | 1pi bright blue | 6.50 | 3.00 |
| **164** | A21 | 2pi blue black (C) | 75.00 | 30.00 |
| *a.* | | Imperf. | | |
| | | *Nos. 151-164 (14)* | 696.50 | 238.00 |

Stamps of 1901-05 Overprinted in Carmine or Blue

The overprint was applied to 18 denominations in four settings with change of city name, producing individual sets for each city: "MONASTIR," "PRISTINA," "SALONIKA" and "USKUB."

**1911, June 26** *Perf. 12, 13½*

| | | | | |
|---|---|---|---|---|
| **165** | A16 | 5pa bister | 2.50 | 3.75 |
| **166** | A16 | 10pa yellow green | 2.50 | 3.75 |
| **167** | A16 | 20pa magenta | 6.00 | 7.50 |
| **168** | A16 | 1pi violet blue | 6.00 | 7.50 |
| **169** | A16 | 2pi gray blue | 6.00 | 7.50 |
| **170** | A16 | 5pi ocher | 40.00 | 60.00 |
| **171** | A16 | 25pi dark green | 60.00 | 75.00 |
| **172** | A16 | 50pi yellow | 100.00 | 125.00 |
| **173** | A17 | 5pa purple | 2.50 | 3.75 |
| **174** | A17 | 10pa green | 2.50 | 3.75 |
| **175** | A17 | 20pa carmine | 6.00 | 7.50 |
| **176** | A17 | 1pi blue | 6.00 | 7.50 |
| **177** | A17 | 2pi orange | 6.00 | 7.50 |
| **178** | A17 | 5pi lilac rose | 40.00 | 60.00 |
| **179** | A17 | 25pi chocolate | 85.00 | 125.00 |
| **180** | A17 | 50pi yellow brown | 100.00 | 125.00 |
| **181** | A18 | 2½pi red violet | 65.00 | 100.00 |
| **182** | A18 | 10pi orange brown | 60.00 | 60.00 |
| | | *Nos. 165-182 (18)* | 596.00 | 790.00 |

Sultan's visit to Macedonia. The Arabic overprint reads: "Souvenir of the Sultan's Journey, 1329." Values same for all cities. See Nos. P69-P81.

General Post Office, Constantinople
A22

**1913, Mar. 14** ***Perf. 12***

| No. | Type | Denom. | Color | Unused | Used |
|---|---|---|---|---|---|
| **237** | A22 | 2pa | olive green | 1.00 | .50 |
| **238** | A22 | 5pa | ocher | 1.00 | .50 |
| **239** | A22 | 10pa | blue green | 1.00 | .50 |
| **240** | A22 | 20pa | carmine rose | 1.00 | .50 |
| **241** | A22 | 1pi | ultra | 1.00 | .50 |
| **242** | A22 | 2pi | indigo | 2.00 | .50 |
| **243** | A22 | 5pi | dull violet | 3.50 | .50 |
| **244** | A22 | 10pi | dull red | 6.00 | 1.00 |
| **245** | A22 | 25pi | gray green | 22.50 | 22.50 |
| **246** | A22 | 50pi | orange brown | 85.00 | 125.00 |

See Nos. J53-J58. For overprints and surcharges see Nos. 247-250, 328-339, 344, 407-414, 529-538, 568, B15-B16, B33-B36, Turkey in Asia 68, Thrace 10, 10A, 11, 11A, 12, N82.

Overprinted in Carmine or Blue

| No. | Type | Denom. | Color | Unused | Used |
|---|---|---|---|---|---|
| **247** | A22 | 10pa | blue green (C) | 1.00 | .50 |
| **248** | A22 | 20pa | car rose (Bl) | 1.00 | .50 |
| **249** | A22 | 1pi | ultra (C) | 1.00 | .50 |
| **250** | A22 | 2pi | indigo (C) | 17.50 | 7.50 |
| | | | *Nos. 237-250 (14)* | 144.50 | 161.00 |

Mosque of Selim, Adrianople — A23

**1913, Oct. 23** **Engr.**

| No. | Type | Denom. | Color | Unused | Used |
|---|---|---|---|---|---|
| **251** | A23 | 10pa | green | 1.50 | 1.00 |
| **252** | A23 | 20pa | red | 2.50 | 2.00 |
| **253** | A23 | 40pa | blue | 6.00 | 3.00 |
| | | | *Nos. 251-253 (3)* | 10.00 | 6.00 |

Recapture of Adrianople (Edirne) by the Turks.

See Nos. 592, J59-J62. For overprints and surcharge see Nos. 415-417, 539-540, J59-J62, J67-J70, J83-J86, Thrace N84.

Obelisk of Theodosius in the Hippodrome
A24

Column of Constantine
A25

Leander's Tower — A26

One of the Seven Towers — A27

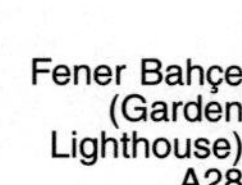

Fener Bahçe (Garden Lighthouse)
A28

The Castle of Europe on the Bosporus
A29

Mosque of Sultan Ahmed — A30

Monument to the Martyrs of Liberty
A31

Fountains of Suleiman
A32

Cruiser "Hamidie"
A33

View of Kandili on the Bosporus
A34

War Ministry (Later Istanbul University)
A35

Sweet Waters of Europe Park
A36

Mosque of Suleiman
A37

The Bosporus
A38

Sultan Ahmed's Fountain
A39

Sultan Mohammed V — A40

Designs A24-A39: Views of Constantinople.

**1914, Jan. 14** **Litho.**

| No. | Type | Denom. | Color | Unused | Used |
|---|---|---|---|---|---|
| **254** | A24 | 2pa | red lilac | .50 | .40 |
| **255** | A25 | 4pa | dark brown | .50 | .40 |
| **256** | A26 | 5pa | violet brown | .50 | .40 |
| **257** | A27 | 6pa | dark blue | .50 | .40 |
| | | | **Engr.** | | |
| **258** | A28 | 10pa | green | 2.00 | .40 |
| **259** | A29 | 20pa | red | 1.75 | .40 |
| **260** | A30 | 1pi | blue | .50 | .40 |
| ***b.*** | | | Booklet pane of 2+2 labels | | |
| **261** | A31 | 1½pi | car & blk | 1.00 | .40 |
| **262** | A32 | 1¾pi | sl & red brn | 1.00 | .40 |
| **263** | A33 | 2pi | green & blk | 2.00 | .40 |
| **264** | A34 | 2½pi | org & ol grn | 1.50 | .40 |
| **265** | A35 | 5pi | dull violet | 3.00 | .40 |
| **266** | A36 | 10pi | red brown | 7.00 | .40 |
| **267** | A37 | 25pi | olive green | 125.00 | 5.50 |
| **268** | A38 | 50pi | carmine | 6.00 | 2.25 |
| **269** | A39 | 100pi | deep blue | 75.00 | 27.50 |
| | | | Cut cancellation | | 12.00 |
| **270** | A40 | 200pi | green & blk | 550.00 | *400.00* |
| | | | Cut cancellation | | 25.00 |
| | | | *Nos. 254-270 (17)* | 777.75 | 440.45 |

See Nos. 590-591, 593-598.

For overprints and surcharges see Nos. 271-287, 419, 541, 552-553, 574A, 601, 603-604, P174, Turkey in Asia 1-3, 5-9, 73-74, Thrace N77, N78.

Stamps of Preceding Issue Overprinted in Red or Blue

| No. | Type | Denom. | Color | Unused | Used |
|---|---|---|---|---|---|
| **271** | A28 | 10pa | green (R) | 2.00 | .50 |
| **272** | A29 | 20pa | red (Bl) | 10.00 | .50 |
| **273** | A30 | 1pi | blue (R) | 2.00 | .50 |
| **275** | A32 | 1¾pi | sl & red brn (Bl) | 2.00 | 1.25 |
| **276** | A33 | 2pi | green & blk (R) | 50.00 | 3.25 |
| | | | *Nos. 271-276 (5)* | 66.00 | 6.00 |

No. 261 Surcharged

**1914, July 23**

| No. | Type | Denom. | Color | Unused | Used |
|---|---|---|---|---|---|
| **277** | A31 | 1pi on 1½pi | car & blk | 3.25 | 2.50 |
| ***a.*** | | | "1330" omitted | 2.50 | 1.50 |
| ***b.*** | | | Double surcharge | | |
| ***c.*** | | | Triple surcharge | 5.00 | 5.00 |

7th anniv. of the Constitution. The surcharge reads "10 July, 1330, National fête" and has also the numeral "1" at each side, over the original value of the stamp.

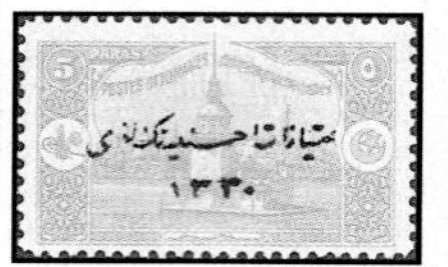

Stamps of 1914 Overprinted in Black or Red

| No. | Type | Denom. | Color | Unused | Used |
|---|---|---|---|---|---|
| **278** | A26 | 5pa | violet brn (Bk) | 1.75 | .50 |
| **279** | A28 | 10pa | green (R) | 3.25 | .50 |
| **280** | A29 | 20pa | red (Bk) | 4.00 | .50 |
| **281** | A30 | 1pi | blue (R) | 10.00 | 1.50 |
| **282** | A33 | 2pi | grn & blk (R) | 15.00 | 1.50 |
| **283** | A35 | 5pi | dull violet (R) | 50.00 | 4.25 |
| **284** | A36 | 10pi | red brown (R) | 190.00 | 65.00 |
| | | | *Nos. 278-284 (7)* | 274.00 | 73.75 |

This overprint reads "Abolition of the Capitulations, 1330".

No. 269 Surcharged

**1915**

| No. | Type | Denom. | Color | Unused | Used |
|---|---|---|---|---|---|
| **286** | A39 | 10pi on 100pi | | 62.50 | 22.50 |
| ***a.*** | | | Inverted surcharge | — | — |

No. 270 Surcharged

| No. | Type | Denom. | Color | Unused | Used |
|---|---|---|---|---|---|
| **287** | A40 | 25pi on 200pi | | 25.00 | 8.00 |

Preceding Issues Overprinted in Carmine or Black

**1915**

**On Stamps of 1892**

| No. | Type | Denom. | Color | Unused | Used |
|---|---|---|---|---|---|
| **288** | A10 | 10pa | gray green | 1.00 | .50 |
| ***a.*** | | | Inverted overprint | 7.50 | 7.50 |
| **289** | A13 | 2pi | brown orange | 1.50 | .50 |
| ***a.*** | | | Inverted overprint | 7.50 | 7.50 |
| **290** | A14 | 5pi | dull violet | 4.00 | .50 |
| ***a.*** | | | On No. 99a | 17.00 | 17.00 |

**On Stamp of 1897**

| No. | Type | Denom. | Color | Unused | Used |
|---|---|---|---|---|---|
| **291** | A10 | 5pa on 10pa | gray grn | 1.00 | .50 |
| ***a.*** | | | Inverted overprint | 5.00 | 5.00 |
| ***b.*** | | | On No. 100a | 10.00 | 10.00 |

**On Stamps of 1901**

| No. | Type | Denom. | Color | Unused | Used |
|---|---|---|---|---|---|
| **292** | A16 | 5pa | bister | 1.00 | .50 |
| **293** | A16 | 1pi | violet blue | 3.00 | .50 |
| **294** | A16 | 2pi | gray blue | 2.50 | .50 |
| **295** | A16 | 5pi | ocher | 20.00 | .50 |
| **296** | A16 | 25pi | dark green | 50.00 | 20.00 |
| **297** | A17 | 5pa | purple | 1.00 | .50 |
| **298** | A17 | 10pa | green | 1.50 | .50 |
| **299** | A17 | 20pa | carmine | 1.50 | .50 |
| ***a.*** | | | Inverted overprint | 7.50 | 7.50 |
| **300** | A17 | 1pi | blue | 1.50 | .50 |
| ***a.*** | | | Inverted overprint | 5.00 | 5.00 |
| **301** | A17 | 2pi | orange | 2.00 | .50 |
| ***a.*** | | | Inverted overprint | 7.50 | 7.50 |
| ***b.*** | | | Double ovpt. (R and Bk) | 5.00 | 5.00 |
| **302** | A17 | 5pi | lilac rose | 2.50 | .50 |
| **303** | A17 | 25pi | brown | 12.50 | 2.00 |

**On Stamps of 1905**

| No. | Type | Denom. | Color | Unused | Used |
|---|---|---|---|---|---|
| **304** | A18 | 5pa | ocher | 1.00 | .50 |
| **305** | A18 | 10pa | dull green | 1.00 | .50 |
| ***a.*** | | | Inverted overprint | 5.00 | 5.00 |
| **306** | A18 | 20pa | carmine | 1.00 | .50 |
| ***a.*** | | | Inverted overprint | 5.00 | 5.00 |
| **307** | A18 | 1pi | brt blue | 1.50 | .50 |
| ***a.*** | | | Inverted overprint | 5.00 | 5.00 |
| **308** | A18 | 2pi | slate | 2.50 | .50 |
| ***a.*** | | | Inverted overprint | 10.00 | 10.00 |
| **309** | A18 | 2½pi | red violet | 1.50 | .50 |
| **310** | A18 | 5pi | brown | 2.00 | .50 |
| ***a.*** | | | Inverted overprint | 10.00 | 10.00 |
| **311** | A18 | 10pi | orange brown | 12.50 | .50 |
| **312** | A18 | 25pi | olive green | 50.00 | 8.00 |

**On Stamps of 1906**

| No. | Type | Denom. | Color | Unused | Used |
|---|---|---|---|---|---|
| **313** | A18 | 10pa | dull green | 2.00 | .50 |
| **314** | A18 | 2pi | slate | 5.00 | .50 |
| ***a.*** | | | Inverted overprint | 5.00 | 5.00 |

**On Stamps of 1908**

| No. | Type | Denom. | Color | Unused | Used |
|---|---|---|---|---|---|
| **314B** | A19 | 2pi | blue black | 225.00 | 50.00 |
| **315** | A19 | 2½pi | violet brown | 3.00 | .50 |
| **315A** | A19 | 5pi | dark violet | 100.00 | 35.00 |
| **315B** | A19 | 10pi | red | 15.00 | 7.50 |
| **316** | A19 | 25pi | dark green | 30.00 | 5.00 |
| ***a.*** | | | Inverted overprint | 17.00 | 17.00 |

With Additional Overprint

**316B** A19 2pi blue black 15.00 5.00

### On Stamps of 1909

**317** A21 5pa ocher 1.00 .50
*a.* Inverted overprint 10.00 10.00
*b.* Double overprint 10.00 5.00
**318** A21 20pa car rose 1.00 .50
*a.* Inverted overprint 5.00 5.00
**319** A21 1pi ultra 2.00 .50
*a.* Inverted overprint 5.00 5.00
**320** A21 2pi blue black 2.00 .50
*a.* Inverted overprint 5.00 5.00
**321** A21 2½pi dark brown 67.50 25.00
**322** A21 5pi dark violet .30 .20
*a.* Inverted overprint 6.50 6.50
**323** A21 10pi dull red 10.00 .50
**324** A21 25pi dark green 1,750. 1,200.

With Additional Overprint

**325** A21 20pa carmine rose 2.00 .50
*a.* Inverted overprint 5.00 5.00
**326** A21 1pi ultra 2.00 .50
**327** A21 2pi blue black 3.50 .50

### On Stamps of 1913

**328** A22 5pa ocher 1.00 .50
*a.* Inverted overprint 7.50 7.50
**329** A22 10pa blue green 1.00 .50
*a.* Inverted overprint 10.00 10.00
**330** A22 20pa carmine rose 1.00 .50
*a.* Inverted overprint 7.50 7.50
**331** A22 1pi ultra 1.00 .50
*a.* Inverted overprint 5.00 5.00
**332** A22 2pi indigo 1.50 .50
*a.* Inverted overprint 5.00 5.00
**333** A22 5pi dull violet 3.00 .50
**334** A22 10pi dull red 10.00 .50
*a.* Inverted overprint 10.00 10.00
**335** A22 25pi gray green 30.00 20.00

With Additional Overprint

**336** A22 10pa blue green 1.00 .50
**337** A22 20pa carmine rose 1.00 .50
**338** A22 1pi ultra 2.00 .50
**339** A22 2pi indigo 7.50 3.00
*a.* Inverted overprint 10.00 10.00

See Nos. P121-P133.

Stamps of 1901-13 Overprinted

**1916**

**340** A17 5pa purple 1.00 .50
*a.* 5pa purple, #P43 80.00 80.00
**341** A17 10pa green 1.00 .50
*a.* Double overprint 6.50 6.50
*b.* 10pa yellow green, #103 80.00 80.00
**342** A21 20pa car rose, #153 2.00 .50
*a.* 20pa carmine rose, #162 110.00 110.00
**343** A21 1pi ultra 5.50 1.00
**344** A22 5pi dull violet 10.00 3.00
*Nos. 340-344 (5)* 19.50 5.50

Occupation of the Sinai Peninsula.

Old General Post Office of Constantinople A41

**1916, May 29 Litho.** ***Perf. 12½, 13½***

**345** A41 5pa green .75 .50
**346** A41 10pa carmine .75 .50
**347** A41 20pa ultra .75 .50
**348** A41 1pi violet & blk 1.50 .50
**349** A41 5pi yel brn & blk 20.00 2.50
*Nos. 345-349 (5)* 23.75 4.50

Introduction of postage in Turkey, 50th anniv. For overprints see Nos. 418, B42-B45.

Stamps of 1892-1905 Overprinted

**1916**

**350** A10 10pa gray grn (R) 2.00 2.00
**351** A18 20pa carmine (Bl) 3.75 2.50
**352** A18 1pi blue (R) 10.00 5.00
**353** A18 2pi slate (Bk) 12.50 1.00
**354** A18 2½pi red violet (Bk) 20.00 1.50
*Nos. 350-354 (5)* 48.25 12.00

National Fête Day. Overprint reads "10 Temuz 1332" (July 23, 1916).

Preceding Issues Overprinted or Surcharged in Red or Black:

a

b

**1916**

### On Stamps of 1892-98

**355** A10(a) 10pa gray green 1.00 .50
**355A** A11(a) 20pa violet brown .75 .50
*b.* Inverted overprint 10.00 10.00
**356** A12(a) 1pi gray blue 50.00 50.00
**357** A13(a) 2pi brown org 5.00 1.50
**358** A14(a) 5pi dull violet 50.00 50.00

### On Stamp of 1897

**359** A10(b) 5pa on 10pa gray grn .75 .50

### On Stamps of 1901

**361** A16(a) 5pa bister .75 .50
*a.* Double overprint 7.50 7.50
**362** A16(a) 10pa yel grn 1.00 .50
**363** A16(a) 20pa magenta .75 .50
**364** A16(a) 1pi violet blue 1.00 .50
*a.* Inverted overprint 7.50 7.50
**365** A16(a) 2pi gray blue 5.00 .50
**366** A16(b) 5pi on 25pi dk grn 55.00 55.00
**367** A16(b) 10pi on 25pi dk grn 55.00 55.00
**368** A16(a) 25pi dark green 55.00 55.00
**369** A17(a) 5pa purple 75.00 50.00
**370** A17(a) 10pa green 1.50 1.50
**371** A17(a) 20pa carmine .75 .50
*a.* Inverted overprint 7.50 7.50
**372** A17(a) 1pi blue .75 .50
*a.* Inverted overprint 7.50 7.50
**373** A17(a) 2pi orange 1.50 .50
**374** A17(b) 10pi on 25pi brown 5.00 1.50
**375** A17(b) 10pi on 50pi yel brn 7.50 1.50
**376** A17(a) 25pi brown 7.50 1.50
**377** A17(a) 50pi yel brn 10.00 2.50

### On Stamps of 1905

**378** A18(a) 5pa ocher .75 .50
**379** A18(a) 20pa carmine .75 .50
*a.* Inverted overprint 10.00 5.00
**380** A18(a) 1pi brt blue 2.00 .50
*a.* Inverted overprint 10.00 5.00
**381** A18(a) 2pi slate 1.00 .50
**382** A18(a) 2½pi red violet 7.50 1.50
**383** A18(b) 10pi on 25pi ol grn 7.50 2.50
**384** A18(b) 10pi on 50pi dp vio 7.50 2.00
**385** A18(a) 25pi olive green 7.50 3.00
**386** A18(a) 50pi deep violet 6.00 3.00

### On Stamps of 1906

**387** A18(a) 10pa dull green 1.00 .60
**388** A18(a) 20pa carmine 1.00 .60
**389** A18(a) 1pi brt blue 1.00 .60

### On Stamps of 1908

**390** A19(a) 2½pi violet brown 67.50 67.50
**391** A19(b) 10pi on 25pi dk grn 20.00 12.50
**392** A19(b) 10pi on 50pi red brn 67.50 67.50
**393** A19(b) 25pi on 50pi red brn 67.50 67.50
**394** A19(a) 25pi dark green 7.50 2.50
**395** A19(a) 50pi red brown 50.00 50.00

With Additional Overprint

**396** A19(a) 2pi blue black 67.50 67.50

### On Stamps of 1908-09

**397** A20(a) 5pa ocher 67.50 67.50
**398** A21(a) 5pa ocher .75 2.50
**399** A21(a) 10pa blue green 50.00 50.00
**400** A21(a) 20pa carmine rose 50.00 50.00
**401** A21(a) 1pi ultra 1.00 .50
**402** A21(a) 2pi blue black 3.00 1.50
**403** A21(a) 2½pi dark brown 50.00 50.00
**404** A21(a) 5pi dark violet 50.00 50.00

With Additional Overprint

**405** A21(a) 1pi ultra 67.50 67.50
**406** A21(a) 2pi blue black 50.00 50.00

### On Stamps of 1913

**407** A22(a) 5pa ocher .75 .50
**408** A22(a) 20pa carmine rose 1.50 .50
**409** A22(a) 1pi ultra 1.50 .50
**410** A22(a) 2pi indigo 3.00 1.00
**411** A22(b) 10pi on 50pi org brn 12.50 10.00
**412** A22(a) 25pi gray green 7.50 5.00
**413** A22(a) 50pi orange brown 15.00 12.50

With Additional Overprint

**414** A22(a) 1pi ultra 1.00 1.00

### On Commemorative Stamps of 1913

**415** A23(a) 10pa green 1.25 .50
**416** A23(a) 20pa red 2.00 .50
**417** A23(a) 40pa blue 6.00 2.50

### On Commemorative Stamp of 1916

**418** A41(a) 5pi yel brn & blk 1.00 .50

No. 277 Surcharged in Blue

**419** A31 60pa on 1pi on 1½pi 2.50 3.50
*a.* "1330" omitted 40.00 40.00

See Nos. P134-P152, J67-J70.

Turkish Artillery A42

Mosque at Orta Köy, Constantinople — A43

Lighthouse on Bosporus — A44

Monument to Martyrs of Liberty — A45

Map of the Dardanelles; Sultan Mohammed V — A46

Map of the Dardanelles A47

Istanbul Across the Golden Horn A48

Pyramids of Egypt A49

Dolma Bahçe Palace and Mohammed V — A50

Sentry and Shell — A51

Sultan Mohammed V — A52

**1916-18 Typo.** ***Perf. 11½, 12½***

**420** A42 2pa violet 1.25 .50
**421** A43 5pa orange .75 .50
**424** A44 10pa green .75 1.00

**Engr.**

**425** A45 20pa deep rose .75 .50
**426** A46 1pi dull violet 2.50 .50

**Typo.**

**428** A47 50pa ultra 1.25 .50
**429** A48 2pi org brn & ind 3.00 .50
**430** A49 5pi pale blue & blk 17.50 1.00

**Engr.**

**431** A50 10pi dark green 8.75 5.00
**432** A50 10pi dark violet 32.50 2.50
**433** A50 10pi dark brown 14.00 2.50
**434** A51 25pi carmine, *straw* 2.25 1.50
**437** A52 50pi carmine 5.00 5.00
**438** A52 50pi indigo 2.00 2.50
**439** A52 50pi green, *straw* 2.50 10.00
*Nos. 420-439 (15)* 94.75 34.00

For overprints and surcharges see Nos. 541B-541E, 554-560, 565-566, 569-574, 575, 577-578, 579A-580, Turkey in Asia 4, 10, 64-66, Thrace N76, N80, N81. Compare designs A42-A43 with A53-A54.

**Forgeries of Nos. 446-545 abound.**

Preceding Issues Overprinted or Surcharged in Red, Black or Blue:

d

e

f

g

**1917**

### On Stamps of 1865

| | | | | |
|---|---|---|---|---|
| **446** | A5(d) | 20pa yellow (R) | 45.00 | 67.50 |
| *a.* | | Star without rays (R) | 50.00 | 57.50 |
| **447** | A5(d) | 1pi pearl gray (R) | 45.00 | 67.50 |
| *a.* | | Star without rays (R) | 50.00 | 57.50 |
| **448** | A5(d) | 2pi blue (R) | 45.00 | 67.50 |
| **449** | A5(d) | 5pi carmine (Bk) | 45.00 | 67.50 |

### On Stamp of 1867

| | | | | |
|---|---|---|---|---|
| **450** | A5(d) | 5pi rose (Bk) | 45.00 | 67.50 |

### On Stamps of 1870-71

| | | | | |
|---|---|---|---|---|
| **451** | A5(d) | 2pi red (Bl) | 45.00 | 67.50 |
| **452** | A5(d) | 5pi blue (Bk) | 45.00 | 67.50 |
| **453** | A5(d) | 25pi dull rose (Bl) | 45.00 | 67.50 |

### On Stamp of 1874-75

| | | | | |
|---|---|---|---|---|
| **454** | A5(d) | 10pa red violet (Bl) | 45.00 | 67.50 |

### On Stamps of April, 1876

| | | | | |
|---|---|---|---|---|
| **455** | A5(d) | 10pa red lilac (Bl) | 45.00 | 67.50 |
| *a.* | | 10pa red violet (Bl) | 50.00 | 67.50 |
| **457** | A5(d) | 20pa pale green (R) | 45.00 | 67.50 |
| **458** | A5(d) | 1pi yellow (Bl) | 45.00 | 67.50 |

### On Stamps of January, 1876

| | | | | |
|---|---|---|---|---|
| **459** | A5(d) | ¼pi on 10pa rose lil (Bl) | 45.00 | 67.50 |
| **460** | A5(d) | ½pi on 20pa yel grn (R) | 45.00 | 67.50 |
| **461** | A5(d) | 1¼pi on 50pa rose (Bl) | 45.00 | 67.50 |

### On Stamps of September, 1876

| | | | | |
|---|---|---|---|---|
| **462** | A7(d) | 50pa blue & yel (R) | 45.00 | 67.50 |
| **463** | A7(d) | 2pi blk & redsh brn (R) | 45.00 | 67.50 |
| **464** | A7(d) | 25pi claret & rose (Bk) | 45.00 | 67.50 |

### On Stamps of 1880-84

| | | | | |
|---|---|---|---|---|
| **465** | A7(d) | 5pa black & ol (R) | 45.00 | 67.50 |
| **466** | A7(d) | 10pa black & grn (R) | 45.00 | 67.50 |

### On Stamps of 1881-82

| | | | | |
|---|---|---|---|---|
| **467** | A5(d) | 20pa gray (Bl) | 45.00 | 67.50 |
| **468** | A5(d) | 2pi pale sal (Bl) | 45.00 | 67.50 |

### On Stamps of 1884-86

| | | | | |
|---|---|---|---|---|
| **469** | A7(d) | 10pa grn & pale grn (Bk) | 45.00 | 67.50 |
| **470** | A7(d) | 2pi ocher & pale ocher (Bk) | 45.00 | 67.50 |
| **471** | A7(d) | 5pi red brn & pale brn (Bk) | 45.00 | 67.50 |

### On Stamps of 1886

| | | | | |
|---|---|---|---|---|
| **472** | A7(d) | 5pa blk & pale gray (R) | 2.00 | 1.75 |
| *a.* | | Inverted overprint | 30.00 | 30.00 |
| **473** | A7(d) | 2pi org & bl (Bk) | 3.00 | 2.50 |
| *a.* | | Inverted overprint | 35.00 | 35.00 |
| **474** | A7(d) | 5pi grn & pale grn (R) | 45.00 | 67.50 |
| **475** | A7(d) | 25pi bis & pale bis (Bk) | 45.00 | 67.50 |

### On Stamp of 1888

| | | | | |
|---|---|---|---|---|
| **476** | A7(d) | 5pi dk brn & gray (Bk) | 45.00 | 67.50 |

### On Stamps of 1892-98

| | | | | |
|---|---|---|---|---|
| **477** | A11(d) | 20pa vio brn (R) | 4.00 | 3.00 |
| **478** | A13(d) | 2pi brn org (R) | 4.00 | 3.50 |
| *a.* | | Tête bêche pair | 13.50 | 13.50 |

### On Stamps of 1901

| | | | | |
|---|---|---|---|---|
| **479** | A16(d) | 5pa bister (R) | 3.00 | 3.00 |
| *a.* | | Inverted overprint | 20.00 | 20.00 |
| **480** | A16(d) | 20pa mag (Bk) | 2.00 | 1.50 |
| *a.* | | Inverted overprint | 25.00 | 25.00 |
| **481** | A16(d) | 1pi vio bl (R) | 3.00 | 3.00 |
| *a.* | | Inverted overprint | 20.00 | 20.00 |
| **482** | A16(d) | 2pi gray bl (R) | 5.00 | 5.00 |
| **483** | A16(d) | 5pi ocher (R) | 32.50 | 50.00 |
| **484** | A16(e) | 10pi on 50pi yel (R) | 32.50 | 50.00 |
| **485** | A16(d) | 25pi dk grn (R) | 100.00 | 50.00 |
| **486** | A17(d) | 5pa purple (Bk) | 32.50 | 50.00 |
| **487** | A17(d) | 10pa green (R) | 5.00 | 5.00 |
| **488** | A17(d) | 20pa car (Bk) | 2.00 | 1.50 |
| *a.* | | Inverted overprint | 20.00 | 20.00 |
| **489** | A17(d) | 1pi blue (R) | 1.00 | .90 |
| **490** | A17(d) | 2pi org (Bk) | 3.00 | 3.00 |
| *a.* | | Inverted overprint | 20.00 | 20.00 |
| **491** | A17(d) | 5pi lil rose (R) | 32.50 | 50.00 |
| **492** | A17(e) | 10pi on 50pi yel brn (R) | 32.50 | 50.00 |
| **493** | A17(d) | 25pi brown (R) | 5.00 | 5.00 |

### On Stamps of 1905

| | | | | |
|---|---|---|---|---|
| **494** | A18(d) | 5pa ocher (R) | 2.00 | 1.00 |
| *a.* | | Inverted overprint | 20.00 | 20.00 |
| **495** | A18(d) | 10pa dl grn (R) | 32.50 | 50.00 |
| **496** | A18(d) | 20pa car (Bk) | 1.00 | 1.00 |
| *a.* | | Double ovpt., one invtd. | 35.00 | 35.00 |
| *b.* | | Inverted overprint | 35.00 | 35.00 |
| **497** | A18(d) | 1pi blue (R) | 1.50 | 1.00 |
| *a.* | | Inverted overprint | 35.00 | 35.00 |
| **498** | A18(d) | 2pi slate (R) | 5.00 | 5.00 |
| **499** | A18(d) | 2½pi red vio (Bk) | 5.00 | 5.00 |
| *a.* | | Inverted overprint | 20.00 | 20.00 |
| **500** | A18(d) | 5pi brown (R) | 35.00 | 45.00 |
| **501** | A18(d) | 10pi orange brn (R) | 35.00 | 50.00 |
| **502** | A18(e) | 10pi on 50pi dp vio (R) | 35.00 | 50.00 |
| **503** | A18(d) | 25pi ol grn (R) | 35.00 | 50.00 |

### On Nos. 128-131

| | | | | |
|---|---|---|---|---|
| **504** | A18(d) | 10pa dl grn (R) | 1.50 | 1.00 |
| *a.* | | Inverted overprint | 20.00 | 20.00 |
| **505** | A18(d) | 20pa car (Bk) | 1.00 | .75 |
| *a.* | | Double ovpt., one invtd. | 20.00 | 20.00 |
| *b.* | | Inverted overprint | 20.00 | 20.00 |
| **506** | A18(d) | 1pi brt bl (Bk) | 1.00 | .75 |
| *a.* | | Inverted overprint | 20.00 | 20.00 |
| **507** | A18(d) | 1pi brt bl (R) | 1.50 | 1.25 |
| *a.* | | Inverted overprint | 20.00 | 20.00 |
| **508** | A18(d) | 2pi slate (Bk) | 35.00 | 50.00 |
| | | *Nos. 494-508 (15)* | *227.00* | *311.75* |

### On Stamps of 1908

| | | | | |
|---|---|---|---|---|
| **509** | A19(d) | 5pa ocher (R) | 1.50 | 1.25 |
| **510** | A19(d) | 10pa bl grn (R) | 20.00 | 20.00 |
| **510A** | A19(d) | 1pi brt blue (R) | *125.00* | 140.00 |
| **511** | A19(d) | 2pi bl blk (R) | 35.00 | 50.00 |
| **512** | A19(d) | 2½pi violet brn (Bk) | 35.00 | 35.00 |
| **512A** | A19(d) | 10pi red (R) | *150.00* | 225.00 |
| **513** | A19(e) | 10pi on 50pi red brn (R) | 35.00 | 50.00 |
| **514** | A19(d) | 25pi dark green (R) | 35.00 | 50.00 |

With Additional Overprint

| | | | | |
|---|---|---|---|---|
| **514A** | A19(d) | 10pa bl grn (Bk) | 150.00 | 225.00 |
| **515** | A19(d) | 1pi brt bl (Bk) | 35.00 | 50.00 |
| **516** | A19(d) | 2pi bl blk (R) | 5.00 | 5.00 |
| **516A** | A19(d) | 2pi bl blk (Bk) | 35.00 | 67.50 |

### On Stamps of 1908-09

| | | | | |
|---|---|---|---|---|
| **517** | A20(d) | 5pa ocher (R) | 3.00 | 3.00 |
| **518** | A21(d) | 5pa ocher (R) | 2.00 | 1.50 |
| *a.* | | Double overprint | 20.00 | 20.00 |
| *b.* | | Dbl. ovpt., one inverted | 20.00 | 20.00 |
| **519** | A21(d) | 10pa bl grn (R) | 2.00 | 1.50 |
| **520** | A21(d) | 20pa carmine rose (Bk) | 2.00 | 1.50 |
| *a.* | | Double overprint | 35.00 | 35.00 |
| **521** | A21(d) | 1pi ultra (R) | 1.00 | .75 |
| *a.* | | 1p bright blue (R) | 30.00 | 30.00 |
| **522** | A21(d) | 2pi bl blk (R) | 5.00 | 5.00 |
| **523** | A21(d) | 2½pi dk brn (Bk) | 35.00 | 50.00 |
| **524** | A21(d) | 5pi dk vio (R) | 35.00 | 50.00 |
| **525** | A21(d) | 10pi dull red (R) | 35.00 | 50.00 |

With Additional Overprint ب

| | | | | |
|---|---|---|---|---|
| **525A** | A21(d) | 10pa bl grn (Bk) | 175.00 | 225.00 |
| **526** | A21(d) | 1pi ultra (Bk) | 125.00 | 90.00 |
| **527** | A21(d) | 1pi ultra (R) | 2.50 | 2.50 |
| *a.* | | 1pi bright blue (R) | 125.00 | 140.00 |
| **528** | A21(d) | 2pi bl blk (Bk) | 35.00 | 50.00 |

### On Stamps of 1913

| | | | | |
|---|---|---|---|---|
| **529** | A22(d) | 5pa ocher (R) | 1.25 | 1.25 |
| **530** | A22(d) | 10pa bl grn (R) | 35.00 | 50.00 |
| **531** | A22(d) | 20pa car rose (Bk) | 1.50 | 2.50 |
| **532** | A22(d) | 1pi ultra (R) | 1.50 | 3.50 |
| **533** | A22(d) | 2pi indigo (R) | 3.50 | 3.50 |
| **534** | A22(d) | 5pi dl vio (R) | 35.00 | 50.00 |
| **535** | A22(d) | 10pi dl red (Bk) | 45.00 | 50.00 |

With Additional Overprint

| | | | | |
|---|---|---|---|---|
| **536** | A22(d) | 10pa bl grn (Bk) | 1.50 | 1.50 |
| *a.* | | Inverted overprint | 20.00 | 20.00 |
| **537** | A22(d) | 1pi ultra (Bk) | 3.00 | 3.00 |
| *a.* | | Inverted overprint | 20.00 | 20.00 |
| **538** | A22(d) | 2pi indigo (Bk) | 35.00 | 100.00 |

### On Commemorative Stamps of 1913

| | | | | |
|---|---|---|---|---|
| **539** | A23(d) | 10pa green (R) | 5.00 | 5.00 |
| *a.* | | Inverted overprint | 20.00 | 20.00 |
| **540** | A23(d) | 40pa blue (R) | 7.00 | 7.00 |
| *a.* | | Inverted overprint | 20.00 | 20.00 |

### On No. 277, with Addition of New Value

| | | | | |
|---|---|---|---|---|
| **541** | A31 | 60pa on 1pi on 1½pi (Bk) | 1.50 | 1.50 |
| *a.* | | "1330" omitted | 45.00 | 45.00 |

### On Stamps of 1916-18

| | | | | |
|---|---|---|---|---|
| **541B** | A51(f) | 25pi car, *straw* | 5.00 | 5.00 |
| **541C** | A52(g) | 50pi carmine | 17.50 | 17.50 |
| **541D** | A52(g) | 50pi indigo | 35.00 | 50.00 |
| **541E** | A52(g) | 50pi green, *straw* | 15.00 | 27.50 |

### Ovptd. on Eastern Rumelia No. 12

| | | | | |
|---|---|---|---|---|
| **542** | A4(d) | 20pa blk & rose (Bl) | 35.00 | 35.00 |

### Ovptd. in Black on Eastern Rumelia #15-17

| | | | | |
|---|---|---|---|---|
| **543** | A4(d) | 5pa lilac & pale lilac | 45.00 | 45.00 |
| **544** | A4(d) | 10pa green & pale green | 45.00 | 45.00 |
| **545** | A4(d) | 20pa carmine & pale rose | 45.00 | 45.00 |

Some experts question the status of Nos. 510A, 512A and 525A.

See Nos. J71-J86, P153-P172.

Surcharged

**1917**

| | | | | |
|---|---|---|---|---|
| **545A** | A52a | 5pa on 1pi red | .75 | .50 |

It is stated that No. 545A was never issued without surcharge.

See Nos. 548f, 545A, 602.

Turkish Artillery A53

**1917** **Typo.** ***Perf. 11½, 12½***

| | | | | |
|---|---|---|---|---|
| **546** | A53 | 2pa Prussian blue | 100.00 | |

In type A42 the Turkish inscription at the top is in one group, in type A53 it is in two groups. It is stated that No. 546 was never placed in use. Copies were distributed through the Universal Postal Union at Bern.

For surcharges see Nos. 547-548, Turkey in Asia 69-70.

Surcharged

| | | | | |
|---|---|---|---|---|
| **547** | A53 | 5pi on 2pa Prus bl | 12.50 | .90 |
| *a.* | | Inverted surcharge | 9.00 | 9.00 |
| *b.* | | Turkish "5" omitted at lower left | | |

Surcharged

**1918**

| | | | | |
|---|---|---|---|---|
| **548** | A53 | 5pi on 2pa Prus blue | 12.50 | .90 |
| *g.* | | Inverted surcharge | 10.00 | 10.00 |

Top line of surcharge on Nos. 547-548 reads "Ottoman Posts."

For surcharge see Thrace No. N79.

No. 545A Surcharged

**1918**

| | | | | |
|---|---|---|---|---|
| **548A** | A52a | 2pa on 5pa on 1pi red | 1.50 | 1.50 |
| *b.* | | Double surcharge | 10.00 | 10.00 |
| *c.* | | Inverted surcharge | 10.00 | 10.00 |
| *d.* | | Double surcharge inverted | 10.00 | 10.00 |
| *e.* | | Dbl. surch., one inverted | 10.00 | 10.00 |
| *f.* | | In pair with No. 545A | 17.50 | 17.50 |

Enver Pasha and Kaiser Wilhelm II on Battlefield A54

St. Sophia and Obelisk of the Hippodrome A55

**1918** **Typo.** ***Perf. 12, 12½***

| | | | | |
|---|---|---|---|---|
| **549** | A54 | 5pa brown red | 75.00 | |
| **550** | A55 | 10pa gray green | 75.00 | |

The stamps, of which very few saw postal use, were converted into paper money by pasting on thick yellow paper and reperforating.

Values are for copies with original gum. Copies removed from the yellow paper are worth $8 each.

### Armistice Issue

Overprinted in Black or Red

**1919, Nov. 30**

### On Stamps of 1913

| | | | | |
|---|---|---|---|---|
| **552** | A34 | 2½pi org & ol grn | 125.00 | 300.00 |
| **553** | A38 | 50pi carmine | 125.00 | 300.00 |

### On Stamps of 1916-18

| | | | | |
|---|---|---|---|---|
| **554** | A46 | 1pi dull violet (R) | 7.50 | 10.00 |
| **555** | A47 | 50pa ultra (R) | .75 | 1.50 |
| **556** | A48 | 2pi org brn & ind | .75 | 1.50 |

557 A49 5pi pale bl & blk (R) .75 1.50
558 A50 10pi dark green (R) 6.25 10.00
559 A51 25pi carmine, *straw* 6.25 10.00
560 A52 50pi grn, *straw* (R) 6.25 10.00

Fountain in Desert near Sinai — A56

Sentry at Beersheba — A57

Turkish Troops at Sinai A58

**Typo.**

562 A56 20pa claret .75 1.50
563 A57 1pi blue (R) 125.00 150.00
564 A58 25pi slate blue (R) 125.00 150.00
*Nos. 552-564 (12)* 529.25 946.00

The overprint reads: "Souvenir of the Armistice, 30th October 1334." Nos. 562 to 564 are not known to have been regularly issued without overprint.

See No. J87. For overprints and surcharges see Nos. 576, 579, 582, 583-584, 586, Turkey in Asia 71, Thrace N83.

Stamps of 1911-19 Overprinted in Turkish
"Accession to the Throne of His Majesty, 3rd July 1334-1918," the Tughra of Sultan Mohammed VI and sometimes Ornaments and New Values

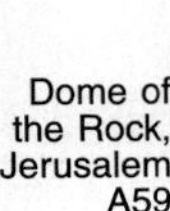

Dome of the Rock, Jerusalem A59

**1919**

565 A42 2pa violet .75 2.50
566 A43 5pa orange .50 .50
567 A21 5pa on 2pa ol grn .50 .50
a. Inverted surcharge 10.00 10.00
568 A22 10pa on 2pa ol grn .50 .50
569 A44 10pa green 1.25 1.50
a. Inverted overprint 25.00 25.00
570 A45 20pa deep rose .75 .50
a. Inverted overprint 12.00 12.00
571 A46 1pi dull violet 1.25 1.00
572 A47 60pa on 50pa ultra 1.25 1.00
573 A48 60pa on 2pi org brn & ind .50 .50
574 A48 2pi orange brn & ind .50 1.00
574A A34 2½pi orange & ol grn 25.00 37.50
575 A49 5pi pale blue & blk .50 1.00
576 A56 10pi on 20pa cl .50 1.00
577 A50 10pi dark brown 2.50 2.50
578 A51 25pi carmine, *straw* 2.00 2.00
579 A57 35pi on 1pi blue 1.50 2.50
579A A52 50pi carmine 25.00 37.50
580 A52 50pi green, *straw* 6.00 5.00
581 A59 100pi on 10pa green 6.00 5.00
582 A58 250pi on 25pi sl bl 6.00 5.00
*Nos. 565-582 (20)* 82.75 108.50

See note after #586. See #J88-J91.
For overprint and surcharge see Nos. 585, Thrace N82.

Surcharged with Ornaments, New Values and

***Perf. 11½, 12½***

583 A56 20pa claret 1.75 10.00
584 A57 1pi deep blue 2.50 17.50
585 A59 60pa on 10pa green 1.50 7.50
586 A58 25pi slate blue 7.50 50.00
a. Inverted overprint 100.00
*Nos. 583-586 (4)* 13.25 85.00

#576, 579, 581, 582, 583-586 were prepared in anticipation of the invasion and conquest of Egypt by the Turks. They were not issued at that time but subsequently received various overprints in commemoration of Sultan Mehmet Sadi's accession to the throne (#565-582) and of the 1st anniv. of this event (#583-586).

For surcharge see Thrace No. N83.

Designs of 1913 Modified

**1920** **Litho.** ***Perf. 11, 12***

590 A26 5pa brown orange 1.00 .50

**Engr.**

591 A28 10pa green 1.00 .50
592 A23 20pa rose 1.00 .50
593 A30 1pi blue green 3.75 .50
594 A32 3pi blue 1.00 .50
595 A34 5pi gray 50.00 .50
596 A36 10pi gray violet 12.50 .50
597 A37 25pi dull violet 5.00 2.50
598 A38 50pi brown 5.00 10.00
*Nos. 590-598 (9)* 80.25 16.00

On most stamps of this issue the designs have been modified by removing the small Turkish word at right of the tughra of the Sultan. In the 3pi and 5pi the values have been altered, while for the 25pi the color has been changed.

For surcharges see Thrace Nos. N77, N78, N84.

Black Surcharge

**1921-22**

600 SP1 30pa on 10pa red vio 1.25 .50
a. Double surcharge 37.50 37.50
b. Imperf.
601 A28 60pa on 10pa green 1.25 .50
a. Double surcharge 22.50 22.50
602 A52a 4½pi on 1pi red 2.50 .50
a. Inverted surcharge 20.00 20.00
603 A32 7½pi on 3pi blue 12.50 1.00
604 A32 7½pi on 3pi bl (R) ('22) 20.00 2.50
a. Double surcharge 30.00 30.00
*Nos. 600-604 (5)* 37.50 5.00

ΕΛΛΗΝΙΚΗ
ΚΑΤΟΧΗ
ΛΕΠΤΑ·50

Turkish Stamps of 1916-21 with Greek surcharge as above in blue or black are of private origin.

**Issues of the Republic**

Crescent and Star — A64

TWO PIASTERS:
Type I — "2" measures 3¼x1¾mm
Type II — "2" measures 2¾x1½mm

FIVE PIASTERS:
Type I — "5" measures 3½x2¼mm
Type II — "5" measures 3x1¾mm

***Perf. 11, 12, 13½, 13½x12***

**1923-25** **Litho.**

605 A64 10pa gray black .25 .25
606 A64 20pa citron .25 .25
607 A64 1pi deep violet .25 .25
a. Slanting numeral in lower left corner .50 .25
608 A64 1½pi emerald .25 1.50
609 A64 2pi bluish grn (I) 2.00 .50
a. 2pi deep green (II) .75 .25
610 A64 3pi yel brn 1.00 .50
611 A64 3¾pi lilac brown 2.50 2.50
612 A64 4½pi carmine .75 1.00
613 A64 5pi purple (I) 3.50 1.50
a. 5pi violet (II) 12.50 1.00
614 A64 7½pi blue 2.50 .50
615 A64 10pi slate 7.50 1.00
a. 10pi blue 7.50 1.00
616 A64 11¼pi dull rose 2.50 2.00
617 A64 15pi brown 10.00 1.00
618 A64 18¾pi myrtle green 4.50 3.00
619 A64 22½pi orange 6.00 2.00
620 A64 25pi black brown 30.00 2.50
621 A64 50pi gray 75.00 4.00
622 A64 100pi dark violet 150.00 8.50
624 A64 500pi deep green 500.00 160.00
Cut cancellation 1.60
*Nos. 605-624 (19)* 798.75 192.75
Set, never hinged 3,000.

#605-610, 612-617 exist imperf. & part perf.

Bridge of Sakarya and Mustafa Kemal — A65

**1924, Jan. 1** ***Perf. 12***

625 A65 1½pi emerald .50 .30
626 A65 3pi purple .60 .50
627 A65 4½pi pale rose 2.00 1.60
628 A65 5pi yellow brown 2.00 1.60
629 A65 7½pi deep blue 2.00 1.60
630 A65 50pi orange 22.50 10.00
631 A65 100pi brown violet 52.50 20.00
632 A65 200pi olive brown 72.50 35.00
*Nos. 625-632 (8)* 154.60 70.60
Set, never hinged 750.00

Signing of Treaty of Peace at Lausanne.

The Legendary Blacksmith and his Gray Wolf — A66

Sakarya Gorge — A67

Fortress of Ankara — A68

Mustafa Kemal Pasha — A69

**1926** **Engr.**

634 A66 10pa slate .50 .20
635 A66 20pa orange .50 .20
636 A66 1g brt rose .50 .20
637 A67 2g green 1.50 .25
638 A67 2½g gray black 2.00 .50
639 A67 3g copper red 2.50 .50
640 A68 5g lilac gray 3.00 .50
641 A68 6g red 1.00 .25
642 A68 10g deep blue 7.50 .50
643 A68 15g deep orange 10.00 1.25
644 A69 25g dk green & blk 15.00 1.25
645 A69 50g carmine & blk 20.00 1.50
646 A69 100g olive grn & blk 35.00 2.00
647 A69 200g brown & blk 90.00 5.50
*Nos. 634-647 (14)* 189.00 14.60
Set, never hinged 800.00

Stamps of 1926 Overprinted in Black, Silver or Gold

**1927, Sept. 9**

648 A66 1g brt rose .50 .50
649 A67 2g green .50 1.00
650 A67 2½g gray black 1.50 2.00
651 A67 3g copper red 2.00 2.50
652 A68 5g lilac gray 2.50 4.00
653 A68 6g red 1.50 1.50
654 A68 10g deep blue 3.50 3.50
655 A68 15g deep orange 5.00 5.00
656 A69 25g dk green & blk (S) 15.00 20.00
657 A69 50g car & blk (S) 27.50 37.50
658 A69 100g ol grn & blk (G) 60.00 75.00
*Nos. 648-658 (11)* 119.50 152.50
Set, never hinged 425.00

Agricultural and industrial exhibition at Izmir, Sept. 9-20, 1927.

The overprint reads: "1927" and the initials of "Izmir Dokuz Eylul Sergisi" (Izmir Exhibition, September 9).

**Second Izmir Exhibition Issue**

Nos. 634-647 Overprinted in Red or Black

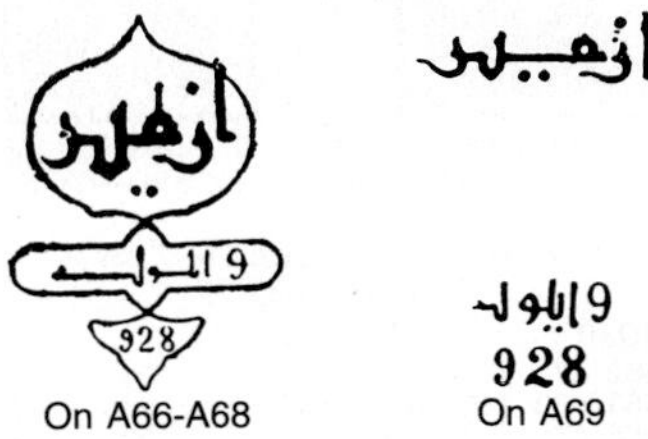


On A66-A68 On A69

**1928, Sept. 9**

659 A66 10pa slate (R) .50 .40
660 A66 20pa orange .50 .40
661 A66 1g brt rose 1.00 .50
662 A67 2g green (R) 1.50 1.50
663 A67 2½g gray blk (R) 1.50 1.50
664 A67 3g copper red 1.50 1.50
665 A68 5g lilac gray (R) 2.00 3.00
666 A68 6g red .50 .50
667 A68 10g deep blue 3.50 3.00
668 A68 15g deep orange 5.00 2.00
669 A69 25g dk grn & blk (R) 15.00 6.25
670 A69 50g car & blk 17.50 20.00
671 A69 100g ol grn & blk (R) 40.00 50.00
672 A69 200g brn & blk (R) 62.50 62.50
*Nos. 659-672 (14)* 152.50 153.05
Set, never hinged 650.00

The overprint reads "Izmir, September 9, 1928."

Nos. 636, 652, 654 Surcharged in Black (#673) or Red (#674-675)

**1929**

| No. | Description | Unused | Used |
|---|---|---|---|
| 673 | A66 20pa on 1g brt rose | .50 | .25 |
| a. | Inverted surcharge | 3.50 | 3.50 |
| 674 | A68 2½k on 5g lilac gray | 1.00 | .50 |
| a. | Inverted surcharge | 7.50 | 7.50 |
| 675 | A68 6k on 10g deep blue | 6.00 | .75 |
| | *Nos. 673-675 (3)* | 7.50 | 1.50 |
| | Set, never hinged | 40.00 | |

Railroad Bridge over Kizil Irmak — A70

A71

A72

A73

Latin Inscriptions
Without umlaut over first "U" of "CUMHURIYETI"

**1929** **Engr.**

| No. | Description | Unused | Used |
|---|---|---|---|
| 676 | A70 2k gray black | 5.00 | 1.00 |
| 677 | A70 2½k green | 3.00 | 1.00 |
| 678 | A70 3k violet brown | 4.00 | 1.50 |
| 679 | A71 6k dark violet | 25.00 | 1.00 |
| 680 | A72 12½k deep blue | 35.00 | 3.75 |
| 681 | A73 50k carmine & blk | 60.00 | 8.75 |
| | *Nos. 676-681 (6)* | 132.00 | 17.00 |
| | Set, never hinged | 400.00 | |

See Nos. 682-691, 694-695, 697, 699. For surcharges & overprints see #705-714, 716-717, 719, 721, 727, 765-766, 770-771, 777, C2, C7.

Sakarya Gorge — A74

Mustafa Kemal Pasha — A75

With umlaut over first "U" of "CUMHURIYETI"

**1930**

| No. | Description | Unused | Used |
|---|---|---|---|
| 682 | A71 10pa green | .25 | .25 |
| 683 | A70 20pa gray violet | .25 | .25 |
| 684 | A70 1k olive green | .50 | .50 |
| 685 | A71 1½k olive black | .50 | .40 |
| 686 | A70 2k dull violet | 3.00 | .50 |
| 687 | A70 2½k deep green | 2.00 | .50 |
| 688 | A70 3k brown orange | 20.00 | 1.50 |
| 689 | A71 4k deep rose | 7.50 | .50 |
| 690 | A72 5k rose lake | 11.50 | .50 |
| 691 | A71 6k indigo | 7.50 | .50 |
| 692 | A74 7½k red brown | .25 | .25 |
| 694 | A72 12½k deep ultra | .75 | .25 |
| 695 | A72 15k deep orange | .75 | .50 |
| 696 | A74 17½k dark gray | .75 | .50 |
| 697 | A72 20k black brown | 50.00 | 2.00 |
| 698 | A74 25k olive brown | 1.00 | 1.00 |
| 699 | A72 30k yellow brown | 1.75 | 1.00 |
| 700 | A74 40k red violet | 1.50 | 1.00 |
| 701 | A75 50k red & black | 3.50 | 1.25 |
| 702 | A75 100k olive grn & blk | 3.50 | 1.25 |
| 703 | A75 200k dk green & blk | 3.75 | 1.50 |
| 704 | A75 500k chocolate & blk | 17.50 | 22.50 |
| | *Nos. 682-704 (22)* | 138.00 | 38.40 |
| | Set, never hinged | 400.00 | |

For surcharges and overprints see Nos. 715, 718, 720, 722-726, 767-769, 772-773, 775-776, 778-780, 823-828, 848-850, C1, C3-C6, C8-C11.

Nos. 682-704 Surcharged in Red or Black:

Sivas
D. Y.
30 ag. 930
1 K.
a

D. Y. Sivas
30 ag. 930
10 P.
b

Sivas
D. Y.
30 ag. 930
40 K.
c

**1930, Aug. 30**

| No. | Description | Unused | Used |
|---|---|---|---|
| 705 | A71(a) 10pa on 10pa (R) | .50 | 1.25 |
| 706 | A70(b) 10pa on 20pa | .50 | 1.50 |
| 707 | A70(b) 20pa on 1ku | 1.00 | 1.25 |
| 708 | A71(a) 1k on 1½k (R) | .50 | 1.25 |
| 709 | A70(b) 1½k on 2k | 1.00 | 1.50 |
| 710 | A70(b) 2k on 2½k (R) | 2.50 | 2.00 |
| 711 | A70(b) 2½k on 3k | 2.00 | 1.50 |
| 712 | A71(a) 3k on 4k | 2.00 | 1.00 |
| 713 | A72(a) 4k on 5k | 2.50 | 4.00 |
| 714 | A71(a) 5k on 6k (R) | 3.50 | 4.00 |
| 715 | A74(a) 6k on 7½k | .75 | .50 |
| 716 | A72(a) 7½k on 12½k (R) | 1.25 | 1.00 |
| 717 | A72(a) 12½k on 15k | 1.25 | 4.00 |
| 718 | A74(b) 15k on 17½k (R) | 5.00 | 4.00 |
| 719 | A72(b) 17½k on 20k (R) | 5.00 | 2.00 |
| 720 | A74(b) 20k on 25k (R) | 7.50 | 2.50 |
| 721 | A72(b) 25k on 30k | 5.00 | 2.50 |
| 722 | A74(b) 30k on 40k | 7.50 | 7.50 |
| 723 | A75(c) 40k on 50k | 15.00 | 7.50 |
| 724 | A75(c) 50k on 100k (R) | 70.00 | 16.00 |
| 725 | A75(c) 100k on 200k (R) | 85.00 | 27.50 |
| 726 | A75(c) 250k on 500k (R) | 75.00 | 35.00 |
| | *Nos. 705-726 (22)* | 294.25 | 129.25 |
| | Set, never hinged | 800.00 | |

Inauguration of the railroad between Ankara and Sivas.

There are numerous varieties in these settings as: "309," "390," "930" inverted, no period after "D," no period after "Y" and raised period before "Y."

No. 685 Surcharged in Red

**1931, Apr. 1**

| No. | Description | Unused | Used |
|---|---|---|---|
| 727 | A71 1k on 1½k olive blk | .60 | .20 |

Olive Tree with Roots Extending to All Balkan Capitals — A76

**1931, Oct. 20** **Engr.** ***Perf. 12***

| No. | Description | Unused | Used |
|---|---|---|---|
| 728 | A76 2½k dark green | .40 | .20 |
| 729 | A76 4k carmine | .50 | .20 |
| 730 | A76 6k steel blue | .50 | .20 |
| 731 | A76 7½k dull red | .50 | .20 |
| 732 | A76 12k deep orange | 1.00 | .25 |
| 733 | A76 12½k dark blue | 1.00 | .25 |
| 734 | A76 30k dark violet | 1.75 | 1.50 |
| 735 | A76 50k dark brown | 3.00 | .75 |
| 736 | A76 100k brown violet | 6.25 | 1.50 |
| | *Nos. 728-736 (9)* | 14.90 | 5.05 |
| | Set, never hinged | 20.00 | |

Second Balkan Conference.

A77

A78

Mustafa Kemal Pasha (Kemal Atatürk) — A79

**1931-42** **Typo.** ***Perf. 11½, 12***

| No. | Description | Unused | Used |
|---|---|---|---|
| 737 | A77 10pa blue green | .20 | .20 |
| 738 | A77 20pa deep orange | .20 | .20 |
| 739 | A77 30pa brt violet ('38) | .25 | .20 |
| 740 | A78 1k dk slate green | .20 | .20 |
| 740A | A77 1½k magenta ('42) | .55 | .20 |
| 741 | A78 2k dark violet | .50 | .20 |
| 741A | A78 2k yel grn ('40) | .25 | .25 |
| 742 | A77 2½k green | .50 | .20 |
| 743 | A78 3k brn org ('38) | 1.50 | .20 |
| 744 | A78 4k slate | 2.50 | .20 |
| 745 | A78 5k rose red | .25 | .25 |
| 745A | A78 5k brown blk ('40) | 2.00 | .50 |
| 746 | A78 6k deep blue | 3.00 | .20 |
| 746A | A78 6k rose ('40) | .80 | .30 |
| 747 | A77 7½k deep rose ('32) | .25 | .20 |
| 747A | A78 8k brt blue ('38) | 3.50 | .20 |
| b. | 8k dark blue ('36) | 3.50 | .20 |
| 748 | A77 10k black brn ('32) | .60 | .20 |
| 748A | A77 10k deep blue ('40) | 7.00 | .60 |
| 749 | A77 12k bister ('32) | .40 | .20 |
| 750 | A79 12½k indigo ('32) | .40 | .20 |
| 751 | A77 15k org yel ('32) | .40 | .20 |
| 752 | A77 20k olive grn ('32) | .40 | .20 |
| 753 | A77 25k Prus blue ('32) | 2.00 | .25 |
| 754 | A77 30k magenta ('32) | 7.50 | .50 |
| 755 | A79 100k maroon ('32) | 200.00 | 5.50 |
| 756 | A79 200k purple ('32) | 3.75 | 2.00 |
| 757 | A79 250k chocolate ('32) | 100.00 | 11.50 |
| | *Nos. 737-757 (27)* | 338.90 | 25.05 |
| | Set, never hinged | 750.00 | |

See Nos. 1015-1033, 1117B-1126. For overprints see Nos. 811-816.

Symbolizing 10th Anniversary of Republic — A80

President Atatürk — A81

**1933, Oct. 29** ***Perf. 10***

| No. | Description | Unused | Used |
|---|---|---|---|
| 758 | A80 1½k blue green | 1.25 | 1.00 |
| 759 | A80 2k olive brown | 1.25 | 1.00 |
| 760 | A81 3k red brown | 1.25 | 1.00 |
| 761 | A81 6k deep blue | 1.25 | 1.00 |
| 762 | A80 12½k dark blue | 3.25 | 2.50 |
| 763 | A80 25k dark brown | 8.00 | 5.00 |
| 764 | A81 50k orange brown | 20.00 | 15.00 |
| | *Nos. 758-764 (7)* | 36.25 | 26.50 |
| | Set, never hinged | 55.00 | |

10th year of the Turkish Republic. The stamps were in use for three days only.

Nos. 682, 685, 692, 694, 696-698, 702 Overprinted or Surcharged in Red:

**1934, Aug. 26** ***Perf. 12***

| No. | Description | Unused | Used |
|---|---|---|---|
| 765 | A71 10pa green | .50 | 1.00 |
| 766 | A71 1k on 1½k | 1.00 | .75 |
| 767 | A74 2k on 25k | 1.50 | 1.25 |
| 768 | A74 5k on 7½k | 5.00 | 5.00 |
| 769 | A74 6k on 17½k | 2.50 | 2.00 |
| 770 | A72 12½k deep ultra | 7.50 | 5.00 |
| 771 | A72 15k on 20k | 50.00 | 45.00 |
| 772 | A74 20k on 25k | 35.00 | 37.50 |
| 773 | A75 50k on 100k | 40.00 | 37.50 |
| | *Nos. 765-773 (9)* | 143.00 | 135.00 |
| | Set, never hinged | 600.00 | |

Izmir Fair, 1934.

Nos. 696, 698, 701-704 Surcharged in Black

**1936, Oct. 26**

| No. | Description | Unused | Used |
|---|---|---|---|
| 775 | A74 4k on 17½k | 1.00 | .50 |
| 776 | A74 5k on 25k | 1.00 | .50 |
| 777 | A73 6k on 50k | 1.00 | .50 |
| 778 | A75 10k on 100k | 1.75 | 1.00 |
| 779 | A75 20k on 200k | 5.50 | 2.00 |
| 780 | A75 50k on 500k | 10.00 | 3.25 |
| | *Nos. 775-780 (6)* | 20.25 | 7.75 |
| | Set, never hinged | 67.50 | |

**"1926" in Overprint**

| No. | Description | Unused | Used |
|---|---|---|---|
| 775a | A74 4k on 17½k | 6.50 | 3.75 |
| 776a | A74 5k on 25k | 7.00 | 3.75 |
| 777a | A73 6k on 50k | 7.00 | 3.75 |
| 778a | A75 10k on 100k | 9.00 | 4.50 |
| 779a | A75 20k on 200k | 20.00 | 10.00 |
| 780a | A75 50k on 500k | 55.00 | 27.50 |
| | *Nos. 775a-780a (6)* | 104.50 | 53.25 |
| | Set, never hinged | 250.00 | |

Re-militarization of the Dardanelles.

Hittite Bronze Stag — A82

Thorak's Bust of Kemal Atatürk — A83

**1937, Sept. 20** **Litho.** ***Perf. 12***

| No. | Description | Unused | Used |
|---|---|---|---|
| 781 | A82 3k light violet | 1.75 | 1.25 |
| 782 | A83 6k blue | 3.00 | 2.00 |
| 783 | A82 7½k bright pink | 4.75 | 3.75 |
| 784 | A83 12½k indigo | 10.00 | 7.50 |
| | *Nos. 781-784 (4)* | 19.50 | 14.50 |
| | Set, never hinged | 32.50 | |

2nd Turkish Historical Congress, Istanbul, Sept. 20-30.

Arms of Turkey, Greece, Romania and Yugoslavia — A84

**1937, Oct. 29** ***Perf. 11½***

| No. | Description | Unused | Used |
|---|---|---|---|
| 785 | A84 8k carmine | 6.75 | 3.50 |
| 786 | A84 12½k dark blue | 15.00 | 4.75 |

The Balkan Entente.

Street in Izmir A85

Fig Tree — A87

30pa, View of Fair Buildings. 3k, Tower, Government Square. 5k, Olive branch. 6k, Woman with grapes. 7½k, Woman picking grapes. 8k, Izmir Harbor through arch. 12k, Statue of Pres. Ataturk. 12½k, Pres. Ataturk.

**1938, Aug. 20 Photo. *Perf. 11½***
**Inscribed: "Izmir Enternasyonal Fuari 1938"**

**789** A85 10pa dark brown .50 .60
**790** A85 30pa purple .75 .50
**791** A87 2½k brt green 1.25 1.00
**792** A87 3k brown orange 1.25 .50
**793** A87 5k olive green 2.25 .75
**794** A85 6k brown 5.00 .40
**795** A87 7½k scarlet 5.00 2.50
**796** A87 8k brown lake 3.50 1.50
**797** A87 12k rose violet 6.25 3.50
**798** A87 12½k deep blue 10.00 8.50
*Nos. 789-798 (10)* 35.75 19.75
Set, never hinged 70.00

Izmir International Fair.

President Atatürk Teaching Reformed Turkish Alphabet A95

**1938, Nov. 2**

**799** A95 2½k brt green 1.00 .55
**800** A95 3k orange 1.00 .55
**801** A95 6k rose violet 1.10 .65
**802** A95 7½k deep rose 1.10 1.00
**803** A95 8k red brown 1.40 1.10
**804** A95 12½k brt ultra 2.00 1.25
*Nos. 799-804 (6)* 7.60 5.10
Set, never hinged 18.00

Reform of the Turkish alphabet, 10th anniv.

Army and Air Force A96

Atatürk Driving Tractor — A98

3k, View of Kayseri. 7½k, Railway bridge. 8k, Scout buglers. 12½k, President Ataturk.

**1938, Oct. 29**
**Inscribed: "Cumhuriyetin 15 inc yil donumu hatirasi"**

**805** A96 2½k dark green .45 .35
**806** A96 3k red brown .45 .35
**807** A98 6k bister .75 .35
**808** A96 7½k red 1.25 .90
**809** A96 8k rose violet 4.00 2.50
**810** A98 12½k deep blue 2.25 1.75
*Nos. 805-810 (6)* 9.15 6.20
Set, never hinged 20.00

15th anniversary of the Republic.

Stamps of 1931-38 Overprinted in Black

**1938, Nov. 21 *Perf. 11½x12***

**811** A78 3k brown orange .50 .35
**812** A78 5k rose red .50 .35
**813** A78 6k deep blue .75 .50
**814** A77 7½k deep rose .80 .55
**815** A78 8k dark blue 2.00 .75
*a.* 8k bright blue 225.00 150.00
**816** A79 12½k indigo 3.75 1.75
*Nos. 811-816 (6)* 8.30 4.25
Set, never hinged 15.00

President Kemal Atatürk (1881-1938). The date is that of his funeral.

**Catalogue values for unused stamps in this section, from this point to the end of the section, are for Never Hinged items.**

Turkish and American Flags — A102

Presidents Inönü and F. D. Roosevelt and Map of North America A103

Designs: 3k, 8k, Inonu and Roosevelt. 7½k, 12½k, Kemal Ataturk and Washington.

**1939, July 15 Photo. *Perf. 14***

**817** A102 2½k ol grn, red & bl .25 .20
**818** A103 3k dk brn & bl grn .50 .20
**819** A102 6k purple, red & bl .50 .20
**820** A103 7½k org ver & bl grn 1.00 .40
**821** A103 8k dp cl & bl grn .75 .40
**822** A103 12½k brt bl & bl grn 2.00 .85
*Nos. 817-822 (6)* 5.00 2.25

US constitution, 150th anniversary.

Nos. 698, 702-704 Surcharged in Black

**1939, July 23 Unwmk. *Perf. 13***

**823** A74 3k on 25k .40 .25
**824** A75 6k on 200k .65 .50
**825** A74 7½k on 25k .75 .50
**826** A75 12k on 100k 1.00 .50
**827** A75 12½k on 200k 2.00 .50
**828** A75 17½k on 500k 3.00 1.00
*Nos. 823-828 (6)* 7.80 3.25

Annexation of Hatay.

Railroad Bridge A105

Locomotive A106

Track Through Mountain Pass A107

Design: 12½k, Railroad tunnel, Atma Pass.

**1939, Oct. 20 Typo. *Perf. 11½***

**829** A105 3k lt orange red 3.25 3.25
**830** A106 6k chestnut 3.75 3.75
**831** A107 7½k rose pink 5.25 5.25
**832** A107 12½k dark blue 8.75 8.75
*Nos. 829-832 (4)* 21.00 21.00

Completion of the Sivas to Erzerum link of the Ankara-Erzerum Railroad.

Atatürk Residence in Ankara — A109

Kemal Atatürk — A110

A111

Designs: 5k, 6k, 7½k, 8k, 12½k, 17½k, Various portraits of Ataturk, "1880-1938."

**1939-40 Photo.**

**833** A109 2½k brt green 1.00 .50
**834** A110 3k dk blue gray 1.00 .50
**835** A110 5k chocolate 1.25 .75
**836** A110 6k chestnut 1.25 .75
**837** A110 7½k rose red 3.75 1.00
**838** A110 8k gray green 1.75 1.00
**839** A110 12½k brt blue 2.00 1.50
**840** A110 17½k brt rose 6.50 2.00
*Nos. 833-840 (8)* 18.50 8.00

**Souvenir Sheet**

**841** A111 100k blue black 70.00 100.00

Death of Kemal Ataturk, first anniversary. Size of No. 841: 90x120mm.
Issued: 2½k, 6k, 12½k, 11/11/39; others, 1/3/40.

Namik Kemal A118

Arms of Turkey, Greece, Romania and Yugoslavia A119

**1940, Jan. 3**

**842** A118 6k chestnut 1.25 .60
**843** A118 8k dk olive grn 3.00 1.50
**844** A118 12k brt rose red 3.50 2.00
**845** A118 12½k brt blue 7.50 3.00
*Nos. 842-845 (4)* 15.25 7.10

Birth cent. of Namik Kemal, poet and patriot.

***Perf. 11½***
**1940, Jan. 1 Typo. Unwmk.**

**846** A119 8k light blue 3.00 1.00
**847** A119 10k deep blue 5.50 1.00

The Balkan Entente.

Nos. 703-704 Surcharged in Red or Black

**1940, Aug. 20 *Perf. 12***

**848** A75 6k on 200k dk grn & blk (R) .50 1.00
**849** A75 10k on 200k dk grn & blk .75 1.50
**850** A75 12k on 500k choc & blk 1.25 2.50
*Nos. 848-850 (3)* 2.50 5.00

13th International Izmir Fair.

Map of Turkey and Census Figures A120

**1940, Oct. 1 Typo. *Perf. 11½***

**851** A120 10pa dark blue green .25 .25
**852** A120 3k orange 1.25 1.25
**853** A120 6k carmine rose 1.50 1.50
**854** A120 10k dark blue 2.50 2.50
*Nos. 851-854 (4)* 5.50 5.50

Census of Oct. 20, 1940.

Runner — A121

Pole Vaulter — A122

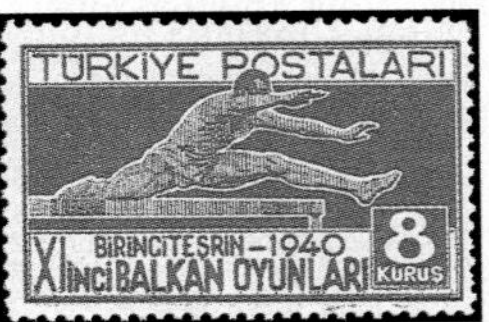

Hurdler A123

Discus Thrower — A124

**1940, Oct. 5**

**855** A121 3k olive green 2.50 2.50
**856** A122 6k rose 7.50 3.50
**857** A123 8k chestnut brown 3.50 4.00
**858** A124 10k dark blue 5.50 10.00
*Nos. 855-858 (4)* 19.00 20.00

11th Balkan Olympics.

Mail Carriers on Horseback A125

Postman of 1840 and 1940 — A126

Old Sailing Vessel and Modern Mailboat — A127

Design: 12k, Post Office, Istanbul.

**1940, Dec. 31 Typo. *Perf. 10***

**859** A125 3k gray green .50 .50
**860** A126 6k rose .75 .75
**861** A127 10k dark blue 1.00 1.00
**862** A127 12k olive brown 1.50 1.50
*Nos. 859-862 (4)* 3.75 3.75

Centenary of the Turkish post.

Harbor Scene A129

Statue of Atatürk — A132

Designs: 3k, 6k, 17½k, Various Izmir Fair buildings. 12k, Girl picking grapes.

**1941, Aug. 20 Litho. *Perf. 11½***
**Inscribed: "Izmir Enternasyonal Fuari 1941"**

**863** A129 30pa dull green .20 .20
**864** A129 3k olive gray .20 .20
**865** A129 6k salmon rose .20 .20
**866** A129 10k blue .30 .30
**867** A129 12k dull brown vio .45 .45
**868** A129 17½k dull brown 1.25 1.25
*Nos. 863-868 (6)* 2.60 2.60

Izmir International Fair, 1941.

Tomb of Barbarossa II — A135

Barbarossa II (Khair ed-Din) — A137

Barbarossa's Fleet in Battle — A136

**1941**

**869** A135 20pa dark violet .20 .20
**870** A136 3k light blue .75 .75
**871** A136 6k rose red 1.25 1.25
**872** A136 10k deep ultra 1.50 1.50
**873** A136 12k dull brn & bis 1.75 1.75
**874** A137 17½k multicolored 2.25 2.25
*Nos. 869-874 (6)* 7.70 7.70

400th death anniv. of Barbarossa II.

President Inönü
A138 A138a

**1942-45 *Perf. 11½x11, 11***

**875** A138 0.25k yellow bis .20 .20
**876** A138 0.50k lt yellow grn .20 .20
**877** A138 1k gray green .20 .20
**877A** A138 1½k brt vio ('45) .20 .20
**878** A138 2k bluish green .30 .20
**879** A138 4k fawn .30 .30
**880** A138 4½k slate .30 .30
**881** A138 5k light blue .35 .20
**882** A138 6k salmon rose .30 .20
**883** A138 6¾k ultra .20 .20
**884** A138 9k blue violet .80 .20
**885** A138 10k dark blue .30 .20
**886** A138 13½k brt pink .30 .20
**887** A138 16k Prus green .50 .20
**888** A138 17½k rose lake .30 .20
**889** A138 20k brown violet .50 .50
**890** A138 27½k orange .50 .50
**891** A138 37k buff .50 .50
**892** A138 50k purple 1.60 .25
**893** A138 100k olive bister 5.00 3.00
**894** A138a 200k brown 17.50 2.50
*Nos. 875-894 (21)* 30.35 10.45

Ankara — A139

Antioch — A141

0.50k, Mohair goats. 1½k, Ankara Dam. 2k, Oranges. 4k, Merino sheep. 4½k, Train. 5k, Tile decorating. 6k, Atatürk statue, Ankara. 6¾k, 10k, Pres. Ismet Inonu. 13½k, Grand National Assembly. 16k, Arnavutkoy, Istanbul. 17½k, Republic monument, Istanbul. 20k, Safety monument, Ankara. 27½k, Post Office, Istanbul. 37k, Monument at Afyon. 50k, "People's House," Ankara. 100k, Atatürk & Inonu. 200k, Pres. Inonu.

**1943, Apr. 1 *Perf. 11***

**896** A139 0.25k citron .20 .20
**897** A139 0.50k brt green .40 .20
**898** A141 1k yellow olive .20 .20
**899** A141 1½k deep violet .20 .20
**900** A139 2k brt blue green .40 .20
**901** A139 4k copper red 2.00 .50
**902** A139 4½k black 2.00 .20
**903** A141 5k sapphire 1.25 .50
**904** A139 6k carmine rose .20 .20
**905** A139 6¾k brt ultra .20 .20
**906** A139 10k dark blue .20 .20
**907** A141 13½k brt red violet .30 .20
**908** A141 16k myrtle green 3.50 .20
**909** A139 17½k brown orange 1.00 .20
**910** A139 20k sepia 1.25 .20
**911** A139 27½k dk orange 1.50 1.00
**912** A139 37k lt yellow brn 1.25 .40
**913** A141 50k purple 10.00 .20
**914** A139 100k dk olive grn 12.50 2.50
**915** A139 200k dark brown 9.00 2.00
*a.* Souvenir sheet 70.00 100.00
*Nos. 896-915 (20)* 47.55 9.70

No. 915a contains one stamp similar to No. 915, perf. 13½ and printed in sepia. Issued Apr. 20.

For surcharge see No. 928.

Girl with Grapes — A158

Entrance to Izmir Fair A159

Fair Building A160

**1943, Aug. 20 Litho. *Perf. 11½***

**916** A158 4½k dull olive .25 .25
**917** A159 6k carmine rose .25 .25
**918** A160 6¾k blue .25 .25
**919** A159 10k dark blue .50 .25
**920** A158 13½k sepia 1.00 1.00
**921** A160 27½k dull gray 1.50 1.75
*Nos. 916-921 (6)* 3.75 3.75

Izmir International Fair.

Soccer Team on Parade A161

Turkish Flag and Soldier — A162

Designs: 6¾k, Bridge. 10k, Hospital. 13½k, View of Ankara. 27½k, President Inonu.

**1943, Oct. 29 *Perf. 11x11½, 11½x11***
**Inscribed: "Cumhuriyetin 20 nci Yildonomu Hatirasi"**

**922** A161 4½k lt olive grn 1.50 1.75
**923** A162 6k rose red .25 .20
**924** A161 6¾k ultra .25 .20
**925** A161 10k violet blue .25 .20
**926** A161 13½k olive .50 .20
**927** A162 27½k lt brown .50 .75
*Nos. 922-927 (6)* 3.25 3.30

Republic, 20th anniv. Nos. 922-927 exist imperf.

No. 905 Surcharged with New Value in Red

**1945 *Perf. 11***

**928** A139 4½k on 6¾k brt ultra .50 .20

Recording Census Data — A167

President Ismet Inönü — A169

**1945, Oct. 21 Litho. *Perf. 11½***

**929** A167 4½k olive black .55 .20
**930** A167 9k violet .60 .20
**931** A167 10k violet blue .60 .20
**932** A167 18k dark red 1.25 .50
*Nos. 929-932 (4)* 3.00 1.10

**Souvenir Sheet**
***Imperf***

**933** A167 1 l chocolate 75.00 100.00

Census of 1945.

***Perf. 11½ to 12½***

**1946, Apr. 1 Unwmk.**

**934** A169 0.25k brown red .20 .20
**935** A169 1k dk slate grn .20 .20
**936** A169 1½k plum .50 .20
**937** A169 9k purple 1.00 .20
**938** A169 10k deep blue 1.50 .20
**939** A169 50k chocolate 5.00 .20
*Nos. 934-939 (6)* 8.40 1.20

U.S.S. Missouri A170

**1946, Apr. 5 *Perf. 11½***

**940** A170 9k dark purple .25 .20
**941** A170 10k dk chalky blue .25 .20
**942** A170 27½k olive green 1.00 2.00
*a.* Imperf., pair 25.00
*Nos. 940-942 (3)* 1.50 2.40

Visit of the USS Missouri to Istanbul, 4/5.

Sower A171

Dove and Flag-Decorated Banderol A172

**1946, June 16 *Perf. 11½ to 12½***

**943** A171 9k violet .25 .20
**944** A171 10k dark blue .40 .20
**945** A171 18k olive green .65 1.00
**946** A171 27½k red orange 1.25 2.50
*Nos. 943-946 (4)* 2.55 3.90

Passing of legislation to distribute state lands to poor farmers.

**1947, Aug. 20 Photo. *Perf. 12***

**947** A172 15k violet & dk bl .40 .25
**948** A172 20k blue & dk blue 1.00 .50
**949** A172 30k brown & gray blk .40 .25
**950** A172 1 l ol grn & dk grn .50 .50
*Nos. 947-950 (4)* 2.30 1.50

Izmir International Fair.

Victory Monument, Afyon Karahisar A173

Ismet Inönü as General A174

Kemal Atatürk as General — A175

**1947, Aug. 30**

**951** A173 10k dk brn & pale brn .50 .30
**952** A174 15k brt violet & gray .35 .20
**953** A175 20k dp blue & gray .55 .20
**954** A173 30k grnsh blk & gray 1.00 .30

**955** A174 60k ol gray & pale brn 1.50 .65
**956** A175 1 l dk green & gray 2.50 1.25
*Nos. 951-956 (6)* 6.40 2.90

25th anniv. of the Battle of Dumlupinar, Aug. 30, 1922.

Grapes and Istanbul Skyline A176

**1947, Sept. 22**

**957** A176 15k rose violet .25 .25
**958** A176 20k deep blue .50 .50
**959** A176 60k dark brown .75 .75
*Nos. 957-959 (3)* 1.50 1.50

International Vintners' Congress, Istanbul.

Approaching Train, Istanbul Skyline and Sirkeci Terminus — A177

**1947, Oct. 9**

**960** A177 15k rose violet .40 .25
**961** A177 20k brt blue .60 .20
**962** A177 60k olive green 1.50 1.25
*Nos. 960-962 (3)* 2.50 1.70

International Railroad Congress, Istanbul.

President Ismet Inönü
A178 A179

**1948 Unwmk. Engr.** ***Perf. 12, 14***

**963** A178 0.25k dark red .20 .20
**964** A178 1k olive black .20 .20
**965** A178 2k brt rose lilac .20 .20
**966** A178 3k red orange .20 .20
**967** A178 4k dark green .20 .20
**968** A178 5k blue .20 .20
**969** A178 10k chocolate .20 .20
**970** A178 12k deep red 1.00 .30
**971** A178 15k violet .20 .20
**972** A178 20k deep blue .30 .20
**973** A178 30k brown 1.50 .30
**974** A178 60k black 4.00 .50
**975** A179 1 l olive green 8.00 .50
**976** A179 2 l dark brown 30.00 5.00
**977** A179 5 l deep plum 17.50 27.50
*Nos. 963-977 (15)* 63.90 35.90

For overprints see Nos. O13-O42.

President Ismet Inönü and Lausanne Conference — A180

Conference Building A180a

**1948, July 23 Photo.** ***Perf. 11½***

**978** A180 15k rose lilac .70 .70
**979** A180a 20k blue .90 .90
**980** A180a 40k gray green 1.10 1.10
**981** A180 1 l brown 1.75 1.75
*Nos. 978-981 (4)* 4.45 4.45

25th anniversary of Lausanne Treaty.

Statue of Kemal Atatürk, Ankara — A181

**1948, Oct. 29**

**982** A181 15k violet .40 .40
**983** A181 20k blue .50 .50
**984** A181 40k gray green 1.10 1.10
**985** A181 1 l brown 2.25 2.25
*Nos. 982-985 (4)* 4.25 4.25

25th anniv. of the proclamation of the republic.

A182 A183

A184

Wrestlers A185

**1949, June 3**

**986** A182 15k rose lilac 2.00 .50
**987** A183 20k blue 2.50 1.00
**988** A184 30k brown 2.50 .50
**989** A185 60k green 3.50 3.00
*Nos. 986-989 (4)* 10.50 5.00

5th European Wrestling Championships, Istanbul, June 3-5, 1949.

Ancient Galley A186

Galleon Mahmudiye A187

Monument to Khizr Barbarossa A188

Designs: 15k, Cruiser Hamidiye. 20k, Submarine Sakarya. 30k, Cruiser Yavuz.

**1949, July 1**

**990** A186 5k violet .75 .50
**991** A187 10k brown .75 .50
**992** A186 15k lilac rose .75 .50
**993** A186 20k gray blue 1.75 .90
**994** A186 30k gray 1.00 .50
**995** A188 40k olive gray 3.50 1.75
*Nos. 990-995 (6)* 8.50 4.65

Fleet Day, July 1, 1949.

A189

UPU Monument, Bern A190

***Perf. 11½***

**1949, Oct. 9 Unwmk. Photo.**

**996** A189 15k violet .50 .25
**997** A189 20k blue .50 .25
**998** A190 30k dull rose .50 .25
**999** A190 40k green 1.00 .50
*Nos. 996-999 (4)* 2.50 1.25

UPU, 75th anniversary.

Istanbul Fair Building A191

**1949, Oct. 1 Litho.** ***Perf. 10***

**1000** A191 15k brown .50 .25
**1001** A191 20k blue .50 .25
**1002** A191 30k olive .60 .50
*Nos. 1000-1002 (3)* 1.60 1.00

Istanbul Fair, Oct. 1-31.

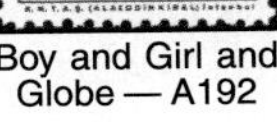

Boy and Girl and Globe — A192

Aged Woman Casting Ballot — A193

Kemal Atatürk and Map A194

**1950, Aug. 13** ***Perf. 11½***

**1003** A192 15k purple .20 .20
**1004** A192 20k deep blue .30 .30

2nd World Youth Council Meeting, 1950. No. 1004 exists imperf. Value $3.

**1950, Aug. 30**

**1005** A193 15k dark brown .25 .25
**1006** A193 20k dark blue .25 .25
**1007** A194 30k dk blue & gray .50 .50
*Nos. 1005-1007 (3)* 1.00 1.00

Election of May 14, 1950.

Hazel Nuts — A195

Symbolical of 1950 Census — A196

Designs: 12k, Acorns. 15k, Cotton. 20k, Symbolical of the fair. 30k, Tobacco.

**1950, Sept. 9**

**1008** A195 8k gray grn & buff .50 .50
**1009** A195 12k magenta 1.00 1.00
**1010** A195 15k brn blk & lt brn .50 .50
**1011** A195 20k dk blue & aqua 1.50 1.50
**1012** A195 30k brn blk & dull org 1.50 1.50
*Nos. 1008-1012 (5)* 5.00 5.00

Izmir International Fair, Aug. 20-Sept. 20.

**1950, Oct. 9 Litho.** ***Perf. 11½***

**1013** A196 15k dark brown .20 .20
**1014** A196 20k violet blue .30 .20

General census of 1950.

Atatürk Types of 1931-42

***Perf. 10x11½, 11½x12***

**1950-51 Typo.**

**1015** A77 10p dull red brn .20 .20
**1016** A77 10p vermilion ('51) .35 .50
**1017** A77 20p blue green 1.00 .25
**1018** A78 1k olive green .25 .20
**1019** A78 2k plum .25 .20
**1020** A78 2k dp yellow ('51) .75 .30
**1021** A78 3k yellow orange .55 .20
**1022** A78 3k gray ('51) .75 .20
**1023** A78 4k green ('51) .75 .20
**1024** A78 5k blue .50 .20
**1025** A78 5k plum ('51) 3.50 .30
**1026** A77 10k brown orange 1.50 .20
**1027** A77 15k purple 1.25 .20
**1028** A77 15k brown carmine 12.00 .25
**1029** A77 20k dark blue 20.00 .25
**1030** A77 30k pink ('51) 17.00 .50
**1031** A79 100k red brown ('51) 2.50 .50
**1032** A79 200k dark brown 10.00 1.00
**1033** A79 200k rose violet ('51) 10.00 1.50
*Nos. 1015-1033 (19)* 83.10 7.15

16th Century Flight of Hezarfen Ahmet Celebi — A197

Plane over Istanbul A198

40k, Biplane over Taurus Mountains.

**1950, Oct. 17 Litho.** ***Perf. 11***

**1034** A197 20k dk green & blue .35 .35
**1035** A197 40k dk brown & blue .55 .55
**1036** A198 60k purple & blue .90 .90
*Nos. 1034-1036 (3)* 1.80 1.80

Regional meeting of the ICAO, Istanbul, Oct. 17.

Farabi
A199

**1950, Dec. 1 Unwmk. *Perf. 11½***
**Multicolored Center**

| No. | Type | Value | Color | Unused | Used |
|---|---|---|---|---|---|
| **1037** | A199 | 15k | blue | .50 | .50 |
| **1038** | A199 | 20k | blue violet | .50 | .50 |
| **1039** | A199 | 60k | red brown | 3.00 | 2.00 |
| **1040** | A199 | 1 l | gold & bl vio | 3.50 | 3.00 |
| | | | *Nos. 1037-1040 (4)* | 7.50 | 6.00 |

Death millenary of Farabi, Arab philosopher.

Mithat Pasha and Security Bank Building — A200

Design: 20k, Agricultural Bank.

**1950, Dec. 21 Photo.**

| No. | Type | Value | Color | Unused | Used |
|---|---|---|---|---|---|
| **1041** | A200 | 15k | rose violet | 1.00 | 1.00 |
| **1042** | A200 | 20k | blue | 1.00 | 1.00 |

3rd Congress of Turkish Cooperatives, Istanbul, Dec. 25, 1950.

Floating a Ship
A201

Lighthouse — A202

**1951, July 1**

| No. | Type | Value | Description | Unused | Used |
|---|---|---|---|---|---|
| **1043** | A201 | 15k | shown | .50 | .50 |
| **1044** | A201 | 20k | Steamship | .50 | .50 |
| **1045** | A201 | 30k | Diver rising | 1.00 | 1.00 |
| **1046** | A202 | 1 l | shown | 2.00 | 2.00 |
| | | | *Nos. 1043-1046 (4)* | 4.00 | 4.00 |

25th anniv. of the recognition of coastal rights in Turkish waters to ships under the Turkish flag.

Mosque of Sultan Ahmed
A203

Henry Carton de Wiart — A204

Designs: 20k, Dolma Bahce Palace. 60k, Rumeli Hisari Fortress.

**1951, Aug. 31 Photo. *Perf. 13½***

| No. | Type | Value | Color | Unused | Used |
|---|---|---|---|---|---|
| **1047** | A203 | 15k | dark green | .25 | .25 |
| **1048** | A203 | 20k | deep ultra | .30 | .30 |
| **1049** | A204 | 30k | brown | .35 | .35 |
| **1050** | A203 | 60k | purple brown | 1.75 | 1.75 |
| | | | *Nos. 1047-1050 (4)* | 2.65 | 2.65 |

40th Interparliamentary Conf., Istanbul.

Allegory of Food and Agriculture
A205

Designs: 20k, Dam. 30k, United Nations Building. 60k, University, Ankara.

**1952, Jan. 3 Unwmk. *Perf. 14***
**Inscribed: "Akdeniz Yetistirme Merkezi. Ankara 1951."**

| No. | Type | Value | Color | Unused | Used |
|---|---|---|---|---|---|
| **1051** | A205 | 15k | green | .50 | .50 |
| **1052** | A205 | 20k | blue violet | .60 | .60 |
| **1053** | A205 | 30k | blue | 1.50 | 1.50 |
| **1054** | A205 | 60k | red | 2.50 | 2.50 |
| *a.* | | | Souvenir sheet of 4 | 75.00 | 75.00 |
| | | | *Nos. 1051-1054 (4)* | 5.10 | 5.10 |

UN Mediterranean Economic Instruction Center.

No. 1054a contains one each of Nos. 1051-1054, imperf., with inscriptions in dark blue gray.

Abdulhak Hamid Tarhan, Poet, Birth Cent. — A206

**1952, Feb. 5 Photo. *Perf. 13½***

| No. | Type | Value | Color | Unused | Used |
|---|---|---|---|---|---|
| **1055** | A206 | 15k | dark purple | .50 | .50 |
| **1056** | A206 | 20k | dark blue | .50 | .50 |
| **1057** | A206 | 30k | brown | .50 | .50 |
| **1058** | A206 | 60k | dark olive grn | 1.75 | 1.75 |
| | | | *Nos. 1055-1058 (4)* | 3.25 | 3.25 |

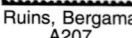

Ruins, Bergama
A207

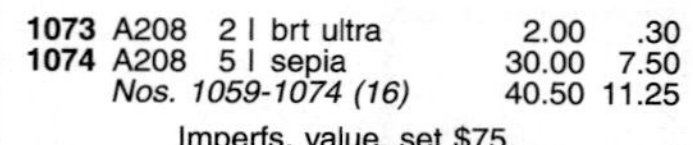


Rumeli Hisari Fortress
A215

Tarsus Cataract
A208

Designs: 2k, Ruins, Milas. 3k, Karatay Gate, Konya. 4k, Kozak plateau. 5k, Urgup. 10k, 12k, 15k, 20k, Kemal Ataturk. 30k, Mosque, Bursa. 40k, Mosque, Istanbul. 75k, Rocks, Urgup. 1 l, Palace, Istanbul. 2 l, Pavilion, Istanbul. 5 l, Museum interior, Istanbul.

**1952, Mar. 15 *Perf. 13½***

| No. | Type | Value | Color | Unused | Used |
|---|---|---|---|---|---|
| **1059** | A207 | 1k | brown orange | .20 | .20 |
| **1060** | A207 | 2k | olive green | .20 | .20 |
| **1061** | A207 | 3k | rose brown | .20 | .20 |
| **1062** | A207 | 4k | blue green | .50 | .50 |
| **1063** | A207 | 5k | brown | .20 | .20 |
| **1064** | A207 | 10k | dark brown | .20 | .20 |
| **1065** | A207 | 12k | brt rose car | .50 | .50 |
| **1066** | A207 | 15k | purple | .25 | .20 |
| **1067** | A207 | 20k | chalky blue | .75 | .20 |
| **1068** | A207 | 30k | grnsh gray | .50 | .20 |
| **1069** | A207 | 40k | slate blue | 3.50 | .20 |
| **1070** | A208 | 50k | olive | .50 | .20 |
| **1071** | A208 | 75k | slate | .50 | .25 |
| **1072** | A208 | 1 l | deep purple | .50 | .20 |
| **1073** | A208 | 2 l | brt ultra | 2.00 | .30 |
| **1074** | A208 | 5 l | sepia | 30.00 | 7.50 |
| | | | *Nos. 1059-1074 (16)* | 40.50 | 11.25 |

Imperfs, value, set $75.

For surcharge & overprint see #1075, 1255.

No. 1059 Surcharged with New Value in Black

**1952, June 1**

| No. | Type | Value | Color | Unused | Used |
|---|---|---|---|---|---|
| **1075** | A207 | 0.50k on 1k | brn org | .25 | .20 |

Technical Faculty Building
A209

**1952, Aug. 20 *Perf. 12x12½***

| No. | Type | Value | Color | Unused | Used |
|---|---|---|---|---|---|
| **1076** | A209 | 15k | violet | .50 | .50 |
| **1077** | A209 | 20k | blue | .75 | .75 |
| **1078** | A209 | 60k | brown | 1.25 | 1.25 |
| | | | *Nos. 1076-1078 (3)* | 2.50 | 2.50 |

8th Intl. Congress of Theoretic and Applied Mechanics.

Turkish Soldier — A210

Pigeons Bandaging Wounded Hand — A212

20k, Soldier with Turkish flag. 30k, Soldier & child with comic book. 60k, Raising Turkish flag.

**1952, Sept. 25 *Perf. 14***

| No. | Type | Value | Color | Unused | Used |
|---|---|---|---|---|---|
| **1079** | A210 | 15k | Prus blue | .30 | .30 |
| **1080** | A210 | 20k | deep blue | .40 | .40 |
| **1081** | A210 | 30k | brown | .60 | .60 |
| **1082** | A210 | 60k | olive blk & car | 1.25 | 1.25 |
| | | | *Nos. 1079-1082 (4)* | 2.55 | 2.55 |

Turkey's participation in the Korean war.

**1952, Oct. 29 *Perf. 12½x12***

20k, Flag, rainbow and ruined homes.

**Dated "1877-1952"**

| No. | Type | Value | Color | Unused | Used |
|---|---|---|---|---|---|
| **1085** | A212 | 15k | dk green & red | .55 | .25 |
| **1086** | A212 | 20k | blue & red | 1.25 | .45 |

Turkish Red Crescent Society, 75th anniv.

Relief From Panel of Aziziye Monument — A213

Aziziye Monument
A214

Design: 40k, View of Erzerum.

**1952, Nov. 9 *Perf. 11***

| No. | Type | Value | Color | Unused | Used |
|---|---|---|---|---|---|
| **1087** | A213 | 15k | purple | .30 | .30 |
| **1088** | A214 | 20k | blue | .50 | .50 |
| **1089** | A214 | 40k | olive gray | .70 | .70 |
| | | | *Nos. 1087-1089 (3)* | 1.50 | 1.50 |

75th anniv. of the Battle of Aziziye at Erzerum.

Troops Entering Constan-tinople — A216

Sultan Mohammed II — A217

Designs: 8k, Soldiers moving cannon. 10k, Mohammed II riding into sea, and Turkish armada. 12k, Landing of Turkish army. 15k, Ancient wall, Constantinople. 30k, Mosque of Faith. 40k, Presenting mace to Patriarch Yenadios. 60k, Map of Constantinople, c. 1574. 1 l, Tomb of Mohammed II. 2.50 l, Portrait of Mohammed II.

**1953, May 29 Photo. *Perf. 11½***
**Inscribed: "Istanbulun Fethi 1453-1953"**

| No. | Type | Value | Color | Unused | Used |
|---|---|---|---|---|---|
| **1090** | A215 | 5k | brt blue | 1.00 | .50 |
| **1091** | A215 | 8k | gray | 1.50 | .50 |
| **1092** | A215 | 10k | blue | .50 | .50 |
| **1093** | A215 | 12k | rose lilac | 1.00 | .50 |
| **1094** | A215 | 15k | brown | .75 | .25 |
| **1095** | A216 | 20k | vermilion | 1.00 | .25 |
| **1096** | A216 | 30k | dull green | 2.00 | 1.00 |
| **1097** | A215 | 40k | violet blue | 3.50 | 1.25 |
| **1098** | A215 | 60k | chocolate | 2.50 | 1.25 |
| **1099** | A215 | 1 l | blue green | 6.00 | 1.75 |

***Perf. 12***

| No. | Type | Value | Color | Unused | Used |
|---|---|---|---|---|---|
| **1100** | A217 | 2 l | multi | 12.50 | 5.00 |
| **1101** | A217 | 2.50 l | multi | 7.50 | 7.50 |
| *a.* | | | Souvenir sheet | 150.00 | 75.00 |
| | | | *Nos. 1090-1101 (12)* | 39.75 | 20.25 |

Conquest of Constantinople by Sultan Mohammed II, 500th anniv.

Ruins of the Odeon, Ephesus
A218

15k, Church of St. John the Apostle. 20k, Shrine of Virgin Mary, Panaya Kapulu. 40k, Ruins of the Double Church. 60k, Shrine of the Seven Sleepers. 1 l, Restored house of the Virgin Mary.

**1953, Aug. 16 Litho. *Perf. 13½***
**Multicolored Center**

| No. | Type | Value | Color | Unused | Used |
|---|---|---|---|---|---|
| **1102** | A218 | 12k | sage green | .25 | .25 |
| **1103** | A218 | 15k | lilac | .20 | .20 |
| **1104** | A218 | 20k | dk slate blue | .25 | .25 |
| **1105** | A218 | 40k | light green | .55 | .55 |
| **1106** | A218 | 60k | violet blue | .75 | .75 |
| **1107** | A218 | 1 l | brown red | 2.25 | 2.25 |
| | | | *Nos. 1102-1107 (6)* | 4.25 | 4.25 |

Pres. Celal Bayar, Mithat Pasha. Herman Schulze-Delitzsch and People's Bank — A219

Design: 20k, Pres. Bayar, Mithat Pasha and University of Ankara.

**1953, Sept. 2 Photo. *Perf. 10½***

| No. | Type | Value | Color | Unused | Used |
|---|---|---|---|---|---|
| **1108** | A219 | 15k | orange brown | .50 | .50 |
| **1109** | A219 | 20k | Prus green | .50 | .50 |

5th Intl. People's Circuit Congress, Istanbul, Sept.

Combined Harvester
A220

Kemal Atatürk — A221

Designs: 15k, Berdan dam. 20k, Military parade. 30k, Diesel train. 35k, Yesilkoy airport.

**1953, Oct. 29** *Perf. 14*

**1110** A220 10k olive bister .20 .20
**1111** A220 15k dark gray .20 .20
**1112** A220 20k rose red .35 .35
**1113** A220 30k olive green .75 .75
**1114** A220 35k dull blue .35 .35
**1115** A221 55k dull purple 1.10 1.10
*Nos. 1110-1115 (6)* 2.95 2.95

Turkish Republic, 30th anniv.

Kemal Atatürk and Mausoleum at Ankara — A222

**1953, Nov. 10**

**1116** A222 15k gray black .30 .25
**1117** A222 20k violet brown .60 .40

15th death anniv. of Kemal Ataturk.

Type of 1931-42
Without umlaut over first "U" of "CUMHURIYETI"

***Perf. 11½x12, 10x11½***

**1953-56** **Typo.** **Unwmk.**

**1117B** A77 20p yellow .30 .20
**1118** A78 1k brown orange .30 .20
**1119** A78 2k rose pink ('53) .25 .20
**1120** A78 3k yellow brn ('53) .25 .20
**1120A** A78 4k slate ('56) 1.50 .40
**1121** A78 5k blue 2.00 .20
**1121A** A78 8k violet ('56) .25 .20
**1122** A77 10k dark olive ('53) .25 .20
**1123** A77 12k brt car rose ('53) .25 .20
**1124** A77 15k fawn .60 .20
**1125** A77 20k rose lilac 3.50 .40
**1126** A77 30k lt blue grn ('54) 1.25 .20
*Nos. 1117B-1126 (12)* 10.70 2.80

Compass and Map
A223

Designs: 20k, Globe, crescent and stars. 40k, Tree symbolical of 14 NATO members.

**1954, Apr. 4** **Photo.** *Perf. 14*

**1127** A223 15k brown 1.50 1.10
**1128** A223 20k violet blue 2.00 1.50
**1129** A223 40k dark green 14.00 12.00
*Nos. 1127-1129 (3)* 17.50 14.60

NATO, 5th anniv.

Industry, Engineering and Agriculture — A224

Justice and Council of Europe Flag — A225

**1954, Aug. 8** **Litho.** *Perf. 10½*

**1130** A224 10k brown 2.75 2.00
**1131** A225 15k dark green 2.50 1.00
**1132** A225 20k blue 2.75 1.00
**1133** A224 30k brt violet 12.00 8.50
*Nos. 1130-1133 (4)* 20.00 12.50

Council of Europe, 5th anniv.

Flag Signals to Plane — A226

Amaury de La Grange and Plane
A227

Design: 45k, Kemal Ataturk and air fleet.

**1954, Sept. 20** *Perf. 12½*

**1134** A226 20k black brown .20 .20
**1135** A227 35k dull violet .25 .20
**1136** A227 45k deep blue .45 .30
*Nos. 1134-1136 (3)* .90 .70

47th Congress of the Intl. Aeronautical Federation, Istanbul, 1954.

Souvenir Sheet

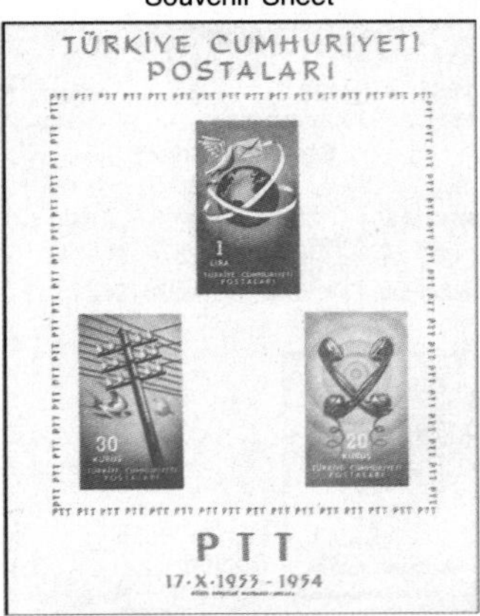

A228

**1954, Oct. 18** *Imperf.*

**1137** A228 Sheet of 3 12.50 5.50
*a.* 20k aquamarine .65 .65
*b.* 30k violet blue .65 .65
*c.* 1 l red violet 1.40 1.40

First anniv. of Law of Oct. 17, 1953, reorganizing the Department of Post, Telephone and Telegraph.

Ziya Gokalp
A229

Kemal Atatürk
A230

**1954, Oct. 25** *Perf. 11*

**1138** A229 15k rose lilac .25 .20
**1139** A229 20k dark green .35 .20
**1140** A229 30k crimson .60 .35
*Nos. 1138-1140 (3)* 1.20 .75

30th death anniv. of Ziya Gokalp, author and historian.

**1955, Mar. 1** *Perf. 12½*

**1141** A230 15k carmine rose .20 .20
**1142** A230 20k blue .20 .20
**1143** A230 40k dark gray .30 .20
**1144** A230 50k blue green .55 .20
**1145** A230 75k orange brown .65 .20
*Nos. 1141-1145 (5)* 1.90 1.00

Relief Map of Dardanelles — A231

Artillery Loaders — A232

30k, Minelayer Nusrat. 60k, Col. Kemal Atatürk.

**1955, Mar. 18** *Perf. 10½*

**1146** A231 15k green .20 .20
**1147** A232 20k orange brown .20 .20
**1148** A231 30k ultra .25 .20
**1149** A232 60k olive gray .80 .40
*Nos. 1146-1149 (4)* 1.45 1.00

Battle of Gallipoli, 40th anniversary.

Aerial Map
A233

**1955, Apr. 14** *Perf. 11*

**1150** A233 15k gray .20 .20
**1151** A233 20k aquamarine .20 .20
**1152** A233 50k brown .35 .20
**1153** A233 1 l purple .80 .30
*Nos. 1150-1153 (4)* 1.55 .90

City Planning Congress, Ankara, 1955.

Carnation — A234

**1955, May 19** **Litho.** *Perf. 10*

**1154** A234 10k shown .50 .50
**1155** A234 15k Tulip .50 .50
**1156** A234 20k Rose .75 .50
**1157** A234 50k Lily 1.75 1.00
*Nos. 1154-1157 (4)* 3.50 2.50

National Flower Show, Istanbul, May 20-Aug. 20.

Battle First Aid Station
A235

30k, Gulhane Military Hospital, Ankara.

**1955, Aug. 28** **Unwmk.** *Perf. 12*

**1158** A235 20k red, lake & gray .25 .20
**1159** A235 30k dp grn & yel grn .50 .20

XVIII Intl. Congress of Military Medicine, Aug. 8-Sept. 1, Istanbul.

Soccer Game
A236

Emblem and Soccer Ball — A237

1 l, Emblem with oak & olive branches.

**1955, Aug. 30** *Perf. 10*

**1160** A236 15k light ultra .50 .20
**1161** A237 20k crimson rose .60 .20
**1162** A236 1 l light green 1.25 .75
*Nos. 1160-1162 (3)* 2.35 1.15

Intl. Military Soccer Championship games, Istanbul, Aug. 30.

Sureté Monument, Ankara
A238

20k, Dolma Bahce Palace. 30k, Police College, Ankara. 45k, Police Martyrs' Monument, Istanbul.

**1955, Sept. 5** *Perf. 10*
**Inscribed: "Enterpol Istanbul 1955"**

**1163** A238 15k blue green .25 .25
**1164** A238 20k brt violet .35 .35
**1165** A238 30k gray black .40 .30
**1166** A238 45k lt brown .80 .50
*Nos. 1163-1166 (4)* 1.80 1.40

24th general assembly of the Intl. Criminal Police, Istanbul, Sept. 5-9.

Early Telegraph Transmitter
A239

Modern Transmitter A240

***Perf. 13½x14, 14x13½***

**1955, Sept. 10** **Photo.**

**1167** A239 15k olive .20 .20
**1168** A240 20k crimson rose .20 .20
**1169** A239 45k fawn .40 .20
**1170** A240 60k ultra .40 .40
*Nos. 1167-1170 (4)* 1.20 1.00

Centenary of telecommunication.

Academy of Science, Istanbul A241

Designs: 20k, University. 60k, Hilton Hotel. 1 l, Kiz Kulesi (Leander's Tower).

**1955, Sept. 12** ***Perf. 13½x14***

**1171** A241 15k yellow orange .25 .25
**1172** A241 20k crimson rose .25 .25
**1173** A241 60k purple .35 .25
**1174** A241 1 l deep blue .65 .45
*Nos. 1171-1174 (4)* 1.50 1.20

10th meeting of the governors of the Intl. Bank of Reconstruction and Development and the Intl. Monetary Fund, Istanbul, Sept. 12-16.

Surlari, Istanbul A242

Mosque of Sultan Ahmed — A243

Congress Emblem — A244

Designs: 30k, Haghia Sophia. 75k, Map of Constantinople, by Christoforo Buondelmonti, 1422.

**1955, Sept. 15** **Litho.** ***Perf. 11½***

**1175** A242 15k grnsh blk & Prus grn .35 .20
**1176** A243 20k vermilion & org .25 .20
**1177** A242 30k sepia & vio brn .25 .20
**1178** A243 75k ultramarine .70 .50
*Nos. 1175-1178 (4)* 1.55 1.10

10th Intl. Congress of Byzantine Research, Istanbul, Sept. 15-21, 1955.

**1955, Sept. 26** ***Perf. 10½x11***

30k, Chalet in Istanbul. 55k, Bridges.

**Inscribed: "Beynelmiel X. Vol Kongresi Istanbul 1955"**

**1179** A244 20k red violet .20 .20
**1180** A244 30k dk grn & yel grn .20 .20
**1181** A244 55k dp bl & brt bl .75 .40
*Nos. 1179-1181 (3)* 1.15 .80

10th International Transportation Congress.

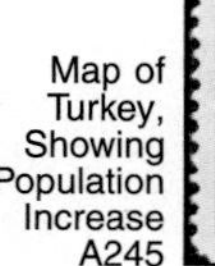

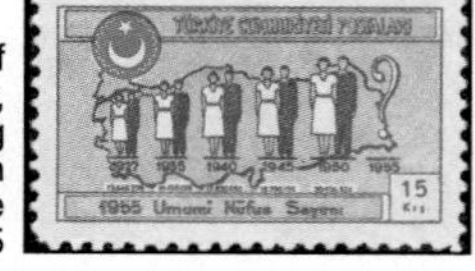


Map of Turkey, Showing Population Increase A245

**1955, Oct. 22** **Unwmk.** ***Perf. 10***

**Map in Rose**

**1182** A245 15k lt & dk gray & red .35 .25
**1183** A245 20k lt & dk vio & red .25 .25
**1184** A245 30k lt & dk ultra & red .30 .25
**1185** A245 60k lt & dk bl grn & red .70 .30
*Nos. 1182-1185 (4)* 1.60 1.05

Census of 1955.

Waterfall, Antalya — A246

Alanya and Seljukide Dockyards A247

Designs: 30k, Theater at Aspendos. 45k, Ruins at Side. 50k, View of Antalya. 65k, St. Nicholas Church at Myra (Demre) and St. Nicholas.

***Perf. 14x13½, 13½x14***

**1955, Dec. 10** **Photo.** **Unwmk.**

**1186** A246 18k bl, ol grn & ultra .25 .25
**1187** A247 20k blue, ultra & brn .25 .25
**1188** A247 30k dl grn, ol bis & grn .25 .25
**1189** A246 45k yel grn & brn 2.25 1.00
**1190** A246 50k Prus grn & ol bis .40 .30
**1191** A247 65k orange ver & blk .50 .40
*Nos. 1186-1191 (6)* 3.90 2.45

Kemal Atatürk — A248

**1955-56** **Litho.** ***Perf. 12½***

**1192** A248 0.50k carmine .20 .20
**1193** A248 1k yellow orange .20 .20
**1194** A248 2k brt blue .20 .20
**1195** A248 3k scarlet .20 .20
**1196** A248 5k lt brown .20 .20
**1197** A248 6k lt blue grn .20 .20
**1198** A248 10k blue green .20 .20
**1199** A248 18k rose violet .20 .20
**1200** A248 20k lt violet bl .25 .20
**1201** A248 25k olive green .30 .20
**1202** A248 30k violet .35 .20
**1203** A248 40k fawn .45 .20
**1204** A248 75k slate blue 1.25 .20
*Nos. 1192-1204 (13)* 4.20 2.60

Issue dates: 3k, 1955. Others, 1956.

Tomb at Nigde — A249

Zubeyde Hanum — A250

**1956, Apr. 12** ***Perf. 10½***

**1205** A249 40k violet bl & bl .20 .20

25th anniv. of the Turkish History Society. The tomb of Hüdavent Hatun, a sultan's daughter, exemplifies Seljukian architecture of the 14th century.

**1956, May 13** ***Perf. 11***

**1206** A250 20k pale brn & dk brn .25 .25

***Imperf***

**1207** A250 20k lt grn & dk grn .75 1.50

Mother's Day; Zubeyde Hanum, mother of Kemal Ataturk.

Shah and Queen of Iran A251

**1956, May 15** **Unwmk.** ***Perf. 11***

**1208** A251 100k grn & pale grn 1.00 1.00

***Imperf***

**1209** A251 100k red & pale grn 7.00 5.00

Visit of the Shah and Queen of Iran to Turkey, May 15.

Erenkoy Sanitarium A252

**1956, July 31** ***Perf. 11***

**1210** A252 50k dk bl grn & pink .40 .20

Anti-Tuberculosis work among PTT employees.

Symbol of Izmir Fair — A253

A254

**1956, Aug. 20** ***Perf. 11***

**1211** A253 45k brt green .20 .20

**Souvenir Sheet**

***Imperf***

**1212** A254 Sheet of 2 3.00 3.00
***a.*** 50k rose red .75 .40
***b.*** 50k bright ultramarine .75 .40

25th Intl. Fair, Izmir, 8/20-9/20. See #C28.

Hands Holding Bottled Serpent — A255

**1956, Sept. 10** **Litho.** ***Perf. 10½***

**1213** A255 25k multicolored .30 .30
***a.*** Tete beche pair 1.25

25th Intl. Anti-Alcoholism Congress, Istanbul Sept. 10-15.

Printed both in regular sheets and in sheets with alternate vertical rows inverted.

Medical Center at Kayseri — A256

Sariyar Dam — A257

**1956, Nov. 1** ***Perf. 12½x12***

**1214** A256 60k violet & yel .20 .20

750th anniv. of the first medical school and clinic in Anatolia.

**1956, Dec. 2** **Litho.** ***Perf. 10½***

**1215** A257 20k vermilion .20 .20
**1216** A257 20k bright blue .20 .20

Inauguration of Sariyar Dam.

Freestyle Wrestling A258

Mehmet Akif Ersoy — A259

Design: 65k, Greco-Roman wrestling.

**1956, Dec. 8** **Unwmk.** ***Perf. 10½***

**1217** A258 40k brt yel grn & brn .50 .35
**1218** A258 65k lt bluish gray & dp car .50 .35

16th Olympic Games, Melbourne, Nov. 22-Dec. 8, 1956.

**1956, Dec. 26**

**1219** A259 20k brn & brt yel grn .25 .20
**1220** A259 20k rose car & lt gray .25 .20
**1221** A259 20k vio bl & brt pink .25 .20
*Nos. 1219-1221 (3)* .75 .60

20th death anniv. of Mehmet Akif Ersoy, author of the Turkish National Anthem.

Each value bears a different verse of the anthem.

Theater in Troy — A260

Trojan Vase — A261

Design: 30k, Trojan Horse.

***Perf. 13½x14, 14x13½***

**1956, Dec. 31** **Photo.** **Unwmk.**

**1222** A260 15k green 1.00 .60
**1223** A261 20k red violet 1.00 .60
**1224** A260 30k chestnut 1.50 .60
*Nos. 1222-1224 (3)* 3.50 1.80

Excavations at Troy.

Mobile Chest X-Ray Unit A262

Kemal Atatürk — A263

**1957, Jan. 1 Litho. *Perf. 12***
**1225** A262 25k ol brn & red .20 .20

Fight against tuberculsois.

**1956-57 *Perf. 12½***
**1226** A263 ½k blue green .20 .20
**1227** A263 1k yellow orange .20 .20
**1228** A263 3k gray olive .20 .20
**1229** A263 5k violet .20 .20
**1230** A263 6k rose car ('57) .35 .20
**1231** A263 10k rose violet .20 .20
**1232** A263 12k fawn ('57) .30 .20
**1233** A263 15k lt violet bl .20 .20
**1234** A263 18k carmine ('57) .30 .20
**1235** A263 20k lt brown .20 .20
**1236** A263 25k lt blue green .20 .20
**1237** A263 30k slate blue .20 .20
**1238** A263 40k olive ('57) .40 .20
**1239** A263 50k orange .35 .20
**1240** A263 60k brt blue ('57) .50 .20
**1241** A263 70k Prus green ('57) 1.75 .25
**1242** A263 75k brown 1.00 .25
*Nos. 1226-1242 (17)* 6.75 3.50

Pres. Heuss of Germany — A264

**1957, May 5 Unwmk. *Perf. 10½***
**1243** A264 40k yellow & brown .20 .20

Visit of Pres. Theodor Heuss of Germany to Turkey, May 5. See No. C29.

View of Bergama and Ruin A265

40k, Dancers in kermis at Bergama.

**1957, May 24**
**1244** A265 30k brown .20 .20
**1245** A265 40k green .25 .20

20th anniv. of the kermis at Bergama (Pergamus).

Symbols of Industry and Flags A266

**1957, July 1 Photo. *Perf. 13½x14***
**1246** A266 25k violet .20 .20
**1247** A266 40k gray blue .20 .20

Turkish-American collaboration, 10th anniv.

Osman Hamdi Bey A267

Hittite Sun Course from Alaça Höyük — A268

**1957, July 6 *Perf. 10½***
**1248** A267 20k beige, pale brn & blk .30 .20
**1249** A268 30k Prussian green .35 .20

75th anniv. of the Academy of Art. The 20k exists with "cancellation" omitted.

King of Afghanistan — A269

**1957, Sept. 1 Litho. *Perf. 10½***
**1250** A269 45k car lake & pink .20 .20

Visit of Mohammed Zahir Shah, King of Afghanistan, to Turkey. See No. C30.

Medical Center, Amasya A270

Design: 65k, Suleiman Medical Center.

**1957, Sept. 29 Unwmk. *Perf. 10½***
**1251** A270 25k vermilion & yellow .20 .20
**1252** A270 65k brt grnsh bl & citron .30 .20

11th general meeting of the World Medical Assoc.

Mosque of Suleiman A271

Architect Mimar Koca Sinan (1489-1587) A272

**1957, Oct. 18 *Perf. 11***
**1253** A271 20k gray green .20 .20
**1254** A272 100k brown .30 .25

400th anniv. of the opening of the Mosque of Suleiman, Istanbul.

No. 1073 Surcharged with New Value and "ISTANBUL Filatelik n. Sergisi 1957"

**1957, Nov. 11 Photo. *Perf. 13½***
**1255** A208 50k on 2 l brt ultra .25 .20

1957 Istanbul Philatelic Exhibition.

Forestation Map of Turkey — A273

25k, Forest & hand planting tree, vert.

**1957, Nov. 18 Litho. *Perf. 10½***
**1256** A273 20k green & brown .20 .20
**1257** A273 25k emerald & bl grn .20 .20

Centenary of forestry in Turkey.

Nos. 1256-1257 each come with two different tabs attached (four tabs in all) bearing various quotations.

A274

A275

**1957, Nov. 23**
**1258** A274 50k pink, vio, red & yel .50 .25

400th death anniv. of Fuzuli (Mehmet Suleiman Ogiou), poet.

**1957, Nov. 28 Photo. *Perf. 14x13½***
**1259** A275 65k dk Prus blue .20 .20
**1260** A275 65k rose violet .20 .20

Benjamin Franklin (1706-1790).

Green Dome, Tomb of Mevlana, at Konya — A276

Mevlana — A278

Konya Museum A277

***Perf. 11x10½, 10½x11***
**1957, Dec. 17 Litho. Unwmk.**
**1261** A276 50k green, bl & vio .20 .20
**1262** A277 100k dark blue .30 .20

**Miniature Sheet**
***Imperf***
**1263** A278 100k multicolored 1.25 1.00

Jalal-udin Mevlana (1207-1273), Persian poet and founder of the Mevlevie dervish order. No. 1263 contains one stamp 32x42mm.

Kemal Atatürk (Double Frame; Serifs) — A279

**1957 Unwmk. *Perf. 11½***
**Size: 18x22mm**
**1264** A279 ½k lt brown .20 .20
**1265** A279 1k lt violet bl .20 .20
**1266** A279 2k black violet .20 .20
**1267** A279 3k orange .20 .20
**1268** A279 5k blue green .20 .20
**1269** A279 6k dk slate grn .20 .20
**1270** A279 10k violet .20 .20
**1271** A279 12k brt green .20 .20
**1272** A279 15k dk blue grn .20 .20
**1273** A279 18k rose carmine .20 .20
**1274** A279 20k brown .20 .20
**1275** A279 25k brown red .20 .20
**1276** A279 30k brt blue .20 .20
**1277** A279 40k slate blue .20 .20
**1278** A279 50k yellow orange .20 .20
**1279** A279 60k black .25 .20
**1280** A279 70k rose violet .25 .20
**1281** A279 75k gray olive .30 .20
**Size: 21x29mm**
**1282** A279 100k carmine .65 .20
**1283** A279 250k olive 1.75 .20
*Nos. 1264-1283 (20)* 6.20 4.00

College Emblem — A280

View of Adana — A281

**1958, Jan. 16 Litho. *Perf. 10½x11***
**1288** A280 20k bister, ind & org .20 .20
**1289** A280 25k dk blue, bis & org .20 .20

"Turkiye" on top of 25k. 75th anniv. of the College of Economics and Commerce, Istanbul.

**1958 Photo. *Perf. 11½***
**Size: 26x20½mm**
**1290** A281 5k Adana .20 .20
**1291** A281 5k Adapazari .20 .20
**1292** A281 5k Adiyaman .20 .20
**1293** A281 5k Afyon .20 .20
**1294** A281 5k Amasya .20 .20
**1295** A281 5k Ankara .20 .20
**1296** A281 5k Antakya .20 .20
**1297** A281 5k Antalya .20 .20
**1298** A281 5k Artvin .20 .20
**1299** A281 5k Aydin .20 .20
**1300** A281 5k Balikesir .20 .20
**1301** A281 5k Bilecik .20 .20
**1302** A281 5k Bingol .20 .20
**1303** A281 5k Bitlis .20 .20
**1304** A281 5k Bolu .20 .20
**1305** A281 5k Burdur .20 .20
**1306** A281 5k Bursa .20 .20
**1307** A281 5k Canakkale .20 .20
**1308** A281 5k Cankiri .20 .20
**1309** A281 5k Corum .20 .20
**1310** A281 5k Denizli .20 .20
**1311** A281 5k Diyarbakir .20 .20
**Size: 32½x22mm**
**1312** A281 20k Adana .20 .20
**1313** A281 20k Adapazari .20 .20
**1314** A281 20k Adiyaman .20 .20
**1315** A281 20k Afyon .20 .20
**1316** A281 20k Amasya .20 .20
**1317** A281 20k Ankara .20 .20
**1318** A281 20k Antakya .20 .20
**1319** A281 20k Antalya .20 .20
**1320** A281 20k Artvin .20 .20
**1321** A281 20k Aydin .20 .20
**1322** A281 20k Balikesir .20 .20
**1323** A281 20k Bilecik .20 .20
**1324** A281 20k Bingol .20 .20
**1325** A281 20k Bitlis .20 .20
**1326** A281 20k Bolu .20 .20
**1327** A281 20k Burdur .20 .20
**1328** A281 20k Bursa .20 .20
**1329** A281 20k Canakkale .20 .20

1330 A281 20k Cankiri .20 .20
1331 A281 20k Corum .20 .20
1332 A281 20k Denizli .20 .20
1333 A281 20k Diyarbakir .20 .20
*Nos. 1290-1333 (44)* 8.80 8.80

**1959**

**Size: 26x20½mm**

1334 A281 5k Edirne .20 .20
1335 A281 5k Elazig .20 .20
1336 A281 5k Erzincan .20 .20
1337 A281 5k Erzurum .20 .20
1338 A281 5k Eskisehir .20 .20
1339 A281 5k Gaziantep .20 .20
1340 A281 5k Giresun .20 .20
1341 A281 5k Gumusane .20 .20
1342 A281 5k Hakkari .20 .20
1343 A281 5k Isparta .20 .20
1344 A281 5k Istanbul .20 .20
1345 A281 5k Izmir .20 .20
1346 A281 5k Izmit .20 .20
1347 A281 5k Karakose .20 .20
1348 A281 5k Kars .20 .20
1349 A281 5k Kastamonu .20 .20
1350 A281 5k Kayseri .20 .20
1351 A281 5k Kirklareli .20 .20
1352 A281 5k Kirsehir .20 .20
1353 A281 5k Konya .20 .20
1354 A281 5k Kutahya .20 .20
1355 A281 5k Malatya .20 .20

**Size: 32½x22mm**

1356 A281 20k Edirne .20 .20
1357 A281 20k Elazig .20 .20
1358 A281 20k Erzincan .20 .20
1359 A281 20k Erzurum .20 .20
1360 A281 20k Eskisehir .20 .20
1361 A281 20k Gaziantep .20 .20
1362 A281 20k Giresun .20 .20
1363 A281 20k Gumusane .20 .20
1364 A281 20k Hakkari .20 .20
1365 A281 20k Isparta .20 .20
1366 A281 20k Istanbul .20 .20
1367 A281 20k Izmir .20 .20
1368 A281 20k Izmit .20 .20
1369 A281 20k Karakose .20 .20
1370 A281 20k Kars .20 .20
1371 A281 20k Kastamonu .20 .20
1372 A281 20k Kayseri .20 .20
1373 A281 20k Kirklareli .20 .20
1374 A281 20k Kirsehir .20 .20
1375 A281 20k Konya .20 .20
1376 A281 20k Kutahya .20 .20
1377 A281 20k Malatya .20 .20
*Nos. 1334-1377 (44)* 8.80 8.80

**1960**

**Size: 26x20½mm**

1378 A281 5k Manisa .20 .20
1379 A281 5k Maras .20 .20
1380 A281 5k Mardin .20 .20
1381 A281 5k Mersin .20 .20
1382 A281 5k Mugla .20 .20
1383 A281 5k Mus .20 .20
1384 A281 5k Nevsehir .20 .20
1385 A281 5k Nigde .20 .20
1386 A281 5k Ordu .20 .20
1387 A281 5k Rize .20 .20
1388 A281 5k Samsun .20 .20
1389 A281 5k Siirt .20 .20
1390 A281 5k Sinop .20 .20
1391 A281 5k Sivas .20 .20
1392 A281 5k Tekirdag .20 .20
1393 A281 5k Tokat .20 .20
1394 A281 5k Trabzon .20 .20
1395 A281 5k Tunceli .20 .20
1396 A281 5k Urfa .20 .20
1397 A281 5k Usak .20 .20
1398 A281 5k Van .20 .20
1399 A281 5k Yozgat .20 .20
1400 A281 5k Zonguldak .20 .20

**Size: 32½x22mm**

1401 A281 20k Manisa .20 .20
1402 A281 20k Maras .20 .20
1403 A281 20k Mardin .20 .20
1404 A281 20k Mersin .20 .20
1405 A281 20k Mugla .20 .20
1406 A281 20k Mus .20 .20
1407 A281 20k Nevsehir .20 .20
1408 A281 20k Nigde .20 .20
1409 A281 20k Ordu .20 .20
1410 A281 20k Rize .20 .20
1411 A281 20k Samsun .20 .20
1412 A281 20k Siirt .20 .20
1413 A281 20k Sinop .20 .20
1414 A281 20k Sivas .20 .20
1415 A281 20k Tekirdag .20 .20
1416 A281 20k Tokat .20 .20
1417 A281 20k Trabzon .20 .20
1418 A281 20k Tunceli .20 .20
1419 A281 20k Urfa .20 .20
1420 A281 20k Usak .20 .20
1421 A281 20k Van .20 .20
1422 A281 20k Yozgat .20 .20
1423 A281 20k Zonguldak .20 .20
*Nos. 1378-1423 (46)* 9.20 9.20
*Nos. 1290-1423 (134)* 26.80 26.80

Ruins at Pamukkale A282

Designs: 25k, Travertines at Pamukkale.

**1958, May 18 Litho. *Perf. 12***
1424 A282 20k brown .20 .20
1425 A282 25k blue .20 .20

"Industry" A283

Symbolizing New Europe A284

**1958, Oct. 10 Unwmk. *Perf. 10½***
1426 A283 40k slate blue .20 .20

National Industry Exhibition.

**Europa Issue**

**1958, Oct. 10**
1427 A284 25k vio & dull pink *.50* .25
1428 A284 40k brt ultra *.50* .25

Letters A285

**1958, Oct. 5**
1429 A285 20k orange & blk .20 .20

Intl. Letter Writing Week, Oct. 5-11.

Atatürk 20th Anniv. Death — A286

**1958, Nov. 10 *Perf. 12***
1430 25k Flame and mausoleum .20 .20
1431 75k Atatürk .25 .20
*a.* A286 Pair, #1430-1431 .45 .25

20th death anniv. of Kemal Ataturk.

Emblem — A288

**1959, Jan. 10 Litho. *Perf. 10***
1432 A288 25k dk violet & yel .20 .20

25th anniv. of the Agricultural Faculty of Ankara University.

Blackboard and School Emblem — A289

**1959, Jan. 15 *Perf. 10½***
1433 A289 75k black & yellow .20 .20

75th anniv. of the establishment of a secondary boys' school in Istanbul.

State Theater, Ankara A290

Design: 25k, Portrait of Sinasi.

**1959, Mar. 30 Unwmk. *Perf. 10½***
1434 A290 20k red brn & emer .20 .20
1435 A290 25k Prus grn & org .20 .20

Centenary of the Turkish theater; Sinasi, writer of the first Turkish play in 1859.

Globe and Stars A291

**1959, Apr. 4 *Perf. 10***
1436 A291 105k red .20 .20
1437 A291 195k green .40 .25

10th anniversary of NATO.

Aspendos Theater A292

**1959, May 1 Litho. *Perf. 10½***
1438 A292 20k bis brn & vio .20 .20
1439 A292 20k grn & ol bis .20 .20

Aspendos (Belkins) Festival.

No. B70 Surcharged in Ultramarine

**1959, May 5**
1440 SP25 105k on 15k + 5k org .35 .20

Council of Europe, 10th anniversary.

Basketball — A293

**1959, May 21 *Perf. 10***
1441 A293 25k red org & dk bl .25 .25

11th European and Mediterranean Basketball Championship.

"Karadeniz" A294

Telegraph Mast — A295

Kemal Atatürk — A296

Designs: 1k, Turkish Airlines' SES plane. 10k, Grain elevator, Ankara. 15k, Iron and Steel Works, Karabück. 20k, Euphrates Bridge, Birecik. 25k, Zonguldak Harbor. 30k, Gasoline refinery, Batman. 40k, Rumeli Hisari Fortress. 45k, Sugar factory, Konya. 55k, Coal mine, Zonguldak. 75k, Railway. 90k, Crane loading ships. 100k, Cement factory, Ankara. 120k, Highway. 150k, Harvester. 200k, Electric transformer.

***Perf. 10½, 11, 11½, 12½, 13½***

**1959-60 Litho. Unwmk.**
1442 A294 1k indigo .20 .20
1443 A294 5k brt blue ('59) .20 .20
1444 A294 10k blue .20 .20
1445 A294 15k brown .50 .20
1446 A294 20k slate green .20 .20
1447 A294 25k violet .20 .20
1448 A294 30k lilac .30 .25
1449 A294 40k blue .50 .20
1450 A294 45k dull violet .50 .20
1451 A294 55k olive brown .50 .20
1452 A295 60k green .65 .20
1453 A295 75k gray olive 2.50 .20
1454 A295 90k dark blue 5.50 .20
1455 A295 100k gray 7.50 .20
1456 A295 120k magenta 2.50 .25
1457 A294 150k orange 2.50 .30
1458 A295 200k yellow green 3.00 .30
1459 A296 250k black brown 3.00 .40
1460 A296 500k dark blue 5.00 .60
*Nos. 1442-1460 (19)* 35.45 4.70

Postage Due Stamps of 1936 Surcharged

**1959, June 1 *Perf. 11½***
1461 D6 20k on 20pa brown .20 .20
1462 D6 20k on 2k lt blue .20 .20
1463 D6 20k on 3k brt vio .20 .20
1464 D6 20k on 5k Prus bl .20 .20
1465 D6 20k on 12k brt rose .20 .20
*Nos. 1461-1465 (5)* 1.00 1.00

Anchor Emblem — A297

Design: 40k, Sea Horse emblem.

**1959, July 4 *Perf. 11***
1466 A297 30k multicolored .20 .20
1467 A297 40k multicolored .20 .20

50th anniv. of the Merchant Marine College.

11th Century Warrior A298

**1959, Aug. 26 Litho. *Perf. 11***
1468 A298 2½ l rose lil & lt bl .70 .50

Battle of Malazkirt, 888th anniversary.

A299

Ornament — A300

Design: 40k, Mosque.

**1959, Oct. 19 Unwmk. *Perf. 12½***

**1469** A299 30k black & red .20 .20
**1470** A299 40k lt blue, blk & ocher .20 .20
**1471** A300 75k dp blue, yel & red .30 .20
*Nos. 1469-1471 (3)* .70 .60

Turkish Artists Congress, Ankara.

Kemal Atatürk — A301

**Litho.; Center Embossed**

**1959, Nov. 10 *Perf. 14***

**1472** A301 500k dark blue 1.50 .75
*a.* Min. sheet of 1, red, imperf. 2.50 1.75

School of Political Science, Ankara A302

Emblem — A303

Crossed Swords Emblem — A304

**1959, Dec. 4 Photo. *Perf. 13½***

**1473** A302 40k green & brown .20 .20
**1474** A302 40k red brown & bl .20 .20
**1475** A303 1 l lt & dk vio & buff .30 .20
*Nos. 1473-1475 (3)* .70 .60

Political Science School, Ankara, cent.

Inscribed: "Kara Harbokulunum 125 Yili"

Design: 40k, Bayonet and flame.

**1960, Feb. 28 Litho. *Perf. 10½***

**1476** A304 30k vermilion & org .20 .20
**1477** A304 40k brown, car & yel .20 .20

125th anniv. of the Territorial War College.

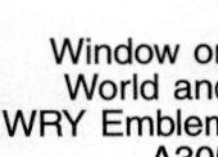

Window on World and WRY Emblem A305

Spring Flower Festival — A306

150k, Symbolic shanties & uprooted oak emblem.

**1960, Apr. 7**

**1478** A305 90k brt grnsh bl & blk .20 .20
**1479** A305 105k yellow & blk .30 .20

World Refugee Year, 7/1/59-6/30/60.

**1960, June 4 Photo. *Perf. 11½***
**Granite Paper**

**1480** A306 30k Carnations .35 .20
**1481** A306 40k Jasmine .40 .20
**1482** A306 75k Rose .60 .20
**1483** A306 105k Tulip .80 .30
*Nos. 1480-1483 (4)* 2.15 .90

Atatürk Square, Nicosia A307

Design: 105k, Map of Cyprus.

**1960, Aug. 16 Litho. *Perf. 10½***

**1484** A307 40k blue & pink .20 .20
**1485** A307 105k blue & yellow .25 .20

Independence of the Republic of Cyprus.

Women and Nest A308

Design: 30k, Globe and emblem.

**1960, Aug. 22 Photo. *Perf. 11½***

**1486** A308 30k lt vio & yel .20 .20
**1487** A308 75k grnsh bl & gray .25 .20

16th meeting of the Women's Intl. Council.

Soccer A309

#1489, Basketball. #1490, Wrestling. #1491, Hurdling. #1492, Steeplechase.

**1960, Aug. 25**

**1488** A309 30k yellow green .40 .40
**1489** A309 30k black .40 .40
**1490** A309 30k slate blue .40 .40
**1491** A309 30k purple .40 .40
**1492** A309 30k brown .40 .40
*a.* Sheet of 25, #1488-1492 17.50 10.00
*Nos. 1488-1492 (5)* 2.00 2.00

17th Olympic Games, Rome, 8/25-9/11.
Printed in sheets of 25 (5x5) with every horizontal and every vertical row containing one of each design. Also printed in normal sheets of 100.

Common Design Types pictured following the introduction.

**Europa Issue, 1960**
Common Design Type

**1960, Sept. 19**
**Size: 33x22mm**

**1493** CD3 75k green & bl grn *.85* .50
**1494** CD3 105k dp bl & lt bl *1.25* .85

Agah Efendi and Front Page of Turcamani Ahval — A310

UN Emblem and Torch — A311

**1960, Oct. 21 Photo. *Perf. 11½***

**1495** A310 40k brown blk & sl .20 .20
**1496** A310 60k brn blk & bis brn .20 .20

Centenary of Turkish journalism.

**1960, Oct. 24 Unwmk.**

Design: 105k, UN headquarters building and UN emblem forming "15," horiz.

**1497** A311 90k brt bl & dk bl .20 .20
**1498** A311 105k lt bl grn & brn .25 .20

15th anniversary of the United Nations.

Army Emblem A312

Tribunal A313

Design: 195k, "Justice," vert.

**1960, Oct. 14 Litho. *Perf. 13***

**1499** A312 40k violet & bister .20 .20
**1500** A313 105k red, gray & brn .25 .20
**1501** A313 195k grn, rose red & brn .45 .20
*Nos. 1499-1501 (3)* .90 .60

Trial of ex-President Celal Bayar and ex-Premier Adnan Menderes.

Revolutionaries and Statue — A314

Prancing Horse, Broken Chain — A315

Designs: 30k, Ataturk and hand holding torch. 105k, Youth, soldier and broken chain.

**1960, Dec. 1 Photo. *Perf. 14½***

**1502** A314 10k gray & blk .20 .20
**1503** A314 30k purple .20 .20
**1504** A315 40k brt red & blk .20 .20
**1505** A314 105k blue blk & red .40 .20
*Nos. 1502-1505 (4)* 1.00 .80

Revolution of May 27, 1960.

Faculty Building A316

Sculptured Head of Atatürk — A317

Designs: 40k, Map of Turkey and sun disk.

**1961, Jan. 9 Litho. *Perf. 13***

**1506** A316 30k slate grn & gray .20 .20
**1507** A316 40k brn blk & bis brn .20 .20
**1508** A317 60k dk green & buff .25 .20
*Nos. 1506-1508 (3)* .65 .60

25th anniv. of the Faculty of Languages, History and Geography, University of Ankara.

Communication and Transportation — A318

40k, Highway construction, telephone & telegraph. 75k, New parliament building, Ankara.

**1961, Apr. 27 Unwmk. *Perf. 13***

**1509** A318 30k dull vio & blk .20 .20
**1510** A318 40k green & black .35 .20
**1511** A318 75k dull blue & blk .45 .20
*Nos. 1509-1511 (3)* 1.00 .60

9th conference of ministers of the Central Treaty Org. (CENTO), Ankara.

Flag and People — A319

Legendary Wolf and Osman Warriors A320

Design: 60k, "Progress" (Atatürk showing youth the way).

**1961, May 27 Litho.**

**1512** A319 30k multicolored .20 .20
**1513** A320 40k sl grn & yel .20 .20
**1514** A319 60k grn, pink & dk red .25 .20
*Nos. 1512-1514 (3)* .65 .60

First anniversary of May 27 revolution.

Rockets A321

Designs: 40k, Crescent and star emblem, "50" and Jet. 75k, Atatürk, eagle and jets, vert.

**1961, June 1**

**1515** A321 30k brn, org yel & blk .20 .20
**1516** A321 40k violet & red .25 .20
**1517** A321 75k slate blk & bis .55 .25
*Nos. 1515-1517 (3)* 1.00 .65

50th anniversary of Turkey's air force.

**Europa Issue, 1961**
Common Design Type

**1961, Sept. 18** *Perf. 13*
**Size: 32x22mm**

| No. | Type | Description | Unused | Used |
|---|---|---|---|---|
| 1518 | CD4 | 30k dk violet bl | *.55* | .35 |
| 1519 | CD4 | 40k gray | *.65* | .35 |
| 1520 | CD4 | 75k vermilion | *1.25* | .60 |
| | | *Nos. 1518-1520 (3)* | 2.45 | 1.30 |

Tulip and Cogwheel A322

Open Book and Olive Branch A324

Torch, Hand and Cogwheel A323

**1961, Oct. 21** **Unwmk.** **Litho.**

| No. | Type | Description | Unused | Used |
|---|---|---|---|---|
| 1521 | A322 | 30k slate, pink & sil | .20 | .20 |
| 1522 | A323 | 75k ultra, org & blk | .35 | .20 |

Technical and professional schools, cent.

**1961, Oct. 29**

| No. | Type | Description | Unused | Used |
|---|---|---|---|---|
| 1523 | A324 | 30k red, blk & olive | .20 | .20 |
| 1524 | A324 | 75k brt blue, blk & grn | .30 | .20 |

Inauguration of the new Parliament.

Kemal Atatürk
A325 A326

**1961-62** **Litho.** *Perf. 10x10½*
**Size: 20x25mm**

| No. | Type | Description | Unused | Used |
|---|---|---|---|---|
| 1525 | A325 | 1k brown org ('62) | .75 | .20 |
| 1526 | A325 | 5k blue | 1.25 | .20 |
| 1527 | A325 | 10k sepia | 2.00 | .20 |
| 1528 | A326 | 10k car rose | 2.00 | .20 |
| 1529 | A325 | 30k dull grn ('62) | 5.75 | .25 |

**Size: 21½x31mm**

| No. | Type | Description | Unused | Used |
|---|---|---|---|---|
| 1530 | A325 | 10 l violet ('62) | 12.00 | 1.50 |
| | | *Nos. 1525-1530 (6)* | 23.75 | 2.55 |

NATO Emblem and Dove — A327

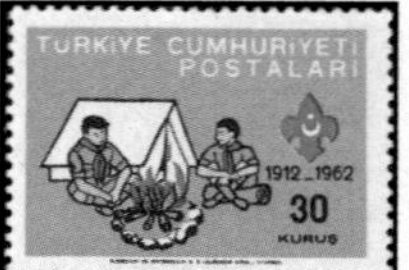
Scouts at Campfire A328

Design: 105k, NATO emblem, horiz.

**1962, Feb. 18** **Unwmk.** *Perf. 13*

| No. | Type | Description | Unused | Used |
|---|---|---|---|---|
| 1545 | A327 | 75k dl bl, blk & sil | .20 | .20 |
| 1546 | A327 | 105k crimson, blk & sil | .30 | .20 |

10th anniv. of Turkey's admission to NATO.

**1962, July 22** **Litho.**

60k, Scouts with flag. 105k, Scouts saluting.

| No. | Type | Description | Unused | Used |
|---|---|---|---|---|
| 1547 | A328 | 30k lt grn, blk & red | .20 | .20 |
| 1548 | A328 | 60k gray, blk & red | .25 | .20 |
| 1549 | A328 | 105k tan, blk & red | .35 | .20 |
| | | *Nos. 1547-1549 (3)* | .80 | .60 |

Turkish Boy Scouts, 50th anniversary.

Soldier Statue — A329

Oxcart from Victory Monument, Ankara A330

Design: 75k, Atatürk.

**1962, Aug. 30** **Unwmk.** *Perf. 13*

| No. | Type | Description | Unused | Used |
|---|---|---|---|---|
| 1550 | A329 | 30k slate green | .20 | .20 |
| 1551 | A330 | 40k gray & sepia | .20 | .20 |
| 1552 | A329 | 75k gray blk & lt gray | .30 | .20 |
| | | *Nos. 1550-1552 (3)* | .70 | .60 |

40th anniv. of Battle of Dumlupinar.

**Europa Issue, 1962**
Common Design Type

**1962, Sept. 17**
**Size: 37x23mm**

| No. | Type | Description | Unused | Used |
|---|---|---|---|---|
| 1553 | CD5 | 75k emerald & blk | *.65* | .40 |
| 1554 | CD5 | 105k red & blk | *.85* | .50 |
| 1555 | CD5 | 195k blue & blk | *1.50* | .65 |
| | | *Nos. 1553-1555 (3)* | 3.00 | 1.55 |

Brown imprint.

Virgin Mary's House, Ephesus A331

20pa Stamp of 1863 A332

40k, Inside view after restoration, horiz. 75k, Outside view, horiz. 105k, Statue of Virgin Mary.

**1962, Dec. 8** **Photo.** *Perf. 13½*

| No. | Type | Description | Unused | Used |
|---|---|---|---|---|
| 1556 | A331 | 30k multicolored | .20 | .20 |
| 1557 | A331 | 40k multicolored | .20 | .20 |
| 1558 | A331 | 75k multicolored | .25 | .20 |
| 1559 | A331 | 105k multicolored | .35 | .20 |
| | | *Nos. 1556-1559 (4)* | 1.00 | .80 |

**1963, Jan. 13** *Perf. 13x13½*

Issue of 1863: 30k, 1pi. 40k, 2pi. 75k, 5pi.

| No. | Type | Description | Unused | Used |
|---|---|---|---|---|
| 1560 | A332 | 10k yellow, brn & blk | .20 | .20 |
| 1561 | A332 | 30k rose, lil & blk | .20 | .20 |
| 1562 | A332 | 40k lt bl, bluish grn & blk | .25 | .20 |
| 1563 | A332 | 75k red brn, rose & blk | .45 | .20 |
| | | *Nos. 1560-1563 (4)* | 1.10 | .80 |

Centenary of Turkish postage stamps. See No. 1601, souvenir sheet.

Starving People A333

Designs: 40k, Sowers. 75k, Hands protecting Wheat Emblem, and globe.

**1963, Mar. 21** **Unwmk.** *Perf. 13*

| No. | Type | Description | Unused | Used |
|---|---|---|---|---|
| 1564 | A333 | 30k dp bl & dk bl | .20 | .20 |
| 1565 | A333 | 40k brn org & brn | .20 | .20 |
| 1566 | A333 | 75k grn & dk grn | .25 | .20 |
| | | *Nos. 1564-1566 (3)* | .65 | .60 |

FAO "Freedom from Hunger" campaign.

Julian's Column, Ankara — A334

Ethnographic Museum A335

10k, Ankara Citadel. 30k, Gazi Institute of Education. 50k, Atatürk's mausoleum. 60k, President's residence. 100k, Ataturk's home, Cankaya. 150k, Parliament building.

**1963** **Litho.** *Perf. 13*

| No. | Type | Description | Unused | Used |
|---|---|---|---|---|
| 1568 | A334 | 1k sl grn & yel grn | .20 | .20 |
| 1569 | A334 | 1k purple | .20 | .20 |
| 1570 | A335 | 5k sepia & buff | .20 | .20 |
| 1571 | A335 | 10k lil rose & pale bl | .40 | .20 |
| 1573 | A335 | 30k black & violet | .90 | .20 |
| 1574 | A335 | 50k blue & yellow | 1.90 | .20 |
| 1575 | A335 | 60k dk blue gray | 2.50 | .40 |
| 1576 | A335 | 100k olive brown | 1.75 | .40 |
| 1577 | A335 | 150k dull green | 8.00 | 1.10 |
| | | *Nos. 1568-1577 (9)* | 16.05 | 3.10 |

Map of Turkey and Atom Symbol A336

Designs: 60k, Symbols of medicine, agriculture, industry and atom. 100k, Emblem of Turkish Atomic Energy Commission.

**1963, May 27** **Unwmk.** *Perf. 13*

| No. | Type | Description | Unused | Used |
|---|---|---|---|---|
| 1584 | A336 | 50k red brn & blk | .20 | .20 |
| 1585 | A336 | 60k grn, dk grn, yel & red | .25 | .20 |
| 1586 | A336 | 100k violet bl & bl | .55 | .30 |
| | | *Nos. 1584-1586 (3)* | 1.00 | .70 |

Turkish nuclear research center, 1st anniv.

Meric Bridge A337

Sultan Murad I — A338

Designs: 10k, Üçserefeli Mosque. 60k, Summerhouse, Edirne Palace.

**1963, June 17**

| No. | Type | Description | Unused | Used |
|---|---|---|---|---|
| 1587 | A338 | 10k dp bl & yel grn | .20 | .20 |
| 1588 | A337 | 30k red org & ultra | .20 | .20 |
| 1589 | A337 | 60k dk bl, red & brn | .20 | .20 |
| 1590 | A338 | 100k multicolored | .65 | .25 |
| | | *Nos. 1587-1590 (4)* | 1.25 | .85 |

600th anniv. of the conquest of Edirne (Adrianople).

Soldier and Rising Sun A339

**1963, June 28**

| No. | Type | Description | Unused | Used |
|---|---|---|---|---|
| 1591 | A339 | 50k red, blk & gray | .20 | .20 |
| 1592 | A339 | 100k red, blk & ol | .30 | .20 |

600th anniversary of the Turkish army.

Plowing A340

Mithat Pasha — A341

Design: 50k, Agriculture Bank, Ankara.

*Perf. 13x13½, 13½x13*
**1963, Aug. 27** **Photo.** **Unwmk.**

| No. | Type | Description | Unused | Used |
|---|---|---|---|---|
| 1593 | A340 | 30k brt yel grn, red brn & grn | .20 | .20 |
| 1594 | A340 | 50k pale vio & Prus bl | .20 | .20 |
| 1595 | A341 | 60k gray & green | .30 | .20 |
| | | *Nos. 1593-1595 (3)* | .70 | .60 |

Centenary of Agriculture Bank, Ankara.

Sports and Exhibition Palace, Istanbul and #5 — A342

Designs: 50k, Sultan Ahmed Mosque & Turkey in Asia #22. 60k, View of Istanbul & Turkey in Asia #87. 100k, Rumeli Hisari Fortress & #679. 130k, Ankara Fortress & #C2.

**1963, Sept. 7** **Litho.** *Perf. 13*

| No. | Type | Description | Unused | Used |
|---|---|---|---|---|
| 1596 | A342 | 10k blk, yel & rose | .20 | .20 |
| a. | | Rose omitted | *37.50* | *37.50* |
| 1597 | A342 | 50k blk, grn & rose lil | .30 | .20 |
| 1598 | A342 | 60k dk brn, dk bl & blk | .35 | .20 |
| 1599 | A342 | 100k dk vio & lil rose | .50 | .20 |
| 1600 | A342 | 130k brn, tan & dp org | .75 | .20 |
| | | *Nos. 1596-1600 (5)* | 2.10 | 1.00 |

"Istanbul 63" Intl. Stamp Exhibition.

Type of 1963 Inscribed: "F.I.P. GÜNÜ"
Souvenir Sheet

Issues of 1863: 10k, 20pa. 50k, 1pi. 60k, 2pi. 130k, 5pi.

**Unwmk.**
**1963, Sept. 13** **Litho.** ***Imperf.***

| No. | Type | Description | Unused | Used |
|---|---|---|---|---|
| 1601 | | Sheet of 4 | 1.50 | 1.25 |
| a. | A332 | 10k yel, brown & blk | .20 | .20 |
| b. | A332 | 50k lilac, pink & blk | .20 | .20 |
| c. | A332 | 60k bluish grn, lt bl & blk | .30 | .20 |
| d. | A332 | 130k red brn, pink & blk | .35 | .20 |

Intl. Philatelic Federation.

**Europa Issue, 1963**
Common Design Type

**1963, Sept. 16**
**Size: 32x24mm**

| No. | Type | Description | Unused | Used |
|---|---|---|---|---|
| 1602 | CD6 | 50k red & black | *.60* | .25 |
| 1603 | CD6 | 130k bl grn, blk & bl | *.80* | .35 |

Atatürk and First Parliament Building A343

Atatürk and: 50k, Turkish flag. 60k, New Parliament building.

**1963, Oct. 29 Photo. Perf. 13½**

1604 A343 30k blk, gold, yel & mar .20 .20
1605 A343 50k dk grn, gold, yel & red .30 .20
1606 A343 60k dk brn, gold & yel .40 .20
*Nos. 1604-1606 (3)* .90 .60

40th anniversary of Turkish Republic.

Atatürk, 25th Death Anniv. — A344

**1963, Nov. 10**

1607 A344 50k red, gold, grn & brn .25 .20
1608 A344 60k red, gold, bl & brn .35 .20

NATO, 15th Anniv. A346

130k, NATO emblem and olive branch.

**1964, Apr. 4 Litho. Perf. 13**

1610 A346 50k grnsh bl, vio bl & red .25 .20
1611 A346 130k red & black .45 .40

12 Stars and Europa with Torch A347

Design: 130k, Torch and stars.

**1964, May 5 Litho. Perf. 12**

1612 A347 50k red brn, yel & vio bl .35 .20
1613 A347 130k vio bl, lt bl & org .60 .40

15th anniversary of Council of Europe.

Recaizade Mahmut Ekrem, Writer — A348

Portraits: 1k, Hüseyin Rahmi Gürpinar, novelist. 5k, Ismail Hakki Izmirli, scientist. 10k, Sevket Dag, painter. 60k, Gazi Ahmet Muhtar Pasha, commander. 100k, Ahmet Rasim, writer. 130k, Salih Zeki, mathematician.

**1964 Litho. Perf. 13½x13**

1614 A348 1k red & blk .20 .20
1615 A348 5k dull grn & blk .20 .20
1616 A348 10k tan & blk .20 .20
1617 A348 50k ultra & dk bl .70 .20
1618 A348 60k gray & blk .80 .20
1619 A348 100k grnsh bl & dk bl .90 .20
1620 A348 130k brt grn & dk grn 4.00 .40
*Nos. 1614-1620 (7)* 7.00 1.60

Mosque of Sultan Ahmed A349

Kiz Kulesi, Mersin — A350

Designs: No. 1622, Zeus Temple, Silifke. No. 1623, View of Amasra. No. 1625, Augustus' Gate and minaret, Ankara.

**1964, June 11 Unwmk. Perf. 13**

1621 A349 50k gray ol & yel grn .20 .20
1622 A349 50k claret & car .20 .20
1623 A349 50k dk bl & vio bl .20 .20
1624 A350 60k sl grn & dk gray .30 .20
1625 A350 60k dk brn & org brn .30 .20
*Nos. 1621-1625 (5)* 1.20 1.00

Kars Castle — A351

Alp Arslan, Conqueror of Kars, 1064 — A352

**1964, Aug. 16 Unwmk. Perf. 13**

1626 A351 50k blk & pale vio .40 .40
1627 A352 130k blk, gold, sal & pale vio 1.25 .60

900th anniversary of conquest of Kars.

**Europa Issue, 1964**

Common Design Type

**1964, Sept. 14 Litho. Perf. 13**

**Size: 22x33mm**

1628 CD7 50k org, ind & sil *.90* .50
1629 CD7 130k lt bl, mag & cit *1.75* .85

Fuat, Resit and Ali Pashas — A353

Design: 60k, Mustafa Resit Pasha, vert.

**1964, Nov. 3 Perf. 13**

**Sizes: 48x33mm (50k, 100k); 22x33mm (60k)**

1630 A353 50k multicolored .30 .20
1631 A353 60k multicolored .40 .20
1632 A353 100k multicolored .60 .30
*Nos. 1630-1632 (3)* 1.30 .70

125th anniversary of reform decrees.

Parachutist — A354

Designs: 90k, Glider, horiz. 130k, Ataturk watching squadron in flight.

**1965, Feb. 16 Litho. Perf. 13**

1633 A354 60k lt bl, blk, red & yel .20 .20
1634 A354 90k bister & multi .30 .20
1635 A354 130k lt blue & multi .50 .20
*Nos. 1633-1635 (3)* 1.00 .60

Turkish Aviation League, 40th anniv.

Emblem A355

Designs: 50k, Radio mast and waves, vert. 75k, Hand pressing button.

**1965, Feb. 24 Unwmk. Perf. 13**

1636 A355 30k multicolored .20 .20
1637 A355 50k multicolored .20 .20
1638 A355 75k multicolored .35 .20
*Nos. 1636-1638 (3)* .75 .60

Telecommunications meeting of the Central Treaty Org., CENTO.

Coast of Ordu — A356

50k, Manavgat Waterfall, Antalya. 60k, Sultan Ahmed Mosque, Istanbul. 100k, Hali Rahman Mosque, Urfa. 130k, Red Tower, Alanya.

**1965, Apr. 5 Litho.**

1639 A356 30k multicolored .20 .20
1640 A356 50k multicolored .25 .20
1641 A356 60k multicolored .25 .20
1642 A356 100k multicolored .45 .20
1643 A356 130k multicolored .65 .20
*Nos. 1639-1643 (5)* 1.80 1.00

ITU Emblem, Old and New Communication Equipment — A357

**1965, May 17 Perf. 13**

1644 A357 50k multicolored .20 .20
1645 A357 130k multicolored .55 .25

ITU, centenary.

ICY Emblem A358

**1965, June 26 Litho. Unwmk.**

1646 A358 100k red org, red brn & brt grn .30 .20
1647 A358 130k gray, lil & ol grn .45 .25

International Cooperation Year.

Hands Holding Book A358a

Map and Flags of Turkey, Iran and Pakistan A358b

**1965, July 21 Unwmk. Perf. 13**

1648 A358a 50k org brn, yel & dk brn .30 .20
1649 A358b 75k dl bl, red, grn blk & org .45 .20

1st anniv. of the signing of the Regional Cooperation Development Pact by Turkey, Iran and Pakistan.

Kemal Ataturk — A359

**1965 Litho. Perf. 12½**

1650 A359 1k brt green .20 .20
1651 A359 5k violet blue .20 .20
1652 A359 10k blue .60 .20
1653 A359 25k gray 1.50 .20
1654 A359 30k magenta 2.00 .20
1655 A359 50k brown 3.00 .25
1656 A359 150k orange 7.50 .50
*Nos. 1650-1656 (7)* 15.00 1.75

**Europa Issue, 1965**

Common Design Type

**1965, Sept. 27 Perf. 13**

**Size: 32x23mm**

1665 CD8 50k gray, ultra & grn *1.25* .70
1666 CD8 130k tan, blk & grn *2.25* 1.40

Map of Turkey and People A360

Designs: 50k, "1965." 100k, "1965," symbolic eye and man, vert.

**Unwmk.**

**1965, Oct. 24 Litho. Perf. 13**

1667 A360 10k multicolored .20 .20
1668 A360 50k grn, blk & lt yel grn .20 .20
1669 A360 100k orange, sl & blk .40 .20
*Nos. 1667-1669 (3)* .80 .60

Issued to publicize the 1965 census.

Plane over Ankara Castle A361

Designs: 30k, Archer and Ankara castle. 50k, Horsemen with spears (ancient game). 100k, Three stamps and medal. 150k, Hands holding book, vert.

**1965, Oct. 25**

1670 A361 10k brt vio, yel & red .20 .20
1671 A361 30k multicolored .20 .20
1672 A361 50k lt gray ol, ind & red .20 .20
1673 A361 100k gray & multi .40 .25
*Nos. 1670-1673 (4)* 1.00 .85

**Souvenir Sheet**

***Imperf***

1674 A361 150k multicolored 1.10 1.00

1st Natl. Postage Stamp Exhibition "Ankara 65."

Resat Nuri Guntekin, Novelist — A362

Portraits: 5k, Besim Omer Akalin, M.D. 10k, Tevfik Fikret, poet. 25k, Tanburi Cemil, composer. 30k, Ahmet Vifik Pasha, playwright. 50k, Omer Seyfettin, novelist. 60k, Kemalettin Mimaroglu, architect. 150k, Halit Ziya Usakligil, novelist. 220k, Yahya Kemal Beyatli, poet.

**1965 Litho. *Perf. 13½x13***
**Black Portrait and Inscriptions**

**1675** A362 1k rose .20 .20
**1676** A362 5k blue .30 .20
**1677** A362 10k buff .30 .20
**1678** A362 25k dull red brn .50 .20
**1679** A362 30k gray .50 .20
**1680** A362 50k orange .75 .20
**1681** A362 60k red lilac .85 .20
**1682** A362 150k lt green 1.10 .20
**1683** A362 220k tan 2.00 .30
*Nos. 1675-1683 (9)* 6.50 1.90

Training Ship Savarona — A363

Designs: 60k, Submarine "Piri Reis." 100k, Cruiser "Alpaslan." 130k, Destroyer "Gelibolu." 220k, Destroyer "Gemlik."

**1965, Dec. 6 Photo. *Perf. 11½***

**1684** A363 50k blue & brown .35 .20
**1685** A363 60k blue & black .50 .20
**1686** A363 100k blue & black .80 .25
**1687** A363 130k blue & vio blk 1.25 .40
**1688** A363 220k blue & indigo 1.75 .65
*Nos. 1684-1688 (5)* 4.65 1.70

First Congress of Turkish Naval Society.

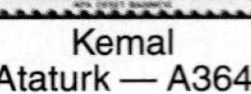

Kemal Ataturk — A364

Halide Edip Adivar, Writer — A365

**1965 Litho. *Perf. 13½***
**Imprint: "Apa Ofset Basimevi"**
**Black Portrait and Inscriptions**

**1689** A364 1k rose lilac .20 .20
**1690** A364 5k lt green .20 .20
**1691** A364 10k blue gray .30 .20
**1692** A364 50k olive bister .50 .20
**1693** A364 150k silver 1.50 .20
*Nos. 1689-1693 (5)* 2.70 1.00

See Nos. 1724-1728.

**1966 Litho. *Perf. 13½***

Portraits: 25k, Huseyin Sadettin Arel, writer and composer. 30k, Kamil Akdik, graphic artist. 60k, Abdurrahman Seref, historian. 130k, Naima, historian.

**1694** A365 25k gray & brn blk .50 .20
**1695** A365 30k rose vio & blk brn .50 .20
**1696** A365 50k blue & black .55 .20
**1697** A365 60k lt grn & blk brn .55 .20
**1698** A365 130k lt vio bl & blk 1.00 .20
*Nos. 1694-1698 (5)* 3.10 1.00

Tiles, Green Mausoleum, Bursa — A366

Tiles: 60k, Spring flowers, Hurrem Sultan Mausoleum, Istanbul. 130k, Stylized flowers, 16th century.

**1966, May 15 Litho. *Perf. 13½x13***

**1699** A366 50k multicolored .50 .20
**1700** A366 60k multicolored .80 .30
**1701** A366 130k multicolored 1.25 .35
*Nos. 1699-1701 (3)* 2.55 .85

On No. 1700 the black ink was applied by a thermographic process and varnished, producing a shiny, raised effect to imitate the embossed tiles of the design source.

Volleyball — A367

View of Bodrum — A368

**1966, May 20 *Perf. 13x13½***

**1702** A367 50k tan & multi .35 .20

4th Intl. Military Volleyball Championship.

**1966, May 25 *Perf. 13x13½, 13½x13***

Views: 30k, Kusadasi. 50k, Anadolu Hisari, Istanbul. 90k, Marmaris. 100k, Izmir.

**1703** A368 10k multi .20 .20
**1704** A368 30k multi .60 .20
**1705** A368 50k multi, horiz. .30 .20
**1706** A368 90k multi .30 .20
**1707** A368 100k multi, horiz. .40 .20
*Nos. 1703-1707 (5)* 1.80 1.00

Inauguration of Keban Dam — A369

Design: 60k, View of Keban Dam area.

**1966, June 10 *Perf. 13½***

**1708** A369 50k multicolored .20 .20
**1709** A369 60k multicolored .40 .20

Visit of King Faisal of Saudi Arabia — A370

**1966, Aug. 29 Litho. *Perf. 13½x13***

**1710** A370 100k car rose & dk car .55 .20

Symbolic Postmark and Stamp — A371

Designs: 60k, Flower made of stamps. 75k, Stamps forming display frames. 100k, Map of Balkan states, magnifying glass and stamp.

**1966, Sept. 3 *Perf. 13½x13***

**1711** A371 50k multicolored .20 .20
**1712** A371 60k multicolored .20 .20
**1713** A371 75k multicolored .40 .20
*Nos. 1711-1713 (3)* .80 .60

**Souvenir Sheet**
***Imperf***

**1714** A371 100k multicolored 1.50 1.25

2nd "Balkanfila" stamp exhibition, Istanbul.

Sultan Suleiman on Horseback — A372

90k, Mausoleum, Istanbul. 130k, Suleiman.

**1966, Sept. 6 *Perf. 13½x13***

**1715** A372 60k multicolored .40 .20
**1716** A372 90k multicolored .70 .25
**1717** A372 130k multicolored 1.40 .40
*Nos. 1715-1717 (3)* 2.50 .85

Sultan Suleiman the Magnificent (1496?-1566). On No. 1717 a gold frame was applied by raised thermographic process.

**Europa Issue, 1966**
Common Design Type

**1966, Sept. 26 Litho. *Perf. 13x13½***
**Size: 22x33mm**

**1718** CD9 50k lt bl, vio bl & blk *1.10* .65
*a.* Black (inscriptions & imprint) omitted *65.00*
**1719** CD9 130k lil, dk red lil & blk *2.25* 1.10

Symbols of Education, Science and Culture — A373

**1966, Nov. 4 Litho. *Perf. 13***

**1720** A373 130k brn, bis brn & yel .45 .20

UNESCO, 20th anniversary.

Middle East University of Technology — A374

Designs: 100k, Atom symbol. 130k, design symbolizing sciences.

**1966, Nov. 15**

**1721** A374 50k multicolored .20 .20
**1722** A374 100k multicolored .30 .20
**1723** A374 130k multicolored .50 .30
*Nos. 1721-1723 (3)* 1.00 .70

10th anniv. of the Middle East University of Technology.

Ataturk Type of 1965
Imprint: "Kiral Matbaasi — Ist"

**1966 Litho. *Perf. 12½***
**Black Portrait and Inscriptions**

**1724** A364 25k yellow .25 .20
**1725** A364 30k pink .30 .20
**1726** A364 50k rose lilac 1.25 .20
**1727** A364 90k pale brown .70 .20
**1728** A364 100k gray 1.00 .20
*Nos. 1724-1728 (5)* 3.50 1.00

Statue of Ataturk, Ankara — A375

Equestrian Statues of Ataturk: No. 1729A, Statue in Izmir. No. 1729B, Statue in Samsun.

**Without Imprint**

**1967 Litho. *Perf. 13x12½***
**Size: 23x16mm**

**1729** A375 10k black & yellow .30 .20

**Inscribed "1967"**
**Imprint: Kiral Matbaasi**
**Size: 22x15mm**

**1729A** A375 10k black & salmon .30 .20
**1729B** A375 10k black & lt grn .30 .20
*Nos. 1729-1729B (3)* .90 .60

Issued for use on greeting cards. See Nos. 1790-1791A, 1911.

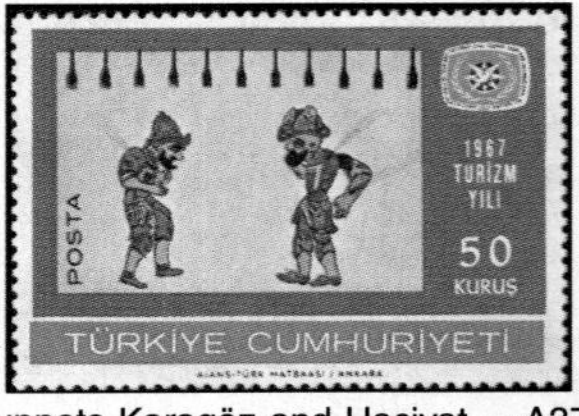

Puppets Karagöz and Hacivat — A376

Intl. Tourist Year Emblem and: 60k, Sword and shield game. 90k, Traditional military band. 100k, raised effect.

***Perf. 13x13½, 13½x13***
**1967, Mar. 30 Litho.**

**1730** A376 50k multicolored .50 .20
**1731** A376 60k multicolored .70 .20
**1732** A376 90k multicolored .90 .25
**1733** A376 100k multicolored 1.40 .35
*Nos. 1730-1733 (4)* 3.50 1.00

Intl. Tourist Year. On No. 1733 the black ink was applied by a thermographic process and varnished, producing a shiny, raised effect.

Woman Vaccinating Child, Knife and Lancet — A377

Fallow Deer — A378

**1967, Apr. 1 *Perf. 13x13½***

**1734** A377 100k multicolored .60 .25

250th anniv. of smallpox vaccination (variolation) in Turkey. The gold was applied by a thermographic process and varnished, producing a shiny, raised effect.

**1967, Apr. 23 Litho. *Perf. 13x13½***

**1735** A378 50k shown .30 .20
**1736** A378 60k Wild goat .40 .20
**1737** A378 100k Brown bear .55 .20
**1738** A378 130k Wild boar .80 .25
*Nos. 1735-1738 (4)* 2.05 .85

Soccer Players and Emblem with Map of Europe — A379

130k, Players at left, smaller emblem.

**1967, May 1 *Perf. 13***

**1739** A379 50k multicolored .65 .20
**1740** A379 130k yellow & multi .85 .30

20th Intl. Youth Soccer Championships.

Sivas Hospital — A380

**1967, July 1 Litho. *Perf. 13***

**1741** A380 50k multicolored .40 .20

750th anniversary of Sivas Hospital.

Selim Sirri Tarcan A381

60k, Olympic Rings, Baron Pierre de Coubertin.

**1967, July 20**

**1742** A381 50k lt blue & multi .25 .20
**1743** A381 60k lilac & multi .25 .20
*a.* Pair, #1742-1743 .50 .40

1st Turkish Olympic competitions.

Ahmed Mithat, Writer — A382

Portraits: 5k, Admiral Turgut Reis. 50k, Sokullu Mehmet, statesman. 100k, Nedim, poet. 150k, Osman Hamdi, painter.

**1967 Litho. *Perf. 12½***

**1744** A382 1k green & blk .40 .20
**1745** A382 5k dp bister & blk .40 .20
**1746** A382 50k brt violet & blk .80 .20
**1747** A382 100k citron & blk 1.50 .20
**1748** A382 150k yellow & blk 2.50 .20
*Nos. 1744-1748 (5)* 5.60 1.00

Ruins of St. John's Church, Ephesus A383

Design: 130k, Inside view of Virgin Mary's House, Ephesus.

**1967, July 26 *Perf. 13***

**1749** A383 130k multicolored .25 .20
**1750** A383 220k multicolored .55 .30

Visit of Pope Paul VI to the House of the Virgin Mary in Ephesus, July 26.

Plate on Firing Grid and Ornaments A384

**1967, Sept. 1**

**1751** A384 50k pale lil, blk, ind & bl .30 .20

5th International Ceramics Exhibition.

View of Istanbul and Emblem A385

**1967, Sept. 4 Litho. *Perf. 13***

**1752** A385 130k dk blue & gray .30 .20

9th Congress of the Intl. Commission of Large Dams.

Stamps, Ornament and Map of Turkey A386

Kemal Ataturk A387

Design: 60k, Grapes and stamps.

**1967**

**1753** A386 50k multicolored .20 .20
**1754** A386 60k multicolored .25 .20
*a.* Souvenir sheet, #1753-1754 1.25 1.25

Intl. Trade Fair, Izmir.

**1967 Litho. *Perf. 11½x12***

**Booklet Stamps**

**1755** A387 10k black & lt ol grn 1.25 .30
*a.* Booklet pane of 10 100.00
*b.* Booklet pane of 25 250.00
**1756** A387 50k black & pale rose 1.25 .30
*a.* Booklet pane of 2 40.00
*b.* Bklt. pane, 5 #1755, 4 #1756 + label 35.00

Symbolic Water Cycle — A388

Human Rights Flame — A390

Child and Angora Cat, Man with Microscope — A389

**1967, Dec. 1 Litho. *Perf. 13***

**1757** A388 90k lt grn, blk & org .25 .20
**1758** A388 130k lilac, blk & org .30 .25

Hydrological Decade (UNESCO), 1965-74.

**1967, Dec. 23 *Perf. 13***

60k, Horse and man with microscope.

**1759** A389 50k multicolored .35 .20
**1760** A389 60k multicolored .45 .25

125th anniv. of Turkish veterinary medicine.

**1968, Jan. 1 *Perf. 13x13½***

**1761** A390 50k rose lil, dk bl & org .20 .20
**1762** A390 130k lt bl, dk bl & red org .35 .20

International Human Rights Year.

Archer on Horseback — A391

Miniatures, 16th Century: 50k, Investiture. 60k, Sultan Suleiman the Magnificent receiving an ambassador, vert. 100k, Musicians.

***Perf. 13x13½, 13½x13***

**1968, Mar. 1 Litho.**

**1763** A391 50k multicolored .50 .50
**1764** A391 60k multicolored 1.00 1.00
**1765** A391 90k multicolored 1.25 1.25
**1766** A391 100k multicolored 1.50 1.50
*Nos. 1763-1766 (4)* 4.25 4.25

Kemal Ataturk — A392

**1968 Litho. *Perf. 12½***

**1767** A392 1k dk & lt blue .20 .20
**1768** A392 5k dk & lt green .20 .20
**1769** A392 50k org brn & yel 1.50 .20
**1770** A392 200k dk brown & pink 5.00 .25
*Nos. 1767-1770 (4)* 6.90 .85

Law Book and Oak Branch A393

Mithat Pasha and Scroll A394

**1968, Apr. 1 *Perf. 13***

**1771** A393 50k multicolored .35 .35
**1772** A394 60k multicolored .40 .40

Centenary of the Court of Appeal.

**1968, Apr. 1**

Designs: 50k, Scales of Justice. 60k, Ahmet Cevdet Pasha and scroll.

**1773** A393 50k multicolored .25 .20
**1774** A394 60k multicolored .35 .20

Centenary of the Supreme Court.

**Europa Issue, 1968**

Common Design Type

**1968, May 6 Litho. *Perf. 13***

**Size: 31½x23mm**

**1775** CD11 100k pck bl, yel & red *1.75* .75
**1776** CD11 130k green, yel & red *3.25* 1.25

Yacht Kismet — A395

"Fight Usury" A396

**1968, June 15 Litho. *Perf. 13***

**1777** A395 50k lt ultra & multi .50 .50

Round-the-world trip of the yacht Kismet, Aug. 22, 1965-June 14, 1968.

**1968, June 19**

**1778** A396 50k multicolored .35 .35

Centenary of the Pawn Office, Istanbul.

Sakarya Battle and Independence Medal — A397

130k, Natl. anthem & reverse of medal.

**1968, Aug. 30 *Perf. 13x13½***

**1779** A397 50k gold & multi .40 .40
**1780** A397 130k gold & multi .60 .60

Turkish Independence medal. The gold on Nos. 1779-1780 was applied by a thermographic process and varnished, producing a shiny, raised effect.

Ataturk and Galatasaray High School — A398

50k, "100" and old and new school emblems. 60k, Portraits of Beyazit II and Gulbaba.

**1968, Sept. 1 Litho.**

**1781** A398 50k gray & multi .25 .25
**1782** A398 60k tan & multi .50 .50
**1783** A398 100k lt blue & multi .75 .75
*Nos. 1781-1783 (3)* 1.50 1.50

Centenary of Galatasaray High School.

Charles de Gaulle — A399

**1968, Oct. 25 Litho. *Perf. 13***

**1784** A399 130k multicolored .90 .50

Visit of President Charles de Gaulle of France to Turkey.

Kemal Ataturk — A400

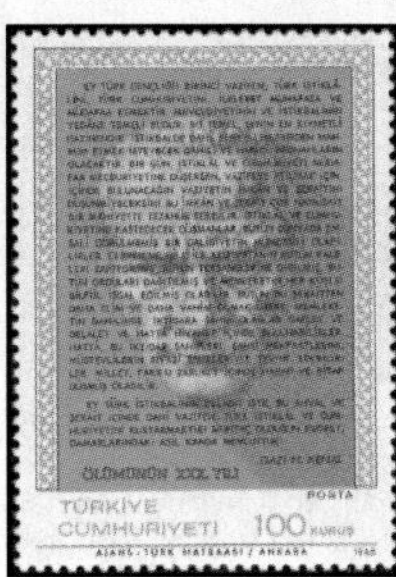


Ataturk and his Speech to Youth — A401

50k, Ataturk's tomb and Citadel of Ankara. 60k, Ataturk looking out a train window. 250k, Framed portrait of Ataturk in military uniform.

**1968, Nov. 10**

**1785** A400 30k orange & blk .30 .20
**1786** A400 50k brt grn & sl grn .30 .20
**1787** A400 60k bl grn & blk .35 .20
**1788** A401 100k blk, gray & brt grn .70 .20
**1789** A401 250k multicolored 1.25 .40
*Nos. 1785-1789 (5)* 2.90 1.20

30th death anniv. of Kemal Ataturk.

Ataturk Statue Type of 1967

Equestrian Statues of Ataturk: No. 1790, Statue in Zonguldak. No. 1791, Statue in Antakya. No. 1791A, Statue in Bursa.

**Imprint: Kiral Matbaasi 1968**

**1968-69 Litho. *Perf. 13x12½***

**Size: 22x15mm**

**1790** A375 10k black & lt blue .25 .20
**1791** A375 10k blk & brt rose lil .25 .20

***Perf. 13½***

**Imprint: Tifdruk Matbaacilik Sanayii A. S. 1969**

**Size: 21x16½mm**

**1791A** A375 10k dk grn & tan ('69) .30 .20
*Nos. 1790-1791A (3)* .80 .60

Ince Minare Mosque, Konya — A402

ILO Emblem A403

Historic Buildings: 10k, Doner Kumbet (tomb), Kayseri. 50k, Karatay Medresse (University Gate), Konya. 100k, Ortakoy Mosque, Istanbul. 200k, Ulu Mosque, Divriki.

**1968-69 Photo. *Perf. 13x13½***

**1792** A402 1k dk brn & buff ('69) .20 .20
**1793** A402 10k plum & dl rose ('69) .30 .20
**1794** A402 50k dk ol grn & gray .40 .20
**1795** A402 100k dk & lt grn ('69) 1.10 .25
**1796** A402 200k dp bl & lt bl ('69) 1.75 .35
*Nos. 1792-1796 (5)* 3.75 1.20

**1969, Apr. 15 Litho. *Perf. 13***

**1797** A403 130k dk red & black .30 .20

ILO, 50th anniv.

Sultana Hafsa, Medical Pioneer A404

**1969, Apr. 26 Litho. *Perf. 13½x13***

**1798** A404 60k multicolored .75 .75

**Europa Issue, 1969**

Common Design Type

**1969, Apr. 28 *Perf. 13***

**Size: 32x23mm**

**1799** CD12 100k dull vio & multi *1.60* .65
**1800** CD12 130k gray grn & multi *2.25* 1.60

Kemal Ataturk — A405

Map of Istanbul — A407

Ataturk and S.S. Bandirma A406

**1969, May 19 Litho. *Perf. 13***

**1801** A405 50k multicolored .25 .25
**1802** A406 60k multicolored .35 .35

50th anniv. of the landing of Kemal Ataturk at Samsun.

**1969, May 31**

**1803** A407 130k vio bl, lt bl, gold & red .35 .20

22nd Congress of the Intl. Chamber of Commerce, Istanbul.

Educational Progress A408

Agricultural Progress A409

Designs: 90k, Pouring ladle and industrial symbols. 100k, Road sign (highway construction). 180k, Oil industry chart and symbols.

**1969 Litho. *Perf. 13½x13***

**1804** A408 1k black & gray .20 .20
**1805** A408 1k black & bis brn .20 .20
**1806** A408 1k black & lt grn .20 .20
**1807** A408 1k black & lt vio .20 .20
**1808** A408 1k black & org red .20 .20
**1809** A409 50k brown & ocher .40 .20
**1810** A409 90k blk & grnsh gray .65 .20
**1811** A408 100k black & org red .90 .20
**1812** A408 180k violet & orange 1.60 .20
*Nos. 1804-1812 (9)* 4.55 1.80

Issued: 1, 100k, 4/8; 50k, 6/11; 90, 180k, 8/15.

Sultan Suleiman Receiving Sheik Abdul Latif — A410

Kemal Ataturk — A411

Designs: 80k, Lady Serving Wine, Safavi miniature, Iran. 130k, Lady on Balcony, Mogul miniature, Pakistan.

**1969, July 21 Litho. *Perf. 13***

**1813** A410 50k yellow & multi .30 .20
**1814** A410 80k yellow & multi .50 .20
**1815** A410 130k yellow & multi .85 .35
*Nos. 1813-1815 (3)* 1.65 .75

5th anniv. of the signing of the Regional Cooperation for Development Pact by Turkey, Iran and Pakistan.

**1969, July 23**

Design: 60k, Ataturk monument and bas-relief showing congress.

**1816** A411 50k black & gray .25 .25
**1817** A411 60k black & grnsh gray .35 .35

50th anniversary, Congress of Erzerum.

Sivas Congress Delegates A412

Design: 50k, Congress Hall.

**1969, Sept. 4 Litho. *Perf. 13***

**1818** A412 50k dk brn & dp rose .25 .25
**1819** A412 60k olive blk & yel .35 .35

50th anniv. of the Congress of Sivas (preparation for the Turkish war of independence).

Bar Dance — A413

Folk Dances: 50k, Candle dance (çaydaçira). 60k, Scarf dance (halay). 100k, Sword dance (kiliç-kalkan). 130k, Two male dancers (zeybek), vert.

**1969, Sept. 9**

**1820** A413 30k brown & multi .20 .20
**1821** A413 50k multicolored .35 .20
**1822** A413 60k multicolored .45 .20
**1823** A413 100k yellow & multi .60 .20
**1824** A413 130k multicolored 1.00 .40
*Nos. 1820-1824 (5)* 2.60 1.20

1914 Airplane "Prince Celaleddin" A414

75k, First Turkish letter carried by air.

**1969, Oct. 18 Litho. *Perf. 13***

**1825** A414 60k dk blue & blue .25 .20
**1826** A414 75k black & bister .35 .20

55th anniv. of the first Turkish mail transported by air.

"Kutadgu Bilig" A415

**1969, Nov. 20 Litho. *Perf. 13***

**1827** A415 130k ol bis, brn & gold .35 .20

900th anniv. of "Kutadgu Bilig," a book about the function of the state, compiled by Jusuf of Balasagun in Tashkent, 1069.

Ataturk's Arrival in Ankara, after a Painting — A416

Design: 60k, Ataturk and his coworkers in automobiles arriving in Ankara, after a photograph.

**1969, Dec. 27 Litho. *Perf. 13***

**1828** A416 50k multicolored .60 .20
**1829** A416 60k multicolored 1.00 .30

50th anniv. of Kemal Ataturk's arrival in Ankara, Dec. 27, 1919.

Bosporus Bridge, Map of Europe and Asia — A417

Design: 60k, View of proposed Bosporus Bridge and shore lines.

**1970, Feb. 20 Litho. *Perf. 13***

**1830** A417 60k gold & multi .75 .30
**1831** A417 130k gold & multi 1.50 .65

Foundation ceremonies for the bridge across the Bosporus linking Europe and Asia.

Kemal Ataturk and Signature A418

Kemal Ataturk A419

**1970 Litho. *Perf. 13***

**1832** A418 1k dp orange & brn .20 .20
**1833** A419 5k silver & blk .20 .20
**1834** A419 30k citron & blk .35 .20
**1835** A418 50k lt olive & blk .45 .20
**1836** A419 50k pink & blk .50 .20
**1837** A419 75k lilac & blk .75 .20
**1838** A419 100k blue & blk 1.00 .20
*Nos. 1832-1838 (7)* 3.45 1.40

Education Year Emblem — A420

Turkish EXPO '70 Emblem — A421

**1970, Mar. 16**

**1839** A420 130k ultra, pink & rose lil .45 .20

International Education Year.

**1970, Mar. 27**

100k, EXPO '70 emblem & Turkish pavilion.

**1840** A421 50k gold & multi .20 .20
**1841** A421 100k gold & multi .30 .20

EXPO '70 International Exhibition, Osaka, Japan, Mar. 15-Sept. 13.

Opening of Grand National Assembly A422

Design: 60k, Session of First Grand National Assembly, 1920.

**1970, Apr. 23**

**1842** A422 50k multicolored .20 .20
**1843** A422 60k multicolored .30 .20

Turkish Grand National Assembly, 50th anniv.

Emblem of Cartographic Service A423

Map of Turkey and Gen. Mehmet Sevki Pasha — A424

Designs: 60k, Plane and aerial mapping survey diagram. 100k, Triangulation point in mountainous landscape.

***Perf. 13½x13 (A423), 13x13½ (A424)***

**1970, May 2** **Litho.**

**1844** A423 50k blue & multi .20 .20
**1845** A424 60k blk, gray grn & brick red .20 .20
**1846** A423 100k multicolored .35 .35
**1847** A424 130k multicolored .60 .50
*Nos. 1844-1847 (4)* 1.35 1.25

Turkish Cartographic Service, 75th anniv.

**Europa Issue, 1970**
Common Design Type

**1970, May 4** ***Perf. 13***
**Size: 37x23mm**

**1848** CD13 100k ver, blk & org *1.50* .75
**1849** CD13 130k dk bl grn, blk & org *3.50* 1.50

Inauguration of UPU Headquarters, Bern — A425

**1970, May 20**

**1850** A425 60k blk & dull blue .25 .20
**1851** A425 130k blk & dl ol grn .45 .20

Lady with Mimosa, by Osman Hamdi (1842-1910) A426

Paintings: No. 1853, Deer, by Seker Ahmet (1841-1907). No. 1854, Portrait of Fevzi Cakmak, by Avni Lifij (d. 1927). No. 1855, Sailboats, by Nazmi Ziya (1881-1937); horiz.

**1970** **Litho.** ***Perf. 13***
**Size: 29x49mm**

**1852** A426 250k multicolored 1.10 .35
**1853** A426 250k multicolored 1.10 .35

**Size: 32x49mm**

**1854** A426 250k multicolored 1.10 .35

**Size: 73½x33mm**

**1855** A426 250k multicolored 1.10 .35
*Nos. 1852-1855 (4)* 4.40 1.40

Issued: #1852-1853, 6/15; #1854-1855, 12/15.

Turkish Folk Art — A427

**1970, June 15**

**1856** A427 50k multicolored .40 .20

3rd National Stamp Exhibition, ANKARA 70, Oct. 28-Nov. 4. Pane of 50, each stamp se-tenant with label. This 50k, in pane of 50 without labels, was re-issued Oct. 28 with Nos. 1867-1869.

View of Fethiye A428

80k, Seeyo-Se-Pol Bridge, Esfahan, Iran. 130k, Saiful Malook Lake, Pakistan.

**1970, July 21** **Litho.** ***Perf. 13***

**1857** A428 60k multicolored .25 .20
**1858** A428 80k multicolored .30 .20
**1859** A428 130k multicolored .45 .25
*Nos. 1857-1859 (3)* 1.00 .65

6th anniv. of the signing of the Regional Cooperation for Development Pact by Turkey, Iran and Pakistan.

Sultan Balim's Tomb — A429

Haci Bektas Veli — A430

30k, Tomb of Haci Bektas Veli, horiz.

**1970, Aug. 16** **Litho.** ***Perf. 13***

**1860** A429 30k multicolored .20 .20
**1861** A429 100k multicolored .40 .20
**1862** A430 180k multicolored .80 .20
*Nos. 1860-1862 (3)* 1.40 .60

700th death anniv. of Haci Bektas Veli, mystic.

Hittite Sun Disk and "ISO" A431

**1970, Sept. 15**

**1863** A431 110k car rose, gold & blk .20 .20
**1864** A431 150k ultra, gold & blk .30 .20

8th General Council Meeting of the Intl. Standardization Org., Ankara.

UN Emblem, People and Globe — A432

Stamp "Flower" and Book — A433

100k, UN emblem and propeller, horiz.

**1970, Oct. 24** **Litho.** ***Perf. 13***

**1865** A432 100k gray & multi .30 .20
**1866** A432 220k multicolored .55 .25

25th anniversary of the United Nations.

**1970, Oct. 28**

Designs: 60k, Ataturk monument and stamps, horiz. 130k, Abstract flower.

**1867** A433 10k multicolored .20 .20
**1868** A433 60k blue & multi .20 .20

**Souvenir Sheet**

**1869** A433 130k dk green & org 2.00 1.50

3rd National Stamp Exhibition, ANKARA 70, Oct. 28-Nov. 4. See note below No. 1856.

InönüBattle Scene — A434

Design: No. 1871, Second Battle of Inönü.

**1971** **Litho.** ***Perf. 13***

**1870** A434 100k multicolored .50 .20
**1871** A434 100k multicolored .50 .20

1st and 2nd Battles of Inönü, 50th anniv. Issue dates: #1870, Jan. 10; #1871, Apr. 1.

Village on River Bank, by Ahmet Sekür — A435

Painting: No. 1872, Landscape, Yildiz Palace Garden, by Ahmet Ragip Bicakcilar.

**1971, Mar. 15** **Litho.** ***Perf. 13***

**1872** A435 250k multicolored 1.25 .40
**1873** A435 250k multicolored 1.25 .40

See #1901-1902, 1909-1910, 1937-1938.

Campaign Against Discrimination A436

**1971, Mar. 21** **Litho.** ***Perf. 13***

**1874** A436 100k multicolored .20 .20
**1875** A436 250k gray & multi .45 .25

Intl. Year against Racial Discrimination.

**Europa Issue, 1971**
Common Design Type

**1971, May 3** **Litho.** ***Perf. 13***
**Size: 31½x22½mm**

**1876** CD14 100k lt bl, cl & mag *2.10* 1.00
**1877** CD14 150k dp org, grn & red *3.50* 1.50

Kemal Ataturk
A437 A438

**1971**

**1878** A437 5k gray & ultra .20 .20
**1879** A437 25k gray & dk red .50 .20
**1880** A438 25k brown & pink .25 .25
**1881** A437 100k gray & violet .75 .20
**1882** A438 100k green & salmon .75 .20
**1883** A438 250k blue & gray 2.00 .20
**1884** A437 400k tan & olive grn 3.50 .25
*Nos. 1878-1884 (7)* 7.95 1.50

Pres. Kemal Gürsel — A439

Mosque of Selim, Edirne — A440

**1971, May 27** **Litho.** ***Perf. 13***

**1885** A439 100k multicolored .35 .20

Revolution of May 27, 1960; Kemal Gürsel (1895-1966), president.

**1971, July 21** **Litho.** ***Perf. 13***

150k, Religious School, Chaharbagh, Iran. 200k, Badshahi Mosque, Pakistan.

**1886** A440 100k multi .25 .20
**1887** A440 150k multi .35 .20
**1888** A440 200k multi, horiz. .50 .20
*Nos. 1886-1888 (3)* 1.10 .60

Regional Cooperation by Turkey, Iran and Pakistan, 7th anniversary.

Alp Arslan and Battle of Malazkirt — A441

Design: 250k, Archers on horseback.

**1971, Aug. 26** **Litho.** ***Perf. 13x13½***

**1889** A441 100k multicolored .75 .20
**1890** A441 250k red, org & blk 1.20 .40

900th anniversary of the Battle of Malazkirt, which established the Seljuk Dynasty in Asia Minor.

Battle of Sakarya — A442

**1971, Sept. 13**

**1891** A442 100k violet & multi .80 .45

50th anniversary of the victory of Sakarya.

Turkey-Bulgaria Railroad — A443

Designs: 110k, Ferry and map of Lake Van. 250k, Turkey-Iran railroad.

**1971**

**1892** A443 100k multicolored .75 .20
**1893** A443 110k multicolored .75 .20
**1894** A443 250k yellow & multi 1.75 .60
*Nos. 1892-1894 (3)* 3.25 1.00

Turkish railroad connections with Bulgaria &Iran. Issued: 110, 250k, 9/27; 100k, 10/4.

Netball and Map of Mediterranean A444

200k, Runner and stadium, vert. 250k, Shot put and map of Mediterranean, vert.

**1971, Oct. 6**

**1895** A444 100k dull vio & blk .35 .20
**1896** A444 200k brn, blk & emer .55 .25

**Souvenir Sheet**

***Imperf***

**1897** A444 250k ol bis & slate grn .95 .85

Mediterranean Games, Izmir.

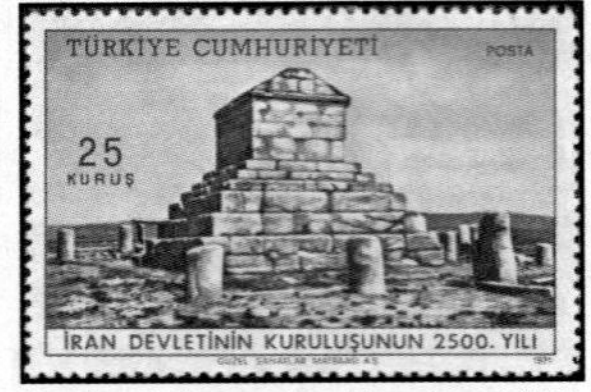


Tomb of Cyrus the Great — A445

Designs: 100k, Harpist, Persian mosaic, vert. 150k, Ataturk and Riza Shah Pahlavi.

**1971, Oct. 13**

**1898** A445 25k lt blue & multi .25 .20
**1899** A445 100k multicolored .65 .20
**1900** A445 150k dk brown & buff 1.10 .25
*Nos. 1898-1900 (3)* 2.00 .65

2500th anniversary of the founding of the Persian empire by Cyrus the Great.

Painting Type of 1971

No. 1901, Sultan Mohammed I and his Staff. No. 1902, Palace with tiled walls.

**1971, Nov. 15** **Litho.** ***Perf. 13***

**1901** A435 250k multicolored 1.25 .40
**1902** A435 250k multicolored 1.25 .40

Yunus Emre — A446

**1971, Dec. 27** **Litho.** ***Perf. 13***

**1903** A446 100k brown & multi .65 .20

650th death anniv. of Yunus Emre, Turkish folk poet.

First Turkish World Map and Book Year Emblem — A447

**1972, Jan. 3** ***Perf. 13***

**1904** A447 100k buff & multi .50 .20

International Book Year.

Doves and NATO Emblem — A448

Fisherman, by Cevat Dereli — A449

**1972, Feb. 18** **Litho.** ***Perf. 13***

**1905** A448 100k dull grn, blk & gray .80 .25
**1906** A448 250k dull bl, blk & gray 1.00 .60

Turkey's membership in NATO, 20th anniv.

**Europa Issue 1972**

Common Design Type

**1972, May 2** **Litho.** ***Perf. 13***

**Size: 22x33mm**

**1907** CD15 110k blue & multi *3.00* 1.00
**1908** CD15 250k brown & multi *4.50* 2.00

Painting Type of 1971

No. 1909, Forest, Seker Ahmet. No. 1910, View of Gebze, Anatolia, by Osman Hamdi.

**1972, May 15** **Litho.**

**1909** A435 250k multicolored 1.25 .35
**1910** A435 250k multicolored 1.25 .35

Ataturk Statue Type of 1967

Design: 25k, Ataturk Statue in front of Ethnographic Museum, Ankara.

Imprint: Ajans - Turk/Ankara 1972

***Perf. 12½x11½***

**1972, June 12** **Litho.**

**Size: 22x15½mm**

**1911** A375 25k black & buff .20 .20

**1972, July 21** **Litho.** ***Perf. 13***

Paintings: 125k, Young Man, by Abdur Rehman Chughtai (Pakistan). 150k, Persian Woman, by Behzad.

**1912** A449 100k gold & multi .60 .20
**1913** A449 125k gold & multi .90 .25
**1914** A449 150k gold & multi 1.00 .35
*Nos. 1912-1914 (3)* 2.50 .80

Regional Cooperation for Development Pact among Turkey, Iran and Pakistan, 8th anniv.

Ataturk and Commanders at Mt. Koca — A450

Designs: No. 1916, Battle of the Commander-in-chief. No. 1917, Turkish army entering Izmir. 110k, Artillery and cavalry.

**1972** **Litho.** ***Perf. 13x13½***

**1915** A450 100k lt ultra & blk .35 .20
**1916** A450 100k pink & multi .50 .20
**1917** A450 100k yellow & multi .50 .20
**1918** A450 110k orange & multi .75 .25
*Nos. 1915-1918 (4)* 2.10 .85

50th anniv. of fight for establishment of independent Turkish republic. Issued: #1915, 1918, 8/26; #1916, 8/30; #1917, 9/9.

"Cancer is Curable" A451

International Railroad Union Emblem — A452

**1972, Oct. 10** **Litho.** ***Perf. 12½x13***

**1919** A451 100k blk, brt bl & red .35 .20

Fight against cancer.

**1972, Dec. 31** **Litho.** ***Perf. 13***

**1920** A452 100k sl grn, ocher & red .30 .20

Intl. Railroad Union, 50th anniv.

Kemal Ataturk — A453

**1972-76** **Litho.** ***Perf. 13½x13***

**Size: 21x26mm**

**1921** A453 5k gray & blue .20 .20
**1922** A453 25k orange ('75) .25 .20
**1923** A453 100k buff & red brn ('73) 1.00 .20
**1924** A453 100k lt gray & gray ('75) .35 .20
**1925** A453 110k lt bl & vio bl .75 .25
**1926** A453 125k dull grn ('73) 1.25 .20
**1927** A453 150k tan & brown 1.00 .20
**1928** A453 150k lt grn & grn ('75) .25 .20
**1929** A453 175k yel & lil ('73) 1.75 .25
**1930** A453 200k buff & red 1.25 .20
**1931** A453 250k pink & pur ('75) .30 .20
**1931A** A453 400k gray & Prus bl ('76) .35 .20
**1932** A453 500k pink & violet 2.00 .50
**1933** A453 500k gray & ultra ('75) .75 .30

**Size: 22x33mm**

***Perf. 13***

**1934** A453 10 l pink & car rose ('75) 1.75 .30
*Nos. 1921-1934 (15)* 13.20 3.60

See Nos. 2060-2061.

**Europa Issue 1973**

Common Design Type

**1973, Apr. 4** **Litho.** ***Perf. 13***

**Size: 32x23mm**

**1935** CD16 110k gray & multi *3.25* 1.75
**1936** CD16 250k multicolored *6.75* 2.75

Painting Type of 1971

Paintings: No. 1937, Beyazit Almshouse, Istanbul, by Ahmet Ziya Akbulut. No. 1938, Flowers, by Suleyman Seyyit, vert.

**1973, June 15** **Litho.** ***Perf. 13***

**1937** A435 250k multicolored .85 .35
**1938** A435 250k multicolored .85 .35

Helmet, Sword and Oak Leaves — A454

Mausoleum of Antiochus I — A455

Design: 100k, Helmet, sword and laurel.

**1973, June 28** ***Perf. 13x12½***

**1939** A454 90k brown, gray & grn .25 .20
**1940** A454 100k brown, lem & grn .25 .20

Army Day.

**1973, July 21** **Litho.** ***Perf. 13***

Designs: 100k, Colossal heads, mausoleum of Antiochus I (69-34 B.C.), Commagene, Turkey. 150k, Statue, Shahdad Kerman, Persia, 3000 B.C. 200k, Street, Mohenjo-daro, Pakistan.

**1941** A455 100k lt blue & multi .25 .20
**1942** A455 150k olive & multi .30 .20
**1943** A455 200k brown & multi .45 .60
*Nos. 1941-1943 (3)* 1.00 1.00

Regional Cooperation for Development Pact among Turkey, Iran and Pakistan, 9th anniv.

Minelayer Nusret A456

Designs: 25k, Destroyer Istanbul. 100k, Speedboat Simsek and Naval College. 250k, Two-masted training ship Nuvid-i Futuh.

**1973, Aug. 1**

**Size: 31½x22mm**

**1944** A456 5k Prus bl & multi .20 .20
**1945** A456 25k Prus bl & multi .20 .20
**1946** A456 100k Prus bl & multi .60 .20

**Size: 48x32mm**

**1947** A456 250k blue & multi 1.50 .25
*Nos. 1944-1947 (4)* 2.50 .85

abu-al-Rayhan al-Biruni A457

Emblem of Darussafaka Foundation A458

**1973, Sept. 4** **Litho.** ***Perf. 13x12½***

**1948** A457 250k multicolored .70 .70

abu-al-Rayhan al-Biruni (973-1048), philosopher and mathematician.

**1973, Sept. 15** ***Perf. 13***

**1949** A458 100k silver & multi .30 .20

Centenary of the educational and philanthropic Darussafaka Foundation.

BALKANFILA IV Emblem — A459

Designs: 110k, Symbolic view and stamps. 250k, "Balkanfila 4."

**1973** **Litho.** ***Perf. 13***

**1950** A459 100k gray & multi .35 .20
**1951** A459 110k multicolored .20 .20
**1952** A459 250k multicolored .45 .20
*Nos. 1950-1952 (3)* 1.00 .60

BALKANFILA IV, Philatelic Exhibition of Balkan Countries, Izmir, Oct. 26-Nov. 5.
Issued: 100k, Sept. 26; 110k, 250k, Oct. 26.

Sivas Shepherd Dog — A460

Kemal Ataturk — A461

**1973, Oct. 4**

**1953** A460 25k shown .20 .20
**1954** A460 100k Angora cat .60 .20

**1973, Oct. 10** **Litho.** ***Perf. 13***

**1955** A461 100k gold & blk brn .40 .20

35th death anniv. of Kemal Ataturk.

Flower and "50" — A462

Ataturk — A463

250k, Torch & "50." 475k, Grain & cogwheel.

**1973, Oct. 29**

**1956** A462 100k purple, red & bl .20 .20
**1957** A462 250k multicolored .45 .20
**1958** A462 475k brt blue & org .70 .35
*Nos. 1956-1958 (3)* 1.35 .75

**Souvenir Sheet**
***Imperf***

**1959** A463 500k multicolored 1.25 .90

50th anniv. of the Turkish Republic. #1959 contains one stamp with simulated perforations.

Bosporus Bridge A464

150k, Istanbul & Bosporus Bridge. 200k, Bosporus Bridge, children & UNICEF emblem, vert.

**1973, Oct. 30** ***Perf. 13***

**1960** A464 100k multicolored .30 .20
**1961** A464 150k multicolored .50 .30
**1962** A464 200k multicolored .55 .30
*Nos. 1960-1962 (3)* 1.35 .80

Inauguration of the Bosporus Bridge from Istanbul to Üsküdar, Oct. 30, 1973; UNICEF; children from East and West brought closer through Bosporus Bridge (No. 1962).

Mevlana's Tomb and Dancers — A465

Jalal-udin Mevlana — A466

**1973, Dec. 1** ***Perf. 13x12½***

**1963** A465 100k blk, lt ultra & grn .30 .20
**1964** A466 250k blue & multi .55 .25

Jalal-udin Mevlana (1207-1273), poet and founder of the Mevlevie dervish order.

Cotton and Ship — A467

Export Products: 90k, Grapes. 100k, Figs. 250k, Citrus fruits. 325k, Tobacco. 475k, Hazelnuts.

**1973, Dec. 10** **Litho.** ***Perf. 13***

**1965** A467 75k black, gray & bl .20 .20
**1966** A467 90k black, olive & bl .30 .20
**1967** A467 100k black, emer & bl .40 .20
**1968** A467 250k blk, brt yel & bl 1.10 .25
**1969** A467 325k blk, yel & bl 1.10 .25
**1970** A467 475k blk, org brn & bl 1.60 .40
*Nos. 1965-1970 (6)* 4.70 1.50

Pres. Inönü — A468

Hittite King, 8th Century B.C. — A469

**1973, Dec. 25** **Litho.** ***Perf. 13***

**1971** A468 100k sepia & buff .30 .20

Ismet Inönü, (1884-1973), first Prime Minister and second President of Turkey.

**1974, Apr. 29** **Litho.** ***Perf. 13***

Europa: 250k, Statuette of a Boy, (2nd millenium B.C.).

**1972** A469 110k multicolored *5.50 1.50*
**1973** A469 250k lt blue & multi *9.50 3.50*

Silver and Gold Figure, 3000 B.C. — A470

Child Care — A471

Archaeological Finds: 175k, Painted jar, 5000 B.C., horiz. 200k, Vessels in bull form, 1700-1600 B.C., horiz. 250k, Pitcher, 700 B.C.

**1974, May 24** **Litho.** ***Perf. 13***

**1974** A470 125k multicolored .35 .20
**1975** A470 175k multicolored .60 .20
**1976** A470 200k multicolored .75 .20
**1977** A470 250k multicolored 1.10 .40
*Nos. 1974-1977 (4)* 2.80 1.00

**1974, May 24**

**1978** A471 110k gray blue & blk .30 .20

Sisli Children's Hospital, Istanbul, 75th anniv.

Anatolian Rug, 15th Century A472

Designs: 150k, Persian rug, late 16th century. 200k, Kashan rug, Lahore.

**1974, July 21** **Litho.** ***Perf. 12½x13***

**1979** A472 100k blue & multi .65 .20
**1980** A472 150k brown & multi 1.00 .20
**1981** A472 200k red & multi 2.00 .25
*Nos. 1979-1981 (3)* 3.65 .65

10th anniversary of the Regional Cooperation for Development Pact among Turkey, Iran and Pakistan.

Dove with Turkish Flag over Cyprus A473

**1974, Aug. 26** **Litho.** ***Perf. 13***

**1982** A473 250k multicolored .80 .40

Cyprus Peace Operation.

Wrestling A474

Arrows Circling Globe A475

90k, 250k, various wrestling holds, horiz.

**1974, Aug. 29**

**1983** A474 90k multicolored .25 .20
**1984** A474 100k multicolored .40 .20
**1985** A474 250k multicolored .70 .25
*Nos. 1983-1985 (3)* 1.35 .65

World Freestyle Wrestling Championships.

**1974, Oct. 9** **Litho.** ***Perf. 13***

UPU Emblem and: 110k, "UPU" in form of dove. 200k, Dove.

**1986** A475 110k bl, gold & dk bl .25 .20
**1987** A475 200k green & brown .30 .20
**1988** A475 250k multicolored .55 .30
*Nos. 1986-1988 (3)* 1.10 .70

Centenary of Universal Postal Union.

"Law Reforms" A476

"National Economy" A477

"Education" A478

**1974, Oct. 29**

**1989** A476 50k blue & black .20 .20
**1990** A477 150k red & multi .25 .20
**1991** A478 400k multicolored .65 .30
*Nos. 1989-1991 (3)* 1.10 .70

Works and reforms of Kemal Ataturk.

Arrows Pointing Up — A479

Cogwheel and Map of Turkey A480

**1974, Nov. 29** **Litho.** ***Perf. 13***

**1992** A479 25k brown & black .20 .20
**1993** A480 100k brown & gray .35 .20

3rd 5-year Development Program (#1992), and industrialization progress (#1993).

Volleyball — A481

**1974, Dec. 30**

**1994** A481 125k shown .25 .20
**1995** A481 175k Basketball .45 .20
**1996** A481 250k Soccer .80 .20
*Nos. 1994-1996 (3)* 1.50 .60

Automatic Telex Network A482

Postal Check
A483

Radio Transmitter and Waves
A484

**1975, Feb. 5** **Litho.** ***Perf. 13***

**1997** A482 5k black & yellow .20 .20
**1998** A483 50k ol grn & org .20 .20
**1999** A484 100k blue & black .30 .20
*Nos. 1997-1999 (3)* .70 .60

Post and telecommunications.

Child Entering Classroom
A485

Children's paintings: 50k, View of village. 100k, Dancing children.

**1975, Apr. 23** **Litho.** ***Perf. 13***

**2000** A485 25k multicolored .20 .20
**2001** A485 50k multicolored .20 .20
**2002** A485 100k multicolored .30 .20
*Nos. 2000-2002 (3)* .70 .60

Karacaoglan Monument in Mut, by Huseyin Gezer — A486

**1975, Apr. 25**

**2003** A486 110k dk grn, bis & red .30 .25

Karacaoglan (1606-1697), musician.

Orange Harvest in Hatay, by Cemal Tollu — A487

Europa: 250k, Yoruk Family on Plateau, by Turgut Zaim.

**1975, Apr. 28**

**2004** A487 110k bister & multi *2.75 1.10*
**2005** A487 250k bister & multi *4.25 2.00*

Porcelain Vase, Turkey
A488

Designs: 200k, Ceramic plate, Iran, horiz. 250k, Camel leather vase, Pakistan.

***Perf. 13½x13, 13x13½***

**1975, July 21** **Litho.**

**2006** A488 110k multicolored 1.00 .30
**2007** A488 200k multicolored 1.50 .50
**2008** A488 250k ultra & multi 1.50 .80
*Nos. 2006-2008 (3)* 4.00 1.60

Regional Cooperation for Development Pact among Turkey, Iran and Pakistan.

Horon Folk Dance — A489

Regional Folk Dances: 125k, Kasik. 175k, Bengi. 250k, Kasap. 325k, Kafkas, vert.

**1975, Aug. 30** **Litho.** ***Perf. 13***

**2009** A489 100k blue & multi .35 .20
**2010** A489 125k green & multi .55 .20
**2011** A489 175k rose & multi .65 .20
**2012** A489 250k multicolored .95 .25
**2013** A489 325k orange & multi 1.50 .40
*Nos. 2009-2013 (5)* 4.00 1.25

Knight Slaying Dragon — A490

The Plunder of Salur Kazan's House — A491

Design: 175k, Two Wanderers, horiz.

**1975, Oct. 15** **Litho.** ***Perf. 13***

**2014** A490 90k multicolored .25 .20
**2015** A490 175k multicolored .40 .30
**2016** A491 200k multicolored .60 .40
*Nos. 2014-2016 (3)* 1.25 .90

Illustrations for tales by Dede Korkut.

Common Carp
A492

**1975, Nov. 27** **Litho.** ***Perf. 12½x13***

**2017** A492 75k Turbot .75 .50
**2018** A492 90k shown 1.00 .60
**2019** A492 175k Trout 1.50 .75
**2020** A492 250k Red mullet 3.00 .85
**2021** A492 475k Red bream 3.75 1.25
*Nos. 2017-2021 (5)* 10.00 3.95

Women's Participation
A493

Insurance Nationalization — A494

Fine Arts — A495

**1975, Dec. 5** ***Perf. 12½x13, 13x12½***

**2022** A493 100k bis, blk & red .20 .20
**2023** A494 110k violet & multi .30 .20
**2024** A495 250k multicolored .40 .20
*Nos. 2022-2024 (3)* .90 .60

Works and reforms of Ataturk.

Ceramic Plate — A496

Europa: 400k, Decorated pitcher.

**1976, May 3** **Litho.** ***Perf. 13***

**2025** A496 200k purple & multi *5.00 2.00*
**2026** A496 400k multicolored *10.00 3.00*

Sultan Ahmed Mosque
A497

**1976, May 10**

**2027** A497 500k gray & multi .80 .40

7th Islamic Conference, Istanbul.

Lunch in the Field
A498

Children's Drawings: 200k, Boats on the Bosporus, vert. 400k, Winter landscape.

**1976, May 19** **Litho.** ***Perf. 13***

**2028** A498 50k multicolored .20 .20
**2029** A498 200k multicolored .25 .20
**2030** A498 400k multicolored .45 .20
*Nos. 2028-2030 (3)* .90 .60

Samsun 76, First National Junior Philatelic Exhibition, Samsun.

Storks, Sultan Marsh
A499

Conservation Emblem and: 200k, Horses, Manyas Lake. 250k, Borabay Lake. 400k, Manavgat Waterfall.

**1976, June 5**

**2031** A499 150k multicolored 2.00 .60
**2032** A499 200k multicolored .65 .20
**2033** A499 250k multicolored 1.10 .20
**2034** A499 400k multicolored 1.25 .25
*Nos. 2031-2034 (4)* 5.00 1.25

European Wetland Conservation Year.

Nasreddin Hodja Carrying Liver — A500

Montreal Olympic Emblem and Flame — A501

Turkish Folklore: 250k, Friend giving recipe for cooking liver. 600k, Hawk carrying off liver and Hodja telling hawk he cannot enjoy liver without recipe.

**1976, July 5** **Litho.** ***Perf. 13***

**2035** A500 150k multicolored .25 .20
**2036** A500 250k multicolored .40 .20
**2037** A500 600k multicolored .95 .35
*Nos. 2035-2037 (3)* 1.60 .75

**1976, July 17**

Designs: 400k, "76," Montreal Olympic emblem, horiz. 600k, Montreal Olympic emblem and ribbons.

**2038** A501 100k red & multi .20 .20
**2039** A501 400k red & multi .50 .25
**2040** A501 600k red & multi .90 .40
*Nos. 2038-2040 (3)* 1.60 .85

21st Olympic Games, Montreal, Canada, 7/17-8/1.

Kemal Ataturk
A502

Designs: 200k, Riza Shah Pahlavi. 250k, Mohammed Ali Jinnah.

**1976, July 21** **Litho.** ***Perf. 13½***

**2041** A502 100k multicolored .25 .20
**2042** A502 200k multicolored .35 .20
**2043** A502 250k multicolored .50 .25
*Nos. 2041-2043 (3)* 1.10 .65

Regional Cooperation for Development Pact among Turkey, Pakistan and Iran, 12th anniversary.

"Ataturk's Army"
A503

Ataturk's Speeches
A504

"Peace at Home and in the World"
A505

**1976, Oct. 29** **Litho.** ***Perf. 13***

**2044** A503 100k black & red .20 .20
**2045** A504 200k gray grn & multi .25 .20
**2046** A505 400k blue & multi .55 .25
*Nos. 2044-2046 (3)* 1.00 .65

Works and reforms of Ataturk.

Hora
A506

**1977, Jan. 19 Litho. *Perf. 13***
**2047** A506 400k multicolored .70 .25

MTA Sismik 1 "Hora" geophysical exploration ship.

Keyboard and Violin Sound Hole — A507

**1977, Feb. 24 Litho. *Perf. 13x13½***
**2048** A507 200k multicolored .40 .20

Turkish State Symphony Orchestra, sesquicentennial.

Ataturk and "100" — A508

Design: 400k, Hand holding ballot.

**1977, Mar. 21 Litho. *Perf. 13***
**2049** A508 200k black & red .25 .20
**2050** A508 400k black & brown .50 .25

Centenary of Turkish Parliament.

Hierapolis (Pamukkale) A509

Europa: 400k, Zelve (mountains and poppies).

**1977, May 2 Litho. *Perf. 13½x13***
**2051** A509 200k multicolored *6.00 2.00*
**2052** A509 400k multicolored *10.00 3.00*

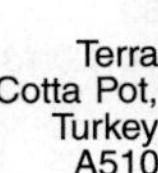
Terra Cotta Pot, Turkey A510

Designs: 225k, Terra cotta jug, Iran. 675k, Terra cotta bullock cart, Pakistan.

**1977, July 21 Litho. *Perf. 13***
**2053** A510 100k multicolored .25 .20
**2054** A510 225k multicolored .75 .25
**2055** A510 675k multicolored 1.50 .55
*a.* Souv. sheet, #2053-2055 *8.00 8.00*
*Nos. 2053-2055 (3)* 2.50 1.00

Regional Cooperation for Development Pact among Turkey, Iran and Pakistan, 13th anniv.

Finn-class Yacht A511

Kemal Ataturk A512

200k, Three yachts. 250k, Symbolic yacht.

**1977, July 28**
**2056** A511 150k lt bl, bl & blk .25 .20
**2057** A511 200k ultra & blue .40 .20
**2058** A511 250k ultra & black .55 .20
*Nos. 2056-2058 (3)* 1.20 .60

European Finn Class Sailing Championships, Istanbul, July 28.

Ataturk Type of 1972

**1977, June 13 Litho. *Perf. 13½x13***
**2060** A453 100k olive .50 .20
**2061** A453 200k brown .75 .25

Imprint: "GUZEL SANATLAR MATBAASI A.S. 1977"

**1977, Sept. 23 Litho. *Perf. 13***
**Size: 20½x22mm**
**2062** A512 200k blue .30 .20
**2063** A512 250k Prussian blue .35 .20

Imprint: "TIFDRUK-ISTANBUL 1978"

**1978, June 28 Photo. *Perf. 13***
**Size: 20x25mm**
**2065** A512 10k brown .20 .20
**2066** A512 50k grnsh gray .20 .20
**2067** A512 1 l fawn .20 .20
**2068** A512 2½ l purple .30 .20
**2069** A512 5 l blue .55 .20
**2072** A512 25 l dl grn & lt bl 2.00 .30
**2073** A512 50 l dp org & tan 3.00 .70
*Nos. 2065-2073 (7)* 6.45 2.00

No. 1832 Surcharged with New Value and Wavy Lines

**1977, Aug. 17**
**2078** A418 10k on 1k dp org & brn .30 .20

"Rationalism" A513

"National Sovereignty" A514

"Liberation of Nations" — A515

**1977, Oct. 29 Litho. *Perf. 13***
**2079** A513 100k multicolored .20 .20
**2080** A514 200k multicolored .20 .20
**2081** A515 400k multicolored .40 .20
*Nos. 2079-2081 (3)* .80 .60

Works and reforms of Ataturk.

Mohammad Allama Iqbal — A516

Trees and Burning Match — A517

**1977, Nov. 9 *Perf. 13x12½***
**2082** A516 400k multicolored .45 .20

Mohammad Allama Iqbal (1877-1938), Pakistani poet and philosopher.

**1977, Dec. 15 Litho. *Perf. 13***

Design: 250k, Sign showing growing tree.

**2083** A517 50k green, blk & red .20 .20
**2084** A517 250k gray, grn & blk .25 .20

Forest conservation. See type A542.

Wrecked Car — A518

Passing on Wrong Side — A519

Traffic Sign, "Slow!" — A520

Two types of 50k:
I — Number on license plate.
II — No number on plate.

Traffic Safety: 250k, Tractor drawing overloaded farm cart. 800k, Accident caused by incorrect passing. 10 l, "Use striped crossings."

**1977-78 *Perf. 13½x13, 13x13½***
**2085** A518 50k ultra, blk & red, II .60 .55
*a.* Type I .70 .55
**2086** A519 150k red, gray & blk .25 .20
**2087** A518 250k ocher, blk & red .50 .20
**2088** A520 500k gray, red & blk .50 .20
**2089** A520 800k multicolored 1.10 .25
**2090** A520 10 l dl grn, blk & brn 1.75 .35
*Nos. 2085-2090 (6)* 4.70 1.75

Issued: 500k, 1977; others, 1978.

Ishak Palace, Dogubeyazit — A521

Europa: 5 l, Anamur Castle.

**1978, May 2 Litho. *Perf. 13***
**2091** A521 2½ l multicolored *7.00 2.50*
**2092** A521 5 l multicolored *12.00 3.50*

Riza Shah Pahlavi — A522

**1978, June 16 Litho. *Perf. 13x13½***
**2093** A522 5 l multicolored .50 .50

Riza Shah Pahlavi (1877-1944) of Iran, birth centenary.

Yellow Rose, Turkey A523

3½ l, Pink roses, Iran. 8 l, Red roses, Pakistan.

**1978, July 21 Litho. *Perf. 13***
**2094** A523 2½ l multi .20 .20
**2095** A523 3½ l multi .30 .20
**2096** A523 8 l multi .70 .25
*Nos. 2094-2096 (3)* 1.20 .65

Regional Cooperation for Development Pact among Turkey, Iran and Pakistan.

Anti-Apartheid Emblem — A524

**1978, Aug. 14 Litho. *Perf. 13½x13***
**2097** A524 10 l multicolored .85 .25

Anti-Apartheid Year.

View of Ankara — A525

Design: 5 l, View of Tripoli, horiz.

***Perf. 13x12½, 12½x13***
**1978, Aug. 17**
**2098** A525 2½ l multi .30 .20
**2099** A525 5 l multi .75 .20

Turkish-Libyan friendship.

Souvenir Sheet

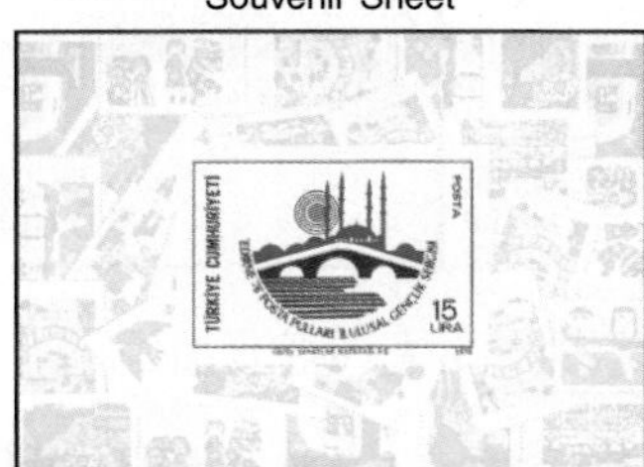

Bridge and Mosque — A526

**1978, Oct. 25 *Imperf.***
**2100** A526 15 l multicolored 1.25 .80

Edirne '78, 2nd Natl. Phil. Youth Exhib.

Independence Medal
A527

Latin Alphabet
A529

Speech Reform
A528

**1978, Oct. 29** ***Perf. 13x13½, 13½x13***

2101 A527 2½ l multi .20 .20
2102 A528 3½ l multi .25 .20
2103 A529 5 l multi .35 .20
*Nos. 2101-2103 (3)* .80 .60

Ataturk's works and reforms.

House on Bosporus, 1699 — A530

Turkish Houses: 2½ l, Izmit, 1774, vert. 3½ l, Kula, 17th cent., vert. 5 l, Milas, 18th-19th cent., vert. 8 l, Safranbolu, 18th-19th cent.

***Perf. 13x12½, 12½x13***

**1978, Nov. 22**

2104 A530 1 l multi .20 .20
2105 A530 2½ l multi .30 .20
2106 A530 3½ l multi .40 .20
2107 A530 5 l multi .60 .20
2108 A530 8 l multi .95 .25
*Nos. 2104-2108 (5)* 2.45 1.05

Carrier Pigeon, Plane, Horseback Rider, Train
A531

Europa: 5 l, Morse key, telegraph and Telex machine. 7½ l, Telephone dial and satellite.

**1979, Apr. 30** **Litho.** ***Perf. 13***

2109 A531 2½ l multicolored *3.00 1.00*
2110 A531 5 l org brn & blk *5.00 1.00*
2111 A531 7½ l brt blue & blk *5.75 1.50*
*Nos. 2109-2111 (3)* *13.75 3.50*

Plowing, by Namik Ismail
A532

Paintings: 7½ l, Potters, by Kamalel Molk, Iran. 10 l, At the Well, by Allah Baksh, Pakistan.

**1979, Sept. 5** **Litho.** ***Perf. 13½x13***

2112 A532 5 l multi .20 .20
2113 A532 7½ l multi .35 .20
2114 A532 10 l multi .55 .25
*Nos. 2112-2114 (3)* 1.10 .65

Regional Cooperation for Development Pact among Turkey, Pakistan and Iran, 15th anniversary.

A533

A534

**1979, Sept. 17** ***Perf. 13***

2115 A533 5 l Colemanite .35 .20
2116 A533 7½ l Chromite .50 .20
2117 A533 10 l Antimonite .80 .20
2118 A533 15 l Sulphur 1.00 .30
*Nos. 2115-2118 (4)* 2.65 .90

10th World Mining Congress.

**1979, Sept. 24**

8-shaped road, train tunnel, plane and emblem.

2119 A534 5 l multicolored .30 .20

European Ministers of Communications, 8th Symposium.

Youth — A535

Secularization
A536

Design: 5 l, National oath.

**1979, Oct. 29** ***Perf. 13x12½, 12½x13***

2120 A535 2½ l multi .20 .20
2121 A536 3½ l multi .20 .20
2122 A535 5 l black & orange .30 .20
*Nos. 2120-2122 (3)* .70 .60

Ataturk's works and reforms.

Poppies — A537

**1979, Nov. 26** **Litho.** ***Perf. 13x13½***

2123 A537 5 l shown .25 .20
2124 A537 7½ l Oleander .45 .20
2125 A537 10 l Late spider orchid .70 .20
2126 A537 15 l Mandrake 1.10 .25
*Nos. 2123-2126 (4)* 2.50 .85

See Nos. 2154-2157.

Kemal Ataturk
A538 A538a

***Perf. 12½x11½, 13x12½(No. 2131)***

**1979-81** **Litho.**

2127 A538 50k olive ('80) .20 .20
2128 A538 1 l grn & lt grn .20 .20
2129 A538 2½ l purple .25 .20
2130 A538 2½ l bl grn & lt bl ('80) .20 .20
2131 A538 2½ l orange ('81) .20 .20
2132 A538 5 l ultra & gray .50 .20
*a.* Sheet of 8 2.75 2.75
2133 A538 7½ l brown .50 .20
2134 A538 7½ l red ('80) .70 .20
2135 A538 10 l rose carmine .80 .20
2136 A538 20 l gray ('80) 1.25 .30
*Nos. 2127-2136 (10)* 4.80 2.10

No. 2132a for Ankara '79 Philatelic Exhibition, Oct. 14-20.
For surcharge see No. 2261.

**1980-82** **Photo.** ***Perf. 13½***

2137 A538a 7½ l red brown .20 .20
*c.* Sheet of 4 2.50 2.50
2137A A538a 10 l brown .65 .20
2138 A538a 20 l lilac .65 .20
2138A A538a 30 l gray .80 .30
2139 A538a 50 l orange red 1.25 .30
2140 A538a 75 l brt green 2.00 .60
2141 A538a 100 l blue 2.50 .75
*Nos. 2137-2141 (7)* 8.05 2.55

No. 2137c for ANTALYA '82 4th Natl. Junior Stamp Show.
Issued: #2137, 7/15/81; #2137c, 10/3/82; 30 l, 9/23/81; others, 12/10/80.
See Nos. 2164-2169.

Turkish Printing, 250th Anniversary — A539

**1979, Nov. 30** **Litho.** ***Perf. 13***

2142 A539 10 l multicolored .60 .45

2nd International Olive Oil Year — A540

***Perf. 12½x13, 13x12½***

**1979, Dec. 20** **Litho.**

2143 A540 5 l shown .20 .20
2144 A540 10 l Globe, oil drop, vert. .45 .20

Uskudarli Hoca Ali Riza Bey (1857-1930), Painter — A541

Europa: 15 l, Ali Sami Boyar (1880-1967), painter. 20 l, Dr. Hulusi Behcet (1889-1948), physician, discovered Behcet skin disease.

**1980, Apr. 28** ***Perf. 13***

2145 A541 7½ l multi *1.75 1.00*
2146 A541 15 l multi *2.50 1.25*
2147 A541 20 l multi *3.25 1.25*
*Nos. 2145-2147 (3)* 7.50 3.50

Forest Conservation
A542

Earthquake Destruction
A543

**1980, July 3** ***Perf. 13½x13***

2148 A542 50k ol grn & red org .30 .20

See type A517. For surcharge see No. 2262.

**1980, Sept. 8** ***Perf. 13***

2149 A543 7½ l shown .30 .25
2150 A543 20 l Seismograph .70 .50

7th World Conference on Earthquake Engineering, Istanbul.

Games' Emblem, Sports — A544

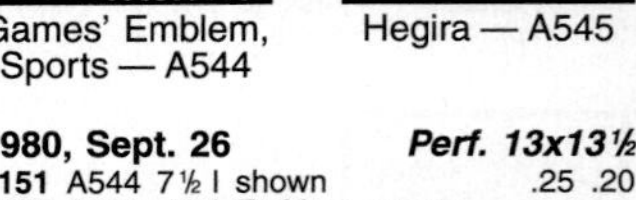

Hegira — A545

**1980, Sept. 26** ***Perf. 13x13½***

2151 A544 7½ l shown .25 .20
2152 A544 20 l Emblem, sports, diff. .70 .20

First Islamic Games, Izmir.

**1980, Nov. 9**

2153 A545 20 l multicolored .80 .40

**Plant Type of 1979**

**1980, Nov. 26** ***Perf. 13***

2154 A537 2½ l Manisa tulip .20 .20
2155 A537 7½ l Ephesian bellflower .50 .20
2156 A537 15 l Angora crocus .75 .20
2157 A537 20 l Anatolian orchid 1.25 .20
*Nos. 2154-2157 (4)* 2.70 .80

Avicenna Treating Patient
A546

Avicenna (Arab Physician), Birth Millenium: 20 l, Portrait, vert.

**1980, Dec. 15**

2158 A546 7½ l multi .40 .20
2159 A546 20 l multi .70 .30

Balkanfila VIII Stamp Exhibition, Ankara
A547

**1981, Jan. 1** **Litho.** ***Perf. 13***

2160 A547 10 l red & black .60 .20

Kemal Ataturk — A548

**1981, Feb. 4** ***Perf. 13***

2163 A548 10 l lilac rose .50 .20

**Ataturk Type of 1980**

**1983-84** ***Perf. 13x13½***

2164 A538a 15 l grnsh blue .25 .20
2165 A538a 20 l orange ('84) .30 .20
2167 A538a 65 l bluish grn .95 .20
2169 A538a 90 l lilac rose 1.25 .20
*Nos. 2164-2169 (4)* 2.75 .80

Issued: #2164, 2167, 2169, 11/30; #2165, 7/25.

Sultan Mehmet the Conqueror (1432-1481) — A549

**1981, May 3** **Litho.** ***Perf. 13x12½***

2173 A549 10 l multicolored .30 .25
2174 A549 20 l multicolored .65 .50

Gaziantep (Folk Dance) A550

Antalya A551

**1981, May 4** **Litho.** ***Perf. 13***
**2175** A550 7½ l shown .25 .20
**2176** A550 10 l Balikesir .35 .20
**2177** A550 15 l Kahramanmaras .55 .25
**2178** A551 35 l shown *4.00 1.10*
**2179** A551 70 l Burdur *5.00 2.25*
*Nos. 2175-2179 (5)* *10.15 4.00*

Nos. 2178-2179 show CEPT (Europa) emblem.

Nos. C40, 1925, 1931A, 2089 Surcharged in Black with New Value and Wavy Lines

**1981, June 3** ***Perf. 13½x13***
**2179A** AP7 10 l on 60k .40 .20
**2180** A453 10 l on 110k .40 .20
**2181** A453 10 l on 400k .40 .20
**2182** A520 10 l on 800k .40 .20
*Nos. 2179A-2182 (4)* 1.60 .80

A552

Kemal Ataturk A553

**1981, June 22** ***Perf. 13x12½***
**2183** A552 7½ l Rug, Bilecik .20 .20
**2184** A552 10 l Embroidery .25 .20
**2185** A552 15 l Drum, zurna players .40 .20
**2186** A552 20 l Embroidered napkin .40 .20
**2187** A552 30 l Rug, diff. .75 .20
*Nos. 2183-2187 (5)* 2.00 1.00

22nd Intl. Turkish Folklore Congress.

**1981, May 19** **Litho.** ***Perf. 14x15***
**2188** A553 2½ l No. 1801 .20 .20
**2189** A553 7½ l No. 1816 .20 .20
**2190** A553 10 l No. 1604 .20 .20
**2191** A553 20 l No. 804 .50 .20
**2192** A553 25 l No. 777 .60 .20
**2193** A553 35 l No. 1959 .75 .20
*Nos. 2188-2193 (6)* 2.45 1.20

**Souvenir Sheet**

**2194** Sheet of 6 11.00 5.50
*a.* A553 2½ l like 2½ l .20 .20
*b.* A553 37½ l like 7½ l .40 .20
*c.* A553 50 l like 10 l .60 .20
*d.* A553 100 l like 20 l 1.25 .40
*e.* A553 125 l like 25 l 1.50 .50
*f.* A553 175 l like 35 l 2.25 .65

Souvenir Sheet

Balkanfila VIII Stamp Exhibition, Ankara — A554

**1981, Aug. 8** **Litho.** ***Perf. 13***
**2195** A554 Sheet of 2 5.00 5.00
*a.* 50 l No. B68 2.50 2.50
*b.* 50 l No. 733 2.50 2.50

5th General Congress of European Physics Society A555

**1981, Sept. 7** ***Perf. 12½x13***
**2196** A555 10 l red & multi .25 .20
**2197** A555 30 l blue & multi .60 .20

World Food Day A556

**1981, Oct. 16**
**2198** A556 10 l multicolored .25 .20
**2199** A556 30 l multicolored .60 .20

Constituent Assembly Inauguration — A557

**1981, Oct. 23** ***Perf. 13***
**2200** A557 10 l multicolored .25 .20
**2201** A557 30 l multicolored .60 .20

Ataturk — A558

Portraits of Ataturk.

**1981-82** ***Perf. 11½x12½, 13 (#2204)***
**2202** A558 1 l green .20 .20
**2203** A558 2½ l purple .20 .20
**2204** A558 2½ l gray & org *.50 .20*
**2205** A558 5 l blue .20 .20
**2206** A558 10 l orange .20 .20
**2207** A558 35 l brown .70 .20
*Nos. 2202-2207 (6)* 2.00 1.20

Issued: #2204, 12/10/81; others, 1/27/82.

Literacy Campaign A559

Energy Conservation A560

**1981, Dec. 24** ***Perf. 13½***
**2217** A559 2½ l Procession .35 .20

**1982, Jan. 11** ***Perf. 13***
**2218** A560 10 l multicolored .45 .20

Magnolias, by Ibrahim Calli (b. 1882) A561

Sultanhan Caravanserai A562

**1982, Mar. 17** ***Perf. 13x13½, 13½x13***
**2219** A561 10 l shown .25 .20
**2220** A561 20 l Fishermen, horiz. .50 .20
**2221** A561 30 l Sewing Woman .65 .20
*Nos. 2219-2221 (3)* 1.40 .60

**Europa Issue**

**1982, Apr. 26** ***Perf. 13x12½***
**2222** A562 30 l shown .75 .25
**2223** A562 70 l Silk Route 1.60 .50
*a.* Min. sheet, 2 each #2222-2223 7.00 7.00
*b.* Pair, #2222-2223 2.50 1.00

1250th Anniv. of Kul-Tigin Monument, Kosu Saydam, Mongolia — A563

**1982, June 9** ***Perf. 13***
**2224** A563 10 l Monument .20 .20
**2225** A563 30 l Kul-Tigin (685-732), Gok-Turkish commander .40 .20

Pendik Shipyard Opening A564

**1982, July 1** ***Perf. 12½x13***
**2226** A564 30 l Ship, emblem .40 .20

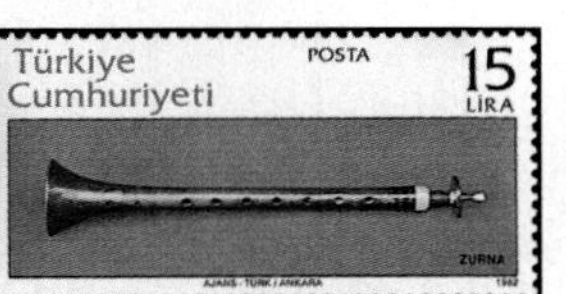

Mountains of Anatolia A565

**1982, July 17** ***Perf. 13***
**2227** A565 7½ l Agri Dagi, vert. .20 .20
**2228** A565 10 l Buzul Dagi .30 .20
**2229** A565 15 l Demirkazik, vert. .50 .20
**2230** A565 20 l Erciyes .70 .20
**2231** A565 30 l Kackar Dagi, vert. .90 .20
**2232** A565 35 l Uludag 1.25 .20
*Nos. 2227-2232 (6)* 3.85 1.20

Beyazit State Library Centenary A566

**1982, Sept. 27**
**2233** A566 30 l multicolored .50 .25

Musical Instruments of Anatolia — A567

**1982, Oct. 13**
**2234** A567 7½ l Davul .30 .20
**2235** A567 10 l Baglama .40 .20
**2236** A567 15 l shown .60 .20
**2237** A567 20 l Kemence .90 .20
**2238** A567 30 l Ney 1.10 .20
*Nos. 2234-2238 (5)* 3.30 1.00

Roman Temple Columns, Sart A568

**1982, Nov. 3**
**2239** A568 30 l multi .75 .35

Family Planning and Mother-Child Health — A569

**1983, Jan. 12** **Litho.** ***Perf. 13***
**2240** A569 10 l Family on map .25 .20
**2241** A569 35 l Mother and child .75 .20

30th Anniv. of Customs Cooperation Council — A570

**1983, Jan. 26**
**2242** A570 45 l multi .75 .20

1982 Constitution — A571

**1983, Jan. 27**
**2243** A571 10 l Ballot box .20 .20
**2244** A571 30 l Open book, scale .35 .20

Manastirli Bey A572

**1983, Mar. 16** **Litho.**
**2245** A572 35 l multi .45 .20

Manastirli Hamdi Bey (1890-1945), telegrapher of news of Istanbul's occupation to Ataturk, 1920.

### Europa Issue

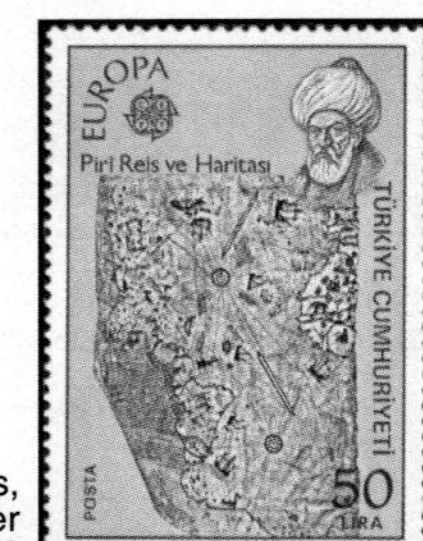
Piri Reis, Geographer A573

**1983, May 5 Litho.** ***Perf. 12½x13***
**2246** A573 50 l shown 15.00 2.50
**2247** A573 100 l Ulug Bey (1394-1449), astronomer 35.00 7.50

Youth Week A574

**1983, May 16**
**2248** A574 15 l multi .25 .20

World Communications Year — A575

**1983, May 16** ***Perf. 13***
**2249** A575 15 l Carrier pigeon, vert. .30 .20
**2250** A575 50 l Phone lines .60 .20
**2251** A575 70 l Emblem, vert. 1.10 .20
*Nos. 2249-2251 (3)* 2.00 .60

50th Anniv. of State Civil Aviation A576

**1983, May 20 Litho.** ***Perf. 13***
**2252** A576 50 l Plane, jet .50 .20
**2253** A576 70 l Airport .70 .20

18th Council of Europe Art Exhibition A577

15 l, Eros, 2nd cent. BC, vert. 35 l, Two-headed duck, Hittite, 14th cent BC. 50 l, Zinc jugs, plate, 16th cent., vert. 70 l, Marcus Aurelius and his wife Faustina the Young, 2nd cent.

**1983, May 22** ***Perf. 13***
**2254** A577 15 l multi .40 .20
**2255** A577 35 l multi .90 .20
**2256** A577 50 l multi 1.00 .20
**2257** A577 70 l multi 1.10 .20
*Nos. 2254-2257 (4)* 3.40 .80

Council of Europe's "The Water's Edge" Campaign — A578

Coastal Views.

**1983, June 1 Litho.** ***Perf. 13x12½***
**2258** A578 10 l Olodeniz .40 .25
**2259** A578 25 l Olympus .40 .25
**2260** A578 35 l Kekova .90 .50
*Nos. 2258-2260 (3)* 1.70 1.00

Nos. 2127, 2148 Surcharged
***Perf. 12½x11½, 13½x13***

**1983, June 8**
**2261** A538 5 l on 50k olive .20 .20
**2262** A542 5 l on 50k ol grn & red org .20 .20

Kemal Ataturk A579

Aga Khan Architecture Award A580

**1983, June 22** ***Perf. 13***
**2263** A579 15 l bl grn & bl .25 .20
*a.* Sheet of 5 + label 1.75 1.25
**2264** A579 50 l green & blue .80 .20
**2265** A579 100 l orange & blue 1.75 .30
*Nos. 2263-2265 (3)* 2.80 .70

For surcharge see No. 2432.

**1983, Sept. 4 Photo.** ***Perf. 11½***
**2266** A580 50 l View of Istanbul .75 .20

60th Anniv. of the Republic A582

**1983, Oct. 29** ***Perf. 13½x13***
**2268** A582 15 l multi .25 .20
**2269** A582 50 l multi .75 .20

Columns, Aphrodisias — A583

**1983, Nov. 2** ***Perf. 13***
**2270** A583 50 l multi 1.00 .75

UNESCO Campaign for Istanbul and Goreme — A584

**1984, Feb. 15 Litho.** ***Perf. 13***
**2271** A584 25 l St. Sophia Basilica .30 .20
**2272** A584 35 l Goreme .45 .20
**2273** A584 50 l Istanbul .60 .20
*Nos. 2271-2273 (3)* 1.35 .60

Natl. Police Org. Emblem A585

**1984, Apr. 10 Litho.** ***Perf. 13***
**2274** A585 15 l multi .30 .25

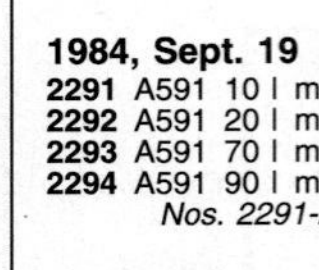
Europa (1959-84) A586

**1984, Apr. 30** ***Perf. 13½x13***
**2275** A586 50 l blue & multi 15.00 2.50
**2276** A586 100 l gray & multi 26.00 5.00

Mete Khan, Hun Ruler, 204 BC, Flag A587

Sixteen States (Hun Rulers and Flags): 20 l, Panu, Western Hun empire (48-216). 50 l, Attila, 375-454. 70 l, Aksunvar, Ak Hun empire, 420-562.

**1984, June 20 Litho.** ***Perf. 13***
**2277** A587 10 l multi .50 .20
**2278** A587 20 l multi .75 .20
**2279** A587 50 l multi 1.75 .20
**2280** A587 70 l multi 3.00 .20
*Nos. 2277-2280 (4)* 6.00 .80

See Nos. 2315-2318, 2349-2352, 2382-2385.

Occupation of Cyprus, 10th Anniv. A588

**1984, July 20 Litho.** ***Perf. 13***
**2281** A588 70 l Dove, olive branch 1.10 .50

Wild Flowers A589

Armed Forces Day A590

**1984, Aug. 1** ***Perf. 11½x12½***
**2282** A589 10 l Marshmallow flower .20 .20
**2283** A589 20 l Red poppy .25 .20
**2284** A589 70 l Sowbread .85 .20
**2285** A589 200 l Snowdrop 2.50 .30
**2286** A589 300 l Tulip 4.00 .40
*Nos. 2282-2286 (5)* 7.80 1.30

See Nos. 2301-2308. For surcharges see Nos. 2465, 2467, 2479-2480.

**1984, Aug. 26** ***Perf. 13½x13***
**2287** A590 20 l Soldier, dove, flag .30 .20
**2288** A590 50 l Sword .50 .20
**2289** A590 70 l Arms, soldier, flag .75 .20
**2290** A590 90 l Map, soldier 1.00 .20
*Nos. 2287-2290 (4)* 2.55 .80

Trees and Wood Products A591

Pres. Ismet Inonu (1884-1973), A592

Seed, Tree and Product: 10 l, Liquidambar, liquidambar grease. 20 l, Oriental spruce, stringed instrument. 70 l, Oriental beech, chair. 90 l, Cedar of Lebanon, ship.

**1984, Sept. 19 Litho.** ***Perf. 13x12½***
**2291** A591 10 l multi .50 .20
**2292** A591 20 l multi .50 .20
**2293** A591 70 l multi 1.00 .20
**2294** A591 90 l multi 1.50 .20
*Nos. 2291-2294 (4)* 3.50 .80

**1984, Sept. 24** ***Perf. 13***
**2295** A592 20 l Portrait .30 .20

First Intl. Turkish Carpet Congress — A593

**1984, Oct. 7** ***Perf. 13x13½***
**2296** A593 70 l Seljukian carpet, 13th cent. .75 .50

Ruins of Ancient City of Harran A594

**1984, Nov. 7** ***Perf. 13½x13***
**2297** A594 70 l Columns, arch 1.25 1.25

Turkish Women's Suffrage, 50th Anniv. A595

**1984, Dec. 5 Litho.** ***Perf. 13***
**2298** A595 20 l Women voting .25 .20

40th Anniv., ICAO — A596

**1984, Dec. 7 Litho.** ***Perf. 13***
**2299** A596 100 l Icarus, ICAO emblem 1.25 1.00

Souvenir Sheet

No. 1047 — A597

**1985, Jan. 13 Litho.** ***Imperf.***
**2300** A597 Sheet of 4, 2 each #a.-b. 4.00 3.00
*a.-b.* 70 l, any single .50 .50

Istanbul '87. No. 2300b has denomination in lower right.

### Flower Type of 1984

**1985** ***Perf. 11½x12½***
**2301** A589 5 l Narcissus .20 .20
***Perf. 12½x13***
**2308** A589 100 l Daisy 1.10 .20

Issue dates: #2301, Feb. 6; #2308, July 31.

Turkish Aviation League, 60th Anniv. A598

**1985, Feb. 16** *Perf. 13*

**2310** A598 10 l Parachutist, glider .30 .25
**2311** A598 20 l Hot air balloon, vert. .70 .50

INTELSAT, 20th Anniv. — A599

**1985, Apr. 3**

**2312** A599 100 l multi 1.50 .75

### Europa Issue

Ulvi Cemal Erkin (1906-1972) and Kosekce — A600

Composers and music: 200 l, Mithat Fenmen (1916-1982) and Concertina.

**1985, Apr. 29** *Perf. 13½x13*

**2313** A600 100 l multi *25.00 3.50*
**2314** A600 200 l multi *35.00 5.00*

### Turkish States Type of 1984

Sixteen States (Kagan rulers and flags): 10 l, Bilge, Gokturk Empire (552-743) and Orhon-Turkish alphabet. 20 l, Bayan, Avar Empire (565-803). 70 l, Hazar, Hazar Empire (651-983). 100 l, Kutlug Kul Bilge, Uygur State (774-1335).

**1985, June 20**

**2315** A587 10 l multi .40 .20
**2316** A587 20 l multi .75 .20
**2317** A587 70 l multi 1.40 .20
**2318** A587 100 l multi 2.75 .20
*Nos. 2315-2318 (4)* 5.30 .80

Intl. Youth Year A601

**1985, Aug. 8**

**2319** A601 100 l multi 1.10 .75
**2320** A601 120 l multi 1.50 1.25

Postal Code Inauguration A602

**1985, Sept. 4** *Perf. 13*

**Background Color**

**2321** A602 10 l pale yel brn .25 .20
**2322** A602 20 l fawn .40 .20
**2323** A602 20 l gray green .40 .20
**2324** A602 20 l brt blue .40 .20
**2325** A602 70 l rose lilac .90 .20
**2326** A602 100 l gray 1.25 .30
*Nos. 2321-2326 (6)* 3.60 1.30

Symposium of Natl. Palaces — A603

**1985, Sept. 25** *Perf. 13½x13*

**2327** A603 20 l Aynalikavak, c. 1703 .35 .20
**2328** A603 100 l Beylerbeyi, 1865 1.40 .20

UN, 40th Anniv. A604

**1985, Oct. 24**

**2329** A604 100 l multi 1.25 1.00

Alanya Fortress and City A605

**1985, Nov. 7**

**2330** A605 100 l multi 1.50 .75

A606

A607

**1985, Nov. 12** *Perf. 13x13½*

**2331** A606 100 l multi 1.25 .75

Turkish Meteorological Service, 60th anniv.

**1985, Dec. 14**

**2332** A607 20 l multi .30 .20

Isik Lyceum, Istanbul, cent.

Ataturk — A608

*Perf. 11½x12½*

**1985, Dec. 18** **Litho.**

**2334** A608 10 l pale bl & ultra .20 .20
**2335** A608 20 l beige & brn .25 .20
**2336** A608 100 l lt pink & claret 1.25 .20
*Nos. 2334-2336 (3)* 1.70 .60

7th Intl. Children's Festival, Ankara A609

Various children's drawings.

**1986, Apr. 23** **Litho.** *Perf. 12½x13*

**2342** A609 20 l multi .30 .25
**2343** A609 100 l multi .85 .25
**2344** A609 120 l multi 1.00 1.00
*Nos. 2342-2344 (3)* 2.15 1.50

### Europa Issue

Pollution A610

**1986, Apr. 28** *Perf. 13*

**2345** A610 100 l shown *12.00 2.50*
**2346** A610 200 l Bandaged leaf *17.50 5.00*

1st Ataturk Intl. Peace Prize — A611

Kirkpinar Wrestling Matches, Edirne — A613

1st Turkish Submarine, Cent. — A612

**1986, May 19** **Litho.** *Perf. 13*

**2347** A611 20 l gold & multi .50 .50
**2348** A611 100 l silver & multi 1.25 .75

### States Type of 1984

Sixteen States (Devleti rulers and flags): 10 l, Bilge Kul Kadir Khan, Kara Khanids State (840-1212). 20 l, Alp-Tekin, Ghaznavids State (963-1183). 100 l, Seldjuk Bey, Seldjuks State (1040-1157). 120 l, Muhammed Harezmsah, Khwarizm-Shahs State (1157-1231).

**1986, June 20**

**2349** A587 10 l multi .30 .20
**2350** A587 20 l multi .60 .20
**2351** A587 100 l multi 1.25 .20
**2352** A587 120 l multi 2.50 .20
*Nos. 2349-2352 (4)* 4.65 .80

**1986, June 16** **Litho.** *Perf. 13*

**2353** A612 20 l Torpedo sub Abdulhamid 1.00 .50

**1986, June 30**

**2354** A613 10 l Oiling bodies .50 .50
**2355** A613 20 l Five wrestlers .50 .50
**2356** A613 100 l Two wrestlers 1.50 1.00
*Nos. 2354-2356 (3)* 2.50 2.00

Organization for Economic Cooperation and Development, 25th Anniv. — A614

**1986, Sept. 30** **Litho.** *Perf. 13½x13*

**2357** A614 100 l multi .60 .25

Automobile, Cent. — A615

**1986, Oct. 15**

**2358** A615 10 l Benz Velocipede, 1886 .75 .50
**2359** A615 20 l Rolls-Royce Silver Ghost, 1906 1.00 .50
**2360** A615 100 l Mercedes Touring Car, 1928 2.00 1.00
**2361** A615 200 l Abstract speeding car 2.75 1.50
*Nos. 2358-2361 (4)* 6.50 3.50

Paintings A616

Celal Bayar (1883-1986), 3rd President — A617

Designs: 100 l, Bouquet with Tulip, by Feyhaman Duran (1886-1970). 120 l, Landscape with Fountain, by H. Avni Lifij (1886-1927), horiz.

**1986, Oct. 22** *Perf. 13½x13, 13x13½*

**2362** A616 100 l multi .70 .40
**2363** A616 120 l multi 2.00 .55

**1986, Oct. 27** *Perf. 13*

**2364** A617 20 l shown .50 .20
**2365** A617 100 l Profile .75 .20

Kubad-Abad Ruins, Beysehir Lake — A618

**1986, Nov. 7** *Perf. 13½x13*

**2366** A618 100 l multi 1.10 .40

Mehmet Akif Ersoy (1873-1936), Composer of the Turkish National Anthem — A619

**1986, Dec. 27** **Litho.** *Perf. 13½x13*

**2367** A619 20 l multi .35 .20

Road Safety A620

Intl. Year of Shelter for the Homeless A622

Butterflies A621

**1987, Feb. 4 Litho. *Perf. 13x13½***
**2368** A620 10 l Use seatbelts .20 .20
**2369** A620 20 l Don't drink alcohol and drive .25 .20
**2370** A620 150 l Observe speed limit 1.10 .20
*Nos. 2368-2370 (3)* 1.55 .60

For surcharges see Nos. 2466, 2477-2478.

**1987, Feb. 25 *Perf. 13½x13***
**2371** A621 10 l Celerio euphorbiae .50 .25
**2372** A621 20 l Vanessa atalanta 1.00 .50
**2373** A621 100 l Euplagia quadripunctaria 4.00 1.75
**2374** A621 120 l Colias crocea 4.50 2.50
*Nos. 2371-2374 (4)* 10.00 5.00

**1987, Mar. 18 Litho. *Perf. 13x13½***
**2375** A622 200 l multi 1.25 .75

Karabuk Iron and Steel Works, 50th Anniv. A623

**1987, Apr. 3 Litho. *Perf. 13½x13***
**2376** A623 50 l Interior .30 .20
**2377** A623 200 l Exterior .80 .20

Natl. Sovereignty — A624

**1987, Apr. 23 *Perf. 13½x13***
**2378** A624 50 l multi .35 .20

Founding of the Turkish state, 67th anniv.

Architecture — A625

Europa: 50 l, Turkish History Institute, 1951-67, designed by Turgut Cansever with Ertur Yener. 200 l, Social Insurance Institute, 1963, designed by Sedad Hakki Eldem.

**1987, Apr. 28 *Perf. 13***
**2379** A625 50 l multi *10.00 2.00*
**2380** A625 200 l multi *25.00 4.00*

92nd Session, Intl. Olympic Committee, Istanbul, May 9-12 — A626

**1987, May 9 Litho. *Perf. 13x13½***
**2381** A626 200 l multi 1.25 .75

Turkish States Type of 1984

Sixteen states (Devleti and Imparatorlugu rulers and flags): 10 l, Batu Khan, Golden Horde State (1227-1502). 20 l, Kutlug Timur Khan, Great Timur Empire (1368-1507). 50 l, Babur Shah, Babur Empire (1526-1858). 200 l, Osman Bey Gasi, Ottoman Empire (1299-1923).

**1987, June 20 *Perf. 12½x13***
**2382** A587 10 l multi .50 .25
**2383** A587 20 l multi 1.00 .30
**2384** A587 50 l multi 1.50 .30
**2385** A587 200 l multi 3.25 1.00
*Nos. 2382-2385 (4)* 6.25 1.85

Album of the Conqueror, Mehmet II, 15th Cent., Topkapi Palace Museum — A627

Untitled paintings by Mehmet Siyah Kalem: 10 l, Two warriors, vert. 20 l, Three men, donkey. 50 l, Blackamoor whipping horse. 200 l, Demon, vert.

***Perf. 13½x13, 13x13½***
**1987, July 1 Litho.**
**2386** A627 10 l multi .75 .40
**2387** A627 20 l multi 1.00 .40
**2388** A627 50 l multi 1.25 .40
**2389** A627 200 l multi 2.00 1.00
*Nos. 2386-2389 (4)* 5.00 2.20

Natl. Palaces A628

**1987, Sept. 25 *Perf. 13½x13***
**2390** A628 50 l Ihlamur, c. 1850 .50 .50
**2391** A628 200 l Kucuksu Pavilion, 1857 1.25 .50

See Nos. 2425-2426.

"Tughra," Suleiman's Calligraphic Signature — A629

Designs: 30 l, Portrait, vert. 200 l, Suleiman Receiving a Foreign Minister, contemporary miniature, vert. 270 l, Bust, detail of bas-relief, The Twenty-Three Law-Givers, entrance to the gallery of the US House of Representatives.

**Litho., Litho. & Engr. (270 l)**
**1987, Oct. 1 *Perf. 13½x13, 13x13½***
**2392** A629 30 l multi .50 .35
**2393** A629 50 l shown .75 .45
**2394** A629 200 l multi 2.00 .80
**2395** A629 270 l multi 2.50 1.10
*Nos. 2392-2395 (4)* 5.75 2.70

Suleiman the Magnificent (1494-1566), sultan of the Turkish Empire (1520-1566). On No. 2395, the gold ink was applied by a thermographic process producing a shiny, raised effect.

A630

Presidents: a, Cemal Gursel (1961-1966). b, Cevdet Sunay (1966-1973). c, Fahri S. Koruturk (1973-1980). d, Kenan Evren (1982-). e, Ismet Inonu (1938-1950). f, Celal Bayar (1950-1960). g, Mustafa Kemal Ataturk (1923-1938).

**1987, Oct. 29 Litho. *Imperf.***
**Souvenir Sheet**
**2396** A630 Sheet of 7 6.00 6.00
*a.-f.* 50 l any single .60 .60
*g.* 100 l multi, 26x37mm .75 .75

A631

**1988, Apr. 9 Litho. *Perf. 13***
**2397** A631 50 l shown *.75 .50*
**2398** A631 200 l Mosque, architectural elements *2.25 1.00*

Joseph (Mimar) Sinan (1489-1588), architect.

Health — A632

**1988, May 4**
**2399** A632 50 l Immunization, horiz. .20 .20
**2400** A632 200 l Fight drug abuse .35 .20
**2401** A632 300 l Safe work conditions, horiz. .50 .20
**2402** A632 600 l Organ donation 1.10 .30
*Nos. 2399-2402 (4)* 2.15 .90

**Europa Issue**

Telecommunications — A633

Transport and communication: 200 l, Modes of transportation, vert.

**1988, May 2 Litho. *Perf. 13, 12½***
**2403** A633 200 l multi *5.00 2.00*
**2404** A633 600 l multi *15.00 3.00*

Steam, Electric and Diesel Locomotives A634

50 l, American Standard steam engine, c. 1850. 100 l, Steam engine produced in Esslingen for Turkish railways, 1913. 200 l, Henschel Krupp steam engine, 1926. 300 l, E 43001 Toshiba electric engine produced in Japan, 1987. 600 l, MTE-Tulomsas #24361 diesel-electric high-speed engine, 1984.

**1988, May 24 *Perf. 13***
**2405** A634 50 l buff, brn & blk 1.00 .50
**2406** A634 100 l buff, brn & blk 2.00 1.00
**2407** A634 200 l buff, brn & blk 3.00 1.75
**2408** A634 300 l buff, brn & blk 3.50 2.00
**2409** A634 600 l buff, brn & blk 5.50 3.25
*Nos. 2405-2409 (5)* 15.00 8.50

Court of Cassation (Supreme Court), 120th Anniv. A635

**1988, July 1 Litho. *Perf. 13½x13***
**2410** A635 50 l multi .50 .30

Bridge Openings — A636

Designs: 200 l, Fatih Sultan Mehmet Bridge, Kavacik-Hisarustu. 300 l, Seto Ohashi (Friendship) Bridges, the Minami and Kita.

**1988, July 3 Litho. *Perf. 13x13½***
**2411** A636 200 l multi 1.25 .75
**2412** A636 300 l multi 2.00 1.00

Telephone System A637

**1988, Aug. 24 Litho. *Perf. 13½x13***
**2413** A637 100 l multi .45 .20

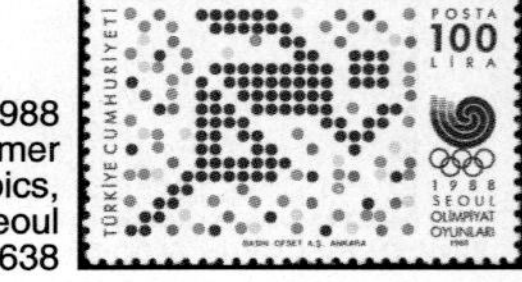

1988 Summer Olympics, Seoul A638

***Perf. 12½x13, 13x12½***
**1988, Sept. 17 Litho.**
**2414** A638 100 l Running .50 .20
**2415** A638 200 l Archery .75 .20
**2416** A638 400 l Weight lifting 1.00 .25
**2417** A638 600 l Gymnastics, vert. 1.50 .35
*Nos. 2414-2417 (4)* 3.75 1.00

Naim Suleymanoglu, 1988 Olympic Gold Medalist, Weight Lifting — A639

**1988, Oct. 5 Litho. *Perf. 13x12½***
**2418** A639 1000 l multi 5.00 2.50

Aerospace Industries A640

**1988, Oct. 28 *Perf. 13½x13, 13x13½***
**2419** A640 50 l Gear, aircraft, vert. .20 .20
**2420** A640 200 l shown .60 .20

Butterflies A641

**1988, Oct. 28 *Perf. 13½x13***
**2421** A641 100 l Gonepteryx rhamni 1.50 .75
**2422** A641 200 l Chazara briseis 3.50 1.25
**2423** A641 400 l Allancastria cerisyi godart 5.00 2.25

2424 A641 600 l Nymphalis antiopa 7.50 3.50
a. Souvenir sheet of 4, #2421-2424 30.00 30.00
*Nos. 2421-2424 (4)* 17.50 7.75

ANTALYA '88.

Natl. Palaces Type of 1987

**1988, Nov. 3 Litho. *Perf. 13***

**2425** A628 100 l Maslak Royal Lodge, c. 1890 .50 .50
**2426** A628 400 l Yildiz Sale Pavilion, 1889 1.00 1.00

Souvenir Sheet

Kemal Ataturk — A642

**1988, Nov. 10 *Perf. 13x13½***

**2427** A642 400 l multi 1.75 1.75

Medicinal Plants of Anatolia A643

**1988, Dec. 14 Litho. *Perf. 13***

**2428** A643 150 l Tilia rubra .45 .20
**2429** A643 300 l Malva silvestris .65 .20
**2430** A643 600 l Hyoscyamus niger 1.25 .20
**2431** A643 900 l Atropa belladonna 2.50 .30
*Nos. 2428-2431 (4)* 4.85 .90

Stamps of 1983-85 Surcharged

***Perf. 13, 11½x12½***

**1989, Feb. 8 Litho.**

**2432** A579 50 l on 15 l No. 2263 .20 .20
**2433** A608 75 l on 10 l No. 2334 .30 .20
**2434** A608 150 l on 20 l No. 2336 .75 .20
*Nos. 2432-2434 (3)* 1.25 .60

Surcharge on No. 2432 is slightly different.

Artifacts in the Museum of Anatolian Civilizations, Ankara — A644

Designs: 150 l, Seated Goddess with Child, neolithic bisque figurine, Hacilar, 6th millennium B.C. 300 l, Lead figurine, Alisar Huyuk, Assyrian Trading Colonies Era, c. 19th cent. B.C. 600 l, Human-shaped vase, Kultepe, Assyrian Trading Colonies Era, 18th cent. B.C. 1000 l, Ivory mountain god, Bogazkoy, Hittite Empire, 14th cent. B.C.

**1989, Feb. 8 Litho. *Perf. 13½x13***

**2435** A644 150 l multi .50 .20
**2436** A644 300 l multi .75 .50
**2437** A644 600 l multi 1.25 1.00
**2438** A644 1000 l multi 2.50 1.50
*Nos. 2435-2438 (4)* 5.00 3.20

See Nos. 2458-2461, 2495-2498, 2520-2523, 2617-2620.

NATO, 40th Anniv. A645

**Wmk. 394**

**1989, Apr. 4 Litho. *Perf. 13½***

**2439** A645 600 l multi .90 .20

**Europa Issue**

Children's Games — A646

***Perf. 13x12½***

**1989, Apr. 23 Wmk. 394**

**2440** A646 600 l Leapfrog *20.00* *3.50*
**2441** A646 1000 l Open the door, Headbezirgan *30.00* *5.00*

Steamships — A647

***Perf. 13½x13***

**1989, July 1 Litho. Wmk. 394**

**2442** A647 150 l Sahilbent 2.50 1.50
**2443** A647 300 l Ragbet 3.75 2.00
**2444** A647 600 l Tari 5.00 2.50
**2445** A647 1000 l Guzelhisar 7.50 3.75
*Nos. 2442-2445 (4)* 18.75 9.75

French Revolution, Bicent. — A648

Kemal Ataturk — A649

**Wmk. 394**

**1989, July 14 Litho. *Perf. 14***

**2446** A648 600 l multi 1.25 .20

**1989, Aug. 16 *Perf. 13x13½***

**2447** A649 2000 l gray & bluish gray 2.00 .50
**2448** A649 5000 l gray & deep red brn 5.00 1.25

See Nos. 2485-2486, 2538-2541. For surcharges see Nos. 2655-2656.

No. 2336 Surcharged in Bright Blue

***Perf. 11½x12½***

**1989, Aug. 31 Litho. Unwmk.**

**2449** A608 500 l on 20 l .70 .20

Photography, 150th Anniv. — A650

**1989, Oct. 17 *Perf. 13½x13***

**2450** A650 175 l Camera .25 .20
**2451** A650 700 l Shutter .85 .20

State Exhibition of Paintings and Sculpture A651

Designs: 200 l, *Manzara*, by Hikmet Onat. 700 l, *Sari Saz*, by Bedri Rahmi Eyuboglu. 1000 l, *Kadin*, by Zuhtu Muridoglu.

***Perf. 13½x13***

**1989, Oct. 30 Litho. Wmk. 394**

**2452** A651 200 l multicolored .25 .20
**2453** A651 700 l multicolored .80 .20
**2454** A651 1000 l multicolored 1.10 .30
*Nos. 2452-2454 (3)* 2.15 .70

Jawaharlal Nehru, 1st Prime Minister of Independent India — A652

**1989, Nov. 14 *Perf. 13½x12½***

**2455** A652 700 l multicolored .80 .20

Sea Turtles A653

**1989, Nov. 16 *Perf. 13½x13***

**2456** A653 700 l Caretta caretta 2.00 1.25
**2457** A653 1000 l Chelonia mydas 4.50 2.50
a. Souv. sheet of 2, #2456-2457 12.00 12.00

**Artifacts Type of 1989**

***Perf. 13x12½, 12½x13***

**1990, Feb. 8 Litho. Wmk. 394**

**2458** A644 100 l Ivory female deity .25 .25
**2459** A644 200 l Ceremonial vessel .40 .40
**2460** A644 500 l Seated goddess pendant .90 .65
**2461** A644 700 l Carved lion 1.50 1.10
*Nos. 2458-2461 (4)* 3.05 2.40

Nos. 2458 and 2460 vert.

Wars of Dardanelles, 1915 — A654

**1990, Mar. 18 *Perf. 13***

**2462** A654 1000 l multicolored .85 .20

EXPO '90 Intl. Garden and Greenery Exposition, Osaka — A655

Illustration reduced.

***Perf. 12½x13***

**1990, Apr. 1 Litho. Wmk. 394**

**2463** 1000 l Bridge at left 1.00 .25
**2464** 1000 l Pavilion at left 1.00 .25
a. A655 Pair, #2463-2464 2.00 .75

Nos. 2301, 2368 and 2284 Surcharged

***Perfs. as Before***

**1990, Apr. 4 Litho.**

**2465** A589 50 l on 5 l #2301 .60 .20
**2466** A620 100 l on 10 l #2368 1.50 .20
**2467** A589 200 l on 70 l #2284 3.50 .25
*Nos. 2465-2467 (3)* 5.60 .65

Grand Natl. Assembly, 70th Anniv. — A657

Europa 1990 — A658

**1990, Apr. 23 *Perf. 13***

**2468** A657 300 l multicolored .50 .50

**1990, May 2**

Post offices.

**2469** A658 700 l Ulus, Ankara *7.50* *2.75*
**2470** A658 1000 l Sirkeci, Istanbul, horiz. *10.00* *3.00*

8th European Supreme Courts Conf. A659

**1990, May 7 Litho. *Perf. 12½x13***

**2471** A659 1000 l multicolored 1.50 .75

Salamandra Salamandra — A660

World Environment Day: No. 2473, Triturus vittatus. No. 2474, Bombina bombina. No. 2475, Hyla arborea, vert.

**1990, June 5 *Perf. 13½x13***

**2472** A660 300 l multicolored .50 .50
**2473** A660 500 l multicolored .50 .50
**2474** A660 1000 l multicolored 1.00 1.00
**2475** A660 1500 l multicolored 1.75 1.75
*Nos. 2472-2475 (4)* 3.75 3.75

Turkey-Japan Relations, Cent. — A661

**1990, June 13 *Perf. 12½x13***

**2476** A661 1000 l multicolored 1.50 1.00

**Traffic Types of 1987 and Nos. 2283-2284 Surcharged**

**1990, June 20 *Perf. 14***

**2477** A620 150 l on 10 l 2.00 .50
**2478** A620 300 l on 20 l 3.00 .50

***Perf. 11½x12½***

**2479** A589 300 l on 70 l #2284 3.00 .75
**2480** A589 1500 l on 20 l #2283 8.75 .75
*Nos. 2477-2480 (4)* 16.75 2.50

Boats in Saintes Marines — A662

Paintings by Vincent Van Gogh (1853-1890): 300 l, Self-portrait, vert. 1000 l, Vase with Sunflowers, vert. 1500 l, Road of Cypress and Stars.

**Wmk. 394**

**1990, July 29 Litho. *Perf. 13***

**2481** A662 300 l multicolored 1.50 1.00
**2482** A662 700 l multicolored 2.75 1.50
**2483** A662 1000 l multicolored 3.25 2.25
**2484** A662 1500 l multicolored 3.50 3.00
*Nos. 2481-2484 (4)* 11.00 7.75

**Ataturk Type of 1989**

**1990, Aug. 1 Unwmk. *Perf. 14***

**2485** A649 500 l gray & olive grn .75 .20
**2486** A649 1000 l gray & rose vio 1.00 .40

A664

A665

***Perf. 13x13½***

**1990, Aug. 22 Wmk. 394**

**2487** A664 300 l multicolored .50 .50

Intl. Literacy Year.

**1990, Oct. 17 Litho. *Perf. 13x13½***

State exhibition of paintings and sculpture by: 300 l, Nurullah Berk. 700 l, Cevat Dereli. 1000 l, Nijad Sirel.

**2488** A665 300 l multicolored .30 .20
**2489** A665 700 l multicolored .60 .25
**2490** A665 1000 l multicolored .90 .35
*Nos. 2488-2490 (3)* 1.80 .80

PTT, 150th Anniv. A666

Past and present communication methods: 200 l, Post rider, truck, train, airplane, ship. 250 l, Telegraph key, computer terminal. 400 l, Telephone switchboard, computerized telephone exchange. 1500 l, Power lines, satellite.

**1990, Oct. 23 *Perf. 14***

**2491** A666 200 l multicolored .20 .20
**2492** A666 250 l multicolored .20 .20
**2493** A666 400 l multicolored .30 .20
**2494** A666 1500 l multicolored 1.10 2.25
*a.* Souv. sheet of 4, #2491-2494 3.00 2.25
*Nos. 2491-2494 (4)* 1.80 2.85

For surcharges see Nos. 2657-2659.

**Artifacts Type of 1989**

300 l, Figurine of a woman, c. 5000-4500 BC. 500 l, Sistrum, c. 2100-2000 BC. 1000 l, Spouted vessel with 3-footed pedestal, c. 2000-1750 BC. 1500 l, Ceremonial vessel, 1900-1700 BC.

**1991, Feb. 8 Litho. *Perf. 13x12½***

**2495** A644 300 l multi .25 .20
**2496** A644 500 l multi .50 .30
**2497** A644 1000 l multi .75 .50
**2498** A644 1500 l multi 1.50 .75
*Nos. 2495-2498 (4)* 3.00 1.75

Nos. 2495-2498 are vert.

Lakes of Turkey A667

**Wmk. 394**

**1991, Apr. 24 Litho. *Perf. 13***

**2499** A667 250 l Abant .20 .20
**2500** A667 500 l Egridir .40 .20
**2501** A667 1500 l Van 1.10 .60
*Nos. 2499-2501 (3)* 1.70 1.00

Europa — A668

**Unwmk.**

**1991, May 6 Litho. *Perf. 13***

**2502** A668 1000 l multicolored *15.00* *3.50*
**2503** A668 1500 l multi, diff. *22.50* *4.00*

Natl. Statistics Day — A669

**1991, May 9 *Perf. 13½x13***

**2504** A669 500 l multicolored .40 .20

Eastern Mediterranean Fiber Optic Cable System — A670

**1991, May 13**

**2505** A670 500 l multicolored .40 .20

European Conf. of Transportation Ministers — A671

**1991, May 22 *Perf. 13***

**2506** A671 500 l multicolored .60 .40

Caricature Art A672

500 l, "Amcabey" by Cemal Nadir Guler. 1000 l, "Abdulcanbaz" by Turhan Selcuk, vert.

**Wmk. 394**

**1991, Sept. 11 Litho. *Perf. 13***

**2507** A672 500 l multicolored .60 .20
**2508** A672 1000 l multicolored 1.00 .50

Ceramics A673

Wall facings: 500 l, 13th cent. Seljuk bird. 1500 l, 16th cent. Ottoman floral pattern.

**1991, Sept. 23 *Perf. 13½x13***

**2509** A673 500 l multicolored .40 .20
**2510** A673 1500 l multicolored 1.25 .60

Symposium on Intl. Protection of Human Rights, Antalya — A674

**1991, Oct. 4 *Perf. 13x12½***

**2511** A674 500 l multicolored .40 .20

Southeastern Anatolia Irrigation and Power Project A675

**1991, Oct. 6 Unwmk. *Perf. 13½x13***

**2512** A675 500 l multicolored .40 .20

Turkish Fairy Tales — A676

Baldboy: 500 l, With genie. 1000 l, At party. 1500 l, Plowing field.

**1991, Oct. 9 *Perf. 13x13½***

**2513** A676 500 l multicolored .40 .20
**2514** A676 1000 l multicolored .80 .40
**2515** A676 1500 l multicolored 1.25 .60
*Nos. 2513-2515 (3)* 2.45 1.20

Snakes A677

***Perf. 12½x13***

**1991, Oct. 23 Wmk. 394**

**2516** A677 250 l Eryx jaculus 2.00 .50
**2517** A677 500 l Elaphe quatuor-lineata 3.00 1.00
**2518** A677 1000 l Vipera xanthina 6.00 2.00
**2519** A677 1500 l Vipera kaznakovi 8.00 3.50
*Nos. 2516-2519 (4)* 19.00 7.00

World Environment Day.

**Antiquities Type of 1989**

300 l, Statuette of Mother Goddess, Neolithic, 6000 B.C., vert. 500 l, Hasanoglan statuette, Early Bronze Age, 3000 B.C., vert. 1000 l, Inandik vase, Old Hittite, 18th cent. B.C., vert. 1500 l, Lion statuette, Urartian, 8th cent. B.C., vert.

**Wmk. 394**

**1992, Feb. 12 Litho. *Perf. 13***

**2520** A644 300 l multicolored .25 .20
**2521** A644 500 l multicolored .40 .20
**2522** A644 1000 l multicolored .80 .40
**2523** A644 1500 l multicolored 1.25 .60
*Nos. 2520-2523 (4)* 2.70 1.40

Discovery of America, 500th Anniv. A678

**Wmk. 394**

**1992, May 4 Litho. *Perf. 13***

**2524** A678 1500 l shown *7.00* *2.00*
**2525** A678 2000 l Balloons, vert. *12.50* *3.00*

Europa.

Settlement of Jews in Turkey, 500th Anniv. A679

**1992, May 15 *Perf. 12½x13***

**2526** A679 1500 l multicolored 1.00 1.00

A681

A682

**Wmk. 394**

**1992, June 1 Litho. *Perf. 13***

**2529** A681 500 l multicolored .40 .40

Turkish Court of Accounts, 130th anniv.

**1992, June 4**

**2530** A682 1500 l multicolored .75 .75

Economics Congress, Izmir.

World Environment Day — A683

**1992, June 5 Litho. *Perf. 13***

**2531** A683 500 l Vanellus vanellus .50 .50
**2532** A683 1000 l Oriolus oriolus .75 .50
**2533** A683 1500 l Tadorna tadorna 1.00 .50
**2534** A683 2000 l Halcyon smyrnensis, vert. 1.50 1.00
*Nos. 2531-2534 (4)* 3.75 2.50

Ataturk Type of 1989 and:

Kemal Ataturk — A683a

A683b

10,000 l, Full face. 100,000 l, Facing left.

***Perf. 13, 14 (#2539, 2541, 2543-2544A)***

**1992-96 Litho. Unwmk.**

**2538** A649 250 l gold, brn & org 1.25 .20
**2539** A649 5000 l gold & vio 1.50 .40
**2540** A649 10,000 l gold & blue 3.75 1.90

2541 A649 20,000 l gold & lil rose 6.50 1.60
2542 A683a 50,000 l multi 3.50 1.75
2543 A683b 50,000 l lake & pink 2.00 .90
2544 A683b 100,000 l grn bl & yel org 3.50 1.75
*Nos. 2538-2544 (7)* 22.00 8.50

Issued: 250 l, 10,000 l, 5/28/92; 5000 l, 20,000 l, 9/29/93; #2542, 11/10/94; #2543, 100,000 l, 6/1/96.

For surcharges see Nos. 2655, 2732.

Black Sea Economic Cooperation Summit — A684

**Wmk. 394**

**1992, June 25 Litho. *Perf. 13***

2545 A684 1500 l multicolored .60 .30

1992 Summer Olympics, Barcelona A685

**1992, July 25 Wmk. 394**

2546 A685 500 l Doves .30 .20
2547 A685 1000 l Boxing .40 .25
2548 A685 1500 l Weight lifting .75 .30
2549 A685 2000 l Wrestling 1.50 .45
*Nos. 2546-2549 (4)* 2.95 1.20

Anatolian Folktales — A686

Scenes: 500 l, Woman carrying milk to soldiers. 1000 l, Pouring milk into trough. 1500 l, Soldiers dipping into trough.

***Perf. 13x12½***

**1992, Sept. 23 Litho. Wmk. 394**

2550 A686 500 l multicolored .20 .20
2551 A686 1000 l multicolored .30 .20
2552 A686 1500 l multicolored .50 .25
*Nos. 2550-2552 (3)* 1.00 .65

Turkish Handicrafts — A687

500 l, Embroidered flowers. 1000 l, Dolls in traditional costumes, vert. 3000 l, Saddlebags.

**1992, Oct. 21 *Perf. 13½x13, 13x13½***

2553 A687 500 l multicolored .20 .20
2554 A687 1000 l multicolored .35 .20
2555 A687 3000 l multicolored .95 .50
*Nos. 2553-2555 (3)* 1.50 .90

See Nos. 2585-2588, 2611-2612.

Fruits — A688

**Wmk. 394**

**1992, Nov. 25 Litho. *Perf. 13***

2556 A688 500 l Cherries .25 .20
2557 A688 1000 l Peaches .50 .20
2558 A688 3000 l Grapes 1.00 .45
2559 A688 5000 l Apples 2.00 .75
*Nos. 2556-2559 (4)* 3.75 1.60

See Nos. 2565-2568.

Famous Men — A689

Designs: No. 2560, Sait Faik Abasiyanik (1906-54), writer. No. 2561, Fikret Mualla Saygi (1904-67), artist. No. 2562, Cevat Sakir Kabaagacli (1886-1973), author. No. 2563, Muhsin Ertugrul (1892-1979), actor and producer. No. 2564, Asik Veysel Satiroglu (1894-1973), composer.

***Perf. 14, 13½x13 (#2561, 2564)***

**1992, Dec. 30 Litho.**

2560 A689 T multicolored .65 .20
2561 A689 T multicolored .65 .20
2562 A689 M multicolored .90 .20
2563 A689 M multicolored .90 .20
2564 A689 M multicolored .90 .20
*Nos. 2560-2564 (5)* 4.00 1.00

Value on day of issue: Nos. 2560-2561, 500 l. Nos. 2562-2564, 1000 l.

See Nos. 2577-2581.

**Fruit Type of 1992**

**Wmk. 394**

**1993, Apr. 28 Litho. *Perf. 13***

2565 A688 500 l Bananas .50 .30
2566 A688 1000 l Oranges .50 .50
2567 A688 3000 l Pears 1.00 .75
2568 A688 5000 l Pomegranates 2.00 1.40
*Nos. 2565-2568 (4)* 4.00 2.95

Europa — A690

Sculptures by: 1000 l, Hadi Bara. 3000 l, Zuhtu Muridoglu.

**1993, May 3**

2569 A690 1000 l multicolored *1.25 .60*
2570 A690 3000 l multicolored *2.25 1.00*

A691

**Wmk. 394**

**1993, July 6 Litho. *Perf. 13***

2571 A691 2500 l lt bl, dk bl & gold .75 .50

Economic Cooperation Organization Meeting, Istanbul.

Houses — A692

**1993, July 7**

Various houses from Black Sea region.

2572 A692 1000 l multicolored .50 .20
2573 A692 2500 l multi, horiz. .50 .40
2574 A692 3000 l multicolored 1.00 .60
2575 A692 5000 l multi, horiz. 1.00 .80
*Nos. 2572-2575 (4)* 3.00 2.00

See Nos. 2604-2607, 2631-2634, 2647-2650, 2676-2679.

Hodja Ahmet Yesevi (1093-1166), Poet — A693

**1993, July 28**

2576 A693 3000 l lt bl, dk bl & gold .65 .30

**Famous Men Type of 1992**

Designs: No. 2577, Haci Arif Bey (1831-84), composer. No. 2578, Neyzen Tevfik Kolayli (1878-1953), poet. No. 2579, Munir Nurettin Selcuk (1900-81), composer, musician. No. 2580, Cahit Sitki Taranci (1910-56), poet. No. 2581, Orhan Veli Kanik (1914-50), writer.

***Perf. 14, 13½x13 (2578-2580)***

**1993, Aug. 4 Litho. Unwmk.**

2577 A689 T brown & red brown .65 .20
2578 A689 T brown & red brown .65 .20
2579 A689 M brown & red brown .90 .20
2580 A689 M brown & red brown .90 .20
2581 A689 M brown & red brown .90 .20
*Nos. 2577-2581 (5)* 4.00 1.00

Value on day of issue: Nos. 2577-2578, 500 l. Nos. 2579-2581, 1000 l.

Istanbul, Proposed Site for 2000 Olympics A694

**1993, Aug. 11 *Perf. 12½x13***

2582 A694 2500 l multicolored .80 .40

Protection of Mediterranean Sea Against Pollution — A695

**Unwmk.**

**1993, Oct. 12 Litho. *Perf. 13***

2583 A695 1000 l Amphora on sea floor .20 .20
2584 A695 3000 l Dolphin jumping .50 .25

**Handicrafts Type of 1992**

***Perf. 12½x13, 13x12½***

**1993, Oct. 21 Wmk. 394**

2585 A687 1000 l Painted rug .20 .20
2586 A687 2500 l Earrings .40 .20
2587 A687 5000 l Money purse, vert. .80 .40
*Nos. 2585-2587 (3)* 1.40 .80

Republic, 70th Anniv. — A696

**1993, Oct. 29 Wmk. 394 *Perf. 13***

2588 A696 1000 l multicolored .40 .40

Civil Defence Organization — A697

***Perf. 12½x13***

**1993, Nov. 25 Unwmk.**

2589 A697 1000 l multicolored .40 .40

Turksat Satellite — A698

Natl. Water Project — A699

Designs: 1500 l, Satellite, globe, map of Turkey. 5000 l, Satellite transmissions to areas in Europe and Asia.

***Perf. 13x13½***

**1994, Jan. 21 Litho. Wmk. 394**

2590 A698 1500 l multicolored .20 .20
2591 A698 5000 l multicolored .55 .20

**1994, Feb. 28 *Perf. 13x12½***

2592 A699 1500 l multicolored .40 .30

Native Cuisine A700

***Perf. 12½x13***

**1994, Mar. 23 Litho. Wmk. 394**

2593 A700 1000 l Ezogel in corbasi .50 .50
2594 A700 1500 l Mixed dolma .50 .50
2595 A700 3500 l Shish kebabs .50 .50
2596 A700 5000 l Baklava 1.00 .50
*Nos. 2593-2596 (4)* 2.50 2.00

Europa A701

1500 l, Marie Curie (1867-1934), chemist, vert. 5000 l, Albert Einstein (1879-1955), physicist.

**Unwmk.**

**1994, May 2 Litho. *Perf. 13***

2597 A701 1500 l multicolored *.50 .50*
2598 A701 5000 l multicolored *1.50 1.50*

World Environment Day — A703

Views of: 6000 l, Antalya. 8500 l, Mugla, vert.

**Wmk. 394**

**1994, June 5 Litho.** ***Perf. 13***
**2602** A703 6000 l multicolored 1.00 .75
**2603** A703 8500 l multicolored 1.60 1.00

### Houses Type of 1993

2500 l, 2-story housing complex. 3500 l, 3-story home with balconies. 6000 l, Tri-level country home. 8500 l, 2-story home.

**1994, July 7**
**2604** A692 2500 l multi, horiz. .40 .40
**2605** A692 3500 l multi, horiz. .40 .40
**2606** A692 6000 l multi, horiz. .40 .40
**2607** A692 8500 l multi, horiz. 1.25 .40
*Nos. 2604-2607 (4)* 2.45 1.60

Tourism A704

**1994, Aug. 3**
**2608** A704 5000 l Hiking .50 .30
**2609** A704 10,000 l Rafting 1.00 .50

Project of the Year 2001 A705

**1994, Aug. 27**
**2610** A705 2500 l multicolored .50 .50

### Handicrafts Type of 1992

Designs: 7500 l, Kusak pattern used on 18th cent. clothing, vert. 12,000 l, Pacalik pattern used on 19th cent. clothing.

**1994, Oct. 21**
**2611** A687 7500 l multicolored 1.00 .50
**2612** A687 12,500 l multicolored 1.50 1.50

Mushrooms — A706

**1994, Nov. 16**
**2613** A706 2500 l Morchella conica .50 .50
**2614** A706 5000 l Agaricus bernardii .75 .75
**2615** A706 7500 l Lactarius deliciosus 1.25 1.25
**2616** A706 12,500 l Macrolepiota procera 2.50 2.50
*Nos. 2613-2616 (4)* 5.00 5.00

See Nos. 2637-2640.

### Antiquities Type of 1989

Lydian Treasures, 6th cent. B.C.: 2500 l, Silver pitcher, vert. 5000 l, Silver incense burner, vert. 7500 l, Gold, glass necklace. 12,500 l, Gold brooch.

**1994, Dec. 7**
**2617** A644 2500 l multicolored .50 .35
**2618** A644 5000 l multicolored .70 .40
**2619** A644 7500 l multicolored 1.10 .60
**2620** A644 12,500 l multicolored 2.00 .80
*Nos. 2617-2620 (4)* 4.30 2.15

Nevruz, New Day A707

**1995, Mar. 21**
**2621** A707 3500 l multicolored .40 .40

Europa — A708

**1995, May 5**
**2622** A708 3500 l Flowers *1.00 1.00*
**2623** A708 15,000 l Olive branch *2.00 2.00*

Istanbul '96 World Stamp Exhibition — A709

a, 7000 l, Buildings. b, 25,000 l, Tower, buildings. c, 7000 l, Mosque, city along harbor. c, 25,000 l, Residential area, mosque, harbor.

**1995, May 24**
**2624** A709 Block of 4, #a.-d. 5.00 2.50

Nos. 2624a-2624b and 2624c-2624d are each continuous designs.

European Nature Conservation Year — A710

**1995, June 5**
**2625** A710 5000 l Field of poppies .30 .20
**2626** A710 15,000 l Trees .85 .40
**2627** A710 25,000 l Mountain valley 1.40 .70
*Nos. 2625-2627 (3)* 2.55 1.30

A711

A712

**1995, Feb. 1**
**2628** A711 15,000 l red & blue 1.25 1.25

Motion Pictures, cent.

**1995, Apr. 23**
**2629** A712 5000 l multicolored .40 .40

1sh Conference of the Moslem Women Parliamentaries, Pakistan.

### Houses Type of 1993

5000 l, 2-story block house. 10,000 l, Tower of part-stone house. 15,000 l, Interior view of 2-story house, horiz. 20,000 l, Three unit-connecting apartment, horiz.

**1995, July 7**
**2631** A692 5000 l multicolored .75 .35
**2632** A692 10,000 l multicolored 1.00 .35
**2633** A692 15,000 l multicolored 1.10 .50
**2634** A692 20,000 l multicolored 1.25 1.00
*Nos. 2631-2634 (4)* 4.10 2.20

UN, 50th Anniv. — A713

**1995, Oct. 24**
**2635** A713 15,000 l shown .80 .40
**2636** A713 30,000 l UN emblem, "50" 1.60 .80

### Mushroom Type of 1994

Designs: 5000 l, Amanita phalloides. 10,000 l, Lepiota helveola. 20,000 l, Gyromitra esculenta. 30,000 l, Amanita gemmata.

**1995, Nov. 16**
**2637** A706 5000 l multicolored .50 .50
**2638** A706 10,000 l multicolored .80 .80
**2639** A706 20,000 l multicolored 1.75 1.75
**2640** A706 30,000 l multicolored 2.00 2.00
*Nos. 2637-2640 (4)* 5.05 5.05

Children's Rights A714

6,000 l, Rainbow, hearts, flower, sun in sky. 10,000 l, Child's hand drawing letter "A."

**1996, Mar. 13**
**2641** A714 6,000 l multicolored .40 .40
**2642** A714 10,000 l multicolored 1.10 1.00

Fauna — A715

Designs: a, 5,000 l, Bee. b, 10,000 l, Dog. c, 15,000 l, Rooster. d, 30,000 l, Fish.

**1996, Apr. 10** **Unwmk.**
**2643** A715 Sheet of 4, #a.-d. 5.00 5.00

Instanbul '96.

Famous Women A716

***Perf. 12½x13***
**1996, May 5 Litho. Unwmk.**
**2644** A716 10,000 l Nene Hatun 1.50 1.50
**2645** A716 40,000 l Halide Edip Adivar 3.00 3.00

Europa.

World Environment Day — A717

**Unwmk.**
**1996, June 3 Litho.** ***Perf. 13***
**2646** A717 50,000 l multicolored 1.75 .90

### Houses Type of 1993

Designs: 10,000 l, Tri-level block house, horiz. 15,000 l, Two story with bay window, gate at entrance to side courtyard, horiz. 25,000 l, Two story townhouse, double wooden doors at bottom. 50,000 l, Flat-roofed, two-story townhouse.

**1996, July 7** ***Perf. 13***
**2647** A692 10,000 l multicolored .35 .20
**2648** A692 15,000 l multicolored .60 .30
**2649** A692 25,000 l multicolored .90 .45
**2650** A692 50,000 l multicolored 1.75 .90
*Nos. 2647-2650 (4)* 3.60 1.85

1996 Summer Olympic Games, Atlanta — A718

a, 10,000 l, Archery. b, 15,000 l, Wrestling. c, 25,000 l, Weight lifting. d, 50,000 l, Hurdles.

**1996, July 19**
**2651** A718 Sheet of 4, #a.-d. 6.50 6.50

ISTANBUL '96. Exists imperf.

Turkish Press, 50th Anniv. A719

**1996, July 24** ***Perf. 12½x13***
**2652** A719 15,000 l multicolored .60 .30

Euro '96, European Soccer Championships, Great Britain — A720

**1996, June 8** ***Perf. 13***
**2653** A720 15,000 l Player, vert. .60 .30
**2654** A720 50,000 l Soccer ball, flags 1.75 .90

Nos. 2447, 2491, 2493-2494, 2538 Surcharged in Orange or Deep Violet Blue

or

***Perfs., Printing Methods as Before***
**1996, July 22**
**2655** A649 T on 250 l #2538 (O) .75 .20
**2656** A649 T on 2000 l #2447 .75 .20

**2657** A666 M on 200 l #2491 1.10 .20
**2658** A666 M on 400 l #2493 1.10 .20
**2659** A666 M on 1500 l #2494 1.10 .20
*Nos. 2655-2659 (5)* 4.80 1.00

Nos. 2655-2656 and 2657-2659 had face values of 10,000 l and 15,000 l on day of issue.

See No. 2732.

Methods of Transportation — A721

a, 25,000 l, Airplane (b). b, 50,000 l, Helicopter, ship (d). c, 75,000 l, Train. d, 100,000 l, Bus (c).

**Unwmk.**

**1996, Sept. 27 Litho. *Perf. 13***
**2660** A721 Sheet of 4, #a.-d. 10.00 10.00

Istanbul '96.

New Year A722

**Unwmk.**

**1996, Oct. 23 Litho. *Perf. 13***
**2661** A722 15,000 l multicolored .55 .30

Social and Cultural Heritage A723

10,000 l, Public Library, Bayezit, Amasya. 15,000 l, Mosque and hospital, Divrigi.

**1996, Dec. 17 Litho. *Perf. 13***
**2662** A723 10,000 l multicolored .30 .30
**2663** A723 15,000 l multicolored .50 .50

Stories and Legends — A724

Europa: 25,000 l, Little children dressed in flowers and leaves riding a giant peacock. 70,000 l, Genie, man being riding a giant bird.

**1997, May 5 Litho. *Perf. 13***
**2664** A724 25,000 l multicolored *1.25 1.25*
**2665** A724 70,000 l multicolored *2.50 2.50*

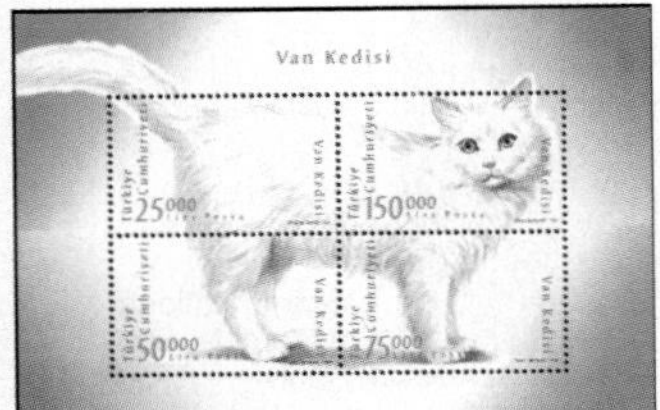

White Cat — A725

Designs: a, 25,000 l, Tail, hindquarters. b, 50,000 l, Back legs. c, 75,000 l, Front legs. d, 150,000 l, Face.

**1997, Apr. 23**
**2666** A725 Sheet of 4, #a.-d. 7.50 7.50

Language Day — A726

**1997, May 13 Litho. *Perf. 13***
**2667** A726 25,000 l multicolored .50 .50

World Environment Day — A727

**1997, June 5**
**2668** A727 35,000 l multicolored .60 .60

Orchids — A728

Designs: 25,000 l, Ophrys tenthredinifera. 70,000 l, Ophrys apifera.

**1997, May 28**
**2669** A728 25,000 l multicolored .60 .20
**2670** A728 70,000 l multicolored 1.40 .45

25th Intl. Istanbul Festival A729

**1997, June 13 *Perf. 13½***

**Background Color**

**2671** A729 15,000 l blue .20 .20
**2672** A729 25,000 l pink .50 .50
**2673** A729 70,000 l blue green 1.25 1.25
**2674** A729 75,000 l purple 1.50 1.50
**2675** A729 100,000 l green blue 2.00 2.00
*Nos. 2671-2675 (5)* 5.45 5.45

**House Type of 1993**

Inscribed: 25,000 l, Bir Urfa Evi, vert. 40,000 l, Bir Mardin Evi. 80,000 l, Bir Diyarbakir Evi. 100,000 l, Kemaliye'de Bir Ev, vert.

**1997, July 7 Litho. *Perf. 13***
**2676** A692 25,000 l multicolored .40 .40
**2677** A692 40,000 l multicolored .80 .80
**2678** A692 80,000 l multicolored 1.50 1.50
**2679** A692 100,000 l multicolored 2.00 2.00
*Nos. 2676-2679 (4)* 4.70 4.70

A730

A731

Flowers: 40,000 l, Lilium candidum. 100,000 l, Euphorbia pulcherima.

**1997, Sept. 8 Litho. *Perf. 13***
**2680** A730 40,000 l multicolored .85 .20
**2681** A730 100,000 l multicolored 1.90 .50

**1997, Sept. 13**

World Air Games: No. 2682, Hang gliding. No. 2683, Sailplane. No. 2684, Man pointing up at biplanes. No. 2685, Hot air balloon.

**2682** A731 40,000 l multicolored .80 .80
**2683** A731 40,000 l multicolored .80 .80
**2684** A731 100,000 l multicolored 2.25 2.25
**2685** A731 100,000 l multicolored 3.00 3.00
*Nos. 2682-2685 (4)* 6.85 6.85

Forestry Congress A732

**1997, Oct. 13 Litho. *Perf. 13***
**2686** A732 50,000 l multicolored 1.00 1.00

15th European Gymnastics Congress — A733

**1997, Oct. 13**
**2687** A733 100,000 l multicolored 2.00 2.00

Traditional Women's Headcovers A734

**1997, Nov. 19 Litho. *Perf. 13***
**2688** A734 50,000 l Gaziantep 1.00 .50
**2689** A734 50,000 l Canakkale 1.00 .50
**2690** A734 100,000 l Isparta 1.75 1.00
**2691** A734 100,000 l Bursa 1.75 1.00
*Nos. 2688-2691 (4)* 5.50 3.00

See Nos. 2711-2714, 2748-2751, 2765-2768.

1998 Winter Olympic Games, Nagano — A735

Slalom skiers: No. 2692, #1 on bib. No. 2693, #119 on bib.

**1998, Feb. 7 Litho. *Perf. 13***
**2692** 125,000 l multicolored 2.00 2.00
**2693** 125,000 l multicolored 2.00 2.00
***a.*** A735 Pair, #2692-2693 4.25 4.25

Intl. Year of the Ocean — A736

Designs: a, 50,000 l, Turtle, jellyfish. b, 75,000 l, Fish, octopus. c, 125,000 l, Coral, crab. d, 125,000 l, Fish, coral, starfish.

**1998, Apr. 18 Litho. *Perf. 13***
**2694** A736 Sheet of 4, #a.-d. 6.00 6.00

Dardenelles Campaign — A737

Memorial Statues: #2695, "Mother with Children," Natl. War Memorial, Wellington. #2696, "With Great Respect to the Mehmetcik, Gallipoli" (Turkish soldier carrying wounded ANZAC).

**1998, Mar. 18 Litho. *Perf. 13***
**2695** A737 125,000 l multicolored 1.10 1.10
**2696** A737 125,000 l multicolored 1.10 1.10

See New Zealand Nos. 1490-1491.

A738

A739

Europa (National Festivals and Holidays): 100,000 l, Kemal Ataturk, natl. flag, people celebrating. 150,000 l, Ataturk, natl. flag, children of different races celebrating together.

**1998, May 5**
**2697** A738 100,000 l multicolored *1.25 1.25*
**2698** A738 150,000 l multicolored *2.25 2.25*

**1998, May 1 Litho. *Perf. 13***

Tulips: 50,000 l, Sylvestris. 75,000 l, Armena (pink). 100,000 l, Armena (violet). 125,000 l, Saxatilis.

**2699** A739 50,000 l multicolored .65 .65
**2700** A739 75,000 l multicolored 1.10 1.10
**2701** A739 100,000 l multicolored 1.25 1.25
**2702** A739 125,000 l multicolored 2.00 2.00
*Nos. 2699-2702 (4)* 5.00 5.00

**Souvenir Sheet**

World Environment Day — A740

Owls: a, Two on branches. b, One flying, one standing.

**1998, June 5 Litho. *Perf. 13½***
**2703** A740 150,000 l Sheet of 2, #a.-b. 4.00 4.00

Contemporary Arts — A741

75,000 l, Couple dancing. 100,000 l, Man playing cello. 150,000 l, Ballerina.

**1998, Aug. 14 Litho. *Perf. 13***
**2704** A741 75,000 l multi .70 .35
**2705** A741 100,000 l multi, vert. .90 .45
**2706** A741 150,000 l multi, vert. 1.40 .70
*Nos. 2704-2706 (3)* 3.00 1.50

Kemal Ataturk — A742

**1998, Aug. 20 Litho. *Perf. 13***
**2707** A742 150,000 l cl & brn 1.25 .50
**2708** A742 175,000 l bl & rose brn 1.75 .65
**2709** A742 250,000 l brn & cl 2.25 .95
**2710** A742 500,000 l brn & dk bl 5.00 1.90
*Nos. 2707-2710 (4)* 10.25 4.00

Traditional Headcovers Type of 1997

**1998, Nov. 24 Litho. *Perf. 13***
**2711** A734 75,000 l Afyon .70 .35
**2712** A734 75,000 l Ankara .70 .35
**2713** A734 175,000 l Mus 1.60 .80
**2714** A734 175,000 l Mugla 1.60 .80
*Nos. 2711-2714 (4)* 4.60 2.30

Turkish Republic, 75th Anniv. — A743

275,000 l, Flag, silhouette of Ataturk.

**1998, Oct. 29 Litho. *Perf. 13***
**2715** A743 175,000 l shown 1.75 .90
*a.* Souvenir sheet of 1, imperf. 1.75 1.25
**2716** A743 275,000 l red & blk 2.75 1.40
*a.* Souvenir sheet of 1, imperf. 2.75 2.00

Nos. 2715a, 2716a have simulated perforations.

Famous People A744

#2717, Ihap Hulusi Görey (1898-1986). #2718, Bedia Muvahht (1897-1993). No. 2719, Feza Gürsey (1921-92). #2720, Haldun Taner (1915-86). #2721, Vasfi Riza Zobu (1902-92).

**1998, Dec. 31 Photo. *Perf. 13***
**2717** A744 M gray bl, bl & plum 1.25 .25
**2718** A744 M lil, dp lil & plum 1.25 .25
**2719** A744 T org, brn & plum 1.50 .40
**2720** A744 T gray vio, vio & plum 1.50 .40
**2721** A744 T grn, blk & plum 1.50 .40
*Nos. 2717-2721 (5)* 7.00 1.70

On day of issue, Nos. 2717-2718 were valued at 50,000 l each, and Nos. 2719-2721 were valued at 75,000 l each.

NATO, 50th Anniv. A745

**1999, Apr. 4 Litho. *Perf. 13***
**2722** A745 200,000 l multicolored 2.00 1.50

Ottoman Empire, 700th Anniv. A746

Designs: No. 2723, Man on horse surrounded by people in buildings. No. 2724, Man on horse, three men in foreground. No. 2725, Men seated.

No. 2726, Man on white horse, castle. No. 2727, Group of women, horiz.

**1999, Apr. 12**
**2723** A746 175,000 l multicolored 1.50 1.10
**2724** A746 175,000 l multicolored 1.50 1.10
**2725** A746 175,000 l multicolored 1.50 1.10
*Nos. 2723-2725 (3)* 4.50 3.30

**Size: 79x119mm, 119x79mm**
***Imperf***
**2726** A746 200,000 l multicolored 1.50 1.50
**2727** A746 200,000 l multicolored 1.50 1.50

Europa A747

Natl. Parks: 175,000 l, Köprülü Canyon, vert. 200,000 l, Kackarlar.

***Perf. 13¼x13, 13x13¼***
**1999, May 5 Litho.**
**2728** A747 175,000 l multicolored 2.00 2.00
**2729** A747 200,000 l multicolored 2.00 2.00

World Environment Day — A748

No. 2730: a, 100,000 l, Tetrax tetrax. 200,000 l, Hoplopterus spinosus.

No. 2731: a, 100,000 l, Marbled duck. b, 200,000 l, Sitta kruperi.

**1999, June 3 Litho. *Perf. 13¼***
**2730** A748 Sheet of 2, #a.-b. 2.50 2.50
**2731** A748 Sheet of 2, #a.-b. 2.50 2.50

See Nos. 2763-2764.

No. 2538 Surcharged in Violet Blue

**1999 Litho. *Perf. 13***
**2732** A649 T on 250 l #2537 .75 .40

No. 2732 sold for 50,000 l on day of issue.

Souvenir Sheet

National Congress During the War for Independence — A749

Designs: a, 100,000 l, Ataturk, two other men, building. b, 100,000 l, Ataturk, two other men seated. c, 200,000 l, Two men standing in front of building. d, 200,000 l, Ataturk standing in front of building.

***Perf. 13¼x13***
**1999, June 22 Litho. Unwmk.**
**2733** A749 Sheet of 4, #a.-d. 4.00 4.00

Art — A750

**1999, July 8 Litho. *Perf. 13x13¼***
**2734** A750 250,000 l shown 1.50 .75
**2735** A750 250,000 l multi, diff. 1.50 .75

Tourism — A751

***Perf. 13x13¼, 13¼x13***
**1999, Sept. 19 Litho.**

No. 2736, Temple to Zeus. No. 2737, Antakya Archaelogical Museum, horiz. No. 2738, Golf course, Antalya. No. 2739, Sailboat off Bodrum.

**2736** A751 125,000 l multi 1.00 1.00
**2737** A751 125,000 l multi 1.00 1.00
**2738** A751 225,000 l multi 1.50 1.50
**2739** A751 225,000 l multi 1.50 1.50
*Nos. 2736-2739 (4)* 5.00 5.00

Dams A752

225,000 l, Cubuk 1. 250,000 l, Atatürk.

**1999, Sept. 19 Litho. *Perf. 13¼x13***
**2740** A752 225,000 l multi 1.50 1.50
**2741** A752 250,000 l multi 1.50 1.50

Kemal Atatürk — A753

**1999, Sept. 27 Litho. *Perf. 13¾***
**2742** A753 225,000 l grn & brn 2.50 .55
**2743** A753 250,000 l brn & lil 2.50 .65
**2744** A753 500,000 l pink & grn 3.75 1.40
**2745** A753 1,000,000 l bl & red 6.25 2.75
*Nos. 2742-2745 (4)* 15.00 5.35

Thanks for Earthquake Rescue Efforts — A754

Designs: 225,000 l, Hands holding wreckage, flowers, vert. 250,000 l, Rescuers, handclasp.

***Perf. 13¼x13, 13x13¼***
**1999, Oct. 15 Litho.**
**2746** A754 225,000 l multi 1.10 .55
**2747** A754 250,000 l multi 1.40 .65

**Women's Headcovers Type of 1997**
**1999, Nov. 24 Litho. *Perf. 13¼***
**2748** A734 150,000 l Manisa .80 .40
**2749** A734 150,000 l Nigde .80 .40
**2750** A734 250,000 l Antalya 1.40 .65
**2751** A734 250,000 l Amasya 1.40 .65
*Nos. 2748-2751 (4)* 4.40 2.10

Caravansaries — A755

**1999, Dec. 24 Litho. *Perf. 13¼x13***
**2752** A755 150,000 l Sarapsa .65 .25
**2753** A755 250,000 l Obruk 1.00 .45

Millennium A756

Designs: 275,000 l, Earth, brain, satellite. 300,000 l, Monachus monachus.

**2000, Feb. 1 Litho. *Perf. 13¼***
**2754** A756 275,000 l multi 2.00 2.00
**2755** A756 300,000 l multi 2.00 2.00

Merchant Ships A757

125,000 l, Bug. 150,000 l, Gülcemal. 275,000 l, Nusret. 300,000 l, Bandirma.

**2000, Mar. 16**
**2756** A757 125,000 l multi .55 .55
**2757** A757 150,000 l multi .65 .65
**2758** A757 275,000 l multi 1.75 1.75
**2759** A757 300,000 l multi 2.00 2.00
*Nos. 2756-2759 (4)* 4.95 4.95

Grand National Assembly, 80th Anniv. — A758

***Perf. 13x13¼, 13¼x13***
**2000, Apr. 23 Litho.**
**2760** A758 275,000 l shown 1.00 1.00
**2761** A758 300,000 l Sprouts, horiz. 1.10 1.10

**Europa, 2000**
Common Design Type

**2000, May 9** ***Perf. 13x13¼***
**2762** CD17 300,000 l multi 2.00 2.00

**World Environment Day Type of 1999**
Souvenir Sheets

No. 2763, 275,000 l: a, Aquila heliaca. b, Picus viridis.
No. 2764, 275,000 l: a, Oxyura leucocephala. b, Recurvirostra avosetta.

**2000, June 5** **Litho.** ***Perf. 13¼***
**Sheets of 2, #a-b**
**2763-2764** A748 Set of 2 5.00 5.00

**Women's Headcover Type of 1997**

Designs: No. 2765, 275,000 l, Trabzon. No. 2766, 275,000 l, Tunceli. No. 2767, 275,000 l, Corum. No. 2768, 275,000 l, Izmir.

**2000, July 15**
**2765-2768** A734 Set of 4 5.00 5.00

Souvenir Sheet

Nomadic Life A759

a, Woman at loom, woman seated. b, Women & containers. c, Women, 2 goats, carpet on tent rope. d, Woman, children, 6 goats, carpet on rope.

**2000**
**2769** Sheet of 4 5.50 5.50
*a.-d.* A759 300,000 l Any single 1.00 1.00

Military Leaders — A760

Designs: 100,000 l, Gen. Yakup Sevki Subasi. 200,000 l, Lt. Gen. Musa Kazim Karabekir (c. 1882-1948). 275,000 l, Marshal Mustafa Fevzi Cakmak (1876-1950). 300,000 l, Gen. Cevat Cobanli (1871-1938).

**2000**
**2770-2773** A760 Set of 4 4.50 4.50

2000 Summer Olympics, Sydney A761

Designs: 125,000 l, Rhythmic gymnastics. 150,000 l, Swimming. 275,000 l, High jump. 300,000 l, Archery.

**2000**
**2774-2777** A761 Set of 4 4.00 4.00

Crocuses — A762

Designs: 250,000 l, Crocus chrysanthus. 275,000 l, Crocus olivieri. 300,000 l, Crocus biflorus. 1,250,000 l, Crocus sativus.

**2000, Oct. 9** **Litho.** ***Perf. 13¾x14***
**2778-2781** A762 Set of 4 8.25 3.75

Architecture — A763

Designs: 200,000 l, Arslan Baba. 275,000 l, Karasaç Ana. 300,000 l, Hoca Ahmet Yesevi.

**2000, Oct. 19** **Litho.** ***Perf. 13¼x13***
**2782-2784** A763 Set of 3 4.00 4.00

Turksat 2A — A764

Women's Clothing — A765

**2001, Jan. 25** **Litho.** ***Perf. 13x13¾***
**2785** A764 200,000 l multi 1.25 1.25

**2001, Mar. 19**

Designs: No. 2786, 200,000 l, Afyon. No. 2787, 200,000 l, Balikesir. No. 2788, 325,000 l, Kars. No. 2789, 325,000 l, Tokat.

**2786-2789** A765 Set of 4 3.00 3.00

**Women's Headcovers Type of 1997**

Designs: 200,000 l, Mersin-Silifke. 250,000 l, Sivas. 425,000 l, Aydin. 450,000 l, Hakkari.

**2001, Apr. 16** **Litho.** ***Perf. 13¼***
**2790-2793** A734 Set of 4 3.50 3.50

Europa — A766

Waterfalls: 450,000 l, Düdenbasi. 500,000 l, Yerköprü.

**2001, May 5** ***Perf. 13***
**2794-2795** A766 Set of 2 3.00 3.00

Aviators A767

Designs: 250,000 l, Capt. Ismail Hakki Bey. 300,000 l, Lieut. Nuri Bey. 450,000 l, Lieut. Sadik Bey. 500,000 l, Capt. Fethi Bey.

**2001, May 15**
**2796-2799** A767 Set of 4 5.00 5.00

**World Environment Day Type of 1999**

No. 2800, 300,000 l: a, Turdus pilaris. b, Carduelis carduelis.
No. 2801, 450,000 l: a, Merops apiaster. b, Upupa epops.

**2001, June 5** ***Perf. 13¼***
**Sheets of 2, #a-b**
**2800-2801** A748 Set of 2 5.00 5.00

Kemal Ataturk — A768

Medicinal Plants — A769

Ataturk (1881-1938) and: 300,000 l, Turkish flag. 450,000 l, Birthplace

**2001, May 19** **Litho.** ***Perf. 13***
**2802-2803** A768 Set of 2 2.00 2.00

**2001, June 27** ***Perf. 13¾***

Designs: 250,000 l, Myrtus communis. 300,000 l, Achillea millefolium. 450,000 l, Hypericum perforatum. 500,000 l, Rosa moyesii. 1,750,000 l, Crataegus oxyacantha.

**2804-2808** A769 Set of 5 10.00 2.25

Horses A770

Designs: 300,000 l, Horse and foal. No. 2810, 450,000 l, Three horses. No. 2811, 450,000 l, Two horses galloping. 500,000 l, Horse, vert.

**2001, July 16** ***Perf. 13***
**2809-2812** A770 Set of 4 4.50 4.50

**Merchant Ships Type of 2000**

Designs: 250,000 l, Resitpasa. No. 2814, 300,000 l, Mithatpasa. No. 2815, 300,000 l, Gülnihal, 500,000 l, Aydin.

**2001, Sept. 3** ***Perf. 13¼***
**2813-2816** A757 Set of 4 3.75 3.75

Architecture A771

Designs: No. 2817, 300,000 l, Sirvansahlar Palace, Baku, Azerbaijan. No. 2818, 300,000 l, Sultan Tekes Mausoleum, Urgench, Uzbekistan. 450,000 l, Timur Mausoleum, Samarkand, Uzbekistan. 500,000 l, While Tlightning Mausoleum, Bursa.

**2001, Oct. 15**
**2817-2820** A771 Set of 4 4.00 4.00

Sultan Nevruz A772

**2002, Mar. 21** **Litho.** ***Perf. 13¼***
**2821** A772 400,000 l multi 1.10 1.10

**Women's Clothing Type of 2001**

Designs: 350,000 l, Kastamonu. 400,000 l, Canakkale. 500,000 l, Amasya-Ilisu. 600,000 l, Elazig.

**2002, Apr. 16** ***Perf. 13x13¼***
**2822-2825** A765 Set of 4 4.50 4.50

Europa — A773

**2002, May 5** **Litho.** ***Perf. 13x13¼***
**2826** A773 500,000 l multi 1.50 1.50

2002 World Cup Soccer Championships, Japan and Korea — A774

Designs: 400,000 l, Players, referee. 600,000 l, Crowd, player making scissors kick.

**2002, May 31** **Litho.** ***Perf. 13¼x13***
**2827-2828** A774 Set of 2 2.50 2.50

Famous Men — A775

Designs: 100,000 l, Muzaffer Sarisözen (1898-1963), musician. 400,000 l, Arif Nihat Asya (1904-75), writer. 500,000 l, Vedat Tek (1873-1942), architect. 600,000 l, Hilmi Ziya Ulken (1901-74), philosopher. 2,500,000 l, Ibrahim Calli (1882-1960), painter.

**2002, June 3** ***Perf. 13¾x14***
**2829-2833** A775 Set of 5 11.00 3.75

Souvenir Sheet

Wild Cats — A776

No. 2834: a, Panthera pardus tulliana. b, Lynx lynx. c, Panthera tigris. d, Caracal caracal.

**2002, June 20** ***Perf. 13¼x13***
**2834** A776 400,000 l Sheet of 4, #a-d 4.50 4.50

Souvenir Sheet

Shells — A777

Various shells: a, 400,000 l. b, 500,000 l. c, 600,000 l. d, 750,000 l.

**2002, June 25**
**2835** A777 Sheet of 4, #a-d 6.00 6.00

Third Place Finish of Turkish Team in World Cup Soccer Championships — A778

Designs: 400,000 l, Players in action. 700,000 l, Team photo.

**2002, July 29** ***Perf. 13x13¼***
**2836-2837** A778 Set of 2 2.75 2.75

String Instruments A779

Designs: 450,000 l, Violin. 700,000 l, Bass.

**2002, Oct. 10** ***Perf. 13¼x13***
**2838-2839** A779 Set of 2 3.00 3.00

**Merchant Ships Type of 2000**

Designs: 450,000 l, Ege. 500,000 l, Ayvalik. No. 2842, 700,000 l, Karadeniz. No. 2843, 700,000 l, Marakaz.

**2002, Nov. 4** **Litho.** ***Perf. 13***
**2840-2843** A757 Set of 4 5.00 5.00

Souvenir Sheet

Turkish and Hungarian Buildings — A780

No. 2844: a, 450,000 l, Gazi Kassim Pasha Mosque, Pécs, Hungary. b, 700,000 l, Rakoczi House, Tekirdag, Turkey.

**2002, Dec. 2** **Litho.** ***Perf. 13¼***
**2844** A780 Sheet of 2, #a-b 3.00 3.00

See Hungary Nos. 3819-3820.

BJK Soccer Team, Cent. — A781

Team emblem and: 500,000 l, Eagle, Turkish and team flags. 700,000 l, Eagle, stadium. 750,000 l, Soccer players. 1,000,000 l, Eagle's head.

**2003, Mar. 3** ***Perf. 13x13¼***
**2845-2848** A781 Set of 4 6.50 6.50

A782

A783

Europa: 500,000 l, Travel poster. 700,000 l, Ankara State Theater poster.

**2003, May 9** **Litho.** ***Perf. 13***
**2849-2850** A782 Set of 2 3.00 3.00

**2003, May 29**

Conquest of Constantinople, 550th Anniv.: No. 2851, 500,000 l, Leaders at table. No. 2852, 500,000 l, Sultan Mehmet II seated. 700,000 l, Robe. 1,500,000 l, Sultan Mehmet II and cartouche.

**2851-2854** A783 Set of 4 6.00 6.00

Souvenir Sheet

World Environment Day — A784

No. 2855: a, Gazella subgutturosa. b, Cervus elaphus. c, Capreolus capreolus. d, Cervus dama.

**2003, June 5**
**2855** A784 500,000 l Sheet of 4, #a-d 4.50 4.50

Zodiac A785

**2003, June 19** ***Perf. 13¼***
**2856** A785 500,000 l multi 1.00 1.00

**Women's Clothing Type of 2001**

Designs: No. 2857, 500,000 l, Sivas. No. 2858, 500,000 l, Gaziantep. No. 2859, 700,000 l, Erzincan. No. 2860, 700,000 l, Ankara-Beypazari.

**2003, July 8** ***Perf. 13***
**2857-2860** A765 Set of 4 5.50 5.50

Fruit Blossoms — A786

Blossoms: 500,000 l, Ayva cicegi (quince). 700,000 l, Erik cicegi (plum). 750,000 l, Kiraz cicegi (cherry) . 1,000,000 l, Nar cicegi (pomegranate). 3,000,000 l, Portakal cicegi (orange).

**2003, July 25** ***Perf. 13¾x14***
**2861-2865** A786 Set of 5 12.00 6.50

Brass Instruments A787

Designs: 600,000 l, French horn. 800,000 l, Trumpet.

**2003, Sept. 23** **Litho.** ***Perf. 13¼x13***
**2866-2867** A787 Set of 2 3.00 3.00

Republic of Turkey, 80th Anniv. A788

Kemal Ataturk, flag and: No. 2868, 600,000 l, Cavalry. No. 2869, 600,000 l, Buildings.

**2003, Oct. 29** **Litho.** ***Perf. 13¼x13***
**2868-2869** A788 Set of 2 2.50 2.50

Navy Ships A789

Designs: No. 2870, 600,000 l, Karadeniz. No. 2871, 600,000 l, Gediz. No. 2872, 700,000 l, Salihreis. No. 2873, 700,000 l, Kocatepe.

**2003, Nov. 14**
**2870-2873** A789 Set of 4 6.00 6.00

Agriculture Bank, 140th Anniv. — A790

**2003, Nov. 20** ***Perf. 13x13¼***
**2874** A790 600,000 l multi 1.25 1.25

Buildings Associated with Kemal Ataturk — A791

Designs: 600,000 l, House, Trabzon. 700,000 l, Museum, Sakarya. 800,000 l, House, Selanik. 1,000,000 l, Museum, Ankara.

**2003, Dec. 12**
**2875-2878** A791 Set of 4 5.50 5.50

PTT Bank — A792

**2004, Mar. 3** ***Perf. 14***
**2879** A792 600,000 l multi .95 .45

**Women's Clothing Type of 2001**

Designs: 600,000 l, Edirne. No. 2881, 700,000 l, Tunceli. No. 2882, 700,000 l, Burdur. 800,000 l, Trabzon.

**2004, Apr. 30** ***Perf. 13x13¼***
**2880-2883** A765 Set of 4 5.00 5.00

Europa — A793

Designs: 700,000 l, Skier, windsurfer. 800,000 l, Tourist at archaeological ruins, ships.

**2004, May 9**
**2884-2885** A793 Set of 2 3.00 3.00

Souvenir Sheet

World Environment Day — A794

No. 2886: a, Falco tinnunculus. b, Buteo buteo. c, Aquila chrysaetos. d, Milvus migrans.

**2004, June 5** ***Perf. 13¼x13***
**2886** A794 700,000 l Sheet of 4, #a-d 5.00 5.00

Caravansaries — A795

Designs: 600,000 l, Mamahatun Caravansary, Erzincan. 700,000 l, Cardak Caravasary, Denizli.

**2004, June 7**
**2887-2888** A795 Set of 2 2.50 2.50

Gendarmerie, 165th Anniv. — A796

**2004, June 14** ***Perf. 13x13¼***
**2889** A796 600,000 l multi .80 .40

Birds — A797

Designs: 100,000 l, Regulus regulus. 250,000 l, Sylvia rueppelli. 600,000 l, Hippolais polyglotta. 700,000 l, Passer domesticus. 800,000 l, Emberiza bruniceps. 1,000,000 l, Fringilla coelebs. 1,500,000 l, Phoenicurus phoenicurus. 3,500,000 l, Erithacus rubecula.

**20004, July 23** ***Perf. 14***

| | | | | |
|---|---|---|---|---|
| **2890** | A797 | 100,000 l multi | .20 | .20 |
| **2891** | A797 | 250,000 l multi | .35 | .20 |
| **2892** | A797 | 600,000 l multi | .80 | .40 |
| **2893** | A797 | 700,000 l multi | .95 | .50 |
| **2894** | A797 | 800,000 l multi | 1.10 | .55 |
| **2895** | A797 | 1,000,000 l multi | 1.40 | .70 |
| **2896** | A797 | 1,500,000 l multi | 2.10 | 1.00 |
| **2897** | A797 | 3,500,000 l multi | 4.75 | 2.40 |
| | *Nos. 2890-2897 (8)* | | 11.65 | 5.95 |

2004 Summer Olympics, Athens A798

Designs: 600,000 l, Wrestling. No. 2899, 700,000 l, Weight lifting. No. 2900, 700,000 l, Women's track and field, vert. 800,000 l, Wrestling, diff.

***Perf. 13¼x13, 13x13¼***

**2004, Aug. 13**

**2898-2901** A798 Set of 4 5.00 5.00

Souvenir Sheet

Navy Submarines — A799

No. 2902: a, 600,000 l, 18 Mart. b, 700,000 l, Preveze. c, 700,000 l, Anafartalar. d, 800,000 l, Atilay.

**2004, Sept. 14** ***Perf. 13x13¼***

**2902** A799 Sheet of 4, #a-d 5.00 5.00

Piri Reis (1465-1554), Admiral and Map Compiler — A800

**2004, Sept. 20**

**2903** A800 600,000 l multi 1.00 1.00

Waterfalls A801

Designs: 600,000 l, Kapuzbasi Waterfall. 700,000 l, Sudüsen Waterfall, vert.

**2004, Oct. 19** ***Perf. 13x13¼, 13¼x13***

**2904-2905** A801 Set of 2 3.00 3.00

Buildings Associated With Kemal Ataturk — A802

Designs: 600,000 l, Ataturk Summer House, Bursa. No. 2907, 700,000 l, Ataturk House Museum, Erzurum. No. 2908, 700,000 l, Ataturk House, Havza. 800,000 l, State Railways Director's Building, Ankara.

**2004, Nov. 8** **Litho.** ***Perf. 13¼x13***

**2906-2909** A802 Set of 4 5.00 5.00

Souvenir Sheet

Turkish Stars Aerobatics Team — A803

No. 2910: a, 600,000 l, Two airplanes. b, 700,000 l, Five airplanes. c, 800,000 l, Seven airplanes flying upwards. d, 900,000 l, Seven airplanes flying left.

**2004, Dec. 7** **Litho.** ***Perf. 13¼x13***

**2910** A803 Sheet of 4, #a-d 6.00 6.00

Provinces A804

**2005, Jan. 1** **Litho.** ***Perf. 14***

| | | | | | |
|---|---|---|---|---|---|
| **2914** | A804 | 1k | Adana | .20 | .20 |
| **2915** | A804 | 5k | Adiyaman | .20 | .20 |
| **2916** | A804 | 10k | Afyon | .20 | .20 |
| **2917** | A804 | 25k | Agri | .35 | .20 |
| **2918** | A804 | 50k | Amasya | .70 | .35 |
| **2919** | A804 | 60k | Ankara | .85 | .40 |
| **2920** | A804 | 60k | Bitlis | .85 | .40 |
| **2921** | A804 | 70k | Antalya | 1.00 | .50 |
| **2922** | A804 | 70k | Bolu | 1.00 | .50 |
| **2923** | A804 | 80k | Artvin | 1.10 | .55 |
| **2924** | A804 | 80k | Burdur | 1.10 | .55 |
| **2925** | A804 | 90k | Aydin | 1.25 | .60 |
| **2926** | A804 | 1 l | Balikesir | 1.50 | .75 |
| **2927** | A804 | 1.50 l | Bilecik | 2.25 | 1.10 |
| **2928** | A804 | 3.50 l | Bingol | 5.00 | 2.50 |
| **2929** | A804 | 3.50 l | Bursa | 5.00 | 2.50 |
| | *Nos. 2914-2929 (16)* | | | 22.55 | 11.50 |

A805 A806

Designs: 60k, Batiburnu Lighthouse, Canakkale. 70k, Zonguldak Lighthouse, Zonguldak.

**2005, Mar. 18** **Litho.** ***Perf. 13x13¼***

**2930-2931** A805 Set of 2 2.00 1.00

**2005, Apr. 1**

Marmaris Intl. Maritime Festival: 70k, Sailboat. 80k, Sailboat, sun on horizon.

**2932-2933** A806 Set of 2 2.25 1.10

A807 A808

**2005, Apr. 10**

**2934** A807 70k multi 1.10 .55

Turkish Police, 160th anniv.

**2005, Apr. 23**

Grand National Assembly, 85th anniv.: 60k, Torch, star and crescent. 70k, Crescent and fireworks over Grand National Assembly.

**2935-2936** A808 Set of 2 1.90 .95

Europa — A809

**2005, May 9**

**2937** A809 70k multi 1.10 .55

Caftans of Sultans — A810

Caftan of Sultan: No. 2938, 70k, Ahmed I (shown). No. 2939, 70k, Ahmed I, diff. No. 2940, 70k, Murad III. No. 2941, 70k, Selim.

**2005, May 20**

**2938-2941** A810 Set of 4 4.25 2.10

Souvenir Sheet

World Environment Day — A811

No. 2942: a, 60k, Pagellus bogaraveo. b, 70k, Epinephelus guaza. c, 70k, Merlanyus euxinus. d, 80k, Maena smaris.

**2005, June 5** **Litho.** ***Perf. 13¼x13***

**2942** A811 Sheet of 4, #a-d 4.25 2.10

Tapestries & Carpets — A812

Designs: 60k, Carpet from Hereke region, Turkey. 70k, L'humanité Assaillie par les Sept Pechés Capitaux tapestry, Belgium.

**2005, June 22** **Litho.** ***Perf. 13x13¼***

**2943-2944** A812 Set of 2 2.00 1.00

See Belgium Nos. 2098-2099.

World Architecture Congress, Istanbul — A813

**2005, July 3**

**2945** A813 70k multi 1.10 .55

Mosaics A814

Designs: 60k, Akelos. No. 2947, 70k, Oceanos and Tethys. No. 2948, 70k, Achilles. 80k, Menad.

**2005, July 5** ***Perf. 13¼x13***

**2946-2949** A814 Set of 4 4.25 2.10

Clocks — A815

Designs: 60k, Musical clock, 1770. 70k, Clock, 1867.

**2005, July 20** ***Perf. 13x13¼***

**2950-2951** A815 Set of 2 2.00 1.00

Turkish Grand Prix, Istanbul — A816

**2005, Aug. 19** **Litho.** ***Perf. 13x13¼***

**2952** A816 70k multi 1.10 .55

Philanthropic Businessmen — A817

Designs: 60k, Sakip Sabanci (1933-2004). 70k, Vehbi Koç (1901-96).

**2005, Sept. 21** **Litho.** ***Perf. 13¼x13***

**2953-2954** A817 Set of 2 2.00 1.00

Provinces
A818

**2005, Sept. 28** *Perf. 13¾*

| | | | | |
|---|---|---|---|---|
| **2955** A818 | 50k Canakkale | .75 | .35 |
| **2956** A818 | 60k Cankiri | .90 | .45 |
| **2957** A818 | 60k Corum | .90 | .45 |
| **2958** A818 | 60k Denizli | .90 | .45 |
| **2959** A818 | 60k Diyarbakir | .90 | .45 |
| **2960** A818 | 60k Edirne | .90 | .45 |
| **2961** A818 | 60k Elazig | .90 | .45 |
| **2962** A818 | 70k Erzincan | 1.10 | .55 |
| **2963** A818 | 70k Erzurum | 1.10 | .55 |
| **2964** A818 | 70k Eskisehir | 1.10 | .55 |
| **2965** A818 | 70k Gaziantep | 1.10 | .55 |
| **2966** A818 | 70k Giresun | 1.10 | .55 |
| **2967** A818 | 70k Gumushane | 1.10 | .55 |
| **2968** A818 | 1 l Hakkari | 1.50 | .75 |
| **2969** A818 | 1.50 l Hatay | 2.25 | 1.10 |
| **2970** A818 | 2.50 l Isparta | 3.75 | 1.90 |
| *Nos. 2955-2970 (16)* | | 20.25 | 10.10 |

Mevlana Jalal ad-Din ar-Rumi (1207-73), Islamic Philosopher
A819

**2005, Sept. 30** *Perf. 13x13¼*
**2971** A819 70k multi 1.10 .55

See Iran No. 2911 and Syria No. 1574.

Galatasaray Sports Club, Cent. — A820

Club emblem and: No. 2972, 60k, Soccer stadium crowd, lion and "100." No. 2973, 70k, Soccer stadium, trophy.
No. 2974: a, 60k, Man, lion and "100." b, 70k, Club emblem, building. c, 80k, Soccer players. d, 1 l, Soccer players with trophy.

**2005, Oct. 11** *Perf. 13x13¼*
**2972-2973** A820 Set of 2 1.90 .95

**Souvenir Sheet**
*Perf. 13¼x13*

**2974** A820 Sheet of 4, #a-d 4.50 2.25

No. 2974 contains four 41x26mm stamps.

Start of Negotiations for Turkish Admission to European Union — A821

**2005, Nov. 3** *Perf. 13¼x13*
**2975** A821 70k multi 1.10 .55

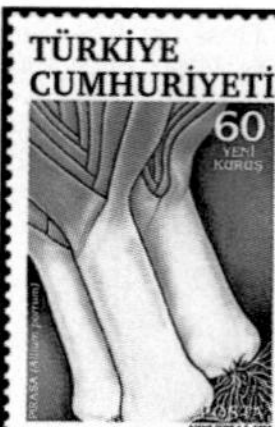
Vegetables — A824

Designs, 60k, Allium porrum (leeks). 70k, Allium sativum (garlic). 80k, Allium cepa (onions).

**2005, Nov. 21 Litho.** *Perf. 13x13¼*
**2978-2980** A824 Set of 3 3.25 1.60

Europa Stamps, 50th Anniv. (in 2006) — A825

Designs: No. 2981, 60k, Vignette of #1907. No. 2982, 70k, Vignette of #1628. 80k, Vignette of #B120. 1 l, Vignette of #1719.
No. 2985, horiz.: a, 10k, #1520. b, 25k, #1800. c, 60k, #1553. d, 70k, #1775.
No. 2986, horiz.: a, 10k, #1493. b, 25k, #1936. c, 60k, #1602. d, 70k, #1876.

**2005, Dec. 15 Litho.** *Perf. 13x13¼*
**2981-2984** A825 Set of 4 4.75 2.40

**Souvenir Sheets**
*Perf. 13¼x13*

**2985** A825 Sheet of 4, #a-d 2.50 1.25

*Imperf*

**2986** A825 Sheet of 4, #a-d 2.50 1.25

2006 Winter Olympics, Turin
A826

Designs: 60k, Speed skating. 70k, Skiing.

**2006, Feb. 10** *Perf. 13¼x13*
**2987-2988** A826 Set of 2 2.00 1.00

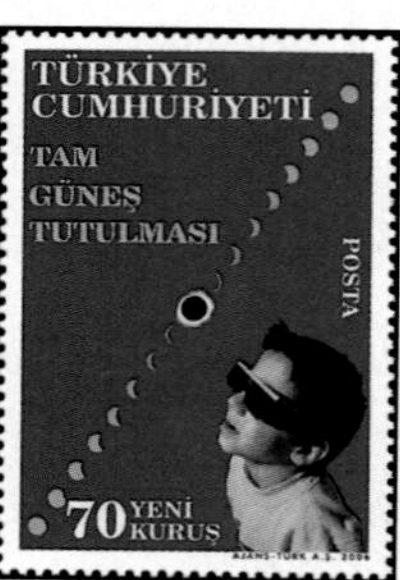
March 29 Total Solar Eclipse
A827

**2006, Mar. 29 Litho.** *Perf. 13¼x13*
**2989** A827 70k multi 1.10 .55

Support for Education
A828

**2006, Apr. 10**
**2990** A828 60k multi .95 .45

Karaoglan, Cartoon Hero — A829

Karaoglan: 60k, With bow and arrow. No. 2992, 70k, Attacking swordsman. No. 2993, 70k, On horseback. 80k, On horseback, diff.

**2006, Apr. 20** *Perf. 13x13¼*
**2991-2994** A829 Set of 4 4.25 2.10

Izzet Baysal (1907-2000), Architect — A830

**2006, May 11 Litho.** *Perf. 13¼x13*
**2995** A830 60k multi .85 .45

A831

A832

A833

A834

A835

A836

A837

A838

A839

Kemal Ataturk (1881-1938) — A840

**2006, May 19**

| | | | |
|---|---|---|---|
| **2996** | Block of 10 | 7.50 | 3.75 |
| *a.* | A831 60k multi | .75 | .35 |
| *b.* | A832 60k multi | .75 | .35 |
| *c.* | A833 60k multi | .75 | .35 |
| *d.* | A834 60k multi | .75 | .35 |
| *e.* | A835 60k multi | .75 | .35 |
| *f.* | A836 60k multi | .75 | .35 |
| *g.* | A837 60k multi | .75 | .35 |
| *h.* | A838 60k multi | .75 | .35 |
| *i.* | A839 60k multi | .75 | .35 |
| *j.* | A840 60k multi | .75 | .35 |

Europa — A841

**2006, May 30** *Perf. 13x13¼*
**2997** A841 70k multi .90 .45

Miniature Sheet

World Environment Day — A842

No. 2998: a, 25k, Parched earth. b, 50k, Tree. c, 60k, Tree, diff. d, 70k, Forest.

**2006, June 5**
**2998** A842 Sheet of 4, #a-d 2.75 1.40

Intl. Year of Deserts and Desertification.

2006 World Cup Soccer Championships, Germany — A843

Designs: No. 2999, 70k, Player dribbling ball. No. 3000, 70k, Player kicking ball, horiz.

**2006, June 9** *Perf. 13x13¼, 13¼x13*
**2999-3000** A843 Set of 2 1.90 .95

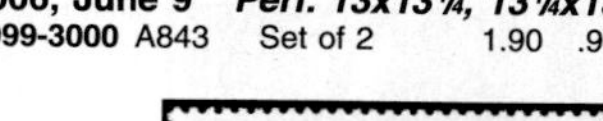

Airplanes
A844

Designs: 60k, Deperdussin monoplane. No. 3002, 70k, Bleriot monoplane. No. 3003, 70k, R. E. P. monoplane.

**2006, June 22** ***Perf. 13¼x13***
**3001-3003** A844 Set of 3 2.60 1.40

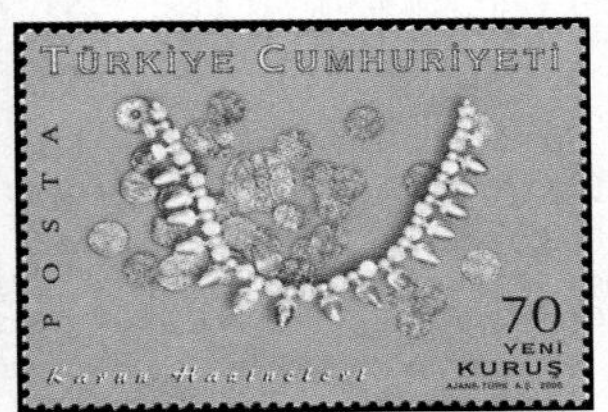

Treasures of Karun — A845

Designs: No. 3004, 70k, Bracelet and coins. No. 3005, 70k, Winged sun disc pectoral and bracelet. 80k, Lion's head bracelets.

**2006, July 10** ***Perf. 13x13¼***
**3004-3006** A845 Set of 3 2.75 1.40

Provinces A846

**2006, Sept. 11** ***Perf. 13¼x13***

| | | | | | |
|---|---|---|---|---|---|
| **3007** | A846 | 10k | Kahramanmaras | .20 | .20 |
| **3008** | A846 | 10k | Manisa | .20 | .20 |
| **3009** | A846 | 50k | Kirsehir | .70 | .35 |
| **3010** | A846 | 50k | Kocaeli | .70 | .35 |
| **3011** | A846 | 60k | Izmir | .80 | .40 |
| **3012** | A846 | 60k | Konya | .80 | .40 |
| **3013** | A846 | 60k | Mardin | .80 | .40 |
| **3014** | A846 | 60k | Mugla | .80 | .40 |
| **3015** | A846 | 70k | Istanbul | .95 | .50 |
| **3016** | A846 | 70k | Mersin | .95 | .50 |
| **3017** | A846 | 1 l | Kastamonu | 1.40 | .70 |
| **3018** | A846 | 1 l | Kirklareli | 1.40 | .70 |
| **3019** | A846 | 1.60 l | Kayseri | 2.25 | 1.10 |
| **3020** | A846 | 2 l | Malatya | 2.75 | 1.40 |
| **3021** | A846 | 4 l | Kars | 5.50 | 2.75 |
| **3022** | A846 | 4 l | Kutahya | 5.50 | 2.75 |
| | | | *Nos. 3007-3022 (16)* | 25.70 | 13.10 |

Scenes From Movie, "Selvi Boylum Al Yazmalim" — A847

Various scenes: 60k, 70k.

**2006, Sept. 16** ***Perf. 13x13¼***
**3023-3024** A847 Set of 2 1.75 .85

Turkish Railroads, 150th Anniv. A848

Designs: 60k, Steam locomotive. 70k, Electric train.

**2006, Sept. 23** ***Perf. 13¼x13***
**3025-3026** A848 Set of 2 1.75 .85

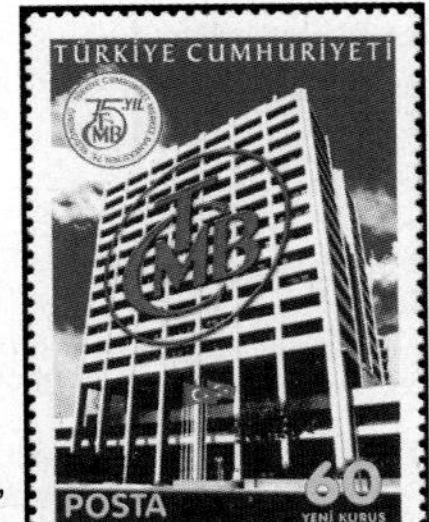

Central Bank, 75th Anniv. A849

**2006, Oct. 3**
**3027** A849 60k multi .80 .40

Intl. Telecommunications Union Conference, Antalya — A850

Conference emblem and: 60k, Globe with spotlight on Turkey. 70k, Map with lines drawn to Turkey.

**2006, Nov. 6** ***Perf. 13x13¼***
**3028-3029** A850 Set of 2 1.90 .95

Turkish Atomic Energy Authority, 50th Anniv. A852

**2006, Nov. 22** **Litho.** ***Perf. 13¼x13***
**3031** A852 60k multi .85 .40

Geothermal Resources — A853

Designs: 60k, Four steam clouds. 70k, Steam leaving smokestack.

**2006, Dec. 11**
**3032-3033** A853 Set of 2 1.90 .95

---

## SEMI-POSTAL STAMPS

Regular Issues Overprinted in Carmine or Black

Overprint reads: "For War Orphans"

***Perf. 12, 13½ and Compound***

**1915** **Unwmk.**

### On Stamps of 1905

**B1** A18 10pa dull grn (#119) .75 .50
**B2** A18 10pi orange brown 12.50 .80

### On Stamp of 1906

**B3** A18 10pa dull grn (#128) 40.00 25.00

### On Stamps of 1908

**B4** A19 10pa blue green 1.50 .75
**B5** A19 5pi dark violet 75.00 12.50
*Nos. B1-B5 (5)* 129.75 39.55

With Additional Overprint

**B6** A19 10pa blue green 240.00 175.00

### On Stamps of 1909

**B7** A21 10pa blue green 1.00 .75
*a.* Inverted overprint 22.50 22.50
*b.* Double overprint, one invtd. 30.00 30.00
**B8** A21 20pa carmine rose 1.00 .75
*a.* Inverted overprint 27.50 27.50
**B9** A21 1pi ultra 1.00 .75
**B10** A21 5pi dark violet 8.75 1.50
*Nos. B7-B10 (4)* 11.75 3.75

With Additional Overprint

**B11** A21 10pa blue green 1.00 .75
*b.* Double overprint, one inverted 5.00 5.00
**B12** A21 20pa carmine rose 1.50 .75
**B13** A21 1pi ultra 2.00 .75

### On Stamps of 1913

**B14** A22 10pa blue green 1.00 .75
*a.* Inverted overprint 22.50 22.50
**B15** A22 1pi ultra 1.00 .75
*a.* Double overprint 5.00 5.00
*Nos. B11-B15 (5)* 6.50 3.75

With Additional Overprint

**B16** A22 10pa blue green 1.25 .75
*a.* Inverted overprint 27.50 27.50

### On Newspaper Stamp of 1908

**B17** A19 10pa blue green 360.00 175.00

### On Newspaper Stamp of 1909

**B18** A21 10pa blue green 1.25 1.00

Regular Issues Overprinted in Carmine or Black

**1916**

### On Stamps of 1901

**B19** A17 1pi blue 1.00 .50
**B20** A17 5pi lilac rose 10.00 1.50

### On Stamps of 1905

**B21** A18 1pi brt blue 7.50 2.00
**B22** A18 5pi brown 7.50 5.00

### On Stamp of 1906

**B23** A18 1pi brt blue 1.00 .75

### On Stamps of 1908

**B24** A19 20pa carmine (Bk) *300.00*
**B25** A19 10pi red 500.00 200.00

With Additional Overprint

**B26** A19 20pa carmine 1.00 .75
**B27** A19 1pi brt blue (C) 20.00 5.00

### On Stamps of 1909

**B28** A21 20pa carmine rose 1.00 .75
**B29** A21 1pi ultra .50 .75
**B30** A21 10pi dull red 175.00 100.00

With Additional Overprint

**B31** A21 20pa carmine rose .75 .50
**B32** A21 1pi ultra 1.00 .75

### On Stamps of 1913

**B33** A22 20pa carmine rose 1.00 .75
**B34** A22 1pi ultra 1.00 .35
*a.* Inverted overprint 5.00 5.00
**B35** A22 10pi dull red 22.50 15.00

With Additional Overprint

**B36** A22 20pa carmine rose 1.00 .75

### On Newspaper Stamps of 1901

**B37** A16 5pi ocher 11.50 6.00
*a.* 5pa bister, No. P37 150.00 150.00

Regular Issues Surcharged in Black

### On Stamp of 1899

**B38** A11 10pa on 20pa vio brn 1.00 .75

### On Stamp of 1905

**B39** A18 10pa on 20pa carmine 1.00 .75

### On Stamp of 1906

**B40** A18 10pa on 20pa carmine .90 .75

### On Newspaper Stamp of 1893-99

**B41** A11 10pa on 20pa violet brn 2.00 1.50
*Nos. B38-B41 (4)* 4.90 3.75

Nos. 346-349 Overprinted

**B42** A41 10pa carmine 1.00 .75
*a.* Inverted overprint 6.75 6.75
**B43** A41 20pa ultra 1.00 .75
*a.* Inverted overprint 6.75 6.75
**B44** A41 1pi violet & blk 1.00 .90
*a.* Inverted overprint 6.75 6.75
**B45** A41 5pi yel brn & blk 1.00 .75
*a.* Inverted overprint 11.00 11.00
*Nos. B42-B45 (4)* 4.00 3.15

Nos. B42-B45 formed part of the Postage Commemoration issue of 1916.

A Soldier's Farewell — SP1

**1917, Feb. 20** **Engr.** ***Perf. 12½***
**B46** SP1 10pa red violet 1.25 .50

For surcharges see Nos. 600, B47.

Stamp of Same Design Surcharged

**B47** SP1 10pa on 20pa car rose 2.00 .50

Badge of the Society — SP9

School Teacher — SP10

Marie Sklodowska Curie — SP16

Kemal Atatürk — SP23

Designs: 2k+2k, Woman farmer. 2½k+2½k, Typist. 4k+4k, Aviatrix and policewoman. 5k+5k, Women voters. 7½k+7½k, Yildiz Palace, Istanbul. 10k+10k, Carrie Chapman Catt. 12½k+12½k, Jane Addams. 15k+15k, Grazia Deledda. 20k+20k, Selma Lagerlof. 25k+25k, Bertha von Suttner. 30k+30k, Sigrid Undset.

**1935, Apr. 17 Photo. *Perf. 11½***

**Inscribed: "XII Congres Suffragiste International"**

| | | | | |
|---|---|---|---|---|
| **B54** | SP9 | 20pa + 20pa brn | .50 | .50 |
| **B55** | SP10 | 1k + 1k rose car | .75 | .50 |
| **B56** | SP10 | 2k + 2k sl bl | 1.00 | .75 |
| **B57** | SP10 | 2½k + 2½k yel grn | 1.00 | .75 |
| **B58** | SP10 | 4k + 4k blue | 1.50 | 1.00 |
| **B59** | SP10 | 5k + 5k dl vio | 2.50 | 2.00 |
| **B60** | SP10 | 7½k + 7½k org red | 2.50 | 2.00 |
| **B61** | SP16 | 10k + 10k org | 2.50 | 2.50 |
| **B62** | SP16 | 12½k + 12½k dk bl | 2.50 | 2.50 |
| **B63** | SP16 | 15k + 15k violet | 5.00 | 5.00 |
| **B64** | SP16 | 20k + 20k red org | 7.50 | 6.25 |
| **B65** | SP16 | 25k + 25k grn | 15.00 | 14.00 |
| **B66** | SP16 | 30k + 30k ultra | 90.00 | 100.00 |
| **B67** | SP16 | 50k + 50k dk sl grn | 175.00 | 150.00 |
| **B68** | SP23 | 100k + 100k brn car | 125.00 | 140.00 |
| | | *Nos. B54-B68 (15)* | 432.25 | 427.75 |
| | | Set, never hinged | 675.00 | |

12th Congress of the Women's Intl. Alliance.

**Catalogue values for unused stamps in this section, from this point to the end of the section, are for Never Hinged items.**

Katip Chelebi — SP24

***Perf. 10½***

**1958, Sept. 24 Litho. Unwmk.**

| | | | | |
|---|---|---|---|---|
| **B69** | SP24 | 50k + 10k gray | .25 | .20 |

Mustafa ibn 'Abdallah Katip Chelebi Hajji Khalifa (1608-1657), Turkish author.

Road Building Machine SP25

Kemal Atatürk — SP26

Ruins, Göreme SP27

Design: 25k+5k, Tanks and planes.

**1958, Oct. 29**

| | | | | |
|---|---|---|---|---|
| **B70** | SP25 | 15k + 5k orange | .20 | .20 |
| **B71** | SP26 | 20k + 5k lt red brn | .20 | .20 |
| **B72** | SP25 | 25k + 5k brt grn | .20 | .20 |
| | | *Nos. B70-B72 (3)* | .60 | .60 |

The surtax went to the Red Crescent Society and to the Society for the Protection of Children.

For surcharge see No. 1440.

**1959, July 8 Litho. *Perf. 10***

| | | | | |
|---|---|---|---|---|
| **B73** | SP27 | 105k + 10k pur & buff | .30 | .20 |

Issued for tourist publicity.

Istanbul SP28

**1959, Sept. 11**

| | | | | |
|---|---|---|---|---|
| **B74** | SP28 | 105k + 10k lt bl & red | .25 | .20 |

15th International Tuberculosis Congress.

Manisa Asylum SP29

Merkez Muslihiddin SP30

Kermis at Manisa: 90k+5k, Sultan Camil Mosque, Manisa, vert.

**1960, Apr. 17 Unwmk. *Perf. 13***

| | | | | |
|---|---|---|---|---|
| **B75** | SP29 | 40k + 5k grn & lt bl | .25 | .20 |
| **B76** | SP29 | 40k + 5k vio & rose lil | .25 | .20 |
| **B77** | SP29 | 90k + 5k dp cl & car rose | .60 | .20 |
| **B78** | SP30 | 105k + 10k multi | .80 | .20 |
| | | *Nos. B75-B78 (4)* | 1.90 | .80 |

Census Symbol — SP32

**1960, Sept. 23 Photo. *Perf. 11½***

**Granite Paper**

| | | | | |
|---|---|---|---|---|
| **B79** | SP31 | 30k + 5k bl & rose pink | .20 | .20 |
| **B80** | SP32 | 50k + 5k grn, dk bl & ultra | .25 | .20 |

Issued for the 1960 Census.

Old Observatory SP33

Fatin Gökmen — SP34

Designs: 30k+5k, Observatory emblem. 75k+5k, Building housing telescope.

**1961, July 1 Litho. *Perf. 13***

| | | | | |
|---|---|---|---|---|
| **B81** | SP33 | 10k + 5k grnsh bl & grn | .25 | .25 |
| **B82** | SP33 | 30k + 5k vio & blk | .75 | .75 |
| **B83** | SP34 | 40k + 5k brown | .25 | .25 |
| **B84** | SP33 | 75k + 5k olive grn | .75 | .75 |
| | | *Nos. B81-B84 (4)* | 2.00 | 2.00 |

Kandill Observatory, 50th anniversary.

Anti-Malaria Work — SP35

UNICEF, 10th anniv.: 30k+5k, Mother and infant, horiz. 75k+5k, Woman distributing pasteurized milk.

**1961, Dec. 11 Unwmk. *Perf. 13***

| | | | | |
|---|---|---|---|---|
| **B85** | SP35 | 10k + 5k Prus green | .20 | .20 |
| **B86** | SP35 | 30k + 5k dull violet | .30 | .20 |
| **B87** | SP35 | 75k + 5k dk olive bis | .60 | .20 |
| | | *Nos. B85-B87 (3)* | 1.10 | .60 |

Malaria Eradication Emblem, Map and Mosquito SP36

**1962, Apr. 7 Litho.**

| | | | | |
|---|---|---|---|---|
| **B88** | SP36 | 30k + 5k dk & lt brn | .20 | .20 |
| **B89** | SP36 | 75k + 5k blk & lil | .20 | .20 |

WHO drive to eradicate malaria.

Poinsettia SP37

Wheat and Census Chart SP38

Flowers: 40k+10k, Bird of paradise flower. 75k+10k, Water lily.

**1962, May 19 *Perf. 12½x13½***

**Flowers in Natural Colors**

| | | | | |
|---|---|---|---|---|
| **B90** | SP37 | 30k + 10k lt bl & blk | .20 | .20 |
| **B91** | SP37 | 40k + 10k lt bl & blk | .30 | .20 |
| **B92** | SP37 | 75k + 10k lt bl & blk | .80 | .30 |
| | | *Nos. B90-B92 (3)* | 1.30 | .70 |

Inscribed: "Umumi Ziraat Sayimi"

**1963, Apr. 14 Photo. *Perf. 11½***

Design: 60k+5k, Wheat and chart, horiz.

| | | | | |
|---|---|---|---|---|
| **B93** | SP38 | 40k + 5k gray grn & yel | .20 | .20 |
| **B94** | SP38 | 60k + 5k org yel & blk | .20 | .20 |

1961 agricultural census. Two black bars obliterate "Kasim 1960" inscription.

Red Lion and Sun, Red Crescent, Red Cross and Globe SP39

Designs: 60k+10k, Emblems in flowers, vert. 100k+10k, Emblems on flags.

**1963, Aug. 1 *Perf. 13***

| | | | | |
|---|---|---|---|---|
| **B95** | SP39 | 50k + 10k multi | .20 | .20 |
| **B96** | SP39 | 60k + 10k multi | .25 | .20 |
| **B97** | SP39 | 100k + 10k multi | .40 | .30 |
| | | *Nos. B95-B97 (3)* | .85 | .70 |

Centenary of International Red Cross.

Angora Goat — SP40

Olympic Torch Bearer — SP41

Animals: 10k+5k, Steppe cattle, horiz. 50k+5k. Arabian horses, horiz. 60k+5k, Three Angora goats. 100k+5k, Montofon cattle, horiz.

**1964, Oct. 4 Litho. *Perf. 13***

| | | | | |
|---|---|---|---|---|
| **B98** | SP40 | 10k + 5k multi | .30 | .20 |
| **B99** | SP40 | 30k + 5k multi | .30 | .20 |
| **B100** | SP40 | 50k + 5k multi | .50 | .20 |
| **B101** | SP40 | 60k + 5k multi | .70 | .20 |
| **B102** | SP40 | 100k + 5k multi | .90 | .20 |
| | | *Nos. B98-B102 (5)* | 2.70 | 1.00 |

Issued for Animal Protection Day.

**1964, Oct. 10 Unwmk.**

Designs: 10k+5k, Running, horiz. 60k+5k, Wrestling. 100k+5k, Discus.

| | | | | |
|---|---|---|---|---|
| **B103** | SP41 | 10k + 5k org brn, blk & red | .30 | .20 |
| **B104** | SP41 | 50k + 5k ol, blk & red | .30 | .20 |
| **B105** | SP41 | 60k + 5k bl, blk & red | .70 | .20 |
| **B106** | SP41 | 100k + 5k vio, blk, red & sil | 1.00 | .30 |
| | | *Nos. B103-B106 (4)* | 2.30 | .90 |

18th Olympic Games, Tokyo, Oct. 10-25.

Map of Dardanelles and Laurel SP42

Designs: 90k+10k, Soldiers and war memorial, Canakkale. 130k+10k, Turkish flag and arch, vert.

**1965, Mar. 18 Litho. *Perf. 13***

| | | | | |
|---|---|---|---|---|
| **B107** | SP42 | 50k + 10k vio, yel & gold | .20 | .20 |
| **B108** | SP42 | 90k + 10k vio bl, bl, yel & grn | .25 | .20 |
| **B109** | SP42 | 130k + 10k dk brn, red & yel | .45 | .40 |
| | | *Nos. B107-B109 (3)* | .90 | .80 |

50th anniversary of Battle of Gallipoli.

Tobacco Plant — SP43

Goddess, Basalt Carving — SP44

50k+5k, Tobacco leaves and Leander's tower, horiz. 100k+5k, Tobacco leaf.

**1965, Sept. 16 Unwmk. *Perf. 13***

**B110** SP43 30k + 5k brn, lt brn & grn .20 .20
**B111** SP43 50k + 5k vio bl, ocher & pur .30 .20
**B112** SP43 100k + 5k blk, ol grn & ocher .50 .25
*Nos. B110-B112 (3)* 1.00 .65

Second International Tobacco Congress.

***Perf. 13½x13, 13x13½***

**1966, June 6 Litho.**

Archaeological Museum, Ankara: 30k+5k, Eagle and rabbit, ivory carving, horiz. 60k+5k, Bronze bull. 90k+5k, Gold pitcher.

**B113** SP44 30k + 5k multi .20 .20
**B114** SP44 50k + 5k multi .30 .20
**B115** SP44 60k + 5k multi .45 .25
**B116** SP44 90k + 5k multi .60 .35
*Nos. B113-B116 (4)* 1.55 1.00

Grand Hotel Ephesus SP45

Designs: 60k+5k, Konak Square, Izmir, vert. 130k+5k, Izmir Fair Grounds.

**1966, Oct. 18 Litho. *Perf. 12***

**B117** SP45 50k + 5k multi .20 .20
**B118** SP45 60k + 5k multi .25 .20
**B119** SP45 130k + 5k multi .55 .35
*Nos. B117-B119 (3)* 1.00 .75

33rd Congress of the Intl. Fair Assoc.

**Europa Issue, 1967**

Common Design Type

**1967, May 2 Litho. *Perf. 13x13½***

**Size: 22x33mm**

**B120** CD10 100k + 10k multi 1.00 1.00
*a.* Dark blue ("Europa") omitted
**B121** CD10 130k + 10k multi 2.50 1.75

Cloverleaf Crossing, Map of Turkey SP46

130k+5k, Highway E5 & map of Turkey.

**1967, June 30 Litho. *Perf. 13***

**B122** SP46 60k + 5k multi .30 .20
**B123** SP46 130k + 5k multi, vert. .60 .30

Inter-European Express Highway, E5.

WHO Emblem SP47

**1968, Apr. 7 Litho. *Perf. 13***

**B124** SP47 130k + 10k lt ultra, blk & yel .35 .20

WHO, 20th anniversary.

Efem Pasha, Dr. Marko Pasha and View of Istanbul — SP48

60k+10k, Omer Pasha, Dr. Abdullah Bey & wounded soldiers. 100k+10k, Ataturk & Dr. Refik Say in front of Red Crescent headquarters, vert.

**1968, June 11 Litho. *Perf. 13***

**B125** SP48 50k + 10k multi .40 .20
**B126** SP48 60k + 10k multi .50 .25
**B127** SP48 100k + 10k multi .80 .40
*Nos. B125-B127 (3)* 1.70 .85

Centenary of Turkish Red Crescent Society.

NATO Emblem and Dove SP49

NATO, 20th anniv.: 130k+10k, NATO emblem and globe surrounded by 15 stars, symbols of the 15 NATO members.

**1969, Apr. 4 Litho. *Perf. 13***

**B128** SP49 50k + 10k brt grn, blk & lt bl .25 .20
**B129** SP49 130k + 10k bluish blk, bl & gold .45 .30

Red Cross, Crescent, Lion and Sun Emblems SP50

Design: 130k+10k, Conference emblem and Istanbul skyline.

**1969, Aug. 29 Litho. *Perf. 13***

**B130** SP50 100k + 10k dk & lt bl & red .30 .20
**B131** SP50 130k + 10k red, lt bl & blk .45 .25

21st Intl. Red Cross Conf., Istanbul.

Erosion Control SP51

60k+10k, Protection of flora (dead tree). 130k+10k, Protection of wildlife (bird of prey).

**1970, Feb. 9 Litho. *Perf. 13***

**B132** SP51 50k + 10k multi .25 .25
**B133** SP51 60k + 10k multi .40 .40
**B134** SP51 130k + 10k multi .95 .95
*Nos. B132-B134 (3)* 1.60 1.60

1970 European Nature Conservation Year.

Globe and Fencer SP52

Design: 130k+10k, Globe, fencer and folk dancer with sword and shield.

**1970, Sept. 13 Litho. *Perf. 13***

**B135** SP52 90k + 10k bl & blk .30 .20
**B136** SP52 130k + 10k ultra, lt bl, blk & org .40 .20

International Fencing Championships.

"Children's Protection" SP53

Designs: 100k+15k, Hand supporting child, vert. 110k+15k, Mother and child.

**1971, June 30 Litho. *Perf. 13***

**Star and Crescent Emblem in Red**

**B137** SP53 50k + 10k lil rose & blk .20 .20
**B138** SP53 100k + 15k brn, rose & blk .25 .20
**B139** SP53 110k + 15k org brn, bis & blk .30 .20
*Nos. B137-B139 (3)* .75 .60

50th anniv. of the Child Protection Assoc.

UNICEF, 25th Anniv. — SP54

"Your Heart is your Health" — SP55

**1971, Dec. 11**

**B140** SP54 100k + 10k multi .25 .20
**B141** SP54 250k + 15k multi .60 .40

**1972, Apr. 7 Litho. *Perf. 13***

**B142** SP55 250k + 25k gray, blk & red .55 .40

World Health Day.

Olympic Emblems, Runners SP56

100k+15k, Olympic rings & motion emblem. 250k+25k, Olympic rings & symbolic track ('72).

**1972, Aug. 26**

**B143** SP56 100k + 15k multi .25 .20
**B144** SP56 110k + 25k multi .35 .20
**B145** SP56 250k + 25k multi .50 .30
*Nos. B143-B145 (3)* 1.10 .70

20th Olympic Games, Munich, 8/26-9/11.

Emblem of Istanbul Technical University SP57

**1973, Apr. 21 Litho. *Perf. 13***

**B146** SP57 100k + 25k multi .35 .20

Istanbul Technical University, 200th anniv.

Dove and "50" SP58

**1973, July 24 Litho. *Perf. 12½x13***

**B147** SP58 100k + 25k multi .35 .20

Peace Treaty of Lausanne, 50th anniversary.

World Population Year — SP59

**1974, June 15 Litho. *Perf. 13***

**B148** SP59 250k + 25k multi .75 .35

Guglielmo Marconi (1874-1937), Italian Electrical Engineer and Inventor SP60

**1974, Nov. 15 Litho. *Perf. 13½***

**B149** SP60 250k + 25k multi .75 .35

Dr. Albert Schweitzer SP61

Africa with South-West Africa SP62

**1975, Jan 14 Litho. *Perf. 13***

**B150** SP61 250k + 50k multi .90 .45

Dr. Albert Schweitzer (1875-1965), medical missionary and music scholar.

**1975, Aug. 26 Litho. *Perf. 13x12½***

**B151** SP62 250k + 50k multi .70 .35

Namibia Day (independence for South-West Africa).

Ziya Gökalp SP63

Spoonbill SP64

**1976, Mar. 23 Litho. *Perf. 13***

**B152** SP63 200k + 25k multi .35 .20

Ziya Gökalp (1876-1924), philosopher.

**1976, Nov. 19 Litho. *Perf. 13***

Birds: 150k+25k, European roller. 200k+25k, Flamingo. 400k+25k, Hermit ibis, horiz.

**B153** SP64 100k + 25k multi .40 .20
**B154** SP64 150k + 25k multi .45 .20
**B155** SP64 200k + 25k multi .85 .25
**B156** SP64 400k + 25k multi 1.50 .35
*Nos. B153-B156 (4)* 3.20 1.00

Decree by Mehmet Bey, and Ongun Holy Bird — SP65

**1977, May 13 Litho. *Perf. 13***

**B157** SP65 200k + 25k grn & blk .40 .20

700th anniv. of Turkish as official language.

10th World Energy Conference SP66

Design: 600k+50k, Conference emblem and globe with circles.

**1977, Sept. 19 Litho. *Perf. 12½***
**B158** SP66 100k + 25k multi .40 .20
**B159** SP66 600k + 50k multi 1.25 .50

Running SP67

Designs: 2½ l+50k, Gymnastics. 5 l+ 50k, Table tennis. 8 l+50k, Swimming.

**1978, July 18 Litho. *Perf. 13***
**B160** SP67 1 l + 50k multi .20 .20
**B161** SP67 2½ l + 50k multi .20 .20
**B162** SP67 5 l + 50k multi .60 .20
**B163** SP67 8 l + 50k multi 1.00 .20
*Nos. B160-B163 (4)* 2.00 .80

GYMNASIADE '78, World School Games, Izmir.

Ribbon and Chain SP68

Design: 5 l+50k, Ribbon and flower, vert.

***Perf. 12½x13, 13x12½***
**1978, Sept. 3 Litho.**
**B164** SP68 2½ l + 50k multi .75 .20
**B165** SP68 5 l + 50k multi 1.00 .20

European Declaration of Human Rights, 25th anniversary.

Children, Head of Ataturk SP69

Black Francolin SP70

IYC Emblem and: 5 l+50k, Children with globe as balloon. 8 l+50k, Kneeling person and child, globe.

**1979, Apr. 23 Litho. *Perf. 13x13½***
**B166** SP69 2½ l + 50k multi .25 .20
**B167** SP69 5 l + 50k multi .40 .20
**B168** SP69 8 l + 50k multi .60 .25
*Nos. B166-B168 (3)* 1.25 .65

International Year of the Child.

**1979, Dec. 3 Litho. *Perf. 13x13½***

#B170, Great bustard. #B171, Crane. #B172, Gazelle. #B173, Mouflon muffelwild.

**B169** SP70 5 l + 1 l multi .80 .20
**B170** SP70 5 l + 1 l multi .80 .20
**B171** SP70 5 l + 1 l multi .80 .20
**B172** SP70 5 l + 1 l multi .80 .20
**B173** SP70 5 l + 1 l multi .80 .20
*a.* Strip of 5, #B169-B173 5.00 5.00

European Wildlife Conservation Year. No. B173a has continuous design.

Flowers, Trees and Sun SP71

Rodolia Cardinalis SP72

Environment Protection: 7½ l+ 1 l Sun, water. 15 l+1 l, Industrial pollution, globe. 20 l+1 l, Flower in oil puddle.

**1980, June 4 Litho. *Perf. 13***
**B174** SP71 2½ l + 1 l multi .20 .20
**B175** SP71 7½ l + 1 l multi .25 .20
**B176** SP71 15 l + 1 l multi .45 .25
**B177** SP71 20 l + 1 l multi .50 .35
*Nos. B174-B177 (4)* 1.40 1.00

**1980, Dec. 3 Litho. *Perf. 13***

Useful Insects: 7½ l+1 l, Bracon hebetor; 15 l+1 l, Calosoma sycophanta; 20 l+1 l, Deraeocoris rutilus.

**B178** SP72 2½ l + 1 l multi .25 .20
**B179** SP72 7½ l + 1 l multi .45 .20
**B180** SP72 15 l + 1 l multi .80 .20
**B181** SP72 20 l + 1 l multi 1.00 .20
*Nos. B178-B181 (4)* 2.50 .80

Intl. Year of the Disabled SP73

TB Bacillus Centenary SP75

Insects SP74

**1981, Mar. 25 Litho. *Perf. 13***
**B182** SP73 10 l + 2½ l multi .30 .20
**B183** SP73 20 l + 2½ l multi .45 .20

**1981, Dec. 16 Litho. *Perf. 13***

Useful Insects: No. B184, Cicindela campestris. No. B185, Syrphus vitripennis. No. B186, Ascalaphus macaronius. No. B187, Empusa fasciata.

**B184** SP74 10 l + 2½ l multi .30 .20
**B185** SP74 20 l + 2½ l multi .50 .20
**B186** SP74 30 l + 2½ l multi .75 .25
**B187** SP74 40 l + 2½ l multi 1.00 .35
*Nos. B184-B187 (4)* 2.55 1.00

See Nos. B190-B194, B196-B200.

**1982, Mar. 24 *Perf. 13x12½***

Portraits: #B188, Dr. Tevfik Saglam (1882-1963). #B189, Robert Koch.

**B188** SP75 10 l + 2½ l multi .30 .20
**B189** SP75 30 l + 2½ l multi .70 .20

### Insect Type of 1981

Useful Insects: 10 l+2½ l, Eurydema spectabile. 15 l+2½ l, Dacus oleae. 20 l+2½ l, Klapperichicen viridissima. 30 l+2½ l, Leptinotarsa decemlineata. 35 l+2½ l, Rhynchites auratus.

**1982, Aug. 18 Litho. *Perf. 13***
**B190** SP74 10 l + 2½ l multi .55 .20
**B191** SP74 15 l + 2½ l multi .75 .20
**B192** SP74 20 l + 2½ l multi .75 .20
**B193** SP74 30 l + 2½ l multi .95 .20
**B194** SP74 35 l + 2½ l multi 1.00 .20
*Nos. B190-B194 (5)* 4.00 1.00

Richard Wagner (1813-1883), Composer — SP76

**1983, Feb. 13**
**B195** SP76 30 l + 5 l multi 1.10 1.00

### Insect Type of 1981

Harmful Insects: 15 l+5 l, Eurygaster Intergriceps Put. 25 l+5 l, Phyllobius nigrofasciatus Pes. 35 l+5 l, Cercopis intermedia Kbm. 50 l+10 l, Graphosoma lineatum (L). 75 l+10 l, Capnodis miliaris (King).

**1983, Sept. 14 Litho. *Perf. 13***
**B196** SP74 15 l + 5 l multi .50 .20
**B197** SP74 25 l + 5 l multi .65 .20
**B198** SP74 35 l + 5 l multi .85 .20
**B199** SP74 50 l + 10 l multi 1.25 .25
**B200** SP74 75 l + 10 l multi 1.75 .40
*Nos. B196-B200 (5)* 5.00 1.25

Topkapi Museum Artifacts SP77

1984 Summer Olympics SP78

**1984, May 30 Litho. *Perf. 13***
**B201** SP77 20 l + 5 l Kaftan, 16th cent. .30 .20
**B202** SP77 70 l + 15 l Ewer .95 .40
**B203** SP77 90 l + 20 l Swords 1.60 .45
**B204** SP77 100 l + 25 l Lock, key 1.90 .55
*Nos. B201-B204 (4)* 4.75 1.60

Surtax was for museum. See Nos. B208-B211, B213-B216, B218-B221.

**1984, July 28**

Designs: 20 l+5 l, Banners, horiz. 70 l+15 l, Medalist Oyunlan. 100 l+20 l, Running, horiz.

**B205** SP78 20 l + 5 l multi .75 .50
**B206** SP78 70 l + 15 l multi .90 .75
**B207** SP78 100 l + 20 l multi 1.50 1.00
*Nos. B205-B207 (3)* 3.15 2.25

### Artifacts Type of 1984

Ceramicware: 10 l+5 l, Iznik plate. 20 l+10 l, Iznik boza pitcher and mug, 16th cent. 100 l+15 l, Du Paquier ewer and basin, 1730. 120 l+20 l, Ching dynasty plate, 1522-1566.

**1985, May 30 Litho. *Perf. 13***
**B208** SP77 10 l + 5 l multi .50 .20
**B209** SP77 20 l + 10 l multi .80 .40
**B210** SP77 100 l + 15 l multi 1.75 1.10
**B211** SP77 120 l + 20 l multi 2.50 1.40
*Nos. B208-B211 (4)* 5.55 3.10

Rabies Vaccine, Cent. — SP79

**1985, July 16 *Perf. 13x13½***
**B212** SP79 100 l + 15 l Pasteur 1.50 1.00

### Artifacts Type of 1984

20 l+5 l, Metal and ceramic incense burner, c. 17th cent. 100 l+10 l, Jade lidded mug decorated with precious gems, 16th cent. 120 l+15 l, Dagger designed by Mahmut I, 1714. 200 l+30 l, Willow buckler, defensive shield, undated.

**1986, May 30 Litho. *Perf. 13x12½***
**B213** SP77 20 l + 5 l multi .50 .25
**B214** SP77 100 l + 10 l multi 1.00 .40
**B215** SP77 120 l + 15 l multi 1.10 .50
**B216** SP77 200 l + 30 l multi 2.25 .75
*Nos. B213-B216 (4)* 4.85 1.90

General Assembly of NATO SP80

**1986, Nov. 13 Litho. *Perf. 13½x13***
**B217** SP80 100 l + 20 l multi 1.25 .40

### Artifacts Type of 1984

Designs: 20 l+5 l, Crystal and gold ewer, 16th cent., vert. 50 l+10 l, Emerald and gold pendant, 17th cent. 200 l+15 l, Sherbet jug, 19th cent., vert. 250 l+30 l, Crystal and gold pen box, 16th cent.

**1987, May 30 Litho. *Perf. 13***
**B218** SP77 20 l + 5 l multi .75 .20
**B219** SP77 50 l + 10 l multi 1.00 .40
**B220** SP77 200 l + 15 l multi 1.25 1.00
**B221** SP77 250 l + 30 l multi 2.00 1.25
*Nos. B218-B221 (4)* 5.00 2.85

15th Intl. Chemotherapy Congress, Istanbul — SP81

**1987, July 19 Litho. *Perf. 13***
**B222** SP81 200 l + 25 l multi .85 .20

Intl. Road Transport Union (IRU) 21st World Congress SP82

**1988, June 13 Litho. *Perf. 12½x13***
**B223** SP82 200 l +25 l multi .55 .20

European Environmental Campaign Balancing Nature and Development — SP83

Designs: 100 l+25 l, Hands, desert reclamation. 400 l+50 l, Eye, road, planted field.

**1988, Oct. 19 Litho. *Perf. 12½x13***
**B224** SP83 100 l +25 l multi .35 .20
**B225** SP83 400 l +50 l multi 1.25 .30

Silkworm Industry SP84

***Perf. 13½x13***
**1989, Apr. 15 Litho. Wmk. 394**
**B226** SP84 150 l +50 l Silkworm .30 .20
**B227** SP84 600 l +100 l Cocoon, strands 1.10 .25

Council of Europe, 40th Anniv. SP85

**1989, May 5 Litho. *Perf. 13***
**B228** SP85 600 l +100 l multi .90 .25

European Tourism Year SP86

**1990, Apr. 26 Wmk. 394**
**B229** SP86 300 l +50 l Antalya .35 .20
**B230** SP86 1000 l +100 l Istanbul 1.10 .30

Fight Against Addictions — SP87

Fight Against: No. B231, Smoking. No. B232, Drugs, horiz.

**1990, June 26 Litho. *Perf. 13***
**B231** SP87 300 l +50 l multi .30 .20
**B232** SP87 1000 l +100 l multi .90 .45

Yunus Emre (died c.1321), Poet
SP88 SP89

**1991, June 26 Litho. *Perf. 13***
**B233** SP88 500 l +100 l multi .50 .25
**B234** SP89 1500 l +100 l multi 1.25 .65

Wolfgang Amadeus Mozart (1756-1791), Composer — SP90

**1991, July 24**
**B235** SP90 1500 l +100 l multi 1.25 .65

Turkish Supreme Court, 30th Anniv. SP91

**1992, Apr. 25**
**B236** SP91 500 l + 100 l multi .50 .25

Scouts Planting Tree SP92

#B238 Mountain climber on rope, vert.

**1992, Dec. 18**
**B237** SP92 1000 l +200 l multi .50 .30
**B238** SP92 3000 l +200 l multi .90 .50

Travertine, Pamukkale — SP93

Different views of rock formations.

**1993, June 6**
**B239** SP93 1000 l +200 l multi .30 .20
**B240** SP93 3000 l +500 l multi .80 .40

Intl. Day for Natural Disaster Reduction SP94

**1993, Oct. 13 *Perf. 12½x13***
**B241** SP94 3000 l + 500 l multi .90 .50

Intl. Olympic Committee, Cent. — SP95

**1994, Aug. 17 *Perf. 13***
**B242** SP95 12,500 l +500 l multi 1.50 1.00

Trees SP96

Designs: No. B243, Platanus orientalis. No. B244, Cupressus sempervirens, vert.

**1994, Nov. 30**
**B243** SP96 7500 l +500 l multi 1.00 .80
**B244** SP96 12,500 l +500 l multi 2.00 1.50

TBMM (Great Natl. Assembly), 75th Anniv. SP97

**1995, Apr. 23**
**B245** SP97 3500 l +500 l multi .25 .20

The Epic of Manas SP98

Designs: No. B246, Lancers charging. No. B247, Abay Kunanbay (1845-1904), poet, vert.

**1995, June 28**
**B246** SP98 3500 l +500 l multi .25 .20
**B247** SP98 3500 l +500 l multi .25 .20

For the People of Bosnia-Herzegovina — SP99

**1996, Feb. 28**
**B248** SP99 10,000 l +2500 l multi .75 .75

Ankara University, 50th Anniv. SP100

**Unwmk.**
**1996, Nov. 20 Litho. *Perf. 13***
**B249** 15,000 l +2500 l multi .65 .30

Fight Against Cancer, 50th Anniv. SP101

**1997, Feb. 18 Litho. *Perf. 12½x13***
**B250** SP101 25,000 l +5000 l multi .65 .30

Pakistan Independence, 50th Anniv. — SP102

Mohammed Ali Jinnah (1876-1948).

**1997, Mar. 23 Litho. *Perf. 13***
**B251** SP102 25,000 l +5000 l multi .60 .30

Universal Declaration of Human Rights SP103

Stylized designs: 75,000 l, Puzzle piece with outlines of people's faces. 175,000 l, Heart-shaped kite with people as tail.

**1998, Dec. 10 Litho. *Perf. 13½***
**B252** SP103 75,000 l +25,000 l 1.00 .50
**B253** SP103 175,000 l +25,000 l 2.00 1.00

GATA 100, Yilinda SP104

**1998, Dec. 30 Litho. *Perf. 13***
**B254** SP104 75,000 l +10,000 l multi .60 .30

Kemal Ataturk's Entry Into War College, Cent. — SP105

**1999, Mar. 13 Litho. *Perf. 13***
**B255** SP105 75,000 l +5,000 l multi .40 .20

Council of Europe, 50th Anniv. SP106

**1999, Apr. 30 Litho. *Perf. 13¼***
**B256** SP106 175,000 l +10,000 l 2.00 1.25

Church, Mosque and Synagogue — SP107

Dancers SP108

**2000, May 25 Litho. *Perf. 13¼***
**B257** SP107 275,000 l +10,000 l 1.50 1.50
**B258** SP108 300,000 l +10,000 l 1.50 1.50

Tombs and Mausoleums — SP109

150,000 l+25,000 l, Usta Sagirt Kumbeti Ahlat, vert. 200,000 l+25,000 l, Kocbasli Mezar Tasi Tunceli. 275,000 l+25,000 l, Isabey Turbesi, Uskup, vert. 300,000 l+25,000 l, Yusuf bin Kuseyr Turbesi, Nahcivan, vert.

**2000**
**B259-B262** SP109 Set of 4 5.00 5.00

Coins SP110

Various coins with background colors of: No. B263, 300,000 l + 25,000 l, Red. No. B264, 300,000 l + 25,000 l, Blue green. 450,000 l + 25,000 l, Dark carmine. 500,000 l + 25,000 l, Blue violet.

**2001, Oct. 1 Litho. *Perf. 13***
**B263-B266** SP110 Set of 4 5.50 5.50

Caravansaries — SP111

Designs: 300,000 l + 25,000 l, Ashab i Kehf Han, Afsin. 500,000 l + 25,000 l, Horozlu Han, Konya.

**2001, Nov. 19** **Litho.** ***Perf. 13***
**B267-B268** SP111 Set of 2 2.75 2.75

Turkey's Admission to NATO, 50th Anniv. SP112

**2002, Feb. 18**
**B269** SP112 400,000 l + 25,000 l 1.10 1.10

Trains SP113

Designs: 500,000 l + 25,000 l, Steam locomotive. 700,000 l + 25,000 l, Electric locomotive.

**2002, Sept. 16** **Litho.** ***Perf. 13¼x13***
**B270-B271** SP113 Set of 2 3.25 3.25

Trains SP114

Designs: 600,000 l+50,000 l, Trolley. 800,000 l+50,000 l, Subway.

**2003, Sept. 9** **Litho.** ***Perf. 13¼x13***
**B272-B273** SP114 Set of 2 2.75 2.75

Ibrahim Hakki Erzurumlu (1703-72), Writer — SP115

**2003, Dec. 24** **Litho.** ***Perf. 13x13¼***
**B274** SP115 600,000 l +50,000 l multi .95 .95

Lighthouses SP116

Designs: 600,000 l + 50,000 l, Kerempe Lighthouse, Kastamonu. 700,000 l + 50,000 l, Taslikburnu Lighthouse, Antalya.

**2004, Apr. 5**
**B275-B276** SP116 Set of 2 3.00 3.00

Scouting — SP117

Designs: 600,000 l + 50,000 l, Girl Scout in foreground. 700,000 l + 50,000 l, Boy Scout in foreground.

**2004, Sept. 30**
**B277-B278** SP117 Set of 2 2.25 2.25

Rotary International, Cent. — SP118

**2005, Feb. 23** **Litho.** ***Perf. 13x13¼***
**B279** SP118 80k +10k multi 1.50 1.50

Intl. Year of Physics SP119

**2005, Sept. 13** **Litho.** ***Perf. 13¼x13***
**B280** SP119 70k +10k multi 1.25 1.25

World Forests Day SP120

**2006, Mar. 21** **Litho.** ***Perf. 13¼x13***
**B281** SP120 60k +10k multi 1.10 1.10

Mehmet Akif Ersoy (1873-1936), Poet — SP121

Ersoy at: 60k+10k, Left. 70k+10k, Right.

**2006, Oct. 13** **Litho.** ***Perf. 13¼x13***
**B282-B283** SP121 Set of 2 2.10 2.10

## AIR POST STAMPS

**Catalogue values for unused stamps in this section are for Never Hinged items.**

Nos. 692, 695, 698, 700 Overprinted or Surcharged in Brown or Blue

**1934, July 15** **Unwmk.** ***Perf. 12***
**C1** A74 7½k (Br) .75 .20
**C2** A72 12½k on 15k (Br) .75 .25
**C3** A74 20k on 25k (Br) .75 .25
**C4** A74 25k (Bl) 1.00 .40
**C5** A74 40k (Br) 2.25 1.25
*Nos. C1-C5 (5)* 5.50 2.35

Regular Stamps of 1930 Surcharged in Brown

**1937**
**C6** A74 4½k on 7½k red brn 5.00 1.00
**C7** A72 9k on 15k dp org 40.00 20.00
**C8** A74 35k on 40k red vio 10.00 4.25
*Nos. C6-C8 (3)* 55.00 25.25

Nos. 698, 703-704 Surcharged in Black

**1941, Dec. 18**
**C9** A74 4½k on 25k 2.00 1.50
**C10** A75 9k on 200k 9.75 8.25
**C11** A75 35k on 500k 6.25 5.25
*Nos. C9-C11 (3)* 18.00 15.00

Plane over Izmir AP1

Planes over: 5k, 40k, Izmir. 20k, 50k, Ankara. 30k, 1 l, Istanbul.

**1949, Jan. 1** **Photo.** ***Perf. 11½***
**C12** AP1 5k gray & vio .25 .25
**C13** AP1 20k bl gray & brn .25 .25
**C14** AP1 30k bl gray & ol brn 1.00 .25
**C15** AP1 40k bl & dp ultra 1.00 1.00
**C16** AP1 50k gray vio & red brn 1.00 .25
**C17** AP1 1 l gray bl & dk grn 3.00 .65
*Nos. C12-C17 (6)* 6.50 2.65

For overprints see Nos. C19-C21.

Plane Over Rumeli Hisari Fortress AP2

**1950, May 19** **Unwmk.**
**C18** AP2 2½ l gray bl & dk grn 22.50 14.00

Nos. C12, C14 and C16 Overprinted in Red

**1951, Apr. 9** ***Perf. 11½***
**C19** AP1 5k gray & vio 1.50 .50
**C20** AP1 30k bl gray & ol brn 2.00 .60
**C21** AP1 50k gray vio & red brn 2.50 .70
*Nos. C19-C21 (3)* 6.00 1.80

Industrial Congress, Ankara, Apr. 9.

Yesilkoy Airport and Plane AP3

Designs: 20k, 45k, Yesilkoy Airport and plane in flight. 35k, 55k, Ankara Airport and plane. 40k, as No. C22.

**1954, Nov. 1** ***Perf. 14***
**C22** AP3 5k red brn & bl 1.00 .25
**C23** AP3 20k brn org & bl .65 .25
**C24** AP3 35k dk grn & bl .65 .25
**C25** AP3 40k dp car & bl .65 .25
**C26** AP3 45k violet & bl 1.50 .25
**C27** AP3 55k black & bl 4.00 .50
*Nos. C22-C27 (6)* 8.45 1.75

Symbol of Izmir Fair — AP4

**1956, Aug. 20** **Litho.** ***Perf. 10½***
**C28** AP4 25k reddish brown .20 .20

25th Intl. Fair at Izmir, Aug. 20-Sept. 20.

Heuss Type of Regular Issue, 1957

**1957, May 5**
**C29** A264 40k sal pink & magenta .25 .20

Zahir Shah Type of Regular Issue, 1957

**1957, Sept. 1**
**C30** A269 25k grn & lt grn .25 .20

Hawk — AP5

Crane — AP6

Birds: 40k, 125k, Swallows. 65k, Cranes. 85k, 195k, Gulls. 245k, Hawk.

**1959, Aug. 13** **Litho.** ***Perf. 10½***
**C31** AP5 40k bright lilac .40 .20
**C32** AP5 65k blue green 2.50 .40
**C33** AP5 85k bright blue .75 .20
**C34** AP5 105k yel & sepia .50 .20
**C35** AP6 125k brt violet .75 .40
**C36** AP6 155k yel green 1.00 .25
**C37** AP6 195k violet blue 1.25 .30
**C38** AP6 245k brn & brn org 2.75 1.00
*Nos. C31-C38 (8)* 9.90 2.95

De Havilland Rapide Biplane AP7

Kestrel — AP8

Designs: 60k, Fokker Friendship transport plane. 130k, DC9-30. 220k, DC-3. 270k, Viscount 794.

**1967, July 13 Litho. *Perf. 13½x13***
**C39** AP7 10k pink & blk .25 .20
**C40** AP7 60k lt grn, red & blk .30 .20
**C41** AP7 130k bl, blk & red .65 .20
**C42** AP7 220k lt brn, blk & red .95 .30
**C43** AP7 270k org, blk & red 1.40 .35
*Nos. C39-C43 (5)* 3.55 1.25

For surcharge see No. 2179A.

**1967, Oct. 10 Litho. *Perf. 13***

Birds: 60k, Golden eagle. 130k, Falcon. 220k, Sparrow hawk. 270k, Buzzard.

**C44** AP8 10k brown & salmon .60 .20
**C45** AP8 60k brown & yellow .45 .20
**C46** AP8 130k brown & lt bl 1.10 .20
**C47** AP8 220k brown & lt grn 1.75 .25
**C48** AP8 270k org brn & gray 2.50 .35
*Nos. C44-C48 (5)* 6.40 1.20

F-104 Jet Plane — AP9

Turkish Air Force Emblem and Jets AP10

Designs: 200k, Victory monument, Afyon, and Jets. 325k, F-104 jets and pilot. 400k, Bleriot XI plane with Turkish flag. 475k, Flight of Hezarfen Ahmet Celebi from Galata Tower to Usküdar.

**1971, June 1 Litho. *Perf. 13***
**C49** AP9 110k multi .50 .20
**C50** AP9 200k multi 1.10 .20
**C51** AP10 250k multi 1.10 .25
**C52** AP9 325k multi 1.75 .25
**C53** AP10 400k multi 1.90 .30
**C54** AP10 475k multi 2.50 .35
*Nos. C49-C54 (6)* 8.85 1.55

The gold ink on No. C51 is applied by a thermographic process which gives a raised and shiny effect.

F-28 Plane — AP11

**1973, Dec. 11 Litho. *Perf. 13***
**C55** AP11 110k shown .45 .25
**C56** AP11 250k DC-10 .90 .30

## POSTAGE DUE STAMPS

Same Types as Regular Issues of Corresponding Dates

**1863 Unwmk. *Imperf.***
**Blue Band**
**J1** A1 20pa blk, *red brn* 100.00 32.50
a. Tête bêche pair 225.00 225.00
b. Without band 50.00
c. Red band 90.00 45.00
**J2** A2 1pi blk, *red brn* 150.00 22.50
a. Tête bêche pair 225.00 225.00
b. Without band 50.00
**J3** A3 2pi blk, *red brn* 500.00 70.00
a. Tête bêche pair 650.00 450.00
**J4** A4 5pi blk, *red brn* 300.00 80.00
a. Tête bêche pair 425.00 425.00
b. Without band 100.00
c. Red band 150.00
*Nos. J1-J4 (4)* 1,050. 205.00

**1865 *Perf. 12½***
**J6** A5 20pa brown 2.50 5.00
**J7** A5 1pi brown 2.50 5.00
b. Half used as 20pa on cover
c. Printed on both sides 25.00
**J8** A5 2pi brown 12.50 25.00
a. Half used as 1pi on cover
**J9** A5 5pi brown 5.00 30.00
a. Half used as 2½pi on cover
**J10** A5 25pi brown 45.00 100.00
*Nos. J6-J10 (5)* 67.50 165.00

Exist imperf. Values, $60 to $100 each.

The 10pa brown is an essay. Value about $2,750.

**1867**
**J11** A5 20pa bister brn 7.50 100.00
**J12** A5 1pi bister brn 7.50
a. With surcharge of 5pi 13.50
b. Imperf., pair 65.00
**J13** A5 2pi fawn 75.00
**J14** A5 5pi fawn 17.50
**J15** A5 25pi bister brn *21,250.*
*Nos. J11-J14 (4)* 107.50

Nos. J12-J15 were not placed in use.

**1869 *Perf. 13½***
**With Yellow-Brown Border**
**J16** A5 20pa bister brn 10.00 10.00
a. Without surcharge
**J17** A5 1pi bister brn 550.00 5.00
a. Without surcharge
**J18** A5 2pi bister brn 800.00 5.00
**J19** A5 5pi bister brn 1.50 12.50
b. Without border
c. Printed on both sides 15.00
**J20** A5 25pi bister brn — —
*Nos. J16-J20 (4)* 1,361. 32.50

**With Brown Border**

Color of border ranges from brown to reddish brown and black brown.

**J21** A5 20pa bister brn 125.00 20.00
a. Inverted surcharge
b. Without surcharge
**J22** A5 1pi bister brn 550.00 12.50
a. Without surcharge
**J23** A5 2pi bister brn 450.00 12.50
a. Inverted surcharge
**J24** A5 5pi bister brn 2.50 15.00
b. Without surcharge
**J25** A5 25pi bister brn 37.50 100.00
*Nos. J21-J25 (5)* 1,165. 160.00

***Pin-perf., Perf. 5 to 11½ and Compound***

**1871**
**With Brick Red Border**
**J26** A5 20pa bister brn 875.00 50.00
**J27** A5 1pi bister brn *5,000.*
**J28** A5 2pi bister brn 110.00 140.00
**J29** A5 5pi bister brn 7.50 25.00

**With Black Brown Border**
**J31** A5 20pa bister brn 150.00 2.50
a. Half used as 10pa on cover
b. Imperf., pair 16.50
c. Printed on both sides 40.00 40.00
**J32** A5 1pi bister brn 225.00 2.50
a. Half used as 20pa on cover
c. Inverted surcharge 50.00 35.00
d. Printed on both sides
**J33** A5 2pi bister brn 6.00 9.00
a. Half used as 1pi on cover
c. Imperf., pair 16.50
**J34** A5 5pi bister brn 2.50 20.00
a. Half used as 2½pi on cover
c. Printed on both sides
**J35** A5 25pi bister brn 40.00 125.00
a. Inverted surcharge
*Nos. J31-J35 (5)* 423.50 *159.00*

**1888 *Perf. 11½ and 13½***
**J36** A7 20pa black 3.00 12.50
**J37** A7 1pi black 3.00 12.50
**J38** A7 2pi black 3.00 15.00
b. Diagonal half used as 1pi
*Nos. J36-J38 (3)* 9.00 40.00

***Imperf***
*J36a* A7 20pa 11.00
*J37a* A7 1pi 11.00
*J38a* A7 2pi 11.00

**1892 *Perf. 13½***
**J39** A11 20pa black 7.00 12.50
**J40** A12 1pi black 22.50 12.50
a. Printed on both sides
**J41** A13 2pi black 17.50 12.50
*Nos. J39-J41 (3)* 47.00 *37.50*

**1901**
**J42** A11 20pa black, *deep rose* 2.50 20.00

**1901**
**J43** A17 10pa blk, *deep rose* 4.00 6.00
**J44** A17 20pa blk, *deep rose* 3.75 8.75
**J45** A17 1pi blk, *deep rose* 3.00 10.00
**J46** A17 2pi blk, *deep rose* 1.75 15.00
*Nos. J43-J46 (4)* 12.50 39.75

**1905 *Perf. 12***
**J47** A18 1pi black, *deep rose* 3.00 10.00
**J48** A18 2pi black, *deep rose* 4.50 20.00

**1908, *Perf. 12, 13½ and Compound***
**J49** A19 1pi black, *deep rose* 80.00 7.50
**J50** A19 2pi black, *deep rose* 12.50 45.00

**1909**
**J51** A21 1pi black, *deep rose* 15.00 *50.00*
**J52** A21 2pi black, *deep rose* *150.00 175.00*
a. Imperf. 65.00

**1913 *Perf. 12***
**J53** A22 2pa blk, *deep rose* 1.00 .50
**J54** A22 5pa blk, *deep rose* 1.00 .50
**J55** A22 10pa blk, *deep rose* 1.00 .50
**J56** A22 20pa blk, *deep rose* 1.00 .50
**J57** A22 1pi blk, *deep rose* 4.50 10.00
**J58** A22 2pi blk, *deep rose* 8.00 17.50
*Nos. J53-J58 (6)* 16.50 29.50

**Adrianople Issue**

Nos. 251-253 Surcharged in Black, Blue or Red

**1913**
**J59** A23 2pa on 10pa green (Bk) 3.25 .35
**J60** A23 5pa on 20pa red (Bl) 3.25 .35
**J61** A23 10pa on 40pa bl (R) 10.00 .80
**J62** A23 20pa on 40pa bl (Bk) 32.50 11.00
*Nos. J59-J62 (4)* 49.00 12.50

For surcharges see Nos. J67-J70, J83-J86.

D1

D2

D3

D4

**1914 Engr.**
**J63** D1 5pa claret 1.25 10.00
**J64** D2 20pa red 1.25 10.00
**J65** D3 1pi dark blue 1.25 10.00
**J66** D4 2pi slate 1.25 10.00
*Nos. J63-J66 (4)* 5.00 40.00

For surcharges and overprints see Nos. J87-J91.

Nos. J59 to J62 Surcharged in Red or Black

**1916**
**J67** A23 10pa on 2pa on 10pa (R) 55.00 55.00
**J68** A23 20pa on 5pa on 20pa 55.00 55.00
**J69** A23 40pa on 10pa on 40pa 55.00 55.00
**J70** A23 40pa on 20pa on 40pa (R) 55.00 55.00
*Nos. J67-J70 (4)* 220.00 220.00

Preceding Issues Overprinted in Red, Black or Blue

**1917**
**On Stamps of 1865**
**J71** A5 20pa red brn (Bl) 45.00 67.50
**J72** A5 1pi red brn (Bl) 45.00 67.50
**J73** A5 2pi bis brn (Bl) 45.00 67.50
**J74** A5 5pi bis brn (Bl) 45.00 67.50
**J75** A5 25pi dk brn (Bl) 45.00 67.50
*Nos. J71-J75 (5)* 225.00 337.50

**On Stamp of 1869**
**Red Brown Border**
**J76** A5 5pi bis brn (R) 45.00 67.50

**On Stamp of 1871**
**Black Brown Border**
**J77** A5 5pi bis brn 75.00 50.00

**On Stamps of 1888**
**J78** A7 1pi black (R) 45.00 67.50
**J79** A7 2pi black (R) 45.00 67.50

**On Stamps of 1892**
**J80** A11 20pa black (R) 2.50 2.50
**J81** A12 1pi black (R) 2.50 2.50
**J82** A13 2pi black (R) 2.50 2.50
*Nos. J80-J82 (3)* 7.50 7.50

**Adrianople Issue**

On Nos. J59 to J62 with Addition of New Value

**J83** A23 10pa on 2pa on 10pa (R) 1.00 1.00
**J84** A23 20pa on 5pa on 20pa (Bk) 1.00 1.00
**J85** A23 40pa on 10pa on 40pa (Bk) 1.50 1.50
a. "40pa" double
**J86** A23 40pa on 20pa on 40pa (R) 3.50 3.50
*Nos. J83-J86 (4)* 7.00 7.00

Nos. J71-J86 were used as regular postage stamps.

**Armistice Issue**

No. J65 Overprinted

**1919, Nov. 30**
**J87** D3 1pi dark blue 125.00 150.00

**Accession to the Throne Issue**

Postage Due Stamps of 1914 Overprinted in Turkish "Accession to the Throne of His Majesty. 3rd July, 1334-1918"

**1919**
**J88** D1 10pa on 5pa claret 25.00 37.50
**J89** D2 20pa red 25.00 37.50
**J90** D3 1pi dark blue 25.00 37.50
**J91** D4 2pi slate 25.00 37.50
*Nos. J88-J91 (4)* 100.00 150.00

Railroad Bridge over Kizil Irmak — D5

Kemal Atatürk — D6

**1926 Engr.**
**J92** D5 20pa ocher 1.00 2.50
**J93** D5 1g red 1.50 5.00
**J94** D5 2g blue green 2.50 5.00
**J95** D5 3g lilac brown 2.50 12.50
**J96** D5 5g lilac 5.00 20.00
*Nos. J92-J96 (5)* 12.50 45.00
Set, never hinged 30.00

**Catalogue values for unused stamps in this section, from this point to the end of the section, are for Never Hinged items.**

**1936 Litho. *Perf. 11½***
**J97** D6 20pa brown .20 .20
**J98** D6 2k light blue .20 .20
**J99** D6 3k bright violet .20 .20
**J100** D6 5k Prussian blue .20 .20
**J101** D6 12k bright rose .35 .20
*Nos. J97-J101 (5)* 1.15 1.00

For surcharges see Nos. 1461-1465.

Local Issues

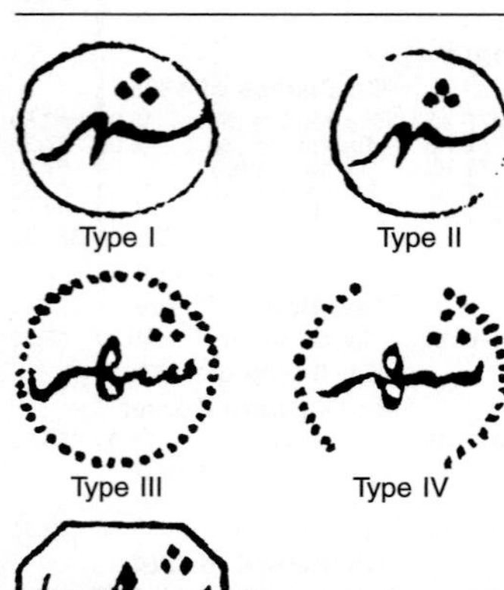

Type I Type II

Type III Type IV

Type V Type VI

During 1873//1882 Turkish stamps with the above overprints were used for local postage in Constantinople (types 1-5) and Mount Athos (type 6).

## MILITARY STAMPS

### For the Army in Thessaly

Tughra and Bridge at Larissa — M1

**1898, Apr. 21 Unwmk. *Perf. 13***

**M1** M1 10pa yellow green 10.00 7.50
**M2** M1 20pa rose 10.00 7.50
**M3** M1 1pi dark blue 10.00 7.50
**M4** M1 2pi orange 10.00 7.50
**M5** M1 5pi violet 10.00 7.50
*Nos. M1-M5 (5)* 50.00 37.50

Issued for Turkish occupation forces to use in Thessaly during the Greco-Turkish War of 1897-98.

Forgeries of Nos. M1-M5 are perf. 11½.

## OFFICIAL STAMPS

**Catalogue values for unused stamps in this section are for Never Hinged items.**

O1

***Perf. 10 to 12 and Compound***

**1948 Typo. Unwmk.**

**O1** O1 10pa rose brown .50 .20
**O2** O1 1k gray green .50 .20
**O3** O1 2k rose violet .50 .20
**O4** O1 3k orange .50 .20
**O5** O1 5k blue 25.00 .90
**O6** O1 10k brown org 7.50 .20
**O7** O1 15k violet 2.50 .20
**O8** O1 20k dk blue 3.00 .20
**O9** O1 30k olive bister 5.00 .80
**O10** O1 50k black 5.00 .80
**O11** O1 1 l bluish grn 5.00 .80
**O12** O1 2 l lilac rose 10.00 1.00
*Nos. O1-O12 (12)* 65.00 5.70

Regular Issue of 1948 Overprinted Type "a" in Black

**1951**

**O13** A178 5k blue .20 .20
**O14** A178 10k chocolate .30 .20
**O15** A178 20k deep blue .60 .20
**O16** A178 30k brown .90 .20
*Nos. O13-O16 (4)* 2.00 .80

Overprint "a" is 15½mm wide. Points of crescent do not touch star. The 0.25k (No. 963) exists with overprint "a" but its status is questionable.

b

c

Overprinted Type "b" in Dark Brown

**1953**

**O17** A178 0.25k dk red .20 .20
**O18** A178 5k blue .30 .20
**O19** A178 10k chocolate .40 .20
**O20** A178 15k violet 1.00 .20
**O21** A178 20k deep blue 6.00 1.00
**O22** A178 30k brown 1.25 .30
**O23** A178 60k black 1.40 .20
*Nos. O17-O23 (7)* 10.55 2.30

Overprint "b" is 14mm wide. Lettering thin with sharp, clean corners.

Overprinted Type "c" in Black or Green Black

**1953-54**

**O23A** A178 0.25k dk red (G Bk) ('53) .25 .20
*f.* Black overprint *4.00 4.00*
*g.* Violet overprint ('53) *4.00 4.00*
**O23B** A178 10k chocolate 12.50 .65
**O23C** A178 15k violet 15.00 1.00
**O23D** A178 30k brown 6.50 .65
**O23E** A178 60k black 8.00 1.00
*Nos. O23A-O23E (5)* 42.25 3.50

Lettering of type "c" heavy with rounded corners.

Small Star — d

Large Star — e

Overprinted or Surcharged Type "d" in Black

**1955**

**O24** A178 0.25k dark red .20 .20
**O25** A178 1k olive black .20 .20
**O26** A178 2k brt rose lil .20 .20
**O27** A178 3k red orange .30 .20
**O28** A178 4k dk green .30 .20
**O29** A178 5k on 15k vio .30 .20
**O31** A178 10k on 15k vio .30 .20
**O32** A178 15k violet .30 .20
**O33** A178 20k deep blue .35 .20
**O35** A179 40k on 1 l ol grn .45 .25
**O36** A179 75k on 2 l dk brn .70 .60
**O37** A179 75k on 5 l dp plum 8.00 8.00
*Nos. O24-O37 (12)* 11.60 10.65

Type "d" is 15x16mm wide. Overprint on Nos. O35-O37 measures 19x22mm. Nos. O29, O31, O35-O37 have two bars and new value added.

Overprinted or Surcharged Type "e" in Black

**1955**

*O25a* A178 1k olive black .20 .20
*O29a* A178 5k on 15k violet .70 .20
**O30** A178 5k blue .65 .25
*O31a* A178 10k on 15k violet *1.00 .25*
*c.* "10" without serif .20 .20
*O33a* A178 20k deep blue .45 .20
**O34** A178 30k brown .30 .20

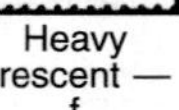

Heavy crescent — f

Thin crescent — g

Overprinted or Surcharged Type "f" in Black

**1957**

*O24b* A178 0.25k dark red .30 .20
*O38b* A178 ½k on 1k ol blk .20 .20
*O25b* A178 1k olive black .20 .20
*O31b* A178 10k on 15k violet .40 .20
*O35b* A179 75k on 1 l olive grn *1.00 .30*
*Nos. O24b-O35b (5)* *2.10 1.10*

Type "f" crescent is larger and does not touch wavy line. The surcharged "10" on No. O31b exists only without serifs. The overprint on O35b measures 17x22½mm.

Overprinted or Surcharged Type "g" in Black

**1957**

**O38** A178 ½k on 1k ol blk .20 .20
**O39** A178 1k ol blk .20 .20
**O40** A178 2k on 4k dk grn .20 .20
**O41** A178 3k on 4k dk grn .20 .20
**O42** A178 10k on 12k dp red .20 .20
*Nos. O38-O42 (5)* 1.00 1.00

The shape of crescent and star on type "g" varies on each value. Overprint measures 14x18mm. The surcharged stamps have two bars and new value added.

O2

O3

O4

**1957 Litho. *Perf. 10½***

**O43** O2 5k blue .25 .20
**O44** O2 10k orange brn .25 .20
**O45** O2 15k lt violet .25 .20
**O46** O2 20k red .25 .20
**O47** O2 30k gray olive .25 .20
**O48** O2 40k brown vio .25 .20
**O49** O2 50k grnsh blk .25 .20
**O50** O2 60k lt yel grn .30 .20
**O51** O2 75k yellow org .50 .25
**O52** O2 100k green .75 .25
**O53** O2 200k deep rose 1.25 .50
*Nos. O43-O53 (11)* 4.55 2.60

**1959 Unwmk. *Perf. 10***

**O54** O2 5k rose .20 .20
**O55** O2 10k ol grn .20 .20
**O56** O2 15k car rose .20 .20
**O57** O2 20k lilac .20 .20
**O58** O2 40k blue .20 .20
**O59** O2 60k orange .25 .20
**O60** O2 75k gray .50 .20
**O61** O2 100k violet .65 .20
**O62** O2 200k red brn 1.10 .65
*Nos. O54-O62 (9)* 3.50 2.25

**1960 Litho. *Perf. 10½***

**O63** O3 1k orange .20 .20
**O64** O3 5k vermilion .20 .20
**O65** O3 10k gray grn .35 .20
**O67** O3 30k red brn .20 .20
**O70** O3 60k green .25 .20
**O71** O3 1 l rose lilac .30 .20
**O72** O3 1½ l brt ultra .95 .20
**O74** O3 2½ l violet 1.50 .35
**O75** O3 5 l blue 3.50 .85
*Nos. O63-O75 (9)* 7.45 2.60

For surcharge see No. O83.

**1962 Typo. *Perf. 13***

**O76** O4 1k olive bister .20 .20
**O77** O4 5k brt green .20 .20
**O78** O4 10k red brown .20 .20
**O79** O4 15k dk blue .20 .20
**O80** O4 25k carmine .30 .20
**O81** O4 30k ultra .20 .20
*Nos. O76-O81 (6)* 1.30 1.20

For surcharge see No. O82.

Nos. O81 and O70 Surcharged

**1963**

**O82** O4 50k on 30k ultra .35 .20

***Perf. 10½***

**Litho.**

**O83** O3 100k on 60k green .50 .20

O5

O6

O7

**1963 Litho. *Perf. 12½***

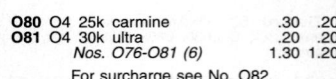

**O84** O5 1k gray .20 .20
**O85** O5 5k salmon .20 .20
**O86** O5 10k green .20 .20
**O87** O5 50k car rose .20 .20
**O88** O5 100k ultra .55 .20
*Nos. O84-O88 (5)* 1.35 1.00

For surcharge see No. O139.

**1964 Unwmk. *Perf. 12½***

**O89** O6 1k gray .20 .20
**O90** O6 5k blue .20 .20
**O91** O6 10k yellow .20 .20
**O92** O6 30k red .40 .20
**O93** O6 50k lt green .50 .20
**O94** O6 60k brown 1.50 .20
**O95** O6 80k pale grnsh bl 3.50 .40
**O96** O6 130k indigo 3.00 .60
**O97** O6 200k lilac 7.50 .80
*Nos. O89-O97 (9)* 17.00 3.00

For surcharge see No. O140.

**1965 Litho. *Perf. 13***

**O98** O7 1k emerald .20 .20
**O99** O7 10k ultra .25 .20
**O100** O7 50k orange .35 .20
*Nos. O98-O100 (3)* .80 .60

For surcharge see No. O141.

Carpet Designs O8

Seljuk Tile, 13th Century O9

1k, Usak. 50k, Bergama. 100k, Ladik. 150k, Seljuk. 200k, Nomad. 500k, Anatolia.

**1966 Litho. *Perf. 13***

**O101** O8 1k orange .20 .20
**O102** O8 50k green .20 .20
**O103** O8 100k brt pink .30 .20
**O104** O8 150k violet blue .65 .20
**O105** O8 200k olive bister .80 .20
**O106** O8 500k lilac 3.00 .40
*Nos. O101-O106 (6)* 5.15 1.40

For surcharge see No. O142.

**1967 Litho. *Perf. 11½x12***

**O107** O9 1k dk bl & lt bl .20 .20
**O108** O9 50k org & dk bl .20 .20
**O109** O9 100k lil & dk bl .20 .20
*Nos. O107-O109 (3)* .60 .60

For surcharge see No. O143.

Leaf Design — O10

**1968 Litho. *Perf. 13***
**O110** O10 50k brn & lt grn .20 .20
**O111** O10 150k blk & dl yel .50 .20
**O112** O10 500k red brn & lt bl 1.60 .20
*Nos. O110-O112 (3)* 2.30 .60

O11

O12

O13

**1969, Aug. 25 Litho. *Perf. 13***
**O113** O11 1k lt grn & red .20 .20
**O114** O11 10k lt grn & bl .20 .20
**O115** O11 50k lt grn & brn .20 .20
**O116** O11 100k lt grn & red vio .40 .20
*Nos. O113-O116 (4)* 1.00 .80

**1971, Mar. 1 Litho. *Perf. 11½x12***
**O117** O12 5k brown & blue .20 .20
**O118** O12 10k vio bl & ver .20 .20
**O119** O12 30k org & vio bl .20 .20
**O120** O12 50k Prus bl & sepia .35 .20
**O121** O12 75k yellow & green .60 .20
*Nos. O117-O121 (5)* 1.55 1.00

**1971, Nov. 15 Litho. *Perf. 11½x12***
**O122** O13 5k lt bl & gray .20 .20
**O123** O13 25k cit & lt brn .20 .20
**O124** O13 100k org & olive .20 .20
**O125** O13 200k dk brn & bis .40 .20
**O126** O13 250k rose lil & vio .60 .20
**O127** O13 500k dk bl & brt bl .95 .45
*Nos. O122-O127 (6)* 2.55 1.45

O14

O15

O16

**1972, Apr. 7 Litho. *Perf. 13***
**O128** O14 5k buff & blue .20 .20
**O129** O14 100k buff & olive .25 .20
**O130** O14 200k buff & carmine .55 .20
*Nos. O128-O130 (3)* 1.00 .60

**1973, Sept 20 Litho. *Perf. 13***
**O131** O15 100k violet & buff .65 .20

**1974, June 17 Litho. *Perf. 13½x13***
**O132** O16 10k sal pink & brn .20 .20
**O133** O16 25k blue & dk brn .20 .20
**O134** O16 50k brt pink & brn .20 .20
**O135** O16 150k lt grn & brn .40 .20
**O136** O16 250k rose & brn .65 .20
**O137** O16 500k yellow & brn 1.25 .25
*Nos. O132-O137 (6)* 2.90 1.25

O17

O18

O19

**1975, Nov. 5 Litho. *Perf. 12½x13***
**O138** O17 100k lt blue & maroon .20 .20

Nos. O84, O89, O98, O101, O107 Surcharged in Red or Black

***Perf. 12½, 13, 11½x12***

**1977, Aug. 17 Litho.**
**O139** O5 5k on 1k gray .20 .20
**O140** O6 5k on 1k gray .20 .20
**O141** O7 5k on 1k emer .20 .20
**O142** O8 5k on 1k org (B) .20 .20
**O143** O9 5k on 1k dk & lt bl .20 .20
*Nos. O139-O143 (5)* 1.00 1.00

**1977, Dec. 29 Litho. *Perf. 13½x13***
**O144** O18 250k lt bl & grn .35 .20

**1978 Photo. *Perf. 13½***
**O145** O19 50k pink & rose .20 .20
**O146** O19 2½ l buff & grnsh blk .25 .20
**O147** O19 4½ l lil rose & sl grn .40 .20
**O148** O19 5 l lt blue & pur .40 .20
**O149** O19 10 l lt grn & grn .85 .20
**O150** O19 25 l yellow & red 2.25 .20
*Nos. O145-O150 (6)* 4.35 1.20

O20

O21

O22

**1979 Litho. *Perf. 13½***
**O151** O20 50k dp org & brn .20 .20
**O152** O20 2½ l bl & dk bl .25 .20

**1979, Dec. 20 Litho. *Perf. 13½***
**O153** O21 50k sal & dk bl .20 .20
**O154** O21 1 l lt grn & red .20 .20
**O155** O21 2½ l lil rose & red .30 .20
**O156** O21 5 l lt bl & mag .30 .20
**O157** O21 7½ l lt lil & dk bl .30 .20
**O158** O21 10 l yel & dk bl .40 .20
**O159** O21 35 l gray & rose ('81) 1.25 .20
**O160** O21 50 l pnksh & dk bl ('81) 1.50 .20
*Nos. O153-O160 (8)* 4.45 1.60

**1981, Oct. 23 Litho. *Perf. 13½***
**O161** O22 5 l yel & red 2.00 .20
**O162** O22 10 l salmon & red 2.50 .20
**O163** O22 35 l gray & rose 3.00 .20
**O164** O22 50 l pink & dk bl 3.50 .20
**O165** O22 75 l pale grn & grn 6.00 .25
**O166** O22 100 l lt bl & dk bl 8.00 .45
*Nos. O161-O166 (6)* 25.00 1.50

O23

O24

**1983-84 Litho. *Perf. 12½x13***
**Background Color**
**O167** O23 5 l yellow 1.00 .20
**O168** O23 15 l yellow bister 1.25 .20
**O169** O23 20 l gray ('84) .50 .20
**O170** O23 50 l sky blue 3.00 .20
**O171** O23 65 l pink 3.75 .20
**O172** O23 70 l pale rose ('84) .75 .20
**O173** O23 90 l bister brn 5.50 .20
**O174** O23 90 l bl gray ('84) 1.10 .20
**O175** O23 100 l lt green ('84) 1.75 .20
**O176** O23 125 l lt green 6.00 .50
**O177** O23 230 l pale salmon ('84) 3.00 .40
*Nos. O167-O177 (11)* 27.60 2.70

For surcharges see Nos. O184, O186-O190.

**1986-87**
**O178** O24 5 l yel & vio .40 .20
**O179** O24 10 l org & vio .40 .20
**O180** O24 20 l gray & vio .40 .20
**O180A** O24 50 l pale blue & dp ultra ('87) .50 .20
**O181** O24 100 l lt yel grn & vio 2.00 .20
**O182** O24 300 l pale vio & vio blue ('87) 2.50 .20
*Nos. O178-O182 (6)* 6.20 1.20

For surcharges see Nos. O183, O185.

Nos. O179, O168, O180, O172, O173, O177 Surcharged in Dark Orange

**1989**
**O183** O24 500 l on 10 l 2.00 .20
**O184** O23 500 l on 15 l 2.00 .20
**O185** O24 500 l on 20 l 2.00 .20
**O186** O23 1000 l on 70 l 3.00 .25
**O187** O23 1000 l on 90 l 3.00 .25
**O188** O23 1250 l on 230 l 4.00 .50
*Nos. O183-O188 (6)* 16.00 1.60

Issued: #O183, O185-O188, 8/9; #O184, 6/7.

Nos. O171 & O174 Surcharged in Black

**1991, Mar. 27**
**O189** O23 100 l on 65 l .40 .20
**O190** O23 250 l on 90 l .80 .20

O25

O26

O27

***Perf. 11½x12½***

**1992, Mar. 24 Litho.**
**O191** O25 3000 l lt brn & dk brn 2.00 .30
**O192** O25 5000 l lt grn & dk grn 6.00 .50

**1992, Dec. 2 Litho. *Perf. 12½x13***
**O193** O26 1000 l bl grn & vio bl .50 .20
**O194** O26 10,000 l vio bl & bl grn 4.50 .50

**1993, Sept. 27 Litho. *Perf. 12½x13***
**O195** O27 1000 l brown & green 1.00 .20
**O196** O27 1500 l brown & green 1.50 .20
**O197** O27 5000 l green & claret 4.00 .40
*Nos. O195-O197 (3)* 6.50 .80

O28

O29

O30

**1994, May 9 Litho. *Perf. 11½x12***
**O198** O28 2500 l pink & violet 1.00 .20
**O199** O28 25,000 l yel & brn 2.75 .50

**1995, Jan. 25**
**O200** O29 3500 l violet & lt vio 1.00 .20
**O201** O29 17,500 l bl grn & lt grn 4.00 .45

**1995, May 17**
**O202** O30 50,000 l ol & apple grn 3.25 1.60

O31

**1995, Nov. 8 Litho. *Perf. 12½x13***
**O203** O31 5000 l salmon & org .75 .20

O32 O32a
O32b O32c

**1996, July 10 Litho. *Perf. 11½x12¼***
**O204** O32 15,000 l bl & red 1.00 .20
**O205** O32a 20,000 l grn & pur 1.50 .25
**O206** O32b 50,000 l pur & grn 2.00 .40
**O207** O32c 100,000 l red & bl 3.00 .75
*Nos. O204-O207 (4)* 7.50 1.60

O33

O34

O35

**1997, Feb. 5 Litho. *Perf. 12½x13***
**O208** O33 25,000 l red & blue .55 .30

**1997, Aug. 4 Litho. *Perf. 12½x13***
**O209** O34 40,000 l multicolored .55 .30
**O210** O35 250,000 l multicolored 3.50 1.75

O36 O37
O38 O39

**1998, June 10 Litho. *Perf. 12½x13***
**O211** O36 40,000 l dk bl & lt bl .40 .20
**O212** O37 100,000 l purple 1.00 .50
**O213** O38 200,000 l brn & pale bl grn 1.90 1.00
**O214** O39 500,000 l brn & pale bl grn 4.75 2.50
*Nos. O211-O214 (4)* 8.05 4.20

O40

O41

O42

**1998, July 29 Litho. *Perf. 12½x13***

| | | | | |
|---|---|---|---|---|
| **O215** | O40 | 75,000 l multicolored | .75 | .30 |

**1999 Litho. *Perf. 11½x12¼***

| | | | | |
|---|---|---|---|---|
| **O216** | O41 | (R) vio & blue grn | 2.50 | .45 |
| **O217** | O42 | (RT) black & pink | 4.50 | .45 |

O43 O44 O45 O46

**2000, Apr. 3 Litho. *Perf. 11½x12¼***

| | | | | |
|---|---|---|---|---|
| **O218** | O43 | 50,000 l blue & pink | .40 | .20 |
| **O219** | O44 | 75,000 l brn & gray | .50 | .20 |
| **O220** | O45 | 500,000 l red brn & lt bl | 3.00 | .40 |
| **O221** | O46 | 1,250,000 l dk bl & buff | 6.00 | 1.00 |
| | | *Nos. O218-O221 (4)* | 9.90 | 1.80 |

O47

***Perf. 11½x12¼***

**2001, Dec. 13 Litho.**

| | | | | |
|---|---|---|---|---|
| **O222** | O47 | R blue & yel org | 1.00 | .20 |

Sold for 300,000 l on day of issue.

O48 O49 O50 O51

O52

***Perf. 11½x12¼***

**2002, Dec. 10 Litho.**

| | | | | |
|---|---|---|---|---|
| **O223** | O48 | 50,000 l multi | .20 | .20 |
| **O224** | O49 | 100,000 l multi | .25 | .20 |
| **O225** | O50 | 250,000 l multi | .50 | .30 |
| **O226** | O51 | 500,000 l multi | 1.00 | .60 |
| **O227** | O52 | 1,500,000 l multi | 3.75 | 1.75 |
| | | *Nos. O223-O227 (5)* | 5.70 | 3.05 |

O53 O54 O55 O56

***Perf. 11½x12¼***

**2003, Aug. 18 Litho.**

| | | | | |
|---|---|---|---|---|
| **O228** | O53 | 500,000 l bl & red | 1.00 | .70 |
| **O229** | O54 | 750,000 l bl & yel | 1.50 | .80 |
| **O230** | O55 | 1,000,000 l bl & grn | 1.50 | 1.00 |
| **O231** | O56 | 3,000,000 l bl & yel | 5.00 | 2.10 |
| | | *Nos. O228-O231 (4)* | 9.00 | 4.60 |

O57

**2003, Oct. 13 Litho. *Perf. 11½x12¼***

| | | | | |
|---|---|---|---|---|
| **O232** | O57 | R pink & purple | 1.25 | .85 |

Sold for 600,000 l on day of issue.

Buildings O58

Designs: 100,000 l, Hamidiye Etfal Children's Sanitorium. 500,000 l, Heating Plant, Silahtaraga. 600,000 l, PTT Headquarters, Ankara, vert. 1,000,000 l, Finance Ministry building, Ankara, vert. 3,500,000 l, Old Post and Telegraph Ministry building, Istanbul.

**2004, Oct. 15 *Perf. 13¼x13, 13x13¼***

| | | | | |
|---|---|---|---|---|
| **O233** | O58 | 100,000 l multi | .20 | .20 |
| **O234** | O58 | 500,000 l multi | .75 | .50 |
| **O235** | O58 | 600,000 l multi | .80 | .60 |
| **O236** | O58 | 1,000,000 l multi | 1.50 | 1.00 |
| **O237** | O58 | 3,500,000 l multi | 5.50 | 2.00 |
| | | *Nos. O233-O237 (5)* | 8.75 | 4.30 |

### Building Type of 2004

Design: 60k, Prime Minister's Building, Ankara.

**2005, Jan. 1 Litho. *Perf. 14***

| | | | | |
|---|---|---|---|---|
| **O238** | O58 | 60k multi | .90 | .90 |

Buildings O59

Designs: 10k, Museum of the Republic, Ankara. 25k, Culture and Tourism Ministry, Ankara. 50k, State Guest House, Ankara. 60k, Sculpture Museum, Ankara. 1 l, Ethnographic Museum, Ankara. 3.50 l, National Library, Ankara.

**2005, July 4 Litho. *Perf. 13¼x13***

**Frame Color**

| | | | | |
|---|---|---|---|---|
| **O239** | O59 | 10k orange | .20 | .20 |
| **O240** | O59 | 25k orange | .35 | .35 |
| **O241** | O59 | 50k yel green | .75 | .75 |
| **O242** | O59 | 60k blue | .90 | .90 |
| **O243** | O59 | 1 l yellow | 1.50 | 1.50 |
| **O244** | O59 | 3.50 l dull org | 5.25 | 5.25 |
| | | *Nos. O239-O244 (6)* | 8.95 | 8.95 |

Kemal Ataturk — O60

Various portraits.

**2006, Apr. 21 Litho. *Perf. 13x13¼***

**Background Color**

| | | | | |
|---|---|---|---|---|
| **O245** | O60 | 10k blue | .20 | .20 |
| **O246** | O60 | 50k brown | .75 | .75 |
| **O247** | O60 | 60k dark red | .95 | .95 |
| **O248** | O60 | 1 l blue green | 1.50 | 1.50 |
| **O249** | O60 | 3.50 l red | 5.50 | 5.50 |
| | | *Nos. O245-O249 (5)* | 8.90 | 8.90 |

## NEWSPAPER STAMPS

N1

Black Overprint

**1879 Unwmk. *Perf. 11½ and 13½***

| | | | | |
|---|---|---|---|---|
| **P1** | N1 | 10pa blk & rose lilac | 225.00 | 225.00 |

Other stamps found with this "IMPRIMES" overprint were prepared on private order and have no official status as newspaper stamps.

Counterfeits exist of No. P1.

The 10pa surcharge, on half of 20pa rose and pale rose was made privately. See note after No. 77.

Regular Issue of 1890 Handstamped in Black

There are two types of this handstamp, varying slightly in size.

**1891 *Perf. 13½, 11½***

| | | | | |
|---|---|---|---|---|
| **P10** | A7 | 10pa grn & gray | 40.00 | 12.50 |
| *a.* | | Imperf. | 22.50 | 12.50 |
| **P11** | A7 | 20pa rose & gray | 75.00 | 15.00 |
| **P12** | A7 | 1pi blue & gray | *200.00* | *150.00* |
| **P13** | A7 | 2pi yel & gray | *500.00* | *400.00* |
| **P14** | A7 | 5pi buff & gray | *1,000.* | *750.00* |
| | | *Nos. P10-P14 (5)* | *1,815.* | *1,327.* |

**Blue Handstamp**

| | | | | |
|---|---|---|---|---|
| *P10b* | A7 | 10pa green & gray | *200.00* | *125.00* |
| *P11a* | A7 | 20pa rose & gray | *300.00* | *250.00* |
| *P12a* | A7 | 1pi blue & gray | *400.00* | *375.00* |
| | | *Nos. P10b-P12a (3)* | *900.00* | *750.00* |

This overprint in red and on 2pi and 5pi in blue is considered bogus.

Same Handstamp on Regular Issue of 1892

**1892 *Perf. 13½***

| | | | | |
|---|---|---|---|---|
| **P25** | A10 | 10pa gray green | *400.00* | *100.00* |
| **P26** | A11 | 20pa rose | *1,250.* | *375.00* |
| **P27** | A12 | 1pi pale blue | *110.00* | *150.00* |
| **P28** | A13 | 2pi brown org | *200.00* | *175.00* |
| **P29** | A14 | 5pi pale violet | *1,800.* | *1,250.* |
| *a.* | | On No. 99a | *500.00* | |
| | | *Nos. P25-P29 (5)* | *3,760.* | *2,050.* |

The handstamps on Nos. P10-P29 are found double, inverted and sideways. Counterfeit overprints comprise most of the copies offered for sale in the marketplace.

Regular Issues of 1892-98 Overprinted in Black

**1893-98**

| | | | | |
|---|---|---|---|---|
| **P30** | A10 | 10pa gray grn | 3.75 | 2.50 |
| **P31** | A11 | 20pa vio brn ('98) | 3.00 | 1.50 |
| *a.* | | 20pa dark pink | .60 | .60 |
| *b.* | | 20pa pink | 225.00 | 15.00 |
| **P32** | A12 | 1pi pale blue | 3.00 | 1.50 |
| **P33** | A13 | 2pi brown org | 27.50 | 12.50 |
| *a.* | | Tete beche pair | | 22.50 |
| **P34** | A14 | 5pi pale violet | 85.00 | 75.00 |
| *a.* | | On No. 99a | 140.00 | 65.00 |
| | | *Nos. P30-P34 (5)* | 122.25 | 93.00 |

For surcharge and overprints see Nos. B41, P134-P136, P153-P154.

No. 95 Surcharged

**1897**

| | | | | |
|---|---|---|---|---|
| **P36** | A10 | 5pa on 10pa gray grn | 4.00 | 2.00 |
| *a.* | | "Cniq" instead of "Cinq" | 15.00 | 15.00 |

For overprint see No. P137.

Nos. 102-107 Overprinted in Black

**1901 *Perf. 12, 13½ and Compound***

| | | | | |
|---|---|---|---|---|
| **P37** | A16 | 5pa bister | 1.00 | 1.00 |
| *a.* | | Inverted overprint | | |
| **P38** | A16 | 10pa yellow grn | 6.25 | 6.25 |
| **P39** | A16 | 20pa magenta | 32.50 | 7.50 |
| **P40** | A16 | 1pi violet blue | 60.00 | 22.50 |
| **P41** | A16 | 2pi gray blue | 42.50 | 37.50 |
| **P42** | A16 | 5pi ocher | 300.00 | 90.00 |
| | | *Nos. P37-P42 (6)* | 442.25 | 164.75 |

For overprints see Nos. B37, P69-P74, P123, P138-P141, P155-P158.

Same Overprint on Nos. 110-115

**1901**

| | | | | |
|---|---|---|---|---|
| **P43** | A17 | 5pa purple | 8.75 | 2.00 |
| **P44** | A17 | 10pa green | 32.50 | 2.50 |
| **P45** | A17 | 20pa carmine | 8.75 | 1.50 |
| *a.* | | Overprinted on back | | |
| **P46** | A17 | 1pi blue | 25.00 | 2.00 |
| **P47** | A17 | 2pi orange | 87.50 | 4.00 |
| *a.* | | Inverted overprint | | |
| **P48** | A17 | 5pi lilac rose | 160.00 | 27.50 |
| | | *Nos. P43-P48 (6)* | 322.50 | 39.50 |

For overprints see Nos. P75-P80, P124-P126, P142-P146, P159-P164.

Same Overprint on Regular Issue of 1905

**1905**

| | | | | |
|---|---|---|---|---|
| **P49** | A18 | 5pa ocher | 2.50 | 1.00 |
| **P50** | A18 | 10pa dull green | 30.00 | 1.50 |
| **P51** | A18 | 20pa carmine | 2.50 | 1.25 |
| **P52** | A18 | 1pi pale blue | 2.50 | 1.25 |
| **P53** | A18 | 2pi slate | 70.00 | 10.00 |
| **P54** | A18 | 5pi brown | 175.00 | 20.00 |
| | | *Nos. P49-P54 (6)* | 282.50 | 35.00 |

For overprints see Nos. P127-P129, P147-P150, P165-P171.

Regular Issue of 1908 Overprinted in Carmine or Blue

**1908**

**P55** A19 5pa ocher (Bl) 10.00 .50
**P56** A19 10pa blue grn (C) 17.50 .50
**P57** A19 20pa carmine (Bl) 22.50 1.00
**P58** A19 1pi brt blue (C) 100.00 2.50
**P59** A19 2pi blue blk (C) 150.00 7.50
**P60** A19 5pi dk violet (C) 200.00 17.50
*Nos. P55-P60 (6)* 500.00 29.50

For overprints see Nos. B17, P130-P131, P151, P172.

Same Overprint on Regular Issue of 1909

**1909**

**P61** A21 5pa ocher (Bl) 3.00 1.00
*a.* Imperf.
**P62** A21 10pa blue grn (C) 8.75 1.50
**P63** A21 20pa car rose (Bl) 60.00 1.75
*a.* Imperf.
**P64** A21 1pi brt blue (C) 100.00 5.00
**P65** A21 2pi blue blk (C) 250.00 30.00
**P66** A21 5pi dk violet (C) 500.00 65.00
*Nos. P61-P66 (6)* 921.75 104.25

For surcharge and overprints see Nos. B18, P67-P68, P81, P132-P133, P152.

No. 151 Surcharged in Blue

**1910** ***Perf. 12, 13½ and Compound***
**P67** A21 2pa on 5pa ocher .75 .75

**1911** ***Perf. 12***
**P68** A21 2pa olive green 1.00 .50

Preceding Newspaper Issues with additional Overprint in Carmine or Blue

The overprint was applied to 13 denominations in four settings with change of city name, producing individual sets for each city: "MONASTIR," "PRISTINA," "SALONIKA" and "USKUB."

**1911, June 26** ***Perf. 12, 13½***
**P69** A16 5pa bister 15.00 22.50
**P70** A16 10pa yellow grn 15.00 22.50
**P71** A16 20pa magenta 15.00 22.50
**P72** A16 1pi violet blue 15.00 22.50
**P73** A16 2pi gray blue 20.00 30.00
**P74** A16 5pi ocher 40.00 60.00
**P75** A17 5pa purple 7.50 12.50
**P76** A17 10pa green 7.50 12.50
**P77** A17 20pa carmine 7.50 12.50
**P78** A17 1pi blue 7.50 12.50
**P79** A17 2pi orange 10.00 15.00
**P80** A17 5pi lilac rose 20.00 30.00
**P81** A21 2pa olive green 2.50 3.75
*Nos. P69-P81 (13)* 182.50 278.75

Values for each of the 4 city sets of 13 are the same.

The note after No. 182 will also apply to Nos. P69-P81.

Newspaper Stamps of 1901-11 Overprinted in Carmine or Black

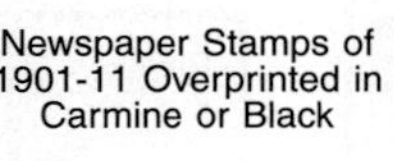

**1915**

### On Stamps of 1893-98

**P121** A10 10pa gray green 6.00 .50
*a.* Inverted overprint 10.00 10.00
**P122** A13 2pi yellow brn 1.50 1.00
*a.* Inverted overprint 10.00 10.00

### On Stamps of 1901

**P123** A16 10pa yellow grn 1.00 .50
**P124** A17 5pa purple 1.00 1.00
**P125** A17 20pa carmine 2.00 1.00
**P126** A17 5pi lilac rose 20.00 5.00

### On Stamps of 1905

**P127** A18 5pa ocher 1.00 .50
*a.* Inverted overprint 7.50 7.50
**P128** A18 2pi slate 17.50 5.00
**P129** A18 5pi brown 10.00 .60

### On Stamps of 1908

**P130** A19 2pi blue blk *1,375. 550.00*
**P131** A19 5pi dk violet 10.00 1.25

### On Stamps of 1909

**P132** A21 5pa ocher 1.00 .50
**P133** A21 5pi dk violet 100.00 35.00
*Nos. P121-P129,P131-P133 (12)* 171.00 51.85

Preceding Newspaper Issues with additional Overprint in Red or Black

**1916**

### On Stamps of 1893-98

**P134** A10 10pa gray green 1.00 .50
**P135** A11 20pa violet brn .50 .50
**P136** A14 5pi dull violet 50.00 50.00

### On Stamp of 1897

**P137** A10 5pa on 10pa gray grn .60 .50

### On Stamps of 1901

**P138** A16 5pa bister .50 .30
**P139** A16 10pa yellow grn .90 .90
**P140** A16 20pa magenta 1.00 .90
*a.* Inverted overprint 10.00 10.00
**P141** A16 1pi violet blue 1.00 1.00
**P142** A17 5pa purple 50.00 50.00
**P143** A17 10pa green 50.00 50.00
**P144** A17 20pa carmine 1.50 .90
**P145** A17 1pi blue 1.50 .90
**P146** A17 2pi orange 1.50 .90

### On Stamps of 1905

**P147** A18 5pa ocher 1.00 .75
**P148** A18 10pa dull green 50.00 50.00
**P149** A18 20pa carmine 50.00 50.00
**P150** A18 1pi pale blue 1.75 1.00

### On Stamp of 1908

**P151** A19 5pa ocher 62.50 62.50

### On Stamp of 1909

**P152** A21 5pa ocher 62.50 62.50
*Nos. P134-P152 (19)* 387.75 384.05

Preceding Newspaper Issues with additional Overprint in Red or Black

**1917**

### On Stamps of 1893-98

**P153** A12 1pi gray (R) 2.50 2.00
**P154** A11 20pa vio brn (R) 3.75 3.75

### On Stamps of 1901

**P155** A16 5pa bister (Bk) 1.50 1.25
*a.* Inverted overprint 20.00 20.00
**P156** A16 10pa yel grn (R) 1.50 1.25
**P157** A16 20pa mag (Bk) 1.50 1.25
**P158** A16 2pi gray bl (R) 40.00 30.00
**P159** A17 5pa purple (Bk) 2.25 2.25
*a.* Inverted overprint 20.00 20.00
*b.* Double overprint 20.00 20.00
*c.* Double ovpt., one inverted 25.00 25.00
**P160** A17 10pa green (R) 22.50 35.00
**P161** A17 20pa car (Bk) 1.50 1.25
**P162** A17 1pi blue (R) 3.00 3.00
**P163** A17 2pi orange (Bk) 2.50 2.50
**P164** A17 5pi lil rose (R) 32.50 50.00

### On Stamps of 1905

**P165** A18 5pa ocher (R) 2.50 2.00
*a.* Inverted overprint 10.00 10.00
**P166** A18 5pa ocher (Bk) 3.00 2.50
*a.* Inverted overprint 10.00 10.00
**P167** A18 10pa dull grn (R) 2.50 2.00
**P168** A18 20pa car (Bk) 2.50 2.00
*a.* Double overprint 15.00 15.00
**P169** A18 1pi blue (R) 2.50 2.00
*a.* Inverted overprint 25.00 25.00
**P170** A18 2pi slate (R) 32.50 50.00
**P171** A18 5pi brown (R) 32.50 50.00

### On Stamp of 1908

**P172** A19 5pa ocher (R) 32.50 50.00
*Nos. P153-P172 (20)* 225.50 294.00

Nos. P153-P172 were used as regular postage stamps.

#P173

#P174

**1919**

### Blue Surcharge and Red Overprint

**P173** A21 5pa on 2pa ol grn .75 .75
*a.* Red overprint double 12.50 5.00
*b.* Blue surcharge double 12.50 5.00

**1920** **Red Surcharge**
**P174** A25 5pa on 4pa brn 1.25 .50

**Catalogue values for unused stamps in this section, from this point to the end of the section, are for Never Hinged items.**

Dove and Citadel of Ankara — N6

**1952-55** **Litho.** ***Perf. 12½***
**P175** N6 0.50k grnsh gray .20 .20
**P176** N6 0.50k violet ('53) .20 .20

***Perf. 10½, 10***

**P177** N6 0.50k red org ('54) .20 .20
**P178** N6 0.50k brown ('55) .20 .20
*Nos. P175-P178 (4)* .80 .80

## POSTAL TAX STAMPS

Map of Turkey and Red Crescent PT1

**1928** **Unwmk.** **Typo.** ***Perf. 14***

### Crescent in Red

**RA1** PT1 ½pi lt brown .30 .20
**RA2** PT1 1pi red violet .30 .20
**RA3** PT1 2½pi orange .30 .20

### Engr.

### Various Frames

**RA4** PT1 5pi dk brown .60 .45
**RA5** PT1 10pi yellow green .75 .55
**RA6** PT1 20pi slate 1.25 .60
**RA7** PT1 50pi dark violet 3.75 1.40
*Nos. RA1-RA7 (7)* 7.25 3.60
Set, never hinged 13.00

The use of these stamps on letters, parcels, etc. in addition to the regular postage, was obligatory on certain days in each year.

For surcharges see Nos. RA16, RA21-RA22.

Cherubs Upholding Star — PT2

**1932**

**RA8** PT2 1k ol bis & red .50 .20
**RA9** PT2 2½k dk brn & red .65 .20
**RA10** PT2 5k green & red .85 .20
**RA11** PT2 25k black & red 2.75 .90
*Nos. RA8-RA11 (4)* 4.75 1.50
Set, never hinged 7.50

For surcharges and overprints see Nos. RA12-RA15, RA28-RA29, RA36-RA38.

No. RA8 Surcharged

**RA12** PT2 20pa on 1k .25 .20
**RA13** PT2 3k on 1k 1.00 .40
*a.* 3 "kruus" 2.50 2.50

By a law of Parliament the use of these stamps on letters and telegraph forms, in addition to the regular fees, was obligatory from Apr. 20-30 of each year. The inscription in the tablet at the bottom of the design states that the money derived from the sale of the stamps is devoted to child welfare work.

No. RA8 Surcharged

**1933**

**RA14** PT2 20pa on 1k ol bis & red .25 .20
**RA15** PT2 3k on 1k ol bis & red 1.00 .60

No. RA5 Surcharged

**RA16** PT1 5k on 10pi yel grn & red .95 .45
*Nos. RA14-RA16 (3)* 2.20 1.25

PT3

PT4

**1933** ***Perf. 11, 11½***
**RA17** PT3 20pa gray vio & red .65 .20
**RA18** PT4 1k violet & red .80 .20
**RA19** PT4 5k dk brown & red 2.50 .50
**RA20** PT3 15k green & red 3.50 .50
*Nos. RA17-RA20 (4)* 7.45 1.40
Set, never hinged 11.00

Nos. RA17 and RA20 were issued in Ankara; Nos. RA18 and RA19 in Izmir.

For overprint see No. RA27.

Nos. RA3, RA1 Surcharged in Black

**1933-34**

**RA21** PT1 1k on 2½pi orange .25 .20
**RA22** PT1 5k on ½pi lt brown .70 .25

Map of Turkey PT5

**1934-35 Crescent in Red *Perf. 12***

| | | | | | |
|---|---|---|---|---|---|
| **RA23** | PT5 | ½k | blue ('35) | .20 | .20 |
| **RA24** | PT5 | 1k | red brown | .20 | .20 |
| **RA25** | PT5 | 2½k | brown ('35) | .50 | .20 |
| **RA26** | PT5 | 5k | blue green ('35) | 1.25 | .20 |
| | | | *Nos. RA23-RA26 (4)* | 2.15 | .80 |
| | | | Set, never hinged | 5.00 | |

Frame differs on No. RA26.

See Nos. RA30-RA35B. For surcharge see No. RA63.

Nos. RA17, RA8-RA9 Overprinted "P.Y.S." in Roman Capitals

**1936 *Perf. 11, 14***

| | | | | | |
|---|---|---|---|---|---|
| **RA27** | PT3 | 20pa | gray vio & red | .40 | .20 |
| **RA28** | PT2 | 1k | ol bis & red | .40 | .20 |
| **RA29** | PT2 | 3k | on 2½k dk brn & red | .75 | .30 |
| | | | *Nos. RA27-RA29 (3)* | 1.55 | |
| | | | Set, never hinged | 12.00 | |

Type of 1934-35, Inscribed "Türkiye Kizilay Cemiyeti"

**1938-46 *Perf. 8½-11½***

Type I — Imprint, "Devlet Basimevi". Crescent red.

Type II — Imprint, "Alaeddin Kiral Basimevi". Crescent carmine.

Type III — Imprint, "Damga Matbaasi". Crescent red.

**Crescent in Red or Carmine**

| | | | | | |
|---|---|---|---|---|---|
| **RA30** | PT5 | ½k | blue (I) | .20 | .20 |
| *a.* | | | Type II | 3.50 | 1.00 |
| *b.* | | | Type III | .30 | .20 |
| **RA31** | PT5 | 1k | red vio (I) | .20 | .20 |
| *a.* | | | Type II | 6.50 | 2.00 |
| *b.* | | | Type III | .30 | .20 |
| **RA32** | PT5 | 2½k | orange (I) | .20 | .20 |
| *a.* | | | Type III | 1.25 | .25 |
| **RA33** | PT5 | 5k | blue grn (I) | .35 | .20 |
| **RA33A** | PT5 | 5k | choc (III) ('42) | 1.00 | .20 |
| **RA34** | PT5 | 10k | pale grn (I) | .95 | .30 |
| *a.* | | | Type III | 1.25 | .30 |
| **RA35** | PT5 | 20k | black (I) | 1.40 | .45 |
| **RA35A** | PT5 | 50k | pur (III) ('46) | 5.00 | .55 |
| **RA35B** | PT5 | 1 l | blue (III) ('44) | 22.50 | 2.50 |
| | | | *Nos. RA30-RA35B (9)* | 31.80 | 4.80 |
| | | | Set, never hinged | 75.00 | |

No. RA9 Surcharged in Black

**1938 *Perf. 14***

| | | | | | |
|---|---|---|---|---|---|
| **RA36** | PT2 | 20pa | on 2½k | .40 | .20 |
| **RA37** | PT2 | 1k | on 2½k | .60 | .20 |

No. RA9 Surcharged in Black

**1938 Unwmk. *Perf. 14***

| | | | | | |
|---|---|---|---|---|---|
| **RA37A** | PT2 | 20pa | on 2½k | .90 | .50 |
| **RA37B** | PT2 | 1k | on 2½k | 1.10 | .65 |

No. RA9 Surcharged "1 Kurus" in Black

**1939 *Perf. 14***

| | | | | | |
|---|---|---|---|---|---|
| **RA38** | PT2 | 1k | on 2½k dk brn & red | .50 | .50 |

Child — PT6

Nurse with Child — PT7

**1940 Typo. *Perf. 12***

**Star in Carmine**

| | | | | | |
|---|---|---|---|---|---|
| **RA39** | PT6 | 20pa | bluish grn | .30 | .20 |
| **RA40** | PT6 | 1k | violet | .30 | .20 |
| **RA41** | PT7 | 1k | lt blue | .30 | .20 |
| **RA42** | PT7 | 2½k | pale red lil | .30 | .20 |
| **RA43** | PT6 | 3k | black | .35 | .20 |
| **RA44** | PT7 | 5k | pale violet | .30 | .20 |
| **RA45** | PT7 | 10k | blue green | 1.00 | .40 |
| **RA46** | PT6 | 15k | dark blue | .75 | .30 |
| **RA47** | PT7 | 25k | olive bister | 2.50 | 1.25 |
| **RA48** | PT7 | 50k | olive gray | 6.00 | 2.50 |
| | | | *Nos. RA39-RA48 (10)* | 12.10 | 5.65 |
| | | | Set, never hinged | 30.00 | |

Soldier and Map of Turkey — PT8

**1941-44 *Perf. 11½***

| | | | | | |
|---|---|---|---|---|---|
| **RA49** | PT8 | 1k | purple | .40 | .20 |
| **RA50** | PT8 | 2k | light blue | 2.50 | .20 |
| **RA51** | PT8 | 3k | chestnut | 2.75 | .50 |
| **RA51A** | PT8 | 4k | mag ('44) | 9.50 | .35 |
| **RA52** | PT8 | 5k | brt rose | 7.75 | 2.50 |
| **RA53** | PT8 | 10k | dk blue | 11.00 | 4.00 |
| | | | *Nos. RA49-RA53 (6)* | 33.90 | 7.75 |
| | | | Set, never hinged | 75.00 | |

The tax was used for national defense.

Baby — PT9

Nurse and Baby — PT13

Nurse and Children PT10

Nurse Feeding Child PT11

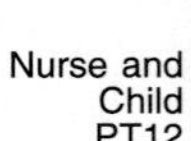

Nurse and Child PT12

Nurse and Child — PT14

President Inonu Holding Child — PT15

Children PT16

**1942 Unwmk. Typo. *Perf. 11½***

**Star in Red**

| | | | | | |
|---|---|---|---|---|---|
| **RA54** | PT9 | 20pa | brt violet | .40 | .20 |
| **RA55** | PT9 | 20pa | chocolate | .40 | .20 |
| **RA56** | PT10 | 1k | dk slate grn | .40 | .20 |
| **RA57** | PT11 | 2½k | yellow grn | .40 | .30 |
| **RA58** | PT12 | 3k | dark blue | .40 | .30 |
| **RA59** | PT13 | 5k | brt pink | .40 | .30 |
| **RA60** | PT14 | 10k | lt blue | .70 | .40 |
| **RA61** | PT15 | 15k | dk red brn | 1.10 | .70 |
| **RA62** | PT16 | 25k | brown | 1.75 | 1.00 |
| | | | *Nos. RA54-RA62 (9)* | 5.95 | 3.60 |

See Nos. RA175, RA179-RA180.

No. RA32 Surcharged with New Value in Brown

**1942 *Perf. 10***

| | | | | | |
|---|---|---|---|---|---|
| **RA63** | PT5 | 1k | on 2½k org & red (I) | .20 | .20 |

Child Eating — PT17

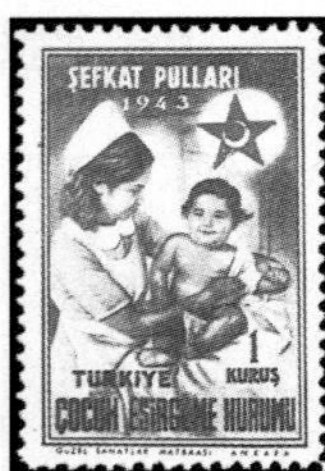

Nurse and Child — PT18

Nurse and Child PT19

Child and Red Star — PT20

President Inönü and Child — PT21

Inscribed: "Sefcat Pullari 23 Nisan 1943 Cocuk Esirgeme Kurumu."

**1943 Star in Red *Perf. 11***

| | | | | | |
|---|---|---|---|---|---|
| **RA64** | PT17 | 50pa | lilac | .20 | .20 |
| **RA65** | PT17 | 50pa | gray green | .25 | .20 |
| **RA66** | PT18 | 1k | lt ultra | .25 | .20 |
| **RA67** | PT19 | 3k | dark red | .30 | .20 |
| **RA68** | PT20 | 15k | cream & blk | 1.50 | .40 |
| **RA69** | PT21 | 100k | brt violet blue | 2.50 | 1.60 |
| *a.* | | | Souvenir sheet, #RA64-RA69, imperf. | 5.50 | 5.50 |
| | | | *Nos. RA64-RA69 (6)* | 5.00 | 2.80 |

Star and Crescent PT23

Hospital PT24

Nurse and Children PT25

Baby PT26

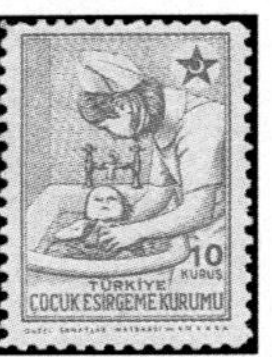

Nurse Bathing Baby — PT27

Nurse Feeding Child — PT28

Baby with Bottle — PT29

Child — PT30

Hospital — PT31

***Perf. 10 to 12 and Compound***

**1943-44**

**Star in Red**

| | | | | | |
|---|---|---|---|---|---|
| **RA71** | PT23 | 20pa | deep blue | .40 | .30 |
| **RA72** | PT24 | 1k | gray green | .40 | .20 |
| **RA73** | PT25 | 3k | pale gray brn | .40 | .20 |
| **RA74** | PT26 | 5k | yellow orange | .70 | .30 |
| **RA75** | PT26 | 5k | violet brn | .30 | .20 |
| **RA76** | PT27 | 10k | red | .40 | .30 |
| **RA77** | PT28 | 15k | red violet | .60 | .40 |
| **RA78** | PT29 | 25k | pale violet | .90 | .50 |
| **RA79** | PT30 | 50k | lt blue | 2.00 | 1.00 |
| **RA80** | PT31 | 100k | lt green | 5.00 | 4.00 |
| | | | *Nos. RA71-RA80 (10)* | 11.10 | 7.40 |
| | | | Set, never hinged | 22.00 | |

For surcharge see No. RA156.

Nurse Holding Baby — PT32

Nurse Feeding Child — PT33

Child — PT34

Star and Crescent PT35

**1945-47 Unwmk. Litho. *Perf. 11½***

**Star in Red**

| | | | | |
|---|---|---|---|---|
| **RA81** | PT32 | 1k lilac brn | .40 | .20 |
| *a.* | | 1k rose violet | .50 | .20 |
| **RA82** | PT33 | 5k yellow grn | .70 | .20 |
| *a.* | | 5k green | .70 | .20 |
| **RA83** | PT34 | 10k red brown | .50 | .20 |
| **RA84** | PT35 | 250k gray black | 9.50 | 3.50 |
| **RA84A** | PT35 | 500k dull vio ('47) | 37.50 | 12.50 |
| | | *Nos. RA81-RA84A (5)* | 48.60 | 16.60 |
| | | Set, never hinged | 90.00 | |

Imprint on No. RA82: "Kagit ve Basim isleri A.S. ist." On No. RA82a: "Guzel Sanatlar Matbaasi — Ankara."

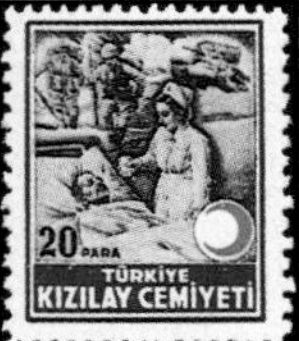
Nurse and Wounded Soldier PT36

President Inönü and Victim of Earthquake PT37

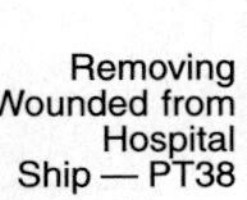

Removing Wounded from Hospital Ship — PT38

Nurse and Soldier — PT39

Feeding the Poor — PT40

Wounded Soldiers on Landing Raft — PT41

Symbolical of Red Crescent Relief — PT42

**1945 *Perf. 12x10, 10x12***

**Crescent in Red**

| | | | | |
|---|---|---|---|---|
| **RA85** | PT36 | 20pa dp bl & brn org | .30 | .20 |
| **RA86** | PT37 | 1k ol grn & ol bis | .30 | .20 |
| **RA87** | PT38 | 2½k dp bl & red | .50 | .20 |
| **RA88** | PT39 | 5k dp bl & red | 1.25 | .30 |
| **RA89** | PT40 | 10k dp bl & lt grn | 1.25 | .40 |
| **RA90** | PT41 | 50k blk & gray grn | 3.00 | 1.00 |
| **RA91** | PT42 | 1 l black & yel | 12.00 | 4.00 |
| | | *Nos. RA85-RA91 (7)* | 18.60 | 6.30 |
| | | Set, never hinged | 45.00 | |

See Nos. RA181-RA182.

Ankara Sanatorium PT43

**1946 *Perf. 12***

| | | | | |
|---|---|---|---|---|
| **RA92** | PT43 | 20k red & lt bl | .65 | .30 |

See No. RA210. For surcharge see No. RA186.

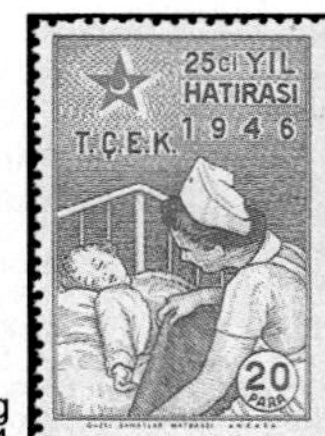
Covering Sleeping Child — PT44

Designs: 1k, Mother and child. 2½k, Nurse at playground. 5k, Doctor examining infant. 15k, Feeding child. 25k, Bathing child. 50k, Weighing baby. 150k, Feeding baby.

**1946 Litho. *Perf. 12½***

**Inscribed: "25ci Yil Hatirasi 1946"**

**Star in Carmine**

| | | | | |
|---|---|---|---|---|
| **RA93** | PT44 | 20pa brown | .35 | .20 |
| **RA94** | PT44 | 1k blue | .35 | .20 |
| **RA95** | PT44 | 2½k carmine | .35 | .20 |
| **RA96** | PT44 | 5k vio brn | .60 | .20 |
| **RA97** | PT44 | 15k violet | .90 | .50 |
| **RA98** | PT44 | 25k gray grn | 1.25 | .60 |
| **RA99** | PT44 | 50k bl grn | 1.75 | 1.50 |
| **RA100** | PT44 | 150k gray brn | 3.25 | 1.75 |
| | | *Nos. RA93-RA100 (8)* | 8.80 | 5.15 |
| | | Set, never hinged | 15.00 | |

For surcharge see No. RA155.

Hospital Ship — PT52

Ambulance Plane — PT53

Hospital Train — PT54

Ambulance PT55

Boy Scout and Red Crescent Flag — PT56

Stretcher Bearers and Wounded Soldier PT57

Nurse and Hospital — PT58

Sanatorium PT59

**1946 *Perf. 11½***

| | | | | |
|---|---|---|---|---|
| **RA101** | PT52 | 1k multi | 1.25 | 1.25 |
| **RA102** | PT53 | 4k multi | 1.25 | 1.25 |
| **RA103** | PT54 | 10k multi | 3.50 | 3.50 |
| **RA104** | PT55 | 25k multi | 4.50 | 4.50 |
| **RA105** | PT56 | 40k multi | 8.50 | 8.50 |
| **RA106** | PT57 | 70k multi | 6.00 | 6.00 |
| **RA107** | PT58 | 1 l multi | 5.50 | 5.50 |
| **RA108** | PT59 | 2½ l multi | 12.50 | 12.50 |
| | | *Nos. RA101-RA108 (8)* | 43.00 | 43.00 |

For overprints see Nos. RA139-RA146.

Souvenir Sheet

Pres. Inönü and Child — PT60

**1946 Unwmk. Typo. *Imperf.***

**Without Gum**

| | | | | |
|---|---|---|---|---|
| **RA109** | PT60 | 250k slate blk, pink & red | 20.00 | 17.50 |

Turkish Society for the Prevention of Cruelty to Children, 25th anniv.

Nurse and Wounded Soldier PT61

Pres. Inönü and Victim of Earthquake PT62

Nurse and Soldier — PT64

Symbolical of Red Crescent Relief — PT67

**1946-47 Litho. *Perf. 11½***

**Crescent in Red**

| | | | | |
|---|---|---|---|---|
| **RA113** | PT61 | 20pa dk bl vio & ol ('47) | .20 | .20 |
| **RA114** | PT62 | 1k dk brn & yel | .45 | .20 |
| **RA115** | PT64 | 5k dp bl & red | .45 | .25 |
| **RA116** | PT67 | 1 l brn blk & yel | 1.90 | 1.25 |
| | | *Nos. RA113-RA116 (4)* | 3.00 | 1.90 |

PT68

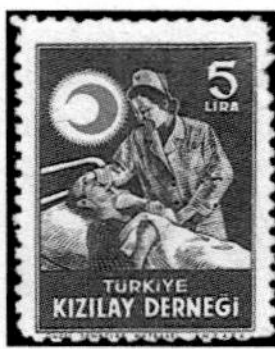
Nurse and Wounded Soldier — PT69

Victory and Soldier — PT70

**1947**

**Crescent in Red**

| | | | | |
|---|---|---|---|---|
| **RA117** | PT68 | 250k brn blk & grn | 5.25 | 2.00 |
| **RA118** | PT69 | 5 l sl gray & org | 8.75 | 3.50 |

**Booklet Pane of One**

***Perf. 11½ (top) x Imperf.***

| | | | | |
|---|---|---|---|---|
| **RA119** | PT70 | 10 l deep blue | 22.50 | — |

Black numerals above No. RA119 indicate position in booklet.

President Inönü and Victim of Earthquake PT71

Nurse and Child PT72

**1947 *Perf. 11½***

| | | | | |
|---|---|---|---|---|
| **RA120** | PT71 | 1k dk brn, pale bl & red | .20 | .20 |
| **RA121** | PT72 | 2½k bl vio & car | .20 | .20 |

See Nos. RA221-RA223. For surcharge see No. RA154.

Nurse Offering Encouragement PT73

Plant with Broken Stem PT74

***Perf. 8½, 11½x10, 11x10½***

**1948-49 Typo. Unwmk.**

**Crescent in Red**

| | | | | |
|---|---|---|---|---|
| **RA122** | PT73 | ½k ultra ('49) | .55 | .20 |
| **RA123** | PT73 | 1k indigo | .20 | .20 |
| **RA124** | PT73 | 2k lilac rose | .20 | .20 |
| **RA125** | PT73 | 2½k org ('49) | .20 | .20 |
| **RA126** | PT73 | 3k bl grn | .20 | .20 |
| **RA127** | PT73 | 4k gray ('49) | .35 | .20 |
| **RA128** | PT73 | 5k blue | .70 | .20 |
| **RA129** | PT73 | 10k pink | 1.25 | .20 |
| **RA130** | PT73 | 25k chocolate | 1.60 | .25 |

***Perf. 10***

| | | | | |
|---|---|---|---|---|
| **RA130A** | PT74 | 50k ultra & bl gray ('49) | 2.25 | .75 |
| **RA130B** | PT74 | 100k grn & pale grn ('49) | 5.25 | 1.00 |
| | | *Nos. RA122-RA130B (11)* | 12.75 | 3.60 |
| | | Set, never hinged | 30.00 | |

For surcharges see Nos. RA151-RA153, RA187.

Nurse and Children — PT75

Various Scenes with Children.

Inscribed: "1948 Cocuk Yili Hatirasi"

**1948 Litho. *Perf. 11***
**Star in Red**

RA131 PT75 20pa dp ultra .20 .20
RA132 PT75 20pa rose lilac .20 .20
RA133 PT75 1k dp Prus bl .30 .20
RA134 PT75 3k dk brn vio .40 .25
RA135 PT75 15k slate black 1.25 1.00
RA136 PT75 30k orange 2.75 2.50
RA137 PT75 150k yellow grn 3.75 3.50
RA138 PT75 300k brown red 5.75 5.50
*Nos. RA131-RA138 (8)* 14.60 13.35
Set, never hinged 30.00

No. RA136 is arranged horizontally. For overprints and surcharges see Nos. RA199-RA206.

**Catalogue values for unused stamps in this section, from this point to the end of the section, are for Never Hinged items.**

Nos. RA101 to RA108 Overprinted in Carmine

**1949 *Perf. 11½***

RA139 PT52 1k multi 10.00 10.00
RA140 PT53 4k multi 10.00 10.00
RA141 PT54 10k multi 10.00 10.00
RA142 PT55 25k multi 10.00 10.00
RA143 PT56 40k multi 20.00 20.00
RA144 PT57 70k multi 10.00 10.00
RA145 PT58 1 l multi 10.00 10.00
RA146 PT59 2½ l multi 10.00 10.00
*Nos. RA139-RA146 (8)* 90.00 90.00

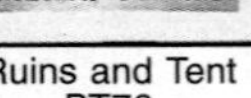

Ruins and Tent PT76 "Protection" PT77

**Booklet Panes of One**

**1949 *Perf. 10 (top) x Imperf.***

RA149 PT76 5k gray, vio gray & red 2.00 1.00
RA150 PT76 10k red vio, sal & red 2.00 1.00

Black numerals above each stamp indicate its position in the booklet.

No. RA124 Surcharged in Black

**1950 Unwmk. *Perf. 8½***

RA151 PT73 20pa on 2k 1.25 1.00

Postal Tax Stamps of 1944-48 Surcharged with New Value in Black or Carmine

***Perf. 8½ to 12½ and Compound***

**1952**

RA152 PT73 20pa on 3k bl grn .50 .25
RA153 PT73 20pa on 4k gray .75 .25
RA154 PT72 1k on 2½k bl vio & car (C) 1.00 1.50
RA155 PT44 1k on 2½k car 2.00 1.00
RA156 PT25 1k on 3k pale gray brn 2.00 1.00
*Nos. RA152-RA156 (5)* 6.25 4.00

Various Symbolical Designs Inscribed "75 iNCi" etc.

**1952 Typo. *Perf. 10***
**Crescent in Carmine**

RA157 PT77 5k bl grn & bl 2.00 1.50
RA158 PT77 15k yel grn, bl & cr 2.00 1.50
RA159 PT77 30k bl, grn & brn 2.00 1.50
RA160 PT77 1 l blk, bl & cr 2.00 1.50
a. Souvenir sheet, #RA157-RA160, imperf. 30.00 30.00
*Nos. RA157-RA160 (4)* 8.00 6.00

Printed in sheets of 20 containing one horizontal row of each value.

Nurse and Children PT78

Design: 1k, Nurse and baby.

**1954 Litho. *Perf. 10½***
**Star in Red**

RA161 PT78 20pa aqua .35 .35
RA162 PT78 20pa yellow .35 .35
RA163 PT12 1k deep blue .80 .80
*Nos. RA161-RA163 (3)* 1.50 1.50

Globe and Flag — PT79

Designs: 5k, Winged nurse in clouds. 10k, Protecting arm of Red Crescent.

**1954**

RA164 PT79 1k multi .20 .20
RA165 PT79 5k multi .50 .20
RA166 PT79 10k car, grn & gray 1.00 .20
*Nos. RA164-RA166 (3)* 1.70 .60

See Nos. RA208, RA211-RA213. For surcharges see Nos. RA187A-RA187B.

Florence Nightingale — PT80


Selimiye Barracks PT81

30k, Florence Nightingale, full-face.

**1954, Nov. 4**
**Crescent in Carmine**

RA167 PT80 20k gray grn & dk brn .50 .50
RA168 PT80 30k dl brn & blk .75 .50
RA169 PT81 50k buff & blk 1.25 .50
*Nos. RA167-RA169 (3)* 2.50 1.50

Arrival of Florence Nightingale at Scutari, cent.

Type of 1942 and

Children Kissing — PT82

Nurse Holding Baby — PT83

**1955, Apr. 23**
**Star in Red**

RA170 PT82 20pa chalky bl .20 .20
RA171 PT82 20pa org brn .20 .20
RA172 PT82 1k lilac .20 .20
RA173 PT82 3k gray bis .20 .20
RA174 PT82 5k orange .20 .20
RA175 PT12 10k green 2.50 .75
RA176 PT83 15k dk blue .25 .20
RA177 PT83 25k brn car 1.50 1.40
RA178 PT83 50k dk gray grn 2.00 1.50
RA179 PT12 2½ l dull brn 375.00 125.00
RA180 PT12 10 l rose lil 875.00 250.00
*Nos. RA170-RA180 (11)* 1,257. 379.85

Types of 1945
Inscribed: "Turkiye Kizilay Dernegi"

**1955 Litho. *Perf. 10½x11½, 10½***
**Crescent in Red**

RA181 PT36 20pa vio brn & lem .25 .25
RA182 PT41 1k blk & gray grn .25 .25

Nurse — PT85

Nurses on Parade PT86

Design: 100k, Two nurses under Red Cross and Red Crescent flags and UN emblem.

***Perf. 10½***

**1955, Sept. 5 Unwmk. Litho.**
**Crescent and Cross in Red**

RA183 PT85 10k blk & pale brn .75 .35
RA184 PT86 15k dk grn & pale yel grn .75 .45
RA185 PT85 100k lt ultra 3.50 1.75
*Nos. RA183-RA185 (3)* 5.00 2.55

Meeting of the board of directors of the Intl. Council of Nurses, Istanbul, Aug. 29-Sept. 5, 1955.

Nos. RA92 and RA130B Surcharged "20 Para"

**1955**

RA186 PT43 20p on 20k .50 .40

**Typo.**

RA187 PT74 20p on 100k (surch. 11½x2mm) .60 .40
c. Surcharge 13½x2½mm 1.00 .75

No. RA164 Surcharged with New Value and Two Bars

**1956 Litho. *Perf. 10½***

RA187A PT79 20p on 1k multi .25 .25
RA187B PT79 2.50k on 1k multi .25 .25

Woman and Children — PT87

Designs: 10k, 25k, 50k, Flag and building. 250k, 5 l, 10 l, Mother nursing baby.

**1956 Litho. *Perf. 10½***
**Star in Red**

RA188 PT87 20pa red org .50 .50
RA189 PT87 20pa gray grn .50 .50
RA190 PT87 1k purple .50 .50
RA191 PT87 1k grnsh bl .50 .50
RA192 PT87 3k lt red brn 1.00 .50
RA193 PT87 10k rose car 2.00 2.00
RA194 PT87 25k brt grn 4.00 2.00
RA195 PT87 50k brt ultra 6.00 2.50
RA196 PT87 250k red lilac 15.00 5.00
RA197 PT87 5 l sepia 35.00 15.00
RA198 PT87 10 l dk sl grn 57.50 30.00
*Nos. RA188-RA198 (11)* 122.50 59.00

Nos. RA131-RA138 Overprinted and Surcharged in Black or Red: "IV. DUNYA Cocuk Gunu 1 Ekim 1956"

**1956, Oct. 1 Unwmk. *Perf. 11***

RA199 PT75 20pa (R) 10.00 10.00
RA200 PT75 20pa 10.00 10.00
RA201 PT75 1k (R) 10.00 10.00
RA202 PT75 3k (R) 10.00 10.00
RA203 PT75 15k (R) 10.00 10.00
RA204 PT75 25k on 30k 10.00 10.00
RA205 PT75 100k on 150k (R) 12.00 12.00
RA206 PT75 250k on 300k 14.00 14.00
*Nos. RA199-RA206 (8)* 86.00 86.00

The tax was for child welfare.

Type of 1954, Redrawn Type of 1946, and

Flower PT88

Children PT89

**1957 Unwmk. *Perf. 10½***
**Crescent in Red**

RA207 PT88 ½k lt ol gray & brn .50 .20
RA208 PT79 1k ol bis, blk & grn .50 .20
RA209 PT88 2½k yel grn & bl grn .50 .20
RA210 PT43 20k red & lt bl 2.75 1.25
RA211 PT79 25k lt gray, blk & grn 2.75 1.25
RA212 PT79 50k bl, dk grn & grn 8.00 1.50
RA213 PT79 100k vio, blk & grn 8.75 3.00
*Nos. RA207-RA213 (7)* 23.75 7.60

No. RA210 inscribed "Turkiye Kizilay Cemiyeti." No. RA92 inscribed ". . . . Dernegi."

**1957 Unwmk. *Perf. 10½***

RA214 PT89 20pa car & red .20 .20
RA215 PT89 20pa grn & red .20 .20
RA216 PT89 1k ultra & car .20 .20
RA217 PT89 3k red org & car 1.50 1.50
*Nos. RA214-RA217 (4)* 2.10 2.10

"Blood Donor and Recipient" PT90

Child and Butterfly PT91

Designs: 75k, Figure showing blood circulation. 150k, Blood transfusion symbolism.

**1957, May 22**

**Size: 24x40mm**

| | | | | |
|---|---|---|---|---|
| **RA218** | PT90 | 25k gray, blk & red | .25 | .20 |

**Size: 22½x37½mm**

| | | | | |
|---|---|---|---|---|
| **RA219** | PT90 | 75k grn, blk & red | .50 | .30 |
| **RA220** | PT90 | 150k yel grn & red | 1.25 | .60 |
| | | *Nos. RA218-RA220 (3)* | 2.00 | 1.10 |

Redrawn Type of 1947

Inscribed: "V Dunya Cocuk Gunu"

**1957 Star in Red *Perf. 10½***

| | | | | |
|---|---|---|---|---|
| **RA221** | PT72 | 100k blk & bis brn | 1.25 | .75 |
| **RA222** | PT72 | 150k blk & yel grn | 1.25 | .75 |
| **RA223** | PT72 | 250k blk & vio | 2.50 | 1.00 |
| | | *Nos. RA221-RA223 (3)* | 5.00 | 2.50 |

The tax was for child welfare.

**1958 Litho. Unwmk.**

Various Butterflies. 50k, 75k horiz.

| | | | | |
|---|---|---|---|---|
| **RA224** | PT91 | 20k gray & red | .75 | .75 |
| **RA225** | PT91 | 25k multi | .75 | .75 |
| **RA226** | PT91 | 50k multi | 1.50 | 1.50 |
| **RA227** | PT91 | 75k grn, yel & blk | 2.00 | 2.00 |
| **RA228** | PT91 | 150k multi | 2.50 | 2.50 |
| | | *Nos. RA224-RA228 (5)* | 7.50 | 7.50 |

Florence Nightingale — PT92

**1958**

**Crescent in Red**

| | | | | |
|---|---|---|---|---|
| **RA229** | PT92 | 1 l bluish green | .40 | .25 |
| **RA230** | PT92 | 1½ l gray | .60 | .50 |
| **RA231** | PT92 | 2½ l blue | .80 | .60 |
| | | *Nos. RA229-RA231 (3)* | 1.80 | 1.35 |

Turkey stopped issuing postal tax stamps in June, 1958. Similar stamps of later date are private charity stamps issued by the Red Crescent Society and the Society for the Protection of Children.

## POSTAL TAX AIR POST STAMPS

### Air Fund Issues

These stamps were obligatory on all air mail for 21 days a year. Tax for the Turkish Aviation Society: 20pa for a postcard, 1k for a regular letter, 2 1/2k for a registered letter, 3k for a telegram, 5k-50k for a package, higher values for air freight. Postal tax air post stamps were withdrawn Aug. 21, 1934 and remainders destroyed later that year.

Biplane PTAP1

***Perf. 11, Pin Perf.***

**1926 Unwmk. Litho.**

**Type PTAP1**

**Size: 35x25mm**

| | | | |
|---|---|---|---|
| **RAC1** | 20pa brn & pale grn | 2.25 | .30 |
| **RAC2** | 1g blue grn & buff | 1.25 | .30 |

**Size: 40x29mm**

| | | | |
|---|---|---|---|
| **RAC3** | 5g vio & pale grn | 5.00 | 1.00 |
| **RAC4** | 5g car lake & pale grn | 25.00 | 15.00 |
| | *Nos. RAC1-RAC4 (4)* | 33.50 | 16.60 |
| | Set, never hinged | 275.00 | |

PTAP2

PTAP3

**1927-29**

**Type PTAP2**

| | | | |
|---|---|---|---|
| **RAC5** | 20pa dl red & pale grn | .50 | .20 |
| **RAC6** | 1k green & yel | .45 | .20 |

**Type PTAP3**

***Perf. 11½***

| | | | |
|---|---|---|---|
| **RAC7** | 2k dp cl & yel grn | .60 | .35 |
| **RAC8** | 2½k red & yel grn | 4.50 | 1.60 |
| **RAC9** | 5k dk bl gray & org | .45 | .45 |
| **RAC10** | 10k dk grn & rose | 3.75 | 1.25 |
| **RAC11** | 15k green & yel | 3.75 | 1.00 |
| **RAC12** | 20k ol brn & yel | 5.00 | 2.00 |
| **RAC13** | 50k dk bl & cob bl | 8.00 | 4.50 |
| **RAC14** | 100k car & lt bl | 110.00 | 80.00 |
| | *Nos. RAC5-RAC14 (10)* | 137.00 | 91.55 |
| | Set, never hinged | 825.00 | |

#RAC1, RAC5, RAC7 and RAC11 Surcharged in Black (RAC15-RAC16, RAC18-RAC19) or Red (Others)

**1930-31**

| | | | |
|---|---|---|---|
| **RAC15** | 1k ("Bir kurus") on RAC1 | 200.00 | 75.00 |
| **RAC16** | 1k ("Bir Kurus") on RAC5 | .75 | .50 |
| **RAC17** | 100pa ("Yuz Para") on RAC7 | 1.00 | .75 |
| **RAC18** | 5k ("Bes Kurus") on RAC5 | 5.00 | 1.50 |
| **RAC19** | 5k ("5 Kurus") on RAC5 | 1.00 | .75 |
| **RAC20** | 10k ("On kurus") on RAC7 | 1.50 | 1.25 |
| **RAC21** | 50k ("Elli kurus") on RAC7 | 8.00 | 4.00 |
| **RAC22** | 1 l ("Bir lira") on RAC7 | *25.00* | *9.00* |
| **RAC23** | 5 l ("Bes lira") on RAC11 | *2,000.* | *400.00* |
| | *Nos. RAC15-RAC23 (9)* | *2,242.* | *492.75* |
| | Set, never hinged | 5,000. | |

PTAP4

PTAP5

**1931-32 Litho. *Perf. 11½***

| | | | | |
|---|---|---|---|---|
| **RAC24** | PTAP4 | 20pa black | 5.00 | 1.75 |

**Typo.**

| | | | | |
|---|---|---|---|---|
| **RAC25** | PTAP5 | 1k brown car ('32) | 1.00 | .50 |
| **RAC26** | PTAP5 | 5k red ('32) | 2.00 | .75 |
| **RAC27** | PTAP5 | 10k green ('32) | 3.00 | 1.50 |
| | | *Nos. RAC24-RAC27 (4)* | 11.00 | 4.50 |

PTAP6

**1933**

**Type PTAP6**

| | | | |
|---|---|---|---|
| **RAC28** | 10pa ("On Para") grn | 3.50 | 2.00 |
| **RAC29** | 1k ("Bir Kurus") red | 8.00 | 2.75 |
| **RAC30** | 5k ("Bes Kurus") lil | 12.00 | 3.00 |
| | *Nos. RAC28-RAC30 (3)* | 23.50 | 7.75 |

# TURKEY IN ASIA

'tər-kē in 'ā-zhə

(Anatolia)

40 Paras = 1 Piaster

This designation, which includes all of Turkey in Asia Minor, came into existence during the uprising of 1919, led by Mustafa Kemal Pasha. Actually there was no separation of territory, the Sultan's sovereignty being almost immediately reduced to a small area surrounding Constantinople. The formation of the Turkish Republic and the expulsion of the Sultan followed in 1923. Subsequent issues of postage stamps are listed under Turkey (Republic).

### Issues of the Nationalist Government

Turkish Stamps of 1913-18 Surcharged in Black or Red

(The Surcharge reads "Angora 3 Piastres")

**1920 Unwmk. *Perf. 12***

**On Stamps of 1913**

| | | | | |
|---|---|---|---|---|
| **1** | A24 | 3pi on 2pa red lilac | 2.50 | 3.50 |
| **2** | A25 | 3pi on 4pa dk brn | 37.50 | *37.50* |
| **3** | A27 | 3pi on 6pa dk bl | 250.00 | *150.00* |

**On Stamp of 1916-18**

| | | | | |
|---|---|---|---|---|
| **4** | A42 | 3pi on 2pa vio (Bk) | 15.00 | 10.00 |
| | | *Nos. 1-4 (4)* | 305.00 | 201.00 |

Turkish Stamps of 1913-18 Handstamped in Black or Red

(The Surch. reads "Post, Piastre 3")

**1921 *Perf. 12***

**On Stamps of 1913**

| | | | | |
|---|---|---|---|---|
| **5** | A24 | 3pi on 2pa red lilac | 25.00 | 25.00 |
| *a.* | | On No. 1 | 45.00 | 67.50 |
| **6** | A25 | 3pi on 4pa dk brown | 30.00 | 30.00 |
| *a.* | | On No. 2 | 150.00 | 160.00 |
| **7** | A25 | 3pi on 4pa dk brn (R) | 150.00 | 175.00 |
| *a.* | | On No. 2 | 150.00 | 160.00 |
| **8** | A27 | 3pi on 6pa dk blue | 125.00 | 150.00 |
| *a.* | | On No. 3 | 275.00 | 300.00 |
| **9** | A27 | 3pi on 6pa dk bl (R) | 62.50 | 75.00 |
| *a.* | | On No. 3 | 100.00 | 125.00 |

**On Stamps of 1916-18**

| | | | | |
|---|---|---|---|---|
| **10** | A42 | 3pi on 2pa vio (R) | 62.50 | 75.00 |
| *a.* | | On No. 4 | 90.00 | 110.00 |
| | | *Nos. 5-10 (6)* | 455.00 | 530.00 |

**Turkish Revenue Stamps Handstamped in Turkish "Osmanli Postalari, 1336" (Ottoman Post, 1920).**

عثمانلی پوسته لری
١٣٣٦

Dash at upper left is set high. Bottom (date) line is 8½mm long.

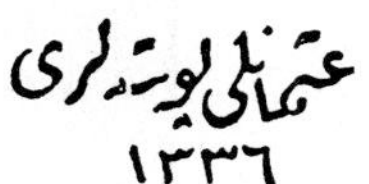

Dash at upper left is set lower. Bottom (date) line is 10mm long.

عثمانلی پوسته لری
١٣٣٦

Dash at upper left is set lower. Bottom (date) line is 9mm long.

Religious Tribunals Revenue — R1

| | | | | |
|---|---|---|---|---|
| **12** | R1 | 1pi green (a, b, c) | 750.00 | 300.00 |
| **13** | R1 | 5pi ultra (a, b) | *16,000.* | *15,500.* |
| **14** | R1 | 50pi gray grn (a, b, c) | 25.00 | 35.00 |
| | | Cut cancellation | | 1.50 |
| **15** | R1 | 100pi buff (a) | 140.00 | 90.00 |
| *a.* | | 100pi yellow (a) | 90.00 | 67.50 |
| | | Cut cancellation | | 7.50 |
| **16** | R1 | 500pi orange (a) | 225.00 | 150.00 |
| | | Cut cancellation | | 19.00 |
| **17** | R1 | 1000pi brown (a) | 3,000. | *1,750.* |
| | | Cut cancellation | | 175.00 |

See Nos. 29-32.

Court Costs Revenue — R2

Black Overprint

| | | | | |
|---|---|---|---|---|
| **18** | R2 | 10pa green (b, c) | 110.00 | 100.00 |
| **19** | R2 | 1pi ultra (a, c) | — | *15,000.* |
| **20** | R2 | 5pi rose (c) | *15,000.* | — |
| **21** | R2 | 50pi ocher (a, b, c) | 50.00 | 50.00 |
| *a.* | | 50pi yellow (a, b, c) | 12.00 | 16.00 |
| | | Cut cancellation, #21, 21a | | 2.00 |
| **22** | R2 | 100pi brown (a) | 150.00 | 100.00 |
| | | Cut cancellation | | 20.00 |
| **23** | R2 | 500pi slate (a) | 325.00 | 325.00 |
| | | Cut cancellation | | 20.00 |

See Nos. 24, 33-39.

Notary Public Revenue R3

Design R2 Overprinted "Katibi Adliye Masus dur" in Red

| | | | | |
|---|---|---|---|---|
| **24** | R3 | 50pi ocher (a) | 1,250. | 150.00 |
| | | Cut cancellation | | 20.00 |

Laborer's Passport Tax Stamp — R4

Notary Public Revenue — R5

Black Overprint

**25** R4 2pi emerald (a, c) — *20,000.*
**26** R5 100pi yellow brn (a) 1,250. 150.00
Cut cancellation 20.00

See Nos. 46-48.

Theater Tax Stamp — R6

Land Registry Revenue — R7

**27** R6 20pa black *5,000.* *5,000.*
**28** R7 2pi blue black *6,250.* *6,250.*

See Nos. 40, 45.

Hejaz Railway Tax Stamp — R8

***Perf. 11½***

**28A** R8 2pi dk red & bl (b) 1,750. *1,750.*

**Turkish Revenue Stamps Overprinted in Turkish "Osmanli Postalari, 1337" (Ottoman Post, 1921)**

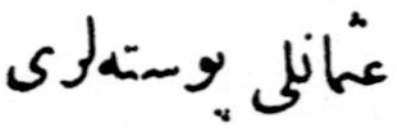


١٣٣٧ On #29-63

***Perf. 12***

**29** R1 10pa slate 16.00 13.50
*a.* Handstamped overprint 100.00 *50.00*
*b.* Double overprint
**30** R1 1pi green 27.50 18.00
*a.* Inverted overprint 35.00 22.50
*b.* Handstamped overprint *3,250.* *3,250.*
**31** R1 5pi ultra 27.50 13.50
*a.* "1337" inverted 100.00 90.00
*b.* Half used as 2½pi on cover
*c.* Handstamped overprint 875.00 875.00
*Nos. 29-31 (3)* 71.00 45.00

**Handstamped Overprint**

**32** R1 50pi green *6,250.* *6,250.*

Design R2 Overprinted

**33** R2 10pa green 22.50 22.50
*a.* Handstamped overprint 3,500. *3,500.*
**34** R2 1pi ultra 45.00 22.50
*a.* Handstamped overprint 875.00 875.00
**35** R2 5pi red 22.50 22.50
*a.* Inverted overprint
*b.* "1337" inverted *100.00* 100.00
*c.* Half used as 2½pi on cover
*d.* Handstamped overprint 6,750. 6,750.

**36** R2 50pi ocher, handtamped ovpt. 500.00 100.00
Cut cancellation 10.00
*Nos. 33-36 (4)* 590.00 167.50

Design R3 Overprinted
Additional Turkish Overprint in Red or Black

**37** R3 10pa green (R) *90.00* 57.50
**38** R3 1pi ultra (R) 67.50 45.00
**39** R3 5pi rose (Bk) 67.50 45.00
*a.* "1337" inverted *200.00* *200.00*
*b.* Handstamped overprint *6,250.* *6,250.*
*Nos. 37-39 (3)* 225.00 147.50

Design R7 Overprinted

**40** R7 2pi blue black 110.00 100.00
*a.* Handstamped overprint *5,000.* *5,000.*

R12

**1921** ***Perf. 12***

**Overprinted in Black**

**41** R12 5pi green 150.00 125.00
Cut cancellation 15.00
*a.* Handstamped overprint *5,000.* *5,000.*

Museum Tax Stamp R13

**Overprinted in Black**

**42** R13 1pi ultra 400.00 400.00
*a.* Handstamped overprint *5,000.* *5,000.*
**43** R13 5pi deep green 450.00 450.00
*a.* Handstamped overprint *5,000.* *5,000.*

**Handstamped Overprint**

**44** R13 5pi dark vio *6,250.* *6,250.*

The overprint variety "337" for "1337" exists on Nos. 42-43.

Design R6 Overprinted
***Perf. 12, 12½***

**45** R6 20pa black 12.50 4.25
*a.* Date 4½mm high 15.00
*b.* "337" for "1337" 25.00

Design R5 Overprinted

**46** R5 10pa green 25.00 25.00
*a.* Overprint 21mm long
*b.* "131" for "1337"
**47** R5 1pi ultra 37.50 25.00
*a.* "13" for "1337" *50.00* *50.00*
*b.* "131" for "1337" *50.00* *50.00*
*c.* Inverted overprint *90.00* *90.00*
*d.* Handstamped overprint *4,000.* *4,000.*
**48** R5 5pi red 62.50 25.00
*a.* Inverted overprint *90.00* *90.00*
*b.* "131" for "1337" *85.00* *85.00*
*c.* Handstamped overprint *4,000.* *4,000.*
*Nos. 46-48 (3)* 125.00 75.00

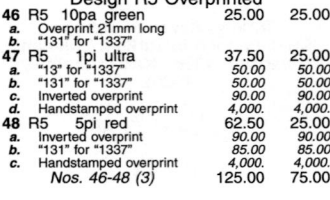

R16

***Perf. 11½, 11½x11***

**Overprinted in Black**

**49** R16 10pa pink 4.00 1.50
*a.* Imperf.
*b.* Date "1237" 5.00 2.00
*d.* Inverted overprint
*e.* Handstamped overprint *1,750.* *1,750.*
**50** R16 1pi yellow 10.00 5.00
*a.* Overprint 18mm long 10.00 5.00
*b.* Date "1332" 12.00
*c.* Date "1317"
*d.* Inverted overprint
*e.* Handstamped overprint *1,750.* *1,750.*
**51** R16 2pi yellow grn 12.50 5.00
*a.* Date "1237" 15.00
*b.* Date "1317"
*c.* Imperf.
*d.* Inverted overprint 40.00 9.00
*e.* Handstamped overprint — —
**52** R16 5pi red 20.00 1.00
*a.* Horiz. pair, imperf. vert.
*b.* Inverted overprint 25.00 7.50
*c.* Double overprint 30.00 12.50
*d.* Date "1332" 45.00
*e.* Half used as 2½pi on cover
*f.* Overprint 18mm long 20.00 7.50
*g.* Handstamped overprint *1,750.* *1,750.*
*Nos. 49-52 (4)* 46.50 12.50

Design R8 Overprinted
TURKISH INSCRIPTIONS:

20 Paras 1 Piaster

2 Piasters

5 Piasters

**1921** ***Perf. 11½***

**Dark Red & Blue**

**53** R8 20pa on 1pi 75.00 75.00
**54** R8 1pi on 1pi 4.00 3.00
**55** R8 2pi on 1pi 4.00 3.00
*a.* Inverted surcharge
**56** R8 5pi on 1pi 6.00 5.00
*Nos. 53-56 (4)* 89.00 86.00

See No. 57.

No. 54 Overprinted

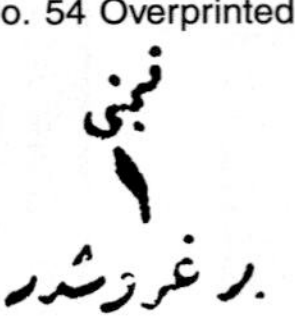


**57** R8 1pi on 1pi dk red & bl 45.00 45.00

Hejaz Railway Tax Stamp — R19

**Overprinted in Black**

**58** R19 1pi grn & brn red 4.00 3.00
*a.* Double overprint
*b.* Handstamped overprint

The errors "1307," "1331" and "2337" occur once in each sheet of Nos. 53-58.

Naval League Labels — R20

**1921** ***Perf. 12x11½***

**Overprinted in Black**

**59** R20 1pa orange 10.00 15.00
*a.* Date "1327" 15.00 3.50
**60** R20 2pa indigo 10.00 15.00
**61** R20 5pa green 12.50 17.50
**62** R20 10pa brown 25.00 30.00
**63** R20 40pa red brown 175.00 190.00
*Nos. 59-63 (5)* 232.50 267.50

The error "2337" occurs on all values of this issue.

The Naval League stamps have pictures of three Turkish warships. They were sold for the benefit of sailors of the fleet but did not pay postage until they were overprinted in 1921.

Turkish Stamps of 1915-20 Overprinted

a

اطنه
١ كانون اول
١٣٣٧

b

The overprints on Nos. 64-77 read "Adana December 1st, 1921." This issue commemorated the withdrawal of the French from Cilicia.

On No. 71 the lines of the overprint are further apart than on Nos. 68-70 and 73-74.

**1921** ***Perf. 12***

**64** A44 (a) 10pa grn (424) 6.00 6.00
**65** A45 (a) 20pa deep rose (425) 6.00 6.00
*a.* Inverted overprint 17.00
**66** A51 (a) 25pi car, *straw* (434) 15.00 20.00
*a.* Double overprint
*b.* Inverted overprint 37.50 37.50
*Nos. 64-66 (3)* 27.00 32.00

**On Newspaper Stamp of 1915**

**67** A21 (a) 5pa och (P132) 90.00 150.00

**On Stamp of 1915**

**68** A22 (b) 5pa och (328) 350.00 400.00

**On Stamps of 1917-18**

**69** A53 (b) 5pi on 2pa (547) 12.50 15.00
**70** A53 (b) 5pi on 2pa (548) 12.50 15.00

**On Stamp of 1919**

**71** A57 (b) 35pi on 1pi bl (Bk; 579) 40.00 45.00
*a.* Inverted surcharge

**On Newspaper Stamp of 1915**

**72** A21 (b) 5pa och (P132) *200.00* *200.00*

On No. 72 the overprint is vertical, half reading up and half reading down.

**On Stamps of 1920**

**73** A32 (b) 3pi blue (594) 10.00 10.00
**74** A36 (b) 10pi gray vio (596) 12.50 15.00

**On Postage Due Stamps of 1914**

**75** D1 (a) 5pa claret (J63) 350.00 350.00
**76** D2 (a) 20pa red (J64) 350.00 400.00
*a.* Inverted overprint
**77** D3 (b) 1pi dk bl (J65) 350.00 400.00
*a.* Inverted overprint *750.00* *750.00*
*Nos. 75-77 (3)* 1,050. 1,150.

Withdrawal of the French from Cilicia. Forged overprints exist.

Pact of Revenge, Burning Village at Top — A21

Izmir Harbor — A22

Mosque of Selim, Adrianople A23

Mosque of Selim, Konya — A24

Soldier — A25

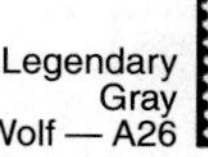

Legendary Gray Wolf — A26

Snake Castle and Seyhan River, Adana — A27

Parliament Building at Sivas — A28

A29

Mosque at Urfa — A30

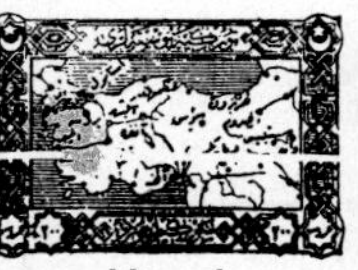

Map of Anatolia — A31

Declaration of Faith from the Koran — A32

**1922** **Litho.** ***Perf. 11½***

| | | | | | |
|---|---|---|---|---|---|
| **78** | A21 | 10pa | violet brn | 1.00 | .25 |
| **79** | A22 | 20pa | blue grn | 1.00 | .25 |
| **80** | A23 | 1pi | dp blue | 1.00 | .25 |
| **81** | A24 | 2pi | red brown | 3.00 | .50 |
| **82** | A25 | 5pi | dk blue | 3.00 | .50 |
| **83** | A26 | 10pi | dk brown | 12.50 | .75 |
| **84** | A27 | 25pi | rose | 15.00 | 1.00 |
| **85** | A28 | 50pi | indigo | 1.00 | 15.00 |
| **86** | A29 | 50pi | dk gray | 1.00 | 1.25 |
| **87** | A30 | 100pi | violet | 75.00 | 5.00 |
| | | | Cut cancellation | | 1.25 |
| **88** | A31 | 200pi | slate | 200.00 | 62.50 |
| | | | Cut cancellation | | 1.50 |
| **89** | A32 | 500pi | green | 125.00 | 27.50 |
| | | | Cut cancellation | | 3.00 |
| | | | *Nos. 78-89 (12)* | 438.50 | 114.75 |
| | | | Set, never hinged | 2,000. | |

***Imperf***

| | | | | |
|---|---|---|---|---|
| *79a* | A22 | 20pa | 25.00 | *30.00* |
| *80a* | A23 | 1pi | 15.00 | *20.00* |
| *82a* | A25 | 5pi | 15.00 | *20.00* |
| *84a* | A27 | 25pi | 35.00 | *30.00* |
| *85a* | A28 | 50pi | 27.50 | *30.00* |

Stamps of Type A23 Overprinted

**1922**

| | | | | | |
|---|---|---|---|---|---|
| **90** | A23 | 1pi | deep blue | 7.00 | 15.00 |
| **91** | A23 | 5pi | deep blue | 7.00 | 20.00 |
| **92** | A23 | 10pi | brown | 7.00 | 20.00 |
| **93** | A23 | 25pi | rose | 10.00 | 25.00 |
| **94** | A23 | 50pi | slate | 12.50 | 25.00 |
| **95** | A23 | 100pi | violet | 17.50 | 37.50 |
| **96** | A23 | 200pi | black vio | 17.50 | 50.00 |
| **97** | A23 | 500pi | blue green | 25.00 | 75.00 |
| | | | *Nos. 90-97 (8)* | 103.50 | |
| | | | Set, never hinged | 200.00 | |

Withdrawal of the French from Cilicia and the return of the Kemalist Natl. army. The overprint reads: "Adana, Jan. 5, 1922."

No. 90-97 without overprint were presented to some high government officials.

First Parliament House, Ankara — A33

**1922** **Litho.**

| | | | | | |
|---|---|---|---|---|---|
| **98** | A33 | 5pa | violet | .50 | 2.50 |
| **99** | A33 | 10pa | green | 1.00 | 2.50 |
| **100** | A33 | 20pa | pale red | 1.50 | 2.00 |
| **101** | A33 | 1pi | brown org | 10.00 | 1.50 |
| **102** | A33 | 2pi | red brown | 20.00 | 4.25 |
| **103** | A33 | 3pi | rose | 2.50 | .50 |
| ***a.*** | | | Arabic "13" in right corner | 10.00 | 7.50 |
| ***b.*** | | | Thin grayish paper | 55.00 | 7.50 |
| | | | *Nos. 98-103 (6)* | 35.50 | 13.25 |
| | | | Set, never hinged | 90.00 | |

Nos. 98-103, 103b exist imperf. In 1923 several stamps of Turkey and Turkey in Asia were overprinted in Turkish for advertising purposes. The overprint reads: "Izmir Economic Congress, 17 Feb., 1339."

## POSTAGE DUE STAMPS

D1

**1922** **Litho.** ***Perf. 11½***

| | | | | | |
|---|---|---|---|---|---|
| **J1** | D1 | 20pa | dull green | .50 | 5.00 |
| ***a.*** | | | Imperf. | | — |
| **J2** | D1 | 1pi | gray green | .50 | 5.00 |
| **J3** | D1 | 2pi | red brown | 1.50 | 17.50 |
| **J4** | D1 | 3pi | rose | 3.50 | 25.00 |
| **J5** | D1 | 5pi | dark blue | 4.50 | 55.00 |
| | | | *Nos. J1-J5 (5)* | 10.50 | |
| | | | Set, never hinged | 55.00 | |

# TURKISH REPUBLIC OF NORTHERN CYPRUS

'tər-kish ri-'pə-blik of 'nor-thə,r,n 'sī-prəs

LOCATION — Northern 40% of the Island of Cyprus in the Mediterranean Sea off the coast of Turkey.

Established following Turkish invasion of Cyprus in 1974. On Nov. 15, 1983 Turkey declared the Turkish Republic of Northern Cyprus to be independent. No other country has recognized this country.

1000 Milliemes = 1 Pound
100 Kurus = 1 Turkish Lira (1978)

**Catalogue values for all unused stamps in this country are for Never Hinged items.**

Letters bearing these stamps enter international mail via the Turkish Post Office.

**Watermark**

Wmk. 390

Republic of Turkey, 50th Anniv.
A1 A2

Designs: 3m, Woman sentry. 5m, Military parade. 10m, Flag bearers. 15m, Anniversary emblem. 20m, Ataturk statue. 50m, Painting, "The Fallen." 70m, Turkish flag, map of Cyprus.

***Perf. 12x11½, 11½x12***

**1974, July 27** **Litho.** **Unwmk.**

| | | | | | |
|---|---|---|---|---|---|
| **1** | A1 | 3m | multicolored | 37.50 | 37.50 |
| **2** | A2 | 5m | multicolored | .35 | .20 |
| **3** | A1 | 10m | multicolored | .50 | .20 |
| **4** | A2 | 15m | multicolored | .60 | .50 |
| **5** | A1 | 20m | multicolored | .70 | .70 |
| **6** | A1 | 50m | multicolored | 3.00 | 2.75 |
| **7** | A2 | 70m | multicolored | 27.50 | 15.00 |
| | | | *Nos. 1-7 (7)* | 70.15 | 56.85 |

First day covers are dated 1/29/73.

Nos. 5, 3 Surcharged

**1975, Mar. 3** ***Perf. 12x11½***

| | | | | | |
|---|---|---|---|---|---|
| **8** | A1 | 30m on 20m, #5 | | *1.25* | *1.00* |
| **9** | A1 | 100m on 10m, #3 | | *3.00* | *2.25* |

Surcharge appears in different positions.

Historical Sites and Landmarks A3

Designs: 3m, Namik Kemal's bust, Famagusta. 5m, 30m, Kyrenia Harbor. 10m, Ataturk Statue, Nicosia. 15m, St. Hilarion Castle. 20m, Ataturk Square, Nicosia. 25m, Coastline, Famagusta. 50m, Lala Mustafa Pasha Mosque, Famagusta vert. 100m, Kyrenia Castle. 250m, Kyrenia Castle, exterior walls. 500m, Othello Tower, Famagusta vert.

**1975-76** ***Perf. 13***

| | | | | | |
|---|---|---|---|---|---|
| **10** | A3 | 3m | pink & multi | .40 | .30 |
| **11** | A3 | 5m | bl & multi | .40 | .30 |
| **12** | A3 | 10m | pink & multi | .45 | .40 |
| **13** | A3 | 15m | pink & multi | .50 | .40 |
| **14** | A3 | 15m | bl & multi | .50 | .40 |
| **15** | A3 | 20m | pink & multi | 3.00 | .40 |
| **16** | A3 | 20m | bl & multi | .40 | .40 |
| **17** | A3 | 25m | pink & multi | .60 | .50 |
| **18** | A3 | 30m | pink & multi | .90 | .75 |
| **19** | A3 | 50m | pink & multi | 1.50 | 1.00 |
| **20** | A3 | 100m | pink & multi | 1.75 | 1.25 |
| **21** | A3 | 250m | pink & multi | 2.50 | 1.75 |
| **22** | A3 | 500m | pink & multi | 3.50 | 3.00 |
| | | | *Nos. 10-22 (13)* | 16.40 | 10.85 |

Issued: #10, 12-13, 15, 17-22, 4/21; #11, 14, 16, 8/2/76. #1, 14, 16 have different inscriptions and "1976."

For surcharges see Nos. 28-29.

Peace in Cyprus — A4

Designs: 50m, Map, olive branch, severed chain. 150m, Map, globe, olive branch, vert.

**1975, July 20** ***Perf. 13½x13, 13x13½***

| | | | | | |
|---|---|---|---|---|---|
| **23** | A4 | 30m | multicolored | .40 | .25 |
| **24** | A4 | 50m | multicolored | .50 | .35 |
| **25** | A4 | 150m | multicolored | 1.10 | 1.00 |
| | | | *Nos. 23-25 (3)* | 2.00 | 1.60 |

Europa — A5

Paintings: 90m, Pomegranates by I.V. Guney. 100m, Harvest Time by F. Direkoglu.

**1975, Dec. 29** ***Perf. 13***

| | | | | | |
|---|---|---|---|---|---|
| **26** | A5 | 90m | multicolored | *2.00* | *1.00* |
| **27** | A5 | 100m | multicolored | *3.00* | *1.50* |

Nos. 19, 20 Surcharged

**1976, Apr. 28** ***Perf. 13***

| | | | | |
|---|---|---|---|---|
| **28** | A3 | 10m on 50m, #19 | .50 | .50 |
| **29** | A3 | 30m on 100m, #20 | 1.25 | 1.25 |

Europa — A6

Olympic Games, Montreal — A8

Fruits — A7

**1976, May 3**

| | | | | | |
|---|---|---|---|---|---|
| **30** | A6 | 60m | Expectation | *.75* | *.30* |
| **31** | A6 | 120m | Man in Meditation | *1.50* | *.65* |

**1976, June 28**

| | | | | | |
|---|---|---|---|---|---|
| **32** | A7 | 10m | Ceratonia siliqua | .20 | .20 |
| **33** | A7 | 25m | Citrus nobilis | .30 | .20 |
| **34** | A7 | 40m | Fragaria vesca | .40 | .20 |
| **35** | A7 | 60m | Citrus sinensis | .50 | .30 |
| **36** | A7 | 80m | Citrus limon | .75 | .45 |
| | | | *Nos. 32-36 (5)* | 2.15 | 1.35 |

For surcharges see Nos. 66-69.

**1976, July 17**

Design: 100m, Olympic rings, doves, horiz.

| | | | | | |
|---|---|---|---|---|---|
| **37** | A8 | 60m | multicolored | .40 | .20 |
| **38** | A8 | 100m | multicolored | .70 | .35 |

Liberation Monument — A9

**1976, Nov. 1** *Perf. 13x13½*

| | | | | |
|---|---|---|---|---|
| **39** | A9 | 30m multi | .30 | .20 |
| **40** | A9 | 150m multi, diff. | .65 | .45 |

Europa — A10

**1977, May 2** *Perf. 13*

| | | | | |
|---|---|---|---|---|
| **41** | A10 | 80m Salamis Bay | *2.00* | *.75* |
| **42** | A10 | 100m Kyrenia Port | *3.00* | *1.25* |

Handicrafts A11

**1977, June 27**

| | | | | |
|---|---|---|---|---|
| **43** | A11 | 15m Pottery | .20 | .20 |
| **44** | A11 | 30m Gourds, vert. | .20 | .20 |
| **45** | A11 | 125m Baskets | .30 | .30 |
| | | *Nos. 43-45 (3)* | .70 | .70 |

Landmarks A12

Designs: 20m, Arap Ahmet Pasha Mosque, Nicosia, vert. 40m, Paphos Castle. 70m, Bekir Pasha aqueduct, Larnaca. 80m, Sultan Mahmut library, Nicosia.

**1977, Dec. 2** *Perf. 13x13½, 13½x13*

| | | | | |
|---|---|---|---|---|
| **46** | A12 | 20m multicolored | .20 | .20 |
| **47** | A12 | 40m multicolored | .30 | .20 |
| **48** | A12 | 70m multicolored | .40 | .25 |
| **49** | A12 | 80m multicolored | .60 | .40 |
| | | *Nos. 46-49 (4)* | 1.50 | 1.05 |

Namik Kemal (1840-1888), Writer — A13

**1977, Dec. 21** *Perf. 13*

| | | | | |
|---|---|---|---|---|
| **50** | A13 | 30m Bust, home | .20 | .20 |
| **51** | A13 | 140m Portrait, vert. | .50 | .50 |

Social Security — A14

Europa — A15

Designs: 275k, Man with sling, crutch. 375k, Woman with children.

**1978, Apr. 17** *Perf. 13x13½*

| | | | | |
|---|---|---|---|---|
| **52** | A14 | 150k blk, bl & yel | .30 | .20 |
| **53** | A14 | 275k blk, grn & red org | .40 | .20 |
| **54** | A14 | 375k blk, red org & bl | .70 | .25 |
| | | *Nos. 52-54 (3)* | 1.40 | .65 |

**1978, May 2** *Perf. 13x13½, 13½x13*

225k, Oratory in Buyuk Han, Nicosia. 450k, Reservoir, Selimiye Mosque, Nicosia.

| | | | | |
|---|---|---|---|---|
| **55** | A15 | 225k multi | *3.25* | *1.00* |
| **56** | A15 | 450k multi, horiz. | *6.50* | *1.50* |

Transportation A16

**1978, July 10** *Perf. 13½x13*

| | | | | |
|---|---|---|---|---|
| **57** | A16 | 75k Roadway | .30 | .20 |
| **58** | A16 | 100k Hydrofoil | .40 | .20 |
| **59** | A16 | 650k Airplane | .70 | .70 |
| | | *Nos. 57-59 (3)* | 1.40 | 1.10 |

National Oath — A17

Kemal Ataturk — A18

**1978, Sept. 13**

| | | | | |
|---|---|---|---|---|
| **60** | A17 | 150k Dove, olive branch | .25 | .20 |
| **61** | A17 | 225k Stylized pen, vert. | .35 | .20 |
| **62** | A17 | 725k Stylized dove | .65 | .65 |
| | | *Nos. 60-62 (3)* | 1.25 | 1.05 |

**1978, Nov. 10**

| | | | | |
|---|---|---|---|---|
| **63** | A18 | 75k bl grn & lt grn | .20 | .20 |
| **64** | A18 | 450k brn & buff | .20 | .20 |
| **65** | A18 | 650k Prus bl & lt bl | .30 | .30 |
| | | *Nos. 63-65 (3)* | .70 | .70 |

Nos. 33-36 Surcharged

**1979, June 4**

| | | | | |
|---|---|---|---|---|
| **66** | A7 | 50k on 25m | .25 | .20 |
| **67** | A7 | 1 l on 40m | .30 | .20 |
| **68** | A7 | 3 l on 60m | .25 | .20 |
| **69** | A7 | 5 l on 80m | .50 | .25 |
| | | *Nos. 66-69 (4)* | 1.30 | .85 |

Souvenir Sheet

Turkish Invasion of Cyprus, 5th Anniv. — A19

Illustration reduced.

**1979, July 2** *Imperf.*

| | | | | |
|---|---|---|---|---|
| **70** | A19 | 15 l multicolored | 3.50 | 3.25 |

Europa A20

Communications: 3 l, Stamps, building, map. 8 l, Early and modern telephones, globe, satellite.

**1979, Aug. 20** **Litho.** *Perf. 13*

| | | | | |
|---|---|---|---|---|
| **71** | A20 | 2 l multicolored | *1.50* | *.40* |
| **72** | A20 | 3 l multicolored | *2.00* | *.65* |
| **73** | A20 | 8 l multicolored | *4.25* | *1.00* |
| | | *Nos. 71-73 (3)* | 7.75 | 2.05 |

Intl. Consultative Radio Committee, 50th Anniv. — A21

**1979, Sept. 24**

| | | | | |
|---|---|---|---|---|
| **74** | A21 | 2 l blue & multi | .20 | .20 |
| **75** | A21 | 5 l gray & multi | .25 | .20 |
| **76** | A21 | 6 l green & multi | .35 | .30 |
| | | *Nos. 74-76 (3)* | .80 | .70 |

Intl. Year of the Child A22

Childrens' drawings of children.

**1979, Oct. 29**

| | | | | |
|---|---|---|---|---|
| **77** | A22 | 1½ l multi, vert. | .20 | .20 |
| **78** | A22 | 4½ l multicolored | .35 | .30 |
| **79** | A22 | 6 l multi, vert. | .45 | .40 |
| | | *Nos. 77-79 (3)* | 1.00 | .90 |

Press reports in Jan. 1980 state that the 1979 UPU Congress declared Turkish Cyprus stamps invalid for international mail.

A23

Europa — A24

Anniv. and events: 2½ l, Lala Mustafa Pasha Mosque, Famagusta. 10 l, Arap Ahmet Pasha Mosque, Lefkosa. 20 l, Holy Kaaba, Mosque.

**1980, Mar. 23**

| | | | | |
|---|---|---|---|---|
| **80** | A23 | 2½ l multicolored | .25 | .20 |
| **81** | A23 | 10 l multicolored | .45 | .25 |
| **82** | A23 | 20 l multicolored | .70 | .70 |
| | | *Nos. 80-82 (3)* | 1.40 | 1.15 |

1st Islamic Conference in Turkish Cyprus (2½ l). General Assembly of World Islam Congress (10 l). Moslem year 1400 AH (20 l).

**1980, May 23**

| | | | | |
|---|---|---|---|---|
| **83** | A24 | 5 l Ebu-Suud Efendi | *.75* | *.40* |
| **84** | A24 | 30 l Sultan Selim II | *2.50* | *.80* |

Historic Landmarks A25

Designs: 2½ l, Omer's Shrine, Kyrenia. 3½ l, Entrance gate, Famagusta. 5 l, Funerary monuments, Famagusta. 10 l, Bella Paise Abbey, Kyrenia. 20 l, Selimiye Mosque, Nicosia.

**1980, June 25**

**Blue Paper**

| | | | | |
|---|---|---|---|---|
| **85** | A25 | 2½ l buff & Prus bl | .20 | .20 |
| **86** | A25 | 3½ l pale pink & dk grn | .20 | .20 |
| **87** | A25 | 5 l pale bl grn & dk car | .20 | .20 |
| **88** | A25 | 10 l lt grn & red lil | .25 | .20 |
| **89** | A25 | 20 l buff & dk bl | .40 | .35 |
| | | *Nos. 85-89 (5)* | 1.25 | 1.15 |

For overprints and surcharges see Nos. 198-200.

Cyprus Postage Stamps, Cent. A26

**1980, Aug. 16**

| | | | | |
|---|---|---|---|---|
| **90** | A26 | 7½ l No. 5, vert. | .25 | .20 |
| **91** | A26 | 15 l No. 199 | .35 | .20 |
| **92** | A26 | 50 l Social welfare, vert. | .90 | .80 |
| | | *Nos. 90-92 (3)* | 1.50 | 1.20 |

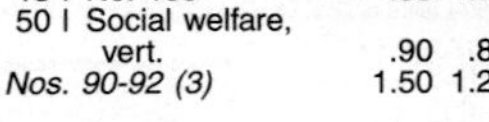

Palestinian Solidarity A27

15 l, Dome of the Rock, entrance, vert.

**1980, Mar. 24**

| | | | | |
|---|---|---|---|---|
| **93** | A27 | 15 l multicolored | .30 | .25 |
| **94** | A27 | 35 l multicolored | .75 | .60 |

World Muslim Congress Statement — A28

**1981, Mar. 24**

| | | | | |
|---|---|---|---|---|
| **95** | A28 | 1 l In Turkish | .20 | .20 |
| **96** | A28 | 35 l In English | .75 | .65 |

Ataturk by Feyhamam Duran — A29

**1981, May 19**

| | | | | |
|---|---|---|---|---|
| **97** | A29 | 20 l multicolored | .65 | .65 |

Printed with se-tenant label promoting Ataturk Stamp Exhibition.

Europa A30

Folk dances.

**1981, June 29**

| | | | | |
|---|---|---|---|---|
| **98** | A30 | 10 l multicolored | *.75* | *.40* |
| **99** | A30 | 30 l multi, diff. | *2.00* | *1.00* |

Souvenir Sheet

Ataturk, Birth Cent. — A31

Illustration reduced.

**1981, July 23** *Imperf.*

| | | | |
|---|---|---|---|
| **100** | A31 150 l multicolored | 2.25 | 1.75 |

No. 100 has simulated perfs.

Flowers A32

Designs: 1 l, Convolvulus althaeoides, vert. 5 l, Cyclamen persicum. 10 l, Mandragara officinarum. 25 l, Papaver rhoeas, vert. 30 l, Arum dioscoridis, vert. 50 l, Chrysanthemum segetum. 100 l, Cistus salyiaefolius, vert. 150 l, Ferula communis.

**1981-82** *Perf. 13*

| | | | | |
|---|---|---|---|---|
| **101** | A32 | 1 l multicolored | .20 | .20 |
| **102** | A32 | 5 l multicolored | .20 | .20 |
| **103** | A32 | 10 l multicolored | .25 | .25 |
| **104** | A32 | 25 l multicolored | .40 | .40 |
| **105** | A32 | 30 l multicolored | .45 | .45 |
| **106** | A32 | 50 l multicolored | .75 | .75 |
| **107** | A32 | 100 l multicolored | 1.50 | 1.50 |
| **108** | A32 | 150 l multicolored | 2.25 | 2.25 |
| | | *Nos. 101-108 (8)* | 6.00 | 6.00 |

Issue dates: 1 l, 10 l, 25 l, 150 l, Sept. 28; 5 l, 30 l, 50 l, 100 l, Jan. 22, 1982.

For surcharge & overprints see #138-141, 201.

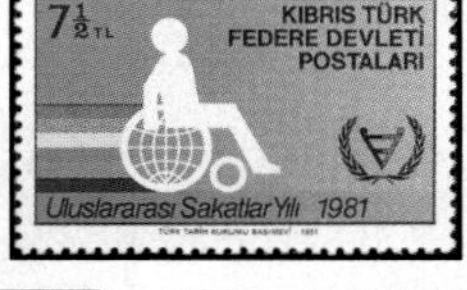


Intl. Year for Disabled Persons A33

Fight Against Apartheid — A34

World Food Day — A35

**1981, Oct. 16**

| | | | | |
|---|---|---|---|---|
| **109** | A33 | 7½ l multicolored | .20 | .20 |
| **110** | A34 | 10 l multicolored | .35 | .30 |
| **111** | A35 | 20 l multicolored | .65 | .50 |
| | | *Nos. 109-111 (3)* | 1.20 | 1.00 |

Palestinian Solidarity A36

**1981, Nov. 29**

| | | | |
|---|---|---|---|
| **112** | A36 10 l multicolored | .25 | .25 |

Royal Wedding of Prince Charles and Lady Diana Spencer — A37

**1981, Nov. 30**

| | | | |
|---|---|---|---|
| **113** | A37 50 l multicolored | 1.00 | .70 |

Souvenir Sheet

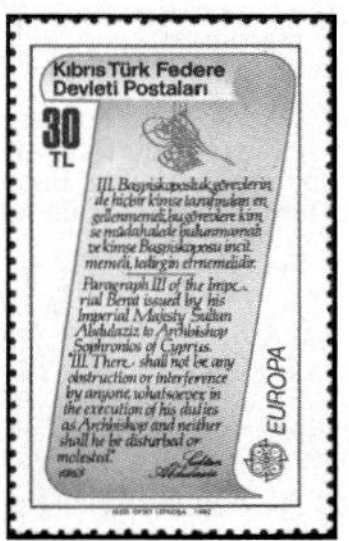


Charter of Cyprus, 1865 — A38

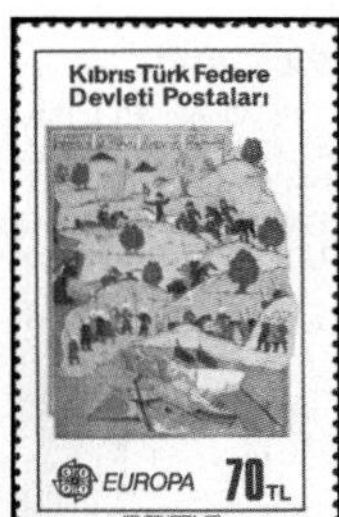


Turkish Forces Landing in Tuzla — A39

**1982, July 30**

| | | | |
|---|---|---|---|
| **114** | Sheet of 4 | *5.00* | *5.00* |
| *a.* | A38 30 l multicolored | *1.00* | *1.00* |
| *b.* | A39 70 l multicolored | *1.00* | *1.00* |

Europa. #114 contains 2 each #114a, 114b.

Buffavento Castle — A40

Windsurfing — A41

Kantara Castle A42

Tourism: 30 l, Shipwreck museum.

*Perf. 12½x12, 12x12½*

**1982, Aug. 20**

| | | | | |
|---|---|---|---|---|
| **116** | A40 | 5 l multicolored | .25 | .20 |
| **117** | A41 | 10 l multicolored | .30 | .25 |
| **118** | A42 | 15 l multicolored | .35 | .30 |
| **119** | A42 | 30 l multicolored | .60 | .40 |
| | | *Nos. 116-119 (4)* | 1.50 | 1.15 |

Art Treasures — A43

Designs: 30 l, The Wedding by Aylin Orek. 50 l, Carob Pickers by Ozden Nazim, vert.

**1982, Dec. 3** *Perf. 13x13½, 13½x13*

| | | | |
|---|---|---|---|
| **120** | A43 30 l multicolored | .30 | .30 |
| **121** | A43 50 l multicolored | .50 | .50 |

Robert Koch, TB Bacillus A44

World Cup Soccer Championships, Spain — A45

Scouting, 75th Anniv. — A46

**1982, Dec. 15** *Perf. 12½*

| | | | | |
|---|---|---|---|---|
| **122** | A44 | 10 l multicolored | .25 | .20 |
| **123** | A45 | 30 l multicolored | .75 | .60 |
| **124** | A46 | 70 l multicolored | 2.00 | 1.50 |
| | | *Nos. 122-124 (3)* | 3.00 | 2.30 |

Paintings A47

30 l, Calloused Hands by Salih Oral. 35 l, Malya-Limassol Bus by Emin Cizenel.

**1983, May 16** *Perf. 13½x13*

| | | | |
|---|---|---|---|
| **125** | A47 30 l multicolored | .90 | .75 |
| **126** | A47 35 l multicolored | 1.25 | 1.00 |

Miniature Sheet

Europa — A48

a, Map by Piri Reis. b, Cyprus seen from Skylab.

**1983, June 30** *Perf. 13*

| | | | |
|---|---|---|---|
| **127** | A48 Sheet of 2 | *60.00* | *60.00* |
| *a.-b.* | 100 l any single | *15.00* | *15.00* |

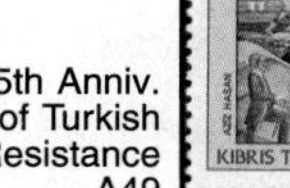

25th Anniv. of Turkish Resistance A49

Designs: 15 l, No. 3. 20 l, Exploitation, Suppression & Resurrection by Aziz Hasan. 25 l, Resistance by Guner Pir.

**1983, Aug. 1** *Perf. 13*

| | | | | |
|---|---|---|---|---|
| **129** | A49 | 15 l multi, vert. | .30 | .30 |
| **130** | A49 | 20 l multi | .45 | .45 |
| **131** | A49 | 25 l multi, vert. | .50 | .50 |
| | | *Nos. 129-131 (3)* | 1.25 | 1.25 |

World Communications Year — A50

**1983, Aug. 1**

| | | | |
|---|---|---|---|
| **132** | A50 30 l shown | .60 | .60 |
| **133** | A50 50 l Letters | 1.00 | 1.00 |

Birds A51

**1983, Oct. 10**

| | | | | |
|---|---|---|---|---|
| **134** | A51 | 10 l Merops apiaster | .25 | .20 |
| **135** | A51 | 15 l Carduelis carduelis | .35 | .20 |
| **136** | A51 | 50 l Erithacus rubecula | 1.00 | .70 |
| **137** | A51 | 65 l Oriolus oriolus | 1.40 | 1.00 |
| *a.* | | Block of 4, #134-137 | 3.50 | 3.00 |
| | | *Nos. 134-137 (4)* | 3.00 | 2.10 |

Nos. 103, 108 Ovptd.

Nos. 101, 104 Ovptd. or Surcharged

**1983, Dec. 7**

| | | | | | |
|---|---|---|---|---|---|
| **138** | A32 | 10 l | multicolored | .20 | .20 |
| **139** | A32 | 15 l | on 1 l multi | .20 | .20 |
| **140** | A32 | 25 l | multicolored | .35 | .35 |
| **141** | A32 | 150 l | multicolored | 2.00 | 2.00 |
| | | | *Nos. 138-141 (4)* | 2.75 | 2.75 |

Europa, 25th Anniv. A52

**1984, May 30** ***Perf. 12x12½***

| | | | | | |
|---|---|---|---|---|---|
| **142** | A52 | 50 l | blk, yel & brn | *1.00* | *.50* |
| **143** | A52 | 100 l | blk, bl & ultra | *2.00* | *1.00* |
| *a.* | | | Pair, #142-143 | *3.25* | *2.75* |

Olympics, Los Angeles A53

***Perf. 12½x12, 12x12½***

**1984, June 19**

| | | | | | |
|---|---|---|---|---|---|
| **144** | A53 | 10 l | Olympic flame, vert. | .20 | .20 |
| **145** | A53 | 20 l | Olympic rings | .20 | .20 |
| **146** | A53 | 70 l | Judo | .60 | .60 |
| | | | *Nos. 144-146 (3)* | 1.00 | 1.00 |

Ataturk Cultural Center A54

***Perf. 12x12½***

**1984, July 20** **Wmk. 390**

| | | | | | |
|---|---|---|---|---|---|
| **147** | A54 | 120 l | blk, yel & brn | .90 | .90 |

Turkish Invasion of Cyprus, 10th Anniv. A55

**1984, July 20**

| | | | | | |
|---|---|---|---|---|---|
| **148** | A55 | 20 l | shown | .40 | .40 |
| **149** | A55 | 70 l | Map, flag, olive branch | .70 | .70 |

Forest Conservation — A56

**1984, Aug. 20**

| | | | | | |
|---|---|---|---|---|---|
| **150** | A56 | 90 l | multicolored | 1.25 | .75 |

Paintings — A57

20 l, Old Turkish Houses in Nicosia by Cevdet Cagdas. 70 l, Scenery by Olga Rauf.

**1984, Sept. 21** ***Perf. 13***

| | | | | | |
|---|---|---|---|---|---|
| **151** | A57 | 20 l | multicolored | .40 | .40 |
| **152** | A57 | 70 l | multicolored | 1.10 | 1.10 |

Proclamation of Turkish Republic of Northern Cyprus — A58

Unanimous Vote by Legislative Assembly — A59

***Perf. 12½x12, 12x12½***

**1984, Nov. 15**

| | | | | | |
|---|---|---|---|---|---|
| **153** | A58 | 20 l | multicolored | .30 | .30 |
| **154** | A59 | 70 l | multicolored | .70 | .70 |

Independence, 1st Anniv.

European Taekwondo Championship, Kyrenia — A60

**1984, Dec. 10**

| | | | | | |
|---|---|---|---|---|---|
| **155** | A60 | 10 l | Competitors | .30 | .20 |
| **156** | A60 | 70 l | Flags | .60 | .55 |

Balance of the Spirit — A61

Paintings by Saulo Mercader: 20 l, The Look, vert.

**1984, Dec. 10** ***Perf. 12½x13, 13x12½***

| | | | | | |
|---|---|---|---|---|---|
| **157** | A61 | 20 l | multicolored | .20 | .20 |
| **158** | A61 | 70 l | multicolored | .50 | .50 |

Visit by Nuremburg Chamber Orchestra A62

**1984, Dec. 10** ***Perf. 12½***

| | | | | | |
|---|---|---|---|---|---|
| **159** | A62 | 70 l | multicolored | .75 | .50 |

Dr. Fazil Kucuk (1906-1984), Politician — A63

70 l, Kucuk reading newspaper, c. 1970.

**1985, Jan.**

| | | | | | |
|---|---|---|---|---|---|
| **160** | A63 | 20 l | multicolored | .20 | .20 |
| **161** | A63 | 70 l | multicolored | .50 | .50 |

Domestic Animals A64

**1985, May 29** ***Perf. 12x12½***

| | | | | | |
|---|---|---|---|---|---|
| **162** | A64 | 100 l | Capra | .55 | .55 |
| **163** | A64 | 200 l | Bos taurus | 1.10 | 1.10 |
| **164** | A64 | 300 l | Ovis aries | 1.60 | 1.60 |
| **165** | A64 | 500 l | Equus asinus | 2.75 | 2.75 |
| | | | *Nos. 162-165 (4)* | 6.00 | 6.00 |

Europa — A65

Paintings — A66

Composers: No. 166, George Frideric Handel (1685-1759). No. 167, Domenico Scarlatti (1685-1757). No. 168, Johann Sebastian Bach (1685-1750). No. 169, Buhurizade Mustafa Itri (1640-1712).

**1985, June 26** ***Perf. 12½x12***

| | | | | | |
|---|---|---|---|---|---|
| **166** | A65 | 20 l | grn & multi | *.30* | *.25* |
| **167** | A65 | 20 l | brn lake & multi | *.30* | *.25* |
| **168** | A65 | 100 l | bl & multi | *1.25* | *.80* |
| **169** | A65 | 100 l | brn & multi | *1.25* | *.80* |
| *a.* | | | Block of 4, #166-169 | *3.75* | *3.75* |

Printed in sheets of 16, containing 4 No. 169a.

**1985, Aug.** ***Perf. 12½x13***

Paintings: 20 l, Pastoral Life by Ali Atakan. 50 l, Woman Carrying Water by Ismet V. Guney.

| | | | | | |
|---|---|---|---|---|---|
| **170** | A66 | 20 l | multicolored | .35 | .35 |
| **171** | A66 | 50 l | multicolored | .55 | .55 |

Intl. Youth Year A67

**Wmk. 390**

**1985, Oct. 29** **Litho.** ***Perf. 12½***

| | | | | | |
|---|---|---|---|---|---|
| **172** | A67 | 20 l | shown | .20 | .20 |
| **173** | A67 | 100 l | Globe, dove | .60 | .60 |

Northern Cyprus Air League — A68

Development of Rabies Vaccine, Cent. — A69

Ismet Inonu (1884-1973), Turkish Pres. — A70

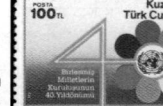

UN, 40th Anniv. A71

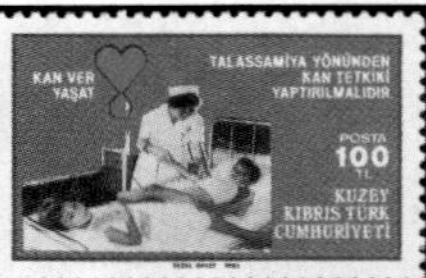

Blood Donor Services A72

**1985, Nov. 29**

| | | | | | |
|---|---|---|---|---|---|
| **174** | A68 | 20 l | multicolored | .20 | .20 |
| **175** | A69 | 50 l | Pasteur | .30 | .30 |
| **176** | A70 | 100 l | brown | .60 | .60 |
| **177** | A71 | 100 l | multicolored | .60 | .60 |
| **178** | A72 | 100 l | multicolored | .60 | .60 |
| | | | *Nos. 174-178 (5)* | 2.30 | 2.30 |

Paintings — A73

20 l, House with Arches by Gonen Atakol. 100 l, Ataturk Square by Yalkin Muhtaroglu.

**1986, June 20** ***Perf. 13***

| | | | | | |
|---|---|---|---|---|---|
| **179** | A73 | 20 l | multicolored | .20 | .20 |
| **180** | A73 | 100 l | multicolored | .40 | .40 |

Miniature Sheet

Europa — A74

**1986, June 20** ***Perf. 12x12½***

| | | | | | |
|---|---|---|---|---|---|
| **181** | A74 | | Sheet of 2 | *16.00* | *16.00* |
| *a.* | | 100 l | Gyps fulvus | *4.00* | *2.00* |
| *b.* | | 200 l | Roadside litter | *8.00* | *4.00* |

Karagoz Puppets — A75

**1986, July 25** ***Perf. 12½x13***

| | | | | | |
|---|---|---|---|---|---|
| **182** | A75 | 100 l | multicolored | .40 | .40 |

Anatolian Artifacts A76

Designs: 10 l, Ring-shaped composite pottery, Kernos, Old Bronze Age (2300-1050 B.C.). 20 l, Bird-shaped lidded pot, Skuru Hill tomb, Morphou, late Bronze Age (1600-1500 B.C.), vert. 50 l, Earthenware jug, Vryse, Kyrenia, Neolithic Age (4000 B.C.). 100 l,

Terra sigillata statue of Artemis, Sea of Salamis, Roman Period (200 B.C.), vert.

**1986, Sept. 15** ***Perf. 12½***
**183** A76 10 l multicolored .20 .20
**184** A76 20 l multicolored .20 .20
**185** A76 50 l multicolored .25 .25
**186** A76 100 l multicolored .50 .50
*Nos. 183-186 (4)* 1.15 1.15

For surcharge see No. 295A.

Defense Forces, 10th Anniv. — A77

World Food Day — A78

World Cup Soccer Championships, Mexico — A79

Halley's Comet A80

**1986, Oct. 13**
**187** A77 20 l multicolored .20 .20
**188** A78 50 l multicolored .30 .30
**189** A79 100 l multicolored .35 .35
**190** A80 100 l multicolored .40 .40
*Nos. 187-190 (4)* 1.25 1.25

Development Projects — A81

**1986, Nov. 17**
**191** A81 20 l Water resources .20 .20
**192** A81 50 l Housing .20 .20
**193** A81 100 l Airport .45 .45
*Nos. 191-193 (3)* .85 .85

Royal Wedding of Prince Andrew and Sarah Ferguson — A82

Anniv. and events: No. 195, Queen Elizabeth II, 60th birthday.

***Perf. 12½x13***

**1986, Nov. 20** **Wmk. 390**
**194** A82 100 l multicolored .35 .35
**195** A82 100 l multicolored .35 .35
*a.* Pair, #194-195 .70 .70

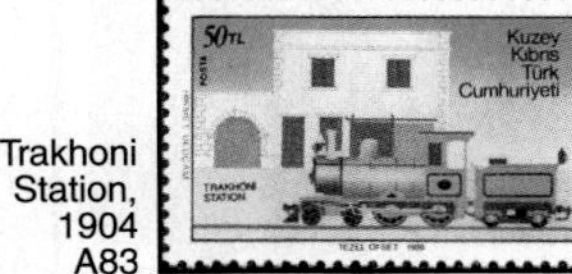


Trakhoni Station, 1904 A83

**1986, Dec. 31**
**196** A83 50 l shown .35 .25
**197** A83 100 l Locomotive #1, 1904 .90 .60

Rail transport, 1904-1951.

Nos. 86, 88-89, 105 Overprinted or Surcharged

a

b

**1987, May 18** **Unwmk.** ***Perf. 13***
**198** A25(a) 10 l on #89 .40 .20
**199** A25(a) 15 l on 3½ l, #86 .40 .20
**200** A25(a) 20 l on #88 .50 .25
**201** A32(b) 30 l on #105 .80 .35
*Nos. 198-201 (4)* 2.10 1.00

Paintings — A84

Folk Dancers — A86

Europa A85

Designs: 50 l, Shepherd by Feridun Isiman. 125 l, Pear Woman by Mehmet Uluhan.

***Perf. 12½x13***

**1987, May 27** **Wmk. 390**
**202** A84 50 l multicolored .35 .20
**203** A84 125 l multicolored .85 .40

**1987, June 30** ***Perf. 12½***

Modern architecture: 50 l, Bauhaus-style house, designed by A. Vural Behaeddin, 1973. 200 l, House, designed by Necdet Turgay, 1979.

**204** A85 50 l multicolored *1.50* .40
**205** A85 200 l multicolored *4.00* *1.75*
*a.* Bklt. pane, 2 each #204-205 *12.00*

No. 205a contains two copies each of Nos. 204-205, printed alternately, with unprinted selvage at each end of the pane, perf between stamps and selvage and imperf on outside edges. Thus, singles from the pane gauge 12½ by imperf.

**1987, Aug. 20**
**206** A86 20 l multicolored .20 .20
**207** A86 50 l multi, diff. .20 .20
**208** A86 200 l multi, diff. .50 .50
**209** A86 1000 l multi, diff. 2.50 2.50
*Nos. 206-209 (4)* 3.40 3.40

For surcharge see No. 295B.

Infantry Regiment, 1st Anniv. — A87

5th Islamic Summit Conf., Kuwait — A88

Pharmaceutical Federation — A89

**1987, Sept. 30**
**210** A87 50 l multicolored .20 .20
**211** A88 200 l multicolored .50 .50
**212** A89 200 l multicolored .50 .50
*Nos. 210-212 (3)* 1.20 1.20

Ahmet Belig Pasha (1851-1924), Egyptian Judge — A90

Mehmet Emin Pasha (1813-1871), Turkish Grand Vizier — A91

Famous men: 125 l, Mehmet Kamil Pasha (1832-1913), grand vizier.

**1987, Oct. 22**
**213** A90 50 l brn & yel .20 .20
**214** A91 50 l multicolored .20 .20
**215** A91 125 l multicolored .35 .30
*Nos. 213-215 (3)* .75 .70

Pres. Rauf Denktash, Turkish Prime Minister Turgut Ozal A92

**1987, Nov. 2**
**216** A92 50 l multi .20 .20

New Kyrenia Harbor A93

**Wmk. 390**

**1987, Nov. 20** **Litho.** ***Perf. 12½***
**217** A93 150 l shown .40 .40
**218** A93 200 l Eastern Mediterranean University .55 .55

Chair Weaver, by Osman Guvenir — A94

Paintings: 20 l, Woman Making Pastry, by Ayhan Mentes, vert. 150 l, Woman Weaving a Rug, by Zekai Yesiladali, vert.

**Wmk. 390**

**1988, May 2** **Litho.** ***Perf. 13***
**219** A94 20 l multi .20 .20
**220** A94 50 l multi .20 .20
**221** A94 150 l multi .45 .35
*Nos. 219-221 (3)* .85 .75

Europa A95

**1988, May 31** ***Perf. 12½***
**222** A95 200 l Tugboat *Piyale Pasha* 2.75 1.00
**223** A95 500 l Satellite dish, broadcast tower, vert. 4.00 1.25

Bayrak Radio and Television Corporation, 25th anniv. (500 l).

Tourism A96

Photographs: 150 l, Nicosia, by Aysel Erduran. 200 l, Famagusta, by Sonia Halliday and Laura Lushington. 300 l, Kyrenia, by Halliday and Lushington.

**1988, June 17**
**224** A96 150 l multi .25 .25
**225** A96 200 l multi .35 .35
**226** A96 300 l multi .50 .50
*Nos. 224-226 (3)* 1.10 1.10

Turkish Prime Ministers — A97

No. 227, Bulent Ecevit, 1970's. No. 228, Bulent Ulusu, Sept. 21, 1980-Dec. 13, 1983. No. 229, Turgut Ozal, from Dec. 13, 1983.

**1988, July 20**
**227** A97 50 l shown .20 .20
**228** A97 50 l multi .20 .20
**229** A97 50 l multi .20 .20
*Nos. 227-229 (3)* .60 .60

Civil Defense A98

**1988, Aug. 8** ***Perf. 12x12½***
**230** A98 150 l multicolored .35 .35

Summer Olympics, Seoul A99

**1988, Sept. 17** ***Perf. 12½***
**231** A99 200 l shown .30 .30
**232** A99 250 l Women's running .40 .40
**233** A99 400 l Seoul .65 .65
*Nos. 231-233 (3)* 1.35 1.35

Sedat Simavi (1896-1953), Turkish Journalist — A100

Intl. Conferences, Kyrenia — A101

North Cyprus Intl. Industrial Fair — A102

Intl. Red. Cross and Red Crescent Organizations, 125th Anniv. — A103

US-USSR Summit Meeting on Nuclear Arms Reduction A104

WHO, 40th Anniv. — A105

**1988, Oct. 17** ***Perf. 12½x12, 12x12½***

**234** A100 50 l olive grn .20 .20
**235** A101 100 l multi .25 .25
**236** A102 300 l multi .55 .55
**237** A103 400 l multi .85 .85
**238** A104 400 l Gorbachev and Reagan .85 .85
**239** A105 600 l multi 1.10 1.10
*Nos. 234-239 (6)* 3.80 3.80

Miniature Sheet

Portraits and Photographs of Kemal Ataturk — A106

b, Holding canteen. c, In uniform. d, Facing left.

**1988, Nov. 10** ***Perf. 12½***

**240** A106 Sheet of 4 2.25 2.00
***a.-d.*** 250 l any single .35 .25

Souvenir Sheet

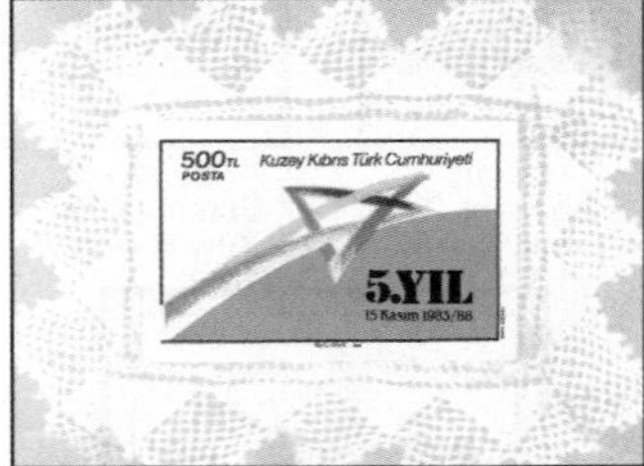
Turkish Republic of Northern Cyprus, 5th Anniv. — A107

**1988, Nov. 15** ***Imperf.***

**241** A107 500 l multicolored 1.50 1.25

Dervis Pasha Mansion, 19th Cent., Nicosia — A108

Designs: 400 l, Gamblers' Inn, 17th cent., Asmaalti Meydani. 600 l, Camii Cedit Mosque, 1902, Paphos, vert.

**1989, Apr. 28** ***Perf. 13***

**242** A108 150 l shown .30 .30
**243** A108 400 l multi .80 .80
**244** A108 600 l multi 1.25 1.25
*Nos. 242-244 (3)* 2.35 2.35

Europa — A109

**1989, May 31** ***Perf. 12½x12***

**245** A109 600 l Girl, doll *2.25 1.00*
**246** A109 1000 l Flying kite *3.25 1.25*
***a.*** Bklt. pane, 2 each #245-246, perf. 12½ *10.50*

Geneva Peace Summit, Aug. 24, 1988 A110

**1989, June 30** ***Perf. 12½***

**247** A110 500 l blk & dark red 1.00 1.00

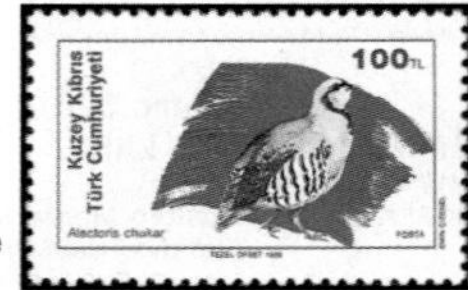
Wildlife A111

**1989, July 31**

**248** A111 100 l Alectoris chukar .20 .20
**249** A111 200 l Lepus cyprius .40 .40
**250** A111 700 l Francolinus francolinus 1.40 1.40
**251** A111 2000 l Vulpes vulpes 4.00 4.00
*Nos. 248-251 (4)* 6.00 6.00

Natl. Development Projects — A112

***Perf. 12½x12, 12x12½***

**1989, Sept. 29**

**252** A112 100 l Road construction .20 .20
**253** A112 150 l Sanitary water supply .30 .30
**254** A112 200 l Afforestation .40 .40
**255** A112 450 l Telecommunications .90 .90
**256** A112 650 l Power station 1.25 1.25
**257** A112 700 l Irrigation ponds 1.40 1.40
*Nos. 252-257 (6)* 4.45 4.45

Nos. 253-256 vert.

Free Port, Famagusta, 15th Anniv. — A113

Turkish Cypriot Post, 25th Anniv. — A114

Saded Newspaper, Cent. — A115

Intl. Marine Organization, 30th Anniv. — A116

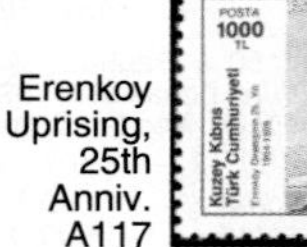
Erenkoy Uprising, 25th Anniv. A117

***Perf. 12x12½, 12½x13 (450 l)***

**1989, Nov. 17**

**258** A113 100 l multicolored .20 .20
**259** A114 450 l multicolored .90 .90
**260** A115 500 l multicolored 1.00 1.00
**261** A116 600 l multicolored 1.25 1.25
**262** A117 1000 l multicolored 2.00 2.00
*Nos. 258-262 (5)* 5.35 5.35

Erdal Inonu A118

Agriculture A119

**1989, Dec. 15** ***Perf. 12½x12***

**263** A118 700 l multicolored 1.40 1.40

Visit of Inonu, Turkish politician, to northern Cyprus.

**1989, Dec. 25** ***Perf. 12x12½, 12½x12***

**264** A119 150 l Mule drawn .30 .30
**265** A119 450 l Ox drawn .90 .90
**266** A119 550 l Millstone, olive press 1.10 1.10
*Nos. 264-266 (3)* 2.30 2.30

Nos. 264-265 horiz.

World Health Day A120

***Perf. 12x12½***

**1990, Apr. 19** **Litho.** **Wmk. 390**

**267** A120 200 l shown .40 .20
**268** A120 700 l Cigarette, heart 1.50 .40

Europa A121

Post offices.

***Perf. 12x12½***

**1990, May 31** **Litho.** **Wmk. 390**

**269** A121 1000 l Yenierenkoy *3.00 1.50*
**270** A121 1500 l Ataturk Meydani *4.50 2.00*
***a.*** Souv. sheet, 2 #269, 2 #270 *18.00 16.00*

World Cup Soccer Championships, Italy — A122

**1990, June 8**

**271** A122 300 l Turkish Cypriot team .65 .65
**272** A122 1000 l Ball, emblem, globe 2.00 2.00

A123

A126

A125

World Environment Day: Birds.

**1990, June 5** ***Perf. 12***

**273** A123 150 l Turdus philomelos *4.00* .75
**274** A123 300 l Sylvia atricapilla *5.75* 1.25
**275** A123 900 l Phoenicurus ochruros *12.00* 2.75
**276** A123 1000 l Phyllosopus collybita *15.00* 5.00
*Nos. 273-276 (4)* 36.75 9.75

For surcharge see No. 386.

**1990, July 31** ***Perf. 13x12½, 12½x13***

Designs: 300 l, Painting by Filiz Ankac. 1000 l , Sculpture by Sinasi Tekman, vert.

**279** A125 300 l multicolored .65 .65
**280** A125 1000 l multicolored 2.00 2.00

**Wmk. 390**

**1990, Aug. 24** **Litho.** ***Perf. 12½***

**281** A126 150 l Amphitheater, Soli .35 .35
**282** A126 1000 l Mosaic, Soli 2.00 2.00

European Tourism Year.

Visit by Turkish President Kenan Evren A127

**1990, Sept. 19**

**283** A127 500 l multicolored 1.00 1.00

Traffic Safety A128

**1990, Sept. 21**

**284** A128 150 l Wear seat belts .35 .35
**285** A128 300 l Obey the speed limit .65 .65
**286** A128 1000 l Obey traffic signals 2.00 2.00
*Nos. 284-286 (3)* 3.00 3.00

A129

Flowers — A130

**1990, Oct. 1**

**287** A129 1000 l multicolored 2.00 2.00

Visit by Turkish Prime Minister Yildirim Akbulut.

***Perf. 12½x12***

**1990, Oct. 31** **Litho.** **Wmk. 390**

**288** A130 150 l Rosularia cypria .35 .20
**289** A130 200 l Silene fraudratrix .40 .20
**290** A130 300 l Scutellaria sibthorpii .65 .20
**291** A130 600 l Sedum lampusae 1.25 .30
**292** A130 1000 l Onosma caespitosum 2.00 .50
**293** A130 1500 l Arabis cypria 3.25 .80
*Nos. 288-293 (6)* 7.90 2.20

For surcharges see Nos. 295C, 387.

Intl. Literacy Year A131

**1990, Nov. 24** ***Perf. 12x12½***

**294** A131 300 l Ataturk as teacher .65 .20
**295** A131 750 l A, b, c, books, map 1.60 .40

Nos. 183, 206, 288 Surcharged

**1991, June 3**

**Perfs. & Printing Methods as Before**

**295A** A76 250 l on 10 l #183 .20 .20
**295B** A86 250 l on 20 l #206 .20 .20
**295C** A130 500 l on 150 l #288 .35 .25
*Nos. 295A-295C (3)* .75 .65

Shape of obliterator varies.

Orchids — A132

**Wmk. 390**

**1991, July 8** **Litho.** ***Perf. 14***

**296** A132 250 l Ophrys lapethica .55 .55
**297** A132 500 l Ophrys kotschyi 1.60 1.60

See Nos. 303-306.

A133

***Perf. 12½x12***

**1991, July 29** **Litho.** **Wmk. 390**

Europa: a, Hermes space shuttle. b, Ulysses probe.

**Miniature Sheet**

**298** A133 2000 l Sheet of 2, #a.-b. *8.00 8.00*

Public Fountains A134

**Wmk. 390**

**1991, Sept. 9** **Litho.** ***Perf. 12***

**299** A134 250 l Kuchuk Medrese .20 .20
**300** A134 500 l Djafer Pasha .35 .35
**301** A134 1500 l Sarayonu Square 1.10 1.10
**302** A134 5000 l Arabahmet Mosque 3.50 3.50
*Nos. 299-302 (4)* 5.15 5.15

Orchid Type of 1991

**1991, Oct. 10** ***Perf. 14***

**303** A132 100 l Serapias levantina .20 .20
**304** A132 500 l Dactylorhiza romana .40 .40
**305** A132 2000 l Orchis simia 1.40 1.40
**306** A132 3000 l Orchis sancta 2.00 2.00
*Nos. 303-306 (4)* 4.00 4.00

Hindiler by Salih M. Cizel — A135

Painting: 500 l, Dusme by Asik Mene.

**Wmk. 390**

**1991, Nov. 5** **Litho.** ***Perf. 13***

**307** A135 250 l multicolored .20 .20
**308** A135 500 l multicolored .25 .25

See type A143. For surcharge see No. 381.

World Food Day A136

Basbakan Mustafa Cagatay (1937-1989) A137

Eastern Mediterranean University — A138

Wolfgang Amadeus Mozart, Death Bicent. A139

**1991, Nov. 20** ***Perf. 12***

**309** A136 250 l multicolored .20 .20
**310** A137 500 l multicolored .30 .30
**311** A138 500 l multicolored .30 .30
**312** A139 1500 l multicolored .85 .85
*Nos. 309-312 (4)* 1.65 1.65

For surcharge see No. 380.

World AIDS Day A140

**1991, Dec. 13** ***Perf. 12***

**313** A140 1000 l multicolored .55 .55

Lighthouses — A141

**1991, Dec. 16** ***Perf. 12x12½***

**314** A141 250 l Canbulat Burcu, Famagusta .20 .20
**315** A141 500 l Yat Limani, Kyrenia .30 .30
**316** A141 1500 l Turizm Limani, Kyrenia .85 .85
*Nos. 314-316 (3)* 1.35 1.35

Tourism A142

Designs: 250 l, Elephant and hippopotamus fossils, Kyrenia. 500 l, Roman fish ponds, Lambusa (58 BC-398 AD). 1500 l, Roman tomb and church, Lambusa (58 BC-1192 AD).

**1991, Dec. 27**

**317** A142 250 l multicolored .20 .20
**318** A142 500 l multicolored .30 .30
**319** A142 1500 l multicolored .85 .85
*Nos. 317-319 (3)* 1.35 1.35

Paintings A143

Designs: 500 l, Ebru, by Arife Kandulu. 3500 l, Nicosia, by Ismet Tartar.

**Wmk. 390**

**1992, Mar. 31** **Litho.** ***Perf. 14***

**320** A143 500 l multicolored .25 .25
**321** A143 3500 l multicolored 1.75 1.75

See type A135.

Tourism A144

No. 322, Ancient building, Famagusta. No. 323, Trap shooting range, Nicosia. 1000 l, Salamis Bay resort, Famagusta. 1500 l, Casino, Kyrenia.

**1992, Apr. 21** ***Perf. 13½x14, 14x13½***

**322** A144 500 l multi .25 .25
**323** A144 500 l multi .25 .25
**324** A144 1000 l multi .50 .50
**325** A144 1500 l multi, vert. .75 .75
*Nos. 322-325 (4)* 1.75 1.75

Souvenir Sheet

Discovery of America, 500th Anniv. — A145

Europa: a, 1500 l, Santa Maria, Nina and Pinta. b, 3500 l, Columbus.

**1992, May 29** ***Perf. 13½x14***

**326** A145 Sheet of 2, #a.-b. *10.00 10.00*

Sea Turtles A146

***Perf. 13½x14***

**1992, June 30 Litho. Wmk. 390**

| | | | | |
|---|---|---|---|---|
| **327** | A146 1000 l | Green turtle | *3.00* | *3.00* |
| **328** | A146 1500 l | Loggerhead turtle | *3.50* | *3.50* |
| *a.* | | Souv. sheet, 2 ea #327-328 | *14.00* | *14.00* |

World Wildlife Fund.

1992 Summer Olympics, Barcelona A147

#329: a, Women's gymnastics, vert. b, Tennis, vert. 1000 l, High jump. 1500 l, Cycling.

**1992, July 25** ***Perf. 14x13½***

| | | | | |
|---|---|---|---|---|
| **329** | A147 500 l | Pair, #a-b. | .75 | .75 |

***Perf. 13½x14***

| | | | | |
|---|---|---|---|---|
| **330** | A147 1000 l | multicolored | .50 | .50 |
| **331** | A147 1500 l | multicolored | .75 | .75 |
| | | *Nos. 329-331 (3)* | 2.00 | 2.00 |

Electric Power Plant, Kyrenia A148

Social Insurance, 15th Anniv. A149

Intl. Federation of Women Artists A150

Veterinary Services A151

***Perf. 13½x14***

**1992, Sept. 30 Litho. Wmk. 390**

| | | | | |
|---|---|---|---|---|
| **332** | A148 500 l | multicolored | .25 | .25 |
| **333** | A149 500 l | multicolored | .25 | .25 |
| **334** | A150 1500 l | multicolored | .75 | .75 |
| **335** | A151 1500 l | multicolored | .75 | .75 |
| | | *Nos. 332-335 (4)* | 2.00 | 2.00 |

Civil Aviation Office, 17th Anniv. A152

Meteorology Office, 18th Anniv. — A153

Mapping, 14th Anniv. A154

***Perf. 13½x14***

**1992, Nov. 20 Litho. Wmk. 390**

| | | | | |
|---|---|---|---|---|
| **336** | A152 1000 l | multicolored | .50 | .50 |
| **337** | A153 1000 l | multicolored | .50 | .50 |
| **338** | A154 1200 l | multicolored | .60 | .60 |
| | | *Nos. 336-338 (3)* | 1.60 | 1.60 |

Native Cuisine A155

Food: 2000 l, Zulbiye (pastry). 2500 l, Cicek Dolmasi (stuffed squash flowers). 3000 l, Tatar Boregi (flaky pastry dish). 4000 l, Seftali kebab (meat dish).

**1992, Dec. 14**

| | | | | |
|---|---|---|---|---|
| **339** | A155 2000 l | multicolored | 1.00 | 1.00 |
| **340** | A155 2500 l | multicolored | 1.25 | 1.25 |
| **341** | A155 3000 l | multicolored | 1.50 | 1.50 |
| **342** | A155 4000 l | multicolored | 2.00 | 2.00 |
| | | *Nos. 339-342 (4)* | 5.75 | 5.75 |

Intl. Conference on Nutrition, Rome. See Nos. 388-390.

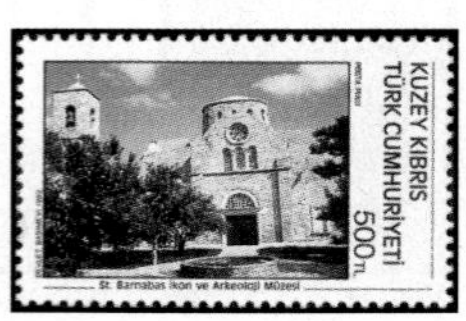


Tourism A156

Designs: 500 l, Church and Monastery of St. Barnabas. 10,000 l, Bowl.

***Perf. 13½x14***

**1993, Apr. 1 Litho. Wmk. 390**

| | | | | |
|---|---|---|---|---|
| **343** | A156 500 l | multi | .25 | .25 |
| **344** | A156 10,000 l | multi | 5.00 | 5.00 |

Souvenir Sheet

KUZEY KIBRIS TÜRK CUMHURİYETİ POSTALARI
Turkish Republic Of Northern Cyprus
EUROPA 2000 TL
EUROPA 3000 TL
ÇAĞDAŞ SANAT CONTEMPORARY ART 1993
KUZEY KIBRIS TÜRK CUMHURİYETİ POSTALARI
Turkish Republic Of Northern Cyprus

Europa — A157

Contemporary paintings by: a, 2000 l, Turksal Ince. b, 3000 l, Ilkay Onsoy.

***Perf. 14x13½***

**1993, May 5 Litho. Wmk. 390**

| | | | | |
|---|---|---|---|---|
| **345** | A157 | Sheet of 2, #a.-b. | *2.00* | *2.00* |

Trees — A158

**1993, June 11** ***Perf. 14x13½***

| | | | | |
|---|---|---|---|---|
| **346** | A158 500 l | Olea europea | .25 | .20 |
| **347** | A158 1000 l | Eucalyptus camaldulensis | .50 | .50 |
| **348** | A158 3000 l | Platanus orientalis | 1.50 | 1.50 |
| **349** | A158 4000 l | Pinus brutia tenore | 2.00 | 2.00 |
| | | *Nos. 346-349 (4)* | 4.25 | 4.20 |

Arabahmet Rehabilitation Project — A159

***Perf. 13½x14***

**1993, Sept. 20 Litho. Wmk. 390**

| | | | | |
|---|---|---|---|---|
| **350** | A159 1000 l | shown | .20 | .20 |
| **351** | A159 3000 l | Homes, diff. | .50 | .50 |

Creation of Turkish Republic of Northern Cyprus, 10th Anniv. A160

Designs: No. 353, Flags changing to dove, vert. 1000 l, Dove flying from flag. 5000 l, Flowers forming "10," map.

***Perf. 13½x14, 14x13½***

**1993, Nov. 15 Litho. Wmk. 390**

| | | | | |
|---|---|---|---|---|
| **352** | A160 500 l | multicolored | .20 | .20 |
| **353** | A160 500 l | multicolored | .20 | .20 |
| **354** | A160 1000 l | multicolored | .20 | .20 |
| **355** | A160 5000 l | multicolored | .80 | .80 |
| | | *Nos. 352-355 (4)* | 1.40 | 1.40 |

Ataturk, 55th Death Anniv. — A161

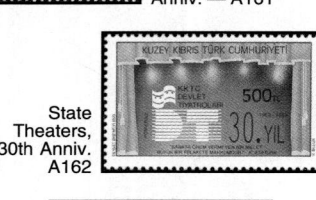


State Theaters, 30th Anniv. A162

Turkish Resistance Organization, 35th Anniv. — A163

Turkish News Agency, 20th Anniv. A164



Tchaikovsky, Death Cent. — A165

***Perf. 14x13½, 13½x14***

**1993, Dec. 27 Litho. Wmk. 390**

| | | | | |
|---|---|---|---|---|
| **356** | A161 500 l | multicolored | .20 | .20 |
| **357** | A162 500 l | multicolored | .20 | .20 |
| **358** | A163 1500 l | multicolored | .30 | .30 |
| **359** | A164 2000 l | multicolored | .40 | .40 |
| **360** | A165 5000 l | multicolored | 1.10 | 1.10 |
| | | *Nos. 356-360 (5)* | 2.20 | 2.20 |

Soyle Falci, by Goral Ozkan A166

Design: 6500 l, Sculpture, IV Hareket, by Senol Özdevrim.

**1994, Mar. 31** ***Perf. 14***

| | | | | |
|---|---|---|---|---|
| **361** | A166 1000 l | multicolored | .20 | .20 |
| **362** | A166 6500 l | multicolored | 1.40 | 1.40 |

Fazil Kucuk (1906-84), Physician and Political Leader — A167

**1994, Apr. 1**

| | | | | |
|---|---|---|---|---|
| **363** | A167 1500 l | multicolored | .30 | .30 |

Souvenir Sheet

Archaeological Discoveries — A168

Europa: a, Neolithic village, Ayios Epectitos Vrysi. b, Neolithic man, early tools found in excavation.

**1994, May 16** ***Perf. 13½***

| | | | | |
|---|---|---|---|---|
| **364** | A168 8500 l | Sheet of 2, #a.-b. | *3.00* | *3.00* |

1994 World Cup Soccer Championships, US — A169

**1994, June 30**

| | | | | |
|---|---|---|---|---|
| **365** | A169 2500 l | Trophy, vert. | .20 | .20 |
| **366** | A169 10,000 l | US map | .80 | .80 |

Turkish Postal Service in Northern Cyprus, 30th Anniv. A170

**1994, June 30**

| | | | | |
|---|---|---|---|---|
| **367** | A170 50,000 l | multicolored | 4.00 | 4.00 |

A171

A172

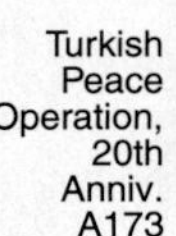

Turkish Peace Operation, 20th Anniv. A173

**1994, July 20** ***Perf. 14***

| | | | | |
|---|---|---|---|---|
| **368** | A171 | 2500 l shown | .20 | .20 |
| **369** | A172 | 5000 l Monument | .40 | .40 |
| **370** | A172 | 7000 l Monument, diff. | .50 | .50 |
| **371** | A173 | 8500 l shown | .65 | .65 |
| | | *Nos. 368-371 (4)* | 1.75 | 1.75 |

First Rural Postal Cancellations, Cent. — A174

Postmarks, stamps: 1500 l, Karpas, Cyprus #131. 2500 l, Gazi Magusa (Famagusta), #71. 5000 l, Bey Keuy, Cyprus #150. 7000 l, Aloa, Cyprus, #179. 8500 l, Pyla, Cyprus #152.

**1994, Aug. 15** ***Perf. 13½***

| | | | | |
|---|---|---|---|---|
| **372** | A174 | 1500 l multicolored | .20 | .20 |
| **373** | A174 | 2500 l multicolored | .20 | .20 |
| **374** | A174 | 5000 l multicolored | .35 | .35 |
| **375** | A174 | 7000 l multicolored | .55 | .55 |
| **376** | A174 | 8500 l multicolored | .70 | .70 |
| | | *Nos. 372-376 (5)* | 2.00 | 2.00 |

Sea Shells — A175

**1994, Nov. 15** ***Perf. 14***

| | | | | |
|---|---|---|---|---|
| **377** | A175 | 2500 l Charonia tritonis | .20 | .20 |
| **378** | A175 | 12,500 l Tonna galea | .70 | .35 |
| **379** | A175 | 12,500 l Cypraea talpa | .70 | .35 |
| | | *Nos. 377-379 (3)* | 1.60 | .90 |

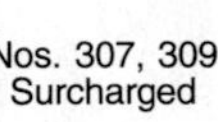

Nos. 307, 309 Surcharged

**1994, Dec. 12** ***Perfs., etc. as Before***

| | | | | |
|---|---|---|---|---|
| **380** | A136 | 1500 l on 250 l multi | .20 | .20 |
| **381** | A135 | 2500 l on 250 l multi | .20 | .20 |

Size and location of surcharge varies.

European Nature Conservation Year — A176

Designs: 2000 l, Donkeys on mountain top. 3500 l, Shoreline. 15,000 l, Donkeys in field.

**1995, Feb. 10** **Wmk. 390** ***Perf. 14***

| | | | | |
|---|---|---|---|---|
| **382** | A176 | 2000 l multicolored | .20 | .20 |
| **383** | A176 | 3500 l multicolored | .20 | .20 |
| **384** | A176 | 15,000 l multicolored | 1.00 | 1.00 |
| | | *Nos. 382-384 (3)* | 1.40 | 1.40 |

Souvenir Sheet

Peace and Freedom — A177

Europa: a, Globe, dove. b, Doves over Europe.
Illustration reduced.

**1995, Apr. 20** ***Perf. 13½x14***

| | | | | |
|---|---|---|---|---|
| **385** | A177 | 15,000 l Sheet of 2, #a.-b. | *2.50* | *2.50* |

Nos. 275 & 290 Surcharged

**1995, Apr. 21** ***Perfs., etc. as Before***

| | | | | |
|---|---|---|---|---|
| **386** | A123 | 2000 l on 900 l #275 | 1.75 | 1.50 |
| **387** | A130 | 3500 l on 300 l #290 | 3.50 | 3.50 |

Size and location of surcharge varies.

Native Cusine Type of 1992

Food: 3500 l, Sini katmeri. 10,000 l, Kolokas musakka, Bullez kizartma. 14,000 l, Enginar dolmasi.

***Perf. 13½x14***

**1995, May 29** **Litho.** **Wmk. 390**

| | | | | |
|---|---|---|---|---|
| **388** | A155 | 3500 l multicolored | .20 | .20 |
| **389** | A155 | 10,000 l multicolored | .55 | .55 |
| **390** | A155 | 14,000 l multicolored | .80 | .80 |
| | | *Nos. 388-390 (3)* | 1.55 | 1.55 |

Butterflies A178

**1995, June 30**

| | | | | |
|---|---|---|---|---|
| **391** | A178 | 3500 l Papilio machaon | .20 | .20 |
| **392** | A178 | 4500 l Charaxes jasius | .20 | .20 |
| **393** | A178 | 15,000 l Cynthia cardui | .70 | .70 |
| **394** | A178 | 30,000 l Vanessa atalanta | 1.40 | 1.40 |
| | | *Nos. 391-394 (4)* | 2.50 | 2.50 |

Visit by Turkish Pres. Suleyman Demirel A179

**1995, Aug. 21** ***Perf. 13½***

| | | | | |
|---|---|---|---|---|
| **395** | A179 | 5000 l multicolored | .25 | .25 |

Tourism A180

Designs: 3500 l, Beach scene, Kyrenia. 7500 l, Sailboats. 15,000 l, Ruins, Famagusta, vert. 20,000 l, St. George Cathedral, Famagusta, vert.

**1995, Aug. 21**

| | | | | |
|---|---|---|---|---|
| **396** | A180 | 3500 l multicolored | .20 | .20 |
| **397** | A180 | 7500 l multicolored | .40 | .40 |
| **398** | A180 | 15,000 l multicolored | .80 | .80 |
| **399** | A180 | 20,000 l multicolored | 1.00 | 1.00 |
| | | *Nos. 396-399 (4)* | 2.40 | 2.40 |

State Printing Office, 20th Anniv. A181

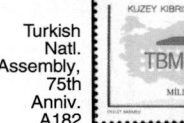

Turkish Natl. Assembly, 75th Anniv. A182

Louis Pasteur (1822-95) A183

UN, 50th Anniv. A184

G. Marconi (1874-1937), Radio, Cent. — A185

Motion Pictures, Cent. — A186

***Perf. 13½x14, 14x13½***

**1995, Nov. 7** **Litho.** **Wmk. 390**

| | | | | |
|---|---|---|---|---|
| **400** | A181 | 3000 l multicolored | .20 | .20 |
| **401** | A182 | 3000 l multicolored | .20 | .20 |
| **402** | A183 | 5000 l multicolored | .25 | .25 |
| **403** | A184 | 22,000 l multicolored | 1.25 | 1.25 |
| **404** | A185 | 30,000 l multicolored | 1.60 | 1.60 |
| **405** | A186 | 30,000 l multicolored | 1.60 | 1.60 |
| | | *Nos. 400-405 (6)* | 5.10 | 5.10 |

A187 A188

Tombstone inscriptions, Orhon and Yenisey river region: 5000 l, Kültigin Heykelinin Basi. 10,000 l, Kültigin Yaziti.

**1995, Dec. 28** ***Perf. 14x13½***

| | | | | |
|---|---|---|---|---|
| **406** | A187 | 5000 l multicolored | .25 | .25 |
| **407** | A187 | 10,000 l multicolored | .55 | .55 |

Reading of Orhon Epitaphs, cent.

**1996, Jan. 31**

| | | | | |
|---|---|---|---|---|
| **408** | A188 | 10,000 l multicolored | .55 | .55 |

Bosnia-Herzegovina.

Fish A189

Designs: 60,000 l, Mullus surmuletus. 10,000 l, Thalassoma pavo. 28,000 l, Diplodus vulgaris. 40,000 l, Epinephelus guaza.

**1996, Mar. 29** ***Perf. 14***

| | | | | |
|---|---|---|---|---|
| **409** | A189 | 6,000 l multicolored | .20 | .20 |
| **410** | A189 | 10,000 l multicolored | .30 | .30 |
| **411** | A189 | 28,000 l multicolored | .80 | .80 |
| **412** | A189 | 40,000 l multicolored | 1.10 | 1.10 |
| | | *Nos. 409-412 (4)* | 2.40 | 2.40 |

Tourism A190

Designs: 100,000 l, Pomegranate tree, vert. 150,000 l, Pomegranate fruit, vert. 250,000 l, Bellapais Monastery. 500,000 l, Folk dancing.

***Perf. 14x13½, 13½x14***

**1996, Apr. 26** **Litho.** **Wmk. 390**

| | | | | |
|---|---|---|---|---|
| **413** | A190 | 100,000 l multi | 2.50 | 2.50 |
| **414** | A190 | 150,000 l multi | 3.75 | 3.75 |
| **415** | A190 | 250,000 l multi | 6.25 | 6.25 |
| **416** | A190 | 500,000 l multi | 12.50 | 12.50 |
| | | *Nos. 413-416 (4)* | 25.00 | 25.00 |

Famous Women A191

Europa: 15,000 l, Beria Remzi Ozoran. 50,000 l, Kadriye Hulusi Hacibulgur.

**1996, May 31** ***Perf. 13½x14***

| | | | | |
|---|---|---|---|---|
| **417** | A191 | 15,000 l multicolored | *.50* | *.50* |
| **418** | A191 | 50,000 l multicolored | *2.00* | *2.00* |

World Environment Day — A192

Designs: a, Older, dying trees in mountainous area. b, Newly-planted trees.

**1996, June 28** ***Perf. 13½***

| | | | | | |
|---|---|---|---|---|---|
| **419** | A192 | 50,000 l | Sheet of 2, #a.-b. | 1.10 | 1.10 |

1996 Summer Olympic Games, Atlanta — A193

a, 15,000 l, Basketball. b, 50,000 l, Javelin. c, 15,000 l, Discus. d, 50,000 l, Volleyball.

**1996, July 31**

| | | | | | |
|---|---|---|---|---|---|
| **420** | A193 | | Sheet of 4, #a.-d. | 3.00 | 3.00 |

Euro '96, European Soccer Championship, Great Britain — A194

**1996, Oct. 31** ***Perf. 13½x14***

| | | | | | |
|---|---|---|---|---|---|
| **421** | A194 | 15,000 l | shown | .40 | .40 |
| **422** | A194 | 35,000 l | Flags, soccer ball | 1.40 | 1.40 |
| ***a.*** | | | Pair, #421-422 | 2.00 | 2.00 |

Civil Defense A195

Security Forces — A196

Nasreddin Hodja A197

Children's Rights A198

***Perf. 13½x14, 14x13½***

**1996, Dec. 23** **Litho.** **Wmk. 390**

| | | | | | |
|---|---|---|---|---|---|
| **423** | A195 | 10,000 l | multicolored | .25 | .25 |
| **424** | A196 | 20,000 l | multicolored | .50 | .50 |
| **425** | A197 | 50,000 l | multicolored | 1.25 | 1.25 |
| **426** | A198 | 75,000 l | multicolored | 1.90 | 1.90 |
| | | | *Nos. 423-426 (4)* | 3.90 | 3.90 |

Paintings — A199

Designs: 25,000 l, Buildings, people, by Lebibe Sonuc. 70,000 l, Woman seated beside plant, by Ruzen Atakan.

**1997, Jan. 31** ***Perf. 14***

| | | | | | |
|---|---|---|---|---|---|
| **427** | A199 | 25,000 l | multicolored | .65 | .65 |
| **428** | A199 | 70,000 l | multicolored | 1.75 | 1.75 |

Mushrooms A200

Natl. Flag on Mountainside A201

Designs: 15,000 l, Amanita phallioides. No. 430, Morchella esculenta. No. 431, Pleurotus eryngii. 70,0000 l, Amanita muscaria.

**1997, Mar. 31**

| | | | | | |
|---|---|---|---|---|---|
| **429** | A200 | 15,000 l | multicolored | .45 | .45 |
| **430** | A200 | 25,000 l | multicolored | .65 | .65 |
| **431** | A200 | 25,000 l | multicolored | .65 | .65 |
| **432** | A200 | 70,000 l | multicolored | 1.75 | 1.75 |
| | | | *Nos. 429-432 (4)* | 3.50 | 3.50 |

**1997, Apr. 23**

| | | | | | |
|---|---|---|---|---|---|
| **433** | A201 | 60,000 l | multicolored | 1.50 | 1.50 |

Stories and Legends A202

Europa: 25,000 l, Woman with broom, children playing, man with donkey. 70,000 l, Well, apple tree, man behind bushes.

**1997, May 30** ***Perf. 13½x14***

| | | | | | |
|---|---|---|---|---|---|
| **434** | A202 | 25,000 l | multicolored | .75 | .75 |
| **435** | A202 | 70,000 l | multicolored | 1.75 | 1.75 |

Visit by Turkish Leaders A203

Designs: 15,000 l, Prime Minister Necmeddin Erbakan, vert. 80,000 l, Pres. Süleyman Demirel.

***Perf. 14x13½, 13½x14***

**1997, June 20**

| | | | | | |
|---|---|---|---|---|---|
| **436** | A203 | 15,000 l | multicolored | .30 | .30 |
| **437** | A203 | 80,000 l | multicolored | 1.50 | 1.50 |

A204

A205

Raptors: No. 438, Aquila chrysaetos. No. 439, Falco eleanorae. 75,000 l, Falco tinnunculus. 100,000 l, Pernis apivorus.

**1997, July 31** ***Perf. 14x13½***

| | | | | | |
|---|---|---|---|---|---|
| **438** | A204 | 40,000 l | multicolored | .55 | .55 |
| **439** | A204 | 40,000 l | multicolored | .55 | .55 |
| **440** | A204 | 75,000 l | multicolored | 1.00 | 1.00 |
| **441** | A204 | 100,000 l | multicolored | 1.40 | 1.40 |
| | | | *Nos. 438-441 (4)* | 3.50 | 3.50 |

**1997, Oct. 28**

Old Coins Used in Cyprus: 25,000 l, 1861 Abdül Aziz gold lira. 40,000 l, 1808 Mahmud II gold rumi. 75,000 l, 1566 Selim II gold lira. 100,000 l, 1909 Mehmed V gold besibirlik.

| | | | | | |
|---|---|---|---|---|---|
| **442** | A205 | 25,000 l | multicolored | .35 | .35 |
| **443** | A205 | 40,000 l | multicolored | .55 | .55 |
| **444** | A205 | 75,000 l | multicolored | 1.00 | 1.00 |
| **445** | A205 | 100,000 l | multicolored | 1.40 | 1.40 |
| | | | *Nos. 442-445 (4)* | 3.30 | 3.30 |

Turk Lisesi, Cent. A206

Scouting, 90th Anniv. A207

Fight Against AIDS — A208

Diesel Engine, Cent. A209

***Perf. 13½x14, 14x13½***

**1997, Dec. 22** **Litho.** **Wmk. 390**

| | | | | | |
|---|---|---|---|---|---|
| **446** | A206 | 25,000 l | multicolored | .30 | .30 |
| **447** | A207 | 40,000 l | multicolored | .50 | .50 |
| **448** | A208 | 100,000 l | multicolored | 1.25 | 1.25 |
| **449** | A209 | 150,000 l | multicolored | 1.75 | 1.75 |
| | | | *Nos. 446-449 (4)* | 3.80 | 3.80 |

Ismet Sevki (1884-1957) and Ahmet Sevki (1874-1959), Photographers — A210

**1998, Jan. 28** ***Perf. 13½x14***

| | | | | | |
|---|---|---|---|---|---|
| **450** | A210 | 40,000 l | shown | .50 | .50 |
| **451** | A210 | 105,000 l | Ahmet Sevki, vert. | 1.25 | 1.25 |

Insects A211

Designs: 40,000 l, Agrion splendens. 65,000 l, Ascalaphus macaronius. 125,000 l, Podalonia hirsuta. 150,000 l, Rhyssa persuasoria.

**1998, Mar. 30**

| | | | | | |
|---|---|---|---|---|---|
| **452** | A211 | 40,000 l | multicolored | .40 | .40 |
| **453** | A211 | 65,000 l | multicolored | .65 | .65 |
| **454** | A211 | 125,000 l | multicolored | 1.25 | 1.25 |
| **455** | A211 | 150,000 l | multicolored | 1.50 | 1.50 |
| | | | *Nos. 452-455 (4)* | 3.80 | 3.80 |

Doors — A212

**1998, Apr. 30** ***Perf. 14x13½***

| | | | | | |
|---|---|---|---|---|---|
| **456** | A212 | 115,000 l | shown | 1.10 | 1.10 |
| **457** | A212 | 140,000 l | Door, steps | 1.40 | 1.40 |

Natl. Festival A213

Europa: 150,000 l, Globe, map of Cyprus, flags, vert.

**1998, May 30** ***Perf. 13½x14, 14x13½***

| | | | | | |
|---|---|---|---|---|---|
| **458** | A213 | 40,000 l | multicolored | .65 | .65 |
| **459** | A213 | 150,000 l | multicolored | 2.10 | 2.10 |

Intl. Year of the Ocean A214

Various marine life.

**1998, June 30** ***Perf. 13½x14***

| | | | | | |
|---|---|---|---|---|---|
| **460** | A214 | 40,000 l | multicolored | .30 | .30 |
| **461** | A214 | 90,000 l | multicolored | .65 | .65 |

Visit by Turkish Prime Minister Mesut Yilmaz A215

**1998, July 20**

| | | | | | |
|---|---|---|---|---|---|
| **462** | A215 | 75,000 l | multicolored | .55 | .55 |

Turkish Pres. Süleyman Demirel — A216

1998 World Cup Soccer Championships, France — A217

Design: 175,000 l, Pres. Demirel, Pres. Rauf R. Denktash, view of ocean, horiz.

**1998, July 25** ***Perf. 13½x14, 14x13½***

**463** A216 75,000 l multicolored .55 .55
**464** A216 175,000 l multicolored 1.25 1.25

Establishment of Yaylacik water program.

**1998, July 31** ***Perf. 13½x14, 13x13½***

75,000 l, Team coming across field, fans in stadium. 175,000 l, Holding up World Cup trophy.

**465** A217 75,000 l multi, horiz. .55 .55
**466** A217 175,000 l multi 1.25 1.25

Visit of Turkish Deputy Prime Minister Bülent Ecevit — A218

Traditional Crafts — A219

**1998, Sept. 5** ***Perf. 14***

**467** A218 200,000 l multicolored 1.50 1.50

**1998, Oct. 26** ***Perf. 13½x14, 14x13½***

**468** A219 50,000 l Kalayci, horiz. .40 .40
**469** A219 75,000 l Sepetci .60 .60
**470** A219 130,000 l Bileyici 1.00 1.00
**471** A219 400,000 l Oymaci, horiz. 3.00 3.00
*Nos. 468-471 (4)* 5.00 5.00

Bayrak Radio & Television, 35th Anniv. A220

Turkish Cyprus, 15th Anniv. A221

Turkish Republic, 75th Anniv. A222

Universal Declaration of Human Rights, 50th Anniv. — A223

No. 476a, 75,000 l, Natl. flag, map of Turkish Cyprus.

**1998, Nov. 15**

**472** A220 50,000 l multicolored .40 .40
**473** A221 75,000 l multicolored .55 .55
**474** A222 75,000 l multicolored .55 .55
**475** A223 175,000 l multicolored 1.25 .65
*Nos. 472-475 (4)* 2.75 2.15

**Souvenir Sheet**

**476** Sheet of 2, #473, #476a 1.10 1.10

A224

**1999, Jan. 15** ***Perf. 14***

**477** A224 75,000 l multicolored .55 .55

Dr. Fazil Kücük (1906-84), politician.

A225

**1999, Jan. 30**

Scene from "Othello," by Verdi: a, Singers standing. b, Singer on floor.

**478** A225 200,000 l Sheet of 2, #a.-b. 1.60 1.60

Snakes A226

Designs: 50,000 l, Malpolon monspessulanus insignitus. 75,000 l, Hierophis jugularis. 195,000 l, Vipera lebetina. 220,000 l, Natrix natrix.

**1999, Mar. 26** ***Perf. 13½x14***

**479** A226 50,000 l multicolored .40 .40
**480** A226 75,000 l multicolored .60 .60
**481** A226 195,000 l multicolored 1.60 1.60
**482** A226 220,000 l multicolored 1.75 1.75
*Nos. 479-482 (4)* 4.35 4.35

Europa A227

**1999, May 17** ***Perf. 14***

**483** A227 75,000 l Sütunlu Cave .75 .75
**484** A227 200,000 l Incirli Cave, vert. 1.75 1.75

Turkish Peace Operation, 25th Anniv. A228

**Wmk. 390**

**1999, July 20** **Litho.** ***Perf. 13¾***

**485** A228 150,000 l shown 1.25 1.25
**486** A228 250,000 l Dove, map, sun 2.00 2.00

Turkish Postal Administration in Cyprus, 35th Anniv. — A229

**1999, Nov. 12** **Litho.** ***Perf. 13¾***

**487** A229 75,000 l multicolored .25 .25

UPU, 125th Anniv. A230

**1999, Nov. 12**

**488** A230 225,000 l multicolored .80 .80

Total Solar Eclipse, Aug. 11 — A231

**1999, Nov. 12**

**489** A231 250,000 l multicolored .90 .90

Destruction of Turkish Heritage in Southern Cyprus — A232

Photos of: 75,000 l, Building, Limassol. 150,000 l, Mosque, Evdim. 210,000 l, Bayraktar Mosque, Nicosia (Lefkosa). 1,000,000 l, Cami-i Kebir Mosque, Paphos (Baf), vert.

**1999, Dec. 3**

**490** A232 75,000 l multi .20 .20
**491** A232 150,000 l multi .55 .55
**492** A232 210,000 l multi .75 .75
**493** A232 1,000,000 l multi 3.75 3.75
*Nos. 490-493 (4)* 5.25 5.25

Millennium A233

Designs: 75,000 l, Cellular phone. 150,000 l, "Welcome 2000." 275,000 l, Computer. 300,000 l, Satellite.

**2000, Mar. 3** **Litho.** ***Perf. 13¾***

**494** A233 75,000 l multi .25 .25
**495** A233 150,000 l multi .50 .50
**496** A233 275,000 l multi .95 .95
**497** A233 300,000 l multi 1.00 1.00
*Nos. 494-497 (4)* 2.70 2.70

Beach Scenes A234

Designs: 300,000 l, Umbrella, pail, shovel, beach ball, sailboats. 340,000 l, Beach chair.

**2000, Apr. 29** **Litho.** ***Perf. 13¾***

**498** A234 300,000 l multi 1.00 1.00
**499** A234 340,000 l multi 1.10 1.10

**Europa, 2000**

**Souvenir Sheet**

**Common Design Type and**

A235

**2000, May 31** **Wmk. 390** ***Perf. 14***

**500** Sheet of 2 1.90 1.90
*a.* CD17 300,000 l multi .95 .95
*b.* A235 300,000 l multi .95 .95

4th Intl. Music Festival, Bellapais Abbey A236

Designs: 150,000 l, Bellapais Abbey. 350,000 l, Blended colors, vert.

**2000, June 21** ***Perf. 13¾***

**501** A236 150,000 l multi .45 .45
**502** A236 350,000 l multi 1.10 1.10

Visit of Turkish Pres. Ahmet N. Sezer — A237

**2000, June 22**

**503** A237 150,000 l multi .45 .45

2000 Summer Olympics, Sydney A238

125,000 l, Torch and Olympic rings, vert. 200,000 l, Runner.

**2000, July 25**

**504-505** A238 Set of 2 .90 .90

**No. 409 Surcharged**

**Method & Perf. as Before**

**2000, Sept. 28** **Wmk. 390**

**506** A189 50,000 l on 6000 l .20 .20

Flora and Fauna — A239

Designs: 125,000 l, Praying mantis on flower. 200,000 l, Butterfly on flower. 275,000 l, Bee on flower. 600,000 l, Snail on flower stem.

**Wmk. 390**

**2000, Oct. 16 Litho. *Perf. 13¾***
**507-510** A239 Set of 4 3.75 3.75

Kerchief Borders A240

Background colors: 125,000 l, Yellow. 200,000 l, Lilac. 265,000 l, Green. 350,000 l, Brown.

**2000, Nov. 28**
**511-514** A240 Set of 4 3.00 3.00

Restored Buildings, Lefkosa A241

Designs: 125,000 l, Lusignan House. 200,000 l, Eaved House.

**Wmk. 390**

**2001, Mar. 28 Litho. *Perf. 13¾***
**515-516** A241 Set of 2 .75 .75

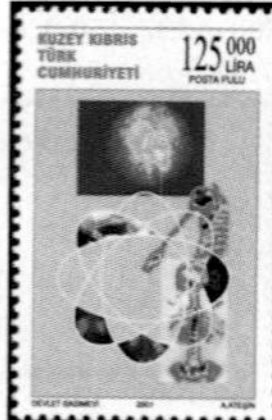

Art — A242

Works by: 125,000 l, Inci Kansu. 200,000 l, Emel Samioglu. 350,000 l, Ozden Selenge, vert. 400,000 l, Ayhatun Atesin.

**2001, Mar. 30**
**517-520** A242 Set of 4 2.50 2.50

Europa — A243

World Environment Day — A244

Designs: 200,000 l, Degirmenlik Reservoir. 500,000 l, Waterfall, Sinar.

**2001, May 31**
**521-522** A243 Set of 2 1.60 1.60

**2001, June 22**

Designs: 125,000 l, Atomic model, x-ray images. 450,000 l, X-ray images, radiation symbol.

**523-524** A244 Set of 2 1.10 1.10

Police Uniforms — A245

Uniforms from: 125,000 l, 1885. 200,000 l, 1933. 500,000 l, 1934. 750,000 l, 1983.

**2001, Aug. 24**
**525-528** A245 Set of 4 2.75 2.75

Automobiles — A246

Designs: 175,000 l, 1954 MG TF. 300,000 l, 1948 Vauxhall 14. 475,000 l, 1922 Bentley. 600,000 l, 1955 Jaguar XK 120.

**Wmk. 390**

**2001, Nov. 2 Litho. *Perf. 13¾***
**529-532** A246 Set of 4 1.90 1.90

Publication of The Genocide Files, by Harry Scott Gibbons — A247

**2001, Dec. 24**
**533** A247 200,000 l multi .30 .30

July 20th Technical School, Cent. A248

**2001, Dec. 24**
**534** A248 200,000 l multi .30 .30

Cartoon Art — A249

Designs: 250,000 l, Chef with grinder and book, by Utku Karsu, vert. 300,000 l, People singing "We Are the World," malnourished Africans, by Musa Kayra. 475,000 l, Can of diet cola airdropped for a malnourished African, by Serhan Gazi, vert. 850,000 l, Child viewing city and painting a country scene, by Mustafa Tozaki, vert.

**Wmk. 390**

**2002, Feb. 28 Litho. *Perf. 13¾***
**535-538** A249 Set of 4 2.60 2.60

Tourism A250

Underwater photographs: 250,000 l, Turtle swimming. 300,000 l, Starfish on coral. 500,000 l, Fish. 750,000 l, Shipwreck.

**2002, Mar. 27**
**539-542** A250 Set of 4 2.50 2.50

Souvenir Sheet

Europa — A251

No. 543: a, Man on stilts. b, Tightrope walker.

**Wmk. 390**

**2002, May 27 Litho. *Perf. 13¾***
**543** A251 600,000 l Sheet of 2, #a-b 1.50 1.50

2002 World Cup Soccer Championships, Japan and Korea — A252

Designs: 300,000 l, Soccer team. 1,000,000 l, "Lift Embargo on Sports."

**2002, June 24**
**544-545** A252 Set of 2 1.60 1.60

Native Costumes — A253

Designs: 250,000 l, Woman. 300,000 l, Man. 425,000 l, Man, diff. 700,000 l, Woman, diff.

**2002, Aug. 8**
**546-549** A253 Set of 4 2.00 2.00

Children's Art — A254

Art by: 300,000 l, M. A. Alpdogan. 600,000 l, S. Avci, vert.

**Wmk. 390**

**2002, Sept. 30 Litho. *Perf. 13¾***
**550-551** A254 Set of 2 .90 .90

Sports Personalities A255

Famous Men A256

Designs: 300,000 l, Sureyya Ayhan, winner of women's 1500m race at 2002 European Track and Field Championships. 1,000,000 l, Park Jung-tae (1944-2002), father of modern taekwondo.

**2002, Oct. 28**
**552-553** A255 Set of 2 1.60 1.60

**2002, Dec. 3**

Designs: 100,000 l, Oguz Karayel (1933-96), soccer player. 175,000 l, Mete Adanir (1961-89), soccer player. 300,000 l, M. Necati Ozkan (1899-1970). 575,000 l, Osman Turkay (1927-2001), poet, horiz.

**554-557** A256 Set of 4 1.40 1.40

Art — A257

Paintings by: 250,000 l, S. Bayraktar. 1,000,000 l, F. Sükan.

**Wmk. 390**

**2003, Feb. 21 Litho. *Perf. 13¾***
**558-559** A257 Set of 2 1.50 1.50

Souvenir Sheet

Europa — A258

Poster art: a, Tree. b, Question mark.

**2003, May 8**
**560** A258 600,000 l Sheet of 2, #a-b 1.60 1.60

Birds A259

Designs: 100,000 l, Oenanthe cypriaca. 300,000 l, Sylvia melanothorax. 500,000 l, Phalacrocorax pygmeus, vert. 600,000 l, Phoenicopterus ruber, vert.

**2003, June 3**
**561-564** A259 Set of 4 2.10 2.10

Chests A260

Chest from: 250,000 l, Seher. 300,000 l, Lapta. 525,000 l, Baf. 1,000,000 l, Karpaz ve Akatu.

***Perf. 13¾x14***

**2003, July 25 Litho. Wmk. 390**
**565-568** A260 Set of 4 3.00 3.00

Flowers — A261

Designs: 150,000 l, Gladiolus triphyllus. 175,000 l, Tulipa cypria. 500,000 l, Ranunculus asiaticus. 525,000 l, Narcissus tazetta.

**2003, Oct. 21 *Perf. 14x13¾***
**569-572** A261 Set of 4 1.75 1.75

National Anniversaries — A262

No. 573 — Kemal Ataturk and flag of: a, Turkey. b, Turkish Republic of Northern Cyprus.

**2003, Nov. 14** ***Perf. 13¾x14***
**573** A262 3,000,000 l Horiz. pair, #a-b 8.50 8.50

Republic of Turkey, 80th anniv. (#573a), Turkish Republic of Northern Cyprus, 20th anniv. (#573b).

Federation of Agricultural Producers, 60th Anniv. A263

**2003, Dec. 12**
**574** A263 300,000 l multi .45 .45

Lions International in Turkish Republic of Northern Cyprus, 40th Anniv. — A263a

**2003, Dec. 12**
**575** A264 500,000 l multi .70 .70

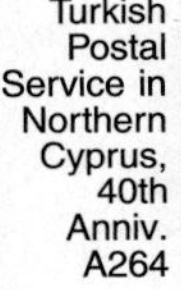

Turkish Postal Service in Northern Cyprus, 40th Anniv. A264

Emblem and: 250,000 l, Mailbox and Nicosia Post Office. 1,500,000 l, Globe, winged envelopes.

***Perf. 13¾x14***
**2004, Apr. 30** **Litho.** **Wmk. 390**
**576-577** A264 Set of 2 2.40 2.40

Souvenir Sheet

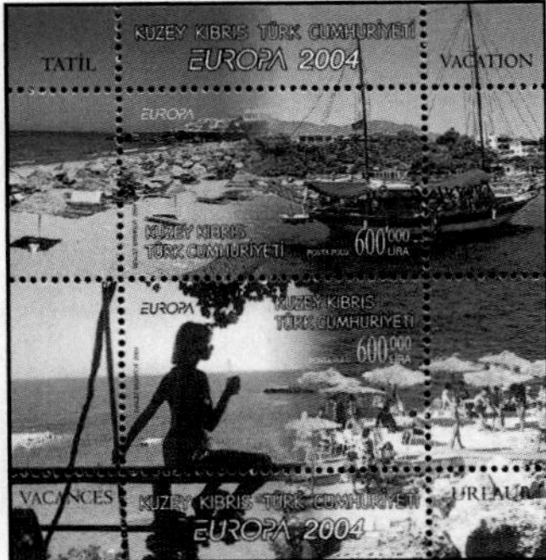


Europa — A265

No. 578: a, Beach, sailboat. b, Woman holding drink, beach.

**2004, May 25**
**578** A265 600,000 l Sheet of 2, #a-b 1.60 1.60

Exists imperf.

Eurasia Postal Union A266

**2004, June 7**
**579** A266 300,000 l multi .40 .40

Flowers — A267

Designs: 250,000 l, Salvia veneris. 300,000 l, Phlomis cypria. 500,000 l, Pimpinella cypria. 600,000 l, Rosularia cypria.

**2004, July 9** ***Perf. 14x13¾***
**580-583** A267 Set of 4 2.40 2.40

Soccer Stadiums A268

Stadium and: 300,000 l, European Soccer Championships emblem. 1,000,000 l, UEFA (European Football Union) 50th anniv. emblem.

**2004, Aug. 20** ***Perf. 13¾x14***
**584-585** A268 Set of 2 1.75 1.75

2004 Summer Olympics, Athens — A269

No. 586, 300,000 l: a, Sailing, handball. b, Boxing, equestrian.
No. 587, 500,000 l: a, Weight lifting, gymnastics. b, Canoeing, tennis.

**2004, Sept. 24** ***Perf. 14x13¾***
**Horiz. pairs, #a-b**
**586-587** A269 Set of 2 2.25 2.25

Eastern Mediterranean University, 25th Anniv. (in 2004) — A270

**2005, Feb. 15** **Litho.** ***Perf. 13¾x14***
**588** A270 15k multi .25 .25

Cyprus Turkish Philatelic Association, 25th Anniv. (in 2004) — A271

**2005, Feb. 15**
**589** A271 30k multi .50 .50

Website for Universities in Turkish Republic of Northern Cyprus — A272

**2005, Feb. 15**
**590** A272 50k multi .80 .80

A273

Tourism A274

**2005, Mar. 9**
**591** A273 10k multi .20 .20
**592** A274 1 l multi 1.60 1.60

Children's Drawings — A275

Drawings of men and women by: 25k, E. Demirci. 50k, E. Oztemiz.

**2005, Apr. 22** ***Perf. 14x13¾***
**593-594** A275 Set of 2 1.10 1.10

Europa — A276

No. 595: a, Woman at left, round table. b, Oven, square table, woman at right.
Illustration reduced.

**2005, May 30** ***Perf. 13¾x14***
**595** A276 60k Pair, #a-b 1.75 1.75
*c.* Souvenir sheet, 2 #595 3.50 3.50

Flowers — A277

Designs: 15k, Fianthus cyprius. 25k, Delphinium caseyi. 30k, Brassica hilarionis. 50k, Limonium albidum.

**2005, July 8** ***Perf. 14x13¾***
**596-599** A277 Set of 4 1.90 1.90

Arts in Towns A278

Designs, 10k, Beach, umbrellas, musical symbols, artist's palette, olive branches, Kyrenia (Girne). 25k, Musical symbols, mosque, Famagusta (Gazimagusa). 50k, Dancers, building, Nicosia (Lefkosa). 1 l, Theater and masks, Kyrenia, Famagusta and Nicosia.

***Perf. 13½x13¾***
**2005, Sept. 9** **Litho.** **Wmk. 390**
**600-603** A278 Set of 4 2.75 2.75

Ercan Airport — A279

**2005, Nov. 23** ***Perf. 13¾x13½***
**604** A279 50k multi .75 .75

University of Northern Cyprus A280

**2005, Nov. 23** ***Perf. 13½x13¾***
**605** A280 1 l multi 1.50 1.50

Europa Stamps, 50th Anniv. A281

Designs: No. 606, 1.40 l, Map of Cyprus. No. 607, 1.40 l, Photo of Cyprus from space, satellite.

**2006, Jan. 6**
**606-607** A281 Set of 2 4.25 4.25
*607a* Souvenir sheet, #606-607 4.25 4.25

No. 607a exists imperf.

**Flowers Type of 2005**

Designs: 15k, Helianthemum obtusifolium. 25k, Iris sisyrhinchium, horiz. 40k, Ranunculus asiaticus, horiz. 50k, Crocus veneris, horiz. 60k, Anemone coronaria, horiz. 70k, Cyclamen persicum.

***Perf. 14x13¾, 13¾x14***
**2006** **Litho.** **Wmk. 390**
**608-613** A277 Set of 6 3.75 3.75

Art — A282

Design: 55k, Sculpture by S. Oztan. 60k, Painting by M. Hastürk.

***Perf. 13¾x13½***
**2006, Apr. 7** **Litho.** **Wmk. 390**
**614-615** A282 Set of 2 1.75 1.75

Dr. Fazil Kucuk (1906-84), Politician — A283

**2006, May 18**

**616** A283 40k multi .50 .50

Kemal Ataturk (1881-1938) A284

**2006, May 18**

**617** A284 1 l multi 1.25 1.25

Europa — A286

Designs: No. 618, 70k, Birds and stars. No. 619, 70k, Pregnant woman, fetus, flags of European countries.

**2006, May 18**

**618-619** A286 Set of 2 1.75 1.75

*619a* Souvenir sheet, #618-619 1.75 1.75

No. 619a exists imperf.

2006 World Cup Soccer Championships, Germany — A287

No. 620: a, 50k, World Cup trophy, map of Germany, mascots, soccer ball and field. b, 1 l, Soccer ball, player, Brandenburg Gate.

**2006, July 7** ***Perf. 13¾x13½***

**620** A287 Pair, #a-b 2.00 2.00

Birds A288

Forest Fire Prevention A289

Designs: 40k, Vanellus vanellus. 50k, Anas platyrhynchos. 60k, Alcedo atthis. 1 l, Himantopus himantopus.

**2006, Sept. 22**

**621-624** A288 Set of 4 3.50 3.50

**2006, Oct. 10** ***Perf. 14x13¾***

**625** A289 50k multi .70 .70

Naci Talat (1945-91), Politician A290

**2006, Oct. 10** ***Perf. 14***

**626** A290 70k multi .95 .95

Eastern Mediterranean Intl. Regatta — A291

**2006, Oct. 10** ***Perf. 14x13¾***

**627** A291 1.50 l multi 2.10 2.10

---

## POSTAL TAX STAMP

Trees — PT1

**1995, July 24** **Litho.** ***Perf. 14***

**RA1** PT1 1000 l black & green 1.50 1.25

---

# TURKMENISTAN

ˌtərk-ˌme-nə-ˈstan

LOCATION — Southern Asia, bounded by Kazakhstan, Uzbekistan, Iran and Afghanistan

GOVT. — Independent republic, member of the Commonwealth of Independent States

AREA — 188,417 sq. mi.

POP. — 4,366,383 (1999 est.)

CAPITAL — Ashgabat

With the breakup of the Soviet Union on Dec. 26, 1991, Turkmenistan and ten former Soviet republics established the Commonwealth of Independent States.

100 Kopecks = 1 Ruble

Manat (1994)

**Catalogue values for all unused stamps in this country are for Never Hinged items.**

Dagdan Necklace, 19th Century — A1

Designs: No. 3, Girl in traditional costume, horiz. No. 4, Akhaltekin horse and rider in native riding dress. No. 5, Mollanepes Theater, horiz. 15r, National arms. No. 7, Pres. Saparmurad Niyazov at left, national flag, horiz. No. 8, Niyazov at right, flag, horiz. No. 9, Map of Turkmenistan.

**1992** **Litho.** ***Perf. 12x12½***

| | | | | |
|---|---|---|---|---|
| 1 | A1 | 50k multicolored | .20 | .20 |

***Perf. 12½***

| | | | | |
|---|---|---|---|---|
| 2 | A1 | 10r multicolored | .25 | .25 |
| 3 | A1 | 10r multicolored | .30 | .30 |
| 4 | A1 | 10r multicolored | .30 | .30 |
| 5 | A1 | 10r multicolored | .30 | .30 |
| 6 | A1 | 15r multicolored | .50 | .50 |
| 7 | A1 | 25r multicolored | .75 | .75 |
| 8 | A1 | 25r multicolored | 1.75 | 1.75 |
| | | *Nos. 1-8 (8)* | 4.35 | 4.35 |

**Size: 112x79mm**

***Imperf***

| | | | | |
|---|---|---|---|---|
| 9 | A1 | 10r multicolored | 6.50 | 6.50 |

Issued: 50k, 1992; #8, 12/8; others, 8/27.
Nos. 2-8 exist imperf.

Nos. 4, 6 Ovptd. with Horse's Head

**1992, Dec. 12**

**Color of Overprint**

| | | | | |
|---|---|---|---|---|
| 10 | A1 | 10r black | 2.00 | 2.00 |
| 11 | A1 | 10r brown | 2.00 | 2.00 |
| 12 | A1 | 10r red | 2.00 | 2.00 |
| 13 | A1 | 10r vermilion | 2.00 | 2.00 |
| 14 | A1 | 10r carmine | 2.00 | 2.00 |
| 15 | A1 | 10r green | 2.00 | 2.00 |
| 16 | A1 | 15r black | 2.00 | 2.00 |
| 17 | A1 | 15r brown | 2.00 | 2.00 |
| 18 | A1 | 15r red | 2.00 | 2.00 |
| 19 | A1 | 15r pink | 2.00 | 2.00 |
| 20 | A1 | 15r blue | 2.00 | 2.00 |
| 21 | A1 | 15r yellow | 2.00 | 2.00 |
| | | *Nos. 10-21 (12)* | 24.00 | 24.00 |

1992 Summer Olympics, Barcelona A2

Designs: a, 1r, Weight lifting. b, 3r, Equestrian. c, 5r, Wrestling. d, 10r, Rowing. e, 15r, Emblem of Turkmenistan Olympic Committee. No. 23, Flags, symbols for modern pentathalon, weight lifting, rowing, gymnastics.

**1992, Dec. 15** **Photo.** ***Perf. 10½x10***

**22** A2 Strip of 5, #a.-e. 6.00 6.00

***Imperf***

**Size: 108x82mm**

**23** A2 15r multicolored 5.50 5.50

For surcharge see No. 33.

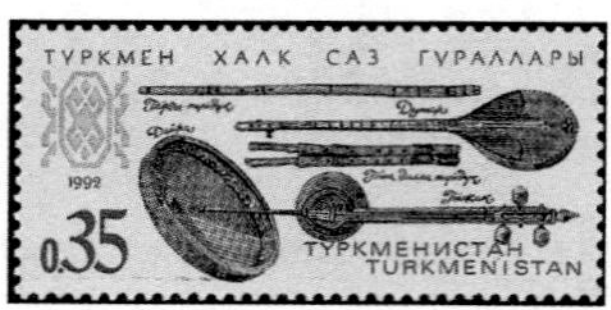


Musical Instruments — A3

**Photo. & Engr.**

**1992, Sept. 13** ***Perf. 12x11½***

**28** A3 35k buff, red brn, gold & black .20 .20

Horse A4

**1992, Aug. 9** **Photo.** ***Perf. 12***

**29** A4 20k shown .20 .20

**30** A4 40k Snake, vert. .25 .25

A5

**1992, Nov. 29** **Litho.** ***Perf. 12x11½***

**31** A5 1r multicolored .25 .25

US Pres. Bill Clinton, Pres. Saparmurad Niyazov — A6

Designs dated: a. 21.30.93. b. 22.03.93. c, 23.03.93. d, 24.03.93. e, 25.03.93.

**1993, Mar. 21** **Litho.** ***Perf. 10½***

**32** A6 100r Strip of 5, #a.-e. 8.50 8.50

Pres. Niyazov's visit to New York City & Washington DC.
Exists imperf.

No. 22 Surcharged

**1993, Apr. 1** **Photo.** ***Perf. 10½x10***

| | | | | |
|---|---|---|---|---|
| **33** | A2 | Strip of 5 | 5.00 | 5.00 |
| *a.* | | 25r on 1r | 1.00 | 1.00 |
| *b.* | | 10r on 3r | .45 | .45 |
| *c.* | | 15r on 5r | .55 | .55 |
| *d.* | | 15r on 10r | .55 | .55 |
| *e.* | | 50r on 15r | 1.75 | 1.75 |

Size of surcharge varies.

Phoca Caspica — A7

World Wildlife Fund A8

Phoca caspica: #34a, 25r, Facing right. #34b, 500r, Facing left. 15r, Lying in snow. 50r, On rocks. 100r, Mother and young. 150r, Swimming.

**1993, Oct. 11** **Litho.** ***Perf. 13½***

| | | | | |
|---|---|---|---|---|
| **34** | A7 | Pair #a.-b. | 3.50 | 3.50 |
| **35** | A8 | 15r multicolored | .50 | .50 |
| **36** | A8 | 50r multicolored | .85 | .85 |
| **37** | A8 | 100r multicolored | 1.50 | 1.50 |

**38** A8 150r multicolored 3.00 3.00
*a.* Bklt. pane, 2 ea #34-38 22.00 22.00
Booklet, #38a 24.00
*Nos. 34-38 (5)* 9.35 9.35

Formation of Tovarishch Society for Exploitation of Turkmen Oil Fields, 115th Anniv. — A9

Designs: 1m, Two men viewing oil field. 1.5m, Early tanker Turkmen. 2m, Oil well. 3m, Alfred Nobel, Ludwig Nobel, Robert Nobel, Petr Bilderling, vert. 5m, Early oil field.

**1994, June 26 Litho. *Perf. 13***

**39** A9 1m multicolored .50 .50
**40** A9 1.5m multicolored .75 .75
**41** A9 2m multicolored 1.00 1.00
**42** A9 3m multicolored 1.25 1.25
*a.* Miniature sheet of 8 + label 10.00 10.00
*Nos. 39-42 (4)* 3.50 3.50

**Souvenir Sheet**

**43** A9 5m multicolored 2.50 2.50

See Azerbaijan Nos. 416-418a.

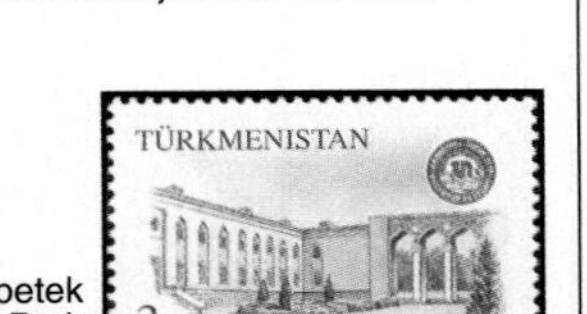


Repetek Natl. Park A10

Designs: 3m, Repetek Institute. No. 45, Desert, camels. No. 46, Echus carinatus. No. 47, Varanus griseus. 20m, Testudo horsfieldi. No. 49, Haloxylon ammodendron.

**1994, Dec. 11 Litho. *Perf. 13***

**44** A10 3m multicolored .50 .50
**45** A10 5m multicolored .55 .55
**46** A10 5m multicolored .55 .55
*a.* Miniature sheet of 8 + label 6.00 6.00
**47** A10 10m multicolored 1.10 1.10
**48** A10 20m multicolored 2.00 2.00
*Nos. 44-48 (5)* 4.70 4.70

**Souvenir Sheet**

**49** A10 10m multicolored 2.00 2.00

Intl. Olympic Committee, Cent. — A11

**1994, Dec. 30 Litho. *Perf. 14***

**50** A11 11.25m multicolored 1.75 1.75

**Souvenir Sheet**

**51** A11 20m multicolored 3.50 3.50

**Miniature Sheet**

Save the Aral Sea — A12

Designs: a, Feis caracal. b, Salmo trutta aralensis. c, Hyaena hyaena. d, Pseudoscaphirhynchus kaufmanni. e, Aspiolucius esocinus.

**1996, Apr. 29 Litho. *Perf. 14***

**52** A12 100m Sheet of 5, #a.-e. 6.50 6.50

Independence, 5th Anniv. — A13

#53, Map of Turkmenistan on globe, vert. #54, Train pulling into station. #55, Natl. Airport, vert. #56, Iranian Pres. Rafsanjani, Turkmenistan Pres. Saparmurad Niyazov, Turkish Pres. Demirel. 500m, UN Secretary-General Boutros Boutros-Gali, Pres. Niyazov, vert. 1000m, Natl. flag, arms.

**1996, Oct. 27 Litho. *Perf. 14***

**53** A13 100m multicolored .25 .25
**54** A13 100m multicolored .40 .40
**55** A13 300m multicolored .75 .75
**56** A13 300m multicolored 1.00 1.00
**57** A13 500m multicolored 1.50 1.50
**58** A13 1000m multicolored 2.75 2.75
*Nos. 53-58 (6)* 6.65 6.65

1996 Summer Olympic Games, Atlanta A14

**1997, May 5 Litho. *Perf. 14x14½***

**59** A14 100m Judo .50 .50
**60** A14 300m Boxing 1.25 1.25
**61** A14 300m Track & field 1.25 1.25
**62** A14 300m Wrestling 1.25 1.25
**63** A14 500m Shooting 2.50 2.50
*Nos. 59-63 (5)* 6.75 6.75

**Souvenir Sheet**

**64** A14 1000m Olympic torch 6.25 6.25

Items inscribed "Turkmenistan" that were not authorized but which have appeared on the market in recent months include:

Single stamps of 100m depicting Princess Diana (3 different stamps), Mother Teresa, Pope John Paul II and Mother Teresa, 50th Anniv. of India, and 50th Anniv. of Pakistan.

Sheets of 4 stamps with denominations of 100m depicting JAPEX 98 / Cats.

Sheets of 9 stamps with denominations of 100m depicting the Titanic, Trains, Golfers, Japanese Armor, Japanese Paper Dolls, and Japanese Art.

Sheets of 6 stamps with denominations of 120m depicting Millennium (8 different sheets).

Sheets of 6 stamps with denominations of 120m depicting Pokémon, and Brad Pitt.

Sheets of 4 stamps with denominations of 195m depicting Greenpeace, Elvis Presley, Birds, Orchids, and Japanese Fashion.

Sheets of 6 stamps with denominations of 195m depicting Marilyn Monroe.

Sheets of 9 stamps with denominations of 195m depicting Cacti, and Minerals.

Sheets of 4 stamps with denominations of 250m depicting Akira Kurosawa.

Sheets of 2 stamps with denominations of 390m depicting Brazilian soccer players from 1998 World Cup.

Sheets of 9 stamps with denominations of 1000m depicting IBRA / Mushrooms (2 different sheets).

Souvenir sheets of 1 stamp with various denominations depicting Hokusai Artwork (2 different sheets), Pope John Paul II (2 different sheets), the Titanic (2 different sheets), 1998 Winter Olympics (2 sheets), Year of the Tiger (2 sheets), 50th Anniv. of Israel, Princess Diana, Queen Mother, Che Guevara, Frank Sinatra, Marilyn Monroe, Elvis Presley, International Year of Older Persons / Bob Hope, 1998 World Cup Soccer Championships, Severiano Ballasteros, Jacques Villeneuve, Leaders of the World / Automobiles, and Maria de Medici / Millennium.

Women's Traditional Clothing — A15

Various costumes.

**1999, July 5 Litho. *Perf. 14***

**65** A15 500m multi .75 .75
**66** A15 1000m multi 1.25 1.25
**67** A15 1200m multi 1.75 1.75
**68** A15 2500m multi 2.25 2.25
**69** A15 3000m multi 3.00 3.00
*Nos. 65-69 (5)* 9.00 9.00

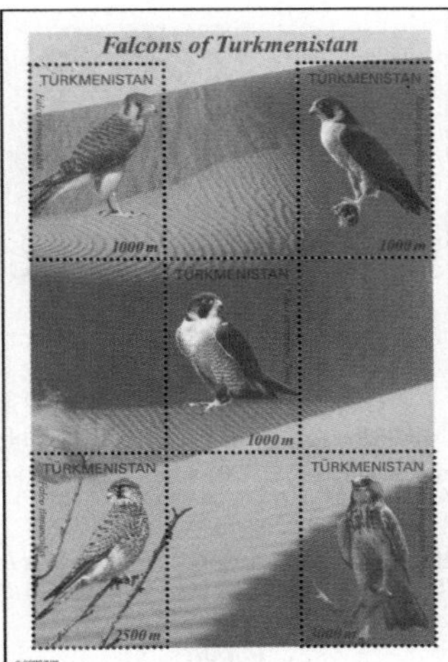


Falcons — A16

a, 1000m, Falco tinnunculus. b, 1000m, Falco peregrinus, looking left. c, 1000m, Falco peregrinus, looking right. d, 2500m, Falco tinnunculus, diff. e, 3000m, Falco peregrinus, diff.

**2000, Mar. 30 Litho. *Perf. 14***

**70** A16 Sheet of 5, #a-e 11.50 11.50

Horn — A17

**2000, Oct. Litho. *Imperf.***

**Self-Adhesive**

**71** A17 A multi 1.25 1.25

Sold for 5000m on day of issue.

UN Resolution on the Permanent Neutrality of Turkmenistan, 5th Anniv. — A18

UN emblem, "5," and flags of Turkmenistan and resolution co-sponsors: a, Afghanistan. b, Armenia. c, Azerbaijan. d, Bangladesh. e, Belarus. f, Colombia. g, Czech Republic. h, Egypt. i, France. j, Georgia. k, India. l, Indonesia. m, Iran. n, Kenya. o, Kyrgyzstan. p, Malaysia. q, Mauritius. r, Pakistan. s, Moldova. t, Russia. u, Senegal. v, Tajikistan. w, Turkey. x, Ukraine.

**2000, Dec. Litho. *Perf. 14***

**72** Sheet of 24 + label 37.50 37.50
*a.-x.* A18 3000m Any single 1.50 1.50

Trade Center Building A19

Flag and Arms A20

**2001, Apr. 24 Litho. *Imperf.***

**Self-Adhesive**

**73** A19 B multi .60 .60
**74** A20 U multi 1.25 1.25

No. 73 sold for 1,200m, No. 74 sold for 3,000m on day of issue.

Horses — A21

No. 75, horiz.: a, Perenli. b, Garader. c, Pyyada. d, Tyllanur. e, Arkadas. f, Yanardag.
No. 76, 5000m, Yanardag, diff., horiz. (denomination at LR). No. 77, 5000m, Yanardag, diff., horiz. (denomination at UR).
No. 78: a, Bitarap. b, Yanardag, diff.

**2001, Aug. 20 Litho. *Perf. 14½x14***

| | | | | |
|---|---|---|---|---|
| **75** | A21 | 3000m Sheet of 6, #a-f | 9.00 | 9.00 |

**Size: 116x90mm**

***Imperf***

| | | | | |
|---|---|---|---|---|
| **76-77** | A21 | Set of 2 | 5.00 | 5.00 |

**Souvenir Sheet**

***Perf. 14x14½***

| | | | | |
|---|---|---|---|---|
| **78** | A21 | 5000m Sheet of 2, #a-b | 5.00 | 5.00 |

Items inscribed "Turkmenistan" that were not authorized by Turkmenistan postal officials but have appeared on the market in recent months include:

Sheets of 9 stamps with denominations of 50m depicting Kim Basinger, Matt Damon, and Pope John Paul II.

Sheets of 9 stamps with denominations of 100m depicting Leading Personalities of the 20th Century.

Sheets of 6 stamps with denominations of 120m depicting Leonardo DiCaprio, and Princess Diana.

Sheets of 8 stamps with denominations of 120m and one label depicting scenes and people from the 20th Century (3 different sheets).

Sheets of 9 stamps with denominations of 120m depicting Princess Diana, Musical group V.I.P., Television show "Xena, Warrior Princess," Elizabeth Taylor, Bruce Lee, Jackie Chan, Tiger Woods, Muhammad Ali, Monaco Grand Prix race cars, Auto racer David Coulthard, Soccer player David Beckham, Euro 2000 European Football Championships, Rugby players, Tennis Stars of the Millennium, Sportsmen of the Millennium, Elephants, Cats, Butterflies, and Pokémon.

Sheets of 2 stamps with denominations of 390m depicting Soccer players from the 1998 World Cup (2 different sheets depicting French and Japanese players).

Souvenir sheets of 1 with denominations of 975m depicting the Mona Lisa, Marilyn Monroe, and Lucille Ball.

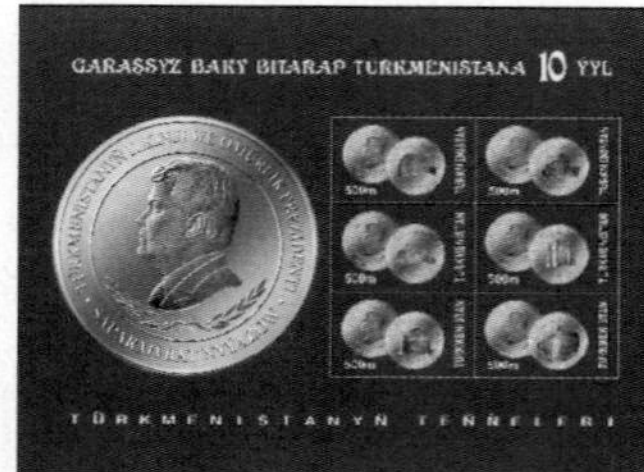

A22

Independence, 10th Anniv. — A23

No. 79 — 500m coins with reverses showing: a, Building with domed roof, coin denomination at right. b, Building with domed roof and tower, coin denomination at left. c, Building with pointed, conical roof. d, Building with archway. e, Building with domed roof on cubic base. f, Statue.
No. 80 — Archaeological sites: a, Soltan Sanjar. b, Nusay. c, Gyz Gala. d, Urgenç. e, Anew. f, Köne Urgenç.
No. 81 — Items in National museum: a, Horn. b, 19th cent. carpet. c, Musical instrument. d, Statue of nude woman. e, Vase. f, 20th cent. decoration.
No. 82, horiz. — Hotels: a, Ahal. b, Gara Altyn. c, Demiryolçy. d, Altyn Suw. e, Köpetdag. f, Aziya.
No. 83 — Buildings: a, Altyn Asyryn Yasayys Jaylary. b, Bitaraplyk Binasy (Arch of Neutrality). c, Türkmendöwletätiyaçlandyrys. d, Random Tower. e, Türkmenbasy Bank. f, Altyn Asyr Söwda Merkezi (Trade Center Building).
No. 84 — Monuments to: a, Oguz Han. b, Seljuk Bay. c, Bayram Han. d, Soltan Sanjar. e, Gorkut Ata. f, Görogly Beg.
No. 85 — Monuments to: a, Sahyrlary Bayram Han. b, Sahyrlary Kemine. c, Sahyrlary Zelili. d, Sahyrlary Seydi. e, Sahyrlary Mollanepes. f, Sahyrlary Mätäji.

**2001 Litho. *Imperf.***

| | | | | |
|---|---|---|---|---|
| **79** | A22 | 500m Sheet of 6, #a-f | 3.00 | 3.00 |
| **80** | A23 | 1000m Sheet of 6, #a-f | 5.00 | 5.00 |
| **81** | A23 | 1200m Sheet of 6, #a-f | 7.00 | 7.00 |
| **82** | A23 | 1250m Sheet of 6, #a-f | 8.00 | 8.00 |
| **83** | A23 | 1250m Sheet of 6, #a-f | 8.00 | 8.00 |
| **84** | A23 | 3000m Sheet of 6, #a-f | 15.00 | 15.00 |
| **85** | A23 | 3000m Sheet of 6, #a-f | 15.00 | 15.00 |
| | | *Nos. 79-85 (7)* | 61.00 | 61.00 |

Issued: Nos. 79-80, 10/17; No. 81, 10/19; Nos. 82-83, 10/23; Nos. 84-85, 10/21.

Mohammed Ali Jinnah (1876-1948), First Governor General of Pakistan — A24

**2001, Dec. 25 Litho. *Perf. 13***

| | | | | |
|---|---|---|---|---|
| **86** | A24 | 500m multi | .90 | .90 |

Birds — A25

No. 87, 3000m: a, Motacilla flava. b, Lanius isabellinus. c, Oenanthe oenanthe. d, Corvus monedula. e, Corvus cornix. f, Upupa pyrrhocorax.
No. 88, 3000m: a, Sylvia communis. b, Cuculus canorus. c, Sylvia curruca. d, Corvus pica. e, Corvus frugilegus. f, Corvus corax.
No. 89, 5000m, Anas crecca. No. 90, 5000m, Riparia riparia.

**2002, Dec. 1 Litho. *Perf. 14***

**Sheets of 6, #a-f**

| | | | | |
|---|---|---|---|---|
| **87-88** | A25 | Set of 2 | 15.00 | 15.00 |

**Souvenir Sheets**

| | | | | |
|---|---|---|---|---|
| **89-90** | A25 | Set of 2 | 4.00 | 4.00 |

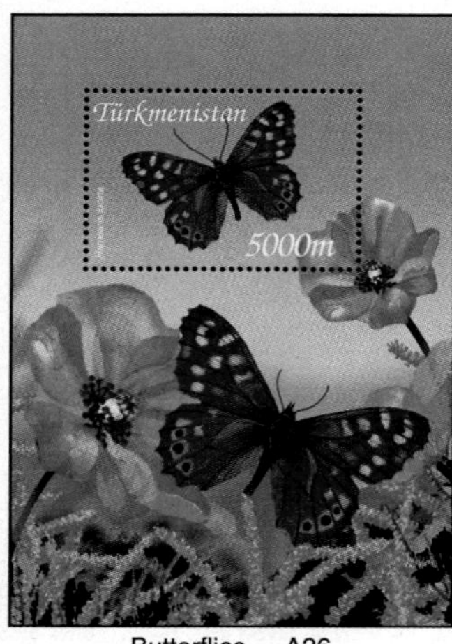

Butterflies — A26

No. 91, 3000m, vert.: a, Vanessa indica. b, Cynthia cardui. c, Pararge aegeria. d, Pieris rapae. e, Lysandra bellargus. f, Anthocharis cardamines.
No. 92, 3000m, vert.: a, Pandoriana pandora. b, Chazara briseis. c, Aphantopus hyperantus. d, Iolana iolas. e, Pararge schakra. f, Maniola jurtina.
No. 93, 5000m, Hamearis lucina. No. 94, 5000m, Quercusia quercus.

**2002, Dec. 1**

**Sheets of 6, #a-f**

| | | | | |
|---|---|---|---|---|
| **91-92** | A26 | Set of 2 | 15.00 | 15.00 |

**Souvenir Sheets**

| | | | | |
|---|---|---|---|---|
| **93-94** | A26 | Set of 2 | 4.00 | 4.00 |

Souvenir Sheet

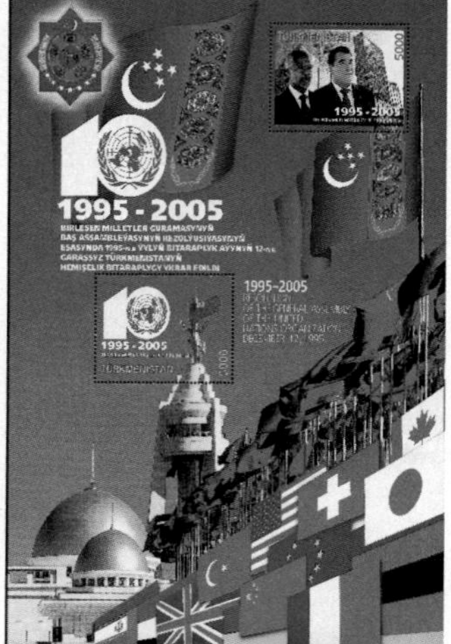

Permanent Neutrality of Turkmenistan, 10th Anniv. — A32

No. 100: a, UN Secretary General Kofi Annan and Turkmenistan Pres. Saparmurad Niyazov. b, Sculpture on building, UN emblem.

**2005, Dec. 1 Litho. *Perf. 11½***

| | | | | |
|---|---|---|---|---|
| **100** | A32 | 5000m Sheet of 2, #a-b | *10.00* | *10.00* |

Souvenir Sheets

A33

A34

A35

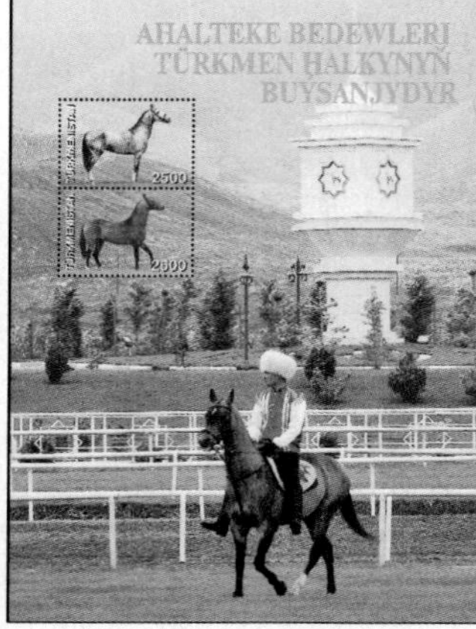

Akhal-Teke Horses — A36

No. 101: a, Horse's head. b, Horse rearing up.
No. 102: a, Pony nursing. b, Horse walking left.
No. 103: a, Horse facing right. b, Horse facing left.
No. 104: a, Gray horse and mountain. b, Brown horse and mountain.

**2005, Dec. 1**

| | | | | |
|---|---|---|---|---|
| **101** | A33 | 2500m Sheet of 2, #a-b | *4.00* | *4.00* |
| **102** | A34 | 2500m Sheet of 2, #a-b | *4.00* | *4.00* |
| **103** | A35 | 2500m Sheet of 2, #a-b | *4.00* | *4.00* |
| **104** | A36 | 2500m Sheet of 2, #a-b | *4.00* | *4.00* |
| | | *Nos. 101-104 (4)* | *16.00* | *16.00* |

Miniature Sheet

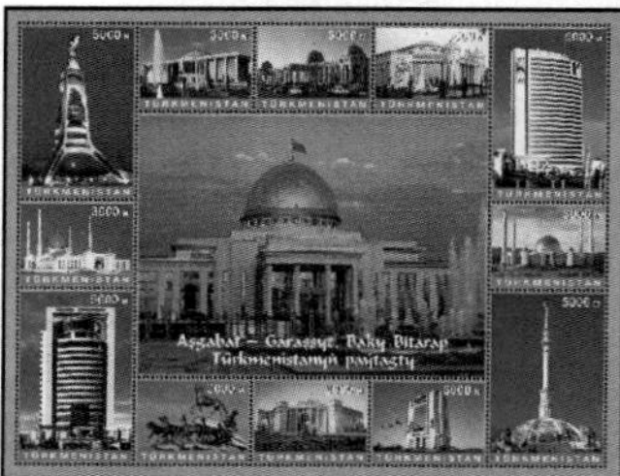

Ashgabat Architecture — A37

No. 105: a, 3000m, Building with dome, fountain at left. b, 3000m, Rukhiyet Palace (building with three green domes, automobiles). c, 3000m, Building with three golden domes and fountain. d, 3000m, Goktepe Mosque (green domes). e, 3000m, Mosque with golden domes. f, 3000m, Statue of Akhal-Teke horses. g, 3000m, Domed building with fence. h, 3000m, Central Bank and flags. i, 5000m, Neutrality Arch at night, vert. j, 5000m, Oil and Gas Ministry Building with flagpoles at right, vert. k, 5000m, President Hotel with flagpoles at left, vert. l, Independence Monument with statues at left and right, vert. Sizes: Nos.

105a-105h, 40x30mm; Nos. 105i-105l, 40x60mm.

**2006** **Litho.** ***Perf. 13x12¾***

| | | | |
|---|---|---|---|
| **105** | A37 | Sheet of 12, #a-l, + label | *17.00 17.00* |

# TURKS AND CAICOS ISLANDS

ˈtərks ənˌdˌ ˈ kā-kəs ˈī-lənds

LOCATION — A group of islands in the West Indies, at the southern extremity of the Bahamas
GOVT. — British colony; a dependency of Jamaica until 1959
AREA — 192 sq. mi.
POP. — 16,863 (1999 est.)
CAPITAL — Grand Turk

12 Pence = 1 Shilling
20 Shillings = 1 Pound
100 Cents = 1 US Dollar (1969)

**Catalogue values for unused stamps in this country are for Never Hinged items, beginning with Scott 90.**

Dependency's Badge
A6 A7

**1900-04 Engr. Wmk. 2 *Perf. 14***

1 A6 ½p green 3.00 *4.50*
2 A6 1p rose 4.00 .85
3 A6 2p black brown 1.10 *1.40*
4 A6 2½p gray blue ('04) 2.00 1.10
*a.* 2½p blue ('00) 8.50 *17.50*
5 A6 4p orange 4.25 *8.00*
6 A6 6p violet 2.75 *7.50*
7 A6 1sh purple brn 3.75 *20.00*

**Wmk. 1**

8 A7 2sh violet 45.00 *67.50*
9 A7 3sh brown lake 62.50 *85.00*
*Nos. 1-9 (9)* 128.35 *195.85*

**1905-08 Wmk. 3**

10 A6 ½p green 5.75 .20
11 A6 1p carmine 18.00 .55
12 A6 3p violet, *yel* ('08) 2.50 *7.00*
*Nos. 10-12 (3)* 26.25 *7.75*

King Edward VII — A8

**1909, Sept. 2 *Perf. 14***

13 A8 ¼p yellow green .85 .45
14 A8 1p carmine 1.40 .45
15 A8 2p gray 3.50 1.60
16 A8 2½p ultra 4.25 4.25
17 A8 3p violet, *yel* 2.75 2.25
18 A8 4p red, *yel* 3.75 *8.00*
19 A8 6p violet 8.00 7.00
20 A8 1sh black, *green* 8.00 *9.50*
21 A8 2sh red, *grn* 40.00 *55.00*
22 A8 3sh black, *red* 40.00 *45.00*
*Nos. 13-22 (10)* 112.50 *133.50*

Turk's-Head Cactus
A9

George V
A10

**1910-11 Wmk. 3**

23 A9 ¼p claret 2.00 1.10
24 A9 ¼p red ('11) .70 .50

See Nos. 36, 44.

**1913-16**

25 A10 ½p yellow green .55 *2.00*
26 A10 1p carmine 1.10 *2.50*
27 A10 2p gray 2.50 *4.00*
28 A10 2½p ultra 2.50 *3.50*
29 A10 3p violet, *yel* 2.50 *12.50*
30 A10 4p scarlet, *yel* 1.10 *11.00*
31 A10 5p olive grn ('16) 7.50 *25.00*
32 A10 6p dull violet 2.75 *4.00*
33 A10 1sh orange 1.75 *5.75*
34 A10 2sh red, *bl grn* 8.50 *30.00*
*a.* 2sh red, *grnsh white* ('19) 30.00 *80.00*
*b.* 2sh red, *emerald* ('21) *55.00* *80.00*
35 A10 3sh black, *red* 17.50 *30.00*
*Nos. 25-35 (11)* 48.25 *130.25*

Issued: 5p, 5/18/16; others, 4/1/13.
For overprints see Nos. MR1-MR13.

**1921, Apr. 23 Wmk. 4**

36 A9 ¼p red 2.75 *17.50*
37 A10 ½p green 3.00 *6.25*
38 A10 1p scarlet 1.10 *6.25*
39 A10 2p gray 1.10 *21.00*
40 A10 2½p ultra 2.00 *8.50*
41 A10 5p olive green 9.00 *57.50*
42 A10 6p dull violet 7.50 *57.50*
43 A10 1sh brown orange 7.50 *32.50*
*Nos. 36-43 (8)* 33.95 *207.00*

A11

A12

Inscribed "Postage"

**1922-26**

44 A9 ¼p gray black ('26) .90 *1.10*
45 A11 ½p green 2.50 *3.75*
46 A11 1p brown .55 *3.75*
47 A11 1½p rose red ('25) 7.50 *18.00*
48 A11 2p gray .55 *5.75*
49 A11 2½p violet, *yel* .55 *2.00*
50 A11 3p ultra .55 *5.75*
51 A11 4p red, *yel* 1.40 *18.00*
52 A11 5p yellow grn 1.00 *25.00*
53 A11 6p dull violet .80 *7.00*
54 A11 1sh orange .90 *21.00*
55 A11 2sh red, *green* 2.25 *10.50*

**Wmk. 3**

56 A11 2sh red, *green* ('25) 29.00 *80.00*
57 A11 3sh black, *red* ('25) 5.75 *32.50*
*Nos. 44-57 (14)* 54.20 *234.10*

Issued: #47, 56-57, 11/24; #44, 10/11; others, 11/20.

Inscribed "Postage and Revenue"

**1928, Mar. 1 Wmk. 4**

60 A12 ½p green .85 .55
61 A12 1p brown .85 .80
62 A12 1½p red .85 *3.75*
63 A12 2p dk gray .85 .55
64 A12 2½p vio, *yel* .85 *5.75*
65 A12 3p ultra .85 *8.00*
66 A12 6p brown vio .85 *8.50*
67 A12 1sh brown org 4.25 *8.50*
68 A12 2sh red, *grn* 7.00 *40.00*
69 A12 5sh green, *yel* 12.50 *40.00*
70 A12 10sh violet, *bl* 57.50 *110.00*
*Nos. 60-70 (11)* 87.20 *226.40*

Common Design Types pictured following the introduction.

**Silver Jubilee Issue**
Common Design Type

**1935, May 6 *Perf. 11x12***

71 CD301 ½p green & blk .35 *.50*
72 CD301 3p ultra & brn 1.75 *3.25*
73 CD301 6p ol grn & lt bl 1.75 *3.75*
74 CD301 1sh brn vio & ind 3.50 2.50
*Nos. 71-74 (4)* 7.35 *10.00*
Set, never hinged 12.00

**Coronation Issue**
Common Design Type

**1937, May 12 *Perf. 13½x14***

75 CD302 ½p deep green .20 .20
76 CD302 2p gray .30 .25
77 CD302 3p brt ultra .40 .25
*Nos. 75-77 (3)* .90 .70
Set, never hinged 1.25

Raking Salt — A13

Salt Industry — A14

**1938-45 Wmk. 4 *Perf. 12½***

78 A13 ¼p black .20 .20
79 A13 ½p green 1.90 .20
80 A13 1p brown .35 .20
81 A13 1½p carmine .35 .20
82 A13 2p gray .55 .25
83 A13 2½p orange 2.00 .90
84 A13 3p ultra .25 .25
85 A13 6p rose violet 4.75 1.40
85A A13 6p blk brn ('45) .20 .20
86 A13 1sh bister 1.90 *8.00*
86A A13 1sh dk ol grn ('45) .20 .20
87 A14 2sh rose car 20.00 13.50
88 A14 5sh green 24.00 15.00
89 A14 10sh dp violet 6.00 *6.75*
*Nos. 78-89 (14)* 62.65 47.25
Set, never hinged 90.00

**Catalogue values for unused stamps in this section, from this point to the end of the section, are for Never Hinged items.**

**Peace Issue**
Common Design Type

**1946, Nov. 4 Engr. *Perf. 13½x14***

90 CD303 2p gray black .20 .20
91 CD303 3p deep blue .25 .20

**Silver Wedding Issue**
Common Design Types

**1948, Sept. 13 Photo. *Perf. 14x14½***

92 CD304 1p red brown .20 .25

***Perf. 11½x11***
**Engr.; Name Typo.**

93 CD305 10sh purple 8.50 *13.00*

Dependency's Badge — A17

Flag and Merchant Ship — A18

Map of the Islands A19

Victoria and George VI A20

**1948, Dec. 14 Engr. *Perf. 12½***

94 A17 ½p green .20 .20
95 A17 2p carmine .25 .20
96 A18 3p deep blue .40 .40
97 A19 6p violet .50 .45
98 A20 2sh ultra & blk .75 *.75*
99 A20 5sh blue grn & blk 2.25 2.00
100 A20 10sh chocolate & blk 3.50 *5.00*
*Nos. 94-100 (7)* 7.85 *9.00*

Cent. of political separation from the Bahamas.

**UPU Issue**
Common Design Types
**Engr.; Name Typo. on 3p, 6p**
***Perf. 13½, 11x11½***

**1949, Oct. 10 Wmk. 4**

101 CD306 2½p red orange .20 .20
102 CD307 3p indigo 1.40 1.40
103 CD308 6p chocolate .55 .55
104 CD309 1sh olive .55 .55
*Nos. 101-104 (4)* 2.70 2.70

Loading Bulk Salt — A21

Dependency's Badge — A22

Designs: 1p, Salt Cay. 1½p, Caicos mail. 2p, Grand Turk. 2½p, Sponge diving. 3p, South Creek. 4p, Map. 6p, Grand Turk Light. 1sh, Government House. 1sh6p, Cockburn Harbor. 2sh, Government offices. 5sh, Salt Loading.

**1950, Aug. 2 Engr. *Perf. 12½***

105 A21 ½p deep green .70 .50
106 A21 1p chocolate .60 *1.00*
107 A21 1½p carmine 1.00 .75
108 A21 2p red orange .50 *.50*
109 A21 2½p olive green .90 .65
110 A21 3p ultra .25 *.50*
111 A21 4p rose car & blk 3.00 .95
112 A21 6p ultra & blk 2.25 .65
113 A21 1sh bl gray & blk 1.00 .50
114 A21 1sh6p red & blk 9.00 4.50
115 A21 2sh ultra & emer 3.25 *4.75*
116 A21 5sh black & ultra 20.00 9.50
117 A22 10sh purple & blk 20.00 *22.50*
*Nos. 105-117 (13)* 62.45 *47.25*

**Coronation Issue**
Common Design Type

**1953, June 2 *Perf. 13½x13***

118 CD312 2p red orange & blk .30 *.75*

M. S. Kirksons A23

Design: 8p, Flamingos in flight.

**1955, Feb. 1 Wmk. 4 *Perf. 12½***

119 A23 5p emerald & blk .50 .50
120 A23 8p yellow brn & blk 2.00 .50

Queen Elizabeth II — A24

Bonefish A25

Pelican and Salinas A26

Designs: 2p, Red grouper. 2½p, Spiny lobster. 3p, Albacore. 4p, Muttonfish snapper. 5p,

Permit. 6p, Conch. 8p, Flamingos. 1sh, Spanish mackerel. 1sh6p, Salt Cay. 2sh, Caicos sloop. 5sh, Cable office. 10sh, Dependency's badge.

***Perf. 13½x14 (1p), 13½x13***

**1957-60 Engr. Wmk. 314**

**121** A24 1p lil rose & dk bl .20 .20
**122** A25 1½p orange & slate .20 .20
**123** A25 2p ol & brn red .20 .20
**124** A25 2½p brt grn & car .20 .20
**125** A25 3p purple & blue .20 .20
**126** A25 4p blk & dp rose .60 .20
**127** A25 5p brown & grn .80 .40
**128** A25 6p ultra & car 1.60 .45
**129** A25 8p black & ver 2.75 .20
**130** A25 1sh blk & dk blue .65 .20
**131** A25 1sh6p vio bl & dk brn 10.00 1.10
**132** A25 2sh lt brn & vio bl 10.00 2.10
**133** A25 5sh brt car & blk 1.60 1.60

***Perf. 14***

**134** A26 10sh purple & blk 10.50 6.75

***Perf. 14x14½***

**Photo.**

**135** A26 £1 dk red & brn 45.00 13.50
*Nos. 121-135 (15)* 84.50 27.50

Issued: £1, 11/1/60; others, 11/25/57.

Map of Islands A27

***Perf. 13½x14***

**1959, July 4 Wmk. 4 Photo.**

**136** A27 6p ol grn & salmon .45 .45
**137** A27 8p violet & salmon .55 .55

Granting of a new constitution.

**Freedom from Hunger Issue**
Common Design Type
***Perf. 14x14½***

**1963, June 4 Wmk. 314**

**138** CD314 8p carmine rose .50 .50

**Red Cross Centenary Issue**
Common Design Type

**1963, Sept. 2 Litho. *Perf. 13***

**139** CD315 2p black & red .20 .20
**140** CD315 8p ultra & red .70 .70

**Shakespeare Issue**
Common Design Type

**1964, Apr. 23 Photo. *Perf. 14x14½***

**141** CD316 8p green .30 .30

**ITU Issue**
Common Design Type
***Perf. 11x11½***

**1965, May 17 Litho. Wmk. 314**

**142** CD317 1p ver & brown .20 .20
**143** CD317 2sh emer & lt blue .80 .80

**Intl. Cooperation Year Issue**
Common Design Type

**1965, Oct. 25 Wmk. 314 *Perf. 14½***

**144** CD318 1p blue grn & claret .20 .20
**145** CD318 8p lt violet & green .60 .60

**Churchill Memorial Issue**
Common Design Type

**1966, Jan. 24 Photo. *Perf. 14***
**Design in Black, Gold and Carmine Rose**

**146** CD319 1p bright blue .20 .20
**147** CD319 2p green .20 .20
**148** CD319 8p brown .40 .40
*a.* Gold impression double 200.00
**149** CD319 1sh6p violet .90 .90
*Nos. 146-149 (4)* 1.70 1.70

**Royal Visit Issue**
Common Design Type

**1966, Feb. 4 Litho. *Perf. 11x12***
**Portraits in Black**

**150** CD320 8p violet blue .30 .30
**151** CD320 1sh6p dk car rose .55 .55

Andrew Symmers Landing with Union Jack — A28

Designs: 8p, Andrew Symmers, his signature, Royal Warrant and Union Jack. 1sh6p, New coat of arms, Royal Cypher and St. Edward's crown.

***Perf. 13½***

**1966, Oct. 1 Unwmk. Photo.**

**152** A28 1p dk blue & dp org .20 .20
**153** A28 8p dk blue, dl yel & car .20 .20
**154** A28 1sh6p multicolored .35 .35
*Nos. 152-154 (3)* .75 .75

200th anniv. of the landing of Andrew Symmers, British agent, establishing the ties with Great Britain.

**UNESCO Anniversary Issue**
Common Design Type
**Wmk. 314**

**1966, Dec. 1 Litho. *Perf. 14***

**155** CD323 1p "Education" .20 .20
**156** CD323 8p "Science" .30 .30
**157** CD323 1sh6p "Culture" .50 .50
*Nos. 155-157 (3)* 1.00 1.00

Turk's-head Cactus — A29

Boat Building A30

Designs: 2p, Donkey cart. 3p, Sisal industry. 4p, Conch industry. 6p, Salt industry. 8p, Skin diving. 1sh, Fishing. 1sh6p, Water skiing. 2sh, Crawfish industry. 3sh, Map of Islands. 5sh, Fishing industry. 10sh, Coat of arms. £1, Queen Elizabeth II.

***Perf. 14½x14, 14x14½***

**1967, Feb. 1 Photo. Wmk. 314**

**158** A29 1p vio, red & yel .20 .30
**159** A30 1½p choc & org yel .20 .30
**160** A29 2p gray, yel & sl .20 .30
**161** A29 3p green & dk brn .20 .30
**162** A30 4p grnsh bl, blk & pink .20 .30
**163** A29 6p blue & dk brn .20 .30
**164** A29 8p aqua, dk bl & yel .20 .30
**165** A30 1sh grnsh bl & red brn .20 .30
**166** A29 1sh6p brt grnsh bl, yel & brn .30 *.50*
**167** A30 2sh multicolored .40 *.70*
**168** A30 3sh grnsh bl & mar .55 *.95*
**169** A30 5sh sky bl, dk bl & yel .95 *1.60*
**170** A30 10sh multicolored 1.90 *3.25*
**171** A29 £1 dk car rose, sil & dk bl 4.00 *7.00*
*Nos. 158-171 (14)* 9.70 16.40

See #181, 217-230. For surcharges see #182-195.

Turks Islands No. 1 A31

Designs: 6p, Turks Islands No. 2 and portrait of Queen Elizabeth on simulated stamp. 1sh, Turks Islands No. 3 (like 1p).

**1967, May 1 Photo. *Perf. 14½***

**172** A31 1p lilac rose & blk .20 .20
**173** A31 6p gray & black .20 .20
**174** A31 1sh Prus blue & blk .45 .45
*Nos. 172-174 (3)* .85 .85

Centenary of Turks Islands stamps.

Human Rights Flame A32

**1968, Apr. 1 *Perf. 14x14½***

**175** A32 1p lt green & multi .20 .20
**176** A32 8p lt blue & multi .20 .20
**177** A32 1sh6p multicolored .45 .45
*Nos. 175-177 (3)* .85 .85

International Human Rights Year.

Martin Luther King, Jr. and Protest March of 1968 A33

**1968, Oct. 1 Photo. Wmk. 314**

**178** A33 2p dk blue, dk & lt brn .20 .20
**179** A33 8p dk car rose, dk & lt brn .20 .20
**180** A33 1sh6p dp vio, dk & lt brn .30 .30
*Nos. 178-180 (3)* .70 .70

Martin Luther King, Jr. (1929-68), American civil rights leader.

Nos. 158-171 Surcharged

**4c**

Designs as before and: ¼c, Coat of arms like 10sh.

***Perf. 14x14½, 14½x14***

**1969, Sept. 8 Photo. Wmk. 314**

**181** A30 ¼c lt gray & multi .20 .20
**182** A29 1c on 1p multi .20 .20
**183** A29 2c on 2p multi .20 .20
**184** A29 3c on 3p multi .20 .20
**185** A30 4c on 4p multi .20 .20
**186** A29 5c on 6p multi .20 .20
**187** A29 7c on 8p multi .20 .20
**188** A30 8c on 1½p multi .20 .20
**189** A30 10c on 1sh multi .20 .20
**190** A29 15c on 1sh6p multi .20 .20
**191** A30 20c on 2sh multi .30 .30
**192** A30 30c on 3sh multi .40 .40
**193** A30 50c on 5sh multi .60 .60
**194** A30 $1 on 10sh multi 1.40 1.40
**195** A29 $2 on £1 multi 6.00 6.00
*Nos. 181-195 (15)* 10.70 10.70

The surcharge is differently arranged on each denomination to fit the design; the old denomination is obliterated with a rectangle on the 8c and 15c.

See Nos. 217-230.

**1969 Wmk. 314 Sideways**

*182a* A29 1c on 1p .20 *.30*
*183a* A29 2c on 2p .20 *.30*
*184a* A29 3c on 3p .20 *.30*
*186a* A29 5c on 6p .20 *.30*
*187a* A29 7c on 8p .20 *.30*
*190a* A29 15c on 1sh6p .30 *.50*
*195a* A29 $2 on £1 3.00 *4.75*
*Nos. 182a-195a (7)* 4.30 6.75

Nativity with John the Baptist — A34

Designs from the Book of Hours of Eleanora, Duchess of Tuscany: 3c, 30c, Flight into Egypt.

***Perf. 13x12½***

**1969, Oct. 20 Litho. Wmk. 314**

**196** A34 1c plum & multi .20 .20
**197** A34 3c dk blue & multi .20 .20
**198** A34 15c olive & multi .25 .25
**199** A34 30c yellow brn & multi .45 .45
*Nos. 196-199 (4)* 1.10 1.10

Christmas.

Coat of Arms — A35

**1970, Feb. 2 Litho. *Perf. 13x12½***

**200** A35 7c brown & multi .20 .20
**201** A35 35c violet blue & multi .75 .75

New Constitution, inaugurated 6/16/69.
See No. 769.

Christ Bearing the Cross, by Dürer — A36

Albrecht Dürer Engravings: 7c, Christ on the Cross. 50c, The Lamentation for Christ.

***Perf. 13½x14***

**1970, Mar. 17 Engr. Wmk. 314**

**202** A36 5c dp blue & blk .20 .20
**203** A36 7c vermilion & blk .20 .20
**204** A36 50c dk brown & multi .75 .75
*Nos. 202-204 (3)* 1.15 1.15

Easter.

Dickens and "Oliver Twist" Scene A37

Charles Dickens and Scene from: 3c, "A Christmas Carol." 15c, "Pickwick Papers." 30c, "The Old Curiosity Shop."

**Litho. & Engr.**

**1970, June 17 *Perf. 13½x13***

**205** A37 1c yel, red brn & blk .20 .20
**206** A37 3c sal pink, sl & blk .20 .20
**207** A37 15c salmon, bl & blk .25 .25
**208** A37 30c lt blue, ol & blk .55 .55
*Nos. 205-208 (4)* 1.20 1.20

Charles Dickens (1812-70), English novelist.

Red Cross Ambulance, 1870 — A38

5c, 30c, Red Cross ambulance, 1970.

**1970, Aug. 4 Litho. *Perf. 13½x14***

**209** A38 1c orange & multi .20 .20
**210** A38 5c ocher & multi .20 .20
**211** A38 15c brt pink & multi .30 .30
**212** A38 30c multicolored .55 .55
*Nos. 209-212 (4)* 1.25 1.25

Centenary of British Red Cross Society.

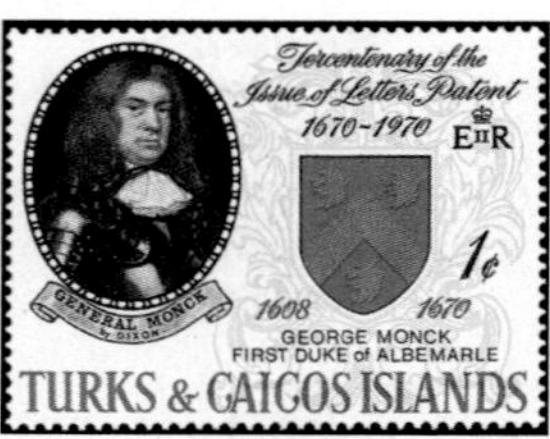


Gen. George Monck, Duke of Albemarle, and his Coat of Arms — A39

Designs: 8c, 35c, Coats of arms of Charles II and Queen Elizabeth II.

**1970, Dec. 1 Litho.** ***Perf. 12½x13½***

**213** A39 1c multicolored .20 .20
**214** A39 8c multicolored .20 .20
**215** A39 10c multicolored .30 .30
**216** A39 35c multicolored 1.00 .95
*Nos. 213-216 (4)* 1.70 1.65

Tercentenary of the issue of Letters Patent to the Six Lords Proprietors.

### Types of 1967
Values in Cents and Dollars

Designs: 1c, Turk's-head cactus. 2c, Donkey cart. 3c, Sisal industry. 4c, Conch industry. 5c, Salt industry. 7c, Skin diving. 8c, Boat building. 10c, Fishing. 15c, Water skiing. 20c, Crawfish industry. 30c, Map of Islands. 50c, Fishing industry. $1, Arms of Colony. $2, Queen Elizabeth II.

***Perf. 14x14½, 14½x14***

**1971, Feb. 2 Photo. Wmk. 314**

**217** A29 1c violet, red & yel .20 .25
**218** A29 2c gray, yel & slate .20 .25
**219** A29 3c green & dk brn .20 .25
**220** A30 4c grnsh bl, blk & pink .20 .25
**221** A29 5c blue & dk brown .20 .25
**222** A29 7c aqua, dk bl & yel .20 .25
**223** A30 8c choc & org yel .20 .25
**224** A30 10c grnsh bl & red brn .25 .30
**225** A29 15c brt grnsh bl, yel & brn .45 .55
**226** A30 20c multicolored .65 .85
**227** A30 30c grnsh bl & mar 1.00 1.25
**228** A30 50c sky bl, dk bl & yel 1.50 1.90
**229** A30 $1 blue & multi 3.00 3.75
**230** A29 $2 dk car rose, sil & dk blue 5.75 7.25
*Nos. 217-230 (14)* 14.00 17.60

The ¼c, released with this set is a shade of No. 181, the background being a greenish, slightly darker gray.

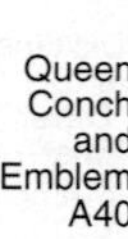

Queen Conch and Emblem A40

Tourist publicity (Sun, Sea and Sand Emblem and): 1c, Seahorse, vert. 15c, American oyster catcher. 30c, Blue Marlin.

***Perf. 14½x14, 14x14½***

**1971, May 2 Litho. Wmk. 314**

**232** A40 1c multicolored .20 .20
**233** A40 3c multicolored .20 .20
**234** A40 15c multicolored .40 .40
**235** A40 30c multicolored .75 .75
*Nos. 232-235 (4)* 1.55 1.55

Pirate Sloop A41

Designs: 3c, Pirates burying treasure. 15c, Marooned pirate. 30c, Buccaneers.

**1971, July 17** ***Perf. 14½x14***

**236** A41 2c multicolored .20 .20
**237** A41 3c multicolored .20 .20
**238** A41 15c multicolored .60 .60
**239** A41 30c multicolored 1.10 1.10
*Nos. 236-239 (4)* 2.10 2.10

A42

Adoration of the Virgin and Child, from Wilton Diptych, French School, c. 1395 — A43

**1971, Oct. 12 Litho.** ***Perf. 14x13½***

**240** A42 2c dull brn & multi .20 .20
**241** A43 2c dull brn & multi .20 .20
**242** A42 8c green & multi .20 .20
**243** A43 8c green & multi .20 .20
**244** A42 15c dk blue gray & multi .30 .30
**245** A43 15c dk blue gray & multi .30 .30
*Nos. 240-245 (6)* 1.40 1.40

Christmas.

Rocket Launch, Cape Canaveral — A44

10c, Space capsule in orbit around earth. 15c, Map of Turks & Caicos Islands & splashdown. 20c, Distinguished Service Medal, vert.

**1972, Feb. 21** ***Perf. 13½***

**246** A44 5c lt blue & blk .20 .20
**247** A44 10c multicolored .20 .20
**248** A44 15c lt green & multi .30 .30
**249** A44 20c blue & multi .40 .40
*Nos. 246-249 (4)* 1.10 1.10

First orbital flight by US astronaut Lt. Col. John H. Glenn, Jr., and splashdown off Turks and Caicos Islands, 10th anniversary.

The Three Crosses, by Rembrandt — A45

Details from Etchings by Rembrandt: 2c, Christ Before Pilate, vert. 30c, Descent from the Cross, vert.

**1972, Mar. 17** ***Perf. 14x13½, 13½x14***

**250** A45 2c lilac & black .20 .20
**251** A45 15c pink & black .30 .30
**252** A45 30c yellow & black .60 .60
*Nos. 250-252 (3)* 1.10 1.10

Easter.

Richard Grenville and "Revenge" — A46

Discoverers and explorers of the Americas: ¼c, Christopher Columbus, Niña, Pinta and Santa Maria, vert. 10c, Capt. John Smith and three-master, vert. 30c, Juan Ponce de León and three-master.

**1972, July 4**

**253** A46 ¼c multicolored .20 .20
**254** A46 8c multicolored 1.00 .20
**255** A46 10c multicolored 1.00 .25
**256** A46 30c multicolored 2.00 .75
*Nos. 253-256 (4)* 4.20 1.40

### Silver Wedding Issue, 1972
Common Design Type

Design: Queen Elizabeth II, Prince Philip, turk's-head cactus and spiny lobster.

***Perf. 14x14½***

**1972, Nov. 20 Photo. Wmk. 314**

**257** CD324 10c ultra & multi .20 .20
**258** CD324 20c multicolored .40 .40

Treasure Hunting, c. 1700 — A47

Designs: 5c, Replica of silver bank medallion, 1687, obverse. 10c, Same, reverse. 30c, Scuba diver, 1973.

***Perf. 14x14½***

**1973, Jan. 18 Litho. Wmk. 314**

**259** A47 3c Prus blue & multi .20 .20
**260** A47 5c plum, silver & blk .20 .20
**261** A47 10c brt rose, silver & blk .20 .20
**262** A47 30c violet blue & multi .65 .65
a. Souvenir sheet of 4, #259-262 2.25 2.25
*Nos. 259-262 (4)* 1.25 1.25

Treasure hunting.

Arms of Jamaica, Turks and Caicos Islands — A48

**1973, Apr. 16 Litho.** ***Perf. 13½x14***

**263** A48 15c buff & multi .35 .35
**264** A48 35c lt green & multi .75 .75

Centenary of annexation to Jamaica.

Sooty Tern — A49

Birds: 1c, Magnificent frigate bird. 2c, Noddy tern. 3c, Blue gray gnatcatcher. 4c, Little blue heron. 5c, Catbird. 7c, Black-whiskered vireo. 8c, Osprey. 10c, Flamingo. 15c, Brown pelican. 20c, Parula warbler. 30c, Northern mockingbird. 50c, Ruby-throated hummingbird. $1, Bahama bananaquit. $2, Cedar waxwing. $5, Painted bunting.

### Wmk. 314 Sideways

**1973, Aug. 1 Litho.** ***Perf. 14***

**265** A49 ¼c yellow & multi .20 .20
**266** A49 1c pink & multi .20 .20
**267** A49 2c orange & multi .20 .20
**268** A49 3c lilac rose & multi .50 .45
**269** A49 4c lt blue & multi .20 .20
**270** A49 5c lt green & multi .35 .20
**271** A49 7c salmon & multi .40 .25
**272** A49 8c blue & multi .50 .45
**273** A49 10c brt blue & multi .60 .60
**274** A49 15c tan & multi .90 .80
**275** A49 20c brt yel & multi 2.40 2.25
**276** A49 30c yellow & multi 2.10 1.90
**277** A49 50c yellow & multi 3.25 3.00
**278** A49 $1 blue & multi 6.25 6.25
**279** A49 $2 gray & multi 13.50 12.50
*Nos. 265-279 (15)* 31.55 29.45

**1974-75 Wmk. 314 Upright**

*266a* A49 1c pink & multi ('75) .45 *.60*
*267a* A49 2c orange & multi .95 *1.25*
*268a* A49 3c lil rose & multi ('75) 1.50 *1.90*
*275a* A49 20c brt yel & multi ('75) 4.75 *6.25*
*Nos. 266a-275a (4)* 7.65 10.00

**1976-77 Wmk. 373**

*265a* A49 ¼c yellow & multi ('77) .20 .20
*266b* A49 1c pink & multi ('77) .20 .20
*267b* A49 2c orange & multi ('77) .20 .20
*268b* A49 3c lilac rose & multi .20 .20
*269a* A49 4c lt bl & multi ('77) .20 .20
*270a* A49 5c lt grn & multi ('77) .20 .20
*273a* A49 10c brt bl & multi ('77) .25 .25
*274a* A49 15c tan & multi ('77) .40 .65
*275b* A49 20c brt yel & multi .50 .80
*276a* A49 30c yel & multi ('77) .75 1.25
*277a* A49 50c yel & multi ('77) 1.25 2.00
*278a* A49 $1 blue & multi ('77) 2.50 4.00
*279b* A49 $2 gray & multi ('77) 5.25 8.00
**279A** A49 $5 yel grn & multi 13.50 21.00
*Nos. 265a-279A (14)* 25.60 39.15

Bermuda Sloop — A50

Old Sailing Ships: 5c, HMS Blanche. 8c, US privateer Grand Turk and packet Hinchinbrooke. 10c, HMS Endymion. 15c, RMS Medina. 20c, HMS Daring.

**1973, July 19 Litho.** ***Perf. 13½***

**280** A50 2c multicolored .20 .20
**281** A50 5c multicolored .20 .20
**282** A50 8c multicolored .40 .40
**283** A50 10c multicolored .55 .55
**284** A50 15c multicolored .85 .85
**285** A50 20c multicolored 1.10 1.10
a. Souvenir sheet of 6, #280-285 3.75 3.75
*Nos. 280-285 (6)* 3.30 3.30

### Princess Anne's Wedding Issue
Common Design Type

**1973, Nov. 14 Wmk. 314** ***Perf. 14***

**286** CD325 12c blue grn & multi .20 .20
**287** CD325 18c slate & multi .25 .25

Lucayan Stool A51

Designs: Lucayan artifacts.

**1974, July 17 Litho.** ***Perf. 14½***

**288** A51 6c shown .20 .20
**289** A51 10c Broken wood bowl .20 .20
**290** A51 12c Greenstone axe .20 .20
**291** A51 18c Wood bowl .25 .25
**292** A51 35c Animal head, fragment of stool .50 .30
a. Souvenir sheet of 5, #288-292 1.40 1.40
*Nos. 288-292 (5)* 1.35 1.15

Carvings made by Lucayan Indians, first inhabitants of the islands.

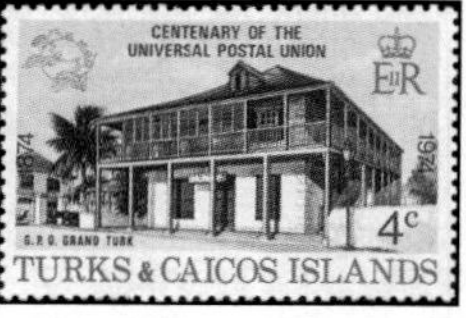


Grand Turk G.P.O. A52

UPU Emblem and: 12c, Map of Turks and Caicos Islands and local mail sloop. 18c, "United Service" (globe and "UPU"). 55c, Design symbolic of the Islands joining the UPU in 1881.

**1974, Oct. 9 Wmk. 314 *Perf. 14***

293 A52 4c yellow & multi .20 .20
294 A52 12c blue & multi .20 .20
295 A52 18c violet & multi .25 .25
296 A52 55c lt blue & multi .75 .75
*Nos. 293-296 (4)* 1.40 1.40

Centenary of Universal Postal Union.

"His Finest Hour" A53

12c, Churchill and Franklin D. Roosevelt.

**1974, Nov. 30 Wmk. 373**

297 A53 12c multicolored .20 .20
298 A53 18c multicolored .35 .35
*a.* Souvenir sheet of 2, #297-298 .70 .70

Sir Winston Churchill (1874-1965).

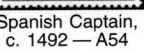

Spanish Captain, c. 1492 — A54

Old Windmill, Salt Cay — A55

Uniforms: 20c, Officer, Royal Artillery, 1783. 25c, Officer, 67th Foot, 1798. 35c, Private, First West India Regiment, 1833.

**1975, Mar. 26 Wmk. 314 *Perf. 14½***

299 A54 5c blue & multi .20 .20
300 A54 20c blue & multi .30 .30
301 A54 25c blue & multi .40 .40
302 A54 35c blue & multi .55 .55
*a.* Souvenir sheet of 4, #299-302 1.75 1.75
*Nos. 299-302 (4)* 1.45 1.45

**1975, Oct. 16 Litho. Wmk. 373**

Salt industry: 10c, Pink salt pans, horiz. 20c, Salt raking at Salt Cay, horiz. 25c, Unprocessed salt ready for shipment.

303 A55 6c violet & multi .20 .20
304 A55 10c lt brown & multi .20 .20
305 A55 20c red & multi .30 .30
306 A55 25c magenta & multi .40 .40
*Nos. 303-306 (4)* 1.10 1.10

Star Coral A56

**1975, Dec. 4 Litho. Wmk. 373**

307 A56 6c shown .20 .20
308 A56 10c Elkhorn coral .30 .25
309 A56 20c Brain coral .60 .50
310 A56 25c Staghorn coral .75 .60
*Nos. 307-310 (4)* 1.85 1.55

Schooner A57

American Bicentennial: 20c, Ship of the line. 25c, Frigate Grand Turk. 55c, Ketch.

**1976, May 28 *Perf. 14x13½***

311 A57 6c orange & multi .20 .20
312 A57 20c violet blue & multi .40 .30
313 A57 25c brown & multi .50 .35
314 A57 55c multicolored .90 .80
*a.* Souvenir sheet of 4, #311-314 2.75 2.75
*Nos. 311-314 (4)* 2.00 1.65

Turks and Caicos Islands No. 151 A58

25c, Turks and Caicos Islands No. 150.

**1976, July 14 Wmk. 373 *Perf. 14½***

315 A58 20c carmine & multi .50 .45
316 A58 25c violet blue & multi .60 .55

Visit of Queen Elizabeth II and Prince Philip to the Caribbean, 10th anniversary.

Virgin and Child, by Carlo Dolci — A59

Christmas: 10c, Virgin and Child with St. John, by Botticelli. 20c, Adoration of the Kings, from Retable by the Master of Paradise. 25c, Adoration of the Kings, illuminated page, French, 15th century.

**1976, Nov. 10 Litho. *Perf. 14x13½***

317 A59 6c multicolored .20 .20
318 A59 10c orange & multi .20 .20
319 A59 20c red lilac & multi .30 .30
320 A59 25c multicolored .35 .35
*Nos. 317-320 (4)* 1.05 1.05

Queen with Regalia — A60

Designs: 6c, Queen presenting Order of British Empire to E. T. Wood, Grand Turk, 1966. 55c, Royal family on balcony of Buckingham Palace. $5, Portrait of Queen from photograph taken during her 1966 visit to Grand Turk.

**1977 Litho. *Perf. 14x13½***

321 A60 6c multicolored .20 .20
322 A60 25c multicolored .35 .35
323 A60 55c multicolored .75 .75
*Nos. 321-323 (3)* 1.30 1.30

**Souvenir Sheet**

***Perf. 14***

324 A60 $5 multicolored 3.25 3.25

25th anniv. of the reign of Elizabeth II.
Nos. 322 and 323 were also issued in booklet panes of 2.
Issued: #321-323, Feb. 7; #324, Dec. 6.

Friendship 7 Capsule — A61

Designs: 3c, Lunar rover, vert. 6c, Tracking Station on Grand Turk. 20c, Moon landing craft, vert. 25c, Col. Glenn's rocket leaving launching pad, vert. 50c, Telstar 1 satellite.

**Wmk. 373**

**1977, June 20 Litho. *Perf. 13½***

325 A61 1c multicolored .20 .20
326 A61 3c multicolored .20 .20
327 A61 6c multicolored .20 .20
328 A61 20c multicolored .25 .25
329 A61 25c multicolored .35 .35
330 A61 50c multicolored .75 .75
*Nos. 325-330 (6)* 1.95 1.95

US Tracking Station on Grand Turk, 25th anniversary.

Adoration of the Kings, 1634 by Rubens — A63

Rubens Paintings: ¼c, Flight into Egypt. 1c, Adoration of the Kings, 1624. 6c, Madonna with Garland. 20c, $1, Virgin and Child Adored by Angels. $2, Adoration of the Kings, 1618.

**1977, Dec. 23**

331 A63 ¼c multicolored .20 .20
332 A63 ½c multicolored .20 .20
333 A63 1c multicolored .20 .20
334 A63 6c multicolored .20 .20
335 A63 20c multicolored .25 .25
336 A63 $2 multicolored 2.10 2.10
*Nos. 331-336 (6)* 3.15 3.15

**Souvenir Sheet**

337 A63 $1 multicolored 1.90 1.90

Christmas and 400th birth anniversary of Peter Paul Rubens (1577-1640).

Map of Turks Island Passage A64

Designs: 20c, Grand Turk lighthouse and sailboat (LUG cargo vessel). 25c, Deepsea fishing yacht. 55c, S.S. Jamaica Planter.

**Wmk. 373, Unwmkd.**

**1978, Feb. 2 Litho. *Perf. 13½***

338 A64 6c multicolored .20 .20
339 A64 20c multicolored .40 .35
340 A64 25c multicolored .50 .45
341 A64 55c multicolored 1.10 1.10
*a.* Souv. sheet of 4, #338-341, unwmkd. 2.50 2.50
*Nos. 338-341 (4)* 2.20 2.10

Turks Island Passage, a major Caribbean shipping route.
No. 341a exists watermarked. Value $50.

Queen Victoria in Coronation Regalia — A65

British Monarchs in Coronation Regalia: 10c, Edward VII. 25c, George V. $2, George VI. $2.50, Elizabeth II.

**1978, June 2 Litho. *Perf. 14***

342 A65 6c multicolored .20 .20
343 A65 10c multicolored .20 .20
344 A65 25c multicolored .30 .30
345 A65 $2 multicolored 1.50 1.50
*Nos. 342-345 (4)* 2.20 2.20

**Souvenir Sheet**

346 A65 $2.50 multicolored 2.00 2.00

25th anniversary of coronation of Queen Elizabeth II. Nos. 342-345 also issued in sheets of 3 plus label, perf. 12.

Wilbur Wright and Flyer 3 A66

Aviation Progress: 6c, Cessna 337 and Wright brothers. 10c, Southeast Airlines' Electra and Orville Wright. 15c, C47 cargo plane on South Caicos runway. 35c, Norman-Britten Islander at Grand Turk airport. $1, Orville Wright and Flyer, 1902. $2, Wilbur Wright and Flyer.

**1978, June 29 Litho. *Perf. 14½***

347 A66 1c multicolored .20 .20
348 A66 6c multicolored .20 .20
349 A66 10c multicolored .20 .20
350 A66 15c multicolored .20 .20
351 A66 35c multicolored .60 .60
352 A66 $2 multicolored 2.10 2.10
*Nos. 347-352 (6)* 3.50 3.50

**Souvenir Sheet**

353 A66 $1 multicolored .85 .85

Queen Elizabeth II — A67

Designs: 15c, Ampulla and anointing spoon. 25c, St. Edward's crown.

***Imperf. x Roulette 5***

**1978, July 24 Litho.**

**Self-adhesive**

354 Souvenir booklet 3.00
*a.* A67 Bklt. pane of 3, 15c, 25c, $2 1.90
*b.* A67 Bklt. pane, 3 each, 15c, 25c 1.10

25th anniv. of coronation of Queen Elizabeth II. #354 contains #354a-354b printed on peelable paper backing with music and text of hymns.

11th Commonwealth Games, Edmonton, Canada, Aug. 3-12 — A68

**1978, Aug. 3 Litho. *Perf. 15***

355 A68 6c shown .20 .20
356 A68 20c Weight lifting .25 .25
357 A68 55c Boxing .70 .70
358 A68 $2 Bicycling 1.50 1.50
*Nos. 355-358 (4)* 2.65 2.65

**Souvenir Sheet**

359 A68 $1 Sprinting 1.40 1.40

Fish A69

**1978-79 Litho. *Perf. 14***

360 A69 1c Indigo hamlet .20 .20
361 A69 2c Tobacco fish .20 .20
362 A69 3c Passing Jack .20 .20
363 A69 4c Porkfish .20 .20
364 A69 5c Spanish grunt .20 .20
365 A69 7c Yellowtail snapper .20 .20
366 A69 8c Foureye butterflyfish .20 .20
367 A69 10c Yellow fin grouper .20 .20
368 A69 15c Beau Gregory .25 .25
369 A69 20c Queen angelfish .35 .35
370 A69 30c Hogfish .50 .50
371 A69 50c Fairy Basslet .85 .85
372 A69 $1 Clown wrasse 1.60 1.60

**373** A69 $2 Stoplight parrotfish 3.50 3.50
**374** A69 $5 Queen triggerfish 8.50 8.50
*Nos. 360-374 (15)* 17.15 17.15

Issue dates: 1c, 3c, 5c, 10c, 15c, 20c, Nov. 17, 1978; others Feb. 6, 1979.
Nos. 368-369, 372-374 exist dated 1983. Value $20.

**1981, Dec. 15** ***Perf. 12½x12***
*360a* A69 1c .20 .20
*364a* A69 5c .20 .20
*367a* A69 10c .20 .20
*369a* A69 20c .45 .45
*371a* A69 50c 1.10 1.10
*372a* A69 $1 2.10 2.10
*373a* A69 $2 4.50 4.50
*374a* A69 $5 11.00 11.00
*Nos. 360a-374a (8)* 19.75 19.75

Virgin with the Goldfinch, by Dürer — A70

Dürer Paintings: 20c, Virgin and Child with St. Anne. 35c, Nativity, horiz. $1, Adoration of the Kings, horiz. $2, Praying Hands.

**1978, Dec. 11** **Litho.** ***Perf. 14***
**375** A70 6c multicolored .20 .20
**376** A70 20c multicolored .20 .20
**377** A70 35c multicolored .45 .45
**378** A70 $2 multicolored 1.75 1.75
*Nos. 375-378 (4)* 2.60 2.60

**Souvenir Sheet**

**379** A70 $1 multicolored 2.40 2.40

Christmas and 450th death anniversary of Albrecht Dürer (1471-1528), German painter.

Ospreys A71

Endangered Species: 20c, Green turtle. 25c, Queen conch. 55c, Rough-toothed dolphin. $1, Humpback whale. $2, Iguana.

**1979, May 17** **Litho.** ***Perf. 14***
**380** A71 6c multicolored .25 .20
**381** A71 20c multicolored .70 .35
**382** A71 25c multicolored .90 .40
**383** A71 55c multicolored 1.90 .90
**384** A71 $1 multicolored 3.50 1.75
*Nos. 380-384 (5)* 7.25 3.60

**Souvenir Sheet**

**385** A71 $2 multicolored 3.50 3.00

The Beloved, by Dante Gabriel Rossetti A72

Paintings and IYC Emblem: 25c, Tahitian Girl, by Paul Gauguin. 55c, Calmady Children, by Sir Thomas Lawrence. $1, Mother and Daughter (detail), by Gauguin. $2, Marchesa Elena Grimaldi, by Van Dyck.

**1979, July 2** **Litho.** ***Perf. 14***
**386** A72 6c multicolored .20 .20
**387** A72 25c multicolored .20 .20
**388** A72 55c multicolored .40 .40
**389** A72 $1 multicolored .80 .80
*Nos. 386-389 (4)* 1.60 1.60

**Souvenir Sheet**

**390** A72 $2 multicolored 1.50 1.50

International Year of the Child.

Stampless Cover and "Medina" — A73

Designs: 20c, Map of Islands and Rowland Hill. 45c, Stamped envelope and "Orinoco." 75c, Paddlewheeler "Shannon" and letter. $1, Royal Packet "Trent," map of Islands. $2, New and old seals.

**1979, Sep. 10** **Litho.** ***Perf. 14***
**391** A73 6c multicolored .20 .20
**392** A73 20c multicolored .25 .25
**393** A73 45c multicolored .60 .60
**394** A73 75c multicolored 1.00 1.00
**395** A73 $1 multicolored 1.20 1.20

***Perf. 12***

**396** A73 $2 multicolored ('80) 3.25 3.25
*a.* Souv. sheet of 1, perf. 14 ('79) 2.00 2.00
*Nos. 391-396 (6)* 6.50 6.50

Nos. 391-395 were issued in sheets of 40, and in sheets of 5 stamps plus label, in changed colors, perf. 12.
No. 396 issued May 6, 1980 in sheet of 5 plus label picturing signal flags and map.

No. 396a overprinted: "BRASILIANA 79"

Souvenir Sheet

**1979, Sept. 10** **Litho.** ***Perf. 14***
**397** A73 $2 multicolored 1.75 1.75

Brasiliana 79 Intl. Philatelic Exhibition, Rio de Janeiro, Sept. 15-23.

Cuneiform Script — A74

Designs: 5c, Egyptian papyrus; Chinese writing. 15c, Greek runner; Roman post horse; Roman ship. 25c, Pigeon post; railway post; steamship postal packet. 40c, Balloon post; first airmail plane; supersonic airmail jet. $1, Original stamp press (3 designs each of 5c, 15c, 25c, 40).

***Imperf. x Roulette 5, Imperf. ($1)***
**1979, Sept. 27** **Litho.**

**Self-adhesive**

**398** Souvenir booklet *6.00*
*a.* A74 Bklt. pane of 1 ($1)
*b.* A74 Bklt. pane, 3 each 5c, 15c
*c.* A74 Bklt. pane, 3 each 25c, 40c

Sir Rowland Hill (1795-1879), originator of penny postage. No. 398 contains 3 booklet panes on peelable paper backing with descriptions of stamp designs.

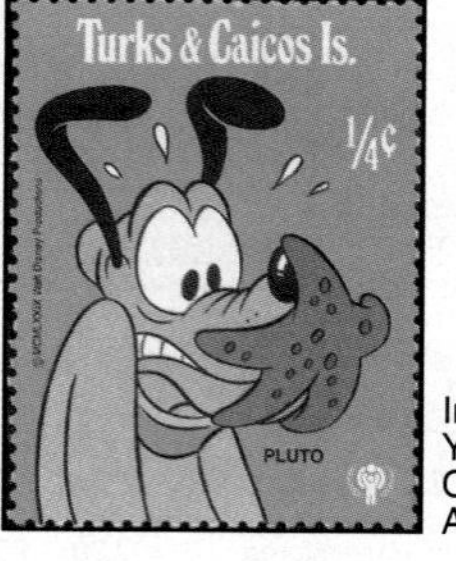

International Year of the Child A74a

Designs: Aquatic scenes.

**1979, Nov. 2** **Litho.** ***Perf. 11***
**399** A74a ¼c Pluto and starfish .20 .20
**400** A74a ½c Minnie Mouse .20 .20
**401** A74a 1c Mickey Mouse skin-diving .20 .20
**402** A74a 2c Goofy riding turtle .20 .20
**403** A74a 3c Donald and dolphin .20 .20
**404** A74a 4c Mickey Mouse and fish .20 .20
**405** A74a 5c Goofy surfing .20 .20
**406** A74a 25c Pluto and lobster .60 .25
**407** A74a $1 Daisy Duck water-skiing 2.50 1.00
*Nos. 399-407 (9)* 4.50 2.65

**Souvenir Sheet**

***Perf. 13½x14***

**408** A74a $1.50 Goofy 1.90 1.50

St. Nicholas, Icon, 17th Century — A75

Icons or Illuminations: 3c, Emperor Otto II, 10th century. 6c, St. John, Book of Lindisfarne. 15c, Christ and angels. 20c, Christ attended by angels, Book of Kells, 9th century. 25c, St. John the Evangelist. 65c, Christ enthroned, 17th century. $1, St. John, 8th century. $2, St. Matthew, Book of Lindisfarne.

**1979, Nov. 26**
**409** A75 1c multicolored .20 .20
**410** A75 3c multicolored .20 .20
**411** A75 6c multicolored .20 .20
**412** A75 15c multicolored .20 .20
**413** A75 20c multicolored .20 .20
**414** A75 25c multicolored .35 .35
**415** A75 65c multicolored .80 .80
**416** A75 $1 multicolored 1.20 1.20
*Nos. 409-416 (8)* 3.35 3.35

**Souvenir Sheet**

**417** A75 $2 multicolored 2.00 2.00

Christina's World, by Andrew Wyeth — A76

Art Treasures: 10c, Ivory leopards, Benin, 19th century. 20c, The Kiss, by Gustav Klimt, vert. 25c, Portrait of a Lady, by Rogier van der Weyden, vert. 80c, Sumerian bull's head harp, 2600 B.C., vert. $1, The Wave, by Hokusai. $2, Holy Family, by Rembrandt, vert.

**1979, Dec. 19** **Litho.** ***Perf. 13½***
**418** A76 6c multicolored .20 .20
**419** A76 10c multicolored .20 .20
**420** A76 20c multicolored .25 .25
**421** A76 25c multicolored .35 .35
**422** A76 80c multicolored 1.00 1.00
**423** A76 $1 multicolored 1.20 1.20
*Nos. 418-423 (6)* 3.20 3.20

**Souvenir Sheet**

**424** A76 $2 multicolored 2.00 2.00

Pied-billed Grebe — A77

**1980, Feb. 20** **Litho.** ***Perf. 14***
**425** A77 20c shown .75 .40
**426** A77 25c Ovenbirds .90 .45
**427** A77 35c Marsh hawks 1.25 .65
**428** A77 55c Yellow-bellied sapsucker 2.00 .90
**429** A77 $1 Blue-winged teals 3.50 1.75
*Nos. 425-429 (5)* 8.40 4.15

**Souvenir Sheet**

**430** A77 $2 Glossy ibis 4.25 4.25

Stamp Under Magnifier, Perforation Gauge, London 1980 Emblem A78

**1980, May 6** **Litho.** ***Perf. 14x14½***
**431** A78 25c shown .35 .35
**432** A78 40c Stamp in tongs, gauge .50 .50

**Souvenir Sheet**

**433** A78 $2 Exhibition Hall 1.75 1.75

London 1980 International Stamp Exhibition, May 6-14.

Trumpet Triton A79

**1980, June 26** **Litho.** ***Perf. 14***
**434** A79 15c shown .30 .30
**435** A79 20c Measled cowry .40 .40
**436** A79 30c True tulip .55 .55
**437** A79 45c Lion's paw .85 .85
**438** A79 55c Sunrise tellin 1.00 1.00
**439** A79 70c Grown cone 1.40 1.40
*Nos. 434-439 (6)* 4.50 4.50

Queen Mother Elizabeth, 80th Birthday — A80

**1980, Aug. 4** **Litho.** ***Perf. 14***
**440** A80 80c multicolored 1.00 1.00

**Souvenir Sheet**

***Perf. 12***

**441** A80 $1.50 multicolored 1.75 1.75

Pinocchio — A81

Christmas: Scenes from Walt Disney's Pinocchio.

**1980, Sept. 25** ***Perf. 11***
**442** A81 ¼c multicolored .20 .20
**443** A81 ½c multicolored .20 .20
**444** A81 1c multicolored .20 .20
**445** A81 2c multicolored .20 .20
**446** A81 3c multicolored .20 .20
**447** A81 4c multicolored .20 .20
**448** A81 5c multicolored .20 .20
**449** A81 75c multicolored 1.10 1.10
**450** A81 $1 multicolored 1.50 1.50
*Nos. 442-450 (9)* 4.00 4.00

**Souvenir Sheet**

**451** A81 $2 multi, vert. 4.50 4.50

Medical Examination, Lions — A82

**1980, Oct. 8 Litho. *Perf. 14***
**452** A82 10c shown .20 .20
**453** A82 15c Scholarships, Kiwanis .20 .20
**454** A82 45c Education, Soroptimists .70 .70
**455** A82 $1 Lobster boat, Rotary 1.25 1.25
*Nos. 452-455 (4)* 2.35 2.35

**Souvenir Sheet**

**456** A82 $2 Funds for schools, Rotary 2.25 2.25

Lions, Rotary, Kiwanis and Soroptimists service organizations; 75th anniv. of Rotary Intl.

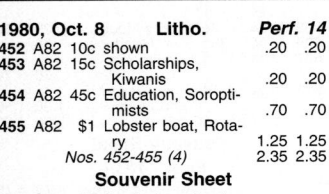

Martin Luther King, Jr. (1929-68) — A83

Human Rights Leaders: 30c, John F. Kennedy. 45c, Roberto Clemente (1934-72), baseball player. 70c, Frank Worrel (1927-67), cricket player. $1, Harriet Tubman (1823-1913), born slave, helped others escape to freedom. $2, Marcus Garvey (1887-1940), Jamaican black nationalist leader.

**1980, Dec. 22 Litho. *Perf. 14***
**457** A83 20c multicolored .25 .25
**458** A83 30c multicolored .35 .35
**459** A83 45c multicolored .55 .55
**460** A83 70c multicolored .90 .90
**461** A83 $1 multicolored 1.25 1.25
*Nos. 457-461 (5)* 3.30 3.30

**Souvenir Sheet**

**462** A83 $2 multicolored 2.00 2.00

Racing Yachts A84

Designs: Racing yachts.

**1981, Jan. 29 Litho. *Perf. 14***
**463** A84 6c multicolored .20 .20
**464** A84 15c multicolored .20 .20
**465** A84 35c multicolored .50 .50
**466** A84 $1 multicolored 1.20 1.20
*Nos. 463-466 (4)* 2.10 2.10

**Souvenir Sheet**

**467** A84 $2 multicolored 2.00 2.00

South Caicos Regatta. No. 467 contains one 28x42mm stamp.

Pluto Listening to Sea Shell — A85

**1981, Feb. 16 *Perf. 13½x14***
**468** A85 10c shown .20 .20
**469** A85 75c Pluto on raft, dolphin 1.00 1.00

**Souvenir Sheet**

**470** A85 $1.50 Pluto 2.75 2.75

50th anniversary of Walt Disney's Pluto.

Night Queen Cactus — A86

**1981, Feb. 10 *Perf. 14***
**471** A86 25c shown .30 .30
**472** A86 35c Ripsaw cactus .40 .40
**473** A86 55c Royal strawberry cactus .65 .65
**474** A86 80c Caicos cactus 1.00 1.00
*Nos. 471-474 (4)* 2.35 2.35

**Souvenir Sheet**

**475** A86 $2 Turks head cactus 2.00 2.00

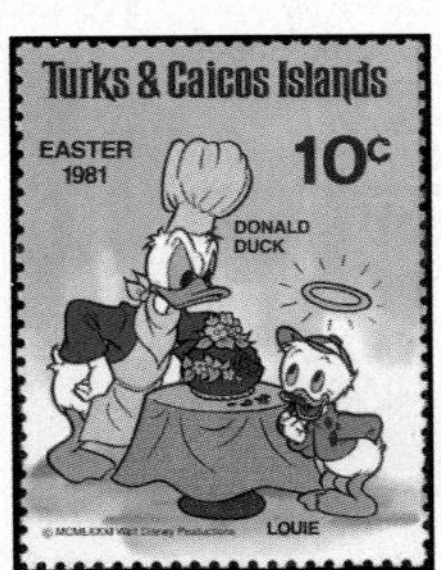


Donald Duck and Louie with Easter Egg — A87

Easter: Various Disney characters with Easter eggs.

**1981, Mar. 20 Litho. *Perf. 11***
**476** A87 10c multicolored .20 .20
**477** A87 25c multicolored .45 .45
**478** A87 60c multicolored 1.25 1.25
**479** A87 80c multicolored 1.50 1.50
*Nos. 476-479 (4)* 3.40 3.40

**Souvenir Sheet**

**480** A87 $4 multicolored 6.25 6.25

Woman with Fan, 1909 — A88

**1981, May 28 Litho. *Perf. 14***
**481** A88 20c shown .20 .20
**482** A88 45c Woman with Pears, 1909 .60 .60
**483** A88 80c The Accordionist, 1911 1.00 1.00
**484** A88 $1 The Aficionado, 1912 1.25 1.25
*Nos. 481-484 (4)* 3.05 3.05

**Souvenir Sheet**

**485** A88 $2 Girl with a Mandolin, 1910 2.75 2.75

Pablo Picasso (1881-1973).

**Royal Wedding Issue**
Common Design Type and

A88a

**1981, June 23 Litho. *Perf. 14***
**486** CD331 35c Couple .20 .20
**487** CD331 65c Kensington Palace .30 .30
**488** CD331 90c Charles .40 .40
*Nos. 486-488 (3)* .90 .90

**Souvenir Sheet**

**489** CD331 $2 Glass coach 1.75 1.75

**Self-adhesive**

***Imperf. x Roulette 5 (20c, $1), Imperf. ($2)***

**1981, July 7**
**490** Booklet 4.00
*a.* A88a Pane of 6 (3x20c, Lady Diana, 3x$1, Charles) 2.25
*b.* A88a Pane of 1, $2, Couple 1.75

Nos. 486-488 also printed in sheets of 5 plus label, perf. 12, in changed colors.

Underwater Marine Biology Observation — A89

**1981, Aug. 21 Litho. *Perf. 14***
**491** A89 15c shown .20 .20
**492** A89 40c Underwater photography .55 .55
**493** A89 75c Diving for wreckage 1.00 1.00
**494** A89 $1 Diver, dolphins 1.25 1.25
*Nos. 491-494 (4)* 3.00 3.00

**Souvenir Sheet**

**495** A89 $2 Diving flag 2.50 2.50

Br'er Rabbit Barricading his Door — A90

Christmas: Scenes from Walt Disney's Uncle Remus.

**1981, Nov. 2 Litho. *Perf. 14x13½***
**496** A90 ¼c multicolored .20 .20
**497** A90 ½c multicolored .20 .20
**498** A90 1c multicolored .20 .20
**499** A90 2c multicolored .20 .20
**500** A90 3c multicolored .20 .20
**501** A90 4c multicolored .20 .20
**502** A90 5c multicolored .20 .20
**503** A90 75c multicolored 1.25 1.25
**504** A90 $1 multicolored 1.75 1.75
*Nos. 496-504 (9)* 4.40 4.40

**Souvenir Sheet**

**505** A90 $2 multicolored 3.50 3.50

Flags of Turks and Caicos Islands A91

Maps of Various Islands: a, Grand Turk. b, Salt Cay. c, South Caicos. d, East Caicos. e, Middle Caicos. f, North Caicos. g, Caicos Cays. h, Providenciales. i, West Caicos.

**1981, Dec. 1 *Perf. 14***
**506** Strip of 10 5.00 5.00
*a.-j.* A91 20c any single .50 .50

Caribbean Buckeyes — A92

Scouting Year — A93

**1982, Jan. 21 Litho. *Perf. 14***
**507** A92 20c shown .35 .35
**508** A92 35c Clench's hairstreaks .65 .65
**509** A92 65c Gulf fritillarys 1.10 1.10
**510** A92 $1 Bush sulphurs 1.90 1.90
*Nos. 507-510 (4)* 4.00 4.00

**Souvenir Sheet**

**511** A92 $2 Turk Isld. leaf butterfly 5.00 5.00

**1982, Feb. 17 Litho. *Perf. 14***
**512** A93 40c Flag ceremony .75 .75
**513** A93 50c Building raft 1.00 1.00
**514** A93 75c Cricket match 1.25 1.25
**515** A93 $1 Nature study 1.60 1.60
*Nos. 512-515 (4)* 4.60 4.60

**Souvenir Sheet**

**516** A93 $2 Baden-Powell, salute 3.50 3.50

1982 World Cup Soccer — A94

Designs: Various soccer players.

**1982, Apr. 30 Litho. *Perf. 14***
**517** A94 10c multicolored .20 .20
**518** A94 25c multicolored .35 .35
**519** A94 45c multicolored .60 .60
**520** A94 $1 multicolored 1.25 1.25
*Nos. 517-520 (4)* 2.40 2.40

**Souvenir Sheet**

**521** A94 $2 multi, horiz. 2.00 2.00

#517-520 issued in sheets of 5 + label.

Phillis Wheatley (1753-1784), Poet, and Washington Crossing Delaware — A95

Washington's 250th Birth Anniv. and F.D. Roosevelt's Birth Centenary: 35c, Washington, Benjamin Banneker (1731-1806), astronomer and mathematician, map. 65c, FDR, George Washington Carver (1864-1943). 80c, FDR with stamp collection. $2, FDR examining Washington stamp.

**1982, May 3 Litho. *Perf. 14***
**522** A95 20c multicolored .25 .25
**523** A95 35c multicolored .50 .50
**524** A95 65c multicolored 1.00 1.00
**525** A95 80c multicolored 1.25 1.25
*Nos. 522-525 (4)* 3.00 3.00

**Souvenir Sheet**

**526** A95 $2 multicolored 3.00 3.00

Second Thoughts, by Norman Rockwell — A96

**1982, June 23 Litho.** ***Perf. 14x13½***

**527** A96 8c shown .20 .20
**528** A96 15c The Proper Gratuity .25 .25
**529** A96 20c Before the Shot .30 .30
**530** A96 25c The Three Umpires .40 .40
*Nos. 527-530 (4)* 1.15 1.15

**Princess Diana Issue**
Common Design Type

**1982 Litho.** ***Perf. 14½x14***

**530A** CD332 8c Sandringham .30 .20
**530B** CD332 35c Wedding 1.40 .55
**530C** CD332 $1.10 Diana 4.50 1.75
*Nos. 530A-530C (3)* 6.20 2.50

**1982, July 1** ***Perf. 14½x14***

**531** CD332 55c Sandringham 1.60 1.00
**532** CD332 70c Wedding 1.60 1.00
**533** CD332 $1 Diana 3.00 1.75
*Nos. 531-533 (3)* 6.20 3.75

Also issued in sheetlets of 5 + label.

**Souvenir Sheet**

**534** CD332 $2 Diana, diff. 6.00 4.00

Skymaster over Caicos Cays — A97

**1982, Aug. 26 Litho.** ***Perf. 14***

**535** A97 8c shown .20 .20
**536** A97 15c Jetstar, Grand Turk .35 .35
**537** A97 65c Helicopter, South Caicos 1.00 1.00
**538** A97 $1.10 Seaplane, Providenciales 1.90 1.90
*Nos. 535-538 (4)* 3.45 3.45

**Souvenir Sheet**

**539** A97 $2 Boeing 727 3.00 3.00

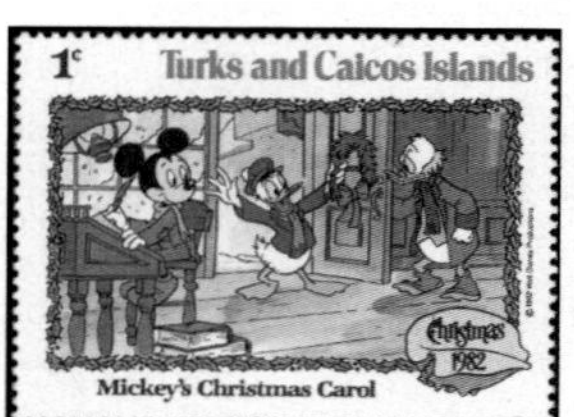


Christmas — A98

Christmas: Scenes from Walt Disney's Mickey's Christmas Carol.

**1982, Dec. 1 Litho.** ***Perf. 13½***

**540** A98 1c multicolored .20 .20
**541** A98 1c multicolored .20 .20
**542** A98 2c multicolored .20 .20
**543** A98 2c multicolored .20 .20
**544** A98 3c multicolored .20 .20
**545** A98 3c multicolored .20 .20
**546** A98 4c multicolored .20 .20
**547** A98 65c multicolored 1.10 1.10
**548** A98 $1.10 multicolored 2.50 1.50
*Nos. 540-548 (9)* 5.00 4.00

**Souvenir Sheet**

**549** A98 $2 multicolored 4.50 4.50

Trams and Locomotives — A99

**1983, Jan. 18 Litho.** ***Perf. 14***

**550** A99 15c West Caicos trolley tram .25 .25
**551** A99 55c West Caicos steam locomotive .90 .90
**552** A99 90c Mule-drawn tram, East Caicos 1.40 1.40
**553** A99 $1.60 Sisal locomotive, East Caicos 2.60 2.60
*Nos. 550-553 (4)* 5.15 5.15

**Souvenir Sheet**

**554** A99 $2.50 Steam engine 4.50 4.50

A99a

**1983, Mar. 14**

**555** A99a 1c Woman crossing guard .20 .20
**556** A99a 8c Wind and solar energy sources .20 .20
**557** A99a 65c Sailing 1.10 1.10
**558** A99a $1 Cricket game 1.75 1.75
*a.* Block or strip of 4, #555-558 3.25 3.25

Commonwealth Day.

Easter — A100

Crucifixion, by Raphael. $2.50 shows entire painting.

**1983, Apr. 7 Litho.** ***Perf. 14***

**559** A100 35c Mary Magdalene, St. John .50 .50
**560** A100 50c Mary .70 .70
**561** A100 95c Angel looking to heaven 1.10 1.10
**562** A100 $1.10 Angel looking to earth 1.25 1.25
*Nos. 559-562 (4)* 3.55 3.55

**Souvenir Sheet**

**563** A100 $2.50 multicolored 5.00 5.00

Piked Whale A101

**1983 Litho.** ***Perf. 14***

**564** A101 50c shown 1.25 1.25
**565** A101 65c Right whale 1.75 1.75
**566** A101 70c Killer whale 1.90 1.90
**567** A101 95c Sperm whale 2.75 2.75
**568** A101 $1.10 Gooseback whale 3.00 3.00
**569** A101 $2 Blue whale 5.25 5.25
**570** A101 $2.20 Humpback whale 6.00 6.00
**571** A101 $3 Longfin pilot whale 8.00 8.00
*Nos. 564-571 (8)* 29.90 29.90

**Souvenir Sheet**

**572** A101 $3 Fin whale 8.00 8.00

Issued: 50c, $2.20, #571, 5/16; 70c, 95c, $2, 6/13; others 7/11. Issued in sheets of 4.

For overprints see Nos. 637-639.

Manned Flight Bicentenary A102

**1983, Aug. 30 Litho.** ***Perf. 14***

**573** A102 25c 1st hydrogen balloon, 1783 .35 .35
**574** A102 35c Friendship 7, 1962 .50 .50
**575** A102 70c Montgolfiere, 1783 .90 .90
**576** A102 95c Columbia space shuttle 1.25 1.25
*Nos. 573-576 (4)* 3.00 3.00

**Souvenir Sheet**

**577** A102 $2 Montgolfiere, Columbia 3.00 3.00

Ships A103

**1985 Litho.** ***Perf. 12½x12***

**578** A103 4c Dug-out canoe .20 .20
**579** A103 5c Santa Maria .20 .20
**580** A103 8c Spanish treasure galleons .20 .20
**581** A103 10c Bermuda sloop .25 .20
**582** A103 20c Privateer Grand Turk .65 .35
**583** A103 25c Nelson's Frigate Boreas .75 .40
**584** A103 30c Warship Endymion 1.10 .60
**585** A103 35c Bark Caesar 1.25 .70
**586** A103 50c Schooner Grapeshot 1.75 .90
**587** A103 65c Invincible 2.40 1.25
**588** A103 95c Magicienne 3.25 1.75
**589** A103 $1.10 Durban 4.00 2.10
**590** A103 $2 Sentinel 6.50 3.50
**591** A103 $3 Minerva 10.00 5.75
**592** A103 $5 Caicos sloop 16.00 8.50
*Nos. 578-592 (15)* 48.50 26.60

Issued: 4c, 8c, 10c, 30c, 65c, $1.10, $5, Mar.; 5c, 20c, 25c, 35c, 50c, 95c, $2, Aug. 12; $3, Dec.

**1983-84** ***Perf. 14***

*578a* A103 4c .20 .20
*579a* A103 5c .20 .20
*580a* A103 8c .20 .20
*581a* A103 10c .25 .20
*582a* A103 20c .80 .60
*583a* A103 25c 1.00 .75
*584a* A103 30c 1.40 .80
*585a* A103 35c 1.60 1.00
*586a* A103 50c 2.10 1.40
*587a* A103 65c 3.00 1.90
*588a* A103 95c 4.00 2.50
*589a* A103 $1.10 4.75 3.00
*590a* A103 $2 8.25 5.50
*591a* A103 $3 13.00 8.50
*592a* A103 $5 19.00 14.50
*Nos. 578a-592a (15)* 59.75 41.25

Issued: 10c, 30c, 65c, $1.10-$3, 10/5/83; 8c, 25c, 50c, 95c, 12/16/83; 4c, 5c, 20c, 35c, $5, 1/9/84.

For overprints see Nos. 744-746.

Christmas A104

Designs: Scenes from Walt Disney's *Oh Christmas Tree.*

**1983, Nov.** ***Perf. 11***

**593** A104 1c Fifer Pig .20 .20
**594** A104 1c Fiddler Pig .20 .20
**595** A104 2c Practical Pig .20 .20
**596** A104 2c Pluto .20 .20
**597** A104 3c Goofy .20 .20
**598** A104 3c Mickey Mouse .20 .20
**599** A104 35c Gyro Gearloose .50 .50
**600** A104 50c Ludwig Von Drake .70 .70
**601** A104 $1.10 Huey, Dewey and Louie 1.50 1.50
*Nos. 593-601 (9)* 3.90 3.90

**Souvenir Sheet**
***Perf. 13½***

**602** A104 $2.50 Around the tree 4.75 4.75

John F. Kennedy (1917-1963), 20th Death Anniv. — A105

**1983, Dec. 22 Litho.** ***Perf. 14***

**603** A105 20c multicolored .30 .30
**604** A105 $1 multicolored 1.60 1.60

Classic Cars A106

**1984, Mar. 15 Litho.** ***Perf. 14***

**605** A106 4c Cadillac V-16, 1933 + label .20 .20
**606** A106 8c Rolls Royce Phantom III, 1937 + label .20 .20
**607** A106 10c Saab 99, 1969 + label .20 .20
**608** A106 25c Maserati Bora, 1973 + label .45 .45
**609** A106 40c Datsun 260Z, 1970 + label .70 .70
**610** A106 55c Porsche 917, 1971 + label 1.00 1.00
**611** A106 80c Lincoln Continental, 1939 + label 1.50 1.50
**612** A106 $1 Triumph TR3A, 1957 + label 1.75 1.75
*Nos. 605-612 (8)* 6.00 6.00

**Souvenir Sheet**

**613** A106 $2 Daimler, 1886 2.75 2.75

125th anniv. of first commercially productive oil well, Drake's Rig, Titusville, Pa. Nos. 605-612 se-tenant with labels showing flags and auto museum names. No. 613 for 150th birth anniv. of Gotlieb Daimler, inventor of high-speed internal combustion engine.

Easter — A107

450th death anniv. of Antonio Allegri Correggio (Various cameo portraits of Correggio, paintings): 15c, Rest on the Flight to Egypt with St. Francis. 40c, St. Luke and St. Ambrose. 60c, Diana and her Chariot. 95c, Deposition of Christ. $2, Nativity with St. Elizabeth and the Infant St. John.

**1984, Apr. 9**

**614** A107 15c multicolored .20 .20
**615** A107 40c multicolored .60 .60
**616** A107 60c multicolored .80 .80
**617** A107 95c multicolored 1.10 1.10
*Nos. 614-617 (4)* 2.70 2.70

**Souvenir Sheet**

**618** A107 $2 multi, horiz. 3.00 3.00

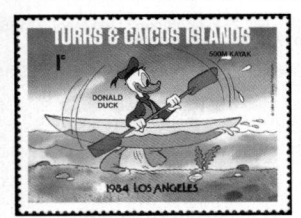

1984 Los Angeles Olympics — A108

Various Disney characters participating in Olympic sports.

**1984, Feb. 21 Litho. *Perf. 14***

**619** A108 1c 500-meter .25 .25
**620** A108 1c Diving .25 .25
**621** A108 2c Single kayak .25 .25
**622** A108 2c 1000-meter kayak .25 .25
**623** A108 3c Highboard diving .25 .25
**624** A108 3c Kayak slalom .25 .25
**625** A108 25c Freestyle swimming .65 .65
**626** A108 75c Water polo 1.90 1.90
**627** A108 $1 Yachting 2.50 2.50
*Nos. 619-627 (9)* 6.55 6.55

**Souvenir Sheet**

**628** A108 $2 Platform diving 6.00 6.00

**1984, Apr. *Perf. 12½x12***

**Same Designs**

*619a* A108 1c .25 .25
*620a* A108 1c .25 .25
*621a* A108 2c .25 .25
*622a* A108 2c .25 .25
*623a* A108 3c .25 .25
*624a* A108 3c .25 .25
*625a* A108 25c .65 .65
*626a* A108 75c 1.90 1.90
*627a* A108 $1 2.50 2.50
*Nos. 619a-627a (9)* 6.55 6.55

**Souvenir Sheet**

*628a* A108 $2 6.00 6.00

Nos. 619a-628a inscribed with Olympic rings emblem. Printed in sheets of 5.

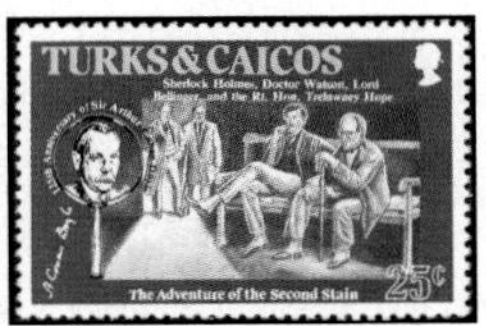


Sir Arthur Conan Doyle (1859-1930) — A109

Scenes from the Adventures of Sherlock Holmes.

**1984, July 16 Litho. *Perf. 14***

**629** A109 25c Second Stain 2.25 1.40
**630** A109 45c Final Problem 3.25 2.25
**631** A109 70c Empty House 4.50 3.50
**632** A109 85c Greek Interpreter 5.50 4.50
*Nos. 629-632 (4)* 15.50 11.65

**Souvenir Sheet**

**633** A109 $2 Doyle, vert. 12.00 14.50

Nos. 567-568, 572 Overprinted with UPU Emblem and: "19TH UPU CONGRESS / HAMBURG, WEST GERMANY./ 1874-1984"

**1984 Litho. *Perf. 14***

**637** A101 95c multicolored 3.50 2.50
**638** A101 $1.10 multicolored 3.50 3.00

**Souvenir Sheet**

**639** A101 $3 multicolored 6.75 6.75

AUSIPEX '84 A110

Darwin, Ship, Map of Australia, Fauna.

**1984, Aug. 22 *Perf. 14x13½***

**640** A110 5c Clown fish .65 .50
**641** A110 35c Monitor lizard 2.25 2.00
**642** A110 50c Rainbow lorikeets 3.00 2.40
**643** A110 $1.10 Koalas 3.75 3.25
*Nos. 640-643 (4)* 9.65 8.15

**Souvenir Sheet**

**644** A110 $2 Grey kangaroo 5.25 5.25

Christmas — A111

Scenes from Walt Disney's The Toy Tinkers.

**1984 Litho. *Perf. 14***

**645** A111 20c multicolored 1.00 .50
**646** A111 35c multicolored 1.40 .70
**647** A111 50c multicolored 2.00 1.00
**648** A111 75c multicolored 2.75 1.75
**649** A111 $1.10 multicolored 3.25 2.50
*Nos. 645-649 (5)* 10.40 6.45

**Souvenir Sheet**

**650** A111 $2 multicolored 4.75 4.75

No. 648 issued in sheets of 8. Issue dates: 75c, Nov. 26, others, Oct. 8.

Audubon Birth Bicentenary A112

Cameo portrait of Audubon, signature and illustrations from Birds of North America.

**1985, Jan. 28 Litho. *Perf. 14***

**651** A112 25c Dendroica magnoliae 2.10 1.00
**652** A112 45c Asio flammeus 3.25 2.10
**653** A112 70c Zenaida macroura 3.75 3.75
**654** A112 85c Progne subis 3.75 4.25
*Nos. 651-654 (4)* 12.85 11.10

**Souvenir Sheet**

**655** A112 $2 Haematopus ostralegus 6.75 6.00

Intl. Civil Aviation Org., 40th Anniv. A113

Pioneers & inventions: 8c, Leonardo da Vinci, 15th century glider wing. 25c, Sir Alliott Verdon Roe, 1949 C. 102 Jet. 65c, Robert H. Goddard, first liquid fuel rocket launch, 1926. $1, Igor Sikorsky, 1939 Sikorsky VS300. $2, Aviator Amelia Earhart, 1937 Lockheed 10E Electra.

**1985, Feb. 21**

**656** A113 8c multicolored .65 .35
**657** A113 25c multicolored 2.00 .45
**658** A113 65c multicolored 3.25 1.75
**659** A113 $1 multicolored 5.00 4.00
*Nos. 656-659 (4)* 10.90 6.55

**Souvenir Sheet**

**660** A113 $2 multicolored 4.50 4.50

Arrival of the Statue of Liberty in New York, Cent. A114

Designs: 20c, Flags of US, France, Franklin, Lafayette. 30c, Designer Frederic A. Bartholdi, engineer Gustave Eiffel, Statue, Eiffel Tower. 65c, Isere, arriving in New York with Statue, 1885. $1.10, Fund raisers Louis Agassiz, H. W. Longfellow, Charles Sumner, Joseph Pulitzer. $2, Dedication day, Oct. 28, 1886.

**1985, Mar. 28**

**661** A114 20c multicolored 1.10 .80
**662** A114 30c multicolored 1.50 .95
**663** A114 65c multicolored 3.25 2.00
**664** A114 $1.10 multicolored 3.50 2.40
*Nos. 661-664 (4)* 9.35 6.15

**Souvenir Sheet**

**665** A114 $2 multicolored 5.00 5.00

Royal Navy A115

Designs: 20c, Sir Edward Hawke, Royal George. 30c, Lord Nelson, H.M.S. Victory. 65c, Adm. Sir George Cockburn, H.M.S. Albion. 95c, Adm. Sir David Beatty, H.M.S. Indefatigable. $2, 18th century naval gunner, cannons.

**1985, Apr. 17**

**666** A115 20c multicolored 2.50 1.75
**667** A115 30c multicolored 2.75 2.50
**668** A115 65c multicolored 4.00 3.50
**669** A115 95c multicolored 5.00 5.50
*Nos. 666-669 (4)* 14.25 13.25

**Souvenir Sheet**

**670** A115 $2 multicolored 6.00 6.00

Intl. Youth Year A116

Anniversaries: 25c, Return of Halley's Comet, 1986. 35c, Mark Twain (1835-1910), Mississippi river boat. 50c, Jakob Grimm (1785-1863), Hansel & Gretel, vert. 95c, Grimm, Rumpelstiltskin, vert. $2, Twain, Grimm, portraits.

**1985, May 17**

**671** A116 25c multicolored 1.25 .40
**672** A116 35c multicolored 2.00 .50
**673** A116 50c multicolored 2.25 .75
**674** A116 95c multicolored 3.25 1.60
*Nos. 671-674 (4)* 8.75 3.25

**Souvenir Sheet**

**675** A116 $2 multicolored 5.00 5.00

Queen Mother, 85th Birthday — A117

Designs: 30c, Queen Mother outside Clarence House, vert. 50c, Visiting Biggin Hill Airfield by helicopter. $1.10, 80th birthday portrait, vert. $2, With Prince Charles at the 1968 Garter Ceremony, Windsor Castle, vert.

**1985, July 15**

**676** A117 30c multicolored .85 .85
**677** A117 50c multicolored 1.25 1.25
**678** A117 $1.10 multicolored 2.75 2.75
*Nos. 676-678 (3)* 4.85 4.85

**Souvenir Sheet**

**679** A117 $2 multicolored 5.00 5.00

George Frideric Handel — A118

Johann Sebastian Bach — A119

Handel or Bach and: 4c, King George II, Zadok the Priest music, 1727. 10c, Queen Caroline, Funeral Anthem, 1737. 15c, Bassoon, Invention No. 3 in D Major. 40c, Natural horn, Invention No. 3 in D Major. 50c, King George I, Water Music, 1714. 60c, Viola d'amore, Invention No. 3 . . . 95c, Clavichord, Invention No. 3 . . . $1.10, Queen Anne, Or la Tromba from Rinaldo. No. 688, Handel, portrait. No. 689, Bach, portrait.

**1985, July 17 *Perf. 15***

**680** A118 4c multicolored .65 .50
**681** A118 10c multicolored 1.00 .50
**682** A119 15c multicolored 1.00 .45
**683** A119 40c multicolored 2.10 .90
**684** A118 50c multicolored 2.75 2.25
**685** A119 60c multicolored 2.50 1.10
**686** A119 95c multicolored 3.00 2.25
**687** A118 $1.10 multicolored 4.75 4.50
*Nos. 680-687 (8)* 17.75 12.45

**Souvenir Sheets**

**688** A118 $2 multicolored 6.75 6.75
**689** A119 $2 multicolored 5.00 4.75

Motorcycle Centenary — A120

Flag of US, UK, Fed. Rep. of Germany or Japan and: 8c, 1915 dual cylinder Harley-Davidson. 25c, 1950 Thunderbird Triumph. 55c, 1985 BMW K100RS. $1.20, 1985 Honda 1100 Shadow. $2, 1885 Daimler Single Track, vert.

**1985, Sept. 4 *Perf. 14***

**690** A120 8c multicolored .80 .30
**691** A120 25c multicolored 1.60 .80
**692** A120 55c multicolored 2.50 1.90
**693** A120 $1.20 multicolored 3.75 *6.00*
*Nos. 690-693 (4)* 8.65 9.00

**Souvenir Sheet**

**694** A120 $2 multicolored 5.00 5.00

Pirates of the Caribbean — A121

Disneyland, 30th Anniv.: No. 695, Fate of Capt. Kidd. No. 696, Pirates imprisoned. No. 697, Bartholomew Roberts, church-going pirate. No. 698, Buccaneers in battle. No. 699, Bride auction. No. 700, Plunder. No. 701, Singing pirates. No. 702, Blackbeard. No. 703, Henry Morgan. No. 704, Mary Read, Anne Bonney.

**1985, Oct. 4 Litho. *Perf. 14***

**695** A121 1c multicolored .30 .30
**696** A121 1c multicolored .30 .30
**697** A121 2c multicolored .30 .30
**698** A121 2c multicolored .30 .30
**699** A121 3c multicolored .30 .30
**700** A121 3c multicolored .30 .30
**701** A121 35c multicolored 2.10 .85
**702** A121 75c multicolored 3.75 *4.25*
**703** A121 $1.10 multicolored 4.25 *5.00*
*Nos. 695-703 (9)* 11.90 11.90

**Souvenir Sheet**

**704** A121 $2.50 multicolored 7.50 7.50

Girl Guides, 75th Anniv. A122

Uniforms of Turks and Caicos and: 10c, Papua New Guinea and China brownies. 40c, Surinam and Korea brownies. 70c, Australia and Canada girl guides. 80c, West Germany and Israel girl guides.

**1985, Nov. 4**

**705** A122 10c multicolored .75 .50
**706** A122 40c multicolored 1.90 1.40
**707** A122 70c multicolored 2.50 *3.00*
**708** A122 80c multicolored 3.00 *3.25*
*Nos. 705-708 (4)* 8.15 8.15

**Souvenir Sheet**

**709** A122 $2 Anniv. emblem 5.00 5.00

Grand Turk Chapter, 35th anniv.

World Wildlife Fund A123

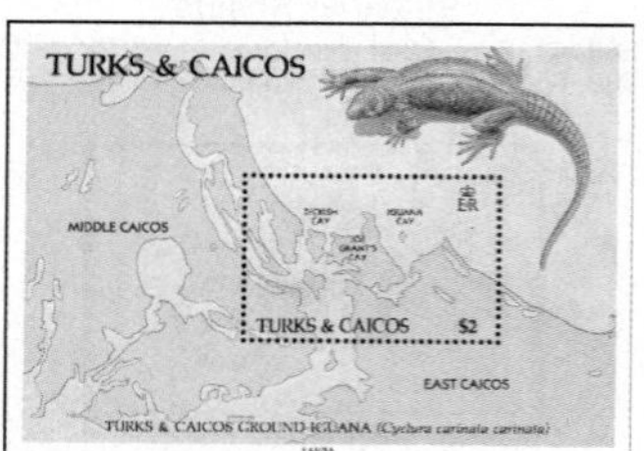

Map of the Islands — A124

Turks & Caicos ground iguanas.

**1986, Nov. 20** ***Perf. 14***

**710** A123 8c multicolored *2.00 1.00*
**711** A123 10c multicolored *2.00 1.00*
**712** A123 20c multicolored *3.25 2.00*
**713** A123 35c multicolored *7.50 6.50*
*Nos. 710-713 (4) 14.75 10.50*

**Souvenir Sheet**

**714** A124 $2 multicolored 13.50 *14.00*

A125

Christmas — A126

Wedding pictures.

**1986, Dec. 19 Litho.** ***Perf. 14***

**715** A125 35c Couple .90 .90
**716** A125 65c Sarah in coach 1.60 1.60
**717** A125 $1.10 Couple, close-up 2.75 2.75
*Nos. 715-717 (3)* 5.25 5.25

**Souvenir Sheet**

**718** A125 $2 In Westminster Abbey 5.75 5.75

Wedding of Prince Andrew and Sarah Ferguson.

**1987, Dec. 9 Litho.** ***Perf. 14***

Illuminations by miniaturist Giorgio Giulio Clovio (1498-1578) from the Farnese Book of Hours: 35c, Prophecy of the Birth of Christ to King Achaz. 50c, The Annunciation. 65c, The Circumcision. 95c, Adoration of the Kings. $2, The Nativity, from the Townley Lectionary.

**719** A126 35c multicolored 1.40 .80
**720** A126 50c multicolored 2.00 1.90
**721** A126 65c multicolored 2.40 2.40
**722** A126 95c multicolored 3.50 *4.00*
*Nos. 719-722 (4)* 9.30 9.10

**Souvenir Sheet**

**723** A126 $2 multicolored 6.25 *7.50*

Accession of Queen Victoria to the Throne of England, 150th Anniv. A127

Ships and memorials: 8c, HMS Victoria, Victoria Cross. 35c, SS Victoria, coin. 55c, Victoria & Albert I, Great Britain No. 1. 95c, Victoria & Albert II, Victoria Public Library, Turks & Caicos. $2, Bark Victoria.

**1987, Dec. 24**

**724** A127 8c multicolored 2.75 1.25
**725** A127 35c multicolored 2.75 2.40
**726** A127 55c multicolored 3.25 3.25
**727** A127 95c multicolored 4.00 5.25
*Nos. 724-727 (4)* 12.75 12.15

**Souvenir Sheet**

**728** A127 $2 multicolored 8.00 *8.00*

US Constitution Bicentennial — A128

Designs: 10c, NJ state flag. 35c, Freedom of Worship, vert. 65c, US Supreme Court, vert. 80c, John Adams, vert. $2, George Mason, vert.

**1987, Dec. 31**

**729** A128 10c multicolored .25 .25
**730** A128 35c multicolored .65 .65
**731** A128 65c multicolored 1.75 1.75
**732** A128 80c multicolored 2.50 2.50
*Nos. 729-732 (4)* 5.15 5.15

**Souvenir Sheet**

**733** A128 $2 multicolored 3.75 *4.25*

Discovery of America, 500th Anniv. (in 1992) A129

4c, Caravel, first sighting of land, Oct. 12, 1492. 25c, Columbus meets with Indians, Oct. 14. 70c, Fleet anchored in harbor, Oct. 15. $1, Landing, Oct. 16. $2, Nina, Pinta and Santa Maria.

**1988, Jan. 20**

**734** A129 4c multicolored .65 .40
**735** A129 25c multicolored 1.25 .80
**736** A129 70c multicolored 3.75 *4.25*
**737** A129 $1 multicolored 3.75 *4.25*
*Nos. 734-737 (4)* 9.40 9.70

**Souvenir Sheet**

**738** A129 $2 multicolored 6.00 6.00

Sea Scouts Salute Jamboree and Australia A130

Australia Bicent.: 8c, Arawak artifact, scouts exploring cave on Middle Caicos, vert. 35c, Santa Maria, scouts rowing to Hawks Nest. 65c, Scouts diving to explore a sunken Spanish galleon, vert. 95c, Plantation worker cutting sisal, scouts exploring plantation ruins. $2, Splashdown of Friendship 7, piloted by John Glenn, Feb. 20, 1962, vert.

**1988, Feb. 12 Litho.** ***Perf. 14***

**739** A130 8c multicolored .20 .20
**740** A130 35c shown .70 .70
**741** A130 65c multicolored 1.25 1.25
**742** A130 95c multicolored 1.90 1.90
*Nos. 739-742 (4)* 4.05 4.05

**Souvenir Sheet**

**743** A130 $2 multicolored 5.25 5.75

Nos. 581, 583 and 590 Ovptd. "40th WEDDING ANNIVERSARY / H.M. QUEEN ELIZABETH II / H.R.H. THE DUKE OF EDINBURGH"

**1988, Mar. 14 Litho.** ***Perf. 14***

**744** A103 10c multicolored .25 .25
**745** A103 25c multicolored .70 .70
**746** A103 $2 multicolored 5.50 5.50
*Nos. 744-746 (3)* 6.45 6.45

A131

A132

**1988, Aug. 29** **Litho.**

**747** A131 8c Soccer .50 .25
**748** A131 30c Yachting .75 .75
**749** A131 70c Cycling 3.25 2.75
**750** A131 $1 Running 2.50 *3.25*
*Nos. 747-750 (4)* 7.00 7.00

**Souvenir Sheet**

**751** A131 $2 Swimming 5.00 5.00

1988 Summer Olympics, Seoul.

**1988, Sept. 5** **Litho.**

Billfish Tournament: 8c, Passenger jet, fishing boat and fisherman reeling-in giant swordfish. 10c, Photographing prize catch. 70c, Fishing boat, lighthouse. $1, Blue marlin. $2, Sailfish.

**752** A132 8c multicolored 1.25 .30
**753** A132 10c multicolored .65 .30
**754** A132 70c multicolored 2.75 *3.00*
**755** A132 $1 multicolored 3.25 *3.75*
*Nos. 752-755 (4)* 7.90 7.35

**Souvenir Sheet**

**756** A132 $2 multicolored 6.00 6.00

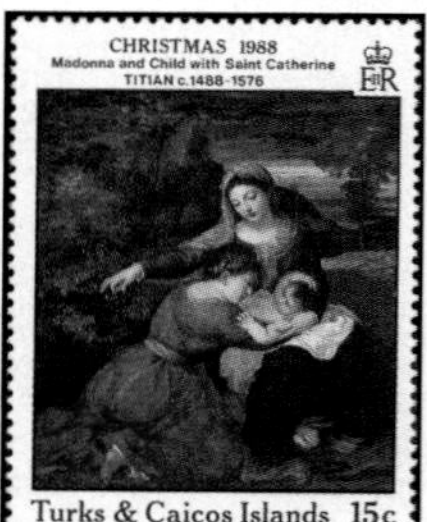

Christmas A133

Paintings by Titian: 15c, Madonna and Child with St. Catherine and the Infant John the Baptist, c. 1530. 25c, Madonna with a Rabbit, c. 1526. 35c, Virgin and Child with Sts. Stephen, Jerome and Mauritius, c. 1520. 40c, The Gypsy Madonna, c. 1510. 50c, The Holy Family and a Shepherd, c. 1510. 65c, Madonna and Child, c. 1510. $3, Madonna and Child with St. John the Baptist and St. Catherine, c. 1530. No. 764, Adoration of the Magi, c. 1560. No. 765, The Annunciation, c. 1560.

**1988, Oct. 24** **Litho.**

**757** A133 15c multicolored .30 .30
**758** A133 25c multicolored .50 .50
**759** A133 35c multicolored .70 .70
**760** A133 40c multicolored .80 .80
**761** A133 50c multicolored 1.00 1.00
**762** A133 65c multicolored 1.25 1.25
**763** A133 $3 multicolored 6.00 6.00
*Nos. 757-763 (7)* 10.55 10.55

**Souvenir Sheets**

**764** A133 $2 multicolored 4.50 4.50
**765** A133 $2 multicolored 4.50 4.50

Visit of Princess Alexandra, 1st Cousin of Queen Elizabeth II — A134

Various portraits and: 70c, Government House. $1.40, Map. $2, Flora, vert.

**1988, Nov. 14 Litho.** ***Perf. 14***

**766** A134 70c multicolored 2.50 2.10
**767** A134 $1.40 multicolored 5.50 *5.75*

**Souvenir Sheet**

**768** A134 $2 multicolored 10.00 10.00

Arms Type of 1970 Without Inscription

***Perf. 14½x15***

**1988, Dec. 15 Litho. Unwmk.**

**769** A35 $10 multicolored 20.00 20.00

Pre-Columbian Societies and Their Customs — A135

UPAE and discovery of America anniv. emblems and: 10c, Hollowing-out tree to make a canoe, vert. 50c, Body painting and statue. 65c, Three islanders with body paint. $1, Canoeing, vert. $2, Petroglyph.

**1989, May 15 Litho.** ***Perf. 14***

**770** A135 10c multicolored .25 .25
**771** A135 50c multicolored 1.25 1.25
**772** A135 65c multicolored 1.50 1.50
**773** A135 $1 multicolored 2.25 2.25
*Nos. 770-773 (4)* 5.25 5.25

**Souvenir Sheet**

**774** A135 $2 multicolored 5.50 *5.75*

Discovery of America 500th anniv. (in 1992).

Souvenir Sheet

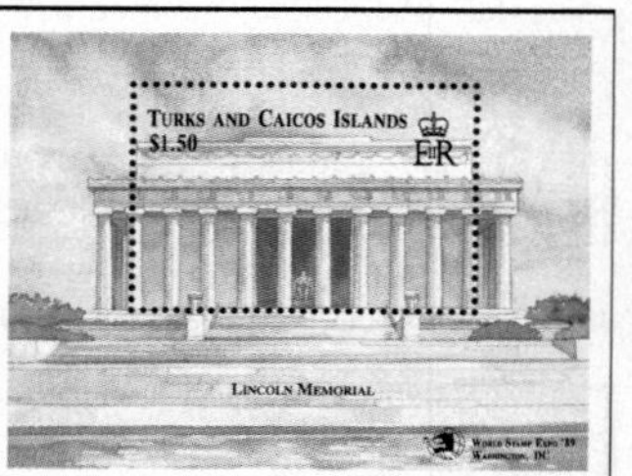

Lincoln Memorial, Washington, D.C. — A136

**1989, Nov. 17 Litho.** ***Perf. 14***

**775** A136 $1.50 multicolored 4.25 4.25

World Stamp Expo '89.

Miniature Sheets

American Presidential Office, 200th Anniv. — A137

US presidents, historic events and monuments.

No. 776: a, Jackson, early train. b, Van Buren, origins of baseball and Moses Fleetwood Walker, 1st black to play professional baseball. c, Harrison, Harrison's "Keep the Ball Rollin'" slogan and parade. d, Tyler, annexation of Texas, 1845. e, Polk, 1st US postage stamps (#2), 1847, and discovery of gold in California, 1849. f, Taylor, Mexican-American War, 1847.

No. 777: a, Hayes, end of Civil War reconstruction. b, Garfield, Garfield leading Union soldiers in the Battle of Shiloh. c, Arthur, opening of the Brooklyn Bridge, 1883. d, Cleveland, Columbian Exposition, 1893 (US #245). e, Benjamin Harrison, Pan-American Union building, map. f, McKinley, Spanish-American War (Rough Riders Monument, by Solon Borglum).

No. 778: a, Hoover, 1933 Olympic Games, Los Angeles and Lake Placid (American sprinter Ralph Metcalf and Norwegian figure skater Sonja Henie). b, Franklin Delano Roosevelt, Roosevelt's support of the March of Dimes (dime, 1946). c, 150th anniv. of inauguration of Washington, New York World's Fair, 1939. d, Truman, founding of the U.N., 1945. e, Eisenhower, invasion of Normandy, 1944. f, Kennedy, Apollo 11 mission, 1969.

**1989, Nov. 19** *Perf. 14*

| | | | |
|---|---|---|---|
| **776** | Sheet of 6 | 7.00 | 7.00 |
| ***a.-f.*** | A137 50c any single | 1.10 | 1.10 |
| **777** | Sheet of 6 | 7.00 | 7.00 |
| ***a.-f.*** | A137 50c any single | 1.10 | 1.10 |
| **778** | Sheet of 6 | 7.00 | 7.00 |
| ***a.-f.*** | A137 50c any single | 1.10 | 1.10 |

Fraser is incorrectly spelled "Frazer" on No. 778c.

Christmas — A138

Religious paintings by Giovanni Bellini: 15c, Madonna and Child. 25c, The Madonna of the Shrubs. 35c, The Virgin and Child. 40c, The Virgin and Child with a Greek Inscription. 50c, The Madonna of the Meadow. 65c, The Madonna of the Pear. 70c, The Virgin and Child, diff. $1, Madonna and Child, diff. No. 787, The Madonna with John the Baptist and Another Saint. No. 788, The Virgin and Child Enthroned.

**1989, Dec. 18**

| | | | | | |
|---|---|---|---|---|---|
| **779** | A138 | 15c | multicolored | .40 | .40 |
| **780** | A138 | 25c | multicolored | .65 | .65 |
| **781** | A138 | 35c | multicolored | .90 | .90 |
| **782** | A138 | 40c | multicolored | 1.10 | 1.10 |
| **783** | A138 | 50c | multicolored | 1.25 | 1.25 |
| **784** | A138 | 65c | multicolored | 1.60 | 1.60 |
| **785** | A138 | 70c | multicolored | 1.75 | 1.75 |
| **786** | A138 | $1 | multicolored | 5.25 | 5.25 |
| | | | *Nos. 779-786 (8)* | 12.90 | 12.90 |

**Souvenir Sheets**

| | | | | | |
|---|---|---|---|---|---|
| **787** | A138 | $2 | multicolored | 6.50 | 6.50 |
| **788** | A138 | $2 | multicolored | 6.50 | 6.50 |

Souvenir Sheet

1st Moon Landing, 20th Anniv. — A139

Flowers — A140

Designs: a, Liftoff. b, Eagle lunar module on Moon's surface. c, Aldrin obtaining soil samples. d, Neil Armstrong walking on Moon. e, Columbia and Eagle in space.

**1990, Jan. 8**

| | | | |
|---|---|---|---|
| **789** | Sheet of 5 | 6.00 | 6.00 |
| ***a.-e.*** | A139 50c any single | 1.10 | 1.10 |

**1990, Jan. 11** **Litho.** *Perf. 14*

| | | | | | |
|---|---|---|---|---|---|
| **790** | A140 | 8c | *Zephyranthes rosea* | .20 | .20 |
| **791** | A140 | 10c | *Sophora tomentosa* | .20 | .20 |
| **792** | A140 | 15c | *Coccoloba uvifera* | .30 | .30 |
| **793** | A140 | 20c | *Encyclia gracilis* | .40 | .40 |
| **794** | A140 | 25c | *Tillandsia streptophylla* | .50 | .50 |
| **795** | A140 | 30c | *Maurandella antirrhiniflora* | .60 | .60 |
| **796** | A140 | 35c | *Tillandsia balbisiana* | .70 | .70 |
| **797** | A140 | 50c | *Encyclia rufa* | 1.00 | 1.00 |
| **798** | A140 | 65c | *Aechmea lingulata* | 1.25 | 1.25 |
| **799** | A140 | 80c | *Asclepias curassavica* | 1.60 | 1.60 |
| **800** | A140 | $1 | *Caesalpinia bahamensis* | 2.00 | 2.00 |
| **801** | A140 | $1.10 | *Capparis cynophallophora* | 2.25 | 2.25 |
| **802** | A140 | $1.25 | *Stachytarpheta jamaicensis* | 2.50 | 2.50 |
| **803** | A140 | $2 | *Cassia biflora* | 4.00 | 4.00 |
| **804** | A140 | $5 | *Clusia rosea* | 10.00 | 10.00 |
| **805** | A140 | $10 | *Opuntia bahamana* | 20.00 | 20.00 |
| | | | *Nos. 790-805 (16)* | 47.50 | 47.50 |

**1994** ***Perf. 12***

| | | | | |
|---|---|---|---|---|
| *790a* | A140 | 8c | .20 | .20 |
| *791a* | A140 | 10c | .20 | .20 |
| *792a* | A140 | 15c | .35 | .35 |
| *793a* | A140 | 20c | .50 | .50 |
| *794a* | A140 | 25c | .60 | .60 |
| *795a* | A140 | 30c | .70 | .70 |
| *796a* | A140 | 35c | .85 | .85 |
| *797a* | A140 | 50c | 1.25 | 1.25 |
| *798a* | A140 | 65c | 1.50 | 1.50 |
| *799a* | A140 | 80c | 1.90 | 1.90 |
| *800a* | A140 | $1 | 2.40 | 2.40 |
| *801a* | A140 | $1.10 | 2.75 | 2.75 |
| *802a* | A140 | $1.25 | 3.00 | 3.00 |
| *803a* | A140 | $2 | 4.75 | 4.75 |
| *804a* | A140 | $5 | 12.00 | 12.00 |
| *805a* | A140 | $10 ('95) | 24.00 | 24.00 |
| | | *Nos. 790a-805a (16)* | 56.95 | 56.95 |

Birds A141

**1990, Feb. 19**

| | | | | | |
|---|---|---|---|---|---|
| **806** | A141 | 10c | Yellow-billed cuckoo | .80 | .50 |
| **807** | A141 | 15c | White-tailed tropic bird | .90 | .50 |
| **808** | A141 | 20c | Kirtland's warbler | 1.10 | .70 |
| **809** | A141 | 30c | Yellow-crowned night heron | 1.40 | .70 |
| **810** | A141 | 50c | West Indian tree duck | 2.00 | 1.00 |
| **811** | A141 | 80c | Yellow-bellied sapsucker | 2.50 | 2.25 |
| **812** | A141 | $1 | American kestrel | 3.50 | *4.00* |
| **813** | A141 | $1.40 | Mockingbird | 3.25 | 2.75 |
| | | | *Nos. 806-813 (8)* | 15.45 | 12.40 |

**Souvenir Sheets**

| | | | | | |
|---|---|---|---|---|---|
| **814** | A141 | $2 | Osprey | 7.00 | 7.00 |
| **815** | A141 | $2 | Yellow warbler | 7.00 | 7.00 |

Fish A142

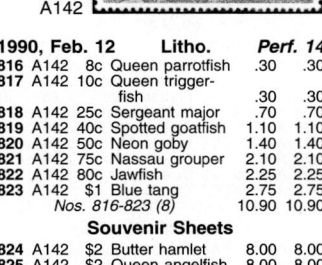

**1990, Feb. 12** **Litho.** *Perf. 14*

| | | | | | |
|---|---|---|---|---|---|
| **816** | A142 | 8c | Queen parrotfish | .30 | .30 |
| **817** | A142 | 10c | Queen triggerfish | .30 | .30 |
| **818** | A142 | 25c | Sergeant major | .70 | .70 |
| **819** | A142 | 40c | Spotted goatfish | 1.10 | 1.10 |
| **820** | A142 | 50c | Neon goby | 1.40 | 1.40 |
| **821** | A142 | 75c | Nassau grouper | 2.10 | 2.10 |
| **822** | A142 | 80c | Jawfish | 2.25 | 2.25 |
| **823** | A142 | $1 | Blue tang | 2.75 | 2.75 |
| | | | *Nos. 816-823 (8)* | 10.90 | 10.90 |

**Souvenir Sheets**

| | | | | | |
|---|---|---|---|---|---|
| **824** | A142 | $2 | Butter hamlet | 8.00 | 8.00 |
| **825** | A142 | $2 | Queen angelfish | 8.00 | 8.00 |

Butterflies A143

**1990, Mar. 19**

| | | | | | |
|---|---|---|---|---|---|
| **826** | A143 | 15c | White peacock | .85 | .60 |
| **827** | A143 | 25c | Cloudless sulphur | 1.00 | .75 |
| **828** | A143 | 35c | Mexican fritillary | 1.40 | .90 |
| **829** | A143 | 40c | Fiery skipper | 1.50 | 1.00 |
| **830** | A143 | 50c | Chamberlain's sulphur | 1.50 | 1.25 |
| **831** | A143 | 60c | Pygmy blue | 1.75 | 1.75 |
| **832** | A143 | 90c | Dusky swallowtail | 3.00 | *3.50* |
| **833** | A143 | $1 | Antillean dagger wing | 3.00 | *3.50* |
| | | | *Nos. 826-833 (8)* | 14.00 | 13.25 |

**Souvenir Sheets**

| | | | | | |
|---|---|---|---|---|---|
| **834** | A143 | $2 | Thomas's blue | 5.50 | 5.50 |
| **835** | A143 | $2 | 9 Queen species | 5.50 | 5.50 |

Nos. 826, 831 and 833 vert.

America Issue A144

Fish, UPAE and discovery of America 500th anniv. emblems.

**1990, Apr. 2**

| | | | | | |
|---|---|---|---|---|---|
| **836** | A144 | 10c | Rock beauty | .65 | .40 |
| **837** | A144 | 15c | Coney | .75 | .55 |
| **838** | A144 | 25c | Red hind | 1.00 | .70 |
| **839** | A144 | 50c | Banded butterflyfish | 1.50 | 1.50 |
| **840** | A144 | 60c | French angelfish | 2.00 | 1.75 |
| **841** | A144 | 75c | Blackbar soldierfish | 2.10 | 2.25 |
| **842** | A144 | 90c | Stoplight parrotfish | 2.25 | 2.75 |
| **843** | A144 | $1 | French grunt | 2.50 | 3.00 |
| | | | *Nos. 836-843 (8)* | 12.75 | 12.90 |

**Souvenir Sheets**

| | | | | | |
|---|---|---|---|---|---|
| **844** | A144 | $2 | Gray angelfish | 5.00 | 5.00 |
| **845** | A144 | $2 | Blue chromis | 5.00 | 5.00 |

Penny Black, 150th Anniv. — A145

British Pillar Boxes — A146

25c, 1p essay in blue, without letters. 35c, Letter Box #1, 1855. 50c, Penfold Box, 1866. 75c, Great Britain #3, essay. $1, 2p blue essay. $1.25, Air mail box, 1935. #852, Great Britain #1. #853, K type box, 1979.

**1990, May 3** **Litho.** *Perf. 14*

| | | | | | |
|---|---|---|---|---|---|
| **846** | A145 | 25c | bluish blk | 1.40 | .90 |
| **847** | A146 | 35c | gray & pale brn | 1.00 | 1.00 |
| **848** | A146 | 50c | gray & dk blue | 1.40 | 1.40 |
| **849** | A145 | 75c | red brown | 3.00 | 2.25 |
| **850** | A145 | $1 | dk blue | 3.75 | 3.75 |
| **851** | A146 | $1.25 | gray & blue | 3.00 | *4.50* |
| | | | *Nos. 846-851 (6)* | 13.55 | 13.80 |

**Souvenir Sheets**

| | | | | | |
|---|---|---|---|---|---|
| **852** | A145 | $2 | black | 6.00 | 6.00 |
| **853** | A146 | $2 | blk & red brn | 6.00 | 6.00 |

Stamp World London '90.

Queen Mother, 90th Birthday — A147

**1990, Aug. 20** **Litho.** *Perf. 14*

| | | | | | |
|---|---|---|---|---|---|
| **854** | A147 | 10c | multicolored | .35 | .30 |
| **855** | A147 | 25c | multi, diff. | .70 | .50 |
| **856** | A147 | 75c | multi, diff. | 1.25 | 1.25 |
| **857** | A147 | $1.25 | multi, diff. | 2.10 | *2.40* |
| | | | *Nos. 854-857 (4)* | 4.40 | 4.45 |

**Souvenir Sheet**

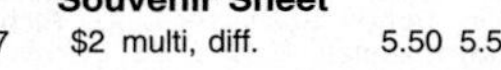

| | | | | | |
|---|---|---|---|---|---|
| **858** | A147 | $2 | multi, diff. | 5.50 | 5.50 |

Birds A148

**1990, Sept. 24** **Litho.** *Perf. 14*

| | | | | | |
|---|---|---|---|---|---|
| **859** | A148 | 8c | Stripe-headed tanager, vert. | .80 | .60 |
| **860** | A148 | 10c | Black-whiskered vireo | .80 | .60 |
| **861** | A148 | 25c | Blue-grey gnatcatcher | 1.10 | .60 |
| **862** | A148 | 40c | Lesser scaup | 2.10 | 1.25 |
| **863** | A148 | 50c | White-cheeked pintail | 2.10 | 1.25 |
| **864** | A148 | 75c | Common stilt | 2.50 | 2.50 |
| **865** | A148 | 80c | Common oystercatcher, vert. | 2.50 | *3.00* |
| **866** | A148 | $1 | Tricolored heron | 3.00 | *3.55* |
| | | | *Nos. 859-866 (8)* | 14.90 | 13.35 |

**Souvenir Sheets**

| | | | | | |
|---|---|---|---|---|---|
| **867** | A148 | $2 | Bahama woodstar | 5.25 | 5.25 |
| **868** | A148 | $2 | American coot | 5.25 | 5.25 |

Christmas A149

Different details from paintings by Rubens: 10c, 50c, 75c, No. 876, Triumph of Christ over Sin and Death. 35c, 45c, 65c, $1.25, No. 877,

St. Theresa Praying for the Souls in Purgatory. Nos. 876-877 show entire painting.

**1990, Dec. 17 Litho. *Perf. 14***

**869** A149 10c multicolored .35 .20
**870** A149 35c multicolored 1.00 .80
**871** A149 45c multicolored 1.10 1.00
**872** A149 50c multicolored 1.25 1.10
**873** A149 65c multicolored 1.75 1.40
**874** A149 75c multicolored 2.00 1.75
**875** A149 $1.25 multicolored 3.00 3.00
*Nos. 869-875 (7)* 10.45 9.25

**Souvenir Sheets**

**876** A149 $2 multicolored 5.25 5.25
**877** A149 $2 multicolored 5.25 5.25

1992 Summer Olympics, Barcelona — A150

**1991, Jan. 17**

**878** A150 10c Kayaking .20 .20
**879** A150 25c Track .60 .60
**880** A150 75c Pole vault 1.75 1.75
**881** A150 $1.25 Javelin 3.00 3.00
*Nos. 878-881 (4)* 5.55 5.55

**Souvenir Sheet**

**882** A150 $2 Baseball 5.75 6.50

No. 878 inscribed Canoeing.

Voyages of Discovery A151

Designs: 5c, Henry Hudson, 1611. 10c, Roald Amundsen (airship), 1926. 15c, Amundsen (ship), 1906. 50c, USS Nautilus, 1958. 75c, Robert Scott, 1911. $1, Richard Byrd, Floyd Bennett, 1926. $1.25, Lincoln Ellsworth, 1935. $1.50, Cook, 1772-75. No. 891, The Nina. No. 892, The search for land.

**1991, Apr. 15 Litho. *Perf. 14***

**883** A151 5c multicolored .55 .40
**884** A151 10c multicolored .55 .40
**885** A151 15c multicolored .85 .55
**886** A151 50c multicolored 1.10 .85
**887** A151 75c multicolored 2.00 1.50
**888** A151 $1 multicolored 2.25 2.00
**889** A151 $1.25 multicolored 3.00 *3.75*
**890** A151 $1.50 multicolored 3.25 *4.25*
*Nos. 883-890 (8)* 13.55 13.70

**Souvenir Sheets**

**891** A151 $2 multicolored 6.50 6.50
**892** A151 $2 multicolored 6.50 6.50

Discovery of America, 500th anniv. (in 1992).

Butterflies A152

**1991, May 13 Litho. *Perf. 14***

**893** A152 5c White peacock .25 .25
**894** A152 25c Orion .70 .70
**895** A152 35c Gulf fritillary 1.00 1.00
**896** A152 45c Caribbean buckeye 1.25 1.25
**897** A152 55c Flambeau 1.50 1.50
**898** A152 65c Malachite 1.75 1.75
**899** A152 70c Florida white 2.00 2.00
**900** A152 $1 Great southern white 2.75 2.75
*Nos. 893-900 (8)* 11.20 11.20

**Souvenir Sheets**

**901** A152 $2 Giant hairstreak 7.50 7.50
**902** A152 $2 Orange-barred sulphur 7.50 7.50

Extinct Animals A153

**1991, June 3**

**903** A153 5c Protohydrochoerus .25 .25
**904** A153 10c Phororhacos .25 .25
**905** A153 15c Prothylacynus .40 .40
**906** A153 50c Borhyaena 1.25 1.25
**907** A153 75c Smilodon 2.00 2.00
**908** A153 $1 Thoatherium 2.50 2.50
**909** A153 $1.25 Cuvieronius 3.25 3.25
**910** A153 $1.50 Toxodon 4.00 4.00
*Nos. 903-910 (8)* 13.90 13.90

**Souvenir Sheets**

**911** A153 $2 Mesosaurus 7.25 7.25
**912** A153 $2 Astrapotherium 7.25 7.25

**Royal Family Birthday, Anniversary**

Common Design Type

**1991 Litho. *Perf. 14***

**913** CD347 10c multicolored .60 .30
**914** CD347 25c multicolored .80 .65
**915** CD347 35c multicolored .95 .80
**916** CD347 45c multicolored 2.25 1.25
**917** CD347 50c multicolored 2.50 1.60
**918** CD347 65c multicolored 1.90 1.90
**919** CD347 80c multicolored 2.25 *2.50*
**920** CD347 $1 multicolored 3.00 *3.50*
*Nos. 913-920 (8)* 14.25 12.50

**Souvenir Sheets**

**921** CD347 $2 Elizabeth, Philip 5.75 *6.25*
**922** CD347 $2 Diana, sons, Charles 7.50 *7.50*

10c, 45c, 50c, $1, No. 922, Charles and Diana, 10th wedding anniv., issued: July 29. Others, Queen Elizabeth II, 65th birthday, issued: June 8.

For overprints see Nos. 1020-1022.

Mushrooms — A154

10c, Pluteus chrysophlebius. 15c, Leucopaxillus gracillimus. 20c, Marasmius haematocephalus. 35c, Collybia subpruinosa. 50c, Marasmius atrorubens, vert. 65c, Leucocoprinus birnbaumii, vert. $1.10, Trogia cantharelloides, vert. $1.25, Boletellus cubensis, vert. No. 931, Gerronema citrinum. No. 932, Pyrrhoglossum pyrrhum, vert.

**1991, June 24 Litho. *Perf. 14***

**923** A154 10c multicolored .30 .30
**924** A154 15c multicolored .45 .45
**925** A154 20c multicolored .60 .60
**926** A154 35c multicolored 1.00 1.00
**927** A154 50c multicolored 1.50 1.50
**928** A154 65c multicolored 1.90 1.90
**929** A154 $1.10 multicolored 3.25 3.25
**930** A154 $1.25 multicolored 3.75 3.75
*Nos. 923-930 (8)* 12.75 12.75

**Miniature Sheets**

**931** A154 $2 multicolored 6.50 *6.75*
**932** A154 $2 multicolored 6.50 *6.75*

Paintings by Vincent Van Gogh — A155

Paintings: 15c, Weaver Facing Left, with Spinning Wheel. 25c, Head of a Young Peasant with Pipe, vert. 35c, The Old Cemetery Tower at Nuenen, vert. 45c, Cottage at Nightfall. 50c, Still Life with Open Bible. 65c, Lane at the Jardin du Luxembourg. 80c, The Pont du Carrousel and the Louvre. $1, Vase with Poppies, Cornflowers, Peonies and Chrysanthemums, vert. No. 941, Entrance to the Public Park. No. 942, Plowed Field.

**1991, Aug. 26 *Perf. 13***

**933** A155 15c multicolored .45 .45
**934** A155 25c multicolored .75 .75
**935** A155 35c multicolored 1.00 1.00
**936** A155 45c multicolored 1.40 1.40
**937** A155 50c multicolored 1.50 1.50
**938** A155 65c multicolored 1.90 1.90
**939** A155 80c multicolored 2.40 2.40
**940** A155 $1 multicolored 3.00 3.00
*Nos. 933-940 (8)* 12.40 12.40

**Size: 107x80mm**

***Imperf***

**941** A155 $2 multicolored 5.75 5.75
**942** A155 $2 multicolored 5.75 5.75

Phila Nippon '91 A156

Japanese steam locomotives.

**1991, Nov. 4 Litho. *Perf. 14***

**943** A156 8c Series 8550 .40 .40
**944** A156 10c C 57 .40 .40
**945** A156 45c Series 4110 1.25 .90
**946** A156 50c C 55 1.25 .90
**947** A156 65c Series 6250 1.75 1.75
**948** A156 80c E 10 2.00 2.00
**949** A156 $1 Series 4500 2.10 2.40
**950** A156 $1.25 C 11 2.75 2.75
*Nos. 943-950 (8)* 11.90 11.50

**Souvenir Sheets**

**951** A156 $2 C 62 5.75 5.75
**952** A156 $2 C 58 5.75 5.75

Christmas A157

Details or entire paintings by Gerard David: 8c, Adoration of the Shepherds. 15c, Virgin and Child Enthroned with Two Angels. 35c, The Annunciation (outside wings). 45c, The Rest on the Flight into Egypt. 50c, The Rest on the Flight into Egypt, diff. 65c, Virgin and Child with Angels. 80c, The Adoration of the Shepherds, diff. $1.25, The Perussis Altarpiece. No. 961, The Adoration of the Kings. No. 962, The Nativity.

**1991, Dec. 23 *Perf. 12***

**953** A157 8c multicolored .30 .30
**954** A157 15c multicolored .45 .45
**955** A157 35c multicolored 1.00 1.00
**956** A157 45c multicolored 1.25 1.25
**957** A157 50c multicolored 1.50 1.50
**958** A157 65c multicolored 1.75 1.75
**959** A157 80c multicolored 2.40 2.40
**960** A157 $1.25 multicolored 3.50 3.50
*Nos. 953-960 (8)* 12.15 12.15

**Souvenir Sheets**

***Perf. 14½***

**961** A157 $2 multicolored 5.75 5.75
**962** A157 $2 multicolored 5.75 5.75

Boy Scouts A160

No. 968, Member of Boy Scout Service Corps at New York World's Fair, 1964-65. No. 969, Lord Robert Baden-Powell, vert. $2, Silver Buffalo Award.

**1992, July 6 Litho. *Perf. 14***

**968** A160 $1 multicolored 3.50 3.50
**969** A160 $1 multicolored 3.50 3.50

**Souvenir Sheet**

**970** A160 $2 multicolored 7.50 7.50

17th World Scout Jamboree, Korea.

Anniversaries and Events — A161

Designs: 25c, Astronaut releasing communications satellite. 50c, Tree with dead side, healthy side. 65c, Emblems, globe, food products. 80c, Fish in polluted, clean water. $1, Runners, Lions Intl. emblem. $1.25, Orbiting quarantine facility modules. No. 977, Planned orbital transfer vehicle for Mars. No. 977A, Industrial pollution, clean beach.

**1992-93 Litho. *Perf. 14***

**971** A161 25c multicolored .75 .75
**972** A161 50c multicolored 1.50 1.50
**973** A161 65c multicolored 1.90 1.90
**974** A161 80c multicolored 2.25 2.25
**975** A161 $1 multicolored 3.00 3.00
**976** A161 $1.25 multicolored 3.50 3.50
*Nos. 971-976 (6)* 12.90 12.90

**Souvenir Sheets**

**977** A161 $2 multicolored 5.00 5.00
**977A** A161 $2 multicolored 5.00 5.00

Intl. Space Year (#971, 976-977). Earth Summit, Rio de Janeiro (#972, 974, 977A). Intl. Conf. on Nutrition, Rome (#973). Lions Intl., 75th anniv. (#975).

Issued: #972, 974, 977A, 1/93; others, 12/92.

**Queen Elizabeth II's Accession to the Throne, 40th Anniv.**

Common Design Type

**1992, Feb. 6 Litho. *Perf. 14***

**978** CD348 10c multicolored .50 .50
**979** CD348 20c multicolored .95 .95
**980** CD348 25c multicolored 1.10 1.10
**981** CD348 35c multicolored 1.10 1.10
**982** CD348 50c multicolored 1.60 1.60
**983** CD348 65c multicolored 1.90 1.90
**984** CD348 80c multicolored 2.00 2.00
**985** CD348 $1.25 multicolored 2.25 2.25
*Nos. 978-985 (8)* 11.40 11.40

**Souvenir Sheets**

**986** CD348 $2 Queen at left, boat dock 5.50 5.50
**987** CD348 $2 Queen at right, shoreline 5.50 5.50

Spanish Art — A162

Paintings: 8c, St. Monica, by Luis Tristan. 20c, 45c, The Vision of Ezekiel: The Resurrection of the Flesh (different details) by Francisco Collantes. 50c, The Martyrdom of St. Philip, by Jose de Ribera. 65c, St. John the Evangelist, by Juan Ribalta. 80c, Archimedes by Jose de Ribera. $1, St. John the Baptist in the Desert by de Ribera. $1.25, The Martyrdom of St. Philip (detail), by de Ribera. No. 996, The Baptism of Christ by Juan Fernandez Navarrete. No. 997, Battle between Christians and Moors at El Sotillo, by Francisco de Zurbaran.

**1992, May 26 Litho. *Perf. 13***

**988** A162 8c multicolored .20 .20
**989** A162 20c multicolored .45 .45
**990** A162 45c multicolored 1.10 1.10
**991** A162 50c multicolored 1.10 1.10
**992** A162 65c multicolored 1.40 1.40
**993** A162 80c multicolored 1.75 1.75
**994** A162 $1 multicolored 2.25 2.25
**995** A162 $1.25 multicolored 2.75 2.75
*Nos. 988-995 (8)* 11.00 11.00

**Size: 95x120mm**

***Imperf***

**996** A162 $2 multicolored 5.50 5.50
**997** A162 $2 multicolored 5.50 5.50

Granada '92.

Discovery of America, 500th Anniv. A163

Commemorative coins, scenes of first voyage: 10c, Nina, ship. 15c, Pinta, ship. 20c, Santa Maria, Columbus' second coat of arms. 25c, Fleet at sea, ships. 30c, Landfall, sailing ship. 35c, Setting sail, Columbus departing. 50c, Columbus sighting New World, Columbus. 65c, Columbus exploring Caribbean, ship. 80c, Claiming land for Spain, Columbus, priest and cross. $1.10, Columbus exchanging gifts with native, Columbus, native.

No. 1008, Coins like #998-1000. No. 1009, Coins like #1004, 1006-1007.

**1992, Oct. Litho. *Perf. 14***

**998** A163 10c multicolored .40 .40
**999** A164 15c multicolored .60 .60
**1000** A164 20c multicolored .60 .60
**1001** A164 25c multicolored .85 .85
**1002** A164 30c multicolored .85 .85
**1003** A164 35c multicolored 1.00 1.00
**1004** A164 50c multicolored 1.10 1.10
**1005** A164 65c multicolored 1.60 1.60
**1006** A164 80c multicolored 1.60 1.60
**1007** A164 $1.10 multicolored 1.75 1.75
*Nos. 998-1007 (10)* 10.35 10.35

**Souvenir Sheets**

**1008** A164 $2 multicolored 6.00 6.00
**1009** A164 $2 multicolored 6.00 6.00

Christmas A164

Details or entire paintings by Simon Bening: 8c, Nativity. 15c, Circumcision. 35c, Flight to Egypt. 50c, Massacre of the Innocents.

By Dirk Bouts: 65c, The Annunciation. 80c, The Visitation. $1.10, The Adoration of the Angels. $1.25, The Adoration of the Wise Men. No. 1018, The Virgin and Child. No. 1019, The Virgin Seated with the Child.

**1992, Nov. Litho. *Perf. 13½x14***

**1010** A164 8c multicolored .35 .35
**1011** A164 15c multicolored .70 .70
**1012** A164 35c multicolored 1.00 1.00
**1013** A164 50c multicolored 1.25 1.25
**1014** A164 65c multicolored 1.75 1.75
**1015** A164 80c multicolored 2.10 2.10
**1016** A164 $1.10 multicolored 2.40 2.40
**1017** A164 $1.25 multicolored 2.40 2.40
*Nos. 1010-1017 (8)* 11.95 11.95

**Souvenir Sheets**

**1018** A164 $2 multicolored 6.50 6.50
**1019** A164 $2 multicolored 6.50 6.50

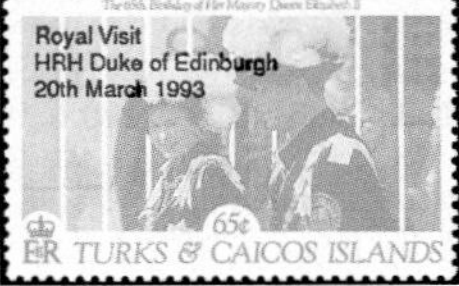


Nos. 915, 918 & 921 Ovptd. in Red or Black

**1993, Mar. 20 Litho. *Perf. 14***

**1020** CD347 35c on #915 1.00 1.00
**1021** CD347 65c on #918 2.00 2.00

**Souvenir Sheet**

**1022** CD347 $2 on #921 (Bk) 5.00 5.00

Miniature Sheet

Coronation of Queen Elizabeth II, 40th Anniv. — A165

Designs: a, 15c, Chalice and paten from royal collection. b, 50c, Official coronation photograph. c, $1, Coronation ceremony. d, $1.25, Queen, Prince Philip.

$2, New Portrait.

**1993, June 2 Litho. *Perf. 13½x14***

**1023** A165 Sheet, 2 ea #a.-d. 12.50 12.50

**Souvenir Sheet**

***Perf. 14***

**1024** A165 $2 multicolored 5.00 5.00

No. 1024 contains one 28x42mm stamp.

Christmas A166

Details or entire woodcut, Mary, Queen of the Angels, by Durer: 8c, 20c, 35c, $1.25.

Details or entire paintings by Raphael: 50c, $1, Virgin and Child with St. John the Baptist. 65c, The Canagiani Holy Family. 80c, The Holy Family with the Lamb.

Each $2: No. 1033, Mary, Queen of the Angels, by Durer. No. 1034, The Canagiani Holy Family, diff., by Raphael.

***Perf. 13½x14, 14x13½***

**1993, Dec. Litho.**

**1025-1032** A166 Set of 8 12.50 12.50

**Souvenir Sheets**

**1033-1034** A166 Set of 2 11.00 11.00

Dinosaurs A167

8c, Omphalosaurus. 15c, Coelophysis. 20c, $2 (#1043), Triceratops. 35c, $2 (#1044), Dilophosaurus. 50c, Pterodactylus. 65c, Elasmosaurus. 80c, Stegosaurus. $1.25, Euoplocephalus.

**1993, Nov. 15 Litho. *Perf. 14***

**1035-1042** A167 Set of 8 9.25 9.25

**Souvenir Sheets**

**1043-1044** A167 Set of 2 10.00 10.00

Birds A168

Designs: 10c, Killdeer. 15c, Yellow-crowned night heron, vert. 35c, Northern mockingbird. 50c, Eastern kingbird, vert. 65c, Magnolia warbler. 80c, Cedar waxwing, vert. $1.10, Ruby-throated hummingbird. $1.25, Painted bunting, vert. No. 1053, American kestrel. No. 1054, Ruddy duck.

**1993, Dec.**

**1045** A168 10c multicolored .30 .30
**1046** A168 15c multicolored .45 .45
**1047** A168 35c multicolored 1.10 1.10
**1048** A168 50c multicolored 1.50 1.50
**1049** A168 65c multicolored 2.10 2.10
**1050** A168 80c multicolored 2.40 2.40
**1051** A168 $1.10 multicolored 3.25 3.25
**1052** A168 $1.25 multicolored 3.75 3.75
*Nos. 1045-1052 (8)* 14.85 14.85

**Souvenir Sheets**

**1053** A168 $2 multicolored 5.25 5.25
**1054** A168 $2 multicolored 5.25 5.25

Fish A169

Designs: 10c, Bluehead wrasse. 20c, Honeycomb cowfish. 25c, Glasseye snapper. 35c, Spotted drum. 50c, Jolthead porgy. 65, Smallmouth grunt. 80c, Peppermint bass. $1.10, Indigo hamlet.

Each $2: No. 1063, Bonnethead shark. No. 1064, Sharpnose shark.

**1993, Dec. 15**

**1055-1062** A169 Set of 8 10.00 10.00

**Souvenir Sheets**

**1063-1064** A169 Set of 2 9.50 9.50

1994 World Cup Soccer Championships, US — A170

Designs: 8c, Segio Goycoechea, Argentina. 10c, Bado Illgner, Germany. 50c, Nico Claesen, Belgium. 65c, West German team. 80c, Cameroun team. $1, Santin, Francescoli, Uruguay; Cuciuffo, Argentina. $1.10, Sanchez, Mexico.

Each $2: No. 1072, Imre Garaba, Hungary, vert. No. 1073, Pontiac Silverdome.

**1994, Sept. 26 Litho. *Perf. 14***

**1065-1071** A170 Set of 7 10.00 10.00

**Souvenir Sheets**

**1072-1073** A170 Set of 2 9.00 9.00

Mushrooms — A171

Designs: 5c, Xerocomus guadelupae, vert. 10c, Volvariella volvacea, vert. 35c, Hygrocybe atrosquamosa. 50c, Pleurotus ostreatus. 65c, Marasmius pallescens. 80c, Coprinus plicatilis, vert. $1.10, Bolbitius vitellinus. $1.50, Pyroglossum lilaceipes, vert.

Each $2: No. 1082, Lentinus edodes. No. 1083, Russula cremeolilacina, vert.

**1994, Oct. 10**

**1074-1081** A171 Set of 8 12.00 12.00

**Souvenir Sheets**

**1082-1083** A171 Set of 2 9.50 9.50

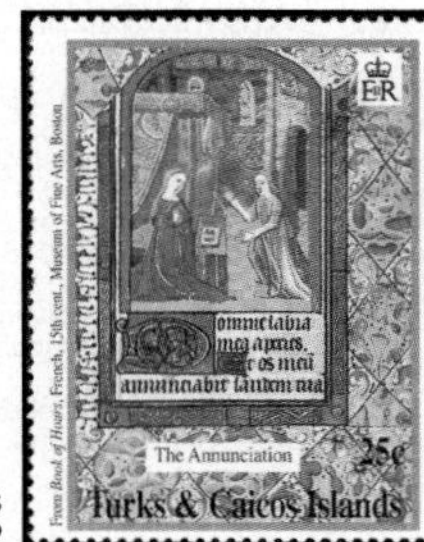


Christmas A172

Illustrations from French Book of Hours: 25c, The Annunciation. 50c, The Visitation. 65c, Annunciation to the Shepherds. 80c, The Nativity. $1, Flight into Egypt.

$2, The Adoration of the Magi.

**1994, Dec. 5 Litho. *Perf. 14***

**1084-1088** A172 Set of 5 9.25 9.25

**Souvenir Sheet**

**1089** A172 $2 multicolored 5.75 5.75

Butterflies A173

Designs: 15c, Dryas julia. 20c, Urbanus proteus. 25c, Colobura dirce. 50c, Papilio homerus. 65c, Chiodes catillus. 80c, Eurytides zonaria. $1, Hypolymnas misippus. $1.25, Phoebis avellaneda.

Each $2: No. 1098, Eurema adamsi. No. 1099, Morpho peleides.

**1994, Dec. 12**

**1090-1097** A173 Set of 8 10.50 10.50

**Souvenir Sheets**

**1098-1099** A173 Set of 2 9.50 9.50

D-Day, 50th Anniv. A174

Designs: 10c, Gen. Montgomery, British landing on Juno Beach. 15c, Adm. Sir Bertram Ramsay, British commandos at Sword Beach. 35c, Gun crew aboard HMS Belfast. 50c, Montgomery, Eisenhower, Tedder review battle scene. 65c, Gen. Eisenhower, 101st Airborne Div. paratroopers. 80c, Gen. Omar Bradley, US landings on Omaha Beach. $1.10, Second wave of US troops on D-Day. $1.25, Supreme Commander Eisenhower presents Operation Overload.

Each $2: No. 1108, Eisenhower, Montgomery seated at table. No. 1109, Beachhead secured.

**1994, Dec. 19**

**1100-1107** A174 Set of 8 12.00 12.00

**Souvenir Sheets**

**1108-1109** A174 Set of 2 9.00 9.00

Orchids A175

Designs: 8c, Cattleya deckeri. 20c, Epidendrum carpophorum. 25c, Epidendrum ciliare. 50c, Encyclia phoenicea. 65c, Bletia patula. 80c, Brassia caudata. $1, Brassavola nodosa. $1.25, Bletia purpurea.

Each $2: No. 1118, Ionopsis utricularioides. No. 1119, Vanilla planifolia.

**1995, Jan. 5**

**1110-1117** A175 Set of 8 12.00 12.00

**Souvenir Sheets**

**1118-1119** A175 Set of 2 10.00 10.00

Miniature Sheet of 12

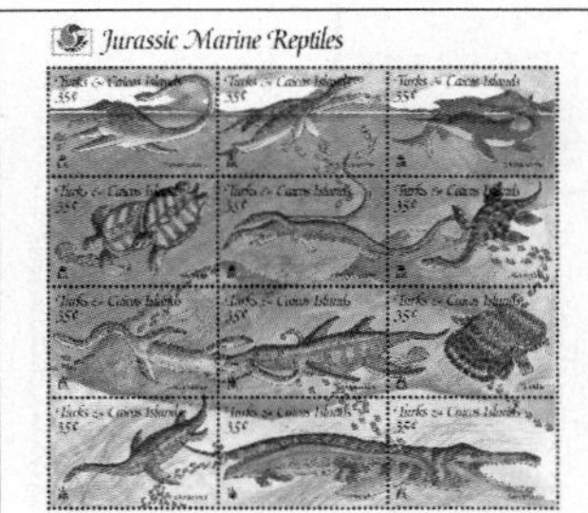


PHILAKOREA '94 — A176

Jurassic marine reptiles: a, Elasmosaurus. b, Plesiosaurus. c, Ichthyosaurus. d, Arcfielon. e, Askeptosaurus. f, Macroplata. g, Ceresiosaurus. h, Lipoleurodon. i, Henodus. j, Muraenosaurus. k, Placodus. l, Kronosaurus.

**1995, Jan. 23**

**1120** A176 35c #1120a-1120 l 10.50 10.50

First Manned Moon Landing, 25th Anniv. A177

Designs: 10c, Apollo XI in flight. 20c, Simulated moon landing. 25c, Painting, Astronauts on the Moon, by Kovales. 35c, First foot, footprint on moon. 50c, Aldrin, solar wind experiment. 65c, Armstrong, Aldrin setting up flag on moon. 80c, Command module Columbia in Lunar orbit. $1.10, Recovery of Apollo XI in Pacific.

Each $2: No. 1129, Lift-off at Cape Canaveral, vert. No. 1130, Moon rock on display in Houston.

**1995, Jan. 9 Litho. *Perf. 14***

**1121-1128** A177 Set of 8 9.00 9.00

**Souvenir Sheets**

**1129-1130** A177 Set of 2 9.00 9.00

Intl. Olympic Committee, Cent. — A178

Summer, Winter Olympic events: 8c, Fencing. 10c, Speed skating. 15c, Diving. 20c, Cycling. 25c, Ice hockey. 35c, Figure skating. 50c, Soccer. 65c, Bobsled. 80c, Super giant slalom. $1.25, Equestrian.

Each $2: #1141, Gymnastics. #1142, Downhill skiing.

**1995, Feb. 6**

**1131-1140** A178 Set of 10 12.00 12.00

**Souvenir Sheets**

**1141-1142** A178 Set of 2 9.00 9.00

Domestic Cats A179

Various cats, kittens: 15c, 20c, 35c, 50c, 65c, 80c, $1, $1.25.

Each $2: No. 1151, Two sleeping. No. 1152, Kitten, ladybugs in flowers.

**1995, July 3 Litho. *Perf. 14***

**1143-1150** A179 Set of 8 12.00 12.00

**Souvenir Sheets**

**1151-1152** A179 Set of 2 10.00 10.00

Birds — A180

A180a

10c, Belted kingfisher. 15c, Clapper rail. 20c, American redstart. 25c, Roseate tern. 35c, Purple gallinule. 45c, Ruddy turnstone. 50c, Barn owl. 60c, Brown booby. 80c, Great blue heron. $1, Antillean nighthawk. $1.25, Thick-billed vireo. $1.40, American flamingo. $2, Wilson's plover. $5, Blue-winged teal. $10, Reddish egret.

**1995, Aug. 2 Litho. *Perf. 13***

| | | | | |
|---|---|---|---|---|
| **1153** | A180 | 10c multi | .20 | .20 |
| **1154** | A180 | 15c multi | .35 | .35 |
| **1155** | A180 | 20c multi | .45 | .45 |
| **1156** | A180 | 25c multi | .60 | .60 |
| **1157** | A180 | 35c multi | .80 | .80 |
| **1158** | A180 | 45c multi | 1.00 | 1.00 |
| **1159** | A180 | 50c multi | 1.10 | 1.10 |
| **1160** | A180 | 60c multi | 1.40 | 1.40 |
| **1161** | A180 | 80c multi | 1.90 | 1.90 |
| **1162** | A180 | $1 multi | 2.25 | 2.25 |
| **1163** | A180 | $1.25 multi | 3.00 | 3.00 |
| **1164** | A180 | $1.40 multi | 3.25 | 3.25 |
| **1165** | A180 | $2 multi | 4.50 | 4.50 |
| **1166** | A180 | $5 multi | 11.50 | 11.50 |
| **1166A** | A180a | $10 multi | 22.50 | 22.50 |
| *Nos. 1153-1166A (15)* | | | 54.80 | 54.80 |

Queen Mother, 95th Birthday A181

No. 1167: a, Drawing. b, Wearing crown jewels. c, Formal portrait. d, Blue dress with pearls.

$2, Green blue outfit.

**1995, Aug. 4 *Perf. 13½x14***

**1167** A181 50c Block or strip of 4, #a.-d. 4.75 4.75

**Souvenir Sheet**

**1168** A181 $2 multicolored 4.50 4.50

No. 1167 was issued in sheets of 8 stamps.

VE Day, 50th Anniv. A182

Designs: 10c, "Big Three" meet at Yalta. 15c, Allied war prisoners released. 20c, American, Soviets meet at Elbe River. 25c, Death of Franklin D. Roosevelt. 60c, US 9th Army confirms cease fire. 80c, New York City celebrates VE Day. $1, Nuremberg War Crimes trials begin.

$2, Big Ben, US Capitol, St. Basil's Cathedral.

**1995, Aug. 14 Litho. *Perf. 14***

**1169-1175** A182 Set of 7 8.00 8.00

**Souvenir Sheet**

**1176** A182 $2 multicolored 4.50 4.50

Miniature Sheet of 9

Singapore '95 — A183

Diving equipment, each 60c: No. 1177a, Wm. James, scuba, 1825. b, Rouquayrol apparatus, 1864. c, Fluess oxygen rebreathing apparatus, 1878. d, Armored diving suit, 1900. e, Jim Janett explores sunken Lusitania in Peress armored diving suit, 1935. f, Cousteau-Gagnan aqualung, 1943. g, Underwater camera, 1955. h, Sylvia Earle dives to 1,520 ft. in Jim suit, 1979. i, Spider propeller-driven rigid suit, 1984.

Each $2: No. 1178, Helmet diver, 1935. No. 1179, Jacques-Yves Cousteau.

**1995, Sept. 1 *Perf. 14½***

**1177** A183 Sheet of 9, #a.-i. 12.50 12.50

**Souvenir Sheets**

**1178-1179** A183 Set of 2 9.00 9.00

Christmas A184

Details or entire paintings, by Piero di Cosimo (1462-1521): 20c, Madonna and Child with Young St. John. 25c, Adoration of the Child. 60c, Madonna and Child with Young St. John, St. Margaret, and An Angel. $1, Madonna and Child with An Angel.

$2, Madonna and Child with Angels and Saints.

**1995, Dec. 29 Litho. *Perf. 14***

**1180-1183** A184 Set of 4 4.75 4.75

**Souvenir Sheet**

**1184** A184 $2 multicolored 4.50 4.50

UN, 50th Anniv. — A185

Designs: 15c, Rights of women and children. 60c, Peace. 80c, Human rights. $1, Education.

Each $2: No. 1189, Flags of nations forming "50." No. 1190, Tractor, portions of UN, FAO emblems.

**1996, Feb. 26 Litho. *Perf. 14***

**1185-1188** A185 Set of 4 5.75 5.75

**Souvenir Sheets**

**1189-1190** A185 Set of 2 10.00 10.00

Queen Elizabeth II, 70th Birthday A186

No. 1191: a, Portrait. b, Wearing blue hat. c, In uniform, on horseback.

$2, As younger woman wearing white and yellow hat.

**1996, Apr. 21 Litho. *Perf. 13½x14***

**1191** A186 80c Strip of 3, #a.-c. 4.75 4.75

**Souvenir Sheet**

**1192** A186 $2 multicolored 4.75 4.75

No. 1191 was issued in sheets of 9 stamps.

History of Underwater Exploration A187

No. 1193, each 55c: a, Glaucus, God of Divers, 2500BC. b, Alexander the Great decends to ocean bottom, 332BC. c, Salvage diver, 1430. d, Borelli's rebreathing device, 1680. e, Edmond Halley's diving bell, 1690. f, John Lethbridge's diving machine, 1715. g, Klingert's diving apparatus, 1789. h, Drieberg's triton, 1808. i, Seibe's diving helmet, 1819.

No. 1194, each 60c: a, Jim Jarrat in "Iron Man" armored diving suit explores Lusitania, 1935. b, Cousteau, team excavate first shipwreck using scuba gear, 1952. c, Oldest shipwreck ever found, coast of Turkey, 1959. d, Swedish warship Vasa raised, 1961. e, Mel Fisher discovers Spanish galleon Atocha, 1971. f, Whydah, first pirate ship found, is discovered by Barry Clifford, 1984. g, Dr. Robert Ballard, using robot sub Argo finds battleship Bismarck, 1989. h, Radeau "Land Tortoise" scuttled in 1758 during French and Indian War found in Lake George, NY, 1991. i, Deep-diving nuclear submarine recovers ancient Roman shipwreck cargo, 1994.

Each $2: No. 1195, Arab diver Issa, 12th cent. No. 1196, Pearl diver in Caribbean, 1498. No. 1197, Diver in Newtsuit investigates Edmund Fitzgerald. No. 1198, Submarine Alvin explores Titanic, 1985.

**1996, May 13 Litho. *Perf. 14***

**1193** A187 Sheet of 9, #a.-i. 10.00 10.00

**1194** A187 Sheet of 9, #a.-i. 11.00 11.00

**Souvenir Sheets**

**1195-1198** A187 Set of 4 20.00 20.00

CHINA '96 (Nos. 1193, 1195-1196). CAPEX '96 (Nos. 1194, 1197-1198).

1996 Summer Olympics, Atlanta A188

Olympic gold medals for: No. 1199, Equestrian. No. 1200, Cycling. No. 1201, Fencing. No. 1202, Gymnastics. No. 1203, Hurdles. No. 1204, Pole vault. No. 1205, Sprints. No. 1206, Swimming. No. 1207, Diving. No. 1208, Running.

**1996, May 27 *Perf. 13½***

**1199-1208** A188 55c Set of 10 11.00 11.00

*1208a* Sheet of 10, #1199-1208 11.00

Nos. 1199-1208 issued in sheets as well as in No. 1208a.

A189

A190

James A.G.S. McCartney (1945-80), 1st Chief Minister of Turks & Caicos Islands,

**1996, July 8 Litho. *Perf. 14***

**1209** A189 60c multicolored 1.25 1.25

Ministerial Government, 20th anniv.

No. 1209 was issued in sheets of 9.

**1996, Sept. 8 Litho. *Perf. 14***

Working Dogs: No. 1210: a, Space research. b, Racing. c, Rescue. d, Military. e, Sporting. f, Companion. g, Hearing ear. h, Sled. i, Police. j, Guarding. k, Watch. l, Security.

Each $2: No. 1211, Guide. No. 1212, Sheep dog.

**1210** A190 25c Sheet of 12, #a.-l. 7.75 7.75

**Souvenir Sheets**

**1211-1212** A190 Set of 2 11.00 11.00

Winnie the Pooh, Christmas A191

Designs: 15c, Pooh trying to stay awake. 20c, Piglet, star. 35c, Ribbons and bows. 50c, Jingle bells. 60c, "Pooh loves Christmas." 80c, "Big hearts come in bouncy packages." $1, Santa Pooh. $1.25, "My most favorite."

No. 1221, Piglet, cookie. No. 1222, Piglet placing star atop tree.

**1996, Nov. 25 Litho. *Perf. 13½x14***

**1213-1220** A191 Set of 8 10.50 10.50

**Souvenir Sheets**

**1221** A191 $2 multicolored 5.00 5.00
**1222** A191 $2.60 multicolored 6.50 6.50

Flowers — A192

A193

No. 1223: a, Giant milkweed. b, Geiger tree. c, Passion flower. d, Hibiscus.

No. 1224: a, Yellow elder. b, Prickly poppy. c, Frangipani. d, Seaside mahoe.

Each $2: No. 1225, Chain of love. No. 1226, Firecracker.

**1997, Feb. 10 Litho. *Perf. 14***

**1223** A192 20c Strip or block of 4, #a.-d. 3.25 3.25
**1224** A192 60c Strip or block of 4, #a.-d. 4.75 4.75

**Souvenir Sheets**

**1225-1226** A192 Set of 2 9.00 9.00

Nos. 1223-1224 were each issued in sheets of 8 stamps.

**1997, Mar. 24 Litho. *Perf. 14***

UNICEF, 50th Anniv.: a, Dove flying right. b, Three children. c, Dove flying left. d, Boy with dog, girl holding cat.

**1227** A193 60c Sheet of 4, #a.-d. 6.00 6.00

Souvenir Sheets

UNESCO, 50th Anniv. — A194

Canterbury Cathedral: No. 1228, View from rear. No. 1229, Interior view. Illustration reduced.

**1997, Mar. 24 Litho. *Perf. 14***

**1228** A194 $2 multicolored 4.50 4.50
**1229** A194 $2 multicolored 4.50 4.50

Queen Elizabeth II, Prince Philip, 50th Wedding Anniv. A195

Designs: a, Queen waving. b, Royal arms. c, Queen, Prince riding in car. d, Prince, Queen seated. e, Windsor Castle. f, Prince Philip.

$2, Wedding portrait.

**1997, Apr. 21 Litho. *Perf. 14***

**1230** A195 60c Sheet of 6, #a.-f. 9.00 9.00

**Souvenir Sheet**

**1231** A195 $2 multicolored 5.75 5.75

Heinrich von Stephan (1831-97), Founder of UPU A196

Portrait of Von Stephan and: No. 1232: a, British mail coach, 1700's. b, UPU emblem. c, Space shuttle, future transport.

$2, Von Stephan, Hemerodrome, messenger of ancient Greece.

**1997, July 1 Litho. *Perf. 14***

**1232** A196 50c Sheet of 3, #a.-c. 3.75 3.75

**Souvenir Sheet**

**1233** A196 $2 multicolored 5.00 5.00

PACIFIC 97.

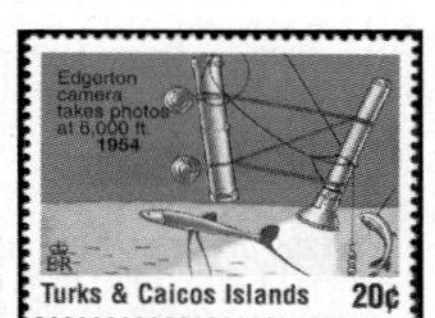

Underwater Exploration A197

No. 1234: a, Edgerton camera taking photos at 6,000 ft., 1954. b, Conshelf Habitat, 1963. c, Sealab II, 1965. d, Research Habitat, Tektite, 1970. e, Discovery of Galapagos Volcanic Rift, 1974. f, Epaulard, robot survey craft, 1979. g, Sea life discovered thriving in undersea oil field, 1995. h, Deep flight, 1996, one-man research vessel. i, Sea ice is studied from above, under sea, Okhotsk Tower, off Japan, 1996.

Each $2: No. 1235, Coelacanth. No. 1236, John Williamson makes first underwater movies, 1914.

**1997, Aug. 21 Litho. *Perf. 14***

**1234** A197 20c Sheet of 9, #a.-i. 5.50 5.50

**Souvenir Sheets**

**1235-1236** A197 Set of 2 10.00 10.00

Stampshow 97.

Christmas A198

Entire paintings or details: 15c, Adoration of an Angel, by Studio of Fra Angelico. 20c, Scenes from the Life of St. John the Baptist, by Master of Saint Severin. 35c, Archangel Gabriel, by Masolino de Panicale. 50c, 60c, Jeremiah with Two Angels, by Gherardo Starnina (diff. angels). 80c, The Annunciation, by Giovanni di Palo di Grazia. $1, The Annunciation, by Carlo di Bracceso. $1.25, The Nativity, by Benvenuto di Giovanni Guasta.

Each $2: No. 1245, The Wilton Diptych (right panel), by unknown English or French artist, c. 1395. No. 1246, Adoring Angels, from The Journey of the Magi, by Benozzo Gozzoli.

**1997, Dec. 8 Litho. *Perf. 14***

**1237-1244** A198 Set of 8 11.50 11.50

**Souvenir Sheets**

**1245-1246** A198 Set of 2 10.00 10.00

World Wildlife Fund — A199

Snapper: a, Blackfin. b, Dog. c, Cubera. d, Mahogany.

**1998, Feb. 24 Litho. *Perf. 14***

**1247** A199 25c Block of 4, #a.-d. 3.00 3.00

No. 1247 was issued in sheets of 16 stamps.

Intl. Year of the Reef.

Marine Life — A200

Underwater photographs: 20c, Spotted flamingo tongue. 50c, Feather duster. 60c, Squirrel fish. 80c, Queen angelfish. $1, Barracuda. $1.25, Fairy basslet.

Each $2: No. 1254, Rough file clam. No. 1255, Spotted cleaning shrimp.

**1998, May 1 Litho. *Perf. 14***

**1248-1253** A200 Set of 6 9.75 9.75

**Souvenir Sheets**

**1254-1255** A200 Set of 2 9.50 9.50

A201

A202

Stylized designs showing symbol for earth, water, and - #1256: a, Dove. b, Crab. c, Fish. d, Clover leaf.

$2, Symbol for earth and water.

**1998, July 30 Litho. *Perf. 14***

**1256** A201 50c Sheet of 4, #a.-d. 4.50 4.50

**Souvenir Sheet**

**1257** A201 $2 multicolored 5.50 5.50

Intl. Year of the Ocean.

**Royal Air Force, 80th Anniv.**

Common Design Type Re-Inscribed

Designs: 20c, SE 5A. 50c, Sopwith Camel. 60c, Supermarine Spitfire. 80c, Avro Lancaster. $1, Panavia Tornado. $1.25, Hawker Hurricane.

Each $2: No. 1264, Hawker Siddeley Harrier. No. 1265, Avro Vulcan.

**1998, Aug. 18 Litho. *Perf. 14***

**1258-1263** CD350 Set of 6 9.50 9.50

**Souvenir Sheets**

**1264-1265** CD350 Set of 2 10.00 10.00

**1998, July 30 Litho. *Perf. 14***

Anniversaries and Events: 20c, University of the West Indies, 50th anniv. 60c, UNESCO, World Summit Program. 80c, Universal Declaration of Human Rights. $1, John Glenn's return to space.

$2, NASA Space Shuttle leaving launching pad.

**1266-1269** A202 Set of 4 6.25 6.25

**Souvenir Sheet**

**1270** A202 $2 multicolored 5.50 5.50

A203

A204

**1998, Aug. 31**

**1271** A203 60c multicolored 1.25 1.25

Diana, Princess of Wales (1961-97). No. 1271 was issued in sheets of 6.

**1998, Nov. 30 Litho. *Perf. 14***

Paintings by Sister Thomasita Fessler — #1272: a, Magi's Visit. b, Flight Into Egypt. c, Wedding Feast. d, Maria. e, Annunciation & Visitation. f, Nativity. $2, Queen of Mothers.

**1272** A204 50c Sheet of 6, #a.-f. 7.00 7.00

**Souvenir Sheet**

**1273** A204 $2 multicolored 4.50 4.50

Christmas. Nos. 1272e-1272f are each 58x48mm.

Coral Gardens A205

No. 1274: a, Flamingos in flight. b, Sailboats. c, Seagulls, lighthouse. d, House along shore, seagulls. e, Pillar coral, yellowtail snapper (f). f, Elliptical star coral. g, Porkfish. h, Spotted eagle ray. i, Large ivory coral. j, Mustard hill coral, shy hamlet. k, Blue crust coral. l. Fused staghorn coral. m, Queen angelfish, massive starlet coral. n, Pinnate spiny sea fan. o, Knobby star coral, squirrelfish. p, Lowridge cactus coral, juvenile porkfish. q, Orange telesto coral. r, Spanish hogfish (q), Knobby ten-ray star coral. s, Boulder brain coral, clown wrasse. t, Rainbow parrotfish, regal sea fan. u, Great star coral, bluestriped grunt. v, Stinging coral, blue tang. w, Lavender thin finger coral. x, Juvenile french grunt (w), brilliant sea fingers.

Each $2: No. 1275, Sea fan. No. 1276, Elkhorn coral.

**1999, June 7 Litho. *Perf. 14¼x14½***

**1274** A205 20c Sheet of 24, #a.-x. 13.50 13.50

**Souvenir Sheets**

**1275-1276** A205 Set of 2 10.00 10.00

Wedding of Prince Edward and Sophie Rhys-Jones — A206

Portraits — #1277: a, Couple facing forward. b, Edward. c, Sophie. d, Couple walking arm in arm.
Each $2: No. 1278, Couple facing forward. No. 1279, Couple facing each other.

**1999, June 19 Litho. *Perf. 14***
**1277** A206 60c Sheet of 4, #a.-d. 5.75 5.75

**Souvenir Sheets**

**1278-1279** A206 Set of 2 9.50 9.50

Queen Mother (b. 1900) A207

Designs: a, At age 7. b, At age 19. c, At wedding. d, With daughters. e, With King George VI during World War II. f, In 1958. g, At age 60. h, In 1970. i, With Princes Charles and William, 1983. j, Current photograph.

**1999, Aug. 4 Litho. *Perf. 13½x13¾***
**1280** A207 50c Sheet of 10, #a.-j. 10.00 10.00

Stamp inscription on No. 1280f is incorrect.
No. 1280 was reissued in 2002 with added inscription in margin, "Good Health and Happiness to her Majesty The Queen Mother on her 101st Birthday."

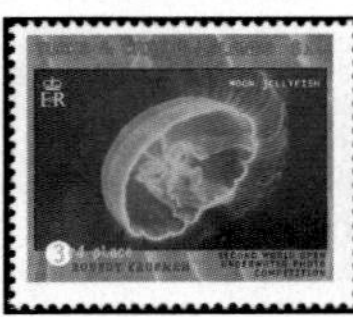

2nd World Underwater Photography Competition Winners A208

No. 1281: a, 10c, Painted tunicates (8th place). b, 20c, Peacock flounder (7th). c, 50c, Squirt anemone shrimps (6th). d, 60c, Juvenile drum (5th). e, 80c, Batwing coral crab (4th). f, $1, Moon jellyfish (3rd).
Each $2: No. 1282, Christmas tree worms (2nd). No. 1283, Longhorn nudibranch (1st).

**1999, Oct. 11 Litho. *Perf. 14¼x13¾***
**1281** A208 Sheet of 6, #a.-f. 8.50 8.50
*g.* As No. 1281, with corrected pictures 6.50 6.50

Issued: No. 1281g, 11/6/00.
On No. 1281, the illustrations for the 10c and 20c stamps are incorrect, with the 10c stamp inscribed "Painted tunicates," but depicting a peacock flounder, and the 20c stamp inscribed "Peacock flounder," but depicting painted tunicates. The pictures were switched on No. 1281g, making the inscriptions match the pictures.

**Souvenir Sheets**
***Perf. 13¾***

**1282-1283** A208 Set of 2 10.00 10.00

Nos. 1282-1283 each contain one 50x38mm stamp.

Christmas A209

Paintings by Anthony Van Dyck: 20c, The Mystic Marriage of Saint Catherine. 50c, Rest on the Flight into Egypt. No. 1286, $2, Holy Family with Saints John and Elizabeth.
No. 1287, The Madonna of the Rosary.

**1999, Dec. 7 *Perf. 13¾***
**1284-1286** A209 Set of 3 6.50 6.50

**Souvenir Sheet**

**1287** A209 $2 multicolored 5.00 5.00

Millennium A210

***Perf. 14½x14¼***
**1999, Nov. 15 Litho.**
**1288** A210 20c silver & multi .40 .40
**1289** A210 $1 gold & multi 2.00 2.00

Millennium A211

Globe, clock and: No. 1290: a, London. b, Turks & Caicos Islands. c, New York. d, Rome. e, Jerusalem. f, Paris.
Each $2: No. 1291, Flag of Islands. No. 1292, Arms of Islands.

**2000, Jan. 18 Litho. *Perf. 14x13¾***
**1290** A211 50c Sheet of 6, #a.-f. 6.00 6.00

**Souvenir Sheets**

**1291-1292** A211 Set of 2 10.00 10.00

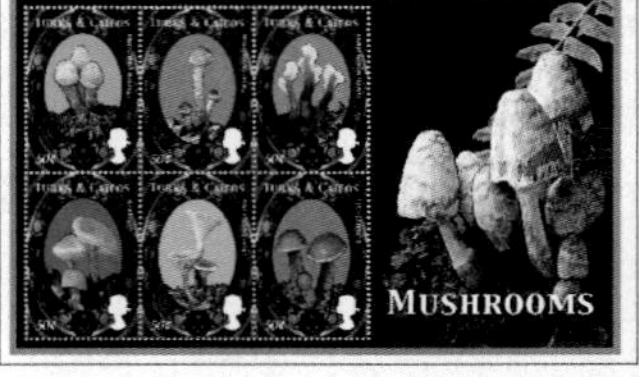

Mushrooms — A212

No. 1293, vert.: a, Pholiota squarroides. b, Psilocybe squamosa. c, Spathularia velutipes. d, Russula. e, Clitocybe clavipes. f, Boletus frostii.
No. 1294, Strobilurus conigenoides. No. 1295, Stereum ostrea.
Illustration reduced.

**2000, July 6 Litho. *Perf. 14***
**1293** A212 50c Sheet of 6, #a-f 9.00 9.00

**Souvenir Sheets**

**1294-1295** A212 $2 Set of 2 11.00 11.00

Souvenir Sheet

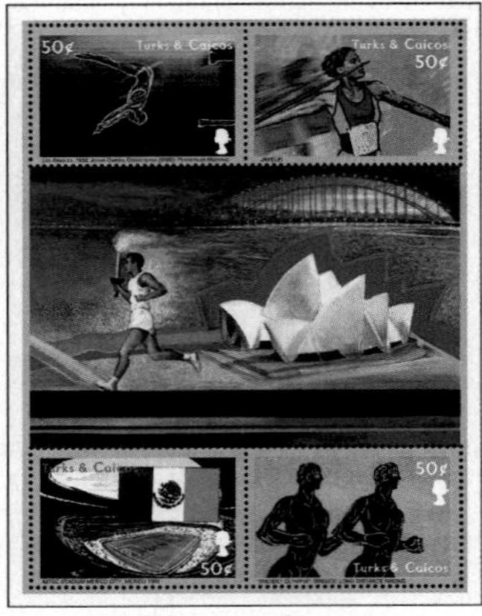

2000 Summer Olympics, Sydney — A213

No. 1296: a, Johan Gabriel Oxenstierna. b, Javelin. c, Aztec Stadium, Mexico City and Mexican flag. d, Ancient Greek runners.

**2000, Sept. 25**
**1296** A213 50c Sheet of 4, #a-d 5.50 5.50

Birds A214

Designs: No. 1297, Chickadee. No. 1298, Scrub turkey. No. 1299, Sickle-bill gull.
No. 1300: a, Egret. b, Tern. c, Osprey. d, Great blue heron. e, Pelican. f, Bahama pintail.
No. 1301, Flamingo, vert. No. 1302, Macaw, vert.

**2000, Oct. 2**
**1297-1299** A214 50c Set of 3 3.75 3.75
**1300** A214 60c Sheet of 6, #a-f 9.25 9.25

**Souvenir Sheets**

**1301-1302** A214 $2 Set of 2 10.50 10.50

Dogs and Cats — A215

No. 1303, 60c: a, Airedale terrier. b, Beagle. c, Dalmatian. d, Chow chow. e, Chihuahua. f, Pug.
No. 1304, 80c: a, Egyptian mau. b, Manx. c, Burmese. d, Korat. e, Maine coon cat. f, American shorthair.
No. 1305, $2, Collie. No. 1306, $2, Devon rex.

**2000, Nov. 13 Litho. *Perf. 14***
**Sheets of 6, #a-f**

**1303-1304** A215 Set of 2 21.00 21.00

**Souvenir Sheets**

**1305-1306** A215 Set of 2 11.00 11.00

Battle of Britain, 60th Anniv. A216

Designs: No. 1307, 50c, Douglas Robert Stewart Bader. No. 1308, 50c, Alan Christopher "Al" Deere. No. 1309, 50c, James Edgar "Johnny" Johnson. No. 1310, 50c, Edgar James "Cobber" Kain. No. 1311, 50c, James Harry "Ginger" Lacey. No. 1312, 50c, Air Vice-marshal Trafford Leigh. No. 1313, 50c, Adolph Gysbert "Sailor" Malan. No. 1314, Air Vice-marshal Keith Park.
No. 1315, each 50c: a, Winston Churchill. b, Barrage balloon. c, Heinkel He-111 Casa 2 111E. d, Soldier's farewell kiss to son. e, Hawker Hurricane. f, Dr, Jocelyn Henry Temple Peakins, clergyman in Home Guard. g, RAF fighter pilots scramble after an alert. h, Civilian volunteers scan the skies.
No. 1316, $2, Churchill, British flag. No. 1317, $2, London children.

**2000, Dec. 4 *Perf. 14***
**Stamps + labels**

**1307-1314** A216 Set of 8 11.50 11.50
**1315** A216 Sheet of 8, #a-h 11.50 11.50

**Souvenir Sheets**

**1316-1317** A216 Set of 2 11.50 11.50

Butterflies — A217

No. 1318, 50c: a, Clorinde. b, Blue night. c, Small lace-wing. d, Mosaic. e, Monarch. f, Grecian shoemaker.
No. 1319, 50c: a, Giant swallowtail. b, Common morpho. c, Tiger pierid. d, Banded king shoemaker. e, Figure-of-eight. f, Polydamas swallowtail.
No. 1320, $2, Orange-barred sulphur. No. 1321, $2, White peacock.

**2000, Dec. 11 Litho.**
**Sheets of 6, #a-f**

**1318-1319** A217 Set of 2 15.00 15.00

**Souvenir Sheets**

**1320-1321** A217 Set of 2 11.00 11.00

Ships A218

Designs: No. 1322, 60c, Neptune. No. 1323, 60c, Eagle. No. 1324, 60c, Gloria. No. 1325, 60c, Clipper ship, vert.
No. 1326, 60c: a, Viking long ship. b, Henri Grace à Dieu. c, Golden Hind. d, Endeavor. e, Anglo-Norman. f, Libertad.
No. 1327, 60c: a, Northern European cog. b, Carrack. c, Mayflower. d, Queen Anne's Revenge. e, Holkar. f, Amerigo Vespucci.
No. 1328, $2, USS Constitution, vert. No. 1329, $2, Denmark, vert.

**2001, May 15 Litho. *Perf. 14***
**1322-1325** A218 Set of 4 4.75 4.75

**Sheets of 6, #a-f**

**1326-1327** A218 Set of 2 14.50 14.50

**Souvenir Sheets**

**1328-1329** A218 Set of 2 8.00 8.00

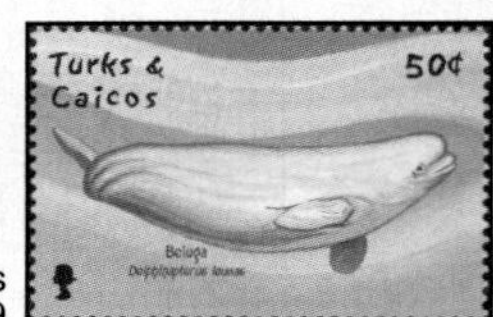

Whales A219

Designs: No. 1330, 50c, Beluga. No. 1331, 50c, Killer. No. 1332, 50c, Dwarf sperm. No. 1333, 50c, Shortfin pilot.

No. 1334, 50c: a, Bowhead. b, Two killer. c, Pygmy sperm. d, Right. e, Sperm. f, California gray.

No. 1335, 50c: a, Narwhal. b, One killer (in air). c, Bryde's. d, Belugas. e, Sperm (and starfish). f, Pilot.

No. 1336, $2, Cuvier's beaked. No. 1337, $2, Humpback (with calf).

**2001, May 15**

| | | | | |
|---|---|---|---|---|
| **1330-1333** | A219 | Set of 4 | 4.00 | 4.00 |

**Sheets of 6, #a-f**

| | | | | |
|---|---|---|---|---|
| **1334-1335** | A219 | Set of 2 | 12.00 | 12.00 |

**Souvenir Sheets**

| | | | | |
|---|---|---|---|---|
| **1336-1337** | A219 | Set of 2 | 8.00 | 8.00 |

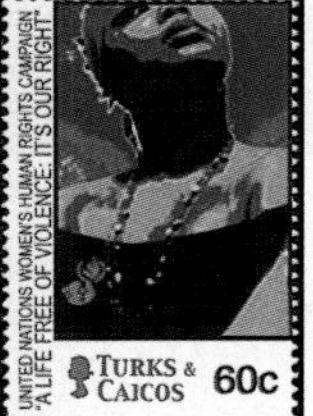


UN Women's Human Rights Campaign — A220

Designs: 60c, Woman. 80c, Woman, bird, torch.

**2001, June 18 Litho. *Perf. 14***

| | | | | |
|---|---|---|---|---|
| **1338-1339** | A220 | Set of 2 | 3.00 | 3.00 |

Phila Nippon '01 — A221

Designs: No. 1340, 60c, Autumn Moon in Mirror, by Suzuki Harunobu. No. 1341, 60c, Rikaku II as a Fisherman, by Hirosada. No. 1342, 60c, Musical Party, by Hishikawa Moronobu. No. 1343, 60c, Kannon and Four Farmers, by H. Gatto. No. 1344, 60c, Rain in Fifth Month, by Kunisada I. No. 1345, 60c, The Lives of Women, by Kuniyoshi Utagawa.

**2001, July 30 *Perf. 12x12¼***

| | | | | |
|---|---|---|---|---|
| **1340-1345** | A221 | Set of 6 | 7.25 | 7.25 |

Queen Victoria (1819-1901) — A222

No. 1346, 60c, oval frames: a, Wearing white headcovering. b, Wearing crown as young woman. c, Wearing black hat. d, Wearing crown as old woman.

No. 1347, 60c, rectangular frames: a, Wearing white headcovering. b, Holding flowers. c, Wearing white dress. d, Wearing crown, white dress with blue sash.

No. 1348, $2, Brown orange background. No. 1349, $2, Holding umbrella.

**2001, July 2 *Perf. 14***

**Sheets of 4, #a-d**

| | | | | |
|---|---|---|---|---|
| **1346-1347** | A222 | Set of 2 | 9.75 | 9.75 |

**Souvenir Sheets**

| | | | | |
|---|---|---|---|---|
| **1348-1349** | A222 | Set of 2 | 8.00 | 8.00 |

Queen Elizabeth II, 75th Birthday — A223

No. 1350: a, In pink hat. b, With crown looking left. c, In green hat. d, With crown looking forward. e, In red orange hat. f, With crown and veil.

$2, Wearing robe.

**2001, July 2**

| | | | | |
|---|---|---|---|---|
| **1350** | A223 | 60c Sheet of 6, #a-f | 7.25 | 7.25 |

**Souvenir Sheet**

| | | | | |
|---|---|---|---|---|
| **1351** | A223 | $2 multi | 4.00 | 4.00 |

Butterflies — A224

Designs: 10c, Cuban mimic. 15c, Gundlach's swallowtail, vert. 20c, Graphium androcles. 25c, Eastern black swallowtail. 35c, Papilio velvois, vert. 45c, Schaus swallowtail, vert. 50c, Pipevine swallowtail, vert. 60c, Euploea mniszecki, vert. 80c, Poey's black swallowtail, vert. $1, Graphium encelades, vert. $1.25, Jamaican ringlet. $1.40, Eastern tiger swallowtail. $2, Graphium milon, vert. $5, Palamedes swallowtail. $10, Zebra swallowtail.

***Perf. 14x14¾, 14¾x14***

**2001, Sept. 27**

| | | | | |
|---|---|---|---|---|
| **1352** | A224 | 10c multi | .20 | .20 |
| **1353** | A224 | 15c multi | .30 | .30 |
| **1354** | A224 | 20c multi | .40 | .40 |
| **1355** | A224 | 25c multi | .50 | .50 |
| **1356** | A224 | 35c multi | .70 | .70 |
| **1357** | A224 | 45c multi | .90 | .90 |
| **1358** | A224 | 50c multi | 1.00 | 1.00 |
| **1359** | A224 | 60c multi | 1.25 | 1.25 |
| **1360** | A224 | 80c multi | 1.60 | 1.60 |
| **1361** | A224 | $1 multi | 2.00 | 2.00 |
| **1362** | A224 | $1.25 multi | 2.50 | 2.50 |
| **1363** | A224 | $1.40 multi | 2.75 | 2.75 |
| **1364** | A224 | $2 multi | 4.00 | 4.00 |
| **1365** | A224 | $5 multi | 10.00 | 10.00 |
| **1366** | A224 | $10 multi | 20.00 | 20.00 |
| | | *Nos. 1352-1366 (15)* | 48.10 | 48.10 |

25c, 35c, $5, $10 exist dated "2003."

Reign of Queen Elizabeth II, 50th Anniv. — A225

No. 1367: a, Crossing Place Trail, Middle Caicos. b, Wades Green Plantation, North Caicos. c, Underwater scenery, Grand Turk. d, St. Thomas Anglican Church, Grand Turk. e, Ripsaw band, Grand Turk. f, Basketweaving.

No. 1368: a, Visit of Princess Royal, 1960. b, Visit of Queen Elizabeth II, 1966. c, Visit of Princess Alexandra, 1988. d, Visit of Duke of Edinburgh, 1993. e, Visit of Prince Andrew, 2000.

No. 1369: a, Salt Industry, 1952-62. b, Space splashdown, 1962-72. c, Ministerial government system, 1972-82. d, Quincentennial of Columbus' landfall, 1982-92. e, National Museum, 1992-2002.

**2002, June 1 Litho. *Perf. 14¼***

| | | | | |
|---|---|---|---|---|
| **1367** | | Sheet of 6 | 3.00 | 3.00 |
| *a.-f.* | A225 | 25c Any single | .50 | .50 |

***Perf. 13¾***

| | | | | |
|---|---|---|---|---|
| **1368** | | Sheet of 5 | 6.25 | 6.25 |
| *a.-e.* | A225 | 60c Any single | 1.25 | 1.25 |

***Perf. 13¾x14¼***

| | | | | |
|---|---|---|---|---|
| **1369** | | Sheet of 5 | 8.00 | 8.00 |
| *a.-e* | A225 | 80c Any single | 1.60 | 1.60 |

No. 1368 contains five 31x31mm stamps; No. 1369 contains five 30x34mm stamps.

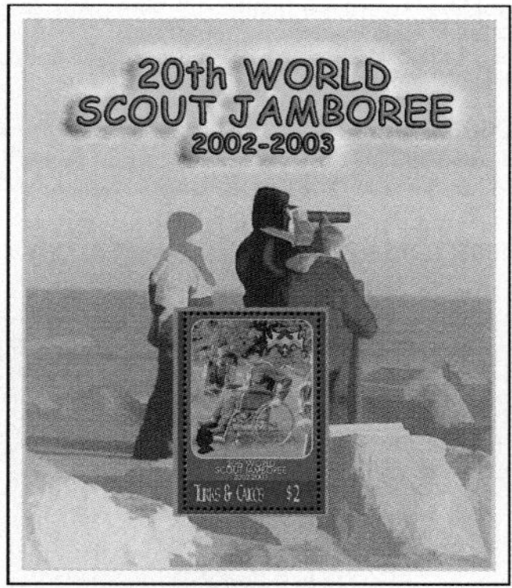


20th World Scout Jamboree, Thailand — A226

No. 1370: a, Scout with mallet and chisel. b, Scout with rifle. c, Scout hanging on rope above water. d, Scouts and lantern.

$2, Handicapped Scouts.

**2002, July 15 *Perf. 14***

| | | | | |
|---|---|---|---|---|
| **1370** | A226 | 80c Sheet of 4, #a-d | 6.50 | 6.50 |

**Souvenir Sheet**

| | | | | |
|---|---|---|---|---|
| **1371** | A226 | $2 multi | 4.00 | 4.00 |

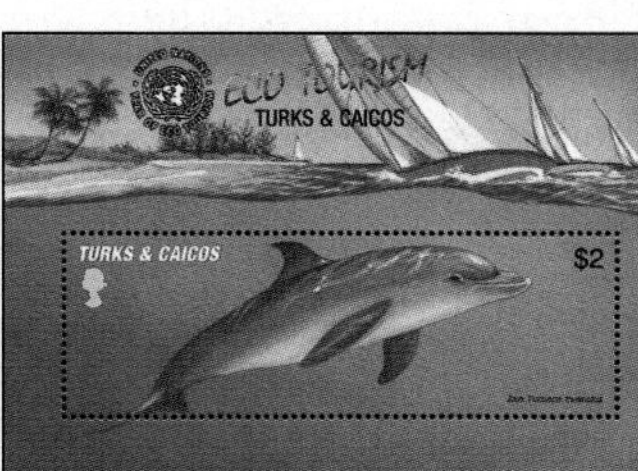


Intl. Year of Ecotourism — A227

No. 1372, vert.: a, Humpback whale. b, Water sports. c, Regattas. d, Queen angelfish. e, Manta ray. f, Turtle.

$2, Jojo dolphin.

**2002, July 15**

| | | | | |
|---|---|---|---|---|
| **1372** | A227 | 60c Sheet of 6, #a-f | 7.25 | 7.25 |

**Souvenir Sheet**

| | | | | |
|---|---|---|---|---|
| **1373** | A227 | $2 multi | 4.00 | 4.00 |

No. 1372 contains six 28x42mm stamps.

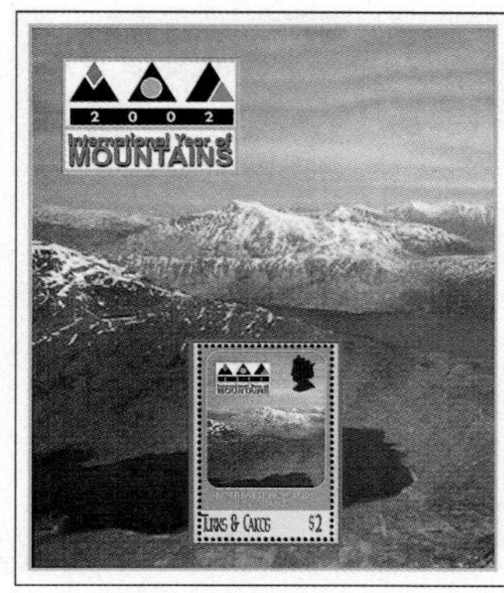


Intl. Year of Mountains — A228

No. 1374: a, Devil's Peak, South Africa. b, Mt. Drakensburg, South Africa. c, Mt. Blanc, France. d, Roan Mountain, US. e, Mt. Sefton, New Zealand. f, Mt. Cook, New Zealand.

$2, Northwest Highlands, Scotland.

**2002, July 22**

| | | | | |
|---|---|---|---|---|
| **1374** | A228 | 80c Sheet of 6, #a-f | 9.75 | 9.75 |

**Souvenir Sheet**

| | | | | |
|---|---|---|---|---|
| **1375** | A228 | $2 multi | 4.00 | 4.00 |

United We Stand — A229

**2002, Aug. 5**

| | | | | |
|---|---|---|---|---|
| **1376** | A229 | 50c multi | 1.00 | 1.00 |

Printed in sheets of 4.

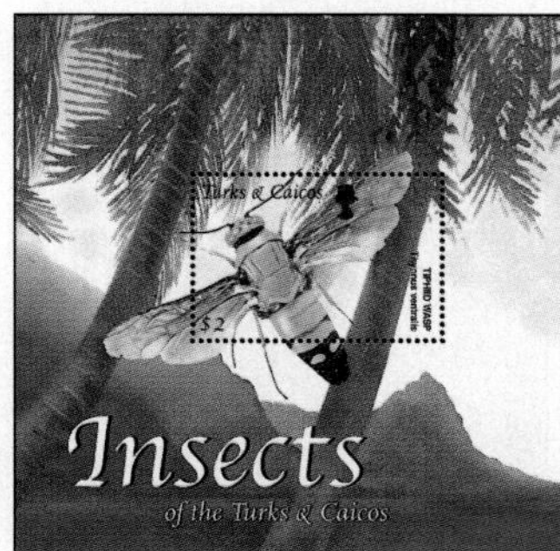


Insects and Birds — A230

No. 1377, 60c: a, Hawk moth. b, Burnet moth. c, Mammoth wasp. d, Branch-boring beetle. e, Flower mantid, Pseudocrebotra species. f, Flower mantid, Creobroter species.

No. 1378, 60c: a, Sooty tern. b, Magnificent frigatebird. c, American white pelican. d, Northern shoveler. e, Baltimore oriole. f, Roseate spoonbill.

No. 1379, $2, Tiphiid wasp. No. 1380, $2, Greater flamingo, vert.

**2002, Aug. 12 *Perf. 14***

**Sheets of 6, #a-f**

| | | | | |
|---|---|---|---|---|
| **1377-1378** | A230 | Set of 2 | 14.50 | 14.50 |

**Souvenir Sheets**

| | | | | |
|---|---|---|---|---|
| **1379-1380** | A230 | Set of 2 | 8.00 | 8.00 |

Queen Mother Elizabeth (1900-2002) — A231

No. 1381: a, Without hat. b, With hat.

**2002, Oct. 21**

**1381** A231 80c Sheet, 2 each #a-b 6.50 6.50

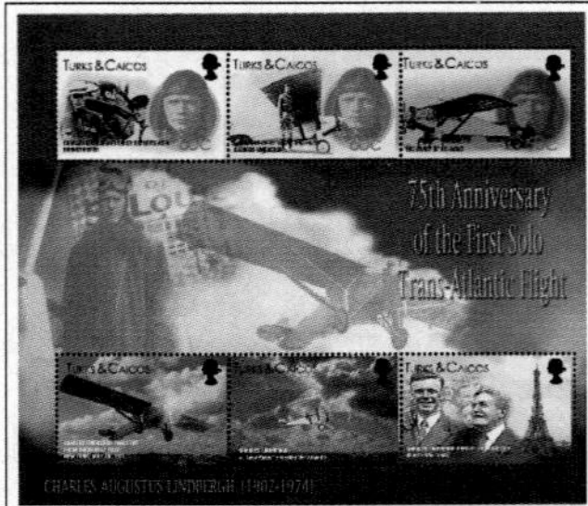


First Nonstop Solo Transatlantic Flight, 75th Anniv. — A232

No. 1382: a, Charles Lindbergh's early exploits as a barnstormer. b, Lindbergh standing in front of Spirit of St. Louis. c, Spirit of St. Louis. d, Take-off from Roosevelt Field. e, Crossing the Atlantic. f, Arrival and welcome in Paris.

**2002, Nov. 18 Litho. *Perf. 14***

**1382** A232 60c Sheet of 6, #a-f 7.25 7.25

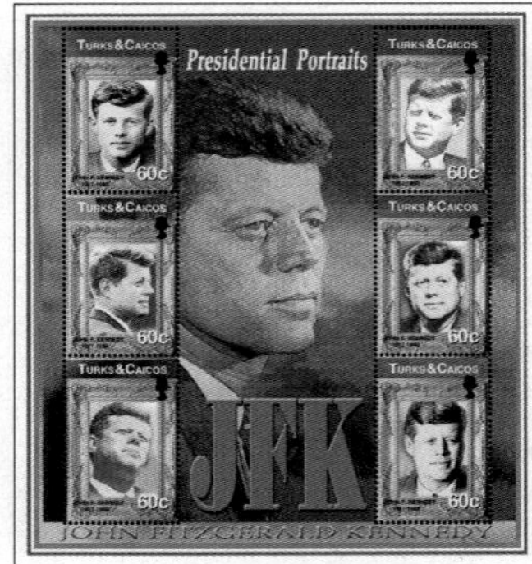


Pres. John F. Kennedy (1917-63) — A233

No. 1383 — Portrait color: a, Orange brown. b, Red violet. c, Greenish gray. d, Blue violet. e, Purple. f, Dull brown.

**2002, Nov. 18**

**1383** A233 60c multi 7.25 7.25

Christmas A234

Designs: 20c, Madonna and Child, by Giovanni Bellini, vert. 25c, Adoration of the Magi, by Correggio. 60c, Transfiguration of Christ, by Bellini, vert. 80c, Polyptych of St. Vincent Ferrer, by Bellini, vert. $1, Miraculous Mass, by Simone Martini, vert.

$2, Christ in Heaven with Four Saints, by Domenico Ghirlandaio.

**2002, Nov. 25**

**1384-1388** A234 Set of 5 5.75 5.75

**Souvenir Sheet**

**1389** A234 $2 multi 4.00 4.00

Japanese Art — A235

Designs: 25c, Nagata no Taro Nagamune, by Kuniyoshi Utagawa. 35c, Danjuro Ichikawa VII, by Kunisada Utagawa. 60c, Nagata no Taro Nagamune, by Kuniyoshi Utagawa, diff. $1, Nagata no Taro Nagamune, by Kuniyoshi Utagawa, diff.

No. 1394 — Scroll of Actors, by Chikanobu Toyohara and others: a, Smiling man holding fan. b, Man holding sword at mouth. c, Man holding sword vertically. d, Man with tree branch above head.

$2, Two Women by a River, by Chikanobu Hashimoto.

**2003, June 17 Litho. *Perf. 14¼***

**1390-1393** A235 Set of 4 4.50 4.50

**1394** A235 80c Sheet of 4, #a-d 6.50 6.50

**Souvenir Sheet**

**1395** A235 $2 multi 4.00 4.00

Rembrandt Paintings A236

Designs: 25c, Portrait of a Young Man Resting His Chin on His Hand. 50c, A Woman at an Open Door. No. 1398, $1, The Return of the Prodigal Son. No. 1399, $1, Portrait of an Elderly Man.

No. 1400: a, Nicolaas van Bambeeck. b, Agatha Bas, Wife of Nicolaas van Bambeeck. c, Portrait of a Man Holding His Hat. d, Saskia in a Red Hat.

$2, Christ Driving the Money Changers from the Temple.

***Perf. 14¼, 13¼ (#1400)***

**2003, June 17**

**1396-1399** A236 Set of 4 5.50 5.50

**1400** A236 60c Sheet of 4, #a-d 5.00 5.00

**Souvenir Sheet**

**1401** A236 $2 multi 4.00 4.00

Paintings by Joan Miró — A237

Designs: 25c, Portrait of a Young Girl. 50c, Table with Glove. 60c, Self-portrait, 1917. $1, The Farmer's Wife.

No. 1406: a, Portrait of Ramon Sunyer. b, Self-portrait, 1919. c, Portrait of a Spanish Dancer. d, Portrait of Joana Obrador.

No. 1407, Flowers and Butterfly. No. 1408, Still Life of the Coffee Grinder, horiz.

**2003, June 17 *Perf. 14¼***

**1402-1405** A237 Set of 4 4.75 4.75

**1406** A237 80c Sheet of 4, #a-d 6.50 6.50

***Imperf***

**Size: 104x83mm**

**1407** A237 $2 multi 4.00 4.00

**Size: 83x104mm**

**1408** A237 $2 multi 4.00 4.00

Caribbean Community, 30th Anniv. — A238

**2003, July 4 *Perf. 14***

**1409** A238 60c multi 1.25 1.25

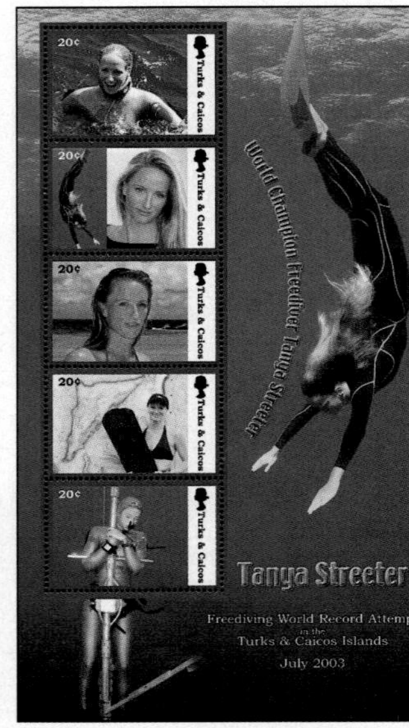


Tanya Streeter, World Champion Freediver — A239

No. 1410: a, Wearing wetsuit in water. b, Diving underwater, portrait. c, Wearing bathing suit at shore. d, Standing in front of map. e, Holding on to diving apparatus.

**2003, July 15**

**1410** A239 20c Sheet of 5, #a-e 2.00 2.00

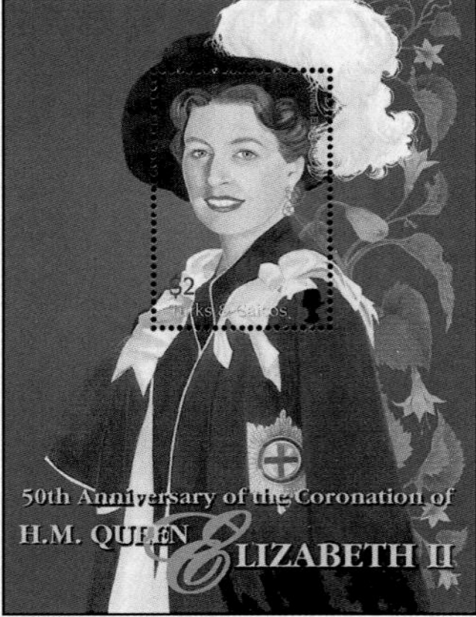


Coronation of Queen Elizabeth II, 50th Anniv. — A240

No. 1411: a, Wearing crown and white robe. b, Wearing lilac dress. c, Wearing tiara and red dress.

$2, Wearing hat and blue cape. $5, Profile portrait.

**2003, Aug. 25**

**1411** A240 80c Sheet of 3, #a-c 5.00 5.00

**Souvenir Sheets**

**1412-1413** A240 Set of 2 14.00 14.00

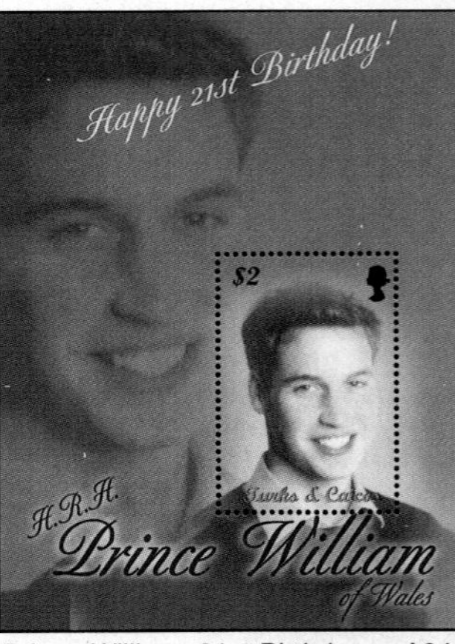


Prince William, 21st Birthday — A241

No. 1414: a, Portrait in blue. b, Pink background. c, Purple background.

$2, Dark blue background.

**2003, Aug. 25**

**1414** A241 $1 Sheet of 3, #a-c 6.00 6.00

**Souvenir Sheet**

**1415** A241 $2 multi 4.00 4.00

Tour de France Bicycle Race, Cent. — A242

No. 1416: a, Eddy Merckx, 1974. b, Bernard Thévenet, 1975. c, Lucien Van Impe, 1976. d, Thévenet, 1977.

$2, Bernard Hinault, 1979.

**2003, Aug. 25 *Perf. 13¾x14¼***

**1416** A242 $1 Sheet of 4, #a-d 8.00 8.00

**Souvenir Sheet**

**1417** A242 $2 multi 4.00 4.00

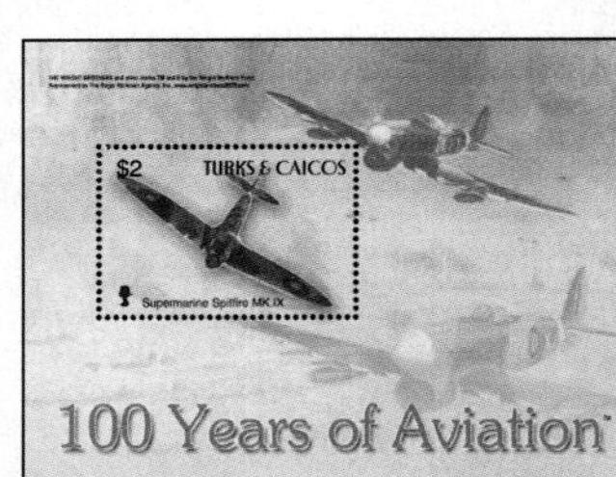


Powered Flight, Cent. — A243

No. 1418: a, Vought F4U Corsair. b, Messerschmidt Me 262. c, A6M. d, Hawker Hurricane.

$2, Supermarine Spitfire Mk IX.

**2003, Aug. 25 *Perf. 14***

**1418** A243 60c Sheet of 4, #a-d 5.00 5.00

**Souvenir Sheet**

**1419** A243 $2 multi 4.00 4.00

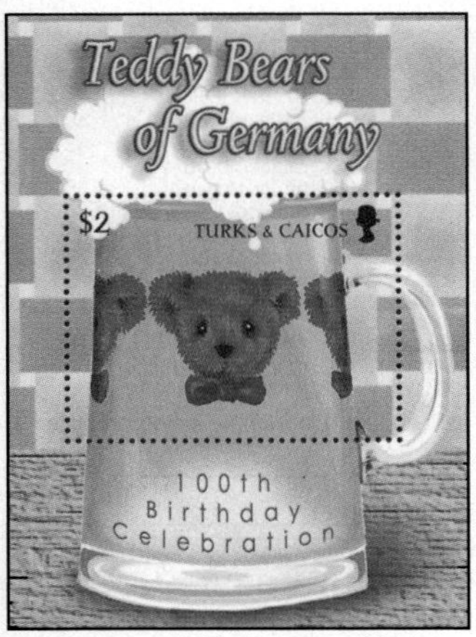


German Teddy Bears — A244

No. 1420, vert.: a, Bear with red and yellow uniform. b, Bear with dress. c, Bear with violin case. d, Bear with sword.
$2, Bear on beer mug.

**2003, Aug. 25** ***Perf. 12x12¼***
**1420** A244 50c Sheet of 4, #a-d 4.00 4.00

**Souvenir Sheet**
***Perf. 12¼x12***

**1421** A244 $2 multi 4.00 4.00

Butterflies A245

Designs: 50c, Papilio thersites. 60c, Papilio andraemon. 80c, Papilio pelaus. $1, Consul hippona.
$2, Papilio pelaus, diff.

**2003, Nov. 17** ***Perf. 14***
**1422-1425** A245 Set of 4 6.00 6.00

**Souvenir Sheet**

**1426** A245 $2 multi 4.00 4.00

Orchids A246

Designs: 50c, Laelia anceps. 60c, Laelia briegeri. 80c, Laelia fidelensis. $1, Laelia cinnabarina.
$2, Laelia rubescens.

**2003, Nov. 17**
**1427-1430** A246 Set of 4 6.00 6.00

**Souvenir Sheet**

**1431** A246 $2 multi 4.00 4.00

Dogs A247

Designs: 50c, Beagle. 60c, Sabueso Espanol, vert. 80c, Basset hound, vert. $1, Jack Russell terrier, vert.
$2, Dachshund.

**2003, Nov. 17**
**1432-1435** A247 Set of 4 6.00 6.00

**Souvenir Sheet**

**1436** A247 $2 multi 4.00 4.00

Cats A248

Designs: 50c, Persian. 60c, Cymric. 80c, Main Coon, vert. $1, Tiffany.
$2, Kurile Island bobtail.

**2003, Nov. 17**
**1437-1440** A248 Set of 4 6.00 6.00

**Souvenir Sheet**

**1441** A248 $2 multi 4.00 4.00

Christmas A249

Paintings: 25c, Madonna of the Harpies, by Andrea del Sarto. 60c, Madonna and Child with St. John, by del Sarto. 80c, Madonna and Child with St. Joseph and St. Peter Martyr, by del Sarto. $1, Madonna and Child with the Angels, by del Sarto.
$2, Montefeltro Altarpiece, by Piero della Francesca.

**2003, Nov. 24** ***Perf. 14¼***
**1442-1445** A249 Set of 4 5.50 5.50

**Souvenir Sheet**

**1446** A249 $2 multi 4.00 4.00

Marine Life — A250

Photographs from underwater photography contest: Nos. 1447, 1452a, 25c, Golden Rough Head Blennie, by Rand McMeins. Nos. 1448, 1452b, 50c, Octopus at Night, by Marc Van Driessche. Nos. 1449, 1452c, 60c, Sea Turtle, by Mike Nebel. Nos. 1450, 1452d, 80c, Juvenile Octopus, by Amber Blecker. Nos. 1451, 1452e, $1, School of Horse Eye Jacks, by Blecker.
$2, Coral Reef, by Keith Kaplan, vert.

***Perf. 12, 12¾ (#1452)***
**2006, June 1** **Litho.**

**Stamps With Thin "Shadow" Frame**

**1447-1451** A250 Set of 5 6.50 6.50

**Miniature Sheet**
**Stamps With Thick "Shadow" Frame**

**1452** A250 Sheet of 5, #a-e 6.50 6.50

**Souvenir Sheet**

**1453** A250 $2 multi 4.00 4.00

Washington 2006 World Philatelic Exhibition. (Nos. 1452-1453). The perforation tips at the tops of the stamps on Nos. 1452a-1452e are all white, gradiating to blue on the lower halves of the stamps, while the perforation tips on Nos. 1447-1451 show other colors. The shadow frames at the bottom of Nos 1452a-1452e are 1mm thick and about ½mm thick on Nos. 1447-1451. The distances between the bottom of the denomination and the top of the country name differ on Nos. 1452a-1452e from those found on Nos. 1447-1451. No. 1447 has incorrect spelling, "Ruogh," in inscription, while No. 1452a has word correctly spelled as "Rough."

Queen Elizabeth II, 80th Birthday — A251

No. 1454 — Various depictions of Queen Elizabeth II: a, 50c. b, 60c. c, 80c. d, $1.
$6, Wearing crown.

**2006, Sept. 12** **Litho.** ***Perf. 13½***
**1454** A251 Sheet of 4, #a-d 6.00 6.00

**Souvenir Sheet**

**1455** A251 $6 multi 12.00 12.00

Christmas — A252

The Birth of Christ and Adoration of the Shepherds, by Peter Paul Rubens: Nos. 1456, 1460a, 25c, Praying shepherd. Nos. 1457, 1460b, 60c, Infant Jesus. Nos. 1458, 1460c, 80c, Heads of two shepherds. Nos. 1459, 1460d, $1, Virgin Mary.
$6, Our Lady, The Christ Child and Saints, by Rubens, vert.

**2006, Dec. 27** ***Perf. 13¼x13½***

**Stamps With Painting Title**

**1456-1459** A252 Set of 4 5.50 5.50

**Stamps Without Painting Title**

**1460** A252 Sheet of 4, #a-d 5.50 5.50

**Souvenir Sheet**
***Perf. 13½x13¼***

**1461** A252 $6 multi 12.00 12.00

## WAR TAX STAMPS

Regular Issue of 1913-16 Overprinted

**1917** **Wmk. 3** ***Perf. 14***

**Black Overprint at Bottom of Stamp**

**MR1** A10 1p carmine .20 *1.75*
 *a.* Double overprint 200.00 *275.00*
 *b.* "TAX" omitted
 *c.* Pair, one without ovpt.
**MR2** A10 3p violet, *yel* 1.40 *5.75*
 *a.* Double overprint 110.00

Black Overprint at Top or Middle of Stamp

**1917**
**MR3** A10 1p carmine .20 *1.40*
 *a.* Inverted overprint 55.00
 *b.* Double overprint 50.00 *62.50*
 *c.* Pair, one without overprint 625.00
**MR4** A10 3p violet, *yel* .70 *2.00*
 *a.* Double overprint 50.00
 *b.* Dbl. ovpt., one inverted 375.00

Same Overprint in Violet or Red

**1918-19**
**MR5** A10 1p car (V) ('19) .20 *1.10*
 *a.* Double overprint 24.00
 *b.* "WAR" omitted 175.00
**MR6** A10 3p violet, *yel* (R) 11.00 *30.00*
 *a.* Double overprint 375.00

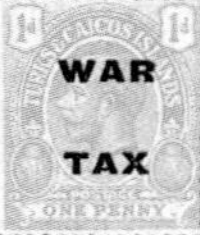


Regular Issue of 1913-16 Overprinted in Black

**1918**
**MR7** A10 1p carmine .20 *1.40*
**MR8** A10 3p violet, *yel* 2.75 *4.25*

Same Overprint in Red

**1919**
**MR9** A10 3p violet, *yel* .20 *2.75*

Regular Issue of 1913-16 Overprinted in Black

**MR10** A10 1p carmine .20 *1.10*
 *a.* Double overprint 160.00 *190.00*
**MR11** A10 3p violet, *yel* .35 *3.00*

WAR

Regular Issue of 1913-16 Overprinted

TAX

**MR12** A10 1p carmine .20 2.75
 *a.* Double overprint *100.00*
**MR13** A10 3p violet, *yel* .55 *3.00*

## CAICOS

**Catalogue values for all unused stamps in this country are for Never Hinged items.**

Turks & Caicos Nos. 360, 364, 366, 369, 371-373 Ovptd. with Black Bar and "CAICOS ISLANDS"

**Unwmk.**

**1981, July 24** **Litho.** ***Perf. 14***
**1** A69 1c Indigo hamlet .20 .20
**2** A69 5c Spanish grunt .20 .20
**3** A69 8c Foureye butterflyfish .20 .20
**4** A69 20c Queen angelfish .40 .40
**5** A69 50c Fairy basslet .95 .95
**6** A69 $1 Clown wrasse 1.90 1.90
**7** A69 $2 Stoplight parrotfish 3.75 3.75
 *Nos. 1-7 (7)* 7.60 7.60

Common Design Types pictured following the introduction.

**Royal Wedding Issue**
Common Design Type
Turks & Caicos Nos. 486-489 Ovptd. with Black Bar and "Caicos Islands"

**1981, July 24**
**8** CD331 35c Charles & Diana .35 .35
**9** CD331 65c Kensington Palace .65 .65
**10** CD331 90c Prince Charles .90 .90
 *Nos. 8-10 (3)* 1.90 1.90

**Souvenir Sheet**

**11** CD331 $2 Glass coach 5.00 5.00

***Roulette x Imperf. (#12a), Imperf. (#12b)***

**1981, Oct. 29**

**Self-Adhesive**

**12** Souvenir booklet 27.50
 *a.* A88a Pane, 3 each 20c, Diana, $1, Charles) 15.00
 *b.* A88a Pane of 1 $2, Couple 10.00

Nos. 8-11 exist with overprint in all capital letters, values about the same. Nos. 8-10, in both overprint types, also exist in sheets of 5 plus label in changed colors, perf. 12.

Hawksbill turtle
C1

**1983-84** ***Perf. 14***

**13** C1 8c Diver with lobster and conch shell .30 .30
**14** C1 10c shown .30 .30
**15** C1 20c Stone idol, Arawak Indians .65 .65
**16** C1 35c Sloop construction 1.10 1.10
**17** C1 50c Marine biology 1.60 1.60
**18** C1 95c 707 Jetliner 3.25 3.25
**19** C1 $1.10 15th cent. Spanish ship 3.75 3.75
**20** C1 $2 British soldier, Fort St. George 6.75 6.75
**21** C1 $3 Pirates Anne Bonny, Calico Jack 10.00 10.00
*Nos. 13-21 (9)* 27.70 27.70

Issued: #13-19, 6/6/83; #20-21, 5/18/84.
For overprints see Nos. 47-49.

Christmas Type of Turks and Caicos

Walt Disney characters in Santa Claus is Coming to Town.

**1983, Nov. 7** ***Perf. 11***

**22** A104 1c Chip 'n Dale .40 .40
**23** A104 1c Goofy & Patch .40 .40
**24** A104 2c Morty, Ferdie & Pluto .40 .40
**25** A104 2c Morty .40 .40
**26** A104 3c Donald, Huey, Dewey & Louie .40 .40
**27** A104 3c Goofy & Louie .40 .40
**28** A104 50c Uncle Scrooge 2.50 2.50
**29** A104 70c Mickey Mouse & Ferdie 3.50 3.50
**30** A104 $1.10 Pinocchio, Jiminy Cricket and Figaro 5.00 5.00
*Nos. 22-30 (9)* 13.40 13.40

**Souvenir Sheet**

***Perf. 13½x14***

**31** A104 $2 Morty & Ferdie, fireplace 6.75 6.75

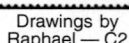

Drawings by Raphael — C2

1984 Summer Olympics, Los Angeles — C3

Designs: 35c, Leda and the Swan. 50c, Study of Apollo for Parnassus. 95c, Study of two figures for The Battle of Ostia. $1.10, Study for the Madonna of the Goldfinch. $2.50, The Garvagh Madonna.

**1983, Dec. 15** ***Perf. 14***

**32** C2 35c multicolored 1.10 1.10
**33** C2 50c multicolored 1.60 1.60
**34** C2 95c multicolored 3.00 3.00
**35** C2 $1.10 multicolored 3.50 3.50
*Nos. 32-35 (4)* 9.20 9.20

**Souvenir Sheet**

**36** C2 $2.50 multicolored 6.00 6.00

500th birth anniv. of Raphael.

**1984, Mar. 1**

**37** C3 4c High jump .20 .20
**38** C3 25c Archery .50 .50
**39** C3 65c Cycling 1.25 1.25
**40** C3 $1.10 Soccer 2.25 2.25
*Nos. 37-40 (4)* 4.20 4.20

**Souvenir Sheet**

**41** C3 $2 Show jumping, horiz. 4.75 4.75

Easter — C4

Walt Disney characters: 35c, Horace Horsecollar, Clarabelle Cow. 45c, Mickey, Minnie & Chip. 75c, Gyro Gearloose, Chip 'n Dale. 85c, Mickey, Chip 'n Dale. $2.20, Donald sailing with nephews.

**1984, Apr. 15** ***Perf. 14x13½***

**42** C4 35c multicolored 1.00 1.00
**43** C4 45c multicolored 1.25 1.25
**44** C4 75c multicolored 2.10 2.10
**45** C4 85c multicolored 2.50 2.50
*Nos. 42-45 (4)* 6.85 6.85

**Souvenir Sheet**

**46** C4 $2.20 mulitcolored 7.50 7.50

Nos. 18-19 Ovptd. with emblem and "Universal Postal Union 1874-1984"

**1984, June 19** ***Perf. 14***

**47** C1 95c multicolored 1.90 1.90
**48** C1 $1.10 multicolored 2.25 2.25

No. 20 Ovptd. "AUSIPEX 1984"

**1984, Aug. 22**

**49** C1 $2 multicolored 4.00 4.00

Columbus' First Landfall — C5

**1984, Sept. 21**

**50** C5 10c Sighting manatees .50 .50
**51** C5 70c Fleet 3.50 3.50
**52** C5 $1 West Indies landing 5.00 5.00
*Nos. 50-52 (3)* 9.00 9.00

**Souvenir Sheet**

**53** C5 $2 Fleet, map 5.00 5.00

Columbus' first landing, 492nd anniv.

Christmas C6

Walt Disney characters: 20c, Santa Claus, Donald and Mickey. 35c, Donald at refrigerator. 50c, Donald, Micky riding toy train. 75c, Donald carrying presents. $1.10, Huey, Louie, Dewey and Donald singing carols. $2, Donald as Christmas tree.

***Perf. 13½x14, 12x12½ (75c)***

**1984, Nov. 26**

**54** C6 20c multicolored .80 .80
**55** C6 35c multicolored 1.40 1.40
**56** C6 50c multicolored 2.00 2.00
**57** C6 75c multicolored 3.00 3.00
**58** C6 $1.10 multicolored 4.50 4.50
*Nos. 54-58 (5)* 11.70 11.70

**Souvenir Sheet**

***Perf. 13½x14***

**59** C6 $2 multicolored 6.25 6.25

No. 57 printed in sheets of 8.

Audubon Birth Bicentenary — C7

**1985, Feb. 12** ***Perf. 14***

**60** C7 20c Thick-billed vireo .85 .85
**61** C7 35c Black-faced grassquit 1.50 1.50
**62** C7 50c Pearly-eyed thrasher 2.10 2.10
**63** C7 $1 Greater Antillean bullfinch 4.25 4.25
*Nos. 60-63 (4)* 8.70 8.70

**Souvenir Sheet**

**64** C7 $2 Stripe-headed tanagers 5.00 5.00

No. 64 exists imperf.

Intl. Youth Year — C8

**1985, May 8**

**65** C8 16c Education .30 .30
**66** C8 35c Health .70 .70
**67** C8 70c Love 1.40 1.40
**68** C8 90c Peace 1.75 1.75
*Nos. 65-68 (4)* 4.15 4.15

**Souvenir Sheet**

**69** C8 $2 Peace dove, child 5.25 5.25

UN 40th anniv.

Intl. Civil Aviation Org., 40th Anniv. C9

**1985, May 26**

**70** C9 35c DC-3 1.60 1.60
**71** C9 75c Convair 440 3.50 3.50
**72** C9 90c TCNA Islander 4.25 4.25
*Nos. 70-72 (3)* 9.35 9.35

**Souvenir Sheet**

**73** C9 $2.20 Hang glider 7.50 7.50

Queen Mother, 85th Birthday Type of Turks & Caicos

**1985, July 7**

**74** A117 35c Wearing green hat .85 .85
**75** A117 65c With Princess Anne, horiz. 1.50 1.50
**76** A117 95c Wearing white hat 2.25 2.25
*Nos. 74-76 (3)* 4.60 4.60

**Souvenir Sheet**

**77** A117 $2 Inspecting guardsmen 4.75 4.75

Mark Twain, 150th Birth Anniv. — C10

Walt Disney characters in Tom Sawyer, Detective (Intl. Youth Year): 8c, Mickey and Goofy as Tom and Huck reading reward poster. 35c, Meeting Jake Dunlap. 95c, Spying on Jubiter Dunlap. $1.10, With Pluto finding body. No. 86, Unmasking Jubiter Dunlap.

Walt Disney characters portraying Six Soldiers of Fortune (The Brothers Grimm, Bicent.): 16c, Donald receiving his meager pay. 25c, Donald meets Horace Horsecollar as strong man. 65c, Donald meets Mickey the marksman. $1.35, Goofy wins footrace against Princess Daisy. No. 87, Soldiers with sack of gold.

**1985, Dec. 5** ***Perf. 14x13½***

**78** C10 8c multicolored .40 .40
**79** C10 16c multicolored .65 .65
**80** C10 25c multicolored 1.00 1.00
**81** C10 35c multicolored 1.50 1.50
**82** C10 65c multicolored 2.50 2.50
**83** C10 95c multicolored 4.00 4.00
**84** C10 $1.10 multicolored 4.75 4.75
**85** C10 $1.35 multicolored 5.75 5.75
*Nos. 78-85 (8)* 20.55 20.55

**Souvenir Sheet**

**86** C10 $2 multicolored 7.50 7.50
**87** C10 $2 multicolored 7.50 7.50

Stamps are no longer being produced for Caicos.

## TURKS ISLANDS

'tərks 'ī-ləndz

LOCATION — West Indies, at the southern extremity of the Bahamas
GOVT. — Former dependency of Jamaica
POP. — 2,000 (approx.)
CAPITAL — Grand Turk

In 1848 the Turks Islands together with the Caicos group, lying to the northwest, were made a British colony. In 1873 the Colony became a dependency under the government of Jamaica although separate stamp issues were continued. Postage stamps inscribed Turks and Caicos Islands have been used since 1900.

12 Pence = 1 Shilling

Values for unused stamps are for examples with original gum as defined in the catalogue introduction. Very fine examples of Nos. 1-42 will have generally rough perforations that cut into the design on one or more sides due to the narrow spacing of the stamps on the plates and imperfect perforating methods. Stamps with perfs clear of the design on all four sides are extremely scarce and will command substantially higher prices.

Because of the printing and imperfect perforating methods, stamps are often found scissor separated. Prices will not be adversely affected on those stamps where the scissor cut does not remove the perforations.

**Watermark**

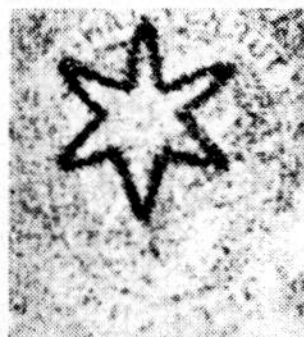
Wmk. 5 — Small Star

Queen Victoria — A1

***Perf. 11½ to 13***

**1867** **Unwmk.** **Engr.**

**1** A1 1p rose 62.50 62.50
**2** A1 6p gray black 110.00 *140.00*
**3** A1 1sh slate blue 105.00 67.50
*Nos. 1-3 (3)* 277.50 270.00

***Perf. 11 to 13x14 to 15***

**1873-79 Wmk. 5**

4 A1 1p lake 57.50 57.50
5 A1 1p dull red ('79) 62.50 67.50
*a.* Horiz. pair, imperf. btwn. *19,000.*
*b.* Perf. 11-12 *1,100.*
6 A1 1sh violet 5,750. *2,250.*

Stamps offered as No. 6 are often copies from which the surcharge has been removed.

Stamps of 1867-79 Surcharged in Black:

a b

c

d e

12 settings of the ½p, 9 of 2½p, and 6 of 4p.

**1881 Unwmk. *Perf. 11 to 13***

7 (a) ½p on 6p gray blk 85.00 *140.00*
7A (b) ½p on 6p gray blk 80.00 *120.00*
8 (b) ½p on 1sh slate bl 110.00 *180.00*
*a.* Double surcharge *5,750.*
8B (c) ½p on 1sh slate bl *11,000.*
*c.* Without fraction bar

***Perf. 11 to 13x14 to 15***

**Wmk. 5**

9 (a) ½p on 1p dull red 150.00 200.00
*a.* Double surcharge
10 (b) ½p on 1p dull red 55.00 *90.00*
11 (c) ½p on 1p dull red 210.00 *275.00*
*a.* Double surcharge 4,250.
12 (d) ½p on 1p dull red 260.00
*a.* Without fraction bar 1,150.
*b.* Double surcharge
13 (e) ½p on 1p dull red 600.00
14 (a) ½p on 1sh violet 175.00 225.00
*a.* Double surcharge 4,000.
15 (b) ½p on 1sh violet 140.00 *225.00*
*a.* Without fraction bar 625.00
16 (c) ½p on 1sh violet 105.00 *190.00*

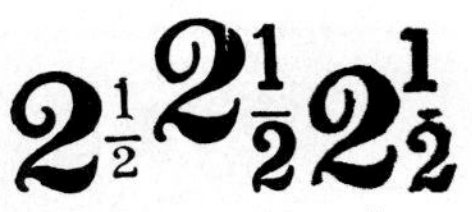

f g h

***Perf. 11 to 13***

**Unwmk.**

17 (f) 2½p on 6p gray blk *9,500.*
18 (g) 2½p on 6p gray blk 375.00 *450.00*
*a.* Horiz. pair, imperf. between *19,000.*
*b.* Double surcharge *9,500.*
19 (h) 2½p on 6p gray blk 175.00 *325.00*
*a.* Double surcharge *9,500.*

i

j

***Perf. 11 to 13x14 to 15***

**Wmk. 5**

20 (i) 2½p on 1sh violet *2,600.*
21 (h) 2½p on 1sh violet 625.00 *950.00*
22 (j) 2½p on 1sh violet *9,500.*

k

l

m n

***Perf. 11 to 13***

**Unwmk.**

24 (k) 2½p on 6p gray blk *8,500.*
25 (k) 2½p on 1sh slate bl *15,000.*
26 (l) 2½p on 1sh slate bl 850.00
27 (m) 2½p on 1sh slate bl *2,200.*
*a.* Without fraction bar *8,000.*
28 (n) 2½p on 1sh slate bl *6,500.*

o

***Perf. 11 to 13x14 to 15***

**Wmk. 5**

29 (l) 2½p on 1p dull red 600.00
30 (o) 2½p on 1p dull red 1,350.
31 (l) 2½p on 1sh violet 850.00
*a.* Double surcharge of "½" *4,000.*
32 (o) 2½p on 1sh violet 1,350.
*b.* Double surcharge of "½" *5,750.*

p

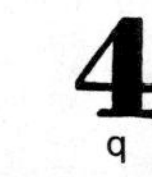

q

r

***Perf. 11 to 13***

**Unwmk.**

33 (p) 4p on 6p gray black 85.00 120.00
34 (q) 4p on 6p gray black 375.00 *475.00*
35 (r) 4p on 6p gray black 475.00 *350.00*

Copies of No. 33 with top of "4" painted in are sometimes offered as No. 35.

***Perf. 11 to 13x14 to 15***

**Wmk. 5**

36 (r) 4p on 1p dull red 950.00 625.00
*a.* Inverted surcharge 3,250.
37 (p) 4p on 1p dull red 850.00 550.00
*a.* Inverted surcharge
38 (p) 4p on 1sh violet 450.00 *625.00*
39 (q) 4p on 1sh violet *2,750.*

**Wmk. Crown and C C (1)**

**1881 Engr. *Perf. 14***

40 A1 1p brown red 67.50 95.00
*a.* Diagonal half used as ½p on cover
41 A1 6p olive brown 110.00 170.00
42 A1 1sh slate green 170.00 140.00
*Nos. 40-42 (3)* 347.50 405.00

A2

A3

**1881 Typo.**

43 A2 4p ultramarine 140.00 67.50

**1882-95 Engr. Wmk. 2**

44 A1 1p orange brn ('83) 77.50 35.00
*a.* Half used as ½p on cover 4,750.
45 A1 1p car lake ('89) 1.75 *2.25*
46 A1 6p yellow brn ('89) 2.25 3.00
47 A1 1sh black brn ('87) 3.50 3.00
*a.* 1sh deep brown 3.50 3.00

**Typo.**

**Die A**

48 A2 ½p dull green ('85) 2.50 4.00
*a.* ½p blue green ('82) 10.50 25.00
49 A2 2½p red brown ('82) 21.00 15.00
50 A2 4p gray ('84) 20.00 2.75
*a.* Half used as 2p on cover 4,750.

**Die B**

51 A2 ½p gray green ('94) 2.75 2.00
52 A2 2½p ultra ('93) 2.75 2.75
53 A2 4p dk vio & bl ('95) 11.00 15.00

For explanation of dies A and B see back of this volume.

**1887 Engr. *Perf. 12***

54 A1 1p carmine lake 14.00 3.25

No. 49 Surcharged in Black

**1889**

55 A2 1p on 2½p red brown 10.00 *11.00*
*a.* Double surcharge
*b.* Double surcharge, one inverted
*c.* "One" omitted 1,800.
*d.* Half used as ½p on cover 5,500.

No. 55c caused by the misplacement of the surcharge. Stamps also exist from the same sheet reading "Penny One."

No. 50 Surcharged in Black

Two types of surcharge:
Type I — Upper bar continuous across sheet.
Type II — Upper bar breaks between stamps.

**1893**

56 A2 ½p on 4p gray (I) 160.00 150.00
*a.* Type II 2,600. 1,150.

This surcharge exists in five settings.

**1894 Typo.**

57 A3 5p olive grn & carmine 6.00 *16.50*
*a.* Diag. half used as 2½p on cover *4,250.*

## TUVALU

tü-'vä-,ü

LOCATION — A group of islands in the Pacific Ocean northeast of Australia.
GOVT. — Independent state in the British Commonwealth
AREA — 9½ sq. mi.
POP. — 10,588 (1999 est.)
CAPITAL — Funafuti

Tuvalu, formerly Ellice Islands, consists of nine islands.

Australian dollar

**Catalogue values for all unused stamps in this country are for Never Hinged items.**

**Watermark**

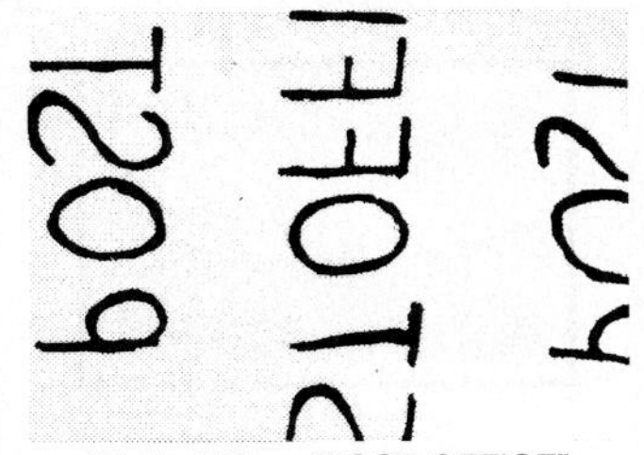

Wmk. 380 — "POST OFFICE"

**Gilbert and Ellice Islands Types of 1971**

Overprinted "TUVALU" and Bar in Violet Blue or Silver (35c)

**Wmk. 373**

**1976, Jan. 1 Litho. *Perf. 14***

1 A18 1c 1.25 .60
2 A19 2c 1.60 .85
*a.* Wmk. 314 sideways 240.00 25.00
*b.* Wmk. 314 upright 1,500. 140.00
3 A19 3c Wmk. 314 2.50 1.25
*a.* Wmk. 373 .80 .55
4 A19 4c 1.60 .90
5 A19 5c Wmk. 314 1.60 *1.25*
6 A18 6c 1.60 .85
7 A18 8c Wmk. 314 1.60 *1.25*
8 A18 10c Wmk. 314 1.60 *1.60*
9 A18 15c 2.50 1.00
10 A19 20c 1.60 *1.25*
11 A19 25c Wmk. 314 10.50 3.50
*a.* Wmk. 373 .90 .75
12 A19 35c 2.50 1.40
13 A18 50c 1.60 *1.25*
*a.* Wmk. 314 47.50 22.50
14 A18 $1 1.60 *1.60*
*a.* Wmk. 314 110.00 70.00
15 A18 $2 2.10 1.60
*Nos. 1-15 (15)* 35.75 20.15

Men from Gilbert and Ellice — A1

Designs: 10c, Map of Gilbert and Ellice Islands, vert. 35c, Gilbert and Ellice canoes.

**1976, Jan. 1 Wmk. 373**

16 A1 4c multicolored .60 .75
17 A1 10c multicolored .80 .90
18 A1 35c multicolored 1.10 1.25
*Nos. 16-18 (3)* 2.50 2.90

Separation of the Gilbert and Ellice Islands.

50c Coin and Octopus — A2

New coinage: 10c, 10c-coin and red-dyed crab. 15c, 20c-coin and flyingfish. 35c, $1-coin and green turtle.

**Wmk. 373**

**1976, Apr. 21 Litho. *Perf. 14***

19 A2 5c bister & multi .30 .30
20 A2 10c ultra & multi .85 .65
21 A2 15c blue & multi 1.25 .80
22 A2 35c lt green & multi 2.25 1.40
*Nos. 19-22 (4)* 4.65 3.15

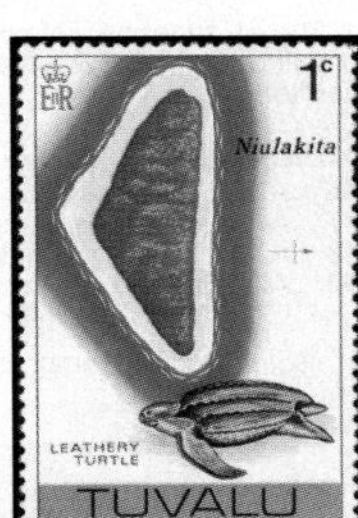


Map of Niulakita, Leathery Turtle — A3

Te Ano Game A4

2c, Map of Nukulaelae and sleeping mat. 4c, Map of Nui and talo vegetable. 5c, Map of Nanumanga and grass dancing skirt. 6c, Map of Nukufetau and coconut crab. 8c, Map of Funafuti and banana tree. 10c, Map of Tuvalu Islands. 15c, Map of Niutao and flyingfish. 20c, Map of Vaitupu and maneapa (house). 25c, Map of Nanumea and palu fish hook. 50c, Canoe pole fishing. $1, Reef fishing by flare. $2, House. $5, Colony Ship M.V. Nivanga.

**1976 Wmk. 373 Litho. *Perf. 13½***

23-37 A3 Set of 15 65.00 18.00

Issue dates: $5, Sept. 1; others July 1.
See #58-70. For overprints see #85-91.

New Testament
A5

Designs: 20c, Lotolelei Church, Nanumea. 25c, Kelupi Church, Nui. 30c, Mataloa o Tuvalu Church, Vaitupu. 35c, Palataiso o Keliso Church, Nanumanga.

***Perf. 14x14½***

**1976, Oct. 6 Litho. Wmk. 373**

**38-42** A5 Set of 5 7.50 6.00

Christmas 1976. Printed in sheets of 10 stamps and 2 labels.

Prince Philip Carried Ashore at Vaitupu — A6

Designs: 15c, Queen and Prince Philip on Buckingham Palace balcony. 50c, Queen Leaving Buckingham Palace for coronation.

**1977, Feb. 9 Litho. *Perf. 13½x14***

| | | | | |
|---|---|---|---|---|
| **43** | A6 | 15c multicolored | 1.75 | 1.50 |
| **44** | A6 | 35c multicolored | 2.25 | *2.50* |
| **45** | A6 | 50c multicolored | 3.50 | 3.50 |
| *a.* | | Souv. sheet, #43-45, perf. 15 | 8.00 | 6.50 |
| | | *Nos. 43-45 (3)* | 7.50 | 7.50 |

25th anniv. of the reign of Elizabeth II.

Health (Microscope) — A7

20c, Education (blackboard). 30c, Fruit growing (palm). 35c, Map of South Pacific Territory.

**1977, May 4 Litho. *Perf. 13½x14***

| | | | | |
|---|---|---|---|---|
| **46** | A7 | 5c lilac & multi | .65 | .50 |
| **47** | A7 | 20c orange & multi | .65 | .50 |
| **48** | A7 | 30c yellow grn & multi | .65 | .50 |
| **49** | A7 | 35c lt blue & multi | .95 | .65 |
| | | *Nos. 46-49 (4)* | 2.90 | 2.15 |

South Pacific Commission, 30th anniv.

Swearing-in Ceremony and Scout Emblem — A8

Designs (Scout Emblem and): 20c, Scouts in outrigger canoe. 30c, Scouts under sun shelter. 35c, Lord Baden-Powell.

***Perf. 13½x14***

**1977, Aug. 10 Litho. Wmk. 373**

| | | | | |
|---|---|---|---|---|
| **50** | A8 | 5c multicolored | .55 | .55 |
| **51** | A8 | 20c multicolored | .55 | .55 |
| **52** | A8 | 30c multicolored | .85 | .85 |
| **53** | A8 | 35c multicolored | .85 | .85 |
| | | *Nos. 50-53 (4)* | 2.80 | 2.80 |

Scouting in Tuvalu (Ellice Islands), 50th anniv.

Hurricane Beach and Coral — A9

Designs: 20c, Boring apparatus on "Porpoise," vert. 30c, Map of islands showing line of dredgings to prove Darwin's theory, vert. 35c, Charles Darwin and "Beagle."

***Perf. 13½***

**1977, Nov. 2 Unwmk. Litho.**

| | | | | |
|---|---|---|---|---|
| **54** | A9 | 5c multicolored | .75 | .75 |
| **55** | A9 | 20c multicolored | .75 | .75 |
| **56** | A9 | 30c multicolored | 1.10 | .90 |
| **57** | A9 | 35c multicolored | 1.10 | .90 |
| | | *Nos. 54-57 (4)* | 3.70 | 3.30 |

1896-97 Royal Soc. of London Expeditions to explore coral reefs by dredging and boring.

**Types of 1976**

Designs: 30c, Fatele, local dance. 40c, Screw pine. Others as before.

**1977-78 Unwmk. *Perf. 13½***

| | | | | |
|---|---|---|---|---|
| **58** | A3 | 1c multicolored | .35 | .35 |
| **59** | A3 | 2c multicolored | .35 | .35 |
| **60** | A3 | 4c multicolored | .35 | .35 |
| **61** | A3 | 5c multicolored | .35 | .35 |
| **62** | A3 | 6c multicolored | .35 | .35 |
| **63** | A3 | 8c multicolored | .35 | .35 |
| **64** | A3 | 10c multicolored | .35 | .35 |
| **66** | A3 | 20c multicolored | 2.50 | 1.75 |
| **67** | A3 | 25c multicolored | 1.75 | .60 |
| **68** | A4 | 30c multicolored | .70 | .70 |
| **69** | A4 | 40c multicolored | .95 | 1.00 |
| **70** | A4 | $5 multicolored | 7.00 | 7.00 |
| | | *Nos. 58-70 (12)* | 15.35 | 13.50 |

Issued: #58, 61, 63-64, 67, 1977; others, 1978.

Pacific Pigeon — A10

Wild Birds of Tuvalu: 20c, Reef heron. 30c, Fairy tern. 40c, Lesser frigate bird.

***Perf. 14x13½***

**1978, Jan. 25 Litho. Unwmk.**

| | | | | |
|---|---|---|---|---|
| **73** | A10 | 8c lilac & multi | 1.60 | .90 |
| **74** | A10 | 20c ocher & multi | 2.00 | 1.25 |
| **75** | A10 | 30c dull green & multi | 2.50 | 1.75 |
| **76** | A10 | 40c brt green & multi | 2.50 | 2.00 |
| | | *Nos. 73-76 (4)* | 8.60 | 5.90 |

Lawedua — A11

Ships: 20c, Tug Wallacia. 30c, Freighter Cenpac Rounder. 40c, Pacific Explorer.

**1978, Apr. 5 Unwmk. *Perf. 13½x14***

| | | | | |
|---|---|---|---|---|
| **77** | A11 | 8c multicolored | .20 | .20 |
| **78** | A11 | 20c multicolored | .35 | .35 |
| **79** | A11 | 30c multicolored | .55 | .45 |
| **80** | A11 | 40c multicolored | .70 | .65 |
| | | *Nos. 77-80 (4)* | 1.80 | 1.65 |

Canterbury Cathedral — A12

Designs: 30c, Salisbury Cathedral. 40c, Wells Cathedral. $1, Hereford Cathedral.

**1978, June 2 Litho. *Perf. 13½x14***

| | | | | |
|---|---|---|---|---|
| **81** | A12 | 8c multicolored | .25 | .25 |
| **82** | A12 | 30c multicolored | .25 | .25 |
| **83** | A12 | 40c multicolored | .25 | .25 |
| **84** | A12 | $1 multicolored | .65 | .65 |
| *a.* | | Souv. sheet, #81-84, perf. 15 | 1.25 | 1.25 |
| | | *Nos. 81-84 (4)* | 1.40 | 1.40 |

25th anniv. of coronation of Elizabeth II. #81-84 were also issued in bklt. panes of 2.

Types of 1976 Overprinted: "INDEPENDENCE 1ST OCTOBER 1978"

**1978, Oct. 1 Litho. *Perf. 13½***

| | | | | |
|---|---|---|---|---|
| **85** | A3 | 8c multicolored | .25 | .25 |
| **86** | A3 | 10c multicolored | .25 | .25 |
| **87** | A3 | 15c multicolored | .25 | .25 |
| **88** | A3 | 20c multicolored | .25 | .25 |
| **89** | A4 | 30c multicolored | .25 | .25 |
| **90** | A4 | 35c multicolored | .25 | .25 |
| **91** | A4 | 40c multicolored | .30 | .30 |
| | | *Nos. 85-91 (7)* | 1.80 | 1.80 |

Independence, Oct. 1, 1978. Overprint in 3 lines on vert. stamps, 1 line on horiz.

White Frangipani — A13

Wild Flowers: 20c, Zephyrantes rosea. 30c, Gardenia taitensis. 40c, Clerodendron inerme.

**1978, Oct. 4 Unwmk. *Perf. 14***

| | | | | |
|---|---|---|---|---|
| **92** | A13 | 8c multicolored | .25 | .25 |
| **93** | A13 | 20c multicolored | .25 | *.30* |
| **94** | A13 | 30c multicolored | .35 | *.40* |
| **95** | A13 | 40c multicolored | .50 | *.70* |
| | | *Nos. 92-95 (4)* | 1.35 | 1.65 |

Squirrelfish — A14

Fish: 2c, Yellow-banded goatfish. 4c, Imperial angelfish. 5c, Rainbow butterfly. 6c, Blue angelfish. 8c, Blue striped snapper. 10c, Orange clownfish. 15c, Chevroned coralfish. 20c, Fairy cod. 25c, Clown triggerfish. 30c, Long-nosed butterfly. 35c, Yellowfin tuna. 40c, Spotted eagle ray. 45c, Black-tipped rock cod. 50c, Hammerhead shark. 70c, Lionfish, vert. $1, White-barred triggerfish, vert. $2, Beaked coralfish, vert. $5, Tiger shark, vert.

**1979, Jan. 24 Litho. *Perf. 14***

| | | | | |
|---|---|---|---|---|
| **96** | A14 | 1c multicolored | .20 | .20 |
| **97** | A14 | 2c multicolored | .20 | .20 |
| **98** | A14 | 4c multicolored | .20 | .20 |
| **99** | A14 | 5c multicolored | .20 | .20 |
| **100** | A14 | 6c multicolored | .20 | .20 |
| **101** | A14 | 8c multicolored | .20 | .20 |
| **102** | A14 | 10c multicolored | .20 | .20 |
| **103** | A14 | 15c multicolored | .20 | .20 |
| **104** | A14 | 20c multicolored | .20 | .20 |
| **105** | A14 | 25c multicolored | .20 | .20 |
| **106** | A14 | 30c multicolored | .25 | .25 |
| **107** | A14 | 35c multicolored | .30 | .30 |
| **108** | A14 | 40c multicolored | .35 | .35 |
| **108A** | A14 | 45c multicolored | 1.90 | 1.25 |
| **109** | A14 | 50c multicolored | .55 | .55 |
| **110** | A14 | 70c multicolored | .60 | .60 |
| **111** | A14 | $1 multicolored | .80 | .80 |
| **112** | A14 | $2 multicolored | 1.90 | 1.90 |
| **113** | A14 | $5 multicolored | 4.50 | 4.50 |
| | | *Nos. 96-113 (19)* | 13.15 | 12.50 |

No. 108A issued June 16, 1981.

#101, 104, 106, 108 and #102, 105, 107, 108A were also issued in booklet panes of 4.

For surcharge & overprints see #150, O1-O19.

Capt. Cook
A15

Designs: 30c, Flag raising on new island. 40c, Observation of transit of Venus. $1, Death of Capt. Cook.

**1979, Feb. 14 *Perf. 14x14½***

| | | | | |
|---|---|---|---|---|
| **114** | A15 | 8c multicolored | .20 | .20 |
| **115** | A15 | 30c multicolored | .20 | .20 |
| **116** | A15 | 40c multicolored | .20 | .20 |
| **117** | A15 | $1 multicolored | .40 | .40 |
| *a.* | | Strip of 4, #114-117 | 2.75 | 2.75 |

Bicentenary of death of Capt. James Cook (1728-1779). Nos. 114-117 printed se-tenant horizontally in sheets of 12 (4x3) with gutters between horizontal rows.

Grumman Goose over Nukulaelae — A16

Grumman Goose over: 20c, Vaitupu. 30c, Nui. 40c, Funafuti.

**1979, May 16 Litho. *Perf. 14x13½***

| | | | | |
|---|---|---|---|---|
| **118** | A16 | 8c multicolored | .35 | .35 |
| **119** | A16 | 20c multicolored | .35 | .35 |
| **120** | A16 | 30c multicolored | .45 | *.55* |
| **121** | A16 | 40c multicolored | .65 | .65 |
| | | *Nos. 118-121 (4)* | 1.80 | 1.90 |

Inauguration of internal air service.

Hill, Tuvalu No. 16, Letterbox, London, 1855 — A17

Hill, Stamps of Tuvalu and: 40c, No. 17, Penny Black. $1, No. 18, mail coach.

**1979, Aug. 20 Litho. *Perf. 13½x14***

| | | | | |
|---|---|---|---|---|
| **122** | A17 | 30c multicolored | .30 | .30 |
| **123** | A17 | 40c multicolored | .30 | .30 |
| **124** | A17 | $1 multicolored | .75 | .75 |
| *a.* | | Souvenir sheet of 3, #122-124 | 1.75 | 1.75 |
| | | *Nos. 122-124 (3)* | 1.35 | 1.35 |

Sir Rowland Hill (1795-1879), originator of penny postage.

Boy — A18

Designs: Children of Tuvalu.

**1979, Oct. 20 Litho. *Perf. 14***

| | | | | |
|---|---|---|---|---|
| **125** | A18 | 8c multicolored | .25 | .25 |
| **126** | A18 | 20c multicolored | .25 | .25 |
| **127** | A18 | 30c multicolored | .30 | .30 |
| **128** | A18 | 40c multicolored | .35 | .35 |
| | | *Nos. 125-128 (4)* | 1.15 | 1.15 |

International Year of the Child.

Cowry Shells A19

**1980, Feb. Litho. *Perf. 14***

| | | | | |
|---|---|---|---|---|
| **129** | A19 | 8c *Cypraea Argus* | .25 | .25 |
| **130** | A19 | 20c *Cypraea scurra* | .25 | .25 |
| **131** | A19 | 30c *Cypraea carneola* | .35 | .35 |
| **132** | A19 | 40c *Cypraea aurantium* | .50 | .50 |
| | | *Nos. 129-132 (4)* | 1.35 | 1.35 |

Philatelic Bureau, Funafuti, Tuvalu No. 28, Arms, London 1980 Emblem — A20

Coat of Arms, London 1980 Emblem and: 20c, Gilbert and Ellice #41, Nukulaelae cancel, Tuvalu #24. 30c, US airmail cover. $1, Map of Tuvalu.

**1980, Apr. 30 Litho. *Perf. 13½x14***

| | | | | |
|---|---|---|---|---|
| **133** | A20 | 10c multicolored | .30 | .30 |
| **134** | A20 | 20c multicolored | .30 | .30 |
| **135** | A20 | 30c multicolored | .35 | .35 |
| **136** | A20 | $1 multicolored | .95 | .95 |
| *a.* | | Souvenir sheet of 4, #133-136 | 2.00 | 2.00 |
| | | *Nos. 133-136 (4)* | 1.90 | 1.90 |

London 80 Intl. Stamp Exhib., May 6-14.

Queen Mother Elizabeth, 80th Birthday — A21

**1980, Aug. 14 Litho. *Perf. 14***

| | | | | |
|---|---|---|---|---|
| **137** | A21 | 50c multicolored | .50 | .50 |

Issued in sheets of 10 plus 2 labels.

Aethaloessa Calidalis — A22

**1980, Aug. 20 Litho. *Perf. 14***

| | | | | |
|---|---|---|---|---|
| **138** | A22 | 8c *shown* | .20 | .20 |
| **139** | A22 | 20c *Parotis suralis* | .20 | .20 |
| **140** | A22 | 30c *Dudua aprobola* | .30 | .30 |
| **141** | A22 | 40c *Decadarchis simulans* | .40 | .40 |
| | | *Nos. 138-141 (4)* | 1.10 | 1.10 |

Air Pacific Heron (First Regular Air Service to Tuvalu, 1964) — A23

Aviation Anniversaries: 20c, Hawker Siddeley 748 (air service to Tuvalu). 30c, Sunderland Flying Boat (War time service to Funafuti, 1945. 40c, Orville Wright and Flyer (Wright brothers' first flight, 1903).

**1980, Nov. 5 Litho. *Perf. 14***

| | | | | |
|---|---|---|---|---|
| **142** | A23 | 8c multicolored | .25 | .25 |
| **143** | A23 | 20c multicolored | .25 | .25 |
| **144** | A23 | 30c multicolored | .35 | .25 |
| **145** | A23 | 40c multicolored | .50 | .45 |
| | | *Nos. 142-145 (4)* | 1.35 | 1.20 |

Hypolimnas Bolina Elliciana — A24

**1981, Feb. 3 Litho. *Perf. 14½***

| | | | | |
|---|---|---|---|---|
| **146** | A24 | 8c shown | .30 | .30 |
| **147** | A24 | 20c Hypolimnas, diff. | .35 | .35 |
| **148** | A24 | 30c Hypolimnas, diff. | .45 | .45 |
| **149** | A24 | 40c Junonia vallida | .75 | .75 |
| | | *Nos. 146-149 (4)* | 1.85 | 1.85 |

No. 109 Surcharged

**1981, Feb. 24 Litho. *Perf. 14***

| | | | | |
|---|---|---|---|---|
| **150** | A14 | 45c on 50c multicolored | .60 | .60 |

Elizabeth, 1809 A25

**Wmk. 373**

**1981, May 13 Litho. *Perf. 14***

| | | | | |
|---|---|---|---|---|
| **151** | A25 | 10c shown | .25 | .25 |
| **152** | A25 | 25c Rebecca, 1819 | .25 | .25 |
| **153** | A25 | 35c Independence II, 1821 | .35 | .35 |
| **154** | A25 | 40c Basilisk, 1872 | .45 | .45 |
| **155** | A25 | 45c Royalist, 1890 | .50 | .50 |
| **156** | A25 | 50c Olivebank, 1920 | .65 | .65 |
| | | *Nos. 151-156 (6)* | 2.45 | 2.45 |

See Nos. 216-221, 353-356, 410-413.

Prince Charles, Lady Diana, Royal Yacht Charlotte A25a

Prince Charles and Lady Diana — A25b

Illustration A25b is reduced.

**Wmk. 380**

**1981, July 10 Litho. *Perf. 14***

| | | | | |
|---|---|---|---|---|
| **157** | A25a | 10c Couple, Carolina | .20 | .20 |
| *a.* | | Blkt. pane of 4, perf. 12, unwmkd. | .30 | |
| **158** | A25b | 10c Couple | .40 | .40 |
| **159** | A25a | 45c Victoria and Albert III | .25 | .25 |
| **160** | A25b | 45c like #158 | .50 | .50 |
| *a.* | | Blkt. pane of 2, perf. 12, unwmkd. | .50 | |
| **161** | A25a | $2 Britannia | 1.00 | 1.00 |
| **162** | A25b | $2 like #158 | 2.75 | 2.75 |
| | | *Nos. 157-162 (6)* | 5.10 | 5.10 |

Royal wedding. Issued in sheets of 7 (6 design A25a; 1 design A25b). Set of 3 $12.
For surcharges see Nos. B1-B2.

Souvenir Sheet

**1981, Dec. Litho. *Perf. 12***

| | | | | |
|---|---|---|---|---|
| **163** | A25b | $1.50 Couple | .85 | .85 |

Admission to UPU — A26

**Wmk. Harrison's, London**

**1981, Nov. 19 Engr. *Perf. 14½x14***

| | | | | |
|---|---|---|---|---|
| **164** | A26 | 70c dark blue | .50 | .50 |
| **165** | A26 | $1 dark red brown | .75 | .75 |
| *a.* | | Souv. sheet of 2, #164-165, unwmkd. | 2.00 | 2.00 |

Amatuku Maritime School — A27

**1982, Feb. 17 Litho. *Perf. 13½x14***

| | | | | |
|---|---|---|---|---|
| **166** | A27 | 10c Map | .35 | .35 |
| **167** | A27 | 25c Motorboat | .35 | .35 |
| **168** | A27 | 35c School, dock | .45 | .45 |
| **169** | A27 | 45c Flag, ship | .65 | .65 |
| | | *Nos. 166-169 (4)* | 1.80 | 1.80 |

A27a

**Wmk. 380**

**1982, May 19 Litho. *Perf. 14***

| | | | | |
|---|---|---|---|---|
| **170** | A27a | 10c Caroline of Brandenburg-Ansbach, 1714 | .20 | .20 |
| **171** | A27a | 45c Brandenburg-Ansbach arms | .25 | .25 |
| **172** | A27a | $1.50 Diana | 1.00 | 1.00 |
| | | *Nos. 170-172 (3)* | 1.45 | 1.45 |

21st birthday of Princess Diana, July 1.

#170-172 Overprinted: "ROYAL BABY"

**1982, July 14 Litho. *Perf. 14***

| | | | | |
|---|---|---|---|---|
| **173** | A27a | 10c multicolored | .30 | .30 |
| **174** | A27a | 45c multicolored | .30 | .30 |
| **175** | A27a | $1.50 multicolored | .90 | .90 |
| | | *Nos. 173-175 (3)* | 1.50 | 1.50 |

Birth of Prince William of Wales, June 21.

Scouting Year — A28

**1982, Aug. 18**

| | | | | |
|---|---|---|---|---|
| **176** | A28 | 10c Emblems | .25 | .25 |
| **177** | A28 | 25c Campfire | .40 | .35 |
| **178** | A28 | 35c Parade | .55 | .40 |
| **179** | A28 | 45c Scout | .70 | .45 |
| | | *Nos. 176-179 (4)* | 1.90 | 1.45 |

Visit of Queen Elizabeth II and Prince Philip — A29

**1982, Oct. 26 Litho. *Perf. 14***

| | | | | |
|---|---|---|---|---|
| **180** | A29 | 25c Arms, Duke of Edinburgh's Personal Standard | .25 | .25 |
| **181** | A29 | 45c Flags | .50 | .50 |
| **182** | A29 | 50c Queen Elizabeth II, maps | .55 | .55 |
| *a.* | | Souvenir sheet of 3, #180-182 | 1.50 | 1.50 |
| | | *Nos. 180-182 (3)* | 1.30 | 1.30 |

Handicrafts — A30

1c, Fisherman's hat, lures, hooks. 2c, Cowrie shell handbags. 5c, Wedding & baby food baskets. 10c, Canoe model. 15c, Women's sun hats. 20c, Climbing rope. 25c, Pandanus baskets. 30c, Tray, coconut stands. 35c, Pandanus pillows, shell necklaces. 40c, Round baskets, fans. 45c, Reef sandals, fish trap. 50c, Rat trap, vert.. 60c, Waterproof boxes, vert.. $1, Pump drill, adze, vert. $2, Fisherman's hat, canoe bailers, vert. $5, Fishing rod, lures, scoop nets, vert.

**1983-84 Litho. *Perf. 14***

| | | | | |
|---|---|---|---|---|
| **183** | A30 | 1c multicolored | .35 | .25 |
| **184** | A30 | 2c multicolored | .35 | .25 |
| **185** | A30 | 5c multicolored | .35 | .25 |
| **186** | A30 | 10c multicolored | .35 | .25 |
| **186A** | A30 | 15c multicolored | 2.50 | *2.75* |
| **187** | A30 | 20c multicolored | .35 | .25 |
| **188** | A30 | 25c multicolored | .35 | .25 |
| **188A** | A30 | 30c multicolored | 2.25 | 2.25 |
| **189** | A30 | 35c multicolored | .50 | .40 |
| **190** | A30 | 40c multicolored | .35 | *.55* |
| **191** | A30 | 45c multicolored | .40 | *.65* |
| **192** | A30 | 50c multicolored | .50 | .70 |
| **192A** | A30 | 60c multicolored | 3.25 | 2.25 |
| **193** | A30 | $1 multicolored | .50 | *.70* |
| **194** | A30 | $2 multicolored | .70 | *.85* |
| **195** | A30 | $5 multicolored | 1.10 | *1.25* |
| | | *Nos. 183-195 (16)* | 14.15 | 13.85 |

Issued: 15c, 1984; others, 3/14/83.
For surcharges & overprints see #207, 230, O20-O32.

Commonwealth Day — A31

**Wmk. 373**

**1983, Mar. 14 Litho. *Perf. 14***

| | | | | |
|---|---|---|---|---|
| **196** | A31 | 20c Fishing industry | .35 | .20 |
| **197** | A31 | 35c Traditional dancing | .35 | .30 |
| **198** | A31 | 45c Satellite view | .45 | .40 |
| **199** | A31 | 50c First container ship | .60 | .50 |
| | | *Nos. 196-199 (4)* | 1.75 | 1.40 |

Dragonflies — A32

**1983, May 25 Wmk. 380**

| | | | | |
|---|---|---|---|---|
| **200** | A32 | 10c Pantala flavescens | .25 | .25 |
| **201** | A32 | 35c Anax guttatus | .65 | .65 |
| **202** | A32 | 40c Tholymis tillarga | .75 | .75 |
| **203** | A32 | 50c Diplacodes bipunctata | .85 | .85 |
| | | *Nos. 200-203 (4)* | 2.50 | 2.50 |

Boys Brigade Centenary — A33

**1983, Aug. 10** **Wmk. 373**

**204** A33 10c Running, emblem .30 .30
**205** A33 35c Canoeing .75 .75
**206** A33 $1 Officer, boys 1.75 *1.75*
*Nos. 204-206 (3)* 2.80 2.80

No. 193 Surcharged in Black

**1983, Aug. 26** **Wmk. 380**

**207** A30 60c on $1 multi 1.00 .60

First Manned Flight Bicentenary — A34

**1983, Sept. 21** **Wmk. 373**

**208** A34 25c Montgolfier balloon, vert. .40 .40
**209** A34 35c McKinnon Turbo Goose .50 .50
**210** A34 45c Beechcraft Super King Air 200 .60 .60
**211** A34 50c Double Eagle II Balloon, vert. .70 .70
*a.* Souvenir sheet of 4, #208-211 3.00 3.00
*Nos. 208-211 (4)* 2.20 2.20

World Communications Year — A35

**1983, Nov. 18** **Wmk. 380**

**212** A35 25c Conch Shell Trumpet, vert. .25 .25
**213** A35 35c Radio Operator, vert. .40 .40
**214** A35 45c Teleprinter .55 .55
**215** A35 50c Transmitting station .60 .60
*Nos. 212-215 (4)* 1.80 1.80

**Ship Type of 1981**

**1984, Feb. 16** **Wmk. 380**

**216** A25 10c Titus, 1897 .25 .25
**217** A25 20c Malaita, 1905 .25 .25
**218** A25 25c Aymeric, 1906 .30 .30
**219** A25 35c Anshun, 1965 .40 .40
**220** A25 45c Beaverbank, 1970 .50 .50
**221** A25 50c Benjamin Bowring, 1981 .65 .65
*Nos. 216-221 (6)* 2.35 2.35

---

**Leaders of the World**

**Large quantities of some Leaders of the World issues were sold at a fraction of face value when the printer was liquidated.**

---

Historic Locomotives — A36

*Perf. 12½x13*

**1984, Feb. 29** **Unwmk.**

**Se-tenant Pairs, #a.-b.**

**a. — Side and front views.**

**b. — Action scene.**

**222** A36 1c Class GS-4, US, 1941 .25 .25
**223** A36 15c AD-60, Australia, 1952 .30 .30
**224** A36 40c C38, Australia, 1943 .90 .90
**225** A36 60c Achilles England, 1892 1.25 1.25
*Nos. 222-225 (4)* 2.70 2.70

See Nos. 235-246, 291-294, 320-323.

**No. 191 Surcharged**

**Wmk. 380**

**1984, Feb. 1** **Litho.** ***Perf. 14***

**230** A30 30c on 45c multi .55 .55

For overprint see No. O25.

Beach Flowers A38

**1984, May 30**

**231** A38 25c Ipomoea pes-caprae .50 .50
**232** A38 45c Ipomoea macrantha .75 .75
**233** A38 50c Triumfetta procumbens .95 .95
**234** A38 60c Portulaca quadrifida 1.25 1.25
*Nos. 231-234 (4)* 3.45 3.45

**Train Type of 1984**

**1984** **Litho.** ***Perf. 12½x13***

**Se-tenant Pairs, #a.-b.**

**a. — Side and front views.**

**b. — Action scene.**

**235** A36 1c Class 9700, Japan, 1897 .45 .45
**236** A36 10c Casey Jones, US, 1896 .45 .45
**237** A36 15c Class 2310K, France, 1909 .45 .45
**238** A36 15c Triplex, US, 1914 .45 .45
**239** A36 20c Class 370, Gt. Britain, 1981 .45 .45
**240** A36 25c Class 4F, Gt. Britain, 1924 .60 .60
**241** A36 30c Glass 640, Italy, 1907 .70 .70
**242** A36 40c Tornado, Gt. Britain, 1888 .90 .90
**243** A36 50c Broadlands, Gt. Britain, 1967 1.25 1.25
**244** A36 60c Locomotion, Gt. Britain, 1825 1.60 1.60
**245** A36 $1 C57, Japan, 1937 2.40 2.40
**246** A36 $1 Class 4500, France, 1906 2.40 2.40
*Nos. 235-246 (12)* 12.10 12.10

Issued: #235, 237, 241, 245, 10/4; others, 6/27.

15th South Pacific Forum A38a

**1984, Aug. 21** **Litho.** ***Perf. 14***

**255** A38a 60c National flag .55 .55
**256** A38a 60c Tuvalu crest .55 .55

Ausipex '84 A38b

**1984, Aug. 21** ***Perf. 14***

**257** A38b 60c Exhib. emblem .55 .55
**258** A38b 60c Royal Exhibi. Building .55 .55

A. Shrewsbury Playing Cricket — A39

Cricket players in action or portrait.

**1984, Nov. 5** **Litho.** ***Perf. 12½***

**Se-tenant Pairs #a.-b.**

**259** A39 5c shown .35 .35
**260** A39 30c H. Verity 1.00 1.00
**261** A39 50c E.H. Hendren 1.00 1.00
**262** A39 60c J. Briggs 1.25 1.25
*Nos. 259-262 (4)* 3.60 3.60

Drawings, Christmas 1984 — A40

**1984, Nov. 14** **Litho.** ***Perf. 14½x14***

**267** A40 15c By Eli Faalata .30 .30
**268** A40 40c By Toakai Niutao .40 .40
**269** A40 50c By Falesa Teuila .50 .50
**270** A40 60c By Piuani Talie .65 .65
*Nos. 267-270 (4)* 1.85 1.85

Classic Automobiles — A41

Sketch listed first followed by angled view.

**1984, Dec. 7** **Litho.** ***Perf. 12½x13***

**Se-tenant Pairs, #a.-b.**

**a. — Side and front views.**

**b. — Action scene.**

**271** A41 1c Morris Minor, 1949 .50 .50
**272** A41 15c Studebaker Avanti, 1963 .50 .50
**273** A41 50c Chevrolet International Six, 1929 1.25 1.25
**274** A41 $1 Allard J2, 1950 2.50 2.50
*Nos. 271-274 (4)* 4.75 4.75

See Nos. 299-302, 332-339, 396-396E, 414-425.

John J. Audubon — A42

#279a, Common flicker. #279b, Say's phoebe. #280a, Townsend's warbler. #280b, Bohemian waxwing. #281a, Prothonotary warbler. #281b, Worm-eating warbler. #282a, Broad-winged hawk. #282b, Northern harrier.

**1985, Feb. 12** **Litho.** ***Perf. 12½***

**279** A42 1c Pair, #a.-b. .35 .35
**280** A42 25c Pair, #a.-b. .75 .75
**281** A42 50c Pair, #a.-b. 1.50 1.50
**282** A42 70c Pair, #a.-b. 1.90 1.90
*Nos. 279-282 (4)* 4.50 4.50

Birds and Eggs A43

**1985, Feb. 27** ***Perf. 14***

**287** A43 15c Black-naped tern .40 .30
**288** A43 40c Black noddy 1.00 .75
**289** A43 50c White-tailed tropicbird 1.10 .85
**290** A43 60c Sooty tern 1.50 1.10
*Nos. 287-290 (4)* 4.00 3.00

**Train Type of 1984**

**1985, Mar. 19** ***Perf. 12½***

**Se-tenant Pairs, #a.-b.**

**a. — Side and front views.**

**b. — Action scene.**

**291** A36 5c Churchward, U.K. .35 .35
**292** A36 10c Class K.F., China .35 .35
**293** A36 30c Class 99.77, East Germany .90 .90
**294** A36 $1 Pearson, U.K. 3.00 3.00
*Nos. 291-294 (4)* 4.60 4.60

**Automobile Type of 1984**

**1985, Apr. 3**

**Se-tenant Pairs, #a.-b.**

**a. — Side and front views.**

**b. — Action scene.**

**299** A41 1c Rickenbacker, 1923 .50 .50
**300** A41 20c Detroit-Electric, 1914 .50 .50
**301** A41 50c Packard Clipper, 1941 1.25 1.25
**302** A41 70c Audi Quattro, 1982 1.90 1.90
*Nos. 299-302 (4)* 4.15 4.15

World War II Aircraft A44

**1985, May 29** **Litho.** ***Perf. 14***

**307** A44 15c Curtiss P-40N 1.75 1.00
**308** A44 40c Consolidated B-24D Liberator 2.00 1.50
**309** A44 50c Lockheed PV-1 Ventura 2.00 1.75
**310** A44 60c Douglas C-54 Skymaster 2.00 1.75
*a.* Souvenir sheet of 4, #307-310 6.00 4.00
*Nos. 307-310 (4)* 7.75 6.00

Queen Mother, 85th Birthday — A45

#310a, Facing right. #310b, Facing left. #311a, 317a, Facing right. #311b, 317b, Facing front. #312a, 316a, Waving to crowd. #312b, 316b, Facing front. #313a, Facing front. #313b, Facing left. #314a, As a young woman. #314b, as Queen Consort.

**1985-86** **Litho.** ***Perf. 12½***

**311** A45 5c Pair, #a.-b. .45 .45
**312** A45 30c Pair, #a.-b. .70 .70
**313** A45 60c Pair, #a.-b. 1.40 1.40
**314** A45 $1 Pair, #a.-b. 2.10 2.10
*Nos. 311-314 (4)* 4.65 4.65

**Souvenir Sheets**

**315** A45 $1.20 #a.-b. 2.50 2.50
**316** A45 $2 #a.-b. 6.25 6.25
**317** A45 $3 #a.-b. 8.75 8.75

Issued: #316-317, 6/10/86; others, 7/4/85.

**Train Type of 1984**

**1985, Sept. 18**

**Se-tenant Pairs, #a.-b.**

**a. — Side and front views.**

**b. — Action scene.**

**320** A36 10c 1936 Green Arrow, U.K. .40 .40
**321** A36 40c 1982 G.M. (EMD) SD-50, US 1.10 1.10
**322** A36 65c 1932 DRG Flying Hamburger, Germany 1.50 1.50
**323** A36 $1 1908 JNR Class 1070, Japan 1.60 1.60
*Nos. 320-323 (4)* 4.60 4.60

Girl Guides, 75th Anniv. — A46

**1985, Aug. 28 Litho. *Perf. 15***

**328** A46 15c Playing guitar .35 .25
**329** A46 40c Camping .70 .70
**330** A46 50c Flag bearer .85 .85
**331** A46 60c Guides' salute 1.00 1.00
***a.*** Souvenir sheet of 4, #328-331 3.25 3.25
*Nos. 328-331 (4)* 2.90 2.80

**Car Type of 1984**

5c, 1929 Cord L-29, US. 10c, 1932 Horch 670 V-12, Germany. 15c, 1901 Lanchester, UK. 35c, 1950 Citroen 2 CV, France. 40c, 1957 MGA, UK. 55c, 1962 Ferrari 250-GTO, Italy. $1, 1932 Ford V-8, US. $1.50, 1977 Aston Martin-Lagonda, UK.

**1985, Oct. 8 *Perf. 12½***

**a. — Side and front views.**

**b. — Action scene.**

**332-339** A41 Set of 8 pairs 7.75 7.75

Crabs A47

**1986, Jan. 7 *Perf. 15***

**348** A47 15c Stalk-eyed ghost .35 .35
**349** A47 40c Red and white painted .90 .90
**350** A47 50c Red-spotted 1.10 1.10
**351** A47 60c Red hermit 1.40 1.40
*Nos. 348-351 (4)* 3.75 3.75

**Souvenir Sheet of 2**

Events — A48

#352a, American and Soviet flags, chess board & knight. #352b, Rotary Intl. emblem.

**1986, Mar. 19 Litho. *Perf. 13x12½***

**352** A48 $3 #a.-b. 7.00 7.00

Fischer and Karpov, world chess champions; Rotary Intl., 80th anniv.

No. 352 exists with plain or decorated border.

**Ship Type of 1981**

**1986, Apr. 14 *Perf. 15***

**353** A25 15c Messenger of Peace .25 .25
**354** A25 40c John Wesley .75 .75
**355** A25 50c Duff .90 .90
**356** A25 60c Triton 1.00 1.00
*Nos. 353-356 (4)* 2.90 2.90

Queen Elizabeth II, 60th Birthday — A49

Various portraits.

**1986, Apr. 21 *Perf. 12½***

**357** A49 10c multicolored .40 .40
**358** A49 90c multicolored .60 .60
**359** A49 $1.50 multicolored 1.00 1.00
**360** A49 $3 multi, vert. 2.00 2.00
*Nos. 357-360 (4)* 4.00 4.00

**Souvenir Sheet**

**361** A49 $4 multicolored 5.00 5.00

Peace Corps, 25th Anniv. A50

**1986, May 22 *Perf. 14***

**362** A50 50c multicolored .85 .85

For overprint see No. 374.

A51

A52

**1986, May 22 *Perf. 14x13½***

**363** A51 60c multicolored .90 .90

AMERIPEX '86.

**1986, June 30 Litho. *Perf. 15***

Players and teams.

**364** A52 1c So. Korea .20 .20
**365** A52 5c France .20 .20
**366** A52 10c W. Germany, 1974 .20 .20
**367** A52 40c Italy .45 .45

**Size: 60x40mm**

***Perf. 13x12½***

**368** A52 60c W. Germany vs. Holland, 1974 .55 .55
**369** A52 $1 Canada .95 .95
**370** A52 $2 No. Ireland 2.10 2.10
**371** A52 $3 England 2.75 2.75
*Nos. 364-371 (8)* 7.40 7.40

**Souvenir Sheets**

**372** A52 $1.50 like #369 2.10 2.10
**373** A52 $2.50 like #370 3.50 3.50

1986 World Cup Soccer Championships. Nos. 366 and 368 picture emblem; others picture character trademark.

**No. 362 Ovptd. with STAMPEX '86 Emblem**

**1986, Aug. 4 Litho. *Perf. 14***

**374** A50 50c multicolored .70 .70

A53

Wedding of Prince Andrew and Sarah Ferguson — A54

#381a, Andrew, vert. #381b, Couple, vert. #382a, Andrew. #382b, Princess Diana, Sarah.

***Perf. 12½***

**1986, July 18 Litho. Unwmk.**

**381** A53 60c Pair, #a.-b. 1.25 1.25
**382** A53 $1 Pair, #a.-b. 2.50 2.50

**Souvenir Sheet**

***Perf. 13x12½***

**383** A54 $6 Newlyweds 5.75 5.75

No. 382a pictures Westminster Abbey in LR.

For overprints see Nos. 389-390.

Geckos A55

**1986, July 30 Litho. *Perf. 14***

**384** A55 15c Mourning gecko .40 .30
**385** A55 40c Oceanic stump-toed 1.10 .85
**386** A55 50c Azure-tailed skink 1.40 1.10
**387** A55 60c Moth skink 1.90 1.50
*Nos. 384-387 (4)* 4.80 3.75

**Souvenir Sheet**

South Pacific Forum, 15th Anniv. A56

Flags and maps: a, Australia. b, Cook Islands. c, Micronesia. d, Fiji. e, Kiribati. f, Nauru. g, New Zealand. h, Niue. i, Papua New Guinea. j, Solomon Islands. k, Tonga. l, Tuvalu. m, Vanuatu. n, Western Samoa.

**Wmk. 380**

**1986, Aug. 4 Litho. *Perf. 15***

**388** Sheet of 14 + label 7.00 7.00
***a.-n.*** A56 40c any single .50 .50

No. 388 has center label picturing Executive Committee headquarters, Suva, Fiji.

**Nos. 381-382 Ovptd. "Congratulations to T.R.H. The Duke & Duchess of York" in Silver**

**1986 Unwmk. *Perf. 12½***

**389** A53 60c Pair, #a.-b. 1.75 1.75
**390** A53 $1 Pair, #a.-b. 2.75 2.75

Exist tete-beche.

**Car Type of 1984**

15c, 1953 Cooper, UK. 40c, 1964 Rover 2000, UK. 50c, 1930 Ruxton, US. 60c, 1950 Jowett Jupiter, UK. 90c, 1964 Cobra Daytona Coupe, US. $1.50, 1903 Packard Model F "Old Pacific," US.

**1986, Oct. Litho. *Perf. 12½***

**Se-tenant Pairs, #a.-b.**

**a. — Side and front views.**

**b. — Action scene.**

**391-396** A41 Set of 6 pairs 7.75 7.75

Marine Life A57

**1986, Nov. 5 Unwmk. *Perf. 14***

**397** A57 15c Sea star .75 .75
**398** A57 40c Pencil urchin 1.25 1.25
**399** A57 50c Fragile coral 1.40 1.40
**400** A57 60c Pink coral 1.60 1.60
*Nos. 397-400 (4)* 5.00 5.00

See Nos. 465-468, 524-527.

**Souvenir Sheets**

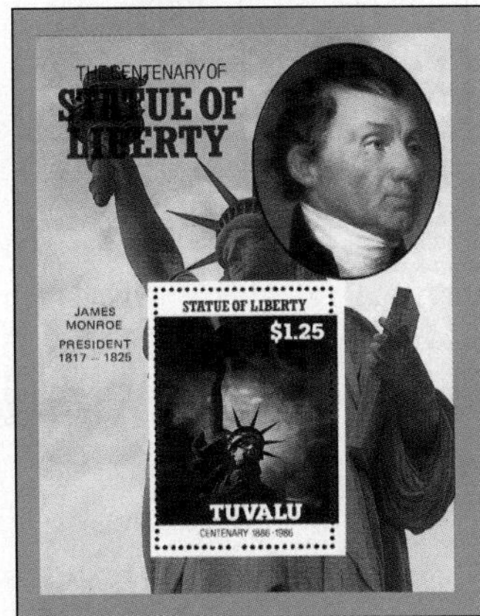


Statue of Liberty, Cent. — A58

Various views of the statue.

**1986, Nov. 24**

**401** A58 $1.25 multicolored 1.10 1.10
**402** A58 $1.50 multicolored 1.50 1.50
**403** A58 $1.80 multicolored 1.90 1.90
**404** A58 $2 multicolored 2.10 2.10
**405** A58 $2.25 multicolored 2.40 2.40
**406** A58 $2.50 multicolored 2.50 2.50
**407** A58 $3 multicolored 3.25 3.25
**408** A58 $3.25 multicolored 3.50 3.50
**409** A58 $3.50 multicolored 4.00 4.00
*Nos. 401-409 (9)* 22.25 22.25

**Ships Type of 1981**

**1987, Feb. 4 Unwmk. *Perf. 14***

**410** A25 15c Southern Cross IV .75 .75
**411** A25 40c John Williams VI 1.60 1.60
**412** A25 50c John Williams IV 1.75 1.75
**413** A25 60c M.S. Southern Cross 1.75 1.75
*Nos. 410-413 (4)* 5.85 5.85

**Car Type of 1984**

1c, 1938 Talbot-Lago, France. 2c, 1930 Dupont Model G, US. 5c, 1950 Riley RM, U.K. 10c, 1915 Chevrolet Baby Grand, US. 20c, 1968 Shelby Mustang GT 500 KR, US. 30c, 1952 Ferrari 212 Export Barchetta, Italy. 40c, 1912 Peerless Model 48-Six, US. 50c, 1954 Sunbeam Alpine, U.K. 60c, 1969 Matra-Ford MS80, France. 70c, 1934 Squire 1-Litre, U.K. 75c, 1931 Talbot 105, U.K. $1, 1928 Plymouth Model Q, US.

*Perf. 12½*

**1987, May 7 Litho. Unwmk.**

**Se-tenant Pairs, #a.-b.**

**a. — Side and front views.**

**b. — Action scene.**

**414-425** A41 Set of 12 pairs, #a.-b. 8.75 8.75
*425c* Souv. sheet of 2 3.75 3.75

Ferns — A59

**1987, July 7 Wmk. 380 *Perf. 14***

**438** A59 15c Nephrolepis saligna .20 .20
**439** A59 40c Asplenium nidus .70 .70
**440** A59 50c Microsorum scolopendria .85 .85
**441** A59 60c Pteris tripartita 1.00 1.00
*Nos. 438-441 (4)* 2.75 2.75

**Souvenir Sheet**

**442** A59 $1.50 Psilotum nudum 2.50 2.50

A60

#443a, 444b, 445a, 456b, Flowers, all diff. #443b, 444a, 445b, 456a, Woman wearing fou, all diff.

**1987, Aug. 12 Wmk. 380**

**443** A60 15c Pair, #a.-b. .40 .40
**444** A60 40c Pair, #a.-b. 1.10 1.10
**445** A60 50c Pair, #a.-b. 1.25 1.25
**446** A60 60c Pair, #a.-b. 1.60 1.60
*Nos. 443-446 (4)* 4.35 4.35

Crayfish and Coconut Crabs A61

**Wmk. 380**

**1987, Nov. 11 Litho. *Perf. 14***

**451** A61 40c Coconut crabs .80 .60
**452** A61 50c Painted crayfish 1.00 .75
**453** A61 60c Ocean crayfish 1.10 .90
*Nos. 451-453 (3)* 2.90 2.25

Photograph of Queen Victoria, 1897, by Downey — A62

60c, Elizabeth and Philip on their wedding day, 1947. 80c, Elizabeth, Charles, Philip, c. 1950. $1, Elizabeth, Anne, 1950. $2, Elizabeth, 1970. $3, Elizabeth, children, 1950.

**1987, Nov. 20 Unwmk. *Perf. 15***

**454-458** A62 Set of 5 5.00 5.00

**Souvenir Sheet**

**459** A62 $3 red org & blk 4.25 4.25

Accession of Queen Victoria to the throne of England, sesquicentennial; wedding of Queen Elizabeth II and Prince Philip, 40th anniv.

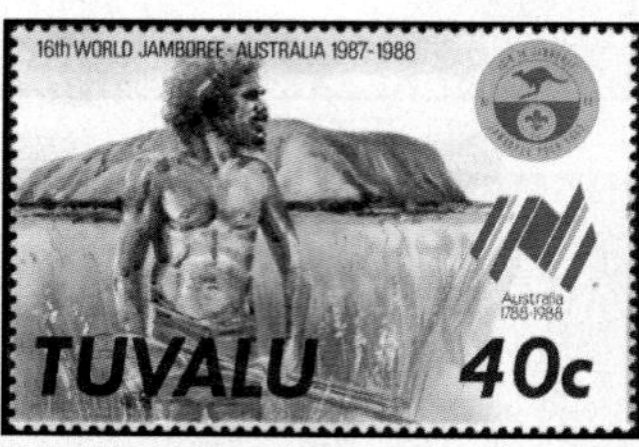


16th World Scout Jamboree, Australia, 1987-88 — A63

Jamboree and Australia bicentennial emblems plus: 40c, Aborigine, Ayer's Rock. 60c, Capt. Cook, by Dance, and HMS Endeavor. $1, Scout and Scout Park Arch. $1.50, Koala and kangaroo. $2.50, Lord and Lady Baden-Powell.

*Perf. 13x12½*

**1987, Dec. 2 Litho. Unwmk.**

**460** A63 40c multicolored .55 .55
**461** A63 60c multicolored .80 .80
**462** A63 $1 multicolored 1.50 1.50
**463** A63 $1.50 multicolored 2.10 2.10
*Nos. 460-463 (4)* 4.95 4.95

**Souvenir Sheet**

**464** A63 $2.50 multicolored 3.75 3.75

**Marine Life Type of 1986**

**Unwmk.**

**1988, Feb. 29 Litho. *Perf. 15***

**465** A57 15c Spanish dancer .50 .25
**466** A57 40c Hard corals 1.25 .60
**467** A57 50c Feather stars 1.50 .75
**468** A57 60c Staghorn corals 1.75 .90
*Nos. 465-468 (4)* 5.00 2.50

Birds A64

**1988, Mar. 2 *Perf. 15***

**469** A64 5c Jungle fowl .20 .20
**470** A64 10c White tern .20 .20
**471** A64 15c Brown noddy .20 .20
**472** A64 20c Phoenix petrel .20 .20
**473** A64 25c Pacific golden plover .25 .25
**474** A64 30c Crested tern .30 .30
**475** A64 35c Sooty tern .35 .35
**476** A64 40c Bristle-thighed curlew .40 .40
**477** A64 45c Eastern bar-tailed godwit .45 .45
**478** A64 50c Reef heron .50 .50
**479** A64 55c Greater frigatebird .55 .55
**480** A64 60c Red-footed booby .65 .65
**481** A64 70c Red-necked stint .75 .75
**482** A64 $1 New Zealand long-tailed cuckoo 1.25 1.25
**483** A64 $2 Red-tailed tropicbird 2.25 2.25
**484** A64 $5 Banded rail 5.50 5.50
*Nos. 469-484 (16)* 14.00 14.00

For overprints see Nos. 676-679, 796-799, O33-O48.

Intl. Red Cross and Red Crescent Organizations, 125th Annivs. — A65

*Perf. 12½*

**1988, May 9 Litho. Unwmk.**

**485** A65 15c Jean-Henri Dunant .30 .30
**486** A65 40c Junior Red Cross .35 .35
**487** A65 50c Care for the handicapped .55 .55
**488** A65 60c First aid training .60 .60
*Nos. 485-488 (4)* 1.80 1.80

**Souvenir Sheet**

**489** A65 $1.50 Lecture 1.90 1.90

A66

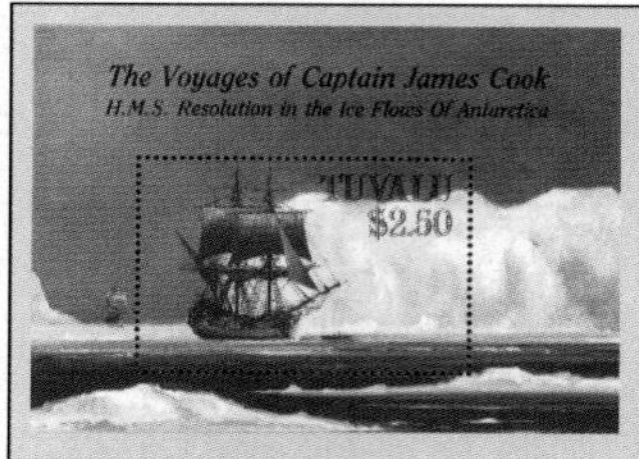


Voyages of Capt. Cook — A67

Designs: 20c, HMS *Endeavour* (starboard side). 40c, *Endeavour* (stern). 50c, Landing, Tahiti, 1769, vert. 60c, Maori chief, vert. 80c, *Resolution* and native Hawaiian sail ship. $1, Cook, by Sir Nathaniel Dance-Holland (1735-1811), vert. $2.50, Antarctic icebergs surrounding the *Resolution*. Illustration A67 reduced.

**1988, June 15 Litho. *Perf. 12½***

**490-495** A66 Set of 6 5.75 5.75

**Souvenir Sheet**

**496** A67 $2.50 shown 4.25 4.25

Fungi — A68

**1988, July 25 Litho. *Perf. 15***

**497** A68 40c Ganoderma applanatum .95 .95
**498** A68 50c Pseudoepicoccum cocos 1.25 1.25
**499** A68 60c Rigidoporus zonalis 1.40 1.40
**500** A68 90c Rigidoporus microporus 2.10 2.10
*Nos. 497-500 (4)* 5.70 5.70

See Nos. 520-523.

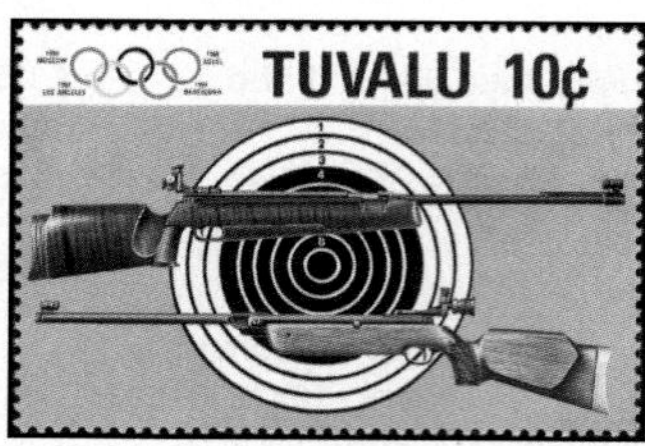


1988 Summer Olympics, Seoul — A69

*Perf. 12½*

**1988, Aug. 19 Litho. Unwmk.**

**501** A69 10c Rifles, target .35 .35
**502** A69 20c Judo .55 .55
**503** A69 40c One-man kayak 1.25 1.25
**504** A69 60c Swimming 1.90 1.90
**505** A69 80c Yachting 2.40 2.40
**506** A69 $1 Balance beam 3.25 3.25
*Nos. 501-506 (6)* 9.70 9.70

Natl. Independence, 10th Anniv. — A70

**Wmk. 380**

**1988, Sept. 28 Litho. *Perf. 14***

**507** A70 60c Queen Elizabeth in boat 1.00 1.00
*a.* Souvenir sheet of 1 1.00 1.00
**508** A70 90c In sedan chair 1.40 1.40
*a.* Souvenir sheet of 1 1.40 1.40
**509** A70 $1 shown 1.60 1.60
*a.* Souvenir sheet of 1 1.60 1.60
**510** A70 $1.20 Seated at dais 2.00 2.00
*a.* Souvenir sheet of 1 2.00 2.00
*Nos. 507-510 (4)* 6.00 6.00

Nos. 507-508 and 510 vert.

Christmas — A71

**Unwmk.**

**1988, Dec. 5 Litho. *Perf. 14***

**511** A71 15c Mary .30 .30
**512** A71 40c Christ child .70 .70
**513** A71 60c Joseph 1.10 1.10
*Nos. 511-513 (3)* 2.10 2.10

**Souvenir Sheet**

**514** A71 $1.50 Heraldic angel 2.75 2.75

Palm-frond or Pandanus-leaf Skirts — A72

**1989, Mar. 31 Litho. *Perf. 14***

**515** A72 40c multi 1.10 1.10
**516** A72 50c multi, diff. 1.25 1.25
**517** A72 60c multi, diff. 1.50 1.50
**518** A72 90c multi, diff. 2.25 2.25
*Nos. 515-518 (4)* 6.10 6.10

**Souvenir Sheet**

**519** A72 $1.50 multi, vert. 3.75 3.75

**Fungi Type of 1988**

**1989, May 24 Litho. *Perf. 14***

**520** A68 40c Trametes muelleri 1.00 1.00
**521** A68 50c Pestalotiopsis palmarum 1.25 1.25
**522** A68 60c Trametes cingulata 1.50 1.50
**523** A68 90c Schizophyllum commune 2.40 2.40
*Nos. 520-523 (4)* 6.15 6.15

**Marine Life Type of 1986**

**1989, July 31 Litho. *Perf. 14***

**524** A57 40c Pennant coralfish .90 .90
**525** A57 50c Anemone fish 1.10 1.10
**526** A57 60c Batfish 1.25 1.25
**527** A57 90c Threadfin coralfish 2.25 2.25
*a.* Miniature sheet of 4, #524-527 6.25 6.25
*Nos. 524-527 (4)* 5.50 5.50

Souvenir Sheet

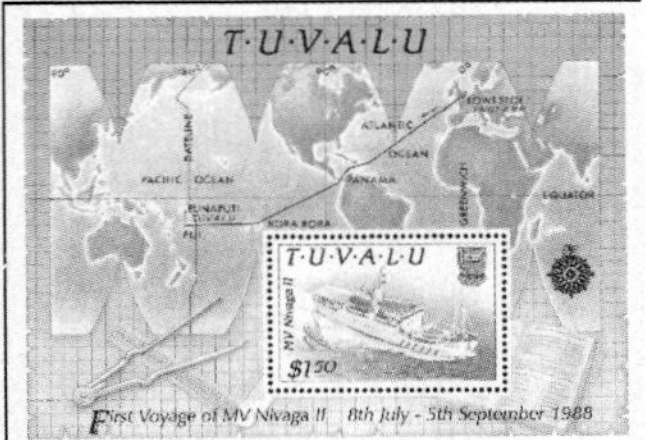

Maiden Voyage of M.V. *Nivaga II*, 1988 — A73

**1989, Oct. 9** **Litho.** ***Perf. 14***

**528** A73 $1.50 multicolored 2.75 2.75

Christmas — A74

Tropical Trees — A75

**Unwmk.**

**1989, Nov. 29** **Litho.** ***Perf. 14***

**529** A74 40c Conch shell .95 .95
**530** A74 50c Flower bouquet 1.25 1.25
**531** A74 60c Germinated coconut 1.50 1.50
**532** A74 90c Shell jewelry 2.10 2.10
*Nos. 529-532 (4)* 5.80 5.80

**1990, Feb. 28** **Litho.** ***Perf. 14½***

**533** A75 15c *Cocus nucifera* .50 .50
**534** A75 30c *Rhizophora samoensis* .95 .95
**535** A75 40c *Messerschmidia argentea* 1.25 1.25
**536** A75 50c *Pandanus tectorius* 1.60 1.60
**537** A75 60c *Hernandia nymphaeifolia* 1.90 1.90
**538** A75 90c *Pisonia grandis* 3.00 3.00
*Nos. 533-538 (6)* 9.20 9.20

Penny Black, 150th Anniv. A76

**1990, May 3** **Litho.** ***Perf. 14***

**539** A76 15c multicolored .90 .90
**540** A76 40c multicolored 2.25 2.25
**541** A76 90c multicolored 5.50 5.50
*Nos. 539-541 (3)* 8.65 8.65

**Souvenir Sheet**

**542** A76 $2 multicolored 8.50 8.50

Stamp World London '90.

World War II Ships A77

Designs: 15c, Japanese merchant conversion, 1940. 30c, USS Unimak, seaplane tender, 1944. 40c, Amagari, Japanese Hubuki class, 1942. 50c, AO-24 USS Platte, Nov. 1, 1943. 60c, Japanese Shumushu Class (Type A) escort. 90c, CV-22 USS Independence.

**1990**

**543-548** A77 Set of 6 15.00 15.00

Flowers — A78

**1990, Sept. 21** **Litho.** ***Perf. 14½***

**549** A78 15c Erythrina fusca .30 .30
**550** A78 30c Capparis cordifolia .55 .55
**551** A78 40c Portulaca pilosa .75 .75
**552** A78 50c Cordia subcordata .95 .95
**553** A78 60c Scaevola taccada 1.10 1.10
**554** A78 90c Suriana maritima 1.75 1.75
*Nos. 549-554 (6)* 5.40 5.40

UN Development Program, 40th Anniv. — A79

**1990, Nov. 20** **Litho.** ***Perf. 14***

**555** A79 40c Surveyor 1.40 1.40
**556** A79 60c Communications station 2.10 2.10
**557** A79 $1.20 Fishing boat *Te Tautai* 4.00 4.00
*Nos. 555-557 (3)* 7.50 7.50

Christmas A80

Seashells — A81

**1990, Nov. 20**

**558** A80 15c Mary and Joseph .50 .50
**559** A80 40c Nativity 1.40 1.40
**560** A80 60c Shepherds 2.10 2.10
**561** A80 90c Three Kings 3.25 3.25
*Nos. 558-561 (4)* 7.25 7.25

**1991, Jan. 18** **Litho.** ***Perf. 14***

**562** A81 40c Murex ramosus 1.25 1.25
**563** A81 50c Conus marmoreus 1.75 1.75
**564** A81 60c Trochus niloticus 2.00 2.00
**565** A81 $1.50 Cypraea mappa 4.50 4.50
*Nos. 562-565 (4)* 9.50 9.50

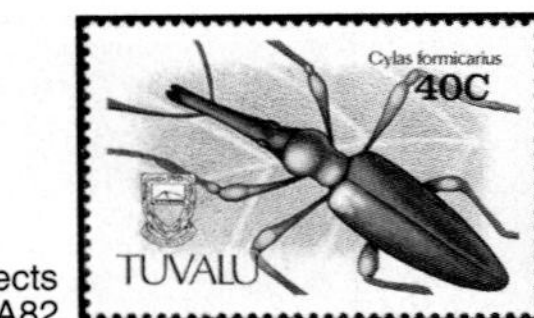

Insects A82

**1991, Mar. 22** **Litho.** ***Perf. 14***

**566** A82 40c Cylas formicarius 1.60 1.60
**567** A82 50c Heliothis armiger 2.10 2.10
**568** A82 60c Spodoptera litura 2.50 2.50
**569** A82 $1.50 Agrius convolvuli 6.00 6.00
*Nos. 566-569 (4)* 12.20 12.20

A83

A84

Endangered marine life.

**1991, May 31** **Litho.** ***Perf. 14***

**570** A83 40c Green turtle 1.40 1.40
**571** A83 50c Humpback whale 1.60 1.60
**572** A83 60c Hawksbill turtle 2.10 2.10
**573** A83 $1.50 Sperm whale 4.75 4.75
*Nos. 570-573 (4)* 9.85 9.85

**1991, July 31** **Litho.** ***Perf. 14***

**574** A84 40c Soccer 1.75 1.75
**575** A84 50c Volleyball 2.10 2.10
**576** A84 60c Lawn tennis 2.75 2.75
**577** A84 $1.50 Cricket 6.25 6.25
*Nos. 574-577 (4)* 12.85 12.85

9th South Pacific Games.

World War II Ships A85

**1991, Oct. 15** **Litho.** ***Perf. 14***

**578** A85 40c USS Tennessee 3.25 2.50
**579** A85 50c IJN Haguro 3.50 3.25
**580** A85 60c HMS Achilles 4.50 3.75
**581** A85 $1.50 USS North Carolina 9.50 9.50
*Nos. 578-581 (4)* 20.75 19.00

A86

A87

Christmas: various traditional dance costumes.

**1991, Dec. 13**

**582** A86 40c multicolored 1.60 1.60
**583** A86 50c multicolored 2.10 2.10
**584** A86 60c multicolored 2.50 2.50
**585** A86 $1.50 multicolored 6.25 6.25
*Nos. 582-585 (4)* 12.45 12.45

**1992, Jan. 29** **Litho.** ***Perf. 14***

Constellations.

**586** A87 40c Southern Fish 1.60 1.60
**587** A87 50c Scorpio 2.10 2.10
**588** A87 60c Sagittarius 2.50 2.50
**589** A87 $1.50 Southern Cross 6.00 6.00
*Nos. 586-589 (4)* 12.20 12.20

British Annexation of the Gilbert & Ellice Islands, Cent. — A88

**1992, Mar. 23** **Litho.** ***Perf. 14***

**590** A88 40c King George VI 1.90 1.90
**591** A88 50c King George V 2.25 2.25
**592** A88 60c King Edward VII 2.75 2.75
**593** A88 $1.50 Queen Victoria 7.00 7.00
*Nos. 590-593 (4)* 13.90 13.90

Discovery of America, 500th Anniv. A89

Columbus and: 40c, Queen Isabella & King Ferdinand of Spain. 50c, Polynesians. 60c, South American Indians. $1.50, North American Indians.

**1992, May 22** **Litho.** ***Perf. 14***

**594** A89 40c black & dk blue 1.00 1.00
**595** A89 50c black & dk plum 1.25 1.25
**596** A89 60c black & dk green 1.50 1.50
**597** A89 $1.50 black & dk purple 3.75 3.75
*Nos. 594-597 (4)* 7.50 7.50

World Columbian Stamp Expo '92, Chicago.

Fish A90

Designs: 15c, Bluespot butterflyfish. 20c, Pink parrotfish. 25c, Stripe surgeonfish. 30c, Moon wrasse, 35c, Harlequin filefish. 40c, Bird wrasse. 45c, Black-finned pigfish. 50c, Blue-green chromis. 60c, Hump-headed Maori wrasse. 70c, Ornate coralfish, vert. 90c, Saddled butterflyfish, vert. $1, Vagabond butterflyfish, vert. $2, Longfin bannerfish, vert. $3, Moorish idol, vert.

**1992, July 15**

**598-611** A90 Set of 14 17.00 17.00

For overprints & surcharge see #629-632, 716.

1992 Summer Olympics, Barcelona — A91

**1992, July 27** **Litho.** ***Perf. 14***

| | | | | |
|---|---|---|---|---|
| **612** | A91 | 40c Discus | 1.00 | 1.00 |
| **613** | A91 | 50c Javelin | 1.25 | 1.25 |
| **614** | A91 | 60c Shotput | 1.60 | 1.60 |
| **615** | A91 | $1.50 Track & field | 4.00 | 4.00 |
| | | *Nos. 612-615 (4)* | 7.85 | 7.85 |

**Souvenir Sheet**

| | | | | |
|---|---|---|---|---|
| **616** | A91 | $2 Olympic stadium | 5.00 | 5.00 |

Blue Coral A92

Various views of blue coral.

**1992, Sept. 1**

| | | | | |
|---|---|---|---|---|
| **617** | A92 | 10c multicolored | 1.50 | 1.50 |
| **618** | A92 | 25c multicolored | 3.25 | 3.25 |
| **619** | A92 | 30c multicolored | 3.25 | 3.25 |
| **620** | A92 | 35c multicolored | 4.00 | 4.00 |
| | | *Nos. 617-620 (4)* | 12.00 | 12.00 |

World Wildlife Fund.

Christmas — A93

Wild Flowers — A94

Designs: 40c, Fishermen seeing angel. 50c, Fishermen sailing canoes toward island. 60c, Adoration of the fishermen. $1.50, Flowers, shell necklaces.

**1992, Dec. 25** **Litho.** ***Perf. 14***

| | | | | |
|---|---|---|---|---|
| **621** | A93 | 40c multicolored | .75 | .75 |
| **622** | A93 | 50c multicolored | .95 | .95 |
| **623** | A93 | 60c multicolored | 1.10 | 1.10 |
| **624** | A93 | $1.50 multicolored | 2.75 | 2.75 |
| | | *Nos. 621-624 (4)* | 5.55 | 5.55 |

**1993, Feb. 2** **Litho.** ***Perf. 14***

| | | | | |
|---|---|---|---|---|
| **625** | A94 | 40c Calophyllum inophyllum | 1.00 | 1.00 |
| **626** | A94 | 50c Hibiscus tiliaceus | 1.25 | 1.25 |
| **627** | A94 | 60c Lantana camara | 1.50 | 1.50 |
| **628** | A94 | $1.50 Plumeria rubra | 3.50 | 3.50 |
| | | *Nos. 625-628 (4)* | 7.25 | 7.25 |

Nos. 601, 603, & 605-606 Ovptd.

**1992, Sept. 1** **Litho.** ***Perf. 14***

| | | | | |
|---|---|---|---|---|
| **629** | A90 | 30c on #601 | 1.25 | 1.25 |
| **630** | A90 | 40c on #603 | 1.50 | 1.50 |
| **631** | A90 | 50c on #605 | 2.10 | 2.10 |
| **632** | A90 | 60c on #606 | 2.50 | 2.50 |
| | | *Nos. 629-632 (4)* | 7.35 | 7.35 |

World War II in the Pacific, 50th Anniv. A95

**1993, Apr. 23** **Litho.** ***Perf. 14***

| | | | | |
|---|---|---|---|---|
| **633** | A95 | 40c Japanese bombers | 1.60 | 1.60 |
| **634** | A95 | 50c Anti-aircraft gun, vert. | 2.00 | 2.00 |
| **635** | A95 | 60c Using flame thrower | 2.40 | 2.40 |
| **636** | A95 | $1.50 Map of Funafuti Atoll, vert. | 6.50 | 6.50 |
| | | *Nos. 633-636 (4)* | 12.50 | 12.50 |

**Souvenir Sheet**

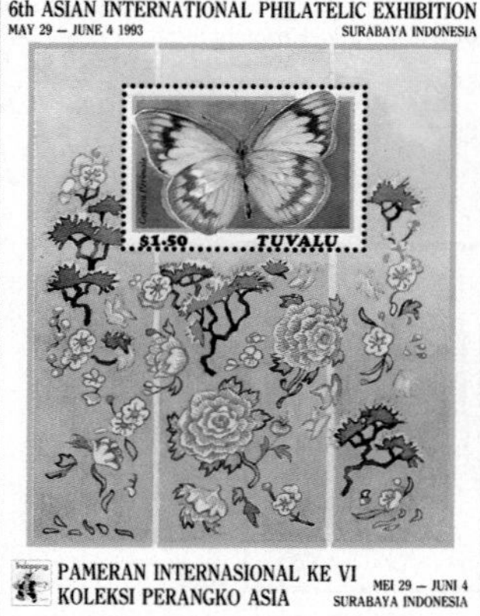

Indopex '93 — A96

**1993, May 29** ***Perf. 14x14½***

| | | | | |
|---|---|---|---|---|
| **637** | A96 | $1.50 Cepora perimale | 5.25 | 5.25 |

Marine Life A97

**1993, June 29** **Litho.** ***Perf. 14***

| | | | | |
|---|---|---|---|---|
| **638** | A97 | 40c Giant clam | .90 | .90 |
| **639** | A97 | 50c Anemone crab | 1.10 | 1.10 |
| **640** | A97 | 60c Octopus | 1.40 | 1.40 |
| **641** | A97 | $1.50 Green turtle | 3.25 | 3.25 |
| | | *Nos. 638-641 (4)* | 6.65 | 6.65 |

Coronation of Queen Elizabeth II, 40th Anniv. — A98

Queen: 40c, Riding in parade with Prince Phillip. 50c, Drinking coconut milk. 60c, Holding umbrella. $1.50, With natives. $2, Coronation ceremony.

**1993, July 5**

| | | | | |
|---|---|---|---|---|
| **642** | A98 | 40c multicolored | .95 | .95 |
| **643** | A98 | 50c multicolored | 1.25 | 1.25 |
| **644** | A98 | 60c multicolored | 1.50 | 1.50 |
| **645** | A98 | $1.50 multicolored | 3.50 | 3.50 |
| | | *Nos. 642-645 (4)* | 7.20 | 7.20 |

**Souvenir Sheet**

| | | | | |
|---|---|---|---|---|
| **646** | A98 | $2 multicolored | 8.75 | 8.75 |

**Souvenir Sheet**

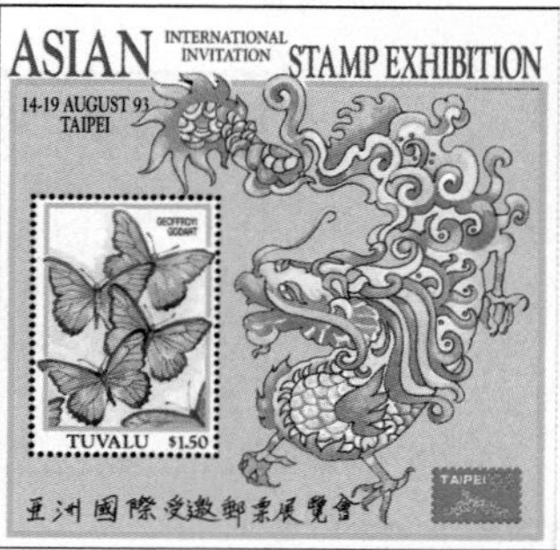

Taipei '93 — A99

Illustration reduced.

**Litho. & Typo.**

**1993, Aug. 14** ***Perf. 14½x14***

| | | | | |
|---|---|---|---|---|
| **647** | A99 | $1.50 Geoffroyi godart | 5.00 | 5.00 |

**Souvenir Sheet**

Bangkok '93 — A100

Illustration reduced.

**1993, Oct. 1** **Litho.** ***Perf. 14x14½***

| | | | | |
|---|---|---|---|---|
| **648** | A100 | $1.50 Paradisea staudinger | 3.00 | 3.00 |

Greenhouse Effect — A101

Christmas — A102

Beach scene with: 40c, Sun at UR. 50c, Sun at UL. 60c, Crab on beach. $1.50, Sea gull in flight.

**1993, Nov. 2** **Litho.** ***Perf. 13½***

| | | | | |
|---|---|---|---|---|
| **649** | A101 | 40c multicolored | .75 | .75 |
| **650** | A101 | 50c multicolored | 1.00 | 1.00 |
| **651** | A101 | 60c multicolored | 1.25 | 1.25 |
| **652** | A101 | $1.50 multicolored | 3.00 | 3.00 |
| *a.* | | Souvenir sheet of 4, #649-652, perf. 14½x14 | 7.25 | 7.25 |
| | | *Nos. 649-652 (4)* | 6.00 | 6.00 |

**1993, Dec. 6** **Litho.** ***Perf. 13½***

| | | | | |
|---|---|---|---|---|
| **653** | A102 | 40c shown | .90 | .90 |
| **654** | A102 | 50c Candle, flowers | 1.10 | 1.10 |
| **655** | A102 | 60c Angel, flowers | 1.40 | 1.40 |
| **656** | A102 | $1.50 Palm tree, candles | 3.25 | 3.25 |
| | | *Nos. 653-656 (4)* | 6.65 | 6.65 |

**Souvenir Sheet**

Hong Kong '94 — A103

Illustration reduced.

**1994, Feb. 18** ***Perf. 14½x14***

| | | | | |
|---|---|---|---|---|
| **657** | A103 | $2 Monarch | 6.25 | 6.25 |

Scenic Views A104

**1994, Feb. 18** **Litho.** ***Perf. 14***

| | | | | |
|---|---|---|---|---|
| **658** | A104 | 40c shown | 1.00 | 1.00 |
| **659** | A104 | 50c Beach, trees, diff. | 1.10 | 1.10 |
| **660** | A104 | 60c Boats, ocean | 1.40 | 1.40 |
| **661** | A104 | $1.50 Boats, beach | 3.75 | 3.75 |
| | | *Nos. 658-661 (4)* | 7.25 | 7.25 |

New Year 1994 (Year of the Dog) — A105

**1994, Apr. 23** **Litho.** ***Perf. 14***

| | | | | |
|---|---|---|---|---|
| **662** | A105 | 40c Irish setter | 1.00 | 1.00 |
| **663** | A105 | 50c Golden retriever | 1.10 | 1.10 |
| **664** | A105 | 60c West Highland terrier | 1.40 | 1.40 |
| **665** | A105 | $1.50 German shepherd | 3.75 | 3.75 |
| | | *Nos. 662-665 (4)* | 7.25 | 7.25 |

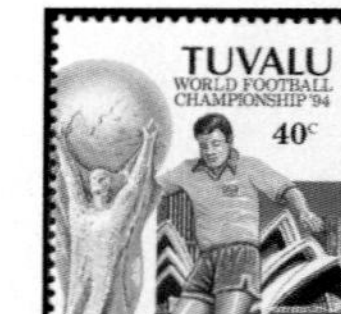

A106

**1994, June 7**

| | | | | |
|---|---|---|---|---|
| **666** | A106 | 40c Australia | .65 | .65 |
| **667** | A106 | 50c England | .85 | .85 |
| **668** | A106 | 60c Argentina | 1.00 | 1.00 |
| **669** | A106 | $1.50 Germany | 2.50 | 2.50 |
| | | *Nos. 666-669 (4)* | 5.00 | 5.00 |

**Souvenir Sheet**

| | | | | |
|---|---|---|---|---|
| **670** | A106 | $2 US | 7.25 | 7.25 |

1994 World Cup Soccer Championships, US.

A107

**1994, Aug. 16** **Litho.** ***Perf. 14***

Seashells.

| | | | | |
|---|---|---|---|---|
| **671** | A107 | 40c Umbonium giganteum | 1.00 | 1.00 |
| **672** | A107 | 50c Turbo petholatus | 1.25 | 1.25 |
| **673** | A107 | 60c Planaxis savignyi | 1.50 | 1.50 |
| **674** | A107 | $1.50 Hydatina physis | 3.75 | 3.75 |
| | | *Nos. 671-674 (4)* | 7.50 | 7.50 |

**Souvenir Sheet**

PHILAKOREA '94 — A108

Illustration reduced.

**1994, Aug. 16**

| | | | | |
|---|---|---|---|---|
| **675** | A108 | $1.50 Pekinese dog | 4.75 | 4.75 |

Nos. 469-470, 476-477 Ovptd.

**1994, Aug. 31 Litho. *Perf. 15***

**676** A64 5c multicolored .35 .35
**677** A64 10c multicolored .35 .35
**678** A64 40c multicolored 1.00 1.00
**679** A64 45c multicolored 1.10 1.10
*Nos. 676-679 (4)* 2.80 2.80

First Manned Moon Landing, 25th Anniv. — A109

a, 40c, Saturn V. b, 50c, Apollo 11. c, 60c, Neil Armstrong. d, $1.50, Splash-down.

**1994, Oct. 31 *Perf. 14***

**680** A109 Strip of 4, #a.-d. 7.25 7.25

Christmas — A110

40c, Boys playing in water. 50c, Islanders, fish being gathered. 60c, People seated under canopy, food. $1.50, Traditional dancers.

**1994, Dec. 15 Litho. *Perf. 14***

**681** A110 40c multicolored .95 .95
**682** A110 50c multicolored 1.10 1.10
**683** A110 60c multicolored 1.40 1.40
**684** A110 $1.50 multicolored 3.50 3.50
*Nos. 681-684 (4)* 6.95 6.95

New Year 1995 (Year of the Boar) A111

40c, One pig. 50c, Pig, piglet. 60c, Three pigs. $1.50, Sow nursing litter.

**1995, Jan. 30 Litho. *Perf. 14***

**685-688** A111 Set of 4 5.50 5.50

FAO, 50th Anniv. A112

40c, Men with vegetables in wheelbarrow. 50c, Man with sack of vegetables. 60c, Girl cleaning vegetables. $1.50, Girl mixing food.

**1995, Mar. 31 Litho. *Perf. 14***

**689-692** A112 Set of 4 6.75 6.75

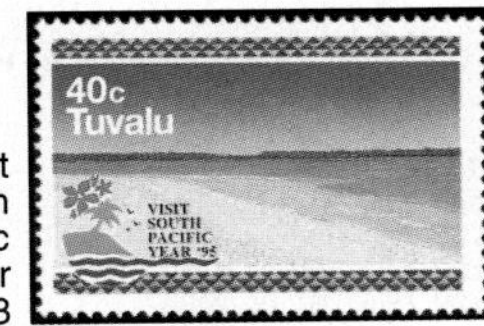


Visit South Pacific Year A113

**1995, May 26 Litho. *Perf. 14***

**693** A113 40c shown .75 .75
**694** A113 50c Sailboat .95 .95
**695** A113 60c Hut 1.10 1.10
**696** A113 $1.50 Home, beach 2.75 2.75
*Nos. 693-696 (4)* 5.55 5.55

Pacific Coastal Orchids A114

40c, Dendrobium comptonii. 50c, Dendrobium aff. involutum. 60c, Dendrobium rarum. $1.50, Grammatophyllum scriptum.

**1995, July 28 Litho. *Perf. 14***

**697-700** A114 Set of 4 7.25 7.25

Souvenir Sheet

Jakarta '95, Asian World Stamp Exhibition — A116

Illustration reduced.

**1995, Aug. 19 Litho. *Perf. 12***

**702** A116 $1 Traditional dancer 2.50 2.50

For overprint see No. 702.

Souvenir Sheet

Singapore '95 World Stamp Exhibition — A117

Illustration reduced.

**1995, Sept. 1**

**703** A117 $1 Phalaenopsis amabillis 2.75 2.75

End of World War II, 50th Anniv. A118

40c, Soldier with sub-machine gun, map of Japan, Tuvalu. 50c, Soldier holding rifle, landing exercise on beach. 60c, US Marine, offshore air and sea battle. $1.50, Soldier firing rifle, atomic mushroom cloud.

**1995, Aug. 19 Litho. *Perf. 14***

**704-707** A118 Set of 4 9.75 9.75

Souvenir Sheet

UN, 50th Anniv. — A119

a, Rowing in outrigger canoes. b, UN New York headquarters. Illustration reduced.

**1995, Oct. 24 *Perf. 14½***

**708** A119 $1 Sheet of 2, #a.-b. 4.25 4.25

Christmas — A120

Scores and verses to Christmas carols and: 40c, Map of island, "Silent Night." 50c, Boy carolers, "O Come All Ye Faithful." 60c, Girl carolers, "The First Noel." $1.50, Angel, "Hark the Herald Angels Sing."

**1995, Dec. 15 Litho. *Perf. 14***

**709-712** A120 Set of 4 6.50 6.50

Miniature Sheet

Independence, First Tuvalu Postage Stamps, 20th Anniv. — A121

a, 40c, #16. b, 60c, #17. c, $1, #18.

**1996, Jan. 1 Litho. *Perf. 14***

**713** A121 Sheet of 3, #a.-c. 5.25 5.25

Miniature Sheet

New Year 1996 (Year of the Rat) — A122

Stylized rats: a, Looking right. b, Facing left, drinking from container.

**1996, Feb. 23 Litho. *Perf. 14x14½***

**714** A122 50c Sheet of 2, #a.-b. 2.50 2.50
*c.* Ovptd. in sheet margin 2.50 2.50
*d.* With added inscription in sheet margin 2.50 2.50

No. 714c is overprinted in sheet margin with exhibition emblem of Hongpex '96.

No. 714d is inscribed in sheet margin with two exhibition emblems of China '96. Issued: 5/18.

No. 702 Ovptd. in Gold

**1996, Mar. 21 Litho. *Perf. 12***

**715** A116 $1 multicolored 1.75 1.75

No. 715 also contains same overprint in sheet margin.

No. 604 Surcharged in Black, Red & Blue

**1996, Oct. 21 Litho. *Perf. 14***

**716** A90 $1 on 45c multi 1.60 1.60

1996 Summer Olympic Games, Atlanta A123

**1996, Sept. 11 Litho. *Perf. 14***

**717** A123 40c Beach volleyball .60 .60
**718** A123 50c Swimming .75 .75
**719** A123 60c Weight lifting .90 .90
**720** A123 $1.50 David Tua, boxer 2.25 2.25
*Nos. 717-720 (4)* 4.50 4.50

UNICEF, 50th Anniv. A124

**1996, Oct. 28**

**721** A124 40c Immunization .60 .60
**722** A124 50c Education for life .75 .75
**723** A124 60c Water tank project .90 .90
**724** A124 $1.50 Hydroponic farm 2.25 2.25
*Nos. 721-724 (4)* 4.50 4.50

Christmas A125

Designs: 40c, Magi following star. 50c, Shepherds seeing star. 60c, Adoration of the Magi. $1.50, Nativity scene.

**1996, Nov. 25 *Perf. 14½***

**725** A125 40c multicolored .70 .70
**726** A125 50c multicolored .85 .85
**727** A125 60c multicolored 1.00 1.00
**728** A125 $1.50 multicolored 2.50 2.50
*Nos. 725-728 (4)* 5.05 5.05

Fish
A126

**1997, Mar. 15** *Perf. 14*

**729** A126 25c Bluetail mullet .40 .40
**730** A126 30c Queen fish leatherskin .45 .45
**731** A126 40c Paddletail .60 .60
**732** A126 45c Long-nose emperor .70 .70
Complete bklt., 4 ea #729-732 8.75
**733** A126 50c Long-snouted unicornfish .75 .75
**734** A126 55c Brigham's snapper .80 .80
**735** A126 60c Red bass .90 .90
**736** A126 70c Red jobfish 1.00 1.00
**737** A126 90c Leopard flounder 1.40 1.40
**738** A126 $1 Red snapper 1.50 1.50
**739** A126 $2 Longtail snapper 3.00 3.00
*a.* Souv. sheet of 1, wmk. 373 3.00 3.00
**740** A126 $3 Black trevally 4.50 4.50
*Nos. 729-740 (12)* 16.00 16.00

No. 739a for return of Hong Kong to China, July 1, 1997.

Souvenir Sheet

New Year 1997 (Year of the Ox) — A127

**1997, June 20** **Litho.** *Perf. 14*

**741** A127 $2 multicolored 5.25

Hong Kong '97.

Ducks and Drakes
A128

**1997, May 29** **Litho.** *Perf. 14*

**742** A128 40c White pekin .60 .60
**743** A128 50c Muscovy .75 .75
**744** A128 60c Pacific black .90 .90
**745** A128 $1.50 Mandarin 2.25 2.25
*Nos. 742-745 (4)* 4.50 4.50

PACIFIC 97.

Domestic Cats — A129

40c, Korat king. 50c, Long-haired ginger kitten. 60c, Shaded cameo. $1.50, American Maine coon.

**1997, June 20**

**746** A129 40c multicolored .70 .70
**747** A129 50c multicolored .85 .85
**748** A129 60c multicolored 1.00 1.00
**749** A129 $1.50 multicolored 2.50 2.50
*Nos. 746-749 (4)* 5.05 5.05

Queen Elizabeth II and Prince Philip, 50th Wedding Anniv. — A130

Designs: No. 750, Queen, Prince standing in open vehicle. No. 751, Queen in yellow hat. No. 752, Queen holding umbrella. No. 753, Queen reading, Prince up close. No. 754, Three pictures of Queen. No. 755, Prince in top hat, Queen.

$2, Queen, Prince riding in open carriage, horiz.

**Wmk. 373**

**1997, Oct. 1** **Litho.** *Perf. 14½*

**750** 40c multicolored .60 .60
**751** 40c multicolored .60 .60
*a.* A130 Pair, #750-751 1.25 1.25
**752** 50c multicolored .75 .75
**753** 50c multicolored .75 .75
*a.* A130 Pair, #752-753 1.50 1.50
**754** 60c multicolored .85 .85
**755** 60c multicolored .85 .85
*a.* A130 Pair, #754-755 1.75 1.75
*Nos. 750-755 (6)* 4.40 4.40

**Souvenir Sheet**

**756** A130 $2 multicolored 3.50 3.50

No. 756 contains one 38x32mm stamp.

Traditional Activities — A131

Christmas: 40c, Turtle hunting. 50c, Pole fishing. 60c, Canoe racing. $1.50, Traditional dance.

*Perf. 13½x13*

**1997, Nov. 25** **Litho.** **Wmk. 373**

**757** A131 40c multicolored .60 .60
**758** A131 50c multicolored .75 .75
**759** A131 60c multicolored .90 .90
**760** A131 $1.50 multicolored 2.25 2.25
*Nos. 757-760 (4)* 4.50 4.50

Souvenir Sheet

New Year 1998 (Year of the Tiger) — A132

Illustration reduced.

**1998, Feb. 2** **Litho.** *Perf. 13*

**761** A132 $1.40 multicolored 2.25 2.25

**Diana, Princess of Wales (1961-97)**

Common Design Type

Designs: a, Wearing red evening dress. b, Wearing black evening dress. c, Wearing tiara. d, With collar up on coat.

*Perf. 14½x14*

**1998, Mar. 31** **Litho.** **Wmk. 373**

**762** CD355 80c Sheet of 4, #a.-d. 4.50 4.50

No. 762 sold for $3.20 + 20c, with surtax from international sales being donated to the Princess Diana Memorial Fund and surtax from national sales being donated to designated local charity.

**Royal Air Force, 80th Anniv.**

Common Design Type of 1993 Re-inscribed

Designs: 40c, Hawker Woodcock. 50c, Vickers Victoria. 60c, Bristol Brigand $1.50, De Haviland DHC 1 Chipmunk.

No. 767: a, Sopwith Pup. b, Armstrong Whitworth FK8. c, North American Harvard. d, Vultee Vengeance.

**Wmk. 384**

**1998, Apr. 1** **Litho.** *Perf. 13½*

**763** CD350 40c multicolored .70 .70
**764** CD350 50c multicolored .80 .80
**765** CD350 60c multicolored 1.00 1.00
**766** CD350 $1.50 multicolored 2.50 2.50
*Nos. 763-766 (4)* 5.00 5.00

**Souvenir Sheet**

**767** CD350 $1 Sheet of 4, #a.-d. 6.00 6.00

Ships
A133

Designs: 40c, "Los Reyes," "Santiago," 1567. 50c, "Morning Star," missionary topsail schooner, 1867. 60c, "The Light," brigantine of Church of the Resurrection, 1870. $1.50, New Zealand missionary schooner, 1900.

**Wmk. 373**

**1998, May 19** **Litho.** *Perf. 14*

**768** A133 40c multicolored .50 .50
**769** A133 50c multicolored .60 .60
**770** A133 60c multicolored .75 .75
**771** A133 $1.50 multicolored 1.75 1.75
*Nos. 768-771 (4)* 3.60 3.60

Dolphins and Porpoises — A134

40c, Bottlenose dolphin. 50c, Dall's porpoise. 60c, Harbor porpoise. $1.50, Common dolphin.

*Perf. 13½x13*

**1998, Aug. 21** **Litho.** **Wmk. 384**

**772** A134 40c multicolored .55 .55
**773** A134 50c multicolored .75 .75
**774** A134 60c multicolored .90 .90
**775** A134 $1.50 multicolored 2.25 2.25
*Nos. 772-775 (4)* 4.45 4.45

Greenpeace, Save Our Seas
A135

Marine life: 20c, Bleached platygyra daedalea, psammocora digitata. 30c, Bleached acropora robusta. 50c, Bleached acropora hyacinthus. $1, Bleached acropora danai, montastrea curta.

$1.50, Bleached seriatopora, bleached stylophora.

**Wmk. 373**

**1998, Nov. 6** **Litho.** *Perf. 14½*

**776** A135 20c multicolored .30 .30
**777** A135 30c multicolored .55 .55
**778** A135 50c multicolored .90 .90
**779** A135 $1 multicolored 1.60 1.60
*Nos. 776-779 (4)* 3.35 3.35

**Souvenir Sheet**

**780** A135 $1.50 multicolored 2.25 2.25

Intl. Year of the Ocean (#780).

Christmas — A136

40c, Flight into Egypt. 50c, Angel speaking to shepherds. 60c, Nativity. $1.50, Adoration of the Magi.

**1998, Nov. 20** *Perf. 14½x14*

**781** A136 40c multicolored .55 .55
**782** A136 50c multicolored .70 .70
**783** A136 60c multicolored .80 .80
**784** A136 $1.50 multicolored 2.00 2.00
*Nos. 781-784 (4)* 4.05 4.05

Independence, 20th Anniv. — A137

Stamps on stamps, Prime Ministers: 40c, #722, Bikenibeu Paeniu. 60c, Kamuta Latasi. 90c, Tomasi Puapua. $1.50, Design like #166, Toaripi Lauti.

**Wmk. 384**

**1998, Oct. 1** **Litho.** *Perf. 14*

**785** A137 40c multicolored .55 .55
**786** A137 60c multicolored .85 .85
**787** A137 90c multicolored 1.25 1.25
**788** A137 $1.50 multicolored 2.00 2.00
*a.* Souvenir sheet, #785-788 4.75 4.75
*Nos. 785-788 (4)* 4.65 4.65

Souvenir Sheet

New Year 1999 (Year of the Rabbit) — A138

Illustration reduced.

*Perf. 14½x14*

**1999, Feb. 16** **Litho.** **Wmk. 373**

**789** A138 $2 multicolored 3.25 3.25

Australia '99, World Stamp Expo
A139

Maritime history: 40c, Heemskerck, 1642. 50c, HMS Endeavour, 1769. 90c, PS Sophie Jane, 1831. $1.50, P&O SS Chusan, 1852.

$2, HM Brig "Supply."

**1999, Mar. 19** *Perf. 14*

**790** A139 40c multicolored .60 .60
**791** A139 50c multicolored .70 .70
**792** A139 90c multicolored 1.40 1.40
**793** A139 $1.50 multicolored 2.10 2.10
*Nos. 790-793 (4)* 4.80 4.80

**Souvenir Sheet**

**794** A139 $2 multicolored 2.50 2.50

Nos. 472, 475, 479, 482 Ovptd.

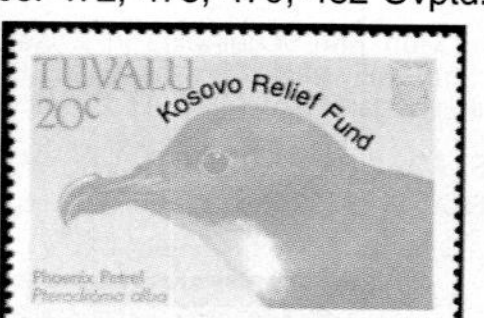


**1999, June 11** **Litho.** *Perf. 15*

**796** A64 20c on #472 .30 .30
**797** A64 35c on #475 .50 .50
**798** A64 55c on #479 .80 .80
**799** A64 $1 on #482 1.40 1.40
*Nos. 796-799 (4)* 3.00 3.00

50% of the sales of Nos. 796-799 will be donated to the Kosovo Relief Fund.

### 1st Manned Moon Landing, 30th Anniv.

Common Design Type

40c, Lift-off. 60c, Lunar module prepares to touchdown. 90c, Ascent stage approaches Command module. $1.50, Recovery.
$2, Looking at earth from moon.

*Perf. 14x13¾*

**1999, July 20 Litho. Wmk. 384**

| | | | |
|---|---|---|---|
| **800** CD357 | 40c multicolored | .60 | .60 |
| **801** CD357 | 60c multicolored | .80 | .80 |
| **802** CD357 | 90c multicolored | 1.40 | 1.40 |
| **803** CD357 | $1.50 multicolored | 2.10 | 2.10 |
| | *Nos. 800-803 (4)* | 4.90 | 4.90 |

**Souvenir Sheet**

*Perf. 14*

| | | | |
|---|---|---|---|
| **804** CD357 | $2 multicolored | 2.50 | 2.50 |

No. 804 contains one circular stamp 40mm in diameter.

### Queen Mother's Century

Common Design Type

Queen Mother: 40c, With King George VI inspecting bomb damage. 60c, With daughters at Balmoral. 90c, With Princes Harry and William, 95th birthday. $1.50, As colonel-in-chief of Queen's Dragoon Guards.
$2, Age 6 photo, photo of Yuri Gagarin.

**Wmk. 384**

**1999, Aug. 16 Litho. *Perf. 13½***

| | | | |
|---|---|---|---|
| **805** CD358 | 40c multicolored | .60 | .60 |
| **806** CD358 | 60c multicolored | .85 | .85 |
| **807** CD358 | 90c multicolored | 1.40 | 1.40 |
| **808** CD358 | $1.50 multicolored | 2.10 | 2.10 |
| | *Nos. 805-808 (4)* | 4.95 | 4.95 |

**Souvenir Sheet**

| | | | |
|---|---|---|---|
| **809** CD358 | $2 multicolored | 4.25 | 4.25 |

Flowers — A141

No. 810: a, Fetai. b, Ateate. c, Portulacacae lueta. d, Tamoloc. e, Beach pea. f, Pomegranate (red letters).
No. 811: a, Cup of gold. b, Rock rose. c, Bower plant. d, Lavender star. e, Hybrid mandevilla. f, Pomegranate (white letters).
No. 812, Scrambled eggs, vert.

*Perf. 13¾*

**1999, Nov. 22 Litho. Unwmk.**

| | | | |
|---|---|---|---|
| **810** A141 | 90c Sheet of 6, #a.-f. | 6.75 | 6.75 |
| **811** A141 | 90c Sheet of 6, #a.-f. | 6.75 | 6.75 |

**Souvenir Sheet**

| | | | |
|---|---|---|---|
| **812** A141 | $3 multi | 5.25 | 5.25 |

A142

Millennium — A143

No. 813, Lady of peace with frame.
No. 814: a, Like No. 813, no frame. b, Olive branch. c, Dove. d. Lion. e, Lamb. f, War crowning peace.
No. 815: Sun on horizon, clock, computer keyboard.

*Perf. 14½x14¼*

**1999, Dec. 31 Litho.**

| | | | |
|---|---|---|---|
| **813** A142 | 90c multi | 1.10 | 1.10 |
| **814** A142 | 90c Sheet of 6, #a.-f. | 7.75 | 7.75 |

**Souvenir Sheet**

*Perf. 14*

| | | | |
|---|---|---|---|
| **815** A143 | $2 multi | 2.75 | 2.75 |

No. 813 printed in sheets of 6.

Worldwide Fund for Nature — A144

Sand tiger shark: a, 10c, Close-up of head. b, 30c, Facing left. c, 50c, Swimming above seaweed. d, 60c, Three sharks.

*Perf. 13¼x13½*

**2000, Feb. 7 Litho. Unwmk.**

| | | | |
|---|---|---|---|
| **816** A144 | Strip of 4, #a.-d. | 3.00 | 3.00 |
| *e.* | Souvenir sheet, 2 #816 | 9.50 | 9.50 |

**Souvenir Sheet**

**Stamps Without WWF Emblem**

| | | | |
|---|---|---|---|
| **817** A144 | Sheet of 4, #a.-d | 2.75 | 2.75 |

Marine Life and Birds — A145

Illustration reduced.
No. 818, each 90c: a, Common tern. b, White-tailed tropicbird. c, Red emperor snapper. d, Clown triggerfish. e, Longfin bannerfish. f, Harlequin tuskfish.
No. 819, each 90c: a, Wilson's storm petrel. b, Common dolphin. c, Spotted seahorse. d, Threeband demoiselle. e, Coral hind. f, Palette surgeonfish.
No. 820, each 90c: a, Great frigatebird. b, Brown booby. c, Dugong. d, Red knot. e, Common starfish. f, Hawksbill turtle.
No. 821, each 90c: a, Manta ray. b, White shark. c, Hammerhead shark. d, Tiger shark. e, Great barracuda. f, Leatherback turtle.
No. 822, each 90c: a, Whale shark. b, Sixspot grouper. c, Bluestreak cleaner wrasse. d, Lemon shark. e, Spotted trunkfish. f, Longnosed butterflyfish.
No. 823, each 90c: a, Chevroned butterflyfish. b, Mandarinfish. c, Bicolor angelfish. d, Copperbanded butterflyfish. e, Clown anemonefish. f, Lemonpeel angelfish.
Each $3: No. 824, Picassofish. No. 825, Pygmy parrotfish. No. 826, Sailfish.

**2000, Mar. 8 *Perf. 14***

**Sheets of 6, #a.-f.**

| | | | |
|---|---|---|---|
| **818-823** A145 | Set of 6 | 45.00 | 45.00 |

**Souvenir Sheets**

| | | | |
|---|---|---|---|
| **824-826** A145 | Set of 3 | 11.00 | 11.00 |

Butterflies — A146

Illustration reduced.
No. 827, each 90c: a, Birdwing. b, Tailed emperor. c, Orchid swallowtail. d, Union Jack. e, Long-tailed blue. f, Common Jezebel.
No. 828, each 90c: a, Caper white. b, Common Indian crow. c, Eastern flat. d, Cairns birdwing. e, Monarch. f, Meadow argus.
No. 829, each 90c, horiz.: a, Glasswing. b, Leftwing. c, Moth butterfly. d, Blue triangle. e, Beak. f, Plane.
Each $3: No. 830, Great egg-fly. No. 831, Palmfly, horiz.

**2000, May 1 Sheets of 6, #a.-f.**

| | | | |
|---|---|---|---|
| **827-829** A146 | Set of 3 | 22.50 | 22.50 |

**Souvenir Sheets**

| | | | |
|---|---|---|---|
| **830-831** A146 | Set of 2 | 7.50 | 7.50 |

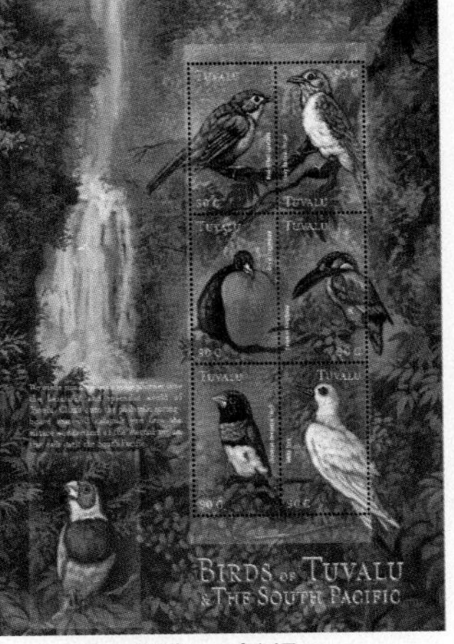


Birds — A147

#832, each 90c: a, Red-billed leiothrix. b, Gray shrike-thrush. c, Great frigatebird. d, Common kingfisher. e, Chestnut-breasted finch. f, White tern.
#833, each 90c: a, White-collared kingfisher. b, Scaled petrel. c, Superb blue wren. d, Osprey. e, Great cormorant. f, Peregrine falcon.
#834, each 90c: a, Rainbow lorikeet. b, White-throated tree creeper. c, White-tailed kingfisher. d, Golden whistler. e, Black-bellied plover. f, Beach thick-knee.
Each $3: #835, Morepork. #836, Broad-billed prion, horiz.
Illustration reduced.

**2000, June 1 Litho. *Perf. 14***

**Sheets of 6, #a-f**

| | | | |
|---|---|---|---|
| **832-834** A147 | Set of 3 | 22.50 | 22.50 |

**Souvenir Sheets**

| | | | |
|---|---|---|---|
| **835-836** A147 | Set of 2 | 7.50 | 7.50 |

Dogs and Cats — A148

No. 837: a, Fox terrier. b, Collie. c, Boston terrier. d, Pembroke Welsh corgi. e, Pointer. f, Dalmatian.
No. 838, vert.: a, Dalmatian. b, Boston terrier. c, Fox terrier. d, Pointer. e, Pembroke Welsh corgi. f, Collie.
No. 839, vert. (denominations in orange): a, Ticked taboy oriental shorthair. b, Balinese. c, Somali. d, Chinchilla Persian. e, Tonkinese. f, Japanese bobtail.
No. 840, vert. (denominations in green): a, Lilac oriental shorthair. b, Balinese. c, Somali. d, Chinchilla Persian. e, Tonkinese. f, Japanese bobtail.
No. 841, Scottish terrier. No. 842, Oriental shorthair, vert.
Illustration reduced.

**2000, July 3 Litho. *Perf. 14***

**Sheets of 6, #a-f**

| | | | |
|---|---|---|---|
| **837-840** A148 | 90c Set of 4 | 22.50 | 22.50 |

**Souvenir Sheets**

| | | | |
|---|---|---|---|
| **841-842** A148 | $3 Set of 2 | 7.75 | 7.75 |

Birds and Animals — A149

No. 843, horiz.: a, Brown noddy. b, Great frigatebird. c, Emperor angelfish. d, Common dolphin. e, Hermit crab. f, Threadfin butterflyfish.
No. 844, horiz.: a, Red-footed booby. b, Red-tailed tropicbird. c, Black-bellied plover. d, Common tern. e, Ruddy turnstone. f, Sanderling.
$3, Great frigatebird.
Illustration reduced.

**2000, Aug. 3**

**Sheets of 6, #a-f**

| | | | |
|---|---|---|---|
| **843-844** A149 | 90c Set of 2 | 14.50 | 14.50 |

**Souvenir Sheet**

| | | | |
|---|---|---|---|
| **845** A149 | $3 Great frigatebird | 3.75 | 3.75 |

New Year 2000 and 2001 (Years of the Dragon and Snake) A150

Designs: 40c, Dragon. 60c, Snake. 90c, Snake, diff. $1.50, Dragon, diff.

**2001, Jan. 15 Litho. *Perf. 13½x13¼***

| | | | |
|---|---|---|---|
| **846-849** A150 | Set of 4 | 5.25 | 5.25 |

Motofoua Secondary School Fire, 1st Anniv.
A151

Fire trucks: 60c, Anglo specialist rescue uUnit. 90c, Anglo 4800 water/foam tender. $1.50, Bronto 33-2T1 combined telescopic ladder/hydralulic platform. $2, Anglo 450 LRX water tender.
$3, Wormold "Arrestor" ARFFV.

**2001, Mar. 9 Litho. *Perf. 13¼***
**850-853** A151 Set of 4 14.50 14.50

**Souvenir Sheet**

**854** A151 $3 multi 7.75 7.75

.tv Corporation
A152

Palm fronds, satellite dish and: 40c, Woman. 60c, Dancers. 90c, Man. $1.50, Child.
$2, Map.

**2001, May 30 Litho. *Perf. 14¼x14½***
**855-858** A152 Set of 4 5.75 5.75

**Souvenir Sheet**

**859** A152 $2 multi 3.25 3.25

Souvenir Sheet

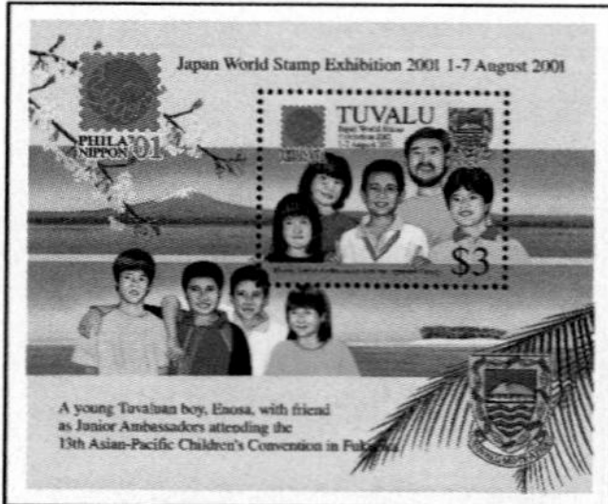


Phila Nippon '01 — A153

**2001, Aug. 1 *Perf. 13***
**860** A153 $3 multi 4.00 4.00

No. 805 Surcharged in Gold like No. 861 and Nos. 806-808 Overprinted in Gold

**Wmk. 384**

**2001, Aug. 4 Litho. *Perf. 13½***
**860A** CD358 60c multi .65 .65
**860B** CD358 90c multi .95 .95
**860C** CD358 $1.50 multi 1.60 1.60
**860D** CD358 $2 on 40c multi 2.25 2.25
*Nos. 860A-860D (4)* 5.45 5.45

No. 809 Surcharged in Gold

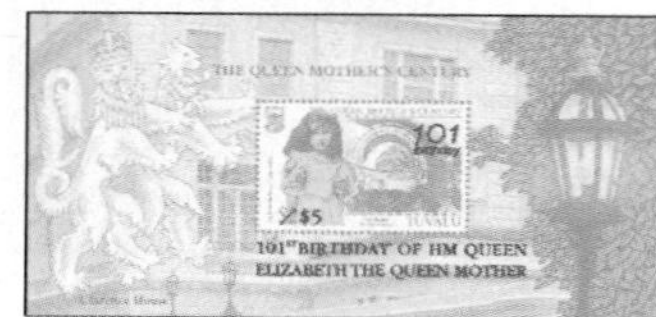


**2001, Aug. 4 Wmk. 384 *Perf. 13½***

**Souvenir Sheet**

**861** CD358 $5 on $2 multi 5.50 5.50

Fauna
A154

Designs: 25c, Mosquito. 30c, Giant African snail. 40c, Cockroach. 45c, Stick insect. 50c, Green stink bug. 55c, Dragonfly. 60c, Monarch caterpillar. 70c, Coconut beetle. 90c, Honeybee. $1, Monarch butterfly. 42, Common eggfly butterfly. $3, Painted lady butterfly.

**Unwmk.**

**2001, Oct. 31 Litho. *Perf. 13***

| | | | | |
|---|---|---|---|---|
| **862** | A154 | 25c multi | .25 | .25 |
| **863** | A154 | 30c multi | .30 | .30 |
| **864** | A154 | 40c multi | .40 | .40 |
| **865** | A154 | 45c multi | .45 | .45 |
| **866** | A154 | 50c multi | .50 | .50 |
| **867** | A154 | 55c multi | .55 | .55 |
| **868** | A154 | 60c multi | .60 | .60 |
| **869** | A154 | 70c multi | .70 | .70 |
| **870** | A154 | 90c multi | .90 | .90 |
| **871** | A154 | $1 multi | 1.00 | 1.00 |
| **872** | A154 | $2 multi | 2.00 | 2.00 |
| **873** | A154 | $3 multi | 3.00 | 3.00 |
| | | *Nos. 862-873 (12)* | 10.65 | 10.65 |

United We Stand — A155

Statue of Liberty and Tuvalu flag: No. 874, $2, Blue background. No. 875, $2, Yellow background.

**2002, Jan. 10 *Perf. 14***
**874-875** A155 Set of 2 4.25 4.25

Paintings Depicting Chapter Scenes From "The Tale of Genji" — A156

No. 876, 40c — Chapter: a, 1. b, 2. c, 3. d, 4. e, 5. f, 6.
No. 877, 60c — Chapter: a, 8, b, 9. c, 10. d, 11. e, 12. f, 13.
No. 878, 90c — Chapter: a, 15. b, 16, c, 17. d, 18. e, 19, f, 20.
No. 879, $4 — Chapter 7. No. 880, $4, Chapter 14. No. 881, $4, Chapter 21.

**2002, Apr. 24 Litho. *Perf. 14¼***

**Sheets of 6, #a-f**

**876-878** A156 Set of 3 12.50 12.50

***Imperf***

**879-881** A156 Set of 3 13.00 13.00

Nos. 876-878 each contain six 37x50mm stamps.

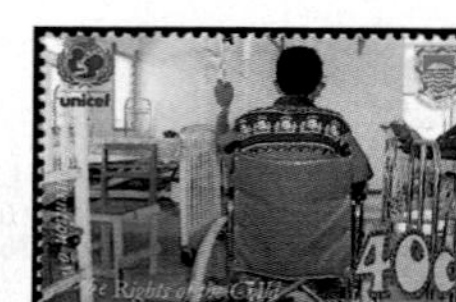


UN Special Session on Children and Convention on Rights of the Child
A157

Designs: 40c, Boy in wheelchair. 60c, Boy and girl sitting near fence. 90c, Nauti Primary School, Funafuti. $4, Mother and child.
No. 886: a, Taulosa Karl. b, Simalua Jacinta Enele.

**2002, May 8 Litho. *Perf. 13¼x13½***
**882-885** A157 Set of 4 6.50 6.50

**Souvenir Sheet**

**886** A157 $1 Sheet of 2, #a-b 2.25 2.25

Reign of Queen Elizabeth II, 50th Anniv. — A158

No. 887: a, Princes William and Harry. b, Queen in blue green suit. c, Queen and Prince Philip. d, Queen wearing red hat.
$4, Queen on horseback.

**2002, June 17 *Perf. 14¼***
**887** A158 $1.50 Sheet of 4, #a-d 6.75 6.75

**Souvenir Sheet**

**888** A158 $4 multi 4.50 4.50

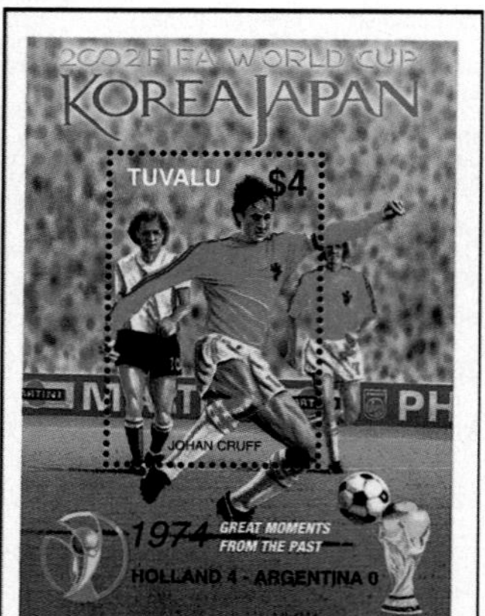


2002 World Cup Soccer Championships, Japan and Korea — A159

No. 889: a, Tom Finney. b, Poster from 1974 World Cup. c, Portuguese player and flag. d, Uruguayan player and flag. e, Suwon World Cup Stadium, Seoul (56x42mm).
$4, Johann Cruyff.

**2002, July 15 *Perf. 14***
**889** A159 90c Sheet of 5, #a-e 5.00 5.00

**Souvenir Sheet**

**890** A159 $4 multi 4.25 4.25

Queen Mother Elizabeth (1900-2002) — A160

No. 891: a, 60c, Wearing tiara (lilac shading at UL) (26x29mm). b, 60c, Wearing tiara (lilac shading at UR) (26x29mm). c, 90c, In crowd, holding bouquet of flowers (lilac shading at UL) (28x23mm). d, 90c, Receiving flowers from children (lilac shading at UR) (28x23mm). e, 90c, With teddy bear (lilac shading at UL) (28x23mm). f, With man, woman and children (lilac shading at UR) (28x23mm). g, Color photograph (40x29mm).
No. 892, $2, lilac shading at UL: a, As child, with another young girl. b, As older woman.
No. 893, $2, lilac shading at UR: a, Smelling flower. b, Wearing brooch.

***Perf. Compound x14¼ (60c), 13¼x10¾ (90c), 13¼x14¼ ($1.50)***

**2002, Aug. 12**
**891** A160 Sheet of 7, #a-g 6.75 6.75

**Souvenir Sheets**

***Perf. 14¾***

**892-893** A160 Set of 2 8.50 8.50

20th World Scout Jamboree, Thailand — A161

No. 894 — Merit badges: a, Citizenship in the World. b, First Aid. c, Personal Fitness. d, Environmental Science.
$5, Lord Robert Baden-Powell.

**2002, Oct. 2 *Perf. 14¼***
**894** A161 $1.50 Sheet of 4, #a-d 6.50 6.50

**Souvenir Sheet**

**895** A161 $5 multi 5.50 5.50

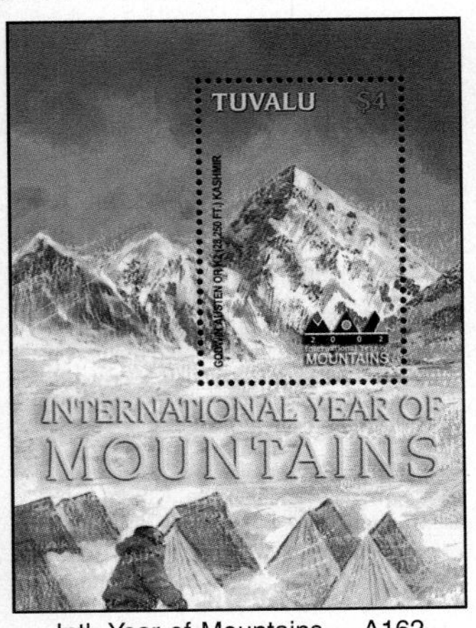


Intl. Year of Mountains — A162

No. 896, horiz.: a, Mt. Fitzroy, Chile. b, Mt. Foraker, US. c, Mt. Fuji, Japan. d, Mt. Malaku, Nepal and China.
$4, Mt. Godwin Austen, Kashmir.

**2002, Oct. 2**
**896** A162 $1.50 Sheet of 4, #a-d 6.50 6.50

**Souvenir Sheet**

**897** A162 $4 multi 4.50 4.50

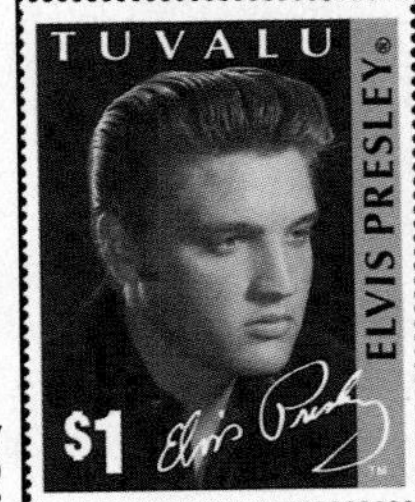


Elvis Presley (1935-77) A163

**2002, Dec. 27 Litho. *Perf. 14¼***
**898** A163 $1 multi 1.10 1.10

No. 898 was printed in sheets of 6.

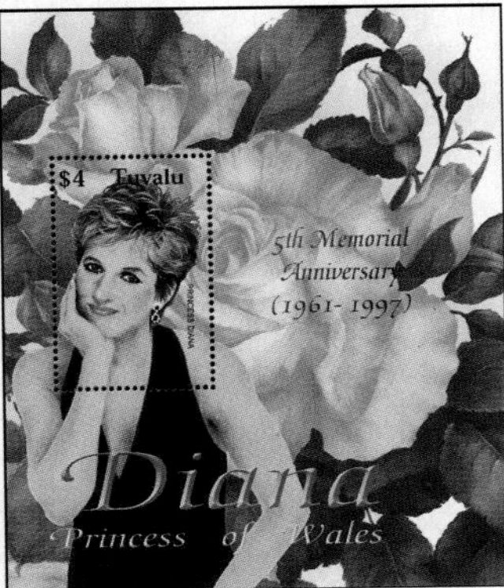


Princess Diana (1961-97) — A164

No. 899 — Diana wearing: a, Black dress, no necklace. b, Black dress, choker necklace. c, Blue dress. d, Blue green scarf. e, Pink blouse, hand at chin. f, Pink dress.
$4, Black dress, hand on chin.

**2002, Dec. 27** ***Perf. 14***
**899** A164 $1 Sheet of 6, #a-f 7.00 7.00

**Souvenir Sheet**

**900** A164 $4 multi 4.50 4.50

Year of the Horse (in 2002) — A165

Various horses: 40c, 60c, 90c, $2.
No. 905: a, Head of horse, seahorse. b, Heads of horse, three seahorses.

**2003, Jan. 23** ***Perf. 13¼***
**901-904** A165 Set of 4 4.75 4.75

**Souvenir Sheet**

**905** A165 $1.50 Sheet of 2, #a-b 3.50 3.50

New Year 2003 (Year of the Ram) — A166

No. 906: a, Green and black background. b, White background. c, Blue background.

**2003, Feb. 1** ***Perf. 14x13¾***
**906** A166 75c Vert. strip of 3, #a-c 2.75 2.75

No. 906 printed in sheets containing two strips.

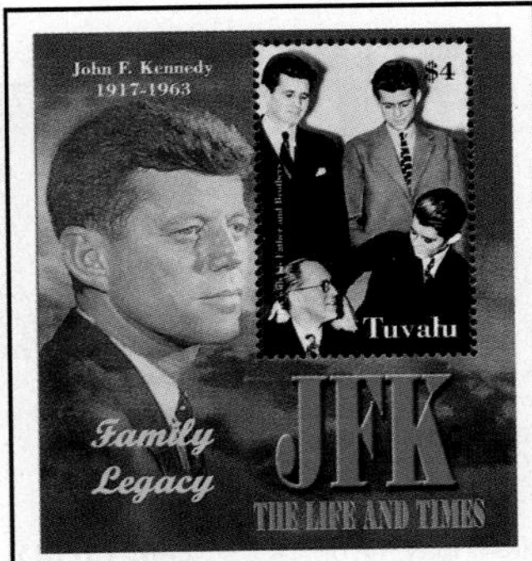


Pres. John F. Kennedy (1917-63) — A167

No. 907: a, In Solomon Islands, 1943. b, On PT 109, 1942. c, Receiving medal for gallantry, 1944. d, Campaigning for Senate, 1952.
$4, With father and brothers.

**2003, Mar. 24** ***Perf. 14***
**907** A167 $1.75 Sheet of 4, #a-d 8.50 8.50

**Souvenir Sheet**

**908** A167 $4 multi 5.00 5.00

Powered Flight, Cent. — A168

No. 909, $1.75: a, Orville Wright in early plane, 1903. b, Wilbur Wright and King Alfonso XIII of Spain, 1909. c, Wilbur Wright's plane, 1908. d, Gabriel Voisin's plane piloted by Léon Delagrange, 1907.
No. 910, $1.75: a, Voisin's motor boat powered glider, 1905. b, Trajan Vuia's single winged plane, 1906. c, Santos-Dumont's biplane, 1906. d, Orville Wright circles parade ground, 1908.
No. 911, $4, Wright Brothers biplane in flight, 1908. No. 912, $4, Glenn Curtiss pilots June Bug, 1908.

**2003, May 19 Litho. *Perf. 14***

**Sheets of 4, #a-d**

**909-910** A168 Set of 2 19.00 19.00

**Souvenir Sheets**

**911-912** A168 Set of 2 10.50 10.50

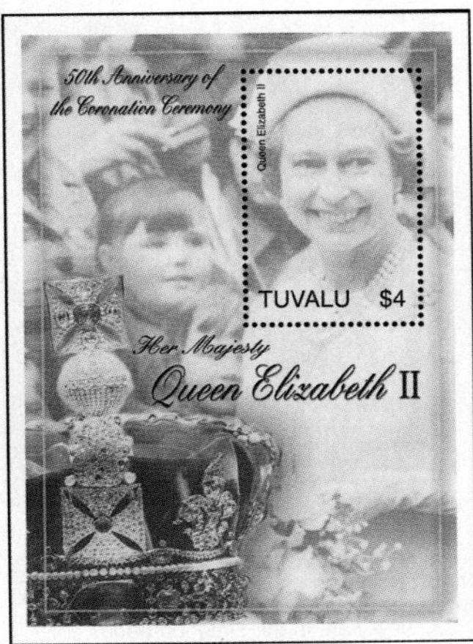


Coronation of Queen Elizabeth II, 50th Anniv. — A169

No. 913: a, Wearing gray dress. b, Wearing tiara. c, Wearing yellow hat.
$4, Wearing hat and pearl necklace.

**2003, Aug. 11**
**913** A169 $2 Sheet of 3, #a-c 8.00 8.00

**Souvenir Sheet**

**914** A169 $4 multi 5.25 5.25

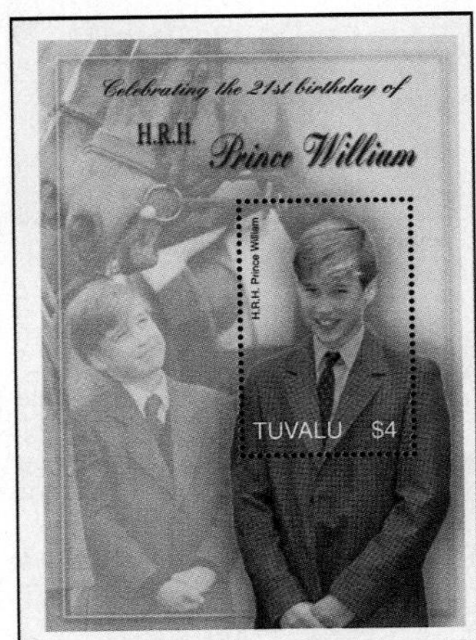


Prince William, 21st Birthday — A170

No. 915: a, Wearing school cap. b, Wearing blue shirt. c, Wearing polo helmet.
$4, Wearing suit and tie.

**2003, Aug. 11**
**915** A170 $1.50 Sheet of 3, #a-c 6.00 6.00

**Souvenir Sheet**

**916** A170 $4 multi 5.25 5.25

General Motors Automobiles — A171

No. 917, $1 — Corvettes: a, Yellow 1979. b, Red 1979. c, Silver 1979. d, 1980.
No. 918, $1.50 — Cadillacs: a, 1931 V-16 Sport Phaeton. b, 1959 Eldorado convertible. c, 1979 Seville Elegante. d, 1983 Seville Elegante.
No. 919, $4, 1990 Corvette. No. 920, $4, 1954 Cadillac Coupe de Ville.

**2003, Sept. 8** ***Perf. 13¾***

**Sheets of 4, #a-d**

**917-918** A171 Set of 2 13.50 13.50

**Souvenir Sheets**

**919-920** A171 Set of 2 10.50 10.50

Corvettes, 50th anniv.; Cadillacs, 100th anniv.

Tour de France Bicycle Race, Cent. — A172

No. 921: a, Gastone Nencini, 1960. b, Jacques Anquetil, 1961. c, Anquetil, 1962. d, Anquetil, 1963.
$4, Jan Janssen, 1968.

**2003, Oct. 6** ***Perf. 13¾x13¼***
**921** A172 $1 Sheet of 4, #a-d 5.50 5.50

**Souvenir Sheet**

**922** A172 $4 multi 5.50 5.50

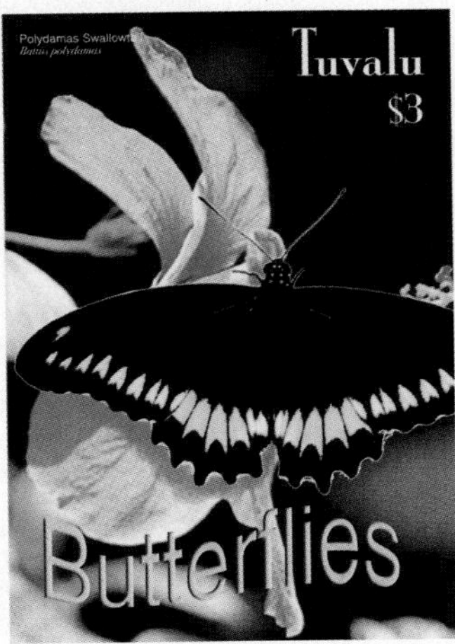


Butterflies — A173

No. 923, horiz.: a, Malachite. b, White M hairstreak. c, Giant swallowtail. d, Bahamian swallowtail.
$3, Polydamas swallowtail.

**2003, Dec. 16** ***Perf. 14***
**923** A173 $1.25 Sheet of 4, #a-d 7.75 7.75

***Imperf***

**924** A173 $3 multi 4.50 4.50

No. 923 contains four 42x28mm stamps.

Flowers — A174

No. 925: a, Rhododendron. b, Golden Artist tulip. c, Golden Splendor lily. d, Flamingo flower.
$3, Candy Bianca rose.

**2003, Dec. 16** ***Perf. 14***
**925** A174 $1.25 Sheet of 4, #a-d 7.75 7.75

***Imperf***

**926** A174 $3 multi 4.50 4.50

No. 925 contains four 28x42mm stamps.

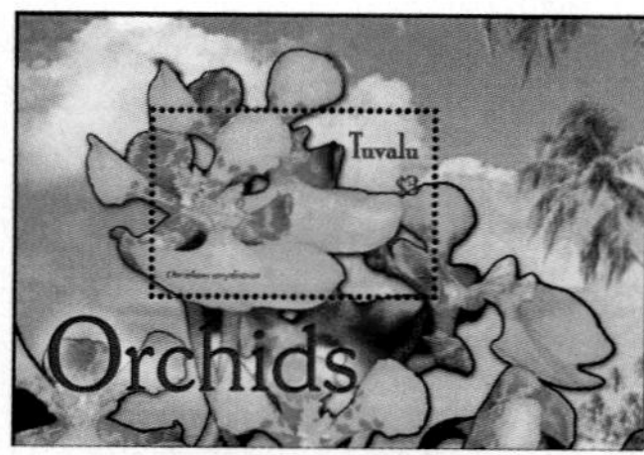

Orchids — A175

No. 927, vert.: a, Dimerandra emarginata. b, Oncidium lanceanum. c, Isochilus linearis. d, Oeceoclades maculata.
$3, Oncidium ampliatum.

**2003, Dec. 16** ***Perf. 14***
**927** A175 $1.25 Sheet of 4, #a-d 7.75 7.75

**Souvenir Sheet**

**928** A175 $3 multi 4.50 4.50

Birds — A176

No. 929: a, Blue-gray gnatcatcher. b, White-eyed vireo. c, Clapper rail. d, Sandhill crane.
$3, Grasshopper sparrow.

**2003, Dec. 16**
**929** A176 $1.25 Sheet of 4, #a-d 7.75 7.75

**Souvenir Sheet**

**930** A176 $3 multi 4.50 4.50

New Year 2004 (Year of the Monkey) A177

Paintings by Chang Dai-chen: 75c, Monkey and Old Tree. $1.50, Two Monkeys.

**2004, Jan. 4** ***Perf. 13½***
**931** A177 75c multi 1.25 1.25

**Souvenir Sheet**

**932** A177 $1.50 multi 2.40 2.40

No. 931 printed in sheets of 4.

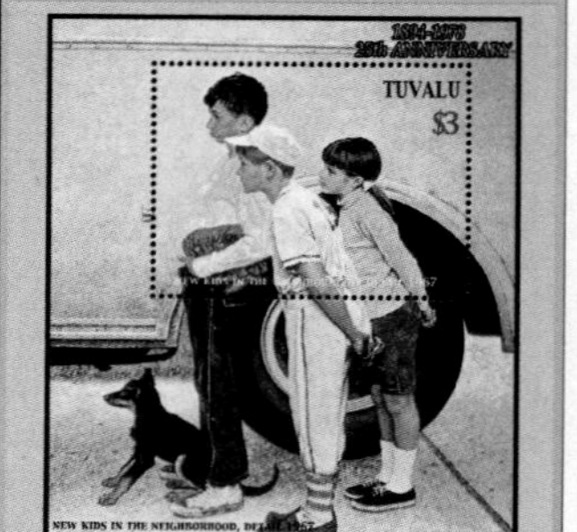

Paintings by Norman Rockwell — A178

No. 933, vert.: a, 100th Year of Baseball. b, The Locker Room (The Rookie). c, The Dugout. d, Game Called Because of Rain.
$3, New Kids in the Neighborhood.

**2004, Jan. 30** ***Perf. 14¼***
**933** A178 $1.25 Sheet of 4, #a-d 7.75 7.75

**Souvenir Sheet**

**934** A178 $3 multi 4.75 4.75

2004 AmeriStamp Expo, Norfolk, Va. (#933).

Paintings by Pablo Picasso (1881-1973) — A179

No. 935, vert.: a, Seated Woman. b, Woman in Armchair. c, Bust of Françoise. d, Head of a Woman.
$4, Françoise Gilot with Paloma and Claude.

**2004, Mar. 1** **Litho.** ***Perf. 14¼***
**935** A179 $1.50 Sheet of 4, #a-d 9.25 9.25

***Imperf***

**936** A179 $4 multi 6.25 6.25

No. 935 contains four 37x50mm stamps.

Paintings by Paul Gauguin (1848-1903) A180

Designs: 50c, Les Seins aux Fleurs Rouges. 60c, Famille Tahitienne. No. 939, $1, Tahitiennes sur la Plage. $2, Jeune Fille à L'Eventail.

No. 941, $1: a, Nafea Faa Ipoipo. b, Le Cheval Blanc. c, Pape Moe. d, Contes Barbares.
$4, Femmes de Tahiti, horiz.

**2004, Mar. 1** ***Perf. 14¼***
**937-940** A180 Set of 4 6.25 6.25
**941** A180 $1 Sheet of 4, #a-d 6.25 6.25

***Imperf***

**Size: 93x73mm**

**942** A180 $4 multi 6.25 6.25

Paintings in the Hermitage, St. Petersburg, Russia A181

Designs: 50c, Philadelphia and Elizabeth Wharton, by Anthony Van Dyck. 80c, A Glass of Lemonade, by Gerard Terborch. $1, A Mistress and Her Servant, by Pieter de Hooch. $1.20, Portrait of a Man and His Three Sons, by Bartholomaeus Bruyn the Elder.
$4, The Milkmaid's Family, by Louis le Nain, horiz.

**2004, Mar. 1** ***Perf. 14¼***
**943-946** A181 Set of 4 5.50 5.50

***Imperf***

**Size: 80x68mm**

**947** A181 $4 multi 6.25 6.25

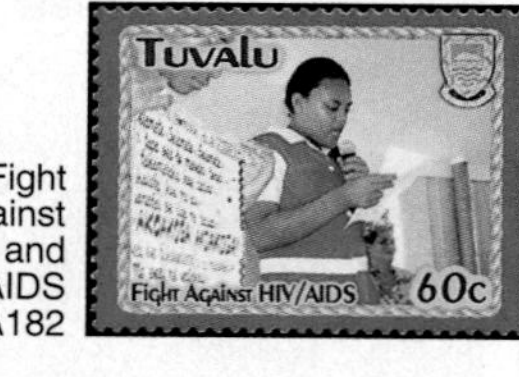

Fight Against HIV and AIDS A182

Designs: 60c, Speaker at conference. 90c, Speaker and dais. $1.50, People standing in front of banner. $2, People seated at dais.
$3, Conference participants.

**2004, May 17** ***Perf. 13x13½***
**948-951** A182 Set of 4 7.00 7.00

**Souvenir Sheet**

**952** A182 $3 multi 4.25 4.25

**Souvenir Sheet**

Inauguration of Republic of China President Chen Shui-bian — A183

No. 953: a, Pres. Chen Shui-bian. b, Saufatu Sopoanga, Prime Minister of Tuvalu.

**2004, May 20** ***Perf. 13½x13¼***
**953** A183 $2 Sheet of 2, #a-b 5.50 5.50

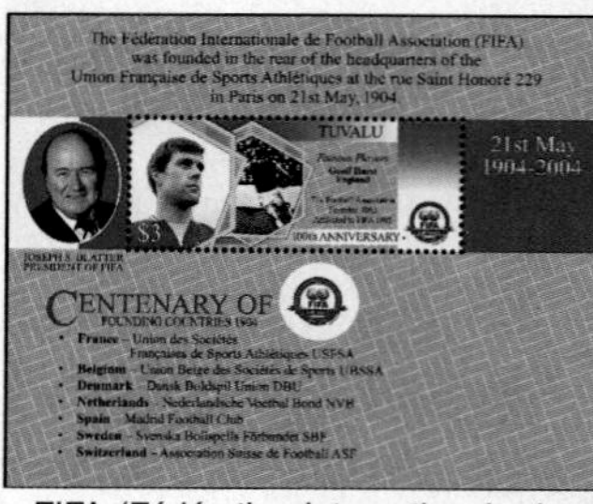

FIFA (Fédération Internationale de Football Association), Cent. — A184

No. 954: a, Sebastiano Rossi. b, Clarence Seedorf. c, Zico. d, Jack Charlton.
$3, Geoff Hurst.

***Perf. 12¾x12½***

**2004, Nov. 29** **Litho.**
**954** A184 $1 Sheet of 4, #a-d 6.25 6.25

**Souvenir Sheet**

**955** A184 $3 multi 4.75 4.75

**Miniature Sheet**

World Peace — A185

No. 956: a, Alfred Nobel. b, Doves. c, Nelson Mandela.

**2005, Jan. 14** ***Perf. 12¾***
**956** A185 $1.50 Sheet of 3, #a-c 7.00 7.00

**Miniature Sheet**

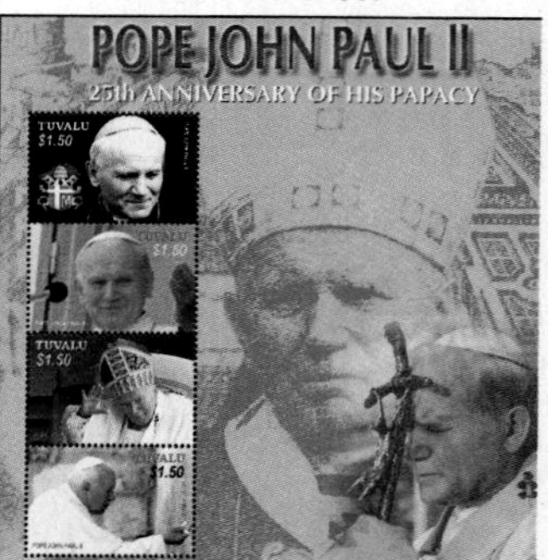

Election of Pope John Paul II, 25th Anniv. (in 2003) — A186

No. 957: a, With papal arms. b, At microphone. c, Wearing miter. d, Placing prayer in Wailing Wall, Jerusalem.

**2005, Jan. 14**
**957** A186 $1.50 Sheet of 4, #a-d 9.25 9.25

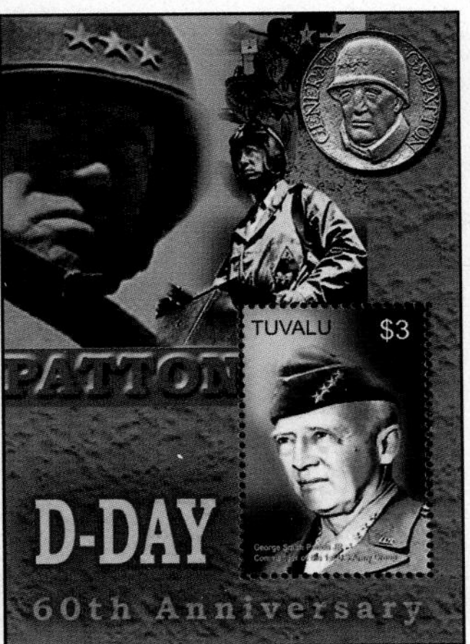


D-Day, 60th Anniv. (in 2004) — A187

No. 958: a, Gen. George C. Marshall. b, Adm. Sir Ramsay Bertram Home. c, Gen. Walter Bedell Smith. d, Field Marshal Alan Francis Brooke.
$3, Gen. George S. Patton.

**2005, Jan. 14**
**958** A187 $1.50 Sheet of 4, #a-d 9.25 9.25

**Souvenir Sheet**

**959** A187 $3 multi 4.75 4.75

Dogs — A188

Designs: 20c, Rat terrier. 75c, Large Spanish hound. $1, Lundehund. $2, Beagle harrier. $3, Old Danish pointer.

**2005, Apr. 26 Litho.** ***Perf. 13¾x13¼***
**960-963** A188 Set of 4 6.25 6.25

**Souvenir Sheet**

**964** A188 $3 multi 4.75 4.75

Marine Life — A189

No. 965: a, Striped-face unicornfish. b, Great barracuda. c, Blue-ringed octopus. d, Giant clam.
$3, Humpback whale.

**2005, Apr. 26** ***Perf. 13¼x13¾***
**965** A189 $1 Sheet of 4, #a-d 6.25 6.25

**Souvenir Sheet**

**966** A189 $3 multi 4.75 4.75

Medicinal Plants — A190

No. 967: a, Common toadflax. b, Pomegranate. c, Black horehound. d, Agnus castus
$3, Black henbane.

**2005, Apr. 26** ***Perf. 13¾x13¼***
**967** A190 $1 Sheet of 4, #a-d 6.25 6.25

**Souvenir Sheet**

**968** A190 $3 multi 4.75 4.75

Insects — A191

No. 969, vert.: a, Louse fly. b, Predacious dung beetle. c, Ladybug. d, Mosquito.
$3, House fly.

**2005, Apr. 26** ***Perf. 13¾x13¼***
**969** A191 $1 Sheet of 4, #a-d 6.25 6.25

**Souvenir Sheet**
***Perf. 13¼x13¾***

**970** A191 $3 multi 4.75 4.75

Pope John Paul II (1920-2005) and Queen Elizabeth II — A192

**2005, July 12** ***Perf. 13½***
**971** A192 $4 multi 6.25 6.25

Battle of Trafalgar, Bicent. — A193

No. 972: a, HMS Victory collides with French ship Redoubtable. b, Admiral Horatio Nelson. c, HMS Victory leads the British fleet. d, Nelson breaths his last breath.
$3, Admiral Cuthbert Collingwood.

**2005, July 28** ***Perf. 12***
**972** A193 $1.50 Sheet of 4, #a-d 9.25 9.25

**Souvenir Sheet**

**973** A193 $3 multi 4.75 4.75

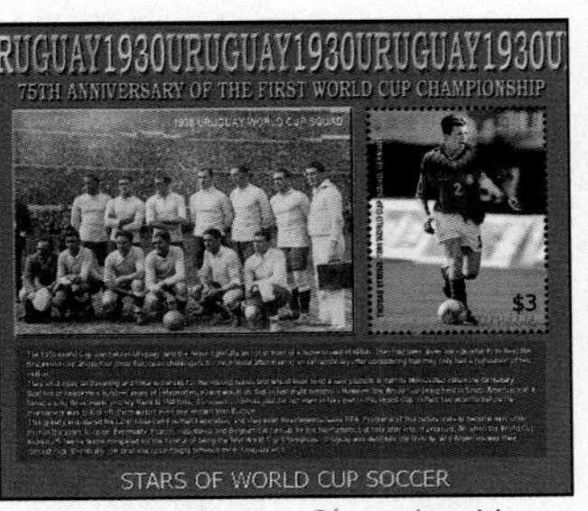


World Cup Soccer Championships, 75th Anniv. — A194

No. 974: a, Thomas Berthold. b, Bobby Charlton. c, Klaus Augenthaler.
$3, Thomas Strunz.

**2005, July 28** ***Perf. 13¼***
**974** A194 $2 Sheet of 3, #a-c 9.25 9.25

**Souvenir Sheet**
***Perf. 12***

**975** A194 $3 multi 4.75 4.75

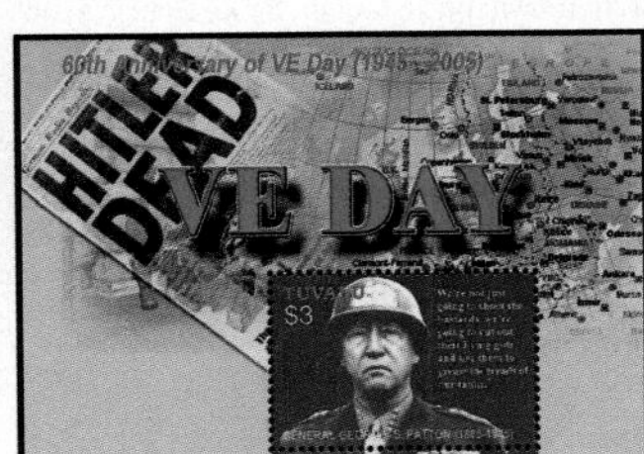


End of World War II, 60th Anniv. — A195

No. 976, $2: a, Sir Winston Churchill. b, Gen. Charles de Gaulle. c, Newspaper report on death of Adolf Hitler.
No. 977, $2: a, Pres. Harry S. Truman. b, Newspaper report on end of war. c, Gen. Dwight D. Eisenhower.
No. 978, $3, Gen. George S. Patton. No. 979, $3, Brig. Gen. Paul W. Tibbets, Jr. and Enola Gay.

**2005, Sept. 21** ***Perf. 12¾***

**Sheets of 3, #a-c**

**976-977** A195 Set of 2 18.50 18.50

**Souvenir Sheets**

**978-979** A195 Set of 2 9.25 9.25

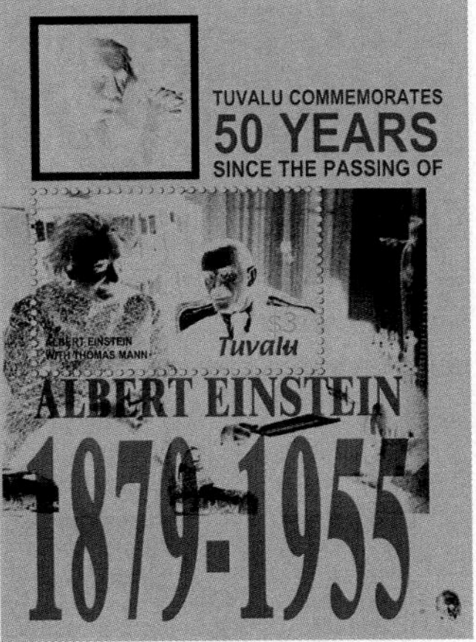


Albert Einstein (1879-1955), Physicist — A196

No. 981 — Einstein and: a, Hendrik Lorentz. b, Fritz Haber. c, David Ben-Gurion.
$3, Einstein with Thomas Mann.

**2005, Sept. 21**
**980** A196 $2 Sheet of 3, #a-c 9.25 9.25

**Souvenir Sheet**

**981** A196 $3 multi 4.50 4.50

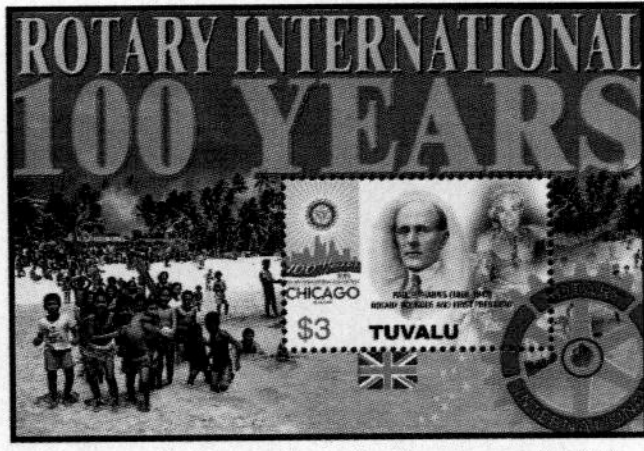


Rotary International, Cent. — A197

No. 982: a, Child. b, Hand holding pills. c, Children.
$3, Paul P. Harris, founder.

**2005, Nov. 28**
**982** A197 $2 Sheet of 3, #a-c 9.25 9.25

**Souvenir Sheet**

**983** A197 $3 multi 4.50 4.50

Hans Christian Andersen (1805-75), Author — A198

No. 984: a, Andersen seated. b, Sculpture of Andersen. c, Head of Andersen.
$3, Statue of Andersen.

**2005, Nov. 28**
**984** A198 $2 Sheet of 3, #a-c 9.25 9.25

**Souvenir Sheet**

**985** A198 $3 multi 4.50 4.50

A199

Elvis Presley (1935-77) — A200

No. 987 — Presley and: a, Gable and top of column of house. b, Roofline of house. c, Bottom of column of house. d, Archway of house.

**2006, Jan. 30** ***Perf. 13½***

| | | | | |
|---|---|---|---|---|
| **986** | A199 | $3 multi | 4.50 | 4.50 |
| **987** | A200 | $3 Sheet of 4, #a-d | 18.00 | 18.00 |

No. 986 printed in sheets of 4.

National Basketball Association Players and Team Emblems — A201

No. 988, 35c: a, Emblem of Detroit Pistons. b, Chauncey Billups.

No. 989, 35c: a, Emblem of New Jersey Nets. b, Rodney Buford.

No. 990, 35c: a, Emblem of Boston Celtics. b, Ricky Davis.

No. 991, 35c: a, Emblem of Miami Heat. b, Udonis Haslem

No. 992, 35c: a, Emblem of Indiana Pacers, horiz. b, Stephen Jackson.

No. 993, 35c: a, Emblem of Minnesota Timberwolves. b, Wally Szczerbiak.

**2006, Jan. 30** ***Perf. 13¼***

**Sheets of 12, 2 #a, 10 #b**

| | | | | |
|---|---|---|---|---|
| **988-993** | A201 | Set of 6 | 37.50 | 37.50 |

Souvenir Sheet

2006 World Cup Soccer Championships, Germany — A202

No. 994 — Player and uniform for: a, 90c, Spain. b, $1, South Korea. c, $1.50, France. d, $2, United States.

**2006, June 9** **Litho.** ***Perf. 13¼***

| | | | | |
|---|---|---|---|---|
| **994** | A202 | Sheet of 4, #a-d | 8.25 | 8.25 |

Corals A203

Designs: 10c, Montipora aequituberculata. 25c, Montipora capricornis. 30c, Montipora verrucosa. 40c, Acropora caroliniana. 50c, Acropora aculeus. 60c, Acropora anthocercis. 65c, Acropora granulosa. 80c, Acropora rosaria. 90c, Acropora cerealis. $1, Acropora yongei. $2, Acropora echinata. $5, Astreopora myriophthalma.

**2006, Oct. 12** ***Perf. 12¾***

| | | | | |
|---|---|---|---|---|
| **995** | A203 | 10c multi | .20 | .20 |
| **996** | A203 | 25c multi | .40 | .40 |
| **997** | A203 | 30c multi | .45 | .45 |
| **998** | A203 | 40c multi | .60 | .60 |
| **999** | A203 | 50c multi | .75 | .75 |
| **1000** | A203 | 60c multi | .90 | .90 |
| **1001** | A203 | 65c multi | 1.00 | 1.00 |
| **1002** | A203 | 80c multi | 1.25 | 1.25 |
| **1003** | A203 | 90c multi | 1.40 | 1.40 |
| **1004** | A203 | $1 multi | 1.50 | 1.50 |
| **1005** | A203 | $2 multi | 3.00 | 3.00 |
| **1006** | A203 | $5 multi | 7.50 | 7.50 |
| | *Nos. 995-1006 (12)* | | 18.95 | 18.95 |

Miniature Sheets

Pres. John F. Kennedy (1917-63) — A204

No. 1007, $1.30: a, On PT109, 1942. b, Receiving medal for gallantry, 1944. c, Portrait with brown background. d, In Ensign's uniform, 1941.

No. 1008, $1.30: a, Wearing bow tie. b, Wearing tan suit. c, With Eleanor Roosevelt. d, Portrait and U.S. Capitol.

**2006, Sept. 21** **Litho.** ***Perf. 13½***

**Sheets of 4, #a-d**

| | | | | |
|---|---|---|---|---|
| **1007-1008** | A204 | Set of 2 | 15.50 | 15.50 |

Queen Elizabeth II, 80th Birthday — A205

No. 1009: a, As child holding dog. b, Wearing crown and holding scepter. c, Wearing jacket. d, Wearing sash and tiara.

$3, Wearing crown.

**2006, Sept. 21**

| | | | | |
|---|---|---|---|---|
| **1009** | A205 | $1.30 Sheet of 4, #a-d | 7.75 | 7.75 |

**Souvenir Sheet**

| | | | | |
|---|---|---|---|---|
| **1010** | A205 | $3 multi | 4.50 | 4.50 |

Space Achievements — A206

No. 1011 — Space Shuttle Discovery's return to space: a, Nose of Shuttle, open cargo doors, text in white reading down. b, Tail of Shuttle, stars, Earth, text in red reading across. c, Tail and wings of Shuttle, open cargo doors, text in red reading down. d, Astronaut on robotic arm. e, Head-on view of Shuttle nose, text in red reading across. f, Robotic arm, text in red and white.

No. 1012 — International Space Station: a, Top of rocket boosters. b, Space Station, text in white reading across. c, Space Shuttle. d, Space Station, text in white reading up.

$3, Calipso Satellite.

**2006**

| | | | | |
|---|---|---|---|---|
| **1011** | A206 | $1 Sheet of 6, #a-f | 9.50 | 9.50 |
| **1012** | A206 | $1.30 Sheet of 4, #a-d | 7.75 | 7.75 |

**Souvenir Sheet**

| | | | | |
|---|---|---|---|---|
| **1013** | A206 | $3 multi | 4.50 | 4.50 |

Issued: No. 1011, 12/21; Nos. 1012-1013, 9/21.

Miniature Sheet

Wolfgang Amadeus Mozart (1756-91), Composer — A207

No. 1014: a, Mozart gazing out window. b, Mozart family, 1780. c, Mozart, 1763. d, Art deco illustration of the young Mozart.

**2006, Oct. 26**

| | | | | |
|---|---|---|---|---|
| **1014** | A207 | $1.30 Sheet of 4, #a-d | 8.00 | 8.00 |

Rembrandt (1606-69), Painter A208

Designs: 10c, Woman in Bed. 20c, The Flight into Egypt. 35c, The Suicide of Lucretia. 95c, Esther Preparing to Intercede with Ahasuerus. $1, Rembrandt's Mother. $2, Child with Dead Peacock.

$3, The Abduction of Ganymede.

**2006, Nov. 9** ***Perf. 14¼***

| | | | | |
|---|---|---|---|---|
| **1015-1020** | A208 | Set of 6 | 7.25 | 7.25 |

***Imperf***

**Size: 76x106mm**

| | | | | |
|---|---|---|---|---|
| **1021** | A208 | $3 multi | 4.75 | 4.75 |

Worldwide Fund for Nature (WWF) — A209

Various Pygmy killer whales.

**2006, Nov. 9** ***Perf. 13½***

| | | | |
|---|---|---|---|
| **1022** | Horiz. strip of 4 | 11.00 | 11.00 |
| *a.* | A209 40c Four whales | .65 | .65 |
| *b.* | A209 60c Two whales | .95 | .95 |
| *c.* | A209 90c Four whales, diff. | 1.40 | 1.40 |
| *d.* | A209 $5 Two whales, diff. | 8.00 | 8.00 |
| *e.* | Miniature sheet, 2 each #1022a-1022d | 22.00 | 22.00 |

Butterflies — A210

No. 1023: a, Tailed jay. b, Ixias undatus. c, Hebomoia leucippe detanii. d, Rajah Brooke's birdwing.

$3, Painted lady.

**2006, Nov. 23**

| | | | | |
|---|---|---|---|---|
| **1023** | A210 | $1 Sheet of 4, #a-d | 6.50 | 6.50 |

**Souvenir Sheet**

| | | | | |
|---|---|---|---|---|
| **1024** | A210 | $3 multi | 4.75 | 4.75 |

Birds — A211

No. 1025: a, Reed warbler. b, Indian pitta. c, Gurney's pitta. d, Northern shrike.

$3, Black-backed fairy wren.

**2006, Nov. 23**

| | | | | |
|---|---|---|---|---|
| **1025** | A211 | $1 Sheet of 4, #a-d | 6.50 | 6.50 |

**Souvenir Sheet**

| | | | | |
|---|---|---|---|---|
| **1026** | A211 | $3 multi | 4.75 | 4.75 |

## SEMI-POSTAL STAMPS

Nos. 159-160 Surcharged and Overprinted: "TONGA CYCLONE / RELIEF / 1982" in 1 or 3 Lines

**Wmk. 380**

**1982, May 20 Litho. *Perf. 14***

**B1** A25a 45c + 20c multi .45 .45
**B2** A25b 45c + 20c multi .45 .45

## POSTAGE DUE STAMPS

Arms of Tuvalu — D1

**1981, May 13 Litho. *Perf. 14***

**J1** D1 1c brt rose lil & blk .30 .30
**J2** D1 2c grnsh bl & blk .30 .30
**J3** D1 5c yellow brn & blk .30 .30
**J4** D1 10c blue grn & blk .30 .30
**J5** D1 20c chocolate & blk .30 .30
**J6** D1 30c orange & blk .30 .30
**J7** D1 40c ultra & blk .30 .30
**J8** D1 50c yellow grn & blk .40 .40
**J9** D1 $1 brt lilac & blk .65 .65
*Nos. J1-J9 (9)* 3.15 3.15

**1982-83 *Perf. 14x15***

*J1a* D1 1c bright rose lilac & black .20 .20
*J2a* D1 2c greenish blue & black .20 .20
*J3a* D1 5c yellow brown & black .20 .20
*J4a* D1 10c blue green & black .20 .20
*J5a* D1 20c chocolate & black .25 .25
*J6a* D1 30c orange & black .40 .30
*J7a* D1 40c ultra & black .50 .35
*J8a* D1 50c yellow green & black .60 .45
*J9a* D1 $1 bright lilac & black .95 .65
*Nos. J1a-J9a (9)* 3.50 2.80

Issued: 1c-20c, 11/25/82 (inscribed "1982"); 30c-$1, 5/25/83 (inscribed "1983").

## OFFICIAL STAMPS

Nos. 96-113 Overprinted: "OFFICIAL"

**1981 Litho. Unwmk. *Perf. 14***

**O1** A14 1c multicolored .25 .25
**O2** A14 2c multicolored .25 .25
**O3** A14 4c multicolored .25 .25
**O4** A14 5c multicolored .25 .25
**O5** A14 6c multicolored .25 .25
**O6** A14 8c multicolored .25 .25
**O7** A14 10c multicolored .25 .25
**O8** A14 15c multicolored .25 .25
**O9** A14 20c multicolored .25 .25
**O10** A14 25c multicolored .30 .30
**O11** A14 30c multicolored .35 .35
**O12** A14 35c multicolored .40 .40
**O13** A14 40c multicolored .50 .50
**O14** A14 45c multicolored .55 .55
**O15** A14 50c multicolored .60 .60
**O16** A14 70c multicolored .80 .80
**O17** A14 $1 multicolored 1.10 1.10
**O18** A14 $2 multicolored 2.40 2.40
**O19** A14 $5 multicolored 5.75 5.75
*Nos. O1-O19 (19)* 15.00 15.00

No. 193 Surcharged and Overprinted "OFFICIAL"

**Wmk. 380**

**1983, Aug. Litho. *Perf. 14***

**O20** A30 60c on $1 multi .75 .75

Nos. 185-186A, 188, 230, 188A-195 Overprinted: "OFFICIAL"

**1984 Litho. Wmk. 380 *Perf. 14***

**O21** A30 5c multicolored .20 *.35*
**O22** A30 10c multicolored .20 *.35*
**O23** A30 15c multicolored .20 *.65*
**O24** A30 25c multicolored .30 *.55*
**O25** A30 30c on 45c multi .65 .65
**O25A** A30 30c multicolored .40 *.65*
**O26** A30 35c multicolored .50 *.70*
**O27** A30 40c multicolored .55 *.70*
**O28** A30 45c multicolored .65 *.70*
**O29** A30 50c multicolored .65 *.65*
**O29A** A30 60c multicolored .75 *.90*
**O30** A30 $1 multicolored .95 .90
**O31** A30 $2 multicolored 1.50 1.00
**O32** A30 $5 multicolored 3.50 2.25
*Nos. O21-O32 (14)* 11.00 11.00

Issued: #O23, O29A, Apr. 30; others Feb. 1.

Nos. 469-484 Overprinted "OFFICIAL"

**1989, Feb. 22 Litho. *Perf. 15***

**O33** A64 5c multicolored .20 .20
**O34** A64 10c multicolored .20 .20
**O35** A64 15c multicolored .20 .20
**O36** A64 20c multicolored .25 .25
**O37** A64 25c multicolored .30 .30
**O38** A64 30c multicolored .40 .40
**O39** A64 35c multicolored .45 .45
**O40** A64 40c multicolored .50 .50
**O41** A64 45c multicolored .60 .60
**O42** A64 50c multicolored .65 .65
**O43** A64 55c multicolored .70 .70
**O44** A64 60c multicolored .75 .75
**O45** A64 70c multicolored .90 .90
**O46** A64 $1 multicolored 1.25 1.25
**O47** A64 $2 multicolored 2.50 2.50
**O48** A64 $5 multicolored 6.50 6.50
*Nos. O33-O48 (16)* 16.35 16.35

**For the following islands all are types of Tuvalu unless otherwise specified.**
**See note following Tuvalu No. 221.**

**Leaders of the World**
**Large quantities of some Leaders of the World sets, including unissued stamps, were sold at a fraction of face value when the printer was liquidated.**

## FUNAFUTI

**Catalogue values for all unused stamps in this country are for Never Hinged items.**

### Locomotive Type of 1984

***Perf. 12½x13***

**1984-86 Litho. Unwmk.**

**Se-tenant Pairs, #a.-b.**
**a. — Side and front views.**
**b. — Action scene.**

1 5c 1919 Class C51, Japan .50 .50
2 5c 1935 F.C.C. Andes Class, Peru .50 .50
3 15c 1934 Kolhapur Class, UK .50 .50
4 15c 1941 V.R. Class H, Australia .50 .50
5 15c 1885 S.A.R. Class Y, Australia .50 .50
6 20c 1951 Class 4, UK .50 .50
7 20c 1928 Class U, UK .50 .50
8 25c 1923 Eryri Cog, UK .60 .60
9 30c 1927 Royal Scot Class, UK .80 .80
10 35c 1828 Lancashire Witch, UK .90 .90
11 35c 1906 NY, NH & H RR Class EP-1, US .90 .90
12 40c 1942 Springbok Class B1, UK 1.00 1.00
13 40c 1827 Royal George, UK 1.00 1.00
14 40c 1926 Northern Pacific Class A5, US 1.00 1.00
15 40c 1900 Aberdare Class 2600, UK 1.00 1.00
16 50c 1829 Sans Pareil, UK 1.40 1.40
17 50c 1924 EST Class 241A, France 1.40 1.40
18 55c 1911 Class 8K, UK 1.50 1.50
19 60c 1913 Sir Gilbert Claughton, UK 1.75 1.75
20 60c 1920 Sherlock Holmes, UK 1.75 1.75
21 60c 1949 Class K1, UK 1.75 1.75
22 $1 1925 Class P1, UK 2.75 2.75
23 $1 1940 SNCF Class 232R, France 2.75 2.75
24 $1.50 1904 B&O Class DD-1 4.25 4.25
*Nos. 1-24 (24)* 30.00 30.00

Issued: #3, 6, 9, 12, 16, 19, 4/16/84; 1, 4, 8, 10, 13, 18, 20, 22, 12/24/84; 2, 5, 11, 14, 17, 23, 4/29/85; 7, 15, 21, 24, 12/30/86.
1986 stamps not inscribed "Leaders of the World."

### Automobile Type of 1984

**1984-87**

**Se-tenant Pairs, #a.-b.**
**a. — Side and front views.**
**b. — Action scene.**
**Design A41**

25 1c 1957 Triumph TR3A, UK .20 .20
26 1c 1932 Nash Special 8 Convertible, US .20 .20
27 10c 1937 Cord 812 Supercharged, US .20 .20
28 10c 1925 AC Six, UK .20 .20
29 20c 1924 Alfa Romeo P2, Italy .40 .40
30 30c 1935 Aston Martin Ulster, UK .60 .60
31 40c 1948 Morgan 4+4, UK .85 .85
32 40c 1906 Renault GP, France .85 .85
33 55c 1903 Cadillac Model A 1.10 1.10
34 60c 1971 Porsche 917K, Germany 1.25 1.25
35 60c 1913 Simplex 75HP, US 1.25 1.25
36 75c 1939 Delahaye Type 165, France 1.50 1.50
37 80c 1938 Opel Admiral, Germany 1.60 1.60
38 $1 1936 Jaguar SS 100, UK 2.00 2.00
39 $1 1965 Aston Martin DB5, UK 2.00 2.00
40 $1.50 1977 Porsche 935 3.25 3.25
*Nos. 25-40 (16)* 17.45 17.45

Issued: #25, 27, 31, 38, 9/13/84; 26, 30, 33, 34, 2/8/85; 28-29, 32, 35-37, 39-40, 8/27/87.
1987 stamps not inscribed "Leaders of the World."

### Queen Mother Type of 1985

Hats: #45a, Blue feathered. #45b, White. #46a, 50a, Pink. #46b, 50b, Tiara. #47a, 51a, Blue. #47b, 51b, Blue with veil covering face. #48a, Blue. #48b, Tiara. #49a, Headband. #49b, Hat.

**1985-86 *Perf. 13x12½***

**45** A45 5c Pair, #a.-b. .45 .45
**46** A45 25c Pair, #a.-b. .70 .70
**47** A45 80c Pair, #a.-b. 2.10 2.10
**48** A45 $1.05 Pair, #a.-b. 2.50 2.50
*Nos. 45-48 (4)* 5.75 5.75

**Souvenir Sheets of 2**

**49** A45 $1.05 #a.-b. 3.50 3.50
**50** A45 $2 #a.-b. 3.75 3.75
**51** A45 $3 #a.-b. 5.75 5.75

Issued: #45-49, 8/26; #50-51, 1/3/86.

### Elizabeth II 60th Birthday Type

**1986, Apr. 21 *Perf. 13x12½, 12½x13***

**52** A49 10c Trooping the colors .20 .20
**53** A49 50c Tiara .55 .55
**54** A49 $1.50 As young woman, 1952 1.75 1.75
**55** A49 $3.50 Tiara, diff., vert. 3.75 3.75
*Nos. 52-55 (4)* 6.25 6.25

**Souvenir Sheet**

**56** A49 $5 Scarf 6.25 6.25

### Royal Wedding Type of 1986

#59a, Andrew holding rifle, vert. #59b, Sarah Ferguson, vert. #60a, Couple. #60b, Prince Philip and Andrew.

**1986, July 23**

**59** A53 60c Pair, #a.-b. 1.25 1.25
**60** A53 $1 Pair, #a.-b. 2.00 2.00

**Souvenir Sheet**

**61** A56 $4 Newlyweds 5.25 5.25

Nos. 59-60 Ovptd. in Silver "Congratulations to T.R.H. The Duke & Duchess of York"

**1986, July 23**

**62** A53 60c Pair, #a.-b. 1.40 1.40
**63** A53 $1 Pair, #a.-b. 2.25 2.25

Royal Anniversaries — A1

**1987 *Perf. 15***

**66** A1 20c Queen Victoria .20 .20
**67** A1 50c George VI, Family .55 .55
**68** A1 75c Elizabeth .85 .85
**69** A1 $1.20 Elizabeth, Philip 1.40 1.40
**70** A1 $1.75 Elizabeth, diff. 2.00 2.00
*Nos. 66-70 (5)* 5.00 5.00

**Souvenir Sheet**

**71** A1 $3 Elizabeth, Family 3.25 3.25

Elizabeth's 40th wedding anniv., Queen Victoria's accession to the throne, sesquicentennial.

### Summer Olympics Type of 1988

**1988, Aug. 19 *Perf. 13x12½***

**72** A69 10c Hurdles .20 .20
**73** A69 20c High jump .25 .25
**74** A69 40c Running .50 .50
**75** A69 50c Discus .60 .60
**76** A69 80c Pole vault 1.00 1.00
**77** A69 90c Javelin 1.10 1.10
*Nos. 72-77 (6)* 3.65 3.65

## NANUMAGA

### Automobile Type of 1984

***Perf. 12½x13***

**1984-87 Litho. Unwmk.**

**Se-tenant Pairs, #a.-b.**
**a. — Side and front views.**
**b. — Action scene.**
**Design A41**

1 5c 1903 De Dion-Bouton Single Cylinder .25 .25
2 5c 1955 Ford Thunderbird .25 .25
3 5c 1966 Lotus Elan, UK .25 .25
4 10c 1915 Stutz Bearcat .25 .25
5 10c 1915 Dodge 4-Cylinder Touring Car .25 .25
6 10c 1976 Jaguar XJ-S, UK .25 .25
7 10c 1928 Morgan Super Sports, UK .25 .25
8 15c 1906 Spyker, Holland .40 .40
9 20c 1957 Dual-Ghia, US .50 .50
10 25c 1966 Lamborghini P400 Miura Coupe, Italy .65 .65
11 25c 1947 Kaiser Traveler, US .65 .65
12 25c 1951 Lancia Aurelia, Italy .65 .65
13 30c 1963 Chevrolet Corvette Coupe .80 .80
14 40c 1949 Jaguar XK 120, UK 1.10 1.10
15 40c 1930 Renault Reinastella, France 1.10 1.10
16 50c 1938 Alvis Speed 25, UK 1.25 1.25
17 60c 1956 Studebaker Golden Hawk 1.60 1.60
18 75c 1909 Alco, US 2.00 2.00
19 $1 1966 Shelby GT-350 Coupe, US 2.75 2.75
20 $1 1968 Mercedes 300 SEL, Germany 2.75 2.75
21 $1 1953 BRM V-16, UK 2.75 2.75
22 $1 1910 Lozier Briarcliff, US 2.75 2.75
*Nos. 1-22 (22)* 23.45 23.45

Issued: #1, 4, 10, 14, 19, 6/11/84; #2, 5, 16, 20, 12/24/84; #6, 11, 18, 21, 7/23/85; #3, 7-9, 12, 15, 17, 22, 8/6/87.
1987 stamps not inscribed "Leaders of the World."

British Monarchs — A2

**1984, Nov. 27 *Perf. 13x12½***

**Se-tenant Pairs, #a.-b.**
**a. — Left stamp.**
**b. — Right stamp.**

**23** A2 10c Richard I .40 .40
**24** A2 20c Richard I, diff. .60 .60
**25** A2 30c Third Crusade 1.00 1.00
**26** A2 40c Alfred the Great 1.25 1.25
**27** A2 50c Alfred, diff. 1.50 1.50
**28** A2 $1 Battle of Edington 3.25 3.25
*Nos. 23-28 (6)* 8.00 8.00

**Locomotive Type of 1984**

**1985, Apr. 3** ***Perf. 12½x13***
**Se-tenant Pairs, #a.-b.**
**a. — Side and front views.**
**b. — Action scene.**
**Design A36**

**29** 10c 1906 NYC & HR Class S .25 .25
**30** 25c 1884 T.R. Class B, Australia .70 .70
**31** 50c 1902 Decapod, UK 1.25 1.25
**32** 60c 1846 Coppernob, UK 1.50 1.50
*Nos. 29-32 (4)* 3.70 3.70

Flowers — A3

#33a, Tecophilaea cyanocrocus. #33b, Lilium pardalinum. #34a, Canarina abyssinica. #34b, Vanda coerulea. #35a, Lathyrus maritimus. #35b, Narcissus tazetta. #36a, Bauera sessiflora. #36b, Thelymitra venosa.

**1985, May 3** ***Perf. 13x12½***
**33** A3 25c Pair, #a.-b. .60 .60
**34** A3 30c Pair, #a.-b. .70 .70
**35** A3 40c Pair, #a.-b. 1.00 1.00
**36** A3 50c Pair, #a.-b. 1.25 1.25
*Nos. 33-36 (4)* 3.55 3.55

**Queen Mother Type of 1985**

Hats: #45a, White. #45b, Blue feathered. #46a, 50a, Violet blue wide-brimmed. #46b, 50b, Blue green wide-brimmed. #47a, 51a, Tiara. #47b, 51b, Light blue. #48a, Dark blue. #48b, Black.
#49a, As young girl. #49b, As young woman.

**1985-86**
**45** A45 15c Pair, #a.-b. .50 .50
**46** A45 55c Pair, #a.-b. 2.10 2.10
**47** A45 65c Pair, #a.-b. 2.25 2.25
**48** A45 90c Pair, #a.-b. 3.25 3.25
*Nos. 45-48 (4)* 8.10 8.10

**Souvenir Sheets of 2**
**49** A45 $1.15 #a.-b. 3.75 3.75
**50** A45 $2.10 #a.-b. 4.50 4.50
**51** A45 $2.50 #a.-b. 5.00 5.00

Issued: #41-49, 9/5; 50-51, 1/3/86.

**Elizabeth II 60th Birthday Type**

**1986, Apr. 21** ***Perf. 13x12½, 12½x13***
**52** A49 5c White hat .35 .35
**53** A49 $1 As young woman 1.10 1.10
**54** A49 $1.75 Tam 2.00 2.00
**55** A49 $2.50 Tiara, vert. 2.75 2.75
*Nos. 52-55 (4)* 6.20 6.20

**Souvenir Sheet**
**56** A49 $4 Portrait 6.25 6.25

World Cup Soccer Championships, Mexico — A4

Players and teams from participating countries.

***Perf. 12½x13, 13x12½***
**1986, June 30**
**57** A4 1c Uruguay, vert. .25 .25
**58** A4 5c Morocco, vert. .25 .25
**59** A4 5c Hungary, vert. .25 .25
**60** A4 10c Poland, vert. .25 .25
**61** A4 20c Argentina, vert. .25 .25
**62** A4 35c Bulgaria .25 .25
**63** A4 50c Portugal, vert. .30 .30
**64** A4 60c Belgium .40 .40
**65** A4 75c France .50 .50
**66** A4 $1 Canada, vert. .75 .75
**67** A4 $2 Germany 1.40 1.40
**68** A4 $4 Scotland, vert. 2.75 2.75
*Nos. 57-68 (12)* 7.60 7.60

**Royal Wedding Type of 1986**

#71a, Prince Andrew, vert. #71b, Sarah Ferguson, vert. #72a, Prince Philip, Andrew. #72b, Prince Andrew.

**1986, July 23**
**71** A53 60c Pair, #a.-b. 1.50 1.50
**72** A53 $1 Pair, #a.-b. 2.50 2.50

**Souvenir Sheet**
**73** A56 $4 Couple 5.25 5.25

Nos. 71-72 Ovptd. in Silver "Congratulations to T.R.H. The Duke & Duchess of York"

**1986, Oct. 26**
**74** A53 60c Pair, #a.-b. 1.40 1.40
**75** A53 $1 Pair, #a.-b. 2.25 2.25

Royal Anniversaries — A5

**1987, Oct. 15** ***Perf. 15***
**78** A5 15c Queen Victoria .20 .20
**79** A5 35c Princesses Margaret and Elizabeth .40 .40
**80** A5 60c Elizabeth holding Princess Anne .65 .65
**81** A62 $1.50 Elizabeth, Philip 1.75 1.75
**82** A62 $1.75 Elizabeth wearing tiara 2.00 2.00
*Nos. 78-82 (5)* 5.00 5.00

**Souvenir Sheet**
**83** A5 $3 Elizabeth 3.25 3.25

Elizabeth's 40th wedding anniv.; Victoria's accession to the throne, sesquicentennial.

---

**NANUMEA**

**Locomotive Type of 1984**
***Perf. 12½x13***
**1984-85** **Litho.** **Unwmk.**
**Se-tenant Pairs, #a.-b.**
**a. — Side and front views.**
**b. — Action scene.**
**Tuvalu Design A36**

**1** 1c 1940 Class E94, Germany .30 .30
**2** 15c 1946 Class 2251, UK .40 .40
**3** 20c 1941 Bantam Cock Class V4, UK .60 .60
**4** 30c 1902 Class C1, UK .95 .95
**5** 35c 1952 S.N.C.F. CC 7121, France 1.10 1.10
**6** 40c 1903 La France Frenchmen Class, UK 1.25 1.25
**7** 50c 1929 5700 Class, UK 1.60 1.60
**8** 50c 1954 S.N.C.F. Class BB 1200, France 1.60 1.60
**9** 60c 1881 Fairlight Class G, UK 1.90 1.90
**10** 60c 1928 V.R. Class S, Australia 1.90 1.90
*Nos. 1-10 (10)* 11.60 11.60

Issued: #2-4, 6-7, 9, 4/30; others, 2/8/85.

**Cricket Players Type of 1984**

**1984, Oct. 9** ***Perf. 13x12½***
**Se-tenant Pairs, #a.-b.**
**Tuvalu Design A39**
**11** 1c J.A. Snow .40 .40
**12** 10c C.J. Tavare .40 .40
**13** 40c G.B. Stevenson 1.10 1.10
**14** $1 P. Carrick 2.50 2.50
*Nos. 11-14 (4)* 4.40 4.40

**Automobile Type of 1984**

**1985-86** ***Perf. 12½x13***
**Se-tenant Pairs, #a.-b.**
**a. — Side and front views.**
**b. — Action scene.**
**Tuvalu Design A41**

**15** 5c 1965 Humber Super-snipe, UK .25 .25
**16** 10c 1934 Singer 9, UK .25 .25
**17** 15c 1948 Holden FX 2.1 Liter Sedan, Australia .40 .40
**18** 20c 1953 Buick Skylark .55 .55
**19** 20c 1951 Simca Aronde, France .55 .55
**20** 35c 1967 Toyota 2000 GT, Japan 1.10 1.10
**21** 40c 1960 Elva Courier, UK 1.25 1.25
**22** 50c 1952 Bentley Continental, UK 1.60 1.60
**23** 50c 1938 Hispano-Suiza V12 Saoutchik Cabriolet, Spain/France 1.60 1.60
**24** 50c 1913 Peugeot Bebe, France 1.60 1.60
**25** 60c 1935 Bluebird V (LSR), UK 1.75 1.75
**26** 60c 1978 Mazda RX7, Japan 1.75 1.75
**27** 75c 1970 Lola T70, UK 2.10 2.10
**28** $2 1908 Locomobile, US 6.25 6.25
*Nos. 15-28 (14)* 21.00 21.00

Issued: #15, 21-22, 25, 1/14; #17-18, 23, 26, 2/22; #16, 19-20, 24, 27-28, 12/30/86.

Cats — A6

#29a, American short-hair. #29b, Turkish Angora. #30a, Korat. #30b, American Maine Coon. #31a, Himalayan. #31b, Shaded Cameo. #32a, Long-haired ginger. #32b, Siamese Seal Point.

**1985, May 28** ***Perf. 13x12½***
**29** A6 5c Pair, #a.-b. .30 .30
**30** A6 30c Pair, #a.-b. .80 .80
**31** A6 50c Pair, #a.-b. 1.25 1.25
**32** A6 $1 Pair, #a.-b. 2.50 2.50
*Nos. 29-32 (4)* 4.85 4.85

**Queen Mother Type of 1985**

Hats: #41a, 47a, Light gray. #41b, 47b, Light blue. #42a, Lavender. #42b, Blue. #43a, Purple. #43b, Pink. #44a, 46a, Blue. #44b, 46b, Blue flowered. #45a, Feathered. #45b, Veiled.

**1985-86**
**41** A45 5c Pair, #a.-b. .25 .25
**42** A45 30c Pair, #a.-b. .80 .80
**43** A45 75c Pair, #a.-b. 2.10 2.10
**44** A45 $1.05 Pair, #a.-b. 2.75 2.75
*Nos. 41-44 (4)* 5.90 5.90

**Souvenir Sheets of 2**
**45** A45 $1.20 #a.-b. 4.00 4.00
**46** A45 $1 #a.-b. 2.00 2.00
**47** A45 $4 #a.-b. 8.00 8.00

Issued: #41-45, 9/5; 46-47, 1/10/86.

**Elizabeth II 60th Birthday Type**

**1986, Apr. 21** ***Perf. 13x12½, 12½x13***
**48** A49 10c As teenager .30 .30
**49** A49 80c As young woman .80 .80
**50** A49 $1.75 Red hat 1.75 1.75
**51** A49 $3 Tiara, vert. 3.00 3.00
*Nos. 48-51 (4)* 5.85 5.85

**Souvenir Sheet**
**52** A49 $4 Green print hat 4.75 4.75

1986 World Cup Soccer Championships, Mexico — A7

**1986, June 10** ***Perf. 13x12½***
**53** A7 1c Italy, 1934 .25 .25
**54** A7 2c Italy, 1938 .25 .25
**55** A7 5c Uruguay, 1950 .25 .25
**56** A7 10c Brazil, 1958 .25 .25
**57** A7 25c Argentina vs. Holland, 1978 .25 .25
**58** A7 40c Brazil vs. Czechoslovakia, 1962 .30 .30
**59** A7 50c Uruguay vs. Argentina, 1930 .40 .40
**60** A7 75c West Germany vs. Hungary, 1954 .60 .60
**61** A7 90c Brazil, 1970 .70 .70
**62** A7 $1 West Germany, 1974 .80 .80
**63** A7 $2.50 Italy vs. West Germany, 1982 2.00 2.00
**64** A7 $4 England, 1966 3.25 3.25
*Nos. 53-64 (12)* 9.30 9.30

**Royal Wedding Type of 1986**

**1986, July 23** ***Perf. 13x12½, 12½x13***
**65** A53 60c Prince Andrew in jeep, vert. .55 .55
**66** A53 60c Sarah Ferguson, vert. .55 .55
**67** A53 $1 Couple .85 .85
**68** A53 $1 Prince Andrew, Princess Anne and parents .85 .85
*Nos. 65-68 (4)* 2.80 2.80

**Souvenir Sheet**
**69** A56 $4 Newlyweds 5.25 5.25

Nos. 65-68 Ovptd. in Silver "Congratulations to T.R.H. The Duke & Duchess of York"

#70a, Prince Andrew in jeep. #70b, Sarah Ferguson. #71a, Couple. #71b, Prince Andrew, Princess Anne and parents.

**1986, Oct. 28**
**70** A53 60c Pair, #a.-b. 1.40 1.40
**71** A53 $1 Pair, #a.-b. 2.25 2.25

**Elizabeth 40th Wedding Anniv. Type**

**1987, Oct. 15** ***Perf. 15***
**74** A62 40c Victoria .45 .45
**75** A62 60c Elizabeth & Philip, wedding portrait .70 .70
**76** A62 80c Elizabeth, Philip & Prince Charles .90 .90
**77** A62 $1 Elizabeth, Princess Anne 1.10 1.10
**78** A62 $2 Elizabeth 2.25 2.25
*Nos. 74-78 (5)* 5.40 5.40

**Souvenir Sheet**
**79** A62 $3 Royal family, diff. 4.25 4.25

Queen Victoria's accession to the throne, 150th anniv.

---

**NIUTAO**

**Automobile Type of 1984**
***Perf. 12½x13***
**1984-85** **Litho.** **Unwmk.**
**Se-tenant Pairs, #a.-b.**
**a. — Side and front views.**
**b. — Action scene.**
**Tuvalu Design A41**

**1** 15c 1930 Bentley 4½ Liter Supercharged, UK .40 .40
**2** 20c 1935 Wolseley Hornet Special, UK .55 .55
**3** 25c 1920 Crossley 25/30HP, UK .70 .70
**4** 30c 1976 Cadillac Eldorado 7-Liter V-8 .85 .85
**5** 40c 1968 Austin Mini Cooper, UK 1.25 1.25
**6** 40c 1958 BMW 507 Cabriolet, W. Germany 1.25 1.25
**7** 50c 1963 Porsche 365C Cabriolet, W. Germany 1.50 1.50
**8** 60c 1971 Tyrrell Ford 001, UK 1.75 1.75
*Nos. 1-8 (8)* 8.25 8.25

Issued: #1, 4-5, 7, 4/16; #2-3, 6, 8, 5/2/85.

**Locomotive Type of 1984**

**1984-85**
**Se-tenant Pairs, #a.-b.**
**a. — Side and front views.**
**b. — Action scene.**
Tuvalu Design A36

**9** 5c 1830 Planet, UK .25 .25
**10** 10c 1863 Prince, UK .25 .25
**11** 10c 1943 Gordon Austerity Class, UK .25 .25
**12** 20c 1830 Northumbrian, UK .55 .55
**13** 30c 1879 Merddin Emrys, UK .80 .80
**14** 40c 1829 Agenoria, UK 1.10 1.10
**15** 45c 1909 Atchison, Topeka & Santa Fe, 1301 1.25 1.25
**16** 50c 1897 Class 6200, Japan 1.50 1.50
**17** 60c 1938 F.M.S.R. Class O, Malaya 1.60 1.60

18 75c 1880 1F, UK 2.10 2.10
19 $1 1908 Class E550, Italy 3.00 3.00
20 $1.20 1914 J.N.R. Class 6760, Japan 3.50 3.50
*Nos. 9-20 (12)* 16.15 16.15

Issue dates: Nos. 9-10, 12, 14, 16, 19, Sept. 17; Nos. 11, 13, 15, 18, 20, Aug. 21, 1985.

### Cricket Players Type of 1984

**1985, Jan. 7** ***Perf. 13x12½***

**Se-tenant Pairs, #a.-b.**

**a. — Head.**

**b. — Action scene.**

**Tuvalu Design A39**

21 1c S.G. Hinks .25 .25
22 15c C. Penn .50 .50
23 50c T.M. Alderman 1.75 1.75
24 $1 K.B.S. Jarvis 3.50 3.50
*Nos. 21-24 (4)* 6.00 6.00

### Audubon Bicentennial Type

#25a, Purple finch. #25b, White-throated sparrow. #26a, Anna's hummingbird. #26b, Smith's longspur. #27a, White-tailed kite. #27b, Harris' hawk. #28a, Northern oriole. #28b, Great crested flycatcher.

**1985, Apr. 4**

25 A42 5c Pair, #a.-b. .20 .20
26 A42 15c Pair, #a.-b. .40 .40
27 A42 25c Pair, #a.-b. .65 .65
28 A42 $1 Pair, #a.-b. 2.75 2.75
*Nos. 25-28 (4)* 4.00 4.00

### Queen Mother Type of 1985

Hat: #37a, Light blue. #37b, Yellow. #38a, 43a, Black. #38b, 43b, Blue. #39a, Tiara. #39b, Pink. #40a, 42a, White. #40b, 42b, Blue. #41a, As young woman. #41b, Feathered.

**1985-86**

37 A45 15c Pair, #a.-b. .40 .40
38 A45 35c Pair, #a.-b. 1.00 1.00
39 A45 70c Pair, #a.-b. 2.00 2.00
40 A45 95c Pair, #a.-b. 2.75 2.75
*Nos. 37-40 (4)* 6.15 6.15

**Souvenir Sheets**

41 A45 $1.05 #a.-b. 2.50 2.50
42 A45 $1.50 #a.-b. 3.50 3.50
43 A45 $4 #a.-b. 8.75 8.75

Issued: #37-41, 9/4; #42-43, 1/10/86.

### Elizabeth II 60th Birthday Type

**1986, Apr. 21** ***Perf. 13x12½, 12½x13***

44 A49 5c White & gray hat .30 .30
45 A49 60c Infant .60 .60
46 A49 $1.50 Flowered white hat 1.50 1.50
47 A49 $3.50 Tiara, vert. 3.75 3.75
*Nos. 44-47 (4)* 6.15 6.15

**Souvenir Sheet**

48 A49 $5 With tiara, diff. 7.75 7.75

For overprints see Nos. 58-62.

### Royal Wedding Type

#51a, Couple, vert. #51b, Sarah Ferguson, vert. #52a, Prince Andrew. #52b, Sarah in evening gown.

**1986, July 23** ***Perf. 12½x13, 13x12½***

51 A53 60c Pair, #a.-b. 1.00 1.00
52 A53 $1 Pair, #a.-b. 2.00 2.00

**Souvenir Sheet**

53 A56 $4 Newlyweds 5.25 5.25

Nos. 51-52 Ovptd. in Silver "Congratulations to T.R.H. The Duke & Duchess of York"

**1986, Oct. 28**

54 A53 60c Pair, #a.-b. 1.40 1.40
55 A53 $1 Pair, #a.-b. 2.25 1.10

Nos. 44-48 Ovptd. in Gold "40th WEDDING ANNIVERSARY OF H.M. QUEEN ELIZABETH II"

**1987, Mar.** ***Perf. 13x12½, 12½x13***

58 A49 5c multicolored .20 .20
59 A49 60c multicolored .75 .75
60 A49 $1.50 multicolored 1.90 1.90
61 A49 $3.50 multicolored 4.50 4.50
*Nos. 58-61 (4)* 7.35 7.35

**Souvenir Sheet**

62 A49 $5 multicolored 6.25 6.25

## NUI

### Locomotives Type of 1984

**1984-88** **Litho.** ***Perf. 12½x13***

**Se-tenant Pairs, #a.-b.**

**a. — Side and front views.**

**b. — Action scene.**

**Tuvalu Design A36**

1 5c 1911 Class 8800, Japan .20 .20
2 5c 1932 Soviet Union Railways Class SU .20 .20
3 10c 1847 Jenny Lind Type, UK .20 .20
4 10c 1907 Victorian Government Railways Class A2, Australia .20 .20
5 15c same, 1950 Class R .30 .30
6 15c 1913 Class 9600, Japan .30 .30
7 20c 1934 LMS Stanier Tilbury Class 4P, UK .40 .40
8 25c 1924 Jinty Class 3, UK .55 .55
9 25c 1928 Boston & Albany Class D12 .55 .55
10 25c 1847 Iron Duke Class, UK .55 .55
11 25c 1917 Wabash Railroad Class L .55 .55
12 30c 1943 South Australian Government Railways 520 Class .65 .65
13 35c 1885 Tennant Class 1463, UK .75 .75
14 40c 1947 No. 10000, UK .85 .85
15 40c 1848 Padarn Railway Fire Queen, UK .85 .85
16 50c 1935 Princess Margaret Rose Class 8P, UK 1.10 1.10
17 50c 1932 Soviet Union Railways Class IS 1.10 1.10
18 60c 1973 D.B. Class ET403, W. Germany 1.25 1.25
19 60c 1916 E. Tenn. & W. N. Carolina R.R. No. 10 1.25 1.25
20 75c 1973 D.B. Class 151, W. Germany 1.60 1.60
21 75c 1909 Tasmanian Goverment Railways Class K Garratt 1.60 1.60
22 $1 1927 B&O President Class 2.25 2.25
23 $1 1832 Mohawk & Hudson Railroad Experiment 2.25 2.25
24 $1.25 1934 Union Pacific Railroad, M-10000 Streamliner 2.75 2.75
*Nos. 1-24 (24)* 22.25 22.25

Issued: #5, 8, 12, 16, 3/19; #1, 6, 9, 22, 2/22/85; #3, 10, 13, 14, 18, 20, 23, 24, 8/7/87; #2, 4, 7, 11, 15, 17, 19, 21, 1/29/88.

1987 and 1988 stamps not inscribed "Leaders of the World."

### British Monarchs Type of Nanumaga

**1984, July 18** ***Perf. 13x12½***

**Se-tenant Pairs, #a.-b.**

25 A2 1c Queen Anne .40 .40
26 A2 5c Henry V .40 .40
27 A2 15c Henry V, diff. .40 .40
28 A2 40c Queen Anne, diff. 1.00 1.00
29 A2 50c Queen Anne, diff. 1.50 1.50
30 A2 $1 Henry V, diff. 2.50 2.50
*Nos. 25-30 (6)* 6.20 6.20

### Automobile Type of 1984

**1985** ***Perf. 12½x13***

**Se-tenant Pairs, #a.-b.**

**a. — Side and front views.**

**b. — Action scene.**

**Tuvalu Design A41**

31 5c 1909 Buick .25 .25
32 15c 1966 Oldsmobile Toronado .35 .35
33 25c 1947 Railton Mobil Special, UK .70 .70
34 30c 1924 Opel Laubfrosch, Germany .75 .75
35 40c 1966 Jensen FF, UK 1.00 1.00
36 40c 1963 Lotus-Climax GP MK 25, UK 1.00 1.00
37 50c 1910 Delaunay Belleville, France 1.40 1.40
38 60c 1956 Jensen 541, UK 1.50 1.50
39 90c 1924 Hispano-Suiza H6 Boulogne, France 2.25 2.25
40 $1.10 1972 Citroen-Maserati S.M. Coupe, France 2.75 2.75
*Nos. 31-40 (10)* 11.95 11.95

Issued: #33-35, 37, 4/2; #31-32, 36, 38-40, 10/9.

### Cricket Players Type of 1984

**1985, May 27** ***Perf. 13x12½***

**Se-tenant Pairs, #a.-b.**

**Tuvalu Design A39**

41 1c S.C. Goldsmith .20 .20
42 40c S.N.V. Waterton 1.00 1.00
43 60c A. Sidebottom 1.40 1.40
44 70c A.A. Metcalfe 1.90 1.90
*Nos. 41-44 (4)* 4.50 4.50

### Queen Mother Type of 1985

#49a, 54a, Purple. #49b, 54b, Tiara. #50a, Light blue. #50b, Lavender. #51a, Violet. #51b, White. #52a, 55a, Light blue. #52b, 55b, Tiara. #53a, White. #53b, Black.

**1985-86**

49 A45 5c Pair, #a.-b. .20 .20
50 A45 50c Pair, #a.-b. 1.25 1.25
51 A45 75c Pair, #a.-b. 2.00 2.00
52 A45 85c Pair, #a.-b. 2.25 2.25
*Nos. 49-52 (4)* 5.70 5.70

**Souvenir Sheets of 2**

53 A45 $1.15 #a.-b. 3.50 3.50
54 A45 $1.50 #a.-b. 3.00 3.00
55 A45 $3.50 #a.-b. 7.50 7.50

Issued: #49-53, 9/4; 54-55, 1/8/86.

### Elizabeth II 60th Birthday Type

**1986, Apr. 21** ***Perf. 13x12½, 12½x13***

56 A49 10c Feathered hat .20 .20
57 A49 80c As young woman .80 .80
58 A49 $1.75 Tiara 1.75 1.75
59 A49 $3 Tiara, diff., vert. 3.00 3.00
*Nos. 56-59 (4)* 5.75 5.75

**Souvenir Sheet**

60 A49 $4 Portrait 6.25 6.25

### Royal Wedding Type of 1986

#63a, Couple, vert. #63b, Prince Andrew, vert. #64a, Couple, Queen Elizabeth II. #64b, Andrew as young boy.

**1986, July 23** ***Perf. 12½x13, 13x12½***

63 A53 60c Pair, #a.-b. 1.10 1.10
64 A53 $1 Pair, #a.-b. 1.75 1.75

**Souvenir Sheet**

65 A56 $4 Sarah in wedding dress 6.25 6.25

Nos. 63-64 Ovptd. in Silver "Congratulations to T.R.H. The Duke & Duchess of York"

**1986, Oct. 28**

66 A53 60c Pair, #a.-b. 1.40 1.40
67 A53 $1 Pair, #a.-b. 2.25 2.25

### Elizabeth 40th Wedding Anniv. Type of Funafuti

**1987, Oct. 15** ***Perf. 15***

70 A1 20c Queen Victoria .20 .20
71 A1 50c George VI, Family .60 .60
72 A1 75c Elizabeth .85 .85
73 A1 $1.20 Elizabeth, Philip 1.40 1.40
74 A1 $1.75 Elizabeth, diff. 2.00 2.00
*Nos. 70-74 (5)* 5.05 5.05

**Souvenir Sheet**

75 A1 $3 Elizabeth, Family 3.50 3.50

Queen Victoria's accession to the throne, sesquicentennial.

## NUKUFETAU

### Automobile Type of 1984

***Perf. 12½x13***

**1984-85** **Litho.** **Unwmk.**

**Se-tenant Pairs, #a.-b.**

**a. — Side and front views.**

**b. — Action scene.**

**Tuvalu Design A41**

1 5c 1904 Mercedes 28 PS, Germany .25 .25
2 10c 1966 Ford GT40 Mark II .25 .25
3 10c 1911 Vauxhall Prince Henry, UK .25 .25
4 15c 1956 Lincoln Continental Mark II .40 .40
5 20c 1950 Bristol 400, UK .50 .50
6 25c 1913 Morris Oxford "Bullnose," UK .75 .75
7 30c 1923 Austin Seven Tourer .80 .80
8 50c 1921 Bugatti Type 13 "Brescia," France 1.50 1.50
9 50c 1967 Monteverdi, Switzerland 1.50 1.50
10 60c 1925 Lancia Lambda, Italy 1.60 1.60
11 60c 1938 Panhard Dynamic, France 1.60 1.60
12 75c 1960 A.C. Ace, UK 2.00 2.00
13 $1.50 1950 Land Rover Model 80, UK 4.50 4.50
*Nos. 1-13 (13)* 15.90 15.90

Issued; #2, 6-8, 10, 5/23; others, 6/26/85.

### British Monarchs Type of Nanumaga

**1984, Nov. 27** ***Perf. 13x12½***

**Se-tenant Pairs, #a.-b.**

14 A2 1c Mary II .50 .50
15 A2 10c Mary II, diff. .50 .50
16 A2 30c Mary II, diff. .85 .85
17 A2 50c Henry IV 1.60 1.60
18 A2 60c Henry IV, diff. 1.90 1.90
19 A2 $1 Henry IV, diff. 3.00 3.00
*Nos. 14-19 (6)* 8.35 8.35

### Cricket Players Type of 1984

**1985, Jan. 7**

**Se-tenant Pairs, #a.-b.**

20 A39 1c D.G. Aslett .35 .35
21 A39 10c N.R. Taylor .35 .35
22 A39 55c S. Oldham 1.75 1.75
23 A39 $1 C.W.J. Athey 3.75 3.75
*Nos. 20-23 (4)* 6.20 6.20

### Locomotive Type of 1984

**1985-88**

**Se-tenant Pairs, #a.-b.**

**a. — Side and front views.**

**b. — Action scene.**

**Tuvalu Design A36**

24 1c 1900 Class XV, Germany .20 .20
25 5c 1859 ECR Class Y, UK .20 .20
26 10c 1923 Nord Super Pacific, France .20 .20
27 10c 1905 LNWR Experiment Class, UK .20 .20
28 15c 1941 SR Merchant Navy Class, UK .30 .30
29 20c 1830 S. Carolina Railroad Best Friend of Charleston .40 .40
30 25c 1941 SR No. 1, UK .55 .55
31 30c 1987 Class 89, UK .65 .65
32 40c 1923 Southern Pacific Railroad Class 4300, US .85 .85
33 50c 1956 New South Wales Government Railways Class 46 1.10 1.10
34 60c 1953 D.B. Class V200, Germany 1.25 1.25
35 60c 1936 Union Railroad Class S-7, US 1.25 1.25
36 60c 1877 Phildelphia & Reading Railroad Camelback 1.25 1.25
37 70c 1968 J.N.R. Class 381, Japan 1.50 1.50
38 $1 1933 Rio Grande Southern Railroad Galloping Goose Railcar, US 2.25 2.25
*a.* Souvenir sheet of 2 2.50 2.50
39 $1.50 1935 Chicago, Milwaukee, St. Paul & Pacific Class A 3.25 3.25
*Nos. 24-39 (16)* 15.40 15.40

Issued: #24, 26, 34, 37, 4/2/85; #29, 32, 35, 39, 3/20/86; #25, 27-28, 30-31, 33, 36, 38, 38a, 9/10/87.

1986 and 1987 stamps not inscribed "Leaders of the World."

### Queen Mother Type of 1985

Hat: #44a, Wide-brimmed blue. #44b, Tiara. #45a, Tiara. #45b, Lavender. #46a, Blue. #46b, White stole. #47a, 50a, White. #47b, 50b, Blue. #48a, 49a, White. #48b, 49b, Wide-brimmed.

**1985, Sept. 5** ***Perf. 13x12½***

44 A45 10c Pair, #a.-b. .20 .20
45 A45 45c Pair, #a.-b. 1.00 1.00
46 A45 65c Pair, #a.-b. 1.60 1.60
47 A45 $1 Pair, #a.-b. 2.50 2.50
*Nos. 44-47 (4)* 5.30 5.30

**Souvenir Sheets of 2**

48 A45 $1.10 #a.-b. 3.75 3.75
49 A45 $1.75 #a.-b. 4.00 4.00
50 A45 $3 #a.-b. 6.75 6.75

**Elizabeth II 60th Birthday Type**

**1986, Apr. 21** ***Perf. 13x12½, 12½x13***

**51** A49 5c Scarf .35 .35
**52** A49 40c Tiara .40 .40
**53** A49 $2 Bareheaded 1.90 1.90
**54** A49 $4 Tiara, vert. 4.25 4.25
*Nos. 51-54 (4)* 6.90 6.90

**Souvenir Sheet**

**55** A49 $5 Blue hat 6.25 6.25

For overprints see Nos. 65-69.

**Royal Wedding Type of 1986**

#58a, Couple, vert. #58b, Andrew, vert. #59a, Andrew, parents. #59b, Andrew.

**1986, July 22**

**58** A53 60c Pair, #a.-b. 1.25 1.25
**59** A53 $1 Pair, #a.-b. 2.00 2.00

**Souvenir Sheet**

**60** A56 $4 Wedding ceremony 5.25 5.25

Nos. 58-59 Ovptd. in Silver "Congratulations to T.R.H. The Duke & Duchess of York"

**1986, Oct. 28**

**61** A53 60c Pair, #a.-b. 1.40 1.40
**62** A53 $1 Pair, #a.-b. 2.25 2.25

Nos. 51-55 Ovptd. in Gold "40th WEDDING ANNIVERSARY OF H.M. QUEEN ELIZABETH II"

**1987, Oct. 15**

**65** A49 5c multicolored .20 .20
**66** A49 40c multicolored .50 .50
**67** A49 $2 multicolored 2.50 2.50
**68** A49 $4 multicolored 5.00 5.00
*Nos. 65-68 (4)* 8.20 8.20

**Souvenir Sheet**

**69** A49 $5 multicolored 6.25 6.25

## NUKULAELAE

**Locomotive Type of 1984**

***Perf. 12½x13***

**1984-86 Litho. Unwmk.**

**Se-tenant Pairs, #a.-b.**

**a. — Side and front views.**

**b. — Action scene.**

**Tuvalu Design A36**

**1** 5c 1891 Calbourne Class 02, UK .25 .25
**2** 5c 1912 K.P.E.V. Class T18, Germany .25 .25
**3** 10c 1942 SNCF Class 141P, France .25 .25
**4** 10c 1962 Class 47, UK .25 .25
**5** 15c 1941 Union Pacific Big Boy, US .25 .25
**6** 15c 1955 DRB 83-10, Germany .25 .25
**7** 20c 1940 S.N.C.F. 160-A-1, France .45 .45
**8** 25c 1901 Class AEG High Speed Railcar, Germany .50 .50
**9** 25c 1839 Albion Railroad Samson, Canada .50 .50
**10** 40c 1907 Saint Class, UK .90 .90
**11** 40c 1900 Nord De Glehn Atlantic, France .90 .90
**12** 40c 1851 Folkstone Class, UK .90 .90
**13** 50c 1914 J.N.R. Class 8620, Japan 1.10 1.10
**14** 50c 1936 Class 8F, UK 1.10 1.10
**15** 80c 1857 Shannon, UK 1.90 1.90
**16** $1 1948 Class A1, UK 2.40 2.40
**17** $1 1955 E.A.R. Class 59, Kenya 2.40 2.40
**18** $1 1897 V.R. Class Na, Australia 2.40 2.40
**19** $1 1859 Undine Class, UK 2.40 2.40
**20** $1.50 1935 Turbomotive, UK 3.50 3.50
*Nos. 1-20 (20)* 22.85 22.85

Issued: #1, 5, 10, 16, 5/23; #2, 7, 11, 17, 12/12; #3, 8, 13, 18, 3/24/85; #4, 6, 9, 12, 14, 15, 19-20, 7/11/86.

1986 stamps not inscribed "Leaders of the World."

**Cricket Players Type of 1984**

**1984, Aug. 8** ***Perf. 13x12½***

**Se-tenant Pairs, #a.-b.**

**21** A39 5c D.B. Close .20 .20
**22** A39 15c G. Boycott .40 .40
**23** A39 30c D.L. Bairstow .95 .95
**24** A39 $1 T.G. Evans 3.00 3.00
*Nos. 21-24 (4)* 4.55 4.55

**Automobile Type of 1984**

**1985** ***Perf. 12½x13***

**Se-tenant Pairs, #a.-b.**

**a. — Side and front views.**

**b. — Action scene.**

**Tuvalu Design A41**

**25** 5c 1924 Bugatti Type 35, France .30 .30
**26** 10c 1908 Sizaire-Naudin, France .30 .30
**27** 25c 1965 Sunbeam Tiger, UK .65 .65
**28** 35c 1907 Napier 60HP Touring Car, UK .90 .90
**29** 35c 1975 BMW 2002 TII, Germany .90 .90
**30** 50c 1910 Austro-Daimler Prince Henry, Austria 1.40 1.40
**31** 50c 1927 La Salle, US 1.40 1.40
**32** 70c 1901 Oldsmobile Curved Dash Buckboard 1.90 1.90
**33** 75c 1955 Rover 90, UK 2.10 2.10
**34** $1 1948 Chrysler Town & Country 2.50 2.50
*Nos. 25-34 (10)* 12.35 12.35

Issue dates: #25, 28, 30, 32, Feb. 8; #26-27, 29, 31, 33-34, July 23.

Dogs — A8

#35a, Hungarian vizsla. #35b, Bearded collie. #36a, Bernese mountain dog. #36b, Boxer. #37a, Labrador retriever. #37b, Shetland sheepdog. #38a, Welsh springer spaniel. #38b, Scottish terrier.

**1985, Apr. 30**

**35** A8 5c Pair, #a.-b. .20 .20
**36** A8 20c Pair, #a.-b. .45 .45
**37** A8 50c Pair, #a.-b. 1.10 1.10
**38** A8 70c Pair, #a.-b. 1.60 1.60
*Nos. 35-38 (4)* 3.35 3.35

**Queen Mother Type of 1985**

Hat: #47a, Purple. #47b, Blue. #48a, 52a, Tiara. #48b, 52b, Lavender. #49a, 53a, Pink. #49b, 53b, Dark blue. #50a, Light purple. #50b, Light blue. #51a, As young girl. #51b, Lace.

**1985-86**

**47** A45 5c Pair, #a.-b. .20 .20
**48** A45 25c Pair, #a.-b. .55 .55
**49** A45 85c Pair, #a.-b. 2.00 2.00
**50** A45 $1 Pair, #a.-b. 2.50 2.50
*Nos. 47-50 (4)* 5.25 5.25

**Souvenir Sheets of 2**

**51** A45 $1.20 #a.-b. 3.00 3.00
**52** A45 $1.20 #a.-b. 2.50 2.50
**53** A45 $3.50 #a.-b. 7.25 7.25

Issued: #46-51, 9/4; #52-53, 1/8/86.

**Elizabeth II 60th Birthday Type**

**1986, Apr. 21** ***Perf. 13x12½, 12½x13***

**54** A49 10c White hat .25 .25
**55** A49 $1 As young woman 1.00 1.00
**56** A49 $1.50 In orange dress 1.50 1.50
**57** A49 $3 Tiara, vert. 3.00 3.00
*Nos. 54-57 (4)* 5.75 5.75

**Souvenir Sheet**

**58** A49 $4 In brown dress 6.25 6.25

**Royal Wedding Type of 1986**

#61a, Andrew, vert. #61b, Couple, vert. #62a, Sarah Ferguson and Princess Diana. #62b, Andrew.

**1986, July 23** ***Perf. 12½x13, 13x12½***

**61** A53 60c Pair, #a.-b. 1.25 1.25
**62** A53 $1 Pair, #a.-b. 2.00 2.00

**Souvenir Sheet**

**63** A56 $4 Sarah in wedding dress 5.25 5.25

Nos. 61-62 Ovptd. in Silver "Congratulations to T.R.H. The Duke & Duchess of York"

**1986, Oct. 28**

**64** A53 60c Pair, #a.-b. 1.40 1.40
**65** A53 $1 Pair, #a.-b. 2.25 2.25

**Queen Elizabeth II 40th Wedding Anniv. Type of Nanumaga**

**1987, Oct. 15** ***Perf. 15***

**68** A5 15c Queen Victoria .20 .20
**69** A5 35c Princesses Margaret and Elizabeth .40 .40
**70** A5 60c Elizabeth holding Princess Anne .65 .65
**71** A5 $1.50 Elizabeth, Philip 1.75 1.75
**72** A5 $1.75 Elizabeth wearing tiara 2.00 2.00
*Nos. 68-72 (5)* 5.00 5.00

**Souvenir Sheet**

**73** A5 $3 Elizabeth 3.50 3.50

Queen Victoria's accession to the throne, sesquicentennial.

## VAITUPU

**Automobile Type of 1984**

***Perf. 12½x13***

**1984-85 Litho. Unwmk.**

**Se-tenant Pairs, #a.-b.**

**a. — Side and front views.**

**b. — Action scene.**

**Tuvalu Design A41**

**1** 5c 1961 Lotus Elite, UK .35 .35
**2** 15c 1950 MG TD Midget, UK .35 .35
**3** 15c 1932 Hillman Minx, UK .35 .35
**4** 15c 1905 White Model E Steam Car, US .35 .35
**5** 25c 1935 Auburn Supercharged 851, US .75 .75
**6** 25c 1981 Renault RE20, France .75 .75
**7** 30c 1928 Lea-Francis Hyper .85 .85
**8** 30c 1940 Packard Darrin .85 .85
**9** 30c 1938 Graham, US .85 .85
**10** 40c 1968 Chevrolet Camaro 1.25 1.25
**11** 40c 1957 Renault Dauphine-Gordini, France 1.25 1.25
**12** 50c 1930 Packard Eight 1.60 1.60
**13** 50c 1926 Miller Special, US 1.60 1.60
**14** 60c 1950 Healey Silverstone, UK 1.90 1.90
**15** 60c 1970 De Tomaso Pantera, Italy 1.90 1.90
**16** $1 1927 Bentley 3-Liter, UK 3.00 3.00
*Nos. 1-16 (16)* 17.95 17.95

Issued: #2, 5, 7, 12, Mar. 19; #1, 3, 6, 8, 10, 13-14, 16, Dec. 12; #4, 9, 11, 15, Apr. 4, 1985.

**British Monarchs Type of Nanumaga**

**1984, July 18** ***Perf. 13x12½***

**Se-tenant Pairs, #a.-b.**

**17** A2 1c Richard III .35 .35
**18** A2 5c Charles I .35 .35
**19** A2 15c Charles I, diff. .35 .35
**20** A2 40c Richard III, diff. 1.00 1.00
**21** A2 50c Richard III, diff. 1.25 1.25
**22** A2 $1 Charles I, diff. 2.50 2.50
*Nos. 17-22 (6)* 5.80 5.80

**Locomotive Type of 1984**

**1985-87** ***Perf. 12½x13***

**Se-tenant Pairs, #a.-b.**

**a. — Side and front views.**

**b. — Action scene.**

**Tuvalu Design A36**

**23** 5c 1929 D.R.G. V3201, Germany .20 .20
**24** 10c 1841 G.W.R. Leo Class, UK .20 .20
**25** 10c 1937 New York Central Railroad Class J3a .20 .20
**26** 15c 1949 Richmond, Fredericksburg & Potomac Railroad Class E8 .30 .30
**27** 25c 1845 Columbine, UK .55 .55
**28** 25c 1954 BR Class 2MT, UK .55 .55
**29** 25c 1980 Amtrak Class AEM-7 .55 .55
**30** 35c 1981 Via Rail LRC Class MPA-27a, Canada .75 .75
**31** 45c 1983 British Columbia Railway Class GF6C .95 .95
**32** 50c 1888 D&H Class B, India 1.10 1.10
**33** 60c 1936 D.R. Class 45, Germany 1.25 1.25
**34** 65c 1904 Northern Pacific Railway Class W, US 1.40 1.40
**35** 80c 1855 W. & A. R.R. General, US 1.75 1.75
**36** 85c 1938 Chicago & North Western Railway Class E-4 1.90 1.90
**37** $1 1911 J.N.R. Class 9020 Mallet, Japan 2.25 2.25
**38** $1 1977 Chicago Regional Transportation Authority Class F40 2.25 2.25
*Nos. 23-38 (16)* 16.15 16.15

Issued: #24, 27, 32-33, 3/7/85; #23, 28, 35, 37, 1/16/86; #25-26, 29-31, 34, 36, 38, 9/10/87.

1986 and 1987 stamps not inscribed "Leaders of the World."

A9

Butterfly illustrations by Roger V. Vigurs: #39a, Marpesia petreus. #39b, Pseudolycaena marsyas. #40a, Charaxes jasius. #40b, Junonia coenia. #41a, Palaeochrysophanus hippothoe. #41b, Sticopthalma camadeva. #42a, Phoebis avellaneda. #42b, Apatura iris.

**1985, Mar. 12** ***Perf. 13x12½***

**39** A9 5c Pair, #a.-b. .20 .20
**40** A9 15c Pair, #a.-b. .45 .45
**41** A9 50c Pair, #a.-b. 1.50 1.50
**42** A9 75c Pair, #a.-b. 2.25 2.25
*Nos. 39-42 (4)* 4.40 4.40

**Queen Mother Type of 1985**

Hat: #51a, 57a, Light blue. #51b, 57b, White. #52a, Tiara. #52b, Lavender. #53a, 56a, Violet. #53b, 56b, Green. #54a, Blue. #54b, Pink. #55a, Looking up. #55b, Looking forward.

**1985-86**

**51** A45 15c Pair, #a.-b. .30 .30
**52** A45 40c Pair, #a.-b. .95 .95
**53** A45 65c Pair, #a.-b. 1.50 1.50
**54** A45 95c Pair, #a.-b. 2.40 2.40
*Nos. 51-54 (4)* 5.15 5.15

**Souvenir Sheets of 2**

**55** A45 $1.10 #a.-b. 3.75 3.75
**56** A45 $2 #a.-b. 4.00 4.00
**57** A45 $2.50 #a.-b. 5.50 5.50

Issued: #51-55, 8/28; 56-57, 1/8/86.

**Elizabeth II 60th Birthday Type**

**1986, Apr. 21** ***Perf. 13x12½, 12½x13***

**58** A49 5c Green hat .35 .35
**59** A49 60c As young woman .55 .55
**60** A49 $2 Flowered hat 1.90 1.90
**61** A49 $3.50 Tiara, vert. 3.25 3.25
*Nos. 58-61 (4)* 6.05 6.05

**Souvenir Sheet**

**62** A49 $5 Straw hat 6.25 6.25

For overprints see Nos. 72-76.

**Royal Wedding Type of 1986**

#65a, Andrew, vert. #65b, Sarah Ferguson, vert. #66a, Charles, Andrew. #66b, Couple.

**1986, July 18** ***Perf. 12½x13, 13x12½***

**65** A53 60c Pair, #a.-b. 1.25 1.25
**66** A53 $1 Pair, #a.-b. 2.00 2.00

**Souvenir Sheet**

**67** A56 $4 Newlyweds 5.25 5.25

Nos. 65-66 Ovptd. in Silver "Congratulations to T.R.H. The Duke & Duchess of York"

**1986, Oct. 28**

**68** A53 60c Pair, #a.-b. 1.40 1.40
**69** A53 $1 Pair, #a.-b. 2.25 2.25

Nos. 58-62 Ovptd. in Gold "40th WEDDING ANNIVERSARY OF H.M. QUEEN ELIZABETH II"

**1987, Oct. 15** ***Perf. 13x12½, 12½x13***

**72** A49 5c multicolored .20 .20
**73** A49 60c multicolored .75 .75
**74** A49 $2 multicolored 2.50 2.50
**75** A49 $3 multicolored 3.75 3.75
*Nos. 72-75 (4)* 7.20 7.20

**Souvenir Sheet**

**76** A49 $5 multicolored 6.25 6.25

## UBANGI-SHARI

ü-ˈbaŋ-g̦ē ˈshär-ē

### (Ubangi-Shari-Chad)

LOCATION — In Western Africa, north of the equator
GOVT. — French Colony
AREA — 238,767 sq. mi.
POP. — 833,916
CAPITAL — Bangui

In 1910 French Congo was divided into the three colonies of Gabon, Middle Congo and Ubangi-Shari and officially named "French Equatorial Africa." Under that name in 1934 the group, with the territory of Chad included, became a single administrative unit. See Gabon.

100 Centimes = 1 Franc

Stamps of Middle Congo Overprinted in Black

**1915-22 Unwmk. *Perf. 14x13½***
**Chalky Paper**

1 A1 1c ol gray & brn .25 .25
a. Double overprint 160.00
b. Imperf. 47.50
2 A1 2c violet & brn .25 .25
3 A1 4c blue & brn .45 .45
4 A1 5c dk grn & bl .45 .45
5 A1 5c yel & bl ('22) .75 .75
6 A1 10c carmine & bl .85 .85
7 A1 10c dp grn & bl grn ('22) .80 .80
8 A1 15c brn vio & rose 1.25 1.25
9 A1 20c brown & blue 3.00 3.00

No. 8 is on ordinary paper.

Overprinted

10 A2 25c blue & grn 1.40 1.40
11 A2 25c bl grn & gray ('22) 1.00 1.00
12 A2 30c scarlet & grn 1.10 1.10
13 A2 30c dp rose & rose ('22) 1.00 1.00
14 A2 35c vio brn & bl 4.00 4.00
15 A2 40c dl grn & brn 5.25 5.25
16 A2 45c vio & red 5.25 5.25
17 A2 50c bl grn & red 5.00 5.00
18 A2 50c blue & grn ('22) .90 .90
19 A2 75c brown & bl 11.00 11.00
20 A3 1fr dp grn & vio 11.00 11.00
21 A3 2fr vio & gray grn 12.50 12.50
22 A3 5fr blue & rose 32.50 32.50
*Nos. 1-22 (22)* 99.95 99.95

For surcharges see Nos. B1-B2.

Types of Middle Congo, 1907-22, Overprinted in Black or Red

**1922**

23 A1 1c violet & grn .45 .45
a. Overprint omitted 150.00
b. Imperf. 30.00
24 A1 2c grn & salmon .60 .60
25 A1 4c ol brn & brn .85 .85
a. Overprint omitted 175.00
26 A1 5c indigo & rose .85 .65
27 A1 10c dp grn & gray grn 1.40 1.40
28 A1 15c lt red & dl bl 1.50 1.50
29 A1 20c choc & salmon 4.50 4.50

Overprinted

30 A2 25c vio & salmon 6.50 6.50
31 A2 30c rose & pale rose 2.40 2.40
32 A2 35c vio & grn 4.00 4.00
33 A2 40c ind & vio (R) 4.00 4.00
34 A2 45c choc & vio 4.00 4.00
35 A2 50c dk bl & pale bl 2.40 2.40
36 A2 60c on 75c vio, *pnksh* 3.00 3.00
37 A2 75c choc & sal 4.75 4.75
38 A3 1fr grn & dl bl (R) 7.50 7.50
a. Overprint omitted
39 A3 2fr grn & salmon 9.75 9.75
40 A3 5fr grn & ol brn 16.50 16.50
*Nos. 23-40 (18)* 74.95 74.75

Stamps of 1922 Issue with Additional Overprint in Black, Blue or Red

**1924-33**

41 A1 1c vio & grn (Bl) .25 .25
a. "OUBANGUI CHARI" omitted 100.00
42 A1 2c grn & sal (Bl) .25 .25
a. "OUBANGUI CHARI" omitted 125.00
b. Double overprint 115.00
43 A1 4c ol brn & brn (Bl) .35 .35
a. Double overprint (Bl + Bk) 150.00
b. "OUBANGUI CHARI" omitted 180.00
44 A1 5c ind & rose .35 .35
a. "OUBANGUI CHARI" omitted 100.00
45 A1 10c dp grn & gray grn .45 .45
46 A1 10c red org & bl ('25) .65 .65
47 A1 15c sal & dl bl .75 .75
48 A1 15c sal & dl bl (Bl) ('26) .55 .55
49 A1 20c choc & salmon (Bl) .85 .85

On Nos. 41-49 the color in ( ) refers to the overprint "Afrique Equatoriale Francaise."

50 A2 25c vio & salmon (Bl) .60 .60
a. Imperf.
51 A2 30c rose & pale rose (Bl) .30 .30
52 A2 30c choc & red ('25) .60 .60
a. "OUBANGUI CHARI" omitted 115.00
53 A2 30c dk grn & grn ('27) 1.00 1.00
54 A2 35c vio & grn (Bl) .60 .60
a. "OUBANGUI CHARI" omitted
55 A2 40c ind & vio (Bl) .60 .60
56 A2 45c choc & vio (Bl) .75 .75
57 A2 50c dk bl & pale bl (R) .40 .40
58 A2 50c gray & bl vio ('25) (R) 1.10 1.10
59 A2 60c on 75c dk vio, *pnksh* (R) .40 .40
60 A2 65c org brn & bl ('28) 1.25 1.25
61 A2 75c choc & sal (Bl) 1.40 1.40
62 A2 75c dp bl & lt bl ('25) (R) .90 .90
a. "OUBANGUI CHARI" omitted 115.00
63 A2 75c rose & dk brn ('28) 2.00 2.00
64 A2 90c brn red & pink ('30) 4.00 4.00
65 A3 1fr grn & ind (Bk + Bl) .60 .60
66 A3 1fr grn & ind (R + Bl) 1.10 1.10
67 A3 1.10fr bister & bl ('28) 2.00 2.00
68 A3 1.25fr mag & lt grn ('33) 7.50 7.50
69 A3 1.50fr ultra & bl ('30) 5.50 5.50
70 A3 1.75fr dk brn & dp buff ('33) 9.25 9.25
71 A3 2fr grn & red 1.10 1.10
a. "OUBANGUI CHARI" omitted 950.00 750.00
72 A3 3fr red vio ('30) 4.75 4.75
73 A3 5fr grn & ol brn (Bl) 3.50 3.50
*Nos. 41-73 (33)* 55.65 55.65

On Nos. 65, 66 the first overprint color refers to OUBANGUI CHARI.
For surcharges see Nos. 74-81.

Types of 1924 Issue Surcharged with New Values in Black or Red

**1925-26**

74 A3 65c on 1fr vio & ol 1.75 1.75
a. "65" omitted 100.00
75 A3 85c on 1fr vio & ol 1.75 1.75
a. "AFRIQUE EQUATORIALE FRANCAISE" omitted 100.00
b. Double surcharge 115.00
76 A3 1.25fr on 1fr dk bl & ultra (R) ('26) 1.00 1.00
a. "1f25" omitted 125.00 125.00

Bars cover old denomination on No. 76.

Types of 1924 Issue Surcharged with New Values and Bars

**1927**

77 A2 90c on 75c brn red & rose red 1.75 1.75
78 A3 1.50fr on 1fr ultra & bl 1.75 1.75
79 A3 3fr on 5fr org brn & dl red 2.60 2.60
80 A3 10fr on 5fr ver & vio 15.00 14.00
81 A3 20fr on 5fr vio & gray 22.50 21.00
*Nos. 77-81 (5)* 43.60 41.10

Common Design Types pictured following the introduction.

### Colonial Exposition Issue
Common Design Types

**1931 Engr. *Perf. 12½***
**Name of Country Typo. in Black**

82 CD70 40c deep green 4.25 4.25
83 CD71 50c violet 4.25 4.25
84 CD72 90c red orange 4.25 4.25
a. Imperf. 80.00
85 CD73 1.50fr dull blue 4.25 4.25
*Nos. 82-85 (4)* 17.00 17.00

### SEMI-POSTAL STAMPS

Regular Issue of 1915 Surcharged

**1916 Unwmk. *Perf. 14x13½***
**Chalky Paper**

B1 A1 10c + 5c car & blue 2.40 2.40
a. Inverted surch. 100.00 100.00
b. Double surcharge 100.00 100.00
c. Double surch., one invtd. 130.00 130.00
d. Vertical surcharge 100.00 100.00
e. No period under "C" 12.00 12.00

Regular Issue of 1915 Surcharged in Carmine

B2 A1 10c + 5c car & blue 1.40 1.40

### POSTAGE DUE STAMPS

Postage Due Stamps of France Overprinted

**1928 Unwmk. *Perf. 14x13½***

J1 D2 5c light blue 1.25 1.25
J2 D2 10c gray brown 1.40 1.40
J3 D2 20c olive green 1.60 1.60
J4 D2 25c bright rose 1.60 1.60
J5 D2 30c light red 1.60 1.60
J6 D2 45c blue green 1.60 1.60
J7 D2 50c brown violet 2.10 *2.10*
J8 D2 60c yellow brown 2.40 *2.40*
J9 D2 1fr red brown 3.00 *3.00*
J10 D2 2fr orange red 4.25 *4.25*
J11 D2 3fr bright violet 4.25 *4.25*
*Nos. J1-J11 (11)* 25.05 25.05

Landscape D3

Emile Gentil — D4

**1930 Typo.**

J12 D3 5c dp bl & olive .70 .70
J13 D3 10c dk red & brn .90 .90
J14 D3 20c green & brn 1.00 1.00
J15 D3 25c lt bl & brn 1.10 1.10
J16 D3 30c bis brn & Prus bl 2.25 2.25
J17 D3 45c Prus bl & ol 2.50 2.50
J18 D3 50c red vio & brn 4.50 4.50
J19 D3 60c gray lil & bl blk 4.75 4.75
J20 D4 1fr bis brn & bl blk 4.25 4.25
J21 D4 2fr violet & brown 5.25 5.25
J22 D4 3fr dp red & brn 6.00 6.00
*Nos. J12-J22 (11)* 33.20 33.20

Stamps of Ubangi-Shari were replaced in 1936 by those of French Equatorial Africa.

# UGANDA

ü-ˈgan-də

LOCATION — East Africa, at the Equator and separated from the Indian Ocean by Kenya and Tanzania
GOVT. — Independent state
AREA — 91,343 sq. mi.
POP. — 21,619,700 (1999 est.)
CAPITAL — Kampala

Stamps of 1898-1902 were replaced by those issued for Kenya, Tanganyika and Uganda. Uganda became independent October 9, 1962.

Cowries (50 = 4 Pence)
16 Annas = 1 Rupee (1896)
100 Cents = 1 Shilling (1962)

**Catalogue values for unused stamps in this country are for Never Hinged items, beginning with Scott 79 in the regular postage section and Scott J1 in the postage due section.**

Unused values for Nos. 1-68 are for copies without gum. Very fine examples will be evenly cut and will show at least two full typewritten framelines.

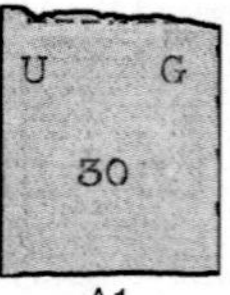
A1

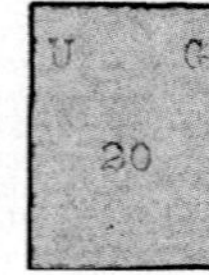
A2

Nos. 1-53 were produced with a typewriter by Rev. Ernest Millar of the Church Missionary Society. They were 20-26mm wide, with nine stamps in a horizontal row. Later two more were added to each row, and the stamps became narrower, 16-18mm.

Rev. Millar got a new typewriter in 1895, and the stamps he typed on it have a different appearance. A violet ribbon in the machine, inserted late in 1895, resulted in Nos. 35-53.

Nos. 1-53 are on thin, tough, white paper, laid horizontally with traces of a few vertical lines.

**Forgeries of Nos. 1-53 are known.**

**Without Gum**
**Wide Letters**
**Typewritten on Thin Laid Paper**
**Stamps 20 to 26mm wide**

**1895 Unwmk. *Imperf.***

1 A1 10(c) black *5,750.* 3,750.
2 A1 20(c) black *5,250.* *1,600.*
3 A1 30(c) black *1,800.* *1,800.*
4 A1 40(c) black *3,250.* 1,550.
5 A1 50(c) black *1,550.* *1,300.*
6 A1 60(c) black *2,100.* 2,100.

**Surcharged with New Value in Black, Pen-written**

10 A1 10 on 50(c) black —
11 A1 15 on 10(c) black —
12 A1 15 on 20(c) black —
13 A1 15 on 40(c) black —
14 A1 15 on 50(c) black —
15 A1 25 on 50(c) black —
16 A1 50 on 60(c) black —

**Stamps 16 to 18mm wide**

17 A1 5(c) black *1,750.* *1,100.*
18 A1 10(c) black *1,750.* *1,500.*
19 A1 15(c) black *1,150.* *1,500.*
20 A1 20(c) black *1,500.* *750.*
21 A1 25(c) black *1,100.* *1,100.*
22 A1 30(c) black *8,750.* *8,750.*
23 A1 40(c) black *8,000.* *8,000.*
24 A1 50(c) black *3,750.* *5,750.*
25 A1 60(c) black *7,500.*

**Narrow Letters**
**Stamps 16 to 18mm wide**

26 A2 5(c) black *1,000.*
27 A2 10(c) black *1,000.*
28 A2 15(c) black *1,000.*
29 A2 20(c) black *800.*
30 A2 25(c) black *1,000.*
31 A2 30(c) black *1,100.*
32 A2 40(c) black *1,100.*
33 A2 50(c) black *950.*
34 A2 60(c) black *1,900.*
35 A2 5(c) violet *575.* *575.*
36 A2 10(c) violet *550.* *550.*
37 A2 15(c) violet *700.* *500.*
38 A2 20(c) violet *425.* *325.*
39 A2 25(c) violet *800.* *800.*
40 A2 30(c) violet *1,100.* *800.*
41 A2 40(c) violet *925.* *925.*
42 A2 50(c) violet *1,000.* 1,150.
43 A2 100(c) violet *3,250.* 3,750.

As a favor to a philatelist, 35c and 45c denominations were made in black and violet. They were not intended for postal use and no rate called for those denominations.

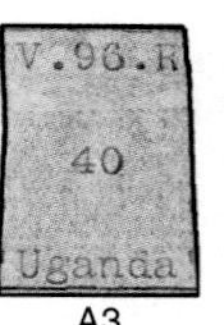
A3

A4

**1896**

44 A3 5(c) violet *550.* *950.*
45 A3 10(c) violet *500.* *575.*
46 A3 15(c) violet *550.* *950.*
47 A3 20(c) violet *325.* *275.*
48 A3 25(c) violet *325.*
49 A3 30(c) violet *575.* *1,150.*
50 A3 40(c) violet *625.* *1,150.*
51 A3 50(c) violet *700.* *900.*
52 A3 60(c) violet *1,600.*
53 A3 100(c) violet *1,500.* 2,250.

Overprinted "L" in Black

**1896 Typeset White Paper**

54 A4 1a black (thin "1") 200.00 175.00
a. Small "O" in "POSTAGE" 1,350. 1,000.
55 A4 2a black 110.00 *140.00*
a. Small "O" in "POSTAGE" 475.00 *525.00*
56 A4 3a black 275.00 *350.00*
a. Small "O" in "POSTAGE" 1,500. *1,800.*
57 A4 4a black 110.00 *175.00*
a. Small "O" in "POSTAGE" 525.00

**Yellowish Paper**

58 A4 8a black 210.00 *250.00*
a. Small "O" in "POSTAGE" 1,250. *1,500.*
59 A4 1r black 425.00 *475.00*
a. Small "O" in "POSTAGE" 1,750.
60 A4 5r black 37,500. 37,500.

Without Overprint

**White Paper**

61 A4 1a black (thin "1") 125.00 110.00
a. Small "O" in "POSTAGE" 700.00 625.00
62 A4 1a black (thick "1") 21.00 *27.50*
a. Small "O" in "POSTAGE" 90.00 *110.00*
63 A4 2a black 29.00 *32.50*
a. Small "O" in "POSTAGE" 110.00 *140.00*
64 A4 3a black 30.00 *35.00*
a. Small "O" in "POSTAGE" 125.00 *160.00*
65 A4 4a black 30.00 *35.00*
a. Small "O" in "POSTAGE" 110.00 *140.00*

**Yellowish Paper**

66 A4 8a black 32.50 *35.00*
a. Small "O" in "POSTAGE" 140.00 *160.00*
67 A4 1r black 87.50 *110.00*
a. Small "O" in "POSTAGE" 350.00 *450.00*
68 A4 5r black 250.00 *400.00*
a. Small "O" in "POSTAGE" 850.00 *1,050.*

Queen Victoria
A5 A6

**1898-1902 Engr. Wmk. 2 *Perf. 14***

69 A5 1a red 2.25 *2.50*
70 A5 1a car rose ('02) 2.25 1.10
71 A5 2a brown 4.00 *8.00*
72 A5 3a gray 13.00 *30.00*
73 A5 4a dark green 7.00 *7.50*
74 A5 8a olive gray 9.00 *27.50*

**Wmk. 1**

75 A6 1r ultra 45.00 *47.50*
76 A6 5r brown 80.00 *110.00*
*Nos. 69-76 (8)* 162.50 *234.10*

A7

**1902 Wmk. 2 Black Overprint**

77 A7 ½a yellow green 2.25 1.60
a. Inverted overprint *2,000.*
b. Double overprint *2,250.*
c. Pair, one without overprint *4,750.*

**Red Overprint**

78 A7 2½a dark blue 3.25 *3.50*
a. Double overprint 750.00

**Catalogue values for unused stamps in this section, from this point to the end of the section, are for Never Hinged items.**

Ripon Falls and Speke Monument
A8

**Wmk. 314**

**1962, July 28 Engr. *Perf. 14***

79 A8 30c vermilion & blk .25 .25
80 A8 50c violet & blk .25 .25
81 A8 1.30sh green & blk .45 .45
82 A8 2.50sh ultra & blk 1.60 1.60
*Nos. 79-82 (4)* 2.55 2.55

Cent. of the discovery of the source of the Nile by John Hanning Speke.

**Independent State**

Murchison Falls — A9

Mulago Hospital, X-Ray Service
A10

Designs: 10c, Tobacco growing. 15c, Coffee growing. 20c, Ankole cattle. 30c, Cotton growing. 50c, Mountains of the Moon. 1.30sh, Rubaga and Namirembe Cathedrals and Kibuli Mosque. 2sh, Makerere College and students. 5sh, Copper mining. 10sh, Cement factory. 20sh, Parliament.

***Perf. 14½x14, 14x14½***

**1962, Oct. 9 Photo. Unwmk.**

83 A9 5c Prus green .25 .25
84 A9 10c red brown .25 .25
85 A9 15c grn, blk & car .25 .25
86 A9 20c bister & pur .25 .25
87 A9 30c brt blue .25 .25
88 A9 50c bluish grn & blk .25 .25
89 A10 1sh bl grn, sep & red .25 .25
90 A10 1.30sh pur & ocher .40 .25
91 A10 2sh grnsh bl, blk & dk car .50 .30
92 A10 5sh dk green & red 1.25 .65
93 A10 10sh red brn & slate 2.50 1.30
94 A10 20sh blue & pale brn 7.00 3.50
*Nos. 83-94 (12)* 13.40 7.75

Uganda's independence, Oct. 9, 1962.

Crowned Crane — A11

**1965, Feb. 20 Photo. *Perf. 14½***

95 A11 30c bl grn, blk, yel & red .25 .20
96 A11 1sh30c ultra, blk, yel & red .75 .50

Intl. Trade Fair at Lugogo Stadium, Kampala, Feb. 20-28.

Black Bee-eater
A12

African Jacana
A13

Arms of Uganda and Birds: 15c, Orange weaver. 20c, Narina trogon. 30c, Sacred ibis. 40c, Blue-breasted kingfisher. 50c, Whale-headed stork. 65c, Black-winged red bishop. 1sh, Ruwenzori turaco. 1.30sh, African fish eagle. 2.50sh, Great blue turaco. 5sh, Lilac-breasted roller. 10sh, Black-collared lovebird. 20sh, Crowned crane.

***Perf. 14½x14, 14x14½***

**1965, Oct. 9 Photo. Unwmk.**

**Birds in Natural Colors**

**Size: 17x21mm, 21x17mm**

97 A12 5c lt vio bl & blk .25 .25
98 A13 10c dull blue & red .25 .25
99 A12 15c dk brown & org .25 .25
100 A12 20c bister & brt grn .25 .25
101 A13 30c hn brn & blk 1.75 .25
102 A12 40c lt yel grn & red 1.00 .40
103 A12 50c dp pur & gray .30 .25
104 A13 65c gray & brick red 2.40 1.30

***Perf. 14½***

**Size: 41x25mm, 25x41mm**

105 A13 1sh lt blue & blk .60 .25
106 A12 1.30sh yel & red brn 6.00 .25
107 A13 2.50sh brt yel grn & blk 4.75 .40
108 A12 5sh lil gray & vio bl 7.50 2.50
109 A13 10sh lt brown & blk 12.00 6.75
110 A13 20sh olive grn & blk 22.00 22.00
*Nos. 97-110 (14)* 59.30 35.35

Parliament Building — A14

13th Commonwealth Parliamentary Assoc. Conf.: 30c, Animal carvings from entrance hall of Uganda Parliament. 50c, Arms of Uganda. 2.50sh, Parliament Chamber.

**1967, Oct. 26 Photo. *Perf. 14½***

111 A14 30c multicolored .20 .20
112 A14 50c multicolored .20 .20
113 A14 1.30sh multicolored .35 .30
114 A14 2.50sh multicolored .70 .60
*Nos. 111-114 (4)* 1.45 1.30

Cordia Abyssinica
A15

Black-galled Acacia
A16

Flowers: 10c, Grewia similis. 15c, Cassia didymobotrya. 20c, Coleus barbatus. 30c, Ochna ovata. 40c, Ipomoea spathulata (morning glory). 50c, Spathodea nilotica (flame tree). 60c, Oncoba spinosa. 70c, Carissa edulis. 1.50sh, Clerodendrum myricoides (blue butterfly bush). 2.50sh, Acanthus arboreus. 5sh, Kigelia aethiopium (sausage tree). 10sh, Erythrina abyssinica (Uganda coral). 20sh, Monodora myristica.

***Perf. 14½x14***

**1969, Oct. 9 Photo. Unwmk.**

115 A15 5c multicolored .20 .20
116 A15 10c multicolored .20 .20
117 A15 15c multicolored .20 .20
118 A15 20c multicolored .20 .20
119 A15 30c multicolored .20 .20
120 A15 40c gray & multi .20 .20
121 A15 50c tan & multi .20 .20
122 A15 60c multicolored .20 .20
123 A15 70c multicolored .20 .20

*Perf. 14*

| | | | | |
|---|---|---|---|---|
| 124 | A16 | 1sh multicolored | .35 | *.20* |
| 125 | A16 | 1.50sh multicolored | .55 | *.20* |
| 126 | A16 | 2.50sh multicolored | .70 | *.20* |
| 127 | A16 | 5sh multicolored | 1.25 | *.20* |
| 128 | A16 | 10sh multicolored | 3.00 | *.55* |
| 129 | A16 | 20sh tan & multi | 7.75 | *1.25* |
| | | *Nos. 115-129 (15)* | 15.40 | *4.40* |

Values of Nos. 124-129 are for canceled-to-order stamps. Cancellations were printed on Nos. 128-129. Postally used copies sell for higher prices.

Nos. 125-126, 129 Surcharged

**1975, Sept. 29 Photo. *Perf. 14***

| | | | | |
|---|---|---|---|---|
| 130 | A16 | 2sh on 1.50sh multi | 1.25 | 1.25 |
| 131 | A16 | 3sh on 2.50sh multi | 25.00 | 25.00 |
| 132 | A16 | 40sh on 20sh multi | 10.00 | 10.00 |
| | | *Nos. 130-132 (3)* | 36.25 | 36.25 |

Millet — A17

Ugandan Crops: 20c, Sugar cane. 30c, Tobacco. 40c, Onions. 50c, Tomatoes. 70c, Tea. 80c, Bananas. 1sh, Corn. 2sh, Pineapple. 3sh, Coffee. 5sh, Oranges. 10sh, Peanuts. 20sh, Cotton. 40sh, Beans.

**1975, Oct. 9 Photo. *Perf. 14x14½***

**Size: 21x17mm**

**Multicolored, Name Panel as follows**

| | | | | |
|---|---|---|---|---|
| 133 | A17 | 10c lt brown | .20 | .20 |
| 134 | A17 | 20c blue | .20 | .20 |
| 135 | A17 | 30c vermilion | .20 | .20 |
| 136 | A17 | 40c lilac | .20 | .20 |
| 137 | A17 | 50c olive | .20 | .20 |
| 138 | A17 | 70c brt green | .20 | .20 |
| 139 | A17 | 80c purple | .20 | .20 |

***Perf. 14½***

**Size: 41x25mm**

| | | | | |
|---|---|---|---|---|
| 140 | A17 | 1sh ocher | .20 | .20 |
| 141 | A17 | 2sh slate | .35 | .25 |
| 142 | A17 | 3sh blue | .55 | .40 |
| 143 | A17 | 5sh yellow green | .70 | .55 |
| 144 | A17 | 10sh brown red | 1.40 | 1.10 |
| 145 | A17 | 20sh rose lilac | 2.75 | 2.25 |
| 146 | A17 | 40sh orange | 5.75 | 4.25 |
| | | *Nos. 133-146 (14)* | 13.10 | 10.40 |

See #195-198. For surcharge & overprints see #175, 203-206, 227-244, 253-257.

Communications Type of Tanzania 1976

Designs: 50c, Microwave tower. 1sh, Cordless switchboard and operators, horiz. 2sh, Telephones of 1880, 1930 and 1976. 3sh, Message switching center, horiz.

**1976, Apr. 15 Litho. *Perf. 14½***

| | | | | |
|---|---|---|---|---|
| 147 | A6a | 50c blue & multi | .20 | .20 |
| 148 | A6a | 1sh red & multi | .20 | .20 |
| 149 | A6a | 2sh yellow & multi | .35 | .25 |
| 150 | A6a | 3sh multicolored | .50 | .40 |
| *a.* | | Souvenir sheet of 4 | 1.75 | 1.75 |
| | | *Nos. 147-150 (4)* | 1.25 | 1.05 |

Telecommunications development in East Africa. No. 150a contains 4 stamps similar to Nos. 147-150 with simulated perforations.

Olympics Type of Tanzania 1976

Designs: 50c, Akii Bua, Ugandan hurdler. 1sh, Filbert Bayi, Tanzanian runner. 2sh, Steve Muchoki, Kenyan boxer. 3sh, Olympic torch, flags of Kenya, Tanzania and Uganda.

**1976, July 5 Litho. *Perf. 14½***

| | | | | |
|---|---|---|---|---|
| 151 | A6b | 50c blue & multi | .20 | .20 |
| 152 | A6b | 1sh red & multi | .25 | .20 |
| 153 | A6b | 2sh yellow & multi | .45 | .40 |
| 154 | A6b | 3sh blue & multi | .70 | .60 |
| *a.* | | Souv. sheet of 4, #151-154, perf. 13 | 7.50 | 5.25 |
| | | *Nos. 151-154 (4)* | 1.60 | 1.40 |

21st Olympic Games, Montreal, Canada, July 17-Aug. 1.

Railway Type of Tanzania 1976

Designs: 50c, Tanzania-Zambia Railway. 1sh, Nile Bridge, Uganda. 2sh, Nakuru Station, Kenya. 3sh, Class A locomotive, 1896.

**1976, Oct. 4 Litho. *Perf. 14***

| | | | | |
|---|---|---|---|---|
| 155 | A6c | 50c lilac & multi | .20 | .20 |
| 156 | A6c | 1sh emerald & multi | .40 | .20 |
| 157 | A6c | 2sh brt rose & multi | .80 | .45 |
| 158 | A6c | 3sh yellow & multi | 1.25 | .65 |
| *a.* | | Souv. sheet, #155-158, perf 13 | 3.50 | 3.50 |
| | | *Nos. 155-158 (4)* | 2.65 | 1.50 |

Rail transport in East Africa.

Fish Type of Tanzania 1977

**1977, Jan. 10 Litho. *Perf. 14½***

| | | | | |
|---|---|---|---|---|
| 159 | A6d | 50c Nile perch | .20 | .20 |
| 160 | A6d | 1sh Tilapia | .30 | .20 |
| 161 | A6d | 3sh Sailfish | .85 | .60 |
| 162 | A6d | 5sh Black marlin | 1.25 | 1.00 |
| *a.* | | Souvenir sheet of 4, #159-162 | 6.00 | 5.50 |
| | | *Nos. 159-162 (4)* | 2.60 | 2.00 |

Festival Type of Tanzania 1977

Festival Emblem and: 50c, Masai tribesmen bleeding cow. 1sh, Dancers from Uganda. 2sh, Makonde sculpture, Tanzania. 3sh, Tribesmen skinning hippopotamus.

**1977, Jan. 15 *Perf. 13½x14***

| | | | | |
|---|---|---|---|---|
| 163 | A6e | 50c multicolored | .20 | .20 |
| 164 | A6e | 1sh multicolored | .25 | .20 |
| 165 | A6e | 2sh multicolored | .45 | .40 |
| 166 | A6e | 3sh multicolored | .70 | .60 |
| *a.* | | Souvenir sheet of 4, #163-166 | 2.60 | 2.25 |
| | | *Nos. 163-166 (4)* | 1.60 | 1.40 |

2nd World Black and African Festival, Lagos, Nigeria, Jan. 15-Feb. 12.

Rally Type of Tanzania 1977

Safari Rally Emblem and: 50c, Automobile passing through village. 1sh, Winner at finish line. 2sh, Car passing through washout. 5sh, Car, elephants and Mt. Kenya.

**1977, Apr. 5 Litho. *Perf. 14***

| | | | | |
|---|---|---|---|---|
| 167 | A6f | 50c multicolored | .20 | .20 |
| 168 | A6f | 1sh multicolored | .20 | .20 |
| 169 | A6f | 2sh multicolored | .45 | .30 |
| 170 | A6f | 5sh multicolored | 1.10 | .85 |
| *a.* | | Souvenir sheet of 4, #167-170 | 2.00 | 2.00 |
| | | *Nos. 167-170 (4)* | 1.95 | 1.55 |

25th Safari Rally, Apr. 7-11.

Church Type of Tanzania 1977

Designs: 50c, Rev. Canon Apolo Kivebulaya. 1sh, Uganda Cathedral. 2sh, Early grass-topped Cathedral. 5sh, Early tent congregation, Kigezi.

**1977, June 30 Litho. *Perf. 14***

| | | | | |
|---|---|---|---|---|
| 171 | A6g | 50c multicolored | .20 | .20 |
| 172 | A6g | 1sh multicolored | .20 | .20 |
| 173 | A6g | 2sh multicolored | .40 | .30 |
| 174 | A6g | 5sh multicolored | 1.00 | .75 |
| *a.* | | Souvenir sheet of 4, #171-174 | 2.00 | 2.00 |
| | | *Nos. 171-174 (4)* | 1.80 | 1.45 |

Church of Uganda, centenary.

Type of 1975 Surcharged with New Value and 2 Bars

**1977, Aug. 22 Photo. *Perf. 14x14½***

| | | | | |
|---|---|---|---|---|
| 175 | A17 | 80c on 60c bananas | .30 | .20 |

No. 175 was not issued without surcharge.

Wildlife Type of Tanzania 1977

Wildlife Fund Emblem and: 50c, Pancake tortoise. 1sh, Nile crocodile. 2sh, Hunter's hartebeest. 3sh, Red colobus monkey. 5sh, Dugong.

**1977, Sept. 26 Litho. *Perf. 14x13½***

| | | | | |
|---|---|---|---|---|
| 176 | A6h | 50c multicolored | .30 | .25 |
| 177 | A6h | 1sh multicolored | .50 | .40 |
| 178 | A6h | 2sh multicolored | 2.25 | 1.00 |
| 179 | A6h | 3sh multicolored | 3.25 | 1.40 |
| 180 | A6h | 5sh multicolored | 3.25 | 2.50 |
| *a.* | | Souvenir sheet of 4, #177-180 | 8.50 | 6.00 |
| | | *Nos. 176-180 (5)* | 9.55 | 5.55 |

Endangered species.

Soccer Type of Tanzania

Soccer Cup and: 50c, Soccer scene and Joe Kadenge. 1sh, Mohammed Chuma receiving trophy, and his portrait. 2sh, Shot on goal and Omari S. Kidevu. 5sh, Backfield defense and Polly Ouma.

**1978, May 3 Litho. *Perf. 14x13½***

| | | | | |
|---|---|---|---|---|
| 181 | A8a | 50c green & multi | .20 | .20 |
| 182 | A8a | 1sh lt brown & multi | .20 | .20 |
| 183 | A8a | 2sh lilac & multi | .40 | .30 |
| 184 | A8a | 5sh dk blue & multi | 1.10 | .75 |
| *a.* | | Souvenir sheet of 4, #181-184 | 2.25 | 2.25 |
| | | *Nos. 181-184 (4)* | 1.90 | 1.45 |

World Soccer Cup Championships, Argentina, June 1-25.
See Nos. 203-206.

Crop Type of 1975

Designs as before.

**1978, June Litho. *Perf. 14½***

**Size: 41x25mm**

**Multicolored, Name Panel as follows**

| | | | | |
|---|---|---|---|---|
| 195 | A17 | 5sh blue | .50 | .25 |
| 196 | A17 | 10sh rose lilac | .95 | .50 |
| 197 | A17 | 20sh brown | 1.90 | 1.00 |
| 198 | A17 | 40sh deep orange | 3.75 | 2.10 |
| | | *Nos. 195-198 (4)* | 7.10 | 3.85 |

Shot Put A18

**1978, July 10 Litho. *Perf. 14***

| | | | | |
|---|---|---|---|---|
| 199 | A18 | 50c shown | .20 | .20 |
| 200 | A18 | 1sh Broad jump | .20 | .20 |
| 201 | A18 | 2sh Running | .40 | .40 |
| 202 | A18 | 5sh Boxing | 1.00 | 1.00 |
| *a.* | | Souv. sheet, #199-202, perf 12 | 2.75 | 2.75 |
| | | *Nos. 199-202 (4)* | 1.80 | 1.80 |

Commonwealth Games, Edmonton, Canada, Aug. 3-12.
For overprints see Nos. 249-252.

Soccer Type of 1978 Inscribed: "WORLD CUP 1978"

Designs: 50c, Backfield defense and Polly Ouma. 2sh, Shot on goal and Omari S. Kidevu. 5sh, Soccer scene and Joe Kadenge. 10sh, Mohammed Chuma receiving trophy, and his portrait.

**1978, Sept. 11 *Perf. 14x13½***

| | | | | |
|---|---|---|---|---|
| 203 | A8a | 50c dk blue & multi | .20 | .20 |
| 204 | A8a | 2sh lilac & multi | .45 | .35 |
| 205 | A8a | 5sh green & multi | 1.00 | .90 |
| 206 | A8a | 10sh lt brown & multi | 2.00 | 1.75 |
| *a.* | | Souv. sheet of 4, #203-206, perf. 12 | 4.00 | 4.00 |
| | | *Nos. 203-206 (4)* | 3.65 | 3.20 |

World Cup Soccer Championship winners.

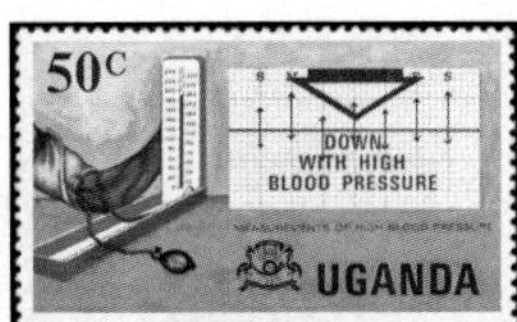

Blood Pressure Gauge and Chart — A19

**1978, Sept. 25 Litho. *Perf. 14***

| | | | | |
|---|---|---|---|---|
| 207 | A19 | 50c shown | .20 | .20 |
| 208 | A19 | 1sh Heart | .20 | .20 |
| 209 | A19 | 2sh Retina | .40 | .35 |
| 210 | A19 | 5sh Kidneys | 1.00 | .95 |
| *a.* | | Souvenir sheet of 4, #207-210 | 2.00 | 2.00 |
| | | *Nos. 207-210 (4)* | 1.80 | 1.70 |

World Health Day and Hypertension Month.

Cattle Unloaded from Plane A20

Flyer 1 and: 1.50sh, "Islander" on runway, Kampala. 2.70sh, Coffee loaded on transport jet. 10sh, Concorde.

**1978, Dec. 16**

| | | | | |
|---|---|---|---|---|
| 211 | A20 | 1sh multicolored | .20 | .20 |
| 212 | A20 | 1.50sh multicolored | .25 | .20 |
| 213 | A20 | 2.70sh multicolored | .45 | .40 |
| 214 | A20 | 10sh multicolored | 1.90 | 1.40 |
| *a.* | | Souvenir sheet of 4, #211-214 | 3.00 | 3.00 |
| | | *Nos. 211-214 (4)* | 2.80 | 2.20 |

75th anniversary of 1st powered flight.
For overprints see Nos. 258-261.

Elizabeth II Leaving Owen Falls Dam — A21

Designs: 1.50sh, Coronation regalia. 2.70sh, Coronation ceremony. 10sh, Royal family on balcony of Buckingham Palace.

**1979, Mar. 1 Litho. *Perf. 12½x12***

| | | | | |
|---|---|---|---|---|
| 215 | A21 | 1sh multicolored | .20 | .20 |
| 216 | A21 | 1.50sh multicolored | .20 | .20 |
| 217 | A21 | 2.70sh multicolored | .35 | .30 |
| 218 | A21 | 10sh multicolored | 1.40 | 1.10 |
| *a.* | | Souvenir sheet of 4, #215-218 | 2.40 | 2.40 |
| | | *Nos. 215-218 (4)* | 2.15 | 1.80 |

25th anniv. of coronation of Elizabeth II.
For overprints see Nos. 245-248.

Bishop Joseph Kiwanuka A22

Designs: 1.50sh, Lubaga Cathedral. 2.70sh, Ugandan pilgrims and St. Peter's, Rome. 10sh, Friar Lourdel-Mapeera, missionary.

**1979, Feb. 15 *Perf. 14***

| | | | | |
|---|---|---|---|---|
| 219 | A22 | 1sh multicolored | .20 | .20 |
| 220 | A22 | 1.50sh multicolored | .20 | .20 |
| 221 | A22 | 2.70sh multicolored | .35 | .30 |
| 222 | A22 | 10sh multicolored | 1.40 | 1.10 |
| *a.* | | Souvenir sheet of 4, #219-222 | 2.40 | 2.40 |
| | | *Nos. 219-222 (4)* | 2.15 | 1.80 |

Ugandan Catholic Church, centenary.
See No. 274. For overprints see Nos. 262-265.

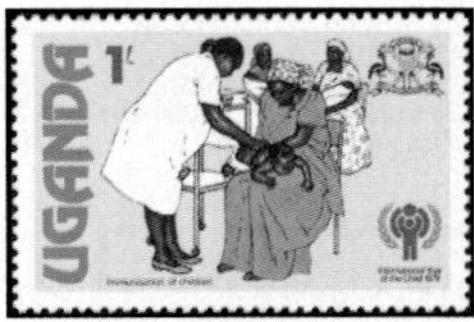

Child Receiving Vaccination — A23

IYC Emblem and: 1.50sh, Handicapped children playing. 2.70sh, Ugandan IYC emblem. 10sh, Teacher and pupils.

**1979, July 16 Litho. *Perf. 14***

| | | | | |
|---|---|---|---|---|
| 223 | A23 | 1sh multicolored | .20 | .20 |
| 224 | A23 | 1.50sh multicolored | .20 | .20 |
| 225 | A23 | 2.70sh multicolored | .25 | .25 |
| 226 | A23 | 10sh multicolored | 1.10 | .90 |
| *a.* | | Souvenir sheet of 4, #223-226 | 2.00 | 2.00 |
| | | *Nos. 223-226 (4)* | 1.75 | 1.55 |

International Year of the Child.
For overprints see Nos. 266-269.

Nos. 133-146, 195-198, 215-218 Overprinted: "UGANDA / LIBERATED / 1979"

**1979, July 12 Photo. *Perf. 14x14½***

**Size: 21x17mm**

| | | | | |
|---|---|---|---|---|
| 227 | A17 | 10c multicolored | .20 | .20 |
| 228 | A17 | 20c multicolored | .20 | .20 |
| 229 | A17 | 30c multicolored | .20 | .20 |
| 230 | A17 | 40c multicolored | .20 | .20 |
| 231 | A17 | 50c multicolored | .20 | .20 |
| 232 | A17 | 70c multicolored | .20 | .20 |
| 233 | A17 | 80c multicolored | .20 | .20 |

***Perf. 14½***

**Size: 41x25mm**

| | | | | |
|---|---|---|---|---|
| 234 | A17 | 1sh multicolored | .20 | .20 |
| 235 | A17 | 2sh multicolored | .25 | .20 |
| 236 | A17 | 3sh multicolored | .40 | .30 |
| 237 | A17 | 5sh multicolored | .55 | .45 |
| 238 | A17 | 10sh multicolored | 1.10 | .90 |
| 239 | A17 | 20sh multicolored | 2.25 | 2.00 |
| 240 | A17 | 40sh multicolored | 4.50 | 3.75 |
| | | *Nos. 227-240 (14)* | 10.65 | 9.20 |

**1979 Litho. Perf. 14½**
**Multicolored, name panel as follows**

**241** A17 5sh blue .75 .55
**242** A17 10sh rose lilac 1.40 1.10
**243** A17 20sh brown 2.60 2.25
**244** A17 40sh deep orange 5.25 4.50
*Nos. 241-244 (4)* 10.00 8.40

**1979, July 12 Litho. Perf. 12½x12**

**245** A21 1sh multicolored .20 .20
**246** A21 1.50sh multicolored .20 .20
**247** A21 2.70sh multicolored .25 .25
**248** A21 15sh on 10sh multi 1.60 1.10
*a.* Souvenir sheet of 4 3.00
*Nos. 245-248 (4)* 2.25 1.75

No. 248a contains Nos. 245-247 and a 15sh in design of No. 218. Issued Aug. 1.

Nos. 199-202; 203, 204-206; 211-214; 219-222, 223-226 Overprinted: "UGANDA LIBERATED 1979"

**1979, Aug. 1 Litho. Perf. 14**

**249** A18 50c multicolored .20 .20
**250** A18 1sh multicolored .20 .20
**251** A18 2sh multicolored .35 .25
**252** A18 5sh multicolored .85 .75

Type A17 of Kenya

**1979, Aug. 1 Perf. 14x13½**

**253** A17 50c multi .20 .20
**255** A17 2sh multi (#204) .30 .25
**256** A17 5sh multi .85 .70
**257** A17 10sh multi 1.75 1.40

Overprint exists on No. 183.

**1979, Aug. 1 Perf. 14**

**258** A20 1sh multicolored .20 .20
**259** A20 1.50sh multicolored .30 .25
**260** A20 2.70sh multicolored .60 .50
**261** A20 10sh multicolored 2.10 1.75

**1979, Aug. 1**

**262** A22 1sh multicolored .20 .20
**263** A22 1.50sh multicolored .25 .20
**264** A22 2.70sh multicolored .45 .40
**265** A22 10sh multicolored 1.60 1.40

**1979, Aug. 16**

**266** A23 1sh multicolored .20 .20
**267** A23 1.50sh multicolored .25 .20
**268** A23 2.70sh multicolored .50 .45
**269** A23 10sh multicolored 1.75 1.60
*a.* Souvenir sheet of 4, #266-269 2.75 2.75
*Nos. 249-269 (20)* 13.10 11.30

ITU Emblem, Radio Waves A24

**1979, Sept. 11**

**270** A24 1sh lt gray & multi .20 .20
**271** A24 1.50sh orange & multi .20 .20
**272** A24 2.70sh yellow & multi .20 .20
**273** A24 10sh blue & multi .90 .75
*Nos. 270-273 (4)* 1.50 1.35

50th anniv. of Intl. Radio Consultative Committee (CCIR) of the ITU.

No. 222a Redrawn and Inscribed: FREEDOM OF WORSHIP DECLARED
Souvenir Sheet

**1979, Sept. Perf. 12**

**274** Sheet of 4 2.25 2.25
*a.* A22 1sh No. 219 .20 .20
*b.* A22 1.50sh No. 220 .20 .20
*c.* A22 2.70sh No. 221 .35 .35
*d.* A22 10sh No. 222 1.40 1.25

In top panel of margin scrolls and coat of arms have been replaced by inscription.

A25

**1979, Nov. 12 Litho. Perf. 14**

**275** A25 1sh #110 .20 .20
**276** A25 1.50sh #112 .20 .20
**277** A25 2.70sh #94 .40 .35
**278** A25 10sh #69 1.50 1.25
*a.* Souvenir sheet of 4, #275-278 2.25 2.25
*Nos. 275-278 (4)* 2.30 2.00

Sir Rowland Hill (1795-1879), originator of penny postage.
For overprints see Nos. 293-296.

Thomson's Gazelle — A26

Designs: 10c, Impalas. 20c, Large-spotted genet. 50c, Bush babies. 80c, Wild hunting dogs. 1sh, Lions. 1.50sh, Mountain gorillas. 2sh, Zebras. 2.70sh, Leopards. 3.50sh, Black rhinoceroses. 5sh, Defassa waterbucks. 10sh, African black buffaloes. 20sh, Hippopotami. 40sh, African elephants.

**1979, Dec. 3 Litho. Perf. 14**
**Size: 21x17mm**

**279** A26 10c multicolored .20 .20
**280** A26 20c multicolored .20 .20
**281** A26 30c multicolored .20 .20
**282** A26 50c multicolored .20 .20
**283** A26 80c multicolored .20 .20

**Size: 39x25mm**

**284** A26 1sh multicolored .20 .20
**285** A26 1.50sh multicolored .20 .20
**286** A26 2sh multicolored .25 .20
**287** A26 2.70sh multicolored .30 .30
**288** A26 3.50sh multicolored .40 .35
**289** A26 5sh multicolored .60 .55
**290** A26 10sh multicolored 1.10 1.00
**291** A26 20sh multicolored 2.50 2.10
**292** A26 40sh multicolored 5.25 4.25
*Nos. 279-292 (14)* 11.80 10.15

Nos. 284, 286, 289 reissued inscribed 1982. See Nos. 400-406. For surcharges see Nos. 386-392.

Nos. 275-278a Overprinted: "LONDON 1980"

**1980, May 6 Litho. Perf. 14**

**293** A25 1sh multicolored .20 .20
**294** A25 1.50sh multicolored .20 .20
**295** A25 2.70sh multicolored .40 .35
**296** A25 10sh multicolored 1.40 1.40
*a.* Souvenir sheet of 4, #293-296 2.25 2.25
*Nos. 293-296 (4)* 2.20 2.15

London 80 Intl. Stamp Exhib., May 6-14.

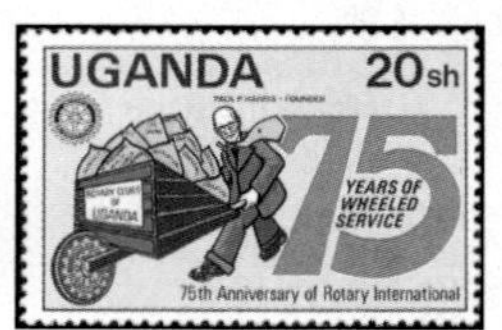


Paul Harris Wheeling Rotary Cart A27

**1980, Aug. Litho. Perf. 14**

**297** A27 1sh Rotary emblem, vert. .20 .20
**298** A27 20sh shown 2.10 1.60
*a.* Souvenir sheet of 2, #297-298 3.00

Rotary International, 75th anniversary.

Soccer, Flags of Olympic Participants, Flame — A28

**1980, Dec. 29 Litho. Perf. 14**

**299** A28 1sh shown .20 .20
**300** A28 2sh Relay race .20 .20
**301** A28 10sh Hurdles .80 .80
**302** A28 20sh Boxing 1.60 1.60
*Nos. 299-302 (4)* 2.80 2.80

**Souvenir Sheet**

**303** Sheet of 4 3.00 3.00
*a.* A28 2.70sh like #299 .20 .20
*b.* A28 3sh like #300 .25 .20
*c.* A28 5sh like #301 .40 .35
*d.* A28 25sh like 302 2.10 1.75

22nd Summer Olympic Games, Moscow, July 19-Aug. 3.

Nos. 299-303 Overprinted with Sport, Winner and Country

**1980, Dec. 29**

**304** A28 1sh multicolored .20 .20
**305** A28 2sh multicolored .20 .20
**306** A28 10sh multicolored .80 .80
**307** A28 20sh multicolored 1.60 1.60
*Nos. 304-307 (4)* 2.80 2.80

**Souvenir Sheet**

**308** Sheet of 4 3.00 3.00
*a.* A28 2.70sh like #304 .20 .20
*b.* A28 3sh like #305 .25 .20
*c.* A28 5sh like #306 .40 .35
*d.* A28 25sh like #307 2.10 1.75

Souvenir Sheet

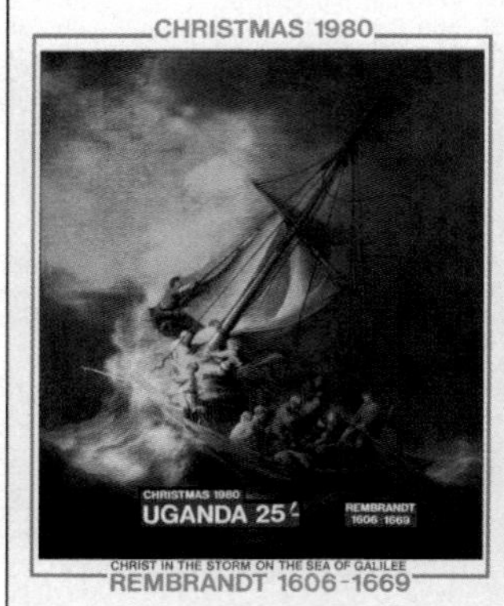


Christ in the Storm on the Sea of Galilee, by Rembrandt — A29

**1980, Dec. 31 Imperf.**

**309** A29 25sh multicolored 6.00 5.25

Christmas 1980.

Heinrich von Stephan and UPU Emblem A30

**1981, June 2 Litho. Perf. 14**

**310** A30 1sh shown .20 .20
**311** A30 2sh UPU headquarters .30 .25
**312** A30 2.70sh Mail plane, 1935 .40 .35
**313** A30 10sh Mail train, 1927 1.40 1.25
*a.* Souvenir sheet of 4, #310-313 3.50 3.50
*Nos. 310-313 (4)* 2.30 2.05

Von Stephan (1831-97), UPU founder.

Common Design Types pictured following the introduction.

**Royal Wedding Issue**
Common Design Type

**1981 Litho. Perf. 14**

**314** CD331 10sh Couple .20 .20
*a.* 10sh on 1sh .20 .20
**315** CD331 50sh Tower of London .30 .25
*a.* 50sh on 5sh .30 .25
**316** CD331 200sh Prince Charles 1.50 1.25
*a.* 200sh on 20sh 1.50 1.25
*Nos. 314-316 (3)* 2.00 1.70
*Nos. 314a-316a (3)* 2.00 1.70

**Souvenir Sheet**

**317** CD331 250sh Royal mews 1.50 1.50
*a.* 250sh on 25sh, light orange 1.50 1.50

Royal wedding. Issue dates: surcharges, July 13; others, July 29. Nos. 314-316 also issued in sheets of 5 plus label, perf. 12, in changed colors.
For overprints see Nos. 342-345.

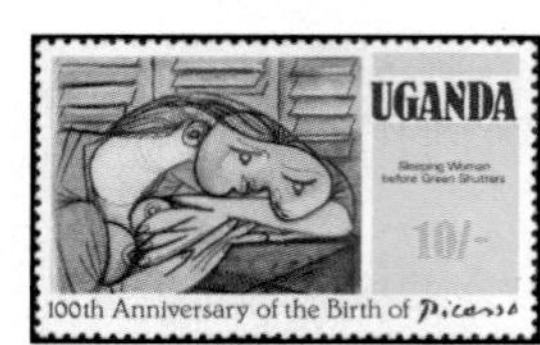


Sleeping Woman Before Green Shutters, by Picasso — A31

Picasso Birth Centenary: 20sh, Bullfight. 30sh, Nude Asleep on a Landscape. 200sh, Interior with a Girl Drawing. 250sh, Minotaur.

**1981, Sept. 21 Litho. Perf. 14**

**318** A31 10sh multicolored .20 .20
**319** A31 20sh multicolored .35 .30
**320** A31 30sh multicolored .50 .40
**321** A31 200sh multicolored 3.50 2.75

**Size: 120x146mm**
***Imperf***

**322** A31 250sh multicolored 5.00 4.00
*Nos. 318-322 (5)* 9.55 7.65

Intl. Year of the Disabled A32

**1981, Dec. Perf. 15**

**323** A32 1sh Sign language .20 .20
**324** A32 10sh Teacher in wheelchair .20 .20
**325** A32 50sh Retarded children .80 .65
**326** A32 200sh Blind man 3.25 2.60
*a.* Souvenir sheet of 4, #323-326 5.25 4.50
*Nos. 323-326 (4)* 4.45 3.65

1982 World Cup Soccer A33

Designs: Various soccer players.

**1982, Jan. 11 Litho. Perf. 14**

**327** A33 1sh multicolored .20 .20
**328** A33 10sh multicolored .20 .20
**329** A33 50sh multicolored .85 .75
**330** A33 200sh multicolored 3.50 3.00
*Nos. 327-330 (4)* 4.75 4.15

**Souvenir Sheet**

**331** A33 250sh World Cup 4.50 4.50

TB Bacillus Centenary — A34

**1982, June 14 Litho.**

**332** A34 1sh Koch .35 .30
**333** A34 10sh Microscope .60 .35
**334** A34 50sh Inoculation 2.75 1.40
**335** A34 100sh Virus under microscope 5.75 2.75
*Nos. 332-335 (4)* 9.45 4.80

**Souvenir Sheet**

**336** A34 150sh Medical School 5.00 3.00

Peaceful Uses of Outer Space A35

**1982, May 17 Litho. Perf. 15**

**337** A35 5sh Mpoma Satellite Earth Station .35 .35
**338** A35 10sh Pioneer II .35 .35
**339** A35 50sh Columbia space shuttle 1.60 1.40
**340** A35 100sh Voyager II, Saturn 3.25 2.75
*Nos. 337-340 (4)* 5.55 4.85

**Souvenir Sheet**

**341** A35 150sh Columbia shuttle 5.25 4.50

Nos. 314-317 Overprinted: "21st BIRTHDAY / HRH Princess of Wales / JULY 1 1982"

**1982, July 7** *Perf. 14*

**342** CD331 10sh multicolored .20 .20
**343** CD331 50sh multicolored .55 .45
**344** CD331 200sh multicolored 2.25 1.75
*Nos. 342-344 (3)* 3.00 2.40

**Souvenir Sheet**

**345** CD331 250sh multicolored 4.50 4.00

Also issued in sheets of 5 + label in changed colors, perf. 12x12½.

20th Anniversary of Independence
A 150sh souvenir sheet showing the Coat of Arms was not issued.

Hornbill — A36

**1982, July 12**

**346** A36 1sh shown .25 .25
**347** A36 20sh Superb starling .70 .60
**348** A36 50sh Bateleur eagle 1.60 1.40
**349** A36 100sh Saddle-bill stork 3.50 2.90
*Nos. 346-349 (4)* 6.05 5.15

**Souvenir Sheet**

**350** A36 200sh Laughing dove 12.50 11.00

Scouting Year A37

**1982, Aug. 23**

**351** A37 5sh Scouts .45 .45
**352** A37 20sh Trophy presentation .95 .75
**353** A37 50sh Helping disabled 2.40 2.10
**354** A37 100sh First aid instruction 4.75 4.25
*Nos. 351-354 (4)* 8.55 7.55

**Souvenir Sheet**

**355** A37 150sh Baden-Powell 6.00 5.25

For overprints see Nos. 376-380.

Franklin D. Roosevelt (1882-1945) — A38

Roosevelt and Washington: 50sh, 200sh, Inaugurations. No. 358, Mount Vernon. No. 359, Hyde Park.

**1982, Sept.** *Litho.*

**356** A38 50sh multicolored .70 .60
**357** A38 200sh multicolored 2.75 2.40

**Souvenir Sheets**

**358** A38 150sh multicolored 2.00 1.90
**359** A38 150sh multicolored 2.00 1.90

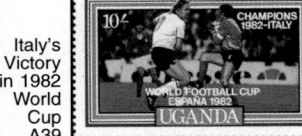

Italy's Victory in 1982 World Cup A39

**1982, Oct.** *Litho.* *Perf. 14½*

**359A** A39 10sh Players .20 .20
**359B** A39 200sh Team 3.00 3.00

**Souvenir Sheet**

**359C** A39 250sh Globe 3.00 3.00

— A39a

**1983, Mar. 14** *Litho.* *Perf. 14*

**360** A39a 5sh Dancers .20 .20
**361** A39a 20sh Traditional currency .30 .30
**362** A39a 50sh Village .70 .70
**363** A39a 100sh Drums 1.40 1.40
*Nos. 360-363 (4)* 2.60 2.60

Commonwealth Day.

St. George and the Dragon, by Raphael A40

**1983, Apr.**

**364** A40 5sh shown .20 .20
**365** A40 20sh St. George and the Dragon, 1505 .35 .35
**366** A40 50sh Moses Parts the Red Sea .90 .90
**367** A40 200sh Expulsion of Heliodorus 3.25 3.25
*Nos. 364-367 (4)* 4.70 4.70

**Souvenir Sheet**

**368** A40 250sh Leo the Great and Attila, 1513 3.25 3.25

A41

7th Non-aligned Summit Conference — A42

**1983, Aug. 15** *Litho.* *Perf. 14½*

**369** A41 5sh multicolored .20 .20
**370** A42 200sh multicolored 2.00 2.00

African Elephants and World Wildlife Emblem A43

5sh, Three adults with elephant bones. 10sh, Three adults walking. 30sh, Elephants standing in water hole. 70sh, Adults with calf.

**1983, Aug. 22** *Perf. 15*

**371** A43 5sh multicolored *1.25 1.25*
**372** A43 10sh multicolored *2.00 2.00*
**373** A43 30sh multicolored *4.75 4.75*
**374** A43 70sh multicolored *12.00 12.00*
*Nos. 371-374 (4)* *20.00 20.00*

Nos. 371-374 were reprinted in 1990, perf 14. Value $25.

**Souvenir Sheet**

**375** A43 300sh Zebras, vert. *8.00 7.00*

No. 375 does not have the WWF emblem. See Nos. 948-953.

Nos. 351-355 Overprinted or Surcharged: "BOYS BRIGADE CENTENARY 1883-1983"

**1983, Sept. 19** *Litho.* *Perf. 14*

**376** A37 5sh multicolored .20 .20
**377** A37 20sh multicolored .20 .20
**378** A37 50sh multicolored .55 .55
**379** A37 400sh on 100sh multi 4.50 4.50
*Nos. 376-379 (4)* 5.45 5.45

**Souvenir Sheet**

**380** A37 150sh multicolored 1.75 1.75

World Communications Year — A44

Designs: 20sh, Mpoma Satellite Earth Station. 50sh, Railroad, Computer Operator. 70sh, Filming Lions. 100sh, Pilots, Radio Communications. 300sh, Communications Satellite.

**1983, Oct. 3** *Litho.* *Perf. 15*

**381** A44 20sh multicolored .25 .25
**382** A44 50sh multicolored .80 .80
**383** A44 70sh multicolored 1.10 1.10
**384** A44 100sh multicolored 1.60 1.60
*Nos. 381-384 (4)* 3.75 3.75

**Souvenir Sheet**

**385** A44 300sh multicolored 3.50 3.50

Nos. 279, 281-285, 289 Surcharged

**1983, Nov. 7** *Litho.* *Perf. 14*

**386** A26 100sh on 10c multi
**387** A26 135sh on 1sh multi
**388** A26 175sh on 30c multi
**389** A26 200sh on 50c multi
**390** A26 400sh on 80c multi
**391** A26 700sh on 5sh multi
**392** A26 1000sh on 1.50sh
*Nos. 386-392 (7)* 18.00 18.00

World Food Day A45

**1984, Jan. 12** *Litho.* *Perf. 14*

**393** A45 10sh Plowing .50 .50
**394** A45 200sh Banana crop 5.75 5.75

Christmas — A46

**1983, Dec. 12** *Litho.* *Perf. 14*

**395** A46 10sh Navitity .20 .20
**396** A46 50sh Sheperds and Angel .40 .40
**397** A46 175sh Flight into Egypt 1.25 1.25
**398** A46 400sh Angels Blowing Trumpets 3.00 3.00
*Nos. 395-398 (4)* 4.85 4.85

**Souvenir Sheet**

**399** A46 300sh Three Kings 2.25 2.25

Animal Type of 1979

**1983, Dec. 19**

**400** A26 100sh like No. 284 .70 .70
**401** A26 135sh like No. 285 .85 .85
**402** A26 175sh like No. 286 1.00 1.00
**403** A26 200sh like No. 287 1.40 1.40
**404** A26 400sh like No. 288 3.00 3.00
**405** A26 700sh like No. 292 4.75 4.75
**406** A26 1000sh like No. 291 6.50 6.50
*Nos. 400-406 (7)* 18.20 18.20

1984 Summer Olympics A48

**1983** *Perf. 14½*

**417** A48 5sh Ruth Kyalisiima .20 .20
**418** A48 115sh Javelin .50 .50
**419** A48 155sh Wrestling .65 .65
**420** A48 175sh Rowing .85 .85
*Nos. 417-420 (4)* 2.20 2.20

**Souvenir Sheet**

**421** A48 500sh Akii-Bua 2.40 2.40

For overprints see Nos. 458-462.

Intl. Civil Aviation Org., 40th Anniv. A49

**1984, Sept.**

**422** A49 5sh Passenger service .55 .55
**423** A49 115sh Cargo service 1.75 1.75
**424** A49 155sh Police airwing 2.40 2.40
**425** A49 175sh Soroti Flying School plane 3.50 3.50
*Nos. 422-425 (4)* 8.20 8.20

**Souvenir Sheet**

**426** A49 250sh Hot air balloon 4.75 4.75

Butterflies A50

**1984, Oct.** *Litho.* *Perf. 14½*

**427** A50 5sh Silver-barred Charaxes .35 .35
**428** A50 115sh Western Emperor Swallowtail 2.75 2.75
**429** A50 155sh African Giant Swallowtail 3.75 3.75
**430** A50 175sh Blue Salamis 4.50 4.50
*Nos. 427-430 (4)* 11.35 11.35

**Souvenir Sheet**

**431** A50 250sh Veinted Yellow 5.50 5.00

Freshwater Fish — A51

**1985** *Litho.* *Perf. 15*

**432** A51 5sh Nothobranchius taeniopygus .45 .45
**433** A51 10sh Bagrus dogmac .65 .45
**434** A51 50sh Polypterus senegalus 1.25 .35
**435** A51 100sh Clarias 1.25 .35
**436** A51 135sh Mormyrus kannume 2.00 1.10
**437** A51 175sh Synodontis victoriae 2.00 1.90
**438** A51 205sh Haplochromis brownae 2.00 *2.25*
**439** A51 400sh Lates niloticus 2.00 *2.50*
**440** A51 700sh Protopterus aethiopicus 2.00 *3.00*
**441** A51 1000sh Barbus radcliffii 2.00 *3.00*
**442** A51 2500sh Malapterus electricus 2.25 *4.00*
*Nos. 432-442 (11)* 17.85 19.35

Issued: #432-435, 437-441, 4/1; #436, 442, 6/10.

For overprints see Nos. 490-494.

Easter A52

**1985, May 13 Litho. *Perf. 14***
**443** A52 5sh The Last Supper .30 .30
**444** A52 115sh Jesus confronts doubting Thomas 1.50 1.50
**445** A52 155sh Crucifixion 1.60 *2.10*
**446** A52 175sh Pentecost 2.10 *2.75*
*Nos. 443-446 (4)* 5.50 6.65

**Souvenir Sheet**
**447** A52 250sh Last prayer in garden 1.00 1.25

UN Child Survival Campaign A53

**1985, July 1**
**448** A53 5sh Mother breastfeeding .35 .35
**449** A53 115sh Growth monitorization 2.00 2.00
**450** A53 155sh Immunization 2.50 2.50
**451** A53 175sh Oral rehydration therapy 2.75 2.75
*Nos. 448-451 (4)* 7.60 7.60

**Souvenir Sheet**
**452** A53 500sh Expectant Mother, food 5.50 5.50

Audubon Birth Bicent. — A54 UN Decade for Women — A56

**1985, July**
**453** A54 115sh Acrocephalus schoenobaenus 2.10 1.75
**454** A54 155sh Ardeola ibis 2.50 1.90
**455** A54 175sh Galerida cristata 2.10 2.50
**456** A54 500sh Aythya fuligula 3.50 *5.00*
*Nos. 453-456 (4)* 10.20 11.15

**Souvenir Sheet**
**457** A54 1000sh Strix aluco 11.50 11.50

See Nos. 469-473.

### Nos. 417-421 Ovptd. or Surcharged with Winners Names, Medals and Countries in Gold

Gold medalists: 5sh, Benita Brown-Fitzgerald, US, 100-meter hurdles. 115sh, Arto Haerkoenen, Finland, javelin. 155sh, Atsuji Miyahara, Japan, 115-pound Greco-Roman wrestling. 100sh, West Germany, quadruple sculls. 1200sh, Edwin Moses, US, 400-meter hurdles.

**1985, July *Perf. 15***
**458** A48 5sh multicolored .25 .25
**459** A48 115sh multicolored .35 .35
**460** A48 155sh multicolored .50 .50
**461** A48 1000sh on 175sh multi 3.00 3.00
*Nos. 458-461 (4)* 4.10 4.10

**Souvenir Sheet**
**462** A48 1200sh on 500sh multi 3.50 3.50

**1985 Litho. *Perf. 14***

5sh, Natl. Women's Day, Mar. 8. 115sh, Girl Guides 75th anniv., horiz. 155sh, Mother Theresa, 1979 Nobel Peace Prize laureate. 1000sh, Queen Mother. #467, Queen Mother inspecting troops. #468, like 115sh, horiz.

**463** A56 5sh multicolored .20 .20
**464** A56 115sh multicolored 1.75 1.60
**465** A56 155sh multicolored 2.90 2.50
**466** A56 1000sh multicolored 1.40 1.75
*Nos. 463-466 (4)* 6.25 6.05

**Souvenir Sheets**
**467** A56 1500sh multicolored 3.50 3.50
**468** A56 1500sh multicolored 5.00 5.00

Issued: #466-467, Aug. 21; others, Nov. 1.

### Audubon Type of 1985

**1985, Dec. 23 *Perf. 12½x12***
**469** A54 5sh Rock ptarmigan .65 .40
**470** A54 155sh Sage grouse 2.25 2.00
**471** A54 175sh Lesser yellowlegs 2.25 *2.50*
**472** A54 500sh Brown-headed cowbird 3.75 *4.50*
*Nos. 469-472 (4)* 8.90 9.40

**Souvenir Sheet**
***Perf. 14***
**473** A54 1000sh Whooping crane 9.50 9.50

UN, 40th Anniv. A57

Designs: 10sh, Forest resources, vert. 180sh, UN Peace-keeping Force. 200sh, Emblem, UN Development Project. 250sh, Intl. Peace Year. 2000sh, Natl., UN flags, vert. 2500sh, Flags, UN Building, New York, vert.

**1986, Feb. *Perf. 15***
**474** A57 10sh multicolored .25 .25
**475** A57 180sh multicolored .35 .35
**476** A57 200sh multicolored .45 .45
**477** A57 250sh multicolored .55 .55
**478** A57 2000sh multicolored 4.25 4.25
*Nos. 474-478 (5)* 5.85 5.85

**Souvenir Sheet**
**479** A57 2500sh multicolored 3.00 *3.25*

1986 World Cup Soccer Championships, Mexico — A58

Various soccer plays.

**1986, Mar. *Perf. 14***
**480** A58 10sh multicolored .30 .30
**481** A58 180sh multicolored 1.00 .60
**482** A58 250sh multicolored 1.10 .75
**483** A58 2500sh multicolored 6.25 *7.00*
*Nos. 480-483 (4)* 8.65 8.65

**Souvenir Sheet**
**484** A58 3000sh multicolored 5.75 5.75

No. 484 contains vert. stamp.
For overprints see Nos. 514-518.

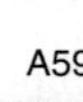
A59

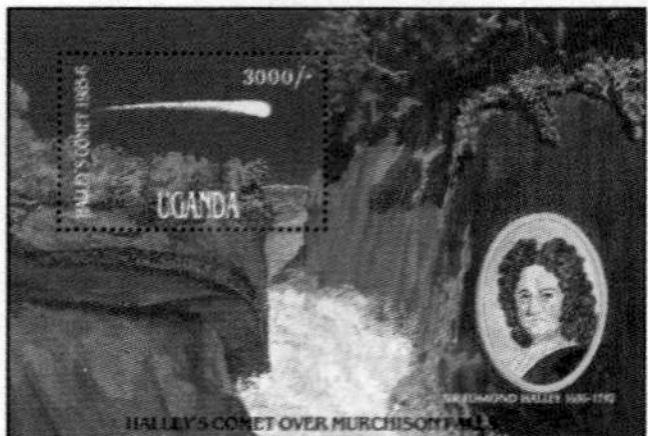

Halley's Comet — A60

Designs: 50sh, Arecibo radio telescope, Puerto Rico, and Tycho Brahe (1546-1601), Danish astronomer. 100sh, Recovery of Astronaut John Glenn, US space capsule, Caribbean, 1962. 140sh, Adoration of the Magi, 1301, by Giotto (1276-1337). 2500sh, Sighting, 1835, Davy Crockett at The Alamo.

**1986, Mar. Litho. *Perf. 14***
**485** A59 50sh multicolored .30 .25
**486** A59 100sh multicolored .45 .25
**487** A59 140sh multicolored .70 .45
**488** A59 2500sh multicolored 5.50 *6.75*
*Nos. 485-488 (4)* 6.95 7.70

**Souvenir Sheet**
**489** A60 3000sh multicolored 6.00 6.00

For overprints see Nos. 519-523.

### Nos. 437, 440-442 and 468 Ovptd. "NRA LIBERATION / 1986" in Silver or Black

**1986, Apr. *Perf. 15***
**490** A51 175sh multi 1.50 1.25
**491** A51 700sh multi 4.00 4.00
**492** A51 1000sh multi (Bk) 4.50 4.50
**493** A51 2500sh multi (Bk) 7.00 *8.25*
*Nos. 490-493 (4)* 17.00 18.00

**Souvenir Sheet**
***Perf. 14***
**494** A56 1500sh multi (Bk) 5.75 4.75

No. 494 ovptd. in one line in margin. A 400sh also exists with silver overprint. All stamps exist with overprint colors transposed.

### Queen Elizabeth II, 60th Birthday
Common Design Type

**1986, Apr. 21 *Perf. 14***
**495** CD339 100sh At London Zoo, c. 1938 .25 .25
**496** CD339 140sh At the races, 1970 .25 .25
**497** CD339 2500sh Sandringham, 1982 4.25 4.25
*Nos. 495-497 (3)* 4.75 4.75

**Souvenir Sheet**
**498** CD339 3000sh Engagement, 1947 4.50 4.50

AMERIPEX '86 — A61

**1986, May 22 *Perf. 15***
**499** A61 50sh Niagara Falls .30 .30
**500** A61 100sh Jefferson Memorial .30 .30
**501** A61 250sh Liberty Bell .50 .50
**502** A61 1000sh The Alamo 1.90 1.90
**503** A61 2500sh George Washington Bridge 4.50 4.50
*Nos. 499-503 (5)* 7.50 7.50

**Souvenir Sheet**
**504** A61 3000sh Grand Canyon 3.50 3.50

Statue of Liberty, cent.

A62

Statue of Liberty, Cent. — A63

Tall ships, Operation Sail: 50sh, Gloria, Colombia, vert. 100sh, Mircea, Romania, vert. 140sh, Sagres II, Portugal. 2500sh, Gazela Primero, US.

**1986, July *Perf. 14***
**505** A62 50sh multicolored .75 .60
**506** A62 100sh multicolored 1.00 .60
**507** A62 140sh multicolored 1.75 1.25
**508** A62 2500sh multicolored 7.75 *9.25*
*Nos. 505-508 (4)* 11.25 11.70

**Souvenir Sheet**
**509** A63 3000sh multicolored 4.25 4.25

### Royal Wedding Issue, 1986
Common Design Type

Designs: 50sh, Prince Andrew and Sarah Ferguson. 140sh, Andrew and Princess Anne. 2500sh, At formal affair. 3000sh, Couple diff. Nos. 510-512 horiz.

**1986, July 23**
**510** CD340 50sh multicolored .25 .25
**511** CD340 140sh multicolored .25 .25
**512** CD340 2500sh multicolored 3.75 *4.50*
*Nos. 510-512 (3)* 4.25 5.00

**Souvenir Sheet**
**513** CD340 3000sh multicolored 4.75 4.75

### Nos. 480-484 Ovptd. or Surcharged "WINNERS Argentina 3 W. Germany 2" in Gold in 2 or 3 Lines

**1986, Sept. 15 Litho. *Perf. 14***
**514** A58 50sh on 10sh multi .20 .20
**515** A58 180sh multicolored .25 .20
**516** A58 250sh multicolored .30 .30
**517** A58 2500sh multicolored 3.75 *3.25*
*Nos. 514-517 (4)* 4.50 3.95

**Souvenir Sheet**
**518** A58 3000sh multicolored 5.75 5.75

### Nos. 485-489 Ovptd. with Halley's Comet Emblem

**1986, Oct. 15 Litho. *Perf. 14***
**519** A59 50sh multicolored .30 .30
**520** A59 100sh multicolored .50 .35
**521** A59 140sh multicolored .70 .60
**522** A59 2500sh multicolored 7.00 *8.00*
*Nos. 519-522 (4)* 8.50 9.25

**Souvenir Sheet**
**523** A60 3000sh multicolored 6.00 6.00

Christian Martyrs A64

Designs: 50sh, St. Kizito. 150sh, St. Kizito educating Ganda converts. 200sh, Execution of Bishop James Hannington. 1000sh, Mwanga's execution of converts, cent. 1500sh, King Mwanga sentencing Christians to death.

**1986, Oct. 15**
**524** A64 50sh multicolored .20 .20
**525** A64 150sh multicolored .20 .20
**526** A64 200sh multicolored .35 .35
**527** A64 1000sh multicolored 1.50 1.50
*Nos. 524-527 (4)* 2.25 2.25

**Souvenir Sheet**
**528** A64 1500sh multicolored 2.25 2.25

A65

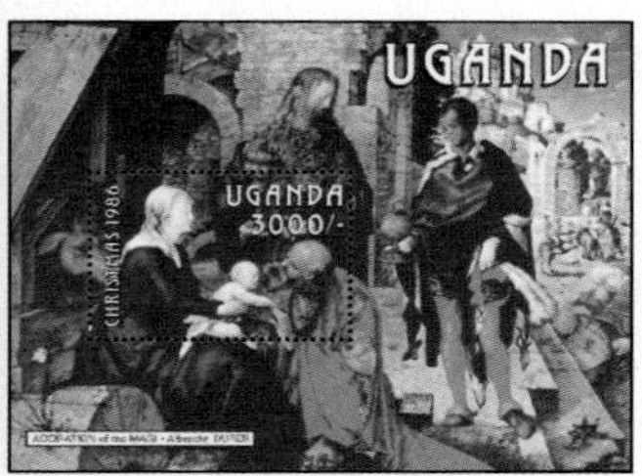


Christmas — A66

Paintings by Albrecht Durer and Titian: 50sh, Madonna of the Cherries. 150sh, Madonna and Child, vert. 200sh, Assumption of the Virgin, vert. 2500sh, Praying Hands, vert. No. 533, Adoration of the Magi. No. 534, Presentation of the Virgin in the Temple.

**1986, Nov. 26 Litho. *Perf. 14***

**529** A65 50sh multicolored .20 .20
**530** A65 150sh multicolored .45 .20
**531** A65 200sh multicolored .60 .25
**532** A65 2500sh multicolored 4.25 *5.50*
*Nos. 529-532 (4)* 5.50 6.15

**Souvenir Sheets**

**533** A66 3000sh multicolored 4.75 4.75
**534** A66 3000sh multicolored 4.75 4.75

Birds and Animals A67

**1987 *Perf. 15***

**535** A67 2sh Red-billed firefinch .40 .35
**536** A67 5sh African pygmy kingfisher .55 .35
**537** A67 10sh Scarlet-chested sunbird .80 .35
**538** A67 25sh White rhinoceros 1.25 .95
**539** A67 35sh Lion 1.25 1.25
**540** A67 45sh Cheetahs 1.50 *1.75*
**541** A67 50sh Cordon bleu 1.75 *2.10*
**542** A67 100sh Giant eland 2.75 *3.50*
*Nos. 535-542 (8)* 10.25 10.60

**Souvenir Sheets**

**543** A67 150sh Carmine bee-eaters 4.75 4.75
**544** A67 150sh Cattle egret, zebra 4.75 4.75

Issue dates: Nos. 535-537, 541, 543, Nov. 2; Nos. 538-540, 542-544, July 22.

Transportation Innovations — A68

**1987, Aug. 14**

**545** A68 2sh Eagle, 1987 .30 .30
**546** A68 3sh Bremen, 1928 .30 .30
**547** A68 5sh Winnie Mae, 1933 .35 .35
**548** A68 10sh Voyager, 1986 .50 .50
**549** A68 15sh Chanute biplane glider, 1896 .80 .80
**550** A68 25sh Norge, 1926 1.10 1.10
**551** A68 35sh Curtis biplane, USS Pennsylvania, 1911 1.75 1.75
**552** A68 45sh Freedom 7, 1961 2.00 2.00
**553** A68 100sh Concorde, 1976 5.75 *6.75*
*Nos. 545-553 (9)* 12.85 13.85

1988 Summer Olympics, Seoul A69

Flags and athletes.

**1987, Oct. 5 *Perf. 14½x14***

**554** A69 5sh Torch bearer .25 .25
**555** A69 10sh Swimming .30 .30
**556** A69 50sh Cycling 1.40 1.40
**557** A69 100sh Gymnastic rings 2.75 2.75
*Nos. 554-557 (4)* 4.70 4.70

**Souvenir Sheet**

**558** A69 150sh Boxing 4.25 *4.50*

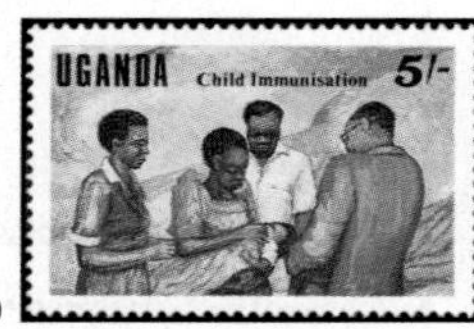


A70

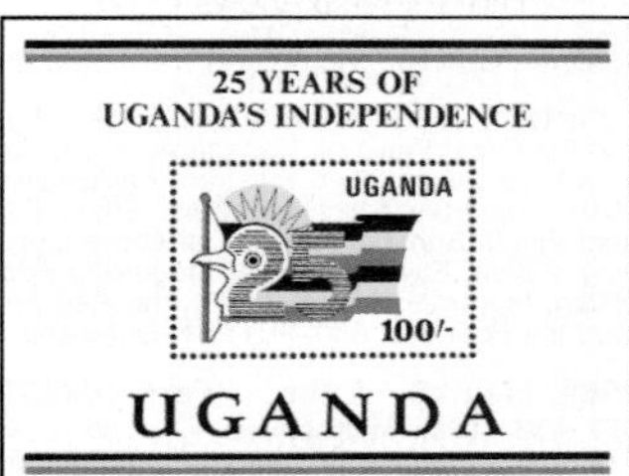


Natl. Independence, 25th Anniv. — A71

**1987, Oct. 8**

**559** A70 5sh shown .25 .25
**560** A70 10sh Mulago Hospital .45 .45
**561** A70 25sh Independence Monument 1.00 1.00
**562** A70 50sh High Court 1.90 1.90
*Nos. 559-562 (4)* 3.60 3.60

**Souvenir Sheet**

**563** A71 100sh shown 3.25 3.25

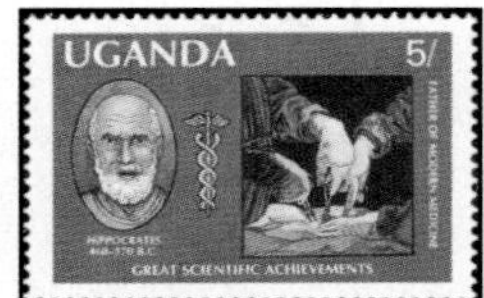


A72

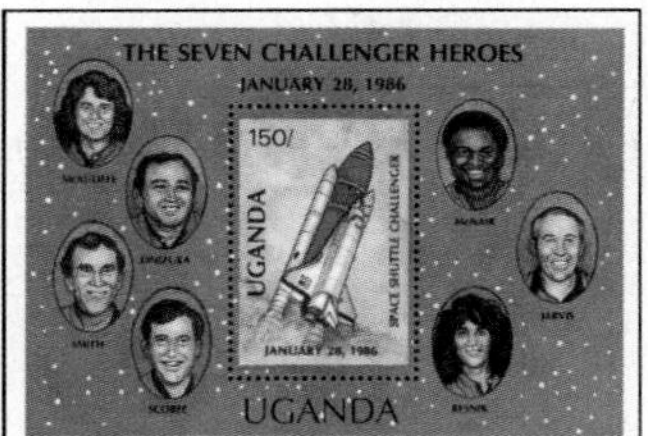


Science and Space — A73

Birds — A74

Designs: 5sh, Hippocrates, father of modern medicine, caduceus and surgeons. 25sh, Albert Einstein and Theory of Relativity equation. 35sh, Sir Isaac Newton and Optics Theory. 45sh, Karl Benz (1844-1929), German engineer, automobile pioneer, and the Mercedes-Benz sports coupe and manufacturers' emblems.

**1987, Nov. 2 *Perf. 14½x14***

**564** A72 5sh multicolored .70 .70
**565** A72 25sh multicolored 2.75 2.75
**566** A72 35sh multicolored 3.25 3.25
**567** A72 45sh multicolored 4.00 4.00
*Nos. 564-567 (4)* 10.70 10.70

**Souvenir Sheet**

***Perf. 14x14½***

**568** A73 150sh shown 6.00 6.00

**1987, Nov. 2 Litho. *Perf. 14***

**569** A74 5sh Golden-backed weaver .65 *.70*
**570** A74 10sh Hoopoe 1.50 1.25
**571** A74 15sh Red-throated bee-eater 1.60 1.25
**572** A74 25sh Lilac-breasted roller 2.10 1.75
**573** A74 35sh Pygmy goose 2.25 2.00
**574** A74 45sh Scarlet-chested sunbird 2.50 2.50
**575** A74 50sh Crowned crane 2.50 2.50
**576** A74 100sh Long-tailed fiscal shrike 4.50 *4.75*
*Nos. 569-576 (8)* 17.60 16.70

**Souvenir Sheets**

**577** A74 150sh African barn owl, horiz. 5.00 5.00
**578** A74 150sh African fish-eagle, horiz. 5.00 5.00

14th World Boy Scout Jamboree, Australia, 1987-88 — A75

Activities: 5sh, Stamp collecting, Uganda Nos. 84 and 116. 25sh, Planting trees, Natl. flag. 35sh, Canoeing on Lake Victoria. 45sh, Hiking and camping. 150sh, Logo of 1987 jamboree and natl. Boy Scout organization emblem.

**1987, Nov. 20**

**579** A75 5sh multicolored .30 .30
**580** A75 25sh multicolored 1.25 1.25
**581** A75 35sh multicolored 1.75 1.75
**582** A75 45sh multicolored 2.10 2.10
*Nos. 579-582 (4)* 5.40 5.40

**Souvenir Sheet**

**583** A75 150sh multicolored 5.00 5.00

Christmas A76

The life of Christ and the Virgin pictured on bas-reliefs, c. 1250, and a tapestry from France: 5sh, The Annunciation. 10sh, The Nativity. 50sh, Flight into Egypt. 100sh, The Adoration of the Magi. 150sh, The Mystic Wine Tapestry.

**1987, Dec. 18**

**584** A76 5sh multicolored .25 .25
**585** A76 10sh multicolored .25 .25
**586** A76 50sh multicolored 1.60 *1.75*
**587** A76 100sh multicolored 3.00 *3.50*
*Nos. 584-587 (4)* 5.10 5.75

**Souvenir Sheet**

**588** A76 150sh multicolored 5.00 5.00

Locomotives — A77

Designs: 5sh, Class 12 2-6-2T light shunter. 10sh, Class 92 1Co-Co1 diesel electric. 15sh, Class 2-8-2. 25sh, Class 2-6-2T light shunter. 35sh, Class 4-8-0. 45sh, Class 4-8-2. 50sh, Class 4-8-4+4-8-4 Garratt. 100sh, Class 87 1Co-Co1 diesel electric. No. 597, Class 59 4-8-2+2-8-4 Garratt. No. 598, Class 31 2-8-4.

**1988, Jan. 18**

**589** A77 5sh multicolored .25 .25
**590** A77 10sh multicolored .45 .45
**591** A77 15sh multicolored .70 .65
**592** A77 25sh multicolored 1.00 1.00
**593** A77 35sh multicolored 1.60 1.25
**594** A77 45sh multicolored 2.00 1.75
**595** A77 50sh multicolored 2.10 1.90
**596** A77 100sh multicolored 5.00 3.00
*Nos. 589-596 (8)* 13.10 10.25

**Souvenir Sheets**

**597** A77 150sh multicolored 5.25 5.25
**598** A77 150sh multicolored 5.25 5.25

Minerals — A78

**1988, Jan. 18**

**599** A78 1sh Columbite-tantalite .20 .20
**600** A78 2sh Galena .20 .20
**601** A78 5sh Malachite .20 .20
**602** A78 10sh Cassiterite .35 .35
**603** A78 35sh Ferberite 1.25 1.25
**604** A78 50sh Emerald 1.75 1.75
**605** A78 100sh Monazite 3.25 3.25
**606** A78 150sh Microcline 5.00 5.00
*Nos. 599-606 (8)* 12.20 12.20

1988 Summer Olympics, Seoul A79

**1988, May 16 Litho. *Perf. 14***

**607** A79 5sh Hurdles .30 .30
**608** A79 25sh High jump .55 *.75*
**609** A79 35sh Javelin .60 *.75*
**610** A79 45sh Long jump .85 *1.00*
*Nos. 607-610 (4)* 2.30 2.80

**Souvenir Sheet**

**611** A79 150sh Medals, five-ring emblem 2.25 2.25

For overprints see Nos. 651-655.

Flowers A80

**1988, July 28 Litho. *Perf. 15***

**612** A80 5sh Spathodea campanulata .25 .20
**613** A80 10sh Gloriosa simplex .25 .20
**614** A80 20sh Thevetica peruviana, vert. .35 .25
**615** A80 25sh Hibiscus schizopetalus .35 .35
**616** A80 35sh Aframomum sceptrum .35 *.40*
**617** A80 45sh Adenium obesum .35 *.50*
**618** A80 50sh Kigelia africana, vert. .45 *.60*
**619** A80 100sh Clappertonia ficifolia .65 *1.00*
*Nos. 612-619 (8)* 3.00 3.50

**Souvenir Sheets**

**620** A80 150sh Costus spectabiis 1.50 1.50
**621** A80 150sh Canarina abyssinica, vert. 1.50 1.50

Intl. Red Cross, 125th Anniv. A81

**1988, Oct. 28 Litho. *Perf. 14***

**622** A81 10sh "AIDS" .30 .30
**623** A81 40sh Immunize children 1.00 1.00
**624** A81 70sh Relief distribution 2.10 2.10
**625** A81 90sh First aid 2.75 2.75
*Nos. 622-625 (4)* 6.15 6.15

**Souvenir Sheet**

**626** A81 150sh Jean-Henri Dunant, vert. 3.25 3.25

Paintings by Titian — A82

Designs: 10sh, Portrait of a Lady, c. 1508. 20sh, Portrait of a Man, 1507. 40sh, Portrait of Isabella d'Este, c. 1534. 50sh, Portrait of Vincenzo Mosti, 1520. 70sh, Pope Paul III Farnese, c. 1545. 90sh, Violante, 1515. 100sh, Lavinia, Titian's Daughter, c. 1565. 250sh, Portrait of Dr. Parma, c. 1515. No. 635, The Speech of Alfonso D'Avalos, c. 1540. No. 636, Cain and Abel.

**1988, Oct. 31** *Perf. 14*

**627** A82 10sh multicolored .25 .25
**628** A82 20sh multicolored .40 .40
**629** A82 40sh multicolored .60 .60
**630** A82 50sh multicolored .75 .75
**631** A82 70sh multicolored .85 .85
**632** A82 90sh multicolored 1.00 1.00
**633** A82 100sh multicolored 1.25 1.25
**634** A82 250sh multicolored 2.40 2.40
*Nos. 627-634 (8)* 7.50 7.50

**Souvenir Sheets**

**635** A82 350sh multicolored 4.75 4.75
**636** A82 350sh multicolored 4.75 4.75

Game Preserves — A83

Designs: 10sh, Giraffes, Kidepo Valley Natl. Park. 25sh, Zebras, Lake Mburo Natl. Park. 100sh, African buffalo, Murchison Falls Natl. Park. 250sh, Pelicans, Queen Elizabeth Natl. Park. 350sh, Roan antelopes, Lake Mburo Natl. Park.

**1988, Nov. 18** **Litho.** *Perf. 14*

**637** A83 10sh multicolored .45 .20
**638** A83 25sh multicolored 1.25 .50
**639** A83 100sh multicolored 2.55 *2.75*
**640** A83 250sh multicolored 7.00 *8.50*
*Nos. 637-640 (4)* 11.25 11.95

**Souvenir Sheet**

**641** A83 350sh multicolored 4.25 4.25

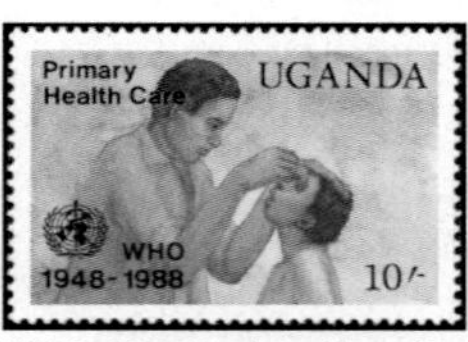


WHO 40th Anniv., Alma Ata Declaration 10th Anniv. — A84

**1988, Dec. 1**

**642** A84 10sh Primary health care .25 .25
**643** A84 25sh Mental health .45 .45
**644** A84 45sh Rural health care .75 .75
**645** A84 100sh Dental care 1.75 1.75
**646** A84 200sh Postnatal care 3.25 3.25
*Nos. 642-646 (5)* 6.45 6.45

**Souvenir Sheet**

**647** A84 350sh Conference Hall, Alma-Ata, USSR 4.00 4.00

Miniature Sheet

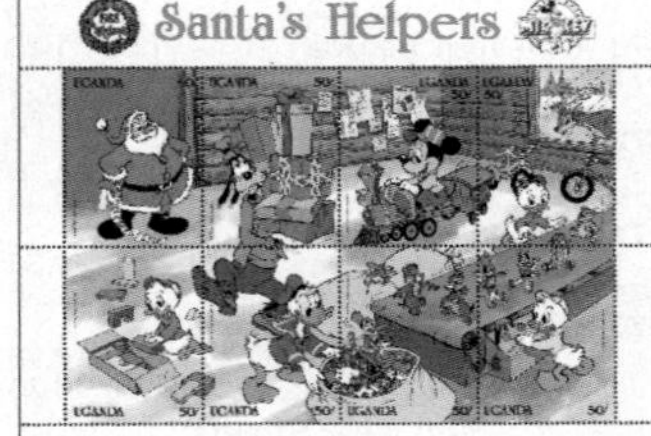


Christmas, Mickey Mouse 60th Birthday — A85

Walt Disney characters: No. 648a, Santa Claus. b, Goofy. c, Mickey Mouse. d, Huey at conveyor belt. e, Dewey packing building blocks. f, Donald Duck. g, Chip-n-Dale. h, Louie at conveyor belt controls. No. 649, Preparing reindeer for Christmas eve flight. No. 650, Mickey loading sleigh with toys, horiz.

**1988, Dec. 2** *Perf. 13½x14, 14x13½*

**648** Sheet of 8 10.00 10.00
*a.-h.* A85 50sh any single .80 .80

**Souvenir Sheets**

**649** A85 350sh multicolored 5.75 5.75
**650** A85 350sh multicolored 5.75 5.75

Nos. 607-611 Ovptd. or Surcharged to Honor Olympic Winners

5sh: "110 M HURDLES / R. KINGDOM / USA"
25sh: "HIGH JUMP / G. AVDEENKO / USSR"
35sh: "JAVELIN / T. KORJUS / FINLAND"
300sh: "LONG JUMP / C. LEWIS / USA"

**1989, Jan. 30** **Litho.** *Perf. 14*

**651** A79 5sh multicolored .25 .25
**652** A79 25sh multicolored .30 .30
**653** A79 35sh multicolored .35 .35
**654** A79 300sh on 45sh multi 3.25 3.25
*Nos. 651-654 (4)* 4.15 4.15

**Souvenir Sheet**

**655** A79 350sh on 150sh multi 5.00 5.00

1990 World Cup Soccer Championships, Italy — A86

Various action scenes.

**1989, Apr. 24** **Litho.** *Perf. 14*

**656** A86 10sh multi, vert. .35 .35
**657** A86 25sh multicolored .55 .55
**658** A86 75sh multicolored 1.60 1.60
**659** A86 200sh multi, vert. 4.00 4.00
*Nos. 656-659 (4)* 6.50 6.50

**Souvenir Sheet**

**660** A86 300sh multicolored 4.50 4.50

Mushrooms — A87

**1989, Aug. 14** **Litho.** *Perf. 14*

**661** A87 10sh Suillus granulatus .60 .60
**662** A87 15sh Omphalotus olearius .75 .75
**663** A87 45sh Oudemansiella radicata 1.50 1.50
**664** A87 50sh Clitocybe nebularis 1.50 1.50
**665** A87 60sh Macrolepiota rhacodes 1.60 1.60
**666** A87 75sh Lepista nuda 1.90 1.90
**667** A87 150sh Suillus luteus 3.50 3.50
**668** A87 200sh Agaricus campestris 3.75 3.75
*Nos. 661-668 (8)* 15.10 15.10

**Souvenir Sheets**

**669** A87 350sh Schizophyllum commune 8.00 8.00
**670** A87 350sh Bolbitius vitellinus 8.00 8.00

"The Thirty-six Views of Mt. Fuji" — A88

Prints by Hokusai (1760-1849): 10sh, Fuji and the Great Wave off Kanagawa. 15sh, Fuji from Lake Suwa. 20sh, Fuji from Kajikazawa. 60sh, Fuji from Shichirigahama. 90sh, Fuji from Ejiri in Sunshu. 120sh, Fuji Above Lightning. 200sh, Fuji from Lower Meguro in Edo. 250sh, Fuji from Edo. No. 679, The Red Fuji from the Foot. No. 680, Fuji from Umezawa.

**1989, May 15** **Litho.** *Perf. 14x13½*

**671** A88 10sh multicolored .35 .35
**672** A88 15sh multicolored .35 .35
**673** A88 20sh multicolored .35 .35
**674** A88 60sh multicolored .90 .90
**675** A88 90sh multicolored 1.40 1.40
**676** A88 120sh multicolored 2.00 2.00
**677** A88 200sh multicolored 3.25 3.25
**678** A88 250sh multicolored 4.00 4.00
*Nos. 671-678 (8)* 12.60 12.60

**Souvenir Sheets**

**679** A88 500sh multicolored 6.25 6.25
**680** A88 500sh multicolored 6.25 6.25

Hirohito (1901-1989), Showa emperor, and Akihito, Heisei emperor of Japan.

PHILEXFRANCE '89 — A89

**1989, July 7** **Litho.** *Perf. 14*

**681** A89 20sh No. 1 .55 .55
**682** A89 70sh No. 10 1.40 1.40
**683** A89 100sh No. 48 1.60 1.60
**684** A89 250sh No. 67 3.25 3.25
*a.* Souvenir sheet of 4, #681-684 10.50 10.50
*Nos. 681-684 (4)* 6.80 6.80

No. 684a sold for 500sh.

2nd All African Scout Jamboree, Aug. 3-15 — A90

**1989, Aug. 3** **Litho.** *Perf. 14*

**685** A90 10sh Fatal child ailments .35 .35
**686** A90 70sh Raising poultry 1.75 1.75
**687** A90 90sh Immunization 2.10 2.10
**688** A90 100sh Brick-making 2.10 2.10
*Nos. 685-688 (4)* 6.30 6.30

**Souvenir Sheet**

**689** A90 500sh Natl. emblem, vert. 5.75 5.75

Scouting, 75th anniv.
For surcharges see Nos. 1301-1304.

Miniature Sheet

Wildlife at Waterhole — A91

Designs: a, Saddle-billed stork. b, White pelican. c, Marabou stork. d, Egyptian vulture, giraffes. e, Bateleur eagle, antelope. f, African elephant. g, Giraffe. h, Goliath heron. i, Black rhinoceros, zebras. j, Zebras, oribi. k, African fish eagle. l, Hippopotamus. m, Black-backed jackal, white pelican. n, Cape buffalo. o, Olive baboon. p, Bohor reedbuck. q, Lesser flamingo, serval. r, Shoebill stork. s, Crowned crane. t, Impala. No. 691, Lion. No. 692, Long-crested eagle.

**1989, Sept. 12** *Perf. 14½x14*

**690** Sheet of 20 22.00 22.00
*a.-t.* A91 30sh any single .60 .60

**Souvenir Sheets**

**691** A91 500sh multicolored 5.75 5.75
**692** A91 500sh multicolored 5.75 5.75

1st Moon Landing, 20th Anniv. — A92

Butterflies — A93

Quotations and scenes from the Apollo 11 mission.

**1989, Oct. 20** **Litho.** *Perf. 14*

**693** A92 10sh Launch vehicle, Moon .30 .30
**694** A92 20sh Eagle lower stage on Moon .30 .30
**695** A92 30sh Columbia .55 .55
**696** A92 50sh Eagle landing .75 .75
**697** A92 70sh Aldrin on Moon 1.10 1.10
**698** A92 250sh Armstrong on ladder 3.75 3.75
**699** A92 300sh Eagle ascending 4.25 4.25
**700** A92 350sh Aldrin, diff. 5.00 5.00
*Nos. 693-700 (8)* 16.00 16.00

**Souvenir Sheets**

**701** A92 500sh Liftoff 5.25 5.25
**702** A92 500sh Parachute landing 5.25 5.25

Nos. 693-697 and 699 horiz.

**1989, Nov. 13**

**"UGANDA" in Black**

**703** A93 5sh Ioalus pallene .65 .65
**704** A93 10sh Hewitsonia boisduvali .70 .70
**705** A93 20sh Euxanthe wakefeildi 1.10 1.10
**706** A93 30sh Papilio echerioides 1.25 1.25
**707** A93 40sh Acraea semivitrea 1.40 1.40
**708** A93 50sh Colotis antevippe 1.40 1.40
**709** A93 70sh Acraea perenna 1.75 1.75
**710** A93 90sh Charaxes cynthia 1.75 1.75
**711** A93 100sh Euphaedra neophroa 1.75 1.75
**712** A93 150sh Cymothoe beckeri 2.25 2.25
**713** A93 200sh Vanessula milca 2.25 2.25
**714** A93 400sh Mimacraea marshalli 3.25 3.25
**715** A93 500sh Axiocerses amanga 3.50 3.50
**716** A93 1000sh Precis hierta 4.50 4.50
*Nos. 703-716 (14)* 27.50 27.50

See Nos. 826-839 for "UGANDA" in blue.

Explorers of Africa A94

Designs: 10sh, John Speke (1827-64), satellite view of Lake Victoria. 25sh, Sir Richard Burton (1821-90), satellite view of Lake Tanganyika. 40sh, Richard Lander (1804-34), bronze ritual figure of the Bakota tribe. 90sh, Rene Caillie (1799-1838), mosque. 125sh, Dorcas gazelle and Sir Samuel Baker (1821-93), discoverer of Lake Albert. 150sh, Phoenician galley and Necho II (d. 595 B.C.), king of Egypt credited by Herodotus with sending an expedition to circumnavigate Africa. 250sh, Vasco da Gama (c. 1460-1524), 1st European to sail around the Cape of Good Hope, and caravel. 300sh, Sir Henry Stanley (1841-1904), discoverer of Lake Edward, and Lady Alice . No. 725, Dr. David Livingstone (1813-73), discoverer of Victoria Falls, and steam launch Ma-Robert. No. 726, Mary Kingsley (1862-1900), ethnologist, and tail-spot climbing perch.

**1989, Nov. 15 Litho. *Perf. 14***

| No. | Type | Value | Description | Unused | Used |
|---|---|---|---|---|---|
| **717** | A94 | 10sh | multicolored | .40 | .40 |
| **718** | A94 | 25sh | multicolored | .45 | .45 |
| **719** | A94 | 40sh | multicolored | .75 | .75 |
| **720** | A94 | 90sh | multicolored | 1.60 | 1.60 |
| **721** | A94 | 125sh | multicolored | 2.25 | 2.25 |
| **722** | A94 | 150sh | multicolored | 2.75 | 2.75 |
| **723** | A94 | 250sh | multicolored | 4.50 | 4.50 |
| **724** | A94 | 300sh | multicolored | 5.50 | 5.50 |
| | | | *Nos. 717-724 (8)* | 18.20 | 18.20 |

**Souvenir Sheets**

| No. | Type | Value | Description | Unused | Used |
|---|---|---|---|---|---|
| **725** | A94 | 500sh | multicolored | 6.50 | 6.50 |
| **726** | A94 | 500sh | multicolored | 6.50 | 6.50 |

Anniversaries and Events — A95

**1989, Dec. 12**

| No. | Type | Value | Description | Unused | Used |
|---|---|---|---|---|---|
| **727** | A95 | 10sh | Bank emblem | .25 | .25 |
| **728** | A95 | 20sh | Satellite dishes, arrows | .25 | .25 |
| **729** | A95 | 75sh | Nehru | 2.10 | 2.10 |
| **730** | A95 | 90sh | Pan-American Dixie Clipper | 2.10 | 2.10 |
| **731** | A95 | 100sh | Locomotion, Stephenson | 2.10 | 2.10 |
| **732** | A95 | 150sh | Concorde cockpit | 3.50 | 3.50 |
| **733** | A95 | 250sh | Wapen von Hamburg, Leopoldus Primus | 3.50 | 3.50 |
| **734** | A95 | 300sh | Concorde cockpit, crew | 4.25 | 4.25 |
| | | | *Nos. 727-734 (8)* | 18.05 | 18.05 |

**Souvenir Sheets**

| No. | Type | Value | Description | Unused | Used |
|---|---|---|---|---|---|
| **735** | A95 | 500sh | Storming of the Bastille | 5.75 | 5.75 |
| **736** | A95 | 500sh | Emperor Frederick I Barbarossa, charter | 5.75 | 5.75 |

African Development Bank 25th anniv. (10sh); World Telecommunications Day, May 17 (20sh); Birth cent. of Jawaharlal Nehru, 1st prime minister of independent India (75sh); 1st scheduled transatlantic airmail flight, 50th anniv. (90sh); 175th anniv. of the invention of the 1st steam locomotive by George Stephenson and opening of the Stockton & Darlington Railway in 1825 (100sh); 1st test flight of the Concorde, 20th anniv. (150sh, 300sh); Port of Hamburg, 800th anniv. (250sh, No. 736); and French revolution bicent. (No. 735).

Christmas — A96 Orchids — A97

Religious paintings by Fra Angelico: 10sh, Madonna and Child. 20sh, Adoration of the Magi. 40sh, Virgin and Child Enthroned with Saints. 75sh, The Annunciation. 100sh, St. Peter Martyr triptych center panel. 150sh, Virgin and Child Enthroned with Saints, diff. 250sh, Virgin and Child Enthroned. 350sh, Annalena Altarpiece. No. 745, Bosco ai Frati Altarpiece. No. 746, Madonna and Child with Twelve Angels.

**1989, Dec. 18**

| No. | Type | Value | Description | Unused | Used |
|---|---|---|---|---|---|
| **737** | A96 | 10sh | multicolored | .25 | .25 |
| **738** | A96 | 20sh | multicolored | .25 | .25 |
| **739** | A96 | 40sh | multicolored | .55 | .55 |
| **740** | A96 | 75sh | multicolored | .90 | .90 |
| **741** | A96 | 100sh | multicolored | 1.10 | 1.10 |
| **742** | A96 | 150sh | multicolored | 1.50 | 1.50 |
| **743** | A96 | 250sh | multicolored | 2.10 | 2.10 |
| **744** | A96 | 350sh | multicolored | 2.40 | 2.40 |
| | | | *Nos. 737-744 (8)* | 9.05 | 9.05 |

**Souvenir Sheets**

| No. | Type | Value | Description | Unused | Used |
|---|---|---|---|---|---|
| **745** | A96 | 500sh | multicolored | 4.00 | 4.00 |
| **746** | A96 | 500sh | multicolored | 4.00 | 4.00 |

**1989, Dec. 18**

| No. | Type | Value | Description | Unused | Used |
|---|---|---|---|---|---|
| **747** | A97 | 10sh | Aerangis kotschyana | .25 | .25 |
| **748** | A97 | 15sh | Angraecum infundibulare | .25 | .25 |
| **749** | A97 | 45sh | Cyrtorchis chailluana | .60 | .60 |
| **750** | A97 | 50sh | Aerangis rhodosticta | .65 | .65 |
| **751** | A97 | 100sh | Eulophia speciosa | 1.25 | 1.25 |
| **752** | A97 | 200sh | Calanthe sylvatica | 2.75 | 2.75 |
| **753** | A97 | 250sh | Vanilla imperialis | 3.25 | 3.25 |
| **754** | A97 | 350sh | Polystachya vulcanica | 4.50 | 4.50 |
| | | | *Nos. 747-754 (8)* | 13.50 | 13.50 |

**Souvenir Sheets**

| No. | Type | Value | Description | Unused | Used |
|---|---|---|---|---|---|
| **755** | A97 | 500sh | Ansellia africana | 5.75 | 5.75 |
| **756** | A97 | 500sh | Ancistrochilus rothschildianus | 5.75 | 5.75 |

For overprints see Nos. 782-786A.

EXPO '90, Osaka — A98

Flowering trees.

**1990, Apr. 17 Litho. *Perf. 14***

| No. | Type | Value | Description | Unused | Used |
|---|---|---|---|---|---|
| **757** | A98 | 10sh | Thevetia peruviana | .30 | .30 |
| **758** | A98 | 20sh | Acanthus eminens | .30 | .30 |
| **759** | A98 | 90sh | Gnidia glauca | .80 | .80 |
| **760** | A98 | 150sh | Oncoba spinosa | 1.10 | 1.10 |
| **761** | A98 | 175sh | Hibiscus rosa-sinensis | 1.25 | 1.25 |
| **762** | A98 | 400sh | Jacaranda mimosifolia | 2.00 | 2.00 |
| **763** | A98 | 500sh | Erythrina abyssinica | 2.25 | 2.25 |
| **764** | A98 | 700sh | Bauhinia purpurea | 2.50 | 2.50 |
| | | | *Nos. 757-764 (8)* | 10.50 | 10.50 |

**Souvenir Sheets**

| No. | Type | Value | Description | Unused | Used |
|---|---|---|---|---|---|
| **765** | A98 | 1000sh | Delonix regia | 6.75 | 6.75 |
| **766** | A98 | 1000sh | Cassia didymobatrya | 6.75 | 6.75 |

World War II Milestones — A99

Designs: 5sh, Allies penetrate west wall, Dec. 3, 1944. 10sh, VE Day, May 8, 1945. 20sh, US forces capture Okinawa, June 22, 1945. 75sh, DeGaulle named commander of all French forces, Apr. 4, 1944. 100sh, US troops invade Saipan, June 15, 1944. 150sh, Allied troops launch Operation Market Garden, Sept. 17, 1944. 200sh, Gen. MacArthur returns to Philippines, Oct. 20, 1944. 300sh, US victory at Coral Sea, May 8, 1942. 350sh, First battle of El Alamein, July 1, 1942. 500sh, Naval battle at Guadalcanal, Nov. 12, 1942. 1000sh, Battle of Britain.

**1990, June 8 Litho. *Perf. 14***

| No. | Type | Value | Description | Unused | Used |
|---|---|---|---|---|---|
| **767** | A99 | 5sh | multicolored | .35 | .35 |
| **768** | A99 | 10sh | multicolored | .35 | .35 |
| **769** | A99 | 20sh | multicolored | .35 | .35 |
| **770** | A99 | 75sh | multicolored | .75 | .75 |
| **771** | A99 | 100sh | multicolored | 1.00 | 1.00 |
| **772** | A99 | 150sh | multicolored | 1.50 | 1.50 |
| **773** | A99 | 200sh | multicolored | 2.00 | 2.00 |
| **774** | A99 | 300sh | multicolored | 3.25 | 3.25 |
| **775** | A99 | 350sh | multicolored | 3.50 | 3.50 |
| **776** | A99 | 500sh | multicolored | 5.00 | 5.00 |
| | | | *Nos. 767-776 (10)* | 18.05 | 18.05 |

**Souvenir Sheet**

| No. | Type | Value | Description | Unused | Used |
|---|---|---|---|---|---|
| **777** | A99 | 1000sh | multicolored | 7.50 | 7.50 |

Queen Mother, 90th Birthday — A100

**1990, July 5**

| No. | Type | Value | Description | Unused | Used |
|---|---|---|---|---|---|
| **778** | | 250sh | Hands clasped | 1.00 | 1.00 |
| **779** | | 250sh | Facing left | 1.00 | 1.00 |
| **780** | | 250sh | Holding dog | 1.00 | 1.00 |
| *a.* | A100 | | Strip of 3, #778-780 | 4.25 | 4.25 |
| | | | *Nos. 778-780 (3)* | 3.00 | 3.00 |

**Souvenir Sheet**

| No. | Type | Value | Description | Unused | Used |
|---|---|---|---|---|---|
| **781** | A100 | 1000sh | like No. 778 | 4.25 | 4.25 |

Nos. 747-754 Ovptd. in Silver

Nos. 755-756 Ovptd. in Silver in Sheet Margin

**1990 Litho. *Perf. 14***

| No. | Type | Value | Description | Unused | Used |
|---|---|---|---|---|---|
| **782** | A97 | 10sh | on No. 747 | .85 | .85 |
| **782A** | A97 | 15sh | on No. 748 | .85 | .85 |
| **782B** | A97 | 45sh | on No. 749 | 1.25 | 1.25 |
| **783** | A97 | 50sh | on No. 750 | 1.25 | 1.25 |
| **783A** | A97 | 100sh | on No. 751 | 1.60 | 1.60 |
| **784** | A97 | 200sh | on No. 752 | 2.10 | 2.10 |
| **785** | A97 | 250sh | on No. 753 | 2.10 | 2.10 |
| **785A** | A97 | 350sh | on No. 754 | 2.50 | 2.50 |
| | | | *Nos. 782-785A (8)* | 12.50 | 12.50 |

**Souvenir Sheet**

| No. | Type | Value | Description | Unused | Used |
|---|---|---|---|---|---|
| **786** | A97 | 500sh | on No. 755 | 5.75 | 5.75 |
| **786A** | A97 | 500sh | on No. 756 | 5.75 | 5.75 |

Issue dates: 15sh, 45sh, 100sh, 350sh, No. 786A, Nov.; others, July 30.

Pan African Postal Union, 10th Anniv. A101

Designs: 750sh, UN Conference on the least developed countries, Paris, Sept. 3-14.

**1990, Aug. 3 Litho. *Perf. 14***

| No. | Type | Value | Description | Unused | Used |
|---|---|---|---|---|---|
| **787** | A101 | 80sh | multicolored | 1.00 | 1.00 |

**Souvenir Sheet**

| No. | Type | Value | Description | Unused | Used |
|---|---|---|---|---|---|
| **788** | A101 | 750sh | multicolored | 4.50 | 4.50 |

Great Britain No. O1 — A102

Designs: 50sh, Canada #12. 100sh, Baden #4b. 150sh, Switzerland #3L1. 200sh, US #C3a. 300sh, Western Australia #1. 500sh, Uganda #29. 600sh, Great Britain #2. No. 797, Uganda #29. No. 798, Sir Rowland Hill.

**1990, Aug. 6 Litho. *Perf. 14***

| No. | Type | Value | Description | Unused | Used |
|---|---|---|---|---|---|
| **789** | A102 | 25sh | multicolored | .30 | .30 |
| **790** | A102 | 50sh | multicolored | .55 | .55 |
| **791** | A102 | 100sh | multicolored | 1.00 | 1.00 |
| **792** | A102 | 150sh | multicolored | 1.25 | 1.25 |
| **793** | A102 | 200sh | multicolored | 1.40 | 1.40 |
| **794** | A102 | 300sh | gray & black | 1.90 | 1.90 |
| **795** | A102 | 500sh | multicolored | 2.10 | 2.10 |
| **796** | A102 | 600sh | multicolored | 2.10 | 2.10 |
| | | | *Nos. 789-796 (8)* | 10.60 | 10.60 |

**Souvenir Sheets**

**Size: 108x77mm**

| No. | Type | Value | Description | Unused | Used |
|---|---|---|---|---|---|
| **797** | A102 | 1000sh | multicolored | 10.50 | 10.50 |

**Size: 119x85mm**

| No. | Type | Value | Description | Unused | Used |
|---|---|---|---|---|---|
| **798** | A102 | 1000sh | scarlet & blk | 10.50 | 10.50 |

Penny Black, 150th anniversary. Nos. 797-798, Stamp World London '90.

Birds A103

**1990, Sept. 3 Litho. *Perf. 14***

| No. | Type | Value | Description | Unused | Used |
|---|---|---|---|---|---|
| **799** | A103 | 10sh | African jacana | .90 | .90 |
| **800** | A103 | 15sh | Ground hornbill | .90 | .90 |
| **801** | A103 | 45sh | Kori bustard, vert. | 1.10 | 1.10 |
| **802** | A103 | 50sh | Secretary bird | 1.10 | 1.10 |
| **803** | A103 | 100sh | Egyptian geese | 1.75 | 1.75 |
| **804** | A103 | 300sh | Goliath heron, vert. | 3.00 | 3.00 |
| **805** | A103 | 500sh | Ostrich, vert. | 4.00 | 4.00 |
| **806** | A103 | 650sh | Saddlebill stork, vert. | 4.25 | 4.25 |
| | | | *Nos. 799-806 (8)* | 17.00 | 17.00 |

**Souvenir Sheets**

| No. | Type | Value | Description | Unused | Used |
|---|---|---|---|---|---|
| **807** | A103 | 1000sh | Volturine guinea fowl, vert. | 5.75 | 5.75 |
| **808** | A103 | 1000sh | Lesser flamingo, vert. | 5.75 | 5.75 |

World Cup Soccer Championships, Italy — A104

Players from various national teams.

**1990, Sept. 24**

| No. | Type | Value | Description | Unused | Used |
|---|---|---|---|---|---|
| **809** | A104 | 50sh | Cameroun | .30 | .30 |
| **810** | A104 | 100sh | Egypt | .60 | .60 |
| **811** | A104 | 250sh | Ireland | 1.50 | 1.50 |
| **812** | A104 | 600sh | West Germany | 3.75 | 3.75 |
| | | | *Nos. 809-812 (4)* | 6.15 | 6.15 |

**Souvenir Sheets**

| No. | Type | Value | Description | Unused | Used |
|---|---|---|---|---|---|
| **813** | A104 | 1000sh | Sweden | 5.25 | 5.25 |
| **814** | A104 | 1000sh | Scotland | 5.25 | 5.25 |

WHO, Promote Better Health — A105

Walt Disney characters in scenes promoting improved health: 10sh, Mickey, Minnie Mouse having a good breakfast. 20sh, Huey, Dewey and Louie looking before crossing street. 50sh, Mickey, Donald Duck against smoking. 90sh, Mickey saving Donald from choking. 100sh, Mickey, Goofy using seat belts. 250sh, Mickey, Minnie avoiding drugs. 500sh, Donald, Daisy exercising. 600sh, Mickey showing bicycle safety. No. 823, Mickey, friends at doctor's office. No. 824, Mickey, friends walking.

**1990, Oct. 19 Litho. *Perf. 13½x13***

| | | | | | |
|---|---|---|---|---|---|
| **815** | A105 | 10sh | multicolored | .30 | .30 |
| **816** | A105 | 20sh | multicolored | .30 | .30 |
| **817** | A105 | 50sh | multicolored | .45 | .45 |
| **818** | A105 | 90sh | multicolored | .75 | .75 |
| **819** | A105 | 100sh | multicolored | .85 | .85 |
| **820** | A105 | 250sh | multicolored | 1.90 | 1.90 |
| **821** | A105 | 500sh | multicolored | 4.25 | 4.25 |
| **822** | A105 | 600sh | multicolored | 5.00 | 5.00 |
| | *Nos. 815-822 (8)* | | | 13.80 | 13.80 |

**Souvenir Sheets**

| | | | | | |
|---|---|---|---|---|---|
| **823** | A105 | 1000sh | multicolored | 6.00 | 6.00 |
| **824** | A105 | 1000sh | multicolored | 6.00 | 6.00 |

Butterfly Type of 1989
"Uganda" in Blue

**1990-92 Litho. *Perf. 14***

| | | | | | |
|---|---|---|---|---|---|
| **826** | A93 | 10sh | like #704 | .65 | .65 |
| **827** | A93 | 20sh | like #705 | .75 | .75 |
| **828** | A93 | 30sh | like #706 | .75 | .75 |
| **829** | A93 | 40sh | like #707 | .75 | .75 |
| **830** | A93 | 50sh | like #708 | 1.00 | 1.00 |
| **831** | A93 | 70sh | like #709 | 1.00 | 1.00 |
| **832** | A93 | 90sh | like #710 | 1.10 | 1.10 |
| **833** | A93 | 100sh | like #711 | 1.10 | 1.10 |
| **834** | A93 | 150sh | like #712 | 1.50 | 1.50 |
| **835** | A93 | 200sh | like #713 | 1.90 | 1.90 |
| **836** | A93 | 400sh | like #714 | 2.25 | 2.25 |
| **837** | A93 | 500sh | like #715 | 2.25 | 2.25 |
| **838** | A93 | 1000sh | like #716 | 4.50 | 4.50 |
| **839** | A93 | 2000sh | like #716 | 11.00 | 11.00 |
| **839A** | A93 | 3000sh | Euphaedra eusemoides | 13.50 | 13.50 |
| **839B** | A93 | 4000sh | Acraea natalica | 14.50 | 14.50 |
| **839C** | A93 | 5000sh | Euphaedra themis | 14.50 | 14.50 |
| | *Nos. 826-839C (17)* | | | 73.00 | 73.00 |

Issue dates: 50sh, 400sh, 500sh, 1000sh, 1991. 3000sh, 4000sh, Jan. 2, 1992. Nos. 827, 833, 835 and 839 exist dated 1991.

This is an expanding set, numbers may change.

Christmas A106

Details from paintings by Rubens: 10sh, 500sh, The Baptism of Christ. 20sh, 150sh, 400sh, 600sh, St. Gregory the Great and Other Saints. 100sh, Saints Nereus, Domitilla and Achilleus. 300sh, Saint Augustine. No. 853, Victory of Eucharistic Truth Over Heresy, horiz. No. 854, Triumph of Faith, horiz.

**1990, Dec. 17 Litho. *Perf. 14***

| | | | | | |
|---|---|---|---|---|---|
| **845** | A106 | 10sh | multicolored | .25 | .25 |
| **846** | A106 | 20sh | multicolored | .25 | .25 |
| **847** | A106 | 100sh | multicolored | .90 | .90 |
| **848** | A106 | 150sh | multicolored | 1.25 | 1.25 |
| **849** | A106 | 300sh | multicolored | 2.00 | 2.00 |
| **850** | A106 | 400sh | multicolored | 2.10 | 2.10 |
| **851** | A106 | 500sh | multicolored | 2.25 | 2.25 |
| **852** | A106 | 600sh | multicolored | 2.50 | 2.50 |
| | *Nos. 845-852 (8)* | | | 11.50 | 11.50 |

**Souvenir Sheets**

| | | | | | |
|---|---|---|---|---|---|
| **853** | A106 | 1000sh | multicolored | 6.25 | 6.25 |
| **854** | A106 | 1000sh | multicolored | 6.25 | 6.25 |

Natl. Census A107

Design: 1000sh, Counting on fingers, houses, people.

**1990, Dec. 28 Litho. *Perf. 14***

| | | | | | |
|---|---|---|---|---|---|
| **855** | A107 | 20sh | multicolored | .50 | .50 |

**Souvenir Sheet**

| | | | | | |
|---|---|---|---|---|---|
| **856** | A107 | 1000sh | multicolored | 6.25 | 6.25 |

Wetlands Fauna — A108

No. 857:a, Damselfly. b, Purple gallinule. c, Sitatunga. d, Purple heron. e, Bushpig. f, Vervet monkey. g, Long reed frog. h, Malachite kingfisher. i, Marsh mongoose. j, Painted reed frog. k, Jacana. l, Charaxes butterfly. m, Nile crocodile. n, Herald snake. o, Dragonfly. p, Lungfish.

No. 858, Nile monitor, horiz.

**1991, Jan. 1 Litho. *Perf. 14***

| | | | | | |
|---|---|---|---|---|---|
| **857** | A108 | 70sh | Sheet of 16, #a.-p. | 17.00 | 17.00 |

**Souvenir Sheet**

| | | | | | |
|---|---|---|---|---|---|
| **858** | A108 | 1000sh | multi | 9.50 | 9.50 |

Fish A109

Designs: 10sh, Haplochromis limax. 20sh, Notobranchius palmqvisti. 40sh, Distichodus affinis. 90sh, Haplochromis sauvagei. 100sh, Aphyosemion calliurum. 350sh, Haplochromis johnstoni. 600sh, Haplochromis dichrourus. 800sh, Hemichromis bimaculatus. No. 867, Haplochromis sp. No. 868, Aphyosemion striatum.

**1991, Jan. 18 Litho. *Perf. 14***

| | | | | | |
|---|---|---|---|---|---|
| **859** | A109 | 10sh | multicolored | .30 | .30 |
| **860** | A109 | 20sh | multicolored | .30 | .30 |
| **861** | A109 | 40sh | multicolored | .30 | .30 |
| **862** | A109 | 90sh | multicolored | .55 | .55 |
| **863** | A109 | 100sh | multicolored | .65 | .65 |
| **864** | A109 | 350sh | multicolored | 1.60 | 1.60 |
| **865** | A109 | 600sh | multicolored | 3.25 | 3.25 |
| **866** | A109 | 800sh | multicolored | 4.00 | 4.00 |
| | *Nos. 859-866 (8)* | | | 10.95 | 10.95 |

**Souvenir Sheets**

| | | | | | |
|---|---|---|---|---|---|
| **867** | A109 | 1000sh | multicolored | 7.50 | 7.50 |
| **868** | A109 | 1000sh | multicolored | 7.50 | 7.50 |

1992 Summer Olympics, Barcelona — A110

**1991, Feb. 25 Litho. *Perf. 14***

| | | | | | |
|---|---|---|---|---|---|
| **869** | A110 | 20sh | Women's hurdles | .30 | .30 |
| **870** | A110 | 40sh | Long jump | .30 | .30 |
| **871** | A110 | 125sh | Table tennis | .90 | .90 |
| **872** | A110 | 250sh | Soccer | 2.00 | 2.00 |
| **873** | A110 | 500sh | 800-meter race | 3.75 | 3.75 |
| | *Nos. 869-873 (5)* | | | 7.25 | 7.25 |

**Souvenir Sheets**

| | | | | | |
|---|---|---|---|---|---|
| **874** | A110 | 1200sh | Women's 4x100-meter relay, horiz. | 7.00 | 7.00 |
| **875** | A110 | 1200sh | Opening ceremony, horiz. | 7.00 | 7.00 |

Trains A111

Designs: 10sh, 10th Class, Zimbabwe. 20sh, 12th Class, Zimbabwe. 80sh, Tribal class, Tanzania and Zambia. 200sh, 4-6-0 Type, Egypt. 300sh, Mikado, Sudan. 400sh, Mountain class Garrat, Uganda. 500sh, Mallet Type, Uganda. 1000sh, 5 F 1 Electric locomotive, South Africa. No. 884, 4-8-2 Type, Zimbabwe. No. 885, Atlantic type, Egypt. No. 886, 4-8-2 Type, Angola. No. 887, Mallet Compound Type, Natal.

**1991, Apr. 2 Litho. *Perf. 14***

| | | | | | |
|---|---|---|---|---|---|
| **876** | A111 | 10sh | multicolored | .30 | .30 |
| **877** | A111 | 20sh | multicolored | .30 | .30 |
| **878** | A111 | 80sh | multicolored | .50 | .50 |
| **879** | A111 | 200sh | multicolored | 1.40 | 1.40 |
| **880** | A111 | 300sh | multicolored | 2.10 | 2.10 |
| **881** | A111 | 400sh | multicolored | 2.75 | 2.75 |
| **882** | A111 | 500sh | multicolored | 3.25 | 3.25 |
| **883** | A111 | 1000sh | multicolored | 6.50 | 6.50 |
| | *Nos. 876-883 (8)* | | | 17.10 | 17.10 |

**Souvenir Sheets**

| | | | | | |
|---|---|---|---|---|---|
| **884** | A111 | 1200sh | multicolored | 5.50 | 5.50 |
| **885** | A111 | 1200sh | multicolored | 5.50 | 5.50 |
| **886** | A111 | 1200sh | multicolored | 5.50 | 5.50 |
| **887** | A111 | 1200sh | multicolored | 5.50 | 5.50 |

Even though Nos. 886-887 have the same issue date as Nos. 876-885, their dollar value was lower when they were released.

Phila Nippon '91 — A112

Walt Disney characters in Japan: 10sh, Scrooge McDuck celebrating Ga-No-Iwai. 20sh, Mickey removes shoes before entering Minnie's home. 70sh, Cartman Goofy leading horse. 80sh, Daisy, Minnie exchange gifts. 300sh, Minnie kneels at entrance to home. 400sh, Mickey, Donald in volcanic sand bath. 500sh, Clarabelle Cow enjoys incense burning. 1000sh, Mickey, Minnie writing New Year cards. No. 896, Mickey, Donald and Goofy in public bath. No. 897, Mickey and friends playing Japanese music.

**1991, May 29 Litho. *Perf. 14x13½***

| | | | | | |
|---|---|---|---|---|---|
| **888** | A112 | 10sh | multicolored | .25 | .25 |
| **889** | A112 | 20sh | multicolored | .25 | .25 |
| **890** | A112 | 70sh | multicolored | .45 | .45 |
| **891** | A112 | 80sh | multicolored | .50 | .50 |
| **892** | A112 | 300sh | multicolored | 1.75 | 1.75 |
| **893** | A112 | 400sh | multicolored | 2.25 | 2.25 |
| **894** | A112 | 500sh | multicolored | 2.75 | 2.75 |
| **895** | A112 | 1000sh | multicolored | 5.00 | 5.00 |
| | *Nos. 888-895 (8)* | | | 13.20 | 13.20 |

**Souvenir Sheets**

| | | | | | |
|---|---|---|---|---|---|
| **896** | A112 | 1200sh | multicolored | 7.50 | 7.50 |
| **897** | A112 | 1200sh | multicolored | 7.50 | 7.50 |

17th World Scout Jamboree, Korea — A113

Designs: 20sh, Lord Baden-Powell. 80sh, Scouts collecting stamps. 100sh, Scout encampment, NY World's Fair, 1939. 150sh, Cover of 1st Scout Handbook. 300sh, Cooking over campfire. 400sh, Neil Armstrong, Edwin Aldrin, 1st scouts on moon. 500sh, Hands raised for Scout Pledge. 1000sh, Statue to Unknown Scout, Gilwell Park, England. No. 906, William D. Boyce, Lord Baden-Powell, Rev. L. Hadley. No. 907, 17th Jamboree Emblem.

**1991, May 27 *Perf. 14***

| | | | | | |
|---|---|---|---|---|---|
| **898** | A113 | 20sh | multicolored | .30 | .30 |
| **899** | A113 | 80sh | multicolored | .45 | .45 |
| **900** | A113 | 100sh | multicolored | .55 | .55 |
| **901** | A113 | 150sh | grn & blk | .80 | .80 |
| **902** | A113 | 300sh | multicolored | 1.60 | 1.60 |
| **903** | A113 | 400sh | multicolored | 2.25 | 2.25 |
| **904** | A113 | 500sh | multicolored | 2.75 | 2.75 |
| **905** | A113 | 1000sh | multicolored | 5.25 | 5.25 |
| | *Nos. 898-905 (8)* | | | 13.95 | 13.95 |

**Souvenir Sheets**

| | | | | | |
|---|---|---|---|---|---|
| **906** | A113 | 1200sh | multicolored | 7.50 | 7.50 |
| **907** | A113 | 1200sh | cream & blk | 7.50 | 7.50 |

For surcharge see No. 1305.

Paintings by Vincent Van Gogh — A114

Paintings: 10sh, Snowy Landscape with Arles in the Background. 20sh, Peasant Woman Binding Sheaves, vert. 60sh, The Drinkers. 80sh, View of Auvers. 200sh, Mourning Man, vert. 400sh, Still Life: Vase with Roses. 800sh, The Raising of Lazarus. 1000sh, The Good Samaritan, vert. No. 916, First Steps. No. 917, Village Street and Steps in Auvers with Figures.

**1991, June 26 Litho. *Perf. 13½***

| | | | | | |
|---|---|---|---|---|---|
| **908** | A114 | 10sh | multicolored | .20 | .20 |
| **909** | A114 | 20sh | multicolored | .20 | .20 |
| **910** | A114 | 60sh | multicolored | .30 | .30 |
| **911** | A114 | 80sh | multicolored | .40 | .40 |
| **912** | A114 | 200sh | multicolored | 1.00 | 1.00 |
| **913** | A114 | 400sh | multicolored | 2.00 | 2.00 |
| **914** | A114 | 800sh | multicolored | 4.00 | 4.00 |
| **915** | A114 | 1000sh | multicolored | 5.00 | 5.00 |
| | *Nos. 908-915 (8)* | | | 13.10 | 13.10 |

**Size: 102x76mm**

***Imperf***

| | | | | | |
|---|---|---|---|---|---|
| **916** | A114 | 1200sh | multicolored | 7.00 | 7.00 |
| **917** | A114 | 1200sh | multicolored | 7.00 | 7.00 |

**Royal Family Birthday, Anniversary**
Common Design Type

**1991, July 5 Litho. *Perf. 14***

| | | | | | |
|---|---|---|---|---|---|
| **918** | CD347 | 20sh | multi | .25 | .25 |
| **919** | CD347 | 70sh | multi | .40 | .40 |
| **920** | CD347 | 90sh | multi | .65 | .65 |
| **921** | CD347 | 100sh | multi | .70 | .70 |
| **922** | CD347 | 200sh | multi | 1.25 | 1.25 |
| **923** | CD347 | 500sh | multi | 3.00 | 3.00 |
| **924** | CD347 | 600sh | multi | 3.75 | 3.75 |
| **925** | CD347 | 1000sh | multi | 6.00 | 6.00 |
| | *Nos. 918-925 (8)* | | | 16.00 | 16.00 |

**Souvenir Sheets**

| | | | | | |
|---|---|---|---|---|---|
| **926** | CD347 | 1200sh | Elizabeth, Philip | 6.00 | 6.00 |
| **927** | CD347 | 1200sh | Sons, Diana, Charles | 7.50 | 7.50 |

20sh, 100sh, 200sh, 1000sh, No. 927, Charles and Diana, 10th wedding anniversary. Others, Queen Elizabeth II, 65th birthday.

Charles de Gaulle, Birth Cent. A115

Designs: 20sh, Portrait, vert. 70sh, Liberation of Paris, 1944, vert. 90sh, With King George VI, 1940, vert. 100sh, Reviewing Free French forces, 1940. 200sh, Making his appeal on BBC, 1940. 500sh, In Normandy, 1944. 600sh, At Albert Hall, 1940. 1000sh, Becoming President of France, 1959, vert. No. 936, Entering Paris, 1944, vert. No. 937, With Eisenhower, 1942.

**1991, July 15 *Perf. 14***

| | | | | | |
|---|---|---|---|---|---|
| **928** | A115 | 20sh | multicolored | .20 | .20 |
| **929** | A115 | 70sh | multicolored | .35 | .35 |
| **930** | A115 | 90sh | multicolored | .45 | .45 |
| **931** | A115 | 100sh | multicolored | .50 | .50 |

**932** A115 200sh multicolored 1.00 1.00
**933** A115 500sh multicolored 2.50 2.50
**934** A115 600sh multicolored 3.00 3.00
**935** A115 1000sh multicolored 5.00 5.00
*Nos. 928-935 (8)* 13.00 13.00

### Souvenir Sheets

**936** A115 1200sh multicolored 6.00 6.00
**937** A115 1200sh multicolored 6.00 6.00

Mushrooms
A116

Designs: 20sh, Volvariella bingensis. 70sh, Agrocybe broadwayi. 90sh, Camarophyllus olidus. 140sh, Marasmius arborescens. 180sh, Marasmiellus subcinereus. 200sh, Agaricus campestris. 500sh, Chlorophyllum molybdites. 1000sh, Agaricus bingensis. No. 946, Leucocoprinus cepaestipes, horiz. No. 947, Laccaria lateritia, horiz.

**1991, July 19 Litho. *Perf. 14***

**938** A116 20sh multicolored .30 .30
**939** A116 70sh multicolored .50 .50
**940** A116 90sh multicolored .65 .65
**941** A116 140sh multicolored 1.00 1.00
**942** A116 180sh multicolored 1.25 1.25
**943** A116 200sh multicolored 1.40 1.40
**944** A116 500sh multicolored 3.50 3.50
**945** A116 1000sh multicolored 7.00 7.00
*Nos. 938-945 (8)* 15.60 15.60

### Souvenir Sheets

**946** A116 1200sh multicolored 6.50 6.50
**947** A116 1200sh multicolored 6.50 6.50

World Wildlife Type of 1983

**1991, Aug. 1**

**948** A43 100sh as No. 371 1.00 1.00
**949** A43 140sh as No. 372 1.40 1.40
**950** A43 200sh as No. 373 1.90 1.90
**951** A43 600sh as No. 374 5.50 5.50
*Nos. 948-951 (4)* 9.80 9.80

### Souvenir Sheets

***Perf. 13x12½***

**952** A43 1200sh Giraffe 11.00 11.00
**953** A43 1200sh Rhinoceros 11.00 11.00

World Wildlife Fund. Nos. 952-953 do not have the WWF emblem.

Flowers in Royal Botanical Gardens, Kew — A118

No. 954: a, Cypripedium calceolus. b, Rhododendron thomsonii. c, Ginkgo biloba. d, Magnolia campbellii. e, Wisteria sinensis. f, Clerodendrum ugandense. g, Eulophia horsfallii. h, Aerangis rhodosticta. i, Abelmoschus moschatus. j, Gloriosa superba. k, Carissa edulis. l, Ochna kirkii. m, Canarina abyssinica. n, Nymphaea caerulea. o, Ceropegia succulenta. p, Strelitzia reginae. q, Strongylodon macrobotrys. r, Victoria amazonica. s, Orchis militaris. t, Sophora microphylla.

No. 955 - Royal Botanic Gardens, Melbourne, Australia: a, Anigozanthos manglesii. b, Banksia grandis. c, Clianthus formosus. d, Gossypium sturtianum. e, Callistemon lanceolatus. f, Saintpaulia ionantha. g, Calodendrum capense. h, Aloe ferox. i, Bolusanthus speciousus. j, Lithops schwantesii k, Protea repens. l, Plumbago capensis. m, Clerodendrum thomsoniae. n, Thunbergia alata. o, Schotia latifolia. p, Epacris impressa. q, Acacia pycnantha. r, Telopea speciosissima. s, Wahlenbergia gloriosa. t, Eucalyptus globulus.

No. 956, The Pagoda, Kew. No. 957, Temple of the Winds, Melbourne.

**1991, Nov. 25 Litho. *Perf. 14½***

**954** A118 100sh Sheet of 20, #a.-t. 17.00 17.00
**955** A118 90sh Sheet of 20, #a.-t. 11.00 11.00

### Souvenir Sheets

**956** A118 1400sh multicolored 9.50 9.50
**957** A118 1400sh multicolored 7.00 7.00

No. 956 contains one 30x38mm stamp.

While Nos. 955 and 957 have the same issue date as Nos. 954 and 956, their dollar value was lower when released. Numbers have been reserved for additional values in this set.

Christmas
A120

Paintings by Piero Della Francesca: 20sh, Madonna with Child and Angels. 50sh, The Baptism of Christ. 80sh, Polyptych of Mercy. 100sh, The Madonna of Mercy. 200sh, The Legend of the True Cross: The Annunciation. 500sh, Pregnant Madonna. 1000sh, Polyptych of St. Anthony: The Annunciation. 1500sh, The Nativity. No. 968, The Brera Altarpiece. No. 969, Polyptych of St. Anthony.

**1991, Dec. 18 Litho. *Perf. 12***

**960** A120 20sh multicolored .20 .20
**961** A120 50sh multicolored .25 .25
**962** A120 80sh multicolored .40 .40
**963** A120 100sh multicolored .50 .50
**964** A120 200sh multicolored 1.00 1.00
**965** A120 500sh multicolored 2.50 2.50
**966** A120 1000sh multicolored 5.00 5.00
**967** A120 1500sh multicolored 7.50 7.50
*Nos. 960-967 (8)* 17.35 17.35

### Souvenir Sheets

***Perf. 14½***

**968** A120 1800sh multicolored 9.00 9.00
**969** A120 1800sh multicolored 9.00 9.00

Boy Scouts
A121

Designs: 20sh, Boy Scout Monument, Silver Bay, NY and Ernest Thompson Seton, first chief scout. 50sh, Tree house and Daniel Beard, Boy Scout pioneer, vert. 1500sh, Boy Scout emblem.

**1992, Jan. 6 Litho. *Perf. 14***

**970** A121 20sh multicolored .50 .50
**971** A121 50sh multicolored .65 .65

### Souvenir Sheet

**972** A121 1500sh multicolored 7.50 7.50

YMCA-Boy Scouts partnership, Lord Robert Baden-Powell, 50th death anniv. in 1991 (#970) and 17th World Scout Jamboree, Korea (#971-972).

A number has been reserved for an additional value in this set.

Balloons
A122

Balloons: a, Modern Hot Air. b, Sport. c, Pro Juventute. d, Blanchard's. e, Nadar's Le Geant. f, First trans-Pacific balloon crossing. g, Montgolfier's. h, Paris, Double Eagle II, used in first trans-Atlantic balloon crossing. i, Tethered.

**1992, Jan. 6 Litho. *Perf. 14***

**974** A122 200sh Sheet of 9, #a.-i. 10.50 10.50

Japanese Attack on Pearl Harbor, 50th Anniv. (in 1991)
A123

Designs: a, Japanese bombers attack USS Vestal. b, Japanese Zero fighter. c, Zeros over burning USS Arizona. d, Battleship Row, USS Nevada under way. e, Japanese Val dive bomber. f, US Dauntless dive bomber attacking Hiryu. g, Japanese planes over Midway Island. h, US Buffalo fighter plane. i, US Wildcat fighters over carrier. j, USS Yorktown and Hammann torpedoed by Japanese submarine.

**1992, Jan. 6 *Perf. 14½x15***

**975** A123 200sh Sheet of 10, #a.-j. 13.50 13.50

Battle of Midway, 50th anniv. (#975f-975j). Inscription for No. 975i incorrectly describes fighters as Hellcats.

Anniversaries and Events — A124

Designs: 400sh, Glider No. 8. 500sh, Man breaking pieces from Berlin Wall. 700sh, Portrait of Mozart and scene from "The Magic Flute." 1200sh, Electric locomotive.

**1992, Jan. 6 Litho. *Perf. 14***

**976** A124 400sh multicolored 2.00 2.00
**977** A124 500sh multicolored 2.50 2.50
**978** A124 700sh multicolored 3.50 3.50
*Nos. 976-978 (3)* 8.00 8.00

### Souvenir Sheet

**979** A124 1200sh multicolored 6.00 6.00

Otto Lillienthal, hang glider, cent. (in 1991) (#976). Brandenburg Gate, Bicent. (#977), Wolfgang Amadeus Mozart, death bicent. (#978), Trans-Siberian Railway, cent. (#979).

Walt Disney Characters on World Tour — A125

Designs: 20sh, Safari surprise in Africa. 50sh, Pluto's tail of India. 80sh, Donald's calypso beat in Caribbean. 200sh, Goofy pulling rickshaw in China. 500sh, Minnie, Mickey on camel in Egypt. 800sh, Wrestling, Japanese style. 1000sh, Goofy bullfighting in Spain. 1500sh, Mickey scoring in soccer game. No. 988, Daisy singing opera in Germany. No. 989, Mickey and Pluto as Cossack dancers in Moscow.

**1992, Feb. *Perf. 13***

**980** A125 20sh multi .30 .30
**981** A125 50sh multi .30 .30
**982** A125 80sh multi .30 .30
**983** A125 200sh multi .70 .70
**984** A125 500sh multi 1.75 1.75
**985** A125 800sh multi 3.00 3.00
**986** A125 1000sh multi 3.50 3.50
**987** A125 1500sh multi 5.25 5.25
*Nos. 980-987 (8)* 15.10 15.10

### Souvenir Sheets

**988** A125 2000sh multi, vert. 7.50 7.50
**989** A125 2000sh multi, vert. 7.50 7.50

## Queen Elizabeth II's Accession to the Throne, 40th Anniv.

Common Design Type

**1992, Feb. 6 Litho. *Perf. 14***

**990** CD348 100sh multi .50 .50
**991** CD348 200sh multi 1.00 1.00
**992** CD348 500sh multi 2.50 2.50
**993** CD348 1000sh multi 5.00 5.00
*Nos. 990-993 (4)* 9.00 9.00

### Souvenir Sheets

**994** CD348 1800sh Queen, waterfalls 9.00 9.00
**995** CD348 1800sh Queen, dam 9.00 9.00

Dinosaurs
A126

**1992, Apr. 8 Litho. *Perf. 14***

**996** A126 50sh Kentrosaurus .35 .35
**997** A126 200sh Iguanodon .65 .65
**998** A126 250sh Hypsilophodon 1.25 1.25
**999** A126 300sh Brachiosaurus 1.00 1.00
**1000** A126 400sh Peloneustes 1.75 1.75
**1001** A126 500sh Pteranodon 1.60 1.60
**1002** A126 800sh Tetralophodon 2.50 2.50
**1003** A126 1000sh Megalosaurus 4.50 4.50
*Nos. 996-1003 (8)* 13.60 13.60

### Souvenir Sheets

**1004** A126 2000sh like #1003 7.50 7.50
**1005** A126 2000sh like #998 7.50 7.50

Nos. 1004-1005 printed in continuous design.

While Nos. 997, 999, 1001-1002, 1005 have the same release date as Nos. 996, 998, 1000, 1003-1004, their value in relation to the dollar was lower when they were released.

Easter
A127

Paintings: 50sh, The Entry into Jerusalem (detail), by Giotto. 100sh, Pilate and the Watch from psalter of Robert de Lisle. 200sh, The Kiss of Judas (detail), by Giotto. 250sh, Christ Washing the Feet of the Disciples, illumination from Life of Christ. 300sh, Christ Seized in the Garden from Melissande Psalter. 500sh, Doubting Thomas, illumination from Life of Christ. 1000sh, The Marys at the Tomb (detail), artist unknown. 2000sh, The Ascension, from 14th century Florentine illuminated manuscript.

Limoge enamels: No. 1014, Agony at Gethsemane. No. 1015, The Piercing of Christ's Side.

**1992 Litho. *Perf. 13½x14***

**1006** A127 50sh multi .25 .25
**1007** A127 100sh multi .35 .35
**1008** A127 200sh multi .75 .75
**1009** A127 250sh multi .85 .85
**1010** A127 300sh multi 1.00 1.00
**1011** A127 500sh multi 1.75 1.75
**1012** A127 1000sh multi 3.50 3.50
**1013** A127 2000sh multi 7.00 7.00
*Nos. 1006-1013 (8)* 15.45 15.45

### Souvenir Sheets

**1014** A127 2500sh multi 7.50 7.50
**1015** A127 2500sh multi 7.50 7.50

Musical Instruments
A128

**1992, July 20 Litho. *Perf. 14***

**1016** A128 50sh Adungu .25 .25
**1017** A128 100sh Endingidi .35 .35
**1018** A128 200sh Akogo .75 .75
**1019** A128 250sh Nanga .85 .85
**1020** A128 300sh Engoma 1.00 1.00
**1021** A128 400sh Amakondere 1.40 1.40

| | | | | | |
|---|---|---|---|---|---|
| **1022** | A128 | 500sh | Akaky-enkye | 1.75 | 1.75 |
| **1023** | A128 | 1000sh | Ennanga | 3.50 | 3.50 |
| | | | *Nos. 1016-1023 (8)* | 9.85 | 9.85 |

Discovery of America, 500th Anniv. A129

Designs: 50sh, World map, 1486. 100sh, Map of Africa, 1508. 150sh, New World, 1500. 200sh, Nina, astrolabe. 600sh, Quadrant, Pinta. 800sh, Hour glass. 900sh, 15th century compass. 2000sh, World map, 1492. No. 1032, 1490 Map by Henricus Martellus, 1490. No. 1033, Sections of 1492 globe.

| **1992, July 24** | | | **Litho.** | | ***Perf. 14*** |
|---|---|---|---|---|---|
| **1024** | A129 | 50sh | multi | .30 | .30 |
| **1025** | A129 | 100sh | multi | .30 | .30 |
| **1026** | A129 | 150sh | multi | .30 | .30 |
| **1027** | A129 | 200sh | multi | .85 | .85 |
| **1028** | A129 | 600sh | multi | 2.50 | 2.50 |
| **1029** | A129 | 800sh | multi | 3.25 | 3.25 |
| **1030** | A129 | 900sh | multi | 3.50 | 3.50 |
| **1031** | A129 | 2000sh | multi | 2.75 | 2.75 |
| | | | *Nos. 1024-1031 (8)* | 13.75 | 13.75 |

**Souvenir Sheets**

| | | | | | |
|---|---|---|---|---|---|
| **1032** | A129 | 2500sh | multi, vert. | 7.25 | 7.25 |
| **1033** | A129 | 2500sh | multi | 5.00 | 5.00 |

World Columbian Stamp Expo '92, Chicago.

While Nos. 1024-1026, 1031 and 1033 have the same issue date as Nos. 1027-1030 and 1032, their value in relation to the dollar was lower when they were released.

Hummel Figurines — A130

1992 Summer Olympics, Barcelona — A131

No. 1042: a, Like #1034. b, Like #1035. c, Like #1036. d, Like #1037.

No. 1043: a, Like #1039. b, Like #1038. c, Like #1040. d, Like #1041.

| **1992, Aug. 28** | | | **Litho.** | | ***Perf. 14*** |
|---|---|---|---|---|---|
| **1034** | A130 | 50sh | Little Laundry Girl | .25 | .25 |
| **1035** | A130 | 200sh | Scrub Girl | .80 | .80 |
| **1036** | A130 | 250sh | Sweeper Girl | .90 | .90 |
| **1037** | A130 | 300sh | Little Mother | 1.10 | 1.10 |
| **1038** | A130 | 600sh | Little Mountaineer | 1.60 | 1.60 |
| **1039** | A130 | 900sh | Little Knitter | 2.25 | 2.25 |
| **1040** | A130 | 1000sh | Little Cowboy | 2.75 | 2.75 |
| **1041** | A130 | 1500sh | Little Astronomer | 5.50 | 5.50 |
| | | | *Nos. 1034-1041 (8)* | 15.15 | 15.15 |

**Souvenir Sheets**

| | | | | | |
|---|---|---|---|---|---|
| **1042** | A130 | 500sh | Sheet of 4, #a.-d. | 7.25 | 7.25 |
| **1043** | A130 | 500sh | Sheet of 4, #a.-d. | 7.25 | 7.25 |

While Nos. 1034, 1038-1040, 1043 have the same release date as Nos. 1035-1037, 1041-1042, their value in relation to the dollar was lower when they were released.

| **1992** | | | **Litho.** | | ***Perf. 14*** |
|---|---|---|---|---|---|
| **1044** | A131 | 50sh | Javelin | .35 | .35 |
| **1045** | A131 | 100sh | High jump, horiz. | .35 | .35 |
| **1046** | A131 | 200sh | Pentathlon (Fencing) | .65 | .65 |
| **1047** | A131 | 250sh | Volleyball | .80 | .80 |
| **1048** | A131 | 300sh | Women's platform diving | 1.00 | 1.00 |
| **1049** | A131 | 500sh | Team cycling | 1.60 | 1.60 |
| **1050** | A131 | 1000sh | Tennis | 3.25 | 3.25 |
| **1051** | A131 | 2000sh | Boxing, horiz. | 6.50 | 6.50 |
| | | | *Nos. 1044-1051 (8)* | 14.50 | 14.50 |

**Souvenir Sheets**

| | | | | | |
|---|---|---|---|---|---|
| **1052** | A131 | 2500sh | Baseball | 7.50 | 7.50 |
| **1053** | A131 | 2500sh | Basketball | 7.50 | 7.50 |

Wild Animals A132

| **1992, Sept. 25** | | | **Litho.** | | ***Perf. 14*** |
|---|---|---|---|---|---|
| **1054** | A132 | 50sh | Spotted hyena | .25 | .25 |
| **1055** | A132 | 100sh | Impala | .25 | .25 |
| **1056** | A132 | 200sh | Giant forest hog | .45 | .45 |
| **1057** | A132 | 250sh | Pangolin | .55 | .55 |
| **1058** | A132 | 300sh | Golden monkey | .70 | .70 |
| **1059** | A132 | 800sh | Serval | 1.75 | 1.75 |
| **1060** | A132 | 1000sh | Bush genet | 2.25 | 2.25 |
| **1061** | A132 | 3000sh | Defassa waterbuck | 6.75 | 6.75 |
| | | | *Nos. 1054-1061 (8)* | 12.95 | 12.95 |

**Souvenir Sheets**

| | | | | | |
|---|---|---|---|---|---|
| **1062** | A132 | 2500sh | Mountain gorilla | 6.50 | 6.50 |
| **1063** | A132 | 2500sh | Hippopotamus | 6.50 | 6.50 |

Birds — A133

Designs: 20sh, Red necked falcon. 30sh, Yellow-billed hornbill. 50sh, Purple heron. 100sh, Regal sunbird. 150sh, White-brown robin chat. 200sh, Shining-blue kingfisher. 250sh, Great blue turaco. 300sh, Emerald cuckoo. 500sh, Abyssinian roller. 800sh, Crowned crane. 1000sh, Doherty's bush shrike. 2000sh, Splendid glossy starling. 3000sh, Little bee eater. 4000sh, Red-headed lovebird.

| **1992, Aug.** | | | **Litho.** | | ***Perf. 15x14*** |
|---|---|---|---|---|---|
| **1064** | A133 | 20sh | multi | .20 | .20 |
| **1065** | A133 | 30sh | multi | .20 | .20 |
| **1066** | A133 | 50sh | multi | .20 | .20 |
| **1067** | A133 | 100sh | multi | .20 | .20 |
| **1068** | A133 | 150sh | multi | .30 | .30 |
| **1069** | A133 | 200sh | multi | .40 | .40 |
| **1070** | A133 | 250sh | multi | .50 | .50 |
| **1071** | A133 | 300sh | multi | .55 | .55 |
| **1072** | A133 | 500sh | multi | 1.00 | 1.00 |
| **1073** | A133 | 800sh | multi | 1.60 | 1.60 |
| **1074** | A133 | 1000sh | multi | 2.00 | 2.00 |
| **1075** | A133 | 2000sh | multi | 4.00 | 4.00 |
| **1076** | A133 | 3000sh | multi | 6.00 | 6.00 |
| **1076A** | A133 | 4000sh | multi | 8.00 | 8.00 |
| | | | *Nos. 1064-1076A (14)* | 25.15 | 25.15 |

Issued: 3000sh, Oct.; others, Aug.?

Walt Disney's Goofy, 60th Anniv. — A134

Scenes from Disney animated films: 50sh, Hawaiian Holiday, 1937, vert. 100sh, The Nifty Nineties, 1941, vert. 200sh, Mickey's Fire Brigade, 1935, vert. 250sh, The Art of Skiing, 1941. 300sh, Mickey's Amateurs, 1937. 1000sh, Boat Builders, 1938. 1500sh, The Olympic Champ, 1942, vert. 2000sh, The Olympic Champ, 1942, vert. No. 1085, Goofy and Wilbur, 1939. No. 1086, Goofy's family tree, vert.

***Perf. 13½x14, 14x13½***

| **1992, Nov. 2** | | | | | **Litho.** |
|---|---|---|---|---|---|
| **1077** | A134 | 50sh | multi | .25 | .25 |
| **1078** | A134 | 100sh | multi | .25 | .25 |
| **1079** | A134 | 200sh | multi | .50 | .50 |
| **1080** | A134 | 250sh | multi | .65 | .65 |
| **1081** | A134 | 300sh | multi | .80 | .80 |
| **1082** | A134 | 1000sh | multi | 2.50 | 2.50 |
| **1083** | A134 | 1500sh | multi | 4.00 | 4.00 |
| **1084** | A134 | 2000sh | multi | 5.25 | 5.25 |
| | | | *Nos. 1077-1084 (8)* | 14.20 | 14.20 |

**Souvenir Sheets**

| | | | | | |
|---|---|---|---|---|---|
| **1085** | A134 | 3000sh | multi | 7.50 | 7.50 |
| **1086** | A134 | 3000sh | multi | 7.50 | 7.50 |

Souvenir Sheet

UN Headquarters, New York City — A135

| **1992, Oct. 28** | | | **Litho.** | | ***Perf. 14*** |
|---|---|---|---|---|---|
| **1087** | A135 | 2500sh | multi | 5.50 | 5.50 |

Postage Stamp Mega Event '92, NYC.

Christmas A136

Details or entire paintings by Zurbaran: 50sh, The Annunciation (angel at left). 200sh, The Annunciation (angel at right). 250sh, The Virgin of the Immaculate Conception. 300sh, The Virgin of the Immaculate Conception (detail). 800sh, 900sh, The Holy Family with Saints Anne, Joachim and John the Baptist (800sh, entire, 900sh, detail). 1000sh, Adoration of the Magi (entire). 2000sh, Adoration of the Magi. No. 1096, The Virgin of the Immaculate Conception (Virgin with arms outstretched). No. 1097, The Virgin of the Immaculate Conception (Virgin with arms folded).

| **1992, Nov. 16** | | | **Litho.** | | ***Perf. 13½x14*** |
|---|---|---|---|---|---|
| **1088** | A136 | 50sh | multi | .30 | .30 |
| **1089** | A136 | 200sh | multi | .50 | .50 |
| **1090** | A136 | 250sh | multi | .70 | .70 |
| **1091** | A136 | 300sh | multi | .85 | .85 |
| **1092** | A136 | 800sh | multi | 2.25 | 2.25 |
| **1093** | A136 | 900sh | multi | 2.50 | 2.50 |
| **1094** | A136 | 1000sh | multi | 2.75 | 2.75 |
| **1095** | A136 | 2000sh | multi | 5.50 | 5.50 |
| | | | *Nos. 1088-1095 (8)* | 15.35 | 15.35 |

**Souvenir Sheets**

| | | | | | |
|---|---|---|---|---|---|
| **1096** | A136 | 2500sh | multi | 7.50 | 7.50 |
| **1097** | A136 | 2500sh | multi | 7.50 | 7.50 |

World Health Organization — A137

Anniversaries and Events — A138

Designs: 50sh, Improving household food security. 200sh, Continue to breastfeed. 250sh, At four months old, give breast milk and soft food. No. 1101, Drink water from a safe and protected source. No. 1102, Jupiter, Voyager 2. No. 1103, Mother holding baby. No. 1104, Impala. No. 1105, Zebra. No. 1106, Count Ferdinand von Zeppelin, zeppelin. 2000sh, Neptune, Voyager 2. 3000sh, Count Zeppelin, zeppelin, diff. No. 1109, Voyager 2, Jupiter, diff. No. 1110, Wart hog. No. 1111, Doctor examining child, Lions Intl. emblem. No. 1112, Count Zeppelin, balloon.

| **1992** | | | **Litho.** | | ***Perf. 14*** |
|---|---|---|---|---|---|
| **1098** | A137 | 50sh | multi | .20 | .20 |
| **1099** | A137 | 200sh | multi | .40 | .40 |
| **1100** | A137 | 250sh | multi | .50 | .50 |
| **1101** | A137 | 300sh | multi | .60 | .60 |
| **1102** | A138 | 300sh | multi | .60 | .60 |
| **1103** | A137 | 800sh | multi | 1.60 | 1.60 |
| **1104** | A138 | 800sh | multi | 2.00 | 2.00 |
| **1105** | A138 | 1000sh | multi | 2.50 | 2.50 |
| **1106** | A138 | 1000sh | multi | 2.00 | 2.00 |
| **1107** | A138 | 2000sh | multi | 4.00 | 4.00 |
| **1108** | A138 | 3000sh | multi | 6.00 | 6.00 |
| | | | *Nos. 1098-1108 (11)* | 20.40 | 20.40 |

**Souvenir Sheets**

| | | | | | |
|---|---|---|---|---|---|
| **1109** | A138 | 2500sh | multi | 5.75 | 5.75 |
| **1110** | A138 | 2500sh | multi | 5.00 | 5.00 |
| **1111** | A138 | 2500sh | multi | 5.00 | 5.00 |
| **1112** | A138 | 2500sh | multi | 5.00 | 5.00 |

WHO (#1098-1101, 1103). Intl. Space Year (#1102, 1107, 1109). Earth Summit, Rio de Janeiro (#1104-1105, 1110). Count Zeppelin, 75th anniv. of death (#1106, 1108, 1112). Lions Intl., 75th anniv. (#1111).

Issue dates: Nos. 1098-1103, 1106, 1109, 1112, Nov.; others, Dec.

1993 Visit of Pope John Paul II to Uganda A139

A139a

Designs: 50sh, Cathedral in Kampala, site of Papal Mass, Kampala, hands releasing doves. 200sh, Site of Papal Mass, Pope. 250sh, Ugandan man, Pope. 300sh, Three Ugandan Catholic leaders, Pope. 800sh, Pope waving, Ugandan map and flag. 900sh, Ugandan woman, Pope wearing mitre. 1000sh, Pope, Ugandan flag, site of Papal Mass. 2000sh, Ugandan flag, Pope waving.

No. 1121, Pope at door of airplane, vert. No. 1122, Pope delivering message at podium, vert.

No. 1123, Pope John Paul II. No. 1124, Pope with hands raised.

| **1993, Feb. 1** | | | **Litho.** | | ***Perf. 14*** |
|---|---|---|---|---|---|
| **1113** | A139 | 50sh | multi | .30 | .30 |
| **1114** | A139 | 200sh | multi | .50 | .50 |
| **1115** | A139 | 250sh | multi | .60 | .60 |
| **1116** | A139 | 300sh | multi | .70 | .70 |
| **1117** | A139 | 800sh | multi | 1.75 | 1.75 |
| **1118** | A139 | 900sh | multi | 1.90 | 1.90 |
| **1119** | A139 | 1000sh | multi | 2.25 | 2.25 |
| **1120** | A139 | 2000sh | multi | 4.50 | 4.50 |
| | | | *Nos. 1113-1120 (8)* | 12.50 | 12.50 |

**Souvenir Sheets**

| | | | | | |
|---|---|---|---|---|---|
| **1121** | A139 | 3000sh | multi | 7.25 | 7.25 |
| **1122** | A139 | 3000sh | multi | 7.25 | 7.25 |

**Embossed**

*Embossed* ***Perf. 12***

| | | | | | |
|---|---|---|---|---|---|
| **1123** | A139a | 5000sh | gold | 20.00 | 20.00 |

**Souvenir Sheet**

***Imperf***

| | | | | | |
|---|---|---|---|---|---|
| **1124** | A139a | 5000sh | gold | 20.00 | 20.00 |

Miniature Sheet

Louvre Museum, Bicent. A140

Details or entire paintings by Rembrandt: No. 1125a, Self-Portrait with an Easel. b, Birds of Paradise. c, The Beef Carcass. d, The Supper at Emmaus. e, Hendrickje Stoffels. f, Titus, Son of the Artist. g, The Holy Family (left). h, The Holy Family (right).
2500sh, Philosopher in Meditation, horiz.

**1993, Apr. 5 Litho. *Perf. 12***

**1125** A140 500sh Sheet of 8, #a.-h. + label 11.25 11.25

**Souvenir Sheet**

***Perf. 14½***

**1126** A140 2500sh multi 7.00 7.00

Dogs A141

**1993, May 28 Litho. *Perf. 14***

| | | | | | |
|---|---|---|---|---|---|
| **1127** | A141 | 50sh | Afghan hound | .45 | .45 |
| **1128** | A141 | 100sh | Newfoundland | .45 | .45 |
| **1129** | A141 | 200sh | Siberian huskies | .80 | .80 |
| **1130** | A141 | 250sh | Briard | 1.00 | 1.00 |
| **1131** | A141 | 300sh | Saluki | 1.40 | 1.40 |
| **1132** | A141 | 800sh | Labrador retriever, vert. | 3.50 | 3.50 |
| **1133** | A141 | 1000sh | Greyhound | 4.00 | 4.00 |
| **1134** | A141 | 1500sh | Pointer | 6.50 | 6.50 |
| | *Nos. 1127-1134 (8)* | | | 18.10 | 18.10 |

**Souvenir Sheets**

**1135** A141 2500sh Cape hunting dog 11.00 11.00
**1136** A141 2500sh Norwegian elkhound 11.00 11.00

Miniature Sheet

Coronation of Queen Elizabeth II, 40th Anniv. A142

No. 1137: a, 50sh, Official coronation photograph. b, 200sh, Orb, Rod of Equity & Mercy. c, 500sh, Queen during coronation ceremony. d, 1500sh, Queen Elizabeth II, Princess Margaret.
2500sh, The Crown, by Grace Wheatley, 1959.

**1993, June 2 Litho. *Perf. 13½x14***

**1137** A142 Sheet, 2 each #a.-d. 13.50 13.50

**Souvenir Sheet**

***Perf. 14***

**1138** A142 2500sh multicolored 7.00 7.00

No. 1138 contains one 28x42mm stamp.

Miniature Sheet

Taipei '93 — A143

Funerary objects: No. 1139a, Tomb guardian god. b, Civil official. c, Tomb guardian god, diff. d, Civil official, diff. e, Chimera. f, Civil official, diff.
2500sh, Statue of Sacred Mother, Ceremonial Hall, Taiyuan, Shanxi.

**1993, Sept. 22 Litho. *Perf. 14x13½***

**1139** A143 600sh Sheet of 6, #a.-f. 8.50 8.50

**Souvenir Sheet**

**1140** A143 2500sh multicolored 8.00 8.00

With Bangkok '93 Emblem

Thai sculpture: No. 1141a, Standing Buddha, 13th-15th cent. b, Crowned Buddha, 13th cent. c, Thepanom, 15th cent. d, Crowned Buddha, 12th cent. e, Four-armed Avalokitesvara, 9th cent. f, Lop Buri standing Buddha, 13th cent.
2500sh, Buddha, interior of Wat Mahathat.

**1993, Sept. 22**

**1141** A143 600sh Sheet of 6, #a.-f. 8.50 8.50

**Souvenir Sheet**

**1142** A143 2500sh multicolored 8.00 8.00

With Indopex '93 Emblem
Miniature Sheet

Japanese Wayang Puppets, Indonesia: No. 1143a, Bupati karma, Prince of Wangga. b, Rahwana. c, Sondjeng Sandjata. d, Raden Damar Wulan. e, Klitik figure. f, Hanaman.
2500sh, Candi Mendut in Kedu Plain, Java, Indonesia.

**1993, Sept. 22 Litho. *Perf. 13½x14***

**1143** A143 600sh Sheet of 6, #a.-f. 8.50 8.50

**Souvenir Sheet**

**1144** A143 2500sh multicolored 8.00 8.00

A144

A145

**1993, Oct. 1 Litho. *Perf. 14***

| | | | | | |
|---|---|---|---|---|---|
| **1145** | A144 | 50sh | Gutierrez, Voeller | .35 | .35 |
| **1146** | A144 | 200sh | Tomas Brolin | .60 | .60 |
| **1147** | A144 | 250sh | Gary Lineker | .75 | .75 |
| **1148** | A144 | 300sh | Munoz, Butragueno | .85 | .85 |
| **1149** | A144 | 800sh | Carlos Valderrama | 2.40 | 2.40 |
| **1150** | A144 | 900sh | Diego Maradona | 2.55 | 2.55 |
| **1151** | A144 | 1000sh | Pedro Troglio | 3.00 | 3.00 |
| **1152** | A144 | 2000sh | Enzo Scifo | 6.00 | 6.00 |
| | *Nos. 1145-1152 (8)* | | | 16.50 | 16.50 |

**Souvenir Sheets**

**1153** A144 2500sh Brazil coaches 7.25 7.25
**1154** A144 2500sh De Napoli, Skuhravy, horiz. 7.25 7.25

1994 World Cup Soccer Championships, US.

**1993, Nov. 3 *Perf. 14***

Cathedrals of the World: 50sh, York Minster, England. 100sh, Notre Dame, Paris. 200sh, Little Metropolis, Athens. 250sh, St. Patrick's, New York. 300sh, Ulm, Germany. 800sh, St. Basil's, Moscow. 1000sh, Roskilde, Denmark. 2000sh, Seville, Spain. No. 1163, Namirembe, Uganda. No. 1163A, St. Peter's, Vatican City.

| | | | | | |
|---|---|---|---|---|---|
| **1155** | A145 | 50sh | multi | .35 | .35 |
| **1156** | A145 | 100sh | multi | .35 | .35 |
| **1157** | A145 | 200sh | multi | .65 | .65 |
| **1158** | A145 | 250sh | multi | .70 | .70 |
| **1159** | A145 | 300sh | multi | .95 | .95 |
| **1160** | A145 | 800sh | multi | 2.50 | 2.50 |
| **1161** | A145 | 1000sh | multi | 3.25 | 3.25 |
| **1162** | A145 | 2000sh | multi | 6.25 | 6.25 |
| | *Nos. 1155-1162 (8)* | | | 15.00 | 15.00 |

**Souvenir Sheets**

**1163** A145 2500sh multi 7.50 7.50
**1163A** A145 2500sh multi 7.50 7.50

Christmas A146

Details or entire woodcut, The Virgin with Carthusian Monks, by Durer: 50sh, 200sh, 300sh, 2000sh.
Details or entire paintings by Raphael: 100sh, 800sh, Sacred Family. 250sh, The Virgin of the Rose. 1000sh, Holy Family (Virgin with Beardless Joseph).
No. 1172, 2500sh, The Virgin with Carthusian Monks, by Durer. No. 1173, 2500sh, Sacred Family, by Raphael.

**1993, Nov. 19 Litho. *Perf. 13½x14***

**1164-1171** A146 Set of 8 13.50 13.50

**Souvenir Sheets**

**1172-1173** A146 Set of 2 16.00 16.00

Mickey Mouse, Friends with Dinosaurs — A147

Disney characters depicted with: 50sh, Stegosaurus. 100sh, Pterandom. 200sh, Mamenchisaurus. 250sh, Rock painting. 300sh, Dino "sails." 500sh, Diplodocus. 800sh, Mamenshisaurus, diff. 1000sh, Triceratops.
No. 1182, 2500sh, Tyrannosaurus rex, Mickey. No. 1183, 2500sh, Minnie, Mickey, mamenchisaurus, diff.

**1993, Dec. 22 Litho. *Perf. 14x13½***

**1174-1181** A147 Set of 8 13.50 13.50

**Souvenir Sheets**

**1182-1183** A147 Set of 2 13.00 13.00

Rinderpest Campaign A148 — Picasso (1881-1973) A149

**1993, Dec. 29 *Perf. 14***

**1184** A148 200sh multicolored .35 .35

**1993, Dec. 29**

Paintings: 100sh, Woman in Yellow, 1907. 250sh, Gertrude Stein, 1906. 2500sh, Woman by a Window, 1956.

**1185-1186** A149 Set of 2 .50 .50

**Souvenir Sheet**

**1187** A149 2500sh multicolored 7.00 7.00

Copernicus (1473-1543) — A150

Polska '93 — A151

Telescopes: 500sh, Early. 1000sh, Modern. 2500sh, Copernicus.

**1993, Dec. 29**

**1188-1189** A150 Set of 2 2.50 2.50

**Souvenir Sheet**

**1190** A150 2500sh multicolored 7.00 7.00

**1993, Dec. 29**

Paintings: 800sh, Creation of the World, by S. I. Witkiewicz par J. Gloqowski, 1921. 1000sh, For the Right to Work, by Andrezej Strumillo, 1952. 2500sh, Temptation of St. Anthony I, by S. I. Witkiewicz (1908-21), horiz.

**1191-1192** A151 Set of 2 3.00 3.00

**Souvenir Sheet**

**1193** A151 2500sh multicolored 4.25 4.25

World Meteorological Day — A152

Fruits and Crops — A153

Designs: 50sh, Weather station, horiz. 200sh, Observatory at Meteorological Training School, Entebbe. 250sh, Satellite receiver at National Meteorological Center, horiz. 300sh, Reading temperatures, National Center, Entebbe, horiz. 400sh, Automatic weather station. 800sh, Destruction by hail storm, horiz. 2500sh, Barograph, horiz.

**1993, Dec. 29**

**1194-1199** A152 Set of 6 3.75 3.75

**Souvenir Sheet**

**1200** A152 2500sh multicolored 4.25 4.25

**1993, Dec. 29**

Designs: 50sh, Passiflora edulis. 100sh, Helianthus annus. 150sh, Musa sapientum. 200sh, Vanilla fragrans. 250sh, Ananas comosus. 300sh, Artocarpus heterophyllus. 500sh, Sorghum bo\icolor. 800sh, Zea mays.
No. 1209, 2000sh, Sesamum indicum. No. 1210, 2000sh, Coffea canephora.

**1201-1208** A153 Set of 8 4.50 4.50

**Souvenir Sheets**

**1209-1210** A153 Set of 2 8.50 8.50

Automotive Anniversaries — A154

No. 1211: a, 1903 Model A Ford, Henry Ford. b, Model T Snowmobile at 1932 Winter Olympics, Jack Shea. c, Lee Iacocca, Ford Mustang at New York World's Fair. d, Jim Clark, Lotus-Ford winning 1965 Indianapolis 500 race.

No. 1212: a, 1994 Mercedes Benz S600 Coupe. b, 1955 Mercedes Benz W196 Grand Prix Champion car, Juan Manuel Fangio. c, 1938 Mercedes Benz W125 road speed record holder, Rudolph Caracciola. d, Carl Benz, 1893 Benz Viktoria.

No. 1213, Carl Benz, vert. No. 1214, Henry Ford, vert.

**1994, Jan. 18 Litho. *Perf. 14***

**1211** A154 700sh Strip of 4, #a.-d. 6.25 6.25
**1212** A154 800sh Strip of 4, #a.-d. 7.25 7.25

**Souvenir Sheets**

**1213** A154 2500sh multicolored 4.50 4.50
**1214** A154 2500sh multicolored 4.50 4.50

First Ford motor, cent. (#1211, #1214). First Benz four-wheel car, cent. (#1212, #1213).

A155

Hong Kong '94 — A156

Stamps, religious shrines, Repulse Bay: No. 1215, Hong Kong #531. No. 1216, #1163.

Snuff boxes, Qing Dynasty: No. 1217a, Glass painted enamel with pavilion. b, Porcelain with floral design. c, Porcelain with quail design. d, Porcelain with openwork design. e, Agate with pair of dogs. f, Agate with man on donkey.

**1994, Feb. 18 Litho. *Perf. 14***

**1215** A155 500sh multicolored .90 .90
**1216** A155 500sh multicolored .90 .90
*a.* Pair, #1215-1216 1.75 1.75

**Miniature Sheet**

**1217** A156 200sh Sheet of 6, #a.-f. 2.25 2.25

Nos. 1215-1216 issued in sheets of 5 pairs. No. 1216a is continuous design.

New Year 1994 (Year of the Dog) (#1217e).

Miniature Sheet

1994 World Cup Soccer Championships, US — A157

Designs: No. 1218a, Georges Grun, Belgium. b, Oscar Ruggeri, Argentina. c, Frank Rijkaard, Holland. d, Magid "Tyson" Musisi, Uganda. e, Donald Keeman, Holland. f, Igor Shallmov, Russia.

No. 1219, 2500sh, RFK Stadium, Washington DC. No. 1220, 2500sh, Ruud Gullit, Holland.

**1994, June 27 Litho. *Perf. 14***

**1218** A157 500sh Sheet of 6, #a.-f. 5.50 5.50

**Souvenir Sheets**

**1219-1220** A157 Set of 2 9.00 9.00

Heifer Project Intl., 50th Anniv. A158

**1994, June 29 Litho. *Perf. 14***

**1221** A158 100sh multicolored .20 .20

Moths — A159

Native Crafts — A160

Designs: 100sh, Lobobunaea goodii. 200sh, Bunaeopsis hersilia. 300sh, Rufoglanis rosea. 350sh, Acherontia atropos. 400sh, Rohaniella pygmaea. 450sh, Euchloron megaera. 500sh, Epiphora rectifascia. 1000sh, Polyphychus coryndoni.

Lobobunaea goodii: No. 1230, 2500sh, Wings down. No. 1231, 2500sh, Wings extended.

**1994, July 13**

**1222-1229** A159 Set of 8 6.75 6.75

**Souvenir Sheets**

**1230-1231** A159 Set of 2 10.00 10.00

**1994, July 18**

Designs: 100sh, Wood stool. 200sh, Wood & banana fiber chair. 250sh, Raffia & palm leaves basket. 300sh, Wool tapestry showing tree planting. 450sh, Wool tapestry showing hair grooming. 500sh, Wood sculpture, drummer. 800sh, Decorated gourds. 1000sh, Lady's bag made from bark cloth.

No. 1240, 2500sh, Raffia baskets. No. 1241, 2500sh, Papyrus hats.

**1232-1239** A160 Set of 8 7.00 7.00

**Souvenir Sheets**

**1240-1241** A160 Set of 2 10.00 10.00

Cats — A161

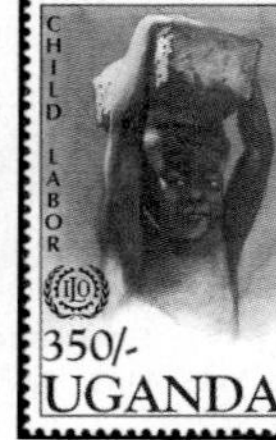

ILO, 75th Anniv. — A162

Cat, historic landmark: 50sh, Turkish angora, Blue Mosque, Turkey, horiz. 100sh, Japanese bobtail, Mt. Fuji, Japan, horiz. 200sh, Norwegian forest cat, windmill, Holland, horiz. 300sh, Egyptian mau, pyramids, Egypt. 450sh, Rex, Stonehenge, England. 500sh, Chartreux, Eiffel Tower, France, horiz. 1000sh, Burmese, Shwe Dagon Pagoda, Burma. 1500sh, Maine coon, Pemaquid Point Lighthouse, Maine.

No. 1250, 2500sh, Russian blue, horiz. No. 1251, 2500sh, Manx, horiz.

**1994, July 22**

**1242-1249** A161 Set of 8 8.25 8.25

**Souvenir Sheets**

**1250-1251** A161 Set of 2 10.00 10.00

**1994, July 29**

**1252** A162 350sh multicolored .70 .70

PHILAKOREA '94 — A163

Designs: 100sh, Eight story Sari pagoda, Paekyangsa. 350sh, Ch'omsongdae (Natl. treasure). 1000sh, Pulguksa Temple exterior.

2500sh, Bronze mural, Pagoda Park, Seoul.

**1994, Aug. 8**

**1253-1255** A163 Set of 3 3.00 3.00

**Souvenir Sheet**

**1256** A163 2500sh multicolored 5.00 5.00

Intl. Year of the Family A164

**1994, Aug. 11**

**1257** A164 100sh multicolored .20 .20

D-Day, 50th Anniv. A165

Designs: 300sh, Mulberry Harbor pierhead moves into position. 1000sh, Mulberry Harbor floating bridge lands armor.

2500sh, Ships, Mulberry Harbor.

**1994, Aug. 11**

**1258** A165 300sh multicolored .60 .60
**1259** A165 1000sh multicolored 2.00 2.00

**Souvenir Sheet**

**1260** A165 2500sh multicolored 5.00 5.00

A166

Intl. Olympic Committee, Cent. — A167

Designs: 350sh, John Akii-bua, Uganda, 100-meter hurdles, 1972. 900sh, Heike Herkel, Germany, high jump, 1992.

2500sh, Aleksei Urmanov, Russia, figure skating, 1994.

**1994, Aug. 11**

**1261** A166 350sh multicolored .70 .70
**1262** A167 900sh multicolored 1.75 1.75

**Souvenir Sheet**

**1263** A166 2500sh multicolored 5.00 5.00

First Manned Moon Landing, 25th Anniv. A168

No. 1264 — Project Mercury astronauts: a, 50sh, Alan B. Shepard, Jr., Freedom 7. b, 100sh, M. Scott Carpenter, Aurora 7. c, 200sh, Virgil I. Grissom, Liberty Bell 7. d, 300sh, L. Gordon Cooper, Jr., Faith 7. e, 400sh, Walter M. Schirra, Jr., Sigma 7. f, 500sh, Donald K. Slayton, Apollo-Soyuz, 1975. g, John H. Glenn, Jr., Friendship 7.

3000sh, Apollo 11 anniv. emblem.

**1994, Aug. 11**

**1264** A168 Sheet of 7, #a.-g, + 2 labels 4.25 4.25

**Souvenir Sheet**

**1265** A168 3000sh multicolored 6.00 6.00

A169

Disney's The Lion King — A169a

No. 1266: a, Baby Simba. b, Mufasa, Simba, Sarabi. c, Young Simba, Nala. d, Timon. e, Rafiki. f, Pumbaa. g, Hyenas. h, Scar. i, Zazu.

No. 1267: a, Rafiki, Mufasa. b, Rafiki, Mufasa, Sarabi. c, Rafiki, Simba. d, Scar, Zazu. e, Rafiki seeing vision. f, Simba, Scar. g, Simba, Nala. h, Simba trying on mane. i, Simba, Nala, Zazu.

No. 1268: a, Scar plots evil plan. b, Mufasa rescues Simba. c, Destroying Mufasa. d, Simba escaping hyenas. e, Timon, Pumbaa, Simba. f, Simba, Timon, Pumbaa sing Hakuna Matata. g, Rafiki. h, Simba, Nala. i, Simba seeing reflection.

No. 1269, 2500sh, Simba, Timon. No. 1270, 2500sh, Characters of the Lion King, vert. No. 1271, 2500sh, Simba's colorful animal kingdon.

No. 1271A, Mufasa, Simba. No. 1271B, Mufasa, Simba on back, standing on rock.

Illustration A169a reduced.

***Perf. 14x13½, 13½x14***

**1994, Sept. 30**

**1266** A169 100sh Sheet of 9, #a.-i. 1.75 1.75
**1267** A169 200sh Sheet of 9, #a.-i. 3.75 3.75
**1268** A169 250sh Sheet of 9, #a.-i. 4.50 4.50
*Nos. 1266-1268 (3)* 10.00 10.00

**Souvenir Sheets**

**1269-1271** A169 Set of 3 15.00 15.00

**Litho. & Embossed**

***Perf. 11½***

**1271A** A169a 5000sh gold
**1271B** A169a 5000sh gold

Sierra Club, Cent. — A170

No. 1272, horiz.: a, 200sh, Cheetahs. b, 250sh, Cheetah kittens. c, 300sh, African wild dog. d, 500sh, African wild dog. e, 600sh, Grevy's zebra. f, 800sh, Chimpanzee. g, 1000sh, Grevy's zebra.

No. 1273: a, 100sh, Chimpanzee. b, 200sh, Chimpanzee. c, 250sh, African wild dog. d, 300sh, Cheetah. e-f, 500sh, 600sh, Gelada baboon. g, 800sh, Grevy's zebra. h, 1000sh, Gelada baboon.

**1994, Nov. 9**

**1272** A170 Sheet of 7, #a.-g. + label 8.00 8.00
**1273** A170 Sheet of 8, #a.-h. 8.25 8.25

ICAO, 50th Anniv. A171

Designs: 100sh, Entebbe Intl. Airport terminal building. 250sh, Entebbe control tower.

**1994, Nov. 14** **Litho.** ***Perf. 14***

**1274** A171 100sh multicolored .20 .20
**1275** A171 250sh multicolored .55 .55

Environmental Protection — A172

Designs: 100sh, Stop poaching. 250sh, Waste disposals. 350sh, Overfishing is a threat. 500sh, Deforestation.

**1994, Nov. 15**

**1276-1279** A172 Set of 4 2.50 2.50

Christmas A173

Paintings: 100sh, Adoration of the Christ Child, by Fillipino Lippi. 200sh, The Holy Family Rests on the Flight into Egypt, by Annibale Carracci. 300sh, Madonna with Christ Child ant St. John, by Piero di Cosimo. 350sh, The Conestabile Madonna, by Raphael. 450sh, Madonna and Child with Angels, after Antonio Rossellino. 500sh, Madonna and Child with St. John, by Raphael. 900sh, Madonna and Child, by Luca Signorelli. 1000sh, Madonna with the Child Jesus, St. John and an Angel, in style of Pier Francesco Fiorentino.

No. 1288, 2500sh, The Madonna of the Magnificat, by Sandro Botticelli. No. 1289, 2500sh, Adoration of the Magi, by Fra Angelico & Filippo Lippi.

**1994, Dec. 5** **Litho.** ***Perf. 13½x14***

**1280-1287** A173 Set of 8 8.50 8.50

**Souvenir Sheets**

**1288-1289** A173 Set of 2 11.00 11.00

Tintoretto (1518-94) A174

Details or entire paintings: 100sh, Self-portrait. 300sh, A Philosopher. 400sh, The Creation of the Animals, horiz. 450sh, The Feast of Belshazzar, horiz. 500sh, The Raising of the Brazen Serpent. 1000sh, Elijah Fed by the Angel.

No. 1296, 2000sh, Finding of Moses. No. 1297, 2000sh, Moses Striking Water from a Rock.

**1995, Feb. 7** **Litho.** ***Perf. 13½***

**1290-1295** A174 Set of 6 5.75 5.75

**Souvenir Sheets**

**1296-1297** A174 Set of 2 8.50 8.50

Birds A175

No. 1298: a, White-faced tree duck. b, European shoveler. c, Hartlaub's duck. d, Milky eagle-owl. e, Avocet. f, African fish eagle. g, Spectacled weaver. h, Black-headed gonolek. i, Great crested grebe. j, Red-knobbed coot. k, Woodland kingfisher. l, Pintail. m, Squacco heron. n, Purple gallinule. o, African darter. p, African jacana.

No. 1299, 2500sh, Fulvous tree duck. No. 1300, 2500sh, Pygmy goose.

**1995, Apr. 24** **Litho.** ***Perf. 14***

**1298** A175 200sh Sheet of 16, #a.-p. 7.00 7.00

**Souvenir Sheets**

**1299-1300** A175 Set of 2 11.00 11.00

Nos. 685-688, 906 Surcharged

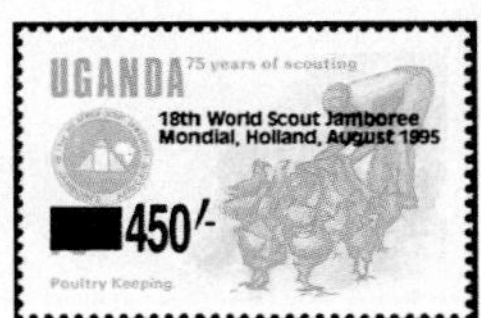


**1995, June 1** **Litho.** ***Perf. 14***

**1301** A90 100sh on #688 multi .20 .20
**1302** A90 450sh on 70sh #686 1.00 1.00
**1303** A90 800sh on 90sh #687 1.75 1.75
**1304** A90 1500sh on 10sh #685 3.25 3.25
*Nos. 1301-1304 (4)* 6.20 6.20

**Souvenir Sheet**

**1305** A113 2500sh on 1200sh multi 5.50 5.50

UN, 50th Anniv. — A176

Designs: 1000sh, Hands releasing butterflies, dragonfly, dove.

No. 1308, Infant's hand holding adult's finger.

**1995, July 6** **Litho.** ***Perf. 14***

**1306** A176 450sh shown 1.25 1.25
**1307** A176 1000sh multicolored 2.75 2.75

**Souvenir Sheet**

**1308** A176 2000sh multicolored 4.50 4.50

FAO, 50th Anniv. — A177

No. 1309 — Corn huskers: a, 350sh, Young woman. b, 500sh, Old woman, girl. c, 1000sh, Woman with baby on back.

2000sh, Boy beside bore well for livestock, irrigation.

**1995, July 6**

**1309** A177 Strip of 3, #a.-c. 4.00 4.00

**Souvenir Sheet**

**1310** A177 2000sh multicolored 4.50 4.50

A178

End of World War II, 50th Anniv. A179

No. 1311: a, Russian 152mm gun fires into center of Berlin. b, Soviets capture Moltke Bridge. c, Emperor William Memorial Church, now war memorial. d, Brandenburg Gate falls to Russian tanks. e, US B-17's continue to devastate industrial Germany. f, Soviet tanks enter Berlin. g, Hitler's chancellery lies in ruins. h, Reichstag burns.

Flags of countries each forming "VJ:" No. 1312a, Australia. b, Great Britain. c, New Zealand. d, US. e, China. f, Canada.

No. 1313, Waving Soviet flag from atop building in Berlin. No. 1314, US flag, combat soldier.

**1995, July 6**

**1311** A178 500sh Sheet of 8, #a.-h. + label 9.00 9.00
**1312** A179 600sh Sheet of 6, #a.-f. + label 8.00 8.00

**Souvenir Sheets**

**1313** A178 2500sh multicolored 5.50 5.50
**1314** A179 2500sh multicolored 5.50 5.50

No. 1313 contains one 56x42mm stamp.

Rotary Intl., 90th Anniv. — A180

Rotary emblem and: No. 1315, Paul Harris. No. 1316, Natl. flag.

**1995, July 6** **Litho.** ***Perf. 14***

**1315** A180 2000sh multicolored 4.50 4.50

**Souvenir Sheet**

**1316** A180 2000sh multicolored 4.50 4.50

Queen Mother, 95th Anniv. A181

No. 1317: a, Drawing. b, Waving. c, Formal portrait. d, Green blue outfit.

2500sh, Pale blue outfit.

**1995, July 6** ***Perf. 13½x14***

**1317** A181 500sh Block or strip of 4, #a.-d. 4.50 4.50

**Souvenir Sheet**

**1318** A181 2500sh multicolored 5.50 5.50

No. 1317 was issued in sheets of 8 stamps.

Sheets of Nos. 1317-1318 exist with with black border and text "In Memoriam/1900-2002" in sheet margins.

Dinosaurs A182

Designs: 150sh, Velociraptor. 200sh, Psittacosaurus. 350sh, Dilophosaurus. 400sh, Kentrosaurus. 500sh, Stegosaurus. 1500sh, Pterodaustro.

No. 1325, vert: a, Archaeopteryx. b, Quetzalcoatlus. c, Pteranodon (b, d). d, Brachiosa (g, h). e, Tsintaosaur. f, Allosaur (g-h). g, Tyranosaur (f, i-k). h, Apatosaur (l). i, Giant dragonfly. j, Dimorphodon. k, Triceratops (l). l, Compsognathus.

No. 1326, 2000sh, Parasaurolophus. No. 1327, 2000sh, Shunosaurus.

**1995, July 15** ***Perf. 14***

**1319-1324** A182 Set of 6 6.75 6.75
**1325** A182 300sh Sheet of 12, #a.-l. 8.00 8.00

**Souvenir Sheets**

**1326-1327** A182 Set of 2 9.00 9.00

Reptiles — A183

**1995** **Litho.** ***Perf. 14x15***

| | | | | |
|---|---|---|---|---|
| **1328** | 50sh | Rough scaled bush viper | .20 | .20 |
| **1329** | 100sh | Pygmy python | .20 | .20 |
| **1330** | 150sh | Three horned chameleon | .30 | .30 |
| **1331** | 200sh | African rock python | .40 | .40 |
| **1332** | 350sh | Nile monitor | .70 | .70 |
| **1333** | 400sh | Savannah monitor | .85 | .85 |
| **1334** | 450sh | Bush viper | .95 | .95 |
| **1335** | 500sh | Nile crocodile | 1.00 | 1.00 |

**Size: 38x24mm**

***Perf. 14***

| | | | | |
|---|---|---|---|---|
| **1336** | 700sh | Bell's hinged tortoise | 1.40 | 1.40 |
| **1337** | 900sh | Rhinoceros viper | 1.90 | 1.90 |
| **1338** | 1000sh | Gaboon viper | 2.00 | 2.00 |
| **1339** | 2000sh | Spitting cobra | 4.00 | 4.00 |
| **1340** | 3000sh | Leopard tortoise | 6.25 | 6.25 |
| **1341** | 4000sh | Puff adder | 8.25 | 8.25 |
| **1341A** | 5000sh | Common house gecko | 10.00 | 10.00 |
| **1341B** | 6000sh | Dwarf chameleon | 12.00 | 12.00 |
| **1341C** | 10,000sh | Boomslang | 20.00 | 20.00 |
| | | *Nos. 1328-1341C (17)* | 70.40 | 70.40 |

Issued: 5000sh, 6000sh, 10,000sh, 11/20; others, 8/21.

Compare with Nos. 1550-1552.

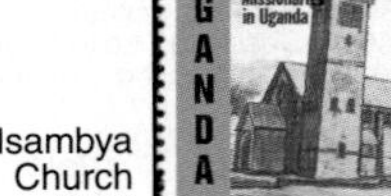


Nsambya Church A184

Designs: 450sh, Namilyango College. 500sh, Intl. Cooperative Alliance, cent. 1000sh, UN Volunteers, 25th anniv.

**1995, Sept. 7** **Litho.** ***Perf. 14***

**1342-1345** A184 Set of 4 4.50 4.50

Mill Hill Missionaries in Uganda, cent. (#1342-1343).

Scenic Landscapes & Waterfalls of Uganda — A185

Designs: No. 1346, 50sh, Bwindi Forest. No. 1347, 50sh, Sipi Falls, vert. No. 1348, 100sh, Karamoja. No. 1349, 100sh, Murchison Falls. No. 1350, 450sh, Sunset, Lake Mburo Natl. Park. No. 1351, 450sh, Bujagali Falls. No. 1352, 500sh, Sunset, Gulu District. No. 1353, 500sh, Two Falls, Murchison. No. 1354, 900sh, Kabale District. No. 1355, 900sh, Falls, Rwenzoris, vert. No. 1356, 1000sh, Rwenzori Mountains. No. 1357, 1000sh, Falls, Rwenzoris, diff., vert.

**1995, Sept. 14**
**1346-1357** A185 Set of 12 12.50 12.50

1996 Summer Olympics, Atlanta A186

Athletes: 50sh, Peter Rono, runner. 350sh, Reiner Klimke, dressage. 450sh, German cycling team. 500sh, Grace Birungi, runner. 900sh, Francis Ogola, track. 1000sh, Nyakana Godfrey, welter-weight boxer.
No. 1364, 2500sh, Rolf Dannenberg, discus, vert. No. 1365, 2500sh, Sebastian Coe, runner.

**1995, Sept. 21**
**1358-1363** A186 Set of 6 7.25 7.25
**Souvenir Sheets**
**1364-1365** A186 Set of 2 11.00 11.00

Domestic Animals A187

No. 1366: a, Peafowl (e). b, Pouter pigeon. c, Rock dove. d, Rouen duck. e, Guinea fowl. f, Donkey. g, Shetland pony. h, Palomino. i, Pigs. j, Border collie. k, Merino sheep. l. Milch goat. m, Black dutch rabbit. n, Lop rabbit. o, Somali cat (p). p, Asian cat.
No. 1367, 2500sh, Saddle bred horses. No. 1368, 2500sh, Oxen.

**1995, Oct. 2**
**1366** A187 200sh Sheet of 16, #a.-p. 7.00 7.00
**Souvenir Sheets**
**1367-1368** A187 Set of 2 11.00 11.00

Boy Scouts at Immunization Centers — A188

Designs: 150sh, Dressing children for weighing, vert. 350sh, Helping mothers carry children, vert. 450sh, Checking health cards. 800sh, Assisting in immunization. 1000sh, Weighing children, vert.

**1995, Oct. 18 Litho. *Perf. 14***
**1369-1373** A188 Set of 5 6.00 6.00

Establishment of Nobel Prize Fund, Cent. — A189

No. 1374, 300sh: a, Hideki Yukawa, physics, 1949. b, F.W. DeKlerk, peace, 1993. c, Nelson Mandela, peace, 1993. d, Odysseus Elytis, literature, 1979. e, Ferdinand Buisson, peace, 1927. f, Lev Landau, physics, 1962. g, Halldor Laxness, literature, 1955. h, Wole Soyinka, literature, 1986. i, Desmond Tutu, peace, 1984. j, Susumu Tonegawa, physiology or medicine, 1987. k, Louis de Broglie, physics, 1929. l, George Seferis, literature, 1963.
No. 1375, 300sh: a, Hermann Staudinger, chemistry, 1953. b, Fritz Haber, chemistry, 1918. c, Bert Sakmann, physiology or medicine, 1991. d, Adolf O.R. Windaus, chemistry, 1928. e, Wilhelm Wien, physics, 1911. f, Ernest Hemingway, literature, 1954. g, Richard M. Willstätter, chemistry, 1915. h, Stanley Cohen, physiology or medicine, 1986. i, J. Hans D. Jensen, physics, 1963. j, Otto H. Warburg, physiology or medicine, 1931. k, Heinrich O. Wieland, chemistry, 1927. l, Albrecht Kossel, physiology or medicine, 1910.
No. 1376, 2000sh, Werner Forssmann, physiology or medicine, 1956. No. 1377, 2000sh, Nelly Sachs, literature, 1966.

**1995, Oct. 31**
**Sheets of 12, #a-l**
**1374-1375** A189 Set of 2 16.00 16.00
**Souvenir Sheets**
**1376-1377** A189 Set of 2 9.00 9.00

Christmas A190

Details or entire paintings of the Madonna and Child, by: 150sh, Hans Holbein the Younger. 350sh, Procaccini. 500sh, Pisanello. 1000sh, Crivelli. 1500sh, Le Nain.
No. 1383, 2500sh, The Holy Family, by Andrea Del Sarto. No. 1384, 2500sh, Madonna and Child, by Bellini.

**1995, Nov. 30 Litho. *Perf. 13½x14***
**1378-1382** A190 Set of 5 7.75 7.75
**Souvenir Sheets**
**1383-1384** A190 Set of 2 10.00 10.00

Orchids — A191

Designs: 150sh, Ansellia africana. 450sh, Satyricum crassicaule. 500sh, Polystachya cultriformis. 800sh, Disa erubescens.
No. 1389: a, Aerangis iuteoalba. b, Satyrium sacculatum. c, Bolusiella maudiae. d, Habenaria attenuata. e, Cyrtorchis arcuata. f, Eulophia angolensis. g, Tridactyle bicaudata. h, Eulophia horsfallii. i, Diaphananthe fragrantissima.
No. 1390, 2500sh, Diaphananthe pulchella. No. 1391, 2500sh, Rangaeris amaniensis.

**1995, Dec. 8 *Perf. 14***
**1385-1388** A191 Set of 4 3.75 3.75
**Miniature Sheet**
**1389** A191 350sh Sheet of 9, #a.-i. 6.25 6.25
**Souvenir Sheets**
**1390-1391** A191 Set of 2 10.00 10.00

New Year 1996 (Year of the Rat) A192

Rat eating: a, Purple grapes. b, Radishes. c, Corn. d, Squash.
2000sh, Green grapes.

**1996, Jan. 29 Litho. *Perf. 14***
**1392** A192 350sh Block of 4, #a.-d. 2.75 2.75
*e.* Miniature sheet, No. 1392 2.75 2.75
**Souvenir Sheet**
**1393** A192 2000sh multicolored 4.00 4.00

No. 1392 issued in sheets of 16 stamps.

**Miniature Sheet**

Wildlife A193

No. 1394: a, 150sh, Wild dogs. b, 200sh, Fish eagle. c, 250sh, Hippopotamus. d, 350sh, Leopard. e, 400sh, Lion. f, 450sh, Lioness. g, 500sh, Meerkat. h, 550sh, Black rhinoceros.
No. 1395: a, 150sh, Gorilla. b, 200sh, Cheetah. c, 250sh, Elephant. d, 350sh, Thomson's gazelle. e, 400sh, Crowned crane. f, 450sh, Sattlebill. g, 500sh, Vulture. h, 550sh, Zebra.
No. 1396, 2000sh, Giraffe, vert. No. 1397, 2000sh, Gray heron.

**1996, Mar. 27 Litho. *Perf. 14***
**1394** A193 Sheet of 8, #a.-h. 5.75 5.75
**1395** A193 Sheet of 8, #a.-h. 6.00 6.00
**Souvenir Sheets**
**1396-1397** A193 Set of 2 8.00 8.00

Disney Characters on the Orient Express — A194

Designs: 50sh, From London to Constantinople via Calais. 100sh, From Paris to Athens. 150sh, Ticket for the Pullman. 200sh, Pullman Corridor. 250sh, Dining car. 300sh, Staff beyond reproach. 600sh, Fun in the Pullman. 700sh, 1901 Unstoppable train enters the buffet in Frankfurt station. 800sh, 1929 passage detained five days by snowstorm. 900sh, Filming "Murder on the Orient Express."
No. 1408, 2500sh, Donald Duck in engine. No. 1409, 2500sh, Mickey, Goofy, Minnie waving from back of train.

**1996, Apr. 15 *Perf. 14x13½***
**1398-1407** A194 Set of 10 8.25 8.25
**Souvenir Sheets**
**1408-1409** A194 Set of 2 10.00 10.00

Paintings by Qi Baishi (1864-1957) A195

No. 1410: a, 50sh, Autumn Pond. b, 100sh, Partridge and Smartweed. c, 150sh, Begonias and Mynah. d, 200sh, Chrysanthemums, Cocks and Hens. e, 250sh, Crabs. f, 300sh, Wisterias and Bee. g, 350sh, Smartweed and Ink-drawn Butterflies. h, 400sh, Lotus and Mandarin Ducks. i, 450sh, Lichees and Locust. j, 500sh, Millet and Preying Mantis.
No. 1411: a, Locust, flowers. b, Crustaceans.

**1996, May 8 Litho. *Perf. 15x14***
**1410** A195 Sheet of 10, #a.-j. 6.00 6.00
**Souvenir Sheet**
***Perf. 14***
**1411** A195 800sh Sheet of 2, #a.-b. 3.50 3.50

No. 1411 contains two 48x34mm stamps. The captions on Nos. 1410c and 1410d are transposed.
CHINA '96, 9th Asian Intl. Philatelic Exhibition.
See Nos. 1475-1476.

Queen Elizabeth II, 70th Birthday — A196

No. 1412: a, Portrait. b, As young woman, wearing crown jewels. c, Wearing red hat, coat.
2000sh, Portrait, diff.

**1996, July 10 *Perf. 13½x14***
**1412** A196 500sh Strip of 3, #a.-c. 3.00 3.00
**Souvenir Sheet**
**1413** A196 2000sh multicolored 4.00 4.00

No. 1412 was issued in sheets of 9 stamps.

Jerusalem, 3000th Anniv. — A197

No. 1414: a, 300sh, Knesset Menorah. b, 500sh, Jerusalem Theater. c, 1000sh, Israel Museum.
2000sh, Grotto of the Nativity.

**1996, July 10 *Perf. 14***
**1414** A197 Sheet of 3, #a.-c. 3.50 3.50
**Souvenir Sheet**
**1415** A197 2000sh multicolored 4.00 4.00

For overprint see Nos. 1556-1557.

Radio, Cent. A198

Entertainers: 200sh, Ella Fitzgerald. 300sh, Bob Hope. 500sh, Nat "King" Cole. 800sh, Burns & Allen.
2000sh, Jimmy Durante.

**1996, July 10 *Perf. 13½x14***
**1416-1419** A198 Set of 4 3.50 3.50
**Souvenir Sheet**
**1420** A198 2000sh multicolored 4.00 4.00

Mushrooms A199

No. 1421: a, 150sh, Coprinus disseminatus. b, 300sh, Caprinus radians. c, 350sh, Hygrophorus coccineus. d, 400sh, Marasmius siccus. e, 450sh, Cortinarius collinitus. f, 500sh, Cortinarius cinnabarinus. g, 550sh, Coltricia cinnamomea. h, 1000sh, Mutinus elegans.
No. 1422, 2500sh, Inocybe soroia. No. 1423, 2500sh, Flammulina velutipes.

**1996, June 24** ***Perf. 14***
**1421** A199 Sheet of 8, #a.-h. 7.50 7.50

**Souvenir Sheets**
**1422-1423** A199 Set of 2 10.00 10.00

Butterflies A200

No. 1424: a, 50sh, Catopsilia philea. b, 100sh, Dione vanillae. c, 150sh, Metemorpha dido. d, 200sh, Papilio sesotris. e, 250sh, Papilio neophilus. f, 300sh, Papilio thoas. g, 350sh, Diorina periander. h, 400sh, Morpho cipris. i, 450sh, Catonephele numilia. j, 500sh, Heliconius doris. k, 550sh, Prepona antimache. l, 600sh, Eunica alcmena.
No. 1425, 2500sh, Caligo martia. No. 1426, 2500sh, Heliconius doris.

**1996, June 26**
**1424** A200 Sheet of 12, #a.-l. 7.75 7.75

**Souvenir Sheets**
**1425-1426** A200 Set of 2 10.00 10.00

UNICEF, 50th Anniv. A201

Designs: 450sh, Two children. 500sh, Two children wearing hats. 550sh, Boy in classroom.
2000sh, Mother and child, vert.

**1996, July 10** **Litho.** ***Perf. 14***
**1427-1429** A201 Set of 3 3.00 3.00

**Souvenir Sheet**
**1430** A201 2000sh multicolored 4.00 4.00

UNESCO, 50th Anniv. — A202

Natl. Parks: 450sh, Darien, Panama. 500sh, Los Glaciares, Argentina. 550sh, Tubbatha Reef Marine Park, Philippines.
2500sh, Rwenzori Mountains, Uganda.

**1996, July 10**
**1431-1433** A202 Set of 3 3.00 3.00

**Souvenir Sheet**
**1434** A202 2500sh multicolored 5.00 5.00

Trains — A203

No. 1435: a, Loco Type B.B.B., Japan, 1968. b, Stephenson's "Rocket," 1829. c, "Austria," 1843. d, 19th cent. type. e, Loco Anglo-Indian, India, 1947. f, Type CoCo DB, Germany.
No. 1436: a, "Lady of Lynn," Great Western, England. b, Chinese type, 1930. c, Meyer-Ritson, Chile. d, Union Pacific "Centennial," US. e, "581" Japanese Natl. Railway, Japan, 1968. f, Co.Co. Series "120" DB, Germany.
No. 1437, 2500sh, Mallard, Great Britain. No. 1438, 2500sh, "99" Type 1-5-0, Germany.

**1996, July 25**
**1435** A203 450sh Sheet of 6, #a.-f. 5.50 5.50
**1436** A203 550sh Sheet of 6, #a.-f. 6.50 6.50

**Souvenir Sheets**
**1437-1438** A203 Set of 2 10.00 10.00

Uganda Post Office, Cent. A204

Designs: 150sh, Emblem. 450sh, Post bus service. 500sh, Modern mail transportation means. 550sh, "100," #48, #59.

**1996, Aug. 30** **Litho.** ***Perf. 14***
**1439-1442** A204 Set of 4 3.25 3.25

Fruits A205

Designs: 150sh, Mango, vert. 350sh, Orange, vert. 450sh, Paw paw, vert. 500sh, Avocado, vert. 550sh, Watermelon.

**1996, Oct. 8** **Litho.** ***Perf. 14***
**1443-1447** A205 Set of 5 4.00 4.00

Christmas A206

Details or entire paintings: 150sh, Annunciation, by Lorenzo Di Credi. 350sh, Madonna of the Loggia (detail), by Botticelli. 400sh, Virgin in Glory with Child and Angels, by Lorenzetti P. 450sh, Adoration of the Child, by Filippino Lippi. 500sh, Madonna of the Loggia, by Botticelli. 550sh, The Strength, by Bottticelli.
No. 1454, 2500sh, Holy Allegory, by Giovanni Bellini, horiz. No. 1455, 2500sh, The Virgin on the Throne with Child and Saints, by Ghirlandaio, horiz.

**1996, Nov. 18** ***Perf. 13½x14***
**1448-1453** A206 Set of 6 4.75 4.75

**Souvenir Sheets**
***Perf. 14x13½***
**1454-1455** A206 Set of 2 10.00 10.00

Sylvester Stallone in Movie, "Rocky III" — A207

**1996, Nov. 21** **Litho.** ***Perf. 14***
**1456** A207 800sh Sheet of 3 4.75 4.75

1996 Summer Olympic Games, Atlanta A208

Scenes from first Olympic Games in US, St. Louis, 1904: 350sh, Steamboat race, stadium. 450sh, Boxer George Finnegan. 500sh, Quadriga race (ancient games). 800sh, John Flanagan, hammer throw, vert.

**1996, Dec. 8**
**1457-1460** A208 Set of 4 4.25 4.25

Traditional Attire — A209

Designs: 150sh, Western region, vert. 350sh, Karimo Jong women, vert. 450sh, Ganda. 500sh, Acholi.
No. 1465, vert. — Headdresses: a, Acholi. b, Alur. c, Bwola dance. d, Madi. e, Karimojong. f, Karimojong with feathers.

**1997, Jan. 2**
**1461-1464** A209 Set of 4 3.00 3.00
**1465** A209 300sh Sheet of 6, #a.-f. 3.50 3.50

New Year 1997 (Year of the Ox) A210

Paintings of oxen: Nos. 1466a, 1467b, Walking left. Nos. 1466b, 1467b, Calf nursing. Nos. 1466c, 1467d, Calf lying down, adult. Nos. 1466d, 1467c, Adult lying down.
1500sh, Calf, vert.

**1997, Jan. 24** **Litho.** ***Perf. 14***
**1466** A210 350sh Strip of 4, #a.-d. 2.75 2.75
**1467** A210 350sh Sheet of 4, #a.-d. 2.75 2.75

**Souvenir Sheet**
**1468** A210 1500sh multicolored 3.00 3.00

No. 1466 was issued in sheets of 4 vert. strips.

World Wildlife Fund — A211

No. 1469 — Rothschild's giraffe: a, Running. b, One bending neck across another's back. c, Head up close. d, Young giraffe, adult facing opposite directions.
2500sh, like #1469d, horiz.

**1997, Feb. 12**
**1469** A211 300sh Strip of 4, #a.-d. 2.25 2.25

**Souvenir Sheet**
**1470** A211 2500sh multicolored 5.00 5.00

No. 1469 was issued in sheets of 4 strips with each strip in a different order.
No. 1470 does not have the WWF emblem.

Souvenir Sheet

Mural from Tomb in Xian — A212

Illustration reduced.

**1996, May 8** **Litho.** ***Perf. 14***
**1471** A212 500sh multicolored 1.00 1.00

China '96. No. 1471 was not available until March 1997.

Promulgation of the Constitution, Oct. 8, 1995 — A213

Designs: 150sh, shown. 350sh, Scroll. 550sh, Closed book, vert.

**1997, Feb. 25** ***Perf. 14x13½***
**1472-1474** A213 Set of 3 2.10 2.10

Paintings Type of 1996

No. 1475 — Paintings by Wu Changshuo (1844-1927): a, 50sh, Red Plum Blossom and Daffodil. b, 100sh, Peony. c, 150sh, Rosaceae. d, 200sh, Pomegranate. e, 250sh, Peach, Peony, and Plum Blossom. f, 300sh, Calyx canthus. g, 350sh, Chrysanthemum. h, 400sh, Calabash. i, 450sh, Chrysanthemum, diff. j, 500sh, Cypress tree.
No. 1476: a, 550sh, Litchi. b, 1000sh, Water lily.

**1997, Mar. 5** ***Perf. 14x15***
**1475** A195 Sheet of 10, #a.-j. 5.50 5.50

**Souvenir Sheet**
***Perf. 14***
**1476** A195 Sheet of 2, #a.-b. 3.00 3.00

Hong Kong '97. No. 1476 contains two 51x38mm stamps.

Summer Olympic Winners — A214

No. 1477: a, 150sh, Sohn Kee-chung, marathon, 1936. b, 200sh, Walter Davis, high jump, 1952. c, 250sh, Roland Matthes, swimming, 1968. d, 300sh, Akii Bua, 400m hurdles, 1972. e, 350sh, Wolfgang Nordwig, pole vault, 1972. f, 400sh, Wilma Rudolph, 4x100m relay, 1960. g, 450sh, Abebe Bikila, marathon, 1964. h, 500sh, Edwin Moses, 400m hurdles, 1984. i, 550sh, Randy Williams, long jump, 1972.
No. 1478: a, 150sh, Bob Hayes, 100m, 1964. b, 200sh, Rod Milburn, 110m hurdles, 1972. c, 250sh, Filbert Bayi, running, 1976. d, 300sh, H. Kipchoge Keino, steeple chase, 1972. e, 350sh, Ron Ray, running, 1976. f, 400sh, Joe Frazier, boxing, 1976. g, 450sh, Carl Lewis, 100m race, 1984. h, 500sh, Gisela

Mauermayer, discus, 1936. i, 550sh, Dietmar Mogenburg, high jump, 1984.

**1997, Mar. 3 Litho. *Perf. 14***
**Sheets of 9, #a-i**

**1477-1478** A214 Set of 2 12.50 12.50

No. 1478h is inscribed shot put in error.

Disney's "Toy Story" — A215

No. 1479, vert.: a, Woody. b, Buzz Lightyear. c, Bo Peep. d, Hamm. e, Slinky. f, Rex.
No. 1480: a, Woody on Andy's bed. b, "Get this wagon train a-movin." c, Bo Peep, blocks. d, Buzz Lightyear. e, Slinky, Rex. f, Woody hides. g, Buzz, Woody. h, Rex, Slinky, Buzz. i, Buzz, Woody on bed.
No. 1481: a, Woody telling Buzz he's sheriff. b, Green Army on alert. c, Woody, Buzz compete. d, Woody sights alien. e, Buzz ponders fate. f, "The Cla-a-a-a-a-a-w." g, Intergalactic emergency. h, Buzz, Woody argue at gas station. i, Buzz, Woody give chase.
No. 1482, 2000sh, Woody spots an intruder, vert. No. 1483, 2000sh, Andy's toys, vert. No. 1484, 2000sh, Buzz Lightyear in space, vert.

**1997, Apr. 2 *Perf. 14x13½, 13½x14***

**1479** A215 100sh Sheet of 6, #a.-f. 1.25 1.25
**1480** A215 150sh Sheet of 9, #a.-i. 2.75 2.75
**1481** A215 200sh Sheet of 9, #a.-i. 3.50 3.50

**Souvenir Sheets**

**1482-1484** A215 Set of 3 12.00 12.00

Man in Space A216

No. 1484A: b, Pioneer 10. c, Voyager 1. d, Viking Orbiter. e, Pioneer, Venus 1. f, Mariner 9. g, Galileo Entry Probe. h, Mariner 10. i, Voyager 2.
No. 1485: a, Sputnik 1. b, Apollo. c, Soyuz. d, Intelsat 1. e, Manned maneuvering unit. f, Skylab. g, Telstar 1. h, Hubble telescope.
No. 1486, Space shuttle Challenger. No. 1486A, Mars Viking Lander Robot.

**1997, Apr. 16 Litho. *Perf. 14***

**1484A** A216 250sh Sheet of 8, #b.-i. 4.25 4.25
**1485** A216 300sh Sheet of 8, #a.-h. 4.75 4.75

**Souvenir Sheet**

**1486** A216 2000sh multicolored 4.00 4.00
**1486A** A216 2000sh multicolored 4.25 4.25

No. 1486 contains one 34x61mm stamp, No. 1486A one 61x35mm stamp.

Deng Xiaoping (1904-97), Chinese Leader — A217

Designs: a, 500sh. b, 550sh. c, 1000sh. 2000sh, Portrait, diff.

**1997, May 9**

**1487** A217 Sheet of 3, #a.-c. 4.00 4.00

**Souvenir Sheet**

**1488** A217 2000sh multicolored 4.00 4.00

Environmental Protection — A218

No. 1489: a-d, Various water hyacinths.
No. 1490: a, Buffalo. b, Uganda kob. c, Guinea fowl. d, Malibu stork.
2500sh, Gorilla.

**1997, May 14**

**1489** A218 500sh Sheet of 4, #a.-d. 4.00 4.00
**1490** A218 550sh Sheet of 4, #a.-d. 4.50 4.50

**Souvenir Sheet**

**1491** A218 2500sh multicolored 5.00 5.00

Queen Elizabeth II, Prince Philip, 50th Wedding Anniv. A219

No. 1492: a, Queen. b, Royal arms. c, Queen in purple outfit, Prince. d, Prince, Queen in white hat. e, Buckingham Palace. f, Prince Philip.
2000sh, Queen in wedding dress.

**1997, June 2 Litho. *Perf. 14***

**1492** A219 200sh Sheet of 6, #a.-f. 2.50 2.50

**Souvenir Sheet**

**1493** A219 2000sh multicolored 4.00 4.00

Paul E. Harris (1868-1947), Founder of Rotary, Intl. — A220

Designs: 1000sh, Combating hunger, Harris. 2500sh, First Rotarians, Gustavus H. Loehr, Sylvester Schiele, Hiram E. Shorey, Paul E. Harris.

**1997, June 2**

**1494** A220 1000sh multicolored 2.00 2.00

**Souvenir Sheet**

**1495** A220 2500sh multicolored 5.00 5.00

Heinrich von Stephan (1831-97) A221

No. 1496 — Portrait of Von Stephan and: a, Chinese post boat. b, UPU emblem. c, Russian special post.
2500sh, Von Stephan, French postman on stilts.

**1997, June 2**

**1496** A221 800sh Sheet of 3, #a.-c. 4.75 4.75

**Souvenir Sheet**

**1497** A221 2500sh multicolored 5.00 5.00

PACIFIC 97.

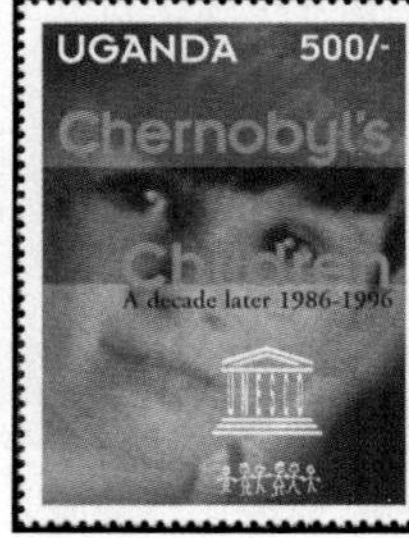

Chernobyl Disaster, 10th Anniv. A222

Designs: 500sh, UNESCO. 700sh, Chabad's Children of Chernobyl.

**1997, May 21 Litho. *Perf. 14x13½***

**1498** A222 500sh multicolored 1.00 1.00
**1499** A222 700sh multicolored 1.50 1.50

1998 Winter Olympic Games, Nagano A223

Designs: 350sh, Men's slalom, vert. 450sh, Two-man bobsled, vert. 800sh, Women's slalom. 2000sh, Men's speed skating.
No. 1504: a, Ski jumping. b, Giant slalom. c, Cross-country skiing. d, Ice hockey. e, Man, pairs figure skating. f, Woman, pairs figure skating.
No. 1505, 2500sh, Downhill skiing. No. 1506, 2500sh, Women's figure skating.

**1997, June 23 Litho. *Perf. 14***

**1500-1503** A223 Set of 4 7.25 7.25
**1504** A223 500sh Sheet of 6, #a.-f. 6.25 6.25

**Souvenir Sheets**

**1505-1506** A223 Set of 2 10.00 10.00

Makerere University, 75th Anniv. — A224

Designs: 150sh, Main building, administration block. 450sh, East African School of Librarianship, vert. 500sh, Buyana stock farm. 550sh, Ceramic dish, School of Architectural and Fine Arts.

**1997, July 31 *Perf. 14x13½, 13½x14***

**1507-1510** A224 Set of 4 4.00 4.00

Mahatma Gandhi (1869-1948) A225

Various portraits.

**1997, Oct. 5 Litho. *Perf. 14***

**1511** A225 600sh multicolored 1.25 1.25
**1512** A225 700sh multicolored 1.40 1.40

**Souvenir Sheet**

**1513** A225 1000sh multicolored 2.00 2.00

1998 World Cup Soccer Championships, France — A226

No. 1514, vert: a, 200sh, Fritz Walter, Germany. b, 300sh, Daniel Passarella, Argentina. c, 450sh, Dino Zoff, Italy. d, 500sh, Bobby Moore, England. e, 600sh, Diego Maradona, Argentina. f, 550sh, Franz Beckenbauer, West Germany.
No. 1515 — Argentina vs. West Germany, Mexico City, 1986: a, d, e, f, h, Action scenes. b, Azteca Stadium. c, Argentine player holding World Cup. g, Argentina team picture.
No. 1516 — Top tournament scorers: a, Paulo Rossi. b, Mario Kempes. c, Gerd Muller. d, Grzegorz Lato. e, Ademir. f, Eusebio Ferreica da Silva. g, Salvatore (Toto) Schillaci. h, Leonidas da Silva. i, Gary Lineker.
No. 1517, 2000sh, England, 1966. No. 1518, 2000sh, W. Germany, 1990.

**1997, Oct. 3 Litho. *Perf. 14***

**1514** A226 Sheet of 6, #a.-f. 10.50 10.50
**1515** A226 250sh Sheet of 8, #a.-h. 8.00 8.00
**1516** A226 250sh Sheet of 9, #a.-i. + label 9.00 9.00

**Souvenir Sheets**

**1517-1518** A226 Set of 2 8.50 8.50

Diana, Princess of Wales (1961-97) A227

**1997, Dec. 1**

**1519** A227 60sh multicolored 1.25 1.25

No. 1519 was issued in sheets of 6.

Christmas A228

Sculpture, entire paintings or details: 200sh, Putto and Dolphin, by Andrea del Verrocchio. 300sh, The Fall of the Rebel Angels, by Pieter Bruegel the Elder. 400sh, The Immaculate Conception, by Murillo. 500sh, Music-making Angel, by Rosso Fiorentino. 600sh, Cupid and Psyche, by Adolphe-William Bouguereau. 700sh, Cupid and Psyche, by Antonio Canova.
No. 1526, 2500sh, Virgin, Angels from The Assumption of the Virgin, by El Greco. No. 1527, 2500sh, Angel from The Assumption of the Virgin, by El Greco.

**1997, Dec. 1**

**1520-1525** A228 Set of 6 5.50 5.50

**Souvenir Sheets**

**1526-1527** A228 Set of 2 10.00 10.00

New Year 1998 (Year of the Tiger) A229

Various paintings of tigers: No. 1528: a, Looking backward. b, Jumping. c, Lying, looking forward. d, Lying, mouth open.
1500sh, On cliff.

**1998, Jan. 16 Litho. *Perf. 13½***

**1528** A229 350sh Sheet of 4, #a.-d. 2.75 2.75

**Souvenir Sheet**

**1529** A229 1500sh multicolored 3.00 3.00

Tourist Attractions — A230

Designs: 300sh, Namugongo Martyrs Shrine, vert. 400sh, Kasubi Tombs. 500sh, Tourist boat, Kazinga Channel. 600sh, Elephant. 700sh, Bujagali Falls, Jinja.

**1998, Feb. 6 Litho. *Perf. 14***

**1530-1534** A230 Set of 5 5.00 5.00

Mother Teresa (1910-97) — A231

No. 1535: a-h, Various portraits. 2000sh, With Diana, Princess of Wales (1961-97).

**1998, Feb. 9 Litho. *Perf. 14***

**1535** A231 300sh Sheet of 8, #a.-h. 4.75 4.75

**Souvenir Sheet**

**1536** A231 2000sh multicolored 4.00 4.00

Nos. 1535a, 1535d-1535e, 1535h are each 22x36mm.

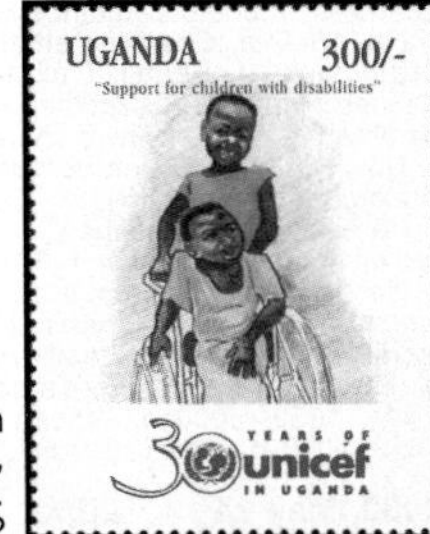


UNICEF in Uganda, 30th Anniv. A232

Designs: 300sh, "Support for children with disabilities." 400sh, "Safeguard children against polio." 600sh, "Sanitation... responsibility for all." 700sh, "Children's right to basic education."

**1998, Mar. 6 *Perf. 13½x14***

**1537-1540** A232 Set of 4 4.50 4.50

Dinosaurs — A233

Designs, horiz: 300sh, Pteranodon. 400sh, Diplodocus. 500sh, Lambeosaurus. 600sh, Centrosaurus. 700sh, Parasaurolophus.

No. 1546: a, Cetiosaurus. b, Brontosaurus. c, Brachiosaurus. d, Deinonychus. e, Dimetrodon. f, Megalosaurus.

No. 1547, 2500sh, Tyrannosaurus. No. 1548, 2500sh, Iguanodon.

**1998, Mar. 24 Litho. *Perf. 14***

**1541-1545** A233 Set of 5 5.00 5.00

**1546** A233 600sh Sheet of 6, #a.-f. 7.25 7.25

**Souvenir Sheets**

**1547-1548** A233 Set of 2 10.00 10.00

Nos. 1547-1548 each contain one 43x57mm stamp.

Writers — A234

No. 1549: a, Rita Dove. b, Mari Evans. c, Sterling A. Brown. d, June Jordan. e, Stephen Henderson. f, Zora Neale Hurston.

**1998, Apr. 6**

**1549** A234 300sh Sheet of 6, #a.-f. 3.75 3.75

Reptiles — A235

Designs: 300sh, Armadillo girdled lizard. 600sh, Spotted sandveld lizard. 700sh, Bell's ringed tortoise.

**1998, Apr. 21 *Perf. 13½***

**1550** A235 300sh multicolored .60 .60

**1551** A235 600sh multicolored 1.25 1.25

**1552** A235 700sh multicolored 1.40 1.40

*Nos. 1550-1552 (3)* 3.25 3.25

Compare with Nos. 1328-1335.

Mickey Mouse, 70th Birthday — A236

No. 1553 — Scenes from cartoon, "Runaway Brain:" a, Mickey afraid of shadow. b, Mickey petting Pluto, newspaper. c, Mickey playing computer game, Pluto. d, Mickey, Minnie running. e, Mickey as target of experiment. f, Minnie being held captive by Pete on top of skyscraper. g, Mickey throwing lasso. h, Mickey surrounding Pete with rope. i, Mickey, Minnie holding onto rope above skyscrapers.

No. 1554, 3000sh, Mickey, Minnie embracing on top of skyscraper. No. 1555, 3000sh, Mickey, Minnie kissing on raft, vert.

**1998, May 4 Litho. *Perf. 14x13½***

**1553** A236 400sh Sheet of 9, #a.-i. 7.25 7.25

**Souvenir Sheets**

**1554-1555** A236 Set of 2 12.00 12.00

Nos. 1414-1415 Ovptd.

**1998, May 13 Litho. *Perf. 14***

**1556** A197 Sheet of 3, #a.-c. (#1414) 3.50 3.50

**Souvenir Sheet**

**1557** A197 2000sh multi (#1415) 4.00 4.00

Sheet margins of Nos. 1556-1557 each contain additional overprint, "ISRAEL 98 — WORLD STAMP EXHIBITION/TEL-AVIV 13-21 MAY 1998."

Sailing Ships A237

No. 1558, 1000sh: a, Fishing schooner. b, Chesapeake oyster boat. c, Java Sea schooner.

No. 1559, 1000sh: a, Santa Maria, 15th cent. galleon. b, Mayflower, 15th cent. galleon. c, Bark.

No. 1560, 3000sh, Boat with lateen sails. No. 1561, 3000sh, Thames River barge, vert.

**1998, June 2 Litho. *Perf. 13x13½***

**Sheets of 3, #a-c + Label**

**1558-1559** A237 Set of 2 12.00 12.00

**Souvenir Sheets**

**1560-1561** A237 Set of 2 12.00 12.00

Nos. 1560-1561 are continuous designs.

Aircraft A238

No. 1562: a, US F4F Wildcat. b, Japanese Zero. c, British Spitfire. d, British Harrier. e, S3A Viking. f, US Corsair.

No. 1563: a, Dornier Do-X transatlantic flyer, 1929. b, German Zucker mail rocket, 1930. c, X-15 Rocket Plane, 1955. d, Goddard's Rocket, 1930's. e, Wright brothers' flight, 1903. f, 160R Sikorsky helicopter, 1939.

No. 1564, 2500sh, P40 Tomahawk. No. 1565, 2500sh, SH346 Seabat.

**1998, July 24 Litho. *Perf. 14***

**1562** A238 500sh Sheet of 6, #a.-f. 6.00 6.00

**1563** A238 600sh Sheet of 6, #a.-f. 7.25 7.25

**Souvenir Sheets**

**1564-1565** A238 Set of 2 10.00 10.00

Flowers of the Mediterranean — A239

No. 1566, vert: a, Onosma. b, Rhododendron luteum. c, Paeonia mascula. d, Geranium macorrhizum. e, Cyclamen graecum. f, Lilium rhodopaedum. g, Narcissus pseudonarcissus. h, Paeonia rhodia. i, Aquilegia amaliae.

No. 1567: a, Paeonia peregrina. b, Muscari comutatum. c, Sternbergia. d, Dianthus. e, Verbascum. f, Aubrieta gracilis. g, Galanthus nivalis. h, Campanula incurva. i, Crocus sieberi.

No. 1568, 2000sh, Paeonia parnassica, vert. No. 1569, 2000sh, Pancratium maritimum, vert.

**1998, Sept. 23 Litho. *Perf. 14***

**1566** A239 300sh Sheet of 9, #a.-i. 5.50 5.50

**1567** A239 600sh Sheet of 9, #a.-i. 11.00 11.00

**Souvenir Sheets**

**1568-1569** A239 Set of 2 8.00 8.00

Christmas A240

Birds: 300sh, Bohemian waxwing. 400sh, House sparrow. 500sh, Black-capped chickadee. 600sh, Eurasian bullfinch. 700sh, Painted bunting. 1000sh, Northern cardinal.

No. 1576, 2500sh, Winter wren, vert. No. 1577, 2500sh, Red-winged blackbird, vert.

**1998, Dec. 3 Litho. *Perf. 14***

**1570-1575** A240 Set of 6 7.00 7.00

**Souvenir Sheets**

**1576-1577** A240 Set of 2 10.00 10.00

Diana, Princess of Wales (1961-97) A241

**1998, Dec. 28 Litho. *Perf. 14½***

**1578** A241 700sh multicolored 2.00 2.00

Picasso A242

Paintings: 500sh, Woman Reading, 1935, vert. 600sh, Portrait of Dora Maar, 1937, vert. 700sh, Des Moiselles D'Avignon, 1907.

2500sh, Night Fishing at Antibes, 1939, vert.

**1998, Dec. 28 *Perf. 14½x13, 13x14½***

**1579-1581** A242 Set of 3 3.75 3.75

**Souvenir Sheet**

**1582** A242 2500sh multicolored 5.25 5.25

Gandhi — A243

**1998, Dec. 28 *Perf. 14***

**1583** A243 600sh Portrait 1.25 1.25

**Souvenir Sheet**

**1584** A243 2500sh Family portrait, horiz. 5.25 5.25

No. 1583 was issued in sheets of 4.

1998 World Scouting Jamboree, Chile — A244

No. 1585: a, Cub Scouts greet Pres. Eisenhower, Georgia, 1956. b, Uncle Dan Beard at 90th birthday party, 1990. c, Future Vice President Hubert Humphrey leads South Dakota troop, 1934.

2000sh, Young scout, tamed beaver, vert.

**1998, Dec. 28**

**1585** A244 700sh Sheet of 3, #a.-c. 6.00 6.00

**Souvenir Sheet**

**1586** A244 2000sh multicolored 4.00 4.00

New Year 1999 (Year of the Rabbit) A245

No. 1587 — Rabbits: a, White. b, With carrot. c, Brown & white. e, Black & white.

**1999, Jan. 4**

**1587** A245 350sh Sheet of 4, #a.-d. 2.50 2.50

**Souvenir Sheet**

**1588** A245 1500sh Rabbit, diff. 2.50 2.50

Uganda Post Office A246

**1999, Jan. 18**

**1589** A246 300sh multicolored 1.75 1.75

Traditional Hairstyles — A247

Hairstyle, region: 300sh, Iru, Bairu. 500sh, Enshunju, Bahima. 550sh, Elemungole, Karamojong. 600sh, Longo, Langi. 700sh, Ekikuura, Bahima.

**1999, Feb. 1**

**1590-1594** A247 Set of 5 5.25 5.25

Marine Life A248

No. 1595: a, Wolfish. b, Equal sea star. c, Purple sea urchin. d, Mountain crab.

No. 1596: a, Blue marlin. b, Arctic tern. c, Common dolphin. d, Blacktip shark. e, Manta ray. f, Blackedge moray. g, Loggerhead turtle. h, Sailfin tang. i, Two-spotted octopus.

No. 1597, 2500sh, Sea nettle jellyfish. No. 1598, 2500sh, Decatopecten striatus.

**1999, Mar. 15 Litho. *Perf. 14***

**1595** A248 500sh Sheet of 4, #a.-d. 3.25 3.25

**1596** A248 500sh Sheet of 9, #a.-i. 9.00 9.00

**Souvenir Sheets**

**1597-1598** A248 each 8.50 8.50

Intl. Year of the Ocean.

Intl. Year of the Elderly A249

Designs: 300sh, Income generating activity. 500sh, Learning from each other. 600sh, Leisure time for the aged. 700sh, Distributing food to the aged.

**1999, July 19 Litho. *Perf. 13x13½***

**1599-1602** A249 Set of 4 3.00 3.00

First Manned Moon Landing, 30th Anniv. — A250

No. 1603: a, Apollo 11 launch. b, Apollo 11 command and service modules. c, Edwin E. Aldrin, Jr. on lunar module ladder. d, Saturn V ready to launch. e, Lunar module descending. f, Aldrin on moon.

No. 1604: a, Freedom 7. b, Gemini 4. c, Apollo 11 command and service modules, diff. d, Vostok 1. e, Saturn V. f, Lunar module on moon.

No. 1605, 3000sh, Aldrin with scientific experiment. No. 1606, 3000sh, Command module re-entry.

**1999, Nov. 24 Litho. *Perf. 13¾***

**1603** A250 600sh Sheet of 6, #a.-f. 4.75 4.75

**1604** A250 700sh Sheet of 6, #a.-f. 5.50 5.50

**Souvenir Sheets**

**1605-1606** A250 Set of 2 8.00 9.00

Queen Mother (b. 1900) — A251

No. 1607: a, With stole. b, At wedding. c, With tiara (black and white photo). d, With tiara (color photo).

3000sh, Visiting Cambridge, 1961.

**1999, Nov. 24 *Perf. 14***

**1607** A251 1200sh Sheet of 4, #a.-d. 6.50 6.50

**Souvenir Sheet**

***Perf. 13¾***

**1608** A251 3000sh multicolored 4.00 4.00

No. 1608 contains one 38x51mm stamp.

Hokusai Paintings A252

No. 1609: a, Dragon Flying Over Mount Fuji (dragon). b, Famous Poses From the Kabuki Theater (one figure). c, Kitsune No Yomeiri. d, Dragon Flying Over Mount Fuji (Mount Fuji). e, Famous Poses From the Kabuki Theater (two figures). f, Girl Holding Cloth.

3000sh, Japanese Spaniel.

**1999, Nov. 24 Litho. *Perf. 13¾***

**1609** A252 700sh Sheet of 6, #a.-f. 5.50 5.50

**Souvenir Sheet**

**1610** A252 3000sh multicolored 4.00 4.00

Birds — A253

Designs: 300sh, African penduline tit. 1000sh, Yellow-fronted tinkerbird. 1200sh, Zebra waxbill. 1800sh, Sooty anteater chat.

No. 1615: a, Gray-headed kingfisher. b, Green-headed sunbird. c, Speckled pigeon. d, Gray parrot. e, Barn owl. f, Gray crowned crane. g, Shoebill. h, Black heron.

No. 1616: a, Scarlet-chested sunbird. b, Lesser honeyguide. c, African palm swift. d, Swamp flycatcher. e, Lizard buzzard. f, Osprey. g, Cardinal woodpecker. h, Pearl-spotted owlet.

No. 1617: a, Fox's weaver. b, Chin-spot flycatcher. c, Blue swallow. d, Purple-breasted sunbird. e, Knob-billed duck. f, Red-collared widowbird. g, Ruwenzori turaco. h, African cuckoo hawk.

No. 1618, 3000sh, Four-banded sandgrouse. No. 1619, 3000sh, Paradise whydah.

**1999, Dec. 6 *Perf. 14***

**1611-1614** A253 Set of 4 5.75 5.75

**1615** A253 500sh Sheet of 8, #a.-h. 5.25 5.25

**1616** A253 600sh Sheet of 8, #a.-h. 6.50 6.50

**1617** A253 700sh Sheet of 8, #a.-h. 7.50 7.50

**Souvenir Sheets**

**1618-1619** A253 Set of 2 8.00 8.00

Primates — A254

Designs: 300sh, L'hoesti monkey. 400sh, Blue monkey. 500sh, Patas monkey. 600sh, Red-tailed monkey. 700sh, Black and white colobus. 1000sh, Mountain gorilla.

2500sh, Olive baboon.

**1999, Nov. 19 Litho. *Perf. 13½x14***

**1620-1625** A254 Set of 6 4.75 4.75

**Souvenir Sheet**

**1626** A254 2500sh multicolored 3.50 3.50

Butterflies A255

Designs: 300sh, Epiphora bauhiniae, vert. 400sh, Phylloxiphia formosa. 500sh, Bunaea alcinoe, vert. 600sh, Euchloron megaera. 700sh, Argema mimosae, vert. 1800sh, Denephila nerii.

3000sh, Lobobunaea angasana.

***Perf. 13½x13¼, 13¼x13½***

**2000, Jan. 19 Litho.**

**1627-1632** A255 Set of 6 5.75 5.75

**Souvenir Sheet**

**1633** A255 3000sh multi 4.00 4.00

A256

A257

UPU, 125th anniv. (in 1999): 600sh, Postman, two women, girl. 700sh, Woman, girl, mail box. 1200sh, Postman in horse-drawn wagon.

**2000, Jan. 28 Litho. *Perf. 14***

**1634-1636** A256 Set of 3 3.50 3.50

**2000, Feb. 18**

No. 1637, 600sh — Orchids: a, Angraecum eichcerianum. b, Angraecum leonis. c, Arpophyllum giganteum. d, Bulbophyllum barbigerum. e, Angraecum ciryamae. f, Aerangis ellisii. g, Disa umiflora. h, Eulophia alta. i, Ancistrochilius stylosa.

No. 1638, 600sh: a, Eulophia paivenna. b, Ansellia gigantea. c, Anglaecopsis gracillima. d, Bonatea steudneri. e, Bulbophyllum falcatum. f, Aerangis citrata. g, Eulophiella elisabethae. h, Aerangis rhodosticta. i, Angraecum scottianum.

No. 1639, 700sh: a, Grammangis ellisii. b, Eulophia stenophylia. c, Oeoniella polystachys. d, Cymbidiella humblotti. e, Polystachya bella. f, Vanilla polycepis. g, Eulophileea roemplerana. h, Habenaria englerana. i, Ansellia frallana.

No. 1640, 700sh: a, Eulophia orthoplectra. b, Cirrhopetalum umbellatum. c, Eulophiella rolfei. d, Eulophia porphyroglossa. e, Eulopia petersii. f, Cyrtorchis arcuata. g, Eurychone rothschildiana. h, Eulophia quartiniana. i, Eulophia stenophylia (one flower).

No. 1641, 3000sh, Polystachya tayloriana, horiz. No. 1642, 3000sh, Ancistrochilus rothschildianus, horiz. No. 1643, 3000sh, Calanthe corymbosa, horiz. No. 1644, 3000sh, Cymbidiella rhodochila, horiz.

**Sheets of 9, #a.-i.**

**1637-1638** A257 Set of 2 14.50 14.50

**1639-1640** A257 Set of 2 17.00 17.00

**Souvenir Sheets**

**1641-1644** A257 Set of 4 16.00 16.00

Butterflies — A258

Designs: 300sh, Short-tailed admiral. 400sh, Guineafowl. 1200sh, Club-tailed charaxes. 1800sh, Cymothoe egesta.

No. 1649: a, Charaxes anrticlea. b, Epitola posthumus. c, Beautiful monarch. d, Blue-banded nymph. e, Euxanthe crossleyi. f, African map. g, Western blue charaxes. h, Noble.

No. 1650: a, Green-veined charaxes. b, Ansorge's leaf butterfly. c, Crawshay's sapphire blue. d, Palla ussheri. e, Friar. f, Blood-red cymothoe. g, Mocker. h, Charaxes eupale.

No. 1651: a, Aeraea pseudolycia. b, Veined yellow. c, Buxton's hairstreak. d, Iolaus isomenias. e, Veined swallowtail. f, Figtree blue. g, Scarlet tip. h, Precis octavia.

No. 1652, 3000sh, African monarch. No. 1653, 3000sh, Kigezi swordtail.

**2000, May 24 Litho. *Perf. 14***

**1645-1648** A258 Set of 4 4.50 4.50

**1649** A258 500sh Sheet of 8, #a-h 4.75 4.75

**1650** A258 600sh Sheet of 8, #a-h 5.75 5.75

**1651** A258 700sh Sheet of 8, #a-h 6.75 6.75

**Souvenir Sheets**

**1652-1653** A258 Set of 2 7.00 7.00

The Stamp Show 2000, London (Nos. 1649-1653).

Popes — A259

No. 1654: a, Agapetus II (946-55). b, Alexander II (1061-73). c, Anastasius IV (1153-54). d, Benedict VIII (1012-24). e, Benedict VII (974-83). f, Calixtus II (1119-24).
No. 1655, Celestine III (1191-98).
Illustration reduced.

**2000, June 28** ***Perf. 13¾***

**1654** A259 900sh Sheet of 6, #a-f 6.50 6.50

**Souvenir Sheet**

**1655** A259 3000sh multi 3.50 3.50

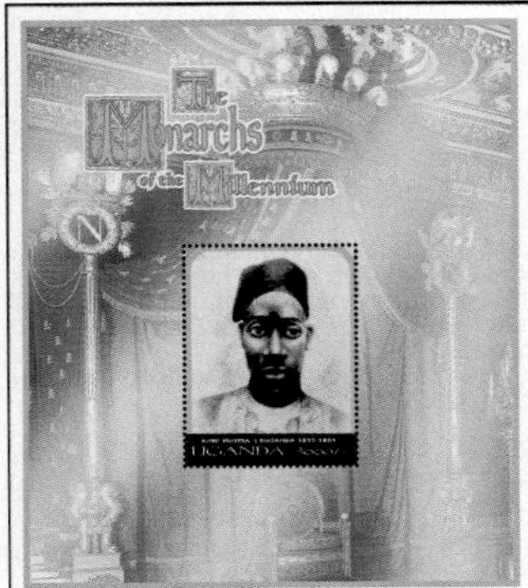

Monarchs — A260

No. 1655A: b, Philip II of France (1180-1223). c, Richard I of England (1189-99). d, William I of England (1066-87).
No. 1656: a, Boris III of Bulgaria (1918-43). b, Holy Roman Emperor Charles V (1519-58). c, Pedro II of Brazil (1831-89). d, Empress Elizabeth of Austria (1854-98). e, Francis Joseph of Austria (1848-1916). f, Frederick I of Bohemia (1619-20).
No. 1657, Mutesa I of Buganda (1191-98). No. 1657A, Cwa II Kabaleega.
Illustration reduced.

**2000, June 28** ***Perf. 13¾***

**1655A** A260 900sh Sheet of 3, #b-d 3.25 3.25
**1656** A260 900sh Sheet of 6, #a-f 6.50 6.50

**Souvenir Sheets**

**1657** A260 3000sh multi 3.50 3.50
**1657A** A260 3000sh multi 3.50 3.50

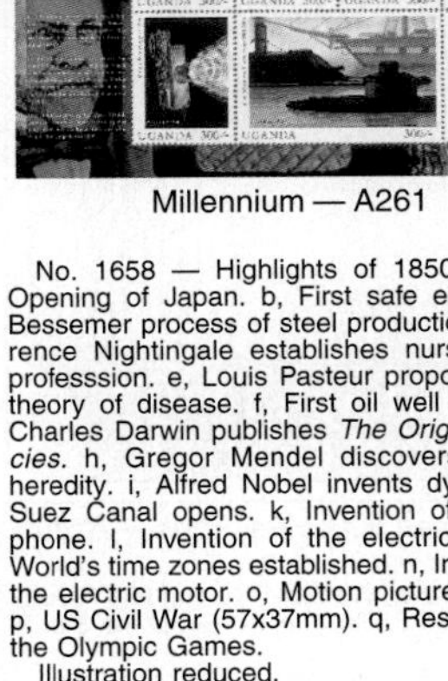

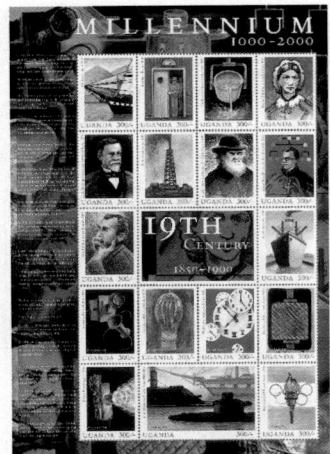

Millennium — A261

No. 1658 — Highlights of 1850-1900: a, Opening of Japan. b, First safe elevator. c, Bessemer process of steel production. d, Florence Nightingale establishes nursing as a professsion. e, Louis Pasteur proposes germ theory of disease. f, First oil well drilled. g, Charles Darwin publishes *The Origin of Species*. h, Gregor Mendel discovers laws of heredity. i, Alfred Nobel invents dynamite, j, Suez Canal opens. k, Invention of the telephone. l, Invention of the electric light. m, World's time zones established. n, Invention of the electric motor. o, Motion pictures appear. p, US Civil War (57x37mm). q, Restoration of the Olympic Games.
Illustration reduced.

**2000, June 28** ***Perf. 12¾x12½***

**1658** A261 300sh Sheet of 17, #a-q + label 6.00 6.00

Millennium — A262

Designs: 300sh, Education for all. 600sh, Nile River. 700sh, Non-traditional exports. 1800sh, Tourism.

**2000, July 24** ***Perf. 14½***

**1659-1662** A262 Set of 4 4.00 4.00

Common Market for Eastern and Southern Africa A263

Designs: 500sh, Border checkpoint before and after COMESA treaty. 1400sh, Open border checkpoint.

**2000, July 24**

**1663-1664** A263 Set of 2 2.25 2.25

Modern British Commonwealth, 50th Anniv. — A264

Designs: 600sh, Flags. 1200sh, Map.

**2000, July 24**

**1665-1666** A264 Set of 2 2.10 2.10

Trains A265

Designs: 300sh, Kenya Railways A 60 Class 4-8-2+2-8-4. 400sh, Mozambique Railways Baldwin 2-8-0. 600sh, Uganda Railways 73 Class German locomotive. 700sh, South Africa Railways Baby Garratt. 1200sh, Uganda Railways 82 Class French locomotive. 1400sh, East Africa Railway Beyer Garratt 4-8-2+2-8-4. 1800sh, Rhodesian Railways 2-8-2+2-8-2 Beyer Garratt. 2000sh, East African Railways Garratt.
No. 1675, 700sh: a, Uganda Railways 36 Class German locomotive. b, South African Railways Class 19D 4-8-2. c, Algeria Railways Garratt 4-8-2+2-8-4. d, Cameroon Railways French locomotive. e, South Africa railways electric freight locomotive. f, Rhodesia Railways 14A Class 2-8-2. g, British-built Egyptian railways locomotive. h, Uganda Railways 73 Class German locomotive, diff.
No. 1676, 700sh: a, 36 Class German locomotive (no counrtry specified). b, Rhodesian Railways 12th Class locomotive. c, Rhodesian Railways Garratt. d, 62 Class German locomotive. e, South Africa Railways Beyer Garratt. f, Sudan Railways locomotive. g, Nigerian Railways locomotive. h, 4-8-0 South Africa Railways.
No. 1677, 3500sh, East African Railways locomotive. No. 1678, 3500sh, Rhodesian Railways Alco 2-8-0. No. 1679, 3500sh, Egyptian State Railways 4-8-2.

**2000, Aug. 14** ***Perf. 14***

**1667-1674** A265 Set of 8 10.00 10.00

**Sheets of 8, #a-h**

**1675-1676** A265 Set of 2 13.50 13.50

**Souvenir Sheets**

**1677-1679** A265 Set of 3 13.00 13.00

Nos. 1677-1679 each contain one 56x42mm stamp.

Christmas — A266

Artwork by: 300sh, Drateru Fortunate Oliver, vert. 400sh, Brenda Tumwebaze. 500sh, Joseph Mukiibi, vert. 600sh, Paul Serunjogi. 700sh, Edward Maswere. 1200sh, Ndeba Harriet. 1800sh, Jude Kasagga, vert.
No. 1687, 3000sh, Nicole Kwiringira, vert. No. 1688, 3000sh, Michael Tinkamanyire, vert.

**2000, Dec. 14** **Litho.** ***Perf. 14***

**1680-1686** A266 Set of 7 6.50 6.50

**Souvenir Sheets**

**1687-1688** A266 Set of 2 7.00 7.00

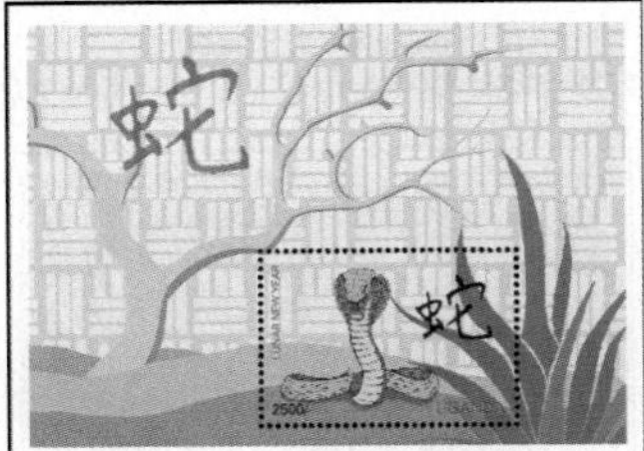

New Year 2001 (Year of the Snake) — A267

No. 1689: a, Snake with tongue out. b, Snake wrapped around person. c, Snake with open mouth. d, Snake hanging from branch.

**2001, Jan. 5**

**1689** A267 600sh Sheet of 4, #a-d 2.75 2.75

**Souvenir Sheet**

**1690** A267 2500sh shown 2.75 2.75

Wildlife — A268

No. 1691: a, Bongo, horiz. b, Black rhinoceros, horiz. c, Leopard.
No. 1692, 3000sh, Parrot. No. 1693, 3000sh, Mountain gorillas, horiz.

***Perf. 13¼x13¾, 13¾x13¼***

**2001, Feb. 5**

**1691** A268 600sh Strip of 3, #a-c 2.00 2.00

**Souvenir Sheets**

**1692-1693** A268 Set of 2 6.75 6.75

Holy Year 2000 — A269

Designs: 300sh, Holy Family. 700sh, Madonna and Child. 1200sh, Nativity, horiz.

**2001, Apr. 4** **Litho.** ***Perf. 13¼***

**1694-1696** A269 Set of 3 2.50 2.50

East African School of Library and Information Science, Makerere University, Kampala — A270

Nairobi University, Kenya — A271

Universities and Flags on Map — A272

Design: 1200sh, Nkrumah Hall, University of Dar es Salaam, Tanzania.

**2001, Apr. 23**

**1697** A270 300sh multi .35 .35
**1698** A271 400sh multi .45 .45
**1699** A270 1200sh multi 1.40 1.40
**1700** A272 1800sh multi 2.10 2.10
*Nos. 1697-1700 (4)* 4.30 4.30

World Meteorological Organization, 50th Anniv. (in 2000) — A273

Designs: 300sh, Anemometer, vert. 2000sh, Tropical sun recorder.

**2001, May 28**
**1701-1702** A273 Set of 2 2.60 2.60

UN High Commissioner for Refugees — A274

Designs: 300sh, Ensure crop production. 600sh, Ensure community participation. 700sh, Ensure improved skills. 1800sh, Ensure improved health and water services.

**2001, June 15**
**1703-1706** A274 Set of 4 4.00 4.00

Phila Nippon '01, Japan — A275

Designs: 600sh, Kikunojo Segawa I and Danjuro Ichikawa as Samurai, by Kiyonobu II. 700sh, Kamezo Tchimura as a Warrior, by Kiyohiro. 1000sh, Danjuro Ichikawa as Shirobei, by Kiyomitsu. 1200sh, Actor Sangoro Arashi, by Shunsho. 1400sh, Koshiro Matsumoto IV as Sukenari Juro, by Kiyonaga. 2000sh, Pheasant on Pine Branch, by Kiyomasu II.
3500sh, Tale of Ise, by Eishi.

**2001, Aug. 1 Litho. *Perf. 14***
**1707-1712** A275 Set of 6 7.75 7.75

**Souvenir Sheet**

**1713** A275 3500sh multi 4.00 4.00

Cats and Dogs — A276

Designs: 400sh, Tabby British shorthair. 900sh, Turkish cat.
No. 1716, 600sh, horiz.: a, Blue and cream shorthair. b, Manx. c, Angora. d, Red and white British shorthair. e, Turkish cat, diff. f, Egyptian mau.
No. 1717, 1400sh, horiz.: a, Red tabby shorthair. b, Japanese bobtail. c, Siamese. d, Tabby Persian. e, Black and white Persian. f, Blue Russian.
No. 1718, 3500sh, Blue-eyed British shorthair. No. 1719, 3500sh, Calico American shorthair.

**2001, Aug. 23**
**1714-1715** A276 Set of 2 1.50 1.50

**Sheets of 6, #a-f**

**1716-1717** A276 Set of 2 13.50 13.50

**Souvenir Sheets**

**1718-1719** A276 Set of 2 8.00 8.00

**2001, Aug. 23**

Designs: 1100sh, German shepherd. 1200sh, Irish setter.
No. 1722, 700sh, horiz.: a, Rottweiler. b, Flat-coated retriever. c, Samoyed. d, Poodle. e, Maltese. f, Irish terrier.
No. 1723, 1300sh, horiz: a, English sheepdog. b, German shepherd, diff. c, Great Dane. d, Boston terrier. e, Bull terrier. f, Australian terrier.
No. 1724, 3500sh, Bloodhound. No. 1725, 3500sh, Pointer, horiz.

**1720-1721** A276 Set of 2 2.60 2.60

**Sheets of 6, #a-f**

**1722-1723** A276 Set of 2 13.50 13.50

**Souvenir Sheets**

**1724-1725** A276 Set of 2 8.00 8.00

APS Stampshow, Chicago (#1723).

Royal Navy Submarines, Cent. — A277

No. 1726, vert.: a, HMS Tribune. b, HMS Royal Oak. c, HMS Invincible. d, HMS Dreadnought. e, HMS Ark Royal. f, HMS Cardiff.

**2001, Aug. 27**
**1726** A277 1000sh Sheet of 6, #a-f 6.75 6.75

**Souvenir Sheet**

**1727** A277 3500sh HMS Triad 4.00 4.00

Queen Victoria (1819-1901) — A278

No. 1728: a, Wearing tiara. b, Wearing white head covering, looking right. c, Wearing black hat. d, Wearing red dress with blue sash. e, Wearing white head covering, looking left. f, With hand on chin.
3500sh, Wearing black, hat, diff.

**2001, Aug. 27**
**1728** A278 1000sh Sheet of 6, #a-f 6.75 6.75

**Souvenir Sheet**

**1729** A278 3500sh multi 4.00 4.00

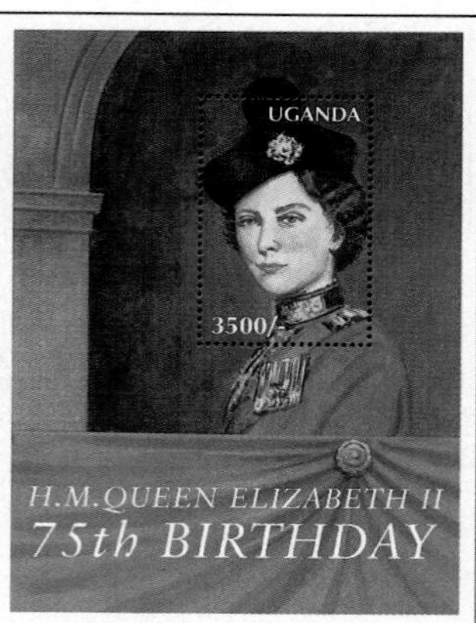


Queen Elizabeth II, 75th Birthday — A279

No. 1730: a, In 1926. b, In 1931. c, In 1939. d, In 1955. e, In 1963. f, In 1999.
3500sh, Wearing cap.

**2001, Aug. 27**
**1730** A279 1000sh Sheet of 6, #a-f 6.75 6.75

**Souvenir Sheet**

**1731** A279 3500sh multi 4.00 4.00

Toulouse-Lautrec Paintings — A280

No. 1732: a, Woman Combing Her Hair. b, The Toilette. c, The English Girl at the Star in Le Havre.
3500sh, Ambassadeurs: Aristide Bruant.

**2001, Aug. 27 Litho. *Perf. 13¾***
**1732** A280 1500sh Sheet of 3, #a-c 5.25 5.25

**Souvenir Sheet**

**1733** A280 3500sh multi 4.00 4.00

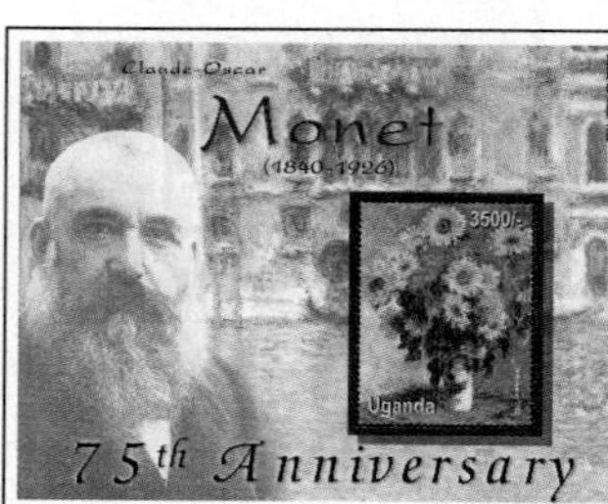


Monet Paintings — A281

No. 1734, horiz.: a, Storm, Belle-Ile Coast. b, The Manneporte, Etretat. c, The Rocks at Pourville, Low Tide. d, The Wild Sea.
3500sh, Sunflowers.

**2001, Aug. 27**
**1734** A281 1200sh Sheet of 4, #a-d 5.50 5.50

**Souvenir Sheet**

**1735** A281 3500sh multi 4.00 4.00

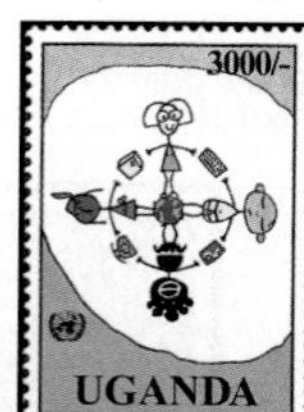


Year of Dialogue Among Civilizations A282

***Perf. 13¾x13¼***

**2001, Nov. 16 Litho.**
**1736** A282 3000sh multi 3.50 3.50

Intl. Volunteers Year A283

Designs: 300sh, Ebola outbreak. 700sh, Save life, donate blood. 2000sh, Collective effort for clean water.

**2001, Nov. 16 *Perf. 13¼x13¾***
**1737-1739** A283 Set of 3 3.50 3.50

Mushrooms — A284

Designs: 300sh, Amanita excelsa. 500sh, Coprinus cinereus. 600sh, Scleroderma aurantium. 700sh, Armillaria mellea. 1200sh, Leopiota procera. 2000sh, Flammulina velutipes.
3000sh, Amanita phalloides.

**2001, Nov. 26 *Perf. 14½***
**1740-1745** A284 Set of 6 6.25 6.25

**Souvenir Sheets**

**1746** A284 3000sh multi 3.50 3.50
**1746A** A284 3000sh multi 3.50 3.50

Christmas — A285

Musical instruments: 400sh, Single skin long drum. 800sh, Animal horn trumpet, horiz. 1000sh, Bugisu clay drum. 1200sh, Musical bow. 1400sh, Pan pipes. 2000sh, Log xylophones, horiz.
No. 1753, 3500sh, Eight-stringed giant bow harp. No. 1754, Nativity scene, horiz.

**2001 *Perf. 13¾x13¼, 13¼x13¾***
**1747-1752** A285 Set of 6 8.00 8.00

**Souvenir Sheets**

**1753-1754** A285 Set of 2 8.25 8.25

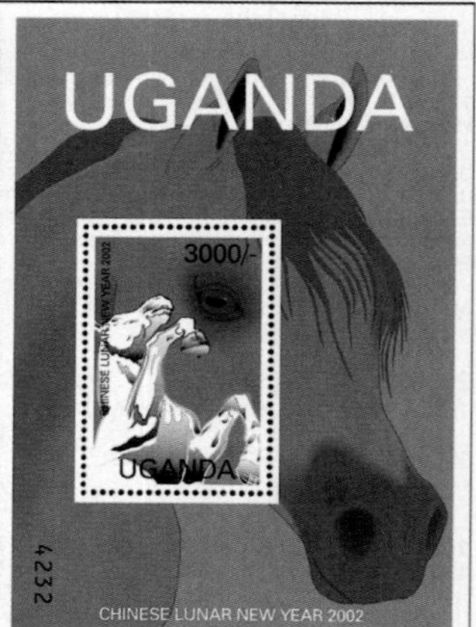


New Year 2002 (Year of the Horse) — A286

No. 1755: a, White horse facing left. b, Dark brown and gray brown horse facing right with all feet on ground. c, Tan and brown horse facing right, with two feet raised.
3000r, Rearing horse.

**2002, May 8 Litho. *Perf. 14x14¼***
**1755** A286 1200sh Sheet of 3, #a-c 4.00 4.00

**Souvenir Sheet**

**1756** A286 3000sh multi 3.25 3.25

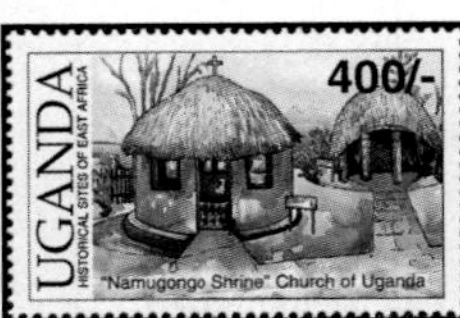

Historic Sites of East Africa A287

Designs: 400sh, Namugongo Shrine Church, Uganda. 800sh, Maruhubi Palace Ruins, Zanzibar, Tanzania. 1200sh, Kings' Burial Grounds, Mparo, Uganda. 1400sh, Old Law Courts, Mombasa, Kenya, vert.

**2002, May 8** ***Perf. 14½***
**1757-1760** A287 Set of 4 4.25 4.25

Reign of Queen Elizabeth II, 50th Anniv. — A288

No. 1761: a, Wearing blue dress. b, Wearing blue and red hat. c, Without hat. d, Wearing blue hat.
3500sh, Wearing brown hat.

**2002, June 17** ***Perf. 14¼***
**1761** A288 1500sh Sheet of 4, #a-d 6.75 6.75

**Souvenir Sheet**

**1762** A288 3500sh multi 4.00 4.00

8th Intl. Interdisciplinary Congress on Women, Kampala — A289

Designs: 400sh, Women, building. 1200sh, Makerere University arms, vert.

***Perf. 13¼x13¾, 13¾x13¼***
**2002, July 8**
**1763-1764** A289 Set of 2 1.75 1.75

United We Stand — A290

**2002, July 15** ***Perf. 13¾x13¼***
**1765** A290 1500sh multi 1.75 1.75

Printed in sheets of 4.

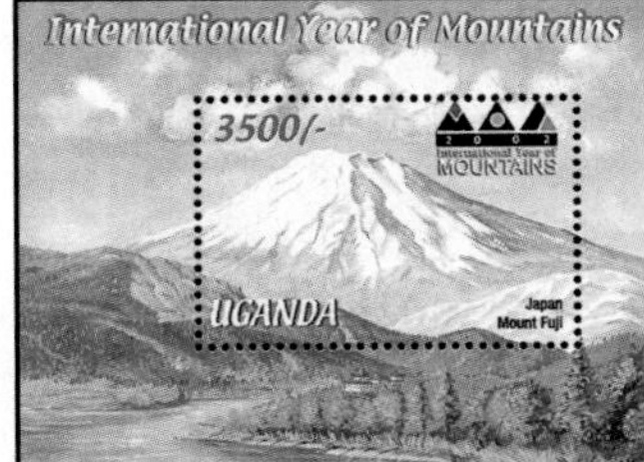

Intl. Year of Mountains — A291

No. 1766: a, Tateyama, Japan. b, Mt. Nikko, Japan. c, Mt. Hodaka, Japan.
3500sh, Mt. Fuji, Japan.

**2002, July 15** ***Perf. 13¼x13¾***
**1766** A291 2000sh Sheet of 3, #a-c 6.75 6.75

**Souvenir Sheet**

**1767** A291 3500sh multi 4.00 4.00

2002 Winter Olympics, Salt Lake City — A292

Designs: No. 1768, 1200sh, Cross-country skiing. No. 1769, 1200sh, Ski jumping.

**2002, July 15** ***Perf. 13¾x13¼***
**1768-1769** A292 Set of 2 2.75 2.75
*1769a* Souvenir sheet, #1768-1769 2.75 2.75

20th World Scout Jamboree, Thailand — A293

No. 1770: a, Scout in forest, 1930s. b, Scout saluting. c, Scouts hiking. d, Scout badge.
3500sh, Lord Robert Baden-Powell.

**2002** ***Perf. 13¼x13¾***
**1770** A293 1400sh Sheet of 4, #a-d 6.25 6.25

**Souvenir Sheet**

***Perf. 13¾x13¼***

**1771** A293 3500sh multi 4.00 4.00

Mammals, Insects, Flowers and Mushrooms — A294

Designs: 400sh, Ceratotherium simum. 800sh, Macrotermes subhyalinus. No. 1774, 1200sh, Gloriosa superba. 1400sh, Cyptotrama asprata.
No. 1776, 1000sh, horiz. — Insects: a, Nudaurelia cytherea. b, Locusta migratoria. c, Anacridium aegyptium. d, Sternotomis bohemanni. e, Papilio dardanus. f, Mantis polyspilota.
No. 1777, 1000sh, horiz. — Mushrooms: a, Termitomyces microcarpus. b, Agaricus trisulphuratus. c, Macrolepiota zeyheri. d, Lentinus stupeus. e, Lentinus sajor-caju. f, Lentinus velutinus.
No. 1778, 1200sh, horiz. — Flowers: a, Canarina eminii. b, Vigna unguiculata. c, Gardenia ternifolia. d, Canavalia rosea. e, Hibiscus calyphyllus. f, Nymphaea lotus.
No. 1779, 1200sh, horiz. — Mammals: a, Kobus kob. b, Alcelaphus buselaphus. c, Damaliiscus lunatus. d, Papio anubis. e, Panthera leo. f, Phacochoerus africanus.
No. 1780, 4000sh, Glossina austeni, horiz. No. 1781, 4000sh, Podoscypha parvula, horiz. No. 1782, 4000sh, Abutilon grandiflorum, horiz. No. 1783, 4000sh, Kobus ellipsiprymnus.

**2002, Nov. 6** **Litho.** ***Perf. 14***
**1772-1775** A294 Set of 4 4.25 4.25

**Sheets of 6, #a-f**

**1776-1779** A294 Set of 4 30.00 30.00

**Souvenir Sheets**

**1780-1781** A294 Set of 4 17.50 17.50

A295

Pres. John F. Kennedy (1917-63) — A296

Various photos.

**2002, Dec. 30**
**1784** A295 1200sh Sheet of 4, #a-d 5.25 5.25
**1785** A296 1400sh Sheet of 4, #a-d 6.00 6.00

A297

Pres. Ronald Reagan — A298

Various photos.

**2002, Dec. 30**
**1786** A297 1200sh Sheet of 4, #a-d 5.25 5.25
**1787** A298 1400sh Sheet of 4, #a-d 6.00 6.00

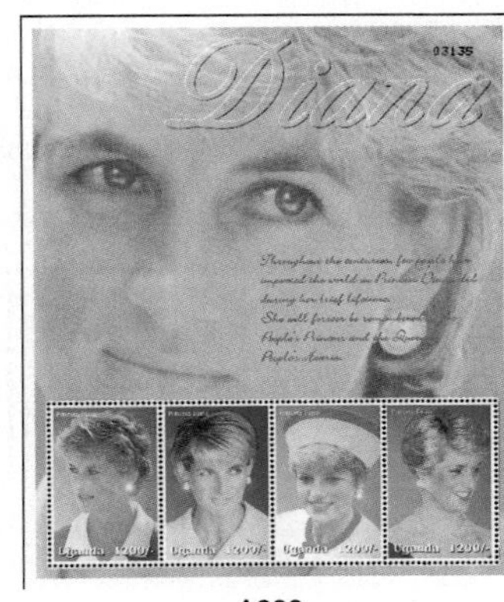

A299

Princess Diana (1961-97) — A300

**2002, Dec. 30**
**1788** A299 1200sh Sheet of 4, #a-d 5.25 5.25
**1789** A300 2000sh Sheet of 4, #a-d 8.75 8.75

New Year 2003 (Year of the Ram) — A301

No. 1790: a, Ram on stage. b, Ram on hill. c, Ram on hill, six ram's heads. d, Six rams. e, Ram in field. f, Ram on mountainside.

**2003, Feb. 1** ***Perf. 14¼x14***
**1790** A301 1000sh Sheet of 6, #a-f 6.50 6.50

Japanese Art — A302

Designs: 400sh, Beauty Arranging Her Hair, by Eisen Keisai. 1000sh, Geishas, by Tsukimaro Kitagawa. 1200sh, Woman Behind a Screen, by Chikanobu Toyohara. 1400sh, Geishas, by Kitagawa, diff.

No. 1795: a, Scene in a Villa (basin in foreground), by Kinichika Toyohara. b, Scene in a Villa (screen at left), by Kunichika Toyohara. c, Visiting a Flower Garden (two people), by Kunisada Utagawa. d, Visiting a Flower Garden (one person), by Utagawa.
5000sh, Woman and Children, by Chikakazu.

**2003, May 26 Litho. *Perf. 14¼***
**1791-1794** A302 Set of 4 4.00 4.00
**1795** A302 1200sh Sheet of 4, #a-d 4.75 4.75

**Souvenir Sheet**
**1796** A302 5000sh multi 5.00 5.00

Rembrandt Paintings A303

Designs: 400sh, Jacob Blessing the Sons of Joseph. 1000sh, A Young Woman in Profile With Fan. 1200sh, The Apostle Peter Kneeling. 1400sh, The Painter Hendrick Martensz Sorgh.
No. 1801: a, Portrait of Margaretha de Geer. b, Portrait of a White Haired Man. c, Portrait of Nicolaes Ruts. d, Portrait of Catrina Hooghsaet.
5000sh, Joseph Accused by Potiphar's Wife.

**2003, May 26**
**1797-1800** A303 Set of 4 4.00 4.00
**1801** A303 1400sh Sheet of 4, #a-d 5.75 5.75

**Souvenir Sheet**
**1802** A303 5000sh multi 5.00 5.00

Paintings of Joan Miró — A304

Designs: 400sh, Group of Personages in the Forest. 800sh, Nocturne. 1200sh, The Smile of a Tear. 1400sh, Personage Before the Sun.
No. 1807, vert: a, Man's Head III. b, Catalan Peasant by Moonlight. c, Woman in the Night. d, Seated Woman.
No. 1808, 3500sh, Self-portrait II. No. 1809, 3500sh, Woman with Three Hairs, Birds and Constellations.

**2003, May 26 *Perf. 14¼***
**1803-1806** A304 Set of 4 3.75 3.75
**1807** A304 1400sh Sheet of 4, #a-d 5.75 5.75

***Imperf***
**Size: 103x82mm**
**1808-1809** A304 Set of 2 7.00 7.00

Buganda Princess Katrina-Sarah Ssangalyambogo, 2nd Birthday — A305

Princess and: 400sh, Bulange (government office building). 1200sh, Twekobe (palace), vert. 1400sh, Drummer, vert.

***Perf. 13x13¼, 13¼x13***
**2003, June 16**
**1810-1812** A305 Set of 3 3.00 3.00

Coronation of Queen Elizabeth II, 50th Anniv. — A306

No. 1813: a, As toddler. b, As young woman, wearing flowered hat. c, Wearing robe and feathered hat.
3500sh, Wearing crown.

**2003, July 15 *Perf. 14***
**1813** A306 2000sh Sheet of 3, #a-c 6.00 6.00

**Souvenir Sheet**
**1814** A306 3500sh multi 3.50 3.50

Prince William, 21st Birthday — A307

No. 1815: a, Wearing cap. b, Wearing blue striped shirt. c, Wearing white shirt.
5000sh, With hand on chin.

**2003, July 15**
**1815** A307 2000sh Sheet of 3, #a-c 6.00 6.00

**Souvenir Sheet**
**1816** A307 5000sh multi 5.00 5.00

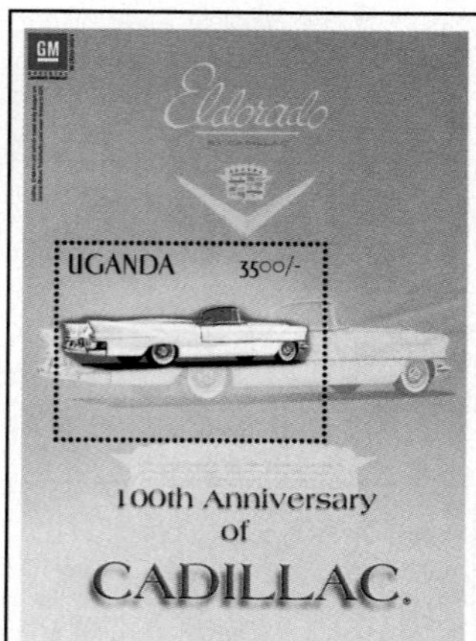
General Motors Automobiles — A308

No. 1817, 1200sh — Cadillacs: a, 1979 Seville Elegante. b, 1998 Eldorado Touring Coupe. c, 2002 Escalade. d, 1983 Seville Elegante.
No. 1818, 1400sh — Corvettes: a, 1970. b, 1972. c, 1982 Collector Edition. d, 1977.
No. 1819, 3500sh, Cadillac Eldorado convertible, 1950s. No. 1820, 3500sh, 1982 Collector Edition Corvette, diff.

**2003, July 15 *Perf. 14¼***
**Sheets of 4, #a-d**
**1817-1818** A308 Set of 2 10.50 10.50

**Souvenir Sheets**
**1819-1820** A308 Set of 2 7.00 7.00

Millennium Development Goals — A309

Designs: No. 1821, 400sh, Promote gender equity and empower women. No. 1822, 400sh, Improve maternal health. 600sh, Ensure environmental sustainability. 1000sh, Reduce child mortality. No. 1825, 1200sh, Eradicate extreme poverty and hunger. No. 1826, 1200sh, Combat HIV, AIDS, malaria and other diseases. 1400sh, Achieve universal primary education. 2000sh, Develop a global partnership for development.

**2003, Oct. 24 *Perf. 14½***
**1821-1828** A309 Set of 8 8.25 8.25

Dances and Costumes — A310

Dances: 400sh, Entogoro. 800sh, Karimojong. 1400sh, Teso.
No. 1832 — Costumes: a, Kiga. b, Acholi. c, Karimojong. d, Ganda.

**2003, Nov. 10 *Perf. 14***
**1829-1831** A310 Set of 3 2.75 2.75
**1832** A310 1200sh Sheet of 4, #a-d 5.00 5.00

Christmas — A311

Dances: 300sh, Journey to Bethlehem. 400sh, Shepherds and angels. 1200sh, Nativity. 1400sh, Adoration of the Magi.
3000sh, Holy Family.

**2003, Nov. 10**
**1833-1836** A311 Set of 4 3.50 3.50

**Souvenir Sheet**
**1837** A311 3000sh multi 3.25 3.25

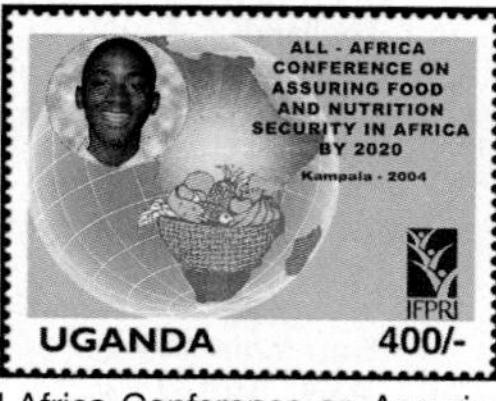
All-Africa Conference on Assuring Food and Nutrition Security in Africa by 2020, Kampala — A312

Map of Africa, food basket, Intl. Food Policy Research Institute emblem and: 400sh, Boy. 1400sh, Boy, diff.

**2004, Aug. 31 Litho. *Perf. 14¼***
**1838-1839** A312 Set of 2 2.10 2.10

Straight Talk Foundation — A313

Child and: 400sh, "Pioneers in Adolescent Health Communication." 1200sh, "Communication for Better Adolescent Health," vert.

**2004, Sept. 22**
**1840-1841** A313 Set of 2 1.90 1.90

Campaign Against Child Labor — A314

Inscriptions: 400sh, "Stop Child Domestic Labor." 2000sh, "Keep the Community Informed."

**2004, Sept. 22**
**1842-1843** A314 Set of 2 2.75 2.75

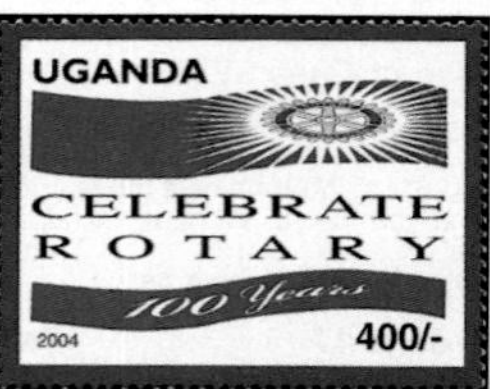
Rotary International, Cent. (in 2005) — A315

Rotary emblem and: 400sh, "Celebrate Rotary." 1200sh, "A Century of Service / A New Century of Success," vert.

**2004, Sept. 22**
**1844-1845** A315 Set of 2 1.90 1.90

New Year 2005 (Year of the Rooster) — A316

No. 1846 — Rooster shades: a, Blue. b, Orange. c, Purple. d, Red.
5000sh, Yellow.

**2005, Apr. 4 Litho. *Perf. 14***
**1846** A316 1200sh Sheet of 4, #a-d 5.50 5.50

**Souvenir Sheet**
**1847** A316 5000sh multi 5.75 5.75

Fight Against Tuberculosis, HIV and Leprosy — A317

WHO emblem and: No. 1848, 400sh, Ill man in blanket. No. 1849, 400sh, Doctor holding arm of ill man. No. 1850, 400sh, Mother and infant. No. 1851, 400sh, Infant in blanket. No. 1852, 400sh, Leper with artificial leg. No. 1853, 400sh, Leper wearing crucifix.

**2005, May 31** ***Perf. 13x12¾***

| | | | | |
|---|---|---|---|---|
| **1848-1853** | A317 | Set of 6 | 2.75 | 2.75 |

Fish A319

Designs: 400sh, Synodontis afrofischeri. 600sh, Protopterus aethiopicus. 1100sh, Clarias gariepinus. 1200sh, Rastrineobola agentea. 1600sh, Bagrus docmac. 2000sh, Schilbe mystus.

No. 1874: a, Mormyrus kannume. b, Barbus jacksonni. c, Bagrus docmac, diff. d, Labeo victorianus.

**2005, Oct. 6** **Litho.** ***Perf. 13¼***

| | | | | |
|---|---|---|---|---|
| **1868-1873** | A319 | Set of 6 | 7.50 | 7.50 |

**Souvenir Sheet**

| | | | | |
|---|---|---|---|---|
| **1874** | A319 | 1000sh Sheet of 4, #a-d | 4.50 | 4.50 |

Western Union in Africa, 10th Anniv. — A320

Designs: 400sh, Map of Africa, olive branches. 1600sh, Globe. 2000sh, Globe and flags, vert.

**2006, July 20** **Litho.** ***Perf. 14¼***

| | | | | |
|---|---|---|---|---|
| **1875-1877** | A320 | Set of 3 | 4.50 | 4.50 |

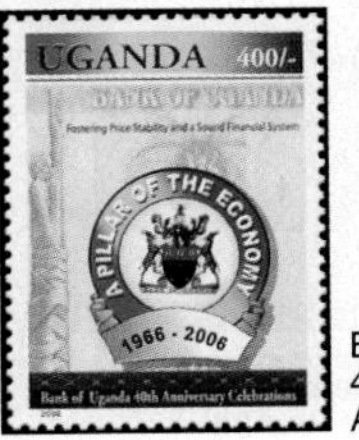

Bank of Uganda, 40th Anniv. — A321

Designs: 400sh, Bank emblem. 600sh, Bank emblem, building, wildlife. 1600sh, Bank emblem, Tilapia nilotica. 2000sh, Bank emblem, mountain gorilla.

**2006, Oct. 3** ***Perf. 13¼***

| | | | | |
|---|---|---|---|---|
| **1878-1881** | A321 | Set of 4 | 5.00 | 5.00 |

Wetlands A322

Designs: 400sh, Cattle and herdsman at water, Ramsar Convention emblem. 1600sh, People and birds near stream. 2000sh, Fishermen at Lake George.

**2006** ***Perf. 13x13½***

| | | | | |
|---|---|---|---|---|
| **1882-1884** | A322 | Set of 3 | 4.50 | 4.50 |

### SEMI-POSTAL STAMPS

**Catalogue values for all unused stamps in this section are for never Hinged items.**

PAPU (Pan African Postal Union), 18th Anniv. — SP1

**1998, Jan. 18** **Litho.** ***Perf. 14***

| | | | | |
|---|---|---|---|---|
| **B1** | SP1 | 300sh +150sh Mountain gorilla | .90 | .90 |

### POSTAGE DUE STAMPS

**Catalogue values for unused stamps in this section are for Never Hinged items.**

Type of Kenya, 1967

***Perf. 14x13½***

**1967, Jan. 3** **Litho.** **Unwmk.**

| | | | | | |
|---|---|---|---|---|---|
| **J1** | D1 | 5c | red | .20 | *2.75* |
| **J2** | D1 | 10c | green | .20 | *2.75* |
| **J3** | D1 | 20c | dark blue | .25 | *3.50* |
| **J4** | D1 | 30c | reddish brown | .45 | *4.50* |
| **J5** | D1 | 40c | red lilac | .65 | *5.00* |
| **J6** | D1 | 1sh | orange | 2.00 | *12.50* |
| | | | *Nos. J1-J6 (6)* | 3.75 | 31.00 |

**1970, Mar. 31** ***Perf. 14x15***

| | | | | | |
|---|---|---|---|---|---|
| *J1a* | D1 | 5c | red | .20 | *.75* |
| *J2a* | D1 | 10c | green | .20 | *.75* |
| *J3a* | D1 | 20c | dark blue | .25 | *2.50* |
| *J4a* | D1 | 30c | reddish brown | .30 | *3.00* |
| *J5a* | D1 | 40c | red lilac | .50 | *3.50* |
| | | | *Nos. J1a-J5a (5)* | 1.45 | 10.50 |

**1973** ***Perf. 15***

| | | | | | |
|---|---|---|---|---|---|
| *J1b* | D1 | 5c | red | .20 | .75 |
| *J2b* | D1 | 10c | green | .20 | .75 |
| *J3b* | D1 | 20c | dark blue | .45 | 2.00 |
| *J4b* | D1 | 30c | reddish brown | .60 | 3.00 |
| *J5b* | D1 | 40c | red lilac | 1.00 | 4.50 |
| *J6b* | D1 | 1sh | orange | 2.50 | 8.00 |
| | | | *Nos. J1b-J6b (6)* | 4.95 | 19.00 |

Nos. J1-J6 Overprinted in Black: "LIBERATED / 1979"

**1979, Dec.** **Litho.** ***Perf. 14***

| | | | | | |
|---|---|---|---|---|---|
| **J7** | D1 | 5c | red | .20 | *.45* |
| **J8** | D1 | 10c | green | .20 | *.45* |
| **J9** | D1 | 20c | violet blue | .20 | *.45* |
| **J10** | D1 | 30c | reddish brown | .20 | *.65* |
| **J11** | D1 | 40c | red lilac | .25 | *.65* |
| **J12** | D1 | 1sh | orange | .70 | *.75* |
| | | | *Nos. J7-J12 (6)* | 1.75 | 3.40 |

Wildlife — D2

**1985, Mar. 11** **Litho.** ***Perf. 15x14***

| | | | | | |
|---|---|---|---|---|---|
| **J13** | D2 | 5sh | Lion | .20 | *.55* |
| **J14** | D2 | 10sh | African buffalo | .20 | *.55* |
| **J15** | D2 | 20sh | Kob antelope | .35 | *.80* |
| **J16** | D2 | 40sh | Elephant | .75 | *1.25* |
| **J17** | D2 | 50sh | Zebra | .75 | *1.25* |
| **J18** | D2 | 100sh | Rhinoceros | 1.00 | *2.00* |
| | | | *Nos. J13-J18 (6)* | 3.25 | 6.40 |

# UKRAINE

yü-ˈkrān

LOCATION — In southeastern Europe, bordering on the Black Sea
GOVT. — Republic
AREA — 231,900 sq. mi.
POP. — 48,760,474 (2001)
CAPITAL — Kyiv

Following the collapse of the Russian Empire, a national assembly met at Kyiv and declared the Ukrainian National Republic on Jan. 22, 1918. During three years of civil war, the Ukrainian army, as well as Bolshevik, White Russian, Allied and Polish armies, fought back and forth across the country. By November, 1920, Ukraine was finally occupied by Soviet forces, and Soviet stamps were used from that time, until the recreation of the independent Ukraine on Dec. 26, 1991.

200 Shahiv = 100 Kopiyok (Kopecks) = 1 Karbovanets (Ruble)
100 Shahiv = 1 Hryvnia
100 Kopecks = 1 Ruble (1992)
100 Kopiyok = 1 Karbovanets (1992)
100 Kopiyok = 1 Hryvnia (1996)

**Catalogue values for unused stamps in this country are for Never Hinged items, beginning with Scott 100 in the regular postage section, Scott B9 in the semi-postal section, and Scott F1 in the registration section.**

**Watermarks**

Wmk. 116 — Crosses and Circles

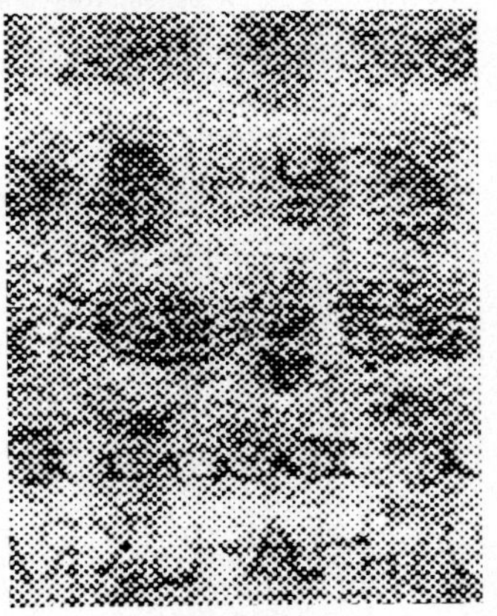
Wmk. 399

Republic's Trident Emblem — A1

Ukrainian Peasant — A2

Allegorical Ukraine — A3

Trident — A4

Inscription of Value — A5

**1918, July** **Typo.** ***Imperf.***

**Thin Paper**

| | | | | |
|---|---|---|---|---|
| **1** | A1 10sh buff | | .20 | *.25* |
| **2** | A2 20sh brown | | .20 | *.25* |
| **3** | A3 30sh ultra | | .20 | *.25* |
| *a.* | 30sh blue | | .65 | *1.25* |
| **4** | A4 40sh green | | .20 | *.25* |
| **5** | A5 50sh red | | .20 | *.25* |
| | | *Nos. 1-5 (5)* | 1.00 | *1.25* |

The stamps of this issue exist perforated or pin-perforated unofficially.

Forgeries of this set exist on a very thin, glossy paper.

These designs were earlier (April, 1918) utilized for money tokens, printed on thin cardboard, perforated 11½, and bearing an inscription on the reverse "Circulates on par with coins" in Ukrainian. These tokens exist favor canceled but were not postage stamps. Value uncanceled, $6 each.

Stamps of Russia Overprinted in Violet, Black, Blue, Red, Brown or Green

This trident-shaped emblem was taken from the arms of the Grand Prince Volodymyr and adopted as the device of the Ukrainian Republic.

In the early months of independence, Russian stamps were commonly used, but the influx of large quantities of stamps from Russia made it necessary to take measures to protect postal revenue. In August, 1918, local post offices were ordered to send their existing stocks of Russian stamps to regional centers, where they were overprinted with the trident arms. Unoverprinted Russian stamps were declared invalid after October 1, although they were often accepted for use.

This overprint was handstamped, typographed or lithographed. It was applied in various cities in the Ukraine and there are numerous types.

Nos. 6-47 represent the basic Russian stamps that received these overprints. Values are for the most common overprint variety.

For a more detailed listing of these overprints, see the Scott Classic Specialized Catalogue.

The basic Russian stamps to which Trident overprints were applied:

A8

A9

A11

A12

A13

A14

A15

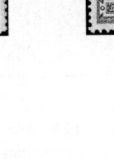

On Stamps of 1902-03

**1918** **Wmk. 168** ***Perf. 13½***

| | | | | |
|---|---|---|---|---|
| **6** | A12 | 3½r black & gray | 25.00 | *30.00* |
| **7** | A12 | 7r black & yellow | 20.00 | *25.00* |

On Stamps of 1909-18
Lozenges of Varnish on Face
***Perf. 14, 14½x15***
**Unwmk.**

| | | | | | |
|---|---|---|---|---|---|
| **8** | A14 | 1k | orange | .20 | *.25* |
| **9** | A14 | 2k | green | .20 | *.25* |
| **10** | A14 | 3k | red | .20 | *.25* |
| **11** | A15 | 4k | carmine | .20 | *.25* |
| **12** | A14 | 5k | claret | .20 | *.25* |
| **13** | A14 | 7k | light blue | .20 | *.25* |
| **14** | A15 | 10k | dark blue | .20 | *.25* |
| **15** | A11 | 14k | blue & rose | .20 | *.40* |
| **16** | A11 | 15k | red brn & bl | .20 | *.25* |
| **17** | A8 | 20k | blue & car | .20 | *.25* |
| **18** | A11 | 25k | grn & gray vio | .20 | *.25* |
| **19** | A11 | 35k | red brn & grn | .20 | *.25* |
| **20** | A8 | 50k | violet & grn | .20 | *.25* |
| **21** | A11 | 70k | brown & org | .20 | *.25* |

***Perf. 13½***

| | | | | | |
|---|---|---|---|---|---|
| **22** | A9 | 1r | lt brn, brn & org | .35 | *.60* |
| **23** | A12 | 3½r | mar & lt grn | .75 | *1.75* |
| **24** | A13 | 5r | dk bl, grn & pale bl | 5.00 | *7.00* |
| **25** | A12 | 7r | dk grn & pink | 6.00 | *8.00* |
| **26** | A13 | 10r | scar, yel & gray | 7.00 | *10.00* |
| | | | *Nos. 6-26 (21)* | 66.90 | *86.00* |

On Stamps of 1917
***Perf. 14, 14½x15***

| | | | | | |
|---|---|---|---|---|---|
| **27** | A14 | 10k | on 7k light blue | .25 | *.30* |
| **28** | A11 | 20k | on 14k bl & rose | .20 | *.25* |

On Stamps of 1917-18
***Imperf***

| | | | | | |
|---|---|---|---|---|---|
| **29** | A14 | 1k | orange | .20 | *.25* |
| **30** | A14 | 2k | gray green | .20 | *.25* |
| **31** | A14 | 3k | red | .20 | *.25* |
| **32** | A15 | 4k | carmine | .20 | *.25* |
| **33** | A14 | 5k | claret | .75 | *1.00* |
| **34** | A11 | 15k | red brn & bl | .20 | *.25* |
| **35** | A8 | 20k | bl & car | .50 | *1.50* |
| **36** | A11 | 25k | grn & gray vio | 50.00 | — |
| **37** | A11 | 35k | red brn & grn | .20 | *.25* |
| **38** | A8 | 50k | violet & grn | .25 | *.75* |
| **39** | A11 | 70k | brown & org | .20 | *.25* |
| **40** | A9 | 1r | pale brn, brn & red org | .30 | *.35* |
| **41** | A12 | 3½r | mar & lt grn | .45 | *1.00* |
| **42** | A13 | 5r | dk bl, grn & pale bl | .50 | *1.25* |
| **43** | A12 | 7r | dk grn & pink | 1.50 | *1.75* |
| **44** | A13 | 10r | scar, yel & gray | 40.00 | *50.00* |
| | | | *Nos. 29-44 (16)* | 95.65 | *59.35* |

On Postal Savings Bank Stamps

**Wmk. 171** **Litho.**
***Perf. 14, 14½x14¾***

| | | | | |
|---|---|---|---|---|
| **45** | 1k red, *buff* | .75 | *15.00* |
| **46** | 5k green, *buff* | 7.00 | *70.00* |
| **47** | 10k brown, *buff* | 1.75 | *200.00* |
| | *Nos. 45-47 (3)* | 9.50 | *285.00* |

Nos. 45-47 were used and accepted as postage stamps during stamp shortages.

The trident overprint was applied by favor to Russia Nos. 88-104, 110-111, the Romanov issue.

For surcharges see Russian Offices in the Turkish Empire Nos. 320-339.

A6

**1919, Jan.** **Litho.**

| | | | |
|---|---|---|---|
| **48** | A6 20hr red & green | 3.00 | *20.00* |

Because of its high face value, No. 48 was used primarily on money transfer forms or parcel receipts.

Nos. 1 and 5 Surcharged

**1919** **Unwmk.** ***Imperf.***

| | | | |
|---|---|---|---|
| **49** | A1 35k on 10sh buff | 7.50 | *15.00* |
| **50** | A5 70k on 50sh red | 20.00 | *35.00* |
| *a.* | Surcharge inverted | 50.00 | |

Some authorities state that Nos. 49-50 were issued by the Soviets in the Ukraine in April 1919.

Excellent forged surcharges exist.

Nos. 1-5 surcharged in grivni (hryven) with the Polish eagle were sold as Polish occupation issues. They are of private origin.

Nos. 1-3 and 5 overprinted diagonally as above ("South Russia") are believed to be of private origin.

A lithographed set of 14 stamps (1hr-200hr) of these types, perf. 11½, was prepared in 1920, but never placed in use. Value, set $3.

All values exist imperf., some with inverted centers. Trial printings exist on various papers, including inverted, multiple, omitted and misaligned center vignettes. These are from the printer's waste.

This set handstamped "VILNA UKRAINA / 1921" and 6 values additionally overprinted "DOPLATA" are of private origin.

In 1923 the Ukrainian government-in-exile in Warsaw prepared an 11-value set, consisting of the 10h, 20h and 40h denominations surcharged and overprinted with the Cyrillic "UPP," supposedly intended as a Field Post issue for a planned invasion of the Ukraine. The invasion never occurred, and the stamps were never issued.

For German stamps overprinted "Ukraine" see Russia Nos. N29-N48.

**Catalogue values for unused stamps in this section, from this point to the end of the section, are for Never Hinged items.**

Cossacks in Ukraine, 500th Anniv. — A20

Design: No. 101, Ukrainian emigrants to Canada.

**1992, Mar. 1** **Litho.** ***Perf. 12***

| | | | |
|---|---|---|---|
| **100** | A20 15k multicolored | .60 | .60 |
| **101** | A20 15k multicolored | .60 | .60 |

Ukrainian emigration to Canada, centennial (No. 101). Dated 1991.

Mykola V. Lysenko (1842-1912), Composer — A21

**1992, Mar. 22** ***Perf. 13***

| | | | |
|---|---|---|---|
| **102** | A21 1r multicolored | .50 | .50 |

Numerous trident overprints on Soviet stamps exist. Many of them are legitimate local issues and were in official use. Locally produced stamps also exist.

Ukrainian Girl — A22

**1992** **Litho.** ***Perf. 12x12½***

| | | | | |
|---|---|---|---|---|
| **118** | A22 | 50k bright blue | .20 | .20 |
| **119** | A22 | 70k bister | .20 | .20 |
| **121** | A22 | 1kb yellow green | .20 | .20 |
| **122** | A22 | 2kb purple | .20 | .20 |
| **124** | A22 | 5kb blue | .20 | .20 |
| **126** | A22 | 10kb red | .50 | .50 |
| **128** | A22 | 20kb green | 1.25 | 1.25 |
| **130** | A22 | 50kb brown | 1.75 | 1.75 |
| | | *Nos. 118-130 (8)* | 4.50 | 4.50 |

Issued: Nos. 124, 126, 128, 130, 5/16; 118-119, 121-122, 6/17.

Mykola I. Kostomarov (1817-1885), Writer — A23

**1992, May 16** **Photo.** ***Perf. 12x11½***

| | | | |
|---|---|---|---|
| **133** | A23 20k olive green | .60 | .60 |

1992 Summer Olympics, Barcelona
A24 A25

**1992, July 25** **Litho.** ***Perf. 13***

| | | | |
|---|---|---|---|
| **134** | A24 3kb yel green & multi | .35 | .35 |
| **135** | A25 4kb multicolored | .50 | .50 |
| **136** | A24 5kb buff & multi | .65 | .65 |
| | *Nos. 134-136 (3)* | 1.50 | 1.50 |

World Forum of Ukrainians, Kyiv — A26

**1992, Aug. 19** **Litho.** ***Perf. 13***

| | | | |
|---|---|---|---|
| **137** | A26 2kb multicolored | .50 | .50 |

Declaration of Independence from the Soviet Union — A27

**1992, Aug. 19** ***Perf. 13½x13***

| | | | |
|---|---|---|---|
| **138** | A27 2kb multicolored | .50 | .50 |

Souvenir Sheet

Union of Ukrainian Philatelists, 25th Anniv. — A28

**1992, Aug. 21** ***Perf. 12***

| | | | |
|---|---|---|---|
| **139** | A28 2kb multicolored | .75 | 1.00 |

Intl. Letter Writing Week A29

**1992, Oct. 4** ***Perf. 13x13½***

| | | | |
|---|---|---|---|
| **140** | A29 5kb multicolored | .60 | .60 |

World Congress of Ukrainian Lawyers, Kyiv — A30

**1992, Oct. 18** **Litho.** ***Perf. 13***

| | | | |
|---|---|---|---|
| **141** | A30 15kb multicolored | 1.00 | 1.00 |

Ukrainian Diaspora in Austria
A31

*Perf. 13½x14½*

**1992, Nov. 27** **Litho.**
**142** A31 5kb multicolored .70 .70

Embroidery
A32

**1992, Nov. 16** **Litho.** ***Perf. 11½x12***
**143** A32 50k black & orange .50 .50

Mohyla Academy, Kyiv, 360th Anniv.
A33

**1992, Nov. 27** **Litho.** ***Perf. 12x12½***
**144** A33 1.50kb multicolored .50 .50

Souvenir Sheet

Ukrainian Medal Winners, 1992 Summer Olympics, Barcelona — A34

**1992, Dec. 14** **Litho.** ***Perf. 14***
**145** A34 10kb multicolored 3.75 3.75

Coats of Arms — A35

**1993, Feb. 15** **Litho.** ***Perf. 14x13½***
**148** A35 3kb Lviv .70 .70
**150** A35 5kb Kyiv 1.10 1.10

See No. 292.

Cardinal Joseph Slipyj (1892-1984)
A36

**1993, Feb. 17** **Litho.** ***Perf. 14x13½***
**166** A36 15kb multicolored 1.00 1.00

1st Vienna-Cracow-Lviv-Kyiv Air Mail Flight, 75th Anniv. — A37

**1993, Mar. 31** ***Perf. 13½x14***
**167** A37 35kb Biplane .75 .75
**168** A37 50kb Jet 1.10 1.00

Easter
A39

**1993, Apr. 8** **Litho.** ***Perf. 13½***
**169** A39 15kb multicolored 1.00 *1.00*

UN Declaration of Human Rights, 45th Anniv. — A40

Design: 5kb, Country Wedding in Lower Austria, by Ferdinand Georg Waldmuller.

*Perf. 14½x13½*

**1993, June 11** **Litho.**
**170** A40 5kb multicolored 1.25 1.25

A41

A41a

A41b

A41c

A41d

A41e

A41f

A41g

A41h

Villagers at Work: 50kb, #177, Reaper with scythe. 100kb, #185, Ox carts. #173A, 200kb, 500kb, Reaper with sickle. #173B, Farmer with oxen. 150kb, 300kb, #184, Shepherd. #183, Bee keeper. #184A, Fisherman. #186, Potter.

(Illustrations A41a-A41h help identify the Cyrillic characters, not the designs.)

***Perf. 12x12½, 14 (#173B, 183, 184A, 186)***

**1993-98** **Litho.**

| | | | | | |
|---|---|---|---|---|---|
| **171** | A41 | 50kb | green | .20 | .20 |
| **172** | A41 | 100kb | blue | .20 | .20 |
| **173** | A41c | (100kb) | brown | .30 | .30 |
| **174** | A41e | (100kb) | magenta | .35 | .35 |
| **175** | A41 | 150kb | red | .20 | .20 |
| **176** | A41 | 200kb | orange | .25 | .25 |
| **177** | A41d | (250kb) | green | .50 | .50 |
| **178** | A41 | 300kb | violet | .25 | .25 |
| **179** | A41 | 500kb | brown | .30 | .30 |
| **180** | A41f | (1800kb) | org brn | .50 | .50 |
| **181** | A41a | (5000kb) | red | 2.50 | 2.50 |
| **182** | A41g | (5300kb) | blue | 1.25 | 1.25 |
| **183** | A41b | (10,000kb) | blue | .40 | .20 |
| *a.* | Perf. 14 | | | 2.25 | 2.25 |
| **184** | A41h | (17,000kb) | red brn | 2.25 | 2.25 |
| | *Nos. 171-184 (14)* | | | 9.45 | |

Nos. 174, 181 issued for domestic letter rate; Nos. 177, 180 for letters within the Commonwealth of Independent States; Nos. 183-184 for mail abroad, surface and airmail. Actual amounts sold for varied with inflation. No. 183a sold for 30k on date of issue and was used for the domestic rate..

Issued: 50, 100, 150, 200, 300, 500kb, 12/18/93; #181, 183a, 5/28/94; #173, 177, 7/2/94; #174, 182, 10/15/94; #180, 184, 11/12/94; #183, 12/30/98.

Famine Deaths, 60th Anniv. — A42

**1993, Sept. 12** **Litho.** ***Perf. 12***
**188** A42 75kb brown .70 .70

First Ukrainian Postage Stamp, 75th Anniv.
A43

**1993, Oct. 9**
**189** A43 100kb blue & brown .70 .70

Stamp Day.

Liberation of Kyiv, 50th Anniv.
A44

**1993, Nov. 6** **Litho.** ***Perf. 12***
**190** A44 75kb multicolored .70 .70

A45

A46

**1994, Jan. 15** **Litho.** ***Perf. 12***
**191** A45 200kb black & red .70 .70

Ahapit, Kyivan Rus physician, Middle Ages.

**1994, Feb. 19** ***Perf. 12x12½***

Endangered species: No. 192, Erythronium dens, canis. No. 193, Cypripedium calceolus.

**192** A46 200kb multicolored .60 .60
**193** A46 200kb multicolored .60 .60

Independence Day — A47

Illustration reduced.

**1994, Sept. 3** **Litho.** ***Imperf.***
**194** A47 5000kb multicolored 1.50 2.50

No. 194 has simulated perforations.

Kyiv University
A47a

**Litho. & Engr.**

**1994, Sept. 24** ***Perf. 13x13½***
**194A** A47a 10,000kb multicolored 1.00 1.00

**Souvenir Sheet**

***Perf. 12½x13***

**194B** A47a 25,000kb multicolored 2.50 2.50

No. 194B contains one 40x27mm stamp.

Liberation of Soviet Areas, 50th Anniv.
A48

Battle maps and: a, Katyusha rockets, liberation of Russia. b, Fighter planes, liberation of Ukraine. c, Combined offensive, liberation of Belarus.

**1994, Oct. 8** **Litho.** ***Perf. 12½x12***
**195** A48 500kb Block of 3, #a.-c., + label 1.25 1.25

See Russia No. 6213, Belarus No. 78.

Excavation of Trypillia culture, Cent. — A49

1st Books Printed in Ukrainian, 500th Anniv. — A50

**1994, Dec. 17 Litho. *Perf. 12x12½***
**196** A49 4000kb multicolored .35 .35

**1994, Dec. 17 *Perf. 13½***
**197** A50 4000kb multicolored .35 .35

Sofiyivka Natural Park, Bicent. A51

**1994, Dec. 17 *Perf. 12½x12***
**198** A51 5000kb multicolored .35 .35

Ilya Y. Repin (1844-1930), Painter — A52

**1994, Dec. 17 *Perf. 12x12½***
**199** A52 4000kb multicolored .35 .35

City of Uzhhorod, 1100th Anniv. — A53

**1995, Jan. 28 Litho. *Perf. 12***
**200** A53 5000kb multicolored .25 .25

Ivan Franko (1856-1916), Writer — A54

Ivan Puliuj (1845-1918), Physicist — A55

No. 203, Lesia Ukrainka (1871-1913), poet.

**1995, Feb. 2 *Perf. 13½***
**201** A54 3000kb multicolored .35 .35
**202** A55 3000kb multicolored .40 .40
**203** A54 3000kb multicolored .35 .35
*Nos. 201-203 (3)* 1.10

Falco Peregrinus — A56

**1995, Apr. 15 Litho. *Perf. 12***
**204** A56 5000kb shown .45 .45
**205** A56 10,000kb Grus grus .50 .50

Maksym T. Rylskyi (1895-1964), Writer — A57

**1995, Apr. 15 *Perf. 13½x14***
**206** A57 50,000kb multicolored .95 .95

End of World War II, 50th Anniv. — A58

**1995, May 9 Litho. *Perf. 13½***
**207** A58 100,000kb multicolored 1.75 1.75

Artek, Intl. Children's Camp A59

**1995, June 16 Litho. *Perf. 13½***
**208** A59 5000kb multicolored .35 .35

Famous Writers A60

Design: 1000kb, Ivan Kotliarevskyi (1769-1838), depiction of his poem, "Eneida." 3000kb, Taras Shevchenko (1814-61), his book, "Kobzar."

**1995, July 8**
**209** A60 1000kb multicolored .30 .30
**210** A60 3000kb multicolored .30 .30

Hetman Petro Konashevych-Sahaidachny — A61

**1995, July 22 Litho. *Perf. 13½***
**211** A61 30,000kb multicolored .60 .60

Arms of Luhansk — A62

**1995 Litho. *Perf. 13½***
**212** A62 10,000kb shown .35 .35
**213** A62 10,000kb Chernihiv .25 .25

Issued: No. 212, 9/15; No. 213, 10/22.

Hetman Bohdan Khmelnytsky (Khmelnytskyi; 1593?-1657) — A63

**1995, Sept. 23 Litho. *Perf. 12½x12***
**214** A63 40,000kb multi .85 .85

Hetman Ivan Mazepa (1640?-1709) — A64

**1995, Oct. 14 *Perf. 13½***
**215** A64 30,000kb multi .65 .65

A65

A66

**1995, Oct. 14**
**216** A65 50,000kb multi 1.25 1.25

European Nature Protection Year.

**1995, Oct. 22**
**217** A66 50,000kb multi 1.10 1.25

Intl. Children's Day.

UN, 50th Anniv. A67

**1995, Oct. 24 *Perf. 12x12½***
**218** A67 50,000kb multi 1.10 1.10

A68 A69

**1995, Dec. 9 *Perf. 13½***
**219** A68 50,000kb multi 1.10 1.10

Ivan Karpenko-Karyi, playwright, actor.

**1995, Dec. 23**
**220** A69 50,000kb multi .90 .90

Mikhailo Hrushevskyi, 1st Ukrainian president.

P. Safarik (1795-1861), Writer — A70

**1995, Dec. 27**
**221** A70 30,000kb green .75 .75

Trolleybus A71

Streetcar A72

City Bus — A73

**1995, Dec. 27 Litho. *Perf. 14***
**222** A71 (1000kb) blue violet .20 .20
**223** A72 (2000kb) green *2.00* 2.00
**224** A73 (3000kb) red .20 .20
*Nos. 222-224 (3)* *2.40*

The postal rate that No. 223 paid was sharply increased greatly affecting the cost of the stamp at the post offices.

No. 222 also exists dated "2003" and "2006."

Taras Shevchenko University Astronomical Observatory, Kyiv, 150th Anniv. — A74

a, 20,000 l, Early astronomical instruments. b, 30,000 l, Telescope. c, 50,000 l, Observatory, sun.

**1996, Jan. 13 *Perf. 12***
**225** A74 Strip of 3, #a.-c. 1.90 1.90

Souvenir Sheet

1994 Winter Olympics, Lillehammer — A75

Medalists: a, 40,000kb, Valentina Tserbe, bronze, biathlon. b, 50,000kb, Oksana Bayul, gold, figure skating.

**1996, Jan. 13**
**226** A75 Sheet of 2, #a.-b. 2.25 3.50

Ahatanhel Krymskyi (1871-1942), Writer — A76

Kharkiv Zoo, Cent. — A77

**1996, Jan. 15** *Perf. 13½*
**227** A76 20,000kb bister & brown .70 .70

**1996, Mar. 23** *Perf. 12½x12*
**228** A77 20,000kb multicolored .60 .60

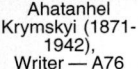

Ivan S. Kozlovskyi (1900-93), Opera Singer — A78

**1996, Mar. 23** *Perf. 13½*
**229** A78 20,000kb multicolored .45 .45

Motion Pictures, Cent. A79

Oleksandr Dovzhenko, film maker, house.

**1996, Mar. 23** *Perf. 12½x12*
**230** A79 4000kb multicolored .50 .50

No. 230 was issued se-tenant with two labels showing scenes from films.

Chernobyl Nuclear Disaster, 10th Anniv. — A80

**1996, Apr. 26** **Litho.** *Perf. 13½*
**231** A80 20,000kb multicolored .60 .60

Symyrenky Family A81

Vasyl Fedorovych (1835-1915), Volodymyr Levkovych (1891-1938), Levko Platonovych (1855-1920).

**1996, May 25**
**232** A81 20,000kb multicolored .40 .40

Vasil Stefanyk (1871-1936), Writer — A82

**1996, June 29**
**233** A82 20,000kb multicolored .45 .45

Mykola M. Myklukho-Maklai (1846-88), Explorer, Philologist — A83

**Litho. & Engr.**

**1996, July 17** *Perf. 13½*
**234** A83 40,000kb multicolored .65 .65

1996 Summer Olympic Games, Atlanta — A84

Modern Olympic Games, Cent. A85

**1996, July 19** **Litho.** *Perf. 13½*
**235** A84 20,000kb Wrestling .45 .45
**236** A84 40,000kb Handball .90 .90
**237** A85 40,000kb Greek athletes .90 .90
*Nos. 235-237 (3)* 2.25

**Souvenir Sheet**

*Perf. 12*

**238** A84 100,000kb Gymnast 1.75

Independence, 5th Anniv. — A86

First Ukrainian Satellite, "Sich-1" — A87

**1996, Aug. 24** *Perf. 13½*
**239** A86 20,000kb multicolored .40 .40

**1996, Aug. 31**
**240** A87 20,000kb multicolored .50 .50

Locomotives — A88

Designs: 20,000kb, Steam, class OD. 40,000kb, Diesel class 2 TE-116.

**1996, Aug. 31**
**241** A88 20,000kb multicolored .50 .50
**242** A88 40,000kb multicolored 1.00 1.00
*a.* Pair, #241-242 1.50 1.50

Airplanes Designed by O.K. Antonov (1906-84) A89

No. 243, Glider A-15, portrait of Antonov. No. 244, AN-2. No. 245, AN-124. No. 246, AN-225.

**1996, Sept. 14**
**243** A89 20,000kb multicolored .60 .60
**244** A89 20,000kb multicolored .60 .60
**245** A89 40,000kb multicolored 1.00 1.00
**246** A89 40,000kb multicolored 1.00 1.00
*a.* Block of 4, #243-246 3.50 3.50

Ivan Piddubnyi (1871-1949), Wrestler — A90

**1996, Nov. 16**
**247** A90 40k multicolored .70 .70

First Ukrainian Antarctic Expedition A91

**1996, Nov. 23**
**248** A91 20k multicolored 1.75 1.75

A92 A93

Flowers: 20k, Leontopodium alpinum. 40k, Narcissus anqustifolius.

**1996, Nov. 23**
**249** A92 20k multicolored .45 .45
**250** A92 40k multicolored .75 .75
*a.* Pair, #249-250 + label 1.40 1.40

**1996, Dec. 7** **Litho.** *Perf. 13½*
**251** A93 20k multicolored .45 .45

UNESCO, 50th anniv.

Viktor S. Kosenko, Composer, Birth Cent. A94

**1996, Dec. 21** **Litho.** *Perf. 13½*
**252** A94 20k multicolored .40 .40

St. Sophia's Cathedral, Kyiv — A95

Illinska (St. Elijah) Church, Subotiv A96

St. George Church, Drohobych A97

#256, Troitska Cathedral, Novomoskovsk.

**1996, Dec. 25**
**253** A95 20k multicolored .40 .40
**254** A96 20k multicolored .40 .40
**255** A97 20k multicolored .40 .40
**256** A97 20k multicolored .40 .40
*a.* Block of 4, #253-256 1.75 1.75

UNICEF, 50th Anniv. A98

**1996, Dec. 31**
**257** A98 20k multicolored .40 .40

Petro Mohyla (1596-1647), Metropolitan of Kyiv — A99

**1996, Dec. 31**
**258** A99 20k multicolored .40 .40

Wild Animals — A100

**1997, Mar. 22** **Litho.** *Perf. 13½*
**259** A100 20k Lynx lynx .50 .50
**260** A100 20k Ursos arctos .50 .50
*a.* Pair, #259-260 + label 1.25 1.25

Cathedral of the Exaltation of the Holy Cross, Poltava, 17th Cent. A101

Designs: No. 262, St. George's Cathedral, Lviv, 18th cent. No. 263, Protection Fortified Church, Sutkivtsi, 14-15th cent.

**1997, Apr. 19 Litho. *Perf. 13½***

**261** A101 20k multicolored .40 .40
**262** A101 20k multicolored .40 .40
**263** A101 20k multicolored .40 .40
*Nos. 261-263 (3)* 1.20

Legendary Founders of Kyiv — A101a

Europa: a, Kyi (holding staff and shield) and Shchek (holding sword). b, Khoriv (holding sword, leaning on shield) and sister, Lybid.

**1997, May 6 Litho. & Engr. *Perf. 13***

**264** A101a 40k Sheet of 2, #a.-b. 2.00 3.00

4th Natl. Philatelic Exhibition, Cherkasy A102

Design: Statue of Taras Shevchenko, stamps, exhibition hall.

**1997, May 17 Litho. *Perf. 13½***

**265** A102 10k multicolored .40 .40

Yurii V. Kondratiuk (1897-1942), Space Pioneer — A103

**1997, June 21 *Perf. 12½x12***

**266** A103 20k multicolored .40 .40

Constitution, 1st Anniv. — A104

**1997, June 28 *Perf. 13½***

**267** A104 20k multicolored .40 .40

Midsummer Festival of Ivan Kupalo — A104a

**1997, July 5 Litho. *Perf. 13½***

**268** A104a 20k multicolored .50 .50

Princess Olha A105

Sultana Roksoliana A106

**1997, July 12 Litho. *Perf. 13½***

**269** A105 40k multicolored .65 .65
**270** A106 40k multicolored .65 .65

First Ukrainian Emigration to Argentina, Cent. A107

Design: Monument to poet Taras Shevchenko, Buenos Aires.

**1997, Aug. 16 Litho. *Perf. 13½***

**271** A107 20k multicolored .40 .40

For Exceptional Service — A108

Order of Yaroslav the Wise — A109

Medals for: No. 273, Military Service. 30k, Bravery. 40k, Order of Bohdan Khmelnytsky. No. 276, Honored Service.

No. 277: a, Medal hanging from chain. b, 8-point star.

Illustration A109 reduced.

**Litho. & Engr.**

**1997, Aug. 20 *Perf. 13½***

**272** A108 20k multicolored .40 .40
**273** A108 20k multicolored .40 .40
**274** A108 30k multicolored .60 .60
**275** A108 40k multicolored .85 .85
**276** A108 60k multicolored 1.25 1.25
*a.* Strip of 5, #272-276 3.75 3.75

**Souvenir Sheet**

***Perf. 13***

**277** A109 60k Sheet of 2, #a.-b. 3.00 3.00

Nos. 277a-277b are each 35x50mm.

Hetman — A110

No. 278, Dmytro "Baida" Vyshnevetskyj (?-1563), boats, archers. No. 279, Pylyp Orlyk (1672-1742), Stockholm harbor, crowd in Thessaloniki street.

**1997, Sept. 13 Litho. *Perf. 12½x12***

**278** A110 20k multicolored .40 .40
**279** A110 20k multicolored .40 .40

See Nos. 357-358, 376-377.

Solomiia Krushelnytska (Salomea Krusceniski, 1872-1952), Actress, Singer — A111

**1997, Sept. 23 Litho. *Perf. 13½***

**280** A111 20k multicolored .40 .40

Airplanes A112

Designs: 20k, Antonov An-74 TK-200. 40k, Antonov An-38-100.

**1997, Oct. 30**

**281** A112 20k multicolored .30 .30
**282** A112 40k multicolored .65 .65

Ships A113

**1997, Dec. 6 Litho. *Perf. 13½***

**283** A113 20k Zavyietnyj, 1903 .30 .30
**284** A113 40k Serhii Korolev, 1970, Academician .65 .65

A114

**1997, Dec. 6 Litho. *Perf. 12x12½***

**285** A114 40k multi + label 1.40 1.40

Participation of Ukrainian astronaut in US space shuttle mission.

A115

**1997, Dec. 20 *Perf. 13½***

Vasyl Krychevskyi (1872-1952), painter, architect.

**286** A115 10k multicolored .40 .40

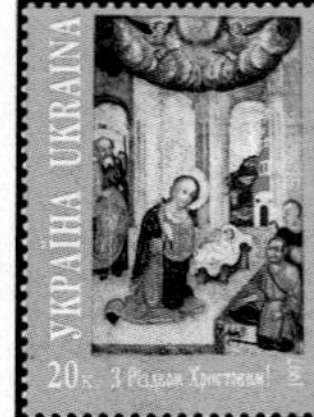

Christmas — A116

**1997, Dec. 20**

**287** A116 20k multicolored .40 .40

Traditional Handicrafts A117

Region: #288, Rooster, Dnipropetrovsk. #289, Vest, Chernivtsi. #290, Ram, Poltava. #291, Molded design, Ivano-Frankivsk.

**1997, Dec. 20**

**288** A117 20k multicolored .30 .30
**289** A117 20k multicolored .30 .30
**290** A117 40k multicolored .70 .70
**291** A117 40k multicolored .70 .70
*Nos. 288-291 (4)* 2.00

***Perf. 11½***

*288a* 20k .35 .35
*289a* 20k .35 .35
*290a* 40k .75 .75
*291a* 40k .75 .75
*b.* Sheet, 2 each #288a-291a 4.50

Nos. 288-291 have colored border. Nos. 288a-291a do not.

Arms Type of 1993

Arms of Transcarpathia (Zakarpattya).

**1997, Dec. 30 Litho. *Perf. 13½***

**292** A35 20k multicolored .45 .45

A118 A119

Wildlife: a, 20k, Skylark. b, 40k, White-tailed eagle. c, 20k, Black stork. d, 40k, Long-eared hedgehog. e, 20k, Garden dormouse. f, 40k, Wild boar.

**1997, Dec. 30 Litho. *Perf. 11½***

**293** A118 Sheet of 6, #a.-f. 3.75 3.75

**Litho. & Engr.**

**1997, Dec. 20 *Perf. 13½***

**294** A119 60k multicolored 1.10 1.10

Hryhorii Skovoroda (1722-94), philosopher.

A120

A121

**1998, Jan. 6 Litho. *Perf. 13½***

**295** A120 20k multicolored .50 .50

Volodymyr Sosiura (1898-1965), poet.

**1998, Feb. 14 Litho. *Perf. 13½***

**296** A121 20k Figure skating .55 .55
**297** A121 20k Biathlon .55 .55

1998 Winter Olympic Games, Nagano.

Bilhorod Dnistrovskyi Fortress, 2500th Anniv. — A122

**1998, Apr. 21 Litho. *Perf. 13½***
**298** A122 20k multicolored .50 .50

UKRFILEKS 98 Natl. Philatelic Exhibition, Sevastopol — A123

Design: Frigate, "Hetman Sahaidachnyi."

**1998, Apr. 28 Litho. *Perf. 13½***
**299** A123 30k multi + label .75 .75

European Bank of Reconstruction and Development — A124

Obverse, reverse of Ukrainian coins: a, 1k, Gold, 11th cent. b, 1k, Silver, 11th cent. c, 60k, 500h St. Sophia Cathedral gold coin. d, 60k, 200h Taras Shevchenko gold coin. e, 30k, 1,000,000k Bohdan Khmelnytsky silver coin. f, 30k, 10h Petro Mohyla silver coin.

**Litho. & Engr.**

**1998, May 8 *Perf. 13½***
**300** A124 Sheet of 6, #a.-f. 7.75 7.75

Ivan Kupalo Natl. Festival — A125

**1998, May 16 Litho. *Perf. 13½***
**301** A125 40k multicolored .60 .60

Europa.

Souvenir Sheet

Askania Nova Nature Preserve, Cent. — A126

a, 40k, Deer. b, 60k, Przewalski horses. Illustration reduced.

**1998, May 16 Litho. *Perf. 11½***
**302** A126 Sheet of 2, #a.-b. 2.50 2.50

Paintings from Lviv Picture Gallery — A127

Designs: No. 303, Portrait of Maria Theresa, by J.E. Liotard. No. 304, Man with a Cello, by Gerard von Honthorst. 40k, Madonna and Child, 17th cent. Lviv School.

1.20h, Madonna and Child and Two Saints, by 16th cent. Italian school.

**1998, June 20 *Perf. 13½***
**303** A127 20k multicolored .35 .35
**304** A127 20k multicolored .35 .35
**305** A127 40k multicolored .70 .70
*a.* Strip of 3, #303-305 1.50 1.50

**Souvenir Sheet**

**306** A127 1.20h multicolored 2.00 2.00

Souvenir Sheet

Polytechnical Institute, Kyiv, Cent. — A128

Illustration reduced.

**1998, June 27 Litho. *Perf. 11½***
**307** A128 1h multicolored 1.25 1.50

Askold & Dyr A129

**Litho. & Engr.**

**1998, July 4 *Perf. 13½***
**308** A129 3h multi + label 4.00 4.00

Hetman Bohdan Khmelnytsky A130

Designs: a, 30k, Battle scene, denomination LR. b, 2k, Portrait of Khmelnytsky. c, 30k, Battle scene, denomination LL. d, 40k, denomination LR. e, 60k, Battle scene. f, 40k, Battle scene, denomination LL.

**1998, July 25 Litho. & Engr.**
**309** A130 Sheet of 6, #a.-f. 6.00 6.00

Ukrainian uprising, 350th anniv.

Town of Halych, 1100th Anniv. A131

**1998, Aug. 8 Litho.**
**310** A131 20k multicolored .50 .50

Queen Anna Yaroslavna (1024?-75) A132

**1998, Aug. 8**
**311** A132 40k multicolored .60 .60

Yurii Lysianskyi (1773-1837), Explorer — A133

**1998, Aug. 13**
**312** A133 40k multicolored .60 .60

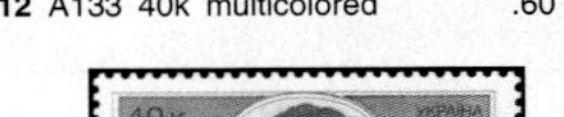

Natalia Uzhvii (1898-1986), Stage Actress — A134

**1998, Sept. 8 Litho. *Perf. 13½***
**313** A134 40k multicolored .45 .45

Polytechnical Institute, Kyiv, Cent. — A135

Designs: 10k, W.L. Kirpichov, first president. No. 315, E.O. Paton, bridge. No. 316, S.P. Timoschenko, mathematical formula. 30k, Igor I. Sikorsky, biplane. 40k, Sergei P. Korolev, rocket, satellite.

**1998, Sept. 10 *Perf. 12½x12***
**314** A135 10k multicolored .20 .20
**315** A135 20k multicolored .20 .20
**316** A135 20k multicolored .20 .20
**317** A135 30k multicolored .35 .35
**318** A135 40k multicolored .40 .40
*a.* Strip of 5, #314-318 1.40 1.40

A136 A137

**1998, Sept. 19 Litho. *Perf. 13½***
**319** A136 10k multicolored .35 .35

World Post Day.

**1998, Sept.19**
**320** A137 20k multicolored .45 .45

Ukrainian book, 1000th anniv.

Church Architecture A138

Designs: No. 321, Church of the Transfiguration, Chernihiv, 11th cent. No. 322, Church of the Holy Protection, Kharkiv, 17th cent.

**1998, Sept. 21**
**321** A138 20k multicolored .60 .60
**322** A138 20k multicolored .60 .60

World Wildlife Fund A139

Branta ruficollis: a, f, 20k, Adults. b, g, 30k, Female on nest. c, h, 40k, Female with goslings. d, i, 60k, Adults, goslings.

**1998, Oct. 10 Litho. *Perf. 13½***
**323** A139 Block of 4, #a.-d. 2.75 2.75
*e.* Block of 4, perf. 11½, #f.-i. 3.00 3.00
*j.* Sheet of 2, #323e 6.00

Antonov Airplanes A140

**1998, Nov. 28 Litho. *Perf. 13½***
**324** A140 20k Antonov 140 .45 .45
**325** A140 40k Antonov 70 .60 .60

**Hetman Type of 1997**

Design: Petro Doroshenko (1627-98).

**1998, Nov. 28 Litho. *Perf. 12½x12***
**326** A141 20k multicolored .40 .40

Borys D. Hrinchenko (1863-1910), Writer — A142

**1998, Dec. 4 Litho. *Perf. 13½***
**327** A142 20k multicolored .40 .40

Christmas — A143

**1998, Dec. 11**
**328** A143 30k multicolored .45 .45

Ukrainians in Australia, 50th Anniv. A144

**1998, Dec. 20**
**329** A144 40k multicolored .40 .40

Illintsi Meteor Impact Area A145

**1998, Dec. 25**
**330** A145 40k multicolored .70 .70

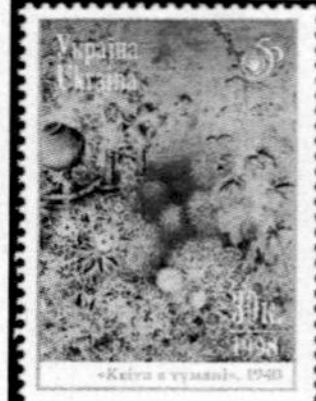

Universal Declaration of Human Rights, 50th Anniv. — A146

Paintings of various flowers by Kateryna Bilokur (1900-61): 30k, 1940. 50k, 1959.

**1998, Dec. 25**
**331** A146 30k multicolored .45 .45
**332** A146 50k multicolored .65 .65
*a.* Pair, #331-332 +label 1.10 1.10

Serhii Paradzhanov (1924-90), Film Director — A147

**1999, Feb. 27 Litho. *Perf. 13½***
**333** A147 40k multi + label .50 .50

Volodymyr Ivasiuk (1949-79), Composer A148

**1999, Mar. 4**
**334** A148 30k multicolored .40 .40

Scythian Gold A149

**1999, Mar. 20**
**335** A149 20k Clasp .25 .25
**336** A149 40k Boar .45 .45
**337** A149 50k Young elk .50 .50
**338** A149 1h Necklace 1.00 1.00
*a.* Block of 4, #335-338 2.25 2.25

Spring Easter Dance — A150

**1999, Apr. 7**
**339** A150 30k multicolored .45 .45

A151

Synevyr Natl. Park: a, 50k, Wooden monuments on bank of Tereblyia River. b, 1h, Thymallus thymallus, river scene.

**1999, Apr. 24**
**340** A151 Pair, #a.-b. 1.25 1.25

Europa.

A152

**1999, May 13**
**341** A152 40k multicolored .45 .45

Panas Myrnyi (1849-1920), writer.

Honoré de Balzac (1799-1850), Writer — A153

**1999, May 20**
**342** A153 40k multicolored .45 .45

Council of Europe, 50th Anniv. A154

**1999, May 22**
**343** A154 40k multicolored .45 .45

Aleksandr Pushkin (1799-1837), Poet — A155

**1999, June 6**
**344** A155 40k + label .45 .45

Sailboats — A156

No. 345: a, Bark (Baidak), double sails, one man at tiller. b, Cossack (Chaika), single sail, rowers.

**1999, June 26**
**345** A156 30k Pair, #a.-b. 1.00 1.00

**Souvenir Sheet**

Yaroslav the Wise — A157

**1999, July 2 Litho. *Perf. 11½***
**346** A157 1.20h multicolored 1.50 2.50

Principality of Halytsko-Volynskyi, 800th Anniv. — A158

**1999, July 27 *Perf. 13½***
**347** A158 50k multicolored .75 .75

A159

A160

Designs: a, 30k, Icon of St. George. b, 60, Girl in a Red Hat, by O.O. Murashko.

**1999, July 27**
**348** A159 Pair, #a.-b. + label 1.10 1.10

Natl. Museum of Art, Cent.

**1999, Aug. 7**
**349** A160 30k Bee on flower .50 .50

Bee keeping in Ukraine.

A161

A162

**1999, Aug. 14 Litho. *Perf. 13½***
**350** A161 30k multicolored .45 .45

UPU, 125th anniv.

**1999, Aug. 14**
**351** A162 30k multicolored .45 .45

Poltava, 1100th anniv.

Presidential Medals — A163

Designs: 30k, Order of Princess Olga. No. 353: a, Medal with trident. b, Medal with star.

**1999, Aug. 17 Litho. & Engr.**
**352** A163 30k multicolored .40 .40

**Souvenir Sheet of 2**

**353** A163 2.50h #a.-b. 5.75 5.75

No. 353 contains two 35x50mm stamps.

Polish-Ukrainian Cooperation in Nature Conservation — A164

a, Cervus elaphus. b, Felis silvestris.

**1999, Sept. 22 Litho. *Perf. 13½***
**354** A164 1.40h Pair, #a.-b. 2.00 2.00

See Poland Nos. 3477-3478.

National Bank — A165

**1999, Sept. 28 Litho. & Engr.**
**355** A165 3h multicolored 2.50 2.50

**Souvenir Sheet**

**356** A165 5h multicolored 3.75 3.75

**Hetman Type of 1997**

Designs: No. 357, Ivan Vyhovskyi (d. 1664), cavalry in water. No. 358, Pavlo Polubotok (1660-1724), ships in water.

**1999 Litho. *Perf. 12¼x12***
**357** A110 30k multi .40 .40
**358** A110 30k multi .40 .40

Issued: No. 357, 11/20; No. 358, 12/22.

A166

Christmas A167

**1999, Nov. 26 Wmk. 399 *Perf. 13½***

**359** A166 30k multi .40 .40

**Unwmk.**

**360** A167 60k multi .60 .60

Children's Art — A168

a, Spacecraft, alien creatures. b, Elephant in space. c, Rocket and space car on planet.

**1999, Nov. 30 Unwmk. *Perf. 11½***

**361** A168 10k Strip of 3, #a.-c. .50 .50

Fauna A169

Designs: a, 40k, Desmana moschata. b, 60k, Gyps fulvus. c, 40k, Lucanus cervus.

**1999, Dec. 9 *Perf. 13½***

**362** A169 Strip of 3, #a.-c. 1.50 1.50

Church of St. Andrew, Kyiv — A170

**1999, Dec. 12**

**363** A170 60k multi + label .80 .80

Mushrooms A171

Designs: a, 30k, Armillariella mellea. b, 30k, Paxillus atrotomentosus. c, 30k, Pleurotus ostratus. d, 40k, Cantharellus cibarius. e, 60k, Agaricus campester.

**1999, Dec. 15 *Perf. 11½***

**364** A171 Sheet of 5, #a.-e., + label 3.25 3.25

New Year 2000 — A172

**1999, Dec. 18 *Perf. 13½***

**365** A172 50k multi + label .65 .65

Motor Vehicles — A173

a, Kraz-65032 truck. b, Tavriia Nova car.

**1999, Dec. 18 Litho.**

**366** A173 30k Pair, #a.-b. .85 .85

Works of Maria Prymachenko — A174

Denomination colors: a, Green. b, Violet.

**1999, Dec. 22**

**367** A174 30k Pair, #a.-b., + central label .60 .60

Halshka Hulevychivna, Philanthropist A175

**1999, Dec. 25 *Perf. 13½***

**368** A175 30k multi .40 .40

Zoogeographic Endowment Fund — A176

Animals from: a, 10k, Carpathian Reserve. b, 30k, Polissia Reserve. c, 40k, Kaniv Reserve. d, 60k, Trakhtemyriv Reserve. e, 1h, Askaniia-Nova Reserve (ram, birds). f, 1h, Kara-Dag Reserve (birds).

**1999, Dec. 28 *Perf. 11½***

**369** A176 Sheet of 6, #a.-f. 3.00 *4.00*

Christianity, 2000th Anniv. — A177

Designs: a, Mother of God mosaic, St. Sofia Cathedral, Kyiv, 11th cent. b, Christ Pantocrator fresco, Church of the Savior's Transfiguration, Polotsk, Belarus, 12th cent. c, Volodymyr Madonna, Tretiakov Gallery, Moscow, 12th cent.

**2000, Jan. 5 Litho. *Perf. 11½***

**370** A177 80k Sheet of 3, #a.-c. 2.00 *2.50*

Souvenir Sheet

Opera and Ballet Theaters — A178

No. 371: a, National Academic, Kyiv. b, Odessa State, Odessa. c, Kharkov State Academic, Kharkov. d, Ivan Franko State Academic, Lviv.

Illustration reduced.

**2000, Jan. 29 Litho. *Perf. 11½***

**371** A178 40k Sheet of 4, #a.-d. 5.00 5.00

Kyiv Bridges — A179

No. 372: a, 10k, Moscow Bridge. b, 30k, Y. O. Paton Bridge. c, 40k, Pedestrian park bridge. d, 60k, Subway bridge.

Illustration reduced.

**2000, Jan. 29 *Perf. 12¼x12***

**372** A179 Block of 4, #a.-d. 1.50 1.50

Souvenir Sheet

Peresopnytsia Gospel — A180

Illustration reduced.

**2000, Feb. 8 *Perf. 11½***

**373** A180 1.50h multi 1.40 *1.50*

A181 A182

**2000, Feb. 11 *Perf. 13½***

**374** A181 30k multi .40 .40

Oksana Petrusenko (1900-40), opera singer

**2000, Feb. 18**

**375** A182 40k multi .40 .40

Marusia Churai, 17th cent. singer

**Hetman Type of 1997**

Designs: No. 376, Danylo Apostol (1654-1734), church, burning castle. No. 377, Ivan Samoylovych (d. 1690), tent, winter scene.

**2000 *Perf. 12¼x12***

**376** A110 30k multi .40 .40

**377** A110 30k multi .40 .40

Issued: No. 376, 2/22; No. 377, 3/3.

World Meteorological Organization, 50th Anniv. — A183

**2000, Mar. 10 Litho. *Perf. 13½***

**378** A183 30k multi .40 .40

**Europa, 2000**

Common Design Type

**2000, Mar. 29 Litho. *Perf. 13½***

**379** CD17 3h multi 1.75 1.75

Souvenir Sheets

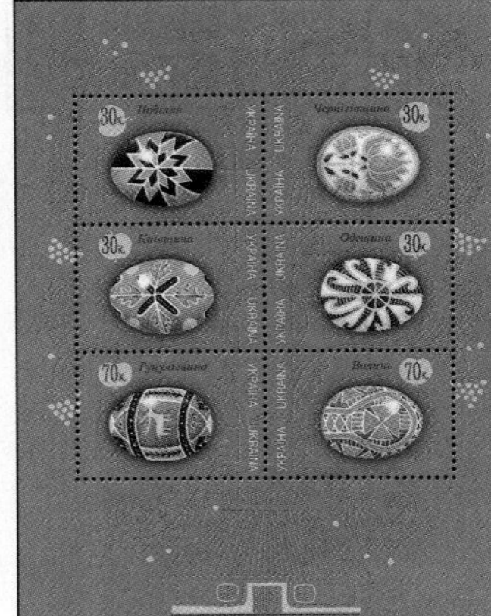

Easter Eggs — A184

No. 380: a, 30k, Egg with black and red star design, Podillia region. b, 30k, Flower egg, Chernihiv region. c, 30k, Egg with leaf design, Kyiv region. d, 30k, Egg with green, white and yellow geometric design, Odesa region. e, 70k, Egg with reindeer design, Hutsulschyna region. f, 70k, Egg with cross design, Volyn region.

**2000, Apr. 28 *Perf. 11½***

**380** A184 Sheet of 6, #a-f 2.25 *2.50*

Stamp Exhibitions — A185

No. 381: a, Woman in native costume, Austria #2. b, Man in native costume, Great Britain #1.
Illustration reduced.

**2000, May 20**
**381** A185 80k Sheet of 2, #a-b 1.25 1.25

WIPA 2000 Stamp Exhibition, Vienna; The Stamp Show 2000, London.

Donetsk Oblast — A186

City of Kyiv — A187

**2000** ***Perf. 12¼x12***
**382** A186 30k multi .40 .40
**383** A187 30k multi .40 .40

Regional and administrative areas.
Issued: No. 382, 5/26; No. 383, 5/28.

6th Natl. Philatelic Exhibition, Donetsk — A188

**2000, May 28 Litho.** ***Perf. 12¼x12***
**384** A188 30k multi .40 .40

City of Ostroh, 900th Anniv. — A189

**2000, June 16 Litho.** ***Perf. 13½***
**385** A189 30k multi .40 .40

2000 Summer Olympics, Sydney — A190

**2000, June 26**
**386** A190 30k High jump .30 .30
**387** A190 30k Boxing .30 .30
**388** A190 70k Yachting .50 .50
**389** A190 1h Rhythmic gymnastics .90 .90
*Nos. 386-389 (4)* 2.00 2.00

Petro Prokopovych (1775-1850), Apiarist — A191

**2000, July 12 Litho.** ***Perf. 13½***
**390** A191 30k multi .40 .40

Shipbuilding — A192

Illustration reduced.

**2000, July 14**
**391** A192 Pair 1.00 1.00
***a.*** 40k Ship St. Paul .35 .35
***b.*** 70k Ship St. Nicholas .60 .60

Tetiana Pata (1884-1976), Artist — A193

No. 392: a, Leafy Plants with Flowers, 1950s. b, Viburnum Berries and Bird, 1957.
Illustration reduced.

**2000, July 21**
**392** A193 Horiz. pair, #a-b + central label .75 .75
***a.-b.*** 40k Any single .35 .35

Dubno, 900th Anniv. — A194

**2000, July 26**
**393** A194 30k multi .45 .45

Harvest Festival — A195

**2000, Aug. 4**
**394** A195 30k multi .50 .50

Souvenir Sheet

Presidential Symbols — A196

Designs: a, Flag. b, Mace. c, Seal. d, Badge.

**2000, Aug. 18 Litho.** ***Perf. 11½***
**395** A196 60k Sheet of 4, #a-d 1.75 1.75

**Regional and Administrative Areas**

Volynska Oblast — A197

Autonomous Republic of Crimea — A198

**2000** ***Perf. 12¼x12***
**396** A197 30k multi .45 .45
**397** A198 30k multi .55 .55

Issued: No. 396, 8/23; No. 397, 10/20.

Kyiv Post Office, 225th Anniv. — A199

Illustration reduced.

**2000, Sept. 3** ***Perf. 11½***
**398** A199 30k multi .45 .45

Endangered Amphibians — A200

No. 399: a, 30k, Triturus vulgaris. b, 70k, Salamandra salamandra.
Illustration reduced.

**2000, Sept. 8** ***Perf. 13½***
**399** A200 Pair, #a-b 1.00 1.00

Yurij Drohobych (1450-94), Writer A201

**2000, Sept. 12**
**400** A201 30k multi .40 .40

Souvenir Sheet

Carpathian National Park — A202

No. 401: a, Mt. Breskul, 1911 meters. b, Mt. Hoberla, 2061 meters.

**2000, Sept. 15** ***Perf. 11½***
**401** A202 80k Sheet of 2, #a-b 1.50 1.50

Flowers — A203

Designs: a, Marigolds. b, Chamomiles. c, Hollyhocks. d, Poppies. e, Periwinkles. f, Cornflowers. g, Morning glories. h, Martagon lilies. i, Peonies. j, Bluebells.

**2000, Oct. 6**
**402** A203 30k Sheet of 10, #a-j 4.00 4.00

Children's Folk Tales — A204

Designs: a, "Ivasyk and Telesyk," (boy in boat, witch). b, "The Crooked Duck," (couple with duck). c, "The Cat and the Rooster."

**2000, Nov. 3**
**403** 30k Horiz. strip of 3 .90 .90
***a.-c.*** A204 Any single .30 .30

New Year 2001 A205

**2000, Nov. 24**
**404** A205 30k multi .45 .45

St. Onufius' Church, Lviv — A206

Church of Christ's Birth, Velyke — A207

Design: 70k, Church of the Resurrection, Sumy.

**2000, Dec. 8** ***Perf. 13½***
**405** A206 30k multi .25 .25
**406** A207 30k multi .25 .25
**407** A207 70k multi .45 .45
*Nos. 405-407 (3)* .95 .95

Souvenir Sheet

St. Vladimir (c. 956-1015), Kyivan Prince — A208

**2000, Dec. 15** ***Perf. 11½***
**408** A208 2h multi 1.75 1.75

Dmytro Rostovskyi (1651-1709), Religious Leader — A209

**2001, Jan. 16 Litho.** ***Perf. 13½***
**409** A209 75k multi .50 .50

Love — A210

**2001, Jan. 26**
**410** A210 30k multi .20 .20

Souvenir Sheet

Prince Danylo Romanovych (1201-64) — A211

**2001, Feb. 1** ***Perf. 11½***
**411** A211 3h multi 2.00 2.00

**Hetman Type of 1997**

Designs: 30k, Yuryi Khmelnytski (1641-85), as monk in Turkish prison, Kamianets-Podilskyi fortifications. 50k, Mykhailo Khanenko (1620-80), leading troops, relinquishing power.

**2001, Feb. 20** ***Perf. 12¼x12***
**412-413** A110 Set of 2 .55 .55

Invention of the Telephone, 125th Anniv. A212

**2001, Mar. 6** ***Perf. 13½***
**414** A212 70k multi .50 .50

Children's Art — A213

Art by: 10k, Alyna Nochvaj. 30k, Olyia Pynych. 40k, Dasha Chemberzhi.

**2001, Mar. 7** ***Perf. 11½***
**415-417** A213 Set of 3 .55 .55

Hollyhocks A214

Marigolds A215

Sunflower A216

Viburnum Opulus Berries A217

Wheat — A218

**2001, Apr. 4 Litho.** ***Perf. 13¾***

| | | | | | |
|---|---|---|---|---|---|
| **418** | A214 | (10k) | multi | .20 | .20 |
| **419** | A215 | (30k) | multi | .20 | .20 |
| **420** | A216 | (71k) | multi | .50 | .50 |
| **421** | A217 | (2.66h) | multi | 1.75 | 1.75 |
| **422** | A218 | (3.65h) | multi | 2.50 | 2.50 |
| | *Nos. 418-422 (5)* | | | 5.15 | 5.15 |

**2006, Oct. 9** ***Perf. 11½,***
**Dated 2006**

| | | | | | |
|---|---|---|---|---|---|
| *418a* | A214 | (10k) | multi | .20 | .20 |
| *419a* | A215 | (30k) | multi | .20 | .20 |
| *420a* | A216 | (71k) | multi | .35 | .35 |
| *421a* | A217 | (2.66h) | multi | 1.25 | 1.25 |
| *422a* | A218 | (3.65h) | multi | 1.90 | 1.90 |
| | *Nos. 418a-422a (5)* | | | 3.90 | 3.90 |

Nos. 420, 422 exist dated "2004." Nos. 421, 422 exist dated "2005" and "2006."

Nos. 418a-422a were issued only in No. F2b.

See Nos. 453-454.

Folktales — A219

No. 423: a, The Fox and Wolf (fox on sleigh, fish). b, The Mitten (bear, fox, wolf, rabbit mouse, frog). c, Sirko the Dog (wolf with bottle, dog).
Illustration reduced.

**2001, Apr. 14** ***Perf. 13½***
**423** A219 30k Horiz. strip of 3, #a-c .60 .60

Ships — A220

No. 424: a, 20k, Twelve Apostles. b, 30k, Three Priests.
Illustration reduced.

**2001, Apr. 20**
**424** A220 Horiz. pair, #a-b .35 .35

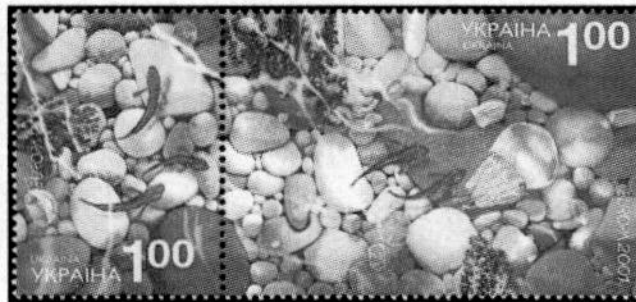

Europa — A221

Fish, jellyfish, seaweed: a, 28x40mm. b, 56x40mm.
Illustration reduced.

**2001, Apr. 27**
**425** A221 1h Horiz. pair, #a-b 1.40 1.40

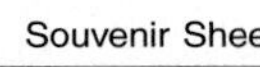

Holy Trinity A222

**2001, May 15**
**426** A222 30k multi .25 .25

Souvenir Sheet

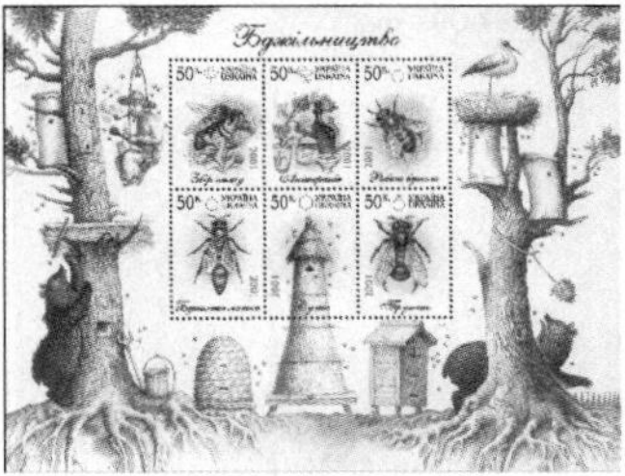

Apiculture — A223

No. 427: a, Bee on flower. b, Plant cutting, jar of honey, bowl of pollen, jars. c, Worker on honeycomb. d, Queen. e, Hive. f, Drone.

**2001, May 22** ***Perf. 11½***
**427** A223 50k Sheet of 6, #a-f 2.10 3.50

Souvenir Sheet

Kyievo-Pecherska Monastery, 950th Anniv. — A224

**2001, May 25**
**428** A224 1.50h multi 1.00 1.00

Visit of Pope John Paul II, June 23-27 A225

**2001, June 15** ***Perf. 13½***
**429** A225 3h multi 2.10 2.10

**Regional and Administrative Areas**

Zakarpatska Oblast — A226

Kharkivska Oblast — A227

**2001** ***Perf. 12¼x12***
**430** A226 30k multi .25 .25
**431** A226 30k multi .25 .25

Issued: No. 430, 6/29; No. 431, 8/18.

**Regional and Administrative Areas**

Chernihivska Oblast — A228

Kirovohradska Oblast — A229

**2001 Litho.** ***Perf. 12¼x12***
**432** A228 30k multi .25 .25
**433** A229 30k multi .25 .25

Issued: No. 432, 9/21; No. 433, 9/22.

Souvenir Sheet

Icons From Khanenko Art Museum — A230

No. 434: a, 20k, Virgin and Child, 28x40mm. b, 30k, St. John the Baptist, 28x40mm. c, Saints Serhyi and Bacchus, 56x40mm.

**2001, July 12 Litho.** ***Perf. 11½***
**434** A230 Sheet of 3, #a-c .75 1.50

Endangered Species A231

No. 435: a, Milvus milvus. b, Scirtopoda telum.

**2001, July 24** ***Perf. 13***
**435** A231 1h Vert. pair, #a-b 1.50 1.50

Dmytro Bortnianskyi (1751-1825), Composer — A232

**2001, July 26**
**436** A232 20k multi .20 .20

Soccer — A233

**2001, Aug. 10**
**437** A233 50k multi .35 .35

Souvenir Sheet

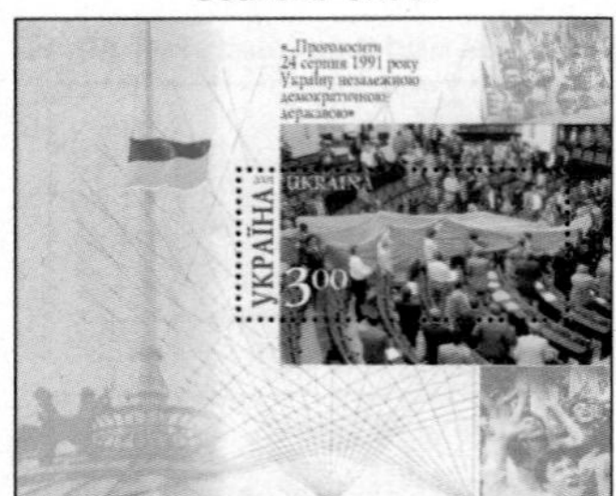

Independence, 10th Anniv. — A234

**2001, Aug. 15** ***Perf. 11½***
**438** A234 3h multi 2.25 2.25

7th Natl. Philatelic Exhibition, Dnipropetrovsk — A235

**2001, Oct. 7** **Litho.** ***Perf. 12¼x12***
**439** A235 30k multi .25 .25

Year of Dialogue Among Civilizations A236

**2001, Oct. 9** ***Perf. 13***
**440** A236 70k multi .50 .50

Souvenir Sheet

Black Sea Marine Life — A237

No. 441: a, 30k, Seahorses. b, 70k, Dolphins, birds.

**2001, Oct. 19** ***Perf. 11½***
**441** A237 Sheet of 2, #a-b .75 1.50

Christmas — A238

**2001, Nov. 9** ***Perf. 12¼x12***
**442** A238 30k multi .25 .25

St. Nicholas A239

**2001, Nov. 16** ***Perf. 13***
**443** A239 30k multi .25 .25

Happy New Year — A240

**2001, Nov. 23**
**444** A240 30k multi .25 .25

Poets — A241

No. 445: a, Taras Shevchenko (1814-61), Ukrainian poet. b, Akakii Tsereteli (1840-1915), Georgian poet.

**2001, Dec. 19**
**445** A241 40k Horiz. pair, #a-b .60 .60

See Georgia No. 276.

**Regional Costumes**

Kyivshchyna Region — A242

Chernihivshchyna Region — A243

Poltavshchyna Region — A244

No. 446: a, 20k, Two women. b, 50k, Man and woman.
No. 447: a, 20k, Musicians and girl. b, 50k, Bride and groom, boy.
No. 448: a, 20k, Priest and family. b, 50k, Two women.

**2001, Dec. 20** ***Perf. 13¼***
**446** A242 Horiz. pair, #a-b .50 .50
**447** A243 Horiz. pair, #a-b .50 .50
**448** A244 Horiz. pair, #a-b .50 .50
*c.* Souvenir sheet, #446-448, perf. 11½ 1.50 1.50
*Nos. 446-448 (3)* 1.50 1.50

**Hetman Type of 1997**

Designs: No. 449, 40k, Pavlo Teteryia (d. 1670) holding scepter, people in town, horsemen and carriage heading for town. No. 450, 40k, Demyian Mnohohrishnyi, receiving scepter, boats in river. No. 451, 40k, Ivan Briukhovetskyi (d. 1668), battle scenes.

**2002, Jan. 17** ***Perf. 12¼x12***
**449-451** A110 Set of 3 .85 .85

Scythian Military History — A245

No. 452: a, Archer on horseback. b, Swordsman in battle. c, Commander on horseback, warrior. d, Female warrior.
Illustration reduced.

**2002, Jan. 29** ***Perf. 13***
**452** A245 40k Block of 4, #a-d 1.10 1.10

**Flower Type of 2001 and**

Periwinkle — A246

**2002** **Litho.** ***Perf. 13¾***
**453** A246 5k multi .20 .20
*a.* Perf. 11½, dated "2006" .20 .20
**454** A214 10k multi .20 .20
*a.* Perf. 11½, dated "2006" .20 .20

Issued: 5k, 2/1; 10k, 2/26; Nos. 453a-454a, 10/9/06. Nos. 453a-454a were issued only in No. F2b.
No. 453 exists dated "2004," "2005" and "2006." No. 454 exist sdated "2005."

Sporting Achievements — A247

Designs: No. 455, 40k, Zhanna Pintusevich-Block winning 100-meter dash at 2001 World Track and Field Championships. No. 456, 40k, Swimmer at 2000 Summer Olympics.

**2002, Feb. 15** ***Perf. 13***
**455-456** A247 Set of 2 .50 .50

**Regional and Administrative Areas**

Kyivska Oblast — A248

**2002, Feb. 18** ***Perf. 12¼x12***
**457** A248 40k multi .25 .25

Shipbuilding — A249

No. 458: a, Frigate Sizopol and coast. b, Brigantine Perseus.
Illustration reduced.

**2002, Feb. 22** ***Perf. 13½***
**458** A249 40k Horiz. pair, #a-b .55 .55

Issuance of First Stamp After Independence, 10th Anniv. — A250

**2002, Mar. 1**
**459** A250 40k No. 100 .25 .25

Leonid Hlibov (1827-93), Writer — A251

**2002, Mar. 4** **Litho.** ***Perf. 13¼***
**460** A251 40k multi .25 .25

Ruslan Ponomariov, Winner of 16th World Chess Championships — A252

**2002, Mar. 29** ***Perf. 13½***
**461** A252 3.50h multi 1.75 1.75

Souvenir Sheet

Europa — A253

No. 462: a, Lion. b, Tiger, horiz.

**2002, Apr. 4** *Perf. 11½*
**462** A253 1.75h Sheet of 2, #a-b 1.75 2.50

Palm Sunday — A254

**2002, Apr. 19** *Perf. 13½*
**463** A254 40k multi .25 .25

Worldwide Fund for Nature (WWF) — A255

Various views of Elaphe situla: a, 40k. b, 70k. c, 80k. d, 2.50h.
Illustration reduced.

**2002, May 25** *Perf. 13½*
**464** A255 Block of 4, #a-d 2.25 2.25
*e.* Perf. 11½ 2.25 2.25

Souvenir Sheet

Opera and Ballet Theaters — A256

No. 465: a, Donetsk (tree at center). b, Dnipropetrovsk (trees at side).

**2002, May 31** *Perf. 11½*
**465** A256 1.25h Sheet of 2, #a-b 1.25 2.00

**Flower Type of 2001 and**

Blue Cornflower A257

Lilac A258

**2002** **Litho.** *Perf. 13¾*
**466** A215 30k multi .20 .20
*a.* Perf. 11½, dated "2006" .20 .20
**467** A257 45k multi .30 .30
*a.* Perf. 11½, dated "2006" .20 .20
**468** A258 (80k) multi .55 .55
*a.* Perf. 11½, dated "2006" .40 .40

Issued: 30k, 6/1; 45k, 9/18; (80k), 7/5.
Nos. 466-468 exist dated "2004." Nos. 466, 467 exist dated "2005" and "2006."
Nos. 466a-468a issued 10/9/06. Nos. 466a-468a were issued only in No. F2b.

**Regional and Administrative Areas**

Luhanska Oblast — A259

Chernivetska Oblast — A260

Odeska Oblast — A261

Cherkaska Oblast — A262

Sumska Oblast — A263

**2002** *Perf. 12¼x12*
**469** A259 40k multi .25 .25
**470** A260 40k multi .25 .25
**471** A261 45k multi .30 .30
**472** A262 45k multi .30 .30
**473** A263 45k multi .30 .30
*Nos. 469-473 (5)* 1.40 1.40

Issued: No. 469, 6/2; No. 470, 6/27; No. 471, 9/20. No. 472, 10/9; No. 473, 10/21.

Endangered Species A264

No. 474: a, Phalacrocorax aristotelis. b, Phocoena phocoena.

**2002, June 14** **Litho.** *Perf. 13*
**474** A264 70k Pair, #a-b .90 .90

Mykola Leontovich (1877-1921), Composer — A265

**2002, June 21** *Perf. 13½*
**475** A265 40k multi .25 .25

Souvenir Sheet

Black Sea Nature Reserve — A266

No. 476: a, Haematopus ostralegus (40x28mm). b, Larus genei (40x28mm). c, Iris pumila (22x26mm). d, Numenius arquata (26x22mm). e, Charadrius alexandrinus (26x22mm).

**2002, July 13** *Perf. 11½*
**476** A266 50k Sheet of 5, #a-e 1.50 2.50

Folk Tales — A267

No. 477: a, Fox and Pancake. b, Mr. Cat. c, Speckled Chicken.
Illustration reduced.

**2002, July 19** *Perf. 14¼x14*
**477** A267 40k Horiz. strip of 3, #a-c .80 .80

Art of Hanna Sobachko-Shostak — A268

No. 478: a, Cage for Starlings, 1963 (peach background). b, Vase with Flowers, 1964 (red background). c, Chamomile Flowers, 1964 (yellow background).

**2002, Aug. 9** *Perf. 14x14¼*
**478** Horiz. strip of 3 .90 .90
*a.-c.* A268 45k Any single .30 .30

Space Pioneers — A269

Designs: 40k, Yurii V. Kondratiuk (1897-1942). 45k, Mykhailo Yianhel (1911-71). 50k, Mykola Kybalchych (1853-81). 70k, Serhii Korolov (1907-66).

**2002, Aug. 23** *Perf. 12¼x12*
**479-482** A269 Set of 4 1.25 1.25

Marine Life — A270

No. 483: a, Phoca caspica. b, Huso huso ponticus.
Illustration reduced.

**2002, Sept. 6** *Perf. 14x14¼*
**483** A270 75k Horiz. pair, #a-b 1.00 1.00

See Kazakhstan No. 386.

Khotyn, 1000th Anniv. — A271

**2002, Sept. 21** *Perf. 12¼x12*
**484** A271 40k multi .25 .25

Odesaphil 2002 Stamp Exhibition, Odesa — A272

**2002, Oct. 5** **Litho.** *Perf. 14¼x14*
**485** A272 45k multi .30 .30

Paintings of Kyiv by Taras Shevchenko (1814-61) — A273

Designs: 45k, Askold's Tomb. 75k, Dnieper River Shoreline. 80k, St. Alexander's Church.

*Perf. 13¾x14½*
**2002, Nov. 15** **Litho.**
**486-488** A273 Set of 3 1.25 1.25

Happy New Year — A274

**2002, Nov. 22** *Perf. 14x14¼*
**489** A274 45k multi .30 .30

**Regional Costumes**

Vinychyna Region — A275

Cherkashchyna Region — A276

Ternopilska Region — A277

No. 490: a, Family, rainbow. b, Family, fruit tree.
No. 491: a, Four girls holding hands. b, Couple gathering crops.
No. 492: a, Priest blessing family. b, People with Easter baskets.

**2002, Dec. 6** *Perf. 13¼*

**490** A275 45k Horiz. pair, #a-b .55 .55
**491** A276 45k Horiz. pair, #a-b .55 .55
**492** A277 45k Horiz. pair, #a-b .55 .55
*c.* Souvenir sheet, #490-492, perf. 11½ 1.75 1.75
*Nos. 490-492 (3)* 1.65 1.65

Folk Tales — A278

No. 493: a, Koza-Dezera (cow on bridge). b, The Straw Bull. c, The Fox and Crane.
Illustration reduced.

**2003, Jan. 17 Litho.** *Perf. 14¼x14*

**493** A278 45k Horiz. strip of 3, #a-c .75 .75

Speed Skating A279

**2003, Jan. 24** *Perf. 14x14¼*

**494** A279 65k multi .35 .35

Military History — A280

No. 495: a, War with Goths, 4th cent. (soldier with spear and shield) b, Battles with Huns, 5th cent. (archer). c, Balkan campaigns, 6th cent. (soldier with hatchet). d, Battles with the Avars, 6th cent. (soldier with spears).
Illustration reduced.

**2003, Feb. 7**

**495** A280 45k Block of 4, #a-d 1.00 1.00

Shipbuilding — A281

No. 496: a, Steamship Grozny (denomination at left. b, Steamship Odessa (denomination at right).
Illustration reduced.

**2003, Feb. 14**

**496** A281 1h Horiz. pair, #a-b 1.10 1.10

Mikola Arkas (1853-1909), Composer — A282

**2003, Feb. 21**

**497** A282 45k multi .25 .25

Souvenir Sheet

Javorivsky National Nature Park — A283

No. 498: a, 1h, Alcede atthis (32x44mm). b, 1h, Cypripedium calceolus (36x41mm). c, 1.50h, Eudia pavonia, horiz. (44x32mm)

**2003, Mar. 3** *Perf. 11½*

**498** A283 Sheet of 3, #a-c 1.90 3.00

Europa — A284

Poster by Oleksiy Shtanko: a, Virgin Mary with dove. b, Guardian angel.
Illustration reduced.

**2003, Mar. 21** *Perf. 11½*

**499** A284 1.75h Horiz. pair, #a-b 2.25 2.25
*c.* Booklet pane, 2 #499 + central label 4.50 —
Complete booklet, #499c 4.50

**Space Pioneers Type of 2002**

Designs: 45k, Olkeksandr Zasiadko (1779-1837). 65k, Kostyantin Konstantinov (1817-71). 70k, Valyntyn Hlushko (1908-89). 80k, Volodymyr Chelomei (1914-84).

**2003, Apr. 11 Litho.** *Perf. 13¾x14½*

**500-503** A269 Set of 4 1.40 1.40

Ukrainian Red Cross Society, 85th Anniv. — A285

**2003, Apr. 18**

**504** A285 45k multi .25 .25

**Regional and Administrative Areas**

Dnipropetrovska Oblast — A286

Lvivska Oblast — A287

Khmelnytska Oblast — A288

Mykolayivska Oblast — A289

Zaporizhiya Oblast — A290

**2003**

**505** A286 45k multi .25 .25
**506** A287 45k multi .25 .25
**507** A288 45k multi .25 .25
**508** A289 45k multi .25 .25
**509** A290 45k multi .25 .25
*Nos. 505-509 (5)* 1.25 1.25

Issued: No. 505, 4/21; No. 506, 5/8; No. 507, 9/8; No. 508, 10/4; No. 509, 10/11.

**Hetman Type of 1997**

Designs: No. 510, 45k, Ivan Skoropadskiy (1646-1722) wearing robe, serfs in field, subjects bowing. No. 511, 45k, Kyrylo Rozumovskiy (1728-1803) holding scepter, attack of palace, palace ruins.

**2003, May 22**

**510-511** A110 Set of 2 .50 .50

Souvenir Sheet

Volodymyr Monomakh (1053-1125), Grand Prince of Kyiv — A291

**2003, May 28** *Perf. 11½*

**512** A291 3.50h multi 1.90 1.90

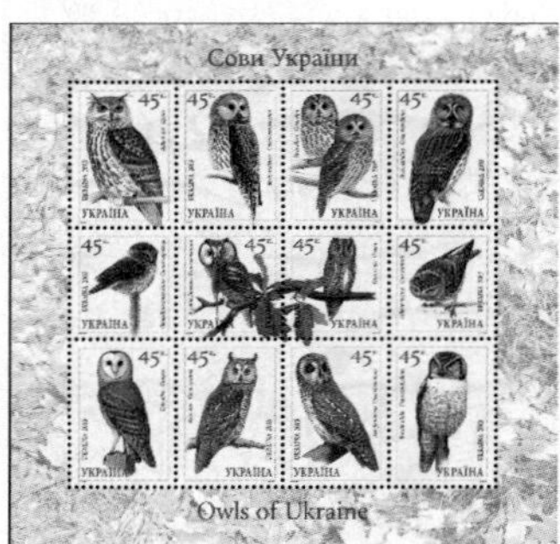

Owls — A292

No. 513: a, Bubo bubo. b, Strix uralensis. c, Strix aluco. d, Strix nebulosa. e, Glaucidium passerinum. f, Aegolius funereus. g, Otus scops. h, Athene noctua. i, Tyto alba. j, Asio otus. k, Asio flammeus. l, Surnia ulula. Size of # 513e-513h: 25x27mm; others: 25x36mm.

**2003, June 14**

**513** A292 45k Sheet of 12, #a-l 2.75 4.50

Oleksandr Myshuha (1853-1922), Opera Singer — A293

**2003, June 20** *Perf. 13¼*

**514** A293 45k multi .25 .25

Sweet Pea — A294

**2003, July 4** *Perf. 13¾*

**515** A294 65k multi .35 .35
*a.* Perf. 11½, dated "2006" .25 .25

No. 515 exists dated "2004" and "2005."
No. 515a issued 10/9/06. No. 515a was issued only in No. F2b.

**Paintings Type of 2002**

Paintings of Kyiv: No. 516, 45k, Podil, by Mykhailo Sazhyn, 1840. No. 517, 45k, Kyiv-Pecherska Monastery, by Vasyl Timm, 1857. No. 518, 45k, Ruins of St. Irene Monastery, by Sazhyn, 1846. No. 519, 45k, View of Old City from Yaroslav Embankment, by Timm, 1854.

**2003, July 18** *Perf. 13¾x14½*

**516-519** A273 Set of 4 1.00 1.00

Customs and Traditions — A295

No. 520: a, Celebration of the Harvest (Church, flowers and insects). b, Ascension (Church, fruit).

**2003, July 25** *Perf. 14¼x14*

**520** A295 45k Horiz. pair, #a-b .50 .50

Borys Hmyryia (1903-69), Composer A296

**2003, Aug. 5** *Perf. 14x14¼*

**521** A296 45k multi .25 .25

Souvenir Sheet

Manyiavskyi Monastery — A297

No. 522: a, Denomination at LL. b, Denomination at LR.

**2003, Aug. 15** *Perf. 11x11½*

**522** A297 1.25h Sheet of 2, #a-b 1.40 2.50

Yevpatoriya, 2500th Anniv. — A298

**2003, Aug. 29** *Perf. 13¾x14½*

**523** A298 45k multi .25 .25

Ancient Trade Routes — A299

No. 524: a, Arrival of Scandinavian seamen in rowboat, coin of Danish King Svend Estridsen. b, Silver coin of Prince Volodymyr Sviatoslavovych, Slavic warship with sail.

**2003, Sept. 17** *Perf. 11½*

**524** A299 80k Vert. pair, #a-b, + central label .90 .90
- *c.* Booklet pane, #524 2.40 —
- *d.* Booklet pane, #524a 1.25 —
- *e.* Booklet pane, #524b 1.25 —
- Complete booklet, #524c, 524d, 524e 5.00

Hryhoryi Kvitka-Osnovyianenko (1778-1843), Writer — A300

**2003, Nov. 14 Litho.** *Perf. 14¼x14*

**525** A300 45k multi .25 .25

Famine of 1932-33 — A301

**2003, Nov. 21** *Perf. 13¾x14½*

**526** A301 45k multi .25 .25

Christmas A302

**Litho. with Foil Application**

**2003, Nov. 25** *Perf. 13¼x13½*

**527** A302 45k multi .25 .25

New Year's Greetings A303

**2003, Nov. 25 Litho.** *Perf. 13½*

**528** A303 45k multi .25 .25

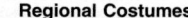

**Regional Costumes**

Kharkiv Region — A304

Sumy Region — A305

Donetsk Region — A306

No. 529: a, Women, religious icons. b, Family, lute.
No. 530: a, Woman, men. b, Group of women.
No. 531: a, Family, sled. b, Workers in field.

**2003, Dec. 19** *Perf. 13¼*

**529** A304 45k Horiz. pair, #a-b .50 .50
**530** A305 45k Horiz. pair, #a-b .50 .50
**531** A306 45k Horiz. pair, #a-b .50 .50
- *c.* Souvenir sheet, #529-531, perf. 11½ 1.50 1.50

Unification of Ukraine and Western Ukraine, 85th Anniv. — A307

**2004, Jan. 22 Litho.** *Perf. 13¾x14½*

**532** A307 45k multi .25 .25

Stanislav Ludkevych (1879-1979), Composer A308

**2004, Jan. 24** *Perf. 13¼*

**533** A308 45k multi .25 .25

Possessions of Hetman Bohdan Khmelnytsky — A309

No. 534: a, Flag. b, Mace. c, Cap. d, Watercup decorated with leaves. e, Tankard. f, Sword.

**Litho. With Foil Application**

**2004, Jan. 29** *Perf. 11½*

**534** A309 45k Sheet of 6, #a-f 1.50 2.50

Shipbuilding — A310

No. 535: a, 1h, Oil tanker Kriti Amber (55x26mm). b, 2.50h, Anti-submarine ship Mikolayiv (55x29mm). c, 3.50h Aircraft carrier Admiral Kuznetzov (55x40mm).

**2004, Feb. 21 Litho.** *Perf. 11½*

**535** A310 Sheet of 3, #a-c 4.00 6.00

**Regional and Administrative Areas**

Ternopilska Oblast — A311

**2004, Mar. 3** *Perf. 13¾x14½*

**536** A311 45k multi .25 .25

Membership in UNESCO, 50th Anniv. — A312

**2004, Mar. 19** *Perf. 14¼x14*

**537** A312 45k multi .25 .25

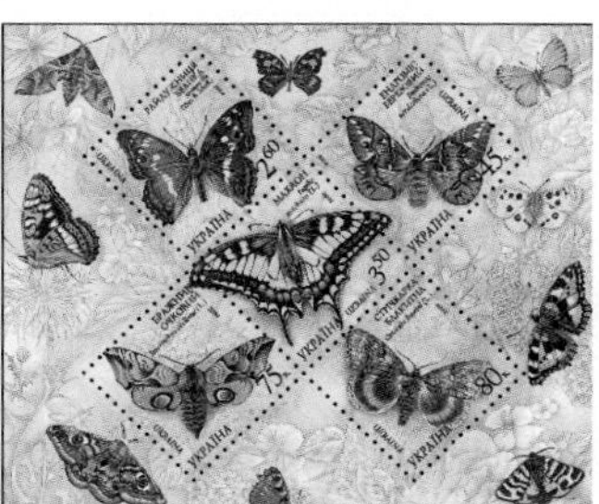
Butterflies — A313

No. 538: a, 45k, Endromis versicolora. b, 75k, Smerinthus ocellatus. c, 80k, Catocala fraxini. d, 2.60h, Apatura ilia. e, 3.50h, Papilio machaon.

**2004, Mar. 6** *Perf. 8*

**538** A313 Sheet of 5, #a-e 4.50 7.00

Famous Ukrainians A314

Designs: No. 539, 45k, Serhyi Lyfar (1904-86), ballet dancer and choreographer. No. 540, 45k, Maria Zankovetska (1854-1934), actress. No. 541, 45k, Mykhaylo Maksymovych (1804-73), historian.

**2004 Litho.** *Perf. 14x14¼*

**539-541** A314 Set of 3 .75 .75

Issued: No. 539, 4/2, Nos. 540-541, 7/23.

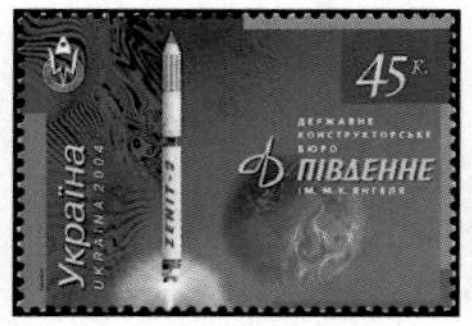
Zenit-1 Rocket A315

**2004, Apr. 14**

**542** A315 45k multi .25 .25

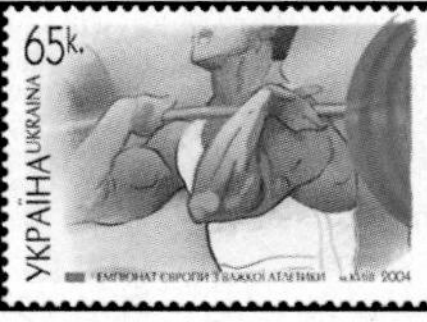
European Weight Lifting Championships, Kyiv — A316

**2004, Apr. 20**

**543** A316 65k multi .35 .35

**Miniature Sheet**

Europa — A317

No. 544: a, 45k, Lastivchyne Hnizdo (22x33mm). b, 75k, Carpathian Mountains (22x33mm). c, 2.61h, Khotyn Castle (29x33mm). d, 3.52h, Pecherska Lavra (39x28mm).

**2004, Apr. 23** *Perf. 11½*

**544** A317 Sheet of 4, #a-d 4.00 6.00

UEFA (European Football Union), 50th Anniv. — A318

**2004, May 17** *Perf. 14¼x14*

**545** A318 3.52h multi 2.00 2.00

FIFA (Fédération Internationale de Football Association), Cent. — A319

No. 546: a, 45k, Player #11. b, 75k, Player #6. c, 80k, Fan. d, 2.61h, Two women players.
Illustration reduced.

**2004, May 17** ***Perf. 13¼***
**546** A319 Block of 4, #a-d 2.60 2.60

Symon Petlura (1879-1926), Political Leader — A320

**2004, May 21**
**547** A320 45k multi .25 .25

**Painting Type of 2002**

Designs: No. 548, 45k, Kiev with St. Andrew's Church, by unknown artist, 1889. No. 549, 45k, Fountain Near the Golden Gate, by Petro Levchenko, 1910. No. 550, 45k, Spring in Kurenivka, by Abram Manevych, 1914-15. No. 551, 45k, St. Michael's Cathedral From the South, by Mykola Burachek, 1919.

**2004, June 11** ***Perf. 13¾x14½***
**548-551** A273 Set of 4 1.00 1.00

Folktales — A321

No. 552: a, The Cat. b, Ivasyk Telesyk. c, The Fat Man.
Illustration reduced.

**2004, June 18** ***Perf. 14¼x14***
**552** A321 45k Horiz. strip of 3, #a-c .75 .75

2004 Summer Olympics, Athens A322

**2004, June 26** ***Perf. 14x14¼***
**553** A322 2.61h multi 1.40 1.40

**Regional and Administrative Areas**

Rovenska Oblast — A323

Khersonska Oblast — A324

Poltavska Oblast — A325

**2004** ***Perf. 13¾x14½***
**554** A323 45k multi .25 .25
**555** A324 45k multi .25 .25
**556** A325 45k multi .25 .25

Issued: No. 554, 7/16; No. 555, 8/20; No. 556, 9/22.

Balaklava, 2500th Anniv. — A327

***Perf. 13¾x14½***
**2004, Aug. 14** **Litho.**
**557** A327 45k multi .25 .25

Kharkiv, 350th Anniv. — A328

**2004, Aug. 20** ***Perf. 14¼x14***
**558** A328 45k multi .25 .25

Bridges — A329

No. 559: a, Inhulskyi Bridge (open drawbridge). b, Darnytska Bridge (three arches above roadway). c, B. M. Preobrazhenskoho Bridge (arches below roadway). d, Southern Buh Bridge (swing bridge).

**2004, Aug. 25** ***Perf. 13¾x14½***
**559** A329 45k Block of 4, #a-d 1.00 1.00

No. 194B Surcharged

**Litho. & Engr.**
**2004, Sept. 15** ***Perf. 12½x13***
**560** A47a 2.61h on 25,000kb multi 1.50 1.50

Taras Shevchenko University, 170th anniv.

Kirovohrad, 250th Anniv. — A330

***Perf. 13¾x14¼***
**2004, Sept. 17** **Litho.**
**561** A330 45k multi .25 .25

Military History — A331

No. 562: a, Infantryman of Prince Oleg, 10th cent. b, National militia, 11th-12th cent. c, Archer on horseback, 12th cent. d, Cavalryman for Danylo Halyts, 13th cent.
Illustration reduced.

**2004, Oct. 15** ***Perf. 14x14¼***
**562** A331 45k Block of 4, #a-d 1.00 1.00

Miniature Sheet

Birds of the Danube Nature Reserve — A332

No. 563: a, 45k, Cygnus olor. b, 75k, Phalacrocorax pygmaeus. c, 80k, Egretta alba. d, 2.61h, Anser anser. e, 3.52h, Platalea leucordia.

**2004, Oct. 26** ***Perf. 11½***
**563** A332 Sheet of 5, #a-e 4.50 7.00

Intl. Space Station, Khartron Systems Emblem A333

1516 Battle Between Cossacks and Tartars Using Fiery Projectiles A334

**2004, Nov. 12** ***Perf. 14x14¼***
**564** A333 45k multi .25 .25
**565** A334 45k multi .25 .25

Christmas A335

No. 566: a, Magi facing right ("2" in background). b, Magi facing left ("5" in background). c, Nativity ("0" in background).

**Litho. With Foil Application**
**2004, Nov. 26** ***Perf. 13¼***
**566** Horiz. strip of 4, #a-b, 2 #c 1.00 1.00
*a.-c.* A335 45k Any single, gold & multi .25 .25

Numbers in background of strip of 4 read "2005."

New Year's Greetings A336

No. 567: a, Santa Claus, large trees at left ("2" in background). b, Santa Claus, large trees at right ("5" in background). c, Tree and gifts ("0" in background).

**2004, Nov. 26**
**567** Horiz. strip of 4, #a-b, 2 #c 1.00 1.00
*a.-c.* A336 45k Any single, silver & multi .25 .25

Numbers in background of strip of 4 read "2005."

Ukrainian and Iranian Aircraft — A337

No. 568: a, Antonov-140, Ukraine (denomination at left). b, Iran-140, Iran (denomination at right).

**2004, Nov. 30** **Litho.** ***Perf. 11½***
**568** Horiz. pair + central label .90 .90
*a.-b.* A337 80k Either single .45 .45

See Iran No.

**Regional Costumes**

Lvivshchyna Region — A338

Ivano-Frankivshchyna Region — A339

Hutsulshchyna Region — A340

No. 569: a, Family, rooster. b, Family, pitcher.
No. 570: a, Musicians. b, Dancers at wedding.
No. 571: a, Men, child, lamb. b, Family, cradle.

**2004, Dec. 10** ***Perf. 13¼***
**569** A338 60k Horiz. pair, #a-b .70 .70
**570** A339 60k Horiz. pair, #a-b .70 .70
**571** A340 60k Horiz. pair, #a-b .70 .70
*c.* Miniature sheet, #569-571, perf. 11½ 2.10 2.10

Poppy — A341

**2005, Jan. 14 Litho. *Perf. 13¾***

572 A341 1h multi .55 .55
a. Perf. 11½, dated "2006" .40 .40

No. 572 exists dated "2006."

No. 572a issued 10/9/06. No. 572a was issued only in No. F2b.

November - December 2004 Protests Against Rigged Elections — A342

**2005, Jan. 23 *Perf. 11½***

573 A342 45k multi .25 .25

Printed in sheets of 7 + label.

**Famous Ukrainians Type of 2004**

Design: No. 574, Pavlo Virskyi (1905-75), choreographer. No. 575, Volodymyr Vynnychenko (1880-1951), writer and statesman.

**2005 Litho. *Perf. 14x14¼***

574 A314 45k multi .25 .25
575 A314 45k multi .25 .25

Issued. No. 574, 2/4; No. 575, 7/15.

Miniature Sheet

Moths — A343

No. 576: a, 45k, Acherontia atropos. b, 75k, Catocala sponsa. c, 80k, Staurophora celsia. d, 2.61h, Marumba quercus. e, Saturnia pyri.

**2005, Feb. 11 *Perf. 11½***

576 A343 Sheet of 5, #a-d 4.50 4.50

**Regional and Administrative Areas**

Vinnytska Oblast — A344

**2005, Feb. 23 *Perf. 13¾x14½***

577 A344 45k multi .25 .25

**Regional and Administrative Areas**

Sevastopol City — A345

Ivano-Frankivska Oblast — A346

Zhitomyrska Oblast — A347

**2005 Litho. *Perf. 13¾x14½***

578 A345 45k multi .25 .25
579 A345 45k multi .25 .25
580 A347 70k multi .40 .40
*Nos. 578-580 (3)* .90 .90

Issued: No. 578, 6/11; No. 579, 7/16; 70k, 9/10.

Paintings by Ivan Aivazovskyi A348

No. 581: a, Sea — Koktebel, 1853. b, Towers on the Rock Near the Bosporus, 1859.

**2005, Mar. 4 Litho. *Perf. 14x14¼***

581 Horiz. pair, #a-b, + central label .50 .50
a.-b. A348 45k Either single .25 .25

The Shepherd, by Heorhyi Yakutovych (1930-2000) — A349

**Litho. & Engr.**

**2005, Mar. 26 *Perf. 11½***

582 A349 3.52h silver & gray blue 2.00 2.00

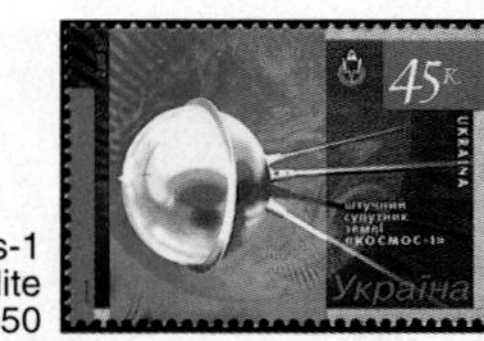

Cosmos-1 Satellite A350

Zenit-2 Rocket A351

Designs: No. 585, Dnepr rocket. No. 586, Cyclone-3 rocket.

**2005, Apr. 12 Litho. *Perf. 14x14¼***

583 A350 45k shown .25 .25
584 A351 45k shown .25 .25
585 A351 45k multi .25 .25
586 A351 45k multi .25 .25
*Nos. 583-586 (4)* 1.00 1.00

A352

End of World War II, 60th Anniv. — A353

**2005 *Perf. 14x14¼***

587 A352 45k multi .25 .25

**Souvenir Sheet**

***Perf. 11½***

588 A353 80k multi .45 .45

Issued: 45k, 4/22; 80k, 5/7. No. 587 issued in sheets of 8 + central label.

Ninth Intl. Philatelic Exhibition, Kyiv — A354

**2005, May 17 *Perf. 13¾x14½***

589 A354 45k multi .25 .25

**Painting Type of 2002**

Paintings of Kyiv: 45k, New Street, by Serhyi Shyshko, 1966. 75k, Park in Winter, by Shyshko, 1960. 80k, Sacred Sophia, by Yuryi Khymych, 1965. 1h, Khreshchatyk Boulevard, by Khymych, 1967, vert.

***Perf. 13¾x14½, 14½x13¾***

**2005, May 18**

590-593 A273 Set of 4 1.75 1.75

Ruslana, Winner of 2004 Eurovision Song Contest — A355

Logo for 2005 Eurovision Song Contest A356

**2005, May 19 *Perf. 11½***

594 A355 45k multi .25 .25
595 A356 2.50h multi 1.40 1.40

Europa — A357

Nos. 596 and 597: a, 2.61h, Bowl of borscht, beets, onions, garlic, tomatoes, pepper, beans, lard, parsley and dill. b, 3.52h, Lidded tureen, cabbage, carrots, onion, garlic, pepper Illustration reduced.

**2005, May 20 *Perf. 11½***

**Stamp Size: 45x32mm**

596 A357 Horiz. pair, #a-b 3.50 3.50

**Booklet Stamps**

**Stamp Size: 40x27mm**

***Perf. 14x14¼***

597 A357 Horiz. pair, #a-b 6.00 6.00
c. Booklet pane, 2 #597 12.00 —
Complete booklet, #597c 12.00

Complete booklet sold for 19.38h.

Development of the Cyrillic Alphabet — A358

**Litho. & Embossed**

**2005, May 21 *Perf. 14¼x14***

598 A358 45k multi .25 .25

Souvenir Sheet

Flora and Fauna in Karadazkyi Nature Reserve — A359

No. 599: a, 45k, Falco cherrug (33x40mm). b, 70k, Ascalaphus macaronius (29x35mm). c, 2.50h, Tursiops truncatus ponticus (33x33mm). d, 3.50h, Martes foina (49x33mm).

**2005, July 28 Litho. *Perf. 11½***

599 A359 Sheet of 4, #a-d 4.25 4.25

World Summit on the Information Society, Tunis A360

**2005, Aug. 12 *Perf. 14x14¼***

600 A360 2.50h multi 1.40 1.40

Series Ov Locomotive — A361

Series C Locomotive — A362

Series Shch Locomotive — A363

Series Ye Locomotive — A364

**2005, Aug. 31**

| | | | |
|---|---|---|---|
| 601 A361 70k multi | .40 | .40 |
| 602 A362 70k multi | .40 | .40 |
| 603 A363 70k multi | .40 | .40 |
| 604 A364 70k multi | .40 | .40 |
| *Nos. 601-604 (4)* | 1.60 | 1.60 |

Nos. 601-604 were each printed in sheets of 11 + label.

Sumy, 350th Anniv. — A365

**2005, Sept. 2**

605 A365 45k multi .25 .25

Nasturtium A366

Water Lily A367

Violets — A368

Wild Rose — A369

**2005** ***Perf. 13¾***

| | | |
|---|---|---|
| 606 A366 25k multi | .20 | .20 |
| a. Perf. 11½, dated "2006" | .20 | .20 |
| 607 A367 70k multi | .40 | .40 |
| a. Perf. 11½, dated "2006" | .30 | .30 |
| 608 A368 (1.53h) multi | 1.10 | 1.10 |
| a. Perf. 11½, dated "2006" | .80 | .80 |
| 609 A369 (2.55h) multi | 1.90 | 1.90 |
| a. Perf. 11½, dated "2006" | 1.40 | 1.40 |
| *Nos. 606-609 (4)* | 3.60 | 3.60 |

Issued: 25k, 9/8; 70k, 9/12; #608, 12/16; #609, 11/24.

Nos. 606-609 exist dated "2006."

Nos. 606a-609a issued 10/9/06. Nos. 606a-609a were issued only in No. F2b.

Horses — A370

No. 610: a, Novoolexandrivskyi heavy draft horse (brown horse facing left with four-line inscription). b, Orlov-Rostopchin (white horse). c, Ukrainian riding horse (brown horse facing left with three-line inscription). d, Thoroughbred (brown horse facing right).

Illustration reduced.

**2005, Sept. 15** ***Perf. 11½***

610 A370 70k Block of 4, #a-d 1.60 1.60

"Safety - Green Light" A371

"Give a Helping Hand" A372

"No to Drugs" A373

**2005, Oct. 14** ***Perf. 14x14¼***

| | | |
|---|---|---|
| 611 Horiz. strip of 3 | 1.25 | 1.25 |
| a. A371 70k multi | .40 | .40 |
| b. A372 70k multi | .40 | .40 |
| c. A373 70k multi | .40 | .40 |

Military History — A374

No. 612: a, Commander Bobrok Volnyets at Battle of Kulikovo, 1380. b, Artillerymen and riflemen, 14th-15th cent. c, Knight Ivanko Sushyk at Grunwald, 1410. d, Prince Konstiantyn Ostrozkyi at Orsha, 1512.

Illustration reduced.

**2005, Oct. 21**

612 A374 70k Block of 4, #a-d 1.60 1.60

**Famous Ukrainians Type of 2004**

Designs: No. 613, Dmytro Yiavornytskyi (1855-1940), historian. No. 614, Oleg Antonov (1906-84), aircraft designer.

**2005-06** **Litho.**

| | | |
|---|---|---|
| 613 A314 70k multi | .45 | .45 |
| 614 A314 70k multi | .45 | .45 |

Issued: #613, 11/7; #614, 2/7/06.

Christmas A375

**Litho. With Foil Application**

**2005, Nov. 11** ***Perf. 13¼***

615 A375 70k multi .45 .45

New Year's Day — A376

**2005, Nov. 11** **Litho.**

616 A376 70k multi .45 .45

St. Barbara's Church, Vienna, Austria — A377

**2005, Dec. 9** ***Perf. 14¼x14***

617 A377 75k multi + label .50 .50

Lviv National Museum, Cent. — A378

No. 618: a, Archangel Michael, by unknown artist (denomination at right). b, Dalmatynka, by Teofil Kopystynskyi (denomination at left).

Illustration reduced.

**2005, Dec. 13** **Litho.**

618 A378 70k Horiz. pair, #a-b, + central label .85 .85

**Regional Costumes**

Zhytomyrshchyna Region — A379

Rivnenshchyna Region — A380

Volyn Region — A381

No. 619: a, Family and dog, St. Basil's Day. b, Man and woman, St. Zosyma's Day.

No. 620: a, People with animals, St. George's Day. b, Men, women and musician, Sts. Peter and Paul's Day.

No. 621: a, People with buckets, Annunciation Day. b, Family and cat, St. Nicholas's Day.

**2005, Dec. 20** ***Perf. 13¼***

| | | |
|---|---|---|
| 619 A379 70k Horiz. pair, #a-b | .85 | .85 |
| 620 A380 70k Horiz. pair, #a-b | .85 | .85 |
| 621 A381 70k Horiz. pair, #a-b | .85 | .85 |
| c. Miniature sheet, #619-621, perf. 11½ | 2.60 | 2.60 |

Europa Stamps, 50th Anniv. — A382

Designs: Nos. 622a, 623a, 1.30h, 50th anniversary emblem. Nos. 622a, 622b, 2.50h, CEPT emblem.

**2006, Jan. 5** **Litho.** ***Perf. 13¼***

**With Names of Designers at Right of Stamps**

622 A382 Vert. pair, #a-b 2.25 2.25

**Souvenir Sheet**

**Without Names of Designers at Right of Stamps**

***Perf. 11½***

623 A382 Sheet of 2, #a-b 2.25 2.25

Art by Hryhoryi Narbut (1886-1920) — A383

**Litho. & Engr.**

**2006, Mar. 10** ***Perf. 11½***

624 A383 3.33h multi 1.90 1.90

Printed in sheets of 11 + label.

Miniature Sheet

Traditional Women's Headdresses — A384

No. 625: a, Drawing of woman wearing fur hat. b, Woman, facing left, wearing black hat with brown ribbon. c, Drawing of woman facing left, wearing undecorated head covering. d, Woman wearing large floral head covering. e, Woman wearing red kerchief. f, Woman wearing small floral head covering. g, Woman wearing white kerchief with red dots. h, Woman wearing brown kerchief with knot in front. i, Drawing of woman, facing right, wearing undecorated head covering. j, Woman wearing floral headcovering with thin black edge. k, Woman wearing kerchief with floral pattern. l, Woman wearing small floral head covering with ribbon.

**2006, Mar. 30** **Litho.** ***Perf. 11½***

625 A384 70k Sheet of 12, #a-l 5.00 5.00

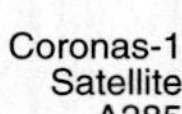

Coronas-1 Satellite A385

Designs: No. 627, Welding in space. No. 628, International observation of Comet Galileo.

**2006, Apr. 12** ***Perf. 14x14¼***

**Color of Panel Denomination Panel**

**626** A385 85k gray .50 .50
**627** A385 85k red brown .50 .50
**628** A385 85k dull brown .50 .50
*Nos. 626-628 (3)* 1.50 1.50

Europa — A386

Designs: Nos. 629a, 630a, 2.50h, Earth and Saturn. Nos. 629b, 630b, 3.50h, Earth and Jupiter.
Illustration reduced.

**2006, Apr. 28** ***Perf. 11½***

**Top Cyrillic Inscription in Black**

**629** A386 Horiz. pair, #a-b 3.50 3.50

**Top Cyrillic Inscription in Red**

**630** A386 Booklet pane of 2, #a-b + 2 labels 7.25 7.25
Complete booklet, #630 7.25

Nos. 630a-630b are 52x26mm. No. 630 sold for 11.52h.

2006 World Cup Soccer Championships, Germany — A387

Designs: 2.50k, Ukrainian soccer players. 3.50k, Soccer ball.

**2006, May 4**

**631-632** A387 Set of 2 3.50 3.50

Georgia, Ukraine, Azerbaijan and Moldova Summit, Kiev A388

**2006, May 23** ***Perf. 14x14¼***

**633** A388 70k multi .45 .45

Paintings of Kiev — A389

Designs: No. 634, 70k, Zaborovskyi Gate, by Boris Tulin, 1987 (shown). No. 635, 70k, Olha Basystiuk Sings, by Tulin, 1987. No. 636, 70k, Kiev-Peherska Lavra, by Oleksandr Hubarev, 1990. No. 637, 70k, Andrew's Alley, by Hubarev, 1983.

**2006, May 24** ***Perf. 13¾x14¼***

**634-637** A389 Set of 4 1.60 1.60

Souvenir Sheet

Lviv, 750th Anniv. — A390

No. 638 — View of Lviv, 1618 and: a, 70k, Coat of arms (38x31mm). b, 2.50h, Coin (69x31mm).

**2006, June 16** ***Perf. 11½***

**638** A390 Sheet of 2, #a-b 1.90 1.90

Miniature Sheet

Fauna of Shatskyi National Park — A391

No. 639: a, Lanius excubitor (28x40mm). b, Lynx lynx (33x35mm). c, Anguilla anguilla (41x29mm). d, Bufo calamita (28x29mm). e, Mustela erminea (45x29mm).

**2006, July 14**

**639** A391 70k Sheet of 5, #a-e 2.00 2.00

Miniature Sheet

Cossack Hetmen — A392

No. 640: a, Ivan Bohun (denomination at UL). b, Ivan Honta (denomination at UR). c, Ivan Pidkova (denomination at LL). d, Ivan Sirko (denomination at LR).

**Litho. & Engr. With Foil Application**

**2006, Aug. 18**

**640** A392 3.50h Sheet of 4, #a-d 7.25 7.25

**Famous Ukrainians Type of 2004**

Design: Ivan Franko (1856-1916), writer.

**2006, Aug. 27 Litho.** ***Perf. 14x14¼***

**641** A314 70k multi .45 .45

Series L Locomotive — A393

Series SO Locomotive — A394

Series YS Locomotive — A395

Series FD Locomotive — A396

**2006, Sept. 15**

**642** A393 70k multi .45 .45
**643** A394 70k multi .45 .45
**644** A395 70k multi .45 .45
**645** A396 70k multi .45 .45
*Nos. 642-645 (4)* 1.80 1.80

Each stamp printed in sheets of 11 + label.

Tenth Natl. Philatelic Exhibition, Lviv — A397

**2006, Oct. 6** **Litho. & Embossed**

**646** A397 70k multi .45 .45

Miltary History — A398

No. 647: a, Cossack-siroma, 16th-17th cent. b, Naval campaigns of 16th-18th cents. c, Khmelnychna national liberation movement (soldiers aiming guns), 17th cent. d, Haidamachnya national liberation movement (soldier with sword), 17th cent.
Illustration reduced.

**2006, Nov. 3 Litho.** ***Perf. 14x14¼***

**647** A398 70k Block of 4, #a-d 1.50 1.50

Horses in Sports — A399

No. 648: a, Dressage. b, Horse racing. c, Harness racing. d, Show jumping.
Illustration reduced.

**2006, Nov. 17** ***Perf. 11½***

**648** A399 70k Block of 4, #a-d 1.50 1.50

Printed in sheets containing two each of Nos. 648a-648d.

St. Nicholas's Day — A400

No. 649: a, Children following angel. b, Angel and St. Nicholas.

**Litho. With Foil Application**

**2006, Nov. 17** ***Perf. 13¼***

**649** A400 70k Horiz. pair, #a-b .75 .75

Christmas — A401

**2006, Nov. 24** ***Perf. 14¼x14***

**650** A401 70k multi .40 .40

**Regional Costumes**

Zaporizhzha Region — A403

Khersonshchyna Region — A404

Odeshchyna Region — A405

No. 652: a, People with flags, candle, and swords, St. Michael's Day. b, People and horses, Assumption Day.
No. 653: a, Women and spinning wheel, St. Catherine's Day. b, Men and oxen, St. Elias's Day.
No. 654: a, People and pig, St. Barbara and St. Sava's Day. b, People and fish, St. Boris and St. Hlib's Day.

**2006, Dec. 15** **Litho.** ***Perf. 13¼***

**652** A403 70k Horiz. pair, #a-b .75 .75
**653** A404 70k Horiz. pair, #a-b .75 .75
**654** A405 70k Horiz. pair, #a-b .75 .75
*c.* Miniature sheet, #652-654, perf. 11½ 2.25 2.25

## SEMI-POSTAL STAMPS

### Ukrainian Soviet Socialist Republic

"Famine" — SP1

Taras H. Shevchenko SP2

"Death" Stalking Peasant — SP3

"Ukraine" Distributing Food — SP4

***Perf. 14½x13½, 13½x14½***

**1923, June Litho. Unwmk.**

| | | | | |
|---|---|---|---|---|
| **B1** | SP1 | 10k + 10k gray bl & blk | .75 | *5.00* |
| **B2** | SP2 | 20k + 20k vio brn & org brn | .75 | *5.00* |
| **B3** | SP3 | 90k + 30k db & blk, *straw* | .75 | *5.00* |
| **B4** | SP4 | 150k + 50k red brn & blk | .75 | *5.00* |
| | | *Nos. B1-B4 (4)* | 3.00 | *20.00* |

**Imperf., Pairs**

| | | | | |
|---|---|---|---|---|
| *B1a* | SP1 | 10k + 10k | 80.00 | 100.00 |
| *B2a* | SP2 | 20k + 20k | 80.00 | 100.00 |
| *B3a* | SP3 | 90k + 30k | 80.00 | 100.00 |
| *B4a* | SP4 | 150k + 50k | 80.00 | 100.00 |

The values of these stamps are in karbovanets, which by 1923 converted to rubles at 100 to 1.

**Wmk. 116**
**Same Colors**

| | | | | |
|---|---|---|---|---|
| **B5** | SP1 | 10k + 10k | *40.00* | *60.00* |
| **B6** | SP2 | 20k + 20k | *40.00* | *60.00* |
| *a.* | | Imperf., pair | 2,000. | |
| **B7** | SP3 | 90k + 30k | *30.00* | *60.00* |
| **B8** | SP4 | 150k + 50k | *30.00* | *60.00* |
| | | *Nos. B5-B8 (4)* | *140.00* | *240.00* |

**Catalogue values for unused stamps in this section, from this point to the end of the section, are for Never Hinged items.**

Mercy and Health Fund — SP5

**1994, Jan. 15 Litho. *Perf. 12***

**B9** SP5 150kb +20kb multi .35

Third Natl. Philatelic Exhibition, Lviv — SP6

**1995, Sept. 23 Litho. *Perf. 13½***

**B10** SP6 50,000kb +5000kb multi 1.00

Souvenir Sheet

Zymnenska Icon of Madonna and Child — SP7

Illustration reduced.

**1999, Sept. 4 Litho. *Perf. 11½***

**B11** SP7 1.20h +10k multicolored .90 .90

Intl. Year of the Elderly.

## REGISTRATION STAMP

**Catalogue values for unused stamps in this section are for Never Hinged items.**

Trident — R1

**2001, Apr. 1 Litho. *Perf. 13¾***

| | | | |
|---|---|---|---|
| **F1** R1 (10.84h) multi | | 7.25 | 7.25 |
| *a.* Perf. 11½, dated "2006" | | 5.25 | 5.25 |

No. F1a issued 10/9/06. No. F1a was issued only in No. F2b.

Trident With Frame — R2

**2005-06 Litho. *Perf. 13¾***

| | | |
|---|---|---|
| **F2** R2 (10.10h) multi | 5.75 | 5.75 |
| *a.* Perf. 11½, dated "2006" | 4.50 | 4.50 |
| *b.* Sheet of 18, #418a-422a, 453a-454a, 466a-468a, 515a, 572a, 606a-609a, F1a, F2a | 18.00 | 18.00 |

Issued: No. F2, 10/28/05; No. F2a, 10/9/06. No. F2 exists dated "2006." No. F2a was issued only in No. F2b. No. F2b sold for 35.41h and exists imperf.

## MILITARY STAMPS

### COURIER FIELD POST ISSUE

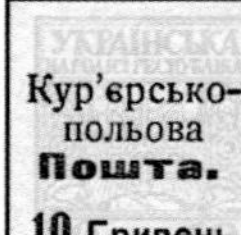

Nos. 1-5, 48 Surcharged

**1920, Aug. 26**

| | | | | |
|---|---|---|---|---|
| **M1** | A1 | 10hr on 10sh buff | 15.00 | — |
| *a.* | | Inverted surcharge | 60.00 | |
| **M2** | A2 | 10hr on 20sh brown | 30.00 | — |
| **M3** | A3 | 10hr on 30sh ultramarine | 35.00 | — |
| **M4** | A4 | 10hr on 40sh green | 40.00 | — |
| *a.* | | Inverted surcharge | 160.00 | |
| **M5** | A5 | 10hr on 50sh red | 35.00 | — |
| **M6** | A1 | 20hr on 10sh buff | 40.00 | — |
| **M7** | A2 | 20hr on 20sh brown | 10.00 | — |
| *a.* | | Inverted surcharge | 40.00 | |
| **M8** | A3 | 20hr on 30sh ultramarine | 30.00 | — |
| *a.* | | Inverted surcharge | 120.00 | |
| **M9** | A4 | 20hr on 40sh green | 30.00 | — |
| **M10** | A5 | 20hr on 50sh red | 30.00 | — |
| *a.* | | Inverted surcharge | 120.00 | |
| **M11** | A1 | 40hr on 10sh buff | 150.00 | — |
| **M12** | A2 | 40hr on 20sh brown | 75.00 | — |
| **M13** | A3 | 40hr on 30sh ultramarine | 300.00 | — |
| **M14** | A4 | 40hr on 40sh green | 150.00 | — |
| **M15** | A5 | 40hr on 50sh red | 300.00 | — |
| **M16** | A6 | 40hr on 20hr red & green | — | — |

Nos. M1-M16 were prepared to facilitate communications between the Ukrainian government-in-exile at Tarnow, Poland, and its military units in the field.

Only two copies of No. M16 are known, one unused and one used on cover.

Forged surcharges and cancellations exist.

# UMM AL QIWAIN

'um-al-kī-'wīn

LOCATION — Oman Peninsula, Arabia, on Arabian Gulf
GOVT. — Sheikdom under British protection
AREA — 300 sq. mi.
POP. — 5,700

Umm al Qiwain is one of six Persian Gulf sheikdoms to join the United Arab Emirates which proclaimed independence Dec. 2, 1971. See United Arab Emirates.

100 Naye Paise = 1 Rupee
100 Dirham = 1 Riyal (1967)

**Catalogue values for all unused stamps in this country are for Never Hinged items.**

Sheik Ahmed bin Rashid al Mulla and Gazelles A1

**Photogravure and Lithographed**
**1964, June 29 Unwmk. *Perf. 14***

**Size: 35x22mm**

| | | | | |
|---|---|---|---|---|
| **1** | A1 | 1np shown | .20 | .20 |
| **2** | A1 | 2np Snake | .20 | .20 |
| **3** | A1 | 3np Hyena | .20 | .20 |
| **4** | A1 | 4np Conspicuous triggerfish | .20 | .20 |
| **5** | A1 | 5np Fish | .20 | .20 |
| **6** | A1 | 10np Silver angelfish | .20 | .20 |
| **7** | A1 | 15np Palace | .20 | .20 |
| **8** | A1 | 20np Umm al Qiwain | .20 | .20 |
| **9** | A1 | 30np Tower | .20 | .20 |

**Size: 42x26mm**

| | | | | |
|---|---|---|---|---|
| **10** | A1 | 40np as 1np | .20 | .20 |
| **11** | A1 | 50np as 2np | .20 | .20 |
| **12** | A1 | 70np as 3np | .65 | .20 |
| **13** | A1 | 1r as 4np | .80 | .25 |
| **14** | A1 | 1.50r as 4np | 1.00 | .30 |
| **15** | A1 | 2r as 10np | 1.25 | .50 |

**Size: 52x33mm**

| | | | | |
|---|---|---|---|---|
| **16** | A1 | 3r as 15np | 2.40 | 1.50 |
| **17** | A1 | 5r as 20np | 4.00 | 2.75 |
| **18** | A1 | 10r as 30np | 7.00 | 4.50 |
| | | *Nos. 1-18 (18)* | 19.30 | 12.20 |

National Stadium, Tokyo, and Discobolus — A2

Designs: 1r, 2r, National Stadium, Tokyo. 1.50r, Indoor swimming arena. 3r, Komazawa Gymnasium. 4r, Stadium entrance.

**1964, Nov. 25 Photo. *Perf. 14***

| | | | | |
|---|---|---|---|---|
| **19** | A2 | 50np multi | .20 | .20 |
| **20** | A2 | 1r multi | .40 | .20 |
| **21** | A2 | 1.50r multi | .50 | .20 |
| **22** | A2 | 2r multi | .80 | .20 |
| **23** | A2 | 3r multi | 1.00 | .35 |
| **24** | A2 | 4r multi | 2.00 | .50 |
| **25** | A2 | 5r multi | 2.75 | .65 |
| | | *Nos. 19-25 (7)* | 7.65 | 2.30 |

18th Olympic Games, Tokyo, Oct. 10-25, 1964. Perf. and imperf. souvenir sheets contain 4 stamps similar to #22-25 in changed colors. Size: 145x115mm.

A3

A4

Designs: 10np, Pres. Kennedy's funeral cortege leaving White House. 15np, Mrs. Kennedy with children, and Robert Kennedy following coffin. 50np, Horse-drawn caisson. 1r, Presidents Truman and Eisenhower, and Margaret Truman Daniels. 2r, Pres. Charles de Gaulle, Emperor Haile Selassie, Chancellor Ludwig Erhart, Sir Alec Douglas-Home and King Frederick IX. 3r, Kennedy family on steps of St. Matthew's Cathedral. 5r, Honor guard at tomb. 7.50r, Portrait of Pres. John F. Kennedy.

***Perf. 14½***
**1965, Jan. 20 Unwmk. Photo.**
**Black Design with Gold Inscriptions**

**Size: 29x44mm**

| | | | | |
|---|---|---|---|---|
| **26** | A3 | 10np pale blue | .20 | .20 |
| **27** | A3 | 15np pale yellow | .20 | .20 |
| **28** | A3 | 50np pale green | .20 | .20 |
| **29** | A3 | 1r pale pink | .30 | .20 |
| **30** | A3 | 2r pale green | .60 | .20 |

**Size: 33x51mm**

| | | | | |
|---|---|---|---|---|
| **31** | A3 | 3r pale gray | 1.00 | .20 |
| **32** | A3 | 5r pale blue | 1.75 | .30 |
| **33** | A3 | 7.50r pale yellow | 2.50 | .50 |
| | | *Nos. 26-33 (8)* | 6.75 | 2.00 |

Pres. John F. Kennedy. A souvenir sheet contains 2 stamps similar to Nos. 32-33 with pale green (5r) and pale salmon (7.50r) backgrounds, size: 29x44mm. Size of sheet: 114x70mm.

**1969, Nov. 19 Litho. *Perf. 14½***

Designs: 10d, Astronaut on Moon. 20d, Landing module approaching moon. 30d, Apollo XII on launching pad. 50d, Commanders Charles Conrad, Jr., Alan L. Bean, Richard F. Gordon, Jr., earth and moon, horiz. 75d, Earth and Apollo XII, horiz. 1r, Sheik Ahmed, rocket and lunar landing module, horiz.

| | | | |
|---|---|---|---|
| **34** | A4 | 10d multi | .20 |
| **35** | A4 | 20d multi | .20 |
| **36** | A4 | 30d multi | .20 |

| | | | | |
|---|---|---|---|---|
| 37 | A4 | 50d emerald & multi | .25 | |
| 38 | A4 | 75d purple & multi | .40 | |
| 39 | A4 | 1r dk bl & multi | .60 | |
| | | *Nos. 34-39 (6)* | 1.85 | |

US Apollo XII moon landing mission, 11/14-24/69.

Two imperf. souvenir sheets of 3 exist, containing stamps similar to Nos. 34-36 and Nos. 37-39.

A5 A7

A6

**1970, May 29 Litho. *Perf. 14***

| | | | | |
|---|---|---|---|---|
| 40 | A5 | 10d James A. Lovell | .20 | |
| 41 | A5 | 30d Fred W. Haise, Jr. | .20 | |
| 42 | A5 | 50d John L. Swigert, Jr. | .20 | |
| a. | | Souv. sheet of 3, #40-42 | .40 | |
| | | *Nos. 40-42 (3)* | .60 | |

Safe return of the crew of Apollo 13.

**1970, Aug. 14 Litho. *Perf. 13½x14***

Designs: 5d, 1.25r, EXPO '70 Emblem. 10d, 20d, Japanese Pavilion.

| | | | | |
|---|---|---|---|---|
| 43 | A6 | 5d yellow & multi | .20 | |
| 44 | A6 | 10d blue & multi | .20 | |
| 45 | A6 | 20d red & multi | .20 | |
| 48 | A6 | 1.25r red & multi | .25 | |
| | | *Nos. 43-48 (4)* | .85 | |

EXPO '70 Intl. Exhib., Osaka, Japan, Mar. 15-Sept. 13, 1970.

A 40d and 1r, showing the Emperor and Empress of Japan, and a souvenir sheet containing these and Nos. 43-45, 48 were prepared, but not issued.

**1970, Oct. 12 Litho. *Perf. 14½x14***

Uniforms: 10d, Private, North Lancashire Regiment. 20d, Royal Navy seaman. 30d, Officer, North Lancashire (Loyal) Regiment. 50d, Private, York and Lancaster Regiment. 75d, Royal Navy officer. 1r, Officer, York and Lancaster Regiment.

| | | | | |
|---|---|---|---|---|
| 49 | A7 | 10d multi | .20 | |
| 50 | A7 | 20d multi | .25 | |
| 51 | A7 | 30d multi | .35 | |
| a. | | Souv. sheet of 3, #49-51 | 1.50 | |
| 52 | A7 | 50d buff & multi | .70 | |
| 53 | A7 | 75d multi | 1.00 | |
| 54 | A7 | 1r buff & multi | 1.50 | |
| a. | | Souv. sheet of 3, #52-54 | 3.50 | |
| | | *Nos. 49-54 (6)* | 4.00 | |

British landings on the Trucial Coast, 150th anniv.

Stamps of Umm al Qiwain were replaced in 1972 by those of United Arab Emirates.

### AIR POST STAMPS

Type of Regular Issue, 1964

**Photogravure and Lithographed**

**1965 Unwmk. *Perf. 14***

**Size: 42x26mm**

| | | | | |
|---|---|---|---|---|
| C1 | A1 | 15np as #1 | .20 | .20 |
| C2 | A1 | 25np as #2 | .20 | .20 |
| C3 | A1 | 35np as #3 | .20 | .20 |
| C4 | A1 | 50np as #4 | .60 | .20 |
| C5 | A1 | 75np as #5 | 1.00 | .20 |
| C6 | A1 | 1r as #6 | 1.25 | .20 |

**Size: 52x33mm**

| | | | | |
|---|---|---|---|---|
| C7 | A1 | 2r as #7 | 2.00 | .40 |
| C8 | A1 | 3r as #8 | 3.00 | .70 |
| C9 | A1 | 5r as #9 | 4.00 | 1.00 |
| | | *Nos. C1-C9 (9)* | 12.45 | 3.30 |

Issued: #C7-C9, Nov. 6; others, Oct. 18.

### AIR POST OFFICIAL STAMPS

Type of Regular Issue, 1964

**Photogravure and Lithographed**

**1965, Dec. 22 Unwmk. *Perf. 14***

**Size: 42x26mm**

| | | | | |
|---|---|---|---|---|
| CO1 | A1 | 75np as #6 | .50 | .20 |

**Size: 52x33mm**

| | | | | |
|---|---|---|---|---|
| CO2 | A1 | 2r as #7 | 1.00 | .40 |
| CO3 | A1 | 3r as #8 | 1.25 | .50 |
| CO4 | A1 | 5r as #9 | 2.25 | 1.00 |
| | | *Nos. CO1-CO4 (4)* | 5.00 | 2.10 |

### OFFICIAL STAMPS

Type of Regular Issue, 1964

**Photogravure and Lithographed**

**1965, Dec. 22 Unwmk. *Perf. 14***

**Size: 42x26mm**

| | | | | |
|---|---|---|---|---|
| O1 | A1 | 25np as #1 | .30 | .20 |
| O2 | A1 | 40np as #2 | .40 | .20 |
| O3 | A1 | 50np as #3 | .60 | .20 |
| O4 | A1 | 75np as #4 | 1.00 | .20 |
| O5 | A1 | 1r as #5 | 1.25 | .25 |
| | | *Nos. O1-O5 (5)* | 3.55 | 1.05 |

# UNITED ARAB EMIRATES

yu-ˌnī-təd ˈar-əb i-ˈmiˌə̧r-əts

(Trucial States)

LOCATION — Arabia, on Arabian Gulf
GOVT. — Federation of sheikdoms
AREA — 32,300 sq. mi.
POP. — 2,377,453 (1995)
CAPITAL — Abu Dhabi

The UAE was formed Dec. 2, 1971, by the union of Abu Dhabi, Ajman, Dubai, Fujeira, Sharjah and Umm al Qiwain. Ras al Khaima joined in Feb. 1972.

1,000 Fils = 1 Dinar
100 Fils = 1 Dirham (1973)

**Catalogue values for all unused stamps in this country are for Never Hinged items.**

Abu Dhabi Nos. 56-67 Overprinted

دولة الامارات العربية المتحدة

## UAE

**1972, Aug. Litho. Unwmk. *Perf. 14***

| | | | | |
|---|---|---|---|---|
| 1 | A10 | 5f multicolored | 3.00 | 3.00 |
| 2 | A10 | 10f multicolored | 3.00 | 3.00 |
| 3 | A10 | 25f multicolored | 4.50 | 4.50 |
| 4 | A10 | 35f multicolored | 6.00 | 6.00 |
| 5 | A10 | 50f multicolored | 10.00 | 10.00 |
| 6 | A10 | 60f multicolored | 11.00 | 11.00 |
| 7 | A10 | 70f multicolored | 15.00 | 15.00 |
| 8 | A10 | 90f multicolored | 18.00 | 18.00 |
| 9 | A11 | 125f multicolored | 60.00 | 60.00 |
| 10 | A11 | 150f multicolored | 80.00 | 80.00 |
| 11 | A11 | 500f multicolored | 190.00 | 190.00 |
| 12 | A11 | 1d multicolored | 375.00 | 375.00 |
| | | *Nos. 1-12 (12)* | 775.50 | 775.50 |

The overprint differs.

#1-12 were used in Abu Dhabi. #2-3 were placed on sale later in Dubai & Sharjah.

Map and Flag of UAE A1

Almagta Bridge, Abu Dhabi — A2

Designs: 10f, Like 5f. 15f, 35f, Coat of arms of UAE (eagle). 75f, Khor Fakkan, Sharjah. 1d, Steel Clock Tower, Dubai. 1.25d, Buthnah Fort, Fujeira. 2d, Alfalaj Fort, Umm al Qiwain. 3d, Khor Khwair, Ras al Khaima. 5d, Palace of Sheik Rashid bin Humaid al Nuaimi, Ajman. 10d, Sheik Zaid bin Sultan al Nahayan, Abu Dhabi.

**1973, Jan. 1 Unwmk. *Perf. 14½***

**Size: 41x25mm**

| | | | | |
|---|---|---|---|---|
| 13 | A1 | 5f multicolored | .20 | .20 |
| 14 | A1 | 10f multicolored | .20 | .20 |
| 15 | A1 | 15f blue & multi | .45 | .20 |
| 16 | A1 | 35f olive & multi | .75 | .30 |

***Perf. 14x15***

**Size: 45x29½mm**

| | | | | |
|---|---|---|---|---|
| 17 | A2 | 65f multicolored | 1.25 | 1.25 |
| 18 | A2 | 75f multicolored | 1.50 | 1.25 |
| 19 | A2 | 1d multicolored | 2.00 | 1.25 |
| 20 | A2 | 1.25d multicolored | 4.25 | 2.00 |
| 21 | A2 | 2d multicolored | 47.50 | 12.50 |
| 22 | A2 | 3d multicolored | 8.75 | 6.75 |
| 23 | A2 | 5d multicolored | 10.50 | 7.00 |
| 24 | A2 | 10d multicolored | 22.50 | 15.00 |
| | | *Nos. 13-24 (12)* | 99.85 | 47.90 |

For surcharge see No. 68.

Festival Emblem A3

**1973, Mar. 27 Litho. *Perf. 13½x14***

| | | | | |
|---|---|---|---|---|
| 25 | A3 | 10f shown | 7.50 | .30 |
| 26 | A3 | 1.25d Trophy | 17.50 | 10.00 |

National Youth Festival, Mar. 27.

Pedestrian Crossing in Dubai — A4

35f, Traffic light school crossing sign, vert. 1.25d, Traffic policemen with car & radio, vert.

**1973, Apr. 1 *Perf. 13½x14, 14x13½***

| | | | | |
|---|---|---|---|---|
| 27 | A4 | 35f green & multi | 4.00 | 2.00 |
| 28 | A4 | 75f blue & multi | 8.00 | 4.00 |
| 29 | A4 | 1.25d violet & multi | 12.50 | 7.50 |
| | | *Nos. 27-29 (3)* | 24.50 | 13.50 |

Traffic Week, Apr. 1-7.

Human Rights Flame and People — A5

**1973, Dec. 10 Litho. *Perf. 14½x14***

| | | | | |
|---|---|---|---|---|
| 30 | A5 | 35f blue, blk & org | 1.25 | .80 |
| 31 | A5 | 65f red, blk & org | 6.00 | 2.00 |
| 32 | A5 | 1.25d olive, blk & org | 9.00 | 4.00 |
| | | *Nos. 30-32 (3)* | 16.25 | 6.80 |

25th anniversary of the Universal Declaration of Human Rights.

UPU and Arab Postal Union Emblems — A6

**1974, Aug. 5 Litho. *Perf. 14x14½***

| | | | | |
|---|---|---|---|---|
| 33 | A6 | 25f multicolored | 2.00 | 1.00 |
| 34 | A6 | 60f emerald & multi | 4.00 | 2.00 |
| 35 | A6 | 1.25d lt brown & multi | 7.50 | 4.50 |
| | | *Nos. 33-35 (3)* | 13.50 | 7.50 |

Centenary of Universal Postal Union.

Health Care — A7

Education — A8

Designs: 65f, Construction. 1.25d, UAE flag, UN and Arab League emblems.

**1974, Dec. 2 Litho. *Perf. 13½***

| | | | | |
|---|---|---|---|---|
| 36 | A7 | 10f multicolored | 1.10 | .40 |
| 37 | A8 | 35f multicolored | 3.25 | 1.10 |
| 38 | A8 | 65f blue & brown | 3.00 | 1.50 |
| 39 | A8 | 1.25d multicolored | 7.00 | 3.50 |
| | | *Nos. 36-39 (4)* | 14.35 | 6.50 |

Third National Day.

Arab Man and Woman Holding Candle over Book — A9

Man and Woman Reading Book — A10

**1974, Dec. 27 *Perf. 14x14½, 14½x14***

| | | | | |
|---|---|---|---|---|
| 40 | A9 | 35f deep ultra & multi | 2.75 | .60 |
| 41 | A10 | 65f orange brn & multi | 3.50 | 1.25 |
| 42 | A10 | 1.25d gray & multi | 7.50 | 2.50 |
| | | *Nos. 40-42 (3)* | 13.75 | 4.35 |

World Literacy Day.

Oil De-gassing Station — A11

50f, Off-shore drilling platform. 100f, Underwater storage tank. 125f, Oil production platform.

**1975, Mar. 10 Litho. *Perf. 13x13½***

| | | | | |
|---|---|---|---|---|
| **43** | A11 | 25f multicolored | 1.50 | .50 |
| **44** | A11 | 50f multicolored | 3.00 | 1.00 |
| **45** | A11 | 100f multicolored | 7.50 | 2.50 |
| **46** | A11 | 125f multicolored | 11.00 | 4.00 |
| *a.* | | Souvenir sheet of 4, #43-46 | 40.00 | 27.50 |
| | | *Nos. 43-46 (4)* | 23.00 | 8.00 |

9th Arab Petroleum Conference.

Three stamps to commemorate the 2nd Gulf Long Distance Swimming Championship were prepared in June, 1975, but not issued. Value $500.

Jabal Ali Earth Station — A12

Jabal Ali Earth Station: 35f, 65f, Communications satellite over globe.

**1975, Nov. 8 Litho. *Perf. 13***

| | | | | |
|---|---|---|---|---|
| **47** | A12 | 15f multicolored | 1.00 | .30 |
| **48** | A12 | 35f multicolored | 3.50 | .75 |
| **49** | A12 | 65f multicolored | 3.50 | 1.00 |
| **50** | A12 | 2d multicolored | 11.00 | 3.00 |
| | | *Nos. 47-50 (4)* | 19.00 | 5.05 |

Various Scenes — A13

Sheik Hamad, Fujeira Ruler — A14

Supreme Council Members (Sheikdom rulers): 60f, Sheik Rashid bin Humaid al Naimi, Ajman. 80f, Sheik Ahmed bin Rashid al Mulla, Umm al Qiwain. 90f, Sheik Sultan bin Mohammed al Qasimi, Sharjah. 1d, Sheik Saqr bin Mohammed al Qasimi, Ras al Khaima. 140f, Sheik Rashid bin Said al Maktum, Dubai. 5d, Sheik Zaid bin Sultan al Nahayan, Abu Dhabi.

**1975, Dec. 2 Litho. *Perf. 14***

| | | | | |
|---|---|---|---|---|
| **51** | A13 | 10f multicolored | .75 | .20 |
| **52** | A14 | 35f multicolored | 2.00 | .75 |
| **53** | A14 | 60f multicolored | 3.00 | 1.50 |
| **54** | A14 | 80f multicolored | 4.00 | 2.50 |
| **55** | A14 | 90f multicolored | 4.50 | 2.75 |
| **56** | A14 | 1d multicolored | 4.50 | 3.00 |
| **57** | A14 | 140f multicolored | 7.50 | 3.75 |
| **58** | A14 | 5d multicolored | 30.00 | 15.00 |
| | | *Nos. 51-58 (8)* | 56.25 | 29.45 |

Fourth National Day.

Students and Lamp of Learning — A15

Arab Literacy Day: 15f, Lamp of learning.

**1976, Feb. 8 Litho. *Perf. 14***

| | | | | |
|---|---|---|---|---|
| **59** | A15 | 15f orange & multi | 1.25 | .30 |
| **60** | A15 | 50f ultra & multi | 2.25 | 1.25 |
| **61** | A15 | 3d multicolored | 12.50 | 7.00 |
| | | *Nos. 59-61 (3)* | 16.00 | 8.55 |

Children Crossing Street — A16

Traffic Week: 15f, Traffic lights and signals, vert. 80f, Road and traffic lights.

***Perf. 14½x14, 14x14½***

**1976, Apr. 1 Litho.**

| | | | | |
|---|---|---|---|---|
| **62** | A16 | 15f brt blue & multi | 2.00 | 1.00 |
| **63** | A16 | 80f blue & multi | 8.00 | 3.75 |
| **64** | A16 | 140f ocher & multi | 17.50 | 10.00 |
| | | *Nos. 62-64 (3)* | 27.50 | 14.75 |

Waves and Ear Phones, ITU Emblem, Coat of Arms — A17

**1976, May 17 Litho. *Perf. 14***

| | | | | |
|---|---|---|---|---|
| **65** | A17 | 50f gray grn & multi | 1.50 | .60 |
| **66** | A17 | 80f pink & multi | 3.25 | 1.50 |
| **67** | A17 | 2d tan & multi | 6.50 | 3.00 |
| | | *Nos. 65-67 (3)* | 11.25 | 5.10 |

International Telecommunications Day.

No. 18 Surcharged

**1976 Litho. *Perf. 14x15***

| | | | | |
|---|---|---|---|---|
| **68** | A2 | 50f on 75f multi | *70.00* | *22.50* |

Coat of Arms — A18

**1976, Aug. 15 Litho. *Perf. 11½***

| | | | | |
|---|---|---|---|---|
| **69** | A18 | 5f dull rose | .25 | *.25* |
| **70** | A18 | 10f golden brown | .25 | .20 |
| **71** | A18 | 15f orange | .40 | .25 |
| **72** | A18 | 35f dull red brn | .65 | .20 |
| **73** | A18 | 50f bright lilac | .85 | .20 |
| **74** | A18 | 60f bister | .95 | .20 |
| **75** | A18 | 80f yellow green | 1.25 | .30 |
| **76** | A18 | 90f ultra | 1.40 | .50 |
| **77** | A18 | 1d blue | 2.00 | .50 |
| **78** | A18 | 140f olive green | 2.50 | 1.10 |
| **79** | A18 | 150f rose violet | 2.50 | 1.25 |
| **80** | A18 | 2d slate | 3.50 | 1.75 |
| **81** | A18 | 5d blue green | 9.00 | 4.25 |
| **82** | A18 | 10d lilac rose | 17.50 | 8.75 |
| | | *Nos. 69-82 (14)* | 43.00 | 19.70 |

See Nos. 91-104.

Sheik Zaid — A19

**1976, Dec. 12 Litho. *Perf. 13***

| | | | | |
|---|---|---|---|---|
| **83** | A19 | 15f rose & multi | 4.50 | .50 |
| **84** | A19 | 140f blue & multi | 10.00 | 4.00 |

5th National Day.

Symbolic Falcon and Globe — A20

**1976, Dec. 15 *Perf. 14x13½***

| | | | | |
|---|---|---|---|---|
| **85** | A20 | 80f yellow & multi | 6.00 | 1.50 |
| **86** | A20 | 2d red & multi | 11.00 | 6.00 |

International Falconry Congress, Abu Dhabi, Dec. 1976.

A21

A22

**1976, Dec. 30 Litho. *Perf. 13***

| | | | | |
|---|---|---|---|---|
| **87** | A21 | 50f multicolored | 5.00 | 1.50 |
| **88** | A21 | 80f multicolored | 10.00 | 3.00 |

Mohammed Ali Jinnah (1876-1948), 1st Governor General of Pakistan.

**1977, Apr. 12 Litho. *Perf. 13½x14***

APU emblem, members' flags.

| | | | | |
|---|---|---|---|---|
| **89** | A22 | 50f multicolored | 6.00 | 1.50 |
| **90** | A22 | 80f multicolored | 9.00 | 3.50 |

Arab Postal Union, 25th anniversary.

Arms Type of 1976

**1977, July 25 Litho. *Perf. 11½***

| | | | | |
|---|---|---|---|---|
| **91** | A18 | 5f dull rose & blk | .35 | .30 |
| **92** | A18 | 10f gldn brn & blk | .35 | .30 |
| **93** | A18 | 15f dull org & blk | .50 | .40 |
| **94** | A18 | 35f lt brown & blk | 1.25 | .45 |
| **95** | A18 | 50f brt lilac & blk | 1.50 | .50 |
| **96** | A18 | 60f bister & blk | 1.60 | .55 |
| **97** | A18 | 80f yel grn & blk | 1.60 | .55 |
| **98** | A18 | 90f ultra & blk | 2.50 | .85 |
| **99** | A18 | 1d blue & blk | 3.75 | 1.25 |
| **100** | A18 | 140f ol grn & blk | 5.50 | 1.75 |
| **101** | A18 | 150f rose vio & blk | 6.00 | 2.00 |
| **102** | A18 | 2d slate & blk | 9.00 | 3.00 |
| **103** | A18 | 5d bl grn & blk | 20.00 | 7.50 |
| **104** | A18 | 10d lil rose & bl | 35.00 | 22.50 |
| | | *Nos. 91-104 (14)* | 88.90 | 41.90 |

Man Reading Book, UAE Arms, UN Emblem A23

**1977, Sept. 8 Litho. *Perf. 14x13½***

| | | | | |
|---|---|---|---|---|
| **105** | A23 | 50f green, brn & gold | 2.00 | .50 |
| **106** | A23 | 3d blue & multi | 8.00 | 3.50 |

International Literacy Day.

A set of three stamps for the 6th Natl. Day was withdrawn from sale on the day of issue, Dec. 2, 1977. Value, $850.

Post Horn and Sails — A24

**1979, Apr. 14 Photo. *Perf. 12x11½***

| | | | | |
|---|---|---|---|---|
| **107** | A24 | 50f multicolored | 1.25 | 1.00 |
| **108** | A24 | 5d multicolored | 8.50 | 6.00 |

Gulf Postal Organization, 2nd Conf., Dubai.

Arab Achievements — A25

**1980, Mar. 22 Litho. *Perf. 14x14½***

| | | | | |
|---|---|---|---|---|
| **109** | A25 | 50f multicolored | .75 | .50 |
| **110** | A25 | 140f multicolored | 2.25 | 1.25 |
| **111** | A25 | 3d multicolored | 4.50 | 2.75 |
| | | *Nos. 109-111 (3)* | 7.50 | 4.50 |

9th National Day — A26

**1980, Dec. 2 Litho. *Perf. 13½***

| | | | | |
|---|---|---|---|---|
| **112** | A26 | 15f multicolored | .60 | .35 |
| **113** | A26 | 50f multicolored | 2.00 | 1.00 |
| **114** | A26 | 80f multicolored | 2.50 | 1.50 |
| **115** | A26 | 150f multicolored | 3.75 | 2.25 |
| | | *Nos. 112-115 (4)* | 8.85 | 5.10 |

**Souvenir Sheet**

***Perf. 13½x14***

| | | | | |
|---|---|---|---|---|
| **116** | A26 | 3d multicolored | 15.00 | 15.00 |

Family on Graph — A27

Hegira (Pilgrimage Year) — A28

**1980, Dec. 15**

117 A27 15f shown .80 .35
118 A27 80f Symbols 2.75 1.25
119 A27 90f like #118 3.50 2.25
120 A27 2d like #117 7.25 5.00
*Nos. 117-120 (4)* 14.30 8.85

1980 population census.

**1980, Dec. 18** ***Perf. 14x13½***

121 A28 15f multicolored .50 .25
122 A28 80f multicolored 2.00 1.25
123 A28 90f multicolored 2.75 1.50
124 A28 140f multicolored 4.25 2.50
*Nos. 121-124 (4)* 9.50 5.50

**Souvenir Sheet**

125 A28 2d multicolored 11.50 11.50

No. 125 contains one 36x57mm stamp.

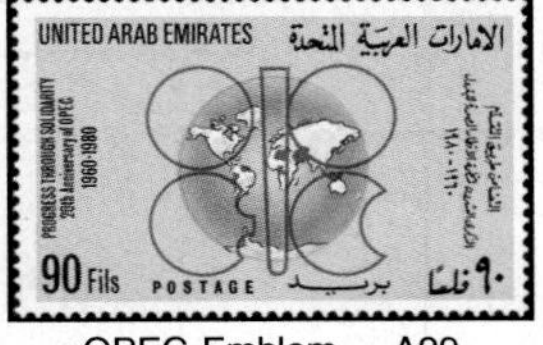


OPEC Emblem — A29

**1980, Dec. 21** ***Perf. 14***

126 A29 50f Men holding OPEC emblem, vert. 1.25 .50
127 A29 80f like #126 2.00 1.25
128 A29 90f shown 2.25 1.50
129 A29 140f like #128 4.00 2.25
*Nos. 126-129 (4)* 9.50 5.50

**Souvenir Sheet**

130 A29 3d like #128 16.00 16.00

Traffic Week — A30

15f, 80f, Crossing guard, students, traffic light. 50f, 5d, Crossing guard, traffic light and signs.

**1981, Mar. 26** **Litho.** ***Perf. 14½***

131 A30 15f multicolored .65 .30
132 A30 50f multicolored 1.25 .75
133 A30 80f multicolored 2.50 1.50
134 A30 5d multicolored 11.00 7.50
*Nos. 131-134 (4)* 15.40 10.05

Size of Nos. 131 and 133: 25½x35mm.

10th Natl. Day — A31

**1981, Dec. 2** **Litho.** ***Perf. 15x14***

135 A31 25f Cogwheel .75 .40
136 A31 150f Soldiers 5.00 2.50
137 A31 2d UN emblem 6.50 3.00
*Nos. 135-137 (3)* 12.25 5.90

Intl. Year of the Disabled — A32

***Perf. 14½x14, 14x14½***

**1981, Dec. 26** **Litho.**

138 A32 25f Couple .75 .35
139 A32 45f Man in wheelchair, vert. 1.50 1.10
140 A32 150f like #139 5.00 2.50
141 A32 2d like #138 7.50 3.25
*Nos. 138-141 (4)* 14.75 7.20

Natl. Arms — A33

**1982-86**

142 A33 5f multicolored .20 .20
143 A33 10f multicolored .20 .20
144 A33 15f multicolored .20 .20
145 A33 25f multicolored .20 .20
145A A33 35f multicolored .20 .20
146 A33 50f multicolored .40 .40
147 A33 75f multicolored .60 .60
148 A33 100f multicolored .90 .90
149 A33 110f multicolored 1.00 1.00
150 A33 125f multicolored 1.50 1.40
151 A33 150f multicolored 1.75 1.25
151A A33 175f multicolored 2.00 1.25

**Size: 23x27mm**

***Perf. 13***

152 A33 2d multicolored 2.00 1.50
152A A33 250f multicolored 2.25 1.25
153 A33 3d multicolored 3.25 1.75
154 A33 5d multicolored 5.50 3.00
155 A33 10d multicolored 12.00 7.50
156 A33 20d multicolored 22.50 12.50
157 A33 50d multicolored 45.00 22.50
*Nos. 142-157 (19)* 101.65 57.80

Issued: 35f, 175f, 250f, 12/15/84; 50d, 2/6/86; others, 3/7/82.

6th Arab Gulf Soccer Championships — A34

**1982, Apr. 4** **Litho.** ***Perf. 14***

167 A34 25f Emblem, flags 1.00 .50
168 A34 75f Eagle, soccer ball, stadium, vert. 3.00 2.00
169 A34 125f Players, vert. 4.00 2.50
170 A34 3d like 75f, vert. 9.00 6.50
*Nos. 167-170 (4)* 17.00 11.50

2nd Disarmament Meeting A35

**1982, Oct. 24** **Litho.** ***Perf. 13x13½***

171 A35 25f multicolored .60 .25
172 A35 75f multicolored 1.90 1.10
173 A35 125f multicolored 3.25 2.25
174 A35 150f multicolored 3.75 2.75
*Nos. 171-174 (4)* 9.50 6.35

11th Natl. Day — A36

Designs: 25f, 150f, Skyscraper, communications tower, natl. crest, castle turret, open book, flag. 75f, 125f, Sun, bird, vert.

**1982, Dec. 2** **Litho.** ***Perf. 14½***

175 A36 25f multicolored .50 .35
176 A36 75f multicolored 2.25 1.50
177 A36 125f multicolored 3.00 2.00
178 A36 150f multicolored 3.50 2.50
*Nos. 175-178 (4)* 9.25 6.35

A37

A38

**1983, Dec. 20** **Litho.** ***Perf. 14x14½***

179 A37 25f multicolored .75 .25
180 A37 150f multicolored 3.25 1.50
181 A37 2d multicolored 4.50 2.75
182 A37 3d multicolored 6.50 3.50
*Nos. 179-182 (4)* 15.00 8.00

World Communications Year.

**1983, Jan. 8** **Litho.** ***Perf. 14½***

Arab Literacy Day: 25f, 75f, Oil lamp, open Koran. 35f, 3d, Scribe.

183 A38 25f multicolored *42.50 60.00*
184 A38 35f multicolored 1.50 .80
185 A38 75f multicolored *42.50 55.00*
186 A38 3d multicolored 10.00 5.00

Nos. 183 and 185 withdrawn from sale on day of issue because of an error in Koranic inscription.

INTELSAT, 20th Anniv. — A39

**1984, Nov. 24** **Litho.** ***Perf. 14½***

187 A39 2d multicolored 5.50 5.00
188 A39 2.50d multicolored 8.00 7.00

13th Natl. Day A40

Flag, portrait of an Emir and building or view from each capital.

**1984, Dec. 2** ***Perf. 14½x13½***

189 A40 1d Building, pavilion 2.50 1.50
190 A40 1d Fortress, cannon 2.50 1.50
191 A40 1d Port, boats 2.50 1.50
192 A40 1d Fortress 2.50 1.50
193 A40 1d Oil refinery 2.50 1.50
194 A40 1d Building, garden 2.50 1.50
195 A40 1d Oil well, palace 2.50 1.50
*Nos. 189-195 (7)* 17.50 10.50

Tidy Week — A41

A42

**1985, Mar. 15** ***Perf. 12½***

196 A41 5d multicolored 11.50 10.00

**1985, Sept. 10** ***Perf. 13½x14½***

197 A42 2d multicolored 6.50 4.00
198 A42 250f multicolored 9.00 6.00

World Junior Chess Championships, Sharjah, Sept. 10-27.

14th Natl. Day — A43

**1985, Dec. 2** ***Perf. 14x13½***

199 A43 50f multicolored .75 .50
200 A43 3d multicolored 6.50 4.00

Population Census — A44

**1985, Dec. 16**

201 A44 50f multicolored 1.00 .50
202 A44 1d multicolored 2.75 1.25
203 A44 3d multicolored 7.00 3.25
*Nos. 201-203 (3)* 10.75 5.00

Intl. Youth Year A45

**1985, Dec. 23** ***Perf. 14½***

204 A45 50f Silhouettes, sapling, vert. .90 .60
205 A45 175f Globe, open book 2.75 1.50
206 A45 2d Youth carrying world, vert. 3.50 2.00
*Nos. 204-206 (3)* 7.15 4.10

Women and Family Day — A46

**1986, Mar. 21** *Perf. 13½*

| | | | | |
|---|---|---|---|---|
| **207** | A46 1d multicolored | | 1.50 | 1.00 |
| **208** | A46 3d multicolored | | 4.00 | 3.00 |

General Postal Authority, 1st Anniv. A47

Designs: 50f, 250f, Posthorn, map, natl. flag, globe. 1d, 2d, Emblem, globe, vert.

**1986, Apr. 1**

| | | | |
|---|---|---|---|
| **209** | A47 50f multicolored | .60 | .50 |
| **210** | A47 1d multicolored | 1.25 | .80 |
| **211** | A47 2d multicolored | 3.25 | 2.25 |
| **212** | A47 250f multicolored | 3.50 | 2.75 |
| | *Nos. 209-212 (4)* | 8.60 | 6.30 |

United Arab Shipping Co., 10th Anniv. A48

**1986, Aug. 20** *Perf. 13x13½*

| | | | |
|---|---|---|---|
| **213** | A48 2d shown | 4.50 | 2.75 |
| **214** | A48 3d Ship's bow, vert. | 5.50 | 3.75 |

A49

A51

Hawk — A50

**1986, Sept. 1** *Perf. 13½x13*

| | | | |
|---|---|---|---|
| **215** | A49 250f multicolored | 4.25 | 1.65 |
| **216** | A49 3d multicolored | 5.25 | 1.90 |

Emirates Telecommunications Corp., Ltd., 10th anniv.

**1986, Sept. 9 Photo.** *Perf. 15x14*

**Booklet Stamps**

**Background Color**

| | | | |
|---|---|---|---|
| **217** | A50 50f pale green | .75 | .75 |
| **218** | A50 75f pink | 1.25 | 1.25 |
| **219** | A50 125f gray | 2.00 | 2.00 |
| *a.* | Bklt. pane, 75f, 125f, 2 50f | 8.00 | |
| | *Nos. 217-219 (3)* | 4.00 | 4.00 |

**1986, Oct. 25** *Perf. 13½*

| | | | |
|---|---|---|---|
| **220** | A51 50f Jet, camel | 1.75 | 1.25 |
| **221** | A51 175f Jet | 5.50 | 4.25 |

Emirates Airlines, 1st anniv.

State Crests, GCC Emblem A52

**1986, Nov. 2** *Perf. 13*

| | | | |
|---|---|---|---|
| **222** | A52 50f shown | .80 | .60 |
| **222A** | A52 175f like no. 223 | 2.75 | 2.25 |
| **223** | A52 3d Tree, emblem | 4.50 | 4.25 |
| | *Nos. 222-223 (3)* | 8.05 | 7.10 |

Gulf Cooperation Council supreme council 7th session, Abu Dhabi, Nov. 1986. No. 222A incorrectly inscribed "1.75f."

15th Natl. Day — A53

**1986, Dec. 2 Litho.** *Perf. 13½*

| | | | |
|---|---|---|---|
| **224** | A53 50f shown | 1.00 | .50 |
| **225** | A53 1d like 50f | 2.25 | 1.50 |
| **226** | A53 175f Flag, emblem | 4.00 | 2.50 |
| **227** | A53 2d like 175f | 4.50 | 3.00 |
| | *Nos. 224-227 (4)* | 11.75 | 7.50 |

27th Chess Olympiad, Dubai — A54

**1986, Nov. 14** *Perf. 12½*

| | | | |
|---|---|---|---|
| **228** | A54 50f Skyscraper, vert. | 1.25 | .75 |
| **229** | A54 2d shown | 5.00 | 4.00 |
| **230** | A54 250f Tapestry, diff. | 6.50 | 5.00 |
| *a.* | Souv. sheet, #228-230, perf 13 | 16.00 | 16.00 |
| | *Nos. 228-230 (3)* | 12.75 | 9.75 |

No. 230a exists imperf. Value, $35.

Arab Police Day — A55

**1986, Dec. 18** *Perf. 13½*

| | | | |
|---|---|---|---|
| **231** | A55 50f multicolored | 1.75 | 1.00 |
| **232** | A55 1d multicolored | 3.00 | 2.50 |

A56

A57

**1987, Mar. 15**

| | | | |
|---|---|---|---|
| **233** | A56 50f multicolored | 1.75 | 1.00 |
| **234** | A56 1d multicolored | 3.00 | 2.50 |

Municipalities and Environment Week.

**1987, Apr. 10**

| | | | |
|---|---|---|---|
| **235** | A57 200f multicolored | 3.50 | 3.50 |
| **236** | A57 250f multicolored | 4.00 | 4.00 |

UAE Flight Information Region, 1st anniv.

A58

A59

**1987, May 25**

| | | | |
|---|---|---|---|
| **237** | A58 50f Water | 1.00 | 1.00 |
| **238** | A58 2d Solar energy, oil well | 8.50 | 8.50 |

Conservation.

**1987, June 23**

| | | | |
|---|---|---|---|
| **239** | A59 1d multicolored | 1.75 | 1.75 |
| **240** | A59 3d multicolored | 4.50 | 4.50 |

United Arab Emirates University, 10th anniv.

1st Shipment of Crude Oil from Abu Dhabi, 25th Anniv. — A60

**1987, July 4** *Perf. 13*

| | | | |
|---|---|---|---|
| **241** | A60 50f Oil rig | .75 | .75 |
| **242** | A60 1d Drilling well, vert. | 1.75 | 1.75 |
| **243** | A60 175f Crew, drill | 2.75 | 2.75 |
| **244** | A60 2d Oil tanker | 3.00 | 3.00 |
| | *Nos. 241-244 (4)* | 8.25 | 8.25 |

Arab Palm Tree and Date Day — A61

**1987, Sept. 15 Litho.** *Perf. 14x15*

| | | | |
|---|---|---|---|
| **245** | A61 50f shown | .90 | .90 |
| **246** | A61 1d Tree, fruit, diff. | 1.60 | 1.60 |

A62

A63

**1987, Nov. 21 Litho.** *Perf. 13x13½*

| | | | |
|---|---|---|---|
| **247** | A62 2d multicolored | 2.75 | 2.75 |
| **248** | A62 250f multicolored | 3.25 | 3.25 |

Intl. Year of Shelter for the Homeless.

**1987, Dec. 15** *Perf. 13½*

| | | | |
|---|---|---|---|
| **249** | A63 1d multicolored | 2.00 | 2.00 |
| **250** | A63 2d multicolored | 4.00 | 4.00 |

Salim Bin Ali Al-Owais (b. 1887), poet.

UN Child Survival Campaign A64

Abu Dhabi Intl. Airport, 6th Anniv. A65

**1987, Oct. 25 Litho.** *Perf. 13*

| | | | |
|---|---|---|---|
| **251** | A64 50f Growth monitoring | .60 | .50 |
| **252** | A64 1d Immunization | 1.25 | 1.00 |
| **253** | A64 175f Oral rehydration therapy | 2.00 | 1.75 |
| **254** | A64 2d Breast feeding, horiz. | 2.25 | 1.90 |
| | *Nos. 251-254 (4)* | 6.10 | 5.15 |

**1988, Jan. 2**

| | | | |
|---|---|---|---|
| **255** | A65 50f Control tower | .85 | .85 |
| **256** | A65 50f Terminal interior | .85 | .85 |
| **257** | A65 100f Aircraft over airport | 2.00 | 2.00 |
| **258** | A65 100f Aircraft at gates | 2.00 | 2.00 |
| | *Nos. 255-258 (4)* | 5.70 | 5.70 |

Natl. Arts Festival A66

**1988, Mar. 21 Litho.** *Perf. 13½*

| | | | |
|---|---|---|---|
| **259** | A66 50f multicolored | 1.00 | 1.00 |
| **260** | A66 250f multicolored | 3.50 | 3.50 |

Youth Cultural Festival A67

Winning children's drawings of a design contest sponsored by the Ministry of Education and the Sharjah Cultural and Information Department.

*Perf. 13x13½, 13½x13*

**1988, May 25 Litho.**

**261** A67 50f Net fisherman .75 .50
**262** A67 1d Woman 1.40 1.25
**263** A67 1.75d Youth as flower 2.25 2.00
**264** A67 2d Recreation 2.75 2.50
*Nos. 261-264 (4)* 7.15 6.25

Palestinian Uprising — A68

**1988, June 28 Litho.** *Perf. 13½*

**265** A68 2d multicolored 2.75 2.25
**266** A68 250f multicolored 3.50 2.75

A69

Banks — A70

**1988, July 16 Litho.** *Perf. 13½*

**267** A69 50f multicolored 2.25 2.25
**268** A70 50f multicolored 2.25 2.25

Abu Dhabi Natl. Bank, Ltd., 20th anniv. (No. 267); Natl. Bank of Dubai, Ltd., 25th anniv. (No. 268).

Port Rashid, Dubai, 16th Anniv. — A71

**1988, Aug. 31 Litho.** *Perf. 13½*

**269** A71 50f Ground transportation .60 .60
**270** A71 1d Piers 1.25 1.25
**271** A71 175f Ship at dock 2.50 2.50
**272** A71 2d Ship, unloading cranes 2.75 2.75
*Nos. 269-272 (4)* 7.10 7.10

1988 Summer Olympics, Seoul — A72

**1988, Sept. 17** *Perf. 15x14½*

**273** 2d Swimming 3.25 3.25
**274** 250f Cycling 4.00 4.00
*a.* A72 Pair, #273-274 7.50 7.50

Ras Al Khaima Natl. Museum, 1st Anniv. — A74

**1988, Nov. 19 Litho.** *Perf. 14*

**275** A74 50f Vase, vert. .60 .50
**276** A74 3d Gold crown 3.00 2.50

18th Arab Scout Conference, Nov. 29-Dec. 3, Abu Dhabi — A75

**1988, Nov. 29** *Perf. 12½*

**277** A75 1d multicolored 1.20 1.20

10th Arbor Day — A76

*Perf. 13½x13, 13x13½*

**1989, Mar. 6 Litho.**

**278** A76 50f Ghaf, vert. .60 .60
**279** A76 100f Palm 1.25 1.25
**280** A76 250f Dahlia blossom 2.75 2.75
*Nos. 278-280 (3)* 4.60 4.60

Sharjah Intl. Airport, 10th Anniv. A77

**1989, Apr. 21 Litho.** *Perf. 13½*

**281** A77 50f multicolored .75 .75
**282** A77 100f multicolored 1.75 1.75

Postal Service, 80th Anniv. A78

**1989, Aug. 19 Litho.** *Perf. 13x13½*

**283** A78 50f Seaplane 1.00 1.00
**284** A78 3d Ship 6.50 6.50

Al-Ittihad Newspaper, 20th Anniv. — A79

**1989, Oct. 20 Litho.** *Perf. 13½*

**285** A79 50f shown .75 .75
**286** A79 1d Al Ittihad Press 1.25 1.25

Gulf Investment Corporation, 5th Anniv. — A80

**1989, Nov. 25**

**287** A80 50f multicolored .65 .65
**288** A80 2d multicolored 3.00 3.00

Child on Crutches, Hands — A81

Bank Building — A82

Designs: 2d, Crouched youth, cracked earth, bread in hand, horiz.

**1989, Dec. 5** *Perf. 15x14, 14x15*

**289** A81 2d multicolored 2.75 2.75
**290** A81 250f shown 3.25 3.25

Intl. Volunteer's Day, Red Crescent Soc.

**1989, Dec. 20** *Perf. 13½*

**291** A82 50f Emblem, architecture .75 .75
**292** A82 1d shown 1.25 1.25

Commercial Bank of Dubai, Ltd., 20th Anniv.

Astrolabe, Manuscript Page and Ship of Bin Majid, 15th Cent. Navigator and Writer A83

**1989, Dec. 25** *Perf. 13x13½, 13½x13*

**293** A83 1d shown 1.25 1.25
**294** A83 3d Ship, page, vert. 4.25 4.25

Heritage revival.

A84

Falcon — A85

**1990, Jan. 17** *Perf. 13½*

**295** A84 50f multicolored .75 .75
**296** A84 1d multicolored 1.90 1.90

3rd Al Ain festival.

**1990, Feb. 17 Litho.** *Perf. 11½*

**Granite Paper**

**297** A85 5f multicolored .20 .20
**298** A85 20f multicolored .20 .20
**299** A85 25f multicolored .20 .20
**301** A85 50f multicolored .45 .40
**302** A85 100f multicolored 2.25 1.25
**303** A85 150f multicolored 3.75 1.75
**304** A85 175f multicolored 4.00 2.00

**Size: 21x26mm**

*Perf. 11½x12*

**306** A85 2d multicolored 5.00 2.75
**307** A85 250f multicolored 5.50 3.00
**309** A85 3d multicolored 7.00 3.50
**310** A85 5d multicolored 10.00 6.00
**311** A85 10d multicolored 20.00 12.00
**312** A85 20d multicolored 35.00 21.00
**313** A85 50d multicolored 90.00 55.00
*Nos. 297-313 (14)* 183.55 109.25

A86

A87

**1990, Mar. 10 Litho.** *Perf. 13½*

**316** A86 50f multicolored .60 .60
**317** A86 250f multicolored 2.50 2.50

Children's cultural festival.

**1990, Aug. 5 Litho.** *Perf. 14x15*

**318** A87 175f shown 1.90 1.90
**319** A87 2d Starving child 2.50 2.50

Red Crescent Society.

Dubai Chamber of Commerce and Industry, 25th Anniv. A88

**1990, July 1** *Perf. 13*

**320** A88 50f multicolored .75 .75
**321** A88 1d multicolored 1.50 1.50

World Cup Soccer Championships, Italy — A89

UAE emblem, character trademark and: 1d, Leaning Tower of Pisa, desert, vert. 2d, Soccer ball, vert. 250f, Circle of flags. 3d, Map, vert.

**1990, June 8** *Perf. 13½*

**322** A89 50f multicolored .75 .75
**323** A89 1d multicolored 1.50 1.50
**324** A89 2d multicolored 3.00 3.00
**325** A89 250f multicolored 4.00 4.00
*Nos. 322-325 (4)* 9.25 9.25

**Souvenir Sheet**

*Perf. 12½*

**326** A89 3d multicolored 7.00 7.00

A90

A91

**1990, Sept. 22 Litho. *Perf. 13½***

**327** A90 50f shown .75 .75
**328** A90 1d Emblem, 30 years 2.25 2.25
**329** A90 175f Emblem, drop of oil 3.50 3.50
*Nos. 327-329 (3)* 6.50 6.50

Organization of Petroleum Exporting Countries (OPEC), 30th anniv.

**1990, Aug. 25 *Perf. 14x14½***

Flowers.

**330** A91 50f Argyrolobeum roseum .90 .90
**331** A91 50f Lamranthus roseus .90 .90
**332** A91 50f Centavrea pseudo sinaica .90 .90
**333** A91 50f Calotropis procera .90 .90
*a.* Souvenir sheet of 4, #330-333 4.50 4.50
**334** A91 50f Nerium oleander .90 .90
**335** A91 50f Catharanthus roseus .90 .90
**336** A91 50f Hibiscus rosa sinensis .90 .90
**337** A91 50f Bougainvillea glabra .90 .90
*a.* Souvenir sheet of 4, #334-337 4.50 4.50
*Nos. 330-337 (8)* 7.20 7.20

A92

A93

**1990, Oct. 8 Litho. *Perf. 13***

**338** A92 50f Water pollution .50 .50
**339** A92 3d Air pollution 3.25 3.25

Environmental pollution.

**1990, Dec. 2 *Perf. 13½***

**340** A93 50f shown .50 .50
**341** A93 175f Bank building, horiz. 3.25 3.25

Central Bank, 10th anniv.

Intl. Conference on High Salinity Tolerant Plants — A94

**1990, Dec. 8 *Perf. 13x13½***

**342** A94 50f Tree .50 .50
**343** A94 250f Water, trees 2.75 2.75

Grand Mosque, Abu Dhabi — A95

2d, Al Jumeirah Mosque, Dubai, vert.

***Perf. 13½x13, 13x13½***

**1990, Nov. 26**

**344** A95 1d multicolored 1.10 1.10
**345** A95 2d multicolored 4.50 4.50

A96

A98

A97

**1991, Jan. 16 Litho. *Perf. 13x13½***

**346** A96 50f multicolored .80 .80
**347** A96 2d multicolored 2.25 2.25

Abu Dhabi Intl. Fair.

**1991, May 17 Litho. *Perf. 14x13½***

**348** A97 2d multicolored 3.00 3.00
**349** A97 3d multicolored 4.50 4.50

World Telecommunications Day.

**1991, June 18 *Perf. 13½***

**350** A98 1d Sheikh Saqr Mosque 1.50 1.50
**351** A98 2d King Faisal Mosque 3.25 3.25

Children's Paintings A99

Designs: 50f, Celebration. 1d, Women waving flags. 175f, Women playing blind-man's buff. 250f, Women dancing for men.

**1991, July 15 Litho. *Perf. 14x13½***

**352** A99 50f multicolored .60 .45
**353** A99 1d multicolored 1.25 .90
**354** A99 175f multicolored 2.25 2.00
**355** A99 250f multicolored 2.75 2.25
*Nos. 352-355 (4)* 6.85 5.60

Fish A100

**1991, Aug. 5 Litho. *Perf. 13½x14***

**356** A100 50f Yellow marked butterflyfish .60 .60
**357** A100 50f Golden trevally .60 .60
**358** A100 50f Two banded porgy .60 .60
**359** A100 50f Red snapper .60 .60
**360** A100 1d Three banded grunt 1.25 1.25
**361** A100 1d Rabbit fish 1.25 1.25
**362** A100 1d Black bream 1.25 1.25
**363** A100 1d Greasy grouper 1.25 1.25
*a.* Min. sheet of 8, #356-363 8.50 8.50
*Nos. 356-363 (8)* 7.40 7.40

A101

A103

A102

Intl. Aerospace Exhibition, Dubai: 175f, Jet fighter over Dubai Intl. Airport. 2d, Fighter silhouette over airport.

**1991, Nov. 3 Litho. *Perf. 13½***

**364** A101 175f multicolored 2.25 2.25
**365** A101 2d multicolored 2.50 2.50

**1991, Oct. 7 *Perf. 13***

Sheikh Rashid Bin Said Al Maktum (1912-90), Ruler of Dubai and: 50f, Airport, vert. 175f, City skyline, vert. 2d, Waterfront, satellite dish.

**366** A102 50f multicolored .50 .50
**367** A102 1d multicolored 1.10 1.10
**368** A102 175f multicolored 2.00 2.00
**369** A102 2d multicolored 2.25 2.25
*Nos. 366-369 (4)* 5.85 5.85

**1991, Oct. 8 Litho. *Perf. 13½***

**370** A103 50f multicolored .75 .75
**371** A103 1d multicolored 1.75 1.75

Civil Defense Day.

A104

A105

A106

20th Natl. Day — A107

#374, Emir at left, fortress, cannon. #377, Fortress on rocky outcropping. #378, Emir at right, fortress, cannon. 3d, Sheikh Said bin Sultan al Nahayan, Defense Forces.

**1991, Dec. 2 Litho. *Perf. 13***

**372** A104 75f multicolored 1.20 1.20
**373** A105 75f multicolored 1.20 1.20
**374** A105 75f multicolored 1.20 1.20
**375** A106 75f multicolored 1.20 1.20
**376** A107 75f multicolored 1.20 1.20
**377** A107 75f multicolored 1.20 1.20
**378** A107 75f multicolored 1.20 1.20

***Imperf***

**Size: 70x90mm**

**378A** A107 3d multicolored 8.00 8.00
*Nos. 372-378A (8)* 16.40 16.40

On Nos. 372-378 portions of the design were applied by a thermographic process producing a shiny, raised effect.

A108

A109

**1991, Nov. 16 *Perf. 13½***

**379** A108 50f lt green & multi .45 .45
**380** A108 3d orange & multi 3.75 3.75

Gulf Cooperaton Council, 10th anniv.

**1992, Jan. 15 Litho. *Perf. 13½***

**381** A109 175f pink & multi 2.20 2.20
**382** A109 250f lt blue & multi 2.50 2.50

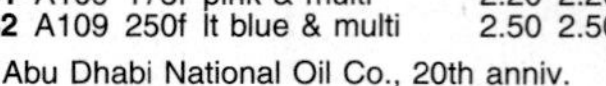

Abu Dhabi National Oil Co., 20th anniv.

Al-Jahli Castle Al-Ain A110

**1992, Apr. 20 Litho. *Perf. 13½***

**383** A110 2d multicolored 2.00 2.00
**384** A110 250f multicolored *60.00 60.00*

Expo '92, Seville.

No. 384 was withdrawn because of poor rendition of Arabic word for "postage."

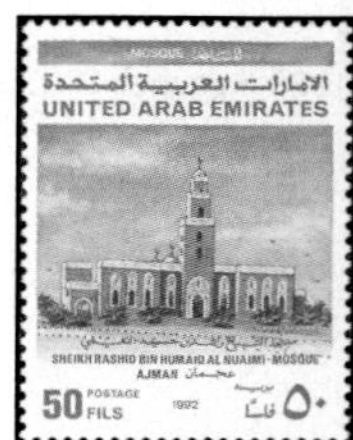


A111

A112

Mosques: 50f, Sheikh Rashid bin Humaid al Nuaimi, Ajman. 1d, Sheikh Ahmed Bin Rashid Al Mualla, Umm Al Quwain.

**1992, Mar. 26** ***Perf. 14x13½***
**385** A111 50f multicolored .80 .80
**386** A111 1d multicolored 1.60 1.60

See Nos. 417-418.

**1992, Apr. 20** ***Perf. 13½x13***
**387** A112 1d shown 1.75 1.75
**388** A112 3d Ear with hearing aid 4.00 4.00

Week of the deaf child.

Zayed Seaport, 20th Anniv. — A113

**1992, June 28** **Litho.** ***Perf. 13½***
**389** A113 50f Aerial view .50 .50
**390** A113 1d Cargo transport 1.25 1.25
**391** A113 175f Ship docked 2.25 2.25
**392** A113 2d Map 2.50 2.50
*Nos. 389-392 (4)* 6.50 6.50

1992 Summer Olympics, Barcelona
A114

**1992, July 25** **Litho.** ***Perf. 14x13½***
**393** A114 50f Yachting .50 .50
**394** A114 1d Running 1.00 1.00
**395** A114 175f Swimming 2.00 2.00
**396** A114 250f Cycling 2.25 2.25
*Nos. 393-396 (4)* 5.75 5.75

**Souvenir Sheet**

**396A** A114 3d Equestrian 5.75 5.75

Children's Paintings
A115

**1992, Aug. 15** ***Perf. 13½x14***
**397** A115 50f Playing soccer .50 .50
**398** A115 1d Playing in field 1.00 1.00
**399** A115 2d Playground 2.25 2.25
**400** A115 250f Children among trees 3.00 3.00
*Nos. 397-400 (4)* 6.75 6.75

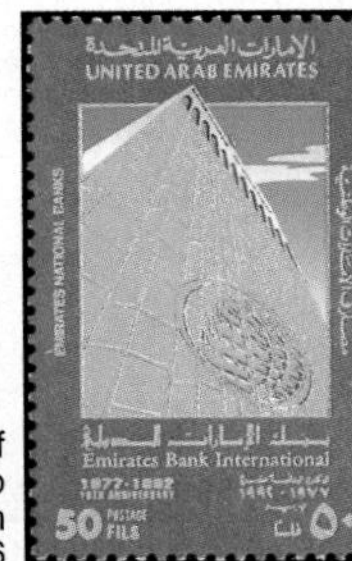

Intl. Bank of United Arab Emirates, 15th Anniv. — A116

Design: 175f, Bank emblem.

**Litho. & Embossed**

**1992, Sept. 9** ***Perf. 11***
**401** A116 50f gold & multi .65 .65

**Size: 35x41mm**

***Perf. 11½***

**402** A116 175f lake, gold & vio 2.00 2.00

Traditional Musical Instruments — A116a

**1992, Oct. 17** **Litho.** ***Perf. 13½***
**402A** A116a 50f Tambourah, vert. .60 .60
**402B** A116a 50f Oud, vert. .60 .60
**402C** A116a 50f Rababah, vert. .60 .60
*g.* Sheet, #402A-402C, perf. 12¾ 1.75 1.75
**402D** A116a 1d Mizmar, shindo 1.20 1.20
**402E** A116a 1d Tabel, hibban 1.20 1.20
**402F** A116a 1d Marwas, duff 1.20 1.20
*h.* Sheet, #402D-402F, perf. 12¾ 3.50 3.50
*Nos. 402A-402F (6)* 5.40 5.40

Camels
A117

Designs: 50f, Race. 1d, Used for transportation, vert. 175f, Harnessed for obtaining water from well. 2d, Roaming free, vert.

**1992, Dec. 23** **Litho.** ***Perf. 13½***
**403** A117 50f multicolored .50 .30
**404** A117 1d multicolored 1.20 .65
**405** A117 175f multicolored 2.25 1.10
**406** A117 2d multicolored 2.50 1.25
*Nos. 403-406 (4)* 6.45 3.30

A118

A119

**1992, Dec. 21**
**407** A118 50f multicolored 1.25 1.25
**408** A118 2d yellow & multi 5.50 5.50

Gulf Cooperation Council, 13th session.

**1993, Jan. 28** **Litho.** ***Perf. 13½***
**409** A119 2d shown 2.50 2.50
**410** A119 250f Building, fishing boat 4.25 4.25

Dubai Creek Golf and Yacht Club.

A120

A121

**1993, Jan. 16**
**411** A120 50f Golf, horiz. .70 .70
**412** A120 1d Fishing 1.40 1.40
**413** A120 2d Boating, horiz. 2.75 2.75
**414** A120 250f Motor vehicle touring, horiz. 3.50 3.50
*Nos. 411-414 (4)* 8.35 8.35

Tourism.

**1993, Mar. 27** **Litho.** ***Perf. 14x13½***
**415** A121 50f violet & multi .70 .70
**416** A121 3d red brown & multi 3.75 3.75

Natl. Youth Festival.

Mosque Type of 1992

**1993, Feb. 16** ***Perf. 13½***

50f, Thabit bin Khalid Mosque, Fujeira. 1d, Sharq al Morabbah Mosque, Al Ain.

**417** A111 50f multicolored 1.25 1.25
**418** A111 1d multicolored 2.50 2.50

Shells
A122

**1993, Apr. 3** **Litho.** ***Perf. 13***
**419** A122 25f Conus textile .35 .35
**420** A122 50f Pinctada radiata .50 .50
**421** A122 100f Murex scolopax 1.00 1.00
**422** A122 150f Natica pulicaris 1.50 1.50
**423** A122 175f Lambis truncata sebae 2.00 2.00
**424** A122 200f Cardita bicolor 2.25 2.25
**425** A122 250f Cypraea grayana 2.75 2.75
**426** A122 300f Cymatium trilineatum 3.75 3.75
*Nos. 419-426 (8)* 14.10 14.10

Campaign Against Drugs
A123

Design: 1d, Skull, drugs, vert.

**1993, Aug. 21** **Litho.** ***Perf. 13½***
**427** A123 50f multicolored 1.60 1.60
**428** A123 1d multicolored 2.25 2.25

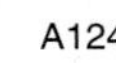
A124

A125

Natl. Bank of Abu Dhabi, 25th Anniv.: 50f, Abu Dhabi skyline, bank emblem. 1d, Bank emblem. 175f, Bank building, emblem. 2d, Skyline, emblem, diff.

**Litho. & Typo.**

**1993, Sept. 15** ***Perf. 11½***
**429** A124 50f silver & multi .50 .50
**430** A124 1d silver & multi 1.00 1.00
**431** A124 175f silver & multi 2.25 2.25
**432** A124 2d silver & multi 2.50 2.50
*Nos. 429-432 (4)* 6.25 6.25

**1993, Nov. 10** **Litho.** ***Perf. 13½***

Dubai Ports Authority: 50f, Aerial view of port. 1d, Loading cargo. 2d, Aerial view, diff. 250f, Globe.

**433** A125 50f purple & multi .55 .55
**434** A125 1d green & multi 1.25 1.25
**435** A125 2d orange & multi 2.75 2.75
**436** A125 250f pink & multi 3.50 3.50
*Nos. 433-436 (4)* 8.05 8.05

Natl. Day
A126

Children's paintings: 50f, Soldiers saluting flag. 1d, Two women sitting, one standing, flag, vert. 175f, Flag, boat. 2d, Flags atop castle tower.

**1993, Dec. 2** **Litho.** ***Perf. 13½***
**437** A126 50f multicolored .60 .60
**438** A126 1d multicolored 1.50 1.50
**439** A126 175f multicolored 2.75 2.75
**440** A126 2d multicolored 3.00 3.00
*Nos. 437-440 (4)* 7.85 7.85

Archaeological Discoveries — A127

Designs: 50f, Tomb. 1d, Rectangular artifact. 175f, Animal-shaped artifact. 250f, Bowl.

**1993, Dec. 15** ***Perf. 14x13½***
**441** A127 50f multicolored .60 .60
**442** A127 1d multicolored 1.40 1.40
**443** A127 175f multicolored 2.50 2.50
**444** A127 250f multicolored 3.25 3.25
*Nos. 441-444 (4)* 7.75 7.75

10th Childrens' Festival, Sharjah
A128

Children's paintings: 50f, Children with balloons, flags. 1d, Children playing, three trees. 175f, Child with picture, girls with balloons. 2d, House, children playing outdoors.

**1994, Mar. 19** **Litho.** ***Perf. 13x13½***
**445** A128 50f green & multi .55 .55
**446** A128 1d blue & multi 1.40 1.40
**447** A128 175f red violet & multi 2.25 2.25
**448** A128 2d carmine & multi 2.50 2.50
*Nos. 445-448 (4)* 6.70 6.70

Arabian Horses A129

50f, Brown horse on hind feet, vert. 1d, White horse. 175f, Head of brown horse, vert. 250f, Head of white and brown horse.

**1994, Jan. 25** ***Perf. 13x13½, 13½x13***

**449** A129 50f multicolored .55 .55
**450** A129 1d multicolored 1.20 1.20
**451** A129 175f multicolored 2.25 2.25
**452** A129 250f multicolored 3.00 3.00
*Nos. 449-452 (4)* 7.00 7.00

10th Conference of Arab Towns, Dubai A130

***Perf. 13x13½, 13½x13***

**1994, May 15** **Litho.**

**453** A130 50f Map, city, vert. .55 .55
**454** A130 1d shown 2.25 2.25

Pilgrimage to Mecca — A131

**1994, Apr. 29** **Litho.** ***Perf. 13x13½***

**455** A131 50f shown .75 .75
**456** A131 2d Holy Ka'aba 3.00 3.00

Intl. Year of the Family A132

Intl. Olympic Committee, Cent. A133

Arab Housing Day — A134

Writers Assoc., 10th Anniv. — A135

**1994, June 15** ***Perf. 13x13½***

**457** A132 1d multicolored 1.40 1.40
**458** A133 1d multicolored 1.40 1.40

***Perf. 13½x13***

**459** A134 1d multicolored 1.40 1.40
**460** A135 1d multicolored 1.40 1.40
*Nos. 457-460 (4)* 5.60 5.60

Archaeological Finds, Al Qusais, Dubai — A136

Designs: 50f, Lidded pitcher, vert. 1d, Pointed-handle pitcher. 175f, Pitcher, arm-shaped handle. 250f, Short round vase.

**1994, Aug. 16** **Litho.** ***Perf. 13½***

**461** A136 50f multicolored .55 .55
**462** A136 1d multicolored 1.30 1.30
**463** A136 175f multicolored 2.20 2.20
**464** A136 250f multicolored 3.00 3.00
*Nos. 461-464 (4)* 7.05 7.05

Environmental Protection — A137

Designs: 50f, Arabian leopard. 1d, Gordon's wildcat. 2d, Caracal. 250f, Sand cat.

**1994, Oct. 10** **Litho.** ***Perf. 13½***

**465** A137 50f multicolored .55 .55
**466** A137 1d multicolored 1.50 1.50
**467** A137 2d multicolored 3.25 3.25
**468** A137 250f multicolored 4.00 4.00
*Nos. 465-468 (4)* 9.30 9.30

12th Arab Gulf Soccer Championships, Abu Dhabi — A138

**1994, Nov. 3** **Litho.** ***Perf. 13½***

**469** A138 50f Ball, emblem, vert. .55 .55
**470** A138 3d Soccer players 3.75 3.75

Birds A139

50f, Merops orientalis. 175f, Halcyon chloris. 2d, Dromas ardeola. 250f, Coracias benghalensis. 3d, Phoenicopterus ruber.

**1994, Dec. 12**

**471** A139 50f multicolored .55 .55
**472** A139 175f multicolored 3.00 3.00
**473** A139 2d multicolored 3.25 3.25
**474** A139 250f multicolored 5.00 5.00
*Nos. 471-474 (4)* 11.80 11.80

**Souvenir Sheet**

**475** A139 3d multi, vert. 7.50 7.50

Archaeological Finds, Mulaiha, Sharjah — A140

Designs: 50f, Front of carved horse, vert. 175f, Ancient coin, vert. 2d, Inscription on metal, vert. 250f, Inscription on stone.

**1995, Jan. 25** **Litho.** ***Perf. 13½***

**476** A140 50f multicolored .45 .45
**477** A140 175f multicolored 1.75 1.75
**478** A140 2d multicolored 2.25 2.25
**479** A140 250f multicolored 2.50 2.50
*Nos. 476-479 (4)* 6.95 6.95

Natl. Dances A141

**1995, Feb. 14**

**480** A141 50f Al-Naashat .45 .45
**481** A141 175f Al-Ayaalah 2.00 2.00
**482** A141 2d Al-Shahhoh 2.25 2.25
*Nos. 480-482 (3)* 4.70 4.70

A142

A143

**1995, Mar. 19** **Litho.** ***Perf. 13½***

**483** A142 50f Helicopters .45 .45
**484** A142 1d Emblem 1.25 1.25
**485** A142 175f Warships, horiz. 2.50 2.50
**486** A142 2d Artillery, horiz. 3.00 3.00
*Nos. 483-486 (4)* 7.20 7.20

Intl. Defense Exhibition & Conf., Abu Dhabi.

**1995, Mar. 22**

**487** A143 1d Arab League emblem 1.25 1.25
**488** A143 2d FAO emblem 2.75 2.75
**489** A143 250f UN emblem 3.50 3.50
*Nos. 487-489 (3)* 7.50 7.50

50th Anniv. of Arab League, FAO & UN.

General Post Office Authority, 10th Anniv. — A144

**1995, Apr. 1**

**490** A144 50f multicolored .75 .75

First Gulf Cooperation Council Philatelic Exhibition, Abu Dhabi — A145

**1995, Apr. 11** **Litho.** ***Perf. 13½***

**491** A145 50f multicolored .75 .75

Traditional Games, Ajman Museum — A146

50f, Boy with hoop, stick. 175f, Girl on swing. 2d, Boy, girl playing stick game within marked boundary. 250f, Two girls playing game with stones.

**1995, Aug. 28** **Litho.** ***Perf. 13½x13***

**492** A146 50f multicolored .45 .45
**493** A146 175f multicolored 1.90 1.90
**494** A146 2d multicolored 2.25 2.25
**495** A146 250f multicolored 2.50 2.50
*Nos. 492-495 (4)* 7.10 7.10

A147

A148

Birds: 50f, Falco naumanni. 175f, Phalacrocorax nigrogularis. 2d, Cursorius cursor. 250f, Upupa epops.

**1995, Sept. 25**

**496** A147 50f multicolored .50 .50
**497** A147 175f multicolored 2.00 2.00
**498** A147 2d multicolored 2.25 2.25
**499** A147 250f multicolored 2.50 2.50
*Nos. 496-499 (4)* 7.25 7.25

See Nos. 528-532.

**1995, Nov. 20**

Natl. Census: 50f, Stylized family, building. 250f, Mosque, skyscrapers, stylized family.

**500** A148 50f multicolored .45 .45
**501** A148 250f multicolored 2.25 2.25

National Day A149

Children's paintings: 50f, People wearing feathered headdresses, palm trees, building. 175f, Girls with flags, balloons, flowers. 2d, Trees, family in front of house holding balloons, flags. 250f, Groups of children along street watching parade of cars.

**1995, Dec. 2** ***Perf. 13x13½***

**502** A149 50f multicolored .45 .45
**503** A149 175f multicolored 1.25 1.25
**504** A149 2d multicolored 1.40 1.40
**505** A149 250f multicolored 1.75 1.75
*Nos. 502-505 (4)* 4.85 4.85

Environmental Protection — A150

**1996, Jan. 25 Litho. *Perf. 13x13½***

**506** A150 50f Dugong dugon .50 .50
**507** A150 2d Delphinus delphis 1.50 1.50
**508** A150 3d Megaptera novaeangliae 2.25 2.25
*a.* Souvenir sheet, #506-508 4.75 4.75
*Nos. 506-508 (3)* 4.25 4.25

A151

A152

**1996, Feb. 27 *Perf. 13½***

**509** A151 50f shown .50 .50
**510** A151 3d Building, beach 2.75 2.75

Hobie Cat 16 World Sailing Championships.

**1996, Apr. 15**

Archaeological Finds, Fujeira Museum: 50f, Two-handled pitcher. 175f, Kettle. 250f, Bracelet. 3d, Metal ornament, horiz.

**511** A152 50f multicolored .50 .50
**512** A152 175f multicolored 1.25 1.25
**513** A152 250f multicolored 2.25 2.25
**514** A152 3d multicolored 2.75 2.75
*Nos. 511-514 (4)* 6.75 6.75

1996 Summer Olympic Games, Atlanta A153

***Perf. 13½x14, 14x 13½***

**1996, July 19 Litho.**

**515** A153 50f Shooting .50 .50
**516** A153 1d Cycling, vert. .80 .80
**517** A153 250f Running, vert. 2.00 2.00
**518** A153 350f Swimming 2.50 2.50
*Nos. 515-518 (4)* 5.80 5.80

Women's Union, 21st Anniv. A154

***Perf. 14x13½, 13½x14***

**1996, Aug. 15**

**519** A154 50f Emblem, vert. .50 .50
**520** A154 3d shown 2.75 2.75

A155

A156

**1996, Sept. 15 *Perf. 14x13½***

**521** A155 1d shown .75 .75
**522** A155 250f Soccer player 2.00 2.00

11th Asian Soccer Cup Championship.

**1996, Oct. 15 *Perf. 13½***

UN Campaign Against Illegal Use of Drugs: 50f, World with snake around it. 3d, Half of man's face, half of skull, hypodermic needle, pills.

**523** A156 50f multicolored .70 .70
**524** A156 3d multicolored 2.50 2.50

Sheikh Saeed Al-Maktoum House, Cent. — A157

Designs: 250f Sheikh Saeed, close-up view of house. 350f, Overall view of house.

**1996, Nov. 12 Litho. *Perf. 13x13½***

**525** A157 50f multicolored .50 .50
**526** A157 250f multicolored 1.75 1.75
**527** A157 350f multicolored 2.50 2.50

Bird Type of 1995

Designs: 50f, Pterocles exustus. 150f, Otus brucei. 250f, Hypocolus ampelinus. 3d, Irania gutturalis. 350f, Falco concolor.

**1996, Nov. 18 *Perf. 14x13½***

**528** A147 50f multicolored .35 .35
**529** A147 150f multicolored 1.25 1.25
**530** A147 250f multicolored 2.25 2.25
**531** A147 3d multicolored 3.00 3.00
**532** A147 350f multicolored 3.25 3.25

Children's Paintings A158

50f, Face. 1d, Boats. 250f, Flowers. 350f, Woman in long dress, palm tree, tent.

***Perf. 14x13½, 13½x14***

**1996, Nov. 19**

**533** A158 50f multi, vert. .35 .35
**534** A158 1d multi .80 .80
**535** A158 250f multi, vert. 2.25 2.25
**536** A158 350f multi, vert. 2.75 2.75

Sheik Zaid bin Sultan al Nahayan, Accession to the Throne of Abu Dhabi, 30th Anniv. A158a

A159

Sheik and: 50f, 250f, Flowers. 1d, 350f, Date palm.

**1996, Dec. 2 Photo. *Perf. 12***

**537** A158a 50f red & multi .40 .40
**538** A158a 1d olive & multi .65 .65
**539** A158a 250f purple & multi 1.60 1.60
**540** A158a 350f gray & multi 2.25 2.25
*Nos. 537-540 (4)* 4.90 4.90

**Photo. & Embossed**

***Imperf***

**Size: 90x70mm**

**541** A159 5d On horseback, gazelles 5.00 5.00

Anniversaries A160

Natl. Day, 25th Anniv. — A161

**Photo. & Embossed**

**1996, Dec. 2 *Perf. 12***

**542** A160 50f red violet & multi .30 .30
**543** A160 1d silver & multi .90 .90

Sheik Zaid bin Sultan al Nahayan's accession to the throne of Abu Dhabi, 30th anniv., Creation of United Arab Emirates, 25th anniv.

**1996, Dec. 2**

50f, 150f, Seven rulers of United Arab Emirates. 1d, 3d, Heraldic eagle, national flag. 5d, Score of Natl. Anthem.

**Granite Paper**

**544** A161 50f green & multi .50 .50
**545** A161 1d multicolored .75 .75
**546** A161 150f tan & multi 1.00 1.00
**547** A161 3d multicolored 2.00 2.00
*Nos. 544-547 (4)* 4.25 4.25

**Photo. & Embossed**

***Imperf***

**Size: 70x90mm**

**547A** A161 5d multicolored 4.75 4.75

Butterflies A162

**1997, Jan. 28 Litho. *Perf. 14x13½***

**548** A162 50f Agrodiaetus loewii .50 .50
**549** A162 1d Papilio machaon 1.00 1.00
**550** A162 150f Orithya 1.75 1.75
**551** A162 250f Chrysippus 3.00 3.00
*Nos. 548-551 (4)* 6.25 6.25

Dubai Shopping Festival A163

***Perf. 13¼x13¾, 13¾x13¼***

**1997, Feb. 22 Litho.**

**552** A163 50f shown .45 .45
**553** A163 250f Shopping bag, vert. 2.25 2.25

Intl. Defense Exhibition & Conference A164

50f, Helicopter airlifting jeep. 1d, Emblem. 250f, Artillery, emblem. 350f, Ships, emblem.

**1997, Mar. 16 Litho. *Perf. 13½***

**554** A164 50f multicolored .40 .40
**555** A164 1d multicolored .75 .75
**556** A164 250f multicolored 1.90 1.90
**557** A164 350f multicolored 2.50 2.50
*Nos. 554-557 (4)* 5.55 5.55

Emirates Bank Group, 20th Anniv. — A165

***Perf. 13¾x13¼***

**1997, Mar. 23 Litho.**

**568** A165 50f multi .55 .55
**569** A165 1d buff & multi 1.20 1.20
*a.* Souv. sheet, #568-569, imperf. 3.75 3.75

No. 569a sold for 5d.

Technical Education and National Development Conference A166

**1997, Apr. 6 *Perf. 13¾x13¼***

**570** A166 50f shown .50 .50
**571** A166 250f Emblem 2.50 2.50

Sharjah Heritage A167

Designs: 50f, Coins. 3d, Museum.

**1997, June 17 Litho. *Perf. 13½***

**572** A167 50f multicolored .60 .60
**573** A167 3d multicolored 2.75 2.75

Emirates Philatelic Association A168

*Perf. 13¾x13¼, 13¼x13¾*

**1997, June 24** **Litho.**

**574** A168 50f shown .45 .45
**575** A168 250f Stamps, horiz. 2.25 2.25

Children's Paintings A169

50f, Cats. 1d, Children playing. 250f, Children, moon, vert. 3d, Abstract.

**1997, Sept. 15** **Litho.** ***Perf. 13½***

**576** A169 50f multicolored .50 .50
**577** A169 1d multicolored .90 .90
**578** A169 250f multicolored 2.00 2.00
**579** A169 3d multicolored 2.50 2.50
*Nos. 576-579 (4)* 5.90 5.90

Reunion, by Sheikha Hassan Maktoum al Maktoum — A170

Mindscape, by Sarah Majid al Futtaim A170a

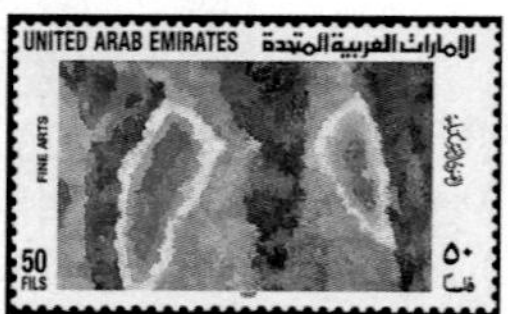
Blue Musings, by Maha Abdulla Al Mazroui — A170b

The Pause, by Khulood Mattar Rashid A170c

The Seas I, by Sheikha Sawsan Abdulaziz Al Qasimi — A170d

Still Life, by Sheikha Bodour Sultan Al Qasimi A170e

The Opening, by Tina Ahmed and Others — 170f

Illustration A170f reduced.

**1997, Oct. 25** **Litho.** ***Perf. 13¾***

**580** A170 50f multi .65 .65
**581** A170a 50f multi .65 .65
**582** A170b 50f multi .65 .65
**583** A170c 50f multi .65 .65
**584** A170d 50f multi .65 .65
**585** A170e 50f multi .65 .65
*Nos. 580-585 (6)* 3.90 3.90

***Imperf***

**586** A170f 5d multi 4.75 4.75

Intl. Aerospace Exhibition, Dubai A171

*Perf. 13½x13¾*

**1997, Nov. 16** **Litho.**

**587** A171 250f Jet fighter 2.50 2.50
**588** A171 3d VTOL airplane 3.25 3.25

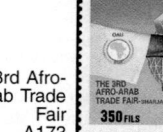

26th National Day A172

Sheikh Zaid bin Sultan al Nahayan and: 50f, Gardens. 1d, Trees and mountains. 150f, Water, trees and mountains. 250f, Roadway.

**1997, Dec. 2** **Litho.** ***Perf. 13½x13¾***

**589** A172 50f multi .45 .45
**590** A172 1d multi .75 .75
**591** A172 150f multi 1.20 1.20
**592** A172 250f multi 1.75 1.75
*Nos. 589-592 (4)* 4.15 4.15

3rd Afro-Arab Trade Fair A173

*Perf. 13x13¼, 13¼x13*

**1997, Dec. 6** **Litho.**

**593** A173 150f Emblem, vert. 1.20 1.20
**594** A173 350f Handshake 2.50 2.50

Arthropods A174

50f, Blepharopsis mendica. 150f, Galeodes sp. 250f, Crocothemis arythraea. 350f, Xylocopa aestuans.

**1998, Feb. 25** **Litho.** ***Perf. 13¼***

**595** A174 50f multicolored .45 .45
**596** A174 150f multicolored 1.25 1.25
**597** A174 250f multicolored 2.10 2.10
**598** A174 350f multicolored 3.00 3.00
*Nos. 595-598 (4)* 4.50

ISAF World Sailing Championship — A175

Various sailboats.

*Perf. 13¼x13, 13x13¼*

**1998, Mar. 2** **Litho.**

**599** A175 50f multi, vert. .45 .45
**600** A175 1d multi 1.25 1.25
**601** A175 250f multi 2.10 2.10
**602** A175 3d multi, vert. 3.00 3.00
*Nos. 599-602 (4)* 6.80 6.80

A176

A177

Triple Intl. Defense Exhibition & Conf., Abu Dhabi: 50f, Combat soldiers in protective gear, horiz. 1d, Emblem over world map, skyline of Abu Dhabi. 150f, Electronic gear. 350f, Missile battery, electronic warfare components.

**1998, Mar. 15** **Litho.** ***Perf. 13½***

**603** A176 50f multicolored .45 .45
**604** A176 1d multicolored 1.25 1.25
**605** A176 150f multicolored 2.10 2.10
**606** A176 350f multicolored 3.00 3.00
*Nos. 603-606 (4)* 6.80 6.80

**1998, Apr. 20** **Litho.** ***Perf. 13½***

**607** A177 50f shown .50 .50
**608** A177 3d Emblem, monument 3.75 3.75

Sharjah, 1998 Arab cultural capital.

World Environment Day — A178

**1998, May 17** **Litho.** ***Perf. 13½***

**609** A178 1d Landscape, oryx 1.75 1.75
**610** A178 350f multicolored 3.00 3.00

Henna A179

Various designs painted on hands.

**1998, Sept. 9** **Litho.** ***Perf. 13½***

**611** A179 50f multicolored .45 .45
**612** A179 1d multicolored .70 .70
**613** A179 150f multicolored 1.10 1.10
**614** A179 2d multicolored 1.40 1.40
**615** A179 250f multicolored 1.75 1.75
**616** A179 3d multicolored 2.10 2.10
*Nos. 611-616 (6)* 7.50 7.50

Art — A180

**1998, Oct. 20** **Litho.** ***Perf. 13½***

**617** A180 50f Fish .45 .45
**618** A180 1d shown .80 .80
**619** A180 250f Mosque, palm trees, vert. 2.00 2.00
**620** A180 350f Door, jar 3.00 3.00
*Nos. 617-620 (4)* 4.20

27th National Day A181

**1998, Dec. 2** **Litho.** ***Perf. 13x13¼***

**621** A181 50f Mountain road .45 .45
**622** A181 350f Boat, city skyline 4.25 4.25

Flowers — A182

Designs: 25f, Indigofera arabica. 50f, Centaureum pulchellum. 75f, Lavandula citriodora. 1d, Taverniera glabra. 150f, Convolvulus deserti. 2d, Capparis spinosa. 250f, Rumex vesicrius. 3d, Anagallis arvensis. 350f, Tribulus arabicus. 5d, Reichardia tinitana.

**1998, Dec. 8** **Litho.** ***Perf. 13¼x13¾***

**623** A182 25f multicolored .20 .20
**624** A182 50f multicolored .30 .30
**625** A182 75f multicolored .40 .40
**626** A182 1d multicolored .55 .55
**627** A182 150f multicolored .85 .85
**628** A182 2d multicolored 1.10 1.10
**629** A182 250f multicolored 1.40 1.40
**630** A182 3d multicolored 1.75 1.75
**631** A182 350f multicolored 1.90 1.90
**632** A182 5d multicolored 2.75 2.75
*Nos. 623-632 (10)* 11.20 11.20

Arthropods A183

50f, Anthia duodecimguttata. 150f, Daphnis nerii. 250f, Acorypha glaucopsis. 350f, Androctonus crassicauda.

**1999, Mar. 15** **Litho.** ***Perf. 13½x14***

**633** A183 50f multicolored .50 .50
**634** A183 150f multicolored 1.25 1.25
**635** A183 250f multicolored 2.50 2.50
**636** A183 350f multicolored 4.00 4.00
*Nos. 633-636 (4)* 8.25 8.25

Intl. Day for Monuments and Sites A184

**1999, Apr. 18** **Litho.** ***Perf. 13x13½***

**637** A184 150f shown 1.50 1.50
**638** A184 250f Fort 2.75 2.75

UPU, 125th Anniv. — A185

**1999 Litho. *Perf. 13½x13***
**639** A185 50f shown 1.00 1.00
**640** A185 350f Emblem, "125" 2.75 2.75

***Imperf***
**Size: 90x70mm**
**641** A185 5d Hemispheres 6.00 6.00

Environmental Protection — A186

Marine life: 50f, Lamprometra klunzingeri. 150f, Pelagia noctiluca. 250f, Hexabranchus sanguineus. 3d, Siphonochalina siphonella.

**1999, Nov. 3 Litho. *Perf. 13½x14***
**642** A186 50f multi .55 .55
**643** A186 150f multi 1.75 1.75
**644** A186 250f multi 3.00 3.00
**645** A186 3d multi 3.50 3.50
*Nos. 642-645 (4)* 8.80 8.80

Handicrafts A187

Designs: 50f, Lacemaking. 1d, Embroidery. 250f, Woman with wickerwork. 350f, Finished wickerwork.

**1999, Nov. 8 *Perf. 14x13½***
**646** A187 50f multi .50 .50
**647** A187 1d multi 1.25 1.25
**648** A187 250f multi 3.00 3.00
**649** A187 350f multi 4.50 4.50
*Nos. 646-649 (4)* 9.25 9.25

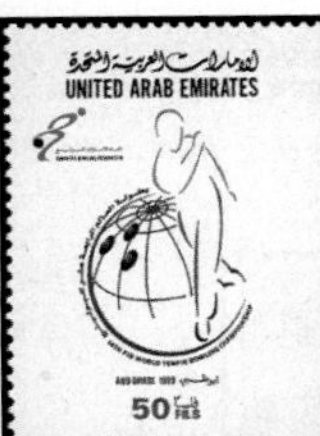
14th Pro World Ten-pin Bowling Championships A188

Designs: 50f, Emblem. 250f, Bowler, pins, Abu Dhabi skyline.

**1999, Nov. 16 Litho. *Perf. 14x13½***
**650-651** A188 Set of 2 3.25 3.25

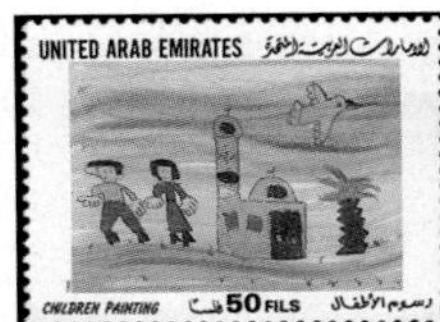
Children's Art — A189

Art by: 50f, Nooran Khaleefa. 1d, Khawla Al Hawal. 150f, Khawla Salem. 250f, Fatimah Ibrahim.

**1999, Dec. 15 *Perf. 13x13½***
**652-655** A189 Set of 4 5.75 5.75

Millennium A190

Falcon and "2000" in: 50f, Gray and silver. 250f, Blue and gold.

**1999, Dec. 22 *Perf. 13½x13***
**656-657** A190 Set of 2 2.75 2.75

Dubai Ports and Customs, Cent. A191

50f, Old building. 3d, Modern building.

**2000, Jan. 26 *Perf. 13x13½***
**658-659** A191 Set of 2 3.75 3.75

Intl. Desertification Conference, Dubai — A192

**2000, Feb. 12 *Perf. 13½x13***
**660** A192 250f multi 2.50 2.50

Environmental Protection — A193

Designs: 50f, Palm trees, Al Gheel. 250f, Aggah Beach.

**2000, Feb. 29 Litho. *Perf. 13x13½***
**661** A193 50f multi .50 .50
**662** A193 250f multi 2.25 2.25

2000 Summer Olympics, Sydney A194

Emblem and: 50f, Swimmer. 2d, Runner. 350f, Shooter.

**2000, Sept. 16 Litho. *Perf. 13x13½***
**663-665** A194 Set of 3 4.25 4.25

Dubai Intl. Holy Koran Award — A195

50f, Medal on ribbon of flags. 250f, Sheikh Zaid bin Sultan al Nahayan and UAE flag.

**2000, Sept. 23 *Perf. 13½x13***
**666-667** A195 Set of 2 4.25 4.25

World Meteorological Organization, 50th Anniv. — A196

Designs: 50f, Barometer and modern map. 250f, Gauge's pointer and old map .

**2000**
**668-669** A196 Set of 2 4.25 4.25

Expansion of Dubai Intl. Airport A197

Denominations: 50f, 350f.

**2000, Nov. 4 Litho. *Perf. 13x13½***
**670-671** A197 Set of 2 5.75 5.75

Development and Environment A198

Designs: 50f, Smile. 250f, Flower. 3d, Heart as leaf. 350f, Heart as globe.

**2001, Mar. 20 Litho. *Perf. 13¼x13***
**672-675** A198 Set of 4 10.00 10.00

Dubai Millennium, Winner of 2000 Dubai World Cup A199

Designs: 3d, Horse's head. 350f, Horse at track.

**2001, Mar. 24 *Perf. 13x13¼***
**676-677** A199 Set of 2 9.50 9.50

Sultan Bin Ali Al Owais (1925-2000), Poet — A200

Designs: 50f, Calligraphy. 1d, Portrait.

**2001, Apr. 30 *Perf. 13¼x13***
**678-679** A200 Set of 2 3.75 3.75

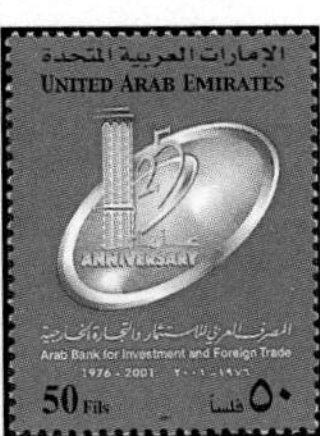
Arab Bank for Investment and Foreign Trade, 25th Anniv. — A201

Designs: 50f, Emblem. 1d, Emblem, diff.

**2001, July 7 Litho. *Perf. 13¼x13***
**680-681** A201 Set of 2 2.75 2.75

7th GCC Postage Stamp Exhibition, Dubai — A202

**2001, July 10**
**682** A202 50f multi 1.75 1.75

Traditional Boats A203

Designs: 50f, Shahoof. 250f, Bagarah. 3d, Sam'aa. 350f, Jalboot.

**2001, Aug. 25 *Perf. 14x13¼***
**683-686** A203 Set of 4 10.00 10.00

Year of Dialogue Among Civilizations A204

Designs: 50f, Emblem. 250f, Branch with multicolored leaves.

**2001, Oct. 9 *Perf. 13¼x13***
**687-688** A204 Set of 2 3.75 3.75

Emirates Post A205

Falcons and inscription: 50f, Changing. 250f, Growing. 3d, Achieving.

**2001, Sept. 15 *Perf. 13x13¼***
**689-691** A205 Set of 3 7.50 7.50

Children's Art — A206

Designs: 1d, Mosque. 250f, Boatbuilding. 3d, Man pouring coffee, vert. 350f, Falconry.

***Perf. 14x13¼, 13¼x14***
**2001, Nov. 12 Litho.**
**692-695** A206 Set of 4 10.50 10.50

Unification of Armed Forces, 25th Anniv. — A207

**2001, Dec. 30** ***Perf. 13¼x13***
**696** A207 1d multi 2.75 2.75

Intl. Water Resources and Management Conference, Dubai — A208

**2002, Feb. 2**
**697** A208 50f multi 2.00 2.00

UAE University, 25th Anniv. — A209

Background colors: 50f, Blue. 1d, Red.

**2002, Mar. 25** ***Perf. 13¼x14***
**698-699** A209 Set of 2 2.75 2.75

Arabian Saluki A210

Various salukis: 50f, 150f, 250f, 3d.

**2002, Apr. 29 Litho.** ***Perf. 13½x13¼***
**700-703** A210 Set of 4 10.50 10.50

Emirates Post, 1st Anniv. — A211

"1" and: 50f, Ring of text. 3d, Emblem.

**2002, May 29** ***Perf. 13¼x13***
**704** A211 50f blue 2.00 2.00

**Souvenir Sheet**

***Perf. 14¼***

**705** A211 3d multi 4.75 4.75

No. 705 contains one 45x35mm stamp.

Rashid Bin Salim Al-Suwaidi Al-Khadhar (1905-80), Poet A212

Designs: 50f, Text. 250f, Portrait.

**2002, July 17 Litho.** ***Perf. 13½x13¼***
**706-707** A212 Set of 2 6.50 6.50

Children's Creativity A213

Designs: 50f, Antelope and boat, by Amna al-Bloushi. 1d, Children, by Fahd al-Habsi. 2d, Earth holding flower, by Hana Mohammed. 250f, Fish, by Hatem al-Dhaheri. 3d, Child holding Earth, by Abdulla Ridha. 350f, Stick figures, by Yousef al-Sind. 5d, Emblem of Latifa Bint Mohammed Award for Childhood Creativity (29x39mm).

***Perf. 13x13¼, 13¼x13 (5d)***

**2002, Oct. 9**
**708-714** A213 Set of 7 17.50 17.50

Sheikh Hamdan Bin Rashid Al-Maktoum Award for Medical Sciences A214

Designs: 50f, Award, emblem, sand dunes. 250f, Caduceus, map.

**2002, Oct. 21** ***Perf. 13x13¼***
**715-716** A214 Set of 2 4.75 4.75

31st National Day — A215

Landmarks in the Emirates: Nos. 717, 724a, 50f, Ajman. Nos. 718, 724b, 50f, Sharjah. Nos. 719, 724c, 50f, Dubai. Nos. 720, 724d, 50f, Abu Dhabi. Nos. 721, 724e, 50f, Ras al Khaima. Nos. 722, 724f, Fujeira. Nos. 723, 724g, Umm al Qiwain.

**2002, Dec. 2 Litho.** ***Perf. 13¼x14***
**717-723** A215 Set of 7 7.50 7.50

**Souvenir Sheet**

**Litho. & Embossed**

***Imperf***

**724** Sheet of 7 7.50 7.50
***a.-g.*** A215 50f Any single 1.00 1.00

No. 724 sold for 5d.

Thuraya Satellite Communications A216

Denominations: 25f, 250f.

**2002 Litho.** ***Perf. 14***
**725-726** A216 Set of 2 2.75 2.75

Issued: 25f, 1/27; 250f, 1/6.

**Falcon Type of 1990**

**2003-04 Litho.** ***Perf. 11½***

**Granite Paper**

**726A** A85 125f multi .90 .90

**Size: 21x26mm**

***Perf. 11½x11¾***

**726B** A85 225f multi 1.50 1.50
**726C** A85 275f multi 2.00 2.00
**726D** A85 325f multi 2.75 2.75
**726E** A85 375f multi 1.90 1.90
**726F** A85 4d multi 2.25 2.25
**726G** A85 6d multi 3.00 3.00
*Nos. 726A-726G (7)* 14.30 14.30

Issued: 125f, 2/23; 225f, 11/24/04; 275f, 325f, 375f, 4/13; 4d, 6d, 9/16.

Items in Al Ain National Museum A217

Designs: 50f, Jar from Hili tombs. 275f, Pottery from Umm an-Nar tombs. 4d, Bronze axe. 6d, Soapstone vessel.

**2003, Feb. 25** ***Perf. 14x13½***
**727-730** A217 Set of 4 11.50 11.50

National Bank of Dubai, 40th Anniv. A218

Panel color: 50f, Blue. 4d, Orange. 6d, Red.

**2003, Apr. 15 Litho.** ***Perf. 14x13¼***
**731-733** A218 Set of 3 10.50 10.50

Miniature Sheet

Wildlife — A218a

No. 733A: b, Arabian leopard. c, Blanford's fox. d, Caracal. e, Cheetah. f, Gordon's wild cat. g, Striped hyena. h, Jackal. i, White-tailed mongoose. j, Ruppell's fox. k, Sand cat. l, Small spotted genet. m, Arabian wolf.

**2003, June 10 Litho.** ***Perf. 14½***
**733A** A218a 50f Sheet of 12, #b-m 3.25 3.25

Coins A219

Designs: 50f, Dirham of Caliph Al Walid bin Abdul Malik. 125f, Arab Sasanian Dirham of Caliph Abdul Malik Bin Marwan. 275f, Dinar of Al Mustansir Billah Al Fatimi. 375f, Dinar of Caliph Abdul Malik bin Marwan.
5d, Dirham of Caliph Muhammed Al Ameen to mark election of Mousa Al Natiq Bilhaq.

**2003, July 20 Litho.** ***Perf. 13¼x13¾***
**734-737** A219 Set of 4 7.50 7.50

**Size: 106x73mm**

***Imperf***

**738** A219 5d multi 20.00 20.00

Sheikh Zaid bin Sultan al Nahayan, 37th Anniv. of Accession as Ruler of Abu Dhabi A220

Sheikh Zaid and: 50f, Camel and sand dune. 175f, Modern buildings.

**2003, Aug. 6 Litho.** ***Perf. 13***
**739-740** A220 Set of 2 2.75 2.75

World Youth Soccer Championships, United Arab Emirates — A221

**2003, Sept. 7** ***Perf. 13x13¼***
**741** A221 375f multi 3.75 3.75

World Bank Boards of Governors Annual Meetings, Dubai — A222

Emblem and: 50f, Emirates Tower. 175f, Falcon. 275f, Mosque domes, horiz. 375f, Dhow. 5d, English and Arabic text.

***Perf. 13¼x13, 13x13¼***

**2003, Sept. 23 Litho.**
**742-745** A222 Set of 4 8.50 8.50

***Imperf***

**Size: 118x74mm**

**746** A222 5d multi 6.75 6.75

Peace A223

Dove and: 50f, Zakharafs. 225f, Door and wind tower. 275f, Columns. 325f, Water taxi.

**2003, Oct. 1** ***Perf. 13x13¼***
**747-750** A223 Set of 4 9.50 9.50

Traditional Housing A224

Designs: 50f, Palm frond house. 175f, Mud house. 275f, Stone house. 325f, Tent.

**2003, Oct. 20** ***Perf. 13½x14***
**751-754** A224 Set of 4 7.50 7.50

Falcons — A225

Designs: 50f, Peregrine falcon. 125f, Hybrid gyr-peregrine falcon. 275f, Gyrfalcon. 375f, Saker falcon.

**2003, Nov. 17** ***Perf. 13¼x14***
**755-758** A225 Set of 4 5.75 5.75

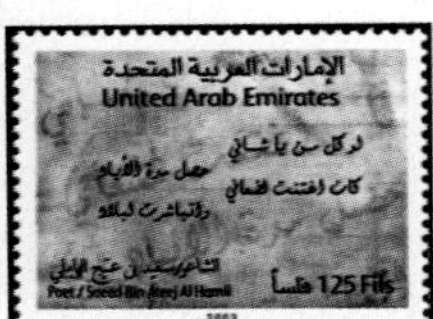

Poetry of Saeed Bin Ateej Al Hamli (1875-1919) A226

Poetry: 125f, Four short lines. 175f, Four long lines.

**2003, Dec. 29** ***Perf. 13x13¼***
**759-760** A226 Set of 2 3.25 3.25

Mohammed Bin Saeed Bin Ghubash (1899-1969), Religious Scholar — A227

Designs: 50f, Portrait. 175f, Books.

**2004, Apr. 5** **Litho.** ***Perf. 13¼x14***
**761-762** A227 Set of 2 3.25 3.25

Fourth Family Meeting — A228

Color of hands: 375f, Orange. 4d, Purple.

**2004, Apr. 19**
**763-764** A228 Set of 2 5.25 5.25

FIFA (Fédération Internationale de Football Association), Cent. — A229

**2004, May 21** **Litho.** ***Perf. 13x13¼***
**765** A229 375f multi 2.75 2.75

Handicrafts by Special Needs Persons — A230

Designs: 50f, Handcrafted vase. 125f, Painting. 275f, Framed branch. 5d, Pottery artwork.

**2004, June 29** ***Perf. 13¼x13***
**766-769** A230 Set of 4 5.25 5.25

2004 Summer Olympics, Athens A231

Olympic rings and: 50f, Track athlete. 125f, Rifle shooter. 275f, Swimmer. 375f, 2004 Athens Olympics emblem, torch bearer.

**2004, Aug. 13** **Litho.** ***Perf. 13x13¼***
**770-773** A231 Set of 4 4.50 4.50

Endangered or Extinct Persian Gulf Marine Life — A232

Designs: 50f, Black finless porpoise. 175f, Serranidae. 275f, Whale shark. 375f, Dugongidae.

**2004, Sept. 26** ***Perf. 14***
**774-777** A232 Set of 4 4.75 4.75
*777a* Booklet pane, 2 each #774-777 9.50 —
Complete booklet, #777a 9.50

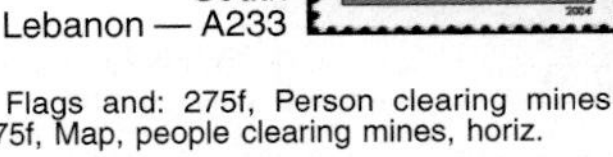

Operation Emirates Solidarity for Mine Clearance in South Lebanon — A233

Flags and: 275f, Person clearing mines. 375f, Map, people clearing mines, horiz.

**2004, Oct. 25** ***Perf. 13x12¾, 12¾x13***
**778-779** A233 Set of 2 3.50 3.50

Sheik Dr. Sultan bin Mohammed al-Qassimi, Ruler of Sharjah — A234

Color of denomination: 50f, Orange brown. 125f, Green. 275f, Red brown. 4d, Blue.

**2004, Nov. 30** ***Perf. 13½x14***
**780-783** A234 Set of 4 4.75 4.75

Traditional Women's Clothing — A235

Designs: 50f, Drawers. 125f, Robe. 175f, Gown. 225f, Jalabia. 275f, Scarf. 375f, Yashmak.

**2004, Dec. 29** **Litho.** ***Perf. 14***
**784-789** A235 Set of 6 6.75 6.75
*789a* Booklet pane, #784-789 6.75 6.75
Complete booklet, #789a 6.75

Dubai Aluminum, 25th Anniv. A236

Designs: 50f, Smelting complex. 275f, Smelting complex, sheikhs (brown background). 375f, Like 275f, blue background.

**2005, Jan. 8** ***Perf. 13***
**790-792** A236 Set of 3 4.00 4.00

10th Dubai Shopping Festival — A237

Designs: 50f, Emblem. 125f, Emblem, diff. 275f, Emblem and "10," green background. 375f, Emblem and "10," red background.

**2005, Jan. 12** ***Perf. 13¼x13***
**793-796** A237 Set of 4 4.50 4.50

2nd Intl. Gathering of Scouting and Belonging, Sharjah — A238

Designs: 50f, Emblem. 375f, Scouts and truck.

**2005, Apr. 1** **Litho.** ***Perf. 13¼x14***
**797-798** A238 Set of 2 2.40 2.40

Shaikha Fatima Bint Mubarak, Women's Rights Activist — A239

**2005, Apr. 10** ***Perf. 14½***
**799** A239 50f multi .30 .30

Al Majedi Bin Dhaher, 17th Century Poet A240

Poetry and: 50f, Sand. 175f, Bricks.

**2005, May 30** **Litho.** ***Perf. 14½***
**800-801** A240 Set of 2 1.25 1.25

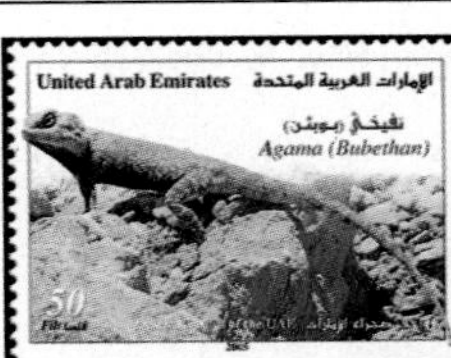

Reptiles A241

Designs: 50f, Agama. 125f, Desert monitor. 225f, Sand lizard. 275f, Dune sand gecko. 375f, Spiny-tailed lizard. 5d, Sand skink.

**2005, Aug. 2** ***Perf. 13¾***
**802-807** A241 Set of 6 8.50 8.50
*807a* Booklet pane, #802-807 8.50 —
Complete booklet, #807a 8.50

Accession of Sheik Khalifa Bin Zayed Al Nahyan, 1st Anniv. — A242

Sheik Khalifa: 50f, With a child. 175f, With another sheik. 275f, With another sheik, diff. 375f, Kissing sheik.

**2005, Nov. 3** **Litho.** ***Perf. 14x13¼***
**808-811** A242 Set of 4 4.75 4.75
*811a* Sheet of 4, #808-811 5.50 5.50

No. 811a sold for 10d.

2005 Census — A243

Emblem at: 50f, Bottom. 375f, Left, horiz.

***Perf. 13¼x13, 13x13¼***
**2005, Nov. 10**
**812-813** A243 Set of 2 2.40 2.40

Desert Plants A244

Designs: 50f, Leptadenia pyrotechnica. 125f, Lycium shawii. 225f, Calotropis procera. 275f, Prosopis cineraria. 325f, Zizyphus spina-christi. 375f, Acacia tortilis.

**2005, Nov. 27** **Litho.** ***Perf. 13½***
**814-819** A244 Set of 6 7.50 7.50
*819a* Booklet pane, #814-819 7.50 —
Complete booklet, #819a 7.50

34th National Day — A245

Children's art: 50f, Flower in Arabic script, by Shaimaa Mohammed Al Halabi. 125f, Ring of children, by Muaz Jamal Ahmed Hassan, horiz. 275f, Hands, by Pithani Srinidhi. 375f,

Doves, flag and plants, by Lina Abu Baker Mukhtar, horiz.

**2005, Dec. 2** ***Perf. 14¼***

**820-823** A245 Set of 4 4.50 4.50

Pearl Diving Tools A246

Designs: 50f, F'ttam (nose clip). 125f, Al Khabet (finger protectors). 175f, Al Dayeen (basket). 275f, Sea rock (diver's weight). 375f, Diver's outfit.

**2005, Dec. 21** ***Perf. 14***

**824-828** A246 Set of 5 5.50 5.50

A souvenir sheet containing Nos. 824-828 with pearl halves affixed to each stamp sold for 100d.

Gulf Cooperation Council Day for Autistic Children — A247

**2006, Apr. 4** **Litho.** ***Perf. 13***

**829** A247 4d multi 2.25 2.25

Souvenir Sheet

Hamad Bin Khalifa Abu Shehab (1932-2002), Poet — A248

No. 830: a, 1d, Head. b, 2d, Hands, poetry in Arabic text.

**2006, Apr. 26** ***Perf. 14¼***

**830** A248 Sheet of 2, #a-b 1.75 1.75

A249

Gulf Cooperation Council, 25th Anniv. — A250

Illustration A250 reduced.

**Litho. with Foil Application**

**2006, May 25** ***Perf. 14***

**831** A249 1d multi .55 .55

***Imperf***

**Size: 165x105mm**

**832** A250 5d multi 2.75 2.75

See Bahrain Nos. 628-629, Kuwait Nos. 1646-1647, Oman Nos. 477-478, Qatar Nos. 1007-1008, and Saudi Arabia No. 1378.

Dubai Police, 50th Anniv. — A251

**2006, June 1** ***Perf. 13¼x13***

**833** A251 1d multi .55 .55

19th Asian Stamp Exhibition, Dubai A252

Designs: 1d, shown. 4d, Four towers.

**Litho. With Foil Application**

**2006, June 24** ***Perf. 13¾***

**834-835** A252 Set of 2 2.75 2.75

Dubai Intl. Holy Koran Award, 10th Anniv. A253

**2006, July 24** **Litho.** ***Perf. 14x13½***

**836** A253 1d multi .55 .55

Al Raha Beach Developments — A254

Designs: 1d, Khor Al Raha. 2d, Al Lissaily. 350f, Al Wateed (40x40mm). 4d, Al Bandar (40x40mm).

**2006, Sept. 18** **Litho.** ***Perf. 13***

**837-840** A254 Set of 4 5.75 5.75

UPU Strategy Conference, Dubai — A255

Designs: 1d, Green arrows. 4d, Blue and green arrows.

**Litho. & Embossed**

**2006, Sept. 27** ***Perf. 14x13½***

**841-842** A255 Set of 2 2.75 2.75

12th Gulf Cooperation Council Postage Stamp Exhibition A256

**2006, Nov. 13** **Litho.** ***Perf. 13¼x13***

**843** A256 1d multi .55 .55

35th National Day — A257

**2006, Dec. 1**

**844** A257 1d multi .55 .55

A souvenir sheet containing one stamp sold for 10d.

Sheikh Mohammed bin Rashid al Maktoum, Prime Minister — A258

Sheikh Mohammed: 1d, Wearing kaffiyeh. 4d, Wearing polo helmet (44x53mm).

**Litho. With 3-Dimensional Plastic Affixed**

**2006, Dec. 2** ***Serpentine Die Cut 9***

**Self-Adhesive**

**845-846** A258 Set of 2 2.75 2.75

---

# UPPER SENEGAL AND NIGER

ˈə-pər ˌse-nə-gäl and ˈnī-jər

LOCATION — In Northwest Africa, north of French Guinea and Ivory Coast

GOVT. — A former French Colony

AREA — 617,600 sq. mi.

POP. — 2,474,142

CAPITAL — Bamako

In 1921 the name of this colony was changed to French Sudan and postage stamps so inscribed were placed in use.

100 Centimes = 1 Franc

Gen. Louis Faidherbe A1

Oil Palms — A2

Dr. N. Eugène Ballay — A3

***Perf. 14x13½***

**1906-07** **Unwmk.** **Typo.**

**Name of Colony in Red or Blue**

| | | | | | |
|---|---|---|---|---|---|
| **1** | A1 | 1c | slate | 1.25 | 1.25 |
| **2** | A1 | 2c | brown | 1.40 | 1.25 |
| **3** | A1 | 4c | brn, *gray bl* | 2.00 | 1.25 |
| **4** | A1 | 5c | green | 5.00 | 2.25 |
| **5** | A1 | 10c | car (B) | 5.00 | 2.40 |
| **6** | A1 | 15c | vio ('07) | 4.00 | 4.00 |
| **7** | A2 | 20c | bluish gray | 5.00 | 3.75 |
| **8** | A2 | 25c | bl, *pnksh* | 15.00 | 3.75 |
| **9** | A2 | 30c | vio brn, *pnksh* | 6.25 | 4.50 |
| **10** | A2 | 35c | blk, *yellow* | 5.00 | 3.75 |
| **11** | A2 | 40c | car, *az* (B) | 8.50 | 6.00 |
| **12** | A2 | 45c | brn, *grnsh* | 9.50 | 8.00 |
| **13** | A2 | 50c | dp vio | 9.50 | 8.00 |
| **14** | A2 | 75c | bl, *org* | 9.50 | 9.50 |
| **15** | A3 | 1fr | blk, *azure* | 22.50 | 20.00 |
| **16** | A3 | 2fr | bl, *pink* | 42.50 | 42.50 |
| **17** | A3 | 5fr | car, *straw* (B) | 87.50 | 87.50 |
| | | | *Nos. 1-17 (17)* | 239.40 | 209.65 |

Camel with Rider — A4

**1914-17** ***Perf. 13½x14***

| | | | | | |
|---|---|---|---|---|---|
| **18** | A4 | 1c | brn vio & vio | .25 | .25 |
| **19** | A4 | 2c | gray & brn vio | .25 | .25 |
| **20** | A4 | 4c | black & blue | .25 | .25 |
| **21** | A4 | 5c | yel grn & bl grn | .75 | .35 |
| **22** | A4 | 10c | red org & rose | 2.00 | 1.60 |
| **23** | A4 | 15c | choc & org ('17) | 1.75 | .60 |
| **24** | A4 | 20c | brn vio & blk | 1.90 | 1.10 |
| **25** | A4 | 25c | ultra & bl | 1.25 | 1.10 |
| **26** | A4 | 30c | ol brn & brn | 1.50 | 1.10 |
| **27** | A4 | 35c | car rose & vio | 2.40 | 1.60 |
| **28** | A4 | 40c | gray & car rose | 2.00 | .80 |
| **29** | A4 | 45c | bl & ol brn | 1.75 | 1.60 |
| **30** | A4 | 50c | black & green | 2.00 | 1.60 |
| **31** | A4 | 75c | org & ol brn | 2.00 | 1.60 |
| **32** | A4 | 1fr | brown & brn vio | 2.00 | 1.60 |
| **33** | A4 | 2fr | green & blue | 2.50 | 2.25 |
| **34** | A4 | 5fr | violet & black | 11.00 | 9.50 |
| | | | *Nos. 18-34 (17)* | 35.55 | 27.15 |

See Burkina Faso for types of this issue that escaped overprinting.

For surcharge see No. B1.

## SEMI-POSTAL STAMP

Regular Issue of 1914 Surcharged in Red

**1915** **Unwmk.** ***Perf. 13½x14***

| No. | Type | Description | Unused | Used |
|---|---|---|---|---|
| **B1** | A4 | 10c + 5c red orange & rose | 1.50 | 1.50 |

## POSTAGE DUE STAMPS

Natives — D1

D2

**1906** **Unwmk.** **Typo.** ***Perf. 14x13½***

| No. | Type | Description | Unused | Used |
|---|---|---|---|---|
| **J1** | D1 | 5c green, *greenish* | 3.00 | 2.25 |
| **J2** | D1 | 10c red brown | 6.50 | 6.00 |
| **J3** | D1 | 15c dark blue | 8.75 | 8.00 |
| **J4** | D1 | 20c black, *yellow* | 12.00 | 4.25 |
| **J5** | D1 | 50c violet | 21.50 | 20.00 |
| **J6** | D1 | 60c black, *buff* | 15.00 | 15.00 |
| **J7** | D1 | 1fr black, *pinkish* | 30.00 | 26.00 |
| | | *Nos. J1-J7 (7)* | 96.75 | 81.50 |

**1914**

| No. | Type | Description | Unused | Used |
|---|---|---|---|---|
| **J8** | D2 | 5c green | .95 | .95 |
| **J9** | D2 | 10c rose | .95 | .95 |
| **J10** | D2 | 15c gray | .95 | .95 |
| **J11** | D2 | 20c brown | 1.10 | 1.10 |
| **J12** | D2 | 30c blue | 1.85 | 1.85 |
| **J13** | D2 | 50c black | 1.50 | 1.50 |
| **J14** | D2 | 60c orange | 5.50 | 5.50 |
| **J15** | D2 | 1fr violet | 5.50 | 5.50 |
| | | *Nos. J8-J15 (8)* | 18.30 | 18.30 |

Stamps of Upper Senegal and Niger were superceded in 1921 by those of French Sudan.

# UPPER SILESIA

ˈə-pər sīˈlē-zh͏ē-ə

LOCATION — Formerly in eastern Germany and prior to World War I a part of Germany.

A plebiscite held under the terms of the Treaty of Versailles failed to determine the status of the country, the voting resulting about equally in favor of Germany and Poland. Accordingly, the League of Nations divided the territory between Germany and Poland.

100 Pfennig = 1 Mark
100 Fennigi = 1 Marka

### Plebiscite Issues

A1

***Perf. 14x13½***

**1920, Feb. 20** **Typo.** **Unwmk.**

| No. | Type | Description | Unused | Used |
|---|---|---|---|---|
| **1** | A1 | 2½pf slate | .40 | *.55* |
| **2** | A1 | 3pf brown | .40 | *.85* |
| **3** | A1 | 5pf green | .30 | *.35* |
| **4** | A1 | 10pf dull red | .40 | *.90* |
| **5** | A1 | 15pf violet | .20 | *.40* |
| **6** | A1 | 20pf blue | .20 | *.40* |
| *a.* | | Imperf., pair | 275.00 | — |
| *b.* | | Half used as 10pf on cover | | 85.00 |
| **7** | A1 | 50pf violet brn | 3.50 | *6.50* |
| **8** | A1 | 1m claret | 5.00 | *9.25* |
| **9** | A1 | 5m orange | 4.25 | *9.25* |
| | | *Nos. 1-9 (9)* | 14.65 | *28.45* |
| | | Set, never hinged | 45.00 | |

Black Surcharge

| 5 Pf. | 5 Pf. | 5 Pf. | 5 Pf. |
|---|---|---|---|
| I | II | III | IV |

| No. | Type | Description | Unused | Used |
|---|---|---|---|---|
| **10** | A1 | 5pf on 15pf vio (I) | 13.00 | *42.50* |
| | | Never hinged | 35.00 | |
| *a.* | | Type II | 13.00 | *42.50* |
| *b.* | | Type III | 13.00 | *42.50* |
| *c.* | | Type IV | 13.00 | *42.50* |
| **11** | A1 | 5pf on 20pf blue (I) | .65 | *2.00* |
| | | Never hinged | 1.60 | |
| *a.* | | Type II | .80 | *2.25* |
| *b.* | | Type III | 1.00 | *2.50* |
| *c.* | | Type IV | 1.25 | *3.25* |

Red Surcharge

| 10 Pf. | 10 Pf. | 10 Pf. | 10 Pf. |
|---|---|---|---|
| I | II | III | IV |

| No. | Type | Description | Unused | Used |
|---|---|---|---|---|
| **12** | A1 | 10pf on 20pf bl (I) | .65 | *1.60* |
| | | Never hinged | 1.60 | |
| *a.* | | Type II | .65 | *1.60* |
| *b.* | | Type III | .65 | *1.60* |
| *c.* | | Type IV | .65 | *1.60* |
| *d.* | | Imperf. | 50.00 | |

Black Surcharge

| 50 Pf. | 50 Pf. | 50 Pf. | 50 Pf. | 50 Pf. |
|---|---|---|---|---|
| I | II | III | IV | V |

| No. | Type | Description | Unused | Used |
|---|---|---|---|---|
| **13** | A1 | 50pf on 5m org (I) | 14.00 | *42.50* |
| | | Never hinged | 80.00 | |
| *a.* | | Type II | 15.00 | *45.00* |
| *b.* | | Type III | 16.00 | *80.00* |
| *c.* | | Type IV | 16.00 | *80.00* |
| *d.* | | Type V | 25.00 | *100.00* |

Nos. 10-13 are found with many varieties including surcharges inverted, double and double inverted.

Dove with Olive Branch Flying over Silesian Terrain — A2

A3

**1920, Mar. 26** **Typo.** ***Perf. 13½x14***

| No. | Type | Description | Unused | Used |
|---|---|---|---|---|
| **15** | A2 | 2½pf gray | .25 | *.40* |
| **16** | A2 | 3pf red brown | .25 | *.40* |
| **17** | A2 | 5pf green | .25 | *.40* |
| **18** | A2 | 10pf dull red | .25 | *.40* |
| **19** | A2 | 15pf violet | .25 | *.40* |
| **20** | A2 | 20pf blue | .65 | *1.60* |
| **21** | A2 | 25pf dark brown | .25 | *.40* |
| **22** | A2 | 30pf orange | .25 | *.40* |
| **23** | A2 | 40pf olive green | .25 | *1.00* |

***Perf. 14x13½***

| No. | Type | Description | Unused | Used |
|---|---|---|---|---|
| **24** | A3 | 50pf gray | .25 | *.40* |
| **25** | A3 | 60pf blue | .25 | *1.60* |
| **26** | A3 | 75pf deep green | .85 | *2.00* |
| **27** | A3 | 80pf red brown | .65 | *1.00* |
| **28** | A3 | 1m claret | .50 | *.40* |
| **29** | A3 | 2m dark brown | .50 | *.40* |
| **30** | A3 | 3m violet | .70 | *.40* |
| **31** | A3 | 5m orange | 2.75 | *4.00* |
| | | *Nos. 15-31 (17)* | 9.10 | 15.60 |
| | | Set, never hinged | 40.00 | |

Nos. 18-28 Overprinted in Black or Red

**1921, Mar. 20**

| No. | Type | Description | Unused | Used |
|---|---|---|---|---|
| **32** | A2 | 10pf dull red | 3.25 | *10.00* |
| **33** | A2 | 15pf violet | 3.25 | *10.00* |
| **34** | A2 | 20pf blue | 4.50 | *14.00* |
| **35** | A2 | 25pf dk brn (R) | 12.00 | *32.50* |
| **36** | A2 | 30pf orange | 9.00 | *20.00* |
| **37** | A2 | 40pf olive grn (R) | 11.00 | *20.00* |

Overprinted

| No. | Type | Description | Unused | Used |
|---|---|---|---|---|
| **38** | A3 | 50pf gray (R) | 11.00 | *27.50* |
| **39** | A3 | 60pf blue | 12.00 | *22.50* |
| **40** | A3 | 75pf deep green | 12.00 | *27.50* |
| **41** | A3 | 80pf red brown | 19.00 | *35.00* |
| **42** | A3 | 1m claret | 22.50 | *65.00* |
| | | *Nos. 32-42 (11)* | 119.50 | *284.00* |
| | | Set, never hinged | 625.00 | |

Inverted or double overprints exist on Nos. 32-33, 35-40. Counterfeit overprints exist.

Type of 1920 and Surcharged

**1922, Mar.**

| No. | Type | Description | Unused | Used |
|---|---|---|---|---|
| **45** | A3 | 4m on 60pf ol grn | .80 | *1.60* |
| **46** | A3 | 10m on 75pf red | .80 | *2.50* |
| **47** | A3 | 20m on 80pf orange | 6.25 | *13.00* |
| | | *Nos. 45-47 (3)* | 7.85 | *17.10* |
| | | Set, never hinged | 25.00 | |

Stamps of the above design were a private issue not recognized by the Inter-Allied Commission of Government. Value, set of 7, $32.50 unused, $72.50 never hinged, $150 used.

## OFFICIAL STAMPS

German Stamps of 1905-20 Handstamped in Blue

**1920, Feb.** **Wmk. 125** ***Perf. 14, 14½***

### On Stamps of 1906-19

| No. | Type | Description | Unused | Used |
|---|---|---|---|---|
| **O1** | A22 | 2pf gray | 1.10 | *1.25* |
| **O3** | A22 | 2½pf gray | .55 | *.65* |
| **O4** | A16 | 3pf brown | .55 | *.65* |
| **O5** | A16 | 5pf green | .55 | *.65* |
| **O6** | A22 | 7½pf orange | .55 | *.65* |
| **O7** | A16 | 10pf car rose | .55 | *.65* |
| **O8** | A22 | 15pf dk violet | .55 | *.65* |
| **O9** | A16 | 20pf blue violet | .55 | *.65* |
| **O10** | A16 | 25pf org & blk, *yel* | 5.25 | *6.50* |
| **O11** | A16 | 30pf org & blk, *buff* | .55 | *.65* |
| **O12** | A22 | 35pf red brown | .55 | *.65* |
| **O13** | A16 | 40pf lake & blk | .55 | *.65* |
| **O14** | A16 | 50pf vio & blk, *buff* | .55 | *.65* |
| **O15** | A16 | 60pf magenta | .55 | *.65* |
| **O16** | A16 | 75pf green & blk | .55 | *.65* |
| **O17** | A16 | 80pf lake & blk, *rose* | 6.50 | *8.00* |
| **O18** | A17 | 1m car rose | 1.10 | *1.25* |
| **O19** | A21 | 2m gray blue | 5.25 | *6.50* |

### On National Assembly Stamps of 1919-20

| No. | Type | Description | Unused | Used |
|---|---|---|---|---|
| **O25** | A23 | 10pf car rose | .90 | *1.10* |
| **O26** | A24 | 15pf choc & bl | 1.60 | *2.00* |
| **O27** | A25 | 25pf green & red | 3.25 | *4.00* |
| **O28** | A25 | 30pf red vio & red | 2.50 | *3.00* |

### On Semi-Postal Stamps of 1919

| No. | Type | Description | Unused | Used |
|---|---|---|---|---|
| **O30** | A16 | 10pf + 5pf carmine | 6.50 | *8.00* |
| **O31** | A22 | 15pf + 5pf dk vio | 6.50 | *8.00* |
| | | *Nos. O1-O31 (24)* | 47.60 | *58.05* |

### Red Handstamp

| No. | Type | Description | Unused | Used |
|---|---|---|---|---|
| *O5a* | A16 | 5pf | 10.00 | *14.00* |
| *O8a* | A22 | 15pf | 6.50 | *10.00* |
| *O9a* | A16 | 20pf | 6.50 | *10.00* |
| *O13a* | A16 | 40pf | 20.00 | *30.00* |
| *O16a* | A16 | 75pf | 20.00 | *30.00* |
| *O26a* | A24 | 15pf | 1.10 | *1.25* |
| | | *Nos. O5a-O26a (6)* | 64.10 | *95.25* |

Values of Nos. O1-O31 are for reprints made with a second type of handstamp differing in minor details from the original (example: period after "S" is round instead of the earlier triangular form). Originals are scarce. Counterfeits exist.

Germany No. 65C with this handstamp is considered bogus by experts.

Local Official Stamps of Germany, 1920, Overprinted

**1920, Apr.** ***Perf. 14***

| No. | Type | Description | Unused | Used |
|---|---|---|---|---|
| **O32** | LO2 | 5pf green | .30 | *.45* |
| **O33** | LO3 | 10pf carmine | .30 | *.45* |
| **O34** | LO4 | 15pf violet brn | .30 | *.45* |
| **O35** | LO5 | 20pf deep ultra | .30 | *.45* |
| **O36** | LO6 | 30pf orange, *buff* | .30 | *.45* |
| **O37** | LO7 | 50pf violet, *buff* | .50 | *1.40* |
| **O38** | LO8 | 1m red, *buff* | 6.00 | *10.00* |
| | | *Nos. O32-O38 (7)* | 8.00 | *13.65* |

Same Overprint on Official Stamps of Germany, 1920-21

**1920-21**

| No. | Type | Description | Unused | Used |
|---|---|---|---|---|
| **O39** | O1 | 5pf green | 1.00 | *2.40* |
| **O40** | O2 | 10pf carmine | .20 | .20 |
| **O41** | O3 | 15pf violet brn | .20 | .20 |
| **O42** | O4 | 20pf deep ultra | .20 | .20 |
| **O43** | O5 | 30pf orange, *buff* | .20 | .20 |
| **O44** | O6 | 40pf carmine rose | .20 | .20 |
| **O45** | O7 | 50pf violet, *buff* | .20 | .20 |
| **O46** | O8 | 60pf red brown | .20 | .20 |
| **O47** | O9 | 1m red, *buff* | .20 | .20 |
| **O48** | O10 | 1.25m dk blue, *yel* | .20 | .20 |
| **O49** | O11 | 2m dark blue | 7.00 | *8.00* |
| **O50** | O12 | 5m brown, *yel* | .20 | .20 |

**1922, Feb.** **Wmk. 126**

| No. | Type | Description | Unused | Used |
|---|---|---|---|---|
| **O51** | O11 | 2m dark blue | .20 | .20 |
| | | *Nos. O39-O51 (13)* | 10.20 | *12.60* |

This overprint is found both horizontal and vertical, reading up or down. It also exists on most values inverted, double and double, one inverted.

# URUGUAY

ˈyur-ə-ˌgwā

LOCATION — South America, between Brazil and Argentina and bordering on the Atlantic Ocean
GOVT. — Republic
AREA — 68,037 sq. mi.
POP. — 3,137,668 (1996)
CAPITAL — Montevideo

120 Centavos = 1 Real
8 Reales = 1 Peso
100 Centesimos = 1 Peso (1859)
1000 Milesimos = 1 Peso (1898)

### Watermarks

Wmk. 187 — R O in Diamond

Wmk. 188 — REPUBLICA O. DEL URUGUAY

Wmk. 189 — Caduceus

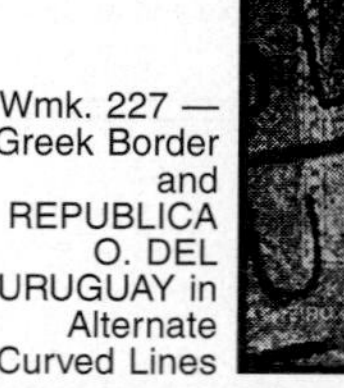

Wmk. 227 — Greek Border and REPUBLICA O. DEL URUGUAY in Alternate Curved Lines

Wmk. 327 — Coat of Arms

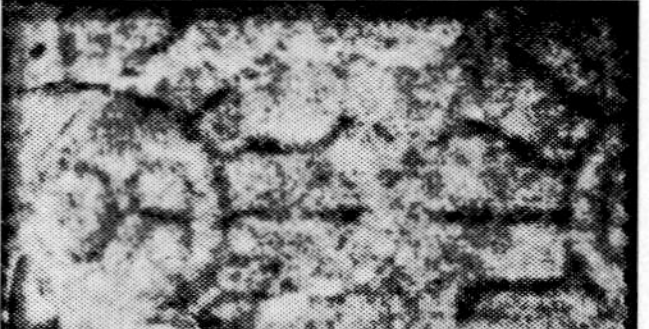

Wmk. 332 — Large Sun and R O U

**Catalogue values for unused stamps in this country are for Never Hinged items, beginning with Scott 534 in the regular postage section, Scott B5 in the semi-postal section, Scott C113 in the airpost section, Scott CB1 in the airpost semi-postal section, Scott E9 in the special delivery section, and Scott Q64 in the parcel post section.**

### Carrier Issues

Issued by Atanasio Lapido, Administrator-General of Posts

"El Sol de Mayo"
A1 A1a

**Unwmk.**

**1856, Oct. 1 Litho. *Imperf.***

| | | | |
|---|---|---|---|
| **1** | A1 | 60c blue | 350. |
| **2** | A1 | 80c green | 325. |
| **3** | A1 | 1r vermilion | 300. |

**1857, Oct. 1**

| | | | |
|---|---|---|---|
| **3B** | A1a | 60c blue | *2,500.* |

Nos. 1-3d were spaced very closely on the stone. Very fine examples will have clear margins on three sides and touching or slightly cut into the frames on the fourth (consult the grading illustrations in the catalogue introduction). All genuinely used examples are pen canceled. Certification by a recognized authority is recommended.

Stamps with tiny faults, such as small thin spots, sell for about 75% of the values of sound copies.

See Nos. 410-413, 771A.

A2

**1858, Mar.**

| | | | | |
|---|---|---|---|---|
| **4** | A2 | 120c blue | 250. | — |
| *c.* | | Tête bêche pair | | *7,500.* |
| **5** | A2 | 180c green | 100.00 | *200.00* |
| *c.* | | Thick paper | 450.00 | — |
| *d.* | | Tête bêche pair | | |
| **6** | A2 | 240c dull ver | 150.00 | *1,500.* |
| *c.* | | 180c in stone of 240c | | — |
| *d.* | | Thick paper (dull ver) | — | |
| *e.* | | 240c setenant with a vacant place | *5,000.* | |
| | | *Nos. 4-6 (3)* | 500.00 | *1,700.* |

### Government Issues

A3

A4

**1859, June 26**

**Thin Numerals**

| | | | | |
|---|---|---|---|---|
| **7** | A3 | 60c lilac | 25.00 | 20.00 |
| *a.* | | 60c gray lilac | 25.00 | 20.00 |
| **8** | A3 | 80c yellow | 190.00 | 35.00 |
| *a.* | | 80c orange | 275.00 | 50.00 |
| **9** | A3 | 100c brown lake | 55.00 | 45.00 |
| *a.* | | 100c brown rose | 55.00 | 45.00 |
| **10** | A3 | 120c blue | 35.00 | 15.00 |
| *a.* | | 120c slate blue | 50.00 | 17.50 |
| **11** | A3 | 180c green | 15.00 | 17.50 |
| **12** | A3 | 240c vermilion | 50.00 | 50.00 |
| | | *Nos. 7-12 (6)* | 370.00 | *182.50* |

**1860**

**Thick Numerals**

| | | | | |
|---|---|---|---|---|
| **13** | A4 | 60c dull lilac | 15.00 | 8.00 |
| *a.* | | 60c gray lilac | 17.50 | 10.00 |
| *b.* | | 60c brown lilac | 17.50 | 12.00 |
| *c.* | | 60c red lilac | 17.50 | 12.00 |
| *d.* | | As "a," fine impression (1st printing) | 70.00 | 40.00 |
| **14** | A4 | 80c yellow | 20.00 | 16.00 |
| *a.* | | 80c orange | 45.00 | 18.00 |
| **15** | A4 | 100c rose | 45.00 | 35.00 |
| *a.* | | 100c carmine | 45.00 | 35.00 |
| **16** | A4 | 120c blue | 21.00 | 16.00 |
| **17** | A4 | 180c yellow grn | 175.00 | 225.00 |
| *a.* | | 180c deep green | 225.00 | 250.00 |
| | | *Nos. 13-17 (5)* | 276.00 | *300.00* |

No. 13 was first printed (1860) in sheets of 192 (16x12) containing 24 types. The impressions are very clear; paper is whitish and of better quality than that of the later printings. In the 1861-62 printings, the layout contains 12 types and the subjects are spaced farther apart.

Coat of Arms — A5

**1864, Apr. 13**

| | | | | |
|---|---|---|---|---|
| **18** | A5 | 6c rose | 12.00 | 7.00 |
| *a.* | | 6c carmine | 32.50 | 25.00 |
| *b.* | | 6c red | 32.50 | 25.00 |
| *c.* | | 6c brick red | 32.50 | 25.00 |
| **20** | A5 | 6c salmon | 300.00 | *385.00* |
| **21** | A5 | 8c green | 17.00 | 17.00 |
| *a.* | | Tête bêche pair | 775.00 | |
| **22** | A5 | 10c yellow | 25.00 | 20.00 |
| *a.* | | 10c ocher | 25.00 | 20.00 |
| **23** | A5 | 12c blue | 15.00 | 15.00 |
| *a.* | | 12c dark blue | 25.00 | 15.00 |
| *b.* | | 12c slate blue | 30.00 | 50.00 |

No. 20, which is on thicker paper, was never placed in use.

Stamps of 1864 Surcharged in Black

**1866, Jan. 1**

| | | | | |
|---|---|---|---|---|
| **24** | A5 | 5c on 12c blue | 20.00 | *42.50* |
| *a.* | | 5c on 12c slate blue | 25.00 | *45.00* |
| *b.* | | Inverted surcharge | 150.00 | |
| *c.* | | Double surcharge | 150.00 | |
| *d.* | | Pair, one without surcharge | | |
| *e.* | | Triple surcharge | 55.00 | |
| **25** | A5 | 10c on 8c brt grn | 20.00 | *42.50* |
| *a.* | | 10c on 8c dl grn | 20.00 | *42.50* |
| *b.* | | Tête bêche pair | 300.00 | |
| *c.* | | Double surcharge | 150.00 | |
| **26** | A5 | 15c on 10c ocher | 20.00 | *67.50* |
| *a.* | | 15c on 10c yellow | 20.00 | *67.50* |
| *b.* | | Inverted surcharge | 150.00 | |
| *c.* | | Double surcharge | 150.00 | |
| **27** | A5 | 20c on 6c rose | 27.00 | *67.50* |
| *a.* | | 20c on 6c rose red | 30.00 | *50.00* |
| *b.* | | Inverted surcharge | 150.00 | |
| *c.* | | Double surcharge | 150.00 | |
| *d.* | | Pair, one without surcharge | | |
| **28** | A5 | 20c on 6c brick red | *350.00* | |
| *a.* | | Double surcharge | 400.00 | |
| | | *Nos. 24-27 (4)* | 87.00 | *220.00* |

Many counterfeits exist.
No. 28 was not issued.

Coat of Arms and Numeral of Value — A7

A8

A8a

A8b

A8c

ONE CENTESIMO:

Type I — The wavy lines behind "CENTESIMO" are clear and distinct. Stamps 4mm apart.

Type II — The wavy lines are rough and blurred. Stamps 3mm apart.

**1866, Jan. 10** ***Imperf.***

| | | | | |
|---|---|---|---|---|
| **29** | A7 | 1c black (type II) | 4.00 | *15.00* |
| *a.* | | 1c black (type I) | 4.00 | *15.00* |
| **30** | A8 | 5c blue | 4.00 | 2.00 |
| *a.* | | 5c dull blue | 4.00 | 2.00 |
| *b.* | | 5c ultramarine | 25.00 | 10.00 |
| *c.* | | Numeral with white flag | 25.00 | 12.00 |
| *d.* | | "ENTECIMOS" | 25.00 | 12.00 |
| *e.* | | "CENTECIMO" | 25.00 | 12.00 |
| *f.* | | "CENTECIMOS" with small "S" | 25.00 | 12.00 |
| *g.* | | Pelure paper | 100.00 | 100.00 |
| *h.* | | Thick paper | | |
| **31** | A8a | 10c yellow green | 15.00 | 5.00 |
| *a.* | | 10c blue green | 17.00 | 6.00 |
| *b.* | | "I" of "CENTECIMOS" omitted | 27.50 | 14.00 |
| *c.* | | "CENIECIMOS" | 27.50 | 14.00 |
| *d.* | | "CENTRCIMOS" | 27.50 | 14.00 |
| **32** | A8b | 15c orange yel | 25.00 | 9.00 |
| *a.* | | 15c yellow | 25.00 | 9.00 |
| **33** | A8c | 20c rose | 30.00 | 10.00 |
| *a.* | | 20c lilac rose | 30.00 | 10.00 |
| *b.* | | Thick paper | 35.00 | 15.00 |
| | | *Nos. 29-33 (5)* | 78.00 | 41.00 |

See Nos. 34-38. For overprint see No. O11.

*Engraved plates were prepared for Nos. 30 to 33 but were not put in use. The stamps were printed from lithographic transfers from the plate. In 1915 a few reprints of the 15c were made from the engraved plate by a California philatelic society, each sheet being numbered and signed by officers of the society; then the plate was defaced.*

**1866-67** ***Perf. 8½ to 13½***

| | | | | |
|---|---|---|---|---|
| **34** | A7 | 1c black | 5.00 | 20.00 |
| **35** | A8 | 5c blue | 5.00 | 1.00 |
| *a.* | | 5c dark blue | 5.00 | 1.00 |
| *b.* | | Numeral with white flag | 15.00 | 8.00 |
| *c.* | | "ENTECIMOS" | 15.00 | 8.00 |
| *d.* | | "CENTECIMO" | 15.00 | 8.00 |
| *e.* | | "CENTECIMOS" with small "S" | 15.00 | 8.00 |
| *f.* | | Pelure paper | 90.00 | 20.00 |
| **36** | A8a | 10c green | 12.00 | 4.00 |
| *a.* | | 10c yellow green | 14.00 | 4.00 |
| *b.* | | "CENIECIMOS" | 20.00 | 10.00 |
| *c.* | | "I" of "CENTECIMOS" omitted | 20.00 | 10.00 |
| *d.* | | "CENTRCIMOS" | 20.00 | 10.00 |
| *e.* | | Pelure paper | 90.00 | 20.00 |
| **37** | A8b | 15c orange yel | 21.00 | 6.00 |
| *a.* | | 15c yellow | 21.00 | 6.00 |
| *b.* | | Thin paper | 25.00 | 10.00 |
| **38** | A8c | 20c rose | 25.00 | 10.00 |
| *a.* | | 20c brown rose | 25.00 | 10.00 |
| *b.* | | Thin paper | 30.00 | 15.00 |
| *c.* | | Thick paper | 30.00 | 15.00 |
| | | *Nos. 34-38 (5)* | 68.00 | 41.00 |

A9

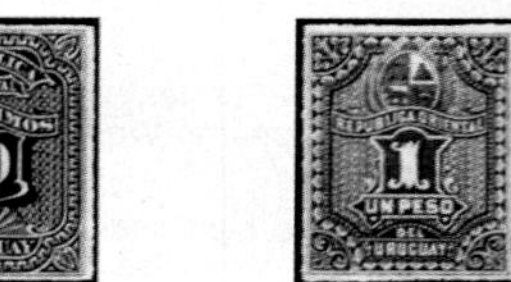

A10

A11

A12

**1877-79 Engr.** ***Rouletted 8***

| | | | | |
|---|---|---|---|---|
| **39** | A9 | 1c red brown | .55 | .40 |
| **40** | A10 | 5c green | .65 | .40 |
| *a.* | | Thick paper | 4.00 | 2.00 |
| **41** | A11 | 10c vermilion | 1.00 | .65 |
| **42** | A11 | 20c bister | 1.10 | .65 |
| **43** | A11 | 50c black | 7.00 | 3.00 |
| **43A** | A12 | 1p blue ('79) | 35.00 | 20.00 |
| | | *Nos. 39-43A (6)* | 45.30 | 25.10 |

The first printing of the 1p had the coat of arms smaller with quarterings reversed. These "error" stamps were not issued, and all were ordered burned. A copy is known to have been in a celebrated Uruguayan collection and a few others exist.

See No. 44. For overprints and surcharges see Nos. 52-53, O1-O8, O10, O19.

**1880, Nov. 10 Litho.** ***Rouletted 6***

| | | | | |
|---|---|---|---|---|
| **44** | A9 | 1c brown | .40 | .40 |
| *a.* | | Imperf., pair | 10.00 | |
| *b.* | | Rouletted 12½ | 2.50 | |

Joaquin Suárez — A13

**1881, Aug. 25** ***Perf. 12½***

**45** A13 7c blue 1.75 1.75
- *a.* Imperf., pair 9.00 9.00

For overprint see No. O9.

Devices from Coat of Arms
A14 A14a

**1882, May 15**

**46** A14 1c green 1.25 1.25
- *a.* 1c yellow green 4.00 2.00
- *b.* Imperf., pair 13.00

**47** A14a 2c rose 1.00 .75
- *a.* Imperf., pair 15.00

These stamps bear numbers from 1 to 100 according to their position on the sheet.

Counterfeits of Nos. 46 and 47 are plentiful.

See Nos. 1132-1133. For overprints see Nos. 54, O12-O13, O20.

Coat of Arms
A15 A16

Gen. Máximo Santos — A17 General José Artigas — A18

***Perf. 12, 12x12½, 12x13, 13x12***

**1883, Mar. 1**

**48** A15 1c green 1.25 1.00
**49** A16 2c red 1.50 1.25
**50** A17 5c blue 2.50 1.75
**51** A18 10c brown 3.00 2.10
*Nos. 48-51 (4)* 8.25 6.10

**Imperf., Pairs**

*48a* A15 1c 7.00
*49a* A16 2c 7.00
*50a* A17 5c 6.50
*51a* A18 10c 11.00

For overprints see Nos. O14-O18.

No. 40 Overprinted in Black

**1883**

**Provisorio**

**1883, Sept. 24** ***Rouletted 8***

**52** A10 5c green 1.00 .75
- *a.* Double overprint 15.00 15.00
- *b.* Overprint reading down 6.00 6.00
- *c.* "Provisorio" omitted 7.00 7.00
- *d.* "1883" omitted 4.50 4.50

No. 52 with overprint in red is a color essay.

No. 41 Surcharged in Black

**1884, Jan. 15**

**53** A11 1c on 10c ver .50 .50
- *a.* Small figure "1" 4.25 4.25
- *b.* Inverted surcharge 4.25 4.25
- *c.* Double surcharge 8.00 5.00

No. 47 Overprinted in Black

***Perf. 12½***

**54** A14a 2c rose .75 .75
- *a.* Double overprint 14.00
- *b.* Imperf., pair 40.00

A22 A23

**Thick Paper**

**1884, Jan. 25** **Litho.** **Unwmk.**

**55** A22 5c ultra 2.00 1.00
- *a.* Imperf., pair 7.50 4.00

**Thin Paper**

***Perf. 12½, 13 and Compound***

**56** A23 5c blue 1.50 .70
- *a.* Imperf., pair 14.00

For overprints see Nos. O21-O22.

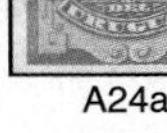

A24 A24a

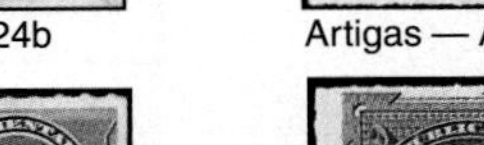

A24b Artigas — A25

Santos — A26 A27

A28

**1884-88** **Engr.** ***Rouletted 8***

**57** A24 1c gray .80 .50
**58** A24 1c olive .75 .40
**59** A24 1c green .65 .40
**60** A24a 2c vermilion .40 .25
**60A** A24a 2c rose ('88) .40 .25
**61** A24b 5c deep blue .80 .30
**61A** A24b 5c blue, *blue* 2.00 .85
**62** A24b 5c violet ('86) .50 .20
**63** A24b 5c lt bl ('88) .50 .20
**64** A25 7c dk brown 2.00 .85
**65** A25 7c org ('88) 2.00 .75
**66** A26 10c olive brn .80 .35
**67** A27 20c red violet 2.00 1.00
**68** A27 20c bis brn ('88) 2.00 1.00
**69** A28 25c gray violet 4.00 1.50
**70** A28 25c ver ('88) 3.00 1.00
*Nos. 57-70 (16)* 22.60 9.80

Water dissolves the blue in the paper of No. 61A.

For overprints see Nos. 73, 98-99, O23-O34, O36-O39, O61.

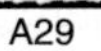

A29 A30

**1887, Oct. 17** **Litho.** ***Rouletted 9***

**71** A29 10c lilac 2.50 1.25
- *a.* 10c gray lilac 3.00 1.25

For overprint see No. O40.

**1888, Jan. 1** **Engr.** ***Rouletted 8***

**72** A30 10c violet .60 .25

For overprint see No. O35.

No. 62 Overprinted in Black

**1889, Oct. 14**

**73** A24b 5c violet .40 .40
- *a.* Inverted overprint 8.00 6.00
- *b.* Inverted "A" for "V" in "Provisorio" 4.00 4.00

No. 73 with overprint in red is a color essay.

Coat of Arms — A32 Numeral of Value — A33

A34 A35

A36 A37

Justice A38 Mercury A39

A40

***Perf. 12½ to 15½ and Compound***

**1889-1901** **Engr.**

**74** A32 1c green .50 .20
- *a.* Imperf., pair 13.00

**75** A32 1c dull bl ('94) .50 .20
**76** A33 2c rose .50 .20
**77** A33 2c red brn ('94) .55 .25
**78** A33 2c org ('99) .55 .25
**79** A34 5c dp blue .50 .20
**80** A34 5c rose ('94) .55 .20
**81** A35 7c bister brn 1.00 .30
**82** A35 7c green ('94) 4.75 2.75
**83** A35 7c car ('00) 4.00 1.75
**84** A36 10c blue grn 3.50 .85
- *a.* Printed on both sides 20.00

**85** A36 10c org ('94) 3.25 .60
**86** A37 20c orange 2.50 .60
**87** A37 20c brown ('94) 4.75 1.75

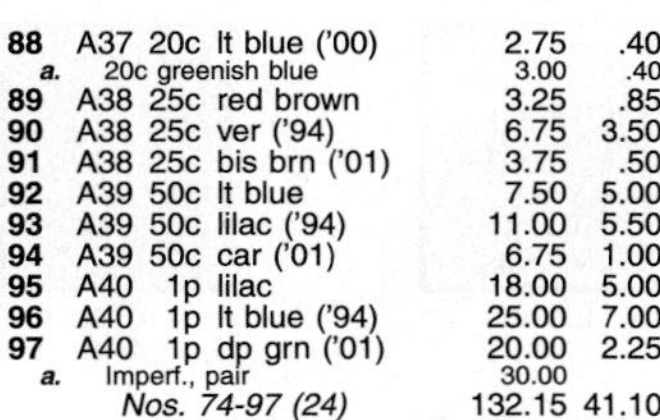

**88** A37 20c lt blue ('00) 2.75 .40
- *a.* 20c greenish blue 3.00 .40

**89** A38 25c red brown 3.25 .85
**90** A38 25c ver ('94) 6.75 3.50
**91** A38 25c bis brn ('01) 3.75 .50
**92** A39 50c lt blue 7.50 5.00
**93** A39 50c lilac ('94) 11.00 5.50
**94** A39 50c car ('01) 6.75 1.00
**95** A40 1p lilac 18.00 5.00
**96** A40 1p lt blue ('94) 25.00 7.00
**97** A40 1p dp grn ('01) 20.00 2.25
- *a.* Imperf., pair 30.00

*Nos. 74-97 (24)* 132.15 41.10

For surcharges and overprints see Nos. 100-101, 142, 180, 185, C1-C3, O41-O60, O89-O91, O108-O109.

Nos. 59 and 62 Overprinted in Red

a b

**1891-92** ***Rouletted 8***

**98** A24 (a) 1c green ('92) .40 .40
- *a.* Inverted overprint 6.00 6.00
- *b.* Double overprint 7.75 7.75
- *c.* Double ovpt., one invtd. 3.00 2.50
- *d.* "PREVISORIO" 4.00 4.00

**99** A24b (b) 5c violet .20 .20
- *a.* "1391" 4.00 2.75
- *b.* Double overprint 4.00 2.75
- *c.* Inverted overprint 4.00 2.75
- *d.* Double ovpt., one invtd. 5.00 3.00

Nos. 86 and 81 Surcharged in Black or Red

c d

***Perf. 12½ to 15½ and Compound***

**1892**

**100** A37 (c) 1c on 20c org (Bk) .40 .40
- *a.* Inverted surcharge 3.00 3.00

**101** A35 (d) 5c on 7c bis brn (R) .40 .40
- *a.* Inverted surcharge 1.00 1.00
- *b.* Double surcharge, one invtd. 3.00 3.00
- *c.* Double surcharge 3.00 3.00
- *d.* Vertical surcharge 10.00
- *e.* "PREVISORIO" 3.00 3.00
- *f.* "Cinco" omitted 4.50

No. 101 with surcharge in green is a color essay.

Several surcharge errors of date and misspelling of "Centésimos" exist. Value $15.

A45 A46

Arms A47 Peace A48

**1892** **Engr.**

**102** A45 1c green .50 .20
**103** A46 2c rose .50 .20
**104** A47 5c blue .50 .20
**105** A48 10c orange 2.00 .85
*Nos. 102-105 (4)* 3.50 1.45

Issued: 1c, 2c, 3/9; 5c, 4/19; 10c, 12/15.

Liberty
A49

Arms
A50

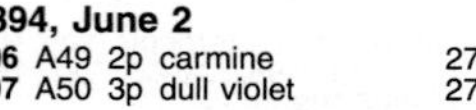

**1894, June 2**

| No. | Type | Description | Unused | Used |
|---|---|---|---|---|
| 106 | A49 | 2p carmine | 27.50 | 17.00 |
| 107 | A50 | 3p dull violet | 27.50 | 17.00 |

Gaucho
A51

Solis Theater
A52

Locomotive
A53

Bull's Head
A54

Ceres — A55

Sailing
Ship — A56

Liberty
A57

Mercury
A58

Coat of
Arms — A59

Montevideo
Fortress — A60

Cathedral in
Montevideo
A61

***Perf. 12 to 15½ and Compound***

**1895-99**

| No. | Type | Description | Unused | Used |
|---|---|---|---|---|
| 108 | A51 | 1c bister | .50 | .20 |
| 109 | A51 | 1c slate bl ('97) | .50 | .20 |
| a. | | Printed on both sides | 14.00 | |
| 110 | A52 | 2c blue | .50 | .20 |
| 111 | A52 | 2c claret ('97) | .50 | .20 |
| 112 | A53 | 5c red | .50 | .20 |
| 113 | A53 | 5c green ('97) | .65 | .20 |
| a. | | Imperf., pair | 3.50 | |
| 114 | A53 | 5c grnsh bl ('99) | 1.00 | .40 |
| 115 | A54 | 7c deep green | 7.75 | 2.50 |
| 116 | A54 | 7c orange ('97) | 3.50 | 1.25 |
| 117 | A55 | 10c brown | 2.00 | .50 |
| 118 | A56 | 20c green & blk | 7.00 | .85 |
| 119 | A56 | 20c cl & blk ('97) | 4.75 | .60 |
| 120 | A57 | 25c red brn & blk | 5.50 | 1.50 |
| a. | | Center inverted | | 2,000. |
| 121 | A57 | 25c pink & bl ('97) | 3.50 | .60 |
| 122 | A58 | 50c blue & blk | 7.00 | 3.50 |
| 123 | A58 | 50c grn & brn ('97) | 5.00 | 1.25 |

| No. | Type | Description | Unused | Used |
|---|---|---|---|---|
| 124 | A59 | 1p org brn & blk | 14.00 | 5.50 |
| 125 | A59 | 1p yel brn & bl ('97) | 9.50 | 3.50 |
| 126 | A60 | 2p violet & grn | 32.50 | 20.00 |
| 127 | A60 | 2p bis & car ('97) | 9.50 | 2.00 |
| 128 | A61 | 3p carmine & blue | 32.50 | 20.00 |
| 129 | A61 | 3p lil & car ('97) | 12.50 | 2.50 |
| | | *Nos. 108-129 (22)* | 160.65 | 67.65 |

All values of this issue exist imperforate but they were not issued in that form.

For overprints and surcharges see Nos. 138-140, 143, 145, 147, O62-O78.

President Joaquin Suárez
A62 A63

Statue of President
Suárez — A64

***Perf. 12½ to 15 and Compound***

**1896, July 18**

| No. | Type | Description | Unused | Used |
|---|---|---|---|---|
| 130 | A62 | 1c brown vio & blk | .25 | .20 |
| 131 | A63 | 5c pale bl & blk | .25 | .20 |
| 132 | A64 | 10c lake & blk | 1.00 | .30 |
| | | *Nos. 130-132 (3)* | 1.50 | .70 |

Dedication of Pres. Suárez statue.

For overprints and surcharge see Nos. 133-135, 144, 146, 152, O79-O81.

Same Overprinted in Red:

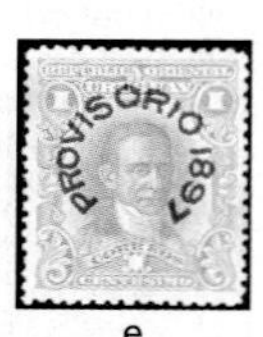

e

f

**1897, Mar. 1**

| No. | Type | Description | Unused | Used |
|---|---|---|---|---|
| 133 | A62 (e) | 1c brn vio & blk | .40 | .40 |
| a. | | Inverted overprint | 6.00 | 6.00 |
| 134 | A63 (e) | 5c pale blue & blk | .50 | .40 |
| a. | | Inverted overprint | 9.50 | 6.00 |
| 135 | A64 (f) | 10c lake & blk | 1.00 | .60 |
| a. | | Inverted overprint | 12.00 | 9.50 |
| b. | | Double overprint | 7.50 | |
| | | *Nos. 133-135 (3)* | 1.90 | 1.40 |

"Electricity" — A68

**1897-99** **Engr.**

| No. | Type | Description | Unused | Used |
|---|---|---|---|---|
| 136 | A68 | 10c red | 1.75 | .40 |
| 137 | A68 | 10c red lilac ('99) | .75 | .50 |

For overprints see Nos. 141, O82-O83.

Regular Issues
Overprinted in Red or
Blue

**1897, Sept. 26**

| No. | Type | Description | Unused | Used |
|---|---|---|---|---|
| 138 | A51 | 1c slate bl (R) | .80 | .60 |
| a. | | Inverted overprint | 4.75 | 4.75 |
| 139 | A52 | 2c claret (Bl) | 1.25 | 1.25 |
| a. | | Inverted overprint | 4.75 | 4.75 |
| 140 | A53 | 5c green (Bl) | 1.75 | 1.60 |
| a. | | Inverted overprint | 7.75 | 7.75 |
| b. | | Double overprint | | |
| 141 | A68 | 10c red (Bl) | 2.75 | 2.75 |
| a. | | Inverted overprint | 17.00 | 17.00 |
| | | *Nos. 138-141 (4)* | 6.55 | 6.20 |

Commemorating the Restoration of Peace at the end of the Civil War.

Issue for use only on the days of the National Fête, Sept. 26-28, 1897.

Regular Issues
Surcharged in Black,
Blue or Red

**1898, July 25**

| No. | Type | Description | Unused | Used |
|---|---|---|---|---|
| 142 | A32 | ½c on 1c bl (Bk) | .40 | .40 |
| a. | | Inverted surcharge | 3.00 | 3.00 |
| 143 | A51 | ½c on 1c bis (Bl) | .40 | .40 |
| a. | | Inverted surcharge | 3.00 | |
| b. | | Double surcharge | 2.50 | |
| 144 | A62 | ½c on 1c brn vio & blk (R) | .40 | .40 |
| 145 | A52 | ½c on 2c blue (Bk) | .40 | .40 |
| 146 | A63 | ½c on 5c pale bl & blk (R) | .40 | .40 |
| a. | | Double surcharge | 6.25 | |
| 147 | A54 | ½c on 7c dp grn (R) | .40 | .40 |
| | | *Nos. 142-147 (6)* | 2.40 | 2.40 |

The 2c red brown of 1894 (#77) was also surcharged like #142-147 but was not issued. Value $12.

Liberty — A69

Statue of
Artigas — A70

**1898-99** **Litho.** ***Perf. 11, 11½***

| No. | Type | Description | Unused | Used |
|---|---|---|---|---|
| 148 | A69 | 5m rose | .25 | .25 |
| 149 | A69 | 5m purple ('99) | .25 | .25 |

**1899-1900** **Engr.** ***Perf. 12½, 14, 15***

| No. | Type | Description | Unused | Used |
|---|---|---|---|---|
| 150 | A70 | 5m lt blue | .25 | .25 |
| 151 | A70 | 5m orange ('00) | .25 | .25 |

No. 135 With
Additional Surcharge
in Black

**1900, Dec. 1**

| No. | Type | Description | Unused | Used |
|---|---|---|---|---|
| 152 | A64 | 5c on 10c lake & blk | .50 | .25 |
| a. | | Black bar covering "1897" omitted | 15.00 | |

Cattle — A72

Girl's
Head — A73

Shepherdess — A74

***Perf. 13½ to 16 and Compound***

**1900-10** **Engr.**

| No. | Type | Description | Unused | Used |
|---|---|---|---|---|
| 153 | A72 | 1c yellow green | .40 | .20 |
| 154 | A73 | 5c dull blue | .80 | .20 |
| 155 | A73 | 5c slate grn ('10) | .80 | .20 |
| 156 | A74 | 10c gray violet | 1.00 | .20 |
| | | *Nos. 153-156 (4)* | 3.00 | .80 |

For surcharges and overprints see Nos. 179, 184, O84, O86, O88, O106-O107.

Eros and
Cornucopia
A75

Basket of Fruit
A76

**1901, Feb. 11**

| No. | Type | Description | Unused | Used |
|---|---|---|---|---|
| 157 | A75 | 2c vermilion | .50 | .20 |
| 158 | A76 | 7c brown orange | 1.75 | .25 |

For surcharges and overprints see Nos. 197-198, O85, O87, O105.

General
Artigas — A78

Cattle — A79

Eros — A80

Cow — A81

Shepherdess
A82

Numeral
A83

Justice — A84

**1904-05** **Litho.** ***Perf. 11½***

| No. | Type | Description | Unused | Used |
|---|---|---|---|---|
| 160 | A78 | 5m orange | .40 | .20 |
| a. | | 5m yellow | .40 | .20 |
| 161 | A79 | 1c green | .50 | .20 |
| a. | | Imperf., pair | 3.50 | |
| 162 | A80 | 2c dp orange | .20 | .20 |
| a. | | 2c orange red | .20 | .20 |
| b. | | Imperf., pair | 3.00 | |
| 163 | A81 | 5c blue | .80 | .20 |
| a. | | Imperf., pair | 3.50 | |
| 164 | A82 | 10c dk violet ('05) | .50 | .20 |
| 165 | A83 | 20c gray grn ('05) | 2.50 | .50 |
| 166 | A84 | 25c olive bis ('05) | 3.25 | .80 |
| | | *Nos. 160-166 (7)* | 8.15 | 2.30 |

For overprints see Nos. 167-169, O92-O98, O101-O103.

Overprinted Diagonally
in Carmine or Black

**1904, Oct. 15**

| No. | Type | Description | Unused | Used |
|---|---|---|---|---|
| 167 | A79 | 1c green (C) | .40 | .40 |
| 168 | A80 | 2c deep orange (Bk) | .65 | .40 |
| 169 | A81 | 5c dark blue (C) | 1.25 | .60 |
| | | *Nos. 167-169 (3)* | 2.30 | 1.40 |

End of the Civil War of 1904. In the first overprinting, "Paz 1904" appears at a 50-degree angle; in the second, at a 63-degree angle.

A85

A86

**1906, Feb. 23** **Litho.** **Unwmk.**

| No. | Type | Description | Unused | Used |
|---|---|---|---|---|
| 170 | A85 | 5c dark blue | 1.10 | .20 |
| a. | | Imperf., pair | 6.00 | |

**1906-07**

| No. | Type | Description | Unused | Used |
|---|---|---|---|---|
| 171 | A86 | 5c deep blue | .30 | .30 |
| 172 | A86 | 7c orange brn ('07) | .70 | .50 |
| 173 | A86 | 50c rose | 5.00 | 1.25 |
| | | *Nos. 171-173 (3)* | 6.00 | 2.05 |

Cruiser "Montevideo" — A87

**1908, Aug. 23 Typo. *Rouletted 13***

**174** A87 1c car & dk grn 2.00 1.50
**175** A87 2c green & dk grn 2.00 1.50
**176** A87 5c org & dk grn 2.00 1.50
*Nos. 174-176 (3)* 6.00 4.50

**Center Inverted**

*174a* A87 1c 300.00 300.00
*175a* A87 2c 300.00 300.00
*176a* A87 5c 300.00 300.00
*Nos. 174a-176a (3)* 900.00 900.00

**Imperf., Pairs**

*174b* A87 1c 30.00
*175b* A87 2c 30.00
*176b* A87 5c 30.00

Independence of Uruguay, declared Aug. 25, 1825. Counterfeits exist.
For surcharges and overprints see Nos. 186, O99-O100, O104, O110.

View of the Port of Montevideo — A88

**Wmk. 187**

**1909, Aug. 24 Engr. *Perf. 11½***

**177** A88 2c lt brown & blk 1.25 1.00
**178** A88 5c rose red & blk 1.25 1.00

Issued to commemorate the opening of the Port of Montevideo, Aug. 25, 1909.

Nos. 156, 91 Surcharged

***Perf. 14 to 16***

**1909, Sept. 13 Unwmk.**

**179** A74 8c on 10c dull vio .75 .20
*a.* "Contesimos" 4.00 2.00
**180** A38 23c on 25c bis brn 1.75 .60

Centaur — A89

**Wmk. 187**

**1910, May 22 Engr. *Perf. 11½***

**182** A89 2c carmine red .60 .40
**183** A89 5c deep blue .60 .40

Cent. of Liberation Day, May 25, 1810.
The 2c in deep blue and 5c in carmine red were prepared for collectors.

Stamps of 1900-06 Surcharged

g

h

i

***Perf. 14 to 16, 11½***

**1910, Oct. 6 Unwmk.**

**Black Surcharge**

**184** A72 (a) 5m on 1c yel grn .20 .20
*a.* Inverted surcharge 4.50 3.75

**Dark Blue Surcharge**

**185** A39 (b) 5c on 50c dull red .40 .20
*a.* Inverted surcharge 4.50 4.50

**Blue Surcharge**

**186** A86 (c) 5c on 50c rose .80 .45
*a.* Double surcharge 20.00
*b.* Inverted surcharge 10.00 8.75
*Nos. 184-186 (3)* 1.40 .85

Artigas A90

"Commercial Progress" A91

**1910, Nov. 21 Engr. *Perf. 14, 15***

**187** A90 5m dk violet .20 .20
**188** A90 1c dp green .20 .20
**189** A90 2c orange red .20 .20
**190** A90 5c dk blue .20 .20
**191** A90 8c gray blk .40 .20
**192** A90 20c brown .60 .20
**193** A91 23c dp ultra 2.75 .40
**194** A91 50c orange 4.00 1.25
**195** A91 1p scarlet 7.50 1.25
*Nos. 187-195 (9)* 16.05 4.10

See Nos. 199-210. For overprints see Nos. 211-213, O118-O124.

Symbolical of the Posts — A92

**1911, Jan. 6 Wmk. 187 *Perf. 11½***

**196** A92 5c rose car & blk .80 .60

1st South American Postal Cong., at Montevideo, Jan. 1911.

No. 158 Surcharged in Red or Dark Blue

***Perf. 14 to 16***

**1911, May 17 Unwmk.**

**197** A76 2c on 7c brn org (R) .40 .40
**198** A76 5c on 7c brn org (Bl) .40 .20
*a.* Inverted surcharge 8.50 8.50

Centenary of the battle of Las Piedras, won by the forces under Gen. Jose Gervasio Artigas, May 8, 1811.

Types of 1910

FOUR AND FIVE CENTESIMOS:
Type I — Large numerals about 3mm high.
Type II — Small numerals about 2¼mm high.

**1912-15 Typo. *Perf. 11½***

**199** A90 5m violet .20 .20
*a.* 5m purple .20 .20
**200** A90 5m magenta .20 .20
*a.* 5m dull rose .20 .20
**201** A90 1c green ('13) .20 .20
**202** A90 2c brown org .20 .20
**203** A90 2c rose red ('13) .20 .20
*a.* 2c deep red ('14) .20 .20
**204** A90 4c org (I) ('14) .20 .20
*a.* 4c orange (II) ('15) .20 .20
*b.* 4c yellow (II) ('13) .20 .20
**205** A90 5c dull bl (I) .40 .20
*a.* 5c blue (II) .40 .20
**206** A90 8c ultra ('13) .50 .20
**207** A90 20c brown ('13) 1.40 .20
*a.* 20c chocolate 1.40 .20
**208** A91 23c dk blue ('15) 3.50 .60
**209** A91 50c orange ('14) 3.50 1.50
**210** A91 1p vermilion ('15) 10.50 1.25
*Nos. 199-210 (12)* 21.00 5.15

Stamps of 1912-15 Overprinted

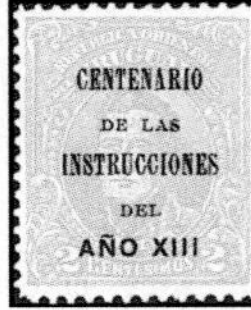


**1913, Apr. 4**

**211** A90 2c brown orange .85 .50
*a.* Inverted overprint 5.00 4.50
**212** A90 4c yellow .85 .50
**213** A90 5c blue .85 .50
*Nos. 211-213 (3)* 2.55 1.50

Cent. of the Buenos Aires Cong. of 1813.

Liberty Extending Peace to the Country — A93

**1918, Jan. 3 Litho.**

**214** A93 2c green & red .85 .50
**215** A93 5c buff & blue .85 .50

Promulgation of the Constitution.

Statue of Liberty, New York Harbor A94

Harbor of Montevideo A95

***Perf. 14, 15, 13½***

**1919, July 15 Engr.**

**217** A94 2c carmine & brn .55 .20
**218** A94 4c orange & brn .55 .20
**219** A94 5c blue & brn .80 .40
**220** A94 8c org brn & ind .80 .40
**221** A94 20c ol bis & blk 2.00 .80
**222** A94 23c green & blk 4.00 1.25
*Nos. 217-222 (6)* 8.70 3.25

Peace at end of World War I.
Perf 13½ used only on 2c, 20c, 23c.

**1919-20 Litho. *Perf. 11½***

**225** A95 5m violet & blk .20 .20
**226** A95 1c green & blk .20 .20
**227** A95 2c red & blk .20 .20
**228** A95 4c orange & blk .35 .20
**229** A95 5c ultra & slate .40 .20
**230** A95 8c gray bl & lt brn .50 .20
**231** A95 20c brown & blk 1.60 .35
**232** A95 23c green & brn 2.75 .65
**233** A95 50c brown & blue 5.00 2.00
**234** A95 1p dull red & bl 10.00 3.00
*Nos. 225-234 (10)* 21.20 7.20

For overprints see Nos. O125-O131.

José Enrique Rodó — A96

Mercury — A97

**1920, Feb. 28 Engr. *Perf. 14, 15***

**235** A96 2c car & blk .55 .40
**236** A96 4c org & bl .65 .50
**237** A96 5c bl & brn .75 .55
*Nos. 235-237 (3)* 1.95 1.45

Issued to honor José Enrique Rodó, author.
For surcharges see Nos. P2-P4.

**1921-22 Litho. *Perf. 11½***

**238** A97 5m lilac .20 .20
**239** A97 5m gray blk ('22) .20 .20
**240** A97 1c lt grn .20 .20
**241** A97 1c vio ('22) .20 .20
**242** A97 2c fawn .40 .20
**243** A97 2c red ('22) .40 .20
**244** A97 3c bl grn ('22) .60 .20
**245** A97 4c orange .40 .20
**246** A97 5c ultra .50 .20
**247** A97 5c choc ('22) .60 .20
**248** A97 12c ultra ('22) 2.40 .60
**249** A97 36c ol grn ('22) 7.75 2.75
*Nos. 238-249 (12)* 13.85 5.35

See Nos. 254-260. For overprint and surcharge see Nos. E1, P1.

Dámaso A. Larrañaga (1771-1848), Bishop, Writer, Scientist and Physician — A98

**1921, Dec. 10 Unwmk.**

**250** A98 5c slate 1.25 1.00

Mercury Type of 1921-22

**1922-23 Wmk. 188**

**254** A97 5m gray blk .20 .20
**255** A97 1c violet ('23) .20 .20
*a.* 1c red violet .20 .20
**256** A97 2c pale red .25 .20
**257** A97 2c deep rose ('23) .30 .20
**259** A97 5c yel brn ('23) .65 .20
**260** A97 8c salmon pink ('23) 1.00 .90
*Nos. 254-260 (6)* 2.60 1.90

Equestrian Statue of Artigas — A99

**Unwmk.**

**1923, Feb. 26 Engr. *Perf. 14***

**264** A99 2c car & sepia .40 .25
**265** A99 5c vio & sepia .40 .25
**266** A99 12c blue & sepia .40 .25
*Nos. 264-266 (3)* 1.20 .75

Southern Lapwing A100

Battle Monument A101

***Perf. 12½, 11½x12½***

**1923, June 25 Litho. Wmk. 189**

**Size: 18x22½mm**

**267** A100 5m gray .20 .20
**268** A100 1c org yel .20 .20
**269** A100 2c lt vio .20 .20
**270** A100 3c gray grn .40 .20
**271** A100 5c lt bl .40 .20
**272** A100 8c rose red .80 .50
**273** A100 12c dp bl .80 .50
**274** A100 20c brn org 2.00 .50
**275** A100 36c emerald 4.00 1.75
**276** A100 50c orange 6.75 2.75
**277** A100 1p brt rose 32.50 20.00
**278** A100 2p lt grn 47.50 20.00
*Nos. 267-278 (12)* 95.75 47.00

See #285-298, 309-314, 317-323, 334-339. For surcharges and overprints see Nos. 345-348, O132-O148, P5-P7.

**1923, Oct. 12 Wmk. 188 *Perf. 11½***

**279** A101 2c dp grn .55 .40
**280** A101 5c scarlet .55 .40
**281** A101 12c dk bl .55 .40
*Nos. 279-281 (3)* 1.65 1.20

Unveiling of the Sarandi Battle Monument by José Luis Zorrilla, Oct. 12, 1923.

"Victory of Samothrace" — A102

**Unwmk.**

**1924, July 29 Typo. *Perf. 11***

**282** A102 2c rose 20.00 10.00
**283** A102 5c mauve 20.00 10.00
**284** A102 12c brt bl 20.00 10.00
*Nos. 282-284 (3)* 60.00 30.00

Olympic Games. Sheets of 20 (5x4).

Five hundred sets of these stamps were printed on yellow paper for presentation purposes. They were not on sale at post offices. Value for set, $650.

Lapwing Type of 1923
First Redrawing
Imprint: "A. BARREIRO Y RAMOS"

**1924, July 26 Litho. *Perf. 12½, 11½***

**Size: 17¼x21½mm**

**285** A100 5m gray blk .20 .20
**286** A100 1c fawn .20 .20
**287** A100 2c rose lil .30 .20
**288** A100 3c gray grn .20 .20
**289** A100 5c chalky blue .20 .20
**290** A100 8c pink .50 .20
**291** A100 10c turq blue .40 .20
**292** A100 12c slate blue .50 .25
**293** A100 15c lt vio .50 .20
**294** A100 20c brown .75 .30
**295** A100 36c salmon 3.00 .70
**296** A100 50c greenish gray 5.00 2.00
**297** A100 1p buff 12.00 4.00
**298** A100 2p dl vio 20.00 10.00
*Nos. 285-298 (14)* 43.75 18.85

Landing of the 33 "Immortals" Led by Juan Antonio Lavalleja — A103

***Perf. 11, 11½***

**1925, Apr. 19 Wmk. 188**

**300** A103 2c salmon pink & blk 1.40 .80
**301** A103 5c lilac & blk 1.40 .80
**302** A103 12c blue & blk 1.40 .80
*Nos. 300-302 (3)* 4.20 2.40

Cent. of the landing of the 33 Founders of the Uruguayan Republic.

Legislative Palace — A104

***Perf. 11½***

**1925, Aug. 24 Unwmk. Engr.**

**303** A104 5c vio & blk 1.25 .80
**304** A104 12c bl & blk 1.25 .80

Dedication of the Legislative Palace.

General Fructuoso Rivera — A105

**Wmk. 188**

**1925, Sept. 24 Litho. *Perf. 11***

**305** A105 5c light red .50 .40

Centenary of Battle of Rincón. See No. C9.

Battle of Sarandí A106

**1925, Oct. 12 *Perf. 11½***

**306** A106 2c bl grn 1.25 1.00
**307** A106 5c dl vio 1.25 1.00
**308** A106 12c dp bl 1.25 1.00
*Nos. 306-308 (3)* 3.75 3.00

Centenary of the Battle of Sarandi.

Lapwing Type of 1923
Second Redrawing
Imprint: "Imprenta Nacional"

**1925-26 *Perf. 11, 11½, 10½***

**Size: 17½x21¾mm**

**309** A100 5m gray blk 1.00 .25
**310** A100 1c dl vio 1.25 .25
**311** A100 2c brt rose 1.60 .25
**312** A100 3c gray grn 1.25 .40
**313** A100 5c dl bl ('26) 2.00 .25
**314** A100 12c slate blue 4.00 .40
*Nos. 309-314 (6)* 11.10 1.80

The design differs in many small details from that of the 1923-24 issues. These stamps may be readily identified by the imprint and perforation.

Lapwing Type of 1923
Third Redrawing
Imprint: "Imp. Nacional" at center

**1926-27 *Perf. 11, 11½, 10½***

**Size: 17½x21¾mm**

**317** A100 5m gray .40 .20
**318** A100 1c lt vio ('27) 2.40 .55
**319** A100 2c red 1.75 .40
**320** A100 3c gray grn 2.40 .65
**321** A100 5c lt bl .75 .20
**322** A100 8c pink ('27) 3.50 .80
**323** A100 36c rose buff 8.00 4.00
*Nos. 317-323 (7)* 19.20 6.80

These stamps may be distinguished from preceding stamps of the same design by the imprint.

**Philatelic Exhibition Issue**

Post Office at Montevideo A107

**Unwmk.**

**1927, May 25 Engr. *Imperf.***

**330** A107 2c green 4.75 3.50
*a.* Sheet of 4 20.00 20.00
**331** A107 5c dull red 4.75 3.50
*a.* Sheet of 4 20.00 20.00
**332** A107 8c dark blue 4.75 3.50
*a.* Sheet of 4 20.00 20.00
*Nos. 330-332 (3)* 14.25 10.50

Printed in sheets of 4 and sold at the Montevideo Exhibition. Lithographed counterfeits exist.

Lapwing Type of 1923
Fourth Redrawing
Imprint: "Imp. Nacional" at right

***Perf. 11, 11½***

**1927, May 6 Litho. Wmk. 188**

**Size: 17¾x21¾mm**

**334** A100 1c gray vio .40 .25
**335** A100 2c vermilion .40 .25
**336** A100 3c gray grn .80 .35
**337** A100 5c blue .40 .25
**338** A100 8c rose 3.00 .80
**339** A100 20c gray brn 4.00 1.60
*Nos. 334-339 (6)* 9.00 3.50

The design has been slightly retouched in various places. The imprint is in italic capitals and is placed below the right numeral of value.

No. 292 Surcharged in Red

Inauguración
Ferrocarril
SAN CARLOS
a ROCHA
14/1/928
**5 cts. 5**

**1928, Jan. 13 Unwmk. *Perf. 11½***

**345** A100 2c on 12c slate blue 2.00 2.00
**346** A100 5c on 12c slate blue 2.00 2.00
**347** A100 10c on 12c slate blue 2.00 2.00
**348** A100 15c on 12c slate blue 2.00 2.00
*Nos. 345-348 (4)* 8.00 8.00

Issued to celebrate the inauguration of the railroad between San Carlos and Rocha.

General Rivera — A108

**1928, Apr. 19 Engr. *Perf. 12***

**349** A108 5c car rose .50 .35

Centenary of the Battle of Las Misiones.

Artigas (7 dots in panels below portrait.) — A109

Imprint:
"Waterlow & Sons. Ltd., Londres"

***Perf. 11, 12½, 13x13½, 12½x13, 13x12½***

**1928-43**

**Size: 16x19½mm**

**350** A109 5m black .20 .20
**350A** A109 5m org ('43) .20 .20
**351** A109 1c dk vio .20 .20
**352** A109 1c brn vio ('34) .20 .20
**352A** A109 1c vio bl ('43) .20 .20
**353** A109 2c dp grn .20 .20
**353A** A109 2c brn red ('43) .20 .20
**354** A109 3c bister .20 .20
**355** A109 3c dp grn ('32) .20 .20
**355A** A109 3c brt grn ('43) .20 .20
**356** A109 5c red .20 .20
**357** A109 5c ol grn ('33) .20 .20
**357A** A109 5c dl pur ('43) .20 .20
**358** A109 7c car ('32) .20 .20
**359** A109 8c dk bl .20 .20
**360** A109 8c brn ('33) .20 .20
**361** A109 10c orange .25 .20
**362** A109 10c red org ('32) .60 .40
**363** A109 12c dp bl ('32) .40 .20
**364** A109 15c dl bl .40 .20
**365** A109 17c dk vio ('32) .80 .20
**366** A109 20c ol brn .65 .20
**367** A109 20c red brn ('33) 1.25 .50
**368** A109 24c car rose .90 .35
**369** A109 24c yel ('33) .80 .40
**370** A109 36c ol grn ('33) 1.40 .50
**371** A109 50c gray 2.40 1.25
**372** A109 50c blk ('33) 3.50 1.60
**373** A109 50c blk brn ('33) 3.00 1.25
**374** A109 1p yel grn 7.00 4.00
*Nos. 350-374 (30)* 26.55 14.45

**1929-33 *Perf. 12½***

**Size: 22 to 22½x28½ to 29½mm**

**375** A109 1p ol brn ('33) 6.00 4.00
**376** A109 2p dk grn 17.00 9.00
**377** A109 2p dl red ('32) 20.00 16.00
**378** A109 3p dk bl 25.00 17.00
**379** A109 3p blk ('32) 23.00 20.00
**380** A109 4p violet 28.00 17.00
**381** A109 4p dk ol grn ('32) 23.00 20.00
**382** A109 5p car brn 32.50 23.00
**383** A109 5p red org ('32) 30.00 20.00
**384** A109 10p lake ('33) 92.50 70.00
**385** A109 10p dp ultra ('33) 92.50 70.00
*Nos. 375-385 (11)* 389.50 286.00

See Nos. 420-423, 462. See type A135.

Equestrian Statue of Artigas — A110

**1928, May 1**

**386** A110 2p Prus bl & choc 16.00 7.75
**387** A110 3p dp rose & blk 23.00 12.00

Symbolical of Soccer Victory — A111

Gen. Eugenio Garzón — A112

**1928, July 29**

**388** A111 2c brn vio 16.00 9.25
**389** A111 5c dp red 16.00 9.25
**390** A111 8c ultra 16.00 9.25
*Nos. 388-390 (3)* 48.00 27.75

Uruguayan soccer victories in the Olympic Games of 1924 and 1928. Printed in sheets of 20, in panes of 10 (5x2).

**1928, Aug. 25 *Imperf.***

**391** A112 2c red 1.40 1.40
*a.* Sheet of 4 6.50 6.50
**392** A112 5c yel grn 1.40 1.40
*a.* Sheet of 4 6.50 6.50
**393** A112 8c dp bl 1.40 1.40
*a.* Sheet of 4 6.50 6.50
*Nos. 391-393 (3)* 4.20 4.20

Dedication of monument to Garzon. Issued in sheets of 4. Lithographed counterfeits exist.

Black River Bridge A113

Gauchos Breaking a Horse — A114

Peace A115

Montevideo A116

Liberty and Flag of Uruguay A117

Liberty with Torch and Caduceus A118

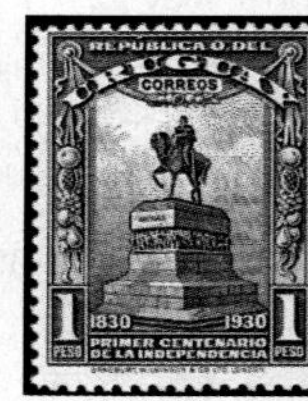

Statue of Artigas A124

Artigas Dictating Instructions for 1813 Congress A119

Seascape
A120

Montevideo Harbor, 1830 — A121

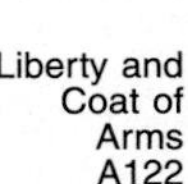

Liberty and Coat of Arms
A122

Montevideo Harbor, 1930 — A123

**1930, June 16** — *Perf. 12½, 12*

| No. | Type | Description | Unused | Used |
|---|---|---|---|---|
| 394 | A113 | 5m gray blk | .20 | .20 |
| 395 | A114 | 1c dk brn | .20 | .20 |
| 396 | A115 | 2c brn rose | .20 | .20 |
| 397 | A116 | 3c yel grn | .20 | .20 |
| 398 | A117 | 5c dk bl | .20 | .20 |
| 399 | A118 | 8c dl red | .35 | .20 |
| 400 | A119 | 10c dk vio | .50 | .35 |
| 401 | A120 | 15c bl grn | .65 | .50 |
| 402 | A121 | 20c indigo | .80 | .65 |
| 403 | A122 | 24c red brn | 1.10 | .80 |
| 404 | A123 | 50c org red | 3.00 | 2.00 |
| 405 | A124 | 1p black | 6.00 | 3.00 |
| 406 | A124 | 2p bl vio | 14.00 | 8.50 |
| 407 | A124 | 3p dk red | 20.00 | 14.00 |
| 408 | A124 | 4p red org | 23.00 | 19.00 |
| 409 | A124 | 5p lilac | 35.00 | 22.50 |
| | | *Nos. 394-409 (16)* | 105.40 | 72.50 |

Cent. of natl. independence and the promulgation of the constitution.

Type of 1856 Issue
Values in Centesimos

**Wmk. 227**

**1931, Apr. 11** — **Litho.** — ***Imperf.***

| No. | Type | Description | Unused | Used |
|---|---|---|---|---|
| 410 | A1 | 2c gray blue | 3.00 | 2.00 |
| *a.* | | Sheet of 4 | 15.00 | 15.00 |
| 411 | A1 | 8c dull red | 3.00 | 2.00 |
| *a.* | | Sheet of 4 | 15.00 | 15.00 |
| 412 | A1 | 15c blue black | 3.00 | 2.00 |
| *a.* | | Sheet of 4 | 15.00 | 15.00 |

**Wmk. 188**

| No. | Type | Description | Unused | Used |
|---|---|---|---|---|
| 413 | A1 | 5c light green | 3.00 | 2.00 |
| *a.* | | Sheet of 4 | 15.00 | 15.00 |
| | | *Nos. 410-413 (4)* | 12.00 | 8.00 |

Sold only at the Philatelic Exhibition, Montevideo, Apr. 11-15, 1931. Issued in sheets of 4.

Juan Zorrilla de San Martin, Uruguayan Poet — A125

**1932, June 6** — **Unwmk.** — *Perf. 12½*

| No. | Type | Description | Unused | Used |
|---|---|---|---|---|
| 414 | A125 | 1½c brown violet | .20 | .20 |
| 415 | A125 | 3c green | .20 | .20 |
| 416 | A125 | 7c dk blue | .25 | .20 |
| 417 | A125 | 12c lt blue | .40 | .25 |
| 418 | A125 | 1p deep brown | 20.00 | 13.00 |
| | | *Nos. 414-418 (5)* | 21.05 | 13.85 |

Semi-Postal Stamp No. B2 Surcharged

**1932, Nov. 1** — *Perf. 12*

| No. | Type | Description | Unused | Used |
|---|---|---|---|---|
| 419 | SP1 | 1½c on 2c + 2c dp grn | .35 | .35 |

Artigas Type of 1928
Imprint: "Imprenta Nacional" at center

**1932-35** — **Litho.** — *Perf. 11, 12½*

**Size: 15¾x19¼mm**

| No. | Type | Description | Unused | Used |
|---|---|---|---|---|
| 420 | A109 | 5m lt brown ('35) | .20 | .20 |
| 421 | A109 | 1c pale violet ('35) | .20 | .20 |
| 422 | A109 | 15m black | .25 | .20 |
| 423 | A109 | 5c bluish grn ('35) | .50 | .20 |
| | | *Nos. 420-423 (4)* | 1.15 | .80 |

Gen. J. A. Lavalleja
A126

Flag of the Race and Globe
A127

**1933, July 12** — **Engr.** — *Perf. 12½*

| No. | Type | Description | Unused | Used |
|---|---|---|---|---|
| 429 | A126 | 15m brown lake | .20 | .20 |

*Perf. 11, 11½, 11x11½*

**1933, Aug. 3** — **Litho.**

| No. | Type | Description | Unused | Used |
|---|---|---|---|---|
| 430 | A127 | 3c blue green | .50 | .25 |
| 431 | A127 | 5c rose | .50 | .25 |
| 432 | A127 | 7c lt blue | .50 | .25 |
| 433 | A127 | 8c dull red | 1.00 | .55 |
| 434 | A127 | 12c deep blue | .65 | .25 |
| 435 | A127 | 17c violet | 1.75 | .80 |
| 436 | A127 | 20c red brown | 3.50 | 1.60 |
| 437 | A127 | 24c yellow | 3.50 | 1.75 |
| 438 | A127 | 36c orange | 5.00 | 2.40 |
| 439 | A127 | 50c olive gray | 5.50 | 3.00 |
| 440 | A127 | 1p bister | 13.00 | 6.25 |
| | | *Nos. 430-440 (11)* | 35.40 | 17.35 |

Raising of the "Flag of the Race" and of the 441st anniv. of the sailing of Columbus from Palos, Spain, on his first voyage to America.

Sower
A128

Juan Zorrilla de San Martin
A129

**1933, Aug. 28** — **Unwmk.** — *Perf. 11½*

| No. | Type | Description | Unused | Used |
|---|---|---|---|---|
| 441 | A128 | 3c blue green | .25 | .20 |
| 442 | A128 | 5c dull violet | .40 | .25 |
| 443 | A128 | 7c lt blue | .40 | .25 |
| 444 | A128 | 8c deep red | .80 | .50 |
| 445 | A128 | 12c ultra | 2.00 | 1.00 |
| | | *Nos. 441-445 (5)* | 3.85 | 2.20 |

3rd Constituent National Assembly.

**1933, Nov. 9** — **Engr.** — *Perf. 12½*

| No. | Type | Description | Unused | Used |
|---|---|---|---|---|
| 446 | A129 | 7c slate | .20 | .20 |

Albatross Flying over Map of the Americas — A130

**1933, Dec. 3** — **Typo.** — *Perf. 11½*

| No. | Type | Description | Unused | Used |
|---|---|---|---|---|
| 447 | A130 | 3c green, blk & brn | 2.75 | 2.00 |
| 448 | A130 | 7c turq bl, brn & blk | 1.60 | .80 |
| 449 | A130 | 12c dk bl, gray & ver | 2.40 | 1.60 |
| 450 | A130 | 17c ver, gray & vio | 5.00 | 2.75 |
| 451 | A130 | 20c yellow, bl & grn | 6.00 | 3.50 |
| 452 | A130 | 36c red, blk & yel | 7.75 | 5.50 |
| | | *Nos. 447-452 (6)* | 25.50 | 16.15 |

7th Pan-American Conf., Montevideo. Issued in sheets of 6. Value, $200. For overprints see Nos. C61-C62.

General Rivera — A131

**1934, Feb.** — **Engr.** — *Perf. 12½*

| No. | Type | Description | Unused | Used |
|---|---|---|---|---|
| 453 | A131 | 3c green | .20 | .20 |

Stars Representing the Three Constitutions — A132

**1934, Mar. 23** — **Typo.**

| No. | Type | Description | Unused | Used |
|---|---|---|---|---|
| 454 | A132 | 3c yellow grn & grn | .60 | .40 |
| 455 | A132 | 7c org red & red | .60 | .40 |
| 456 | A132 | 12c ultra & blue | 2.00 | .80 |

*Perf. 11½*

| No. | Type | Description | Unused | Used |
|---|---|---|---|---|
| 457 | A132 | 17c brown & rose | 2.50 | 1.25 |
| 458 | A132 | 20c yellow & gray | 3.50 | 1.60 |
| 459 | A132 | 36c dk vio & bl grn | 3.50 | 1.60 |
| 460 | A132 | 50c black & blue | 7.00 | 3.25 |
| 461 | A132 | 1p dk car & vio | 16.00 | 6.75 |
| | | *Nos. 454-461 (8)* | 35.70 | 16.05 |

First Year of Third Republic.

Artigas Type of 1928
Imprint: "Barreiro & Ramos S. A."

**1934, Nov. 28** — **Litho.**

| No. | Type | Description | Unused | Used |
|---|---|---|---|---|
| 462 | A109 | 50c brown black | 6.00 | 2.50 |

"Uruguay" and "Brazil" Holding Scales of Justice
A133

Florencio Sánchez
A134

**1935, May 30** — **Unwmk.** — *Perf. 11*

| No. | Type | Description | Unused | Used |
|---|---|---|---|---|
| 463 | A133 | 5m brown | .80 | .40 |
| 464 | A133 | 15m black | .40 | .20 |
| 465 | A133 | 3c green | .40 | .20 |
| 466 | A133 | 7c orange | .40 | .20 |
| 467 | A133 | 12c ultra | .80 | .60 |
| 468 | A133 | 50c yellow green | 4.00 | 2.50 |
| | | *Nos. 463-468 (6)* | 6.80 | 4.10 |

Visit of President Vargas of Brazil.

**1935, Nov. 7**

| No. | Type | Description | Unused | Used |
|---|---|---|---|---|
| 469 | A134 | 3c green | .20 | .20 |
| 470 | A134 | 7c brown | .20 | .20 |
| 471 | A134 | 12c blue | .55 | .35 |
| | | *Nos. 469-471 (3)* | .95 | .75 |

Florencio Sanchez (1875-1910), author.

Artigas (6 dots in panels below portrait) — A135

Imprint: "Imprenta Nacional" at center

**1936-44** — *Perf. 11, 12½*

| No. | Type | Description | Unused | Used |
|---|---|---|---|---|
| 474 | A135 | 5m org brn ('37) | .20 | .20 |
| 475 | A135 | 5m lt brown ('39) | .20 | .20 |
| 476 | A135 | 1c lt violet ('37) | .20 | .20 |
| 477 | A135 | 2c dk brown ('37) | .20 | .20 |
| 478 | A135 | 2c green ('39) | .20 | .20 |
| 479 | A135 | 5c brt blue ('37) | .20 | .20 |
| 480 | A135 | 5c bluish grn ('39) | .40 | .20 |
| 481 | A135 | 12c dull blue ('38) | .40 | .20 |
| 482 | A135 | 20c fawn | 1.40 | .35 |
| 482A | A135 | 20c rose ('44) | 1.00 | .40 |
| 483 | A135 | 50c brown black | 3.00 | .80 |

**Size: 21½x28½mm**

| No. | Type | Description | Unused | Used |
|---|---|---|---|---|
| 483A | A135 | 1p brown | 8.50 | 3.00 |
| 483B | A135 | 2p blue | 14.00 | 12.00 |
| 483C | A135 | 3p gray black | 20.00 | 16.00 |
| | | *Nos. 474-483C (14)* | 49.90 | 34.15 |

See Nos. 488, 576. See type A109.

Power Dam on Black River — A136

**1937-38**

| No. | Type | Description | Unused | Used |
|---|---|---|---|---|
| 484 | A136 | 1c dull violet | .20 | .20 |
| 485 | A136 | 10c blue | .50 | .20 |
| 486 | A136 | 15c rose | 1.25 | .65 |
| 487 | A136 | 1p choc ('38) | 6.25 | 2.50 |
| | | *Nos. 484-487 (4)* | 8.20 | 3.55 |

Imprint: "Imprenta Nacional" at right

**1938**

| No. | Type | Description | Unused | Used |
|---|---|---|---|---|
| 488 | A135 | 1c bright violet | .40 | .20 |

International Law Congress, 1889 — A137

**1939, July 16** — **Litho.** — *Perf. 12½*

| No. | Type | Description | Unused | Used |
|---|---|---|---|---|
| 489 | A137 | 1c brown orange | .20 | .20 |
| 490 | A137 | 2c dull green | .25 | .20 |
| 491 | A137 | 5c rose ver | .25 | .20 |
| 492 | A137 | 12c dull blue | .65 | .40 |
| 493 | A137 | 50c lt violet | 2.50 | 1.50 |
| | | *Nos. 489-493 (5)* | 3.85 | 2.50 |

50th anniversary of the Montevideo Congress of International Law.

Artigas
A138 — A138a

**1939-43** — **Litho.** — **Unwmk.**

**Size: 15¾x19mm**

| No. | Type | Description | Unused | Used |
|---|---|---|---|---|
| 494 | A138 | 5m dl brn org ('40) | .20 | .20 |
| 495 | A138 | 1c lt blue | .20 | .20 |
| 496 | A138 | 2c lt violet | .20 | .20 |
| 497 | A138 | 5c violet brn | .20 | .20 |
| 498 | A138 | 8c rose red | .25 | .20 |
| 499 | A138 | 10c green | .50 | .20 |
| 500 | A138 | 15c dull blue | 1.25 | .60 |

**Size: 24x29½mm**

| No. | Type | Description | Unused | Used |
|---|---|---|---|---|
| 501 | A138 | 1p dull brn ('41) | 2.50 | 1.00 |
| 502 | A138 | 2p dl rose vio ('40) | 7.00 | 3.00 |
| 503 | A138 | 4p orange ('43) | 9.25 | 4.00 |
| 504 | A138 | 5p ver ('41) | 14.00 | 6.00 |
| | | *Nos. 494-504 (11)* | 35.55 | 15.80 |

See No. 578.

Redrawn: Horizontal lines in portrait background

**1940-44**

**Size: 17x21mm**

| No. | Type | Description | Unused | Used |
|---|---|---|---|---|
| 505 | A138a | 5m brn org ('41) | .20 | .20 |
| 506 | A138a | 1c lt blue | .20 | .20 |
| 507 | A138a | 2c lt violet ('41) | .20 | .20 |
| 508 | A138a | 5c violet brn | .20 | .20 |
| 509 | A138a | 8c sal pink ('44) | .20 | .20 |
| 510 | A138a | 10c green ('41) | .40 | .20 |
| 511 | A138a | 50c olive bis ('42) | 6.25 | 1.75 |
| 511A | A138a | 50c yel grn ('44) | 4.75 | 1.75 |
| | | *Nos. 505-511A (8)* | 12.40 | 4.70 |

See Nos. 568-575, 577, 601, 632, 660-661. For surcharges see Nos. 523, 726.

Juan Manuel Blanes, Artist
A139

Francisco Acuna de Figueroa
A140

**1941, Aug. 11 Engr. *Perf. 12½***

| | | | | |
|---|---|---|---|---|
| **512** A139 | 5m ocher | .25 | .20 |
| **513** A139 | 1c henna brown | .25 | .20 |
| **514** A139 | 2c green | .25 | .20 |
| **515** A139 | 5c rose carmine | .60 | .20 |
| **516** A139 | 12c deep blue | 1.25 | .60 |
| **517** A139 | 50c dark violet | 4.75 | 3.25 |
| | *Nos. 512-517 (6)* | 7.35 | 4.65 |

**1942, Mar. 18 Unwmk.**

| | | | |
|---|---|---|---|
| **518** A140 | 1c henna brown | .20 | .20 |
| **519** A140 | 2c deep green | .20 | .20 |
| **520** A140 | 5c rose carmine | .25 | .20 |
| **521** A140 | 12c deep blue | 1.00 | .40 |
| **522** A140 | 50c dark violet | 3.25 | 2.50 |
| | *Nos. 518-522 (5)* | 4.90 | 3.50 |

Issued in honor of Francisco Acuna de Figueroa, author of the National anthem.

No. 506 Surcharged in Red

**1943, Jan. 27**

**523** A138a 5m on 1c lt bl .25 .20

Coat of Arms — A141

Clio — A142

**1943, Mar. 12 Litho.**

| | | | |
|---|---|---|---|
| **524** A141 | 1c on 2c dl vio brn (R) | .20 | .20 |
| **525** A141 | 2c on 2c dl vio brn (V) | .20 | .20 |
| *a.* | Inverted surcharge | 20.00 | 20.00 |

Nos. 524-525 are unissued stamps surcharged. See Nos. 546-555, Q67, Q69, Q74-Q76.

**1943, Aug. 24**

| | | | |
|---|---|---|---|
| **526** A142 | 5m lt violet | .20 | .20 |
| **527** A142 | 1c lt ultra | .20 | .20 |
| **528** A142 | 2c brt rose | .50 | .20 |
| **529** A142 | 5c buff | .50 | .20 |
| | *Nos. 526-529 (4)* | 1.40 | .80 |

100th anniversary of the Historic and Geographic Institute of Uruguay.

Swiss Colony Monument
A143

YMCA Seal
A144

Overprinted "1944" and Surcharged in Various Colors

**1944, May 18**

| | | | |
|---|---|---|---|
| **530** A143 | 1c on 3c dull grn (R) | .20 | .20 |
| **531** A143 | 5c on 7c brn red (B) | .20 | .20 |
| **532** A143 | 10c on 12c dk bl (Br) | .65 | .25 |
| | *Nos. 530-532 (3)* | 1.05 | .65 |

Founding of the Swiss Colony, 50th anniv.

**1944, Sept. 8**

**533** A144 5c blue .20 .20

100th anniv. of the YMCA.

**Catalogue values for unused stamps in this section, from this point to the end of the section, are for Never Hinged items.**

"La Educación del Pueblo"
A145

José Pedro Varela
A146

A147

Monument
A148

***Perf. 11½***

**1945, June 13 Litho. Unwmk.**

| | | | |
|---|---|---|---|
| **534** A145 | 5m brt green | .20 | .20 |
| **535** A146 | 1c dp brown | .20 | .20 |

***Perf. 12½***

| | | | |
|---|---|---|---|
| **536** A147 | 2c rose red | .20 | .20 |
| **537** A148 | 5c blue | .20 | .20 |
| *a.* | Perf. 11½ | .20 | .20 |
| | *Nos. 534-537 (4)* | .80 | .80 |

José Pedro Varela, author, birth cent.

Santiago Vazquez
A149

Silvestre Blanco
A150

Eduardo Acevedo
A151

Bruno Mauricio de Zabala
A152

José Pedro Varela — A153

José Ellauri — A154

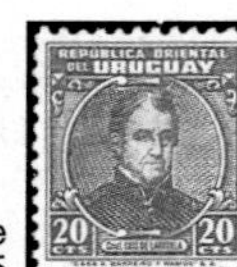
Gen. Luis de Larrobla — A155

**Engraved (5m, 5c, 10c); Lithographed**

**1945-47 *Perf. 10½, 11, 11½, 12½***

| | | | |
|---|---|---|---|
| **538** A149 | 5m purple ('46) | .20 | .20 |
| **539** A150 | 1c yel brn ('46) | .20 | .20 |
| **540** A151 | 2c brown vio | .20 | .20 |
| **541** A152 | 3c grn & dp grn ('47) | .20 | .20 |
| **542** A153 | 5c brt carmine | .20 | .20 |
| **543** A154 | 10c ultra | .40 | .20 |
| **544** A155 | 20c dp grn & choc ('47) | 1.25 | .50 |
| | *Nos. 538-544 (7)* | 2.65 | 1.70 |

No. C86A Surcharged in Blue

**1946, Jan. 9 *Perf. 12½***

**545** AP7 20c on 68c pale vio brn 1.25 .60

Inauguration of the Black River Power Dam. See No. C120.

Type A141 Overprinted

**1946-51 Unwmk. Litho. *Perf. 12½***

| | | | |
|---|---|---|---|
| **546** A141 | 5m orange ('49) | .20 | .20 |
| *a.* | Inverted overprint | | |
| **547** A141 | 2c dl vio brn ('47) | .20 | .20 |
| **548** A141 | 3c green | .20 | .20 |
| **549** A141 | 5c ultra ('51) | .20 | .20 |
| **550** A141 | 10c orange brn | .35 | .20 |
| **551** A141 | 20c dk green | .65 | .25 |
| **552** A141 | 50c brown | 2.00 | 1.00 |
| **553** A141 | 3p lilac rose | 7.00 | 4.50 |
| | *Nos. 546-553 (8)* | 10.80 | 6.75 |

Type A141 Surcharged

**1947-48**

| | | | |
|---|---|---|---|
| **554** A141 | 2c on 5c ultra ('48) | .20 | .20 |
| **555** A141 | 3c on 5c ultra | .20 | .20 |

Statue of Ariel — A158

Bas-relief
A160

Bust of José Enrique Rodó — A159

Bas-relief
A161

***Perf. 12½***

**1948, Jan. 30 Unwmk. Engr.**

**Center in Orange Brown**

| | | | |
|---|---|---|---|
| **556** A158 | 1c grnsh gray | .20 | .20 |
| **557** A159 | 2c purple | .20 | .20 |
| **558** A160 | 3c green | .20 | .20 |
| **559** A161 | 5c red violet | .25 | .20 |
| **560** A160 | 10c dp orange | .35 | .20 |
| **561** A161 | 12c ultra | .40 | .20 |
| **562** A158 | 20c rose violet | .80 | .25 |
| **563** A159 | 50c dp carmine | 2.50 | .90 |
| | *Nos. 556-563 (8)* | 4.90 | 2.35 |

Dedication of the Rodó monument.

View of the Port, Paysandú — A162

Arms of Paysandú
A163

**1948, Oct. 9 Litho.**

| | | | |
|---|---|---|---|
| **564** A162 | 3c blue green | .25 | .20 |
| **565** A163 | 7c ultra | .40 | .25 |

Exposition of Industry and Agriculture, Paysandú, October-November 1948.

Santa Lucia River Highway Bridge
A164

**1948, Dec. 10**

| | | | |
|---|---|---|---|
| **566** A164 | 10c dark blue | .80 | .20 |
| **567** A164 | 50c green | 2.50 | 1.00 |

Redrawn Artigas Types of 1940, 1936, 1939

**1948-51 Litho. *Perf. 12½***

| | | | |
|---|---|---|---|
| **568** A138a | 5m gray ('49) | .20 | .20 |
| **569** A138a | 1c rose vio ('50) | .20 | .20 |
| **570** A138a | 2c orange | .20 | .20 |
| **571** A138a | 2c choc ('50) | .20 | .20 |
| **572** A138a | 3c blue green | .20 | .20 |
| **572A** A138a | 7c violet blue | .20 | .20 |
| **573** A138a | 8c rose car ('49) | .20 | .20 |
| **574** A138a | 10c orange brn ('51) | .20 | .20 |
| **575** A138a | 12c blue ('51) | .20 | .20 |
| **576** A135 | 20c violet | .30 | .20 |
| **577** A138a | 20c rose pink ('51) | .55 | .20 |

**Size: 18x21¾mm**

| | | | |
|---|---|---|---|
| **578** A138 | 1p lilac rose ('51) | 1.10 | .25 |
| | *Nos. 568-578 (12)* | 3.75 | 2.45 |

Nos. 571-572A also exist perf. 11.

Plowing
A165

Mounted Cattle Herder
A166

**1949, Apr. 29 Unwmk. *Perf. 12½***
**579** A165 3c green .20 .20
**580** A166 7c blue .40 .20

4th Regional American Conf. of Labor, 1949.

Cannon, Rural and Urban Views — A167

Symbolical of Soccer Matches — A168

**1950, Oct. 11 Litho.**
**581** A167 1c lilac rose .25 .20
**582** A167 3c green .25 .20
**583** A167 7c deep blue .25 .20
*Nos. 581-583 (3)* .75 .60

200th anniv. of the founding of Cordón, a district of Montevideo.

**1951, Mar. 20 *Perf. 12½, 11***
**584** A168 3c green 1.00 .25
**585** A168 7c violet blue 2.25 .80

4th World Soccer Championship, Rio de Janeiro.

Gen. José Artigas — A169

Flight of the People A170

1c, 2c, 5c, Various equestrian portraits of Artigas. 7c, Dictating instructions. 8c, In congress. 10c, Artigas' flag. 14c, At the citadel. 20c, Arms of Artigas. 50c, In Paraguay. 1p, Bust.

**Engraved and Photogravure**

**1952, Jan. 7 Unwmk. *Perf. 13½***
**586** A169 5m slate .20 .20
**587** A169 1c bl & blk .20 .20
**588** A169 2c pur & red brn .20 .20
**589** A170 3c aqua & dk brn .20 .20
**590** A169 5c red org & blk .20 .20
**591** A170 7c ol & blk .25 .20
**592** A170 8c car & blk .35 .20
**593** A170 10c choc, brt ultra & crim .35 .20
**594** A169 14c dp bl .35 .20
**595** A169 20c org yel, dp ultra & car .80 .20
**596** A169 50c org brn & blk 1.60 .40
**597** A169 1p bl gray & cit 3.00 1.25
*Nos. 586-597 (12)* 7.70 3.65

Centenary (in 1950) of the death of Gen. José Artigas.

Plane and Stagecoach A171

**1952, Oct. 9 Photo. *Perf. 13½x13***
**598** A171 3c bl grn .20 .20
**599** A171 7c blk brn .20 .20
**600** A171 12c ultra .30 .20
*Nos. 598-600 (3)* .70 .60

75th anniv. (in 1949) of the UPU.

Redrawn Artigas Type of 1940-44

**1953, Feb. 23 Litho. *Perf. 11***
**Size: 24x29½mm**
**601** A138a 2p fawn 11.00 8.50

Franklin D. Roosevelt — A172

**1953, Apr. 9 Engr. *Perf. 13½***
**602** A172 3c green .20 .20
**603** A172 7c ultra .25 .20
**604** A172 12c blk brn .40 .25
*Nos. 602-604 (3)* .85 .65

5th Postal Cong. of the Americas & Spain.

Ceibo, Natl. Flower — A173

Horse Breaking — A174

Legislature Building A175

"Island of Seals" (Southern Sea Lions) — A176

Fair Entrance — A177

Designs: 2c, 10c, 5p, Ombu tree. 3c, 50c, Passion Flower. 7c, 3p, Montevideo fortress. 12c, 2p, Outer gate, Montevideo.

***Perf. 13x13½, 13½x13, 12½x13, 13x12½***
**Photo. (5m, 3c, 20c, 50c); Engr.**

**1954, Jan. 14 Unwmk.**
**605** A173 5m multi .20 .20
**606** A174 1c car & blk .20 .20
**607** A174 2c brn & grn .20 .20
**608** A173 3c multi .20 .20
**609** A175 5c pur & red brn .20 .20
**610** A173 7c brn & grn .20 .20
**611** A176 8c car & ultra .40 .20
**612** A174 10c org & grn .35 .20
**613** A175 12c dp ultra & dk brn .25 .20
**614** A174 14c rose lil & blk .25 .20
**615** A173 20c grn, brn, gray & car .70 .20
**616** A173 50c car & multi 2.00 .20
**617** A175 1p car & red brn 2.50 1.00
**618** A175 2p car & blk brn 4.00 1.60
**619** A173 3p lil & grn 4.75 2.00
**620** A176 4p dp brn & dp ultra 13.00 5.00
**621** A174 5p vio bl & grn 10.00 4.00
*Nos. 605-621 (17)* 39.40 16.00

For surcharges see Nos. 637-639, 750, C299.

**1956, Jan. 19 Litho. *Perf. 11***
**622** A177 3c pale olive green .25 .20
**623** A177 7c blue .25 .20
*Nos. 622-623,C166-C168 (5)* 2.00 1.30

First Exposition of National Products.

José Batlle y Ordonez, Birth Centenary A178

Design: 7c, Full length portrait.

***Perf. 13½***
**1956, Dec. 15 Wmk. 90 Photo.**
**624** A178 3c rose red .20 .20
**625** A178 7c sepia .25 .20
*Nos. 624-625,C169-C172 (6)* 1.95 1.50

Same Surcharged with New Values

**1957-58**
**626** A178 5c on 3c ('58) .20 .20
**627** A178 10c on 7c .25 .20
*a.* Surcharge inverted 20.00 20.00

Diver — A179

Eduardo Acevedo — A180

Design: 10c, Swimmer at start, horiz.

***Perf. 10½, 11½***
**1958, Feb. 15 Litho. Unwmk.**
**628** A179 5c brt bl grn .20 .20
**629** A179 10c brt bl .35 .20

14th South American swimming meet, Montevideo.

**1958, Mar. 19 *Perf. 11½, 10½***
**630** A180 5c lt ol grn & blk .20 .20
**631** A180 10c ultra & blk .25 .20

Eduardo Acevedo (1856-1948), lawyer, legislator, minister of foreign affairs, birth cent.

Artigas Type of 1940-44

**1958, Sept. 25 Litho. *Perf. 11***
**632** A138a 5m blue .25 .20

Baygorria Hydroelectric Works — A181

**1958, Oct. 30 Unwmk. *Perf. 11***
**633** A181 5c yel grn & blk .20 .20
**634** A181 10c brn org & blk .20 .20
**635** A181 1p bl gray & blk .65 .25
**636** A181 2p rose & blk 1.25 .55
*Nos. 633-636 (4)* 2.30 1.20

Nos. 608, 610 and 605 Surcharged Similarly to

**Photogravure and Engraved**

**1958-59 *Perf. 13x13½***
**637** A173 5c on 3c multi ('59) .30 .20
**638** A173 10c on 7c brn & grn .30 .20
**639** A173 20c on 5m multi .30 .20
*Nos. 637-639 (3)* .90 .60

Gabriela Mistral — A182

Carlos Vaz Ferreira — A183

**Wmk. 327**
**1959, July 6 Litho. *Perf. 11½***
**640** A182 5c green .20 .20
**641** A182 10c dark blue .20 .20
**642** A182 20c red .20 .20
*Nos. 640-642 (3)* .60 .60

Gabriela Mistral, Chilean poet and educator.

**1959, Sept. 3 *Perf. 11***
**643** A183 5c blk & lt bl .25 .20
**644** A183 10c blk & ocher .25 .20
**645** A183 20c blk & ver .25 .20
**646** A183 50c blk & vio .35 .25
**647** A183 1p blk & grn .55 .25
*Nos. 643-647 (5)* 1.65 1.10

Ferreira (1872-1958), educator and author.

A184

A185

**Wmk. 332**
**1960, May 16 Litho. *Perf. 12***
**648** A184 3c red lil & blk .20 .20
**649** A184 5c dp vio & blk .20 .20
**650** A184 10c brt bl & blk .20 .20
**651** A184 20c chocolate & blk .25 .20
**652** A184 1p gray & blk .40 .20
**653** A184 2p org & blk 1.00 .20
**654** A184 3p olive grn & blk 1.60 .40
**655** A184 4p yel brn & blk 2.00 .75
**656** A184 5p brt red & blk 2.50 .75
*Nos. 648-656 (9)* 8.35 3.10

Dr. Martin C. Martinez (1859-1940), statesman.

**1960, June 6 Wmk. 332 *Perf. 12***
**657** A185 10c Uprooted oak emblem .25 .20

Issued to publicize World Refugee Year, July 1, 1959-June 30, 1960. See No. C207.

Revolutionists and Cabildo, Buenos Aires — A186

**1960, Nov. 4 Litho. *Perf. 12***
**658** A186 5c bl & blk .20 .20
**659** A186 10c bl & ocher .20 .20
*Nos. 658-659,C208-C210 (5)* 1.10 1.00

150th anniv. of the May Revolution of 1810.

Artigas Type of 1940-44

**1960-61 Wmk. 332 *Perf. 11***
**660** A138a 2c gray .20 .20
**661** A138a 50c brn ('61) .20 .20

Gen. Manuel Oribe (1796?-1857), Revolutionary Leader, Pres. of Uruguay (1835-38) — A187

**1961, Mar. 4 Litho. *Perf. 12***

**671** A187 10c brt bl & blk .25 .20
**672** A187 20c bis & blk .25 .20
**673** A187 40c grn & blk .25 .20
*Nos. 671-673 (3)* .75 .60

Cavalry Charge A188

**1961, June 12 Wmk. 332 *Perf. 12***

**674** A188 20c bl & blk .20 .20
**675** A188 40c emer & blk .30 .20

150th anniversary of the revolution.

Welfare, Justice and Education — A189

Gen. José Fructuoso Rivera — A190

**1961, Aug. 14 Wmk. 322 *Perf. 12***

**676** A189 2c bister & lilac .35 .20
**677** A189 5c bister & orange .35 .20
**678** A189 10c bister & scarlet .35 .20
**679** A189 20c bister & yel grn .35 .20
**680** A189 50c bister & light vio .35 .20
**681** A189 1p bister & blue .35 .20
**682** A189 2p bister & citron 1.00 .25
**683** A189 3p bister & gray 1.40 .65
**684** A189 4p bister & light bl 2.40 .80
**685** A189 5p bister & chocolate 2.50 1.25
*Nos. 676-685 (10)* 9.40 4.15

Inter-American Economic and Social Conference of the Organization of American States, Punta del Este, August, 1961. See Nos. C233-C244.

**Wmk. 332**

**1962, May 29 Litho. *Perf. 12***

**686** A190 10c brt red & blk .20 .20
**687** A190 20c bis & blk .20 .20
**688** A190 40c grn & blk .20 .20
*Nos. 686-688 (3)* .60 .60

Issued to honor Gen. José Fructuoso Rivera (1790-1854), first President of Uruguay.

Spade, Grain, Swiss "Scarf" and Hat — A191

Bernardo Prudencio Berro — A192

**1962, Aug. 1 Wmk. 332 *Perf. 12***

**689** A191 10c bl, blk & car .20 .20
**690** A191 20c lt grn, blk & car .25 .20
*Nos. 689-690,C245-C246 (4)* 1.05 .90

Swiss Settlement in Uruguay, cent.

**1962, Oct. 22 Litho. *Perf. 12***

**691** A192 10c grnsh bl & blk .20 .20
**692** A192 20c yel brn & blk .25 .25

Pres. Bernardo P. Berro (1803-1868).

Damaso Larrañaga A193

**1963, Jan. 24 Wmk. 332 *Perf. 12***

**693** A193 20c lt bl grn & dk brn .20 .20
**694** A193 40c tan & dk brn .25 .25

Damaso Antonio Larranaga (1771-1848), teacher, writer and founder of National Library.

Rufous-bellied Thrush — A194

Birds: 50c, Rufous ovenbird. 1p, Chalk-browed mockingbird. 2p, Rufous-collared sparrow.

**1963, Apr. 1 Wmk. 332 *Perf. 12***

**695** A194 2c rose, brn & blk .20 .20
**696** A194 50c lt brn & blk .65 .20
**697** A194 1p tan, brn & blk 1.60 .20
**698** A194 2p lt brn, blk & gray 3.00 .80
*Nos. 695-698 (4)* 5.45 1.40

Thin frame on No. 696, no frame on No. 698.

UPAE Emblem A195

**1963, May 31 Litho.**

**699** A195 20c ultra & blk .50 .20
*Nos. 699,C252-C253 (3)* .95 .60

50th anniv. of the founding of the Postal Union of the Americas and Spain, UPAE. For surcharge see No. C321.

Wheat Emblem — A196

Anchors — A197

**1963, July 8 Wmk. 332 *Perf. 12***

**700** A196 10c grn & yel .25 .20
**701** A196 20c brn & yel .30 .20
*Nos. 700-701,C254-C255 (4)* 1.15 1.00

FAO "Freedom from Hunger" campaign.

**1963, Aug. 16**

**702** A197 10c org & vio .25 .20
**703** A197 20c dk red & gray .30 .20
*Nos. 702-703,C256-C257 (4)* 1.35 1.00

Voyage around the world by the Uruguayan sailing vessel "Alferez Campora," 1960-63.

Large Intestine, Congress Emblem A198

**1963, Dec. 9 Litho.**

**704** A198 10c lt grn, blk & dk car .25 .20
**705** A198 20c org, yel, blk & dk car .30 .20

1st Uruguayan Proctology Cong., Montevideo, Dec. 9-15.

Red Cross Centenary Emblem A199

Imprint: "Imp. Nacional"

**1964, June 5 Wmk. 332 *Perf. 12***

**706** A199 20c blue & red .25 .20
**707** A199 40c gray & red .30 .20

Centenary of International Red Cross.

No. 706 exists with imprint missing. Value $4.

Luis Alberto de Herrera A200

**1964, July 22 Litho. Unwmk.**

**708** A200 20c dl grn, bl & blk .20 .20
**709** A200 40c lt bl, bl & blk .20 .20
**710** A200 80c yel org, bl & blk .20 .20
**711** A200 1p lt vio, bl & blk .40 .25
**712** A200 2p gray, bl & blk .60 .50
*Nos. 708-712 (5)* 1.60 1.35

Herrera (1873-1959), leader of Herrerista party and member of National Government Council.

Nile Gods Uniting Upper and Lower Egypt (Abu Simbel) A201

**1964, Oct. 30 Wmk. 332 *Perf. 12***

**713** A201 20c multi .25 .20
*Nos. 713,C266-C267 (3)* 1.15 .90

UNESCO world campaign to save historic monuments in Nubia. See No. C267a.

Pres. John F. Kennedy A202

**1965, Mar. 5 Wmk. 327 *Perf. 11½***

**714** A202 20c gold, emer & blk .25 .20
*a.* Gold omitted

**715** A202 40c gold, redsh brn & blk .30 .20
*a.* Gold omitted
*Nos. 714-715,C269-C270 (4)* 1.15 1.00

Tete Beche Pair of 1864, No. 21a A203

**1965, Mar. 19 Wmk. 332 *Perf. 12***

**716** A203 40c black & green .25 .20

1st Rio de la Plata Stamp Show, sponsored jointly by the Argentine and Uruguayan philatelic associations, Montevideo, Mar. 19-28. See No. C271.

Benito Nardone A204

40c, Benito Nardone before microphone.

**1965, Mar. 25 Litho.**

**717** A204 20c blk & emer .25 .20
**718** A204 40c blk & emer, vert. .30 .20

1st anniversary of the death of Benito Nardone, president of the Council of Government.

Artigas Quotation — A205

40c, Artigas bust, quotation. 80c, José Artigas.

***Perf. 12x11½***

**1965, May 17 Litho. Wmk. 327**

**719** A205 20c bl, yel & red .25 .20
**720** A205 40c vio bl, cit & blk .25 .20
**721** A205 80c brn, yel, red & bl .35 .20
*Nos. 719-721,C273-C275 (6)* 1.80 1.40

José Artigas (1764-1850), leader of the independence revolt against Spain.

Soccer A206

Designs: 40c, Basketball. 80c, Bicycling. 1p, Woman swimmer.

**1965, Aug. 3 Litho. Wmk. 327**

**722** A206 20c grn, org & blk .30 .20
**723** A206 40c hn brn, cit & blk .30 .20
**724** A206 80c gray, red & blk .30 .20
**725** A206 1p bl, yel grn & blk .30 .20
*Nos. 722-725,C276-C281 (10)* 3.90 2.80

18th Olympic Games, Tokyo, 10/10-25/64.

No. 572A Surcharged in Red

**1965 Unwmk. *Perf. 12½***

**726** A138a 10c on 7c vio bl .25 .20

No. B5 Surcharged:

**1966, Jan. 25 Wmk. 327 *Perf. 11½***
**727** SP2 4c on 5c + 10c grn & org .25 .20

Association of Uruguayan Architects, 50th anniv.

Winston Churchill A207

**Wmk. 332**

**1966, Apr. 29 Litho. *Perf. 12***
**728** A207 40c car, dp ultra & brn .25 .20

Sir Winston Spencer Churchill, statesman and World War II leader. See No. C284.

Arms of Rio de Janeiro and Sugar Loaf Mountain A208

**1966, June 9 Litho. Wmk. 332**
**729** A208 40c emer & brn .25 .20

400th anniversary of the founding of Rio de Janeiro. See No. C285.

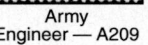

Army Engineer — A209

Daniel Fernandez Crespo — A210

**1966, June 17 Litho.**
**730** A209 20c blk, red, vio bl & yel .25 .20

50th anniversary of the Army Engineers Corps.

**1966, Sept. 16 Wmk. 332 *Perf. 12***

Portraits: No. 732, Washington Beltran. No. 733, Luis Batlle Berres.

**731** A210 20c lt bl & blk .25 .20
**732** A210 20c lt bl & dk brn .25 .20
**733** A210 20c brick red & blk .25 .20
*Nos. 731-733 (3)* .75 .60

Issued to honor political leaders.

Old Printing Press — A211

**1966, Oct. 14 Photo. *Perf. 12***
**734** A211 20c tan, grnsh gray & dk brn .25 .20

50th anniversary of State Printing Office.

Fireman A212

**1966 Litho.**
**735** A212 20c red & blk .40 .25

Issued to publicize fire prevention. Printed with alternating red and black labels inscribed: "Prevengase del fuego! Del pueblo y para el pueblo."

No. 716 Overprinted in Red: "Segunda Muestra y / Jornadas Rioplatenses / de Filatelia / Abril 1966 / Centenario del Sello / Escudito Resellado"

**1966, Nov. 4**
**736** A203 40c blk & grn .25 .20

2nd Rio de la Plata Stamp Show, Buenos Aires, Apr. 1966, and cent. of Uruguay's 1st surcharged issue. See No. C298.

General Leandro Gomez — A213

#738, Gen. Juan Antonio Lavalleja. #739, Aparicio Saravia, revolutionary, on horseback.

**Wmk. 332**

**1966, Nov. 24 Litho. *Perf. 12***
**737** A213 20c slate, blk & dp bl .30 .25
**738** A213 20c red, blk & bl .30 .25
**739** A213 20c blue & blk, horiz. .30 .25
*Nos. 737-739 (3)* .90 .75

Montevideo Planetarium A214

**1967, Jan. 13 Wmk. 332 *Perf. 12***
**740** A214 40c pink & blk .30 .20

10th anniv. of the Montevideo Municipal Planetarium. See No. C301.

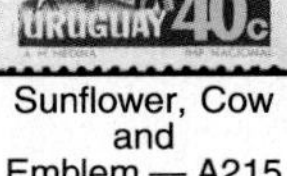

Sunflower, Cow and Emblem — A215

Church of San Carlos — A216

**1967, Jan. 13 Litho.**
**741** A215 40c dk brn & yel .30 .20

Young Farmers' Movement, 20th anniv.

**1967, Apr. 17 Wmk. 332 *Perf. 12***
**742** A216 40c lt bl, blk & dk red .25 .20

Bicentenary of San Carlos.

Eduardo Acevedo A217

**1967, Apr. 17**
**743** A217 20c grn & brn .20 .20
**744** A217 40c org & grn .25 .20

Issued to honor Eduardo Acevedo, lawyer, legislator and Minister of Foreign Affairs.

Arms of Carmelo A218

José Enrique Rodó A219

**1967, Aug. 11 Litho. *Perf. 12***
**745** A218 40c lt & dk bl & ocher .25 .20

Founding of Carmelo, 150th anniv.

**1967, Oct. 6 Wmk. 332 *Perf. 12***

2p, Portrait of Rodó and sculpture, horiz.

**746** A219 1p gray, brn & blk .25 .20
**747** A219 2p rose claret, blk & tan .25 .20

50th anniversary of the death of José Enrique Rodó, author.

Senen M. Rodriguez and Locomotive A220

**1967, Oct. 26 Litho. *Perf. 12***
**748** A220 2p ocher & dk brn .35 .20

Centenary of the founding of the first national railroad company.

Child and Map of Americas A221

Cocoi Heron A222

**1967, Nov. 10 Wmk. 332 *Perf. 12***
**749** A221 1p vio & red .25 .20

Inter-American Children's Institute, 40th anniv.

No. 610 Surcharged in Red

***Perf. 13x13½***

**1967, Nov. 10 Engr. Unwmk.**
**750** A173 1p on 7c brn & grn .25 .20

**1968-70 Wmk. 332 Litho. *Perf. 12***

Birds: 1p, Great horned owl. 3p, Brown-headed gull, horiz. No. 754, White-faced tree duck, horiz. No. 754A, Black-tailed stilts. 5p, Wattled jacanas, horiz. 10p, Snowy egret, horiz.

**751** A222 1p dl yel & brn 2.00 .40
**752** A222 2p bl grn & blk 2.00 .40
**753** A222 3p org, gray & blk ('69) 1.50 .35
**754** A222 4p brn, tan & blk 3.25 .60
**754A** A222 4p ver & blk ('70) 1.50 .35
**755** A222 5p lt red brn, blk & yel 3.75 .60
**756** A222 10p lil & blk 6.75 .80
*Nos. 751-756 (7)* 20.75 3.50

Concord Bridge, Presidents of Uruguay, Brazil A223

**1968, Apr. 3**
**757** A223 6p brown .25 .20

Opening of Concord Bridge across the Uruguay River by Presidents Jorge Pacheco Areco of Uruguay and Arthur Costa e Silva of Brazil.

Soccer Player and Trophy — A224

**1968, May 29 Litho.**
**758** A224 1p blk & yel .25 .20

Victory of the Penarol Athletic Club in the Intercontinental Soccer Championships of 1966.

St. John Bosco, Symbols of Education and Industry A225

**1968, July 31 Wmk. 332 *Perf. 12***
**759** A225 2p brn & blk .25 .20

75th anniv. of the Don Bosco Workshops of the Salesian Brothers.

Sailors' Monument, Montevideo A226

Designs: 6p, Lighthouse and buoy, vert. 12p, Gunboat "Suarez" (1860).

**1968, Nov. 12 Litho. *Perf. 12***
**760** A226 2p gray ol & blk .20 .20
**761** A226 6p lt grn & blk .20 .20
**762** A226 12p brt bl & blk .20 .20
*Nos. 760-762,C340-C343 (7)* 1.50 1.40

Sesquicentennial of National Navy.
For surcharge see No. Q101.

Oscar D. Gestido A227

**1968, Dec. 6 Wmk. 332 *Perf. 12***
**763** A227 6p brn, dp car & bl .25 .20

First anniversary of the death of President Oscar D. Gestido.

Gearwheel, Grain and Two Heads
A228

**1969, Mar. 17 Litho. *Perf. 12***
**764** A228 2p blk & ver .25 .20

25th anniversary of Labor University.

Bicyclists
A229

**1969, Mar. 21 Wmk. 332**
**765** A229 6p dk bl, org & emer .30 .20

1968 World Bicycle Championships. See No. C347.

Gymnasts and Club Emblem
A230

**1969, May 8 Wmk. 332 *Perf. 12***
**766** A230 6p blk & ver .30 .20

75th anniversary of L'Avenir Athletic Club.

Baltasar Brum (1883-1933)
A231

Former presidents: No. 768, Tomas Berreta (1875-1947).

**1969 Litho. *Perf. 12***
**767** A231 6p rose red & blk .25 .20
**768** A231 6p car rose & blk .25 .20

Fair Emblem — A232

**1969, Aug. 15 Wmk. 332 *Perf. 12***
**769** A232 2p multi .25 .20

Issued to publicize the 2nd Industrial World's Fair, Montevideo, 1970.

Diesel Locomotive
A233

Design: No. 771, Old steam locomotive and modern railroad cars.

**1969, Sept. 19 Litho. Wmk. 332**
**770** A233 6p car, blk & ultra .30 .25
**771** A233 6p car, blk & ultra .30 .25
*e.* Pair, #770-771 .60 .60

Centenary of Uruguayan railroads. No. 771e has continuous design and label between pairs.

For surcharges see Nos. Q102-Q103.

Souvenir Sheet

Diligencia Issue, 1856 — A233a

**1969, Oct. 1 *Imperf.***
**771A** A233a Sheet of 3 8.00 8.00
*b.* 60p blue 2.00 2.00
*c.* 80p green 2.50 2.50
*d.* 100p red 3.00 3.00

Stamp Day 1969. No. 771A contains stamps similar to No. 1-3, with denominations in pesos.

No. 771A was re-issued Apr. 15, 1972, with black overprint for 15th anniv. of 1st Lufthansa flight from Uruguay to Germany and the Munich Olympic Games. Value $27.50.

"Combat" and Sculptor Belloni — A234

**1969, Oct. 22 Wmk. 332 *Perf. 12***
**772** A234 6p olive, slate grn & blk .25 .20

José L. Belloni (1882- ), sculptor.

Reserve Officers' Training Center Emblem
A235

Design: 2p, Training Center emblem, and officer in uniform and as civilian.

**1969, Nov. 5 Litho.**
**773** A235 1p yel & dk bl .25 .20
**774** A235 2p dk brn & lt bl .25 .20

Reserve Officers' Training Center, 25th anniv.

Map of Americas and Sun — A236

Stylized Pine — A237

**1970, Apr. 20 Wmk. 332 *Perf. 12***
**775** A236 10p dp bl & gold .25 .20

11th meeting of the governors of the Inter-American Development Bank, Punta del Este.

**1970, May 14**
**776** A237 2p red, blk & brt grn .25 .20

2nd National Forestry and Wood Exhibition.

Artigas' Ancestral Home in Sauce
A238

**1970, June 18 Wmk. 332 *Perf. 12***
**777** A238 15p ver, ultra & blk .30 .25

Map of Uruguay, Sun and Sea
A239

**1970, July 8 Litho.**
**778** A239 5p greenish blue .25 .20

Issued for tourist publicity.

EXPO '70 Emblem, Mt. Fuji and Uruguay Coat of Arms
A240

EXPO '70 Intl. Exhibition, Osaka, Japan, 3/15-9/13: No. 780, Geisha. No. 781, Sun Tower. No. 782, Youth pole.

**1970, Aug. 5 Wmk. 332 *Perf. 12***
**779** A240 25p grn, slate bl & yel .30 .30
**780** A240 25p org, slate bl & grn .30 .30
**781** A240 25p yel, slate bl & pur .30 .30
**782** A240 25p pur, slate bl & org .30 .30
*a.* Block of 4, #779-782 1.25 1.25

Cobbled Street in Colonia del Sacramento
A241

Mother and Son by Edmundo Prati in Salto — A242

**1970, Oct. 21 Litho. *Perf. 12***
**783** A241 5p blk & multi .25 .20

290th anniv. of the founding of Colonia del Sacramento, the 1st European settlement in Uruguay.

**1970, Nov. 4 Litho.**
**784** A242 10p grn & blk .35 .30

Issued to honor mothers.

URUEXPO Emblem
A243

**1970, Dec. 9 Wmk. 332 *Perf. 12***
**785** A243 15p bl, brn org & vio .30 .30

URUEXPO '70, National Philatelic Exposition, Montevideo, Sept. 26-Oct. 4.

Children Holding Hands, and UNESCO Emblem — A244

Children's Drawings: No. 786, Two girls holding hands, vert. No. 788, Boy sitting at school desk, vert. No. 789, Astronaut and monster.

**1970, Dec. 29 Litho. *Perf. 12½***
**786** A244 10p multi .20 .20
**787** A244 10p multi .20 .20
**788** A244 10p dp car & multi .20 .20
**789** A244 10p bl & multi .20 .20
*a.* Block of 4, #786-789 + 2 labels .80 .80

International Education Year.

Alfonso Espinola (1845-1905), Physician, Professor and Philanthropist
A245

**1971, Jan. 13 Wmk. 332 *Perf. 12***
**790** A245 5p dp org & blk .25 .20

Exposition Poster — A246

**1971 Litho. *Perf. 12***
**791** A246 15p multi .25 .20

Uruguay Philatelic Exposition, 1971, Montevideo, March 26-Apr. 19.

5c Coin of 1840, Obverse
A247

Design: #793, 1st coin of Uruguay, reverse.

**1971, Apr. 16 Wmk. 332 *Perf. 12***
**792** A247 25p bl, brn & blk .55 .55
**793** A247 25p bl, brn & blk .45 .45
*a.* Pair, #792-793 1.25 1.25

Numismatists' Day.

Domingo Arena, Lawyer and Journalist — A248

**1971, May 3 Wmk. 332 *Perf. 12***
**794** A248 5p dk car .25 .20

National Anthem A249

**1971, May 19** **Litho.**
**795** A249 15p bl, blk & yel .30 .30

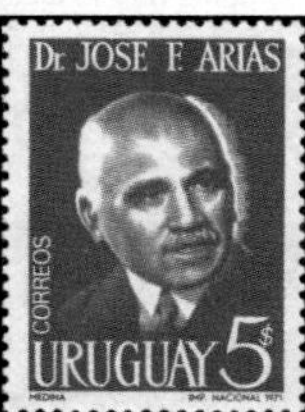


José F. Arias, Physician — A250

**1971, May 25** **Wmk. 332** ***Perf. 12***
**796** A250 5p sepia .25 .20

Eduardo Fabini, Bar from "Campo" A251

**1971, June 2** **Litho.**
**797** A251 5p dk car rose & blk .30 .30

Eduardo Fabini (1882-1950), composer, and 40th anniversary of first radio concert.

José E. Rodó, UPAE Emblem A252

**1971, July 15** **Wmk. 332** ***Perf. 12***
**798** A252 15p ultra & blk .25 .20

José Enrique Rodó (1871-1917), writer, first Uruguayan delegate to Congress of the Postal Union of the Americas and Spain.

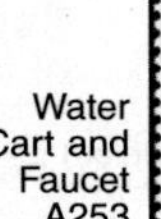

Water Cart and Faucet A253

**1971, July 17**
**799** A253 5p ultra & multi .25 .20

Centenary of Montevideo's drinking water system.

Sheep and Cloth A254

Design: 15p, Sheep, cloth and bale of wool.

**1971, Aug. 7**
**800** A254 5p grn & gray .20 .20
**801** A254 15p dk bl, grnsh bl & gray .25 .20

Wool Promotion.

José Maria Elorza and Merilin Sheep A255

**1971, Aug. 10**
**802** A255 5p lt bl, grn & blk .20 .20

José Maria Elorza, developer of the Merilin sheep.

Criollo Horse A256

**1971, Aug. 11**
**803** A256 5p blk, gray bl & org .25 .20

Bull and Ram A257

**1971, Aug. 13**
**804** A257 20p red, grn, blk & gold .40 .35

Centenary of Rural Association of Uruguay; 19th International Cattle Breeding Exposition, and 66th National Cattle Championships at Prado, Aug. 1971.

Symbol of Liberty and Order A258

20p, Policemen, flag of Uruguay and emblem.

**1971**
**805** A258 10p gray, blk & bl .25 .20
**806** A258 20p dk bl, blk, lt bl & gold .30 .25

To honor policemen killed on duty. Issue dates: 10p, Sept. 9; 20p, Nov. 4.

10p Banknote of 1896 — A259

Design: No. 808, Reverse of 10p note.

**1971, Sept. 23**
**807** A259 25p dl grn, gold & blk .40 .40
**808** A259 25p dl grn, gold & blk .40 .40
*a.* Pair, #807-808 + label 1.00 1.00

75th anniversary of Bank of the Republic.

Farmer and Arms of Durazno A260

**1971, Oct. 11**
**809** A260 20p gold, bl & blk .25 .20

Sesquicentennial of the founding of Durazno.

Emblem and Laurel — A261

**1971, Oct. 20**
**810** A261 10p vio bl, gold & red .25 .20

Winners of Liberator's Cup, American Soccer Champions, 1971.

For surcharge see No. 825.

Voter Casting Ballot — A262

Design: 20p, Citizens voting, horiz.

**1971, Nov. 22** **Wmk. 332** ***Perf. 12***
**811** A262 10p bl & blk .25 .20
**812** A262 20p bl & blk .25 .20

Universal, secret and obligatory franchise.

Map of Uruguay on Globe A263

**1971, Dec. 23**
**813** A263 20p lt bl & vio brn .25 .20

7th Littoral Expo., Paysandu, 3/26-4/11.

Juan Lindolfo Cuestas — A264

**1971, Dec. 27**
**814** A264 10p shown .20 .20
**815** A264 10p Julio Herrera y Obes .20 .20
**816** A264 10p Claudio Williman .20 .20
**817** A264 10p José Serrato .20 .20
**818** A264 10p Andres Martinez Truebá .20 .20
*a.* Horiz. strip of 5, #814-818 1.25 1.25

Presidents of Uruguay.

Souvenir Sheet

Uruguay No. 4, Cathedral of Montevideo and Plaza de la Constitucion — A265

**1972, Jan. 17** ***Imperf.***
**819** A265 120p brn, bl & dp rose 1.00 1.00

Stamp Day 1971 (release date delayed). See Nos. 834-835, 863.

Bartolomé Hidalgo — A266

Missa Solemnis, by Beethoven — A267

**1972, Feb. 28** ***Perf. 12***
**820** A266 5p lt brn, blk & red .25 .20

Bartolomé Hidalgo (1788-1822), Uruguayan-Argentine poet.

**1972, Apr. 20** **Litho.** **Wmk. 332**
**822** A267 20p lil, emer & blk .25 .20

12th Choir Festival of Eastern Uruguay.

Dove and Wounded Bird — A268

Columbus Arch, Colon — A269

**1972, May 9**
**823** A268 10p ver & multi .25 .20

To honor Dionision Disz (age 9), who died saving his sister.

**1972, June 21**
**824** A269 20p red, bl & blk .25 .20

Centenary of Colon, now suburb of Montevideo.

No. 810 Surcharged in Silver

(Surcharge 69mm wide)

**1972, June 30**
**825** A261 50p on 10p multi .25 .25

Winners of the 1971 Intl. Soccer Cup.

Tree Planting — A270

"Collective Housing" — A271

**1972, Aug. 5 Wmk. 332 *Perf. 12***
**826** A270 20p grn & blk .25 .20

Afforestation program.

**1972, Sept. 30 Litho.**
**827** A271 10p dp bl & multi .25 .20

Publicity for collective housing plan.

Amethyst A272

Uruguayan Gem Stones: 9p, Agate. 15p, Chalcedony.

**1972, Oct. 7**
**828** A272 5p gray & multi .25 .25
**829** A272 9p gray bl & multi .25 .25
**830** A272 15p gray grn & multi .30 .30
*Nos. 828-830 (3)* .80 .80

Uniform of 1830 — A273

Design: 20p, Lancer.

**1972, Nov. 21 Litho.**
**831** A273 10p multi .25 .20
**832** A273 20p rose red & multi .25 .25

Red Cross and Map of Uruguay A274

**1972, Dec. 11 Wmk. 332 *Perf. 12***
**833** A274 30p multi .30 .25

75th anniv. of the Uruguayan Red Cross.

Stamp Day Type of 1972
Souvenir Sheets

Designs: 200p, Coat of arms type of 1864 similar to Nos. 18, 20-21, but 60p, 60p and 80p. 220p, Similar to Nos. 22-23, but 100p and 120p.

**1972, Dec. 20 *Imperf.***
**834** A265 200p multi 1.25 .60
**835** A265 220p multi 1.50 .75

Stamp Day 1972. 1st printed cancellations, 200th anniv., #834; Decree establishing regular postal service, cent., #835.

Scales of Justice, Olive Branch A275

**1972, Dec. 27 Wmk. 332 *Perf. 12***
**836** A275 10p gold, dk & lt bl .25 .20

Civil Rights Law for Women, 25th anniv.

Gen. José Artigas A276

Hand Holding Cup; Grain, Map of Americas A277

**1972-74 Wmk. 332 Litho. *Perf. 12***
**837** A276 5p yel ('74) .20 .20
**838** A276 10p dk bis ('74) .20 .20
**839** A276 15p emer ('74) .20 .20
**840** A276 20p lilac ('73) .20 .20
**841** A276 30p lt bl ('73) .20 .20
**842** A276 40p dp org ('73) .20 .20
**843** A276 50p ver ('73) .20 .20
**844** A276 75p ap grn ('73) .20 .20
**845** A276 100p emerald .20 .20
**846** A276 150p choc ('73) .20 .20
**847** A276 200p dk bl ('73) .35 .30
**848** A276 250p pur ('73) .40 .35
**849** A276 500p gray ('73) 1.00 .60
**849A** A276 1000p blue ('73) 2.00 1.25
*Nos. 837-849A (14)* 5.75 4.50

For surcharges see Nos. 929-932.

**1973, Jan. 9**
**850** A277 30p rose red, yel & blk .25 .20

Intl. Institute for Agricultural Research, 39th anniv.

Elbio Fernandez and José P. Varela — A278

**1973, Jan. 16**
**851** A278 10p dl grn, gold & blk .25 .20

Society of Friends of Public Education, cent.

Map of Americas, "1972" and Columbus A279

**1973, Jan. 30**
**852** A279 50p purple .20 .20

Tourist Year of the Americas 1972.

Carlos Maria Ramirez, Scales and Books A280

**1973, Feb. 15**
**853** A280 10p shown .20 .20
**854** A280 10p Justino Jimenez de Arechaga .20 .20
**855** A280 10p Juan Andres Ramirez .20 .20
**856** A280 10p Justino E. Jimenez de Arechaga .20 .20
*a.* Horiz. strip, #853-856 + label 1.00 1.00

Professorship of Constitutional Rights, cent.

Provincial Map of Uruguay A281

**1973, Feb. 27 Litho. *Perf. 12½x12***
**857** A281 20p bl & multi .25 .20

See No. 1167.

Francisco de los Santos A282

**1973, May 16 Wmk. 332 *Perf. 12***
**858** A282 20p grn & blk .25 .20

Soldiers' Day and Battle of Piedras. Santos was a courier who went through enemy lines.

No. C319 Surcharged with New Value and: "HOMENAJE AL 4 CENTENARIO DE CORDOBA . ARGENTINA . 1973"

**1973, May 9 Litho. *Imperf.***
**Souvenir Sheet**

**859** AP57 100p on 5p multi .75 .75

Founding of Cordoba in Argentina, 400th anniv.

Friar, Indians, Church — A283

**1973, July 25 *Perf. 12***
**860** A283 20p lt ultra, pur & blk .25 .20

Villa Santo Domingo Soriano, first Spanish settlement in Uruguay.

Symbolic Fish A284

**1973, Aug. 15**
**861** A284 100p bl & multi .30 .25

First station of Oceanographic and Fishery Service, Montevideo.

A285

Herrera — A286

Sun over flower in Italian colors.

**1973, Sept.**
**862** A285 100p multi .20 .20

Italian Chamber of Commerce of Uruguay.

Stamp Day Type of 1972
Souvenir Sheet

Design: 240p, Thin numeral sun type of 1859 and street scene.

**Wmk. 332**
**1973, Oct. 1 Litho. *Imperf.***
**863** A265 240p grn, org & blk 1.50 1.50

Stamp Day 1973.

**1973, Nov. 12 *Perf. 12***
**866** A286 50p gray, brn & dk brn .20 .20

Centenary of the birth of Luis Alberto de Herrera.

Emblem of Social Coordination Volunteers A287

**Wmk. 352**
**1973, Nov. 19 Litho. *Perf. 12***
**867** A287 50p bl & multi .25 .20

Festival of Nations, Montevideo.

Arm with Arteries and Heart A288

**1973, Nov. 22**
**868** A288 50p blk, red & pink .20 .20

3rd Cong. of the Pan-American Federation of Blood Donors, Montevideo, Nov. 23-25.

Madonna, by Rafael Perez Barradas — A289

**1973, Dec. 10 Litho. Wmk. 332**

**869** A289 50p grn, gray & yel grn .30 .20

Christmas 1973.

Nicolaus Copernicus — A290

**1973, Dec. 26 Litho.**

**870** A290 50p grn & multi .25 .20

500th anniversary of the birth of Nicolaus Copernicus (1473-1543), Polish astronomer.

Praying Hands and Andes — A291

75p, Statue of Christ on mountain, and flower.

**1973, Dec. 26 Litho.**

**871** A291 50p blk, lt grn & ultra .20 .20
**872** A291 75p bl, blk & org .25 .20

Survival and rescue of victims of airplane crash.

OAS Emblem and Map of Americas A292

**1974, Jan. 14 Wmk. 332 *Perf. 12***

**873** A292 250p gray & multi .60 .40

25th anniversary of the Organization of American States (OAS).

Scout Emblems and Flame A293

**1974, Jan. 21**

**874** A293 250p multi .60 .40

1st Intl. Boy Scout Games, Montevideo, 1974.

Hector Suppici Sedes and Car — A294

**1974, Jan. 28 *Perf. 12***

**875** A294 50p sep, grn & blk .30 .25

70th anniversary of the birth of Hector Suppici Sedes (1903-1948), automobile racer.

Three Gauchos — A295

**1974, Mar. 20 Litho. Wmk. 332**

**876** A295 50p multi .25 .20

Centenary of the publication of "Los Tres Gauchos Orientales" by Antonio D. Lussich.

Rifle, Target and Swiss Flag A296

**1974, Apr. 2**

**877** A296 100p multi .25 .20

Centenary of the Swiss Rifle Association.

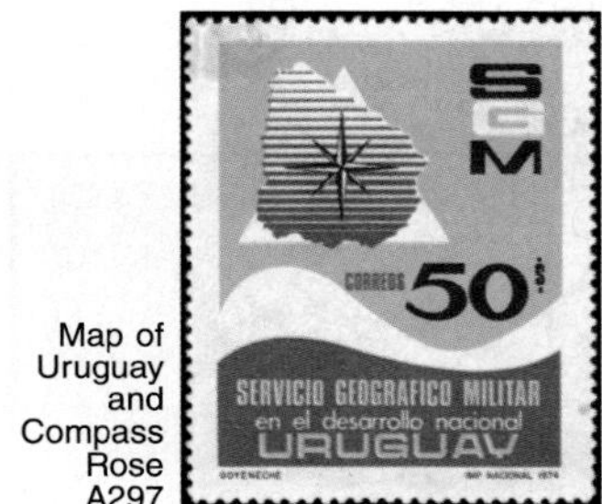

Map of Uruguay and Compass Rose A297

**1974, Apr. 23 Litho.**

**878** A297 50p multi .25 .20

Military Geographical Service.

Montevideo Stadium Tower — A298

Design: 75p, Soccer player, Games' emblem, horiz. 1000p, similar to 75p.

**1974, May 7 Wmk. 332 *Perf. 12***

**879** A298 50p multi .20 .20
**880** A298 75p multi .20 .20
**881** A298 1000p multicolored 20.00 7.75

World Cup Soccer Championship, Munich, June 13-July 7.

No. 881 had limited distribution. A souvenir sheet of one No. 881 was not valid for postage.

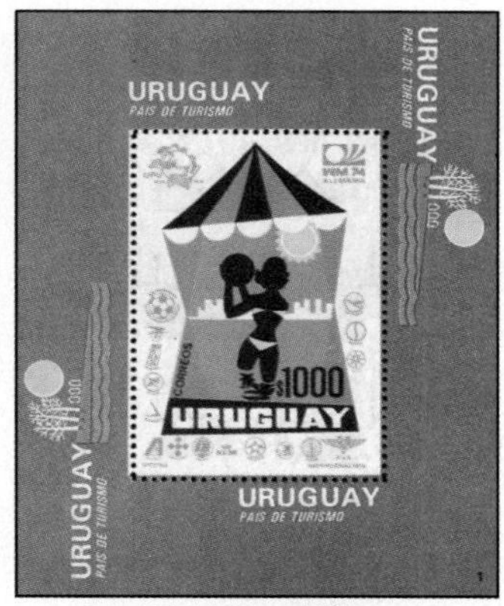

Tourism — A299

**Wmk. 332**

**1974, June 6 Litho. *Perf. 12***

**882** A299 1000p multicolored 35.00 35.00

No. 882 had limited distribution.

Old and New School and Founders A300

**1974, May 21**

**883** A300 75p black & bister .25 .20

Centenary of the Osimani-Llerena Technical School at Salto, founded by Gervasio Osimani and Miguel Llerena.

Gardel and Score — A301

Volleyball and Net — A302

**Wmk. 332**

**1974, June 24 Litho. *Perf. 12***

**884** A301 100p multi .35 .25

Carlos Gardel (1887-1935), singer and motion picture actor. See No. 1173.

**1974, July 11 Wmk. 332 *Perf. 12***

**885** A302 200p lil, yel & blk .30 .25

First anniversary of Women's Volleyball championships, Montevideo, 1973.

"Protect your Heart" — A303

Portrait and Statue — A304

**1974, July 24 Litho.**

**886** A303 75p ol grn, yel & red .25 .20

Heart Foundation publicity.

**1974, Aug. 5**

**887** A304 75p dk & lt bl .25 .20

Centenary (in 1973) of the founding of San José de Mayo by Eusebio Vidal.

A305

A306

Artigas statue, Buenos Aires, flags of Uruguay and Argentina.

**1974, Aug. 13 *Perf. 12½***

**888** A305 75p multi .30 .20

Unveiling of Artigas monument, Buenos Aires.

**1974, Sept. 24 Wmk. 332 *Perf. 12***

**889** A306 100p Radio tower and waves .20 .20

50th anniv. of Broadcasting in Uruguay.

URUEXPO 74 Emblem — A307

URUEXPO Emblem and Old Map of Montevideo Bay — A308

**1974**

**890** A307 100p blk, dk bl & red .20 .20
**891** A308 300p sepia, red & grn .50 .50

URUEXPO 74 Philatelic Exhibition, 10th anniversary of Philatelic Circle of Uruguay (100p) and 250th anniversary of fortification of Montevideo.

Issue dates: 100p, Oct. 1; 300p, Oct. 19.

Letters and UPU Emblem
A309

UPU Cent.: 200p, UPU emblem, letter, and globe.

**1974, Oct. 9**

**892** A309 100p lt bl & multi .20 .20
**893** A309 200p lil, blk & gold .30 .20
*Nos. 892-893,C395-C396 (4)* 2.10 2.00

A 1000p souvenir sheet was not valid for postage. Value $45.

Artigas Statue and Map of Lavalleja
A310

**1974, Oct. 17** ***Perf. 12***

**894** A310 100p ultra & multi .30 .20

Unveiling of Artigas statue in Minas, Lavalleja.

Ship in Dry Dock, Arsenal's Emblem
A312

**1974, Nov. 15 Litho. Wmk. 332**

**896** A312 200p multi .30 .30

Centenary of Naval Arsenal, Montevideo.

Globe Hydrogen Balloon — A313

**1974, Nov. 20**

**897** A313 100p shown .25 .20
**898** A313 100p Farman biplane .25 .20
**899** A313 100p Castaibert monoplane .25 .20
**900** A313 100p Bleriot monoplane .25 .20
*a.* Strip of 4, #897-900 1.50 1.50
**901** A313 150p Military and civilian pilots' emblems .25 .20
**902** A313 150p Nieuport biplane .25 .20
**903** A313 150p Breguet-Bidon fighter .25 .20
**904** A313 150p Caproni bomber .25 .20
*a.* Strip of 4, #901-904 1.50 1.50
*Nos. 897-904 (8)* 2.00 1.60

Aviation pioneers.

Sugar Loaf Mountain and Summit Cross — A314

**1974, Nov. 30**

**905** A314 150p multi .25 .20

Cent. of the founding of Sugar Loaf City.

Adoration of the Kings — A315

**1974** ***Perf. 12***

**906** A315 100p shown .20 .20
**907** A315 150p Three Kings .20 .20
*Nos. 906-907,C400 (3)* .70 .60

Christmas 1974. See No. C401. Issue dates: 100p, Dec. 17; 150p, Dec. 19.

Nike, Fireworks, Rowers and Club Emblem — A316

**1975, Jan. 27 Litho. Wmk. 332**

**908** A316 150p gray & multi .20 .20

Centenary of Montevideo Rowing Club.

Treaty Signing, by José Zorilla de San Martin — A317

**1975, Feb. 12** ***Perf. 12***

**909** A317 100p multi .30 .20

Commercial Treaty between Great Britain and Uruguay, 1817.

Rose — A318

**1975, Mar. 18 Litho. Wmk. 332**

**910** A318 150p multi .60 .40

Bicentenary of city of Rosario.

"The Oath of the 33," by Juan M. Blanes — A319

**1975, Apr. 16** ***Perf. 12***

**911** A319 150p gold & multi .35 .20

Sesquicentennial of liberation movement.

Ship, Columbus and Ancient Map — A320

**1975, Oct. 9 Litho. Wmk. 332**

**912** A320 1p gray & multi 1.25 .80

Hispanic Stamp Day.

Leonardo Olivera and Santa Teresa Fort — A321

Artigas as Young and Old Man
A322

**1975 Litho. Wmk. 332** ***Perf. 12***

**913** A321 10c org & multi .20 .20
**914** A322 50c vio bl & multi .50 .40

Sesquicentennial of the capture of Fort Santa Teresa (10c) and of Uruguay's declaration of independence (50c).
Issue dates: 10c, Oct. 20; 50c, Oct. 17.

Battle of Rincon, by Diogenes Hequet — A323

#916, Artigas' Home, Ibiray, Paraguay. 25c, Battle of Sarandi, by J. Manuel Blanes.

**1975 Litho.**

**915** A323 15c ol & blk .20 .20
**916** A323 15c ol & multi .20 .20
**917** A323 25c ol & multi .30 .30
*Nos. 915-917 (3)* .70 .70

Uruguayan independence. Nos. 915 and 917, 150th anniversary of Battles of Rincon and Sarandi. No. 916, 50th anniversary of school at Artigas mansion.
Issued: #915, 10/23; #916, 11/18; #917, 11/28.

"En Familia," by Sanchez
A324

Florencio Sanchez
A325

Plays by Sanchez: #919, Barranca Abajo. #920, M'Hijo el Doctor. #921, Canillita.

**1975, Oct. 31 Wmk. 332** ***Perf. 12***

**918** A324 20c gray, red & blk .30 .20
**919** A324 20c bl, grn & blk .30 .20
**920** A324 20c red, bl & blk .30 .20
**921** A324 20c grn, gray & blk .30 .20
**922** A325 20c multi .30 .20
*a.* Block of 5 stamps + 4 labels 2.50

Florencio Sanchez (1875-1910), dramatist, birth centenary. Nos. 918-922 printed se-tenant in sheets of 30 stamps and 20 labels.

Maria Eugenia Vaz Ferreira
A326

Design: No. 924, Julio Herrera y Reissig.

**1975**

**923** A326 15c yel, blk & brn .20 .20
**924** A326 15c org, blk & maroon .20 .20

Maria Eugenia Vaz Ferreira (1875-1924), poetess, and Julio Herrera y Reissig (1875-1910), poet, birth anniversaries.
Issue dates: #923, Dec. 9; #924, Dec. 29.

A327

Virgin and Child — A328

Fireworks — A329

**1975**

**925** A327 20c bl & multi .30 .30
**926** A328 30c blk & multi .45 .45
**927** A329 60c multi .60 .60
*Nos. 925-927 (3)* 1.35 1.35

Christmas 1975.
Issued: 20c, 12/16; 30c, 12/15; 60c, 12/11.

Col. Lorenzo Latorre (1840-1916), Pres. of Uruguay (1876-80)
A330

**1975, Dec. 30** *Perf. 12*
**928** A330 15c multi .30 .20

Nos. 840, 842-843, 849A Surcharged

**1975**

**929** A276 10c on 20p lilac .25 .25
**930** A276 15c on 40p orange .25 .25
**931** A276 50c on 50p ver .45 .45
**932** A276 1p on 1000p blue .95 .95
*Nos. 929-932 (4)* 1.90 1.90

There are two surcharge types for Nos. 929 and 930. Values are the same.

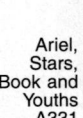

Ariel, Stars, Book and Youths
A331

**1976, Jan. 12 Litho. Wmk. 332**
**933** A331 15c grn & multi .20 .20

75th anniversary of publication of "Ariel," by Jose Enrique Rodo (1872-1917), writer.

Water Sports — A332

Telephone
A333

**1976, Mar. 12 Litho. Wmk. 332**
**934** A332 30c multi .25 .20

23rd South American Swimming, Diving and Water Polo Championships.

**1976, Apr. 9** *Perf. 12*
**935** A333 83c multi .45 .30

Centenary of first telephone call by Alexander Graham Bell, Mar. 10, 1876.

"Plus Ultra" and Columbus' Ships — A334

**Wmk. 332**

**1976, May 10 Litho.** *Perf. 12*
**936** A334 63c gray & multi .50 .30

Flight of Dornier "Plus Ultra" from Spain to South America, 50th anniversary.

A335

A336

Dornier "Wal" and Boeing 727, hourglass.

**1976, May 24**
**937** A335 83c gray & multi .75 .30

Lufthansa German Airline, 50th anniv.

**1976, June 3** *Perf. 11½*

Designs: 10c, Olympics. 15c, Telephone, cent. 25c, UPU, cent., UN #2. 50c, World Cup Soccer Championships, Argentina, 1978.

**938** A336 10c shown *1.40 .50*
**939** A336 15c multicolored *1.40 .50*
**940** A336 25c multicolored *1.40 .50*
**941** A336 50c multicolored *1.40 .50*
*Nos. 938-941 (4)* 5.60 2.00

Nos. 938-941 had limited distribution.
A souvenir sheet containing one each, Nos. 938-941, was not valid for postage. Value $25.

Louis Braille
A340

**1976, June 7**
**942** A340 60c blk & brn .75 .30

Sesquicentennial of the invention of the Braille system of writing for the blind by Louis Braille (1809-1852).

Signing of US Declaration of Independence
A341

**1976, June 21**
**943** A341 1.50p multi 1.75 1.40

American Bicentennial.

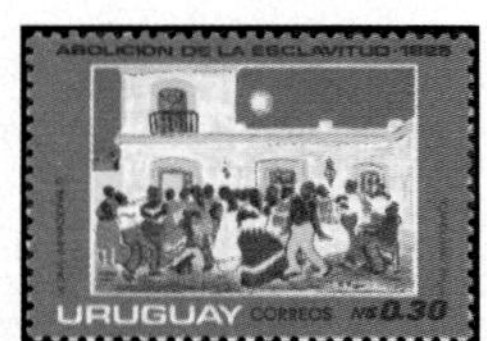


The Candombe, by P. Figari — A342

**Wmk. 332**

**1976, July 29 Litho.** *Perf. 12*
**944** A342 30c ultra & multi .25 .20

Abolition of slavery, sesquicentennial.

Gen. Fructuoso Rivera Statue
A343

**1976, Aug. 2**
**945** A343 5p on 10p multi 3.50 1.75

No. 945 was not issued without surcharge.

General Accounting Office — A344

**Wmk. 332**

**1976, Aug. 24 Litho.** *Perf. 12*
**946** A344 30c bl, blk & brn .30 .20

National General Accounting Office, sesquicentennial.

Old Pump, Emblem and Flame — A345

**1976, Sept. 6**
**947** A345 20c red & blk .20 .20

First official fire fighting service, centenary.

Southern Lapwing
A346

Mburucuya Flower
A347

Spearhead
A348

Figurine
A349

La Yerra, by J. M. Blanes
A350

The Gaucho, by Blanes
A351

Artigas — A352

Designs: 15c, Ceibo flower.

**1976-79 Litho. Wmk. 332** *Perf. 12*

**948** A346 1c violet .20 .20
**949** A347 5c lt grn .20 .20
**950** A347 15c car rose .20 .20
**951** A348 20c gray .20 .20
**952** A349 30c gray blue .20 .20
**953** A352 45c brt bl ('79) .20 .20
**954** A350 50c grnsh bl ('77) .20 .20
**955** A351 1p dk brn ('77) .40 .20
**956** A352 1p brt yel ('79) .20 .20
**957** A352 1.75p bl grn ('79) .30 .30
**958** A352 1.95p gray ('79) .30 .30
**959** A352 2p dl grn ('77) .95 .40
**960** A352 2p lil rose ('79) .40 .35
**961** A352 2.65p vio ('79) .40 .40
**962** A352 5p dk bl 3.00 2.00
**963** A352 10p brn ('77) 5.75 2.00
*Nos. 948-963 (16)* 13.10 7.55

"Diligencia" Uruguay No. 1 — A353

**Wmk. 332**

**1976, Sept. 26 Litho.** *Perf. 12*
**964** A353 30c bister, red & blue .30 .20

Philatelic Club of Uruguay, 50th anniv.

Games' Emblem — A354

**1976, Oct. 26 Litho.** *Perf. 12*
**965** A354 83c gray & multi .75 .40

5th World University Soccer Championships.

World Cup Soccer Championships, Argentina — A355

Anniversaries and Events: 30c, 1976 Summer Olympics, Montreal. 50c, Viking spacecraft. 80c, Nobel prizes, 75th anniv.

**1976, Nov. 12** ***Perf. 12***

| | | | | |
|---|---|---|---|---|
| **966** | A355 | 10c multicolored | 1.60 | .80 |
| **967** | A355 | 30c multicolored | 1.60 | .80 |
| **968** | A355 | 50c multicolored | 1.60 | .80 |
| **969** | A355 | 80c multicolored | 1.60 | .80 |
| | | *Nos. 966-969 (4)* | 6.40 | 3.20 |

Nos. 966-969 had limited distribution. See Nos. C424-C425.

Eye and Spectrum A356

**1976, Nov. 24**

**970** A356 20c blk & multi .30 .20

Foresight prevents blindness.

Map of Montevideo, 1748 — A357

45c, Montevideo Harbor, 1842. 70c, First settlers, 1726. 80c, Coin with Montevideo arms, vert. 1.15p, Montevideo's first coat of arms, vert.

**Wmk. 332**

**1976, Dec. 30** **Litho.** ***Perf. 12***

| | | | | |
|---|---|---|---|---|
| **971** | A357 | 30c multi | .30 | .20 |
| **972** | A357 | 45c multi | .45 | .20 |
| **973** | A357 | 70c multi | .60 | .35 |
| **974** | A357 | 80c multi | .85 | .35 |
| **975** | A357 | 1.15p multi | 1.40 | .45 |
| | | *Nos. 971-975 (5)* | 3.60 | 1.55 |

Founding of Montevideo, 250th anniversary.

Symbolic of Flight A358

**1977, May 7** **Litho.** ***Perf. 12***

**976** A358 80c multi .75 .50

50th anniversary of Varig airlines.

Artigas Mausoleum — A359

**1977, June 17** **Litho.** ***Perf. 12***

**977** A359 45c multi .45 .30

A360

A361

**1977, July 5** **Wmk. 332**

**978** A360 45c Map of Uruguay, arch .45 .30

Centenary of Salesian Brothers' educational system in Uruguay.

**1977, July 21**

Anniversaries and events: 20c, Werner Heisenberg, Nobel Prize for Physics. 30c, World Cup Soccer Championships, Uruguay Nos. 282, 390. 50c, Lindbergh's trans-Atlantic flight, 50th anniv. 1p, Rubens 400th birth anniv.

| | | | | |
|---|---|---|---|---|
| **979** | A361 | 20c shown | 1.25 | .80 |
| **980** | A361 | 30c multicolored | 1.25 | .80 |
| **981** | A361 | 50c multicolored | 1.25 | .80 |
| **982** | A361 | 1p multicolored | 1.25 | .80 |
| *a.* | | Strip, 2 ea #979-982 + 2 labels | — | — |
| | | *Nos. 979-982 (4)* | 5.00 | 3.20 |

Nos. 979-982 had limited distribution.

A souvenir sheet containing Nos. 979-982, imperf., was not valid for postage. It sold for 8p. See Nos. C426-C427.

Children — A362

Windmills — A364

"El Sol de Mayo" A363

**1977, Aug. 10** **Litho.** ***Perf. 12***

**983** A362 45c multi .45 .30

Interamerican Children's Inst., 50th anniv.

**1977, Oct. 1** **Litho.** ***Perf. 12***

**984** A363 45c multi .35 .35

Stamp Day 1977.

**1977, Sept. 29** **Wmk. 332**

**985** A364 70c yel, car & blk .55 .35

Spanish Heritage Day.

Souvenir Sheet

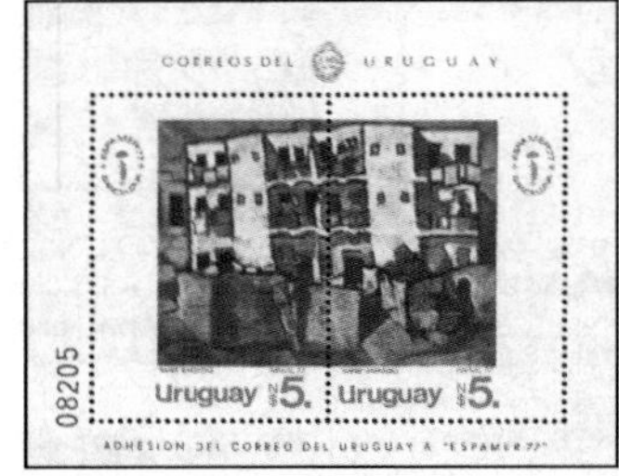


View of Sans (Barcelona), by Barradas — A365

**1977, Oct. 7** **Litho.** ***Perf. 12***

| | | | | |
|---|---|---|---|---|
| **986** | A365 | Sheet of 2 | 6.50 | 6.50 |
| *a.-b.* | | 5p, single stamp | 3.00 | 3.00 |

ESPAMER '77 Philatelic Exhibition, Barcelona, Oct. 7-13.

Planes, UN Emblem, Globe A366

**1977, Oct. 17**

**987** A366 45c multi .25 .20

30th anniv. of Civil Aviation Organization.

Holy Family — A367

Santa Claus — A368

**1977, Dec. 1** **Wmk. 332**

| | | | | |
|---|---|---|---|---|
| **988** | A367 | 45c multi | .25 | .20 |
| **989** | A368 | 70c blk, yel & red | .25 | .20 |

Christmas 1977.

Map of Rio Negro Province A369

**1977, Dec. 16**

**990** A369 45c multi .20 .20

Rio Negro Dam; development of argiculture, livestock and beekeeping. See Nos. 1021-1033.

Mail Collection A370

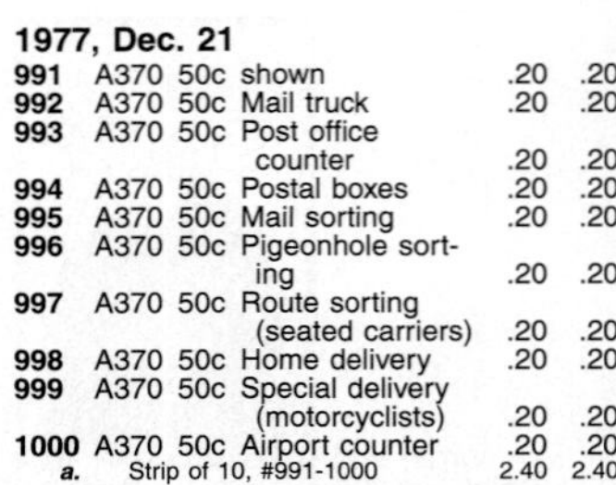

**1977, Dec. 21**

| | | | | |
|---|---|---|---|---|
| **991** | A370 | 50c shown | .20 | .20 |
| **992** | A370 | 50c Mail truck | .20 | .20 |
| **993** | A370 | 50c Post office counter | .20 | .20 |
| **994** | A370 | 50c Postal boxes | .20 | .20 |
| **995** | A370 | 50c Mail sorting | .20 | .20 |
| **996** | A370 | 50c Pigeonhole sorting | .20 | .20 |
| **997** | A370 | 50c Route sorting (seated carriers) | .20 | .20 |
| **998** | A370 | 50c Home delivery | .20 | .20 |
| **999** | A370 | 50c Special delivery (motorcyclists) | .20 | .20 |
| **1000** | A370 | 50c Airport counter | .20 | .20 |
| *a.* | | Strip of 10, #991-1000 | 2.40 | 2.40 |

Uruguayan postal service, 150th anniv.

Edison's Phonograph, 1877 — A371

**1977, Dec. 30**

**1001** A371 50c vio brn & yel .20 .20

Centenary of invention of the phonograph.

"R", Rainbow and Emblem A372

**1977, Dec. 30** **Wmk. 332**

**1002** A372 50c multi .20 .20

World Rheumatism Year.

Emblem and Diploma A373

**1978, Mar. 27** **Litho.** ***Perf. 12***

**1003** A373 50c multi .25 .20

50th anniversary of Military College.

Erhard Schon by Albrecht Durer (1471-1528) — A374

Painting: 50c, Self-Portrait by Peter Paul Rubens (1577-1640).

**1978, June 13** ***Perf. 12½***

| | | | | |
|---|---|---|---|---|
| **1004** | A374 | 25c blk & brn | *1.00* | *.95* |
| **1005** | A374 | 50c brn & blk | *1.75* | *1.40* |

Nos. 1004-1005 had limited distribution. See Nos. C430-C432.

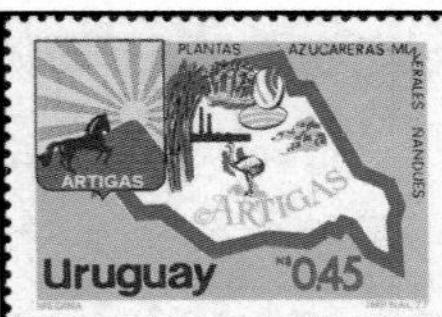


Map and Arms of Artigas Department — A375

**Wmk. 332**

**1978, June 16 Litho. *Perf. 12***
**1006** A375 45c multi .30 .20

Souvenir Sheet

Anniversaries — A376

Designs: 2p, Papilio thoas. No. 1007b, "100." No. 1007c, Argentina '78 emblem and globes. 5p, Model T Ford.

**Wmk. 332**

**1978, Aug. 24 Litho. *Perf. 12***
**1007** A376 Sheet of 4 18.00 18.00
***a.*** 2p multi 1.75 1.75
***b.*** 4p multi 3.50 3.50
***c.*** 4p multi 3.50 3.50
***d.*** 5p multi 4.25 4.25

75th anniv. of 1st powered flight; URUEXPO '78 Phil. Exhib.; Parva Domus social club, cent.; 11th World Cup Soccer Championship, Argentina, June 1-25; Ford motor cars, 75th anniv.

Visiting Angels, by Solari — A377

Designs (Details from No. 1008b): No. 1008a, Second angel. No. 1008c, Third angel.

**1978, Sept. 13 Unwmk.**
**1008** Strip of 3 1.60 1.60
***a.*** A377 1.50p, 19x30mm .30 .30
***b.*** A377 1.50p, 38x30mm .30 .30
***c.*** A377 1.50p, 19x30mm .30 .30

Solari, Uruguayan painter.

Bernardo O'Higgins A378

#1010, José de San Martin and monument.

**1978 Wmk. 332**
**1009** A378 1p multi .25 .20
**1010** A378 1p multi .25 .20

Benardo O'Higgins (1778-1842 and José de San Martin (1778-1850), South American liberators.

Issued: #1009, Sept. 13; #1010, Oct. 10.

Telephone Dials A379

**1978, Sept. 25**
**1011** A379 50c multi .30 .20

Automation of telephone service.

Symbolic Stamps A380

Iberian Tile Pattern — A381

**1978, Oct. 31**
**1012** A380 50c multi .25 .20
**1013** A381 1p multi .25 .20

Stamp Day (50c) and Spanish heritage (1p).

Boeing 727 A382

**1978, Nov. 27**
**1014** A382 50c multi .50 .20

Inauguration of Boeing 727 flights by PLUNA Uruguayan airlines, Nov. 1978.

Angel Blowing Horn — A383

**1978, Dec. 7**
**1015** A383 50c multi .20 .20
**1016** A383 1p multi .30 .20

Christmas 1978.

A384

A385

**1978, Dec. 15 *Perf. 12½***
**1017** A384 1p Flag flying on Plaza of the Nation .25 .20

**Wmk. 332**

**1978, Dec. 27 Litho. *Perf. 12***
**1018** A385 1p blk, red & yel .30 .20

Horacio Quiroga (1868-1928), short story writer.

Arch, Olympic Rings, Lake Placid and Moscow Emblems A386

7p, Olympic Rings, Lake Placid '80 emblem.

**1979, Apr. 28 Litho. *Perf. 12***
**1019** A386 5p multi 1.75 1.40
**1020** A386 7p multi 2.00 1.00

81st Session of Olympic Organizing Committee, Apr. 3-8 (5p), and 13th Winter Olympic Games, Lake Placid, NY, Feb. 12-24.

**Souvenir Sheets**

**1021** Sheet of 4 *30.00 30.00*
***a.*** A386 3p similar to #1019
***b.*** A386 5p Olympic rings
***c.*** A386 7p Rider looking back
***d.*** A386 10p Rider facing forward
**1022** Sheet of 4 *30.00 30.00*
***a.*** A386 3p similar to #1020
***b.*** A386 5p Uruguay '79
***c.*** A386 7p World Chess Olympics '78
***d.*** A386 10p Sir Rowland Hill, Great Britain stamp

No. 1022d shows Great Britain No. 836, but with 11p denomination. No. 1021c-1021d have continuous design.

Nos. 1021-1022 had limited distribution. Except for No. 1022d, singles were sold for postal use in 1980. Nos. 1021-1022 exist imperf.

Map and Arms of Paysandu A387

Map and Arms of Maldonado A388

**1979-81**
**1023** A387 45c shown .20 .20
**1024** A387 45c Salto .20 .20
**1025** A388 45c shown .20 .20
**1026** A387 45c Cerro Largo .20 .20
**1027** A387 50c Treinta y Tres .20 .20
**1028** A387 50c Durazno ('80) .20 .20
**1029** A388 2p Rocha ('81) .35 .35
**1030** A388 2p Flores .35 .35
*Nos. 1023-1030 (8)* 1.90 1.90

See No. 990.

Sapper with Pickax, 1837 — A389

Army Day: No. 1039, Artillery man with cannon, 1830.

**1979, May 18 Litho. *Perf. 12***
**1038** A389 5p multi 1.90 1.00
**1039** A389 5p multi 1.90 1.00

Madonna and Child by Durer A390

Anniversaries and events: 80c, World Cup Soccer Championships, Spain. 1.30p, Sir Rowland Hill, Greece No. 117.

**1979, June 18 *Perf. 12***
**1040** A390 70c brn & gray *6.50 3.25*
**1041** A390 80c multicolored *5.00 2.75*
**1042** A390 1.30p multicolored *5.00 2.75*
*Nos. 1040-1042 (3)* 16.50 8.75

Nos. 1040-1042 had limited distribution.

Issued in sheets of 24 containing 6 blocks of 4 with margin around. See #C437-C438.

Salto Dam A391

**1979, June 19**
**1043** A391 2p multi .45 .30

Crandon Institute Emblem, Grain A392

**1979, July 19**
**1044** A392 1p vio bl & bl .30 .20

Crandon Institute (private Methodist school), centenary.

IYC Emblem, Smiling Kites — A393

Cinderella A394

**1979**
**1045** A393 2p multi .55 .25
**1046** A394 2p multi .55 .25

International Year of the Child. Issue dates: No. 1045, July 23; No. 1046, Aug. 29.

Uruguay Coat of Arms 150th Anniversary — A395

**1979, Sept. 6**
**1047** A395 8p multi 2.75 1.40

Virgin and Child — A396

Symbols, by Torres-Garcia A397

**Wmk. 332**
**1979, Nov. 19 Litho. *Perf. 12***
**1048** A396 10p multi 2.75 1.60

Christmas 1979; Intl. Year of the Child.

**1979, Nov. 12**
**1049** A397 10p yel & blk 2.75 1.60

J. Torres-Garcia (1874-1948), painter.

UPU and Brazilian Postal Emblems — A398

**1979, Oct. 11**
**1050** A398 5p multi 1.25 .80

18th UPU Congress, Rio, Sept.-Oct.

Dish Antenna and Sun — A400

***Perf. 12x11½***
**1979, Nov. 26 Litho. Wmk. 332**
**1052** A400 10p multi 2.75 1.25

Telecom '79, 3rd World Telecommunications Exhibition, Geneva, Sept. 20-26.

Spanish Heritage Day — A401

**1979, Dec. 3 *Perf. 12***
**1053** A401 10p multi 2.75 1.60

Silver Coin Centenary A402

Designs: Obverse and reverse of coins in denominations matching stamps.

**1979, Dec. 26**
**1054** A402 10c multi .20 .20
**1055** A402 20c multi .20 .20
**1056** A402 50c multi .20 .20
**1057** A402 1p multi .40 .20
*Nos. 1054-1057 (4)* 1.00 .80

Souvenir Sheet

Security Agent — A403

**1980, Jan. 10**
**1058** Sheet of 4 3.50 3.50
*a.* A403 1p Police emblem .30 .30
*b.* A403 2p shown .50 .50
*c.* A403 3p Policeman, 1843 .75 .75
*d.* A403 4p Cadet, 1979 1.00 1.00

Police force sesquicentennial.

Light Bulb, Thomas Edison — A404

**1980, Jan. 18**
**1059** A404 2p multi .40 .30

Centenary of electric light (1979).

Bass and Singer — A405

**1980, Jan. 30**
**1060** Sheet of 4 3.00 3.00
*a.* A405 2p Radio waves .65 .65
*b.* A405 2p shown .65 .65
*c.* A405 2p Ballerina .65 .65
*d.* A405 2p Television waves .65 .65

Performing Arts Society, 50th anniversary.

Stamp Day — A406

La Leyenda Patria — A407

**1980, Feb.**
**1061** A406 1p multi .35 .20

**1980, Feb. 26**
**1062** A407 1p multi .30 .20

Printers' Association, 50th Anniversary A408

**1980, Feb.**
**1063** A408 1p multi .35 .20

Lufthansa Cargo Container Service Inauguration — A409

**1980, Apr. 12 Unwmk. *Perf. 12½***
**1064** A409 2p multi .60 .25

Conf. Emblem, Banners — A410

Man, Woman and Birds — A411

**1980, Apr. 28 Wmk. 332 *Perf. 12***
**1065** A410 2p multi .60 .35

8th World Hereford Conf., Punta del Este and Livestock Exhib., Prado/Montivideo.

**1980 Litho. *Perf. 12***
**1066** A411 1p multi .30 .20

International Year of the Child (1979).

Latin-American Lions, 9th Forum — A412

**1980, May 6 Wmk. 332 *Perf. 12***
**1067** A412 1p multi .30 .20

Souvenir Sheet

Rifleman, 1814 — A413

**1980, May 16**
**1068** Sheet of 4 4.00 4.00
*a.* A413 2p shown .80 .80
*b.* A413 2p Cavalry officer, 1830 .80 .80
*c.* A413 2p Private Liberty Dragoons, 1826 .80 .80
*d.* A413 2p, Artigas Militia officer, 1815 .80 .80

Army Day, May 18.

Arms of Colonia — A414

Colonia, 1680 A415

**1980, June 17 Litho. *Perf. 12***
**1069** A414 50c multi 1.50 .20

**Souvenir Sheet**

**1070** Sheet of 4 1.40 1.40
*a.* A415 1p shown .25 .25
*b.* A415 1p 1680, diff. .25 .25
*c.* A415 1p 1980 .25 .25
*d.* A415 1p 1980, diff. .25 .25

Colonia, 300th anniversary.

Rotary Emblem on Globe — A416

Hand Putting Out Cigarette — A417

**1980, July 8**
**1071** A416 5p multi 1.50 .90

Rotary International, 75th anniversary.

**1980, Sept. 8** **Photo.**
**1072** A417 1p multi .25 .20

World Health Day and anti-smoking campaign.

Artigas — A418

Christmas 1980 A419

**Wmk. 332**

| **1980-85** | **Litho.** | | *Perf. 12½* | |
|---|---|---|---|---|
| **1073** A418 | 10c | blue ('81) | .20 | .20 |
| **1074** A418 | 20c | orange | .20 | .20 |
| **1075** A418 | 50c | red | .20 | .20 |
| **1076** A418 | 60c | yellow | .20 | .20 |
| **1077** A418 | 1p | gray | .45 | .25 |
| **1078** A418 | 2p | brown | .85 | .30 |
| **1079** A418 | 3p | brt grn | 1.50 | .35 |
| **1080** A418 | 4p | brt bl ('82) | 1.75 | .45 |
| **1081** A418 | 5p | green ('82) | .95 | .25 |
| **1082** A418 | 6p | brt org ('85) | .35 | .20 |
| **1083** A418 | 7p | lil rose ('82) | 4.50 | .75 |
| **1084** A418 | 10p | blue ('82) | 1.75 | .35 |
| **1085** A418 | 12p | blk ('85) | .95 | .25 |
| **1086** A418 | 15.50p | emer ('85) | 1.25 | .30 |
| **1087** A418 | 20p | dk vio ('82) | 3.75 | .75 |
| **1088** A418 | 30p | lt brn ('82) | 5.50 | .75 |
| **1089** A418 | 50p | gray bl ('82) | 9.00 | 1.90 |
| | *Nos. 1073-1089 (17)* | | 33.35 | 7.65 |

**1980, Dec. 15** **Litho.** *Perf. 12*
**1090** A419 2p multi .50 .25

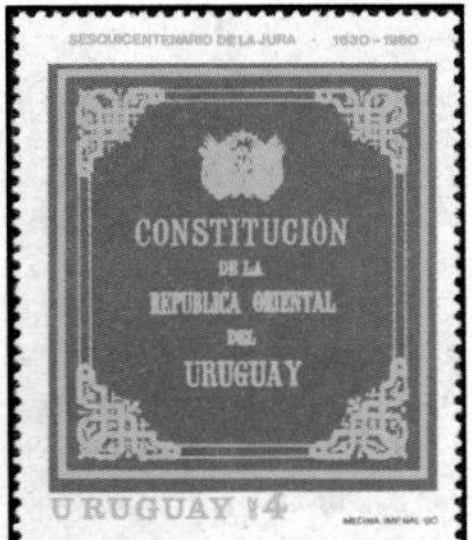

Constitution Title Page — A420

**1980, Dec. 23** *Perf. 12½*
**1091** A420 4p brt bl & gold 1.25 .65

Sesquicentennial of Constitution.

A421

A422

**1980, Dec. 30** *Perf. 12*
**1092** A421 5p Montevideo Stadium 1.75 1.00
**1093** A421 5p Soccer gold cup 1.75 1.00

**Size: 25x79mm**

**1094** A421 10p Flags 1.75 1.00
*a.* Souv. sheet of 3, #1092-1094 9.00 9.00
*Nos. 1092-1094 (3)* 5.25 3.00

Soccer Gold Cup Championship, Montevideo.

**1981, Jan. 27**
**1095** A422 2p multi .60 .20

Spanish Heritage Day.

UPU Membership Centenary — A423

**1981, Feb. 6**
**1096** A423 2p multi .60 .20

Alexander von Humboldt (1769-1859), German Explorer and Scientist — A424

**1981, Feb. 19**
**1097** A424 2p multi .60 .25

Intl. Education Congress and Fair, Montevideo (1980) — A425

**1981, Mar. 31**
**1098** A425 2p multi .60 .20

Hand Holding Gold Cup — A426

Eighth Notes on Map of Americas — A427

**1981, Apr. 8**
**1099** A426 2p multi .60 .25
**1100** A426 5p multi 1.40 .50

1980 victory in Gold Cup Soccer Championship.

**1981, Apr. 28**
**1101** A427 2p multi .60 .20

Inter-American Institute of Musicology, 40th anniv.

World Tourism Conference, Manila, Sept. 27, 1980 — A428

**Wmk. 332**
**1981, June 1** **Litho.** *Perf. 12*
**1102** A428 2p multi .60 .25

Inauguration of PLUNA Flights to Madrid — A429

**1981, May 12**
**1103** A429 2p multi .40 .25
**1104** A429 5p multi .95 .45
**1105** A429 10p multi 1.90 .95
*Nos. 1103-1105 (3)* 3.25 1.65

Army Day — A430

Natl. Atomic Energy Commission, 25th Anniv. — A431

**Wmk. 332**
**1981, May 18** **Litho.** *Perf. 12*
**1106** A430 2p Cavalry soldier, 1843 .60 .25
**1107** A430 2p Infantryman, 1843 .60 .25

**1981, July 20**
**1108** A431 2p multi .60 .25

Europe-South American Soccer Cup — A432

**1981, Aug. 4**
**1109** A432 2p multi .80 .25

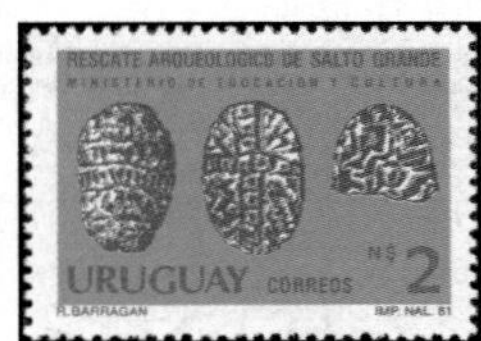

Stone Tablets, Salto Grande Excavation — A433

**1981, Sept. 10**
**1110** A433 2p multi .60 .25

10th Lavalleja Week — A434

**1981, Oct. 3**
**1111** A434 4p multi 1.40 .45

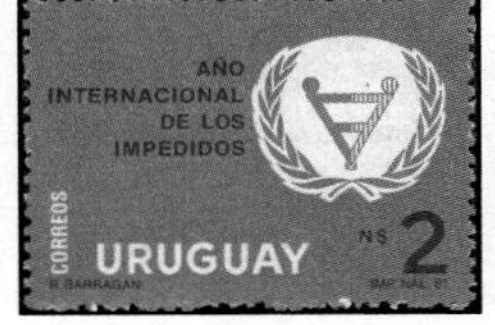

Intl. Year of the Disabled A435

**Wmk. 332**
**1981, Oct. 26** **Litho.** *Perf. 12*
**1112** A435 2p multi .60 .25

UN Environmental Law Meeting Montevideo, Oct. 28-Nov. 6 — A436

**1981, Oct. 28**
**1113** A436 5p multi 1.40 .45

A437

A439

**1981, Oct. 13**
**1114** A437 2p multi .60 .25

50th anniv. of ANCAP (Natl. Administration of Combustible Fuels, Alcohol and Cement).

Souvenir Sheets

Uruguay 81 Intl. Philatelic Exhibition — A438

No. 1114A: b, Copa de Oro trophy. c, Soccer player kicking ball.
No. 1115: a, Chess pieces. b, Prince Charles and Lady Diana, flags of Uruguay and Great Britain.

**Wmk. 332**
**1981, Nov. 23 Litho. *Perf. 12***
**1114A** A438 5p Sheet of 2, #b-c *23.00 23.00*
**1115** A438 5p Sheet of 2, #a-b *25.00 25.00*

1982 World Cup Soccer Championships, Spain (No. 1114Ac), World Chess Championships, Atlanta (No. 1115a); Wedding of Prince Charles and Lady Diana (No. 1115b). Nos. 1114A-1115 exist imperf., which were not valid for postage.

**1981, Dec. 5 *Perf. 12***
**1116** A439 2p multi .65 .25

Topographical Society sesqu. See No. 1407.

Bank of Uruguay, 85th Anniv. — A440

**1981, Dec. 17 *Perf. 12½***
**1117** A440 2p multi .60 .25

Palmar Dam — A441

**1981, Dec. 22 *Perf. 12***
**1118** A441 2p multi .65 .25

Christmas 1981 A442

**1981, Dec. 23**
**1119** A442 2p multi .60 .25

Pres. Joaquin Suarez Bicentenary A443

**1982, Mar. 15**
**1120** A443 5p multi 1.60 .50

Artillery Captain, 1872, Army Day — A444

Cent. (1981) of Pinocchio, by Carlo Collodi — A445

**Wmk. 332**
**1982, May 18 Litho. *Perf. 12***
**1121** A444 3p shown 1.00 .25
**1122** A444 3p Florida Battalion, 1865 1.00 .25

See Nos. 1136-1137.

**1982, June 17**
**1123** A445 2p multi .60 .25

2nd UN Conference on Peaceful Uses of Outer Space, Vienna, Aug. 9-21 — A446

**1982, June 3**
**1124** A446 3p multi 1.25 .70

World Food Day A447

**1982**
**1125** A447 2p multi .60 .20

25th Anniv. of Lufthansa's Uruguay-Germany Flight — A448

**1982, Apr. 14 Unwmk. *Perf. 12½***
**1126** A448 3p Lockheed L-1049-G Super Constellation 1.00 .40
**1127** A448 7p Boeing 747 2.25 .80

American Air Forces Cooperation System — A449

**1982, Apr. 14 Wmk. 332 *Perf. 12***
**1128** A449 10p Emblem 2.65 .80

Juan Zorilla de San Martin (1855-1931), Painter — A450

**1982, Aug. 18 *Perf. 12½***
**1129** A450 3p Self-portrait .80 .40

165th Anniv. of Natl. Navy — A451

**1982, Nov. 15 *Perf. 12***
**1130** A451 3p Navy vessel Capitan Miranda 1.00 .40

Natl. Literacy Campaign — A452

Stamp Day — A453

**1982, Nov. 30**
**1131** A452 3p multi .80 .35

**1982, Dec. 23 *Perf. 12½***
**1132** A453 3p like #46 .30 .20
**1133** A453 3p like #47 .30 .20
*a.* Pair, #1132-1133 1.10 1.10

These stamps bear numbers from 1 to 100 according to their position on the sheet.

Christmas 1982 — A454

**1983, Jan. 4 *Perf. 12***
**1134** A454 3p multi .50 .25

Eduardo Fabini (1882-1950), Composer — A455

**1983, May 10**
**1135** A455 3p gold & brn .50 .20

Army Day Type of 1982

**1983, May 18**
**1136** A444 3p Military College cadet, 1885 .45 .20
**1137** A444 3p 2nd Cavalry Regiment officer, 1885 .45 .20

Visit of King Juan Carlos and Queen Sofia of Spain, May — A456

**1983, May 20 Unwmk.**
**1138** A456 3p Santa Maria, globe .80 .40
**1139** A456 7p Profiles, flags 1.75 .80

Size of No. 1138: 29x39mm.

Brasiliana '83 Emblem — A457

80th Anniv. of First Automobile in Uruguay — A458

Opening of UPAE Building, Montevideo A459

Jose Cuneo (1887-1977), Painter — A460

1982 World Cup A461

Graf Zeppelin Flight Over Montevideo, 50th Anniv. (1984) — A462

J.W. Goethe (1749-1832), 150th Death Anniv. — A463

First Space Shuttle Flight A464

**1983 Litho. Wmk. 332 *Perf. 12***

| | | | |
|---|---|---|---|
| **1140** A457 3p multi | 1.00 | 1.00 |
| **1141** A458 3p multi | 1.00 | 1.00 |
| **1142** A459 3p multi | 1.00 | 1.00 |
| **1143** A460 3p multi | 1.00 | 1.00 |
| *a.* Souvenir sheet of 4 | 6.00 | 6.00 |
| **1144** A461 7p multi | 1.50 | 1.50 |
| **1145** A462 7p multi | 1.50 | 1.50 |
| **1146** A463 7p multi | 1.50 | 1.50 |
| **1147** A464 7p multi | 1.50 | 1.50 |
| *a.* Souvenir sheet of 4 | 10.00 | 10.00 |
| *Nos. 1140-1147 (8)* | 10.00 | 10.00 |

No. 1143a contains stamps similar to Nos. 1140-1143. No. 1147a stamps similar to Nos. 1144-1147. Nos. 1143a and 1147a for URUEXPO '83 and World Communications Year.

Issued: #1142, 6/8; #1143, 1146, 9/29; #1143a, 1147a, 6/9; #1140, 7/22; #1144, 12/13; #1146, 9/20; #1145, 12/8.

Bicentenary of City of Minas — A465

**Wmk. 332**

**1983, Oct. 17 Litho. *Perf. 12***

**1148** A465 3p Founder .65 .20

World Communications Year — A466

**1983, Nov. 30**

**1149** A466 3p multi .25 .20

Garibaldi Death Centenary A467

**1983, Dec. 5**

**1150** A467 7p multi 1.00 .40

Christmas 1983 A468

**Lithographed and Embossed (Braille)**

**1983, Dec. 21 *Perf. 12½***

**1151** A468 4.50p multi .55 .25

50th Anniv. of Automatic Telephones — A469

**1983, Dec. 27 *Perf. 12***

**1152** A469 4.50p multi .50 .20

Simon Bolivar, Battle Scene A470

**Wmk. 332**

**1984, Mar. 28 Litho. *Perf. 12***

**1153** A470 4.50p brn & gldn brn 1.10 .40

Gen. Leandro Gomez — A471

**1984, Jan. 2**

**1154** A471 4.50p multi .40 .25

American Women's Day — A472

Reunion Emblem A473

**1984, Feb. 18**

**1155** A472 4.50p Flags, emblem .40 .25

**1984, Mar. 23**

**1156** A473 10p multi .95 .45

Intl. Development Bank Governors, 25th annual reunion, Punta del Este.

50th Anniv. of Radio Club of Uruguay (1983) A474

**1984, Apr. 11**

**1157** A474 7p multi .60 .30

A475

A476

**1984, Feb. 7 Litho. *Perf. 12***

**1158** A475 4.50p multi .40 .25

Intl. Maritime Org., 25th anniv.

**1984, May 2 Litho. *Perf. 12***

**1159** A476 4.50p multi .40 .25

1930 World Soccer Championships, Montevideo.

Department of San Jose de Mayo, 200th Anniv. — A477

**1984, May 9 Litho. *Perf. 12***

**1160** A477 4.50p multi .40 .25

Tourism, 50th Anniv. A478

**1984, May 15 Litho. *Perf. 12***

**1161** A478 4.50p multi .40 .25

Military Uniforms — A479

Artigas on the Plains — A480

**1984, June 19 Litho. *Perf. 12***

**1162** A479 4.50p Artillery Regiment, 1895 .45 .20

**1163** A479 4.50p Cazadores, 2nd battalion .45 .20

**1984, July 2 Litho. *Perf. 12***

**1164** A480 4.50p bl & blk .40 .25

**1165** A480 8.50p bl & redsh brn .75 .40

A. Penarol Soccer Club A481

**1984, Aug. 21 Litho. *Perf. 12***

**1166** A481 4.50p Championship trophy .45 .25

Provincial Map Type of 1973

**1984, Sept. 21 Litho. *Perf. 12***

**1167** A281 4.50p multi .40 .25

Childrens Council, 50th Anniv. A482

**1984, Oct. 11 Litho. *Perf. 12***

**1168** A482 4.50p multi .40 .25

Christmas
A483

A484

**1984 Litho. *Perf. 12***
**1169** A483 6p multi .60 .30

**1985, Feb. 13 Litho. *Perf. 12***
**1170** A484 4.50p multi .40 .25

1st Jr. World Basketball Championships.

Don Bruno
Mauricio de
Zabala, 300th
Birth
Anniv. — A485

**1985, Apr. 16 Litho. *Perf. 12***
**1171** A485 4.50p multi .60 .20

Intl. Olympic Committee, 90th
Anniv. — A486

Design: Olympic rings, Los Angeles and Sarajevo 1984 Games emblems.

**1985, May 22 *Perf. 12½***
**1172** A486 12p multi 1.00 .50

Carlos Gardel,
(1890-1935),
Entertainer
A487

Catholic Circle of
Workers,
Cent. — A488

**1985, June 21 *Perf. 12***
**1173** A487 6p lt gray, red brn & bl .35 .20

**Wmk. 332**

**1985, June 21 Litho. *Perf. 12***
**1174** A488 6p Cross, clasped hands .20 .20

Icarus, by Hans Erni — A489

**1985, July Photo. Wmk. 332**
**1175** A489 4.50p multi .25 .20

Intl. Civil Aviation Org., 40th anniv.

American Air
Forces
Cooperation
System, 25th
Anniv. — A490

**1985, July**
**1176** A490 12p Emblem, flags .30 .20

FUNSA, Natl. Investment Funds Corp.,
50th Anniv. — A491

**1985, July 31 Litho. Wmk. 332**
**1177** A491 6p multi .25 .20

Intl. Youth
Year
A492

**1985, Aug. 28**
**1178** A492 12p mar & blk .30 .20

Installation of Democratic
Government — A493

**1985, Aug. 30**
**1179** A493 20p brt pur, yel ocher & dk grnsh bl .80 .35

Intl. Book
Fair — A494

**1985**
**1180** A494 20p multi .80 .35

Military
School,
Cent.
A495

**1985, Nov. 29 Litho. *Perf. 12***
**1181** A495 10p multi .40 .20

Department of
Flores,
Cent. — A496

Day of Hispanic
Solidarity — A498

Christmas
1985
A497

**1985, Dec. 9**
**1182** A496 6p Map, arms .20 .20

**1985, Dec. 23**
**1183** A497 10p multi .40 .20
**1184** A497 22p multi .60 .30

**1985, Dec. 27**
**1185** A498 12p Isabel Monument .30 .20

3rd Inter-American Agricultural
Congress — A499

**Wmk. 332**

**1986, Jan. 7 Photo. *Perf. 12***
**1186** A499 12p blk, dl yel & red .30 .20

UPU Day
A500

**1986, Jan. 14 Litho. *Perf. 12***
**1187** A500 15.50p multi .45 .25

1985
Census
A501

**1986, Jan. 21**
**1188** A501 10p multi .25 .20

Conaprole, 50th Anniv. — A502

**1986, Jan. 25**
**1189** A502 10p gold, brt ultra & bl .30 .20

UN, 40th
Anniv.
A503

**Wmk. 332**

**1986, Feb. 26 Litho. *Perf. 12***
**1190** A503 20p multi .45 .25

Brokers and
Auctioneers
Assoc., 50th
Anniv. — A504

**1986, Mar. 19**
**1191** A504 10p multi .20 .20

Gen. Manuel Ceferino
Oribe (1792-1857),
President — A505

Portraits: Nos. 1196, 1200, 2p, 7p, 15p, 20p, Oribe. Nos. 1195, 1209, 1211, 3p, Lavalleja. Nos. 1199, 1208, 1210, 30p, 100p, 200p, Artigas. No. 1198, 17p, 22p, 26p, 45p, 75p, Rivera.

**1986-89 *Perf. 12½***

| | | | | | |
|---|---|---|---|---|---|
| **1192** | A505 | 1p | dl grn | .20 | .20 |
| **1193** | A505 | 2p | scarlet | .20 | .20 |
| **1194** | A505 | 3p | ultra | .20 | .20 |
| **1195** | A505 | 5p | dark blue | .20 | .20 |
| **1196** | A505 | 5p | violet blue | .20 | .20 |
| **1197** | A505 | 7p | tan | .20 | .20 |
| **1198** | A505 | 10p | lilac rose | .25 | .20 |
| **1199** | A505 | 10p | brt green | .20 | .20 |
| **1200** | A505 | 10p | bluish grn | .20 | .20 |
| **1201** | A505 | 15p | dull blue | .20 | .20 |
| **1202** | A505 | 17p | deep blue | .25 | .20 |
| **1203** | A505 | 20p | light brown | .20 | .20 |
| **1204** | A505 | 22p | violet | .20 | .20 |
| **1205** | A505 | 26p | olive blk | .30 | .20 |
| **1206** | A505 | 30p | pale org | .30 | .25 |

| | | | | |
|---|---|---|---|---|
| **1207** | A505 | 45p dark red | .30 | .20 |
| **1208** | A505 | 50p dp bis | .55 | .45 |
| **1209** | A505 | 50p bright pink | .20 | .20 |
| **1210** | A505 | 60p dark gray | .75 | .45 |
| **1211** | A505 | 60p orange | .20 | .20 |
| **1211A** | A505 | 75p red orange | .30 | .25 |
| **1211B** | A505 | 100p dl red brn | 1.10 | .60 |
| **1211C** | A505 | 200p brt yel grn | 1.50 | .75 |
| | *Nos. 1192-1211C (23)* | | 8.20 | 6.15 |

The 22p is airmail.

Issued: 1p, 7p, 4/18; #1195, 30p, 6/16; #1198, 22p, 9/24; #1208, 8/5; 100p, 7/2; 2p, 6/16/87; 3p, #1210, 8/14/87; #1199, 17p, 8/4/87; 26p, 9/2/87; 15p, 9/9/88; 45p, 12/20/88; 200p, 10/19/88; #1211A, 5/19/89; #1211, 7/27/89; #1196, 1203, 8/15/89; #1209, 12/12/89; #1200, 1989.

See Nos. 1321-1329.

Italian Chamber of Commerce in Uruguay — A506

**1986, May 5** *Perf. 12*
**1212** A506 20p multi .60 .20

A507

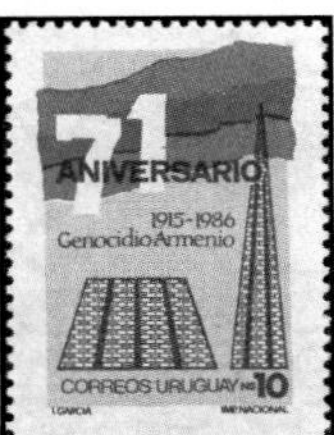


A508

**1986, May 28** **Photo.** *Perf. 12*
**1213** A507 20p multi .50 .30

1986 World Cup Soccer Championships, Mexico.

**Wmk. 332**

**1986, May 19** **Litho.** *Perf. 12*
**1214** A508 10p multi .20 .20

Genocide of the Armenian people, 71st anniv.

A509

A510

**1986, June 16**
**1215** A509 10p multi .20 .20

El Dia Newspaper, cent.

**1986, July 14**
**1216** A510 20p Garcia, Peruvian flag .40 .20

State visit of Pres. Alan Garcia of Peru.

Simon Bolivar, Gen. Sucre, Map A511

**1986, July 24**
**1217** A511 20p multi .45 .25

State visit of Pres. Jaime Lusinchi of Venezuela.

State Visit of Pres. Jose Sarney of Brazil — A512

Zelmar Michelini, Assassinated Liberal Senator — A513

**1986, July 31**
**1218** A512 20p multi .30 .20

**1986, Aug. 21**
**1219** A513 10p vio bl & rose lake .20 .20

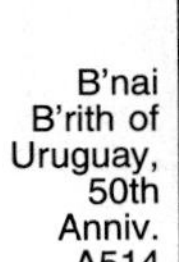


B'nai B'rith of Uruguay, 50th Anniv. A514

**1986, Sept. 10**
**1220** A514 10p red, gold & red brn .25 .20

General Agreement on Tariffs & Trade (GATT) Committee Meeting, Punta del Este — A515

**1986, Sept. 15**
**1221** A515 10p multi .20 .20

Scheduled Flights between Uruguay and Spain, 40th Anniv. — A516

**1986, Sept. 22**
**1222** A516 20p multi .30 .20

Fish Exports A517

**1986, Oct. 1**
**1223** A517 20p multi .30 .20

Wool Exports A518

**1986, Oct. 15**
**1224** A518 20p multi .30 .20

Pres. Blanco, Natl. and Dominican Flags A519

**1986, Oct. 29**
**1225** A519 20p multi .25 .20

State visit of Pres. Salvador Jorge Blanco of the Dominican Republic.

State Visit of Pres. Sandro Pertini of Italy — A520

State Visit of Pres. Raul Alfonsin of Argentina A521

**1986, Oct. 31**
**1226** A520 20p grn & buff .25 .25

**1986, Nov. 10**
**1227** A521 20p multi .30 .20

Hispanic Solidarity Day A522

Design: Felipe and Santiago, the patron saints of Montevideo, and cathedral.

**Wmk. 332**

**1987, Jan. 12** **Litho.** *Perf. 12*
**1228** A522 10p rose lake & blk .20 .20

JUVENTUS, 50th Anniv. (in 1986) — A523

**1987, Jan. 28**
**1229** A523 10p brt yel, blk & ultra .20 .20

Juventus, a Catholic sports, culture and leisure organization.

Hector Gutierrez Ruiz (1934-1976), Politician — A524

Intl. Symposium on Science and Technology A525

**1987, Feb. 23**
**1230** A524 10p brn & deep mag .20 .20
**1231** A525 20p multi .25 .25

Ruiz represented Uruguay at an earlier science and technology symposium.

Visit of Pope John Paul II to La Plata Region — A526

Dr. Jose F. Arias (1885-1985), Founder of the University of Crafts — A527

**1987, Mar. 31**
1232 A526 50p blk & deep org .75 .40

**1987, Apr. 28**
1233 A527 10p multi .20 .20

Jewish Community in Uruguay, 70th Anniv. — A528

**1987, July 8**
1234 A528 10p blk, org & brt bl .25 .20

Pluna Airlines, 50th Anniv. (in 1986) A529

**1987, Sept. 16**
1235 A529 10p Dragon Fly .20 .20
1236 A529 20p Douglas DC-3 .25 .20
1237 A529 25p Vickers Viscount .30 .20
1238 A529 30p Boeing 707 .40 .25
*Nos. 1235-1238 (4)* 1.15 .85

Artigas Antarctic Station A530

**1987, Sept. 28**
1239 A530 20p multi .25 .20

Uruguay Mortgage Bank, 75th Anniv. A531

**1987, Oct. 14**
1240 A531 26p multi .30 .25

Exports — A532

**1987, Oct. 28**
1241 A532 51p Beef .70 .40
1242 A532 51p Milk products .70 .40

Christmas 1987 — A533

**1987, Dec. 21**
1243 A533 17p Nativity, vert. .40 .20
1244 A533 66p shown .80 .50

State Visit of Jose Napoleon Duarte, President of El Salvador — A534

VARIG Airlines, 60th Anniv. (in 1987) — A535

**1988, Jan. 12**
1245 A534 20p brt olive grn & Prus blue .25 .20

**1988, Feb. 9**
1246 A535 66p blk, blue & brt yel .85 .85

Post Office Stamp Foundation A536

**Wmk. 332**
**1988, Feb. 9 Litho. *Perf. 12***
1247 A536 30p on 10+5p brt blue, blk & yel .25 .20

No. 1247 not issued without surcharge.

Intl. Peace Year A537

**1988, Feb. 11**
1248 A537 10p multi .20 .20

Euskal Erria, 75th Anniv. (in 1987) — A538

**1988, Mar. 9**
1249 A538 66p multi .60 .40

Basque-Uruguayan diplomatic relations.

Air Force, 75th Anniv. A539

**1988, Mar. 11**
1250 A539 17p multi .25 .20

Interamerican Children's Institute, 60th Anniv. — A540

**Wmk. 332**
**1988, Mar. 28 Litho. *Perf. 12***
1251 A540 30p apple grn, blk & grn .30 .20

State Hydroelectric Works (UTE), 75th Anniv. — A541

**1988, Apr. 20**
1252 A541 17p shown .20 .20
1253 A541 17p Baygorria Dam .20 .20
1254 A541 51p Gabriel Terra Dam .55 .25
1255 A541 51p Constitucion Dam .55 .25
1256 A541 66p Dams on map .80 .40
*Nos. 1252-1256 (5)* 2.30 1.30

Dated 1987.



Postal Union of America and Spain (UPAE), 75th Anniv. (in 1987) A542

**1988, May 10**
1257 A542 66p multi .55 .45

Israel, 40th Anniv. A543

**1988, May 17**
1258 A543 66p lt ultra & blk .55 .35

Postal Messenger of Peace — A544

**1988, May 24**
1259 A544 66p multi .55 .35

Portrait, *La Cumparsita* Tango — A545

Firemen, Cent. — A546

**1988, June 7**
1260 A545 17p Parade, horiz. .40 .20
1261 A545 51p Score 1.25 .55

Gerardo H. Matos Rodrigues, composer.

**1988, June 21**
1262 A546 17p Pablo Banales, founder .25 .20
1263 A546 26p Fireman, 1900 .30 .25
1264 A546 34p Emblem, horiz. .40 .30
1265 A546 51p Merry Weather fire engine, 1907, horiz. .60 .40
1266 A546 66p Fire pump, 1888, horiz. .95 .60

**Size: 44x24½mm**
1267 A546 100p Ladder truck, 1921 1.50 1.00
*Nos. 1262-1267 (6)* 4.00 2.75

*Capitan Miranda* Trans-world Voyage, Cent. — A547

**1988, July 28**
1268 A547 30p multi .30 .20

Exports A548

**1988**
1269 A548 30p Citrus fruit .25 .20
1270 A548 45p Rice .55 .25
1271 A548 55p Footwear .60 .30
1272 A548 55p Leather and furs .60 .35
*Nos. 1269-1272 (4)* 2.00 1.10

Issued: 30p, #1272, 9/14; 45p, #1271, 8/23.

Natl. Museum of Natural History, 150th Anniv. — A549

30p, *Usnea densirostra* fossil. 90p, *Toxodon platensis* bone, Quaternary period.

**1988, Sept. 20**

**1273** A549 30p blk, yel & red brn .40 .25

**1274** A549 90p blk, ultra & beige .95 .55

*a.* Pair, #1273-1274 2.00 2.00

Battle of Carpinteria, 150th Anniv. (in 1986) — A550

**1988, Nov. 23**

**1275** A550 30p multi .25 .20

Horiz. row contains two stamps, label, then two more stamps.

A551

A552

**1988, Dec. 21**

**1276** A551 115p multi .95 .95

Christmas.

**1988, Dec. 27**

Paintings: a, *Manolita Pina, 1920,* by J. Torres Garcia. b, *78 Squares and Rectangles,* by J.P. Costigliolo. c, Print publicizing an exhibition of works by Pedrero Figari, 1945. d, *Self-portrait, 1947,* by J. Torres Garcia.

**1277** Block or strip of 4 + label 3.25 3.25

*a.-d.* A552 115p any single .75 .50

No. 1277 can be collected as a vert. or horiz. strip of 4, or block of 4, with label.

Spanish Heritage Day A553

**1989, Jan. 9**

**1278** A553 90p multi .65 .40

**1279** A553 115p multi .95 .50

Armenian Organization Hnchakian, Cent. — A554

**Wmk. 332**

**1989, June 7 Litho. *Perf. 12***

**1280** A554 210p red, yel & blue 1.40 .55

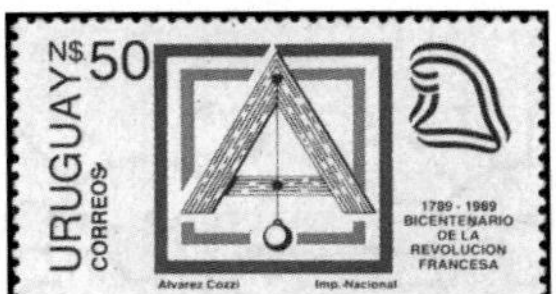


French Revolution, Bicentennial — A555

**1989, July 3**

**1281** A555 50p Plumb line, frame .25 .20

**1282** A555 50p Liberty tree .25 .20

**1283** A555 210p Eye in sunburst 1.10 .45

**1284** A555 210p Liberty 1.10 .45

*Nos. 1281-1284 (4)* 2.70 1.30

Use Postal Codes — A556

**1989, July 25**

**1285** A556 50p Montevideo Dept. map .25 .20

**1286** A556 210p National map, vert. .95 .30

3rd Pan American Milk Congress A557

**1989, Aug. 24**

**1287** A557 170p sky blue & ultra .95 .35

A558

A559

**Wmk. 332**

**1989, Aug. 29 Photo. *Perf. 12***

**1288** A558 170p multicolored .85 .30

Joaquin Jose da Silva Xavier.

**1989, Aug. 31**

**1289** A559 210p blk, red & bl 1.00 .35

Inter-Parliamentary Union Conf., London.

FAO Emblem, Map, Citrus Slice — A560

**1989, Sept. 11**

**1290** A560 180p multicolored .70 .30

8th Conf., Intergovernmental Group on Citrus Fruits.

UN Decade for the Disabled — A561

**1989, Oct. 4**

**1291** A561 50p shown .30 .20

**1292** A561 210p Disabled people .85 .35

America Issue — A562

Nacurutu artifact and UPAE emblem.

**1989, Oct. 11 *Perf. 12½***

**1293** A562 60p multicolored .45 .20

**1294** A562 180p multicolored 1.10 .45

City of Pando, Bicentennial — A563

**1989, Dec. 27 Litho. *Perf. 12***

**1295** A563 60p multicolored .25 .20

Christmas A564

**1989, Dec. 19**

**1296** A564 70p Virgin of Trienta y Tres .35 .20

**1297** A564 210p Barradas, horiz. .95 .45

Charity Hospital, Bicent. (in 1988) — A565

**1990, Jan. 23 Wmk. 332**

**1298** A565 60p multicolored .60 .60

Provincial Arms and Maps A566

**1990**

**1299** A566 70p Soriano .30 .30

**1300** A566 70p Florida, vert. .35 .35

**1301** A566 90p Canelones .40 .40

**1302** A566 90p Lavalleja, vert. .40 .40

**1303** A566 90p San Jose, vert. .40 .40

**1304** A566 90p Rivera .40 .40

*Nos. 1299-1304 (6)* 2.25 2.25

Dated 1989.

Writers — A567

Designs: a, Luisa Luisi (1883-1940). b, Javier de Viana (1872-1926). c, Delmira Agustini (1886-1914). d, J. Zorrilla de San Martin (1855-1931). e, Alfonsina Storni (1892-1938). f, Julio Casal (1889-1954). g, Juana de Ibarbourou (1895-1979). h, Carlos Roxlo (1861-1926).

**1990, Mar. 20**

**1320** Block of 8 + 2 labels 4.25 4.25

*a.-b.* A567 60p any single .25 .25

*c.-d.* A567 75p any single .30 .30

*e.-f.* A567 170p any single .70 .70

*g.-h.* A567 210p any single .95 .95

Printed in sheets of 4 blocks of 4 separated by vert. and horiz. rows of 5 labels. Position of denomination varies to form border around each block.

Dated 1989.

Portraits Type of 1986

25p, 30p, Lavalleja. 60p, 90p, Rivera. 100p, 150p, 300p, 500p, 1000p, Artigas.

**1990 Litho. Wmk. 332 *Perf. 12½***

**1321** A505 25p orange .20 .20

**1322** A505 30p ultra .20 .20

**1323** A505 60p purple .20 .20

**1324** A505 90p org red .45 .30

**1325** A505 100p brown .35 .35

**1326** A505 150p dk blue green .70 .50

**1327** A505 300p blue 1.25 1.00

**1328** A505 500p orange red 2.00 1.00

**1329** A505 1000p red 4.25 3.00

*Nos. 1321-1329 (9)* 9.60 6.75

Issued: 30p, 60p, 7/17; 90p, 3/24; 150p, 6/22; 300p, 7/5; 500p, 3/22; 1000p, 7/24.

A568

A569

**1990, Apr. 3** ***Perf. 12***
**1346** A568 70p multicolored .35 .35

City of Mercedes, bicent. Dated 1989.

**1990, Apr. 24**
**1347** A569 210p multicolored .95 .95

Intl. Agricultural Development Fund, 10th anniv. Dated 1989.

Traffic Safety — A570

Designs: a, Bus, car. b, Don't drink and drive. c, Cross on the green light. d, Obey traffic signs.

**1990, May 28**
**1348** A570 70p Block of 4, #a.-d. .95 .95

General Artigas A571

**1990, June 18**
**1349** A571 60p red & blue .35 .35

A572

A573

**1990, June 26**
**1350** A572 70p multicolored .30 .30

Intl. Mothers' Day. Dated 1989.

**1990, July 10**

Treaty of Montevideo, 1889: a, Gonzalo Ramirez. b, Ildefonso Garcia. c, Flags at left. d, Flags at right.

**1351** A573 60p Block of 4, #a.-d. 1.25 1.25

Nos. 1351c-1351d printed in continuous design. Dated 1989.

Microphone, Tower — A574

b, Newspaper boy. c, Television camera. d, Books.

**1990, Sept. 26**
**1352** A574 70p Block of 4, #a.-d. 1.50 1.50

Carlos Federico Saez (1878-1901) — A575

Portraits: b, Pedro Blanes Viale (1879-1926). c, Edmundo Prati (1889-1970). d, Jose L. Zorrilla de San Martin (1891-1975).

**1990, Dec. 26**
**1353** Block of 4 2.75 2.75
***a.-b.*** A575 90p any single .40 .40
***c.-d.*** A575 210p any single .90 .90

Prevent Forest Fires — A576

**Wmk. 332**
**1990, Oct. 26** **Litho.** ***Perf. 12***
**1354** A576 70np multicolored 1.50 1.50

America Issue — A577

**1990, Nov. 6**
**1355** A577 120p Odocoileus bezoarticus .60 .60
**1356** A577 360p Peltophorum dubium, vert. 1.75 1.75

Army Corps of Engineers, 75th Anniv. — A578

**1991, Jan. 21**
**1357** A578 170p multicolored .85 .85

The Nativity by Brother Juan B. Maino — A579

**1990, Dec. 24**
**1358** A579 170p bister & multi .85 .85
**1359** A579 830p silver & multi 4.25 4.25

Organization of American States, Cent. (in 1989) A580

**Wmk. 332**
**1991, Mar. 21** **Litho.** ***Perf. 12***
**1360** A580 830p bl, blk & yel 3.50 3.50

Prevention of AIDS — A581

**1991, Mar. 8**
**1361** A581 170p bl & multi .85 .85
**1362** A581 830p grn & multi 4.25 4.25

Carnival — A582

**1991, Feb. 19**
**1363** A582 170p multicolored .85 .85

Education — A583

Expanding youth's horizons: a, Stone ax, megalithic monument. b, Wheel, pyramids. c, Printing press, solar system. d, Satellite, diagram.

**Wmk. 332**
**1991, Apr. 23** **Litho.** ***Perf. 12***
**1364** Block of 4 2.40 2.40
***a.-b.*** A583 120p any single .30 .30
***c.-d.*** A583 330p any single .95 .95

Natl. Cancer Day — A584

**1991, June 17**
**1365** A584 360p red & black .95 .95

A585

Exports of Uruguay — A586

***Perf. 12½x13, 13x12½***
**1991** **Litho.** **Wmk. 332**
**1366** A585 120p Textiles .30 .30
**1367** A586 120p Clothing .40 .25
**1368** A585 400p Semiprecious stones, granite 1.25 1.25
*Nos. 1366-1368 (3)* 1.95 1.80

Issued: #1366, 400p, 4/23; #1367, 6/26.

7th Pan American Maccabiah Games — A587

**1991, July 4** ***Perf. 12½x13***
**1369** A587 1490p multicolored 4.00 4.00

Dornier Wal, Route Map — A588

**1991, July 5** ***Perf. 12***
**1370** A588 1510p multicolored 3.50 3.50

Espamer '91.

Entrance to Sacramento Colony A589

Railroads and Trains: 540p, 825p, First locomotive, 1869. 600p, like 360p. 800p, Entrance to Sacramento Colony. 1510p, 2500p, Horse-drawn streetcar.

**Wmk. 332**
**1991-2002** **Litho.** ***Perf. 12***
**1378** A589 360p ol bis & yel .95 .60
**1378A** A589 540p dk bl & gray 1.40 .95
**1379** A589 600p brn, yel & blk .95 .85

**1379A** A589 800p grn & yel grn .95 .95
**1379B** A589 825p bl, gray & blk 1.40 1.25
**1380** A589 1510p ol bis & emer 4.25 3.00
**1382** A589 2500p ol bis, emer & blk 3.50 3.00
*Nos. 1378-1382 (7)* 13.40 10.60

Issued: 360p, 540p, 1510p, July 19; 825p, Feb. 11, 1992; 2500p, May 29, 2002; 600p, June 18, 1992; 800p, Feb. 9, 1993.

For surcharges, see Nos. 2011B, 2059.

Sagrada Family College, Cent. — A590

College of the Immaculate Heart of Mary, Cent. — A591

**Wmk. 332**

**1991, June 26 Litho. *Perf. 12***
**1383** A590 360p multicolored .75 .75
**1384** A591 1370p multicolored 3.00 3.00

Constitutional Oath — A592

**1991, July 17**
**1385** A592 360p multicolored .80 .80

Swiss Confederation, 700th Anniv. — A593

**1991, Aug. 1 *Perf. 13x12½***
**1386** A593 1510p multicolored 4.25 4.25

**Souvenir Sheet**

***Perf. 12***

**1387** A593 3000p multicolored 9.00 9.00

Photography, 150th Anniv. — A594

***Perf. 12½x13***

**1991, Sept. 12 Litho. Wmk. 332**
**1388** A594 1370p multi 2.50 2.50

Actors Society of Uruguay, 50th Anniv. — A595

**1991, Aug. 24 *Perf. 12***
**1389** A595 450p blk & red .85 .85

CREA (Agriculture Association), 25th Anniv. — A596

**1991, Sept. 14 *Perf. 12½x13***
**1390** A596 450p multicolored .85 .85

Whitbread Around the World Race — A597

**1991, Aug. 20 *Perf. 13x12½***
**1391** A597 1510p multicolored 3.00 3.00

Amerigo Vespucci (1454-1512) — A598

America Issue: 450p, First landing at River Plate, 1602, vert.

**1991, Oct. 11 *Perf. 12***
**1392** A598 450p yel & brn .85 .85
**1393** A598 1740p ol & brn 3.00 3.00

Automobiles — A599

Designs: 350p, Gladiator, 1902. 1370p, E.M.F., 1909. 1490p, Renault, 1912. 1510p, Clement-Bayard, 1903, vert.

**1991, Oct. 18 *Perf. 12½x13, 13x12½***
**1394** A599 360p multicolored .85 .85
**1395** A599 1370p multicolored 3.00 3.00
**1396** A599 1490p multicolored 3.00 3.00
**1397** A599 1510p multicolored 3.50 3.50
*Nos. 1394-1397 (4)* 10.35 10.35

Team Nacional Montevideo, Winners of Toyota and Europe-South America Soccer Cups — A600

**Wmk. 332**

**1991, Nov. 8 Litho. *Perf. 12***
**1398** A600 450p shown 1.00 1.00
**1399** A600 450p Emblem, trophy, vert. 1.00 1.00

Margarita Xirgu (1888-1969), Actress — A601

**1991, Oct. 4**
**1400** A601 360p yel & brn .65 .65

INTERPOL, 60th Congress A602

**1991, Oct. 30**
**1401** A602 1740p multicolored 3.00 3.00

Maria Auxiliadora Institute, Cent. — A603

**1991, Nov. 11**
**1402** A603 450p multicolored .85 .85

Technological Laboratory, 25th Anniv. — A604

**1991, Nov. 11**
**1403** A604 1570p dk bl & lt bl 2.75 2.75

The Table by Zoma Baitler — A605

**1991, Oct. 18**
**1404** A605 360p multicolored .65 .65

World Food Day A606

**1991,Oct. 16 *Perf. 12½x13***
**1405** A606 1740p multicolored 3.00 3.00

Ships A607

Designs: a, Steam yacht, Gen. Rivera. b, Coast Guard cutter, Salto. c, Cruiser, Uruguay. d, Tanker, Pte. Oribe.

**Wmk. 332**

**1991, Oct. 4 Litho. *Perf. 12***
**1406** Block of 4 9.00 9.00
***a.-b.*** A607 450p any single 1.00 1.00
***c.-d.*** A607 1570p any single 3.25 3.25

Topographical Society Type of 1981

**1991, Dec. 3 *Perf. 12½***
**1407** A439 550p multi .75 .75

Topographical Society, 160th anniv.

World AIDS Day — A608

**1991, Dec. 1**
**1408** A608 550p bl, blk & brt yel .95 .95
**1409** A608 2040p lt grn, blk & lil 3.50 3.50

Export Industries A609

**Wmk. 332**

**1991, Mar. 20 Litho. *Perf. 12½***
**1410** A609 120p multicolored .20 .20

Christmas A610

**1991, Dec. 24** ***Perf. 12***
**1411** A610 550p Angel .75 .75
**1412** A610 2040p Adoration of the Angels 2.75 2.75

Muscians — A611

Designs: No. 1413a, Francisco Canaro. No. 1413b, Anibal Troilo. No. 1414a, Juan de Dios Filiberto. No. 1414b, Pintin Castellanos.

**Wmk. 332**
**1992, Jan. 20** **Photo.** ***Perf. 12***
**1413** A611 450p Pair, #a.-b. 1.50 1.50
**1414** A611 450p Pair, #a.-b. 1.50 1.50

Patricio Aylwin, Pres. of Chile — A612

***Perf. 11½x12***
**1992, Mar. 23** **Litho.** **Unwmk.**
**1415** A612 550p multicolored .65 .65

Penarol, Winners of Liberator's Cup in Club Soccer — A612a

La Paz City, 120th Anniv. — A612b

***Perf. 13x12½***
**1992, May 29** **Litho.** **Wmk. 332**
**1415A** A612a 600p yel & blk .70 .70

**Souvenir Sheet**
***Perf. 12***
**1415B** A612a 3000p yel & blk 3.75 3.75

**1992, May 25** ***Perf. 13x12½***
**1415C** A612b 550p multicolored .65 .65

World No-Smoking Day — A613

**Wmk. 332**
**1992, May 31** **Litho.** ***Perf. 12***
**1416** A613 2500p multicolored 3.00 3.00

United Nations World Health Day A614

**Wmk. 332**
**1992, July 28** **Litho.** ***Perf. 13***
**1417** A614 2500p bl, lt bl & red 3.00 3.00

Mercosur A615

**1992, Aug. 5** **Photo.** ***Perf. 12***
**1418** A615 2500p multicolored 2.75 2.75

Olymphilex '92, Barcelona — A616

**Wmk. 332**
**1992, Aug. 8** **Photo.** ***Perf. 12***
**1419** A616 2900p multicolored 3.50 3.50

Discovery of America, 500th Anniv. — A617

***Perf. 11½x12, 12x11½***
**1992, Oct. 10** **Litho.** **Unwmk.**
**1420** A617 700p Ship, masts, vert. 1.00 1.00
**1421** A617 2900p Globe, ship 3.50 3.50

Jose Pedro Varela Natl. Teachers College, 50th Anniv. A618

**1992, Oct. 22** ***Perf. 12x11½***
**1422** A618 700p multicolored .75 .75

22nd Regional FAO Conference — A619

Designs: 2500p, Emblems. 2900p, Emblems, children with food basket.

**1992, Sept. 28**
**1423** A619 2500p multicolored 2.50 2.50
**1424** A619 2900p multicolored 3.00 3.00

Intl. Conf. on Nutrition, Rome, Italy (#1424).

Cesar Vallejo (1892-1938), Poet — A620

**1992, Sept. 30**
**1425** A620 2500p brn & dk brn 2.50 2.50

A621

A622

**1992, Oct. 26** ***Perf. 11½x12***
**1426** A621 700p gray, red & blk .75 .75

Assoc. of Wholesalers and Retailers, cent.

***Perf. 11½x12***
**1992, Oct. 10** **Litho.** **Unwmk.**
**1427** A622 700p black, blue & grn 1.25 1.25

Monument to Columbus, cent.

A623

A624

Ruins and lighthouse, Colonia del Sacramento.

**1992, Oct. 10**
**1428** A623 700p multicolored 1.25 1.25

Discovery of America, 500th anniv.

**1992, Oct. 19**
**1429** A624 700p red lil, rose lil & blk 1.25 1.25

Columbus Philanthropic Society, cent.

A625

A626

**1992, Oct. 19**
**1430** A625 2900p multicolored 3.00 3.00

Judaism in the Americas, 500th anniv.

**1992, Oct. 30**
**1431** A626 2900p multicolored 3.00 3.00

Lebanon Society of Uruguay, 50th anniv.

Pan American Health Organization, 90th Anniv. — A627

***Perf. 12x11½***
**1992, Dec. 15** **Litho.** **Unwmk.**
**1432** A627 3200p blk, bl & yel 3.00 3.00

22nd Lions Club Forum for Latin America and the Caribbean — A628

**1992, Dec. 2**
**1433** A628 2700p multicolored 2.50 2.50

Christmas A629

**1992, Dec. 1** ***Perf. 11½x12***

**1434** A629 800p Nativity scene .75 .75
**1435** A629 3200p Star in sky 3.00 3.00

General Manuel Oribe, Birth Bicent. A630

Designs: No. 1436, Oribe, Oriental College. No. 1437, Oribe in military dress uniform, vert.

***Perf. 12x11½, 11½x12***

**1992, Dec. 8** **Litho.** **Unwmk.**

**1436** A630 800p multicolored .75 .75
**1437** A630 800p multicolored .75 .75

Logosofia, 60th Anniv. — A631

**1992, Dec. 29** ***Perf. 12x11½***

**1438** A631 800p blue & yellow .75 .75

Immigrants' Day — A632

**1992, Dec. 4** ***Perf. 11½x12***

**1439** A632 800p black & green .75 .75

ANDEBU, 70th Anniv. — A633

Caritas of Uruguay, 30th Anniv. A634

**1992, Dec. 22** **Photo.** ***Perf. 12x11½***

**1440** A633 2700p Satellite 2.50 2.50
**1441** A634 3200p Map, huts by water 3.00 3.00

A635

A636

**1992, Dec. 18** ***Perf. 11½x12***

**1442** A635 800p brown & yellow .75 .75

Jose H. Molaguero S. A., 50th anniv.

***Perf. 11½x12***

**1993, Mar. 1** **Litho.** **Unwmk.**

**1443** A636 80c multicolored .65 .65

Wilson Ferreira Aldunate.

Economic Science and Accountancy College, Cent. — A637

***Perf. 12x11½***

**1993, Apr. 15** **Photo.** **Unwmk.**

**1444** A637 1p multicolored 1.00 1.00

Souvenir Sheet

Polska '93, Intl. Philatelic Exhibition — A638

a, Lech Walesa. b, Pope John Paul II.

**1993, May 3** ***Perf. 11½x12***

**1445** A638 2p Sheet of 2, #a.-b. 4.50 4.50

A639

A639a

A639b

A639c

A639d

A639e

A639f

A639g

A639h

Design A639g shows the Postal Administration Tower.

ONE PESO (Letter Box — A639):
Type I — "Bugon vecinal 1879" 21½mm, letter box 23½mm high.
Type II — "Bugon vecinal 1879" 22mm, letter box 22½mm high.
Type III — "Bugon vecinal 1879" 19½mm, letter box 21mm high.
There are other differences among the three types.

**Wmk. 332**

**1993-99** **Litho.** ***Perf. 12½***

| | | | | |
|---|---|---|---|---|
| **1446** | A639 | 50c gray ol & yel | .20 | .20 |
| **1447** | A639 | 1p lt brn & yel (I) | .40 | .40 |
| *a.* | | Type II | .50 | .50 |
| *b.* | | Type III, unwatermarked | .25 | .25 |
| *c.* | | Type III, photo., unwmkd. | .25 | .25 |
| **1448** | A639a | 1p org yel & bl | .80 | .80 |

***Perf. 12***

| | | | | |
|---|---|---|---|---|
| **1449** | A639b | 1p org & bl | .55 | .55 |
| **1450** | A639c | (1.20p) blue | .60 | .60 |
| **1451** | A639c | (1.40p) green | .65 | .65 |
| **1452** | A639d | 1.40p yel & bl | .65 | .65 |
| **1453** | A639c | (1.60p) red | 1.00 | 1.00 |
| **1454** | A639 | 1.80p bl & yel | 1.10 | 1.10 |
| **1455** | A639c | (1.80p) brown | 1.00 | 1.00 |
| **1456** | A639c | (2p) gray | 1.00 | 1.00 |
| **1457** | A639c | (2.30p) lilac | 1.25 | 1.25 |
| **1458** | A639 | 2.60p bl, yel & grn | 1.25 | 1.25 |
| **1459** | A639e | (2.60p) grn & yel | 1.25 | 1.25 |
| **1460** | A639e | (2.90p) bl & yel | 1.25 | 1.25 |
| **1460A** | A639e | (3p) gray & brt yel grn | .85 | .85 |
| *b.* | | Unwmkd. | .85 | .85 |
| **1461** | A639e | (3.10p) red & pink | .90 | .90 |
| **1462** | A639e | (3.20p) rose brn & lt brn | 2.75 | 2.75 |
| **1462A** | A639e | (3.50p) pur & lt bl | — | — |
| **1462B** | A639e | (3.80p) brt blue | | |
| **1463** | A639e | (4p) bis & yel, litho. | .95 | .95 |
| **1464** | A639f | 5p bl & yel, perf. 12½ | 2.00 | 2.00 |
| **1465** | A639g | 6p blue & blk | 1.40 | 1.40 |
| **1465A** | A639f | 7p blue & yel | 2.70 | 2.70 |
| **1465B** | A639 | 7.50p vio & yel | 3.00 | 3.00 |
| **1465C** | A639h | 8p bl & yel | 3.00 | 3.00 |
| | | *Nos. 1446-1462,1463-1465C (24)* | 30.50 | 30.50 |

The design of Nos. 1460A, 1462-1463 does not include "PORTE MINIMO." There are minor design differences between #1464 and 1465A.

Issued: #1448, 4/15/93; #1450, 8/2/93; #1451, 12/1/93; #1452, 1/4/94; #1453, 4/4/94; #1455, 8/1/94; #1454 8/9/94; #1449, 10/3/94; 1456, 12/1/94. #1457, 4/1/95; #1458, (2.60p), 8/10/95; 50c, #1447, 8/27/96; #1460, (3.10p), (3.50p), 4/1/96; 7.50p, 5/21/96; 5p, 1997; (3.80p), 5/9/97; #1463, 8/1/97; 6p, 8/13/97; (3.50p), 7/28/98; (3p), 2/1/99. #1460Ab, 1999.

Interior Fire Service, 50th Anniv. — A640

15th Congress of UPAEP — A641

***Perf. 11½x12***

**1993, May 28** **Litho.** **Unwmk.**

**1466** A640 1p multicolored .75 .75

**1993, June 21**

**1467** A641 3.50p multicolored 2.50 2.50

Uruguayan Navy, 175th Anniv. — A642

Sailing ship, Pedro Campbell, first admiral.

***Perf. 12x11½***

**1993, June 28** **Litho.** **Wmk. 332**

**1468** A642 1p multicolored .90 .90

Intl. University Society, 25th Anniv. — A643

**1993, July 2**

**1469** A643 1p multicolored .90 .90

Automobile Club of Uruguay, 75th Anniv. — A644

**1993, July 19** **Photo.** **Unwmk.**

**1470** A644 3.50p 1910 Hupmobile 2.50 2.50

Uruguay Battalion in UN Peacekeeping Force, Cambodia — A645

***Perf. 12x11½***

**1993, Aug. 6** **Litho.** **Unwmk.**

**1471** A645 1p multicolored .90 .90

Souvenir Sheet

Brasiliana '93 — A646

World Cup Soccer Champions: a, Uruguay, 1930, 1950. b, Brazil, 1958, 1962, 1970.

**1993, July 28** ***Perf. 11½x12***
**1472** A646 2.50p Sheet of 2, #a.-b. 3.75 3.75

State Television Channel 5, 30th Anniv. — A647

**1993, Aug. 19** ***Perf. 12x11½***
**1473** A647 1.20p multicolored .90 .90

ANDA, 60th Anniv. A648

***Perf. 12½***
**1993, Sept. 24** **Litho.** **Unwmk.**
**1474** A648 1.20p multicolored .85 .85

Natl. Police Academy, 50th Anniv. A649

**1993, Sept. 24**
**1475** A649 1.20p multicolored .90 .90

Newspaper Diario El Pais, 75th Anniv. — A650

***Perf. 12½***
**1993, Sept. 30** **Litho.** **Unwmk.**
**1476** A650 1.20p multicolored 1.00 1.00

Latin American Conference on Rural Electrification — A651

**1993, Oct. 11**
**1477** A651 3.50p multicolored 2.50 2.50

B'nai B'rith, 150th Anniv. A652

**1993, Oct. 13**
**1478** A652 3.70p multicolored 2.75 2.75

A653

Fauna — A654

**1993** **Photo.** **Wmk. 332** ***Perf. 12½***

| | | | | | |
|---|---|---|---|---|---|
| **1482** | A653 | 20c | Seriema bird | .45 | .20 |
| **1484** | A653 | 30c | Dragon bird | .60 | .25 |
| **1486** | A653 | 50c | Anteaters, horiz. | 1.00 | .40 |
| **1492** | A654 | 1.20p | Giant armadillo | 1.25 | 1.25 |
| | | | *Nos. 1482-1492 (4)* | 3.30 | 2.10 |

Issued: 1.20p, 8/3/93; 20c, 30c, 50c, 10/22/93.

This is an expanding set. Numbers may change.

For surcharge, see No. 2011A.

America Issue A655

***Perf. 12½***
**1993, Oct. 6** **Litho.** **Unwmk.**
**1504** A655 1.20p Caiman latirostris .85 .85
**1505** A655 3.50p Athene cunicularia, vert. 2.50 2.50

Souvenir Sheet

Whitbread Trans-Global Yacht Race — A656

**1993, Oct. 22** ***Perf. 11½x12***
**1506** A656 5p multicolored 3.50 3.50

Beatification of Mother Francisca Rubatto — A657

Intl. Year of Indigenous People — A658

**1993, Oct. 29** **Wmk. 332** ***Perf. 12***
**1507** A657 1.20p multicolored 1.25 1.25

***Perf. 13x12½***
**1993, Oct. 29** **Unwmk.**
**1508** A658 3.50p multicolored 2.50 2.50

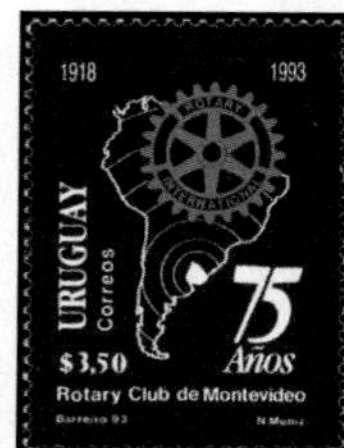


Rotary Club of Montevideo, 75th Anniv. — A658a

***Perf. 12½***
**1993, Nov. 10** **Litho.** **Unwmk.**
**1508A** A658a 3.50p dk bl & bis 3.00 3.00

Rhea Americana A659

**1993, Dec. 20** **Litho.** ***Perf. 12***

| | | | | | |
|---|---|---|---|---|---|
| **1509** | A659 | 20c | shown | .70 | .35 |
| **1510** | A659 | 20c | With chicks | .80 | .40 |
| **1511** | A659 | 50c | Head | 1.25 | .75 |
| **1512** | A659 | 50c | Two walking | 1.25 | .75 |
| | | | *Nos. 1509-1512 (4)* | 4.00 | 2.25 |

World Wildlife Fund.

Children's Rights Day A660

**1994, Jan. 4** ***Perf. 12½***
**1513** A660 1.40p multicolored .95 .95

Independence of Lebanon, 50th Anniv. — A661

**1993, Nov. 22**
**1514** A661 3.70p multicolored 2.50 2.50

Eduardo Victor Haedo — A662

**1993, Nov. 24**
**1515** A662 1.20p multicolored .85 .85

Christmas A663

Intl. AIDS Day — A664

**1993, Dec. 7**
**1516** A663 1.40p shown .90 .90
**1517** A663 4p Nativity, diff. 2.75 2.75

**1993, Dec. 1**
**1518** A664 1.40p multicolored 1.90 1.90

Souvenir Sheets of 4 & 2

Anniversaries & Events — A665

Designs: No. 1519a, Switzerland #3L1, 1913 Swiss private air mail stamp. b, Germany #C40, Uruguay #C426c. c, Uruguay #C372, US #C76. d, Uruguay #C282a, US #C104.

No. 1520a, Switzerland Types A1, A2. b, Switzerland #B541.

**1993, Nov. 18**
**1519** A665 1p #a.-d. 8.50 8.50
**1520** A665 2.50p #a.-b. 8.50 8.50

Swiss postage stamps, 150th anniv. (#1519a, 1520). Dr. Hugo Eckener, 125th anniv. of birth (#1519b). First man on moon, 25th anniv. (#1519c). 1994 World Cup Soccer Championships, US (#1519d).

Nos. 1519-1520 exist imperf. Value $25.

17th Inter-American Naval Conference — A666

**1994, Mar. 21** **Litho.** ***Perf. 12½***
**1521** A666 3.70p multicolored 2.50 2.50

A667

A668

1994, Mar. 11 *Perf. 12½*
**1522** A667 4p multicolored 2.75 2.75

5th World Sports Congress, Punta del Este.

**Unwmk.**

**1994, Apr. 4 Litho. *Perf. 12***
**1523** A668 3.90p multicolored 2.50 2.50

Latin America Youth Organization, 7th conference.

A669

A670

**1994, Apr. 18**
**1524** A669 4.30p multicolored 2.75 2.75

4th World Congress on Merino Wool.

**1994, Apr. 28** *Perf. 12½*
**1525** A670 4.30p multicolored 2.75 2.75

ILO, 75th anniv.

Miniature Sheet

1994 Winter Olympic Medal Winners A671

Designs: a, Katja Seizinger. b, Markus Wasmeier. c, Vreni Schneider. d, Gustav Weder.

**1994, May 6** *Perf. 12*
**1526** A671 1.25p Sheet of 4, #a.-d. 8.00 8.00

No. 1526 exists demonitized and imperf on paper with watermark 322. This item was sold with No. 1526 and has a matching serial number.

Miniature Sheet

1994 World Cup Soccer Championships, US — A672

a, Soccer ball, flags of Uruguay, Brazil. b, Ball, flags of Italy, Argentina. c, Ball, flags of Germany, Great Britain. d, Olympic Rings.

**1994, May 16**
**1527** A672 1.25p Sheet of 4, #a.-d. 8.00 8.00

Uruguay, Olympic soccer gold medalists, 1924-1928 (#1527d).
See note after No. 1526.

Clemente Estable (1894-1976), Biologist — A673

**1994, May 23 Litho. *Perf. 12½***
**1528** A673 1.60p olive & black 1.00 1.00

Electoral Court, 70th Anniv. — A674

**1994, June 7**
**1529** A674 1.60p multicolored 1.00 1.00

Natl. Commission to Prevent Tapeworms — A675

*Perf. 12½*

**1994, June 17 Litho. Unwmk.**
**1530** A675 1.60p multicolored .95 .95

Souvenir Sheet

Cesareo L. Berisso, First Aviator to Land at Natl. Airport, Carrasco — A676

**1994, June 21** *Perf. 12*
**1531** A676 5p multicolored 3.00 3.00

Intl. Cooperatives, 150th Anniv. — A677

**1994, July 1** *Perf. 12½*
**1532** A677 4.30p multicolored 2.50 2.50

Commission on Integration of Regional Electricity, 30th Anniv. — A678

**1994, July 8**
**1533** A678 1.60p multicolored .95 .95

Abate Pierre A679

*Perf. 12½*

**1994, Aug. 5 Litho. Unwmk.**
**1534** A679 4.80p multicolored 2.75 2.75

Intl. Year of the Family A680

**1994, July 28**
**1535** A680 4.80p multicolored 2.75 2.75

The Man of Lugano, by Goffredo Sommavilla (1850-1944) — A681

*Perf. 12½*

**1994, Aug. 15 Litho. Unwmk.**
**1536** A681 4.80p multicolored 2.75 2.75

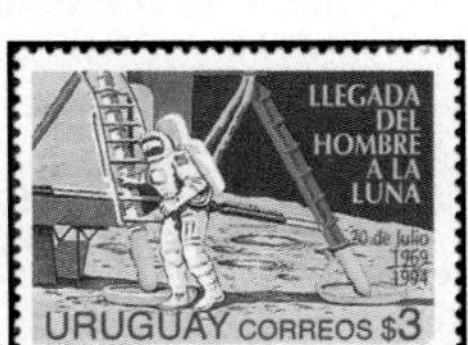
First Manned Moon Landing, 25th Annvi. A682

**1994, July 20**
**1537** A682 3p multicolored 2.00 2.00

Intl. Olympic Committee, Cent. — A683

**1994, Aug. 23**
**1538** A683 4.80p multicolored 3.00 3.00

Elbio Fernandez School, 125th Anniv. A684

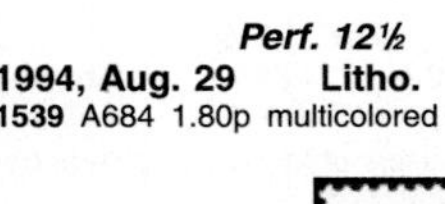

*Perf. 12½*

**1994, Aug. 29 Litho. Unwmk.**
**1539** A684 1.80p multicolored 1.00 1.00

A685

A686

**1994, Sept. 10** *Perf. 12*
**1540** A685 1.80p black & blue 1.25 1.25

Gral. Aparicio Saravia, 90th Death Anniv.

**1994, Sept. 30** *Perf. 12½*
**1541** A686 4.80p multicolored 2.50 2.50

6th Latin American Urban Congress.

General Assoc. of Uruguayan Authors, 65th Anniv. — A687

*Perf. 12½*

**1994, Sept. 26 Litho. Unwmk.**
**1542** A687 1.80p multicolored .95 .95

America Issue A688

**1994, Oct. 10**
**1543** A688 1.80p Stagecoach 1.25 1.25
**1544** A688 4.80p Paddle steamer 3.50 3.50

A689

A690

*Perf. 12½*

**1994, Oct. 28 Litho. Unwmk.**

**1545** A689 2p multicolored 1.10 1.10

Assoc. of Directors of Marketing, 50th anniv.

**1994, Nov. 25**

**1546** A690 2p multicolored 1.10 1.10

YMCA in Uruguay, 85th anniv.

Lottery, 55th Anniv. A691

**1994, Nov. 21**

**1547** A691 2p multicolored 1.10 1.10

First Intl. Seminar to Promote Roads in Uruguay, Punta del Este A692

**1994, Oct. 14**

**1548** A692 2p multicolored 1.10 1.10

Uruguayan Press Assoc., 50th Anniv. — A693

**1994, Oct. 24**

**1549** A693 2p multicolored 1.10 1.10

Miniature Sheet

Natl. Mint, 150th Anniv. A694

Portions of old coin press and: a, Mint building. b, 1844 Copper coin. c, 1844 Silver coin. d, Montevideo silver peso.

**1994, Oct. 17** ***Perf. 12***

**1550** A694 1.50p Sheet of 4, #a.-d. 7.00 7.00

No. 1550 exists demonitized and imperf. on paper with watermark 332. This item was sold with No. 1550 and has matching serial numbers.

Miniature Sheet

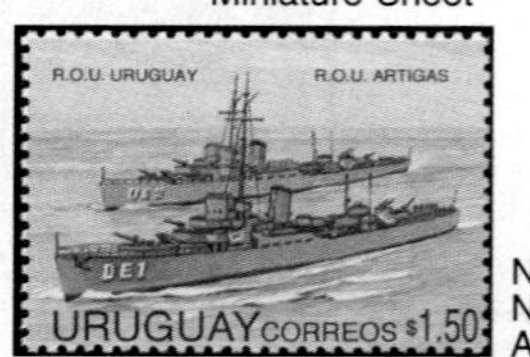

Natl. Navy A695

Ships: a, ROU Uruguay, ROU Artigas. b, ROU Fortuna. c, ROU Uruguay. d, ROU Cte. Pedro Campbell.

**1994, Nov. 15**

**1551** A695 1.50p Sheet of 4, #a.-d. 7.00 7.00

Latin American Peace Movement, 25th Anniv. — A696

**1994, Nov. 15** ***Perf. 12½***

**1552** A696 4.30p multicolored 2.40 2.40

4th Conference of the Latin American and Caribbean Organization of High Fiscal Entities, Montevideo — A697

**1994, Dec. 5**

**1553** A697 5.50p multicolored 3.00 3.00

Christmas A698

**1994, Dec. 2**

**1554** A698 2p shown 1.10 1.10

**1555** A698 5.50p Star, tree, house 3.00 3.00

Uruguayan Red Cross & Red Crescent Societies, 75th Anniv. — A699

*Perf. 12½*

**1994, Dec. 20 Litho. Unwmk.**

**1556** A699 5p multicolored 2.50 2.50

City Post Office — A700

**1995-97 Litho. Wmk. 332** ***Perf. 12***

| | | | | |
|---|---|---|---|---|
| **1557** | A700 | 20c yellow green | .35 | .35 |
| **1565** | A700 | 10p brown | 4.75 | 4.75 |
| **1566** | A700 | 10p dark brown | 2.75 | 2.75 |

**Unwmk.**

| | | | | |
|---|---|---|---|---|
| **1566A** | A700 | 10p claret & black | 2.75 | 2.75 |
| | | *Nos. 1557-1566A (4)* | 10.60 | 10.60 |

Issued: 20c, 1/11/95; 10p, 5/21/96; #1566, 1566A, 1997.

Denomination has no decimal places on Nos. 1566-1566A.

This is an expanding set. Number may change.

Naval Aviation, 70th Anniv. A704

*Perf. 12½*

**1995, Feb. 7 Litho. Unwmk.**

**1567** A704 2p multicolored 1.10 1.10

World Tourism Organization — A705

Designs: No. 1568, Ranch house, sheep herders. No. 1569, Water recreation park. No. 1570, Native wildlife. No. 1571, Beach resort.

**1995, Feb. 13**

| | | | | |
|---|---|---|---|---|
| **1568** | A705 | 5p multicolored | 3.00 | 3.00 |
| **1569** | A705 | 5p multicolored | 3.00 | 3.00 |
| **1570** | A705 | 5p multicolored | 3.00 | 3.00 |
| **1571** | A705 | 5p multicolored | 3.00 | 3.00 |
| | | *Nos. 1568-1571 (4)* | 12.00 | 12.00 |

17th World Conference of Lifeguard Services — A706

**1995, Feb. 15**

**1572** A706 5p multicolored 2.50 2.50

Rotary Intl., 90th Anniv. A707

**1995, Feb. 22**

**1573** A707 5p multicolored 2.50 2.50

ICAO, 50th Anniv. A708

**1995, Mar. 14**

**1574** A708 5p multicolored 2.50 2.50

Pietro Mascagni (1863-1945), Composer — A709

*Perf. 12½*

**1995, Mar. 30 Litho. Unwmk.**

**1575** A709 5p multicolored 2.50 2.50

Miniature Sheet

Butterflies A710

Designs: a, Phoebis neocypris. b, Diogas erippus. c, Euryades duponcheli. d, Automeris coresus.

**1995, June 15 Litho.** ***Perf. 12½***

**1576** A710 5p Sheet of 4, #a.-d. 10.00 10.00

Wild Dog A711

**1995, May 17 Litho.** ***Perf. 12½***

**1577** A711 2.30p multicolored 1.25 1.25

America Cup Soccer Championships A712

Game scenes, flags of participating countries, match sites: a, Paysandu. b, Rivera. c, Ball (no site). d, Montevideo. e, Maldonado.

**1995, July 4**

**1578** A712 2.30p Strip of 5, #a.-e. 5.25 5.25

No. 1578 is a continuous design.

FAO, 50th Anniv. — A713

**1995, July 7**

**1579** A713 5.50p multicolored 2.50 2.50

UN Peace-Keeping Missions — A714

**1995, July 14 Litho.** ***Perf. 12½***

**1580** A714 2.30p multicolored 1.25 1.25

Visit of Italy's Pres. Oscar Luigi Scalfaro A715

**1995, July 21**

**1581** A715 5.50p multicolored 2.50 2.50

A716

A717

**1995, July 24**
**1582** A716 5p multicolored 2.25 2.25

Rotary Intl., 90th anniv.

**1995, Sept. 22**
**1583** A717 2.60p multicolored 1.25 1.25

Jose Pedro Varela, 150th birth anniv.

Miniature Sheet

Shells A718

a, Zidona dufresnei. b, Boccinanops duartei. c, Dorsanum moniliferum. d, Olivancillaria uretai.

**1995, Aug. 4**
**1584** A718 5p Sheet of 4, #a.-d. 15.00 15.00

America Issue A719

Designs: 3p, Dicksonia sellowiana, vert. 6p, Chrysocyon brachyurus.

**Unwmk.**

**1995, Oct. 10 Litho. *Perf. 12***
**1585** A719 3p multicolored 1.40 1.40
**1586** A719 6p multicolored 2.75 2.75

Carlos Gardel, Musician A720

**1995, Sept. 4 *Perf. 12½***
**1587** A720 5.50p blue & black 2.50 2.50

Flowers — A721

Designs: a, Notocactus roseinflorus. b, Verbena chamaedryfolia. c, Bauhinia candicans. d, Tillandsia aeranthos. e, Eichhornia crassipes.

**1995, Sept. 12**
**1588** A721 3p Strip of 5, #a.-e. 8.50 8.50

Miniature Sheet

Uruguay's Artigas Antarctic Scientific Research Base, 10th Anniv. A722

Designs: a, 2.50p, Albatross. b, 4p, Fairchild FAU572. c, 4p, ROU Vanguard. d, 2.50p, PTS/M Amphibian transporter.

**1995, Oct. 13**
**1589** A722 Sheet of 4, #a.-d. 8.00 8.00

Uruguayan Antarctic Institute, 20th anniv.

No. 1589 exists demonitized and imperf. on paper with watermark 332. This item was sold with No. 1589 and has matching serial numbers.

Holocaust Memorial — A723

**1995, Sept. 27 Litho. *Perf. 13x12½***
**1590** A723 6p multicolored 4.00 4.00

UN, 50th Anniv. — A724

**1995, Oct. 24 Litho. *Perf. 12***
**1591** A724 6p multicolored 3.25 3.25

Early Locomotives — A725

No. 1592, Beyer & Peacock, 1876. No. 1593, Criollo, 1895. No. 1594, Beyer & Peacock, 1910.

**1995, Nov. 7**
**1592** A725 3p multicolored 1.40 1.40
**1593** A725 3p multicolored 1.40 1.40
**1594** A725 3p multicolored 1.40 1.40
*Nos. 1592-1594 (3)* 4.20 4.20

Uruguayan Navy, 178th Anniv. — A726

No. 1595, Sailing ship, Artiguista. No. 1596, ROU Pte. Rivera. No. 1597, ROU Montevideo.

**1995, Nov. 15 *Perf. 12½***
**1595** A726 3p multicolored 1.40 1.40
**1596** A726 3p multicolored 1.40 1.40
**1597** A726 3p multicolored 1.40 1.40
*Nos. 1595-1597 (3)* 4.20 4.20

Motion Pictures, Cent. A727

**1995, Dec. 13**
**1598** A727 6p Lumiere Brothers 3.25 3.25

A728

Christmas A729

**1995, Dec. 15**
**1599** A728 2.90p multicolored 1.25 1.25
**1600** A729 6.50p multicolored 3.00 3.00

Modern Olympic Games, Cent. A730

Designs: a, Equestrian event, Atlanta 1996. b, Ski jumper, Nagano 1988. c, Torch bearer, Sydney 2000. d, Skier, Salt Lake City 2002.

**1996, Jan. 30 Litho. *Perf. 12½***
**1601** A730 2.50p Sheet of 4, #a.-d. 8.00 8.00

Latin America Philatelic Exposition.

No. 1601 exists demonitized and imperf. on paper with watermark 332. This item was sold with No. 1601 and has matching serial numbers.

Carnival Personalities A732

**1996, Feb. 16 Litho. *Perf. 12½***
**1603** A732 2.90p Rosa Luna 1.25 1.25
**1604** A732 2.90p Pepino 1.25 1.25
**1605** A732 2.90p Santiago Luz 1.25 1.25
*Nos. 1603-1605 (3)* 3.75 3.75

Golf in Uruguay A733

Designs: a, Cantegril Country Club. b, Cerro Golf Club. c, Fay Crocker. d, Lago Golf Club. e, Golf Club of Uruguay.

**1996, Feb. 27**
**1606** A733 2.90p Strip of 5, #a.-e. 12.00 12.00

No. 1606 was issued in sheets of 25 stamps.

Famous People, Events A734

Designs: a, Statue, Cardinal Barbieri (1892-1979). b, Yitzhak Rabin (1922-95), Nobel Peace Prize. c, Soccer players, First World Cup Soccer Championship, Grand Park Central, July 13, 1930. d, Robert Stolz (1880-1975), composer.

**1996, Mar. 8**
**1607** A734 2.50p Sheet of 4, #a.-d. 5.75 5.75

Philatelic Academy of Uruguay. The Stamp of Today, SODRE TV Chanel 5, 10th anniv.

Montevideo, Capital of Latin American Culture — A735

**1996, Mar. 5**
**1608** A735 2.90p Solis Theater, 1837 1.25 1.25
*a.* Booklet pane of 3 *5.00*
Complete booklet, #1608a *5.00*

General Census A736

**1996, Apr. 29**
**1609** A736 3.20p multicolored 1.25 1.25

1998 World Cup Soccer Championships, France — A737

a, Player in early uniform, Olympic champions, 1924-28, world cup champions, 1930-50, older trophy. b, Trophy, player. d, Two children playing, UNICEF emblem, soccer emblems. e, Olympic rings, two players, eliminations for Atlanta '96.

**1996, Apr. 10**
**1610** A737 2.50p Sheet of 4, #a.-d. 6.50 6.50

Latin America Philatelic Exposition.

No. 1610 exists demonitized and imperf. on paper with watermark 332. This item was sold with No. 1610 and has matching serial numbers.

Bones from Indian Burial Grounds — A738

**1996, Apr. 18**
**1611** A738 3.20p multicolored 1.25 1.25

Alfredo Zitarrosa (1936-89), Guitarist A739

**1996, Mar. 15** ***Perf. 12***
**1612** A739 3p multicolored 1.50 1.50

Prehistoric Animals — A740

Designs: a, Glyptodon claripes. b, Macrauchenia patachonica. c, Toxodon platensis. d, Glossotherium robostum. e, Titanosaurus.

**1996, Apr. 18** ***Perf. 12½***
**1613** A740 3.20p Strip of 5, #a.-e. 8.00 8.00

No. 1613 was issued in sheets of 25 stamps.

Taking Care of Planet Earth, Everyone's Responsibility, by Soraya Campanella — A741

**Unwmk.**
**1996, June 5** **Litho.** ***Perf. 12***
**1614** A741 3.20p multicolored 1.50 1.50

Souvenir Sheet

Calidris Canutus — A742

**1996, May 28** ***Perf. 12½***
**1615** A742 12p multicolored 9.00 9.00

CAPEX '96.

Early Methods of Transportation — A743

Designs: a, 1912 Dion-Buton omnibus. b, 1928 Ford Model A. c, 1940 Raleigh bicycle. d, 1926 Magirus firetruck. e, 1917 Hotchkiss ambulance.

**1996, May 21**
**1616** A743 3.20p Strip of 5, #a.-e. 7.50 7.50

No. 1616 was issued in sheets of 25 stamps.

Sailing Ships A744

Designs: a, Our Lady of Encina, 1726. b, San Francisco. c, Ships of E. Moreau. d, Bold Lady. e, Our Lady of the Light.

**1996, June 17** **Litho.** ***Perf. 12½***
**1617** A744 3.20p Strip of 5, #a.-e. 7.50 7.50

No. 1617 was issued in sheets of 25 stamps.

Landscape in Las Flores, by Carmelo de Arzadun — A745

**1996, July 15** **Litho.** ***Perf. 12½***
**1618** A745 3.50p multicolored 1.40 1.40

Jewish Community in Uruguay, 80th Anniv. — A746

**1996, July 29**
**1619** A746 7.50p multicolored 3.00 3.00

A747

Scientists from Uruguay A748

No. 1620, Enrique Legrand (1861-1939). No. 1621, Victor Bertullo (1919-79). No. 1622, Tomas Beno Hirschfeld (1939-86). No. 1623, Miguel C. Rubino (1886-1945).

**1996, July 30**
**1620** A747 3.50p multicolored 1.40 1.40
**1621** A747 3.50p multicolored 1.40 1.40
**1622** A748 3.50p multicolored 1.40 1.40
**1623** A748 3.50p multicolored 1.40 1.40
*Nos. 1620-1623 (4)* 5.60 5.60

Bank of Uruguay, Cent. — A749

**1996, Sept. 9** ***Perf. 12***
**1624** A749 3.50p 10p note 1.40 1.40
*a.* Booklet pane, #1624 2.00
**1625** A749 3.50p 500p note 1.40 1.40
*a.* Booklet pane, #1625 2.00
Complete bklt., #1624a, 1625a 4.00

Souvenir Sheet

Otto Lilienthal (1848-1896) — A750

Illustration reduced.

**1996, Aug. 30**
**1626** A750 12p multicolored 4.75 4.75

AEROFILA '96.

Scientists A751

No. 1627, Albert Einstein. No. 1628, Aristotle. No. 1629, Isaac Newton.

**1996, Sept. 3** ***Perf. 12½***
**1627** A751 7.50p multicolored 3.00 3.00
**1628** A751 7.50p multicolored 3.00 3.00
**1629** A751 7.50p multicolored 3.00 3.00
*Nos. 1627-1629 (3)* 9.00 9.00

National Heritage — A752

Designs: No. 1630, Map of Gorriti Island showing locations of Spanish forts, 18th cent. No. 1631, Narbona Church, 18th cent.

***Perf. 13x12½***
**1996, Sept. 12** **Litho.** **Unwmk.**
**1630** A752 3.50p multicolored 1.40 1.40
**1631** A752 3.50p multicolored 1.40 1.40

Rural Assoc., 125th Anniv. A753

**1996, Sept. 20** ***Perf. 12½x13***
**1632** A753 3.50p multicolored 1.50 1.50

Marine Life A754

a, Carchardon carcharias. b, Alopias vulpinus. c, Notorynchus cepedianus. d, Squatina dumerili.

**1996, Sept. 23**
**1633** A754 3.50p Sheet of 4, #a.-d. 5.50 5.50

Istanbul '96.

Sports Champions from Uruguay — A755

Designs: a, Angel Rodriguez, boxing, 1917. b, Leandro Noli, cycling, 1939. c, Eduardo G. Risso, rowing, 1948. d, Estrella Puente, javelin, 1949. e, Oscar Moglia, basketball, 1956.

**1996, Oct. 1**
**1634** A755 3.50p Strip of 5, #a.-e. 8.50 8.50

Traditional Costumes A756

America issue: 3.50p, Gaucho. 7.50p, Woman of the campana.

**1996, Oct. 11** ***Perf. 13x12½***
**1635** A756 3.50p multicolored 1.40 1.40
**1636** A756 7.50p multicolored 3.00 3.00

3rd Space Conference of the Americas — A757

**1996, Nov. 4** **Wmk. 332** ***Perf. 12***
**1637** A757 3.50p multicolored 1.75 1.75

Comic Strips, Cent. A758

"Peloduro," by Julio E. Suarez.

**1996, Nov. 7**
**1638** A758 4p multicolored 1.75 1.75

Health Institute, Cent. A759

**1996, Nov. 20**
**1639** A759 4p multicolored 1.75 1.75

Church of the 7th Day Adventists in Uruguay, Cent. — A760

**Wmk. 332**
**1996, Nov. 26 Litho. *Perf. 12½***
**1640** A760 3.50p multicolored 1.40 1.40

Felix de Azara (1746-1811), Naturalist — A761

**1996, Nov. 20 *Perf. 12***
**1641** A761 4p multicolored 1.75 1.75

Fish A762

Designs: No. 1642, Cynolebia nigripinnis. No. 1643, Cynolebia viarius.

**Unwmk.**
**1997, Feb. 24 Litho. *Die Cut***
**Self-Adhesive**
**1642** A762 4p multicolored 1.60 1.60
**1643** A762 4p multicolored 1.60 1.60

Popular Festivals A763

#1644, Natl. Folklore Festival, Durazno. #1645, Traditional Gaucho Festival, Tacuarembo.

**1997 Wmk. 332 *Perf. 12½***
**1644** A763 4p multi 1.60 1.60
**1645** A763 4p multi, vert. 1.60 1.60

Issued: #1644, 1/30; #1645, 3/10.
See Nos. 1653-1656.

Mushrooms — A764

Designs: a, Tricholoma nudum. b, Agaricus xanthodermus. c, Russula sardonia. d, Microsporum canis. e, Polyporus versicolor.

**1997, Feb. 7**
**1646** A764 4p Strip of 5, #a.-e, 10.00 10.00

No. 1646 was issued in sheets of 25 stamps.

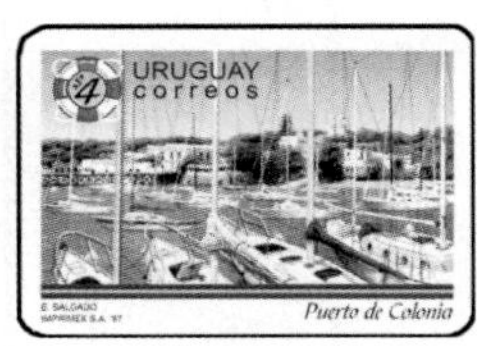

Ports A765

No. 1647, Colonia. No. 1648, Punta del Este. No. 1649, Santiago Vázquez. No. 1650, Buceo.

**1997, Feb. 28 Litho. *Die Cut***
**Self-Adhesive**
**1647** A765 4p multicolored 1.60 1.60
**1648** A765 4p multicolored 1.60 1.60
**1649** A765 4p multicolored 1.60 1.60
**1650** A765 4p multicolored 1.60 1.60
*Nos. 1647-1650 (4)* 6.40 6.40

Artigas' Lancers, Bicent. A766

**1997, Mar. 10 Wmk. 332 *Perf. 12½***
**1651** A766 4p multicolored 1.60 1.60

Military Academy, 50th Anniv. — A767

**1997, Mar. 13**
**1652** A767 4p multicolored 1.60 1.60

Popular Festivals Type of 1997

Coat of arms and: No. 1653, Performers under outdoor pavilion, Beer Week. No. 1654, Ruben Lena, bridge, river, Olimar River Festival, vert. No. 1655, Guitar, man on horse, Festival de Minas Y Abril. No. 1656, Family around person on horseback, Roosevelt Park.

**1997 Litho.**
**1653** A763 5p multicolored 2.00 2.00
**1654** A763 5p multicolored 2.00 2.00
**1655** A763 5p multicolored 2.00 2.00

***Die Cut***
**Unwmk.**
**Self-Adhesive**
**1656** A763 5p multicolored 2.00 2.00
*Nos. 1653-1656 (4)* 8.00 8.00

Lions Intl. (#1656). Issued: #1653, 3/23; #1654, 3/24; #1655, 4/26; #1656, 3/21.

United Mobile Coronary Unit (UCM), 20th Anniv. A768

**1997, Apr. 4 Unwmk. *Die Cut***
**Self-Adhesive**
**1657** A768 5p multicolored 2.00 2.00

UNICEF, 50th Anniv. — A769

**1997, Apr. 8 *Die Cut***
**Self-Adhesive**
**1658** A769 5p multicolored 2.00 2.00

Lighthouses A770

Various birds and: a, Anchorena Tower, 1920. b, Farallón Lighthouse, 1870. c, José Ignacio Lighthouse, 1877. d, Santa Maria Lighthouse, 1874. e, Vigía Tower, 18th cent.

**1997, Apr. 22 *Die Cut***
**Self-Adhesive**
**1659** A770 5p Strip of 5, #a.-e. 13.00 13.00

Prehistoric Animals A771

Designs: a, Devincenzia gallinali. b, Smilodon populator. c, Mesosaurus tenuidens. d, Doedicurus clavicaudatus. e, Artigasia magna.

**1997, May 5 *Die Cut***
**Self-Adhesive**
**1660** A771 5p Strip of 5, #a.-e. 13.00 13.00

A772

Ecclesiastical Provinces — A772a

#1661, Church, diocese of Salto. #1662, Church, diocese of Melo. #1663, Bishop Jacinto Vera, 1st bishop of Montevideo. #1664, Msgr. Mariano Soler, 1st archbishop of Montevideo.

**Wmk. 332**
**1997, May 9 Litho. *Perf. 12½***
**1661** A772 5p multicolored 2.00 2.00
**1662** A772 5p multicolored 2.00 2.00
**1663** A772a 5p multicolored 2.00 2.00
**1664** A772a 5p multicolored 2.00 2.00
*Nos. 1661-1664 (4)* 8.00 8.00

Youth Stamp Collecting A773

Designs: a, 2p, Boy, "Philately?" b, 2p, Boy thinking of stamps. c, 2p, Girl with soccer ball, boy. d, 1p, Boy looking at stamps in album. e, 1p, Boy with tongs and magnifying glass.

**1997, May 25 Unwmk.**
**1665** A773 Strip of 5, #a.-e. 4.00 4.00

PACIFIC 97 — A774

**1997, May 29 *Perf. 12***
**1666** A774 10p Rynchops niger 4.00 4.00

Maccio Theater of San Jose, 85th Anniv. A775

**1997, June 5 Wmk. 332 *Perf. 12½***
**1667** A775 5p multicolored 2.00 2.00

Inter-American Institute of Children, 70th Anniv. — A776

**1997, June 9 Unwmk.**
**1668** A776 5p multicolored 2.00 2.00

Colony of Sacramento — A777

**1997, July 4**
**1669** A777 5p multicolored 2.00 2.00

Punta del Este, 90th Anniv. A778

**1997, July 1**
**1670** A778 5p multicolored 2.00 2.00

Uruguayan Comics — A779

Scenes from comics by: No. 1671, Julio E. Suarez (Peloduro). No. 1672, Geoffrey Foladori.

*Perf. 12½*

**1997, June 30 Litho. Unwmk.**

**1671** A779 5p multicolored 1.50 1.50
**1672** A779 5p multicolored 1.50 1.50

Zionism, Cent. A780

Design: Theodor Herzl (1860-1904), founder of Zionist movement.

**1997, July 17**

**1673** A780 5p multicolored 1.50 1.50

Children's Painting A781

Geranoaetus Melanoleucus A782

**1997, July 21 Litho. *Die Cut***

**Self-Adhesive**

**1674** A781 15p multicolored 4.50 4.50
**1675** A782 25p multicolored 7.75 7.75
*a.* Type II ('04) 2.00 2.00

Type I stamps have printer's name at right, designer's name at left, and have an eagle's head that is rounder, with its edge making a sharper angle with the right margin than on type II. Type II stamps have the printer's name at left and the designer's name at right.

No. 1675a issued 2004. No. 1675a also exists dated "2005."

Nos. 1674, 1675 exist dated 1999.

See Nos. 1840, 1850, 1853, 1855.

Isolation of Acetylsalicylic Acid from Willow Trees, Cent. — A783

**1997, Aug. 12 Litho. *Perf. 12½***

**1676** A783 6p multicolored 1.40 1.40
*a.* Booklet pane of 2 4.50
Complete booklet, #1676a 4.50

Department of Salto — A784

**1997, Aug. 26**

**1677** A784 6p multicolored 1.75 1.75

Felix Mendelssohn (1809-47) — A785

No. 1679, Johannes Brahms (1833-97).

**1997, Sept. 1**

**1678** A785 6p multicolored 1.60 1.60
**1679** A785 6p multicolored 1.60 1.60
*a.* Pair, #1678-1679 3.50 3.50

Natural History Museum of Montevideo, 160th Anniv. — A786

Designs: a, Lucas Kraguevich, paleontologist. b, Jose Arechavaleta, botantist. c, Garibaldi J. Devincenzi, zoologist. d, Antonio Taddei, archaelogist.

**1997, Sept. 3**

**1680** A786 6p Strip of 4, #a.-d. 5.75 5.75

Mercosur (Common Market of Latin America) A787

**1997, Sept. 26 *Perf. 12***

**1681** A787 11p multicolored 3.00 3.00

See Argentina, No. 1975; Bolivia No. 1019; Brazil, No. 2646; Paraguay, No. 2564.

Souvenir Sheet

Passiflora Coerulea — A788

Illustration reduced.

**1997, Sept. 26 *Perf. 12½***

**1682** A788 15p multicolored 4.25 4.25

1st Philatelic Exhibition of Mercosur countries.

Heinrich von Stephan (1831-97) A789

**1997, Oct. 9**

**1683** A789 11p multicolored 3.00 3.00

Souvenir Sheet

Spanish-Uruguayan Monument — A790

Illustration reduced.

**1997, Oct. 9**

**1684** A790 15p Monument 4.00 4.00

Philatelic Exhibition, Spain 1997.

America Issue — A791

Designs: 6p, Woman carrying mail. 11p, Man delivering letters.

**1997, Oct. 10**

**1685** A791 6p multicolored 1.60 1.60
**1686** A791 11p multicolored 3.00 3.00

Artigas Scientific Base, Antarctica — A792

**1997, Oct. 15 *Perf. 12***

**1687** A792 6p Pygoscelis papua 1.60 1.60

Painting, by Domingo Laporte (1855-1928) — A793

**1997, Oct. 21 *Perf. 12½***

**1688** A793 6p multicolored 1.75 1.75

Galicia House, 80th Anniv. A794

**1997, Oct. 24**

**1689** A794 6p multicolored 1.75 1.75

3rd Intl. Congress of Aeronautical and Space History, Montevideo — A795

*Perf. 12½*

**1997, Oct. 27 Litho. Unwmk.**

**1690** A795 6p Arme 2 Biplane 1.75 1.75

1st Biennial Interparliamentary Exhibition of MERCOSUR Paintings, Montevideo — A796

**1997, Oct. 28**

**1691** A796 11p multicolored 3.00 3.00

Souvenir Sheet

Pope John Paul II, Holy Year 2000 — A797

Illustration reduced.

**1997, Nov. 7**

**1692** A797 10p multicolored 6.50 6.50

Third Intl. Assembly Punta del Este, and of arrival of first Polish colonists at River Plate, cent.

Uruguayan Navy, 180th Anniv. — A798

**1997, Nov. 14**

**1693** A798 6p multicolored 1.75 1.75

Shanghai '97 Intl. Stamp and Coin Exhibition A799

No. 1694: a, 3.50p, Front and back of 1 peso coin. b, 3.50p, Chinese flag, Hong Kong harbor, flower, junk. c, 4p, Michael Schumacher, Formula 1 driving champion, Ferrari. d, 4p, Sojourner on Mars, Pathfinder Mission.

No. 1695: a, 3.50p, Martina Hingis, 1997 Wimbledon Ladies' champion. b, 3.50p, Jan Ullrich, 1997 Tour de France winner. c, 4p, Soccer players, 1998 World Cup Soccer Championship, France. d, 4p, Ski jumper, 1998 Winter Olympic Games, Nagano.

**1997, Nov. 19**

**1694** A799 Sheet of 4, #a.-d. 4.25 4.25
**1695** A799 Sheet of 4, #a.-d. 4.25 4.25

Christmas A800

**1997, Nov. 20**

**1696** A800 6p Magi 1.75 1.75
**1697** A800 11p Madonna & Child 3.00 3.00

Uruguayan Sportsmen — A801

Designs: a, Adesio Lombardo, Olympic bronze medalist, basketball, Helsinki, 1952. b, Guillermo Douglas, Olympic bronze medalist, single sculls, Rome, 1932. c, Obdulio Varela, soccer player on 1950 World Cup championship team. d, Atilio Francois, silver medalist, 1947 World Cycling Championships, Paris. e, Juan López Testa, South American 100 meters champion, 1947.

**1997, Nov. 26**
**1698** A801 6p Strip of 5, #a.-e. 8.50 8.50

Mevifil '97, 1st Intl. Exhibition of Philatelic Audio-Visual and Computer Systems — A802

**1997, Dec. 1** ***Perf. 12***
**1699** A802 11p multicolored 3.00 3.00

INDEPEX '97 A803

Early vehicles, inventors: a, 1st Land Rover, 1947. b, Henry Ford (1863-1947), Model A. c, Robert Bosch (1861-1942), inventor of automotive components. d, Rudolf Diesel (1858-1913), patented first diesel engine, 1897.

**1997, Dec. 8** ***Perf. 12½***
**1700** A803 6p Strip of 4, #a.-d. 6.50 6.50

Naval Academy of Uruguay, 90th Anniv. A804

**1997, Dec. 12**
**1701** A804 6p multicolored 1.60 1.60

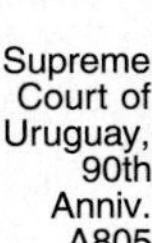

Supreme Court of Uruguay, 90th Anniv. A805

**1997, Dec. 12**
**1702** A805 6p multicolored 1.60 1.60

Uruguayan Post Office, 170th Anniv. — A806

**1997, Dec. 19**
**1703** A806 6p multicolored 1.60 1.60

MEVIR (Movement for Eradication of Unsanitary Rural Housing), 90th Anniv. — A807

Design: Homes, Dr. A. Gallinal, logo.

**1997, Dec. 26**
**1704** A807 6p multicolored 1.60 1.60

Construction Projects — A808

a, Preparation. b, Planning. c, Execution.

**1997, Dec. 29** ***Perf. 12***
**1705** A808 6p Strip of 3, #a.-c. 5.00 5.00
*d.* Booklet pane, #1705 6.00
Complete booklet, #1705d 6.00

Souvenir Sheet

1897 Revolution, Cent. — A809

Design: Gen. Antonio "Chiquito" Saravia and Col. Diego Lamas. Illustration reduced.

**1997, Dec. 30** ***Perf. 12½***
**1706** A809 15p multicolored 4.00 4.00

Painting by Héctor Ragni (b. 1898) — A810

**1998, Feb. 6**
**1707** A810 6p multicolored 1.60 1.60

Naval Station, Montevideo — A811

**1998, Feb. 13**
**1708** A811 6p multicolored 1.60 1.60

Native Trees — A812

a, Butia capitata. b, Grove of butia capitata. c, Grove of phytolacca dioica. d, Phytolacca dioica.

**1998, Mar. 20** ***Perf. 12***
**1709** A812 6p Block of 4, #a.-d. 7.00 7.00

Museum of Humor — A813

Cartoons: No. 1710, by Oscar Abín. No. 1711, by Emilio Cortinas.

**1998, Mar. 13** ***Perf. 12½***
**1710** A813 6p multicolored 1.60 1.60
**1711** A813 6p multicolored 1.60 1.60
*a.* Pair, #1710-1711 3.25 3.25

Wilson Ferreira Aldunate (1919-88) A814

**1998, Mar. 17** ***Perf. 12***
**1712** A814 6p multicolored 1.60 1.60

Fossilized Animals — A815

Designs: a, Testudinites sellowi. b, Proborhyaena gigantea. c, Propachyrucos schiaffinos. d, Stegomastodon platensis.

**1998, Mar. 26**
**1713** A815 6p Block of 4, #a.-d. 7.00 7.00

Israel '98, State of Israel, 50th Anniv. — A816

**1998, Mar. 31** ***Perf. 12***
**1714** A816 12p multicolored 3.25 3.25

Birds — A820

a, Plyborus plancus. b, Cygnus melancoryphus. c, Platalea ajaja. d, Theristicus caudatus.

**1998, Apr. 30**
**1718** A820 6p Block of 4, #a.-d. 6.25 6.25

Organization of American States, 50th Anniv. — A821

**1998, Apr. 14 Litho.** ***Perf. 12¾x12½***
**1719** A821 12p multi 3.00 3.00

61st World Congress of Sports Journalism A822

**1998, Apr. 21 Litho.** ***Perf. 12***
**1720** A822 6p multicolored 1.60 1.60

Land Settlement Institute, 50th Anniv. — A823

**1998, Apr. 22 Litho. *Perf. 12¾x12½***
**1721** A823 6p multi 1.50 1.50

Souvenir Sheet

Intl. Topical Philatelic Exhibition, Nueva Helvecia A824

Cross and: a, 3.50p, Switzerland #5, Uruguay #1. b, 3.50p, Obverse and reverse of Euro coin. c, 4p, Olympic rings and mountain. d, 4p, Space station.

**1998, May 12 *Perf. 12½x12¾***
**1722** A824 Sheet of 4, #a.-d. 3.75 3.75

Swiss Republic, bicent.

Souvenir Sheet

Whales A825

a, 3.50p, Balaeneoptera physalus (b). b, 3.50p, Balaeneoptera acutorostrata. c, 4p, Megaptera novaeangliae (d). d, 4p, Eubalaena australis (c).

**1998, May 15 Litho. *Perf. 12½***
**1723** A825 Sheet of 4, #a.-d. 3.75 3.75

Ambiente '98, Maia, Portugal; Intl. Year of the Ocean; Expo '98, Lisbon.

1983 Labor Day Democracy Demonstrations — A826

***Perf. 12¼x12¾***
**1998, May 27 Litho. Wmk. 332**
**1724** A826 6p brn & blk 1.50 1.50

See Nos. 1740, 1775.

Street Cars — A827

Historic Montevideo trams: a, English "La Comercial," 1906. b, German Transatlantica Co., 1907. c, Transatlantica, 1908. d, Transatlantica double decker, 1916.

**1998, May 29 Litho. *Perf. 12***
**1725** A827 6p Block of 4, #a.-d. 6.25 6.25

Juvalux '98 — A828

Wildcats: a, Felis colocola. b, Felis pardalis. c, Felis wiedil. d, Panthera onca.

**Unwmk.**
**1998, June 18 Litho. *Perf. 12***
**1726** A828 6p Block of 4, #a.-d. 6.00 6.00

Ships A829

a, "Sirus." b, Gunboat "18 de Julio." c, Transport, "Maldonado." d, "Instituto de Pesca No. 1."

**1998, June 25 Litho. *Perf. 12***
**1727** A829 6p Block of 4, #a.-d. 6.00 6.00

Jesuit Mission Church, Calera de las Huérfanas A830

***Perf. 12½x12¾***
**1998, July 24 Litho. Unwmk.**
**1728** A830 12p multi 3.00 3.00

Monument to the Peace of 1872, San José de Mayo, 125th Anniv. — A831

**1998, July 31 *Perf. 12¾x12½***
**1729** A831 6p multi 1.50 1.50

155mm Artillery Unit No. 5, Cent. A832

**1998, Aug. 7 *Perf. 12½x12¾***
**1730** A832 6p multi 1.50 1.50

Butterflies — A833

**1998, Aug. 14 Litho. *Perf. 12***
**1731** A833 6p Eacles imperialis 1.50 1.50
**1732** A833 6p Protoparce luceti-us 1.50 1.50
***a.*** Pair, #1731-1732 3.00 3.00

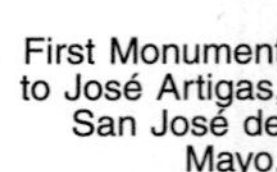

First Monument to José Artigas, San José de Mayo, Cent. — A834

***Perf. 12¾x12½***
**1998, Aug. 24 Litho.**
**1733** A834 6p multi 1.50 1.50

A835

A836

**1998, Aug. 28**
**1734** A835 6p multi 1.50 1.50

Dr. Mauricio López Lombo (1918-93), zoo founder.

**1998, Aug. 31**
**1735** A836 6p multi 1.50 1.50

Falleri-Balzo Music Conservatory, Montevideo, cent.

José Fernández Vergara (1810-1906), Founder of Pueblo Vergara — A837

**1998, Sept. 8**
**1736** A837 6p multi 1.50 1.50

Souvenir Sheet

El Pais Newspaper, 80th Anniv. — A838

Illustration reduced.

**1998, Sept. 14 *Perf. 12½x12¾***
**1737** A838 12p multi 3.00 3.00

Collective Medical Assistance Institute, 145th Anniv. — A839

**1998, Sept. 24 *Perf. 12¾x12½***
**1738** A839 6p multi 1.50 1.50

Postal Link Between Montevideo and Corunna, Spain, 230th Anniv. — A840

**1998, Sept. 24**
**1739** A840 12p multi 3.00 3.00

Espamer '98, Buenos Aires.

**Democracy Demonstration Type**

6p, March of the Social and Cultural Assoc. of Public School Students, 9/25/83.

***Perf. 12½x12¾***
**1998, Sept. 25 Wmk. 332**
**1740** A826 6p brn & blk 1.50 1.50

Iberoamericana '98 Philatelic Exhibition, Maia, Portugal — A841

Airplanes: a, Junkers J52. b, Spad VII. c, Ansaldo SVA-10. d, Neybar.

**Unwmk.**
**1998, Oct. 2 Litho. *Perf. 12***
**1741** A841 6p Block of 4, #a.-d. 6.00 6.00

Death of Chilean Pres. Salvador Allende, 25th Anniv. A842

***Perf. 12¼x12¾***
**1998, Oct. 2 Litho. Unwmk.**
**1742** A842 12p multi 3.00 3.00

50th Anniv. of Enrique Rodríguez Fabregat (1885-1976) as UN Commissioner for Palestine — A843

**1998, Oct. 5 *Perf. 12¾x12½***
**1743** A843 6p multi 1.50 1.50

Radio Carve, 70th Anniv. A844

**1998, Oct. 7 Litho.** ***Perf. 12½x12¾***
**1744** A844 6p multi 1.50 1.50

World Post Day A845

**1998, Oct. 9 Litho.** ***Perf. 12½x12¾***
**1745** A845 12p multi 3.00 3.00

Ilsapex '98, Johannesburg.

America Issue — A846

Famous women: 6p, Julia Guarino (1897-1985), first woman architect in South America. 12p, Dr. Paulina Luisi (1875-1950).

**1998, Oct. 9 Litho.** ***Perf. 12***
**1746** A846 6p multi 1.50 1.50
**1747** A846 12p multi 3.00 3.00

Assoc. of Inland Pharmacies, 50th Anniv. — A847

**1998, Oct. 10** ***Perf. 12½x12¾***
**1748** A847 6p multi 1.50 1.50

Postal Services A847a

***Serpentine Die Cut 11¼***
**1998, Oct. 15 Litho. Unwmk.**
**Self-Adhesive**
**1748A** A847a 25p multi 6.00 6.00

Exists dated 1999.

Classic Vehicles — A848

Designs: a, 1950 Lancia fire engine. b, 1946 Maserati San Remo. c, 1954 Alfa Romeo trolley bus. d, 1936 Fiat Topolino.

**1998, Oct. 23 Litho.** ***Perf. 12***
**1749** A848 6p Block of 4, #a.-d. 6.25 6.25

Italia'98.

Artists A849

Designs: No. 1750, Sculpture, "Motherhood," and self-portrait of Nerses Ounanian (1920-57). No. 1751, Illustrations from book "Piquín y Chispita," by Serafin J. Garcia (1905-85), vert. No. 1752, Musical score by Héctor M. Artola (1903-82), vert.

***Perf. 12½x12¾, 12¾x12½***
**1998, Oct. 27 Litho.**
**1750** A849 6p multi 1.50 1.50
**1751** A849 6p multi 1.50 1.50
**1752** A849 6p multi 1.50 1.50
*Nos. 1750-1752 (3)* 4.50 4.50

Juvenalia '98 — A850

**1998, Oct. 30 Litho.** ***Perf. 12¾x12½***
**1753** A850 6p multi 1.50 1.50

Souvenir Sheet

Uruguay-Germany Philatelic Exhibition, Montevideo — A851

Designs: a, 3.50p, Zeppelin cover, Zeppelin NT. b, 3.50p, Germany #1592, Germany Berlin #9N584, German Democratic Republic #2791, mail box. c, 4p, Brandenburg Gate, Volkswagen Beetle, Konrad Adenauer. d, 4p, Airplane, German mark note and coin.

**1998, Nov. 6 Litho.** ***Perf. 12½x12¾***
**1754** A851 Sheet of 4, #a.-d. 3.75 3.75

IBRA '99, 150th anniv. of German stamps (#1754a, 1754b), 50th anniv. of Federal Republic of Germany (#1754c), 50th anniv. of German mark (#1754d).

16th Congress of Expenditure Control Boards — A852

**1998, Nov. 9**
**1755** A852 12p blue & silver 3.00 3.00

Uruguayan Chamber of Industries, Cent. — A853

**1998, Nov. 9**
**1756** A853 6p multi 1.50 1.50

Flowers — A854

***Serpentine Die Cut 11¼***
**1998-99 Litho.**
**Self-Adhesive**
**1757** A854 1p Oxalis pudica .25 .25
**1760** A854 4p Oxalis pudica (white) .90 .90
**1761** A854 5p Oxalis pudica (purple) .70 .70
**1762** A854 6p Eugenia uniflora 1.50 1.50
**1763** A854 7p Eugenia uniflora 1.60 1.60
**1765** A854 9p Eugenia uniflora 5.00 5.00
**1766** A854 10p Aechmea recurvata 2.50 2.50
**1770** A854 14p Acca sellowiana 3.25 3.25
**1771** A854 50p Acca sellowiana 8.75 8.75
*Nos. 1757-1770 (8)* 15.70 15.70

Issued: 7p, 2/4/99; 4p, 12/23/99; 14p, 8/6/99; 1p, 6p, 10p, 50p, 1998. 9p, 1999. 5p, 2/19/02.

No. 1757 exists dated 1999, 2000, 2001, 2002. No. 1766 exists dated 1999. No. 1766 exists dated 2003.

Christmas — A855

Designs: 6p, The Virgin's Descent to Reward St. Ildefons' Writings (detail), by El Greco. 12p, St. Peter's Tears (detail), by Bartolomé Esteban Murillo.

**1998, Nov. 23 Litho.** ***Perf. 12***
**1772** A855 6p multi 1.50 1.50
**1773** A855 12p multi 3.00 3.00

Paso Del Molina Neighborhood of Montevideo, 250th Anniv. — A856

**1998, Nov. 26** ***Perf. 12½x12¾***
**1774** A856 6p multi 1.50 1.50

**Labor Day Type**

6p, Proclamation at the Obelisk, 11/27/83.

***Perf. 12¼x12¾***
**1998, Nov. 27 Litho. Wmk. 332**
**1775** A826 6p brn & blk 1.50 1.50

Morosoli Cultural Awards — A857

***Perf. 12¾x12½***
**1998, Nov. 27 Litho. Unwmk.**
**1776** A857 6p multi 1.50 1.50

Universal Declaration of Human Rights, 50th Anniv. — A858

**1998, Dec. 10** ***Perf. 12½x12¾***
**1777** A858 6p multi 1.50 1.50

Uruguayan Olympic Committee, 75th Anniv. — A859

**1998, Dec. 15** ***Perf. 12***
**1778** A859 6p multi 1.50 1.50

Uruguayan Sportsmen A860

Designs: a, Juan Lopez (1907-83), soccer coach. b, Hector Scarone (1899-1967), soccer player. c, Leandro Gomez Harley (1902-79), basketball player, hurdler. d, Liberto Corney (1905-55), boxer.

**1998, Dec. 15** ***Perf. 12¾x12½***
**1779** A860 6p Block of 4, #a.-d. 6.00 6.00

Famous Uruguayans — A861

Designs: No. 1780: Dr. Roberto Caldeyro Barcia (1921-96), physiologist. No. 1781, Dr. José Verocay (1876-1923), pathologist. No. 1782, Dr. José L. Duomarco (1905-85), medical researcher.

***Perf. 12¼x12¾***
**1998, Dec. 18 Litho. Unwmk.**
**1780** A861 6p multi 1.50 1.50
**1781** A861 6p multi 1.50 1.50
**1782** A861 6p multi 1.50 1.50
*Nos. 1780-1782 (3)* 4.50 4.50

Emile Zola's "J'accuse" Letter, Cent. (in 1998) A862

**1999, Jan. 4 Litho.** ***Perf. 12½x12¾***
**1783** A862 14p multicolored 3.50 3.50

Las Cañas Resort, Fray Bentos A863

**1999, Feb. 26**
**1784** A863 7p multicolored 1.60 1.60

Rio de la Plata Boundary Treaty, 25th Anniv. A864

**1999, Mar. 15**
**1785** A864 7p multicolored 1.60 1.60

Famous Uruguayans — A865

Designs: No. 1786, Joaquin Torres Garcia (1874-1949), painter. No. 1787, Luis Ernesto Aroztegui (1930-94), textile artist. No. 1788, Juan José Morosoli (1899-1957), writer.

**1999, Mar. 26**
**1786** A865 7p multicolored 2.50 2.50
**1787** A865 7p multicolored 2.50 2.50
**1788** A865 7p multicolored 2.50 2.50
*Nos. 1786-1788 (3)* 7.50 7.50

Birds and Flowering Trees A866

a, Psidium cattleianum, Pipraeidea melanonota. b, Tabebuia ipe, Chlorostilbon aureoventris. c, Duranta repens, Tangara preciosa. d, Citharexylum montevidense, Tachuris rubigastra.

**1999, Apr. 14 Litho.** ***Perf. 12¼x12¾***
**1789** A866 7p Block of 4, #a.-d. 6.00 6.00

Carriages A867

Designs: a, Break de chasse. b, Mylord. c, Coupé trois quarts. d, Break de champ.

**1999, Apr. 29 Litho.** ***Perf. 12½x12¾***
**1790** A867 7p Block of 4, #a.-d. 6.50 6.50

National Soccer Team, Cent. — A868

Designs: a, B. Céspedes, M. Nebel, C. Céspedes, team's first field. b, H. Castro, P. Cea, A. Ciocca, team flag. c, R. Porta, A García, S. Gambetta, team headquarters.

**1999, May 5 Litho.** ***Perf. 12***
**1791** A868 7p Strip of 3, #a.-c. 5.75 5.75
Complete booklet, #1791 6.75

Children's Millennium Stamp Design Contest Winners A869

Designs: a, By Stefani Andrea Furtado. b, By Pilar Trujillo. c, By Lucia Lavie. d, By Cecilia Chopitea.

**1999, May 6 Litho.** ***Perf. 12½x12¾***
**1792** A869 7p Block of 4, #a.-d. 6.50 6.50

Jorge Chebataroff (1909-84), Geographer, Botanist — A870

**1999, May 14**
**1793** A870 7p multicolored 1.60 1.60

Formation of Infantry Brigade No. 1, 60th Anniv. A871

Paintings: No. 1794, Infantry Battalion No. 2 at Battle of Montecaseros, 1852. No. 1795, Infantry Brigade No. 1 at Battle of Estero Bellaco, 1866. No. 1796, Infantry Battalion No. 1 at Battle of Boquerón, 1866.

**1999, May 18**
**1794** A871 7p multicolored 1.75 1.75
**1795** A871 7p multicolored 1.75 1.75
**1796** A871 7p multicolored 1.75 1.75
*Nos. 1794-1796 (3)* 5.25 5.25

Villa de la Restauracion, 150th Anniv. — A872

**1999, May 24** ***Perf. 12¾x12½***
**1797** A872 7p multicolored 1.75 1.75

Souvenir Sheet

Barcelona, Spain Soccer Team, Cent. — A873

Illustration reduced.

**1999, May 28 Litho.** ***Perf. 12½x12¾***
**1798** A873 15p multi 3.25 3.25

1st Festival of Film Critics, Montevideo A874

**1999, June 2** ***Perf. 12¾x12¼***
**Booklet Stamp**
**1799** A874 7p multi 1.60 1.60
*a.* Booklet pane, 2 #1799 3.25
Complete booklet, #1799a 3.25

Philex France 99 A875

Horses: a, Arabian. b, Quarter horse. c, Thoroughbred. d, Shetland pony.

***Perf. 12½x12¾***
**1999, June 10 Litho.**
**1800** A875 7p Block of 4, #a.-d. 6.25 6.25

Publication "Marcha," 60th Anniv. — A876

***Perf. 12¼x12¾***
**1999, June 23 Litho.**
**1801** A876 7p multi 1.60 1.60

Permanent Home for "Espacio Ciencia" Science Exhibits — A877

**1999, July 2** ***Perf. 12¾x12¼***
**1802** A877 7p multi 1.60 1.60

Artigas Antarctic Scientific Base, 25th Anniv. A878

**1999, July 12** ***Perf. 12¼x12¾***
**1803** A878 7p multi 1.60 1.60

Republic of Uruguay University, 150th Anniv. A879

**1999, July 19**
**1804** A879 7p yel & blk 1.60 1.60

UNESCO Regional Office, 50th Anniv. — A880

**1999, July 20** ***Perf. 12¾x12¼***
**1805** A880 7p multi 1.60 1.60

The Last Charruas — A881

a, One seated, one standing. b, Two seated.

**1999, July 22 Litho.** ***Perf. 12¾x12½***
**1806** A881 7p Pair, #a.-b. 3.25 3.25

Souvenir Sheet

Millennium A882

a, 3.50p, Apollo space program. b, 3.50p, Soccer players, 2000 Olympic Games, Sydney. c, 4p, Centenary of Zeppelins. d, 4p, #C60.

**1999, July 30 Litho.** ***Perf. 12½x12¾***
**1807** A882 Sheet of 4, #a.-d. 5.75 5.75

UPU, 125th anniv., Bangkok 2000, Espana 2000, WIPA 2000, Hanover World's Fair.

El Galpón Theater, Montevideo, 50th Anniv. — A883

**1999, Aug. 3** ***Perf. 12¾x12¼***
**1808** A883 7p multi 1.60 1.60

China 1999 World Philatelic Exhibition — A884

Sea planes: a, Piper J-3. b, Short Sunderland.

**1999, Aug. 18** ***Perf. 12¼x12¾***
**1809** A884 7p Pair, #a.-b. 3.25 3.25

Dogs — A885

Designs: a, Cocker spaniel. b, German shepherd. c, Dalmatian. d, Basset hound.

*Perf. 12¾x12½*

**1999, Aug. 24** **Litho.**
**1810** A885 7p Block of 4, #a.-d. 6.00 6.00

Insects & Flowers A886

a, Halictidae, Oxalis sp. b, Apanteles sp., Epidendrum paniculosum. c, Metabolosia univita, Baccharis trimera. d, Compositae, Cantarido.

*Perf. 12½x12¾*

**1999, Sept. 10** **Litho.**
**1811** A886 7p Block of 4, #a.-d. 6.00 6.00

A887

A888

Uruguayan Artists: No. 1812, Orlando Aldama (1904-87), writer. No. 1813, Julio Martínez Oyanguren (1901-73), guitarist.

*Perf. 12¾x12½*

**1999, Sept. 13** **Litho.**
**1812** A887 7p multi 1.60 1.60
**1813** A887 7p multi 1.60 1.60

*Perf. 12¾x12¼*

**1999, Sept. 18** **Litho.**
**1814** A888 7p multi 1.60 1.60

Cultural heritage of Mercosur countries.

First Uruguayan Participation in Olympics, Paris, 1924 — A889

Designs: a, Poster, medal. b, Medal, medal-winning soccer team.

**1999, Sept. 30** *Perf. 12¼x12¾*
**1815** A889 7p Pair, #a.-b. 3.25 3.25

Intl. Year of Older Persons A890

**1999, Oct. 1** **Litho.** *Perf. 12¼x12¾*
**1816** A890 7p multi 1.60 1.60

Philatelic Witches Sabbath, by Mariano Barbasán — A891

**1999, Oct. 1** *Perf. 12*
**1817** A891 7p multi 1.60 1.60

Stamp Day.

America Issue, A New Millennium Without Arms — A892

7p, Arms in trash can. 14p, Earth, satellites.

**1999, Oct. 6** *Perf. 13¾x12¼*
**1818** A892 7p multi 1.60 1.60
**1819** A892 14p multi 3.25 3.25

Inter-American Development Bank, 40th Anniv. — A893

**1999, Oct. 6** *Perf. 12¼x12¾*
**1820** A893 7p multi 1.60 1.60

Winner of Older Person's Stamp Design Contest A894

**1999, Oct. 8**
**1821** A894 7p multi 1.60 1.60

El Ceibo Society, 50th Anniv. A895

**1999, Oct. 8**
**1822** A895 7p multi 1.60 1.60

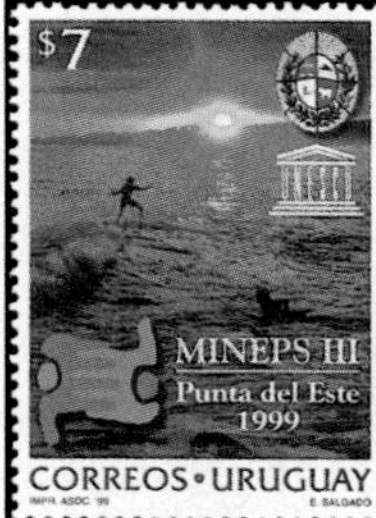
Third Intl. Conference of Ministers for Sports, Punta del Este — A896

**1999, Oct. 13** *Perf. 12*
**1823** A896 7p multi 1.60 1.60

Souvenir Sheets

Official Service of Broadcasting, Television and Entertainment — A897

Illustration reduced.
No. 1824: a, 4p, Television cameraman. b, 4p, Building. c, 3p, Radio studio. d, 3p, Film cameraman.
No. 1825: a, 4p, Symphony orchestra. b, 4p, Chamber music group. c, 3p, Chorus. d, 3p, Ballet dancers.

**1999, Oct. 22** *Perf. 12¼x12¾*
**1824** A897 Sheet of 4, #a.-d. 3.25 3.25
**1825** A897 Sheet of 4, #a.-d. 3.25 3.25

Uruguayan Standards Institute, 60th Anniv. — A898

**1999, Nov. 3**
**1826** A898 7p multi 1.60 1.60

A899

A900

**1999, Nov. 3** *Perf. 12¾x12¼*
**1827** A899 7p multi 1.60 1.60

Vice-President Hugo Batalla (1926-98).

**1999, Nov.12**

Cover of 4/29/29 Mundo Uruguayo magazine.

**1828** A900 7p multi 1.60 1.60

Exhibition of art and design from the 1920s, Blanes Museum, Montevideo.

Millennium — A901

Illustration reduced.
No. 1829 — Various buildings and: a, "1999." b, "2000."

**1999, Nov. 23** **Litho.** *Perf. 12*
**1829** A901 3.50p Pair, #a.-b. 1.60 1.60

Celmar Poumé (1924-83), Cartoonist A902

**1999, Nov. 26** *Perf. 12¾x12¼*
**1830** A902 7p multi 1.60 1.60

Christmas A903

9p, Tree with ornaments. 18p, Carolers.

*Perf. 12¼x12¾, 12¾x12¼*

**1999, Dec. 3**
**1831** A903 9p multi 2.00 2.00
**1832** A903 18p multi, vert. 4.00 4.00

Tannat Wines, 20th Anniv. — A904

**1999, Dec. 9** *Perf. 12*
**1833** A904 9p shown 2.00 2.00
**1834** A904 9p Wine drinker 2.00 2.00

New Maldonado Department Governmental Building — A905

**1999, Dec. 11** *Perf. 12¼x12¾*
**1835** A905 9p multi 2.00 2.00

### Types of 1997 and

Crow's Gorge Nature Reserve A907

Design: 2p, Penitente Waterfall, vert. 5p, Bird. 10p, Crow's Gorge Nature Reserve. No. 1841, Gruta del Palacio, vert. 100p, Sierra de los Caracoles.

***Serpentine Die Cut 11¼, Die Cut (#1836A, 1840, 1850, 1853)***

**2000-04** **Litho.**

**Self-Adhesive**

| | | | | |
|---|---|---|---|---|
| **1836** | A907 | 2p multi | .30 | .30 |
| **1836A** | A908 | 5p multi | .45 | .45 |
| **1837** | A907 | 10p multi | .85 | .85 |
| **1838** | A907 | 11p multi | 2.00 | 2.00 |
| **1840** | A781 | 20p multi | 4.50 | 4.50 |
| **1841** | A907 | 20p multi | 5.00 | 5.00 |
| **1850** | A782 | 32p multi | 7.25 | 7.25 |
| **1853** | A782 | 80p multi | 18.00 | 18.00 |
| **1854** | A907 | 100pmulti | 14.00 | 14.00 |
| **1855** | A782 | 100pmulti | 7.50 | 7.50 |
| | *Nos. 1836-1855 (10)* | | 59.85 | 59.85 |

Issued: 32p, 1/20. No. 1840, 80p, 12/12. 11p, 3/16/01. No. 1841, 4/26/01. 2p, 8/1/01. No. 1854, 2/13/02. No. 1855, 10/5/04. 5p, 12/1; 10p, 10/18; No. 1855A, 9/26. This is an expanding set. Numbers may change.

No. 1855 has straight numerals in denomination.

No. 1836 exists dated "2002." No. 1841 exists dated "2006."

50th Anniv of Artistic Career of Carlos Páez Vilaró — A916

**2000, Jan. 15** **Litho.** ***Perf. 12***
**1856** A916 9p multi 2.00 2.00

Orchids — A917

No. 1857: a, 5p, Laelia purpurata. b, 4p, Cattleya corcovado. c, 4p, Cattleya sp. "hybrid." d, 5p, Laelia tenebrosa.

**2000, Mar. 3**
**1857** A917 Block of 4, #a.-d. 4.00 4.00

Lighthouses — A918

No. 1858: a, 5p, Isla de Flores, 1828. b, 4p, Punta del Este, 1860. c, 4p, Cabo Polonio, 1881. d, 5p, Punta Brava, 1876.

**2000, Mar. 14**
**1858** A918 Block of 4, #a.-d. 4.00 4.00

Carlos Quijano (1900-84), Economics Journalist — A919

**2000, Mar. 30** ***Perf. 12¼x12¾***
**1859** A919 9p multi 2.00 2.00

The Gold Rush, Starring Charlie Chaplin, 75th Anniv. A920

**2000, Apr. 7** **Litho.** ***Perf. 12¼x12¾***
**1860** A920 18p multi 4.00 4.00

Lubrapex 2000 Stamp Show, Brazil.

El Cordón Neighborhood of Montevideo, 250th Anniv. — A921

**2000, Apr. 10** **Litho.** ***Perf. 12¼x12¾***
**1861** A921 9p multi 2.00 2.00

Mural "Espina de la Cruz," by Children of Mercedes — A922

a, 5p, Branches. b, 4p, Two red flowers.

**2000, Apr. 26** ***Perf. 12¼x12***
**1862** A922 Pair, #a-b 2.00 2.00

Francisco García y Santos (1856-1921), Government Official — A923

**2000, May 2** ***Perf. 12¾x12¼***
**1863** A923 9p multi 2.00 2.00

Uruguayan Notaries Assoc., 125th Anniv. — A924

**2000, May 9** **Litho.** ***Perf. 12¾x12¼***
**1864** A924 9p multi 2.00 2.00

Intl. Museum Day — A925

**2000, May 18** **Litho.** ***Perf. 12¾x12¼***
**1865** A925 9p multi 2.00 2.00

Stampin' the Future Children's Stamp Design Contest Winners — A926

Artwork by: a, 5p, Helena Perez. b, 4p, Maria Pia Pereyra. c, 4p, Virginia Regueiro. d, 5p, Blanca E. Lima.
Illustration reduced.

**2000, June 2** **Litho.** ***Perf. 12***
**1866** A926 Block of 4, #a-d 4.00 4.00

Club Soriano, 90th Anniv. A927

**2000, June 9** **Litho.** ***Perf. 12¼x12¾***
**1867** A927 9p multi 2.00 2.00

Antonio Rupenian, Founder of Radio Armenia — A928

**2000, June 16** ***Perf. 12¾x12¼***
**1868** A928 18p multi 4.00 4.00

"1900 Generation" Writers, Cent. — A929

***Perf. 12¾x12¼***

**2000, June 22** **Litho.**
**1869** A929 9p multi 2.00 2.00

Cacti — A930

No. 1870: a, 5p, Notocactus ottonis. b, 4p, Echinopsis multiplex.

**2000, July 4** ***Perf. 12¼***
**1870** A930 Horiz. pair, #a-b 2.00 2.00

Uruguayan Soccer Association, Cent. — A931

No. 1871: a, 5p, Players marching. b, 4p, Team photo. c, 4p, Stadium, World Cup. d, 5p, Players in action, World Cup.
Illustration reduced.

**2000, July 14** **Litho.** ***Perf. 12¼x12***
**1871** A931 Block of 4, #a-d 8.75 8.75

Opera Anniversaries — A932

No. 1872: a, 9p, Scene from Carmen, composer Georges Bizet. b, 9p, Scene from Tosca, composer Giacomo Puccini.
Illustration reduced.

**2000, July 20**
**1872** A932 Pair, #a-b 4.00 4.00

Carmen, 125th anniv.; Tosca, cent.

Latin American Integration Association, 20th Anniv. — A933

**2000, Aug. 11** ***Perf. 12¾x12¼***
**1873** A933 18p multi 4.00 4.00

Naval Aviation, 75th Anniv. A934

**2000, Aug. 18** ***Perf. 12¼x12¾***
**1874** A934 9p multi 2.00 2.00

ORT, 120th Anniv. A935

**2000, Aug. 28**
**1875** A935 9p multi 2.00 2.00

Luis de la Robla (1780-1844), First Postmaster General — A936

**2000, Aug. 28** ***Perf. 12¾x12¼***
**1876** A936 9p multi 2.00 2.00

Gonzalo Rodriguez (1971-99), Race Car Driver — A937

a, 9p, Rodriguez, dark blue car. b, 9p, Rodriguez holding trophy, light blue car.
Illustration reduced.

**2000, Sept. 11** ***Perf. 12x12¼***
**1877** A937 Pair, #a-b 4.00 4.00

Gen. José Artigas (1764-1850) A938

**2000, Sept. 22** **Litho.** ***Perf. 12¼***
**1878** A938 9p multi + label 1.60 1.60

España 2000 Intl. Philatelic Exhibition — A939

Birds: a, 5p, Donacospiza albifrons. b, 4p, Geositta cunicularia. c, 4p, Phacellodomus striaticollis. d, 5p, Cacicus chrysopterus.

Illustration reduced.

**2000, Sept. 27** ***Perf. 12***
**1879** A939 Block of 4, #a-d 3.25 3.25

Soka Gakkai International, 25th Anniv. — A940

**2000, Oct. 2** ***Perf. 12¼x12¾***
**1880** A940 18p multi 3.25 3.25

America Issue, Fight Against AIDS — A941

No. 1881: a, 9p, Tic-tac-toe game with condoms and crosses. b, 18p, Syringe and red ribbon.

**2000, Oct. 10** ***Perf. 12¼***
**1881** A941 Horiz. pair, #a-b 4.75 4.75

Mercosur Cultural Heritage Day — A942

**2000, Oct. 14** ***Perf. 12¾x12¼***
**1882** A942 18p multi 3.25 3.25

Dragon, by Luis Mazzey (1895-1983) — A943

**2000, Oct. 19** ***Perf. 12¼x12¾***
**1883** A943 9p multi 1.60 1.60

Fire Fighters A944

Designs: No. 1884, 9p, At car crash. No. 1885, 9p, Searching for victims, vert.

***Perf. 12¼x12¾, 12¾x12¼***
**2000, Oct. 26**
**1884-1885** A944 Set of 2 3.25 3.25

Prof. Julio Ricaldoni (1906-93), Structural Engineer A945

**2000, Nov. 13** ***Perf. 12¼x12¾***
**1886** A945 9p multi 1.60 1.60

29th Conference on Structural Engineering, Punta del Este.

Training Ship "Capitan Miranda," 70th Anniv. A946

**2000, Nov. 15**
**1887** A946 9p multi 1.60 1.60

Holy Roman Emperor Charles V (1500-58) A947

**2000, Nov. 22** **Litho.**
**1888** A947 22p multi 4.00 4.00

Christmas A948

Designs: 11p, Fireworks. 22p, Holy Family.

**2000, Dec. 1**
**1889-1890** A948 Set of 2 5.75 5.75

Sarandi del Yi, 125th Anniv. — A949

**2000, Dec. 14** ***Perf. 12¾x12¼***
**1891** A949 11p multi 2.00 2.00

Forest Fire Prevention Service A950

**2001, Feb. 9** **Litho.** ***Perf. 12½x12¾***
**1892** A950 11p multi 2.00 2.00

Amphibians and Reptiles — A951

No. 1893: a, Phyllomedusa iheringii. b, Acanthochelys spixii. c, Phrynops hilarii. d, Scinax sqalirostris.

**2001, Feb. 15** ***Perf. 12***
**1893** A951 11p Block of 4, #a-d 8.00 8.00

Paysandú Rowing Club, Cent. A952

**2001, Feb. 28** ***Perf. 12½x12¾***
**1894** A952 11p multi 2.00 2.00

17th Congress of Latin American Confederation of Congress Organizers A953

**2001, Mar. 2** ***Perf. 12¾x12½***
**1895** A953 11p multi 2.00 2.00

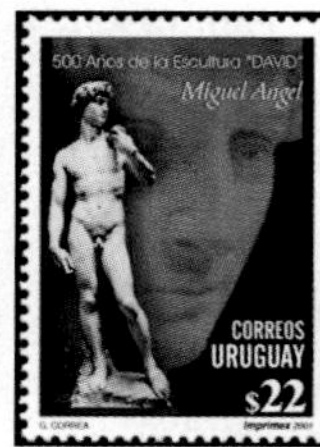

City of Belén, Bicent. — A954

**2001, Mar. 14**
**1896** A954 11p multi 2.00 2.00

David, by Michelangelo, 500th Anniv. — A955

**2001, Mar. 22**
**1897** A955 22p multi 4.00 4.00

Uruguayan Society of Performers, 50th Anniv. — A956

**2001, Mar. 26** ***Perf. 12½x12¾***
**1898** A956 11p multi 2.00 2.00

Casal Catalá, 75th Anniv. — A957

**2001, Apr. 20** ***Perf. 12¾x12½***
**1899** A957 11p multi 2.00 2.00

Universidad Mayor de la República Engineering Faculty, 85th Anniv. — A958

**2001, Apr. 30**
**1900** A958 11p blue 2.00 2.00

Rodolfo V. Tálice (1899-1999), Biologist — A959

**2001, May 2** ***Perf. 12½x12¾***
**1901** A959 11p multi 2.00 2.00

Montevideo Lions Club, 50th Anniv. — A960

**2001, May 14** ***Perf. 12¾x12½***
**1902** A960 11p multi 2.00 2.00

Invention of the Telephone, 125th Anniv. A961

**2001, May 22** ***Perf. 12½x12¾***
**1903** A961 22p multi 4.00 4.00

Snakes — A962

No. 1904: a, Philodryas olfersii. b, Bothrops alternatus.
Illustration reduced.

**2001, May 28** ***Perf. 12***
**1904** A962 11p Horiz. pair, #a-b 4.00 4.00

Juan Manuel Blanes (1830-1901), Painter — A963

**2001, June 8 Litho.** ***Perf. 12½x12¾***
**1905** A963 11p multi 1.75 1.75

Start of Pediatrics Teaching by Dr. Luis Morquio, Cent. — A964

**2001, June 15** ***Perf. 12¾x12½***
**1906** A964 11p multi 1.75 1.75

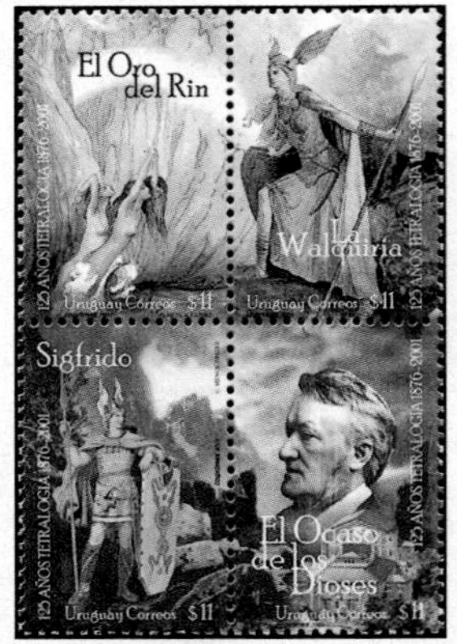


The Ring of the Nibelung, by Richard Wagner — A965

No. 1907: a, The Rhinegold (El Oro del Rin). b, The Valkyrie (La Walquiria). c, Siegfried (Sigfrido). d, The Twilight of the Gods (El Ocaso de los Dioses).

**2001, June 29** ***Perf. 12***
**1907** A965 11p Block of 4, #a-d 6.50 6.50

Intl. Organization for Migration, 50th Anniv. — A966

**2001, July 5** ***Perf. 12¾x12½***
**1908** A966 22p blue & black 3.25 3.25

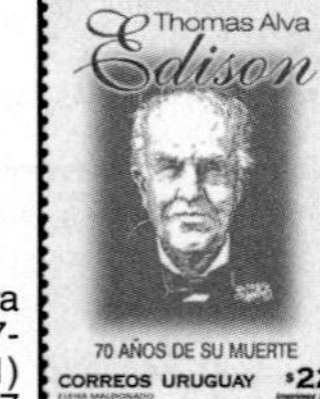


Thomas Alva Edison (1847-1931) A967

**2001, July 12**
**1909** A967 22p multi 3.25 3.25

Laying of Foundation Stone for Montevideo Port, Cent. — A968

**2001, July 18** ***Perf. 12½x12¾***
**1910** A968 11p multi 1.75 1.75

Fowl — A969

No. 1911: a, New Hampshire. b, Orpington-Buff. c, Araucanas. d, Leghorn-Light brown.
Illustration reduced.

**2001, July 30** ***Perf. 12***
**1911** A969 11p Block of 4, #a-d 6.75 6.75

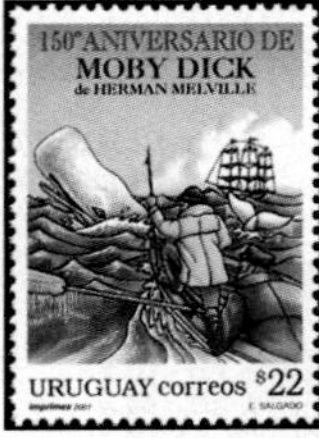


Moby Dick, by Herman Melville, 150th Anniv. — A970

**2001, Aug. 2** ***Perf. 12¾x12½***
**1912** A970 22p multi 3.25 3.25

Bernardo González Pecotche (1901-63), Founder of Logosophy A971

**2001, Aug. 7** ***Perf. 12***
**1913** A971 11p multi 1.75 1.75

First Concorde Flight, 25th Anniv. A972

**2001, Aug. 10** ***Perf. 12½x12¾***
**1914** A972 22p multi 3.25 3.25

Rose Varieties — A973

No. 1915: a, Louis Philippe. b, Souvenir de Mme. Léonie Viennot. c, Kronenbourg. d, Lady Hillingdon.

**2001, Aug. 16** ***Perf. 12***
**1915** A973 11p Block of 4, #a-d 6.75 6.75

Apiculture — A974

No. 1916: a, Apiculturists. b, Bee on flower.
Illustration reduced.

**2001, Sept. 12**
**1916** A974 12p Horiz. pair, #a-b 3.50 3.50

Town of Dolores, Bicent. — A975

**2001, Sept. 21** ***Perf. 12¾x12½***
**1917** A975 12p multi 1.75 1.75

Uruguay Philatelic Club, 75th Anniv. A976

Sun and inscription: No. 1918, 12p, "75 Años." No. 1919, 12p, "1er Presidente / Dr. Miguel A. Paez Formoso."

**2001, Sept. 26** ***Perf. 12½x12¾***
**1918-1919** A976 Set of 2 3.50 3.50

America Issue - UNESCO World Heritage Sites — A977

Buildings from Historic Quarter of Colonia del Sacramento: a, 12p, Basilica del Santisimo. b, 24p, San Benito de Palermo Chapel.

**2001, Sept. 28** ***Perf. 12***
**1920** A977 Horiz. pair, #a-b 5.25 5.25

Carlos Amoretti, 50th Anniv. as Artist A978

**2001, Oct. 2** ***Perf. 12½x12¾***
**1921** A978 12p multi 1.75 1.75

Town of Sauce, 150th Anniv. — A979

**2001, Oct. 12** ***Perf. 12¾x12½***
**1922** A979 12p multi 1.75 1.75

Uruguay - Japan Diplomatic Relations, 80th Anniv. A980

***Perf. 12¼x12¾***
**2001, Sept. 24** **Litho.**
**1923** A980 24p multi 3.50 3.50

Prevention of Illegal Drug Use A981

**2001, Oct. 16**
**1924** A981 12p multi 1.75 1.75

Year of Dialogue Among Civilizations A982

**2001, Oct. 23** ***Perf. 12¾x12¼***
**1925** A982 24p multi 3.50 3.50

Honorary Committee for Fighting Cancer — A983

**2001, Oct. 29**
**1926** A983 12p multi 1.75 1.75

Ultimas Noticias Newspaper, 20th Anniv. — A984

**2001, Oct. 31**
**1927** A984 12p multi 1.75 1.75

Sauce Basketball Club, 50th Anniv. A985

**2001, Nov. 9** ***Perf. 12¼x12¾***
**1928** A985 12p multi 1.75 1.75

Blood Donor's Day — A986

**2001, Nov. 12** ***Perf. 12¾x12¼***
**1929** A986 12p multi 1.75 1.75

Juan Zorilla de San Martín (1855-1931), Writer — A987

**2001, Nov. 13** ***Perf. 12¼x12¾***
**1930** A987 12p multi 1.75 1.75

Uruguayan Navy's Hydrographic Ship "Oyarvide" — A988

**2001, Nov. 14**
**1931** A988 12p multi 1.75 1.75

Uruguayan Visit of Rotary Intl. President Richard King and Wife Cherie — A989

**2001, Nov. 20** ***Perf. 12¾x12¼***
**1932** A989 24p multi 3.50 3.50

Peñarol Athletic Club, 110th Anniv. — A990

**2001, Nov. 22** ***Perf. 12***
**1933** A990 12p multi 1.75 1.75

Julio Sosa (1926-64), Tango Singer — A991

**2001, Nov. 26** ***Perf. 12¾x12¼***
**1934** A991 12p multi 1.75 1.75

José Nasazzi (1901-68), Soccer Player — A992

**2001, Nov. 29**
**1935** A992 12p multi 1.75 1.75

Christmas — A993

Paintings of Adoration of the Shepherds, by: 12p, José Ribera. 24p, Anton Raphael Mengs.

**2001, Dec. 6**
**1936-1937** A993 Set of 2 5.25 5.25

Church of San Carlos, Bicent. — A994

**2001, Dec. 7**
**1938** A994 12p multi 1.75 1.75

National Museum of Visual Arts, 90th Anniv. — A995

**2001, Dec. 12** ***Perf. 12***
**1939** A995 12p multi 1.75 1.75

State Insurance Bank, 90th Anniv. — A996

**2001, Dec. 20** ***Perf. 12¾x12¼***
**1940** A996 12p multi 1.75 1.75

Guettarda Uruguensis — A997

**2001, Dec. 21** ***Perf. 12¼x12¾***
**1941** A997 24p multi 3.50 3.50

St. Josemaría Escrivá de Balaguer (1902-75) — A998

Balaguer and quotes: a, "El trabajo es. . ." b, "Quieres de verdad. . ." c, "La santidad. . ." d, "Que busques. . ."
Illustration reduced.

**2002, Jan. 9** ***Perf. 12***
**1942** A998 12p Block of 4, #a-d 7.00 7.00

Uruguayan Association of Directors of Carnivals and Folk Festivals, 50th Anniv. — A999

Feet of: a, Ringmaster. b, Clown. c, Acrobat.

**2002, Mar. 8** **Litho.** ***Perf. 12½***
**Self-Adhesive**

**1943** Booklet pane of 3 3.25 3.25
***a.-b.*** A999 6p Either single .80 .80
***c.*** A999 12p black 1.60 1.60
Booklet, #1943 3.50

Christianity in Armenia, 1700th Anniv. A1000

**2002, Apr. 23** ***Perf. 12***
**1944** A1000 12p multi 1.50 1.50

New Year 2003 (Year of the Horse) — A1001

**2002, May 14** ***Perf. 12¾x12¼***
**1945** A1001 24p multi 3.00 3.00

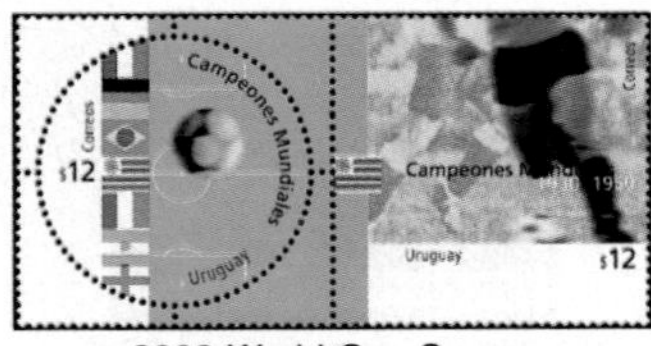
2002 World Cup Soccer Championships, Japan and Korea — A1002

No. 1946: a, Flags, soccer ball, and field (38mm diameter). b, Soccer players, years of Uruguayan championships.
Illustration reduced.

**2002, May 21** ***Perf. 12¾***
**1946** A1002 12p Horiz. pair, #a-b 2.75 2.75

See Argentina No. 2184, Brazil No. 2840, France No. 2891, Germany No. 2163 and Italy No. 2526.

Book Day — A1003

**2002, May 24** ***Perf. 12¾x12¼***
**1947** A1003 12p multi 1.40 1.40

Inter-American Children's Institute, 75th Anniv. — A1004

**2002, June 10** ***Perf. 12¼x12¾***
**1948** A1004 12p multi 1.40 1.40

Department of Tacuarembó, 165th Anniv. — A1005

**2002, June 14**
**1949** A1005 12p multi 1.40 1.40

Cerro de Montevideo Lighthouse, Bicent. — A1006

Designs: 12p, Old lighthouse. 24p, New lighthouse, vert.

***Perf. 12¼x12¾, 12¾x12¼***
**2002, June 24**
**1950-1951** A1006 Set of 2 3.75 3.75

Villa Constitución, 150th Anniv. — A1007

**2002, July 11** ***Perf. 12¼x12¾***
**1952** A1007 12p multi 1.00 1.00

"We Are United" A1008

**2002, July 17**
**1953** A1008 6p multi .50 .50

Printed in sheets of 3 + label. Value $2.

Natural Uruguay A1009

**2002, July 22** **Litho.**
**1954** A1009 24p blue & orange 2.40 2.40

Montevideo Botanical Gardens, Cent. — A1010

No. 1955: a, Botanical Gardens building, Erythrina cristigalli. b, Rhodophiala bifida. c, Prof. Atilio Lombardo and Tillandsia arequitae. d, Heteropterys dumetorum.

**2002, July 31** ***Perf. 12***
**1955** Horiz. strip of 4 4.25 4.25
***a.-d.*** A1010 12p Any single 1.00 1.00

Montevideo Wanderers Soccer Team, Cent. — A1011

**2002, Aug. 1** ***Perf. 12¾x12¼***
**1956** A1011 12p black 1.10 1.10

Sportsmen — A1012

Designs: No. 1957, 12p, Lorenzo Fernández, soccer player. No. 1958, 12p, Josè Leandro Andrade, soccer player. No. 1959, 12p, Alvaro Gestido, soccer player. No. 1960, 12p, César L. Gallardo, fencer. No. 1961, 12p, Pedro Petrone, soccer player.

**2002, Aug. 16** ***Perf. 12¼x12¾***
**1957-1961** A1012 Set of 5 5.25 5.25

Elvis Presley (1935-77) A1013

**2002, Aug. 19** ***Perf. 12¾x12¼***
**1962** A1013 24p multi 2.10 2.10

Agustín Bisio (1894-1952), Poet — A1014

**2002, Aug. 30** ***Perf. 12¾x12¼***
**Self-Adhesive**
**1963** A1014 12p multi 1.10 1.10

City of Artigas, 150th Anniv. — A1015

**2002, Sept. 12** ***Perf. 12¾x12¼***
**Self-Adhesive**
**1964** A1015 12p multi 1.10 1.10

Uruguayan Cooperative Society of Bus Services, 65th Anniv. — A1016

**2002, Sept. 16** ***Perf. 12¼x12¾***
**1965** A1016 12p multi 1.10 1.10

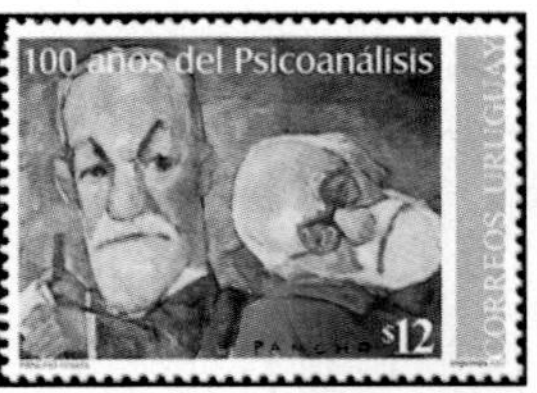
Psychoanalysis, Cent. — A1017

**2002, Sept. 20** ***Perf. 12***
**1966** A1017 12p multi 1.10 1.10

24th Latin American Psychoanalysis Congress, Montevideo.

Horacio Arredondo (1888-1967), Historical Preservationist, and San Miguel Fort — A1018

**2002, Sept. 20** ***Perf. 12¼x12¾***
**1967** A1018 12p multi 1.10 1.10

Paso del Rey Barracks Natl. Historic Monument — A1019

**2002, Sept. 23** ***Perf. 12***
**1968** A1019 12p multi 1.10 1.10

Intl. Year of Ecotourism — A1020

**2002, Sept. 24** **Litho.**
**1969** A1020 12p multi 1.10 1.10

Uruguayan Postal Services, 175th Anniv. — A1021

Designs: No. 1970, Postal Services headquarters, Montevideo. No. 1971, Letter box.

**2002, Oct. 9** ***Perf. 12¾x12¼***
**1970** A1021 12p multi 1.10 1.10

**Souvenir Sheet**
***Imperf***
**1971** A1021 12p multi 1.10 1.10

First Equestrian Statue of Brig. Gen. Juan Antonio Lavalleja, Cent. — A1022

**2002, Oct. 11** ***Perf. 12¾x12¼***
**1972** A1022 12p multi 1.10 1.10

America Issue — Youth, Education and Literacy A1023

"ANALFABETISMO" in: 12p, Word search puzzle. 24p, Bowl of alphabet soup.

**2002, Oct. 16** ***Perf. 12¼x12¾***
**1973-1974** A1023 Set of 2 3.25 3.25

Christmas A1024

**2002, Nov. 4** ***Perf. 12¾x12¼***
**1975** A1024 12p multi 1.10 1.10

Association of Uruguayan Pharmacies, 65th Anniv. — A1025

**2002, Nov. 8** **Litho.**
**1976** A1025 12p multi 1.10 1.10

Tannat Wine — A1026

**2002, Nov. 13**
**1977** A1026 12p multi 1.10 1.10

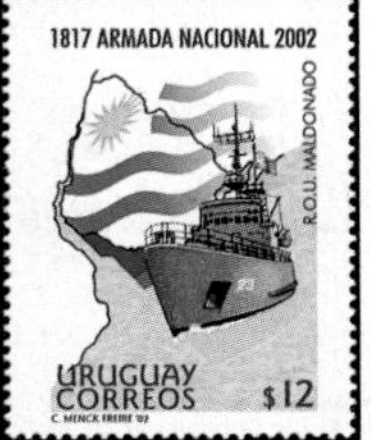


Uruguayan Navy, 185th Anniv. — A1027

**2002, Nov. 13** ***Perf. 13½***
**1978** A1027 12p multi 1.10 1.10

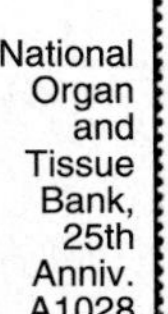

National Organ and Tissue Bank, 25th Anniv. A1028

**2002, Nov. 15**
**1979** A1028 12p multi 1.10 1.10

Taxis in Uruguay, Cent. A1029

**2002, Nov. 25** ***Perf. 12¼x12¾***
**1980** A1029 12p multi 1.10 1.10

Brig. Gen. Manuel Oribe (1792-1857) A1030

**2002, Nov. 28** ***Perf. 12¾x12¼***
**1981** A1030 12p multi 1.10 1.10

George Harrison (1943-2001), Rock Musician A1031

**2002, Nov. 29** ***Perf. 13½***
**1982** A1031 24p multi 3.00 3.00

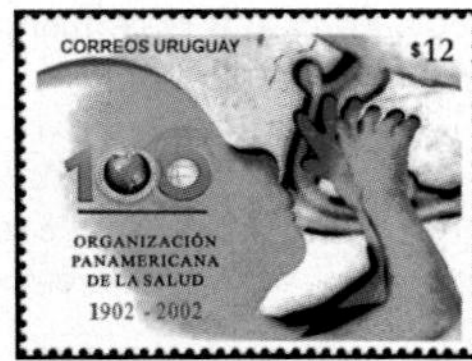


Pan-American Health Organization, Cent. — A1032

**2002, Dec. 2**
**1983** A1032 12p multi 1.10 1.10

Uruguayan Participation in U.N. Peace Keeping Missions, 50th Anniv. — A1033

**2002, Dec. 6** ***Perf. 12¼x12¾***
**1984** A1033 12p multi 1.10 1.10

Alfredo Testoni (1919-2000), Artist — A1034

**2002, Dec. 9** ***Perf. 13½***
**1985** A1034 12p multi 1.10 1.10

Mercosur A1035

Designs: 12p, Ship and coastline. 24p, Beach.

**2002, Dec. 12**
**1986-1987** A1035 Set of 2 3.25 3.25

Battle of Ituzaingó, 175th Anniv. A1036

**2002, Dec. 17** **Litho.**
**1988** A1036 12p multi 1.10 1.10

Battle of Juncal, 175th Anniv. A1037

**2002, Dec. 17**
**1989** A1037 12p multi 1.10 1.10

Village of Juanicó, 130th Anniv. A1038

**2002, Dec. 23** ***Perf. 12¼x12¾***
**1990** A1038 12p multi 1.10 1.10

Uruguay on World Map A1039

**2003, Jan. 17** **Litho.** ***Perf. 12¼x12¾***
**1991** A1039 12p multi 1.10 1.10

Busqueda Weekly, 30th Anniv. A1040

**2003, Jan. 29**
**1992** A1040 12p multi 1.10 1.10

Water Goddess Iemanja — A1041

**2003, Jan. 29** ***Perf. 12¾x12¼***
**1993** A1041 12p multi 1.10 1.10

Uruguay - People's Republic of China Diplomatic Relations, 15th Anniv. — A1042

**2003, Jan. 31** ***Perf. 12***
**1994** A1042 12p multi 1.10 1.10

New Year 2003 (Year of the Ram) — A1043

**2003, Feb. 7** ***Perf. 12¾x12¼***
**1995** A1043 5p multi .45 .45

Explorers A1044

Explorers and maps of their voyages: a, Christopher Columbus, 4th voyage, 1502. b, Juan Díaz de Solís, 1516. c, Sebastian Cabot, 1526-30. d, Hernando Arias de Saavedra, 1597-1618.

**2003, Feb. 14** ***Perf. 12***
**1996** Horiz. strip of 4 3.50 3.50
***a.-d.*** A1044 12p Any single .85 .85

Communications Services Regulatory Union, 2nd Anniv. — A1045

**2003, Feb. 21** ***Perf. 12¼x12¾***
**1997** A1045 12p multi 1.10 1.10

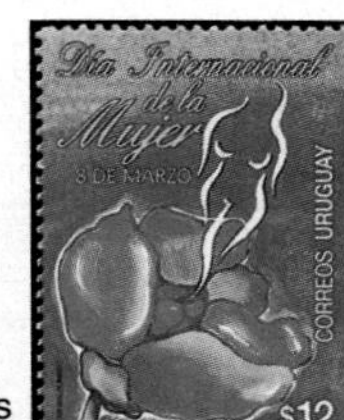


Intl. Women's Day — A1046

**2003, Mar. 7** ***Perf. 12¾x12¼***
**1998** A1046 12p multi 1.10 1.10

City of Treinta y Tres, 150th Anniv. A1047

**2003, Mar. 10** ***Perf. 12¼x12¾***
**1999** A1047 12p multi 1.10 1.10

Butterflies — A1048

No. 2000: a, Heliconius erato. b, Junonia evarete. c, Dryadula phaetusa. d, Parides perrhebus.

**2003, Mar. 18** ***Perf. 12***
**2000** A1048 12p Block of 4, #a-d 5.00 5.00

First Presidency of José Batlle y Ordóñez, Cent. — A1049

No. 2001 — Batlle y Ordóñez: a, Wearing overcoat. b, Wearing presidential sash. c, With head on hand. d, Wearing white jacket.

**2003, Mar. 25** ***Perf. 12***
**2001** Horiz. strip of 4 3.50 3.50
***a.-d.*** A1049 12p Any single .85 .85

Rural Women's Crafts A1050

No. 2002: a, Basket weaving. b, Knitting. c, Pottery making. d, Food canning. e, Jewelry making.

**2003, Mar. 23 Litho.** ***Perf. 12***
**2002** Horiz. strip of 5 5.50 5.50
***a.-e.*** A1050 12p Any single 1.10 1.10

Farruco's Chapel — A1051

**2003, Apr. 4 Litho.** ***Perf. 12¾x12¼***
**2003** A1051 12p multi 1.10 1.10

Natural Foods A1052

**2003, Apr. 9** ***Perf. 12¼x12¾***
**2004** A1052 12p multi 1.10 1.10

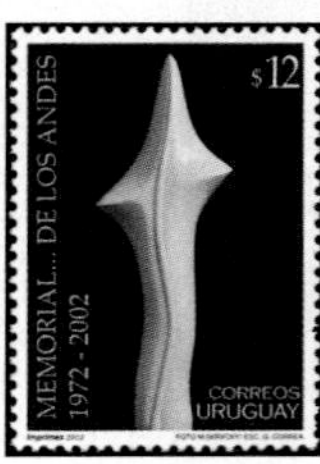

Cerros Azules Caiman Farm A1053

***Serpentine Die Cut 11¼***
**2003, Apr. 10**
**Self-Adhesive**
**2005** A1053 12p multi 1.10 1.10

Memorial to 1972 Airplane Crash in the Andes — A1054

**2003, Apr. 22** ***Perf. 12¾x12¼***
**2006** A1054 12p multi 1.10 1.10

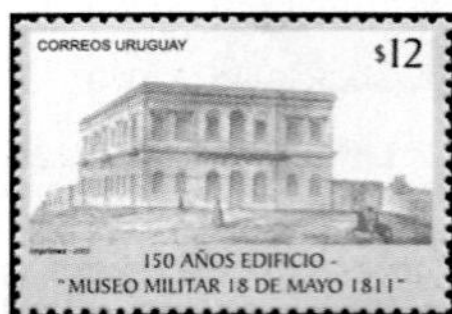

Military Center — A1055

**2003, May 21**
**2007** A1055 12p multi 1.10 1.10

May 18, 1811 Military Museum, 150th Anniv. A1056

**2003, May 26** ***Perf. 12***
**2008** A1056 12p multi 1.10 1.10

Casa de Ximénes and Las Bóvedas, Montevideo Historical District — A1057

**2003, May 30** ***Perf. 12¼***
**2009** A1057 14p multi 1.40 1.40

Wilson Ferreira Aldunate (1919-88), Politician — A1058

No. 2010: a, Brown background. b, Green background. c, Dark violet background, text at right. d, Light violet background, text at left. Illustration reduced.

**2003, June 16 Litho.** ***Perf. 12***
**2010** A1058 14p Block of 4, #a-d 4.75 4.75

Olympic Soccer Gold Medal, 75th Anniv. A1059

**2003, June 18**
**2011** A1059 14p multi 1.10 1.10

Nos. 1382, 1492 Overprinted in Gold

**Methods, Perfs and Watermarks as Before**

**2003, June 18**
**2011A** A654 (14p) on 1.20p #1492 1.50 1.50
**2011B** A589 (36p) on 2500p #1382 4.50 4.50

Compare No. 2011A with No. 2055.

Richard Anderson College, 70th Anniv. — A1060

**2003, July 15**
**2012** A1060 14p multi 1.10 1.10

Santa Isabel del Paso de los Toros, Cent. — A1061

**2003, July 17**
**2013** A1061 14p multi 1.10 1.10

National Association of Affiliates, 70th Anniv. — A1062

**2003, July 24**
**2014** A1062 14p multi 1.10 1.10

Jesús María College, Carrasco, 50th Anniv. — A1063

**2003, Aug. 4**
**2015** A1063 14p multi 1.10 1.10

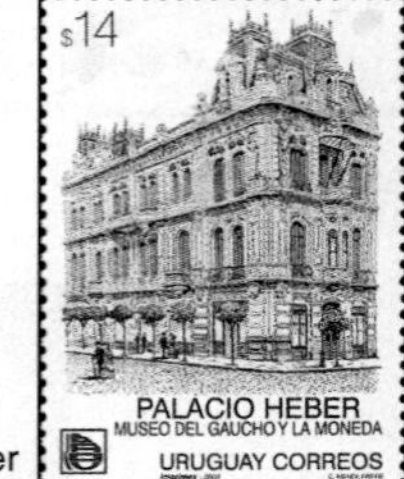

Philatelic Academy of Uruguay, 25th Anniv. A1064

**2003, Aug. 5**
**2016** A1064 14p multi 1.10 1.10

Palacio Heber A1065

**2003, Aug. 14**
**2017** A1065 14p multi 1.10 1.10

Parva Domus Magna Quies, 125th Anniv. — A1066

**2003, Aug. 15**
**2018** A1066 14p multi 1.10 1.10

Security Dept. Commission of Interior Ministry, 4th Anniv. — A1067

**2003, Aug. 18**
**2019** A1067 14p multi 1.10 1.10

First International Victory of Uruguayan Soccer Team, Cent. — A1068

**2003, Sept. 12** ***Perf. 12½x12¾***
**2020** A1068 14p multi 1.10 1.10

Lauro Ayestarán (1913-66), Musicologist — A1069

**2003, Sept. 19** ***Perf. 12***
**2021** A1069 14p multi 1.10 1.10

Asociacion Española Primera de Socorros Mutuos Hospital, 150th Anniv. A1070

**2003, Sept. 19** ***Perf. 12½x12¾***
**2022** A1070 14p multi 1.10 1.10

Dr. Manuel Quintela Clinical Hospital, 50th Anniv. A1071

**2003, Sept. 23** ***Perf. 12***
**2023** A1071 14p multi 1.10 1.10

Society of Friends of Public Education, 135th Anniv. — A1072

**2003, Sept. 24**
**2024** A1072 14p multi 1.10 1.10

Association of Uruguayan Newspaper Reporters, 45th Anniv. — A1073

**2003, Sept. 29** ***Perf. 12½x12¾***
**2025** A1073 14p multi 1.10 1.10

Pres. Fructoso Rivera (c. 1788-1854) A1074

**2003, Oct. 1** ***Perf. 12***
**2026** A1074 14p multi 1.60 1.60

Naval Club, 75th Anniv. A1075

**2003, Oct. 1** ***Perf. 12½x12¾***
**2027** A1075 14p multi 1.10 1.10

Malos Pensamientos Radio Program — A1076

**2003, Oct. 3**
**2028** A1076 14p multi 1.10 1.10

Successes in Intl. Events by Milton Wynants, Cyclist — A1077

**2003, Oct. 7** ***Perf. 12¾x12½***
**2029** A1077 14p multi 1.10 1.10

Ente Nazionale Assistenza Sociale in Uruguay, 50th Anniv. — A1078

**2003, Oct. 9** ***Perf. 12½x12¾***
**2030** A1078 14p multi 1.10 1.10

City of Cardona, Cent. — A1079

**2003, Oct. 10** ***Perf. 12***
**2031** A1079 14p multi 1.10 1.10

Construction League of Uruguay, 84th Anniv. — A1080

**2003, Oct. 14** ***Perf. 12¾x12½***
**2032** A1080 14p multi 1.10 1.10

María Tsakos Foundation, 25th Anniv. — A1081

**2003, Oct. 15**
**2033** A1081 14p multi 1.10 1.10

America Issue — Flora and Fauna A1082

Designs: 14p, Prosopis affinis. 36p, Agouti paca paca.

**2003, Oct. 22** ***Perf. 12½x12¾***
**2034-2035** A1082 Set of 2 3.75 3.75

Independence of Lebanon, 60th Anniv. — A1083

**2003, Oct. 24**
**2036** A1083 14p olive grn & red 1.10 1.10

Souvenir Sheet

Masons in Uruguay, 147th Anniv. — A1084

**2003, Oct. 29** ***Perf. 12¾x12½***
**2037** A1084 14p multi 1.10 1.10

Cacho Bochinche Television Show, 30th Anniv. A1085

**2003, Oct. 29** ***Perf. 12½x12¾***
**2038** A1085 14p multi 1.10 1.10

Morenada, 50th Anniv. — A1086

**2003, Oct. 29**
**2039** A1086 14p multi 1.10 1.10

Brig. Gen. Juan A. Lavalleja (c. 1786-1853) A1087

**2003, Oct. 30** ***Perf. 12***
**2040** A1087 14p multi 1.10 1.10

Souvenir Sheet

Election of Pope John Paul II, 25th Anniv. — A1088

No. 1089 — Uruguayan flag and: a, Pope John Paul II, Vatican arms. b, Polish eagle, map of Latin America.

**2003, Oct. 31**
**2041** A1088 12p Sheet of 2, #a-b 2.00 2.00

Union of Latin American Polish Societies and Organizations, 10th anniv. (#2041b).

Souvenir Sheet

2006 World Cup Soccer Championships, Germany — A1089

No. 2042 — World Cup trophy and: a, Uruguayan flag, J. A. Schiaffino. b, German flag, Fritz Walter.

**2003, Oct. 31**
**2042** A1089 12p Sheet of 2, #a-b 2.00 2.00

Christmas A1090

**2003, Nov. 7** ***Perf. 12¾x12½***
**2043** A1090 14p multi 1.10 1.10

Italian Chamber of Commerce of Uruguay, 120th Anniv. A1091

**2003, Nov. 10** ***Perf. 12½x12¾***
**2044** A1091 14p multi 1.10 1.10

Visit of Manuel Fraga Iribarne, President of Spanish Autonomous Community of Galicia — A1092

**2003, Nov. 10**
**2045** A1092 14p multi 1.10 1.10

San Gregorio de Polanco, 150th Anniv. A1093

**2003, Nov. 14**
**2046** A1093 14p multi 1.10 1.10

United Biblical Society, Bicent. A1094

**2003, Nov. 24**
**2047** A1094 14p multi 1.10 1.10

R.O.U. Paysandu A1095

**2003, Nov. 25** ***Perf. 12***
**2048** A1095 14p multi 1.10 1.10

University Culture Foundation, 35th Anniv. — A1096

**2003, Nov. 28**
**2049** A1096 14p multi 1.10 1.10

Uruguayan Air Force, 50th Anniv. A1097

**2003, Dec. 4**
**2050** A1097 14p multi 1.10 1.10

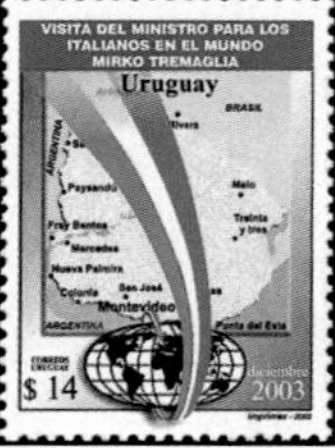

Visit of Mirko Tremaglia, Italian Minister for Italians Abroad — A1098

**2003, Dec. 15**
**2051** A1098 14p multi 1.10 1.10

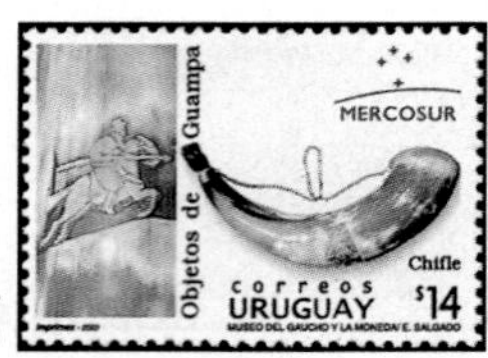

Mercosur A1099

Designs: 14p, Horn. 36p, Silver stirrup.

**2003, Dec. 16**
**2052-2053** A1099 Set of 2 5.00 5.00

Powered Flight, Cent. A1100

**2003, Dec. 19**
**2054** A1100 14p multi 1.10 1.10

**Nos. 1378, 1382, 1458 and 1492 Surcharged in Black or Blue Violet**

j

k

**Methods and Perfs. as Before**

**2004** **Wmk. 332**

| | | | | |
|---|---|---|---|---|
| **2055** | A654(j) | 1p on 1.20p #1492 | .25 | .25 |
| **2056** | A639(j) | 2p on 2.60p #1458 (BV) | .25 | .25 |
| **2057** | A589(k) | 5p on 2500p #1382 | .40 | .40 |
| **2058** | A589(k) | 10p on 360p #1378 | .70 | .70 |
| **2059** | A589(k) | 50p on 825p #1379B | 3.50 | 3.50 |
| | | *Nos. 2055-2059 (5)* | 5.10 | 5.10 |

Issued: Nos. 2055-2056, 1/19; Nos. 2057-2058, 2/16; No. 2059, 3/23. Obliterator on Nos. 2055 and 2056 covers the centesimos portion of the denomination.

Compare No. 2055 with No. 2011A.

Birds — A1101

No. 2060: a, Puffinius gravis. b, Macronectes halli. c, Daption capense. d, Diamedea melanophrys.

Illustration reduced.

**Unwmk.**

**2004, Jan. 22** **Litho.** ***Perf. 12***
**2060** A1101 14p Block of 4, #a-d 6.00 6.00

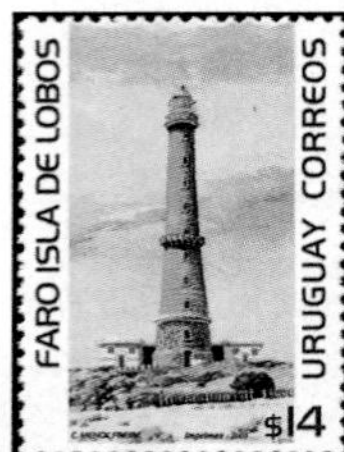

Isla de Lobos Lighthouse A1102

No. 2061: a, Isla de Flores Lighthouse. b, Farallon Lighthouse. c, La Panela Lighthouse. d, Banco Ingles Floating Lighthouse.

**2004, Feb. 10** **Litho.** ***Perf. 12***
**2061** A1102 10p Block of 4, #a-d 3.00 3.00
**2062** A1102 14p shown 1.00 1.00

Abitab, 10th Anniv. — A1103

**Unwmk.**

**2004, Feb. 12** **Litho.** ***Perf. 12***
**2063** A1103 14p multi 1.10 1.10

National Naval Prefecture, 175th Anniv. — A1104

**2004, Feb. 20** **Litho.** ***Perf. 12***
**2064** A1104 14p multi 1.10 1.10

Maté Containers — A1105

No. 2065: a, Maté de Cáliz. b, Maté de Plata Colonial. c, Maté de Calabaza.

Illustration reduced.

**2004, Mar. 4**
**2065** A1105 5p Strip of 3, #a-c 1.25 1.25

33 Orientales Mechanized Infantry Battalion No. 10, Cent. — A1106

**2004, Mar. 12**
**2066** A1106 14p multi 1.10 1.10

Intl. Water Day A1107

**2004, Mar. 25**
**2067** A1107 14p multi 1.10 1.10

Regional Energy Integration Commission, 40th Anniv. — A1108

**2004, Mar. 25**
**2068** A1108 14p multi 1.10 1.10

Grenadier Guards, 80th Anniv. — A1109

**2004, Apr. 1**
**2069** A1109 14p multi 1.10 1.10

Expansion of La Teja Refinery — A1110

**2004, Apr. 2**
**2070** A1110 14p multi 1.10 1.10

Florida Infantry Battalion No. 1, 175th Anniv. A1111

**2004, Apr. 16**
**2071** A1111 14p multi 1.10 1.10

Tribute to Servicemen — A1112

**2004, May 26**
**2072** A1112 14p multi 1.10 1.10

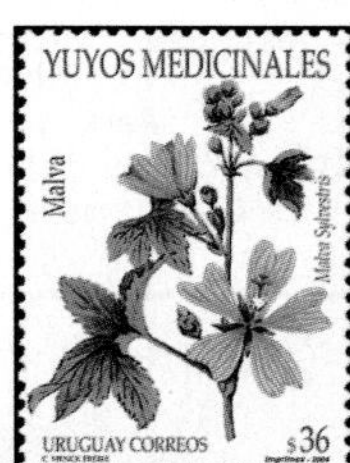

Medicinal Plants — A1113

No. 2073: a, Malva sylvestris. b, Achyrocline satureiodes, c, Baccharis trimera. d, Mentha x piperita.

**2004, June 3**
**2073** Strip of 4 9.75 9.75
*a.-d.* A1113 36p Any single 2.40 2.40

Map and Arms of Montevideo Department — A1114

**2004, June 17**
**2074** A1114 14p multi 1.10 1.10
*a.* Booklet pane of 2 2.40 —
Complete booklet, #2074a 2.40

No. 2074a sold for 35p.

Carlos Gardel (1890-1935), Singer — A1115

**2004, June 24** **Litho.** ***Perf. 12***
**2075** A1115 14p multi 1.10 1.10

Campaign Against Illegal Drugs — A1116

**2004, June 25** **Litho.** ***Perf. 12***
**2076** A1116 14p multi 1.10 1.10

Renán Rodríguez, Politician — A1117

**2004, Aug. 10**
**2077** A1117 14p multi 1.10 1.10

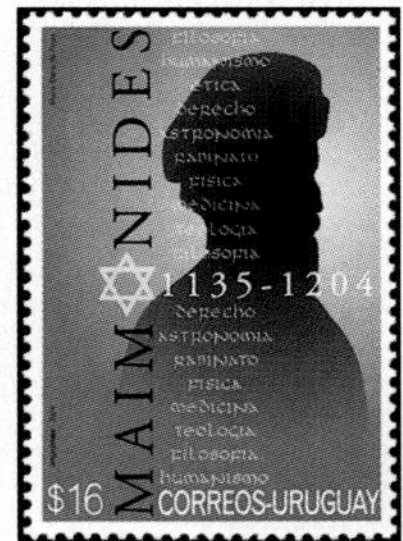

Maimonides (1135-1204), Philosopher A1118

**2004, Aug. 12**
**2078** A1118 16p multi 1.25 1.25

Galician Center, Montevideo, 125th Anniv. — A1119

**2004, Aug. 30**
**2079** A1119 16p multi 1.25 1.25

1904 Battles of Gen. Aparicio Saravia — A1120

No. 2080 — Battle of: a, Illescas. b, Fray-Marcos. c, Paso del Parque. d, Masoller.

**2004, Sept. 8**
**2080** Block of 4 3.00 3.00
*a.-d.* A1120 10p Any single .75 .75

Highway Patrol, 50th Anniv. A1121

**2004, Sept. 15** ***Perf. 12½x12¾***
**2081** A1121 16p multi 1.25 1.25

Joaquín Torres García (1874-1949), Painter — A1122

**2004, Sept. 19**
**2082** A1122 16p multi 1.25 1.25

Magisterial Cooperative, 75th Anniv. — A1123

**2004, Sept. 22**
**2083** A1123 16p multi 1.25 1.25

Army Administrative Corps, Cent. — A1124

**2004, Sept. 22**
**2084** A1124 16p multi 1.25 1.25

FIFA (Fédération Internationale de Football Association), Cent. — A1125

**2004, Oct. 5** ***Perf. 12***
**2085** A1125 37p multi 2.75 2.75

Uruguay - Republic of Korea Diplomatic Relations, 40th Anniv. — A1126

**2004, Oct. 7**
**2086** A1126 16p multi 1.25 1.25

Montevideo Cathedral, Bicent. — A1127

**2004, Oct. 19** **Litho.** ***Perf. 12***
**2087** A1127 16p multi 1.25 1.25

Montevideo Council Building — A1128

**2004, Oct. 22** **Litho.** ***Perf. 12***
**2088** A1128 16p multi 1.25 1.25

Tomás Toribio House — A1129

**2004, Oct. 22**
**2089** A1129 16p multi 1.25 1.25

America Issue - Environmental Protection — A1130

Dirty and clean: 16p, Water. 37p, Birds.

**2004, Oct. 26**
**2090-2091** A1130 Set of 2 4.00 4.00

Armored Infantry Batallion No. 13, Cent. — A1131

**2004, Nov. 16**
**2092** A1131 16p multi 1.25 1.25

Corner Store, 18th Cent. A1132

**2004, Nov. 22**
**2093** A1132 16p multi 1.25 1.25

PriceWaterhouseCoopers in Uruguay, 85th Anniv. — A1133

**2004, Dec. 7**
**2094** A1133 16p multi 1.25 1.25

Review of Court Clerks, Cent. — A1134

**2004, Dec. 8**
**2095** A1134 16p multi 1.25 1.25

Christmas A1135

**2004, Dec. 14**
**2096** A1135 16p multi 1.25 1.25

Water Conservation A1136

**2004, Dec. 21**
**2097** A1136 37p multi 3.00 3.00

Souvenir Sheet

Punta del Este — A1137

**2004, Dec. 27**
**2098** A1137 16p multi 1.25 1.25

1912 Orenstein & Kopell Locomotive — A1138

***Serpentine Die Cut 11¼***
**2004, Dec. 28**
**Self-Adhesive**
**2099** A1138 30p multi 2.75 2.75

Rotary International, Cent. — A1139

**2005, Feb. 23 Litho. *Perf. 12***
**2100** A1139 37p multi 4.50 4.50

Bridges — A1140

No. 2101: a, Chuy del Tacuari Bridge. b, Barra Bridge, Maldonado. c, Mauá Bridge Yaguarón River. d, Castells Bridge, Víboras. Illustration reduced.

**2005, Mar. 18**
**2101** A1140 16p Block of 4, #a-d 6.75 6.75

Ninth Meeting of Latin American Energy Regulators — A1141

**2005, Apr. 5**
**2102** A1141 16p multi 1.25 1.25

"Liberating Dragoons" Ninth Mechanized Cavalry Regiment, Cent. — A1142

**2005, Apr. 11**
**2103** A1142 16p multi 1.25 1.25

Armenian Genocide, 90th Anniv. — A1143

**2005, Apr. 25**
**2104** A1143 16p multi 1.25 1.25

Fingerprint Analysis in Uruguay, Cent. — A1144

**2005, Apr. 26**
**2105** A1144 16p multi 1.25 1.25

No. 1446 Surcharged

**Wmk. 332**
**2005, May 27 Litho. *Perf. 12½***
**2106** A639 2p on 50c #1446 .25 .25

Fountains A1145

Designs: No. 2107, 10p, Constitution Plaza Fountain. No. 2108, 10p, Botanical Garden Fountain. No. 2109, 10p, Athlete's Fountain, Rodó Park. 37p, Cordier Fountain, Prado, horiz.

**2005, June 8 Litho. *Perf. 12***
**2107-2110** A1145 Set of 4 5.75 5.75

Catholic Circle, 120th Anniv. A1146

**2005, June 9**
**2111** A1146 16p multi 1.40 1.40

SOS Children's Villages, 45th Anniv. A1147

**2005, June 23**
**2112** A1147 16p multi 1.40 1.40

St. John the Baptist College, 75th Anniv. A1148

**2005, June 24**
**2113** A1148 16p multi 1.40 1.40

Souvenir Sheet

Death of Pope John Paul II and Election of Pope Benedict XVI — A1149

No. 2114: a, Cross and statue of Pope John Paul II, Montevideo. b, Pope Benedict XVI.

***Perf. 12x11¾***
**2005, July 15 Litho. Unwmk.**
**2114** A1149 10p Sheet of 2, #a-b 1.75 1.75

Medical Association Assistance Center, 70th Anniv. — A1150

**2005 *Perf. 12***
**2115** A1150 16p multi 1.40 1.40

**Inscribed "Correos Uruguay" at Right**
***Perf. 12¾x12½***
**2116** A1150 16p multi 1.40 1.40

Issued: No. 2115, 7/19; No. 2116, 8/4.

Seminary College, 125th Anniv. A1151

Designs: No. 2117, 16p, St. Ignatius of Loyola, college building. No. 2118, 16p, College building.

**2005, July 29 *Perf. 12***
**2117-2118** A1151 Set of 2 2.75 2.75

General Liber Seregni (1916-2004) — A1152

No. 2119 — Inscriptions: a, Vocacion. b, Comienzo. c, Liberacion. d, Reconocimiento. Illustration reduced.

**2005**
**2119** A1152 16p Block of 4, #a-d 5.50 5.50
*e.* Booklet pane, #2119 5.25 —
Complete booklet, #2119e 7.00

Issued: No. 2119, 8/1; No. 2119e, 10/11.

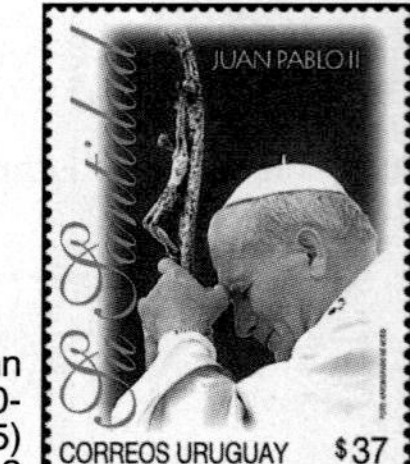

Pope John Paul II (1920-2005) A1153

**2005, Aug. 11 *Perf. 13½x13¾***
**2120** A1153 37p multi 3.25 3.25

Europa Stamps, 50th Anniv. A1154

Designs: 16p, Landscape, by C. De Arzadun, Spain #1263. 37p, The Emus, by De Arzadun, Spain, #1126, vert.

***Perf. 13¾x13½, 13½x13¾***
**2005, Aug. 11 Litho.**
**2121-2122** A1154 Set of 2 4.50 4.50

Urutem 2005 Philatelic Exhibition A1155

**2005, Aug. 15 Litho. *Perf. 12***
**2123** A1155 16p multi 1.40 1.40

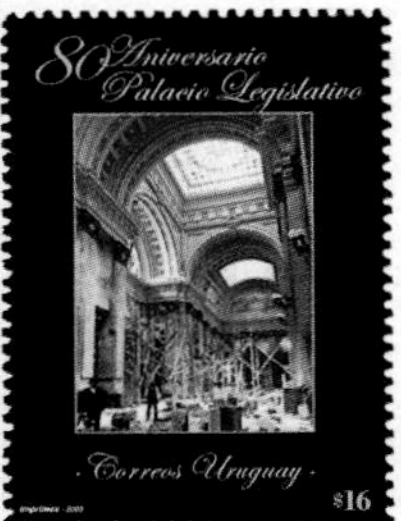


Legislative Palace, 80th Anniv. A1156

**2005, Aug. 24 Litho. *Perf. 12***
**2124** A1156 16p multi 1.40 1.40

Estadio Centenario, 75th Anniv. — A1157

Children's art: No. 2125, $16, Stadium, by Jonatan Belón. No. 2126, 16p, "75" made with flag and soccer field, by Sofia Arca.

**2005, Aug. 30**
**2125-2126** A1157 Set of 2 2.75 2.75

Carlos Solé, Soccer Broadcaster — A1158

**2005, Sept. 20**
**2127** A1158 16p multi 1.40 1.40

World Cup Soccer Championships, 75th Anniv. — A1159

Designs: No. 2128, 16p, Parade of athletes. No. 2129, 16p, Handshake before match. No. 2130, 16p, Awarding of World Cup. 37p, Flags of Germany and Uruguay, emblem of 2006 World Cup Soccer Championships, Germany.

**2005, Oct. 3**
**2128-2131** A1159 Set of 4 7.25 7.25

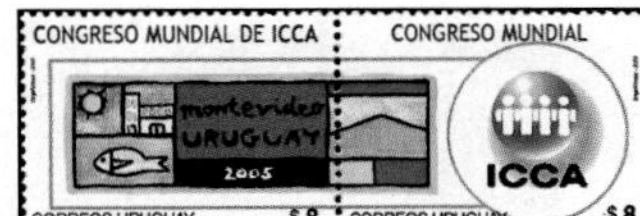


44th Congress of Intl. Congress and Convention Association, Montevideo — A1160

No. 2132: a, Fish sun and buildings. b, Association emblem.
Illustration reduced.

**2005, Nov. 4 Litho. *Perf. 12***
**2132** A1160 8p Horiz. pair, #a-b 1.40 1.40

Uruguay River Fish — A1161

No. 2133: a, Rhamdia sapo. b, Odontesthes bonariensis. c, Hoplias malabaricus. d, Pygocentrus nattereri.
Illustration reduced.

**2005, Nov. 22**
**2133** A1161 16p Block of 4, #a-d 5.50 5.50

El Escolar Magazine, 50th Anniv. — A1162

**2005, Nov. 23**
**2134** A1162 16p multi 1.40 1.40

Customhouse Brokers Association, 70th Anniv. — A1163

**2005, Nov. 25**
**2135** A1163 16p multi 1.40 1.40

Detail From Mural, *Oficios,* by Julio Alpuy — A1164

**2005, Dec. 1**
**2136** A1164 16p multi 1.40 1.40

Writers — A1165

Designs: 16p, Juan Zorilla de San Martin (1855-1931). 37p, Constancio C. Vigil (1876-1954).

**2005, Dec. 9**
**2137-2138** A1165 Set of 2 4.50 4.50

Commercial and Industrial Center of Salto, Cent. — A1166

**2005, Dec. 12**
**2139** A1166 16p multi 1.40 1.40

Central Español Soccer Team, Cent. A1167

**2005, Dec. 12**
**2140** A1167 16p multi 1.40 1.40

Christmas — A1168

**2005, Dec. 12**
**2141** A1168 16p multi 1.40 1.40

Montevideo Atheneum, 137th Anniv. — A1169

**2005, Dec. 14 Litho.**
**2142** A1169 16p multi 1.40 1.40

1924 Paris Olympics, 80th Anniv. (in 2004) A1170

Designs: No. 2143, 16p, Andrés Mazali, soccer gold medalist. No. 2144, 16p, Juan Pedro Cea, soccer gold medalist. No. 2145, 16p, Alfredo Ghierra, soccer gold medalist. 37p, Urn showing soccer players, vert.

**2005, Dec. 20 *Perf. 12***
**2143-2146** A1170 Set of 4 7.25 7.25

America Issue, Fight Against Poverty — A1171

Designs: 16p, Children, teacher and school. 37p, Men with shovel.

**2005, Dec. 22**
**2147-2148** A1171 Set of 2 4.50 4.50

Capitán Miranda, 75th Anniv. — A1172

No. 2149: a, Capitán Miranda in 1930. b, Capitán Miranda in 2005. c, Capt. Francisco P. Miranda (1869-1925). d, Crests of ships Capitán Miranda, Cádiz, and Montevideo.
Illustration reduced.

**2005, Dec. 28**
**2149** A1172 16p Block of 4, #a-d 5.50 5.50

No. 1492 Surcharged in Brown

**2005? Photo. Wmk. 332 *Perf. 12½***
**2150** A654 1p on 1.20p #1492 .25 .25

Obliterator on No. 2150 covers the "20" of original denomination. Compare with Nos. 2055 and 2011A.

Maldonado, 250th Anniv. — A1173

Designs: No. 2151, 16p, San Fernando Cathedral. No. 2152, 16p, Dragoon Quarters.

**2006, Feb. 22 Litho. *Perf. 12***
**2151-2152** A1173 Set of 2 2.75 2.75

Alfredo Zitarrosa (1936-89), Singer — A1174

Zitarrosa and: No. 2153, 16p, Guitar, violin. No. 2154, 16p, Guitar, violin, vert.

**2006, Mar. 10**
**2153-2154** A1174 Set of 2 2.75 2.75

Solís Theater, 150th Anniv. — A1175

**2006, Mar. 28**
**2155** A1175 16p multi 1.40 1.40

Diario Español Newspaper, Cent. — A1176

**2006, May 15**

**2156** A1176 16p multi 1.40 1.40

Public Enterprise Day — A1177

**2006, May 19**

**2157** A1177 16p black 1.40 1.40

Assassinated Politicians — A1178

Designs: No. 2158, 16p, Héctor Gutiérrez Ruiz (1934-76). No. 2159, 16p, Zelmar Michelini (1924-76). No. 2160, 16p, Michelini and Gutiérrez Ruiz.

**2006, June 1**

**2158-2160** A1178 Set of 3 4.00 4.00

SODRE Symphonic Orchestra, 75th Anniv. — A1179

**2006, June 20**

**2161** A1179 16p black 1.40 1.40

Masons in Uruguay, 150th Anniv. — A1180

**2006, Aug. 15**

**2162** A1180 16p multi 1.40 1.40

Horse Breeds — A1181

No. 2163: a, Appaloosa. b, Percheron. c, Belgian Heavy Draft. d, Criollo.

Illustration reduced.

**2006, Aug. 18**

**2163** A1181 16p Block of 4, #a-d 5.50 5.50

First Uruguayan Postage Stamps, 150th Anniv. — A1182

**2006, Sept. 29**

**2164** A1182 16p multi 1.40 1.40

Eladio Dieste (1917-2000), Architect — A1183

**2006, Oct. 3**

**2165** A1183 16p multi 1.40 1.40

Syndical Unification Congress, 40th Anniv. — A1184

No. 2166: a, Marchers with banner. b, Marchers with flag.

Illustration reduced.

**2006, Oct. 3**

**2166** A1184 16p Horiz. pair, #a-b 2.75 2.75



Diplomatic Relations Between Uruguay and the Sovereign Military Order of Malta, 40th Anniv. A1185

**2006, Oct. 4**

**2167** A1185 16p multi 1.40 1.40

Paysandú, 250th Anniv. — A1186

**2006, Oct. 12**

**2168** A1186 16p multi 1.40 1.40

Dr. Washington Beltrán (1914-2003), Politician A1187

**2006, Oct. 25**

**2169** A1187 16p multi 1.40 1.40

16th Ibero-American Summit, Montevideo — A1188

**2006, Nov. 1** Litho. *Perf. 12*

**2170** A1188 37p multi 3.25 3.25

Salto, 250th Anniv. A1189

**2006, Nov. 7** Litho. *Perf. 12*

**2171** A1189 16p multi 1.40 1.40

Channel 10, 50th Anniv. — A1190

**2006, Nov. 8** Litho. *Perf. 12*

**2172** A1190 16p multi 1.40 1.40

America Issue, Energy Conservation — A1191

No. 2173: a, 16p, Screw-in fluorescent light bulbs. b, 37p, Solar panels.

Illustration reduced.

**2006, Nov. 17** Litho. *Perf. 12*

**2173** A1191 Horiz. pair, #a-b 4.50 4.50

Sports A1192

Designs: No. 2174, 16p, Indoor soccer. No. 2175, 16p, Handball. No. 2176, 16p, Rugby. No. 2177, 16p, Tennis.

**2006, Nov. 30**

**2174-2177** A1192 Set of 4 5.25 5.25

Christmas A1193

**2006, Dec. 7**

**2178** A1193 37p multi 3.00 3.00

Musical Instruments A1194

Designs: 15p, Guitar. 37p, Drum, horiz.

**2006, Dec. 11**

**2179-2180** A1194 Set of 2 4.25 4.25

Ocean Liners and Ports — A1195

No. 2181: a, Queen Mary 2, Montevideo. b, Costa Fortuna, Montevideo. c, Zuiderman, Montevideo. d, Star Princess, Punta del Este.

Illustration reduced.

**2006, Dec. 18**

**2181** A1195 37p Block of 4, #a-d 12.50 12.50

Uruguayan Lottery, 150th Anniv. — A1196

**2006, Dec. 22** Litho. *Perf. 12*

**2182** A1196 15p multi 1.25 1.25

Optimist Class Yacht World Championships — A1197

**2006, Dec. 28** Litho. *Perf. 12*

**2183** A1197 37p multi 3.00 3.00

Uruguay Post Emblem A1198

***Serpentine Die Cut 11¼***

**2006, Dec. 29 Litho.**

**Self-Adhesive**

| | | | | |
|---|---|---|---|---|
| **2184** | A1198 | 15p multi | 1.25 | 1.25 |

No. 1492 Surcharged in Golden Brown

No. 1454 Surcharged in Black and Silver

**Methods, Perfs, and Watermarks As Before**

**2007, Jan. 24**

| | | | | |
|---|---|---|---|---|
| **2185** | A654 | 1p on 1.20p #1492 | .20 | .20 |
| **2186** | A639 | 2p on 1.80p #1454 | .20 | .20 |

Compare No. 2185 with Nos. 2011A, 2055 and 2150.

Punta del Este, Cent. — A1199

**Unwmk.**

**2007, Jan. 26 Litho. *Perf. 12***

| | | | | |
|---|---|---|---|---|
| **2187** | A1199 | 37p multi | 3.25 | 3.25 |

Julia Arévalo (1898-1985), Politician — A1201

**2007, Mar. 8 Litho. *Perf. 12***

| | | | | |
|---|---|---|---|---|
| **2189** | A1201 | 15p multi | 1.25 | 1.25 |

## SEMI-POSTAL STAMPS

Indigent Old Man — SP1

**Unwmk.**

**1930, Nov. 13 Engr. *Perf. 12***

| | | | | |
|---|---|---|---|---|
| **B1** | SP1 | 1c + 1c dark violet | .20 | .20 |
| **B2** | SP1 | 2c + 2c deep green | .20 | .20 |
| **B3** | SP1 | 5c + 5c red | .30 | .30 |
| **B4** | SP1 | 8c + 8c gray violet | .30 | .30 |
| | | *Nos. B1-B4 (4)* | 1.00 | 1.00 |

The surtax on these stamps was for a fund to assist the aged.

For surcharge see No. 419.

**Catalogue values for unused stamps in this section, from this point to the end of the section, are for Never Hinged items.**

Dam, Child and Rising Sun — SP2

**Wmk. 327**

**1959, Sept. 29 Litho. *Perf. 11½***

| | | | | |
|---|---|---|---|---|
| **B5** | SP2 | 5c + 10c green & org | .20 | .20 |
| **B6** | SP2 | 10c + 10c dk bl & org | .20 | .20 |
| **B7** | SP2 | 1p + 10c purple & org | .40 | .40 |
| | | *Nos. B5-B7,CB1-CB2 (5)* | 1.35 | 1.35 |

National recovery. For surcharges see Nos. 727, Q100.

Souvenir Sheet

Taipei '96, Intl. Philatelic Exhibition — SP3

Illustration reduced.

**Unwmk.**

**1996, Oct. 21 Litho. *Perf. 12***

| | | | | |
|---|---|---|---|---|
| **B8** | SP3 | 7p +3p multi | 6.00 | 6.00 |

Gen. Artigas Central Railway Station, Montevideo, Cent. — SP4

a, Baldwin, 1889. b, Hudswell Clarke, 1895. c, Luis Andreoni, engineer. d, Hawthorn Leslie, 1914. e, General Electric, 1954.

***Perf. 12½***

**1997, July 15 Litho. Unwmk.**

| | | | | |
|---|---|---|---|---|
| **B9** | SP4 | 4p +1p, Strip of 5, #a.-e. | 10.00 | 10.00 |

Diana, Princess of Wales (1961-97) — SP5

Designs: No. B10, In protective clothing. No. B11, In blue blouse. No. B12, In white.

**1998, Jan. 15 Litho. *Perf. 12½***

| | | | | |
|---|---|---|---|---|
| **B10** | SP5 | 2p +1p multi | 2.00 | 2.00 |
| **B11** | SP5 | 2p +1p multi | 2.00 | 2.00 |

**Souvenir Sheet**

***Perf. 12***

| | | | | |
|---|---|---|---|---|
| **B12** | SP5 | 12p +3p multi | 10.00 | 10.00 |

No. B12 contains one 35x50mm stamp.

## AIR POST STAMPS

No. 91 Overprinted in Dark Blue, Red or Green

**1921-22 Unwmk. *Perf. 14***

| | | | | |
|---|---|---|---|---|
| **C1** | A38 | 25c bister brn (Bl) | 15.00 | 12.00 |
| *a.* | | Black overprint | *625.00* | *625.00* |
| **C2** | A38 | 25c bister brn (R) | 6.50 | 5.00 |
| *a.* | | Inverted overprint | *77.50* | *77.50* |
| **C3** | A38 | 25c bister brn (G) ('22) | 6.50 | 5.00 |
| | | *Nos. C1-C3 (3)* | 28.00 | 22.00 |

This overprint also exists in light yellow green.

No. C1a was not issued. Some authorities consider it an overprint color trial.

AP2

**Wmk. 188**

**1924, Jan. 2 Litho. *Perf. 11½***

| | | | | |
|---|---|---|---|---|
| **C4** | AP2 | 6c dark blue | 2.50 | 2.50 |
| **C5** | AP2 | 10c scarlet | 3.50 | 3.00 |
| **C6** | AP2 | 20c deep green | 5.00 | 5.00 |
| | | *Nos. C4-C6 (3)* | 11.00 | 10.50 |

Heron — AP3

**1925, Aug. 24 *Perf. 12½***

**Inscribed "MONTEVIDEO"**

| | | | | |
|---|---|---|---|---|
| **C7** | AP3 | 14c blue & blk | 30.00 | 14.00 |

**Inscribed "FLORIDA"**

| | | | | |
|---|---|---|---|---|
| **C8** | AP3 | 14c blue & blk | 30.00 | 14.00 |

These stamps were used only on Aug. 25, 1925, the cent. of the Assembly of Florida, on letters intended to be carried by airplane between Montevideo and Florida, a town 60 miles north. The stamps were not delivered to the public but were affixed to the letters and canceled by post office clerks. Later uncanceled copies came on the market.

One authority believes Nos. C7-C8 served as registration stamps on these two attempted special flights.

Gaucho Cavalryman at Rincón — AP4

**1925, Sept. 24 *Perf. 11***

| | | | |
|---|---|---|---|
| **C9** | AP4 | 45c blue green | 15.00 |

Centenary of Battle of Rincon. Used only on Sept. 24. No. C9 was affixed and canceled by post office clerks.

Albatross — AP5

**1926, Mar. 3 Wmk. 188 *Imperf.***

| | | | | |
|---|---|---|---|---|
| **C10** | AP5 | 6c dark blue | 1.50 | 1.50 |
| **C11** | AP5 | 10c vermilion | 2.00 | 2.00 |
| **C12** | AP5 | 20c blue green | 2.50 | 2.50 |
| **C13** | AP5 | 25c violet | 4.00 | 4.00 |
| | | *Nos. C10-C13 (4)* | 10.00 | 10.00 |

Excellent counterfeits exist.

**1928, June 25 *Perf. 11***

| | | | | |
|---|---|---|---|---|
| **C14** | AP5 | 10c green | 2.50 | 2.00 |
| **C15** | AP5 | 20c orange | 4.00 | 3.00 |
| **C16** | AP5 | 30c indigo | 4.00 | 3.00 |
| **C17** | AP5 | 38c green | 7.00 | 6.00 |
| **C18** | AP5 | 40c yellow | 8.00 | 6.00 |
| **C19** | AP5 | 50c violet | 9.00 | 7.00 |
| **C20** | AP5 | 76c orange | 17.00 | 15.00 |
| **C21** | AP5 | 1p red | 20.00 | 18.00 |
| **C22** | AP5 | 1.14p indigo | 45.00 | 40.00 |
| **C23** | AP5 | 1.52p yellow | 70.00 | 65.00 |
| **C24** | AP5 | 1.90p violet | 90.00 | 75.00 |
| **C25** | AP5 | 3.80p red | 200.00 | 150.00 |
| | | *Nos. C14-C25 (12)* | 476.50 | 390.00 |

Counterfeits of No. C25 exist.

**1929, Aug. 23 Unwmk.**

| | | | | |
|---|---|---|---|---|
| **C26** | AP5 | 4c olive brown | 4.00 | 3.00 |

The design was redrawn for Nos. C14-C26. The numerals are narrower, "CENTS" is 1mm high instead of 2½mm and imprint letters touch the bottom frame line.

Pegasus AP6

**1929-43 Engr. *Perf. 12½***

**Size: 34x23mm**

| | | | | |
|---|---|---|---|---|
| **C27** | AP6 | 1c red lilac ('30) | .40 | .40 |
| **C28** | AP6 | 1c dk blue ('32) | .40 | .40 |
| **C29** | AP6 | 2c yellow ('30) | .40 | .40 |
| **C30** | AP6 | 2c olive grn ('32) | .40 | .40 |
| **C31** | AP6 | 4c Prus bl ('30) | .70 | .70 |
| **C32** | AP6 | 4c car rose ('32) | .70 | .70 |
| **C33** | AP6 | 6c dull vio ('30) | .70 | .70 |
| **C34** | AP6 | 6c red brn ('32) | .70 | .70 |
| **C35** | AP6 | 8c red orange | 3.00 | 2.50 |
| **C36** | AP6 | 8c gray ('30) | 4.00 | 3.00 |
| **C36A** | AP6 | 8c brt grn ('43) | 2.50 | 2.00 |
| **C37** | AP6 | 16c indigo | .50 | .50 |
| **C38** | AP6 | 16c rose ('30) | 3.25 | 3.00 |
| **C39** | AP6 | 24c claret | 4.25 | 3.50 |
| **C40** | AP6 | 24c brt vio ('30) | 3.00 | 2.50 |
| **C41** | AP6 | 30c bister | 3.00 | 2.75 |
| **C42** | AP6 | 30c dk grn ('30) | 2.00 | 1.50 |
| **C43** | AP6 | 40c dk brown | 5.50 | 5.00 |
| **C44** | AP6 | 40c yel org ('30) | 6.00 | 5.00 |
| **C45** | AP6 | 60c blue green | 5.00 | 3.25 |
| **C46** | AP6 | 60c emer ('30) | 8.50 | 7.00 |
| **C47** | AP6 | 60c dp org ('31) | 3.00 | 2.00 |
| **C48** | AP6 | 80c dk ultra | 8.00 | 7.00 |
| **C49** | AP6 | 80c green ('30) | 15.00 | 12.00 |
| **C50** | AP6 | 90c light blue | 8.00 | 6.00 |
| **C51** | AP6 | 90c dk olive grn ('30) | 15.00 | 12.00 |
| **C52** | AP6 | 1p car rose ('30) | 10.00 | 7.50 |
| **C53** | AP6 | 1.20p olive grn | 22.00 | 20.00 |
| **C54** | AP6 | 1.20p dp car ('30) | 30.00 | 26.00 |
| **C55** | AP6 | 1.50p red brown | 25.00 | 20.00 |
| **C56** | AP6 | 1.50p blk brn ('30) | 20.00 | 15.00 |
| **C57** | AP6 | 3p deep red | 40.00 | 35.00 |
| **C58** | AP6 | 3p ultra ('30) | 30.00 | 25.00 |
| **C59** | AP6 | 4.50p black | 75.00 | 55.00 |
| **C60** | AP6 | 4.50p violet ('30) | 45.00 | 35.00 |
| **C60A** | AP6 | 10p dp ultra ('43) | 17.00 | 12.00 |
| | | *Nos. C27-C60A (36)* | 417.90 | 335.40 |

See Nos. C63-C82. For surcharges see Nos. C106-C112, C114.

Nos. 450, 452 Overprinted in Red

**1934, Jan. 1** *Perf. 11½*
**C61** A130 17c ver, gray & vio 20.00 15.00
*a.* Sheet of 6 140.00
*b.* Gray omitted 150.00
*c.* Double overprint 150.00
**C62** A130 36c red, blk & yel 20.00 15.00
*a.* Sheet of 6 140.00

7th Pan-American Conference, Montevideo.

Pegasus Type of 1929

**1935 Engr. *Perf. 12½***
**Size: 31½x21mm**
**C63** AP6 15c dull yellow 2.50 2.00
**C64** AP6 22c brick red 1.50 1.40
**C65** AP6 30c brown violet 2.50 2.00
**C66** AP6 37c gray lilac 1.40 1.00
**C67** AP6 40c rose lake 2.00 1.40
**C68** AP6 47c rose 4.00 3.50
**C69** AP6 50c Prus blue 1.40 .80
**C70** AP6 52c dp ultra 4.00 3.50
**C71** AP6 57c grnsh blue 2.00 1.75
**C72** AP6 62c olive green 1.75 .80
**C73** AP6 87c gray green 5.00 4.00
**C74** AP6 1p olive 3.50 2.25
**C75** AP6 1.12p brown red 3.50 2.25
**C76** AP6 1.20p bister brn 15.00 12.00
**C77** AP6 1.27p red brown 15.00 13.00
**C78** AP6 1.62p rose 10.00 9.00
**C79** AP6 2p brown rose 17.00 14.00
**C80** AP6 2.12p dk slate grn 17.00 14.00
**C81** AP6 3p dull blue 15.00 13.00
**C82** AP6 5p orange 60.00 60.00
*Nos. C63-C82 (20)* 184.05 161.65

Counterfeits exist.

Power Dam on Black River — AP7

Imprint: "Imp. Nacional" at center

**1937-41 Litho.**
**C83** AP7 20c lt green ('38) 5.50 4.00
**C84** AP7 35c red brown 8.00 6.50
**C85** AP7 62c blue grn ('38) .80 .30
**C86** AP7 68c yel org ('38) 2.00 1.50
**C86A** AP7 68c pale vio brn ('41) 1.75 .70
**C87** AP7 75c violet 7.50 5.00
**C88** AP7 1p dp pink ('38) 2.50 1.75
**C89** AP7 1.38p rose ('38) 25.00 20.00
**C90** AP7 3p dk blue ('40) 17.00 12.00
*Nos. C83-C90 (9)* 70.05 51.75

**Imprint at left**
**C91** AP7 8c pale green ('39) .60 .50
**C92** AP7 20c lt green ('38) 2.00 1.50

For surcharge and overprint see Nos. 545, C120.

Plane over Sculptured Oxcart — AP8

**1939-44** *Perf. 12½*
**C93** AP8 20c slate .50 .40
**C94** AP8 20c lt violet ('43) .80 .80
**C95** AP8 20c blue ('44) .60 .40
**C96** AP8 35c red 1.00 .80
**C97** AP8 50c brown org 1.00 .30
**C98** AP8 75c deep pink 1.10 .20
**C99** AP8 1p dp blue ('40) 3.25 .60
**C100** AP8 1.38p brt vio 5.50 2.25
**C101** AP8 1.38p yel org ('44) 5.00 4.00
**C102** AP8 2p blue 8.00 1.40
*a.* Perf. 11 7.00 1.10
**C103** AP8 5p rose lilac 10.00 2.25
**C104** AP8 5p bl grn ('44) 15.00 7.00
**C105** AP8 10p rose ('40) 100.00 65.00
*Nos. C93-C105 (13)* 151.75 85.40

Counterfeits exist. They are perf 13, rather than 12½.
For surcharges see Nos. C116-C119.

Nos. C68, C71, C75, C73, C77-C78, C80 Surcharged in Red or Black

**1944, Nov. 22**
**C106** AP6 40c on 47c 1.00 1.00
**C107** AP6 40c on 57c (R) 1.00 1.00
**C108** AP6 74c on 1.12p 1.00 1.00
**C109** AP6 79c on 87c 2.00 2.00
**C110** AP6 79c on 1.27p 3.00 3.00
**C111** AP6 1.20p on 1.62p 2.00 2.00
**C112** AP6 1.43p on 2.12p (R) 2.00 2.00
*Nos. C106-C112 (7)* 12.00 12.00

**Catalogue values for unused stamps in this section, from this point to the end of the section, are for Never Hinged items.**

Legislature Building AP9

**Unwmk.**
**1945, May 11 Engr. *Perf. 11***
**C113** AP9 2p ultra 4.00 2.00

Type of 1929, Surcharged in Violet

**1945, Aug. 14** *Perf. 12½*
**C114** AP6 44c on 75c brown 1.00 .50

Allied Nations' victory in Europe.

"La Eolo" AP10

**1945, Oct. 31** *Perf. 11*
**C115** AP10 8c green 2.00 1.00

Nos. C97 and C101 Surcharged in Violet, Black or Blue

**1945-46** *Perf. 12½*
**C116** AP8 14c on 50c (V) ('46) 1.00 .50
*a.* Inverted surcharge 37.50
**C117** AP8 23c on 1.38p 1.00 .50
*a.* Inverted surcharge 75.00
**C118** AP8 23c on 50c 1.00 .50
*a.* Inverted surcharge 75.00
**C119** AP8 1p on 1.38p (Bl) 1.00 .50
*a.* Inverted surcharge 75.00
*Nos. C116-C119 (4)* 4.00 2.00

Victory of the Allied Nations in WWII.

No. C85 Overprinted in Black

**1946, Jan. 9**
**C120** AP7 62c blue green 2.00 1.00

Issued to commemorate the inauguration of the Black River Power Dam.

AP11

Black Overprint

**1946-49 Litho.**
**C121** AP11 8c car rose .20 .20
*a.* Inverted overprint
**C122** AP11 50c brown .40 .20
*a.* Double overprint 25.00
**C123** AP11 1p lt bl .65 .25
**C124** AP11 2p ol ('49) 3.50 2.00
**C125** AP11 3p lil rose 4.50 3.00
**C126** AP11 5p rose car 8.50 6.00
*Nos. C121-C126 (6)* 17.75 11.65

Four-Motored Plane — AP12

National Airport AP13

**1947-49** *Perf. 11½, 12½*
**C129** AP12 3c org brn ('49) .20 .20
**C130** AP12 8c car rose ('49) .20 .20
**C131** AP12 14c ultra .20 .20
**C132** AP12 23c emerald .20 .20
**C133** AP13 1p car & brn ('49) 1.25 .40
**C134** AP13 3p ultra & brn ('49) 2.75 1.60
**C135** AP13 5p grn & brn ('49) 8.00 4.00
**C136** AP13 10p lil rose & brn 12.00 6.00
*Nos. C129-C136 (8)* 24.80 12.80

Counterfeits exist, perf 11¼. Design size of genuine copies is 34½x24mm, while forgeries are 33½x23½mm.
See Nos. C145-C164. For surcharges see Nos. C206, Q94.

AP14

School of Architecture, University of Uruguay AP15

Black Overprint

**1948, June 9** *Perf. 12½*
**C137** AP14 12c blue .20 .20
**C138** AP14 24c Prus grn .30 .20
**C139** AP14 36c slate blue .45 .30
*Nos. C137-C139 (3)* .95 .70

**1949, Dec. 7**

Designs: 27c, Medical School. 31c, Engineering School. 36c, University.

**C141** AP15 15c carmine .20 .20
**C142** AP15 27c chocolate .20 .20
**C143** AP15 31c dp ultra .40 .20
**C144** AP15 36c dull green .60 .30
*Nos. C141-C144 (4)* 1.40 .90

Founding of the University of Uruguay, cent.

Plane Type of 1947-49

**1952-59 Unwmk. *Perf. 11, 12½***
**C145** AP12 10c blk ('54) .20 .20
**C146** AP12 10c lt red ('58) .20 .20
*a.* Imperf., pair 30.00
**C147** AP12 15c org brn .20 .20
*a.* Vert. pair, imperf btwn. 42.50
**C148** AP12 20c lil rose ('54) .25 .20
**C149** AP12 21c purple .30 .20
**C150** AP12 27c yel grn ('57) .30 .20
**C151** AP12 31c chocolate .45 .20
**C152** AP12 36c ultra .30 .20
**C153** AP12 36c blk ('58) .30 .20
**C154** AP12 50c lt bl ('57) .60 .50
**C155** AP12 50c bl blk ('58) .50 .20
**C156** AP12 62c dl sl bl ('53) .70 .50
**C157** AP12 65c rose ('53) .70 .50
**C158** AP12 84c org ('59) 1.00 .70
**C159** AP12 1.08p vio brn 1.60 .80
**C160** AP12 2p Prus bl 2.50 1.40
**C161** AP12 3p red org 3.00 1.75
**C162** AP12 5p dk gray grn 6.50 4.00
**C163** AP12 5p gray ('57) 3.50 2.50
**C164** AP12 10p dp grn ('55) 17.00 12.50
*Nos. C145-C164 (20)* 40.10 27.15

Planes and Show Emblem AP16

**Unwmk.**
**1956, Jan. 5 Litho. *Perf. 11***
**C166** AP16 20c ultra .35 .35
**C167** AP16 31c olive grn .45 .25
**C168** AP16 36c car rose .70 .30
*Nos. C166-C168 (3)* 1.50 .90

First Exposition of National Products.

Type of Regular Issue and

José Batlle y Ordonez AP17

Designs: 10c, Full-face portrait without hand. 36c, Portrait facing right.

***Perf. 13½***
**1956, Dec. 15 Wmk. 90 Photo.**
**C169** A178 10c magenta .30 .20
**C170** A178 20c grnsh blk .30 .20
**C171** AP17 31c brown .30 .30
**C172** A178 36c bl grn .60 .40
*Nos. C169-C172 (4)* 1.50 1.10

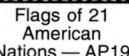

Stamp of 1856 and Stagecoach — AP18

**1956, Dec. 15 Litho.**
**C173** AP18 20c grn, bl & pale yel .45 .30
**C174** AP18 31c brn, bl & lt bl .55 .30
**C175** AP18 36c dp claret & bl .65 .30
*Nos. C173-C175 (3)* 1.65 .90

1st postage stamps of Uruguay, cent.

Flags of 21 American Nations — AP19

Men and Torch of Freedom — AP20

***Perf. 11, 11½ (No. C177)***
**1958, June 19 Unwmk.**
**C176** AP19 23c blue & blk .30 .20
**C177** AP19 34c green & blk .45 .20
**C178** AP19 44c cerise & blk .45 .30
*Nos. C176-C178 (3)* 1.20 .70

Organization of American States, 10th anniv.

**1958, Dec. 10** *Perf. 11*
**C179** AP20 23c blk & blue .25 .20
**C180** AP20 34c blk & yel grn .35 .20
**C181** AP20 44c blk & org red .65 .35
*Nos. C179-C181 (3)* 1.25 .75

10th anniversary of the signing of the Universal Declaration of Human Rights.

"Flight" from Monument to Fallen Aviators — AP21

**1959** **Litho.** *Perf. 11*
**Size: 22x37½mm**
**C182** AP21 3c bis brn & blk .25 .20
**C183** AP21 8c brt lil & blk .25 .20
**C184** AP21 38c black .25 .20
**C185** AP21 50c citron & blk .25 .20
**C186** AP21 60c vio & blk .25 .20
**C187** AP21 90c ol grn & blk .30 .25
**C188** AP21 1p blue & blk .40 .25
**C189** AP21 2p ocher & blk 1.40 .55
**C190** AP21 3p grn & blk 1.50 .95
**C191** AP21 5p vio brn & blk 2.00 1.50
**C192** AP21 10p dp rose car & blk 6.50 4.25
*Nos. C182-C192 (11)* 13.35 8.75

See Nos. C211-C222. For surcharge see No. Q97.

Alberto Santos-Dumont — AP22

**1959, Feb. 13** **Wmk. 327** *Perf. 11½*
**C193** AP22 31c multi .25 .20
**C194** AP22 36c multi .25 .20

Airplane flight of Alberto Santos-Dumont, Brazilian aeronaut, in 1906 in France.

Girl and Waves AP23

Designs: 38c, 60c, 1.05p, Compass and map of Punta del Este.

**1959, Mar. 6** *Perf. 11½*
**C195** AP23 10c ocher & lt bl .20 .20
**C196** AP23 38c grn & bis .20 .20
**C197** AP23 60c lilac & bister .30 .20
**C198** AP23 90c red org & grn .40 .25
**C199** AP23 1.05p blue & bister .60 .45
*Nos. C195-C199 (5)* 1.70 1.30

50th anniv. of Punta del Este, seaside resort.

Torch, YMCA Emblem and Chrismon AP24

**Wmk. 327**
**1959, Dec. 22** **Litho.** *Perf. 11½*
**C200** AP24 38c emer, blk & gray .30 .25
**C201** AP24 50c bl, blk & gray .35 .20
**C202** AP24 60c red, blk & gray .45 .40
*Nos. C200-C202 (3)* 1.10 .85

50th anniv. of the YMCA in Uruguay.

José Artigas and George Washington AP25

Refugees and WRY Emblem AP26

**1960, Mar. 2** *Perf. 11½x12*
**C203** AP25 38c red & blk .20 .20
**C204** AP25 50c brt bl & blk .25 .20
**C205** AP25 60c dp grn & blk .40 .20
*Nos. C203-C205 (3)* .85 .60

Pres. Eisenhower's visit to Uruguay, Feb. 1960.
No. C204 exists imperforate, but was not regularly issued in this form.

No. C150 Surcharged

**1960, Apr. 8** **Unwmk.** *Perf. 11*
**C206** AP12 20c on 27c yel grn .25 .20
*a.* Perf. 12½ .25 .20

**1960, June 6** **Wmk. 332**
**Size: 24x35mm**
**C207** AP26 60c brt lil rose & blk .35 .20

World Refugee Year, 7/1/59-6/30/60.

Type of Regular Issue, 1960
**Wmk. 332**
**1960, Nov. 4** **Litho.** *Perf. 12*
**C208** A186 38c bl & ol grn .20 .20
**C209** A186 50c bl & ver .20 .20
**C210** A186 60c bl & pur .30 .20
*Nos. C208-C210 (3)* .70 .60

Type of 1959 Redrawn with Silhouette of Airplane Added
**1960-61** **Litho.** *Perf. 12*
**C211** AP21 3c blk & pale vio .30 .20
**C212** AP21 20c blk & crimson .30 .20
**C213** AP21 38c blk & pale bl .30 .20
**C214** AP21 50c blk & buff .30 .20
**C215** AP21 60c blk & dp grn .40 .20
**C216** AP21 90c blk & rose .45 .20
**C217** AP21 1p blk & gray .60 .20
**C218** AP21 2p blk & yel grn .85 .20
**C219** AP21 3p blk & red lil 1.10 .25
**C220** AP21 5p blk & org ver 1.60 .50
**C221** AP21 10p blk & yel 3.00 1.00
**C222** AP21 20p blk & dk bl ('61) 5.75 2.25
*Nos. C211-C222 (12)* 14.95 5.60

Pres. Gronchi and Flag Colors AP27

**1961, Apr. 17** **Wmk. 332** *Perf. 12*
**C223** AP27 90c multi .25 .20
**C224** AP27 1.20p multi .30 .25
**C225** AP27 1.40p multi .35 .35
*Nos. C223-C225 (3)* .90 .80

Visit of President Giovanni Gronchi of Italy to Uruguay, April, 1961.

Carrasco National Airport AP28

**1961, May 16** **Wmk. 332** *Perf. 12*
**Building in Gray**
**C226** AP28 1p lt vio .25 .20
**C227** AP28 2p ol gray .45 .20
**C228** AP28 3p orange .75 .40
**C229** AP28 4p purple .90 .45
**C230** AP28 5p aqua 1.25 .60
**C231** AP28 10p lt ultra 2.40 1.00
**C232** AP28 20p maroon 3.75 2.00
*Nos. C226-C232 (7)* 9.75 4.85

Type of Regular "CIES" Issue, 1961
**1961, Aug. 3** **Litho.** **Wmk. 332**
**C233** A189 20c blk & org .30 .20
**C234** A189 45c blk & grn .30 .20
**C235** A189 50c blk & gray .30 .20
**C236** A189 90c blk & plum .30 .20
**C237** A189 1p blk & dp rose .40 .20
**C238** A189 1.40p blk & lt vio .50 .20
**C239** A189 2p blk & bister .55 .25
**C240** A189 3p blk & lt bl .85 .30
**C241** A189 4p blk & yellow 1.25 .55
**C242** A189 5p blk & blue 1.50 .85
**C243** A189 10p blk & yel grn 2.75 1.50
**C244** A189 20p blk & dp pink 5.75 2.75
*Nos. C233-C244 (12)* 14.75 7.40

Swiss Flag, Plow, Wheat Sheaf AP29

**1962, Aug. 1** **Wmk. 332** *Perf. 12*
**C245** AP29 90c car, org & blk .25 .20
**C246** AP29 1.40p car, bl & blk .35 .30

Cent. of the Swiss Settlement in Uruguay.

Red-crested Cardinal — AP30

Birds: 45c, White-capped tanager, horiz. 90c, Vermilion flycatcher. 1.20p, Great kiskadee, horiz. 1.40p, Fork-tailed flycatcher.

**1962, Dec. 5** **Litho.** *Perf. 12*
**C247** AP30 20c gray, blk & red .20 .20
**C248** AP30 45c multi .35 .20
**C249** AP30 90c crim rose, blk & lt brn .75 .20
**C250** AP30 1.20p lt bl, blk & yel .60 .20
**C251** AP30 1.40p blue & sepia 1.10 .25
*Nos. C247-C251 (5)* 3.00 1.05

No frame on #C248, thin frame on #C251. See #C258-C263. For surcharge see #C320.

Type of Regular UPAE Issue, 1963
**1963, May 31** **Wmk. 332** *Perf. 12*
**C252** A195 45c bluish grn & blk .20 .20
**C253** A195 90c magenta & blk .25 .20

Freedom from Hunger Type of Regular Issue
**1963, July 9** **Wmk. 332** *Perf. 12*
**C254** A196 90c red & yel .25 .25
**C255** A196 1.40p violet & yel .35 .35

"Alferez Campora" AP31

**1963, Aug. 16** **Litho.**
**C256** AP31 90c dk grn & org .30 .20
**C257** AP31 1.40p ultra & yel .50 .40

Voyage around the world by the Uruguayan sailing vessel "Alferez Campora," 1960-63.

Bird Type of 1962

Birds: 1p, Glossy cowbird (tordo). 2p, Yellow cardinal. 3p, Hooded siskin. 5p, Sayaca tanager. 10p, Blue and yellow tanager. 20p, Scarlet-headed marsh-bird. All horizontal.

**1963, Nov. 15** **Wmk. 332** *Perf. 12*
**C258** AP30 1p vio bl, blk & brn org .45 .20
**C259** AP30 2p lt brn, blk & yel 1.00 .25
**C260** AP30 3p yel, brn & blk 1.50 .40
**C261** AP30 5p emer, bl grn & blk 2.40 .50
**C262** AP30 10p multi 5.00 1.00
**C263** AP30 20p gray, org & blk 10.50 5.50
*Nos. C258-C263 (6)* 20.85 7.85

Frame on Nos. C260-C263.

Pres. Charles de Gaulle AP32

2.40p, Flags of France and Uruguay.

**1964, Oct. 9** **Litho.** *Perf. 12*
**C264** AP32 1.50p multi .35 .20
**C265** AP32 2.40p multi .65 .35

Charles de Gaulle, Pres. of France, Oct. 1964.

Submerged Statue of Ramses II — AP33

Design: 2p, Head of Ramses II.

**1964, Oct. 30** **Litho.** **Wmk. 332**
**C266** AP33 1.30p multi .30 .25
**C267** AP33 2p bis, red brn & brt bl .60 .45
*a.* Souv. sheet of 3, #713, C266-C267, imperf. 1.60 1.60

UNESCO world campaign to save historic monuments in Nubia.

National Flag AP34

**1965, Feb. 18** **Wmk. 332** *Perf. 12*
**C268** AP34 50p gray, dk bl & yel 6.50 4.00

Kennedy Type of Regular Issue
**1965, Mar. 5** **Wmk. 327** *Perf. 11½*
**C269** A202 1.50p gold, lil & blk .25 .25
**C270** A202 2.40p gold, brt bl & blk .35 .35

Issue of 1864, No. 23 — AP35

6c, 8c, 10c denominations of 1864 issue.

**Wmk. 332**
**1965, Mar. 19** **Litho.** *Perf. 12*
**C271** Sheet of 10 2.25 2.25
**"URUGUAY" at bottom**
*a.* AP35 1p blue & black .25 .25
*b.* AP35 1p brick red & black .25 .25
*c.* AP35 1p green & black .25 .25
*d.* AP35 1p ocher & black .25 .25
*e.* AP35 1p carmine & black .25 .25
**"URUGUAY" at top**
*f.* AP35 1p blue & black .25 .25

*g.* AP35 1p brick red & black .25 .25
*h.* AP35 1p green & black .25 .25
*i.* AP35 1p ocher & black .25 .25
*j.* AP35 1p carmine & black .25 .25

1st Rio de la Plata Stamp Show, sponsored jointly by the Argentine and Uruguayan philatelic associations, Montevideo, Mar. 19-28. No. C271 contains two horizontal rows of stamps and two rows of labels; Nos. C271a-C271e are in first row, Nos. C271f-C271j in second row. Adjacent labels in top and bottom rows.

For overprint see No. C298.

National Arms — AP36

Artigas Monument AP37

**1965, Apr. 30 Wmk. 332 *Perf. 12***
**C272** AP36 20p multi 1.75 1.00

Type of Regular Issue and AP37.

Designs: 1.50p, Artigas and wagontrain. 2.40p, Artigas quotation.

***Perf. 11½x12, 12x11½***
**1965, May 17 Litho. Wmk. 327**
**C273** AP37 1p multi .20 .20
**C274** A205 1.50p multi .30 .25
**C275** A205 2.40p multi .45 .35
*Nos. C273-C275 (3)* .95 .80

José Artigas (1764-1850), leader of the independence revolt against Spain.

Olympic Games Type of Regular Issue

Designs: 1p, Boxing. 1.50p, Running. 2p, Fencing. 2.40p, Sculling. 3p, Pistol shooting. 20p, Olympic rings.

**1965, Aug. 3 Litho. *Perf. 12x11½***
**C276** A206 1p red, gray & blk .20 .20
**C277** A206 1.50p emer, bl & blk .20 .20
**C278** A206 2p dk car, bl & blk .30 .25
**C279** A206 2.40p lt ultra, org & blk .45 .30
**C280** A206 3p lil, yel & blk .60 .35
**C281** A206 20p dk vio bl, pink & lt bl .95 .70
*Nos. C276-C281 (6)* 2.70 2.00

Souvenir Sheet

Designs: 5p, Stamp of 1924, No. 284. 10p, Stamp of 1928, No. 389.

**C282** Sheet of 2 1.75 1.75
*a.* 5p buff, blue & black .55 .55
*b.* 10p blue, black & rose red .80 .80

18th Olympic Games, Tokyo, 10/10-25/64.

ITU Emblem and Satellite AP38

**1966, Jan. 25 Wmk. 332 *Perf. 12***
**C283** AP38 1p bl, bluish blk & ver .25 .20

Cent. of the ITU (in 1965).

Winston Churchill — AP39

**1966, Apr. 29 Wmk. 332 *Perf. 12***
**C284** AP39 2p car, brn & gold .45 .20

Rio de Janeiro Type of Regular Issue

**1966, June 9 Wmk. 332 *Perf. 12***
**C285** A208 80c dp org & brn .25 .20

International Cooperation Year Emblem AP40

**1966, June 9 Litho.**
**C286** AP40 1p bluish grn & blk .25 .20

UN International Cooperation Year.

President Zalman Shazar of Israel AP41

**1966, June 21 Wmk. 327**
**C287** AP41 7p multi .45 .25

Visit of Pres. Zalman Shazar of Israel.

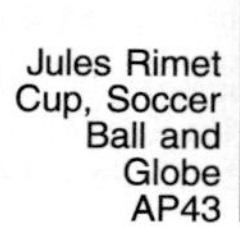

Crested Screamer — AP42

**1966, July 7 Wmk. 327 *Perf. 12***
**C288** AP42 100p bl, blk, red & gray 6.00 1.75

Jules Rimet Cup, Soccer Ball and Globe AP43

**1966, July 11 Litho.**
**C289** AP43 10p dk pur, org & lil .60 .25

World Cup Soccer Championship, Wembley, England, July 11-30.

Bulls AP44

**1966 Wmk. 327, 332 (10p)**
**C290** AP44 4p Hereford .20 .20
**C291** AP44 6p Holstein .20 .20
**C292** AP44 10p Shorthorn .45 .25
**C293** AP44 15p Aberdeen Angus .75 .30
**C294** AP44 20p Norman 1.40 .45
**C295** AP44 30p Jersey 1.75 .75
**C296** AP44 50p Charolais 3.00 1.25
*Nos. C290-C296 (7)* 7.75 3.40

Issued to publicize Uruguayan cattle. Issued: 4p, 50p, 8/13; 6p, 30p, 8/29; 10p, 15p, 20p, 9/26.

Boiso Lanza, Early Plane and Space Capsule AP45

**1966, Oct. 14 Litho. *Perf. 12***
**C297** AP45 25p ultra, blk & lt bl .75 .45

Issued to honor Capt. Juan Manuel Boiso Lanza, pioneer of military aviation.

No. C271 Overprinted: "CENTENARIO DEL SELLO / ESCUDITO RESELLADO"

**1966, Nov. 4 Wmk. 332**
**C298** Sheet of 10 2.25 2.25

**"URUGUAY" at bottom**

*a.-e.* AP35 1p each .25 .25

**"URUGUAY" at top**

*f.-j.* AP35 1p each .25 .25

2nd Rio de la Plata Stamp Show, Buenos Aires, Apr. 1966, sponsored by the Argentine and Uruguayan philatelic associations, and for the cent. of Uruguay's 1st surcharged issue. The addition of black numerals makes the designs resemble the surcharged issue of 1866, Nos. 24-28.

Labels in top row are overprinted "SEGUNDA MUESTRA 1966," in bottom row "SEGUNDAS JORNADAS 1966" and "CENTENARIO DEL SELLO / ESCUDITO RESELLADO" in both rows. One label each in top and bottom rows is overprinted "BUENOS AIRES / ABRIL 1966."

No. 613 Surcharged in Dark Blue

***Perf. 12½x13***
**1966, Dec. 17 Engr. Unwmk.**
**C299** A175 1p on 12c .25 .20

Philatelic Club of Uruguay, 40th anniv.

Dante Alighieri — AP46 Planetarium Projector — AP47

**Wmk. 332**
**1966, Dec. 27 Litho. *Perf. 12***
**C300** AP46 50c sepia & bister .25 .20

Dante Alighieri (1265-1321), Italian poet.

**1967, Jan. 13 Wmk. 332 *Perf. 12***
**C301** AP47 5p dl bl & blk .45 .25

Montevideo Municipal Planetarium, 10th anniv.

Archbishop Makarios and Map of Cyprus AP48

**1967, Feb. 14 Wmk. 332 *Perf. 12***
**C302** AP48 6.60p rose lil & blk .25 .20

Visit of Archbishop Makarios, president of Cyprus, Oct. 21, 1966.

Dr. Albert Schweitzer Holding Fawn — AP49

**1967, Mar. 31 Litho. Wmk. 332**
**C303** AP49 6p grn, blk, brn & sal .50 .50

Albert Schweitzer (1875-1965), medical missionary.

Corriedale Ram AP50

Various Rams: 4p, Ideal. 5p, Romney Marsh. 10p, Australian Merino.

**1967, Apr. 5**
**C304** AP50 3p red org, blk & gray 1.40 .20
**C305** AP50 4p emer, blk & gray 1.40 .20
**C306** AP50 5p ultra, blk & gray 1.40 .20
**C307** AP50 10p yel, blk & gray 1.40 .40
*Nos. C304-C307 (4)* 5.60 1.00

Uruguayan sheep raising.

Flag of Uruguay and Map of the Americas AP51

**1967, Apr. 8**
**C308** AP51 10p dk gray, bl & gold .35 .20

Meeting of American Presidents, Punta del Este, Apr. 10-12.

Numeral Stamps of 1866, Nos. 30-31 AP52

Design: 6p, Nos. 32-33; diff. frame.

**Wmk. 332**
**1967, May 10 Litho. *Perf. 12***
**C309** AP52 3p bl, yel grn & blk .20 .20
*a.* Souvenir sheet of 4 1.00 1.00
**C310** AP52 6p bis, dp rose & blk .35 .25
*a.* Souvenir sheet of 4 1.75 1.75

Cent. of the 1866 numeral issue. Nos. C309a-C310a each contain 4 stamps similar to Nos. C309 and C310 respectively (the arrangement of colors differs in the souvenir sheets).

Ansina, Portrait by Medardo Latorre — AP53

**1967, May 17**

**C311** AP53 2p gray, dk bl & red .25 .20

Issued to honor Ansina, servant of Gen. José Artigas.

Plane Landing AP54

**1967, May 30**

**C312** AP54 10p red, bl, blk & yel .35 .25

30th anniv. (in 1966) of PLUNA Airline.

Shooting for Basket — AP55

Basketball Game — AP56

Basketball Players in Action: No. C314, Driving (ball shoulder high). No. C315, About to pass (ball head high). No. C316, Ready to pass (ball held straight in front). No. C317, Dribbling with right hand.

**1967, June 9**

**C313** AP55 5p multi .30 .25
**C314** AP55 5p multi .30 .25
**C315** AP55 5p multi .30 .25
**C316** AP55 5p multi .30 .25
**C317** AP55 5p multi .30 .25
***a.*** Strip of 5, Nos. C313-C317 1.75 1.50

**Souvenir Sheet**

**C318** AP56 10p org, brt grn & blk 1.75 1.75

5th World Basketball Championships, Montevideo, May 1967.
For overprint see No. C349.

José Artigas, Manuel Belgrano, Flags of Uruguay and Argentina — AP57

**Wmk. 332**

**1967, June 19 Litho. *Imperf.***

**C319** AP57 5p bl, grn & yel 1.00 1.00

3rd Rio de la Plata Stamp Show, Montevideo, Uruguay, June 18-25.
For surcharge see No. 859.

Nos. C248 and C252 Surcharged in Gold

**1967, June 22 *Perf. 12***

**C320** AP30 5.90p on 45c multi .25 .20
**C321** A195 5.90p on 45c multi .25 .20

Don Quixote and Sancho Panza, Painted by Denry Torres — AP58

**1967, July 10**

**C322** AP58 8p bister brn & brn .30 .25

Issued in honor of Miguel de Cervantes Saavedra (1547-1616), Spanish novelist.
For surcharge see No. C356.

Stone Axe — AP59

Railroad Crossing AP60

Designs: 15p, Headbreaker stones. 20p, Spearhead. 50p, Birdstone. 75p, Clay pot. 100p, Ornitholite (ritual sculpture), Balizas, horiz. 150p, Lasso weights (boleadores). 200p, Two spearheads.

**1967-68 Wmk. 332 *Perf. 12***

**C323** AP59 15p gray & blk .20 .20
**C324** AP59 20p gray & blk .20 .20
**C325** AP59 30p gray & lt gray .45 .20
**C326** AP59 50p gray & blk .60 .20
**C327** AP59 75p brn & blk 1.00 .35
**C328** AP59 100p gray & blk 1.40 .60
**C329** AP59 150p gray & blk ('68) 1.75 .60
**C330** AP59 200p gray & blk ('68) 2.40 1.25
*Nos. C323-C330 (8)* 8.00 3.60

**1967, Dec. 4**

**C331** AP60 4p blk, yel & red .25 .20

10th Pan-American Highway Congress, Montevideo.

Lions Emblem and Map of South America — AP61

**1967, Dec. 29**

**C332** AP61 5p pur, yel & emer .30 .20

50th anniversary of Lions International.

Boy Scout AP62

**1968, Jan. 24 Litho.**

**C333** AP62 9p sepia & brick red .40 .25

Issued in memory of Robert Baden-Powell, founder of the Boy Scout organization.

Sun, UN Emblem and Transportation Means — AP63

**1968, Feb. 29 Wmk. 332 *Perf. 12***

**C334** AP63 10p gray, yel, lt & dk bl .25 .20

Issued for International Tourist Year.

Octopus AP64

Marine Fauna: 20p, Silversides. 25p, Characin. 30p, Catfish, vert. 50p, Squid, vert.

**1968 Wmk. 332 *Perf. 12***

**C335** AP64 15p lt grn, bl & blk .70 .20
**C336** AP64 20p brn, grn & bl .70 .20
**C337** AP64 25p multi 1.00 .20
**C338** AP64 30p bl, grn & blk 1.25 .50
**C339** AP64 50p dp org, grn & dk bl 2.00 .65
*Nos. C335-C339 (5)* 5.65 1.75

Issued: 30p, 50p, 10/10; 15p, 20p, 25p, 11/5.

Navy Type of Regular Issue

Designs: 4p, Naval Air Force. 6p, Naval arms. 10p, Signal flags, vert. 20p, Corsair (chartered by General Artigas).

**1968, Nov. 12 Litho.**

**C340** A226 4p bl, blk & red .20 .20
**C341** A226 6p multi .20 .20
**C342** A226 10p lt ultra, red & yel .20 .20
**C343** A226 20p ultra & blk .30 .20
*Nos. C340-C343 (4)* .90 .80

Rowing AP65

**1969, Feb. 11 Wmk. 332 *Perf. 12***

**C344** AP65 30p shown .35 .20
**C345** AP65 50p Running .65 .30
**C346** AP65 100p Soccer 1.00 .45
*Nos. C344-C346 (3)* 2.00 .95

19th Olympic Games, Mexico City, 10/12-27/68.

Bicycling Type of Regular Issue

Designs: 20p, Bicyclist and globe, vert.

**1969, Mar. 21 Wmk. 332 *Perf. 12***

**C347** A229 20p bl, pur & yel .30 .20

"EFIMEX 68" and Globe AP66

**1969, Apr. 10 Wmk. 332 *Perf. 12***

**C348** AP66 20p dk grn, red & bl .30 .20

EFIMEX '68, International Philatelic Exhibition, Mexico City, Nov. 1-9, 1968.

No. C318 Overprinted with Names of Participating Countries, Emblem, Bars, etc. and "CAMPEONATO MUNDIAL DE VOLEIBOL"

**1969, Apr. 25**

**Souvenir Sheet**

**C349** AP56 10p org, brt grn & blk .45 .45

Issued to commemorate the World Volleyball Championships, Montevideo, Apr. 1969.

Book, Quill and Emblem — AP67

Automobile Club Emblem — AP68

**1969, Sept. 16 Litho. *Perf. 12***

**C350** AP67 30p grn, org & blk .45 .25

10th Congress of Latin American Notaries.

**1969, Oct. 7 Wmk. 332 *Perf. 12***

**C351** AP68 10p ultra & red .25 .20

50th anniv. (in 1968) of the Uruguayan Automobile Club.

ILO Emblem AP69

**1969, Oct. 29 Litho. *Perf. 12***

**C352** AP69 30p dk bl grn & blk .40 .25

50th anniv. of the ILO.

Exhibition Emblem — AP70

**1969, Nov. 15 Wmk. 332 *Perf. 12***

**C353** AP70 20p ultra, yel & grn .30 .20

ABUEXPO 69 Philatelic Exhibition, San Pablo, Brazil, Nov. 15-23.

Rotary Emblem and Hemispheres AP71

**1969, Dec. 6 *Perf. 12***

**C354** AP71 20p ultra, bl & bis .50 .25

South American Regional Rotary Conference and the 50th anniv. of the Montevideo Rotary Club.

Dr. Luis Morquio — AP72

**1969, Dec. 22 Litho. Wmk. 332**

**C355** AP72 20p org red & brn .25 .20

Centenary of the birth of Dr. Luis Morquio, pediatrician.

No. C322 Surcharged "FELIZ AÑO 1970 / 6.00 / PESOS"

**1969, Dec. 24**

**C356** AP58 6p on 8p bis brn & brn .25 .20

Issued for New Year 1970.

Mahatma Gandhi and UNESCO Emblem AP73

**1970, Jan. 26 Wmk. 332 *Perf. 12***

**C357** AP73 100p lt bl & brn 3.00 .80

Mohandas K. Gandhi (1869-1948), leader in India's fight for independence.

Evaristo C. Ciganda — AP74

Giuseppe Garibaldi — AP75

**1970, Mar. 10 Litho.**

**C358** AP74 6p brt grn & brn .25 .20

Ciganda, author of the 1st law for teachers' pensions, birth cent.

**1970, Apr. 7 Unwmk. *Perf. 12***

**C359** AP75 20p rose car & pink .25 .20

Centenary of Garibaldi's command of foreign legionnaires in the Uruguayan Civil War.

Fur Seal AP76

Designs: 20p, Rhea, vert. 30p, Common tegu (lizard). 50p, Capybara. 100p, Mulita armadillo. 150p, Puma. 200p, Nutria.

**1970-71 Wmk. 332 *Perf. 12***

| | | | | |
|---|---|---|---|---|
| **C361** | AP76 | 20p pur, emer & blk | .75 | .20 |
| **C362** | AP76 | 30p emer, yel & blk | .75 | .25 |
| **C363** | AP76 | 50p dl yel & brn | 1.50 | .45 |
| **C365** | AP76 | 100p org, sep & blk | 2.00 | .65 |
| **C366** | AP76 | 150p emer & brn | 1.50 | .75 |
| **C367** | AP76 | 200p brt rose, brn & blk ('71) | 3.75 | 1.90 |
| **C368** | AP76 | 250p gray, bl & blk | 4.75 | 2.00 |
| | | *Nos. C361-C368 (7)* | 15.00 | 6.20 |

Soccer and Mexican Flag AP77

**1970, June 2 Litho. *Perf. 12***

**C369** AP77 50p multi .60 .45

9th World Soccer Championships for the Jules Rimet Cup, Mexico City, 5/30-6/21.

"U N" and Laurel — AP78

**1970, June 26 Wmk. 332 *Perf. 12***

**C370** AP78 32p dk bl & gold .50 .25

25th anniversary of the United Nations.

Eisenhower and US Flag — AP79

**1970, July 14 Litho.**

**C371** AP79 30p gray, vio bl & red .40 .25

Issued in memory of Gen. Dwight David Eisenhower, 34th Pres. of US (1890-1969).

Neil A. Armstrong Stepping onto Moon — AP80

**1970, July 21**

**C372** AP80 200p multi 3.00 1.25

1st anniv. of man's 1st landing on the moon.

Flag of the "Immortals" — AP81

**1970, Aug. 24 Wmk. 332 *Perf. 12***

**C373** AP81 500p bl, blk & red 4.50 4.50

The 145th anniversary of the arrival of the 33 "Immortals," the patriots, who started the revolution for independence.

Congress Emblem with Map of South America AP82

**1970, Sept. 16 Unwmk. *Perf. 12***

**C374** AP82 30p bl, dk bl & yel .30 .25

Issued to publicize the 5th Pan-American Congress of Rheumatology, Punta del Este.

Souvenir Sheet

Types of First Air Post Issue — AP83

**1970, Oct. 1 Wmk. 332 *Perf. 12½***

| | | | | |
|---|---|---|---|---|
| **C375** | AP83 | Sheet of 3 | 3.00 | 3.00 |
| *a.* | | 25p brown (Bl) | .90 | .90 |
| *b.* | | 25p brown (R) | .90 | .90 |
| *c.* | | 25p brown (G) | .90 | .90 |

Stamp Day. #C375 contains 3 stamps similar to #C1-C3, but with denominations in pesos.

Flags of ALALC Countries — AP84

**1970, Nov. 23 Litho. *Perf. 12***

**C376** AP84 22p multi .30 .25

For the Latin-American Association for Free Trade (Asociación Latinoamericana de Libre Comercio).

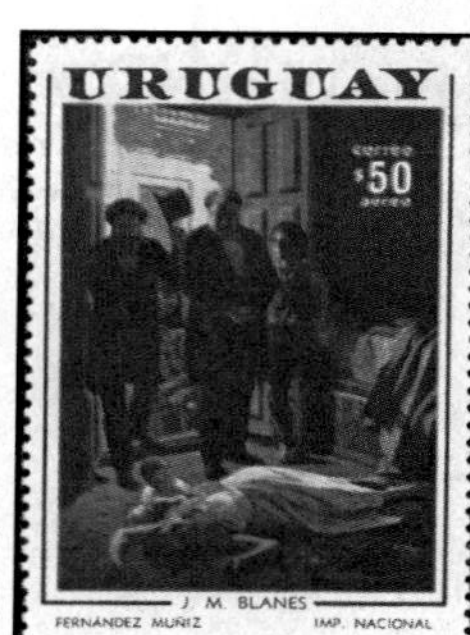


Yellow Fever, by J. M. Blanes AP85

**1971, June 8 Wmk. 332 *Perf. 12***

**C377** AP85 50p blk, dk red brn & yel .55 .30

Juan Manuel Blanes (1830-1901), painter.

Racial Equality, UN Emblem AP86

**1971, June 28 Litho.**

**C378** AP86 27p blk, pink & bis .35 .25

Intl. Year Against Racial Discrimination.

Congress Emblem with Maps of Americas AP87

**1971, July 6 Wmk. 332 *Perf. 12***

**C379** AP87 58p dl grn, blk & org .45 .35

12th Pan-American Congress of Gastroenterology, Punta del Este, Dec. 5-10, 1971.

Committee Emblem AP88

**1971, Nov. 29**

**C380** AP88 30p bl, blk & yel .30 .25

Inter-governmental Committee for European Migration.

Llama and Mountains AP89

Munich Olympic Games Emblem — AP90

**1971, Dec. 30**

**C381** AP89 37p multi .45 .35

EXFILIMA '71, Third Inter-American Philatelic Exposition, Lima, Peru, Nov. 6-14.

**1972, Feb. 1 *Perf. 11½x12***

Designs (Munich '72 Emblem and): 100p, Torchbearer. 500p, Discobolus.

| | | | | |
|---|---|---|---|---|
| **C382** | AP90 | 50p blk, red & org | .30 | .20 |
| **C383** | AP90 | 100p multi | .55 | .40 |
| **C384** | AP90 | 500p multi | 2.75 | 2.00 |
| | | *Nos. C382-C384 (3)* | 3.60 | 2.60 |

20th Olympic Games, Munich, 8/26-9/11.

Retort and WHO Emblem — AP91

Ship with Flags Forming Sails — AP92

**1972, Feb. 22 *Perf. 12***

**C385** AP91 27p multi .25 .20

50th anniversary of the discovery of insulin by Frederick G. Banting and Charles H. Best.

**1972, Mar. 6 Wmk. 332**

**C386** AP92 37p multi .30 .25

Stamp Day of the Americas.

1924 and 1928 Gold Medals, Soccer — AP93

Design: 300p, Olympic flag, Motion and Munich emblems, vert.

**1972, June 12 Litho. *Perf. 12***

| | | | |
|---|---|---|---|
| **C387** | AP93 100p bl & multi | .45 | .45 |
| **C388** | AP93 300p multi | 1.40 | 1.40 |

20th Olympic Games, Munich, 8/26-9/11.

Cross AP94

**1972, Aug. 10**

| | | | |
|---|---|---|---|
| **C389** | AP94 37p vio & gold | .25 | .20 |

Dan A. Mitrione (1920-70), slain US official.

Interlocking Squares and UN Emblem — AP95

**1972, Aug. 16**

| | | | |
|---|---|---|---|
| **C390** | AP95 30p gray & multi | .25 | .20 |

3rd UN Conf. on Trade and Development (UNCTAD III), Santiago, Chile, Apr.-May 1972.

Brazil's "Bull's-eye," 1843 — AP96

**Wmk. 332**

**1972, Aug. 26 Litho. *Perf. 12***

| | | | |
|---|---|---|---|
| **C391** | AP96 50p grn, yel & bl | .25 | .20 |

4th Inter-American Philatelic Exhibition, EXFILBRA, Rio de Janeiro, Aug. 26-Sept. 2.

Map of South America, Compass Rose — AP97

**1972, Sept. 28**

| | | | |
|---|---|---|---|
| **C392** | AP97 37p multi | .30 | .20 |

Uruguay's support for extending territorial sovereignty 200 miles into the sea.

Adoration of the Kings and Shepherds, by Rafael Perez Barradas — AP98

**1972, Oct. 12**

| | | | |
|---|---|---|---|
| **C393** | AP98 20p lemon & multi + label | .40 | .25 |

Christmas 1972 and first biennial exhibition of Uruguayan painting, 1970.

WPY Emblem AP99

**Wmk. 332**

**1974, Aug. 20 Litho. *Perf. 12***

| | | | |
|---|---|---|---|
| **C394** | AP99 500p gray & red | .75 | .60 |

World Population Year 1974.

Soccer, Olympics and UPU Emblems AP100

Anniversaries and events: No. C398a, 17th UPU Congress, Lausanne. No. C398b, World Soccer Federation, 1st South American president. No. C398c, 1976 Summer and Winter Olympics, Innsbruck and Montreal.

**1974, Aug. 30**

| | | | |
|---|---|---|---|
| **C395** | AP100 200p grn & multi | .80 | .80 |
| **C396** | AP100 300p org & multi | .80 | .80 |
| **C397** | AP100 500p multicolored | 8.50 | 8.50 |

**Souvenir Sheet**

| | | | |
|---|---|---|---|
| **C398** | Sheet of 3 | *70.00* | *70.00* |
| *a.-c.* | AP100 500p any single | *20.00* | *20.00* |

Centenary of Universal Postal Union. Nos. C397-C398 had limited distribution.

Mexico No. O1 and Mexican Coat of Arms AP101

**Wmk. 332**

**1974, Oct. 15 Litho. *Perf. 12***

| | | | |
|---|---|---|---|
| **C399** | AP101 200p multi | .25 | .20 |

EXFILMEX '74 5th Inter-American Philatelic Exhibition, Mexico City, Oct. 26-Nov. 3.

**Christmas Type of 1974**

240p, Kings following star. 2500p, Virgin & Child.

**1974**

| | | | |
|---|---|---|---|
| **C400** | A315 240p multi | .30 | .20 |

**Miniature Sheet**

| | | | |
|---|---|---|---|
| **C401** | A315 2500p multi | 3.00 | 3.00 |

Issued: 240p. Dec. 27; 2500p, Dec. 31.

Spain No. 1, Colors of Spain and Uruguay — AP102

**1975, Mar. 4**

| | | | |
|---|---|---|---|
| **C402** | AP102 400p multi | .35 | .25 |

Espana 75, International Philatelic Exhibition, Madrid, Apr. 4-13.

**Souvenir Sheet**

Nos. C253, 893 and C402 — AP103

**Wmk. 332**

**1975, Apr. 4 Litho. *Perf. 12***

| | | | |
|---|---|---|---|
| **C403** | AP103 Sheet of 3 | 5.00 | 5.00 |
| *a.* | 1000p No. C253 | 1.50 | 1.50 |
| *b.* | 1000p No. 893 | 1.50 | 1.50 |
| *c.* | 1000p No. C402 | 1.50 | 1.50 |

Espana 75 Intl. Phil. Exhib., Madrid, Apr. 4-13.

1976 Summer & Winter Olympics, Innsbruck & Montreal AP104

**1975, May 16 *Perf. 12***

| | | | |
|---|---|---|---|
| **C404** | AP104 400p shown | .80 | .60 |
| **C405** | AP104 600p Flags, Olympic rings | 1.10 | .95 |

**Souvenir Sheets**

| | | | |
|---|---|---|---|
| **C406** | Sheet of 2 | 42.50 | 42.50 |
| *a.* | AP104 500p Montreal emblem | 12.50 | 12.50 |
| *b.* | AP104 1000p Innsbruck emblem | 27.50 | 27.50 |
| **C407** | Sheet of 2 | 42.50 | 42.50 |
| *a.* | AP104 500p Emblems, horiz. | 12.50 | 12.50 |
| *b.* | AP104 1000p Flags, horiz. | 27.50 | 27.50 |

Nos. C404-C407 had limited distribution.

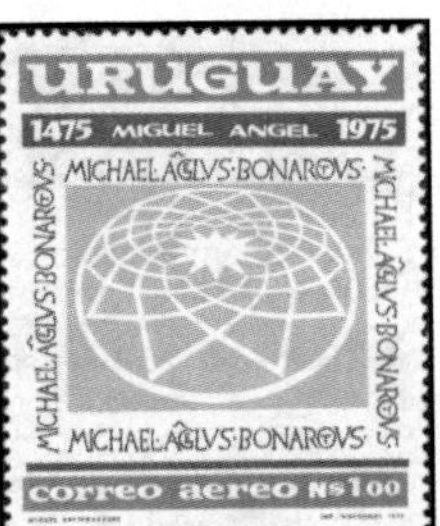

Floor Design for Capitol, Rome AP105

**1975, Aug. 15**

| | | | |
|---|---|---|---|
| **C408** | AP105 1p multi | .85 | .85 |

500th birth anniversary of Michelangelo Buonarroti (1475-1564), Italian sculptor, painter and architect.

Apollo-Soyuz Space Mission, USA & Uruguay Independence — AP106

Anniversaries and events: 15c, Apollo-Soyuz spacecraft. 20c, Apollo-Soyuz spacecraft. 25c, Artigas monument, vert. 30c, George Washington, Pres. Artigas. No. C412, Early Aircraft, vert. No. C413a, Apollo spacecraft, astronauts. No. C413b, US and Uruguayan Declarations of Independence. No. C413c, Modern aircraft. No. C413d, UN Secretaries General. No. C414c, Boiso Lanza, aviation pioneer. 1p, Flags of UN and Uruguay.

**1975, Sept. 29**

| | | | |
|---|---|---|---|
| **C409** | AP106 10c multicolored | 1.10 | .85 |
| **C410** | AP106 15c multicolored | 1.60 | 1.25 |
| **C411** | AP106 25c multicolored | 2.00 | 1.40 |
| **C412** | AP106 50c multicolored | 2.75 | 1.75 |
| | *Nos. C409-C412 (4)* | 7.45 | 5.25 |

**Souvenir Sheets**

| | | | |
|---|---|---|---|
| **C413** | Sheet of 4 | 37.50 | 37.50 |
| *a.-d.* | AP106 40c any single | 8.00 | 8.00 |
| **C414** | Sheet of 4 | 37.50 | 37.50 |
| *a.* | AP106 20c multicolored | 1.50 | 1.50 |
| *b.* | AP106 30c multicolored | 3.75 | 3.75 |
| *c.* | AP106 50c multicolored | 6.50 | 6.50 |
| *d.* | AP106 1p multicolored | 14.00 | 14.00 |

Nos. C409-C414 had limited distribution.

Sun, Uruguay No. C59 and other Stamps — AP108

**Wmk. 332**

**1975, Oct. 13 Litho. *Perf. 12***

| | | | |
|---|---|---|---|
| **C415** | AP108 1p blk, gray & yel | 2.00 | 1.00 |

Uruguayan Stamp Day.

Montreal Olympic Emblem and Argentina '78 — AP109

Flags of US and Uruguay — AP110

UPU and UPAE Emblems AP111

**Wmk. 332**

**1975, Oct. 14 Litho. *Perf. 11½***

| | | | |
|---|---|---|---|
| **C416** | AP109 1p multi | 1.40 | .60 |
| **C417** | AP110 1p multi | 1.40 | .60 |
| **C418** | AP111 1p multi | 1.40 | .60 |
| *a.* | Souvenir sheet of 3 | 14.00 | 14.00 |
| | *Nos. C416-C418 (3)* | 4.20 | 1.80 |

EXFILMO '75 and ESPAMER '75 Stamp Exhibitions, Montevideo, Oct. 10-19. No.

C418a contains 3 stamps similar to Nos. C416-C418, 2p each.

Ocelot AP112

Orchid: #C416, Oncidium bifolium.

**1976, Jan. Litho. *Perf. 12***

**C419** AP112 50c vio bl & multi .40 .30
**C420** AP112 50c emer & multi .40 .30

Souvenir Sheets

Olympics, Soccer, Telecommunications and UPU — AP113

**1976, June 3 *Perf. 11½***

**C422** Sheet of 3 50.00 50.00
*a.* AP113 30c Soccer player 6.00 6.00
*b.* AP113 70c Alexander Graham Bell 14.00 14.00
*c.* AP113 1p UPU emblem, UN #5 20.00 20.00
**C423** Sheet of 3 50.00 50.00
*a.* AP113 40c Discus thrower 6.00 6.00
*b.* AP113 60c Telephone, cent. 9.00 9.00
*c.* AP113 2p UPU emblem, UN #11 25.00 25.00

Nos. C422-C423 had limited distribution.

Anniversaries and Events Type of 1976
Souvenir Sheets

20c, Frederick Passy, Henri Dunant. 35c, Nobel prize, 75th anniv. 40c, Viking spacecraft. 60c, 1976 Summer Olympics, Montreal. 75c, US space missions. 90c, 1976 Summer Olympics, diff.
World Cup Soccer Championships, Argentina: 1p, Uruguay, 1930 champions. 1.50p, Uruguay, 1950 champions.

**1976, Nov. 12 *Perf. 12***

**C424** Sheet of 4 37.50 37.50
*a.* A355 20c multicolored 2.50 2.50
*b.* A355 40c multicolored 4.50 4.50
*c.* A355 60c multicolored 6.50 6.50
*d.* A355 1.50p multicolored 16.00 16.00
**C425** Sheet of 4 37.50 37.50
*a.* A355 35c multicolored 5.00 5.00
*b.* A355 75c multicolored 7.00 7.00
*c.* A355 90c multicolored 8.00 8.00
*d.* A355 1p multicolored 10.00 10.00

Nos. C424-C425 had limited distribution.

Nobel Prize Type of 1977
Souvenir Sheets

Anniversaries and events: 10c, World Cup Soccer Championships. 40c, Victor Hess, Nobel Prize in Physics. 60c, Max Plank, Nobel Prize in Physics. 80c, Graf Zeppelin, Concorde. 90c, Virgin and Child by Rubens. 1.20p, World Cup Soccer Championships, diff. 1.50p, Eduardo Bonilla, Count von Zeppelin. 2p, The Nativity by Rubens.

**1977, July 21**

**C426** Sheet of 4 35.00 35.00
*a.* A361 10c multicolored 1.00 1.00
*b.* A361 60c multicolored 4.00 4.00
*c.* A361 80c multicolored 6.00 6.00
*d.* A361 2p multicolored 14.00 14.00
**C427** Sheet of 4 35.00 35.00
*a.* A361 40c multicolored 2.50 2.50
*b.* A361 90c multicolored 6.50 6.50
*c.* A361 1.20p multicolored 7.50 7.50
*d.* A361 1.50p multicolored 11.00 11.00

Nos. C426-C427 had limited distribution.

Uruguay Natl. Postal System, 150th Anniv. AP114

**1977, July 27**

**C428** AP114 8p multicolored 10.00 10.00

**Souvenir Sheet**

**C429** AP114 10p multicolored 15.00 15.00

No. C428, imperf., was not valid for postage. Souvenir sheets sold in the package with No. C429 were not valid for postage.
For overprint see No. C435.

Paintings Type of 1978

Paintings: 1p, St. George Slaying Dragon by Durer. 1.25p, Duke of Lerma by Rubens. No. 432a, Madonna and Child by Durer. No. 432b, Holy Family by Rubens. No. 432c, Flight from Egypt by Francisco de Goya (1746-1828).

**1978, June 13 *Perf. 12½***

**C430** A374 1p brn & blk 3.25 3.25
**C431** A374 1.25p blk & brn 3.50 3.50

**Souvenir Sheet**

**C432** Sheet of 3 18.00 18.00
*a.-c.* A374 1p any single 5.00 5.00

Nos. C430-C432 had limited distribution.

Souvenir Sheet

ICAO, 30th Anniv. and 1st Powered Flight, 75th Anniv. — AP115

Designs: a, Concorde, Dornier DO-x. b, Graf Zeppelin, Wright Brothers' Flyer. c, Space shuttle and De Pinedo's plane.

**1978, June 13**

**C433** Sheet of 3 22.50 22.50
*a.-c.* AP115 1p any single 6.00 6.00

No. C433 had limited distribution.

Souvenir Sheet

World Cup Soccer Championships, Argentina — AP116

**1978, June 13 *Perf. 12***

**C434** Sheet of 3 45.00 45.00
*a.* AP116 50c multicolored 4.00 4.00
*b.* AP116 1.50p multicolored 11.00 11.00
*c.* AP116 2p multicolored 16.00 16.00

No. C434 had limited distribution.

No. C428 Overprinted in Black

**1978, Aug. 28**

**C435** AP114 8p multicolored 6.00 3.00

No. C435 had limited distribution.

**Madonna and Child Type of 1979**

Various Madonna and Child etchings by Albrecht Dürer with Intl. Year of the Child emblem at: a, UL. b, UR.

**Wmk. 332**

**1979, June 18 Litho. *Perf. 12½***

**C436** A390 1.50p Sheet of 2, #a-b 22.50 22.50

No. C436 had limited distribution.

Boiso Lanza, Wright Brothers AP117

75th anniv. of powered flight.

**1979, June 18 *Perf. 12½***

**C437** AP117 1.80p multicolored 2.75 1.50

No. C437 had limited distribution.
Issued in sheet of 24 containing 6 blocks of 4r with margin around. See Nos. 1040-1042.

Souvenir Sheet

1982 World Cup Soccer Championships, Spain — AP118

**1979, June 18 *Perf. 12***

**C438** Sheet of 3 32.50 32.50
*a.* AP118 50c Jules Rimet cup 2.50 2.50
*b.* AP118 2.50p Uruguay flag 10.00 10.00
*c.* AP118 3p Espana '82 14.00 14.00

No. C438 had limited distribution.

**AIR POST SEMI-POSTAL STAMPS**

**Catalogue values for unused stamps in this section are for Never Hinged items.**

Type of Semi-Postal Stamps, 1959

**Wmk. 327**

**1959, Dec. 29 Litho. *Perf. 11½***

**CB1** SP2 38c + 10c brown & org .25 .25
**CB2** SP2 60c + 10c gray grn & org .30 .30

Issued for national recovery.

**SPECIAL DELIVERY STAMPS**

No. 242 Overprinted **MENSAJERIAS**

**1921, Aug. Unwmk. *Perf. 11½***

**E1** A97 2c fawn .55 .20
*a.* Double overprint 3.25

Caduceus — SD1

Imprint: "IMP. NACIONAL."

**1922, Dec. 2 Litho. Wmk. 188**
**Size: 21x27mm**

**E2** SD1 2c light red .40 .20

**1924, Oct. 1**

**E3** SD1 2c pale ultra .40 .20

**1928 Unwmk. *Perf. 11***

**E4** SD1 2c light blue .40 .20

Imprint: "IMPRA. NACIONAL."

**1928-36 Wmk. 188**
**Size: 16½x19½mm.**

**E5** SD1 2c black, *green* .20 .20

**Unwmk.**

**E6** SD1 2c blue green ('29) .20 .20

***Perf. 11½, 12½***

**E7** SD1 2c blue ('36) .20 .20
*Nos. E5-E7 (3)* .60 .60

**1944, Oct. 23 *Perf. 12½***

**E8** SD1 2c salmon pink .25 .20

**Catalogue values for unused stamps in this section, from this point to the end of the section, are for Never Hinged items.**

**1947, Nov. 19**

**E9** SD1 2c red brown .20 .20

No. E9 Surcharged with New Value

**1957, Oct. 30**

**E10** SD1 5c on 2c red brown .20 .20

**LATE FEE STAMPS**

Galleon and Modern Steamship — LF1

**Wmk. Crossed Keys in Sheet**

**1936, May 18 Litho. *Perf. 11***

**I1** LF1 3c green .20 .20
**I2** LF1 5c violet .20 .20
**I3** LF1 6c blue green .20 .20
**I4** LF1 7c brown .25 .25
**I5** LF1 8c carmine .50 .50
**I6** LF1 12c deep blue .65 .65
*Nos. I1-I6 (6)* 2.00 2.00

## POSTAGE DUE STAMPS

D1

**1902 Unwmk. Engr.** ***Perf. 14 to 15***
**Size: 21¼x18½mm**

J1 D1 1c blue green .40 .20
J2 D1 2c carmine .40 .20
J3 D1 4c gray violet .65 .20
J4 D1 10c dark blue .95 .25
J5 D1 20c ocher 1.50 .80
*Nos. J1-J5 (5)* 3.90 1.65

Surcharged in Red

**1904**
J6 D1 1c on 10c dk bl .80 .80
a. Inverted surcharge 7.75 7.75

**1913-15 Litho.** ***Perf. 11½***
**Size: 22½x20mm**

J7 D1 1c lt grn .50 .20
J8 D1 2c rose red .50 .25
J9 D1 4c dl vio .65 .25
J10 D1 6c dp brn .80 .40

**Size: 21¼x19mm**

J11 D1 10c dl bl .80 .40
*Nos. J7-J11 (5)* 3.25 1.50

Imprint: "Imprenta Nacional"

**1922**
**Size: 20x17mm**

J12 D1 1c bl grn .20 .20
J13 D1 2c red .25 .20
J14 D1 3c red brn .40 .25
J15 D1 4c brn vio .25 .20
J16 D1 5c blue .40 .25
J17 D1 10c gray grn .40 .20
*Nos. J12-J17 (6)* 1.90 1.30

**1926-27 Wmk. 188** ***Perf. 11***
**Size: 20x17mm**

J18 D1 1c bl grn ('27) .40 .20
J19 D1 3c red brn ('27) .40 .20
J20 D1 5c slate blue .40 .20
J21 D1 6c light brown .40 .40
*Nos. J18-J21 (4)* 1.60 1.00

**1929 Unwmk.** ***Perf. 10½, 11***
J22 D1 1c blue green .20 .20
J23 D1 10c gray green .40 .20

Figure of Value Redrawn
(Flat on sides)

**1932 Wmk. 188**
J24 D1 6c yel brn .40 .25

Imprint: "Casa A. Barreiro Ramos S. A."

**1935 Unwmk. Litho.** ***Perf. 12½***
**Size: 20x17mm**

J25 D1 4c violet .40 .25
J26 D1 5c rose .40 .25

Type of 1935
Imprint: "Imprenta Nacional" at right

**1938**
J27 D1 1c blue green .20 .20
J28 D1 2c red brown .20 .20
J29 D1 3c deep pink .20 .20
J30 D1 4c light violet .20 .20
J31 D1 5c blue .20 .20
J32 D1 8c rose .20 .20
*Nos. J27-J32 (6)* 1.20 1.20

## OFFICIAL STAMPS

Regular Issues Handstamped in Black, Red or Blue

Many double and inverted impressions exist of the handstamped overprints on Nos. O1-O83. Prices are the same as for normal stamps or slightly more.

On Stamps of 1877-79

**1880-82 Unwmk.** ***Rouletted 8***
O1 A9 1c red brown 4.00 3.50
O2 A10 5c green 3.00 2.50
O3 A11 20c bister 2.50 2.00
O4 A11 50c black 18.00 15.00
O5 A12 1p blue 20.00 16.00
*Nos. O1-O5 (5)* 47.50 39.00

**On No. 44**
***Rouletted 6***

O6 A9 1c brown ('81) 4.75 4.25

**On Nos. 43-43A**
***Rouletted 8***

O7 A11 50c black (R) 17.00 16.00
O8 A12 1p blue (R) 22.50 20.00

**On Nos. 45, 41, 37a**
***Perf. 12½***

O9 A13 7c blue (R) ('81) 3.25 2.50

***Rouletted 8***

O10 A11 10c ver (Bl) 1.75 1.50

***Perf. 13½***

O11 A8b 15c yellow (Bl) 5.00 4.00

On Nos. 46-47

**1883** ***Perf. 12½***
O12 A14 1c green 6.00 6.00
O13 A14a 2c rose 7.00 7.00

**On Nos. 50-51**
***Perf. 12½, 12x12½, 13***

O14 A17 5c blue (R) 3.00 3.00
a. Imperf., pair 4.50
O15 A18 10c brown (Bl) 5.00 5.00
a. Imperf., pair 6.00

No. 48 Handstamped

**1884** ***Perf. 12½***
O16 A15 1c green 29.00 25.00

Overprinted Type "a" in Black
On Nos. 48-49

**1884** ***Perf. 12, 12x12½, 13***
O17 A15 1c green 29.00 25.00
O18 A16 2c red 10.00 8.00

**On Nos. 53-56**
***Rouletted 8***

O19 A11 1c on 10c ver 1.50 1.25
a. Small "1" (No. 53a) 5.00

***Perf. 12½***

O20 A14a 2c rose 5.00 5.00
O21 A22 5c ultra 5.00 5.00
O22 A23 5c blue 3.75 1.75
*Nos. O17-O22 (6)* 54.25 46.00

On Stamps of 1884-88

**1884-89** ***Rouletted 8***
O23 A24 1c gray 9.25 4.25
O24 A24 1c green ('88) 1.90 .95
O25 A24 1c olive grn 2.50 1.50
O26 A24a 2c vermilion .80 .50
O27 A24a 2c rose ('88) 1.75 .95
O28 A24b 5c slate blue 1.75 .95
O29 A24b 5c slate bl, *bl* 5.00 2.50
O30 A24b 5c violet ('88) 5.00 2.50
O31 A24b 5c lt blue ('89) 5.00 2.50
O32 A25 7c dk brown 5.00 2.50
O33 A25 7c orange ('89) 2.50 1.50
O34 A26 10c olive brn 1.50 .70
O35 A30 10c violet ('89) 12.50 7.50
O36 A27 20c red violet 2.50 1.50
O37 A27 20c bister brn ('89) 12.50 5.50
O38 A28 25c gray violet 3.50 2.50
O39 A28 25c vermilion ('89) 12.50 8.00
*Nos. O23-O39 (17)* 85.45 46.30

The OFICIAL handstamp, type "a," was also applied to No. 73, the 5c violet with "Provisorio" overprint, but it was not regularly issued.

On No. 71

**1887** ***Rouletted 9***
O40 A29 10c lilac 5.00

No. O40 was not regularly issued.

On Stamps of 1889-1899
***Perf. 12½ to 15 and Compound***

**1890-1900**
O41 A32 1c green .80 .20
O43 A32 1c blue ('95) 2.00 2.00
O44 A33 2c rose .80 .20
O45 A33 2c red brn ('95) 2.50 2.50
O46 A33 2c orange ('00) .80 .80
O47 A34 5c deep blue 1.50 1.50
O48 A34 5c rose ('95) 2.00 2.00
O49 A35 7c bister brown 1.25 .80
O50 A35 7c green ('95) 25.00
O51 A36 10c blue green 1.25 .80
O52 A36 10c orange ('95) 25.00
O53 A37 20c orange 1.25 .80
O54 A37 20c brown ('95) 25.00
O55 A38 25c red brown 1.25 .80
O56 A38 25c ver ('95) 55.00
O57 A39 50c lt blue 4.50 4.50
O58 A39 50c lilac ('95) 5.50 5.50
O59 A40 1p lilac 7.00 5.00
O60 A40 1p lt blue ('95) 40.00 22.50

Nos. O50, O52, O54, O56 and O60 were not regularly issued.

On No. 99

**1891** ***Rouletted 8***
O61 A24b 5c violet 1.50 1.25
a. "1391" 9.00

On Stamps of 1895-99
***Perf. 12½ to 15 and Compound***

**1895-1900**
O62 A51 1c bister .60 .60
O63 A51 1c slate blue ('97) 1.25 .55
O64 A52 2c blue .25 .25
O65 A52 2c claret ('97) 1.25 .55
O66 A53 5c red .80 .55
O67 A53 5c green ('97) 1.25 .55
O68 A53 5c grnsh blue ('00) .95 .75
O69 A54 7c deep green .50 .50
O70 A55 10c brown .50 .50
O71 A56 20c green & blk .80 .80
O72 A56 20c claret & blk ('97) 4.50 2.25
O73 A57 25c red brn & blk .80 .80
O74 A57 25c pink & bl ('97) 4.50 2.25
O75 A58 50c blue & blk .95 .95
O76 A58 50c grn & brn ('97) 5.75 2.75
O77 A59 1p org brn & blk 4.75 4.75
O78 A59 1p yel brn & bl ('97) 9.25 5.75
a. Inverted overprint
*Nos. O62-O78 (17)* 38.65 25.10

On Nos. 133-135

**1897, Sept.**
O79 A62 1c brown vio & blk 1.25 1.00
O80 A63 5c pale bl & blk 1.75 1.00
O81 A64 10c lake & blk 1.75 1.10
*Nos. O79-O81 (3)* 4.75 3.10

On Nos. 136-137
***Perf. 12½ to 15 and Compound***

**1897-1900**
O82 A68 10c red 2.50 1.50
O83 A68 10c red lilac ('00) 1.25 1.25

Regular Issue of 1900-01 Overprinted

**1901** ***Perf. 14 to 16***
O84 A72 1c yellow green .50 .20
O85 A75 2c vermilion .60 .20
O86 A73 5c dull blue .60 .20
O87 A76 7c brown orange .85 .50
O88 A74 10c gray violet .90 .55
O89 A37 20c lt blue 7.75 4.00
O90 A38 25c bister brown 1.50 .80
O91 A40 1p deep green 10.00 5.75
a. Inverted overprint 12.50 8.00
*Nos. O84-O91 (8)* 22.70 12.20

Most of the used official stamps of 1901-1928 have been punched with holes of various shapes, in addition to the postal cancellations.

Regular Issue of 1904-05 Overprinted

**1905** ***Perf. 11½***
O92 A79 1c green .50 .20
O93 A80 2c orange red .50 .20
O94 A81 5c deep blue .50 .20
O95 A82 10c dark violet 1.00 .40
O96 A83 20c gray green 3.00 1.00
a. Inverted overprint
O97 A84 25c olive bister 2.00 .80
*Nos. O92-O97 (6)* 7.50 2.80

Regular Issues of 1904-07 Overprinted

**1907, Mar.**
O98 A79 1c green .25 .20
O99 A86 5c deep blue .25 .20
O100 A86 7c orange brown .25 .20
O101 A82 10c dark violet .25 .20
O102 A83 20c gray green .40 .35
a. Inverted overprint 4.00
O103 A84 25c olive bister .50 .40
O104 A86 50c rose .95 .70
*Nos. O98-O104 (7)* 2.85 2.25

Regular Issues of 1900-10 Overprinted

OFICIAL
1910

**1910, July 15** ***Perf. 14½ to 16***
O105 A75 2c vermilion 8.50 4.00
O106 A73 5c slate green 5.00 3.00
O107 A74 10c gray violet 2.50 1.25
O108 A37 20c grnsh blue 2.50 1.25
O109 A38 25c bister brown 4.25 2.40

***Perf. 11½***

O110 A86 50c rose 5.75 2.50
a. Inverted overprint 20.00 15.00
*Nos. O105-O110 (6)* 28.50 14.40

Peace—O1

**1911, Feb. 18 Litho.**
O111 O1 2c red brown .40 .25
O112 O1 5c dark blue .40 .40
O113 O1 8c slate .40 *.60*
O114 O1 20c gray brown .55 *.95*
O115 O1 23c claret .80 *.95*
O116 O1 50c orange 1.50 1.25
O117 O1 1p red 4.00 1.50
*Nos. O111-O117 (7)* 8.05 5.90

Regular Issue of 1912-15 Overprinted

**1915, Sept. 16**
O118 A90 2c carmine .55 .40
O119 A90 5c dark blue .55 .40
O120 A90 8c ultra .55 .40
O121 A90 20c dark brown 1.25 .50
O122 A91 23c dark blue 4.00 3.50
O123 A91 50c orange 6.00 3.50
O124 A91 1p vermilion 8.00 4.00
*Nos. O118-O124 (7)* 20.90 12.70

Regular Issue of 1919 Overprinted

**1919, Dec. 25**
O125 A95 2c red & black .80 .40
a. Inverted overprint 3.50
O126 A95 5c ultra & blk .95 .40
O127 A95 8c gray bl & lt brn .95 .40
a. Inverted overprint 3.50
O128 A95 20c brown & blk 2.00 .80
O129 A95 23c green & brn 2.00 .80
O130 A95 50c brown & bl 4.00 2.00
O131 A95 1p dull red & bl 10.00 4.00
a. Double overprint 15.00
*Nos. O125-O131 (7)* 20.70 8.80

Regular Issue of 1923 Overprinted

**1924 Wmk. 189 *Perf. 12½***

| | | | | |
|---|---|---|---|---|
| **O132** | A100 | 2c violet | .20 | .20 |
| **O133** | A100 | 5c light blue | .20 | .20 |
| **O134** | A100 | 12c deep blue | .30 | .20 |
| **O135** | A100 | 20c buff | .40 | .20 |
| **O136** | A100 | 36c blue green | 1.75 | 1.25 |
| **O137** | A100 | 50c orange | 3.50 | 2.50 |
| **O138** | A100 | 1p pink | 6.25 | 5.00 |
| **O139** | A100 | 2p lt green | 12.00 | 10.00 |
| | | *Nos. O132-O139 (8)* | 24.60 | 19.55 |

Same Overprint on Regular Issue of 1924

**1926-27 Unwmk. *Imperf.***

| | | | | |
|---|---|---|---|---|
| **O140** | A100 | 2c rose lilac | .40 | .20 |
| **O141** | A100 | 5c pale blue | .60 | .20 |
| **O142** | A100 | 8c pink ('27) | .80 | .20 |
| **O143** | A100 | 12c slate blue | .95 | .20 |
| **O144** | A100 | 20c brown | 2.00 | .40 |
| **O145** | A100 | 36c dull rose | 3.00 | .95 |
| | | *Nos. O140-O145 (6)* | 7.75 | 2.15 |

Regular Issue of 1924 Overprinted

**1928 *Perf. 12½***

| | | | | |
|---|---|---|---|---|
| **O146** | A100 | 2c rose lilac | 1.50 | .95 |
| **O147** | A100 | 8c pink | 1.50 | .50 |
| **O148** | A100 | 10c turq blue | 2.00 | .50 |
| | | *Nos. O146-O148 (3)* | 5.00 | 1.95 |

Since 1928, instead of official stamps, Uruguay has used envelopes with "S. O." printed on them, and stamps of many issues which are punched with various designs such as star or crescent.

## NEWSPAPER STAMPS

No. 245 Surcharged

**1922, June 1 Unwmk. *Perf. 11½***

| | | | | |
|---|---|---|---|---|
| **P1** | A97 | 3c on 4c orange | .40 | .40 |
| *a.* | | Inverted surcharge | 9.25 | 9.25 |
| *b.* | | Double surcharge | 2.50 | 2.50 |

Nos. 235-237 Surcharged

**1924, June 1 *Perf. 14½***

| | | | | |
|---|---|---|---|---|
| **P2** | A96 | 3c on 2c car & blk | .40 | .40 |
| **P3** | A96 | 6c on 4c red org & bl | .40 | .40 |
| **P4** | A96 | 9c on 5c bl & brn | .40 | .40 |
| | | *Nos. P2-P4 (3)* | 1.20 | 1.20 |

Nos. 288, 291, 293 Overprinted or Surcharged in Red:

**1926 *Imperf.***

| | | | | |
|---|---|---|---|---|
| **P5** | A100 | 3c gray green | .80 | .25 |
| *a.* | | Double overprint | 1.00 | 1.00 |
| **P6** | A100 | 9c on 10c turq bl | .95 | .40 |
| *a.* | | Double surcharge | 1.00 | 1.00 |
| **P7** | A100 | 15c light violet | 1.25 | .50 |
| | | *Nos. P5-P7 (3)* | 3.00 | 1.15 |

## PARCEL POST STAMPS

Mercury — PP1

Imprint: "IMPRENTA NACIONAL"

***Perf. 11½***

**1922, Jan. 15 Litho. Unwmk.**

**Size: 20x29½mm**

**Inscribed "Exterior"**

| | | | | |
|---|---|---|---|---|
| **Q1** | PP1 | 5c grn, *straw* | .20 | .20 |
| **Q2** | PP1 | 10c grn, *bl gray* | .40 | .20 |
| **Q3** | PP1 | 20c grn, *rose* | 2.00 | .55 |
| **Q4** | PP1 | 30c grn, *grn* | 2.00 | .20 |
| **Q5** | PP1 | 50c grn, *blue* | 3.50 | .40 |
| **Q6** | PP1 | 1p grn, *org* | 5.00 | 1.50 |
| | | *Nos. Q1-Q6 (6)* | 13.10 | 3.05 |

**Inscribed "Interior"**

| | | | | |
|---|---|---|---|---|
| **Q7** | PP1 | 5c grn, *straw* | .25 | .20 |
| **Q8** | PP1 | 10c grn, *bl gray* | .25 | .20 |
| **Q9** | PP1 | 20c grn, *rose* | 1.00 | .25 |
| **Q10** | PP1 | 30c grn, *grn* | 1.40 | .25 |
| **Q11** | PP1 | 50c grn, *blue* | 2.25 | .35 |
| **Q12** | PP1 | 1p grn, *org* | 5.75 | 1.25 |
| | | *Nos. Q7-Q12 (6)* | 10.90 | 2.50 |

Imprint: "IMP. NACIONAL"
Inscribed "Exterior"

**1926, Jan. 20 *Perf. 11½***

| | | | | |
|---|---|---|---|---|
| **Q13** | PP1 | 20c grn, *rose* | 1.75 | .50 |

**Inscribed "Interior"**

***Perf. 11***

| | | | | |
|---|---|---|---|---|
| **Q14** | PP1 | 5c grn, *yellow* | .40 | .20 |
| **Q15** | PP1 | 10c grn, *bl gray* | .50 | .20 |
| **Q16** | PP1 | 20c grn, *rose* | 1.00 | .20 |
| **Q17** | PP1 | 30c grn, *bl grn* | 1.75 | .40 |
| | | *Nos. Q13-Q17 (5)* | 5.40 | 1.50 |

Inscribed "Exterior"

**1926 *Perf. 11½***

| | | | | |
|---|---|---|---|---|
| **Q18** | PP1 | 5c blk, *straw* | .40 | .20 |
| **Q19** | PP1 | 10c blk, *bl gray* | .50 | .20 |
| **Q20** | PP1 | 20c blk, *rose* | 1.10 | .20 |

**Inscribed "Interior"**

| | | | | |
|---|---|---|---|---|
| **Q21** | PP1 | 5c blk, *straw* | .40 | .20 |
| **Q22** | PP1 | 10c blk, *bl gray* | .50 | .20 |
| **Q23** | PP1 | 20c blk, *rose* | 1.00 | .20 |
| **Q24** | PP1 | 30c blk, *bl grn* | 1.75 | .40 |
| | | *Nos. Q18-Q24 (7)* | 5.65 | 1.60 |

PP2

PP3

***Perf. 11, 11½***

**1927, Feb. 22 Wmk. 188**

| | | | | |
|---|---|---|---|---|
| **Q25** | PP2 | 1c dp bl | .20 | .20 |
| **Q26** | PP2 | 2c lt grn | .20 | .20 |
| **Q27** | PP2 | 4c violet | .20 | .20 |
| **Q28** | PP2 | 5c red | .25 | .20 |
| **Q29** | PP2 | 10c dk brn | .40 | .20 |
| **Q30** | PP2 | 20c orange | .60 | .40 |
| | | *Nos. Q25-Q30 (6)* | 1.85 | 1.40 |

See Nos. Q35-Q38, Q51-Q54.

**1928, Nov. 20 *Perf. 11***

**Size: 15x20mm**

| | | | | |
|---|---|---|---|---|
| **Q31** | PP3 | 5c blk, *straw* | .20 | .20 |
| **Q32** | PP3 | 10c blk, *gray blue* | .20 | .20 |
| **Q33** | PP3 | 20c blk, *rose* | .50 | .20 |
| **Q34** | PP3 | 30c blk, *green* | .80 | .20 |
| | | *Nos. Q31-Q34 (4)* | 1.70 | .80 |

Type of 1927 Issue

**1929-30 Unwmk. *Perf. 11, 12½***

| | | | | |
|---|---|---|---|---|
| **Q35** | PP2 | 1c violet | .20 | .20 |
| **Q36** | PP2 | 1c ultra ('30) | .20 | .20 |
| **Q37** | PP2 | 2c bl grn ('30) | .20 | .20 |
| **Q38** | PP2 | 5c red ('30) | .20 | .20 |
| | | *Nos. Q35-Q38 (4)* | .80 | .80 |

Nos. Q35-Q38, and possibly later issues, occasionally show parts of a papermaker's watermark.

PP4

**1929, July 27 Wmk. 188 *Perf. 11***

| | | | | |
|---|---|---|---|---|
| **Q39** | PP4 | 10c orange | .50 | .50 |
| **Q40** | PP4 | 15c slate blue | .50 | .50 |
| **Q41** | PP4 | 20c ol brn | .50 | .50 |
| **Q42** | PP4 | 25c rose red | 1.00 | .50 |
| **Q43** | PP4 | 50c dark gray | 2.00 | 1.00 |
| **Q44** | PP4 | 75c violet | 8.00 | 6.00 |
| **Q45** | PP4 | 1p gray green | 7.50 | 3.00 |
| | | *Nos. Q39-Q45 (7)* | 20.00 | 12.00 |

For overprints see Nos. Q57-Q63.

Ship and Train — PP5

Numeral of Value — PP6

**1938-39 Unwmk. *Perf. 12½***

| | | | | |
|---|---|---|---|---|
| **Q46** | PP5 | 10c scarlet | .40 | .20 |
| **Q47** | PP5 | 20c dk bl | .60 | .20 |
| **Q48** | PP5 | 30c lt vio ('39) | .95 | .20 |
| **Q49** | PP5 | 50c green | 1.75 | .20 |
| **Q50** | PP5 | 1p brn org | 2.50 | 1.10 |
| | | *Nos. Q46-Q50 (5)* | 6.20 | 1.90 |

See #Q70-Q73, Q80, Q88-Q90, Q92-Q93, Q95.

Type of 1927 Redrawn

**1942-55? Litho. *Perf. 12½***

| | | | | |
|---|---|---|---|---|
| **Q51** | PP2 | 1c vio ('55) | | |
| **Q52** | PP2 | 2c bl grn | .20 | .20 |
| **Q54** | PP2 | 5c lt red ('44) | .20 | .20 |

The vertical and horizontal lines of the design have been strengthened, the "2" redrawn, etc. No. Q51 has oval "O" in CENTESIMO, 2¼mm from frame line at right; No. Q35 has round "O" 1¾mm from frame line.

**1943, Apr. 28 Engr.**

| | | | | |
|---|---|---|---|---|
| **Q55** | PP6 | 1c dk car rose | .20 | .20 |
| **Q56** | PP6 | 2c grnsh blk | .20 | .20 |

Parcel Post Stamps of 1929 Overprinted in Black

**1943, Dec. 15 Wmk. 188 *Perf. 11***

| | | | | |
|---|---|---|---|---|
| **Q57** | PP4 | 10c orange | 1.00 | .50 |
| **Q58** | PP4 | 15c slate blue | 1.00 | .50 |
| **Q59** | PP4 | 20c olive brn | 1.00 | .50 |
| **Q60** | PP4 | 25c rose red | 1.50 | 1.00 |
| **Q61** | PP4 | 50c dk gray | 2.50 | 2.00 |
| **Q62** | PP4 | 75c violet | 5.00 | 4.00 |
| **Q63** | PP4 | 1p gray grn | 8.00 | 4.50 |
| | | *Nos. Q57-Q63 (7)* | 20.00 | 13.00 |

**Catalogue values for unused stamps in this section, from this point to the end of the section, are for Never Hinged items.**

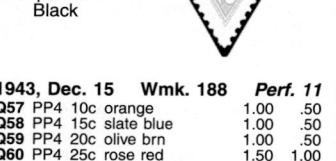

Bank of the Republic — PP7

University — PP8

***Perf. 12½***

**1945, Sept. 5 Litho. Unwmk.**

| | | | | |
|---|---|---|---|---|
| **Q64** | PP7 | 1c green | .20 | .20 |
| **Q65** | PP8 | 2c brt vio | .20 | .20 |

See Nos. Q77-Q79, Q84.

Custom House — PP9

Type A141 Overprinted

**1946, Dec. 11 *Perf. 11½***

| | | | | |
|---|---|---|---|---|
| **Q66** | PP9 | 5c yel brn & bl | .20 | .20 |

Red Overprint

**1946, Dec. 27 *Perf. 12½***

| | | | | |
|---|---|---|---|---|
| **Q67** | A141 | 1p light blue | .70 | .20 |

See Nos. Q69, Q76.

Mail Coach — PP11

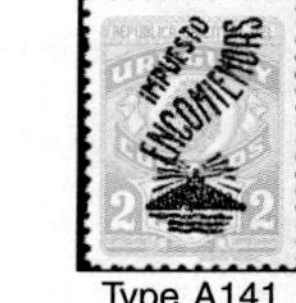

Type A141 Overprinted

**1946, Dec. 23**

| | | | | |
|---|---|---|---|---|
| **Q68** | PP11 | 5p red & ol brn | 12.00 | 5.00 |

Black Overprint

**1947**

| | | | | |
|---|---|---|---|---|
| **Q69** | A141 | 2c dull violet brn | .20 | .20 |

See Nos. Q74-Q76.

Type of 1938

**1947-52 Unwmk. *Perf. 12½***

| | | | | |
|---|---|---|---|---|
| **Q70** | PP5 | 5c brown org ('52) | .20 | .20 |
| **Q71** | PP5 | 10c violet | .20 | .20 |
| **Q72** | PP5 | 20c vermilion | .25 | .20 |
| **Q73** | PP5 | 30c blue | .50 | .20 |
| | | *Nos. Q70-Q73 (4)* | 1.15 | .80 |

Type of 1947
Black Overprint

**1948-49**

| | | | | |
|---|---|---|---|---|
| **Q74** | A141 | 1c rose lilac ('49) | .20 | .20 |
| **Q75** | A141 | 5c ultra | .20 | .20 |
| **Q76** | A141 | 5p rose carmine | 4.00 | 1.75 |
| | | *Nos. Q74-Q76 (3)* | 4.40 | 2.15 |

Types of 1945

**1950**

| | | | | |
|---|---|---|---|---|
| **Q77** | PP8 | 1c vermilion | .20 | .20 |
| **Q78** | PP7 | 2c chalky blue | .20 | .20 |

**1952 *Perf. 11***

| | | | | |
|---|---|---|---|---|
| **Q79** | PP7 | 10c blue green | .20 | .20 |

Type of 1938-39

**1954 *Perf. 12½***

| | | | | |
|---|---|---|---|---|
| **Q80** | PP5 | 20c carmine | .20 | .20 |

Custom House — PP13

1p, State Railroad Administration Building.

**1955 Unwmk. Litho. *Perf. 12½***

| | | | | |
|---|---|---|---|---|
| **Q81** | PP13 | 5c brown | .20 | .20 |
| **Q82** | PP13 | 1p light ultra | 2.00 | 1.50 |

See Nos. Q83, Q85-Q86, Q96. For surcharge see No. Q87.

Types of 1945 and 1955

Design: 20c, Solis Theater.

**1956-57 *Perf. 11***

| | | | | |
|---|---|---|---|---|
| **Q83** | PP13 | 5c gray ('57) | .30 | .20 |
| **Q84** | PP7 | 10c lt olive grn | .20 | .20 |
| **Q85** | PP13 | 20c yellow | .20 | .20 |
| **Q86** | PP13 | 20c lt red brn ('57) | .20 | .20 |
| | | *Nos. Q83-Q86 (4)* | .90 | .80 |

No. Q83 Surcharged with New Value in Red

**1957**

| | | | | |
|---|---|---|---|---|
| **Q87** | PP13 | 30c on 5c gray | .20 | .20 |

Type of 1938-39

**1957-60 Wmk. 327 *Perf. 11***

**Q88** PP5 20c lt blue ('59) .20 .20

**Unwmk.**

**Q89** PP5 30c red lilac .20 .20

***Perf. 12½***

**Q90** PP5 1p dk blue ('60) .25 .25
*Nos. Q88-Q90 (3)* .65 .65

Nos. Q88 and Q93 are in slightly larger format-17¼x21mm instead of 16x19½mm.

National Printing Works PP14

**1960, Mar. 23 Wmk. 327 *Perf. 11***

**Q91** PP14 30c yellow green .20 .20

Type of 1938-39

**1962-63 Wmk. 332 *Perf. 11***

**Q92** PP5 50c slate green .20 .20

***Perf. 10½***

**Q93** PP5 1p blue grn ('63) .50 .50

No. C158 Surcharged

**1965 Unwmk. *Perf. 11***

**Q94** AP12 5p on 84c orange .35 .20

For use on regular and air post parcels.

Types of 1938-55

1p, State Railroad Administration Building.

**1966 Litho. *Perf. 10½***

**Q95** PP5 10c blue green .20 .20

**Wmk. 327**

**Q96** PP13 1p brown .20 .20

No. C184 Surcharged in Red

**1966 Unwmk. *Perf. 11***

**Q97** AP21 1p on 38c black .20 .20

Plane and Bus — PP15

Design: 20p, Plane facing left and bus; "Encomiendas" on top.

**Wmk. 332**

**1969, July 8 Litho. *Perf. 12***

**Q98** PP15 10p blk, crim & bl grn .20 .20
**Q99** PP15 20p bl, blk & yel .40 .20

No. B7 Surcharged

**1971, Feb. 3 Wmk. 327 *Perf. 11½***

**Q100** SP2 60c on 1p + 10c 1.25 .60

No. 761 Surcharged in Red

**1971, Nov. 12 Wmk. 332 *Perf. 12***

**Q101** A226 60c on 6p lt grn & blk .45 .25

Nos. 770-771 Surcharged

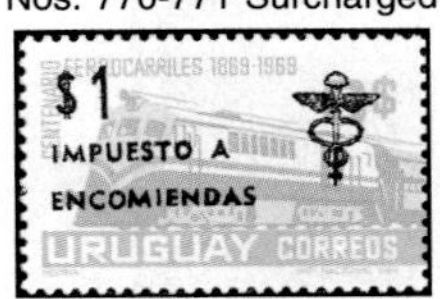


**1972, Nov. 6 Litho. *Perf. 12***

**Q102** A233 1p on 6p multi (#770) 1.00 .55
**Q103** A233 1p on 6p multi (#771) 1.00 .55
*a.* Pair, #Q102-Q103 2.00 1.10

See note after No. 771.

Parcels and Arrows PP16

Old Mail Truck PP17

Designs: Early means of mail transport.

**1974 Wmk. 332 Litho. *Perf. 12***

**Q104** PP16 75p shown .20 .20
**Q105** PP17 100p shown .40 .25
**Q106** PP17 150p Steam engine .95 .95
**Q107** PP17 300p Side-wheeler .90 .55
**Q108** PP17 500p Plane 1.40 .80
*Nos. Q104-Q108 (5)* 3.85 2.75

Issue dates: 75p, Feb. 13; others, Mar. 6.

---

## UZBEKISTAN

ˌuz-ˌbe-ki-ˈstan

LOCATION — Central Asia, bounded by Kazakhstan, Turkmenistan, Tajikistan, Afghanistan and Kyrgyzstan

GOVT. — Independent republic, member of the Commonwealth of Independent States

AREA — 172,741 sq. mi.

POP. — 25,155,064 (2001 est.)

CAPITAL — Tashkent (Toshkent)

With the breakup of the Soviet Union on Dec. 26, 1991, Uzbekistan and ten former Soviet republics established the Commonwealth of Independent States.

100 Kopecks = 1 Ruble
100 Tiyin = 1 Sum

**Catalogue values for all unused stamps in this country are for Never Hinged items.**

Princess Nadira (1792-1842) — A1

***Perf. 11½x12***

**1992, May 7 Unwmk. Photo.**

**1** A1 20k multicolored .30 .30

Melitaea Acreina A2

**1992, Aug. 31 Litho. *Perf. 12***

**2** A2 1r multicolored .25 .25

Independence from Soviet Union, 1st Anniv. — A3

**1992, Sept. 25 Photo. *Perf. 12***

**3** A3 1r multicolored .25 .25

Khiva Mosque, 19th Cent. — A4

**1992, Oct. 20 *Perf. 11½***

**4** A4 50k multicolored .20 .20

Samarkand — A5

**1992, Oct. 28 Litho. *Perf. 13x13½***

**5** A5 10r multicolored .40 .40

Winner of 1992 Aga Khan Award for Architecture.

Samovar, 19th Cent. — A6

**1992, Nov. 20 *Perf. 12x11½***

**6** A6 50k multicolored .35 .35

Fauna A7

Designs: 1r, Teratoscincus scincus. No. 8, Naja oxiana. No. 9, Ondatra zibethica, vert. 3r, Pandion haliaetus, vert. 5r, Remiz pendulinus, vert. 10r, Dryomys nitedula, vert. 15r, Varanus griseus. 20r, Cervus elaphus baktrianus.

**1993, Mar. 12 Litho. *Perf. 12***

**7** A7 1r multicolored .20 .20
**8** A7 2r multicolored .20 .20
**9** A7 2r multicolored .20 .20
**10** A7 3r multicolored .20 .20
**11** A7 5r multicolored .20 .20
**12** A7 10r multicolored .35 .35
**13** A7 15r multicolored .75 .75
*Nos. 7-13 (7)* 2.10 2.10

**Souvenir Sheet**

**14** A7 20r multicolored .75 .75

**Russia Nos. 4596-4600, 5838, 5841-5843, 5984 Surcharged in Vio Bl, Brt Bl, Bl, Red, Blk and Grn**

a

**Methods and perfs as before**

**1993**

**15** A2765 2r on 1k (#5838, BB) *.30 .30*
**16** A2138 8r on 4k (#4599, Bl) *.25 .25*
**17** A2138 15r on 2k (#4597) *2.50 2.50*
**18** A2765 15r on 2k (#5984) *2.50 2.50*
**19** A2765 15r on 3k (#5839, R) *2.50 2.50*
**20** A2765 15r on 4k (#4520, V) *2.50 2.50*
**21** A2765 15r on 4k (#5840, R) *2.50 2.50*
**22** A2765 15r on 5k (#5841) *2.50 2.50*
**23** A2139 15r on 6k (#4600, R) *2.50 2.50*
**24** A2765 15r on 7k (#5985a, R) *2.50 2.50*
**25** A2765 15r on 10k (#5842) *2.50 2.50*
**26** A2765 15r on 15k (#5843, R) *2.50 2.50*
**27** A2138 20r on 4k (#4599, Bk) *.45 .45*
**28** A2139 30r on 3k (#4598, G) *.45 .45*
**28A** A2138 100r on 1k (#4596, R) *.65 .65*
**29** A2138 500r on 1k (#4596, Bl) *3.50 3.50*
*Nos. 15-29 (16)* *30.60 30.60*

No. 18 exists imperf. Numbers have been reserved for additional stamps with uncertain status.

Flag and Coat of Arms — A8

***Perf. 12x12½, 11½x12 (#33)***

**1993, June 10 Litho.**

**30** A8 8r multicolored .20 .20
**31** A8 15r multicolored .25 .25
**33** A8 50r multicolored .70 .70
**34** A8 100r multicolored 1.50 1.50
*Nos. 30-34 (4)* 2.65 2.65

No. 33 is 19x26½mm.

Flowers — A9

**1993, Sept. 10 *Perf. 12***

**38** A9 20r Dianthus uzbekistanicus .20 .20
**39** A9 20r Colchicum kesselringii .20 .20
**40** A9 25r Crocus alatavicus .30 .30
**41** A9 25r Salvia bucharica .30 .30

42 A9 30r Tulipa kaufmanniana .35 .35
43 A9 30r Tulipa greigii .35 .35
*Nos. 38-43 (6)* 1.70 1.70

**Souvenir Sheet**

44 A9 50r Tulip 1.00 1.00

Coat of Arms — A10

**1994, July 2 Litho. *Perf. 12***

45 A10 1t green .20 .20

***Perf. 11½x12***

46 A10 75s claret .25 .25

**1995 Litho. *Perf. 14***

47 A10 2s green .80 .80

**Size: 20x33mm**

48 A10 3s carmine .80 .80
49 A10 6s carmine 1.25 1.25
49A A10 15s blue *2.00 2.00*

**Denomination Shown with Decimal**

50 A10 3s carmine .25 .25
51 A10 6s blue 1.25 1.25
*Nos. 45-51 (8)* 6.80 6.80

Issued: 15s, 12/26; others, 4/18.
See Nos. 151A-154, 228-237.

Statue of Tamerlane, Tashkent — A10a

**1994, Sept. 1 Litho. *Perf. 12½x12***

52 A10a 20t multicolored .20 .20

Bakhouddin, 675th Anniv. — A11

**1994, Aug. 1 *Perf. 12½x12***

55 A11 100s multi + label .25 .25

**Souvenir Sheet**

President's Cup Intl. Tennis Tournament, Tashkent — A12

**1994, June 3 *Perf. 12x12½***

56 A12 500s multicolored 1.00 1.00

Ulugh Beg (1394-1449), Astronomer — A13

30t, Portals of Samarkand. 35t, Portals of Bukhara. 40t, Globe, astrolabe. 45t, Statue. 60t, Portrait.

**1994, Sept. 15 Litho. *Perf. 12x12½***

57 A13 30t multi + label .20 .20
58 A13 35t multi + label .20 .20
59 A13 40t multi + label .20 .20
60 A13 45t multi + label .40 .40
*Nos. 57-60 (4)* 1.00 1.00

**Souvenir Sheet**

61 A13 60t multicolored .75 .75

**Russia Nos. 4596, 5113, 5839, 5840, 5843, 5984 Surcharged in Red Violet or Red**

b

**Methods and perfs as before**

**1995, Jan.**

61A A2138(a) 2s on 1k (#4596, R) *1.50 1.50*
61B A2765(a) 2s on 3k (#5839, R) *1.50 1.50*
61C A2765(b) 200s on 2k (#5984) *1.50 1.50*
61D A2765(b) 200s on 4k (#5840) *1.50 1.50*
61E A2436(b) 200s on 5k (#5113) *1.50 1.50*
61F A2765(b) 200s on 15k (#5843) *1.50 1.50*
*Nos. 61A-61F (6) 9.00 9.00*

No. 61C exists imperf.

**Souvenir Sheet**

End of World War II, 50th Anniv. — A14

**1995, May 8 Litho. *Perf. 12***

62 A14 20s multicolored 2.25 2.25

**Souvenir Sheet**

UPU — A15

**1995, Sept. 21**

63 A15 20s multicolored 1.75 1.75

Capra Falconeri A16

**1995, Aug. 15 *Perf. 12½***

64 A16 6s shown .70 .50
65 A16 10s Three on mountain 1.00 .75
66 A16 10s Up close 1.00 .75
67 A16 15s Lying down 1.75 1.25
*Nos. 64-67 (4)* 4.45 3.25

World Wildlife Fund.

Intl. Tennis Tournament, Tashkent '95 — A17

**1995, Aug. 25 *Perf. 14***

68 A17 10s multicolored 1.25 1.25

Silk Road Architecture A19

Designs: 6s, Mosque, 15th cent. No. 71, Blue-domed mosque, ruins, 15th cent. No. 72, Mosque with 4 minarets, 19th cent. No. 73, Cylindrical-style mosque, 19th cent.
20s, Map of mosque sites, camel, mosque.

**1995, Aug. 28 Litho. *Perf. 12x12½***

70 A19 6s multicolored 1.00 1.00
71 A19 10s multicolored 2.00 2.00
72 A19 10s multicolored 2.00 2.00
73 A19 15s multicolored 3.00 3.00
*Nos. 70-73 (4)* 8.00 8.00

**Souvenir Sheet**

74 A19 20s multicolored 5.00 5.00

Folktales — A20

6s, Man wrestling with creature, woman spilling bowls. #76, Man looking at stork, nest of eggs. #77, Women watching man cut into watermelon full of gold coins. #78, Creature carrying woman. 15s, Man holding beads, parrot.

**1995, Aug. 24**

75 A20 6s multi + label 1.25 1.25
76 A20 10s multicolored 1.75 1.75
77 A20 10s multicolored 1.75 1.75
78 A20 10s multicolored 1.75 1.75
79 A20 15s multicolored 2.50 2.50
*Nos. 75-79 (5)* 9.00 9.00

Moths A21

6s, Karanasa abramovi. #81, Colias romanovi. #82, Parnassius delphius. #83, Neohipparchia fatua. #84, Chasara staudingeri. #85, Colias wiskotti. 15s, Parnassius tianschanicus.
20s, Colias christophi.

**1995, Oct. 10 *Perf. 12½x12***

80 A21 6s multicolored 1.25 1.25
81 A21 10s multicolored 2.00 2.00
82 A21 10s multicolored 2.00 2.00
83 A21 10s multicolored 2.00 2.00
84 A21 10s multicolored 2.00 2.00
85 A21 10s multicolored 2.00 2.00
86 A21 15s multicolored 3.00 3.00
*Nos. 80-86 (7)* 14.25 14.25

**Souvenir Sheet**

87 A21 20s multicolored 3.00 3.00

Aircraft A22

**1995, Oct. 10**

88 A22 6s JIN-2 1.25 1.25
89 A22 10s IL-76 2.00 2.00
90 A22 10s KA-22 2.00 2.00
91 A22 10s AN-8 2.00 2.00
92 A22 10s AN-22 2.00 2.00
93 A22 10s AN-12 2.00 2.00
94 A22 15s IL-114 3.25 3.25
*Nos. 88-94 (7)* 14.50 14.50

**Souvenir Sheet**

95 A22 20s like No. 94 3.00 3.00

Wildlife from Tashkent Zoo — A23

Designs: 6s, Camelus ferus. No. 97, Aegupius monachus. No. 98, Ursus arctos isabellinus. No. 99, Zebra. No. 100, Macaca mulatta. No. 101, Pelecanus crispus. 15s, Loxodonta africana.
20s, Capra falconeri.

**1995, Nov. 30 *Perf. 12x12½***

96 A23 6s multicolored 1.00 1.00
97 A23 10s multicolored 1.75 1.75
98 A23 10s multicolored 1.75 1.75
99 A23 10s multicolored 1.75 1.75
100 A23 10s multicolored 1.75 1.75
101 A23 10s multicolored 1.75 1.75
102 A23 15s multicolored 2.50 2.50
*Nos. 96-102 (7)* 12.25 12.25

**Souvenir Sheet**

103 A23 20s multicolored 3.00 3.00

Wild Animals A24

Designs: 10s, Ovis ammon bocharensis. No. 105, Ovis ammon severtzov. No. 106, Cervus elaphus bactrianus. No. 107, Capra sibirica. No. 108, Ovis ammon karelini. No. 109, Ovis ammon cycloceros. 20s, Saiga tatarica.
25s, Gazella subgutturosa.

**1996, Feb. 16 *Perf. 12½x12***

104 A24 10s multicolored 1.00 1.00
105 A24 15s multicolored 1.50 1.50
106 A24 15s multicolored 1.50 1.50
107 A24 15s multicolored 1.50 1.50
108 A24 15s multicolored 1.50 1.50
109 A24 15s multicolored 1.50 1.50
110 A24 20s multicolored 2.25 2.25
*Nos. 104-110 (7)* 10.75 10.75

**Souvenir Sheet**

111 A24 25s multicolored 2.75 2.75

Painting A25

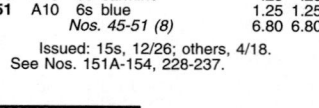

**1995, Oct. Litho. *Perf. 12x12½***

112 A25 15s multicolored 1.50 1.50

Souvenir Sheet

Save the Aral Sea — A26

a, 15s, Felis caracal. b, 15s, Salmo trutta aralensis. c, 20s, Hyaena hyaena. d, 20t, Pseudoscaphirynchus kaufmanni. e, 25t, Aspiolucius esocinus.

**1996, May 15** *Perf. 14*
**113** A26 Sheet of 5, #a.-e. 5.00 5.00

See Kazakhstan #145, Kyrgyzstan #107, Tadjikistan #91, Turkmenistan #52.

1996 Summer Olympic Games, Atlanta A27

**1996, June 23 Litho.** *Perf. 12½x12*

| | | | | |
|---|---|---|---|---|
| **114** | A27 | 6s Soccer | .50 | .50 |
| **115** | A27 | 10s Equestrian event | 1.00 | 1.00 |
| **116** | A27 | 15s Boxing | 1.25 | 1.25 |
| **117** | A27 | 20s Cycling | 2.00 | 2.00 |
| | | *Nos. 114-117 (4)* | 4.75 | 4.75 |

Souvenir Sheet

Tamerlane (1336-1405) — A28

**1996, Aug. 31 Litho.** *Perf. 14*
**118** A28 20s multicolored 4.50 4.50
*a.* Inscribed "1336-1404," perf 12x12½ *5.50 5.50*

Issued: No. 118a, 8/9/96.

Souvenir Sheet

Independence Day — A29

Illustration reduced.

**1996, Aug. 27 Litho.** *Perf. 12x12½*
**119** A29 20s multicolored 1.75 1.75

Tashkent Tennis Cup Championship A30

**1996, Sept. 2 Litho.** *Perf. 14*
**121** A30 12s green 3.00 3.00

A31

A32

**1996, Sept. 18** *Perf. 14*
**122** A31 15s Faijzulla Khodjaev 2.25 2.25

**1996, Oct. 14 Litho.** *Perf. 14*
**123** A32 15s black & buff 2.25 2.25

Abdurauf Fitrat (1886-1996).

Futuristic Space Travel — A33

9s, Shuttle-type vehicle. #126, Vehicle in front of sun. #127, Sun's rays, vehicle traveling left. #128, Large vehicle, sun in distance. #129, Saucer-shaped vehicle landing on planet. 25s, Two men in cockpit.
30s, Two different space vehicles.

**1997, Mar. 17**

| | | | | |
|---|---|---|---|---|
| **124** | A33 | 9s multi, vert. | .75 | .75 |
| **125** | A33 | 15s shown | 1.25 | 1.25 |
| **126** | A33 | 15s multi | 1.25 | 1.25 |
| **127** | A33 | 15s multi | 1.25 | 1.25 |
| **128** | A33 | 15s multi, vert. | 1.25 | 1.25 |
| **129** | A33 | 15s multi, vert. | 1.25 | 1.25 |
| **130** | A33 | 25s multi, vert. | 1.50 | 1.50 |
| | | *Nos. 124-130 (7)* | 8.50 | 8.50 |

**Souvenir Sheet**

**131** A33 30s multi, vert. 3.00 3.00

Fairy Tales A34

#132, Genie. #133, Bird. #134, Child holding mirror in front of couple. #135, Ape. #136, Face of creature, horse. #137, Large bird attacking deer. 30s, Two people kneeling before throne.
35s, Man on horse.

**1997, Apr. 18**

| | | | | |
|---|---|---|---|---|
| **132** | A34 | 15s multicolored | 1.00 | 1.00 |
| **133** | A34 | 15s multicolored | 1.00 | 1.00 |
| **134** | A34 | 20s multicolored | 1.25 | 1.25 |
| **135** | A34 | 20s multicolored | 1.25 | 1.25 |
| **136** | A34 | 25s multicolored | 1.50 | 1.50 |
| **137** | A34 | 25s multicolored | 1.50 | 1.50 |
| **138** | A34 | 30s multicolored | 2.00 | 2.00 |
| | | *Nos. 132-138 (7)* | 9.50 | 9.50 |

**Souvenir Sheet**

**139** A34 35s multicolored 3.50 3.50

Abdulhamid Sulaymon, Birth Cent. — A35

**1997, June 20**
**140** A35 6s lilac, black & gray 2.00 2.00

Pantera Pardus Tullianus A36

Designs: No. 142, Yawning. No. 143, Stretching. 25s, Walking on fallen tree.
30s, With mouth open.

**1997, May 28**

| | | | | |
|---|---|---|---|---|
| **141** | A36 | 9s multicolored | .75 | .75 |
| **142** | A36 | 15s multicolored | 1.25 | 1.25 |
| **143** | A36 | 15s multicolored | 1.25 | 1.25 |
| **144** | A36 | 25s multicolored | 2.25 | 2.25 |
| | | *Nos. 141-144 (4)* | 5.50 | 5.50 |

**Souvenir Sheet**

**145** A36 30s multicolored 2.50 2.50

No. 145 contains one 30x40mm stamp.

Sites on Silk Road A37

In Bukhara: No. 146, Ancient citadel. No. 147, Tomb of Ismail Samani, vert.
In Khiva: No. 148, Minaret, vert. No. 149, Fortress wall with open door.
No. 150, Mosque, Bukhara. No. 151, Minaret, Khiva, diff., vert.

**1997 Litho.** *Perf. 14*

| | | | | |
|---|---|---|---|---|
| **146** | A37 | 15s multicolored | *1.00* | 1.00 |
| **147** | A37 | 15s multicolored | *1.00* | 1.00 |
| **148** | A37 | 15s multicolored | *1.00* | 1.00 |
| **149** | A37 | 15s multicolored | *1.00* | 1.00 |
| | | *Nos. 146-149 (4)* | *4.00* | 4.00 |

**Souvenir Sheets**

| | | | | |
|---|---|---|---|---|
| **150** | A37 | 30s multicolored | *2.25* | 2.25 |
| **151** | A37 | 30s multicolored | *2.25* | 2.25 |

Issued: Nos. 146-147, 150, 10/7; Nos. 148-149, 151, 10/8.

Arms Type of 1994 Redrawn

**1998 Litho.** *Perf. 14*

**Size: 14x22mm**

| | | | | |
|---|---|---|---|---|
| **151A** | A10 | 2s green | .30 | .30 |
| **152** | A10 | 3s carmine | .50 | .50 |
| **153** | A10 | 6s green | .65 | .65 |
| **153A** | A10 | 12s green | 2.25 | 2.25 |
| **153B** | A10 | 15s red | 1.25 | 1.25 |
| **154** | A10 | 45s blue | 3.25 | 3.25 |
| | | *Nos. 151A-154 (6)* | 8.20 | 8.20 |

Nos. 152-154 have country name "O'ZBEKISTON" at top and " "POCHTA 1998" at bottom.
#152, 153 exist dated 1999.
Issued: 6s, 2/25; 12s, 15s, 45s, 3/25; 2s, 4/16; 3s, 4/17.

Intl. Tennis Tournament, Tashkent A38

Emblem and: No. 155, President's Cup. No. 156, Tennis player. No. 157, Camel.

**1997 Litho.** *Perf. 14*

| | | | | |
|---|---|---|---|---|
| **155** | A38 | 6s blue & grn | *1.25* | *1.25* |
| **156** | A38 | 6s blue & grn | *1.25* | *1.25* |
| **157** | A38 | 6s blue & grn | *1.25* | *1.25* |
| | | *Nos. 155-157 (3)* | *3.75* | *3.75* |

Automobiles — A39

a, 9s, Tico. b, 12s, Damas. c, 15s, Nexia.

**1997, Sept. 19 Litho.** *Perf. 14*
**158** A39 Block of 3, #a.-c. + label 2.75 2.75

Tennis Tournament A40

Sharq Taronlalari Intl. Music Festival A41

**1998, Aug. 17 Litho.** *Perf. 14*
**159** A40 15s multicolored 1.25 1.25

**1998, July 15**
**160** A41 15s multicolored 1.00 1.00

Berdaq Monument A42

Kamoliddin Behzod, Poet A43

**1998, Aug. 17**
**161** A42 15s blue & brown .75 .75

**1998, Aug. 17**
**162** A43 15s multicolored 1.00 1.00

Imam Al-Buxoriy A44

Ahmad Al-Fargoni A45

**1998, June 26**
**163** A44 15s multicolored .75 .75

**1998, June 26**
**164** A45 15s multicolored 1.00 1.00

Folktales — A46

Designs: a, 8s, Woman holding baby. b, 10s, "Alpomish" over rainbow. c, 15s, Three men seated before fire. d, 15s, Man talking to man with sword. e, 18s, Man riding horse. f, 18s, Knight with longbow, squire with arrow. g, 20s, Swordmaker at work. h, 20s, Man fighting lion. i, 25s, Man, woman walking arm in arm.

**1998, Nov. 27 Litho. *Perf. 14***
165 A46 Sheet of 9, #a.-i. 5.50 5.50

No. 165 is a continuous design.

**Arms Type of 1994 Redrawn**

**1999-2001 Litho. *Perf. 14***
**Size: 14x23mm**

| | | | | |
|---|---|---|---|---|
| 167 | A10 | 5s blue green | .40 | .40 |
| 168 | A10 | 6s green | .85 | .85 |
| 168A | A10 | 10s dk green | .40 | .40 |
| *d.* | | 10s emerald, dated "2004" | .40 | .40 |
| 168B | A10 | 15s lt blue | .70 | .70 |
| 168C | A10 | 17s dk blue | .75 | .75 |
| 169 | A10 | 30s blue | .85 | .85 |
| 170 | A10 | 40s rose | .50 | .50 |
| 170A | A10 | 45s rose | 1.50 | 1.50 |
| *a.* | | 45s carmine, dated 2001 | 1.75 | 1.75 |
| 171 | A10 | 60s rose car | 1.50 | 1.50 |
| | | *Nos. 167-171 (9)* | 7.45 | 7.45 |

Issued: 6s, 3/22/99. 15s, 17s, 30s, 45s, 12/5/00. 5s, 60s, 1/17/01; No. 168A, 40s, 2/5/01. No. 168Ad, 6/15/04.

Nos. 167-171 have country name "O'ZBEKISTON" at top and "POCHTA" and year at bottom. Stamps issued in 2001 are inscribed "2000." No. 170 exists dated "2001." No. 167 exists dated "2004" and "2005."

No. 168 is inscribed "6 so'm." No. 153 is inscribed "6-00."

Trains — A47

Locomotives: #172, OV steam, 1897-1917. #173, EA steam, 1931-35. 28s, FD steam, 1931-41. 36s, SO steam, 1934-52. #176, VL-22 electric. #177, KCh. 69s, TEP-6.

**1999, May 11 Litho. *Perf. 14***

| | | | | |
|---|---|---|---|---|
| 172 | A47 | 18s multicolored | .50 | .50 |
| 173 | A47 | 18s multicolored | .50 | .50 |
| 174 | A47 | 28s multicolored | .75 | .75 |
| 175 | A47 | 36s multicolored | .85 | .85 |
| 176 | A47 | 56s multicolored | 1.25 | 1.25 |
| 177 | A47 | 56s multicolored | 1.25 | 1.25 |
| 178 | A47 | 69s multicolored | 1.50 | 1.50 |
| | | *Nos. 172-178 (7)* | 6.60 | 6.60 |

A48

A49

Designs: 18s, Horse rearing.
No. 180, horiz.: a, 36s, Robed rider on horse. b, 28s, White horse. c, 69s, Jockey on race horse.
75s, Black horse, horiz.

**1999, May 25**
179 A48 18s multicolored 1.25 1.25
180 A48 Vert. strip of 3, #a.-c. 3.25 3.25

**Souvenir Sheet**
181 A48 75s multicolored 3.25 3.25

No. 180 printed in sheets of 8 stamps containing 2 strips and one each of Nos. 180a and 180c.

**1999, June 8**

Story of Badal Qorachi — #182: a, 18s, Woman, deer. b, 18s, Two archers on horses. c, 28s, Archer on horse. d, 36s, White giant. e, 56s, Black giant. f, 56s, Troll, cat, bones. g, Man, woman.
75s, Woman on sofa, demon, horiz.

182 A49 Sheet of 7, #a.-g. + label *3.75 3.75*

**Souvenir Sheet**
183 A49 75s multicolored *2.00 2.00*

A50

A51

Reptiles: No. 184, Trapelus sanguinolentus.
No. 185, horiz.: a, 18s, Eremias arguta. b, 18s, Vipera ursinii. c, 28s, Phrynocephalus mystaceus. d, 36s, Agkistrodon halys. e, 56s, Eumeces schneideri. f, 69s, Vipera lebetina.
75s, Two lizards, horiz.

**1999, June 22**
184 A50 56s multicolored *.75 .75*
185 A50 Sheet of 6, #a.-f. *3.75 3.75*

**Souvenir Sheet**
186 A50 75s multicolored *2.25 2.25*

**1999, July 7**
187 A51 45s light green & black *1.40 1.40*

UPU, 125th anniv.

A52

A53

**1999, July 21**
188 A52 30s green & claret *1.00 1.00*

Muhammadrizo Erniyozbek ogli-Ogahiy, poet.

**1999, Oct. 22 Litho. *Perf. 14x13¾***

Birds of Prey: No. 189, Circaetus qallicus. No. 190, Falco tinnunculus. No. 191, Aquila chrysaetos. No. 192, Gyps fulvus. 36s, Falco cherrug. 56s, Gypaetus barbatus. 60s, Pandion haliaetus.
75s, Bird, hatchlings.

| | | | | |
|---|---|---|---|---|
| 189 | A53 | 15s multi | .50 | .50 |
| 190 | A53 | 15s multi | .50 | .50 |
| 191 | A53 | 18s multi | .60 | .60 |
| 192 | A53 | 18s multi | .60 | .60 |
| 193 | A53 | 36s multi | .90 | .90 |
| 194 | A53 | 56s multi | 1.25 | 1.25 |
| 195 | A53 | 60s multi | 1.50 | 1.50 |
| | | *Nos. 189-195 (7)* | 5.85 | 5.85 |

**Souvenir Sheet**
196 A53 75s multi *2.25 2.25*

A54

A55

Soccer.

**1999, Nov. 8**

| | | | | |
|---|---|---|---|---|
| 197 | A54 | 15s Two players | .50 | .50 |
| 198 | A54 | 18s Two players, diff. | .50 | .50 |
| 199 | A54 | 28s Two players, diff. | .60 | .60 |
| 200 | A54 | 28s Player, goalie | .60 | .60 |
| 201 | A54 | 36s Player, goalie, diff. | 1.00 | 1.00 |
| 202 | A54 | 56s Two players, diff. | 1.25 | 1.25 |
| 203 | A54 | 69s Two players, diff. | 1.60 | 1.60 |
| | | *Nos. 197-203 (7)* | 6.05 | 6.05 |

**Souvenir Sheet**
***Perf. 13¾x14***
204 A54 75s Two players, horiz. *2.25 2.25*

**1999, Dec. 13 Litho. *Perf. 14x13¾***

Prehistoric Animals: a, 28s, Meqaneura. b, 28s, Mesosaurus. c, 36s, Rhamphorhynchus. d, 36s, Styracosaurus albertensis. e, 56s, Trachodon annectens. f, 56s, Tarbosaurus bataar. g, 69s, Arsinoitherium. h, 75s, Phororhacos.

205 A55 Sheet of 8, #a.-h. *8.50 8.50*

Uzbek National Circus — A56

28s, Woman and lion. # 207, 36s, Acrobat with bow and arrow. #208, 36s, Acrobat. #209, 56s, Clown on horse. #210, 56s, Two riders on horse. 69s, Wire walker.
100s, Woman, camels, llamas, horiz.

**2000. Jan. 4 *Perf. 14***

| | | | | |
|---|---|---|---|---|
| 206 | A56 | 28s multi | .50 | .50 |
| 207 | A56 | 36s multi | .50 | .50 |
| 208 | A56 | 36s multi | .50 | .50 |
| 209 | A56 | 56s multi | 1.00 | 1.00 |
| 210 | A56 | 56s multi | 1.00 | 1.00 |
| 211 | A56 | 69s multi | 1.25 | 1.25 |
| | | *Nos. 206-211 (6)* | 4.75 | 4.75 |

**Souvenir Sheet**
212 A56 100s multi *2.00 2.00*

Horses — A57

Designs: 69s, Horses pulling carriage.
No. 214: a, 36s, Horse in dressage competition. b, 36s, Horse jumping fences. c, 56s, Horses in race. d, 56s, Horse jumping steeplechase fence. e, 75s, Horse with sulky. f, 75s, Race winner.

**2000, Feb. 1**
213 A57 69s multi *1.00 1.00*

**Sheet of 6**
214 A57 #a.-f. *6.00 6.00*

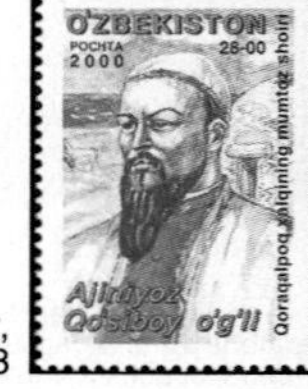
Ajiniyoz Qo'siboy, Poet — A58

**2000, Mar. 31 Litho. *Perf. 14***
215 A58 28s multi *.90 .90*

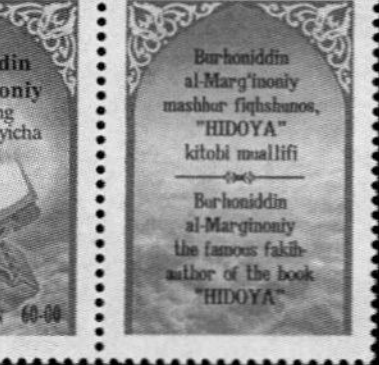
Famous Uzbek Writers — A59

Designs: No. 216, 60s, Burhoniddin al Marg'inoniy. No. 217, 60s, Imam Abu mansur al-Moturidiy, horiz.

**2000, Oct. 24**
**Stamp + label**
216-217 A59 Set of 2 *2.25 2.25*

UN High Commissioner for Refugees, 50th Anniv. — A60

**2000, Dec. 11**
218 A60 125s multi + label *2.00 2.00*

Bats A61

Designs: 15s, Tadarida teniotis. 30s, Otonycteris hemrichi. 45s, Nyctalus lasiopterus, vert. 50s, Muotis frater, vert. 60s, Rhinolophus hipposideros, vert. 90s, Barbastella leucomelas, vert. 125s, Nyctalus noctula, vert.
160s, Unidentified bat, vert.

**2001, Feb. 23 *Perf. 13¾x14, 14x13¾***
219-225 A61 Set of 7 *4.75 4.75*

**Souvenir Sheet**
226 A61 160s multi *2.75 2.75*

Dated 2000.

Native Costumes — A62

**2001, Feb. 26** ***Perf. 14x13¾***

**227** Horiz. strip of 5 + label *6.00 6.00*
- ***a.*** A62 45s multi *.50 .50*
- ***b.*** A62 50s multi, diff. *.60 .60*
- ***c.*** A62 60s multi, diff. *.70 .70*
- ***d.*** A62 90s multi, diff. *1.00 1.00*
- ***e.*** A62 125s multi, diff. *1.50 1.50*

Dated 2000.

### Arms Type of 1994 Redrawn

**2001-05** **Litho.** ***Perf. 14***

**Size: 14x23mm**

**228** A10 15s emerald *.40 .40*
**229** A10 17s dull green *.40 .40*
**230** A10 20s dull green *.40 .40*
**231** A10 25s bright blue *.40 .40*
**232** A10 30s sky blue *.40 .40*
**232A** A10 30s green *.50 .50*
- ***b.*** light green, dated "2005" *.50 .50*

**233** A10 33s gray blue *.50 .50*
**234** A10 45s red *.75 .75*
**235** A10 50s rose *.90 .90*
**236** A10 60s rose pink *1.10 1.10*
**237** A10 100s rose *1.50 1.50*
*Nos. 228-237 (11)* *7.25 7.25*

Issued: 15s, 17s, 25s, 33s, 50s, 60s, 100s, 4/3; 20s, 30s, 4/11; 45s, 6/22. No. 232A, 5/26/03; No. 232Ab, 3/25/05.

No. 237 exists dated "2003." No. 232A exists dated "2004."

Ali Shir Nava'i (1441-1501), Poet — A63

**2001, Apr. 11**

**238** Horiz. strip of 5 + label *6.00 6.00*
- ***a.*** A63 60s Hayrat ul-abror *.75 .75*
- ***b.*** A63 70s Farhod va Shirin *.75 .75*
- ***c.*** A63 85s Layli va Majnun *.90 .90*
- ***d.*** A63 90s Sab'ai sayyora *.90 .90*
- ***e.*** A63 125s Saddi Iskandariy *1.25 1.25*

World Environment Day — A64

**2001, June 20**

**239** A64 100s multi *1.10 1.10*

Avesto, 2700th Anniv. — A65

**2001, June 20**

**240** A65 160s multi *1.75 1.75*

Souvenir Sheet

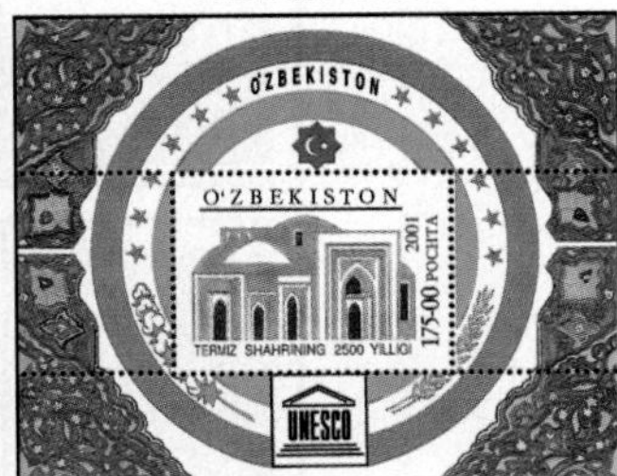


Termiz, 2500th Anniv. — A66

**2001, June 20**

**241** A66 175s multi *2.75 2.75*

Souvenir Sheet

Independence, 10th Anniv. — A67

**2001, June 20**

**242** A67 175s multi *2.75 2.75*

Souvenir Sheet

Regional Communications Cooperation — A68

**2001, June 20**

**243** A68 175s multi *2.75 2.75*

### 10th Anniv. of Independence Issue

Vertical Label

Horizontal Label

Tourist Hotel — A69

Monuments — A70

Inauguration of Pres. Islam Karimov — A71

Pres. Karimov at United Nations A72

Pres. Karimov at Istanbul Summit A73

Hirmon A74

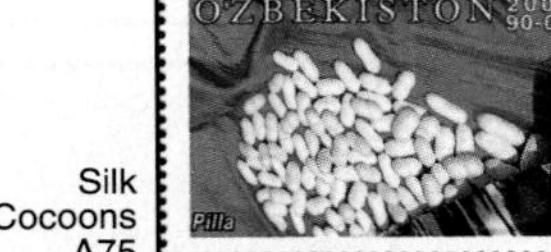


Silk Cocoons A75

Fergana Refinery A76

Power Station A77

Daewoo Auto Factory A78

Securities Exchange A79

Kamchik Tunnel A80

Pres. Karimov and US Pres. Clinton A81

Pres. Karimov and Russian Pres. Vladimir Putin A82

Pres. Karimov and Japanese Emperor Akihito A83

Pres. Karimov and Chinese Pres. Jiang Zemin A84

Pres. Karimov and German Chancellor Gerhard Schröder A85

Pres. Karimov and French Pres. Jacques Chirac A86

Pres. Karimov and British Prime Minister John Major A87

Pres. Karimov and Iranian Pres. Ali Mohammad Khatami — A88

Pres. Karimov and Egyptian Pres. Hosni Mubarak A89

Pres. Karimov and Italian Pres. Carlos Ciampi A90

Pres. Karimov and Indian Pres. Kocheril Narayanan
A91

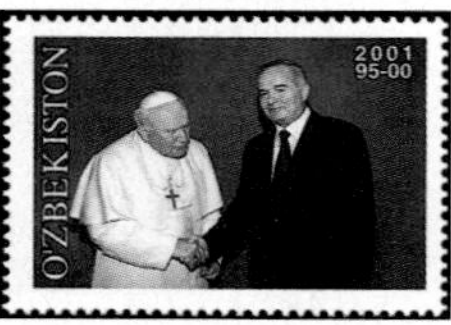

Pres. Karimov and Pope John Paul II — A92

Textile Workers
A93

Shurtan Gas Complex — A94

Muborak Refinery — A95

Oil Pipeline — A96

Solar Collector
A97

Soldiers with Flag
A98

Missiles
A99

Soldiers Training
A100

Kurash Sports Complex
A101

New Year's Celebration — A102

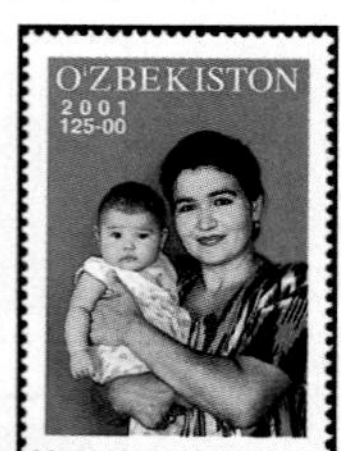

Mother and Child — A103

Wedding
A104

Bukhara Refinery — A105

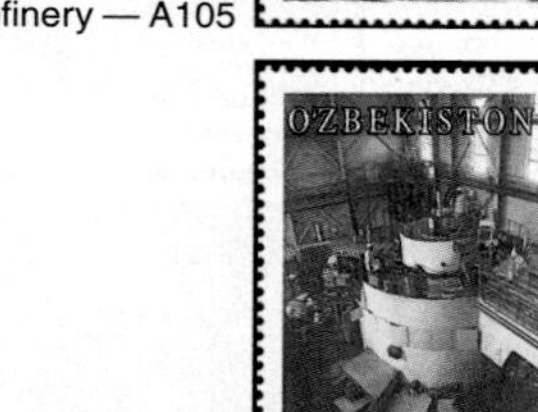

Nuclear Power Plant — A106

A70 Designs: No. 245, Zahriddin Bobur Monument. No. 246, Amir Temur Monument. No. 247, Al-Motorudi Monument. No. 248, Al-Marginoniy Monument. No. 249, Jaloliddin Manguberdi Monument. No. 250, Al-Bukhoriy Monument. No. 273, Alisher Navoi Monument. No 274, Berdaq Monument. No. 284, Alpomish Monument. No. 288, Al-Fargoniy Monument.

**2001 Litho. *Perf. 14x13¾, 13¾x14***
**Stamp + Label with Same Orientation**

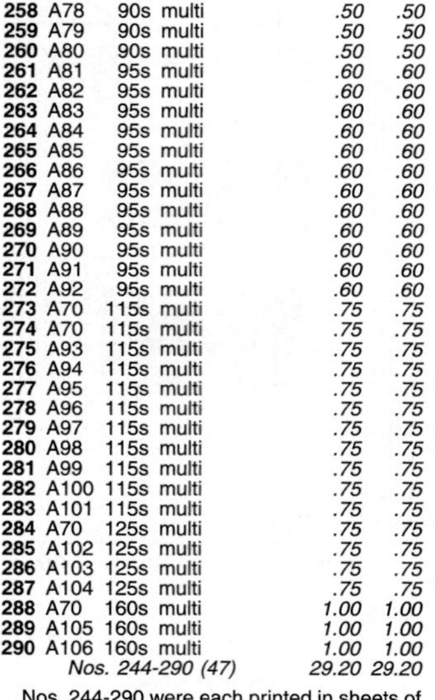

| No. | Design | Value | Color | Unused | Used |
|---|---|---|---|---|---|
| **244** | A69 | 60s | multi | .35 | .35 |
| **245** | A70 | 60s | multi | .35 | .35 |
| **246** | A70 | 70s | multi | .35 | .35 |
| **247** | A70 | 75s | multi | .35 | .35 |
| **248** | A70 | 75s | multi | .35 | .35 |
| **249** | A70 | 85s | multi | .50 | .50 |
| **250** | A70 | 90s | multi | .50 | .50 |
| **251** | A71 | 90s | multi | .50 | .50 |
| **252** | A72 | 90s | multi | .50 | .50 |
| **253** | A73 | 90s | multi | .50 | .50 |
| **254** | A74 | 90s | multi | .50 | .50 |
| **255** | A75 | 90s | multi | .50 | .50 |
| **256** | A76 | 90s | multi | .50 | .50 |
| **257** | A77 | 90s | multi | .50 | .50 |
| **258** | A78 | 90s | multi | .50 | .50 |
| **259** | A79 | 90s | multi | .50 | .50 |
| **260** | A80 | 90s | multi | .50 | .50 |
| **261** | A81 | 95s | multi | .60 | .60 |
| **262** | A82 | 95s | multi | .60 | .60 |
| **263** | A83 | 95s | multi | .60 | .60 |
| **264** | A84 | 95s | multi | .60 | .60 |
| **265** | A85 | 95s | multi | .60 | .60 |
| **266** | A86 | 95s | multi | .60 | .60 |
| **267** | A87 | 95s | multi | .60 | .60 |
| **268** | A88 | 95s | multi | .60 | .60 |
| **269** | A89 | 95s | multi | .60 | .60 |
| **270** | A90 | 95s | multi | .60 | .60 |
| **271** | A91 | 95s | multi | .60 | .60 |
| **272** | A92 | 95s | multi | .60 | .60 |
| **273** | A70 | 115s | multi | .75 | .75 |
| **274** | A70 | 115s | multi | .75 | .75 |
| **275** | A93 | 115s | multi | .75 | .75 |
| **276** | A94 | 115s | multi | .75 | .75 |
| **277** | A95 | 115s | multi | .75 | .75 |
| **278** | A96 | 115s | multi | .75 | .75 |
| **279** | A97 | 115s | multi | .75 | .75 |
| **280** | A98 | 115s | multi | .75 | .75 |
| **281** | A99 | 115s | multi | .75 | .75 |
| **282** | A100 | 115s | multi | .75 | .75 |
| **283** | A101 | 115s | multi | .75 | .75 |
| **284** | A70 | 125s | multi | .75 | .75 |
| **285** | A102 | 125s | multi | .75 | .75 |
| **286** | A103 | 125s | multi | .75 | .75 |
| **287** | A104 | 125s | multi | .75 | .75 |
| **288** | A70 | 160s | multi | 1.00 | 1.00 |
| **289** | A105 | 160s | multi | 1.00 | 1.00 |
| **290** | A106 | 160s | multi | 1.00 | 1.00 |
| | *Nos. 244-290 (47)* | | | *29.20* | *29.20* |

Nos. 244-290 were each printed in sheets of 2 stamps and 2 labels.

Uzbekistan Arms — A107

Uzbekistan Flag — A108

Motor Vehicles
A109

Central Bank Building — A110

Bank Association Building — A111

Tashkent Khokimiyat Building
A112

Central Trade Center Building
A113

Shurtan Gas Complex
A114

Shurtan Gas Complex
A115

Couple with Baby
A116

Children
A117

Farm Equipment
A118

Airplanes
A119

Constitution
A120

Majlis Hall — A121

Gold Ingots and Coins
A122

Muruntay Gold Mine
A123

Independence Day Celebrations — A124

Independence Day Celebrations — A125

A109 Designs: No. 292a, Nexia. No. 292b, Damas. No. 293a, Tico. No. 293b, Matiz.

A118 Designs: No. 298a, Case 2022 cotton picker. No. 298b, SHR-100 tractor.

A119 Designs: No. 299a, IL-76 MF cargo plane. No. 299b, IL-114-100 passenger plane.

| | | | |
|---|---|---|---|
| **291** | Pair with central label | *1.00* | *1.00* |
| ***a.*** | A107 90s multi | *.50* | *.50* |
| ***b.*** | A108 90s multi | *.50* | *.50* |
| **292** | Pair with central label | *1.00* | *1.00* |
| ***a.-b*** | A109 90s Any single | *.50* | *.50* |
| **293** | Pair with central label | *1.00* | *1.00* |
| ***a.-b.*** | A109 90s multi | *.50* | *.50* |
| **294** | Pair with central label | *1.00* | *1.00* |
| ***a.*** | A110 90s multi | *.50* | *.50* |
| ***b.*** | A111 90s multi | *.50* | *.50* |
| **295** | Pair with central label | *1.00* | *1.00* |
| ***a.*** | A112 90s multi | *.50* | *.50* |
| ***b.*** | A113 90s multi | *.50* | *.50* |
| **296** | Pair with central label | *1.75* | *1.75* |
| ***a.*** | A114 115s multi | *.80* | *.80* |
| ***b.*** | A115 115s multi | *.80* | *.80* |
| **297** | Pair with central label | *1.75* | *1.75* |
| ***a.*** | A116 125s multi | *.80* | *.80* |
| ***b.*** | A117 125s multi | *.80* | *.80* |
| **298** | Pair with central label | *2.00* | *2.00* |
| ***a.-b.*** | A118 160s Any single | *.90* | *.90* |
| **299** | Pair with central label | *1.25* | *1.25* |
| ***a.*** | A119 90s multi | *.50* | *.50* |
| ***b.*** | A119 115s multi | *.70* | *.70* |
| **300** | Pair with central label | *1.10* | *1.10* |
| ***a.*** | A120 115s multi | *.70* | *.70* |
| ***b.*** | A121 60s multi | *.35* | *.35* |
| **301** | Pair with central label | *1.25* | *1.25* |
| ***a.*** | A122 115s multi | *.70* | *.70* |
| ***b.*** | A123 90s multi | *.40* | *.40* |
| **302** | Pair with central label | *1.25* | *1.25* |
| ***a.*** | A124 125s multi | *.75* | *.75* |
| ***b.*** | A125 90s multi | *.50* | *.50* |
| | *Nos. 291-302 (12)* | *15.35* | *15.35* |

Nos. 291-302 printed in sheets of four stamps and two labels (two pairs).

Theater
A126

Theater
A127

Theater
A128

Medals — A129

Combine
A130

Combine
A131

Pres. Karimov and Farmers
A132

Soldier Taking Oath Before Flag
A133

Man and Soldier Embracing
A134

Frontier Guards and Dog
A135

Athletes — A136

Soldiers in Formation
A137

Diver Training
A138

Decontamination Training — A139

Modern Architecture — A140

Armed Forces — A141

Archaeology — A142

High School — A143

Uzbekistan on World Map — A144

A129 Designs: No. 304a, Dostelik. No. 304b, I Darajali "Shon-Sharaf." No. 304c, II Darajali "Shon-Sharaf." No. 305a, I Darajali Sog'lom Avlod Uchun. No. 305b, II Darajali Sog'lom Avlod Uchun. No. 305c, Mehnat Shuhrati. No. 306a, Jaloliddin Manguberdi. No. 306b, Buyuk Xizmatlari Uchun. No. 306c, El-Yurt Hurmati. No. 307a, Oltin Yildiz. No. 307b, Mustaqillik. No. 307c, Amir Temur.

A136 Designs: No. 310a, Muhammadqodir Abdullayev. No. 310b, Lina Cheryazova. No. 310c, Artur Grigoryan. No. 312a, 160s, Armen Bagdasarov. No. 312b, 160s, Rustam Qosimjonov. No. 312c, 115s, Otabek Kosimov. No. 312d, 115s, Iroda To'laganova. No. 312e, 100s, Dilshod Muxtorov. No. 312e, 115s, Oksana Chusovitina.

No. 313: a, Temuriylar Tarixi Muzeyi (Amir Temur Museum). b, Oqsaroy. c, Oliy Majlis. d, Motamsaro Ona (Monument to Grieving Mother). e, Shahidlar Xotirasi (Respect Monument). f, Interkontinental mehmonxonasi (Intercontinental Hotel). g, Milliy Bank (National Bank). h, Yunusobod Sport Majmuasi (Yunusobod Sport Complex).

No. 314: a, 60s, Infantrymen, tank. b, 70s, Airplane and crew. c, 80s, Helicopter and crew. d, 90s, Soldier directing tank with flags. e, 90s, Minesweeper. f, 115s, Soldiers in classroom. g, 160s, Tanks. h, 60s, Artillery.

No. 315: a, 75s, Pot. b, 75s, Artifact with arch. c, 75s, Artifact with hole at top and side. d, 80s, Broken pot. e, 80s, Anthropomorphic figure with arms. f, 80s, Buddha. g, 80s, Costumed figure. h, 80s, Disk. i, 80s, Anthropomorphic figure missing arm. j, 80s, Box. k, 80s, Face.

| | | | |
|---|---|---|---|
| **303** | Strip of 3 + label | *1.50* | *1.50* |
| ***a.*** | A126 90s multi | *.50* | *.50* |
| ***b.*** | A127 90s multi | *.50* | *.50* |
| ***c.*** | A128 90s multi | *.50* | *.50* |
| **304** | Strip of 3 + label | *2.75* | *2.75* |
| ***a.-c.*** | A129 160s Any single | *.85* | *.85* |
| **305** | Strip of 3 + label | *2.75* | *2.75* |
| ***a.-c.*** | A129 160s Any single | *.85* | *.85* |
| **306** | Strip of 3 + label | *2.75* | *2.75* |
| ***a.-c.*** | A129 160s Any single | *.85* | *.85* |
| **307** | Strip of 3 + label | *2.75* | *2.75* |
| ***a.-c.*** | A129 160s Any single | *.85* | *.85* |
| **308** | Strip of 3 + label | *2.75* | *2.75* |
| ***a.*** | A130 160s multi | *.85* | *.85* |
| ***b.*** | A131 160s multi | *.85* | *.85* |
| ***c.*** | A132 160s multi | *.85* | *.85* |
| **309** | Strip of 3 + label | *1.75* | *1.75* |
| ***a.*** | A133 60s multi | *.35* | *.35* |
| ***b.*** | A134 80s multi | *.50* | *.50* |
| ***c.*** | A135 90s multi | *.60* | *.60* |
| **310** | Strip of 3 + label | *2.50* | *2.50* |
| ***a.*** | A136 160s multi | *1.00* | *1.00* |
| ***b.-c*** | A136 115s Any single | *.70* | *.70* |
| **311** | Block of 3 + label | *1.75* | *1.75* |
| ***a.*** | A137 115s multi | *.70* | *.70* |
| ***b.*** | A138 80s multi | *.50* | *.50* |
| ***c.*** | A139 70s multi | *.40* | *.40* |
| | *Nos. 303-311 (9)* | *21.25* | *21.25* |

### Sheets

| | | | | |
|---|---|---|---|---|
| **312** | A136 | Sheet of 6, #a-f, + 3 labels | *4.50* | *4.50* |
| **313** | A140 | 115s Sheet of 8, #a-h, + label | *6.00* | *6.00* |
| **314** | A141 | Sheet of 8, #a-h, + label | *4.50* | *4.50* |
| **315** | A142 | Sheet of 11, #a-k, + label | *5.25* | *5.25* |

### Souvenir Sheets

| | | | |
|---|---|---|---|
| **316** | A143 160s multi | *1.25* | *1.25* |
| **317** | A144 175s multi | *1.75* | *1.75* |

Labels have same orientation as stamps and are at left side of strips on Nos. 303-310, and at UR on No. 311. No. 312 contains three different labels.

Commonwealth of Independent States, 10th Anniv. — A145

**2001, Nov. 8** ***Perf. 13¾x14***

| | | | |
|---|---|---|---|
| **318** | A145 60s multi | *.90* | *.90* |

Artwork of Oral Tansiqboyev — A146

No. 319: a, 100s, Mening Qo'shig'im (My Song). b, 125s, Angren-Qo'qon Tog'yo'li (Angren-Kokand Mountain Road).

Illustration reduced.

**2001, Nov. 8**

| | | | | |
|---|---|---|---|---|
| **319** | A146 | Pair, #a-b, with central label | *2.25* | *2.25* |

Flowers — A147

Designs: 45s, Zygophyllum bucharicum. 50s, Viola hissarica. 60s, Bergenia hissarica. 70s, Eremurus hilariae. 85s, Salvia korolkowii. 90s, Lamyropappus schakaptaricus. 145s, Punica granatum.
175s, Undescribed flowers.

**2002, May 10 Litho. *Perf. 14x13¾***
**320-326** A147 Set of 7 *4.75 4.75*

**Souvenir Sheet**

**327** A147 175s multi *2.00 2.00*

Hominids — A148

No. 328: a, 40s, Dryopithecus maior. b, 45s, Homo erectus modjokertensis. c, 50s, Pithecanthropus erectus. d, 60s, Australopithecus afarensis. e, 70s, Zinjanthropus boisei. f, 85s, Homo sapiens neanderthalensis. g, 90s, Sinanthropus pekinensis. h, 125s, Protanthropus heidelbergensis. i, 160s, Homo sapiens fossilis.

**2002, May 10 *Perf. 13¾x14***
**328** A148 Sheet of 9, #a-i, + 3 labels *5.00 5.00*

Protection of Ozone Layer — A149

**2002, June 7 Litho. *Perf. 13¾x14***
**329** A149 40s multi *.90 .90*

Souvenir Sheet

City of Shahrisabz, 2700th Anniv. — A150

**2002, June 14 *Perf. 14***
**330** A150 30s multi *.90 .90*

Uzbek Sports
A151

Designs: 45s, Chavgon. 50s, Poyga. 60s, Kamondan otish. 70s, Qiz quvmoq. 85s, Ro'molcha olish. 90s, Kurash. 145s, Uloq.
175s, Ro'molcha olish, diff.

**2002, July 26 *Perf. 13¾x14***
**331-337** A151 Set of 7 *4.75 4.75*

**Souvenir Sheet**

**338** A151 175s multi *1.75 1.75*

Ancient Coins — A152

No. 339: a, 30s, Silver tetradrachm of Eucratides I c. 171-135 BC, obverse. b, 45s, As "a," reverse. c, 60s, Silver coin of Buxoro, obverse. d, 90s, As "c," reverse. e, 125s, Silver miri of Tamerlane, 1370-1405, obverse. f, 160s, As "e," reverse.
Illustration reduced.

**2002, Aug. 1**
**339** A152 Block of 6, #a-f *4.75 4.75*

City of Nukus, 70th Anniv. — A153

**2002, Oct. 2**
**340** A153 100s multi *1.25 1.25*

Iris Varieties — A154

Designs: 15s, Qoraqum. 30s, Solnechniy zaychik. 45s, Simfoniya. 50s, Chimyon. 60s, Ikar. 90s, Babye leto. 125s, Toshkent.
160s, Askiya.

**2002, Oct. 2 *Perf. 14x13¾***
**341-347** A154 Set of 7 *4.50 4.50*

**Souvenir Sheet**

**348** A154 160s multi *2.00 2.00*

---

Uzbekistan postal officials have declared the following items as "illegal:"
Sheets of eight stamps depicting Trains (4 different sheets with denominations of 56s, 75s, 95s and 125s);
Sheets of six stamps with various denominations depicting Birds (2 different), Animals, Year of the Snake, Chiroptera, Lizards, Chess;
Sheets of one label and five stamps with various denominations depicting Perissodactyla;
Souvenir sheets of one depicting Trains (8 different 36s sheets, 4 different 56s sheets, 2 different 75s sheets).

---

G'afur G'ulom (1903-66), Poet — A155

**2003, May 4 Litho. *Perf. 13¾x14***
**349** A155 1000s brown *5.25 5.25*

**European Bank Annual Meeting Issue**

Vertical Label

Horizontal Label

National Bank, Tashkent — A156

Kaltaminor Minaret, Khiva — A157

Aloqabank, Tashkent A158

Pres Karimov and European Bank for Reconstruction and Development Pres. Jean Lemierre — A159

Islamkhodja Minaret, Khiva — A160

East Gates, Khiva — A161

Samanid Museum, Bukhara — A162

Ark, Bukhara — A163

Women's Traditional Dress — A164

Women's Traditional Dress — A165

Women's Traditional Dress — A166

Women's Traditional Dress — A167

Women's Traditional Dress — A168

A157 Designs: 630s, Gumbazi Sayyidon Mausoleum, Shahrisabz. 920s, Go'ri Amir Mausoleum, Samarqand. 970s, Chorminor Madrasasi, Bukhara. 1330s, Registon, Samarqand, horiz.

**2003, May 4** ***Perf. 14x13¾, 13¾x14***

**Stamp + Label with Same Orientation**

**350** A156 520s multi *4.00 4.00*
**351** A157 520s multi *4.00 4.00*
**352** A157 630s multi *4.50 4.50*
**353** A157 920s multi *7.00 7.00*
**354** A157 970s multi *7.50 7.50*
**355** A158 970s multi *7.50 7.50*
**356** A157 1330s multi *10.00 10.00*
**357** A159 1330s multi *10.00 10.00*
**358** Horiz. pair with central label *8.50 8.50*
*a.* A160 580s multi *4.00 4.00*
*b.* A161 520s multi *4.00 4.00*
**359** Horiz. pair with central label *14.00 14.00*
*a.* A162 1170s multi *9.00 9.00*
*b.* A163 630s multi *4.50 4.50*
**360** Horiz. strip of 5 with flanking label *17.50 17.50*
*a.* A164 240s multi *1.75 1.75*
*b.* A165 320s multi *2.50 2.50*
*c.* A166 520s multi *4.00 4.00*
*d.* A167 580s multi *4.00 4.00*
*e.* A168 630s multi *4.50 4.50*

**Types of 2001-02**

**Stamp + Label with Same Orientation**

**361** A110 520s multi *4.00 4.00*
**362** A111 580s multi *4.00 4.00*
**363** Horiz. pair with central label *8.50 8.50*
*a.* A74 170s multi *1.25 1.25*
*b.* A93 920s multi *7.00 7.00*
**364** Horiz. pair with central label *6.00 6.00*
*a.* A107 240s multi *1.75 1.75*
*b.* A108 520s multi *4.00 4.00*
**365** Horiz. pair with central label *6.50 6.50*
*a.* A114 630s multi *4.50 4.50*
*b.* A115 240s multi *1.75 1.75*
**366** Horiz. pair with central label *6.50 6.50*
*a.* A122 520s multi *4.00 4.00*
*b.* A123 320s multi *2.50 2.50*
**367** Horiz. pair with flanking label *8.50 8.50*
*a.* A152 520s Like #339a *4.00 4.00*
*b.* A152 520s Like #339b *4.00 4.00*
**368** Horiz. pair with flanking label *8.50 8.50*
*a.* A152 580s Like #339c *4.00 4.00*
*b.* A152 580s Like #339d *4.00 4.00*
**369** Horiz. pair with flanking label *9.50 9.50*
*a.* A152 630s Like #339e *4.50 4.50*
*b.* A152 630s Like #339f *4.50 4.50*
**370** A140 Sheet of 8 + central label *37.50 37.50*
*a.* 520s Like #313a *4.00 4.00*
*b.* 970s Like #313b *7.50 7.50*
*c.* 580s Like #313c *4.00 4.00*
*d.* 630s Like #313d *4.50 4.50*
*e.* 320s Like #313e *2.50 2.50*
*f.* 630s Like #313f *4.50 4.50*
*g.* 920s Toshkent shahar hokimiyati (mayor's house) *7.00 7.00*
*h.* 240s Like #313h *1.75 1.75*

**Type of 2001 Redrawn**

**371** Horiz. pair with central label *12.00 12.00*
*a.* A109 630s Like #292a *4.50 4.50*
*b.* A109 970s Like #293b *7.50 7.50*
*Nos. 350-371 (22) 206.00 206.00*

Famous Men — A169

Designs: 125s, Komil Yormatov, film director. 500s, Jo'raxon Sultonov, singer.

**2003, July 8** ***Perf. 13¾x14***
**372-373** A169 Set of 2 *4.50 4.50*

Birds — A170

Designs: No. 374, 100s, Ciconia ciconia asiatica. No. 375, 100s, Ciconia nigra. No. 376, 125s, Platalea leucorodia. No. 377, 125s, Phoenicopterus ruber.

**2003, Sept. 17** ***Perf. 14x13¾***
**374-377** A170 Set of 4 *4.50 4.50*

Caps — A171

Designs: No. 378, 100s, Kula-tung. No. 379, 100s, Erkaklar do'ppisi. No. 380, 100s, Bayram do'ppisi. No. 381, 125s, Ayollar do'ppisi. No. 382, 125s, Ayollar taxya-do'ppisi. No. 383, 155s, Erkaklar do'ppisi, diff. No. 384, 155s, Bolalar bayram do'ppisi.

**2003, Oct. 7**
**378-384** A171 Set of 7 *6.25 6.25*

Paintings — A172

No. 385: a, Tong. Onalik, by R. Ahmedov. b, Baxt, by S. Ayitbayev.

**2003, Nov. 19**
**385** A172 970s Horiz. pair, #a-b *7.75 7.75*

See Kazakhstan No. 434.

Abuxoliq G'ijduvoniy, Bukhara, 900th Anniv. — A173

Illustration reduced.

**2003, Nov. 28** ***Perf. 13¾x14***
**386** A173 125s multi + label *1.25 1.25*

**Souvenir Sheet**

2004 Summer Olympics, Athens — A174

**2004, June 15** **Litho.** ***Perf. 14x13¾***
**387** A174 205s multi *1.25 1.25*

Ma'murjon Uzoqov (1904-63), Singer — A175

Abdulla Qodiriy (1894-1938), Writer — A176

**2004, Oct. 11** ***Perf. 14***
**388** A175 100s lt blue & blk *.75 .75*
**389** A176 125s lt blue & blk *.95 .95*

Grapes — A177

Designs: 60s, Kaltak. No. 391, 100s, Oq husayni. No. 392, 100s, Kattaqo'rg'on. No. 393, 125s, Echkemar. No. 394, 125s, Qizil Xurmoni. 155s, Qora Andijon. 210s, Parkent.

**2004, Oct. 11** ***Perf. 14x13¾***
**390-396** A177 Set of 7 *6.25 6.25*

Jewelry of 19th and 20th Centuries A178

Inscriptions: 60s, Tumor, Samarqand. No. 398, 100s, Tumor, Toshkent. No. 399, 100s, Qi'ltiqtumor, Qo'qon. No. 400, 125s, Tumor, Buxoro. No. 401, 125s, Bo'yintumor, Toshkent. 155s, Qo'ltiqtumor, Buxoro. 210s, Tumor, Buxoro, diff.

**2004, Oct. 18**
**397-403** A178 Set of 7 *6.50 6.50*

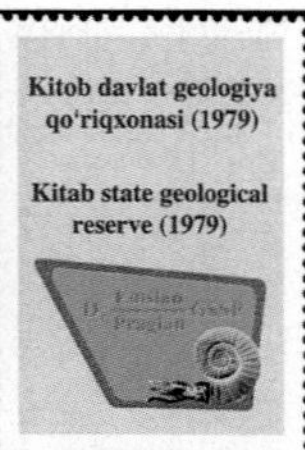

Kitab State Geological Reserve, 25th Anniv. — A179

**2004, Dec. 1**
**404** A179 100s multi + label *.85 .85*

**Arms Type of 1994 Redrawn**

**2004-06** **Litho.** ***Perf. 14***

**Size: 14x23mm**

**405** A10 35s green *.20 .20*
**406** A10 60s green *.30 .30*
*a.* light green, dated "2005" *.30 .30*
**407** A10 65s green *.35 .35*
**408** A10 125s dark blue *.50 .50*
**409** A10 200s red *.70 .70*
**410** A10 250s blue *.90 .90*
**411** A10 290s red *1.00 1.00*
**412** A10 350s blue *1.25 1.25*
**413** A10 430s red *1.50 1.50*
**414** A10 2500s red *8.50 8.50*
**415** A10 3700s blue *12.00 12.00*
*Nos. 405-415 (11) 27.20 27.20*

Issued: No. 406, 6/15; Nos. 406a, 408, 4/15/05; others, 1/5/06. Nos. 405, 407, 409-415 are dated "2005," though issued in 2006.

Oybek (1905-68), Writer — A180

**2005, Apr. 25** **Litho.** ***Perf. 14x13¾***
**416** A180 125s multi *.85 .85*

**Miniature Sheet**

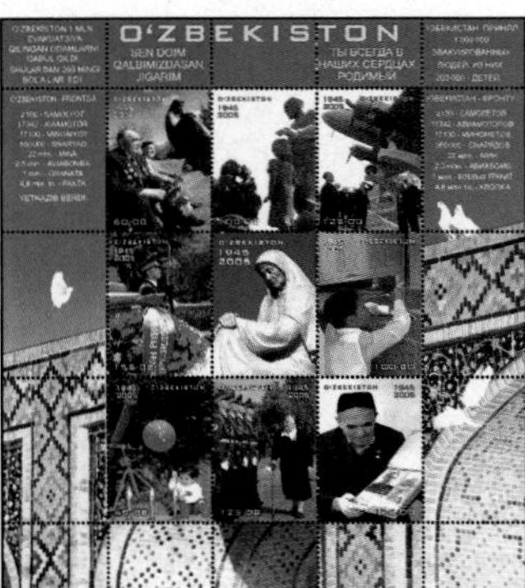

End of World War II, 60th Anniv. — A181

No. 417: a, 60s, Veterans at war memorial. b, 60s, Child with balloon at memorial. c, 100s, Sculptures. d, 100s, Child looking at memorial. e, 125s, Veterans looking at airplane sculpture. f, 125s, Woman passing soldiers. g, 155s, Soldier and floral display. h, 155s, Man looking at scrapbook.

**2005, May 6**
**417** A181 Sheet of 8, #a-h, + central label *6.25 6.25*

Tashkent University of Information Technologies, 50th Anniv. — A182

Illustration reduced.

**2005, May 25** ***Perf. 13¾x14***
**418** A182 125s multi + label *.85 .85*

Qarshi, 2700th Anniv. — A183

**2005, Aug. 1**
**419** A183 125s multi *1.00 1.00*

Doves — A184

No. 420: a, 85s, Qopqon-chinni. b, 85s, Ruyan. c, 100s, Novvoti. d, 100s, Oq kaptar. e, 125s, Juk. f, 125s, Chelkar. g, 155s, Udi. h, 155s, Gulsor.
210s, Buxoro kaptari.

**2005, Sept. 15**
**420** A184 Sheet of 8, #a-h *4.75 4.75*

**Souvenir Sheet**
**421** A184 210s multi *2.00 2.00*

Miniature Sheet

Toreutic Art — A185

No. 422: a, 60s, Teapot with ribbed ornamentation. b, 60s, Teapot with round ornamentation. c, 100s, Teapot, diff. d, 125s, Teapot, diff. 155s, Teapot-samovar. 340s, Teapot with square lid.

**2005, Oct. 25**
**422** A185 Sheet of 6, #a-f *6.25 6.25*

Ma'mun Academy, 1000th Anniv. — A186

**2005, Dec. 15** ***Perf. 13¾x14***
**423** A186 430s multi *2.25 2.25*

Paintings A187

Designs: No. 424, 200s, Ko'i, by V. I. Yenin. No. 425, 200s, Osuda Kun, by B. Boboyev, vert. No. 426, 250s, Samarqand, Navro'z, by G. Abdurahmanov, vert. No. 427, 250s, Qo'qondagi Choyxona, by J. Umarbekov, vert. No. 428, 300s, Oqtosh, by R. Ahmedov, vert. No. 429, 300s, Yoz, by Y. P. Melnikov, vert. 350s, Kuz, by N. Qo'ziboyev, vert.

**2006, Jan. 3** ***Perf. 13¾x14, 14x13¾***
**424-430** A187 Set of 7 *8.00 8.00*

Dated 2005.

Rustam Qosimjonov, Intl. Chess Federation World Champion — A188

**2006, Jan. 5** ***Perf. 13¾x14***
**431** A188 200s multi *1.00 1.00*

Dated 2005.

Medalists at 2004 Summer Olympics, Athens — A189

Designs: No. 432, 200s, Artur Taymazov, 120kg freestyle wrestling gold medalist. No. 433, 200s, Aleksandr Doxturushvili, 74kg Greco-Roman wrestling gold medalist. 250s, Magomed Ibragimov, 96kg freestyle wrestling silver medalist. 350s, O'tkir Haydarov and Bahodir Sultonov, 81kg and 54kg boxing bronze medalists, horiz.

**2006, Jan. 5** ***Perf. 14x13¾, 13¾x14***
**432-435** A189 Set of 4 *5.50 5.50*

Dated 2005.

2006 Winter Olympics, Turin — A190

Designs: 1540s, Skiing. 2155s, Figure skating.

**2006, May 19** **Litho.** ***Perf. 14x13¾***
**436-437** A190 Set of 2 11.50 11.50

Musical Instruments A191

Designs: 200s, Tanbur and Qashqar rubobi. 250s, Surnay and Tor. 290s, Surnay and Doira. 350s, Nay and Dutor. 410s, G'ijjak. 430s, Nog'om. 580s, Tanbur and Chang.

**2006, May 19**
**438-444** A191 Set of 7 10.00 10.00

Dogs A192

Designs: 350s, Labrador retriever. 540s, Cocker spaniel. 600s, German shepherd. 780s, Asian sheepdog.
1150s, Collie and German shepherd.

**2006, May 19** ***Perf. 13¾x14***
**445-448** A192 Set of 4 6.50 6.50

**Souvenir Sheet**
**449** A192 1150s multi 2.75 2.75

Souvenir Sheet

2006 World Cup Soccer Championships, Germany — A193

**2006, May 19** ***Perf. 14x13¾***
**450** A193 720s multi 2.75 2.75

Fish — A194

No. 451: a, 45s, Salmo trutta aralensis. b, 90s, Acipenser nudiventris. c, 250s, Pseudoscaphirhynchus kaufmanni. 300s, Barbus brachcephalus.
1010s, Aspiolucius esocinus.

**2006, July 10** ***Perf. 13¾x14***
**451** A194 Sheet of 4, #a-d 2.75 2.75

**Souvenir Sheet**
**452** A194 1010s multi 3.25 3.25

Bell Tower, Tashkent A195

Alisher Navoiy Theater A196

**2006, Aug. 10** ***Perf. 14x13¾***
**453** A195 55s green .30 .30

***Perf. 13¾x14***
**454** A196 90s emerald .40 .40

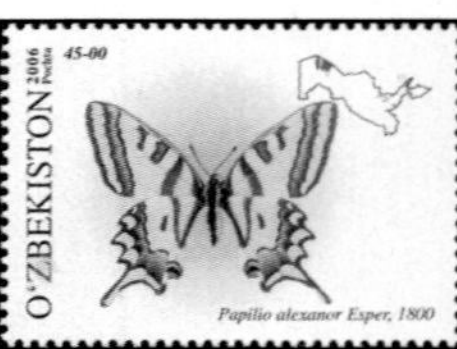
Butterflies A197

Designs: 45s, Papilio alexanor. 90s, Parnassius mnemosyne. 200s, Parnassius apollonius. 250s, Parnassius maximinus. 300s, Parnassius honrathi. No. 460, 350s, Hypermnestra helios. No. 461, 350s, Parnassius charltonius.
1010s, Parnassius actius.

**2006, Aug. 10** ***Perf. 13¾x14***
**455-461** A197 Set of 7 5.00 5.00

**Souvenir Sheet**
**462** A197 1010s multi 3.75 3.75

**15th Anniv. of Independence Issue**

Horizontal Label

Vertical Label

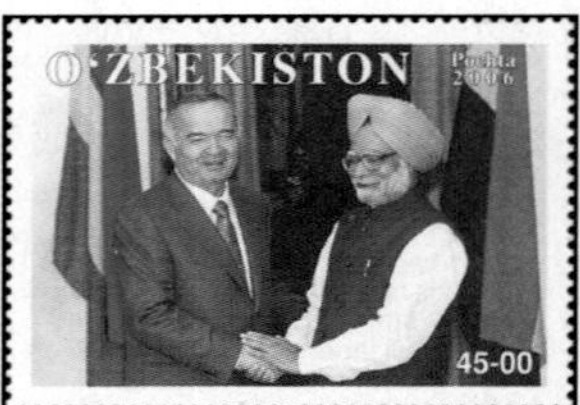
Pres. Islam Karimov and Indian Prime Minister Manmohan Singh — A198

School and Children, Kokand — A199

House of Children's Creativity — A200

Senate Chamber — A201

Emblem of 2005 Intl. Cotton Fair, Tashkent, and Cotton Boll — A202

Pres. Karimov and People's Republic of China Chairman Hu Jintao — A203

Pres. Karimov and Latvian Pres. Vaire Vike-Fraiberg — A204

Qungirot Soda Factory — A205

Leaders at Shanghai Cooperation Organization Summit, Tashkent — A206

Cement Factory A207

Railroad Construction — A208

Pres. Karimov and Graduates of Vaseda University — A209

Monument of Independence and Humanism — A210

Mine — A211

Bronze Smelter — A212

Festival — A213

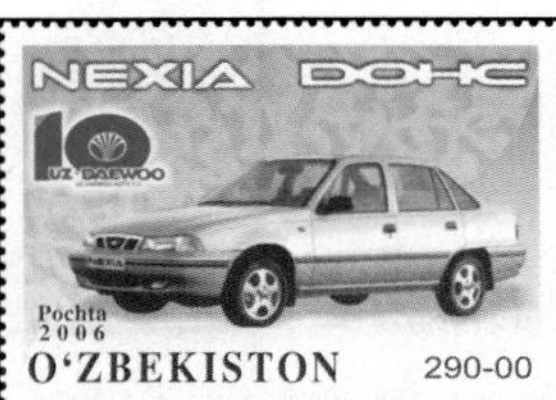

Daewoo Nexia DOHC — A214

Kurash A215

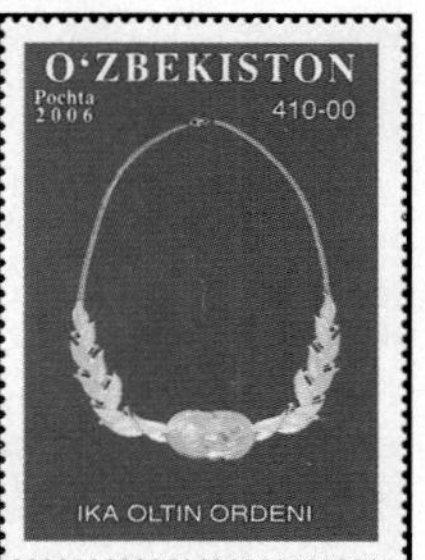

Intl. Kurash Association Medal A216

Pres. Karimov and Cotton Pickers — A217

Pres. Karimov and Cotton Pickers — A218

Pres. Karimov and Farmers — A219

Roads — A220

Textiles — A221

Military — A222

Sports — A223

A198 Designs — Pres. Karimov and: No. 466, Malaysian King Tuanku Syed Sirajuddin. No. 470, Writer Said Akhmad. No. 474, Slovenian Pres. Janez Drnovsek. No. 477, Russian Pres. Vladimir Putin. No. 480, South Korean Pres. Roh Moo-hyun. No. 483, Uzbek labor leader.

A200 Designs: No. 469, Humanism Arch. No. 478, Medical School, Margilan. No. 484, Tashkent Railway Station. No. 486, Senate Building.

A206 Design: No. 482, Leaders at Euro-Asian Economic Union meeting.

A207 Design: No. 481, Angren Coal Mine.

A213 Design: No. 489b, 90s, Festival, diff.

A214 Design: No. 490b, 200s, Daewoo Damas II.

A215 Designs: No. 491b, 90s, Kurash, diff. No. 491c, 100s, Kurash, diff.

A216 Designs: No. 492b, 580s, FILA Wrestling medal. No. 492c, 720s, National Olympic Committee medal.

No. 494: a, 90s, Winding mountain road. b, 180s, Road construction. c, 55s, Highway.

No. 495: a, 410s, Workers and textile mill machinery. b, 580s, Women holding skeins of thread. c, 250s, Textile mill machinery.

No. 496: a, 410s, Soldiers in joint Uzbekistan-Russia anti-terrorism exercises, flags. b, 100s, Graduation of cadets. c, 250s, Soldiers at desks.

No. 497: a, 580s, Pres. Karimov and student athletes. b, 45s Stadium. c, 55s, Swimming meet. d, 90s, Athletes with medals. e, 200s, Karate. f, 250s, Soccer. g, 100s, Synchronized swimming. h, 290s, Equestrian event.

***Perf. 13¾x14, 14x13¾***

**2006, Aug. 25**

**Stamp + Label With Same Orientation**

| No. | Type | Value | Color | Unused | Used |
|---|---|---|---|---|---|
| **463** | A198 | 45s | multi | .60 | .60 |
| **464** | A199 | 45s | multi | .60 | .60 |
| **465** | A200 | 45s | multi | .60 | .60 |
| **466** | A198 | 55s | multi | .60 | .60 |
| **467** | A201 | 90s | multi | .60 | .60 |
| **468** | A202 | 90s | multi | .60 | .60 |
| **469** | A200 | 95s | multi | .60 | .60 |
| **470** | A198 | 100s | multi | .60 | .60 |
| **471** | A203 | 200s | multi | 1.00 | 1.00 |
| **472** | A204 | 200s | multi | 1.00 | 1.00 |
| **473** | A205 | 200s | multi | 1.00 | 1.00 |
| **474** | A198 | 250s | multi | 1.25 | 1.25 |
| **475** | A206 | 250s | multi | 1.25 | 1.25 |
| **476** | A207 | 250s | multi | 1.25 | 1.25 |
| **477** | A198 | 290s | multi | 1.50 | 1.50 |
| **478** | A200 | 290s | multi | 1.50 | 1.50 |
| **479** | A208 | 290s | multi | 1.50 | 1.50 |
| **480** | A198 | 350s | multi | 1.50 | 1.50 |
| **481** | A207 | 350s | multi | 1.50 | 1.50 |
| **482** | A206 | 410s | multi | 2.00 | 2.00 |
| **483** | A198 | 430s | multi | 2.10 | 2.10 |
| **484** | A200 | 430s | multi | 2.10 | 2.10 |
| **485** | A209 | 580s | multi | 3.00 | 3.00 |

**486** A200 720s multi 3.75 3.75
**487** A210 1010s multi 5.25 5.25
*Nos. 463-487 (25) 37.25 37.25*

**Pairs**

**488** Horiz. pair with central label 1.20 1.20
*a.* A211 45s multi .60 .60
*b.* A212 45s multi .60 .60
**489** Horiz. pair with central label 1.20 1.20
*a.* A213 45s multi .60 .60
*b.* A213 45s multi .60 .60
**490** Horiz. pair with central label 2.50 2.50
*a.* A214 290s multi 1.50 1.50
*b.* A214 200s multi 1.00 1.00
*Nos. 488-490 (3) 4.90 4.90*

**Strips**

**491** Strip of 3 + label 3.25 3.25
*a.* A215 430s multi 2.10 2.10
*b.* A215 90s multi .60 .60
*c.* A215 100s multi .60 .60
**492** Strip of 3 + label 9.00 9.00
*a.* A216 410s multi 2.00 2.00
*b.* A216 580s multi 3.00 3.00
*c.* A216 720s multi 3.75 3.75
**493** Strip of 3 + label 3.00 3.00
*a.* A217 200s multi 1.00 1.00
*b.* A218 250s multi 1.25 1.25
*c.* A219 90s multi .60 .60
*Nos. 491-493 (3) 15.25 15.25*

**Sheets**

**494** A220 Sheet of 3, #a-c, + label 1.60 1.60
**495** A221 Sheet of 3, #a-c, + label 6.00 6.00
**496** A222 Sheet of 3, #a-c, + label 3.75 3.75
**497** A223 Sheet of 8, #a-h, + label 8.25 8.25
*Nos. 494-497 (4) 19.60 19.60*

Nos. 463-475, 477-480, 482-486 were printed in sheets of 2 stamps and 2 labels. Nos. 476, 481 and 487 were printed in sheets of 5 stamps and 5 labels. Nos. 488-490 were printed in sheets of 4 stamps and 2 labels (2 pairs).

National Flag, 15th Anniv. — A224

Illustration reduced.

**2006, Nov. 1** ***Perf. 13¾x14***
**498** A224 600s multi + label 2.00 2.00

Miniature Sheet

Intl. Year of Deserts and Desertification — A225

No. 499: a, 45s, Oxyura leucocephala. b, 250s, Haliaeetus albicilla. c, 350s, Phalcrocorax pygmaeus. d, 350s, Marmaronetta angustirostris.

**2006, Nov. 1**
**499** A225 Sheet of 4, #a-d 3.75 3.75

Roses — A226

Designs: 45s, Rosa divina. 90s, Rosa maracandica. 250s, Rosa persica. 350s, Rosa vassilczencoi.
600s, Rosa divina, diff.

**2006, Nov. 1** ***Perf. 14x13¾***
**500-503** A226 Set of 4 3.75 3.75

**Souvenir Sheet**

**504** A226 600s multi 1.75 1.75

Souvenir Sheet

Year of Charity and Medical Workers — A227

**2006, Nov. 17** ***Perf. 13¾x14***
**505** A227 720s multi 2.25 2.25

Souvenir Sheet

Regional Communications Commonwealth, 15th Anniv. — A228

**2006, Nov. 17**
**506** A228 1010s multi 3.50 3.50

## VANUATU

ˌvan-ˌwä-ˈtü

LOCATION — Island group in south Pacific Ocean northeast of New Caledonia
GOVT. — Republic
AREA — 5,700 sq. mi.
POP. — 189,036 (1999 est.)
CAPITAL — Port Vila

The Anglo-French condominium of New Hebrides (Vol. 4) became the independent state of Vanuatu July 30, 1980.

Hebrides franc Vatu (1981)

**Catalogue values for all unused stamps in this country are for Never Hinged items.**

Erromango Is. and Kaori Tree — A44

Designs: 10fr, Archipelago and man making copra. 15fr, Espiritu Santo Island and cattle. 20fr, Efate Island and Post Office, Vila. 25fr, Malakula Island and headdresses. 30fr, Aoba and Maewo Islands and pig tusks. 35fr, Pentecost Island and land diving. 40fr, Tanna Island and Prophet John Frum's Red Cross. 50fr, Shepherd Island and canoe with sail. 70fr, Banks Island and dancers. 100fr, Ambrym Island and carvings. 200fr, Aneityum Island and decorated baskets. 500fr, Torres Islands and fishing with bow and arrow.

**Wmk. 373**

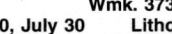

**1980, July 30 Litho.** ***Perf. 14***
**280** A44 5fr multicolored .20 .20
**281** A44 10fr multicolored .20 .20
**282** A44 15fr multicolored .35 .30
**283** A44 20fr multicolored .45 .40
**284** A44 25fr multicolored .55 .45
**285** A44 30fr multicolored .70 .60
**286** A44 35fr multicolored .80 .65
**287** A44 40fr multicolored .80 .75
**288** A44 50fr multicolored .85 .90
**289** A44 70fr multicolored 1.60 1.25
**290** A44 100fr multicolored 1.60 1.00
**291** A44 200fr multicolored 1.75 1.75
**292** A44 500fr multicolored 3.25 3.75
*Nos. 280-292 (13) 13.10 12.20*

**Inscribed in French**

**Unwmk.**

*280a* A44 5fr multicolored .35 .20
*281a* A44 10fr multicolored .45 .20
*282a* A44 15fr multicolored .50 .30
*283a* A44 20fr multicolored .55 .35
*284a* A44 25fr multicolored .60 .40
*285a* A44 30fr multicolored .60 .50
*286a* A44 35fr multicolored .65 .60
*287a* A44 40fr multicolored .95 .70
*288a* A44 50fr multicolored 1.10 .80
*289a* A44 70fr multicolored 1.50 1.10
*290a* A44 100fr multicolored 1.60 1.25
*291a* A44 200fr multicolored 1.90 2.00
*292a* A44 500fr multicolored 4.25 4.00
*Nos. 280a-292a (13) 15.00 12.40*

Rotary Emblem — A52 Kiwanis Emblem — A53

**1980, Sept. 16** **Wmk. 373**
**293** A52 10fr Emblem, horiz. .20 .20
**294** A52 40fr shown .65 .65

**Inscribed in French**

**Unwmk.**

*293a* A52 10fr multicolored .20 .20
*294a* A52 40fr multicolored .85 .85

75th anniv. of Rotary Intl. and 8th anniv. of Port Vila Rotary Club (40fr).

**1980, Sept. 16** **Wmk. 373**
**295** A53 10fr shown .20 .20
**296** A53 40fr Emblem, horiz. .50 .50

**Inscribed in French**

**Unwmk.**

*295a* A53 10fr multicolored .25 .20
*296a* A53 40fr multicolored 1.00 .85

New Zealand District Kiwanis Convention, Port Vila, Sept. 16-18.

Christmas A54

Erythrura Trichroa — A55

Paintings: 10fr, Virgin and Child, by Michael Pacher. 15fr, Virgin and Child, by Hans Memling. 30fr, Rest on the Flight to Egypt, by Adriaen van der Werff.

**1980, Nov. 12** **Wmk. 373**
**297** A54 10fr multicolored .20 .20
**298** A54 15fr multicolored .25 .25
**299** A54 30fr multicolored .55 .55
*Nos. 297-299 (3) 1.00 1.00*

**1981, Feb. 18**
**300** A55 10fr shown .45 .25
**301** A55 20fr Chalcophaps indica .90 .55
**302** A55 30fr Pachycephala pectoralis 1.25 .90
**303** A55 40fr Ptilinopus tannensis 1.60 1.10
*Nos. 300-303 (4) 4.20 2.80*

Duke of Edinburgh's 60th Birthday — A56

**1981, June 10** ***Perf. 14x14½***
**304** A56 15v Tribesman, portrait .20 .20
**305** A56 25v Portrait .30 .30
**306** A56 35v Family .45 .45
**307** A56 45v shown .60 .60
*Nos. 304-307 (4) 1.55 1.55*

**Common Design Types**
pictured following the introduction.

**Royal Wedding Issue**
Common Design Type

**1981, July 29**
**308** CD331 15v Bouquet .25 .25
**309** CD331 45v Charles .55 .55
**310** CD331 75v Couple .80 .80
*Nos. 308-310 (3) 1.60 1.60*

First Anniv. of Independence — A57

**1981, July 19**
**311** A57 15v Map, flag, vert. .20 .20
**312** A57 25v Emblem .20 .20
**313** A57 45v Anthem .45 .45
**314** A57 75v Arms, vert. .65 .65
*Nos. 311-314 (4) 1.50 1.50*

Christmas A58

Designs: Children's drawings.

**Wmk. 373**

**1981, Nov. 11 Litho.** ***Perf. 14***
**315** A58 15v Three kings .20 .20
**316** A58 25v Girl holding lamb, vert. .30 .30
**317** A58 35v Butterfly-angel .40 .40
**318** A58 45v Gift bearer, vert. .60 .60
*a.* Souvenir sheet, #315-318 1.75 1.75
*Nos. 315-318 (4) 1.50 1.50*

Broadbills — A59

Orchids — A60

**1982, Feb. 8** *Perf. 14½x14*

**319** A59 15v shown .75 .75
**320** A59 20v Rainbow lorries 1.00 1.00
**321** A59 25v Buff-bellied flycatchers 1.25 1.25
**322** A59 45v Fantails 2.25 2.25
*Nos. 319-322 (4)* 5.25 5.25

***Perf. 14x13½, 13½x14***

**1982, June 15**

**323** A60 1v Flickengeria comata .20 .50
**324** A60 2v Calanthe triplicata .25 .55
**325** A60 10v Dendrobium sladei .30 .30
**326** A60 15v Dendrobium mohlianum .40 .25
**327** A60 20v Dendrobium macrophyllum .50 .30
**328** A60 25v Dendrobium purpureum .80 .50
**329** A60 30v Robiquetia mimus .90 .80
**330** A60 35v Dendrobium mooreanum 1.00 .90
**331** A60 45v Spathoglottis plicata 1.25 1.00
**332** A60 50v Dendrobium seemannii 1.50 1.25
**333** A60 75v Dendrobium conanthum 2.25 1.90
**334** A60 100v Dendrobium macranthum 2.75 2.00
**335** A60 200v Coelogyne lamellata 3.25 3.00
**336** A60 500v Bulbophyllum longiscapum 6.50 6.75
*Nos. 323-336 (14)* 21.85 20.00

Nos. 330-333, 336 horiz.

For surcharges see Nos. 383, 512, 551-554, 586-589A, B1.

Scouting Year A61

**Wmk. 373**

**1982, Sept. 1** **Litho.** *Perf. 14*

**337** A61 15v Around campfire .40 .40
**338** A61 20v First aid .45 .45
**339** A61 25v Signal tower .60 .60
**340** A61 45v Building raft 1.10 1.10
**341** A61 75v Scout sign 1.75 1.75
*Nos. 337-341 (5)* 4.30 4.30

Christmas — A62

Details from Nativity painting. 35v, 45v horiz.

**1982, Nov. 16**

**342** A62 15v multicolored .35 .35
**343** A62 25v multicolored .50 .50
**344** A62 35v multicolored .75 .75
**345** A62 45v multicolored 1.00 1.00
*a.* Souvenir sheet of 4, #342-345 3.25 3.25
*Nos. 342-345 (4)* 2.60 2.60

Hypolimnas Octocula A63

**1983, Jan. 17** *Perf. 14½*

**346** Pair 2.40 1.75
*a.* A63 15v shown 1.10 .85
*b.* A63 15v Euploea sylvester 1.10 .85
**347** Pair 2.75 2.25
*a.* A63 20v Polyura sacco 1.25 1.10
*b.* A63 20v Papilio canopus 1.25 1.10
**348** Pair 3.50 2.50
*a.* A63 25v Parantica pumila 1.75 1.25
*b.* A63 25v Luthrodes cleotas 1.75 1.25
*Nos. 346-348 (3)* 8.65 6.50

A64

**1983, Mar. 14** *Perf. 13½x14*

**349** A64 15v Pres. Sokomanu .20 .20
**350** A64 20v Fisherman .25 .25
**351** A64 25v Herdsman, cattle .30 .30
**352** A64 75v Flags, map .90 .90
*Nos. 349-352 (4)* 1.65 1.65

Commonwealth Day. 20v, 75v inscribed in French.

Economic Zone — A65

a, Thunnus albacares. b, Map. c, Matthew Isld. d, Hunter Isld. e, Epinephelus morrhua, etelis carbunculus. f, Katsuwonus pelamis.

***Perf. 14x13½***

**1983, May 23** **Litho.** **Wmk. 373**

**353** Sheet of 6 3.00 3.00
*a.-f.* A65 25v multicolored .50 .50

Manned Flight Bicentenary — A66

Balloons or Airships: 15v, Montgolfiere, 1783. 20v, J.A.C. Charles 1st hydrogen balloon, 1783. 25v, Blanchard & Jeffries 1st English Channel crossing, 1785. 35v, H. Giffard's 1st mechanically powered airship, 1852. 40v, Renard and Krebs' airship, 1884. 45v, Graf Zeppelin's 1st transworld flight, 1929.

**1983, Aug. 4** **Litho.** *Perf. 14*

**354** A66 15v multi, vert. .30 .30
**355** A66 20v multi, vert. .35 .35
**356** A66 25v multi, vert. .45 .45
**357** A66 35v multi .60 .60
**358** A66 40v multi .70 .70
**359** A66 45v multi .85 .85
*Nos. 354-359 (6)* 3.25 3.25

For overprint see No. 372.

World Communications Year — A67

**1983, Oct. 10** **Litho.** **Wmk. 373**

**360** A67 15v Mail transport, Bauerfield Airport .25 .25
**361** A67 20v Switchboard operator .35 .35
**362** A67 25v Telex operator .50 .50
**363** A67 45v Satellite earth station .90 .90
*a.* Souv. sheet of 4, #360-363 + 3 labels 5.00 5.00
*Nos. 360-363 (4)* 2.00 2.00

No. 363a issued for WCY and 75th anniv. of New Hebrides stamps.

Local Fungi — A68

**1984, Jan. 9** **Litho.** *Perf. 14*

**364** A68 15v Cymatoderma elegans, vert. .95 .95
**365** A68 25v Lignosus rhinoceros, vert. 1.10 1.10
**366** A68 35v Stereum ostrea 1.60 1.60
**367** A68 45v Ganoderma boninenze, vert. 2.10 2.10
*Nos. 364-367 (4)* 5.75 5.75

**Lloyd's List Issue**

Common Design Type

**1984, Apr. 30** **Litho.** *Perf. 14½x14*

**368** CD335 15v Port Vila .30 .30
**369** CD335 20v Induna .45 .45
**370** CD335 25v Air Vanuatu jet .60 .60
**371** CD335 45v Brahman Express 1.10 1.10
*Nos. 368-371 (4)* 2.45 2.45

No. 359 Overprinted "UPU CONGRESS / HAMBURG"

**1984, June 11** **Wmk. 373** *Perf. 14*

**372** A66 45v multicolored .90 .90

Cattle A69

**1984, July 3** **Litho.** *Perf. 14*

**373** A69 15v Charolais .30 .30
**374** A69 25v Charolais-Afrikaner .45 .45
**375** A69 45v Friesian .85 .85
**376** A69 75v Charolais-Brahman 1.40 1.40
*Nos. 373-376 (4)* 3.00 3.00

Ausipex '84 — A70

Ships.

**1984, Sept. 7**

**377** A70 25v Makambo .80 .55
**378** A70 45v Rockton 1.40 1.00
**379** A70 100v Waroonga 2.50 *4.00*
*a.* Souvenir sheet of 3, #377-379 4.75 *5.00*
*Nos. 377-379 (3)* 4.70 5.55

Christmas A71

**1984, Nov. 19** **Litho.** **Wmk. 373**

**380** A71 25v Father Christmas, child in hospital .50 .30
**381** A71 45v Nativity .95 .75
**382** A71 75v Father Christmas, children 1.50 1.50
*Nos. 380-382 (3)* 2.95 2.55

No. 323 Surcharged with 2 Black Bars

**1985, Jan. 22** **Litho.** *Perf. 14x13½*

**383** A60 5v on 1v multi .75 .50

Ceremonial Dance Costumes — A71a

Audubon Birth Bicent. — A72

**1985, Jan. 22** *Perf. 14*

**384** A71a 20v Ambrym Island .35 .35
**385** A71a 25v Pentecost Island .50 .50
**386** A71a 45v Women's Grade Ceremony, S.W. Malakula .85 .85
**387** A71a 75v Same, men's 1.25 1.25
*Nos. 384-387 (4)* 2.95 2.95

**Wmk. 373**

**1985, Mar. 26** **Litho.** *Perf. 14*

Peregrine falcons.

**388** A72 20v multicolored 1.10 1.10
**389** A72 35v multicolored 1.40 1.40
**390** A72 45v multicolored 1.60 1.60
**391** A72 100v multicolored 2.75 *2.75*
*Nos. 388-391 (4)* 6.85 6.85

**Queen Mother 85th Birthday**

Common Design Type

***Perf. 14½x14***

**1985, June 7** **Wmk. 384**

**392** CD336 5v Wedding photo .25 .25
**393** CD336 20v 80th birthday celebration .50 .50
**394** CD336 35v At Ancona, Italy .65 .65
**395** CD336 55v Holding Prince Henry 1.00 1.00
*Nos. 392-395 (4)* 2.40 2.40

**Souvenir Sheet**

**396** CD336 100v At Covent Garden Opera 2.75 2.75

EXPO '85, Tsukuba — A73

35v, Mala naval patrol boat. 45v, Japanese fishing fleet, Port Vila. 55v, Mobile Force Band. 100v, Prime Minister Walter H. Lini.

**1985, July 26** **Wmk. 373** *Perf. 14*

**397** A73 35v multicolored .75 .45
**398** A73 45v multicolored .95 .70
**399** A73 55v multicolored 1.00 .85
**400** A73 100v multicolored 1.10 *1.75*
*a.* Souvenir sheet of 4, #397-400 4.75 4.75
*Nos. 397-400 (4)* 3.80 3.75

Natl. independence, 5th anniv.

Intl. Youth Year A74

Children's drawings.

**1985, Sept. 16** **Wmk. 373** *Perf. 14*

**401** A74 20v Alain Lagaliu .55 .55
**402** A74 30v Peter Obed .65 .65
**403** A74 50v Mary Estelle 1.10 1.10
**404** A74 100v Abel M rani 1.75 1.75
*Nos. 401-404 (4)* 4.05 4.05

Natl. and UN Flags, Map
A75

**1985, Sept. 24 Litho. *Perf. 14***
**405** A75 45v multicolored 1.25 1.10

Admission of Vanuatu to UN, 4th anniv.

Sea Slugs — A76

Scuba Diving — A77

**1985, Nov. 11 Wmk. 373 *Perf. 14½***
**406** A76 20v Chromodoris elisa bethina .50 .50
**407** A76 35v Halgerda aurantiomaculata .95 .95
**408** A76 55v Chromodoris kuniei 1.40 1.40
**409** A76 100v Notodoris minor 2.50 2.50
*Nos. 406-409 (4)* 5.35 5.35

Nos. 407-408 horiz. See Nos. 497-500.

**1986, Jan. 22 Wmk. 384 *Perf. 14***
**410** A77 30v shown .90 .55
**411** A77 35v Volcanic eruption 1.10 .60
**412** A77 55v Land diving 1.10 .95
**413** A77 100v Wind surfing 1.40 *2.10*
*Nos. 410-413 (4)* 4.50 4.20

See No. 479.

**Queen Elizabeth II 60th Birthday**
Common Design Type

Designs: 20v, With Prince Charles and Princess Anne, 1951. 35v, At christening of Prince William, the Music Room, Buckhingham Palace, 1982. 45v, State visit, 1985. 55v, State visit to Mexico, 1974. 100v, Visiting Crown Agents' offices, 1983.

**1986, Apr. 21 Litho. *Perf. 14x14½***
**414** CD337 20v scar, blk & sil .35 .35
**415** CD337 35v ultra & multi .60 .60
**416** CD337 45v green & multi .70 .70
**417** CD337 55v violet & multi .90 .90
**418** CD337 100v multicolored 1.75 1.75
*Nos. 414-418 (5)* 4.30 4.30

For overprints & surcharges see #465-469, B2-B6.

AMERIPEX '86 — A78

**1986, May 19 Wmk. 373 *Perf. 14***
**419** A78 45v SS President Coolidge .95 .65
**420** A78 55v As troop ship, 1942 1.10 .80
**421** A78 135v Site of sinking, 1942 2.00 2.00
*a.* Souvenir sheet of 3, #419-421 4.75 4.25
*Nos. 419-421 (3)* 4.05 3.45

Halley's Comet
A79

**1986, June 23 Wmk. 384 *Perf. 14½***
**422** A79 30v Comet, deity statue 1.25 1.25
**423** A79 45v Family sighting comet 1.50 1.50
**424** A79 55v Comet over SW Pacific 1.75 1.75
**425** A79 100v Edmond Halley, manuscript 2.40 2.40
*Nos. 422-425 (4)* 6.90 6.90

Coral
A80

**1986, Oct. 27 Wmk. 373 *Perf. 14***
**426** A80 20v Daisy .75 .75
**427** A80 45v Organ pipe 1.75 1.75
**428** A80 55v Sea fan 2.10 2.10
**429** A80 135v Soft 5.25 5.25
*Nos. 426-429 (4)* 9.85 9.85

Intl. Peace Year
A81

**1986, Nov. 3 Litho. *Perf. 14***
**430** A81 30v Children of the world .70 .70
**431** A81 45v Child praying 1.00 1.00
**432** A81 55v UN building, negotiators 1.25 1.25
**433** A81 135v Peoples working in harmony 3.25 3.25
*Nos. 430-433 (4)* 6.20 6.20

Automotives
A82

**1987, Jan. 22**
**434** A82 20v Datsun 240Z, 1969 .40 .40
**435** A82 45v Model A Ford, 1927 .80 .80
**436** A82 55v Unic, 1924-25 .95 .95
**437** A82 135v Citroen DS19, 1975 2.25 2.25
*Nos. 434-437 (4)* 4.40 4.40

IRHO Coconut Research Station, 25th Anniv.
A83

**1987, May 13 *Perf. 14½x14***
**438** A83 35v Nursery .65 .65
**439** A83 45v Cocos nucifera tree .95 .95
**440** A83 100v Cocos nucifera fruit 1.60 1.60
**441** A83 135v Station 2.00 2.00
*Nos. 438-441 (4)* 5.20 5.20

Fish — A84

***Perf. 14x14½***
**1987, July 15 Wmk. 384**
**442** A84 1v Cirrhitichthys aprinus .25 .25
**443** A84 5v Zanclus cornutus .25 .25
**444** A84 10v Canthigaster cinctus .25 .25
**445** A84 15v Amphiprion rubrocinctus .30 .30
**446** A84 20v Acanthurus lineatus .45 .45
**447** A84 30v Thalassoma hardwicki .60 .60
**448** A84 35v Anthias tuka .65 .65
**449** A84 40v Adioryx microstomus .75 .75
**450** A84 45v Balistoides conspicillum .95 .95
**451** A84 50v Xyrichtys taeniouris 1.00 1.00
**452** A84 55v Hemitaurich-thys polyepis 1.10 1.10
**453** A84 65v Pterois volitans 1.25 1.25
**454** A84 100v Paracirrhites forsteri 2.25 2.25
**455** A84 300v Balistapus undulatus 6.25 6.25
**456** A84 500v Chaetodon ephippium 8.50 8.50
*Nos. 442-456 (15)* 24.80 24.80

Insects
A85

**1987, Sept. 22 Wmk. 373 *Perf. 14***
**457** A85 45v Xylotrupes gideon 1.00 1.00
**458** A85 55v Phyllodes imperialis 1.10 1.10
**459** A85 65v Cyphogaster 1.50 1.50
**460** A85 100v Othreis fullonia 2.25 2.25
*Nos. 457-460 (4)* 5.85 5.85

Christmas Carols — A86

**1987, Nov. 10 *Perf. 13½x14***
**461** A86 20v Away in a Manger .40 .40
**462** A86 45v Once in Royal David's City .90 .90
**463** A86 55v While Shepherds Watched Their Flocks 1.10 1.10
**464** A86 65v We Three Kings of Orient Are 1.25 1.25
*Nos. 461-464 (4)* 3.65 3.65

Nos. 414-418 Ovptd. in Silver:
"40TH WEDDING ANNIVERSARY"

***Perf. 14x14½***
**1987, Dec. 9 Litho. Wmk. 384**
**465** CD337 20v scar, blk & sil .60 .60
**466** CD337 35v ultra & multi .75 .75
**467** CD337 45v green & multi 1.00 1.00
**468** CD337 55v violet & multi 1.10 1.10
**469** CD337 100v multicolored 1.90 1.90
*Nos. 465-469 (5)* 5.35 5.35

World Wildlife Fund — A87

Dugongs.

**1988, Feb. 29 *Perf. 13x13½***
**470** A87 5v Mother, calf 1.25 .45
**471** A87 10v Adult 2.00 .45
**472** A87 20v Two adults 2.50 1.25
**473** A87 45v Herd 4.50 3.25
*Nos. 470-473 (4)* 10.25 5.40

Australia Bicentennial
A88

Burns Philip emblem, bicent. emblem and steamships.

**1988, May 18 Wmk. 373 *Perf. 12***
**474** A88 20v S.S. Tambo .40 .40
**475** A88 45v S.S. Induna .85 .85
**476** A88 55v S.S. Morinda 1.00 1.00
**477** A88 65v S.S. Marsina 1.10 1.10
*Nos. 474-477 (4)* 3.35 3.35

Capt. James Cook (1728-1779), Explorer — A89

***Perf. 14 on 2 or 3 Sides***
**1988, July 29 Wmk. 384**
**478** A89 45v black & red .90 .90

SYDPEX '88. No. 478 printed in panes of 10 plus 5 center labels picturing a map of Vanuatu, HMS Resolution, exhibition emblem, HMS Endeavour or a map of Australia.

Tourism Type of 1986
Souvenir Sheet
**Wmk. 373**

**1988, Aug. 24 Litho. *Perf. 14***
**479** Sheet of 2 4.00 4.00
*a.* A77 55v like No. 412 1.00 1.00
*b.* A77 100v like No. 413 2.00 2.00

EXPO '88. Nos. 479a-479b are dated 1988 and "Vanuatu" is inscribed in violet blue.

1988 Summer Olympics, Seoul — A90

**1988, Sept. 19 *Perf. 13½x14***
**480** A90 20v Boxing .25 .25
**481** A90 45v Track events .80 .80
**482** A90 55v Signing Olympic agreement .95 .95
**483** A90 65v Soccer 1.10 1.10
*Nos. 480-483 (4)* 3.10 3.10

**Souvenir Sheet**
**484** A90 150v Tennis 3.25 3.25

Intl. Tennis Federation, 75th anniv. (150v).

**Lloyds of London, 300th Anniv.**
Common Design Type

Designs: 20v, Lloyds new building, 1988. 55v, Cargo ship Shirrabank, horiz. 65v, Adela, horiz. 145v, Excursion steamer General Slocum on fire in New York Harbor, 1904.

**1988, Oct. 25 Wmk. 384 *Perf. 14***
**485** CD341 20v multicolored .50 .50
**486** CD341 55v multicolored 1.25 1.25
**487** CD341 65v multicolored 1.40 1.40
**488** CD341 145v multicolored 3.50 3.50
*Nos. 485-488 (4)* 6.65 6.65

FAO — A91

***Perf. 14½x14, 14x14½***
**1988, Nov. 14**
**489** A91 45v Tending crops 1.10 1.10
**490** A91 55v Fishing, vert. 1.25 1.25
**491** A91 65v Animal husbandry, vert. 1.25 1.25
**492** A91 120v Produce market 1.60 1.60
*Nos. 489-492 (4)* 5.20 5.20

Christmas A92

Carols: 20v, Silent Night, Holy Night. 45v, Angels From the Realms of Glory. 65v, O Come All Ye Faithful. 155v, In That Poor Stable How Charming Jesus Lies.

**1988, Dec. 1 Litho. *Perf. 14½x14***

| | | | |
|---|---|---|---|
| **493** A92 20v multicolored | .40 | .40 |
| **494** A92 45v multicolored | .65 | .65 |
| **495** A92 65v multicolored | .80 | .80 |
| **496** A92 155v multicolored | 2.10 | 2.10 |
| *Nos. 493-496 (4)* | 3.95 | 3.95 |

Marine Life Type of 1985

Shrimp.

**1989, Feb. 1 *Perf. 14***

| | | |
|---|---|---|
| **497** A76 20v Periclimenes brevicarpalis | .40 | .40 |
| **498** A76 45v Lysmata grabhami | .95 | .95 |
| **499** A76 65v Rhynchocinetes | 1.25 | 1.25 |
| **500** A76 150v Stenopus hispidus | 2.75 | 2.75 |
| *Nos. 497-500 (4)* | 5.35 | 5.35 |

Economic & Social Commission for Asia and the Pacific (ESCAP) A93

***Perf. 12x12½***

**1989, Apr. 5 Litho. Wmk. 373**

| | | |
|---|---|---|
| **501** A93 20v Consolidated Catalina | 1.00 | 1.00 |
| **502** A93 45v Douglas DC-3 | 1.50 | 1.50 |
| **503** A93 55v Embraer EMB110 Bandeirante | 1.60 | 1.60 |
| **504** A93 200v Boeing 737-300 | 5.00 | 5.00 |
| *Nos. 501-504 (4)* | 9.10 | 9.10 |

Inauguration of the Sydney-Noumea-Espiritu Santo Service, 1948 (20v).

PHILEXFRANCE '89 — A94

Exhibition emblem and: No. 505a, Porte de Versailles Hall Number 1. No. 505b, Eiffel Tower. No. 506, Revolt of French Troops, Nancy, 1790.

**1989, July 5 Wmk. 373 *Perf. 12***

| | | |
|---|---|---|
| **505** A94 Pair | 5.75 | 5.75 |
| ***a.-b.*** 100v any single | 2.75 | 2.75 |

**Souvenir Sheet**

***Perf. 14***

**Wmk. 384**

| | | |
|---|---|---|
| **506** A94 100v multicolored | 2.25 | 2.25 |

French revolution, bicent.

**Moon Landing, 20th Anniv.**

Common Design Type

Apollo 17: 45v, Command module in space. 55v, Harrison Schmitt, Gene Cerman and Ron Evans. 65v, Mission emblem. 120v, Liftoff. 100v, Recovery of Apollo 11 crew after spashdown.

**1989, July 20 Wmk. 384 *Perf. 14***

**Size of Nos. 508-509: 29x29mm**

| | | |
|---|---|---|
| **507** CD342 45v multicolored | 1.60 | 1.60 |
| **508** CD342 55v multicolored | 1.60 | 1.60 |
| **509** CD342 65v multicolored | 1.90 | 1.90 |
| **510** CD342 120v multicolored | 3.25 | 3.25 |
| *Nos. 507-510 (4)* | 8.35 | 8.35 |

**Souvenir Sheet**

| | | |
|---|---|---|
| **511** CD342 100v multicolored | 3.25 | 3.25 |

No. 324 Surcharged

***Perf. 14x13½***

**1989, Oct. 18 Litho. Wmk. 373**

| | | |
|---|---|---|
| **512** A60 100v on 2v multi | 4.00 | 4.00 |

STAMPSHOW '89, Melbourne.

World Stamp Expo '89 — A95

***Perf. 14x13½***

**1989, Nov. 6 Litho. Wmk. 384**

| | | |
|---|---|---|
| **513** A95 65v New Hebrides #256 | 3.75 | 3.75 |

**Souvenir Sheet**

| | | |
|---|---|---|
| **514** Sheet of 2 | 10.50 | 10.50 |
| ***a.*** A95 65v New Hebrides #254 | 4.00 | 4.00 |
| ***b.*** A95 100v The White House (detail) | 6.00 | 6.00 |

A96

A97

Flora.

***Perf. 12½x12***

**1990, Jan. 5 Wmk. 373**

| | | |
|---|---|---|
| **515** A96 45v Alocasia macrorrhiza | .95 | .95 |
| **516** A96 55v Acacia spirorbis | 1.10 | 1.10 |
| **517** A96 65v Metrosideros collina | 1.40 | 1.40 |
| **518** A96 145v Hoya australis | 3.25 | 3.25 |
| *Nos. 515-518 (4)* | 6.70 | 6.70 |

**1990, Apr. 30 *Perf. 13x13½***

Stamp World London '90 Exhibition emblem and simulated stamps or stamps on stamps: 45v, Kava (simulated stamps). 65v, Luganville P.O. exterior, interior (simulated stamps). 100v, Propeller plane, 19th cent. packet (simulated stamps). 150v, New Hebrides #187-188, first day cancellation. 200v, Great Britain #1, Vanuatu #281.

| | | |
|---|---|---|
| **519** A97 45v multicolored | .95 | .95 |
| **520** A97 65v multicolored | 1.60 | 1.60 |
| **521** A97 100v multicolored | 2.25 | 2.25 |
| **522** A97 200v multicolored | 4.25 | 4.25 |
| *Nos. 519-522 (4)* | 9.05 | 9.05 |

**Souvenir Sheet**

| | | |
|---|---|---|
| **523** A97 150v multicolored | 7.75 | 7.75 |

Penny Black, 150th anniv. No. 523 margin pictures first day cancel and cachet.

Independence, 10th Anniv. — A98

25v, Natl. Council of Women Emblem. 50v, Pres. Frederick Kalomuana Timakata. 55v, Preamble to Constitution. 65v, Vanuaaku Pati flag. 80v, Reserve Bank. 150v, Prime Minister Walter H. Lini.

**1990, July 30 *Perf. 14***

| | | |
|---|---|---|
| **524** A98 25v multicolored | .50 | .50 |
| **525** A98 50v multicolored | 1.10 | 1.10 |
| **526** A98 55v multicolored | 1.25 | 1.25 |
| **527** A98 65v multicolored | 1.40 | 1.40 |
| **528** A98 80v multicolored | 1.75 | 1.75 |
| *Nos. 524-528 (5)* | 6.00 | 6.00 |

**Souvenir Sheet**

| | | |
|---|---|---|
| **529** A98 150v multi | 6.75 | 6.75 |

Minature Sheet

Charles De Gaulle (1890-1970) — A99

**Wmk. 373**

**1990, Nov. 22 Litho. *Perf. 14***

| | | |
|---|---|---|
| **530** Sheet, 2 ea #530c-530f + 2 labels | 20.00 | 20.00 |
| ***a.*** A99 20v At Bayeux, after D-day landing | 3.75 | 3.75 |
| ***b.*** A99 25v Alsace, 1945 | 3.75 | 3.75 |
| ***c.*** A99 30v Portrait | 1.50 | 1.50 |
| ***d.*** A99 45v Spitfire, Biggin Hill, 1942 | 1.60 | 1.60 |
| ***e.*** A99 55v Casablanca, 1943 | 1.75 | 1.75 |
| ***f.*** A99 65v Day of Glory, Paris, 1944 | 1.90 | 1.90 |

Christmas — A100

**1990, Dec. 5 *Perf. 13***

| | | |
|---|---|---|
| **531** Strip of 5 | 5.50 | 5.50 |
| ***a.*** A100 25v Angel facing right | .55 | .55 |
| ***b.*** A100 50v Shepherds | .85 | .85 |
| ***c.*** A100 65v Nativity | .95 | .95 |
| ***d.*** A100 70v The Three Kings | 1.00 | 1.00 |
| ***e.*** A100 80v Angel facing left | 1.00 | 1.00 |

Butterflies A101

***Perf. 14x14½***

**1991, Jan. 9 Wmk. 384**

| | | |
|---|---|---|
| **532** A101 25v Parthenos sylvia | .70 | .70 |
| **533** A101 55v Euploea leucostictos | 1.40 | 1.40 |
| **534** A101 80v Lampides boeticus | 1.90 | 1.90 |
| **535** A101 150v Danaus plexippus | 3.50 | 3.50 |
| *Nos. 532-535 (4)* | 7.50 | 7.50 |

Art Festival — A102

Phila Nippon '91 — A103

**Wmk. 373**

**1991, May 2 Litho. *Perf. 13½***

| | | |
|---|---|---|
| **536** A102 25v Dance | .55 | .55 |
| **537** A102 65v Weaving | 1.50 | 1.50 |
| **538** A102 80v Carving | 1.90 | 1.90 |
| **539** A102 150v Music | 3.50 | 3.50 |
| *Nos. 536-539 (4)* | 7.45 | 7.45 |

**Elizabeth & Philip, Birthdays**

Common Design Types

**Wmk. 384**

**1991, June 17 Litho. *Perf. 14½***

| | | |
|---|---|---|
| **540** CD345 65v multicolored | 1.00 | 1.00 |
| **541** CD346 70v multicolored | 1.10 | 1.10 |
| ***a.*** Pair, #540-541 + label | 2.50 | 2.50 |

**Wmk. 373**

**1991, Nov. 15 Litho. *Perf. 14½***

Birds: 50v, White-collared kingfisher. 55v, Green palm lorikeet. 80v, Scarlet robin. 100v, Pacific swallow. 150v, Reef heron.

| | | |
|---|---|---|
| **542** A103 50v multicolored | 1.10 | 1.10 |
| **543** A103 55v multicolored | 1.10 | 1.10 |
| **544** A103 80v multicolored | 1.75 | 1.75 |
| **545** A103 100v multicolored | 2.10 | 2.10 |
| *Nos. 542-545 (4)* | 6.05 | 6.05 |

**Souvenir Sheet**

| | | |
|---|---|---|
| **546** A103 150v multicolored | 3.25 | 3.25 |

Fight Against AIDS A104

Designs: 25v, Multiple partners, unsafe sex can spread AIDS. 65v, AIDS victim and care giver. 80v, AIDS kills, shark. 150v, Children's playground.

**1991, Nov. 29 Wmk. 384 *Perf. 14***

| | | |
|---|---|---|
| **547** A104 25v multicolored | .70 | .70 |
| **548** A104 65v multicolored | 1.25 | 1.25 |
| **549** A104 80v multicolored | 1.60 | 1.60 |
| **550** A104 150v multicolored | 3.00 | 3.00 |
| *Nos. 547-550 (4)* | 6.55 | 6.55 |

Nos. 324-326 & 329 Surcharged

***Perf. 14x13½***

**1991, June 12 Litho. Wmk. 373**

| | | |
|---|---|---|
| **551** A60 20v on 2v #324 | .55 | .55 |
| **552** A60 60v on 10v #325 | 1.75 | 1.75 |
| **553** A60 70v on 15v #326 | 2.10 | 2.10 |
| **554** A60 80v on 30v #329 | 2.25 | 2.25 |
| *Nos. 551-554 (4)* | 6.65 | 6.65 |

**Queen Elizabeth II's Accession to the Throne, 40th Anniv.**

Common Design Type

**1992, Feb. 6 Wmk. 384 *Perf. 14***

| | | |
|---|---|---|
| **555** CD349 20v multicolored | .35 | .35 |
| **556** CD349 25v multicolored | .45 | .45 |
| **557** CD349 60v multicolored | .95 | .95 |
| **558** CD349 65v multicolored | 1.00 | 1.00 |

**Wmk. 373**

| | | |
|---|---|---|
| **559** CD349 70v multicolored | 1.00 | 1.00 |
| *Nos. 555-559 (5)* | 3.75 | 3.75 |

New Hebrides Participation in World War II — A105

Designs: 50v, Grumman F4F-4 Wildcat. 55v, Douglas SBD-3 Dauntless. 65v, Consolidated PBY-5A Catalina. 80v, USS Hornet. 200v, Vought-Sikorsky OS2U-3.

***Perf. 13½x14***

**1992, May 22 Litho. Wmk. 373**

**560** A105 50v multicolored 2.25 2.25
**561** A105 55v multicolored 2.25 2.25
**562** A105 65v multicolored 2.50 2.50
**563** A105 80v multicolored 3.50 3.50
*Nos. 560-563 (4)* 10.50 10.50

**Souvenir Sheet**

**564** A105 200v multicolored 11.50 11.50

World Columbian Stamp Expo, Chicago (No. 564).
See Nos. 590-594, 664-667.

Vanuatu's Membership in the World Meteorological Organization, 10th Anniv. — A106

Designs: 25v, Meteorological station, Port Vila. 60v, Cyclone near Vanuatu seen by Japanese satellite GMS 4. 80v, Weather chart showing cyclone. 105v, Cyclone warning broadcast by radio.

**1992, June 20** ***Perf. 14***

**565** A106 25v multicolored .60 .60
**566** A106 60v multicolored 1.50 1.50
**567** A106 80v multicolored 1.75 1.75
**568** A106 105v multicolored 2.10 2.10
*Nos. 565-568 (4)* 5.95 5.95

1992 Melanesian Cup — A107

**1992, July 20** ***Perf. 13½x14***

**569** A107 20v Soccer team, trophy .55 .55
**570** A107 65v Soccer players 1.50 1.50
**571** A107 70v Men's track 1.75 1.75
**572** A107 80v Women's track 1.75 1.75
*Nos. 569-572 (4)* 5.55 5.55

1992 Summer Olympics, Barcelona (#571-572).
For surcharges see Nos. 621-622.

World Food Day — A108

Designs: 20v, "Breast is best." 70v, Central Hospital, Port Vila. 80v, "Give your children a healthy future." 150v, Nutritious food.

**1992, Oct. 16 Wmk. 384** ***Perf. 14***

**573** A108 20v green & brown .40 .40
**574** A108 70v brown & green 1.10 1.10
**575** A108 80v green & brown 1.40 1.40
**576** A108 150v brown & green 2.25 2.25
*Nos. 573-576 (4)* 5.15 5.15

Turtles A109

**1992, Dec. 15** ***Perf. 14x14½***

**577** A109 55v Leatherback turtle 1.60 1.60
**578** A109 65v Loggerhead turtle 1.75 1.75
**579** A109 70v Hawksbill turtle 2.25 2.25
**580** A109 80v Green turtle 3.00 3.00
*Nos. 577-580 (4)* 8.60 8.60

**Souvenir Sheet**

**581** A109 200v Green turtle hatchlings 5.50 5.50

Hibiscus — A110

Designs: 25v, Light pink hibiscus rosa-sinensis. 55v, Hibiscus tiliaceus. 80v, Red hibiscus rosa-sinensis. 150v, Dark pink hibiscus rosa-sinensis.

**Wmk. 384**

**1993, Mar. 3 Litho.** ***Perf. 14***

**582** A110 25v multicolored .50 .50
**583** A110 55v multicolored 1.10 1.10
**584** A110 80v multicolored 1.50 1.50
**585** A110 150v multicolored 2.75 2.75
*Nos. 582-585 (4)* 5.85 5.85

Nos. 331, 333-335 Surcharged

***Perf. 13½x14, 14x13½***

**1993, Apr. 21 Litho. Wmk. 373**

**586** A60 40v on 45v #331 .80 .80
**587** A60 55v on 75v #333 1.10 1.10
**588** A60 65v on 100v #334 1.25 1.25
**589** A60 150v on 200v #335 3.00 3.00
*Nos. 586-589 (4)* 6.15 6.15

Size and location of surcharge varies.

No. 326 Surcharged

**1993, June 1**

**589A** A60 20v on 35v #326 1.10 1.10

World War II Type of 1992

20v, Grumman F6F-3 Hellcat. 55v, Lockheed P-38F Lightning. 65v, GrummanTBF-1 Avenger. 80v, USS Essex. 200v, Douglas C-47 Dakota.

**1993, June 30** ***Perf. 13½***

**590** A105 20v multicolored .80 .80
**591** A105 55v multicolored 2.25 2.25
**592** A105 65v multicolored 2.75 2.75
**593** A105 80v multicolored 3.25 3.25
*Nos. 590-593 (4)* 9.05 9.05

**Souvenir Sheet**

**594** A105 200v multicolored 9.00 9.00

Island Scenes A111

Designs: 5v, Iririki Island, Port Vila. 10v, Iririki Island, yachts. 15v, Court House, Port Vila. 20v, Two girls, Pentecost Island. 25v, Women dancers, Tanna Island. 30v, Market, Port Vila. 45v, Man with canoe, Erakor Island, vert. 50v, Coconut trees, Champagne Beach. 55v, Coconut trees, North Efate Islands. 60v, Fish (Banks Group). 70v, Sea fan, Tongoa Island, vert. 75v, Espiritu Santo Island. 80v, Sailboat at sunset, Port Vila Bay, vert. 100v, Mele Waterfall, vert. 300v, Yasur Volcano, Tanna Island, vert. 500v, Erakor Island.

**1993, July 7** ***Perf. 14x14½, 14½x14***

**595** A111 5v multicolored .20 .20
**596** A111 10v multicolored .20 .20
**597** A111 15v multicolored .25 .25
**598** A111 20v multicolored .35 .35
**599** A111 25v multicolored .40 .40
**600** A111 30v multicolored .50 .50
**601** A111 45v multicolored .75 .75
**602** A111 50v multicolored .80 .80
**603** A111 55v multicolored .90 .90
**604** A111 60v multicolored 1.00 1.00
**605** A111 70v multicolored 1.10 1.10
**606** A111 75v multicolored 1.25 1.25
**607** A111 80v multicolored 1.25 1.25
**608** A111 100v multicolored 1.60 1.60
**609** A111 300v multicolored 4.75 4.75
**610** A111 500v multicolored 8.00 8.00
*Nos. 595-610 (16)* 23.30 23.30

For surcharges see Nos. 619-620, 742-745A.

Shells — A112

**Wmk. 373**

**1993, Sept. 15 Litho.** ***Perf. 14½***

**611** A112 55v Trochus niloticus 1.25 1.25
**612** A112 65v Lioconcha castrensis 1.60 1.60
**613** A112 80v Turbo petholatus 2.00 2.00
**614** A112 150v Pleuroploca trapezium 3.75 3.75
*Nos. 611-614 (4)* 8.60 8.60

See Nos. 632-635, 654-657.

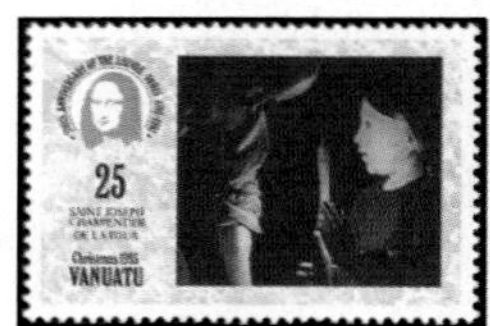


Louvre Museum, Bicent. A113

Paintings by De La Tour: 25v, St. Joseph the Carpenter. 55v, The Newborn. 80v, Adoration of the Shepherds (detail). 150v, Adoration of the Shepherds (entire).

**Wmk. 373**

**1993, Nov. 10 Litho.** ***Perf. 14***

**615** A113 25v multicolored .50 .50
**616** A113 55v multicolored 1.10 1.10
**617** A113 80v multicolored 1.60 1.60
**618** A113 150v multicolored 3.25 3.25
*Nos. 615-618 (4)* 6.45 6.45

Nos. 570, 572, 598, 600 Surcharged

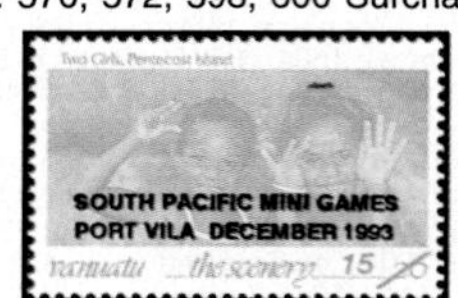


**1993, Dec. 6 Litho. Wmk. 373**

**Perfs. as Before**

**619** A111 15v on 20v #598 .30 .30
**620** A111 25v on 30v #600 .45 .45
**621** A107 55v on 65v #570 1.00 1.00
**622** A107 70v on 80v #572 1.25 1.25
*Nos. 619-622 (4)* 3.00 3.00

Service Organizations A114

Intl. Year of the Family A115

Hong Kong '94: 25v, Kiwanis Intl., Charity Races, vert. 60v, Lions Intl. Twin Otter on mercy mission. 75v, Rotary Intl. fighting malaria, vert. 150v, Red Cross blood donar service. 200v, Emblems of service organizations.

***Perf. 14x15, 15x14***

**1994, Feb. 18 Litho. Wmk. 373**

**623** A114 25v multicolored .45 .45
**624** A114 60v multicolored 1.10 1.10
**625** A114 75v multicolored 1.40 1.40
**626** A114 150v multicolored 2.75 2.75
*Nos. 623-626 (4)* 5.70 5.70

**Souvenir Sheet**

**627** A114 200v multicolored 3.75 3.75

**1994, Mar. 2** ***Perf. 14***

**628** A115 25v vio & rose brn .45 .45
**629** A115 60v ver & dk grn 1.10 1.10
**630** A115 90v green & sepia 1.60 1.60
**631** A115 150v brn & vio bl 2.75 2.75
*Nos. 628-631 (4)* 5.90 5.90

Shell Type of 1993

**1994, May 31 Litho.** ***Perf. 12***

**632** A112 60v Cyprea argus 1.50 1.50
**633** A112 70v Conus marmoreus 1.75 1.75
**634** A112 85v Lambis chiragra 2.25 2.25
**635** A112 155v Chicoreus brunneus 4.00 4.00
*Nos. 632-635 (4)* 9.50 9.50

Tourism — A116

Designs: a, 25v, Slit gong (drum), traditional hut. b, 75v, Volcano, boats. c, 90v, Sailboats, airplane, green palm lorikeet. d, 200v, Helicopter, woman with tray of fruit.

**1994, July 27 Litho.** ***Perf. 13½***

**636** A116 Strip of 4, #a.-d. 8.75 8.75

Anemonefish — A117

**1994, Aug. 16 Litho.** ***Perf. 12***

**637** A117 55v Pink 2.25 2.25
**638** A117 70v Clark's 3.00 3.00
**639** A117 80v Red & black 3.25 3.25
**640** A117 140v Orange-fin 6.00 6.00
*a.* Souvenir sheet of 1 4.75 4.75
*Nos. 637-640 (4)* 14.50 14.50

Philakorea '94 (#640a).

ICAO, 50th Anniv. — A118

Designs: 25v, 1950 Qantas Catalina. 60v, 1956 Tai Douglas DC3. 75v, 1966 New Hebrides Airways Drover. 90v, 1994 Air Vanuatu Boeing 737.

**1994, Dec. 7**

**641** A118 25v multicolored .55 .55
**642** A118 60v multicolored 1.50 1.50
**643** A118 75v multicolored 1.75 1.75
**644** A118 90v multicolored 2.25 2.25
*Nos. 641-644 (4)* 6.05 6.05

Hibiscus A119

**1995, Feb. 1 Litho. *Perf. 12***

**645** A119 25v The Path .50 .50
**646** A119 60v Old Frankie 1.25 1.25
**647** A119 90v Fijian white 1.90 1.90
**648** A119 200v Surf rider 4.25 4.25
*Nos. 645-648 (4)* 7.90 7.90

Lizards A120

Designs: 25v, Emoia nigromarginata. 55v, Nactus multicarinatus. 70v, Lepidodactylus. 80v, Emoia caerulocauda. 140v, Emoia sanfordi.

**1995, Apr. 12**

**649** A120 25v multicolored .55 .55
**650** A120 55v multicolored 1.25 1.25
**651** A120 70v multicolored 1.60 1.60
**652** A120 80v multicolored 1.75 1.75
**653** A120 140v multicolored 3.25 3.25
*Nos. 649-653 (5)* 8.40 8.40

Shell Type of 1993

**1995, June 1**

**654** A112 25v Epitonium scalare .65 .65
**655** A112 55v Strombus latissimus 1.50 1.50
**656** A112 90v Conus bullatus 2.25 2.25
**657** A112 200v Pterynotus pinnatus 5.25 5.25
*Nos. 654-657 (4)* 9.65 9.65

Anniversaries — A121

Designs: 25v, Girls wearing traditional head pieces. 55v, Stylized picture of natives dancing, vert. 60v, Children, doves, natl. flag, UN flag, vert. 75v, Embroidered tapestry of native, vert. 90v, Troops parading. 140v, Group in traditional ceremony.

***Perf. 14x13½, 13½x14***

**1995, July 28 Litho.**

**658** A121 25v multicolored .55 .55
**659** A121 55v multicolored 1.25 1.25
**660** A121 60v multicolored 1.25 1.25
**661** A121 75v multicolored 1.75 1.75
**662** A121 90v multicolored 1.90 1.90
**663** A121 140v multicolored 3.00 3.00
*a.* Souvenir sheet of 1 3.25 3.25
*Nos. 658-663 (6)* 9.70 9.70

UN, 50th anniv. (#660). Singapore 95 (#663a). Others, independence, 15th anniv.

World War II Type of 1992

**1995, Sept. 1 Litho. *Perf. 12½***

**664** A105 60v SB2C Helldiver 2.10 2.10
**665** A105 70v Spitfire Mk VIII 2.40 2.40
**666** A105 75v F4U-1A Corsair 2.40 2.40
**667** A105 80v PV1 Ventura 2.75 2.75
*Nos. 664-667 (4)* 9.65 9.65

**Souvenir Sheet**

***Perf. 13½***

**667A** A105 140v Japanese surrender, USS Missouri 6.25 6.25

No. 667A for Singapore 95.

Artifacts — A122

Ambae money mat and: a, 25v, Rambaramp mortuary effigy, Malakula. b, 60v, Wusi pot, Espiritu Santo. c, 75v, Slit gong, Efate Island. d, 90v, Tapa cloth, Erromango Island.

Nos. 668e, 668f, like No. 668d.

Illustration reduced.

**1995, Nov. 22 Litho. *Perf. 13½x13***

**668** A122 Strip of 4, #a.-d. 4.75 4.75
*e.* 90v Perf. 14 1.60 1.60
*f.* Souvenir sheet, #668e 2.25 2.25

No. 668f, 9th Asian Intl. Philatelic Exhibition, Beijing.

Issued: Nos. 668e, 668f, Dec. 1995.

See No. 720.

Fishing A123

**1996, Feb. 1 Litho. *Perf. 14***

**669** A123 55v Cast net 1.10 1.10
**670** A123 75v Reef 1.40 1.40
**671** A123 80v Deep water, vert. 1.50 1.50
**672** A123 140v Game, vert. 2.75 2.75
*Nos. 669-672 (4)* 6.75 6.75

Flying Foxes A124

No. 673, Notopteris macdonaldi, facing left. No. 674, Pteropus anetianus, green leaves on tree, vert. No. 675, Pteropus anetianus, diff., vert. No. 676, Notopteris macdonaldi, diff.

No. 677, vert: a, 90v, Pteropus tonganus. b, 140v, Pteropus tonganus, diff.

**1996, Apr. 3 Litho. *Perf. 14***

**673** A124 25v multicolored .95 .75
**674** A124 25v multicolored .95 .75
**675** A124 25v multicolored .95 .75
**676** A124 25v multicolored .95 .75
*Nos. 673-676 (4)* 3.80 3.00

**Souvenir Sheet**

**677** A124 Sheet of 2, #a.-b. 6.00 6.00

World Wildlife Fund (Nos. 673-676). 9th Asian Intl. Philatelic Exhibition (No. 677).

UNICEF, 50th Anniv. A125

**Unwmk.**

**1996, June 5 Litho. *Perf. 14***

**678** A125 55v Immunizations 1.25 1.25
**679** A125 60v Breast feeding 1.40 1.40

Radio, Cent. A126

60v, Airplane, radio signal. 75v, Radio Vanuatu. 80v, Guglielmo Marconi. 90v, Ship, radio signal.

**1996, June 5 *Perf. 14½***

**680** A126 60v multicolored 1.10 1.10
**681** A126 75v multicolored 1.25 1.25
**682** A126 80v multicolored 1.40 1.40
**683** A126 90v multicolored 1.60 1.60
*a.* Block of 4, #680-683 6.25 6.25

Modern Olympic Games, Cent. — A127

Designs: 25v, Marie Kapalu, Tawai Keiruan, Baptiste Firiam, Tava Kalo, 1996 athletes from Vanuatu. 70v, 1996 Athletes in training. 75v, 1950's Athletes. 200v, 1896 Athletes.

**1996, July 17 Litho. *Perf. 14***

**684** A127 25v multicolored .50 .50
**685** A127 70v multicolored 1.50 1.50
**686** A127 75v multicolored 1.50 1.50
**687** A127 200v multicolored 4.50 4.50
*Nos. 684-687 (4)* 8.00 8.00

Christmas A128

Children of various races holding candles in front of churches: a, 25v, Presbyterian, Roman Catholic. b, 60v, Church of Christ. c, 75v, 7th Day Adventist, Apostolic. d, 90v, Anglican.

**1996, Sept. 11 Litho. *Perf. 14***

**688** A128 Strip of 4, #a.-d. 5.00 5.00

No. 688 is a continuous design.

Hibiscus A129

**1996, Nov. 13 Litho. *Perf. 13½***

**689** A129 25v Lady Cilento .55 .55
**690** A129 60v Kinchen's Yellow 1.25 1.25
**691** A129 90v D.J. O'Brien 1.90 1.90
**692** A129 200v Cuban Variety 4.25 4.25
*a.* Sheet of 2, #689, #692 5.25 5.25
*Nos. 689-692 (4)* 7.95 7.95

Hong Kong '97. No. 692a issued 2/12/97.

Diving A130

Designs: 70v, Coral Garden. 75v, Lady of the President Coolidge. 90v, "Boris," Queensland grouper. 140v, Wreck of the President Coolidge.

**1997, Jan. 15 Litho. *Perf. 14½x14***

**693** A130 70v multicolored 1.40 1.40
**694** A130 75v multicolored 1.40 1.40
**695** A130 90v multicolored 1.75 1.75
**696** A130 140v multicolored 2.75 2.75
*a.* Souvenir sheet, #694, 696 5.25 5.25
*b.* Souvenir sheet, #693-696 11.00 11.00
*Nos. 693-696 (4)* 7.30 7.30

Pacific '97 (#696a).

Birds A131

25v, Sharp-tailed sandpiper. 55v, Crested tern. 60v, Little pied cormorant. 75v, Brown booby. 80v, Reef heron. 90v, Red-tailed tropic bird.

**1997, June 4 Litho. *Perf. 13½x14***

**697** A131 25v multi .55 .55
**698** A131 55v multi 1.10 1.10
**699** A131 60v multi 1.25 1.25
**700** A131 75v multi 1.50 1.50
**701** A131 80v multi, vert. 1.50 1.50
**702** A131 90v multi, vert. 1.75 1.75
*Nos. 697-702 (6)* 7.65 7.65

Air Vanuatu, 10th Anniv. A132

Designs: 25v, Pilot at controls. 60v, Airplane being serviced, cargo loaded. 90v, Serving drinks to passengers. 200v, Passengers leaving plane upon arrival at Vanuatu.

**1997, Apr. 2 *Perf. 14½x14***

**703** A132 25v multicolored .50 .50
**704** A132 60v multicolored 1.25 1.25
**705** A132 90v multicolored 1.90 1.90
**706** A132 200v multicolored 4.00 4.00
*Nos. 703-706 (4)* 7.65 7.65

No. 704 is 81x31mm.

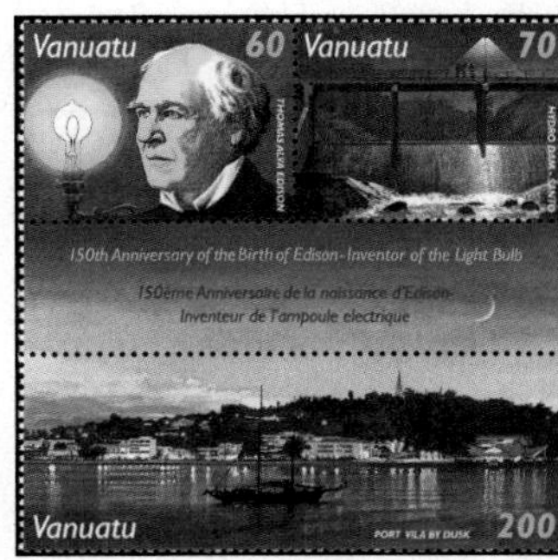


Thomas A. Edison (1847-1931) — A133

Designs: 60v, Light bulb, Edison. 70v, Hydro dam, Santo. 200v, Port Vila by dusk.

**1997, Aug. 27 Litho. *Perf. 12***

**707** A133 60v multicolored 1.10 1.10
**708** A133 70v multicolored 1.25 1.25
**709** A133 200v multicolored 3.50 3.50
*a.* Block of 3, #707-709 + label 6.75 6.75

No. 709 is 80x30mm.

Fish — A134

Designs: 25v, Yellow-faced angelfish. 55v, Flame angelfish. 60v, Lemonpeel angelfish. 70v, Emperor angelfish. 140v, Multi-barred angelfish.

**1997, Nov. 12 Litho. *Perf. 14x13½***

| | | | | |
|---|---|---|---|---|
| **710** | A134 | 25v multicolored | .45 | .45 |
| **711** | A134 | 55v multicolored | 1.10 | 1.10 |
| **712** | A134 | 60v multicolored | 1.25 | 1.25 |
| **713** | A134 | 70v multicolored | 1.40 | 1.40 |
| **714** | A134 | 140v multicolored | 2.75 | 2.75 |
| | | *Nos. 710-714 (5)* | 6.95 | 6.95 |

Architecture in Vanuatu A135

Designs: 30v, Fale-Espiritu Santo. 65v, Natl. Cultural Center. 80v, University of the South Pacific. 200v, Chief's Nakamal.

**1998, Feb. 11 Litho. *Perf. 14½x14***

| | | | | |
|---|---|---|---|---|
| **715** | A135 | 30v multicolored | .50 | .50 |
| **716** | A135 | 65v multicolored | 1.10 | 1.10 |
| **717** | A135 | 80v multicolored | 1.25 | 1.25 |
| **718** | A135 | 200v multicolored | 3.25 | 3.25 |
| | | *Nos. 715-718 (4)* | 6.10 | 6.10 |

**Diana, Princess of Wales (1961-97)**

Common Design Type

Various portraits: a, 75v. b, 85v. c, 145v.

**1998, Mar. 31 Litho. *Perf. 14½x14***

| | | | | |
|---|---|---|---|---|
| **718A** | CD355 | 95v multicolored | 1.40 | 1.40 |

**Sheet of 4**

| | | | | |
|---|---|---|---|---|
| **719** | CD355 | #a.-c., 718A | 7.50 | 7.50 |

No. 719 sold for 400v + 50v, with surtax from international sales being donated to The Diana, Princess of Wales Memorial Fund and surtax from national sales being donated to designated local charity.

Artifacts Type of 1995

Tribal masks: a, 30v, South West Malakula. b, 65v, North Ambrym. c, 75v, Gana Island Banks. d, 85v, Uripiv Island, Malakula. e, 95v, Vao Island, Malakula, and Central South Pentecost.

**1998, June 3 Litho. *Perf. 14½***

| | | | | |
|---|---|---|---|---|
| **720** | A122 | Strip of 5, #a.-e. | 7.25 | 7.25 |

Butterflies — A136

30v, Danaus plexippus. 60v, Hypolimnas bolina. 65v, Eurema hecabe. 75v, Nymphalidae. 95v, Precis villida. 205v, Tirumala hamata.

**1998, July 23 Litho. *Die Cut***

**Self-Adhesive**

| | | | | |
|---|---|---|---|---|
| **721** | A136 | 30v multicolored | .60 | .60 |
| **722** | A136 | 60v multicolored | 1.25 | 1.25 |
| **723** | A136 | 65v multicolored | 1.50 | 1.50 |
| **724** | A136 | 75v multicolored | 1.75 | 1.75 |
| **725** | A136 | 95v multicolored | 2.00 | 2.00 |
| **726** | A136 | 205v multicolored | 3.75 | 3.75 |
| *a.* | | Souvenir sheet of 1 | 5.50 | 5.50 |
| | | *Nos. 721-726 (6)* | 10.85 | 10.85 |

Singpex '98 (#726a).

Volcanoes — A137

30v, Yasur, Tanna. 60v, Marum & Benbow, Ambrym. 75v, Gaua. 80v, Lopevi. 145v, Ambae.

**1998, Oct. 23 Litho. *Perf. 15x14***

| | | | | |
|---|---|---|---|---|
| **728** | A137 | 30v multicolored | .50 | .50 |
| **729** | A137 | 60v multicolored | 1.00 | 1.00 |
| **730** | A137 | 75v multicolored | 1.25 | 1.25 |
| **731** | A137 | 80v multicolored | 1.25 | 1.25 |
| **732** | A137 | 145v multicolored | 2.50 | 2.50 |
| | | *Nos. 728-732 (5)* | 6.50 | 6.50 |

Early Explorers A138

Explorer, ship: 34v, Pedro Fernandez de Quiros, San Pedro y Paulo, 1606. 73v, Louis-Antoine de Bougainville, Boudeuse, 1768. 84v, Capt. James Cook, HMS Resolution, 1774. 90v, Jean-Fancois de Galaup de la Perousse, Astrolabe, 1788. 96v, Jules Sebastien-Cesar Dumont d'Urville, Astrolabe, "1788."

**1999, Feb. 17 Litho. *Perf. 14***

| | | | | |
|---|---|---|---|---|
| **733** | A138 | 34v multicolored | .55 | .55 |
| **734** | A138 | 73v multicolored | 1.25 | 1.25 |
| **735** | A138 | 84v multicolored | 1.40 | 1.40 |
| *a.* | | Souv. sheet, #733-735 | 3.25 | 3.25 |
| **736** | A138 | 90v multicolored | 1.40 | 1.40 |
| **737** | A138 | 96v multicolored | 1.50 | 1.50 |
| *a.* | | Souv. sheet, #734, 736-737 | 4.00 | 4.00 |
| | | *Nos. 733-737 (5)* | 6.10 | 6.10 |

No. 735a was released for Australia '99 World Stamp Expo on 3/19/99; No. 737a for PhilexFrance 99.

Birds — A139

34v, Vanuatu kingfisher. 67v, Shining cuckoo. 73v, Peregrine falcon. 107v, Rainbow lorikeet.

**1999, May 12 Litho. *Perf. 14***

| | | | | |
|---|---|---|---|---|
| **738** | A139 | 34v multicolored | .85 | .85 |
| **739** | A139 | 67v multicolored | 1.50 | 1.50 |
| | | Booklet, 5 #739 | 9.00 | |
| **740** | A139 | 73v multicolored | 1.75 | 1.75 |
| **741** | A139 | 107v multicolored | 2.50 | 2.50 |
| *a.* | | Sheet of 1 | 5.50 | 5.50 |
| *b.* | | Sheet of 1 with China 1999 emblem in margin | 4.50 | 4.50 |
| | | *Nos. 738-741 (4)* | 6.60 | 6.60 |

Issued: #741b, 8/18.

Nos. 601, 603-605, 608 Surcharged

***Perf. 14½x14, 14x14½***

**1998-2000 Litho.**

| | | | | |
|---|---|---|---|---|
| **742** | A111 | 1v on 100v #608 | .20 | .20 |
| **742A** | A111 | 2v on 45v #601 | .20 | .20 |
| **743** | A111 | 2v on 55v #603 | .20 | .20 |
| **744** | A111 | 3v on 60v #604 | .20 | .20 |
| **744A** | A111 | 3v on 75v #606 | .20 | .20 |
| **745** | A111 | 4v on 45v #601 | .20 | .20 |
| **745A** | A111 | 5v on 70v #605 | | |
| **745B** | A111 | 34v on 20v #598 | .50 | .50 |
| **745C** | A111 | 67v on 300v #609 | 1.00 | 1.00 |
| | | *Nos. 742-745C (8)* | 2.70 | 2.70 |

Issued: No. 742, No. 742A, 743, 744, 745, 745A, 12/18/98; No. 744A, 4/27/99; Nos. 745B, 745C, 2/17/00.

Ceremonial Dancers — A140

1v, Banks Islands. 2v, Small Nambas, Laman-Malakula. 3v, Small Nambas, Malakula. 5v, Smol Bag Theatre. 107v, South West Bay, Malakula. 200v, Big Nambas, Malakula. 500v, Pentacost.

**1999, July 14 *Perf. 14***

| | | | | |
|---|---|---|---|---|
| **746** | A140 | 1v multicolored | .20 | .20 |
| **747** | A140 | 2v multicolored | .20 | .20 |
| **748** | A140 | 3v multicolored | .20 | .20 |
| **749** | A140 | 5v multicolored | .20 | .20 |
| **750** | A140 | 107v multicolored | 1.60 | 1.60 |
| **751** | A140 | 200v multicolored | 3.25 | 3.25 |
| **752** | A140 | 500v multicolored | 7.75 | 7.75 |
| | | *Nos. 746-752 (7)* | 13.40 | 13.40 |

Poisonous Fish — A141

Designs: 34v, Pterois antennata. 84v, Pterois antennata, diff. 90v, Pterois volitans. 96v, Pterois volitans, diff.

**1999, Oct. 13 Litho. *Perf. 14¼***

| | | | | |
|---|---|---|---|---|
| **753** | A141 | 34v multi | .65 | .65 |
| **754** | A141 | 84v multi | 1.50 | 1.50 |
| **755** | A141 | 90v multi | 1.75 | 1.75 |
| **756** | A141 | 96v multi | 1.90 | 1.90 |
| | | *Nos. 753-756 (4)* | 5.80 | 5.80 |

Millennium A142

Designs: a, 34v, Fish. b, 68v, Girl, land diver, vert. c, 84v, Fetish, vert. d, 90v, Bird, flowers. e, 96v, Man with conch shell.

**1999, Dec. 1 *Perf. 14½***

| | | | | |
|---|---|---|---|---|
| **757** | A142 | Sheet of 5, #a.-e. | 6.50 | 6.50 |

Souvenir Sheet

Queen Mother, 100th Birthday — A143

a, 107v, As child. b, 100v, As old woman. Illustration reduced.

**Litho. with Foil Application**

**2000, May 22 *Perf. 13¼***

| | | | | |
|---|---|---|---|---|
| **758** | A143 | Sheet of 2, #a-b | 3.50 | 3.50 |

The Stamp Show 2000, London.

Intelsat A144

Designs: 10v, Launch vehicle. 34v, Port Vila ground station. 100v, Intelsat 802 over Vaunatu. 225v, Intelsat and Tam Tam drum.

**Litho. with Foil Application**

**2000, June 21 *Die Cut Perf. 10***

**Self-Adhesive**

| | | | | |
|---|---|---|---|---|
| **759-762** | A144 | Set of 4 | 6.25 | 6.25 |
| *762a* | | Souvenir sheet, #760, 762 | 4.50 | 4.50 |

World Stamp Expo 2000, Anaheim (#762a).

Independence, 20th Anniv., UN Peace Year — A145

Artwork: 34v, Abstract painting by Sero Kuautonga. 67v, Tapa cloth by Moses Pita. 73v, Tapestry by Juliet Pita. 84v, Natora wood carving by Emmannuel Watt. 90v, Watercolor by Joseph John.

**2000, July 29 Litho. *Perf. 13¾x13¼***

| | | | | |
|---|---|---|---|---|
| **763-767** | A145 | Set of 5 | 6.25 | 6.25 |
| | | Booklet, 5 #764 | 6.00 | |

2000 Summer Olympics, Sydney — A146

Designs: 56v, Runner. 67v, Weight lifter. 90v, High jumper. 96v, Boxer.

**2000, Sept. 15 *Perf. 13¼x13***

| | | | | |
|---|---|---|---|---|
| **768-771** | A146 | Set of 4 | 5.50 | 5.50 |
| | | Booklet, 5 #769 | 6.00 | |

Dolphins — A147

34v, Common. 73v, Spotted. 84v, Spinner. 107v, Bottlenose.

**2000, Nov. 30 Litho. *Perf. 12½***

| | | | | |
|---|---|---|---|---|
| **772-775** | A147 | Set of 4 | 5.25 | 5.25 |
| *775a* | | Souvenir sheet, #774-775 | 4.00 | 4.00 |

Hong Kong 2001 Stamp Exhibition (#775a).

Birds — A148

Designs: 35v, Cardinal honeyeater. 60v, Vanuatu white-eye. 90v, Santo Mountain starling. 100v, Royal parrotfinch. 110v, Vanuatu Mountain honeyeater.

**2001, Feb. 1 Litho. *Perf. 14***

| | | | | |
|---|---|---|---|---|
| **776-780** | A148 | Set of 5 | 5.50 | 5.50 |
| *780a* | | Horiz. strip, #776-780 | 5.75 | 5.75 |

Exports — A149

Designs: 35v, Vanilla. 75v, Cacao. 90v, Coffee. 110v, Copra.

**2001, Apr. 11 *Perf. 13¼x13***

| | | | | |
|---|---|---|---|---|
| **781-784** | A149 | Set of 4 | 5.75 | 5.75 |

Whales A150

Designs: 60v, Sperm. 80v, Humpback, vert. 90v, Blue.

***Perf. 14½x14¾, 14¾x14½***

**2001, July 18 Litho.**

| | | | | |
|---|---|---|---|---|
| **785-787** | A150 | Set of 3 | 3.75 | 3.75 |
| *787a* | | Souvenir sheet, #785-787, perf. 14½ | 3.75 | 3.75 |

See New Caledonia No. 874.

**Ceremonial Dancers Type of 1999**

Designs: 35v, Snake dance, Banks Islands, horiz. 100v, Toka Dance, Tanna, horiz. 300v, Rom Dance, Ambryn, horiz. 1000v, Brasive Dance, Futuna, horiz.

**2001, Sept. 12 Litho. *Perf. 13x13¼***

| | | | | |
|---|---|---|---|---|
| **788** | A140 | 35v multi | .70 | .70 |
| **789** | A140 | 100v multi | 1.90 | 1.90 |
| **790** | A140 | 300v multi | 5.75 | 5.75 |

**Litho. With Foil Application**

| | | | | |
|---|---|---|---|---|
| **791** | A140 | 1000v multi | 19.00 | 19.00 |
| | | *Nos. 788-791 (4)* | 27.35 | 27.35 |

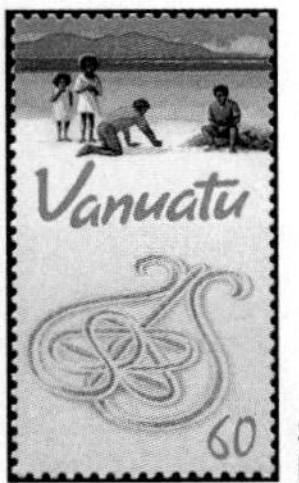

Sand Drawings — A151

Various sand drawings and: a, Four people on beach. b, Man standing in canoe in water. c, Man sitting on canoe, man rowing canoe. d, Canoe, shelter.

***Perf. 12¾x13½***

**2001, Nov. 28 Litho.**

| | | | | |
|---|---|---|---|---|
| **792** | A151 | 60v multi | 1.00 | 1.00 |
| **792A** | A151 | 90v multi | 1.50 | 1.50 |
| **792B** | A151 | 110vmulti | 1.90 | 1.90 |
| **792C** | A151 | 135vmulti | 2.40 | 2.40 |
| ***Cd.*** | | Horiz. strip of 4 + central label | 8.00 | 8.00 |

Intl. Year of Ecotourism A152

Designs: Nos. 793, 798a, 35v, Mount Yasur, Pentecost Island land diver, dancers. Nos. 794, 798b, 60v Dancers, man making kava. Nos. 795, 798c, 75v, Siri Falls, flowers, birds, vert. Nos. 796, 798d, 110v, Kayakers, scuba diver, vert. Nos. 797, 798e, 135v, Beach bungalows, tourists.

**2002, Jan. 30 Litho. *Perf. 14***

**Stamps + Label**

| | | | | |
|---|---|---|---|---|
| **793-797** | A152 | Set of 5 | 7.25 | 7.25 |

**Souvenir Sheet**

**Without Labels**

***Perf. 14½x14¾***

| | | | | |
|---|---|---|---|---|
| **798** | A152 | Sheet of 5, #a-e | 7.25 | 7.25 |

Nos. 793, 794, and 797 are 38x26mm and Nos. 795-796 are 26x38mm, while Nos. 798a, 798b, and 798e are 37x25mm and Nos. 798c-798d are 25x37mm.

Horses A153

Designs: 35v, Working horses. 60v, Cattle roundup. 75v, Horse racing. 80v, Tourism and horses. 200v, Wild Tanna horse.

**2002, Mar. 27 *Perf. 14¾x14***

| | | | | |
|---|---|---|---|---|
| **799-803** | A153 | Set of 5 | 6.25 | 6.25 |
| *803a* | | Souvenir sheet of 1 | 2.75 | 2.75 |
| *803b* | | Souvenir sheet of 1 with Philakorea 2002 emblem | 3.00 | 3.00 |

Issued: No. 803b, 7/31/02.

Soccer A154

Designs: 35v, Children's soccer. 80v, Under 17 soccer. 110v, Women's soccer. 135v, International soccer.

**2002, May 31 Litho. *Perf. 13¾***

| | | | | |
|---|---|---|---|---|
| **804-807** | A154 | Set of 4 | 5.50 | 5.50 |

Value is for stamps with surrounding selvage.

Reforestation — A155

No. 808: a, Girl with seedling of Artocarpus atilis. b, Boy and man planting seedling of Endospermum medullosum. c, Canoe carver with Gyrocarpus americanus log. d, Mother and child with Dracontomelon vitiense fruit.

***Serpentine Die Cut***

**2002, July 31 Litho.**

**Self-Adhesive**

| | | | | |
|---|---|---|---|---|
| **808** | | Horiz. strip of 4 | 4.25 | |
| *a.* | A155 | 35v multi | .50 | .50 |
| *b.* | A155 | 60v multi | .90 | .90 |
| *c.* | A155 | 90v multi | 1.25 | 1.25 |
| *d.* | A155 | 110v multi | 1.60 | 1.60 |

Dugongs A156

Designs: 35v, Pair nuzzling. 75v, Pair swimming. 80v, One swimming. 135v, One on ocean floor.

**2002, Sept. 25 Litho. *Perf. 13¾***

| | | | | |
|---|---|---|---|---|
| **812-815** | A156 | Set of 4 | 4.75 | 4.75 |
| *815a* | | Souvenir sheet, #814-815 | 3.25 | 3.25 |

Orchids — A157

Designs: 35v, Dendrobium gouldii. 60v, Dendrobium polysema. 90v, Dendrobium spectabile. 110v, Flickingeria comata.

**2002, Nov. 27 Litho. *Perf. 13¼***

| | | | | |
|---|---|---|---|---|
| **816-819** | A157 | Set of 4 | 4.50 | 4.50 |

Year of Cattle — A158

Cattle Breeds: 35v, Limousin. 80v, Charolais. 110v, Simmental. 135v, Red Brahman.

**2003, Jan. 29 *Perf. 13***

| | | | | |
|---|---|---|---|---|
| **820-823** | A158 | Set of 4 | 5.75 | 5.75 |

Pentecost Island Land Divers — A159

Designs: 35v, Diver on platform. 80v, Diver in air. 110v, Dancers, platform. 200v, Diver and platform (35x90mm).

**2003, Mar. 26 *Perf. 13¾x13¼***

| | | | | |
|---|---|---|---|---|
| **824-827** | A159 | Set of 4 | 6.75 | 6.75 |
| *827a* | | Souvenir sheet of 1 | 3.25 | 3.25 |

Snorkeling A160

Various people snorkeling: 35v, 80v, 90v, 110v, 135v. 80v and 90v are vert.

**2003, May 28 Litho. *Perf. 13¾***

| | | | | |
|---|---|---|---|---|
| **828-832** | A160 | Set of 5 | 7.50 | 7.50 |
| *832a* | | Souvenir sheet, #828-832, perf. 13¼ | 7.50 | 7.50 |

Natanggura Palm — A161

Half of palm nut and: 35v, Man planting palm tree, carved dolphins. 80v, Man weaving thatch for roof, carved turtle. 90v, Carver, carved lizard. 135v, Carvers, carved fish.

**2003, July 23 *Perf. 13¾x13¼***

| | | | | |
|---|---|---|---|---|
| **833-836** | A161 | Set of 4 | 5.75 | 5.75 |

Opening of Underwater Post Office in May 2003 — A162

**2003, Sept. 24 *Perf. 13¾***

| | | | | |
|---|---|---|---|---|
| **837** | A162 | 90v multi | 1.60 | 1.60 |

Sea Horses — A163

Designs: 60v, Hippocampus kuda. 90v, Hippocampus histrix. 200v, Hippocampus bargibanti.

**2003, Sept. 24**

| | | | | |
|---|---|---|---|---|
| **838-840** | A163 | Set of 3 | 6.00 | 6.00 |
| *840a* | | Souvenir sheet of 1 | 3.50 | 3.50 |

Moths A164

Designs: 35v, Daphnis hypothous. 90v, Hippotion celerio. 110v, Euchromia creusa. 135v, Eudocima salaminia.

**2003, Nov. 26 *Perf. 13½***

| | | | | |
|---|---|---|---|---|
| **841-844** | A164 | Set of 4 | 6.50 | 6.50 |

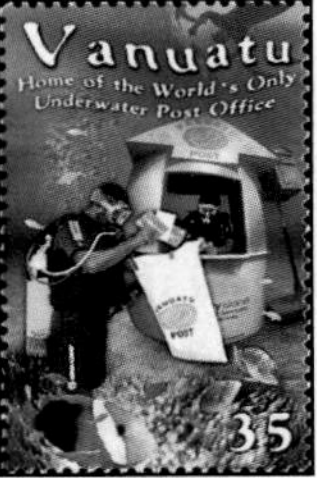

Activities at Underwater Post Office — A165

Designs: 35v, Workers placing mail in bag. 80v, Swimmer placing mail in mail box. 110v, Swimmer at counter. 220v, Clerk at counter, swimmer near mail box.

**2004, Jan. 30** ***Perf. 13¾x13½***

**845-848** A165 Set of 4 8.25 8.25
*848a* Souvenir sheet of 1 4.00 4.00

2004 Hong Kong Stamp Expo (#848a).

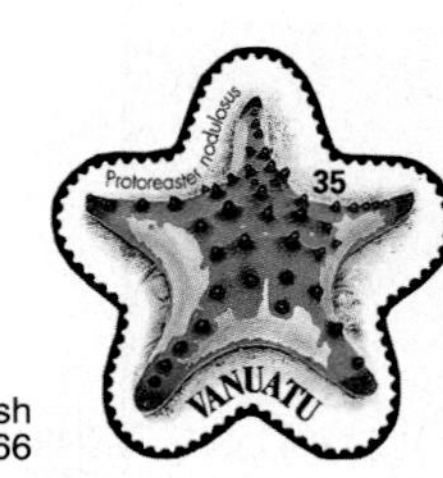


Starfish
A166

Designs: 35v, Protoreaster nodulosus. 60v, Linckia laevigata. 90v, Fromia monilis. 250v, Echinaster callosus.

***Serpentine Die Cut***

**2004, Apr. 28** **Litho.**

**Self-Adhesive**

**849-852** A166 Set of 4 7.75 7.75

Red-tailed
Tropicbird
A167

Designs: 35v, Adult and juvenile. 50v, Adult and chick, vert. 75v, Adult flying above juvenile, vert. 135v, Adult in flight. 200v, Adult pair.

**2004, July 14** **Litho.** ***Perf. 13¾***

**853-857** A167 Set of 5 8.75 8.75
*857a* Souvenir sheet, #853-857, perf. 13½ 8.75 8.75

Musket Cove to Port Vila Yacht Race, 25th Anniv. — A168

Various yachts: 35v, 80v, 90v, 200v. 80v and 200v are vert.

**2004, Sept. 18** ***Perf. 14¼***

**858-861** A168 Set of 4 7.00 7.00
*861a* Souvenir sheet of 1 3.50 3.50

See Fiji Nos. 1024-1027

Miniature Sheet

Marine Life — A169

No. 862: a, Red and black anemonefish. b, Longfin bannerfish. c, Goldman's sweetlips. d, Green turtle. e, Clark's anemonefish. f, Harlequin sweetlips. g, Yellowtail coris. h, Emperor angelfish. i, Hairy red hermit crab, leaf oyster. j, Spotfin lionfish. k, Yellow-lipped sea krait. l, Clam.

***Serpentine Die Cut 13¼***

**2004, Nov. 24** **Litho.**

**Self-Adhesive**

**862** A169 35v Sheet of 12, #a-l 8.00 8.00

Christmas
A170

***Serpentine Die Cut 13***

**2004, Nov. 24**

**Self-Adhesive**

**863** A170 80v multi 1.50 1.50

Sunsets
A171

Designs: 60v, Sailboat. 80v, Man with raised arm, vert. 90v, Sailboats, vert. 135v, Man blowing conch shell.

**2005, Jan. 19** ***Perf. 14x14½, 14½x14***

**864-867** A171 Set of 4 6.75 6.75

Miniature Sheet

Lapita People — A172

No. 868: a, 50v, Man holding tool, vert. b, 70v, People cleaning fish. c, 110v, People tending fire and carrying animal to fire. d, 200v, Women making baskets, mother and child, vert.

**2005, Mar. 2** ***Perf. 13¼***

**868** A172 Sheet of 4, #a-d 8.25 8.25

Pacific Explorer 2005 World Stamp Expo, Sydney.

Volcano
Post
A173

Mail box on Mount Yasur and: 35v, Five tourists. 80v, Native woman. 100v, Three postal workers. 250v, Postal worker removing mail.

**2005, May 31** **Litho.** ***Perf. 14x14¼***

**869-872** A173 Set of 4 8.50 8.50
*872a* Souvenir sheet of 1 4.50 4.50

Souvenir Sheet

Independence, 25th Anniv. — A174

No. 873: a, 35v, Vanuatu natives celebrating. b, 50v, Soldiers raising Vanuatu flag, 1980. c, 400v, Children and statue of family.

**2005, July 30** **Litho.** ***Perf. 13***

**873** A174 Sheet of 3, #a-c 8.75 8.75

Miniature Sheet

Corals — A175

No. 874: a, Lace coral. b, Star coral. c, Sun coral (Tubastraea sp.). d, Plate coral. e, Brown anthelia. f, Bubble coral. g, Flowerpot coral. h, Cup coral. i, Daisy coral. j, Sun coral (Tubastraea diaphana). k, Mushroom-feather coral. l, Sun coral (Tubastraea micrantha).

***Serpentine Die Cut 13½x13¼***

**2005, Sept. 7** **Litho.**

**Self-Adhesive**

**874** A175 35v Sheet of 12, #a-l 7.75 7.75

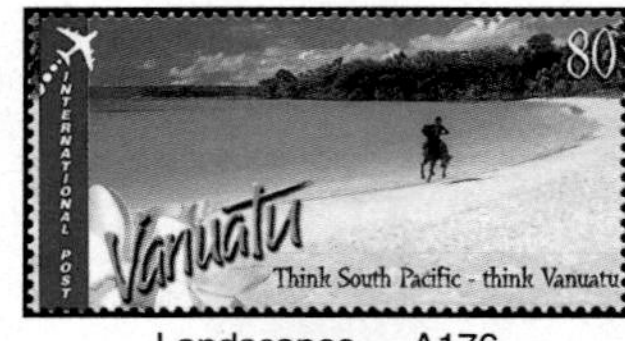


Landscapes — A176

Designs: 80v, Horse and rider on beach. 90v, Palm trees. 110v, Waterfall. 135v, Harbor.

**2005, Nov. 16** **Litho.** ***Perf. 14¼x14***

**875-878** A176 Set of 4 7.50 7.50

Miniature Sheet

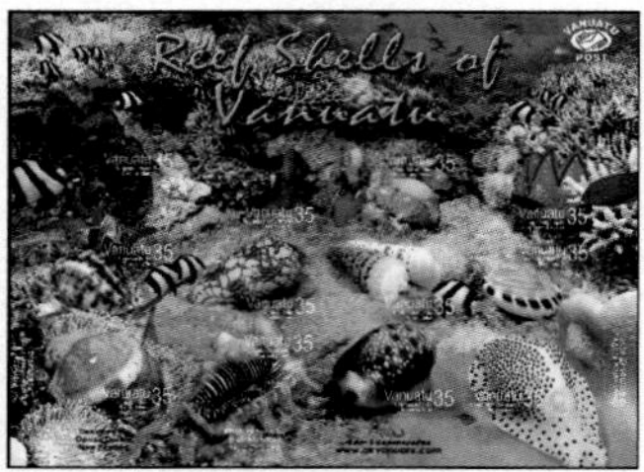


Reef Shells — A177

No. 879: a, Crocus clam. b, Pearl oyster. c, Gold-ringer cowrie. d, Cock-a-comb oyster. e, Tiger cowrie. f, Textile cone. g, Marlinspike. h, Vibex bonnet. i, Erosa cowrie. j, Scorpion conch. k, Honey cowrie. l, Umbilical ovula.

***Serpentine Die Cut 13½***

**2006, Feb. 8**

**Self-Adhesive**

**879** A177 35v Sheet of 12, #a-l 7.50 7.50

Queen
Elizabeth
II, 80th
Birthday
A178

Queen: 50v, As young woman in Army uniform. 100v, Without hat. No. 882, 110v, With blue hat. No. 883, 200v, With yellow hat.

No. 884: a, 110v, Like 100v. b, 200v, Like No. 882.

**2006, Apr. 21** **Litho.** ***Perf. 14***

**With White Frames**

**880-883** A178 Set of 4 8.25 8.25

**Souvenir Sheet**

**Without White Frames**

**884** A178 Sheet of 2, #a-b 5.75 5.75

Souvenir Sheet

Arrival in Vanuatu of Pedro Fernandez de Quiros, 400th Anniv. — A179

**2006, May 10** ***Perf. 13¼***

**885** A179 350v multi 6.50 6.50

2006 World Cup Soccer Championships, Germany — A180

Various soccer players, 2006 World Cup emblem on soccer jersey: 35v, 80v, 110v, 135v.

**2006, June 9** **Litho.** ***Die Cut***

**Self-Adhesive**

**886-889** A180 Set of 4 6.50 6.50
*889a* Souvenir sheet, #886-889 6.50 6.50

Flowers
A181

Designs: 5v, Passiflora foetida. 10v, Hibiscus rosa-sinensis. 20v, Cereus undatus. 40v, Strelitzia reginae. 50v, Spathodea campanulata. 70v, Delonix regia. 90v, Hibiscus hilaceus. 100v, Nymphaea sp. 150v, Plumeria obtusa. 500v, Allamanda cathartica. 1000v, Thunbergia grandiflora.

***Serpentine Die Cut 11¾***

**2006, July 1**

**Self-Adhesive**

| | | | | |
|---|---|---|---|---|
| **890** | A181 | 5v multi | .20 | .20 |
| **891** | A181 | 10v multi | .20 | .20 |
| **892** | A181 | 20v multi | .35 | .35 |
| **893** | A181 | 40v multi | .70 | .70 |
| **894** | A181 | 50v multi | .90 | .90 |
| **895** | A181 | 70v multi | 1.25 | 1.25 |
| **896** | A181 | 100v multi | 1.75 | 1.75 |
| **897** | A181 | 150v multi | 2.75 | 2.75 |
| **898** | A181 | 500v multi | 9.00 | 9.00 |
| **899** | A181 | 1000v multi | 18.00 | 18.00 |

**Inscribed "International Post" at Left**

| | | | | |
|---|---|---|---|---|
| **900** | A181 | 5v multi | .20 | .20 |
| **901** | A181 | 10v multi | .20 | .20 |
| **902** | A181 | 20v multi | .35 | .35 |
| **903** | A181 | 50v multi | .90 | .90 |
| **904** | A181 | 90v multi | 1.60 | 1.60 |
| **905** | A181 | 100v multi | 1.75 | 1.75 |
| **906** | A181 | 500v multi | 9.00 | 9.00 |
| **907** | A181 | 1000v multi | 18.00 | 18.00 |
| | | *Nos. 890-907 (18)* | 67.10 | 67.10 |

Miniature Sheet

Worldwide Fund for Nature (WWF) — A182

No. 908: a, 70v, Giant grouper and coral. b, 90v, Giant grouper and smaller fish. c, 100v, Juvenile giant groupers. d, 150v, Giant grouper, smaller fish, diff.

**2006, Oct. 4** **Litho.** ***Perf. 13¼***

**908** A182 Sheet, 2 each #a-d 15.00 15.00

Shipwreck of the SS President Coolidge — A183

Designs: 90v, Diver, corals. 100v, Divers, fish. 130v, Shipwreck, fish. 150v, Ship sinking, sailors leaving ship (85x30mm).

**2006, Nov. 29** **Litho.** ***Perf. 13¼***
**909-912** A183 Set of 4 9.00 9.00

**Shipwreck Type of 2006**
Souvenir Sheet

No. 913: a, 90v, Like #909. b, 100v, Like #910. c, 130v, Like #911. d, 150v, Like #912.

**2006, Nov. 29** **Litho.** ***Perf. 13¼***
**Stamps Without "International Post"**
**913** A183 Sheet of 4, #a-d 9.00 9.00

### SEMI POSTAL STAMPS

Nos. 324 and 414-418 Surcharged "Hurricane Relief Fund"

**Wmk. 373 (No. B1), 384**
***Perf. 14x13½, 14x14½***

**1987, May 12** **Litho.**

| | | | | |
|---|---|---|---|---|
| **B1** | A60 | 20v +10v on 2v | 1.40 | 1.40 |
| **B2** | CD337 | 20v +10v | 1.40 | 1.40 |
| **B3** | CD337 | 35v +15v | 2.40 | 2.40 |
| **B4** | CD337 | 45v +20v | 2.75 | 2.75 |
| **B5** | CD337 | 55v +25v | 5.25 | 5.25 |
| **B6** | CD337 | 100v +50v | 5.75 | 5.75 |
| | | *Nos. B1-B6 (6)* | 18.95 | 18.95 |

Old value of #B1 obliterated by 2 horizontal bars. Surcharge indicated by text "Surcharge +10."

# VATICAN CITY

'va-ti-kən 'si-tē

LOCATION — Western Italy, directly outside the western boundary of Rome

GOVT. — Independent state subject to certain political restrictions under a treaty with Italy

AREA — 108.7 acres

POP. — 870 (1999 est.)

100 Centesimi = 1 Lira

100 Cents = 1 Euro (2002)

**Catalogue values for unused stamps in this country are for Never Hinged items, beginning with Scott 68 in the regular postage section, Scott C1 in the airpost section, Scott E3 in the special delivery section, and Scott J7 in the postage due section.**

### Watermarks

Wmk. 235 — Crossed Keys

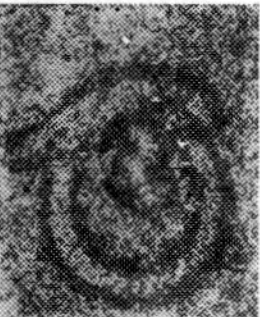

Wmk. 277 — Winged Wheel

Papal Arms — A1

Pope Pius XI — A2

**Unwmk.**

**1929, Aug. 1 Engr. *Perf. 14***

**Surface-Colored Paper**

| No. | Type | Denom. | Color | Unused | Used |
|---|---|---|---|---|---|
| **1** | A1 | 5c | dk brn & pink | .20 | .25 |
| **2** | A1 | 10c | dk grn & lt grn | .25 | .30 |
| **3** | A1 | 20c | violet & lilac | .55 | .40 |
| **4** | A1 | 25c | dk bl & lt bl | .70 | .45 |
| **5** | A1 | 30c | indigo & yellow | .80 | .60 |
| **6** | A1 | 50c | ind & sal buff | 1.25 | .65 |
| **7** | A1 | 75c | brn car & gray | 1.60 | 1.00 |
| | | | **Photo.** | | |
| | | | **White Paper** | | |
| **8** | A2 | 80c | carmine rose | 1.25 | .40 |
| **9** | A2 | 1.25 l | dark blue | 2.00 | .75 |
| **10** | A2 | 2 l | olive brown | 3.75 | 1.40 |
| **11** | A2 | 2.50 l | red orange | 3.25 | 2.50 |
| **12** | A2 | 5 l | dk green | 3.75 | *8.50* |
| **13** | A2 | 10 l | olive blk | 8.00 | *11.50* |
| | | | *Nos. 1-13,E1-E2 (15)* | 53.35 | *52.20* |
| | | | Set, never hinged | 150.00 | |

The stamps of Type A1 have, in this and subsequent issues, the words "POSTE VATICANE" in rows of colorless letters in the background.

For surcharges and overprints see Nos. 14, 35-40, 61-67, J1-J6, Q1-Q13.

No. 5 Surcharged in Red

**1931, Oct. 1**

| No. | Type | Description | Unused | Used |
|---|---|---|---|---|
| **14** | A1 | 25c on 30c ind & yel | 2.10 | 1.40 |
| | | Never hinged | 6.75 | |

Arms of Pope Pius XI — A5

Vatican Palace and Obelisk — A6

Vatican Gardens — A7

Pope Pius XI A8

St. Peter's Basilica A9

**1933, May 31 Engr. Wmk. 235**

| No. | Type | Denom. | Color | Unused | Used |
|---|---|---|---|---|---|
| **19** | A5 | 5c | copper red | .20 | .20 |
| *a.* | | | Imperf., pair | 250.00 | *275.00* |
| **20** | A6 | 10c | dk brn & blk | .20 | .20 |
| **21** | A6 | 12½c | dp grn & blk | .20 | .20 |
| **22** | A6 | 20c | orange & blk | .20 | .20 |
| *a.* | | | Vertical pair imperf. between and at bottom | 250.00 | 250.00 |
| **23** | A6 | 25c | dk olive & blk | .20 | .20 |
| *a.* | | | Imperf., pair | 150.00 | 175.00 |
| **24** | A7 | 30c | blk & dk brn | .20 | .20 |
| **25** | A7 | 50c | viot & dk brn | .20 | .20 |
| **26** | A7 | 75c | brn red & dk brn | .20 | .20 |
| **27** | A7 | 80c | rose & dk brn | .20 | .20 |
| **28** | A8 | 1 l | violet & blk | 3.25 | 2.75 |
| **29** | A8 | 1.25 l | dk bl & blk | 11.00 | 5.00 |
| **30** | A8 | 2 l | dk brn & blk | 27.50 | 20.00 |
| **31** | A8 | 2.75 l | dk vio & blk | 32.50 | *40.00* |
| **32** | A9 | 5 l | blk brn & grn | .20 | .25 |
| **33** | A9 | 10 l | dk blue & dk grn | .20 | .30 |
| **34** | A9 | 20 l | blk & dp grn | .25 | .35 |
| | | | *Nos. 19-34,E3-E4 (18)* | 77.40 | 71.35 |
| | | | Set, never hinged | 210.00 | |

Nos. 8-13 Surcharged in Black

**1934, June 16 Unwmk.**

| No. | Type | Description | Unused | Used |
|---|---|---|---|---|
| **35** | A2 | 40c on 80c | 3.25 | 1.90 |
| **36** | A2 | 1.30 l on 1.25 l | 57.50 | 37.50 |
| *a.* | | Small figures "30" in "1.30" | *10,000.* | *7,250.* |
| | | Never hinged | 12,500. | |
| **37** | A2 | 2.05 l on 2 l | 125.00 | 14.00 |
| *a.* | | No comma btwn. 2 & 0 | 275.00 | 20.00 |
| | | Never hinged | 850.00 | |
| **38** | A2 | 2.55 l on 2.50 l | 82.50 | 150.00 |
| *a.* | | No comma btwn. 2 & 5 | 150.00 | 275.00 |
| | | Never hinged | 475.00 | |
| **39** | A2 | 3.05 l on 5 l | 275.00 | 275.00 |
| **40** | A2 | 3.70 l on 10 l | 250.00 | *400.00* |
| *a.* | | No comma btwn. 3 & 7 | — | — |
| | | *Nos. 35-40 (6)* | 793.25 | 878.40 |
| | | Set, never hinged | 2,300. | |

A second printing of Nos. 36-40 was made in 1937. The 2.55 l and 3.05 l of the first printing and 1.30 l of the second printing sell for more.

The status of No. 40a has been questioned. The editors would like to examine an authenticated copy of this variety.

Forged surcharges of Nos. 35-40 are plentiful.

Tribonian Presenting Pandects to Justinian I A10

Pope Gregory IX Promulgating Decretals A11

**1935, Feb. 1 Photo.**

| No. | Type | Denom. | Color | Unused | Used |
|---|---|---|---|---|---|
| **41** | A10 | 5c | red orange | 1.25 | .75 |
| **42** | A10 | 10c | purple | 1.25 | .75 |
| **43** | A10 | 25c | green | 12.50 | 12.50 |
| **44** | A11 | 75c | rose red | 45.00 | 27.50 |
| **45** | A11 | 80c | dark brown | 35.00 | 21.00 |
| **46** | A11 | 1.25 l | dark blue | 45.00 | 20.00 |
| | | | *Nos. 41-46 (6)* | 140.00 | 82.50 |
| | | | Set, never hinged | 500.00 | |

Intl. Juridical Congress, Rome, 1934.

Doves and Bell — A12

Allegory of Church and Bible — A13

St. John Bosco — A14

St. Francis de Sales — A15

**1936, June 22**

| No. | Type | Denom. | Color | Unused | Used |
|---|---|---|---|---|---|
| **47** | A12 | 5c | blue green | .75 | 1.00 |
| **48** | A13 | 10c | black | .75 | 1.00 |
| **49** | A14 | 25c | yellow green | 40.00 | 8.50 |
| **50** | A12 | 50c | rose violet | .75 | 1.00 |
| **51** | A13 | 75c | rose red | 40.00 | 40.00 |
| **52** | A14 | 80c | orange brn | 1.50 | 2.00 |
| **53** | A15 | 1.25 l | dark blue | 2.00 | 2.00 |
| **54** | A15 | 5 l | dark brown | 2.00 | *6.25* |
| | | | *Nos. 47-54 (8)* | 87.75 | 61.75 |
| | | | Set, never hinged | 300.00 | |

Catholic Press Conference, 1936.

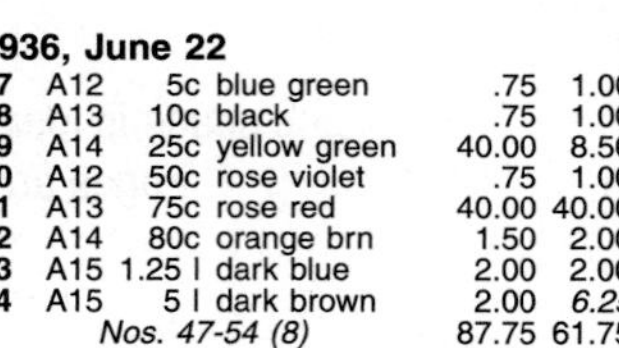

Crypt of St. Cecilia in Catacombs of St. Calixtus A16

Basilica of Sts. Nereus and Achilleus in Catacombs of St. Domitilla A17

**1938, Oct. 12 *Perf. 14***

| No. | Type | Denom. | Color | Unused | Used |
|---|---|---|---|---|---|
| **55** | A16 | 5c | bister brown | .20 | .20 |
| **56** | A16 | 10c | deep orange | .20 | .20 |
| **57** | A16 | 25c | deep green | .25 | .25 |
| **58** | A17 | 75c | deep rose | 5.50 | 5.50 |
| **59** | A17 | 80c | violet | 17.00 | 17.00 |
| **60** | A17 | 1.25 l | blue | 22.50 | 22.50 |
| | | | *Nos. 55-60 (6)* | 45.65 | 45.65 |
| | | | Set, never hinged | 125.00 | |

Intl. Christian Archaeological Congress, Rome, 1938.

### Interregnum Issue

Nos. 1-7 Overprinted in Black

**1939, Feb. 20 *Perf. 14***

| No. | Type | Denom. | Color | Unused | Used |
|---|---|---|---|---|---|
| **61** | A1 | 5c | dk brn & pink | 27.50 | 6.00 |
| **62** | A1 | 10c | dk grn & lt grn | .30 | .20 |
| **63** | A1 | 20c | violet & lilac | .30 | .20 |
| **64** | A1 | 25c | dk bl & lt bl | 3.00 | *3.50* |
| **65** | A1 | 30c | indigo & yellow | .60 | .20 |
| *a.* | | | Pair, one without ovpt. | *1,300.* | |
| **66** | A1 | 50c | indigo & sal buff | .60 | .20 |
| **67** | A1 | 75c | brn car & gray | .60 | .20 |
| | | | *Nos. 61-67 (7)* | 32.90 | 10.50 |
| | | | Set, never hinged | 92.50 | |

**Catalogue values for unused stamps in this section, from this point to the end of the section, are for Never Hinged items.**

Coronation of Pope Pius XII — A18

**1939, June 2 Photo.**

| No. | Type | Denom. | Color | Unused | Used |
|---|---|---|---|---|---|
| **68** | A18 | 25c | green | 2.25 | .30 |
| **69** | A18 | 75c | rose red | .50 | .45 |
| **70** | A18 | 80c | violet | 6.25 | 3.00 |
| **71** | A18 | 1.25 l | deep blue | .50 | .45 |
| | | | *Nos. 68-71 (4)* | 9.50 | 4.20 |

Coronation of Pope Pius XII, Mar. 12, 1939.

Arms of Pope Pius XII — A19

Pope Pius XII

A20 A21

**Wmk. 235**

**1940, Mar. 12 Engr. *Perf. 14***

| No. | Type | Denom. | Color | Unused | Used |
|---|---|---|---|---|---|
| **72** | A19 | 5c | dark carmine | .20 | .20 |
| **73** | A20 | 1 l | purple & blk | .20 | .20 |
| **74** | A21 | 1.25 l | slate bl & blk | .20 | .20 |
| *a.* | | | Imperf., pair | *450.00* | *500.00* |
| **75** | A20 | 2 l | dk brn & blk | 1.40 | .85 |
| **76** | A21 | 2.75 l | dk rose vio & blk | 2.00 | 1.75 |
| | | | *Nos. 72-76 (5)* | 4.00 | 3.20 |

See #91-98. For surcharges see #102-109.

A22

A23

Picture of Jesus inscribed "I have Compassion on the Multitude."

**1942, Sept. 1 Photo. Unwmk.**

**77** A22 25c dk blue green .20 .20
**78** A22 80c chestnut brown .20 .20
**79** A22 1.25 l deep blue .20 .20
*Nos. 77-79 (3)* .60 .60

See Nos. 84-86, 99-101.

**1942, Jan. 16**

Consecration of Archbishop Pacelli by Pope Benedict XV.

**80** A23 25c myr grn & gray grn .20 .20
**81** A23 80c dk brn & yel grn .20 .20
**82** A23 1.25 l sapphire & vio bl .20 .20
*a.* Name and value panel omitted
**83** A23 5 l vio blk & gray blk .20 .25
*Nos. 80-83 (4)* .80 .85

25th anniv. of the consecration of Msgr. Eugenio Pacelli (later Pope Pius XII) as Archbishop of Sardes.

Type of 1942
Inscribed MCMXLIII

**1944, Jan. 31**

**84** A22 25c dk blue green .20 .20
**85** A22 80c chestnut brown .20 .20
**86** A22 1.25 l deep blue .20 .20
*Nos. 84-86 (3)* .60 .60

Raphael Sanzio — A24

Designs: 80c, Antonio da Sangallo. 1.25 l, Carlo Maratti. 10 l, Antonio Canova.

**1944, Nov. 21 Wmk. 235 Photo.**

**87** A24 25c olive & green .30 .20
**88** A24 80c cl & rose vio .60 .25
*a.* Dbl. impression of center *750.00*
**89** A24 1.25 l bl vio & dp bl .60 .25
*a.* Imperf., pair *650.00 900.*
**90** A24 10 l bister & ol brn 1.25 .75
*Nos. 87-90 (4)* 2.75 1.45

400th anniv. of the Pontifical Academy of the Virtuosi of the Pantheon.

Types of 1940

**1945, Mar. 5 Engr. Unwmk.**

**91** A19 5c gray .20 .20
*a.* Imperf., pair 200.00
**92** A19 30c brown .20 .20
*a.* Imperf., pair 120.00
**93** A19 50c dark green .20 .20
**94** A21 1 l brown & blk .20 .20
**95** A21 1.50 l rose car & blk .20 .20
*a.* Imperf., pair 325.00
**96** A21 2.50 l dp ultra & blk .20 .20
**97** A20 5 l rose vio & blk .20 *.25*
**98** A20 20 l gray grn & blk .25 *.30*
*Nos. 91-98,E5-E6 (10)* 2.25 2.35

Nos. 91-96 exist in pairs imperf. between, some vertical, some horizontal. Value, each $150.

Pair imperf. vertically exist of 30c and 50c (value $50), and of 5 lire (value $90).

Type of 1942
Inscribed MCMXLIV
**Wmk. 277**

**1945, Sept. 12 Photo. *Perf. 14***

**99** A22 1 l dk blue green .20 .20
**100** A22 3 l dk carmine .20 .20
*a.* Jesus image omitted 100.00 100.00
**101** A22 5 l deep ultra .20 .20
*Nos. 99-101 (3)* .60 .60

Nos. 99-101 exist in pairs imperf. between, both horizontal and vertical. Value, each $140.

Pairs imperf. horizontally exist of 3 lire (value $50) and 5 lire (value $60).

Nos. 91 to 98 Surcharged with New Values and Bars in Black or Blue

Two types of 25c on 30c:
I — Surcharge 16mm wide.
II — Surcharge 19mm wide.

Two types of 1 l on 50c:
I — Surcharge bars 5mm wide.
II — Bars 4mm wide.

**1946, Jan. 9 Unwmk. *Perf. 14***

**102** A19 20c on 5c .20 .20
**103** A19 25c on 30c (I) .20 .20
*a.* Type II .40 .20
*b.* Inverted surcharge (II) 350.00 350.00
**104** A19 1 l on 50c (I) .20 .20
*a.* Type II 5.00 3.50
**105** A21 1.50 l on 1 l (Bl) .20 .20
*a.* Double surcharge 175.00
**106** A21 3 l on 1.50 l .20 .20
**107** A21 5 l on 2.50 l .40 .20
**108** A20 10 l on 5 l 1.10 .55
**109** A20 30 l on 20 l 3.25 1.50
*Nos. 102-109,E7-E8 (10)* 14.25 6.75

Nos. 102, 105-109 exist in horizontal pairs, imperf. between. Value, each $150.

Vertical pairs imperf. between exist of Nos. 102, 106-107 (value, each $150) and of No. 104a (value $250).

Nos. 102, 104-108 exist in pairs imperf. vertically or horizontally, or both. Value $40 to $60.

Nos. 102-108 exist in pairs, one without surcharge. Value, Nos. 102-105, each $150; Nos. 106-108, each $200.

St. Vigilio Cathedral, Trent — A28

St. Angela Merici — A29

Designs: 50c, St. Anthony Zaccaria. 75c, St. Ignatius of Loyola. 1 l, St. Cajetan Thiene. 1.50 l, St. John Fisher. 2 l, Christoforo Cardinal Madruzzi. 2.50 l, Reginald Cardinal Pole. 3 l, Marello Cardinal Cervini. 4 l, Giovanni Cardinal del Monte. 5 l, Emperor Charles V. 1 l, Pope Paul III.

***Perf. 14, 14x13½***

**1946, Feb. 21 Photo. Unwmk.**

**Centers in Dark Brown**

**110** A28 5c olive bister .20 .20
**111** A29 25c purple .20 .20
**112** A29 50c brown orange .20 .20
**113** A29 75c black .20 .20
**114** A29 1 l dk violet .20 .20
**115** A29 1.50 l red orange .20 .20
**116** A29 2 l yellow green .20 .20
**117** A29 2.50 l deep blue .20 .20
**118** A29 3 l brt carmine .20 .20
**119** A29 4 l ocher .20 .20
**120** A29 5 l brt ultra .20 .20
**121** A29 10 l dp rose car .20 .20
*Nos. 110-121,E9-E10 (14)* 2.80 2.80

Council of Trent (1545-63), 400th anniv.

Vertical pairs imperf. between exist of Nos. 110-111, 114, 116-117 (value, each $150); Nos. 113, 119 (value, each $100); Nos. 115, 118 (value, each $75).

Horizontal pairs imperf. between exist of #121 (value $200); #113, 117 (value $150).

Basilica of St. Agnes — A40

Basilica of the Holy Cross in Jerusalem A41

Pope Pius XII A42

Basilicas: 3 l, St. Clement, 5 l, St. Prassede. 8 l, St. Mary in Cosmedin. 16 l, St. Sebastian. 25 l, St. Lawrence. 35 l, St. Paul. 40 l, St. Mary Major.

***Perf. 14, 14x13½***

**1949, Mar. 7 Photo. Wmk. 235**

**122** A40 1 l dark brown .20 .20
**123** A40 3 l violet .20 .20
**124** A40 5 l deep orange .20 .20
*a.* Perf. 14x13½ 15.00 4.50
**125** A40 8 l dp blue grn .20 .20

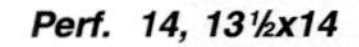
***Perf. 14, 13½x14***

**126** A41 13 l dull green 6.00 5.00
**127** A41 16 l dk olive brn .20 .20
*a.* Perf. 14 .75 .25
**128** A41 25 l car rose 4.75 .65
**129** A41 35 l red violet 26.00 12.00
*a.* Perf. 13½x14 55.00 8.25
**130** A41 40 l blue .20 .20
*a.* Perf. 13½x14 .25 .25

**Engr.**
***Perf. 14***

**131** A42 100 l sepia 3.00 3.00
*Nos. 122-131,E11-E12 (12)* 88.95 45.10

All values come in two perfs except the 100 l.

Jesus Giving St. Peter the Keys to Heaven — A43

Cathedrals of St. Peter, St. Paul, St. John Lateran and St. Mary Major — A44

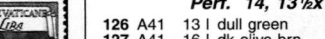

Pope Boniface VIII Proclaiming Holy Year in 1300 — A45

Pope Pius XII in Ceremony of Opening the Holy Door — A46

**Wmk. 277**

**1949, Dec 21 Photo. *Perf. 14***

**132** A43 5 l red brn & brn .20 .20
**133** A44 6 l ind & yel brn .20 .20
**134** A45 8 l ultra & dk grn .75 .35
**135** A46 10 l green & slate .25 .25
**136** A43 20 l dk grn & red brn 1.25 .25
**137** A44 25 l sepia & dp blue .60 .25
**138** A45 30 l grnsh blk & rose lil 1.50 1.00
**139** A46 60 l blk brn & brn rose 1.00 1.00
*Nos. 132-139 (8)* 5.75 3.50

Holy Year, 1950.

Palatine Guard and Statue of St. Peter — A47

**1950, Sept. 12**

**140** A47 25 l sepia 8.25 2.50
**141** A47 35 l dark green 3.25 2.50
**142** A47 55 l red brown 1.90 2.50
*Nos. 140-142 (3)* 13.40 7.50

Centenary of the Palatine Guard.

Pope Pius XII Making Proclamation A48

Crowd at the Basilica of St. Peter — A49

**1951, May 8 Unwmk.**

**143** A48 25 l chocolate 8.50 .75
**144** A49 55 l bright blue 3.50 *10.50*

Proclamation of the Roman Catholic dogma of the Assumption of the Virgin Mary, Nov. 1, 1950.

A50

Pope Pius X — A51

***Perf. 14x13½***

**1951, June 3 Photo. Wmk. 235**

**Background of Medallion in Gold**

**145** A50 6 l purple .20 .20
**146** A50 10 l Prus green .20 .20
**147** A51 60 l blue 5.50 5.50
**148** A51 115 l brown 15.00 15.00
*Nos. 145-148 (4)* 20.90 20.90

Council of Chalcedon A52

Pope Leo I Remonstrating with Attila the Hun — A53

**1951, Oct. 31 Engr. *Perf. 14x13½***

**149** A52 5 l dk gray green .50 .25
*a.* Pair, imperf. horiz. *350.00*
**150** A53 25 l red brown 3.00 1.75
*a.* Horiz. pair, imperf. btwn. *700.00* *700.00*
**151** A52 35 l carmine rose 8.00 3.00
**152** A53 60 l deep blue 22.50 10.00
**153** A52 100 l dark brown 30.00 25.00
*Nos. 149-153 (5)* 64.00 40.00

Council of Chalcedon, 1500th anniv.

No. 126 Surcharged with New Value and Bars in Carmine

**1952, Mar. 15 *Perf. 14***

**154** A41 12 l on 13 l dull grn 1.75 1.00
*a.* Perf. 13½x14 1.75 1.00
*b.* Pair, one without surcharge 300.00 300.00

Roman States Stamp and Stagecoach — A54

**1952, June 9 Engr. *Perf. 13***

**155** A54 50 l sep & dp bl, *cr* 5.00 3.25
*a.* Souvenir sheet 140.00 100.00

1st stamp of the Papal States, cent.
#155a contains 4 stamps similar to #155, with papal insignia and inscription in purple. Singles from the souvenir sheet differ slightly from #155. The colors are closer to black and blue, and the cream tone of the paper is visible on the back.

St. Maria Goretti — A55

St. Peter — A56

***Perf. 13½x14***

**1953, Feb. 12 Photo. Wmk. 235**

**156** A55 15 l dp brown & vio 4.25 2.00
**157** A55 35 l dp rose & brn 3.25 2.00

Martyrdom of St. Maria Goretti, 50th anniv.

***Perf. 13½x13, 14***

**1953, Apr. 23 Engr.**

Designs: 5 l, Pius XII and Roman sepulcher. 10 l, St. Peter and Tomb of the Apostle. 12 l, Sylvester I and Constantine Basilica. 20 l, Julius II and Bramante's plans. 25 l, Paul III and the Apse. 35 l, Sixtus V and dome. 45 l, Paul V and facade. 60 l, Urban VIII and the canopy. 65 l, Alexander VII and colonnade. 100 l, Pius VI and the sacristy.

**158** A56 3 l dk red brn & blk .20 .20
**159** A56 5 l slate & blk .20 .20
**160** A56 10 l dk green & blk .20 .20
**161** A56 12 l chestnut & blk .20 .20
**162** A56 20 l violet & blk .20 .20
**163** A56 25 l dk brown & blk .20 .20
**164** A56 35 l dk carmine & blk .20 .20
**165** A56 45 l olive brn & blk .20 .20
**166** A56 60 l dk blue & blk .20 .20
**167** A56 65 l car rose & blk .20 .20
**168** A56 100 l rose vio & blk .20 .20
*Nos. 158-168,E13-E14 (13)* 2.75 2.65

St. Clare of Assisi — A57

Peter Lombard Medal — A59

Virgin Mary and St. Bernard A58

**Unwmk.**

**1953, Aug. 12 Photo. *Perf. 13***

**169** A57 25 l aqua, yel brn & vio brn 2.00 1.00
**170** A57 35 l brn red, yel brn & vio brn 14.00 9.00

Death of St. Clare of Assisi, 700th anniv.

**1953, Nov. 10**

**171** A58 20 l ol grn & dk vio brn .75 .50
**172** A58 60 l brt bl & ol grn 7.25 4.00

Death of St. Bernard of Clairvaux, 800th anniv.

**1953, Dec. 29**

**173** A59 100 l lil rose, bl, dk grn & yel 32.50 20.00

Peter Lombard, Bishop of Paris 1159.

Pope Pius XI and Vatican City — A60

**1954, Feb. 12 Wmk. 235**

**174** A60 25 l bl, red brn & cr 1.25 1.00
**175** A60 60 l yel brn & dp bl 3.00 2.50

Signing of the Lateran Pacts, 25th anniv.

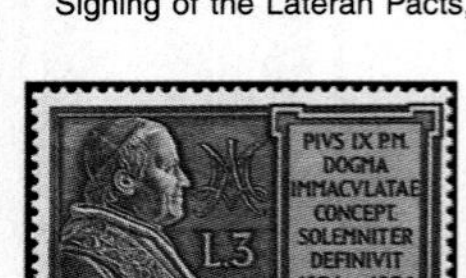

Pope Pius IX A61

Portraits: (At left) - 6 l, 20 l, Pope Pius IX. (At right) — 4 l, 12 l, 35 l, Pope Pius XII.

**1954, May 26 Engr. *Perf. 13***

**176** A61 3 l violet .20 .20
**177** A61 4 l carmine .20 .20
**178** A61 6 l plum .20 .20
**179** A61 12 l blue green 1.00 .20
**180** A61 20 l red brown .90 .85
**181** A61 35 l ultra 2.25 2.25
*Nos. 176-181 (6)* 4.75 3.90

Marian Year; centenary of the dogma of the Immaculate Conception.

St. Pius X — A62

**1954, May 29 Photo.**

**Colors (except background): Yellow and Plum**

**182** A62 10 l dark brown .25 .25
**183** A62 25 l violet 2.50 1.25
**184** A62 35 l dk slate gray 4.25 *2.50*
*Nos. 182-184 (3)* 7.00 *4.00*

Canonization of Pope Pius X, May 20, 1954.
#182-184 exist imperf. Value, each pair $800.

Basilica of St. Francis of Assisi A63

**1954, Oct. 1 Photo. *Perf. 14***

**185** A63 20 l dk vio gray & cr 2.00 1.75
**186** A63 35 l dk brown & cream 1.50 1.40

Consecration of the Basilica of St. Francis of Assisi, 200th anniv.

St. Augustine A64

**1954, Nov. 13**

**187** A64 35 l blue green 1.00 .90
**188** A64 50 l redsh brown 1.90 1.75

1600th birth anniv. of St. Augustine.

Madonna of the Gate of Dawn, Vilnius — A65

**1954, Dec. 7**

189 A65 20 l pink & multi 1.00 .75
190 A65 35 l blue & multi 7.50 3.75
191 A65 60 l multicolored 12.50 5.75
*Nos. 189-191 (3)* 21.00 10.25

Issued to mark the end of the Marian Year.

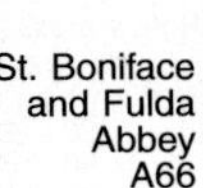

St. Boniface and Fulda Abbey A66

**1955, Apr. 28 Engr. *Perf. 13***

192 A66 10 l grnsh gray .20 .20
193 A66 35 l violet .60 .60
*a.* Imperf., pair 100.00
194 A66 60 l brt blue green .70 .70
*Nos. 192-194 (3)* 1.50 1.50

1200th death anniv. of St. Boniface.

Pope Sixtus II and St. Lawrence A67

Pope Nicholas V A68

**Wmk. 235**

**1955, June 27 Photo. *Perf. 14***

195 A67 50 l carmine 3.75 2.00
196 A67 100 l deep blue 2.50 2.00

Fra Angelico (1387-1455), painter. Design is from a Fra Angelico fresco.

**1955, Nov. 28**

197 A68 20 l grnsh bl & ol brn .20 .20
198 A68 35 l rose car & ol brn .35 .25
199 A68 60 l yel grn & ol brn .70 .35
*Nos. 197-199 (3)* 1.25 .80

Death of Pope Nicholas V, 500th anniv.

St. Bartholomew and Church of Grottaferrata A69

Capt. Gaspar Roust A70

**1955, Dec. 29**

200 A69 10 l brown & gray .20 .20
201 A69 25 l car rose & gray .80 .30
202 A69 100 l dk green & gray 2.00 1.50
*Nos. 200-202 (3)* 3.00 2.00

900th death anniv. of St. Bartholomew, abbot of Grottaferrata.

**1956, Apr. 27 Engr. *Perf. 13***

6 l, 50 l, Guardsman. 10 l, 60 l, Two drummers.

203 A70 4 l dk carmine rose .20 .20
204 A70 6 l deep orange .20 .20
205 A70 10 l deep ultra .20 .20
206 A70 35 l brown .55 .40
207 A70 50 l violet .75 .60
208 A70 60 l blue green .85 .65
*Nos. 203-208 (6)* 2.75 2.25

450th anniv. of the Swiss Papal Guard.

St. Rita of Cascia — A71

Pope Paul III Confirming Society of Jesus — A72

**1956, May 19 Photo. *Perf. 14***

209 A71 10 l gray green .20 .20
210 A71 25 l olive brown .60 .60
211 A71 35 l ultra .45 .45
*Nos. 209-211 (3)* 1.25 1.25

500th death anniv. of St. Rita of Cascia.

**1956, July 31 Engr. *Perf. 13***

212 A72 35 l dk red brown .55 .55
213 A72 60 l blue gray 1.10 1.00

400th death anniv. of St. Ignatius of Loyola, founder of the Society of Jesus.

St. John of Capistrano A73

**1956, Oct. 30 *Perf. 14***

214 A73 25 l slate blk & grn 2.25 1.25
215 A73 35 l dk brn car & brn 1.00 .75

5th cent. of the death of St. John of Capistrano, leader in the war against the Turks.

Black Madonna of Czestochowa — A74

St. Domenico Savio — A75

**1956, Dec. 20**

216 A74 35 l dk blue & blk .25 .25
217 A74 60 l green & ultra .60 .55
218 A74 100 l brn & dk car rose 1.00 .85
*Nos. 216-218 (3)* 1.85 1.65

300th anniv. of the proclamation of the Madonna of Czestochowa as "Queen of Poland."

**1957, Mar. 21 Wmk. 235 *Perf. 13½***

6 l, 60 l, Sts. Domenico Savio and John Bosco.

219 A75 4 l red brown .20 .20
220 A75 6 l brt carmine .20 .20
221 A75 25 l green .20 .20
222 A75 60 l ultra 1.40 1.10
*Nos. 219-222 (4)* 2.00 1.70

Death cent. of St. Domenico Savio.

Cardinal Capranica and College A76

Design: 10 l, 100 l, Pope Pius XII.

**1957, June 27 Engr. *Perf. 13***

223 A76 5 l dk carmine rose .20 .20
224 A76 10 l pale brown .20 .20
225 A76 35 l grnsh black .20 .20
226 A76 100 l ultra .50 .50
*Nos. 223-226 (4)* 1.10 1.10

500th anniv. of Capranica College, oldest seminary in the world.

Pontifical Academy of Science A77

**1957, Oct. 9 Photo. *Perf. 14***

227 A77 35 l dk blue & green .55 .55
228 A77 60 l brown & ultra .80 .55

Pontifical Academy of Science, 20th anniv.

Mariazell A78

High Altar — A79

**1957, Nov. 14 Engr. *Perf. 13½***

229 A78 5 l green .20 .20
230 A79 15 l slate .20 .20
231 A78 60 l ultra .70 .25
232 A79 100 l violet .90 .85
*Nos. 229-232 (4)* 2.00 1.50

Mariazell shrine, Austria, 800th anniv.

Apparition of the Virgin Mary — A80

Designs: 10 l, 35 l, Sick man and basilica. 15 l, 100 l, St. Bernadette.

***Perf. 13x14***

**1958, Feb. 21 Wmk. 235**

233 A80 5 l dark blue .20 .20
234 A80 10 l blue green .20 .20
235 A80 15 l reddish brown .20 .20
236 A80 25 l rose carmine .20 .20
237 A80 35 l gray brown .20 .20
238 A80 100 l violet .20 .20
*Nos. 233-238 (6)* 1.20 1.20

Centenary of apparition of the Virgin Mary at Lourdes and the establishment of the shrine.

Pope Pius XII — A81

Statue of Pope Clement XIII by Canova — A82

60 l, 100 l, Vatican pavilion at Brussels fair.

**1958, June 19 Engr. *Perf. 13***

239 A81 35 l claret .30 .25

***Perf. 13x14***

240 A81 60 l fawn .55 .55
241 A81 100 l violet 1.75 1.25
242 A81 300 l ultra 1.40 1.10
*a.* Souvenir sheet of 4, #239-242 20.00 15.00
*Nos. 239-242 (4)* 4.00 3.15

Universal and Intl. Exposition, Brussels.

**1958, July 2 *Perf. 14***

Statues: 10 l, Clement XIV. 35 l, Pius VI. 100 l, Pius VII.

243 A82 5 l brown .20 .20
244 A82 10 l carmine rose .20 .20
245 A82 35 l blue gray .25 .25
246 A82 100 l dark blue .85 .85
*Nos. 243-246 (4)* 1.50 1.50

Antonio Canova (1757-1822), sculptor.

**Interregnum Issue**

St. Peter's Keys and Papal Chamberlain's Insignia — A83

**Wmk. 235**

**1958, Oct. 21 Photo. *Perf. 14***

247 A83 15 l brn blk, *yel* 1.40 1.00
248 A83 25 l brown black .20 .20
249 A83 60 l brn blk, *pale vio* .20 .20
*Nos. 247-249 (3)* 1.80 1.40

Pope John XXIII — A84

Pope Pius XI — A85

Design: 35 l, 100 l, Coat of Arms.

**1959, Apr. 2 Photo. *Perf. 14***

250 A84 25 l car rose, bl & buff .20 .20
251 A84 35 l multicolored .20 .20
252 A84 60 l rose car, bl & ocher .20 .20
253 A84 100 l multicolored .20 .20
*Nos. 250-253 (4)* .80 .80

Coronation of Pope John XXIII, 11/4/58.

**1959, May 25 Wmk. 235 *Perf. 14***

254 A85 30 l brown .20 .20
255 A85 100 l violet blue .20 .20

Lateran Pacts, 30th anniversary.

St. Lawrence A86

Radio Tower and Archangel Gabriel A87

Portraits of Saints: 25 l, Pope Sixtus II. 50 l, Agapitus. 60 l, Filicissimus. 100 l, Cyprianus. 300 l, Fructuosus.

**1959, May 25**

| | | | | | |
|---|---|---|---|---|---|
| **256** | A86 | 15 l | red, brn & yel | .25 | .20 |
| **257** | A86 | 25 l | lilac, brn & yel | .25 | .20 |
| **258** | A86 | 50 l | Prus bl, blk & yel | .25 | .20 |
| **259** | A86 | 60 l | ol grn, brn & bis | .25 | .20 |
| **260** | A86 | 100 l | maroon, brn & yel | .25 | .20 |
| **261** | A86 | 300 l | bis brn & dk brn | .50 | .35 |
| | | | *Nos. 256-261 (6)* | 1.75 | 1.35 |

Martyrs of Emperor Valerian's persecutions.

**1959, Oct. 27 Photo. *Perf. 14***

| | | | | | |
|---|---|---|---|---|---|
| **262** | A87 | 25 l | rose, org yel & dk brn | .20 | .20 |
| **263** | A87 | 60 l | multicolored | .20 | .20 |

2nd anniv. of the papal radio station, St. Maria di Galeria.

St. Casimir, Palace and Cathedral, Vilnius A88

**1959, Dec. 14 Engr. Wmk. 235**

| | | | | | |
|---|---|---|---|---|---|
| **264** | A88 | 50 l | brown | .20 | .20 |
| **265** | A88 | 100 l | dull green | .25 | .20 |

500th anniv. (in 1958) of the birth of St. Casimir, patron saint of Lithuania.

Nativity by Raphael — A89

**1959, Dec. 14 Engr. *Perf. 13½***

| | | | | | |
|---|---|---|---|---|---|
| **266** | A89 | 15 l | dark gray | .20 | .20 |
| **267** | A89 | 25 l | magenta | .20 | .20 |
| **268** | A89 | 60 l | bright ultra | .20 | .20 |
| | | | *Nos. 266-268 (3)* | .60 | .60 |

St. Antoninus — A90

Transept of Lateran Basilica — A91

25 l, 110 l, St. Antoninus preaching.

***Perf. 13x14***

**1960, Feb. 29 Wmk. 235**

| | | | | | |
|---|---|---|---|---|---|
| **269** | A90 | 15 l | ultra | .20 | .20 |
| **270** | A90 | 25 l | turquoise | .20 | .20 |
| **271** | A90 | 60 l | brown | .30 | .25 |
| **272** | A90 | 110 l | rose claret | .60 | .35 |
| | | | *Nos. 269-272 (4)* | 1.30 | 1.00 |

5th cent. of death of St. Antoninus, bishop of Florence.

**1960, Feb. 29 Photo. *Perf. 14***

| | | | | | |
|---|---|---|---|---|---|
| **273** | A91 | 15 l | brown | .20 | .20 |
| **274** | A91 | 60 l | black | .40 | .20 |

Roman Diocesan Synod, February, 1960.

Flight into Egypt by Fra Angelico — A92

Cardinal Sarto's Departure from Venice — A93

Designs: 10 l, 100 l, St. Peter Giving Alms to the Poor, by Masaccio. 25 l, 300 l, Madonna of Mercy, by Piero della Francesca.

**1960, Apr. 7 Wmk. 235 *Perf. 14***

| | | | | | |
|---|---|---|---|---|---|
| **275** | A92 | 5 l | green | .20 | .20 |
| **276** | A92 | 10 l | gray brown | .20 | .20 |
| **277** | A92 | 25 l | deep carmine | .20 | .20 |
| **278** | A92 | 60 l | lilac | .20 | .20 |
| **279** | A92 | 100 l | ultra | 1.90 | 1.50 |
| **280** | A92 | 300 l | Prus green | .65 | .40 |
| | | | *Nos. 275-280 (6)* | 3.35 | 2.70 |

World Refugee Year, 7/1/59-6/30/60.

**1960, Apr. 11 Engr. *Perf. 13½***

35 l, Pope John XXIII praying at coffin of Pope Pius X. 60 l, Body of Pope Pius X returning to Venice.

| | | | | | |
|---|---|---|---|---|---|
| **281** | A93 | 15 l | brown | .25 | .25 |
| **282** | A93 | 35 l | rose carmine | .60 | .60 |
| **283** | A93 | 60 l | Prus green | 1.25 | .85 |
| | | | *Nos. 281-283 (3)* | 2.10 | 1.70 |

Return of the body of Pope Pius X to Venice.

Feeding the Hungry A94

"Acts of Mercy," by Della Robbia: 10 l, Giving drink to the thirsty. 15 l, Clothing the naked. 20 l, Sheltering the homeless. 30 l, Visiting the sick. 35 l, Visiting prisoners. 40 l, Burying the dead. 70 l, Pope John XXIII.

**1960, Nov. 8 Photo. *Perf. 14***
**Centers in Brown**

| | | | | | |
|---|---|---|---|---|---|
| **284** | A94 | 5 l | red brown | .20 | .20 |
| **285** | A94 | 10 l | green | .20 | .20 |
| **286** | A94 | 15 l | slate | .20 | .20 |
| **287** | A94 | 20 l | rose carmine | .20 | .20 |
| **288** | A94 | 30 l | violet blue | .20 | .20 |
| **289** | A94 | 35 l | violet brown | .20 | .20 |
| **290** | A94 | 40 l | red orange | .20 | .20 |
| **291** | A94 | 70 l | ocher | .20 | .20 |
| | | | *Nos. 284-291,E15-E16 (10)* | 2.00 | 2.00 |

Holy Family by Gerard van Honthorst A95

**1960, Dec. 6 Wmk. 235 *Perf. 14***

| | | | | | |
|---|---|---|---|---|---|
| **292** | A95 | 10 l | slate grn & slate blk | .20 | .20 |
| **293** | A95 | 15 l | sepia & ol blk | .20 | .20 |
| **294** | A95 | 70 l | grnsh bl & dp bl | .30 | .20 |
| | | | *Nos. 292-294 (3)* | .70 | .60 |

St. Vincent de Paul — A96

St. Meinrad — A97

Designs: 70 l, St. Louisa de Marillac. 100 l, St. Louisa and St. Vincent.

**1960, Dec. 6**

| | | | | | |
|---|---|---|---|---|---|
| **295** | A96 | 40 l | dull violet | .20 | .20 |
| **296** | A96 | 70 l | dark gray | .30 | .20 |
| **297** | A96 | 100 l | dk red brown | .70 | .30 |
| | | | *Nos. 295-297 (3)* | 1.20 | .70 |

Death of St. Vincent de Paul, 300th anniv.

**1961, Feb. 28 *Perf. 14***

Designs: 40 l, Statue of Our Lady of Einsiedeln. 100 l, Einsiedeln monastery, horiz.

| | | | | | |
|---|---|---|---|---|---|
| **298** | A97 | 30 l | dark gray | .45 | .20 |
| **299** | A97 | 40 l | lt violet | 1.50 | .40 |
| **300** | A97 | 100 l | brown | 1.50 | .85 |
| | | | *Nos. 298-300 (3)* | 3.45 | 1.45 |

Death of St. Meinrad, 1,100th anniv.; Einsiedeln Abbey, Switzerland.

Pope Leo the Great Defying Attila — A98

**Wmk. 235**
**1961, Apr. 6 Photo. *Perf. 14***

| | | | | | |
|---|---|---|---|---|---|
| **301** | A98 | 15 l | rose brown | .20 | .20 |
| **302** | A98 | 70 l | Prus green | .25 | .25 |
| **303** | A98 | 300 l | brown black | 1.75 | .55 |
| | | | *Nos. 301-303 (3)* | 2.20 | 1.00 |

Death of Pope Leo the Great (St. Leo Magnus), 1,500th anniv. The design is from a marble bas-relief in St. Peter's Basilica.

St. Paul Arriving in Rome, 61 A.D. — A99

10 l, 30 l, Map showing St. Paul's journey to Rome. 20 l, 200 l, First Basilica of St. Paul, Rome.

**1961, June 13 Wmk. 235 *Perf. 14***

| | | | | | |
|---|---|---|---|---|---|
| **304** | A99 | 10 l | Prus green | .20 | .20 |
| **305** | A99 | 15 l | dl red brn & gray | .20 | .20 |
| **306** | A99 | 20 l | red org & gray | .20 | .20 |
| **307** | A99 | 30 l | blue | .20 | .20 |
| **308** | A99 | 75 l | org brn & gray | .30 | .30 |
| **309** | A99 | 200 l | blue & gray | 1.60 | 1.10 |
| | | | *Nos. 304-309 (6)* | 2.70 | 2.20 |

Arrival of St. Paul in Rome, 1,900th anniv.

1861 and 1961 Mastheads A100

70 l, Editorial offices. 250 l, Rotary press.

**1961, July 4**

| | | | | | |
|---|---|---|---|---|---|
| **310** | A100 | 40 l | red brn & blk | .20 | .20 |
| **311** | A100 | 70 l | blue & blk | .40 | .30 |
| **312** | A100 | 250 l | yellow & blk | 1.90 | 1.10 |
| | | | *Nos. 310-312 (3)* | 2.50 | 1.60 |

Centenary of L'Osservatore Romano, Vatican's newspaper.

St. Patrick's Purgatory, Lough Derg — A101

Arms of Roncalli Family — A102

10 l, 40 l, St. Patrick, marble sculpture.

**Wmk. 235**
**1961, Oct. 6 Photo. *Perf. 14***

| | | | | | |
|---|---|---|---|---|---|
| **313** | A101 | 10 l | buff & slate grn | .20 | .20 |
| **314** | A101 | 15 l | blue & sepia | .20 | .20 |
| **315** | A101 | 40 l | yellow & bl grn | .25 | .20 |
| **316** | A101 | 150 l | Prus bl & red brn | .70 | .50 |
| | | | *Nos. 313-316 (4)* | 1.35 | 1.10 |

Death of St. Patrick, 1,500th anniv.

**1961, Nov. 25**

Designs: 25 l, Church at Sotto il Monte. 30 l, Santa Maria in Monte Santo, Rome. 40 l, Church of San Carlo al Corso, Rome (erroneously inscribed with name of Basilica of Sts. Ambrosius and Charles, Milan). 70 l, Altar, St. Peter's, Rome. 115 l, Pope John XXIII.

| | | | | | |
|---|---|---|---|---|---|
| **317** | A102 | 10 l | gray & red brn | .20 | .20 |
| **318** | A102 | 25 l | ol bis & sl grn | .20 | .20 |
| **319** | A102 | 30 l | vio bl & pale pur | .20 | .20 |
| **320** | A102 | 40 l | lilac & dk blue | .20 | .20 |
| **321** | A102 | 70 l | gray grn & org brn | .30 | .20 |
| **322** | A102 | 115 l | choc & slate | .70 | .45 |
| | | | *Nos. 317-322 (6)* | 1.80 | 1.45 |

80th birthday of Pope John XXIII.

"The Adoration" by Lucas Chen — A103

Draining of Pontine Marshes Medal by Pope Sixtus V, 1588 — A104

**1961, Nov. 25**

**Center Multicolored**

| No. | Type | Description | Unused | Used |
|---|---|---|---|---|
| **323** | A103 | 15 l bluish green | .20 | .20 |
| **324** | A103 | 40 l gray | .20 | .20 |
| **325** | A103 | 70 l pale lilac | .30 | .20 |
| | | *Nos. 323-325 (3)* | .70 | .60 |

Christmas.

**1962, Apr. 7 Wmk. 235 *Perf. 14***

40 l, 300 l, Map of Pontine Marshes showing 18th cent. drainage under Pope Pius VI.

| No. | Type | Description | Unused | Used |
|---|---|---|---|---|
| **326** | A104 | 15 l dark violet | .20 | .20 |
| **327** | A104 | 40 l rose carmine | .20 | .20 |
| **328** | A104 | 70 l brown | .20 | .20 |
| **329** | A104 | 300 l dull green | .65 | .40 |
| | | *Nos. 326-329 (4)* | 1.25 | 1.00 |

WHO drive to eradicate malaria.

"The Good Shepherd" A105

Wheatfield (Luke 10:2) — A106

**1962, June 2 Photo.**

| No. | Type | Description | Unused | Used |
|---|---|---|---|---|
| **330** | A105 | 10 l lilac & black | .20 | .20 |
| **331** | A106 | 15 l blue & ocher | .20 | .20 |
| **332** | A105 | 70 l lt green & blk | .25 | .30 |
| **333** | A106 | 115 l fawn & ocher | 1.25 | 1.10 |
| **334** | A105 | 200 l brown & black | 2.00 | 1.40 |
| | | *Nos. 330-334 (5)* | 3.90 | 3.20 |

Issued to honor the priesthood and to stress its importance as a vocation.

"The Good Shepherd" is a fourth-century statue in the Lateran Museum, Rome.

St. Catherine of Siena — A107

Paulina M. Jaricot — A108

**1962, June 12**

| No. | Type | Description | Unused | Used |
|---|---|---|---|---|
| **335** | A107 | 15 l brown | .20 | .20 |
| **336** | A107 | 60 l brt violet | .30 | .25 |
| **337** | A107 | 100 l blue | .60 | .40 |
| | | *Nos. 335-337 (3)* | 1.10 | .85 |

Canonization of St. Catherine of Siena, 500th anniv. The portrait is from a fresco by Il Sodoma, Church of St. Dominic, Siena.

**1962, July 5**

**Portrait Multicolored**

| No. | Type | Description | Unused | Used |
|---|---|---|---|---|
| **338** | A108 | 10 l pale violet | .20 | .20 |
| **339** | A108 | 50 l dull green | .20 | .20 |
| **340** | A108 | 150 l gray | .80 | .50 |
| | | *Nos. 338-340 (3)* | 1.20 | .90 |

Paulina M. Jaricot (1799-1862), founder of the Society for the Propagation of the Faith.

Sts. Peter and Paul A109

Design: 40 l, 100 l, "The Invincible Cross," relief from sarcophagus.

**Wmk. 235**

**1962, Sept. 25 Photo. *Perf. 14***

| No. | Type | Description | Unused | Used |
|---|---|---|---|---|
| **341** | A109 | 20 l lilac & brown | .20 | .20 |
| **342** | A109 | 40 l lt brown & blk | .20 | .20 |
| **343** | A109 | 70 l bluish grn & brn | .20 | .20 |
| **344** | A109 | 100 l sal pink & blk | .20 | .20 |
| | | *Nos. 341-344 (4)* | .80 | .80 |

6th Congress of Christian Archeology, Ravenna, Sept. 23-28.

"Faith" by Raphael — A110

Designs: 10 l, "Hope." 15 l, "Charity." 25 l, Arms of Pope John XXIII and emblems of the Four Evangelists. 30 l, Ecumenical Congress meeting in St. Peter's. 40 l, Pope John XXIII on throne. 60 l, Statue of St. Peter. 115 l, The Holy Ghost as a dove (symbolic design).

**Photo.; Center Engr. on 30 l**

**1962, Oct. 30**

| No. | Type | Description | Unused | Used |
|---|---|---|---|---|
| **345** | A110 | 5 l brt blue & blk | .20 | .20 |
| **346** | A110 | 10 l green & blk | .20 | .20 |
| **347** | A110 | 15 l ver & sepia | .20 | .20 |
| **348** | A110 | 25 l ver & slate | .20 | .20 |
| **349** | A110 | 30 l lilac & blk | .20 | .20 |
| **350** | A110 | 40 l dk carmine & blk | .20 | .20 |
| **351** | A110 | 60 l dk grn & dp org | .20 | .20 |
| **352** | A110 | 115 l crimson | .20 | .20 |
| | | *Nos. 345-352 (8)* | 1.60 | 1.60 |

Vatican II, the 21st Ecumenical Council of the Roman Catholic Church, which opened Oct. 11, 1962. Nos. 345-347 show "the Three Theological Virtues" by Raphael.

Nativity Scene A111

Set in India, following a design by Marcus Toano.

**1962, Dec. 4**

**Center Multicolored**

| No. | Type | Description | Unused | Used |
|---|---|---|---|---|
| **353** | A111 | 10 l gray | .20 | .20 |
| **354** | A111 | 15 l brown | .20 | .20 |
| **355** | A111 | 90 l dull green | .30 | .20 |
| | | *Nos. 353-355 (3)* | .70 | .60 |

Miracle of the Loaves and Fishes by Murillo — A112

Pope John XXIII — A113

Design: 40 l, 200 l, "The Miraculous Catch of Fishes" by Raphael.

**Wmk. 235**

**1963, Mar. 21 Photo. *Perf. 14***

| No. | Type | Description | Unused | Used |
|---|---|---|---|---|
| **356** | A112 | 15 l brn & dk brn | .20 | .20 |
| **357** | A112 | 40 l rose red & blk | .20 | .20 |
| **358** | A112 | 100 l blue & dk brn | .20 | .20 |
| **359** | A112 | 200 l bl grn & blk | .20 | .20 |
| | | *Nos. 356-359 (4)* | .80 | .80 |

FAO "Freedom from Hunger" campaign.

**1963, May 8**

| No. | Type | Description | Unused | Used |
|---|---|---|---|---|
| **360** | A113 | 15 l red brown | .20 | .20 |
| **361** | A113 | 160 l black | .40 | .20 |

Awarding of the Balzan Peace Prize to Pope John XXIII.

**Interregnum Issue**

Keys of St. Peter and Papal Chamberlain's Insignia — A114

**1963, June 15 Wmk. 235 *Perf. 14***

| No. | Type | Description | Unused | Used |
|---|---|---|---|---|
| **362** | A114 | 10 l dk brown | .20 | .20 |
| **363** | A114 | 40 l dk brown, *yel* | .20 | .20 |
| **364** | A114 | 100 l dk brown, *vio* | .20 | .20 |
| | | *Nos. 362-364 (3)* | .60 | .60 |

Pope Paul VI — A115

St. Cyril — A116

Design: 40 l, 200 l, Arms of Pope Paul VI.

**1963, Oct. 16 Engr. *Perf. 13x14***

| No. | Type | Description | Unused | Used |
|---|---|---|---|---|
| **365** | A115 | 15 l black | .20 | .20 |
| **366** | A115 | 40 l carmine | .20 | .20 |
| **367** | A115 | 115 l redsh brown | .20 | .20 |
| **368** | A115 | 200 l slate blue | .40 | .25 |
| | | *Nos. 365-368 (4)* | 1.00 | .85 |

Coronation of Pope Paul VI, June 30, 1963.

**Wmk. 235**

**1963, Nov. 22 Photo. *Perf. 14***

Designs: 70 l, Map of Hungary, Moravia and Poland, 16th century. 150 l, St. Methodius.

| No. | Type | Description | Unused | Used |
|---|---|---|---|---|
| **369** | A116 | 30 l violet black | .20 | .20 |
| **370** | A116 | 70 l brown | .30 | .20 |
| **371** | A116 | 150 l rose claret | .40 | .20 |
| | | *Nos. 369-371 (3)* | .90 | .60 |

1100th anniv. of the beginning of missionary work among the Slavs by Sts. Cyril and Methodius. The pictures of the saints are from 16th century frescoes in St. Clement's Basilica, Rome.

African Nativity Scene — A117

Church of the Holy Sepulcher, Jerusalem A118

**1963, Nov. 22**

| No. | Type | Description | Unused | Used |
|---|---|---|---|---|
| **372** | A117 | 10 l brn & pale brn | .20 | .20 |
| **373** | A117 | 40 l ultra & brown | .20 | .20 |
| **374** | A117 | 100 l gray olive & brn | .25 | .20 |
| | | *Nos. 372-374 (3)* | .65 | .60 |

The design is after a sculpture by the Burundi artist Andreas Bukuru.

**1964, Jan. 4 Wmk. 235 *Perf. 14***

15 l, Pope Paul VI. 25 l, Nativity Church, Bethlehem. 160 l, Well of the Virgin Mary, Nazareth.

| No. | Type | Description | Unused | Used |
|---|---|---|---|---|
| **375** | A118 | 15 l black | .20 | .20 |
| **376** | A118 | 25 l rose brown | .20 | .20 |
| **377** | A118 | 70 l brown | .20 | .20 |
| **378** | A118 | 160 l ultra | .20 | .20 |
| | | *Nos. 375-378 (4)* | .80 | .80 |

Visit of Pope Paul VI to the Holy Land, Jan. 4-6.

St. Peter from Coptic Church at Wadi-es-Sebua, Sudan — A119

Design: 20 l, 200 l, Trajan's Kiosk, Philae.

**1964, Mar. 10 Photo.**

| No. | Type | Description | Unused | Used |
|---|---|---|---|---|
| **379** | A119 | 10 l ultra & red brn | .20 | .20 |
| **380** | A119 | 20 l multicolored | .20 | .20 |
| **381** | A119 | 70 l gray & red brn | .20 | .20 |
| **382** | A119 | 200 l gray & multi | .20 | .20 |
| | | *Nos. 379-382 (4)* | .80 | .80 |

UNESCO world campaign to save historic monuments in Nubia.

Pietà by Michelangelo A120

Isaiah by Michelangelo A121

Designs: 15 l, 100 l, Pope Paul VI. 250 l, Head of Mary from Pietà.

**1964, Apr. 22 Wmk. 235 *Perf. 14***

| No. | Type | Description | Unused | Used |
|---|---|---|---|---|
| **383** | A120 | 15 l violet blue | .20 | .20 |
| **384** | A120 | 50 l dark brown | .20 | .20 |
| **385** | A120 | 100 l slate blue | .20 | .20 |
| **386** | A120 | 250 l chestnut | .20 | .20 |
| | | *Nos. 383-386 (4)* | .80 | .80 |

New York World's Fair, 1964-65.

**1964, June 16 Engr. *Perf. 13½x14***

| No. | Type | Description | Unused | Used |
|---|---|---|---|---|
| **387** | A121 | 10 l Michelangelo, after Jacopino del Conte | .20 | .20 |
| **388** | A121 | 25 l Isaiah | .20 | .20 |
| **389** | A121 | 30 l Delphic Sibyl | .20 | .20 |
| **390** | A121 | 40 l Jeremiah | .20 | .20 |
| **391** | A121 | 150 l Joel | .20 | .20 |
| | | *Nos. 387-391 (5)* | 1.00 | 1.00 |

Michelangelo Buonarroti (1475-1564). Designs are from the Sistine Chapel.

The Good Samaritan A122

*Perf. 14x13½*

**1964, Sept. 22 Engr. Wmk. 235**

**392** A122 10 l red brown & red .20 .20
**393** A122 30 l dark blue & red .20 .20
**394** A122 300 l gray & red .25 .20
*Nos. 392-394 (3)* .65 .60

Cent. (in 1963) of the founding of the Intl. Red Cross.

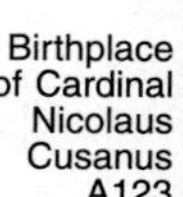

Birthplace of Cardinal Nicolaus Cusanus A123

Design: 200 l, Cardinal's sepulcher, Church of San Pietro in Vincoli, Rome.

**1964, Nov. 16 Wmk. 235**

**395** A123 40 l dull blue grn .20 .20
**396** A123 200 l rose red .30 .20

German cardinal Nicolaus Cusanus (Nicolaus Krebs of Kues) (1401-1464).

Japanese Nativity Scene by Kimiko Koseki — A124

Pope Paul VI and Map of India and Southeast Asia — A125

**1964, Nov. 16 Photo. *Perf. 14***

**397** A124 10 l multicolored .20 .20
*a.* Yellow omitted
**398** A124 15 l black & multi .20 .20
**399** A124 135 l bister & multi .25 .20
*Nos. 397-399 (3)* .65 .60

**1964, Dec. 2**

Designs: 15 l, Pope Paul VI at prayer. 25 l, Eucharistic Congress altar, Bombay, horiz. 60 l, Gateway of India, Bombay, horiz.

**400** A125 15 l dull violet .20 .20
**401** A125 25 l green .20 .20
**402** A125 60 l brown .20 .20
**403** A125 200 l dull violet .20 .20
*Nos. 400-403 (4)* .80 .80

Trip of Pope Paul VI to India, Dec. 2-5, 1964.

Uganda Martyrs — A126

Dante by Raphael — A127

Various groups of Martyrs of Uganda.

*Perf. 13½x14*

**1965, Mar. 16 Engr. Wmk. 235**

**404** A126 15 l Prus green .20 .20
**405** A126 20 l brown .20 .20
**406** A126 30 l ultra .20 .20
**407** A126 75 l black .20 .20
**408** A126 100 l rose red .20 .20
**409** A126 160 l violet .20 .20
*Nos. 404-409 (6)* 1.20 1.20

Canonization of 22 African martyrs, 10/18/64.

**Photogravure and Engraved**

**1965, May 18 *Perf. 13½x14***

Designs: 40 l, Dante and the 3 beasts at entrance to the Inferno. 70 l, Dante and Virgil at entrance to Purgatory. 200 l, Dante and Beatrice in Paradise. (40 l, 70 l, 200 l, by Botticelli.)

**410** A127 10 l bis brn & dk brn .20 .20
**411** A127 40 l rose & dk brn .20 .20
**412** A127 70 l lt grn & dk brn .20 .20
**413** A127 200 l pale bl & dk brn .20 .20
*Nos. 410-413 (4)* .80 .80

Birth of Dante Alighieri, 700th anniv.

St. Benedict by Perugino A128

Pope Paul VI Addressing UN Assembly A129

Design: 300 l, View of Monte Cassino.

**1965, July 2 Photo. *Perf. 14***

**414** A128 40 l brown .20 .20
**415** A128 300 l dark green .30 .20

Conferring of the title Patron Saint of Europe upon St. Benedict by Pope Paul VI; restoring of the Abbey of Monte Cassino.

**1965, Oct. 4 Wmk. 235 *Perf. 14***

30 l, 150 l, UN Headquarters and olive branch.

**416** A129 20 l brown .20 .20
**417** A129 30 l sapphire .20 .20
**418** A129 150 l olive green .20 .20
**419** A129 300 l rose violet .25 .20
*Nos. 416-419 (4)* .85 .80

Visit of Pope Paul VI to the UN, NYC, Oct. 4.

Peruvian Nativity Scene A130

Cartographer A131

**1965, Nov. 25 Engr. *Perf. 13½x14***

**420** A130 20 l rose claret .20 .20
**421** A130 40 l red brown .20 .20
**422** A130 200 l gray green .20 .20
*Nos. 420-422 (3)* .60 .60

**1966, Mar. 8 Photo. *Perf. 14***

Designs: 5 l, Pope Paul VI. 10 l, Organist. 20 l, Painter. 30 l, Sculptor. 40 l, Bricklayer. 55 l, Printer. 75 l, Plowing farmer. 90 l, Blacksmith. 130 l, Scholar.

**423** A131 5 l sepia .20 .20
**424** A131 10 l violet .20 .20
**425** A131 15 l brown .20 .20
**426** A131 20 l gray green .20 .20
**427** A131 30 l brown red .20 .20
**428** A131 40 l Prus green .20 .20
**429** A131 55 l dark blue .20 .20
**430** A131 75 l dk rose brown .20 .20
**431** A131 90 l carmine rose .20 .20
**432** A131 130 l black .20 .20
*Nos. 423-432,E17-E18 (12)* 2.40 2.40

The Pope's portrait is from a bas-relief by Enrico Manfrini; the arts and crafts designs are bas-reliefs by Mario Rudelli from the chair in the Pope's private chapel.

King Mieszko I and Queen Dabrowka A132

Designs: 25 l, St. Adalbert (Wojciech) and Cathedrals of Wroclaw and Gniezno. 40 l, St. Stanislas, Skalka Church, Wawel Cathedral and Castle, Cracow. 50 l, Queen Jadwiga (Hedwig), Holy Gate with Our Lady of Mercy, Vilnius, and Jagellon University Library, Cracow. 150 l, Black Madonna of Czestochowa, cloister and church of Bright Mountain, Czestochowa, and St. John's Cathedral, Warsaw. 220 l, Pope Paul VI blessing students and farmers.

*Perf. 14x13½*

**1966, May 3 Engr. Wmk. 235**

**433** A132 15 l black .20 .20
**434** A132 25 l violet .20 .20
**435** A132 40 l brick red .20 .20
**436** A132 50 l claret .20 .20
**437** A132 150 l slate blue .20 .20
**438** A132 220 l brown .20 .20
*Nos. 433-438 (6)* 1.20 1.20

Millenium of Christianization of Poland.

Pope John XXIII Opening Vatican II Council A133

Nativity, Sculpture by Scorzelli A134

Designs: 15 l, Ancient Bible on ornate display stand. 55 l, Bishops celebrating Mass. 90 l, Pope Paul VI greeting Patriarch Athenagoras I. 100 l, Gold ring given to participating bishops. 130 l, Pope Paul VI carried in front of St. Peter's.

**1966, Oct. 11 Photo. *Perf. 14***

**439** A133 10 l red & black .20 .20
**440** A133 15 l brown & green .20 .20
**441** A133 55 l blk & brt rose .20 .20
**442** A133 90 l slate grn & blk .20 .20
**443** A133 100 l green & ocher .20 .20
**444** A133 130 l orange brn & brn .20 .20
*Nos. 439-444 (6)* 1.20 1.20

Conclusion of Vatican II, the 21st Ecumenical Council of the Roman Catholic Church, Dec. 8, 1965.

**1966, Nov. 24 Wmk. 235 *Perf. 14***

**445** A134 20 l plum .20 .20
**446** A134 55 l slate green .20 .20
**447** A134 225 l yellow brown .20 .20
*Nos. 445-447 (3)* .60 .60

St. Peter, Fresco, Catacombs, Rome — A135

Cross, People and Globe — A136

Designs: 20 l, St. Paul, fresco from Catacombs, Rome. 55 l, Sts. Peter and Paul, glass painting, Vatican Library. 90 l, Baldachin by Bernini, St. Peter's, Rome. 220 l, Interior of St. Paul's, Rome.

*Perf. 13½x14*

**1967, June 15 Photo. Unwmk.**

**448** A135 15 l multi .20 .20
**449** A135 20 l multi .20 .20
**450** A135 55 l multi .20 .20
**451** A135 90 l multi .20 .20
**452** A135 220 l multi .20 .20
*Nos. 448-452 (5)* 1.00 1.00

Martyrdom of the Apostles Peter and Paul, 1,900th anniv.

**1967, Oct. 13 Wmk. 235 *Perf. 14***

**453** A136 40 l carmine rose .20 .20
**454** A136 130 l brt blue .20 .20

3rd Congress of Catholic Laymen, Rome, Oct. 11-18.

Sculpture of Shepherd Children of Fatima — A137

Nativity, 9th Century Painting on Wood — A138

Designs: 50 l, Basilica at Fatima. 200 l, Pope Paul VI praying before statue of Virgin of Fatima.

**1967, Oct. 13 *Perf. 13½x14***

**455** A137 30 l multi .20 .20
**456** A137 50 l multi .20 .20
**457** A137 200 l multi .20 .20
*Nos. 455-457 (3)* .60 .60

Apparition of the Virgin Mary to 3 shepherd children at Fatima, 50th anniv.

**Christmas Issue**

**1967, Nov. 28 Photo. Unwmk.**

**458** A138 25 l purple & multi .20 .20
**459** A138 55 l gray & multi .20 .20
**460** A138 180 l green & multi .20 .20
*Nos. 458-460 (3)* .60 .60

Pope Paul VI — A139

Holy Infant of Prague — A140

Designs: 55 l, Monstrance from fresco by Raphael. 220 l, Map of South America.

**1968, Aug. 22 Wmk. 235 *Perf. 14***

**461** A139 25 l blk & dk red brn .20 .20
**462** A139 55 l blk, gray & ocher .20 .20
**463** A139 220 l blk, lt bl & sep .20 .20
*Nos. 461-463 (3)* .60 .60

Visit of Pope Paul VI to the 39th Eucharistic Congress in Bogotá, Colombia, Aug. 22-25.

**Engraved and Photogravure**

**1968, Nov. 28 *Perf. 13½x14***

**464** A140 20 l plum & pink .20 .20
**465** A140 50 l vio & pale vio .20 .20
**466** A140 250 l dk bl & lt bluish gray .20 .20
*Nos. 464-466 (3)* .60 .60

The Resurrection, by Fra Angelico de Fiesole — A141

Pope Paul VI with African Children — A142

**Easter Issue**

*Perf. 13½x14*

**1969, Mar. 6 Engr. Wmk. 235**

| | | | | |
|---|---|---|---|---|
| **467** | A141 | 20 l dk carmine & buff | .20 | .20 |
| **468** | A141 | 90 l green & buff | .20 | .20 |
| **469** | A141 | 180 l ultra & buff | .20 | .20 |
| | | *Nos. 467-469 (3)* | .60 | .60 |

Common Design Types pictured following the introduction.

**Europa Issue**

Common Design Type

*Perf. 13½x14*

**1969, Apr. 28 Photo. Wmk. 235**

**Size: 36½x27mm**

| | | | | |
|---|---|---|---|---|
| **470** | CD12 | 50 l gray & lt brn | .20 | .20 |
| **471** | CD12 | 90 l vermilion & lt brn | .20 | .20 |
| **472** | CD12 | 130 l olive & lt brn | .20 | .20 |
| | | *Nos. 470-472 (3)* | .60 | .60 |

*Perf. 13½x14*

**1969, July 31 Photo. Wmk. 235**

Designs: 55 l, Pope Paul VI and African bishops. 250 l, Map of Africa with Kampala, olive branch and compass rose.

| | | | | |
|---|---|---|---|---|
| **473** | A142 | 25 l bister & brown | .20 | .20 |
| **474** | A142 | 55 l dk red & brown | .20 | .20 |
| **475** | A142 | 250 l multicolored | .20 | .20 |
| | | *Nos. 473-475 (3)* | .60 | .60 |

Visit of Pope Paul VI to Uganda, 7/31-8/2.

Pope Pius IX — A143

Mt. Fuji and EXPO '70 Emblem — A144

Designs: 50 l, Chrismon, emblem of St. Peter's Circle. 220 l, Pope Paul VI.

*Perf. 13½x14*

**1969, Nov. 18 Engr. Wmk. 235**

| | | | | |
|---|---|---|---|---|
| **476** | A143 | 30 l red brown | .20 | .20 |
| **477** | A143 | 50 l dark gray | .20 | .20 |
| **478** | A143 | 220 l deep plum | .20 | .20 |
| | | *Nos. 476-478 (3)* | .60 | .60 |

Centenary of St. Peter's Circle, a lay society dedicated to prayer, action and sacrifice.

**1970, Mar. 16 Photo. Unwmk.**

EXPO '70 Emblem and: 25 l, EXPO '70 emblem. 40 l, Osaka Castle. 55 l, Japanese Virgin and Child, by Domoto in Osaka Cathedral. 90 l, Christian Pavilion.

| | | | | |
|---|---|---|---|---|
| **479** | A144 | 25 l gold, red & blk | .20 | .20 |
| **480** | A144 | 40 l red & multi | .20 | .20 |
| **481** | A144 | 55 l brown & multi | .20 | .20 |
| **482** | A144 | 90 l gold & multi | .20 | .20 |
| **483** | A144 | 110 l blue & multi | .20 | .20 |
| | | *Nos. 479-483 (5)* | 1.00 | 1.00 |

EXPO '70 Intl. Exhibition, Osaka, Japan, Mar. 15-Sept. 13.

Centenary Medal, Jesus Giving St. Peter the Keys — A145

Designs: 50 l, Coat of arms of Pope Pius IX. 180 l, Vatican I Council meeting in St. Peter's, obverse of centenary medal.

**Engr. & Photo.; Photo. (50 l)**

**1970, Apr. 29** ***Perf. 13x14***

| | | | | |
|---|---|---|---|---|
| **484** | A145 | 20 l orange & brown | .20 | .20 |
| **485** | A145 | 50 l multicolored | .20 | .20 |
| **486** | A145 | 180 l ver & brn | .30 | .25 |
| | | *Nos. 484-486 (3)* | .70 | .65 |

Centenary of the Vatican I Council.

Christ, by Simone Martini A146

25 l, Christ with Crown of Thorns, by Rogier van der Weyden. 50 l, Christ, by Albrecht Dürer. 90 l, Christ, by El Greco. 180 l, Pope Paul VI.

**1970, May 29 Photo.** ***Perf. 14x13***

| | | | | |
|---|---|---|---|---|
| **487** | A146 | 15 l gold & multi | .20 | .20 |
| **488** | A146 | 25 l gold & multi | .20 | .20 |
| **489** | A146 | 50 l gold & multi | .20 | .20 |
| **490** | A146 | 90 l gold & multi | .20 | .20 |
| **491** | A146 | 180 l gold & multi | .25 | .20 |
| | | *Nos. 487-491 (5)* | 1.05 | 1.00 |

Ordination of Pope Paul VI, 50th anniv.

Adam, by Michelangelo; UN Emblem — A147

Pope Paul VI — A148

UN Emblem and: 90 l, Eve, by Michelangelo. 220 l, Olive branch.

**1970, Oct. 8 Photo.** ***Perf. 13x14***

| | | | | |
|---|---|---|---|---|
| **492** | A147 | 20 l multi | .20 | .20 |
| **493** | A147 | 90 l multi | .20 | .20 |
| **494** | A147 | 220 l multi | .25 | .20 |
| | | *Nos. 492-494 (3)* | .65 | .60 |

25th anniversary of the United Nations.

**1970, Nov. 26 Photo. Unwmk.**

Designs: 55 l, Holy Child of Cebu, Philippines. 100 l, Madonna and Child, by Georg Hamori, Darwin Cathedral, Australia. 130 l, Cathedral of Manila. 220 l, Cathedral of Sydney.

| | | | | |
|---|---|---|---|---|
| **495** | A148 | 25 l multi | .20 | .20 |
| **496** | A148 | 55 l multi | .20 | .20 |
| **497** | A148 | 100 l multi | .20 | .20 |
| **498** | A148 | 130 l multi | .20 | .20 |
| **499** | A148 | 220 l multi | .25 | .20 |
| | | *Nos. 495-499 (5)* | 1.05 | 1.00 |

Visit of Pope Paul VI to the Far East, Oceania and Australia, Nov. 26-Dec. 5.

Angel Holding Lectern — A149

Madonna and Child by Francesco Ghissi — A150

Sculptures by Corrado Ruffini: 40 l, 130 l, Crucified Christ surrounded by doves. 50 l, like 20 l.

**1971, Feb. 2** ***Perf. 13x14***

| | | | | |
|---|---|---|---|---|
| **500** | A149 | 20 l multicolored | .20 | .20 |
| **501** | A149 | 40 l dp orange & multi | .20 | .20 |
| **502** | A149 | 50 l purple & multi | .20 | .20 |
| **503** | A149 | 130 l multicolored | .25 | .20 |
| | | *Nos. 500-503 (4)* | .85 | .80 |

Intl. year against racial discrimination.

**1971, Mar. 26 Photo.** ***Perf. 14***

Paintings: Madonna and Child, 40 l, by Sassetta (Stefano di Giovanni); 55 l, Carlo Crivelli; 90 l, by Carlo Maratta. 180 l, Holy Family, by Ghisberto Ceracchini.

| | | | | |
|---|---|---|---|---|
| **504** | A150 | 25 l gray & multi | .20 | .20 |
| **505** | A150 | 40 l gray & multi | .20 | .20 |
| **506** | A150 | 55 l gray & multi | .20 | .20 |
| **507** | A150 | 90 l gray & multi | .20 | .20 |
| **508** | A150 | 180 l gray & multi | .20 | .20 |
| | | *Nos. 504-508 (5)* | 1.00 | 1.00 |

St. Dominic, Sienese School — A151

St. Stephen, from Chasuble, 1031 — A152

Portraits of St. Dominic: 55 l, by Fra Angelico. 90 l, by Titian. 180 l, by El Greco.

**1971, May 25 Unwmk.** ***Perf. 13x14***

| | | | | |
|---|---|---|---|---|
| **509** | A151 | 25 l multi | .20 | .20 |
| **510** | A151 | 55 l multi | .20 | .20 |
| **511** | A151 | 90 l multi | .20 | .20 |
| **512** | A151 | 180 l multi | .25 | .20 |
| | | *Nos. 509-512 (4)* | .85 | .80 |

St. Dominic de Guzman (1170-1221), founder of the Dominican Order.

**1971, Nov. 25**

180 l, Madonna as Patroness of Hungary, 1511.

| | | | | |
|---|---|---|---|---|
| **513** | A152 | 50 l multi | .20 | .20 |
| **514** | A152 | 180 l black & yellow | .30 | .20 |

Millenium of the birth of St. Stephen (975?-1038), king of Hungary.

Bramante A153

Designs: 25 l, Bramante's design for dome of St. Peter's. 130 l, Design for spiral staircase.

**1972, Feb. 22 Engr.** ***Perf. 13½x14***

| | | | | |
|---|---|---|---|---|
| **515** | A153 | 25 l dull yellow & blk | .20 | .20 |
| **516** | A153 | 90 l dull yellow & blk | .20 | .20 |
| **517** | A153 | 130 l dull yellow & blk | .25 | .20 |
| | | *Nos. 515-517 (3)* | .65 | .60 |

Bramante (real name Donato d'Agnolo; 1444-1514), architect.

St. Mark in Storm, 12th Century Mosaic — A154

Map of Venice, 1581 — A155

Design: 180 l, St. Mark's Basilica, Painting by Emilio Vangelli.

**Unwmk.**

**1972, June 6 Photo.** ***Perf. 14***

| | | | | |
|---|---|---|---|---|
| **518** | A154 | 25 l lt brown & multi | .20 | .20 |
| **519** | A155 | Block of 4 | 1.00 | .60 |
| *a.-d.* | | 50 l, UL, UR, LL, LR, each | .25 | .20 |
| **520** | A154 | 180 l lt blue & multi | 1.10 | .65 |
| *a.* | | Souvenir sheet, #518-520 | 2.50 | 2.50 |
| | | *Nos. 518-520 (3)* | 2.30 | 1.45 |

UNESCO campaign to save Venice.

Gospel of St. Matthew, 13th Century, French A156

Illuminated Initials from: 50 l, St. Luke's Gospel, Biblia dell'Aracoeli 13th century, French. 90 l, Second Epistle of St. John, 14th century, Bologna. 100 l, Apocalypse of St. John, 14th century, Bologna. 130 l, Book of Romans, 14th century, Central Italy.

**1972, Oct. 11** ***Perf. 14x13½***

| | | | | |
|---|---|---|---|---|
| **521** | A156 | 30 l multi | .20 | .20 |
| **522** | A156 | 50 l multi | .20 | .20 |
| **523** | A156 | 90 l multi | .20 | .20 |
| **524** | A156 | 100 l multi | .20 | .20 |
| **525** | A156 | 130 l multi | .35 | .25 |
| | | *Nos. 521-525 (5)* | 1.15 | 1.05 |

Intl. Book Year. Illustrations are from illuminated medieval manuscripts.

Luigi Orione A157

Design: 180 l, Lorenzo Perosi and music from "Hallelujah."

**1972, Nov. 28 Photo. *Perf. 14x13½***

**526** A157 50 l rose, lilac & blk .20 .20
**527** A157 180 l orange, grn & blk .30 .20

Secular priests Luigi Orione (1872-1940), founder of CARITAS, Catholic welfare organization; and Lorenzo Perosi (1872-1956), composer.

Cardinal Bessarion A158

Eucharistic Congress Emblem — A159

40 l, Reading Bull of Union between the Greek and Latin Churches, 1439, from bronze door of St. Peter's. 130 l, Coat of arms from tomb, Basilica of Holy Apostles, Rome.

***Perf. 13x14***

**1972, Nov. 28 Wmk. 235 Engr.**

**528** A158 40 l dull green .20 .20
**529** A158 90 l carmine .25 .20
**530** A158 130 l black .20 .20
*Nos. 528-530 (3)* .65 .60

Johannes Cardinal Bessarion (1403?-1472), Latin Patriarch of Constantinople, who worked for union of the Greek and Latin Churches. Portrait by Cosimo Rosselli in Sistine Chapel.

**1973, Feb. 27 Photo. Unwmk.**

Designs: 75 l, Head of Mary (Pietà), by Michelangelo. 300 l, Melbourne Cathedral.

**531** A159 25 l violet & multi .20 .20
**532** A159 75 l olive & multi .20 .20
**533** A159 300 l multicolored .50 .40
*Nos. 531-533 (3)* .90 .80

40th Intl. Eucharistic Congress, Melbourne, Australia, Feb. 18-25.

St. Teresa — A160

Copernicus A161

Designs: 25 l, St. Teresa's birthplace, Alençon. 220 l, Lisieux Basilica.

**1973, May 23 Engr. & Photo.**

**534** A160 25 l black & pink .20 .20
**535** A160 55 l black & yellow .20 .20
**536** A160 220 l black & lt blue .40 .25
*Nos. 534-536 (3)* .80 .65

St. Teresa of Lisieux and of the Infant Jesus (1873-1897), Carmelite nun.

**1973, June 19 Engr. *Perf. 14***

Designs: 20 l, 100 l, View of Torun.

**537** A161 20 l dull green .20 .20
**538** A161 50 l brown .20 .20
**539** A161 100 l lilac .20 .20
**540** A161 130 l dark blue .30 .20
*Nos. 537-540 (4)* .90 .80

Nicolaus Copernicus (1473-1543), Polish astronomer.

St. Wenceslas A162

**1973, Sept. 25 Photo. *Perf. 14***

**541** A162 20 l shown .20 .20
**542** A162 90 l Arms of Prague Diocese .20 .20
**543** A162 150 l Spire of Prague Cathedral .25 .20
**544** A162 220 l St. Adalbert .35 .20
*Nos. 541-544 (4)* 1.00 .80

Millenium of Prague Latin Episcopal See.

St. Nerses Shnorali — A163

25 l, Church of St. Hripsime. 90 l, Armenian khatchkar, a stele with cross and inscription.

**Engr. & Litho.**

**1973, Nov. 27 *Perf. 13x14***

**545** A163 25 l tan & dk brown .20 .20
**546** A163 90 l lt violet & blk .20 .20
**547** A163 180 l lt green & sepia .35 .20
*Nos. 545-547 (3)* .75 .60

Armenian Patriarch St. Nerses Shnorali (1102-1173).

Noah's Ark, Rainbow and Dove (Mosaic) — A164

Design: 90 l, Lamb drinking from stream, and Tablets of the Law (mosaic).

**1974, Apr. 23 Litho. *Perf. 13x14***

**548** A164 50 l gold & multi .20 .20
**549** A164 90 l gold & multi .30 .20

Centenary of the Universal Postal Union.

"And There was Light" — A165

St. Thomas Aquinas Teaching — A166

Designs: 25 l, Noah's Ark, horiz. 50 l, The Annunciation. 90 l, Nativity (African). 180 l, Hands holding grain (Spanish inscription: The Lord feeds his people), horiz. Designs chosen through worldwide youth competition in connection with 1972 Intl. Book Year.

***Perf. 13x14, 14x13***

**1974, Apr. 23 Photo.**

**550** A165 15 l brown & multi .20 .20
**551** A165 25 l yellow & multi .20 .20
**552** A165 50 l blue & multi .20 .20
**553** A165 90 l green & multi .20 .20
**554** A165 180 l rose & multi .25 .20
*Nos. 550-554 (5)* 1.05 1.00

"The Bible: the Book of Books."

**Engr. & Litho.**

**1974, June 18 Unwmk. *Perf. 13x14***

Designs: 50 l, Students (left panel). 220 l, Students (right panel). Designs from a painting in the Convent of St. Mark in Florence, by an artist from the School of Fra Angelico.

**Sizes: 50 l, 220 l, 20x36mm, 90 l, 26x36mm**

**555** A166 50 l dk brown & gold .20 .20
**556** A166 90 l dk brown & gold .20 .20
**557** A166 220 l dk brown & gold .40 .25
***a.*** Strip of 3, #555-557 .70 .55

St. Thomas Aquinas (1225-1274), scholastic philosopher.

St. Bonaventure A167

Woodcuts: 40 l, Civita Bagnoregio. 90 l, Tree of Life (13th century).

**1974, Sept. 26 Photo. *Perf. 13x14***

**558** A167 40 l gold & multi .20 .20
**559** A167 90 l gold & multi .25 .20
**560** A167 220 l gold & multi .30 .20
*Nos. 558-560 (3)* .75 .60

St. Bonaventure (Giovanni di Fidanza; 1221-1274), scholastic philosopher.

Christ, St. Peter's Basilica — A168

Pope Paul VI Giving his Blessing — A169

Holy Year 1975: 10 l, Christus Victor, Sts. Peter and Paul. 30 l, Christ. 40 l, Cross surmounted by dove. 50 l, Christ enthroned. 55 l, St. Peter. 90 l, St. Paul. 100 l, St. Peter. 130 l, St. Paul. 220 l, Arms of Pope Paul VI. Designs of 10 l, 25 l, are from St. Peter's; 30 l, 40 l, from St. John Lateran; 50 l, 55 l, 90 l, from St. Mary Major; 100 l, 130 l, from St. Paul outside the Walls.

**1974, Dec. 19 Photo. *Perf. 13x14***

**561** A168 10 l multi .20 .20
**562** A168 25 l multi .20 .20
**563** A168 30 l multi .20 .20
**564** A168 40 l multi .20 .20
**565** A168 50 l multi .20 .20
**566** A168 55 l multi .20 .20
**567** A168 90 l multi .20 .20
**568** A168 100 l multi .20 .20
**569** A168 130 l multi .20 .20
**570** A169 220 l multi .25 .20
**571** A169 250 l multi .30 .25
*Nos. 561-571 (11)* 2.35 2.25

Pentecost, by El Greco — A170

**1975, May 22 Engr. *Perf. 13x14***

**572** A170 300 l car rose & orange .60 .40

Fountain, St. Peter's Square — A171

Fountains of Rome: 40 l, Piazza St. Martha, Apse of St. Peter's. 50 l, Borgia Tower and St. Peter's. 90 l, Belvedere Courtyard. 100 l, Academy of Sciences. 200 l, Galleon.

**Litho. & Engr.**

**1975, May 22 *Perf. 14***

**573** A171 20 l buff & blk .20 .20
**574** A171 40 l pale violet & blk .20 .20
**575** A171 50 l salmon & blk .20 .20
**576** A171 90 l pale citron & blk .20 .20
**577** A171 100 l pale green & blk .20 .20
**578** A171 200 l pale blue & blk .30 .25
*Nos. 573-578 (6)* 1.30 1.25

European Architectural Heritage Year.

Miracle of Loaves and Fishes, Gilt Glass A172

Designs: 150 l, Painting of Christ, from Comodilla Catacomb. 200 l, Raising of Lazarus. All works from 4th century.

***Perf. 14x13½***

**1975, Sept. 25 Photo. Unwmk.**

**579** A172 30 l multi .20 .20
**580** A172 150 l brown & multi .25 .20
**581** A172 200 l green & multi .45 .30
*Nos. 579-581 (3)* .90 .70

9th Intl. Congress of Christian Archaeology.

Investiture of First Librarian Bartolomeo Sacchi by Pope Sixtus IV
A173

Designs: 100 l, Pope Sixtus IV and books in old wooden press, from Latin Vatican Codex 2044, vert. 250 l, Pope Sixtus IV visiting Library, fresco in Hospital of the Holy Spirit. Design of 70 l is from fresco by Melozzo di Forli in Vatican Gallery.

***Perf. 14x13½, 13½x14***

**1975, Sept. 25 Litho. & Engr.**

**582** A173 70 l gray & lilac .20 .20
**583** A173 100 l lt yellow & grn .25 .20
**584** A173 250 l gray & red .55 .30
*Nos. 582-584 (3)* 1.00 .70

Founding of the Vatican Apostolic Library, 500th anniv.

Mt. Argentario Monastery
A174

St. Paul of the Cross, by Giovanni Della Porta — A175

Design: 300 l, Basilica of Sts. John and Paul and burial chapel of Saint.

**1975, Nov. 27 Photo. *Perf. 14x13½***

**585** A174 50 l multi .20 .20
**586** A175 150 l multi .25 .20
**587** A174 300 l multi .45 .25
*Nos. 585-587 (3)* .90 .65

Bicentenary of death of St. Paul of the Cross, founder of the Passionist religious order in 1737.

Praying Women, by Fra Angelico — A176

International Women's Year: 200 l, Seated women, by Fra Angelico.

**1975, Nov. 27 *Perf. 13½x14***

**588** A176 100 l multi .20 .20
**589** A176 200 l multi .40 .25

Virgin and Child in Glory, by Titian
A177

Design: 300 l, The Six Saints, by Titian. Designs from "The Madonna in Glory with the Child Jesus and Six Saints."

**1976, May 13 Engr. *Perf. 14x13½***

**590** A177 100 l rose magenta .25 .20
**591** A177 300 l rose magenta .50 .40
***a.*** Pair, #590-591 .75 .60

Titian (1477-1576), painter.

A178

A179

Designs: 150 l, Eucharist, wheat and globe. 200 l, Hands Holding Eucharist. 400 l, Hungry mankind reaching for the Eucharist.

**1976, July 2 Photo. *Perf. 13½x14***

**592** A178 150 l gold, red & bl .20 .20
**593** A178 200 l gold & blue .25 .25
**594** A178 400 l gold, grn & brn .40 .40
*Nos. 592-594 (3)* .85 .85

41st Intl. Eucharistic Congress, Philadelphia, PA, Aug. 1-8.

**1976, Sept. 30 Photo. *Perf. 13½x14***

Details from Transfiguration by Raphael: 30 l, Moses Holding Tablets. 40 l, Transfigured Christ. 50 l, Prophet Elijah with book. 100 l, Apostles John and Peter. 150 l, Group of women. 200 l, Landscape.

**595** A179 30 l ocher & multi .20 .20
**596** A179 40 l red & multi .20 .20
**597** A179 50 l violet & multi .20 .20
**598** A179 100 l multicolored .20 .20
**599** A179 150 l green & multi .25 .20
**600** A179 200 l ocher & multi .35 .25
*Nos. 595-600 (6)* 1.40 1.25

St. John's Tower
A180

Roman Views: 100 l, Fountain of the Sacrament. 120 l, Fountain at entrance to the gardens. 180 l, Basilica, Cupola of St. Peter's and Sacristy. 250 l, Borgia Tower and Sistine Chapel. 300 l, Apostolic Palace and Courtyard of St. Damasius.

**Litho. & Engr.**

**1976, Nov. 23 *Perf. 14***

**601** A180 50 l gray & black .20 .20
**602** A180 100 l salmon & dk brn .20 .20
**603** A180 120 l citron & dk grn .20 .20
**604** A180 180 l pale gray & blk .20 .20
**605** A180 250 l yellow & brn .25 .20
**606** A180 300 l pale lilac & mag .30 .25
*Nos. 601-606 (6)* 1.35 1.25

The Lord's Creatures
A181

70 l, Brother Sun. 100 l, Sister Moon and Stars. 130 l, Sister Water. 170 l, Praise in infirmities and tribulations. 200 l, Praise for bodily death. Designs are illustrations by Duilio Cambellotti for "The Canticle of Brother Sun," by St. Francis.

**1977, Mar. 10 Photo. *Perf. 14x13½***

**607** A181 50 l multi .20 .20
**608** A181 70 l multi .20 .20
**609** A181 100 l multi .20 .20
**610** A181 130 l multi .20 .20
**611** A181 170 l multi .20 .20
**612** A181 200 l multi .25 .20
*Nos. 607-612 (6)* 1.25 1.20

St. Francis of Assisi, 750th death anniv.

Sts. Peter and Paul
A182

Design: 350 l, Pope Gregory XI and St. Catherine of Siena. Designs are after fresco by Giorgio Vasari.

**1977, May 20 Engr. *Perf. 14***

**613** 170 l black .30 .20
**614** 350 l black .50 .30
***a.*** A182 Pair, #613-614 .85 .60

Return of Pope Gregory XI from Avignon, 600th anniv.

Dormition of the Virgin — A183

**1977, July 5 Photo. *Perf. 13½x14***

Design: 400 l, Virgin Mary in Heaven. Both designs after miniatures in Latin manuscripts, Vatican Library.

**615** A183 200 l multi .30 .20
**616** A183 400 l multi .55 .30

Feast of the Assumption.

The Nile Deity, Roman Sculpture — A184

Sculptures: 120 l, Head of Pericles. 130 l, Roman Couple Joining Hands. 150 l, Apollo Belvedere, head. 170 l, Laocoon, head. 350 l, Apollo Belvedere, torso.

**1977, Sept. 29 *Perf. 14x13½***

**617** A184 50 l multi .20 .20
**618** A184 120 l multi .20 .20
**619** A184 130 l multi .20 .20
**620** A184 150 l multi .20 .20
**621** A184 170 l multi .20 .20
**622** A184 350 l multi .30 .30
*Nos. 617-622 (6)* 1.30 1.30

Classical sculptures in Vatican Museums.

Creation of Man and Woman — A185

Designs: 70 l, Three youths in the furnace. 100 l, Adoration of the Kings. 130 l, Raising of Lazarus. 200 l, The Good Shepherd. 400 l, Chrismon, Cross, sleeping soldiers (Resurrection). Designs are bas-reliefs from Christian sarcophagi, 250-350 A.D., found in Roman excavations.

**1977, Dec. 9 Photo. *Perf. 14x13½***

**623** A185 50 l multi .20 .20
**624** A185 70 l multi .20 .20
**625** A185 100 l multi .20 .20
**626** A185 130 l multi .20 .20
**627** A185 200 l multi .20 .20
**628** A185 400 l multi .35 .25
*Nos. 623-628 (6)* 1.35 1.25

Madonna with the Parrot and Rubens Self-portrait
A186

**1977, Dec. 9 *Perf. 13½x14***

**629** A186 350 l multi .50 .50

Peter Paul Rubens (1577-1640).

Pope Paul VI, by Lino Bianchi Barriviera
A187

Design: 350 l, Christ's Face, by Pericle Fazzini and arms of Pope Paul VI.

**1978, Mar. 9 Photo. *Perf. 14***

**630** A187 350 l multi .50 .30
**631** A187 400 l multi .50 .40

80th birthday of Pope Paul VI.

Pope Pius IX (1792-1878)
A188

Designs: 130 l, Arms of Pope Pius IX. 170 l, Seal of Pius IX, used to sign definition of Dogma of Immaculate Conception.

**Litho. & Engr.**

**1978, May 9 *Perf. 13x14***

**632** A188 130 l multi .20 .20
**633** A188 170 l multi .30 .20
**634** A188 200 l multi .35 .20
*Nos. 632-634 (3)* .85 .60

**Interregnum Issues**

Keys of St. Peter and Papal Chamberlain's Insignia
A189 A190

**1978, Aug. 23 Photo. *Perf. 14***

**635** A189 120 l purple & lt green .30 .20
**636** A189 150 l purple & salmon .35 .20
**637** A189 250 l purple & yellow .35 .20
*Nos. 635-637 (3)* 1.00 .60

**1978, Oct. 12 Photo. *Perf. 14***

**638** A190 120 l black & multi .25 .20
**639** A190 200 l black & multi .25 .20
**640** A190 250 l black & multi .25 .20
*Nos. 638-640 (3)* .75 .60

Pope John Paul I, Pope from Aug. 26 to Sept. 28, 1978 — A191

Pope John Paul I: 70 l, Sitting on his throne. 250 l, Walking in Vatican garden. 350 l, Giving blessing, horiz.

**1978, Dec. 11** ***Perf. 13x14, 14x13***

**641** A191 70 l multi .20 .20
**642** A191 120 l multi .25 .25
**643** A191 250 l multi .30 .30
**644** A191 350 l multi .40 .40
*Nos. 641-644 (4)* 1.15 1.15

Arms of Pope John Paul II A192

Designs: 250 l, Pope John Paul II raising hand in blessing. 400 l, Jesus giving keys to St. Peter.

**Litho. & Engr.**

**1979, Mar. 22** ***Perf. 14x13***

**645** A192 170 l black & multi .25 .25
**646** A192 250 l black & multi .30 .30
**647** A192 400 l black & multi .55 .45
*Nos. 645-647 (3)* 1.10 1.00

Inauguration of pontificate of Pope John Paul II.

Martyrdom of St. Stanislas A193

St. Basil the Great Instructing Monk A194

Designs: 150 l, St. Stanislas appearing to the people. 250 l, Gold reliquary, 1504, containing saint's head. 500 l, View of Cracow Cathedral.

**1979, May 18** **Photo.** ***Perf. 14***

**648** A193 120 l multi .20 .20
**649** A193 150 l multi .20 .20
**650** A193 250 l multi .35 .30
**651** A193 500 l multi .75 .65
*Nos. 648-651 (4)* 1.50 1.35

900th anniversary of martyrdom of St. Stanislas (1030-1079), patron saint of Poland.

**Engr. & Photo.**

**1979, June 25** ***Perf. 13½x14***

St. Basil the Great, 16th cent. of death: 520 l, St. Basil the Great visiting the sick.

**652** A194 150 l multi .20 .20
**653** A194 520 l multi .85 .70

Father Secchi, Solar Protuberance, Spectrum and Meteorograph — A195

Father Angelo Secchi (1818-1878), astronomer, solar protuberance, spectrum and: 220 l, Spectroscope. 300 l, Telescope.

**Litho. & Engr.**

**1979, June 25** ***Perf. 14x13½***

**654** A195 180 l multi .25 .25
**655** A195 220 l multi .35 .30
**656** A195 300 l multi .40 .30
*Nos. 654-656 (3)* 1.00 .85

Vatican City A196

Papal Arms and Portraits: 70 l, Pius XI. 120 l, Pius XII. 150 l, John XXIII. 170 l, Paul VI. 250 l, John Paul I. 450 l, John Paul II.

**1979, Oct. 11** **Photo.** ***Perf. 14x13½***

**657** A196 50 l multi .20 .20
**658** A196 70 l multi .20 .20
**659** A196 120 l multi .20 .20
**660** A196 150 l multi .20 .20
**661** A196 170 l multi .25 .25
**662** A196 250 l multi .30 .30
**663** A196 450 l multi .65 .50
*Nos. 657-663 (7)* 2.00 1.85

Vatican City State, 50th anniversary.

Infant, by Andrea Della Robbia, IYC Emblem — A197

IYC Emblem and Della Robbia Bas Reliefs, Hospital of the Innocents, Florence.

**Engr. & Photo.**

**1979, Nov. 27** ***Perf. 13½x14***

**664** A197 50 l multi .20 .20
**665** A197 120 l multi .20 .20
**666** A197 200 l multi .30 .20
**667** A197 350 l multi .50 .40
*Nos. 664-667 (4)* 1.20 1.00

International Year of the Child.

Abbot Desiderius Giving Codex to St. Benedict — A198

Illuminated Letters and Illustrations, Codices, Vatican Apostolic Library: 100 l, St. Benedict writing the Rule. 150 l, Page from the Rule. 220 l, Death of St. Benedict. 450 l, Montecassino (after painting by Paul Bril).

**1980, Mar. 21** **Photo.** ***Perf. 14x13½***

**668** A198 80 l multi .20 .20
**669** A198 100 l multi .20 .20
**670** A198 150 l multi .25 .25
**671** A198 220 l multi .30 .30
**672** A198 450 l multi .60 .55
*Nos. 668-672 (5)* 1.55 1.50

St. Benedict of Nursia (patron saint of Europe), 1500th birth anniversary.

Bernini, Medallion Showing Baldacchino in St. Peter's — A199

Gian Lorenzo Bernini (1598-1680), Architect (Self-portrait and Medallion): 170 l, St. Peter's Square with third wing (never built). 250 l, Bronze chair, Doctors of the Church. 350 l, Apostolic Palace stairway.

**1980, Oct. 16** **Litho.** ***Perf. 14x13½***

**673** A199 80 l multicolored .20 .20
**674** A199 170 l multicolored .25 .25
**675** A199 250 l multicolored .35 .30
**676** A199 350 l multicolored .55 .35
*Nos. 673-676 (4)* 1.35 1.10

St. Albertus Magnus on Mission of Peace — A200

**1980, Nov. 18** **Litho.** ***Perf. 13½x14***

**677** A200 300 l shown .40 .30
**678** A200 400 l As bishop .55 .40

St. Albertus Magnus, 700th death anniv.

Communion of the Saints — A201

**1980, Nov. 18** ***Perf. 14x13½***

**679** A201 250 l shown .35 .25
**680** A201 500 l Christ and saints .65 .60

Feast of All Saints.

Guglielmo Marconi and Pope Pius XI, Vatican Radio Emblem, Vatican Arms A202

Designs: 150 l, Microphone, Bible text. 200 l, St. Maria di Galeria Radio Center antenna, Archangel Gabriel statue. 600 l, Pope John Paul II.

**1981, Feb. 12** **Photo.** ***Perf. 14x13½***

**681** A202 100 l shown .20 .20
**682** A202 150 l multicolored .25 .20
**683** A202 200 l multicolored .30 .25
**684** A202 600 l multicolored .80 .65
*Nos. 681-684 (4)* 1.55 1.30

Vatican Radio, 50th anniversary.

Virgil Seated at Podium, Vergilius Romanus — A203

**1981, Apr. 23** **Litho.** ***Perf. 14***

**685** A203 350 l multicolored .75 .65
**686** A203 600 l multicolored 1.40 1.10

2000th birth anniversary of Virgil.
Issued in sheets of 16 stamps plus 9 labels.

Congress Emblem A204

Congress Emblem and: 150 l, Virgin appearing to St. Bernadette. 200 l, Pilgrims going to Lourdes. 500 l, Bishop and pilgrims.

**1981, June 22** **Photo.**

**687** A204 80 l multicolored .20 .20
**688** A204 150 l multicolored .20 .20
**689** A204 200 l multicolored .30 .30
**690** A204 500 l multicolored .60 .60
*Nos. 687-690 (4)* 1.30 1.30

42nd Intl. Eucharistic Congress, Lourdes, France, July 16-23.

Intl. Year of the Disabled A205

**1981, Sept. 29** **Photo.** ***Perf. 14x13½***

**691** A205 600 l multicolored .90 .80

Jan van Ruusbroec, Flemish Mystic, 500th Birth Anniv. — A206

**Litho. & Engr.**

**1981, Sept. 29** ***Perf. 13½x14***

**692** A206 200 l shown .35 .35
**693** A206 300 l Portrait .45 .45

1980 Journeys of Pope John Paul II — A207

**1981, Dec. 3** **Photo.** ***Perf. 13½x14½***

**694** A207 50 l Papal arms .20 .20
**695** A207 100 l Map of Africa .20 .20
**696** A207 120 l Crucifix .20 .20
**697** A207 150 l Communion .20 .20
**698** A207 200 l African bishop .20 .20
**699** A207 250 l Visiting sick .30 .30
**700** A207 300 l Notre Dame, France .40 .40
**701** A207 400 l UNESCO speech .50 .50
**702** A207 600 l Christ of the Andes, Brazil .90 .90
**703** A207 700 l Cologne Cathedral, Germany 1.00 1.00
**704** A207 900 l John Paul II 1.10 1.10
*Nos. 694-704 (11)* 5.20 5.20

700th Death Anniv. of St. Agnes of Prague — A208

Designs: 700 l, Handing order to Grand Master of the Crosiers of the Red Star. 900 l, Receiving letter from St. Clare.

**1982, Feb. 16** **Photo.** ***Perf. 13½x14***

**705** A208 700 l multicolored 1.00 1.00
**706** A208 900 l multicolored 1.10 1.10

Pueri Cantores A209

St. Teresa of Avila (1515-1582) A210

Luca Della Robbia (1400-1482), Sculptor: No. 708, Pueri Cantores, diff. No. 709, Virgin in Prayer (44x36mm).

**Photo. & Engr.**

**1982, May 21** *Perf. 14*

**707** A209 1000 l multicolored 1.25 1.10
**708** A209 1000 l multicolored 1.25 1.10
**709** A209 1000 l multicolored 1.25 1.10
*a.* Strip of 3, #707-709 4.00 3.50

**1982, Sept. 23** **Photo.**

Sketches of St. Teresa by Riccardo Tommasi-Ferroni.

**710** A210 200 l multicolored .25 .25
**711** A210 600 l multicolored .80 .80
**712** A210 1000 l multicolored 1.25 1.25
*Nos. 710-712 (3)* 2.30 2.30

Christmas A211

Nativity Bas-Reliefs: 300 l, Wit Stwosz, Church of the Virgin Mary, Cracow. 450 l, Enrico Manfrini.

**Photo. & Engr.**

**1982, Nov. 23** *Perf. 14*

**713** A211 300 l multicolored .45 .45
**714** A211 450 l multicolored .65 .65

400th Anniv. of Gregorian Calendar — A212

Sculpture Details, Tomb of Pope Gregory XIII, Vatican Basilica.

**1982, Nov. 23** **Engr.** *Perf. 13½x14*

**715** A212 200 l Surveying the globe .25 .25
**716** A212 300 l Receiving Edict of Reform .40 .40
**717** A212 700 l Presenting edict .90 .90
*a.* Souvenir sheet of 3, #715-717 2.50 2.50
*Nos. 715-717 (3)* 1.55 1.55

Souvenir Sheets

Greek Vase — A213

**1983, Mar. 10** **Litho.** *Perf. 13½x14*

**718** Sheet of 6 3.25 2.00
*a.* A213 100 l shown .20 .20
*b.* A213 200 l Italian vase .35 .25
*c.* A213 250 l Female terra-cotta bust .50 .30
*d.* A213 300 l Marcus Aurelius bust .55 .35
*e.* A213 350 l Bird fresco .65 .45
*f.* A213 400 l Pope Clement VIII vestment .75 .45

**1983, June 14** **Litho.** *Perf. 13½x14*

**719** Sheet of 6 3.50 3.50
*a.* A213 100 l Horse's head, Etruscan terra cotta .20 .20
*b.* A213 200 l Horseman, Greek fragment .25 .20
*c.* A213 300 l Male head, Etruscan .30 .20
*d.* A213 400 l Apollo Belvedere head .50 .25
*e.* A213 500 l Moses, Roman fresco .55 .35
*f.* A213 1000 l Madonna and Child, by Bernardo Daddi 1.25 .70

**1983, Nov. 10** **Litho.** *Perf. 13½x14*

**720** Sheet of 6 4.00 4.00
*a.* A213 150 l Greek cup, Oedipus and the Sphinx .25 .20
*b.* A213 200 l Etruscan bronze statue of a child .30 .20
*c.* A213 350 l Emperor Augustus marble statue .40 .25
*d.* A213 400 l Good Shepherd marble statue .55 .30
*e.* A213 500 l St. Nicholas Saving a ship by G. da Fabriano .70 .40
*f.* A213 1200 l The Holy face by G. Rouault 1.50 1.00

Vatican Collection: The Papacy and Art - US 1983 exhibition, New York, Chicago, San Francisco.

Extraordinary Holy Year, 1983-84 (1950th Anniv. of Redemption) A214

Sketches by Giovanni Hajnal.

**1983, Mar. 10** **Photo. & Engr.**

**721** A214 300 l Crucifixion .45 .30
**722** A214 350 l Christ the Redeemer .55 .40
**723** A214 400 l Pope .45 .45
**724** A214 2000 l Holy Spirit 2.75 2.75
*Nos. 721-724 (4)* 4.20 3.90

Theology, by Raphael (1483-1517) A215

St. Casimir of Lithuania (1458-1484) A217

Gregor Johann Mendel (1822-1884), Biologist — A216

Allegories, Room of the Segnatura.

**1983, June 14**

**725** A215 50 l shown .20 .20
**726** A215 400 l Poetry .60 .60
**727** A215 500 l Justice .70 .70
**728** A215 1200 l Philosphy 1.75 1.75
*Nos. 725-728 (4)* 3.25 3.25

**Photo. & Engr.**

**1984, Feb. 28** *Perf. 14x13½*

Phases of pea plant hybridization.

**729** A216 450 l multicolored .60 .45
**730** A216 1500 l multicolored 2.00 1.50

**1984, Feb. 28** *Perf. 14*

**731** A217 550 l multicolored .90 .55
**732** A217 1200 l multicolored 2.00 1.25

Pontifical Academy of Sciences — A218

**1984, June 18** **Litho. & Engr.**

**733** A218 150 l shown .25 .20
**734** A218 450 l Secret Archives .65 .55
**735** A218 550 l Apostolic Library .85 .65
**736** A218 1500 l Observatory 2.25 1.75
*Nos. 733-736 (4)* 4.00 3.15

Papal Journeys A218a

**1984-85** **Photo.** *Perf. 13½x14½*

**737** A218a 50 l Pakistan .20 .20
**738** A218a 100 l Philippines .20 .20
**739** A218a 150 l Guam .30 .20
**740** A218a 250 l Japan .45 .30
**741** A218a 300 l Alaska .55 .50
**742** A218a 400 l Africa .80 .50
**743** A218a 450 l Portugal .90 .60
*a.* Bklt. pane, 4 ea #738, 741-743 + 4 labels ('85) 12.00
**744** A218a 550 l Grt. Britain 1.10 .70
**745** A218a 1000 l Argentina 2.00 1.40
**746** A218a 1500 l Switzerland 3.00 1.90
**747** A218a 2500 l San Marino 4.00 3.25
**748** A218a 4000 l Spain 8.00 5.25
*Nos. 737-748 (12)* 21.50 15.00

Issued: Nos. 737-748, 10/2/84; No. 743a, 3/14/85.

St. Damasus I (b. 304) A219

St. Damasus I and: 200 l, Sepulchre of Sts. Marcellinus and Peter. 500 l, Epigraph of St. Januarius. 2000 l, Basilica, Church of the Martyrs Simplicius, Faustinus and Beatrice.

**1984, Nov. 27** **Photo.** *Perf. 14x13½*

**749** A219 200 l multicolored .35 .25
**750** A219 500 l multicolored .90 .60
**751** A219 2000 l multicolored 3.75 2.25
*Nos. 749-751 (3)* 5.00 3.10

St. Methodius (d. 885) — A220

St. Methodius and: 500 l, Madonna and Christ. 600 l, St. Cyril, carrying the body of St. Clement I. 1700 l, Sts. Benedict and Cyril, patrons of Europe.

**Photo. & Engr.**

**1985, May 7** *Perf. 13½x14*

**752** A220 500 l multicolored .90 .50
**753** A220 600 l multicolored 1.10 .60
**754** A220 1700 l multicolored 3.25 1.60
*Nos. 752-754 (3)* 5.25 2.70

St. Thomas More (1477-1535) — A221

St. Thomas More (from a portrait by Hans Holbein) and: 250 l, map of British Isles. 400 l, Frontispiece of Utopia. 2000 l, Frontispiece of Domenico Regi's biography of More.

**Litho. & Engr.**

**1985, May 7** *Perf. 14x13½*

**755** A221 250 l multicolored .45 .25
**756** A221 400 l multicolored .80 .40
**757** A221 2000 l multicolored 3.75 2.00
*Nos. 755-757 (3)* 5.00 2.65

St. Gregory VII (c. 1020-85) A222

Designs: 150 l, Eagle from Byzantine door, St. Paul's Basilica, Rome. 450 l, St. Gregory blessing. 2500 l, Sarcophagus.

*Perf. 13½x14, 14x13½*

**1985, June 18** **Photo.**

**758** A222 150 l multi, vert. .25 .20
**759** A222 450 l multi, vert. .75 .45
**760** A222 2500 l multicolored 4.00 2.50
*Nos. 758-760 (3)* 5.00 3.15

43rd Intl. Eucharistic Congress — A223

Emblem, host, cross and: 100 l, Outline map of Africa. 400 l, Altar and Assembly of Bishops. 600 l, African chalice. 2300 l, African Christian family.

**Photo. & Engr.**

**1985, June 18** *Perf. 13½x14*

**761** A223 100 l multicolored .20 .20
**762** A223 400 l multicolored .60 .40
**763** A223 600 l multicolored .90 .55
**764** A223 2300 l multicolored 3.50 2.00
*Nos. 761-764 (4)* 5.20 3.15

Concordat Agreement Ratification A224

**1985, Oct. 15** **Photo.** *Perf. 14x13½*

**765** A224 400 l Papal arms, map of Italy .65 .35

Coaches A225

**1985, Oct. 15** **Litho. & Engr.**

**766** A225 450 l dp lil rose & int bl .75 .35
**767** A225 1500 l brt bl & dp lil rose 2.00 1.40
*a.* Souvenir sheet of 2, #766-767, perf. 13½x12½ 3.25 3.25

Italia '85.

Intl. Peace Year 1986 — A226

Biblical and gospel texts: 50 l, Isaiah 2:4. 350 l, Isaiah 52:7. 450 l, Matthew 5:9. 650 l, Luke 2:14. 2000 l, Message for World Peace, speech of Pope John Paul II, Jan. 1, 1986.

**1986, Apr. 14 Photo. *Perf. 14***

**768** A226 50 l multicolored .20 .20
**769** A226 350 l multicolored .55 .30
**770** A226 450 l multicolored .80 .40
**771** A226 650 l multicolored 1.10 .60
**772** A226 2000 l multicolored 3.50 2.00
*Nos. 768-772 (5)* 6.15 3.50

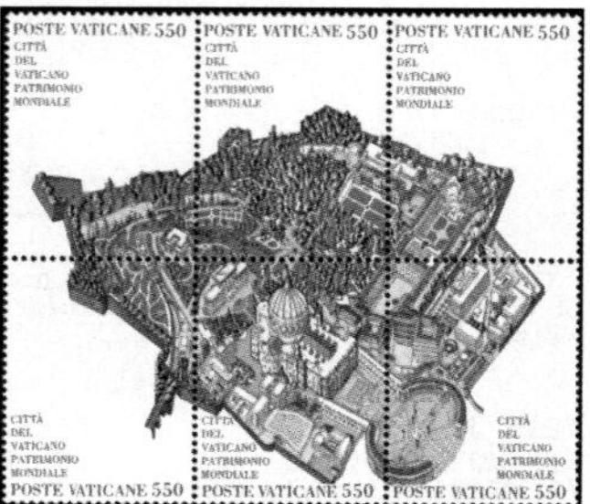


Vatican City — A227

**1986, Apr. 14 *Perf. 13½x14***

**773** A227 Block of 6 6.75 3.00
***a.-f.*** 550 l, any single 1.10 .50

UNESCO World Heritage Campaign. No. 773 has continuous design.

Patron Saints of the Sick — A228

Conversion of St. Augustine (354-430) in 387 — A230

Pontifical Academy of Sciences, 50th Anniv. A229

Designs: No. 774, St. Camillus de Lellis rescuing invalid during Tiber flood, by Pierre Subleyras (1699-1749). No. 775, St. John of God with invalids, by Gomez Moreno (1834-1918). 2000 l, Pope John Paul II visiting the sick.

**Litho. & Engr.**

**1986, June 12 *Perf. 13½x14***

**774** A228 700 l multicolored 1.25 .60
**775** A228 700 l multicolored 1.25 .60
**776** A228 2000 l multicolored 3.50 1.90
*Nos. 774-776 (3)* 6.00 3.10

**Litho. & Engr.**

**1986, Oct. 2 *Perf. 14x13½***

School of Athens (details), by Raphael: 1500 l, Scribes. 2500 l, Students learning math.

**777** A229 1500 l multicolored 2.75 1.50
**778** A229 2500 l multicolored 4.25 2.50

**1987, Apr. 7 Photo. *Perf. 13½x14***

Religious art: 300 l, St. Augustine reading St. Paul's Epistles, fresco by Benozzo Gozzoli (1420-1498), Church of St. Augustine, San Gimignano. 400 l, Baptism of St. Augustine, painting by Bartolomeo di Gentile (1470-1534), Vatican Art Gallery. 500 l, Ecstasy of St. Augustine, fresco by Benozzo Gozzoli, Church of St. Augustine. 2200 l, St. Augustine, detail of Disputa del Sacramento, fresco by Raphael (1483-1520), Room of the Segnatura, Apostolic Palace.

**779** A230 300 l multicolored .50 .30
**780** A230 400 l multicolored .70 .45
**781** A230 500 l multicolored .85 .50
**782** A230 2200 l multicolored 3.75 2.25
*Nos. 779-782 (4)* 5.80 3.50

A231

Christianization Anniversaries A232

Seals: 700 l, Church of Riga, 1234-1269. 2400 l, Marian Basilica of the Assumption, Aglona, 1780.

**1987, June 2 Photo. *Perf. 13½x14***

**783** A231 700 l multicolored 1.40 .95
**784** A231 2400 l multicolored 4.75 3.25

Christianization of Latvia, 800th anniv.

**1987, June 2 *Perf. 13½x14***

Designs: 200 l, Christ, statue in the Lithuanian Chapel, Vatican Crypt. 700 l, Two Angels and Our Lady Holding the Body of Christ, by a Lithuanian artist. 3000 l, Lithuanian shrine.

**785** A232 200 l multicolored .30 .25
**786** A232 700 l multicolored 1.10 .75
**787** A232 3000 l multicolored 4.50 3.00
*Nos. 785-787 (3)* 5.90 4.00

Christianization of Lithuania, 600th anniv.

OLYMPHILEX '87, Rome, Aug. 29-Sept. 9 — A233

Details of mosaic from the Baths of Caracalla: 400 l, Judge. 500 l, Athlete. 600 l, Athlete, diff. 2000 l, Athlete, diff.

**Litho. & Engr.**

**1987, Aug. 29 *Perf. 14***

**788** A233 400 l multicolored .65 .45
**789** A233 500 l multicolored .85 .55
**790** A233 600 l multicolored 1.00 .65
**791** A233 2000 l multicolored 3.25 2.25
*Nos. 788-791 (4)* 5.75 3.90

**Souvenir Sheet**

**792** Sheet of 4 + 4 labels 5.75 5.75
***a.*** A233 400 l like No. 788 .65 .65
***b.*** A233 500 l like No. 789 .80 .80
***c.*** A233 600 l like No. 780 1.00 1.00
***d.*** A233 2000 l like No. 791 3.25 3.25

Stamps from souvenir sheet have a Greek border in blue surrounding vignettes (pictured). Nos. 788-791 have single line border in blue. No. 792 has 4 labels picturing the papal arms, a goblet, a crown and the exhibition emblem.

Inauguration of the Philatelic and Numismatic Museum — A235

Designs: 400 l, Philatelic department, Vatican City, No. 1. 3500 l, Numismatic department, 1000-lire coin of 1986.

**1987, Sept. 29 Photo. *Perf. 14x13½***

**793** A235 400 l multicolored .60 .45
**794** A235 3500 l multicolored 5.50 3.75

Journeys of Pope John Paul II, 1985-86 A236

Designs: 50 l, Venezuela, Peru, Ecuador and Trinidad & Tobago, 1985. 250 l, The Netherlands, Luxembourg, Belgium, 1985. 400 l, Togo, Ivory Coast, Cameroun, Central Africa, Zaire, Kenya and Morocco, 1985. 500 l, Liechtenstein, 1986. 4000 l, Bangladesh, Singapore, Fiji, New Zealand, Australia and Seychelles, 1986.

**1987, Oct. 27 Photo. *Perf. 14x13½***

**795** A236 50 l multicolored .20 .20
**796** A236 250 l multicolored .65 .45
**797** A236 400 l multicolored 1.10 .70
**798** A236 500 l multicolored 1.25 .85
**799** A236 600 l multicolored 1.60 1.00
**800** A236 700 l multicolored 1.90 1.25
**801** A236 2500 l multicolored 6.75 4.50
**802** A236 4000 l multicolored 11.00 7.25
*Nos. 795-802 (8)* 24.45 16.20

A237

A238

Transfer of St. Nicholas Relics from Myra to Bari, 900th anniv.: 500 l, Arrival of relics at Bari. 700 l, Act of charity, three improverished women. 3000 l, Miraculous rescue of ship.

**1987, Dec. 3 *Perf. 13½x14***

**803** A237 500 l multicolored 2.00 1.25
**804** A237 700 l multicolored 3.00 2.00
**805** A237 3000 l multicolored 12.50 8.00
*Nos. 803-805 (3)* 17.50 11.25

St. Nicholas of Bari (c. 270-352), bishop of Myra. Legend of Santa Claus originated because of his charitable works. Printed in sheets of 8 + 16 se-tenant labels picturing Santa Claus.

**1988, Apr. 19 Photo.**

Children and: 500 l, Sister of the Institute of the Daughters of Mary Help of Christians. 1000 l, St. John Bosco. 2000 l, Salesian lay brother. Printed in a continuous design.

**806** Strip of 3 5.25 4.00
***a.*** A238 500 l multicolored .70 .50
***b.*** A238 1000 l multicolored 1.50 1.00
***c.*** A238 2000 l multicolored 3.00 2.00

St. John Bosco (1815-1888), educator.

A239

A240

**1988, June 16 Photo. *Perf. 13½x14***

**807** A239 50 l Annunciation .20 .20
**808** A239 300 l Nativity .40 .25
**809** A239 500 l Pentecost .65 .40
**810** A239 750 l Assumption 1.10 .60
**811** A239 1000 l Mother of the Church 1.40 .80
**812** A239 2400 l Refuge of Sinners 3.25 1.90
*Nos. 807-812 (6)* 7.00 4.15

Marian Year, 1987-88.

**1988, June 16**

Baptism of the Rus' of Kiev, Millennium: 450 l, "Prince St. Vladimir the Great," from a 15th cent. icon. 650 l, Cathedral of St. Sophia, Kiev. 2500 l, "Mother of God in Prayer," from a mosaic at the cathedral.

**813** A240 450 l multicolored .75 .45
**814** A240 650 l multicolored 1.00 .65
**815** A240 2500 l multicolored 3.75 2.25
*Nos. 813-815 (3)* 5.50 3.35

Paintings by Paolo Veronese (1528-1588) — A241

Designs: 550 l, Marriage of Cana (Madonna and Christ) the Louvre, Paris. 650 l, Self-portrait of the Artist, Villa Barbaro of Maser, Treviso. 3000 l, Marriage of Cana (woman and two men).

***Perf. 13½x14, 14x13½***

**1988, Sept. 29 Photo. & Engr.**

**816** A241 550 l multicolored .80 .45
**817** A241 650 l multi, horiz. .95 .55
**818** A241 3000 l multicolored 4.25 2.50
*Nos. 816-818 (3)* 6.00 3.50

Christmas A242

Luke 2:14 and: 50 l, Angel facing LR. 400 l, Angel facing UR. 500 l, Angel facing LL. 550 l, Shepherds. 850 l, Nativity. 1500 l, Magi.

**1988, Dec. 12 Photo. *Perf. 13½x14***

**819** A242 50 l multicolored .20 .20
**820** A242 400 l multicolored .60 .30
**821** A242 500 l multicolored .70 .35
**822** A242 550 l multicolored .80 .40
**823** A242 850 l multicolored 1.25 .60
**824** A242 1500 l multicolored 2.25 1.00
*Nos. 819-824 (6)* 5.80 2.85

### Souvenir Sheet

**825** Sheet of 6 — 5.75 5.75
- *a.* A242 50 l gold & multi — .20 .20
- *b.* A242 400 l gold & multi — .60 .30
- *c.* A242 500 l gold & multi — .70 .35
- *d.* A242 550 l gold & multi — .80 .40
- *e.* A242 850 l gold & multi — 1.25 .60
- *f.* A242 1500 l gold & multi — 2.25 1.00

No. 825 has continuous design.

Feast of the Visitation, 600th Anniv. — A243

Illuminations: 550 l, The Annunciation. 750 l, The Visitation (Virgin and St. Elizabeth). 2500 l, Mary, Elizabeth and infants.

**1989, May 5 Photo. *Perf. 13½x14***

**826** A243 550 l multicolored .80 .40
**827** A243 750 l multicolored 1.10 .55
**828** A243 2500 l multicolored 3.75 1.90
*Nos. 826-828 (3)* 5.65 2.85

### Souvenir Sheet

Gregorian Egyptian Museum, 150th Anniv. — A244

Designs: 400 l, Apis. 650 l, Isis and Apis dicephalous bust. 750 l, Statue of the physician Ugiahorresne. 2400 l, Pharaoh Mentuhotep.

**Litho. & Engr.**

**1989, May 5 *Perf. 14x13½***

**829** Sheet of 4 — 6.00 6.00
- *a.* A244 400 l multicolored — .55 .30
- *b.* A244 650 l multicolored — .90 .50
- *c.* A244 750 l multicolored — 1.10 .55
- *d.* A244 2400 l multicolored — 3.25 1.75

A245

A246

Birds from engravings by Eleazar Albin in *Histoire Naturelle des Oiseaux,* 1750.

**1989, June 13 Photo. *Perf. 12***

**Granite Paper**

**830** A245 100 l Parrot .20 .20
**831** A245 150 l Green woodpecker .20 .20
**832** A245 200 l Crested and common wrens .25 .20
**833** A245 350 l Kingfisher .45 .25
**834** A245 500 l Red grosbeak of Virginia .65 .30
**835** A245 700 l Bullfinch .90 .45
**836** A245 1500 l Lapwing plover 2.00 1.00
**837** A245 3000 l French teal 4.00 2.00
*Nos. 830-837 (8)* 8.65 4.60

**Photo. & Engr.**

**1989, Sept. 29 *Perf. 13½x14***

Symbols of the Eucharist.

**838** A246 550 l shown .80 .40
**839** A246 850 l multi, diff. 1.25 .65
**840** A246 1000 l multi, diff. 1.50 .75
**841** A246 2500 l multi, diff. 3.75 1.90
*Nos. 838-841 (4)* 7.30 3.70

44th Intl. Eucharistic Cong., Seoul, Oct. 5-8.

Ecclesiastical Hierarchy in the US, Bicent. — A247

Designs: 450 l, Basilica of the Assumption of the Blessed Virgin Mary, Baltimore. 1350 l, John Carroll (1735-1815), 1st bishop of Baltimore and the US. 2400 l, Cathedral of Mary Our Queen, Baltimore.

**1989, Nov. 9 Photo. *Perf. 12***

**842** A247 450 l multicolored .65 .40
**843** A247 1350 l multicolored 2.00 1.25
**844** A247 2400 l multicolored 3.50 2.00
*Nos. 842-844 (3)* 6.15 3.65

Papal Journeys 1988 A248

Papal arms, Pope John Paul II and maps: 50 l, Uruguay, Bolivia, Peru and Paraguay, May 7-19. 550 l, Austria, June 23-27. 800 l, Zimbabwe, Botswana, Lesotho, Swaziland and Mozambique, Sept. 10-19. 1000 l, France, Oct. 8-11. 4000 l, Pastoral visits in Italy, 1978-1988.

**1989, Nov. 9 *Perf. 14x13½***

**845** A248 50 l multicolored .20 .20
**846** A248 550 l multicolored .80 .50
**847** A248 800 l multicolored 1.10 .70
**848** A248 1000 l multicolored 1.50 .90
**849** A248 4000 l multicolored 5.75 3.50
*Nos. 845-849 (5)* 9.35 5.80

St. Angela Merici (c. 1474-1540) A249

Designs: 700 l, The vision of the mystical stair, Prophecy of the Ursulines. 800 l, Evangelical counsel. 2800 l, Ursulines mission continued.

**1990, Apr. 5 Photo. *Perf. 13½x14***

**850** A249 700 l multicolored 1.25 .80
**851** A249 800 l multicolored 1.40 .95
**852** A249 2800 l multicolored 4.75 3.25
*Nos. 850-852 (3)* 7.40 5.00

Caritas Intl., 40th Anniv. A250

Designs: 450 l, Abraham. 650 l, Three visitors. 800 l, Abraham and Sarah. 2000 l, Three visitors at Abraham's table.

**1990, June 5 Photo. *Perf. 12x11½***

**Granite Paper**

**853** A250 450 l multicolored .75 .45
**854** A250 650 l multicolored 1.10 .70
**855** A250 800 l multicolored 1.25 .85
**856** A250 2000 l multicolored 3.25 2.00
*Nos. 853-856 (4)* 6.35 4.00

### Souvenir Sheet

**857** Sheet of 4 — 6.00 6.00
- *a.* A250 450 l like #853 — .65 .50
- *b.* A250 650 l like #854 — 1.00 .65
- *c.* A250 800 l like #855 — 1.25 .85
- *d.* A250 2000 l like #856 — 3.00 2.00

Nos. 853-856 have a single line border in gold. Nos. 857a-857d have no border line.

No. 857 with "Pro Terremotati 1997" overprinted in sheet margin exists in limited quantities, sold for 8000 l to assist earthquake victims in Umbria and Marche, but was not officially issued by Vatican postal authorities. Value $25.

A251

A252

**1990, June 5 *Perf. 13½x14***

**858** A251 300 l Ordination of St. Willibrord .50 .30
**859** A251 700 l Stay in Antwerp 1.10 .70
**860** A251 3000 l Leaving belongings, death 4.75 3.25
*Nos. 858-860 (3)* 6.35 4.25

1300th anniv. of ministry of St. Willibrord.

**1990, Oct. 2**

Diocese of Beijing-Nanking, 300th Anniv.: 500 l, Lake Beijing. 750 l, Church of the Immaculate Conception, Beijing, 1650. 1500 l, Lake Beijing, diff. 2000 l, Church of the Redeemer, Beijing, 1703.

**861** A252 500 l multicolored .70 .45
**862** A252 750 l multicolored 1.10 .70
**863** A252 1500 l multicolored 2.25 1.40
**864** A252 2000 l multicolored 2.75 1.90
*Nos. 861-864 (4)* 6.80 4.45

Christmas A253

Details from painting by Sebastiano Mainardi.

**1990, Nov. 27 Photo. *Perf. 13***

**865** A253 50 l Choir of Angels .20 .20
**866** A253 200 l St. Joseph .30 .30
**867** A253 650 l Holy Child 1.10 1.10
**868** A253 750 l Madonna 1.25 1.25
**869** A253 2500 l Nativity scene, vert. 4.00 4.00
*Nos. 865-869 (5)* 6.85 6.85

Paintings of the Sistine Chapel — A254

Different details from lunettes: 50 l, 100 l, Eleazar. 150 l, 250 l, Jacob. 350 l, 400 l, Josiah. 500 l, 650 l, Asa. 800 l, 1000 l, Zerubbabel. 2000 l, 3000 l, Azor.

**1991, Apr. 9 Photo. *Perf. 11½***

**Granite Paper**

**870** A254 50 l multicolored .20 .20
**871** A254 100 l multicolored .20 .20
- *a.* Booklet pane of 6 .75

**872** A254 150 l multicolored .20 .20
- *a.* Booklet pane of 6 1.25

**873** A254 250 l multicolored .35 .35
**874** A254 350 l multicolored .45 .45
**875** A254 400 l multicolored .50 .50
**876** A254 500 l multicolored .70 .70
**877** A254 650 l multicolored .90 .90
- *a.* Booklet pane of 6 5.50

**878** A254 800 l multicolored 1.00 1.00
**879** A254 1000 l multicolored 1.40 1.40
**880** A254 2000 l multicolored 2.75 2.75
**881** A254 3000 l multicolored 4.00 4.00
*Nos. 870-881 (12)* 12.65 12.65

Encyclical Rerum Novarum, Cent. A255

Arms of Pope Leo XIII and: 600 l, Title page of Encyclical. 750 l, Allegory of Church's interest in workers, employers. 3500 l, Pope Leo XIII (1878-1903).

**1991, May 23 Engr. *Perf. 14x13½***

**882** A255 600 l blue & dk grn .90 .90
**883** A255 750 l sage grn & rose car 1.10 1.10
**884** A255 3500 l brt pur & dk bl 5.25 5.25
*Nos. 882-884 (3)* 7.25 7.25

Vatican Observatory, Cent. — A256

Canonization of St. Bridget, 600th Anniv. — A257

Designs: 750 l, Astrograph for making photographic sky map, 1891. 1000 l, Zeiss Double Astrograph, Lake Castelgandolfo, 1935, horiz. 3000 l, New telescope, Vatican Observatory, Mt. Graham, Arizona, 1991.

***Perf. 11½x12, 12x11½***

**1991, Oct. 1 Photo.**

**Granite Paper**

**885** A256 750 l multicolored 1.10 1.10
**886** A256 1000 l multicolored 1.50 1.50
**887** A256 3000 l multicolored 4.50 4.50
*Nos. 885-887 (3)* 7.10 7.10

**1991, Oct. 1 *Perf. 12½x13***

Designs: 1500 l, Receiving Madonna's revelations. 2000 l, Receiving Christ's revelations.

**888** A257 1500 l multicolored 2.25 2.25
**889** A257 2000 l multicolored 3.25 3.25

Journeys of Pope John Paul II, 1990 — A258

Pope John Paul II and: 200 l, Cathedral of Immaculate Conception, Ouagadougou, Burkina Faso. 550 l, St. Vitus' Cathedral,

Prague. 750 l, Our Lady of Guadaloupe's Basilica, Mexico. 1500 l, Ta' Pinu Sanctuary, Gozo. 3500 l, Cathedral of Christ the King, Gitega, Burundi.

**Litho. & Engr.**

**1991, Nov. 11** *Perf. 13½x14*

**890** A258 200 l green & multi .30 .30
**891** A258 550 l org brn & multi .85 .85
**892** A258 750 l claret & multi 1.10 1.10
**893** A258 1500 l dk brn & multi 2.25 2.25
**894** A258 3500 l grn bl & multi 5.50 5.50
*Nos. 890-894 (5)* 10.00 10.00

West Africa, Jan. 25-Feb. 1 (200 l); Czechoslovakia, Apr. 21-22 (550 l); Mexico, Curacao, May 6-14 (750 l); Malta, May 25-27 (1500 l); Tanzania, Burundi, Rwanda, Ivory Coast, Sept. 1-10 (3500 l).

A259

A260

Special Assembly for Europe of Synod of Bishops: 300 l, Colonnade of St. Peter's Basilica. 500 l, St. Peter's Basilica and Square. 4000 l, Colonnade of St. Peter's Basilica, Apostolic Palace.

**1991, Nov. 11 Engr.** *Perf. 12½x13*

**895** A259 300 l olive & blk .45 .45
**896** A259 500 l olive & blk .80 .80
**897** A259 4000 l olive & blk 6.00 6.00
*a.* Strip of 3, #895-897 8.00 8.00

No. 897a has continous design.

**1992, Mar. 24 Photo.** *Perf. 11½x12*

Discovery and Evangelization of America, 500th Anniv.: 500 l, Christopher Columbus. 600 l, Saint Peter Claver. 850 l, La Virgen de los Reyes Catolicos. 1000 l, Bishop Bartolome de las Casas. 2000 l, Father Junipero Serra. Charts: 1500 l, New World. 2500 l, Old World.

**Granite Paper**

**898** A260 500 l multicolored .75 .75
**899** A260 600 l multicolored .90 .90
**900** A260 850 l multicolored 1.25 1.25
**901** A260 1000 l multicolored 1.50 1.50
**902** A260 2000 l multicolored 3.00 3.00
*Nos. 898-902 (5)* 7.40 7.40

**Souvenir Sheet**

***Perf. 12***

**903** A260 Sheet of 2 6.00 6.00
*a.* 1500 l multicolored 2.25 2.25
*b.* 2500 l multicolored 3.75 3.75

Piero Della Francesca (d. 1492), Painter — A261

St. Giuseppe Benedetto Cottolengo (1786-1842) A262

Frescoes: 300 l, 750 l (detail), Our Lady of Childbirth. 1000 l, 3000 l (detail), Resurrection.

**1992, May 15 Photo.** *Perf. 13½x14*

**904** A261 300 l multicolored .40 .40
**905** A261 750 l multicolored 1.10 1.10
**906** A261 1000 l multicolored 1.40 1.40
**907** A261 3000 l multicolored 4.25 4.25
*Nos. 904-907 (4)* 7.15 7.15

**1992, May 15** *Perf. 11½x12*

St. Giuseppe Benedetto Cottolengo: 650 l, Comforting the sick. 850 l, With Little House of Divine Providence.

**Granite Paper**

**908** A262 650 l multicolored 1.00 1.00
**909** A262 850 l multicolored 1.40 1.40

A263

A264

Plants of the New World: a, Frumentum indicum. b, Solanum pomiferum. c, Opuntia. d, Cacaos, cacavifera. e, Solanum tuberosum, capsicum, mordens. f, Ananas sagitae folio.

**1992, Sept. 15 Photo.** *Perf. 11½x12*

**Granite Paper**

**910** Block of 6 7.50 7.50
*a.-f.* A263 850 l any single 1.25 1.25

**1992, Oct. 12** *Perf. 12½x13*

**911** A264 700 l multicolored 1.00 1.00

4th General Conference of the Latin American Episcopacy.

Christmas A265

Mosaics from Basilica of St. Maria Maggiore, Rome: 600 l, The Annunciation. 700 l, Nativity. 1000 l, Adoration of the Magi. 1500 l, Presentation to the Temple.

**1992, Nov. 24 Photo.** *Perf. 11½*

**Granite Paper**

**912** A265 600 l multicolored .90 .90
**913** A265 700 l multicolored 1.00 1.00
**914** A265 1000 l multicolored 1.40 1.40
**915** A265 1500 l multicolored 2.10 2.10
*Nos. 912-915 (4)* 5.40 5.40

St. Francis Healing Man from Ilerda, by Giotto di Bondone (1266-1337) — A266

**1993, Jan. 9 Litho.** *Perf. 13½x14*

**916** A266 1000 l multi + label 1.25 1.25

Prayer Meeting for Peace in Europe, Assisi.

Architecture of Vatican City and Rome — A267

Buildings: 200 l, St. Peter's Basilica, Vatican City. 300 l, St. John Lateran Basilica, Rome. 350 l, St. Mary Major's Basilica, Rome. 500 l, St. Paul's Basilica, Rome. 600 l, Apostolic Palace, Vatican. 700 l, Lateran Apostolic Palace, Rome. 850 l, Papal Palace, Castel Gandolfo. 1000 l, Chancery Palace, Rome. 2000 l, Palace of the Propagation of the Faith, Rome. 3000 l, St. Calixtus Palace, Rome.

**1993, Mar. 23 Photo.** *Perf. 12x11½*

**Granite Paper**

**917** A267 200 l multicolored .25 .25
*a.* Booklet pane of 4 1.10
**918** A267 300 l multicolored .40 .40
*a.* Booklet pane of 4 1.60
**919** A267 350 l multicolored .50 .50
*a.* Booklet pane of 4 2.00
**920** A267 500 l multicolored .65 .65
*a.* Booklet pane of 4 2.75
**921** A267 600 l multicolored .80 .80
**922** A267 700 l multicolored .95 .95
**923** A267 850 l multicolored 1.10 1.10
**924** A267 1000 l multicolored 1.40 1.40
**925** A267 2000 l multicolored 2.75 2.75
**926** A267 3000 l multicolored 4.00 4.00
*Nos. 917-926 (10)* 12.80 12.80

A268

Congress emblem, Vatican arms and: 500 l, Cross, grape vines. 700 l, Cross, hands breaking bread. 1500 l, Hands lifting chalice. 2500 l, Wheat, banner.

**1993, May 22 Litho.** *Perf. 14x13½*

**927** A268 500 l multicolored .60 .60
**928** A268 700 l multicolored .90 .90
**929** A268 1500 l multicolored 1.90 1.90
**930** A268 2500 l multicolored 3.00 3.00
*Nos. 927-930 (4)* 6.40 6.40

45th Intl. Eucharistic Congress, Seville.

A269

**1993, May 22 Engr.** *Perf. 13½x14*

Traditio Legis Sarcophagus, St. Peter's Basilica: a, 200 l, Sacrifice of Isaac. b, 750 l, Apostle Peter receiving law from Jesus, Apostle Paul. c, 3000 l, Christ watching servant pouring water on Pilate's hands.

**931** A269 Triptych, #a.-c. 5.00 5.00

Ascension Day, May 20.

Contemporary Art — A270

Europa: 750 l, Crucifixion, by Felice Casorati (1886-1963). 850 l, Rouen Cathedral, by Maurice Utrillo (1883-1955).

**1993, Sept. 29 Photo.** *Perf. 13*

**932** A270 750 l multicolored .95 .95
**933** A270 850 l multicolored 1.00 1.00

Death of St. John of Nepomuk, 600th Anniv. — A271

2000 l, Buildings in Prague, Charles Bridge.

**1993, Sept. 29 Litho.** *Perf. 13½x14*

**934** A271 1000 l multicolored 1.25 1.25
**935** A271 2000 l multicolored 2.50 2.50

Travels of Pope John Paul II — A272

Visits to: 600 l, Senegal, Gambia, Guinea. 1000 l, Angola, St. Thomas and Prince. 5000 l, Dominican Republic.

**1993, Nov. 23 Photo.** *Perf. 12x11½*

**Granite Paper**

**936** A272 600 l multicolored .70 .70
**937** A272 1000 l multicolored 1.25 1.25
**938** A272 5000 l multicolored 5.75 5.75
*Nos. 936-938 (3)* 7.70 7.70

Hans Holbein the Younger (1497?-1543), Painter — A273

Details or entire paintings: 700 l, 1000 l, Madonna of Solothurn. 1500 l, Self-portrait.

**Litho. & Engr.**

**1993, Nov. 23** *Perf. 13½x14*

**939** A273 700 l multicolored .85 .85
**940** A273 1000 l multicolored 1.25 1.25
**941** A273 1500 l multicolored 1.75 1.75
*Nos. 939-941 (3)* 3.85 3.85

Synod of Bishops, Special Assembly for Africa A274

Designs: 850 l, Stylized crosier, dome with cross, vert. 1000 l, Crucifix, dome of St. Peter's Basilica, crosiers, African landscape.

***Perf. 12½x13, 13x12½***

**1994, Apr. 8 Photo.**

**942** A274 850 l multicolored 1.10 1.10
**943** A274 1000 l multicolored 1.25 1.25

The Restored Sistine Chapel — A275

Frescoes, by Michelangelo: Creation of the Sun and Moon: No. 944, Sun. No. 945, God pointing toward moon. Creation of Man: No. 946, Adam, No. 947, God. Original Sin: No. 948, Adam, Eve taking apple from serpent. No. 949, Adam, Eve forced from Garden of

Eden. The Flood: No. 950, People on dry ground. No. 951, People on stone outcropping.
4000 l, Detail of Last Judgment, Christ and the Virgin.

**1994, Apr. 8 Photo. *Perf. 11½***

| | | | | |
|---|---|---|---|---|
| **944** | 350 l multicolored | | .40 | .40 |
| **945** | 350 l multicolored | | .40 | .40 |
| *a.* | A275 Pair, #944-945 | | .80 | .80 |
| **946** | 500 l multicolored | | .60 | .60 |
| **947** | 500 l multicolored | | .60 | .60 |
| *a.* | A275 Pair, #946-947 | | 1.25 | 1.25 |
| **948** | 1000 l multicolored | | 1.25 | 1.25 |
| **949** | 1000 l multicolored | | 1.25 | 1.25 |
| *a.* | A275 Pair, #948-949 | | 2.50 | 2.50 |
| **950** | 2000 l multicolored | | 2.50 | 2.50 |
| **951** | 2000 l multicolored | | 2.50 | 2.50 |
| *a.* | A275 Pair, 950-951 | | 5.00 | 5.00 |
| | *Nos. 944-951 (8)* | | 9.50 | 9.50 |

**Souvenir Sheet**

***Perf. 12***

**952** A275 4000 l multicolored 5.00 5.00

No. 952 contains one 36x54mm stamp.

European Inventions, Discoveries — A276

Europa: 750 l, Progess from wheel to atom traced by white thread. 850 l, Galileo in center of solar system, scientific instruments.

**1994, May 31 Litho. *Perf. 13x13½***

| | | | | |
|---|---|---|---|---|
| **953** | A276 | 750 l multicolored | .95 | .95 |
| **954** | A276 | 850 l multicolored | 1.10 | 1.10 |

Intl. Year of the Family — A277

Stained glass: 400 l, God creating man and woman. 750 l, Family under names of four Evangelists. 1000 l, Parents teaching son. 2000 l, Young man comforting elderly couple.

**1994, May 31 Photo. *Perf. 13x14***

| | | | | |
|---|---|---|---|---|
| **955** | A277 | 400 l multicolored | .50 | .50 |
| **956** | A277 | 750 l multicolored | .95 | .95 |
| **957** | A277 | 1000 l multicolored | 1.25 | 1.25 |
| **958** | A277 | 2000 l multicolored | 2.50 | 2.50 |
| | | *Nos. 955-958 (4)* | 5.20 | 5.20 |

Giovanni da Montecorvino (1247-1328), Missionary — A278

**1994, Sept. 27 Litho. *Perf. 14***

**959** A278 1000 l multicolored 1.40 1.40

Evangelization of China, 700th anniv.

13th Intl. Convention of Christian Archaeology, Split, Croatia — A279

Mosaics from Euphrasian Basilica, Parentium, Croatia, 6th Cent.: 700 l, Bishop Euphrasius, Archdeacon Claudius, Claudius' son. 1500 l, Madonna and Child, two angels. 3000 l, Christ, Apostles Peter & Paul.

**1994, Sept. 27 *Perf. 13x14***

| | | | | |
|---|---|---|---|---|
| **960** | A279 | 700 l multicolored | 1.00 | 1.00 |
| **961** | A279 | 1500 l multicolored | 2.00 | 2.00 |
| **962** | A279 | 3000 l multicolored | 4.25 | 4.25 |
| | | *Nos. 960-962 (3)* | 7.25 | 7.25 |

Travels of Pope John Paul II — A280

Designs: 600 l, Benin, Uganda, Sudan. 700 l, Albania. 1000 l, Spain. 2000 l, Jamaica, Mexico, US. 3000 l, Lithuania, Latvia, Estonia.

**1994, Nov. 18 Engr. *Perf. 13***

| | | | | |
|---|---|---|---|---|
| **963** | A280 | 600 l multicolored | .85 | .85 |
| **964** | A280 | 700 l multicolored | 1.00 | 1.00 |
| **965** | A280 | 1000 l multicolored | 1.40 | 1.40 |
| **966** | A280 | 2000 l multicolored | 2.75 | 2.75 |
| **967** | A280 | 3000 l multicolored | 4.25 | 4.25 |
| | | *Nos. 963-967 (5)* | 10.25 | 10.25 |

Christmas A281

The Nativity, by Il Tintoretto: 700 l, The Holy Family. No. 969, The Holy Family, two women. No. 970, Adoration of the shepherds.

**1994, Nov. 18 Photo. *Perf. 11½***

**Granite Paper**

**968** A281 700 l multicolored 1.00 1.00

**Size: 45x27mm**

| | | | | |
|---|---|---|---|---|
| **969** | A281 | 1000 l multicolored | 1.40 | 1.40 |
| **970** | A281 | 1000 l multicolored | 1.40 | 1.40 |
| *a.* | | Pair, #969-970 | 2.80 | 2.80 |
| | | *Nos. 968-970 (3)* | 3.80 | 3.80 |

Peace and Freedom A282

**1995, Mar. 25 Photo. *Perf. 14x13***

| | | | | |
|---|---|---|---|---|
| **971** | A282 | 750 l shown | .90 | .90 |
| **972** | A282 | 850 l Hands clasp, dove | 1.00 | 1.00 |

Europa.

Shrine of Loreto, 700th Anniv. — A283

Details of artworks from vaults of Sacristy: 600 l, St. Mark's, Angel with chalice, by Melozzo da Forli. 700 l, St. Mark's, Angel with lamb, by da Forli. 1500 l, 2500 l, St. John's, Music making angels, by Luca Signorelli.
No. 977, Marble carving showing Holy House of Loreto.

**1995, Mar. 25 *Perf. 11½***

| | | | | |
|---|---|---|---|---|
| **973** | A283 | 600 l multicolored | .70 | .70 |
| **974** | A283 | 700 l multicolored | .80 | .80 |
| **975** | A283 | 1500 l multicolored | 1.75 | 1.75 |
| **976** | A283 | 2500 l multicolored | 3.00 | 3.00 |
| | | *Nos. 973-976 (4)* | 6.25 | 6.25 |

**Souvenir Sheet**

**977** A283 3000 l multicolored 3.50 3.50

No. 977 contains one 36x36mm stamp.

Radio, Cent. A284

Designs: 850 l, Guglielmo Marconi, transmitting equipment. 1000 l, Archangel Gabriel, Pope John Paul II, Marconi broadcasting station, Vatican City.

**1995, June 8 Photo. *Perf. 14***

| | | | | |
|---|---|---|---|---|
| **978** | A284 | 850 l multicolored | 1.00 | 1.00 |
| **979** | A284 | 1000 l multicolored | 1.25 | 1.25 |

See Germany No. 1990, Ireland Nos. 973-974, Italy Nos. 2038-2039, San Marino Nos. 1336-1337.

A285

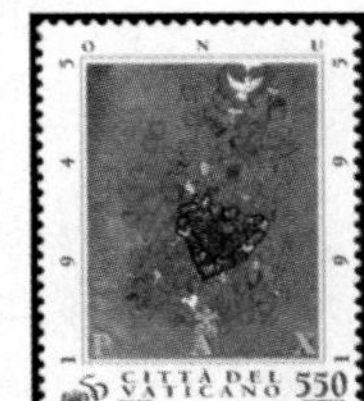


A286

European Nature Conservation Year (Scenes in Vatican Gardens & Castel Gandolfo: 200 l, Fountain of the Triton, arches of rhyncospernum jasminoides. 300 l, Avenue of roses, Palazzo Barberini. 400 l, Statue of Apollo Citaredo. 550 l, Ruins of Domitian's Villa, Avenue of roses. 750 l, Acer negundo, Viale dell'Osservatorio. 1500 l, Belvedere garden. 2000 l, Fountain of the Eagle, Quercus ilex. 3000 l, Avenue of cypresses, equestrian statue.

**1995, June 8 *Perf. 12***

**Granite Paper**

| | | | | |
|---|---|---|---|---|
| **980** | A285 | 200 l multicolored | .25 | .25 |
| **981** | A285 | 300 l multicolored | .35 | .35 |
| *a.* | | Booklet pane of 3 | 1.00 | |
| **982** | A285 | 400 l multicolored | .50 | .50 |
| *a.* | | Booklet pane of 3 | 1.50 | |
| **983** | A285 | 550 l multicolored | .70 | .70 |
| *a.* | | Booklet pane of 3 | 2.25 | |
| **984** | A285 | 750 l multicolored | .90 | .90 |
| *a.* | | Booklet pane of 3 | 2.75 | |
| | | Complete booklet, #981a, 982a, 983a, 984a | 7.50 | |
| **985** | A285 | 1500 l multicolored | 1.90 | 1.90 |
| **986** | A285 | 2000 l multicolored | 2.50 | 2.50 |
| **987** | A285 | 3000 l multicolored | 3.75 | 3.75 |
| | | *Nos. 980-987 (8)* | 10.85 | 10.85 |

**1995, Oct. 3 Photo. *Perf. 13½x13***

Paintings of peace, by Paolo Guiotto: 550 l, Small hearts flying from large heart. 750 l, Stylized faces. 850 l, Doves in flight. 1250 l, Lymph reaching to smallest branches. 2000 l, Explosion of colors, people.

| | | | | |
|---|---|---|---|---|
| **988** | A286 | 550 l multicolored | .70 | .70 |
| **989** | A286 | 750 l multicolored | .95 | .95 |
| **990** | A286 | 850 l multicolored | 1.10 | 1.10 |
| **991** | A286 | 1250 l multicolored | 1.50 | 1.50 |
| **992** | A286 | 2000 l multicolored | 2.50 | 2.50 |
| | | *Nos. 988-992 (5)* | 6.75 | 6.75 |

UN, 50th anniv.

A287

A288

St. Anthony of Padua (1195-1231): 750 l, St. John of God (1495-1550). 3000 l, St. Philip Neri (1515-95).

**Litho. & Engr.**

**1995, Oct. 3 *Perf. 13½x14***

| | | | | |
|---|---|---|---|---|
| **993** | A287 | 500 l green & brown | .65 | .65 |
| **994** | A287 | 750 l violet & green | .95 | .95 |
| **995** | A287 | 3000 l magenta & black | 3.75 | 3.75 |
| | | *Nos. 993-995 (3)* | 5.35 | 5.35 |

**1995, Nov. 20 Photo. *Perf. 12x11½***

Scenes depicting life of Jesus Christ from illuminated manuscripts: 400 l, The Annunciation. 850 l, Nativity. 1250 l, Flight into Egypt. 2000 l, Jesus among the teachers.

**Granite Paper**

| | | | | |
|---|---|---|---|---|
| **996** | A288 | 400 l multicolored | .50 | .50 |
| **997** | A288 | 850 l multicolored | 1.10 | 1.10 |
| **998** | A288 | 1250 l multicolored | 1.60 | 1.60 |
| **999** | A288 | 2000 l multicolored | 2.50 | 2.50 |
| | | *Nos. 996-999 (4)* | 5.70 | 5.70 |

Towards the Holy Year 2000.

Travels of Pope John Paul II A289

Designs: 1000 l, Giving greeting in Croatia, statue of Blessed Lady, Zagreb Cathedral. 2000 l, In Italy, lighthouse in Genoa, Orvieto Cathedral, Valley of Temples in Agrigento.

**1995, Nov. 20 Litho. *Perf. 14½x14***

| | | | | |
|---|---|---|---|---|
| **1000** | A289 | 1000 l multicolored | 1.25 | 1.25 |
| **1001** | A289 | 2000 l multicolored | 2.50 | 2.50 |

Religious Anniversaries A290

Designs: 1250 l, Angel holding crosses, Union of Brest-Litovsk, 400th anniv. 2000 l, Cross with branches, Latin episcopal mitre, Byzantine mitre, Union of Uzhorod, 350th anniv.

**1996, Mar. 16 Photo. *Perf. 13½x14***

| | | | | |
|---|---|---|---|---|
| **1002** | A290 | 1250 l multicolored | 1.60 | 1.60 |
| **1003** | A290 | 2000 l multicolored | 2.50 | 2.50 |

A291

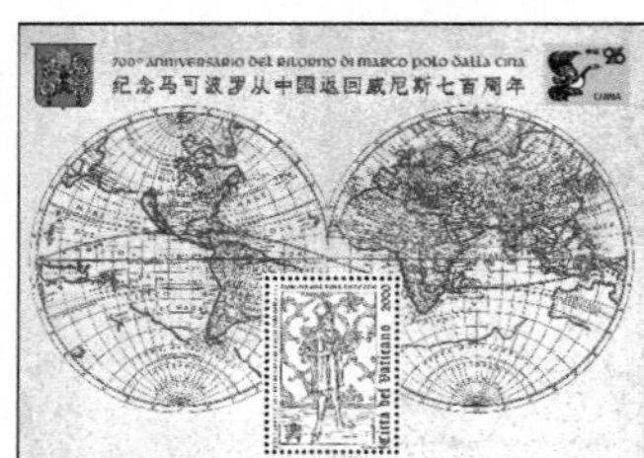

Marco Polo's Return from China, 700th Anniv. — A292

Designs from miniatures, Bodleian Library, Oxford: 350 l, Marco Polo delivering Pope Gregory X's letter to Great Khan. 850 l, Great Khan dispensing alms to poor in Cambaluc. 1250 l, Marco Polo receiving golden book from Great Khan. 2500 l, Marco Polo in Persia listening to story of three Kings who go to Bethlehem to adore Jesus.

2000 l, Stylized portrait of Marco Polo drawn from first printed edition of "I1 Milione." Illustration reduced.

**1996, Mar. 15** *Perf. 11½*

**Granite Paper**

| | | | | | |
|---|---|---|---|---|---|
| **1004** | A291 | 350 l | multicolored | .45 | .45 |
| **1005** | A291 | 850 l | multicolored | 1.10 | 1.10 |
| **1006** | A291 | 1250 l | multicolored | 1.60 | 1.60 |
| **1007** | A291 | 2500 l | multicolored | 3.25 | 3.25 |
| | | | *Nos. 1004-1007 (4)* | 6.40 | 6.40 |

**Souvenir Sheet**

*Perf. 12x11½*

| | | | | | |
|---|---|---|---|---|---|
| **1008** | A292 | 2000 l | black | 2.50 | 2.50 |

A293

A294

Famous Women: 750 l, Gianna Baretta Molla (1922-62), physician. 850 l, Sister Edith Stein (1891-1942).

**1996, May 7** **Engr.** *Perf. 13x14*

| | | | | | |
|---|---|---|---|---|---|
| **1009** | A293 | 750 l | blue | 1.00 | 1.00 |
| **1010** | A293 | 850 l | brown | 1.10 | 1.10 |

**1996, May 7** **Photo.** *Perf. 13*

Modern Olympic Games, Cent.: a, Statue of athlete. b, Athlete's torso. c, Hand. d, Statue of athlete reaching upward. e, Hercules.

| | | | |
|---|---|---|---|
| **1011** | Strip of 5 | 8.00 | 8.00 |
| ***a.-e.*** | A294 1250 l any single | 1.60 | 1.60 |

Ordination of Pope John Paul II, 50th Anniv. A295

Designs: 500 l, Wawel Cathedral, Krakow. 750 l, Pope John Paul II giving blessing. 1250 l, Basilica of St. John Lateran, Rome.

**1996, Oct. 12** **Litho.** *Perf. 14*

| | | | | | |
|---|---|---|---|---|---|
| **1012** | A295 | 500 l | multicolored | .65 | .65 |
| **1013** | A295 | 750 l | multicolored | 1.00 | 1.00 |
| **1014** | A295 | 1250 l | multicolored | 1.60 | 1.60 |
| | | | *Nos. 1012-1014 (3)* | 3.25 | 3.25 |

Life of Jesus Christ from Illuminated Manuscripts A296

Designs: 550 l, Baptism of Jesus at River Jordan. 850 l, Temptation in the desert. 1500 l, Cure of the leper. 2500 l, Jesus the teacher.

**1996, Oct. 12** **Photo.** *Perf. 12x11½*

| | | | | | |
|---|---|---|---|---|---|
| **1015** | A296 | 550 l | multicolored | .75 | .75 |
| **1016** | A296 | 850 l | multicolored | 1.10 | 1.10 |
| **1017** | A296 | 1500 l | multicolored | 2.00 | 2.00 |
| **1018** | A296 | 2500 l | multicolored | 3.25 | 3.25 |
| | | | *Nos. 1015-1018 (4)* | 7.10 | 7.10 |

Christmas — A297

Nativity, by Murillo (1618-82).

**1996, Nov. 20** **Litho.** *Perf. 13½*

| | | | | | |
|---|---|---|---|---|---|
| **1019** | A297 | 750 l | multicolored | 1.00 | 1.00 |

St. Celestine V (1215-96) A298

#1021, St. Alfonso Maria De'Liguori (1696-1787).

**1996, Nov. 20** *Perf. 13½x14*

| | | | | | |
|---|---|---|---|---|---|
| **1020** | A298 | 1250 l | multicolored | 1.60 | 1.60 |
| **1021** | A298 | 1250 l | multicolored | 1.60 | 1.60 |

Travels of Pope John Paul II, 1995 A299

Designs: 250 l, Jan. 11-21, Philippines, Papua New Guinea, Australia, Sri Lanka. 500 l, May 20-22, Czech Republic, Poland. 750 l, June 3-4, Belgium. 1000 l, June 30-July 3, Slovakia. 2000 l, Sept. 14-20, Cameroun, South Africa, Kenya. 5000 l, Oct. 4-9, UN headquarters, NY, US.

**1996, Nov. 20** *Perf. 14x13½*

| | | | | | |
|---|---|---|---|---|---|
| **1022** | A299 | 250 l | blue & multi | .35 | .35 |
| **1023** | A299 | 500 l | blue green & multi | .65 | .65 |
| **1024** | A299 | 750 l | green & multi | 1.00 | 1.00 |
| **1025** | A299 | 1000 l | brown & multi | 1.25 | 1.25 |
| **1026** | A299 | 2000 l | gray & multi | 2.50 | 2.50 |
| **1027** | A299 | 5000 l | pink & multi | 6.75 | 6.75 |
| | | | *Nos. 1022-1027 (6)* | 12.50 | 12.50 |

Papal Carriages and Automobiles A300

Designs: 50 l, Touring carriage. 100 l, Graham Paige. 300 l, Festive traveling carriage. 500 l, Citroen Lictoria VI. 750 l, Grand touring carriage. 850 l, Mercedes Benz. 1000 l, Festive half carriage. 1250 l, Mercedes Benz 300SEL. 2000 l, Touring carriage, diff. 4000 l, Fiat "Pope mobile."

**1997, Mar. 20** **Photo.** *Perf. 12*

**Granite Paper**

| | | | | | |
|---|---|---|---|---|---|
| **1028** | A300 | 50 l | multicolored | .20 | .20 |
| **1029** | A300 | 100 l | multicolored | .20 | .20 |
| **1030** | A300 | 300 l | multicolored | .35 | .35 |
| **1031** | A300 | 500 l | multicolored | .60 | .60 |
| **1032** | A300 | 750 l | multicolored | .90 | .90 |
| **1033** | A300 | 850 l | multicolored | 1.00 | 1.00 |
| **1034** | A300 | 1000 l | multicolored | 1.10 | 1.10 |
| **1035** | A300 | 1250 l | multicolored | 1.50 | 1.50 |
| **1036** | A300 | 2000 l | multicolored | 2.25 | 2.25 |
| **1037** | A300 | 4000 l | multicolored | 4.75 | 4.75 |
| | | | *Nos. 1028-1037 (10)* | 12.85 | 12.85 |

A301

A302

Swiss Guard: 750 l, Guard in traditional attire. 850 l, Guard in armor with sword in front of iron gate.

**1997, Mar. 20** **Litho.** *Perf. 13½*

| | | | | | |
|---|---|---|---|---|---|
| **1038** | A301 | 750 l | multicolored | .90 | .90 |
| **1039** | A301 | 850 l | multicolored | 1.00 | 1.00 |
| ***a.*** | | | Strip of 2 + 2 labels | 1.90 | 1.90 |

Europa.

**1997, Apr. 23** **Engr.** *Perf. 14*

| | | | | | |
|---|---|---|---|---|---|
| **1040** | A302 | 850 l | deep violet | 1.00 | 1.00 |

St. Adalbert (956-997). See Germany No. 1964, Poland No. 3337, Czech Republic No. 3012, Hungary No. 3569.

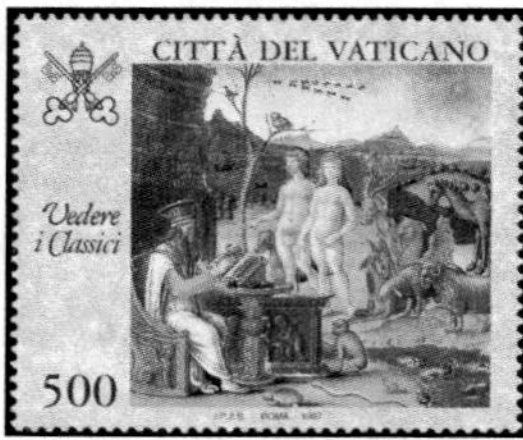


A303

"Looking at the Classics," Museum Exhibition — A304

Pictures from texts of Latin and Greek classics: 500 l, Aristotle observing and describing various species from man to insect, from his "De Historia Animalium." 750 l, Bacchus riding dragon, from "Metamorphoses" by Ovid. 1250 l, General haranguing his soldiers, from "Iliad" by Homer. 2000 l, Hannibal leaving Canne, two horsemen, foot soldier, from "Ab Urbe Condita" by Titus Livius.

Masks from "Comedies," by Terrence: No. 1045: a, Man, woman. b, Two women. c, Two men.

**1997, Apr. 23** **Photo.** *Perf. 14*

| | | | | | |
|---|---|---|---|---|---|
| **1041** | A303 | 500 l | multicolored | .60 | .60 |
| **1042** | A303 | 750 l | multicolored | .90 | .90 |
| **1043** | A303 | 1250 l | multicolored | 1.50 | 1.50 |
| **1044** | A303 | 2000 l | multicolored | 2.40 | 2.40 |
| | | | *Nos. 1041-1044 (4)* | 5.40 | 5.40 |

*Perf. 13½*

| | | | | | |
|---|---|---|---|---|---|
| **1045** | A304 | 1000 l | Sheet of 3, #a.-c. | 3.50 | 3.50 |

A305

A306

46th Intl. Eucharistic Congress, Wroclaw, Poland: 650 l, Elements of the Eucharist, chalice, consecrated Host, arms of Wroclaw. 1000 l, The Last Supper, fish, Congress emblem. 1250 l, Wroclaw Cathedral, sheaf of wheat, holy spirit descending on church. 2500 l, "IHS" symbol of Christ on cross, doves, world with two hands on it.

**1997, May 27** **Photo.** *Perf. 13*

| | | | | | |
|---|---|---|---|---|---|
| **1046** | A305 | 650 l | multicolored | .75 | .75 |
| **1047** | A305 | 1000 l | multicolored | 1.10 | 1.10 |
| **1048** | A305 | 1250 l | multicolored | 1.40 | 1.40 |
| **1049** | A305 | 2500 l | multicolored | 2.75 | 2.75 |
| | | | *Nos. 1046-1049 (4)* | 6.00 | 6.00 |

**1997, Sept. 15** **Litho.** *Perf. 13x14*

| | | | | | |
|---|---|---|---|---|---|
| **1050** | A306 | 900 l | multicolored | 1.00 | 1.00 |

Pope Paul VI (1897-1978).

No. 1050 was printed se-tenant with 4 labels.

St. Ambrose (d. 397) — A307

Towards the Holy Year 2000 — A308

**1997, Sept. 15** **Photo.** *Perf. 13x14*

| | | | | | |
|---|---|---|---|---|---|
| **1051** | A307 | 800 l | multicolored | .90 | .90 |

**1997, Sept. 15** *Perf. 12*

Illustrations of Christ's miracles: 400 l, Healing of paralyzed man. 800 l, Calming of the tempest. 1300 l, Multiplication of bread and fish. 3600 l, Peter's confession and conferment of primacy.

**Granite Paper**

| | | | | | |
|---|---|---|---|---|---|
| **1052** | A308 | 400 l | multicolored | .45 | .45 |
| **1053** | A308 | 800 l | multicolored | .90 | .90 |
| **1054** | A308 | 1300 l | multicolored | 1.90 | 1.90 |
| **1055** | A308 | 3600 l | multicolored | 4.25 | 4.25 |
| | | | *Nos. 1052-1055 (4)* | 7.50 | 7.50 |

1996 Travels of Pope John Paul II — A309

Designs: 400 l, Central & South America, Feb. 5-12. 900 l, Tunisia, Apr. 14. 1000 l, Slovenia , May 17-19. 1300 l, Germany, June 21-23. 2000 l, Hungary, Sept. 6-7. 4000 l, France, Sept. 19-22.

**1997, Nov. 11 Litho. *Perf. 14x13½***

**1056** A309 400 l multicolored .50 .50
**1057** A309 900 l multicolored 1.00 1.00
**1058** A309 1000 l multicolored 1.25 1.25
**1059** A309 1300 l multicolored 1.50 1.50
**1060** A309 2000 l multicolored 2.25 2.25
**1061** A309 4000 l multicolored 4.75 4.75
*Nos. 1056-1061 (6)* 11.25 11.25

Christmas — A310

Detail from "The Nativity," by Benozzo Gozzoli (1420-97).

**1997, Nov. 11 Photo. *Perf. 14***

**1062** A310 800 l multicolored .95 .95

Feasts of Sts. Peter and Paul, June 29th — A311

**1998, Mar. 24 Photo. *Perf. 13***

**1063** A311 800 l St. Peter .90 .90
**1064** A311 900 l St. Paul 1.00 1.00

Europa.

The Popes of the Holy Years 1300-1525 A312

Designs: 200 l, Boniface VIII, 1300. 400 l, Clement VI, 1350. 500 l, Boniface IX, 1390, 1400. 700 l, Martin V, 1423. 800 l, Nicholas V, 1450. 900 l, Sixtus IV, 1475. 1300 l, Alexander VI, 1500. 3000 , Clement VII, 1525.

**1998, Mar. 24 Litho. *Perf. 14***

**1065** A312 200 l multicolored .25 .25
**1066** A312 400 l multicolored .45 .45
**1067** A312 500 l multicolored .60 .60
**1068** A312 700 l multicolored .80 .80
**1069** A312 800 l multicolored .90 .90
**1070** A312 900 l multicolored 1.00 1.00
**1071** A312 1300 l multicolored 1.50 1.50
**1072** A312 3000 l multicolored 3.50 3.50
*Nos. 1065-1072 (8)* 9.00 9.00

Nos. 1065-1072 were each printed se-tenant with a label picturing the respective papal arms.

See Nos. 1095-1102, 1141-1150.

A313

A314

**Litho. & Engr.**

**1998, May 19 *Perf. 13½x14***

**1073** A313 900 l Face on Shroud 1.00 1.00
**1074** A313 2500 l Cathedral of Turin 2.75 2.75

Exposition of the Shroud of Turin.

**1998, May 19 Photo. *Perf. 12***

Frescoes of Angels, by Melozzo da Forli (1438-94), Basilica of Sts. Apostles, Rome: Angels playing various musical instruments.

**Granite Paper**

**1075** A314 450 l multicolored .60 .60
**1076** A314 650 l multicolored .75 .75
**1077** A314 800 l multicolored .90 .90
**1078** A314 1000 l multicolored 1.10 1.10
**1079** A314 1300 l multicolored 1.50 1.50
**1080** A314 2000 l multicolored 2.25 2.25
*Nos. 1075-1080 (6)* 7.10 7.10

Towards Holy Year 2000 A315

Episodes from the Life of Christ: 500 l, Triumphal entry into Jerusalem. 800 l, Washing of the feet. 1300 l, The Last Supper. 3000 l, Crucifixion.

**1998, May 19 *Perf. 12***

**Granite Paper**

**1081** A315 500 l multicolored .60 .60
**1082** A315 800 l multicolored .90 .90
**1083** A315 1300 l multicolored 1.50 1.50
**1084** A315 3000 l multicolored 3.25 3.25
*Nos. 1081-1084 (4)* 6.25 6.25

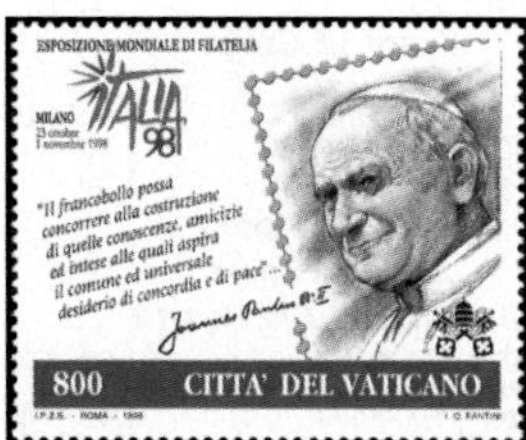


Italia '98 A316

**1998, Oct. 23 Photo. *Perf. 14***

**1085** A316 800 l Pope John Paul II 1.00 1.00

See Italy No. 2259 and San Marino No. 1430.

The Good Shepherd — A317 Christian Sculptures — A318

**1998, Oct. 25 *Perf. 12 Vert.***

**Granite Paper**

**Booklet Stamp**

**1086** A317 900 l multicolored 1.10 1.10
*a.* Booklet pane of 5 5.50
Complete booklet, #1086a 5.50

Italia '98.

**1998, Oct. 25 *Perf. 12***

Designs: a, 600 l, Peter's denial. b, 900 l, Praying woman. c, 1000 l, Christ and the Cyrenean. 2000 l, Christ with the Cross and Two Apostles.

**Granite Paper**

**1087** A318 Sheet of 4, #a.-d. 5.50 5.50

Italia '98. Margin is embossed.

Christmas — A319

**1998, Dec. 1 Litho. *Perf. 14x13½***

**1088** A319 800 l multicolored 1.00 1.00

See Croatia No. 381.

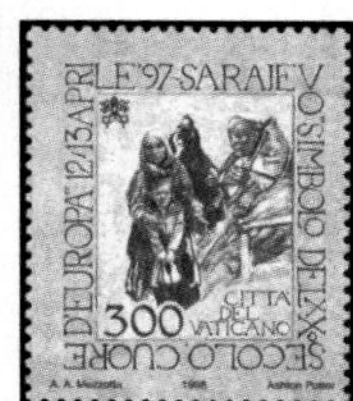


1997 Travels of Pope John Paul II — A320

Designs: 300 l, Sarajevo, 4/12-13/97. 600 l, Prague, 4/25-27/97. 800 l, Beirut, 5/10-11/97. 900 l, Poland, 5/21-6/10/97. 1300 l, Paris, 8/21-24/97. 5000 l, Rio de Janeiro, 10/2-6/97.

**1998, Dec. 1 *Perf. 12½***

**1089** A320 300 l brown .35 .35
**1090** A320 600 l green .70 .70
**1091** A320 800 l brown 1.00 1.00
**1092** A320 900 l violet blue 1.10 1.10
**1093** A320 1300 l org brn 1.60 1.60
**1094** A320 5000 l org brn 6.00 6.00
*Nos. 1089-1094 (6)* 10.75 10.75

Popes of the Holy Years Type of 1998

Popes: 300 l, Julius III, 1550. 600 l, Gregory XIII, 1575. 800 l, Clement VIII, 1600. 900 l, Urban VIII, 1625. 1000 l, Innocent X, 1650. 1300 l, Clement X, 1675. 1500 l, Innocent XII, 1700. 2000 l, Benedict XIII, 1725.

**1999, Mar. 23 Litho. *Perf. 14***

**1095** A312 300 l multicolored .35 .35
**1096** A312 600 l multicolored .65 .65
**1097** A312 800 l multicolored .90 .90
**1098** A312 900 l multicolored 1.00 1.00
**1099** A312 1000 l multicolored 1.10 1.10
**1100** A312 1300 l multicolored 1.40 1.40
**1101** A312 1500 l multicolored 1.60 1.60
**1102** A312 2000 l multicolored 2.25 2.25
*Nos. 1095-1102 (8)* 9.25 9.25

Nos. 1095-1102 were each printed se-tenant with a label picturing the respective papal arms.

Flowers from Vatican Gardens and Papal Villa, Castelgandolfo A321

Europa: 800 l, John Paul II Rose. 900 l, Water lilies.

**1999, Mar. 23 Litho. *Perf. 12½x13***

**1103** A321 800 l multicolored .90 .90
**1104** A321 900 l multicolored 1.00 1.00
*a.* Pair, #1103-1104 + label 1.90 1.90

Padre Pio de Pietrelcina (1887-1968) — A322

#1106: a, 1st church, San Giovanni Rotondo. b, New church, San Giovanni Rotondo. c, Like #1105.

**1999, Apr. 27 Litho. *Perf. 14x13***

**1105** A322 800 l multicolored .90 .90

**Souvenir Sheet**

***Perf. 13x13½***

**1106** A322 Sheet of 3 2.10 2.10
*a.* 300 l multi, vert. .35 .35
*b.* 600 l multi, vert. .70 .70
*c.* 900 l multi 1.00 1.00

Nos. 1106a-1106b are 30x40mm, No. 1106c is 60x40mm.

A323

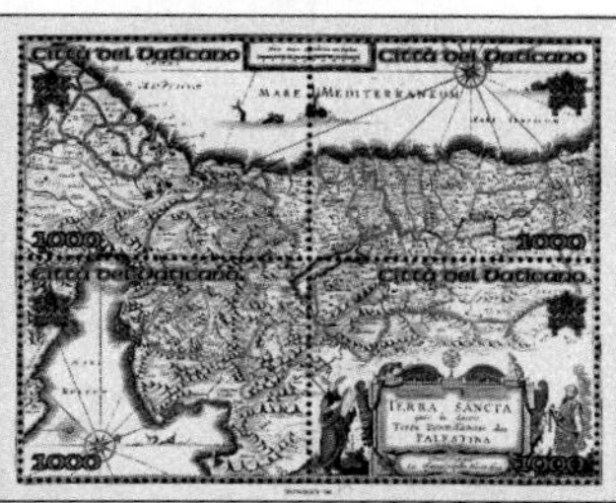

Holy Places in Palestine — A324

Nos. 1107-1111: 19th cent. watercolors, Pontifical Lateran University Library.

Map of Holy Land from "Geographia Blaviana," 17th cent - #1112: a, Mediterranean Sea, denomination, LL. b, Mediterranean Sea, denomination LR. c, Red Sea, Holy Land. d, Inscription indentifying map.

**1999, May 25 Photo. *Perf. 11½***

**Granite Paper**

**1107** A323 200 l Bethlehem .20 .20
**1108** A323 500 l Nazareth .55 .55
**1109** A323 800 l Lake of Tiberias .85 .85
**1110** A323 900 l Jerusalem 1.00 1.00
**1111** A323 1300 l Mount Tabor 1.40 1.40
*Nos. 1107-1111 (5)* 4.00 4.00

***Perf. 12x11¾***

**1112** A324 1000 l Sheet of 4, #a.-d. 4.25 4.25

Towards Holy Year 2000 A325

Events from life of Christ: 400 l, Deposition from the Cross. 700 l, Resurrection. 1300 l, Pentecost. 3000 l, Last Judgement.

**1999, May 25** ***Perf. 12x11¾***
**Granite Paper**

**1113** A325 400 l multicolored .45 .45
**1114** A325 700 l multicolored .75 .75
**1115** A325 1300 l multicolored 1.40 1.40
**1116** A325 3000 l multicolored 3.25 3.25
*Nos. 1113-1116 (4)* 5.85 5.85

Kosovo 1999 — A326

**1999, May 25** ***Perf. 12¼***
**Granite Paper**

**1117** A326 3600 l black 4.00 4.00

Proceeds from sale of stamp benefits victims of the fighting in Kosovo.

1998 Travels of Pope John Paul II — A327

600 l, Cuba, June 21-26. 800 l, Nigeria, Mar. 21-23. 900 l, Austria, June 19-21. 1300 l, Croatia, Oct. 2-4. 2000 l, Italy, Oct. 20.

**1999, Oct. 12** **Litho.** ***Perf. 14x13½***

**1118** A327 600 l multicolored .70 .70
**1119** A327 800 l multicolored .90 .90
**1120** A327 900 l multicolored 1.00 1.00
**1121** A327 1300 l multicolored 1.50 1.50
**1122** A327 2000 l multicolored 2.25 2.25
*Nos. 1118-1122 (5)* 6.35 6.35

Council of Europe, 50th Anniv. — A328

**1999, Oct. 12** **Photo.** ***Perf. 11¾***
**Granite Paper**

**1123** A328 1200 l multicolored 1.40 1.40

Christmas A329

The Birth of Christ, by Giovanni di Pietro: 500 l, Joseph (detail). 800 l, Christ (detail). 900 l, Mary (detail). 1200 l, Entire painting.

***Perf. 13¼x12½***
**1999, Nov. 24** **Litho.**

**1124** A329 500 l multi .50 .50
**1125** A329 800 l multi .80 .80
**1126** A329 900 l multi .90 .90
**1127** A329 1200 l multi 1.25 1.25
*Nos. 1124-1127 (4)* 3.45 3.45

Opening of the Holy Door for Holy Year 2000 A330

Various panels of Holy Door. Stamps on No. 1136 lack white border.

**1999, Nov. 24** **Photo.** ***Perf. 11¾x12***
**Granite Paper**

**1128** A330 200 l multi .20 .20
**1129** A330 300 l multi .30 .30
**1130** A330 400 l multi .40 .40
**1131** A330 500 l multi .50 .50
**1132** A330 600 l multi .60 .60
**1133** A330 800 l multi .75 .75
**1134** A330 1000 l multi 1.00 1.00
**1135** A330 1200 l multi 1.25 1.25
*Nos. 1128-1135 (8)* 5.00 5.00

**Souvenir Sheet**

**1136** Sheet of 8, #a.-h. 5.25 5.25
*a.* A330 200 l Like #1128 .20 .20
*b.* A330 300 l Like #1129 .30 .30
*c.* A330 400 l Like #1130 .40 .40
*d.* A330 500 l Like #1131 .50 .50
*e.* A330 600 l Like #1132 .60 .60
*f.* A330 800 l Like #1133 .80 .80
*g.* A330 1000 l Like #1134 1.00 1.00
*h.* A330 1200 l Like #1135 1.25 1.25

Holy Year 2000 — A331

Designs: 800 l, St. Peter's Basilica. 1000 l, Basilica of St. John Lateran. 1200 l, Basilica of St. Mary Major. 2000 l, Basilica of St. Paul.

**2000, Feb. 4** **Photo.** ***Perf. 11¾***
**Granite Paper**

**1137** A331 800 l multi .75 .75
**1138** A331 1000 l multi 1.00 1.00
**1139** A331 1200 l multi 1.25 1.25
**1140** A331 2000 l multi 2.00 2.00
*Nos. 1137-1140 (4)* 5.00 5.00

**Popes of the Holy Year Type of 1998**

Designs: 300 l, Benedict XIV, 1750. 400 l, Pius VI, 1775. 500 l, Leo XII, 1825. 600 l, Pius IX, 1875. 700 l, Leo XIII, 1900. 800 l, Pius XI, 1925. 1200 l, Pius XII, 1950. 1500 l, Paul VI, 1975. No. 1149, John Paul II with miter, 2000. No. 1150, John Paul II with hand on chin, 2000.

**2000, Feb. 4** **Litho.** ***Perf. 13¾***

**1141** A312 300 l multi + label .30 .30
**1142** A312 400 l multi + label .40 .40
**1143** A312 500 l multi + label .50 .50
**1144** A312 600 l multi + label .60 .60
**1145** A312 700 l multi + label .70 .70
**1146** A312 800 l multi + label .75 .75
**1147** A312 1200 l multi + label 1.25 1.25
**1148** A312 1500 l multi + label 1.50 1.50
**1149** A312 2000 l multi + label 2.00 2.00
*Nos. 1141-1149 (9)* 8.00 8.00

**Souvenir Sheet**

**1150** A312 2000 l multi 2.00 2.00

No. 1150 contains one label.

Christianity in Iceland, 1000th Anniv. A332

**2000, Feb. 4** ***Perf. 13¼x13¾***

**1151** A332 1500 l multi 1.50 1.50

See Iceland Nos. 900-901.

**Europa, 2000**
Common Design Type

**2000, May 9** **Litho.** ***Perf. 13¼x13***

**1152** CD17 1200 l multi 1.25 1.25

Printed in sheets of 10, with left and right side selvage of Priority Mail etiquettes.

Pope John Paul II, 80th Birthday — A333

800 l, Pope. 1200 l, Black Madonna of Jasna Gora. 2000 l, Pope's silver cross.

**2000, May 9** **Engr.** ***Perf. 13x12¾***

**1153** A333 800 l purple .75 .75
**1154** A333 1200 l dark blue 1.25 1.25
**1155** A333 2000 l green 2.00 2.00
*Nos. 1153-1155 (3)* 4.00 4.00

See Poland Nos. 3520-3522.

Restored Sistine Chapel Frescoes — A334

Designs: 500 l, The Calling of St. Peter and St. Andrew, by Domenico Ghirlandaio. 1000 l, The Trials of Moses, by Sandro Botticelli. 1500 l, The Donation of the Keys, by Pietro Perugino. 3000 l, The Worship of the Golden Calf, by Cosimo Rosselli.

***Perf. 11½x11¾***
**2000, May 9** **Photo.** **Blue Frame**
**Granite Paper**

**1156** A334 500 l multi .50 .50
**1157** A334 1000 l multi 1.00 1.00
**1158** A334 1500 l multi 1.50 1.50
**1159** A334 3000 l multi 3.00 3.00
*Nos. 1156-1159 (4)* 6.00 6.00

20th World Youth Day — A335

Various photos of Pope John Paul II and youth.

***Perf. 13¾x13¼***
**2000, June 19** **Litho.**
**Color of Cross**

**1160** A335 800 l red .80 .80
**1161** A335 1000 l green 1.00 1.00
**1162** A335 1200 l violet 1.10 1.10
**1163** A335 1500 l orange 1.50 1.50

**Booklet Stamp**
**Self-Adhesive**
***Serpentine Die Cut 12***

**1164** A335 1000 l green 1.00 1.00
*a.* Booklet of 4 + 4 labels 4.00
*Nos. 1160-1164 (5)* 5.40 5.40

47th Intl. Eucharistic Congress A336

**2000, June 19** ***Perf. 13x12½***

**1165** A336 1200 l multi 1.10 1.10

Beatification of Pope John XXIII — A337

**2000, Sept. 1** **Photo.** ***Perf. 13¼x14***

**1166** A337 1200 l multi 1.10 1.10

1999 Travels of Pope John Paul II — A338

#1167: a, Mexico, 1/22-28. b, Romania, 5/7-9. c, Poland, 6/17. d, Slovenia, 9/19. e, India and Georgia, 11/5-9.

**2000, Sept. 1** ***Perf. 11¾***
**Granite Paper**

**1167** Horiz. strip of 5 4.50 4.50
*a.-e.* A338 1000 l Any single .90 .90

Christmas A339

Frescoes in Basilica of St. Francis, Assisi, by Giotto: 800 l, Nativity. 1200 l, Infant Jesus. 1500 l, Mary. 2000 l, Joseph.

**2000, Nov. 7** **Photo.** ***Perf. 11¾x11½***
**Granite Paper**

**1168-1171** A339 Set of 4 5.00 5.00

**Sistine Chapel Restoration Type of 2000**

Paintings: 800 l, The Baptism of Christ, by Pietro Perugino. 1200 l, The Passage of the Red Sea, by Biagio d'Antonio. 1500 l, The Punishment of Core, Datan and Abiron, by Sandro Botticelli. 4000 l, The Sermon on the Mount, by Cosimo Rosselli.

***Perf. 11½x11¾***
**2001, Feb. 15** **Photo.**
**Granite Paper**
**Red Frame**

**1172-1175** A334 Set of 4 7.00 7.00

Christian Conversion of Armenia, 1700th Anniv. — A340

Scenes from illuminated code of 1569: 1200 l, St. Gregory prepares to give King Tiridates human features. 1500 l, St. Gregory makes Agatangel write history of Armenians. 2000 l, St. Gregory and King Tiridates meet Emperor Constantine and Pope Sylvester I.

**2001, Feb. 15** ***Perf. 11¾***
**Granite Paper**

**1176-1178** A340 Set of 3 4.50 4.50

Year of Dialogue Among Civilizations A341

**2001, May 22 Litho. *Perf. 14¼x14***
**1179** A341 1500 l multi 1.40 1.40

Europa — A342

Designs: 800 l, Hands holding water above earth. 1200 l, Hand catching water.

**2001, May 22 *Perf. 13½x13¼***
**1180-1181** A342 Set of 2 1.75 1.75

Giuseppe Verdi (1813-1901), Composer A343

Verdi and: 800 l, Score from Nabucco. 1500 l, Costumes from Aida. 2000 l, Scenery from Othello.

**2001, May 22 *Perf. 13¼x14¼***
**1182-1184** A343 Set of 3 3.75 3.75

2000 Travels of Pope John Paul II — A344

Designs: 500 l, Mount Sinai, Feb. 26. 800 l, Mount Nebo, Mar. 20. 1200 l, The Last Supper, Mar. 23. 1500 l, Holy Sepulchre, Mar. 26. 5000 l, Fatima, May 12.
3000 l, Western Wall.

**2001, Sept. 25 Litho. *Perf. 13¼***
**1185-1189** A344 Set of 5 8.50 8.50

**Souvenir Sheet**

***Perf. 13¼x14***

**1190** A344 3000 l multi 2.75 2.75

No. 1190 contains one 35x26mm stamp.

Remission of Debts of Poor Countries A345

Various panels by Carlo di Camerino: 200 l, 400 l, 800 l, 1000 l, 1500 l.

**2001, Sept. 25 Photo. *Perf. 13***
**1191-1195** A345 Set of 5 3.75 3.75

Giuseppe Toniolo Institute for Higher Studies, 80th Anniv. — A346

**Litho. & Embossed**

**2001, Nov. 22 *Perf. 12¾***
**1196** A346 1200 l red & blue 1.10 1.10

Etruscan Museum Gold Objects — A347

Designs: 800 l, Parade fibula. 1200 l, Earrings. 1500 l, Vulci fibula. 2000 l, Head of Medusa.

**2001, Nov. 22 Photo. *Perf. 13½***
**1197-1200** A347 Set of 4 5.25 5.25

Christmas A348

Artwork by Egino G. Weinert: 800 l, The Annunciation. 1200 l, The Nativity. 1500 l, Adoration of the Magi.

**2001, Nov. 22 Litho. *Perf. 13x13¼***
**1201-1203** A348 Set of 3 3.25 3.25
*1202a* Booklet pane of 4 + 4 etiquettes 4.50
Booklet, #1202a 4.50

100 Cents = 1 Euro (€)

Depictions of Virgin Mary in Vatican Basilica — A349

Designs: 8c, Our Lady of Women in Labor. 15c, Our Lady with People Praying. 23c, Our Lady at the Tomb of Pius XII. 31c, Our Lady of the Fever. 41c, Our Lady of the Slap. 52c, Mary Immaculate. 62c, Our Lady Help of Christians. 77c, Virgin of the Deesis. €1.03, L'Addolorata. €1.55, Presentation of Mary at the Temple.

**2002, Mar. 12 Litho. *Perf. 13¼x13***

| | | | | |
|---|---|---|---|---|
| **1204** | A349 | 8c multi | .20 | .20 |
| **1205** | A349 | 15c multi | .35 | .35 |
| **1206** | A349 | 23c multi | .55 | .55 |
| **1207** | A349 | 31c multi | .75 | .75 |
| **1208** | A349 | 41c multi | 1.00 | 1.00 |
| **1209** | A349 | 52c multi | 1.20 | 1.20 |
| **1210** | A349 | 62c multi | 1.50 | 1.50 |
| **1211** | A349 | 77c multi | 1.80 | 1.80 |
| **1212** | A349 | €1.03 multi | 2.40 | 2.40 |
| **1213** | A349 | €1.55 multi | 3.50 | 3.50 |
| | | *Nos. 1204-1213 (10)* | 13.25 | 13.25 |

Pontifical Ecclesiastical Academy, 300th Anniv. — A350

No. 1214: a, Pope Clement XI. b, Academy building (46x33mm). c, Pope John Paul II.

**2002, Mar. 12 Engr. *Perf. 13¼x13***
**1214** A350 Horiz. strip of 3 5.50 5.50
***a.-c.*** 77c Any single 1.80 1.80

**Sistine Chapel Restoration Type of 2000**

Designs: 26c, The Temptation of Christ, by Sandro Botticelli. 41c, The Last Supper, by Cosimo Rosselli. 77c, Moses' Journey in Egypt, by Pietro Perugino. €1.55, The Last Days of Moses, by Luca Signorelli.

***Perf. 11½x11¾***

**2002, June 13 Photo.**

**Granite Paper**

**1215-1218** A334 Set of 4 7.00 7.00

Europa — A351

Christ and the Circus, by Aldo Carpi: 41c, Entire painting. 62c, Detail.

**2002, June 13 *Perf. 13¼***
**1219-1220** A351 Set of 2 2.40 2.40

Roman States Postage Stamps, 150th Anniv. — A352

Designs: 41c, Regina Viarum, Roman States #11. 52c, Cassian Way, Roman States #25. €1.03, Vatican walls, Vatican City #2. €1.55, St. Peter's Basilica.

**2002, June 13 *Perf. 13x13¼***
**1221-1223** A352 Set of 3 4.50 4.50

**Souvenir Sheet**

***Perf.***

**1224** A352 €1.55 multi 3.60 3.60

No. 1224 contains one 31mm diameter stamp.

St. Leo IX (1002-54), Pope A353

Designs: 41c, Portrait. 62c, In procession, receiving papal miter. €1.29, Reading from scroll, as prisoner of Normans.

**2002, Sept. 26 Litho. *Perf. 13x13¼***
**1225-1227** A353 Set of 3 5.50 5.50

Cimabue (1240-1302), Artist — A354

Designs: 26c, Crucifix. 62c, Jesus Christ. 77c, Virgin Mary. €1.03, St. John.

**2002, Sept. 26 Photo. *Perf. 13¼x14***
**1228-1231** A354 Set of 4 6.25 6.25

Nativity, by Pseudo Ambrogio di Baldese — A355

**2002, Nov. 21 Photo. *Perf. 13***
**1232** A355 41c multi .95 .95

See New Zealand No. 1834.

2001 Travels of Pope John Paul II — A356

Designs: 41c, Greece, Syria and Malta, May 4-9. 62c, Ukraine, June 23-27. €1.55, Armenia and Kazakhstan, Sept. 22-27.

**2002, Nov. 21 Litho. *Perf. 13x13¼***
**1233-1235** A356 Set of 3 6.00 6.00
*1234a* Booklet pane, 4 #1234 + 4 etiquettes 5.75
Booklet, #1234a 5.75

A357

Pontificate of John Paul II, 25th Anniv. — A358

No. 1236: a, Election as Pope, 1978. b, In Poland, 1979. c, In France, 1980. d, Assassination attempt, 1981. e, At Fatima, Portugal, 1982. f, Extraordinary Holy Year, 1983. g, At Quirinale Palace, Rome, 1984. h, World Youth Day, 1985. i, At synagogue, Rome, 1986. j, Pentecost vigil, 1987. k, At European Parliament, Strasbourg, France, 1988. l, Meeting with Mikhail Gorbachev, 1989. m, At Guinea-Bissau leper colony, 1990. n, At European Bishops' Synod, 1991. o, Publication of Catechism of the Catholic Church, 1992. p, Praying for the Balkans in Assisi, 1993. q, At Sistine Chapel, 1994. r, At UN Headquarters for 50th anniv. celebrations, 1995. s, In Germany, 1996. t, In Sarajevo, Bosnia & Herzegovina, 1997. u, In Cuba, 1998. v, Opening Holy Doors, 1999. w, World Youth Day, 2000. x, Closing Holy Doors, 2001. y, Addressing Italian Parliament, 2002.

**2003, Mar. 20 Litho. *Perf. 13x13¼***
**1236** Sheet of 25 24.00 24.00
***a.-y.*** A357 41c Any single .95 .95

**Etched on Silver Foil**

***Die Cut Perf. 12½x13***

**Self-Adhesive**

**1237** A358 €2.58 Pope John Paul II 6.00 6.00

Cancels can be easily removed from No. 1237.
See Poland Nos. 3668-3669.

Martyrdom of St. George, 1700th Anniv. A359

**2003, May 6 Litho. & Engr.** ***Perf. 13***
**1238** A359 62c multi 1.50 1.50

Europa — A360

Poster art for: 41c, 1975 Holy Year. 62c, Exhibition of Slav codices, incunabula and rare books at Sistine Hall, 1985.

**2003, May 6 Litho.** ***Perf. 13¼x13***
**1239-1240** A360 Set of 2 2.40 2.40

Masterpieces by Beato Angelico in Niccolina Chapel — A361

Designs: 41c, Diaconal Consecration of St. Lawrence. 62c, St. Stephen Preaching. 77c, Trial of St. Lawrence. €1.03, Stoning of St. Stephen.

**2003, May 6 Photo.** ***Perf. 13¼***
**1241-1244** A361 Set of 4 6.50 6.50

Beatification of Mother Teresa of Calcutta — A362

***Perf. 13½x13¼***
**2003, Sept. 23 Litho.**
**1245** A362 41c multi + label .95 .95

Printed in sheets of 5 + 5 different labels.

19th Century Artists — A363

Designs: 41c, Blessed Are the Pure at Heart, by Paul Gauguin. 62c, The Pietà, by Vincent van Gogh.

***Perf. 13¼x13½***
**2003, Sept. 23 Photo.**
**1246** A363 41c multi .95 .95
**1247** A363 62c multi 1.50 1.50
*a.* Booklet pane of 4 + 4 etiquettes 6.00 —
Complete booklet, #1247a 6.00

Animals in Vatican Basilica Art A364

Designs: 21c, Dragon. 31c, Camel. 77c, Horse. €1.03, Leopard.

**2003, Sept. 23**
**1248-1251** A364 Set of 4 5.50 5.50

Canonization of Josemaría Escrivá de Balaguer, Oct. 6, 2003 — A365

**2003, Nov. 18 Litho.** ***Perf. 14x13¼***
**1252** A365 41c multi 1.00 1.00

2002 Travels of Pope John Paul II — A366

Designs: 62c, Bulgaria and Azerbaijan, May 22-26. 77c, Canada, Guatemala and Mexico, July 23-Aug. 2. €2.07, Poland, Aug. 16-19.

**2003, Nov. 18** ***Perf. 13x13¼***
**1253-1255** A366 Set of 3 8.50 8.50

Christmas A367

**2003, Nov. 18**
**Stamp With White Border**
**1256** A367 41c multi 1.00 1.00
**Souvenir Sheet**
**Stamp Without White Border**
**1257** A367 41c multi 1.00 1.00

Death of Pope Paul VI, 25th anniv. (#1257).

St. Pius V (1504-72) A368

Altarpiece by Grazio Cossoli in Chapel of the Rosary, Santa Croce di Bosco Marengo: 4c, Detail depicting St. Pius V and flag. €2, Entire altarpiece.

**Litho. & Silk Screened**
**2004, Mar. 18** ***Perf. 13¼x13***
**1258-1259** A368 Set of 2 5.00 5.00

2003 Travels of Pope John Paul II — A369

Designs: 60c, Spain, May 3-4. 62c, Bosnia & Herzegovina, June 22. 80c, Croatia, June 5-9. €1.40, Slovakia, Sept. 11-14.

**2004, Mar. 18 Litho.**
**1260-1263** A369 Set of 4 8.50 8.50

Papal Visits to Poland — A370

No. 1264, 45c: a, Pope with hand on chin. b, Pope praying. c, Pope carrying crucifix. d, Pope with crucifix against head.

No. 1265, 62c: a, Pope holding crucifix, diff. b, Pope with arm raised. c, Pope, wearing white, seated. d, Pope, wearing red cape, seated.

**Litho. (Labels Litho. & Embossed)**
**2004, Mar. 18**
**Sheets of 4, #a-d, + 8 Labels**
**1264-1265** A370 Set of 2 10.50 10.50

Children AIDS Victims — A371

**2004, June 3 Photo.** ***Perf. 13¼x13***
**1266** A371 45c multi + label 1.10 1.10

Printed in sheets of 6 + 6 stamp-sized labels (with different text) and 1 large central label.

Europa — A372

Paintings of: 45c, Men on horses. 62c, People in garden.

**2004, June 3 Litho.** ***Perf. 12¾x13¼***
**1267-1268** A372 Set of 2 2.60 2.60

Flags and One-Euro Coins — A373

**2004, June 3 Litho.** ***Perf. 13½***

| | | | | | |
|---|---|---|---|---|---|
| **1269** | A373 | 4c | Austria | .20 | .20 |
| **1270** | A373 | 8c | Belgium | .20 | .20 |
| **1271** | A373 | 15c | Finland | .35 | .35 |
| **1272** | A373 | 25c | France | .60 | .60 |
| **1273** | A373 | 30c | Germany | .70 | .70 |
| **1274** | A373 | 40c | Greece | .95 | .95 |
| **1275** | A373 | 45c | Vatican City | 1.10 | 1.10 |
| **1276** | A373 | 60c | Ireland | 1.40 | 1.40 |
| **1277** | A373 | 62c | Italy | 1.50 | 1.50 |
| **1278** | A373 | 70c | Luxembourg | 1.75 | 1.75 |
| **1279** | A373 | 80c | Monaco | 1.90 | 1.90 |
| **1280** | A373 | €1 | Netherlands | 2.40 | 2.40 |
| **1281** | A373 | €1.40 | Portugal | 3.50 | 3.50 |
| **1282** | A373 | €2 | San Marino | 4.75 | 4.75 |
| **1283** | A373 | €2.80 | Spain | 6.75 | 6.75 |
| | *Nos. 1269-1283 (15)* | | | 28.05 | 28.05 |

48th Intl. Eucharistic Congress A374

Designs: 45c, Hands breaking bread over chalice. 65c, Hand raising eucharist.

**2004, Sept. 16 Litho.** ***Perf. 13x13¼***
**1284-1285** A374 Set of 2 2.75 2.75

Contemporary Religious Art in Vatican Museum Collection — A375

Designs: 45c, Still Life with Bottles, by Giorgio Morandi. 60c, The Fall of an Angel, by Marino Marini. 80c, Landscape with Houses, by Ezio Pastorio. 85c, Tuscan Countryside, by Giulio Cesare Vinzio.

**2004, Sept. 16 Photo.** ***Perf. 14x13¼***
**1286** A375 45c multi 1.10 1.10
**1287** A375 60c multi 1.50 1.50
*a.* Perf. 13½x13¼ 1.50 1.50
*b.* Booklet pane of 4 #1287a + 4 etiquettes 6.00 —
Complete booklet, #1287b 6.00
**1288** A375 80c multi 2.00 2.00
**1289** A375 85c multi 2.10 2.10
*Nos. 1286-1289 (4)* 6.70 6.70

Petrarch (1304-74), Poet
A376

**2004, Nov. 18 Photo. *Perf. 13¼x13***
**1290** A376 60c multi 1.60 1.60

Christmas
A377

**2004, Nov. 18 Litho. *Perf. 13¼***
**1291** A377 80c multi 2.25 2.25

**Interregnum Issue**

Arms of St. Peter and Papal Chamberlain's Insignia — A378

Inscription colors: 60c, Blue. 62c, Red. 80c, Green.

**2005, Apr. 12 Litho. *Perf. 13½x13***
**1292-1294** A378 Set of 3 5.25 5.25

Pope Benedict XVI — A379

Pope Benedict XVI wearing: 45c, Stole. 62c, White vestments. 80c, Miter.

**2005, June 2 Litho. *Perf. 13¼x13***
**1295-1297** A379 Set of 3 4.75 4.75

Coronation of Pope Benedict XVI, Apr. 19, 2005.

20th World Youth Day
A380

**2005, June 2**
**1298** A380 62c multi 1.50 1.50

See Germany No. 2343.

Europa
A381

Ceramic plates depicting fish painted by Pablo Picasso with background colors of: 62c, Orange. 80c, Blue.

**2005, June 2 *Perf. 12½***
**1299-1300** A381 Set of 2 3.50 3.50

Ratification of Modifications to Italy-Vatican Concordat, 20th Anniv. — A382

Arms of Vatican City and Italy and: 45c, Pen. €2.80, Map.

**2005, June 9 Photo. *Perf. 13¼***
**1301-1302** A382 Set of 2 8.00 8.00

See Italy Nos. 2677-2678.

Resurrection of Christ, by Perugino — A383

Various painting details: 60c, 62c, 80c, €1. €2.80, Jesus Christ.

**2005, June 9 *Perf. 14x13¼***
**1303-1306** A383 Set of 4 7.50 7.50

**Souvenir Sheet**

***Perf. 13¼x13¾***

**1307** A383 €2.80 multi 6.75 6.75

No. 1307 contains one 29x60mm stamp.

Dinner at Emmaus, by Primo Conti
A384

**2005, Nov. 10 Litho. *Perf. 13x13¼***
**1308** A384 62c multi 1.50 1.50

Eleventh General Assembly of the Synod of Bishops.

2004 Journeys of Pope John Paul II — A385

Designs: 45c, Bern, Switzerland, June 5-6. 80c, Lourdes, France, Aug. 14-15. €2, Loreto, Italy, Sept. 5.

**2005, Nov. 10**
**1309-1311** A385 Set of 3 7.75 7.75

The Annunciation, by Raphael — A386

Designs: Nos. 1312, 1314a, Drawing of Angel, Painting of Virgin Mary. Nos. 1313, 1314b, Painting of Angel, drawing of Virgin Mary.

**Litho. & Engr.**

**2005, Nov. 10 *Perf. 13x13¼***
**1312** A386 62c multi 1.50 1.50
**1313** A386 €1 multi 2.40 2.40

**Souvenir Sheet**

**1314** A386 €1.40 Sheet of 2, #a-b 6.75 6.75

See France No. 3153.

Swiss Papal Guards, 500th Anniv.
A387

Designs: 62c, Guard and drummers. 80c, Guards and St. Peter's Basilica.

**2005, Nov. 22 Litho. *Perf. 14x14¼***
**1315-1316** A387 Set of 2 3.50 3.50

Nos. 1315-1316 each issued in sheets of 6. See Switzerland Nos. 1224-1225.

Christmas
A388

Details from Adoration of the Shepherds, by François Le Moyne: 45c, Shepherds and sheep. 62c, Angel. 80c, Madonna and Child.

**2005, Nov. 22 *Perf. 13¼x13***
**1317-1319** A388 Set of 3 4.50 4.50
*1319a* Booklet pane of 4 #1319 7.50 —
Complete booklet, #1319a 7.50

Europa
A389

Designs: 62c, Praying hands, church, mosque and synagogue. 80c, Handshake, classroom.

**2006, Mar. 16 Litho. *Perf. 13x13¼***
**1320-1321** A389 Set of 2 3.50 3.50

Jesuits
A390

Designs: 45c, Blessed Peter Faber (1506-46). 60c, St. Ignatius of Loyola (1491-1556). €2, St. Francis Xavier (1506-52).

**2006, Mar. 16**
**1322-1324** A390 Set of 3 7.50 7.50

Andrea Mantegna (c. 1430-1506), Painter
A391

Designs: 60c, Madonna and Child. 85c, Saints Gregory and John the Baptist. €1, Saints Peter and Paul.

No. 1328 — San Zeno Polyptych: a, Country name at right. b, Country name at left.

**2006, Mar. 16 Photo. *Perf. 12¾***
**1325-1327** A391 Set of 3 6.00 6.00

**Souvenir Sheet**

***Perf. 13¼x13***

**1328** A391 €1.40 Sheet of 2, #a-b 6.75 6.75

No. 1328 contains two 21x37mm stamps.

Wolfgang Amadeus Mozart (1756-91), Composer
A392

**Litho. & Engr.**

**2006, June 22 *Perf. 14x14¼***
**1329** A392 80c multi 2.10 2.10

2005 Travels of Pope Benedict XVI — A393

Designs: 62c, National Eucharistic Congress, Bari, Italy, May 21-29. €1.40, World Youth Day, Cologne, Germany, Aug. 16-21.

**2006, June 22 Litho. *Perf. 13¼x13***
**1330-1331** A393 Set of 2 5.25 5.25

St. Peter's Basilica, 500th Anniv. — A394

No. 1332, 45c — 1506 medallion depicting: a, Allegory of architecture (denomination at LL). b, Architect Donato Bramante (denomination at UR).
No. 1333, 60c — 1506 medallion depicting: a, Pope Julius II (denomination at LL). b, Bramante's plan for St. Peter's Basilica (denomination at UR).

**Litho. & Embossed**
**2006, June 22 *Perf. 14***
**Horiz. Pairs, #a-b**
**1332-1333** A394 Set of 2 5.50 5.50

Intl. Year of Deserts and Desertification — A395

Designs: 62c, Flowers, child on parched earth. €1, Trees, child and cattle.

**2006, Oct. 12 Litho. *Perf. 13½x13¼***
**1334-1335** A395 Set of 2 4.25 4.25

Diplomatic Relations Between Vatican City and Singapore, 25th Anniv. — A396

Designs: 85c, Merlion and St. Peter's Basilica. €2, Flags of Singapore and Vatican City.

**2006, Oct. 12 *Perf. 13½x13***
**1336-1337** A396 Set of 2 7.25 7.25

See Singapore Nos. 1232-1233.

Vatican Musum, 500th Anniv. A397

Heads from Laocoon sculpture: 60c, Son of Laocoon. 65c, Laocoon. €1.40, Son of Laocoon, diff.
€2.80, Laocoon, horiz.

**Litho. & Embossed**
**2006, Oct. 12 *Perf. 13x13¼***
**1338-1340** A397 Set of 3 6.75 6.75

**Souvenir Sheet**
***Perf. 13 Horiz.***
**1341** A397 €2.80 multi 7.00 7.00

No. 1341 contains one 80x30mm stamp.

Christmas A398

Stained glass from Pope's private chapel: 60c, Shepherds. 65c, Holy Family. 85c, Magi and Star of Bethlehem.

**2006, Oct. 12 Litho. *Perf. 13¼x13***
**1342-1344** A398 Set of 3 5.25 5.25
*1343a* Booklet pane of 4 #1343 6.50 —
Complete booklet, #1343a 6.50

## SEMI-POSTAL STAMPS

### Holy Year Issue

Cross and Orb
SP1 SP2

***Perf. 13x13½***
**1933, Apr. 1 Unwmk. Engr.**
**B1** SP1 25c + 10c green 3.50 *3.50*
**B2** SP1 75c + 15c scarlet 6.25 *11.50*
**B3** SP2 80c + 20c red brown 22.50 16.00
**B4** SP2 1.25 l + 25c ultra 7.00 *12.00*
*Nos. B1-B4 (4)* 39.25 *43.00*
Set, never hinged 100.00

## AIR POST STAMPS

> **Catalogue values for unused stamps in this section are for Never Hinged items.**

Statue of St. Peter AP1

Dove of Peace over Vatican AP2

Elijah's Ascent into Heaven AP3

Our Lady of Loreto and Angels Moving the Holy House AP4

**Wmk. 235**
**1938, June 22 Engr. *Perf. 14***
**C1** AP1 25c brown .20 .20
**C2** AP2 50c green .20 .20
**C3** AP3 75c lake .20 .20
**C4** AP4 80c dark blue .20 .20
**C5** AP1 1 l violet .45 .45
**C6** AP2 2 l ultra 1.00 .60
**C7** AP3 5 l slate blk 2.25 1.50
**C8** AP4 10 l dk brown vio 2.25 1.90
*Nos. C1-C8 (8)* 6.75 5.25

Dove of Peace Above St. Peter's Basilica — AP5

House of Our Lady of Loreto — AP6

Birds Circling Cross — AP7

**1947, Nov. 10 Photo.**
**C9** AP5 1 l rose red .20 .20
**C10** AP6 4 l dark brown .20 .20
**C11** AP5 5 l brt ultra .20 .20
**C12** AP7 15 l brt purple .90 .50
**C13** AP6 25 l dk blue green 3.50 .40
**C14** AP7 50 l dk gray 5.00 1.50
**C15** AP7 100 l red orange 25.00 2.00
*Nos. C9-C15 (7)* 35.00 5.00

Nos. C13-C15 exist imperf. Value, each pair $1,000.

Archangel Raphael and Young Tobias AP8

**1948, Dec. 28 Engr. *Perf. 14***
**C16** AP8 250 l sepia 25.00 10.00
**C17** AP8 500 l ultra 450.00 275.00
Set, hinged 300.00

Angels and Globe AP9

**1949, Dec. 3**
**C18** AP9 300 l ultra 20.00 5.00
**C19** AP9 1000 l green 100.00 47.50
Set, hinged 75.00

UPU, 75th anniversary.

Franciscus Gratianus AP10

Dome of St. Peter's Cathedral AP11

**1951, Dec. 20 *Perf. 14x13***
**C20** AP10 300 l deep plum 240.00 150.00
**C21** AP10 500 l deep blue 35.00 17.50
Set, hinged 175.00

Publication of unified canon laws, 800th anniv.

**1953, Aug. 10 *Perf. 13***
**C22** AP11 500 l chocolate 21.00 2.50
**C23** AP11 1000 l deep ultra 62.50 12.50
Set, hinged 40.00

See Nos. C33-C34.

Archangel Gabriel by Melozzo da Forli — AP12

Obelisk of St. John Lateran — AP13

Archangel Gabriel: 10 l, 35 l, 100 l, Annunciation by Pietro Cavallini. 15 l, 50 l, 300 l, Annunciation by Leonardo da Vinci.

**1956, Feb. 12 Wmk. 235**
**C24** AP12 5 l gray black .20 .20
**C25** AP12 10 l blue green .20 .20
**C26** AP12 15 l deep orange .20 .20
**C27** AP12 25 l dk car rose .20 .20
**C28** AP12 35 l carmine .25 .20
**C29** AP12 50 l olive brown .20 .20
**C30** AP12 60 l ultra 2.75 2.25
**C31** AP12 100 l orange brown .20 .20
**C32** AP12 300 l deep violet .50 .20
*Nos. C24-C32 (9)* 4.70 3.85

Type of 1953

**1958 *Perf. 13½***
**C33** AP11 500 l grn & bl grn 7.50 4.00
*a.* Perf. 14 1,200. 700.00
**C34** AP11 1000 l dp mag .75 .75
*a.* Perf. 14 .75 .75

**1959, Oct. 27 Engr. *Perf. 13½x14***

Obelisks, Rome: 10 l, 60 l, St. Mary Major. 15 l, 100 l, St. Peter. 25 l, 200 l, Piazza del Popolo. 35 l, 500 l, Trinita dei Monti.

**C35** AP13 5 l dull violet .20 .20
**C36** AP13 10 l blue green .20 .20
**C37** AP13 15 l dk brown .20 .20
**C38** AP13 25 l slate grn .20 .20
**C39** AP13 35 l ultra .20 .20
**C40** AP13 50 l yellow grn .20 .20
**C41** AP13 60 l rose carmine .20 .20
**C42** AP13 100 l bluish black .20 .20
**C43** AP13 200 l brown .20 .20
**C44** AP13 500 l orange brn .30 .20
*Nos. C35-C44 (10)* 2.10 2.00

Archangel Gabriel by Filippo Valle — AP14

Jet over St. Peter's Cathedral AP15

**1962, Mar. 13** **Wmk. 235**

| | | | | |
|---|---|---|---|---|
| C45 | AP14 | 1000 l brown | 1.25 | .75 |
| C46 | AP14 | 1500 l dark blue | 1.75 | 1.25 |

**1967, Mar. 7** **Photo.** ***Perf. 14***

Designs: 40 l, 200 l, Radio tower and statue of Archangel Gabriel (like A87). 90 l, 500 l, Aerial view of St. Peter's Square and Vatican City.

| | | | | |
|---|---|---|---|---|
| C47 | AP15 | 20 l brt violet | .20 | .20 |
| C48 | AP15 | 40 l black & pink | .20 | .20 |
| C49 | AP15 | 90 l sl bl & dk gray | .20 | .20 |
| C50 | AP15 | 100 l black & salmon | .20 | .20 |
| C51 | AP15 | 200 l vio blk & gray | .20 | .20 |
| C52 | AP15 | 500 l dk brn & lt brn | .25 | .20 |
| | | *Nos. C47-C52 (6)* | 1.25 | 1.20 |

Archangel Gabriel by Fra Angelico — AP16

**1968, Mar. 12** **Engr.** ***Perf. 13½x14***

| | | | | |
|---|---|---|---|---|
| C53 | AP16 | 1000 l dk car rose, *cr* | 1.00 | .75 |
| C54 | AP16 | 1500 l black, *cr* | 1.75 | 1.50 |

St. Matthew, by Fra Angelico AP17

The Evangelists, by Fra Angelico from Niccolina Chapel: 300 l, St. Mark. 500 l, St. Luke. 1000 l, St. John.

**Engr. & Photo.**
***Perf. 14x13½***

**1971, Sept. 30** **Unwmk.**

| | | | | |
|---|---|---|---|---|
| C55 | AP17 | 200 l blk & pale grn | .20 | .20 |
| C56 | AP17 | 300 l black & bister | .20 | .20 |
| C57 | AP17 | 500 l black & salmon | .85 | .60 |
| C58 | AP17 | 1000 l black & pale lil | 1.00 | .75 |
| | | *Nos. C55-C58 (4)* | 2.25 | 1.75 |

AP18

AP19

Seraph, mosaic from St. Mark's Basilica, Venice.

**Litho. & Engr.**

**1974, Feb. 21** ***Perf. 13x14***

| | | | | |
|---|---|---|---|---|
| C59 | AP18 | 2500 l multicolored | 2.50 | 2.00 |

**Litho. & Engr.**

**1976, Feb. 19** ***Perf. 13x14***

Last Judgment, by Michelangelo: 500 l, Angel with Trumpet. 1000 l, Ascending figures. 2500 l, Angels with trumpets.

| | | | | |
|---|---|---|---|---|
| C60 | AP19 | 500 l sal, bl & brn | 1.25 | 1.10 |
| C61 | AP19 | 1000 l sal, bl & brn | 1.50 | 1.10 |
| C62 | AP19 | 2500 l sal, bl & brn | 2.00 | 1.50 |
| | | *Nos. C60-C62 (3)* | 4.75 | 3.70 |

Radio Waves, Antenna, Papal Arms AP20

**1978, July 11** **Engr.** ***Perf. 14x13***

| | | | | |
|---|---|---|---|---|
| C63 | AP20 | 1000 l multicolored | 1.00 | .70 |
| C64 | AP20 | 2000 l multicolored | 2.00 | 1.40 |
| C65 | AP20 | 3000 l multicolored | 3.00 | 1.90 |
| | | *Nos. C63-C65 (3)* | 6.00 | 4.00 |

10th World Telecommunications Day.

Pope John Paul II Shaking Hands, Arms of Dominican Republic AP21

**1980** **Litho. & Engr.** ***Perf. 14x13½***

| | | | | |
|---|---|---|---|---|
| C66 | AP21 | 200 l shown | .25 | .25 |
| C67 | AP21 | 300 l Mexico | .30 | .30 |
| C68 | AP21 | 500 l Poland | .60 | .60 |
| C69 | AP21 | 1000 l Ireland | 1.10 | 1.10 |
| C70 | AP21 | 1500 l US | 1.75 | 1.75 |
| C71 | AP21 | 2000 l UN | 2.00 | 2.00 |
| C72 | AP21 | 3000 l with Dimitrios I, Turkey | 3.50 | 3.50 |
| | | *Nos. C66-C72 (7)* | 9.50 | 9.50 |

Issued: 3000 l, Sept. 18; others June 24.

World Communications Year — AP22

Designs: 2000 l, Moses Explaining The Law to the People by Luca Signarelli. 5000 l, Paul Preaching in Athens, Tapestry of Raphael design.

**1983, Nov. 10** ***Perf. 14***

| | | | | |
|---|---|---|---|---|
| C73 | AP22 | 2000 l multicolored | 3.00 | 3.00 |
| C74 | AP22 | 5000 l multicolored | 6.75 | 6.75 |

Journeys of Pope John Paul II, 1983-84 AP23

Designs: 350 l, Central America, the Caribbean, 1983. 450 l, Warsaw Cathedral, Our Lady of Czestochowa, Poland, 1983. 700 l, Statue of Our Lady, Lourdes, France, 1983. 1000 l, Mariazell Sanctuary, St. Stephen's Cathedral, Austria, 1983. 1500 l, Asia, the Pacific, 1984. 2000 l, Einsiedeln Basilica, St. Nicholas of Flue, Switzerland, 1984. 2500 l, Quebec's Notre Dame Cathedral, five crosses of the Jesuit martyrs, Canada, 1984. 5000 l, Saragossa, Spain, Dominican Republic and Puerto Rico, 1984.

**1986, Nov. 20** **Photo.** ***Perf. 14x13½***

| | | | | |
|---|---|---|---|---|
| C75 | AP23 | 350 l multicolored | .50 | .50 |
| C76 | AP23 | 450 l multicolored | .65 | .65 |
| C77 | AP23 | 700 l multicolored | 1.00 | 1.00 |
| C78 | AP23 | 1000 l multicolored | 1.50 | 1.50 |
| C79 | AP23 | 1500 l multicolored | 2.25 | 2.25 |
| C80 | AP23 | 2000 l multicolored | 3.25 | 3.25 |
| C81 | AP23 | 2500 l multicolored | 4.00 | 4.00 |
| C82 | AP23 | 5000 l multicolored | 8.00 | 8.00 |
| | | *Nos. C75-C82 (8)* | 21.15 | 21.15 |

Papal Journeys Type of 1986

Designs: 450 l, Horseman, shepherdess, St. Peter's Basilica, Cathedral of Santiago in Chile, and the Sanctuary of Our Lady of Lujan, Argentina. 650 l, Youths and the Cathedral of Speyer, Federal Republic of Germany. 1000 l, St. Peter's Basilica, Altar of Gdansk, flowers and thorns. 2500 l, Crowd and American skyscrapers. 5000 l, Tepee at Fort Simpson, Canada, and American Indians.

**1988, Oct. 27** **Photo.** ***Perf. 14x13½***

| | | | | |
|---|---|---|---|---|
| C83 | AP23 | 450 l multicolored | .65 | .65 |
| C84 | AP23 | 650 l multicolored | .95 | .95 |
| C85 | AP23 | 1000 l multicolored | 1.50 | 1.50 |
| C86 | AP23 | 2500 l multicolored | 3.50 | 3.50 |
| C87 | AP23 | 5000 l multicolored | 7.25 | 7.25 |
| | | *Nos. C83-C87 (5)* | 13.85 | 13.85 |

Uruguay, Chile and Argentina, Mar. 30-Apr. 14, 1987 (450 l); Federal Republic of Germany, Apr. 30-May 4, 1987 (650 l); Poland, June 8-14, 1987 (1000 l); US, Sept. 10-19, 1987 (2500 l); and Canada, Sept. 20, 1987 (5000 l).

Journeys of Pope John Paul II, 1989 AP24

**1990, Nov. 27** **Photo.** ***Perf. 12***
**Granite Paper**

| | | | | |
|---|---|---|---|---|
| C88 | AP24 | 500 l Africa | .80 | .80 |
| C89 | AP24 | 1000 l Scandinavia | 1.60 | 1.60 |
| C90 | AP24 | 3000 l Santiago de Compostela, Spain | 5.00 | 5.00 |
| C91 | AP24 | 5000 l Asia | 8.00 | 8.00 |
| | | *Nos. C88-C91 (4)* | 15.40 | 15.40 |

Madagascar, Reunion, Zambia and Malawi, Apr. 28-May 6 (500 l); Norway, Iceland, Finland, Denmark and Sweden, June 1-10 (1000 l); Korea, Indonesia and Mauritius, Oct. 6-16 (5000 l).

Travels of Pope John Paul II, 1991 AP25

**1992, Nov. 24** **Photo.** ***Perf. 14***

| | | | | |
|---|---|---|---|---|
| C92 | AP25 | 500 l multicolored | .65 | .65 |
| C93 | AP25 | 1000 l multicolored | 1.40 | 1.40 |
| C94 | AP25 | 4000 l multicolored | 5.25 | 5.25 |
| C95 | AP25 | 6000 l multicolored | 8.00 | 8.00 |
| | | *Nos. C92-C95 (4)* | 15.30 | 15.30 |

Portugal, May 10-13 (500 l); Poland, June 1-9 (1000 l); Poland, Hungary, Aug. 13-20 (4000 l); Brazil, Oct. 12-21 (6000 l).

## SPECIAL DELIVERY STAMPS

Pius XI SD1

**Unwmk.**

**1929, Aug. 1** **Photo.** ***Perf. 14***

| | | | | |
|---|---|---|---|---|
| E1 | SD1 | 2 l carmine rose | 14.00 | 11.50 |
| E2 | SD1 | 2.50 l dark blue | 12.00 | 12.00 |

For overprints see Nos. Q14-Q15.

**Catalogue values for unused stamps in this section, from this point to the end of the section, are for Never Hinged items.**

Aerial View of Vatican City SD2

**1933** **Wmk. 235** **Engr.**

| | | | | |
|---|---|---|---|---|
| E3 | SD2 | 2 l rose red & brn | .35 | .35 |
| E4 | SD2 | 2.50 l dp blue & brn | .35 | *.55* |

**1945** **Unwmk.**

| | | | | |
|---|---|---|---|---|
| E5 | SD2 | 3.50 l dk car & ultra | .30 | .30 |
| E6 | SD2 | 5 l ultra & green | .30 | .30 |

Nos. E5 and E6 Surcharged with New Values and Bars in Black

**1946, Jan. 9**

| | | | | |
|---|---|---|---|---|
| E7 | SD2 | 6 l on 3.50 l dk car & ultra | 4.25 | 1.75 |
| E8 | SD2 | 12 l on 5 l ultra & grn | 4.25 | 1.75 |

Vertical pairs imperf. between exist of No. E7 (value $150) and No. E8 (value $200).

Bishop Matteo Giberti SD3

Design: 12 l, Gaspar Cardinal Contarini.

**1946, Feb. 21** **Photo.**
**Centers in Dark Brown**

| | | | | |
|---|---|---|---|---|
| E9 | SD3 | 6 l dark green | .20 | .20 |
| E10 | SD3 | 12 l copper brown | .20 | .20 |

See note after No. 121.
#E9-E10 exist imperf and part perf.

Basilica of St. Peter SD5

Design: 80 l, Basilica of St. John.

**1949, Mar. 7** **Wmk. 235** ***Perf. 14***

| | | | | |
|---|---|---|---|---|
| E11 | SD5 | 40 l slate gray | 10.50 | 3.25 |
| *a.* | | Perf. 13½x14 | 21.00 | 7.50 |
| E12 | SD5 | 80 l chestnut brown | 37.50 | 20.00 |
| *a.* | | Perf. 13½x14 | 40.00 | 22.50 |

St. Peter and His Tomb — SD6

85 l, Pius XII and Roman sepulcher.

***Perf. 13½x13, 14***

**1953, Apr. 23** **Engr.**

| | | | | |
|---|---|---|---|---|
| E13 | SD6 | 50 l blue grn & dk brn | .20 | .20 |
| E14 | SD6 | 85 l dp orange & dk brn | .35 | .25 |

Arms of Pope John XXIII SD7

**1960** **Photo.** ***Perf. 14***

| | | | | |
|---|---|---|---|---|
| E15 | SD7 | 75 l red & brown | .20 | .20 |
| E16 | SD7 | 100 l dk blue & brown | .20 | .20 |

Pope Paul VI by Enrico Manfrini — SD8

Design: 150 l, Papal arms.

**1966, Mar. 8 Wmk. 235 *Perf. 14***
**E17** SD8 150 l black brown .20 .20
**E18** SD8 180 l brown .20 .20

## POSTAGE DUE STAMPS

Regular Issue of 1929 Overprinted in Black and Brown

**1931, Sept. 15 Unwmk. *Perf. 14***
**J1** A1 5c dk brown & pink .20 .20
*a.* Double frame
**J2** A1 10c dk grn & lt grn .20 .20
*a.* Frame omitted *675.00*
**J3** A1 20c violet & lilac 5.75 2.00

Surcharged

**J4** A1 40c on 30c indigo & yel 1.50 *4.00*

Surcharged

**J5** A2 60c on 2 l olive brn 27.50 18.00
**J6** A2 1.10 l on 2.50 l red org 3.75 *16.00*
*Nos. J1-J6 (6)* 38.90 *40.40*
Set, never hinged 100.00

In addition to the surcharges, #J4-J6 are overprinted with ornamental frame as on #J1-J3.

**Catalogue values for unused stamps in this section, from this point to the end of the section, are for Never Hinged items.**

Papal Arms
D1 D2

**Unwmk.**

**1945, Aug. 16 Typo. *Perf. 14***
**J7** D1 5c black & yellow .20 .20
**J8** D1 20c black & lilac .20 .20
**J9** D1 80c black & salmon .20 .20
**J10** D1 1 l black & green .20 .20
**J11** D1 2 l black & blue .20 .20
**J12** D1 5 l black & gray .20 .20
*a.* Imperf., pair 125.00 125.00
*Nos. J7-J12 (6)* 1.20 1.20

A second type of Nos. J7-J12 exists, in which the colored lines of the background are thicker.
The 20c and 5 lire exist in horizontal pairs imperf. vertically. Value, each $100.
The 20c exists in horizontal pairs imperf. between. Value $275.

***Perf. 13½x13***

**1954, Apr. 30 Wmk. 235 Engr.**
**J13** D2 4 l black & rose .20 .20
**J14** D2 6 l black & green .30 .30
**J15** D2 10 l black & yellow .20 .20
**J16** D2 20 l black & blue .45 .30
**J17** D2 50 l black & ol brn .20 .20
**J18** D2 70 l black & red brn .20 .20
*Nos. J13-J18 (6)* 1.55 1.40

Papal Arms — D3

**Photo. & Engr.**

**1968, May 28 Wmk. 235 *Perf. 14***
**J19** D3 10 l black, *grysh bl* .20 .20
**J20** D3 20 l black, *pale bl* .20 .20
**J21** D3 50 l black, *pale lil rose* .20 .20
**J22** D3 60 l black, *gray* .20 .20
**J23** D3 100 l black, *dull yel* .20 .20
**J24** D3 180 l black, *bluish lil* .20 .20
*Nos. J19-J24 (6)* 1.20 1.20

## PARCEL POST STAMPS

Regular Issue of 1929 Overprinted

**1931 Unwmk. *Perf. 14***
**Q1** A1 5c dk brown & pink .40 .30
**Q2** A1 10c dk grn & lt grn .40 .30
**Q3** A1 20c violet & lilac 4.75 5.50
**Q4** A1 25c dk bl & lt bl 6.25 4.25
**Q5** A1 30c indigo & yel 9.25 4.25
**Q6** A1 50c indigo & sal buff 9.25 4.25
**Q7** A1 75c brn car & gray 2.75 2.75

Overprinted

**Q8** A2 80c carmine rose 1.60 1.90
**Q9** A2 1.25 l dark blue 2.75 2.00
**Q10** A2 2 l olive brown .55 .85
*a.* Inverted overprint 325.00 475.00
**Q11** A2 2.50 l red orange .55 .85
*a.* Double overprint 225.00
*b.* Inverted overprint 500.00
**Q12** A2 5 l dark green .55 .85
**Q13** A2 10 l olive black .55 .85
*a.* Double overprint 325.00

Special Delivery Stamps of 1929 Overprinted Vertically

**Q14** SD1 2 l carmine rose .55 .85
**Q15** SD1 2.50 l dark blue .55 .85
*Nos. Q1-Q15 (15)* 40.70 30.60
Set, never hinged 95.00

# VENEZUELA

ˌve-nə-ˈzwā-lə

LOCATION — Northern coast of South America, bordering on the Caribbean Sea
GOVT. — Republic
AREA — 352,143 sq. mi.
POP. — 23,203,466 (1999 est.)
CAPITAL — Caracas

100 Centavos = 8 Reales = 1 Peso
100 Centesimos = 1 Venezolano (1879)
100 Centimos = 1 Bolivar (1880)

**Watermark**

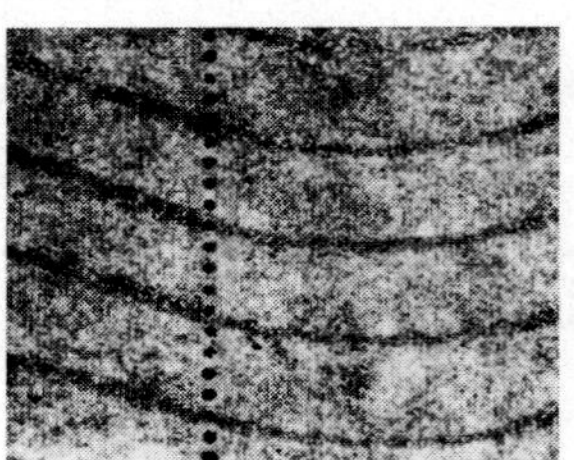

Wmk. 346

**Catalogue values for unused stamps in this country are for Never Hinged items, beginning with Scott 743 in the regular postage section, Scott B2 in the semi-postal section, Scott C709 in the airpost section, and Scott E1 in the special delivery section.**

Coat of Arms — A1

Fine Impression
No Dividing Line Between Stamps

**Unwmk.**

**1859, Jan. 1 Litho. *Imperf.***
**1** A1 ½r yellow 23.00 9.25
*a.* ½r orange 27.00 11.00
*b.* Greenish paper *225.00*
**2** A1 1r blue 325.00 20.00
*a.* Half used as ½r on cover *400.00*
**3** A1 2r red 42.50 15.00
*a.* 2r dull rose red 55.00 17.00
*b.* Half used as 1r on cover 450.00
*c.* Greenish paper 225.00 140.00
*Nos. 1-3 (3)* 390.50 44.25

Coarse Impression

**1859-62**

**Thick Paper**

**4** A1 ½r orange ('61) 12.00 4.00
*a.* ½r yellow ('59) 500.00 30.00
*b* ½r olive yellow 750.00 35.00
*c.* Bluish paper 575.00
*d.* ½r dull rose (error)
**5** A1 1r blue ('62) 20.00 12.50
*a.* 1r pale blue 35.00 15.00
*b.* 1r dark blue 35.00 15.00
*c.* Half used as ½r on cover *400.00*
*d.* Bluish paper 200.00
**6** A1 2r red ('62) 30.00 20.00
*a.* 2r dull rose 42.50 20.00
*b.* Tête bêche pair *5,000.* *3,500.*
*c.* Half used as 1r on cover *400.00*
*d.* Bluish paper *225.00*
*Nos. 4-6 (3)* 62.00 36.50

In the fine impression, the background lines of the shield are more sharply drawn. In the coarse impression, the shading lines at each end of the scroll inscribed "LIBERTAD" are usually very heavy. Stamps of the coarse impression are closer together, and there is usually a dividing line between them.
Nos. 1-3 exist on thick paper and on bluish paper. Nos. 1-6 exist on pelure paper.
The greenish paper varieties (Nos. 1b and 3c) and the bluish paper varieties were not regularly issued.

Arms — A2 Eagle — A3

**1862 Litho.**
**7** A2 ¼c green 20.00 110.00
**8** A2 ½c dull lilac 30.00 *190.00*
*a.* ½c violet 40.00 210.00
**9** A2 1c gray brown 42.50 225.00
*Nos. 7-9 (3)* 92.50 *525.00*

Counterfeits are plentiful. Forged cancellations abound on Nos. 7-17.

**1863-64**
**10** A3 ½c pale red ('64) 55.00 *125.00*
*a.* ½c red 60.00 *125.00*
**11** A3 1c slate ('64) 62.50 *160.00*
**12** A3 ½r orange 7.75 3.50
**13** A3 1r blue 17.00 8.50
*a.* 1r pale blue 30.00 13.00
*b.* Half used as ½r on cover *400.00*

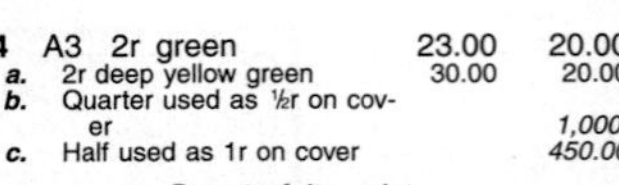

**14** A3 2r green 23.00 20.00
*a.* 2r deep yellow green 30.00 20.00
*b.* Quarter used as ½r on cover *1,000.*
*c.* Half used as 1r on cover *450.00*

Counterfeits exist.

Redrawn

**1865**
**15** A3 ½r orange 4.00 2.50
*a.* ½r yellow 4.00 2.50

The redrawn stamp has a broad "N" in "FEDERACION." "MEDIO REAL" and "FEDERACION" are in thin letters. There are 52 instead of 49 pearls in the circle.
The status of No. 15 has been questioned.

A4 Simón Bolívar — A5

**1865-70**
**16** A4 ½c yel grn ('67) 200.00 300.00
**17** A4 1c bl grn ('67) 200.00 *250.00*
**18** A4 ½r brn vio (thin paper) 9.25 2.00
**19** A4 ½r lil rose ('70) 9.25 2.50
*a.* ½r brownish rose 9.25 3.00
*b.* Tête bêche pair 110.00 *150.00*
**20** A4 1r vermilion 42.50 15.00
*a.* Half used as ½r on cover *200.00*
**21** A4 2r yellow 160.00 77.50
*a.* Half used as 1r on cover *750.00*
*b.* Quarter used as ½r on cover *1,000.*
*Nos. 16-21 (6)* 621.00 *647.00*

This issue is known unofficially rouletted.
Postal forgeries exist of the ½r.
For overprints see Nos. 37-48.

Overprinted in Very Small Upright Letters "Bolivar Sucre Miranda dash> Decreto de 27 de Abril de 1870", or "Decreto de 27 de Junio 1870" in Slanting Letters

(The "Junio" overprint is continuously repeated, in four lines arranged in two pairs, with the second line of each pair inverted.)

| | | | |
|---|---|---|---|
| Un | 1 | Siete | 7 |
| Dos | 2 | Nueve | 9 |
| Tres | 3 | Quince | 15 |
| Cuatro | 4 | Veinte | 20 |
| Cinco | 5 | Cincuenta | 50 |

**1871-76 Litho.**
**22** A5 1c yellow 1.50 .40
*a.* 1c orange 2.10 .45
*b.* 1c brown orange ('76) 2.10 .30
*c.* 1c pale buff ('76) 2.10 .45
*d.* Laid paper 1.00 .75
**23** A5 2c yellow 2.00 .45
*a.* 2c orange 4.00 .45
*b.* 2c brown orange 3.50 .75
*c.* 2c pale buff ('76) 3.50 .45
*d.* Laid paper 3.50 .55
*e.* Frame inverted *4,000.* *3,000.*
**24** A5 3c yellow 3.00 .75
*a.* 3c orange 3.00 1.40
*b.* 3c pale buff ('76) 5.50 1.75
**25** A5 4c yellow 4.00 .75
*a.* 4c orange 4.50 1.25
*b.* 4c brown orange ('76) 4.50 1.25
*c.* 4c buff ('76) 4.50 1.25
**26** A5 5c yellow 4.00 .75
*a.* 5c orange 4.00 .90
*b.* 5c pale buff ('76) 4.00 .90
*c.* Laid paper 7.50 .90
**27** A5 1r rose 4.00 2.00
*a.* 1r pale red 4.00 2.00
*b.* Laid paper 6.00 2.50
*c.* Half used as ½r on cover *1,800.*
**28** A5 2r rose 4.50 2.00
*a.* 2r pale red 4.50 2.00
*b.* Laid paper 12.00 2.50
**29** A5 3r rose 6.00 2.00
*a.* 3r pale red 6.00 2.00
**30** A5 5r rose 5.75 1.00
*a.* 5r pale red 5.75 1.00
**31** A5 7r rose 22.50 4.00
*a.* 7r pale red 22.50 4.00
**32** A5 9r green 22.50 4.25
*a.* 9r olive green 22.50 6.00
**33** A5 15r green 55.00 8.50
*a.* 15r gray green ('76) 55.00 8.50
*b.* Frame inverted *8,000.* *6,500.*
**34** A5 20r green 77.50 20.00
*a.* Laid paper 110.00 35.00
**35** A5 30r green 375.00 110.00
*a.* 30r gray green ('76) 600.00 160.00
*b.* Double overprint
**36** A5 50r green 1,200. 300.00
*a.* 50r gray green ('76)
*Nos. 22-34 (13)* 212.25 46.85
*Nos. 22-35 (14)* 587.25 156.85

These stamps were made available for postage and revenue by official decree, and were the only stamps sold for postage in Venezuela from Mar., 1871 to Aug., 1873.

Due to lack of canceling stamps, the majority of specimens were canceled with pen marks. Fiscal cancellations were also made with the pen. The values quoted are for pen-canceled copies.

Different settings were used for the different overprints. Stamps with the upright letters were issued in 1871. Those with the slanting letters in one double line were issued in 1872-73. Specimens with the slanting overprint in two double lines were issued starting in 1874 from several different settings, those of 1877-78 showing much coarser impressions of the design than the earlier issues. The 7r and 9r are not known with this overprint. Stamps on laid paper (1875) are from a separate setting.

Stamps and Types of 1866-67 Overprinted in Two Lines of Very Small Letters Repeated Continuously Overprinted "Estampillas de Correo - Contrasena"

**1873, July 1**

**37** A4 ½r pale rose 70.00 13.00
*a.* ½r rose 70.00 13.00
*b.* Inverted overprint 125.00 50.00
*c.* Tête bêche pair *2,750. 2,000.*
**38** A4 1r vermilion 85.00 25.00
*a.* Inverted overprint 400.00 175.00
*b.* Half used as ½r on cover *550.00*
**39** A4 2r yellow 300.00 125.00
*a.* Inverted overprint 400.00 175.00
*b.* Half used as 1r on cover *12,000.*
*Nos. 37-39 (3)* 455.00 163.00

Overprinted "Contrasena — Estampillas de Correo"

**1873, Nov.**

**40** A4 1c gray lilac 30.00 32.50
*a.* Inverted overprint 6.50 *17.00*
**41** A4 2c green 125.00 90.00
*a.* Inverted overprint 40.00 50.00
**42** A4 ½r rose 72.50 13.00
*a.* Inverted overprint 30.00 4.00
*b.* ½r pink 60.00 11.00
**43** A4 1r vermilion 85.00 23.00
*a.* Inverted overprint 35.00 9.00
*b.* Half used as ½r on cover *300.00*
**44** A4 2r yellow 325.00 160.00
*a.* Inverted overprint 110.00 50.00
*b.* Half used as 1r on cover *1,500.*
*Nos. 40-44 (5)* 637.50 318.50

Overprinted "Contrasena — Estampilla de Correos"

**1875**

**45** A4 ½r rose 85.00 10.00
*a.* Inverted overprint 125.00 25.00
*b.* Double overprint 160.00 90.00
**46** A4 1r vermilion 160.00 15.00
*a.* Inverted overprint 200.00 80.00
*b.* Tête bêche pair *3,500. 3,000.*
*c.* Half used as ½r on cover *250.00*

Overprinted "Estampillas de correo — Contrasena"

**1876-77**

**47** A4 ½r rose 77.50 9.25
*a.* ½r pink 65.00 7.50
*b.* Inverted overprint 65.00 7.50
*c.* Both lines of overprint read "Contrasena" 75.00 17.50
*d.* Both lines of overprint read "Estampillas de correo" 75.00 17.50
*e.* Double overprint 125.00 35.00
**48** A4 1r vermilion ('77) 92.50 23.00
*a.* Inverted overprint 85.00 24.00
*b.* Tête bêche pair *2,250. 2,500.*
*c.* Half used as ½r on cover *250.00*

On Nos. 47 and 48 "correo" has a small "c" instead of a capital. Nos. 45 and 46 have the overprint in slightly larger letters than the other stamps of the 1873-76 issues.

Simón Bolívar
A6 A7

Overprinted "Decreto de 27 Junio 1870" Twice, One Line Inverted

**1879** ***Imperf.***

**49** A6 1c yellow 4.00 1.00
*a.* 1c orange 5.00 1.50
*b.* 1c olive yellow 5.50 1.75
**50** A6 5c yellow 3.50 .50
*a.* 5c orange 2.50 .75
*b.* Double overprint 20.00 10.00
**51** A6 10c blue 5.00 .50
**52** A6 30c blue 7.75 1.00
**53** A6 50c blue 7.75 1.00
**54** A6 90c blue 40.00 12.00
**55** A7 1v rose red 77.50 18.00
**56** A7 3v rose red 130.00 55.00
**57** A7 5v rose red 225.00 77.50
*Nos. 49-57 (9)* 500.50 166.50

In 1879 and the early part of 1880 there were no regular postage stamps in Venezuela and the stamps inscribed "Escuelas" were permitted to serve for postal as well as revenue purposes. Postally canceled copies are extremely scarce. Values quoted are for stamps with cancellations of banks or business houses or with pen cancellations. Copies with pen marks removed are sometimes offered as unused stamps, or may have fraudulent postal cancellations added.

Nos. 49-57 exist without overprint. These probably are revenue stamps.

A8 A9

**1880** ***Perf. 11***

**58** A8 5c yellow 1.50 .50
*a.* 5c orange 1.50 .50
*b.* Printed on both sides 150.00 85.00
**59** A8 10c yellow 2.50 .60
*a.* 10c orange 2.50 .60
**60** A8 25c yellow 2.50 .60
*a.* 25c orange 2.75 .70
*b.* Printed on both sides 110.00 52.50
*c.* Impression of 5c on back *175.00* 90.00
**61** A8 50c yellow 4.75 .80
*a.* 50c orange 5.25 .85
*b.* Half used as 25c on cover 400.00
*c.* Printed on both sides 150.00 90.00
*d.* Impression of 25c on back 150.00 90.00
**62** A9 1b pale blue 12.00 1.40
**63** A9 2b pale blue 17.00 1.75
**64** A9 5b pale blue 40.00 5.75
*a.* Half used as 2½b on cover —
**65** A9 10b rose red 200.00 70.00
**66** A9 20b rose red 1,200. 200.00
**67** A9 25b rose red *5,000.* 500.00
*Nos. 58-65 (8)* 280.25 81.40

See note on used values below No. 57.

Bolívar — A10

**1880** **Litho.** ***Perf. 11***

**Thick or Thin Paper**

**68** A10 5c blue 15.00 7.25
*a.* Printed on both sides 225.00 140.00
**69** A10 10c rose 20.00 12.00
*a.* 10c carmine 20.00 12.00
*b.* Double impression 90.00 75.00
*c.* Horiz. pair, imperf. btwn. 75.00 75.00
**70** A10 10c scarlet 20.00 12.00
*a.* Horiz. pair, imperf. btwn. 75.00 75.00
**71** A10 25c yellow 15.00 7.25
*b.* Thick paper 20.00 10.00
**72** A10 50c brown 92.50 40.00
*a.* 50c deep brown 92.50 40.00
*b.* Printed on both sides 225.00 140.00
**73** A10 1b green 140.00 50.00
*a.* Horiz. pair, imperf. btwn. 300.00 300.00
*Nos. 68-73 (6)* 302.50 128.50

Nos. 68 to 73 were used for the payment of postage on letters to be sent abroad and the Escuelas stamps were then restricted to internal use.

Counterfeits of this issue exist in a great variety of shades as well as in wrong colors. They are on thick and thin paper, white or toned, and imperf. or perforated 11, 12 and compound. They are also found tête bêche. Counterfeits of Nos. 68 to 72 inclusive often have a diagonal line across the "S" of "CENTS" and a short line from the bottom of that letter to the frame below it. Originals of No. 73 show parts of a frame around "BOLIVAR."

Simón Bolívar
A11 A12

A13

A14

A15

**1882, Aug. 1** **Engr.** ***Perf. 12***

**74** A11 5c blue .70 .35
**75** A12 10c red brown .70 .35
**76** A13 25c yellow brown 1.00 .40
*a.* Printed on both sides 50.00 27.50
**77** A14 50c green 2.40 .70
**78** A15 1b violet 3.25 1.75
*Nos. 74-78 (5)* 8.05 3.55

Nos. 75-78 exist imperf. Value, set $32.50.

See Nos. 88, 92-95. For surcharges and overprints see Nos. 100-103, 108-112.

A16

A17

A18

A19

A20

A21

A22 A23

**1882-88**

**79** A16 5c blue green .20 .20
**80** A17 10c brown .20 .20
**81** A18 25c orange .20 .20
**82** A19 50c blue .20 .20
**83** A20 1b vermilion .25 .20
**84** A21 3b dull vio ('88) .25 .20
**85** A22 10b dark brn ('88) 1.25 .80
**86** A23 20b plum ('88) 1.50 .95
*Nos. 79-86 (8)* 4.05 2.95

By official decree, dated Apr. 14, 1882, stamps of types A11 to A15 were to be used for foreign postage and those of types A16 to A23 for inland correspondence and fiscal use.

Issue date: Nos. 79-83, Aug. 1.

See Nos. 87, 89-91, 96-99. For surcharges and overprints see Nos. 104-107, 114-122.

**1887-88** **Litho.** ***Perf. 11***

**87** A16 5c gray green .25 .20
**88** A13 25c yellow brown 42.50 15.00
**89** A18 25c orange .40 .35
**90** A20 1b orange red ('88) 3.50 .75
*Nos. 87-90 (4)* 46.65 16.30

***Perf. 14***

**91** A16 5c gray green 70.00 22.50

Stamps of type A16, perf. 11 and 14, are from a new die with "ESCUELAS" in smaller letters. Stamps of the 1887-88 issue, perf. 12, and a 50c dark blue, perf. 11 or 12, are believed by experts to be from printer's waste.

Counterfeits of No. 91 have been made by perforating printers waste of No. 96.

***Rouletted 8***

**92** A11 5c blue 40.00 17.00
**93** A13 25c yel brown 15.00 10.00
**94** A14 50c green 15.00 10.00
**95** A15 1b purple 30.00 20.00
*Nos. 92-95 (4)* 100.00 57.00

**1887-88**

**96** A16 5c green .20 .20
**97** A18 25c orange .20 .20
**98** A19 50c dark blue .70 .70
**99** A21 3b purple ('88) 3.00 3.00
*Nos. 96-99 (4)* 4.10 4.10

The so-called imperforate varieties of Nos. 92 to 99, and the pin perforated 50c dark blue, type A19, are believed to be from printer's waste.

Stamps of 1882-88 Handstamp Surcharged in Violet

**1892** ***Perf. 12***

**100** A11 25c on 5c blue *40.00 40.00*
**101** A12 25c on 10c red brn *16.00 16.00*
**102** A13 1b on 25c yel brn *16.00 16.00*
**103** A14 1b on 50c green *20.00 20.00*
*Nos. 100-103 (4)* *92.00 92.00*

See note after No. 107.

**1892**

**104** A16 25c on 5c bl grn *10.00 6.00*
**105** A17 25c on 10c brown *10.00 6.00*
**106** A18 1b on 25c orange *15.00 12.00*
**107** A19 1b on 50c blue *23.00 12.00*
*Nos. 104-107 (4)* *58.00 36.00*

Counterfeits of this surcharge abound.

Stamps of 1882-88 Overprinted in Red or Black:

**1893**

**108** A11 5c blue (R) .55 .25
*a.* Inverted overprint 3.25 3.25
*b.* Double overprint 16.00 16.00
**109** A12 10c red brn (Bk) .90 .90
*a.* Inverted overprint 4.00 4.00
*b.* Double overprint 16.00 16.00
**110** A13 25c yel brn (R) .80 .50
*a.* Inverted overprint 5.25 5.25
*b.* Double overprint 16.00 16.00
*c.* 25c yel brn (Bk) *500.00 500.00*
**111** A14 50c green (R) 1.25 .80
*a.* Inverted overprint 5.25 5.25
*b.* Double overprint 27.50 27.50
**112** A15 1b pur (R) 3.00 1.20
*a.* Inverted overprint 10.00 10.00
*Nos. 108-112 (5)* 6.50 3.65

**1893**

**114** A16 5c bl grn (R) .20 .20
*a.* Inverted overprint 3.25 3.25
*b.* Double overprint 5.25 5.25
**115** A17 10c brn (R) .20 .20
*a.* Inverted overprint 3.25 3.25
**116** A18 25c org (R) .20 .20
*a.* Inverted overprint 3.25 3.25
**117** A18 25c org (Bk) 5.75 2.75
*a.* Inverted overprint 8.25 5.00
**118** A19 50c blue (R) .20 .20
*a.* Inverted overprint 3.25 3.25
**119** A20 1b ver (Bk) .60 .40
*a.* Inverted overprint 4.00 4.00
**120** A21 3b dl vio (R) .90 .40
*a.* Double overprint 8.25 8.25
**121** A22 10b dk brn (R) 3.50 2.25
*a.* Double overprint 10.00 10.00
*b.* Inverted overprint 20.00 20.00
**122** A23 20b plum (Bk) 3.00 3.00
*a.* Double overprint 10.00 20.00
*b.* Inverted overprint
*Nos. 114-122 (9)* 14.55 9.60

Counterfeits exist.

Simón Bolívar
A24 A25

**1893** **Engr.**
**123** A24 5c red brn .90 .25
**124** A24 10c blue 3.25 1.25
**125** A24 25c magenta 15.00 .50
**126** A24 50c brn vio 4.25 .55
**127** A24 1b green 5.75 1.25
*Nos. 123-127 (5)* 29.15 3.80

Many shades exist in this issue, but their values do not vary.

**1893**
**128** A25 5c gray .20 .20
**129** A25 10c green .20 .20
**130** A25 25c blue .20 .20
**131** A25 50c orange .20 .20
**132** A25 1b red vio .20 .20
**133** A25 3b red .55 .20
**134** A25 10b dl vio .90 .80
**135** A25 20b red brn 4.25 2.75
*Nos. 128-135 (8)* 6.70 4.75

By decree of Nov. 28, 1892, the stamps inscribed "Correos" were to be used for external postage and those inscribed "Instruccion" were for internal postage and revenue purposes.

For surcharge see No. 230.

---

After July 1, 1895, stamps inscribed "Escuelas" or "Instruccion" were no longer available for postage. Stamps of design A25 in shades different than those listed were printed after 1895.

---

Landing of Columbus
A26

**1893** ***Perf. 12***
**136** A26 25c magenta 11.00 .60

4th cent. of the discovery of the mainland of South America, also participation of Venezuela in the Intl. Exhib. at Chicago in 1893.

Map of Venezuela
A27

**1896** **Litho.**
**137** A27 5c yel grn 3.00 2.75
*a.* 5c apple green 3.00 2.75
**138** A27 10c blue 4.00 3.00
**139** A27 25c yellow 4.00 5.50
*a.* 25c orange 4.00 5.50
*b.* Tête bêche pair 125.00 125.00
**140** A27 50c rose red 52.50 27.00
*a.* 50c red 52.50 52.50
*b.* Tête bêche pair 375.00 375.00
**141** A27 1b violet 40.00 27.00
*Nos. 137-141 (5)* 103.50 65.25

Gen. Francisco Antonio Gabriel de Miranda (1752-1816).

These stamps were in use from July 4 to Nov. 4, 1896. Later usage is known.

There are many forgeries of this issue. They include faked errors, imperforate stamps and many tête bêche. The paper of the originals is thin, white and semi-transparent. The gum is shiny and crackled. The paper of the reprints is often thick and opaque. The gum is usually dull, smooth, thin and only slightly adhesive.

Bolívar — A28

**1899-1901** **Engr.**
**142** A28 5c dk grn 1.00 .25
**143** A28 10c red 1.25 .40
**144** A28 25c blue 1.50 .55
**145** A28 50c gray blk 2.00 1.00
**146** A28 50c org ('01) 1.75 .50
**147** A28 1b yel grn 32.50 15.00
**149** A28 2b orange 375.00 225.00
*Nos. 142-147,149 (7)* 415.00 242.70

Stamps of 1899 Overprinted in Black

**1900**
**150** A28 5c dk grn 1.25 .40
*a.* Inverted overprint 4.75 4.75
**151** A28 10c red 1.25 .40
*a.* Inverted overprint 6.50 6.50
*b.* Double overprint 10.50 10.50
**152** A28 25c blue 7.75 1.25
*a.* Inverted overprint 13.00 13.00
**153** A28 50c gray blk 4.00 .55
*a.* Inverted overprint 12.00 12.00
**154** A28 1b yel grn 1.75 .80
*a.* Double overprint 13.00 13.00
*b.* Inverted overprint 12.00 12.00
**155** A28 2b orange 2.75 2.25
*a.* Inverted overprint 35.00 35.00
*b.* Double overprint 32.50 32.50
*Nos. 150-155 (6)* 18.75 5.65

Initials are those of R. T. Mendoza.

Counterfeit overprints exist, especially of inverted and doubled varieties.

Bolivar Type of 1899-1903 Overprinted

**1900**
**156** A28 5c dk grn 200.00 200.00
**157** A28 10c red 200.00 200.00
**158** A28 25c blue 350.00 175.00
**159** A28 50c yel orange 23.00 1.60
**160** A28 1b slate 1.25 1.00
*a.* Without overprint 4,000. —
*Nos. 156-160 (5)* 774.25 577.60

Overprinted

**1900, Aug. 14**
**161** A28 5c green 7.75 .55
**162** A28 10c red 7.00 1.00
**163** A28 25c blue 7.75 1.00
*Nos. 161-163 (3)* 22.50 2.55

**Inverted Overprint**

*161a* A28 5c 9.25 6.50
*162a* A28 10c 9.25 6.50
*163a* A28 25c 12.00 7.25
*Nos. 161a-163a (3)* 30.50 20.25

Overprint exists on each value without "Castro" or without "1900."

Type of 1893 Surcharged

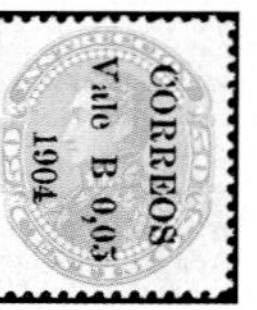

**1904, Jan.** ***Perf. 12***
**230** A25 5c on 50c green .80 .60
*a.* "Vele" 23.00 23.00
*b.* Surcharge reading up 1.00 .50
*c.* Double surcharge 18.00 18.00

Gen. José de Sucre — A35

Pres. Cipriano Castro — A37

**1904-09** **Engr.**
**231** A35 5c bl grn .50 .20
**232** A35 10c carmine .55 .20
**233** A35 15c violet .90 .40
**234** A35 25c dp ultra 6.50 .40
**235** A35 50c plum 1.00 .50
**236** A35 1b plum 1.10 .50
*Nos. 231-236 (6)* 10.55 2.20

Issued: 15c, Dec. 1909; others, July 1, 1904.

**1905, July 5** **Litho.** ***Perf. 11½***
**245** A37 5c vermilion 3.25 3.25
*a.* 5c carmine 5.00 5.00
**246** A37 10c dark blue 5.50 4.25
**247** A37 25c yellow 2.00 1.50
*Nos. 245-247 (3)* 10.75 9.00

National Congress. Issued for interior postage only. Valid only for 90 days.

Various part-perforate varieties of Nos. 245-247 exist. Value, $15-$30.

Liberty — A38

**1910, Apr. 19** **Engr.** ***Perf. 12***
**249** A38 25c dark blue 13.00 .60

Centenary of national independence.

Francisco de Miranda
A39

Rafael Urdaneta
A40

Bolívar — A41

**1911** **Litho.** ***Perf. 11½x12***
**250** A39 5c dp grn .50 .20
**251** A39 10c carmine .50 .20
**252** A40 15c gray 5.75 .40
**253** A40 25c dp bl 3.25 .60
*a.* Imperf., pair 40.00 50.00
**254** A41 50c purple 3.50 .40
**255** A41 1b yellow 3.50 1.50
*Nos. 250-255 (6)* 17.00 3.30

The 50c with center in blue was never issued although copies were postmarked by favor.

The centers of Nos. 250-255 were separately printed and often vary in shade from the rest of the design. In a second printing of the 5c and 10c, the entire design was printed at one time.

Redrawn

**1913**
**255A** A40 15c gray 3.50 2.25
**255B** A40 25c deep blue 2.00 .65
**255C** A41 50c purple 2.00 .65
*Nos. 255A-255C (3)* 7.50 3.55

The redrawn stamps have two berries instead of one at top of the left spray; a berry has been added over the "C" and "S" of "Centimos"; and the lowest leaf at the right is cut by the corner square.

Simón Bolívar
A42 A43

**1914, July** **Engr.** ***Perf. 13½, 14, 15***
**256** A42 5c yel grn 37.50 .55
**257** A42 10c scarlet 35.00 .50
**258** A42 25c dark blue 5.75 .25
*Nos. 256-258 (3)* 78.25 1.30

Printed by the American Bank Note Co.

Different frames.

**1915-23** ***Perf. 12***
**259** A43 5c green 4.25 .25
**260** A43 10c vermilion 10.00 .60
**261** A43 10c claret ('22) 10.00 .90
**262** A43 15c dull ol grn 9.25 .60
**263** A43 25c ultra 6.50 .25
*a.* 25c blue 13.00 .60
**264** A43 40c dull green 23.00 11.50
**265** A43 50c dp violet 6.50 .80
**266** A43 50c ultra ('23) 17.00 4.75
**267** A43 75c lt blue 57.50 23.00
*a.* 75c greenish blue 57.50 23.00
**268** A43 1b dark gray 35.00 5.25
*Nos. 259-268 (10)* 179.00 47.90

See Nos. 269-285. For surcharges see Nos. 307, 309-310.

Type of 1915-23 Issue
Printed by Waterlow & Sons, Ltd.
Re-engraved

**1924-39** ***Perf. 12½***
**269** A43 5c orange brn .55 .20
*a.* 5c yellow brown .55 .20
*b.* Horiz. pair, imperf. btwn. 25.00 40.00
**270** A43 5c green ('39) 12.00 1.00
**271** A43 7½c yel grn ('39) 1.25 .40
**272** A43 10c dk green .25 .20
**273** A43 10c dk car ('39) 4.00 .25
**274** A43 15c olive grn 2.25 .50
**275** A43 15c brown ('27) .30 .20
**276** A43 25c ultra 2.25 .25
**277** A43 25c red ('28) .25 .20
*a.* Horiz. pair, imperf. btwn. 50.00 85.00
**278** A43 40c dp blue ('25) .55 .25
**279** A43 40c slate bl ('39) 7.75 1.25
**280** A43 50c dk blue .55 .25
**281** A43 50c dk pur ('39) 7.75 .85
**282** A43 1b black .55 .25
**283** A43 3b yel org ('25) 1.75 .95
**284** A43 3b red org ('39) 12.00 4.25
**285** A43 5b dull vio ('25) 16.00 8.50
*Nos. 269-285 (17)* 70.00 19.75

***Perf. 14***

*269c* A43 5c 7.00 2.00
*272a* A43 10c 7.00 2.00
*274a* A43 15c 8.25 2.75
*276a* A43 25c 12.00 4.75
*280a* A43 50c 35.00 14.00
*282a* A43 1b 42.50 27.00
*Nos. 269c-282a (6)* 111.75 52.50

The re-engraved stamps may readily be distinguished from the 1915 issue by the perforation and sometimes by the colors. The designs differ in many minor details which are too minute for illustration or description.

Bolívar and Sucre
A44

***Perf. 11½x12, 12***

**1924, Dec. 1** **Litho.**
**286** A44 25c grayish blue 2.75 .55

**Redrawn**

**286A** A44 25c ultra 3.50 .85

Centenary of the Battle of Ayacucho.

The redrawn stamp has a whiter effect with less shading in the faces. Bolívar's ear is clearly visible and the outline of his aquiline nose is broken.

A45

A46

Revenue Stamps Surcharged in Black or Red

**1926** *Perf. 12, 12½*

**287** A45 5c on 1b ol grn .65 .40
- *a.* Double surcharge 8.00 8.00
- *b.* Pair, one without surcharge 12.00 12.00
- *c.* Inverted surcharge 8.00 8.00

**288** A46 25c on 5c dk brn (R) .65 .40
- *a.* Inverted surcharge 8.00 8.00
- *b.* Double surcharge 8.00 8.00

View of Ciudad Bolívar and General J.V. Gómez — A47

**1928, July 21** **Litho.** *Perf. 12*

**289** A47 10c deep green 1.00 .65
- *a.* Imperf., pair 40.00

25th anniversary of the Battle of Ciudad Bolívar and the foundation of peace in Venezuela.

Simón Bolívar
A48 A49

**1930, Dec. 9**

**290** A48 5c yellow 1.00 .35
**291** A48 10c dark blue 1.00 .25
**292** A48 25c rose red 1.00 .25
*Nos. 290-292 (3)* 3.00 .85

**Imperf., Pairs**

*290a* A48 5c 5.25 5.25
*291a* A48 10c 6.50 6.50
*292a* A48 25c 10.50 10.50

Death centenary of Simón Bolívar (1783-1830), South American liberator.

Nos. 290-292 exist part-perforate, including pairs imperf. between, imperf. horiz., imperf. vert. Value range, $6-12.

Various Frames
Bluish Winchester Security Paper

**1932-38** **Engr.** *Perf. 12½*

**293** A49 5c violet .50 .20
**294** A49 7½c dk green ('37) 1.00 .40
**295** A49 10c green .60 .20
**296** A49 15c yellow 1.50 .25
**297** A49 22½c dp car ('38) 3.50 .50
**298** A49 25c red 1.25 .20
**299** A49 37½c ultra ('36) 4.50 2.00
**300** A49 40c indigo 4.50 .25
**301** A49 50c olive grn 4.50 .40
**302** A49 1b lt blue 6.00 .70
**303** A49 3b brown 40.00 13.00
**304** A49 5b yellow brn 50.00 17.00
*Nos. 293-304 (12)* 117.85 35.10

For surcharges see Nos. 308, 318-319, C223.

Arms of Bolívar — A50

**1933, July 24** **Litho.** *Perf. 11*

**306** A50 25c brown red 3.00 2.40
- *a.* Imperf., pair 32.50 32.50

150th anniv. of the birth of Simón Bolívar. Valid only to Aug. 21.

Stamps of 1924-32 Surcharged in Black: (Blocks of Surcharge in Color of stamps)

**1933**

**307** A43 7½c on 10c grn .50 .25
- *a.* Double surcharge 2.50 2.50
- *b.* Inverted surcharge 4.25 4.25

**308** A49 22½c on 25c (#298) 2.00 .85
**309** A43 22½c on 25c (#277) 1.50 1.50
- *a.* Double surcharge 10.00 10.00

**310** A43 37½c on 40c dp bl 2.00 .95
- *a.* Double surcharge 11.50 11.50
- *b.* Inverted surcharge 10.00 10.00

*Nos. 307-310 (4)* 6.00 3.55

Nurse and Child — A51

River Scene — A52

Gathering Cacao Pods — A53

Cattle Raising A54

Plowing A55

***Perf. 11, 11½ or Compound***

**1937, July 1** **Litho.**

**311** A51 5c deep violet .55 .35
**312** A52 10c dk slate grn .55 .20
**313** A53 15c yellow brn 1.00 .55
**314** A51 25c cerise 1.00 .35
**315** A54 50c yellow grn 6.50 4.25
**316** A55 3b red orange 12.00 7.75
**317** A51 5b lt brown 23.00 15.00
*Nos. 311-317 (7)* 44.60 28.45

Nos. 311-317 exist imperforate. Value for set $75. Nos. 311-315 exist in pairs, imperf. between; value range, $20-$30.

For overprints and surcharges see Nos. 321-324, 345, 376-377, 380-384.

No. 300 Surcharged in Black

**1937, July** *Perf. 12½*

**318** A49 25c on 40c indigo 7.75 .95
- *a.* Double surcharge 16.00 16.00
- *b.* Inverted surcharge 13.00 13.00
- *c.* Triple surcharge 32.50 32.50

Surcharged

**319** A49 25c on 40c indigo 400.00 325.00
- *a.* Double surcharge

A56

**1937, Oct. 28** **Litho.** *Perf. 10½*

**320** A56 25c blue 1.25 .45

Acquisition of the Port of La Guaira by the Government from the British Corporation, June 3, 1937. Exists imperf. See Nos. C64-C65.

A redrawn printing of No. 320, with top inscription beginning "Nacionalización . . ." was prepared but not issued. Value, $40.

For surcharge see No. 385.

Stamps of 1937 Overprinted in Black

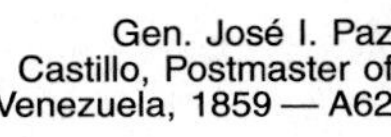

**1937, Dec. 17** *Perf. 11, 11½*

**321** A51 5c deep violet 5.75 3.25
**322** A52 10c dk slate grn 1.75 .75
- *a.* Inverted overprint 13.00 13.00

**323** A51 25c cerise 1.50 .55
- *a.* Inverted overprint 16.00 16.00

**324** A55 3b red orange 375.00 225.00
*Nos. 321-324 (4)* 384.00 229.55

Part-perforate pairs exist of Nos. 321-322 and 324. Value range, $12.50 to $125.

See Nos. C66-C78.

Gathering Coffee Beans — A57

Simón Bolívar — A58

Post Office, Caracas — A59

**1938** **Engr.** *Perf. 12*

**325** A57 5c green .40 .20
**326** A57 5c deep green .40 .20
**327** A58 10c car rose .70 .20
**328** A58 10c dp rose .70 .20
**329** A59 15c dk violet 1.40 .25
**330** A59 15c olive grn .85 .25
**331** A58 25c lt blue .40 .20
**332** A58 25c dk blue .40 .20
**333** A58 37½c dk blue 8.50 4.00
**334** A58 37½c lt blue 2.75 .85
**335** A59 40c sepia 20.00 7.75
**336** A59 40c black 17.00 7.75
**337** A57 50c olive grn 27.50 7.75
**338** A57 50c dull violet 9.25 .85
**339** A58 1b dp brown 12.00 5.50
**340** A58 1b black brown 17.00 1.50
**341** A57 3b orange 92.50 50.00
**342** A59 5b black 15.00 7.75
*Nos. 325-342 (18)* 226.75 95.40

See Nos. 400 and 412.

Teresa Carreño — A60

Bolívar Statue — A61

**1938, June 12** *Perf. 11½x12*

**343** A60 25c blue 5.75 .60

Teresa Carreno, Venezuelan pianist, whose remains were repatriated Feb. 14, 1938.

For surcharge see No. 386.

**1938, July 24** *Perf. 12*

**344** A61 25c dark blue 6.50 .60

"The Day of the Worker."

For surcharge see No. 387.

Type of 1937 Surcharged in Black

**1938** **Litho.** *Perf. 11, 11½*

**345** A51 40c on 5b lt brn 8.50 4.50
- *a.* Inverted surcharge 21.00 21.00

Gen. José I. Paz Castillo, Postmaster of Venezuela, 1859 — A62

**1939, Apr. 19** **Engr.** *Perf. 12½*

**348** A62 10c carmine 2.50 .70

80th anniv. of the first Venezuelan stamp.

View of Ojeda A63

**1939, June 24** **Photo.**

**349** A63 25c dull blue 9.25 .75

Founding of city of Ojeda.

Cristóbal Mendoza A64

Diego Urbaneja A65

**1939, Oct. 14** **Engr.** *Perf. 13*

**350** A64 5c green .40 .20
**351** A64 10c dk car rose .40 .20
**352** A64 15c dull lilac 1.00 .25
**353** A64 25c brt ultra .80 .20
**354** A64 37½c dark blue 15.00 6.25
**355** A64 50c lt olive grn 16.00 4.00
**356** A64 1b dark brown 6.50 3.50
*Nos. 350-356 (7)* 40.10 14.60

Mendoza (1772-1839), postmaster general.

**1940-43** *Perf. 12*

**357** A65 5c Prus green .45 .20
**357A** A65 7½c dk bl grn ('43) .65 .25
**358** A65 15c olive .80 .25
**359** A65 37½c deep blue 1.25 .60
**360** A65 40c violet blue .95 .30
**361** A65 50c violet 5.50 1.40
**362** A65 1b dk violet brn 2.75 .75
**363** A65 3b scarlet 8.00 3.25
*Nos. 357-363 (8)* 20.35 7.00

See Nos. 399, 408, 410 and 411. For surcharges see Nos. 396, C226.

Battle of Carabobo, 1821 — A67

**1940, June 13**
**365** A67 25c blue 6.00 .70

Birth of General JoséAntonio Páez, 150th anniv.

"Crossing the Andes" by Tito Salas — A68

**1940, June 13**
**366** A68 25c dark blue 6.00 .70

Death cent. of General Francisco Santander.

Monument and Urn containing Ashes of Simón Bolívar — A69

Bed where Simón Bolívar was Born — A70

Designs: 15c, "Christening of Bolivar" by Tito Salas. 20c, Bolivar's birthplace, Caracas. 25c, "Bolivar on Horseback" by Salas. 30c, Patio of Bolivar House, Caracas. 37½c, Patio of Bolivar's Birthplace. 50c, "Rebellion of 1812" by Salas.

**1940-41**
**367** A69 5c turq green .25 .20
**368** A70 10c rose pink .25 .20
**369** A69 15c olive .60 .20
**370** A70 20c blue ('41) 1.00 .20
**371** A69 25c lt blue .60 .20
**372** A70 30c plum ('41) 1.50 .25
**373** A70 37½c dk blue 3.00 1.00
**374** A70 50c purple 2.00 .50
*Nos. 367-374 (8)* 9.20 2.75

110th anniv. of the death of Simón Bolívar.
See #397, 398, 403, 405-407, 409. For surcharges see #375, 401-402, C224, C237-C238.

No. 371 Surcharged In Black

**1941**
**375** A69 20c on 25c lt blue .60 .20
*a.* Inverted surcharge 10.00 10.00

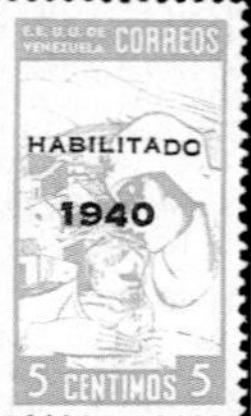


Nos. 311-312 Overprinted in Black

**1941** ***Perf. 11½***
**376** A51 5c deep violet 2.00 .50
*a.* Double overprint 10.00 8.25
*b.* Vert. pair, imperf. btwn. 14.00 14.00
*c.* Inverted overprint 20.00 16.00
**377** A52 10c dk slate grn 1.00 .30
*a.* Double overprint 13.00 13.00

Symbols of Industry A77

Caracas Cathedral A78

**1942, Dec. 17** **Litho.** ***Perf. 12***
**378** A77 10c scarlet 1.00 .25
*a.* Imperf., pair 22.50 22.50

Grand Industrial Exposition, Caracas.

**1943** **Engr.**
**379** A78 10c rose carmine .75 .20

See No. 404.

Stamps of 1937 Overprinted in Black

**1943** ***Perf. 11, 11½***
**380** A51 5c deep violet 16.00 9.50
**381** A52 10c dk slate grn 6.00 4.00
**382** A54 50c yellow green 8.00 4.50
**383** A55 3b red orange 45.00 22.00
*Nos. 380-383 (4)* 75.00 40.00

Issued for sale to philatelists & sold only in sets.

Stamps of 1937-38 Surcharged in Black

**1943** ***Perf. 11½, 10½, 12***
**384** A51 20c on 25c cerise 27.50 27.50
**385** A56 20c on 25c blue 70.00 70.00
**386** A60 20c on 25c dk blue 13.50 13.50
**387** A61 20c on 25c dk blue 13.50 13.50
*a.* Inverted surcharge 42.50 42.50
*Nos. 384-387 (4)* 124.50 124.50

Issued for sale to philatelists & sold only in sets.

Souvenir Sheet

A79

**1944, Aug. 22** **Litho.** ***Perf. 12***
**Flags in Red, Yellow, Blue & Black**
**388** A79 Sheet of 4 35.00 35.00
*a.* 5c Prussian green 3.00 .80
*b.* 10c rose 4.50 .80
*c.* 20c ultramarine 4.50 1.75
*d.* 1b rose lake 6.00 2.25

80th anniv. of Intl. Red Cross and 37th anniv. of Venezuela's joining.
No. 388 exists imperf. Value $60.

Antonio José de Sucre — A80

**1945, Mar. 3** **Engr.** **Unwmk.**
**389** A80 5c orange yellow 1.00 .50
**390** A80 10c dark blue 1.50 .80
**391** A80 20c rose pink 2.00 .80
*Nos. 389-391,C206-C215 (13)* 16.30 10.90

Birth of Antonio de Sucre, 150th anniv.

Andrés Bello — A81

Gen. Rafael Urdaneta — A82

**1946, Aug. 24**
**392** A81 20c deep blue .65 .35
**393** A82 20c deep blue .65 .35
*Nos. 392-393,C216-C217 (4)* 3.50 1.10

80th anniversary of the death of Andrés Bello (1780?-1865), educator and writer, and the centenary of the death of Gen. Rafael Urdaneta.

Allegory of the Republic — A83

**1946, Oct. 18** **Litho.** ***Perf. 11½***
**394** A83 20c greenish blue .70 .30
*Nos. 394,C218-C221 (5)* 5.10 3.50

Anniversary of Revolution of October, 1945. Exists imperf.

Anti-tuberculosis Institute, Maracaibo — A84

**1947, Jan. 12**
**395** A84 20c ultra & yellow .70 .30
*Nos. 395,C228-C231 (5)* 6.15 4.70

12th Pan-American Health Conf., Caracas, Jan. 1947. Exists imperf. and part perf.

No. 362 Surcharged in Green

**396** A65 15c on 1b dk vio brn .70 .30
*a.* Inverted surcharge 6.00 5.00
*Nos. 396,C223-C227 (6)* 30.50 23.95

Types of 1938-40

**1947** **Engr.**
**397** A69 5c green .20 .20
**398** A70 30c black 1.00 .50
**399** A65 40c red violet .95 .25
**400** A59 5b deep orange 40.00 18.00
*Nos. 397-400 (4)* 42.15 18.95

In 1947 a decree authorized the use of 5c and 10c revenue stamps of the above type for franking correspondence. Other denominations were also used unofficially.
For surcharges see Nos. 876-883.

Nos. 398 and 373 Surcharged in Red

**1947** **Unwmk.** ***Perf. 12***
**401** A70 5c on 30c black .40 .20
*a.* Inverted surcharge 5.00 5.00
**402** A70 5c on 37½c dk bl .45 .20
*a.* Inverted surcharge 5.00 5.00

Types of 1938-43

**1947-48**
**403** A69 5c brt ultra .20 .20
**404** A78 10c red .20 .20
**405** A69 15c rose car .50 .20
**406** A69 25c violet .40 .20
**407** A70 30c dk vio brn ('48) .50 .20
**408** A65 40c orange ('48) .50 .20
**409** A70 50c olive green .95 .20
**410** A65 1b deep blue 1.75 .20
**411** A65 3b gray 3.50 .90
**412** A59 5b chocolate 13.00 5.00
*Nos. 403-412 (10)* 21.50 7.50

M. S. Republica de Venezuela A85

Imprint: "American Bank Note Company"

**1948-50** **Engr.** ***Perf. 12***
**413** A85 5c blue .20 .20
**414** A85 7½c red org ('49) .50 .30
*a.* Booklet pane of 20
**415** A85 10c car rose .40 .20
*a.* Booklet pane of 10
**416** A85 15c gray ('50) .40 .20
**417** A85 20c sepia .30 .20
**418** A85 25c violet ('49) .40 .20
**419** A85 30c orange ('50) 2.75 1.60
**420** A85 37½c brown ('49) 1.25 1.00
**421** A85 40c olive ('50) 1.75 1.25
**422** A85 50c red violet ('49) .50 .20
**423** A85 1b gray green 1.25 .40
*Nos. 413-423 (11)* 9.70 5.75

Grand Colombian Merchant Fleet. See Nos. 632-634, C256-C271, C554-C556. For surcharges see Nos. 450-451.

Santos Michelena — A86

Christopher Columbus — A87

**1949, Apr. 25** *Perf. 12½*
**424** A86 5c ultra .20 .20
**425** A86 10c carmine .40 .20
**426** A86 20c sepia 1.60 .60
**427** A86 1b green 5.25 2.75
*Nos. 424-427,C272-C277 (10)* 15.45 9.00

Centenary of the death of Santos Michelena, Finance Minister, and the 110th anniversary of the Postal Convention of Bogota.

**1949-50** **Engr.**
**428** A87 5c deep ultra .35 .20
**429** A87 10c carmine 1.25 .40
**430** A87 20c dark brown 1.50 .50
**431** A87 1b green 4.00 1.75
*Nos. 428-431,C278-C283 (10)* 15.40 7.15

450th anniversary (in 1948) of Columbus' discovery of the American mainland.
Issued: 5c, 10c, 1949; 20c, 1b, Jan. 1950.

Arms of Venezuela A88

**1948**
**432** A88 5c blue 1.25 .65
**433** A88 10c red 1.50 .75

The 20c and 1b, type A88, and six similar air post stamps were prepared but not issued. Value, set of 8, about $125.

Gen. Francisco de Miranda — A89

**1950, Mar. 28** **Unwmk.** *Perf. 12*
**434** A89 5c blue .20 .20
**435** A89 10c green .35 .20
**436** A89 20c sepia .70 .30
**437** A89 1b rose carmine 3.25 1.50
*Nos. 434-437 (4)* 4.50 2.20

Bicentenary of birth of General Francisco de Miranda.

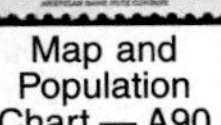
Map and Population Chart — A90

Alonso de Ojeda — A91

**1950, Sept. 1**
**438** A90 5c blue .20 .20
**439** A90 10c gray .20 .20
**440** A90 15c sepia .20 .20
**441** A90 25c green .30 .20
**442** A90 30c red .40 .20
**443** A90 50c violet .80 .30
**444** A90 1b red brown 2.00 1.00
*Nos. 438-444,C302-C310 (16)* 8.90 5.70

8th National Census of the Americas.

**1950, Dec. 18** **Photo.** *Perf. 11½*
**445** A91 5c deep blue .20 .20
**446** A91 10c deep red .25 .20
**447** A91 15c slate gray .30 .20
**448** A91 20c ultra 1.25 .50
**449** A91 1b blue green 5.00 2.50
*Nos. 445-449 (5)* 7.00 3.60
*Nos. 445-449,C316-C321 (11)* 13.90 7.15

450th anniversary (in 1949) of the discovery of the Gulf of Maracaibo.

Nos. 414 and 420 Surcharged in Black

**1951** **Unwmk.** *Perf. 12*
**450** A85 5c on 7½c red org .30 .20
**451** A85 10c on 37½c brn .30 .20
*a.* Inverted surcharge 16.00 16.00

Telegraph Stamps Surcharged in Black or Red

**1951, June** **Engr.**
**Grayish Security Paper**
**452** 5c on 5c brown .20 .20
**453** 10c on 10c green .25 .20
**454** 20c on 1b blk (R) .50 .20
**455** 25c on 25c carmine .65 .25
**456** 30c on 2b ol grn (R) .85 .65
*Nos. 452-456 (5)* 2.45 1.50

The 5c and 10c surcharges include quotation marks on each line and values are expressed "Bs. 0.05" etc.

Bolivar Statue, New York — A92

**1951, July 13** *Perf. 12*
**457** A92 5c green .20 .20
**458** A92 10c car rose .40 .20
**459** A92 20c ultra .40 .20
**460** A92 30c slate gray .50 .25
**461** A92 40c deep green .70 .25
**462** A92 50c red brown 1.50 .50
**463** A92 1b gray black 4.75 2.50
*Nos. 457-463 (7)* 8.45 4.10
*Nos. 457-463,C322-C329 (15)* 15.65 7.45

Relocation of the equestrian statue of Simon Bolivar in NYC, Apr. 19, 1951.

Arms of Carabobo and "Industry" — A93

**1951** **Unwmk.** **Photo.** *Perf. 11½*
**464** A93 5c green .20 .20
**465** A93 10c red .20 .20
**466** A93 15c brown .25 .20
**467** A93 20c ultra .35 .20
**468** A93 25c orange brn .40 .20
**469** A93 30c blue .85 .35
**470** A93 35c purple 3.25 2.75
*Nos. 464-470 (7)* 5.50 4.10

Issue dates: 5c, 10c, Oct. 8; others, Oct. 29.

**Arms of Zulia and "Industry"**
**471** A93 5c green .20 .20
**472** A93 10c red .30 .20
**473** A93 15c brown .65 .30
**474** A93 20c ultra .85 .40
**475** A93 50c brown org 5.25 3.75
**476** A93 1b dp gray grn 1.75 .65
**477** A93 5b rose violet 3.75 2.50
*Nos. 471-477 (7)* 12.75 8.00

Issued: 5c, 10c, Sept. 8; others, Sept. 20.

**Arms of Anzoategui and Globe**
**478** A93 5c green .20 .20
**479** A93 10c red .20 .20
**480** A93 15c brown .65 .30
**481** A93 20c ultra 1.10 .20
**482** A93 40c red orange 2.25 1.10
**483** A93 45c rose violet 6.75 3.75
**484** A93 3b blue gray 2.50 1.25
*Nos. 478-484 (7)* 13.65 7.00

Issue date: Nov. 9.

**Arms of Caracas and Buildings**
**485** A93 5c green .40 .20
**486** A93 10c red .50 .20
**487** A93 15c brown 1.25 .30
**488** A93 20c ultra 2.50 .30
**489** A93 25c orange brn 3.75 .65
**490** A93 30c blue 3.25 .75
**491** A93 35c purple 32.50 19.00
*Nos. 485-491 (7)* 44.15 21.40

Issued: 5c, 10c, June 20; others, Aug. 6.

**Arms of Tachira and Agricultural Products**
**492** A93 5c green .20 .20
**493** A93 10c red .40 .20
**494** A93 15c brown .75 .25
**495** A93 20c ultra 1.75 .45
**496** A93 50c brown org 110.00 14.00
**497** A93 1b dp gray grn 1.75 .65
**498** A93 5b dull purple 4.50 2.50
*Nos. 492-498 (7)* 119.35 18.25

Issue date: Aug. 9.

**Arms of Venezuela and Statue of Simon Bolivar**
**499** A93 5c green .30 .20
**500** A93 10c red .25 .20
**501** A93 15c brown 2.25 .45
**502** A93 20c ultra 2.25 .30
**503** A93 25c orange brn 3.75 .85
**504** A93 30c blue 3.75 .85
**505** A93 35c purple 20.00 15.00
*Nos. 499-505 (7)* 32.55 17.85

Issue date: Aug. 6.

**1952**
**Arms of Miranda and Agricultural Products**
**506** A93 5c green .20 .20
**507** A93 10c red .20 .20
**508** A93 15c brown .45 .20
**509** A93 20c ultra .50 .20
**510** A93 25c orange brn .65 .30
**511** A93 30c blue 1.10 .50
**512** A93 35c purple 6.50 4.50
*Nos. 506-512 (7)* 9.60 6.10

**Arms of Aragua and Stylized Farm**
**513** A93 5c green .20 .20
**514** A93 10c red .20 .20
**515** A93 15c brown .40 .20
**516** A93 20c ultra .40 .20
**517** A93 25c orange brn .90 .25
**518** A93 30c blue .90 .40
**519** A93 35c purple 5.00 3.75
*Nos. 513-519 (7)* 8.00 5.20

Issue date: 20c, 30c, Mar. 24.

**Arms of Lara, Agricultural Products and Rope**
**520** A93 5c green .20 .20
**521** A93 10c red .20 .20
**522** A93 15c brown .30 .20
**523** A93 20c ultra .70 .20
**524** A93 25c orange brn .80 .50
**525** A93 30c blue 1.50 .40
**526** A93 35c purple 6.25 3.75
*Nos. 520-526 (7)* 9.95 5.45

Issue date: 20c, 30c, Mar. 24.

**Arms of Bolivar and Stylized Design**
**527** A93 5c green .20 .20
**528** A93 10c red .20 .20
**529** A93 15c brown .30 .20
**530** A93 20c ultra .65 .20
**531** A93 40c red orange 2.50 .85
**532** A93 45c rose violet 6.50 4.50
**533** A93 3b blue gray 3.00 2.00
*Nos. 527-533 (7)* 13.35 8.15

Issue date: 20c, Mar. 24.

**Arms of Sucre, Palms and Seascape**
**534** A93 5c green .20 .20
**535** A93 10c red .20 .20
**536** A93 15c brown .75 .20
**537** A93 20c ultra .75 .20
**538** A93 40c red orange 2.50 .65
**539** A93 45c rose violet 9.00 5.50
**540** A93 3b blue gray 2.25 1.50
*Nos. 534-540 (7)* 15.65 8.45

**Arms of Trujillo Surrounded by Stylized Tree**
**541** A93 5c green .20 .20
**542** A93 10c red .20 .20
**543** A93 15c brown 1.10 .20
**544** A93 20c ultra 1.10 .25
**545** A93 50c brown orange 6.25 3.00
**546** A93 1b dp gray green 1.50 .55
**547** A93 5b dull purple 3.75 1.90
*Nos. 541-547 (7)* 14.10 6.30

**1953-54**
**Map of Delta Amacuro and Ship**
**548** A93 5c green .20 .20
**549** A93 10c red .20 .20
**550** A93 15c brown .30 .20
**551** A93 20c ultra .50 .20
**552** A93 40c red orange 1.60 1.00
**553** A93 45c rose violet 7.50 4.50
**554** A93 3b blue gray 2.00 1.50
*Nos. 548-554 (7)* 12.30 7.80

**Arms of Falcon and Stylized Oil Refinery**
**555** A93 5c green .20 .20
**556** A93 10c red .20 .20
**557** A93 15c brown .40 .20
**558** A93 20c ultra .40 .20
**559** A93 50c brown orange 2.00 1.00
**560** A93 1b dp gray grn 1.25 .80
**561** A93 5b dull purple 3.75 2.00
*Nos. 555-561 (7)* 8.20 4.60

Issue date: 20c, Feb. 13.

**Arms of Guarico and Factory**
**562** A93 5c green .20 .20
**563** A93 10c red .20 .20
**564** A93 15c brown .40 .20
**565** A93 20c ultra .45 .20
**566** A93 40c red orange 2.25 1.40
**567** A93 45c rose violet 5.50 2.75
**568** A93 3b blue gray 2.25 1.25
*Nos. 562-568 (7)* 11.25 6.20

Issue date: 20c, Feb. 13.

**Arms of Merida and Church**
**569** A93 5c green .20 .20
**570** A93 10c red .20 .20
**571** A93 15c brown .25 .20
**572** A93 20c ultra .65 .20
**573** A93 50c brown orange 3.00 1.25
**574** A93 1b dp gray green .80 .55
**575** A93 5b dull purple 3.00 1.60
*Nos. 569-575 (7)* 8.10 4.20

Issue date: 20c, Feb. 2.

**Arms of Monagas and Horses**
**576** A93 5c green .20 .20
**577** A93 10c red .20 .20
**578** A93 15c brown .30 .20
**579** A93 20c ultra .45 .25
**580** A93 40c red orange 2.00 .75
**581** A93 45c rose violet 6.25 3.75
**582** A93 3b blue gray 2.50 2.00
*Nos. 576-582 (7)* 11.90 7.35

**Arms of Portuguesa and Forest**
**583** A93 5c green .20 .20
**584** A93 10c red .20 .20
**585** A93 15c brown .25 .20
**586** A93 20c ultra .50 .20
**587** A93 50c brown org 2.75 1.75
**588** A93 1b dp gray grn .70 .30
**589** A93 5b dull purple 3.00 2.00
*Nos. 583-589 (7)* 7.60 4.85

Issue date: 5c, 10c, Feb. 2.

**Map of Amazonas and Orchid**
**590** A93 5c green .50 .20
**591** A93 10c red .50 .20
**592** A93 15c brown 1.10 .20
**593** A93 20c ultra 3.00 .30
**594** A93 40c red orange 3.50 1.00
**595** A93 45c rose violet 5.50 2.75
**596** A93 3b blue gray 8.00 3.00
*Nos. 590-596 (7)* 22.10 7.65

Issue date: Jan. 1954.

**Arms of Apure, Horse and Bird**
**597** A93 5c green .20 .20
**598** A93 10c red .20 .20
**599** A93 15c brown .35 .20
**600** A93 20c ultra 1.75 .20
**601** A93 50c brown org 2.25 1.75
**602** A93 1b dp gray grn .75 .65
**603** A93 5b dull purple 4.50 2.50
*Nos. 597-603 (7)* 10.00 5.70

Issue date: Jan. 1954.

**Arms of Barinas, Cow and Horse**
**604** A93 5c green .20 .20
**605** A93 10c red .20 .20
**606** A93 15c brown .25 .20
**607** A93 20c ultra 1.75 .25
**608** A93 50c brown org 2.00 1.25
**609** A93 1b dp gray grn .50 .25
**610** A93 5b dull purple 4.50 2.25
*Nos. 604-610 (7)* 9.40 4.60

Issue date: Jan. 1954.

**Arms of Cojedes and Cattle**
**611** A93 5c green .20 .20
**612** A93 10c red .20 .20
**613** A93 15c brown .20 .20
**614** A93 20c ultra .20 .20
**615** A93 25c orange brown .90 .25
**616** A93 30c blue 1.40 .40
**617** A93 35c purple 1.75 1.10
*Nos. 611-617 (7)* 4.85 2.55

Issue date: Dec, 17, 1953.

**Arms of Nueva Esparta and Fish**
**618** A93 5c green .20 .20
**619** A93 10c red .20 .20
**620** A93 15c brown .45 .20

**621** A93 20c ultra .50 .20
**622** A93 40c red orange 2.25 .85
**623** A93 45c rose vio 5.50 3.25
**624** A93 3b blue gray 2.50 1.75
*Nos. 618-624 (7)* 11.60 6.65

Issue date: Jan. 1954.

**Arms of Yaracuy and Tropical Foliage**

**625** A93 5c green .40 .20
**626** A93 10c red .20 .20
**627** A93 15c brown .30 .20
**628** A93 20c ultra .45 .20
**629** A93 25c orange brn .65 .30
**630** A93 30c blue .75 .25
**631** A93 35c purple 1.75 1.10
*Nos. 625-631 (7)* 4.50 2.45
*Nos. 464-631 (168)* 420.40 180.85

Issue date: Jan. 1954.
See Nos. C338-C553.

Ship Type of 1948-50, Redrawn
Coil Stamps
Imprint: "Courvoisier S.A."

**1952 Unwmk. Photo. *Perf. 11½x12***

**632** A85 5c green .65 .20
**633** A85 10c car rose 1.10 .20
**634** A85 15c gray 3.75 .20
*Nos. 632-634,C554-C556 (6)* 9.50 1.20

Juan de Villegas and Cross of Father Yepez — A94

Virgin of Coromoto and Child — A95

**1952, Sept. 14 *Perf. 11½***

**635** A94 5c green .20 .20
**636** A94 10c red .50 .20
**637** A94 20c dk gray bl .80 .25
**638** A94 40c dp org 3.75 1.50
**639** A94 50c brown 2.00 .85
**640** A94 1b violet 3.75 1.00
*Nos. 635-640 (6)* 11.00 4.00
*Nos. 635-640,C557-C564 (14)* 22.90 8.90

Founding of the city of Barquisimeto by Juan de Villegas, 400th anniv.

**1952-53 *Perf. 11½x12***

**Size: 17x26mm**

**641** A95 1b rose pink 6.00 1.00

**Size: 26½x41mm**

**642** A95 1b rose pink ('53) 4.50 1.00

**Size: 36x55mm**

**643** A95 1b rose pink ('53) 2.00 .75
*Nos. 641-643 (3)* 12.50 2.75

300th anniv. of the appearance of the Virgin Mary to a chief of the Coromoto Indians.
Issue date: No. 641, Oct. 6.

Telegraph Stamps Surcharged in Black or Red

**1952, Nov. 24 Engr. *Perf. 12***

**Grayish Security Paper**

**644** 5c on 25c car .25 .20
**645** 10c on 1b blk (R) .25 .20

Surcharged

**1952, Dec.**

**646** 20c on 25c car .30 .20
**647** 30c on 2b ol grn 1.90 1.25
**648** 40c on 1b blk (R) .75 .40
**649** 50c on 3b red org 2.50 1.50
*Nos. 646-649 (4)* 5.45 3.35

Post Office, Caracas — A96

***Perf. 13x12½***

**1953-54 Unwmk. Photo.**

**650** A96 5c green .20 .20
*a.* Bklt. pane of 10
**651** A96 7½c brt green .35 .25
**652** A96 10c rose carmine .25 .20
*a.* Bklt. pane of 10
**653** A96 15c gray .40 .20
**654** A96 20c ultra .25 .20
**655** A96 25c magenta .40 .20
**656** A96 30c blue 1.90 .25
**657** A96 35c brt red vio .85 .25
**658** A96 40c orange 1.25 .40
**659** A96 45c violet 1.90 .65
**660** A96 50c red orange 1.25 .40
*Nos. 650-660 (11)* 9.00 3.20

Issued: 20c, 30c, 45c, 3/11; 7½c, 25c, 50c, 6/53; 5c, 10c, 2/54; 15c, 1954.
See Nos. C565-C575, C587-C589.

Type of 1953-54 Inscribed "Republica de Venezuela"

A96a

**1955**

**661** A96a 5c green .20 .20
**662** A96a 10c rose car .20 .20
**663** A96a 15c gray .20 .20
**664** A96a 20c ultra .25 .20
**665** A96a 30c blue .65 .40
**666** A96a 35c brt red vio .65 .20
**667** A96a 40c orange 1.00 .25
**668** A96a 45c violet 1.25 .50
*Nos. 661-668 (8)* 4.40 2.15
*Nos. 661-668,C597-C606 (18)* 10.80 5.40

Arms of Valencia and Industrial Scene — A97

Coat of Arms — A98

**1955, Mar. 26 Engr. *Perf. 12***

**669** A97 5c brt grn .20 .20
**670** A97 20c ultra .40 .20
**671** A97 25c reddish brn .65 .20
**672** A97 50c vermilion 1.00 .25
*Nos. 669-672,C590-C596 (11)* 4.85 2.40

Founding of Valencia del Rey, 400th anniv.

**1955, Dec. 9 Unwmk. *Perf. 11½***

**673** A98 5c green .30 .20
**674** A98 20c ultra 1.00 .20
**675** A98 25c rose car .80 .20
**676** A98 50c orange 1.00 .20
*Nos. 673-676,C607-C612 (10)* 5.85 2.15

1st Postal Convention, Caracas, 2/9-15/54.

Book and Map of the Americas — A99

Simon Bolivar — A100

**1956 Photo. *Perf. 11½***

**Granite Paper**

**677** A99 5c lt grn & bluish grn .20 .20
**678** A99 10c lil rose & rose vio .20 .20
**679** A99 20c ultra & dk bl .20 .20
**680** A99 25c gray & lil gray .25 .20
**681** A99 30c lt bl & bl .25 .20
**682** A99 40c bis brn & brn .30 .20
**683** A99 50c ver & red brn .65 .30
**684** A99 1b lt pur & vio 1.00 .50
*Nos. 677-684 (8)* 3.05 2.00
*Nos. 677-684,C629-C635 (15)* 5.55 3.65

Book Festival of the Americas, 11/15-30/56.

**Engraved, Center Embossed**

**1957-58 Unwmk. *Perf. 13½***

**685** A100 5c brt bl grn .20 .20
**686** A100 10c red .20 .20
**687** A100 20c lt slate bl .40 .20
**688** A100 25c rose lake .40 .20
**689** A100 30c vio blue .50 .20
**690** A100 40c red orange .75 .20
**691** A100 50c orange yel 1.00 .50
*Nos. 685-691 (7)* 3.45 1.70
*Nos. 685-691,C636-C642 (14)* 7.30 3.40

150th anniv. of the Oath of Monte Sacro and the 125th anniv. of the death of Simon Bolivar (1783-1830).
Issued: 10c, 50c, 1958; others, 11/15/57.

Hotel Tamanaco, Caracas A101

**1957-58 Engr. *Perf. 13***

**692** A101 5c green .20 .20
**693** A101 10c carmine .20 .20
**694** A101 15c black .25 .20
**695** A101 20c dark blue .30 .20
**696** A101 25c dp claret .30 .20
**697** A101 30c dp ultra .50 .20
**698** A101 35c purple .30 .20
**699** A101 40c orange .40 .20
**700** A101 45c rose violet .50 .20
**701** A101 50c yellow .70 .25
**702** A101 1b dk slate grn 1.00 .40
*Nos. 692-702 (11)* 4.65 2.45
*Nos. 692-702,C643-C657 (26)* 13.95 7.00

Issued: 5c, 10c, Oct. 10, 1957; others, 1958.
For surcharge see No. 878.

Main Post Office, Caracas — A102

**1958, May 14 Litho. *Perf. 14***

**703** A102 5c emerald .20 .20
**704** A102 10c rose red .20 .20
**705** A102 15c gray .20 .20
**706** A102 20c lt bl .20 .20
**707** A102 35c red lilac .20 .20
**708** A102 45c brt vio 1.25 .85
**709** A102 50c yellow .30 .20
**710** A102 1b lt ol grn .75 .40
*Nos. 703-710 (8)* 3.30 2.45
*Nos. 703-710,C658-C670 (21)* 12.30 8.60

See Nos. 748-750, C658-C670, C786-C792.
For surcharges see Nos. 865, C807, C856-C861.

Main Post Office, Caracas A103

**1958, Nov. 17 Engr. *Perf. 11½x12***

**711** A103 5c green .25 .20
**712** A103 10c rose red .40 .20
**713** A103 15c black .50 .20
*Nos. 711-713,C671-C673 (6)* 2.25 1.20

Arms of Merida — A104

**1958, Oct. 9 Photo. *Perf. 14x13½***

**714** A104 5c green .20 .20
**715** A104 10c bright red .20 .20
**716** A104 15c greenish gray .20 .20
**717** A104 20c blue .20 .20
**718** A104 25c magenta .40 .20
**719** A104 30c violet .20 .20
**720** A104 35c light purple .25 .20
**721** A104 40c orange .60 .20
**722** A104 45c deep rose lilac .30 .20
**723** A104 50c bright yellow .50 .20
**724** A104 1b gray green 1.50 .50
*Nos. 714-724 (11)* 4.55 2.50
*Nos. 714-724,C674-C689 (27)* 12.85 7.15

400th anniversary of the founding of the city of Merida. For surcharge see No. 873.

Arms of Trujillo, Bolivar Monument and Trujillo Hotel — A105

**1959, Nov. 17 Unwmk. *Perf. 14***

**725** A105 5c emerald .20 .20
**726** A105 10c rose .20 .20
**727** A105 15c gray .20 .20
**728** A105 20c blue .20 .20
**729** A105 25c brt pink .25 .20
**730** A105 30c lt ultra .40 .20
**731** A105 35c lt pur .40 .20
**732** A105 45c rose lilac .50 .25
**733** A105 50c yellow .50 .20
**734** A105 1b lt ol grn 1.25 .65
*Nos. 725-734 (10)* 4.10 2.50
*Nos. 725-734,C690-C700 (21)* 8.75 5.25

Founding of the city of Trujillo, 400th anniv.

Stadium A106

**1959 Mar. 10 Litho. *Perf. 13½***

**735** A106 5c brt grn .25 .20
**736** A106 10c rose pink .25 .20
**737** A106 20c blue .45 .20
**738** A106 30c dk bl .55 .20
**739** A106 50c red lilac .85 .20
*Nos. 735-739 (5)* 2.35 1.00
*Nos. 735-739,C701-C705 (10)* 4.20 2.25

8th Central American and Caribbean Games, Caracas, Nov. 29-Dec. 14, 1958.
#735-739 exist imperf. Value, pair $25.

Stamp of 1859, Mailman and José Ignacio Paz Castillo A107

Stamp of 1859 and: 50c, Mailman on horseback and Jacinto Gutierrez. 1b, Plane, train and Miguel Herrera.

**1959, Sept. 15 Engr. *Perf. 13½x14***

**740** A107 25c org yel .50 .25
**741** A107 50c blue .50 .25
**742** A107 1b rose red 1.25 .45
*Nos. 740-742,C706-C708 (6)* 3.90 1.85

Centenary of Venezuelan postage stamps.

**Catalogue values for unused stamps in this section, from this point to the end of the section, are for Never Hinged items.**

Alexander von Humboldt — A108

Newspaper, 1808, and View of Caracas, 1958 — A109

**1960, Feb. 9 Unwmk. *Perf. 13½***

**743** A108 5c grn & yel grn .35 .25
**744** A108 30c vio bl & vio .95 .25
**745** A108 40c org & brn org 1.25 .40
*Nos. 743-745,C709-C711 (6)* 5.25 1.65

Centenary of the death of Alexander von Humboldt, German naturalist and geographer.

Post Office Type of 1958

**1960, July Litho. *Perf. 14***

**748** A102 25c yellow .20 .20
**749** A102 30c light blue .25 .20
**750** A102 40c fawn .55 .20
*Nos. 748-750 (3)* 1.00 .60

**1960, June 6 Litho. *Perf. 14***

**751** A109 10c rose & blk .40 .20
**752** A109 20c lt blue & blk .65 .20
**753** A109 35c lilac & blk 1.00 .70
*Nos. 751-753,C712-C714 (6)* 6.45 2.75

150th anniv. (in 1958) of the 1st Venezuelan newspaper, Gazeta de Caracas.

Agustin Codazzi A110

National Pantheon — A111

**1960, June 15 Engr. Unwmk.**

**754** A110 5c brt green .20 .20
**755** A110 15c gray .65 .20
**756** A110 20c blue .50 .20
**757** A110 45c purple .65 .30
*Nos. 754-757,C715-C720 (10)* 5.65 2.55

Centenary (in 1959) of the death of Agustin Codazzi, geographer.
For surcharges see Nos. 869, C884.

**1960, May 9 Litho.**

**Pantheon in Bister**

**758** A111 5c emerald .20 .20
**759** A111 20c brt blue .50 .20
**760** A111 25c light olive .80 .20
**761** A111 30c dull blue .95 .25
**762** A111 40c fawn 1.40 .45
**763** A111 45c lilac 1.25 .45
*Nos. 758-763 (6)* 5.10 1.75
*Nos. 758-763,C721-C734 (20)* 23.20 6.75

For surcharges see Nos. C894-C895.

Andres Eloy Blanco, Poet (1896-1955) A112

**1960, May 21 Unwmk. *Perf. 14***

**Portrait in Black**

**764** A112 5c emerald .25 .20
**765** A112 30c dull blue .30 .20
**766** A112 50c yellow .65 .25
*Nos. 764-766,C735-C737 (6)* 4.10 1.45

For surcharge see No. C874.

Independence Meeting of April 19, 1810, Led by Miranda — A113

**1960, Aug. 19 Litho. *Perf. 13½***

**Center Multicolored**

**767** A113 5c brt green .50 .20
**768** A113 20c blue 1.00 .25
**769** A113 30c violet blue 1.40 .35
*Nos. 767-769,C738-C740 (6)* 6.40 1.80

150th anniversary of Venezuela's Independence.
See Nos. 812-814, C804-C806. For surcharge see No. C893.

Drilling for Oil — A114

**1960, Aug. 26 Engr. *Perf. 14***

**770** A114 5c grn & slate grn 1.75 .65
**771** A114 10c dk car & brn .65 .25
**772** A114 15c gray & dull pur .85 .30
*Nos. 770-772,C741-C743 (6)* 5.60 2.10

Issued to publicize Venezuela's oil industry.

Luisa Cáceres de Arismendi A115

**Unwmk.**

**1960, Oct. 21 Litho. *Perf. 14***

**Center Multicolored**

**773** A115 20c light blue 1.25 .35
**774** A115 25c citron 1.00 .40
**775** A115 30c dull blue 1.40 .50
*Nos. 773-774,C744-C746 (5)* 6.70 2.35

Death of Luisa Càceres de Arismendi, 94th anniv.

José Antonio Anzoategui — A116

**1960, Oct. 29 Engr.**

**776** A116 5c emerald & gray ol .30 .20
**777** A116 15c ol gray & dl vio .45 .20
**778** A116 20c blue & gray vio .60 .20
*Nos. 776-778,C747-C749 (6)* 3.20 1.50

140th anniversary (in 1959) of the death of General José Antonio Anzoategui.

Antonio José de Sucre — A117

**Unwmk.**

**1960, Nov. 18 Litho. *Perf. 14***

**Center Multicolored**

**779** A117 10c deep rose .40 .20
**780** A117 15c gray brown .50 .25
**781** A117 20c blue .70 .35
*Nos. 779-781,C750-C752 (6)* 4.85 2.05

130th anniversary of the death of General Antonio José de Sucre.

Bolivar Peak, Merida — A118

Designs: 15c, Caroni Falls, Bolivar. 35c, Cuacharo caves, Monagas.

**1960, Mar. 22 *Perf. 14***

**782** A118 5c emerald & grn 1.00 1.00
**783** A118 15c gray & dk gray 3.25 3.25
**784** A118 35c rose lil & lil 2.75 2.75
*Nos. 782-784,C753-C755 (6)* 12.70 12.70

Buildings and People — A119

**1961 Litho. Unwmk.**

**Building in Orange**

**785** A119 5c emerald .20 .20
**786** A119 10c carmine .20 .20
**787** A119 15c gray .20 .20
**788** A119 20c blue .20 .20
**789** A119 25c lt red brown .25 .20
**790** A119 30c dull blue .25 .20
**791** A119 35c red lilac .35 .20
**792** A119 40c fawn .55 .25
**793** A119 45c brt violet .70 .30
**794** A119 50c yellow .55 .20
*Nos. 785-794 (10)* 3.45 2.15

1960 national census. See #C756-C770. For surcharge see No. 866.

Rafael Maria Baralt — A120

Yellow-headed Parrot — A121

**1961, Mar. 11 Engr. *Perf. 14***

**795** A120 5c grn & slate grn .20 .20
**796** A120 15c gray & dull red brn .40 .20
**797** A120 35c rose lilac & lt vio .60 .20
*Nos. 795-797,C771-C773 (6)* 3.55 1.60

Rafael Maria Baralt, statesman, death cent.

**1961, Sept. 6 Litho. *Perf. 14½***

**798** A121 30c shown 1.00 .40
**799** A121 40c Snowy egret 1.40 .40
**800** A121 50c Scarlet ibis 2.25 .70
*Nos. 798-800,C776-C778 (6)* 7.30 3.30

Juan J. Aguerrevere — A122

**1961, Oct. 21 Unwmk. *Perf. 14***

**801** A122 25c dark blue .25 .20
*a.* Souvenir sheet, imperf. 1.40 1.40

Centenary of the founding of the Engineering Society of Venezuela, Oct. 28, 1861.
No. 801a sold for 1b.
No. 801a exists with "Valor: Bs 1,00" omitted at lower left corner. Value, $7.

Battle of Carabobo, 1821 — A123

**1961, Dec. 1 *Perf. 14***

**Center Multicolored**

**802** A123 5c emerald & blk .20 .20
**803** A123 40c brown & blk .60 .25
*Nos. 802-803,C779-C784 (8)* 15.05 4.90

140th anniversary of Battle of Carabobo.

Oncidium Papilio Lindl. — A124

Orchids: 10c, Caularthron bilamellatum. 20c, Stanhopea Wardii Lodd. 25c, Catasetum pileatum. 30c, Masdevallia tovarensis. 35c, Epidendrum Stamfordianum Batem, horiz. 50c, Epidendrum atropurpureum Willd. 3b, Oncidium falcipetalum Lindl.

***Perf. 14x13½, 13½x14***

**1962, May 30 Litho. Unwmk.**

**Orchids in Natural Colors**

**804** A124 5c black & orange .20 .20
**805** A124 10c blk & brt grnsh bl .20 .20
**806** A124 20c black & yel grn .50 .20
**807** A124 25c black & lt blue .70 .20
**808** A124 30c black & olive .80 .20
**809** A124 35c black & yellow .90 .25
**810** A124 50c black & gray 1.00 .30
**811** A124 3b black & vio 6.00 2.50
*Nos. 804-811 (8)* 10.30 4.05
*Nos. 804-811,C794-C803 (18)* 25.30 9.30

For surcharges see Nos. 872, C885-C887.

Independence Type of 1960

Signing Declaration of Independence.

**1962, June 11 *Perf. 13½***

**Center Multicolored**

**812** A113 5c emerald .30 .20
**813** A113 20c blue .50 .20
**814** A113 25c yellow .75 .30
*a.* Souv. sheet, #812-814, imperf 3.25 3.25
*Nos. 812-814,C804-C806 (6)* 5.85 1.95

150th anniv. of the Venezuelan Declaration of Independence, July 5, 1811.
No. 814a sold for 1.50b.

Shot Put A125

**1962, Nov. 30 Litho. *Perf. 13x14***

**815** A125 5c shown .25 .20
**816** A125 10c Soccer .25 .20
**817** A125 25c Swimming .35 .20
***a.*** Souv. sheet, #815-817, imperf 2.75 2.75
*Nos. 815-817,C808-C810 (6)* 3.35 1.80

1st Natl. Games, Caracas, 1961. The stamps are arranged so that two pale colored edges of each stamp join to make a border around blocks of four.

No. 817a sold for 1.40b.

For surcharge see No. C899.

Vermilion Cardinal — A126

Malaria Eradication Emblem, Mosquito and Map — A127

Birds: 10c, Great kiskadee. 20c, Glossy black thrush. 25c, Collared trogons. 30c, Swallow tanager. 40c, Long-tailed sylph. 3b, Black-necked stilt.

**1962, Dec. 14 *Perf. 14x13½***

**Birds in Natural Colors, Black Inscription**

**818** A126 5c brt yellow grn .25 .20
**819** A126 10c violet blue .25 .20
**820** A126 20c lilac rose .50 .20
**821** A126 25c dull brown .60 .20
**822** A126 30c lemon .75 .20
**823** A126 40c lilac 1.00 .30
**824** A126 3b fawn 7.00 3.00
*Nos. 818-824 (7)* 10.35 4.30
*Nos. 818-824,C811-C818 (15)* 25.05 10.60

For surcharges see Nos. 868, C880-C882.

**Lithographed and Embossed**

***Perf. 13½x14***

**1962, Dec. 20 Wmk. 346**

**825** A127 50c brown & black .65 .25

WHO drive to eradicate malaria. See Nos. C819-C819a.

White-tailed Deer A128

Designs: 10c, Collared peccary. 35c, Collared titi (monkey). 50c, Giant Brazilian otter. 1b, Puma. 3b, Capybara.

***Perf. 13½x14***

**1963, Mar. 13 Litho. Unwmk.**

**Multicolored Center; Black Inscriptions**

**826** A128 5c green .20 .20
**827** A128 10c orange .20 .20
**828** A128 35c red lilac .25 .20
**829** A128 50c blue .55 .25
**830** A128 1b rose brown 2.75 1.40
**831** A128 3b yellow 5.50 3.50
*Nos. 826-831 (6)* 9.45 5.75
*Nos. 826-831,C820-C825 (12)* 23.75 11.00

For surcharges see #870-871, C888-C889.

Fisherman and Map of Venezuela A129

Cathedral of Bocono A130

**1963, Mar. 21**

**832** A129 25c pink & ultra .25 .20
*Nos. 832,C826-C827 (3)* 1.30 .90

FAO "Freedom from Hunger" campaign.

**1963, May 30 Wmk. 346**

**833** A130 50c brn, red & grn, *buff* .55 .20

400th anniversary of the founding of Bocono. See No. C828.

St. Peter's Basilica, Rome A131

**1963, June 11 *Perf. 14x13½***

**834** A131 35c dk bl, brn & buff .45 .20
**835** A131 45c dk grn, red brn & buff .50 .20
*Nos. 834-835,C829-C830 (4)* 3.15 1.10

Vatican II, the 21st Ecumenical Council of the Roman Catholic Church.

National Flag — A132

**1963, July 29 Unwmk. *Perf. 14***

**836** A132 30c gray, red, yel & bl 1.00 .20

Centenary of Venezuela's flag and coat of arms. See No. C831.

Lake Maracaibo Bridge — A133

Map, Soldier and Emblem — A134

***Perf. 13½x14***

**1963, Aug. 24 Wmk. 346**

**837** A133 30c blue & brown .35 .20
**838** A133 35c bluish grn & brn .40 .20
**839** A133 80c blue grn & brn .85 .35
*Nos. 837-839,C832-C834 (6)* 5.10 2.00

Opening of bridge over Lake Maracaibo. For surcharge see No. 875.

**1963, Sept. 10 Unwmk.**

**840** A134 50c red, bl & grn, *buff* .50 .20

25th anniversary of the armed forces. See No. C835. For surcharge see No. C862.

Dag Hammarskjold and World Map — A135

***Perf. 14x13½***

**1963, Sept. 25 Unwmk.**

**841** A135 25c dk bl, bl grn & ocher .25 .20
**842** A135 55c grn, grnsh bl & ocher 1.00 .30
*Nos. 841-842,C836-C837 (4)* 3.45 1.45

"1st" anniv. of the death of Dag Hammarskjold, Secretary General of the UN, 1953-61.

See #C837a. For surcharges see #867, C875-C876.

Dr. Luis Razetti — A136

Dr. Francisco A. Risquez — A137

**1963, Oct. 10 Litho.**

**843** A136 35c blue, ocher & brn .45 .20
**844** A136 45c mag, ocher & brn .65 .20
*Nos. 843-844,C838-C839 (4)* 4.00 1.75

Dr. Luis Razetti, physician, birth cent.

**1963, Dec. 31 *Perf. 11½x12***

Design: 20c, Dr. Carlos J. Bello.

**845** A137 15c multicolored .20 .20
**846** A137 20c multicolored .30 .20
*Nos. 845-846,C840-C841 (4)* 2.00 1.10

Cent. of the Intl. Red Cross.

Oil Field Workers — A138

Pedro Gual — A139

10c, Oil refinery. 15c Crane & building construction. 30c, Cactus, train & truck. 40c, Tractor.

**1964, Feb. 5 Litho. *Perf. 14x13½***

**847** A138 5c multi .25 .20
**848** A138 10c multi .25 .20
**849** A138 15c multi .30 .20
**850** A138 30c multi .50 .25
**851** A138 40c multi .55 .25
*Nos. 847-851 (5)* 1.85 1.10
*Nos. 847-851,C842-C846 (10)* 3.35 2.10

Department of Industrial Development, cent.

**1964, Mar. 20 Unwmk. *Perf. 14***

**852** A139 40c lt olive green .55 .20
**853** A139 50c lt red brown .70 .25
*Nos. 852-853,C847-C848 (4)* 3.00 1.05

Pedro Gual (1784-1862), statesman.

Carlos Arvelo — A140

**1964, Apr. 17 Engr. *Perf. 14x13½***

**854** A140 1b dull bl & gray 1.40 .45

Centenary of the death of Dr. Carlos Arvelo (1784-1862), chief physician of Bolivar's revolutionary army, director of Caracas Hospital, rector of Central University and professor of pathology.

For surcharge see No. 874.

Foundry Ladle and Molds A141

**1964, May 22 *Perf. 14x13½***

**855** A141 20c multicolored .30 .20
**856** A141 50c multicolored .55 .20
*Nos. 855-856,C849-C850 (4)* 3.00 1.15

Orinoco Steel Mills.

Romulo Gallegos, Novelist, 80th Birthday — A142

**Unwmk.**

**1964, Aug. 3 Litho. *Perf. 12***

**857** A142 5c dk & lt green .20 .20
**858** A142 10c bl & pale bl .20 .20
**859** A142 15c dk & lt red lil .30 .20
*Nos. 857-859,C852-C854 (6)* 2.35 1.25

Angel Falls, Bolivar State A143

Tourist Publicity: 10c, Tropical landscape, Sucre State. 15c, San Juan Peaks, Guarico. 30c, Net fishermen, Anzoategui. 40c, Mountaineer, Merida.

**1964, Oct. 22 *Perf. 13½x14***

**860** A143 5c multi .20 .20
**861** A143 10c multi .20 .20
**862** A143 15c multi .20 .20
**863** A143 30c multi .40 .20
**864** A143 40c multi .60 .20
*Nos. 860-864 (5)* 1.60 1.00

Issues of 1958-64 Surcharged in Black, Dark Blue or Lilac

**1965**

**865** A102 5c on 1b (#710) .40 .20
**866** A119 10c on 45c (#793) .20 .20
**867** A135 15c on 55c (#842) .20 .20
**868** A126 20c on 3b (#824) .20 .20
**869** A110 25c on 45c (#757) (DB) .20 .20

**870** A128 25c on 1b (#830) .25 .20
**871** A128 25c on 3b (#831) .30 .20
**872** A124 25c on 3b (#811) (L) .20 .20
**873** A104 30c on 1b (#724) .25 .20
**874** A140 40c on 1b (#854) .60 .20
**875** A133 60c on 80c (#839) .75 .25
*Nos. 865-875 (11)* 3.55 2.25

Lines of surcharge arranged variously; old denomination obliterated with bars on Nos. 867, 870-872. See Nos. C856-C899.

Revenue Stamps of 1947 Surcharged in Red or Black

Imprint: "American Bank Note Co."

**1965 Engr. *Perf. 12, 13½ (No. 882)***
**876** R1 5c on 5c emerald .20 .20
**877** R1 5c on 20c red brn .20 .20
**878** R1 10c on 10c brn ol .20 .20
**879** R1 15c on 40c grn .20 .20
**880** R1 20c on 3b dk bl (R) .30 .20
**881** R1 25c on 5b vio bl (R) .60 .25
**882** R1 25c on 5b vio bl (R) (Imprint: "Bundesdruckerei Berlin") .30 .20
**883** R1 60c on 3b dk bl (R) .75 .25
*Nos. 876-883 (8)* 2.75 1.70

Type R1 is illustrated above No. 401.

John F. Kennedy and Alliance for Progress Emblem A144

**1965, Aug. 20 Photo. *Perf. 12x11½***
**884** A144 20c gray .35 .20
**885** A144 40c bright lilac .55 .20
*Nos. 884-885 (2)* .90 .40

Map of Venezuela and Guiana by Codazzi, 1840 — A145

Protesilaus Leucones — A146

Maps of Venezuela and Guiana: 15c, by Juan M. Restrepo, 1827, horiz. 40c, by L. de Surville, 1778.

**1965, Nov. 5 Litho. *Perf. 13½***
**886** A145 5c multi .20 .20
**887** A145 15c multi .30 .20
**888** A145 40c multi .55 .20
*a.* Souv. sheet, #886-888, imperf 6.00 6.00
*Nos. 886-888,C905-C907 (6)* 2.70 1.30

Issued to publicize Venezuela's claim to part of British Guiana.
No. 888a sold for 85c.

**1966, Jan. 25 Litho. *Perf. 13½x14***
**Various Butterflies in Natural Colors**
**Black Inscriptions**
**889** A146 20c lt olive grn 1.25 .25
**890** A146 30c lt yellow grn 2.50 .25
**891** A146 50c yellow 3.75 .30
*Nos. 889-891,C915-C917 (6)* 14.50 2.30

Ship and Map of Atlantic Ocean A147

**1966, Mar. 10 Litho. *Perf. 13½x14***
**892** A147 60c brown, bl & blk 1.40 .45

Bicentenary of the first maritime mail.

"El Carite" Dance — A148

Various Folk Dances

***Perf. 14x13½***
**1966, Apr. 5 Litho. Unwmk.**
**893** A148 5c gray & multi .20 .20
**894** A148 10c orange & multi .20 .20
**895** A148 15c lemon & multi .30 .20
**896** A148 20c lilac & multi .40 .20
**897** A148 25c brt pink & multi .55 .25
**898** A148 35c yel grn & multi .60 .30
*Nos. 893-898,C919-C924 (12)* 9.00 3.60

Type of Air Post Stamps and

Arturo Michelena, Self-portrait A149

Paintings: 1b, Penthesileia, battle scene. 1.05b, The Red Cloak.

***Perf. 12½x12, 12x12½***
**1966, May 12 Litho. Unwmk.**
**899** A149 95c sepia & buff .80 .60
**900** AP74 1b multi 1.00 .60
**901** AP74 1.05b multi 1.25 .60
*Nos. 899-901,C927-C929 (6)* 6.30 3.30

Arturo Michelena (1863-1898), painter. Miniature sheets of 12 exist.

Construction Worker and Map of Americas — A150

Designs: 20c, as 10c. 30c, 65c, Labor monument. 35c, Machinery worker and map of Venezuela. 50c, Automobile assembly line.

**1966, July 6 Litho. *Perf. 14x13½***
**902** A150 10c yellow & blk .20 .20
**903** A150 20c lt grnsh bl & blk .25 .20
**904** A150 30c lt blue & vio .25 .20
**905** A150 35c lemon & olive .35 .20
**906** A150 50c brt rose & claret .50 .25
**907** A150 65c salmon pink & brn .65 .30
*Nos. 902-907 (6)* 2.20 1.35

2nd Conference of Ministers of Labor of the Organization of American States.

Velvet Cichlid A151

**1966, Aug. 31 Litho. *Perf. 13½x14***
**908** A151 15c shown .25 .20
**909** A151 25c Perch cichlid .35 .20
**910** A151 45c Piranha .95 .30
*Nos. 908-910,C933-C935 (6)* 5.75 1.90

Nativity — A152

Rubén Dario — A154

Satellite, Radar, Globe, Plane and Ship A153

**1966, Dec. 9 Litho. *Perf. 13½x14***
**911** A152 65c violet & blk .80 .30

Christmas 1966.

**1966, Dec. 28 *Perf. 13½x14***
**912** A153 45c multi .65 .25

Ministry of Communications, 30th anniv.

**1967 Litho.**
**913** A154 70c gray bl & dk bl 1.00 .45

Rubén Dario (pen name of Felix Rubén Garcia Sarmiento, 1867-1916), Nicaraguan poet, newspaper correspondent and diplomat.

Old Building and Arms, University of Zulia A155

***Perf. 13½x14***
**1967, Apr. 21 Litho. Unwmk.**
**914** A155 80c gold, blk & car 1.00 .45

University of Zulia founding, 75th anniv.

Front Page and Printing Press — A156

**1968, June 27 Photo. *Perf. 14x13½***
**915** A156 1.50b emer, blk & brn 1.50 .60

Newspaper Correo del Orinoco, 150th anniv.

Boll Weevil A157

Insect Pests: 20c, Corn borer, vert. 90c, Tobacco caterpillar.

***Perf. 14x13½, 13½x14***
**1968, Aug. 30 Litho.**
**916** A157 20c multicolored .50 .20
**917** A157 75c olive & multi 1.50 .25
**918** A157 90c multicolored 2.10 .35
*Nos. 916-918,C989-C991 (6)* 7.10 1.40

Guayana Substation A158

Designs: 45c, Guaira River Dam, horiz. 50c, Macagua Dam and power plant, horiz. 80c, Guri River Dam and power plant.

**1968, Nov. 8 Litho.**
**919** A158 15c fawn & multi .20 .20
**920** A158 45c dl yel & multi .50 .20
**921** A158 50c bl grn & multi .75 .25
**922** A158 80c blue & multi 1.10 .50
*Nos. 919-922 (4)* 2.55 1.15

Electrification program.

House and Piggy Bank A159

**1968, Dec. 6 Litho. *Perf. 13½x14***
**923** A159 45c blue & multi .60 .25

National Savings System.

Nursery and Child Planting Tree A160

Designs: 15c, Child planting tree (vert.; this design used as emblem on entire issue). 30c, Waterfall, vert. 45c, Logging. 55c, Fields and village, vert. 75c, Palambra (fish).

***Perf. 14x13½, 13½x14***
**1968, Dec. 19 Litho.**
**924** A160 15c multicolored .30 .20
**925** A160 20c multicolored .30 .20
**926** A160 30c multicolored .35 .20
**927** A160 45c multicolored .50 .20
**928** A160 55c multicolored 1.10 .30
**929** A160 75c multicolored .75 .20
*Nos. 924-929 (6)* 3.30 1.30
*Nos. 924-929,C1000-C1005 (12)* 9.50 3.70

Issued to publicize nature conservation.

Colorada Beach, Sucre A161

Designs: 45c, Church of St. Francis of Yare, Miranda. 90c, Stilt houses, Zulia.

**1969, Jan. 24 *Perf. 13½x14***
**930** A161 15c multicolored .20 .20
**931** A161 45c multicolored .55 .20
**932** A161 90c multicolored .80 .50
*Nos. 930-932,C1006-C1008 (6)* 2.55 1.50

Tourist publicity. For souvenir sheet see No. C1007a.

Bolivar Addressing Congress of Angostura — A162

**1969, Feb. 15 Litho. *Perf. 11***

**933** A162 45c multicolored .60 .25

Sesquicentennial of the Congress of Angostura (Ciudad Bolivar).

Martin Luther King, Jr. — A163

**1969, Apr. 1 Litho. *Perf. 13½***

**934** A163 1b bl, red & dk brn 1.00 .30

Rev. Dr. Martin Luther King, Jr. (1929-1968), American civil rights leader and recipient of the Nobel Peace Prize, 1964.

Tabebuia A164

Trees: 65c, Erythrina poeppigiana. 90c, Platymiscium.

**1969, May 30 Litho. *Perf. 13½x14***

**935** A164 50c multicolored .75 .20
**936** A164 65c gray & multi 1.00 .25
**937** A164 90c pink & multi 1.50 .40
*Nos. 935-937,C1009-C1011 (6)* 5.35 1.45

Issued to publicize nature conservation.

Still Life with Pheasant, by Rojas — A165

Paintings by Cristobal Rojas (1858-1890): 25c, On the Balcony, vert. 45c, The Christening. 50c, The Empty Place (family). 60c, The Tavern. 1b, Man's Arm, vert.

***Perf. 14x13½, 13½x14***

**1969, June 27 Litho. Unwmk.**

**Size: 32x42mm, 42x32mm**

**938** A165 25c gold & multi .25 .20
**939** A165 35c gold & multi .45 .20
**940** A165 45c gold & multi .75 .25
**941** A165 50c gold & multi .85 .30
**942** A165 60c gold & multi 1.10 .35

***Perf. 11***

**Size: 26x53mm**

**943** A165 1b gold & multi 1.60 .60
*Nos. 938-943 (6)* 5.00 1.90

ILO Emblem A166

**1969, July 28 *Perf. 13½***

**944** A166 2.50b fawn & blk 2.00 1.25

50th anniv. of the ILO.

Charter and Coat of Arms A167

Industrial Complex A168

**1969, Aug. 26 Litho. *Perf. 13½***

**945** A167 45c ultra & multi .65 .25
**946** A168 1b multicolored 1.00 .35

Industrial development.

House with Arcade, Carora — A169

Designs: 25c, Ruins of Pastora Church. 55c, Chapel of the Cross. 65c, House of Culture.

**1969, Sept. 8 *Perf. 13x14½***

**947** A169 20c multicolored .20 .20
**948** A169 25c multicolored .30 .20
**949** A169 55c multicolored .75 .20
**950** A169 65c multicolored 1.00 .35
*Nos. 947-950 (4)* 2.25 1.00

400th anniversary of city of Carora.

Simon Bolivar in Madrid — A170

Designs: 10c, Bolivar's wedding, Madrid, 1802, horiz. 35c, Bolivar monument. Madrid.

***Perf. 13½x14, 14x13½***

**1969, Oct. 28 Litho.**

**951** A170 10c multicolored .20 .20
**952** A170 15c brn red & blk .30 .20
**953** A170 35c multicolored .40 .20
*a.* Souvenir sheet of 2 2.00 2.00
*Nos. 951-953 (3)* .90 .60

Bolivar's sojourn in Spain. No. 953a contains 2 imperf. stamps similar to Nos. 952-953 with simulated perforation. Sold for 75c.

"Birds in the Woods" — A171

Design: 45c, "Children in Summer Camp." Both designs are after children's paintings.

**1969, Dec. 12 Litho. *Perf. 12½***

**954** A171 5c emerald & multi .20 .20
**955** A171 45c red & multi .65 .30

Issued for Children's Day.

Map of Great Colombia A172

**1969, Dec. 16 Litho. *Perf. 11½***

**956** A172 45c multicolored .55 .20

150th anniversary of the founding of the State of Great Colombia.

St. Anthony's, Clarines A173

Churches: 30c, Church of the Conception, Caroni. 40c, St. Michael's, Burbusay. 45c, St. Anthony's, Maturin. 75c, St. Nicholas, Moruy. 1b, Coro Cathedral.

**1970, Jan. 15 *Perf. 14***

**957** A173 10c pink & multi .20 .20
**958** A173 30c emerald & multi .25 .20
**959** A173 40c yellow & multi .55 .20
**960** A173 45c gray bl & multi .75 .25
*a.* Souvenir sheet of 1, imperf. 1.50 1.50
**961** A173 75c yellow & multi 1.00 .35
**962** A173 1b orange & multi 1.25 .45
*Nos. 957-962 (6)* 4.00 1.65

Colonial architecture.
No. 960a sold for 75c.

A174

A175

Design: Seven Hills of Valera.

**1970, Feb. 13 Litho. *Perf. 13x14½***

**963** A174 95c multicolored 1.10 .35

Sesquicentennial of the city of Valera.

**1970, July 29 Litho. *Perf. 14x13½***

Flowers: 20c, Monochaetum Humboldtianum. 25c, Symbolanthus vasculosis. 45c, Cavedishia splendens. 1b, Befaria glauca.

**964** A175 20c multicolored .50 .20
**965** A175 25c multicolored .80 .20
**966** A175 45c multicolored 1.10 .40
**967** A175 1b multicolored 1.60 .55
*Nos. 964-967,C1049-C1052 (8)* 8.50 2.55

Battle of Boyaca, by Martin Tovar y Tovar A176

**1970, Aug. 7 *Perf. 13½x14***

**968** A176 30c multicolored .35 .20

150th anniversary of Battle of Boyaca.

Our Lady of Belén de San Mateo — A177

Designs: 35c, Pastoral Cross of Archbishop Silvestre Guevera y Lira, 1867. 40c, Our Lady of Valle. 90c, Virgin of Chiquinquira. 1b, Our Lady of Socorro de Valencia.

**1970, Sept. 1 *Perf. 14x13½***

**969** A177 35c gray & multi .45 .20
**970** A177 40c gray & multi .55 .20
**971** A177 60c gray & multi .80 .30
*a.* Souvenir sheet of 1, imperf. 1.40 1.40
**972** A177 90c gray & multi .95 .40
**973** A177 1b gray & multi 1.25 .50
*Nos. 969-973 (5)* 4.00 1.60

The designs are from sculptures and paintings in various Venezuelan churches.
No. 971a sold for 75c.

Venezuela No. 22 and EXFILCA Emblem — A178

Designs: 20c, EXFILCA emblem and flags of participating nations, vert. 70c, Venezuela No. C13 and EXFILCA emblem, vert.

**1970, Nov. 28 Litho. *Perf. 11***

**974** A178 20c yellow & multi .30 .20
**975** A178 25c dk blue & multi .35 .20
**976** A178 70c brown & multi .75 .30
*a.* Souvenir sheet of 1, imperf. 1.40 1.40
*Nos. 974-976 (3)* 1.40 .70

EXFILCA 70, 2nd Interamerican Philatelic Exhibition, Caracas, Nov. 27-Dec. 6. No. 976a is a hexagon with each side 50mm long. Sold for 85c.

Guardian Angel, by Juan Pedro Lopez — A179

**1970, Dec. 1 Litho. *Perf. 14½x13½***

**977** A179 45c dull yellow & multi .55 .25

Christmas 1970.

Jet and 1920 Plane A180

**1970, Dec. 10** ***Perf. 13x14***

**978** A180 5c blue & multi .25 .20

Venezuelan Air Force, 50th anniversary.

Question Mark Full of Citizens — A181

**1971, Apr. 30 Litho.** ***Perf. 14x13½***

**Light Green, Red & Black**

**979** Block of 4 3.50 2.00
- *a.* A181 30c frame L & T .85 .40
- *b.* A181 30c frame T & R .85 .40
- *c.* A181 30c frame L & B .85 .40
- *d.* A181 30c frame B & R .85 .40

National Census, 1971. Sheet of 20 contains 5 No. 979 and 5 blocks of 4 labels. See No. C1054.

Battle of Carabobo A182

**1971, June 21** ***Perf. 13½x14***

**980** A182 2b blue & multi 1.75 1.00

Sesquicentennial of Battle of Carabobo.

Map of Federal District — A183

State maps. 25c, 55c, 85c, 90c, vert.

**1971 Litho.** ***Perf. 13½x14, 14x13½***

**981** A183 5c shown .40 .20
**982** A183 15c Monagas .40 .20
**983** A183 20c Nueva Esparta .40 .20
**984** A183 25c Portuguesa .40 .20
**985** A183 45c Sucre .45 .20
**986** A183 55c Tachira .55 .20
**987** A183 65c Trujillo .65 .20
**988** A183 75c Yaracuy .75 .30
**989** A183 85c Zulia .95 .30
**990** A183 90c Amazonas 1.50 .30
**991** A183 1b Federal Dependencies 1.60 .55
*Nos. 981-991 (11)* 8.05 2.85
*Nos. 981-991,C1035-C1048 (25)* 19.20 6.85

Issued: 5c, 7/15; 15c, 20c, 8/16; 25c, 45c, 9/15; 55c, 65c, 10/15; 75c, 85c, 11/15; 90c, 1b, 12/15.

Madonna and Child A184

Luis Daniel Beauperthuy A185

Design: #993, Madonna & Jesus in manger.

**1971, Dec. 1** ***Perf. 11***

**992** A184 25c multicolored .50 .20
**993** A184 25c multicolored .50 .20
- *a.* Pair, #992-993 1.00 .50

Christmas 1971. Printed checkerwise.

**1971, Dec. 10** ***Perf. 14x13½***

**994** A185 1b vio bl & multi 1.00 .50

Dr. Luis Daniel Beauperthuy, scientist.

Globe in Heart Shape — A186

Flags of Americas and Arms of Venezuela A187

**1972, Apr. 7 Litho.** ***Perf. 14x13½***

**995** A186 1b red, ultra & blk .75 .45

"Your heart is your health," World Health Day 1972.

**1972, May 16 Litho.** ***Perf. 14x13½***

Designs: 4b, Venezuelan flag. 5b, National anthem. 10b, Araguaney, national tree. 15b, Map, North and South America. All show flags of American nations in background.

**996** A187 3b multicolored 4.00 1.00
**997** A187 4b multicolored 4.25 1.75
**998** A187 5b multicolored 4.75 2.25
**999** A187 10b multicolored 9.00 3.00
**1000** A187 15b multicolored 13.00 4.25
*Nos. 996-1000 (5)* 35.00 12.25

"Venezuela in America."

Parque Central Complex A188

#1002, Front view ("Parque Central" on top). #1003, Side view ("Parque Central" at right).

**1972, July 25** ***Perf. 11½***

**1001** A188 30c yellow & multi .25 .20
**1002** A188 30c blue & multi .25 .20
**1003** A188 30c red & multi .25 .20
- *a.* Strip of 3, #1001-1003 1.40 1.40

Completion of "Parque Central" middle-income housing project, Caracas.

Mahatma Gandhi — A189

**1972, Oct. 2 Litho.** ***Perf. 13½x14***

**1004** A189 60c multicolored .75 .40

103rd birthday of Mohandas K. Gandhi (1869-1948), leader in India's fight for independence, advocate of non-violence.

Children Playing Music — A190

Christmas: #1006, Children roller skating.

**1972, Dec. 5 Litho.** ***Perf. 13½x14***

**1005** 30c multicolored .25 .20
**1006** 30c multicolored .25 .20
- *a.* A190 Pair, #1005-1006 .70 .70

Indigo Snake A191

Snake: 15c, South American chicken snake. 25c, Venezuelan lance-head. 30c, Coral snake. 60c, Casabel rattlesnake. 1b, Boa constrictor.

**1972, Dec. 15 Litho.** ***Perf. 13½x14***

**1007** A191 10c black & multi .50 .35
**1008** A191 15c black & multi .50 .35
**1009** A191 25c black & multi .70 .35
**1010** A191 30c black & multi .80 .35
**1011** A191 60c black & multi 1.50 .40
**1012** A191 1b black & multi 2.25 .60
*Nos. 1007-1012 (6)* 6.25 2.40

Copernicus — A192

Sun — A193

Designs: 5c, Model of solarcentric system. 15c, Copernicus' book "De Revolutionibus."

**1973, Feb. 19 Litho.** ***Perf. 13½x14***

**1013** 5c multicolored .20 .20
**1014** 10c multicolored .35 .20
**1015** 15c multicolored .50 .20
- *a.* A192 Strip of 3, #1013-1015 1.10 .90

**1973 Litho.** ***Perf. 13½***

Designs: Planetary system.

**Size: 26½x29mm**

**1016** A193 5c shown .25 .25
**1017** A193 5c Earth .25 .25
**1018** A193 20c Mars .55 .25
**1019** A193 20c Saturn .40 .25
**1020** A193 30c Asteroids .45 .25
**1021** A193 40c Neptune .55 .25
**1022** A193 50c Venus .80 .40
**1023** A193 60c Jupiter .95 .45
**1024** A193 75c Uranus 1.10 .55
**1025** A193 90c Pluto 1.40 .80
**1026** A193 90c Moon 2.00 .80
**1027** A193 1b Mercury 2.25 .95

**Size: 27x55mm**

***Perf. 12***

**1028** A193 10c Orbits and Saturn .25 .25
**1029** A193 15c Sun, Mercury, Venus, Earth .40 .25
**1030** A193 15c Jupiter, Uranus, Neptune, Pluto .45 .25
- *a.* Strip of 3, #1028-1030 1.10 1.10

*Nos. 1016-1030 (15)* 12.05 6.20

10th anniversary of Humboldt Planetarium. No. 1030a has continuous design showing solar system.

Issue dates: Nos. 1016, 1018, 1021, 1023-1025, Mar. 15; others Mar. 30.

OAS Emblem, Map of Americas — A194

**1973, Apr. 30 Litho.** ***Perf. 13½x14***

**1031** A194 60c multicolored .45 .25

Organization of American States, 25th anniv.

José Antonio Paez — A195

Street of the Lancers, Puerto Cabello — A196

Designs: 10c, Paez in uniform. 30c, Paez and horse, from old print. 2b, Paez at Battle of Centauro, horiz. 10c, 2b are after contemporary paintings.

**1973** ***Perf. 14x13½, 13½x14***

**1032** A195 10c gold & multi .20 .20
**1033** A195 30c red, blk & gold .25 .20
**1034** A195 50c bl, vio bl & dk brn .45 .25
**1035** A196 1b multicolored .90 .45
**1036** A195 2b gold & multi 1.50 .90
*Nos. 1032-1036 (5)* 3.30 2.00

Gen. José Antonio Paez (1790-1873), leader in War of Independence, President of Venezuela. The 1b for the sesquicentenary of the fall of Puerto Cabello.

Issue dates: Nos. 1033-1034, May 6; Nos. 1032, 1036, June 13; No. 1035, Nov. 8.

José P. Padilla, Mariano Montilla, Manuel Manrique — A197

1b, Naval battle. 2b, Line-up for naval battle.

**1973, July 27 Litho. *Perf. 12½***

| | | | | |
|---|---|---|---|---|
| **1037** | A197 | 50c multicolored | .35 | .20 |
| **1038** | A197 | 1b multicolored | .75 | .35 |
| **1039** | A197 | 2b multicolored | 1.50 | .75 |
| | | *Nos. 1037-1039 (3)* | 2.60 | 1.30 |

150th anniv. of the Battle of Maracaibo.

Bishop Ramos de Lora — A198

Plane, Ship, Margarita Island — A199

**1973, Aug. 1 Photo. *Perf. 14x13½***

| | | | | |
|---|---|---|---|---|
| **1040** | A198 | 75c gold & dk brn | .60 | .25 |

Sesquicentennial of the birth of Ramos de Lora (1722-1790), first Bishop of Merida de Maracaibo and founder of the Colegio Seminario, the forerunner of the University of the Andes.

**1973, Sept. 8 Litho. *Perf. 14x13½***

| | | | | |
|---|---|---|---|---|
| **1041** | A199 | 5c multicolored | .20 | .20 |

Establishment of Margarita Island as a free port.

Map of Golden Road and Waterfall — A200

Designs (Road Map and): 10c, Scarlet macaw. 20c, Church ruins. 50c, 60c, Indian mountain sanctuary. 90c, Colonial church. 1b, Flags of Venezuela and Brazil.

**1973, Oct. 1 Litho. *Perf. 13***

| | | | | |
|---|---|---|---|---|
| **1042** | A200 | 5c black & multi | .25 | .25 |
| **1043** | A200 | 10c black & multi | .25 | .25 |
| **1044** | A200 | 20c black & multi | .80 | .25 |
| **1045** | A200 | 50c black & multi | .85 | .35 |
| **1046** | A200 | 60c black & multi | .85 | .35 |
| **1047** | A200 | 90c black & multi | 1.30 | .40 |
| **1048** | A200 | 1b black & multi | 1.60 | .55 |
| | | *Nos. 1042-1048 (7)* | 5.90 | 2.40 |

Completion of the Golden Road from Santa Elena de Uairen, Brazil, to El Dorado, Venezuela.

Issued: 50c, 60c, Oct. 30; others Oct. 1.

Gen. Paez Dam and Power Station — A201

**1973, Oct. 14 *Perf. 14x13½***

| | | | | |
|---|---|---|---|---|
| **1049** | A201 | 30c multicolored | .30 | .20 |

Opening of the Gen. José Antonio Paez Dam and Power Station.

Child on Slide — A202

Designs: No. 1051, Fairytale animals. No. 1052, Children's book. No. 1053, Children disembarking from plane for vacation.

**1973, Dec. 4 Litho. *Perf. 12***

| | | | | |
|---|---|---|---|---|
| **1050** | A202 | 10c multicolored | .25 | .20 |
| **1051** | A202 | 10c multicolored | .25 | .20 |
| **1052** | A202 | 10c multicolored | .25 | .20 |
| **1053** | A202 | 10c multicolored | .25 | .20 |
| | | *Nos. 1050-1053 (4)* | 1.00 | .80 |

Children's Foundation Festival.

King Following Star — A203

Christmas: No. 1055, Two Kings.

**1973, Dec. 5 Litho. *Perf. 14x13½***

| | | | | |
|---|---|---|---|---|
| **1054** | | 30c multicolored | .45 | .20 |
| **1055** | | 30c multicolored | .45 | .20 |
| *a.* | A203 | Pair, #1054-1055 | 1.00 | 1.00 |

Regional Map of Venezuela A204

**1973, Dec. 13 *Perf. 13½x14***

| | | | | |
|---|---|---|---|---|
| **1056** | A204 | 25c multicolored | .40 | .20 |

Introduction of regionalization.

Map of Carupano and Revelers — A206



Handicraft A205

Designs: 35c, Industrial park. 45c, Cog wheels and chimney.

**1973, Dec. 18 *Perf. 14x13½***

| | | | | |
|---|---|---|---|---|
| **1057** | A205 | 15c blue & multi | .20 | .20 |
| **1058** | A205 | 35c multicolored | .30 | .20 |
| **1059** | A205 | 45c yellow & multi | .50 | .20 |
| | | *Nos. 1057-1059 (3)* | 1.00 | .60 |

Progress in Venezuela and jobs for the handicapped.

**1974, Feb. 22 *Perf. 13½x14***

| | | | | |
|---|---|---|---|---|
| **1060** | A206 | 5c multicolored | .25 | .20 |

10th anniversary of Carupano Carnival.

Congress Emblem — A207

**1974, May 20 Litho. *Perf. 13½***

| | | | | |
|---|---|---|---|---|
| **1061** | A207 | 50c multicolored | .50 | .20 |

9th Venezuelan Engineering Congress, Maracaibo, May 19-25.

Waves and "M" A208

Designs: Under-water photographs of deep-sea fish and marine life.

**1974, June 20 Litho. *Perf. 12½***

| | | | | |
|---|---|---|---|---|
| **1062** | A208 | 15c multicolored | .40 | .20 |
| **1063** | A208 | 35c multicolored | .60 | .20 |
| **1064** | A208 | 75c multicolored | .75 | .25 |
| **1065** | A208 | 80c multicolored | .75 | .35 |
| | | *Nos. 1062-1065 (4)* | 2.50 | 1.00 |

3rd UN Conference on the Law of the Sea, Caracas, June 20-Aug. 29.

Pupil and New School — A209

"Pay your Taxes" Campaign: 10c, 15c, 20c, like 5c. 25c, 30c, 35c, 40c, Suburban housing development. 45c, 50c, 55c, 60c, Highway and overpass. 65c, 70c, 75c, 80c, Playing field (sport). 85c, 90c, 95c, 1b, Operating room. All designs include Venezuelan coat of arms, coins and banknotes.

**1974 *Perf. 13½***

| | | | | |
|---|---|---|---|---|
| **1066** | A209 | 5c blue & multi | .25 | .25 |
| **1067** | A209 | 10c ultra & multi | .25 | .25 |
| **1068** | A209 | 15c violet & multi | .25 | .25 |
| **1069** | A209 | 20c lilac & multi | .25 | .25 |
| **1070** | A209 | 25c multicolored | .25 | .25 |
| **1071** | A209 | 30c multicolored | .50 | .25 |
| **1072** | A209 | 35c multicolored | .25 | .25 |
| **1073** | A209 | 40c olive & multi | .40 | .25 |
| **1074** | A209 | 45c multicolored | .40 | .25 |
| **1075** | A209 | 50c green & multi | .40 | .25 |
| **1076** | A209 | 55c multicolored | .70 | .40 |
| **1077** | A209 | 60c multicolored | .55 | .30 |
| **1078** | A209 | 65c bister & multi | 1.30 | .60 |
| **1079** | A209 | 70c multicolored | .60 | .25 |
| **1080** | A209 | 75c multicolored | .70 | .30 |
| **1081** | A209 | 80c brown & multi | .70 | .30 |
| **1082** | A209 | 85c ver & multi | .70 | .30 |
| **1083** | A209 | 90c multicolored | .85 | .30 |
| **1084** | A209 | 95c multicolored | 1.50 | .95 |
| **1085** | A209 | 1b multicolored | .85 | .40 |
| | | *Nos. 1066-1085 (20)* | 11.65 | 6.60 |

Bolivar at Battle of Junin A210

**1974, Aug. 6 Litho. *Perf. 13½x14***

| | | | | |
|---|---|---|---|---|
| **1086** | A210 | 2b multicolored | 1.50 | .75 |

Sesquicentennial of the Battle of Junin.

Globe and UPU Emblem — A211

50c, Postrider, sailing ship, steamer and jet.

**1974, Oct. 9 *Perf. 12***

| | | | | |
|---|---|---|---|---|
| **1087** | A211 | 45c dk blue & multi | .35 | .20 |
| **1088** | A211 | 50c black & multi | .45 | .20 |

Centenary of Universal Postal Union.

Rufino Blanco-Fombona — A212

Portraits of Blanco-Fombona and his books.

**1974, Oct. 16 Litho. *Perf. 12½***

| | | | | |
|---|---|---|---|---|
| **1089** | A212 | 10c gray & multi | .20 | .20 |
| **1090** | A212 | 30c yellow & multi | .20 | .20 |
| **1091** | A212 | 45c multicolored | .30 | .20 |
| **1092** | A212 | 90c buff & multi | .50 | .25 |
| | | *Nos. 1089-1092 (4)* | 1.20 | .85 |

Centenary of the birth of Rufino Blanco-Fombona (1874-1944), writer.

Children A213

**1974, Nov. 29 Litho. *Perf. 13½***

| | | | | |
|---|---|---|---|---|
| **1093** | A213 | 70c blue & multi | .60 | .25 |

Children's Foundation Festival.

General Sucre — A214

Globe with South American Map and Flags — A215

Battle of Ayacucho — A216

1b, Map of South America with battles marked.

**1974, Dec. 9** ***Perf. 14x13½, 13½x14***

| | | | | |
|---|---|---|---|---|
| **1094** | A214 | 30c multicolored | .20 | .20 |
| **1095** | A215 | 50c multicolored | .30 | .25 |
| **1096** | A215 | 1b multicolored | .65 | .30 |
| **1097** | A216 | 2b multicolored | 1.25 | .65 |
| | | *Nos. 1094-1097 (4)* | 2.40 | 1.40 |

Sesquicentennial of the Battle of Ayacucho.

Adoration of the Shepherds, by J. B. Mayno — A217

**1974, Dec. 16** **Photo.** ***Perf. 14x13½***

| | | | | |
|---|---|---|---|---|
| **1098** | | 30c Shepherd | .30 | .25 |
| **1099** | | 30c Madonna & Child | .30 | .25 |
| *a.* | A217 | Pair, #1098-1099 | .90 | .90 |

Christmas 1974.

Road Building, 1905 and El Ciempies Overpass, 1972 — A219

Designs: 20c, 1b, Jesus Muñoz Tebar, first Minister of Public Works. 25c, Bridges on Caracas-La Guaira Road, 1912 and 1953. 40c, View of Caracas, 1874 and 1974. 70c, Tucacas Railroad Station, 1911, and projected terminal, 1974. 80c, Anatomical Institute, Caracas, 1911, and Social Security Hospital, 1969. 85c, Quininari River Bridge, 1804, and Orinoco River Bridge, 1967.

**1974, Dec. 18** **Litho.** ***Perf. 12½***

| | | | | |
|---|---|---|---|---|
| **1100** | A219 | 5c ultra & multi | .20 | .20 |
| **1101** | A219 | 20c ocher & blk | .25 | .20 |
| **1102** | A219 | 25c blue & multi | .30 | .20 |
| **1103** | A219 | 40c yellow & multi | .30 | .20 |
| **1104** | A219 | 70c green & multi | 1.40 | .25 |
| **1105** | A219 | 80c multicolored | 1.10 | .30 |
| **1106** | A219 | 85c orange & multi | 1.50 | .30 |
| **1107** | A219 | 1b red & black | 1.60 | .50 |
| | | *Nos. 1100-1107 (8)* | 6.65 | 2.15 |

Centenary of the Ministry of Public Works.

Women and IWY Emblem — A220

**1975, Oct. 8** **Litho.** ***Perf. 13½x14***

| | | | | |
|---|---|---|---|---|
| **1108** | A220 | 90c multicolored | .60 | .35 |

International Women's Year.

Scout Emblem and Tents — A221

**1975, Nov. 11** **Litho.** ***Perf. 13½x14***

| | | | | |
|---|---|---|---|---|
| **1109** | A221 | 20c multicolored | .20 | .20 |
| **1110** | A221 | 80c multicolored | .50 | .25 |

14th World Boy Scout Jamboree, Lillehammer, Norway, July 29-Aug. 7.

Adoration of the Shepherds — A222

**1975, Dec. 5** **Litho.** ***Perf. 13½x14***

| | | | | |
|---|---|---|---|---|
| **1111** | | 30c multicolored | .25 | .25 |
| **1112** | | 30c multicolored | .25 | .25 |
| *a.* | A222 | Pair, #1111-1112 | .85 | .85 |

Christmas 1975.

Bolivar's Tomb — A224

Design: 1.05b, National Pantheon.

**1976, Feb. 2** **Engr.** ***Perf. 14x13½***

| | | | | |
|---|---|---|---|---|
| **1113** | A224 | 30c gray & ultra | .20 | .20 |
| **1114** | A224 | 1.05b sepia & car | .50 | .25 |

Centenary of National Pantheon.

Bolivia Flag Colors A225

**1976, Mar. 22** **Litho.** ***Perf. 13½***

| | | | | |
|---|---|---|---|---|
| **1115** | A225 | 60c multicolored | .35 | .20 |

Sesquicentennial of Bolivia's independence.

Aerial Map Survey — A226

**1976, Apr. 8** ***Perf. 13½x12½***

| | | | | |
|---|---|---|---|---|
| **1116** | A226 | 1b black & vio bl | .50 | .25 |

Natl. Cartographic Institute, 40th anniv.

Gen. Ribas' Signature A227

José Felix Ribas A228

**1976, Apr. 26** **Photo.** ***Perf. 12½x13***

| | | | | |
|---|---|---|---|---|
| **1117** | A227 | 40c red & green | .30 | .20 |

***Perf. 13½***

| | | | | |
|---|---|---|---|---|
| **1118** | A228 | 55c multicolored | .40 | .20 |

Gen. José Felix Ribas (1775-1815), independence hero, birth bicentenary.

Musicians of the Chacao School, by Armandio Barrios — A229

Lamas's Colophon A230

**1976, May 13** **Litho.** ***Perf. 13½***

| | | | | |
|---|---|---|---|---|
| **1119** | A229 | 75c multicolored | .40 | .25 |

**Photo.** ***Perf. 12½x13***

| | | | | |
|---|---|---|---|---|
| **1120** | A230 | 1.25b buff, red & gray | .70 | .35 |

José Angel Lamas (1775-1814), composer, birth bicentenary.

Bolivar, by José Maria Espinoza — A231

**1976** **Engr.** ***Perf. 12***

**Size: 18x22½mm**

| | | | | |
|---|---|---|---|---|
| **1121** | A231 | 5c green | .20 | .20 |
| **1122** | A231 | 10c lilac rose | .20 | .20 |
| **1123** | A231 | 15c brown | .20 | .20 |
| **1124** | A231 | 20c black | .20 | .20 |
| **1125** | A231 | 25c yellow | .20 | .20 |
| **1126** | A231 | 30c violet bl | .20 | .20 |
| **1127** | A231 | 45c dk purple | .20 | .20 |
| **1128** | A231 | 50c orange | .20 | .20 |
| **1129** | A231 | 65c blue | .25 | .20 |
| **1130** | A231 | 1b vermilion | .30 | .25 |

**Size: 26x32mm**

***Perf. 12x11½***

| | | | | |
|---|---|---|---|---|
| **1131** | A231 | 2b gray | .65 | .25 |
| **1132** | A231 | 3b violet blue | .95 | .40 |
| **1133** | A231 | 4b yellow | 1.25 | .55 |
| **1134** | A231 | 5b orange | 1.50 | .75 |
| **1135** | A231 | 10b dull purple | 3.50 | 1.40 |
| **1136** | A231 | 15b blue | 5.25 | 2.00 |
| **1137** | A231 | 20b vermilion | 6.50 | 2.75 |
| | | *Nos. 1121-1137 (17)* | 21.75 | 10.15 |

Issued: 5c-1b, May 17; 2b-20b, July 15.

Coil Stamps

**1978, May 22** ***Perf. 13½ Horiz.***

**Size: 18x22½mm**

| | | | | |
|---|---|---|---|---|
| **1138** | A231 | 5c green | .20 | .20 |
| **1139** | A231 | 10c lilac rose | .20 | .20 |
| **1140** | A231 | 15c brown | .20 | .20 |
| **1141** | A231 | 20c black | .20 | .20 |
| **1142** | A231 | 25c yellow | .20 | .20 |
| **1143** | A231 | 30c violet blue | .20 | .20 |
| **1144** | A231 | 45c dk purple | .20 | .20 |
| **1144A** | A231 | 50c orange | .25 | .20 |
| **1144B** | A231 | 65c blue | .25 | .20 |
| **1144C** | A231 | 1b vermilion | .40 | .20 |
| | | *Nos. 1138-1144C (10)* | 2.30 | 2.00 |

Black control number on back of every fifth stamp.

See Nos. 1305-1307, 1362-1366, 1401-1409, 1482, 1484, 1487, 1490. Compare with designs A405-A406.

Maze A232

Central University A233

Faculty Emblems A234

**1976, June 1** **Litho.** ***Perf. 12½x13***

| | | | | |
|---|---|---|---|---|
| **1145** | A232 | 30c multicolored | .20 | .20 |
| **1146** | A233 | 50c yel, org & blk | .25 | .20 |
| **1147** | A234 | 90c black & yellow | .55 | .35 |
| | | *Nos. 1145-1147 (3)* | 1.00 | .75 |

Central University of Venezuela, 250th anniv.

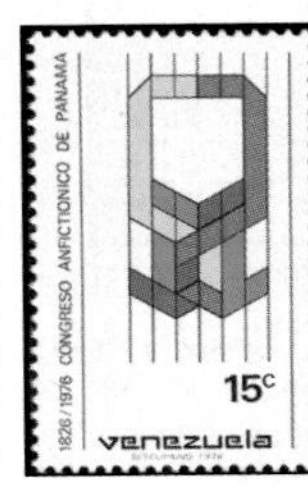


"Unity" — A235

Washington, US Bicent. Emblem A236

Designs: 45c, 1.25b, similar to 15c.

**1976, June 29** **Litho.** ***Perf. 12½***

| | | | | |
|---|---|---|---|---|
| **1148** | A235 | 15c multicolored | .20 | .20 |
| **1149** | A235 | 45c multicolored | .25 | .20 |
| **1150** | A235 | 1.25b multicolored | .55 | .35 |
| | | *Nos. 1148-1150 (3)* | 1.00 | .75 |

Amphictyonic Cong. of Panama, Sesqui.

**1976, July 4** **Engr.** ***Perf. 14***

US Bicentennial Emblem and: No. 1152, Jefferson. No. 1153, Lincoln. No. 1154, F. D. Roosevelt. No. 1155, J. F. Kennedy.

| | | | | |
|---|---|---|---|---|
| **1151** | A236 | 1b red brn & blk | .60 | .30 |
| **1152** | A236 | 1b green & blk | .60 | .30 |
| **1153** | A236 | 1b purple & blk | .60 | .30 |
| **1154** | A236 | 1b blue & blk | .60 | .30 |
| **1155** | A236 | 1b olive & blk | .60 | .30 |
| | | *Nos. 1151-1155 (5)* | 3.00 | 1.50 |

American Bicentennial.

Valve — A237

Ornament A239

Nativity, by Barbaro Rivas — A238

Computer drawings of valves & pipelines.

**1976, Nov. 8 Photo. *Perf. 123½x14***

**1156** A237 10c multicolored .20 .20
**1157** A237 30c multicolored .20 .20
**1158** A237 35c multicolored .20 .20
**1159** A237 40c multicolored .20 .20
**1160** A237 55c multicolored .25 .20
**1161** A237 90c multicolored .45 .25
*Nos. 1156-1161 (6)* 1.50 1.25

Nationalization of the oil industry.

**1976, Dec. 1 Litho. *Perf. 13x14***

**1162** A238 30c multicolored .40 .25

Christmas 1976.

**Lithographed and Embossed**

**1976, Dec. 15 *Perf. 14x13½***

**1163** A239 60c yellow & black .35 .20

Declaration of Bogota (economic agreements of Andean countries), 10th anniv.

Coat of Arms of Barinas — A240

**1977, May 25 Photo. *Perf. 12½x13***

**1164** A240 50c multicolored .35 .20

400th anniv. of the founding of Barinas.

Crucified Christ, Patron Saint of La Grita — A241

**1977, Aug. 6 Litho. *Perf. 13***

**1165** A241 30c multicolored .30 .25

Founding of La Grita, 400th anniv. (in 1976).

Symbolic City — A242

**1977, Aug. 26 Litho. *Perf. 13½***

**1166** A242 1b multicolored .50 .25

450th anniversary of the founding of Coro.

Communications Symbols — A243

**1977, Sept. 30 Litho. *Perf. 13½x14***

**1167** A243 85c multicolored .50 .20

9th Interamerican Postal and Telecommunications Staff Congress, Caracas, Sept. 26-30.

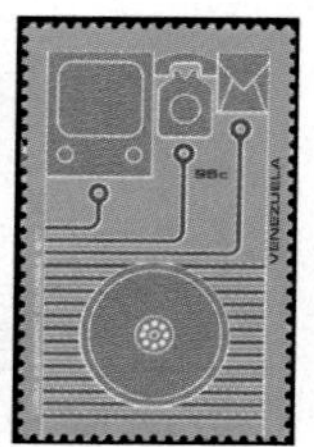

Cable Connecting with TV, Telephone and Circuit Box — A244

**1977, Oct. 12 Litho. *Perf. 14***

**1168** A244 95c multicolored .50 .20

Inauguration of Columbus underwater cable linking Venezuela and the Canary Islands.

"Venezuela" A245

Designs: "Venezuela" horizontal on 50c, 1.05b; reading up on 80c, 1.25b; reading down on 1.50b.

**1977, Nov. 26 Photo. *Perf. 13½x13***

**1169** A245 30c brt yel & blk .20 .20
**1170** A245 50c dp org & blk .25 .20
**1171** A245 80c gray & blk .45 .20
**1172** A245 1.05b red & blk .50 .20
**1173** A245 1.25b yel & blk .60 .20
**1174** A245 1.50b gray & blk .75 .25
*Nos. 1169-1174 (6)* 2.75 1.25

Iron industry nationalization, 1st anniv.

Juan Pablo Duarte — A246

Nativity, Colonial Sculpture — A247

**1977, Dec. 8 Engr. *Perf. 11x13***

**1175** A246 75c black & lilac .50 .20

Duarte (1813-76), leader in liberation struggle.

**1977, Dec. 15 Litho. *Perf. 13***

**1176** A247 30c green & multi .25 .20

Christmas 1977.

OPEC Emblem — A248

**1977, Dec. 20**

**1177** A248 1.05b brt & lt bl & blk .60 .20

50th Conference of Oil Producing and Exporting Countries, Caracas.

Bicyclist A249

**1978, Jan. 16 Litho. *Perf. 13½x13***

**1178** A249 5c Racing bicyclists .20 .20
**1179** A249 1.25b shown .60 .20

World Bicycling Championships, San Cristobal, Tachira, Aug. 22-Sept. 4.

Profiles A250

**1978, Apr. 21 Litho. *Perf. 13½x14***

**1180** A250 70c blk, gray & lil .35 .20

Language Day.
Issued in tete-beche pairs. Value $2.75.

Magnetic Computer Tape and Satellite A251

**1978, May 17 Litho. *Perf. 14***

**1184** A251 75c violet blue .40 .20

10th World Telecommunications Day.

"1777-1977" — A252

Goya's Carlos III as Computer Print — A253

**1978, June 23 Litho. *Perf. 12***

**1185** A252 30c multicolored .20 .20
**1186** A253 1b multicolored .55 .20

200th anniversary of Venezuelan unification.

**Bolivar Bicentenary**

Juan Vicente Bolivar y Ponte, Father of Simon Bolivar — A254

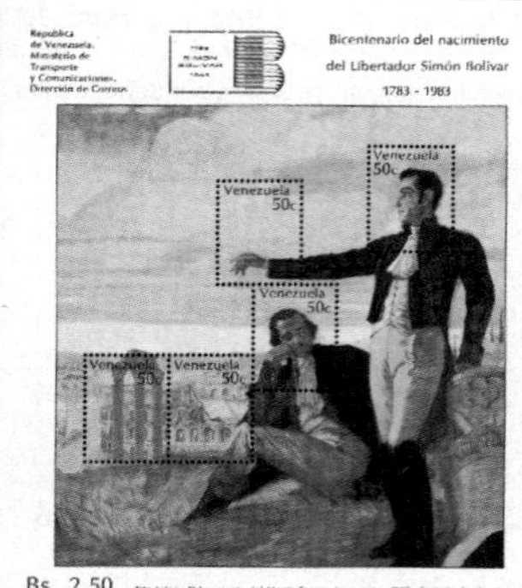

The Oath on Monte Sacro, Rome, by Tito Salas — A255

Designs: 30c, Bolivar as infant in nursemaid's arms (detail from design of No. 1189). No. 1189, Baptism of the Liberator, by Tito Salas, 1929.

Illustration A255 is reduced.

**1978, July 24 Engr. *Perf. 12½***

**1187** A254 30c emerald & blk .20 .20
**1188** A254 1b multicolored .55 .25

**Souvenir Sheet**

**Litho.**

***Perf. 14***

**1189** A255 Sheet of 5 32.50 32.50
*a.* 50c, single stamp 1.25 1.25

**1978, Dec. 17 Engr. *Perf. 12½***

Designs: 30c, Bolivar at 25. 1b, Simon Rodriguez. No. 1192, shown. (Bolivar's tutor).

**1190** A254 30c multicolored .20 .20
**1191** A254 1b rose red & blk .30 .20

**Souvenir Sheet**

**Litho.**

***Perf. 14***

**1192** A255 Sheet of 5 16.00 16.00
*a.* 50c, single stamp .75 .75

Size of souvenir sheet stamps: 20x24mm. Size of #1189: 154x130mm; #1192: 130x155mm.

**1979, July 24 Engr. *Perf. 12½***

Designs: 30c, Alexander Sabes Petion, president of Haiti. 1b, Bolivar's signature.

No. 1195: a, Partial map of Jamaica, horiz. b, Partial map of Jamaica, vert. c, Bolivar, 1816. d, Luis Brion. e, Petion.

**1193** A254 30c org, vio & blk .30 .20
**1194** A254 1b red org & blk .45 .20

**Souvenir Sheet**

**Litho.**

***Perf. 14***

**1195** A255 Sheet of 5 3.25 3.25
*a.-e.* 50c, any single .30 .30

Size of souvenir sheet stamps: 26x20, 20x26mm.

**1979, Dec. 17 Engr. *Perf. 12½***

Designs: 30c, Bolivar. 1b, Slave. No. 1198, Freeing of the Slaves, by Tito Salas. (30c, 1b, details from design of No. 1198.)

**1196** A254 30c multicolored .20 .20
**1197** A254 1b multicolored .30 .20

**Souvenir Sheet**

**Litho.**

***Perf. 14***

**1198** A255 Sheet of 5 5.00 5.00
*a.* 50c, single stamp .90 .90

Simon Bolivar, birth centenary. Size of souvenir sheet stamps: 22x28mm.

See Nos. 1228-1230, 1264-1266, 1276-1284, 1294-1296, 1317-1322.

"T" and "CTV" — A256

Symbolic Design — A257

Designs: Different arrangement of letters "T" and "CTV" for "Confederacion de Trabajeros Venezolanos."

**1978, Sept. 27 Photo. *Perf. 13x13½***

**1199** Strip of 5 .75 .75
*a.-e.* A256 30c, single stamp .20 .20
**1200** Strip of 5 1.60 1.60
*a.-e.* A256 95c, single stamp .25 .20

Workers' Day.

**1978, Oct. 3 Litho. *Perf. 14***

**1201** A257 50c dark brown .50 .25

Rafael Rangel, physician and scientist, birth centenary.

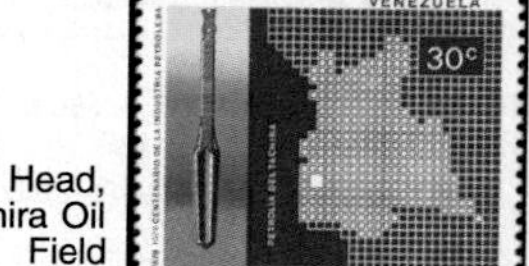

Drill Head, Tachira Oil Field Map — A258

"P" as Pipeline A259

**1978, Nov. 2 Litho. *Perf. 13½***

| | | | | |
|---|---|---|---|---|
| **1202** | A258 | 30c multicolored | .25 | .20 |
| **1203** | A259 | 1.05b multicolored | .55 | .25 |

Centenary of oil industry.

Star — A260

**1978, Dec. 6 Litho. *Perf. 14***

| | | | | |
|---|---|---|---|---|
| **1204** | A260 | 30c multicolored | .25 | .20 |

Christmas 1978.

"P T" — A261

**1979, Feb. 8 Litho. *Perf. 12½***

| | | | | |
|---|---|---|---|---|
| **1205** | A261 | 75c black & red | .25 | .20 |

Creation of Postal and Telegraph Institute.

"Dam Holding Back Water" A262

**1979, Feb. 15 Photo. *Perf. 13½***

| | | | | |
|---|---|---|---|---|
| **1206** | A262 | 2b silver, gray & blk | .65 | .35 |

Guri Dam, 10th anniversary.

San Martin, by E. J. Maury — A263

60c, San Martin, by Mercedes. 70c, Monument, Guayaquil. 75c, San Martin's signature.

**1979, Feb. 25 *Perf. 12½x13***

| | | | | |
|---|---|---|---|---|
| **1207** | A263 | 40c blue, blk & yel | .20 | .20 |
| **1208** | A263 | 60c blue, blk & yel | .25 | .20 |
| **1209** | A263 | 70c blue, blk & yel | .35 | .20 |
| **1210** | A263 | 75c blue, blk & yel | .35 | .25 |
| | | *Nos. 1207-1210 (4)* | 1.15 | .85 |

José de San Martin (1778-1850), South American liberator.

"Rotary" — A264

**1979, Aug. 7 Litho. *Perf. 14x13½***

| | | | | |
|---|---|---|---|---|
| **1211** | A264 | 85c gold & blk | .30 | .20 |

Rotary Club of Caracas, 50th anniversary.

Our Lady of Coromoto Appearing to Children A265

**Engraved and Lithographed**

**1979, Aug. 23 *Perf. 13***

| | | | | |
|---|---|---|---|---|
| **1212** | A265 | 55c black & dp org | .25 | .20 |

Canonization of Our Lady of Coromoto, 25th anniv.

London Residence, Coat of Arms, Miranda — A266

**1979, Oct. 23 Litho. *Perf. 14½x14***

| | | | | |
|---|---|---|---|---|
| **1213** | A266 | 50c multicolored | .25 | .20 |

Francisco de Miranda (1750-1816), Venezuelan independence fighter.

O'Leary, Maps of South America and United Kingdom A267

**1979, Nov. 6**

| | | | | |
|---|---|---|---|---|
| **1214** | A267 | 30c multicolored | .25 | .20 |

Daniel O'Leary (1801-1854), writer.

A268 A269

IYC Emblem and: 79c, Boy holding nest. 80c, Boys in water, bridge.

**1979, Nov. 20 Litho. *Perf. 14½x14***

| | | | | |
|---|---|---|---|---|
| **1215** | A268 | 70c lt blue & blk | .25 | .20 |
| **1216** | A268 | 80c multicolored | .30 | .20 |

International Year of the Child.

**1979, Dec. 1 Litho. *Perf. 13***

| | | | | |
|---|---|---|---|---|
| **1217** | A269 | 30c multicolored | .25 | .20 |

Christmas 1979.

Caudron Bomber, EXFILVE Emblem A270

EXFILVE Emblem and: No. 1219, Stearman biplane. No. 1220, UH-1H helicopter. No. 1221, CF-5 jet fighter.

**1979, Dec. 15 *Perf. 11x11½***

| | | | | |
|---|---|---|---|---|
| **1218** | A270 | 75c multicolored | .25 | .20 |
| **1219** | A270 | 75c multicolored | .25 | .20 |
| **1220** | A270 | 75c multicolored | .25 | .20 |
| **1221** | A270 | 75c multicolored | .25 | .20 |
| *a.* | | Block of 4, #1218-1221 | 1.25 | .60 |

Venezuelan Air Force, 59th anniv.; EXFILVE 79, 3rd Natl. Philatelic Exhibition, Dec. 7-17.

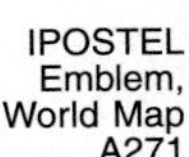

IPOSTEL Emblem, World Map A271

**1979, Dec. 27 *Perf. 11½***

| | | | | |
|---|---|---|---|---|
| **1222** | A271 | 75c multicolored | .30 | .20 |

Postal and Telegraph Institute, introduction of new logo.

Queen Victoria, Hill — A272

**1980, Feb. 13 Litho. *Perf. 12½***

| | | | | |
|---|---|---|---|---|
| **1223** | A272 | 55c multicolored | .25 | .20 |

Sir Rowland Hill (1795-1879), originator of penny postage.

Dr. Augusto Pi Suner, Physiologist, Birth Centenary — A273

**1980, Mar. 14 Litho. *Perf. 11½***

| | | | | |
|---|---|---|---|---|
| **1224** | A273 | 80c multicolored | .30 | .20 |

Spanish Seed Leaf — A274

Juan Lovera (1778-1841), Artist — A275

**Lithographed and Engraved**

**1980, Mar. 27 *Perf. 13***

| | | | | |
|---|---|---|---|---|
| **1225** | A274 | 50c multicolored | .50 | .20 |

Pedro Loefling (1729-56), Swedish botanist.

**1980, May 25 Litho. *Perf. 13½***

| | | | | |
|---|---|---|---|---|
| **1226** | A275 | 60c blue & dp org | .25 | .20 |
| **1227** | A275 | 75c violet & org | .30 | .20 |

Bolivar Bicentenary Type of 1978

30c, Signing of document. 1b, House of Congress. #1230, Angostura Congress, by Tito Salas.

**1980, July 24 Engr. *Perf. 12½***

| | | | | |
|---|---|---|---|---|
| **1228** | A254 | 30c multicolored | .20 | .20 |
| **1229** | A254 | 1b multicolored | .40 | .20 |

**Souvenir Sheet**

**Litho.**

***Perf. 14***

| | | | | |
|---|---|---|---|---|
| **1230** | A255 | Sheet of 5 | 3.25 | 3.25 |
| *a.* | | 50c, single stamp | .20 | .20 |

Simon Bolivar (1783-1830), revolutionary. Size of souvenir sheet stamps: 25x20mm, 20x25mm.

Dancing Girls, by Armando Reveron — A276

Bernardo O'Higgins — A277

**1980, Aug. 17 Litho. *Perf. 13***

| | | | | |
|---|---|---|---|---|
| **1231** | A276 | 50c shown | .20 | .20 |

**Size: 25x40mm**

| | | | | |
|---|---|---|---|---|
| **1232** | A276 | 65c Portrait | .45 | .25 |

Armando Reveron (1889-1955), artist.

**Lithographed and Engraved**

**1980, Aug. 22 *Perf. 13x14***

| | | | | |
|---|---|---|---|---|
| **1233** | A277 | 85c multicolored | .60 | .25 |

Bernardo O'Higgins (1776-1842), Chilean soldier and statesman.

School Ship Simon Bolivar A278

Frigate Mariscal Sucre A279

***Perf. 11½ (#1234), 11x11½***

**1980, Sept. 13 Litho.**

| | | | | |
|---|---|---|---|---|
| **1234** | A278 | 1.50b shown | 1.25 | .40 |
| **1235** | A279 | 1.50b shown | 1.25 | .40 |
| **1236** | A279 | 1.50b Submarine Picua | 1.25 | .40 |
| **1237** | A279 | 1.50b Naval Academy | 1.25 | .40 |
| | | *Nos. 1234-1237 (4)* | 5.00 | 1.60 |

"Picuda" is misspelled on stamp.

Workers Holding OPEC Emblem A280

20th Anniv. of OPEC (Organization of Petroleum Exporting Countries): #1239, Emblem.

**1980, Sept. 14 Litho. *Perf. 12x11½***

| | | | | |
|---|---|---|---|---|
| **1238** | A280 | 1.50b multicolored | .50 | .25 |
| **1239** | A280 | 1.50b multicolored | .50 | .25 |

Death of Simon Bolivar A281

**1980, Dec. 17 Litho. *Perf. 11x11½***

| | | | | |
|---|---|---|---|---|
| **1240** | A281 | 2b multicolored | 1.25 | .40 |

Simon Bolivar, 150th anniversary of death.

A282

A283

**Lithographed and Engraved**

**1980, Dec. 17** ***Perf. 13x12½***
**1241** A282 2b multicolored .75 .35

Gen. José Antonio Sucre, 150th anniv. of death.

**1980, Dec. 19 Litho.** ***Perf. 14x13½***
**1242** A283 1b Nativity by Rubens .35 .25

Christmas 1980.

Helen Keller's Initials (Written and Braille) — A284

**Lithographed and Embossed**

**1981, Feb. 12** ***Perf. 12½***
**1243** A284 1.50b multicolored .45 .25

Helen Keller (1880-1968), blind and deaf writer and lecturer.

John Baptiste de la Salle — A285

San Felipe City, 250th Anniv. — A286

**1981, May 15 Litho.** ***Perf. 11½x11***
**1244** A285 1.25b multicolored .40 .20

Christian Brothers' 300th anniv.

**1981, May 1** ***Perf. 11½***
**1245** A286 3b multicolored .75 .35

Municipal Theater of Caracas Centenary A287

**1981, June 28 Litho.** ***Perf. 12***
**1246** A287 1.25b multicolored 1.40 .25

A288

A290

A289

**1981, Sept. 15 Litho.** ***Perf. 11½***
**1247** A288 2b multicolored .60 .20

UPU membership centenary.

**1981, Oct. 14 Litho.**
**1248** A289 1b multicolored .30 .20

11th natl. population and housing census.

**1981, Dec. 3 Litho.** ***Perf. 11½***
**1249** A290 95c multicolored .35 .20

9th Bolivar Games, Barquisimeto.

19th Cent. Bicycle A291

**1981, Dec. 5 Photo.** ***Perf. 13x14***
**1250** A291 1b shown .55 .35
**1251** A291 1.05b Locomotive, 1926 .55 .35
**1252** A291 1.25b Buick, 1937 .80 .40
**1253** A291 1.50b Coach 1.00 .50
*Nos. 1250-1253 (4)* 2.90 1.60

See Nos. 1289-1292, 1308-1311.

Christmas 1981 A292

**1981, Dec. 21 Litho.** ***Perf. 11½***
**1254** A292 1b multicolored .30 .20

50th Anniv. of Natural Science Society — A293

**1982, Jan. 21** ***Perf. 11½***
**1255** A293 1b Mt. Autana .30 .20
**1256** A293 1.50b Sarisarinama .45 .25
**1257** A293 2b Guacharo Cave .60 .30
*Nos. 1255-1257 (3)* 1.35 .75

20th Anniv. of Constitution A294

**1982, Jan. 28 Photo.** ***Perf. 13x13½***
**1258** A294 1.85b gold & blk .60 .25

A295

A296

**1982, Feb. 19 Litho.** ***Perf. 13½***
**1259** A295 3b multicolored .90 .40

20th anniv. of agricultural reform.

**1982, Mar. 12 Litho.** ***Perf. 13½***
**1260** A296 1b blue & dk blue .30 .20

Jules Verne (1828-1905), science fiction writer.

Natl. Anthem Centenary (1981) A297

**1982, Mar. 26** ***Perf. 11½***
**1261** A297 1b multicolored .30 .20

1300th Anniv. of Bulgaria A298

6th Natl. 5-Year Plan, 1981-85 A299

**1982, June 2 Litho.** ***Perf. 13½***
**1262** A298 65c multicolored .20 .20

**1982, June 11**
**1263** A299 2b multicolored .40 .20

Bolivar Types of 1978

**1982, July 24 Engr.** ***Perf. 12½***
**1264** A254 30c Juan José Rondon .20 .20
**1265** A254 1b José Antonio Anzoategui .20 .20

**Souvenir Sheet**

**Litho.**

***Perf. 14***

**1266** A255 Sheet of 5 3.00 3.00
*a.-e.* 50c, any single .20 .20

Single stamps of No. 1266 show details from Battle of Boyaca, by Martin Tovar y Tovar. Size of souvenir sheet stamps: 19x26mm, 26x19mm.

Cecilio Acosta (1818-1881), Writer — A299a

**1982, Aug. 13 Litho.** ***Perf. 11½***
**1266F** A299a 3b multicolored .45 .25

Aloe A300

**1982, Oct. 14 Photo.** ***Perf. 13***
**1267** A300 1.05b shown .65 .35
**1268** A300 2.55b Tortoise 1.75 .35
**1269** A300 2.75b Tara amarilla tree 2.00 .35
**1270** A300 3b Guacharo bird 2.25 .40
*Nos. 1267-1270 (4)* 6.65 1.45

Andres Bello (1781-1865), Statesman and Reformer — A301

**1982, Nov. 20 Litho.** ***Perf. 12***
**1271** A301 1.05b multicolored .45 .20
**1272** A301 2.55b multicolored .95 .30
**1273** A301 2.75b multicolored .95 .30
**1274** A301 3b multicolored 1.25 .35
*Nos. 1271-1274 (4)* 3.60 1.15

Christmas 1982 — A302

Design: Holy Family creche figures by Francisco J. Cardozo, 18th cent.

**Photogravure and Engraved**

**1982, Dec. 7** ***Perf. 13½***
**1275** A302 1b multicolored .20 .20

Bolivar Types of 1978

**1982-83 Engr.** ***Perf. 12½***
**1276** A254 30c Victory Monument, Carabobo .20 .20
**1277** A254 30c Monument to the Meeting plaque .20 .20
**1278** A254 30c Antonio de Sucre .20 .20
**1279** A254 1b Jose Antonio Paez .35 .20
**1280** A254 1b Sword hilt, 1824 .35 .20
**1281** A254 1b Guayaquil Monument .35 .20
*Nos. 1276-1281 (6)* 1.65 1.20

**Souvenir Sheets**

**Litho.**

***Perf. 14***

**1282** A255 Sheet of 5 3.25 3.25
*a.-e.* 50c, any single .20 .20
**1283** A255 Sheet of 5 3.25 3.25
*a.-e.* 50c, any single .20 .20
**1284** A255 Sheet of 5 3.25 3.25
*a.-e.* 50c, any single .20 .20

No. 1282: Battle of Carabobo by Martin Tovar y Tovar; No. 1283, Monument to the Meeting; No. 1284, Battle of Ayacucho, by Martin Tovar y Tovar.

Issue dates: Nos. 1276-1277, 1279, 1281-1283, Dec. 17; others, Apr. 18, 1983.

Gen. Jose Francisco Bermudez — A303

Antonio Nicolas Briceno, Liberation Hero A304

*Perf. 13x13½, 15x14*

**1982, Dec. 23** **Litho.**

| | | | | |
|---|---|---|---|---|
| **1285** | A303 3b multicolored | | 1.10 | .30 |
| **1286** | A304 3b multicolored | | 1.10 | .30 |

25th Anniv. of 1958 Reforms A305

**1983, Jan. 23** *Perf. 10½x10*

| | | | |
|---|---|---|---|
| **1287** | A305 3b multicolored | .65 | .30 |

A306

A307

**1983, Mar. 20** **Photo.** *Perf. 13½x13*

| | | | |
|---|---|---|---|
| **1288** | A306 4b olive & red | .65 | .30 |

25th anniv. of Judicial Police Technical Dept.

Transportation Type of 1981

*Perf. 13½x14½*

**1983, Mar. 28** **Photo.**

| | | | |
|---|---|---|---|
| **1289** | A291 75c Lincoln, 1923 | .75 | .30 |
| **1290** | A291 80c Locomotive, 1889 | .75 | .30 |
| **1291** | A291 85c Willys truck, 1927 | .90 | .30 |
| **1292** | A291 95c Cleveland motor-cycle, 1920 | .90 | .30 |
| | *Nos. 1289-1292 (4)* | 3.30 | 1.20 |

**1983, May 17** **Photo.** *Perf. 13x12½*

| | | | |
|---|---|---|---|
| **1293** | A307 2.85b multicolored | .45 | .30 |

World Communications Year.

Bolivar Type of 1978

Designs: 30c; Flags of Colombia, Peru, Chile, Venezuela, and Buenos Aires. 1b; Equestrian Statue of Bolivar.

**Photo. & Engr. (#1294), Engr. (#1295)**

**1983, July 25** *Perf. 12½*

| | | | |
|---|---|---|---|
| **1294** | A254 30c multicolored | .35 | .20 |
| **1295** | A254 1b multicolored | .40 | .20 |

**Souvenir Sheet**

**Litho.**

*Perf. 14*

| | | | |
|---|---|---|---|
| **1296** | A255 Sheet of 5 | 3.50 | 3.25 |
| ***a.-e.*** | 50c, any single | .20 | .20 |

Single stamps of No. 1296 show details of "The Liberator on the Silver Mountain of Potosi" Size of souvenir sheet stamps, 20x25mm.

9th Pan-American Games
A308 A309

Designs: #1303a, baseball. b, cycle wheel. c, boxing glove. d, soccer ball. e, target.

**Lithographed and Engraved**

**1983, Aug. 25** *Perf. 13*

| | | | |
|---|---|---|---|
| **1297** | A308 2b shown | .40 | .20 |
| **1298** | A308 2b Swimming | .40 | .20 |
| **1299** | A308 2.70b Cycling | .50 | .40 |
| **1300** | A308 2.70b Fencing | .50 | .40 |
| **1301** | A308 2.85b Runners | .55 | .50 |
| **1302** | A308 2.85b Weightlifting | .55 | .50 |
| | *Nos. 1297-1302 (6)* | 2.90 | 2.20 |

**Souvenir Sheet**

| | | | |
|---|---|---|---|
| **1303** | Sheet of 5 | 11.00 | 11.00 |
| ***a.-e.*** | A309 1b, any single | 11.00 | 11.00 |

#1303 for Copan '83. Size: 167x121mm.

25th Anniv. of Cadafe (State Electricity Authority) — A310

**1983, Oct. 27** **Litho.** *Perf. 14*

| | | | |
|---|---|---|---|
| **1304** | A310 3b multicolored | 1.00 | .45 |

Bolivar Type of 1976

**1983, Sept. 29** **Engr.** *Perf. 12*

**Size: 26x32mm**

| | | | |
|---|---|---|---|
| **1305** | A231 25b blue green | 6.25 | 3.00 |
| **1306** | A231 30b brown | 7.50 | 3.75 |
| **1307** | A231 50b brt rose lilac | 11.50 | 6.25 |
| | *Nos. 1305-1307 (3)* | 25.25 | 13.00 |

Transportation Type of 1981

Various views of Caracas Metro.

**1983, Dec.** **Photo.** *Perf. 13½x14½*

| | | | |
|---|---|---|---|
| **1308** | A291 55c multicolored | .50 | .30 |
| **1309** | A291 75c multicolored | .50 | .30 |
| **1310** | A291 95c multicolored | .50 | .30 |
| **1311** | A291 2b multicolored | 1.10 | .45 |
| | *Nos. 1308-1311 (4)* | 2.60 | 1.35 |

Christmas 1983 A311

**1983, Dec. 1** **Litho.** *Perf. 13x14*

| | | | |
|---|---|---|---|
| **1312** | A311 1b Nativity | .25 | .25 |

Scouting Year (1982) A312

**Lithographed and Engraved**

**1983, Dec. 14** *Perf. 12½x13*

| | | | |
|---|---|---|---|
| **1313** | A312 2.25p Pitching tent | .40 | .25 |
| **1314** | A312 2.55b Planting tree | .40 | .25 |
| **1315** | A312 2.75b Mountain climbing | .45 | .25 |
| **1316** | A312 3b Camp site | .45 | .25 |
| | *Nos. 1313-1316 (4)* | 1.70 | 1.00 |

Bolivar Type of 1976

Designs: No. 1317, Title page of "Opere de Raimondo Montecuccoli" (most valuable book in Caracas University Library). No. 1318, Pedro Gual, Congress of Panama delegate, 1826. No. 1319, Jose Maria Vargas (b. 1786), University of Caracas pres. No. 1320, José Faustino Sanchez Carrion, Congress of Panama delegate, 1826.

**1984** **Engr.** *Perf. 12½*

| | | | |
|---|---|---|---|
| **1317** | A254 30c multicolored | .25 | .20 |
| **1318** | A254 30c multicolored | .25 | .20 |
| **1319** | A254 1b multicolored | .25 | .20 |
| **1320** | A254 1b multicolored | .25 | .20 |
| | *Nos. 1317-1320 (4)* | 1.00 | .80 |

**Souvenir Sheets**

**Litho.**

*Perf. 14*

| | | | |
|---|---|---|---|
| **1321** | A255 Sheet of 5 | 3.00 | 2.75 |
| ***a.-e.*** | 50c, any single | .20 | .20 |
| **1322** | A255 Sheet of 5 | 3.25 | 3.25 |
| ***a.-e.*** | 50c, any single | .20 | .20 |

Single stamps of No. 1321 show details of Arts, Science and Education, fresco by Hector Poleo; 1322, Map of South America, 1829. Size of souvenir sheet stamps: 20x30mm; 27x20mm.

Issued: #1317, 1319, 1321, 1/19; others, 1/20.

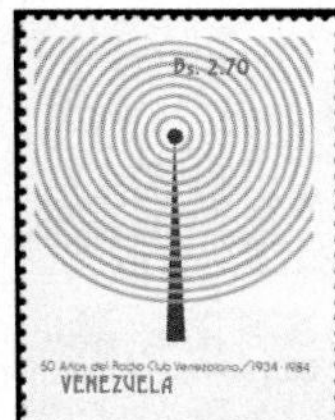
Radio Waves — A313

Intelligentsia for Peace — A314

**1984, Jan. 30** **Litho.** *Perf. 14x13*

| | | | |
|---|---|---|---|
| **1323** | A313 2.70b multicolored | .40 | .20 |

Radio Club of Venezuela, 50th anniv.

**1984, Jan. 31**

| | | | |
|---|---|---|---|
| **1324** | A314 1b Doves | .20 | .20 |
| **1325** | A314 2.70b Profile | .40 | .20 |
| **1326** | A314 2.85b Flower, head | .40 | .20 |
| | *Nos. 1324-1326 (3)* | 1.00 | .60 |

President Romulo Gallegos (1884-1969) A315

Gallegos: No. 1327, Portrait as a young man in formal dress. No. 1328, Portrait, 1948.

**1984-85** **Litho.** *Perf. 11½*

| | | | |
|---|---|---|---|
| **1327** | A315 1.70b royal bl, dl bl, beige & blk | .40 | .25 |
| **1328** | A315 1.70b ocher, org brn & buff | .40 | .25 |

Issued: #1327, 10/12/84; #1328, 1/18/85.

See Nos. 1335-1336.

Pan-American Union of Engineering Associations, 18th Convention A316

**1984, Oct. 28**

| | | | |
|---|---|---|---|
| **1329** | A316 2.55b pale buff, dk bl | .65 | .20 |

Christmas 1984 A317

**1984, Dec. 3**

| | | | |
|---|---|---|---|
| **1330** | A317 1b multicolored | .30 | .20 |

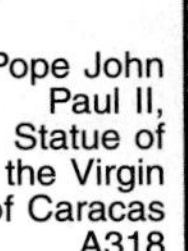
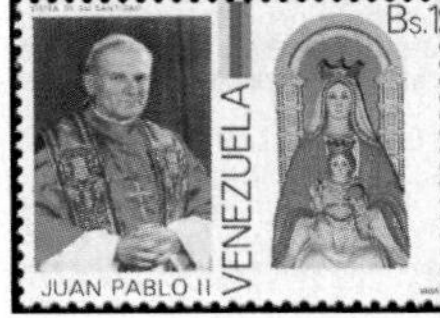
Pope John Paul II, Statue of the Virgin of Caracas A318

**1985, Jan. 26** **Litho.** *Perf. 12*

| | | | |
|---|---|---|---|
| **1331** | A318 1b multicolored | .80 | .25 |

Papal visit, 1985.

Pascua City Bicent. A319

**1985, Feb. 10**

| | | | |
|---|---|---|---|
| **1332** | A319 1.50b multicolored | .40 | .25 |

Dr. Mario Briceno-Iragory (b. 1897), Historian — A320

**1985, Oct.** **Litho.** *Perf. 12*

| | | | |
|---|---|---|---|
| **1333** | A320 1.25b silver & ver | .30 | .20 |

Natl. St. Vincent de Paul Soc., Cent. — A321

**1985, July**

| | | | |
|---|---|---|---|
| **1334** | A321 1b dk ol bis, ver & buff | .40 | .20 |

Gallegos Memorial Type of 1984-85

Designs: Gallegos, diff.

**1985, Aug. 8**

| | | | |
|---|---|---|---|
| **1335** | A315 1.70b gray grn, dk gray grn & dl gray grn | .30 | .20 |
| **1336** | A315 1.70b grn, sage grn & dl grn | .30 | .20 |

Dated 1984.

Latin American Economic System, 10th Anniv. A322

**1985, Aug. 15**

**1337** A322 4b black & red 1.40 .60

Miniature Sheet

Virgin Mary, Birth Bimillennium A323

Statues: a, Virgin of the Divine Shepherd. b, Chiquinquira Madonna. c, Coromoto Madonna. d, Valley Madonna. e, Virgin of Perpetual Succor. f, Virgin of Peace. g, Immaculate Conception Virgin. h, Soledad Madonna. i, Virgin of Consolation. j, Nieves Madonna.

**1985, Sept. 9**

**1338** Sheet of 10 6.00 6.00
*a.-j.* A323 1b, any single .40 .20

OPEC, 25th Anniv. A324

**1985, Sept. 13**

**1339** A324 6b multicolored 1.10 .60

Opening of the Museum of Contemporary Art, Caracas — A325

**1985, Oct. 24** ***Perf. 13½***

**1340** A325 3b multicolored .55 .30

Dated 1983.

UN, 40th Anniv. A326

**1985, Nov. 15** ***Perf. 12***

**1341** A326 10b brt blue & ver 1.50 .90

Intl. Youth Year A327

**1985, Nov. 26**

**1342** A327 1.50b multicolored .30 .20

Christmas 1985 — A328

Nativity: a, Sheperds. b, Holy Family, Magi. Se-tenant in a continuous design.

**1985, Dec. 2**

**1343** A328 Pair 1.25 1.25
*a.-b.* 2b, any single .60 .20

Dr. Luis Maria Drago (b. 1859), Politician A329

**1985, Dec. 20** ***Perf. 13½***

**1344** A329 2.70b tan, ver & sepia .50 .35

Dated 1984.

Miniature Sheet

Natl. Oil Industry, 10th Anniv. A330

Designs: a, Industry emblem. b, Isla Oil Refinery. c, Bariven oil terminal. d, Pequiven refinery. e, Corpoven drilling rig. f, Maraven offshore rig. g, Intevep labs. h, Meneven refinery. i, Lagoven refinery. j, Emblem, early drilling rig.

**1985, Dec. 13** ***Perf. 12***

**1345** Sheet of 10 12.00 12.00
*a.-b.* A330 1b multi .25 .25
*c.-d.* A330 2b multi .55 .25
*e.-f.* A330 3b multi 1.00 .35
*g.-h.* A330 4b multi 1.25 .40
*i.-j.* A330 5b multi 1.50 .50

Simon Bolivar Memorial Coins — A331

**1985, Dec. 18**

**1346** A331 2b multicolored .35 .25
**1347** A331 2.70b multicolored .50 .30
**1348** A331 3b multicolored .55 .35
*Nos. 1346-1348 (3)* 1.40 .90

Dated 1984.

Guayana Development Corp., 25th Anniv. — A332

**1985, Dec. 27**

**1349** A332 2b Guayana City .35 .25
**1350** A332 3b Orinoco Steel Mill .55 .35
**1351** A332 5b Raul Leoni-Guri Hydro-electric Dam .90 .60
*Nos. 1349-1351 (3)* 1.80 1.20

Miniature Sheet

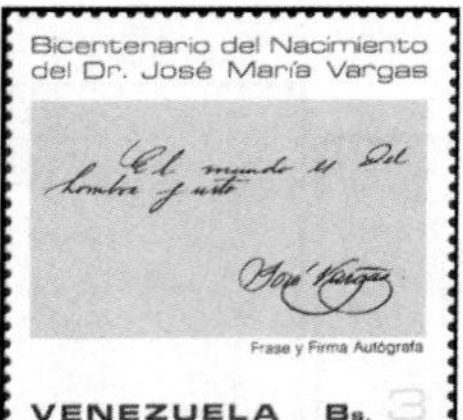


A333

Dr. Jose Vargas (1786-1854) — A334

Designs: No. 1352a, Handwriting and signature. b, Portrait, 1874, by Martin Tovar y Tovar. c, Statue, Palace of the Academies. d, Flags, EXFILBO '86 emblem. e, Vargas do Caracas Hospital. f, Frontispiece of lectures manual, 1842. g, Portrait, 1986, by Alirio Palacios. h, Gesneria vargasii. i, Bolivar-Vargas commemorative medal, 1955, 6th Natl. Medical Sciences Cong. j, Portrait, anonymous, 19th cent.

No. 1353a, Portrait, facing front. b, Portrait, facing left, Nos. 1352a, 1352d, 1352e, 1352h and 1352i have horizontal vignettes.

**1986, Mar. 10** **Litho.** ***Perf. 12***

**1352** Sheet of 10 7.75 7.75
*a.-j.* A333 3b, any single .65 .30

**Souvenir Sheet**

***Imperf***

**1353** Sheet of 2 10.00 10.00
*a.-b.* A334 15b, any single 4.50 .75

EXFILBO '86, Mar. 10-17, Caracas, 1st Bolivarian exhibition.

Youths Painting School Wall A335

**1986, May 12** ***Perf. 12***

**1354** A335 3b shown .50 .25
**1355** A335 5b Repairing desk .90 .25

Founding and maintenance of educational institutions.

Francisco Miranda's Work for American Liberation, Bicent. (1981) A336

**Lithographed and Engraved**

**1986, Apr. 18** ***Perf. 13***

**1356** A336 1.05b multicolored .20 .20

Dated 1983.

INDULAC, 45th Anniv. A337

**1986, June 27** **Litho.** ***Perf. 12***

**1357** A337 2.55b Milk trucks, vert. .30 .20
**1358** A337 2.70b Map, vert. .35 .20
**1359** A337 3.70b Milk processing plant .40 .20
*Nos. 1357-1359 (3)* 1.05 .60

Industria Lactea (INDULAC), Venezuelan milk processing company.

Miniature Sheet

Viasa Venezuelan Airlines, 25th Anniv. A338

a, Commemorative coin. b, Douglas DC-8 ascending. c, DC-8 taxiing. d, Boeing 747 in flight. e, DC-10 tails. f, Map of hemispheres. g, DC-10 taking off. h, Rear of DC-10 & DC8 on runway. i, DC-9 over mountains. j, Crew in cockpit.

**1986, Aug. 11** **Litho.** ***Perf. 12***

**1360** Sheet of 10 8.00 8.00
*a.-e.* A338 3b, any single .50 .35
*f.-j.* A338 3.25b, any single .55 .35

Miniature Sheet

Romulo Betancourt (1908-1981), President — A339

a, i, Portrait with natl. flag. b, j, Seated in armchair, smoking pipe. c, h, Wearing hat, text. d, f, Wearing sash of office. e, g, Reading.

**1986, Sept. 28**

**1361** Sheet of 10 10.00 10.00
*a.-e.* A339 2.70b, any single .50 .20
*f.-j.* A339 3b, any single .60 .25

Redrawn Bolivar Type of 1976

**1986, Sept. 29** **Litho.** ***Perf. 12½***

**1362** A231 25c red .35 .25
**1363** A231 50c blue .35 .25
**1364** A231 75c pink .35 .25
**1365** A231 1b orange .35 .25
**1366** A231 2b brt yellow grn .40 .25
*Nos. 1362-1366 (5)* 1.80 1.25

Nos. 1362-1366 inscribed Armitano.

For surcharges see Nos. 1453-1464.

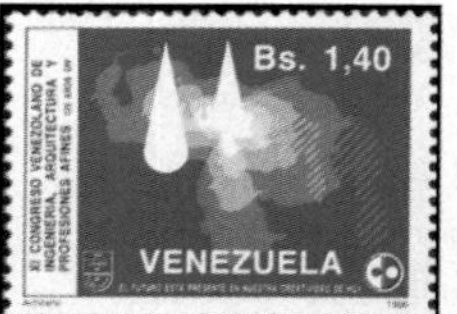


Re-opening of Zulia University, 40th Anniv. — A340

**1986, Sept. 29**

**1367** A340 2.70b shown .30 .25
**1368** A340 2.70b Library entrance .30 .25
*a.* Pair, #1367-1368 .60 .60



11th Congress of Architects, Engineers and Affiliated Professionals — A341

**1986, Oct. 3**

**1369** A341 1.40b multicolored .20 .20
**1370** A341 1.55b multicolored .20 .20
*a.* Pair, #1369-1370 1.50 1.50

Fauna and Flora A342

**1986, Sept. 12 Photo. *Perf. 13½***

1371 A342 70c Priodontes maximus .65 .55
1372 A342 85c Espeletia angustifolia .65 .55
1373 A342 2.70b Crocodylus intermedius .65 .55
1374 A342 3b Brownea grandiceps .80 .60
*Nos. 1371-1374 (4)* 2.75 2.25

Miniature Sheet

State Visit of Pope John Paul II — A343

**1986, Oct. 22 *Perf. 12***

1375 Sheet of 10 6.00 6.00
*a.* A343 1b Pope, mountains .20 .20
*b.* A343 2b Bridge .30 .20
*c.* A343 3b Kissing the ground .40 .20
*d.* A343 3b Statue of Our Lady .40 .20
*e.* A343 4b Crosier, buildings .60 .20
*f.* A343 5.25b Waterfall .80 .25

#1375 contains 2 each #1375a-1375b, 1375e-1375f and one each #1375c-1375d.

Miniature Sheet

Children's Foundation, 20th Anniv. A344

Children's drawings: a, Three children. b, Hearts, children, birds. c, Child, animals. d, Animals, house. e, Landscape. f, Child, flowers on table. g, Child holding ball. h, Children, birds. i, Lighthouse, port. j, Butterfly in flight.

**1986, Nov. 10**

1376 Sheet of 10 4.75 4.75
*a.-e.* A344 2.55b, any single .35 .20
*f.-j.* A344 2.70b, any single .35 .20

Christmas — A345

Creche figures carved by Eliecer Alvarez.

**1986, Nov. 10**

1377 2b shown .25 .20
1378 2b Virgin and child .25 .20
*a.* A345 Pair, #1377-1378 .50 .50

City Police, 25th Anniv. A346

Emblem and: a, Emergency medical aid, helicopter. b, Security at sporting event. c, Bar code. d, Cadets in front of police academy. e, Motorcycle police.

**1986, Dec. 10**

1379 Strip of 5 4.00 4.00
*a.-e.* A346 2.70b, any single .50 .25

Folk Art A347

**Lithographed and Engraved**

**1987, Jan. 31 *Perf. 13***

1380 A347 2b Musical instrument .30 .20
1381 A347 2b Fabric .30 .20
1382 A347 3b Ceramic pot .40 .20
1383 A347 3b Basket work .40 .20
*Nos. 1380-1383 (4)* 1.40 .80

Dated 1983. Nos. 1380, 1382 show Pre-Hispanic art.

Discovery of the Tubercle Bacillus by Robert Koch, Cent. (in 1982) A348

**Lithographed and Engraved**

**1987, Feb. 27 *Perf. 14x14½***

1384 A348 2.55b multicolored .55 .20

Dated 1983.

Miniature Sheet

Easter 1987 A349

Paintings and sculpture: a, Arrival of Jesus in Jerusalem. b, Christ at the Column. c, Jesus of Nazareth. d, The Descent. e, The Solitude. f, The Last Supper. g, Christ Suffering. h, The Crucifixion. i, Christ Entombed. j, The Resurrection.

**1987, Apr. 2 Litho. *Perf. 12***

1385 Sheet of 10 17.50 17.50
*a.-e.* A349 2b, any single 1.00 .25
*f.-j.* A349 2.25b, any single 1.10 .25

World Neurochemistry Congress — A350

3b, Bolivar and Bello, outdoor sculpture by Marisol Escobar. 4.25b, Retinal neurons.

**1987, May 8 Litho. *Perf. 12***

1386 A350 3b multicolored .50 .20
1387 A350 4.25b multicolored .60 .20
*a.* Pair, #1386-1387 3.00 3.00

Miniature Sheet

Tourism A351

Hotels: a, f, Barquisimeto Hilton. b, g, Lake Hotel Intercontinental, Maracaibo. c, h, Macuto Sheraton, Caraballeda. d, i, Melia Caribe, Caraballeda. e, j, Melia, Puerto la Cruz.

**1987, May 29 Litho. *Perf. 12***

1388 Sheet of 10 15.00 15.00
*a.-e.* A351 6b, any single .65 .25
*f.-j.* A351 6.50b, any single, diff. .65 .25

Natl. Institute of Canalization, 35th Anniv. — A352

**1987, June 25 Litho. *Perf. 12***

1389 A352 2b Map of Amazon territory waterways .20 .20
1390 A352 4.25b Apure and Bolivar states waterways .35 .25
*g.* Pair, #1389-1390 1.00 1.00

Vincente Emilion Sojo (1887-1974), Composer — A352a

2b, Academy of Fine Arts, Caracas. 4b, Sojos directing choir. 5b, Hymn to Bolivar score. 6b, Sojo, score on blackboard. 7b, Portrait, signature.

**1987, July 1 Litho. *Perf. 12***

1390A Strip of 5 37.50 37.50
*b.* A352a 2b tan & sepia 1.25 1.25
*c.* A352a 4b tan & sepia 2.00 1.40
*d.* A352a 5b tan & sepia 2.00 1.40
*e.* A352a 6b tan & sepia 3.25 2.00
*f.* A352a 7b tan & sepia 4.00 2.00

Printed in sheets of 10 containing two strips of five, black control number (UR).

Simon Bolivar University, 20th Anniv. A353

Designs: a, Bolivar statue by Roca Rey, 1973. b, Outdoor sculpture of solar panels by Alejandro Otero, 1972. c, Rectory, 1716. d, Laser. e, Owl, sculpture, 1973.

**1987, July 9 Litho. *Perf. 12***

1391 Strip of 5 15.00 15.00
*a.* A353 2b multicolored 1.00 .50
*b.* A353 3b multicolored 1.50 .50
*c.* A353 4b multicolored 2.00 .60
*d.* A353 5b multicolored 2.50 1.00
*e.* A353 6b multicolored 3.00 1.00

Miniature Sheet

Ministry of Transportation and Communication — A354

Designs: a, Automobiles. b, Ship. c, Train, Cathedral. d, Letters, telegraph key. e, Communication towers. f, Highway. g, Airplane. h, Locomotive, rail caution signs. i, Satellite dish. j, Satellite in orbit.

**1987, July 16**

1392 Sheet of 10 7.50 7.50
*a.-e.* A354 2b any single .20 .20
*f.-j.* A354 2.25b any single .20 .20

Nos. 1392a and 1392f, 1392b and 1392g, 1392c and 1392h, 1392d and 1392i, 1392e and 1392j have continuous designs.

Miniature Sheet

Venezuela Navigation Company, 70th Anniv. A355

Designs: a, Corporate headquarters. b, Fork lift. c, Ship's Superstructure. d, Engine room. e, The Zulia. f, The Guarico. g, Ship's officer on the bridge. h, Bow of supertanker. i, Loading dock. j, Map of sea routes.

**1987, July 31 Litho. *Perf. 12***

1393 Sheet of 10 6.25 6.25
*a.-b.* A355 2b, any single .20 .20
*c.-d.* A355 3b, any single .25 .20
*e.-f.* A355 4b, any single .30 .20
*g.-h.* A355 5b, any single .40 .20
*i.-j.* A355 6b, any single .45 .25

Nos. 1393a, 1393c, 1393e, 1393g and 1393i in vertical strip; No. 1393b, 1393d, 1393f, 1393h and 1393j in vertical strip.

Miniature Sheet

Natl. Guard, 50th Anniv. A356

a, f, Air-sea rescue. b, g, Traffic control. c, h, Environment and nature protection. d, i, Border control. e, j, Industrial security.

**1987, Aug. 6**

1394 Sheet of 10 40.00 40.00
*a.-e.* A356 2b, any single 1.25 .25
*f.-j.* A356 4b, any single 3.00 .50

Discovery of America, 500th Anniv. (in 1992) A357

20th cent. paintings (details): 2b, Departure from Port of Palos, by Jacobo Borges. 7b, Discovery of America, by Tito Salas. 11.50b, El Padre de las Casas, Protector of the Indians, by Salas. 12b, Trading in Venezuela at the Time of the Conquest, by Salas. 12.50b, Defeat of Guaicaipuro, by Borges.

**1987, Oct. Litho. *Perf. 12***

1395 Strip of 5 8.00 8.00
*a.* A357 2b multi .20 .20
*b.* A357 7b multi .60 .30
*c.* A357 11.50b multi 1.00 .45
*d.* A357 12b multi 1.10 .55
*e.* A357 12.50b multi 1.25 .55

Christmas 1987 — A358

Paintings and sculpture representing the Spanish Colonial School, 18th cent.: 2b, *The Annunciation,* by Juan Pedro Lopez (1724-1787). 3b, *Nativity,* by Jose Francisco Rodriguez (1767-1818). 5.50b, *Adoration of the Magi,* anonymous. 6b, *Flight into Egypt,* by Lopez.

**1987, Nov. 17 Litho. *Perf. 12***

1396 Block of 4 6.75 6.75
*a.* A358 2b multi .25 .25
*b.* A358 3b multi .30 .25
*c.* A358 5.50b multi .50 .30
*d.* A358 6b multi .60 .30

### Miniature Sheet

Sidor Mills, 25th Anniv. — A359

Natl. steel production: a-d, Exterior view of steel plant (in a continuous design). e, Tower bearing the SIDOR emblem. f, Furnaces and molten steel flowing down gutters. g, Pooring steel rods. h, Slab mill. i, Steel rod production, diff. j, Anniv. emblem.

**1987, Nov. 23**

**1397** Sheet of 10 — 7.75 7.75
*a.* A359 2b multi — .20 .20
*b.* A359 6b multi — .60 .30
*c.* A359 7b multi — .70 .35
*d.* A359 11.50b multi — 1.10 .55
*e.* A359 12b black — 1.25 .60
*f.* A359 2b multi — .20 .20
*g.* A359 6b multi — .60 .30
*h.* A359 7b multi — .70 .35
*i.* A359 11.50b multi — 1.10 .55
*j.* A359 12b multi — 1.25 .60

Meeting of 8 Latin American Presidents, 1st Anniv. — A360

**1987, Nov. 26**

**1398** A360 6b multi — .60 .30

Pequiven Petrochemical Co., 10th Anniv. — A361

**1987, Dec. 1**

**1399** Strip of 5 — 7.75 7.75
*a.* A361 2b Plastics — .20 .20
*b.* A361 6b Refined oil products — .60 .30
*c.* A361 7b Fertilizers — .70 .30
*d.* A361 11.50b Installations — 1.10 .55
*e.* A361 12b Expansion — 1.25 .60

St. John Bosco (1815-88) A362

Portrait of Bosco and: 2b, Map, children. 3b, National Church, Caracas. 4b, Vocational training (printer's apprentice). 5b, Church of Mary Auxiliadora. 6b, Missionary school (nun teaching children).

**1987, Dec. 8**

**1400** Strip of 5 — 4.00 4.00
*a.* A362 2b multi — .20 .20
*b.* A362 3b multi — .30 .20
*c.* A362 4b multi — .40 .20
*d.* A362 5b multi — .45 .25
*e.* A362 6b multi — .60 .30

### Redrawn Bolivar Type of 1976

**1987, Dec. 31 — Litho. — *Perf. 12½***

**1401** A231 3b emerald grn — .35 .20
**1402** A231 4b gray — .50 .20
**1403** A231 5b vermilion — .65 .25
**1404** A231 10b dark olive bister — 1.50 .50
**1405** A231 15b rose claret — 2.25 .80
**1406** A231 20b bright blue — 2.75 1.00
**1407** A231 25b olive bister — 3.50 1.50
**1408** A231 30b dark violet — 4.25 1.75
**1409** A231 50b carmine — 7.00 2.75
*Nos. 1401-1409 (9)* — 22.75 8.95

Nos. 1401-1409 inscribed Armitano.

29th Assembly of Inter-American Development Bank Governors — A363

**1988, Mar. 18 — Litho. — *Perf. 12***

**1410** A363 11.50b multi — 1.00 .55

### Miniature Sheet

Republic Bank, 30th Anniv. A364

Bank functions and finance projects: a, Personal banking at branch. b, Capital for labor. c, Industrial projects. d, Financing technology. e, Exports and imports. f, Financing agriculture. g, Fishery credits. h, Dairy farming development. i, Construction projects. j, Tourism trade development.

**1988, Apr. 11**

**1411** Sheet of 10 — 10.00 10.00
*a.-e.* A364 2b any single — .35 .20
*f.-j.* A364 6b any single — .50 .25

No. 1411 contains two strips of five.

Anti-Polio Campaign Day of Victory, May 25 — A365

Design: Polio victims pictured on bronze relief, Rotary and campaign emblems.

**1988, May 20 — Litho. — *Perf. 12***

**1412** A365 11.50b multi — 1.00 .45

Carlos Eduardo Frias (1906-1986), Founder of the Natl. Publicity Industry — A366

**1988, May 27 — Litho. — *Perf. 12***

**1414** A366 Pair — 4.00 4.00
*a.* 4b multi — .35 .25
*b.* 10b multi — .75 .45

Publicity Industry, 50th anniv.

Venalum Natl. Aluminum Corp., 10th Anniv. — A367

Designs: 2b, Factory interior. 6b, Electric smelter. 7b, Aluminum pipes. 11.50b, Aluminum blocks moved by crane. 12b, Soccer team, aluminum equipment on playing field.

**1988, June 10**

**1415** Strip of 5 — 9.00 9.00
*a.* A367 2b multi — .30 .20
*b.* A367 6b multi — .80 .25
*c.* A367 7b multi — .90 .25
*d.* A367 11.50b multi — 1.50 .55
*e.* A367 12b multi — 1.50 .55

Nature Conservation — A368

Birds: 2b, Carduelis cucullata. 6b, Eudocimus ruber. 11.50b, Harpia harpyja. 12b, Phoenicopterus ruber ruber. 12.50b, Pauxi pauxi.

**1988, June 17 — Litho. — *Perf. 12***

**1416** Strip of 5 — 6.00 6.00
*a.* A368 2b multi — .25 .20
*b.* A368 6b multi — .60 .25
*c.* A368 11.50b multi — 1.10 .45
*d.* A368 12b multi — 1.25 .40
*e.* A368 12.50b multi — 1.25 .45

Army Day — A369

Military uniforms: a, Simon Bolivar in dress uniform, 1828. b, Gen.-in-Chief Jose Antonio Paez in dress uniform, 1821. c, Liberation Army division gen., 1810. d, Brig. gen., 1820. e, Artillery corpsman, 1836. f, Alferez Regiment parade uniform, 1988. g, Division Gen. No. 1 dress uniform, 1988. h, Line Infantry Regiment, 1820. i, Promenade Infantry, 1820. j, Light Cavalry, 1820.

**1988, June 20**

**1417** Sheet of 10 — 15.00 15.00
*a., f.* A369 2b multi — .30 .20
*b., g.* A369 6b multi — .75 .25
*c., h.* A369 7b multi — .90 .25
*d., i.* A369 11.50b multi — 1.50 .45
*e., j.* A369 12b multi — 1.60 .45

Scabbard, Sword and Signature A370

Paintings by Tito Salas: 4.75b, *The General's Wedding.* 6b, Portrait. 7b, *Battle of Valencia.* 12b, *Retreat from San Carlos.*

**1988, July 1 — Litho. — *Perf. 12***

**1418** Strip of 5 — 7.50 7.50
*a.* A370 2b shown — .35 .25
*b.* A370 4.75b multi — .65 .25
*c.* A370 6b multi — .75 .25
*d.* A370 7b multi — 1.25 .30
*e.* A370 12b multi — 2.75 .45

General Rafael Urdaneta (b. 1788).

General Santiago Marino (b. 1788), by Martin Tovar y Tovar — A371

**1988, July**

**1419** A371 4.75b multi — .45 .25

1988 Summer Olympics, Seoul — A372

**1988, Aug. 2**

**1420** A372 12b multi — .90 .45

Electric Industry, Cent. A373

Buildings, 1888: 2b, 1st Office. 4.75b, Jaime Carrillo and electrical plant. 10b, Bolivar Plaza. 11.50b, Baralt Theater. 12.50b, Central Thermoelectric Plant, Ramon Lagoon, 1988.

**1988, Oct. 25 — Litho. — *Perf. 12***

**1421** Strip of 5 — 6.50 6.50
*a.* A373 2b multi — .20 .20
*b.* A373 4.75b multi — .40 .20
*c.* A373 10b multi — .80 .35
*d.* A373 11.50b multi — .90 .45
*e.* A373 12.50b multi — 1.00 .45

Christmas — A374

Designs: 4b, Nativity (left side), by Tito Salas, 1936. 6b, Christ child, anonymous, 17th cent. 15b, Nativity (right side).

**1988, Dec. 9**

**1422** 4b multi — .30 .20
**1423** 6b multi — .45 .25
**1424** 15b multi — 1.25 .60
*a.* A374 Strip, #1423, 2 ea #1422, 1424 — 7.00 7.00

### Miniature Sheet

Marian Year — A375

Icons: a, Our Lady of Copacabana, Bolivia. b, Our Lady of Chiquinquira, Colombia. c, Our Lady of Coromoto, Venezuela. d, Our Lady of the Clouds, Ecuador. e, Our Lady of Antigua, Panama. f, Our Lady of the Evangelization, Peru. g, Our Lady of Lujan, Argentina. h, Our Lady of Altagracia, Dominican Republic. i, Our Lady of Aparecida, Brazil. j, Our Lady of Guadalupe, Mexico.

**1988, Aug. 15 — Litho. — *Perf. 12***

**1425** Sheet of 10 — 8.75 8.75
*a.-e.* A375 4.75b any single — .35 .20
*f.-j.* A375 6b any single — .40 .25

Juan Manuel Cagigal Observatory, Cent. — A376

Designs: 2b, Bardou refracting telescope. 4.75b, Universal theodolite AUZ-27. 6b, Bust of Cagigal. 11.50b, Boulton cupola and night sky over Caracas in September. 12b, Satellite photographing Hurricane Allen.

**1989, Sept. 5**

**1426** Strip of 5 6.75 6.75
*a.* A376 2b multicolored .25 .25
*b.* A376 4.75b multicolored .45 .25
*c.* A376 6b multicolored .60 .30
*d.* A376 11.50b multicolored 1.00 .50
*e.* A376 12b multicolored 1.10 .60

Comptroller-General's Office, 50th Anniv. — A377

**1988, Oct. 14** **Litho.** ***Perf. 12***

**1427** A377 10b multi .75 .40

Portrait of Founder Juan Pablo Rojas Paul, by Cristobal Rojas, 1890 — A378

**1989, Oct. 21** **Litho.** ***Perf. 12***

**1428** A378 6b Commemorative medal .40 .25
**1429** A378 6.50b shown .45 .25
*a.* Pair, #1428-1429 1.00 1.00

Natl. History Academy, cent.

Portrait of Ricardo A379

Paintings: No. 1430, Simon Bolivar and Dr. Mordechay Ricardo. No. 1430A, The Octagon. Nos. 1430-1430A printed in continuous design completing the painting *The Liberator in Curacao,* by John de Pool.

**1989, Jan. 27** **Litho.** ***Perf. 12***

**1430** A379 10b multi .75 .40
**1430A** A379 10b multi .75 .40
**1430B** A379 11.50b shown 1.10 .50
*c.* Strip of 5, #1430B, 2 ea #1430-1430A 9.25 9.25

Convention with Holy See, 25th Anniv. — A380

Designs: a, Raul Leoni, constitutional president, 1964-69. b, Cardinal Quintero, archbishop of Caracas, 1960-80. c, Arms of Cardinal Lebrun, archbishop of Caracas since 1980. d, Arms of Luciano Storero, titular archbishop of Tigimma. e, Pope Paul VI.

**1989, May 4** **Litho.** ***Perf. 12***

**1431** Strip of 5 4.00 4.00
*a.-b.* A380 4b any single .30 .20
*c.-d.* A380 12b any single .85 .55
*e.* A380 16b any single 1.10 .75

Bank of Venezuela, Cent. A381

Designs: a, *Cocoa Harvest,* by Tito Salas, 1946. b, *Teaching a Boy How to Grow Coffee,* by Salas, 1946. c, Bank headquarters, Caracas. d, Archive of the Liberator, Caracas. e, Aforestation campaign (seedling). f, Aforestation campaign (five youths planting seedlings). g, 50-Bolivar bank note (left side). h, 50-Bolivar bank note (right side). i, 500-Bolivar bank note (left side). j, 500-Bolivar bank note (right side).

**1989, Aug. 1**

**1432** Sheet of 10 8.50 8.50
*a.-f.* A381 4b any single .25 .20
*g.-j.* A381 8b any single .60 .35

Nos. 1432g-1432h and 1432i-1432j printed in continuous designs.

America Issue — A382

UPAE emblem and pre-Columbian votive bisque artifacts: 6b, Vessel. 24b, Statue of a man.

**1989**

**1433** A382 6b multicolored .80 .25
**1434** A382 24b multicolored 3.50 1.75
*a.* Pair, #1433-1434 5.00 5.00

Christmas A383

a, Shepherds, sheep. b, Angel appears to 3 shepherds. c, Holy Family. 12b, Two witnesses. 15b, Adoration of the kings.

**1989** **Litho.** ***Perf. 12***

**1435** Strip of 5 11.50 11.50
*a.* A383 5b shown .40 .25
*b.-c.* A383 6b any single .45 .25
*d.* A383 12b multicolored 1.00 .45
*e.* A383 15b multicolored 1.10 .60

Miniature Sheets

Bank of Venezuela, 20th Anniv. — A384

Tree and arms: No. 1436: a, Tabebuia chrysantha, national. b, Ceiba pentandra, Federal District. c, Myrospermum frutescens, Anzoategui. d, Pithecellobium saman, Aragua. e, Cedrela odorata, Barinas. f, Diptenyx punctata, Bolivar. g, Licania pyrofolia, Apure. h, Sterculia apetala, Carabobo.

No. 1437: a, Tabebuia rosea, Cojedes. b, Prosopis juliflora, Falcon. c, Copernicia tectorum, Guarico. d, Erythrina poeppigiana, Merida. e, Brawnea leucantha, Miranda. f, Mauritia flexuosa, Monagas. g, Malpighia glabra, Lara. h, Guaicum officinale, Nueva Esparta.

No. 1438: a, Swietenia macrophylla, Portuguesa. b, Platymiscium diadelphum, Sucre. c, Prumnopitys montana de Laub, Tachira. d, Roystonea venezuelana, Yaracuy. e, Cocos nucifera, Zulia. f, Hevea benthamiana, Federal Territory of Amazonas. g, Erythrina fusca, Trujillo. h, Rhizophora mangle, Territory of the Amacuro Delta.

**1990, June 27** **Litho.** ***Perf. 12***

**1436** Sheet of 8 + 2 labels 17.00 17.00
*a.-f.* A384 10b any single .50 .25
*g.* A384 40b multicolored 2.00 1.00
*h.* A384 50b multicolored 2.50 1.25
**1437** Sheet of 8 + 2 labels 17.00 17.00
*a.-f.* A384 10b any single .50 .25
*g.* A384 40b multicolored 2.00 1.00
*h.* A384 50b multicolored 2.50 1.25
**1438** Sheet of 8 + 2 labels 17.00 17.00
*a.-f.* A384 10b any single .50 .25
*g.* A384 40b multicolored 2.00 1.00
*h.* A384 50b multicolored 2.50 1.25

Central Bank of Venezuela, 50th Anniv. A385

Designs: a, Santa Capilla Headquarters, 1943. b, Headquarters, 1967. c, Left half of 500b Bank Note, 1940. d, Right half of 500b Bank Note, 1940. e, Sun of Peru decoration, 1825. f, Medals Ayacucho, 1824, Boyaca, 1820 and Liberators of Quito, 1822. g, Swords of Peru, 1825. h, Cross pendant, Bucaramanga, 1830. i, Medallion of George Washington, 1826. j, Portrait of Gen. O'Leary.

**1990, Oct. 15**

**1439** Sheet of 10 10.50 10.50
*a.-f.* A385 10b any single .50 .30
*g.-h.* A385 15b any single .75 .35
*i.* A385 40b multicolored 2.00 1.00
*j.* A385 50b multicolored 2.50 1.25

University of Zulia, Cent. A386

Designs: a, Dr. Francisco Ochoa, founder. b, Dr. Jesus E. Lossada, President, 1946-47. c, Soil conservation. d, Developing alternative automotive fuels. e, Organ transplants.

**1990, Sept. 18** **Litho.** ***Perf. 12***

**1440** Strip of 5 8.00 8.00
*a.-b.* A386 10b any single .50 .30
*c.-d.* A386 15b any single .75 .35
*e.* A386 20b multicolored 1.10 .55

Christmas A387

Paintings: a, St. Joseph and Child by Juan Pedro Lopez. b, The Nativity by Lopez. c, The Return from Egypt by Matheo Moreno. d, The Holy Family by unknown artist. e, The Nativity (oval painting) by Lopez.

**1990, Nov. 25**

**1441** Strip of 5 7.50 7.50
*a.-c.* A387 10b any single .50 .30
*d.-e.* A387 20b any single 1.10 .55

OPEC, 30th Anniv. — A388

a, Globe. b, Square emblem. c, Circular emblem. d, Diamond emblem. e, Flags.

**1990, Dec. 21** **Litho.** ***Perf. 12***

**1442** Strip of 5 5.50 5.50
*a.-b.* A388 10b any single .50 .30
*c.* A388 20b multicolored 1.10 .55
*d.* A388 30b multicolored 1.50 .75
*e.* A388 40b multicolored 2.00 1.10

America Issue — A389

**1990, Dec. 12** **Litho.** ***Perf. 12***

**1443** A389 10b Lake dwelling .50 .30
**1444** A389 40b Coastline 2.00 1.00
*a.* Pair, #1443-1444 4.00 4.00

Exfilve '90, Caracas — A389a

Designs: 40b, Bank of Venezuela 1000b note. 50b, Bank of Caracas 100b note.

**1990, Nov. 16** **Litho.** ***Imperf.***

**1444B** A389a 40b multicolored 2.25 2.25
**1444C** A389a 50b multicolored 2.75 2.75

No. 1444B, Bank of Venezuela, cent. No. 1444C, Bank of Caracas, cent.

St. Ignatius of Loyola (1491-1556) A390

Designs: a, Jesuit quarters, Caracas. b, Death mask. c, Statue by Francisco de Vergara, 18th century. d, Statue of Our Lady of Montserrat, 11th century.

**1991, Apr. 12** **Litho.** ***Perf. 12***

**1445** Strip of 4 + label 12.50 12.50
*a.-b.* A390 12b any single .55 .30
*c.* A390 40b multicolored 2.00 .90
*d.* A390 50b multicolored 2.25 1.10

Venezuelan-American Cultural Center, 50th Anniv. — A391

Designs: a, Elisa Elvira Zuloaga (1900-1980), painter & engraver. b, Gloria Stolk (1912-1979), writer. c, Caroline Lloyd (1924-1980), composer. d, Jules Waldman (1912-1990), publisher. e, William Coles (1908-1978), attorney.

**1991, July 4** **Litho.** ***Perf. 12***

**1446** Strip of 5 12.50 12.50
*a.-c.* A391 12b any single .55 .30
*d.* A391 40b multicolored 2.00 1.00
*e.* A391 50b multicolored 2.25 1.10

Miniature Sheet

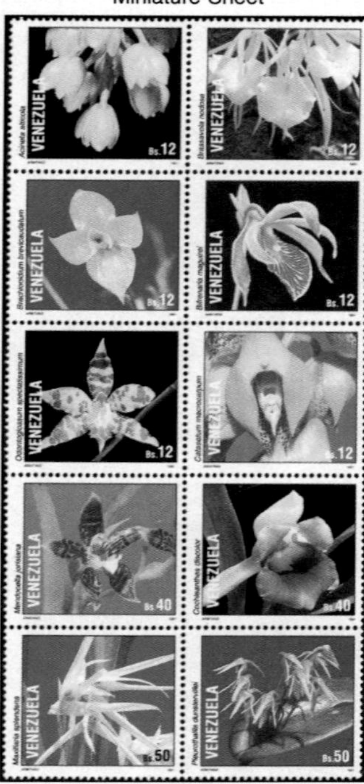

Orchids — A392

Designs: No. 1447a, 12b, Acineta alticola. b, 12b, Brassavola nodosa. c, 12b, Brachionidium brevicaudatum. d, 12b, Bifrenaria maguirei. e, 12b, Odontoglossum spectatissimum. f, 12b, Catasetum macrocarpum. g, 40b, Mendocella jorisiana. h, 40b, Cochleanthes discolor. i, 50b, Maxillaria splendens. j, 50b, Pleurothallis dunstervillei. No. 1448, Cattleya violacea.

**1991, Aug. 22 Litho. *Perf. 12***

**1447** A392 Sheet of 10, #a.-j. 15.00 15.00

**Souvenir Sheet**

**1448** A392 50b multicolored 12.00 12.00

No. 1448 contains one 42x37mm stamp. No. 1447 exists imperf. Value $45.

See Nos. 1499-1500, 1508-1509.

Democratic Action Party, 50th Anniv. — A393

Designs: a, People voting. b, Agricultural reform. c, Students and teachers. d, Nationalization of the petroleum industry.

**1991, Sept. 13 Litho. *Perf. 12***

**1449** A393 12b Block of 4, #a.-d. 2.00 2.00

America Issue A394

**1991, Oct. 24**

**1450** A394 12b Terepaima Chief .45 .25

**1451** A394 40b Paramaconi Chief 2.00 1.25

*a.* Pair, #1450-1451 2.75 2.75

Children's Foundation, 25th Anniv. — A395

Children's drawings: a, 12b, Children in house. b, 12b, Playground. c, 12b, Carnival. d, 12b, Woman and girl walking by pond. e, 12b, Boy in hospital. f, 12b, Five children around tree. g, 40b, Two girls in colorful room. h, 40b, Classroom. i, 50b, Three children. j, 50b, Four children dancing.

**1991, Oct. 31 Litho. *Perf. 12***

**1452** A395 Sheet of 10, #a.-j. 12.00 12.00

Nos. 1362-1364 Surcharged

**1991 Litho. *Perf. 12½***

| | | | | |
|---|---|---|---|---|
| **1453** | A231 | 5b on 25c red | .25 | .20 |
| **1454** | A231 | 5b on 75c pink | .25 | .20 |
| **1455** | A231 | 10b on 25c red | .50 | .25 |
| **1456** | A231 | 10b on 75c pink | .50 | .25 |
| **1457** | A231 | 12b on 50c blue | .65 | .35 |
| **1458** | A231 | 12b on 75c pink | .65 | .35 |
| **1459** | A231 | 20b on 50c blue | 1.00 | .50 |
| **1460** | A231 | 20b on 75c pink | 1.00 | .50 |
| **1461** | A231 | 40b on 50c blue | 2.00 | 1.00 |
| **1462** | A231 | 40b on 75c pink | 2.00 | 1.00 |
| **1463** | A231 | 50b on 50c blue | 2.50 | 1.25 |
| **1464** | A231 | 50b on 75c pink | 2.50 | 1.25 |
| | | *Nos. 1453-1464 (12)* | 13.80 | 7.10 |

Christmas A396

Children's art work: a, 10b, Wise men. b, 12b, Holy Family. c, 20b, Statues of Holy Family. d, 25b, Shepherds. e, 30b, Holy Family, cow, donkey.

**1991, Nov. 14 Litho. *Perf. 12***

**1465** A396 Strip of 5, #a.-e. 6.75 6.75

Souvenir Sheet

Exfilve '91, Caracas — A397

**1991, Nov. 29 Litho. *Perf. 12***

**1466** A397 50b No. 136 2.10 2.10

Discovery of America, 500th Anniv. (in 1992) A398

a, 12b, Coat of arms of Columbus. b, 12b, Santa Maria. c, 12b, Map by Juan de la Cosa. d, 40b, Sighting land. e, 50b, Columbus with Queen Isabella and King Ferdinand II.

**1991, Dec. 12 Litho. *Perf. 12***

**1468** A398 Strip of 5, #a.-e. 4.75 4.75

**1992, Mar. 15**

Designs: No. 1469a, 12b, Emblem for discovery of America Commission. b, 12b, Venezuelan pavillion, Expo '92. c, 12b, 15th century map of Spain. d, 12b, Portrait of Columbus, by Susy Dembo. e, 12b, Encounter, by Ivan Jose Rojas. f, 12b, 0x500 America, by Annella Armas. g, 40b, Imago-Mundi, by Alessandro Grechi. h, 40b, Long Journey, by Gloria Fiallo. i, 50b, Playa Dorado, by Carlos Riera. j, 50b, Irminaoro, by Erasmo Sanches Cedeno. No. 1470, Untitled work, by Muaricio Sanchez.

**1469** A398 Sheet of 10, #a.-j. 12.00 12.00

**1470** A398 50b multicolored 2.25 2.25

Expo '92, Seville. No. 1470 contains one 38x42mm stamp.

Protection of Nature — A399

Turtles: No. 1471a, Geochelone carbonaria, facing left. b, Geochelone carbonaria, facing right. c, Podocnemis expansa, facing left. d, Podocnemis expansa, swimming.

**1992, June 12 Litho. *Perf. 12***

**1471** A399 12b Block of 4, #a.-d. 4.75 2.50

World Wildlife Fund.

Miniature Sheet

Beatification of Josemaria Escriva — A400

Designs: a, 18b, Teaching in Venezuela, 1975. b, 18b, Celebrating mass. c, 18b, Parents, Jose Escriva and Dolores Albas. d, 18b, Text with autograph. e, 18b, Kissing feet of Madonna. f, 18b, Commemorative medallion. g, 60b, With Pope Paul VI. h, 60b, At desk, writing. i, 75b, Portrait. j, 75b, Portrait in St. Peter's Square, 1992.

**1992, Oct. 2 Litho. *Perf. 12***

**1472** A400 Sheet of 10, #a.-j. 12.00 12.00

Electrification of Southern Regions A401

Designs: a, 12b, Roof of native hut. b, 12b, Transmission lines and towers. c, 12b, Horses running through pond. d, 40b, Workmen under tower. e, 50b, Baskets, crafts.

**1992, July 15 Litho. *Perf. 12***

**1473** A401 Strip of 5, #a.-e. 4.50 4.50

Miniature Sheet

Artwork, by Mateo Manaure — A402

Color of background: a, 12b, Red. b, 12b, Red violet. c, 12b, Gray. d, 12b, Violet brown. e, 40b, Brown. f, 40b, Blue. g, 50b, Blue violet. h, 50b, Black.

**1993, July 23**

**1474** A402 Sheet of 8, #a.-h. + 2 labels 6.00 6.00

Bank of Maracaibo, 110th anniv.

Discovery of America, 500th Anniv. — A403

Paintings: a, 18b, The Third Trip, by Elio Caldera. b, 60b, Descontextura, by Juan Pablo Nascimiento.

**1992, Nov. 20 Litho. *Perf. 12***

**1476** A403 Pair, #a.-b. 2.40 2.40

Christmas A404

Artwork by Lucio Rivas: a, 18b, Adoration of the Shepherds. b, 75b, Adoration of the Magi.

100b, Flight into Egypt.

**1992, Dec. 3 Litho. *Perf. 12***

**1477** A404 Pair, #a.-b. 2.75 2.75

**Souvenir Sheet**

**1478** A404 100b multicolored 2.75 2.75

No. 1478 contains one 42x38mm stamp.

Redrawn Bolivar Type of 1976 and

A405

A406

Designs: 5b, Natl. Pantheon. 10b, Victory Monument, Carabobo. 20b, Jose Antonio Paez. 25b, Luisa Caceres de Arismendi. 35b, Ezequiel Zamora. 40b, Cristobal Mendoza. #1490, Central University. #1491, Jose Felix Ribas. #1494, Manuel Piar. 200b, Simon Bolivar.

**1993-94 Litho. *Perf. 12½***

**Size: 18x22mm**

| | | | | | |
|---|---|---|---|---|---|
| **1479** | A405 | 1b | silver | .25 | .20 |
| **1480** | A405 | 2b | greenish blue | .25 | .20 |
| **1482** | A231 | 5b | red | .25 | .20 |
| **1484** | A231 | 10b | violet | .25 | .20 |
| **1487** | A231 | 20b | olive green | .55 | .25 |
| **1488** | A405 | 25b | red brown | .40 | .30 |
| **1488A** | A405 | 35b | brt yel grn | .60 | .40 |
| **1489** | A405 | 40b | lt blue | .65 | .45 |
| **1490** | A231 | 50b | orange | 1.40 | .60 |
| **1491** | A405 | 50b | lilac rose | .90 | .65 |
| **1493** | A406 | 100b | brown | 2.75 | 1.40 |
| **1494** | A405 | 100b | dark blue | 1.75 | 1.00 |
| **1496** | A405 | 200b | brown | 3.50 | 2.00 |
| | | | *Nos. 1479-1496 (13)* | 13.50 | 7.85 |

Nos. 1479-1493 inscribed Armitano.

See Nos. 1548-1562.

Orchid Type of 1991

Miniature Sheet

Designs: a, 20b, Cattleya percivaliana. b, 20b, Anguloa ruckeri. c, 20b, Chondrorhyncha flaveola. d, 20b, Stenia pallida. e, 20b, Zygosepalum lindeniae. f, 20b, Maxillaria triloris. g, 80b, Stanhopea wardii. h, 80b, Oncidium papilio. i, 100b, Oncidium hastilabium. j, 100b, Sobralia cattleya. 150b, Polycycnis muscifera.

**1993, Apr. 1 Litho. *Perf. 12***

**1499** A392 Sheet of 10, #a.-j. 14.00 14.00

**Souvenir Sheet**

**1500** A392 150b multicolored 6.00 6.00

Miniature Sheet

Settlement of Tovar Colony, 150th Anniv. — A408

Designs: a, 24b, Woman. b, 24b, Children. c, 24b, Catholic Church, 1862. d, 24b, Statue of St. Martin of Tours, 1843. e, 24b, Fruits and vegetables. f, 24b, School, 1916. g, 80b, Home of founder, Augustin Codazzi, 1845. h, 80b, House of colony director, Alexander Benitz, 1845. i, 100b, Breidenbach Mill, 1860. j, 100b, Parade.

**1993, Apr. 12 Litho. *Perf. 12***

**1501** A408 Sheet of 10, #a.-j. 12.50 12.50

Miniature Sheet

19th Pan-American Railways Conference — A409

Designs: a, 24b, Tucacas steam locomotive. b, 24b, Halcon steam locomotive on Las Mostazas Bridge, 1894. c, 24b, Maracaibo locomotive. d, 24b, Tender, rail cars, Palo Grande Station. e, 24b, Fiat diesel locomotive, 1957. f, 24b, GP-9-L diesel locomotive, 1957. g, 80b, GP-15-L diesel locomotive, 1982. h, 80b, Metro subway train, Caracas. i, 100b, Electric locomotive. j, 100b, Passenger cars of electric train.

**1993, May 25 Litho. *Perf. 12***

**1502** A409 Sheet of 10, #a.-j. 18.00 18.00

Nos. 1502c-1502d, 1502i-1502j are continuous designs.

A410

A411

World Day to Stop Smoking: a, 24b, Shown. b, 80b, "No smoking" emblem.

**1993, May 27 Litho. *Perf. 12½x12***

**1503** A410 Pair, #a.-b. 2.75 2.75

**1993, Oct. 7 Litho. *Perf. 12***

America Issue: a, 24b, Amazona barbadensis. b, 80b, Ara macao.

**1504** A411 Pair, #a.-b. 4.75 4.75

Miniature Sheets

Native Indians — A412

Christmas — A413

Designs: No. 1505a, 1b, Two Yanomami children with painted bodies, spear. b, 1b, Yanomami woman preparing food. c, 40b, Two Panare children performing in Katyayinto ceremony. d, 40b, Panare man with nose flute. e, 40b, Taurepan man in canoe. f, 40b, Taurepan girl weaving. g, 40b, Piaroa woman with infant. h, 40b, Piaroa dancers wearing war masks. i, 100b, Hoti man blowing flute. j, 100b, Hoti woman carrying baby, basket over back.

150b, Child blowing traditional whistle.

**1993, Nov. 25 Litho. *Perf. 12***

**1505** A412 Sheet of 10, #a.-j. 9.25 9.25

**Souvenir Sheet**

**1506** A412 150b multicolored 3.25 3.25

**1993, Nov. 30**

Nativity scene: a, f, 24b, Joseph. b, g, 24b, Madonna and Child. c, h, 24b, Shepherd boy, wise man holding gift, lambs. d, i, 80b, Wise man with hands folded, boy. e, j, 100b, Wise man presenting gift, boy with hands folded.

**1507** A413 Sheet of 10, #a.-j. 10.50 10.50

Nos. 1507f-1507j are black, magenta & buff.

Orchid Type of 1991

Miniature Sheet

Designs: a, 35b, Chrysocycnis schlimii. b, 35b, Galeandra minax. c, 35b, Oncidium falcipetalum. d, 35b, Oncidium lanceanum. e, 40b, Sobralia violacea linden. f, 40b, Sobralia infundibuligera. g, 80b, Mendoncella burkei. h, 80b, Phragmipedium caudatum. i, 100b, Phragmipedium kaieteurum. j, 200b, Stanhopea grandiflora.

150b, Epidendrum elongatum.

**1994, May 19 Litho. *Perf. 12***

**1508** A392 Sheet of 10, #a.-j. 16.00 16.00

**Souvenir Sheet**

**1509** A392 150b multicolored 3.25 3.25

No. 1509 contains one 42x37mm stamp.

Miniature Sheet of 10

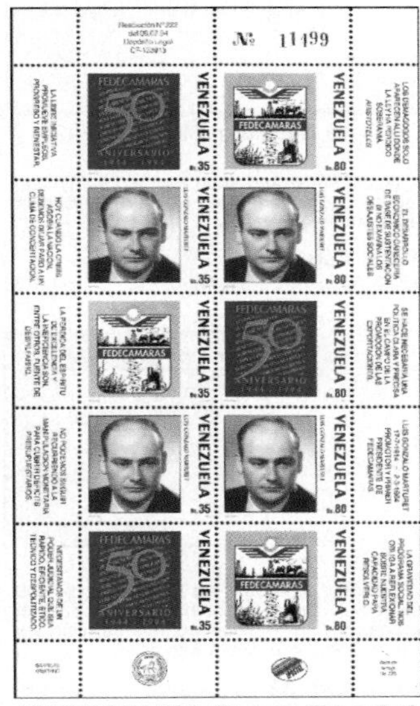


FEDECAMARAS (Federal Council of Production & Commerce Associations), 50th Anniv. — A414

a, 35b; f, 80b, Anniversary emblem. b, 35b; e, 80b, Luis Gonzalo Marturet (1914-64), 1st president. c, 35b; d, 80b, FEDECAMARAS emblem.

**1994, July 17 Litho. *Perf. 12***

**1510** A414 #c, f, 2 ea #a-b, d-e 9.75 9.75

Judicial Service A415

**1994, Sept. 13 Litho. *Perf. 12***

**1511** A415 100b multicolored 1.75 1.75

Miniature Sheet

Christmas A416

Paintings: a, 35b, g, 80b, The Nativity, by follower of Jose Lorenzo de Alvarado. b, 35b, h, 80b, Birth of Christ, 19th cent. c, 35b, i, 80b, The Nativity, diff., by follower of Jose Lorenzo de Alvarado. d, 35b, j, 80b, Adoration of the Magi, 17th cent.. e, 35b, f, 80b, Birth of Christ, by School of Tocuyo.

**1994, Dec. 1**

**1512** A416 Sheet of 10, #a.-j. 9.75 9.75

Miniature Sheet

Antonio Jose de Sucre (1795-1830) — A417

Designs: No. 1513a, 25b, Portrait. b, 25b, Dona Mariana Carcelen Y Larrea Marquesa de Solanda. c, 35b, Top of equestrian monument. d, 35b, Bottom of monument. e, 40b, Painting of Battle of Pichincha, mountains at top. f, 40b, Painting of Battle of Pichincha, battle scent. g, 80b, Painting of Battle of Ayacucho, soldiers on horseback. h, 80b, Painting of Battle of Ayacucho, dead soldiers. i, 100b, Painting of Surrender at Ayachucho, general signing document. j, 100b, Painting of Surrender at Ayachucho, seated general at right.

150b, Portion of mural, Carabobo, by Pedro Centeno Vallenilla.

**1995, Feb. 2**

**1513** A417 Sheet of 10, #a.-j. 9.50 9.50

**Souvenir Sheet**

**1514** A417 150b multicolored 2.50 2.50

Postal Transportation — A418

a, 35b, Post office van. b, 80b, Airplane.

**1995, Mar. 22 Litho. *Perf. 12***

**1515** A418 Pair, #a.-b. 2.10 2.10

No. 1515 issued in sheets of 10 stamps.

Miniature Sheet

St. Jean-Baptiste de La Salle (1651-1719), Educator — A419

Denomination LR: a, 100b, Portrait. b, 35b, Students with microscope, academic education. c, 35b, Soccer players, sports education. d, 35b, Scouts at camp, citizenship education. e, 80b, La Salle College, Caracas.

Denomination LL: f, like #1516e. g, like #1516d. h, like #1516b. i, like #1516c. j, like #1516a.

**1995, May 15**

**1516** A419 Sheet of 10, #a.-j. 7.75 7.75

Miniature Sheet

Founding of Salesian Order, Cent. A420

Designs: a, 35b, St. John Bosco (1815-88), priest with child. b, 35b, Lonely child, Madonna and Child. c, 35b, Man running machine tool. d, 35b, Young men working with electronic instruments. e, 35b, Baseball game. f, 35b, Basketball game. g, 80b, People working in fields. h, 80b, Man looking at chili peppers. i, 100b, Young tribal natives receiving religious training. j, 100b, Tribal native.

**1995, Apr. 26**
**1517** A420 Sheet of 10, #a.-j. 8.75 8.75

Miniature Sheet

Orchids A421

Designs: a, 35b, Maxillaria guareimensis. b, 35b, Paphinia lindeniana. c, 50b, Catasetum longifolium. d, 50b, Anguloa clowesii. e, 35b, Coryanthes biflora. f, 35b, Catasetum pileatum. g, 80b, Maxillaria histrionica. h, 80b, Sobralia ruckeri. i, 35b, Mormodes convolutum. j, 35b, Huntleya lucida.
150b, Catasetum barbatum.

**1995, May 31** **Litho.** ***Perf. 12***
**1518** A421 Sheet of 10, #a.-j. 8.00 8.00

**Souvenir Sheet**

**1519** A421 150b multicolored 2.25 2.25

No. 1519 contains one 42x36mm stamp.
See #1534-1535, 1563-1564, 1587-1588.

CAF (Andes Development Corporation), 25th Anniv. — A422

**1995, June 7**
**1520** A422 80b multicolored 1.25 1.25

Miniature Sheet

Beatification of Mother Maria of San Jose A423

Designs: a, 35b, In formal habit. b, 35b, Pope John Paul II. c, 35b, As young woman distributing Bibles. d, 35b, Doing embroidary work. e, 35b, Statue of Madonna, altar. f, 35b, Kneeling in devotions. g, 80b, Walking with Sisters in hospital. h, 80b, With patient in hospital. i, 100b, Working with children. j, 100b, Helping person seated along road.

**1995, July 2**
**1521** A423 Sheet of 10, #a.-j. 9.25 9.25

Nos. 1521a-1521b, 1521c-1521d, 1521e-1521f, 1521g-1521h, 1521i-1521j are each continuous designs.

UN, 50th Anniv. — A424

Designs: a, People from different countries unfurling UN flag. b, Emblem on UN flag.

**1995, June 26**
**1522** A424 50b Pair, #a.-b. 3.25 3.25

Gen. José Gregorio Monagas (1795-1858), President, Liberator of the Slaves — A425

a, Portrait. b, Slave family with opened chains.

**1995, July 26** **Litho.** ***Perf. 12***
**1523** A425 50b Pair, #a.-b. 1.40 1.40

Slave Rebellion, Bicent. — A426

Jose Leonardo Chirino and: a, Liberty leading the people (after Delacroix). b, Revolutionaries with weapons.

**1995, Aug. 16**
**1524** A426 50b Pair, #a.-b. 1.50 1.50

Venezuelan Red Cross, Cent. A427

Designs: a, 100b, Red Cross flag. b, 80b, Carlos J. Bello Hospital. c, 35b, Surgery scene. d, 35b, Rescue workers carrying victim. e, 35b, Care givers with child.

**1995, Aug. 30**
**1525** A427 Strip of 5, #a.-e. 4.50 4.50

America Issue A428

Environmental protection: a, 35b, Trees, lake. b, 80b, Flowers, hillside.

**1995, Sept. 13** **Litho.** ***Perf. 12***
**1526** A428 Pair, #a.-b. 2.00 2.00

No. 1526 was issued in sheets of 10 stamps.
No. 1526 exists in two types: the heavy border at top is above "America" only: the heavy line extends over the denomination. Values the same.

Miniature Sheet

Native Aboriginals A429

No. 1527: a, 25b, Kuana man seated on post. b, 25b, Kuana woman using stones to do laundry. c, 35b, Guahibo people, one playing flute. d, 35b, Guahibo shaman with child. e, 50b, Uruak man with tree branch. f, 50b, Uruak woman cooking. g, 80b, Warao woman spinning twine. h, 80b, Warao man, woman in boat. i, 100b, Bari men with bows, arrows. j, 100b, Bari man rubbing sticks to make fire.
150b, Young boy with bird.

**1995, Oct. 18**
**1527** A429 Sheet of 10, #a.-j. 8.75 8.75

**Souvenir Sheet**

**1528** A429 150b multicolored 2.40 2.40

See Nos. 1541-1542.

Miniature Sheet

Electricity in Caracas, Cent. A430

Designs: a, 35b, Ricardo Zuloaga, early pioneer. b, 35b, Early electric plant. c, 35b, Substation. d, 35b, 1908 Electric trams. e, 35b, Electric lampposts mandated by Congress, 1908. f, 35b, Lampposts, Bolivar Plaza. g, 80b, Electrical repairman. h, 80b, Lighted cross, Avila. i, 100b, Teresa Carreño Cultural Complex. j, 100b, Ricardo Zuloaga main generator plant.

**1995, Nov. 6**
**1529** A430 Sheet of 10, #a.-j. 9.00 9.00

Miniature Sheet

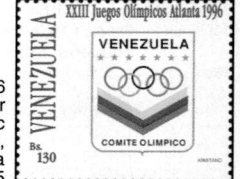


Christmas A431

Designs: a, 35b, The Annunciation. b, 35b, Being turned away at the inn. c, 100b, Birth of Christ in the stable. d, 35b, Angel appearing to shepherds. e, 35b, Three Magi. f, 40b, Christmas pageant. g, 40b, Children skating. h, 100b, Christmas presents. i, 40b, Women preparing food for holidays. j, 40b, Children, mother preparing food for holidays.

**1995, Nov. 15**
**1530** A431 Sheet of 10, #a.-j. 8.50 8.50

Nos. 1530f-1530g, and 1530i-1530j are each continuous designs.

Miniature Sheet

Petroleum Industries of South America (PDVSA), 20th Anniv. A432

a, 35b, PDVSA emblem, 7 petroleum company emblems. b, PDVSA emblem, 6 petroleum company emblems. c, 80b, Oil derrick. d, 80b, Refinery. e, 35b, Oil tanker crossing under bridge. f, 35b, Worker, orimulsion tanks. g, 35b, Two people examining carbon. h, 35b, Semi truck hauling petrochemicals. i, 35b, Filling station. j, 35b, Gas storage tanks.

**1995, Dec. 13** **Litho.** ***Perf. 12***
**1531** A432 Sheet of 10, #a.-j. 9.00 9.00

Miniature Sheet

Town of El Tocuyo, 450th Anniv. A433

Designs: a, 35b, City arms. b, 35b, Workers in sugar cane field. c, Church of Our Lady of Immaculate Conception. d, Statue of Madonna inside church. e, 35b, Ruins of Temple of Santa Domingo. f. 35b, House of Culture. g, 80b, Cactus, vegetation. h, 80b, Cactus up close. i, 100b, Dancers with swords. j, 100b, Man playing guitar.

**1995, Dec. 5**
**1532** A433 Sheet of 10, #a.-j. 9.00 9.00

Miniature Sheet

Vist of Pope John Paul II — A434

Statues of various saints, Pope and: a, 25b, Children. b, 25b, Man, woman. c, 40b, Man, woman, baby. d, 40b, Elderly man. e, 50b, Woman, boy. f, 50b, Sick person. g, 60b, Man in prison. h, 60b, Working man. i, 100b, People of various career fields. j, 100b, Priests, nuns.
200b, Pope John Paul II holding crucifix.

**1996, Jan. 26**
**1533** A434 Sheet of 10, #a.-j. 10.00 10.00

**Souvenir Sheet**

**1533K** A434 200b multicolored 2.50 2.50

Orchid Type of 1995

Designs: a, Epidendrum fimbriatum. b, Myoxanthus reymondii. c, Catasetum pileatum. d, Ponthieva maculata. e, Maxillaria triloris. f, Scaphosepalum breve. g, Cleistes rosea. h, Maxillaria sophronitis. i, Catasetum discolor. j, Oncidium ampliatum.
200b, Odontoglossum naevium.

**1996, May 31** **Litho.** ***Perf. 12***
**1534** A421 60b Sheet of 10, #a.-j. 7.25 7.25

**Souvenir Sheet**

**1535** A421 200b multicolored 2.50 2.50

1996 Summer Olympic Games, Atlanta A435

Designs: a, Emblem of Olympic Committee. b, Swimmer. c, Boxer. d, Cyclist. e, Medal winners.

**1996, June 28** **Litho.** ***Perf. 12***
**1536** A435 130b Strip of 5, #a.-e. 6.50 6.50

No. 1536 was issued in a sheet of 10 stamps.

Use of Automation at Maiquetia Intl. Airport, 25th Anniv. A436

Designs: a, Symbol of automation. b, Map of airport flight routes. c, La Guaira Airdrome, 1929. d, Maiqueitia Airport, 1944. e, Simon Bolivar Airport, 1972. f, Interior view of terminal. g, Airport police, control tower. h, Airport firetruck. i, Airplane at terminal, Simon Bolivar Airport. j, Airplane on taxiway, Simon Bolivar Airport.

**1996, Aug. 4**
**1537** A436 80b Sheet of 10, #a-j 8.50 8.50

America Issue A437

Traditional costumes: a, 60b, Women's. b, 130b, Men's.

**1996, Sept. 10**
**1538** A437 Pair, #a.-b. 2.00 2.00

No. 1538 was issued in sheets of 10 stamps.

Mario Briceño-Iragorry (1897-1958) — A438

Portraits: a, As young man, Trujillo, 1913. b, At University of Mérida, 1919. c, As politician, 1944. d, As writer, 1947. e, As older man, Caracas, 1952.

**1996, Sept. 24**
**1539** A438 80b Strip of 5, #a.-e. 4.25 4.25

No. 1539 was issued in sheets of 10 stamps.

Caracas Rotary Club, 70th Anniv. — A439

**1996, Oct. 3**
**1540** A439 50b multicolored .55 .55

No. 1540 was issued in sheets of 10.

Native Aboriginal Type of 1995

Designs: a, 80b, Yukpa boy working in garden. b, 80b, Paraujanos girl carrying fruit. c, 80b, Kinaroes man, woman bundling cattails. d, 80b, Motilon man with bananas. e, 80b, Chaque mother carrying infant on back. f, 100b, Guajiros man, young woman fixing hair. g, 100b, Mucuchi man carrying pack on back. h, 100b, Mape man with bow and arrow. i, 100b, Macoa working with grain, painted faces. j, 100b, Yaruros man weaving. 200b, Woman breastfeeding infant.

**1996, Oct. 11**
**1541** A429 Sheet of 10, #a.-j. 9.75 9.75

**Souvenir Sheet**

**1542** A429 200b multicolored 2.10 2.10

Souvenir Sheet

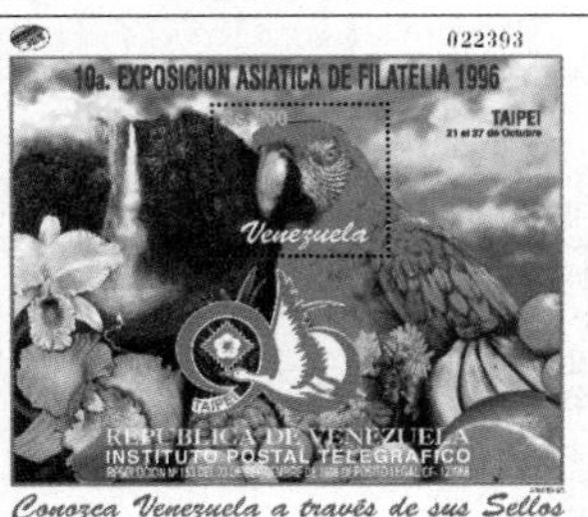
Taipei '96, Intl. Philatelic Exhibition — A440

**1996, Oct. 21 Litho. *Perf. 12***
**1543** A440 200b Ara chloroptera *5.50 5.50*

José Gregorio Hernández (1864-1908), Physician — A441

a, As young boy. b, As student, anatomy drawing. c, Praying, Madonna statue. d, Thinking of the needy. e, In research study. f, As professor of university. g, Comforting sick patient. h, Empty chair at academy. i, Vargas Hospital, statue, portrait of Hernández. j, Hospital named after Hernández, statue.
200b, Portrait of Hernández.

**1996, Oct. 26 Litho. *Perf. 12***
**1544** A441 60b Sheet of 10, #a.-j. 4.50 4.50

**Souvenir Sheet**

**1545** A441 200b multicolored 1.50 1.50

No. 1545 contains one 42x36mm stamp.

Christmas A442

Designs: a, 60b, Child setting up Nativity scene. b, 60b, Three men with guitars, woman. c, 60b, Rooster, people making music. d, 60b, People with painted faces dancing, singing. e, 60b, Men, woman playing drums, instruments. f, 80b, Exchanging gifts of food. g, 80b, Family at table, looking at gift of food. h, 80b, Child in hammock, presents. i, 80b, Parading replica of infant Jesus. j, 80b, Kissing feet of Christ Child.

**1996, Nov. 7**
**1546** A442 Sheet of 10, #a.-j. 5.25 5.25

Andrés Eloy Blanco (1896-1955), Politician, Writer A443

Designs: a, As adolescent. b, As Caracas city official, government building. c, With family. d, With democratic founders. e, As politician, building. f, As President of Constituent Assembly, building. g, As "Poet of Pueblo." h, Lincoln Memorial, as Chancellor of the Republic. i, Author of writings on Spain, sailing ship. j, Map of Spain, sailing ships, conquistador on horseback.

**1997, Feb. 17 Litho. *Perf. 12***
**1547** A443 100b Sheet of 10, #a.-j. 6.25 6.25

Simon Bolivar (1783-1830) — A444

**1997, Mar. 7 Litho. *Perf. 13½x13***

| | | | | | |
|---|---|---|---|---|---|
| **1548** | A444 | 15b | olive | .20 | .20 |
| **1549** | A444 | 20b | brown org | .20 | .20 |
| **1550** | A444 | 40b | dark brown | .25 | .25 |
| **1551** | A444 | 50b | rose claret | .40 | .40 |
| **1552** | A444 | 70b | deep violet | .55 | .55 |
| **1553** | A444 | 90b | deep blue | .80 | .80 |
| **1554** | A444 | 200b | dp grn bl | 1.50 | 1.50 |
| **1555** | A444 | 300b | dp bl grn | 2.00 | 2.00 |
| **1556** | A444 | 400b | gray | 3.00 | 3.00 |
| **1557** | A444 | 500b | pale sepia | 3.50 | 3.50 |
| **1558** | A444 | 600b | pale brown | 3.75 | 3.75 |
| **1559** | A444 | 800b | pale vio brn | 4.75 | 4.75 |
| **1560** | A444 | 900b | slate blue | 5.00 | 5.00 |
| **1561** | A444 | 1000b | dk org brn | 5.25 | 5.25 |
| **1562** | A444 | 2000b | olive bister | 10.00 | 10.00 |
| | | | *Nos. 1548-1562 (15)* | 41.15 | 41.15 |

Orchid Type of 1995

Designs: a, Phragmipedium lindleyanum. b, Zygosepalum labiosum. c, Acacallis cyanea. d, Maxillaria camaridii. e, Scuticaria steelei. f, Aspasia variegata. g, Comparettia falcata. h, Scapyglottis stellata. i, Maxillaria ruffescens. j, Vanilla pompona.
250b, Rodriguezia lanceolata.

**1997, May 30 *Perf. 12***
**1563** A421 165b Sheet of 10, #a.-j. 10.00 10.00

**Souvenir Sheet**

**1564** A421 250b multicolored 1.00 1.00

No. 1564 contains one 42x37mm stamp.

Independence Conspiracy of Gual and España, Bicent. — A445

#1565, José María España, proclamation for independence being read. #1566, España under arrest. #1567, Manuel Gual, soldiers. #1568, Gual fleeing through door, sailing ship, standing on Trinidad. #1569, Revolutionary flag, sailing ship.

**1997, July 16**

| | | | | | |
|---|---|---|---|---|---|
| **1565** | A445 | 165b | multicolored | .70 | .70 |
| **1566** | A445 | 165b | multicolored | .70 | .70 |
| *a.* | | | Pair, #1565-1566 | 1.40 | 1.40 |
| **1567** | A445 | 165b | multicolored | .70 | .70 |
| *a.* | | | Pair, #1566-1567 | 1.40 | 1.40 |
| **1568** | A445 | 165b | multicolored | .70 | .70 |
| *a.* | | | Pair, #1567-1568 | 1.40 | 1.40 |
| **1569** | A445 | 165b | multicolored | .70 | .70 |
| *a.* | | | Pair, #1565, 1569 | 1.40 | 1.40 |
| *b.* | | | Pair, #1568-1569 | 1.40 | 1.40 |

Printed in sheet of 10 containing one each #1566a, 1567a, 1568a, 1569a-1569b.

Treaty of Tlatelolco Banning Use of Nuclear Weapons in Latin America, 30th Anniv. A446

Various stylized designs representing devastation resulting from use of nuclear weapons: a.-e., White inscriptions. f.-j., Black inscriptions.

**1997, July 31**
**1570** A446 140b Sheet of 10, #a.-j. 6.50 6.50

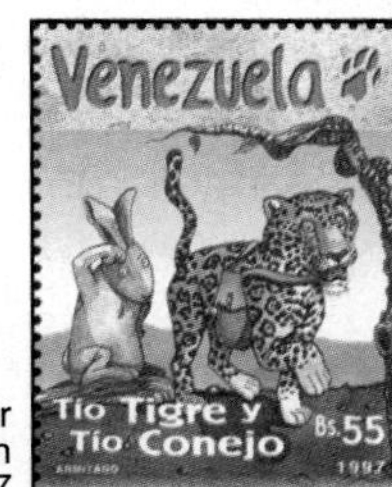
Stories for Children A447

"The Rabbit and the Tiger:" a, Rabbit, tiger carrying satchel. b, Watching rat figure digging. c, Watching turtle on his back. d, Rabbit. e. Rat in net, rabbit. f, Tiger, house, rat. g, Bird, rat, rabbit, bee, beehive. h, Rabbit, turtle. i, Tiger with stick over shoulder. j, Tiger with mouth open, bees.
250b, Rabbit, tiger.

**1997, Aug. 7**
**1571** A447 55b Sheet of 10, #a.-j. 2.75 2.75

**Souvenir Sheet**

**1572** A447 250b multicolored 1.25 1.25

No. 1572 contains one 42x37mm stamp.
The reverse of Nos. 1571a-1571j are each inscribed with parts of the childrens' story.

Unexpected Adventures of a Postman A448

America Issue: 110p, Giving letter to woman with dog. 280p, With motor scooter in rain.

**1997, Aug. 29 Litho. *Perf. 12***

| | | | | | |
|---|---|---|---|---|---|
| **1573** | A448 | 110p | multicolored | .90 | .90 |
| **1574** | A448 | 280p | multicolored | 2.00 | 2.00 |
| *a.* | | | Pair, #1573-1574 | 5.00 | 5.00 |

No. 1574a was issued in sheets of 10 stamps.

Villa of Anauco Villa, Bicent. A449

Designs: a, Inscription. b, Main entrance. c, Entrance corridor. d, Interior patio. e, Exterior corridor leading to kitchen. f, Kitchen. g, Stairs leading to balcony. h, Coach house. i, Stable. j, Outside stable, water trough.

**1997, Sept. 23**
**1575** A449 110b Sheet of 10, #a.-j. 5.00 5.00

Independence in India, 50th Anniv. — A450

Designs: a, 165b, Jawaharlal Nehru. b, 200b, Sardar Patel, flag. c, 165b, Congressional building. d, 200b, Gandhi. e, 165b, Purification at the Ganges. f, 200b, Rabindranath Tagore. g, 165b, Motion picture industry. h, 200b, Traditional music. i, 165b, Insat-1B meteorological satellite. j, 200b, Use of modern technology.
250b, Minarets of Taj Majal.

**1997, Oct. 2**
**1576** A450 Sheet of 10, #a.-j. 8.50 8.50

**Souvenir Sheet**

**1577** A450 250b multicolored 1.60 1.60

Heinrich von Stephan (1831-97) A451

a, 110b, Portrait. b, 280b, UPU emblem.

**1997, Oct. 9 Litho. *Perf. 12***
**1578** A451 Pair, #a.-b. 1.10 1.10

Wicker-work A452

No. 1579: a, Red basket, Ye'Kuana. b, With handles, Ye'Kuana. c, Round, Ye'Kuana. d, Tray, Panare. e, Backpack, Pemon. f, With carrying strap, Yanomami. g, Round (dk brown), diff., Ye'Kuana. h, Tray, Ye'Kuana. i, Oval tray, Panare. j, Wide mouth, Warao.
250b, Square box with lid, Ye'Kuana.

**1997, Oct. 24** ***Perf. 12***
**1579** A452 140b Sheet of 10, #a.-j. 8.00 8.00

**Souvenir Sheet**

**1580** A452 250b multicolored 2.75 2.75

No. 1580 contains one 42x37mm stamp.

Christmas A453

a, Annunciation. b, Mary, St. Elizabeth. c, No room at the inn. d, Nativity. e, Annunciation to shepherds. f, Adoration of the shepherds. g, Magi following star. h, Adoration of the Magi. i, Presentation of Christ child in temple. j, Flight into Egypt.

**1997, Oct. 31**
**1581** A453 110b Sheet of 10, #a.-j. 5.00 5.00

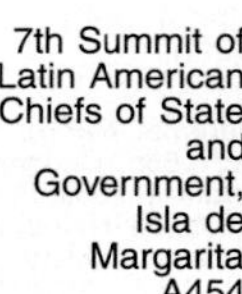

7th Summit of Latin American Chiefs of State and Government, Isla de Margarita A454

a, 165b, j, 200b, Social justice. b, 165b, i, 200b, Free elections. c, 165b, h, 200b, Summit emblem. d, 165b, g, 200b, Truthful information. e, 165b, f, 200b, Human rights.

**1997, Nov. 5**
**1582** A454 Sheet of 10, #a.-j. 5.00 5.00

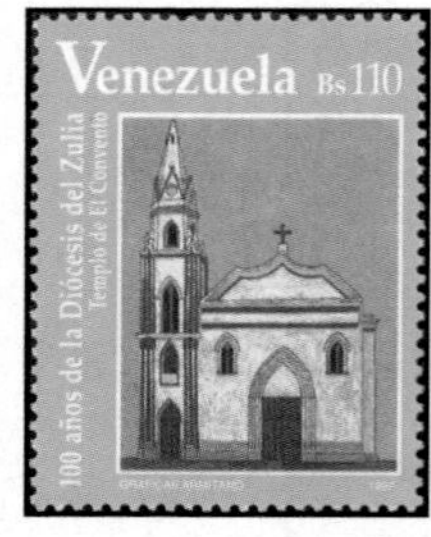


Diocese of Zulia, Cent. A455

Churches: a, Convent. b, Church of St. Ann. c, Reliquary, Chiquinquira. d, Basilica of Chiquinquira and St. John of God. e, Church, Aranza. f, Cathedral, Maracaibo. g, Cathedral, Machiques. h, Archbishop's seal. i, Cathedral, Cabimas. j, Cathedral of the Virgin, San Carlos.

**1997, Dec. 16**
**1583** A455 110b Sheet of 10, #a.-j. 3.00 3.00

Democracy in Venezuela, 40th Anniv. — A456

Designs: a, Commemorative emblem. b, Popular decision. c, Public education. d, Social development. e, Freedom of expression. f, Capital, constitution. g, Popular culture. h, Civil rights. i, Environmental protection. j, Social and civic participation.

**1998, Feb. 19** **Litho.** ***Perf. 12***
**1584** A456 110b Sheet of 10, #a.-j. 4.25 4.25

Discovery of Margarita Island, 500th Anniv. — A457

Map of Margarita Islands and: a, 200b, Angel Rock. b, 265b, Christopher Columbus, ship. c, 200b, Simon Bolivar. d, 200b, Pearl diver. e, 265b, Statue of the Virgin del Valle, church. f, 100b, Mending fish net, fishermen in boats. g, 200b, Gen. Santiago Marino. h, 100b, Petronila Mata, cannon. i, 200b, Gen. Juan Bautista Arismendi. j, 100b, Parrot.
250b, Women weeping at the Lagoon of Martyrs, horiz.

**1998, Mar. 26** **Litho.** ***Perf. 12***
**1585** A457 Sheet of 10, #a.-j. 6.25 6.25

**Souvenir Sheet**

**1586** A457 250b multicolored 1.00 1.00

No. 1586 contains one 42x37mm stamp.

Orchid Type of 1995

a, Oncidium orthostates. b, Epidendrum praetervisum. c, Odontoglossum schilleranum. d, Bletia lansbergii. e, Caularthron bicornutum. f, Darwiniera bergoldii. g, Houlletia tigrina. h, Pleurothallis acuminata. i, Elleanthus lupulinus. j, Epidendrum ferrugineum.
250b, Pleurothallis immersa.

**1998, May 29**
**1587** A421 185b Sheet of 10, #a.-j. 6.50 6.50

**Souvenir Sheet**

**1588** A421 250b multicolored 1.00 1.00

No. 1588 contains one 42x37mm stamp.

Henri Pittier Natl. Park, 60th Anniv. — A458

Fauna: a, 140b, Crax pauxi. b, 150b, Spizaetus ornatus. c, 200b, Touit collaris. d, 200b, Trogon collaris. e, 350b, Cyanocorax yncas. f, 140b, Tersina viridis. g, 150b, Phyllomedusa trinitatis. h, 200b, Morpho peleides. i, 200b, Acrocinus longimanus. j, 350b, Dynastes hercules.

**1998, July 17**
**1589** A453 Sheet of 10, #a.-j. 7.25 7.25

Comptroller General of the Republic, 60th Anniv. — A459

Designs: a, 140b, Gumersindo Torres Millet, founding Comptroller. b, 140b, Luis Antonio Pietri Yépez, first Comptroller of the democracy. c, 140b, View of capitol dome. d, 140b, Colors of flag (service to society). e, 200b, Simon Bolivar, coins. f, 200b, Various numbers on green background. g, 350b, Newspaper headlines (inform the public). h, 350b, Statue of justice (uphold law). i, 350b, Text of duties of the Comptroller General. j, 350b, Emblem, the 6th Assembly of the Latin American and Caribbean States Comptrollers.

**1998, July 29**
**1590** A459 Sheet of 10, #a.-j. 8.25 8.25

Organization of the American States (OAS), 50th Anniv. — A460

a, 140b, Logo of the anniversary. b, 140b, OAS emblem. c, 350b, Flags forming double helix, US flag at center left. d, 150b, Deactivating land mine. e, 150b, Defending human rights. f, 200b, Simon Bolivar, coins. g, 200b, Scroll, quill pen, inkwell. h, 350b, Flags forming double helix, Venezuelan flag at center right. i, 200b, Road sign with map of Americas. j, 200b, Mountain climbers.

**1998, July 30**
**1591** A460 Sheet of 10, #a.-j. 7.25 7.25

Expo '98, Lisbon A461

Designs: a, 140b, Bird, turtle, crab. b, 140b, Fishermen throwing net from boat. c, 150b, Seashells, turtle. d, 150b, Fish. e, 200b, Marine life, denomination, UR. f, 200b, Marine life, denomination LR. g, 200b, Man riding through river on horse. h, 200b, Cattle in river, monkey. i, 350b, Two sea birds. j, 350b, Monkey, waterfall, flower.

**1998, July 31**
**1592** A461 Sheet of 10, #a.-j. 8.00 8.00

18th Central American and Caribbean Games, Maracaibo A462

Figures: a, 150b, Running. b, 200b, Playing basketball. c, 150b, Bowling. d, 200b, Boxing. e, 150b, Cycling. f, 200b, Fencing. g, 150b, Performing gymnastics. h, 200b, Weight lifting. i, 150b, Swimming. j, 200b, Playing tennis.

**1998, Aug. 4**
**1593** A462 Sheet of 10, #a.-j. 6.00 6.00

Discovery of Venezuela, 500th Anniv. — A463

Designs: a, 350b, Christopher Columbus. b, 200b, Juan de la Cosa (1460?-1510), map. c, 200b, Huts built on stilts in water. d, 150b, Women of three different races. e, 140b, 13th cent. artifact. f, 350b, Alonso de Ojeda (1465-1515), map. g, 200b, Detail of map of Jodocus Hondius. h, 200b, Modern city. i, 150b, Various people of modern Venezuela. j, 140b, Statues of Catholic king and queen.

**1998, Aug. 10**
**1594** A463 Sheet of 10, #a.-j. 7.25 7.25

Landing of Christoper Columbus, and Exploration of Amerigo Vespucci, 500th Anniv. A464

**1998, Aug. 12**
**1595** A464 400b multicolored 3.00 3.00

See Italy No. 2252.

Treaty of Amazon Cooperation, 20th Anniv. A465

Designs: a, Casiquiare River, denomination LR. b, Casiquiare River, denomination LL. c, Bactris gasipaes. d, Neblinaria celiae. e, Paracheidon axelrodi. f, Dendrobates leucomelas. g, Nocthocrax urumatum. h, Speothos venaticus. i, Cocuy mountain. j, Neblina Mountains.

**1998, Aug. 20**
**1596** A465 200b Sheet of 10, #a.-j. 8.00 8.00

Children's Story — A466

Cockroach Martinez and Perez Rat: a, Cockroach. b, Burro. c, Parrot. d, Insects with camera, pad. e, Cat. f, Cockroach, pig. g, Goat. h, Cockroach, rat. i, Rat. j, Cockroach, bird.
350b, Cockroach.

**1998, Aug. 21** **Litho.** ***Perf. 12***
**1597** A466 130b Sheet of 10, #a.-j. 5.00 5.00

**Souvenir Sheet**

**1598** A466 350b multicolored 1.25 1.25

State of Israel, 50th Anniv. — A467

a, 350b, Menorah. b, 350b, Moses, Ten Commandments. c, 200b, Theodore Herzl. d, 200b, King David. e, 140b, Blowing of Shofar. f, 350b, Torah. g, 350b, Praying at Wailing Wall. h, 200b, David Ben Gurion. i, 200b, Knesset. j, 140b, Book Museum.

**1998, Sept. 15**

**1599** A467 Sheet of 10, #a.-j. 6.00 6.00

Souvenir Sheet

Comptroller General, 60th Anniv. — A468

**1998, Sept.**

**1600** A468 480b multicolored 1.75 1.75

UPU, 125th Anniv. A469

a, 100b, Customer at window, clerks at left. b, 100b, Scanning bar code, woman at right. c, 100b, Electronic mail. d, 100b, Hybrid mail. e, 100b, Business mail. f, 300b, Like "a," clerks at right. g, 300b, Like "b," woman at left. h, 300b, Like "c," large monitor at right. i, 300b, Like "d," woman at right. j, 300b, Like "e," building with stacks at left.

**1998, Sept. 29**

**1601** A469 Sheet of 10, #a.-j. 7.00 7.00

Legendary Caciques A470

a, Caruao. b, Manaure. c, Guacamayo. d, Tapiaracay. e, Mamacuri. f, Maniacuare. g, Mara. h, Chacao. i, Tamanaco. j, Tiuna. 500b, Indian.

**1998, Oct. 9**

**1602** A470 420b Sheet of 10, #a.-j. 15.00 15.00

**Souvenir Sheet**

**1603** A470 500b multicolored 1.75 1.75

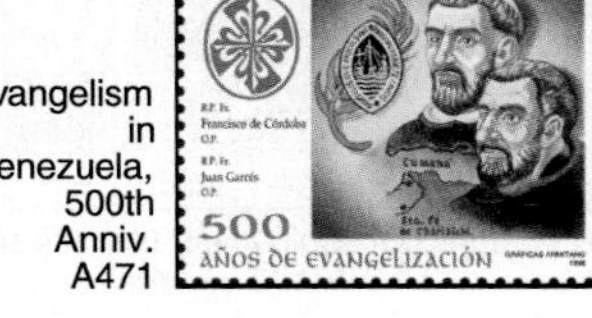

Evangelism in Venezuela, 500th Anniv. A471

No. 1604: a, 100b, Fr. Francisco de Córdoba, Fr. Juan Garcés. b, 100b, Fr. Matías Ruíz Blanco. c, 100b, Fr. Vincente de Requejada. d, 100b, Fr. José Gumilla. e, 100b, Fr. Antonio Gonzáles de Acuña. f, 300b, Fr. Pedro de Córdoba. g, 300b, Fr. Francisco de Pamplona. h, 300b, Fr. Bartolomé Díaz. i, 300b, Fr. Filipe Salvador Gilij. j, 300b, Don Mariano Martí.

350b, Emblem of Papal Nuncio.

**1998, Oct. 24** **Litho.** ***Perf. 12***

**1604** A471 Sheet of 10, #a.-j. 5.50 5.50

**Souvenir Sheet**

**1605** A471 350b multicolored 1.00 1.00

No. 1605 contains one 42x37mm stamp.

Special Olympics, 30th Anniv. A472

180b: a, Carrying torch. b, Giving hug. c, Soccer players. d, Girl holding small flag. e, Girl performing gymnastics.

420b: f, Swimmer. g, Coach walking with athletes. h, Hitting volleyball. i, Particpants cheering. j, Coach instructing girl in softball.

**1998, Oct. 30** **Litho.** ***Perf. 12***

**1606** A472 Sheet of 10, #a.-j. 10.50 10.50

Christmas A473

Children standing in front of windows — 180b: a, Girl holding sparkler. b, Boy holding artist's brush, ornament. c, Girl with kite. d, Boy with pinwheel. e, Girls playing musical instruments.

420b: f, Boy on wagon. g, Girl with yo-yo, doll. h, Boy with bell. i, Girl with spool and thread. j, Boy on skateboard.

**1998, Nov. 4**

**1607** A473 Sheet of 10, #a.-j. 10.50 10.50

America Issue — A474

Famous women: a, 180b, Teresa de la Parra (1889-1936), writer. b, 420b, Teresa Carreño (1853-1917), pianist.

**1998, Nov. 23**

**1608** A474 Pair, #a.-b. 2.25 2.25

William H. Phelps (1875-1965), Ornithologist A475

Portrait of Phelps and — 200b: a, Cephalopterus ornatus. b, Topaza pella. c, Grallaria excelsa phelpsi. d, Chrysolampis mosquitus. e, Tangara xanthogastra phelpsi.

300b: f, Radio transmitter. g, Mt. Phelps. h, Baseball and glove. i, Phelps Library. j, Cash register.

**1998, Dec. 4**

**1609** A475 Sheet of 10, #a.-j. 12.00 12.00

Msgr. Jesús Manuel Jáuregui Moreno (1848-1905) A476

Designs: a, Portrait as younger man. b, Christ on the cross. c, Our Mother of Angels Church. d, Madonna and Child. e, Portrait as older man.

**1999, Jan. 30** **Litho.** ***Perf. 12***

**1610** A476 500b Strip of 5, #a.-e. 8.75 8.75

Holy Sacrament for the Consecration of the Republic of Venezuela, Cent. A477

No. 1612: a, Man, elderly woman. b, Priest. c, Ostensorium (top). d, Boy with basketball, girl. e, Man, woman holding baby. f, Lady doctor. g, Woman. h, Ostensorium (base). i, Soldier. j, Native man holding spear.

500b, Hands of priest holding the Host.

**1999, June 16** **Litho.** ***Perf. 12***

**1611** A477 250b Sheet of 10, #a.-j. 8.25 8.25

**Souvenir Sheet**

**1612** A477 500b multicolored 1.60 1.60

No. 1612 contains one 42x37mm stamp.

Souvenir Sheet

Andino Parliament, 20th Anniv. — A478

**1999** **Litho.** ***Perf. 12***

**1613** A478 500b multi 1.50 1.50

Christmas A479

a, 500b, Betrothal of Joseph, Mary. b, 500b, Annunciation. c, 500b, Elizabeth, Mary. d, 500b, The search for lodging in Bethlehem. e, 500b, Birth of Jesus. f, 300b, Vision of the shepherds. g, 300b, Magi following star. h, 300b, Adoration of the Magi. i, 300b, Flight into Egypt. j, 300b, Slaughter of the innocents.

**1999, Nov. 5** ***Perf. 12x12¼***

**1614** A479 Sheet of 10, #a.-j. 12.00 12.00

**Souvenir Sheet**

Expo 2000, Hanover — A480

Illustration reduced.

**2000, July 8** **Litho.** ***Perf. 12***

**1615** A480 650b multi 2.10 2.10

2nd Summit of Heads of State and Government of OPEC Countries — A481

No. 1616 — Sites in Venezuela: a, 300b, Angel Falls. b, 300b, Llanos, Cojedes. c, 300b, Quebrada Jaspe. d, 300b, Morichal Largo. e, 300b, Auyantepuy, Carrao River. f, 400b, Lake Maracaibo. g, 400b, Humboldt Peak. h, 400b, Mochima. i, 400b, Morichal Largo River. j, 400b, Auyantepuy, from Uruyen.

No. 1617, 550b: a, Saudi Arabia. b, Algeria. c, United Arab Emirates. d, Indonesia. e, Iraq. f, Iran. g, Kuwait. h, Libya. i, Nigeria. j, Qatar.

**2000, Sept. 26** **Litho.** ***Perf. 12***

**Sheets of 10, #a-j**

**1616-1617** A481 Set of 2 27.50 27.50

Christmas — A482

No. 1618: a, 300b, Angel and "Gloria." b, 300b, Angel and "a." c, 650b, Angel and "Dios." d, 300b, Angel and "en los." e, 300b, Angel and "Cielos." f, 300b, Shepherd and lamb. g, 550b, Joseph. h, 650b, Jesus. i, 550b, Mary. j, 300b, Woman with water jar.

**2000, Nov. 29**

**1618** A482 Sheet of 10, #a-j 12.00 12.00

America Issue, A New Millennium Without Arms — A483

No. 1619: a, 300b, Finger in gun barrel. b, 650b, Man in heaven.

**2000, Dec. 14**

**1619** A483 Vert. pair, #a-b 2.75 2.75

Educational Building and Endowment Foundation, 25th Anniv. — A484

No. 1620 — School buildings in: a, Caracas. b, Vargas State. c, Portuguesa State. d, Mérida State. e, Yaracuy State.

**2001, May 9 Litho. *Perf. 12***

**1620** Horiz. strip of 5 4.75 4.75
*a.-c.* A484 300b Any single .85 .85
*d.-e.* A484 400b Any single 1.10 1.10

Orchids — A485

No. 1621: a, 200b, Galeottia jorisiana. b, 200b, Lycaste longipetala. c, 300b, Coryanthes albertinae. d, 300b, Hexisea bidentata. e, 400b, Lycaste macrophylla. f, 400b, Masdevallia maculata. g, 550b, Ada aurantiaca. h, 550f, Kefersteinia graminea. i, 550b, Sobralia liliastrum. j, 550b, Gongora maculata.
650b, Masdevallia tovarensis.

**2001, May 25**

**1621** A485 Sheet of 10, #a-j 20.00 20.00

**Souvenir Sheet**

**1622** A485 650b multi 3.25 3.25

Blessed Josemaría Escrivá de Balaguer (1902-75), Founder of Opus Dei — A486

No. 1623: a, 300b, Portrait. b, 300b, Bell of Nuestra Senora de los Angeles Church. c, 300b, Figure of Infant Jesus. d, 300b, Escrivá with men. e, 550b, Escrivá with women. f, 550f, Escrivá receiving doctorate, 1972. g, 550b, Escrivá with children, 1975. h, 300b, Commemorative plaque, Caracas Cathedral. i, 550b, Color portrait. j, 300b, Beatification ceremony, St. Peter's Square, Vatican City.

**2001, June 8**

**1623** A486 Sheet of 10, #a-j 20.00 20.00

Battle of Carabobo, 180th Anniv. A487

No. 1624: a, Thomas I. Ferriar. b, Bolívar in Buenavista, by Martín Tovar y Tovar. c, Quote by Simón Bolívar. d, Commemorative column. e, Pedro Camejo. f, José Antonio Páez, by Tovar y Tovar. g, Santiago Mariño, by Tovar y Tovar. h, Simón Bolívar, by M. Eberstein. i, Manuel Cedeño, by Tito Salas. j, Ambrosio Plaza, by Salas.

**2001, June 22**

**1624** Sheet of 10 23.00 23.00
*a.-e.* A487 400b Any single 1.10 1.10
*f.-j.* A487 600b Any single 1.60 1.60

Christmas — A488

Holy Family and angel with: a, 200b, Clarinet. b, 200b, Guitar. c, 220b, Lute. d, 220b, Trumpet. e, 280b, Violin. f, 280b, Harp. g, 400b, Bagpipes. h, 400b, Pan pipes. i, 500b, Drum. j, 500b, Stringed instrument.

**2001, Nov. 30 Litho. *Perf. 12***

**1625** A488 Sheet of 10, #a-j 15.00 15.00

Navigational Signaling, 160th Anniv. — A489

Navigational aids: a, Margarita Aqueduct buoy. b, BNFA buoy. c, Punta Brava lighthouse. d, Punta Macolla lighthouse. e, Los Roques lighthouse. f, Isla Redonda lighthouse. g, Punta Faragoza lighthouse. h, Punta Ballena lighthouse. i, Punta Tigre lighthouse. j, Recalada de Güiria lighthouse.

**2002, May 10 Litho. *Perf. 12***

**1626** Sheet of 10 12.00 12.00
*a.-b.* A489 300b Either single .60 .60
*c.-f.* A489 450b Any single .90 .90
*g.-j.* A489 500b Any single 1.00 1.00

Symbolic Incorporation of Guacaipuro into National Pantheon — A490

No. 1627: a, Tiaora and Caycape, sisters of Guacaipuro. b, Guacaipuro defeats Pedro de Miranda. c, Guacaipuro defeated by Juan Rodriguez Suárez. d, Killing in the gold mines. e, Death of Juan Rodriguez Suárez. f, Guacaipuro's escape from cabin fire. g, Death of Guacaipuro. h, Urquía, companion of Guacairpuro. i, Baruta, first son of Guacaipuro. j, Guacaipuro, Cacique of the Teques and Caracas people.

**2002, Oct. 29 Litho. *Perf. 12***

**1627** Sheet of 10 7.75 7.75
*a.* A490 200b multi .30 .30
*b-g.* A490 300b any single .45 .45
*h.* A490 350b multi .55 .55
*i.* A490 400b multi .60 .60
*j.* A490 500b multi .75 .75

Mission Robinson — A491

No. 1628: a, Toddler. b, Boy reading. c, Simón Bolívar and torch. d, Simón "Robinson" Rodriguez, Bolívar's teacher. e, Rodriguez and Eiffel Tower. f, Bolívar and flag. g, Bolívar and Rodriguez reading. h, Bolívar standing and Rodriguez seated. i, Rodriguez, men and women reading. j, Indians reading.

**2003, Sept. 19 Litho. *Perf. 12x12¼***

**1628** A491 Sheet of 10 7.50 7.50
*a.-d.* 300b Any single .35 .35
*e.-f.* 400b Either single .50 .50
*g.-j.* 500b Any single .65 .65

Agricultural, Fishery and Forestry Fund (FONDAFA) — A492

No. 1629: a, Cattle drive. b, Farmer plowing field. c, Row of tractors. d, Farmer tending crops. e, Corn in field. f, Boats. g, Ear of corn. h, Farmer in tractor in field. i, Cacao pods. j, Cacao beans.

**2003, Nov. 7 *Perf. 12***

**1629** A492 Sheet of 10 7.00 7.00
*a.-f.* 300b Any single .35 .35
*g.-h.* 400b Either single .50 .50
*i.-j.* 500b Either single .65 .65

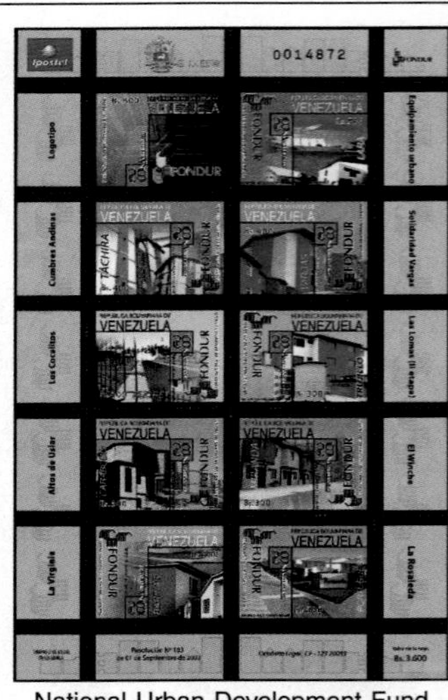

National Urban Development Fund (FONDUR), 28th Anniv. — A493

No. 1630: a, Barinas. b, Portuguesa. c, Carabobo. d, Miranda. e, Sucre. f, Trujillo. g, Táchira. h, Vargas. i, FONDUR emblem. j, Lara.

**2003, Dec. 16 Litho. *Perf. 14¼***

**1630** A493 Sheet of 10 4.50 4.50
*a.-f.* 300b Any single .35 .35
*g.-h.* 400b Either single .50 .50
*i.-j.* 500b Either single .65 .65

Natl. Urban Transportation Fund (FONTUR), 12th Anniv. — A494

No. 1631: a, Av. Uruguay, Lara. b, Carretera del Páramo, Merida. c, Av. Cumanan-Cumanacoa, Sucre. d, Carratera Santa Lucia, Barinas. e, Francissco Fajardo Expressway, Caracas. f, Students. g, Paraiso Tunnel, Caracas. h, VIVEX Module. i, Row of buses. j, Av. Cruz Paredes, Barinas.

**2003, Dec. 18 Litho. *Perf. 14¼***

**1631** A494 Sheet of 10 5.25 5.25
*a.-c.* 300b Any single .35 .35
*d.-f.* 400b Any single .50 .50
*g-j.* 500b Any single .65 .65

Natl. Telecommunications Commission (CONATEL) — A495

No. 1632: a, Three Amazonian children, two dogs and hammock. b, Caracas and mountain. c, Amazonian children with spears. d, Snow-covered Bolivar Peak. e, Amazonian child in canoe aiming arrow. f, Medina Beach. g, Amazonian children aiming arrows skyward.

h, Angel Falls. i, Amazonian children making baskets. j, Coro Dunes.

**2003, Dec. 23 Litho. *Perf. 12***

| | | | |
|---|---|---|---|
| **1632** A495 | Sheet of 10 | 5.25 | 5.25 |
| *a.-d.* | 300b Any single | .35 | .35 |
| *e.-f.* | 400b Either single | .50 | .50 |
| *g.-h.* | 500b Either single | .65 | .65 |
| *i.-j.* | 600b Either single | .75 | .75 |

Foundation for the Development of Community and Municipal Reconstruction (FUNDACOMUN), 42nd Anniv. — A496

No. 1633: a, Miranda. b, Trujillo. c, Mérida. d, Falcón. e, Vargas. f, Esparta. g, Caracas, denomination at left. h, Caracas, denomination at right. i, Barinas. j, Lara.

**2004, Mar. 10 Litho. *Perf. 12***

| | | | |
|---|---|---|---|
| **1633** A496 | Sheet of 10 | 4.50 | 4.50 |
| *a.-c.* | 300b Any single | .30 | .30 |
| *d.-f.* | 400b Any single | .45 | .45 |
| *g.-j.* | 500b Any single | .50 | .50 |

Barrio Adentro Mission — A497

No. 1634: a, Houses on hillside, people in doorway. b, Woman, house, ladder, people in alley. c, Woman, mother and child. d, Family, children. e, Boys playing baseball, boat. f, People near fence, man with cap. g, Man, sand dunes. h, Man with guitar, cows. i, Mountain, woman, cross and statue. j, Indians, river.

**2004, Mar. 24 *Perf. 12***

| | | | |
|---|---|---|---|
| **1634** A497 | Sheet of 10 | 10.50 | 10.50 |
| *a.-b.* | 300b Either single | .30 | .30 |
| *c.-f.* | 500b Any single | .50 | .50 |
| *g.* | 750b multi | .80 | .80 |
| *h.-i.* | 1500b Either single | 1.60 | 1.60 |
| *j.* | 1700b multi | 1.75 | 1.75 |

**Souvenir Sheet**

Design: 1000b, Man pushing wheelbarrow, horiz.

| | | | |
|---|---|---|---|
| **1634K** A497 | 1000b multi | 1.40 | 1.40 |

No. 1634K contains one 41x36mm stamp.

National Housing Institute (INAVI) — A498

No. 1635: a, Apartment block 6, El Silencio. b, El Pilar. c, Central section of apartment block 1, El Silencio. d, La Quiboreña. e, Apartment block 7, El Silencio. f, Santa Ana. g, Apartment block 144, El Silencio. h, La Quiracha. i, Architectural drawings of Caracas buildings. j, Los Peregrinos.

**2004, May 28 Litho. *Perf. 12***

| | | | |
|---|---|---|---|
| **1635** A498 | Sheet of 10 | 4.50 | 4.50 |
| *a.-c.* | 300b Any single | .30 | .30 |
| *d.-f.* | 400b Any single | .45 | .45 |
| *g.-j.* | 500b Any single | .55 | .55 |

National Aquatic Areas and Islands Institute (INEA) — A499

No. 1636: a, INEA emblem. b, INEA emblem and headquarters. c, Marine firefighters, boats. d, Firetruck, marine firefighter moving drum. e, Sunken tugboat Gran Roque. f, Underwater view of Gran Roque. g, Tugboats. h, Large ships at port. i, Starfish, religious statue. j, Boats and birds.

**2004, June 15**

| | | | |
|---|---|---|---|
| **1636** A499 | Sheet of 10 | 7.75 | 7.75 |
| *a.-b.* | 300b Either single | .30 | .30 |
| *c.-f.* | 500b Any single | .55 | .55 |
| *g.* | 600b multi | .60 | .60 |
| *h.* | 1000b multi | 1.00 | 1.00 |
| *i.* | 1500b multi | 1.60 | 1.60 |
| *j.* | 1700b multi | 1.75 | 1.75 |

A500

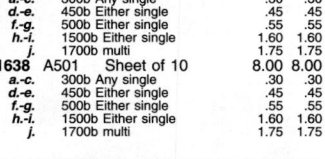

Latin American Parliament, 40th Anniv. — A501

No. 1637: a, Latin American Parliament emblem, 40th anniversary emblem. b, 40th anniversary emblem. c, Latin American Parliament flag and 40th anniversary emblem. d, Flags of member nations. e, Flags and Andrés Townsend Ezcurra. f, Flags and Luis Beltrán Prieto Figueroa. g, Flags and Nelson Carneiro. h, Plenary meeting room, Venezuela. i, Assembly hall, Sao Paolo. j, Latin American Parliament Building, Sao Paolo.

No. 1638: a, Latin American Parliament emblem. b, 40th Anniversary emblem. c, Mérida Session emblem. d, Charter of Social Rights. e, Flags and map of Latin America. f, Flag and map of Panama. g, Táchira Session emblem. h, Bird with ball and chain (social debt). i, Simón Bolivar. j, Constitutional Hypothesis.

**2004, July 12**

| | | | |
|---|---|---|---|
| **1637** A500 | Sheet of 10 | 8.00 | 8.00 |
| *a.-c.* | 300b Any single | .30 | .30 |
| *d.-e.* | 450b Either single | .45 | .45 |
| *f.-g.* | 500b Either single | .55 | .55 |
| *h.-i.* | 1500b Either single | 1.60 | 1.60 |
| *j.* | 1700b multi | 1.75 | 1.75 |
| **1638** A501 | Sheet of 10 | 8.00 | 8.00 |
| *a.-c.* | 300b Any single | .30 | .30 |
| *d.-e.* | 450b Either single | .45 | .45 |
| *f.-g.* | 500b Either single | .55 | .55 |
| *h.-i.* | 1500b Either single | 1.60 | 1.60 |
| *j.* | 1700b multi | 1.75 | 1.75 |

CVG Edelca, 40th Anniv. — A502

No. 1639: a, Macagua Hydroelectric Station and Dam,, Ciudad Guayana. b, Electric transmission towers and lines. c, Electrical power equipment. d, Room, Guri. e, Native people. f, Guri Hydroelectric Station and Dam. g, Streetlights near Macagua Hydroelectric Station and Dam. h, Solar tower, by Alejandro Otero. i, Dam, Ecomuseum, Caroní. j, Gran Sabana.

No. 1640, Guri Hydroelectric Station and Dam.

**2004, July 29**

| | | | |
|---|---|---|---|
| **1639** A502 | Sheet of 10 | 6.50 | 6.50 |
| *a.-b.* | 300b Either single | .30 | .30 |
| *c.* | 400b multi | .45 | .45 |
| *d.-g.* | 500b Any single | .55 | .55 |
| *h.* | 600b multi | .60 | .60 |
| *i.* | 1000b multi | 1.00 | 1.00 |
| *j.* | 1500b multi | 1.60 | 1.60 |

**Souvenir Sheet**

| | | | |
|---|---|---|---|
| **1640** A502 | 1000b multi | 1.00 | 1.00 |

No. 1640 contains one 41x36mm stamp.

United Nations Population Fund — A503

No. 1641 — Inscriptions: a, Los y las adolescentes . . . b, El comporttmiento . . . c, Las niñas tienen . . . d, Los seres humanos . . . e, Promovamos el empoderamiento . . . f, Los derechjos reproductivos . . . g, Por una maternidad sin riesgo. h, El derecho al desarrollo . . . i, Eliminemos la violencia . . . j, El condón protege vidas.

**2004, Sept. 15**

| | | | |
|---|---|---|---|
| **1641** A503 | Sheet of 10 | 8.25 | 8.25 |
| *a.-d.* | 500b Any single | .55 | .55 |
| *e.-j.* | 1000b Any single | 1.00 | 1.00 |

National Parks Institute (INPARQUES) — A504

No. 1642 — Parks and: a, Food. b, Education. c, Recreation. d, Water. e, Landscapes. f, Biodiversity. g, Conservation. h, Electricity. i, Tourism. j, Ethnic people.

**2004, Oct. 11 Litho. *Perf. 14¼x14½***

| | | | |
|---|---|---|---|
| **1642** A504 | Sheet of 10 | 6.50 | 6.50 |
| *a.-b.* | 300b Either single | .30 | .30 |
| *c.* | 400b multi | .40 | .40 |
| *d.-g.* | 500b Any single | .55 | .55 |

| | | | |
|---|---|---|---|
| *h.* | 600b multi | .60 | .60 |
| *i.* | 1000b multi | 1.10 | 1.10 |
| *j.* | 1500b multi | 1.60 | 1.60 |

National Tax and Customs Administration (SENIAT) — A505

No. 1643 — Inscriptions: a, Aporte a la educación, cultura y deporte (children). b, Aporte a la salud. c, Dile no al contrabando. d, Con tus tributos . . . e, Aporte a la educación, cultura y deporte (baseball players). f, Construcción de futuras . . . g, Aporte a la vialidad. h, Bienvenidos a un país . . . i, Aporte a la educación, cultura y deporte (building and palm tree). j, Aporte a la educación, cultura y deporte (modern building and sculpture).

**2004, Oct. 15 Litho. *Perf. 12***

| | | | | |
|---|---|---|---|---|
| **1643** | A505 | Sheet of 10 | 8.25 | 8.25 |
| *a.-d.* | | 500b Any single | .55 | .55 |
| *e.-j.* | | 1000b Any single | 1.00 | 1.00 |

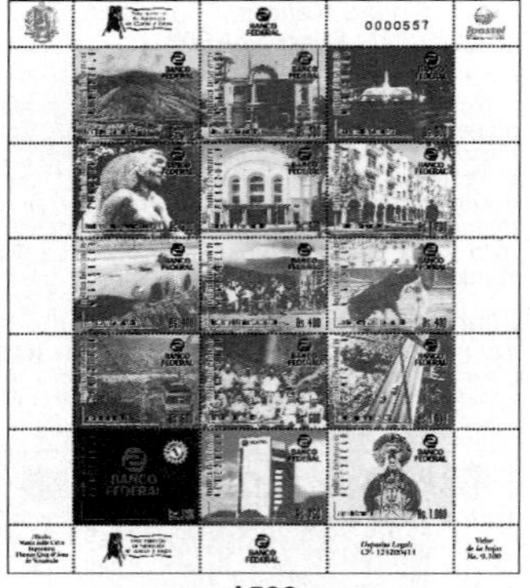

A506

Banco Federal — A507

No. 1644: a, Cerro El Avila, Caracas, 1945. b, Nuevo Circo, Caracas, 1970. c, Plaza Venezuela, Caracas, 1943. d, Sculpture by Francisco Narváez, Caracas, 1940. e, Baralt Theater, Maracaibo, 1883. f, Los Próceres, Caracas, 1956. g, El Paraíso Horse Track, Caracas, 1908. h, Bullfighter Luis Sánchez Olivares, Caracas, 1950. i, Funicular, Mérida, 1954. j, Angel Falls, Bolivar State, 1937. k, Banco Federal emblem, gold star. l, Banco Federal Building (sepia). m, Lake Bridge, Maracaibo, 1962. n, Virgin of Coromoto (sepia). o, El Silencio, Caracas, 1945.

No. 1645: a, San Fernando de Apure Church. b, Caracas Cathedral. c, Coro Cathedral. d, Santa Inés de Cumaná Cathedral. e, Our Lady of Chiquinquirá Basilica. f, Our Lady of Coromoto Basilica. g, St. Rose of Lima Church, Ortíz. h, Mérida Cathedral. i, Our Lady of the Assumption Cathedral. j, San Cristóbal Cathedral. k, Banco Federal emblem, silver star. l, Banco Federal Building (full color). m, Barquisimeto Cathedral. n, Virgin of Coromoto (full color). o, Valencia Cathedral.

**2005, Jan. 20 Litho. *Perf. 14¼x14½***

| | | | | |
|---|---|---|---|---|
| **1644** | A506 | Sheet of 15 | 9.50 | 9.50 |
| *a.-e.* | | 300b Any single | .30 | .30 |
| *f.-h.* | | 400b Any single | .40 | .40 |
| *i.-j.* | | 600b Either single | .60 | .60 |
| *k.-l.* | | 750b Either single | .80 | .80 |
| *m.-n.* | | 1000b Either single | 1.10 | 1.10 |
| *o.* | | 1700b multi | 1.75 | 1.75 |
| **1645** | A507 | Sheet of 15 | 9.50 | 9.50 |
| *a.-e.* | | 300b Any single | .30 | .30 |
| *f.-h.* | | 400b Any single | .40 | .40 |
| *i.-j.* | | 600b Either single | .60 | .60 |
| *k.-l.* | | 750b Either single | .80 | .80 |
| *m.-n.* | | 1000b Either single | 1.10 | 1.10 |
| *o.* | | 1700b multi | 1.75 | 1.75 |

Christmas — A508

No. 1646 — Creche figures from various states: a, Bolívar. b, Falcón. c, Mérida. d, Aragua. e, Miranda. f, Miranda, diff. g, Falcón, diff. h, Zulia. i, Bolívar, diff. j, Trujillo.

**2004, Dec. 23 *Perf. 12***

| | | | | |
|---|---|---|---|---|
| **1646** | A508 | Sheet of 10 | 7.50 | 7.50 |
| *a.-b.* | | 300b Either single | .30 | .30 |
| *c.-d.* | | 400b Either single | .40 | .40 |
| *e.* | | 600b multi | .60 | .60 |
| *f.-g.* | | 750b Either single | .75 | .75 |
| *h.-i.* | | 1000b Either single | 1.10 | 1.10 |
| *j.* | | 1700b multi | 1.75 | 1.75 |

**Souvenir Sheet**

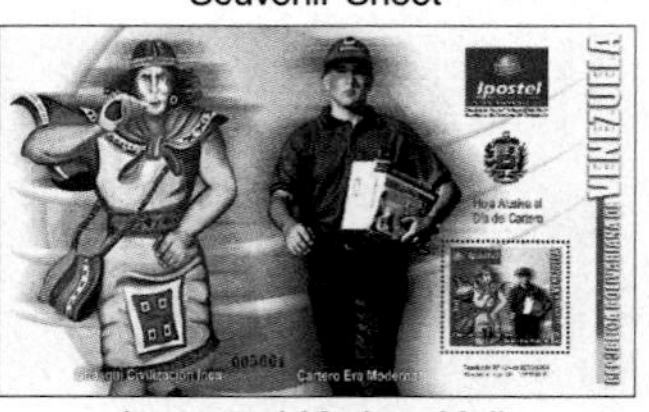

Incan and Modern Mail Deliverers — A509

**2004 *Perf. 12***

| | | | | |
|---|---|---|---|---|
| **1647** | A509 | 1000b multi | 1.10 | 1.10 |

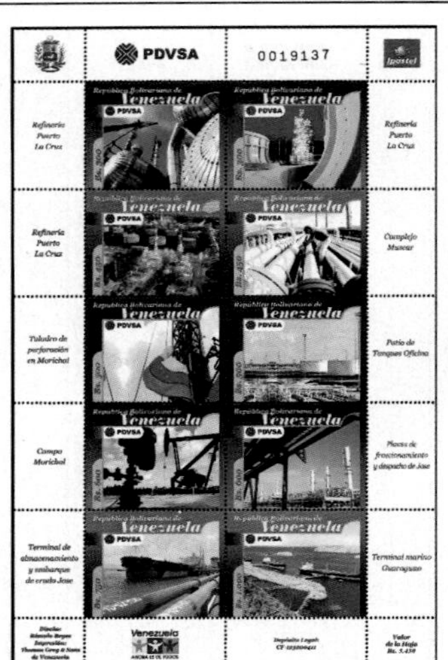

Petróleos de Venezuela, S. A. — A510

No. 1648: a, Crane above turbines, Puerto La Cruz Refinery. b, Night view of tower Puerto La Cruz Refinery. c, Aerial view of Puerto La Cruz refinery. d, Man inspecting pipes. e, Crane and Venezuelan flag. f, Storage tanks. g, Oil wells. h, Refinery towers. i, Oil tanker and pipes. j, Tankers at Guaraguao Marine Terminal.

**2004, Nov. 24 Litho. *Perf. 14¼***

| | | | | |
|---|---|---|---|---|
| **1648** | A510 | Sheet of 10 | 5.75 | 5.75 |
| *a.-b.* | | 300b Either single | .30 | .30 |
| *c.-d.* | | 450b Either single | .45 | .45 |
| *e.-f.* | | 500b Either single | .50 | .50 |
| *g.-h.* | | 600b Either single | .65 | .65 |
| *i.* | | 750b multi | .80 | .80 |
| *j.* | | 1000b multi | 1.10 | 1.10 |

Mountains — A511

Designs: No. 1649, Bolivar Peak, Venezuela. No. 1650, Mt. Damavand, Iran.

**2004 Litho. *Perf. 13***

| | | | | |
|---|---|---|---|---|
| **1649** | A511 | 1700b multi | 1.90 | 1.90 |
| **1650** | A511 | 1700b multi | 1.90 | 1.90 |
| *a.* | | Horiz. pair, #1649-1650 | 3.80 | 3.80 |

No. 1650 has "Republica Bolivariana de Venezuela" overprinted in black over vignette. No. 1650 exists without overprint.

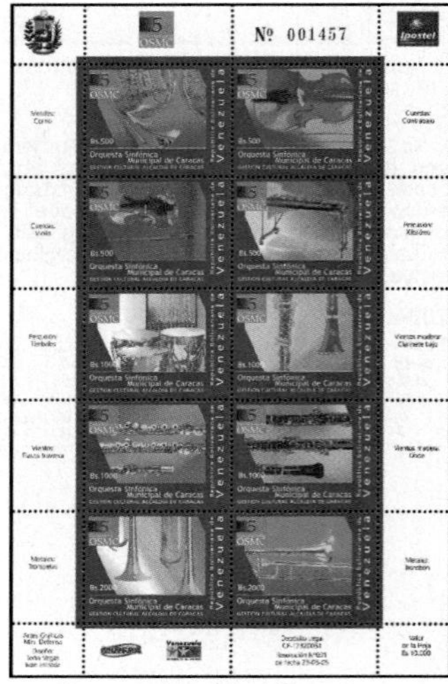

Caracas Municipal Symphony Orchestra, 25th Anniv. — A512

No. 1651: a, French horns. b, Bass (in blue) and bow. c, Violin and bow. d, Marimba. e, Timpani. f, Clarinets. g, Flutes. h, Oboes. i, Trumpets. j, Trombone.

**2005 *Perf. 12***

| | | | | |
|---|---|---|---|---|
| **1651** | A512 | Sheet of 10 | 9.50 | 9.50 |
| *a.-d.* | | 500b Any single | .45 | .45 |
| *e.-h.* | | 1000b Any single | .95 | .95 |
| *i.-j.* | | 2000b Either single | 1.90 | 1.90 |

16th World Youth and Student Festival — A513

No. 1652: a, Festival emblems from 1947-59. b, Festival emblems from 1962-2005. c, Festival emblem and joined arms. d, Festival emblem and text of Simón Bolívar's Vow of Monte Sacro. e, Festival emblem and Bolívar with outstretched arm, signature of Bolívar. f, Festival emblem and broken chain. g, Festival emblem, Bolívar. h, Festival emblem, dove. i, Festival emblem, dove, globe and hands. j, Festival emblem and hands.

1000b, Festival emblem and Bolívar with outstretched arm, horiz.

**2005, Aug. 5 Litho. *Perf. 12***

| | | | | |
|---|---|---|---|---|
| **1652** | A513 | Sheet of 10 | 5.00 | 5.00 |
| *a.-d.* | | 300b Any single | .30 | .30 |
| *e.-i.* | | 500b Any single | .45 | .45 |
| *j.* | | 1500b multi | 1.40 | 1.40 |

**Souvenir Sheet**

***Perf. 12x11¾***

| | | | | |
|---|---|---|---|---|
| **1653** | A513 | 1000b multi | 1.10 | 1.10 |

No. 1653 contains one 41x36mm stamp.

IPOSTEL — A514

No. 1654: a, IPOSTEL emblem, flag, Caracas Post Office. b, Postal vans. c, IPOSTEL emblem on envelope, Caracas Post Office. d, Postal motorcycles. e, Carmelitas Post Office. f, Airplane, postal bicycles. g, Falcón Post Office. h, Mail carriers. i, Zulia Post Office. j, Postal workers in San Martín.

No. 1655: a, Man, IPOSTEL emblem, letters. b, Postal worker, mail sacks. c, Mail on conveyor belt. d, Mail carriers with parcels. e, Postal workers sorting mail. f, Postal workers at Ribas Mission. g, Mail sacks. h, Doctor, medical equipment at Barrio Adentro Mission. i, Postal worker and postal machinery. j, Forklift and Mercal emblem.

**2005, Oct. 10 *Perf. 12***

| | | | | |
|---|---|---|---|---|
| **1654** | A514 | Sheet of 10 | 9.25 | 9.25 |
| *a.-b.* | | 300b Either single | .30 | .30 |
| *c.-d.* | | 400b Either single | .35 | .35 |
| *e.-f.* | | 600b Either single | .55 | .55 |
| *g.-i.* | | 1700b Any single | 1.60 | 1.60 |
| *j.* | | 2000b multi | 1.90 | 1.90 |
| **1655** | A514 | Sheet of 10 | 9.25 | 9.25 |
| *a.-b.* | | 300b Either single | .30 | .30 |
| *c.-d.* | | 400b Either single | .35 | .35 |
| *e.-f.* | | 600b Either single | .55 | .55 |
| *g.-i.* | | 1700b Any single | 1.60 | 1.60 |
| *j.* | | 2000b multi | 1.90 | 1.90 |

Central Bank of Venezuela, 65th Anniv. — A515

No. 1656: a, Bank emblem. b, Caracas branch. c, Maracaibo branch. d, Venezuela Mint. e, Children's economic educational program. f, Numismatic Museum. g, Plaza Juan Pedro López. h, Gold bars. i, Bank notes and printing plates. j, Coins.

**2005, Oct. 20** ***Perf. 12½x13½***

| | | | | |
|---|---|---|---|---|
| **1656** | A515 | Sheet of 10 | 8.50 | 8.50 |
| ***a.-b.*** | | 300b Either single | .30 | .30 |
| ***c.-d.*** | | 400b Either single | .35 | .35 |
| ***e.-f.*** | | 600b Either single | .55 | .55 |
| ***g.-h.*** | | 1500b Either single | 1.40 | 1.40 |
| ***i.-j.*** | | 1700b Either single | 1.60 | 1.60 |

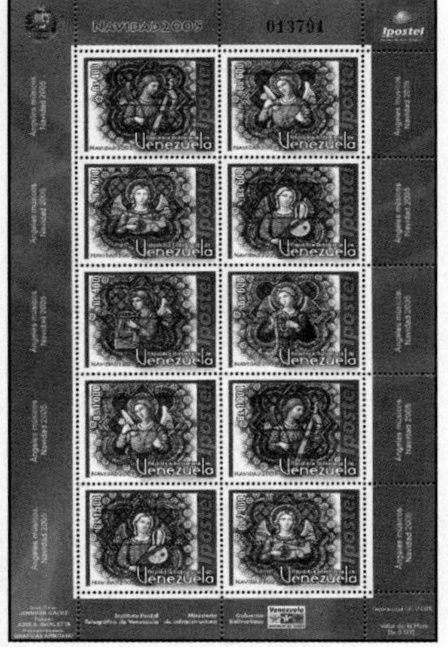

Christmas — A516

No. 1657 — Angel with: a, h, Long-necked stringed instrument with bow. b, j, Lute. c, Harp. d, g, Maracas. e, i, Stringed instrument with bow. f, Horn.

**2005, Dec. 1** ***Perf. 12***

| | | | | |
|---|---|---|---|---|
| **1657** | A516 | Sheet of 10 | 8.00 | 8.00 |
| ***a.-c.*** | | 400b Any single | .35 | .35 |
| ***d.-f.*** | | 600b Any single | .55 | .55 |
| ***g.-h.*** | | 1000b Either single | .95 | .95 |
| ***i.*** | | 1500b multi | 1.40 | 1.40 |
| ***j.*** | | 2000b multi | 1.90 | 1.90 |

National Guard — A517

No. 1658: a, Villa Zoila. b, Troops and building with ornate roof. c, Troops and automobiles. d, Troops saluting. e, Helicopter. f, Troops in inflatable raft. g, Three guardsmen at industrial site. h, Two guardsmen inspecting boxes. i, Guardsman with drug-sniffing dog. j, Guardsman, children.

**2006, Feb. 23**

| | | | | |
|---|---|---|---|---|
| **1658** | A517 | Sheet of 10 | 8.50 | 8.50 |
| ***a.-d.*** | | 300b Any single | .30 | .30 |
| ***e.-f.*** | | 400b Either single | .35 | .35 |
| ***g.-h.*** | | 1500b Either single | 1.40 | 1.40 |
| ***i.-j.*** | | 2000b Either single | 1.90 | 1.90 |

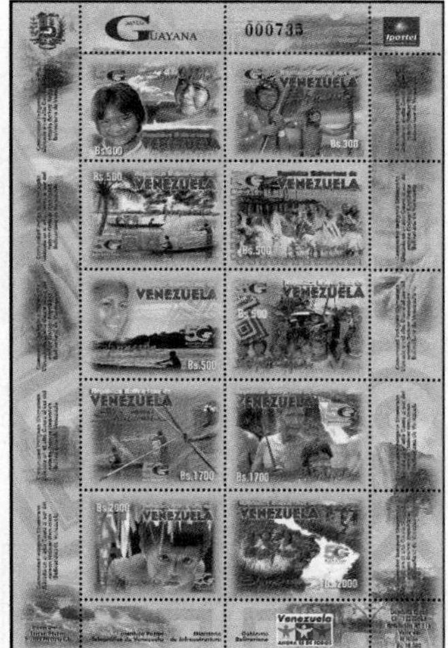

Banco Guayana, 50th Anniv. — A518

No. 1659 — Shimaraña people: a, People with painted faces. b, Archer and man with spear. c, Canoes on water. d, Women near dock. e, Man in canoe, woman's face. f, Children. g, Bow fishermen. h, Men, child, waterfall. i, Child. j, Women, dancer and river.

**2006, Mar. 16**

| | | | | |
|---|---|---|---|---|
| **1659** | A518 | Sheet of 10 | 9.50 | 9.50 |
| ***a.-b.*** | | 300b Either single | .30 | .30 |
| ***c.-f.*** | | 500b Any single | .45 | .45 |
| ***g.-h.*** | | 1700b Either single | 1.60 | 1.60 |
| ***i.-j.*** | | 2000b Either single | 1.90 | 1.90 |

National Tax and Customs Administration (SENIAT) — A519

No. 1660 — Customs buildings in: a, Valencia. b, Puerto Cabello. c, Paraguachón. d, Santa Elena de Uairén. e, Maiquetia (in day). f, Maiquetia (at night). g, Ureña. h, Táchira. i, Barcelona. j, La Guaira.

**2006, Mar. 22**

| | | | | |
|---|---|---|---|---|
| **1660** | A519 | Sheet of 10 | 8.75 | 8.75 |
| ***a.-b.*** | | 400b Either single | .35 | .35 |
| ***c.-d.*** | | 500b Either single | .45 | .45 |
| ***e.-f.*** | | 700b Either single | .65 | .65 |
| ***g.-h.*** | | 1000b Either single | .95 | .95 |
| ***i.-j.*** | | 2000b Either single | 1.90 | 1.90 |

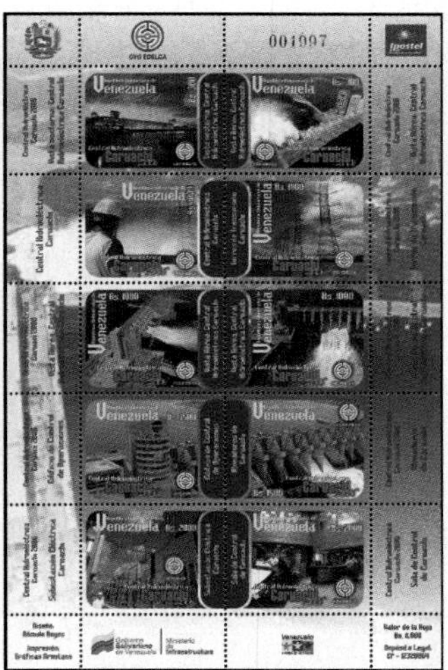

Carauchi Hydroelectric Dam Project — A520

No. 1661: a, Dam at night. b, Aerial view of dam. c, Worker at dam. d, Power lines. e, Aerial view of dam, water flowing to right. f, Aerial view of dam, water flowing straight ahead, descriptive text at left. g, Control tower. h, Spillway. i, Electrical substation. j, Control room.

No. 1662 — Rescued animals: a, Iguana iguana. b, Caluromys philander. c, Paleosuchus palpebrosus. d, Geochelone carbonaria. e, Cebus olivaceus. f, Choloepus didactylus. g, Tupinambis teguixin. h, Lora bejuca. i, Coendou prehensilis. j, Tamandua tetradactyla.

No. 1663, Aerial view of dam, water flowing straight ahead, descriptive text at top.

**2006, Apr. 6**

| | | | | |
|---|---|---|---|---|
| **1661** | A520 | Sheet of 10 | 11.00 | 11.00 |
| ***a.-b.*** | | 300b Either single | .30 | .30 |
| ***c.-f.*** | | 1000b Any single | .95 | .95 |
| ***g.-h.*** | | 1500b Either single | 1.40 | 1.40 |
| ***i.-j.*** | | 2000b Either single | 1.90 | 1.90 |
| **1662** | A520 | Sheet of 10 | 11.00 | 11.00 |
| ***a.-b.*** | | 300b Either single | .30 | .30 |
| ***c.-f.*** | | 1000b Any single | .95 | .95 |
| ***g.-h.*** | | 1500b Either single | 1.40 | 1.40 |
| ***i.-j.*** | | 2000b Either single | 1.90 | 1.90 |

**Souvenir Sheet**

| | | | | |
|---|---|---|---|---|
| **1663** | A520 | 1000b multi | .95 | .95 |

No. 1663 contains one 42x37mm stamp.

141st Extraordinary Meeting of OPEC A521

No. 1664 — Petroleum facilities, meeting emblem and: a, "OPEP". b, Flag of United Arab Emirates flag. c, Flag of Libya. d, Flag of Iraq. e, Flag of Saudi Arabia. f, Flag of Indonesia. g, Flag of Nigeria. h, Flag of Algeria. i, Flag of Iran. j, Flag of Qatar. k, Flag of Venezuela. l, Flag of Kuwait.

**2006, June 1**

| | | | | |
|---|---|---|---|---|
| **1664** | | Sheet of 12 | 10.00 | 10.00 |
| ***a.-b.*** | A521 | 300b Either single | .30 | .30 |
| ***c.-h.*** | A521 | 500b Any single | .45 | .45 |
| ***i.-j.*** | A521 | 1500b Either single | 1.40 | 1.40 |
| ***k.-l.*** | A521 | 2000b Either single | 1.90 | 1.90 |

Caracas Mass Transit — A522

No. 1665: a, Train on Yellow line. b, Yellow line station. c, Plaza Venezuela Station. d, Three trains. e, Train switches. f, Line 4 Tunnel. g, Metro bus. h, Control room. i, Construction of Line 4 Nuevo Circo Station. j, Art by Jesús Soto, Chacaíto Station.

**2006, July 2**

| | | | | |
|---|---|---|---|---|
| **1665** | A522 | Sheet of 10 | 12.00 | 12.00 |
| ***a.-b.*** | | 300b Either single | .30 | .30 |
| ***c.-d.*** | | 500b Either single | .45 | .45 |
| ***e.-f.*** | | 1500b Either single | 1.40 | 1.40 |
| ***g.-j.*** | | 2000b Any single | 1.90 | 1.90 |

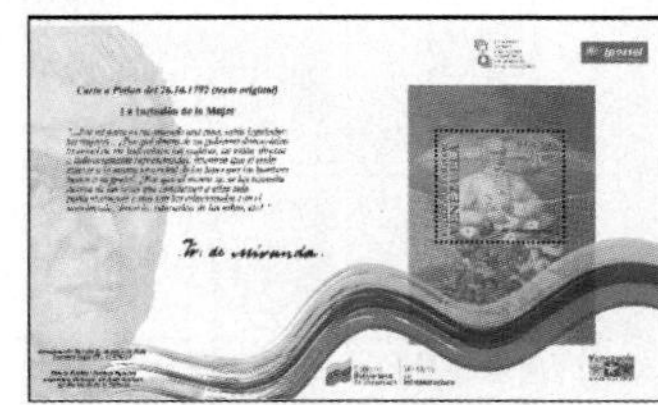

Francisco de Miranda University — A523

No. 1666, vert.: a, Miranda on horse. b, Miranda facing left. c, Nose, mouth and hand of Miranda. d, Statue of Miranda, Venezuelan flag. e, Miranda holding flag. f, Miranda at Venezuelan independence ceremonies. g, Miranda. h, Statues of Miranda. i, Miranda facing right. j, Miranda writing letter, ship.

No. 1667, Like #1666j.

**2006, July 28**

| | | | | |
|---|---|---|---|---|
| **1666** | A523 | Sheet of 10 | 8.75 | 8.75 |
| ***a.-d.*** | | 300b Any single | .30 | .30 |
| ***e.-f.*** | | 500b Either single | .45 | .45 |
| ***g.-h.*** | | 1500b Either single | 1.40 | 1.40 |
| ***i.-j.*** | | 2000b Either single | 1.90 | 1.90 |

**Souvenir Sheet**

| | | | | |
|---|---|---|---|---|
| **1667** | A523 | 1500b multi | 1.40 | 1.40 |

No. 1666 contains ten 35x45mm stamps.

Children's Art — A524

No. 1668: a, Flag of Liberty, by Elimar Sanchez. b, Miranda (Miranda and broken chain), by Gabriel Solano. c, Miranda and Catalina, by Elikarina Sánchez. d, Musical Aspects of Miranda (G clef), by Josmelys Díaz. e, Miranda Playing, by Nasser Sultan. f, Miranda and His Dreams, by Cynthia Urbina. g, Flag of Miranda, by Janem Sultan. h, Miranda Thinking, by Luis Miguel Martínez. i, Miranda and His Family, by Vianny Gonella. j, Diary of Miranda, by José A. Martínez.

**2006**

| | | | | |
|---|---|---|---|---|
| **1668** | A524 | Sheet of 10 | 8.75 | 8.75 |
| *a.-d.* | | 300b Any single | .30 | .30 |
| *e.-f.* | | 500b Either single | .45 | .45 |
| *g.-h.* | | 1500b Either single | 1.40 | 1.40 |
| *i.-j.* | | 2000b Either single | 1.90 | 1.90 |

Souvenir Sheet

CVG EDELCA, 43rd Anniv. — A525

**2006**

| | | | | |
|---|---|---|---|---|
| **1669** | A525 | 3500b multi | 3.25 | 3.25 |

Central University, Caracas — A526

No. 1670: a, Exterior of Engineering Library. b, Interior of Engineering Library. c, Electrical Engineering Building. d, School of Engineering, Metallurgy and Material Sciences, Sculpture by Harry Abend. e, School of Civil Engineering. f, School of Chemical Engineering, Petroleum and Geology, Mines and Geophysics. g, Mural by Alejandro Otero at School of Engineering. h, Machinery at Institute of Materials and Structural Models. i, Fluid Mechanics Institute. j, Aulas Auditorium.

**2006**

| | | | | |
|---|---|---|---|---|
| **1670** | A526 | Sheet of 10 | 17.50 | 17.50 |
| *a.-d.* | | 400b Any single | .35 | .35 |
| *e.-f.* | | 600b Either single | .55 | .55 |
| *g.-h.* | | 3000b Either single | 2.75 | 2.75 |
| *i.-j.* | | 5000b Either single | 4.75 | 4.75 |

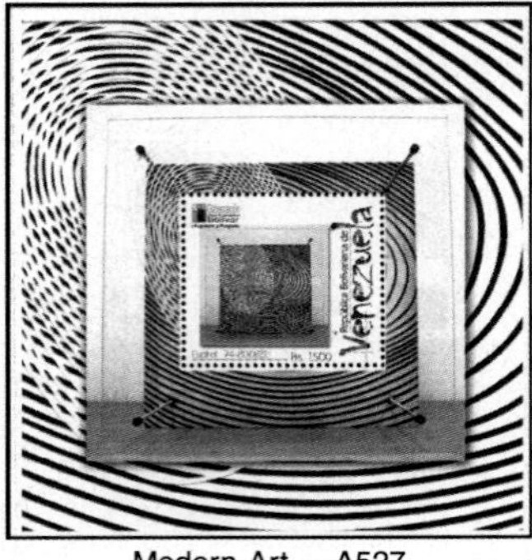

Modern Art — A527

No. 1671: a, Esfera Japón. b, Biface Naranja. c, Repetición y Progresión. d, Repetición Optica No. 2. e, Composición Dinámica. f, Muro Optico. g, Pardelas Interferentes. h, Espiral. i, Ambivalencia Dicembre. j, Estructura Cinética.
1500b, Espiral, diff.

**2006**

| | | | | |
|---|---|---|---|---|
| **1671** | A527 | Sheet of 10 | 6.25 | 6.25 |
| *a.-b.* | | 300b Either single | .30 | .30 |
| *c.-f.* | | 500b Any single | .45 | .45 |
| *g.-j.* | | 1000b Any single | .95 | .95 |

**Souvenir Sheet**

| | | | | |
|---|---|---|---|---|
| **1672** | A527 | 1500b multi | 1.40 | 1.40 |

No. 1671 contains ten 45x35mm stamps.

Transportation — A528

No. 1673: a, Airplane in flight. b, Simón Bolívar Intl. Airport, Maiquetía. c, Highway, Ayacucho. d, Highway, Barquisimeto. e, José Antonio Páez Highway. f, Caracas — La Guaira Viaduct. g, Line 3, Caracas Metro. h, Line 4, Caracas Metro. i, Maracaibo Metro. j, Teques Metro. k, Valencia Metro. l, Caracas — Tuy Medio tram.

**2006**

| | | | | |
|---|---|---|---|---|
| **1673** | A528 | Sheet of 12 | 13.50 | 13.50 |
| *a.-g.* | | 300b Any single | .30 | .30 |
| *h.-j.* | | 2000b Any single | 1.90 | 1.90 |
| *k.-l.* | | 3000b Either single | 2.75 | 2.75 |

A529

Christmas — A530

No. 1674: a, Musicians. b, Toy. c, Top. d, Holiday table setting. e, Food. f, Letter to Baby Jesus. g, Illuminated cross. h, Yo-yo. i, Yo-yo, top and toy. j, Envelope with Holy Family.
No. 1675: a, Nativity. b, Food. c, Letter to Baby Jesus. d, IPOSTEL emblem with Holy Family.

**2006**

| | | | | |
|---|---|---|---|---|
| **1674** | A529 | Sheet of 10 | 9.00 | 9.00 |
| *a.-b.* | | 300b Either single | .30 | .30 |
| *c.-d.* | | 450b Either single | .40 | .40 |
| *e.-f.* | | 550b Either single | .50 | .50 |
| *g.-h.* | | 1000b Either single | .95 | .95 |
| *i.* | | 2000b multi | 1.90 | 1.90 |
| *j.* | | 3000b multi | 2.75 | 2.75 |
| **1675** | A530 | Sheet of 4 | 3.50 | 3.50 |
| *a.-b.* | | 300b Either single | .30 | .30 |
| *c.* | | 1000b multi | .95 | .95 |
| *d.* | | 2000b multi | 1.90 | 1.90 |

## SEMI-POSTAL STAMPS

A 5c green stamp of the Cruzada Venezolana Sanitaria Social portraying Simon Bolivar was overprinted "EE. UU. DE VENEZUELA CORREOS" in 1937.

It is stated that 50,000 copies without control numbers on back were sold by post offices and 147,700 with control numbers on back were offered for sale by the Society at eight times face value.

Bolívar Funeral Carriage SP1

**Unwmk.**

**1942, Dec. 17** **Engr.** ***Perf. 12***

| | | | | |
|---|---|---|---|---|
| **B1** | SP1 | 20c + 5c blue | 4.50 | .50 |

Cent. of the arrival of Simón Bolívar's remains in Caracas. The surtax was used to erect a monument to his memory. See Nos. CB1-CB2.

**Catalogue values for unused stamps in this section, from this point to the end of the section, are for Never Hinged items.**

Red Cross Nurse — SP2

**1975, Dec. 15** **Litho.** ***Perf. 14***

| | | | | |
|---|---|---|---|---|
| **B2** | SP2 | 30c + 15c multi | .30 | .20 |
| **B3** | SP2 | 50c + 25c multi | .45 | .30 |

Surtax for Venezuelan Red Cross.

Carmen América Fernandez de Leoni — SP3

Children in Home — SP4

**1976, June 7** **Litho.** ***Perf. 13½***

| | | | | |
|---|---|---|---|---|
| **B4** | SP3 | 30c + 15c multi | .25 | .20 |
| **B5** | SP4 | 50c + 25c multi | .45 | .30 |

Surtax was for the Children's Foundation, founded by Carmen América Fernandez de Leoni in 1966.

Patient — SP5

**1976, Dec. 8** **Litho.** ***Perf. 14***

| | | | | |
|---|---|---|---|---|
| **B6** | SP5 | 10c + 5c multi | .20 | .20 |
| **B7** | SP5 | 30c + 10c multi | .25 | .20 |

Surtax was for Anti-tuberculosis Society.

## AIR POST STAMPS

Air post stamps of 1930-42 perforated "GN" (Gobierno Nacional) were for official use.

Airplane and Map of Venezuela
AP1 AP2

**1930** **Unwmk.** **Litho.** ***Perf. 12***

| | | | | | |
|---|---|---|---|---|---|
| **C1** | AP1 | 5c | bister brn | .20 | .20 |
| **C2** | AP1 | 10c | yellow | .20 | .20 |
| *a.* | | 10c salmon | | 32.50 | 32.50 |
| **C3** | AP1 | 15c | gray | .20 | .20 |
| **C4** | AP1 | 25c | lilac | .20 | .20 |
| **C5** | AP1 | 40c | olive grn | .20 | .20 |
| *a.* | | 40c slate blue | | 40.00 | |
| *b.* | | 40c slate green | | 40.00 | |
| **C6** | AP1 | 75c | dp red | .25 | .20 |
| **C7** | AP1 | 1b | indigo | .40 | .20 |
| **C8** | AP1 | 1.20b | blue grn | .60 | .30 |
| **C9** | AP1 | 1.70b | dk blue | .75 | .40 |
| **C10** | AP1 | 1.90b | blue grn | .75 | .45 |
| **C11** | AP1 | 2.10b | dk blue | 1.50 | .60 |
| **C12** | AP1 | 2.30b | vermilion | 1.50 | .45 |
| **C13** | AP1 | 2.50b | dk blue | 1.50 | .45 |
| **C14** | AP1 | 3.70b | blue grn | 1.50 | 1.00 |
| **C15** | AP1 | 10b | dull vio | 4.50 | 2.25 |
| **C16** | AP1 | 20b | gray grn | 7.00 | 4.25 |
| | | *Nos. C1-C16 (16)* | | 21.25 | 11.55 |

Nos. C1-C16 exist imperforate or partly perforated. See Nos. C119-C126.

Issued: 10b, June 8; 20b, June 16; others, Apr. 5.

Bluish Winchester Security Paper

**1932, July 12** **Engr.** ***Perf. 12½***

| | | | | | |
|---|---|---|---|---|---|
| **C17** | AP2 | 5c | brown | .40 | .20 |
| **C18** | AP2 | 10c | org yel | .40 | .20 |
| **C19** | AP2 | 15c | gray lilac | .40 | .20 |
| **C20** | AP2 | 25c | violet | .40 | .20 |
| **C21** | AP2 | 40c | ol grn | .80 | .20 |
| **C22** | AP2 | 70c | rose | .55 | .20 |
| **C23** | AP2 | 75c | red org | 1.00 | .20 |
| **C24** | AP2 | 1b | dk bl | 1.10 | .20 |
| **C25** | AP2 | 1.20b | green | 2.25 | .85 |
| **C26** | AP2 | 1.70b | red brn | 4.50 | .55 |
| **C27** | AP2 | 1.80b | ultra | 2.25 | .35 |
| **C28** | AP2 | 1.90b | green | 5.50 | 3.50 |
| **C29** | AP2 | 1.95b | blue | 6.50 | 2.75 |
| **C30** | AP2 | 2b | blk brn | 4.00 | 2.25 |
| **C31** | AP2 | 2.10b | blue | 9.25 | 5.50 |
| **C32** | AP2 | 2.30b | red | 4.00 | 2.25 |
| **C33** | AP2 | 2.50b | dk bl | 5.50 | 1.40 |
| **C34** | AP2 | 3b | dk vio | 5.50 | .85 |
| **C35** | AP2 | 3.70b | emerald | 7.75 | 5.50 |

| | | | | |
|---|---|---|---|---|
| C36 | AP2 | 4b red org | 5.50 | 1.40 |
| C37 | AP2 | 5b black | 6.50 | 2.25 |
| C38 | AP2 | 8b dk car | 13.00 | 4.50 |
| C39 | AP2 | 10b dk vio | 25.00 | 7.75 |
| C40 | AP2 | 20b grnsh slate | 55.00 | 20.00 |
| | | *Nos. C17-C40 (24)* | 167.05 | 63.25 |

Pairs imperf. between exist of the 1b (value $150); the 25c and 4b (value $300 each).

Air Post Stamps of 1932 Surcharged in Black

**1937, June 4**

| | | | | |
|---|---|---|---|---|
| C41 | AP2 | 5c on 1.70b red brn | 11.00 | 7.00 |
| C42 | AP2 | 10c on 3.70b emer | 11.00 | 7.00 |
| C43 | AP2 | 15c on 4b red org | 5.00 | 3.50 |
| C44 | AP2 | 25c on 5b blk | 5.00 | 3.50 |
| C45 | AP2 | 1b on 8b dk car | 4.00 | 3.50 |
| C46 | AP2 | 2b on 2.10b bl | 30.00 | 23.00 |
| | | *Nos. C41-C46 (6)* | 66.00 | 47.50 |

Various varieties of surcharge exist, including double and triple impressions. No. C43 exists in pair imperf. between; value $30 unused, $50 used.

Allegory of Flight AP3

Allegory of Flight AP4

National Pantheon at Caracas AP5

Airplane — AP6

AP7

***Perf. 11, 11½ and Compound***

**1937, July 1** **Litho.**

| | | | | |
|---|---|---|---|---|
| C47 | AP3 | 5c brn org | .30 | .40 |
| C48 | AP4 | 10c org red | .25 | .20 |
| C49 | AP5 | 15c gray blk | .60 | .40 |
| C50 | AP6 | 25c dk vio | .60 | .40 |
| C51 | AP4 | 40c yel grn | 1.10 | .55 |
| C52 | AP3 | 70c red | 1.10 | .40 |
| C53 | AP5 | 75c bister | 2.50 | 1.30 |
| C54 | AP3 | 1b dk gray | 1.50 | .55 |
| C55 | AP4 | 1.20b pck grn | 6.50 | 4.25 |
| C56 | AP3 | 1.80b dk ultra | 3.25 | 2.00 |
| C57 | AP5 | 1.95b lt ultra | 10.00 | 7.75 |
| C58 | AP6 | 2b chocolate | 4.25 | 2.75 |
| C59 | AP6 | 2.50b gray bl | 11.50 | 11.50 |
| C60 | AP4 | 3b lt vio | 6.50 | 4.50 |
| C61 | AP6 | 3.70b rose red | 11.50 | 15.00 |
| C62 | AP5 | 10b red vio | 25.00 | 15.00 |
| C63 | AP3 | 20b gray | 30.00 | 23.00 |
| | | *Nos. C47-C63 (17)* | 116.45 | 89.95 |

All values exist imperf, and all except the 3.70b part-perf.

Counterfeits exist.

For overprints & surcharges see #C66-C78, C114-C118, C164-C167, C169-C172, C174-C180.

**1937, Oct. 28** ***Perf. 11***

| | | | | |
|---|---|---|---|---|
| C64 | AP7 | 70c emerald | 1.40 | .55 |
| C65 | AP7 | 1.80b ultra | 2.25 | 1.00 |

Acquisition of the Port of La Guaira by the Government from the British Corporation, June 3, 1937. Exist imperf.

A redrawn printing of Nos. C64-C65, with lower inscription beginning "Nacionalización . . ." was prepared but not issued. Price, $40 each.

For overprints see Nos. C168, C173.

Air Post Stamps of 1937 Overprinted in Black

**1937, Dec. 17** ***Perf. 11, 11½***

| | | | | |
|---|---|---|---|---|
| C66 | AP4 | 10c org red | 1.00 | .70 |
| *a.* | | Inverted overprint | 15.00 | 12.00 |
| C67 | AP6 | 25c dk vio | 2.00 | 1.00 |
| C68 | AP4 | 40c yel grn | 2.00 | 1.40 |
| C69 | AP3 | 70c red | 1.50 | 1.00 |
| *a.* | | Inverted overprint | 15.00 | 14.00 |
| *b.* | | Double overprint | 20.00 | 16.00 |
| C70 | AP3 | 1b dk gray | 2.00 | 1.40 |
| *a.* | | Inverted overprint | 16.00 | 13.00 |
| *b.* | | Double overprint | 13.00 | |
| C71 | AP4 | 1.20b pck grn | 30.00 | 20.00 |
| *a.* | | Inverted overprint | 77.50 | |
| C72 | AP3 | 1.80b dk ultra | 5.75 | 2.40 |
| C73 | AP5 | 1.95b lt ultra | 7.75 | 4.25 |
| *a.* | | Inverted overprint | 60.00 | 40.00 |
| C74 | AP6 | 2b chocolate | 50.00 | 23.00 |
| *a.* | | Inverted overprint | 100.00 | 90.00 |
| *b.* | | Double overprint | 82.50 | 82.50 |
| C75 | AP6 | 2.50b gray bl | 50.00 | 19.00 |
| *a.* | | Double overprint | 70.00 | |
| *b.* | | Inverted overprint | 100.00 | 82.50 |
| C76 | AP4 | 3b lt vio | 30.00 | 12.00 |
| C77 | AP5 | 10b red vio | 72.50 | 40.00 |
| C78 | AP3 | 20b gray | 77.50 | 47.50 |
| *a.* | | Double overprint | 150.00 | 150.00 |
| | | *Nos. C66-C78 (13)* | 332.00 | 173.65 |

Counterfeit overprints exist on #C77-C78.

View of La Guaira AP8

National Pantheon AP9

Oil Wells AP10

**1938-39** **Engr.** ***Perf. 12***

| | | | | |
|---|---|---|---|---|
| C79 | AP8 | 5c green | 1.00 | .50 |
| C80 | AP8 | 5c dk grn | .20 | .20 |
| C81 | AP9 | 10c car rose | 1.40 | .80 |
| C82 | AP9 | 10c scarlet | .20 | .20 |
| C83 | AP8 | 12½c dull vio | .60 | .55 |
| C84 | AP10 | 15c slate vio | 3.00 | 1.25 |
| C85 | AP10 | 15c dk bl | .85 | .20 |
| C86 | AP8 | 25c dk bl | 3.00 | 1.25 |
| C87 | AP8 | 25c bis brn | .25 | .20 |
| C88 | AP10 | 30c vio ('39) | 2.00 | .20 |
| C89 | AP9 | 40c dk vio | 3.50 | 1.25 |
| C90 | AP9 | 40c redsh brn | 2.50 | .20 |
| C91 | AP8 | 45c Prus grn ('39) | 1.00 | .20 |
| C92 | AP9 | 50c blue ('39) | 1.25 | .20 |
| C93 | AP10 | 70c car rose | .85 | .25 |
| C94 | AP8 | 75c bis brn | 6.00 | 2.00 |
| C95 | AP8 | 75c ol bis | 1.40 | .20 |
| C96 | AP10 | 90c red org ('39) | 1.00 | .20 |
| C97 | AP9 | 1b ol & bis | 7.00 | 2.75 |
| C98 | AP9 | 1b dk vio | 1.25 | .20 |
| C99 | AP10 | 1.20b orange | 20.00 | 5.75 |
| C100 | AP10 | 1.20b green | 2.00 | .55 |
| C101 | AP8 | 1.80b ultra | 2.00 | .55 |
| C102 | AP9 | 1.90b black | 5.50 | 2.75 |
| C103 | AP10 | 1.95b lt bl | 4.25 | 2.50 |
| C104 | AP8 | 2b ol gray | 45.00 | 15.00 |
| C105 | AP8 | 2b car rose | 1.75 | .70 |
| C106 | AP9 | 2.50b red brn | 45.00 | 20.00 |
| C107 | AP9 | 2.50b orange | 10.00 | 2.75 |
| C108 | AP10 | 3b bl grn | 20.00 | 4.75 |
| C109 | AP10 | 3b ol gray | 5.50 | 2.00 |
| C110 | AP8 | 3.70b gray blk | 7.75 | 5.50 |
| C111 | AP10 | 5b red brn ('39) | 7.75 | 2.00 |
| C112 | AP9 | 10b vio brn | 20.00 | 2.40 |
| C113 | AP10 | 20b red org | 57.50 | 25.00 |
| | | *Nos. C79-C113 (35)* | 292.25 | 105.00 |

See Nos. C227a, C235-C236, C254-C255.

For surcharge see No. C227.

Nos. C51, C56, C58-C59, C61 Surcharged

**1938, Apr. 15** ***Perf. 11, 11½***

| | | | | |
|---|---|---|---|---|
| C114 | AP3 | 5c on 1.80b | .85 | .60 |
| *a.* | | Inverted surcharge | 12.50 | 7.50 |
| C115 | AP6 | 10c on 2.50b | 3.00 | 1.40 |
| *a.* | | Inverted surcharge | 10.00 | 7.50 |
| C116 | AP6 | 15c on 2b | 1.40 | 1.10 |
| C117 | AP4 | 25c on 40c | 1.75 | 1.40 |
| C118 | AP6 | 40c on 3.70b | 3.50 | 3.25 |
| | | *Nos. C114-C118 (5)* | 10.50 | 7.75 |

Plane & Map Type of 1930

White Paper; No Imprint

**1938-39** **Engr.** ***Perf. 12½***

| | | | | |
|---|---|---|---|---|
| C119 | AP1 | 5c dk grn ('39) | .25 | .20 |
| C120 | AP1 | 10c org yel ('39) | .55 | .20 |
| C121 | AP1 | 12½c rose vio ('39) | 1.10 | .85 |
| C122 | AP1 | 15c dp bl | .95 | .20 |
| C123 | AP1 | 25c brown | 1.10 | .20 |
| C124 | AP1 | 40c olive ('39) | 2.75 | .40 |
| C125 | AP1 | 70c rose car ('39) | 20.00 | 7.75 |
| C126 | AP1 | 1b dk bl ('39) | 7.75 | 3.00 |
| | | *Nos. C119-C126 (8)* | 34.45 | 12.80 |

Monument to Sucre — AP11

Monuments at Carabobo AP12 AP13

**1938, Dec. 23** ***Perf. 13½***

| | | | | |
|---|---|---|---|---|
| C127 | AP11 | 20c brn blk | .80 | .30 |
| C128 | AP12 | 30c purple | 1.20 | .30 |
| C129 | AP13 | 45c dk bl | 1.75 | .25 |
| C130 | AP11 | 50c lt ultra | 1.50 | .25 |
| C131 | AP13 | 70c dk car | 26.00 | 7.50 |
| C132 | AP12 | 90c red org | 2.50 | .75 |
| C133 | AP13 | 1.35b gray blk | 3.00 | 1.00 |
| C134 | AP11 | 1.40b slate gray | 12.00 | 2.75 |
| C135 | AP12 | 2.25b green | 6.00 | 2.00 |
| | | *Nos. C127-C135 (9)* | 54.75 | 15.10 |

For surcharge see No. C198.

Simón Bolívar and Carabobo Monument AP14

**1940, Mar. 30** ***Perf. 12***

| | | | | |
|---|---|---|---|---|
| C136 | AP14 | 15c blue | .75 | .20 |
| C137 | AP14 | 20c olive bis | .75 | .20 |
| C138 | AP14 | 25c red brn | 2.75 | .40 |
| C139 | AP14 | 40c blk brn | 2.25 | .20 |
| C140 | AP14 | 1b red lilac | 5.00 | .55 |
| C141 | AP14 | 2b rose car | 11.00 | 1.40 |
| | | *Nos. C136-C141 (6)* | 22.50 | 2.95 |

"The Founding of Grand Colombia" AP15

**1940, June 13**

| | | | | |
|---|---|---|---|---|
| C142 | AP15 | 15c copper brown | 1.25 | .45 |

Founding of the Pan American Union, 50th anniv.

Statue of Simón Bolívar, Caracas — AP16

**1940-44**

| | | | | |
|---|---|---|---|---|
| C143 | AP16 | 5c dk grn ('42) | .20 | .20 |
| C144 | AP16 | 10c scar ('42) | .20 | .20 |
| C145 | AP16 | 12½c dull purple | .60 | .25 |
| C146 | AP16 | 15c blue ('43) | .40 | .20 |
| C147 | AP16 | 20c bis brn ('44) | .40 | .20 |
| C148 | AP16 | 25c bis brn ('42) | .40 | .20 |
| C149 | AP16 | 30c dp vio ('43) | .40 | .20 |
| C150 | AP16 | 40c blk brn ('43) | .50 | .20 |
| C151 | AP16 | 45c turq grn ('43) | .50 | .20 |
| C152 | AP16 | 50c blue ('44) | .50 | .20 |
| C153 | AP16 | 70c rose pink | 1.50 | .25 |
| C154 | AP16 | 75c ol bis ('43) | 6.00 | 1.25 |
| C155 | AP16 | 90c red org ('43) | 1.00 | .25 |
| C156 | AP16 | 1b dp red lil ('42) | .50 | .20 |
| C157 | AP16 | 1.20b dp yel grn ('43) | 1.90 | .60 |
| C158 | AP16 | 1.35b gray blk ('42) | 8.00 | 3.75 |
| C159 | AP16 | 2b rose pink ('43) | 1.50 | .20 |
| C160 | AP16 | 3b ol blk ('43) | 2.50 | .60 |
| C161 | AP16 | 4b black | 2.00 | .60 |
| C162 | AP16 | 5b red brn ('44) | 16.00 | 6.25 |
| | | *Nos. C143-162 (20)* | 45.00 | 16.00 |

See #C232-C234, C239-C253. For surcharges see #C225, C873.

Nos. C48, C50-C65 Overprinted

***Perf. 11, 11½ & Compound***

**1943, Dec. 21**

| | | | | |
|---|---|---|---|---|
| C164 | AP4 | 10c orange red | 2.00 | .90 |
| C165 | AP6 | 25c dk violet | 2.00 | .90 |
| C166 | AP4 | 40c yellow grn | 2.00 | .90 |
| C167 | AP3 | 70c red | 2.00 | .90 |
| C168 | AP7 | 70c emerald | 2.00 | .90 |
| C169 | AP5 | 75c bister | 2.00 | .90 |
| C170 | AP3 | 1b dk gray | 2.00 | .90 |
| C171 | AP4 | 1.20b peacock grn | 5.00 | 1.60 |
| C172 | AP3 | 1.80b dk ultra | 5.00 | 1.60 |
| C173 | AP7 | 1.80b dk ultra | 5.00 | 2.50 |
| C174 | AP5 | 1.95b lt ultra | 6.00 | 3.25 |
| C175 | AP6 | 2b chocolate | 6.00 | 3.25 |
| C176 | AP6 | 2.50b gray blue | 5.00 | 3.25 |
| C177 | AP4 | 3b lt violet | 6.00 | 3.25 |
| C178 | AP6 | 3.70b rose red | 52.50 | 45.00 |
| C179 | AP5 | 10b red violet | 12.00 | 10.00 |
| C180 | AP3 | 20b gray | 27.50 | 20.00 |
| | | *Nos. C164-C180 (17)* | 144.00 | 100.00 |
| | | Set, never hinged | 175.00 | |

Issued for sale to philatelists. Nos. C164-C169 were sold only in sets.

Nearly all are known with invtd. ovpt.

Flags of Venezuela and the Red Cross — AP17

Baseball Players — AP18

**1944, Aug. 22 Litho. *Perf. 12***
**Flags in red, yellow, blue and black**

**C181** AP17 5c gray green .20 .20
**C182** AP17 10c magenta .20 .20
**C183** AP17 20c brt blue .25 .20
**C184** AP17 30c violet bl .30 .20
**C185** AP17 40c chocolate .40 .20
**C186** AP17 45c apple green 1.25 .40
**C187** AP17 90c orange 1.00 .40
**C188** AP17 1b gray black 2.00 .40
*Nos. C181-C188 (8)* 5.60 2.20
Set, never hinged 6.25

80th anniv. of the Intl. Red Cross and 37th anniv. of Venezuela's joining the organization.
Nos. C181-C188 exist imperf. and part perf.

**1944, Oct. 12**
**"AEREO" in dark carmine**

**C189** AP18 5c dull vio brn .30 .20
**C190** AP18 10c gray green .50 .20
**C191** AP18 20c ultra .50 .25
**C192** AP18 30c dull rose 1.00 .40
**C193** AP18 45c rose violet 2.00 .70
**C194** AP18 90c red orange 3.50 1.40
**C195** AP18 1b dark gray 4.00 1.40
**C196** AP18 1.20b yellow grn 9.25 7.25
**C197** AP18 1.80b ocher 12.00 9.25
*Nos. C189-C197 (9)* 33.05 21.05
Set, never hinged 42.50

7th World Amateur Baseball Championship Games, Caracas.
Nos. C189-C197 exist imperf, and all but 1b exist part perf. Various errors of "AEREO" overprint exist.

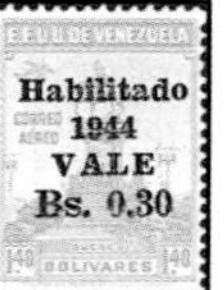


No. C134 Surcharged in Black

**1944, Nov. 17 *Perf. 13½***

**C198** AP11 30c on 1.40b .45 .45
*a.* Double surcharge 32.50 32.50
*b.* Inverted surcharge 12.50 12.50

Charles Howarth — AP19

Antonio José de Sucre — AP20

**1944, Dec. 21 Unwmk. *Perf. 12***

**C199** AP19 5c black .20 .20
**C200** AP19 10c purple .20 .20
**C201** AP19 20c sepia .30 .30
**C202** AP19 30c dull green .35 .30
**C203** AP19 1.20b bister 1.75 1.50
**C204** AP19 1.80b deep ultra 4.00 3.00
**C205** AP19 3.70b rose 3.00 3.00
*Nos. C199-C205 (7)* 9.80 8.50
Set, never hinged 12.50

Cent. of founding of 1st cooperative shop in Rochdale, England, by Charles Howarth.
Nos. C199-C205 exist imperf. and part perf.

**1945, Mar. 3 Engr.**

**C206** AP20 5c orange .20 .20
**C207** AP20 10c violet .20 .20
**C208** AP20 20c grnsh blk .20 .20
**C209** AP20 30c brt green .20 .20
**C210** AP20 40c olive .50 .50
**C211** AP20 45c black brn .75 .50
**C212** AP20 90c redsh brn 1.00 .50
**C213** AP20 1b dp red lil 1.00 .50
**C214** AP20 1.20b black 3.00 2.50
**C215** AP20 2b yellow 4.75 3.50
*Nos. C206-C215 (10)* 11.80 8.80
Set, never hinged 14.50

150th birth anniv. of Antonio Jose de Sucre, Grand Marshal of Ayacucho.

Type of 1946

**1946, Aug. 24 *Perf. 12***

**C216** A81 30c Bello 1.10 .20
**C217** A82 30c Urdaneta 1.10 .20
Set, never hinged 2.75

Allegory of Republic — AP23

***Perf. 11½***

**1946, Oct. 18 Litho. Unwmk.**

**C218** AP23 15c dp violet bl .35 .20
**C219** AP23 20c bister brn .35 .20
**C220** AP23 30c dp violet .45 .30
**C221** AP23 1b brt rose 3.25 2.50
*Nos. C218-C221 (4)* 4.40 3.20
Set, never hinged 4.75

Anniversary of the Revolution of October, 1945. Exist imperf. and part perf.

Nos. 297, 371, C152 and 362 Surcharged in Black

**1947, Jan. *Perf. 12***

**C223** A49 10c on 22½c dp car .25 .20
*a.* Inverted surcharge 4.00 4.00
**C224** A69 15c on 25c lt bl .40 .25
**C225** AP16 20c on 50c blue .40 .25
*a.* Inverted surcharge 5.00 5.00
**C226** A65 70c on 1b dk vio brn .75 .45
*a.* Inverted surcharge 4.00 4.00

Type of 1938 Surcharged in Black

**C227** AP10 20b on 20b org red 28.00 22.50
*a.* Surcharge omitted 92.50 40.00
*Nos. C223-C227 (5)* 29.80 23.65
Set, never hinged 40.00

"J. R. G." are the initials of "Junta Revolucionaria de Gobierno."
Also exist: 20c on #C143, 10c on #371.

Anti-tuberculosis Institute, Maracaibo — AP24

**1947, Jan. 12 Litho.**
**Venezuela Shown on Map in Yellow**

**C228** AP24 15c dark blue .40 .30
**C229** AP24 20c dark brown .40 .30
**C230** AP24 30c violet .40 .30
**C231** AP24 1b carmine 4.25 3.50
*Nos. C228-C231 (4)* 5.45 4.40
Set, never hinged 6.25

12th Pan-American Health Conf., Caracas, Jan. 1947.
Nos. C228-C231 exist imperf., part perf. and with yellow omitted.

Types of 1938-40

**1947, Mar. 17 Engr.**

**C232** AP16 75c orange 7.50 4.50
**C233** AP16 1b brt ultra .70 .25
**C234** AP16 3b red brown 17.50 8.00
**C235** AP10 5b scarlet 15.00 5.00
**C236** AP9 10b violet 20.00 7.50
*Nos. C232-C236 (5)* 60.70 25.25
Set, never hinged 85.00

On Nos. C235 and C236 the numerals of value are in color on a white table.

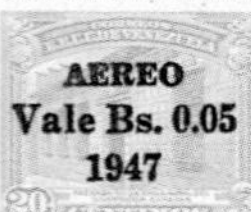


No. 370 Surcharged in Black

**1947, June 20**

**C237** A70 5c on 20c blue .40 .20
**C238** A70 10c on 20c blue .40 .20
*a.* Inverted surcharge 5.00 5.00
Set, never hinged 1.00

Types of 1938-44

**1947-48 Engr.**

**C239** AP16 5c orange .20 .20
**C240** AP16 10c dk green .20 .20
**C241** AP16 12½ bister brn .45 .45
**C242** AP16 15c gray .20 .20
**C243** AP16 20c violet .20 .20
**C244** AP16 25c dull green .20 .20
**C245** AP16 30c brt ultra .45 .20
**C246** AP16 40c green ('48) .20 .20
**C247** AP16 45c vermilion .45 .20
**C248** AP16 50c red violet .25 .20
**C249** AP16 70c dk car 1.00 .45
**C250** AP16 75c purple ('48) .65 .25
**C251** AP16 90c black 1.00 .30
**C252** AP16 1.20b red brn ('48) 1.25 .50
**C253** AP16 3b dp blue 1.75 .50
**C254** AP10 5b olive grn 9.25 5.00
**C255** AP9 10b yellow 8.25 4.75
*Nos. C239-C255 (17)* 25.95 14.00
Set, never hinged 35.00

On Nos. C254 and C255 the numerals of value are in color on a white tablet.
Issue dates: 5c, 10c, Oct. 8. 15c, Dec. 2, 40c, 75c, 1.20b, May 10, 1948. Others, Oct. 27, 1947.

M. S. Republica de Venezuela — AP25

Santos Michelena AP26

Imprint: "American Bank Note Company"

**1948-50 Unwmk. *Perf. 12***

**C256** AP25 5c red brown .20 .20
**C257** AP25 10c deep green .20 .20
**C258** AP25 15c brown .20 .20
**C259** AP25 20c violet brn .25 .20
**C260** AP25 25c brown black .25 .20
**C261** AP25 30c olive green .25 .20
**C262** AP25 45c blue green .45 .25
**C263** AP25 50c gray black .75 .40
**C264** AP25 70c orange 1.25 .40
**C265** AP25 75c brt ultra 2.25 .55
**C266** AP25 90c car lake 1.25 1.25
**C267** AP25 1b purple 1.75 .80
**C268** AP25 2b gray 1.90 1.25
**C269** AP25 3b emerald 7.00 4.00
**C270** AP25 4b deep blue 3.25 4.00
**C271** AP25 5b orange red 13.00 6.00
*Nos. C256-C271 (16)* 34.20 20.10

Issued to honor the Grand-Colombian Merchant Fleet. See Nos. C554-C556.
Issued: 5c, 10c, 15c, 25c, 30c, 1b, 7/9/48; 45c, 75c, 5b, 5/11/50; others, 3/9/49.
For surcharges see Nos. C863-C864.

**1949, Apr. 25**

**C272** AP26 5c orange brn .25 .20
**C273** AP26 10c gray .25 .20
**C274** AP26 15c red orange .50 .50
**C275** AP26 25c dull green 1.00 .80
**C276** AP26 30c plum 1.00 .80
**C277** AP26 1b violet 5.00 2.75
*Nos. C272-C277 (6)* 8.00 5.25

See note after No. 427.

Christopher Columbus AP27

**1948-49 Unwmk. *Perf. 12½***

**C278** AP27 5c brown ('49) .25 .20
**C279** AP27 10c gray .25 .25
**C280** AP27 15c orange ('49) .55 .25
**C281** AP27 25c green ('49) 1.00 .55
**C282** AP27 30c red vio ('49) 1.25 .80
**C283** AP27 1b violet ('49) 5.00 2.25
*Nos. C278-C283 (6)* 8.30 4.30

See note after No. 431.

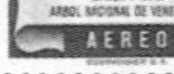

AP28 AP29

Symbols of global air mail.

**1950 *Perf. 12***

**C284** AP28 5c red brown .25 .20
**C285** AP28 10c dk green .25 .20
**C286** AP28 15c olive brn .25 .20
**C287** AP28 25c olive gray .40 .30
**C288** AP28 30c olive grn .55 .30
**C289** AP28 50c black .40 .25
**C290** AP28 60c brt ultra 1.10 .60
**C291** AP28 90c carmine 1.40 .75
**C292** AP28 1b purple 1.90 .50
*Nos. C284-C292 (9)* 6.50 3.30
Set, never hinged 7.50

75th anniv. of the UPU.
Issue dates: 5c, Jan. 28. Others, Feb. 19.

**1950, Aug. 25 Photo. *Perf. 11½***

Araguaney, Venezuelan national tree.

**Foliage in Yellow**

**C293** AP29 5c orange brn .25 .20
**C294** AP29 10c blue grn .25 .20
**C295** AP29 15c deep plum .50 .20
**C296** AP29 25c dk gray grn 4.50 1.25
**C297** AP29 30c red orange 4.75 1.60
**C298** AP29 50c dark gray 2.75 .40
**C299** AP29 60c deep blue 4.50 .80
**C300** AP29 90c red 7.00 1.60
**C301** AP29 1b rose violet 8.00 2.00
*Nos. C293-C301 (9)* 32.50 8.25
Set, never hinged 45.00

Issued to publicize Forest Week, 1950.

Census Type of 1950

**1950, Sept. 1 Engr. *Perf. 12***

**C302** A90 5c olive gray .20 .20
**C303** A90 10c green .20 .20
**C304** A90 15c olive green .20 .20
**C305** A90 25c gray .30 .30
**C306** A90 30c orange .45 .25
**C307** A90 50c lt brown .30 .20
**C308** A90 60c ultra .30 .20
**C309** A90 90c rose carmine 1.10 .45
**C310** A90 1b violet 1.75 1.40
*Nos. C302-C310 (9)* 4.80 3.40

Signing Act of Independence — AP31

**1950, Nov. 17**

**C311** AP31 5c vermilion .35 .20
**C312** AP31 10c red brown .35 .20
**C313** AP31 15c violet .50 .20
**C314** AP31 30c brt blue .70 .25
**C315** AP31 1b green 3.25 1.40
*Nos. C311-C315 (5)* 5.15 2.25

200th anniversary of the birth of Gen. Francisco de Miranda.

Alonso de Ojeda Type of 1950

**1950, Dec. 18 Photo. *Perf. 11½***

**C316** A91 5c orange brn .20 .20
**C317** A91 10c cerise .25 .20
**C318** A91 15c black brn .30 .20
**C319** A91 25c violet .55 .25
**C320** A91 30c orange 1.10 .45
**C321** A91 1b emerald 4.50 2.25
*Nos. C316-321 (6)* 6.90 3.55

Bolivar Statue Type of 1951

**1951, July 13 Engr. *Perf. 12***

**C322** A92 5c purple .40 .20
**C323** A92 10c dull green .45 .20
**C324** A92 20c olive gray .45 .20

**C325** A92 25c olive green .50 .20
**C326** A92 30c vermilion .65 .30
**C327** A92 40c lt brown .65 .30
**C328** A92 50c gray 1.60 .55
**C329** A92 70c orange 2.50 1.40
*Nos. C322-C329 (8)* 7.20 3.35

Queen Isabella I — AP34

**1951, Oct. 12 Photo. *Perf. 11½***
**C330** AP34 5c dk green & buff .30 .20
**C331** AP34 10c dk red & cream .30 .20
**C332** AP34 20c dp blue & gray .50 .20
**C333** AP34 30c dk blue & gray .50 .20
*a.* Souv. sheet of 4, #C330-C333 3.00 2.75
*Nos. C330-C333 (4)* 1.60 .80
Set, never hinged 2.25

500th anniv. of the birth of Queen Isabella I of Spain.

Bicycle Racecourse — AP35

**1951, Dec. 18 Engr. *Perf. 12***
**C334** AP35 5c green .75 .20
**C335** AP35 10c rose carmine .85 .20
**C336** AP35 20c redsh brown .95 .25
**C337** AP35 30c blue 1.25 .35
*a.* Souv. sheet, #C334-C337 11.00 11.00
*Nos. C334-C337 (4)* 3.80 1.00
Set, never hinged 4.00

3rd Bolivarian Games, Caracas, Dec. 1951.

Arms of Carabobo and "Industry" — AP36

**1951 Photo. *Perf. 11½***
**C338** AP36 5c blue green .40 .20
**C339** AP36 7½c gray green .50 .30
**C340** AP36 10c car rose .40 .20
**C341** AP36 15c dark brown .50 .20
**C342** AP36 20c gray blue .55 .20
**C343** AP36 30c deep blue 1.50 .25
**C344** AP36 45c magenta .75 .25
**C345** AP36 60c olive brown 1.40 .55
**C346** AP36 90c rose brown 3.25 1.75
*Nos. C338-C346 (9)* 9.25 3.90

Issue date: Oct. 29.

### Arms of Zulia and "Industry"

**C347** AP36 5c blue green .40 .20
**C348** AP36 10c car rose .40 .20
**C349** AP36 15c dark brown .60 .20
**C350** AP36 30c deep blue 4.00 1.25
**C351** AP36 60c olive brown 2.40 .40
**C352** AP36 1.20b brown car 8.00 5.00
**C353** AP36 3b blue gray 2.75 .75
**C354** AP36 5b purple brn 4.00 2.00
**C355** AP36 10b violet 6.25 4.00
*Nos. C347-C355 (9)* 28.80 14.00

Issued: 5b, 9/8; 5c, 3b, 10b, 10/8; others, 10/29.

### Arms of Anzoategui

**C356** AP36 5c blue green .35 .20
**C357** AP36 10c car rose .35 .20
**C358** AP36 15c dk brown .45 .20
**C359** AP36 25c sepia .55 .20
**C360** AP36 30c deep blue 1.40 .80
**C361** AP36 50c henna brn 1.40 .40
**C362** AP36 60c olive brn 2.00 .25
**C363** AP36 1b purple 2.50 .80
**C364** AP36 2b violet gray 4.25 1.75
*Nos. C356-C364 (9)* 13.25 4.80

Issue date: Nov. 9.

### Arms of Caracas and Buildings

**C365** AP36 5c blue green .70 .30
**C366** AP36 7½c gray green 2.10 .95
**C367** AP36 10c car rose .50 .30
**C368** AP36 15c dk brown 5.00 .65
**C369** AP36 20c gray blue 3.25 .65
**C370** AP36 30c deep blue 5.50 1.25
**C371** AP36 45c magenta 3.25 .75
**C372** AP36 60c olive brn 11.50 1.50
**C373** AP36 90c rose brn 6.50 5.25
*Nos. C365-C373 (9)* 38.30 11.60

Issue date: Aug. 6.

### Arms of Tachira and Agricultural Products

**C374** AP36 5c blue green .30 .30
**C375** AP36 10c car rose .30 .30
**C376** AP36 15c dk brown .85 .30
**C377** AP36 30c deep blue 11.00 1.25
**C378** AP36 60c olive brn 8.50 1.25
**C379** AP36 1.20b brown car 8.50 6.00
**C380** AP36 3b blue gray 2.75 1.25
**C381** AP36 5b purple brn 5.00 2.50
**C382** AP36 10b violet 6.75 5.00
*Nos. C374-C382 (9)* 43.95 18.15

Issue date: Aug. 9.

### Arms of Venezuela and Bolivar Statue

**C383** AP36 5c blue green .40 .20
**C384** AP36 7½c gray grn 1.00 .65
**C385** AP36 10c car rose .30 .20
**C386** AP36 15c dk brown 2.25 .65
**C387** AP36 20c gray blue 3.00 .50
**C388** AP36 30c deep blue 5.50 1.10
**C389** AP36 45c magenta 2.50 .45
**C390** AP36 60c olive brn 11.50 2.25
**C391** AP36 90c rose brn 7.25 5.00
*Nos. C383-C391 (9)* 33.70 11.00

Issue date: Aug. 6.

**1952**

### Arms of Miranda and Agricultural Products

**C392** AP36 5c blue green .30 .20
**C393** AP36 7½c gray grn .50 .30
**C394** AP36 10c car rose .30 .20
**C395** AP36 15c dark brown .60 .20
**C396** AP36 20c gray blue .90 .25
**C397** AP36 30c deep blue 1.75 .40
**C398** AP36 45c magenta 1.60 .20
**C399** AP36 60c olive brn 3.00 .55
**C400** AP36 90c rose brn 13.50 8.00
*Nos. C392-C400 (9)* 22.45 10.30

Issue date: 7½c, 15c, 20c, 30c, Mar. 24.

### Arms of Aragua and Stylized Farm

**C401** AP36 5c blue green .60 .20
**C402** AP36 7½c gray grn .50 .30
**C403** AP36 10c car rose .30 .20
**C404** AP36 15c dk brown 1.75 .25
**C405** AP36 20c gray blue .85 .25
**C406** AP36 30c deep blue 2.50 .30
**C407** AP36 45c magenta 1.90 .25
**C408** AP36 60c olive brn 4.00 .40
**C409** AP36 90c rose brn 15.00 8.00
*Nos. C401-C409 (9)* 27.40 10.15

Issue date: 7½c, 15c, 20c, 30c, Mar. 24.

### Arms of Lara, Agricultural Products and Rope

**C410** AP36 5c blue green .60 .20
**C411** AP36 7½c gray grn .50 .30
**C412** AP36 10c car rose .30 .20
**C413** AP36 15c dk brown .90 .20
**C414** AP36 20c gray blue 1.40 .20
**C415** AP36 30c deep blue 2.75 .40
**C416** AP36 45c magenta 1.40 .35
**C417** AP36 60c olive brn 2.75 .65
**C418** AP36 90c rose brn 15.00 10.00
*Nos. C410-C418 (9)* 25.60 12.50

Issue date: 7½c, 15c, 20c, Mar. 24.

### Arms of Bolivar and Stylized Design

**C419** AP36 5c blue green 3.25 .35
**C420** AP36 10c car rose .30 .20
**C421** AP36 15c dark brown .50 .20
**C422** AP36 25c sepia .40 .20
**C423** AP36 30c deep blue 2.25 .95
**C424** AP36 50c henna brn 1.50 .40
**C425** AP36 60c olive brn 2.50 .55
**C426** AP36 1b purple 2.25 .40
**C427** AP36 2b violet gray 5.25 1.75
*Nos. C419-C427 (9)* 18.20 5.00

Issue date: 15c, 30c, Mar. 24.

### Arms of Sucre, Palms and Seascape

**C428** AP36 5c blue green .30 .20
**C429** AP36 10c car rose .20 .20
**C430** AP36 15c dk brown .40 .20
**C431** AP36 25c sepia 8.50 .20
**C432** AP36 30c deep blue 2.75 .85
**C433** AP36 50c henna brn 1.25 .30
**C434** AP36 60c olive brn 1.60 .65
**C435** AP36 1b purple 2.00 .50
**C436** AP36 2b violet gray 4.50 2.25
*Nos. C428-C436 (9)* 21.50 5.35

Issue date: 15c, 30c, Mar. 24.

### Arms of Trujillo Surrounded by Stylized Tree

**C437** AP36 5c blue green 5.25 .35
**C438** AP36 10c car rose .40 .20
**C439** AP36 15c dk brown 1.50 .20
**C440** AP36 30c deep blue 6.50 1.10
**C441** AP36 60c olive brn 4.75 1.00
**C442** AP36 1.20b rose red 4.25 2.40
**C443** AP36 3b blue gray 2.00 1.00
**C444** AP36 5b purple brn 4.50 1.75
**C445** AP36 10b violet 7.75 4.00
*Nos. C437-C445 (9)* 36.90 12.00

Issue date: 5c, 30c, Mar. 24.

**1953-54**

### Map of Delta Amacuro and Ship

**C446** AP36 5c bl grn .30 .20
**C447** AP36 10c car rose .20 .20
**C448** AP36 15c dk brn .45 .20
**C449** AP36 25c sepia .65 .30
**C450** AP36 30c dp bl 2.50 .75
**C451** AP36 50c hn brn 1.25 .30
**C452** AP36 60c ol brn 1.90 .60
**C453** AP36 1b purple 2.40 .85
**C454** AP36 2b vio gray 4.00 3.00
*Nos. C446-C454 (9)* 13.65 6.40

Issue date: 15c, 30c, Feb. 13.

### Arms of Falcon and Stylized Oil Refinery

**C455** AP36 5c bl grn .50 .25
**C456** AP36 10c car rose .25 .25
**C457** AP36 15c dk brn .50 .25
**C458** AP36 30c dp bl 4.00 1.10
**C459** AP36 60c ol brn 3.00 .85
**C460** AP36 1.20b rose red 3.75 3.50
**C461** AP36 3b bl gray 4.00 2.25
**C462** AP36 5b pur brn 6.50 4.50
**C463** AP36 10b violet 6.50 5.00
*Nos. C455-C463 (9)* 29.00 17.95

Issue date: 10c, 15c, 30c, Feb. 13.

### Arms of Guarico and Factory

**C464** AP36 5c blue grn .30 .20
**C465** AP36 10c car rose .20 .20
**C466** AP36 15c dk brn .45 .20
**C467** AP36 25c sepia .65 .30
**C468** AP36 30c dp bl 2.75 1.10
**C469** AP36 50c hn brn 1.40 .45
**C470** AP36 60c ol brn 1.60 .65
**C471** AP36 1b purple 2.75 .65
**C472** AP36 2b vio gray 4.00 2.10
*Nos. C464-C472 (9)* 14.10 5.85

Issue date: 15c, 30c, Feb. 13.

### Arms of Merida and Church

**C473** AP36 5c bl grn .30 .25
**C474** AP36 10c car rose .25 .25
**C475** AP36 15c dk brn .50 .25
**C476** AP36 30c dp bl 4.50 1.00
**C477** AP36 60c ol brn 2.25 .60
**C478** AP36 1.20b rose red 3.75 2.25
**C479** AP36 3b bl gray 2.25 1.00
**C480** AP36 5b pur brn 4.25 2.25
**C481** AP36 10b violet 6.00 3.75
*Nos. C473-C481 (9)* 24.05 11.60

Issue date: 10c, Feb. 2.

### Arms of Monagas and Horses

**C482** AP36 5c bl grn .25 .20
**C483** AP36 10c car rose .20 .20
**C484** AP36 15c dk brn .40 .20
**C485** AP36 25c sepia .30 .20
**C486** AP36 30c dp bl 3.75 1.00
**C487** AP36 50c hn brn 1.50 .50
**C488** AP36 60c ol brn 1.75 .50
**C489** AP36 1b purple 2.50 .65
**C490** AP36 2b vio gray 3.50 1.75
*Nos. C482-C490 (9)* 14.15 5.20

Issue date: 10c, Feb. 2.

### Arms of Portuguesa and Forest

**C491** AP36 5c bl grn 1.25 .40
**C492** AP36 10c car rose .30 .30
**C493** AP36 15c dk brn .75 .30
**C494** AP36 30c dp bl 3.75 1.75
**C495** AP36 60c ol brn 2.75 .70
**C496** AP36 1.20b rose red 6.50 3.75
**C497** AP36 3b bl gray 2.25 1.25
**C498** AP36 5b pur brn 4.00 2.25
**C499** AP36 10b violet 5.75 4.75
*Nos. C491-C499 (9)* 27.30 15.45

Issue date: 5c, 10c, 30c, Feb. 2.

### Map of Amazonas and Orchid

**C500** AP36 5c bl grn .85 .20
**C501** AP36 10c car rose .20 .20
**C502** AP36 15c dk brn .85 .20
**C503** AP36 25c sepia 1.75 .20
**C504** AP36 30c dp bl 4.50 .45
**C505** AP36 50c hn brn 3.50 .75
**C506** AP36 60c ol brn 4.50 .75
**C507** AP36 1b purple 17.50 2.50
**C508** AP36 2b vio gray 7.00 3.00
*Nos. C500-C508 (9)* 40.65 8.25

Issue date: Jan. 1954

### Arms of Apure, Horse and Bird

**C509** AP36 5c bl grn .60 .30
**C510** AP36 10c car rose .30 .30
**C511** AP36 15c dk brn .60 .30
**C512** AP36 30c dp bl 2.25 1.00
**C513** AP36 60c ol brn 2.10 .50
**C514** AP36 1.20b brn car 3.50 2.50
**C515** AP36 3b bl gray 2.10 1.10
**C516** AP36 5b pur brn 4.25 2.00
**C517** AP36 10b violet 6.00 4.25
*Nos. C509-C517 (9)* 21.70 12.25

Issue date: Jan. 1954.

### Arms of Barinas, Cow and Horse

**C518** AP36 5c bl grn .20 .20
**C519** AP36 10c car rose .20 .20
**C520** AP36 15c dk brn .75 .20
**C521** AP36 30c dp blue 2.50 1.00
**C522** AP36 60c ol brn 2.50 .50
**C523** AP36 1.20b brn car 3.50 1.90
**C524** AP36 3b bl gray 2.25 1.00
**C525** AP36 5b pur brn 3.75 1.25
**C526** AP36 10b violet 5.50 4.00
*Nos. C518-C526 (9)* 21.15 10.25

Issue date: Jan. 1954.

### Arms of Cojedes and Cattle

**C527** AP36 5c bl grn 2.50 .40
**C528** AP36 7½c gray grn .65 .40
**C529** AP36 10c car rose .20 .20
**C530** AP36 15c dk brn .20 .20
**C531** AP36 20c gray bl .50 .20
**C532** AP36 30c dp blue 3.50 .50
**C533** AP36 45c mag 1.25 .30
**C534** AP36 60c ol brn 2.50 .45
**C535** AP36 90c rose brn 3.00 1.75
*Nos. C527-C535 (9)* 14.30 4.40

Issue date: Dec.

### Arms of Nueva Esparta and Fish

**C536** AP36 5c bl grn .40 .20
**C537** AP36 10c car rose .20 .20
**C538** AP36 15c dk brn .65 .20
**C539** AP36 25c sepia 1.10 .25
**C540** AP36 30c dp bl 2.25 .50
**C541** AP36 50c hn brn 2.25 .50
**C542** AP36 60c ol brn 2.25 .30
**C543** AP36 1b purple 3.25 .75
**C544** AP36 2b vio gray 4.50 2.25
*Nos. C536-C544 (9)* 16.85 5.15

Issue date: Jan. 1954.

### Arms of Yaracuy and Tropical Foliage

**C545** AP36 5c bl grn .55 .20
**C546** AP36 7½c gray grn 6.50 6.00
**C547** AP36 10c car rose .30 .20
**C548** AP36 15c dk brn .60 .20
**C549** AP36 20c gray bl 1.00 .20
**C550** AP36 30c dp bl 2.00 .50
**C551** AP36 45c mag 1.40 .30
**C552** AP36 60c ol brn 1.40 .50
**C553** AP36 90c rose brn 3.75 2.50
*Nos. C545-C553 (9)* 17.50 10.60
*Nos. C338-C553 (216)* 573.70 232.10

Issue date: Jan. 1954.

Ship Type of 1948-50 Redrawn
Coil Stamps
Imprint: "Courvoisier S.A."

**1952 Unwmk. *Perf. 12x11½***
**C554** AP25 5c rose brn .85 .20
**C555** AP25 10c org red 1.40 .20
**C556** AP25 15c ol brn 1.75 .20
*Nos. C554-C556 (3)* 4.00 .60

Barquisimeto Type of 1952

**1952, Sept. 14 Photo. *Perf. 11½***
**C557** A94 5c blue green .25 .20
**C558** A94 10c car rose .25 .20
**C559** A94 20c dk blue .40 .20
**C560** A94 25c black brn .60 .20
**C561** A94 30c ultra .75 .20
**C562** A94 40c brown org 3.50 1.50
**C563** A94 50c dk ol grn 1.40 .40
**C564** A94 1b purple 4.75 2.00
*Nos. C557-C564 (8)* 11.90 4.90

Caracas Post Office Type of 1953-54

**1953, Mar. 11 *Perf. 12½***
**C565** A96 7½c yellow grn .20 .20
**C566** A96 15c dp plum .20 .20
**C567** A96 20c slate .20 .20
**C568** A96 25c sepia .35 .20
**C569** A96 40c plum .35 .20
**C570** A96 45c rose vio .35 .20
**C571** A96 50c red orange .55 .20
**C572** A96 70c dk sl grn 1.10 .55
**C573** A96 75c dp ultra 3.75 .80
**C574** A96 90c brown org .90 .45
**C575** A96 1b violet blue .90 .45
*Nos. C565-C575 (11)* 8.85 3.65

See Nos. C587-C589, C597-C606.

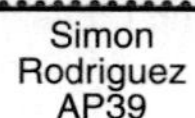

Simon Rodriguez
AP39

Quotation from Bolivar's Manifesto of 1824
AP40

**1954, Feb. 28** ***Perf. 11½***

**C576** AP39 5c blue green .25 .20
**C577** AP39 10c car rose .35 .20
**C578** AP39 20c gray blue .45 .20
**C579** AP39 45c magenta .70 .25
**C580** AP39 65c gray green 2.25 1.00
*Nos. C576-C580 (5)* 4.00 1.85

Centenary of the death of Simon Rodriguez, scholar and tutor of Bolivar.

**1954, Mar. 1** **Unwmk.**

**C581** AP40 15c blk & brn buff .20 .20
**C582** AP40 25c dk red brn & gray .65 .20
**C583** AP40 40c dk red brn & red org .45 .20
**C584** AP40 65c black & blue 1.10 .60
**C585** AP40 80c dk red brn & rose .85 .45
**C586** AP40 1b pur & rose lil 1.75 .35
*Nos. C581-C586 (6)* 5.00 2.00

10th Inter-American Conf., Caracas, Mar. 1954.

P.O. Type of 1953

**1954, Feb.** **Photo.** ***Perf. 12½***

**C587** A96 5c orange .20 .20
**C588** A96 30c red brown 1.90 1.00
**C589** A96 60c bright red 1.90 1.25
*Nos. C587-C589 (3)* 4.00 2.45

Valencia Arms Type of 1955

**1955, Mar. 26** **Engr.** ***Perf. 12***

**C590** A97 5c blue green .20 .20
**C591** A97 10c rose pink .20 .20
**C592** A97 20c ultra .20 .20
**C593** A97 25c gray .20 .20
**C594** A97 40c violet .45 .25
**C595** A97 50c vermilion .45 .25
**C596** A97 60c olive green .90 .25
*Nos. C590-C596 (7)* 2.60 1.55

P.O. Type of 1953 Inscribed: "Republica de Venezuela"

**1955** **Photo.** ***Perf. 12½***

**C597** A96a 5c orange .20 .20
**C598** A96a 10c olive brn .20 .20
**C599** A96a 15c deep plum .20 .20
**C600** A96a 20c slate .25 .20
**C601** A96a 30c red brn .25 .20
**C602** A96a 40c plum .75 .25
**C603** A96a 45c rose violet .75 .40
**C604** A96a 70c dk slate grn 1.90 .85
**C605** A96a 75c deep ultra 1.25 .50
**C606** A9a6 90c brown org .65 .25
*Nos. C597-C606 (10)* 6.40 3.25

Caracas Arms Type of 1955

**1955, Dec. 9** **Unwmk.** ***Perf. 11½***

**C607** A98 5c yellow org .25 .20
**C608** A98 15c claret brn .25 .20
**C609** A98 25c violet blk .25 .20
**C610** A98 40c red .50 .20
**C611** A98 50c red orange .50 .20
**C612** A98 60c car rose 1.00 .35
*Nos. C607-C612 (6)* 2.75 1.35

University Hospital, Caracas
AP43

5c, 10c, 15c, 70c, O'Leary School, Barinas. 25c, 30c, 80c, University Hospital, Caracas. 40c, 45c, 50c, 1b, Caracas-La Guaira Highway. 60c, 65c, 75c, 2b, Towers of Simon Bolivar Center.

**1956-57** **Unwmk.** ***Perf. 11½***

**C613** AP43 5c orange .25 .20
**C614** AP43 10c sepia .25 .20
**C615** AP43 15c claret brown .25 .20
**C616** AP43 20c dark blue .25 .20
**C617** AP43 25c gray black .25 .20
**C618** AP43 30c henna brown .30 .20
**C619** AP43 40c bright crimson .45 .20
**C620** AP43 45c brown violet .30 .20
**C621** AP43 50c deep orange .55 .20
**C622** AP43 60c olive green .55 .20
**C623** AP43 65c bright blue .90 .20
**C624** AP43 70c blue green .95 .25
**C625** AP43 75c ultra 1.00 .35
**C626** AP43 80c carmine rose 1.10 .20
**C627** AP43 1b plum .70 .25
**C628** AP43 2b dark car rose 1.40 .75
*Nos. C613-C628 (16)* 9.45 4.00

Issued: 20c, 40c, 45c, 50c, 1b, 11/5/56; others, 1957.

Book and Flags of American Nations — AP44

**1956-57**

**Granite Paper**

**C629** AP44 5c orange & brn .20 .20
**C630** AP44 10c brn & pale brn .20 .20
**C631** AP44 20c blue & sapphire .20 .20
**C632** AP44 25c gray vio & gray .25 .20
**C633** AP44 40c rose red & pale pur .35 .20
**C634** AP44 45c vio brn & gray brn .45 .20
**C635** AP44 60c olive & gray ol .85 .45
*Nos. C629-C635 (7)* 2.50 1.65

Book Festival of the Americas, 11/15-30/56. Issued: 5c, 40c, 11/15; others, 2/7/57.

Bolivar Type of 1957-58

**Engraved; Center Embossed**

**1957-58** **Unwmk.** ***Perf. 13½***

**C636** A100 5c orange .20 .20
**C637** A100 10c olive gray .20 .20
**C638** A100 20c blue .55 .20
**C639** A100 25c gray black .60 .20
**C640** A100 40c rose red .55 .20
**C641** A100 45c rose lilac .65 .25
**C642** A100 65c yellow brn 1.10 .45
*Nos. C636-C642 (7)* 3.85 1.70

Issued: 45c, 1958; others, Nov. 15, 1957.

Tamanaco Hotel Type of 1957-58

**1957-58** **Engr.** ***Perf. 13***

**C643** A101 5c dull yellow .25 .20
**C644** A101 10c brown .25 .20
**C645** A101 15c chocolate .25 .20
**C646** A101 20c gray blue .25 .20
**C647** A101 25c sepia .25 .20
**C648** A101 30c violet bl .25 .20
**C649** A101 40c car rose .30 .20
**C650** A101 45c claret .35 .20
**C651** A101 50c red org .35 .20
**C652** A101 60c yellow grn .70 .20
**C653** A101 65c orange brn 1.60 .75
**C654** A101 70c slate .90 .35
**C655** A101 75c grnsh blue 1.00 .45
**C656** A101 1b dk claret 1.00 .45
**C657** A101 2b dk gray 1.60 .55
*Nos. C643-C657 (15)* 9.30 4.55

Issue dates: 5c, 10c, Oct. 10; others, 1958. For surcharge see No. C878.

Post Office Type of 1958

**1958, May 14** **Litho.** ***Perf. 14***

**C658** A102 5c dp yellow .20 .20
**C659** A102 10c brown .20 .20
**C660** A102 15c red brn .20 .20
**C661** A102 20c lt blue .20 .20
**C662** A102 25c lt gray .20 .20
**C663** A102 30c lt ultra .20 .20
**C664** A102 40c brt yel grn .20 .20
**C665** A102 50c red orange .20 .20
**C666** A102 60c rose pink .20 .20
**C667** A102 65c red .30 .20
**C668** A102 90c violet .40 .20
**C669** A102 1b lilac .50 .20
**C670** A102 1.20b bister brn 6.00 3.75
*Nos. C658-C670 (13)* 9.00 6.15

See Nos. C786-C792. For surcharges see Nos. C856-C861.

Post Office Type of 1958
Coil Stamps

**1958** **Engr.** ***Perf. 11½x12***

**C671** A103 5c deep yellow .25 .20
**C672** A103 10c brown .35 .20
**C673** A103 15c dark brown .50 .20
*Nos. C671-C673 (3)* 1.10 .60

Merida Type of 1958

**1958, Oct. 9** **Photo.** ***Perf. 13½***

**C674** A104 5c orange yellow .20 .20
**C675** A104 10c gray brown .20 .20
**C676** A104 15c dull red brn .20 .20
**C677** A104 20c chalky blue .20 .20
**C678** A104 25c brown gray .25 .20
**C679** A104 30c violet bl .25 .20
**C680** A104 40c rose car .35 .20
**C681** A104 45c brt lilac .35 .20
**C682** A104 50c red orange .45 .25
**C683** A104 60c lt olive grn .35 .20
**C684** A104 65c henna brn 1.10 .45
**C685** A104 70c gray black .65 .35
**C686** A104 75c brt grnsh bl 1.25 .65
**C687** A104 80c brt vio bl .80 .35
**C688** A104 90c blue green .80 .35
**C689** A104 1b lilac .90 .45
*Nos. C674-C689 (16)* 8.30 4.65

Trujillo Type of 1959

**1958, Nov. 17** **Photo.** ***Perf. 14***

**C690** A105 5c orange yel .20 .20
**C691** A105 10c lt brown .20 .20
**C692** A105 15c redsh brown .20 .20
**C693** A105 20c lt blue .20 .20
**C694** A105 25c pale gray .25 .20
**C695** A105 30c lt vio blue .25 .20
**C696** A105 40c brt yel grn .30 .20
**C697** A105 50c red orange .30 .20
**C698** A105 60c lilac rose .45 .25
**C699** A105 65c vermilion 1.40 .65
**C700** A105 1b lilac .90 .25
*Nos. C690-C700 (11)* 4.65 2.75

Emblem — AP45

**1959, Mar. 10** **Litho.** ***Perf. 13½***

**C701** AP45 5c yellow .25 .20
**C702** AP45 10c red brown .25 .20
**C703** AP45 15c orange .30 .20
**C704** AP45 30c gray .50 .30
**C705** AP45 50c green .55 .35
*Nos. C701-C705 (5)* 1.85 1.25

8th Central American and Caribbean Games, Caracas, Nov. 29-Dec. 14, 1958. Exist imperf. Value, pair $25.

Stamp Centenary Type of 1959

Stamp of 1859 and: 25c, Mailman and José Ignacio Paz Castillo. 50c, Mailman on horseback and Jacinto Gutierrez. 1b, Plane, train and Miguel Herrera.

**1959, Sept. 15** **Engr.** ***Perf. 13½***

**C706** A107 25c orange yel .30 .20
**C707** A107 50c blue .45 .25
**C708** A107 1b rose red .90 .45
*Nos. C706-C708 (3)* 1.65 .90

**Catalogue values for unused stamps in this section, from this point to the end of the section, are for Never Hinged items.**

Alexander von Humboldt Type of 1960

**1960, Feb. 9** **Unwmk.**

**C709** A108 5c ocher & brn .35 .20
**C710** A108 20c brt bl & turq bl .95 .20
**C711** A108 40c ol & ol grn 1.40 .35
*Nos. C709-C711 (3)* 2.70 .75

Newspaper Type of 1960

**1960, June 11** **Litho.** ***Perf. 14***

**C712** A109 5c yellow & blk 1.90 .80
**C713** A109 15c lt red brn & blk 1.00 .30
**C714** A109 65c salmon & blk 1.50 .55
*Nos. C712-C714 (3)* 4.40 1.65

Agustin Codazzi Type of 1960

**1960, June 15** **Engr.**

**C715** A110 5c yel org & brn .20 .20
**C716** A110 10c brn & dk brn .20 .20
**C717** A110 25c gray & blk .40 .20
**C718** A110 30c vio bl & sl .55 .20
**C719** A110 50c org brn & brn .90 .30
**C720** A110 70c gray ol & ol gray 1.40 .55
*Nos. C715-720 (6)* 3.65 1.65

For surcharge see No. C884.

National Pantheon Type of 1960

**1960, May 9** **Litho.**

**Pantheon in Bister**

**C721** A111 5c dp bister .20 .20
**C722** A111 10c red brown .25 .20
**C723** A111 15c fawn .30 .20
**C724** A111 20c lt blue .45 .20
**C725** A111 25c gray 2.40 .25
**C726** A111 30c lt vio bl 2.40 .40
**C727** A111 40c brt yel grn .45 .20
**C728** A111 45c lt violet .70 .20
**C729** A111 60c deep pink .90 .30
**C730** A111 65c salmon .90 .30
**C731** A111 70c gray 1.25 .40
**C732** A111 75c chalky blue 3.75 .70
**C733** A111 80c lt ultra 1.90 .60
**C734** A111 1.20b bister brn 2.25 .85
*Nos. C721-C734 (14)* 18.10 5.00

For surcharges see Nos. C894-C895.

Andres Eloy Blanco Type of 1960

**1960, May 21** ***Perf. 14***

**Portrait in Black**

**C735** A112 20c blue .40 .20
**C736** A112 75c grnsh blue 1.25 .30
**C737** A112 90c brt violet 1.25 .30
*Nos. C735-C737 (3)* 2.90 .80

For surcharge see No. C874.

Independence Type of 1960

**1960, Aug. 19** **Litho.** ***Perf. 13½***

**Center Multicolored**

**C738** A113 50c orange .85 .25
**C739** A113 75c brt grnsh blue 1.25 .40
**C740** A113 90c purple 1.40 .35
*Nos. C738-C740 (3)* 3.50 1.00

Oil Refinery
AP46

**Unwmk.**

**1960, Aug. 26** **Engr.** ***Perf. 14***

**C741** AP46 30c dk bl & sl bl .50 .20
**C742** AP46 40c yel grn & ol .85 .30
**C743** AP46 50c org & red brn 1.00 .40
*Nos. C741-C743 (3)* 2.35 .90

Issued to publicize Venezuela's oil industry.

Luisa Cáceres de Arismendi Type of 1960

**1960, Oct. 21** **Litho.** ***Perf. 14***

**Center Multicolored**

**C744** A115 5c bister .95 .35
**C745** A115 10c redsh brown 1.25 .55
**C746** A115 60c rose carmine 2.25 .70
*Nos. C744-C746 (3)* 4.45 1.60

José Antonio Anzoategui Type of 1960

**1960, Oct. 29** **Engr.**

**C747** A116 25c gray & brown .55 .20
**C748** A116 40c yel grn & ol gray .55 .40
**C749** A116 45c rose cl & dl pur .75 .30
*Nos. C747-C749 (3)* 1.85 .90

Antonio José de Sucre Type of 1960

**Unwmk.**

**1960, Nov. 18** **Litho.** ***Perf. 14***

**Center Multicolored**

**C750** A117 25c gray .75 .30
**C751** A117 30c violet blue 1.10 .40
**C752** A117 50c brown orange 1.40 .55
*Nos. C750-C752 (3)* 3.25 1.25

Type of Regular Issue, 1960

Designs: 30c, Bolivar Peak. 50c, Caroni Falls. 65c, Cuacharo caves.

**1960, Mar. 22** ***Perf. 14***

**C753** A118 30c vio bl & blk bl 1.90 1.90
**C754** A118 50c brn org & brn 1.90 1.90
**C755** A118 65c red org & red brn 1.90 1.90
*Nos. C753-C755 (3)* 5.70 5.70

Cow's Head, Grain, Man and Child
AP47

Arms of San Cristobal
AP48

**1961, Feb. 6 Litho. Unwmk.**
**Cow and Inscription in Black**

**C756** AP47 5c yellow .20 .20
**C757** AP47 10c brown .20 .20
**C758** AP47 15c redsh brn .20 .20
**C759** AP47 20c dull blue .20 .20
**C760** AP47 25c gray .20 .20
**C761** AP47 30c violet bl .25 .20
**C762** AP47 40c yellow grn .30 .20
**C763** AP47 45c lilac .35 .20
**C764** AP47 50c orange .40 .20
**C765** AP47 60c cerise .45 .20
**C766** AP47 65c red orange .60 .20
**C767** AP47 70c gray .90 .30
**C768** AP47 75c brt grnsh bl .85 .25
**C769** AP47 80c brt violet .85 .20
**C770** AP47 90c violet 1.25 .40
*Nos. C756-C770 (15)* 7.20 3.35

9th general census & 3rd agricultural census.
Issued: 5-15c, 30c, 60-65c, 75-80c, 2/6; others, 4/6.
For surcharges see Nos. C865-C866.

Rafael Maria Baralt Type of 1961

**1961, Mar. 11 Engr. *Perf. 14***

**C771** A120 25c gray & sepia .65 .30
**C772** A120 30c dk blue & vio .75 .30
**C773** A120 40c yel grn & ol grn .95 .40
*Nos. C771-C773 (3)* 2.35 1.00

**1961, Apr. 10 Litho.**
**Arms in Original Colors**

**C774** AP48 5c orange & blk .20 .20
**C775** AP48 55c yel grn & blk .65 .25

400th anniversary of San Cristobal.
For surcharge see No. C879.

Bird Type of 1961

Birds: 5c, Troupial. 10c, Golden cock of the rock. 15c, Tropical mockingbird.

**1961, Sept. 6 Unwmk. *Perf. 14½***

**C776** A121 5c multicolored 1.25 .85
**C777** A121 10c multicolored .60 .45
**C778** A121 15c multicolored .80 .50
*Nos. C776-C778 (3)* 2.65 1.80

Charge, Battle of Carabobo — AP49

**1961, Dec. 1 Litho. *Perf. 14***
**Center Multicolored**

**C779** AP49 50c black & ultra .75 .20
**C780** AP49 1.05b black & org 1.75 .50
**C781** AP49 1.50b blk & lil rose 2.00 .50
**C782** AP49 1.90b black & lilac 2.50 1.00
**C783** AP49 2b black & gray 3.25 1.00
**C784** AP49 3b black & grnsh bl 4.00 1.25
*Nos. C779-C784 (6)* 14.25 4.45

140th anniversary of Battle of Carabobo.
For surcharges see Nos. C867-C870.

Arms of Cardinal Quintero
AP50

Archbishop Rafael Arias Blanco — AP51

**1962, Mar. 1 Unwmk.**

**C785** AP50 5c lilac rose .25 .20
*a.* Souv. sheet of 1, imperf. 2.10 1.90

1st Venezuelan Cardinal, José Humberto Quintero.
No. C785a, issued Mar. 23, sold for 1b.

Post Office Type of 1958

**1962, Apr. 12 Litho. *Perf. 13½x14***

**C786** A102 35c citron .25 .20
**C787** A102 55c gray olive .40 .20
**C788** A102 70c bluish green .65 .25
**C789** A102 75c brown orange .80 .20
**C790** A102 80c fawn .80 .30
**C791** A102 85c deep rose 1.25 .45
**C792** A102 95c lilac rose .85 .40
*Nos. C786-C792 (7)* 5.00 2.00

For surcharges see Nos. C856-C861.

**1962, May 10 *Perf. 10½***

**C793** AP51 75c red lilac .80 .30

4th anniversary (in 1961) of the anti-communist pastoral letter of the Archbishop of Caracas, Rafael Arias Blanco.

Orchid Type of 1962

Orchids: 5c, Oncidium volvox. 20c, Cycnoches chlorochilon. 25c, Cattleya Gaskelliana. 30c, Epidendrum difforme, horiz. 40c, Catasetum callosum Lindl, horiz. 50c, Oncidium bicolor Lindl. 1b, Brassavola nodosa Lindl, horiz. 1.05b, Epidendrum lividum Lindl. 1.50b, Schomburgkia undulata Lindl. 2b, Oncidium zebrinum.

***Perf. 14x13½, 13½x14***
**1962, May 30 Litho. Unwmk.**
**Orchids in Natural Colors**

**C794** A124 5c blk & lt grn .20 .20
**C795** A124 20c black .20 .20
**C796** A124 25c black & fawn .55 .20
**C797** A124 30c black & pink .50 .20
**C798** A124 40c black & yel .55 .20
**C799** A124 50c black & lil .75 .20
**C800** A124 1b blk & pale rose 1.00 .35
**C801** A124 1.05b blk & dp org 3.25 1.00
**C802** A124 1.50b blk & pale vio 3.50 1.10
**C803** A124 2b blk & org brn 4.50 1.60
*Nos. C794-C803 (10)* 15.00 5.25

For surcharges see Nos. C885-C887.

Independence Type of 1960

Signing Declaration of Independence.

**1962, June 11 *Perf. 13½***
**Center Multicolored**

**C804** A113 55c olive .60 .20
**C805** A113 1.05b brt rose 2.10 .55
**C806** A113 1.50b purple 1.60 .50
*a.* Souv. sheet of 3, #C804-C806, imperf. 5.00 5.00
*Nos. C804-C806 (3)* 4.30 1.25

No. C806a, issued Oct. 13, sold for 4.10b.
A buff cardboard folder exists with impressions of Nos. 812-814, C804-C806. Perforation is simulated. Sold for 5.60b. Value $10.
For surcharge see No. C893.

No. 710 Surcharged in Rose Carmine: "BICENTENARIO DE UPATA 1762-1962 RESELLADO AEREO VALOR Bs. 2,00"

**1962, July 7 *Perf. 13½x14***

**C807** A102 2b on 1b lt ol grn 2.00 .90

Upata, a village in the state of Bolivar, 200th anniv.

National Games Type of 1962

***Perf. 13x14***
**1962, Nov. 30 Unwmk. Litho.**

**C808** A125 40c Bicycling .40 .25
**C809** A125 75c Baseball .60 .30
**C810** A125 85c Woman athlete 1.50 .65
*a.* Souv. sheet of 3, #C808-C810 imperf. 4.00 3.50
*Nos. C808-C810 (3)* 2.50 1.20

See note after No. 817.
No. C810a sold for 3b.
For surcharge see No. C899.

Bird Type of 1962

Birds: 5c, American kestrel. 20c, Black-bellied tree duck, horiz. 25c, Amazon kingfisher. 30c, Rufous-tailed chachalaca. 50c, Black-and-yellow troupial. 55c, White-naped nightjar. 2.30b, Red-crowned woodpecker. 2.50b, Black-moustached quail-dove.

**1962, Dec. 14 *Perf. 14x13½, 13½x14***
**Birds in Natural Colors; Black Inscription**

**C811** A126 5c car rose .20 .20
**C812** A126 20c brt blue .50 .20
**C813** A126 25c lt gray .60 .20
**C814** A126 30c lt olive .65 .20
**C815** A126 50c violet 1.00 .30
**C816** A126 55c dp orange 1.75 .45
**C817** A126 2.30b dl red brn 5.00 2.25
**C818** A126 2.50b orange yel 5.00 2.50
*Nos. C811-C818 (8)* 14.70 6.30

For surcharges see Nos. C880-C882.

Malaria Eradication Emblem, Mosquito and Map — AP52

**Lithographed and Embossed**
***Perf. 13½x14***
**1962, Dec. 20 Wmk. 346**

**C819** AP52 30c green & blk .55 .25
*a.* Souv. sheet of 2, #825, C819, imperf. 3.00 3.00

WHO drive to eradicate malaria. No. C819a sold for 2b.

Animal Type of Regular Issue

5c, Spectacle bear, vert. 40c, Paca. 50c, Three-toed sloths. 55c, Great anteater. 1.50b, South American tapirs. 2b, Jaguar.

***Perf. 14x13½, 13½x14***
**1963, Mar. 13 Litho. Unwmk.**
**Multicolored Center; Black Inscriptions**

**C820** A128 5c yellow .25 .20
**C821** A128 40c brt green .80 .25
**C822** A128 50c lt violet 1.10 .30
**C823** A128 55c brown olive 1.40 .40
**C824** A128 1.50b gray 4.00 1.60
**C825** A128 2b ultra 6.75 2.50
*Nos. C820-C825 (6)* 14.30 5.25

For surcharges see Nos. C888-C889.

Freedom from Hunger Type of 1963

40c, Map, shepherd. 75c, Map, farmer.

**1963, Mar. 21**

**C826** A129 40c lt yel grn & dl red .45 .30
**C827** A129 75c yellow & brown .60 .40

Arms of Bocono — AP53

**1963, May 30 Wmk. 346**

**C828** AP53 1b multicolored 1.40 .40

400th anniversary of the founding of Bocono.
For surcharge see No. C892.

Papal and Venezuelan Arms
AP54

**1963, June 11 *Perf. 14x13½***
**Arms Multicolored**

**C829** AP54 80c light green 1.10 .30
**C830** AP54 90c gray 1.10 .40

Vatican II, the 21st Ecumenical Council of the Roman Catholic Church.
For surcharges see Nos. C871-C872.

Arms of Venezuela — AP55

**1963, July 29 Unwmk. *Perf. 14***

**C831** AP55 70c gray, red, yel & bl .95 .40

Cent. of Venezuela's flag and coat of arms.
For surcharge see No. C883.

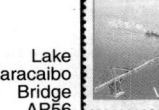

Lake Maracaibo Bridge
AP56

**Wmk. 346**
**1963, Aug. 24 Litho. *Perf. 14***

**C832** AP56 90c grn, brn & ocher 1.25 .40
**C833** AP56 95c blue, brn & och 1.25 .45
**C834** AP56 1b ultra, brn & och 1.00 .40
*Nos. C832-C834 (3)* 3.50 1.25

Opening of bridge over Lake Maracaibo.
For surcharges see Nos. C897-C898.

Armed Forces Type of 1963

**1963, Sept. 10 Unwmk.**

**C835** A134 1b red & bl, *buff* 1.75 .75

For surcharge see No. 862.

Hammarskjold Type of 1963

**1963, Sept. 25 Unwmk. *Perf. 14***

**C836** A135 80c dk bl, lt ultra & ocher .95 .40
**C837** A135 90c dk bl, bl & ocher 1.25 .55
*a.* Souv. sheet of 4, #841-842, C836-C837, imperf. 4.50 4.50

No. C837a sold for 3b.
For surcharges see Nos. C875-C876.

Dr. Luis Razetti, Physician, Birth Cent. — AP57

**1963, Oct. 10 Engr.**

**C838** AP57 95c dk blue & mag 1.40 .60
**C839** AP57 1.05b dk brn & grn 1.50 .75

For surcharges see Nos. C890-C891.

Red Cross Type of 1963

Designs: 40c, Sir Vincent K. Barrington. 75c, Red Cross nurse and child.

**1963, Dec. 31 Litho. *Perf. 11½x12***

**C840** A137 40c multicolored .55 .30
**C841** A137 75c multicolored .95 .40

Development Type of 1964

Designs: 5c, Loading cargo. 10c, Tractor and corn. 15c, Oil field workers. 20c, Oil refinery. 50c, Crane and building construction.

**1964, Feb. 5 Unwmk. *Perf. 14x13½***

**C842** A138 5c multicolored .25 .20
**C843** A138 10c multicolored .25 .20
**C844** A138 15c multicolored .25 .20
**C845** A138 20c multicolored .25 .20
**C846** A138 50c multicolored .50 .20
*Nos. 842-846 (5)* 1.50 1.00

Cent. of the Dept. of Industrial Development and to publicize the Natl. Industrial Expo.

Pedro Gual Type of 1964

**1964, Mar. 20** ***Perf. 14x13½***

**C847** A139 75c dull blue green .75 .25
**C848** A139 1b bright pink 1.00 .35

Blast Furnace and Map of Venezuela — AP58

Arms of Ciudad Bolivar — AP59

**1964, May 22 Litho.** ***Perf. 13½x14***

**C849** AP58 80c multi .90 .35
**C850** AP58 1b multi 1.25 .40

Issued to publicize the Orinoco steel mills.

**1964, May 22** ***Perf. 10½***

**C851** AP59 1b multi 1.25 .70

Bicentenary of Ciudad Bolivar.

AP60

AP61

**1964, Aug. 3 Unwmk.** ***Perf. 11½***

**C852** AP60 30c bister brn & yel .35 .20
**C853** AP60 40c plum & pink .55 .20
**C854** AP60 50c brn & tan .75 .25
*Nos. C852-C854 (3)* 1.65 .65

80th birthday of novelist Romulo Gallegos.

**1964, Nov. 11 Litho.** ***Perf. 14x13½***

**C855** AP61 1b orange & dk vio 1.10 .50

Eleanor Roosevelt and 15th anniv. (in 1963) of the Universal Declaration of Human Rights.
For surcharge see No. C896.

Issues of 1947-64 Surcharged in Black, Dark Blue, Red, Carmine or Lilac with New Value and: "RESELLADO / VALOR"

**1965**

**C856** A102 5c on 55c (#C787) .40 .20
**C857** A102 5c on 70c (#C788) .40 .20
**C858** A102 5c on 80c (#C790) .40 .20
**C859** A102 5c on 85c (#C791) .40 .20
**C860** A102 5c on 90c (#C668) .40 .20
**C861** A102 5c on 95c (#C792) .40 .20
**C862** A134 5c on 1b (#C835) .55 .20
**C863** AP25 10c on 3b (#C269) (C) .40 .20
**C864** AP25 10c on 4b (#C270) (C) .70 .20
**C865** AP47 10c on 70c (#C767) (C) .45 .20
**C866** AP47 10c on 90c (#C770) (C) .40 .20
**C867** AP49 10c on 1.05b (#C780) .60 .20
**C868** AP49 10c on 1.90b (#C782) .40 .20
**C869** AP49 10c on 2b (#C783) .45 .20
**C870** AP49 10c on 3b (#C784) .45 .20
**C871** AP54 10c on 80c (#C829) .40 .20
**C872** AP54 10c on 90c (#C830) .40 .20
**C873** AP16 15c on 3b (#C253) .45 .20
**C874** A112 15c on 90c (#C737) .40 .20
**C875** A135 15c on 80c (#C836) .40 .20
**C876** A135 15c on 90c (#C837) .40 .20
**C877** AP59 15c on 1b (#C851) .45 .20
**C878** A101 20c on 2b (#C657) (R) .55 .20
**C879** AP48 20c on 55c (#C775) (DB) .45 .20

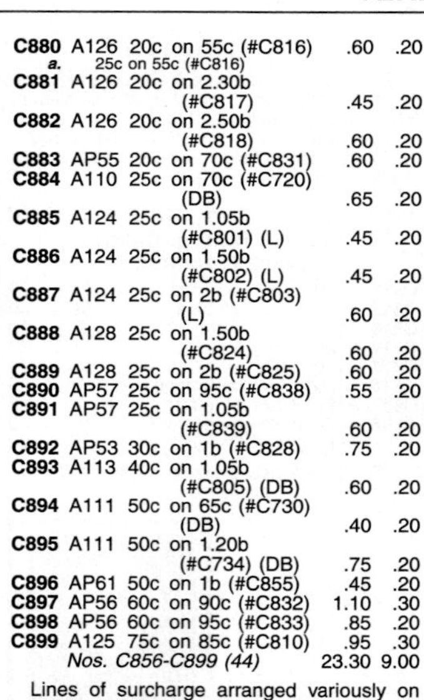

**C880** A126 20c on 55c (#C816) .60 .20
*a.* 25c on 55c (#C816)
**C881** A126 20c on 2.30b (#C817) .45 .20
**C882** A126 20c on 2.50b (#C818) .60 .20
**C883** AP55 20c on 70c (#C831) .60 .20
**C884** A110 25c on 70c (#C720) (DB) .65 .20
**C885** A124 25c on 1.05b (#C801) (L) .45 .20
**C886** A124 25c on 1.50b (#C802) (L) .45 .20
**C887** A124 25c on 2b (#C803) (L) .60 .20
**C888** A128 25c on 1.50b (#C824) .60 .20
**C889** A128 25c on 2b (#C825) .60 .20
**C890** AP57 25c on 95c (#C838) .55 .20
**C891** AP57 25c on 1.05b (#C839) .60 .20
**C892** AP53 30c on 1b (#C828) .75 .20
**C893** A113 40c on 1.05b (#C805) (DB) .60 .20
**C894** A111 50c on 65c (#C730) (DB) .40 .20
**C895** A111 50c on 1.20b (#C734) (DB) .75 .20
**C896** AP61 50c on 1b (#C855) .45 .20
**C897** AP56 60c on 90c (#C832) 1.10 .30
**C898** AP56 60c on 95c (#C833) .85 .20
**C899** A125 75c on 85c (#C810) .95 .30
*Nos. C856-C899 (44)* 23.30 9.00

Lines of surcharge arranged variously on Nos. C856-C899. Old denominations obliterated with bars on Nos. C862, C871-C873, C875-C877, C883, C885-C887, C889, C892, C896-C898. Vertical surcharge on Nos. C865-C866, C871-C872, C874, C878, C896.

Kennedy Type of 1965

**1965, Aug. 20 Photo.** ***Perf. 12x11½***

**C900** A144 60c lt grnsh bl .75 .30
**C901** A144 80c red brn .90 .35

Medical Federation Emblem — AP62

**1965, Aug. 24 Litho.** ***Perf. 13½x14***

**C902** AP62 65c red org & blk 1.10 .55

20th anniversary of the founding of the Medical Federation of Venezuela.

Unisphere and Venezuela Pavilion AP63

**1965, Aug. 31** ***Perf. 14x13½***

**C903** AP63 1b multi 1.00 .30

New York World's Fair, 1964-65.

Andrés Bello (1780?-1865), Educator and Writer — AP64

***Perf. 14x13½***

**1965, Oct. 15 Litho. Unwmk.**

**C904** AP64 80c dk brn & org 1.10 .55

Map Type of 1965

Maps of Venezuela and Guiana: 25c, Map of Venezuela and Guiana by J. Cruz Cano, 1775. 40c, Map stamp of 1896 (No. 140). 75c, Map by the Ministry of the Exterior, 1965 (all horiz.).

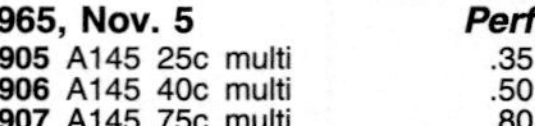

**1965, Nov. 5** ***Perf. 13½***

**C905** A145 25c multi .35 .20
**C906** A145 40c multi .50 .20
**C907** A145 75c multi .80 .30
*a.* Souv. sheet of 3, #C905-C907, imperf. 11.00 11.00
*Nos. C905-C907 (3)* 1.65 .70

#C907a, issued June 7, 1966, sold for 1.65b.

ITU Emblem and Telegraph Poles AP65

**1965, Nov. 19 Litho.** ***Perf. 13½x14***

**C908** AP65 75c blk & ol grn .75 .30

Cent. of the ITU.

Simon Bolivar and Quotation AP66

**1965, Dec. 9** ***Perf. 14x13½***

**C909** AP66 75c lt bl & dk brn .75 .30

Sesquicentennial of Bolivar's Jamaica letter, Sept. 6, 1815.

Children Riding Magic Carpet and Three Kings on Camels — AP67

Fermin Toro — AP68

**1965, Dec. 16** ***Perf. 13½x14***

**C910** AP67 70c yel & vio bl 1.10 .55

Children's Festival, 1965 (Christmas).

**1965, Dec. 22** ***Perf. 14x13½***

**C911** AP68 1b blk & org .90 .30

Death centenary of Fermin Toro (1808-1865), statesman and writer.

Winston Churchill — AP69

**1965, Dec. 29** ***Perf. 14½x13***

**C912** AP69 1b lilac & blk 1.10 .40

Sir Winston Spencer Churchill (1874-1965), statesman and World War II leader.

ICY Emblem, Arms of Venezuela and UN Emblem AP70

**1965, Dec. 30** ***Perf. 13½x14***

**C913** AP70 85c gold & vio blk 1.10 .40

International Cooperation Year, 1965.

OAS Emblem and Map of America — AP71

Farms of 1936 and 1966 — AP72

**1965, Dec. 31** ***Perf. 14x13½***

**C914** AP71 50c bl, blk & gold .90 .30

Organization of American States, 75th anniv.

Butterfly Type of 1966

**1966, Jan. 25 Litho.** ***Perf. 13½x14***

**Various Butterflies in Natural Colors; Black Inscriptions**

**C915** A146 65c lilac 1.75 .40
**C916** A146 85c blue 2.50 .50
**C917** A146 1b salmon pink 2.75 .60
*Nos. C915-C917 (3)* 7.00 1.50

**1966, Mar. 1** ***Perf. 14x13½***

**C918** AP72 55c blk, yel & emer .80 .30

30th anniversary of the Ministry for Agriculture and Husbandry.

Dance Type of 1966

Various folk dances.

**1966, Apr. 5 Litho.** ***Perf. 14***

**C919** A148 40c bl & multi .75 .25
**C920** A148 50c multi .90 .30
**C921** A148 60c vio & multi .60 .20
**C922** A148 70c multi 1.40 .40
**C923** A148 80c red & multi 1.50 .50
**C924** A148 90c ocher & multi 1.60 .60
*Nos. C919-C924 (6)* 6.75 2.25

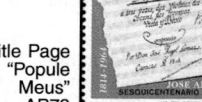

Title Page "Popule Meus" AP73

**1966, Apr. 15** ***Perf. 13½x14***

**C925** AP73 55c yel grn, blk & bis .55 .30
**C926** AP73 95c dp mag, blk & bis .75 .40

150th anniv. (in 1964) of the death of José Angel Lamas, composer of natl. anthem.

Circus Scene, by Michelena — AP74

Paintings by Michelena: 1b, Miranda in La Carraca. 1.05b, Charlotte Corday.

*Perf. 12x12½*

**1966, May 12 Litho. Unwmk.**

| | | | | |
|---|---|---|---|---|
| **C927** | AP74 | 95c multi | .90 | .50 |
| **C928** | AP74 | 1b multi | 1.10 | .50 |
| **C929** | AP74 | 1.05b multi | 1.25 | .50 |
| | | *Nos. C927-C929 (3)* | 3.25 | 1.50 |

Cent. of the birth of Arturo Michelena (1863-1898), painter. Miniature sheets of 12 exist. See Nos. 900-901.

Abraham Lincoln — AP75

**1966, May 31** ***Perf. 13½x14***

| | | | | |
|---|---|---|---|---|
| **C930** | AP75 | 1b gray & blk | .90 | .55 |

Dr. José Gregorio Hernandez AP76

**1966, July 29 Litho.** ***Perf. 14x13½***

| | | | | |
|---|---|---|---|---|
| **C931** | AP76 | 1b brt bl & vio bl | 1.25 | .50 |

Centenary (in 1964) of the birth of Dr. José Gregorio Hernandez, physician.

Dr. Manuel Dagnino and Hospital AP77

**1966, Aug. 16 Litho.** ***Perf. 13½x14***

| | | | | |
|---|---|---|---|---|
| **C932** | AP77 | 1b sl grn & yel grn | 1.10 | .40 |

Founding of Chiquinquira Hospital, cent.

Fish Type of 1966

Fish: 75c, Pearl headstander, vert. 90c, Swordtail characine. 1b, Ramirez's dwarf cichlid.

***Perf. 14x13½, 13½x14***

**1966, Aug. 31**

| | | | | |
|---|---|---|---|---|
| **C933** | A151 | 75c multi | 1.40 | .40 |
| **C934** | A151 | 90c grn & multi | 1.40 | .40 |
| **C935** | A151 | 1b multi | 1.40 | .40 |
| | | *Nos. C933-C935 (3)* | 4.20 | 1.20 |

Rafael Arevalo Gonzalez — AP78

Simon Bolivar, 1816 — AP79

**1966, Sept. 13 Litho.** ***Perf. 13½x14***

| | | | | |
|---|---|---|---|---|
| **C936** | AP78 | 75c yel bis & blk | 1.00 | .40 |

Centenary of the birth of Rafael Arevalo Gonzalez, journalist.

Imprint: "Bundesdruckerei Berlin 1966"

Bolivar Portraits: 25c, 30c, 35c, by José Gil de Castro, 1825. 40c, 50c, 60c, Anonymous painter, 1825. 80c, 1.20b, 4b, Anonymous painter, c. 1829.

**1966**

**Multicolored Center**

| | | | | |
|---|---|---|---|---|
| **C937** | AP79 | 5c lem & blk | .20 | .20 |
| **C938** | AP79 | 10c lt ol grn & blk | .20 | .20 |
| **C939** | AP79 | 20c grn & blk | .20 | .20 |
| **C940** | AP79 | 25c salmon & blk | .20 | .20 |
| **C941** | AP79 | 30c pink & blk | .20 | .20 |
| **C942** | AP79 | 35c dl rose & blk | .25 | .20 |
| **C943** | AP79 | 40c bis brn & blk | .20 | .20 |
| **C944** | AP79 | 50c org brn & blk | .35 | .20 |
| **C945** | AP79 | 60c brn red & blk | .35 | .20 |
| **C946** | AP79 | 80c brt bl & blk | .75 | .30 |
| **C947** | AP79 | 1.20b dl bl & blk | 1.10 | .55 |
| **C948** | AP79 | 4b vio bl & blk | 3.75 | 2.25 |
| | | *Nos. C937-C948 (12)* | 7.75 | 4.90 |

Issued to honor Simon Bolivar.

Issue dates: Nos. C937-C939, Aug. 15; Nos. C940-C942, Sept. 29; others, Oct. 14.

See Nos. C961-C972.

"Justice" — AP80

**1966, Nov. 3 Litho.** ***Perf. 14x13½***

| | | | | |
|---|---|---|---|---|
| **C949** | AP80 | 50c pale lil & red lil | .75 | .30 |

50th anniversary of the Academy of Political and Social Sciences.

Angostura Bridge, Orinoco River — AP81

**1967, Jan. 6 Litho.** ***Perf. 13½x14***

| | | | | |
|---|---|---|---|---|
| **C950** | AP81 | 40c multi | .50 | .20 |

Issued to commemorate the opening of the Angostura Bridge over the Orinoco River.

Pavilion of Venezuela AP82

**1967, Apr. 28 Litho.** ***Perf. 11x13½***

| | | | | |
|---|---|---|---|---|
| **C951** | AP82 | 1b multi | .90 | .30 |

EXPO '67, International Exhibition, Montreal, Apr. 28-Oct. 27, 1967.

Statue of Chief Guaicaipuro AP83

Constellations over Caracas, 1567 and 1967 — AP84

Designs: 45c, Captain Francisco Fajardo. 55c, Diego de Losada, the Founder. 65c, Arms of Caracas. 90c, Map of Caracas, 1578. 1b, Market on Plaza Mayor, 1800.

**1967 Litho.** ***Perf. 14x13½, 13½x14***

| | | | | |
|---|---|---|---|---|
| **C952** | AP83 | 15c multi | .20 | .20 |
| **C953** | AP83 | 45c gold, car & brn | .35 | .20 |
| **C954** | AP83 | 55c multi | .45 | .20 |
| **C955** | AP84 | 60c blk, ultra & sil | .50 | .20 |
| **C956** | AP83 | 65c multi | .65 | .25 |
| **C957** | AP84 | 90c multi | .80 | .30 |
| **C958** | AP84 | 1b multi | .90 | .35 |
| | | *Nos. C952-C958 (7)* | 3.85 | 1.70 |

400th anniv. of the founding of Caracas (1st issue). See Nos. C977-C982 (2nd issue).

Two souvenir sheets each contain single stamps similar to Nos. C952-C953, but with simulated perforation. Sold for 1b each. Size: 80x119mm. Value $45 each.

Issued: 55c, 65c, July 28; others, July 12.

Gen. Francisco Esteban Gomez — AP85

Juan Vicente González — AP86

**1967, July 31 Litho.** ***Perf. 14x13½***

| | | | | |
|---|---|---|---|---|
| **C959** | AP85 | 90c multi | .90 | .40 |

150th anniversary, Battle of Matasiete.

**1967, Oct. 18 Litho.** ***Perf. 14x13½***

| | | | | |
|---|---|---|---|---|
| **C960** | AP86 | 80c ocher & blk | .90 | .30 |

Centenary of the death (in 1866) of Juan Vicente González, journalist.

Bolivar Type of 1966

Imprint: "Druck Bruder Rosenbaum. Wien"

**1967-68 Litho.** ***Perf. 13½x14***

**Multicolored Center**

| | | | | |
|---|---|---|---|---|
| **C961** | AP79 | 5c lemon & blk | .20 | .20 |
| **C962** | AP79 | 10c lemon & blk | .20 | .20 |
| **C963** | AP79 | 20c grn & blk | .30 | .20 |
| **C964** | AP79 | 25c salmon & blk | .25 | .20 |
| **C965** | AP79 | 30c pink & blk | .30 | .20 |
| **C966** | AP79 | 35c dl rose & blk | .30 | .20 |
| **C967** | AP79 | 40c bis brn & blk | .50 | .20 |
| **C968** | AP79 | 50c org brn & blk | 4.00 | .30 |
| **C969** | AP79 | 60c brn red & blk | 1.75 | .80 |
| **C970** | AP79 | 80c brt bl & blk | 1.00 | .40 |
| **C971** | AP79 | 1.20b dl bl & blk | 1.50 | .30 |
| **C972** | AP79 | 4b vio bl & blk | 4.00 | 1.60 |
| | | *Nos. C961-C972 (12)* | 14.30 | 4.80 |

Issue dates: 20c, 30c, 50c, Nov. 24; 5c, 25c, 40c, Feb. 5, 1968; others, Aug, 28, 1967.

Child with Pinwheel AP87

**1967, Dec. 15 Litho.** ***Perf. 14x13½***

| | | | | |
|---|---|---|---|---|
| **C973** | AP87 | 45c multi | .50 | .20 |
| **C974** | AP87 | 75c multi | .65 | .25 |
| **C975** | AP87 | 90c multi | .85 | .30 |
| | | *Nos. C973-C975 (3)* | 2.00 | .75 |

Children's Festival.

Madonna with the Rosebush, by Stephan Lochner AP88

**1967, Dec. 19**

| | | | | |
|---|---|---|---|---|
| **C976** | AP88 | 1b multi | 1.25 | .55 |

Christmas 1967.

Palace of the Academies, Caracas — AP89

Views of Caracas: 50c, St. Theresa's Church, vert. 70c, Federal Legislature. 75c, University City. 85c, El Pulpo highways crossing. 2b, Avenida Libertador.

**1967, Dec. 28** ***Perf. 13½x14, 14x13½***

| | | | | |
|---|---|---|---|---|
| **C977** | AP89 | 10c multi | .20 | .20 |
| **C978** | AP89 | 50c lil & multi | .35 | .20 |
| **C979** | AP89 | 70c multi | .65 | .20 |
| **C980** | AP89 | 75c multi | .75 | .25 |
| **C981** | AP89 | 85c multi | .80 | .30 |
| **C982** | AP89 | 2b multi | 2.25 | .85 |
| | | *Nos. C977-C982 (6)* | 5.00 | 2.00 |

400th anniv. of Caracas (2nd issue).

Dr. José Manuel Nuñez Ponte (1870-1965), Educator — AP90

**1968, Mar. 8 Litho.** ***Perf. 14***

| | | | | |
|---|---|---|---|---|
| **C983** | AP90 | 65c multi | .55 | .25 |

De Miranda and Printing Press AP91

Designs (Miranda Portraits and): 35c, Parliament, London. 45c, Arc de Triomphe, Paris. 70c, Portrait, vert. 80c, Portrait bust and Venezuelan flags, vert.

***Perf. 13½x14, 14x13½***

**1968, June 20 Litho.**

| | | | | |
|---|---|---|---|---|
| **C984** | AP91 | 20c yel brn, grn & brn | .25 | .20 |
| **C985** | AP91 | 35c multi | .40 | .20 |
| **C986** | AP91 | 45c lt bl & multi | .75 | .30 |
| **C987** | AP91 | 70c multi | .90 | .25 |
| **C988** | AP91 | 80c multi | 1.10 | .40 |
| | | *Nos. C984-C988 (5)* | 3.40 | 1.35 |

General Francisco de Miranda (1750?-1816), revolutionist, dictator of Venezuela.

Insect Type of 1968

Insect Pests: 5c, Red leaf-cutting ant, vert. 15c, Sugar cane beetle, vert. 20c, Leaf beetle.

***Perf. 14x13½, 13½x14***

**1968, Aug. 30 Litho.**

| | | | | |
|---|---|---|---|---|
| **C989** | A157 | 5c multi | .50 | .20 |
| **C990** | A157 | 15c multi | 1.00 | .20 |
| **C991** | A157 | 20c gray & multi | 1.50 | .20 |
| | | *Nos. C989-C991 (3)* | 3.00 | .60 |

Three Keys — AP92

**1968, Oct. 17 Litho. *Perf. 14x13½***
**C992** AP92 95c yel, vio & dk grn .95 .35

Natl. Comptroller's Office, 30th anniv.

Fencing — AP93

Designs: 5c, Pistol shooting, vert. 15c, Running. 75c, Boxing. 5b, Sailing, vert.

***Perf. 14x13½, 13½x14***
**1968, Nov. 6 Litho. Unwmk.**
**C993** AP93 5c vio, bl & blk .45 .25
**C994** AP93 15c multi .55 .25
**C995** AP93 30c yel grn, dk grn & blk .70 .25
**C996** AP93 75c multi 1.25 .35
**C997** AP93 5b multi 4.75 1.75
*Nos. C993-C997 (5)* 7.70 2.85

19th Olympic Games, Mexico City, 10/12-27.

Holy Family, by Francisco José de Lerma — AP94

Dancing Children and Stars — AP95

**1968, Dec. 4 Litho. *Perf. 14x13½***
**C998** AP94 40c multi .55 .20

Christmas 1968.

**1968, Dec. 13 Litho. *Perf. 14x13½***
**C999** AP95 80c vio & org .75 .30

Issued for the 5th Children's Festival.

### Conservation Type of 1968

Designs: 15c, Marbled wood-quail, vert. 20c, Water birds, vert. 30c, Woodcarvings and tools, vert. 90c, Brown trout. 95c, Valley and road. 1b, Red-eyed vireo feeding young bronzed cowbird.

***Perf. 13½x14, 14x13½***
**1968, Dec. 19 Litho.**
**C1000** A160 15c multi .40 .30
**C1001** A160 20c multi .40 .30
**C1002** A160 30c multi .50 .30
**C1003** A160 90c multi 1.40 .40
**C1004** A160 95c multi 2.00 .60
**C1005** A160 1b multi 1.50 .50
*Nos. C1000-C1005 (6)* 6.20 2.40

### Tourist Type of 1969

Designs: 15c, Giant cactus and desert, Falcon. 30c, Hotel Humboldt, Federal District. 40c, Cable car and mountain peaks, Merida.

**1969, Jan. 24 *Perf. 13½x14***
**C1006** A161 15c multi .25 .20
**C1007** A161 30c multi .25 .20
*a.* Souv. sheet of 2, #931, C1007, imperf. 1.40 1.40
**C1008** A161 40c multi .50 .20
*Nos. C1006-C1008 (3)* 1.00 .60

### Tree Type of 1969

Trees: 5c, Cassia grandis. 20c, Triplaris caracasana. 25c, Samanea saman.

**1969, May 30 Litho. *Perf. 13½x14***
**C1009** A164 5c lt grn & multi .50 .20
**C1010** A164 20c org & multi .75 .20
**C1011** A164 25c lt vio & multi .85 .20
*Nos. C1009-C1011 (3)* 2.10 .60

Alexander von Humboldt, by Joseph Stieler — AP96

Map of Maracaibo, 1562 — AP97

**1969, Sept. 12 Photo. *Perf. 14***
**C1012** AP96 50c multi .60 .20

Alexander von Humboldt (1769-1859), naturalist and explorer.

***Perf. 13½x13, 13x13½***
**1969, Sept. 30 Litho.**

20c, Ambrosio Alfinger, Alfonso Pacheco, Pedro Maldonado, horiz. 40c, Maracaibo coat of arms. 70c, University Hospital. 75c, Monument to the Indian Mara. 1b, Baralt Square, horiz.

**C1013** AP97 20c lil & multi .25 .20
**C1014** AP97 25c org & multi .30 .20
**C1015** AP97 40c multi .35 .20
**C1016** AP97 70c grn & multi .75 .25
**C1017** AP97 75c brn & multi .90 .30
**C1018** AP97 1b multi 1.10 .40
*Nos. C1013-C1018 (6)* 3.65 1.55

400th anniversary of Maracaibo.

Astronauts Neil A. Armstrong, Edwin E. Aldrin, Jr., Michael Collins and Moonscape AP98

**1969, Nov. 18 Litho. *Perf. 12½***
**C1019** AP98 90c multi 1.25 .50
*a.* Souv. sheet of 1, imperf. 1.90 1.90

See note after US No. C76.

Virgin with the Rosary, 17th Century AP99

Christmas: 80c, Holy Family, Caracas, 18th Cent.

**1969, Dec. 1 Litho. *Perf. 12½***
**C1020** AP99 75c gold & multi .75 .30
**C1021** AP99 80c gold & multi .90 .35
*a.* Pair, #C1020-C1021 1.85 1.85

Simon Bolivar, 1819, by M. N. Bate — AP100

Bolivar Portraits: 45c, 55c, like 15c. 65c, 70c, 75c Drawing by Francois Roulin, 1828. 85c, 90c, 95c, Charcoal drawing by José Maria Espinoza, 1828. 1b, 1.50b, 2b, Drawing by Espinoza, 1830.

**1970, Mar. 16 Litho. *Perf. 14x13½***
**C1022** AP100 15c multi .20 .20
**C1023** AP100 45c bl & multi .40 .20
**C1024** AP100 55c org & multi .55 .20
**C1025** AP100 65c multi .55 .25
**C1026** AP100 70c bl & multi .65 .35
**C1027** AP100 75c org & multi .85 .35
**C1028** AP100 85c multi .95 .35
**C1029** AP100 90c bl & multi 1.00 .40
**C1030** AP100 95c org & multi 1.10 .45
**C1031** AP100 1b multi 1.10 .45
**C1032** AP100 1.50b bl & multi 1.25 .50
**C1033** AP100 2b multi 2.75 1.60
*Nos. C1022-C1033 (12)* 11.35 5.30

Issued to honor Simon Bolivar (1783-1830), liberator and father of his country.

General Antonio Guzmán Blanco and Dr. Martin J. Sanabria AP101

**1970, June 26 Litho. *Perf. 13***
**C1034** AP101 75c brt grn & multi .65 .30

Free obligatory elementary education, cent.

Map of Venezuela with Claim to Part of Guyana — AP102

State map and arms. 55c, 90c, vert.

***Perf. 13½x14, 14x13½***
**1970-71 Litho.**
**C1035** AP102 5c shown .35 .20
**C1036** AP102 15c Apure .35 .20
**C1037** AP102 20c Aragua .40 .20
**C1038** AP102 20c Anzoategui .45 .20
**C1039** AP102 25c Barinas .45 .20
**C1040** AP102 25c Bolivar .45 .20
**C1041** AP102 45c Carabobo .65 .20
**C1042** AP102 55c Cojedes .70 .20
**C1043** AP102 65c Falcon .75 .20
**C1044** AP102 75c Guárico .90 .25
**C1045** AP102 85c Lara 1.10 .30
**C1046** AP102 90c Mérida 1.10 .30
**C1047** AP102 1b Miranda 1.10 .40
**C1048** AP102 2b Delta Amacuro Territory 2.40 .95
*Nos. C1035-C1048 (14)* 11.15 4.00

Issued: 5c, 7/15; 15c, #C1037, 1/18; #C1038-C1039, 2/15/71; #C1040, 45c, 3/15/71; 55c, 65c, 4/15; 75c, 85c, 5/15/71; 90c, 1b, 6/15/71; 2b, 7/15/71.

### Flower Type of 1970

Flowers: 20c, Epidendrum secundum. 25c, Oyedaea verbesinoides. 45c, Heliconia villosa. 1b, Macleania nitida.

**1970, July 29 Litho. *Perf. 14x13½***
**C1049** A175 20c multi .50 .20
**C1050** A175 25c multi .60 .20
**C1051** A175 45c multi 1.50 .35
**C1052** A175 1b multi 1.90 .45
*Nos. C1049-C1052 (4)* 4.50 1.20

Caracciolo Parra Olmedo AP104

**1970, Nov. 16 Photo. *Perf. 12½***
**C1053** AP104 20c bl & multi .30 .20

Sesquicentennial of birth of Caracciolo Parra Olmedo (1819-1900), professor of law, rector of University of Merida.

Census Chart — AP105

**1971, Apr. 30 Litho. *Perf. 13½x14***
**C1054** Block of 4 4.50 2.25
*a.* AP105 70c, frame L & T .80 .30
*b.* AP105 70c, frame T & R .80 .30
*c.* AP105 70c, frame L & B .80 .30
*d.* AP105 70c, frame B & R .80 .30

See note after No. 979.

Cattleya Gaskelliana — AP106

Orchids: 20c, Cattleya percivaliana, vert. 75c, Cattleya mossiae, vert. 90c, Cattleya violacea. 1b, Cattleya lawrenciana.

***Perf. 14x13½, 13½x14***
**1971, Aug. 25**
**C1055** AP106 20c blk & multi .55 .25
**C1056** AP106 25c blk & multi .80 .25
**C1057** AP106 75c blk & multi 1.50 .50
**C1058** AP106 90c blk & multi 2.10 .80
**C1059** AP106 1b blk & multi 2.25 .90
*Nos. C1055-C1059 (5)* 7.20 2.70

40th anniversary of Venezuelan Society of Natural History. Issued in sheets of 5 stamps and one label with Society emblem in blue. Value $20.

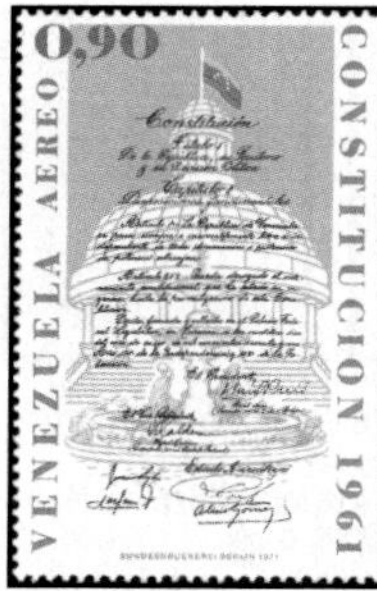


Draft of Constitution Superimposed on Capitol AP107

**1971, Dec. 29 Litho. *Perf. 13½***
**C1060** AP107 90c multi .80 .40

Anniversary of 1961 Constitution.

## AIR POST SEMI-POSTAL STAMPS

King Vulture
SPAP1

**Unwmk.**

| 1942, Dec. 17 | Engr. | *Perf. 12* | |
|---|---|---|---|
| **CB1** SPAP1 15c + 10c org brn | | 2.25 | .60 |
| **CB2** SPAP1 30c + 5c violet | | 2.25 | .75 |
| Set, never hinged | | 7.50 | |

See note after No. B1.

## SPECIAL DELIVERY STAMPS

**Catalogue values for unused stamps in this section are for Never Hinged items.**

SD1

SD2

*Perf. 12½*

| 1949, Mar. 9 | Unwmk. | Engr. | |
|---|---|---|---|
| **E1** SD1 30c red | | .60 | .30 |

**Wmk. 116**

| 1961, Apr. 7 | Litho. | *Perf. 13½* | |
|---|---|---|---|
| **E2** SD2 30c orange | | .55 | .25 |

## REGISTRATION STAMPS

Bolívar — R1

| 1899, May Unwmk. Engr. | *Perf. 12* | |
|---|---|---|
| **F1** R1 25c yellow brown | 3.00 | 2.50 |

No. F1 Overprinted like Nos. 150-155

| 1900 | | |
|---|---|---|
| **F2** R1 25c yellow brown | 1.50 | 1.50 |
| *a.* Inverted overprint | 22.50 | 22.50 |
| *b.* Double overprint | 30.00 | 30.00 |

Counterfeit overprints exist, especially of the varieties.

## OFFICIAL STAMPS

Coat of Arms
O1 O3

**Lithographed, Center Engraved**

| 1898, May 1 Unwmk. | *Perf. 12* | |
|---|---|---|
| **O1** O1 5c bl grn & blk | .80 | .55 |
| **O2** O1 10c rose & blk | .95 | .85 |
| **O3** O1 25c bl & blk | 1.50 | 1.40 |
| **O4** O1 50c yel & blk | 2.50 | 2.25 |
| **O5** O1 1b vio & blk | 2.75 | 2.50 |
| *Nos. O1-O5 (5)* | 8.50 | 7.55 |

Nos. O4 and O5 Handstamp Surcharged in Magenta or Violet

| 1899, Nov. | | |
|---|---|---|
| **O6** O1 5c on 50c yel & blk | 4.75 | 4.50 |
| **O7** O1 5c on 1b vio & blk | 20.00 | 18.00 |
| **O8** O1 25c on 50c yel & blk | 20.00 | 18.00 |
| **O9** O1 25c on 1b vio & blk | 12.00 | 11.00 |
| *Nos. O6-O9 (4)* | 56.75 | 51.50 |

**Inverted Surcharge**

| | | |
|---|---|---|
| *O6a* O1 5c on 50c | 15.00 | 15.00 |
| *O7a* O1 5c on 1b | 40.00 | 40.00 |
| *O8a* O1 25c on 50c | 32.50 | 32.50 |
| *O9a* O1 25c on 1b | 32.50 | 32.50 |
| *Nos. O6a-O9a (4)* | 120.00 | 120.00 |

Nos. O6-O9 exist with double surcharge. Value each $18.50-$37.50.

Many of the magenta overprints have become violet. There are intermediate shades.

Counterfeit overprints exist.

| 1900 | Litho., Center Engr. | |
|---|---|---|
| **O14** O3 5c bl grn & blk | .40 | .40 |
| **O15** O3 10c rose & blk | .55 | .55 |
| **O16** O3 25c bl & blk | .55 | .55 |
| **O17** O3 50c yel & blk | .55 | .55 |
| **O18** O3 1b dl vio & blk | .65 | .65 |
| *Nos. O14-O18 (5)* | 2.70 | 2.70 |

O4

No Stars Above Shield — O5

Imprint: "American Bank Note Co., N.Y."

| 1904, July | Engr. | |
|---|---|---|
| **O19** O4 5c emerald & blk | .25 | .25 |
| **O20** O4 10c rose & blk | .65 | .65 |
| **O21** O4 25c blue & blk | .65 | .65 |
| **O22** O4 50c red brn & blk | 4.25 | 4.25 |
| *a.* 50c claret & black | 4.25 | 4.25 |
| **O23** O4 1b red brn & blk | 2.00 | 2.00 |
| *a.* 1b claret & black | 2.00 | 2.00 |
| *Nos. O19-O23 (5)* | 7.80 | 7.80 |

| 1912 | Lithographed in Caracas | |
|---|---|---|
| **O24** O5 5c grn & blk | .55 | .30 |
| **O25** O5 10c car & blk | .55 | .30 |
| **O26** O5 25c dk bl & blk | .55 | .30 |
| **O27** O5 50c pur & blk | .55 | .40 |
| *a.* Center double | 19.00 | |
| **O28** O5 1b yel & blk | 1.30 | .80 |
| *Nos. O24-O28 (5)* | 3.50 | 2.10 |

Perforated Initials

After 1925, Venezuela's official stamps consisted of regular postage stamps, some commemoratives and air post stamps of 1930-42 punched with "GN" (Gobierno Nacional) in large perforated initials.

## LOCAL STAMPS FOR THE PORT OF CARUPANO

In 1902 Great Britain, Germany and Italy, seeking compensation for revolutionary damages, established a blockade of La Guaira and seized the custom house. Carúpano, a port near Trinidad, was isolated and issued the following provisionals. A treaty effected May 7, 1903, referred the dispute to the Hague Tribunal.

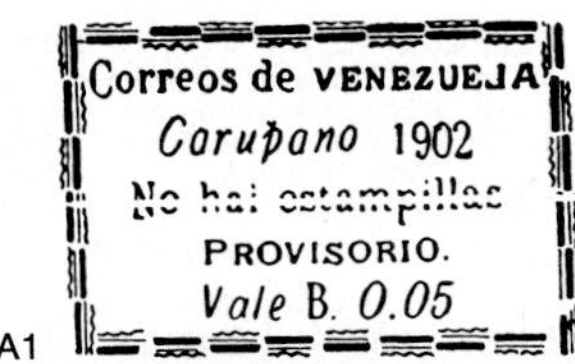

A1

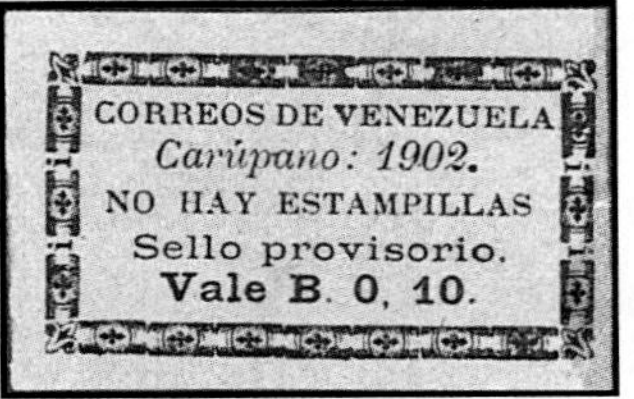

A2

| 1902 | Typeset | *Imperf.* |
|---|---|---|
| **1** A1 5c purple, *orange* | | 27.00 |
| **2** A2 10c black, *orange* | | 40.00 |
| *a.* Tête bêche pair | | 82.50 |
| **3** A1 25c purple, *green* | | 32.50 |
| **4** A1 50c green, *yellow* | | 80.00 |
| **5** A1 lb blue, *rose* | | 100.00 |
| *Nos. 1-5 (5)* | | 279.50 |

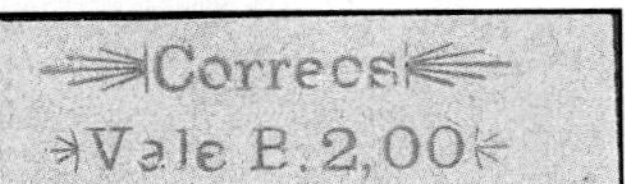

A3

| 1902 | |
|---|---|
| **6** A3 1b black, *yellow* | 200.00 |
| *a.* Tête bêche pair | |


A4

| 1903 | Handstamped | |
|---|---|---|
| **7** A4 5c carmine, *yellow* | 40.00 | 40.00 |
| **8** A4 10c green, *yellow* | 92.50 | 92.50 |
| **9** A4 25c green, *orange* | 45.00 | 45.00 |
| **10** A4 50c blue, *rose* | 45.00 | 45.00 |
| **11** A4 1b violet, *gray* | 45.00 | 45.00 |
| **12** A4 2b carmine, *green* | 45.00 | 45.00 |
| **13** A4 5b violet, *blue* | 45.00 | 45.00 |
| *Nos. 7-13 (7)* | 357.50 | 357.50 |

Dangerous counterfeits exist of Nos. 1-13.

## LOCAL STAMPS FOR THE STATE OF GUAYANA

Revolutionary Steamship "Banrigh" — A1

Control Mark

| 1903 | Typo. | *Perf. 12* | |
|---|---|---|---|
| **1** A1 5c black, *gray* | | 19.00 | 19.00 |
| **2** A1 10c black, *orange* | | 47.50 | 47.50 |
| **3** A1 25c black, *pink* | | 19.00 | 19.00 |
| **4** A1 50c black, *blue* | | 30.00 | 30.00 |
| **5** A1 1b black, *straw* | | 25.00 | 25.00 |
| *Nos. 1-5 (5)* | | 140.50 | 140.50 |

Nos. 1-5 can be found with or without the illustrated control mark which covers four stamps.

Counterfeits include the 10c and 50c in red and are from different settings from the originals. They are on papers differing in colors from the originals. All 5c on granite paper are bogus.

Coat of Arms
A2

| 1903 | |
|---|---|
| **11** A2 5c black, *pink* | 40.00 |
| **12** A2 10c black, *orange* | 50.00 |
| **13** A2 25c black, *gray blue* | 40.00 |
| *a.* 25c black, *blue* | 40.00 |
| **14** A2 50c black, *straw* | 40.00 |
| **15** A2 1b black, *gray* | 30.00 |
| *Nos. 11-15 (5)* | 200.00 |

Postally used examples are very scarce, and are specimens having 9 ornaments in horizontal borders. Nos. 11-15 pen canceled sell for same values as unused.

See note on controls after No. 5.

Counterfeits exist of Nos. 11-15. Stamps with 10 ornaments in horizontal borders are counterfeits.

Nos. 1-5, 11-15 were issued by a group of revolutionists and had a limited local use. The dates on the stamps commemorate the declaration of Venezuelan independence and a compact with Spain against Joseph Bonaparte.

# VIET NAM

vē-'et-'näm

LOCATION — In eastern Indo-China
GOVT. — Kingdom
AREA — 123,949 sq. mi.
POP. — 77,311,210 (1999 est.)
CAPITAL — Hanoi

Viet Nam, which included the former French territories of Tonkin, Annam and Cochin China, became an Associated State of the French Union in 1949. The Communist Viet Minh obtained control of Northern Viet Nam in 1954, and the republic of South Viet Nam was established in October, 1955.

100 Cents (Xu) = 1 Piaster (Dong)

**Catalogue values for unused stamps in this country are for Never Hinged items, beginning with Scott 27 in the regular postage section, Scott B2 in the semi-postal section, Scott C1 in the air-post section, Scott J1 in the postage due section, and Scott M1 in the military section..**

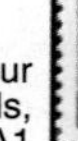

Bongour Falls, Dalat — A1

Emperor Bao-Dai — A2

Designs: 20c, 2pi, 10pi, Imperial palace, Hué. 30c, 15pi, Lake, Hanoi. 50c, 1pi, Temple, Saigon.

***Perf. 13x13½, 13½x13***
**Unwmk.**

**1951, June 6-Oct. 23** **Photo.**

| No. | Type | Value | Unused | Used |
|---|---|---|---|---|
| 1 | A1 | 10c olive green | .20 | .20 |
| 2 | A1 | 20c deep plum | .20 | .20 |
| 3 | A1 | 30c blue | .30 | .40 |
| 4 | A1 | 50c red | .50 | .20 |
| 5 | A1 | 60c brown | .40 | .20 |
| 6 | A1 | 1pi chestnut brn | .40 | .20 |
| 7 | A2 | 1.20pi yellow brn | 4.00 | 5.00 |
| 8 | A1 | 2pi purple | 1.50 | .20 |
| 9 | A2 | 3pi dull blue | 4.00 | .20 |
| 10 | A1 | 5pi green | 5.00 | .70 |
| 11 | A1 | 10pi crimson | 13.50 | .90 |
| 12 | A1 | 15pi red brown | 75.00 | 6.00 |
| 13 | A2 | 30pi blue green | 45.00 | 7.00 |
| | | *Nos. 1-13 (13)* | 150.00 | 21.40 |
| | | Set, never hinged | 250.00 | |

Souvenir booklets exist comprising five gummed sheets of 1 containing Nos. 1, 2, 6, 9, 12, together with commemorative inscriptions. Value, $150.

Empress Nam-Phuong A3

Globe and Lightning Bolt A4

**1952, Aug. 15** ***Perf. 12½***

| No. | Type | Value | Unused | Used |
|---|---|---|---|---|
| 14 | A3 | 30c dk pur, yel & brn | .60 | .35 |
| 15 | A3 | 50c blue, yel & brn | 1.25 | .65 |
| 16 | A3 | 1.50pi ol grn, yel & brn | 2.40 | .30 |
| | | *Nos. 14-16 (3)* | 4.25 | 1.30 |
| | | Set, never hinged | 7.25 | |

For surcharge see No. B1.

**1952, Aug. 24** **Engr.** ***Perf. 13***

| No. | Type | Value | Unused | Used |
|---|---|---|---|---|
| 17 | A4 | 1pi greenish blue | 2.50 | 1.75 |
| | | Never hinged | 4.00 | |

Viet Nam's admission to the ITU, 1st anniv.

Coastal Scene and UPU Emblem A5

**1952, Sept. 12**

| No. | Type | Value | Unused | Used |
|---|---|---|---|---|
| 18 | A5 | 5pi red brown | 2.75 | 1.25 |
| | | Never hinged | 4.75 | |

Viet Nam's admission to the UPU, 1st anniv.

Bao-Dai and Pagoda of Literature, Hanoi — A6

**1952, Nov. 10** ***Perf. 12***

| No. | Type | Value | Unused | Used |
|---|---|---|---|---|
| 19 | A6 | 1.50pi rose violet | 2.50 | .50 |
| | | Never hinged | 4.50 | |

39th birthday of Emperor Bao-Dai.

Crown Prince Bao-Long in Annamite Costume — A7

70c, 80c, 100pi, Prince in Annamite costume. 90c, 20pi, 50pi, Prince in Western uniform.

**1954, June 15** ***Perf. 13***

| No. | Type | Value | Unused | Used |
|---|---|---|---|---|
| 20 | A7 | 40c aqua | .20 | .20 |
| 21 | A7 | 70c claret | .20 | .20 |
| 22 | A7 | 80c black brown | .20 | *.30* |
| 23 | A7 | 90c dark green | .40 | *.80* |
| 24 | A7 | 20pi rose pink | 1.25 | *2.25* |
| 25 | A7 | 50pi violet | 3.75 | *6.25* |
| 26 | A7 | 100pi blue violet | 6.00 | *10.00* |
| | | *Nos. 20-26 (7)* | 12.00 | *20.00* |
| | | Set, never hinged, brown gum | 20.00 | |
| | | Set, never hinged, white gum | 35.00 | |

---

## SOUTH VIET NAM

## (Republic of Viet Nam)

## (Viet Nam Cong Hoa)

GOVT. — Republic
AREA — 66,280 sq. mi.
POP. — 19,600,000 (est. 1973)
CAPITAL — Saigon

**Catalogue values for unused stamps in this section, from this point to the end of the section, are for Never Hinged items. Because of the tropical conditions, never hinged stamps must also be free wrinkles, toning, and any other disturbance.**

Mythological Turtle — A8

**Unwmk.**

**1955, July 20** **Engr.** ***Perf. 13***

| No. | Type | Value | Unused | Used |
|---|---|---|---|---|
| 27 | A8 | 30c claret | 1.25 | .20 |
| 28 | A8 | 50c dark green | 3.00 | .75 |
| 29 | A8 | 1.50pi bright blue | 2.75 | .30 |
| | | *Nos. 27-29 (3)* | 7.00 | 1.25 |
| | | Set, never hinged | 11.50 | |

Refugees on Raft — A9

**1955, Oct. 11**

| No. | Type | Value | Unused | Used |
|---|---|---|---|---|
| 30 | A9 | 70c crimson rose | .85 | .20 |
| 31 | A9 | 80c brown violet | 2.50 | .35 |
| 32 | A9 | 10pi indigo | 5.25 | .50 |
| 33 | A9 | 20pi vio, red brn & org | 16.00 | .75 |
| 34 | A9 | 35pi dk bl, blk brn & yel | 32.50 | 3.75 |
| 35 | A9 | 100pi dk grn, brn vio & org | 72.50 | 6.75 |
| | | *Nos. 30-35 (6)* | 129.60 | 12.30 |

1st anniv. of the flight of the North Vietnamese.

No. 34 is inscribed "Chiên-Dich-Huynh-Dê" (Operation Brotherhood) below design. See No. 54.

Post Office, Saigon — A10

Pres. Ngo Dinh Diem — A11

**1956, Jan. 10** ***Perf. 12***

| No. | Type | Value | Unused | Used |
|---|---|---|---|---|
| 36 | A10 | 60c bluish green | 1.90 | .25 |
| 37 | A10 | 90c violet | 3.50 | .40 |
| 38 | A10 | 3pi red brown | 6.75 | .60 |
| | | *Nos. 36-38 (3)* | 12.15 | 1.25 |

5th anniv. of independent postal service.

**1956** **Engr.** ***Perf. 13x13½***

| No. | Type | Value | Unused | Used |
|---|---|---|---|---|
| 39 | A11 | 20c orange ver | .30 | .20 |
| 40 | A11 | 30c rose lilac | .60 | .20 |
| 41 | A11 | 50c brt carmine | .30 | .20 |
| 42 | A11 | 1pi violet | .60 | .20 |
| 43 | A11 | 1.50pi violet | 1.25 | .20 |
| 44 | A11 | 3pi black brown | 1.25 | .20 |
| 45 | A11 | 4pi dark blue | 1.90 | .20 |
| 46 | A11 | 5pi red brown | 2.50 | .20 |
| 47 | A11 | 10pi blue | 3.00 | .25 |
| 48 | A11 | 20pi gray black | 7.75 | .50 |
| 49 | A11 | 35pi green | 21.00 | 1.10 |
| 50 | A11 | 100pi brown | 45.00 | 4.25 |
| | | *Nos. 39-50 (12)* | 85.45 | 7.70 |

Nos. 36-38 Overprinted

**1956, Aug. 6** ***Perf. 12***

| No. | Type | Value | Unused | Used |
|---|---|---|---|---|
| 51 | A10 | 60c bluish green | .75 | .30 |
| 52 | A10 | 90c violet | 1.50 | .30 |
| 53 | A10 | 3pi red brown | 2.25 | .60 |
| | | *Nos. 51-53 (3)* | 4.50 | 1.20 |

The overprint reads: "Government Post Office Building."

### No. 34 with Black Bar over Inscription below Design

**1956, Aug. 6**

| No. | Type | Value | Unused | Used |
|---|---|---|---|---|
| 54 | A9 | 35pi dk bl, blk brn & yel | 5.50 | 2.75 |

Bamboo — A12

Children — A13

**1956, Oct. 26** **Litho.** ***Perf. 13x13½***

| No. | Type | Value | Unused | Used |
|---|---|---|---|---|
| 55 | A12 | 50c scarlet | .75 | .20 |
| 56 | A12 | 1.50pi rose violet | 1.00 | .20 |
| 57 | A12 | 2pi brt green | 1.25 | .25 |
| 58 | A12 | 4pi deep blue | 3.25 | .35 |
| | | *Nos. 55-58 (4)* | 6.25 | 1.00 |

1st anniv. of the Republic.

**1956, Nov. 7** **Engr.** ***Perf. 13½x14***

| No. | Type | Value | Unused | Used |
|---|---|---|---|---|
| 59 | A13 | 1pi lilac rose | .50 | .20 |
| 60 | A13 | 2pi blue green | .75 | .20 |
| 61 | A13 | 6pi purple | 1.25 | .20 |
| 62 | A13 | 35pi violet blue | 7.00 | 1.25 |
| | | *Nos. 59-62 (4)* | 9.50 | 1.85 |

"Operation Brotherhood."

Hunters on Elephants A14

Loading Cargo A15

Design: 90c, 2pi, 3pi, Mountain dwelling.

**1957, July 7** **Photo.** ***Perf. 13***

| No. | Type | Value | Unused | Used |
|---|---|---|---|---|
| 63 | A14 | 20c yellow grn & pur | .50 | .20 |
| 64 | A14 | 30c bister & dp mag | .60 | .20 |
| 65 | A14 | 90c yel grn & dk brn | .70 | .20 |
| 66 | A14 | 2pi green & ultra | .95 | .20 |
| 67 | A14 | 3pi blue vio & brn | 1.25 | .30 |
| | | *Nos. 63-67 (5)* | 4.00 | 1.10 |

**1957, Oct. 21** ***Perf. 13½x13***

| No. | Type | Value | Unused | Used |
|---|---|---|---|---|
| 68 | A15 | 20c rose violet | .20 | .20 |
| 69 | A15 | 40c lt olive grn | .20 | .20 |
| 70 | A15 | 50c lt carmine rose | .35 | .20 |
| 71 | A15 | 2pi ultra | 1.10 | .20 |
| 72 | A15 | 3pi brt green | 1.50 | .20 |
| | | *Nos. 68-72 (5)* | 3.35 | 1.00 |

9th Colombo Plan Conference, Saigon.

Torch, Map and Constitution A16

Farmers, Tractor and Village A17

**1957, Oct. 26** **Litho.** ***Perf. 13x13½***

| No. | Type | Value | Unused | Used |
|---|---|---|---|---|
| 73 | A16 | 50c black, green & sal | .20 | .20 |
| 74 | A16 | 80c black, brt bl & mag | .20 | .20 |
| 75 | A16 | 1pi black, bl grn & brt car | .35 | .20 |
| 76 | A16 | 4pi blk, ol grn & fawn | .50 | .20 |
| 77 | A16 | 5pi blk, grnsh bl & cit | .75 | .25 |
| 78 | A16 | 10pi black, ultra & rose | 1.50 | .40 |
| | | *Nos. 73-78 (6)* | 3.50 | 1.45 |

Republic of South Viet Nam, 2nd anniv.

**1958, July 7** **Engr.** ***Perf. 13½***

| No. | Type | Value | Unused | Used |
|---|---|---|---|---|
| 79 | A17 | 50c yellow green | .30 | .20 |
| 80 | A17 | 1pi deep violet | .45 | .20 |
| 81 | A17 | 2pi ultra | .75 | .20 |
| 82 | A17 | 10pi brick red | 1.75 | .65 |
| | | *Nos. 79-82 (4)* | 3.25 | 1.25 |

4th anniv. of the government of Ngo Dinh Diem.

Girl and Lantern — A18

A19

**1958, Sept. 27**

| No. | Type | Value | Description | Unused | Used |
|---|---|---|---|---|---|
| **83** | A18 | 30c | yellow | .30 | .20 |
| **84** | A18 | 50c | dk carmine rose | .35 | .20 |
| **85** | A18 | 2pi | dp carmine | .40 | .20 |
| **86** | A18 | 3pi | blue green | .85 | .20 |
| **87** | A18 | 4pi | lt olive green | 1.40 | .20 |
| | | | *Nos. 83-87 (5)* | 3.30 | 1.00 |

Children's Festival.

**1958, Oct. 26** *Perf. 13½*

| No. | Type | Value | Description | Unused | Used |
|---|---|---|---|---|---|
| **88** | A19 | 1pi | dull red brown | .40 | .20 |
| **89** | A19 | 2pi | bluish green | .50 | .20 |
| **90** | A19 | 4pi | rose carmine | .75 | .20 |
| **91** | A19 | 5pi | rose lilac | 1.60 | .35 |
| | | | *Nos. 88-91 (4)* | 3.25 | .95 |

Issued for United Nations Day.

> Most South Viet Nam stamps from 1958 onward exist imperforate in issued and trial colors, and also in small presentation sheets in issued colors.

UNESCO Building, Paris — A20

Cathedral of Hué — A22

Thien Mu Pagoda, Hué — A23

National Museum A24

50c, 2pi, Palace of Independence, Saigon.

Torch and UN Emblem — A21

**1958, Nov. 3** *Perf. 12½x13*

| No. | Type | Value | Description | Unused | Used |
|---|---|---|---|---|---|
| **92** | A20 | 50c | ultra | .30 | .20 |
| **93** | A20 | 2pi | bright red | .40 | .20 |
| **94** | A20 | 3pi | lilac rose | .80 | .20 |
| **95** | A20 | 6pi | violet | 1.25 | .30 |
| | | | *Nos. 92-95 (4)* | 2.75 | .90 |

UNESCO Headquarters in Paris opening, 11/3.

**1958, Dec. 10** **Engr.** *Perf. 13½*

| No. | Type | Value | Description | Unused | Used |
|---|---|---|---|---|---|
| **96** | A21 | 50c | dark blue | .20 | .20 |
| **97** | A21 | 1pi | brown carmine | .25 | .20 |
| **98** | A21 | 2pi | yellow green | .40 | .20 |
| **99** | A21 | 6pi | rose violet | .85 | .35 |
| | | | *Nos. 96-99 (4)* | 1.70 | .95 |

Signing of the Universal Declaration of Human Rights, 10th anniv.

**1958-59** *Perf. 13½*

| No. | Type | Value | Description | Unused | Used |
|---|---|---|---|---|---|
| **100** | A22 | 10c | dk blue gray | .20 | .20 |
| **101** | A23 | 30c | green ('59) | .60 | .20 |
| **102** | A24 | 40c | dk green ('59) | .65 | .20 |
| **103** | A24 | 50c | green ('59) | .65 | .20 |
| **104** | A24 | 2pi | grnsh blue ('59) | 2.00 | .20 |
| **105** | A23 | 4pi | dull purple ('59) | 2.25 | .30 |
| **106** | A24 | 5pi | dk carmine ('59) | 2.40 | .30 |
| **107** | A22 | 6pi | orange brown | 3.25 | .40 |
| | | | *Nos. 100-107 (8)* | 12.00 | 2.00 |

Trung Sisters on Elephants A25

**1959, Mar. 14** **Photo.** *Perf. 13*

| No. | Type | Value | Description | Unused | Used |
|---|---|---|---|---|---|
| **108** | A25 | 50c | multicolored | .60 | .20 |
| **109** | A25 | 2pi | ocher, grn & bl | 1.25 | .20 |
| **110** | A25 | 3pi | emerald, vio & bis | 1.90 | .20 |
| **111** | A25 | 6pi | multicolored | 3.75 | .40 |
| | | | *Nos. 108-111 (4)* | 7.50 | 1.00 |

Sisters Trung Trac and Trung Nhi who resisted a Chinese invasion in 40-44 A.D.

Symbols of Agrarian Reforms A26

**1959, July 7** **Engr.** *Perf. 13*

| No. | Type | Value | Description | Unused | Used |
|---|---|---|---|---|---|
| **112** | A26 | 70c | lilac rose | .30 | .20 |
| **113** | A26 | 2pi | dk grn & Prus bl | .35 | .20 |
| **114** | A26 | 3pi | olive | .60 | .20 |
| **115** | A26 | 6pi | dark red & red | 1.25 | .35 |
| | | | *Nos. 112-115 (4)* | 2.50 | .95 |

5th anniv. of Ngo Dinh Diem's presidency.

Diesel Engine and Map of North and South Viet Nam — A27

**1959, Aug. 7**

| No. | Type | Value | Description | Unused | Used |
|---|---|---|---|---|---|
| **116** | A27 | 1pi | lt violet & grn | .70 | .20 |
| **117** | A27 | 2pi | gray & green | .80 | .20 |
| **118** | A27 | 3pi | grnsh bl & grn | 1.10 | .20 |
| **119** | A27 | 4pi | maroon & grn | 1.90 | .25 |
| | | | *Nos. 116-119 (4)* | 4.50 | .85 |

Re-opening of the Saigon-Dongha Railroad.

Volunteer Road Workers A28

**1959, Oct. 26**

| No. | Type | Value | Description | Unused | Used |
|---|---|---|---|---|---|
| **120** | A28 | 1pi | org brn, ultra & grn | .65 | .20 |
| **121** | A28 | 2pi | violet, org & grn | .85 | .20 |
| **122** | A28 | 4pi | dk bl, bl & bis | 1.90 | .30 |
| **123** | A28 | 5pi | bister, brn & ocher | 2.10 | .45 |
| | | | *Nos. 120-123 (4)* | 5.50 | 1.15 |

4th anniv. of the constitution, stressing communal development.

Boy Scout — A29

**1959, Dec.** **Engr.** *Perf. 13*

| No. | Type | Value | Description | Unused | Used |
|---|---|---|---|---|---|
| **124** | A29 | 3pi | brt yellow grn | .35 | .20 |
| **125** | A29 | 4pi | deep lilac rose | .90 | .20 |
| **126** | A29 | 8pi | dk brn & lil rose | 1.50 | .35 |
| **127** | A29 | 20pi | Prus bl & bl grn | 3.75 | .70 |
| | | | *Nos. 124-127 (4)* | 6.50 | 1.45 |

National Boy Scout Jamboree.

Symbols of Family and Justice A30

**1960**

| No. | Type | Value | Description | Unused | Used |
|---|---|---|---|---|---|
| **128** | A30 | 20c | emerald | .30 | .20 |
| **129** | A30 | 30c | brt grnsh blue | .35 | .20 |
| **130** | A30 | 2pi | orange & maroon | .85 | .20 |
| **131** | A30 | 6pi | car & rose vio | 3.00 | .55 |
| | | | *Nos. 128-131 (4)* | 4.50 | 1.15 |

Issued to commemorate the family code.

Refugee Family and WRY Emblem A31

**1960, Apr. 7** **Engr.** *Perf. 13*

| No. | Type | Value | Description | Unused | Used |
|---|---|---|---|---|---|
| **132** | A31 | 50c | brt lilac rose | .25 | .20 |
| **133** | A31 | 3pi | brt green | .45 | .20 |
| **134** | A31 | 4pi | scarlet | .55 | .25 |
| **135** | A31 | 5pi | dp violet blue | .75 | .35 |
| | | | *Nos. 132-135 (4)* | 2.00 | 1.00 |

World Refugee Year, 7/1/59-6/30/60.

Henri Dunant — A32

**1960, May 8**

**Cross in Carmine**

| No. | Type | Value | Description | Unused | Used |
|---|---|---|---|---|---|
| **136** | A32 | 1pi | dark blue | .45 | .20 |
| **137** | A32 | 3pi | green | 1.40 | .20 |
| **138** | A32 | 4pi | crimson rose | 1.40 | .30 |
| **139** | A32 | 6pi | dp lilac rose | 1.75 | .45 |
| | | | *Nos. 136-139 (4)* | 5.00 | 1.15 |

Centenary (in 1959) of the Red Cross idea.

Model Farm A33

**1960, July 7** *Perf. 13*

| No. | Type | Value | Description | Unused | Used |
|---|---|---|---|---|---|
| **140** | A33 | 50c | ultra | .35 | .20 |
| **141** | A33 | 1pi | dark green | .45 | .20 |
| **142** | A33 | 3pi | orange | .95 | .25 |
| **143** | A33 | 7pi | bright pink | 1.75 | .35 |
| | | | *Nos. 140-143 (4)* | 3.50 | 1.00 |

Establishment of communal rice farming.

Girl With Basket of Rice and Rice Plant A34

**1960, Nov. 21**

| No. | Type | Value | Description | Unused | Used |
|---|---|---|---|---|---|
| **144** | A34 | 2pi | emerald & green | .50 | .20 |
| **145** | A34 | 4pi | blue & ultra | 1.00 | .30 |

Conf. of the UN FAO, Saigon, Nov. 1960.

Map and Flag of Viet Nam — A35

**1960, Oct. 26** **Engr.** *Perf. 13*

| No. | Type | Value | Description | Unused | Used |
|---|---|---|---|---|---|
| **146** | A35 | 50c | grnsh bl, car & yel | .40 | .20 |
| **147** | A35 | 1pi | ultra, car & yel | .55 | .20 |
| **148** | A35 | 3pi | purple, car & yel | .95 | .20 |
| **149** | A35 | 7pi | yel grn, car & yel | 1.60 | .30 |
| | | | *Nos. 146-149 (4)* | 3.50 | .90 |

Fifth anniversary of the Republic.

Agricultural Development Center, Tractor and Plow — A36

**1961, Jan. 3** *Perf. 13*

| No. | Type | Value | Description | Unused | Used |
|---|---|---|---|---|---|
| **150** | A36 | 50c | red brown | .30 | .20 |
| **151** | A36 | 70c | rose lilac | .55 | .20 |
| **152** | A36 | 80c | rose red | .65 | .20 |
| **153** | A36 | 10pi | bright pink | 3.00 | .40 |
| | | | *Nos. 150-153 (4)* | 4.50 | 1.00 |

Plant and Child — A37

Pres. Ngo Dinh Diem — A38

**1961, Mar. 23** *Perf. 13*

| No. | Type | Value | Description | Unused | Used |
|---|---|---|---|---|---|
| **154** | A37 | 70c | light blue | .30 | .20 |
| **155** | A37 | 80c | ultra | .40 | .20 |
| **156** | A37 | 4pi | olive bister | .55 | .20 |
| **157** | A37 | 7pi | grnsh bl & yel grn | 1.25 | .35 |
| | | | *Nos. 154-157 (4)* | 2.50 | .95 |

Child protection.

**1961, Apr. 29** *Perf. 13*

| No. | Type | Value | Description | Unused | Used |
|---|---|---|---|---|---|
| **158** | A38 | 50c | brt ultra | .60 | .20 |
| **159** | A38 | 1pi | red | 1.00 | .20 |
| **160** | A38 | 2pi | lilac rose | 2.00 | .20 |
| **161** | A38 | 4pi | brt violet | 4.00 | .20 |
| | | | *Nos. 158-161 (4)* | 7.60 | .80 |

Second term of Pres. Ngo Dinh Diem.

Boy, Girl and Flaming Torch A39

**1961, July 7** **Engr.** *Perf. 13*

| No. | Type | Value | Description | Unused | Used |
|---|---|---|---|---|---|
| **162** | A39 | 50c | red | .20 | .20 |
| **163** | A39 | 70c | bright pink | .35 | .20 |
| **164** | A39 | 80c | ver & maroon | .45 | .20 |
| **165** | A39 | 8pi | dp claret & mag | 1.25 | .40 |
| | | | *Nos. 162-165 (4)* | 2.25 | 1.00 |

Issued for Youth Day.

Saigon-Bien Hoa Highway Bridge — A40

**1961, July 28**

166 A40 50c yellow green .35 .20
167 A40 1pi orange brown .50 .20
168 A40 2pi dark blue .75 .20
169 A40 5pi brt red lilac 1.40 .20
*Nos. 166-169 (4)* 3.00 .80

Opening of Saigon-Bien Hoa Highway.

Alexandre de Rhodes A41

**1961, Sept. 5**

170 A41 50c rose carmine .35 .20
171 A41 1pi claret .50 .20
172 A41 3pi bister brown .55 .20
173 A41 6pi emerald 1.60 .30
*Nos. 170-173 (4)* 3.00 .90

Alexandre de Rhodes (1591-1660), Jesuit missionary who introduced Roman characters to express the Viet Nam language.

Young Man with Torch, Sage, Pagoda — A42

Temple Dedicated to Confucius — A43

**1961, Oct. 26** ***Perf. 13***

174 A42 50c orange ver .30 .20
175 A42 1pi brt green .55 .20
176 A42 3pi rose red .65 .20
177 A42 8pi rose lilac & brn 2.00 .30
*Nos. 174-177 (4)* 3.50 .90

Moral Rearmament of Youth Movement.

**1961, Nov. 4** **Engr.**

178 A43 1pi brt green .30 .20
179 A43 2pi rose red .45 .20
180 A43 5pi olive 1.25 .25
*Nos. 178-180 (3)* 2.00 .65

15th anniversary of UNESCO.

Earth Scraper Preparing Ground for Model Village — A44

Man Fighting Mosquito and Emblem — A45

**1961, Dec. 11** ***Perf. 13***

181 A44 50c dark green 1.00 .20
182 A44 1pi Prus bl & car lake 1.25 .20
183 A44 2pi olive grn & brn 1.75 .20
184 A44 10pi Prus blue 6.00 .35
*Nos. 181-184 (4)* 10.00 .95

Agrarian reform program.

**1962, Apr. 7** ***Perf. 13***

185 A45 50c brt lilac rose .30 .20
186 A45 1pi orange .40 .20
187 A45 2pi emerald .55 .20
188 A45 6pi ultra 1.25 .40
*Nos. 185-188 (4)* 2.50 1.00

WHO drive to eradicate malaria.

Postal Check Center, Saigon — A46

Madonna of Vang — A47

**1962, May 15** **Engr.** ***Perf. 13***

189 A46 70c dull green .20 .20
190 A46 80c chocolate .30 .20
191 A46 4pi lilac rose .90 .20
192 A46 7pi rose red 2.10 .40
*Nos. 189-192 (4)* 3.50 1.00

Inauguration of postal checking service.

**1962, July 7**

193 A47 50c violet & rose red .25 .20
194 A47 1pi red brn & indigo .35 .20
195 A47 2pi brown & rose car .65 .20
196 A47 8pi green & dk blue 3.25 .25
*Nos. 193-196 (4)* 4.50 .85

Catholic shrine of the Madonna of Vang.

Armed Guards and Village A48

**1962, Oct. 26**

197 A48 50c bright red .35 .20
198 A48 1pi yellow green .55 .20
199 A48 1.50pi lilac rose .70 .20
200 A48 7pi ultra 1.90 .40
*Nos. 197-200 (4)* 3.50 1.00

"Strategic village" defense system.

Gougah Waterfall, Dalat — A49

Trung Sisters' Monument and Vietnamese Women — A50

**1963, Jan. 3**

201 A49 60c orange red .75 .20
202 A49 1pi bluish black 1.00 .20

62nd birthday of Pres. Ngo Dinh Diem; Spring Festival.

**1963, Mar. 1** **Engr.**

203 A50 50c green .20 .20
204 A50 1pi dk carmine rose .30 .20
205 A50 3pi lilac rose .40 .20
206 A50 8pi violet blue 1.10 .40
*Nos. 203-206 (4)* 2.00 1.00

Issued for Women's Day.

Farm Woman with Grain A51

**1963, Mar. 21** ***Perf. 13***

207 A51 50c red .30 .20
208 A51 1pi dk car rose .35 .20
209 A51 3pi lilac rose .50 .20
210 A51 5pi violet .85 .30
*Nos. 207-210 (4)* 2.00 .90

FAO "Freedom from Hunger" campaign.

Common Defense Emblem — A52

Emblem — A53

**1963, July 7** **Engr.** ***Perf. 13***

211 A52 30c bister .45 .20
212 A52 50c lilac rose .55 .20
213 A52 3pi brt green .85 .20
214 A52 8pi red 1.40 .25
*Nos. 211-214 (4)* 3.25 .85

Common defense effort. The inscription says: "Personalism-Common Progress."

**1963, Oct. 26** ***Perf. 13***

215 A53 50c rose red .25 .20
216 A53 1pi emerald .40 .20
217 A53 4pi purple .85 .25
218 A53 5pi orange 1.50 .55
*Nos. 215-218 (4)* 3.00 1.20

The fighting soldiers of the Republic.

Centenary Emblem and Map — A54

**1963, Nov. 17** **Engr.**

**Cross in Deep Carmine**

219 A54 50c Prus blue .35 .20
220 A54 1pi deep carmine .75 .20
221 A54 3pi orange yellow 1.00 .20
222 A54 6pi brown 2.40 .40
*Nos. 219-222 (4)* 4.50 1.00

Centenary of International Red Cross.

Constitution and Scales — A55

**1963, Dec. 10** ***Perf. 13***

223 A55 70c orange .20 .20
224 A55 1pi brt rose .35 .20
225 A55 3pi green .45 .20
226 A55 8pi ocher 1.10 .35
*Nos. 223-226 (4)* 2.10 .95

15th anniv. of the Universal Declaration of Human Rights.

Danhim Hydroelectric Station — A56

**1964, Jan. 15** **Engr.**

227 A56 40c rose red .40 .20
228 A56 1pi bister brown .40 .20
229 A56 3pi violet blue .60 .20
230 A56 8pi olive green 1.10 .45
*Nos. 227-230 (4)* 2.50 1.05

Inauguration of the Danhim Hydroelectric Station.

Atomic Reactor A57

**1964, Feb. 3** ***Perf. 13***

231 A57 80c olive .40 .20
232 A57 1.50pi brown orange .40 .20
233 A57 3pi chocolate .85 .20
234 A57 7pi brt blue 1.10 .40
*Nos. 231-234 (4)* 2.75 1.00

Peaceful uses of atomic energy.

Compass Rose, Barograph and UN Emblem — A58

South Vietnamese Gesturing to North Vietnamese; Map — A59

**1964, Mar. 23** **Engr.**

235 A58 50c bister .20 .20
236 A58 1pi vermilion .25 .20
237 A58 1.50pi rose claret .35 .20
238 A58 10pi emerald 1.10 .40
*Nos. 235-238 (4)* 1.90 1.00

4th World Meteorological Day, Mar. 23.

**1964, July 20** ***Perf. 13***

239 A59 30c dk grn, ultra & mar 1.10 .20
240 A59 50c dk car rose, yel & blk 1.10 .20
241 A59 1.50pi dk bl, dp org & blk 1.10 .35
*Nos. 239-241 (3)* 3.30 .75

10th anniv. of the Day of National Grief, July 20, 1954, when the nation was divided into South and North Viet Nam.

Hatien Beach — A60

**1964, Sept. 7** **Engr.** ***Perf. 13½***

242 A60 20c bright ultra .25 .25
243 A60 3pi emerald 1.00 .30

Revolutionists and "Nov. 1" — A61

Designs: 80c, Soldier breaking chain. 3pi, Broken chain and date: "1-11 1963," vert.

**1964, Nov. 1** **Engr.** ***Perf. 13***

244 A61 50c red lilac & indigo .50 .20
245 A61 80c violet & red brn .55 .20
246 A61 3pi dk blue & red .95 .55
*Nos. 244-246 (3)* 2.00 .95

Anniv. of November 1963 revolution.

Temple, Saigon A62

Designs: 1pi, Royal tombs, Hué. 1.50pi, Fishermen and sailboats at Phan-Thiet beach. 3pi, Temple, Gia-Dhin.

**1964-66** ***Perf. 13***

**Size: 35½x26mm**

247 A62 50c fawn, grn & dl vio .55 .20
248 A62 1pi olive bis & ind .85 .20
249 A62 1.50pi ol gray & dk sl grn .80 .20

**250** A62 3pi vio, dk sl grn & cl 1.60 .40
*Nos. 247-250 (4)* 3.80 1.00

**Coil Stamp**

**Size: 23x17mm**

**250A** A62 1pi ol bis & ind ('66) 6.00 3.50

Issue date: Nos. 247-250, Dec. 2, 1964.

Hung Vuong and Au Co with their Children A63

**1965, Apr. Engr. *Perf. 13***

**251** A63 3pi car lake & org red 1.25 .30
**252** A63 100pi brown vio & vio 11.00 2.25

Mythological founders of Viet Nam, c. 2000 B.C.

ITU Emblem, Insulator and TV Mast — A64

Buddhist Wheel of Life and Flames — A65

**1965, May 17 Engr.**

**253** A64 1pi olive, dp car & bister .45 .20
**254** A64 3pi henna brn, car & lil 1.10 .30

ITU, centenary.

**1965, May 15 *Perf. 13***

1.50pi, Wheel, lotus blossom and world map, horiz. 3pi, Wheel and Buddhist flag.

**Inscribed: "Phat-Giao" (Buddhism)**

**255** A65 50c dark carmine 1.50 .20
**256** A65 1.50pi dk blue & ocher 1.50 .20
**257** A65 3pi org brn & dk brn 2.25 .35
*Nos. 255-257 (3)* 5.25 .75

Anniversary of Buddha's birth.

ICY Emblem and Women of Various Races — A66

Ixora — A67

**1965, June 26**

**258** A66 50c bluish blk & bis .70 .20
**259** A66 1pi dk brn & brn .70 .20
**260** A66 1.50pi dark red & gray 1.10 .30
*Nos. 258-260 (3)* 2.50 .70

International Cooperation Year.

**1965, Sept. 10 Engr. *Perf. 13***

Flowers: 80c, Orchid. 1pi, Chrysanthemum. 1.50pi, Lotus, horiz. 3pi, Plum blossoms.

**261** A67 70c grn, slate grn & red .30 .20
**262** A67 80c dk brn, lil & sl grn .40 .20
**263** A67 1pi dk blue & yellow .50 .20
**264** A67 1.50pi sl grn, dl grn & gray .75 .20
**265** A67 3pi slate grn & org 1.50 .40
*Nos. 261-265 (5)* 3.45 1.20

Student, Dormitory and Map of Thu Duc — A68

**1965, Oct. 15 *Perf. 13***

**266** A68 50c dark brown .20 .20
**267** A68 1pi bright green .20 .20
**268** A68 3pi crimson .50 .20
**269** A68 7pi dark blue violet 1.40 .45
*Nos. 266-269 (4)* 2.30 1.05

Issued to publicize higher education.

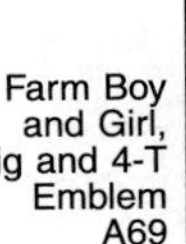

Farm Boy and Girl, Pig and 4-T Emblem A69

4pi, Farm boy with chicken, village and 4-T flag.

**1965, Nov. 25 Engr. *Perf. 13***

**270** A69 3pi emerald & dk red .75 .20
**271** A69 4pi dull violet & plum 1.25 .25

10th anniv. of the 4-T Clubs and the National Congress of Young Farmers.

Basketball A70

Designs: 1pi, Javelin. 1.50pi, Hand holding torch, athletic couple. 10pi, Pole vault.

**1965, Dec. 14 Engr. *Perf. 13***

**272** A70 50c dk car & brn org .40 .20
**273** A70 1pi brn org & red brn .50 .20
**274** A70 1.50pi brt green .75 .20
**275** A70 10pi red lil & brn org 2.10 .50
*Nos. 272-275 (4)* 3.75 1.10

Radio Tower — A71

Loading Hook and Globe — A72

Radio tower, telephone dial, map of Viet Nam.

**1966, Apr. 24 Engr. *Perf. 13***

**276** A71 3pi brt blue & brn .45 .20
**277** A71 4pi purple, red & blk .55 .25

Saigon microwave station.

**1966, June 22 Engr. *Perf. 13***

**278** A72 3pi gray & dk car rose .35 .20
**279** A72 4pi olive & dk purple .45 .20
**280** A72 6pi brt grn & dk blue .75 .30
*Nos. 278-280 (3)* 1.55 .70

Appreciation of the help given by the free world.

Hands Reaching for Persecuted Refugees A73

**1966, July 20**

**281** A73 3pi brn, vio brn & olive .40 .20
**282** A73 7pi claret, vio brn & dk pur .85 .20

Refugees from communist oppression.

Paper Soldiers, Votive Offering A74

Designs: 1.50pi, Man and woman making offerings. 3pi, Floating candles in paper boats. 5pi, Woman burning paper offerings.

**1966, Aug. 30 Engr. *Perf. 13***

**283** A74 50c red, blk & bis brn .60 .20
**284** A74 1.50pi brown, emer & grn 1.00 .20
**285** A74 3pi rose red & lake 1.40 .20
**286** A74 5pi org brn, bis & dk brn 2.00 .30
*Nos. 283-286 (4)* 5.00 .90

Wandering Souls Festival.

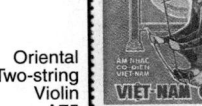

Oriental Two-string Violin A75

Vietnamese Instruments: 3pi, Woman playing 16-string guitar. 4pi, Musicians playing two-string guitars. 7pi, Woman and boy playing flutes.

**1966 Engr. *Perf. 13***

**Size: 35½x26mm**

**287** A75 1pi brown red & brn .75 .20
**288** A75 3pi rose lilac & pur .75 .20
**289** A75 4pi rose brown & brn 1.25 .25
**290** A75 7pi dp blue & vio bl 2.75 .40
*Nos. 287-290 (4)* 5.50 1.05

**Coil Stamp**

**Size: 23x17mm**

**290A** A75 3pi rose lil & pur 7.00 .50
*b.* Booklet pane of 5 —

Nos. 287-290 were issued Sept. 28.

No. 290Ab contains two vertical strip of 5 with selvage at either end. These strips were also sold loose without booklet cover.

WHO Building, Geneva, and Flag — A76

Designs: 50c, WHO Building and emblem, horiz. 8pi, WHO flag and building.

**1966, Oct. 12**

**291** A76 50c purple & carmine .20 .20
**292** A76 1.50pi red brn, vio bl & blk .20 .20
**293** A76 8pi grnsh bl, vio bl & brn 1.00 .50
*Nos. 291-293 (3)* 1.40 .90

Opening of WHO Headquarters, Geneva.

Hand Holding Spade, and Soldiers A77

Soldier and Workers — A78

Designs: 1.50pi, Flag, workers. 4pi, Soldier and cavalryman.

**1966, Nov. 1 Engr. *Perf. 13***

**294** A77 80c dull brn & red brn .35 .20
**295** A77 1.50pi car rose, yel & brn .70 .20
**296** A78 3pi brown & slate grn .70 .20
**297** A78 4pi lilac, black & brn 2.50 .30
*Nos. 294-297 (4)* 4.25 .90

3rd anniv. of the revolution against the government of Pres. Ngo Dinh Diem.

Symbolic Tree and UNESCO Emblem — A79

Designs: 3pi, Globe and olive branches. 7pi, Symbolic temple, horiz.

**1966, Dec. 15 Engr. *Perf. 13***

**298** A79 1pi pink, brn & dk car .60 .20
**299** A79 3pi dp bl, grn & brn org .60 .20
**300** A79 7pi grnsh bl, dk bl & red 1.50 .35
*Nos. 298-300 (3)* 2.70 .75

20th anniv. of UNESCO.

Bitter Melon A80

**1967, Jan. 12 Engr. *Perf. 13***

**301** A80 50c Cashew, vert. 1.00 .20
**302** A80 1.50pi shown 1.50 .20
**303** A80 3pi Sweetsop 1.75 .20
**304** A80 20pi Areca nuts 4.25 .40
*Nos. 301-304 (4)* 8.50 1.00

Phan-Boi-Chau — A81

Designs: 20pi, Phan-Chau-Trinh portrait and addressing crowd.

**1967, Mar. 24 Engr. *Perf. 13***

**305** A81 1pi mar, red brn & dk brn .25 .20
**306** A81 20pi vio, slate grn & blk 1.25 .45

Issued to honor Vietnamese patriots.

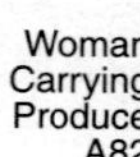

Woman Carrying Produce A82

Labor Day: 1pi, Market scene. 3pi, Two-wheeled horse cart. 8pi, Farm scene with water buffalo.

**1967, May 1** **Engr.** ***Perf. 13***

**307** A82 50c vio bl, dk bl & ultra .20 .20
**308** A82 1pi sl grn & dull pur .20 .20
**309** A82 3pi dk carmine .40 .20
**310** A82 8pi brt car rose & pur .85 .40
*Nos. 307-310 (4)* 1.65 1.00

Potter, Vases and Lamp — A83

Weavers and Potters A84

Designs: 1.50pi, Vase and basket. 35d, Bag and lacquerware.

**1967, July 22** **Engr.** ***Perf. 13***

**311** A83 50c red brn, grn & ultra .20 .20
**312** A83 1.50pi grnsh bl, car & blk .40 .20
**313** A84 3pi red, vio & org brn 1.00 .20
**314** A83 35pi bis brn, blk & dk red 3.00 .60
*Nos. 311-314 (4)* 4.60 1.20

Issued to publicize Vietnamese handicrafts.

Wedding Procession A85

**1967, Sept. 18** **Engr.** ***Perf. 13***

**315** A85 3pi rose cl, dk vio & red 1.50 .25

Symbols of Stage, Music and Art — A86

**Litho. & Engr.**

**1967, Oct. 27** ***Perf. 13***

**316** A86 10pi bl gray, blk & red 1.50 .20

Issued to publicize the Cultural Institute.

"Freedom and Justice" A87

Balloting A88



"Establishment of Democracy" — A89

**1967, Nov. 1** **Photo.**

**317** A87 4pi mag, brn & ocher .75 .20
**318** A88 5pi brown, yel & blk 1.00 .20
**319** A89 30pi dl lil, indigo & red 2.75 .50
*Nos. 317-319 (3)* 4.50 .90

National Day; general elections.

Pagoda and Lions Emblem A90

**1967, Dec. 5** **Photo.** ***Perf. 13½x13***

**320** A90 3pi multicolored 1.50 .80

50th anniversary of Lions International.

Teacher with Pupils and Globe — A91

**1967, Dec. 10** ***Perf. 13x13½***

**321** A91 3pi tan, blk, yel & car 1.50 .25

International Literacy Day, Sept. 8, 1967.

Tractor and Village — A92

Rural Construction Program: 9pi, Bulldozer and home building. 10pi, Wheelbarrow, tractor and new building. 20pi, Vietnamese and Americans working together.

**1968, Jan. 26** **Photo.** ***Perf. 13½***

**322** A92 1pi multicolored .20 .20
**323** A92 9pi lt blue & multi .80 .20
**324** A92 10pi multicolored 1.25 .25
**325** A92 20pi yel, red lil & blk 1.65 .35
*Nos. 322-325 (4)* 3.90 1.00

WHO Emblem — A93

**1968, Apr. 7** **Photo.** ***Perf. 13½***

**326** A93 10pi gray grn, blk & yel 1.50 .80

WHO, 20th anniversary.

Flags of Viet Nam's Allies — A94

Designs: 1.50pi, Flags surrounding SEATO emblem. 3pi, Flags, handclasp, globe and map of Viet Nam. 50pi, Flags and handclasp.

**1968, June 22** **Photo.** ***Perf. 13½***

**327** A94 1pi multicolored .60 .20
**328** A94 1.50pi multicolored 1.25 .20
**329** A94 3pi multicolored 2.40 .20
**330** A94 50pi multicolored 7.75 .95
*Nos. 327-330 (4)* 12.00 1.55

Issued to honor Viet Nam's allies.

Three-wheeled Truck and Tractor — A95

Private Property Ownership: 80c, Farmer, city man and symbols of property. 2pi, Three-wheeled cart, taxi and farmers. 30pi, Taxi, three-wheeled cart and tractor in field.

Inscribed: "HUU-SAN-HOA CONG-NHAN VA NONG-DAN"

**1968, Nov. 1** **Photo.** ***Perf. 13½***

**331** A95 80c multicolored .20 .20
**332** A95 2pi steel blue & multi .20 .20
**333** A95 10pi orange brn & multi .85 .35
**334** A95 30pi gray blue & multi 2.75 1.00
*Nos. 331-334 (4)* 4.00 1.75

Human Rights Flame — A96

Men of Various Races — A97

**1968, Dec. 10** **Photo.** ***Perf. 13½***

**335** A96 10pi multicolored .75 .25
**336** A97 16pi purple & multi 1.50 .30

International Human Rights Year.

UNICEF Emblem, Mother and Child — A98

6pi, Children flying kite with UNICEF emblem.

**1968, Dec. 11**

**337** A98 6pi multicolored 1.00 .25
**338** A98 16pi multicolored 1.25 .40

Workers and Train — A99

1.50pi, 3pi, Crane, train, map of Viet Nam.

**1968, Dec. 15**

**339** A99 1.50pi multicolored .70 .20
**340** A99 3pi org, vio bl & grn .85 .20
**341** A99 9pi multicolored 1.10 .20
**342** A99 20pi multicolored 2.00 .35
*Nos. 339-342 (4)* 4.65 .95

Reopening of Trans-Viet Nam Railroad.

Farm Woman — A100

Vietnamese Women: 1pi, Merchant. 3pi, Nurses, horiz. 20pi, Three ladies.

**1969, Mar. 23** **Engr.** ***Perf. 13***

**343** A100 50c vio bl, lil & ocher .20 .20
**344** A100 1pi grn, bis & dk brn .20 .20
**345** A100 3pi brown, blk & bl .30 .20
**346** A100 20pi lilac & multi 1.40 .55
*Nos. 343-346 (4)* 2.10 1.15

Soldiers and Civilians A101

Family Welcoming Soldier A102

**1969, June 1** **Photo.** ***Perf. 13***

**347** A101 2pi multicolored .20 .20
**348** A102 50pi multicolored 2.25 .50

Pacification campaign.

Man Reading Constitution, Scales of Justice A103

Voters, Torch and Scales A104

**1969, June 9**

**349** A103 1pi yel org, yel & blk .20 .20
**350** A104 20pi multicolored 2.50 .30

Constitutional democracy. Phrase on both stamps: "Democratic and Governed by Law."

Mobile Post Office — A105

Mobile Post Office: 3pi, Window service. 4pi, Child with letter. 20pi, Crowd at window and postmark: "15, 12, 67."

**1969, July 10**

**351** A105 1pi multicolored .20 .20
**352** A105 3pi multicolored .45 .20
**353** A105 4pi multicolored .55 .20
**354** A105 20pi ocher & multi 1.10 .35
*Nos. 351-354 (4)* 2.30 .95

Installation of the first mobile post office in Viet Nam.

Mnong-gar Woman A106

1pi, Djarai woman. 50pi, Bahnar man.

**1969, Aug. 29** **Photo.** ***Perf. 13***
**355** A106 1pi brt pink & multi .75 .20
**356** A106 6pi sky blue & multi 1.75 .20
**357** A106 50pi gray & multi 7.50 .40
*Nos. 355-357 (3)* 10.00 .80

Ethnic minorities in Viet Nam.

Civilians Becoming Soldiers A107

General Mobilization: 3pi, Bayonet training. 5pi, Guard duty. 10pi, Farewell.

**1969, Sept. 20**
**Inscribed: "TONG BONG VIEN"**
**358** A107 1.50pi orange & multi .75 .20
**359** A107 3pi purple & multi 1.60 .20
**360** A107 5pi blk, red & ocher 2.40 .20
**361** A107 10pi pink & multi 3.25 .35
*Nos. 358-361 (4)* 8.00 .95

ILO Emblem and Globe — A108

**1969, Oct. 29** **Photo.** ***Perf. 13***
**362** A108 6pi blue grn, blk & gray .55 .20
**363** A108 20pi red, blk & gray 1.40 .20

ILO, 50th anniversary.

Pegu House Sparrow — A109

Birds: 6pi, Moluccan munia. 7pi, Great hornbill. 30pi, Old world tree sparrow.

**1970, Jan. 15** **Photo.** ***Perf. 12½x14***
**364** A109 2pi blue & multi *.90 .25*
**365** A109 6pi orange & multi *2.00 .50*
**366** A109 7pi org brn & multi *3.00 .50*
**367** A109 30pi blue & multi *11.50 1.50*
*Nos. 364-367 (4)* *17.40 2.75*

Burning House and Family — A110

Design: 20pi, Family fleeing burning house and physician examining child.

**1970, Jan. 31** **Photo.** ***Perf. 13***
**368** A110 10pi multicolored 1.25 .20
**369** A110 20pi multicolored 2.00 .25

Mau Than disaster, 1968.

Vietnamese Costumes — A111

Traditional Costumes: 1pi, Man, woman and priest, vert. 2pi, Seated woman with fan. 100pi, Man and woman.

Inscribed: "Y-PHUC CO TRUYEN"

**1970, Mar. 13** **Photo.** ***Perf. 13***
**370** A111 1pi lt brown & multi .20 .20
**371** A111 2pi pink & multi .20 .20
**372** A111 3pi ultra & multi .20 .20
**373** A111 100pi multicolored 6.00 1.65
*Nos. 370-373 (4)* 6.60 2.25

Issued for the Trung Sisters' Festival.

Building Workers, Pagodas and Bridge A112

Rebuilding of Hué: 20pi, Concrete mixers and scaffolds.

**1970, June 10** **Litho. & Engr.**
**374** A112 6pi multicolored .85 .20
**375** A112 20pi rose lil, brn & bis 1.40 .40

Plower in Rice Field — A113

**1970, Aug. 29** ***Perf. 13***
**376** A113 6pi multicolored 1.75 .45

"Land to the Tiller" agricultural reform program.

New Building and Scaffold A114

Construction Work — A115

**1970, Sept. 15** **Engr.** ***Perf. 13***
**377** A114 8pi pale ol & brn org .50 .20
**378** A115 16pi brn, indigo & yel 1.00 .30

Reconstruction after 1968 Tet Offensive.

Productivity Year Emblem A116

**1970, Oct. 3**
**379** A116 10pi multicolored 1.75 .45

Asian Productivity Year.

Nguyen-Dinh-Chieu — A117

Education Year Emblem — A118

**1970, Nov. 16** **Engr.** ***Perf. 13½***
**380** A117 6pi dull vio, red & brn 1.25 .20
**381** A117 10pi grn, red & dk brn 2.00 .20

Nguyen-Dinh-Chieu (1822-1888), poet.

**Litho. & Engr.**
**1970, Nov. 30** ***Perf. 13***
**382** A118 10pi pale brn, yel & blk 1.75 .65

International Education Year.

Parliament Building A119

Dancers — A120

Design: 6pi, Senate Building.

**1970, Dec.**
**383** A119 6pi lt bl, cit & dk brn .75 .20
**384** A119 10pi multicolored 1.50 .20

6pi issued Dec. 8 for the 6th Cong.; 10pi issued Dec. 9 for the 9th General Assembly of the Asian Interparliamentary Union.

**1971, Jan. 12**

Designs: Various Vietnamese dancers and musicians. 6pi and 7pi horizontal.

**385** A120 2pi ultra & multi .85 .20
**386** A120 6pi pale green & multi 2.40 .20
**387** A120 7pi pink & multi 2.75 .20
**388** A120 10pi brown org & multi 3.00 .45
*Nos. 385-388 (4)* 9.00 1.05

For surcharge see No. 500.

Farmers and Law — A121

Agrarian Reform Law: 3pi, Tractor and law, dated 26.3.1970. 16pi, Farmers, people rejoicing and law book.

**1971, Mar. 26** **Engr.** ***Perf. 13***
**389** A121 2pi vio bl, dk brn & dl org .20 .20
**390** A121 3pi pale grn, brn & dk bl .80 .20
**391** A121 16pi multicolored 3.50 .20
*Nos. 389-391 (3)* 4.50 .60

For surcharge see No. 482.

Courier on Horseback A122

Design: 6pi, Mounted courier with flag.

**Engr. & Photo.**
**1971, June 6** ***Perf. 13***
**392** A122 2pi violet & multi 1.00 .20
**393** A122 6pi tan & multi 3.50 .20

Postal history.

Military and Naval Operations on Vietnamese Coast — A123

**1971, June 19**
**394** A123 3pi multi + label 1.00 .25
**395** A123 40pi multi + label 5.00 .65

Armed Forces Day.

Deer — A124

Rice Harvest A125

**1971, Aug. 20** **Engr.**
**396** A124 9pi shown 1.75 .20
**397** A124 30pi Tiger 5.75 .70

**Litho. & Engr.**
**1971, Sept. 28** ***Perf. 13***

30pi, Threshing and winnowing rice and rice plants. 40pi, Bundling and carrying rice.

**398** A125 1pi multicolored .20 .20
**399** A125 30pi sal pink, dk pur & blk 3.50 .25
**400** A125 40pi sepia, yel & grn 4.25 .30
*Nos. 398-400 (3)* 7.95 .75

For surcharge see No. 496.

Inauguration of UPU Building, Bern — A126

**1971, Nov. 9** **Engr.** ***Perf. 13***
**401** A126 20pi green & multi 3.25 .75

Fish — A127

Various Fish; 2pi vertical.

**1971, Nov. 16** **Photo. & Engr.**
**402** A127 2pi multicolored 1.75 .20
**403** A127 10pi violet & multi 3.25 .20
**404** A127 100pi lilac & multi 24.50 2.40
*Nos. 402-404 (3)* 29.50 2.80

Mailman and Woman on Water Buffalo
A128

Rural Mail: 10pi, Bird carrying letter. 20pi, Mailman with bicycle delivering mail to villagers.

**1971, Dec. 20 Engr. *Perf. 13***
**Inscribed: "PHAT TRIEN BUU-CHINH NONG THON"**

**405** A128 5pi multicolored 1.25 .20
**406** A128 10pi multicolored 2.25 .20
**407** A128 20pi multicolored 4.00 1.25
*Nos. 405-407 (3)* 7.50 1.65

Trawler Fishermen, and Fish — A129

Publicity for Fishing Industry: 7pi, Net fishing from boat. 50d, Trawler with seine.

**1972, Jan. 2 Engr. *Perf. 13***
**408** A129 4pi pink, blk & blue 1.00 .20
**409** A129 7pi lt blue, blk & red 1.50 .20
**410** A129 50pi multicolored 7.50 1.60
*Nos. 408-410 (3)* 10.00 2.00

King Quang Trung (1752-1792) — A130

**1972, Jan. 28 *Perf. 13½***
**411** A130 6pi red & multi 1.10 .20
*a.* Booklet pane of 10 65.00
**412** A130 20pi black & multi 3.50 .50

No. 411a is imperf. horizontally.

Road Workers
A131

**1972, Feb. 4**
**413** A131 3pi multicolored .50 .20
**414** A131 8pi multicolored 1.75 .20

Community development.

Rice Farming
A132

**1972, Mar. 26 Engr. *Perf. 13½***
**415** A132 1pi shown .20 .20
**416** A132 10pi Wheat farming 2.25 .20

Farmers' Day.

Plane over Dalat — A133

**1972, Apr. 18 Engr. & Photo.**
**417** A133 10pi shown 1.25 .25
**418** A133 10pi over Ha-tien 1.25 .25
**419** A133 10pi over Hue 1.25 .25
**420** A133 10pi over Saigon 1.25 .25
*a.* Block of 4, #417-420 10.00 2.00
**421** A133 25pi like No. 417 2.75 .25
**422** A133 25pi like No. 418 2.75 .25
**423** A133 25pi like No. 419 2.75 .25
**424** A133 25pi like No. 420 2.75 .25
*a.* Block of 4, #421-424 21.00 3.50
*Nos. 417-424 (8)* 16.00 2.00

20 years Air Viet Nam.

Scholar
A134

20pi, Teacher, pupils. 50pi, Scholar, scroll.

**1972, May 5 Engr. & Litho.**
**425** A134 5pi multicolored .35 .20
**Engr.**
**426** A134 20pi lt green & multi 1.50 .40
**427** A134 50pi pink & multi 4.00 .60
*Nos. 425-427 (3)* 5.85 1.20

Ancient letter writing art.

Armed Farmer — A135

6pi, Civilian rifleman & Self-defense Forces emblem, horiz. 20pi, Man, woman training with rifles.

**Engr. & Litho.**
**1972, June 15 *Perf. 13***
**428** A135 2pi brt rose & multi 1.25 .25
**429** A135 6pi multicolored 2.00 .25
**430** A135 20pi lt violet & multi 2.75 .25
*Nos. 428-430 (3)* 6.00 .75

Civilian Self-defense Forces.

Hands Holding Safe — A136

**1972, July 10**
**431** A136 10pi lt blue & multi 1.75 .20
**432** A136 25pi lt green & multi 3.25 .40

Treasury Bonds campaign.

Frontier Guard — A137


Soldier Helping Wounded Man — A138

Designs: 10pi, 3 guards and horse, horiz. 40pi, Marching guards, horiz.

**Engr. & Litho.**
**1972, Aug. 14 *Perf. 13***
**433** A137 10pi olive & multi .55 .20
**434** A137 30pi buff & multi 1.40 .25
**435** A137 40pi lt blue & multi 1.90 .45
*Nos. 433-435 (3)* 3.85 .90

Historic frontier guards.

**1972, Sept. 1**

Designs: 16pi, Soldier on crutches and flowers. 100pi, Veterans' memorial, map and flag.

**436** A138 9pi olive & multi .75 .25
**437** A138 16pi yellow & multi 1.00 .25
**438** A138 100pi lt blue & multi 5.50 1.00
*Nos. 436-438 (3)* 7.25 1.50

For surcharge see No. 483.

Tank, Memorial, Flag and Map — A139

Soldiers and Map of Viet Nam — A140

**1972, Nov. 25 Litho. *Perf. 13***
**439** A139 5pi multicolored 8.00 .20
**440** A140 10pi ultra & multi 12.00 .20

Victory at Binh-Long.

Book Year Emblem and Globe — A141

Designs: 4pi, Emblem, books circling globe. 5pi, Emblem, books and globe.

**1972, Nov. 30**
**441** A141 2pi dp carmine & multi .45 .20
**442** A141 4pi blue & multi .75 .20
**443** A141 5pi yellow bister & multi 1.10 .20
*Nos. 441-443 (3)* 2.30 .60

International Book Year.

Liberated Vietnamese Family — A142

Soldiers Raising Vietnamese Flag — A143

**1973, Feb. 18 Litho. *Perf. 13***
**444** A142 10pi yellow & multi 2.00 .20

To celebrate the 200,000th returnee.

**1973, Feb. 24 Litho. *Perf. 13***

Design: 10pi, Victorious soldiers and map of demilitarized zone, horiz.

**445** A143 3pi lilac & multi 1.00 .20
**446** A143 10pi yellow grn & multi 1.50 .20

Victory at Quang Tri.

Satellite, Storm over Viet Nam — A144

**1973, Mar. 23 Litho. *Perf. 12½x12***
**447** A144 1pi lt blue & multi .80 .20

World Meteorological Day.
For surcharge see No. 497.

Farmers with Tractor, Symbol of Law — A145

Farmer Plowing with Water Buffalos
A146

Pres. Thieu Holding Agrarian Reform Law
A147

**1973, Mar. 26 Litho. *Perf. 12½x12***
**448** A145 2pi lt green & multi 2.00 .25
**449** A146 5pi orange & multi 2.00 .25
***Perf. 11***
**450** A147 10pi blue & multi 60.00 10.00
*Nos. 448-450 (3)* 64.00 10.50

3rd anniv. of the agrarian reform law; 5-year plan for rural development.

Value for No. 450 is for stamp with first day cancel. Commercially used copies are worth substantially more.

See No. 475.

INTERPOL Emblem and Headquarters
A148

2pi, INTERPOL emblem. 25pi, INTERPOL emblem, side view of Headquarters.

**1973, Apr. 8 Litho. *Perf. 12½x12***
**451** A148 1pi olive & multi .20 .20
**452** A148 2pi yellow & multi .20 .20
**453** A148 25pi ocher, lilac & brn 2.75 .20
*Nos. 451-453 (3)* 3.15 .60

Intl. Criminal Police Org., 50th anniv.
For surcharge see No. 498.

ITU Emblem and Waves
A149

2pi, Globe and waves. 3pi, ITU emblem.

**1973, May 17**
**454** A149 1pi dull blue & multi .25 .20
**455** A149 2pi brt blue & multi .50 .20
**456** A149 3pi orange & multi .75 .20
*Nos. 454-456 (3)* 1.50 .60

World Telecommunications Day.
For surcharge see No. 499.

Globe, Hand Holding House — A150

Men Building Pylon — A151

Design: 10pi, Fish in net, symbols of agriculture, industry and transportation.

**1973, Nov. 6 Litho. *Perf. 12x12½***
**457** A150 8pi gray & multi .70 .20
**458** A150 10pi vio bl, blk & gray .90 .20
**459** A151 15pi blk, org & lil rose 1.40 .25
*Nos. 457-459 (3)* 3.00 .65

National development.

For surcharge see No. 514.

Water Buffalos
A152

**1973, Dec. 20 Litho. *Perf. 12½x12***

**460** A152 5pi shown .70 .20
**461** A152 10pi Water buffalo 1.00 .20

Human Rights Flame, Three Races
A153

Design: 100pi, Human Rights flame, scales and people, vert.

**1973, Dec. 29 *Perf. 12½x12, 12x12½***

**462** A153 15pi ultra & multi .75 .20
**463** A153 100pi green & multi 2.25 .30

25th anniv. of Universal Declaration of Human Rights.

"25" and WHO Emblem
A154

Design: 15pi, WHO emblem, diff.

**1973, Dec. 31 *Perf. 12½x12***

**464** A154 8pi orange, bl & brn .60 .20
**465** A154 15pi lt brn, bl & brt pink .90 .20

25th anniversary of WHO.
For surcharge see No. 515.

Sampan Ferry
A155

Design: 10pi, Sampan ferry (different).

**1974, Jan. 13 Litho. *Perf. 14x13½***

**466** A155 5pi lt blue & multi 1.25 .20
**467** A155 10pi yellow grn & multi 1.75 .40

Sampan ferry women.

Soldiers of 7 Nations
A156

American War Memorial
A157

Map of South Viet Nam and Allied Flags — A158

Design: No. 469, Soldiers and flags of South Viet Nam, Korea, US, Australia New Zealand, Thailand and Philippines. Same flags shown on 8pi and 60pi.

**1974, Jan. 28 *Perf. 12½x12, 12x12½***

**468** A156 8pi multicolored .40 .20
**469** A156 15pi lt brown & multi .85 .20
**470** A157 15pi multicolored .85 .20
**471** A158 60pi multicolored 2.50 .20
*Nos. 468-471 (4)* 4.60 .80

In honor of South Viet Nam's allies.
For surcharge see No. 516.

Trung Sisters on Elephants Fighting Chinese
A159

**1974, Feb. 27 Litho. *Perf. 12½x12***

**472** A159 8pi green, citron & blk 1.10 .20
**473** A159 15pi dp orange & multi 1.40 .20
**474** A159 80pi ultra, pink & blk 2.75 .20
*Nos. 472-474 (3)* 5.25 .60

Trung Trac and Trung Nhi, queens of Viet Nam, 39-43 A.D. Day of Vietnamese Women.

Pres. Thieu Type of 1973 and

Farmers Going to Work — A160

Woman Farmer Holding Rice — A161

**1974, Mar. 26 Litho. *Perf. 14***

**475** A147 10pi blue & multi .50 .20

***Perf. 12½x12, 12x12½***

**476** A160 20pi yellow & multi .50 .20
**477** A161 70pi blue & multi 5.00 .50
*Nos. 475-477 (3)* 6.00 .90

Agriculture Day. Size of No. 475 is 31x50mm, No. 450 is 34x54mm and printed on thick paper. No. 475 has been extensively redrawn and first line of inscription in bottom panel changed to "26 THANG BA."

Value for No. 477 is for stamp with first day cancel. Commercially used copies are worth substantially more.

Hung Vuong with Bamboo Tallies
A162

Flag Inscribed: Hung Vuong, Founder of Kingdom
A163

**1974, Apr. 2 *Perf. 14x13½***

**478** A162 20pi yellow & multi 1.00 .30
**479** A163 100pi olive & multi 3.50 .50

Hung Vuong, founder of Vietnamese nation and of Hông-Bang Dynasty (2879-258 B.C.).

National Library
A164

New National Library Building: 15pi, Library, right facade and Phoenix.

**1974, Apr. 14**

**480** A164 10pi orange, brn & blk .65 .30
**481** A164 15pi multicolored .85 .40

Nos. 391 and 437 Surcharged with New Value and Two Bars in Red

**1974 *Perf. 13***

**482** A121 25pi on 16pi multi 1.75 .35
**483** A138 25pi on 16pi multi 1.75 .40

Memorial Tower, Saigon — A165

Globe, Crane Lifting Crate — A167

Crane with Flags, Globe and Map of Viet Nam — A166

***Perf. 12x12½, 12½x12***

**1974, June 22 Litho.**

**484** A165 10pi blue & multi .60 .25
**485** A166 20pi multicolored 1.40 .30
**486** A167 60pi yellow & multi 4.50 .35
*Nos. 484-486 (3)* 6.50 .90

International Aid Day.

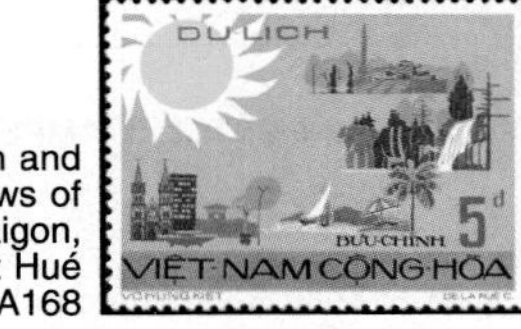

Sun and Views of Saigon, Dalat Hué
A168

Cau-Bong Bridge, Nha Trang
A169

Thien-Mu Pagoda, Hué — A170

**1974, July 12 *Perf. 14x13½, 13½x14***

**487** A168 5pi blue & multi .95 .30
**488** A169 10pi blue & multi .95 .30
**489** A170 15pi yellow & multi 1.50 .30
*Nos. 487-489 (3)* 3.40 .90

Tourist publicity.

Rhynchostylis Gigantea — A171

Orchids: 20pi, Cypripedium caliosum, vert. 200pi, Dendrobium nobile.

**1974, Aug. 18**

**490** A171 10pi blue & multi .30 .20
**491** A171 20pi yellow & multi .35 .25
**492** A171 200pi bister & multi 5.00 1.00
*Nos. 490-492 (3)* 5.65 1.45

Hands Passing Letter, UPU Emblem
A172

UPU Emblem and Woman — A173

UPU Cent.: 30pi, World map, bird, UPU emblem.

***Perf. 12½x12, 12x12½***

**1974, Oct. 9 Litho.**

**493** A172 20pi ultra & multi .25 .20
**494** A172 30pi orange & multi .50 .25
**495** A173 300pi gray & multi 3.25 1.00
*Nos. 493-495 (3)* 4.00 1.45

Nos. 398, 447, 451, 454, 387 Surcharged with New Value and Two Bars in Red

**1974-75**

**496** A125 25pi on 1pi multi *6.25*
**497** A144 25pi on 1pi multi *6.25*
**498** A148 25pi on 1pi multi *6.25*
**499** A149 25pi on 1pi multi *9.00*
**500** A120 25pi on 7pi multi *9.00*
*Nos. 496-500 (5)* *36.75*

Issued: #496, 498, 1/1/75; others, 11/18/74.

Hien Lam Pavilion, Hué
A174

Throne, Imperial Palace, Hué
A175

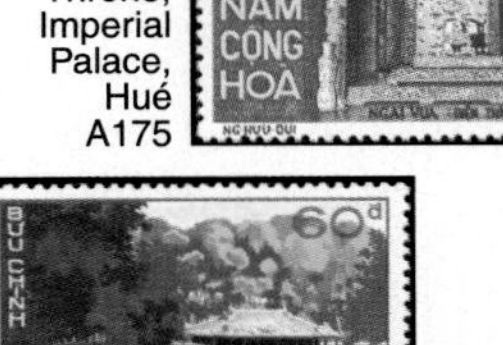

Water Pavilion, Hué
A176

**1975, Jan. 5 Litho. *Perf. 14x13½***

**501** A174 25pi multicolored 1.50 .25
**502** A175 30pi multicolored 2.25 .25
**503** A176 60pi multicolored 2.75 .50
*Nos. 501-503 (3)* 6.50 1.00

Historic sites.

Symbol of Youth, Children Holding Flower — A177

Family and Emblem
A178

**1975, Jan. 14** ***Perf. 11½***

**504** A177 20pi blue & multi 3.50 .30

***Perf. 12½x12***

**505** A178 70pi yellow & multi 3.50 .35

Intl. Conf. on Children & Natl. Development.

Unicorn Dance A179

Boy Lighting Firecracker A180

Bringing New Year Gifts and Wishes — A181

***Perf. 14x13½, 13½x14***

**1975, Jan. 26** **Litho.**

| | | | | |
|---|---|---|---|---|
| **506** | A179 | 20pi multicolored | 2.50 | .25 |
| **507** | A180 | 30pi blue & multi | 3.00 | .30 |
| **508** | A181 | 100pi bister & multi | 7.00 | .50 |
| | | *Nos. 506-508 (3)* | 12.50 | 1.05 |

Lunar New Year, Tet.

A182

A183

A184

Designs: 25pi, Military chief from play "San Hau." 40pi, Scene from "Tam Ha Nam Duong." 100pi, Warrior Luu-Kim-Dinn.

**1975, Feb. 23**

| | | | | |
|---|---|---|---|---|
| **509** | A182 | 25pi rose & multi | 1.25 | .30 |
| **510** | A183 | 40pi lt green & multi | 2.00 | .30 |
| **511** | A184 | 100pi violet & multi | 6.75 | .50 |
| | | *Nos. 509-511 (3)* | 10.00 | 1.10 |

National theater.

Produce, Map of Viet Nam, Ship — A185

Irrigation Project A186

**1975, Mar. 26** **Litho.** ***Perf. 12½x12***

| | | | | |
|---|---|---|---|---|
| **512** | A185 | 10pi multicolored | 1.75 | .20 |
| **513** | A186 | 50pi multicolored | 5.25 | .30 |

Agriculture Day; 5th anniv. of Agrarian Reform Law.

Nos. 457, 464, 468 Surcharged with New Value and Two Bars in Red

**1975**

| | | | | |
|---|---|---|---|---|
| **514** | A150 | 10pi on 8pi multi | 12.00 | 2.00 |
| **515** | A154 | 10pi on 8pi multi | 8.00 | 1.00 |
| **516** | A156 | 25pi on 8pi multi | 8.00 | 1.50 |
| | | *Nos. 514-516 (3)* | 28.00 | 4.50 |

In the 1980's a number of South Viet Nam stamps appeared on the market. These apparently had been printed before the collapse of the Republic but saw no postal use. These include, but are not limited to, sets of two for western electric and for rural electric, one each for history, library, New Year and cows, a set of three for transportation and a set of four for economic development.

## SEMI-POSTAL STAMPS

Type of 1952 Surcharged in Carmine

+50c

***Perf. 12x12½***

**1952, Nov. 10** **Unwmk.**

**B1** A3 1.50pi + 50c bl, yel & brn 4.00 3.25

Never hinged 10.00

The surtax was for the Red Cross.

**Catalogue values for unused stamps in this section, from this point to the end of the section, are for Never Hinged items. Because of the tropical conditions, never hinged stamps must also be free wrinkles, toning, and any other disturbance.**

Sabers and Flag — SP1

**1952, Dec. 21** **Engr.** ***Perf. 13***

**B2** SP1 3.30pi + 1.70pi dp claret 1.50 .50

The surtax was for the Wounded Soldiers' Aid Organization.

X-ray Camera and Patient SP2

**1960, Aug. 1** ***Perf. 13***

**B3** SP2 3pi + 50c bl grn & red 1.00 .60

The surtax was for the Anti-Tuberculosis Foundation.

## AIR POST STAMPS

**Catalogue values for unused stamps in this section, from this point to the end of the section, are for Never Hinged items. Because of the tropical conditions, never hinged stamps must also be free wrinkles, toning, and any other disturbance.**

AP1

AP2

***Perf. 13½x12½***

**1952-53** **Unwmk.** **Photo.**

| | | | | |
|---|---|---|---|---|
| **C1** | AP1 | 3.30pi dk brn red & pale yel grn | 1.00 | .50 |
| **C2** | AP1 | 4pi brown & yellow | 1.50 | .25 |
| **C3** | AP1 | 5.10pi dk vio bl & sal pink | 1.50 | .40 |
| **C4** | AP2 | 6.30pi yellow & car | 1.50 | .50 |
| | | *Nos. C1-C4 (4)* | 5.50 | 1.65 |

Issued: #C2, 11/24/53; others, 3/8/52.

Dragon AP3

Fish — AP4

**1952, Sept. 3** **Engr.** ***Perf. 13***

| | | | | |
|---|---|---|---|---|
| **C5** | AP3 | 40c red | 1.40 | .35 |
| **C6** | AP3 | 70c green | 2.40 | .50 |
| **C7** | AP3 | 80c ultra | 2.40 | .50 |
| **C8** | AP3 | 90c brown | 2.40 | .50 |
| **C9** | AP4 | 3.70pi deep magenta | 5.25 | .75 |
| | | *Nos. C5-C9 (5)* | 13.85 | 2.60 |

Nos. C5-C9 exist imperforate in a souvenir booklet. Value, $175.

### South Viet Nam

Phoenix — AP5

**1955, Sept. 7**

**C10** AP5 4pi violet & lil rose 2.75 .50

Crane Carrying Letter AP6

**1960, Dec. 20.** ***Perf. 13***

| | | | | |
|---|---|---|---|---|
| **C11** | AP6 | 1pi olive | .60 | .25 |
| **C12** | AP6 | 4pi green & dk blue | 1.50 | .25 |
| **C13** | AP6 | 5pi ocher & purple | 1.75 | .35 |
| **C14** | AP6 | 10pi deep magenta | 3.00 | .75 |
| | | *Nos. C11-C14 (4)* | 6.85 | 1.60 |

## POSTAGE DUE STAMPS

**Catalogue values for unused stamps in this section, from this point to the end of the section, are for Never Hinged items. Because of the tropical conditions, never hinged stamps must also be free wrinkles, toning, and any other disturbance.**

Temple Lion D1

Dragon D2

***Perf. 13x13½***

**1952, June 16** **Typo.** **Unwmk.**

| | | | | |
|---|---|---|---|---|
| **J1** | D1 | 10c red & green | .85 | .20 |
| **J2** | D1 | 20c green & yellow | 1.10 | .20 |
| **J3** | D1 | 30c purple & orange | 1.40 | .20 |
| **J4** | D1 | 40c dk grn & sal rose | 1.90 | .25 |
| **J5** | D1 | 50c dp carmine & gray | 2.50 | .30 |
| **J6** | D1 | 1pi blue & silver | 4.25 | .20 |
| | | *Nos. J1-J6 (6)* | 12.00 | 1.35 |

### South Viet Nam

**1955-56**

| | | | | |
|---|---|---|---|---|
| **J7** | D2 | 2pi red vio & org | .40 | .20 |
| **J8** | D2 | 3pi violet & grnsh bl | .55 | .20 |
| **J9** | D2 | 5pi violet & yellow | .60 | .20 |
| **J10** | D2 | 10pi dk green & car | .90 | .20 |
| **J11** | D2 | 20pi red & brt grn ('56) | 2.00 | .50 |
| **J12** | D2 | 30pi brt grn & yel ('56) | 3.00 | .75 |
| **J13** | D2 | 50pi dk red brn & yel ('56) | 6.00 | 1.50 |
| **J14** | D2 | 100pi pur & yel ('56) | 12.00 | 3.50 |
| | | *Nos. J7-J14 (8)* | 25.45 | 7.05 |

Nos. J11-J14 inscribed "BUU-CHINH" instead of "TIMBRE-TAXE."

Atlas Moth — D3

Design: 3pi, 5pi, 10pi, Three butterflies.

**1968, Aug. 20** **Photo.** ***Perf. 13½x13***

| | | | | |
|---|---|---|---|---|
| **J15** | D3 | 50c multicolored | *1.25* | .25 |
| **J16** | D3 | 1pi multicolored | *1.40* | .25 |
| **J17** | D3 | 2pi multicolored | *2.75* | .25 |
| **J18** | D3 | 3pi multicolored | *4.00* | .25 |
| **J19** | D3 | 5pi multicolored | *6.75* | .25 |
| **J20** | D3 | 10pi multicolored | *9.00* | .25 |
| | | *Nos. J15-J20 (6)* | *25.15* | 1.50 |

Nos. J15-J18 Surcharged with New Value and Two Bars in Red

**1974, Oct. 1**

**J21** D3 5pi on 3pi multi .75
**J22** D3 10pi on 50c multi .75
**J23** D3 40pi on 1pi multi 2.75
**J24** D3 60pi on 2pi multi 3.25
*Nos. J21-J24 (4)* 7.50

## MILITARY STAMPS

**Catalogue values for unused stamps in this section, from this point to the end of the section, are for Never Hinged items. Because of the tropical conditions, never hinged stamps must also be free wrinkles, toning, and any other disturbance.**

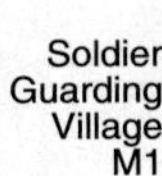

Soldier Guarding Village
M1

***Rouletted 7½***

**1961, June Unwmk. Litho.**

**M1** M1 och, brn, dk grn & blk 4.00 1.00

**1961, Sept. Typo.**

**M2** M1 org yel, dk grn & brn 3.50 1.00

Bottom inscription on No. M1 is black, brown on No. M2.

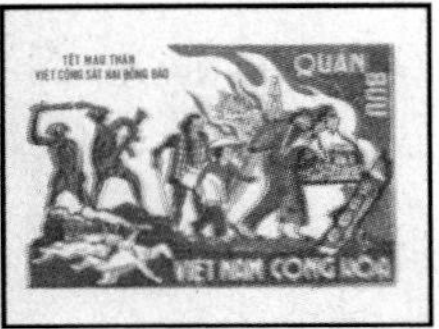


Battle and Refugees
M2

**1969, Feb. 22 Litho. *Imperf.***

**M3** M2 red & green *60.00*
*a.* Booklet pane of 10 *600.00*

## NORTH VIET NAM

LOCATION — In eastern Indo-China
GOVT. — Republic
AREA — 61,293 sq. mi.
POP. — 18,800,000 (1968 est.)
CAPITAL — Hanoi

Beginning in 1946, the Communist Viet Minh fought the French in a guerrilla war that ended with the French defeat at Dien Bien Phu in 1954. In an agreement signed in Geneva on July 21, 1954, Viet Nam was partitioned at the 17th parallel. The government in Hanoi controlled the north, and engaged in another protracted military campaign against American and South Vietnamese forces that led to the official reunification of the country under Communist control on July 2, 1976.

100 Cents (Xu) = 10 Hao = 1 Piaster (Dong)

**All stamps are without gum unless otherwise indicated. Values for stamps with gum are for Never Hinged items.**

**Watermark**

Wmk. 376 — "R de C"

**VIET MINH ISSUES**

Stamps and Types of Indo-China Overprinted or Surcharged

**Printing Methods and Perfs as Before**

**1945-46 Without Gum**

**No. 236 Overprinted "VIET-NAM DAN-CHU CONG-HOA"**

**1L1** A41 1pi yel grn (Yersin) 8.00

**Nos. 238-239 (Rhodes) Overprinted "VIET-NAM DAN-CHU CONG-HOA" with "VN" & "IXIXIXIXIX" Obliterators**

***Perf. 11½***

**1L2** A43 15c dk vio brn, perf. 11½ 1.25
*a.* Perf. 12 1.25
*b.* Perf. 11½, green overprint 2.50
**1L3** A43 30c org brn, perf. 11½ 1.00
*a.* Perf. 13½ 2.00
*b.* Perf. 12 15.00

**No. 242 Overprinted "VIET-NAM DAN-CHU CONG-HOA" with "VN" & "VN.VN" Obliterators**

**1L4** A44 50c dl red (Athlete) 7.00

**No. 241 Overprinted "VIET-NAM DAN-CHU CONG-HOA" with "VN" & "XXXX" Obliterators**

**1L5** A44 10c dk vio brn & yel (Athlete) 18.00

**Nos. 218-222 (Petain) Overprinted "VIET-NAM DAN-CHU CONG-HOA" with "Buu-Chinh" and Wavy Line Obliterators**

**1L6** A32 3c olive brn, perf. 11½ 1.75
*a.* Perf. 12x14 5.00
*b.* Perf. 14 15.00
**1L7** A32 6c rose red 1.00
**1L8** A32 10c dull grn (R) 5.00
**1L9** A32 40c dk bl (R) 3.00
**1L10** A32 40c slate bl (R) 3.00
*Nos. 1L6-1L10 (5)* 13.75

**Nos. 245-246 and Type (Pavie) Overprinted "VIET-NAM DAN-CHU CONG-HOA" with "BUU-CHINH" and Wavy Line & "VN" Obliterators**

**1L11** A46 4c org yel 1.50
**1L12** A46 10c dl grn 1.50
**1L13** A46 20c dark red 1.25
*Nos. 1L11-1L13 (3)* 4.25

**No. 165A Overprinted "VIET-NAM DAN-CHU CONG-HOA" with "BUU CHINH" and Slanted Lines Obliterator**

**1L14** A22 25c dk bl (Planting Rice, R), top line 18 mm wide 60.00
*a.* Top line 20 mm wide 80.00

Nos. 1L14-1L14a issued with gum.

**No. 232 (Courbet) Overprinted "VIET-NAM DAN-CHU CONG-HOA DOC-LAP TU-DO HANH-PHUC"**

**1L15** A39 3c lt brn 1.00
**1L16** A39 6c car rose 2.00

**No. 261 (Lagree) Overprinted Vertically "VIET-NAM DAN-CHU CONG-HOA DOC-LAP TU-DO HANH-PHUC" with "BUU-CHINH" & "III" Obliterator**

**1L17** A52 40c brt bl 1.50

**Nos. 253-255 (Doumer) Overprinted "VIET-NAM DOC-LAP TU-DO HANH-PHUC BUU-CHINH" with Wavy Line Obliterators**

**1L18** A50 2c red vio 1.50
**1L19** A50 4c lt brn 1.25
**1L20** A50 10c yel grn 1.50
*Nos. 1L18-1L20 (3)* 4.25

**Nos. 217, 256-258 (Petain, Charner) Overprinted "VIET-NAM DOC-LAP TU-DO HANH-PHUC BUU-CHINH" with "VN" and Wavy Line Obliterators**

**1L21** A32 1c blk brn 2.00
**1L22** A51 10c green 1.75
**1L23** A51 20c brn red 1.75
**1L24** A51 1pi pale yel grn 7.50
*Nos. 1L21-1L24 (4)* 13.00

**No. 230 and Type (Genouilly) Overprinted "VIET-NAM DOC-LAP TU-DO HANH-PHUC BUU-CHINH" with "X" Obliterator**

**1L25** A37 5c dull brown 1.50
**1L26** A37 6c carmine rose 5.00

**No. 210-212 (Sihanouk) Surcharged with New Value & "X" Obliterators**

**1L27** A28 5d on 1c red org (Bl) 12.50
**1L28** A28 10d on 6c violet (R) 15.00
**1L29** A28 15d on 25c dp ultra (R) 15.00
*Nos. 1L27-1L29 (3)* 42.50

**Nos. 225-226 (Sihanouk) Surcharged with New Value with Wavy Line and Straight Line Obliterators**

**1L30** A34 50xu on 1c brown 3.00
**1L31** A35 2d on 6c car rose 20.00

**Nos. 213-214 (Elephant) Surcharged with New Value, "VIET-NAM DAN-CHU CONG-HOA," Wavy Line and Straight Line Obliterators**

**1L32** A29 2d on 3c reddish brn (G) 12.50
**1L33** A29 4d on 6c crim (G) 12.50

**Nos. 247-248 (Pasquier) Surcharged Vertically with New Value, "VIET NAM DAN CHU CONG HOA," Wavy Line & "X" Obliterators**

**1L34** A47 1d on 5c brn vio 4.00
**1L35** A47 2d on 10c dl grn 6.50

**No. B30 Surcharged with New Value, "VIET-NAM DAN-CHU CONG-HOA," "Binh-si Bi-nan," Wavy Line Obliterator**

**1L36** SP7 5d on 15c+60c brn vio (Cathedral) 25.00

**Nos. 259-260 (Lagree) Surcharged Vertically with New Value, "VIET-NAM DAN CHU CONG HOA BUU-CHINH," Wavy Line & "VN" Obliterators**

**1L37** A52 30xu on 1c dl gray brn (R) 1.75
**1L38** A52 3d on 15c dl rose vio 3.00

**Nos. 243-244 (La Grandiere) Surcharged with New Value, "VIET-NAM DAN CHU CONG HOA BUU CHINH," Wavy Line Obliterator**

**1L39** A45 1d on 5c dk brn (Bl) 12.50
**1L40** A45 4d on 1c dull brn 3.00

**Surcharged with New Value, "VIET-NAM Dan-chu Cong-hoa BUU-CHINH," Wavy & Straight Line Obliterators**

**1L41** A42 30xu on 15c brn vio (Garnier, R) 2.50

**No. 242 (Garnier) Surcharged with New Value, "VIET-NAM DAN CHU CONG HOA BUU-CHINH," Wavy & Straight Line Obliterators**

**1L42** A42 5d on 1c dull ol bis 5.00

**Nos. 249-252 (De Lanessan, Van Vollenhoven) Surcharged with New Value, "VIET-NAM DAN CHU CONG HOA BUU CHINH," Straight Line Obliterators**

**1L43** A49 50xu on 1c dl gray brn 3.00
**1L44** A48 60xu on 1c ol brn 4.50
**1L45** A48 1.60d on 10c green 14.00
**1L46** A49 3d on 15c dl rose vio (Bl) 4.50
*Nos. 1L43-1L46 (4)* 26.00

**Nos. B30-B31 (Cathedral) Surcharged with New Value, "VIET-NAM DAN-CHU CONG-HOA CUU-DOI," Wavy Line Obliterators**

**1L47** SP7 2d on 15c+60c brn vio 22.50
**1L48** SP7 3d on 40c+1.10pi blue 22.50

**No. 234 (Yersin) Surcharged with Added Value, "VIET-NAM DAN-CHU CONGHOA Bao Anh," and Straight Line obliterators**

**1L49** A41 +2d on 6c car rose 9.00

**No. 233 (Behaine) Surcharged with Added Value, "VIET-NAM DAN-CHU CONG-HOA Binh si bi nan," Wavy Line, "V" & "N" Obliterators**

**1L50** A40 +3d on 20c dull red 5.00

**No. 215 (Saigon Fair) Surcharged with Added Value, "VIET-NAM DAN CHU CONG HOA Chong nan mu chu" & Wavy Line**

**1L51** A30 +4d on 6c car rose 9.00

**No. 229 (Natl. Revolution) Surcharged with Added Value, "VIET-NAM DAN-CHU CONGHOA Doi song moi," and "X" Obliterator**

**1L52** A36 +4d on 6c car rose 6.50

**Nos. 213-214 Surcharged with Added Value, "VIET-NAM DAN-CHU CONG-HOA Quoc-Phong" and Wavy Line in Blue**

**1L53** A29 +5d on 3c reddish brown 17.50
**1L54** A29 +10d on 6c crimson 17.50

**Nos. 216, 224 Surcharged with "VIET-NAM DAN-CHU CONG-HOA DAN-SINH" & Straight Lines**

**1L55** A31 30xu +3d on 6c (Nam-Phuong) 3.75

***Perf. 13½***

**1L56** A33 30xu +3d on 6c (Bao-Dai) 3.75
*a.* Perf. 12 50.00

Ho Chi Minh
VM1 VM2

**1946 Litho. Unwmk. *Perf. 11½***

**Without Gum**

**1L57** VM1 1h green .50
**1L58** VM1 3h rose .50
**1L59** VM1 9h yellow bister .50

**With Added Inscription "+PHU THU CUU-QUOC"**

**1L60** VM1 4h +6h Prussian blue 1.50
**1L61** VM1 6h +9h brown violet 1.50
*Nos. 1L57-1L61 (5)* 4.50

**1948 Typo. *Perf. 7 Rough***

**Thin, Rough, Brown Paper**

| | | | |
|---|---|---|---|
| **1L62** | VM2 2d brown | 22.50 | |
| **1L63** | VM2 5d red | 22.50 | |

For surcharge and overprints see Nos. 50, O6-O7.

---

## REPUBLIC OF NORTH VIET NAM

**From 1945-2002, all stamps are without gum unless otherwise indicated. Values for stamps with gum are for Never Hinged items.**

---

**Many North Vietnamese stamps are roughly perforated, especially issues before 1958.**

---

Ho Chi Minh, Map of Vietnam A1

**1951-55 Unwmk. Litho. *Imperf.***

| | | | |
|---|---|---|---|
| **1** | A1 100d brown | 26.00 | *8.25* |
| *a.* | Perf. 11¼ ('55) | 35.00 | *6.75* |
| **2** | A1 100d green | 21.00 | *8.25* |
| *a.* | Perf. 11¼ ('55) | 35.00 | *6.75* |

***Perf. 11¼***

| | | | |
|---|---|---|---|
| **3** | A1 200d red | 30.00 | *8.25* |
| *a.* | Imperf. ('55) | 20.00 | *6.75* |
| | *Nos. 1-3 (3)* | 77.00 | 24.75 |

Nos. 1-3 printed on thin semi-transparent paper.

Nos. 1-3 used values are for cto. Postally used copies are worth about 5 times these values.

Counterfeits exist.

For surcharges, see Nos. 9-14, 36-38, and note before No. J1.

Blacksmith — A2

**1953-55 *Perf. 11¼***

| | | | |
|---|---|---|---|
| **4** | A2 100d violet | 7.00 | 5.25 |
| **5** | A2 500d brown | 10.50 | *14.00* |

Issued: 100d, 6/53. 500d, 2/55.

Georgi Malenkov, Ho Chi Minh, Mao Tse-tung and Flags — A3

**1954-55 *Perf. 11¼***

| | | | |
|---|---|---|---|
| **6** | A3 50d brown & red, *brnish* | 25.00 | *30.00* |
| **7** | A3 100d red | 20.00 | *25.00* |
| **8** | A3 100d yellow & red, *brnish* | 30.00 | *30.00* |
| | *Nos. 6-8 (3)* | 75.00 | *85.00* |

Issued: 50d, 10/54; #7, 1/54; #8, 4/55.

No. 7 printed on thin, white paper.

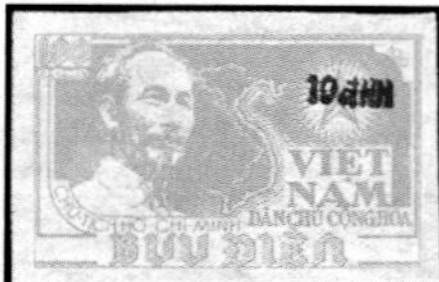

Nos. 1-3 Surcharged in Red or Blue

**1954, Oct. *Imperf.***

| | | | |
|---|---|---|---|
| **9** | A1 10d on 100d brown | 22.50 | *32.50* |
| **10** | A1 10d on 100d green | 22.50 | *32.50* |

***Perf. 11***

| | | | |
|---|---|---|---|
| **11** | A1 20d on 200d red (Bl) | 22.50 | *42.50* |
| | *Nos. 9-11 (3)* | 67.50 | *107.50* |

Nos. 1-3 Surcharged in Black, Red or Blue

**1954, Oct. *Imperf.***

| | | | |
|---|---|---|---|
| **12** | A1 10d on 100d brown (Bk, R or Bl) | 26.00 | *35.00* |
| **13** | A1 10d on 100d green (Bk, R or Bl) | 26.00 | *35.00* |

***Perf. 11***

| | | | |
|---|---|---|---|
| **14** | A1 20d on 200d red (Bk or Bl) | 60.00 | *75.00* |
| | *Nos. 12-14 (3)* | 112.00 | *145.00* |

Nos. 9-14 exist with counterfeit surcharges, counterfeit surcharges on counterfeit stamps, and with fantasy surcharges.

Victory at Dien Bien Phu A4

**1954-56 *Perf. 11¼***

| | | | |
|---|---|---|---|
| **17** | A4 10d red brn & yel brn | 20.00 | *30.00* |
| *a.* | Imperf | 90.00 | *100.00* |
| **18** | A4 50d red & org yel | 20.00 | *30.00* |
| *a.* | Imperf | 20.00 | *40.00* |
| **19** | A4 150d brown & blue | 20.00 | *35.00* |
| *a.* | Imperf | 20.00 | *40.00* |
| | *Nos. 17-19 (3)* | 60.00 | *95.00* |

Issued: Imperfs, 10/54; others, 1956. See #O5.

Used values for Nos. 17-19 are for postally used copies. The 10d exists cto, perf or imperf. Value about 1/10 those shown above.

Liberation of Hanoi — A5

**1955, Jan. 1 *Perf. 11½***

| | | | |
|---|---|---|---|
| **20** | A5 10d lt blue & bl | 7.50 | 8.00 |
| **21** | A5 50d dk grn & grn | 7.50 | 8.00 |
| **22** | A5 150d rose & brn red | 15.00 | 12.00 |
| | *Nos. 20-22 (3)* | 30.00 | 28.00 |

Nos. 20-22 used values are for postally used copies. Cto copies are worth about $1 each.

Land Reform A6

**1955-56 *Perf. 11¼***

| | | | |
|---|---|---|---|
| **23** | A6 5d lt green | 18.00 | 8.50 |
| **24** | A6 10d gray | 18.00 | 8.50 |
| **25** | A6 20d orange | 18.00 | 8.50 |
| **26** | A6 50d rose | 18.00 | 8.50 |
| **27** | A6 100d lt brown | 37.50 | 32.50 |
| | *Nos. 23-27 (5)* | 109.50 | 66.50 |

Issued: 100d, 12/55; 20d, 50d, 2/56; others, 6/56. See Nos. O8-O9.

Return of Government to Hanoi — A7

**1956, Mar. 1 *Perf. 11¼***

| | | | |
|---|---|---|---|
| **28** | A7 1000d violet | 32.50 | 25.00 |
| **29** | A7 1500d dk blue | 32.50 | 25.00 |
| **30** | A7 2000d turquoise | 85.00 | 67.50 |
| **31** | A7 3000d blue green | 160.00 | 210.00 |
| | *Nos. 28-31 (4)* | 310.00 | 327.50 |

Counterfeits exist, often imperf and offered as proofs.

Re-opening of Hanoi-China Railroad — A8

**1956, Mar. 1**

| | | | |
|---|---|---|---|
| **32** | A8 100d dark blue | 40.00 | 16.00 |
| **33** | A8 200d blue green | 40.00 | 16.00 |
| **34** | A8 300d violet | 40.00 | 32.50 |
| **35** | A8 500d lilac brown | 40.00 | *65.00* |
| | *Nos. 32-35 (4)* | 160.00 | 129.50 |

Counterfeits exist, often imperf and offered as proofs.

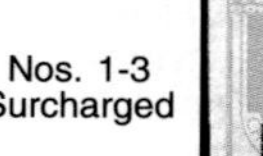

Nos. 1-3 Surcharged

**1954, Oct. *Imperf.***

| | | | |
|---|---|---|---|
| **36** | A1 10d on 100d brown | 35.00 | *50.00* |
| **37** | A1 10d on 100d green | 35.00 | *50.00* |

***Perf. 11***

| | | | |
|---|---|---|---|
| **38** | A1 20d on 200d red | 35.00 | *50.00* |
| | *Nos. 36-38 (3)* | 105.00 | *150.00* |

Nos. 36-38 exist with counterfeit surcharges, counterfeit surcharges on counterfeit stamps, and with fantasy surcharges.

Tran Dang Ninh (1910-55), Guerrilla Leader A9

**1956, July Litho. *Perf. 11¼***

| | | | |
|---|---|---|---|
| **39** | A9 5d bl grn & pale grn | 5.00 | *2.40* |
| **40** | A9 10d lilac & rose | 5.00 | *2.40* |
| **41** | A9 20d gr brn & dk gray | 7.75 | *3.00* |
| **42** | A9 100d dk blue pale bl | 7.75 | *3.00* |
| | *Nos. 39-42 (4)* | 25.50 | *10.80* |

Nos. 39-42 used values are for cto. Postally used value, set $14.

Mac Thi Buoi (1927-51), Guerrilla Leader A10

**1956, Nov. 3 *Perf. 11½***

| | | | |
|---|---|---|---|
| **43** | A10 1000d rose & lilac rose | 100.00 | 100.00 |
| **44** | A10 2000d brown & bister | 100.00 | 100.00 |
| **45** | A10 4000d bl grn & green | 150.00 | 100.00 |
| **46** | A10 5000d ultra & lt blue | 300.00 | *400.00* |
| | *Nos. 43-46 (4)* | 650.00 | *700.00* |

Nos. 43-46 used values are for postally used. Cto value, set $100.

Counterfeits exist, often imperf and offered as proofs.

Bai Thuong Dam — A11

**1956-58 *Perf. 11¼***

| | | | |
|---|---|---|---|
| **47** | A11 100d vio bl & lil brn | 10.00 | *1.90* |
| *a.* | Perf 13 | 10.00 | *1.60* |
| **48** | A11 200d lilac & gr grn | 10.00 | *2.25* |
| *a.* | Perf 13 | 10.00 | *1.90* |
| **49** | A11 300d rose & lil brn | 20.00 | *3.25* |
| *a.* | Perf 13 | 20.00 | *2.75* |
| | *Nos. 47-49 (3)* | 40.00 | 7.40 |

Nos. 47-49 used values are for cto. Postally used copies are worth about 10 times these values.

Issued: #47-49, 12/15/56; #47a-49a, 1958.

No. 1L63 Surcharged

**1956, Dec. Typo. *Perf. 7 Rough***

| | | | |
|---|---|---|---|
| **50** | VM2 50d on 5d dp red, *brnish* | 80.00 | *90.00* |

Reprints and counterfeits exist.

Nam Dinh Textile Mill — A13

**1957, Mar. Litho. *Perf. 12½***

| | | | |
|---|---|---|---|
| **51-53** | A13 100d, 200d, 300d, set of 3 | 27.50 | 3.75 |
| *51a* | Perf. 11½ | 7.50 | 7.50 |

Nos. 51-53 used values are for cto. Postally used value, set $15.

No. 51 also exists perf 11½x12½, imperf and imperf by perf 11½.

Ho Chi Minh — A14

**1957 *Perf. 12½***

| | | | |
|---|---|---|---|
| **54-57** | A14 20d, 60d, 100d, 300d, set of 4 | 24.00 | 21.00 |

Issued: 20d, 60d, 12/13; others, 5/19.

Fourth World Trade Union Congress, Leipzig A15

**1957, Aug. 1 *Perf. 12½***

| | | | |
|---|---|---|---|
| **58** | A15 300d red violet | 10.00 | 3.00 |

See Nos. O17-O20.

Democratic Republic, 12th Anniv. A16

**1957, Sept. 2 *Perf. 13***

| | | | |
|---|---|---|---|
| **59-60** | A16 20d, 100d, set of 2 | 9.00 | 5.00 |

Presidents Voroshilov, Ho Chi Minh — A17

**1957, Nov. 7** ***Perf. 12½***
**61-63** A17 100d, 500d, set of 1000d, 3 47.50 37.50

Russian revolution, 40th anniv.

Anti-illiteracy Campaign — A18

**1958, Jan. 6** ***Perf. 12½***
**64-66** A18 50d, 150d, 1000d, set of 3 40.00 29.00

A19 A20

**1958, Mar. 8**
**67-68** A19 150d, 500d, set of 2 40.00 32.50

Physical education.

**1958, May 1**
**69-70** A20 50d, 150d, set of 2 13.00 8.00

May Day.

Fourth Intl. Congress of Democratic Women, Vienna A21

**1958, May** **Typo.**
**71** A21 150d blue 10.00 9.00

A22

A22a

#72, 150d, #75, 2000d, Basket, lace & cup, vert. #73, 150d, #74, 1000d, Potter.

**1958** **Litho.**
**72-75** A22, A22a Set of 4 29.00 22.50

Arts & Crafts Fair, Hanoi.

Issued: Nos. 72, 75, 6/26; others, 8/19.

Building the Reunification Railway — A23

**1958, July 20**
**76-77** A23 50d, 150d, set of 2 10.00 4.00

August Revolution, 13th Anniv. A24

**1958, Aug. 19**
**78-79** A24 150d, 500d, set of 2 8.00 6.50

Resistance Movement in South Viet Nam, 13th Anniv. A25

**1958, Sept. 23**
**80-81** A25 50d, 150d, set of 2 10.50 5.00

A26

A27

**1958, Oct.**
**82** A26 150d grnsh blue & blk 3.00 1.50

Tran Hung Dao (1253-1300),

**1958, Nov. 7** **Engr.** ***Perf. 11½***

Hanoi Engineering Plant.

**83** A27 150d brown 3.50 1.40

Mutual Aid Teams — A28

**1958, Nov. 7**
**84-85** A28 150d, 500d, set of 2 12.00 4.50

Ngoc Son Temple (Temple of Jade) — A29

**1958, Dec. 1** **Photo.** ***Perf. 12***
**86-87** A29 150d, 2000d, set of 2 32.50 11.00

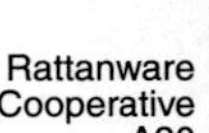

Rattanware Cooperative A30

**1958, Dec. 31**
**88** A30 150d greenish blue 3.50 1.25

Ha Long Bay — A31

**1959, Feb. 8**
**89-90** A31 150d, 350d, set of 2 8.00 3.75

Cam Pha Coal Mines — A32

**1959, Mar. 3** **Engr.** ***Perf. 11½***
**91** A32 150d blue 7.50 .75

Trung Sisters — A33

**1959, Mar. 14** **Litho.** ***Perf. 11***
**92-93** A33 5xu, 8xu, set of 2 9.00 6.25

World Peace Movement, 10th Anniv. — A34

**1959, Apr. 15**
**94** A34 12xu purple, *rose* 2.50 .60

Xuan Quang Dam A35

**1959, May 1**
**95-96** A35 6xu, 12xu, set of 2 8.50 1.50

Phu Loi Massacre A36

**1959, May 15**
**97-98** A36 12xu, 20xu, set of 2 7.00 1.75

Hien Luong Bridge — A37

**1959, July 20**
**99** A37 12xu black & carmine 3.00 1.50

Me Tri Radio Station — A38

**1959, Aug. 10**
**100-101** A38 3xu, 12xu, set of 2 5.00 1.40

Sports A39

Designs: 1xu, Shooting. 6xu, Swimming. 12xu, Wrestling.

**1959, Sept. 2**
**102-104** A39 Set of 3 8.00 3.00

Size of No. 103 is 43x31mm.

People's Republic of China, 10th Anniv. — A40

**1959, Oct. 1**
**105** A40 12xu multicolored 5.00 .70

Fruits — A41

Designs: 3xu, Coconuts. 12xu, Bananas. 30xu, Pineapple.

**1959, Nov. 20**
**106-108** A41 Set of 3 8.00 3.50

People's Army, 15th Anniv. A42

**1959, Dec. 22**
**109** A42 12xu multicolored 3.00 1.60

A43

A44

**1960, Jan. 6**

**110-111** A43 2xu, 12xu, set of 2 5.50 3.00

Vietnamese Workers' Party, 30th Anniv.

**1960, Jan. 6**

Ethnic costumes: 2xu, Ede. 10xu, Meo. No. 114, 12xu, Tay. No. 115, 12xu, Thai.

**112-115** A44 Set of 4 9.00 7.00

Census A45

Designs: 1xu, People. 12xu, Transmitting tower, dam, buildings, workers.

**1960, Feb. 20**

**116-117** A45 Set of 2 4.00 2.75

No. 117 is 37x26mm.

Intl. Women's Day, 50th Anniv. A46

**1960, Mar. 8**

**118** A46 12xu multicolored 2.00 1.75

A47

A48

**1960, Apr. 5**

**119-120** A47 4xu, 12xu, set of 2 62.50 30.00

Hung Vuong Temple.

**1960, Apr. 22**

**121-122** A48 5xu, 12xu, set of 2 5.50

*121a* Souv. sheet of 1, olive brown & blue, imperf. 75.00

Lenin. No. 121a exists on brownish paper.

Election of National Assembly Delegates — A49

**1960, May 3** ***Perf. 11***

**123** A49 12xu multicolored, *rose* 2.00 1.60

A50

A51

**1960, May 8**

**124-125** A50 8xu, 12xu, set of 2 5.00 .95

Viet Nam Red Cross.

**1960, May 19**

Ho Chi Minh, 70th Birthday: Nos. 128, 130, Ho with children.

**126** A51 4xu green & purple
**127** A51 12xu pink & brown
**128** A51 12xu multicolored
*Nos. 126-128 (3)* 8.00 3.00

**Souvenir Sheets**

***Imperf***

**129** A51 10xu yel bis & brn, *rose* 13.50
**130** A51 10xu multicolored 12.00

No. 128 is 25x39mm.

New Constitution A52

**1960, July 7**

**131** A52 12xu lemon & gray 3.00 1.50

National Day, 15th Anniv. A53

**1960, Sept. 2**

**132-133** A53 4xu, 12xu, set of 2 7.50 7.00

Development — A54

Designs: No. 134, Classroom. No. 135, Plowing. No. 136, Factory.

**1960, Sept. 2**

**134-136** A54 12xu Set of 3 13.50

3rd Vietnamese Communist Party Congress — A55

**1960, Sept. 4**

**137-138** A55 1xu, 12xu, set of 2 6.50 3.00

World Federation of Trade Unions, 15th Anniv. — A56

**1960, Oct. 3**

**139** A56 12xu black & vermilion 6.00 5.25

Hanoi, 950th Anniv. A57

**1960, Oct. 10** **Litho.** ***Perf. 11***

**140-141** A57 8xu, 12xu, set of 2 7.50 3.00

*141a* Souv. sheet of 1, imperf. 15.00 14.00

No. 141a exists on brownish paper.

15 Years' Achievements Exhibition — A58

**1960, Oct. 20**

**142-143** A58 2xu, 12xu, set of 2 4.00 2.10

World Federation of Democratic Youth, 15th Anniv. — A59

**1960, Nov. 10**

**144** A59 12xu multicolored 3.50 3.00

Trade Unions, 2nd Natl. Congress A60

**1961, Feb. 10**

**145** A60 12xu multicolored, *rose* 2.50 1.25

Vietnamese Women's Union, 3rd Natl. Congress — A61

**1961, Mar. 8** **Tinted Paper**

**146-147** A61 6xu, 12xu, set of 2 7.00 2.40

Animals — A62

Ly Tu Trong — A63

Designs: 12xu, Rusa unicolor. 20xu, Helarctos malynus. 50xu, Elephas maximus. 1d, Hylobates leucogenys.

**1961, Mar. 8**

**148-151** A62 Set of 4 30.00 13.00

Imperf., #148-151 *60.00* 60.00

**1961, Mar. 18**

**152-153** A63 2xu, 12xu, set of 2 3.75 2.10

Youth Labor Union, 3rd Congress.

Young Pioneers, 20th Anniv. — A64

**1961, May 2**

**154-155** A64 1xu, 12xu, set of 2 4.75 2.50

Intl. Red Cross — A65

**1961, May 8**

**156-157** A65 6xu, 12xu, set of 2 8.00 3.50

Intl. Children's Day — A66

**1961, June 1** ***Perf. 11***

**158-159** A66 4xu, 12xu, set of 2 6.00 3.00

Yuri Gagarin's Space Flight A67

**1961, June 15**

**160-161** A67 6xu, 12xu, set of 2 24.00 10.50

Imperf., #160-161 27.50

Hanoi, Hue and Saigon A68

**1961, July 20**

**162-163** A68 12xu, 3d, set of 2 22.50 17.00

A69 A70

**1961, July 20**
**164-165** A69 12xu, 2d, set of 2 10.00 2.75
Imperf., #164-165 — —

Reunification campaign.

**1961, Aug. 21**
**166-167** A70 2xu, 12xu, set of 2 6.00 2.40

Geological exploration.

Savings Campaign A71

**1961, Aug. 21**
**168-169** A71 3xu, 12xu, set of 2 5.00 1.50

Ancient Towers — A72

Gherman Titov's Space Flight — A73

Designs: 6xu, Thien Mu, Hue. 10xu, Pen Brush, Bac Ninh. No. 172, 12xu, Binh Son, Vinh Phuc. No. 173, 12xu, Cham, Phan Rang.

**1961, Sept. 12**
**170-173** A72 Set of 4 10.00 3.75
Imperf., #170-173 12.00

**1961, Oct. 17**
**174-175** A73 6xu, 12xu, set of 2 8.00 3.75
Imperf., #174-175 12.00

A74 A76

Port of Haiphong — A75

**1961, Oct. 17**
**176** A74 12xu vermilion & black 3.50 2.40

22nd Communist Party Congress, Moscow.

**1961, Nov. 7**
**177-178** A75 5xu, 12xu, set of 2 9.50 3.00

**1961, Nov. 18** ***Perf. 13½***

Musicians: No. 179, 12xu, Flutist. No. 180, 12xu, Cymbalist. 30xu, Dancer with fan. 50xu, Guitarist.

**179-182** A76 Set of 4 16.00 14.00
Imperf., #179-182 20.00
*182a* Souvenir sheet, #179-182 60.00

Stamps on No. 182a are se-tenant and perfed on outside edges of the strip of 4.

5th World Trade Union Congress, Moscow A77

**1961, Dec. 4** ***Perf. 11***
**183** A77 12xu dp red lil & gray 2.00 .80

Natl. Resistance, 15th Anniv. A78

**1961, Dec. 4**
**184-185** A78 4xu, 12xu, set of 2 2.25 2.00

Tet Holiday — A79

Designs: 6xu, Sow, piglets. 12xu, Poultry.

**1962, Jan. 16** **Litho.**
**186-187** A79 Set of 2 9.00 6.00

Tet Tree-Planting Festival — A80

**1962, Jan. 16**
**188-189** A80 12xu, 40xu, set of 2 7.00

Crops — A81

Designs: 2xu, Camellia sinensis. 6xu, Illicium verum. No. 192, 12xu, Coffea arabica. No. 193, 12xu, Ricinus communis. 30xu, Rhus succedanea.

**1962, Mar. 1**
**190-194** A81 Set of 5 24.00 9.50

Folk Dances — A82

Designs: No. 195, 12xu, Rong Chieng. No. 196, 12xu, Bamboo. 30xu, Hat. 50xu, Parasol.

**1962, Mar. 20 Photo. *Perf. 11½x12***
**195-198** A82 Set of 4 20.00 6.00
Imperf., #195-198 20.00

**Souvenir Sheet**

**199** A82 30xu like #195 20.00

First Five Year Plan — A83

Designs: 1xu, Kim Lien Apartments, Hanoi. 3xu, State farm. 8xu, Natl. Institute of Hydraulics.

**1962, Apr. 10 Litho. *Perf. 11***
**200-202** A83 Set of 3 3.50 3.50

A84 A85

Flowers: No. 203, 12xu, Hibiscus rosa sinensis. No. 204, 12xu, Plumeria acutifolia. 20xu, Chrysanthemum indicum. 30xu, Nelumbium nuciferum. 50xu, Ipomoea pulchella.

***Perf. 12½x11½***

**1962, Apr. 10** **Photo.**
**203-207** A84 Set of 5 25.00 11.00
Imperf., #203-207 30.00
*206a* Souvenir sheet of 1 15.00

**1962, May 4 Litho. *Perf. 11***
**208** A85 12xu multicolored 3.00 3.00

3rd Natl. Heroes of Labor Congress.

Harrow A86

Dai Lai Lake A87

**1962, May 25**
**209-210** A86-A87 6xu, 12xu, set of 2 4.00 4.00

Visit by Gherman Titov A88

Titov: 12xu, Waving at children. 20xu, Receiving medal from Ho Chi Minh. 30xu, Wearing space suit.

**1962, June 12**
**211-213** A88 Set of 3 8.00 6.50
Imperf., #211-213 12.00

Anti-Malaria Campaign A89

**1962, July 9**
**214-216** A89 8xu, 12xu, 20xu, set of 3 7.50 3.00

War for Reunification — A90

**1962, July 20**
**217** A90 12xu multicolored 3.00 1.50

Ba Be Lake — A91

Design: No. 219, Ban Gioc Falls, vert.

**1962, Aug. 14**
**218-219** A91 12xu Set of 2 4.00 3.25

A stamp picturing a weight lifter exists, but was not released. Value $100.

King Quang Trung (1752-92) A92

Nguyen Trai (1380-1442) A93

**1962, Sept. 16**
**220-221** A92 3xu, 12xu, set of 2 3.50 2.50

**1962, Sept. 19**
**222-223** A93 3xu, 12xu, set of 2 3.50

Food Crops A94

Designs: 1xu, Peanuts. 4xu, Beans. 6xu, Sweet potatoes. 12xu, Corn. 30xu, Cassava.

**1962, Oct. 10**
**224-228** A94 Set of 5 12.00 5.00
Imperf., #224-228

Animal Husbandry A95

Designs: 2xu, Feeding poultry. No. 230, 12xu, Feeding pigs. No. 231, 12xu, Cattle grazing. No. 232, 12xu, Tending water buffalo.

**1962, Nov. 28**
**229-232** A95 Set of 4 7.00 3.50

A stamp commemorating the 45th anniversary of the Russian Revolution exists, but was not issued. Value $200.

First Five Year Plan A96

#233, Evening classes. #234, Clearing land.

**1962, Dec. 28**
**233-234** A96 12xu Set of 2 5.00 2.00

Flights of Vostok 3 and 4 — A97

12xu, Pavel Popovich, Vostok 4. 20xu, Andrian Nikolayev, Vostok 3. 30xu, Rockets lifting-off, vert.

**1962, Dec. 28** ***Perf. 11***
**235-237** A97 Set of 3 6.00 2.75
Imperf., #235-237 12.00

Guerrilla A98

Hoang Hoa Tham (1846-1913) A99

**1963, Jan. 15**
**238-239** A98 5xu, 12xu, set of 2 2.75 1.50

**1963, Feb. 10**
**240-241** A99 6xu, 12xu, set of 2 3.00 1.40

A100

First Five Year Plan A100a

Designs: No. 242, Fertilizing rice paddy. No. 243, Lam Thao superphosphate plant.

**1963, Feb. 25**
**242-243** A100-A100a 12xu Set of 2 3.50 1.50

Karl Marx — A101

**1963, Mar. 14**
**244-245** A101 3xu, 12xu, set of 2 3.25 1.50

Nos. 244-245 are printed on greenish and rose toned paper respectively.

Fidel Castro, Vietnamese Soldiers A102

**1963, Apr. 17**
**246** A102 12xu multicolored 2.00 1.00

May Day A103

**1963, May 8**
**247** A103 12xu multicolored 2.00 1.00

A104

Intl. Red Cross, Cent. — A105

Design: No. 249, Child, syringe.

**1963, May 8**
**248** A104 12xu grn, blk & red
**249** A104 12xu grn, red & blk
**250** A105 20xu multicolored
*Nos. 248-250 (3)* 7.00

Mars 1 Spacecraft — A106

6xu, 12xu (#252), Mars 1 approaching Mars. 12xu (#253), 20xu, Mars 1 entering orbit, vert.

**1963, May 21**
**251-254** A106 Set of 4 7.00 5.00
Imperf., #251-254 15.00

Fishing Industry A107

Designs: No. 255, Trawler, offshore fish. No. 256, Freshwater fish.

**1963, July 3**
**255-256** A107 12xu Set of 2 10.50 6.00

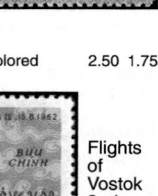

Ho Chi Minh, Nguyen Van Hien — A108

**1963, July 20**
**257** A108 12xu multicolored 2.50 1.75

Flights of Vostok 3, 4 A109

Designs: 12xu, Rockets in orbit. 20xu, Nikolayev. 30xu, Popovich.

**1963, Aug. 11**
**258-260** A109 Set of 3 7.00 6.00
Imperf., #258-260 13.00

First Five Year Plan for Chemical Industry A110

Designs: 3xu, Viet Tri Insecticide Factory. 12xu, Viet Tri Chemical Factory.

**1963, Aug. 11**
**261-262** A110 Set of 2 3.00 2.00

Fish A111

Designs: No. 263, 12xu, Cyprinus carpio. No. 264, 12xu, Myloharyngodon piceus. No. 265, 12xu, Hypophthalmichthys molitrix. 20xu, Ophiocephalus caqua. 30xu, Tilapia mossambica.

**1963, Sept. 10**
**263-267** A111 Set of 5 17.00 7.75
Imperf., #263-267 17.00
*a.* Souvenir Sheet 0f 1, #266 67.50

A112

A113

Birds: #268, 12xu, Francolinus stephenson. #269, 12xu, Acridotheres cristatellus. #270, 12xu, Halcyon smyrneusis. 20xu, Diardigallus diardi, horiz. 30xu, Egretta. 40xu, Psittacula alexandri.

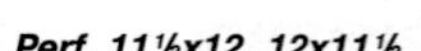

***Perf. 11½x12, 12x11½***

**1963, Oct. 15** **Photo.**
**268-273** A112 Set of 6 35.00 15.00
Imperf., #268-273 45.00

**Souvenir Sheet**

**274** A112 50xu Sheet of 1, like #272 85.00

**1963, Oct. 20** **Litho.** ***Perf. 11***
**275** A113 12xu multicolored 2.00 1.00

World Federation of Trade Unions Congress for Viet Nam.

GANEFO Games A114

#276, 12xu, Swimming. #277, 12xu, Volleyball, vert. #278, 12xu, Soccer, vert. 30xu, High jump.

**1963, Nov. 10**
**276-279** A114 Set of 4 5.00 5.00
Imperf., #276-279 6.00

A115 A116

Flowers: 6xu, Rauwolfia verticillata. No. 281, 12xu, Sophora japonica. No. 282, 12xu, Fibraurea tinctoria. No. 283, 12xu, Chenopodium ambrosioides. 20xu, Momordica cochinchinensis.

**1963, Dec. 3**
**280-284** A115 Set of 5 7.50 3.75
Imperf., #280-284 10.00

**1963, Dec. 20**
**285** A116 12xu multicolored 2.50 1.00

World Day for Viet Nam.



A117

First Five-Year Plan — A118

6xu, Molten cast iron. #287, 12xu, Thai Nguyen Steel & Iron Works. #288, 12xu, Power lines.

**1964, Jan. 25** **Litho.**
**286-288** A117-A118 Set of 3 4.50 1.75

Intl. Quiet Sun Year — A119

**1964, Jan. 25**
**289-290** A119 12xu, 50xu, set of 2 5.00 3.00
Imperf., #289-290 20.00

Flights of Vostok 5 and 6 A120

#291, 12xu, Rockets in orbit. #292, 12xu, Valery Bykovsky. 30xu, Valentina Tereshkova.

**1964, Mar. 25**
**291-293** A120 Set of 3 6.00 5.00
Imperf., #291-293 12.00

A stamp commemorating the anniversary of the founding of the People's Democratic Republic of Korea was printed but not issued.

A121

A122

Flowers: No. 294, 12xu, Persica vulgaris. No. 295, 12xu, Hibiscus mutabilis. No. 296, 12xu, Passiflora hispida. No. 297, 12xu, Saraca dives. 20xu, Michelia champaca. 30xu, Camellia amplexicaulis.

**1964, Apr. 10** ***Perf. 11½x12***
**294-299** A121 Set of 6 13.00 5.00
Imperf., #294-299 15.00

**1964, Apr. 27** ***Perf. 11***

Costumes: 6xu, Peasant, 19th cent. No. 301, 12xu, Woman wearing large hat, 19th cent. No. 302, 12xu, Woman carrying hat.

**300-302** A122 Set of 3 5.00 3.00

Battle of Dien Bien Phu, 10th Anniv. A123

Designs: 3xu, Artillery. 6xu, Machine gun emplacement. Nos. 305, 307c, Bomb disposal. Nos. 306, 307d, Farmer on tractor.

**1964, May 7**
**303** A123 3xu red & black
**304** A123 6xu blue & black
**305** A123 12xu yel org & blk
**306** A123 12xu red lilac & black
*Nos. 303-306 (4)* 7.50 6.00
Imperf., #303-306 11.00

**Souvenir Sheet**

***Imperf***

**307** Sheet of 4 12.50
*a.* A123 3xu orange & black
*b.* A123 6xu yellow green & black
*c.* A123 12xu red, black & orange
*d.* A123 12xu blue & black

Ham Rong Bridge — A124

**1964, May 17**
**308** A124 12xu multicolored 2.50 1.00

Wild Animals A125

Designs: No. 309, 12xu, Panthera tigris, vert. No. 310, 12xu, Pseudaxis axis, vert. No. 311, 12xu, Tapirus indicus. 20xu, Bubalus bubalis. 30xu, Rhinoceros bicornis. 40xu, Bibos banteng.

**1964, June 2** ***Perf. 10½***
**309-314** A125 Set of 6 16.00 13.00
Imperf., #309-314 14.00

Geneva Agreement on Viet Nam, 10th Anniv. A126

Intl. Labor Federation Committee United with People of South Viet Nam — A127

**1964, July 20** ***Perf. 11***
**315-316** A126-A127 12xu Set of 2 3.00 1.50

Nam Bac Ninh Pumping Station A128

**1964, Aug. 25**
**317** A128 12xu blue gray & black 1.75 .80

Liberation of Hanoi, 10th Anniv. — A129

6xu, People cheering soldiers in truck. 12xu, Construction, hammerhead crane.

**1964, Oct. 10**
**318-319** A129 Set of 2 3.50 2.50

Natl. Defense Games — A130

Designs: 5xu, Rowing. No. 321, 12xu, Parachuting, vert. No. 322, 12xu, Gliders, vert. No. 323, 12xu, Shooting.

**1964, Oct. 18**
**320-323** A130 Set of 4 6.50 2.50

Fruits — A131

Designs: No. 324, 12xu, Mangifera indica. No. 325, 12xu, Guarcinia mangostana. No. 326, 12xu, Nephelium litchi. 20xu, Anona squamosa. 50xu, Citrus medica.

**1964, Oct. 31 Photo.** ***Perf. 11½x12***
**324-328** A131 Set of 5 12.50 4.75
Imperf., #324-328 15.00

World Solidarity Conference — A132

Designs: a, Ba Dinh Hall. b, Vietnamese soldier shaking hands with foreign people. c, Fist, planes, submarine.

**1964, Nov. 25 Litho.** ***Perf. 11***
**329** A132 12xu Strip of 3, #a.-c. 4.50 3.00

People's Army, 20th Anniv. A133

Designs: No. 330, Soldiers, flag. No. 331a, Coast guards. No. 331b, Mounted border guards, vert.

**1964, Dec. 22**
**330** A133 12xu multicolored
**331** A133 12xu Pair, #a.-b.
*Nos. 330-331 (2)* 5.00 1.25

Cuban Revolution, 6th Anniv. — A134

Designs: a, Vietnamese, Cuban flags. b, Cuban revolutionaries.

**1965, Jan. 1**
**332** A134 12xu Pair, #a.-b. 4.50 3.00

Economic & Cultural Development of Mountain Region — A135

Designs: 2xu, 3xu, Women pollinating corn. 12xu, Girls walking to school.

**1965, Jan. 1**
**333-335** A135 Set of 3 3.00 2.50
Imperf., #333-335

A136

Vietnamese Worker's Party, 35th Anniv. — A137

Politicians: No. 336a, Le Hong Phong. b, Tran Phu. c, Hoang Van Thu. d, Ngo Gia Tu. e, Nguyen Van Cu.
No. 337a, Party flag. b, Worker, soldier.

**1965 Litho.** ***Perf. 11***
**336** A136 6xu Strip of 5, #a.-e.
**337** A137 12xu Pair, #a.-b.
*Nos. 336-337 (2)* 5.00 4.75

Issued: No. 336, 2/3; No. 337, 1/30.

Transportation Ministers Conference, Hanoi — A138

12xu, 30xu, Nguyen Van Troi, locomotive.

**1965, Mar. 23**
**338-339** A138 Set of 2 7.00 2.00
Imperf., #338-339

Vignette on No. 339 is mirror image of No. 338.

Flight of Voskhod 1 — A139

20xu, Cosmonauts Komarov, Feoktistov, Yegorov, rocket, globe. 1d, Cosmonauts, rocket.

**1965, Mar. 30**
**340-341** A139 Set of 2 9.00 9.00
Imperf., #340-341 11.00

Lenin, 95th Birth Anniv. A140

**1965, Apr. 22** **Litho.**
**342-343** A140 8xu, 12xu, set of 2 4.00

A141

A142

**1965, May 19**
**344-345** A141 6xu, 12xu, set of 2 2.50 1.90

Ho Chi Minh, 75th birthday.

**1965, May 19**
**346** A142 12xu multicolored 2.50 2.00

Afro-Asian Conference, 10th anniv.

Trade Union Conference, Hanoi — A143

Designs: No. 347, Workers solidarity. No. 348, Soldiers, vert. No. 349, Naval battle.

**1965, June 2**
**347-349** A143 12xu Set of 3 4.50

Wild Animals — A144

Designs: No. 350, 12xu, Martes flavigula. No. 351, 12xu, Chrotogale owstoni. No. 352, 12xu, Manis pentadactyla. No. 353, 12xu, Presbytis delacouri, vert. 20xu, Petaurista lylei, vert. 50xu, Nycticebus pygmaeus, vert.

**1965, June 24** **Photo.** ***Perf. 12***
**350-355** A144 Set of 6 17.00 5.50
Imperf., #350-355 25.00

A145

A146

**1965, July 1** ***Perf. 11½x11***
**356** A145 12xu multicolored 3.50 .40

6th Socialist Postal Ministers Conference.

**1965, July 20** **Litho.** ***Perf. 11***

Nguyen Van Troi (1940-64). Denominations: 12xu, 50xu, 4d.

**357-359** A146 Set of 3 9.00 6.00

A147

Insects — A148

Designs: No. 360, 12xu, Tessaratoma papillosa. No. 361, 12xu, Rhynchocoris humeralis. No. 362, 12xu, Poeciliocoris latus. No. 363, 12xu, Tosena melanoptera. 20xu, Cicada. 30xu, Fulgora candelaria.

**1965, July 24** **Photo.**
**360-362** A147 Set of 3
**363-365** A148 Set of 3
*Nos. 360-365 (6)* 12.00 7.00
Imperf., #360-365 18.00

August Revolution, 20th Anniv. A149

**1965, Aug. 19** **Litho.**
**366-367** A149 6xu, 12xu, set of 2 3.00 1.75

Crustaceans — A150

Designs: No. 368, 12xu, Penaeus indicus. No. 369, 12xu, Scylla serrata. No. 370, 12xu, Metapenaeus joyneri. No. 371, 12xu, Neptunus. 20xu, Palinurus japonicus. 50xu, Uca marionis.

**1965, Aug. 19**
**368-373** A150 Set of 6 20.00 8.00
Imperf., #368-373 20.00

500th US Warplane Shot Down — A151

**1965, Aug. 30**
**374** A151 12xu gray green & lilac 7.00 5.50

A152

Completion of 1st Five-Year Plan — A153

#375, Foundry worker. #376, Electricity, irrigation. #377, Public health, education. #377, Students, children playing. #378, Factory worker. #379, Agricultural workers.

**1965**
**375-377** A152 12xu Set of 3 3.50 1.75
**378-380** A153 12xu Set of 3 3.50 1.75
Imperf., #375-380

Issued: #375-377, 9/2; #378-380, 12/25.

Nghe An, Ha Tinh Uprising, 35th Anniv. — A154

**1965, Sept. 12**
**381-382** A154 10xu, 12xu, set of 2 2.50 1.65
Imperf., #381-382

Friendship Between Viet Nam, People's Republic of China, 16th Anniv. — A155

Designs: No. 383, Youth holding flags, Friendship Gate. No. 384, Children waving flags, walking through Gate, vert.

**1965, Oct. 1**
**383-384** A155 12xu Set of 2 10.00 1.75

Flight of Voskhod 2 — A156

#385, 12xu, Konstantin Tsiolkovsky, Sputnik I. #386, 12xu, Voskhod 2, A. Leonov, P. Belyayev. #387, 50xu, Yuri Gagarin. #388, 50xu, Leonov walking in space.

**1965, Oct. 5**
**385-388** A156 Set of 4 8.00 3.25
Imperf., #385-388

A157

A158

Norman R. Morrison, US anti-war demonstration.

**1965, Nov. 22**
**389** A157 12xu black & red 2.50 1.25

**1965, Nov. 25**

Nguyen Du (1765-1820), poet: No. 390, 12xu, Birthplace. No. 391, 12xu, Museum. 20xu, Volume of poems entitled Kieu. 1d, Scene from Kieu.

**390-393** A158 Set of 4 6.00 5.00

A159

Designs: No. 394, 12xu, Ho Chi Minh. No. 395, 12xu, Karl Marx. No. 396, 12xu, Lenin. 50xu, Frederich Engels.

**Litho. & Engr. (#394), Litho.**
**1965, Nov. 28** ***Perf. 11½***
**394-397** A159 Set of 4 6.00 6.00

Nos. 395-397 have white border.

Butterflies A160

#398, 12xu, Cethosia cyane. #399, 12xu, Zelides sarpedon. #400, 12xu, Cethosia. #401, 12xu, Apatura ambica. 20xu, Papilio paris. 30xu, Tros aristolochiae.

**1965, Nov. 28** **Litho.** ***Perf. 11***
**398-403** A160 Set of 6 21.00 6.50
Imperf., #398-403 55.00

South Viet Nam Natl. Liberation Front, 5th Anniv. — A161

**1965, Dec. 20**
**404** A161 12xu lilac 2.50 1.25
Imperf.

1st General Elections, 20th Anniv. — A162

**1966, Jan. 6**
**405** A162 12xu black & red 2.50 1.25

A163

A164

Orchids: No. 406, 12xu, Vanda teres. No. 407, 12xu, Dendrobium meschatum. No. 408, 12xu, Dendrobium nobile. No. 409, 12xu, Dendrobium crystallinum. 20xu, Vandopsis gigantea. 30xu, Dendrobium.

**1966, Jan. 10** ***Perf. 12***
**406-411** A163 Set of 6 12.00 5.50
Imperf., #406-411 20.00

**1966, Jan. 18** ***Perf. 11***
**412** A164 12xu multicolored 2.50 1.00
Imperf.

New Year 1966 (Year of the Horse).

Reptiles A165

#413, 12xu, Physignathus cocincinus. #414, 12xu, Gekko gecko. #415, 12xu, Trionyx sinensis. #416, 12xu, Testudo elongata. 20xu, Varanus salvator. 40xu, Eretmochelys imbricata.

**1966, Feb. 25** ***Perf. 12x11½***
**413-418** A165 Set of 6 12.00 6.00
Imperf., #413-418 20.00

Natl. Sports A166

Designs: No. 419, Archery. No. 420, Wrestling. No. 421, Spear fighting.

**1966, Mar. 25** ***Perf. 11***
**419-421** A166 12xu Set of 3 5.00 2.75

6xu, 12xu, 1d stamps for running, swimming and shooting were printed but not issued.

Youth Labor Union, 35th Anniv. — A167

**1966, Mar. 26**
**422** A167 12xu multicolored 2.00 2.00

1000th US Warplane Shot Down — A168

**1966, Apr. 29**
**423** A168 12xu multicolored 7.50 4.00

May Day — A169

**1966, May 1**
**424** A169 6xu multicolored 2.00 .65

Defending Con Co Island — A170

**1966, June 1**
**425** A170 12xu multicolored 2.50 1.50

A171

A172

**1966, June 1**
**426** A171 12xu red & black 1.75 1.00

Young Pioneers, 25th anniv.

**1966, July 1**

Designs: 3xu, View of Yenan. 12xu, Ho Chi Minh, Mao Tse-Tung.

**427-428** A172 Set of 2 4.00 .75
Imperf., #427-428

Chinese Communist Party, 45th anniv.

A173

A174

Luna 9: 12xu, Flight path to moon. 50xu, In lunar orbit.

**1966, Aug. 5**
**429-430** A173 Set of 2 7.50 3.00
Imperf., #429-430 10.00

**1966, Oct. 10**
**431** A174 12xu multicolored 10.00 3.00

**With Additional Inscription: "NGAY 14.10.1966"**

**431A** A174 12xu multicolored 15.00 3.75
Imperf., #431-431A

1500th US warplane shot down.

Victory in Dry Season Campaign — A175

Designs: 1xu, 12xu (No. 433), Woman guerrilla carrying guns. 12xu (No. 434), Soldier escorting prisoners of war.

**1966, Oct. 15**
**432-434** A175 Set of 3 5.00 2.25
Imperf., #432-434

Vietnamese Women's Union, 20th Anniv. — A176

**1966, Oct. 20**
**435** A176 12xu orange & black 1.00 .70
Imperf.

Birds A177

Designs: No. 436, 12xu, Pitta moluccensis. No. 437, 12xu, Psarisomus dolhousiae. Nos. 438, 12xu, Alcedo atthis, vert. No. 439, 12xu, Oriolus chinensis, vert. 20xu, Upupa epops, vert. 30xu, Oriolus traillii.

**1966, Oct. 31** ***Perf. 12x12½, 12½x12***
**436-441** A177 Set of 6 10.00 5.00
Imperf., #436-441 25.00

GANEFO Asian Games — A178

Designs: No. 442, Soccer. No. 443, Shooting. No. 444, Swimming. No. 445, Running.

**1966, Nov. 25** ***Perf. 11***
**442-445** Set of 4 6.00 4.00
Imperf., #442-445 9.00
*443a* A178 12xu Pair, #442-443
*445a* A178 30xu Pair, #444-445
*Nos. 443a, 445a (4)* 8.50

Ho Chi Minh's Appeal for Natl. Resistance, 20th Anniv. — A179

Designs: No. 446, Flags, workers. No. 447, Soldiers, workers, ships.

**1967, Jan. 30**
**446-447** A179 12xu Set of 2 2.00 1.75

See Nos. 501-504.

Rice Harvest A180

**1967, Jan. 30**
**448** A180 12xu multicolored 1.50 1.40

Bamboo A181

#449, 12xu, Bambusa arundinaceu. #450, 12xu, Arundinaria rolleana. #451, 12xu, Arundinaria racemosa. #452, 12xu, Bambusa bingami. 30xu, Bambusa nutans. 50xu, Dendrocalamus petellaris.

**1967, Feb. 2** ***Perf. 12x11½***
**449-454** A181 Set of 6 9.00 7.25
Imperf., #449-454 12.00

Wild Animals — A182

Designs: No. 455, 12xu, Cuon rutilans. No. 456, 12xu, Arctictis binturong. No. 457, 12xu, Arctonyx collaris. 20xu, Viverra zibetha. 40xu, Macaca speciosa. 50xu, Neofelis nebulosa.

**1967, Mar. 26 Litho.** ***Perf. 12***
**455-460** A182 Set of 6 11.00 6.00
Imperf., #455-460 13.00

2000th US Aircraft Shot Down — A183

**1967, June 7** ***Perf. 11***
**461-462** A183 6xu, 12xu, set of 2 10.00 8.00

Fish A184

#463, 12xu, Saurida filamentosa. #464, 12xu, Scomberomorus niphonius. #465, 12xu, Haplogenys mucronatus. 20xu, Lethrinus haematopterus. 30xu, Formio niger. 50xu, Lutianus erythropterus.

**1967, July 25** ***Perf. 12***
**463-468** A184 Set of 6 11.00 9.75
Imperf., #463-468 13.00

A185 A186

Launch of 1st Chinese ballistic missile: 12xu, Missile, flag, agricultural scene. 30xu, Missile, Gate of Heavenly Peace.

**1967, July 25** ***Perf. 11***
**469-470** A185 Set of 2 7.50 3.00
Imperf., #469-470

**1967, Oct. 15**

Russian October Revolution, 50th anniv.: 6xu, Lenin, revolutionary soldiers. No. 472a, 12xu, Lenin, armed mob. No. 472b, 12xu, Lenin, Marx, Vietnamese soldiers. 20xu, Cruiser Aurora.

**471-473** A186 Set of 4 4.00 3.00

No. 472 is printed se-tenant.

2500th US Warplane Shot Down — A187

Design: No. 475, Plane in flames, vert.

**1967, Nov. 6**
**474-475** A187 12xu Set of 2 9.00 8.00

1st Chinese Hydrogen Bomb Test — A188

Designs: 12xu, Atomic symbol, Gate of Heavenly Peace. 20xu, Chinese lantern, atomic symbol, dove.

**1967, Nov. 20**
**476-477** A188 Set of 2 5.00 3.00
Imperf., #476-477 32.50

No. 477 is 30x35mm.

A189

#478, 12xu, Rifle fire from trenches. #479, 12xu, Militia with captured US pilot. #480, 12xu, Factory anti-aircraft unit. #481, 12xu, Naval anti- aircraft unit. 20xu, Aerial dog-fight. 30xu, Heavy anti-aircraft battery.

**1967, Dec. 19** ***Perf. 12***
**478-483** A189 Set of 6 6.00 4.75

Chickens — A190

Designs: No. 484, 12xu, White spotted cock, hen. No. 485, 12xu, Black hens. No. 486, 12xu, Bantam cock, hen. No. 487, 12xu, Bantam cock. 20xu, Fighting cocks. 30xu, Exotic hen. 40xu, Hen, chicks from Ho region. 50xu, Dong Cao's cock, hen.

**1968, Feb. 29**
**484-491** A190 Set of 8 11.00 5.00
Imperf., #484-491 17.50

Victories of 1966-67 — A191

No. 492: a, Soldier attacking US tank. b, Gunner firing on US ships. c, Burning village. d, Soldier firing mortar.

No. 493: a, Attacking US artillery. b, Escorting US prisoners. c, Interrogating refugees. d, Civilian demonstration.

**1968, Mar. 5** ***Perf. 11***
**492-493** A191 12xu, 2 blocks of 4 6.00 6.00
Imperf., #492-493

Maxim Gorki (1868-1936) — A192

**1968, Mar. 5**
**494** A192 12xu brown & black 1.50 .80
Imperf.

Roses — A193

Designs: No. 495, 12xu, Pale red. No. 496, 12xu, Orange. No. 497, 12xu, Pink. 20xu, Yellow, 30xu, Dark red. 40xu, Lilac.

**1968, Apr. 25 Photo.** ***Perf. 11½x12***
**495-500** A193 Set of 6 12.00 12.00
Imperf., #495-500 16.00

Ho Chi Minh's Appeal for Resistance Type

Values and colors: No. 501, 6xu, greenish blue and yellow. No. 502, 12xu, vermilion. No. 503, 12xu, bright blue. No. 504, 12xu, brownish lilac.

**1968, Apr. 25 Litho.** ***Perf. 11***
**Size: 25x17mm**
**501-504** A179 6xu, 12xu Set of 4 6.00 3.00
Imperf., #501-504

Ho Chi Minh, Flag A195

**1968, May 19**
**505** A195 12xu brown & red 2.00 .50
Imperf.

Karl Marx — A196

**1968, May 19**
**506** A196 12xu olive grn & blk 1.75 .25

3000th US Warplane Shot Down A197

#507: a, 12xu, Anti-aircraft machine gunners. b, 12xu, Women firing anti-aircraft gun.

#508: a, 40xu, Vietnamese plane shooting down US plane. b, 40xu, Anti-aircraft missile.

**1968, May 19**
**507-508** A197 Set of 2 pairs 14.00 10.00
Imperf., #507-508

Handicrafts — A198

6xu, Rattan products. #510, 12xu, Ceramics. #511, 12xu, Bamboo products. 20xu, Ivory carving. 30xu, Lacquerware. 40xu, Silverware.

**1968, July 5** ***Perf. 12***
**509-514** A198 Set of 6 6.50 6.00
Imperf., #509-514 15.00

Martial Arts A199

Designs: No. 515, 12xu, Saber fencing. No. 516, 12xu, Stick fighting. No. 517, 12xu, Dagger fighting. 30xu, Unarmed combat. 40xu, Chinese war sword fighting. 50xu, Duel with swords, shields.

**1968, Nov. 1**
**515-520** A199 Set of 6 10.00 9.00
Imperf., #515-520 16.00

Architecture — A200

Designs: No. 521, 12xu, Khue Van tower, vert. No. 522, 12xu, Bell tower, Keo pagoda, vert. 20xu, Covered bridge, Thay pagoda. 30xu, One-pillar pagoda, Hanoi, vert. 40xu, Gateway, Ninh Phuc pagoda. 50xu, Tay Phuong pagoda.

**1968, Nov. 5**
**521-526** A200 Set of 6 6.00 5.75
Imperf., #521-526 10.00

Foreign Solidarity with Viet Nam — A201

#527, 12xu, Latin American guerrilla, vert. #528, 12xu, Cuban, Vietnamese militia. 20xu, Asian, African, Latin American soldiers, vert.

**1968, Dec. 15 Wmk. 376 *Perf. 12½***
**With Gum**
**527-529** A201 Set of 3 4.00 3.00

Scenes of War A202

Artworks: No. 530, 12xu, Defending the mines. No. 531, 12xu, Plowman with rifle, vert. 30xu, Repairing railway track. 40xu, Wreckage of US aircraft.

**1968, Dec. 15 Wmk. 376 *Perf. 12½***
**With Gum**
**530-533** A202 Set of 4 4.00 3.75

Victories in South Viet Nam — A203

#534, 12xu, Tay Nguyen throwing grenade. #535, 12xu, Gun crews, Tri Thien. #536, 12xu, Nam Ngai shooting down US aircraft. 40xu, Insurgents, Tay Ninh, destroyed US armor. 50xu, Guerrillas preparing bamboo spike booby traps.

**1969, Feb. 16 Unwmk. *Perf. 11½***
**534-538** A203 Set of 5 6.00 6.00

Timber Industry A204

Designs: 6xu, Loading timber trucks. No. 540, 12xu, Log raft running rapids. No. 541, 12xu, Launch towing log raft. No. 542, 12xu, Elephant hauling timber. No. 543, 12xu, Forest protection. 20xu, Water buffalo hauling log. 30xu, Hauling logs by overhead cable.

**1969, Apr. 10**
**539-545** A204 Set of 7 9.00 8.75
Imperf., #539-545 15.00

Scenes of War — A205

Designs: No. 546, 12xu, Young guerrilla. No. 547, 12xu, Scout on patrol. 20xu, Female guerrilla, vert. 30xu, Halt at way station. 40xu, After a skirmish. 50xu, Liberated hamlet.

***Perf. 12½x11½, 11½x12½***
**1969, July 20**
**546-551** A205 Set of 6 8.00 5.50
Imperf., #546-551 15.00

Tet Offensive Battles — A206

Designs: 8xu, 12xu (No. 553), Ben Tre. No. 554, 12xu, Mortar crew, Khe Sanh, vert. No. 555, 12xu, Two soldiers, flag, Hue, vert. No. 556, 12xu, Soldier running toward US Embassy, Saigon, vert.

**1969, July 31 *Perf. 11***
**552-556** A206 Set of 5 3.50 2.25
Imperf., #552-556

Liberation of Hanoi, 15th Anniv. A207

#557, Soldier with flamethrower. #558, Children constructing toy buildings.

**1969, Oct. 10**
**557-558** A207 12xu Set of 2 3.50 1.75
Imperf., #557-558

A208

A209

**1969, Oct. 10**
**559** A208 12xu brn, blk & red 2.50 .80
Imperf.

Bertrand Russell Intl. War Crimes Tribunal, Stockholm and Roskilde.

**1969, Nov. 20 *Perf. 12***

Fruits: No. 560, 12xu, Papaya. No. 561, 12xu, Grapefruit. 20xu, Tangerines. 30xu, Oranges. 40xu, Lychee nuts. 50xu, Persimmons.

**560-565** A209 Set of 6 5.50 2.75
Imperf., #560-565 8.50

Viet Nam Labor Party, 40th Anniv. — A210

Designs: No. 566, Nguyen Ai Quoc. No. 567, Ho Chi Minh. No. 568, Le Hong Phong. No. 569, Tran Phu. No. 570, Nguyen Van Cu.

**1970, Feb. 3 *Perf. 11***
**566-570** A210 12xu Set of 5 5.00 4.00
Imperf., #566-570

Nos. 568-570 are 40x25mm. Nos. 566-567 issued in vert. or horiz. se-tenant pairs. Nos. 568-570 issued in horizontal strips of 3.

Children's Activities — A211

Designs: No. 571, 12xu, Playing with toys. No. 572, 12xu, Three boys at kindergarten. No. 573, 20xu, Tending a garden. No. 574, 20xu, Tending water buffaloes. 30xu, Feeding chickens. 40xu, Piano, violin duet. 50xu, Flying model airplane. 60xu, Walking to school.

**1970, Mar. 8 *Perf. 12***
**571-578** A211 Set of 8 6.50 6.50

For overprints see Nos. 2181-2188.

Lenin, Birth Centenary A212

Designs: 12xu, Making speech. 1d, Portrait.

**1970, Apr. 22 *Perf. 11***
**579-580** A212 Set of 2 4.00 3.75
Imperf., #579-580

Shells A213

No. 581, 12xu, On con lon. No. 582, 12xu, Oc xa cu. 20xu, Oc tien. 1d, Oc tu va.

**1970, Apr. 26 *Perf. 12½x12***
**581-584** A213 Set of 4 6.50 6.00
Imperf., #581-584 10.00

Ho Chi Minh — A214

12xu (#585, 588c, 588g), In 1930 (full face, no beard). 12xu (#586, 588b, 588f), In 1945 (facing right, beard). 2d, 6xu, (#587, 588a, 588e), In 1969 (full face, beard).

**1970, May 19 *Perf. 11***
**585-587** A214 Set of 3 4.75 4.50
Imperf., #585-587

**Souvenir Sheets of 3**

***Imperf***

**588** Types of #585-587, #a.-c., orange background 7.00
**588D** Types of #585-587, #e.-g., pale lilac background 7.50

Stamps in souvenir sheets have white backgrounds. The 6xu stamp is larger than the 2d stamp. Nos. 588a and 588e, 588c and 588g are different colors.

Vietcong Flag A215

**1970, June 6**
**589** A215 12xu multicolored 1.50 .75

Formation of Revolutionary Provisional Government of South Viet Nam, 1st anniv.

Fruits and Vegetables A216

#590, 12xu, Watermelon. #591, 12xu, Pumpkin. 20xu, Cucumber. 50xu, Zucchini. 1d, Melon.

**1970, July 15 *Perf. 12***
**590-594** A216 Set of 5 6.00 6.00
Imperf., #590-594 13.00

Consumer Industries — A217

#595, Coal miners, truck. #596, Power linesman, vert. #597, Textile worker, soldier, vert. #598, Stoker, power plant, vert.

***Perf. 12x11½, 11½x12***
**1970, Aug. 25 Litho. & Engr.**
**595-598** A217 12xu Set of 4 3.25 3.25

Agriculture
A218

**1970, Aug. 25 Litho. *Perf. 11***

**599** A218 12xu multicolored 2.00 .75

Democratic Republic of Viet Nam, 25th Anniv. — A219

Famous people: #600, 12xu, Vo Thi Sau facing firing squad. #601, 12xu, Nguyen Van Troi, captors. #602, 12xu, Phan Din Giot attacking pillbox. #603, 12xu, Ho Chi Minh. 20xu, Nguyen Viet Xuan, troops in battle. 1d, Nguyen Van Be attacking tank with mine.

**1970, Sept. 2**

**600-605** A219 Set of 6 4.00 3.75
Imperf., #600-605

No. 603 is 41x28mm.

Indo-Chinese People's Summit Conf. — A220

**1970, Oct. 25**

**606** A220 12xu multicolored 2.50 .70
Imperf.

Bananas
A221

Designs: No. 607, 12xu, Tay. No. 608, 12xu, Tieu. 50xu, Ngu. 1d, Mat.

**1970, Oct. 25 *Perf. 12***

**607-610** A221 Set of 4 7.00 4.00
Imperf., #607-610 10.00

Friedrich Engels — A222

**1970, Nov. 28 *Perf. 11***

**611-612** A222 12xu, 1d, set of 2 3.25 3.00

Snakes
A223

Designs: 12xu, Akistrodon ciatus. 20xu, Calliophis macclellandii. 50xu, Bungarus faciatus. 1d, Trimeresurus gramineus.

**1970, Nov. 30 Photo. *Perf. 12x11½***

**613-616** A223 Set of 4 6.00 5.00
Imperf., #613-616 20.00

Natl. Liberation Front of South Viet Nam, 10th Anniv. — A224

Design: 6xu, Mother and child, flag, vert.

**1970, Dec. 20 Litho. *Perf. 11***

**617-618** A224 Set of 2 2.50 1.65
Imperf., #617-618

Launching of 1st Chinese Satellite, 1st Anniv. — A225

**1971, Apr. 10**

**619-620** A225 12xu, 50xu Set of 2 5.00 2.00
Imperf., #619-620

Ho Chi Minh
A226

Denominations: 1xu, 3xu, 10xu, 12xu.

**1971, May 19**

**621-624** A226 Set of 4 2.00 1.75
Imperf., #621-624
*624a* Souvenir sheet of 1, imperf. 6.00

No. 624a contains one 52x52mm stamp.

Tay Son Uprising, Bicent. — A227

**1971, June 1**

**625-626** A227 6xu, 12xu, set of 2 2.50 1.65
Imperf., #625-626

Marx, Music for The Internationale — A228

**1971, June 20 *Perf. 12½***

**627** A228 12xu org, blk & red 1.00 .75
Imperf.

Paris Commune, cent.

Hai Thuong Lan Ong, Physician, 250th Birth Anniv.
A229

**1971, July 1**

**628-629** A229 12xu, 50xu Set of 2 3.50 2.00
Imperf., #628-629

Statues from Tay Phuong Pagoda
A230

Designs: No. 630, 12xu, Vasumitri. No. 631, 12xu, Kapimala. No. 632, 12xu, Dhikaca. No. 633, 12xu, Sangkayasheta. 30xu, Bouddha Nandi. 40xu, Rahulata. 50xu, Sangha Nandi. 1d, Cakyamuni.

**1971, July 30 Photo. *Perf. 12***

**630-637** A230 Set of 8 11.00 11.00
Imperf., #630-637 15.00

Ho Chi Minh Working Youth Union, 40th Anniv.
A231

**1971, Sept. 7 Litho. *Perf. 11***

**638** A231 12xu multicolored 1.50 .75
Imperf.

Flight of Luna 16 — A232

Luna 16: No. 639a, 12xu, Return from Moon. No. 639b, 12xu, Flight to Moon. 1d, On Moon.

**1971, Sept. 17**

**639-640** A232 Set of 3 4.00 3.50
Imperf., #639-640 12.00

No. 639 is setenant.

Flight of Luna 17
A233

Designs: No. 641, 12xu, Landing on Moon, vert. No. 642 12xu, On Moon. 1d, Lunakhod 1 crossing lunar crevasse.

**1971, Oct. 15**

**641-643** A233 Set of 3 5.00 5.00
Imperf., #641-643 16.00

Five Tigers
A234

Folk paintings: No. 644, 12xu, White tiger. No. 645, 12xu, Red tiger. No. 646, 12xu, Yellow tiger. 40xu, Green tiger. 50xu, Black tiger. 1d, Five tigers.

**1971, Nov. 25 *Perf. 12***

**644-649** A234 Set of 6 10.00 6.00
Imperf., #644-649 15.00

**Size: 90x119mm**

***Imperf***

**650** A234 1d multicolored 12.00

Chinese Communist Party, 50th Anniv.
A235

**1971, Dec. 1 *Perf. 11***

**651** A235 12xu multicolored 1.50 .40

Mongolian People's Republic, 50th Anniv. — A236

**1971, Dec. 25**

**652** A236 12xu multicolored 1.50 .40

Folk Engravings from Dong Ho — A237

#653a, 12xu, Traditional wrestling. #653b, 12xu, Drum procession. #654a, 12xu, Gathering coconuts, vert. #654b, 12xu, Jealousy, vert. 40xu, Wedding of mice. 50xu, Frog school.

**1972, Jan. 30**

**653-656** A237 Set of 6 10.00 9.00
Imperf., #653-656 10.00

No. 653 is tete-beche.
The 30xu in design of #654a is a proof.

3rd Natl. Trade Unions Congress A238

Designs: 1xu, Workers facing right. 12xu, Workers facing left.

**1972, May 1**
**657-658** A238 Set of 2 2.00 1.25
Imperf., #657-658

Natl. Resistance, 25th Anniv. — A239

Designs: No. 659, Munitions worker. No. 660, Soldier in battle. No. 661, Woman in paddy field. No. 662, Text of Ho Chi Minh's appeal.

**1972, May 5**
**659-662** A239 12xu Set of 4 3.50 1.75
Imperf., #659-662 20.00

Ho Chi Minh's Birthplace A240

Design: No. 664, Home in Hanoi.

**1972, May 19**
**663-664** A240 12xu Set of 2 2.50 1.75
Imperf., #663-664 5.00

A241

A242

**1972, June 20**
**665-666** A241 12xu Set of 2 5.00 2.50
Imperf., #665-666

3500th US warplane shot down.
Added inscription on No. 666 reads "NGAY 20.4.1972."

**1972, Aug. 15**

Georgi Dimitrov (1882-1949), Bulgarian politician: No. 668, Dimitrov at Leipzig Court, 1933.

**667-668** A242 12xu Set of 2 2.50 1.50
Imperf., #667-668 5.00

Birds — A243

Designs: No. 669, 12xu, Lobivanellus indicus. No. 670, 12xu, Anas falcata. 30xu, Bubulcus ibis. 40xu, Gallicrex cinerea. 50xu, Prophyria porphyrio. 1d, Leptoptilos dubius.

**1972, Oct. 12** ***Perf. 12***
**669-674** A243 Set of 6 10.00 8.00
Imperf., #669-674 20.00

A244

A245

4000th US warplane shot down: No. 676, Gunner holding rocket.

**1972, Oct. 19** ***Perf. 11***
**675-676** A244 12xu Set of 2 7.00 1.75
Imperf., #675-676 8.00

**1972, Dec. 1** ***Perf. 12***

Tay Nguyen folk dances: #677, 12xu, Drum. #678, 12xu, Umbrella. #679, 12xu, Shield. 20xu, Horse. 30xu, Ca Dong. 40xu, Rice pounding. 50xu, Khaen. 1d, Cham rong.

**677-684** A245 Set of 8 9.00 8.00
Imperf., #677-684 10.00

Flight of Soyuz 11 A246

Designs: 12xu, Soyuz 11 docking with Salyut laboratory. 1d, Soyuz 11 cosmonauts.

**1972, Dec. 30** ***Perf. 11***
**685-686** A246 Set of 2 3.00 2.75
Imperf., #685-686 7.00

Wild Animals — A247

Designs: 12xu, Cuon alpinus. 30xu, Panthera pardus. 50xu, Felis bengalensis. 1d, Lutra lutra.

**1973, Feb. 15** ***Perf. 12½***
**687-690** A247 Set of 4 7.00 5.00
Imperf., #687-690 17.00

Copernicus A248

Copernicus and: No. 691a, 12xu, Armillary sphere. No. 691b, 12xu, Sun. 30xu, Signature, vert.

**1973, Feb. 17** ***Perf. 11***
**691-692** A248 Set of 3 3.50 3.00
Imperf., #691-692

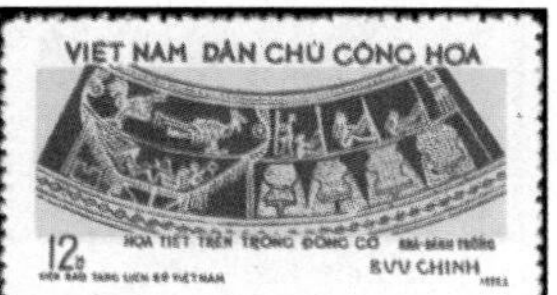

Engravings on Ngoc Lu Bronze Drums — A249

Designs: No. 693, Drummers (Nha Danh Trong). No. 694, Pounding rice (Nha Gia Gao). No. 695, Dancers (Mua). No. 696, War canoe (Thuyen). No. 697, Birds (Chim, Thu).

**1973, Apr. 12**
**693-697** A249 12xu Set of 5 4.00 4.00
Imperf., #693-697

Wild Animals — A250

Designs: 12xu, Tragulus javanicus. 30xu, Capricornis sumatraensis. 50xu, Sus scrofa. 1d, Moschus moschiferus.

**1973, May 25** ***Perf. 12x12½***
**698-701** A250 Set of 4 5.00 5.00
Imperf., 698-701 12.00

Birds A251

#702, 12xu, Pycnonotus jocosus. #703, 12xu, Megalurus palustris. 20xu, Capsychus saularis. 40xu, Rhipidura albicollis. 50xu, Parus major. 1d, Zosterops japonica.

**1973, July 15** ***Perf. 12***
**702-707** A251 Set of 6 7.00 4.00
Imperf., 702-707 15.00

Disabled Soldiers
A252 A252a

**1973, July 27** ***Perf. 11***
**708-709** A252, A252a 12xu Set of 2 2.50
Imperf., #708-709

Three Readiness Youth Movement A253

Designs: No. 710, Road building. No. 711, Open-air class. No. 712, On the march.

**1973, Sept. 2**
**710-712** A253 12xu Set of 3 2.50 1.25
Imperf., #710-712

Democratic People's Republic of Korea, 25th Anniv. — A254

**1973, Sept. 9**
**713** A254 12xu multicolored 1.50 .40
Imperf.

4181st US Warplane Shot Down A255

Designs: No. 714, 12xu, US B-52 hit by air attack. No. 715, 12xu, US B-52, fighter crashing over Haiphong Harbor. No. 716, 12xu, Anti-aircraft battery. 1d, Aircraft wreckage caught in fishing net.

**1973, Oct. 10**
**714-717** A255 Set of 4 7.50 3.75
Imperf., #714-717

Flowers — A256

6xu, 12xu (#719), Chrysanthemum (Cuc). #720, 12xu, Rose. #721, 12xu, Dahlia. #722, 12xu, Chrysanthemum (Bach mi). #723, 12xu, Chrysanthemum (Dai doa).

**1974, Jan. 15**
**718-723** A256 Set of 6 40.00
Imperf., #718-723 70.00

No. 718 may not have been officially released.

Elephants A257

#724, 12xu, Hauling logs. #725, 12xu, War elephant. 40xu, Setting logs in place. 50xu, Circus elephant. 1d, Carrying war supplies.

**1974, Feb. 10** ***Perf. 11½***
**724-728** A257 Set of 5 7.50 7.00
Imperf., #724-728 12.00

Victory at Dien Bien Phu, 20th Anniv. — A258

Designs: a, Dien Bien Phu soldier's badge. b, Soldier waving victory flag.

**1974, May 7** ***Perf. 11***

**729** A258 12xu Pair, #a.-b. 2.50 .70
Imperf. 5.00

Three Responsibilities Women's Movement — A259

Designs: a, Armed worker, peasant. b, Female textile worker.

**1974, June 1**

**730** A259 12xu Pair, #a.-b. 2.50 1.50
Imperf.

A260

A261

Chrysanthemums: No. 731, 12xu, Brown. No. 732, 12xu, Yellow (Vang). 20xu, Ngoc Khong Tuoc. 30xu, White. 40xu, Kim. 50xu, Hong mi. 60xu, Gam. 1d, Lilac.

**1974, June 20** ***Perf. 12x12½***

**731-738** A260 Set of 8 7.00 4.00
Imperf., #731-738 11.00

**1974, Aug. 15** ***Perf. 11***

Industrial plants: No. 739, 12xu, Corchorus capsularis. No. 740, 12xu, Cyperus tojet jormis. 30xu, Morus alba.

**739-741** A261 Set of 3 4.50 2.75
Imperf., #739-741 10.00

Liberation of Hanoi, 20th Anniv. — A262

Designs: a, Woman laying bricks. b, Soldier holding child waving flag.

**1974, Oct. 10**

**742** A262 12xu Pair, #a.-b. 2.50 .80

Solidarity with Chilean Revolution A263

Designs: No. 743, Pres. Salvador Allende, flag. No. 744, Pablo Neruda, poet.

**1974, Oct. 15**

**743-744** A263 12xu Set of 2 2.50 .70
Imperf., #743-744 5.00

Marine Life — A264

Designs: No. 745, 12xu, Rhizostoma. No. 746, 12xu, Loligo. 30xu, Haleotis. 40xu, Pteria martensii. 50xu, Sepia officinalis. 1d, Palinurus japonicus.

**1974, Oct. 25** ***Perf. 12½***

**745-750** A264 Set of 6 7.00 2.50
Imperf., #745-750 12.00

People's Republic of Albania, 30th Anniv. — A265

Designs: a, Natl. arms. b, Albanian, Vietnamese flags, women.

**1974, Nov. 29** ***Perf. 11***

**752** A265 12xu Pair, #a.-b. 2.25 .75
Imperf.

Paris Agreement on Vietnam, 2nd Anniv. — A266

Designs: No. 753, Intl. Conference on Viet Nam in session, 5-line inscription. No. 754, Signing of Paris Agreement, 4-line inscription.

**1975, Jan. 27**

**753-754** A266 12xu Set of 2 2.50 .75
Imperf.

Medicinal Plants — A267

Designs: No. 755, 12xu, Costus speciosus. No. 756, 12xu, Curcuma zedoaria. No. 757, 12xu, Rosa laevigata. 30xu, Erythrina indica. 40xu, Lilium brownii. 50xu, Hibiscus sagittifolius. 60xu, Papaver somniferum. 1d, Belamcanda chinensis.

**1975, Feb. 2** ***Perf. 11½x12***

**755-762** A267 Set of 8 8.00 8.00
Imperf., #755-762 12.50

Vietnamese Labor Party, 45th Anniv. — A268

Designs: No. 763, 12xu, Tran Phu. No. 764, 12xu, Le Hong Phong. No. 765, 12xu, Nguyen Van Cu. No. 766, 12xu, Ngo Gia Tu. 60xu, Ho Chi Minh in 1924, vert.

**1975, Feb. 3** ***Perf. 11***

**763-767** A268 Set of 5 2.75 2.00
Imperf., #763-767 10.00

A269

A270

Fruit: No. 768, 12xu, Achras sapota. No. 769, 12xu, Persica vulgaris. 20xu, Eugenia jambos. 30xu, Chrysophyllum cainito. 40xu, Lucuma mamosa. 50xu, Prunica granitum. 60xu, Durio ziberthinus. 1d, Prunus salicina.

**1975, Apr. 25** ***Perf. 12x12½***

**768-775** A269 Set of 8 7.50 6.00
Imperf., 768-775 12.00

**1975, May 19** ***Perf. 11***

**776-777** A270 12xu, 60xu, set of 2 3.50 1.25
Imperf., #776-777 10.00

Ho Chi Minh, 85th birthday.

People's Republic of Poland, 30th Anniv. A271

**1975, July 5**

**778-781** A271 1xu, 2xu, 3xu, 12xu, set of 4 3.00
Imperf., #778-781

Flags A272

Natl. Arms — A273

Flag of North Viet Nam and: No. 782, Draped flag. No. 783, Flag with star & cresent. No. 784, DDR flag and handshake.

**1975**

**782-785** A272-A273 12xu Set of 4 6.00
Imperf., #782-784

People's Republic of China, 25th anniv. (#782), Republic of Algeria, 20th anniv. (#783), German Democratic Republic, 25th anniv. (#784), liberation of Hungary, 30th anniv. (#785).

Issued: No. 782, 7/5. Nos. 783-785, 8/15.

Independence, 30th Anniv. — A274

#786, Flag. #787, Natl. arms. #788-789, Ho Chi Minh proclaiming independence.

**1975, Sept. 2**

**786-788** A274 12xu Set of 3 3.50 1.25

**Souvenir Sheet**

***Imperf***

**789** A274 20xu multicolored 15.00

No. 789 contains one 45x30mm stamp.

Reptiles A275

#790, 12xu, Dermochelys coriacea. #791, 12xu, Physignathus cocincinus. 20xu, Hydrophis brookii. 30xu, Platysternum megacephalum. 40xu, Leiolepis belliana. 50xu, Python molurus. 60xu, Naja hannah. 1d, Draco maculatus.

**1975, Nov. 25** ***Perf. 12***

**790-797** A275 Set of 8 8.00 7.00
Imperf., #790-797 16.00

Butterflies — A276

#798, 12xu, Pathysa antiphates. #799, 12xu, Danaus plexippus. 20xu, Cynautocera papilionaria. 30xu, Maenas salaminia. 40xu, Papilio machaon. 50xu, Ixias pyrene. 60xu, Eusemia vetula. 1d, Eriboea.

**1976, Jan. 6**

**798-805** A276 Set of 8 9.00 9.00
Imperf., #798-805 25.00

No. 799 misspelled "Danais."

Lan Hoang Thao Orchid A277

**1976, Jan. 25** ***Perf. 11***
**806-807** A277 6xu, 12xu, set of 2 4.00 1.75

See Nos. 854-855.

Wild Animals A278

#808, 12xu, Callosciurus erythraeus. #809, 12xu, Paguma larvata. 20xu, Macaca mulatta. 30xu, Hystrix hodgsoni. 40xu, Nyctereutes procyonoides. 50xu, Selenarctos thibetanus. 60xu, Panthera pardus. 1d, Cynocephalus variegatus.

**1976, Mar. 20** ***Perf. 12***
**808-815** A278 Set of 8 7.00 2.50
Imperf., #808-815 15.00

1st Elections to Unified Natl. Assembly A279

6xu (#816), Map, hand placing ballot in ballot box. 6xu (#817), 12xu, Map, voters.

**1976, Apr. 10** ***Perf. 11***
**816-818** A279 Set of 3 3.50 1.25
Imperf., #816-818

Size of Nos. 817-818 is 35x22mm.
Identical stamps inscribed "Mien Nam Viet Nam" are National Front issues. Same values.

Unified Natl. Assembly, 1st Session A280

Design: 12xu, Inscribed "Doc Lap Thong Nhat Chu Nghia Xa Hoi."

**1976, June 24**
**819-820** A280 6xu, 12xu, set of 2 2.50 .80

Identical stamps inscribed "Mien Nam Viet Nam" are National Front issues. Same values.

A281

A282

**1976, June 24** ***Perf. 12x12½***
**821** A281 12xu multicolored 1.50 .40

Reunification of Viet Nam.

**1976, June 24** ***Perf. 12***

Orchids: No. 822, 12xu, Habenaria rhodocheila. No. 823, 12xu, Dendrobium devonianum. 20xu, Dendrobium tortile. 30xu, Doritis pulcherrima. 40xu, Dendrobium farmeri. 50xu, Dendrobium aggregatum. 60xu, Eria pannea. 1d, Paphiopedilum concolor.

**822-829** A282 Set of 8 8.00 2.00
Imperf., #822-829 10.00

## Socialist Republic of Viet Nam

AREA—128,000 sq. mi.
POP.—77,311,210 (1999 est.0
CAPITAL—Hanoi

Vietnamese Red Cross, 30th Anniv. — A283

**1976, July 27** ***Perf. 11***
**830** A283 12xu multicolored 2.50 .80
Imperf.

Fish — A284

#831, 12xu, Lutjanus sebae. #832, 12xu, Dampieria melanotaenia. 20xu, Therapon theraps. 30xu, Amphiprion bifasciatus. 40xu, Abudefduf sexfasciatus. 50xu, Heniochus acuminatus. 60xu, Amphiprion macrostoma. 1d, Symphorus spilurus.

**1976, Aug. 15** ***Perf. 12***
**831-838** A284 Set of 8 6.00 4.75
Imperf., #831-838 9.00

Viet Nam Worker's Party, 4th Natl. Congress A285

**1976, Nov. 12** ***Perf. 11***
**839-844** A285 2, 3, 5, 10, 12, 20xu, set of 6 3.50 2.50

Viet Nam Communist Party, 4th Natl. Congress — A286

Designs: a, Agriculture, industry. b, Ho Chi Minh, worker, farmer, soldier, scientist.

Design size 24.5mmx35mm

**1976, Dec. 10**
**845** A286 12xu Pair, #a.-b. 2.50 .80
Imperf.

See Nos. 951-954.

Unification of Viet Nam — A287

**1976, Dec. 14**
**846-847** A287 6xu, 12xu, set of 2 2.50 .80
Imperf., #846-847 4.50

General Offensive, 1975 — A288

Designs: 2xu, 50xu, Liberation of Buon Me Thuot. 3xu, 1d, Tanks liberating Da Nang. 6xu, 2d, Tank, soldiers liberating Presidential palace, Saigon.

**1976, Dec. 14**
**848-853** A288 Set of 6 4.50 4.50

Lan Hoang Thao Orchid Type of 1976 Inscribed "VIET NAM" and "1976"

**1976, Dec.** **Litho.** ***Perf. 11***
**854-855** A277 6xu, 12xu Set of 2 45.00 15.00

Dragonflies — A289

#856, 12xu, Ho. #857, 12xu, Bao. 20xu, Canh dom. 30xu, Nuong. 40xu, Suoi. 50xu, Canh vang. 60xu, Canh khoang. 1d, Canh den.

**1977, Jan. 25** ***Perf. 12***
**856-863** A289 Set of 8 7.00 1.50
Imperf., #856-863 16.00

A290

A291

Rare Birds: 12xu (#864), 60xu, Buceros bicornis. 12xu (#865), Ptilolaemus tickelli. 20xu, Berenicornis comatus. 30xu, Aceros undulatus. 40xu, Anthracoceros malabaricus. 50xu, Anthracoceros malayanus. 1d, Aceros nipalensis.

**1977, Apr. 15**
**864-871** A290 Set of 8 7.25 3.25
Imperf., #864-871 9.00

**1977, Apr. 25** ***Perf. 11***

Bronze drum and: 4xu, Thang Long Tower. 5xu, Map. 12xu, Lotus blossom. 50xu, Flag.

**872-875** A291 Set of 4 4.50 2.00
Imperf., #872-875

Natl. Assembly general elections, 1st anniv.

Beetles A292

#876, 12xu, Black-spotted (Dom den). #877, 12xu, Yellow-spotted (Lang vang). 20xu, Veined (Van gach). 30xu, Green (Nhung xanh). 40xu, Green-spotted (Hoa xanh). 50xu, Black (Van den). 60xu, Leopard skin (Da bao). 1d, Nine-spotted (Chin cham).

**1977, June 15** ***Perf. 12½x12***
**876-883** A292 Set of 8 7.00 1.75
Imperf., #876-883 11.00

Wildflowers A293

Designs: No. 884, 12xu, Thevetia peruviana. No. 885, 12xu, Broussonetia papvrifera. 20xu, Aleurites montana. 30xu, Cerbera manghes. 40xu, Cassia multijuga. 50xu, Cassia nodosa. 60xu, Hibiscus schizopetalus. 1d, Lagerstroesnia speciosa.

**1977, Aug. 19** ***Perf. 12x12½***
**884-891** A293 Set of 8 5.00 1.75
Imperf., #884-891 10.00

A294 A295

Dahlias: 6xu (#892), 12xu (#894), Pink. 6xu (#893), 12xu (#895), Orange.

**1977, Sept. 10** ***Perf. 11***
**892-895** A294 Set of 4 3.75 1.75

See Nos. 921-924.

**1977, Sept. 10**

Children drawing map of unified Viet Nam. Denominations: 4xu, 5xu, 10xu, 12xu, 30xu each have different colored border.

**896-900** A295 Set of 5 3.75 3.75

Goldfish A296

Designs: No. 901, 12xu, Dong nai. No. 902, 12xu, Velvet (Hoa nhung). 20xu, Blue Chinese (Tau xanh). 30xu, Dragon-eyed (Mat bong). 40xu, Cam trang. 50xu, Five-colored (Ngu sac). 60xu, Dong nai. 1d, Thap cam.

**1977, Oct. 20** ***Perf. 12***

**901-908** A296 Set of 8 7.50 2.00
Imperf., #901-908 10.00

A297

A298

Russian October Revolution, 60th anniv.: 12xu (No. 909, olive background), 12xu (No. 910, blue background), Ho Chi Minh, Lenin banner. 50xu, Mother holding child with flag. 1d, Workers, farmers, Moscow Kremlin, cruiser Aurora.

**1977, Nov. 7**

**909-912** A297 Set of 4 3.00 2.50

**1978, Jan. 25**

Songbirds: 12xu, Gracula religiosa. No. 914, 20xu, Garrulax canorus. No. 915, 20xu, Streptopelia chinensis. 30xu, Linius schach. 40xu, Garrulax formosus. 50xu, Garrulax chinensis. 60xu, Acridotheres cristatellus. 1d, Garrulax yersini.

**913-920** A298 Set of 8 6.00 1.75
Imperf., #913-920 12.00

Cultivated Flower Type of 1977

5xu, 10xu, Sunflower. 6xu, 12xu, Pansy.

**1978, Mar. 20** ***Perf. 11***

**921-924** A294 Set of 4 4.25 2.40

Intl. Children's Day (June 1977) — A299

**1978, Mar. 20**

**925** A299 12xu multicolored 1.75 .40

Sports A300

#926, 12xu, Discus. #927, 12xu, Long jump. 20xu, Hurdles. 30xu, Hammer throw. 40xu, Shot put. 50xu, Javelin. 60xu, Running. 1d, High jump.

**1978, Apr. 10** ***Perf. 11½***

**926-933** A300 Set of 8 4.50 2.00
Imperf., #926-933 10.00

A301

A302

4th Viet Nam Trade Union Cong.: #934, Trade Union emblem. #935, Ho Chi Minh, workers.

**1978, May 1** ***Perf. 11***

**934-935** A301 10xu Set of 2 2.50 .80

**1978, May 15**

10xu, Ho Chi Minh conducting orchestra. 12xu, Ho Chi Minh's mausoleum, horiz.

**936-937** A302 Set of 2 2.00 .80

No. 937 is 39x23mm.

Young Pioneers' Cultural Palace, Hanoi — A303

**1978, May 29**

**938** A303 10xu multicolored 1.50 .40

Intl. Children's Day.

Sculptures from Tay Phuong Pagoda — A304

Designs: No. 939, 12xu, Sanakavasa. No. 940, 12xu, Parsva. No. 941, 12xu, Punyasas. No. 942, 20xu, Kumarata. No. 943, 20xu, Nagarjuna. 30xu, Yayata. 40xu, Cadiep. 50xu, Ananda. 60xu, Buddhamitra. 1d, Asvagmosa.

**1978, July 1** ***Perf. 12***

**939-948** A304 Set of 10 7.00 3.00
Imperf., #939-948 20.00

Cuban Revolution, 25th Anniv. — A305

**1978, July 20** ***Perf. 11***

**949-950** A305 6xu, 12xu Set of 2 2.50 .80

Types of 1976

6xu (No. 951), 12xu (No. 953), like #845a. 6xu (No. 952), 12xu (No. 952), like #845b.

Design size 18.5mmx23mm

**1978, Aug. 15**

**951-954** A286 Set of 4 4.00 2.00

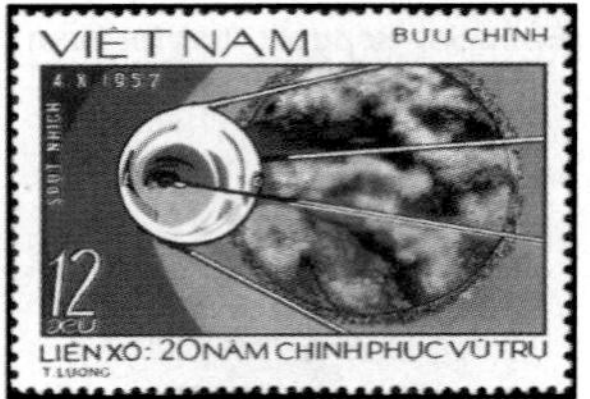

Space Exploration, 20th Anniv. — A306

#955, 12xu, Sputnik. #956, 12xu, Venus 1. 30xu, Spacecraft docking. 40xu, Molniya 1. 60xu, Soyuz. 2d, Cosmonauts Gubarev, Grechko.

**1978, Aug. 28** ***Perf. 12½x12***

**955-960** A306 Set of 6 5.00 1.75
Imperf., #955-960 10.00

World Telecommunications Day — A307

Designs: a, Printed circuit. b, ITU emblem.

**1978, Sept. 25** ***Perf. 11***

**962** A307 12xu Pair, #a.-b. 2.50 .80
Imperf. 15.00

20th Congress of Socialist Postal Ministers — A308

**1978, Sept. 25**

**963** A308 12xu multicolored 1.50 .40

Chrysanthemums — A309

No. 964, 12xu, Tim. No. 965, 12xu, Kim tien. 20xu, Hong. 30xu, Van tho. 40xu, Vang. 50xu, Thuy tim. 60xu, Vang mo. 1d, Nau do.

**1978, Oct. 1** ***Perf. 12***

**964-971** A309 Set of 8 5.50 2.00
Imperf., #964-971 12.00

Dinosaurs A310

Designs: No. 972, 12xu, Plesiosaurus. No. 973, 12xu, Brontosaurus. 20xu, Iguanodon. 30xu, Tyrannosaurus rex. 40xu, Stegosaurus. 50xu, Mosasaurus. 60xu, Triceratops. 1d, Pteranodon.

**1979, Jan. 1** **Litho.** ***Perf. 11½***

**972-979** A310 Set of 8 9.00 2.00
Imperf., #972-979 17.00

No. 977 misspelled "Mozasaurus."

A311

A312

**1979, Jan. 1** ***Perf. 11***

**980** A311 12xu multicolored 1.50 .40
Imperf. 5.00

Socialist Republic of Cuba, 20th anniv.

**1979, Feb. 1**

Quang Trung's victory over the Chinese, 190th Anniv.: #981, Battle plan. #982, Quang Trung.

**981-982** A312 12xu Set of 2 2.50 .80
*a.* Perf 12, #981-982 20.00

Albert Einstein, Physicist A313

Designs: No. 983, 12xu, Einstein. No. 984, 60xu, Equation, sun, planets.

**1979, Mar. 14**

**983-984** A313 12xu, 60xu, set of 2 3.00 1.50

Domestic Animals — A314

10xu, Ram. 12xu, Ox. 20xu, Ewe, lamb. 30xu, White water buffalo, vert. 40xu, Cow. 50xu, Goat. 60xu, Water buffalo, calf. 1d, Young goat, vert.

**1979, Mar. 20** *Perf. 12*
**985-992** A314 Set of 8 5.00 1.50
Imperf., #985-992 7.00

Five Year Plan (1976-80) — A315

#993, 998, Map, emblem. #994, 999, Factory worker. #995, 1000, Peasant woman, tractor. #996, 1001, Soldier. #997, 1002, Man, atom, compass.

**1979** *Perf. 11*
**993-997** A315 6xu Set of 5
**998-1002** A315 12xu Set of 5
*1000a* Perf. 12
*Nos. 993-1002 (10)* 10.00

Issued: Nos. 993-997, 5/1. Nos. 998-1002, 6/1. Nos. 993, 996-1002 on toned paper.

Philaserdica '79, Intl. Stamp Exhibition, Sofia, Bulgaria A316

**1979, May 27** *Perf. 12*
**1003-1004** 12xu, 30xu, set of 2 2.50 .80

Intl. Year of the Child — A317

2xu, Ho Chi Minh, children. 20xu, Nurse, mother, child. 50xu, Children with glider, painting supplies. 1d, Girls of different races.

**1979, June 1** *Perf. 11*
**1005-1008** A317 Set of 4 4.00 3.00

Ornamental Birds — A318

#1009, 12xu, Lophura diardi. #1010, 12xu, Tragopan temminckii. 20xu, Phasianus colchicus. 30xu, Lophura edwardsi. 40xu, Lophura nycthemera, vert. 50xu, Polyplectron germaini, vert. 60xu, Rheinartia ocellata, vert. 1d, Pavo muticus, vert.

**1979, June 16** *Perf. 12*
**1009-1016** A318 Set of 8 6.00 2.10
Imperf., #1009-1016 10.00

Orchids A319

Designs: No. 1017, 12xu, Dendrobium heterocacpum. No. 1018, 12xu, Cymbidium hybridum. 20xu, Rhynchostylis gigantea. 30xu, Dendrobium mobile. 40xu, Aerides falcatum. 50xu, Paphiopedilum callosum. 60xu, Vanda teres. 1d, Dendrobium phalaenopsis.

**1979, Aug. 10** *Perf. 12*
**1017-1024** A319 Set of 8 6.50 1.75
Imperf., #1017-1024 10.00

Cats A320

Designs: No. 1025, 12xu, Meo tam the. No. 1026, 12xu, Meo muop, vert. 20xu, Meo khoang, vert. 30xu, Meo dom van. 40xu, Meo muop dom, vert. 50xu, Meo vang, vert. 60xu, Meo xiem. 1d, Meo van am.

**1979, Nov. 10**
**1025-1032** A320 Set of 8 5.00 3.00
Imperf., #1025-1032 10.00

Vietnamese People's Army, 25th Anniv. — A321

a, People greeting soldiers. b, Frontier guards.

**1979, Dec. 22** *Perf. 11*
**1033** A321 12xu Pair, #a.-b. .80 .80

Roses — A322

Designs: 1xu, 12xu (No. 1036), Red, pink roses. 2xu, 12xu (No. 1037), Single pink rose.

**1980, Jan. 1**
**1034-1037** A322 Set of 4 5.00 2.00

See Nos. 1084-1085.

Aquatic Flowers A323

#1038, 12xu, Nelumbium nuciferum. #1039, 12xu, Nymphala stellata. 20xu, Ipomola reptans. 30xu, Nymphoides indicum. 40xu, Jussiala repens. 50xu, Eichhornia crassipes. 60xu, Monochoria voginalis. 1d, Nelumbo nucifera.

**1980, Jan. 15** *Perf. 12½*
**1038-1045** A323 Set of 8 6.25 3.00
Imperf., #1038-1045 9.00

Vietnamese Communist Party, 50th Anniv. — A324

Designs: No. 1046a, Ho Chi Minh proclaiming independence, 1945. No. 1046b, Peasants with banner, improvised weapons. No. 1047a, Map, soldiers, tanks storming palace. No. 1047b, Soldiers waving flag at Dien Bien Phu. 2d, Ho Chi Minh, soldiers and workers.

**1980, Feb. 3** *Perf. 11*
**1046** A324 12xu Pair, #a.-b.
**1047** A324 20xu Pair, #a.-b.
**1048** A324 2d multicolored
*Nos. 1046-1048 (5)* 4.00 4.00

Lenin, 110th Anniv. of Birth A325

**1980, Apr. 22** *Perf. 12*
**1049-1051** A325 6xu, 12xu, 1d, set of 3 3.25 2.00

1980 Summer Olympics, Moscow A326

#1052, 12xu, Hurdles. #1053, 12xu, Running. 20xu, Team handball. 30xu, Soccer. 40xu, Wrestling. 50xu, Gymnastics, horiz. 60xu, Swimming, horiz. 1d, Sailing, horiz.

**1980, May 1** *Perf. 12x12½, 12½x12*
**1052-1059** A326 Set of 8 6.00 1.75
Imperf., #1052-1059 10.00

A327

A328

Ho Chi Minh, 90th anniv. of birth: 12xu, In 1924. 40xu, As president.

**1980, May 19** *Perf. 11*
**1060-1061** A327 Set of 2 2.00 1.25

**1980, June 15**
**1062** A328 5xu multicolored 1.00 .40

Intl. Children's Day.

Intercosmos '80, Soviet-Vietnamese Space Mission — A329

Designs: No. 1063, 12xu, Cosmonauts. No. 1064, 12xu, Soyuz 37 atop booster. 20xu, Soyuz 37. 40xu, Soyuz docking with Salyut space station. 1d, Soyuz firing retro-rockets. 2d, Parachute landing. 3d, Cosmonauts, Soyuz-Salyut station.

**1980, July 24** *Perf. 12x12½*
**1063-1068** A329 Set of 6 7.00 1.25
Imperf., #1063-1068 10.00

**Souvenir Sheet**

**1069** A329 3d multicolored 6.00
Imperf. 6.75

Saltwater Fish — A330

Designs: No. 1070, 12xu, Rhincodon typus. No. 1071, 12xu, Galeocerdo cuvier. 20xu, Orectolobus japonicus. 30xu, Heterodontus zebra. 40xu, Dasyatis uarnak. 50xu, Pristis microdon. 60xu, Sphyrna lewini. 1d, Myliobatis tobijei.

**1980, Aug. 1** *Perf. 12*
**1070-1077** A330 Set of 8 5.00 1.75
Imperf., #1070-1077 10.00

A331

A332

Post and Telecommunications Office, 35th Anniv.: 12xu, Ho Chi Minh reading newspaper. 20xu, Ho Chi Minh talking on telephone. 50xu, Kim Dong carrying bird in cage. 1d, Dish antenna.

**1980, Aug. 15** **Litho.** *Perf. 12½*
**1078-1081** A331 Set of 4 3.50 3.00

**1980, Aug. 25** *Perf. 11, 12 (#1083)*

Natl. Telecommunications Day: No. 1082, Telephone switchboard operator. No. 1083, Train, map.

**1082-1083** A332 12xu Set of 2 2.00 1.60

Rose Type of 1980

No. 1084, Pink. No. 1085, Red and pink.

**1980, Aug. 25** ***Perf. 11***
**Size: 20x24mm**

**1084-1085** A322 12xu Set of 2 2.00 1.40

For surcharge see No. 1385.

Republic of Vietnam, 35th Anniv. — A333

Designs: No. 1086, 12xu, Ho Chi Minh. No. 1087, 12xu, Natl. arms. 40xu, Pac Bo Cave. 1d, Source of Lenin River, horiz.

**1980, Sept. 2** ***Perf. 12½***

**1086-1089** A333 Set of 4 4.00 4.00

A334

A335

Natl. emblems: 6xu, Arms. No. 1091, 12xu, Flag, horiz. No. 1092, 12xu, Anthem.

**1980, Sept. 20** ***Perf. 12***

**1090-1092** A334 Set of 3 5.00

**1980, Oct. 6** ***Perf. 11***

Nguyen Trai, 600th birth anniv.: 12xu, Nguyen Trai. 50xu, Books, horiz. 1d, Ho Chi Minh reading commemorative stele, Con Son.

**1093-1095** A335 Set of 3 5.00 5.00

For surcharge see No. 1386.

A336

A337

Natl. Women's Union, 50th Anniv.: #1096, Ho Chi Minh, women. #1097, Group of 4 women.

**1980, Oct. 20**

**1096-1097** A336 12xu Set of 2 1.50 .80

**1980, Nov. 20** ***Perf. 12½***

Flowers: No. 1098, 12xu, Ipomoea pulchella. No. 1099, 12xu, Biguoniaceae venusta. 20xu, Petunia hybrida. 30xu, Trapaeolum majus. 40xu, Thunbergia grandiflora. 50xu, Anlamanda cathartica. 60xu, Campsis radicans. 1d, Bougainivillaea spectabilis.

**1098-1105** A337 Set of 8 6.25 1.50
Imperf., #1098-1105 10.00

Ornamental Fish — A338

Designs: No. 1106, 12xu, Betta splendens. No. 1107, 12xu, Symphysodon aequifasciata. 20xu, Poecilobrycon eques. 30xu, Gyrinocheilus aymonieri. 40xu, Barbus tetrazona. 50xu, Pterophyllum eimekei. 60xu, Xiphophorus helleri. 1d, Trichopterus sumatranus.

**1981, Jan. 15** ***Perf. 12***

**1106-1113** A338 Set of 8 6.25 6.25
Imperf., #1106-1113 10.00

26th Soviet Communist Party Congress A339

20xu, Rocket, book. 50xu, Young people, flag.

**1981, Feb. 23** ***Perf. 11***

**1114-1115** A339 Set of 2 2.50 2.00

Animals from Cuc Phuona Natl. Forest — A340

#1116, 12xu, Hylobates concolor. #1117, 12xu, Macaca speciosa. 20xu, Selenarctos thibetanus. 30xu, Cuon alpinus. 40xu, Sus scrofa. 50xu, Cervus unicolor. 60xu, Panthera pardus. 1d, Panthera tigris.

**1981, Apr. 10** ***Perf. 12½x12***

**1116-1123** A340 Set of 8 8.00 1.75
Imperf., #1116-1123 10.00

Doves A341

#1124, 12xu, Treron sieboldi. #1125, 12xu, Ducula aenea, vert. 20xu, Streptopelia tranquebarica, vert. 30xu, Macropygia unchall, vert. 40xu, Ducula badia, vert. 50xu, Treron apicauda. 60xu, Chalcophaps indica. 1d, Seimun treron seimundi.

**1981, June 5** ***Perf. 12***

**1124-1131** A341 Set of 8 5.00 4.00
Imperf., #1124-1131 9.00

Nectar-sucking Birds — A342

Designs: No. 1132, 20xu, Aethopyga siparaja. No. 1133, 20xu, Anthreptes singalensis. 30xu, Aethopyga saturata. 40xu, Aethopyga gouldiae. No. 1136, 50xu, Nectarinia chalcostetha. No. 1137, 50xu, Nectarinia hypogrammica. 60xu, Nectarinia sperata. 1d, Aethopyga nipalensis.

**1981, Aug. 5** ***Perf. 12½x12***

**1132-1139** A342 Set of 8 5.00 1.75
Imperf., #1132-1139 10.00

A343 A343a

**1981, Aug. 5** ***Perf. 11***

**1140** A343 12xu Lotus flower 1.00

**1981, Aug. 5**

Design: Factory militiawoman.

**1140A** A343a 12xu yel & multi 20.00

See Nos. M30-M31.

A344 A345

Fruit: No. 1141, 20xu, Elaeagnus latifolia. No. 1142, 20xu, Fortunella japonica. 30xu, Nephelium lappaceum. 40xu, Averrhoa bilimbi. No. 1145, 50xu, Ziziphus mauritiana. No. 1146, 50xu, Fragaria vesca. 60xu, Bouea oppositifolia. 1d, Syzygium aqueum.

**1981, Oct. 12** ***Perf. 12***

**1141-1148** A344 Set of 8 5.75 1.75
Imperf., #1141-1148 10.00

**1981, Nov. 15** ***Perf. 11***

Planting trees: No. 1149, Ho Chi Minh. No. 1150, Three people.

**1149-1150** A345 30xu Set of 2 1.75 1.00

Tree planting festival.

Bulgaria, 1300th Anniv. A346

**1981, Dec. 9** ***Perf. 11***

**1151-1153** A346 30xu, 50xu, 2d, set of 3 5.50 5.50

Wild Animals — A347

Designs: No. 1154, 30xu, Orangutan. No. 1155, 30xu, Bison bonasus. No. 1156, 40xu, Kangaroo. No. 1157, 40xu, Hippopotamus. No. 1158, 50xu, Rhinoceros sondaicus. No. 1159, 50xu, Giraffe. 60xu, Zebra. 1d, Lion.

**1981, Dec. 9** ***Perf. 12½x12***

**1154-1161** A347 Set of 8 5.00 2.00
Imperf., #1154-1161 9.00

A348

A349

World Food Day: 30xu, 50xu, Woman holding sheaf of rice. 2d, FAO emblem, horiz.

**1982, Jan. 26** ***Perf. 11***

**1162-1164** A348 Set of 3 3.50

**1982, Feb. 19**

**1165-1166** A349 50xu, 5d, set of 2 4.75 4.75

10th World Trade Unions Congress, Havana, Cuba.

5th Vietnamese Communist Party Congress — A350

Designs: No. 1167, 30xu, Ho Chi Minh. No. 1168, 30xu, Hammer, sickle. No. 1169, 30xu, Worker, dam. 50xu, Women harvesting rice. 1d, Ho Chi Minh.

**1982, Feb. 15**

**1167-1170** A350 Set of 4 4.00 2.00

***Imperf***

**Size: 99x61 mm**

**1171** A350 1d multicolored 50.00

Bees & Wasps A351

Designs: No. 1172, 20xu, Ong bove. No. 1173, 20xu, Ong van xanh. 30xu, To vo nau. 40xu, Ong vang. No. 1176, 50xu, Ong dau nau. No. 1177, 50xu, To vo xanh. 60xu, Ong bau. 1d, Ong mat.

**1982, Feb. 25** ***Perf. 12***

**1172-1179** A351 Set of 8 5.00 2.00
Imperf., #1172-1179 10.00

Soccer
A352

#1180, 30xu, 3 players. #1181, 30xu, 2 players. #1182, 40xu, Striped background. #1183, 40xu, grass background. #1184, 50xu, Vertically striped background. #1185, 50xu, Horizonally striped background. 60xu, 1d, Various soccer scenes.

**1982, Apr. 15**
**1180-1187** A352 Set of 8 5.00 2.00
Imperf., #1180-1187 10.00

For overprints see Nos. 2142-2149.

A353

A354

Vietnamese Red Cross, 35th Anniv.: 1d, Red Cross emblem.

**1982, May 15** ***Perf. 11***
**1188-1189** A353 Set of 2 2.50

**1982, May 19** ***Perf. 12***

5th Natl. Women's Congress: No. 1191, Congress emblem, three women.

**1190-1191** A354 12xu Set of 2 2.00

A355

A356

Birds of Prey: No. 1192, 30xu, Microhierax melanoleucos. No. 1193, 30xu, Falco tinnunculus. 40xu, Aviceda leuphotes. No. 1195, 50xu, Icthyophaga nana. No. 1196, 50xu, Milvus korschun. 60xu, Neohierax harmandi, horiz. No. 1198, 1d, Elanus caeruleus, horiz. No. 1199, 1d, Circaetus gallicus.

**1982, June 1**
**1192-1199** A355 Set of 8 8.00 2.25
Imperf., #1192-1199 12.00

**1982, June 1** ***Perf. 11***
**1200-1201** A356 30xu, 3d, set of 2 5.00

Georgi Dimitrov (1882-1949), Bulgarian Communist leader.

Dahlias
A357

Designs (last word or two of Vietnamese inscription): No. 1202, 30xu, Da cam. No. 1203, 30xu, Do. 40xu, Canh se. No. 1205, 50xu, Do nhung. No. 1206, 50xu, Vang. 60xu, Do tuoi. No. 1208, 1d, Bien. No. 1209, 1d, Trang. Various flowers.

**1982, July 15** ***Perf. 12x12½***
**1202-1209** A357 Set of 8 7.00 2.25
Imperf., #1202-1209 12.00

1982 World Cup Soccer Championships, Spain — A358

#1210, 50xu, Ball at bottom right. #1211, 50xu, Ball at right in air. #1212, 50xu, Ball at bottom center. #1213, 1d, 1 player. #1214, 1d, 3 players. 2d, 2 players.

**1982, July 15** ***Perf. 12x12½***
**1210-1215** A358 Set of 6 8.00 8.00
Imperf., #1210-1215 10.00

A359

A360

**1982, July 25** ***Perf. 11***
**1216** A359 30xu Natl. defense 1.50 .80

See No. M32.

**1982, Aug. 15**
**1217** A360 30xu multicolored 1.50

Cuban victory at Giron (Bay of Pigs), 20th anniv.

World Environment Day — A361

#1219, Ho Chi Minh, children planting tree.

**1982, Aug. 15**
**1218-1219** A361 30xu Set of 2 2.00

A362

A363

**1982, Sept. 20**
**1220** A362 30xu multicolored 1.50 .80

Rabindranath Tagore (1861-1941), poet.

**1982, Sept. 25** ***Perf. 12x12½***

Insects: No. 1221, 30xu, Catacanthus incarnatus. No. 1222, 30xu, Sycanus falleni. 40xu, Nezara viridula. No. 1224, 50xu, Lohita grandis. No. 1225, 50xu, Helcomeria spinosa. 60xu, Chrysocoris stollii. No. 1227, 1d, Pterygamia srayi. No. 1228, 1d, Tiarodes ostentans.

**1221-1228** A363 Set of 8 6.75 2.25
Imperf., #1221-1228 11.50

Russian Revolution, 65th Anniv. — A364

Design: No. 1230, Lenin, workers.

**1982, Nov. 7** ***Perf. 11***
**1229-1230** A364 30xu Set of 2 1.75

9th South East Asian Games, New Delhi, India
A365

#1231, 30xu, Table tennis. #1232, 30xu, Swimming. 1d, Wrestling. 2d, Shooting.

**1982, Nov. 19**
**1231-1234** A365 Set of 4 5.50

Fish
A366

Designs: No. 1235, 30xu, Samaris cristatus. No. 1236, 30xu, Tephrinectes sinensis. No. 1237, 40xu, Psettodes erumei. No. 1238, 40xu, Zebrias zebra. No. 1239, 50xu, Cynoglossus puncticeps. No. 1240, 50xu, Pardachirus pavoninus. 60xu, Brachirus orientalis. 1d, Psettina iijimae.

**1982, Dec. 15** ***Perf. 12***
**1235-1242** A366 Set of 8 6.00 1.75
Imperf., #1235-1242 10.00

Socialist Ideals — A367

#1243, 30xu, Agriculture. #1244, 30xu, Industry. 1d, Natl. defense. 2d, Health & education.

**1982, Dec. 25** ***Perf. 11***
**1243-1246** A367 Set of 4 5.50

Founding of Soviet Union, 60th Anniv.
A368

**1982, Dec. 30**
**1247** A368 30xu multicolored 2.50 .80

Sampans
A369

Designs: 30xu, Docked. 50xu, With striped sails. 1d, Sampans on Red River. 3d, With white sails. 5d, With patched sail. 10d, Fast sampan, horiz.

**1983, Jan. 10** ***Perf. 12½***
**1248-1253** A369 Set of 6 7.50
Imperf., #1248-1253 12.50

Locomotives — A370

30xu, Class 231-300. 50xu, Class 230-000. 1d, Class 140-601. 2d, Class 241-000. 3d, Class 141-500. 5d, Class 150-000. 8d, Class 40-300.

**1983, Feb. 20** ***Perf. 13***
**1254-1260** A370 Set of 7 7.50
Imperf., #1254-1260 12.50

1st Manned Balloon Flight, Bicent.
A371

Balloons: 30xu, Montgolfier. 50xu, Yellow. 1d, CA-11. 2d, Hot-air. 3d, Over harbor. 5d, Le Geant. 8d, Ascending. 10d, Montgolfier, diff.

**1983, Mar. 25 Litho. *Perf. 12½***

**1261-1267** A371 Set of 7 8.00
Imperf., #1261-1267 15.00

**Souvenir Sheet**

***Perf. 13***

**1268** A371 10d Sheet of 1 5.50

No. 1268 contains one 32x40mm stamp.

Discovery of Tubercle Bacillus, Cent. — A372

**1983, Mar. 25 *Perf. 11***

**1269** A372 5d multicolored 3.00

Laos-Cambodia-Viet Nam Summit — A373

**1983, Mar. 25**

**1270-1271** A373 50xu, 5d Set of 2 2.75

Cosmonauts — A374

Designs: 30xu, Gubarev, Remek. No. 1273, 50xu, Klimuk, Hermaszewski. No. 1274, 50xu, Bykovsky, Jahn. No. 1275, 1d, Rukavishnikov, Ivanov. No. 1276, 1d, Farcas, Kubasov. No. 1277, 2d, Mendez, Romanenko. No. 1278, 2d, Gorbatko, Tuan. 5d, Dzhanibekov, Gurragcha. 8d, Popov, Prunariu. No. 1281, Gagarin.

**1983, Apr. 1 *Perf. 12½x12***

**1272-1280** A374 Set of 9 9.00
Imperf., #1272-1280 14.00

**Souvenir Sheet**

**1281** A374 10d multicolored 5.00

No. 1281 contains one 36x28mm stamp.

Reptiles A375

Designs: No. 1282, 30xu, Teratolepis fasciata. No. 1283, 30xu, Chamaeleo jacksoni. No. 1284, 50xu, Uromastyx acanthinurus. No. 1285, 80xu, Heloderma suspectum. 1d, Cameleo menle. 2d, Amphibolurus barbatus. 5d, Chlamydosaurus kingi. 10d, Phrynosoma coronatum.

**1983, Apr. 5 *Perf.***

**1282-1289** A375 Set of 8 7.50
Imperf., #1282-1289 13.00

Raphael (1483-1520), Painter — A375a

Designs: 30xu, Virgin Mother Seated on Chair. 50xu, Granduca, the Virgin Mother. 1d, Sistine Madonna. 2d, Marriage of Maria. 3d, The Gardener. 5d, Woman with Veil. 8d, 10d, Self-Portrait.

**1983, Apr. 30 *Perf. 12½***

**1289A-1289G** A375a Set of 7 7.50

**Souvenir Sheet**

***Perf. 13***

**1289H** A375a 10d multicolored 6.50

Chess Pieces — A376

Designs: 30xu, Vietnamese pawns. 50xu, Indian elephant. 1d, Scottish knight, bishop. 2d, Indian elephant, diff. 3d, Knight. 5d, Sailing ship. 8d, Jester, elephant. 10d, Modern pawns.

**1983, May 9 *Perf. 13***

**1290-1296** A376 Set of 7 7.00
Imperf., #1290-1296 12.00

**Souvenir Sheet**

**1297** A376 10d multicolored 7.25

No. 1297 contains one 28x36mm stamp.

**Souvenir Sheet**

TEMBAL '83 World Stamp Exhibition, Basel — A377

**1983, May 21 *Perf. 13***

**1298** A377 10d multicolored 5.00 5.00

1984 Summer Olympics, Los Angeles A378

Designs: 30xu, Long jump. 50xu, Running. 1d, Javelin. 2d, High jump, horiz. 3d, Hurdles, horiz. 5d, Shot put. 8d, Pole vault. 10d, Discus.

**1983, June 13 Litho. *Perf. 13***

**1299-1305** A378 Set of 7 7.50

**Souvenir Sheet**

**1306** A378 10d Sheet of 1 6.25

No. 1306 contains one 32x40mm stamp.

The issuance of this set has been questioned.

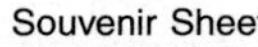

**Souvenir Sheet**

Brasiliana '83, Rio de Janeiro — A379

**1983, July 20 *Perf. 13***

**1307** A379 10d Rhamphastos toco 6.00 5.00

Butterflies A380

Designs: No. 1308, 30xu, Leptocircus meges. No. 1309, 30xu, Terias hecabe. No. 1310, 40xu, Zetides agamemnon. No. 1311, 40xu, Nyctalemon patroclus. No. 1312, 50xu, Papilio chaon. No. 1313, 50xu, Precis almana. 60xu, Thauria lathyi. 1d, Kallima inachus.

**1983, July 30 Litho. *Perf. 12***

**1308-1315** A380 Set of 8 6.25
Imperf., #1308-1315 10.00

**Souvenir Sheet**



Bangkok '83 — A381

**1983, Aug. 4 *Perf. 13***

**1316** A381 10d multicolored 10.00 10.00

Karl Marx (1818-1883) A382

**1983, Oct. 10 *Perf. 11***

**1317-1318** A382 50xu, 10d, set of 2 5.00
Imperf., #1317-1318 50.00

Phu Dong Sports Festival — A383

**1983, Oct. 10**

**1319-1320** A383 30xu, 1d, set of 2 2.00

World Food Day A384

Design: 50xu, Infant, fish. 4d, Family.

**1983, Oct. 10 *Perf. 12½***

**1321-1322** A384 Set of 2 2.50
Imperf., #1321-1322 5.00

Mushrooms A385

#1323, 50xu, Flammulina velutipes. #1324, 50xu, Pleurotus ostreatus. #1325, 50xu, Cantharellus cibarius. #1326, 50xu, Coprinus atramentarius. 1d, Volvariella volvacea. 2d, Agaricus silvaticus. 5d, Morchella esculenta. 10d, Amanita caesarea.

**1983, Oct. 10 *Perf. 12x12½***

**1323-1330** A385 Set of 8 11.00 8.00
Imperf., #1323-1330 11.00

For overprints see Nos. 2150-2157.

World Communications Year — A386

50xu, Letter carrier. 2d, Mail sorting room. 8d, Switchboard operators. #1334, 10d, Radio operator, antenna. #1335, 10d, Telephone, letter, dish antenna, ship.

**1983, Oct. 30 *Perf. 12½***

**1331-1334** A386 Set of 4 4.50

**Souvenir Sheet**

***Perf. 13***

**1335** A386 10d Sheet of 1 3.00

5th Natl. Trade Unions Congress — A387

50xu, Woman with flowers, Vietnam-Soviet Union Friendship Cultural Building. 2d, 30d, Welder.

**1983, Nov. 16 *Perf. 11***

**1336-1338** A387 Set of 3 7.50

Water Birds A388

Designs: No. 1339, 50xu, Ciconia nigra. No. 1340, 50xu, Ardea cinerea. No. 1341, 50xu, Ardea purpurea. No. 1342, 50xu, Ibis leucocephalus. 1d, Grus grus. 2d, Platalea minor. 5d, Nycticorax nycticorax. 10d, Anastomus oscitans.

**1983, Nov. 20** ***Perf. 12x12½***

**1339-1346** A388 Set of 8 9.00 5.00
Imperf., #1339-1346 14.00

No. 1343 inscribed "Grus grue."

World Peace Conference, Prague — A389

Designs: 50xu, Shown. 3d, 5d, 20d, Hands, globe, dove.

**1984, Jan. 15** ***Perf. 11***

**1347-1350** A389 Set of 4 9.00

1984 Winter Olympics, Sarajevo, Yugoslavia — A390

#1351, 50xu, Cross-country skiing, vert. #1352, 50xu, Biathlon, vert. 1d, Speed skating, vert. 2d, Bobsled, vert. 3d, Hockey. 5d, Ski jumping. 6d, Slalom skiing. 10d, Pairs figure skating.

**1984, Jan. 30** ***Perf. 12½***

**1351-1357** A390 Set of 7 7.50
Imperf., #1351-1357 12.00

**Souvenir Sheet**

**1358** A390 10d multicolored 4.50

No. 1358 contains one 40x32mm stamp.

Soviet Union-Vietnamese Projects, 1978-83 — A391

Designs: 20xu (No. 1359), 4d, Hoa Binh Hydro-electric project. 20xu (No. 1360), Vietnamese-Soviet Cultural Palace. 50xu, Thang Long Bridge.

**1984, Jan. 31** ***Perf. 11***

**With Gum**

**1359-1362** A391 Set of 4 55.00

Endangered Animals — A392

Designs: No. 1363, 50xu, Felis marmorata. No. 1364, 50xu, Panthera tigris. No. 1365, 50xu, Panthera pardus. No. 1366, 1d, Hylobates lar. No. 1367, 1d, Nycticebus coucang. No. 1368, 2d, Elephas indidus. No. 1369, 2d, Bos gaurus.

**1984, Feb. 26** ***Perf. 12½x12***

**1363-1369** A392 Set of 7 5.00
Imperf., #1363-1369 14.00

A393

A394

Wildflowers: No. 1370, 50xu, Banhinia variegata. No. 1371, 50xu, Caesalpinia pulcherrima. 1d, Cassia fistula. 2d, Delonix regia. 3d, Artagotrys uncinatus. 5d, Corchorus olitorius. 8d, Banhinia grandiflora.

**1984, Mar. 15** ***Perf. 12x12½***

**1370-1376** A393 Set of 7 7.50
Imperf., #1370-1376 12.50

**Souvenir Sheet**

**1377** A393 10d Delonix regia 4.50

Location of inscriptions differs on Nos. 1373, 1377.

**1984, Mar. 28** ***Perf. 13***

Orchids: No. 1378, 50xu, Cymbidium. No. 1379, 50xu, Brasse cattleya. 1d, Cattleya Dianx. 2d, Cymbidium, diff. 3d, Cymbidium hybridum. 5d, Phoenix winged orchids. 8d, Yellow Queen orchids.

**1378-1384** A394 Set of 7 7.00
Imperf., #1378-1384 10.00

Nos. 1085, 1093 Surcharged

a

b

**1984, Apr. 25** ***Perfs. as before***

**1385** A322(a) 50xu on 12xu #1085 2.00

**1386** A335(b) 50xu on 12xu #1093 2.00

Souvenir Sheet

Espana '84, Madrid — A395

**1984, Apr. 27** ***Perf. 12½***

**1387** A395 10d Ciconia ciconia 5.50

Victory at Dien Bien Phu, 30th Anniv. A396

#1388, 50xu; #1395, 10d, Ho Chi Minh, generals, battle map. #1389, 50xu, Troops, truck. 1d, Civilians carrying provisions. 2d, Man-hauling artillery. 3d, Anti-aircraft battery. 5d, Troops attacking enemy base. 8d, Troops waving flag.

**1984, May 7** ***Perf. 12½***

**1388-1394** A396 Set of 7 6.25

**Souvenir Sheet**

**1395** A396 10d multicolored 4.50

Souvenir Sheet

UPU Congress, Hamburg '84 — A397

**1984, June 19** ***Perf. 13***

**1396** A397 10d Junkers JU-52 3M 5.00

Fish A398

Designs: No. 1397, 30xu, Cypselurus spilopterus. No. 1398, 30xu, Ostracion cornutus. 50xu, Diodon hystrix. 80xu, Chelmon rostratus. 1d, Antennarius tridens. 2d, Pterois russelli. 5d, Mola mola. 10d, Minous monodactylus.

**1984, June 25** **Litho.** ***Perf. 12***

**1397-1404** A398 Set of 8 7.25
Imperf., #1397-1404 10.00

Ornamental Fish — A399

Designs: No. 1405, 50xu, Trichogaster trichopterus. No. 1406, 50xu, Brachydanio rerio. 1d, Macropodus opercularis. 2d, Gymnocorymbus ternetzi. 3d, Hyphessobrycon serpae. 5d, Labeo bicolor. 8d, Batta splendens.

**1984, June 29** ***Perf. 12½***

**1405-1411** A399 Set of 7 6.00
Imperf., #1405-1411 10.00

Vietnamese Trade Union Movement, 55th Anniv. — A400

Designs: No. 1412a, 50xu, House at 15 Hang Non St., Hanoi, vert. No. 1412b, 50xu, Nguyen Duc Canh, vert. 1d, Striking workers. 2d, Ho Chi Minh visiting factory. 3d, Hanoi Mechanical Engineering plant. 5d, Intl. trade union movement.

**1984, July 20** ***Perf. 11***

**1412-1416** A400 Set of 6 5.00

**Souvenir Sheet**

***Imperf***

**1417** A400 2d like #1414 10.00

No. 1412 printed se-tenant. No. 1417 contains one 45x38mm stamp.

Rock Formations, Ha Long Bay — A401

#1418, 50xu, Hang-Bo Nau. #1419, 50xu, Nui Yen Ngua. #1420, 50xu, Hon Dua. #1421, 50xu, Hang Con Gai. #1422, 1d, Hon Coc. #1423, 1d, Hon Ga Choi. 2d, Hon Dinh Huong. 3d, Hon Su Tu. 5d, Hon Am. 8d, Nui Bai Tho.

**1984, July 30** ***Perf. 12½x12***

**1418-1427** A401 Set of 10 7.00
Imperf., #1418-1427 12.50

Dinosaurs — A402

#1428, 50xu, Styracosaurus. #1429, 50xu, Diplodocus. #1430, 1d, Corythosaurus. #1431, 1d, Rhamphyorhynchus. 2d, Seymouria. 3d, Allosaurus. 5d, Dimetrodon. 8d, Brachiosaurus.

**1984, Aug. 30**

**1428-1435** A402 Set of 8 13.50
Imperf., #1428-1435 15.00

Viet Nam-Laos-Cambodia Friendship — A403

**1984, Aug. 30** ***Perf. 11***

**1436-1437** A403 50xu, 10d, set of 2 5.00

Souvenir Sheet

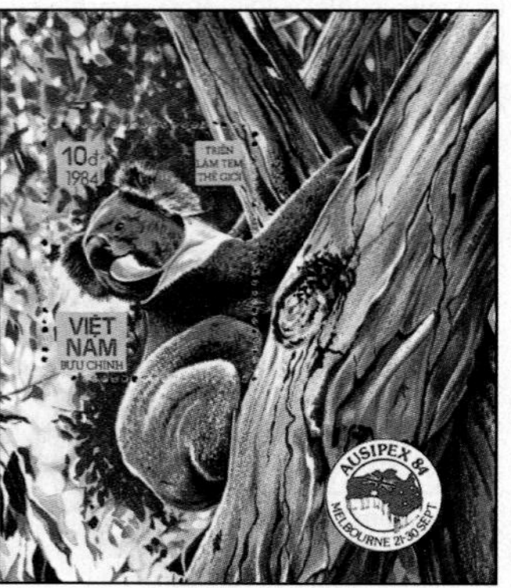


Ausipex '84, Melbourne, Australia — A404

**1984, Sept. 20** ***Perf. 13***
**1438** A404 10d Koala 10.00

Viet Nam-Cambodia Friendship Agreement, 5th Anniv. — A405

50xu, 3d, People, pagoda, statue. 50d, Dancers.

**1984, Sept. 30** ***Perf. 11***
**1439-1441** A405 Set of 3 10.00

Liberation of Hanoi, 30th Anniv. A406

Designs: 50xu, Thang Long Bridge. 1d, Khue Van Gateway. 2d, Ho Chi Minh mausoleum.

**1984, Oct. 5**
**1442-1444** A406 Set of 3 4.00

Vintage Automobiles — A407

#1445, 50xu, Vis-a-Vis, vert. #1446, 50xu, Duc. 1d, Tonneau. 2d, Double phaeton. 3d, Landaulet. 5d, Torpedo. 6d, Coupe de Ville.

**1984, Oct. 30** ***Perf. 12½x13, 13x12½***
**1445-1451** A407 Set of 7 5.00
Imperf., #1445-1451 11.50

Lenin (1870-1924) A408

Paintings of Lenin: 50xu, At his desk. 1d, Standing with revolutionaries. 3d, Speaking at factory. 5d, Meeting with farmers.

**1984, Nov. 15** ***Perf. 12x12½***
**1452-1455** A408 Set of 4 3.50
Imperf., #1452-1455 8.00

UNICEF A409

Paintings: 30xu, Woman, soldiers. 50xu, Mother, children. 1d, Miner, family. 3d, Young girl, vert. 5d, Children playing on ground. 10d, Women, child, vert.

**1984, Dec. 7** ***Perf. 12***
**1456-1461** A409 Set of 6 5.50
Imperf., #1456-1461 10.00

A410 A411

50xu, 30d. Frontier Forces, 25th anniv.

**1984, Dec. 15** ***Perf. 11***
**1462-1463** A410 Set of 2 11.00
Imperf., #1462-1463

See No. M39.

**1984, Dec.** ***Perf. 12½x12***

Flora and Fauna: 20xu, Bubalus bubalis. 30xu, Felis marmorata. No. 1466, 50xu, Hibiscus rosa-sinensis. No. 1467, 50xu, Ailurus fulgens. No. 1468, 50xu, Rosa centifolia. No. 1469, 50xu, Betta splendens. No. 1470, 1d, Chrysanthemum sinense. No. 1471, 1d, Nymphaea ampla. No. 1472, 1d, Pelecanus onocrotalus. No. 1473, 1d, Panthera tigris. No. 1474, 2d, Nycticebus coucang. No. 1475, 2d, Macaca fascicularis. No. 1476, 2d, Dalia coccinea. 5d, Gekko gecko. 10d, Rhytidoceros bicornis.

**1464-1478** A411 Set of 15 12.50
Imperf., #1464-1478 15.00

No. 1466 inscribed "Hybiscus." No. 1470 inscribed "Chrysanthemun."

A412 A413

**1985** ***Perf. 11***
**1479-1480** A412 3d, 5d, set of 2 2.75
Imperf., #1479-1480 30.00

New Year 1985 (Year of the Buffalo). Issued: 3d, 1/21; 5d, 4/30.

**1985, Apr. 26** ***Perf. 11***
**1481** A413 2d Ho Chi Minh .90

Vietnamese Communist Party, 55th anniv.

Military Victory in South Viet Nam, 10th Anniv. A414

Designs: 1d, Soldiers advancing forward. 2d, 10d, Ho Chi Minh, tank, soldiers. 4d, Construction worker. 5d, Map, women.

**1985, Apr. 30** ***Perf. 12½***
**1482-1485** A414 Set of 4 4.50

**Souvenir Sheet**

***Perf. 13***

**1486** A414 10d multicolored 3.75

Cactus A415

Designs: No. 1487, 50xu, Echinocereus knippelianus. No. 1488, 50xu, Lemaireocereus thurberi. 1d, Notocactus haselbergii. 2d, Parodia chrysacanthion. 3d, Pelecyphora pseudopectinata. 5d, Rebutia frebrighii. 8d, Lobivia aurea.

**1985, Apr. 30** ***Perf. 11½***
**1487-1493** A415 Set of 7 7.25
Imperf., #1487-1493 15.00

Vietnamese People's Army, 40th Anniv. — A416

Designs: No. 1494, 50xu, Ho Chi Minh. No. 1495, 50xu, Taking oath on flag. 1d, Anti-aircraft missile. 2d, Soldiers, civilians working together. 3d, Tank entering grounds of presidential palace, Saigon. 5d, Soldier demonstrating use of rifle. 8d, Officers, soldiers, map. 10d, Four soldiers representing branches of military.

**1985, May 6** ***Perf. 12½***
**1494-1500** A416 Set of 7 5.50

**Souvenir Sheet**

**1501** A416 10d multicolored 3.50

A417

A418

End of World War II, 40th Anniv.: 1d, 10d, Victory Monument. 2d, Vietnamese soldier. 4d, Dove, falling American eagle. 5d, Child, doves.

**1985, May 7** ***Perf. 12x12½***
**1502-1505** A417 Set of 4 4.50
Imperf., #1502-1505 12.50

**Souvenir Sheet**

**1506** A417 10d multicolored 3.25

**1985, May 13** ***Perf. 11***

Liberation of Haiphong, 30th anniv.: 2d, Long Chau Lighthouse. 5d, An Duong Bridge, horiz. 10d, To Hieu (1912-44), vert.

**1507-1508** A418 Set of 2 2.25

**Souvenir Sheet**

***Imperf***

**1509** A418 10d multicolored 2.75

Ho Chi Minh, 95th Birth Anniv. — A419

Ho Chi Minh: 1d, At battlefield. 2d, Reading. 4d, 10d, Portrait, vert. 5d, Writing.

**1985, May 19** ***Perf. 12½***
**1510-1513** A419 Set of 4 3.25

**Souvenir Sheet**

***Perf. 13***

**1514** A419 10d multicolored 3.50

No. 1514 contains one 30x36mm stamp.



Motorcycles, Cent. — A420

Designs: No. 1515, 1d, 1895, Germany. No. 1516, 1d, 1898 tricycle, France. No. 1517, 2d, 1913 Harley-Davidson, US. No. 1518, 2d, 1918 Cleveland, US. 3d, 1935 Simplex, US. 4d, 1984 Minarelli, Italy. 6d, 1984 Honda, Japan. 10d, 1984 Honda racing bike.

**1985, June 28** ***Perf. 13***
**1515-1521** A420 Set of 7 5.50
Imperf., #1515-1521 14.00

**Souvenir Sheet**

**1522** A420 10d multicolored 3.25

No. 1522 contains one 32x40mm stamp.

Argentina '85, Buenos Aires — A421

Wild animals: No. 1523, 1d, Aptenodytes pennati, vert. No. 1524, 1d, Dolichotis patagonum, vert. No. 1525, 2d, Panthera onca. No. 1526, 2d, Hydrochoerys capibara. 3d, Peterocnemia pennata, vert. 4d, Priodontes giganteus. 6d, Voltur gryphus. 10d, Lama glama, horiz.

**1985, July 5** ***Perf. 12½***
**1523-1529** A421 Set of 7 8.00
Imperf., #1523-1529 16.00

**Souvenir Sheet**

**With Gum**

***Perf. 13***

**1530** A421 10d multicolored 4.25

No. 1530 contains one 40x32mm stamp.

12th World Youth and Students Festival, Moscow A422

No. 1531, 2d, Youth carrying flags, globe. No. 1532, 2d, Workers, power transmission lines. 4d, Lighthouse, coastal defense. 5d, Intl. festival.

**1985, July 27** ***Perf. 12½***
**1531-1534** A422 Set of 4 5.00
Imperf., #1531-1534 17.50

**Souvenir Sheet**
**With Gum**
***Perf. 13***

**1535** A422 10d like #1531 3.25

Marine Life A423

#1536, 30xu, Nadoa tuberculata. #1537, 30xu, Luidia maculata. #1538, 30xu, Stichopus chloronotus. #1539, 30xu, Holothuria monacaria. #1540, 40xu, Astropyga radiata. #1541, 40xu, Astropecten scoparius. #1542, 40xu, Linckia laevigata.

**1985, July 30** ***Perf. 12***
**1536-1542** A423 Set of 7 7.00
Imperf., #1536-1542 19.00

Socialist Republic of Viet Nam, 40th Anniv. — A424

Designs: 2d, Construction. 3d, Hands shaking, doves. 5d, Flag, military forces. No. 1567, 10d, Flag, Ho Chi Minh.

**1985, Aug. 28** ***Perf. 12½***
**1543-1546** A424 Set of 4 4.50
Imperf., #1543-1546 17.50

**Souvenir Sheet**
***Perf. 13***

**1547** A424 10d like #1543 4.00

No. 1547 contains one 32x40mm stamp.

Vietnamese Police Force, 40th Anniv. — A425

**1985, Aug. 30** ***Perf. 11***
**1548** A425 10d multicolored 4.00

See No. M41.

1st Natl. Sports Festival A426

Designs: 5d, Gymnastics. 10d, Gymnastics, running, swimming.

**1985, Aug. 30**
**1549-1550** A426 Set of 2 4.50

German Railways, 150th Anniv. — A427

Various locomotives: #1551, 1d, Facing left. #1552, 1d, Facing right. #1553, 2d, Facing left. #1554, 2d, Facing right. 3d, 4d, 6d.

**1985, Sept. 13** ***Perf. 12½***
**1551-1557** A427 Set of 7 6.25
Imperf., #1551-1557 10.00

**Souvenir Sheet**
**With Gum**
***Perf. 13***

**1558** A427 10d multicolored 4.50

No. 1558 contains one 32x40mm stamp.

Vietnamese Geological Survey, 30th Anniv. — A428

#1559, Drilling rigs. #1560, Aerial survey.

**1985, Oct. 5** ***Perf. 11***
**1559-1560** A428 1d Set of 2 2.00

Italia '85 A429

Vintage Italian cars: No. 1561, 1d, 1922 Alfa Romeo. No. 1562, 1d, 1932 Bianchi Berlina. No. 1565, 3d, 1912 Itala. No. 1563, 2d, 1928 Isotta Fraschini. No. 1564, 2d, 1930 Bugatti. 4d, 1934 Lancia Augusta. 6d, 1927 Fiat Convertable (top up). 10d, 1927 Fiat Convertable (top down).

**1985, Oct. 25** ***Perf. 13***
**1561-1567** A429 Set of 7 5.50
Imperf., #1561-1567 11.00

**Souvenir Sheet**
**With Gum**

**1568** A429 10d multicolored 3.50

No. 1568 contains one 40x32mm stamp.

Whales A430

Designs: No. 1569, 1d, Balaenoptera musculus. No. 1570, 1d, Balaena borealis. No. 1571, 2d, Orcinus orca. No. 1572, 2d, Delphinus. 3d, Megaptera boops. 4d, Balaenoptera physalus. 6d, Eubalaena glacialis.

**1985, Nov. 15**
**1569-1575** A430 Set of 7 8.50
Imperf., #1569-1575 15.00

1988 World Cup Soccer Championships, Mexico City — A431

Various soccer plays: No. 1576, 1d, From behind goal. No. 1577, 1d, Goalie from side. No. 1578, 2d, From behind goal. No. 1579, 2d, From in front of goal, vert. 3d, vert. 4d, vert. 6d, vert.

**1985, Nov. 30**
**1576-1582** A431 Set of 7 5.00
Imperf., #1576-1582 10.00

**Souvenir Sheet**
***Perf. 13***

**1583** A431 10d multicolored 3.50

No. 1583 contains one 40x32mm stamp.

People's Democratic Republic of Laos, 10th Anniv. — A432

a, Woman, dove. b, Woman dancing, natl. arms.

**1985, Dec. 2** ***Perf. 11***
**1584** A432 1d Pair, #a.-b. 1.40

Traditional Musical Instruments — A433

#1585, 1d, Stone chimes. #1586, 1d, Large bronze drum. #1587, 2d, Flutes. #1588, 2d, Large red drum. 3d, Monochord. 4d, Moon-shaped lute. 6d, Vietnamese two-string violin.

**1985, Dec. 5** ***Perf. 12½x12***
**1585-1591** A433 Set of 7 5.00

A434

A435

Socialist Republic of Viet Nam, 40th Anniv.: No. 1592, 10d, Industry. No. 1593, 10d, Agriculture. 20d, Public health. 30d, Education.

**1985, Dec. 15** ***Perf. 11***
**1592-1595** A434 Set of 4 30.00

**1986, Jan. 6** **Litho.** ***Perf. 11***
**1596-1597** A435 50xu, 1d Set of 2 1.25

1st Natl. Elections, 40th anniv.

A436

A437

**1986, Jan. 6**
**1598** A436 1d multicolored .80

UN 40th anniv.

**1986, Feb. 24** ***Perf. 12½***

Halley's Comet: No. 1599, 2d, Edmond Halley. No. 1600, 2d, Isaac Newton. 3d, Rocket, flags. 5d, Comet.

**1599-1602** A437 Set of 4 3.50
Imperf., #1599-1602 9.00

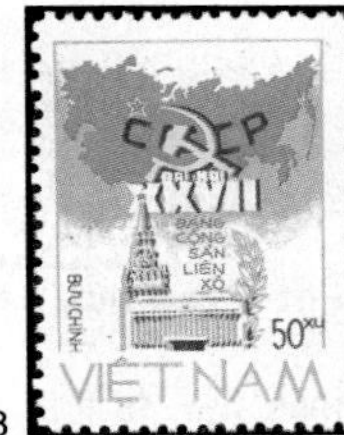
A438

A439

Soviet Communist Party, 27th Congress: 50xu, Kremlin, map. 1d, Lenin banner.

**1986, Feb. 25** ***Perf. 11***
**1603-1604** A438 Set of 2 1.25

**1986, Mar. 1**
**1605** A439 1d Map of Battle of Xuong Giang .90

Le Loi, 600th birth anniv.

1986 World Cup Soccer Championships, Mexico City — A440

Various soccer players in action: No. 1606, 1d, Viet Nam at left. No. 1607, 1d, Viet Nam at right. 2d, Viet Nam at left. No. 1609, 3d, Viet Nam at left. No. 1610, 3d, Viet Nam at right. No. 1611, 5d, Viet Nam at left. No. 1612, 5d, Viet Nam at right.

**1986, Mar. 3** ***Perf. 12½***
**1606-1612** A440 Set of 7 5.50
Imperf., #1606-1612 9.00

**Souvenir Sheet**
***Perf. 13***

**1613** A440 10d multicolored 3.50

No. 1613 contains one 40x32mm stamp.

1st Manned Space Flight, 25th Anniv. A441

#1614, 1d, Konstantin Tsiolkovsky. #1615, 1d, Rocket on transporter. 2d, Yuri Gagarin. #1617, 3d, Valentina Tereshkova, vert. #1618, 3d, Alexei Leonov. #1619, 5d, Apollo-Soyuz, crews. #1620, 5d, Soyuz, Salut space station. 10d, Cosmonauts, vert.

**1986, Apr. 12** ***Perf. 13***

**1614-1620** A441 Set of 7 5.50
Imperf., #1614-1620 10.00

**Souvenir Sheet**

**1621** A441 10d multicolored 3.50

No. 1621 contains one 32x40mm stamp.

Ernst Thalmann (1886-1944), German Politician — A442

**1986, Apr. 16** ***Perf. 11***

**1622** A442 2d red & black .90

May Day — A443

**1986, May 1**

**1623-1624** A443 1d, 5d, set of 2 2.00

Vancouver Expo '86 — A444

Airplanes: No. 1625, 1d, Hawker Hart. No. 1626, 1d, Curtiss Jenny. 2d, PZL-P23. No. 1628, 3d, Yakovlev Yak-11. No. 1629, 3d, Fokker Dr.1. No. 1630, 5d, Boeing P-12 (1920). No. 1631, 5d, Nieuport-Delage NiD.29C1 (1929).

**1986, May 12** ***Perf. 13***

**1625-1631** A444 Set of 7 5.50
Imperf., #1625-1631 8.00

Dam-Strengthening Committee, 40th Anniv. — A445

**1986, May 22** ***Perf. 11***

**1632** A445 1d carmine .60

Bonsai — A446

Designs: No. 1633, 1d, Ficus glomerata. No. 1634, 1d, Ficus benjamina. 2d, Ulmus tonkinensis. No. 1636, 3d, Persica vulgaris. No. 1637, 3d, Streblus asper. No. 1638, 5d, Pinus khasya. No. 1639, 5d, Podocarpus macrophyllus. 10d, Serissa foetida, horiz.

**1986, June 16** ***Perf. 12x12½***

**1633-1639** A446 Set of 7 5.00
Imperf., #1633-1639 14.00

**Souvenir Sheet**

***Perf. 12½x12***

**1640** A446 10d multicolored 3.50

Domestic Cats — A447

Various cats (Background colors): No. 1641, 1d, blue green. No. 1642, 1d, red. 2d, blue. No. 1644, 3d, brown. No. 1645, 3d, blue. No. 1646, 5d, violet. No. 1647, 5d, red, vert.

***Perf. 13x12½, 12½x13***

**1986, June 16**

**1641-1647** A447 Set of 7 5.00
Imperf., #1641-1647 11.00

Traditional Houses A448

Designs: No. 1648, 1d, Thai den. No. 1649, 1d, Nung. 2d, Thai trang. No. 1651, 3d, Tay. No. 1652, 3d, Hmong. No. 1653, 5d, Dao. No. 1654, 5d, Tay nguyen, vert.

***Perf. 12½x12, 12x12½***

**1986, June 20**

**1648-1654** A448 Set of 7 5.00
Imperf., #1648-1654 12.50

**Souvenir Sheet**

***Perf. 12x12½***

**1655** A448 10d like #1654 3.50

Postal Service, 40th Anniv. — A449

Designs: No. 1656, 2d, Telecommunications. No. 1657, 2d, Map, letter carrier. 4d, Soldiers, Nguyen Thi Nghia. 5d, Dish antenna.

**1986, Aug. 15** ***Perf. 13***

**1656-1659** A449 Set of 4 3.25
Imperf., #1656-1659 15.00

A450

Birds: No. 1660, 1d, Merops apiaster. No. 1661, 1d, Cissa chinensis. 2d, Pteruthius erythropterus. No. 1663, 3d, Garrulax leucolophus. No. 1664, 3d, Psarisomus dalhousiae, horiz. No. 1665, 5d, Cyanopica cyanus, horiz. No. 1666, 5d, Motacilla alba. 10d, Copsychus malabaricus.

**1986, Aug. 28** ***Perf. 13***

**1660-1666** A450 Set of 7 5.00
Imperf. #1660-1666 11.50

**Souvenir Sheet**

***Perf. 12½***

**1667** A450 10d multicolored 4.25

No. 1667 contains one 32x40mm stamp. Stockholmia '86.

A451

**1986, Sept. 15** ***Perf. 12x12½***

Domestic fowl: No. 1668, 1d, Plymouth Rock. No. 1669, 1d, Maleagris gallopavo. No. 1670, 2d, Ri. No. 1671, 2d, White Plymouth rock. No. 1672, 3d, Leghorn. No. 1673, 3d, Rhode Island red. No. 1674, 3d, Rhode ri. 5d, Gray Plymouth rock hen.

**1668-1675** A451 Set of 8 5.50
Imperf., #1668-1675 12.50

11th Intl. Trade Unions Congress — A452

**1986, Sept. 16** ***Perf. 12½***

**1676** A452 1d blue & red .80

Artifacts, Hung-Voung Period — A453

Designs: No. 1677, 1d, Seated figure, vert. No. 1678, 1d, Knife hilt in form of female figure, vert. 2d, Bronze axe. No. 1680, 3d, Bronze axe, diff. No. 1681, 3d, Bronze bowl. No. 1682, 5d, Bronze pot (round). No. 1683, 5d, Bronze vase (open top).

**1986, Oct. 15** ***Perf. 12x12½, 12½x12***

**1677-1683** A453 Set of 7 5.00
Imperf., #1677-1683 11.00

**Souvenir Sheet**

***Perf. 12x12½***

**1684** A453 10d like #1677 3.50

Vietnamese Red Cross, 40th Anniv. — A454

**1986, Oct. 20** ***Perf. 12½***

**1685** A454 3d rose & greenish blue .85

Sailing Ships — A455

Various sail and oar-powered ships (sail colors): #1686, 1d, bl, grn, yel. #1687, 1d, org. 2d, yel. #1689, 3d, pur & red. #1690, 3d, bl. #1691, 5d, bl, brn, org. #1692, 5d, org.

***Perf. 12½x12, 12½x13 (#1688)***

**1986, Oct. 20**

**1686-1692** A455 Set of 7 5.50

No. 1688 is 38x47mm.

Butterflies — A456

Designs: No. 1693, 1d, Catopsilia scylla. No. 1694, 1d, Euploea midamus. 2d, Appias nero. No. 1696, 3d, Danaus chrysippus. No. 1697, 3d, Papilio polytes stichius. No. 1698, 5d, Euploea diocletiana. No. 1699, 5d, Charaxes polyxena.

**1986, Nov. 11** ***Perf. 12½***

**1693-1699** A456 Set of 7 5.50
Imperf., #1693-1699 11.00

No. 1696 misspelled "Danais."

Vietnamese Communist Party, 6th Congress — A457

1d, Construction projects. 2d, Natl. defense. 4d, Ho Chi Minh. 5d, Intl. cooperation.

**1986, Nov. 20** ***Perf. 11***

**1700-1703** A457 Set of 4 5.50
*1700a-1703a* Perf. 12½ 50.00
*1702b* Perf. 11x12½ 27.50

**Souvenir Sheet**

***Imperf***

**1704** A457 10d like #1700 3.50

Insects A458

Designs: No. 1705, 1d, Poecilocoris nepalensis. No. 1706, 1d, Bombus americanorum. 2d, Romalea microptera. No. 1708, 3d, Chalcocoris rutilans. No. 1709, 3d, Chrysocoris sellatus. No. 1710, 5d, Paranthrene palmi. No. 1711, 5d, Crocisa crucifera. 10d, Anabrus simplex.

**1986, Nov. 30** ***Perf. 12½***

**1705-1711** A458 Set of 7 5.50
Imperf., #1705-1711 12.50

**Souvenir Sheet**

**1712** A458 10d multicolored 4.00

No. 1712 contains one 32x40mm stamp.

Intl. Peace Year — A459

**1986, Dec. 7** ***Perf. 11***

**1713-1714** A459 1d, 3d, set of 2 1.75

Handicrafts — A460

Designs: No. 1715, 1d, Round dish. No. 1716, 1d, Rattan handbag. 2d, Rattan foot stool. No. 1718, 3d, Bamboo hand basket. No. 1719, 3d, Muong pannier. No. 1720, 5d, Rattan basket with shoulder straps. No. 1721, 5d, Rattan basket with lid. 10d, Tall rattan basket.

**1986, Dec. 10** ***Perf. 11½***

**1715-1721** A460 Set of 7 5.00
Imperf., #1715-1721 9.00

**Souvenir Sheet**

**1722** A460 10d multicolored 3.50

A461

A462

**1986, Dec. 18** ***Perf. 11***

**1723** A461 2d blue green & fawn .90

Natl. Resistance, 40th anniv.

**1986, Dec. 26** ***Perf. 12x12½***

Endangered flora: No. 1724, 1d, Fokienia hodginsii. No. 1725, 1d, Amentotaxus yunnanensis. 2d, Pinus kwangtungensis. No. 1727, 3d, Taxus chinensis. No. 1728, 3d, Cupressus torulosa. No. 1729, 5d, Ducampopinus krempfii. No. 1730, 5d, Tsuga yunnanensis. 10d, Abies nukiangensis.

**1724-1730** A462 Set of 7 5.00
Imperf., #1724-1730 12.00

**Souvenir Sheet**

**1731** A462 10d multicolored 3.50

Elephants — A463

#1732, 1d, Two elephants. #1733, 1d, Female, calf. #1734, 3d, Elephant. #1735, 1d, Elephant facing, vert. #1736, 5d, Man riding elephant, vert. #1737, 5d, Four elephants.

**1986, Dec. 30** ***Perf. 12½***

**1732-1737** A463 Set of 6 5.00
Imperf., #1732-1737 13.50

No. 1737 is 68x27mm.

Vietnamese Legends A464

Designs: a, Son Tinh. b, My Nuong. c-e, Battle between Mountain Genie and Water Genie. f-h, Celebration.

**1987, Jan. 20** ***Perf. 12***

**1738** A464 3d Strip of 8, #a.-h. 7.00
Imperf. 13.50

New Year 1987 (Year of the Cat) — A465

**1987, Jan. 25** ***Perf. 11***

**1739** A465 3d red lilac .80

Natl. Events A466

Ho Chi Minh and: 10d, August revolution, Aug. 19, 1945. 20d, Proclaiming independence, Sept. 9, 1945. 30d, Victory at Dien Bien Phu, July 7, 1954. 50d, Capture of Saigon, Apr. 30, 1975.

**1987, Apr. 10** ***Perf. 11***

**1740-1743** A466 Set of 4 6.25

A467

A468

Champa art: 3d, Temple, Da Nang. 10d, Tower, Na Trang. 15d, Temple, Da Nang (side view). 20d, Dancing girl. 25d, Bust of woman. 30d, Girl playing flute. 40d, Dancing girl, diff.

**1987, June 30** ***Perf. 12x12½***

**1744-1750** A467 Set of 7 7.25
Imperf., #1744-1750 9.50

**Souvenir Sheet**

**1751** A467 50d like #1749 4.00

**1987, July 10** ***Perf. 12½***

Various flowering cacti: 5d, 10d, 15d, 20d, 25d, 30d, 40d.

**1752-1758** A468 Set of 7 5.00

**Souvenir Sheet**

***Perf. 13***

**1759** A468 50d multicolored 3.50

Global Population Reaches 5 Billion — A469

**1987, July 11** ***Perf. 13***

**1760** A469 5d multicolored .50

World Wildlife Fund — A470

Designs: No. 1761, 5d, Concolor gibbon. No. 1762, 5d, Douc monkeys. 15d, Black concolor gibbon. 40d, Douc monkey.

**1987, July 15** ***Perf. 12½***

**1761-1764** A470 Set of 4 7.50
Imperf., #1761-1764 20.00

A471

A472

Western high plateau costumes: 5d, Male Bana. No. 1766, 20d, Female Bana. No. 1767, 20d, Female Gia Rai. No. 1768, 30d, Male Gia Rai. No. 1769, 30d, Male Ede. 40d, Female Ede.

**1987, July 25** ***Perf. 12x12½***

**1765-1770** A471 Set of 6 6.25
Imperf., #1765-1770 10.00

**1987, July 27** ***Perf. 13***

**1771** A472 5d multicolored .75

Day of the Invalids, 40th anniv.

Postal Trade Union, 40th Anniv. A473

Designs: 5d, Letter carrier, jet, truck, train. 30d, Switchboard operator.

**1987, Aug. 30**

**1772-1773** A473 Set of 2 1.75

A474

Paintings by Picasso: No. 1774, 3d, *The Three Musicians.* No. 1775, 20d, War. No. 1776, 20d, Peace. No. 1777, 30d, Child with Dove, vert. No. 1778, 30d, Portrait of Gertrude Stein, vert. 40d, Guernica. 50d, Child as Harlequin.

**1987, Oct. 1** ***Perf. 12½***

**1774-1779** A474 Set of 6 5.50
Imperf., #1774-1779 10.00

**Souvenir Sheet**

**1780** A474 50d multicolored 4.50

No. 1779 is 44x27mm. No. 1780 contains one 40x32mm stamp.

Coral — A475

Designs: 5d, Epanouis. 10d, Acropora. 15d, Rhizopsammia. 20d, Acropora, diff. 25d, Alcyone, 30d, Corollum. 40d, Cristatella.

**1987, Oct. 3** ***Perf. 12x12½***

**1781-1787** A475 Set of 7 7.50
Imperf., #1781-1787 12.50

Intl. Year for Housing for the Homeless A476

**1987, Oct. 5** ***Perf. 13***

**1788** A476 5d greenish bl & blk .75

Russian Revolution, 70th Anniv. — A477

Designs: 5d, 65d, Industry, agriculture. 20d, Lenin. 30d, Construction. 50d, Ho Chi Minh.

**1987, Oct. 6** ***Perf. 13***

**1789-1792** A477 Set of 4 3.50

**Souvenir Sheet**

**1793** A477 65d multicolored 3.25

Hafnia '87 A478

Seaplanes: 5d, PBY-5. 10d, LeO H-246. 15d, Dornier DO-18. 20d, Short Sunderland. 25d, Rohrbach Rostra. 30d, Chetverikov ARK-3. 40d, CANT Z-509. 50d, Curtiss H-16.

**1987, Oct. 12** ***Perf. 13***

**1794-1800** A478 Set of 7 5.00

**Souvenir Sheet**

**1801** A478 50d multicolored 3.25

No. 1801 contains one 40x32mm stamp.

Czechoslovakia-Viet Nam Friendship Agreement, 10th Anniv. — A479

10d, Handshake. 50d, Flags, buildings.

**1987, Oct. 31**

**1802-1803** A479 Set of 2 3.25
Imperf., 1802-1803 17.50

Viet Nam-Soviet Union Cooperation — A480

Designs: 5d, Industry. 50d, Buildings.

**1987, Nov. 3**

**1804-1805** A480 Set of 2 2.75

Mushrooms A481

Designs: 5d, Polyporellus squamosus. 10d, Clitocybe geotropa. 15d, Tricholoma terreum. 20d, Russula aurata. 25d, Collybia fusipes. 30d, Cortinarius violaceus. 40d, Boletus aereus.

**1987, Nov. 10** ***Perf. 12½***

**1806-1812** A481 Set of 7 5.00
Imperf., #1806-1812 10.00

Peace A482

**1987, Nov. 30** ***Perf. 13***

**1813** A482 10d multicolored 1.00

Afro-Asian Solidarity Committee (AAPSO), 30th Anniv. — A483

10d, Hands, dove. 30d, Map, hands, vert.

**1987, Nov. 30**

**1814-1815** A483 Set of 2 1.75
Imperf., #1814-1815 20.00

Victory Over US Bombing Campaign, 15th Anniv. — A484

Designs: 10d, B-52 wreckage. 30d, Children with flowers, wreckage.

**1987, Dec. 26**

**1816-1817** A484 Set of 2 1.75
Imperf., #1816-1817 15.00

Productivity A485

Designs: 5d, Consumer goods. 20d, Agriculture. 30d, Export products.

**1987, Dec. 30**

**1818-1820** A485 Set of 3 2.50

Hoang Sa, Truong Sa Islands A486

Designs: 10d, Ship, sailor. 100d, Maps.

**1988, Jan. 19**

**1821-1822** A486 Set of 2 3.25

Roses — A487

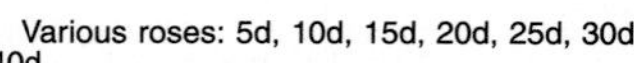

Various roses: 5d, 10d, 15d, 20d, 25d, 30d, 40d.

**1988, Jan. 20** ***Perf. 12½***

**1823-1829** A487 Set of 7 4.50
Imperf., #1823-1829 10.00

**Souvenir Sheet**

***Perf. 13***

**1830** A487 50d multicolored 3.50

Tropical Fish A488

Designs: 5d, Red betta splendens. 10d, Labeo bicolor. 15d, Puntis tetrazona. 20d, Brachydania albolineatus. 25d, Puntis conchonius. 30d, Betta splendens, diff. 40d, Botia lecontei.

**1988, Jan. 20** ***Perf. 13***

**1831-1837** A488 Set of 7 5.00
Imperf., #1831-1837 12.00

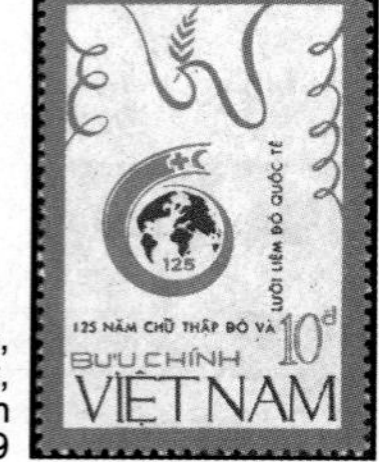

Intl. Red Cross, Red Crescent, 125th Anniv. — A489

**1988, Feb. 17**

**1838** A489 10d multicolored 1.10

Battle of Bach Dang, 700th Anniv. A490

80d, Fleet of ships. 200d, Battle scene.

**1988, Apr. 8**

**1839-1840** A490 Set of 2 3.75

Tourism A491

5d, One-pillar pagoda. 10d, Bach Dang River. 15d, Thien Mu Tower, Hue. 20d, Hgu Hanh Mountain, Da Nang. 25d, Nha Trang beach. 30d, Pren Waterfalls. 40d, Market, Ben Thanh. 50d, Cleft Rocks, Quang Ninh.

**1988, Apr. 20** ***Perf. 12½x12***

**1841-1847** A491 Set of 7 5.50 5.50
Imperf., #1841-1847 10.00

**Souvenir Sheet**

**1848** A491 50d multicolored 3.50

Water Lilies — A492

Designs: 5d, Nymphaea lotus. No. 1850, 10d, Nymphaea pubescens. No. 1851, 10d, Nymphaea nouchali. No. 1852, 20d, Nymphaea rubra. No. 1853, 20d, Nymphaea gigantea. 30d, Nymphaea laydekeri. 50d, Nymphaea capensis.

**1988, Apr. 20** ***Perf. 12x12½***

**1849-1855** A492 Set of 7 5.25
Imperf., #1849-1855 12.50

Offshore Oil Drilling — A493

**1988, Apr. 28** ***Perf. 13***

**1856** A493 1000d multicolored 9.00

A494

Parrots: No. 1857, 10d, Ara araruna. No. 1858, 10d, Psittacula himalayana. No. 1859, 20d, Aprosmictus erythropterus. No. 1860, 20d, Ara chloroptera. No. 1861, 30d, Ara militaris. No. 1862, 30d, Psittacula alexandri. 50d, Loriculus vernalis. 80d, Ara chloroptera, diff.

**1988, May 5** ***Perf. 12x12½***

**1857-1863** A494 Set of 7 5.00
Imperf., #1857-1863 11.00

**Souvenir Sheet**

**1864** A494 80d multicolored 4.00

A495 A496

Membership in Council of Mutual Economic Assistance, 10th Anniv.: 200d, Map. 300d, Headquarters building.

**1988, May 29** ***Perf. 13***

**1865-1866** A495 Set of 2 4.50

**1988, June 1**

**1867** A496 60d multicolored 1.00

Vaccinations against disease.

Problems of Peace and Socialism Magazine, 30th Anniv. — A497

**1988, July 20**

**1868** A497 20d multicolored .90

A498

A499

**1988, Aug. 20**
**1869** A498 150d multicolored 1.50

Pres. Ton Duc Thang, birth cent.

**1988, Aug. 28**

6th Vietnamese Trade Union Congress: 50d, Emblem. 100d, Workers.

**1870-1871** A499 Set of 2 1.75

Children's Paintings A500

#1872, 10d, My Family. #1873, 10d, My House. #1874, 20d, Fishing. #1875, 20d, Flying Kites. #1876, 30d, Girl playing guitar, animals. #1877, 30d, Children in rain, vert. 50d, Girl holding dove, vert. 80d, Family, diff., vert.

***Perf. 12½x12, 12x12½***

**1988, Sept. 25**
**1872-1878** A500 Set of 7 5.50 1.60
Imperf., #1872-1878 7.00

**Souvenir Sheet**

***Perf. 12x12½***

**1879** A500 80d multicolored 3.75

Hydroelectric Plants — A501

Designs: 2000d, Tri An. 3000d, Hoa Binh.

**1988, Sept. 27** ***Perf. 13***
**1880-1881** A501 Set of 2 11.00

A502

A503

**1988, Nov. 3** ***Perf. 13½x13***
**1882** A502 50d multicolored .70

Viet Nam-USSR Friendship Agreement, 10th anniv.

**1988, Dec. 27**

Designs: 100d, Fidel Castro. 300d, Flags, Vietnamese, Cuban people.

**1883-1884** A503 Set of 2 1.75

Cuban revolution, 30th anniv.

Wild Animals A504

Designs: No. 1885, 10d, Bos banteng. No. 1886, 10d, Bos gaurus. No. 1887, 20d, Axis porcinus. No. 1888, 20d, Tapirus indicus. No. 1889, 30d, Capricornis sumatrensis. No. 1890, 30d, Sus scrofa. 50d, Bubalus bubalus. 80d, Rhinoceros sodaicus.

**1988, Dec. 30** ***Perf. 12½***
**1885-1891** A504 Set of 7 5.00
Imperf., #1885-1891 12.50

**Souvenir Sheet**

**1892** A504 80d multicolored 3.50
Imperf. 13.00

Locomotives — A505

Designs: No. 1893, 20d, Kiha 80, Japan. No. 1894, 20d, LRC, Canada. No. 1895, 20d, Hitachi, Japan. No. 1896, 20d, BL-85, USSR. No. 1897, 30d, RC-1, Sweden. No. 1898, 30d, DR-1A, USSR. 50d, T3-136, USSR. 80d, SCNF Z6400.

**1988, Dec. 30** ***Perf. 13***
**1893-1899** A505 Set of 7 5.00
Imperf., #1893-1899 12.50

**Souvenir Sheet**

**1900** A505 80d multicolored 3.50
Imperf. 5.00

No. 1900 contains one 40x32mm stamp.

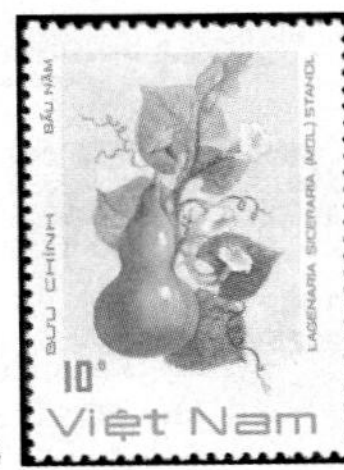


A506

A507

Fruits, vegetables: No. 1901, 10d, Lagenaria siceraria. No. 1902, 10d, Momordica charantia. No. 1903, 20d, Solanum melongena. No. 1904, 20d, Cucurbita moschata. No. 1905, 30d, Luffa cylindrica. No. 1906, 30d, Benincasa hispida. 50d, Lycopercicon esculentum.

**1988, Dec. 30** ***Perf. 12x12½***
**1901-1907** A506 Set of 7 5.00
Imperf., #1901-1907 8.50

**1988, Dec. 30** ***Perf. 13***

Various project spacecraft: No. 1908, 10d, Mars. No. 1909, 10d, Moon. No. 1910, 20d, Saturn. No. 1911, 20d, Inter-planetary. No. 1912, 30d, Venus. No. 1913, 30d, Earth orbital space station. 50d, Cosmos house. 80d, Lander docking with orbiter.

**1908-1914** A507 Set of 7 3.50

**Souvenir Sheet**

**1915** A507 80d multicolored 3.50

Cosmos Day.
No. 1915 contains one 32x40mm stamp.

Shells A508

Designs: No. 1916, 10d, Conus miles. No. 1917, 10d, Strombus lentiginosus. No. 1918, 20d, Nautilus. No. 1919, 20d, Bursa rana. No. 1920, 30d, Turbo petholatus. No. 1921, 30d, Oliva erythros. 50d, Mitra eriscopalis. 80d, Tonna tessellata.

**1988, Dec. 30** ***Perf. 12½x12***
**1916-1922** A508 Set of 7 4.50
Imperf., #1916-1922 13.50

**Souvenir Sheet**

**1923** A508 80d multicolored 3.50

India '89 — A509

Butterflies: No. 1924, 50d, Anaea echemus. No. 1925, 50d, Ascia monuste. No. 1926, 50d, Juniona evarete. No. 1927, 100d, Phoebis avellaneda. No. 1928, 100d, Eurema proterpia. 200d, Papilio palamedes. 300d, Danaus plexippus. 400d, Parides gundlachiamus.

**1989, Jan. 7** ***Perf. 12½***
**1924-1930** A509 Set of 7 4.50
Imperf., #1924-1930 9.00

**Souvenir Sheet**

**1931** A509 400d multicolored 3.00

No. 1931 contains one 40x32mm stamp. Nos. 1924-1930 printed with se-tenant label.

Natl. Day of Cambodia, 10th Anniv. — A510

Designs: 100d, Soldiers, women working in field. 500d, Viet Nam-Cambodia friendship.

**1989, Jan. 7** ***Perf. 13x13½***
**1932-1933** A510 Set of 2 2.75
Imperf., #1932-1933 20.00

India '89 — A511

Designs: No. 1934, 100d, Science, technology. No. 1935, 100d, Agriculture, industry. 300d, Asoka pillar. 600d, Nehru (1889-1964).

**1989, Jan. 20** ***Perf. 13***
**1934-1937** A511 Set of 4 4.00

Battle of Dong Da, Bicent. — A512

Designs: 100d, Festival. 1000d, Quang Trung defeating Qing invaders.

**1989, Feb. 10** ***Perf. 13***
**1938-1939** A512 Set of 2 3.00

Inter-Parliamentary Union, Cent. — A513

Designs: 100d, Vietnamese membership, 10th anniv. 200d, Centennial emblem.

**1989, Mar. 1**
**1940-1941** A513 Set of 2 1.75

Fishing Boats — A513a

Boats from: No. 1942, 10d, Quang Nam. No. 1943, 10d, Quang Tri. No. 1944, 20d, Thua Thien. No. 1945, 20d, Da Nang (sail furled). No. 1946, 30d, Da Nang (under sail). No. 1947, 30d, Quang Tri (under sail). 50d, Hue.

**1989, Mar. 20** ***Perf. 12½x12***
**1942-1948** A513a Set of 7 5.00
Imperf., #1942-1948 10.00

Helicopters — A514

#1949, 10d, Kamov KA-26. #1950, 10d, Boeing Vertol 234. #1951, 20d, Mil MI-10(V10). #1952, 20d, MBB BO 105. #1953, 30d, Kawasaki Hughes 369HS. #1954, 30d, Bell 206B Jet Ranger, 50d, Mil MI-8. 80d, Puma SA330.

**1989, Apr. 12** ***Perf. 12½***
**1949-1955** A514 Set of 7 4.00
Imperf., #1949-1955 10.00

**Souvenir Sheet**

**1956** A514 80d multicolored 3.00
Imperf. 10.00

No. 1956 contains one 40x32mm stamp.

Bicycles A515

#1957, 10d, Bowden Spacelander. #1958, 10d, Rabasa Derbi. #1959, 20d, Huffy. #1960, 20d, Rabasa Derbi. #1961, 30d, VMX-PL. #1962, 30d, Premier. 50d, Columbia RX5.

**1989, May 1** ***Perf. 13***

**1957-1963** A515 Set of 7 4.00
Imperf., #1957-1963 10.00

Turtles — A516

No. 1964, 10d, Cuora trifasciata. No. 1965, 10d, Testudo elegans. No. 1966, 20d, Eretmochelys imbricata. No. 1967, 20d, Platysternon megacephalum. No. 1968, 30d, Dermochelys coriacea. No. 1969, 30d, Chelonia mydas. 50d, Caretta caretta. 80d, Caretta caretta, diff.

**1989, May 1** ***Perf. 12½***

**1964-1970** A516 Set of 7 6.00
Imperf., #1964-1970 11.50

**Souvenir Sheet**

**1971** A516 80d multicolored 3.25
Imperf. 10.00

Finlandia '88 (#1971).

Poisonous Snakes — A517

Designs: No. 1972, 10d, Trimeresurus popeorum. No. 1973, 10d, Trimeresurus mucrosquamatus. No. 1974, 20d, Bungarus fasciatus. No. 1975, 20d, Bungarus candidus. No. 1976, 30d, Calliophis maclellandii. No. 1977, 30d, Ancistrodon acutus. 50d, Ophiophagus hannah, vert.

**1989, May 1**

**1972-1978** A517 Set of 7 5.75
Imperf., #1972-1978 13.50

Pairs Figure Skating — A518

Various figure skaters: No. 1979, 10d, "Viet Nam" at left. No. 1980, 10d, "Viet Nam" at right. No. 1981, 20d, "Viet Nam" at left. No. 1982, 20d, "Viet Nam" at right, horiz. No. 1983, 30d, "Viet Nam" at left. No. 1984, 30d, "Viet Nam" at right, horiz. 50d, "Viet Nam" at left, horiz.

**1989, May 29** ***Perf. 13***

**1979-1985** A518 Set of 7 4.00
Imperf., #1979-1985 10.00

**Souvenir Sheet**

**With Gum**

**1986** A518 80d multi, horiz. 3.50

No. 1986 contains one 40x32mm stamp.

A519

A520

**1989, June 5** ***Perf. 13***

**1987** A519 100d buff .75

Post & Telecommunications.

**1989, July 1** ***Perf. 12***

Ceramics, Li-Tran Period: 50d, Pitcher. No. 1989, 100d, Bowl. No. 1990, 100d, Jug. 200d, Jug, diff. 300d, Vase.

**1988-1992** A520 Set of 5 3.75
Imperf., #1988-1992 6.00

Legend of Giong A521

Designs: 50d, Mother nursing infant. No. 1994, 100d, Giong meets imperial messenger. No. 1995, 100d, Giong riding iron horse, people following. 200d, Giong pulling up bamboo trees. 300d, Giong flying into sky.

**1989, July 1** ***Perf. 12½x12***

**1993-1997** A521 Set of 5 3.50
Imperf., #1993-1997 5.50

French Revolution, Bicent. — A522

Designs: 100d, Emblem. 500d, Liberty leading the people, after Delacroix.

**1989, July 14** ***Perf. 13½x13***

**1998-1999** A522 Set of 2 1.75

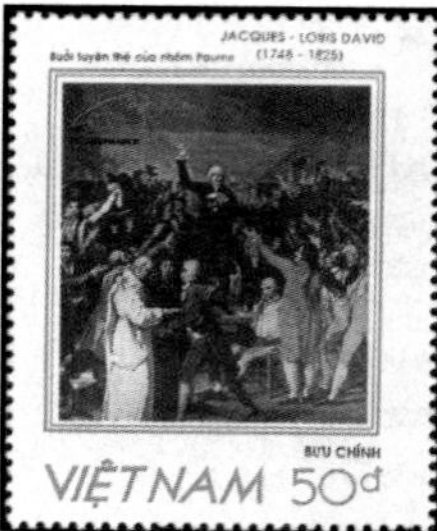


PHILEXFRANCE '89 — A523

Paintings: No. 2000, 50d, Oath of the Tennis Court, by David. No. 2001, 50d, Capture of Louis XVI, horiz. No. 2002, 50d, Liberty, Equality, Fraternity, horiz. No. 2003, 100d, Storming the Bastille. No. 2004, 100d, Death of Marat, by David. 200d, Child and Rabbit, by Prud'hon. 300d, Slave Market, by Gerome, horiz. 400d, Liberty Leading the People, by Delacroix.

**1989, July 14** ***Perf. 13***

**2000-2006** A523 Set of 7 5.00
Imperf., #2000-2006 10.00

**Souvenir Sheet**

**2007** A523 400d multicolored 3.25

No. 2007 contains one 33x44mm stamp.

1990 World Cup Soccer Championships, Italy — A524

Soccer plays: No. 2008, 50d, Dribbling. No. 2009, 50d, Tackling. No. 2010, 50d, Goalie. No. 2011, 100d, Dribbling, diff. No. 2012, 100d, Dribbling, diff., vert. 200d, Preparing to kick, vert. 300d, Heading ball, vert. 400d, Heading ball, diff., vert.

***Perf. 13x12½, 12½x13***

**1989, Aug. 27**

**2008-2014** A524 Set of 7 4.50
Imperf., #2008-2014 11.00

**Souvenir Sheet**

***Perf. 13***

**2015** A524 400d multicolored 3.50

No. 2015 contains one 32x40mm stamp.

Dogs A525

#2016, 50d, Dachshund. #2017, 50d, Beagle. #2018, 50d, English setter, vert. #2019, 100d, German short-haired pointer, vert. #2020, 100d, Basset hounds. 200d, German sheperd, vert. 300d, Beagle, diff.

**1989, Aug. 20** ***Perf. 12½***

**2016-2022** A525 Set of 7 4.50
Imperf., #2016-2022 10.00

No. 2020 is 68x28mm.

Horses A526

#2023, 50d, Tennessee Walking. #2024, 50d, Appaloosa. #2025, 50d, Tersky. #2025, 100d, Kladruber. #2026, 100d, Welsh cob. 200d, Pinto. 300d, Pony and bridle.

**1989, Sept. 23** ***Perf. 13***

**2023-2029** A526 Set of 7 4.50
Imperf., #2023-2029 12.50

No. 2029 is 68x28mm.

Flowers — A527

No. 2030, 50d, Paphiopedilum siamense. No. 2031, 50d, Fuchsia fulgens. No. 2032, 100d, Hemerocallis fulva. No. 2033, 100d, Gloriosa superba. 200d, Strelitzia reginae. 300d, Iris.

**1989, Sept. 23** ***Perf. 12½***

**2030-2035** A527 Set of 6 4.50 2.00
Imperf., #2030-2035 9.00

German Democratic Republic, 40th Anniv. — A528

**1989, Oct. 7** ***Perf. 13***

**2036** A528 200d multicolored .90

Immunization Campaign — A529

#2037, Woman receiving vaccination. #2038, Child receiving oral vaccine. #2039, Clinic.

**1989, Oct. 20**

**2037-2039** A529 100d Set of 3 1.25

Drawings of Everyday Life, 19th Cent. — A530

Designs: 50d, Assembling plow. No. 2041, 100d, Harrowing. No. 2042, 100d, Irrigating. 200d, Fertilizing. 300d, Harvesting.

**1989, Oct. 28** ***Perf. 12x12½***

**2040-2044** A530 Set of 5 3.75 2.40
Imperf., #2040-2044 5.50

Horse Paintings, by Xu Beihong (1895-1953) A531

Various horses: 100d, 200d, 300d, 500d horiz., 800d, 1000d, 1500d.

**1989, Dec. 22** ***Perf. 13***

**2045-2051** A531 Set of 7 5.75
Imperf., #2045-2051 9.00

***Imperf***

**Size: 117x72mm**

**2052** A531 2000d multicolored 5.50
Imperf. 11.00

Vietnamese Communist Party, 60th Anniv. — A532

Designs: 100d, Ho Chi Minh, tank. 500d, Workers, refinery, field.

**1990, Feb. 3** **Litho.** ***Perf. 13***

**2053-2054** A532 Set of 2 2.75
Imperf., #2053-2054 4.50

Ducks — A533

a, 100d, Anas platyrhynchos hybrid. b, 300d, Anas penelope. c, 500d, Anas platyrhynchos. d, 1000d, Anas erythrorhyncha. e, 2000d, Anas platyrhynchos, diff. f, 3000d, Anas undulata.

**1990, Feb. 15**
**2055** A533 Block of 6, #a.-f. 4.50

Trucks A534

100d, Mack. 200d, Volvo F89. 300d, Tatra 915 S1. 500d, Hino KZ30000. 1000d, Iveco. 2000d, Leyland DAF Super Comet. 3000d, Kamaz 53212.

**1990, Feb. 20**
**2056-2062** A534 Set of 7 4.00 1.50
Imperf., #2056-2062 5.50

Architectural Sites, Hue — A535

#2063, 100d, Tu Duc's Mausoleum. #2064, 100d, Hien Nhon Arch. 200d, Ngo Mon Gate. 300d, Thien Mu Temple. 400d, Palace, gateway.

**1990, Feb. 20** ***Perf. 12½x12***
**2063-2066** A535 Set of 4 2.75

**Souvenir Sheet**

**2067** A535 400d multicolored 2.25

Goldfish — A536

Paintings A537

100d, Bulging-eyed, horiz. 300d, Telescopic-eyed, horiz. 500d, Red-headed, horiz. 1000d, Double-tailed. 2000d, Rainbow. 3000d, Comet.

**1990, Mar. 20** ***Perf. 13***
**2068-2073** A536 Set of 6 4.50 1.25
Imperf., #2068-2073 7.00

**1990, Apr. 10**

London '90: 100d, Antonia Zarate, by Goya. 200d, Girl Holding a Paper Fan, by Renoir. 300d, Janet Grizel, by John Russell. 500d, Love Untieing the Belt of Beauty, by Sir Joshua Reynolds. 1000d, Portrait of a Woman, by George Romney. 2000d, Portrait of Madame Ginoux, by Van Gogh. 3000d, Woman in Blue, by Gainsborough. 3500d, Woman in a Straw Hat, by Van Gogh.

**2074-2080** A537 Set of 7 4.50 1.50
Imperf., #2074-2080 7.50

**Souvenir Sheet**

**2081** A537 3500d multicolored 3.50 1.60

1990 World Cup Soccer Championships, Italy — A538

Various soccer players in action: 100d, 200d, 300d, 500d, 1000d, 2000d, 3000d.

**1990, Apr. 19**
**2082-2088** A538 Set of 7 4.00

**Souvenir Sheet**

**2089** A538 3500d multicolored 2.75

No. 2089 contains one 32x40mm stamp.
For overprints see Nos. 2189-2196.

Cats — A539

Dogs — A540

Various cats: 100d, horiz., 200d, 300d, horiz., 500d, 1000d, horiz., 2000d, 3000d.

**1990, May 5**
**2090-2096** A539 Set of 7 4.00

**Souvenir Sheet**

**2097** A539 3500d multicolored 3.25

No. 2097 contains one 44x33mm stamp. Belgica '90 (#2097).

**1990, May 15**

Various dogs: 100d, 200d, 300d, 500d, 1000d, 2000d, 3000d.

**2098-2104** A540 Set of 7 4.00

**Souvenir Sheet**

**2105** A540 3500d Collies 3.25

New Zealand '90.

Ho Chi Minh (1890-1969) A541

Ho Chi Minh and: 100d, Lenin. 300d, Soldiers waving flag. 500d, Hand holding rifle, dove. 1000d, Map. 2000d, Child, dove. 3000d, Stylized globe. 3500d, Flag.

**1990, May 17** ***Perf. 13***
**2106-2111** A541 Set of 6 3.50
Imperf., #2106-2111 5.00

**Souvenir Sheet**

***Perf. 12½x13***

**2112** A541 3500d multicolored 2.50

No. 2112 contains one 33x44mm stamp.

Dinosaurs — A542

100d, Gorgosaurus. 500d, Ceratosaurus. 1000d, Ankylosaurus. 2000d, Ankylosaurus, diff. 3000d, Edaphosaurus.

**1990, June 1** ***Perf. 13***
**2113-2117** A542 Set of 5 5.25 2.25

Columbus' Discovery of America, 500th Anniv. — A543

Designs: 50d, Fleet. No. 2119, 100d, Columbus presenting gifts to natives. No. 2120, 100d, Columbus, priest at Rabida. No. 2121, 100d, Columbus at Court of Ferdinand, Isabella. No. 2122, 200d, Map of Caribbean. No. 2123, 200d, Columbus, arms. 300d, Map of Atlantic. 500d, Teotihuacan pot.

**1990, June 10** ***Perf. 12½***
**2118-2124** A543 Set of 7 5.75

**Souvenir Sheet**

**2125** A543 500d multicolored 2.00

No. 2125 contains one 40x32mm stamp.
For overprints see Nos. 2313-2320.

Sailing Ships A544

Designs: 100d, Viking longship. 500d, Caravel. No. 2128, 1000d, Carrack, 14th-15th cent. No. 2129, 1000d, Flit. No. 2130, 1000d, Carrack, 15th cent., vert. 2000d, Galleon, vert. 3000d, Galleon, diff. 4200d, Egyptian barge.

**1990, June 10** ***Perf. 13***
**2126-2132** A544 Set of 7 5.75
Imperf., #2126-2132 9.00

**Souvenir Sheet**

***Perf. 13x12½***

**2133** A544 4200d multicolored 3.25

No. 2133 contains one 44x33mm stamp.

11th Asian Games, Beijing — A545

Designs: 100d, High jump. 200d, Basketball. 300d, Table tennis. 500d, Volleyball. 1000d, Rhythmic gymnastics. 2000d, Tennis. 3000d, Judo. 3500d, Hurdles.

**1990, June 20** ***Perf. 13***
**2134-2140** A545 Set of 7 5.00 3.25
Imperf., #2134-2140 6.50

**Souvenir Sheet**

***Perf. 12½x13***

**2141** A545 3500d multicolored 2.50

No. 2141 contains one 33x44mm stamp.

Nos. 1180-1187 Ovptd. in Red, Green and Black

**1990, June 22** ***Perf. 12***
**2142-2149** A352 Set of 8 5.00

1990 World Cup Soccer Championships, Italy.

Nos. 1323-1330 Ovptd. in Black and Red

**1990, June 22** ***Perf. 12x12½***
**2150-2157** A385 Set of 8 7.25

Tourism.

Modern Ships A546

100d, Freighter. 300d, Container ship. 500d, Cruise ship. 1000d, Liquified natural gas tanker. 2000d, Ro-Ro ship. 3000d, Ferry.

**1990, July 20** ***Perf. 13***
**2158-2163** A546 Set of 6 5.00
Imperf., #2158-2163 7.50

Post & Telecommunications Dept., 45th Anniv. — A547

Designs: 100d, Dove, ship, plane. 1000d, Satellite antenna.

**1990, Aug. 15** ***Perf. 13x13½***
**2164-2165** A547 Set of 2 .80
Imperf., #2164-2165 2.75

Socialist Republic of Viet Nam, 45th Anniv. — A548

Designs: 100d, Flag, construction projects. 500d, Map, tank, soldiers. 1000d, "VI," ship, communications network. 3000d, Workers, oil rigs. 3500d, Ho Chi Minh.

**1990, Sept. 1** ***Perf. 13***
**2166-2169** A548 Set of 4 3.25
Imperf., #2166-2169 4.00

**Souvenir Sheet**
***Perf. 12½x13***

**2170** A548 3500d multicolored 2.50

No. 2170 contains one 33x44mm stamp. Sixth Vietnamese Communist Party Congress (#2168).

Airships A549

Designs: 100d, Henry Gifford, 1871. 200d, Lebandy, 1910. 300d, Graf Zeppelin. 500d, R-101, 1930. 1000d, Soviet, 1936. 2000d, Tissandier, 1883. 3000d, US Navy. 3500d, "Zodiac," 1931.

**1990, Sept. 10** ***Perf. 12½***
**2171-2177** A549 Set of 7 5.00

**Souvenir Sheet**

**2178** A549 3500d multicolored 2.50 1.00

No. 2178 contains one 40x32mm stamp. Helvetia '90, Stamp World London '90.

Fable of Thach Sanh — A550

Designs: a, 100d, Thach Sanh carrying bundles of wood. b, 300d, Ly Thong. c, 500d, Thach Sanh killing python. d, 1000d, Thach Sanh shooting arrow at eagle. e, 2000d, Thach Sanh in prison. f, 3000d, Thach Sanh, princess.

**1990, Sept. 20** ***Perf. 13***
**2179** A550 Block of 6, #a.-f. 5.00
Imperf. 6.00

Asian-Pacific Postal Training Center, 20th Anniv. — A551

**1990, Sept. 25**
**2180** A551 150d multicolored .45

Nos. 571-578 Ovptd. with Red Cross in Red and "FOR THE FUTURE GENERATION" in various Languages in Black

Language: No. 2181, 12xu, Japanese. No. 2182, 12xu, Italian. No. 2183, 20xu, German. No. 2184, 20xu, Vietnamese. 30xu, English. 40xu, Russian. 50xu, French. 60xu, Spanish.

**1990, Sept. 25** ***Perf. 12***
**2181-2188** A211 Set of 8 5.50

Position of overprint varies.
Use of these stamps at stated face value is unlikely.

Nos. 2082-2089 Ovptd.

**1990, Sept. 25** ***Perf. 13***
**2189-2195** A538 Set of 7 5.00

**Souvenir Sheet**

**2196** A538 3500d multicolored 3.25

Vietnamese Women's Federation, 60th Anniv. — A552

Designs: 100d, Woman carrying rifle. 500d, Women working in field, laboratory.

**1990, Oct. 10**
**2197-2198** A552 Set of 2 .50
Imperf., #2197-2198 3.00

Correggio (1494-1534), Painter — A553

Various paintings of the Madonna and Child: No. 2199, 50xu, shown. No. 2200, 50xu, diff. 1d, 2d, 3d, 5d, 6d.

**1990, Nov. 13** ***Perf. 12½***
**2199-2205** A553 Set of 7 5.50

**Souvenir Sheet**

**2206** A553 10d multicolored 5.50

No. 2206 contains one 32x40mm stamp. Dated "1984." Use of these stamps at stated face value is unlikely.

Protection of Forests — A554

Designs: 200d, Water conservation, healthy forest. 1000d, SOS, prevent forest fires.

**1990, Nov. 15** ***Perf. 13***
**2207-2208** A554 Set of 2 1.25

A555

A555a

Poisonous mushrooms: 200d, Amanita pantherina. 300d, Amanita phalloides. 1000d, Amanita virosa. 1500d, Amanita muscaria. 2000d, Russula emetica. 3000d, Boletus satanas.

**1991, Jan. 21**
**2209-2214** A555 Set of 6 5.50
Imperf., #2209-2214 7.00

**1991, Jan. 31**

1992 Summer Olympics, Barcelona: 200d, Sailing. 300d, Boxing. 400d, Cycling. 1000d, High jump. 2000d, Equestrian. No. 2220, 3000d, Judo. No. 2221, 3000d, Wrestling, horiz. 5000d, Soccer, horiz.

**2215-2221** A555a Set of 7 6.25
Imperf., #2215-2221 7.00

**Souvenir Sheet**

**2222** A555a 5000d multicolored 3.25
Imperf., #2222 5.00

No. 2222 contains one 44x33mm stamp.

Nguyen Binh Khiem (1491-1585), Writer — A556

**1991, Feb. 15**
**2223** A556 200d multicolored .50
Imperf. 2.00

Discovery of America, 500th Anniv. — A557

Sailing ships: 200d, Marisiliana. No. 2225, 400d, Venetian. No. 2226, 400d, Cromster, vert. No. 2227, 2000d, Nina. No. 2228, 2000d, Pinta. 3000d, Howker, vert. 5000d, Santa Maria.
6500d, Portrait of Columbus.

**1991, Feb. 22**
**2224-2230** A557 Set of 7 7.25
Imperf., #2224-2230 6.00

**Souvenir Sheet**

**2231** A557 6500d multicolored 4.00
Imperf. 6.00

Golden Heart Charity — A558

Women wearing traditional costumes: 200d, 500d, 1000d, 5000d.

**1991, Feb. 26**
**2232-2235** A558 Set of 4 3.75
Imperf., #2232-2235 5.00

Sharks A559

Designs: 200d, Carcharhinus melanopterus. 300d, Carcharhinus amblyrhynchos. 400d, Triakis semifasciata. 1000d, Sphyrna mokarran. 2000d, Triaenodon abesus. No. 2241, 3000d, Carcharias laurus. No. 2242, 3000d, Carcharhinus leucas.

**1991, Apr. 6**
**2236-2242** A559 Set of 7 5.50
Imperf., #2236-2242 7.50

Endangered Birds — A560

World Wildlife Fund: 200d, Grus vipio. 300d, Grus antigone chick, vert. 400d, Grus japonensis, vert. 1000d, Grus antigone, adults, vert. 2000d, Grus nigricollis, vert. No. 2248, 3000d, Balearica regulorum, vert. No. 2249, 3000d, Bugeranus leucogerranus.

**1991, Apr. 20**
**2243-2249** A560 Set of 7 6.25
Imperf., #2243-2249 6.00

Shellfish A561

Designs: 200d, 1000d, 2000d, Palinurus, all diff. 300d, Alpheus bellulus. 400d, Periclemenes brevicarpalis. No. 2255, 3000d, Astacus. No. 2256, 3000d, Palinurus, diff.

**1991, Apr. 20**
**2250-2256** A561 Set of 7 5.50
Imperf., #2250-2256 7.00

Young Pioneers, 50th Anniv. — A562

Designs: 200d, shown. 400d, UN Convention on Children's Rights.

**1991, May 15**
**2257-2258** A562 Set of 2 .50
Imperf., #2257-2258 4.00

Rally Cars A563

#2259, 400d, Lada. #2260, 400d, Nissan. 500d, Ford Sierra RS Cosworth. 1000d, Suzuki. 2000d, Mazda 323 4WD. #2264, 3000d, Lancia. #2265, 3000d, Peugeot. 5000d, Peugeot 405.

**1991, May 24**
**2259-2265** A563 Set of 7 5.50
Imperf., #2259-2265 5.00

**Souvenir Sheet**

**2266** A563 5000d multicolored 4.00
Imperf. 5.00

No. 2266 contains one 44x33mm stamp.

Locomotives — A564

#2267, 400d, Puffing Billy, 1811, vert. #2268, 400d, Fusee, 1829, vert. 500d, Stevens, 1825. 1000d, Crampton #80, 1852. 2000d, Locomotion, 1825. #2272, 3000d, Saint-Lo, 1844. #2273, 3000d, Coutances, 1855. 5000d, Atlantic, 1843.

**1991, May 25**

**2267-2273** A564 Set of 7 5.50
Imperf., #2267-2273 8.00

**Souvenir Sheet**

**2274** A564 5000d multicolored 3.25
Imperf. 6.00

No. 2274 contains one 33x44mm stamp.

Frogs A565

World Wildlife Fund: 200d, Dendrobates leucomelas. 400d, Rana esculenta. 500d, Mantella aurantiaca. 1000d, Dendrobates tinctorius. 2000d, Hyla halowelli. No. 2280, 3000d, Agalychnis callidryas. No. 2281, 3000d, Hyla aurea.

**1991, June 12**

**2275-2281** A565 Set of 7 6.00
Imperf., #2275-2281 6.00

7th Vietnamese Communist Party Congress A566

Designs: 200d, Ho Chi Minh, buildings. 300d, Workers. 400d, Mother, children.

**1991, June**

**2282-2284** A566 Set of 3 1.50
Imperf., #2282-2284 4.50

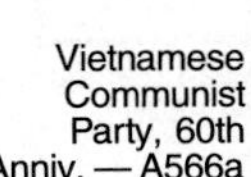

Vietnamese Communist Party, 60th Anniv. — A566a

**1991, June 24 Litho. *Perf. 13***

**2284A** A566a 100d red .75

1992 Winter Olympics, Albertville A567

Designs: 200d, Speed skating, vert. 300d, Free- style skiing, vert. 400d, Bobsled. 1000d, Biathlon. 2000d, Slalom skiing. No. 2290, 3000d, Cross-country skiing, vert. No. 2291, 3000d, Ice dancing, vert. 5000d, Hockey, vert.

**1991, July 15**

**2285-2291** A567 Set of 7 5.50
Imperf., #2285-2291 4.00

**Souvenir Sheet**

**2292** A567 5000d multicolored 3.25
Imperf. 4.00

No. 2292 contains one 33x44mm stamp.

Prehistoric Animals — A568

Designs: a, 200d, Arsinoitherium zitteli. b, 500d, Elephas primigenius. c, 1000d, Baluchitherium. d, 2000d, Deinotherium giganteum. e, 3000d, Brontops. f, 3000d, Uinatherium.

**1991, July 26**

**2293** A568 Block of 6, #a.-f. 6.25

A569

A570

Golden Heart Charity: 200d, Eye, folded hands. 3000d, Tennis player in wheelchair.

**1991, July 27**

**2294-2295** A569 Set of 2 1.75

**1991, Aug. 20**

Chess pieces: 200d, Pawn. 300d, Knight. 1000d, Rook. 2000d, Queen. No. 2300, 3000d, Bishop. No. 2301, 3000d, King. 5000d, Pawn, Knight, King.

**2296-2301** A570 Set of 6 5.50
Imperf., #2296-2301 5.00

**Souvenir Sheet**

**2302** A570 5000d multicolored 3.25
Imperf. 5.00

No. 2302 contains one 33x44mm stamp.

PHILANIPPON '91 — A571

Butterflies: 200d, Attacus atlas. 400d, Morpho cypris. 500d, Troides rotschildi. No. 2306, 1000d, Papilio demetrius. No. 2307, 1000d, Vanessa atalanta. 3000d, Papilio weiskei. 5000d, Apatura ilia substituta. 5500d, Heliconius melpomene.

**1991, Aug. 29**

**2303-2309** A571 Set of 7 5.75
Imperf., #2303-2309 5.00

**Souvenir Sheet**

**2310** A571 5500d multicolored 3.25
Imperf. 5.00

No. 2310 contains one 44x33mm stamp.

Post and Telecommunications Research Institute, 25th Anniv. — A572

**1991, Aug.**

**2311** A572 200d multicolored .50
Imperf. 2.00

**Souvenir Sheet**

**2312** A572 3500d Communications network, horiz. 2.50
Imperf. 5.00

No. 2312 contains one 44x33mm stamp.

Nos. 2118-2125 Ovptd. in Red

**1992, Jan. 15 *Perf. 12½***

**2313-2319** A543 Set of 7 6.50

**Souvenir Sheet**

**2320** A543 500d multicolored 4.00

7th Vietnamese Communist Party Congress A574

200d, Workers, industry, agriculture, atomic energy symbol. 2000d, Map of Asia, hands clasped.

**1992, Feb. 3 Litho. *Perf. 13***

**2322-2323** A574 Set of 2 2.25

1992 Winter Olympics, Albertville — A575

Designs: 200d, Biathlon. 2000d, Hockey. 4000d, Slalom skiing. 5000d, Pairs figure skating. 6000d, Downhill skiing.

**1992, Feb. 5**

**2324-2328** A575 Set of 5 5.50

Miniature Sheet

Columbus' Discovery of America, 500th Anniv. — A576

Designs: a, 4000d, Columbus, flag. b, 6000d, Columbus, natives. c, 8000d, Aboard ship. d, 3000d, Two sailing ships. e, 400d, Columbus' fleet setting sail.
11,000d, Columbus with Ferdinand and Isabella.

**1992, Feb. 12**

**2329** A576 #a.-f. + label 6.25

***Imperf***

**Size: 102x70mm**

**2330** A576 11,000d multicolored 5.00

Airplanes — A577

Designs: 400d, Tupelov TU-154M. 500d, Concorde. 1000d, Airbus A-320. 3000d, Airbus A340-300. 4000d, Boeing Dash 8-400. 5000d, Boeing 747-200. 6000d, McDonnell-Douglas MD-11CF.

**1992, Mar. 6 *Perf. 13***

**2331-2337** A577 Set of 7 5.50

A578

A579

Intl. Decade for Natural Disaster Reduction: 400d, Storm system, weather forecasting equipment. 4000d, Man taking water depth readings.

**1992, Mar. 23**

**2338-2339** A578 Set of 2 1.25

**1992, Mar. 28**

1992 Summer Olympics, Barcelona: 400d, Archery. 600d, Volleyball. 1000d, Wrestling. 3000d, Fencing. 4000d, Running. 5000d, Weight lifting. 6000d, Field hockey. 10,000d, Basketball.

**2340-2346** A579 Set of 7 5.50

**Souvenir Sheet**

**2347** A579 10,000d multicolored 3.50

No. 2347 contains one 32x43mm stamp.

Motorcycles — A580

Designs: 400d, 5000d, Suzuki 500F. 500d, Honda CBR 600F. 1000d, Honda HRC 500F. 3000d, Kawasaki 250F, vert. 4000d, Suzuki RM 250F, vert. 6000d, BMW 1000F. 10,000d, Suzuki RM 250F, diff.

**1992, Apr. 8**
**2348-2354** A580 Set of 7 5.50
**Souvenir Sheet**
**2355** A580 10,000d multicolored 4.50

No. 2355 contains one 33x44mm stamp.

Intl. Space Year A581

400d, Space shuttle launch, vert. 500d, Launch of shuttle Columbia, vert. 3000d, Columbia in space. 4000d, Space station, shuttle Hermes. 5000d, Shuttle Hermes. 6000d, Astronauts, Hubble space telescope, vert.

**1992, Apr. 12**
**2356-2361** A581 Set of 6 5.50

Saigon Post Office, Cent. A582

200d, Main entrance. 10,000d, Facade.

**1992, Apr. 30** ***Perf. 13***
**2362** A582 200d multicolored 1.00
**Souvenir Sheet**
***Perf. 13½***
**2363** A582 10,000d multicolored 2.50

No. 2363 contains one 43x32mm stamp.

European Cup Soccer Championships A583

Various soccer players in action: 200d, 2000d, 4000d, 5000d, 6000d.

**1992, May 14** ***Perf. 13***
**2364-2368** A583 Set of 5 5.00
**Souvenir Sheet**
**2369** A583 9000d multicolored 4.00

No. 2369 contains one 44x33mm stamp.

Spanish Paintings A584

Designs: 400d, Portrait of a Girl, by Zurbaran. 500d, Woman with a Jug, by Murillo. 1000d, Portrait of Maria Aptrickaia, by Velazquez. 3000d, Holy Family with St. Katherine, by de Ribera. 4000d, Madonna and Child with Saints Agnes and Thekla, by El Greco. 5000d, Woman with a Jug, by Goya. 6000d, The Naked Maja, by Goya, horiz. 10,000d, Three Women, by Picasso, horiz.

**1992, May 30**
**2370-2376** A584 Set of 7 5.50
**Souvenir Sheet**
**2377** A584 10,000d multicolored 4.00

No. 2377 contains one 44x33mm stamp. Expo '92, Seville (#2377).

UN Conference on Environmental Protection, 20th Anniv. — A585

Designs: 200d, Clean, polluted water. 4000d, Graph comparing current development pattern with environmentally safe pattern.

**1992, June 1**
**2378-2379** A585 Set of 2 1.25

A586

Flowers — A587

Lighthouses: 200d, Cu Lao Xanh. 3000d, Can Gio. 5000d, Vung Tau. 6000d, Long Chau.

**1992, June 14** ***Perf. 13½x13***
**2380-2383** A586 Set of 4 4.50

Genoa '92.

**1992, June 28** ***Perf. 13***

Designs: 200d, Citrus maxima. 2000d, Nerium indicum. 4000d, Ixora coccinea. 5000d, Cananga oborata. 6000d, Cassia surattensis.

**2384-2388** A587 Set of 5 4.50

Birds — A588

Rodents — A589

Designs: 200d, Ducula spilorrhoa. 2000d, Petrophassa ferruginea. 4000d, Columba livia. 5000d, Lopholaimus antareticus. 6000d, Streptopelia senegalensis, horiz.

**1992, July 3**
**2389-2393** A588 Set of 5 4.50

**1992, July 26**

Designs: 200d, 500d, Cavia porcellus, horiz. 3000d, Hystrix indica, horiz. 4000d, Gerbillus gerbillus. 5000d, Petaurista petaurista. 6000d, Oryctolagus cuniculus.

**2394-2399** A589 Set of 6 5.50

Disabled Soldiers Day, 45th Anniv. A590

**1992, July 27**
**2400** A590 200d multicolored .50

3rd Phu Dong Games A591

**1992, Aug. 1**
**2401** A591 200d multicolored .50

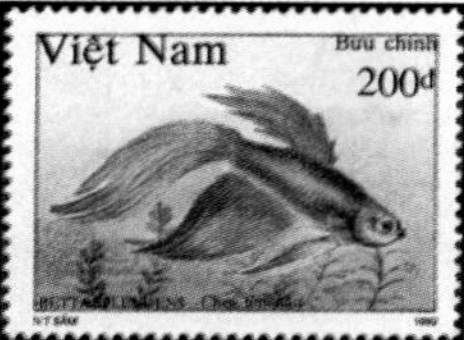
Betta Splendens — A592

Various fish: 200d, 500d, 3000d, 4000d, 5000d, 6000d.

**1992, Aug. 15**
**2402-2407** A592 Set of 6 5.50

1984 Summer Olympics, Los Angeles A592a

Designs: No. 2407A, 50xu, Gymnastics. No. 2407B, 50xu, Soccer, vert. 1d, Wrestling. 2d, Volleyball, vert. 3d, Hurdles. 5d, Basketball, vert. 8d, Weight lifting.
10d, Running, vert.

**1992, Sept. 1** **Litho.** ***Perf. 12½***
**2407A-2407G** A592a Set of 7 4.50 4.50
**Souvenir Sheet**
**2407H** A592a 10d multi 4.50 4.50

Nos. 2407A-2407G were prepared in 1984 but were not released because of Viet Nam's boycott of the 1984 Summer Olympics.

Intl. Planned Parenthood Federation, 40th Anniv. — A593

Designs: 200d, Map showing member's locations, vert. 4000d, Anniv. emblem, map.

**1992, Oct. 1**
**2408-2409** A593 Set of 2 1.25

Hanoi Medical School, 90th Anniv. A594

Designs: 200d, Medical students. 5000d, Alexandre Yersin, school.

**1992, Nov. 20**
**2410-2411** A594 Set of 2 1.50

SOS Children's Villages — A595

Designs: 200d, Adult sheltering child. 5000d, Women, children inside house.

**1992, Dec. 22**
**2412-2413** A595 Set of 2 1.50

17th Southeast Asian Games, Singapore — A596

**1993, Jan. 1**
**2414** A596 200d multicolored .50

Bees A597

Designs: 200d, Apis dorsata. 800d, Apis koschevnikovi. 1000d, Apis laboriosa. 2000d, Apis cerana japonica. 5000d, Apis cerana cerana. 10,000d, Apis mellifera, vert.

**1993, Jan. 15**
**2415-2420** A597 Set of 6 5.50

Fable of Tam Cam — A598

Designs: 200d, Returning from river. 800d, Vision of old man by goldfish pool. 1000d, With unsold rice at market. 3000d, Trying on slipper for prince. 4000d, Rising from lotus flower. 10,000d, Royal couple.

**1993, Jan. 18**
**2421-2426** A598 Set of 6 5.50

New Year 1993 (Year of the Rooster) A599

200d, 5000d, Rooster, hen and chicks.

**1993, Jan. 20**
**2427-2428** A599 Set of 2 1.50

Medicinal Plants A600

Designs: 200d, Atractylodes macrocephala. No. 2430, 1000d, Lonicera japonica. No. 2431, 1000d, Quisqualis indica. 3000d, Rehmannia glutinosa. 12,000d, Gardenia jasminoides.

**1993, Feb. 27**
**2429-2433** A600 Set of 5 5.50

Communications A601

200d, Map, communications equipment. 2500d, Map, Hong Kong-Sri Racha Cable route.

**1993, Mar. 1**
**2434-2435** A601 Set of 2 .75

Asian Animals A602

200d, Ailuropoda melanoleuca. 800d, Panthera tigris. 1000d, Elephas maximus. 3000d, Rhinoceros unicornis. 4000d, Hylobates leucogenys. #2441, 10,000d, Neofelis nebulosa. #2442, 10,000d, Bos sauveli.

**1993, Mar. 10**
**2436-2441** A602 Set of 6 5.00

**Souvenir Sheet**

***Perf. 13½***

**2442** A602 10,000d multicolored 3.25

1994 World Cup Soccer Championships, U.S. — A603

Various soccer players in action.

**1993, Mar. 30** ***Perf. 13***
**2443-2445** A603 200d, 1500d, 7000d, set of 3 2.25

Transportation — A604

Designs: 200d, Wheelbarrow. 800d, Buffalo cart. 1000d, Rickshaw, top up. 2000d, Rickshaw with passenger. 5000d, Rickshaw, top down. 10,000d, Horse-drawn carriage.

**1993, Apr. 6**
**2446-2451** A604 Set of 6 5.00

500Kv Electricity Lines — A605

**1993, May 1**
**2452-2453** 300d, 400d, set of 2 .75

Polska '93 — A606

Paintings: 200d, Sunflowers, by Van Gogh. No. 2455, 1000d, Young Woman, by Modigliani. No. 2456, 1000d, Couple in Forest, by Rousseau. 5000d, Harlequin with Family, by Picasso. No. 2458, 10,000d, Female Model, by Matisse, horiz. No. 2459, 10,000d, Portrait of Dr. Gachet, by Van Gogh.

**1993, May 7** ***Perf. 13***
**2454-2458** A606 Set of 5 5.00

**Souvenir Sheet**

***Perf. 12½***

**2459** A606 10,000d multicolored 3.25

No. 2459 contains one 32x43mm stamp.

Da Lat, Cent. A607

Orchids: 400d, Paphiopedilum hirsutissimum. No. 2461, 1000d, Paphiopedilum malipoense. No. 2462, 1000d, Paphiopedilum gratrixianum. 12,000d, Paphiopedilum hennisianum.

**1993, June 15** ***Perf. 13***
**2460-2463** A607 Set of 4 4.00

Asian Architecture — A608

Landmark buildings from: 400d, Thailand, vert. 800d, Indonesia, vert. 1000d, Singapore, vert. No. 2467, 2000d, Malaysia. No. 2468, 2000d, Cambodia. 6000d, Laos. 8000d, Brunei.

10,000d, Thai Binh, Viet Nam, vert.

**1993, July 10** **Litho.**
**2464-2470** A608 Set of 7 4.75

**Souvenir Sheet**

***Perf. 14x13½***

**2471** A608 10,000d multicolored 3.25 3.25

7th Trade Union Congress — A608a

Designs: 400d, Industry, communications. 5000d, Hand holding hammer, doves, flowers.

**1993, July 28** **Litho.** ***Perf. 13***
**2471A-2471B** A608a Set of 2 1.25

Crabs A609

Designs: 400d, Scylla serrata. 800d, Portunus sanguinotentus. 1000d, Charybdis bimaculata. 2000d, Paralithodes brevipes. 5000d, Portunus pelagicus. 10,000d, Lithodes turritus.

**1993, July 30**
**2472-2477** A609 Set of 6 4.50

Stamp Day A610

5000d, Hand holding stamped envelope.

**1993, Aug. 15**
**2478-2479** A610 Set of 2 1.50

Miniature Sheet

Tennis — A611

Women tennis players: a, 400d. c, 1000d. Male tennis players: b, 1000d. d, 12,000d.

**1993, Sept. 20**
**2480** A611 #a.-d. + 2 labels 4.00

A613

A614

Costumes: 400d, Lo Lo. 800d, Thai. 1000d, Dao Do. 2000d, H'mong. 5000d, Kho Mu. No. 2488, 10,000d, Kinh.

No. 2489, 10,000d, Precious gem stones.

**1993, Oct. 1** ***Perf. 13***
**2483-2488** A613 Set of 6 4.00

**Souvenir Sheet**

***Perf. 13½***

**2489** A613 10,000d multicolored 3.25

Bangkok '93. Issued: Nos. 2483-2488, 10/1/93. No. 2489, 10/10/93.

No. 2489 contains one 43x32mm stamp.

**1994, Jan. 1**

New Year 1994 (Year of the Dog): Various dogs.

**2490-2491** A614 400d, 6000d, set of 2 1.75
Imperf., #2490-2491 4.00

Flowers A615

#2492, 400d, Prunus persica. #2493, 400d, Chrysanthemum morifolium. #2494, 400d, Rosa chinensis. 15,000d, Delonix regia.

**1994**
**2492-2495** A615 Set of 4 5.50

Issued: #2492, 1/4; 15,000d, 4/3; #2493, 7/30; #2494, 10/10.

Chess A616

Designs: 400d, Anatoly Karpov. 1000d, Gary Kasparov. 2000d, Bobby Fischer. 4000d, Emanuel Lasker. No. 2500, 10,000d, Jose Capablanca.

No. 2501, 10,000d, King.

**1994, Jan. 20**

**2496-2500** A616 Set of 5 4.50
Imperf., #2496-2500 8.00

**Souvenir Sheet**

**2501** A616 10,000d multicolored 3.25
Imperf. 4.75

Hong Kong '94 — A617

Festivals: 400d, Hoi Lim. 800d, Cham. 1000d, Tay Nguyen. 12,000d, Nam Bo.

**1994, Feb. 18**

**2502-2505** A617 Set of 4 4.00
Imperf., #2502-2505 6.75

A618

A619

Various opera masks: 400d, 500d, 2000d, 3000d, 4000d, 7000d.

**1994, Mar. 15**

**2506-2511** A618 Set of 6 4.75
Imperf., #2506-2511 8.50

**1994, Mar. 30**

Various gladiolus hybridus: 400d, 2000d, 5000d, 8000d.

**2512-2515** A619 Set of 4 3.75
Imperf., #2512-2515 6.75

Japanese Paintings — A620

Paintings by: 400d, Utamaro. 500d, Harunobu. 1000d, Hokusai. 2000d, Hiroshige. 3000d, Hokusai, diff. 4000d, Utamaro, diff. 8000d, Choki.

**1994, Apr. 9**

**2516-2522** A620 Set of 7 5.25
Imperf., #2516-2522 9.25

Insects — A621

Designs: 400d, Cicindela aurulenta. 1000d, Harmonia octomaculata. 6000d, Cicindela tennipes. 7000d, Collyris.

**1994, Apr. 20**

**2523-2526** A621 Set of 4 3.75
Imperf., #2523-2526 5.50

Victory at Dien Bien Phu, 40th Anniv. A622

Designs: 400d, Soldiers dragging equipment. 3000d, Celebration.

**1994, Apr.**

**2527-2528** A622 Set of 2 .90
Imperf., #2527-2528 1.25

Newspaper "Young Pioneers," 40th Anniv. A623

**1994, May 15** ***Perf. 13x13½***

**2529** A623 400d red & black .45

Crocodiles — A625

Designs: 400d, Crocodylus porosus. 600d, Alligator mississippiensis. 2000d, Crocodylus niloticus. 3000d, Alligator sinensis. 4000d, Caiman yacare. 9000d, Crocodylus johnsoni. 10,000d, Caiman crocodilus.

**1994, June 1** ***Perf. 13x13½***

**2532-2537** A625 Set of 6 5.00
Imperf., #2532-2537 7.50

**Souvenir Sheet**

***Perf. 13½***

**2538** A625 10,000d multicolored 3.25
Imperf. 4.00

No. 2538 contains one 43x32mm stamp.

1994 World Cup Soccer Championships, US — A626

Various soccer players in action: 400d, 600d, 1000d, 2000d, 3000d, 11,000d.

**1994, June 15** ***Perf. 13***

**2539-2544** A626 Set of 6 4.75
Imperf., #2539-2544 8.25

**Souvenir Sheet**

***Perf. 13½***

**2545** A626 10,000d multicolored 3.25
Imperf. 4.75

No. 2545 contains one 32x43mm stamp.

Yersin's Discovery of Plague Bacillus, Cent. A627

**1994, June** ***Perf. 13x13½***

**2546** A627 400d multicolored .60

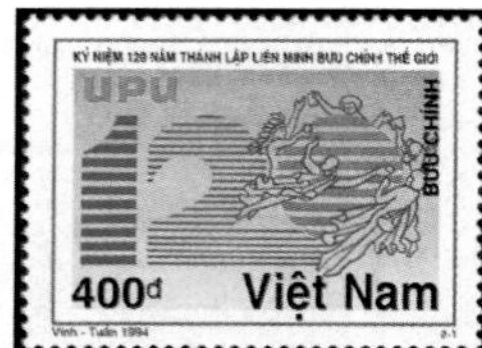


UPU, 120th Anniv. A629

Designs: 400d, UPU emblem, "120." 5000d, World map. 10,000d, UPU emblem, "P," vert.

**1994, Aug. 1** ***Perf. 13***

**2551-2552** A629 Set of 2 1.40

**Souvenir Sheet**

***Perf. 14x13½***

**2553** A629 10,000d multicolored 3.25

PHILAKOREA '94 — A630

Birds: 400d, Numenius arquata. 600d, Oceanites oceanicus. 1000d, Fregata minor. 2000d, Morus capensis. 3000d, Lunda cirrhata. 11,000d, Larus belcheri.

10,000d, Collocalia fuciphaga.

**1994, Aug. 16** ***Perf. 13x13½***

**2554-2559** A630 Set of 6 4.75

**Souvenir Sheet**

***Perf. 13½***

**2560** A630 10,000d multicolored 3.25

No. 2560 contains one 43x32mm stamp.

A631

A632

Bamboo: 400d, Bambusa blumeana. 1000d, Phyllostachys aurea. 2000d, Bambusa vulgaris. 4000d, Tetragonocalamus quadrangularis. 10,000d, Bambusa venticosa.

**1994, Aug. 17** ***Perf. 13½x13***

**2561-2565** A631 Set of 5 5.00

Singpex '94.

**1994, Sept. 20** ***Perf. 13x13½***

Various bridges: 400d, 900d, 8000d.

**2566-2568** A632 Set of 3 2.25

Children's Future A634

Designs: 400d+100d, Boy helping girl in wheelchair with kite. 2000d, Children dancing, vert.

**1994, Oct. 2** **Litho.** ***Perf. 13***

**2572-2573** A634 Set of 2 80

A636

A637

People's Army, 50th Anniv.: 400d, People in formation. 1000d, Soldiers, battle map. 2000d, Ho Chi Minh, child. 4000d, Anti-aircraft battery.

**1994, Dec. 22**

**2576-2579** A636 Set of 4 2.00

**1994, June 25** ***Perf. 13***

Intl. Olympic Committee, Cent.: 400d, Flags. 6000d, Pierre de Coubertin.

**2580-2581** A637 Set of 2 2.75

Việt Nam
BƯU CHÍNH
400d

ICAO, 50th Anniv. A638

Jets: 400d, In flight. 3000d, On ground.

**1994, Dec. 7**

**2582-2583** A638 Set of 2 .90

VIỆT NAM
400d
BƯU CHÍNH

Trams A639

Designs: 400d, With overhead conductor. 900d, Paris tram. 8000d, Philadelphia mail.

**1994, Oct. 10** **Litho.** ***Perf. 13x13½***

**2584-2586** A639 Set of 3 2.25

Liberation of Hanoi, 40th Anniv. A640

Designs: 400d, Greeting soldiers. 2000d, Workers, students, modern technology.

**1994, Oct. 10**

**2587-2588** A640 Set of 2 .70

New Year 1995 (Year of the Boar) A641

Stylized boars: 400d, Adult, five young. 8000d, One eating.

**1995, Jan. 2 Litho. *Perf. 13***
**2589-2590** A641 Set of 2 2.25

A642

A643

Birds: No. 2591, 400d, Pluvialis apricaria, horiz. No. 2592, 400d, Philetairus socius, horiz. No. 2593, 400d, Oxyruncus cristatus, horiz. No. 2594, 400d, Pandion haliaetus. No. 2595, 5000d, Cariama cristata.

**1995, Jan. 20 *Perf. 13x13½, 13½x13***
**2591-2595** A642 Set of 5 1.50

A number has been reserved for a souvenir sheet with this set.

**1995, Feb. 1 *Perf. 13***

Traditional women's attire: 400d, Young women, bicycle. 3000d, Bride. 5000d, Girl in formal dress holding hat.

**2597-2599** A643 Set of 3 1.90

Vietstampex '95 — A644

Owls — A645

**1995, Feb. 18**
**2600** A644 5500d multicolored 1.50

**1995, Mar. 1 *Perf. 13½x13***

Designs: 400d, Ketupa zeylonensis. 1000d, Strix aluco. 2000d, Strix nebulosa. 5000d, Strix seloputo. 10,000d, Otus leucotis. 12,500d, Tyto alba.

**2601-2605** A645 Set of 5 3.75

### Souvenir Sheet

***Perf. 14x13½***

**2606** A645 12,500d multicolored 3.25
Imperf. 4.25

Fish A646

Designs: 400d, Pomacanthus arcuatus. 1000d, Rhinecanthus rectangulus. 2000d, Pygoplites diacanthus. 4000d, Pomacanthus ciliaris. 5000d, Balistes vetula. 9000d, Balistes conspicillum.

**1995, Mar. 20 *Perf. 13***
**2607-2612** A646 Set of 6 4.25

Lenin, 125th Birth Anniv. — A647

**1995, Apr. 22 Litho. *Perf. 13***
**2613** A647 400d red & black .25

End of World War II, 50th Anniv. A648

**1995, May 2 Litho. *Perf. 13***
**2614** A648 400d multicolored .35

A649

A650

1996 Summer Olympics, Atlanta: 400d, Hammer throw. 3000d, Cycling. 4000d, Running. 10,000d, Pole vault.
12,500d, Basketball.

**1995, Apr. 5 Litho. *Perf. 13***
**2615-2618** A649 Set of 4 3.75

### Souvenir Sheet

**2619** A649 12,500d multicolored 3.25

**1995, May 5**

Various balloons: 500d, 1000d, 2000d, 3000d, 4000d, 5000d, 7000d.

**2620-2626** A650 Set of 7 5.00

Finlandia '95, Intl. Philatelic Exhibition, Helsinki.

### Miniature Sheets

Tapirus Indicus — A651

No. 2627a, 400d, With young. b, 1000d, Facing left. c, 2000d, Walking right. d, 4000d, Mouth open, left.
No. 2528a, 4000d, Facing right. b, 4000d, Eating leaves. c, 5000d, In water. d, 6000d, Head protruding out of water.

**1995, Apr. 25**
**2627** A651 Sheet of 4, #a.-d. 2.50
**2628** A651 Sheet of 4, #a.-d. 4.25

World Wildlife Fund (#2627).

### Miniature Sheet

Parachutes — A652

No. 2629: a, 400d, One parachutist descending from sky. b, 2000d, Two descending. c, 3000d, One about to touch ground. d, 9000d, Three men on ground with open parachute.

**1995, May 24**
**2629** A652 Sheet of 4, #a.-d. 3.25

Rhododendrons — A653

Designs: 400d, Fleuryi. 1000d, Sulphoreum. 2000d, Sinofalconeri. 3000d, Lyi. 5000d, Ovatum. 9000d, Tanastylum.

**1995, June 30**
**2630-2635** A653 Set of 6 4.50

### Miniature Sheet

Native Folktale — A654

a, 400d, Brothers and their parents. b, 1000d, Mother saying farewell to her departing sons. c, 3000d, One brother is transformed into a statue. d, 10,000d, Both brothers transformed into statues.

**1995, July 20 Litho. *Perf. 13***
**2636** A654 Sheet of 4, #a.-d. 3.25

A655

A656

400d, Statue of a woman holding child. 3000d, Three women of different races, emblem, horiz.

**1995, Aug. 5**
**2637-2638** A655 Set of 2 .80

Women's Federation of Viet Nam: 65th anniv. (#2637), 1995 Intl. Women's Conf., Beijing (#2638).

**1995, July 26**
**2639** A656 400d multicolored .35

Admission to Assoc. of Southeast Asian Nations (ASEAN).

Natl. Day — A657

#2640, 400d, Ho Chi Minh, people waving flags, dove of peace. #2641, 400d, Ho Chi Minh holding child. #2642, 1000d, Communist symbol, bridge, electrical wire, building. #2643, 1000d, Ho Chi Minh, silhouettes of soldiers, building with flags flying. #2644, 2000d, Soldiers, natl. flag. #2645, 2000d, Antenna, satellite dish, van, olive branch, people on motorcycles.

**1995, Aug. 14**
**2640-2645** A657 Set of 6 1.50

Viet Nam Labor Party, 65th anniv. (No. 2640). Ho Chi Minh, 105th birth anniv. (No. 2641). Evacuation of French troops from North Viet Nam, 40th anniv. (No. 2642). End of war in Viet Nam, 20th anniv. (No 2643). Natl. army, 50th anniv. (No. 2644). Post and Telecommunications Service, 50th anniv. (No. 2645).

Sir Rowland Hill (1795-1879) A658

Design: 4000d, Hill, "penny black."

**1995, Aug. 15**
**2646** A658 4000d multicolored .95

Natl. Sports Games — A659

**1995, Aug. 30**
**2647** A659 400d multicolored .25

Singapore '95 — A660

Orchids: 400d, Paphiopedilum druryi. 2000d, Dendrobium orcraceum. 3000d, Vanda. 4000d, Cattelya. 5000d, Paphiopedilum hirsutissimum. 6000d, Christenosia vietnamica haeger.

12,500d, Angraecum sesquipedale.

**1995, Sept. 1**
**2648-2653** A660 Set of 6 5.25

**Souvenir Sheet**

**2654** A660 12,500d multicolored 3.25

No. 2654 contains one 32x43mm stamp.

Asian Sites — A661

Designs: 400d, Buildings, monuments, tombs, Hue, Viet Nam. 3000d, Walkway over water, Trung Quoc. 4000d, Temple, Macao. 5000d, Kowloon, Hong Kong. 6000d, Pagoda, Dai Bac.

**1995, Sept. 6**
**2655-2659** A661 Set of 5 4.25

UN, 50th Anniv. A662

**1995, Oct. 10**
**2660** A662 2000d multicolored .45

Total Solar Eclipse, Oct. 10, 1995 A663

**1995, Dec. 23 Litho.** ***Perf. 13***
**2661** A663 400d multicolored .35

Paintings of Women A664

Designs: 400d, Woman in white dress, flowers, by To Ngoc Van (1906-54) (4-1). 2000d, Washing hair, by Tran Van Can (1906-94) (4-2). 6000d, Standing beside vase of flowers, by To Ngoc Van (4-3). 8000d, Two women, by Tran Van Can (4-4).

**1995, Nov. 15 Litho.** ***Perf. 13***
**2662-2665** A664 Set of 4 3.75

New Year 1996 (Year of the Rat) — A665

Stylized rats: 400d, One carrying fan, one riding horse. 8000d, Four carrying one in palanquin.

13,000d, Marching in parade, carrying banner.

**1996, Jan. 2 Litho.** ***Perf. 13***
**2666** A665 400d multicolored .20
**2667** A665 8000d multicolored 1.75

**Souvenir Sheet**

**2668** A665 13,000d multi, vert. 2.75

No. 2668 contains one 32x43mm stamp.

Dinosaurs — A666

Designs: 400d, Tsintaosaurus. 1000d, Archaeopteryx. 2000d, Psittacosaurus. 3000d, Hypsilophodon. 13,000d, Parasaurolophus.

**1996, Mar. 6**
**2669-2673** A666 Set of 5 4.50

Kingfishers A667

Designs: 400d, Halcyon smyrnensis. 1000d, Megaceryle alcyon. 2000d, Alcedo Atthis. 4000d, Halcyon coromanda. 12,000d, Ceryle rudis.

**1996, Mar. 11**
**2674-2678** A667 Set of 5 4.50

Flowers A668

Various flowers: No. 2679, 400d, brown (5-1). No. 2680, 400d, claret (5-2). No. 2681, 400d, green (5-3). No. 2682, 400d, blue (5-4). No. 2683, 5000d, red (5-5), vert.

***Perf. 13x13½, 13½x13***

**1996, Jan. 10 Litho.**
**2679-2683** A668 Set of 5 1.25

8th Vietnamese Communist Party Congress — A669

Designs: 400d, Ho Chi Minh (2-1). 3000d, Stylized dove, satellite dish, electrical towers, hammer & sickle, building, olive branch (2-2).

**1996, Feb. 3** ***Perf. 13***
**2684-2685** A669 Set of 2 .75

Asian Sites — A670

Monuments and statues in: 400d, Hanoi. 2000d, Thailand. 3000d, Bhubanesvar, India. 4000d, Kyoto, Japan. 10,000d, Borobudur, Java.

**1996, Feb. 10 Litho.** ***Perf. 13***
**2686-2690** A670 Set of 5 4.50

See Nos. 2773-2777.

Statues — A671

Various statues of men in traditional costumes of early warriors: 400d, 600d, 1000d, 2000d, 3000d, 5000d, 6000d, 8000d.

**1996 Litho.** ***Perf. 13½x13***
**2691-2698** A671 Set of 8 5.50

Central Committee, 50th Anniv. — A672

**1996, May 22** ***Perf. 13***
**2699** A672 400d multicolored .25

UNICEF, 50th Anniv. A673

Designs: 400d, Children of different races, cultures. 7000d, Plant, emblem, water droplets containing representations of education, drinking water, medicine, food.

**1996, May 15**
**2700-2701** A673 Set of 2 1.75

Red Cross of Viet Nam, 50th Anniv. A674

**1996, May 8** ***Perf. 13½***
**2702** A674 3000d Quotation, Ho Chi Minh .75

A675

Traditional Musical Instruments: a, 400d, Mandolin. b, 3000d, Bow and string instrument. c, 4000d, Square-shaped guitar-like instrument. d, 9000d, Zither.

**1996, Apr. 24** ***Perf. 13½x13***
**2703** A675 Sheet of 4, #a.-d. 3.50

China '96 Intl. Philatelic Exhibition.

A676

**1996, May 20** ***Perf. 13***

Insects: 400d, Cincindela japonica. 500d, Calodema wallacei. 1000d, Mylabris oculata. 4000d, Chrysochroa buqueti. 5000d, Ophioniea nigrofasciata. 12,000d, Carabus tauricus.

**2704-2709** A676 Set of 6 5.00

1996 Summer Olympic Games, Atlanta A677

Designs: 2000d, Soccer. 4000d, Sailing. 5000d, Field hockey.

**1996, July 8**
**2710-2712** A677 Set of 3 2.75

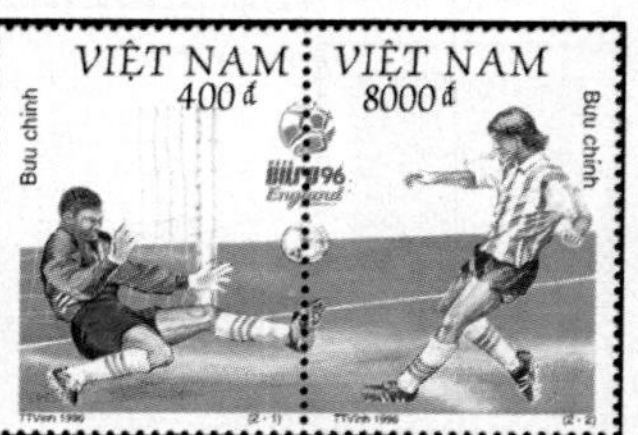

Euro '96, European Soccer Championships, Great Britain — A678

Designs: a, 400d, Net, goalie. b, 8000d, Player making shot on goal.

**1996, June 1**
**2713** A678 Pair, #a.-b. 2.00

No. 2713 is a continuous design.

Aircraft A679

400d, Airbus A320. 1000d, AN-72. 2000d, MD-11F. 6000d, RJ-85. 10,000d, B747-400F. 13,000d, Space shuttle carried by Boeing 747.

**1996, June 1**
**2714-2718** A679 Set of 5 4.50

**Souvenir Sheet**
***Perf. 13½***

**2719** A679 13,000d multicolored 2.75

Stamp Day A680

**1996, Aug. 15** ***Perf. 13***
**2720** A680 400d No. 1L57 (1-1) .25

Paintings by Nguyen Sáng (1923-88) A681

400d, Woman, vase of flowers (2-1). 8000d, Soldiers returning from battle (2-2).

**1996, Sept. 10** ***Perf. 13***
**2721-2722** A681 Set of 2 2.00

Hue School, Cent. — A682

400d, Women walking beside entrance (2-1). 3000d, View of portals, building (2-2).

**1996, Sept. 5**
**2723-2724** A682 Set of 2 .75

Mushrooms A683

Designs: 400d, Aleuria aurantia. 500d, Morchella conica. 1000d, Anthurus archeri. 4000d, Laetiporus serlphureus. 5000d, Filoboletus manipularis. 12,000d, Tremiscus helvelloides.

**1996, Aug. 26** **Litho.** ***Perf. 13***
**2725-2730** A683 Set of 6 5.25

Wild Animals — A684

Designs: a, 400d, Pygathrix nemacus. b, 2000d, Panthera tigris. c, 4000d, Rhinoceros sondaicus. d, 10,000d, Balearica regulorum.

**1996, Oct. 10** **Litho.** ***Perf. 13***
**2731** A684 Sheet of 4, #a.-d. 3.75

Taipei '96.

Campaign Promoting Iodized Salt — A685

**1996, Nov. 2** **Litho.** ***Perf. 13***
**2732** A685 400d multicolored .40

Natl. Liberation Movement, 50th Anniv. — A686

**1996, Dec. 19**
**2733** A686 400d multicolored .40

Fruit — A687

Designs: No. 2734, Hylocereus undatus. No. 2735, Durio zibethinus. No. 2736, Persea americana. No. 2737, Garcinia mangostana. No. 2738, Nephelium lappaceum.

**1997, Jan. 2** ***Perf. 13x13½***
**2734-2738** A687 400d Set of 5 .75

New Year 1997 (Year of the Ox) — A688

Stylized oxen: 400d, Adult, calf. 8000d, Adult.

**1997, Jan. 8** **Litho.** ***Perf. 13***
**2739-2740** A688 Set of 2 2.00

8th Vietnamese Communist Party Congress — A689

**1997, Feb. 3**
**2741** A689 400d multicolored .40

Goldfish A690

Various carassius auratus: 400d, 1000d, 5000d, 7000d, 8000d.

**1997, Feb. 5**
**2742-2746** A690 Set of 5 4.00

**Souvenir Sheet**
***Perf. 13½x14***

**2747** A690 14,000d multicolored 3.00

No. 2747 contains one 43x32mm stamp. Hong Kong '97 (#2747).

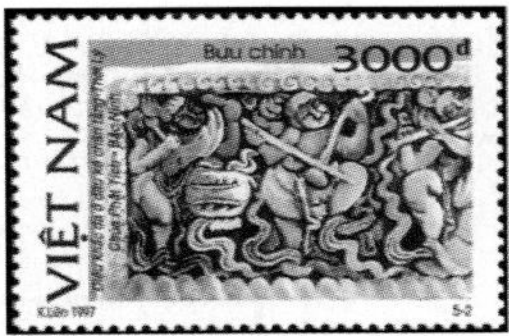
Sculptures from Ly Dynasty — A691

Designs: 400d, Serpents in round figure, vert. 1000d, Dragon head, vert. 3000d, People playing instruments. 5000d, Gargoyle. 10,000d, Dragon-head bowl.

**1997, Mar. 5**
**2748-2752** A691 Set of 5 4.50

Scenes — A692

Designs: 400d, Lake, people in park, Hà Tay. 5000d, Footbridge over river, Lai Chau. 7000d, Houses, fog, trees, Lào Cai.

**1997, Mar. 20**
**2753-2755** A692 Set of 3 3.00

Huynh Thuc Khang (1876-1947) A693

Disabled People in Sports — A694

**1997, Apr. 21** **Litho.** ***Perf. 13½x13***
**2756** A693 400d multi .35

**1997, Apr. 27** ***Perf. 13***

1000d, Tennis. 6000d, Shooting.

**2757-2758** A694 Set of 2 1.60

Wild Animals A695

400d, Chrotogale owstoni. 3000d, Lutra lutra. 4000d, Callosciurus erythraeus. 10,000d, Felis bangalensis.

**1997, May 2**
**2759-2762** A695 Set of 4 3.75

A696

A697

**1997, May 19**
**2763** A696 400d Women's Union .35

**1997, Apr. 15** **Litho.** ***Perf. 13***

Lilium longiflorum ?(Lilies): 400d, Red. 1000d, White. 5000d, Pink & white. 10,000d, Orange.

**2764-2767** A697 Set of 4 3.50

PACIFIC 97 — A698

Suspension bridges: 400d, Golden Gate, San Francisco. 5000d, Raippaluoto. 10,000d, Seto.

**1997, May 12**
**2768-2770** A698 Set of 3 3.25

Children
A699

400d, UN Convention on the Rights of the Child. 5000d, Breast milk is better.

**1997, June 1 Litho. *Perf. 13***
**With Gum**

**2771-2772** A699 Set of 2 1.25 1.25

Asian Sites Type of 1996

Designs: 400d, Pagoda, Hanoi, Viet Nam. 1000d, Ruins of Persepolis, Iran. 3000d, Statue of woman, Iraq. 5000d, Sacred Rock, Kyaikto, Burma. 10,000d, Statue of Buddha lying down, Sr. Lanka.

**1997, June 20 Litho. *Perf. 13***
**2773-2777** A670 Set of 5 4.25

Women's
Costumes
A700

Various costumes: 400d, Woman holding umbrella, San Chay. 2000d, Woman sewing, wearing jacket tied with sash, Dao quain trang. 5000d, Woman pumping water from well provided by UNICEF, Phù Lá. 10,000d, Woman holding hands in air, Kho Me.

**1997, July 8**
**2778-2781** A700 Set of 4 3.75

A701

A702

**1997, July 11**
**2782** A701 400d multicolored .35

Prevention of AIDS.

**1997, Aug. 8 Litho. *Perf. 13***
**2783** A702 400d multicolored .35

ASEAN, 30th anniv.

Monument to War Martyrs & Invalids, 50th Anniv. — A703

**1997, July 25**
**2784** A703 400d multicolored .35

Hibiscus — A704

a, 1000d, Hibiscus rosa sinensis. b, 3000d, Hibiscus schizopetalus. c, 5000d, Hibiscus syriacus (pink). d, 9000d, Hibiscus syriacus (yellow).

**1997, Aug. 1**
**2785** A704 Sheet of 4, #a.-d. 3.75

A705

A706

**1997, Aug. 26 Litho. *Perf. 13***
**2786** A705 400d multicolored .35

Post and Telecommunications Union, 50th anniv.

**1997, Sept. 4**

Sea horses: 400d, 1000d, Hippocampus (diff.). 3000d, Hippocampus guttulatus. 5000d, Hippocampus kelloggi. 6000d, Hippocampus japonicus. 7000d, Hippocampus hippocampus.

**2787-2792** A706 Set of 6 4.75

19th Southeast
Asian
Games — A707

**1997, Oct. 11 Litho. *Perf. 13***
**2793** A707 5000d multicolored 1.25

Handicrafts
A708

Designs: No. 2794, 400d, Lamp. No. 2795, 400d, Two baskets. No. 2796, 400d, Swan-shaped basket. No. 2797, 400d, Deer-shaped basket. 2000d, Basket with handle.

**1998, Jan. 1 Litho. *Perf. 13***
**2794-2798** A708 Set of 5 1.10

7th Francophone Summit, Hanoi — A709

**1997, Sept. 24 Litho. *Perf. 13½x13***
**2799** A709 5000d multicolored 2.25

Birds
A710

400d, Syrmaticus ellioti. 3000d, Lophura diardi. 5000d, Phasianus cholchicus. 6000d, Chrysolophus amherstiae. 8000d, Polyplectron germaini.
14,000d, Lophura imperialis.

**1997, Oct. 15 *Perf. 13***
**2800-2804** A710 Set of 5 4.75

**Souvenir Sheet**
***Perf. 13½***

**2805** A710 14,000d multicolored 2.75

No. 2805 contains one 43x30mm stamp.

New Year
1998 (Year of
the Tiger)
A711

Stylized tigers: 400d, Adult with young. 8000d, Adult.

**1998, Jan. 5 *Perf. 13***
**2806-2807** A711 Set of 2 1.75

Sites in
Vietnam
A712

Designs: No. 2808, 400d, Rocks, lake, Ninh Thuan. No. 2809, 400d, Lake, cavern, Quang Binh. 10,000d, Village of Quang Nam.

**1998, Feb. 2**
**2808-2810** A712 Set of 3 2.10

Communist
Manifesto, 150th
Anniv. — A713

**1998, Feb. 3**
**2811** A713 400d multicolored .35

Bonsai
A714

#2812, 400d, Limonia acidissima. #2813, 400d, Deeringia polysperma. #2814, 400d, Pinus merkusii, vert. 4000d, Barringtonia acutangula, vert. 6000d, Ficus elastica, vert. 10,000d, Wrightia religiosa, vert.
No. 2818, Adenium obesum.

**1998, Mar. 2**
**2812-2817** A714 Set of 6 4.25

**Souvenir Sheet**
***Perf. 13½***

**2818** A714 14,000d multicolored 2.60

No. 2818 contains one 43x32mm stamp.

Tet Offensive,
30th
Anniv. — A715

**1998, Jan. 30 Litho. *Perf. 13***
**2819** A715 400d multicolored .40

Opera — A716

Designs: a, 400d, Thi kính bi oan. b, 1000d, Thi mâu lên chúa. c, 2000d, Thi mâu-gia nô. d, 4000d, Thi me dôp-Xa trúong. e, 6000d, Thi kính bi phat va. f, 9000d, Thi kính xin sua.

**1998, Apr. 20**
**2820** A716 Sheet of 6, #a.-f, 4.50

Raptors A717

Designs: No. 2821, 400d, Pernis apivorus. No. 2822, 400d, Spizaetus ornatus. No. 2823, 400d, Accipter gentilis. 3000d, Buteo buteo. 5000d, Circus melanoleucas. 12,000d, Haliaeetus albicilla.

**1998, May 4 Litho. *Perf. 13***
**2821-2826** A717 Set of 6 4.10

Ho Chi Minh City (Saigon), 300th Anniv. — A718

400d, Tank, natl. flag, Ho Chi Minh as young man, building. 5000d, Monument to Ho Chi Minh, symbols of industry, communications, and transportation.

**1998, Apr. 30**
**2827-2828** A718 Set of 2 1.10

Orchids A719

Designs: 400d, Paphiopedilum appletonianum. 6000d, Paphiopedilum helenae.

**1998, May 18 Litho. *Perf. 13½***
**2829-2830** A719 Set of 2 1.40

Children's Paintings A720

UNICEF: 400d, Children, mother in front of home. 5000d, Children on playground.

**1998, June 1 *Perf. 13***
**2831-2832** A720 Set of 2 1.25

1998 World Cup Soccer Championships, France — A721

Various soccer plays: 400d, 5000d, 7000d.

**1998, June 10**
**2833-2835** A721 Set of 3 2.50

Sculptures of the Tran Dynasty A722

Ornate designs: No. 2836, 400d, Serpent. No. 2837, 400d, Two people. 1000d, Shown. 8000d, Person. 9000d, Face.

**1998, June 15 Litho. *Perf. 13***
**2836-2840** A722 Set of 5 3.50 3.50

A723

**1998, July 13**
**2841** A723 2000d multicolored .70 .70

Intl. Year of the Ocean A724

**1998, Aug. 1 Litho. *Perf. 13***
**2842** A724 400d multicolored .35 .35

Stamp Day — A725

**1998, Aug. 15**
**2843** A725 400d Bell's telephone .35 .35

Ton Duc Thang (1888-1980) A726

**1998, Aug. 20**
**2844** A726 400d multicolored .35 .35

Moths A727

Designs: No. 2845, 400d, Antheraea helferi. No. 2846, 400d, Attacus atlas. 4000d, Argema mittrei, vert. 10,000d, Argema maenas, vert.

**1998, Aug. 22**
**2845-2848** A727 Set of 4 3.25 3.25

Paintings by Te Bach Thach (Qi Baishi; 1863-1957) A728

Various paintings: 400d, Dragonfly & Lotus. 1000d, Chrysanthemum, Cock & Hens. 2000d, Shrimps, 1948. 4000d, Crabs. 6000d, Lotus & Mandarin Ducks. 9000d, Shrimps, 1949.

**1998, Sept. 16**
**2849-2854** A728 Set of 6 4.25 4.25

Legend of the Lake A729

Designs: No. 2855, Turtle with sword leading boat. No. 2856, Lake.

**1998, Oct. 10**
**2855-2856** A729 400d Set of 2 .70 .70

Le Thanh Tong (1442-1497) — A730

**1998, Oct. 12**
**2857** A730 400d multicolored .35 .35

Souvenir Sheet

Italia '98, Intl. Philatelic Exhibition — A731

Milan Cathedral. Illustration reduced.

**1998, Oct. 6 *Perf. 13½***
**2858** A731 16,000d multicolored 3.25 3.00

8th Trade Union Congress A732

**1998, Oct. 15 Litho. *Perf. 13***
**2859** A732 400d multicolored .35 .35

Quy Nhon City, 396th Anniv., Binh Dinh Province, Cent. — A733

**1998, Oct. 20**
**2860** A733 400d multicolored .35 .35

Buoi-Chu Van An Secondary School, 90th Anniv. — A734

Designs: 400d, Students outside school. 5000d, Students listening to speaker.

**1998, Nov. 20**
**2861-2862** A734 Set of 2 1.25 1.25

6th ASEAN Congress, Hanoi — A735

**1998, Dec. Litho. *Perf. 13***
**2863** A735 1000d multicolored .45 .45

Cuban Revolution, 40th Anniv. (in 1999) — A736

**1998, Dec. Litho. *Perf. 13***
**2864** A736 400d multicolored .30 .30

A737

Paintings: 400d, Birds, tree, flowers (Spring). 1000d, Flowers, ducks (Summer). 3000d, Flowers, rooster (Fall). 12,000d, Tree, flowers, deer & fawn (Winter).

**1999, Jan. 4 Litho. *Perf. 13½x13***
**2865-2868** A737 Set of 4 3.00 3.00

A738

New Year 1999 (Year of the Cat): 400d, Cat holding tree branch. 8000d, Two cats. 13,000d, Kittens, ball.

**1999, Jan. 6** ***Perf. 13½***
**2869-2870** A738 Set of 2 1.75 1.75

**Souvenir Sheet**

**2871** A738 13,000d multicolored 2.50 2.50

No. 2871 contains one 32x43mm stamp.

Kites — A739

400d, Large bird with long tail. 5000d, Crescent-shaped. 7000d, Bird with long legs.

**1999 Litho.** ***Perf. 13½x13***
**2872-2874** A739 Set of 3 2.25 2.25

Australia '99, World Stamp Expo A740

Various sailing vessels: #2875, 400d, (4-1). #2876, 400d, (4-2). 7000d, (4-3). 9000d, (4-4).

**1999, Mar. 10 Litho.** ***Perf. 13***
**2875-2878** A740 Set of 4 3.00 3.00

Medicinal Plants A741

Designs: No. 2879, 400d, Kaempferia galanga. No. 2880, 400d, Tacca chantrieri, vert. No. 2881, Alpinia galanga, vert. 6000d, Typhonium trilobatum, vert. 13,000d, Asarum maximum, vert.

**1999, Mar. 15**
**2879-2883** A741 Set of 5 3.75 3.75

Opera Masks A742

Various masks: 400d (6-1). 1000d (6-2). 2000d (6-3). 5000d (6-4). 6000d (6-5). 10,000d (6-6).

**1999, Apr. 16** ***Perf. 13½***
**2884-2889** A742 Set of 6 4.25 4.25

IBRA'99, World Philatelic Exhibition, Nuremberg A743

Octopuses: No. 2890, 400d, Octopus gibertianus. No. 2891, 400d, Philonexis catenulata. 4000d, Paroctopus yendol. 12,000d, Octopus vulgaris.

**1999, Apr. 20**
**2890-2893** A743 Set of 4 3.00 3.00

Landscape Paintings of Southern Viet Nam — A744

#2894, 400d, Sun over lake, Cà Mau. #2895, 400d, Rocks protruding out of water, Kien Giang. 12,000d, Traditional huts, Bac Lieu.

**1999, May 4** ***Perf. 13***
**2894-2896** A744 Set of 3 2.25 2.25

Asia-Pacific Telecommunity, 20th Anniv. — A745

**1999, May 10 Litho.** ***Perf. 13x13¼***
**2897** A745 400d multi .50 .50

Woodpeckers A746

Designs: 400d, Chrysocolaptes lucidus. 1000d, Picumnus innominatus. 3000d, Picus rabieri. 13,000d, Blythipicus pyrrhotis.

**1999, May 18 Litho.** ***Perf. 13***
**2898-2901** A746 Set of 4 3.00 3.00

UNICEF A747

Designs: 400d, Girl, hand. 5000d, Boy carrying factory.

**1999, June 1 Litho.** ***Perf. 13***
**2902-2903** A747 Set of 2 1.00 1.00

Architecture of Late 19th and Early 20th Centuries — A748

Designs: No. 2904, 400d, Government Office Building, Hanoi (3-1). No. 2905, 400d, History Museum, Ho Chi Minh City (3-2). 12,000d, Duc Ba Cathedral (3-3). 15,000d, Theater, Hanoi.

**1999, June 10** ***Perf. 13***
**2904-2906** A748 Set of 3 2.25 2.25

**Souvenir Sheet**

***Perf. 13½x14***

**2907** A748 15,000d multi 2.75 2.75

PhilexFrance '99 (No. 2907). No. 2907 contains one 44x32mm stamp.

Intl. Day to Stop Drug Abuse A749

**1999, June 24 Litho.** ***Perf. 13***
**2908** A749 400d multicolored .35 .35

Da Rang Bridge, Phu Yen A750

**1999, July 1 Litho.** ***Perf. 13***
**2909** A750 400d multi .40 .40

Le Dynasty Sculptures — A751

Designs: No. 2910, 1000d, Man Against Tiger (5-1). No. 2911, 1000d, Phoenix (5-2). 3000d, Playing Chess, vert. (5-3). 7000d, Hostler, vert. (5-4). 9000d, Dragon (5-5).

**1999, July 1**
**2910-2914** A751 Set of 5 3.75 3.75

Birth of World's Six Billionth Person — A752

**1999, Aug. 2**
**2915** A752 400d multi .35 .35

Chinese Landscapes — A753

Designs: 400d, Park, Beijing (4-1). 2000d, Scenic overlook, Anhwei (4-2). 3000d, Park, Shandong, (4-3). 10,000d, Park, Beijing, diff. (4-4).
14,000d, Great Wall of China.

**1999, Aug. 16** ***Perf. 13***
**2916-2919** A753 Set of 4 3.00 3.00

**Souvenir Sheet**

***Perf. 13½x14***

**2920** A753 14,000d multi 2.50 2.50

China 1999 World Philatelic Exhibition (No. 2920). No. 2920 contains one 43x32mm stamp.

Boat Races A754

Races from regions: 400d, North (3-1). 2000d, Central (3-2). 10,000d, South (3-3).

**1999, Sept. 10** ***Perf. 13***
**2921-2923** A754 Set of 3 2.25 2.25

Women's Costumes A755

Various costumes. #2924, 400d (3-1). #2925, 400d (3-2). #2926, 12,000d (3-3).

**1999, Sept. 10**
**2924-2926** A755 Set of 3 2.25 2.25

Buffalo Fighting Festivals A756

Fighting buffaloes: 400d, (2-1). 5000d, (2-2).

**1999, Sept. 15**
**2927-2928** A756 Set of 2 1.00 1.00

Ngo Quyen (898-944), General — A757

**1999, Oct. 21**
**2929** A757 400d multi .35 .35

Nguyen Van Sieu (1799-1872), Teacher, Writer — A758

**1999, Nov. 2 Litho.** ***Perf. 13***
**2930** A758 400d multi .35 .35

Tran Xuan Soan (1849-1923), Anti-colonial Leader — A759

**1999, Nov. 24**
**2931** A759 400d multi .35 .35

United Nations Development Program — A760

Designs: 400d, Mother and child, farmer, fisherman. 8000d, Villagers, buildings.

**1999, Dec. 3**
**2932-2933** A760 Set of 2 1.75 1.75

Viet Nam in the 20th Century — A761

Designs; No. 2934, 400d, Founding of Viet Nam Communist Party (6-1). No. 2935, 400d, Ho Chi Minh's declaration of country's independence (6-2). No. 2936, 1000d, Conquest of South Viet Nam (6-3). No. 2937, 1000d, People, dam, high tension wire tower, atom (6-4). 8000d, People, satellite, satellite dish, dam, high tension wire tower (6-5). 12,000d, Organizations Viet Nam belongs to (6-6).

**2000, Jan. 1 Litho. *Perf. 13***
**With Gum**
**2934-2939** A761 Set of 6 3.75 3.75
*2939a* Sheet, #2934-2939, without gum 4.00 4.00

New Year 2000 (Year of the Dragon) A762

Dragon: 400d, Facing right (2-1). 8000d, Facing right (2-2).

**2000, Jan. 3 *Perf. 13½***
**With Gum**
**2940-2941** A762 Set of 2 1.75 1.75

Intl. Year of Culture and Peace A763

**2000, Jan. 18 With Gum**
**2942** A763 400d multi .35 .35

Viet Nam Communist Party, 70th Anniv. — A764

#2943, Ho Chi Minh (1890-1969), Pres. (8-1). #2944, Tran Phu (1904-31), 1st Gen. Sec. (8-2). #2945, Le Hong Phong (1902-42), Gen. Sec. (8-3). #2946, Ha Huy Tap (1902-41), Gen. Sec. (8-4). #2947, Nguyen Van Cu (1912-41), Gen. Sec. (8-5). #2948, Truong Chinh (1907-88), Gen. Sec. (8-6). #2949, Le Duan (1907-86), Gen. Sec. (8-7). #2950, Nguyen Van Linh (1915-98), Gen. Sec. (8-8).

**2000, Feb. 2 *Perf. 13***
**With Gum**
**2943-2950** A764 400d Set of 8 1.50 1.50

Cockfighting — A765

Postures: No. 2951, 400d, Song long cuoc (4-1). No. 2952, 400d, Long vu da dao (4-2). 7000d, Song long phuong hoang (4-3). 9000d, Nhan o giap chien (4-4).

**2000, Feb. 8 Litho. *Perf. 13***
**2951-2954** A765 Set of 4 3.50 3.50
Imperf., #2951-2954 5.75

Bangkok 2000 Stamp Exhibition A766

Palanquins: 400d, Imperial court roofed palanquin (3-1). 7000d, Palanquin without roof (3-2). 8000d, Roofed palanquin (3-3).
15,000d, Palanquin in procession.

**2000, Mar. 10 With Gum**
**2955-2957** A766 Set of 3 3.25 3.25
**Souvenir Sheet**
**2958** A766 15,000d multi 3.25 3.25

Legend of Lac Long Quan and Au Co — A767

Designs: No. 2959, 400d, Lang Long Quan and Au Co marry (6-1). No. 2960, 400d, Au Co, gives birth to 100 sons (6-2). 500d, Au Co takes 50 children to forest (6-3). 3000d, Lac Long Quan takes 50 children to sea (6-4). 4000d, Eldest son, Hung Vuong ascends to throne (6-5). 11,000d, Vietnamese ethnic groups as descendents (6-6).

**2000, Apr. 4 *Perf. 13½***
**2959-2964** A767 Set of 6 4.00 4.00

Souvenir Sheet

The Stamp Show 2000, London — A768

No. 2965 — Fire engines: a, 400d, Iveco Magirus, Germany. b, 1000d, Hino, Japan. c, 5000d, ZIL 103E, Russia. d, 12,000d, FPS.32 Camiva, France.
Illustration reduced.

**2000, May 15 *Perf. 13***
**2965** A768 Sheet of 4, #a-d 3.50 3.50

Worldwide Fund for Nature A769

Pseudoryx nghetinhensis: No. 2966, 400d, Head, vine (4-1). No. 2967, 400d, In grass (4-2). 5000d, Near pond (4-3). 10,000d, Head, mountains (4-4).

**2000, May 18 *Perf. 13½***
**With Gum**
**2966-2969** A769 Set of 4 6.50 6.50
*2969a* Sheet, 2 each #2966-2969 5.50 5.50

Ho Chi Minh (1890-1969) A770

**2000, May 19 *Perf. 13***
**With Gum**
**2970** A770 400d multi .35 .35

World Stamp Expo 2000, Anaheim A771

Water puppets: No. 2971, 400d, Chu teu (6-1). No. 2972, 400d, Fairy (6-2). No. 2973, 400d, Man plowing field (6-3). 3000d, Female peasant (6-4). 9000d, Drummer (6-5). 11,000d, Fisherman (6-6).

**2000, June 28 *Perf. 13½***
**2971-2976** A771 Set of 6 4.50 4.50

50th Vietnam Youth Volunteers' Day — A772

**2000, July 15 *Perf. 13***
**With Gum**
**2977** A772 400d multi .35 .35

Phu Dong Natl. Youth Sports Festival A773

**2000, July 20 With Gum**
**2978** A773 400d multi .35 .35

Fish A774

Designs: No. 2979, 400d, Cephalopholis miniatus (6-1). No. 2980, 400d, Pomacanthus imperator (6-2). No. 2981, 400d, Epinephelus merra (6-3). 4000d, Zancius cornutus, vert. (6-4). 6000d, Chaetodon ephippium, vert. (6-5). 12,000d, Heniochus acuminatus, vert. (6-6).
15,000d, Chaetodon lunula.

**2000, Aug. 7 *Perf. 13***
**2979-2984** A774 Set of 6 4.00 4.00
**Souvenir Sheet**
***Perf. 13½x13¾***
**2985** A774 15,000d multi 2.75 2.75

Post and Telegraph Dept., 55th Anniv. A775

**2000, Aug. 15 *Perf. 13***
**With Gum**
**2986** A775 400d multi .35 .35

People's Police, 50th Anniv. A776

Designs: 400d, Ho Chi Minh, five policemen. 2000d, Policeman checking documents, vert.

**2000, Aug. 19 Litho. *Perf. 13***
**With Gum**
**2987-2988** A776 Set of 2 .55 .55

Gen. Nguyen Tri Phuong, 200th Anniv. of Birth — A777

**2000, Aug. 31 *Perf. 13½***
**With Gum**
**2989** A777 400d multi .35 .35

UN Right of the Child Conference, 10th Anniv. — A778

Emblem and: 400d, Boy and girl. 5000d, Five children, vert.

**2000, Sept. 8** ***Perf. 13***
**2990-2991** A778 Set of 2 1.25 1.25

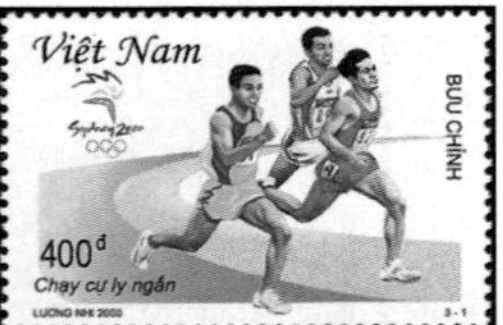

2000 Summer Olympics, Sydney — A779

Designs: 400d, Running. 6000d, Shooting. 7000d, Taekwondo, vert.

**2000, Sept. 15**
**2992-2994** A779 Set of 3 2.25 2.25

Gen. Tran Hung Dao, 700th Anniv. of Death. — A780

**2000, Sept. 17** **With Gum**
**2995** A780 400d multi .35 .35

Birds — A781

Designs: No. 2996, 400d, Leiothrix argentauris. No. 2997, 400d, Pitta ellioti. No. 2998, 400d, Pomatorinus ferruginosus. 5000d, Dicrurus paradiceus, vert. 7000d, Melanochlora sultanea, vert. 10,000d, Stachyris striolata, vert.

**2000, Sept. 28** ***Perf. 13½***
**2996-3001** A781 Set of 6 4.50 4.50

**Souvenir Sheet**

***Perf. 13½x13¾***

**3002** A781 15,000d Trena puella 2.75 2.75

No. 3002 contains one 42x31mm stamp. España 2000 Intl. Philatelic Exhibition (No. 3002).

Vietnam Philately Association, 40th Anniv. — A782

**2000, Oct. 6** ***Perf. 13***

**With Gum**

**3003** A782 400d No. 820 .35 .35

Farmer's Association, 70th Anniv. — A783

**2000, Oct. 14** **With Gum**
**3004** A783 400d multi .35 .35

Women's Union, 70th Anniv. A784

**2000, Oct. 14** **With Gum**
**3005** A784 400d multi .35 .35

Hanoi, 990th Anniv. A785

Designs: 400d, Building, and Ly Thai To, founder of Hanoi. 3000d, Temple, two people, monuments. 10,000d, Peasants with goods, building.
15,000d, People and doves.

**2000, Oct. 15** ***Perf. 13***
**3006-3008** A785 Set of 3 2.25 2.25

**Souvenir Sheet**

***Perf. 13½x13¾***

**3009** A785 15,000d multi 2.75 2.75

Bats — A786

Designs: No. 3010, 400d, Scotmanes ornatus. No. 3011, 400d, Pteropus lylei. 2000d, Rhinolophus paradoxolophus. 6000d, Eonycteris spelaea. 11,000d, Cynopterus sphinx.

**2000, Oct. 16** ***Perf. 13***
**3010-3014** A786 Set of 5 3.25 3.25

Fatherland Front, 70th Anniv. — A787

**2000, Oct. 18** **With Gum**
**3015** A787 400d multi .35 .35

6th Natl. Emulation Congress A788

Designs: 400d, People at work. 3000d, Symbols of industry, vert.

**2000, Nov. 10** **With Gum**
**3016-3017** A788 Set of 2 .90 .90

Flowers A789

Designs: 400d, Oxyspora sp. 5000d, Melanstoma villosa, vert.

**2000, Nov. 15** ***Perf. 13½***

**With Gum**

**3018-3019** A789 Set of 2 1.25 1.25

Hon Khoai Uprising, 60th Anniv. A790

**2000, Dec. 13** ***Perf. 13***

**With Gum**

**3020** A790 400d multi .35 .35

Advent of New Millennium A791

**2001, Jan. 1** **With Gum**
**3021** A791 400d multi .35 .35

New Year 2001 (Year of the Snake) A792

Snake and: 400d, Pink flowers. 8000d, Yellow flowers.

**2001, Jan. 1** ***Perf. 13½***

**With Gum**

**3022-3023** A792 Set of 2 1.60 1.60

Hong Kong 2001 Stamp Exhibition — A793

Fish: 400d, Toxotes microlepis. 800d, Cosmocheilus harmandi. 2000d, Anguilla bicolor pacifica. 3000d, Chitala ornata. 7000d, Megalops cyprinoides. 8000d, Probarbus jullieni.

**2001, Jan. 18** **Litho.** ***Perf. 13***
**3024-3029** A793 Set of 6 3.50 3.50

Nobel Prize, Cent. A794

**2001, Jan. 27** ***Perf. 13½***

**With Gum**

**3030** A794 400d multi .35 .35

Four Seasons — A795

No. 3031: a, 400d, Peach blossoms and birds (spring). b, 800d, Cotton rose and pheasant (summer). c, 4000d, Chrysanthemum and phoenix (autumn). d, 10,000d, Pine tree and cranes (winter).

**2001, Feb. 1** ***Perf. 13¼x13***

**With Gum**

**3031** A795 Sheet of 4, #a-d 2.75 2.75

Wild Fruits — A796

Designs: No. 3032, 400d, Rubus cochinchinensis. No. 3033, 400d, Rhizophora mucronata. No. 3034, 400d, Podocarpus neriifolius. No. 3035, 400d, Magnolia pumila. 15,000d, Taxus chinensis.

**2001, Feb. 8** ***Perf. 13½***

**With Gum**

**3032-3036** A796 Set of 5 2.60 2.60

Landscapes — A797

Designs: No. 3037, 400d, Co Tien Mountain (3-1). No. 3038, 400d, Dong Pagoda, Yen Tu Mountain (3-2). 10,000d, King Dinh Temple (3-3).

**2001, Feb. 23** ***Perf. 13***
**3037-3039** A797 Set of 3 2.00 2.00

Nhan Dan Newspaper, 50th Anniv. — A798

**2001, Mar. 11** **With Gum**
**3040** A798 400d multi .35 .35

Rubies Found in Tan Huong A799

Designs: 400d, 1960-gram ruby. 6000d, 2160-gram "Viet Nam Star."

**2001, Mar. 20** **With Gum**
**3041-3042** A799 Set of 2 1.10 1.10

Ho Chi Minh Youth Union, 70th Anniv. — A800

**2001, Mar. 26 Litho.** ***Perf. 13***
**With Gum**
**3043** A800 400d multi .35 .35

9th Communist Party Congress — A801

Designs: 400d, Ho Chi Minh, flag, map (2-1). 3000d, Hammer and sickle, Ngoc Lu bronze drum head, symbols of technology, vert (2-2).

**2001, Apr. 18** **With Gum**
**3044-3045** A801 Set of 2 .55 .55

Fauna in Cat Tien Natl. Park — A802

Designs: 400d, Arborophila davidi (4-1). 800d, Stichophthalma uemurai (4-2). 3000d, Rhinoceros sondaicus (4-3). 5000d, Crocodylus siamensis (4-4).

**2001, Apr. 30** ***Perf. 13½***
**3046-3049** A802 Set of 4 2.25 2.25

Mushrooms A803

Designs: No. 3050, 400d, Phallus indusiatus (7-1). No. 3051, 400d, Aseroe arachnoidea (7-2). No. 3052, 400d, Phallus tenuis (7-3). 2000d, Phallus impudicus (7-4). 5000d, Phallus rugulosus (7-5). 6000d, Simblum periphragmoides (7-6). 7000d, Mutinus bambusinus (7-7).

**2001, May 2**
**3050-3056** A803 Set of 7 4.00 4.00

A number has been reserved for a souvenir sheet for this set.

**Mushrooms Type of 2001**

Design: 13,000d, Pseudocolus schellenbergiae.

**2001, May 2 Litho.** ***Perf. 13½x13¾***
**3057** A803 13,000d multi 2.75 2.75

No. 3057 contains one 42x31mm stamp.

Ho Chi Minh Young Pioneer's League, 60th Anniv. — A804

**2001, May 15 Litho.** ***Perf. 13***
**With Gum**
**3058** A804 400d multi .35 .35

Viet Minh Front, 60th Anniv. A805

**2001, May 19** **With Gum**
**3059** A805 400d multi .35 .35

Campaign Against Smoking — A806

**2001, May 30** ***Perf. 13¼x13½***
**With Gum**
**3060** A806 800d multi .45 .45

Children A807

Designs: 400d, Two children, UNICEF emblem. 5000d, Five children, UN emblem.

**2001, June 1** ***Perf. 13½***
**3061-3062** A807 Set of 2 1.10 1.10

Children's safety day (#3061); UN Special Session on Children, Washington, DC (#3062).

Diesel Locomotives — A808

Designs: No. 3063, 400d, D18E (6-1). No. 3064, 400d, D4H (6-2). 800d, D11H (6-3). 2000d, D5H (6-4). 6000d, D9E (6-5). 7000d, D12E (6-6).

**2001, June 5** ***Perf. 13***
**3063-3068** A808 Set of 6 3.50 3.50

**Souvenir Sheet**
***Perf. 13½x13¾***
**3069** A808 13,000d D11H, diff. 2.75 2.75

No. 3069 contains one 43x32mm stamp.

Orchids A809

Designs: No. 3070, 800d, Vanda sp. (6-1). No. 3071, 800d, Dendrobium lowianum (6-2). No. 3072, 800d, Phajus wallichii (6-3). No. 3073, 800d, Habenaria medioflexa (6-4). No. 3074, 800d, Arundina graminifolia, vert. (6-5). 12,000d, Calanthe clavata, vert. (6-6).

***Perf. 13½x13¼, 13¼x13½***
**2001, July 5**
**With Gum**
**3070-3075** A809 Set of 6 3.25 3.25

Phila Nippon '01 — A810

Butterflies: No. 3076, 800d, Troides aeacus (6-1). No. 3077, 800d, Inachis io (6-2). No. 3078, 800d, Ancyluris formosissima (6-3). 5000d, Cymothoe sanguris (6-4). 7000d, Taenaris selene (6-5). 10,000d, Trogonoptera brookiana (6-6).
13,000d, Atrophaneura horishanus, vert.

**2001, July 16** ***Perf. 13½x13¼***
**3076-3081** A810 Set of 6 4.00 4.00

**Souvenir Sheet**
***Perf. 13¾x13½***
**3082** A810 13,000d multi 2.75 2.75

No. 3082 contains one 32x42mm stamp.

2002 World Cup Soccer Championships, Japan and Korea — A811

No. 3083: a, 800d, Player with red shirt. b, 3000d, Player with white shirt.

**2001, July 24** ***Perf. 13***
**With Gum**
**3083** A811 Horiz. pair, #a-b .90 .90

Musical Instruments — A812

Designs: No. 3084, 800d, Ho gáo (6-1). No. 3085, 800d, Kenh (6-2). No. 3086, 800d, Dàn tú, vert. (6-3). 2000d, Dàn t'rung, vert. (6-4). 6000d, Trong kinang, vert . (6-5). 9000d, Tính tau, vert. (6-6).

***Perf. 13x13¼, 13¼x13***
**2001, Aug. 4** **Litho.**
**3084-3089** A812 Set of 6 3.25 3.25

Year of Dialogue Among Civilizations — A813

**2001, Oct. 9 Litho.** ***Perf. 13¼x13½***
**With Gum**
**3090** A813 800d multi .45 .45

Tran Huy Lieu (1901-69), Writer — A814

**2001, Nov. 5** ***Perf. 13x12¾***
**With Gum**
**3091** A814 800d multi .45 .45

Nam Cao (1917-51), Writer A815

**2001, Nov. 30** ***Perf. 13x13¼***
**With Gum**
**3092** A815 800d multi .45 .45

A816 A817

**2001** ***Perf. 13½***
**With Gum**
**3093** A816 800d multi .25 .25
**3094** A817 3000d multi .65 .65

New Year 2002 (Year of the Horse) A818

Horse facing: 800d, Right. 8000d, Left. 14,000d, Horse galloping.

**2002, Jan. 2** ***Perf. 13½***
**With Gum**
**3095-3096** A818 Set of 2 1.40 1.40

**Souvenir Sheet**
***Perf. 13½x13¼***
**3097** A818 14,000d multi 2.75 2.75

No. 3097 contains one 42x31mm stamp.

Opera Costumes A819

Designs: No. 3098, 1000d, Giáp Tuong Nam (6-1). No. 3099, 1000d, Giáp Tuong Nu (6-2). 2000d, Giáp Tuong Phan Dien (6-3). 3000d, Long Chan (6-4). 5000d, Giáp Tuong Phien (6-5). 9000d, Lung Xiem Quan Giáp (6-6).

**2002, Jan. 15** ***Perf. 13***
**3098-3103** A819 Set of 6 3.25 3.25

Vo Thi Sáu, Heroine, 50th Anniv. of Death A820

**2002, Jan. 23** ***Perf. 13x13¼***

**3104** A820 1000d multi .45 .45

Program Implementation of 9th Communist Party Congress A821

Designs: 800d, Map, satellite, buildings, dam, power lines, bridge, computer keyboard (2-1). 3000d, Flag, building, doves, people (2-2).

**2002, Feb. 1** ***Perf. 13¼x13***
**With Gum**

**3105-3106** A821 Set of 2 .90 .90

Cacti — A822

Designs: No. 3107, 1000d, Echinocereus albatus (5-1). No. 3108, 1000d, Echinocereus delaetii (5-2). No. 3109, 1000d, Cylindropuntia bigelowii (5-3). 5000d, Echinocereus triglochidatus (5-4). 10,000d, Epiphyllum truncatum (5-5).

**2002, Feb. 18** ***Perf. 13¼x13½***

**3107-3111** A822 Set of 5 3.00 3.00

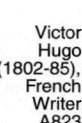

Victor Hugo (1802-85), French Writer A823

**2002, Feb. 26** ***Perf. 13x13¼***
**With Gum**

**3112** A823 1000d multi .45 .45

A824

**2002** **Litho.** ***Perf. 13x13¼***
**With Gum**

**3113** A824 800d multi .45 .45

Birds — A825

Designs: 600d, Actinodura sodangorum (6-1). No. 3115, 800d, Garrulax ngoclinhensis (6-2). No. 3116, 800d, Garrulax pectoralis (6-3). No. 3117, 800d, Pomatorhinus hypoleucos (6-4). 5000d, Minla ignotincta (6-5). 8000d, Minla cyanouroptera (6-6).

**2002, Mar. 15** **Litho.** ***Perf. 13½***
**With Gum**

**3114-3119** A825 Set of 6 2.75 2.75

Landscapes A826

Designs: No. 3120, 800d, Ganh Son, Binh Thuan (3-1). No. 3121, 800d, Dawn over Tung Estuary, Quang Tri (3-2). 10,000d, Sa Huynh Harbor, Quang Ngai (3-3).

**2002, Mar. 15** **With Gum**

**3120-3122** A826 Set of 3 2.00 2.00

Primates — A827

Designs: 600d, Trachypithecus poliocephalus (8-1). 800d, Trachypithecus delacouri (8-2). 1000d, Rhinopithecus avunculus (8-3). 2000d, Pygathrix cinerea (8-4). 4000d, Nomascus concolor (8-5). 5000d, Trachypithecus laotum hatinhensis (8-6). 7000d, Trachypithecus phayrei (8-7). 9000d, Pygathrix nemaeus (8-8).

**2002, Apr. 10**

**3123-3130** A827 Set of 8 4.50 4.50
*3130a* Souvenir sheet, #3123-3130 + label 4.50 4.50

Bui Thi Xuan, 200th Anniv. of Death — A828

**2002, Apr. 13** ***Perf. 13***
**With Gum**

**3131** A828 1000d multi .45 .45

Souvenir Sheet

2002 World Cup Soccer Championships, Japan and Korea — A829

Color of player or players: a, 1000d, Blue. b, 2000d, Red. c, 5000d, Red violet. d, 7000d, Green.

**2002, June 1** **Litho.**
**With Gum**

**3132** A829 Sheet of 4, #a-d 2.75 2.75

Flowers — A830

Designs: 600d, Paphiopedilum concolor (7-1). 800d, Sterculia lanceolata (7-2). 1000d, Schefflera alongensis (7-3). 2000d, Hibiscus tiliaceus (7-4). 3000d, Mussaenda glabra (7-5). 5000d, Boniodendron parviflorum (7-6). 9000d, Bauhinia ornata.

**2002, June 5**

**3133-3139** A830 Set of 7 3.25 3.25

Chau Van Liem, Communist Party Leader, Cent. of Birth — A831

**2002, June 28** **Litho.** ***Perf. 13***
**With Gum**

**3140** A831 800d multi .45 .45

Stamp Day — A832

**2002, July 1** ***Perf. 13x12¾***
**With Gum**

**3141** A832 800d multi + label .45 .45

Tay Nguyen Province A833

**2002, July 10** **Litho.** ***Perf. 13***
**With Gum**

**3142** A833 800d multi .20 .20

Soft-shell Turtles A834

Designs: 800d, Pelochelys bibroni (4-1). 2000d, Pelodiscus sinensis. 5000d, Palea steindachneri. 9000d, Trionyx cartilagineus.

**2002, July 15** **Litho.** ***Perf. 13½***

**3143-3146** A834 Set of 4 2.60 2.60
*3146a* Souvenir sheet, 2 each #3143-3146 5.25 5.25

Viet Nam — Laos Diplomatic Relations, 40th Anniv. A835

**2002, July 18** ***Perf. 13***
**With Gum**

**3147** A835 800d multi .45 .45

Civil Aircraft A836

Designs: 800d, Super King Air B200 in air (4-1). 2000d, Fokker 70 (4-2). 3000d, ATR-72 (4-3). 8000d, Boeing 767-300 (4-4).
14,000d, Super King Air B200 on ground.

**2002, Aug. 1** ***Perf. 13***
**With Gum**

**3148-3151** A836 Set of 4 2.25 2.25

**Souvenir Sheet**
***Perf. 13½x13¾***

**3152** A836 14,000d multi 2.25 2.25

Autumn Festival Lanterns A837

Designs: No. 3153, 800d, Den Ong Sao (4-1). No. 3154, 800d, Den Ong Su (4-2). 2000d, Den Con Tho Om Trang (4-3). 7000d, Den Xep (4-4).

**2002, Aug. 16** ***Perf. 13½***
**With Gum**

**3153-3156** A837 Set of 4 1.50 1.50

Viet Nam Posts and Telecommunications Trade Union, 55th Anniv. — A838

**2002, Aug. 23** ***Perf. 13***
**With Gum**

**3157** A838 800d multi .35 .35

Bridges — A839

Designs: No. 3158, 800d, Cau Long Bien (4-1). No. 3159, 800d, Cau Song Han (4-2). 2000d, Cau Truong Tien (4-3). 10,000d, Cau My Thuan (4-4).

**2002, Sept. 27** *Perf. 13x13¼*
**With Gum**
**3158-3161** A839 Set of 4 2.00 2.00

Communist Party's Ideology and Culture Commission, 72nd Anniv. — A840

**2002, Oct. 10** *Perf. 13*
**With Gum**
**3162** A840 800d multi .35 .35

Hanoi Medical University, Cent. A841

**2002, Nov. 15** **With Gum**
**3163** A841 800d multi .35 .35

Teachers' Day — A842

**2002, Nov. 20** **With Gum**
**3164** A842 800d multi .35 .35

New Year 2003 (Year of the Ram) — A843

Various goats with background colors of: 800d, Rose pink (2-1). 8000d, Orange (2-2).

**2002, Dec. 15** *Perf. 13½*
**With Gum**
**3165-3166** A843 Set of 2 1.25 1.25

Viet Nam — South Korea Diplomatic Relations, 10th Anniv. — A844

Pagoda from: No. 3167, 800d, Viet Nam (2-1). No. 3168, 800d, South Korea (2-2).

**2002, Dec. 21** *Perf. 13*
**With Gum**
**3167-3168** A844 Set of 2 .65 .65

Starting with the 2003 issues, stamps are gummed unless otherwise indicated.

Landscapes — A845

Designs: 800d, Rung Cao Su, Bình Phuoc (3-1). 3000d, Ao Bà Om, Trà Vinh (3-2). 7000d, Mot nhahn song Rach Gam-Xoài Mút, Tien Giang (3-3).

**2003, Feb. 1** **Litho.** *Perf. 13*
**3169-3171** A845 Set of 3 1.40 1.40

Viet Nam Culture Program, 60th Anniv. — A846

**2003, Feb. 3**
**3172** A846 800d multi .30 .30

Viet Nam Cinema Association, 50th Anniv. — A847

**2003, Mar. 1**
**3173** A847 1000d multi .30 .30

Khanh Hoa Province, 350th Anniv. A848

**2003, Mar. 25**
**3174** A848 800d multi .30 .30

Cycle Rickshaws A849

Cycle rickshaws from: 800d, Hanoi. 3000d, Ho Chi Minh City. 8000d, Haiphong.

**2003, Apr. 1**
**3175-3177** A849 Set of 3 1.60 1.60

Adventures of the Cricket — A850

**2003, May 1** *Perf. 13¼x13½*
**3178** Horiz. strip of 6 2.60 2.60
*a.* A850 800d Toi là út. . . (6-1) .20 .20
*b.* A850 1000d Chang bao. . . (6-2) .20 .20
*c.* A850 2000d Toi an han. . . (6-3) .25 .25
*d.* A850 3000d Toi và Trui. . . (6-4) .40 .40
*e.* A850 5000d Mot ngày. . . (6-5) .65 .65
*f.* A850 8000d Tu nay the. . . (6-6) 1.00 1.00

Animals in Ba Vi National Park — A851

Designs: No. 3179, 800d, Manis pentadactyla (4-1). No. 3180, 800d, Petaurista petaurista (4-2). 5000d, Selenarctos thibetanus (4-3). 10,000d, Capricornis sumatraensis (4-4).

**2003, June 5** *Perf. 13½*
**3179-3182** A851 Set of 4 2.25 2.25

22nd South East Asian Games, Viet Nam — A852

Designs: 800d, Soccer (4-1). 2000d, Hurdles (4-2). 3000d, Kayaking (4-3). 7000d, Wrestling (4-4).
10,000d, Games emblem, mascot, stadium.

**2003, July 1** *Perf. 13*
**3183-3186** A852 Set of 4 1.75 1.75
**Souvenir Sheet**
*Perf. 13½x13¾*
**3187** A852 10,000d multi 1.25 1.25

Ninth Congress of Viet Nam Federation of Trade Unions — A853

**2003, July 28** *Perf. 13*
**3188** A853 800d multi .30 .30

Camellias — A854

Designs: 800d, Camellia petelotii (4-1). 1000d, Camellia rubriflora (4-2). 5000d, Camellia vietnamensis (4-3). 6000d, Camellia gilberti (4-4).

**2003, Sept. 1** *Perf. 13½*
**3189-3192** A854 Set of 4 1.75 1.75

Bangkok 2003 World Philatelic Exhibition.

Orchids A855

Designs: 800d, Paphiopedilum dianthum (2-1). 8000d, Pleione bulbocodioides (2-2).

**2003, Oct. 1** *Perf. 13*
**3193-3194** A855 Set of 2 1.10 1.10

Asian Elephants A856

Designs: 800d, Elephant with trunk extended (4-1). 1000d, Elephants and riders (4-2). 2000d, Elephant with trunk down (4-3). 8000d, Two elephants (4-4)

**2003, Oct. 1** *Perf. 13½*
**3195-3198** A856 Set of 4 1.50 1.50
*3198a* Miniature sheet, 2 each #3195-3198 3.00 3.00

My Son World Heritage Site — A857

Various ruins: 800d, (3-1). 3000d, (3-2). 8000d (3-3).
10,000d, Temple (43x32mm).
Illustration reduced.

**2003, Dec. 1** *Perf. 13x13¼*
**3199-3201** A857 Set of 3 1.50 1.50
**Souvenir Sheet**
*Perf. 13½x13¾*
**3202** A857 10,000d multi 1.25 1.25

New Year 2004 (Year of the Monkey) A858

Monkeys and: 800d, Apple tree (2-1). 8000d, Palm leaf (2-2).

**2003, Dec. 1** *Perf. 13½*
**3203-3204** A858 Set of 2 1.10 1.10

Ngo Gia Tu (1908-35), Leader of 1926 Strike — A859

**2003, Dec. 30** *Perf. 13¼x13*
**3205** A859 800d multi .30 .30

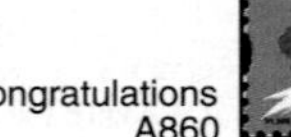

Congratulations A860

Designs: 800d, Flowers (2-1). 8000d, Bird with envelope (2-2).

**2004, Jan. 1** ***Perf. 13 Syncopated***
**3206-3207** A860 Set of 2 1.10 1.10

Shells A861

Designs: 800d, Murex trocheli (3-1). 3000d, Murex haustellum (3-2). 8000d, Chicoreus ramosus (3-3).

**2004, Feb. 1** ***Perf. 13***
**3208-3210** A861 Set of 3 1.50 1.50

Bamboo Lamps — A862

Various lamps with background colors of: 400d, Yellow (3-1). 1000d, Pale green (3-2). 7000d, Buff (3-3).

***Perf. 13 Syncopated***
**2004, Mar. 1** **Litho.**
**3211-3213** A862 Set of 3 1.10 1.10

Hué, UNESCO World Heritage Site — A863

Designs: 800d, Pavilion of Edicts (3-1). 4000d, Ngo Mon Gate (3-2). No. 3216, 8000d, Hien Lam Pavilion (3-3).
No. 3217, 8000d, Thai Hoa Palace.

**2004, Apr. 1** ***Perf. 13***
**Stamp + Label**
**3214-3216** A863 Set of 3 1.75 1.75
**Souvenir Sheet**
***Perf. 13½x13¾***
**3217** A863 8000d multi 1.00 1.00

No. 3217 contains one 42x31mm stamp.

Tran Phu (1904-31), Communist Leader — A864

**2004, May 1** ***Perf. 13***
**3218** A864 800d multi .30 .30

Battle of Dien Bien Phu, 50th Anniv. A865

Designs: 800d, Soldier, flowers (2-1). 5000d, Dancer, flowers.
8000d, Three dancers, flowers.

**2004, May 4** ***Perf. 13***
**3219-3220** A865 Set of 2 .75 .75
**Souvenir Sheet**
***Perf. 13½x13¾***
**3221** A865 8000d multi 1.00 1.00

FIFA (Fédération Internationale de Football Association), Cent. — A866

**2004, May 21** ***Perf. 13***
**3222** A866 800d multi .30 .30

Thieu Nien Newspaper, 50th Anniv. — A867

**2004, June 1**
**3223** A867 800d multi .30 .30

Bonsai — A868

Designs: 800d, Ficus microcarpa (4-1). 2000d, Premna serratifolia (4-2). 3000d, Ficus pilosa (4-3). 8000d, Ficus religiosa (4-4).

**2004, July 1**
**3224-3227** A868 Set of 4 1.75 1.75

2004 World Stamp Championship, Singapore.

2004 Summer Olympics, Athens — A869

Designs: 800d, Hurdles (4-1). 1000d, Swimming, horiz. (4-2). 6000d, Shooting, horiz. (4-3). 7000d, Taekwondo (4-4).

**2004, Aug. 1**
**3228-3231** A869 Set of 4 1.90 1.90

Naming of Country as Viet Nam, Bicent. A870

Designs: 800d, Citadel, Hué, lotus flower (2-1). 5000d, Ho Chi Minh, flag (2-2).

**2004, Sept. 2**
**3232-3233** A870 Set of 2 .75 .75

World Summit on the Information Society, Geneva — A871

**2004, Oct. 9**
**3234** A871 1000d multi .30 .30

Liberation of Hanoi From French, 50th Anniv. — A872

**2004, Oct. 10**
**3235** A872 800d multi .30 .30

Dak Lak Province, Cent. — A873

**2004, Nov. 22**
**3236** A873 800d multi .30 .30

Hoi An, UNESCO World Heritage Site — A874

Designs: 800d, Chua Cau. 8000d, Hoi Quán Phúc Kien.

***Perf. 13¼x13¾ Syncopated***
**2004, Dec. 1**
**3237** A874 800d multi .30 .30
**Souvenir Sheet**
***Perf. 13½x13¾***
**3238** A874 8000d multi 1.00 1.00

No. 3238 contains one 42x31mm stamp.

New Year 2005 (Year of the Rooster) A875

Designs: 800d, Rooster (2-1). 8000d, Hen and chicks.

**2004, Dec. 15** ***Perf. 13***
**3239-3240** A875 Set of 2 1.10 1.10
*3240a* Souvenir sheet, #3239-3240 1.10 1.10

Viet Nam Communist Party, 75th Anniv. — A876

**2005, Feb. 3**
**3241** A876 800d multi .30 .30

Gia Lai Province A877

***Perf. 13¼x13¾ Syncopated***
**2005, Mar. 16** **Litho.**
**3242** A877 800d multi .20 .20

Nha Trang Bay — A878

Designs: 800d, Boat near shore (2-1). 8000d, Road near shore (2-2).

**2005, Apr. 2** ***Perf. 13x12¾***
**Stamp + Label**
**3243-3244** A878 Set of 2 1.10 1.10

Worldwide Fund for Nature (WWF) A879

Various views of Chrotogale owstoni: 800d, (4-1). 3000d, (4-2). 5000d, (4-3). 8000d, (4-4).

**2005, May 2** ***Perf. 13½***
**3245-3248** A879 Set of 4 2.10 2.10
*3248a* Souvenir sheet, #3245-3248, perf. 13x13½ 2.10 2.10

Liberation of Haiphong, 50th Anniv. — A880

Designs: 800d, Burning airplanes at Cat Bi Airport, Haiphong harbor (2-1). 5000d, Nam Trieu Port (2-2).

**2005, May 6** ***Perf. 13x12¾***
**Stamp + Label**
**3249-3250** A880 Set of 2 .75 .75

People's Police, 60th Anniv. A881

Medals and: 800d, Marching police, statue of Ho Chi Minh (2-1). 10,000d, Police helping civilians (2-2).

**2005, Aug. 10** ***Perf. 13***
**3251-3252** A881 Set of 2 1.40 1.40

Posts and Telecommunications Dept., 60th Anniv. — A882

**2005, Aug. 15** *Perf. 13*

**Background Color**

**3253** A882 800d beige .20 .20

**Souvenir Sheet**

***Perf. 13½x13¾***

**3254** A882 8000d gray 1.00 1.00

August Revolution, 60th Anniv. — A883

Crowd with flags in: 1000d, Hanoi (3-1). 2000d, Hué (3-2). 4000d, Saigon (3-3).

**2005, Aug. 19** *Perf. 13*

**3255-3257** A883 Set of 3 .90 .90
*3257a* Souvenir sheet, #3255-3257 .90 .90

Traditional Dress and Houses of Ethnic Groups — A884

No. 3258: a, Ba-na (54-1). b, Bo Y (54-2). c, Brau (54-3). d, Bru-Van Kieu (54-4). e, Cham (54-5). f, Cho-ro (54-6). g, Chu-ru (54-7). h, Chut (54-8). i, Co (54-9). j, Cong (54-10). k, Co-ho (54-11). l, Co Lao (54-12). m, Co-tu (54-13). n, Dao (54-14). o, E-de (54-15). p, Gia-rai (54-16). q, Giay (54-17). r, Gie-Trieng (54-18). s, Ha Nhi (54-19). t, Hoa (54-20). u, Hre (54-21). v, Khang (54-22). w, Khmer (54-23). x, Kho-mu (54-24). y, Kinh (54-25). z, La Chi (54-26). aa, La Ha (54-27). ab, La Hu (54-28). ac, Lao (54-29). ad, Lo Lo (54-30). ae, Lu (54-31). af, Ma (54-32). ag, Mang (54-33). ah, Mnong (54-34). ai, Mong (54-35). aj, Muong (54-36). ak, Ngai (54-37). al, Nung (54-38). am, O Du (54-39). an, Pa Then (54-40). ao, Phu La (54-41). ap, Pu Peo (54-42). aq, Ra-glai (54-43). ar, Ro-mam (54-44). as, San Chay (54-45). at, San Diu (54-46). au, Si La (54-47). av, Ta-oi (54-48). aw, Tay (54-49). ax, Thai (54-50). ay, Tho (54-51). az, Xinh-mun (54-52). ba, Xo-dang (54-53). bb, Xtieng (54-54).

***Perf. 13¾x13¼ Syncopated***

**2005, Aug. 30**

**3258** Sheet of 54 + 2 labels 5.50 5.50
Complete booklet, #3258a-3258bb 5.50
***a.-bb.*** A884 800d Any single .20 .20

Thang Long (Hanoi), 1000th Anniv. A885

People reenacting battles and: 800d, Statue of Gen. Quang Trung, building (3-1). 5000d, Statue of Independence Fighters, building (3-2). No. 3261, 8000d, Statue of Victory Against B-52's, Long Bien Bridge (3-3).

No. 3262, Government officials on dais in Ba Dinh Square.

**2005, Oct. 10** **Litho.** *Perf. 13*

**3259-3261** A885 Set of 3 1.75 1.75

**Souvenir Sheet**

***Perf. 13½x13¾***

**3262** A885 8000d multi 1.00 1.00

New Year 2006 (Year of the Dog) A886

Designs: 800d, Dog and puppies (2-1). 8000d, Dog (2-2).

**2005, Dec. 1** *Perf. 13*

**3263-3264** A886 Set of 2 1.10 1.10
*3264a* Souvenir sheet, #3263-3264 1.10 1.10

National Coat of Arms, 50th Anniv. A887

**2006, Jan. 14** *Perf. 13*

**3265** A887 1000d multi .20 .20

10th Vietnamese Communist Party Congress A888

**2006, Feb. 3**

**3266** A888 800d multi .20 .20

Prime Minister Pham Van Dong (1906-2000) — A889

**2006, Mar. 1**

**3267** A889 800d multi .20 .20

Wolfgang Amadeus Mozart (1756-91), Composer — A890

**2006, Mar. 1**

**3268** A890 2000d multi .25 .25

Léopold Senghor (1906-2001), First President of Senegal — A891

**2006, Mar. 20** **Litho.** *Perf. 13*

**3269** A891 800d multi .20 .20

BirdLife International A892

Designs: 800d, Lophura edwardsi (5-1). 2000d, Arborophila davidi (5-2). 3000d, Lophura hatinhensis (5-3). 5000d, Polyplectron germaini (5-4, 49x23mm). 8000d, Rheinardia ocellata (5-5, 49x23mm).

***Perf. 13¼x14 Syncopated, 13¼x13½ Syncopated (#3273-3274)***

**2006, Apr. 1**

**3270-3274** A892 Set of 5 2.40 2.40
*3274a* Souvenir sheet, #3270-3274 2.40 2.40

2006 World Cup Soccer Championships, Germany — A893

Designs: 800d, One player (1-2). 10,000d, Two players (2-2).

**2006, May 1** **Litho.** *Perf. 13¼x13*

**3275-3276** A893 Set of 2 1.40 1.40

Phong Nha - Ke Bang National Park World Heritage Site — A894

Designs: 800d, Bi Ky Cave (3-1). 4000d, Xuyen Son Cave (3-2). 8000d, Nuoc Moc Stream (3-3).

12,000d, Tien Cave, vert.

**2006, June 1** *Perf. 13x12¾*

**3277-3279** A894 Set of 3 1.60 1.60

**Souvenir Sheet**

***Perf. 13¾x13½***

**3280** A894 12,000d multi 1.50 1.50

No. 3280 contains one 32x43mm stamp.

Animals in Ben En Botanical Gardens A895

Designs: 800d, Nycticebus bengalensis (4-1). 1000d, Neofelis nebulosa, horiz. (4-2). 7000d, Cuon alpinus, horiz. (4-3). 10,000d, Nomascus leucogenys (4-4).

12,000d, Physignathus cocincinus, horiz.

**2006, July 1** *Perf. 13¼x13, 13x13¼*

**3281-3284** A895 Set of 4 2.40 2.40

**Souvenir Sheet**

***Perf. 13½x13¾***

**3285** A895 12,000d multi 1.50 1.50

Flowers — A896

Designs: 800d, Momordica cochinchinensis (4-1). 3000d, Telosma cordata (4-2). 5000d, Momordica charantia (4-3). 8000d, Luffa cylindrica (4-4).

**2006, Aug. 1** *Perf. 13*

**3286-3289** A896 Set of 4 2.10 2.10

Asia-Pacific Economic Cooperation Summit — A897

**2006, Sept. 16**

**3290** A897 8000d multi 1.00 1.00

Cooperation Between Viet Nam and European Union — A898

**2006, Oct. 1** *Perf. 13x13¼*

**3291** A898 800d multi .20 .20

New Year 2007 (Year of the Pig) A899

Designs: 800d, Pig and piglets (2-1). 8000d, Pig (2-2).

**2006, Dec. 15** *Perf. 13*

**3292-3293** A899 Set of 2 1.10 1.10

---

## SEMI-POSTAL STAMPS

World Communications Year — SP1

#B1, Hands holding envelope with ITU emblem. #B2, Satellite dish antenna.

Unwmk.

**1983, Nov. 1 Litho. *Perf. 11***
**B1-B2** SP1 50xu +10xu Set of 2 3.75

## AIR POST STAMP

AP1

Unwmk.

**1959, Nov. 20 Litho. *Perf. 11***
**C1** AP1 20xu blue & black 10.00 7.75

## POSTAGE DUE STAMPS

Nos. 1-4 exist with handstamps of "TT" in a diamond. It is unclear to the editors if these stamps were used.

D1

D2

**1955 Typo. *Perf. 11½***
**J14** D1 50d brown & yellow 15.00 9.00

**1958, Dec. 1 Litho. *Perf. 12½***
**J15** D2 10d purple & red
**J16** D2 20d orange & aqua
**J17** D2 100d gray blue & red
**J18** D2 300d olive grn & red
*Nos. J15-J18 (4)* 15.00 14.00

## MILITARY STAMPS

M1

*Perf. 12½*
**1958, May 1 Litho. Unwmk.**
**M1** M1 multicolored 15.00 9.00

Invalids in Field Paddy
M2

**1959-60 Litho. *Perf. 11***
**M2** M2 org brn & brown
**M3** M2 grey blue & olive
*Nos. M2-M3 (2)* 11.50 4.50

Issued: No. M2, 3/14/59; No. M3, 7/27/60.

Soldier, Train — M3

**1959, July 1**
**M4** M3 bluish green 5.00 1.90

Frontier Guard — M4

**1961, Jan. 3**
**M5** M4 multicolored 15.00 9.75

Naval Patrol
M5

**1962, June 15**
**M6** M5 multicolored 5.75 3.25

Military Medal, Invalid's Badge — M6

**1963, Sept. 10**
**M7** M6 12xu multicolored 4.50 3.75

Rifleman
M7

**1964, Aug.**
**M8** M7 multicolored 5.00 4.00

Rifleman Jumping Wall — M8

**1965**
**M9** M8 red & black
**M10** M8 yellow green & black
*Nos. M9-M10 (2)* 9.00 6.25

Issued: No. M9, 7/1; No. M10, 12/25.

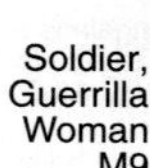

Soldier, Guerrilla Woman
M9

**1966-67**
**M11** M9 greenish blue & vio bl 9.00 7.00

**Redrawn with two boats at right**

**M12** M9 olive & brown bl 13.50 10.50

Issued: #M11, Sept. 25, 1966; #M12, 1967.

Badge of People's Army — M10

**1967, Oct. 7**
**M13** M10 multicolored 2.00 .75

M11

M12

**1968, Nov. 10**
**M14** M11 lilac 1.50 .40

**1969, Nov. 15**
**M15** M12 red & brown red 1.50 .75

M13

**1971, Apr. 27**
**M16** M13 yellow, brown & red 1.50 .75

Nguyen Van Be
M14

Design: No. M18, Nguyen Viet Xuan.

**1971, Oct. 30 *Perf. 11***
**M17** M14 multicolored 1.50 .60

***Perf. 12½***

**M18** M14 black, pink & buff 2.25 1.10

M15

M16

**1973, Dec. 20 *Perf. 11***
**M20** M15 blue, black & buff
*a.* Perf. 12½ 4.50
**M22** M16 olive, red & black
*a.* Perf. 12½ 4.50
*Nos. M20, M22 (2)* 1.00 25

Disabled Veteran in Factory
M17

No. M24, Invalid's Badge, open book, vert.

**1976, July 27**
**M23-M24** M17 Set of 2 2.00 .25

Soldier, Map — M18

Pilot — M19

**1976, Oct. 21**
**M25** M18 red & black 1.00

**1978**

No. M27, Tank driver. No. M28, Seaman.

**M26-M28** M19 Set of 3 5.00 2.00

Issued: No. M26, 6/3; others, 10/10.

M20

Designs: a, Pilot. b, Badge of People's Army.

**1979, Dec. 22**
**M29** M20 Vertical pair, #a.-b. 3.00

Types A343a, A359 and

Ho Chi Minh — M21

#M30, Factory militiawoman. #M31, Soldier, woman pointing. #M32, Militiawoman.

**1981, Aug. 5**
**M30** A343a salmon & multi
**M31** A343a green & multi
**M32** A359 blue & multi
**M33** M21 blue & tan
*Nos. M30-M33 (4)* 4.50 2.25

Size of No. M32: 13x18mm.

M22

**1982, Nov. 9**
**M34** M22 pink & greenish blue 1.50 1.00

M23

**1983, Apr. 30**
**M35** M23 multicolored 2.25 1.10

Victory at Dien Bien Phu, 30th Anniv. M24

**1984, May 5** **Litho.**
**M37** M24 multicolored 1.25

Disabled Soldier Teaching Class — M25

**1984, Nov. 10**
**M38** M25 tan & brown 1.25

Frontier Forces Type of 1984
**1984, Dec. 15**
**M39** A410 multicolored 1.00

M26

**1984, Dec. 22**
**M40** M26 multicolored 2.50

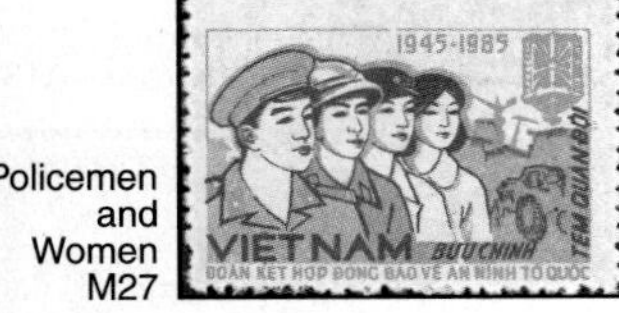

Policemen and Women M27

**1985, Aug. 30**
**M41** M27 multicolored 1.00

M28

**1986, Oct. 1**
**M42** M28 olive brown & black 1.50 .75

M29

**1987, Sept. 23**
**M43** M29 carmine and tan 2.00 1.00

---

## OFFICIAL STAMPS

Harvesting Rice — O1

Denominations in grams or kilograms of rice. Dated 1952.

*Perf. 11¼*
**1953, July** **Litho.** **Unwmk.**
**O1** O1 600g rose 5.50 2.50
**O2** O1 1kg ol brown 6.00 4.00
**O3** O1 2kg orange 8.50 6.50
**O4** O1 5kg gray 15.00 12.00
*Nos. O1-O4 (4)* 35.00 25.00

Dien Bien Phu Type of 1954
**1954-56** ***Perf. 11***
**O5** A4 600g sepia & ocher 18.00 12.50

No. O5 exists perf 6, Value $60; and also imperf, Value $18.
Issued: #O5, 10/54; perf 6, 12/54; imperf, 1956.

Nos. 1L62-1L63 Overprinted

**1955** **Typo.** ***Perf. 7 Rough***
**O6-O7** VM2 100g on 2d, 100g on 5d, set of 2 440.00

Land Reform Type of 1955-56 Inscribed "SU VU" Above Value
**1955** **Litho.** ***Perf. 11***
**O8-O9** A6 40d, 80d, set of 2 32.50 27.50

Cu Chinh Lan (1930-1952) O3

Denominations: 20d, 80d, 100d, 500d, 1000d, 2000d, 3000d.

**1956, June** **Litho.** ***Perf. 11½***
**O10-O16** O3 Set of 7 250.00 225.00

4th World Trade Union Congress Type of 1957 Inscribed "SU VU" Above Value
**1957, Aug. 1** ***Perf. 12½***
**O17-O20** A15 20d, 40d, 80d, 100d, set of 4 20.00 16.00

One-Pillar Pagoda — O4

**1957-58**
**O21** O4 150d green and brown
**O22** O4 150d orange and slate
*Nos. O21-O22 (2)* 26.00 11.00

Nos. O21-O22 exist with and without imprint and designer's name. Issued: No. O21, 12/22/57; No. O22, 3/12/58.

Craft Fair, Hanoi — O5

**1958, May 30**
**O23-O24** O5 150d, 200d, set of 2 8.00 6.00

1st World Congress of Young Workers, Prague — O6

**1958, June 26**
**O25** O6 150d lt olive green & red 3.50 1.75

Soldier, Factory, Crops — O7

**1958, Aug. 19**
**O26-O28** O7 50, 150, 200d, set of 3 11.00 7.00

Opening of New Hanoi Stadium O8

**1958, Dec. 31**
**O29-O32** O8 10d, 20d, 80d, 150d, set of 4 9.50 4.75

Planting Rice — O9

**1962, Sept. 1** ***Perf. 11***
**O33-O35** O9 3, 6, 12xu, set of 3 3.00 2.50

Rural Mail Service O10

**1966, July 1** ***Perf. 11***
**O36-O37** O10 3xu, 6xu, set of 2 1.50 1.00

# VIRGIN ISLANDS

ˈvər-jən ˈī-lənds

LOCATION — West Indies, southeast of Puerto Rico
GOVT. — British colony
AREA — 59 sq. mi.
POP. — 19,107 (1997)
CAPITAL — Road Town

The British Virgin Islands constituted one of the presidencies of the former Leeward Islands colony until it became a colony itself in 1956. For many years stamps of Leeward Islands were used concurrently.

The Virgin Islands group is divided between Great Britain and the United States. See Danish West Indies.

12 Pence = 1 Shilling
20 Shillings = 1 Pound
100 Cents = 1 Dollar (1951)
100 Cents = 1 US Dollar (1962)

**Catalogue values for unused stamps in this country are for Never Hinged items, beginning with Scott 88 in the regular postage section and Scott O1 in the officials section.**

Values for unused stamps are for examples with original gum as defined in the catalogue introduction. However, Nos. 1-2c are valued without gum as the vast majority of examples are found thus.

Virgin and Lamps — A1

St. Ursula — A2

A3

A4

**1866 Litho. Unwmk. *Perf. 12***

**Toned or White Paper**

1 A1 1p green 50.00 *65.00*
 a. Toned paper 52.50 *65.00*
 c. Perf. 15x12, toned paper 6,000. *7,750.*
2 A3 6p rose 65.00 100.00
 a. Large "V" in "VIRGIN" 300.00 *400.00*
 b. White paper 100.00 *120.00*
 c. As "a," white paper 410.00 *525.00*

Copies offered as No. 1c frequently have forged perfs.

**1867-70 *Perf. 15***

3 A1 1p blue grn ('70) 65.00 75.00
4 A1 1p yel grn ('68) 80.00 75.00
 a. Toned paper 92.50 85.00
5 A2 4p lake, *buff* 45.00 65.00
 a. 4p lake, *rose* 55.00 *75.00*
6 A3 6p rose 650.00 650.00
 a. Toned paper ('68) 325.00 *375.00*
7 A4 1sh rose & blk 300.00 *400.00*
 a. Toned paper 300.00 *400.00*
 b. Double lined frame 300.00 *400.00*
 c. As "b," bluish paper 300.00 *400.00*

**Colored Margins**

8 A4 1sh rose & blk 70.00 *87.50*
 a. White paper 70.00 *87.50*
 b. Bluish paper 825.00 *1,000.*
 c. Central figure omitted 92,500.
 *Nos. 3-8 (6)* 1,210. 1,352.

Copies of No. 8c have perfs. trimmed on one or two sides.

**1878 Wmk. 1 *Perf. 14***

9 A1 1p green 90.00 *110.00*

See #16-17, 19-20. For surcharge see #18.

Queen Victoria — A5

**1880 Typo.**

10 A5 1p green 80.00 *95.00*
11 A5 2½p red brown 100.00 *125.00*

**1883-84 Wmk. 2**

12 A5 ½p yellow 92.50 92.50
13 A5 ½p green 6.00 *11.00*
 a. Imperf., pair *1,750.*
14 A5 1p rose 27.50 *32.50*
15 A5 2½p ultra ('84) 3.00 *17.50*
 *Nos. 12-15 (4)* 129.00 *153.50*

No. 13a probably is a plate proof.

**1887 Litho.**

16 A2 4p brick red 40.00 70.00
 a. 4p brown red 50.00 *80.00*
17 A3 6p violet 17.50 *50.00*

No. 8 Handstamp Surcharged in Violet

**1888 Unwmk. *Perf. 15***

18 A4 4p on 1sh dp rose & blk, toned paper 140.00 175.00
 a. Double surcharge *7,500.*
 b. Inverted surcharge *47,500.*
 c. White paper 200.00 *250.00*

**1889 Wmk. 2 *Perf. 14***

19 A1 1p carmine 2.75 *8.25*
20 A4 1sh brown 50.00 *80.00*
 a. 1sh black brown 90.00 *110.00*

St. Ursula with Sheaf of Lilies A7

Edward VII A8

**1899 Engr.**

21 A7 ½p yellow grn 2.75 .60
 a. "PFNNY" 92.50 *140.00*
 b. "F" without cross bar 92.50 *140.00*
 c. Horiz. pair, imperf. between *9,250.*
22 A7 1p red 3.25 2.75
23 A7 2½p ultra 13.00 3.00
24 A7 4p chocolate 4.50 *20.00*
 a. "PENCF" 825. *1,200.*
25 A7 6p dark violet 5.00 3.50
26 A7 7p slate green 9.25 6.50
27 A7 1sh ocher 25.00 *37.50*
28 A7 5sh dark blue 80.00 *95.00*
 *Nos. 21-28 (8)* 142.75 *168.85*

**1904 Typo. Wmk. 3**

29 A8 ½p violet & bl grn .85 .55
30 A8 1p violet & scar 2.75 .45
31 A8 2p violet & bis 6.50 4.00
32 A8 2½p violet & ultra 2.25 2.25
33 A8 3p violet & blk 4.00 2.75
34 A8 6p violet & brn 3.00 2.75
35 A8 1sh green & scar 4.50 *5.50*
36 A8 2sh6p green & blk 27.50 *60.00*
37 A8 5sh green & ultra 52.50 *72.50*
 *Nos. 29-37 (9)* 103.85 150.75

Numerals of 2p, 3p, 1sh and 2sh6p of type A8 are in color on plain tablet.

George V A9

Colony Seal A10

**Die I**

For description of dies I and II see "Dies of British Colonial Stamps" in Table of Contents.

**1913**

**Ordinary Paper**

38 A9 ½p green 1.75 *4.50*
39 A9 1p scarlet 2.50 *16.00*
 a. 1p carmine red 52.50 30.00
40 A9 2p gray 4.50 *27.50*
41 A9 2½p ultra 6.00 *10.00*

**Chalky Paper**

42 A9 3p vio, *yel* 3.00 *7.25*
43 A9 6p dl vio & red vio 5.50 *12.50*
44 A9 1sh blk, *green* 3.50 *10.00*
45 A9 2sh6p blk & red, *bl* 52.50 *55.00*
46 A9 5sh grn & red, *yel* 37.50 *120.00*
 *Nos. 38-46 (9)* 116.75 *262.75*

Numerals of 2p, 3p, 1sh and 2sh6p of type A9 are in color on plain tablet.

**1921 Wmk. 4**

**Die II**

47 A9 ½p green 5.00 *35.00*
48 A9 1p carmine 4.00 *27.50*

For overprints see Nos. MR1-MR2.

**1922 Wmk. 3**

49 A10 3p violet, *yel* .90 *19.00*
50 A10 1sh black, *emerald* .85 *16.00*
51 A10 2sh6p blk & red, *bl* 6.00 *12.50*
52 A10 5sh grn & red, *yel* 35.00 *110.00*
 *Nos. 49-52 (4)* 42.75 *157.50*

**1922-28 Wmk. 4**

53 A10 ½p green .90 *3.00*
54 A10 1p rose red .65 .65
55 A10 1p violet ('27) 1.10 *4.00*
56 A10 1½p rose red ('27) 1.60 *2.75*
57 A10 1½p fawn ('28) 1.90 1.60
58 A10 2p gray 1.10 *6.50*
59 A10 2½p ultra 2.25 *20.00*
60 A10 2½p orange ('23) 1.40 1.75
61 A10 3p dl vio, *yel* ('28) 2.50 *12.50*
62 A10 5p dl lil & ol grn 6.00 *50.00*
63 A10 6p dl vio & red vio 1.60 *7.00*
 a. 6p brown lilac & red violet 1.60 *7.00*
64 A10 1sh blk, *emer* ('28) 2.75 *16.00*
65 A10 2sh6p blk & red, *bl* ('28) 21.00 *52.50*
66 A10 5sh grn & red, *yel* ('23) 21.00 *80.00*
 *Nos. 53-66 (14)* 65.75 *258.25*

The ½, 1, 2 and 2½p are on ordinary paper, the others on chalky.

Numerals of 1½p of type A10 are in color on plain tablet.

Common Design Types pictured following the introduction.

**Silver Jubilee Issue**

Common Design Type

**1935, May 6 Engr. *Perf. 11x12***

69 CD301 1p car & dk blue .50 *1.75*
70 CD301 1½p black & ultra .50 *1.75*
71 CD301 2½p ultra & brn 1.00 *1.75*
72 CD301 1sh brn vio & ind 6.50 *7.25*
 *Nos. 69-72 (4)* 8.50 *12.50*
 Set, never hinged 14.00

**Coronation Issue**

Common Design Type

**1937, May 12 *Perf. 11x11½***

73 CD302 1p dark carmine .20 *.50*
74 CD302 1½p brown .20 *1.50*
75 CD302 2½p deep ultra .35 *.50*
 *Nos. 73-75 (3)* .75 2.50
 Set, never hinged 1.10

King George VI and Seal of the Colony — A11

**1938-47 Photo. *Perf. 14***

76 A11 ½p green .20 .20
77 A11 1p scarlet .20 .20
78 A11 1½p red brown .35 .50
79 A11 2p gray .25 .40
80 A11 2½p ultra .35 .75
81 A11 3p orange .25 .50
82 A11 6p deep violet .90 .40
83 A11 1sh olive bister 1.00 .45
84 A11 2sh6p sepia 7.50 3.50
85 A11 5sh rose lake 10.00 *4.50*
86 A11 10sh brt blue ('47) 5.00 9.75
87 A11 £1 gray blk ('47) 8.00 *16.00*
 *Nos. 76-87 (12)* 34.00 *37.15*
 Set, never hinged 50.00

**Catalogue values for unused stamps in this section, from this point to the end of the section, are for Never Hinged items.**

**Peace Issue**

Common Design Type

***Perf. 13½x14***

**1946, Nov. 1 Engr. Wmk. 4**

88 CD303 1½p red brown .20 .20
89 CD303 3p orange .20 .20

**Silver Wedding Issue**

Common Design Types

**1949, Jan. 3 Photo. *Perf. 14x14½***

90 CD304 2½p brt ultra .25 .25

**Engr.; Name Typo.**

***Perf. 11½x11***

91 CD305 £1 gray black 12.00 12.50

**UPU Issue**

Common Design Types

**Engr.; Name Typo. on Nos. 93 & 94**

**1949, Oct. 10 *Perf. 13½, 11x11½***

92 CD306 2½p ultra .40 .40
93 CD307 3p deep orange 1.00 1.60
94 CD308 6p red lilac .65 .40
95 CD309 1sh olive .65 .40
 *Nos. 92-95 (4)* 2.70 2.80

**University Issue**

Common Design Types

**1951 Engr. *Perf. 14x14½***

96 CD310 3c red brn & gray blk .25 .25
97 CD311 12c purple & black .85 .85

Map of the Islands A12

**1951, Apr. 2 Wmk. 4 *Perf. 14½x14***

98 A12 6c red orange .25 .25
99 A12 12c purple .35 .35
100 A12 24c olive grn .50 .55
101 A12 $1.20 carmine 1.90 1.50
 *Nos. 98-101 (4)* 3.00 2.65

Restoration of the Legislative Council, 1950.

Sombrero Lighthouse — A13

Map of Jost van Dyke — A14

Designs: 3c, Sheep. 4c, Map, Anegada. 5c, Cattle. 8c, Map, Virgin Gorda. 12c, Map, Tortola. 24c, Badge of the Presidency. 60c, Dead Man's Chest. $1.20, Sir Francis Drake Channel. $2.40, Road Town. $4.80, Map, Virgin Islands.

**1952, Apr. 15 *Perf. 12½x13, 13x12½***

102 A13 1c gray black .25 *.65*
103 A14 2c deep green .55 .20
104 A14 3c choc & gray blk .30 *.50*
105 A14 4c red .45 *.65*
106 A14 5c gray blk & rose lake .90 .30
107 A14 8c ultra .55 .55
108 A14 12c purple 1.00 .65
109 A13 24c dk brown 1.10 .20
110 A14 60c blue & ol grn 1.75 *7.00*
111 A14 $1.20 ultra & blk 4.00 *7.50*
112 A14 $2.40 hn brn & dk grn 8.50 8.25
113 A14 $4.80 rose car & bl 14.00 9.00
 *Nos. 102-113 (12)* 33.35 35.45

### Coronation Issue

Common Design Type

**1953, June 2** *Perf. 13½x14*

**114** CD312 2c dk green & blk .25 *.40*

Map of Tortola — A15

Brown Pelican A16

Designs: 1c, Virgin Islands sloop. 2c, Nelthrop Red Poll bull. 3c, Road Harbor. 4c, Mountain travel. 5c, St. Ursula. 8c, Beach scene. 12c, Boat launching. 24c, White Cedar tree. 60c, Skipjack tuna. $1.20, Treasury Square. $4.80, Magnificent frigatebird.

*Perf. 13x12½*

**1956, Nov. 1** **Engr.** **Wmk. 4**

**115** A15 ½c claret & blk .35 .20
**116** A15 1c dk bl & grnsh bl 1.50 .85
**117** A15 2c black & ver .30 .20
**118** A15 3c olive & brt bl .30 .35
**119** A15 4c blue grn & brn .35 .35
**120** A15 5c gray .40 .20
**121** A15 8c dp ultra & org .60 .50
**122** A15 12c car & brt ultra 2.10 .85
**123** A15 24c dull red & grn 1.00 .75
**124** A15 60c yel org & dk bl 8.00 9.50
**125** A15 $1.20 car & yel grn 2.25 8.50

*Perf. 12x11½*

**126** A16 $2.40 vio brn & dl yel 30.00 16.00
**127** A16 $4.80 grnsh bl & dk brn 32.50 16.00
*Nos. 115-127 (13)* 79.65 54.25

Types of 1956 Surcharged

*Perf. 13x12½*

**1962, Dec. 10** **Wmk. 314**

**128** A15 1c on ½c .20 .20
**129** A15 2c on 1c .95 .20
**130** A15 3c on 2c .20 .20
**131** A15 4c on 3c .20 .20
**132** A15 5c on 4c .20 .20
**133** A15 8c on 8c .25 .25
**134** A15 10c on 12c .35 .35
**135** A15 12c on 24c .50 .50
**136** A15 25c on 60c 2.50 1.00
**137** A15 70c on $1.20 .55 2.50

*Perf. 12x11½*

**138** A16 $1.40 on $2.40 9.50 16.00
**139** A16 $2.80 on $4.80 9.50 12.00
*Nos. 128-139 (12)* 24.90 33.60

### Freedom from Hunger Issue

Common Design Type

**1963, June 4** **Photo.** *Perf. 14x14½*

**140** CD314 25c lilac .50 .50

### Red Cross Centenary Issue

Common Design Type

**Wmk. 314**

**1963, Sept. 2** **Litho.** *Perf. 13*

**141** CD315 2c black & red .20 .20
**142** CD315 25c ultra & red .90 .90

### Shakespeare Issue

Common Design Type

**1964, Apr. 23** **Photo.** *Perf. 14x14½*

**143** CD316 10c ultramarine .25 .25

Bonito — A17

Map of Tortola Island — A18

2c, Seaplane at Soper's Hole. 3c, Brown pelican. 4c, Dead Man's Chest (mountain). 5c, Road Harbor. 6c, Fallen Jerusalem Island. 8c, The Baths, Virgin Gorda. 10c, Map of Virgin Islands. 12c, Ferry service, Tortola—St. Thomas. 15c, The Towers. 25c, Plane at Beef Island Airfield. $1, Virgin Gorda Island. $1.40, Yachts, Tortola. $2.80, Badge.

*Perf. 13x12½*

**1964, Nov. 2** **Engr.** **Wmk. 314**

**144** A17 1c gray ol & dk bl .25 1.60
**145** A17 2c rose red & ol .25 .30
**146** A17 3c grnsh bl & sep 3.25 1.60
**147** A17 4c carmine & blk .85 1.60
**148** A17 5c green & blk .70 1.60
**149** A17 6c orange & blk .25 1.10
**150** A17 8c pink & blk .25 .75
**151** A17 10c lt violet & mar 1.25 .30
**152** A17 12c vio bl & Prus grn 2.10 2.25
**153** A17 15c gray & yel grn .35 2.40
**154** A17 25c pur & yel grn 11.50 2.25

*Perf. 13x13½*

**Size: 27x30½mm**

**155** A18 70c bister brn & blk 4.00 5.25
**156** A18 $1 red brn & yel grn 3.25 2.25
**157** A18 $1.40 pink & blue 21.00 10.50

*Perf. 11½x12*

**Size: 27x37mm**

**158** A18 $2.80 rose lilac & blk 21.00 10.50
*Nos. 144-158 (15)* 70.25 44.25

For surcharges & overprints see Nos. 173-175, 190-191.

### ITU Issue

Common Design Type

*Perf. 11x11½*

**1965, May 17** **Litho.** **Wmk. 314**

**159** CD317 4c yellow & bl grn .20 .20
**160** CD317 25c blue & org yel .80 .80

### Intl. Cooperation Year Issue

Common Design Type

**1965, Oct. 25** **Wmk. 314** *Perf. 14½*

**161** CD318 1c blue grn & cl .20 .20
**162** CD318 25c lt violet & grn .65 .65

### Churchill Memorial Issue

Common Design Type

**1966, Jan. 24** **Photo.** *Perf. 14*

**Design in Black, Gold and Carmine Rose**

**163** CD319 1c brt blue .20 .20
**164** CD319 2c green .20 .20
**165** CD319 10c brown .40 .40
**166** CD319 25c violet 1.00 1.00
*Nos. 163-166 (4)* 1.80 1.80

### Royal Visit Issue

Common Design Type

**1966, Feb. 22** **Litho.** *Perf. 11x12*

**167** CD320 4c violet blue .20 .20
**168** CD320 70c dk car rose 2.25 2.25

Stamps of 1866 — A19

Designs: 5c, R.M.S. Atrato, 1866. 25c, Beechcraft mail plane on Beef Island Airfield and 6p stamp (No. 2). 60c, Landing mail at Road Town, 1866, and 1p stamp (No. 1).

*Perf. 12½x13*

**1966, Apr. 25** **Wmk. 314**

**169** A19 5c grn, yel, red & blk .20 .20
**170** A19 10c yel, grn, red, blk & rose .20 .20
**171** A19 25c lt grn, bl, red, blk & rose .50 .50
**172** A19 60c bl, red, blk, & grn 1.00 1.00
*Nos. 169-172 (4)* 1.90 1.90

Centenary of Virgin Islands postage stamps.

Nos. 155, 157-158 Surcharged with New Value and Two Bars

*Perf. 13x12½, 11½x12*

**1966, Sept. 15** **Engr.** **Wmk. 314**

**173** A18 50c on 70c 1.75 1.25
**174** A18 $1.50 on $1.40 3.75 2.75
**175** A18 $3 on $2.80 3.75 4.00
*Nos. 173-175 (3)* 9.25 8.00

### UNESCO Anniversary Issue

Common Design Type

**1966, Dec. 1** **Litho.** *Perf. 14*

**176** CD323 2c "Education" .20 .20
**177** CD323 12c "Science" .25 .25
**178** CD323 60c "Culture" .70 .70
*Nos. 176-178 (3)* 1.15 1.15

Map and Seal of Virgin Islands A20

**Wmk. 314**

**1967, Apr. 18** **Photo.** *Perf. 14½*

**179** A20 2c gold, grn & org .20 .20
**180** A20 10c gold, rose red, grn & org .25 .25
**181** A20 25c gold, red brn, grn & org .25 .25
**182** A20 $1 gold, bl, grn & org .85 .85
*Nos. 179-182 (4)* 1.55 1.55

Introduction of new constitution.

Map of Virgin Islands, Bermuda and C.S. Mercury — A21

10c, Communications center, Chalwell, Virgin Islands. 50c, Cable ship Mercury.

**1967, Sept. 14** **Wmk. 314** *Perf. 14½*

**183** A21 4c green & multi .20 .20
**184** A21 10c dp plum & multi .20 .20
**185** A21 50c bister & multi .45 .45
*Nos. 183-185 (3)* .85 .85

Completion of the Bermuda-Tortola, Virgin Islands, telephone link.

Blue Marlin A22

Designs: 10c, Sergeant fish (cobia). 25c, Peto fish (Wahoo). 40c, Fishing boat, map of Virgin Islands and fishing records.

*Perf. 12½x12*

**1968, Jan. 2** **Photo.** **Wmk. 314**

**186** A22 2c multicolored .20 .20
**187** A22 10c multicolored .25 .25
**188** A22 25c multicolored .50 .50
**189** A22 40c multicolored .80 .80
*Nos. 186-189 (4)* 1.75 1.75

Game fishing in Virgin Islands waters.

Nos. 151 and 154 Overprinted: "1968 / INTERNATIONAL / YEAR FOR / HUMAN RIGHTS"

**1968, July 1** **Engr.** *Perf. 13x12½*

**190** A17 10c lt violet & maroon .20 .20
**191** A17 25c purple & green .30 .30

Martin Luther King, Bible and Sword A23

**1968, Oct. 15** **Litho.** *Perf. 14*

**192** A23 4c dl org, vio & blk .25 .25
**193** A23 25c dl org, gray grn & blk .35 *.50*

Martin Luther King, Jr. (1929-68), American civil rights leader.

DHC-6 Twin Otter A24

Designs: 10c, Hawker Siddeley 748. 25c, Hawker Siddeley Heron. $1, Badge from cap of Royal Engineers.

**1968, Dec. 16** **Unwmk.** *Perf. 14*

**194** A24 2c brn red & multi .20 *.60*
**195** A24 10c grnsh bl, blk & red .20 .20
**196** A24 25c ultra, lt bl, org & blk .40 .20
**197** A24 $1 green & multi 1.60 *2.00*
*Nos. 194-197 (4)* 2.40 3.00

Opening of enlarged Beef Island Airport.

Long John Silver and Jim Hawkins — A25

Tourist and Rock Grouper — A26

Scenes from Treasure Island: 10c, Jim's escape from the pirates, horiz. 40c, The fight with Israel Hands. $1, Treasure trove, horiz.

*Perf. 13½x13, 13x13½*

**1969, Mar. 18** **Photo.** **Wmk. 314**

**198** A25 4c dp car & multi .40 .20
**199** A25 10c multicolored .45 .25
**200** A25 40c ultra & multi .55 .65
**201** A25 $1 black & multi 1.10 2.00
*Nos. 198-201 (4)* 2.50 3.10

Robert Louis Stevenson (1850-94). The Virgin Islands were used as the setting for "Treasure Island."

**1969, Oct. 20** **Litho.** *Perf. 12½*

Tourist Publicity: 10c, Yachts in Road Harbor, Tortola, horiz. 20c, Tourists on beach in Virgin Gorda National Park, horiz. $1, Pipe organ cactus and woman tourist.

**202** A26 2c multicolored .20 *.55*
**203** A26 10c multicolored .20 .20
**204** A26 20c multicolored .35 .25
**205** A26 $1 multicolored 1.75 *2.00*
*Nos. 202-205 (4)* 2.50 3.00

Carib Canoe A27

Ships: 1c, Santa Maria. 2c, H.M.S. Elizabeth Bonaventure. 3c, Dutch buccaneer, 1660. 4c, Thetis (1827 merchant ship). 5c, Henry Morgan's ship. 6c, Frigate Boreas. 8c, Schooner L'Eclair, 1804. 10c, H.M.S. Formidable. 12c, H.M.S. Nymph burning. 15c, Packet Windsor Castle fighting French privateer. 25c, Frigate Astrea, 1808. 50c, H.M.S. Rhone. $1, Tortola sloop. $2, H.M.S. Frobisher. $3, Booker Line Viking (cargo ship). $5, Hydrofoil Sun Arrow.

**Wmk. 314 Sideways**

**1970, Feb. 16** *Perf. 14½*

**206** A27 ½c brn & ocher .20 .20
**207** A27 1c bl, lt grn & vio .20 .20
**208** A27 2c red brn, org & gray .20 .20
**209** A27 3c ver, bl & brn .20 .20
**210** A27 4c brn, bl & vio bl .20 .20
**211** A27 5c grn, pink & blk .20 .20
**212** A27 6c lil, grn & blk .20 .20
**213** A27 8c lt ol, yel & brn .25 .25
**214** A27 10c ocher, bl & brn .30 .35
**215** A27 12c sep, yel & dp cl .45 .55
**216** A27 15c org, grnsh bl & brn .40 .50
**217** A27 25c bl, grnsh gray & pur .60 .75
**218** A27 50c rose car, lt grn & brn 1.25 1.50
**219** A27 $1 brn, sal pink & dk grn 2.50 3.00
**220** A27 $2 gray & yel 5.00 6.25
**221** A27 $3 brn, ol bis & dk bl 7.75 9.50
**222** A27 $5 lil & gray 12.50 15.00
*Nos. 206-222 (17)* 32.40 39.05

For overprints see Nos. 235-236.

**1973, Oct. 17** **Wmk. 314 Upright**

*206a* A27 ½c .85 *5.75*
*209a* A27 3c 2.00 *2.25*
*210a* A27 4c 2.00 *4.25*
*211a* A27 5c 2.00 *2.10*
*214a* A27 10c 2.40 2.40
*215a* A27 12c 3.25 3.25
*Nos. 206a-215a (6)* 12.50 20.00

**Wmk. 314 Sideways**

**1974, Nov. 11** *Perf. 13½*

*207a* A27 1c 1.25 *1.90*
*214b* A27 10c 2.25 2.10
*215b* A27 12c 2.25 3.00
*216a* A27 15c 3.25 3.00
*Nos. 207a-216a (4)* 9.00 10.00

"A Tale of Two Cities," by Dickens A28

Charles Dickens: 10c, "Oliver Twist." 25c, "Great Expectations."

**1970, May 4** **Litho.** *Perf. 14½*

**223** A28 5c blk, gray & pink .20 .20
**224** A28 10c blk, pale yel grn & blue .40 .35
**225** A28 25c blk, yel & lt yel grn .65 *.95*
*Nos. 223-225 (3)* 1.25 1.50

Hospital Visitor A29

10c, Girl Scouts receiving 1st aid training at lake side. 25c, Red Cross & Virgin Islands coat of arms.

**1970, Aug. 10** **Wmk. 314** *Perf. 14*

**226** A29 4c multicolored .20 .20
**227** A29 10c multicolored .30 .20
**228** A29 25c multicolored .75 .70
*Nos. 226-228 (3)* 1.25 1.10

Centenary of British Red Cross.

Mary Read — A30

Pirates: 10c, George Lowther. 30c, Edward Teach (Blackbeard). 60c, Henry Morgan.

**1970, Nov. 16** **Wmk. 314** *Perf. 14*

**229** A30 ½c dp rose & multi .20 .20
**230** A30 10c blue grn & multi .45 .45
**231** A30 30c ultra & multi 1.25 1.25
**232** A30 60c multicolored 1.60 1.60
*Nos. 229-232 (4)* 3.50 3.50

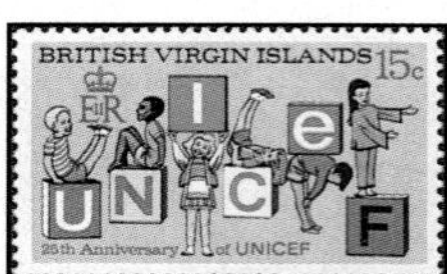


Children Spelling out "UNICEF" A31

**1971, Dec. 13**

**233** A31 15c tan & multi .20 .20
**234** A31 30c lt blue & multi .50 .50

25th anniv. of UNICEF.

Nos. 210 and 217 Dated "1972" and Overprinted: "VISIT OF / H.R.H. / THE / PRINCESS MARGARET"

**1972, Mar. 7** *Perf. 14½*

**235** A27 4c multicolored .20 .20
**236** A27 25c multicolored .30 .40

Seaman, 1800 — A32

10c, Boatswain, 1787-1807. 30c, Captain, 1795-1812. 60c, Admiral in full dress uniform, 1787-95.

**1972, Mar. 17** *Perf. 14x13½*

**237** A32 ½c yellow & multi .20 .20
**238** A32 10c brt pink & multi .40 .40
**239** A32 30c orange & multi 1.10 1.10
**240** A32 60c blue & multi 2.50 2.50
*Nos. 237-240 (4)* 4.20 4.20

INTERPEX, 14th Intl. Stamp Exhib., NYC, Mar. 17-19.

**Silver Wedding Issue, 1972**

Common Design Type

Design: Queen Elizabeth II, Prince Philip, sailfish and "Sir Winston Churchill" yacht.

**1972, Nov. 24** **Photo.** *Perf. 14x14½*

**241** CD324 15c ultra & multi .35 .35
**242** CD324 25c Prus blue & multi .35 .35

Allison Tuna A33

**1972, Dec. 12** **Litho.** *Perf. 13½x14*

**243** A33 ½c Wahoo .20 .20
**244** A33 ½c Blue marlin .20 .20
*a.* Horiz. or vert. pair, #243-244 .20 .20
**245** A33 15c shown .45 .45
**246** A33 25c White marlin .70 .70
**247** A33 50c Sailfish 1.25 1.25
**248** A33 $1 Dolphin 3.00 3.00
*a.* Souvenir sheet of 6, #243-248 12.50 12.50
*Nos. 243-248 (6)* 5.80 5.80

Game fish.

Lettsom House and Medal — A34

Themes from Quaker History: ½c, Dr. John Coakley Lettsom, vert. 15c, Dr. William Thornton, vert. 30c, US Capitol, Washington, DC, and Dr. Thornton who designed it. $1, Library Hall, Philadelphia, and William Penn.

**1973, Mar. 9** **Litho.** *Perf. 13½*

**249** A34 ½c rose & multi .20 .20
**250** A34 10c multicolored .20 .20
**251** A34 15c multicolored .30 .30
**252** A34 30c ultra & multi .60 .60
**253** A34 $1 multicolored 1.90 1.90
*Nos. 249-253 (5)* 3.20 3.20

INTERPEX, 15th Intl. Phil. Exhib., NYC, Mar. 9-11.

Hummingbirds on 1c Coin — A35

Coins and Beach Scenes: 5c, Zenaida doves. 10c, Kingfisher. 25c, Mangrove cuckoos. 50c, Brown pelicans. $1, Magnificent frigate birds.

**1973, June 30** **Wmk. 314** *Perf. 14½*

**254** A35 1c orange & multi .20 *.40*
**255** A35 5c lt blue & multi .70 .20
**256** A35 10c pale ultra & multi 1.00 .20
**257** A35 25c yellow & multi 1.25 .20
**258** A35 50c lt violet & multi 1.40 1.40
**259** A35 $1 ultra & multi 1.75 *2.75*
*Nos. 254-259 (6)* 6.30 5.15

New Virgin Islands coinage.

**Princess Anne's Wedding Issue**

Common Design Type

**1973, Nov. 16** **Wmk. 314** *Perf. 14*

**260** CD325 5c citron & multi .20 .20
**261** CD325 50c blue grn & multi .80 .80

Virgin and Child, by Bernardino Pintoricchio A36

Arms of French Minesweeper Canopus A37

Christmas (Paintings of the Virgin and Child by): 3c, Lorenzo Credi. 25c, Carlo Crivelli. 50c, Bernardino Luini.

**1973, Dec. 7** *Perf. 14x14½*

**262** A36 ½c lt green & multi .20 .20
**263** A36 3c rose & multi .20 .20
**264** A36 25c ocher & multi .50 .50
**265** A36 50c lt blue & multi .95 .95
*Nos. 262-265 (4)* 1.85 1.85

**1974, Mar. 22** **Wmk. 314** *Perf. 14*

**266** A37 5c shown .20 .20
**267** A37 18c USS Saginaw .40 .40
**268** A37 25c HMS Rothesay .50 .50
**269** A37 50c HMCS Ottawa 1.00 1.00
*a.* Souvenir sheet of 4, #266-269 3.00 3.00
*Nos. 266-269 (4)* 2.10 2.10

INTERPEX Phil. Exhib., NYC, Mar. 22-24.

Famous Explorers — A38

**1974, Aug. 19** *Perf. 14½*

**270** A38 5c Columbus .25 .25
**271** A38 10c Sir Walter Raleigh .35 .35
**272** A38 25c Sir Martin Frobisher .40 .40
**273** A38 40c Sir Francis Drake .75 .75
*a.* Souvenir sheet of 4, #270-273 2.00 2.00
*Nos. 270-273 (4)* 1.75 1.75

Sea Shells A39

**1974, Sept. 30** *Perf. 13x13½*

**274** A39 5c Trumpet triton .40 .40
**275** A39 18c West Indian murex .85 .85
**276** A39 25c Bleeding tooth 1.00 1.00
**277** A39 75c Virgin Island latirus 2.50 2.50
*a.* Souvenir sheet of 4, #274-277 5.75 5.75
*Nos. 274-277 (4)* 4.75 4.75

St. Mary, Aldermanbury, London, — A40

Design: 50c, St. Mary, Fulton, Missouri.

**1974, Nov. 30** **Wmk. 373** *Perf. 14*

**278** A40 10c multicolored .20 .20
**279** A40 50c multicolored .50 .50
*a.* Souvenir sheet of 2, #278-279 1.00 1.00

Sir Winston Churchill (1874-1965).

Figurehead from "Boreas" — A41

Figureheads: 18c, The Golden Hind. 40c, Crowned lion from the "Superb." 85c, Warrior, from the "Formidable."

*Perf. 13½x13*

**1975, Mar. 14** **Wmk. 314**

**280** A41 5c multicolored .20 .20
**281** A41 18c multicolored .45 .45
**282** A41 40c multicolored .60 .60
**283** A41 85c multicolored 1.25 1.25
*a.* Souv. sheet of 4, #280-283, perf. 14 3.25 3.25
*Nos. 280-283 (4)* 2.50 2.50

INTERPEX, 17th Phil. Exhib., NYC, Mar. 14-16.

Rock Beauty A42

Designs: Fish.

**1975 Wmk. 373 *Perf. 14***

284 A42 ½c shown .20 .20
285 A42 1c Squirrelfish .55 .65
286 A42 3c Queen trigger-fish 1.40 1.60
287 A42 5c Blue angelfish .35 .45
288 A42 8c Stoplight par-rotfish .35 .45
289 A42 10c Queen angel-fish .35 .45
290 A42 12c Nassau grouper .55 .65
291 A42 13c Blue tang .55 .65
292 A42 15c Sergeant major .55 .65
293 A42 18c Jewfish 1.00 1.25
294 A42 20c Bluehead wrasse .75 .95
295 A42 25c Gray angelfish 1.40 1.60
296 A42 60c Glasseye snap-per 1.60 2.00
297 A42 $1 Blue chromis 2.25 2.75
298 A42 $2.50 French angel-fish 3.75 4.75
299 A42 $3 Queen par-rotfish 5.00 6.00
300 A42 $5 Four-eye butter-flyfish 5.50 6.75
*Nos. 284-300 (17)* 26.10 31.80

Issue dates: $5, Aug. 15. Others, June 16.
½c, 5c, 8c, 10c, 12c, 13c, 15c, 20c reissued dated "1977." Value $4.75.

St. Georges Parish School A43

Designs: 25c, Legislative Council Building. 40c, Mace and gavel of Legislative Council. 75c, Scroll with dates of historical events.

**1975, Nov. 27 Litho. Wmk. 373**

301 A43 5c ultra & multi .20 .20
302 A43 25c green & multi .40 .40
303 A43 40c ocher & multi .50 .50
304 A43 75c ultra & multi .65 .65
*Nos. 301-304 (4)* 1.75 1.75

Restoration of Legislative Council, 25th anniv.

Copper Mine Point A44

Historic Sites: 18c, Dr. Thornton's Ruin, Pleasant Valley. 50c, Callwood distillery. 75c, The Dungeon.

**1976, Mar. 12 Litho. *Perf. 14½***

305 A44 5c red & multi .20 .20
306 A44 18c red & multi .35 .35
307 A44 50c red & multi .70 .70
308 A44 75c red & multi 1.00 1.00
*Nos. 305-308 (4)* 2.25 2.25

Massachusetts Brig Hazard — A45

Designs: 22c, American Privateer Spy. 40c, Continental Navy Frigate Raleigh. 75c, Frigate Alliance and HMS Trepasy.

**1976, May 29 Wmk. 373 *Perf. 14***

309 A45 8c multicolored .35 .20
310 A45 22c multicolored .75 .55
311 A45 40c multicolored 1.40 1.10
312 A45 75c multicolored 2.75 2.00
a. Souvenir sheet of 4, #309-312 7.25 7.25
*Nos. 309-312 (4)* 5.25 3.85

American Bicentennial.

Government House, Tortola — A46

Designs: 15c, Government House, St. Croix, vert. 30c, Flags of US and British Virgin Islands, vert. 75c, Arms of British and US Virgin Islands.

**1976, Oct. 29 Litho. *Perf. 14***

313 A46 8c green & multi .20 .20
314 A46 15c green & multi .20 .20
315 A46 30c green & multi .35 .35
316 A46 75c green & multi .75 .75
*Nos. 313-316 (4)* 1.50 1.50

US and British Virgin Islands Friendship Day, 5th anniversary.

Holy Bible — A47

8c, Queen visiting Agricultural Station, Tortola, 1966. 60c, Presentation of Holy Bible.

**1977, Feb. 7 *Perf. 14x13½***

317 A47 8c silver & multi .20 .20
318 A47 30c silver & multi .30 .30
319 A47 60c silver & multi .50 .50
*Nos. 317-319 (3)* 1.00 1.00

25th anniv. of the reign of Elizabeth II.
For overprints see Nos. 324-326.

Virgin Islands Chart, 1739 — A48

18th Century Maps of Virgin Islands: 22c, 1758. 30c, 1775. 75c, 1779.

**1977, June 12 Wmk. 373 *Perf. 13½***

320 A48 8c multicolored .30 .20
321 A48 22c multicolored .65 .55
322 A48 30c multicolored .85 .75
323 A48 75c multicolored 1.75 1.75
*Nos. 320-323 (4)* 3.55 3.25

Type of 1977 Inscribed: "ROYAL VISIT"

Designs: 5c, Queen visiting Agricultural Station, Tortola, 1966. 25c, Holy Bible. 50c, Presentation of Holy Bible.

**1977, Oct. 26 Litho. *Perf. 14x13½***

324 A47 5c yel brn & multi .20 .20
325 A47 25c dk blue & multi .30 .30
326 A47 50c purple & multi .50 .50
*Nos. 324-326 (3)* 1.00 1.00

Caribbean visit of Queen Elizabeth II.

Divers Checking Equipment — A49

Tourist publicity: 5c, Cup coral inside bow of "Rhone." 8c, Sponge growing on superstructure of "Rhone." 22c, Sponge and cup coral. 30c, Scuba diver searching for sponges in cave. 75c, Marine life.

**1977, Dec. 15 Wmk. 373 *Perf. 13½***

327 A49 ½c multicolored .20 .20
328 A49 5c multicolored .20 .20
329 A49 8c multicolored .20 .20
330 A49 22c multicolored .60 .60
331 A49 30c multicolored .80 .80
332 A49 75c multicolored 1.25 1.25
*Nos. 327-332 (6)* 3.25 3.25

Corals A50

**1978, Feb. 10 *Perf. 14***

333 A50 8c Fire .30 .30
334 A50 15c Staghorn .45 .45
335 A50 40c Brain .85 .85
336 A50 75c Elkhorn 1.90 1.90
*Nos. 333-336 (4)* 3.50 3.50

**Elizabeth II Coronation Anniversary Issue**

Common Design Types
Souvenir Sheet

**1978, June 2 Unwmk. *Perf. 15***

337 Sheet of 6 2.75 2.75
a. CD326 50c Falcon of the Plantagenets .40 .40
b. CD327 50c Elizabeth II .40 .40
c. CD328 50c Iguana .40 .40

No. 337 contains 2 se-tenant strips of Nos. 337a-337c, separated by horizontal gutter.

Lignum Vitae A51

Flowering Trees: 22c, Ginger thomas. 40c, Dog almond. 75c, White cedar.

**1978, Sept. 4 Litho. *Perf. 13x13½***

338 A51 8c multicolored .35 .35
339 A51 22c multicolored .55 .55
340 A51 40c multicolored .75 .75
341 A51 75c multicolored 1.10 1.10
a. Souvenir sheet of 4, #338-341 2.75 2.75
*Nos. 338-341 (4)* 2.75 2.75

Eurema Lisa A52

Butterflies: 22c, Dione vanillae. 30c, Heliconius charitonius. 75c, Hemiargus hanno.

**1978, Dec. 4 Wmk. 373 *Perf. 14***

342 A52 5c multicolored .20 .20
343 A52 22c multicolored 1.00 .80
a. Sheet of 9, 6 #342, 3 #343 3.75 3.75
344 A52 30c multicolored 1.25 1.10
345 A52 75c multicolored 3.25 2.75
*Nos. 342-345 (4)* 5.70 4.85

Spiny Lobsters A53

Conservation: 15c, Iguana, vert. 22c, Hawksbill turtle. 75c, Black coral, vert.

**1979, Feb. 10 Litho.**

346 A53 5c multicolored .20 .20
347 A53 15c multicolored .40 .40
348 A53 22c multicolored .65 .65
349 A53 75c multicolored 1.50 1.50
a. Souvenir sheet of 4, #346-349 3.00 3.00
*Nos. 346-349 (4)* 2.75 2.75

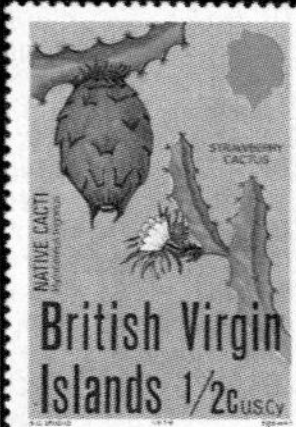

Strawberry Cactus — A54

West Indies Girl and Church — A55

Native Cacti: 5c, Snowy cactus. 13c, Barrel cactus. 22c, Tree cactus. 30c, Prickly pear. 75c, Dildo cactus.

**1979, May 7 Wmk. 373 *Perf. 14***

350 A54 ½c multicolored .20 .20
351 A54 5c multicolored .25 .25
352 A54 13c multicolored .40 .40
353 A54 22c multicolored .50 .50
354 A54 30c multicolored .60 .60
355 A54 75c multicolored .80 .80
*Nos. 350-355 (6)* 2.75 2.75

**1979, July 9 *Perf. 14x14½***

Children and IYC Emblem: 10c, African boy and dancers. 13c, Asian girl and children playing. $1, European girl and bicycle.

356 A55 5c multicolored .20 .20
357 A55 10c multicolored .20 .20
358 A55 13c multicolored .20 .20
359 A55 $1 multicolored .50 .50
a. Souvenir sheet of 4, #356-359 1.40 1.40
*Nos. 356-359 (4)* 1.10 1.10

International Year of the Child.

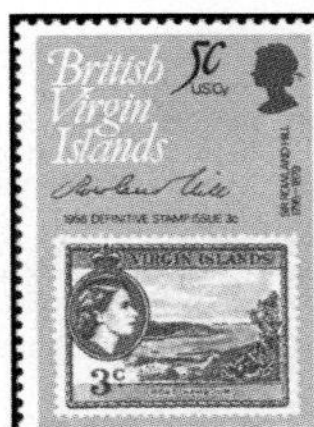
No. 118 — A56

Pencil Urchin — A57

Rowland Hill's Signature and: 13c, Virgin Islands No. 11, horiz. 75c, Unissued Great Britain 2d stamp, 1910, horiz. $1, Virgin Islands No. 8c.

**1979, Oct. 1 Photo. *Perf. 13½***

360 A56 5c multicolored .20 .20
361 A56 13c multicolored .20 .20
362 A56 75c multicolored .85 .85
*Nos. 360-362 (3)* 1.25 1.25

**Souvenir Sheet**

363 A56 $1 multicolored 1.00 1.00

Sir Rowland Hill (1795-1879), originator of penny postage.
For overprints see Nos. 389-390.

**1979-80 Litho. *Perf. 14***

364 A57 ½c Calcified algae .20 .20
365 A57 1c Purple-tipped sea anemone .20 .20
366 A57 3c Starfish .20 .20
367 A57 5c shown .20 .20
368 A57 8c Triton's trumpet .20 .20
369 A57 10c Christmas tree worms .20 .20

**370** A57 13c Flamingo tongue snails .25 *.25*
**371** A57 15c Spider crab .35 .35
**372** A57 18c Sea squirts .35 *.35*
**373** A57 20c Tree tulip .40 .40
**374** A57 25c Rooster tail conch .50 .55
**375** A57 30c Fighting conch .60 .65
**376** A57 60c Mangrove crab 1.25 *1.40*
**377** A57 $1 Coral polyps 2.00 2.10
**378** A57 $2.50 Peppermint shrimp 5.00 5.50
**379** A57 $3 West Indian murex 6.00 6.50
**380** A57 $5 Carpet anemone 10.00 11.00
*Nos. 364-380 (17)* 27.90 30.25

Issued: 5, 8, 10, 15, 20, 25c, $2.50, $3, 12/17; others, 4/1/80.

Nos. 367-368, 370-371, 373, 375 reissued inscribed 1982. Value $8.75.

For overprints see Nos. O1-O15.

Rotary Athletic Meet, Tortola, Emblem A58

**1980, Mar. 3 Litho. *Perf. 13½x14***

**381** A58 8c shown .20 .20
**382** A58 22c Paul P. Harris .25 .25
**383** A58 60c Mount Sage National Park .55 .55
**384** A58 $1 Anniversary emblem 1.00 1.00
*a.* Souvenir sheet of 4, #381-384 2.50 2.50
*Nos. 381-384 (4)* 2.00 2.00

Rotary International, 75th anniv.

Brown Booby, London 1980 Emblem A59

**1980, May 6 Wmk. 373 *Perf. 14***

**385** A59 20c shown .35 .35
**386** A59 25c Magnificent frigatebird .45 .45
**387** A59 50c White-tailed tropic bird .70 .70
**388** A59 75c Brown pelican .95 .95
*a.* Souvenir sheet of 4, #385-388 3.00 3.00
*Nos. 385-388 (4)* 2.45 2.45

London 80 Intl. Stamp Exhib., May 6-14.

Nos. 361-362 Overprinted: "CARIBBEAN COMMONWEALTH PARLIAMENTARY ASSOCIATION MEETING TORTOLA 11-19 JULY 1980"

**1980, July 7 Photo. *Perf. 13½***

**389** A56 13c multicolored .20 .20
**390** A56 75c multicolored .80 .80

Sir Francis Drake — A60

**1980, Sept. 26 Litho. *Perf. 14½***

**391** A60 8c shown .45 .45
**392** A60 15c Queen Elizabeth I .70 .70
**393** A60 30c Drake knighted .85 .85
**394** A60 75c Golden Hinde 1.75 1.75
*a.* Souvenir sheet of 4, #391-394 3.75 3.75
*Nos. 391-394 (4)* 3.75 3.75

400th anniv. of circumnavigation of the world.

Jost Van Dyke A61

**1980, Dec. 1 Wmk. 373 *Perf. 14***

**395** A61 2c shown .20 .20
**396** A61 5c Peter Island .20 .20
**397** A61 13c Virgin Gorda .20 .20
**398** A61 22c Anegada .30 .30
**399** A61 30c Norman Island .35 .35
**400** A61 $1 Tortola 1.00 1.00
*a.* Souvenir sheet of 1 1.50 1.50
*Nos. 395-400 (6)* 2.25 2.25

Dancing Lady — A62

**1981, Mar. 3 Litho. *Perf. 11***

**401** A62 5c shown .30 .30
**402** A62 20c Love in the mist .35 .35
**403** A62 22c Red pineapple .35 .35
**404** A62 75c Dutchman's pipe .90 .90
**405** A62 $1 Maiden apple 1.10 1.10
*Nos. 401-405 (5)* 3.00 3.00

**Royal Wedding Issue**
Common Design Type

**1981, July 22 Litho. *Perf. 14***

**406** CD331 10c Bouquet .20 .20
**407** CD331 35c Charles, Queen Mother .45 .45
**408** CD331 $1.25 Couple 1.50 1.50
*Nos. 406-408 (3)* 2.15 2.15

#406-408 each se-tenant with decorative label.

Duke of Edinburgh's Awards, 25th Anniv. — A63

**1981, Sept. 16 Wmk. 373 *Perf. 14***

**409** A63 10c Stamp collecting .20 .20
**410** A63 15c Running .25 .25
**411** A63 50c Camping .85 .85
**412** A63 $1 Duke of Edinburgh 1.60 1.60
*Nos. 409-412 (4)* 2.90 2.90

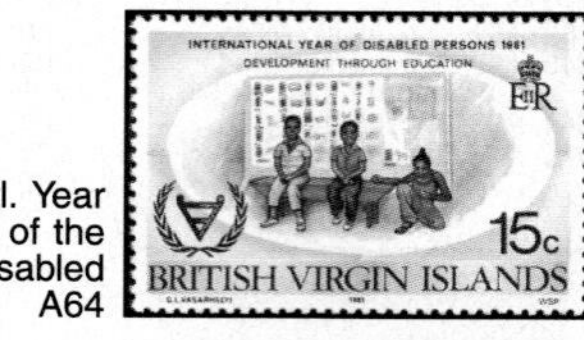


Intl. Year of the Disabled A64

**1981, Oct. 19 Litho. *Perf. 14***

**413** A64 15c Children .30 .30
**414** A64 20c Fort Charlotte Children's Center .40 .40
**415** A64 30c Playing music .60 .60
**416** A64 $1 Center, diff. 2.00 2.00
*Nos. 413-416 (4)* 3.30 3.30

A65

A66

Virgin and Child (Christmas): Details from Adoration of the Shepherds, by Rubens. 50c, horiz.

**1981, Nov. 30 Litho. *Perf. 14***

**417** A65 5c multicolored .20 .20
**418** A65 15c multicolored .25 .25
**419** A65 30c multicolored .50 .50
**420** A65 $1 multicolored 2.00 2.00
*Nos. 417-420 (4)* 2.95 2.95

**Souvenir Sheet**

**421** A65 50c multicolored 1.00 1.00

**1982, Apr. 15 Litho. *Perf. 14x14½***

Hummingbirds on local flora.

**422** A66 15c Green-throated carib, erythrina .45 .45
**423** A66 30c Same, bougainvillea .90 .90
**424** A66 35c Antillean crested hummingbird, granadilla passiflora 1.00 1.00
**425** A66 $1.25 Same, hibiscus 3.50 3.50
*Nos. 422-425 (4)* 5.85 5.85

10th Anniv. of Lions Club of Tortola — A67

**1982, May 3 *Perf. 13½x14***

**426** A67 10c Helping disabled .20 .20
**427** A67 20c Headquarters .35 .35
**428** A67 30c Map .50 .50
**429** A67 $1.50 Emblem 2.50 2.50
*a.* Souvenir sheet of 4, #426-429 3.75 3.75
*Nos. 426-429 (4)* 3.55 3.55

**Princess Diana Issue**
Common Design Type

**1982, July 1 Litho. *Perf. 14***

**430** CD333 10c Arms .20 .20
**431** CD333 35c Diana .55 .55
**432** CD333 50c Wedding .75 .75
**433** CD333 $1.50 Portrait 2.50 2.50
*Nos. 430-433 (4)* 4.00 4.00

10th Anniv. of Air BVI (Natl. Airline) A68

**1982, Sept. 10 Wmk. 373 *Perf. 14***

**434** A68 10c Douglas DC-3 .30 .30
**435** A68 15c Britten-Norman Islander .50 .50
**436** A68 60c Hawker-Siddeley 2.10 2.10
**437** A68 75c Planes 2.50 2.50
*Nos. 434-437 (4)* 5.40 5.40

Scouting Year A69

**1982, Nov. 18**

**438** A69 8c Emblem, Flag raising .20 .20
**439** A69 20c Cub scout, nature study .40 .40
**440** A69 50c Kayak, sea scout 1.00 1.00
**441** A69 $1 Camp Brownsea Is., Baden-Powell 2.00 2.00
*Nos. 438-441 (4)* 3.60 3.60

Commonwealth Day — A70

**1983, Mar. 14 *Perf. 13½x14***

**442** A70 10c Legislature in session .20 .20
**443** A70 30c Wind surfing .50 .50
**444** A70 35c Globe .60 .60
**445** A70 75c Flags 1.25 1.25
*Nos. 442-445 (4)* 2.55 2.55

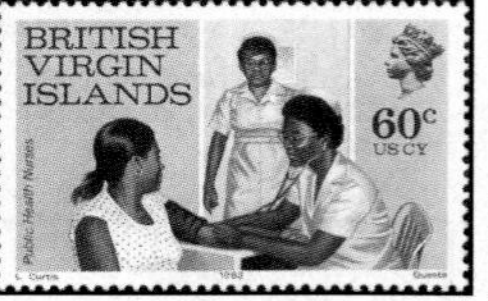


Nursing Week A71

**1983, May 9 Litho. *Perf. 14½***

**446** A71 10c Florence Nightingale (1820-1910), vert. .40 .40
**447** A71 30c Nurse, assistant, vert. 1.10 1.10
**448** A71 60c Public health 2.25 2.25
**449** A71 75c Peebles Hospital 3.00 3.00
*Nos. 446-449 (4)* 6.75 6.75

Boat Building A72

**1983, July 25 *Perf. 14***

**450** A72 15c First stage .35 .35
**451** A72 25c 2nd stage .55 .55
**452** A72 50c Launching 1.10 1.10
**453** A72 $1 First voyage 2.25 2.25
*a.* Souvenir sheet of 4, #450-453 4.25 4.25
*Nos. 450-453 (4)* 4.25 4.25

Manned Flight Bicentenary — A73

**1983, Sept. 15 Wmk. 373 *Perf. 14***

**454** A73 10c Grumman Goose .20 .20
**455** A73 30c De Havilland Heron .50 .50
**456** A73 60c EMB Bandeirante 1.00 1.00
**457** A73 $1.25 Hawker-Siddeley 748 2.00 2.00
*Nos. 454-457 (4)* 3.70 3.70

Christmas — A74

Raphael Paintings.

**1983, Nov. 7 Litho. *Perf. 14½***

**458** A74 8c Madonna & Child with Infant Baptist .20 .20
**459** A74 15c La Belle Jardiniere .30 .30
**460** A74 50c Madonna del Granduca .95 .95
**461** A74 $1 Terranuova Madonna 1.90 1.90
*a.* Souvenir sheet of 4, #458-461 3.50 3.50
*Nos. 458-461 (4)* 3.35 3.35

World Chess Federation, 60th Anniv. — A75

**1984, Feb. 20 Litho. *Perf. 14***

**462** A75 10c Local tournament .55 .55
**463** A75 35c Chess pieces, vert. 1.75 1.75
**464** A75 75c 1980 Olympiad, Winning board, vert. 4.00 4.00
**465** A75 $1 Gold medal 6.00 6.00
*Nos. 462-465 (4)* 12.30 12.30

**Lloyd's List Issue**
Common Design Type

**1984, Apr. 16 Litho. *Perf. 14½x14***

**466** CD335 15c Port Purcell, Tortola .35 .35
**467** CD335 25c Boeing 747 .65 .65
**468** CD335 50c Shipwreck of RMS Rhone 1.25 1.25
**469** CD335 $1 Booker Viking 2.50 2.50
*Nos. 466-469 (4)* 4.75 4.75

Souvenir Sheet

UPU Congress — A76

**1984, May 16 Wmk. 373 *Perf. 14***

**470** A76 $1 Emblem, jet, mailboat 3.00 3.00

1984 Summer Olympics A77

**1984, July 3**

**471** A77 15c Runners .35 .35
**472** A77 15c Runner .35 .35
*a.* Pair, #471-472 1.10 1.10
**473** A77 20c Wind surfers .45 .45
**474** A77 20c Wind surfer .45 .45
*a.* Pair, #473-474 1.40 1.40
**475** A77 30c Yachts .70 .70
**476** A77 30c Yacht .70 .70
*a.* Pair, #475-476 2.10 2.10
*Nos. 471-476 (6)* 3.00 3.00

**Souvenir Sheet**

**477** A77 $1 Torch bearer, vert. 2.25 2.25

Festival (Slavery Abolition Sesquicentennial) — A78

Designs: No. 478: a, Steel band. b, Calypso dancers. c, Dancers (men). d, Woman in traditional dress. e, Parade float.

No. 479 (Sail color of boat(s) in foreground): a, Green & white. b, Red & white, white, purple & white. c, white, yellow & white, blue & white. d, Yellow, red & white. e, Purple & white, white.

Nos. 478 and 479 each in continuous design.

**1984, Aug. 14 *Perf. 13½x14***

**478** Strip of 5, Parade 1.25 1.25
*a.-e.* A78 10c, any single .20 .20
**479** Strip of 5, Regatta 3.50 3.50
*a.-e.* A78 30c, any single .55 .55

Local Boats A79

**1984, Nov. 15 Wmk. 373 *Perf. 13***

**480** A79 10c Sloop .30 .30
**481** A79 35c Fishing boat 1.10 1.10
**482** A79 60c Schooner 2.00 2.00
**483** A79 75c Cargo boat 2.40 2.40
*a.* Souvenir sheet of 4, #480-483 6.25 6.25
*Nos. 480-483 (4)* 5.80 5.80

Four stamps picturing Michael Jackson were printed. The designs were not acceptable to the Virgin Islands so they were not issued. A number of copies had been distributed in advance for publicity purposes.

New Coinage A80

**1985, Jan. 15 Litho. *Perf. 14½***

**484** A80 1c Hawksbill Turtle .20 .20
**485** A80 5c Bonito .20 .20
**486** A80 10c Great Barricuda .20 .20
**487** A80 25c Blue Marlin .65 .65
**488** A80 50c Dolphin 1.25 1.25
**489** A80 $1 Spotfin Butterfly Fish 2.50 2.50
*a.* Miniature sheet of 6, #484-489 5.75 5.75
*Nos. 484-489 (6)* 5.00 5.00

Birds — A81

**1985, July 3 Wmk. 373 *Perf. 14***

**490** A81 1c Boatswain bird .25 .30
**491** A81 2c Night gaulin .25 .30
**492** A81 5c Rain bird .25 .30
**493** A81 8c Mockingbird .25 .30
**494** A81 10c Chinchary .30 .40
**495** A81 12c Wild pigeon .40 .50
**496** A81 15c Bittlin .50 .55
**497** A81 18c Blach witch .55 *.65*
**498** A81 20c Pond shakey .65 .75
**499** A81 25c Killy-killy .80 .90
**500** A81 30c Thrushie 1.00 1.10
**501** A81 35c Marmi dove 1.10 *1.25*
**502** A81 40c Little gaulin 1.40 *1.60*
**503** A81 50c Ground dove 1.60 1.75
**504** A81 60c Blue gaulin 2.00 2.25
**505** A81 $1 Pimleco 3.25 3.75
**506** A81 $2 White booby 7.00 8.00
**507** A81 $3 Cow bird 9.75 11.00
**508** A81 $5 Turtle dove 16.00 19.00
*Nos. 490-508 (19)* 47.30 54.65

For overprints see Nos. O16-O34.

**1987, Oct. 28 Wmk. 384**

*494a* A81 10c .35 .35
*496a* A81 15c .55 .55
*498a* A81 20c .75 .75
*499a* A81 25c .90 .90
*501a* A81 35c 1.25 1.25
*505a* A81 $1 3.75 3.75
*507a* A81 $3 11.00 11.00
*Nos. 494a-507a (7)* 18.55 18.55

Queen Mother, 85th Birthday — A82

Audubon Birth Bicent. — A83

Portraits.

**1985, Aug. 26 Litho. *Perf. 12½***

**509** A82 10c Facing right .20 .20
**510** A82 10c Facing left .20 .20
**511** A82 25c Facing right .45 .45
**512** A82 25c Facing left .45 .45
**513** A82 50c Facing right .90 .90
**514** A82 50c Facing forward .90 .90
**515** A82 75c Facing right 1.25 1.25
**516** A82 75c Facing forward 1.25 1.25
*Nos. 509-516 (8)* 5.60 5.60

Souvenir Sheets

**1985-86 Litho. *Perf. 13x12½***

**517** Sheet of 2 3.50 3.50
*a.-b.* A82 $1 dull grn & multi 1.75 1.75
**518** Sheet of 2 3.50 3.50
*a.-b.* A82 $1 orange & multi 1.60 1.60
**519** Sheet of 2 8.50 8.50
*a.-b.* A82 $2.50 dl yel & multi 4.25 4.25

Issued: #517, 12/18/85; #518-519, 2/18/86.
For overprints see Nos. 528-531.

**1985, Dec. 17 *Perf. 15***

**520** A83 5c Seaside sparrow .20 .20
**521** A83 30c Passenger pigeon .60 .60
**522** A83 50c Yellow-breasted chat 1.00 1.00
**523** A83 $1 American kestrel 2.00 2.00
*Nos. 520-523 (4)* 3.80 3.80

Cruise Ships A84

**1986, Jan. 27**

**524** A84 35c Flying Cloud .75 .75
**525** A84 50c Newport Clipper 1.10 1.10
**526** A84 75c Cunard Countess 1.75 1.75
**527** A84 $1 Sea Goddess 2.40 2.40
*Nos. 524-527 (4)* 6.00 6.00

Nos. 511-512, 515-516 Ovptd. "MIAMI / B.V.I. / INAUGURAL FLIGHT"

**1986, Apr. 17 Litho. *Perf. 12½***

**528** A82 25c on No. 511 .50 .50
**529** A82 25c on No. 512 .50 .50
**530** A82 75c on No. 515 1.50 1.50
**531** A82 75c on No. 516 1.50 1.50
*Nos. 528-531 (4)* 4.00 4.00

Queen Elizabeth II, 60th Birthday — A85

***Perf. 13x12½, 12½x13***

**1986, Apr. 21 Litho.**

**532** A85 12c Portrait, 1958 .20 .20
**533** A85 35c Maundy service .55 .55
**534** A85 $1.50 Contemporary photograph 2.25 2.25
**535** A85 $2 Canberra, 1982, vert. 3.00 3.00
*Nos. 532-535 (4)* 6.00 6.00

**Souvenir Sheet**

**536** A85 $3 Contemporary photograph, diff. 6.00 6.00

Stamps with blue ribbons and frames omitted were from stock sold when the printer was liquidated.

Wedding of Prince Andrew and Sarah Ferguson — A86

**1986, July 23 *Perf. 12½***

**537** A86 35c Couple, vert. .55 .55
**538** A86 35c Sarah, vert. .55 .55
**539** A86 $1 Andrew 1.60 1.60
**540** A86 $1 Sarah, diff. 1.60 1.60
*Nos. 537-540 (4)* 4.30 4.30

Stamps of the same denomination exist se-tenant.

Nos. 537-540 Overprinted "Congratulations to T.R.H. The Duke & Duchess of York" were not issued.

Traditional Rum Production — A87

**1986, July 30 *Perf. 14***

**541** A87 12c Harvesting sugar cane .50 .50
**542** A87 40c Grinding 1.90 1.90
**543** A87 60c Distillery 3.00 3.00
**544** A87 $1 Transport 5.00 5.00
*Nos. 541-544 (4)* 10.40 10.40

**Souvenir Sheet**

**545** A87 $2 Up Spirits ceremony, 19th cent. 8.75 8.75

Souvenir Sheet

Wedding of Prince Andrew and Sarah Ferguson — A88

**1986, Oct. 15 Litho. *Perf. 13x12½***

**546** A88 $4 multicolored 7.50 6.00

Cable-Laying Ships — A89

**1986, Oct. 15 Wmk. 380 *Perf. 12½***

**547** A89 35c Sentinel .70 .70
**548** A89 35c Retriever .70 .70
*a.* Pair, #547-548 1.40 1.40
**549** A89 60c Cable Enterprise 1.25 1.25
**550** A89 60c Mercury 1.25 1.25
*a.* Pair, #549-550 2.50 2.50
**551** A89 75c Recorder 1.50 1.50
**552** A89 75c Pacific Guardian 1.50 1.50
*a.* Pair, #551-552 3.00 3.00

**553** A89 $1 Great Eastern 2.00 2.00
**554** A89 $1 Cable Venture 2.00 2.00
*a.* Pair, #553-554 4.00 4.00
*Nos. 547-554 (8)* 10.90 10.90

**Souvenir Sheets**

**555** Sheet of 2 1.40 1.40
*a.-b.* A89 40c, like #547-548 .70 .70
**556** Sheet of 2 1.75 1.75
*a.-b.* A89 50c, like #549-550 .90 .90
**557** Sheet of 2 2.75 2.75
*a.-b.* A89 80c, like #551-552 1.40 1.40
**558** Sheet of 2 5.25 5.25
*a.-b.* A89 $1.50, like #553-554 2.50 2.50

Cable and wireless in the islands, 20th anniv.

Souvenir Sheets

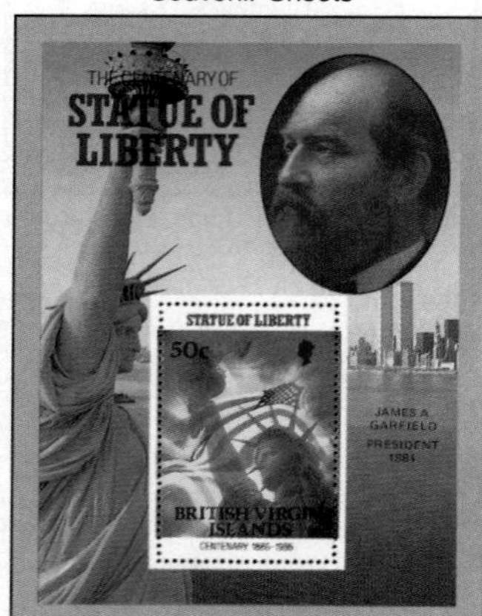


Statue of Liberty, Cent. — A90

Various views of the statue.

**1986, Dec. 15 Litho. *Perf. 14***

**559** A90 50c multicolored .95 .95
**560** A90 75c multicolored 1.60 1.60
**561** A90 90c multicolored 1.75 1.75
**562** A90 $1 multicolored 2.00 2.00
**563** A90 $1.25 multicolored 2.50 2.50
**564** A90 $1.50 multicolored 3.00 3.00
**565** A90 $1.75 multicolored 3.50 3.50
**566** A90 $2 multicolored 3.75 3.75
**567** A90 $2.50 multicolored 5.00 5.00
*Nos. 559-567 (9)* 24.05 24.05

A91

Shipwrecks — A92

**1987, Apr. 15 *Perf. 14***

**572** A91 12c Spanish galleon, 18th cent. .75 .75
**573** A91 35c HMS Astrea, 1808 2.25 2.25
**574** A91 75c RMS Rhone, 1867 4.25 4.25
**575** A91 $1.50 SS Rocus, 1929 9.25 9.25
*Nos. 572-575 (4)* 16.50 16.50

**Souvenir Sheet**

**576** A92 $2.50 Brig Volvart, 1918 17.00 17.00

Natl. Flags, Outline Maps — A93

Botanical Gardens — A94

**1987, May 28**

**577** A93 10c Montserrat .20 .20
**578** A93 15c Grenada .55 .55
**579** A93 20c Dominica .75 .75
**580** A93 25c St. Kitts-Nevis .95 .95
**581** A93 35c St. Vincent and Grenadines 1.25 1.25
**582** A93 50c Virgin Isls. 1.90 1.90
**583** A93 75c Antigua & Barbuda 2.75 2.75
**584** A93 $1 St. Lucia 3.75 3.75
*Nos. 577-584 (8)* 12.10 12.10

11th Meeting of the Organization of Eastern Caribbean States.

**1987, Aug. 12 Wmk. 384**

**585** A94 12c Spider lily .65 .65
**586** A94 35c Barrel cactus 2.10 2.10
**587** A94 $1 Wild plantain 5.75 5.75
**588** A94 $1.50 Little butterfly orchid 8.50 8.50
*Nos. 585-588 (4)* 17.00 17.00

**Souvenir Sheet**

**589** A94 $2.50 White cedar 5.75 5.75

Postal Service Bicent. A95

Designs: 10c, 18th Cent. packet, #7 canceled "A13." 20c, Map of the islands, #22 canceled "A91." 35c, Tortola Post Office and Customs House, and #5 canceled "Tortola De 20 61." $1.50, Mail plane and #154 canceled "Road town No 2 64 Tortola W.I." $2.50, Late 19th cent. steam packet and #10 canceled "A Tortola Ap 12 70."

**1987, Dec. 17 Litho. *Perf. 14½***

**590** A95 10c multicolored .65 .65
**591** A95 20c multicolored 1.25 1.25
**592** A95 35c multicolored 2.25 2.25
**593** A95 $1.50 multicolored 9.75 9.75
*Nos. 590-593 (4)* 13.90 13.90

**Souvenir Sheet**

**594** A95 $2.50 multicolored 7.25 7.25

Paintings by Titian — A96

10c, Salome, 1512. 12c, Man with the Glove, c. 1520-22. 20c, Fabrizio Salvaresio, 1558. 25c, Daughter of Roberto Strozzi, 1542. 40c, Pope Julius II. 50c, Bishop Ludovico Beccadelli, 1552. 60c, Philip II. $1, Empress Isabella of Portugal, 1548. #603, Emperor Charles V at Muhlberg, 1548. #604, Pope Paul III & His Grandsons, 1546.

***Perf. 13½x14***

**1988, Aug. 11 Unwmk.**

**595** A96 10c multicolored .35 .35
**596** A96 12c multicolored .45 .45
**597** A96 20c multicolored .75 .75
**598** A96 25c multicolored .95 .95
**599** A96 40c multicolored 1.60 1.60
**600** A96 50c multicolored 1.90 1.90
**601** A96 60c multicolored 2.40 2.40
**602** A96 $1 multicolored 4.00 4.00
*Nos. 595-602 (8)* 12.40 12.40

**Souvenir Sheet**

**603** A96 $2 multicolored 7.25 7.25
**604** A96 $2 multicolored 7.25 7.25

1st Annual Open Chess Tournament — A97

35c, Pawn & Transporter aircraft over Sir Francis Drake Channel. $1, King & Jose Raul Capablanca (1888-1942), Cuban chess master and world champion from 1921-27. $2, Match scene.

**1988, Aug. 25 Unwmk. *Perf. 14***

**605** A97 35c multicolored 3.75 3.75
**606** A97 $1 multicolored 10.50 10.50

**Souvenir Sheet**

**607** A97 $2 multicolored 12.00 12.00

1988 Summer Olympics, Seoul A98

**1988, Sept. 8**

**608** A98 12c Hurdling .55 .55
**609** A98 20c Windsurfing .95 .95
**610** A98 75c Basketball 3.75 3.75
**611** A98 $1 Tennis 4.75 4.75
*Nos. 608-611 (4)* 10.00 10.00

**Souvenir Sheet**

**612** A98 $2 Running 4.75 4.75

Intl. Red Cross, 125th Anniv. A99

Safety warnings and steps in administering cardiopulmonary resuscitation (CPR): 12c, "Don't swim alone." 30c, "No swimming during electrical storms." 60c, "Don't eat before swimming." $1, "Proper equipment for boating." No. 617a, Turn victim on back. No. 617b, Position victim's chin so breathing passages are not blocked. No. 617c, Mouth-to-mouth resuscitation. No. 617d, Chest compressions. Nos. 617a-617d vert.

**1988, Sept. 26**

**613** A99 12c multicolored .55 .55
**614** A99 30c multicolored 1.40 1.40
**615** A99 60c multicolored 2.75 2.75
**616** A99 $1 multicolored 4.75 4.75
*Nos. 613-616 (4)* 9.45 9.45

**Souvenir Sheet**

**617** Sheet of 4 7.75 7.75
*a.-d.* A99 50c any single 1.00 1.00

#617a-617d has a continuous design.

Visit of Princess Alexandra — A100

World Wildlife Fund — A101

Various photographs of the princess.

**1988, Nov. 9 Litho. *Perf. 14***

**618** A100 40c shown 1.90 1.90
**619** A100 $1.50 multi, diff. 7.00 7.00

**Souvenir Sheet**

**620** A100 $2 multi, diff. 8.25 8.25

**1988, Nov. 15**

Brown pelicans, *Pelecanus Occidentalis.*

**621** A101 10c Pelican in flight .85 .85
**622** A101 12c Perched 1.10 1.10
**623** A101 15c Close-up of head 1.25 1.25
**624** A101 35c Swallowing fish 3.00 3.00
*Nos. 621-624 (4)* 6.20 6.20

Reptiles, Marine Mammals and Birds — A102

20c, Anegada rock iguana. 40c, Virgin gorda dwarf gecko. 60c, Hawksbill turtle. $1, Humpback whale. #629, Northern shoveler, American widgeon & ring-necked ducks. #630, Trunk turtle.

**1988, Nov. 15**

**625** A102 20c multicolored 1.10 1.10
**626** A102 40c multicolored 2.25 2.25
**627** A102 60c multicolored 3.50 3.50
**628** A102 $1 multicolored 5.75 5.75
*Nos. 625-628 (4)* 12.60 12.60

**Souvenir Sheets**

**629** A102 $2 multicolored 10.50 10.50
**630** A102 $2 multicolored 7.75 7.75

Spring Regatta A103

Various yachts.

**1989, Apr. 7 Litho. *Perf. 14***

**631** A103 12c multi, diff., vert. .35 .35
**632** A103 40c shown 1.25 1.25
**633** A103 75c multi, diff., vert. 2.25 2.25
**634** A103 $1 multi, diff. 3.00 3.00
*Nos. 631-634 (4)* 6.85 6.85

**Souvenir Sheet**

**635** A103 $2 multi, diff., vert. 7.75 7.75

Pre-Columbian Societies and Their Customs — A104

**1989, May 18**

**636** A104 10c Hammock .40 .40
**637** A104 20c Making a fire .85 .85
**638** A104 25c Carvers 1.00 1.00
**639** A104 $1.50 Arawak family 6.50 6.50
*Nos. 636-639 (4)* 8.75 8.75

**Souvenir Sheet**

**640** A104 $2 Ritual 8.75 8.75

Discovery of America 500th anniv. (in 1992).

1st Moon Landing, 20th Anniv. A105

Highlights of the Apollo 11 mission: 15c, Lunar surface, mission emblem. 30c, Buzz Aldrin conducting solar wind experiment. 65c, Raising American flag. $1, Recovery of crew after splashdown. $2, Portrait of crew.

**1989, Sept. 28 Litho. *Perf. 14***

**641** A105 15c multicolored .80 .80
**642** A105 30c multicolored 1.60 1.60
**643** A105 65c multicolored 3.25 3.25
**644** A105 $1 multicolored 5.25 5.25
*Nos. 641-644 (4)* 10.90 10.90

**Souvenir Sheet**

***Perf. 13½x14***

**645** A105 $2 multicolored 8.75 8.75

No. 645 contains one 37x46mm stamp.

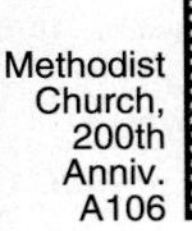

Methodist Church, 200th Anniv. A106

Designs: 12c, Black Harry, Nathaniel Gilbert preaching. 25c, Book symbolizing role of the church in education. 35c, East End Methodist Church, 1810. $1.25, John Wesley, modern youth choir. $2, Thomas Coke.

**1989, Oct. 24 *Perf. 14***

**646** A106 12c multicolored .55 .55
**647** A106 25c multicolored 1.10 1.10
**648** A106 35c multicolored 1.60 1.60
**649** A106 $1.25 multicolored 5.50 5.50
*Nos. 646-649 (4)* 8.75 8.75

**Souvenir Sheet**

**650** A106 $2 multicolored 7.25 7.25

1990 World Cup Soccer Championships, Italy — A107

Various athletes.

**1989, Nov. 6**

**651** A107 5c shown .60 .60
**652** A107 10c multi, diff. .60 .60
**653** A107 20c multi, diff. 1.25 1.25
**654** A107 $1.75 multi, diff. 11.00 11.00
*Nos. 651-654 (4)* 13.45 13.45

**Souvenir Sheet**

**655** A107 $2 Natl. team 10.00 10.00

Princess Alexandra, Sunset House — A108

Royal Yacht Britannia — A109

b, Princess Margaret, Government House. c, Hon. Angus Ogilvy, Little Dix Bay Hotel. d, Princess Diana & her children, Necker Island Resort.

**1990, May 3 Litho. *Perf. 14***

**656** Min. sheet of 4 10.50 10.50
*a.-d.* A108 50c any single 1.00 1.00

**Souvenir Sheet**

**657** A109 $2 multicolored 7.75 7.75

Stamp World London '90.

Audubon's Shearwater — A110

**1990, May 15**

**658** A110 5c shown .20 .20
**659** A110 12c Red-necked pigeon .30 .30
**660** A110 20c Common gallinule .55 .55
**661** A110 25c Green heron .70 .70
**662** A110 40c Yellow warbler 1.10 1.10
**663** A110 60c Smooth-billed ani 1.75 1.75
**664** A110 $1 Antillean crested hummingbird 2.75 2.75
**665** A110 $1.25 Black-faced grassquit 3.50 3.00
*Nos. 658-665 (8)* 10.85 10.35

**Souvenir Sheets**

**666** A110 $2 Egg of royal tern 5.00 5.00
**667** A110 $2 Egg of red-billed tropicbird 5.00 5.00

Blue Tang A111

**1990, June 18**

**668** A111 10c shown .45 .45
**669** A111 35c Glasseye 1.75 1.75
**670** A111 50c Slippery Dick 2.40 2.40
**671** A111 $1 Porkfish 5.00 5.00
*Nos. 668-671 (4)* 9.60 9.60

**Souvenir Sheet**

**672** A111 $2 Yellowtail snapper 7.25 7.25

A112

A113

**1990, Aug. 30 Litho. *Perf. 14***

**673** A112 12c multicolored .40 .40
**674** A112 25c multi, diff. .85 .85
**675** A112 60c multi, diff. 2.10 2.10
**676** A112 $1 multi, diff. 3.50 3.50
*Nos. 673-676 (4)* 6.85 6.85

**Souvenir Sheet**

**677** A112 $2 multi, diff. 5.50 5.50

Queen Mother, 90th birthday.

**1990, Dec. 10 Litho. *Perf. 14***

Various soccer players.

**678** A113 12c multicolored .45 .45
**679** A113 20c multi, diff. .75 .75
**680** A113 50c multi, diff. 1.90 1.90
**681** A113 $1.25 multi, diff. 4.75 4.75
*Nos. 678-681 (4)* 7.85 7.85

**Souvenir Sheet**

**682** A113 $2 multi, diff. 6.75 6.75

World Cup Soccer Championships, Italy.

1992 Summer Olympics, Barcelona A114

**1990, Dec. 20 Litho. *Perf. 14***

**683** A114 12c Judo .60 .60
**684** A114 40c Yachting 1.90 1.90
**685** A114 60c Hurdles 3.00 3.00
**686** A114 $1 Show jumping 5.00 5.00
*Nos. 683-686 (4)* 10.50 10.50

**Souvenir Sheet**

**687** A114 $2 Windsurfing 6.00 6.00

Copper Mine Ruins A115

**1991, Mar. 1 Litho. *Perf. 14***

**688** A115 10c Cyanthea arborea, vert. .35 .35
**689** A115 25c shown .95 .95
**690** A115 35c Mt. Healthy windmill ruin, vert. 1.40 1.40
**691** A115 $2 Baths, Virgin Gorda 8.00 8.00
*Nos. 688-691 (4)* 10.70 10.70

National Park Trust.

Flowers — A116

Butterflies — A117

**1991-92 Litho. *Perf. 14***

**692** A116 1c Haiti Haiti .20 .20
**693** A116 2c Lobster claw .20 .20
**694** A116 5c Frangipani .20 .20
**695** A116 10c Autograph tree .20 .20
**696** A116 12c Yellow allamanda .25 .25
**697** A116 15c Lantana .30 .30
**698** A116 20c Jerusalem thorn .45 .45
**699** A116 25c Turk's cap .55 .55
**700** A116 30c Swamp immortelle .65 .65
**701** A116 35c White cedar .75 .75
**702** A116 40c Mahoe tree .90 .90
**703** A116 45c Pinguin 1.00 1.00
**704** A116 50c Christmas orchid 1.10 1.10
**705** A116 70c Lignum vitae 1.60 1.60
**706** A116 $1 African tulip tree 2.25 2.25
**707** A116 $2 Beach morning glory 4.50 4.50
**708** A116 $3 Organ pipe cactus 6.50 6.50
**709** A116 $5 Tall ground orchid 11.50 11.50
**710** A116 $10 Ground orchid 22.50 22.50
*Nos. 692-710 (19)* 55.60 55.60

Nos. 695, 701, 703 exist dated "1995."

The 70c, $1 and $2 exist perf 12, the $3 prerf 12½. These were issued in Aug. 1995.

Issued: $10, 5/92; others, 5/1/91.

For overprints see Nos. O37-O51.

**1991, June 28 Litho. *Perf. 14***

**711** A117 5c Cloudless sulphur .40 .40
**712** A117 10c Flambeau .40 .40

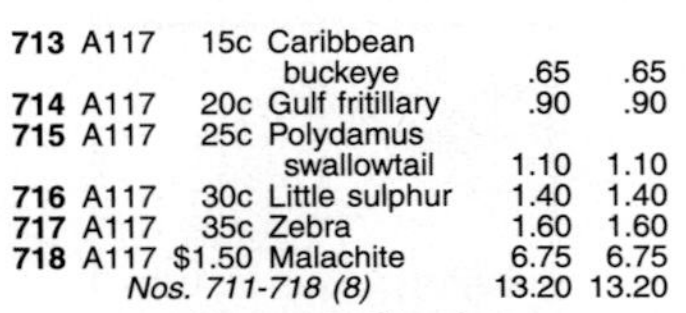

**713** A117 15c Caribbean buckeye .65 .65
**714** A117 20c Gulf fritillary .90 .90
**715** A117 25c Polydamus swallowtail 1.10 1.10
**716** A117 30c Little sulphur 1.40 1.40
**717** A117 35c Zebra 1.60 1.60
**718** A117 $1.50 Malachite 6.75 6.75
*Nos. 711-718 (8)* 13.20 13.20

**Souvenir Sheets**

**719** A117 $2 Monarch, horiz. 8.00 8.00
**720** A117 $2 Red rim, horiz. 8.00 8.00

Voyages of Discovery A118

Ships of explorers: 12c, Ferdinand Magellan, 1519-1521. 50c, Rene-Robert de la Salle, 1682. 75c, John Cabot, 1497-1498. $1, Jacques Cartier, 1534. $2, Columbus' ship, 1493 woodcut, vert.

**1991, Sept. 20 Litho. *Perf. 14***

**721** A118 12c multicolored .50 .50
**722** A118 50c multicolored 2.10 2.10
**723** A118 75c multicolored 3.25 3.25
**724** A118 $1 multicolored 4.25 4.25
*Nos. 721-724 (4)* 10.10 10.10

**Souvenir Sheet**

**725** A118 $2 multicolored 8.00 8.00

Vincent Van Gogh (1853-1890), Painter — A119

Paintings: 15c, Cottage with Decrepit Barn and Stooping Woman. 30c, Paul Gauguin's Armchair, vert. 75c, Breton Women. $1, Vase with Red Gladioli, vert. $2, The Dance Hall in Arles (detail).

**1991, Nov. 1 *Perf. 13***

**726** A119 15c multicolored .70 .70
**727** A119 30c multicolored 1.40 1.40
**728** A119 75c multicolored 3.50 3.50
**729** A119 $1 multicolored 4.75 4.75
*Nos. 726-729 (4)* 10.35 10.35

**Souvenir Sheet**

**730** A119 $2 multicolored 10.00 10.00

Christmas A120

Entire paintings or details by Quinten Massys: 15c, The Virgin and Child Enthroned. 30c, The Virgin and Child Enthroned, diff. 60c, The Adoration of the Magi. $1, Virgin in Adoration. No. 735, The Virgin Standing with Angels. No. 736, The Adoration of the Magi.

**1991, Dec. 12 Litho. *Perf. 12***

**731** A120 15c multicolored .85 .85
**732** A120 30c multicolored 1.75 1.75
**733** A120 60c multicolored 3.50 3.50
**734** A120 $1 multicolored 5.75 5.75
*Nos. 731-734 (4)* 11.85 11.85

**Souvenir Sheets**

***Perf. 14½***

**735** A120 $2 multicolored 6.00 6.00
**736** A120 $2 multicolored 6.00 6.00

Mushrooms — A121

**1992, Jan. 15** ***Perf. 14***

| | | | | | |
|---|---|---|---|---|---|
| **737** | A121 | 12c | Agaricus bisporus, vert. | .80 | .80 |
| **738** | A121 | 30c | Lentinus edodes | 2.00 | 2.00 |
| **739** | A121 | 45c | Hyrocybe acutoconica, vert. | 3.00 | 3.00 |
| **740** | A121 | $1 | Gymnopilus chrysopellus | 6.75 | 6.75 |
| | | | *Nos. 737-740 (4)* | 12.55 | 12.55 |

**Souvenir Sheet**

| | | | | | |
|---|---|---|---|---|---|
| **741** | A121 | $2 | Pleurotus ostreatus | 10.50 | 10.50 |

**Queen Elizabeth II's Accession to the Throne, 40th Anniv.**

Common Design Type

**1992, Feb. 6** **Litho.** ***Perf. 14***

| | | | | | |
|---|---|---|---|---|---|
| **742** | CD348 | 12c | multicolored | .35 | .35 |
| **743** | CD348 | 45c | multicolored | 1.40 | 1.40 |
| **744** | CD348 | 60c | multicolored | 1.90 | 1.90 |
| **745** | CD348 | $1 | multicolored | 3.00 | 3.00 |
| | | | *Nos. 742-745 (4)* | 6.65 | 6.65 |

**Souvenir Sheet**

| | | | | | |
|---|---|---|---|---|---|
| **746** | CD348 | $2 | multicolored | 6.75 | 6.75 |

Discovery of America, 500th Anniv. A122

10c, Queen Isabella. 15c, Columbus' fleet. 20c, Columbus' second coat of arms. 30c, Landing Monument on Watling Island, Columbus' signature. 45c, Columbus. 50c, Flag of Ferdinand & Isabella, Columbus landing on Watling Island. 70c, Convent at La Rabida. $1.50, Replica of Santa Maria at New York World's Fair, 1964-65. #755, Columbus' 2nd fleet. #756, Map.

**1992, May 26** **Litho.** ***Perf. 14***

| | | | | | |
|---|---|---|---|---|---|
| **747** | A122 | 10c | multi, vert. | .35 | .35 |
| **748** | A122 | 15c | multi | .55 | .55 |
| **749** | A122 | 20c | multi, vert. | .75 | .75 |
| **750** | A122 | 30c | multi | 1.10 | 1.10 |
| **751** | A122 | 45c | multi, vert. | 1.60 | 1.60 |
| **752** | A122 | 50c | multi | 1.90 | 1.90 |
| **753** | A122 | 70c | multi, vert. | 2.50 | 2.50 |
| **754** | A122 | $1.50 | multi | 5.75 | 5.75 |
| | | | *Nos. 747-754 (8)* | 14.50 | 14.50 |

**Souvenir Sheet**

| | | | | | |
|---|---|---|---|---|---|
| **755** | A122 | $2 | multicolored | 7.25 | 7.25 |
| **756** | A122 | $2 | multicolored | 7.25 | 7.25 |

1992 Summer Olympics, Barcelona — A123

**1992, Aug.** **Litho.** ***Perf. 14***

| | | | | | |
|---|---|---|---|---|---|
| **757** | A123 | 15c | Basketball | .80 | .80 |
| **758** | A123 | 30c | Tennis | 1.60 | 1.60 |
| **759** | A123 | 60c | Volleyball | 3.50 | 3.50 |
| **760** | A123 | $1 | Soccer | 5.50 | 5.50 |
| | | | *Nos. 757-760 (4)* | 11.40 | 11.40 |

**Souvenir Sheet**

| | | | | | |
|---|---|---|---|---|---|
| **761** | A123 | $2 | Olympic flame | 9.75 | 9.75 |

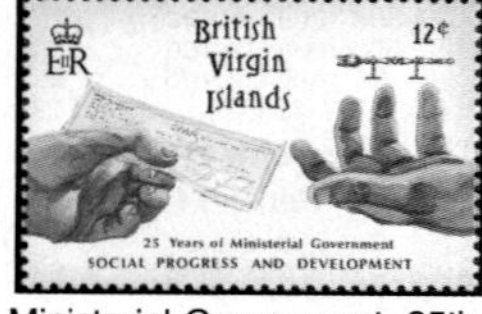

Ministerial Government, 25th Anniv. — A124

Designs: 12c, Social progress and development. 15c, Map of Virgin Islands. 45c, Administration complex. $1.30, International finance.

**1993, Apr.** **Litho.** ***Perf. 14***

| | | | | | |
|---|---|---|---|---|---|
| **762** | A124 | 12c | multicolored | .35 | .35 |
| **763** | A124 | 15c | multicolored | .40 | .40 |
| **764** | A124 | 45c | multicolored | 1.25 | 1.25 |
| **765** | A124 | $1.30 | multicolored | 3.75 | 3.75 |
| | | | *Nos. 762-765 (4)* | 5.75 | 5.75 |

Tourism A125

15c, Swimming from anchored yacht. 30c, Sailboat. 60c, Scuba diver in pink wetsuit. $1, Snorkelers, anchored boat.

#770: a, Trimaran, vert. b, Scuba diver, vert.

**1993, Apr.** **Litho.** ***Perf. 14***

| | | | | | |
|---|---|---|---|---|---|
| **766** | A125 | 15c | multi | .50 | .50 |
| **767** | A125 | 30c | multi, vert. | 1.10 | 1.10 |
| **768** | A125 | 60c | multi | 2.40 | 2.40 |
| **769** | A125 | $1 | multi, vert. | 4.00 | 4.00 |
| | | | *Nos. 766-769 (4)* | 8.00 | 8.00 |

**Souvenir Sheet**

| | | | | | |
|---|---|---|---|---|---|
| **770** | A125 | $1 | Sheet of 2, #a.-b. | 8.25 | 8.25 |

Miniature Sheet

Coronation of Queen Elizabeth II, 40th Anniv. A126

No. 771: a, 12c, Official coronation photograph. b, 45c, Dove atop Rod of Equity and Mercy. c, 60c, Royal family. d, $1, Recent color photo.

**1993, June 2** **Litho.** ***Perf. 13½x14***

| | | | | | |
|---|---|---|---|---|---|
| **771** | A126 | | Sheet, 2 each #a.-d. | 12.50 | 12.50 |

A souvenir sheet containing a $2 stamp was not an authorized issue. Value $10.

Discovery of Virgin Islands, 500th Anniv. A127

3c, Ferdinand and Isabella supporting Columbus. 12c, Departure of Columbus. 15c, Departure of second voyage. 25c, Arms, flag of British Virgin Islands. 30c, Columbus, Santa Maria. 45c, Columbus' second fleet at sea. 60c, Rowing ashore. $1, Landing of Columbus. #781, Natives watching ships. #782, Columbus, two ships of his fleet.

**1993, Sept. 24** **Litho.** ***Perf. 14***

| | | | | | |
|---|---|---|---|---|---|
| **773** | A127 | 3c | multicolored | .25 | .25 |
| **774** | A127 | 12c | multicolored | .35 | .35 |
| **775** | A127 | 15c | multicolored | .45 | .45 |
| **776** | A127 | 25c | multicolored | .75 | .75 |
| **777** | A127 | 30c | multicolored | .95 | .95 |
| **778** | A127 | 45c | multicolored | 1.40 | 1.40 |
| **779** | A127 | 60c | multicolored | 1.90 | 1.90 |
| **780** | A127 | $1 | multicolored | 3.00 | 3.00 |
| | | | *Nos. 773-780 (8)* | 9.05 | 9.05 |

**Souvenir Sheets**

| | | | | | |
|---|---|---|---|---|---|
| **781** | A127 | $2 | multicolored | 4.75 | 4.75 |
| **782** | A127 | $2 | multicolored | 4.75 | 4.75 |

Secondary Education and Library Services, 50th Anniv. — A128

Designs: 5c, Historical documents. 10c, Sporting activities. 15c, Stanley W. Nibbs, educator, vert. 20c, Bookmobile. 30c, Norwell E. Harrigan, educator, vert. 35c, Public library's annual summer program. 70c, Text. $1, High school.

***Perf. 14x13½, 13½x14***

**1993, Dec.** **Litho.**

| | | | | | |
|---|---|---|---|---|---|
| **783** | A128 | 5c | multicolored | .45 | .45 |
| **784** | A128 | 10c | multicolored | .45 | .45 |
| **785** | A128 | 15c | multicolored | .65 | .65 |
| **786** | A128 | 20c | multicolored | .90 | .90 |
| **787** | A128 | 30c | multicolored | 1.25 | 1.25 |
| **788** | A128 | 35c | multicolored | 1.40 | 1.40 |
| **789** | A128 | 70c | multicolored | 2.75 | 2.75 |
| **790** | A128 | $1 | multicolored | 4.25 | 4.25 |
| | | | *Nos. 783-790 (8)* | 12.10 | 12.10 |

Anegada Ground Iguana — A129

5c, Crawling right. 10c, Head up to right. 15c, View from behind. 45c, Head up to left. $2, Head.

**1994, Jan.** **Litho.** ***Perf. 14***

| | | | | | |
|---|---|---|---|---|---|
| **791** | A129 | 5c | multicolored | .55 | .55 |
| **792** | A129 | 10c | multicolored | .55 | .55 |
| **793** | A129 | 15c | multicolored | .70 | .70 |
| **794** | A129 | 45c | multicolored | 2.50 | 2.50 |
| | | | *Nos. 791-794 (4)* | 4.30 | 4.30 |

**Souvenir Sheet**

| | | | | | |
|---|---|---|---|---|---|
| **795** | A129 | $2 | multicolored | 6.25 | 6.25 |

World Wildlife Fund.

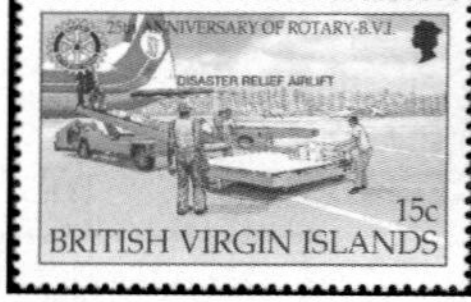

Rotary Club of Virgin Islands, 25th Anniv. A130

Designs: 15c, Disaster relief airlift. 45c, Kids, Sea "Kats." 50c, Donated hospital equipment. 90c, Paul P. Harris (1868-1947), founder of Rotary Intl.

**1994, June 3** **Litho.** ***Perf. 14***

| | | | | | |
|---|---|---|---|---|---|
| **796** | A130 | 15c | multicolored | .45 | .45 |
| **797** | A130 | 45c | multicolored | 1.25 | 1.25 |
| **798** | A130 | 50c | multicolored | 1.50 | 1.50 |
| **799** | A130 | 90c | multicolored | 2.50 | 2.50 |
| | | | *Nos. 796-799 (4)* | 5.70 | 5.70 |

Miniature Sheet of 6

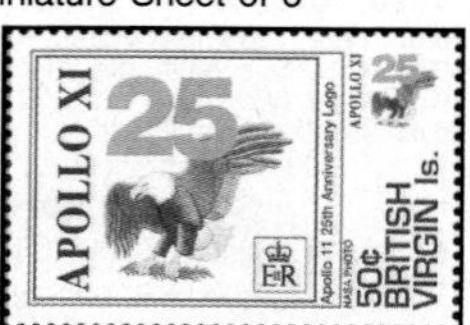

First Manned Moon Landing, 25th Anniv. A131

Designs: No. 800a, Anniversary emblem. b, Lunar landing training vehicle. c, Apollo 11 liftoff, July 16, 1969. d, Lunar module Eagle in flight. e, Moon landing site approached by Eagle. f, 1st step on Moon, July 20, 1969.

No. 801, Mission patch, crew signatures.

**1994, Sept. 30** **Litho.** ***Perf. 14***

| | | | | | |
|---|---|---|---|---|---|
| **800** | A131 | 50c | #a.-f. | 13.50 | 13.50 |

**Souvenir Sheet**

| | | | | | |
|---|---|---|---|---|---|
| **801** | A131 | $2 | multicolored | 9.75 | 9.75 |

A132

A133

Previous champions: 15c, Argentina, 1978. 35c, Italy, 1982. 50c, Argentina, 1986. $1.30, W. Germany, 1990.

$2, US flag, World Cup trophy, horiz.

**1994, Dec. 16** **Litho.** ***Perf. 14***

| | | | | | |
|---|---|---|---|---|---|
| **802** | A132 | 15c | multicolored | .70 | .70 |
| **803** | A132 | 35c | multicolored | 1.75 | 1.75 |
| **804** | A132 | 50c | multicolored | 2.40 | 2.40 |
| **805** | A132 | $1.30 | multicolored | 6.25 | 6.25 |
| | | | *Nos. 802-805 (4)* | 11.10 | 11.10 |

**Souvenir Sheet**

| | | | | | |
|---|---|---|---|---|---|
| **806** | A132 | $2 | multicolored | 8.75 | 8.75 |

1994 World Cup Soccer Championships, US.

**UN, 50th Anniv.**

Common Design Type

Designs: 15c, Peugeot P4 all-purpose light vehicle. 30c, Foden medium tanker. 45c, Sisu all-terrain vehicle. $2, Westland Lynx AH7 helicopter.

**Wmk. 373**

**1995, Oct. 24** **Litho.** ***Perf. 14***

| | | | | | |
|---|---|---|---|---|---|
| **807** | CD353 | 15c | multicolored | .45 | .45 |
| **808** | CD353 | 30c | multicolored | .90 | .90 |
| **809** | CD353 | 45c | multicolored | 1.40 | 1.40 |
| **810** | CD353 | $2 | multicolored | 6.25 | 6.25 |
| | | | *Nos. 807-810 (4)* | 9.00 | 9.00 |

**Wmk. 373**

**1995, Nov. 15** **Litho.** ***Perf. 13***

Anegada Flamingos.

| | | | | | |
|---|---|---|---|---|---|
| **811** | A133 | 15c | Juveniles | .50 | .50 |
| **812** | A133 | 20c | Adults | .75 | .75 |
| **813** | A133 | 60c | Adult feeding | 2.10 | 2.10 |
| **814** | A133 | $1.45 | Adult feeding chick | 5.00 | 5.00 |
| | | | *Nos. 811-814 (4)* | 8.35 | 8.35 |

**Souvenir Sheet**

| | | | | | |
|---|---|---|---|---|---|
| **815** | A133 | $2 | Chicks | 6.25 | 6.25 |

Christmas — A134

Children's paintings: 12c, House with palm trees. 50c, Santa in boat. 70c, Red house, Christmas tree, presents. $1.30, Dove of peace.

**Wmk. 384**

**1995, Dec. 1** **Litho.** ***Perf. 14***

| | | | | | |
|---|---|---|---|---|---|
| **816** | A134 | 12c | multicolored | .50 | .50 |
| **817** | A134 | 50c | multicolored | 2.10 | 2.10 |
| **818** | A134 | 70c | multicolored | 3.00 | 3.00 |
| **819** | A134 | $1.30 | multicolored | 5.50 | 5.50 |
| | | | *Nos. 816-819 (4)* | 11.10 | 11.10 |

Island Scenes A135

Designs: 15c, Seine fishing. 35c, Sandy Spit, Jost Van Dyke. 90c, Map of Jost Van Dyke. $1.50, Foxy's wooden boat regatta.

***Perf. 13½x13***

**1996, Feb. 14** **Litho.** **Wmk. 373**

| | | | | | |
|---|---|---|---|---|---|
| **820** | A135 | 15c | multicolored | .50 | .50 |
| **821** | A135 | 35c | multicolored | 1.25 | 1.25 |
| **822** | A135 | 90c | multicolored | 3.00 | 3.00 |
| **823** | A135 | $1.50 | multicolored | 5.25 | 5.25 |
| | | | *Nos. 820-823 (4)* | 10.00 | 10.00 |

See Nos. 892-896.'

**Queen Elizabeth II, 70th Birthday**

Common Design Type

Queen in various attire, scenes of Virgin Islands: 10c, Government House, Tortola. 30c, Legislative Council Chambers. 45c, Road Harbor. $1.50, Map of Virgin Islands.
$2, Wearing royal crown.

*Perf. 13½x14*

**1996, Apr. 22 Litho. Wmk. 373**

**824** CD354 10c multicolored .20 .20
**825** CD354 30c multicolored .75 .75
**826** CD354 45c multicolored 1.10 1.10
**827** CD354 $1.50 multicolored 3.75 3.75
*Nos. 824-827 (4)* 5.80 5.80

**Souvenir Sheet**

*Perf. 13x13½*

**828** CD354 $2 multicolored 4.75 4.75

Modern Olympic Games, Cent. A136

**Wmk. 373**

**1996, May 22 Litho. Perf. 13**

**829** A136 20c Hurdles .50 .50
**830** A136 35c Volleyball .90 .90
**831** A136 50c Swimming 1.25 1.25
**832** A136 $1 Sailing 2.50 2.50
*Nos. 829-832 (4)* 5.15 5.15

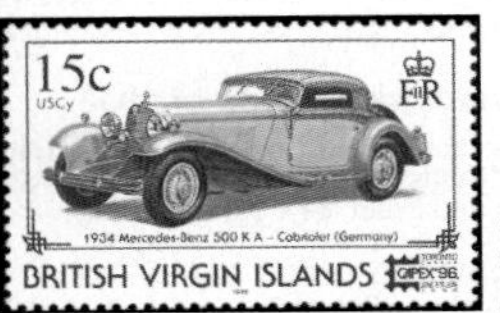


CAPEX '96 A137

Vintage automobiles: 15c, 1934 Mercedes-Benz 500KA Cabriolet. 40c, 1934 Citroen 12. 60c, 1932 Cadillac V-8 Sport Phaeton. $1.35, 1934 Rolls Royce Phantom II.
$2, 1932 Fort Sport Coupe.

**Wmk. 373**

**1996, June 8 Litho. Perf. 13½**

**833** A137 15c multicolored .35 .35
**834** A137 40c multicolored .90 .90
**835** A137 60c multicolored 1.60 1.60
**836** A137 $1.35 multicolored 3.50 3.50
*Nos. 833-836 (4)* 6.35 6.35

**Souvenir Sheet**

**837** A137 $2 multicolored 4.75 4.75

UNICEF, 50th Anniv. A138

Goals of UNICEF for the year 2000: 10c, Educate the child. 15c, Children first. 30c, Children have rights. 45c, No more polio.

*Perf. 14x14½*

**1996, Sept. 16 Litho. Wmk. 373**

**838** A138 10c multicolored .40 .40
**839** A138 15c multicolored .60 .60
**840** A138 30c multicolored 1.25 1.25
**841** A138 45c multicolored 1.90 1.90
*Nos. 838-841 (4)* 4.15 4.15

Girl Guiding in Virgin Islands, 25th Anniv. — A139

Designs: 10c, Rainbows, arts and crafts. 15c, Brownies, community service. 30c, Guides, campfire. 45c, Rangers, H.M. Queen's birthday parade. $2, Lady Baden-Powell, world chief guide.

**Wmk. 373**

**1996, Dec. 30 Litho. Perf. 13½**

**842** A139 10c multicolored .20 .20
**843** A139 15c multicolored .35 .35
**844** A139 30c multicolored .65 .65
**845** A139 45c multicolored 1.00 1.00
**846** A139 $2 multicolored 4.50 4.50
*Nos. 842-846 (5)* 6.70 6.70

Game Fish A140

**1997, Jan. 6 Wmk. 384 Perf. 14**

**847** A140 1c Mackerel .20 .20
**848** A140 10c Wahoo .20 .20
**849** A140 15c Barracuda .30 .30
**850** A140 20c Tarpon .40 .40
**851** A140 25c Tiger shark .50 .50
**852** A140 35c Sailfish .70 .70
**853** A140 40c Dolphin .80 .80
**854** A140 50c Blackfin tuna 1.00 1.00
**855** A140 60c Yellowfin tuna 1.25 1.25
**856** A140 75c Kingfish 1.50 1.50
**857** A140 $1.50 White marlin 3.00 3.00
*a.* Souvenir sheet of 1, wmk. 373 3.50 3.50
**858** A140 $1.85 Amberjack 3.75 3.75
**859** A140 $2 Bonito 4.00 4.00
**860** A140 $5 Bonefish 10.00 10.00
**861** A140 $10 Blue marlin 20.00 20.00
*Nos. 847-861 (15)* 47.60 47.60

No. 857a, Hong Kong '97.

Queen Elizabeth II and Prince Philip, 50th Wedding Anniv. — A141

#862, Prince with horse. #863, Queen Elizabeth II. #864, Queen riding in open carriage. #865, Prince Philip. #866, Queen holding hat down, Prince. #867, Prince Charles on polo pony.
$2, Queen, Prince riding in open carriage, horiz.

**Wmk. 373**

**1997, July 10 Litho. Perf. 13**

**862** 30c multicolored .60 .60
**863** 30c multicolored .60 .60
*a.* A141 Pair, #862-863 1.50 1.50
**864** 45c multicolored .90 .90
**865** 45c multicolored .90 .90
*a.* A141 Pair, #864-865 2.25 2.25
**866** 70c multicolored 1.40 1.40
**867** 70c multicolored 1.40 1.40
*a.* A141 Pair, #866-867 3.75 3.75
*Nos. 862-867 (6)* 5.80 5.80

**Souvenir Sheet**

**868** A141 $2 multicolored 4.75 4.75

Crabs A142

**Wmk. 373**

**1997, Sept. 11 Litho. Perf. 13**

**869** A142 12c Fiddler .30 .30
**870** A142 15c Coral .40 .40
**871** A142 35c Blue 1.00 1.00
**872** A142 $1 Giant hermit 3.00 3.00
*Nos. 869-872 (4)* 4.70 4.70

**Souvenir Sheet**

**873** A142 $2 Arrow 5.75 5.75

Orchids A143

Designs: a, 20c, Psychilis macconnelliae. b, 50c, Tolumnia prionochila. c, 60c, Tetramicra canaliculata. d, 75c, Liparis elata.
$2, Dendrobium crumenatum, vert.

**Wmk. 373**

**1997, Nov. 26 Litho. Perf. 14**

**874** A143 Strip of 4, #a.-d. 4.75 4.75

**Souvenir Sheet**

**875** A143 $2 multicolored 4.75 4.75

World Voyage of Sir Francis Drake A144

Portions of map and: No. 876: a, Francis Drake. b, Drake Coat of Arms. c, Queen Elizabeth I. d, Christopher & Marigold. e, Golden Hinde. f, Swan. g, Cacafuego. h, Elizabeth. i, Maria. j, Drake's Astrolabe. k, Golden Hinde beakhead. l, 16th cent. compass rose.
$2, Modern ship named, "Sir Francis Drake."

**1997, Dec. 13 Perf. 14½**

**876** A144 40c Sheet of 12, #a.-l. 12.00 12.00

**Souvenir Sheet**

**877** A144 $2 multicolored 5.25 5.25

**Diana, Princess of Wales (1961-97)**

Common Design Type

Portraits: a, 15c. b, 45c. c, 70c. d, $1.

*Perf. 14½x14*

**1998, Mar. 31 Litho. Wmk. 373**

**878** CD355 Sheet of 4, #a.-d. 5.75 5.75

No. 878 sold for $2.30 + 20c, with surtax from international sales being donated to the Princess Diana Memorial Fund and surtax from national sales being donated to designated local charity.

**Royal Air Force, 80th Anniv.**

Common Design Type of 1993 Re-inscribed

Designs: 20c, Fairey IIIF. 35c, Supermarine Scapa. 50c, Westland Sea King HAR3. $1.50, BAe Harrier GR7.
No. 883: a, Curtiss H.12 Large America. b, Curtiss JN-4A. c, Bell Airacobra. d, Boulton-Paul Defiant.

*Perf. 13½x14*

**1998, Apr. 1 Litho. Wmk. 373**

**879** CD350 20c multicolored .50 .50
**880** CD350 35c multicolored .95 .95
**881** CD350 50c multicolored 1.40 1.40
**882** CD350 $1.50 multicolored 4.00 4.00
*Nos. 879-882 (4)* 6.85 6.85

**Souvenir Sheet**

**883** CD350 75c Sheet of 4, #a.-d. 8.00 8.00

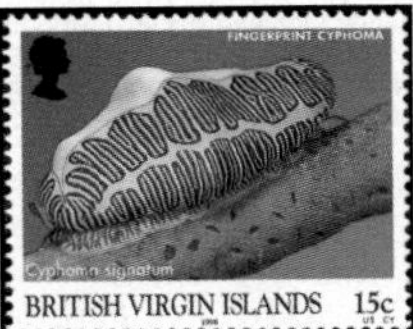


Marine Life — A145

Designs: 15c, Fingerprint cyphoma. 30c, Long spined sea urchin. 45c, Split crown feather duster worm. $1, Upside down jelly.
$2, Giant anemone.

**1998, May 20 Wmk. 384 Perf. 14½**

**884** A145 15c multicolored .55 .55
**885** A145 30c multicolored 1.10 1.10
**886** A145 45c multicolored 1.75 1.75
**887** A145 $1 multicolored 3.75 3.75
*Nos. 884-887 (4)* 7.15 7.15

**Souvenir Sheet**

**888** A145 $2 multicolored 6.25 6.25

No. 888 is a continuous design.

Childrens' Art Festival A146

**Wmk. 373**

**1998, Aug. 25 Litho. Perf. 14**

**889** A146 30c Girl in yellow & red, vert. .75 .75
**890** A146 45c Dancer, vert. 1.10 1.10
**891** A146 $1.30 shown 3.50 3.50
*Nos. 889-891 (3)* 5.35 5.35

Island Scenes Type of 1996

Designs: 12c, Salt pond. 30c, Shipwreck, HMS Rhone. 70c, Traditional house. $1.45, Salt Island.
$2, Gathering salt.

**1998, Oct. 28**

**892** A135 12c multicolored .30 .30
**893** A135 30c multicolored .75 .75
**894** A135 70c multicolored 1.75 1.75
**895** A135 $1.45 multicolored 4.00 4.00
*Nos. 892-895 (4)* 6.80 6.80

**Souvenir Sheet**

**896** A135 $2 multicolored 5.00 5.00

Anniversaries and Events — A147

5c, Classes in computer training, woodworking, electronics. 15c, Students playing musical instruments. 30c, Chapel, Mona Campus, Jamaica. 45c, Plaque on wall, university crest. 50c, Dr. John Coakley Lettsom, map of Little Jost Van Dyke island. $1, Crest of the Medical Society of London, building.

**Wmk. 384**

**1998, Dec. 14 Litho. Perf. 14**

**897** A147 5c multicolored .20 .20
**898** A147 15c multicolored .30 .30
**899** A147 30c multicolored .70 .70
**900** A147 45c multicolored .95 .95
**901** A147 50c multicolored 1.10 1.10
**902** A147 $1 multicolored 2.25 2.25
*Nos. 897-902 (6)* 5.50 5.50

Comprehensive education in Virgin Islands, 30th anniv. (#897-898). University of West Indies, 50th anniv. (#899-900). Founding of the Medical Society of London by Dr. John Coakley Lettsom, 225th anniv. (#901-902).

Lizards A148

Designs: 5c, Rock iguana. 35c, Pygmy gecko. 60c, Slippery back skink. $1.50, Wood slave gecko.
No. 907: a, Doctor lizard. b, Yellow-bellied lizard. c, Man lizard. d, Ground lizard.

*Perf. 14½x14*

**1999, Apr. 30 Litho. Wmk. 373**

**903** A148 5c multicolored .20 .20
**904** A148 35c multicolored .90 .90
**905** A148 60c multicolored 1.60 1.60
**906** A148 $1.50 multicolored 4.00 4.00
*Nos. 903-906 (4)* 6.70 6.70

**Sheet of 4**

**907** A148 75c #a.-d. 7.75 7.75

**Wedding of Prince Edward and Sophie Rhys-Jones**

Common Design Type

*Perf. 13¾x14*

**1999, June 15 Litho. Wmk. 384**

**908** CD356 20c Separate portraits .45 .45
**909** CD356 $3 Couple 7.25 7.25

**1st Manned Moon Landing, 30th Anniv.**

Common Design Type

Designs: 10c, Apollo 11 on launch pad. 40c, Second stage fires. 50c, Artist's rendition of Apollo 11 on moon. $2, Astronauts transfer to lunar module.
$2.50, Looking at earth from moon.

**Perf. 14x13¾**

**1999, July 20 Litho. Wmk. 384**

**910** CD357 10c multicolored .20 .20
**911** CD357 40c multicolored .95 .95
**912** CD357 50c multicolored 1.25 1.25
**913** CD357 $2 multicolored 5.00 5.00
*Nos. 910-913 (4)* 7.40 7.40

**Souvenir Sheet**

**Perf. 14**

**914** CD357 $2.50 multicolored 6.25 6.25

No. 914 contains one 40mm circular stamp.

Shells — A149

Designs: 25c, Measle cowrie. 35c, West Indian top shell. 75c, Zigzag scallop. $1, West Indian fighting conch.

No. 919: a, 5c, Sunrise tellin. b, 10c, King helmet. c, 25c, Like No. 915. d, 35c, Like No. 916. e, 75c, Like No. 917. f, $1, Like No. 918.

**Wmk. 373**

**1999, Nov. 1 Litho. Perf. 14¼**

**915** A149 25c multi .60 .60
**916** A149 35c multi .95 .95
**917** A149 75c multi 1.90 1.90
**918** A149 $1 multi 2.50 2.50
**919** A149 Strip of 6, #a.-f. 6.50 6.50
*Nos. 915-919 (5)* 12.45 12.45

Vignette extends to the top perforations on Nos. 915-918, but does not on stamps from No. 919.

Christmas A150

Churches: 20c, Zion Hill Methodist. 35c, Fat Hogs Bay Seventh Day Adventist. 50c, Ruins of Kingstown St. Philip's Anglican. $1, Road Town St. William's Catholic.

**Perf. 13¼x13**

**1999, Dec. 16 Litho. Wmk. 373**

**920** A150 20c multi .45 .45
**921** A150 35c multi .80 .80
**922** A150 50c multi 1.10 1.10
**923** A150 $1 multi 2.40 2.40
*Nos. 920-923 (4)* 4.75 4.75

British Monarchs — A151

Illustration reduced.

a, Henry VII. b, Lady Jane Grey. c, Charles I. d, William III. e, George III. f, Edward VII.

**Wmk. 373**

**2000, Feb. 29 Litho. Perf. 14**

**924** A151 60c Sheet of 6, #a.-f. 8.75 8.75

The Stamp Show 2000, London.

**Prince William, 18th Birthday**

Common Design Type

William: 20c, As toddler, on chest. 40c, As toddler, standing. 50c, With ski cap & goggles. 60c, Wearing suits & striped shirts. $1, Wearing sweater & bow tie.

**Perf. 14¼x13¾, 13¾x14¼**

**2000, June 21 Litho. Wmk. 373**

**Stamps With White Border**

**925** CD359 20c multi .45 .45
**926** CD359 40c multi, vert. .90 .90
**927** CD359 50c multi, vert. 1.25 1.25
**928** CD359 $1 multi 2.40 2.40
*Nos. 925-928 (4)* 5.00 5.00

**Souvenir Sheet**

**Stamps Without White Border**

**Perf. 14¼**

**929** Sheet of 5 7.25 7.25
*a.* CD359 20c multi .40 .40
*b.* CD359 40c multi .80 .80
*c.* CD359 50c multi 1.00 1.00
*d.* CD359 60c multi 1.25 1.25
*e.* CD359 $1 multi 2.00 2.00

Queen Mother, 100th Birthday — A152

Various photos. Frame color: 15c, Lilac. 35c, Light green. 70c, Pink. $1.50, Light blue.

**Wmk. 373**

**2000, Aug. 4 Litho. Perf. 13¾**

**930-933** A152 Set of 4 7.25 7.25

Flowering Plants and Trees — A153

10c, Red hibiscus. 15c, Pink oleander. 35c, Yellow bell. 50c, Yellow & white frangipani. 75c, Flamboyant. $2, Bougainvillea.

**2000, Sept. 7 Perf. 13½x13¾**

**934-939** A153 Set of 6 9.75 9.75

Millennium — A154

Virgin Islands history: 5c, Site of Emancipation Proclamation. 20c Nurse Mary Louise Davies. 30c, Cheyney University, US, founded by Richard Humphries. 45c, Enid Leona Scatliffe, former chief education officer. 50c, H. Lavity Stoutt Community College. $1 Sir J. Olva Georges.

$2, Victoria Cross of Pvt. Samuel Hodge, vert.

**Wmk. 373**

**2000, Nov. 16 Litho. Perf. 14**

**940-945** A154 Set of 6 6.25 6.25

**Souvenir Sheet**

**946** A154 $2 multi 5.00 5.00

Restoration of the Legislative Council, 50th Anniv. — A155

Virgin Islands Councilmen: 10c, Dr. Q. William Osbourne & Arnando Scatliffe. 15c, H. Robinson O'Neal & A. Austin Henley. 20c, Wilfred W. Smith & John C. Brudenell-Bruce. 35c, Howard R. Penn & I. G. Fonseca. 50c, Carlton L. de Castro & Theodolph H. Faulkner. 60c, Willard W. Wheatley. $1, H. Lavity Stoutt.

**2000, Nov. 22**

**947-953** A155 Set of 7 7.25 7.25

Souvenir Sheet

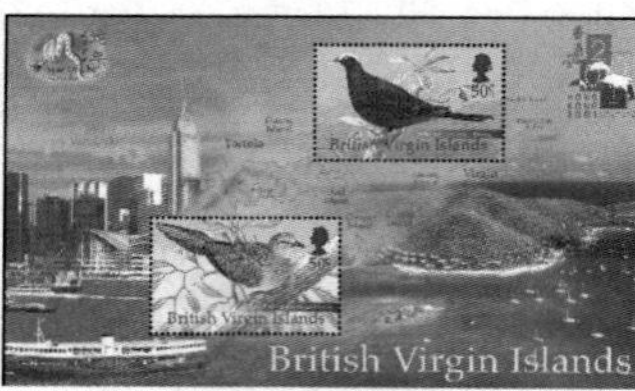


New Year 2001 (Year of the Snake) — A156

No. 954: a, 50c, White-crowned dove. b, 50c, Bar-tailed cuckoo dove.

Illustration reduced.

**2001, Feb. 1 Perf. 14½**

**954** A156 Sheet of 2, #a-b 2.50 2.50

Hong Kong 2001 Stamp Exhibition.

Visiting Royal Navy Ships A157

Designs: 35c, HMS Wistaria, 1923-30. 50c, HMS Dundee, 1934-35. 60c, HMS Eurydice, 1787. 75c, HMS Pegasus, 1787. $1, HMS Astrea, 1807. $1.50 HM Yacht Britannia, 1966.

**Wmk. 373**

**2001, Sept. 28 Litho. Perf. 14**

**955-960** A157 Set of 6 11.50 11.50

Nobel Prizes, Cent. — A158

Nobel laureates: 10c, Fridtjof Nansen, Peace, 1922. 20c, Albert Einstein, Physics, 1921. 25c, Sir Arthur Lewis, Economics, 1979. 40c, Saint-John Perse, Literature, 1960. 70c, Mother Teresa, Peace, 1979. $2, Christian Lous Lange, Peace, 1921.

**2001, Oct. 5**

**961-966** A158 Set of 6 11.00 11.00

**Reign Of Queen Elizabeth II, 50th Anniv. Issue**

Common Design Type

Designs: Nos. 967, 971a, 15c, Princess Elizabeth in uniform. Nos. 968, 971b, 50c, In 1977. Nos. 969, 971c, 60c, Holding flowers. Nos. 970, 971d, 75c, In 1996. No. 971e, $1, 1955 portrait by Annigoni (38x50mm).

**Perf. 14¼x14½, 13¾ (#971e)**

**2002, Feb. 6 Litho. Wmk. 373**

**With Gold Frames**

**967-970** CD360 Set of 4 6.75 6.75

**Souvenir Sheet**

**Without Gold Frames**

**971** CD360 Sheet of 5, #a-e 10.00 10.00

Reptiles in Guinness Book Of World Records A159

Designs: 5c, Estuarine crocodile. 20c, Reticulated python. 30c, Komodo dragon. 40c, Boa constrictor. $1, Dwarf caiman. $2, Sphaerodactylus parthenopion.

$1.50, Head of Sphaerodactylus parthenopion.

**Perf. 13¼x13**

**2002, June 10 Litho. Wmk. 373**

**972-977** A159 Set of 6 10.00 10.00

*977a* Sheet of 6, #972-977 10.00 10.00

**Souvenir Sheet**

**978** A159 $1.50 multi 3.75 3.75

**Queen Mother Elizabeth (1900-2002)**

Common Design Type

Designs: 20c, Wearing tiara (black and white photograph). 60c, Wearing dark blue hat. Nos. 981, 983a, $2, Wearing hat (black and white photograph). Nos. 982, 983b, $3, Wearing pink hat.

**Perf. 13¾x14¼**

**2002, Aug. 5 Litho. Wmk. 373**

**With Purple Frames**

**979-982** CD361 Set of 4 14.50 14.50

**Souvenir Sheet**

**Without Purple Frames**

**Perf. 14½x14¼**

**983** CD361 Sheet of 2, #a-b 12.50 12.50

Royal Navy Ships A160

Designs: 20c, HMS Invincible and HMS Argo. 35c, HMS Boreas and HMS Solebay. 50c, HMS Coventry. $3, HMS Argyll.

**Wmk. 373**

**2002, Aug. 30 Litho. Perf. 14**

**984-987** A160 Set of 4 8.25 8.25

**Island Scenes Type of 1996**

Designs: 5c, Spring Bay. 40c, Devils Bay. 60c, The Baths. 75c, St. Thomas Bay. $1, Savannah and Pond Bay. $2, Trunk Bay.

**2002, Sept. 13**

**988-993** A135 Set of 6 9.75 9.75

West Indian Whistling Duck — A161

Designs: Nos. 994, 998a, 10c, Duckling and eggs. Nos. 995, 998b, 35c, Duck standing on rock, vert. Nos. 996, 998c, 40c, Duck in water, vert. Nos. 997, 998d, 70c, Two ducks. No. 998e, $2, Duck's head.

**Perf. 14¼x13¾, 13¾x14¼**

**2002, Dec. Litho. Wmk. 373**

**Stamps With Brown Border**

**994-997** A161 Set of 4 3.75 3.75

**Souvenir Sheet**

**Stamps Without Brown Border**

**Perf. 14¼x14½ (Horiz. stamps), 14½ (Vert. stamps)**

**998** A161 Sheet of 5, #a-e 8.50 8.50

Birdlife International.

Anniversaries and Events — A162

No. 999, 10c: a, Sprinters. b, Cyclists.

No. 1000, 35c: a, Laser class sailboats. b, Women's long jump.

No. 1001, 50c: a, Bareboat class sailboats. b, Racing Cruiser class sailboats.

No. 1002, $1.35: a, Carlos and Esme Downing, founders of Island Sun newspaper. b, Island Sun newspaper and emblem.

Illustration reduced.

**Wmk. 373**

**2003, Mar. 13 Litho. Perf. 13½**

**Horiz. pairs, #a-b**

**999-1002** A162 Set of 4 9.25 9.25

2002 Commonwealth Games (#999); Admission to Olympic Games, 20th anniv. (#1000); Spring Regatta, 30th anniv. (#1001); Island Sun newspaper, 40th anniv. (#1002).

**Head of Queen Elizabeth II**

Common Design Type

**Wmk. 373**

**2003, June 2 Litho. *Perf. 13¾***

**1003** CD362 $5 multi 10.00 10.00

**Coronation of Queen Elizabeth II, 50th Anniv.**

Common Design Type

Designs: Nos. 1004, 1006a, 15c, Queen in gown. Nos. 1005, 1006b, $5, Royal Family on Buckingham Palace balcony.

***Perf. 14¼x14½***

**2003, June 2 Litho. Wmk. 373**

**Vignettes Framed, Red Background**

**1004-1005** CD363 Set of 2 10.50 10.50

**Souvenir Sheet**

**Vignettes Without Frame, Purple Panel**

**1006** CD363 Sheet of 2, #a-b 10.50 10.50

**Prince William, 21st Birthday**

Common Design Type

Designs: 50c, William in polo uniform at right. $2, William on polo pony at left.

**Wmk. 373**

**2003, June 21 Litho. *Perf. 14¼***

**With Gray Frames**

**1007** CD364 50c multi 1.00 1.00
**1008** CD364 $2 multi 4.00 4.00

**Without Gray Frames**

**1009** Horiz. pair 5.00 5.00
*a.* CD364 50c multi 1.00 1.00
*b.* CD364 $2 multi 4.00 4.00
*Nos. 1007-1009 (3)* 10.00 10.00

Powered Flight, Cent. — A163

Designs: 15c, Douglas DC-4. 20c, Boeing Stearman "Kaydet." 35c, B-25 J Mitchell. 40c, F-4B Phantom. 70c, CH-47 Chinook helicopter. $2, AH-64 Apache helicopter.
Illustration reduced.

***Perf. 13¼x13¾***

**2003, Nov. 15 Litho. Wmk. 373**

**Stamp + Label**

**1010-1015** A163 Set of 6 7.75 7.75

Christmas — A164

Details from Arrival of the English Ambassadors, by Vittore Carpaccio: 20c, Men standing near railing and pillar. 40c, Men, ships in background. $2.50, Seated man.
No. 1019a (36x36mm), Kneeling man delivering message.

***Perf. 13¾x13½***

**2003, Dec. 15 Litho. Wmk. 373**

**1016-1018** A164 Set of 3 6.25 6.25

**Souvenir Sheet**

**1019** A164 Sheet, #1016-1018, 1019a 8.25 8.25
*a.* $1 multi, perf. 13½x13¼ 2.00 2.00

**Game Fish Type of 1997**

***Serpentine Die Cut 12½ on 3 Sides***

**2004, July 1 Litho. Unwmk.**

**Self-Adhesive**

**Booklet Stamps**

**Size: 21x17mm**

**1020** A140 15c Barracuda .30 .30
*a.* Booklet pane of 4 1.20
**1021** A140 20c Tarpon .40 .40
*a.* Booklet pane of 4 1.60
**1022** A140 35c Sailfish .70 .70
*a.* Booklet pane of 4 2.80
Complete booklet, #1020a, 1022a 4.00
**1023** A140 40c Dolphin .80 .80
*a.* Booklet pane of 3 + label 2.40
Complete booklet, #1021a, 1023a 5.25
*Nos. 1020-1023 (4)* 2.20 2.20

Fruit — A165

**2004, July 20 Wmk. 373 *Perf. 13¾***

**1024** A165 15c Pomegranates .30 .30
**1025** A165 20c Cashews .40 .40
**1026** A165 35c Tamarinds .70 .70
**1027** A165 40c Soursop .80 .80
**1028** A165 50c Mangos 1.00 1.00
**1029** A165 $2 Guavaberries 4.00 4.00
**1030** A165 $5 Mamee apples 10.00 10.00
*Nos. 1024-1030 (7)* 17.20 17.20

Virgin Islands Festival, 50th Anniv. — A166

Designs: 10c, Parade. 60c, Horse race. $1, Kayak race. $2.35, Festival Queen.

**Wmk. 373**

**2004, Oct. 26 Litho. *Perf. 13¼***

**1031-1034** A166 Set of 4 8.25 8.25

Sports — A167

Designs: 75c, Women soccer players. $1, Runner.

**2004, Dec. 30 *Perf. 14***

**1035-1036** A167 Set of 2 3.50 3.50

FIFA (Fédération Internationale de Football Association), cent.; 2004 Summer Olympics, Athens.

Caribbean Endemic Bird Festival A168

Designs: 5c, Black and white warbler. 25c, Worm-eating warbler. 35c, Yellow warbler. 50c, Prothonotary warbler.
No. 1041: a, 10c, Prairie warbler. b, 15c, Yellow-rumped warbler. c, 40c, Black-throated blue warbler. d, 60c, Cape May warbler. e, 75c, Northern parula. f, $2.75, Palm warbler.

**Wmk. 373**

**2005, July 8 Litho. *Perf. 13¾***

**1037-1040** A168 Set of 4 2.40 2.40
**1041** A168 Miniature sheet, #1037-1040, 1041a-1041f 12.00 12.00

**Fruit Type of 2004**

**2005, Aug. 25 Wmk. 373**

**1042** A165 1c Hog plum .20 .20
**1043** A165 10c Coco plum .20 .20
**1044** A165 25c Sugar apple .50 .50
**1045** A165 60c Papaya 1.25 1.25
**1046** A165 75c Custard apple 1.50 1.50
**1047** A165 $1 Otaheite gooseberry 2.00 2.00
**1048** A165 $1.50 Guava 3.00 3.00
**1049** A165 $10 Passion fruit 20.00 20.00
*Nos. 1042-1049 (8)* 28.65 28.65

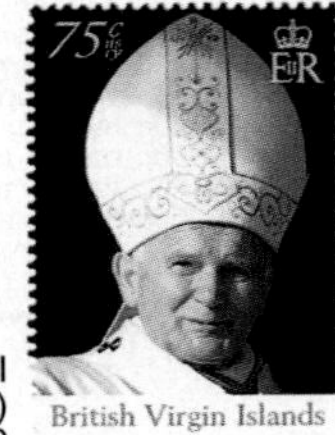


Pope John Paul II (1920-2005) A169

**Wmk. 373**

**2005, Aug. 18 Litho. *Perf. 14***

**1050** A169 75c multi 1.50 1.50

Worldwide Fund for Nature (WWF) — A170

Various depictions of Virgin Islands tree boa: 20c, 30c, 70c, $1.05.

**Wmk. 373**

**2005,Sept. 15 Litho. *Perf. 14***

**1051-1054** A170 Set of 4 4.50 4.50
*1054a* Miniature sheet, 2 each #1051-1054 9.00 9.00

Battle of Trafalgar, Bicent. — A171

Designs: 5c, HMS Colossus. 25c, HMS Boreas. 75c, HMS Victory. $3, Admiral Horatio Nelson, vert.
$2.50, HMS Colossus and French ship.

**2005, Oct. 18 *Perf. 14x14¾, 14¾x14***

**1055-1058** A171 Set of 4 8.25 8.25

**Souvenir Sheet**

***Perf. 13½***

**1059** A171 $2.50 multi 5.00 5.00

No. 1059 contains one 44x44mm stamp.

Christmas A172

Flora: 15c, Century plant. 35c, Poinsettia, horiz. 60c, Inkberry. $2.50, Snow on the mountain, horiz.

**2005, Nov. 3 *Perf. 14¾x14, 14x14¾***

**1060-1063** A172 Set of 4 7.25 7.25

Anniversaries A173

Designs: 20c, Social Security, 25th anniv. 40c, ZBVI radio station, 40th anniv. 50c, Beef Island Airstrip, 50th anniv. $1, Rotary International, cent.

**Wmk. 373**

**2005, Nov. 16 Litho. *Perf. 13¾***

**1064-1067** A173 Set of 4 4.25 4.25

Queen Elizabeth II, 80th Birthday A174

Queen: 15c, As young woman, in uniform. 75c, Wearing white hat. No. 1070, $1.50, Wearing large earrings. No. 1071, $2, Wearing gray hat with large brim.
No. 1072: a, $1.50, Like 75c. b, $2, Like #1070.

***Perf. 14¼x14***

**2006, July 17 Litho. Wmk. 373**

**Stamps With White Frames**

**1068-1071** A174 Set of 4 9.00 9.00

**Souvenir Sheet**

**Stamps Without White Frames**

**1072** A174 Sheet of 2, #a-b 7.00 7.00

## WAR TAX STAMPS

Regular Issue of 1913 Overprinted

**1916-17 Wmk. 3 *Perf. 14***

**Die I**

**MR1** A9 1p scarlet .55 *8.00*
*a.* 1p carmine 2.50 *20.00*
**MR2** A9 3p violet, *yellow* 3.50 *16.00*

## OFFICIAL STAMPS

**Catalogue values for unused stamps in this section are for Never Hinged items.**

Nos. 365-368, 370-380 Overprinted "OFFICIAL" in Silver

**1985, July Litho. *Perf. 14***

**O1** A57 1c multi .25 .55
**O2** A57 3c multi .35 .55
**O3** A57 5c multi .35 .45
**O4** A57 8c multi .45 .45
**O5** A57 13c multi .55 .45
**O6** A57 15c multi .55 .45
**O7** A57 18c multi .85 .70
**O8** A57 20c multi .85 .70
**O9** A57 25c multi 1.00 .85
**O10** A57 30c multi 1.40 1.00
**O11** A57 60c multi 2.00 2.00
**O12** A57 $1 multi 3.25 3.25
**O13** A57 $2.50 multi 5.75 5.75
**O14** A57 $3 multi 8.75 8.75
**O15** A57 $5 multi 11.50 11.50
*Nos. O1-O15 (15)* 37.85 37.40

Nos. 364-380 overprinted in gold and Nos. 364, 369 overprinted in silver exist but were not issued by the Virgin Islands.

Nos. 490-508 Ovptd. "OFFICIAL"

**1986 Litho. *Perf. 14***

**O16** A81 1c multicolored .30 .30
**O17** A81 2c multicolored .30 .30
**O18** A81 5c multicolored .30 .30

**O19** A81 8c multicolored .30 .30
**O20** A81 10c multicolored .30 .30
**O21** A81 12c multicolored .40 .40
**O22** A81 15c multicolored .45 .45
**O23** A81 18c multicolored .55 .55
**O24** A81 20c multicolored .65 .65
**O25** A81 25c multicolored .80 .80
**O26** A81 30c multicolored .95 .95
**O27** A81 35c multicolored 1.10 1.10
**O28** A81 40c multicolored 1.25 1.25
**O29** A81 50c multicolored 1.40 1.40
**O30** A81 60c multicolored 1.60 1.60
**O31** A81 $1 multicolored 2.75 2.75
**O32** A81 $2 multicolored 5.75 5.75
**O33** A81 $3 multicolored 8.50 8.50
**O34** A81 $5 multicolored 15.00 15.00
*Nos. O16-O34 (19)* 42.65 42.65

Issue: 1, 5, 10, 15, 20-35c, $5, 7/3; others, 1/28.

Nos. 694-695, 698, 701-706, 708 Ovptd. "OFFICIAL"

**1991, Sept. Litho. *Perf. 14***
**O37** A116 5c multicolored .20 *.20*
**O38** A116 10c multicolored .20 *.20*
**O41** A116 20c multicolored .45 *.45*
**O44** A116 35c multicolored .80 *.80*
**O45** A116 40c multicolored .90 *.90*
**O46** A116 45c multicolored 1.00 *1.00*
**O47** A116 50c multicolored 1.10 *1.10*
**O48** A116 70c multicolored 1.60 *1.60*
**O49** A116 $1 multicolored 2.25 *2.25*
**O51** A116 $3 multicolored 7.00 *7.00*
*Nos. O37-O51 (10)* 15.50 *15.50*

Ovpt. on Nos. O37-O51 is 19mm long.
Used values are for c-t-o copies.
Nos. O37-O38, O41, O44-O49, O51 were not available unused until mid-1992.
This set was never used in the Virgin Islands.

Nos. 694-695, 698, 700-706, 708 Ovptd. "OFFICIAL"

**1992 Litho. *Perf. 14***
**O55** A116 5c multicolored .20 .20
**O56** A116 10c multicolored .20 .20
**O59** A116 20c multicolored .45 .45
**O61** A116 30c multicolored .70 .70
**O62** A116 35c multicolored .80 .80
**O63** A116 40c multicolored .90 .90
**O64** A116 45c multicolored 1.00 1.00
**O65** A116 50c multicolored 1.10 1.10
**O66** A116 70c multicolored 1.60 1.60
**O67** A116 $1 multicolored 2.25 2.25
**O69** A116 $3 multicolored 7.00 7.00
*Nos. O55-O69 (11)* 16.20 16.20

Ovpt. on Nos. O55-O56, O59, O61-O67, O69 is 15½mm long.

# WALLIS AND FUTUNA ISLANDS

ˈwä-ləs and fə-ˈtü-nə ˈī-ləndz

LOCATION — Group of islands in the South Pacific Ocean, northeast of Fiji
GOVT. — French Overseas Territory
AREA — 106 sq. mi.
POP. — 15,129 (1999 est.)
CAPITAL — Mata-Utu, Wallis Island

100 Centimes = 1 Franc

**Catalogue values for unused stamps in this country are for Never Hinged items, beginning with Scott 127 in the regular postage section, Scott B9 in the semi-postal section, Scott C1 in the air-post section, and Scott J37 in the postage due section.**

New Caledonia Stamps of 1905-28 Overprinted in Black or Red

**1920-28 Unwmk. *Perf. 14x13½***
**1** A16 1c black, *green* .20 .20
*a.* Double overprint 100.00
**2** A16 2c red brown .20 .20
**3** A16 4c blue, *org* .30 .30
**4** A16 5c green .30 .30
**5** A16 5c dull blue ('22) .30 .30
**6** A16 10c rose .45 .45
**7** A16 10c green ('22) .60 .60
**8** A16 10c red, *pink* ('25) 1.75 1.75
**9** A16 15c violet .85 .85
**10** A17 20c gray brown .75 .75
**11** A17 25c blue, *grn* 1.10 1.10
**12** A17 25c red, *yel* ('22) .70 .70
**13** A17 30c brown, *org* 1.25 1.25
**14** A17 30c dp rose ('22) 1.10 1.10
**15** A17 30c red orange ('25) .60 .60
**16** A17 30c lt green ('27) 1.90 1.90
**17** A17 35c black, *yel* (R) .75 .75
**18** A17 40c rose, *grn* .85 .85
**19** A17 45c violet brn, *pnksh* 1.25 1.25
**20** A17 50c red, *org* 1.25 1.25
**21** A17 50c dark blue ('22) 1.50 1.50
**22** A17 50c dark gray ('25) 1.75 1.75
**23** A17 65c deep blue ('28) 5.25 5.25
**24** A17 75c olive green 1.60 1.60

Overprinted

**25** A18 1fr blue, *yel grn* 3.50 3.50
*a.* Triple overprint 150.00
**26** A18 1.10fr orange brn ('28) 4.25 4.25
**27** A18 2fr carmine, *bl* 5.75 5.75
**28** A18 5fr black, *org* (R) 11.50 11.50
*Nos. 1-28 (28)* 51.55 51.55

No. 9 Surcharged New Value and Bars in Various Colors

**1922**
**29** A16 0.01c on 15c violet (Bk) .60 .60
**30** A16 0.02c on 15c violet (Bl) .60 .60
**31** A16 0.04c on 15c violet (G) .60 .60
**32** A16 0.05c on 15c violet (R) .60 .60
*Nos. 29-32 (4)* 2.40 2.40

Stamps and Types of 1920 Surcharged with New Values and Bars in Black or Red

**1924-27**
**33** A18 25c on 2fr car, *bl* .85 .85
**34** A18 25c on 5fr black, *org* .85 .85
**35** A17 65c on 40c rose red, *grn* ('25) 1.40 1.40
**36** A17 85c on 75c ol grn ('25) 1.10 1.10
**37** A17 90c on 75c dp rose ('27) 1.75 1.75
**38** A18 1.25fr on 1fr dp bl (R; '26) .85 .85
**39** A18 1.50fr on 1fr dp bl, *bl* ('27) 3.75 3.75
*a.* Double surcharge 240.00
*b.* Surcharge omitted 210.00
**40** A18 3fr on 5fr red vio ('27) 6.00 6.00
*a.* Surcharge omitted 210.00
*b.* Double surcharge 240.00
**41** A18 10fr on 5fr ol, *lav* ('27) 29.00 *29.00*
**42** A18 20fr on 5fr vio rose, *yel* ('27) 35.00 *35.00*
*Nos. 33-42 (10)* 80.55 80.55

New Caledonia Stamps and Types of 1928-40 Overprinted as in 1920

**1930-40 *Perf. 13½, 14x13, 14x13½***
**43** A19 1c brn vio & indigo .20 .20
*a.* Double overprint 140.00
**44** A19 2c dk brn & yel grn .20 .20
**45** A19 3c brn vio & ind ('40) .20 .20
**46** A19 4c org & Prus grn .20 .20
**47** A19 5c Prus bl & dp ol .20 .20
**48** A19 10c gray lil & dk brn .20 .20
**49** A19 15c yel brn & dp bl .20 .20
**50** A19 20c brn red & dk brn .45 .45
**51** A19 25c dk grn & dk brn .85 .85
**52** A20 30c gray grn & bl grn .85 .85
**53** A20 35c Prus grn & dk grn ('38) .85 .85
*a.* Without overprint 130.00
**54** A20 40c brt red & olive .85 .85
**55** A20 45c dp bl & red org .85 .85
**56** A20 45c bl grn & dl grn ('40) .75 .75
**57** A20 50c violet & brn .85 .85
**58** A20 55c bl vio & rose red ('38) 2.00 2.00
**59** A20 60c vio bl & car ('40) .25 .25
**60** A20 65c org brn & bl 1.75 1.75
**61** A20 70c dp rose & brn ('38) 1.10 1.10
**62** A20 75c Prus bl & ol gray 2.75 2.75
**63** A20 80c dk cl & grn ('38) 1.00 1.00
**64** A20 85c green & brown 3.00 3.00
**65** A20 90c dp red & brt red 2.00 2.00
**66** A20 90c ol grn & rose red ('39) .90 .90
**67** A21 1fr dp ol & sal red 3.25 3.25
**68** A21 1fr rose red & dk car ('38) 1.90 1.90
**69** A21 1fr brn red & grn ('40) .20 .20
**70** A21 1.10fr dp grn & brn 26.00 26.00
**71** A21 1.25fr brn red & grn ('33) 2.75 2.75
**72** A21 1.25fr rose red & dk car ('39) .75 .75
**73** A21 1.40fr dk bl & red org ('40) .90 .90
**74** A21 1.50fr dp bl & bl 1.00 1.00
**75** A21 1.60fr dp grn & brn ('40) 1.40 1.40
**76** A21 1.75fr dk bl & red org ('33) 11.50 11.50
**77** A21 1.75fr vio bl ('38) 1.90 1.90
**78** A21 2fr red org & brn 1.40 1.40
**79** A21 2.25fr vio bl ('39) 1.50 1.50
**80** A21 2.50fr brn & lt brn ('40) 1.50 1.50
**81** A21 3fr magenta & brn 1.40 1.40
**82** A21 5fr dk bl & brn 1.90 1.90
**83** A21 10fr vio & brn, *pnksh* 2.50 2.50
**84** A21 20fr red & brn, *yel* 3.75 3.75
*Nos. 43-84 (42)* 87.95 87.95

For overprints see Nos. 94-126.
For types A19 and A21 of New Caledonia, with "RF," overprinted as above, see Nos. 126A-126F.

Common Design Types pictured following the introduction.

**Colonial Exposition Issue**
Common Design Types

**1931, Apr. 13 Engr. *Perf. 12½***
**Name of Country Typo. in Black**
**85** CD70 40c deep green 7.50 7.50
**86** CD71 50c violet 7.50 7.50
**87** CD72 90c red orange 7.50 7.50
**88** CD73 1.50fr dull blue 7.50 7.50
*Nos. 85-88 (4)* 30.00 30.00

**Colonial Arts Exhibition Issue**
Common Design Type
Souvenir Sheet

**1937 *Imperf.***
**89** CD78 3fr red violet 22.50 *27.50*
Never hinged 27.50

**New York World's Fair Issue**
Common Design Type

**1939, May 10 Engr. *Perf. 12½x12***
**90** CD82 1.25fr carmine lake 2.40 2.40
**91** CD82 2.25fr ultramarine 2.40 2.40

**Petain Issue**
New Caledonia Nos. 216A-216B Overprinted "WALLIS ET FUTUNA" in Lilac or Red

**1941 Engr. *Perf. 12½x12***
**92** A21a 1fr bluish green (L) 1.00
**93** A21a 2.50fr dark blue (R) 1.00

Nos. 92-93 were issued by the Vichy government in France, but were not placed on sale in Wallis & Futuna.
For surcharges, see Nos. B8A-B8B.

Nos. 43-69, 71, 74, 77-78, 80-84 with Additional Overprint in Black

**1941-43 *Perf. 14x13½***
**94** A19 1c 2.50 2.50
**95** A19 2c 2.50 2.50
**96** A19 3c 70.00 70.00
**97** A19 4c 3.25 3.25
**98** A19 5c 3.25 3.25
**99** A19 10c 3.25 3.25
**100** A19 15c 3.25 3.25
**101** A19 20c 4.50 4.50
**102** A19 25c 4.50 4.50
**103** A20 30c 4.50 4.50
**104** A20 35c 3.25 3.25
**105** A20 40c 3.75 3.75
**106** A20 45c #55 3.75 3.75
**107** A20 45c #56 80.00 80.00
**108** A20 50c 3.25 3.25
**109** A20 55c 3.25 3.25
**110** A20 60c 70.00 70.00
**111** A20 65c 3.25 3.25
**112** A20 70c 3.25 3.25
**113** A20 75c 4.50 4.50
**114** A20 80c 3.25 3.25
**115** A20 85c 3.75 3.75
**116** A20 90c #65 3.25 3.25
**117** A21 1fr #68 3.75 3.75
**118** A21 1.25fr #71 3.75 3.75
**119** A21 1.50fr 3.25 3.25
**120** A21 1.75fr #77 3.25 3.25
**121** A21 2fr 3.75 3.75
**122** A21 2.50fr 125.00 125.00
**123** A21 3fr 3.25 3.25
**124** A21 5fr 7.00 7.00
**125** A21 10fr 50.00 50.00
**126** A21 20fr 72.50 72.50
*Nos. 94-126 (33)* 565.50 565.50

Types of New Caledonia Without "RF" overprinted as in 1920

**1944**
**126A** A19 10c gray lil & dk brn .85
**126B** A19 15c yel brn & dp bl 1.10
**126C** A21 1fr brn red & grn 1.50
**126D** A21 1.50fr blue 1.90
**126E** A21 10fr vio & brn, *pnksh* 1.90
**126F** A21 20fr red & brn, *yel* 1.90
*Nos. 126A-126F (6)* 9.15

Nos. 126A-126F were issued by the Vichy government in France, but were not placed on sale in Wallis & Futuna.

**Catalogue values for unused stamps in this section, from this point to the end of the section, are for Never Hinged items.**

Ivi Poo, Bone Carving in Tiki Design
A1

**1944 Unwmk. Photo. *Perf. 11½x12***
**127** A1 5c lt brown .30 .30
**128** A1 10c dp gray blue .30 .30
**129** A1 25c emerald .30 .30
**130** A1 30c dull orange .30 .30
**131** A1 40c dk slate grn .75 .75
**132** A1 80c brown red .75 .75
**133** A1 1fr red violet .40 .40
**134** A1 1.50fr red .40 .40
**135** A1 2fr gray black .50 .50
**136** A1 2.50fr brt ultra .65 .65
**137** A1 4fr dark purple .75 .75
**138** A1 5fr lemon yellow 1.00 1.00
**139** A1 10fr chocolate 1.25 1.25
**140** A1 20fr deep green 1.25 1.25
*Nos. 127-140 (14)* 8.90 8.90

Nos. 127, 129 and 136 Surcharged with New Values and Bars in Black or Carmine

**1946**
**141** A1 50c on 5c lt brown .65 .65
**142** A1 60c on 5c lt brown .65 .65
**143** A1 70c on 5c lt brown .65 .65
**144** A1 1.20fr on 5c lt brown .65 .65
**145** A1 2.40fr on 25c emerald .65 .65
**146** A1 3fr on 25c emerald .65 .65
**147** A1 4.50fr on 25c emerald 1.50 1.50
**148** A1 15fr on 2.50fr (C) 1.75 1.75
*Nos. 141-148 (8)* 7.15 7.15

**Military Medal Issue**
Common Design Type
**Engraved and Typographed**

**1952, Dec. 1 *Perf. 13***
**149** CD101 2fr multicolored 6.00 6.00

Wallis Islander
A2

**Unwmk.**

**1957, June 11 Engr. *Perf. 13***
**150** A2 3fr dk purple & lil rose 1.00 1.00
**151** A2 9fr bl, dl lil & vio brn 1.60 1.60

Imperforates

Most Wallis and Futuna stamps from 1957 onward exist imperforate in issued and trial colors, and also in small presentation sheets in issued colors.

**Flower Issue**
Common Design Type

Design: 5fr, Montrouziera, horiz.

**1958, Aug. 4 Photo. *Perf. 12½x12***
**152** CD104 5fr multicolored 3.00 1.75

**Human Rights Issue**
Common Design Type

**1958, Dec. 10 Engr. *Perf. 13***
**153** CD105 17fr brt bl & dk bl 3.75 3.00

Women Making Tapa Cloth — A3

Kava Ceremony A4

17fr, Dancers. 19fr, Dancers with paddles.

**1960, Sept. 19 Engr. *Perf. 13***
**154** A3 5fr dk brown, grn & org brn 1.50 1.10
**155** A4 7fr dk brown & Prus grn 2.25 1.90
**156** A4 17fr ultra, claret & grn 2.50 2.00
**157** A3 19fr claret & slate 2.75 2.10
*Nos. 154-157 (4)* 9.00 7.10

Map of South Pacific — A4a

**1962, July 18 Photo. *Perf. 13x12***
**158** A4a 16fr multicolored 3.50 3.25

5th South Pacific Conf., Pago Pago, 1962.

Sea Shells — A5

**1962-63 Engr. *Perf. 13***
**Size: 22x36mm**
**159** A5 25c Triton 1.10 1.10
**160** A5 1fr Mitra episcopalis 1.10 1.10
**161** A5 2fr Cypraecassis rufa 2.10 2.10
**162** A5 4fr Murex tenuspina 3.00 3.00
**163** A5 10fr Oliva erythrostoma 6.75 6.75
**164** A5 20fr Cyprae tigris 10.50 10.50
*Nos. 159-164,C18 (7)* 37.05 31.55

**Red Cross Centenary !ssue**
Common Design Type

**1963, Sept. 2 Unwmk. *Perf. 13***
**165** CD113 12fr red lil, gray & car 2.50 2.50

**Human Rights Issue**
Common Design Type

**1963, Dec. 10 Engr.**
**166** CD117 29fr dk red & ocher 5.50 *5.50*

**Philatec Issue**
Common Design Type

**1964, Apr. 15 Unwmk. *Perf. 13***
**167** CD118 9fr dk sl grn, grn & red 2.50 *2.50*

Queen Amelia and Ship "Queen Amelia" A6

**1965, Feb. 15 Photo. *Perf. 12½x13***
**168** A6 11fr multicolored 5.50 5.50

**WHO Anniversary Issue**
Common Design Type

**1968, May 4 Engr. *Perf. 13***
**169** CD126 17fr bl grn, org & lil 4.50 4.50

**Human Rights Year Issue**
Common Design Type

**1968, Aug. 10 Engr. *Perf. 13***
**170** CD127 19fr dk pur, org brn & brt mag 3.00 3.00

Outrigger Canoe A7

**1969, Apr. 30 Photo. *Perf. 13***
**171** A7 1fr multicolored 1.00 1.00
*Nos. 171,C31-C35 (6)* 28.75 14.50

**ILO Issue**
Common Design Type

**1969, Nov. 24 Engr. *Perf. 13***
**172** CD131 9fr orange, brn & bl 2.25 2.25

**UPU Headquarters Issue**
Common Design Type

**1970, May 20 Engr. *Perf. 13***
**173** CD133 21fr lil rose, ind & ol bis 3.25 3.25

No. 157 Surcharged with New Value and Two Bars

**1971 Engr. *Perf. 13***
**174** A3 12fr on 19fr 1.25 1.25

Weight Lifting — A8

**1971, Oct. 25**
**175** A8 24fr shown 4.00 4.00
**176** A8 36fr Basketball 5.00 5.00
*Nos. 175-176,C37-C38 (4)* 18.50 14.50

4th South Pacific Games, Papeete, French Polynesia, Sept. 8-19.

**De Gaulle Issue**
Common Design Type

Designs: 30fr, Gen. de Gaulle, 1940. 70fr, Pres. de Gaulle, 1970.

**1971, Nov. 9 Engr. *Perf. 13***
**177** CD134 30fr blue & black 6.75 4.50
**178** CD134 70fr blue & black 10.50 7.25

Child's Outrigger Canoe A9

Designs: 16fr, Children's canoe race. 18fr, Outrigger racing canoe.

**1972, Oct. 16 Photo. *Perf. 13x12½***
**Size: 35½x26½mm**
**179** A9 14fr dk green & multi 7.25 3.00
**180** A9 16fr dk plum & multi 7.25 3.00
**181** A9 18fr blue & multi 11.00 4.00
*Nos. 179-181,C41 (4)* 55.50 28.00

Outrigger sailing canoes.

Rhinoceros Beetle A10

Insects: 25fr, Cosmopolities sordidus (beetle). 35fr, Ophideres fullonica (moth). 45fr, Dragonfly.

**1974, July 29 Photo. *Perf. 13***
**182** A10 15fr ol & multi 2.50 2.00
**183** A10 25fr ol & multi 3.50 3.00
**184** A10 35fr gray bl & multi 5.00 4.00
**185** A10 45fr multicolored 7.25 6.00
*Nos. 182-185 (4)* 18.25 15.00

Georges Pompidou (1911-74), Pres. of France — A11

**1975, Dec. 1 Engr. *Perf. 13***
**186** A11 50fr ultra & slate 5.00 4.00

Battle of Yorktown and George Washington — A12

American Bicentennial: 47fr, Virginia Cape Battle and Lafayette.

**1976, June 28 Engr. *Perf. 13***
**187** A12 19fr blue, red & olive 2.00 1.25
**188** A12 47fr blue, red & maroon 3.50 3.00

For overprints see Nos. 205-206.

Conus Ammiralis — A13

Sea Shells: 23fr, Cyprae assellus. 43fr, Turbo petholatus. 61fr, Mitra papalis.

**1976, Oct. 1 Engr. *Perf. 13***
**189** A13 20fr multicolored 2.75 2.00
**190** A13 23fr multicolored 2.75 2.00
**191** A13 43fr multicolored 6.00 4.00
**192** A13 61fr ultra & multi 8.50 6.50
*Nos. 189-192 (4)* 20.00 14.50

Father Chanel and Poi Church — A14

32fr, Father Chanel and map of islands.

**1977, Apr. 28 Litho. *Perf. 12***
**193** A14 22fr multicolored 1.50 1.10
**194** A14 32fr multicolored 2.00 1.50

Return of the ashes of Father Chanel, missionary.

Bowl, Mortar and Pestle A15

Handicrafts: 25fr, Wooden bowls and leather bag. 33fr, Wooden comb, club, and boat model. 45fr, War clubs, Futuna. 69fr, Lances.

**1977, Sept. 26 Litho. *Perf. 12½***
**195** A15 12fr multicolored .80 .55
**196** A15 25fr multicolored 1.50 .75
**197** A15 33fr multicolored 1.75 1.00
**198** A15 45fr multicolored 2.25 1.25
**199** A15 69fr multicolored 3.00 2.50
*Nos. 195-199 (5)* 9.30 6.05

Post Office, Mata Utu — A16

50fr, Sia Hospital, Mata Utu. 57fr, Administration Buildings, Mata Utu. 63fr, St. Joseph's Church, Sigave. 120fr, Royal Palace, Mara Utu.

**1977, Dec. 12 Litho. *Perf. 13***
**200** A16 27fr multicolored 1.25 1.00
**201** A16 50fr multicolored 2.00 1.25
**202** A16 57fr multicolored 2.00 1.25
**203** A16 63fr multicolored 2.50 2.00
**204** A16 120fr multicolored 6.50 3.25
*Nos. 200-204 (5)* 14.25 8.75

Nos. 187-188 Overprinted: "JAMES COOK / Bicentenaire de la / découverte des Iles / Hawaii 1778-1978"

**1978, Jan. 20 Engr. *Perf. 13***
**205** A12 19fr multicolored 2.50 2.00
**206** A12 47fr multicolored 5.00 3.00

Bicentenary of the arrival of Capt. Cook in the Hawaiian Islands.

Cruiser Triomphant — A17

Warships: 200fr, Destroyers Cap des Palmes and Chevreuil. 280fr, Cruiser Savorgnan de Brazza.

**1978, June 18 Photo. *Perf. 13x12½***
**207** A17 150fr multicolored 9.00 5.25
**208** A17 200fr multicolored 12.00 7.50
**209** A17 280fr multicolored 16.00 10.00
*Nos. 207-209 (3)* 37.00 22.75

Free French warships serving in the Pacific, 1940-1944.

Solanum Seaforthianum — A18

Flowers: 24fr, Cassia alata. 29fr, Gloriosa superba. 36fr, Hymenocallis littoralis.

**1978, July 11 Photo. *Perf. 13***
**210** A18 16fr multicolored 1.50 .75
**211** A18 24fr multicolored 1.50 .85
**212** A18 29fr multicolored 2.25 1.25
**213** A18 36fr multicolored 3.00 1.50
*Nos. 210-213 (4)* 8.25 4.35

Gray Egret — A19

Birds: 18fr, Red-footed booby. 28fr, Brown booby. 35fr, White tern.

**1978, Sept. 5 Photo. *Perf. 13***
**214** A19 17fr multicolored 1.40 .70
**215** A19 18fr multicolored 1.40 .75
**216** A19 28fr multicolored 2.00 1.10
**217** A19 35fr multicolored 2.75 1.25
*Nos. 214-217 (4)* 7.55 3.80

Traditional Patterns — A20

Designs: 55fr, Corpus Christi procession. 59fr, Chief's honor guard.

**1978, Oct. 3**
**218** A20 53fr multicolored 2.00 1.25
**219** A20 55fr multicolored 2.75 1.50
**220** A20 59fr multicolored 3.00 1.75
*Nos. 218-220 (3)* 7.75 4.50

Human Rights Flame A21

**1978, Dec. 10 Litho. *Perf. 12½***
**221** A21 44fr multicolored 1.25 .75
**222** A21 56fr multicolored 1.75 1.00

30th anniversary of Universal Declaration of Human Rights.

Fishing Boat — A22

Designs: 30fr, Weighing young tuna. 34fr, Stocking young tunas. 38fr, Measuring tuna. 40fr, Angler catching tuna. 48fr, Adult tuna.

**1979, Mar. 19 Litho. *Perf. 12***
**223** A22 10fr multicolored .75 .40
**224** A22 30fr multicolored 1.00 .75
**225** A22 34fr multicolored 1.25 .80
**226** A22 38fr multicolored 1.90 1.10
**227** A22 40fr multicolored 2.10 1.60
**228** A22 48fr multicolored 3.00 1.60
*a.* Souv. sheet of 6, #223-228 + 3 labels 18.00 18.00
*Nos. 223-228 (6)* 10.00 6.25

Tuna tagging by South Pacific Commission.
For surcharge see No. 261.

Boy with Raft and IYC Emblem — A23

Design: 58fr, Girl on horseback.

**1979, Apr. 9 Photo. *Perf. 13***
**229** A23 52fr multicolored 1.75 1.00
**230** A23 58fr multicolored 1.90 1.10

International Year of the Child.

Bombax Ellipticum — A24

64fr, Callophyllum. 76fr, Pandanus odoratissimus.

**1979, Apr. 23 Litho. *Perf. 13***
**231** A24 50fr multicolored 1.40 .85
**232** A24 64fr multicolored 1.90 1.10
**233** A24 76fr multicolored 2.50 1.60
*Nos. 231-233 (3)* 5.80 3.55

Green and Withered Landscapes — A25

**1979, May 28 Photo. *Perf. 13***
**234** A25 22fr multicolored 1.10 .60

Anti-alcoholism campaign.

Flowers — A26

**1979, July 16 Photo. *Perf. 12½x13***
**235** A26 20fr Crinum .60 .30
**236** A26 42fr Passiflora 1.40 .70
**237** A26 62fr Canna indica 2.00 1.00
*Nos. 235-237 (3)* 4.00 2.00

See Nos. 279-281.

Swimming — A27

**1979, Aug. 27 Engr. *Perf. 13***
**238** A27 31fr shown 1.50 1.00
**239** A27 39fr High jump 2.00 1.25

6th South Pacific Games, Suva, Fiji, Aug. 27-Sept. 8.

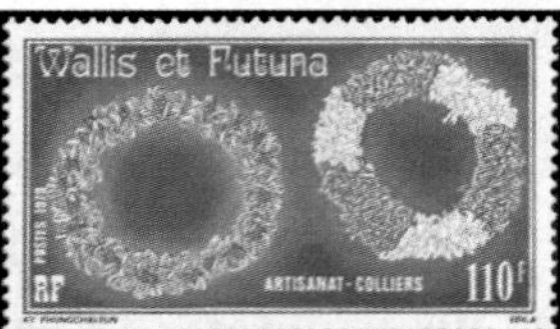


Flower Necklaces — A28

Design: 140fr, Coral necklaces.

**1979, Aug. 27 Litho.**
**240** A28 110fr multicolored 3.00 1.75
**241** A28 140fr multicolored 3.75 2.25

Trees and Birds, by Sutita — A29

Paintings by Local Artists: 65fr, Birds and Mountain, by M. A. Pilioko, vert. 78fr, Festival Procession, by Sutita.

**1979, Oct. 8 *Perf. 13x12½, 12½x13***
**242** A29 27fr multicolored 1.00 .50
**243** A29 65fr multicolored 1.60 .90
**244** A29 78fr multicolored 2.50 1.25
*Nos. 242-244 (3)* 5.10 2.65

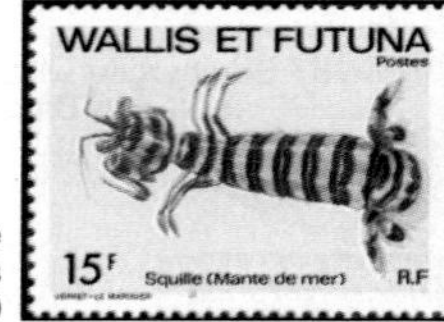


Marine Mantis A30

Marine Life: 23fr, Hexabranchus sanguineus. 25fr, Spondylus barbatus. 43fr, Gorgon coral. 45fr, Linckia laevigata. 63fr, Tridacna squamosa.

**1979, Nov. 5 Photo. *Perf. 13x12½***
**245** A30 15fr multicolored .75 .40
**246** A30 23fr multicolored 1.00 .50
**247** A30 25fr multicolored 1.25 .60
**248** A30 43fr multicolored 1.50 .75
**249** A30 45fr multicolored 1.75 .80
**250** A30 63fr multicolored 2.50 1.25
*Nos. 245-250 (6)* 8.75 4.30

See #294-297. For surcharge see #272.

Transportation Type of 1979

**1980, Feb. 29 Litho. *Perf. 13***
**251** AP32 1fr like No. C87 .30 .20
**252** AP32 3fr like No. C88 .30 .20
**253** AP32 5fr like No. C89 .40 .30
*Nos. 251-253 (3)* 1.00 .70

Radio Station and Tower — A31

**1980, Apr. 21 Litho. *Perf. 13***
**254** A31 47fr multicolored 1.60 1.00

Radio station FR3, 1st anniversary.

Jesus Laid in the Tomb, by Maurice Denis — A32

**1980, Apr. 28 *Perf. 13x12½***
**255** A32 25fr multicolored 1.25 .65

Easter 1980.

Gnathodentex Mossambicus — A33

**1980, Aug. 25 Litho. *Perf. 12½x13***
**256** A33 23fr shown 1.00 .65
**257** A33 27fr Pristipomoides filamentosus 1.25 .75
**258** A33 32fr Etelis carbunculus 1.90 1.00
**259** A33 51fr Cephalopholis wallisi 2.50 1.75
**260** A33 59fr Aphareus rutilans 3.00 2.00
*a.* Vert. strip of 5, Nos. 256-260 10.00 10.00

No. 228 Surcharged:

**1980, Sept. 29 Litho. *Perf. 12***
**261** A22 50fr on 48fr multi 2.00 1.25

Sydpex 80 Philatelic Exhibition, Sydney.

13th World Telecommunications Day — A34

**1981, May 17 Litho. *Perf. 12½***
**262** A34 49fr multicolored 1.50 1.00

Pierre Curie and Laboratory Equipment — A35

**1981, May 25 Litho. *Perf. 13***
**263** A35 56fr multicolored 1.75 1.00

Pierre Curie (1859-1906), discoverer of radioactivity.

Conus Textile A36

Designs: Marine life.

**1981, June 22 *Perf. 12½x13***

**264** A36 28fr Favites .90 .75
**265** A36 30fr Cyanophycees 1.10 .75
**266** A36 31fr Ceratium vultur 1.25 .75
**267** A36 35fr Amphiprion frenatus 1.90 1.00
**268** A36 40fr shown 1.90 1.10
**269** A36 55fr Comatule 2.40 1.25
*a.* Vert. strip of 6, Nos. 264-269 10.00 10.00

No. 269a is from sheet of 24.

60th Anniv. of Anti-tuberculin Vaccine (Developed by Calmette and Guerin) — A37

**1981, July 28 Litho. *Perf. 13***
**270** A37 27fr multicolored 1.10 .65

Intl. Year of the Disabled — A38

**1981, Aug. 17**
**271** A38 42fr multicolored 1.75 1.00

No. 245 Surcharged in Red

**1981, Sept. Photo. *Perf. 13x12½***
**272** A30 5fr on 15fr multi .60 .25

Thomas Edison (1847-1931) and his Phonograph, 1878 — A39

**1981, Sept. 5 Engr. *Perf. 13***
**273** A39 59fr multicolored 2.50 1.25

Battle of Yorktown, 1781 (American Revolution) — A40

**1981, Oct. 19 Engr. *Perf. 13***
**274** A40 66fr Admiral de Grasse 1.75 1.25
**275** A40 74fr Sea battle, vert. 2.25 1.75

200-Mile Zone Surveillance — A41

**1981, Dec. 4 Litho. *Perf. 13***
**276** A41 60fr Patrol boat Dieppoise 1.25 1.00
**277** A41 85fr Protet 2.50 1.75

TB Bacillus Centenary — A42

**1982, Mar. 24 Litho. *Perf. 13***
**278** A42 45fr multicolored 3.00 1.00

Flower Type of 1979 in Changed Colors

**1982, May 3 Photo. *Perf. 12½x13***
**279** A26 1fr like No. 235 .30 .25
**280** A26 2fr like No. 236 .40 .25
**281** A26 3fr like No. 237 .40 .30
*Nos. 279-281 (3)* 1.10 .80

PHILEXFRANCE '82 Intl. Stamp Exhibition, Paris, June 11-21 — A43

**1982, May 12 Engr. *Perf. 13***
**282** A43 140fr No. 25 2.50 1.75

Acanthe Phippium A44

Orchids and rubiaceae (83fr).

**1982, May 24 Litho. *Perf. 12½x13***
**283** A44 34fr shown .85 .70
**284** A44 68fr Acanthe phippium, diff. 1.75 1.40
**285** A44 70fr Spathoglottis pacifica 2.00 1.40
**286** A44 83fr Mussaenda raiateensis 2.25 1.75
*Nos. 283-286 (4)* 6.85 5.25

Scouting Year A45

**1982, June 21 *Perf. 12½***
**287** A45 80fr Baden-Powell 1.75 1.40

Cypraea Talpa A46

Porcelaines shells.

**1982, June 28 *Perf. 12½x13***
**288** A46 10fr shown .30 .20
**289** A46 15fr Cypraea vitellus .70 .30
**290** A46 25fr Cypraea argus .85 .50
**291** A46 27fr Cypraea carneola 1.10 .75
**292** A46 40fr Cypraea mappa 1.40 1.10
**293** A46 50fr Cypraea tigris 1.75 1.25
*Nos. 288-293 (6)* 6.10 4.10

Marine Life Type of 1979

**1982, Oct. 1 Photo. *Perf. 13x12½***
**294** A30 32fr Gorgones milithea 1.00 .50
**295** A30 35fr Linckia laevigata 1.25 .85
**296** A30 46fr Hexabranchus sanguineus 1.50 1.00
**297** A30 63fr Spondylus barbatus 2.25 1.50
*Nos. 294-297 (4)* 6.00 3.85

St. Teresa of Jesus of Avila (1515-1582) — A48

**1982, Nov. 8 Engr. *Perf. 13***
**298** A48 31fr multicolored .90 .55

See No. 315.

Traditional House A49

**1983, Jan. 20 Litho. *Perf. 13***
**299** A49 19fr multicolored .70 .35

Gustave Eiffel (1832-1923), Architect — A50

**1983, Feb. 14 Engr. *Perf. 13***
**300** A50 97fr multicolored 2.75 1.50

A51

A52

**1983, June 28 Engr. *Perf. 13***
**301** A51 92fr Thai dancer, 19th cent. 2.25 1.25

BANGKOK '83 Intl. Stamp Show, Aug. 4-13.

**1983, Aug. 25 Litho. *Perf. 13x13½***
**302** A52 20fr multicolored .70 .35

World Communications Year.

Cone Shells A53

**1983-84 Litho. *Perf. 13½x13***
**303** A53 10fr Conus tulipa .35 .25
**304** A53 17fr Conus capitaneus .55 .35
**305** A53 21fr Conus virgo .55 .35
**306** A53 22fr Strombus lentiginosus .50 .35
**307** A53 25fr Lambis chiragra .55 .45
**308** A53 35fr Strombus dentatus 1.00 .55
**309** A53 39fr Conus vitulinus 1.00 .70
**310** A53 43fr Lambis scorpius 1.25 .55
**311** A53 49fr Strombus aurisdianae 1.60 1.10
**312** A53 52fr Conus marmoreus 1.40 1.10
**313** A53 65fr Conus leopardus 1.75 1.25
**314** A53 76fr Lambis crocata 2.25 1.25
*Nos. 303-314 (12)* 12.75 8.25

Issued: 22, 25, 35, 43, 49, 76fr, 3/23/84; others, 10/14/83.

No. 298 Redrawn with Espana '84 Emblem

**1984, Apr. 27 Engr. *Perf. 13***
**315** A48 70fr multicolored 1.75 1.00

Denis Diderot (1713-1784), Philosopher A54

**1984, May 11**
**316** A54 100fr Portrait, encyclopedia title page 2.40 1.25

Nature Protection (Whale) A55

**1984, June 5 Litho. *Perf. 13x12½***
**317** A55 90fr Orcina orca 2.75 1.25

4th Pacific Arts Festival — A56

**1984, Nov. 30 Litho. *Perf. 13***
**318** A56 160fr Islanders 3.75 2.50

Lapita Pottery — A57

Ethno-Archaeological Museum: Excavation site, reconstructed ceramic bowl.

**1985, Jan. 16 Litho. *Perf. 13***
**319** A57 53fr multicolored 1.40 .75

Seashells A58

**1985, Feb. 11**
**320** A58 2fr Nautilus pompilius .20 .20
**321** A58 3fr Murex bruneus .20 .20
**322** A58 41fr Casmaria erinaceus 1.25 .80
**323** A58 47fr Conus vexillum 1.50 .90
**324** A58 56fr Harpa harpa 1.90 1.00
**325** A58 71fr Murex ramosus 2.25 1.50
*Nos. 320-325 (6)* 7.30 4.60

Victor Hugo, Author (1802-1885) A59

Bat — A60

**1985, Mar. 7 Engr.**
**326** A59 89fr multicolored 2.50 1.25

**1985, Apr. 29 Litho.**
**327** A60 38fr multicolored 2.00 .75

Intl. Youth Year — A61

**1985, May 20 Litho. *Perf. 12½x13***
**328** A61 64fr Children 1.50 .85

UN, 40th Anniv. — A61a

**1985, July 12 Engr. *Perf. 13***
**328A** A61a 49fr Prus grn, dk ultra & red 1.25 .70

Pierre de Ronsard (1524-1585), Poet — A62

**1985, Sept. 16 Engr. *Perf. 13***
**329** A62 170fr brt bl, sep & brn 4.25 2.75

Dr. Albert Schweitzer — A63

**1985, Nov. 22 Engr. *Perf. 13***
**330** A63 50fr blk, dk red lil & org brn 1.60 1.00

World Food Day — A64

**1986, Jan. 23 Litho. *Perf. 12½x13***
**331** A64 39fr Breadfruit 1.25 .60

Flamboyants — A65

**1986, Feb. 13 *Perf. 13x12½***
**332** A65 38fr multicolored 2.00 1.00

Seashells A66

**1986, Apr. 24 Litho. *Perf. 13½x13***
**333** A66 4fr Lambis truncata .30 .30
**334** A66 5fr Charonia tritonis .30 .30
**335** A66 10fr Oliva miniacea .40 .30
**336** A66 18fr Distorsio anus .60 .55
**337** A66 25fr Mitra mitra .95 .60
**338** A66 107fr Conus distans 2.90 1.75
*Nos. 333-338 (6)* 5.45 3.80

Also exists in se-tenant strips of 6 from sheet of 24.

1986 World Cup Soccer Championships, Mexico — A67

**1986, May 20 *Perf. 13x12½***
**339** A67 95fr multicolored 2.50 1.40

UNICEF.

Discovery of Horn Islands, 370th Anniv. — A68

No. 340: a, 8fr, William Schouten, ship. b, 9fr, Jacob LeMaire, ship. c, 155fr, Map of Alo & Alofi.

**1986, June 19 Engr. *Perf. 13***
**340** A68 Strip of 3, #a.-c. 5.50 4.00

James Watt (1736-1819), Inventor, and Steam Engine — A69

**1986, July 11**
**341** A69 74fr blk & dk red 2.40 1.25

La Lorientaise Patrol Boat — A70

7fr, 120fr vertical.

**1986, Aug. 7**
**342** A70 6fr shown .50 .35
**343** A70 7fr Commandant Blaison .50 .35
**344** A70 120fr Balny escort ship 4.00 2.00
*Nos. 342-344 (3)* 5.00 2.70

Rose Laurel — A71

**1986, Oct. 2 Litho. *Perf. 13x12½***
**345** A71 97fr multi 2.50 1.60

Virgin and Child, by Sandro Botticelli A72

**1986, Dec. 12 Litho. *Perf. 12½x13***
**346** A72 250fr multicolored 5.50 3.25

Christmas.

Butterflies — A73

**1987, Apr. 2 Litho. *Perf. 12½***
**347** A73 2fr Papilio montrouzieri .20 .20
**348** A73 42fr Belenois java 1.25 .60
**349** A73 46fr Delias ellipsis 1.40 .60
**350** A73 50fr Danaus pumila 1.60 .75
**351** A73 52fr Luthrodes cleotas 2.00 .85
**352** A73 59fr Precis villida 2.25 1.00
*Nos. 347-352 (6)* 8.70 4.00

World Wrestling Championships — A74

**1987, May 26 Litho. *Perf. 12½***
**353** A74 97fr multi 2.50 1.25

For overprint see No. 360.

Seashells A75

**1987, June 24 Litho. *Perf. 13***
**354** A75 3fr Cymatium pileare .25 .25
**355** A75 4fr Conus textile .30 .30
**356** A75 28fr Cypraea mauritiana 1.00 .60
**357** A75 44fr Bursa bubo 1.10 .80

**358** A75 48fr Cypraea testudinaria 1.25 .85
**359** A75 78fr Cypraecassis rufa 2.10 1.20
*Nos. 354-359 (6)* 6.00 4.00

Also exists in se-tenant strips of 6 from sheet of 24.

No. 353 Overprinted

**1987, Aug. 29 Litho. *Perf. 12½***
**360** A74 97fr multicolored 2.75 1.75

OLYMPHILEX '87, Rome.

Bust of a Girl, by Auguste Rodin (1840-1917) A76

**1987, Sept. 15 Engr. *Perf. 13***
**361** A76 150fr plum 4.25 2.00

See No. 390.

World Post Day — A77

**1987, Oct. 9 Litho. *Perf. 13***
**362** A77 116fr multicolored 2.75 1.40

Birds — A78

**1987, Oct. 28 *Perf. 13x12½***
**363** A78 6fr Anas superciliosa .20 .20
**364** A78 19fr Pluvialis dominica .50 .20
**365** A78 47fr Gallicolumba stairi 1.25 .50
**366** A78 56fr Arenaria interpres 1.60 .85
**367** A78 64fr Rallus philippensis 1.75 .85
**368** A78 68fr Limosa lapponica 2.25 1.00
*Nos. 363-368 (6)* 7.55 3.60

Francis Carco (1886-1958), Painter — A79

Design: Carco and views of the Moulin de la Galette and Place du Tertre, Paris.

**1988, Jan. 29 Litho. *Perf. 13***
**369** A79 40fr multicolored 1.25 .65

Jean-Francois de Galaup (1741-c.1788), Comte de La Perouse, Explorer — A80

Design: Ships *L'Astrolabe* and *La Boussole*, portrait of La Perouse.

**1988, Mar. 21 Engr. *Perf. 13***
**370** A80 70fr org brn, dark blue & olive grn 2.75 1.25

Intl. Red Cross and Red Crescent Organizations, 125th Annivs. — A81

**1988, July 4 Engr. *Perf. 13***
**371** A81 30fr blk, dark red & brt blue grn 2.00 1.00

1988 Summer Olympics, Seoul — A82

**1988, Sept. 1 Engr. *Perf. 13***
**372** A82 11fr Javelin .55 .40
**373** A82 20fr Women's volleyball .75 .55
**374** A82 60fr Windsurfing 1.60 1.10
**375** A82 80fr Yachting 2.25 1.50
*a.* Souv. sheet of 4, #372-375 + 2 labels, gutter between 6.50 6.50
*Nos. 372-375 (4)* 5.15 3.55

Intl. Maritime Organization Emblem and Packet *Escorteur* F727 — A83

**1989, Jan. 26 Litho. *Perf. 13***
**376** A83 26fr multi 1.00 .50

Jean Renoir (1894-1979), Film Director, and Scene from *The Grand Illusion* — A84

**1989, Feb. 16 Engr. *Perf. 13***
**377** A84 24fr brt lil rose, dark vio brn & brt org 1.00 .60

Antoine Becquerel (1788-1878), Physicist — A85

***Perf. 13x12½***
**1988, Nov. 9 Engr. Unwmk.**
**378** A85 18fr blk & dark ultra .75 .40

Futuna Hydroelectric Plant — A86

**Wmk. 385**
**1989, Apr. 13 Litho. *Perf. 13½***
**379** A86 25fr multi .85 .40

A87

A88

**Unwmk.**
**1988, Oct. 26 Litho. *Perf. 13***
**380** A87 17fr multi .75 .40

World Post Day.

**1989, May 17 *Perf. 12½x13***
**381** A88 21fr multi .85 .40

World Telecommunications Day.

Fresco A89

**1989, June 8 *Perf. 12½***
**382** A89 22fr multi .80 .40

PHILEXFRANCE '89 — A90

Declaration of Human Rights and Citizenship, Bicent. — A91

**1989, July 7 Litho. *Perf. 13***
**383** A90 29fr multi 1.00 .50
**384** A91 900fr multi 17.50 14.00
*a.* Souv. sheet of 2, #383-384 + label 24.00 24.00

No. 384 is airmail. No. 384a sold for 1000fr.

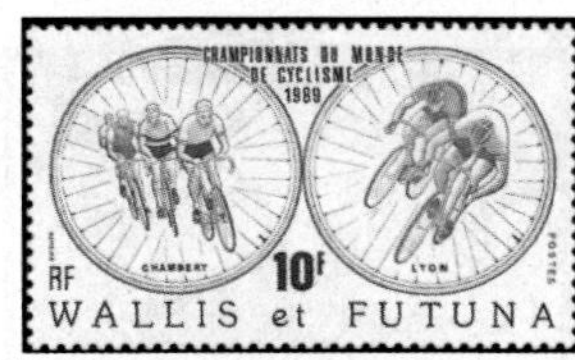

World Cycling Championships — A92

**1989, Sept. 14 Engr. *Perf. 13***
**385** A92 10fr blk, red brn & emer .60 .45

World Post Day — A93

**Unwmk.**
**1989, Oct. 18 Litho. *Perf. 13***
**386** A93 27fr multicolored .80 .40

Landscape — A94

**1989, Nov. 23 Litho. *Perf. 13***
**387** A94 23fr multicolored .80 .40

Star of Bethlehem A95

**1990, Jan. 9 Litho. *Perf. 12½***
**388** A95 44fr multicolored 1.25 .75

Fossilized Tortoise A96

**1990, Feb. 15 Litho. *Perf. 12½x13***
**389** A96 48fr multicolored 2.75 1.25

Sculpture by Auguste Rodin (1840-1917)
A97

**1990, Mar. 15** **Engr.** ***Perf. 13***
**390** A97 200fr royal blue 5.00 2.75

1990 World Cup Soccer Championships, Italy — A98

**1990, Apr. 16** **Litho.**
**391** A98 59fr multicolored 1.50 .90

Orchids
A99

**1990, May 17** **Litho.** ***Perf. 12½***
**392** A99 78fr multicolored 2.50 1.25

Mother's Day

Phaeton — A100

**1990, July 16** ***Perf. 13***
**393** A100 300fr multicolored 8.00 4.00
**394** A100 600fr Island 17.50 8.00

Moana II — A101

**1990, Aug. 16** **Engr.** ***Perf. 13***
**395** A101 40fr shown 1.10 .60
**396** A101 50fr Moana III 1.75 .75

Native Huts
A102

**1990, Sept. 17** **Litho.** ***Perf. 13x12½***
**397** A102 28fr multicolored .90 .45

Stamp Day
A103

**1990, Oct. 16** **Litho.** ***Perf. 12½***
**398** A103 97fr multicolored 2.75 1.50

Wallis Island Pirogue — A104

**1990, Nov. 16** **Litho.** ***Perf. 13x12½***
**399** A104 46fr multicolored 1.50 .60

Best Wishes — A105

**1990, Dec. 17** **Litho.** ***Perf. 13x12½***
**400** A105 100fr multicolored 2.75 1.25

Patrol Boat La Glorieuse — A106

**1991** **Engr.** ***Perf. 13***
**401** A106 42fr La Moqueuse 1.25 .75
**402** A106 52fr shown 1.75 .80

Issue dates: 42fr, Jan. 7; 52fr, Mar. 4.

A107

**1991, Feb. 4** **Litho.** ***Perf. 13***
**403** A107 7fr Breadfruit picker .30 .25
**404** A107 54fr Taro planter 1.50 .70
**405** A107 62fr Spear fisherman 1.60 .75
**406** A107 72fr Native warrior 1.90 .90
**407** A107 90fr Kailao dancer 2.75 1.25
*a.* Souv. sheet of 5, #403-407 9.00 9.00
*Nos. 403-407 (5)* 8.05 3.85

Issued: 7fr, 9/2; 54fr, 5/13; 62fr, 4/1; 72fr, 2/4; 90fr, 11/4.
No. 407a sold for 300fr.

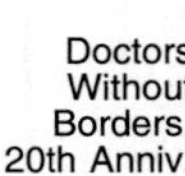
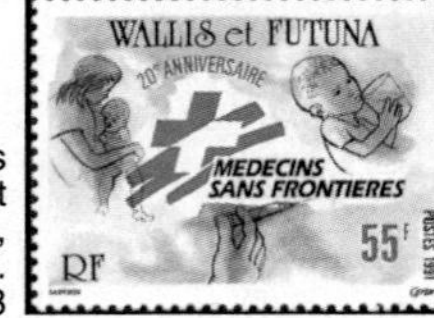


Doctors Without Borders, 20th Anniv.
A108

**1991, Feb. 18** **Litho.** ***Perf. 13½***
**408** A108 55fr multicolored 1.60 .75

Ultralight Aircraft — A108a

**1991, June 24**
**409** A108a 85fr multicolored 2.10 1.00

Portrait of Jean by Auguste Renoir (1841-1919) — A109

**1991, July 8** **Photo.** ***Perf. 12½x13***
**410** A109 400fr multicolored 10.00 5.50

**Litho.**
***Die Cut***
**Self-Adhesive**

**411** A109 400fr multicolored 10.00 5.50

Overseas Territorial Status, 30th Anniv. — A110

**1991, July 29** **Litho.** ***Perf. 13***
**412** A110 102fr multicolored 2.50 1.25

Feast of the Assumption — A111

**1991, Aug. 15** ***Perf. 13x12½***
**413** A111 30fr multicolored 1.00 .50

Amnesty Intl., 30th Anniv.
A113

**1991, Oct. 7** ***Perf. 13x12½***
**414** A113 140fr bl, vio & yel 3.75 2.25

Central Bank for Economic Cooperation, 50th Anniv. — A114

**1991, Dec. 2** **Litho.** ***Perf. 13***
**415** A114 10fr multicolored .50 .30

Flowers
A115

1fr, Monette allamanda cathartica. 4fr, Hibiscus rosa sinensis. 80fr, Ninuphar.

**1991, Dec. 2** ***Perf. 12½x13, 13x12½***
**416** A115 1fr multi .40 .20
**417** A115 4fr multi, vert. .40 .30
**418** A115 80fr multi 1.90 1.10
*Nos. 416-418 (3)* 2.70 1.60

Christmas — A116

**1991, Dec. 16** **Litho.** ***Perf. 13***
**419** A116 60fr multicolored 1.60 .90

Maritime Surveillance — A117

**1992, Jan. 20** **Litho.** ***Perf. 13***
**420** A117 48fr multicolored 1.60 .75

1992 Winter Olympics, Albertville — A118

**1992, Feb. 17** **Litho.** ***Perf. 13***
**421** A118 150fr multicolored 3.50 2.25

Canada '92, Intl. Philatelic Exposition, Montreal — A119

Illustration reduced.

**1992, Mar. 25 Engr. *Perf. 13***
**422** A119 35fr blk, violet & red 1.25 .55

1992 Summer Olympics, Barcelona — A120

**1992, Apr. 15 Engr. *Perf. 13***
**423** A120 106fr bl grn, grn & bl 2.75 1.50

Granada '92, Intl. Philatelic Exposition — A121

Illustration reduced.

**1992, Apr. 17 Engr. *Perf. 12½x12***
**424** A121 100fr multicolored 2.75 1.40

Expo '92, Seville — A122

**1992, Apr. 20 *Perf. 13***
**425** A122 200fr bl grn, ol & red brn 5.00 3.00

Chaetodon Ephippium — A123

Designs: 22fr, Chaetodon auriga. 23fr, Heniochus monoceros. 24fr, Pygoplites diacanthus. 25fr, Chaetodontoplus conspicillatus. 26fr, Chaetodon unimaculatus. 27fr, Siganus punctatus. 35fr, Zebrasoma veliferum. 45fr, Paracanthurus hepatus. 53fr, Siganus vulpinus.

**1992-93 Litho. *Perf. 13***
**426** A123 21fr multicolored .65 .45
**427** A123 22fr multicolored .65 .45
**428** A123 23fr multicolored .65 .45
**429** A123 24fr multicolored .70 .60
**430** A123 25fr multicolored .90 .60
**431** A123 26fr multicolored .90 .60
**432** A123 27fr multicolored .90 .70
**433** A123 35fr multicolored 1.00 .70
**434** A123 45fr multicolored 1.25 .90
**435** A123 53fr multicolored 1.50 .90
*Nos. 426-435 (10)* 9.10 6.35

Issued: 21fr, 26fr, 5/18; 22fr, 7/27; 25fr, 7/27; 23fr, 24fr, 9/14; 35fr, 45fr, 6/21/93; 27fr, 53fr, 9/6/93.

Natives A125

a, 3 warriors. b, 2 warriors. c, Warrior, 2 boats. d, 2 spear fisherman. e, 3 fisherman.

**1992, June 15 Litho. *Perf. 12***
**436** A125 70fr Strip of 5, #a.-e. 10.00 7.00
*f.* Souvenir sheet of 5, #a.-e. 12.50 12.50

#436 has continuous design. #436f sold for 450fr.

Support Ship, "La Garonne" A126

**1992, Oct. 12 Litho. *Perf. 12***
**437** A126 20fr multicolored .75 .40

L'Idylle D'Ixelles, by Auguste Rodin (1840-1917) A127

**1992, Nov. 17 Engr. *Perf. 13***
**438** A127 300fr lilac & dk blue 8.00 5.00

Miribilis Jalapa A128

**1992, Dec. 7 Litho. *Perf. 12½***
**439** A128 200fr multicolored 5.00 3.25

Maritime Forces of the Pacific — A129

**1993, Jan. 27 Litho. *Perf. 13x12½***
**440** A129 130fr multicolored 3.00 2.25

School Art — A130

**1993, Feb. 22 Litho. *Perf. 12***
**441** A130 56fr multicolored 1.60 .75

See Nos. 451-452.

Birds A131

Designs: 50fr, Rallus philippensis swindellsi. 60fr, Porphyrio porphyrio. 110fr, Ptilinopus greyi.

**1993, Mar. 20 *Perf. 13½***
**442** A131 50fr multicolored 1.40 .75
**443** A131 60fr multicolored 1.60 .85
**444** A131 110fr multicolored 3.25 1.75
*Nos. 442-444 (3)* 6.25 3.35

Mother's Day A132

**1993, May 30 Litho. *Perf. 12½***
**445** A132 95fr Hibiscus 2.25 1.25
**446** A132 120fr Siale 2.75 1.75

Admiral Antoine d'Entrecasteaux (1737-1793), French Navigator — A133

**1993, July 12 Engr. *Perf. 13***
**447** A133 170fr grn bl, red brn & blk 4.00 2.50

Taipei '93 — A134

**1993, Aug. 14 Litho. *Perf. 13x12½***
**448** A134 435fr multicolored 12.50 10.00

Churches — A135

**1993, Aug. 15 *Perf. 13***
**449** A135 30fr Tepa, Wallis .75 .60
**450** A135 30fr Vilamalia, Futuna .75 .60

School Art Type of 1993

**1993 Litho. *Perf. 13x13½, 13½x13***
**451** A130 28fr Stylized trees .75 .40
**452** A130 52fr Family, vert. 1.25 .75

Issue dates: 28fr, Oct. 18. 52fr, Nov. 8.

Christmas A136

**1993, Dec, 6 *Perf. 13***
**453** A136 80fr multicolored 1.90 1.25

Traditional Arts and Crafts Exhibition A137

**1994, Mar. 24 Litho. *Perf. 12½***
**454** A137 80fr multicolored 1.90 1.25

Liberation of Paris, 50th Anniv. — A138

**1994, Apr. 21 Engr. *Perf. 13***
**455** A138 110fr black, blue & red 3.00 1.75

Satellite Communications — A139

**1994, June 23 Litho.**
**456** A139 10fr multicolored 1.10 .25

1994 World Cup Soccer Championships, U.S. — A140

**1994, June 23**
**457** A140 105fr multicolored 2.50 1.50

Princesses Ouveennes, 1903 — A141

**1994, July 21 Engr. *Perf. 13***
**458** A141 90fr blue grn, blk & red 2.50 1.25

Symbols of Playing Cards Suits — A142

**1994, Aug. 25 Litho. *Perf. 13***
459 A142 40fr multicolored 1.10 .55

Ultra-Light Aircraft — A143

**1994, Aug. 25**
460 A143 5fr multicolored 1.00 .25

Coconut — A144

**1994, Oct. 13 Litho. *Perf. 13***
461 A144 36fr multicolored 1.00 .55

Parrots A145

**1994, Nov. 17 Litho. *Perf. 13x13½***
462 A145 62fr multicolored 2.00 1.10

Grand Lodge of France, Cent. — A146

**1994, Nov. 24 Engr. *Perf. 13***
463 A146 250fr multicolored 6.50 3.50

Preparing Traditional Meal — A147

**1995, Jan. 25 Litho. *Perf. 13***
464 A147 80fr multicolored 2.40 1.25

Aerial View of Islands A148

**1995, Feb. 21 *Perf. 13x13½, 13½x13***
465 A148 85fr Nukulaelae 2.00 1.25
466 A148 90fr Nukufetau, vert. 2.25 1.40
467 A148 100fr Nukufotu, Nukuloa 2.75 1.50
*Nos. 465-467 (3)* 7.00 4.15

Mua College — A149

**1995, Apr. 11 *Perf. 12***
468 A149 35fr multicolored 1.10 .60

UN, 50th Anniv. — A150

Illustration reduced.

**1995, June 26 Litho. *Perf. 13½***
469 A150 55fr multicolored 1.50 .80

10th South Pacific Games — A151

**1995, Aug. 1 Litho. *Perf. 13***
470 A151 70fr multicolored 1.90 1.00

Local Plants — A152

**1995, Oct. 24 Litho. *Perf. 13½x13***
471 A152 20fr Breadfruit tree .50 .40
472 A152 60fr Tarot 1.50 .75
473 A152 65fr Kava 2.00 1.10
*Nos. 471-473 (3)* 4.00 2.25

See Nos. 478-481, 484-485.

Tapa — A153

**1995, Dec. 12 Litho. *Perf. 13***
474 A153 25fr Native life, vert. .65 .55
475 A153 26fr Fish, sea shells .75 .55

Mothers from the Islands — A154

**1996, Jan. 14 Litho. *Perf. 13½x13***
476 A154 80fr multicolored 2.00 1.10

Golf A155

**1996, Jan. 24 *Perf. 13***
477 A155 95fr multicolored 3.50 1.40

Local Plant Type of 1995

**1996 Litho. *Perf. 13½x13***
478 A152 27fr Cananga odorata .60 .30
479 A152 28fr Mahoaa .75 .40
480 A152 45fr Hibiscus 1.00 .60
481 A152 52fr Ufi 1.25 .70
*Nos. 478-481 (4)* 3.60 2.00

Issued: #479, 481, 3/14; #478, 480, 6/20.

Sanglants Swamp — A156

**1996, June 26 *Perf. 13***
482 A156 53fr multicolored 1.40 .80

Chess — A157

**1996, July 17**
483 A157 110fr multicolored 2.75 1.50

Plant Type of 1995

Designs: 30fr, 48fr, Calladium.

**1996, Sept. 17 Litho. *Perf. 13½x13***
**Background Color**
484 A152 30fr blue green .65 .30
485 A152 48fr lilac 1.10 .60

Francoise Perroton, Missionary — A158

**1996, Oct. 25 *Perf. 13***
486 A158 50fr multicolored 1.50 .75

UNICEF, 50th Anniv. A159

**1996, Dec. 4 Litho. *Perf. 13***
487 A159 25fr multicolored .75 .45

CPS, 50th Anniv. A160

**1997, Feb. 6 Litho. *Perf. 13***
488 A160 7fr multicolored .25 .25

Royal Standards A161

**1997, Feb. 14 Litho. *Perf. 13x13½***
489 A161 56fr King Lavelua 1.10 .55
490 A161 60fr King Tuiagaifo 1.25 .60
491 A161 70fr King Tuisigave 1.40 .65
*Nos. 489-491 (3)* 3.75 1.80

Brasseur de Kava — A162

**1997, Apr. 17 *Perf. 13½x13***
492 A162 170fr multicolored 3.50 1.75

Island Scenes A163

Designs: 10fr, Old man telling stories to children seated around campfire. 36fr, Braiding mat, vert. 40fr, Preparing "Kai'umu" (feast).

***Perf. 13x13½, 13½x13***
**1997, May 20 Litho.**
493 A163 10fr multicolored .20 .20
494 A163 36fr multicolored .80 .50
495 A163 40fr multicolored .90 .60
*Nos. 493-495 (3)* 1.90 1.30

Green Lagoon Turtles A164

**1997, June 18 *Perf. 13x13½***
496 A164 62fr Crawling ashore 1.75 .80
497 A164 80fr Swimming 2.25 1.10

Festival of Avignon — A165

**1997, July 31** **Litho.** ***Perf. 13***
**498** A165 160fr multicolored 3.50 1.75

Berlin Handicapped Sports Festival — A166

**1997, Aug. 12**
**499** A166 35fr multicolored 1.10 .55

D'Uvéa Karate Club — A167

Illustration reduced.

**1997, Oct. 15** **Litho.** ***Perf. 13x13½***
**500** A167 24fr multicolored 1.00 .35

Fight Against AIDS — A168

**1997, Dec. 1** **Litho.** ***Perf. 13***
**501** A168 5fr multicolored 1.25 .30

Christmas — A169

**1997, Dec, 24**
**502** A169 85fr Nativity 2.25 1.10

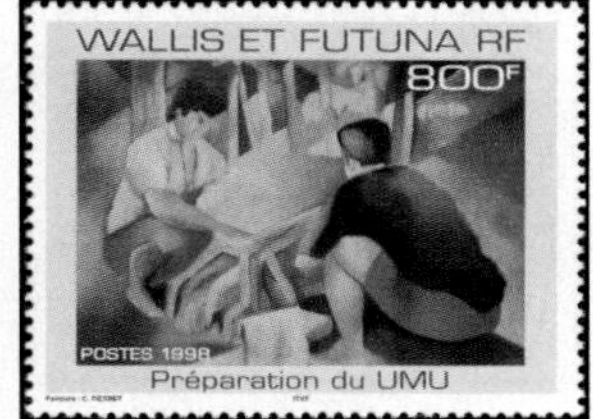
Preparation of UMU — A170

**1998, Jan. 26**
**503** A170 800fr multicolored 16.00 9.00

Orchids — A171

70fr, Vanda T.M.A.. 85fr, Cattleya bow bells. 90fr, Arachnis. 105fr, Cattleya.

**1998, Feb. 18** **Litho.** ***Perf. 13***
**504** A171 70fr multi, vert. 1.50 1.00
**505** A171 85fr multi 1.75 1.25
**506** A171 90fr multi, vert. 1.90 1.25
**507** A171 105fr multi 2.25 1.50
*Nos. 504-507 (4)* 7.40 5.00

Telecom 2000 — A172

**1998, Mar. 24** **Litho.** ***Perf. 13***
**508** A172 7fr multicolored .30 .25

Fishing — A173

Designs: 50fr, Fisherman casting net into lagoon. 52fr, Fisherman sorting catch.

**1998, May 26** **Litho.** ***Perf. 13***
**509** A173 50fr multicolored 1.10 .50
**510** A173 52fr multicolored 1.10 .50

1998 World Cup Soccer Championships, France — A174

**1998, June 10**
**511** A174 80fr multicolored 1.75 1.25

Insects A175

**1998, July 21** **Litho.** ***Perf. 13x13½***
**512** A175 36fr Dragonfly .75 .45
**513** A175 40fr Cicada .80 .55

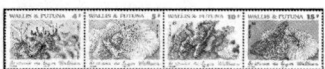

Coral — A176

Various corals: a, 4fr. b, 5fr. c, 10fr. d, 15fr.

**1998** **Litho.** ***Perf. 13x13½***
**514** A176 Strip of 4, #a.-d. 1.50 1.50

52nd Autumn Philatelic Salon — A177

**1998, Nov. 5** **Litho.** ***Perf. 13½***
**515** A177 175fr multicolored 4.00 2.50

World Fight Against AIDS A178

**1998, Dec. 1** ***Perf. 13***
**516** A178 62fr multicolored 1.50 .75

Islet of Nuku Taakimoa A179

**1999, Mar. 22** **Litho.** ***Perf. 13***
**517** A179 130fr multicolored 3.00 1.50

Souvenir Sheet

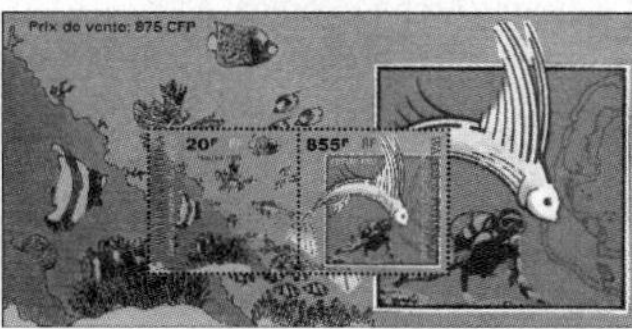
Lagoon Life — A180

a, 20fr, Various fish. b, 855fr, Fish, diver.

**1999, May 17** **Litho.** ***Perf. 13***
**518** A180 Sheet of 2, #a.-b. 17.50 17.50

PhilexFrance '99, World Philatelic Exhibition — A181

**1999, July 2** **Litho.** ***Perf. 13***
**519** A181 200fr multicolored 4.50 3.00

French Senate, Bicent. — A182

**1999, Sept. 20** **Engr.** ***Perf. 13***
**520** A182 125fr multi 2.50 1.25

Territorial Assembly Building — A183

**1999, Aug. 23** **Litho.**
**521** A183 17fr multi .40 .30

Pandanus A184

**1999, Oct. 18**
**522** A184 25fr multi .65 .40

Man Making Canoe A185

**1999, Nov. 8**
**523** A185 55fr multi 1.25 .65

French Postage Stamps, 150th Anniv. — A186

**1999, Dec. 1**
**524** A186 65fr Wallis & Futuna #86 1.50 .75

Millennium — A187

**2000, Jan. 1** **Litho.** ***Perf. 13***
**525** A187 350fr multi 7.50 4.00

Mata'utu Cathedral A188

**2000, Apr. 28 Photo.** ***Perf. 13x13¼***
**526** A188 300fr multi 6.75 3.25

Patrol Boat "La Glorieuse" — A189

**2000, June 5 Engr.** ***Perf. 13x12¾***
**527** A189 155fr multi 3.50 1.75

Sosefo Papilio Makape, First Senator — A190

**2000, June 19** ***Perf. 12¾x13***
**528** A190 115fr multi 2.50 1.25

Overseas Broadcasting Institute — A191

**2000, July 3** ***Perf. 13x12½***
**529** A191 200fr multi 4.50 2.50

Taro Cultivation A192

**2000, July 27 Litho.** ***Perf. 13***
**530** A192 275fr multi 6.00 3.00

Souvenir Sheet

2000 Summer Olympics, Sydney — A193

Traditional games, 85fr: a, Spear throwing. b, Sailing. c, Rowing. d, Volleyball.

**2000, Sept. 15 Litho.** ***Perf. 13***
**531** A193 #a-d + 2 labels 8.00 7.50

8th Pacific Arts Festival A194

**2000, Oct. 23** ***Perf. 13x13¼***
**532** A194 330fr multi 7.25 3.75

Fish — A195

No. 533: a, Coryphaena hippurus. b, Caranx melanpygyus. c, Thunnus albacares.

**2000, Nov. 9 Litho.** ***Perf. 13***
**533** Vert. strip of 3 + 2 labels 9.25 9.25
*a.-c.* A195 115fr Any single 2.50 1.75

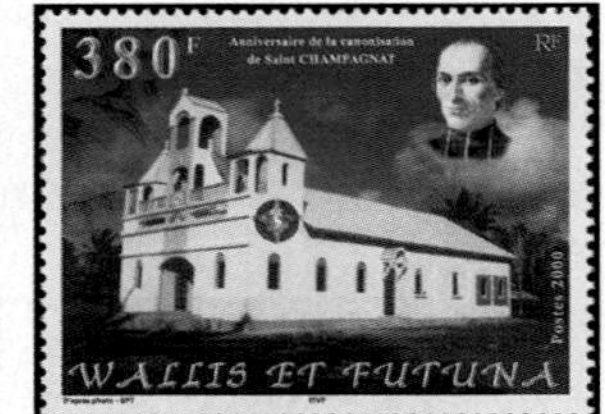

Canonization of St. Marcellin Champagnat, 1st Anniv. — A196

**2000, Nov. 13**
**534** A196 380fr multi 8.25 4.00

Talietumu Archaeological Site — A197

**2000, Dec. 1** ***Perf. 13x13½***
**535** A197 205fr multi 4.50 2.25

Christmas A198

**2000, Dec. 25** ***Perf. 13***
**536** A198 225fr multi 4.75 2.25

Ship "Jacques Cartier" — A199

**2001, Feb. 26 Engr.** ***Perf. 13***
**537** A199 225fr multi 5.00 2.50

Campaign Against Alcoholism A200

**2001, Mar. 14 Litho.** ***Perf. 13¼x13***
**538** A200 75fr multi 1.75 .75

Souvenir Sheet

Tapas — A201

Tapa with: a, Large diamond, shells, map of islands. b, Triangles and diamonds. c, Scenes of native life, fish, shells, boat. d, Overlapping ovals.

**2001, Apr. 14** ***Perf. 13***
**539** A201 90fr Sheet of 4, #a-d, + 2 labels 8.50 8.50

Children's Drawings of Flowers — A202

**2001, May 31**
**540** Horiz. strip of 4 7.00 7.00
*a.* A202 50fr multi 1.00 1.00
*b.* A202 55fr multi 1.00 1.00
*c.* A202 95fr multi 2.00 2.00
*d.* A202 100fr multi 2.00 2.00

Territorial Status, 40th Anniv. A203

**2001, July 29 Litho.** ***Perf. 13***
**541** A203 165fr multi 3.75 1.75

Installation of Mediator, 1st Anniv. A204

**2001, Sept. 26**
**542** A204 800fr multi 17.50 9.00

Year of Dialogue Among Civilizations A205

**2001, Oct. 9**
**543** A205 390fr multi 9.00 4.00

5th Autumn Salon — A206

Birds: a, Dacula pacifica. b, Vini australis. c, Tyto alba.

**2001, Nov. 8**
**544** Vert. strip of 3 + 2 labels 10.00 10.00
*a.-c.* A206 150fr Any single 3.00 2.00

Children's Drawings of Fruit A207

No. 545, 65fr: a, Custard apple (pomme canelle). b, Breadfruit (fruit de pain).

No. 546, 65fr: a, Pineapple. b, Mango.

**2001, Aug. 22 Litho.** ***Perf. 13***
**Vert. Pairs, #a-b**
**545-546** A207 Set of 2 pairs 6.00 4.75

Tomb of Futuna King Fakavelikele — A208

**2001, Dec. 28 Litho.** ***Perf. 13***
**547** A208 325fr multi 7.00 3.25

Finemui-Teesi College — A209

**2002, Jan. 29** ***Perf. 13x13½***
**548** A209 115fr multi 2.50 1.10

Intl. Women's Day — A210

**2002, Mar. 5** **Litho.** ***Perf. 13***
**549** A210 800fr Queen Aloisia 17.50 9.00

Arms of Bishop Pompallier A211

**2002, Apr. 19** **Engr.** ***Perf. 13¼***
**550** A211 500fr multi 11.50 6.00

Uvea Firefighters A212

***Serpentine Die Cut***
**2002, Apr. 28** **Photo.**
**Self-Adhesive**
**551** A212 85fr multi 2.00 1.10

2002 World Cup Soccer Championships, Japan and Korea — A213

**2002, May 31** **Litho.** ***Perf. 13***
**552** A213 65fr multi 1.50 .70

World Environment Day — A214

**2002, June 5** ***Perf. 13x13½***
**553** A214 330fr multi 7.00 4.00

Traditional Buildings A215

Designs: No. 554, 50fr, Building with overhanging roof. No. 555, 50fr, Open-air shelter, vert. No. 556, 55fr, Building with two entry ways. No. 557, 55fr, Building with ladder to roof, vert.

**2002, Aug. 9** **Engr.** ***Perf. 13¼***
**554-557** A215 Set of 4 4.75 2.50

Discovery of the Horn Islands, 1616 A216

No. 558: a, Jacob Lemaire and compass rose. b, Map of Futuna and Alofi Islands. c, William Schouten and ship.

**2002, Aug. 30** **Litho.** ***Perf. 13x13¼***
**558** Horiz. strip of 3 8.50 8.50
***a.-c.*** A216 125fr any single 2.50 2.50
***d.*** Souvenir sheet, #558 9.00 9.00

Landscapes A217

No. 559: a, Utua Bay. b, Liku Bay. c, Kingfisher at Vele. d, Aka'Aka Bay.

**2002, Sept. 20**
**559** Horiz. strip of 4 9.50 9.50
***a.*** A217 95fr multi 1.90 1.50
***b.*** A217 100fr multi 2.00 1.50
***c.*** A217 105fr multi 2.10 1.60
***d.*** A217 135fr multi 2.75 1.75

Enygrus Bibroni — A218

**2002, Oct. 28** **Litho.** ***Perf. 13¼x13***
**560** A218 75fr multi 1.75 .75

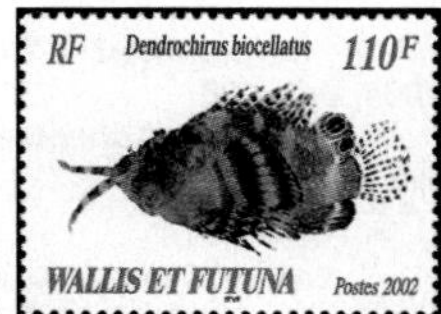


Fish A219

No. 561: a, Dendrochirus biocellatus. b, Discordipina griessingeri. c, Antennacius nummifer. d, Novaculichthys taeniourus.

**2002, Nov. 7** ***Perf. 13x13¼***
**561** Vert. strip of 4 + 3 labels 9.00 9.00
***a.-d.*** A219 110fr Any single 2.25 1.50

Best Wishes A220

**2002, Dec. 5**
**562** A220 140fr multi 2.75 1.40

Last Avro Lancaster Flight to Wallis, 40th Anniv. A221

**2003, Jan. 26** ***Perf. 13***
**563** A221 135fr multi 3.00 1.75

St. Valentine's Day — A222

**2003, Feb. 14** ***Perf. 13***
**564** A222 85fr multi 2.00 1.00

Introduction of the Euro, 1st Anniv. A223

**2003, Feb. 17** ***Perf. 12½x12¾***
**565** A223 125fr multi 2.75 1.50

Values are for examples with surrounding selvage.

Alain Gerbault (1893-1941), Circumnavigator, Aboard Boat "Firecrest" — A224

**2003, Mar. 6** **Engr.** ***Perf. 13¼***
**566** A224 600fr grn & ol grn 11.00 5.50

Postal Art — A225

Various designs.

**2003, Mar. 31** **Litho.** ***Perf. 13***
**567** Horiz. strip of 5 2.25 2.25
***a.*** A225 5fr multi .20 .20
***b.*** A225 10fr multi .20 .20
***c.*** A225 15fr multi .25 .20
***d.*** A225 20fr multi .35 .25
***e.*** A225 40fr multi .75 .40

Coral Reefs A226

Various views.

**2003, Apr. 10** ***Perf. 13x13¼***
**568** Horiz. strip of 4 10.00 10.00
***a.*** A226 95fr multi 1.75 1.75
***b.*** A226 105fr multi 1.90 1.90
***c.*** A226 110fr multi 2.00 2.00
***d.*** A226 115fr multi 2.10 2.10

St. Pierre Chanel (1803-41), Martyred Missionary A227

**2003, Apr. 28** **Engr.** ***Perf. 12¼***
**569** A227 130fr multi 3.00 1.50

2003 Census — A228

**2003, June 12** **Litho.** ***Perf. 13***
**570** A228 55fr multi 1.25 .65

Pacific Legends A229

Legend of the Coconut Palm: 30fr, Eel. 50fr, Coconut palms, split coconut. 60fr, Split and whole coconuts. 70fr, Coconut palms and clouds.

**2003, July 28** **Litho.** ***Perf. 13x13¼***
**571** Horiz. strip of 4 4.75 4.75
***a.*** A229 30fr multi .60 .40
***b.*** A229 50fr multi .95 .75
***c.*** A229 60fr multi 1.10 .85
***d.*** A229 70fr multi 1.25 .95
***e.*** Souvenir sheet, #571a-571d 5.00 5.00

Still Life with Maori Statuette, by Paul Gauguin (1848-1903) A230

No. 573a: Study of Heads of Tahitian Women, by Gauguin.

**2003** ***Perf. 13***
**572** A230 100fr multi 2.40 1.50

**Souvenir Sheet**

**573** Sheet, #572, 573a 4.50 4.50
***a.*** A230 100fr multi 2.00 2.00

Issued: No. 572, 7/31; No. 573, 8/20. See New Caledonia No. 929.

Futuna Waterfalls — A231

**2003, Aug. 6** ***Perf. 13¼x13***
**574** A231 115fr multi 2.50 1.75

Frigate Le Nivose A232

**2003, Sept. 15 Engr. *Perf. 13¼***
**575** A232 325fr multi 7.00 4.00

Bishop Alexandre Poncet (1884-1973) A233

**2003, Sept. 18 Engr. *Perf. 13¼***
**576** A233 205fr multi 4.50 3.00

Arms of Bishop Pierre Bataillon (1810-77) — A234

**2003, Oct. 1 Litho. *Perf. 13¼***
**577** A234 500fr multi 11.00 7.00

2003 Rugby World Cup, Australia A235

**2003, Oct. 10 *Perf. 13***
**578** A235 65fr multi 1.50 .85

Parinari Insularum A236

**2003, Nov. 6 Litho. *Perf. 13¼x13***
**579** A236 250fr multi 5.75 3.50

Goddess Havea Hikule'o — A237

**2004, Jan. 8**
**580** A237 85fr multi 2.00 1.40

People in Canoe A238

**2004, Jan. 13 *Perf. 13***
**581** A238 75fr multi 1.75 1.25

Miniature Sheet

Campaign Against Dengue Fever — A239

No. 582: a, 5fr, Mosquito, crying man. b, 10fr, Mosquitos, man. c, 20fr, Mosquitos, trash. d, 30fr, Mosquitos, sleeping child.

***Perf. 13¼x12¾***
**2004, Feb. 18 Litho.**
**582** A239 Sheet of 4, #a-d 2.00 2.00

Badminton A240

**2004, Mar. 12 *Perf. 13¼x13***
**583** A240 55fr multi 1.50 1.25

Kava Drinkers A241

**2004, Mar. 31 *Perf. 13x13¼***
**584** A241 205fr multi 4.75 4.25

Flora A242

**2004, Apr. 22 *Perf. 13***
**585** Horiz. strip of 4 + central label 2.75 2.75
*a.* A242 15fr Colocasia esculenta .30 .30
*b.* A242 25fr Carrica papaya .50 .50
*c.* A242 35fr Artocarpus altilus .70 .70
*d.* A242 40fr Dioscorea sp. .80 .80

Dispatch Boat Savorgnan de Brazza A243

Gourdou-Leseurre GL 832 Hy No. 5 and Wallis Island — A244

**2004, May 12 Engr. *Perf. 13¼***
**586** A243 300fr multi 6.75 6.00
**587** A244 380fr multi 8.25 7.75

**Souvenir Sheet**
**Litho.**
**588** Sheet of 2 14.00 14.00
*a.* A243 300fr multi 6.00 6.00
*b.* A244 380fr multi 7.75 7.75

First flight over Wallis Island, 68th anniv.

Seaweeds — A245

**2004, June 26 Litho. *Perf. 13***
**589** Horiz. strip of 3 + 2 alternating labels 9.50 9.50
*a.* A245 105fr Turbinaria ornata 2.25 2.25
*b.* A245 155fr Padina melemele 3.25 3.25
*c.* A245 175fr Tubinaria concoides 3.50 3.50

Miniature Sheet

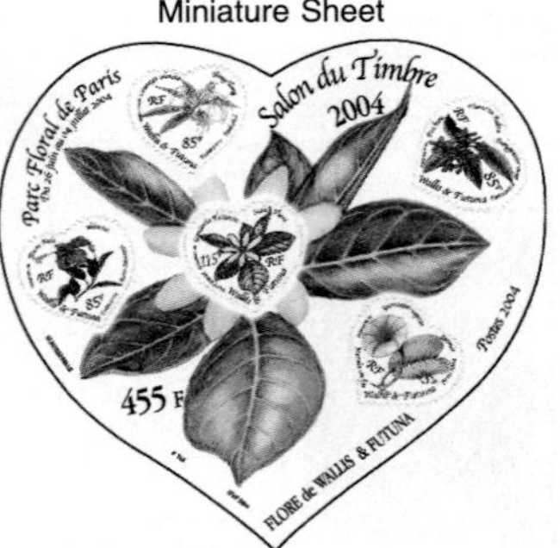
Flowers — A246

No. 590: a, Hibiscus rosa-sinensis. b, Cananga odorata. c, Plumeria rubra. d, Ipomeapes caprae. e, Gardenia taitensis.

***Serpentine Die Cut 14***
**2004, June 26 Photo.**
**Self-Adhesive**
**590** A246 Sheet of 5 9.50
*a.-d.* 85fr Any single 1.75 1.75
*e.* 115fr multi 2.40 2.40

Salon du Timbre 2004, Paris.

Ninth Pacific Arts Festival, Palau A247

**2004, July 22 Litho. *Perf. 13x13¼***
**591** A247 200fr multi 4.50 4.25

Pili'uli Lizard — A248

**2004, July 26 *Perf. 13***
**592** A248 100fr multi 2.25 2.10

Arms of Monsignor Louis Elloy (1829-78) A249

**2004, Sept. 6 Engr. *Perf. 13¼***
**593** A249 500fr multi 11.50 10.50

**No. 517 Redrawn**
**2004, Nov. 10 Litho. *Perf. 13***
**594** A179 115fr multi 2.75 2.50

No. 594 shows a 115fr denomination below an obliterated 130fr denomination, the denomination shown on No. 517. This new denomination is not overprinted. No. 594 also has a 2004 year date, rather than an obliterated 1999 year date.

A250

Traditional Houses — A251

**2004, Nov. 11 *Perf. 13¼x13***
**595** A250 95fr multi 2.25 2.10
**596** A251 130fr multi 3.25 3.00

Nos. 595-596 were printed in sheets containing four of each stamp plus a large central label.

Miniature Sheet

Cone Shells — A252

No. 597: a, Conus eburneus. b, Conus imperialis. c, Conus generalis. d, Gastridium textile.

**2005, Jan. 26 *Perf. 13x13¼***
**597** A252 55fr Sheet of 4, #a-d 4.75 4.75

Miniature Sheet

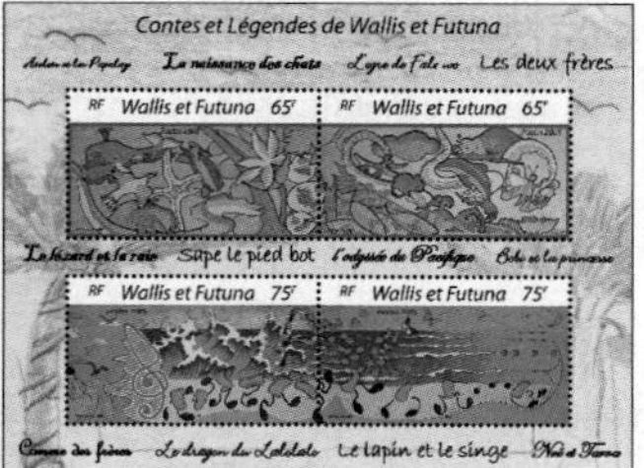


Stories and Legends — A253

No. 598: a, 65fr, Whale, bird, crab, eel, turtle. b, 65fr, Fish, octopus, dolphin, butterfly. c, 75fr, Boy, waves, G clef and musical notes. d, 75fr, Musical notes, butterflies.

**2005, Jan. 31** ***Perf. 13***
**598** A253 Sheet of 4, #a-d 6.25 6.25

Pirogue A254

**2005, Feb. 25 Litho.** ***Perf. 13x13¼***
**599** A254 330fr multi 7.50 7.50

Francophone Week — A255

**2005, Mar. 17**
**600** A255 135fr multi 3.00 3.00

Printed in sheets of 10 + 5 labels. See New Caledonia No. 959.

Family Budget Inquiry A256

**2005, Mar. 31** ***Perf. 12¾***
**601** A256 205fr multi 4.50 4.50

Values are for stamps with surrounding selvage.

Warriors — A257

**2005, Apr. 19** ***Perf. 13½x13***
**602** Horiz. strip of 5 2.50 2.50
*a.* A257 5fr blk, red & maroon .20 .20
*b.* A257 10fr blk, bl & vio blue .20 .20
*c.* A257 20fr blk, pur & indigo .40 .40
*d.* A257 30fr blk & red .65 .65
*e.* A257 50fr blk, lt grn & emerald 1.10 1.10

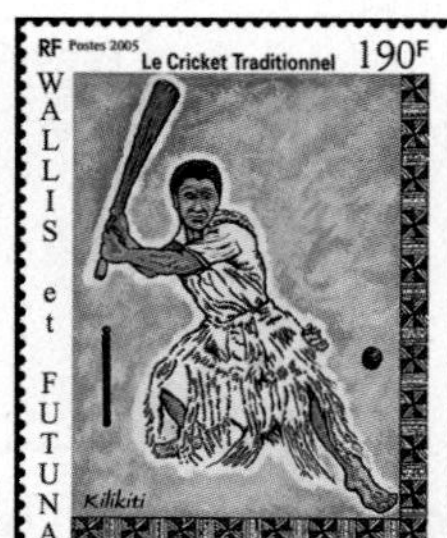


Traditional Cricket A258

**2005, May 16** ***Perf. 13***
**603** A258 190fr multi 4.25 4.00

Butterflies — A259

No. 604: a, 40fr, Papilio montrouzieri. b, 60fr, Danaus pumila.
Illustration reduced.

**2005, June 30** ***Perf. 13x13¼***
**604** A259 Horiz. pair, #a-b 2.50 2.50

Warrior With Spear — A260

***Serpentine Die Cut 11***
**2005, July 14**
**Booklet Stamp**
**Self-Adhesive**

**605** A260 115fr multi 2.50 2.40
*a.* Booklet pane of 10 26.00

Historical Images of Wallis Island — A261

**2005, July 14 Engr.** ***Perf. 13x13¼***
**606** Horiz. pair + central label 7.00 7.00
*a.* A261 155fr Village scene 3.25 3.25
*b.* A261 175fr Family, house 3.75 3.75

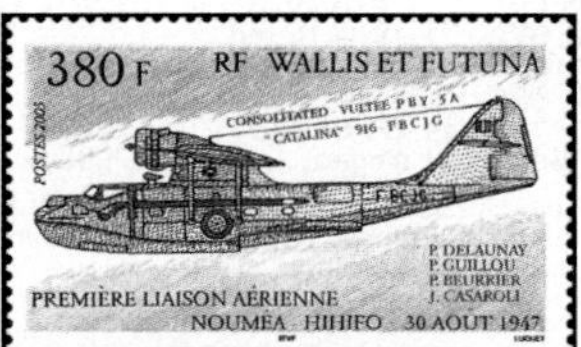


First Noumea to Hihifo Flight, 58th Anniv. — A262

**2005, Aug. 19**
**607** A262 380fr multi 8.50 8.00

Souvenir Sheet

Chelomia Mydas — A263

No. 608 — Green turtle: a, Adult entering water. b, Hatchlings entering water. c, Head. d, Swimming underwater.

**2005, Aug. 19 Litho.** ***Perf. 13x13¼***
**608** A263 85fr Sheet of 4, #a-d 7.25 7.25

Arms of Monsignor Jean Armand Lamaze (1833-1906) A264

**2005, Oct. 5 Engr.** ***Perf. 13¼***
**609** A264 500fr multi 11.00 10.00

Spattoglottis Cinguiculata — A265

**2005, Oct. 30 Litho.** ***Perf. 13***
**610** A265 100fr multi 2.25 2.00

Printed in sheets of 10 + 5 labels.

Design of Wallis and Futuna Islands No. 4 — A266

Design of Wallis and Futuna Islands No. 87 — A267

**2005, Nov. 10 Litho.** ***Perf. 13x13¼***
**611** A266 150fr multi 3.50 3.00
**612** A267 150fr multi 4.00 3.00

59th Autumn Philatelic Show.

Native Child A268

**2006, Mar. 29 Litho.** ***Perf. 13x13¼***
**613** A268 75fr multi 1.75 1.60

Monarchical Flags — A269

Designs: 55fr, Kingdom of Uvea. 65fr, Kingdom of Sigave. 85fr, Kingdom of Alo.

**2006 Litho.** ***Serpentine Die Cut 11***
**Self-Adhesive**
**Booklet Stamps**

**614** A269 55fr multi 1.25 1.25
*a.* Booklet pane of 10 12.50
**615** A269 65fr multi 1.50 1.40
*a.* Booklet pane of 10 15.00
**616** A269 85fr multi 2.00 1.75
*a.* Booklet pane of 10 20.00

Issued: 55fr, 6/17; 65fr, 4/18; 85fr, 3/29.

Haka Mai — A270

**2006** ***Perf. 13¼x13***
**617** A270 190fr multi 4.25 4.25

Removal of Christ from the Cross, by Jean Soane Michon (1926-68) A271

**2006, May 31 Litho.** ***Perf. 13¼x13***
**618** A271 400fr multi 8.50 8.50

2006 World Cup Soccer Championships, Germany A272

**2006, June 9**
**619** A272 100fr multi 2.10 2.10

Mata Vai A273

Mata Tai
A274

**2006, June 17** ***Perf. 13x13¼***
**620** A273 140fr multi 3.00 3.00
**621** A274 200fr multi 4.25 4.25

Historical Images From the 19th Century — A275

**2006, July 13** **Engr.** ***Perf. 13x13¼***
**622** Horiz. pair + central label 15.00 15.00
*a.* A275 330fr Girls dancing 7.00 7.00
*b.* A275 380fr Mua Church 8.00 8.00

Stamp Day — A276

**2006, Aug. 5** **Litho.** ***Perf. 13¼x13***
**623** A276 150fr multi 3.25 3.25

Twin Otter Airplane "Ville de Paris", 20th Anniv. — A277

**2006, Aug. 7** ***Perf. 13***
**624** A277 30fr multi .65 .65

Territorial Rugby Committee — A278

**2006, Sept. 9** ***Perf. 12¾x13½***
**625** A278 10fr multi .25 .25

Uhilamoafa Gravesite
A279

**2006, Sept. 12** ***Perf. 13x13¼***
**626** A279 290fr multi 6.25 6.25

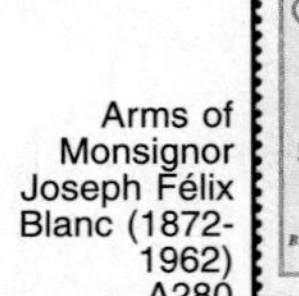
Arms of Monsignor Joseph Félix Blanc (1872-1962)
A280

**2006, Oct. 5** **Engr.** ***Perf. 13¼***
**627** A280 500fr multi 10.50 10.50

Tagaloa, Polynesian Deity — A281

**2006, Nov. 8** **Litho.** ***Perf. 13½x13***
**628** A281 150fr multi 3.50 3.50

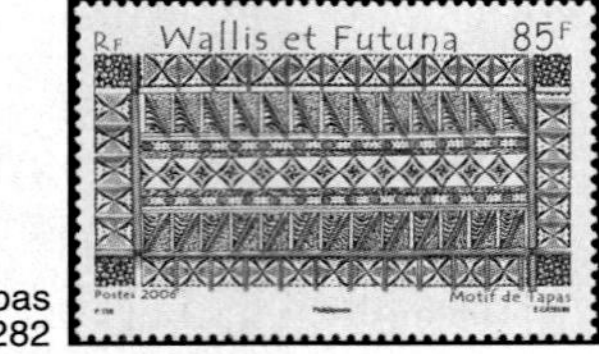
Tapas
A282

No. 629: a, Tapas design (shown). b, Mako à Ono. c, Tauasu à Leava. d, Tapas design, diff.

**Litho. & Engr.**
**2006, Nov. 8** ***Perf. 13x13¼***
**629** Vert. strip of 4 + central label 7.75 7.75
*a.-d.* A282 85fr Any single 1.90 1.90

Souvenir Sheet

Christmas — A283

**2006, Nov. 8** **Litho.** ***Perf. 13***
**630** A283 225fr multi 5.00 5.00

Pio Cardinal Taofinu'u (1923-2006)
A284

**2007, Jan. 19** **Engr.** ***Perf. 12½x13***
**631** A284 800fr multi 17.50 17.50

Telemedicine
A285

**2007, Feb. 28** **Litho.** ***Perf. 13¼x13***
**632** A285 5fr multi .20 .20

Audit Office, Bicent.
A286

**2007, Mar. 19** **Engr.** ***Perf. 13¼***
**633** A286 105fr multi 2.40 2.40

Woman
A287

**2007, Mar. 22** **Litho.** ***Perf. 13***
**634** A287 75fr multi 1.75 1.75

---

## SEMI-POSTAL STAMPS

### French Revolution Issue
Common Design Type

**Unwmk.**
**1939, July 5** **Photo.** ***Perf. 13***
**Name and Value Typo. in Black**

| | | | | |
|---|---|---|---|---|
| **B1** | CD83 | 45c + 25c green | 12.00 | *16.00* |
| **B2** | CD83 | 70c + 30c brown | 12.00 | *16.00* |
| **B3** | CD83 | 90c + 35c red org | 12.00 | *16.00* |
| **B4** | CD83 | 1.25fr + 1fr rose pink | 12.00 | *16.00* |
| **B5** | CD83 | 2.25fr + 2fr blue | 12.00 | *16.00* |
| | | *Nos. B1-B5 (5)* | 60.00 | 80.00 |
| | | Set, never hinged | 95.00 | |

New Caledonia Nos. B10 and B12 Overprinted "WALLIS ET FUTUNA" in Blue or Red, and Common Design Type

**1941** **Photo.** ***Perf. 13½***

| | | | |
|---|---|---|---|
| **B6** | SP2 | 1fr + 1fr red | 1.75 |
| **B7** | CD86 | 1.50fr + 3fr maroon | 1.75 |
| **B8** | SP3 | 2.50fr + 1fr dark blue | 1.75 |
| | | *Nos. B6-B8 (3)* | 5.25 |
| | | Set, never hinged | 5.00 |

Nos. B6-B8 were issued by the Vichy government in France, but were not placed on sale in Wallis & Futuna.

Nos. 92-93
Surcharged in Black or Red

**1944** **Engr.** ***Perf. 12x12½***
**B8A** 50c + 1.50fr on 2.50fr deep blue (R) 1.50
**B8B** + 2.50fr on 1fr green 1.50

Colonial Development Fund.

Nos. B8A-B8B were issued by the Vichy government in France, but were not placed on sale in Wallis & Futuna.

**Catalogue values for unused stamps in this section, from this point to the end of the section, are for Never Hinged items.**

### Red Cross Issue
Common Design Type

**1944** **Photo.** ***Perf. 14½x14***
**B9** CD90 5fr + 20fr red orange 2.50 2.50

The surtax was for the French Red Cross and national relief.

---

## AIR POST STAMPS

**Catalogue values for unused stamps in this section are for Never Hinged items.**

### Victory Issue
Common Design Type
***Perf. 12½***

**1946, May 8** **Unwmk.** **Engr.**
**C1** CD92 8fr dark violet 1.50 1.25

### Chad to Rhine Issue
Common Design Types

**1946**

| | | | | |
|---|---|---|---|---|
| **C2** | CD93 | 5fr dark violet | .90 | .90 |
| **C3** | CD94 | 10fr dk slate grn | 1.00 | 1.00 |
| **C4** | CD95 | 15fr violet brn | 1.25 | 1.25 |
| **C5** | CD96 | 20fr brt ultra | 1.50 | 1.50 |
| **C6** | CD97 | 25fr brown orange | 1.75 | 1.75 |
| **C7** | CD98 | 50fr carmine | 2.50 | 2.50 |
| | | *Nos. C2-C7 (6)* | 8.90 | 8.90 |

Types of New Caledonia Air Post Stamps of 1948, Overprinted in Blue:

**1949, July 4** ***Perf. 13x12½, 12½x13***
**C8** AP2 50fr yel & rose red 6.00 5.00
**C9** AP3 100fr yel & red brn 11.00 8.50

The overprint on No. C9 is in three lines.

### UPU Issue
Common Design Type

**1949, July 4** **Engr.** ***Perf. 13***
**C10** CD99 10fr multicolored 6.00 *5.50*

### Liberation Issue
Common Design Type

**1954, June 6**
**C11** CD102 3fr sepia & vio brn 7.50 6.50

Father Louis Marie Chanel — AP1

**1955, Nov. 21** **Unwmk.** ***Perf. 13***
**C12** AP1 14fr dk grn, grnsh bl & ind 2.25 1.10

Issued in honor of Father Chanel, martyred missionary to the Islands.

View of Mata-Utu, Queen Amelia and Msgr. Bataillon — AP2

33fr, Map of islands and sailing ship.

**1960, Sept. 19 Engr. *Perf. 13***

**C13** AP2 21fr blue, brn & grn 4.00 4.00
**C14** AP2 33fr ultra, choc & bl grn 6.75 4.50

Shell Diver — AP3

**1962, Sept. 20 Unwmk. *Perf. 13***

**C16** AP3 100fr bl, grn & dk red brn 15.00 11.00

**Telstar Issue**

Common Design Type

**1962, Dec. 5**

**C17** CD111 12fr dk pur, mar & bl 2.50 2.50

**Sea Shell Type of Regular Issue**

**1963, Apr. 1 Engr.**

**Size: 26x47mm**

**C18** A5 50fr Harpa ventricosa 12.50 7.00

Javelin Thrower — AP4

**1964, Oct. 10 Engr. *Perf. 13***

**C19** AP4 31fr emer, ver & vio brn 16.00 10.00

18th Olympic Games, Tokyo, Oct. 10-25.

**ITU Issue**

Common Design Type

**1965, May 17 Unwmk. *Perf. 13***

**C20** CD120 50fr multicolored 15.00 11.00

Mata-Utu Wharf — AP5

**1965, Nov. 26 Engr. *Perf. 13***

**C21** AP5 27fr brt bl, sl grn & red brn 4.50 3.00

**French Satellite A-1 Issue**

Common Design Type

Designs: 7fr, Diamant rocket and launching installations. 10fr, A-1 satellite.

**1966, Jan. 17 Engr. *Perf. 13***

**C22** CD121 7fr crim, red & car lake 2.75 2.25
**C23** CD121 10fr car lake, red & crim 2.75 2.25
***a.*** Strip of 2, #C22-C23 + label 6.50 6.50

**French Satellite D-1 Issue**

Common Design Type

**1966, June 2 Engr. *Perf. 13***

**C24** CD122 10fr lake, bl grn & red 2.50 2.50

WHO Headquarters, Geneva, and Emblem — AP6

**1966, July 5 Photo. *Perf. 12½x13***

**C25** AP6 30fr org, maroon & bl 2.75 2.50

New WHO Headquarters, Geneva.

Girl and Boy Reading; UNESCO Emblem — AP7

**1966, Nov. 4 Engr. *Perf. 13***

**C26** AP7 50fr green, org & choc 4.00 3.25

20th anniv. of UNESCO.

Athlete and Pattern AP8

Design: 38fr, Woman ballplayer and pattern.

**1966, Dec. 8 Engr. *Perf. 13x12½***

**C27** AP8 32fr bl, dp car & blk 3.50 2.25
**C28** AP8 38fr emer & brt pink 4.00 2.75

2nd South Pacific Games, Nouméa, 12/8-18.

Samuel Wallis' Ship and Coast of Wallis Island — AP9

**1967, Dec. 16 Photo. *Perf. 13***

**C29** AP9 12fr multicolored 5.50 3.75

Bicentenary of the discovery of Wallis Island.

**Concorde Issue**

Common Design Type

**1969, Apr. 17 Engr. *Perf. 13***

**C30** CD129 20fr black & plum 10.00 7.50

Man Climbing Coconut Palm — AP10

32fr, Horseback rider. 38fr, Men making wooden stools. 50fr, Spear fisherman & man holding basket with fish. 100fr, Women sorting coconuts.

**1969, Apr. 30 Photo. *Perf. 13***

**C31** AP10 20fr multi 2.00 1.00
**C32** AP10 32fr multi 3.50 2.00
**C33** AP10 38fr multi 4.25 2.00
**C34** AP10 50fr multi 6.50 3.25
**C35** AP10 100fr multi 11.50 5.25
*Nos. C31-C35 (5)* 27.75 13.50

No. C14 Surcharged with New Value and Three Bars

**1971 Engr. *Perf. 13***

**C36** AP2 21fr on 33fr multi 3.50 3.00

Pole Vault — AP11

**1971, Oct. 25 Engr. *Perf. 13***

**C37** AP11 48fr shown 4.00 2.00
**C38** AP11 54fr Archery 5.50 3.50

4th South Pacific Games, Papeete, French Polynesia, Sept. 8-19.

South Pacific Commission Headquarters, Noumea — AP12

**1972, Feb. 5 Photo. *Perf. 13***

**C39** AP12 44fr blue & multi 4.50 2.75

South Pacific Commission, 25th anniv.

Round House and Festival Emblem — AP13

**1972, May 15 Engr. *Perf. 13***

**C40** AP13 60fr dp car, grn & pur 6.00 3.50

South Pacific Festival of Arts, Fiji, May 6-20.

Canoe Type of Regular Issue

Design: 200fr, Outrigger sailing canoe race, and island woman.

**1972, Oct. 16 Photo. *Perf. 13x12½***

**Size: 47½x28mm**

**C41** A9 200fr multicolored 30.00 18.00

La Pérouse and "La Boussole" — AP14

Explorers and their Ships: 28fr, Samuel Wallis and "Dolphin." 40fr, Dumont D'Urville and "Astrolabe." 72fr, Bougainville and "La Boudeuse."

**1973, July 20 Engr. *Perf. 13***

**C42** AP14 22fr brn, slate & car 8.00 4.25
**C43** AP14 28fr sl grn, dl red & bl 9.00 4.25
**C44** AP14 40fr brn, ind & ultra 11.50 6.50
**C45** AP14 72fr brown, bl & pur 16.00 8.50
*Nos. C42-C45 (4)* 44.50 23.50

Charles de Gaulle — AP15

**1973, Nov. 9 Engr. *Perf. 13***

**C46** AP15 107fr brn org & dk brn 12.00 4.50

Pres. Charles de Gaulle (1890-1970).

Red Jasmine AP16

Designs: Flowers from Wallis.

**1973, Dec. 6 Photo. *Perf. 13***

**C47** AP16 12fr shown 1.00 .70
**C48** AP16 17fr Hibiscus tiliaceus 1.50 1.25
**C49** AP16 19fr Phaeomeria magnifica 2.00 1.25
**C50** AP16 21fr Hibiscus rosa sinensis 2.50 1.40
**C51** AP16 23fr Allamanda cathartica 3.50 1.90
**C52** AP16 27fr Barringtonia 4.00 2.00
**C53** AP16 39fr Flowers in vase 5.50 3.75
*Nos. C47-C53 (7)* 20.00 12.25

UPU Emblem and Symbolic Design — AP17

**1974, Oct. 9 Engr. *Perf. 13***

**C54** AP17 51fr multicolored 5.50 3.50

Centenary of Universal Postal Union.

Holy Family, Primitive Painting AP18

**1974, Dec. 9 Photo. *Perf. 13***

**C55** AP18 150fr multi 11.00 7.25

Christmas 1974.

Tapa Cloth — AP19

Tapa Cloth: 24fr, Village scene. 36fr, Fish & marine life. 80fr, Marine life, map of islands, village scene.

**1975, Feb. 3 Photo. *Perf. 13***

| | | | | |
|---|---|---|---|---|
| **C56** | AP19 3fr multicolored | .60 | .50 |
| **C57** | AP19 24fr multicolored | 1.50 | 1.10 |
| **C58** | AP19 36fr multicolored | 3.00 | 1.60 |
| **C59** | AP19 80fr multicolored | 6.25 | 4.00 |
| | *Nos. C56-C59 (4)* | 11.35 | 7.20 |

DC-7 in Flight — AP20

Volleyball AP21

**1975, Aug. 13 Engr. *Perf. 13***

**C60** AP20 100fr multicolored 5.00 4.00

First regular air service between Nouméa, New Caledonia, and Wallis.

**1975, Nov. 10 Photo. *Perf. 13***

| | | | | |
|---|---|---|---|---|
| **C61** | AP21 | 26fr shown | 1.50 | .80 |
| **C62** | AP21 | 44fr Soccer | 2.00 | 1.25 |
| **C63** | AP21 | 56fr Javelin | 3.50 | 2.00 |
| **C64** | AP21 | 105fr Spear fishing | 7.25 | 4.50 |
| | | *Nos. C61-C64 (4)* | 14.25 | 8.55 |

5th South Pacific Games, Guam, Aug. 1-10.

Lalolalo Lake, Wallis — AP22

Landscapes: 29fr, Vasavasa, Futuna. 41fr, Sigave Bay, Futuna. 68fr, Gahi Bay, Wallis.

**1975, Dec. 1 Litho. *Perf. 13***

| | | | | |
|---|---|---|---|---|
| **C65** | AP22 10fr grn & multi | 1.00 | .65 |
| **C66** | AP22 29fr grn & multi | 2.00 | 1.25 |
| **C67** | AP22 41fr grn & multi | 3.00 | 1.75 |
| **C68** | AP22 68fr grn & multi | 4.00 | 2.50 |
| | *Nos. C65-C68 (4)* | 10.00 | 6.15 |

Concorde, Eiffel Tower and Sugar Loaf Mountain — AP23

**1976, Jan. 21 Engr. *Perf. 13***

**C69** AP23 250fr multi 20.00 13.50

1st commercial flight of supersonic jet Concorde from Paris to Rio, Jan. 21.

For overprint see No. C73.

Hammer Throw and Stadium — AP24

39fr, Diving, Stadium and maple leaf.

**1976, Aug. 2 Engr. *Perf. 13***

| | | | |
|---|---|---|---|
| **C70** | AP24 31fr multi | 2.25 | 1.50 |
| **C71** | AP24 39fr multi | 3.25 | 2.40 |

21st Olympic Games, Montreal, Canada, July 17-Aug. 1.

De Gaulle Memorial AP25

**Photogravure and Embossed**

**1977, June 18 *Perf. 13***

**C72** AP25 100fr gold & multi 7.00 5.50

5th anniversary of dedication of De Gaulle Memorial at Colombey-les-Deux-Eglises.

No. C69 Overprinted in Dark Brown: "PARIS NEW-YORK / 22.11.77 / 1er VOL COMMERCIAL"

**1977, Nov. 22 Engr. *Perf. 13***

**C73** AP23 250fr multicolored 16.00 12.00

Concorde, 1st commercial flight, Paris-NY.

Balistes Niger — AP26

Fish: 35fr, Amphiprion akindynos. 49fr, Pomacanthus imperator. 51fr, Zanclus cornutus.

**1978, Jan. 31 Litho. *Perf. 13***

| | | | |
|---|---|---|---|
| **C74** | AP26 26fr multi | 1.00 | .65 |
| **C75** | AP26 35fr multi | 1.50 | 1.00 |
| **C76** | AP26 49fr multi | 2.50 | 1.50 |
| **C77** | AP26 51fr multi | 3.00 | 1.75 |
| | *Nos. C74-C77 (4)* | 8.00 | 4.90 |

Map of Wallis and Uvea Islands — AP27

300fr, Map of Futuna and Alofi Islands, horz.

**1978, Mar. 7 Engr.**

| | | | |
|---|---|---|---|
| **C78** | AP27 300fr vio bl & grnsh bl | 12.00 | 8.50 |
| **C79** | AP27 500fr multi | 16.00 | 12.50 |

Father Bataillon, Churches on Wallis and Futuna Islands — AP28

72fr, Monsignor Pompallier, map of Wallis, Futuna and Alofi Islands, outrigger canoe.

**1978, Apr. 28 Litho. *Perf. 13x12½***

| | | | |
|---|---|---|---|
| **C80** | AP28 60fr multi | 1.75 | 1.00 |
| **C81** | AP28 72fr multi | 2.25 | 1.40 |

First French missionaries on Wallis and Futuna Islands.

ITU Emblem — AP29

**1978, May 17 Litho. *Perf. 13***

**C82** AP29 66fr multi 2.50 1.40

10th World Telecommunications Day.

Nativity and Longhouse — AP30

**1978, Dec. 4 Photo. *Perf. 13***

**C83** AP30 160fr multi 6.50 4.00

Christmas 1978.

Popes Paul VI, John Paul I, St. Peter's, Rome — AP31

37fr, Pope Paul VI. 41fr, Pope John Paul I.

***Perf. 12½x13, 13x12½***

**1979, Jan. 31 Litho.**

| | | | | |
|---|---|---|---|---|
| **C84** | AP31 | 37fr multi, vert. | 1.40 | .65 |
| **C85** | AP31 | 41fr multi, vert. | 1.60 | .90 |
| **C86** | AP31 | 105fr multi | 3.75 | 2.00 |
| | | *Nos. C84-C86 (3)* | 6.75 | 3.55 |

In memory of Popes Paul VI and John Paul I.

Monoplane of UTA Airlines AP32

68fr, Freighter Muana. 80fr, Hihifo Airport.

**1979, Feb. 28 *Perf. 13x12½***

| | | | |
|---|---|---|---|
| **C87** | AP32 46fr multi | 1.25 | .75 |
| **C88** | AP32 68fr multi | 1.50 | 1.00 |
| **C89** | AP32 80fr multi | 2.75 | 1.40 |
| | *Nos. C87-C89 (3)* | 5.50 | 3.15 |

Inter-Island transportation.

See Nos. 251-253.

France No. 67 and Eole Weather Satellite — AP33

70fr, Hibiscus & stamp similar to #25. 90fr, Rowland Hill & Penny Black. 100fr, Birds, Kano School, Japan 17th cent. & Japan #9.

**1979, May 7 Photo. *Perf. 13***

| | | | | |
|---|---|---|---|---|
| **C90** | AP33 | 5fr multi | .50 | .30 |
| **C91** | AP33 | 70fr multi, vert. | 2.50 | 1.25 |
| **C92** | AP33 | 90fr multi | 3.00 | 1.75 |
| **C93** | AP33 | 100fr multi | 4.00 | 2.50 |
| | | *Nos. C90-C93 (4)* | 10.00 | 5.80 |

Sir Rowland Hill (1795-1879), originator of penny postage.

Cross of Lorraine and People — AP34

**1979, June 18 Engr. *Perf. 13***

**C94** AP34 33fr multi 1.75 1.25

Map of Islands, Arms of France AP35

**1979, July 19 Photo. *Perf. 13***

**C95** AP35 47fr multi 2.00 1.40

Visit of Pres. Valery Giscard d'Estaing of France.

Capt. Cook, Ships and Island — AP36

**1979, July 28**

**C96** AP36 130fr multi 5.00 3.00

Capt. James Cook (1728-1779).

Telecom Emblem, Satellite, Receiving Station — AP37

**1979, Sept. 20 Litho. *Perf. 13***

**C97** AP37 120fr multi 3.50 2.50

3rd World Telecommunications Exhibition, Geneva, Sept. 20-26.

Virgin of the Crescent Moon, by Albrecht Durer AP38

**1979, Dec. 17 Engr. *Perf. 13***
**C98** AP38 180fr red & blk 6.50 4.50

Christmas 1979. See No. C163.

Rotary International, 75th Anniversary — AP39

**1980, Feb. 29 Litho. *Perf. 13***
**C99** AP39 86fr multi 4.00 2.50

Rochambeau and Troops, US Flag, 1780 — AP40

**1980, May 27 Engr. *Perf. 13***
**C100** AP40 102fr multi 4.00 2.50

Rochambeau's landing at Newport, RI (American Revolution), bicentenary.

National Day, 10th Anniversary — AP41

**1980, July 15 Litho. *Perf. 13***
**C101** AP41 71fr multi 1.50 1.00

Transatlantic Airmail Flight, 50th Anniversary — AP42

**1980, Sept. 22 Engr. *Perf. 13***
**C102** AP42 122fr multi 3.25 2.50

Fleming, Penicillin Bacilli — AP43

**1980, Oct. 20**
**C103** AP43 101fr multi 2.75 1.75

Alexander Fleming (1881-1955), discoverer of penicillin, 25th death anniversary.

Charles De Gaulle, 10th Anniversary of Death — AP44

**1980, Nov. 9 Engr. *Perf. 13***
**C104** AP44 200fr sep & dk ol grn 6.50 5.00

Virgin and Child with St. Catherine, by Lorenzo Lotto — AP45

**1980, Dec. 20 Litho. *Perf. 13x12½***
**C105** AP45 150fr multi 3.50 2.50

Christmas 1980.

Alan B. Shepard and Spacecraft AP46

20th Anniv. of Space Flight: 44fr, Yuri Gagarin.

**1981, May 11 Litho. *Perf. 13***
**C106** AP46 37fr multi 1.00 .50
**C107** AP46 44fr multi 1.25 .60

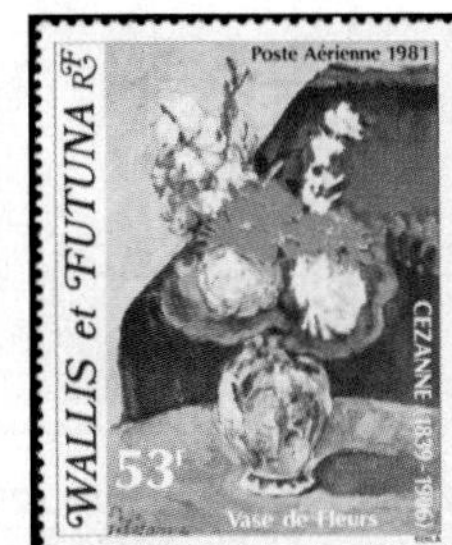

Vase of Flowers, by Paul Cezanne (1839-1906) — AP47

Design: 135fr, Harlequin, by Pablo Picasso.

**1981, Oct. 22 Litho. *Perf. 12½x13***
**C108** AP47 53fr multi 1.75 1.10
**C109** AP47 135fr multi 4.00 2.50

Espana '82 World Cup Soccer — AP48

**1981-82 Engr. *Perf. 13***
**C110** AP48 120fr blk, brn & grn 3.00 1.75
**C110A** AP48 120fr lil, brn & ol grn 3.25 2.50

Issued: #C110, 11/16/81; #C110A,5/13/82.
For overprint see No. C115.

Christmas 1981 — AP49

**1981, Dec. 21 Litho. *Perf. 12½***
**C111** AP49 180fr multi 4.50 3.00

Tapestry, by Pilioho Aloi AP50

**1982, Feb. 22 Litho. *Perf. 12½x13***
**C112** AP50 100fr multi 4.50 2.50

Boats at Collioure, by George Braque (1882-1963) — AP51

**1982, Apr. 13 Litho. *Perf. 12½x13***
**C113** AP51 300fr multi 6.50 4.00

Alberto Santos-Dumont (1873-1932), Aviation Pioneer — AP52

**1982, July 24**
**C114** AP52 95fr multi 3.00 2.00

No. C110 Overprinted with Winner's Name in Blue

**1982, Aug. 26 Engr. *Perf. 13***
**C115** AP48 120fr multi 2.75 2.00

Italy's victory in 1982 World Cup.

French Overseas Possessions Week, Sept. 18-25 — AP53

**1982, Sept. 17 Litho.**
**C116** AP53 105fr Beach 2.00 1.40

Day of the Blind — AP54

**1982, Oct. 18 Engr.**
**C117** AP54 130fr red & blue 3.00 2.00

Christmas 1982 AP55

Adoration of the Virgin, by Correggio.

**1982, Dec. 20 Litho. *Perf. 12½x13***
**C118** AP55 170fr multi 3.50 2.00

Wind Surfing (1984 Olympic Event) — AP56

**1983, Mar. 4 Litho. *Perf. 13***
**C119** AP56 270fr multi 5.50 3.00

World UPU Day — AP57

**1983, Mar. 30 Litho. *Perf. 13***
**C120** AP57 100fr multi 2.00 1.25

Manned Flight Bicentenary AP58

**1983, Apr. 25 Litho. *Perf. 13***
**C121** AP58 205fr Montgolfiere 4.25 2.50

Cat, 1926, by Foujita (d. 1968) AP59

**1983, May 20 Litho. *Perf. 12½x13***
**C122** AP59 102fr multi 3.75 2.00

Pre-Olympic Year — AP60

**1983, July 5 Engr. *Perf. 13***
**C123** AP60 250fr Javelin 4.50 3.00

Alfred Nobel (1833-1896) — AP61

**1983, Aug. 1 Engr. *Perf. 13***
**C124** AP61 150fr multi 3.25 2.00

Nicephore Niepce (1765-1833), Photography Pioneer — AP62

**1983, Sept. 20 Engr. *Perf. 13***
**C125** AP62 75fr dk grn & rose vio 1.75 1.25

Raphael (1483-1520), 500th Birth Anniv. — AP63

**1983, Nov. 10 Litho. *Perf. 12½x13***
**C126** AP63 167fr The Triumph of Galatea 3.75 2.25

Pandanus AP64

**1983, Nov. 30 Litho. *Perf. 13***
**C127** AP64 137fr multi 2.75 2.00

Christmas 1983 AP65

**1983, Dec. 22 Litho. *Perf. 12½x13***
**C128** AP65 200fr Sistine Madonna, by Raphael 3.75 2.50

Steamer Commandant Bory — AP66

**1984, Jan. 9 *Perf. 13***
**C129** AP66 67fr multi 1.50 1.00

1984 Summer Olympics — AP67

**1984, Feb. 3 Litho. *Perf. 13***
**C130** AP67 85fr Weight lifting 1.75 1.00

Frangipani Blossoms AP68

**1984, Feb. 28 *Perf. 12½***
**C131** AP68 130fr multi 2.75 1.40

Easter 1984 AP69

**1984, Apr. 17 Litho. *Perf. 12½x13***
**C132** AP69 190fr Descent from the Cross 3.75 2.25

Homage to Jean Cocteau AP70

**1984, June 30 Litho. *Perf. 13***
**C133** AP70 150fr Portrait 3.25 2.00

Soano Hoatau Tiki Sculpture AP71

Portrait of Alice, by Modigliani (1884-1920) AP72

**1984, July 26**
**C134** AP71 175fr multi 3.50 2.50

**1984, Aug. 20**
**C135** AP72 140fr multi 3.00 2.00

Ausipex '84 — AP73

**1984, Sept. 21 Litho. *Perf. 12½x13***
**C136** AP73 180fr Pilioko Tapestry 3.75 2.00

Se-tenant with label showing exhibition emblem.

Local Dances, by Jean Michon — AP74

**1984, Oct. 11 Photo. *Perf. 13***
**C137** AP74 110fr multi 3.50 2.00

Altar AP75

**1984, Nov. 5 Litho. *Perf. 13x12½***
**C138** AP75 52fr Mount Lulu Chapel 1.50 .90

Christmas 1984 — AP76

**1984, Dec. 21 Litho. *Perf. 13x12½***
**C139** AP76 260fr Tropical Nativity 5.50 3.00

Pilioko Tapestry — AP77

**1985, Apr. 3 Litho. *Perf. 13x12½***
**C140** AP77 500fr multi 9.50 6.00

The Post in 1926, by Utrillo AP78

**1985, June 17 Litho. *Perf. 12½x13***
**C141** AP78 200fr multi 4.50 3.25

Wallis Island Pirogue — AP79

**1985, Aug. 9 *Perf. 13***
**C142** AP79 350fr multi 7.00 4.00

Ship Jacques Cartier — AP80

**1985, Oct. 2 Engr. *Perf. 13x13½***
**C143** AP80 51fr Prus bl, brt bl & dk bl 1.25 .80

Portrait of a Young Woman, by Patrice Nielly AP81

**1985, Oct. 28 Litho. *Perf. 12½x13***
**C144** AP81 245fr multi 5.00 3.00

Nativity, by Jean Michon AP82

**1985, Dec. 19 Litho. *Perf. 12½x13***
**C145** AP82 330fr multi 6.50 4.00

Halley's Comet — AP83

**1986, Mar. 6 Litho. *Perf. 13***
**C146** AP83 100fr multi 2.50 1.40

Cure of Ars, Birth Bicent. — AP84

**1986, Mar. 28 Litho. *Perf. 12½x13***
**C147** AP84 200fr multi 4.00 3.00

French Overseas Territory Status, 25th Anniv. — AP85

**1986, July 29 Engr. *Perf. 13***
**C148** AP85 90fr Queen Amelia 1.75 1.00
**C149** AP85 137fr July 30 Law, Journal of the Republic 2.75 1.50
*a.* Strip of 2, #C148-C149 + label 5.00 5.00

Queen Amelia's request to France for protection, cent.

World Post Day — AP86

**1986, Oct. 9 Litho. *Perf. 13***
**C150** AP86 270fr multi 5.25 3.00

Statue of Liberty, Cent. — AP87

Poi Basilica, 1st Anniv. — AP88

**1986, Oct. 31 Engr.**
**C151** AP87 205fr multi 6.25 3.50

**1987, Apr. 30 Litho. *Perf. 13***
**C152** AP88 230fr Fr. Chanel, basilica 4.50 2.50

Telstar Transmitting to Pleumeur-Bodou, France — AP89

**1987, May 17 Engr. *Perf. 13***
**C153** AP89 200fr gray, brt bl & brn org 4.50 2.50

World Communications Day, 25th anniv. of Telstar.

Piccard, Bathyscaphe Trieste and Stratospheric Balloon — AP90

**1987, Aug. 21 Engr. *Perf. 13***
**C154** AP90 135fr brt ol grn, dk bl & brt bl 3.50 2.50

Auguste Piccard (1884-1962), physicist.

Arrival of First Missionary, 150th Anniv. — AP91

Design: 260fr, Monsignor Bataillon's arrival in 1837, ship and the islands.

**1987, Nov. 8 Engr. *Perf. 13***
**C155** AP91 260fr brt blue, blk & blue grn 5.50 3.50

Christmas 1987 — AP92

**1987, Dec. 15 Litho. *Perf. 13x12½***
**C156** AP92 300fr multi 6.50 3.50

Garros and Bleriot Aircraft — AP93

**1988, Feb. 18 Engr. *Perf. 13***
**C157** AP93 600fr multi 13.00 7.50

Roland Garros (1888-1918), aviator and tennis player.

*Self-portrait with Lace Cravat,* by Maurice Quentin de La Tour (1704-88) AP94

**1988, Apr. 8 Litho.**
**C158** AP94 500fr multi 11.00 6.50

World Telecommunications Day — AP95

**1988, May 5 Litho. *Perf. 12½x13***
**C159** AP95 100fr multi 2.50 1.25

South Pacific Episcopal Conference — AP96

**1988, June 1 Litho. *Perf. 13***
**C160** AP96 90fr Map, bishop 2.25 1.25

Christmas — AP97

**Unwmk.**
**1988, Dec. 15 Litho. *Perf. 13***
**C161** AP97 400fr multi 9.50 5.00

Royal Throne — AP98

**1989, Mar. 11**
**C162** AP98 700fr multi 16.00 7.50

The Virgin of the Crescent Moon Type of 1979

**1989, Dec. 21 Engr. *Perf. 13½x13***
**C163** AP38 800fr plum 18.00 8.50

Christmas 1989.

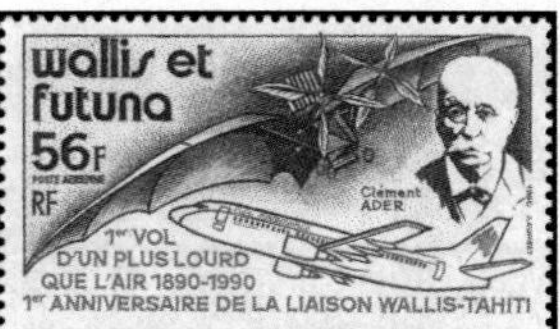


Clement Ader (1841-1926), Aviation Pioneer — AP100

**1990, June 9 Engr. *Perf. 13***
**C164** AP100 56fr multicolored 1.60 1.00

First anniversary of Wallis-Tahiti air link.

Gen. Charles de Gaulle (1890-1979) — AP101

**1990, Nov. 22** ***Perf. 12½x13***
**C165** AP101 1000fr multi 24.00 14.00

Father Louis Marie Chanel, 150th Death Anniv. — AP102

**1991, Apr. 28** **Litho.** ***Perf. 13***
**C166** AP102 235fr multicolored 6.00 3.25

French Open Tennis Championships, Cent. — AP103

Illustration reduced.

**1991, May 24** **Engr.** ***Perf. 13x12½***
**C167** AP103 250fr blk, grn & org 6.50 4.00

Wolfgang Amadeus Mozart, Death Bicent. AP104

**1991, Sept. 23** **Engr.** ***Perf. 13***
**C168** AP104 500fr multicolored 12.50 7.00

World Columbian Stamp Expo '92, Chicago — AP105

**1992, May 22** **Litho.** ***Perf. 13x12½***
**C169** AP105 100fr multicolored 3.00 1.75

**1992, July 15** ***Perf. 13***
**C170** AP105 800fr multicolored 20.00 13.00

Genoa '92.

First French Republic, Bicent. — AP106

**1992, Aug. 17** **Engr.** ***Perf. 13***
**C171** AP106 350fr blk, bl & red 9.00 6.00

Louvre Museum, Bicent. — AP107

**1993, Apr. 12** **Engr.** ***Perf. 13***
**C172** AP107 315fr blue, dk blue & red 8.00 4.00

Nicolaus Copernicus, Heliocentric Solar System — AP108

**1993, May 7** **Engr.** ***Perf. 13***
**C173** AP108 600fr multicolored 15.00 8.00

Polska '93.

Second Year of First French Republic, Bicent. — AP109

**1993, Sept. 22** **Engr.** ***Perf. 13***
**C174** AP109 400fr bl, blk & red 9.50 6.00

Wallis Island Landscape — AP110

**1994, Jan. 26** **Litho.** ***Perf. 13***
**C175** AP110 400fr multicolored 9.25 6.00

Hong Kong '94 — AP111

**1994, Feb. 18** **Litho.** ***Perf. 14x13½***
**C176** AP111 700fr multicolored 16.00 10.00

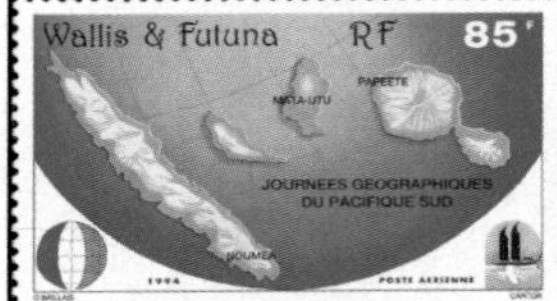

South Pacific Geography Day — AP112

**1994, May 4** **Litho.** ***Perf. 13***
**C177** AP112 85fr multicolored 2.50 1.50

See New Caledonia No. C259.

European Stamp Salon, Paris — AP113

**1994, Sept. 22** **Litho.** ***Perf. 13***
**C178** AP113 300fr multicolored 9.00 4.50

Antoine de Saint-Exupery (1900-44), Aviator, Author — AP114

**1994, Oct. 27** **Engr.** ***Perf. 13***
**C179** AP114 800fr multicolored 18.00 12.00

Christmas AP115

**1994, Dec. 15** **Litho.** ***Perf. 13***
**C180** AP115 150fr multicolored 4.00 2.50

Louis Pasteur (1822-95) — AP116

**1995, Mar. 25** **Litho.** ***Perf. 13***
**C181** AP116 350fr multicolored 9.00 3.50

AP117

AP118

**1995, Apr. 19** ***Perf. 13½x13***
**C182** AP117 115fr multicolored 3.50 1.25

University Teacher's Training Institute of the Pacific. See French Polynesia No. 656.

**1995, May 17** ***Perf. 13***
**C183** AP118 200fr Painting of Cocoa Nuts 5.25 3.00

Intl. Youth Year, 10th Anniv. — AP119

**1995, July 25** **Litho.** ***Perf. 13***
**C184** AP119 450fr multicolored 11.00 6.00

Singapore '95 — AP120

**1995, Aug. 24** **Litho.** ***Perf. 13***
**C185** AP120 500fr multicolored 12.50 5.00

Motion Pictures, Cent. — AP121

Lumiere Brothers, film strip. Illustration reduced.

**1995, Sept. 19**
**C186** AP121 600fr multicolored 15.00 6.00

Charles de Gaulle (1890-1970) — AP122

**1995, Nov. 14** **Engr.** ***Perf. 13***
**C187** AP122 315fr multicolored 8.00 4.00

7th Va'a (Outrigger Canoe) World Championship, Noumea, New Caledonia — AP123

**1996, Apr. 24** **Litho.** ***Perf. 13***
**C188** AP123 240fr multicolored 5.00 3.00

Sisia College — AP124

**1996, May 22** **Litho.** ***Perf. 13½x13***
**C189** AP124 235fr multicolored 5.25 2.75

Radio, Cent. — AP125

**1996, July 25** **Engr.** ***Perf. 13***
**C190** AP125 550fr multicolored 12.50 6.00

Modern Olympic Games, Cent. — AP126

**1996, Aug. 20** **Engr.** ***Perf. 13***
**C191** AP126 1000fr blk & dk bl 24.00 15.00

50th Autumn Stamp Salon AP127

**1996, Oct. 24** **Litho.** ***Perf. 13***
**C192** AP127 175fr multicolored 4.25 2.50

Campaign to Control Alcoholism AP128

**1996, Nov. 19** ***Perf. 13x13½***
**C193** AP128 260fr multicolored 6.25 3.00

Natl. Center for Scientific Research AP129

**1997, Mar. 14** **Litho.** ***Perf. 13***
**C194** AP129 400fr Lapita pottery 9.00 4.50

HIHIFO Air Service — AP130

**1997, July 8** **Litho.** ***Perf. 13***
**C195** AP130 130fr multicolored 3.25 1.50

Sundown Over the Lagoon — AP131

**1997, Sept. 22** **Litho.** ***Perf. 13½x13***
**C196** AP131 300fr multicolored 6.75 4.00

51st Autumn Stamp Salon — AP132

350fr, #C194, 492, 497, 486, C184, C185, 475, C192, C188, 464, 493.
1000fr, Hemispheres, #486, 475, 464, C185, C175, 493, C184, 492, C192, 497, C188, C194, Winged Victory of Samothrace.

**1997, Nov. 6** **Litho.** ***Perf. 13***
**C197** AP132 350fr multi 7.50 4.25

***Imperf***

**C198** AP132 1000fr multi 24.00 24.00

Marshal Jacques Leclerc (1902-47) — AP133

**1997, Nov. 28** **Litho.** ***Perf. 13***
**C199** AP133 800fr multicolored 18.00 10.00

Alphonse Daudet (1840-97), Writer — AP134

**1997, Dec. 16** **Litho.** ***Perf. 13***
**C200** AP134 710fr multi 16.50 10.00

Alofi Beach — AP135

**1998, Apr. 21** **Litho.** ***Perf. 13***
**C201** AP135 315fr multicolored 7.00 4.00

Cricket AP136

**1998, Sept. 22** **Litho.** ***Perf. 13x13½***
**C202** AP136 106fr multicolored 2.75 1.00

Paul Gauguin (1848-1903) — AP137

**1998, Oct. 27** **Litho.** ***Perf. 13***
**C203** AP137 700fr multicolored 16.00 9.00

Garden of Happiness — AP138

**1998, Nov. 17**
**C204** AP138 460fr multicolored 11.00 6.00

Polynesian Dancing AP139

**1998, Dec. 15** **Litho.** ***Perf. 13***
**C205** AP139 250fr multicolored 6.00 3.00

Kava Porter AP140

**1999, Jan. 18**
**C206** AP140 600fr multicolored 14.00 8.00

Shells AP141

95fr, Epitonium scalare. 100fr, Cassis cornuta. 110fr, Charonia tritonis. 115fr, Lambis lambis.

**1999, Feb. 15**
**C207** AP141 95fr multi, vert. 2.25 1.40
**C208** AP141 100fr multi, vert. 2.50 1.50
**C209** AP141 110fr multi 2.75 1.60
**C210** AP141 115fr multi 3.00 1.60
*Nos. C207-C210 (4)* 10.50 6.10

Finemui — AP142

Illustration reduced.

**1999, Apr. 19** **Engr.** ***Perf. 12¾***
**C211** AP142 900fr multicolored 20.00 11.00

Birds of Nuku Fotu AP143

a, 10fr, Airgrettes. b, 20fr, Audubon's. c, 26fr, Fregates. d, 54fr, Paille en queue.

**1999, June 14** **Litho.** ***Perf. 13x13¾***
**C212** AP143 Strip of 4, #a.-d. 2.75 2.50

Wind Song — AP144

**1999, Nov. 22** **Engr.** ***Perf. 13***
**C213** AP144 325fr multi 7.25 4.00

Sunrise Over a Lagoon
AP145

**1999, Dec. 20** **Litho.**

| | | | | |
|---|---|---|---|---|
| **C214** | AP145 | 500fr multi | 12.00 | 7.50 |

First Transport Flight to Futuna, 30th Anniv. — AP146

**2000, Aug. 24** **Litho.** ***Perf. 13***

| | | | | |
|---|---|---|---|---|
| **C215** | AP146 | 350fr multi | 8.50 | 4.00 |

## AIR POST SEMI-POSTAL STAMPS

New Caledonia Nos. CB2-CB3 overprinted "ILES WALLIS ET FUTUNA"

**1942, June 22** **Engr.** ***Perf. 13***

| | | | | |
|---|---|---|---|---|
| **CB1** | SPAP1 | 1.50fr + 3.50fr green | 1.75 | |
| **CB2** | SPAP1 | 2fr + 6fr yellow brown | 1.75 | |

Native children's welfare fund.

Nos. CB1-CB2 were issued by the Vichy government in France, but were not placed on sale in Wallis & Futuna.

### Colonial Education Fund

New Caledonia No. CB4 Common Design Type overprinted "ILES WALLIS ET FUTUNA"

**1942, June 22**

| | | | | |
|---|---|---|---|---|
| **CB3** | CD86a | 1.20fr + 1.80fr blue & red | 1.75 | |

No. CB3 was issued by the Vichy government in France, but was not placed on sale in Wallis & Futuna.

## POSTAGE DUE STAMPS

Postage Due Stamps of New Caledonia, 1906, Overprinted in Black or Red

**1920** **Unwmk.** ***Perf. 13½x14***

| | | | | |
|---|---|---|---|---|
| **J1** | D2 | 5c ultra, *azure* | .85 | .85 |
| **J2** | D2 | 10c brn, *buff* | .90 | .90 |
| **J3** | D2 | 15c grn, *grnsh* | .90 | .90 |
| **J4** | D2 | 20c blk, *yel* (R) | 1.25 | 1.25 |
| *a.* | | Double overprint | 150.00 | |
| **J5** | D2 | 30c carmine rose | 1.40 | 1.40 |
| **J6** | D2 | 50c ultra, *straw* | 2.00 | 2.00 |
| **J7** | D2 | 60c olive, *azure* | 2.50 | 2.50 |
| *a.* | | Double overprint | 110.00 | |
| **J8** | D2 | 1fr grn, *cream* | 3.50 | 3.50 |
| | | *Nos. J1-J8 (8)* | 13.30 | 13.30 |

Type of 1920 Issue Surcharged

**2f**

**1927**

| | | | | |
|---|---|---|---|---|
| **J9** | D2 | 2fr on 1fr brt vio | 15.00 | 15.00 |
| **J10** | D2 | 3fr on 1fr org brn | 15.00 | 15.00 |

Postage Due Stamps of New Caledonia, 1928, Overprinted as in 1920

**1930**

| | | | | |
|---|---|---|---|---|
| **J11** | D3 | 2c sl bl & dp brn | .20 | .20 |
| **J12** | D3 | 4c brn red & bl grn | .20 | .20 |
| **J13** | D3 | 5c red org & bl blk | .20 | .20 |
| **J14** | D3 | 10c mag & Prus bl | .20 | .20 |
| **J15** | D3 | 15c dl grn & scar | .25 | .25 |
| **J16** | D3 | 20c maroon & ol grn | .60 | .60 |
| **J17** | D3 | 25c bis brn & sl bl | .60 | .60 |
| **J18** | D3 | 30c bl grn & ol grn | 1.25 | 1.25 |
| **J19** | D3 | 50c lt brn & dk red | .70 | .70 |
| **J20** | D3 | 60c mag & brt rose | 1.25 | 1.25 |
| **J21** | D3 | 1fr dl bl & Prus grn | 1.25 | 1.25 |
| **J22** | D3 | 2fr dk red & ol grn | 1.25 | 1.25 |
| **J23** | D3 | 3fr vio & brn | 1.25 | 1.25 |
| | | *Nos. J11-J23 (13)* | 9.20 | 9.20 |

Postage Due Stamps of 1930 with Additional Overprint in Black

**1943**

| | | | | |
|---|---|---|---|---|
| **J24** | D3 | 2c sl bl & dp brn | 30.00 | 30.00 |
| **J25** | D3 | 4c brn red & bl grn | 30.00 | 30.00 |
| **J26** | D3 | 5c red org & bl blk | 30.00 | 30.00 |
| **J27** | D3 | 10c mag & Prus bl | 30.00 | 30.00 |
| **J28** | D3 | 15c dl grn & scar | 32.50 | 32.50 |
| **J29** | D3 | 20c mar & ol grn | 32.50 | 32.50 |
| **J30** | D3 | 25c bis brn & sl bl | 32.50 | 32.50 |
| **J31** | D3 | 30c bl grn & ol grn | 32.50 | 32.50 |
| **J32** | D3 | 50c lt brn & dk red | 32.50 | 32.50 |
| **J33** | D3 | 60c mag & brt rose | 32.50 | 32.50 |
| **J34** | D3 | 1fr dl bl & Prus grn | 35.00 | 35.00 |
| **J35** | D3 | 2fr dk red & ol grn | 35.00 | 35.00 |
| **J36** | D3 | 3fr violet & brn | 35.00 | 35.00 |
| | | *Nos. J24-J36 (13)* | 420.00 | 420.00 |

**Catalogue values for unused stamps in this section, from this point to the end of the section, are for Never Hinged items.**

Thalassoma Lunare — D1

Fish: 1fr, Zanclus cornutus, vert. 5fr, Amphiprion percula.

***Perf. 13x13½***

**1963, Apr. 1** **Typo.** **Unwmk.**

| | | | | |
|---|---|---|---|---|
| **J37** | D1 | 1fr yel org, bl & blk | .50 | .50 |
| **J38** | D1 | 3fr red, grnsh bl & grn | 1.25 | *1.60* |
| **J39** | D1 | 5fr org, bluish grn & blk | 2.00 | *2.25* |
| | | *Nos. J37-J39 (3)* | 3.75 | 4.35 |

# WESTERN UKRAINE

ˈwes-tərn yü-ˈkrān

LOCATION — In Eastern Central Europe

GOVT. — A former short-lived independent State

A provisional government was established in 1918 in the eastern part of Austria-Hungary but the area later came under Polish administration.

100 Shahiv (Sotykiv) = 1 Hryvnia
100 Heller = 1 Krone

**Forgeries of almost all Western Ukraine stamps are plentiful. Particularly dangerous forgeries have been noted for the Kolomyia Issue and for the First and Second Stanyslaviv Issues.**

### Lviv Issue

Austria Nos. 145-146, 148, 169 Overprinted

Nos. 1-4A are handstamped with an octagonal overprint that reads "ZAKHIDNO UKR. NARODNA REPUBLYKA" ("Western Ukr National Republic"), framing the image of a rearing crowned lion.

**1918, Nov. 20**

| | | | | |
|---|---|---|---|---|
| **1** | A37 | 3h bright violet | 50.00 | *350.00* |
| *a.* | | Inverted overprint | 125.00 | |
| **2** | A37 | 5h light green | 45.00 | *275.00* |
| *a.* | | Inverted overprint | 125.00 | |
| **3** | A37 | 10h magenta | 35.00 | *275.00* |
| *a.* | | Inverted overprint | 125.00 | |
| **4** | A42 | 20h dark green | 30.00 | *300.00* |
| *a.* | | Inverted overprint | 125.00 | |
| **4A** | A42 | 20h light green | 200.00 | *750.00* |
| | | *Nos. 1-4A (5)* | 360.00 | *1,950.* |

This issue was in circulation for only two days before Lviv was captured by the Poles on Nov. 22. No examples of Nos. 1-4A used in Lviv are known.

The Western Ukrainian National Republic (ZUNR) government evacuated to the city of Ternopil, which became the provisional capital. ZUNR postal operations were set up in other Western Ukrainian cities, and the Lviv Issue was used in Stanyslaviv (earliest known cancellation date, Dec. 8), Khodoriv and Kolomyia.

Nos. 1-4 exist in pairs with both normal and inverted overprints. Value $275.

Overprints in other colors (green, red and violet) are known, but these are probably essays. Violet-black overprints are likely transitional color impressions.

### Kolomyia Issue

Austria Nos. 168, 145, 147, 149 Surcharged

Kolomyia is the main town of the Pokutia region of southwestern Ukraine. Cut off from ZUNR postal officials by wartime conditions and in urgent need of basic value stamps, the Kolomyia postmaster obtained permission from the District Military Command to surcharge remaining Austrian postage stamps to either 5 or 10 sotyks, the equivalent of 5 or 10 heller. These stamps were produced on Dec. 10, under very strict security, by preparing two distinct plates (one for each value) that overprinted 25 stamps at a time (5x5 quarter sections of the Austrian 100-stamp panes). The stamps were placed on sale two days later.

**1918, Dec. 12** **Unwmk.** ***Perf. 12½***

| | | | | |
|---|---|---|---|---|
| **5** | A42 | 5sh on 15h dl red | 75.00 | *100.00* |
| *a.* | | Inverted overprint | 500.00 | *600.00* |
| *b.* | | Double overprint | 500.00 | *600.00* |
| **6** | A37 | 10sh on 3h vio | 80.00 | *100.00* |
| **7** | A37 | 10sh on 6h dp org | *1,200.* | *1,050.* |
| **8** | A37 | 10sh on 12h lt bl | *1,400.* | *1,250.* |
| | | *Nos. 5-8 (4)* | 2,755. | *2,500.* |

10 sotyk on 15 heller values are essays; only six were produced.

All inverted surcharges on Nos. 6-8 are forgeries. Double surcharges are forgeries.

### First Stanyslaviv Issue

Austrian Stamps of 1916-18 Surcharged in Shahiv (shown) and Hryvnia Currency

At the end of December, 1918, the national government again moved, this time to the city of Stanyslaviv (present-day Ivano-Frankivsk). A shortage of qualified postal personnel resulted in a considerable delay in the creation of new ZUNR postage stamps. In the interim, remaining unoverprinted Austrian stamps were used. Finally, on March 18, 1919, 20 different available Austrian definitive stamps were typograph surcharged at the Weidenfeld Printing Shop in Stanyslaviv.

**1919, Mar. 18**

| | | | | |
|---|---|---|---|---|
| **9** | A37 | 3sh on 3h bright violet | 15.00 | *20.00* |
| **10** | A37 | 5sh on 5h light green | 15.00 | *20.00* |
| **11** | A37 | 6sh on 6h deep orange | 30.00 | *50.00* |
| **12** | A37 | 10sh on 10h mag | 25.00 | *35.00* |
| **13** | A37 | 12sh on 12h lt blue | 25.00 | *35.00* |
| *a.* | | Double overprint | 250.00 | *350.00* |
| *b.* | | Double overprint, one on reverse | 75.00 | *175.00* |
| **14** | A42 | 15sh on 15h dull red | 25.00 | *35.00* |
| **15** | A42 | 20sh on 20h deep green | 25.00 | *35.00* |
| **16** | A42 | 30sh on 30h dull violet | 150.00 | *225.00* |
| **17** | A39 | 40sh on 40h olive green | 25.00 | *35.00* |
| **18** | A39 | 50sh on 50h dark green | 25.00 | *35.00* |
| **19** | A39 | 60sh on 60h deep blue | 25.00 | *35.00* |
| **20** | A39 | 80sh on 80h org brn | 25.00 | *35.00* |
| *a.* | | Inverted overprint | 250.00 | *350.00* |
| **21** | A39 | 1hr on 1k car, *yel* | 35.00 | *40.00* |
| **22** | A40 | 2hr on 2k lt blue | 35.00 | *45.00* |
| **23** | A40 | 3hr on 3k claret (on #161) | 2,500. | *2,700.* |
| **24** | A40 | 3hr on 3k car rose (on #165) | 75.00 | 75.00 |
| **25** | A40 | 3hr on 3k car rose (on #173) | 60.00 | 60.00 |
| **26** | A40 | 4hr on 4k dk grn (on #162) | 250.00 | *300.00* |
| **27** | A40 | 4hr on 4k yel grn (on #166) | 45.00 | *50.00* |
| **28** | A40 | 10hr on 10k deep violet | 550.00 | *750.00* |
| *a.* | | Double overprint | 2,500. | *3,000.* |
| | | *Nos. 9-28 (20)* | 3,960. | *4,615.* |

The 25sh on 25h, type A42, in both light and dull blue shades, never received this overprint. All such specimens are fantasies.

### Second Stanyslaviv Issue

The overprinting of a second issue of postage stamps in Stanyslaviv was undertaken in early May. Stamps from several different Austrian stamp series were utilized to create four distinct sets. Most of the stamps available were Austrian postage due, charity or field post stamps.

Same Surcharge on Postage Due Stamps of Bosnia, 1904, but without Asterisks

**1919, May 5**

| | | | | |
|---|---|---|---|---|
| **29** | D1 | 1sh on 1h blk, red & yel | 30.00 | 30.00 |
| *a.* | | Inverted overprint | 60.00 | 60.00 |
| *b.* | | Double overprint | 80.00 | 80.00 |
| **30** | D1 | 2sh on 2h blk, red & yel | 10.00 | *12.00* |
| *a.* | | Inverted overprint | 75.00 | *125.00* |
| **31** | D1 | 3sh on 3h blk, red & yel | 10.00 | *12.00* |
| *a.* | | Inverted overprint | 20.00 | *30.00* |
| **32** | D1 | 4sh on 4h blk, red & yel | 80.00 | 80.00 |
| *a.* | | Inverted overprint | 150.00 | 150.00 |
| *b.* | | Double overprint | 250.00 | 250.00 |
| **33** | D1 | 5sh on 5h blk, red & yel | *2,750.* | *3,000.* |
| **34** | D1 | 6sh on 6h blk, red & yel | 200.00 | *225.00* |
| *a.* | | Inverted overprint | 500.00 | 500.00 |
| *b.* | | Double overprint | 400.00 | *425.00* |
| **35** | D1 | 7sh on 7h blk, red & yel | 20.00 | *25.00* |
| *a.* | | Inverted overprint | 30.00 | *35.00* |
| **36** | D1 | 8sh on 8h blk, red & yel | 15.00 | *20.00* |
| *a.* | | Inverted overprint | 40.00 | *50.00* |
| *b.* | | Vertical overprint | 600.00 | *800.00* |
| *c.* | | As "b," double overprint | 800.00 | *900.00* |
| **37** | D1 | 10sh on 10h blk, red & yel | *900.00* | *1,150.* |
| **38** | D1 | 15sh on 15h blk, red & yel | *350.00* | *350.00* |
| *a.* | | Inverted overprint | 450.00 | *500.00* |
| **39** | D1 | 20sh on 20h blk, red & yel | *5,250.* | |
| *a.* | | Double overprint | 6,500. | *14,000.* |
| **40** | D1 | 50sh on 50h blk, red & yel | *175.00* | *175.00* |
| *a.* | | Inverted overprint | 300.00 | 250.00 |

Nos. 29-40 were created by overprinting Bosnian 1904 postage due stamps, which had been brought to Stanyslaviv by a Ukrainian military officer returning from the Serbian front. The same printing cliché was used as for the First Stanyslaviv Issue, but the asterisk obliterators were removed.

Most of the overprinting was made using 50-stamp panes (half of a sheet). After one half of the pane (25 positions) was overprinted, it would apparently be turned over and its second half overprinted with the same 25-position block, but as an inverted impression. After overprinting, the pane was torn into two equal 25-stamp halves.

Two types of surcharge on No. 61: Shahiv in singular (wara) and in plural (warib). Value the same.

Same Surcharge on Austrian Military Semipostal Stamps of 1918
*Perf. 12½x13*

**41** MSP7 10sh on 10h gray green 100.00 *110.00*
a. Inverted overprint 100.00 *120.00*
b. Double overprint 150.00 *175.00*
**42** MSP8 20sh on 20h magenta 90.00 *85.00*
a. Inverted overprint 85.00 *100.00*
b. Double overprint 120.00 *140.00*
**43** MSP7 45sh on 45h blue 75.00 *85.00*
a. Inverted overprint 65.00 *85.00*

Nos. 41-43 were printed in the same manner as Nos. 29-40.

Same Surcharge on Austrian Military Stamps of 1917
*Perf. 12½*

**44** M3 1sh on 1h grnsh blue *800.00 800.00*
**45** M3 2sh on 2h red org 90.00 90.00
a. Inverted overprint 100.00 100.00
b. Double overprint 175.00 175.00
**46** M3 3sh olive gray 150.00 *160.00*
a. Double overprint 300.00 *325.00*
**47** M3 5sh on 5h olive grn 225.00 225.00
**48** M3 6sh on 6h violet 130.00 *150.00*
**49** M3 10sh on 10h org brn *750.00 850.00*
**50** M3 12sh on 12h blue 450.00 *500.00*
a. Inverted overprint 550.00 *600.00*
**51** M3 15sh on 15h brt rose 425.00 *500.00*
a. Inverted overprint 525.00 *600.00*
**52** M3 20sh on 20h red brn 15.00 *17.00*
a. Inverted overprint 75.00 *120.00*
b. Double overprint 40.00 *45.00*
**53** M3 25sh on 25h ultra *2,750. 3,250.*
**54** M3 30sh on 30h slate *825.00 1,000.*
**55** M3 40sh on 40h olive bis *700.00 700.00*
**56** M3 50sh on 50h deep green 8.00 8.00
a. Inverted overprint 15.00 15.00
b. Double overprint 50.00 50.00
**57** M3 60sh on 60h car rose 800.00 800.00
**58** M3 80sh on 80h dull blue 40.00 40.00
a. Inverted overprint 70.00 *75.00*
**59** M3 90sh on 90h dk vio *800.00 850.00*
**60** M4 2hr on 2k rose, *straw* 12.00 *16.00*
a. Inverted overprint 25.00 *32.50*
b. Imperforate 2,500.
**61** M4 3hr on 3k blue, *grn* 20.00 *22.50*
a. Inverted overprint 24.00 *27.50*
b. Double overprint 55.00 *60.00*
**62** M4 4hr on 4k rose, *grn* 20.00 *22.50*
a. Inverted overprint 24.00 *27.50*
b. Double overprint 55.00 *60.00*
**63** M4 10hr on 10k dl violet, *gray* — —

Two copies exist of No. 63, one unused and one used.

About half of this issue, where several sheets were available for printing, was overprinted in the manner of Nos. 29-43.

Same Surcharge on Austrian Stamps of 1916-18, but with two upper bars

**64** A38 15sh on 36h vio (on #J61) 325.00 *400.00*
a. Double overprint 400.00 *450.00*
**65** A38 50sh on 42h choc (on #J63) 4,500. *5,000.*
**66** A37 3sh on 3h brt violet (on #145) 160.00 160.00
**67** A37 5sh on 5h lt green (on #146) 160.00 160.00
a. Inverted overprint 240.00 240.00
**68** A37 6sh on 6h deep org (on #147) 600.00 600.00
**69** A37 10sh on 10h magenta (on #148) 175.00 175.00
a. Inverted overprint 210.00 210.00
**70** A37 12sh on 12h lt blue (on #149) 350.00 350.00
**71** A38 15sh on 15h rose red (on #150) (on #149) 160.00 160.00
a. Inverted overprint 190.00 190.00
**72** A42 15sh on 15h dull red (on #168) 175.00 175.00
**73** A42 30sh on 30h dull violet (on #171) 160.00 160.00
a. Double overprint 300.00 300.00
**74** A39 40sh on 40h ol grn (on #154) 250.00 250.00
**75** M3 50sh on 50h dp grn (on #M61) 400.00 400.00

The two bars in the surcharge were originally created to obliterate the "PORTO" on Nos. 64 and 65 but were subsequently retained for Nos. 66-75.

**Third Stanyslaviv Issue**

Austrian Stamps of 1916-18 Overprinted

**1919, May**

**76** A37 3h brt violet .50 *1.00*
**77** A37 5h light green .50 *1.00*
**78** A37 6h deep orange .50 *1.00*
**79** A37 10h magenta .50 *1.00*
**80** A37 12h light blue .50 *1.00*
**81** A42 15h dull red .50 *1.00*
**82** A42 20h deep green .50 *1.00*
**83** A42 25h blue .50 *1.00*
**84** A42 30h dull vio .50 *1.00*
**85** A39 40h olive green .75 *1.25*
**86** A39 50h dark green .75 *1.25*
**87** A39 60h deep blue .75 *1.25*
**88** A39 80h orange brn 1.00 *1.25*
**89** A39 90h red violet 1.00 *1.60*
**90** A39 1k car, *yel* 1.25 *4.00*
**91** A40 2k light blue 2.00 *6.00*
**92** A40 3k carmine rose 2.50 *7.50*
**93** A40 4k yellow grn 10.00 *15.00*
**94** A40 10k deep violet 15.00 *40.00*
*Nos. 76-94 (19)* 39.50 *88.10*

Issued: 3h-10h, 15h, 25h-40h, 60h-1k, 5/8; balance of set, 5/13.

A definitive set for Western Ukraine was ordered from the Austrian State Printing Office in March, 1919. Because of the time involved in designing and printing these stamps, Nos. 76-94 were overprinted in Vienna as a provisional issue and were delivered in two shipments. Because travel into and out of Stanyslaviv was becoming more difficult as the month wore on, it was not known whether or not the second shipment, which included the higher values, would arrive. Because of this, the Fourth Stanyslaviv Issue, Nos. 95-103, were overprinted locally.

**Fourth Stanislaviv Issue**

Black Surcharge on Austrian Military Stamps of 1917-18.

**1919, May**

**95** A2 2hr on 2k rose, *straw* 12.00 *14.00*
**96** A2 3hr on 2k rose, *straw* 12.00 *15.00*
**97** A2 3hr on 3k grn, *blue* 80.00 *150.00*
**98** A2 4hr on 2k rose, *straw* 12.00 *15.00*
**99** A2 4hr on 4k rose, *grn* 1,100. *1,600.*
**100** A2 5hr on 2k rose, *straw* 12.00 *15.00*
a. Inverted surcharge 250.00
**101** A2 10hr on 50h dp grn (Austria type M3) 15.00 *35.00*
a. Double surcharge 150.00

Same Surcharge on Austrian Postage Due Stamps of 1916, but without Rosettes and Numerals

**102** D5 1hr ultra 120.00 *175.00*
**103** D5 5hr ultra 1,200. *1,800.*

**REGISTRATION STAMPS**

**Kolomyia Issue**

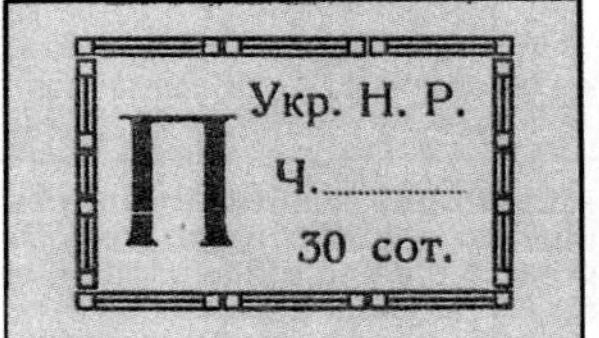


RS1

**Without Gum**

**1918-19 Unwmk. Typeset *Imperf.***

**F1** RS1 30sot black, *rose* 175.00 150.00
**F2** RS1 50sot black, *rose* ('19) 100.00 *125.00*
a. 50sot black, *deep rose* ('19) 100.00 125.00

No. F1 was printed on Dec. 10 and issued Dec. 12, 1918, along with the regular Kolomyia Issue (Nos. 5-8). On Dec. 19, the ZUNR government approved an increase in the registered letter rate to 50 sotyks, effective January 1, 1919. Because of communication disruptions, the Kolomyia post office did not learn of this decree until about January 7, when it ordered new values in the higher denomination (No. F2). F1 continued to be used, usually in combination with 20h of Austrian stamps, until supplies were exhausted, at which point No. F2 was put into use. A second printing of the 50sot value, on darker rose paper, was made in late March.

Nos. F1-F2a were typographed in vertical panes of five stamps by the Wilhelm Brauner Print Ship in Kolomyia.

Forgeries exist.

**OCCUPATION STAMPS**

**Romanian Occupation of Pokutia**

Only the stamps listed below were officially created. Soon after the Romanian occupation ended on Aug. 20, 1919, the C.M.T. handstamps fell into the hands of speculators, and some 37 other Austrian stamps were overprinted. None of these privately-created stamps are known on authentic covers.

Austrian Stamps Surcharged in Dark Violet Blue

**1919, June 14 Unwmk. *Perf. 12½***
**On Stamps of 1916-18**

**N1** A37 40h on 5h lt grn 4.00 *5.00*
**N2** A42 60h on 15h dl red 5.00 *6.00*
**N3** A42 60h on 20h dp grn 2.00 *3.00*
a. Inverted overprint 2,500.
b. Double overprint 20.00
**N4** A42 60h on 25h blue 11.00 *12.00*
a. Inverted overprint 55.00
b. Double overprint 75.00
**N5** A42 60h on 30h dl vio 13.00 14.00
**N6** A39 1k 20h on 50h dk grn 5.00 *6.00*
**N7** A39 1k 20h on 60h dp bl 9.00 *11.00*
**N8** A39 1k 20h on 1k car, *yel* 17.00 19.00

**On Austrian Postage Due Stamps of 1910-1917**

**N9** D4 40h on 5h rose red 18.00 *20.00*
**N10** D3 1k 20h on 25h carmine 150.00 *300.00*
**N11** D4 1k 20h on 25h rose red 150.00 *300.00*
**N12** D4 1k 20h on 30h rose red 1,200. 1,200.
**N13** A38 1k 20h on 50h on 42h choc 1,300. 1,300.

**First Vienna Issue, May 1919:** Lithographed at the Austrian State Printing Office on unwatermarked white paper. Inscribed "Ukrainska Narodnia Respublika Z.O." ("Ukrainian National Republic W(estern) P(rovince)"). Design incorporates the heraldic arms of Ukraine (trident), Kiev (Archangel Michael) and Lviv (lion rampant). 10, 20 and 50 sotyk values imperf; 1 and 10 krone values perf 11½. Not issued. Value, set of 5, $5. Also exists on cream-colored paper.

Arms of Kiev

Arms of Ukraine

Arms of Lviv

**Second Vienna Issue, May 1919:** Lithographed at the Austrian State Printing Office on unwatermarked white paper. Inscribed "Ukrainska Narodnia Republyka Zakhidnia Oblast" ("Ukrainian National Republic Western Province"). Set of 12 values (four of each design), perf 11½ or imperf. Not issued. Value, set of 12: perf $300; imperf $475.

# WEST IRIAN

## (Irian Barat)
## (West New Guinea)

Stamps formerly listed under West Irian now appear in Volume 1, following United Nations, and Volume 3, following Indonesia.

# YEMEN

'ye-mən

LOCATION — Arabian Peninsula, south of Saudi Arabia and bordering on the Red Sea
GOVT. — Republic
AREA — 204,000 sq. mi. (est.)
POP. — 16,942,230 (1999 est.)
CAPITAL — Sana'a (San'a)

40 Bogaches = 1 Imadi
40 Bogaches = 1 Riyal (1962)
100 Fils = 1 Riyal (1978)

The Yemen Arab Republic and the People's Republic of Yemen planned a 30-month unification process scheduled for completion by November 1992. While government ministries merged, both currencies remained valid.

**Catalogue values for unused stamps in this country are for Never Hinged items, beginning with Scott 44 in the regular postage section, Scott C1 in the airpost section.**

### Watermarks

Wmk. 127 — Quatrefoils

Wmk. 258 — Arabic Characters and Y G Multiple

Wmk. 277 — Winged Wheel



### For Domestic Postage

A1

Crossed Daggers and Arabic Inscriptions — A2

**1926 Unwmk. Typo. *Imperf.***
**Laid Paper**
**Without Gum**

| | | | | |
|---|---|---|---|---|
| **1** | A1 | 2½b black | 40.00 | 40.00 |
| **2** | A1 | 2½b black, *orange* | 40.00 | 40.00 |
| **3** | A2 | 5b black | 40.00 | 40.00 |
| | | *Nos. 1-3 (3)* | 120.00 | 120.00 |

No. 2 is known rouletted 7½ or 9.
Type A1 differs from A2 primarily in the inscription in the left dagger blade.
All come on wove paper.

### For Foreign and Domestic Postage

Arabic Inscriptions
A3 A4

**1930-31 Wmk. 127 *Perf. 14***

| | | | | |
|---|---|---|---|---|
| **7** | A3 | ½b orange ('31) | .30 | .20 |
| **8** | A3 | 1b green | .40 | .30 |
| **9** | A3 | 1b yellow grn ('31) | .35 | .25 |
| **10** | A3 | 2b olive grn | .40 | .35 |
| **11** | A3 | 2b olive brn ('31) | .35 | .25 |
| **12** | A3 | 3b dull vio ('31) | .40 | .35 |
| **13** | A3 | 4b red | .60 | .50 |
| **14** | A3 | 4b deep rose ('31) | .50 | .40 |
| **15** | A3 | 5b slate gray ('31) | .90 | .50 |
| **16** | A4 | 6b dull blue | 1.25 | 1.00 |
| **17** | A4 | 6b dp ultra ('31) | 1.00 | .75 |
| **18** | A4 | 8b lilac rose ('31) | 1.40 | 1.00 |
| **19** | A4 | 10b lt brown | 2.00 | 1.40 |
| **20** | A4 | 10b brn org ('31) | 1.75 | 1.00 |
| **21** | A4 | 20b yel grn ('31) | 4.50 | 2.50 |
| **22** | A4 | 1i red brn & lt bl | 8.00 | 6.00 |
| **23** | A4 | 1i lil rose & yel grn ('31) | 8.00 | 6.00 |
| | | *Nos. 7-23 (17)* | 32.10 | 22.75 |

Some values exist imperforate.
For surcharges and overprints see Nos. 30, 59-62, 166-167, 169-171, 174-176.

Flags of Saudi Arabia, Yemen and Iraq — A5

**1939 Litho. Wmk. 258 *Perf. 12½***

| | | | | |
|---|---|---|---|---|
| **24** | A5 | 4b dl rose & ultra | .80 | .50 |
| **25** | A5 | 6b slate bl & ultra | .80 | .50 |
| **26** | A5 | 10b fawn & ultra | 1.40 | .75 |
| **27** | A5 | 14b olive & ultra | 2.25 | 1.25 |
| **28** | A5 | 20b yel grn & ultra | 3.25 | 1.75 |
| **29** | A5 | 1i claret & ultra | 6.50 | 3.50 |
| | | *Nos. 24-29 (6)* | 15.00 | 8.25 |

2nd anniv. of the Arab Alliance. Nos. 24-29 exist imperforate. Value, set $20.
For overprints see Nos. C29-C29D.

No. 7 Handstamped in Black

Three types of surcharge:
a. 11½x16mm
b. 13-13½x15½mm
c. 12x16mm
Values of surcharged stamps are for ordinary copies. Clear, legible surcharges command a premium.

**1939 Wmk. 127 *Perf. 14***

| | | | | |
|---|---|---|---|---|
| **30** | A3 | 4b on ½b orange | *15.00* | *12.50* |

See Nos. 44-48, 59-67, 82, 86-87.

A6

A7

**1940 Wmk. 258 Litho. *Perf. 12½***

| | | | | |
|---|---|---|---|---|
| **31** | A6 | ½b ocher & ultra | .20 | .20 |
| **32** | A6 | 1b lt grn & rose red | .20 | .20 |
| **33** | A6 | 2b bis brn & vio | .20 | .20 |
| **34** | A6 | 3b dl vio & ultra | .25 | .20 |
| **35** | A6 | 4b rose & yel grn | .35 | .30 |
| **36** | A6 | 5b dk gray grn & bis brn | .40 | .35 |
| **37** | A7 | 6b ultra & yel org | .45 | .45 |
| **38** | A7 | 8b claret & dull bl | .55 | .50 |
| **39** | A7 | 10b brn org & yel grn | .75 | .75 |
| **40** | A7 | 14b gray grn & vio | .95 | .80 |
| **41** | A7 | 18b emerald & blk | 1.10 | .90 |
| **42** | A7 | 20b yel ol & cerise | 1.50 | 1.50 |
| **43** | A7 | 1i vio rose, yel grn & brn red | 2.75 | 2.50 |
| | | *Nos. 31-43 (13)* | 9.65 | 8.85 |
| | | Set, never hinged | 20.00 | |

No. 36 was used as a 4b stamp in 1957.
For surcharges see Nos. 44-47.

**Catalogue values for unused stamps in this section, from this point to the end of the section, are for Never Hinged items.**

Nos. 31-34, 36 Handstamped Type "b" in Black

**1946-51 *Perf. 12½***

| | | | | |
|---|---|---|---|---|
| **44** | A6 | 4b on ½b ('51) | *3.50* | *2.50* |
| **45** | A6 | 4b on 1b ('49) | *4.00* | *3.50* |
| **46** | A6 | 4b on 2b ('49) | *4.50* | *3.50* |
| **47** | A6 | 4b on 3b ('49) | *4.50* | *3.50* |

**1945-48 Handstamp Type "a"**

| | | | | |
|---|---|---|---|---|
| *44a* | A6 | 4b on ½b | 4.00 | 3.00 |
| *45a* | A6 | 4b on 1b ('48) | 4.00 | 3.00 |
| *46a* | A6 | 4b on 2b ('48) | 4.50 | 3.50 |
| *47a* | A6 | 4b on 3b ('48) | 5.00 | 3.50 |
| **48** | A6 | 4b on 5b ('46) | 4.00 | 3.00 |

Forged surcharges exist.

A8

**1946**
**Frames in Emerald**

| | | | | |
|---|---|---|---|---|
| **49** | A8 | 4b black | 1.50 | .85 |
| **50** | A8 | 6b lilac rose | 2.25 | 1.50 |
| **51** | A8 | 10b ultra | 3.25 | 1.90 |
| **52** | A8 | 14b olive green | 5.50 | 3.25 |
| | | *Nos. 49-52 (4)* | 12.50 | 7.50 |

Opening of Mutawakkili Hospital. Exist imperforate.
For overprints see Nos. 168, 172-173.

Mocha Coffee Tree — A9

Palace, San'a — A10

**1947-58 Unwmk. Engr. *Perf. 12½***

| | | | | |
|---|---|---|---|---|
| **53** | A9 | ½b yellow brown | .25 | .20 |
| **54** | A9 | 1b purple | .70 | .40 |
| **55** | A9 | 2b ultra | 1.40 | .90 |
| **56** | A10 | 4b red | 2.25 | 1.25 |
| **57** | A10 | 5b gray blue | 2.50 | 1.50 |
| **58** | A9 | 6b yellow green ('58) | 3.50 | 2.00 |
| | | *Nos. 53-58 (6)* | 10.60 | 6.25 |

No. 58 was printed in 1947 but not officially issued until June, 1958.
Additional values, prepared but not issued, were 10b, 20b and 1i, with views of palaces superimposed on flag, and palace square. These were looted from government storehouses during the 1948 revolution and a number of copies later reached collectors. Values, set: unused $20; used (cto) $15.
For surcharges see Nos. 63-65.

Admission of Yemen to the U.N.
10 postage, 5 airmail and 5 postage due stamps for the Admission of Yemen to the UN were not officially issued for use on domestic mail. Pictured on some of the stamps were Truman, Roosevelt, Churchill and the Statue of Liberty. Value, unused: 10v postage, $35; 5v air post, $22; 5v postage due, $14. Covers, scarce and all philatelic, exist to foreign destinations.

Nos. 9, 11, 12 and 15 Handstamped Type "a" in Black

**1949 Wmk. 127 *Perf. 14***

| | | | | |
|---|---|---|---|---|
| **59** | A3 | 4b on 1b yellow grn | 10.00 | 8.00 |
| **60** | A3 | 4b on 2b olive brn | 35.00 | 30.00 |
| **61** | A3 | 4b on 3b dull vio | 12.00 | 10.00 |
| **62** | A3 | 4b on 5b slate gray | 12.00 | 10.00 |

Handstamped type "b" are bogus.

Nos. 53-55 Handstamped Type "b" and "a"

**1949 Unwmk. *Perf. 12½***

| | | | |
|---|---|---|---|
| **63** | A9(b) 4b on ⅛b yel brn | 4.00 | 4.00 |
| **64** | A9(a) 4b on 1b purple | 5.00 | 5.00 |
| *a.* | Handstamp type "b" | 5.00 | 5.00 |
| **65** | A9(a) 4b on 2b ultra | 6.00 | 6.00 |
| *a.* | Handstamp type "b" | 6.00 | 6.00 |
| *b.* | Handstamp 13x15mm | | |

Nos. J1-J2 Handstamped Type "b" in Black

**1953 Wmk. 258**

| | | | |
|---|---|---|---|
| **66** | D1 4b on 1b org & yel grn | *20.00* | *25.00* |
| **67** | D1 4b on 2b org & yel grn | *20.00* | *25.00* |
| *a.* | Handstamp type "c" | *25.00* | *30.00* |
| | *Nos. 59-67 (9)* | 124.00 | 123.00 |

Three minor types of this handstamped 4b surcharge exist. Types "a" and "b" exist inverted, double or horizontal.
Forged surcharges exist.

Parade Ground, San'a — A13

Mosque, San'a A14

Designs: 5b, Flag of Yemen. 6b, Flag & eagle. 8b, Mocha coffee branch. 14b, Walled city of San'a. 20b, 1i, Ta'iz & its citadel.

**1951 Wmk. 277 Photo. *Perf. 14***

| | | | | |
|---|---|---|---|---|
| **68** | A13 | 1b dark brown | .30 | .20 |
| **69** | A13 | 2b red brown | .60 | .20 |
| **70** | A13 | 3b lilac rose | .75 | .35 |
| **71** | A14 | 5b blue & red | 1.25 | .60 |
| **72** | A13 | 6b dk pur & red | 1.40 | .65 |
| **73** | A13 | 8b dk bl & gray grn | 1.50 | .75 |
| **74** | A14 | 10b rose lilac | 1.25 | .85 |
| **75** | A14 | 14b blue green | 2.25 | 1.00 |
| **76** | A14 | 20b rose red | 3.25 | 1.75 |
| **77** | A14 | 1i violet | 7.50 | 3.00 |
| | | *Nos. 68-77 (10)* | 20.05 | 9.35 |
| | | *Nos. 68-77,C3-C9 (17)* | 44.70 | 17.70 |

No. 71 was used as a 4b stamp in 1956. For surcharges see Nos. 82, 86-87.

Palace of the Rock, Wadi Dhahr — A15

Design: 20b, Walls of Ibb.

**Engraved and Photogravure**

**1952 Unwmk. *Perf. 14½, Imperf.***

| | | | | |
|---|---|---|---|---|
| **78** | A15 | 12b choc, bl & dl grn | 6.00 | 6.00 |
| **79** | A15 | 20b dp car, bl & brn | 9.00 | 9.00 |
| | | *Nos. 78-79,C10-C11 (4)* | 35.00 | 35.00 |

Flag and View of San'a (Palace in Background) — A16

**1952**

| | | | | |
|---|---|---|---|---|
| **80** | A16 | 1i red brn, car & gray | 12.50 | 12.50 |

4th anniv. of the accession of King Ahmed, Feb. 18, 1948. See Nos. 81, C12-C13.

Palace in Foreground

**1952**

| | | | | |
|---|---|---|---|---|
| **81** | A16 | 30b red brn, car & dk grn | 11.00 | 11.00 |

Victory of Mar. 13, 1948. See No. C13.

No. 69 Handstamped Type "b" in Black

**1951 (?) Wmk. 277 *Perf. 14***

| | | | | |
|---|---|---|---|---|
| **82** | A13 | 4b on 2b red brown | 5.00 | 5.00 |

Forged surcharges exist. See Nos. 86-87.

Leaning Minaret, Mosque of Ta'iz — A17

Yemen Gate, San'a — A18

**1954 Photo. Unwmk.**

| | | | | |
|---|---|---|---|---|
| **83** | A17 | 4b deep orange | 1.25 | .40 |
| **84** | A17 | 6b deep blue | 2.00 | .60 |
| **85** | A17 | 8b deep blue green | 2.50 | 1.50 |
| | | *Nos. 83-85,C14-C16 (6)* | 19.50 | 6.65 |

Accession of King Ahmed I, 5th anniv.

Nos. 68 and 70 Handstamped Type "b" in Black

**1955 Wmk. 277 *Perf. 14***

| | | | | |
|---|---|---|---|---|
| **86** | A13 | 4b on 1b dk brown | 5.00 | 5.00 |
| *a.* | | Handstamp type "c" | 20.00 | 10.00 |
| **87** | A13 | 4b on 3b lilac rose | 7.50 | 6.00 |

**1956-57 Wmk. 277 *Perf. 14***

| | | | | |
|---|---|---|---|---|
| **87A** | A18 | 1b lt brown | 1.00 | .75 |
| **87B** | A18 | 5b blue green | 1.25 | .75 |
| **87C** | A18 | 10b dark blue ('57) | 1.50 | .85 |
| | | *Nos. 87A-87C (3)* | 3.75 | 2.35 |

Nos. 87A-87C were prepared for official use, but issued for regular postage. The 1b and 5b were used as 4b stamps. A 20b and 1-imadi of type A18 were not issued.

**Arab Postal Union Issue**

Globe — A19

***Perf. 13½x13***

**1957-58 Wmk. 195 Photo.**

| | | | | |
|---|---|---|---|---|
| **88** | A19 | 4b yellow brown | 1.00 | .90 |
| **89** | A19 | 6b green ('58) | 1.40 | 1.10 |
| **90** | A19 | 16b violet ('58) | 2.00 | 1.50 |
| | | *Nos. 88-90 (3)* | 4.40 | 3.50 |

Arab Postal Union founding, July 1, 1954.

**Telecommunications Issue**

Globe, Radio and Telegraph A20

**1959, Mar. Wmk. 318 *Perf. 13x13½***

| | | | | |
|---|---|---|---|---|
| **91** | A20 | 4b vermilion | 1.75 | 1.25 |

Arab Union of Telecommunications.
Exists imperf, Value $6.

**United Arab States Issue**

Flags of UAR and Yemen A21

**1959, Mar. 13**

| | | | | |
|---|---|---|---|---|
| **92** | A21 | 1b dl red brn & blk | .35 | .25 |
| **93** | A21 | 2b dk blue & blk | .45 | .35 |
| **94** | A21 | 4b sl grn, car & blk | .65 | .50 |
| | | *Nos. 92-94,C17-C19 (6)* | 6.55 | 5.05 |

First anniversary of United Arab States.
No. 94 exists imperf. Value $10.

**Arab League Center Issue**

Arab League Center, Cairo A22

***Perf. 13x13½***

**1960, Mar. 22 Wmk. 328**

| | | | | |
|---|---|---|---|---|
| **95** | A22 | 4b dull green & blk | .90 | .90 |

Opening of the Arab League Center and the Arab Postal Museum in Cairo.
Exists imperf. Value $10.

Refugees Pointing to Map of Palestine A23

**1960, Apr. 7 Photo.**

| | | | | |
|---|---|---|---|---|
| **96** | A23 | 4b brown | 1.10 | .75 |
| **97** | A23 | 6b yellow green | 1.75 | 1.25 |

World Refugee Year, 7/1/59-6/30/60.
Exist imperf. Value, set $25.
In 1961 a souvenir sheet was issued containing a 4b gray and 6b sepia in type A18, imperf. Black marginal inscription, "YEMEN 1960," repeated in Arabic. Size: 103x85mm. Value $50.

Torch and Olympic Rings A24

**1960, Dec. Unwmk. *Perf. 14x14½***

| | | | | |
|---|---|---|---|---|
| **98** | A24 | 2b black & lil rose | .55 | .35 |
| **99** | A24 | 4b black & yellow | .85 | .50 |
| **100** | A24 | 6b black & orange | 1.20 | .75 |
| **101** | A24 | 8b brn blk & bl grn | 2.10 | 1.40 |
| **102** | A24 | 20b dk bl, org & vio | 5.00 | 3.00 |
| | | *Nos. 98-102 (5)* | 9.70 | 6.00 |

17th Olympic Games, Rome, 8/25-9/11.
Exist imperf. Value, set $75.
An imperf. souvenir sheet exists, containing one copy of No. 99. Size: 100x60mm. Value $90.

UN Emblem Breaking Chains — A25

**1961 Unwmk. *Perf. 14x14½***

| | | | | |
|---|---|---|---|---|
| **103** | A25 | 1b violet | .35 | .25 |
| **104** | A25 | 2b green | .40 | .30 |
| **105** | A25 | 3b grnsh blue | .50 | .35 |
| **106** | A25 | 4b brt ultra | .55 | .40 |
| **107** | A25 | 6b brt lilac | .70 | .50 |
| **108** | A25 | 14b rose brown | 1.00 | .60 |
| **109** | A25 | 20b brown | 2.00 | 1.60 |
| | | *Nos. 103-109 (7)* | 5.50 | 4.00 |

15th anniversary (in 1960) of UN.
Exist imperf. Value, set $14.
An imperf. souvenir sheet exists, containing one copy of No. 106. Blue marginal inscription. Size: 100x60mm. Value $25.
For overprints see Nos. 137-143.

Cranes and Ship, Hodeida A26

**1961, June Litho. *Perf. 13x13½***

| | | | | |
|---|---|---|---|---|
| **110** | A26 | 4b multicolored | .85 | .40 |
| **111** | A26 | 6b multicolored | 1.40 | .75 |
| **112** | A26 | 16b multicolored | 2.75 | 1.60 |
| | | *Nos. 110-112 (3)* | 5.00 | 2.75 |

Opening of deepwater port at Hodeida.
An imperf. souvenir sheet exists, containing one each of Nos. 110-112. Size: 160x130mm. Value $5.75.
For overprints see Nos. 177, 180.

Alabaster Funerary Mask — A27

Imam's New Palace, San'a — A28

Designs (ancient sculptures from Marib, Sheba): 2b, Horned animal's head, symbolizing Moon God (limestone). 4b, Bronze head of an Emperor 1st or 2nd century. 8b, Statue of Emperor Dhamar Ali. 10b, Statue of a child, 2nd or 3rd century (alabaster). 12b, Stairs in court of Temple of the Moon God. 20b, Alabaster relief, boy riding monster. 1i, Woman with grapes, relief.

**1961, Oct. 14 Photo. *Perf. 11½***

**Granite Paper**

| | | | | |
|---|---|---|---|---|
| **113** | A27 | 1b salmon, blk & gray | .35 | .20 |
| **114** | A27 | 2b purple & gray | .60 | .20 |
| **115** | A27 | 4b pale brn, gray & blk | .80 | .20 |
| **116** | A27 | 8b brt pink & blk | 1.00 | .20 |
| **117** | A27 | 10b yellow & blk | 1.00 | .35 |
| **118** | A27 | 12b lt vio bl & blk | 2.00 | .50 |
| **119** | A27 | 20b gray & blk | 2.40 | .60 |
| **120** | A27 | 1i gray ol & blk | 5.00 | 1.25 |
| | | *Nos. 113-120,C20-C21 (10)* | 16.90 | 5.20 |

Exist imperf. Value, set (10), $25.
For overprints see Nos. 144-145, 147, 151, 153, 156-158, C24, C25.

**1961, Nov. 15 Unwmk.**

8b, Side view of Imam's palace, San'a, horiz. 10b, Palace of the Rock (Dar al-Hajar).

| | | | | |
|---|---|---|---|---|
| **121** | A28 | 4b black & lt bl grn | .35 | .20 |
| **122** | A28 | 8b blk, brt pink & grn | .75 | .45 |
| **123** | A28 | 10b black, sal & grn | .85 | .50 |
| | | *Nos. 121-123,C22-C23 (5)* | 3.90 | 1.95 |

Exist imperf. Value, set (5) $6.
For overprints see #148, 152, 154, C24A, C25A.

Hodeida-San'a Road — A29

**1961, Dec. 25 Litho. *Perf. 13½x13***

**124** A29 4b multicolored .75 .20
**125** A29 6b multicolored .90 .40
**126** A29 10b multicolored 1.50 .50
*Nos. 124-126 (3)* 3.15 1.10

Opening of the Hodeida-San'a highway. A miniature sheet exists containing one each of Nos. 124-126, imperf. Size: 159x129mm. Value $7.

For overprints see Nos. 178-179.

Trajan's Kiosk, Philae, Nubia — A30

**1962, Mar. 1 Photo. *Perf. 11x11½***

**127** A30 4b dk red brown 3.50 1.00
**128** A30 6b blue green 6.25 2.00

Issued to publicize UNESCO's help in safeguarding the monuments of Nubia.

A souvenir sheet exists, containing one each of #127-128, imperf. Size: 100x88½mm. Value $12.50.

Arab League Building, Cairo, and Emblem — A31

**1962, Mar. 22 *Perf. 13½x13***

**129** A31 4b dark green .70 .25
**130** A31 6b deep ultra .85 .40

Arab League Week, Mar. 22-28.

A souvenir sheet exists, containing one each of Nos. 129-130, imperf. Size: 94x80mm. Value $3.50.

For overprints see Nos. 164-165.

Nurses, Mother and Child — A32

Malaria Eradication Emblem — A33

Designs: 4b, Nurse weighing child. 6b, Vaccination. 10b, Weighing infant.

**1962, June 20 Unwmk. *Perf. 11½***

**131** A32 2b multicolored .60 .25
**132** A32 4b multicolored .85 .30
**133** A32 6b multicolored 1.00 .40
**134** A32 10b multicolored 1.75 .50
*Nos. 131-134 (4)* 4.20 1.45

Issued for Child Welfare.

Exist imperf. Value, set $8.

For overprints see Nos. 146, 149-150, 155.

**1962, July 20 *Perf. 13½x13***

**135** A33 4b black & dp org .70 .25
**136** A33 6b dk brown & grn 1.00 .40

WHO drive to eradicate malaria. An imperf. souvenir sheet contains one each of Nos. 135-136. Size: 95x79mm. Value $15.

No. 136 has laurel leaves added and inscription rearranged.

For overprints see Nos. 189-190.

Nos. 103-109 Overprinted

**1962 Photo. Unwmk. *Perf. 14x14½***

**137** A25 1b violet 1.50 1.50
**138** A25 2b green 1.50 1.50
**139** A25 3b greenish blue 1.50 1.50
**140** A25 4b brt ultra 1.50 1.50
**141** A25 6b brt lilac 1.50 1.50
**142** A25 14b rose brown 1.50 1.50
**143** A25 20b brown 1.50 1.50
*Nos. 137-143 (7)* 10.50 10.50

Nos. 113-123 and 131-134 Ovptd. in Dark Green or Dark Red

a

b

**1963, Jan. 1 *Perf. 11½***

**144** A27 (a) 1b No. 113 (G) .20 .20
**145** A27 (a) 2b No. 114 .20 .20
**146** A32 (b) 2b No. 131 .40 .40
**147** A27 (a) 4b No. 115 (G) .40 .40
**148** A28 (a) 4b No. 121 .55 .55
**149** A32 (b) 4b No. 132 (G) .55 .55
**150** A32 (b) 6b No. 133 .70 .70
**151** A27 (a) 8b No. 116 .70 .70
**152** A28 (b) 8b No. 122 (G) 1.00 1.00
**153** A27 (a) 10b No. 117 1.00 1.00
**154** A28 (a) 10b No. 123 1.75 1.75
**155** A32 (b) 10b No. 134 (G) 1.75 1.75
**156** A27 (a) 12b No. 118 1.40 1.40
**157** A27 (a) 20b No. 119 2.00 2.00
**158** A27 (a) 1i No. 120 5.50 5.50
*Nos. 144-158 (15)* 18.10 18.10

For overprints see Nos. C24-C25A.

Proclamation of the Republic A34

UN Freedom From Hunger Campaign A35

**1963, Mar. 15 *Perf. 11x11½***

**159** A34 4b shown .55 .55
**160** A34 6b Flag, tank .85 .85

See Nos. C26-C28.

**1963, Mar. 21 *Perf. 11½x11, 11x11½***

**162** A35 4b Milk cow, horiz. .90
**163** A35 6b shown 1.25

An imperf. souvenir sheet of 2 exists containing one each Nos. 162-163.

For overprints see Nos. 219-220.

Nos. 129-130 Ovptd. in Dark Red

**1963, Sept. 1 *Perf. 13½x13***

**164** A31 4b dark green 7.00 7.00
**165** A31 6b deep ultra 7.00 7.00

Nos. 15-16, 18-23, 50-52 Ovptd. in Black

a

b

**1963, Sept. 1**

**166** A3 (a) 5b No. 15 1.40 1.40
**167** A4 (a) 6b No. 16 1.75 1.75
**168** A8 (b) 6b No. 50 1.75 1.75
**169** A4 (a) 8b No. 18 2.00 2.00
**170** A4 (a) 10b No. 19 2.50 2.50
**171** A4 (a) 10b No. 20 2.50 2.50
**172** A8 (b) 10b No. 51 2.50 2.50
**173** A8 (b) 14b No. 52 7.00 7.00
**174** A4 (a) 20b No. 21 2.75 2.75
**175** A4 (a) 1i No. 22 7.00 7.00
**176** A4 (a) 1i No. 23 5.25 5.25
*Nos. 166-176 (11)* 36.40 36.40

Nos. 111-112 and 125-126 Ovptd. in Black

***Perf. 13x13½, 13½x13***

**1963, Sept. 1 Litho. Unwmk.**

**177** A26 6b No. 111 1.75 1.75
**178** A29 6b No. 125 1.75 1.75
**179** A29 10b No. 126 2.50 2.50
**180** A26 16b No. 112 2.50 2.50

On Nos. 178-179 the bars eliminate old inscription with text of overprint positioned below and to the right of them, on Nos. 177 and 180, the text is slightly left below the bars.

Imperf. souvenir sheets of 2 exist containing Nos. 177 and 180 or Nos. 178-179.

1st Anniv. of the Revolution — A36

***Perf. 11½x11, 11x11½***

**1963, Sept. 26 Photo.**

**186** A36 2b Flag, torch, candle, vert. .35 .30
**187** A36 4b shown .55 .45
**188** A36 6b Flag, grain, chain, vert. .90 .70

Imperf. souvenir sheets of 3 exist containing one each Nos. 186-188.

Red Cross Centenary. Set of six. ¼, ⅓, ½, 4, 8, 20b. Imperf. souv. sheet of two, 4, 8b. Oct. Nos. 6301-6307.

Nos. 135-136 Ovptd. in Black

**1963, Nov. 25 *Perf. 13½x13***

**189** A33 4b black & dp orange 3.00 3.00
**190** A33 6b dk brown & green 4.00 4.00

UN Declaration of Human Rights, 15th Anniv. — A37

**1963, Dec. 10 *Perf. 13½***

**191** A37 4b orange & dk brn vio .55 .55
**192** A37 6b blue grn & blk .75 .75

An imperf. souvenir sheet of 2 exists containing one each Nos. 191-192.

**1964**

Olympic Sports. Set of eight, ¼, ⅓, ½, 1, 1½b, airmail 4, 20b, 1r. Imperf. souv. sheet, 4b. Mar. 30. Nos. 6401-6409.

Bagel Spinning and Weaving Factory Inauguration — A38

**1964, Apr. 10 *Perf. 11x11½, 11½x11***

**193** A38 2b Factory, bobbin, spool, cloth .30 .20
**194** A38 4b Loom machine .40 .30
**195** A38 6b Factory, spool, bolt of cloth .55 .35
**196** A38 16b shown 1.50 1.40

Nos. 193-195 vert. An imperf. souvenir sheet of one exists containing No. 196.

No. 196 is air mail.

Hodeida Airport Inauguration — A39

**1964, Apr. 30 *Perf. 11½x11***

**197** A39 4b Runway .40 .35
**198** A39 6b Runway, terminal .55 .50
**199** A39 10b Aircraft, terminal, ship at sea .75 .55

An imperf. souvenir sheet of one exists containing No. 199.

New York World's Fair. Set of seven, ¼, ⅓, ½, 1, 4b, airmail 16, 20b. Imperf. souv. sheet, 20b. May 10. Nos. 6410-6417.

Summer Olympics, Tokyo. Set of nine, ¼, ⅓, ½, 1, 1½b, airmail, 4, 6, 12, 20b, Imperf. souv. sheet, 20b. June 1. Nos. 6418-6427.

Boy Scouts. Set of nine, ¼, ⅓, ½, 1, 1½b, airmail, 4, 6, 16, 20b. Two souvenir sheets, 16b, perf.; 20b, imperf. June 20. Nos. 6428-6438.

Animals. Set of eleven, ¼, ⅓, ½, 1, 1½b, airmail, 4, 12, 20b, postage due, 4, 12, 20b. Aug. 15. Nos. 6439-6449.

Flowers. Set of eight, ¼, ⅓, ½, 1, 1½b, airmail, 4, 12, 20b. Sept. 1. Nos. 6450-6457.

San'a Intl. Airport Inauguration — A40

**1964, Oct. 1**

**200** A40 1b shown .35 .35
**201** A40 2b Terminal, runway, aircraft .35 .35
**202** A40 4b like 2b .35 .35
**203** A40 8b like 1b .70 .70

An imperf. souvenir sheet of two exists containing one each Nos. 202 and C30.
See No. C30.

Arab Postal Union, 10th Anniv. A41

2nd Arab Summit Conference A42

**1964, Oct. 15** ***Perf. 13½***

**204** A41 4b multicolored .75 .65

See No. C31.

**1964, Nov. 30**

**205** A42 4b shown .75 .65
**206** A42 6b Conference emblem, map 1.00 .80

An imperf. souvenir sheet of 2 exists containing one each Nos. 205-206.
For overprints see Nos. 221-222.

2nd Anniv. of the Revolution A43

Deir Yassin Massacre A44

**1964, Dec. 30**

**207** A43 2b Torch, map .35 .30
**208** A43 4b Revolutionary .70 .50
**209** A43 6b Flag, 2 candles, map .70 .50

An imperf. souvenir sheet of one exists containing No. 209.

**1965**

Birds. Set of eleven, ¼, ½, ¾, 1, 1½, 4b, airmail, 6, 8, 12, 20b, 1r. Imperf. souv. sheet, 20b. Jan. 30. Nos. 6501-6512.

**1965, Apr. 30** ***Perf. 11x11½***

**210** A44 4b red lil & deep blue .80 .60

See No. C32.

Intl. Telecommunications Union (ITU), Cent. — A45

**1965, May 17** ***Perf. 11x11½, 11½x11***

**211** A45 4b red & pale blue, vert. .75 .40
**212** A45 6b org brn & grn 1.00 .55

A souvenir sheet of 1 exists containing #212.

Burning of Algiers Library, 3rd Anniv. A46

**1965, July 7** ***Perf. 11½x11***

**214** A46 4b sepia, red & grn .75 .50

See No. C33.

3rd Anniv. of the Revolution — A47

**1965, Sept. 26**

**215** A47 4b Tractor, corn, grain .75 .50
**216** A47 6b Tractor, tower, buildings 1.00 .55

An imperf. souvenir sheet of one exists containing No. 216.

Intl. Cooperation Year — A48

**1965, Oct. 15** ***Perf. 11x11***

**217** A48 4b shown .80 .60
**218** A48 6b UN building, New York 1.10 .65

An imperf. souvenir sheet of one exists containing No. 218.

John F. Kennedy Memorial. Set of eight, 3x¼, ⅓, ½, 4b, airmail, 8, 12b. Two imperf. souv. sheets, 4, 8b. Nov. 29. Nos. 6513-6522.

Space Exploration. Set of eight, 3x¼, ⅓, ½b, airmail, 4, 8, 16b. Imperf. souv. sheet, 16b. Dec. 29. Nos. 6523-6531.

Nos. 162-163 Overprinted in Black

a

b

**1966, Jan. 15** ***Perf. 11½x11, 11x11½***

**219** A35 4b sal rose & golden brn (a) 1.00 .75
**220** A35 6b brt pur & yel (b) 1.75 1.00

An imperf. souvenir sheet of two exists containing Nos. 219-220.

Communications. Set of eight, 3x¼, ⅓, ½b, airmail, 4, 6, 20b. Imperf. airmail souv. sheet, 20b. Jan. 29. Nos. 6601-6609.

Animals issue of 1965 overprinted in black or red "Prevention of Cruelty to Animals" in English and Arabic. Set of eleven. Souv. sheet, 20b. Mar. 5. Nos. 6610-6621.

Nos. 205-206 Ovptd. in Red or Black

**1966, Mar. 20** ***Perf. 13½***

**221** A42 4b dark green (R) .75 .50
**222** A42 6b orange brown .85 .55

An imperf. souvenir sheet of two exists containing Nos. 221-222 ovptd. in bright pink (4b) or black (6b) with additional inscription at bottom "CASABLANCA / 1965."

Builders of World Peace. Set of nine, 3x¼, ⅓, ½, 4b, airmail, 6, 10, 12b. Two imperf. souvenir sheets, 4, 8b. Mar. 25. Nos. 6622-6632.

Domestic Animals. Set of six, 3x¼, ⅓, ½, 4b. Imperf. souv. sheet, 22b. May 5. Nos. 6633-6639.

Space Exploration issue of 1965 overprinted "Luna IX / 3 February 1966" in English and Arabic. Set of eight. Imperf. souvenir sheet. Nos. 6640-6648.

World Cup Soccer Championship. Set of eight, 3x¼, ⅓, ½b, airmail, 4, 5, 20b. Imperf. souvenir sheet, 20b. May 29. Nos. 6649-6657.

Traffic Day — A49

**1966, June 30** ***Perf. 11x11½***

**223** A49 4b green & ver .75 .50
**224** A49 6b green & ver .85 .55

Space Exploration issue of 1965 overprinted "Surveyor 1 / 2 June 1966" in English and Arabic. Set of five, 3x1b on ¼b, 3b on ⅓b, 4b on ½b. Aug. 15. Nos. 6658-6662.

Revolution, 4th Anniv. Set of three, 2, 4, 6b. Imperf. souv. sheet of 2; 4, 6b. Sept. Nos. 6663-6666.

World's Fair issue of 1964 overprinted "1965 Sana'a." Set of seven. Imperf. souvenir sheet. Nos. 6667-6674.

WHO Headquarters Inauguration. Set of six, 3x¼b, airmail, 4, 8, 16b. Imperf. souvenir sheet, 16b. Nov. 1. Nos. 6675-6681.

Gemini 6-7. Set of eight, 3x¼, ⅓, ½, 2b, airmail, 8, 12b. Imperf. souvenir sheet, 12b. Dec. 1. Nos. 6682-6690.

Gemini 6-7 issue overprinted in red "Gemini IX / Cernan-Stafford / June 1966" in English and Arabic. Set of eight. Imperf. souvenir sheet. Dec. 25. Nos. 6691-6699.

**1967**

Fruit. Set of thirteen, 3x¼, ⅓, ½, 2, 4b, airmail, 6, 8, 10b, postage due, 6, 8, 10b. Feb. 10. Nos. 6701-6713.

Arab League, 25th Anniv. A56

**1970, Oct. 5** **Photo.** ***Perf. 11½x11***

**276** A56 5b org, grn & dark pur .35 —
**277** A56 7b blue, grn & brn .75 —
**278** A56 16b dark olive grn, grn & chalky blue 1.75 —

An imperf souvenir sheet of one exists containing No. 278.

UN, 25th Anniv. A60

**1971, Apr. 4** **Photo.** ***Perf. 11½x11***

**282** A60 5b dark olive grn, grn & dark vio .55 .45
**283** A60 7b blue, grn & dark blue .90 .75

**Souvenir Sheet**

***Imperf***

**284** A60 16b multicolored 2.00 1.50

10th anniv. of Revolution A80

**1972, Nov. 25** **Photo.** ***Perf. 13***

**301** A80 7b lt blue, blk & multi .65 .50
**302** A80 10b gray, blk & multi 1.00 .65
*Nos. 301-302,C40 (3)* 6.65 4.65

For surcharge see No. 318.

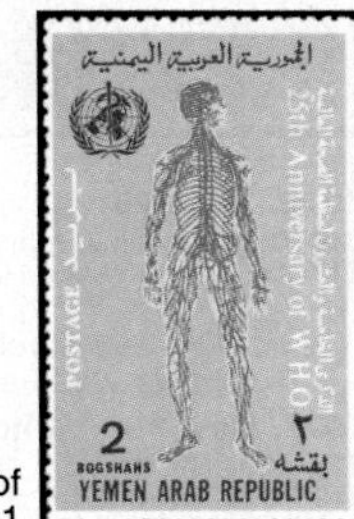


25th Anniv. of WHO — A81

**1972, Dec. 1** **Litho.**

**303** A81 2b lt yel grn & multi .50 .35
**304** A81 21b sky blue & multi 1.40 1.20
**305** A81 37b red lilac & multi 2.25 2.00
*Nos. 303-305 (3)* 4.15 3.55

For surcharge see No. 341A.

Burning of Al-Aqsa Mosque, 2nd Anniv. — A82

**1972, Jan. 1** **Photo.** ***Perf. 13½***

**306** A82 7b lt bl, blk & multi 1.50 .60
**307** A82 18b lt bl, blk & multi 2.50 1.10
*Nos. 306-307,C41 (3)* 6.00 3.10

For surcharges see Nos. 319, 341.

25th Anniv. of UNICEF — A83

**1973, Jan. 15 Photo. *Perf. 13***

**308** A83 7b lt bl, blk & multi 1.00 .65
**309** A83 10b lt bl, blk & multi 1.50 .80
*Nos. 308-309,C42 (3)* 4.25 2.95

For surcharge see No. C46.

UPU Cent. — A84

10th World Hunger Program A85

**1974, Nov. 20 Photo. *Perf. 14***

**310** A84 10b multicolored .75 .40
**311** A84 30b multicolored 2.25 1.50
**312** A84 40b multicolored 3.25 1.90
*Nos. 310-312 (3)* 6.25 3.80

For surcharge see No. 341B.

**1975, Feb. 5 Litho. *Perf. 13½***

**313** A85 10b multicolored .25 .25
**314** A85 30b multicolored .70 .70
**315** A85 63b multicolored 1.25 1.25
*Nos. 313-315 (3)* 2.20 2.20

12th Anniv. of Revolution A86

**1975, Sept. 25**

**316** A86 25f Janad Mosque .50 .35
**317** A86 75f Althawra Hospital 1.00 .65

Nos. 301, 306 surcharged in Black with New Values and Bars

**1975, Nov. 15 Photo. *Perf. 13½***

**318** A80 75f on 7b 2.00 .65
**319** A82 278f on 7b 3.50 1.25
*Nos. 318-319,C46-C48 (5)* 17.75 11.40

Telephone Cent. — A87

Coffee Bean Branch — A88

**1976, Mar. 10 Litho. *Perf. 14½***

**320** A87 25f brt pink & blk .65 .65
**321** A87 75f lt grn & blk 2.00 2.00
**322** A87 160f lt bl & blk 3.25 3.25
*a.* Souvenir sheet of 1 4.00 4.00
*Nos. 320-322 (3)* 5.90 5.90

No. 322a exists both perf. and imperf.

**1976, Apr. 25 *Perf. 14***

**323** A88 1f dull lilac .20 .20
**324** A88 3f pale gray .20 .20
**325** A88 5f lt bl grn .20 .20
**326** A88 10f bis brn .20 .20
**327** A88 25f golden brn .25 .25
**328** A88 50f brt plum .40 .40
**329** A88 75f dull pink .70 .60

**Size: 22x30mm**

***Perf. 14½***

**330** A88 1r sky blue 1.25 .70
**331** A88 1.50r red lilac 1.90 1.40
**332** A88 2r light grn 2.25 1.40
**333** A88 5r yel org 5.00 3.00
*Nos. 323-333 (11)* 12.55 8.55

For surcharges see Nos. 403-407, 592.

2nd Anniv. of Reformation Movement — A89

**1976, June 13 Photo. *Perf. 12x12½***

**334** A89 75f Industrial Park 1.50 1.50
**335** A89 135f Forestry 2.50 2.50

**Souvenir Sheet**

**336** A89 135f Forestry 5.00 5.00

No. 336 contains one stamp (32x47mm).

14th Anniv. of Revolution — A90

3rd Anniv. of Correction Movement — A91

Designs: 25f, Natl. Institute of Public Administration. 75f, Housing and population census. 160f, Sanaa University emblem.

**1976, Sept. 26 Photo. *Perf. 12x12½***

**337** A90 25f buff & multi .60 .60
**338** A90 75f yel bis & multi 1.60 1.60
**339** A90 160f pale grn & multi 3.00 3.00
*Nos. 337-339 (3)* 5.20 5.20

**Souvenir Sheet**

**340** A90 160f pale grn & multi 5.00 5.00

No. 340 contains one stamp (33x49mm).

No. 306 Surcharged in Black with New Value and Bars

**1976**

**341** A82 75f on 7b 1.00 .65

160F

Nos. 304, 312 Surcharged in Black or Red

= =

**1976 Photo. *Perf. 14***

**341A** A81 75f on 21b (R)
**341B** A84 160f on 40b

Size and location of surcharge varies.

**1977 Photo. *Perf. 14***

**342** A91 25f Dish antenna .45 .30
**343** A91 75f Computer, technician 1.25 .65
*a.* Miniature sheet of 1 4.00 4.00

15th Anniv. of September Revolution — A92

**1977 Photo. *Perf. 13½***

**344** A92 25f Sa'ada-San'a Road .45 .35
**345** A92 75f Television, Transmitting tower 1.25 .85
**346** A92 160f like 25f 2.50 2.00
*a.* Souvenir sheet of 1 5.00 5.00
*Nos. 344-346 (3)* 4.20 3.20

25th Anniv. of Arab Postal Union — A93

Pres. Hamdi — A94

**1978 *Perf. 14***

**347** A93 25f lt yel grn & multi .90 .75
**348** A93 60f bis & multi 2.25 1.60
*a.* Miniature sheet of 1 5.00 4.50

**1978 *Perf. 11½***

**349** A94 25f dk grn & blk .35 .35
**350** A94 75f ultra & blk 1.25 1.10
**351** A94 160f brn & blk 2.50 1.90
*a.* Miniature sheet of 1 *15.00* *6.50*
*Nos. 349-351 (3)* 4.10 3.35

30th Anniv. of ICAO (1977) A95

**1979, Nov. 15 Photo. *Perf. 13½***

**352** A95 75f multi 1.90 1.00
**353** A95 135f multi 3.00 1.60
*a.* Miniature sheet of 1 5.00 4.50

Book, World Map, Arab Achievements — A96

**1979, Dec. 1 *Perf. 14***

**354** A96 25f multi .60 .35
**355** A96 75f multi 1.50 1.00
*a.* Souvenir sheet of 1 3.75 3.25

A97

A98

**1980, Jan. 1**

**356** A97 75f multi 1.75 1.00
**357** A97 135f multi, horiz. 2.75 1.60
*a.* Miniature sheet of 1 5.00 4.50

12th World Telecommunications Day, May 17, 1979.

**1980 Photo. *Perf. 14***

Dome of the Rock.

**358** A98 5f brt bl & multi .50 .35
**359** A98 10f yel & multi 1.00 .65

Palestinian fighters and their families.

Argentina World Cup — A99

World Cup emblem and various players.

**1980, Mar. 30**

**360** A99 25f gold & multi .40 .40
**361** A99 30f gold & multi .40 .30
**362** A99 35f gold & multi .50 .40
**363** A99 50f gold & multi .70 .50
*Nos. 360-363,C49-C52 (8)* 6.55 4.80

Issued in sheets of 8.

International Year of the Child — A100

**1980, Apr. 1 *Perf. 13½***

**364** A100 25f Girl, bird 1.60 .50
**365** A100 50f Girl, bird, diff. 2.25 .80
**366** A100 75f Boy, butterfly, flower 2.40 1.25
*Nos. 364-366,C53-C55 (6)* 16.75 6.80

Issued in sheets of 6.

World Scouting Jamboree — A101

**1980, May 1** ***Perf. 13½x14***

**367** A101 25f Fishing .60 .30
**368** A101 35f Troup, aircraft 1.40 .50
**369** A101 40f Mounted bugler, flag 1.40 .50
**370** A101 50f Telescope, night sky 1.50 .65
*Nos. 367-370,C56-C58 (7)* 13.05 5.35

Issued in sheets of 6.

Argentina 1978 World Cup Winners — A102

World cup emblem and various soccer players.

**1980, June 1** ***Perf. 14***

**371** A102 25f gold & multi .45 .25
**372** A102 30f gold & multi .60 .30
**373** A102 35f gold & multi .60 .40
**374** A102 50f gold & multi .90 .40
*Nos. 371-374,C59-C62 (8)* 8.05 4.35

Hegira, 1500th Anniv. — A102A

Designs: 160f, Outside view.

**1980, July 1** ***Perf. 13½***

**375** A102a 25f blk & multi .30 .20
**376** A102a 75f car rose & multi .90 .60
**377** A102a 160f blk & multi 1.90 .75
*a.* Miniature sheet of 1 4.00 4.00
*Nos. 375-377 (3)* 3.10 1.55

17th Anniv. of September Revolution A103

A104

**1980, Sept. 26** ***Perf. 13½***

**378** A103 25f multi .35 .25
**379** A104 75f multi 1.10 .65

**Souvenir Sheet**

**380** 100f multi 3.75 3.75

No. 380 contains one stamp combining designs A103 and A104 (42x34mm).

Al Aqsa Mosque A105

Mosques: 25f, Al-Rawda entrance. 100f, Al-Nabwi. 160f, Al-Haram.

**1980, Nov. 6** **Photo.** ***Perf. 13½***

**381** A105 25f multi .25 .20
**382** A105 75f multi .60 .50
**383** A105 100f multi 1.50 .65
**384** A105 160f multi 2.00 1.00
*Nos. 381-384 (4)* 4.35 2.35

**Souvenir Sheet**

**385** 160f multi 6.00 3.25

Islamic Postal Systems Week and Hegira. No. 385 contains one stamp (109x47mm) combining designs of Nos. 382-384.

Intl. Palestinian Solidarity Day — A106

**1980, Nov. 29**

**386** A106 25f lt bl & multi .40 .25
**387** A106 75f ver & multi 1.10 .90

Inscribed 1979.

9th Arab Archaeological Conference — A107

**1981, Mar. 1** ***Perf. 13½***

**388** A107 75f Al Aamiriya Mosque 1.10 .60
**389** A107 125f Al Hadi Mosque 1.75 .85
*a.* Souvenir sheet of 2, #388-389 3.25 3.25



1980 World Tourism Conference, Manila A108

**1981, Apr. 1**

**390** A108 25f shown .20 .20
**391** A108 75f Mosque, houses .60 .30
**392** A108 100f Columns, horiz. .80 .45
**393** A108 135f Bridge 1.10 .60
**394** A108 160f Vuiew of San'a, horiz. 1.40 .60
*a.* Miniature sheet of 1 4.50 4.50
*Nos. 390-394 (5)* 4.10 2.15

Sir Rowland Hill (1795-1879), Postage Stamp Inventor — A109

**1981, Sept. 15** **Litho.** ***Perf. 14***

**395** A109 25f Portrait, UPU emblem .60
**396** A109 30f Emblem, stamp of 1963 .70
**397** A109 50f Portrait, stamps 1.00
**398** A109 75f Portrait, globe, jet 1.60
**399** A109 100f Portrait, stamp collection 2.25
**400** A109 150f Jets, No. 322 4.00
*Nos. 395-400 (6)* 10.15

**Souvenir Sheets**

**401** A109 200f Portrait, vert. 7.50

***Imperf***

**402** A109 200f Portrait, diff. 7.50

Nos. 398-402 are airmail.

Nos. 323-327 Surcharged

**1981**

**403** A88 125f on 1f 1.00
**404** A88 150f on 3f 1.25
**405** A88 325f on 5f 2.75
**406** A88 350f on 10f 3.25
**407** A88 375f on 25f 3.50
*Nos. 403-407 (5)* 11.75

20th Anniv. of Yemen Airways — A110

**1983, Apr. 1** **Litho.** ***Perf. 14***

**408** A110 75f yel & multi .50 .50
**409** A110 125f red & multi .80 .80
**410** A110 325f bl & multi 2.00 2.00
*Nos. 408-410 (3)* 3.30 3.30

Folk Costumes — A111

**1983, May 1**

**411** A111 50f Woman carrying waterjar 2.00
**412** A111 50f Women, sheep 2.00
**413** A111 50f Man, donkeys 2.00
**414** A111 50f Man in town square 2.00
**415** A111 75f Women, child, well 3.00
**416** A111 75f Scholar 3.00
**417** A111 75f Woman on beach 3.00
**418** A111 75f Camel-drawn plow 3.00
*Nos. 411-418 (8)* 20.00

**Souvenir Sheets**

**419** A111 200f Woman 8.00

***Imperf***

**420** A111 200f Man 8.00

#411-414 vert. #415-420 are airmail.

Sept. 26th Revolution, 20th Anniv. (1982) — A112

**1983, Sept. 26** **Litho.** ***Perf. 14***

**421** A112 100f Communications
**422** A112 150f Literacy
**423** A112 325f Educational development
*a.* Souvenir sheet of 2, #422, 423
**424** A112 400f Independence

World Communications Year — A113

**1983, Dec. 15**

**425** A113 150f lt bl & multi
**426** A113 325f lt grn & multi
*a.* Souvenir sheet of 1

Sept. 26 Revolution, 21st Anniv. — A114

**1984, Apr. 1** **Litho.** ***Perf. 14***

**427** A114 100f shown
**428** A114 150f Fist, statue
**429** A114 325f Gate, tank
*a.* Souvenir sheet of 1

Israel Aggression Day — A115

**1984, Sept. 7**

**430** A115 150f multi 1.50
**431** A115 325f multi 4.00

**Size: 91x120mm**

***Imperf***

**432** A115 325f multi 25.00
*Nos. 430-432 (3)* 30.50

Sept. 26 Revolution, 22nd Anniv. — A116

**1985, Oct. 1**

**433** A116 50f Triumphal Arch
**434** A116 150f San'a Castle walls
**435** A116 325f Stadium, Govt. Palace, San'a
*a.* Souvenir sheet of 1

Intl. Anti-Apartheid Year (1978) — A117

**1985, Jan. 1**

**436** A117 150f dp ver & multi
**437** A117 325f grn & multi
*a.* Souvenir sheet of 1

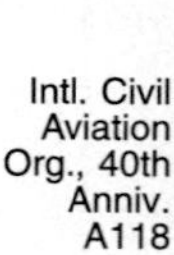

Intl. Civil Aviation Org., 40th Anniv. A118

**1985, Sept. 20**

**438** A118 25f multi
**439** A118 50f multi
**440** A118 150f multi
**441** A118 325f multi
*a.* Souvenir sheet of 1

Arabsat Satellite, 1st Anniv. A119

**1986, Apr. 15 Litho. *Perf. 14***

**442** A119 150f multi 2.50
**443** A119 325f multi 5.50
*a.* Souvenir sheet of 1 8.50

World Telecommunications, 120th Anniv. — A120

**1986, May 1**

**444** A120 150f multi 2.50
**445** A120 325f multi 5.25
*a.* Souvenir sheet of 1 9.00

General People's Conference, 2nd Anniv. — A121

**1986, May 1**

**446** A121 150f multi 2.50
**447** A121 325f multi 4.50
*a.* Souvenir sheet of 1 6.00

A122

A123

**1986, July 1**

**448** A122 150f multi 2.50
**449** A122 325f multi 4.50
*a.* Souvenir sheet of 1 6.00

15th Islamic Foreign Ministers' Conference, San'a, Dec. 18-22, 1984.

**1986, Oct. 1**

**450** A123 150f multi 2.50
**451** A123 325f multi 4.50
*a.* Souvenir sheet of 1 6.00

UN 40th anniv.

Arab League, 39th Anniv. A124

**1986, Nov. 15**

**452** A124 150f multi 2.50
**453** A124 325f multi 4.50

Natl. Arms A125

**1987, Sept. 26 Litho. *Perf. 14***

**454** A125 100f multi .90
**455** A125 150f multi 1.25
**456** A125 425f multi 3.75
*a.* Souvenir sheet of 1 4.00
**457** A125 450f multi 4.00

Sept. 26th Revolution, 25th anniv.
For surcharge see No. 593.

Intl. Youth Year (1985) A126

**1987, Oct. 15 *Perf. 13x13½***

**458** A126 150f multi
**459** A126 425f multi
*a.* Souvenir sheet of 1

For surcharge see No. C150.

Drilling of the Republic's First Oil Well, 1984 A127

**1987, Nov. 1 *Perf. 14***

**460** A127 150f Oil derrick
**461** A127 425f Derrick, refinery
*a.* Souvenir sheet of 1

For surcharge see No. C151.

General Population and Housing Census, 1986 A128

**1987, Dec. 1**

**462** A128 150f multi 2.50
**463** A128 425f multi 4.50
*a.* Souvenir sheet of 1 5.50

For surcharge see No. C152.

1986 World Cup Soccer Championships, Mexico — A129

Designs: 100f, 150f, Match scenes, vert. 425f, Match scene and Pique, character trademark.

**1988, Jan. 1 Litho. *Perf. 14***

**464** A129 100f multi
**465** A129 150f multi, diff.
**466** A129 425f multi
*a.* Souvenir sheet of 1

For surcharge see No. C153.

17th Scouting Conference, San'a — A130

**1988, Mar. 1 Litho. *Perf. 14***

**467** A130 25f Skin diving
**468** A130 30f Table tennis
**469** A130 40f Tennis
**470** A130 50f Two scouts, flag
**471** A130 60f Volleyball
**472** A130 100f Tug-of-war
**473** A130 150f Basketball
**474** A130 425f Archery

**Souvenir Sheet**

**475** A130 425f Scout, emblem, hand sign

For surcharge see No. C154.

San'a Preservation — A131

**1988, May 1 Litho. *Perf. 14***

**476** A131 25f multicolored
**477** A131 50f multicolored
**478** A131 100f multicolored
**479** A131 150f multicolored
**480** A131 425f multicolored
*a.* Souvenir sheet of 1

For surcharge see No. 594.

Battle of Hattin, 800th Anniv. in 1987 A132

**1988 Litho. *Perf. 14***

**482** A132 150f multicolored
**483** A132 425f multicolored
*a.* Souvenir sheet

For surcharge see No. C155.

Arab Telecommunication Day, 1987 — A133

**1988**

**484** A133 100f multicolored
**485** A133 150f multicolored
**486** A133 425f multicolored
*a.* Souvenir sheet

For surcharge see No. C156.

A134

Sept. 26 Revolution, 26th Anniv. — A134a

**1989, Sept. 30**

**487** A134 300f multicolored
**488** A134 375f multicolored
**489** A134a 850f multicolored
**490** A134a 900f multicolored

A souvenir sheet containing one #488 exists.
For surcharges see Nos. 595, 605.

A135

October 14 Revolution, 25th Anniv. — A135a

**1989, Oct. 14**

**491** A135 300f multicolored
**492** A135 375f multicolored
**493** A135a 850f multicolored
**494** A135a 900f multicolored

A souvenir sheet containing one #492 exists.
For surcharges see Nos. 596, 606.

1988 Summer Olympics, Seoul A136

Game emblem and various events: 300f, Table tennis, basketball, track, boxing. 375f,

Soccer game. 850f, Soccer, judo, vert. 900f, Torch bearer.

**1989, Nov. 10 Litho. *Perf. 13x13½***
495 A136 300f multicolored
496 A136 375f multicolored
a. Souvenir sheet
497 A136 850f multicolored
498 A136 900f multicolored

For surcharges see Nos. 597, 607.

Palestinian Uprising A137

**1989, Dec. 9 *Perf. 13x13½, 13½x13***
499 A137 300f shown
500 A137 375f Flag raising, vert.
a. Souvenir sheet of 1
501 A137 850f Burning barricades
502 A137 900f Man waving flag, vert.

For surcharges see Nos. 598, 608.

Arab Cooperation Council — A138

**1990, Feb. 16 Litho. *Perf. 13x13½***
504 A138 300f multicolored
505 A138 375f multicolored
a. Souvenir sheet
506 A138 850f multicolored
507 A138 900f multicolored

For surcharges see Nos. 599, 609.

First Exported Oil — A139

**1990, Mar. 15 *Perf. 14***
508 A139 300f multicolored
509 A139 375f multicolored
a. Souvenir sheet
510 A139 850f multi, diff.
511 A139 900f like 850f

For surcharges see Nos. 600, 610.

Arab Scout Movement, 75th Anniv. A140

**1990, June 15 Litho. *Perf. 13x13½***
512 A140 300f Scouts holding globe
513 A140 375f like No. 512
a. Souvenir sheet of 1
514 A140 850f Oil rig, scouts, globe
515 A140 900f like No. 514

For surcharges see Nos. 601, 611.

Arab Board for Medical Specializations, 10th Anniv. — A141

**1990, Apr. 15 Photo. *Perf. 13½x13***
516 A141 300f brt grn & multi
517 A141 375f lt bl & multi
a. Sheet of 1, perf. 12½
518 A141 850f lt org & multi
519 A141 900f lt vio & multi

For surcharges see Nos. 602, 612.

Immunization Campaign — A142

300f, 375f, Mother feeding infant, vert.

**1990, May 15 *Perf. 13½x13, 13x13½***
520 A142 300f lt bl & multi
521 A142 375f lt org & multi
a. Sheet of 1, perf. 12½
522 A142 850f lt bl grn & multi
523 A142 900f lt lake & multi

No. 521a contains one 26x37mm stamp.
For surcharges see Nos. 603, C157.

UN Development Program, 40th Anniv. — A144

**1990, Oct. 24 Litho. *Perf. 12***
532 A144 150f multicolored

For surcharge see No. 622.

Ducks A145

**1990, Sept. 18 Litho. *Perf. 12***
533 A145 10f Pintail swimming
534 A145 20f Wigeon
535 A145 25f Ruddy shelduck
536 A145 40f Gadwall
537 A145 75f Shelduck, male
538 A145 150f Shoveler
539 A145 600f Teal

**Souvenir Sheet**
540 A145 460f Pintail in flight

For surcharge see No. 623.

Moths and Butterflies A146

**1990, Nov. 3 *Perf. 12½x12***
541 A146 5f Dirphia multicolor
542 A146 20f Automeris io
543 A146 25f Papilio machaon
544 A146 40f Bhutanitis lidderdalii
545 A146 55f Prepona demophon muson
546 A146 75f Agarista agricola
547 A146 700f Attacus edwardsii

**Souvenir Sheet**
***Perf. 12x12½***
548 A146 460f Daphnis nerii, vert.

Prehistoric Animals A147

***Perf. 12x12½, 12½x12***
**1990, Nov. 27**
549 A147 5f Protembolotherium, vert.
550 A147 10f Diatryma, vert.
551 A147 35f Mammuthus
552 A147 40f Edaphosaurus
553 A147 55f Dimorphodon
554 A147 75f Phororhacos
555 A147 700f Ichthyosaurus, vert.

**Size: 61x90mm**
***Imperf***
556 A147 460f Tyrannosaurus, vert.

A148

A149

Various domestic cats.

**1990, Dec. 26 *Perf. 12x12½***
557 A148 5f multicolored
558 A148 15f multicolored
559 A148 35f multicolored
560 A148 55f multicolored
561 A148 60f multicolored
562 A148 150f multicolored
563 A148 600f multicolored

**Size: 70x90mm**
***Imperf***
564 A148 460f multicolored

**1991, Mar. 18 Litho. *Perf. 12x12½***
Mushrooms.
565 A149 50f Boletus aestivalis
566 A149 60f Suillus luteus
567 A149 80f Gyromitra esculenta
568 A149 100f Leccinum scabrum
569 A149 130f Amanita muscaria
570 A149 200f Boletus erythropus
571 A149 300f Leccinum testaceoscabrum

**Size: 70x90mm**
***Imperf***
572 A149 460f Stropharia aeruginosa

Unified Yemen Republic, 1st Anniv. A150

Designs: 300f, 375f, Eagle crest. 850f, 900f, Hand holding flag, map, sun.

**1991, May 22 *Perf. 13x13½***
573 A150 300f pink & multi
574 A150 375f grn bl multi
a. Sheet of 1, perf. 12½
575 A150 850f lt bl & multi
576 A150 900f bl grn & multi

No. 574a contains one 37x27mm stamp.
For surcharges see #604, 613, 624, 627.

Unity Agreement Signed Nov. 30, 1989 — A151

Designs: 300f, 375f, 850f, Fist, flag, map.

**1991, May 22 *Perf. 13½x13***
577 A151 225f multicolored
578 A151 300f multicolored
579 A151 375f multicolored
a. Sheet of 1, perf. 12½
580 A151 650f multicolored
581 A151 850f multicolored

No. 579a contains one 27x37mm stamp.
For surcharges see #614, 617-619, 625.

World Anti-Smoking Day — A153

Designs: 300f, 375f, 850f, Man facing skull smoking cigarette.

**1991, May 31 *Perf. 13x13½***
582 A153 225f multicolored
583 A153 300f multicolored
584 A153 375f multicolored
a. Sheet of 1, perf. 12½
585 A153 650f multicolored
586 A153 850f multicolored

No. 584a contains one 36x26mm stamp.
For surcharges see Nos. 615, 620, 626.

United Nations, 45th Anniv. A154

**1991, June 26 *Perf. 13x13½***
587 A154 5f multicolored
588 A154 8f multicolored
589 A154 10f multicolored
590 A154 12f multicolored

**Souvenir Sheet**
***Perf. 12½***
591 A154 6f multicolored

No. 591 contains one 37x28mm stamp.

### Nos. 329, 456, 480, 489-490, 493-494, 497-498, 501-502, 506-507, 510-511, 514-515, 518-519, 523, 575-576, 581 & 586 Surcharged, "Rials" Spelled Out

**1993, Jan. 1 *Perfs., Etc. as Before***
592 A88 5r on 75f #329
593 A125 8r on 425f #456
594 A131 8r on 425f #480
595 A134a 10r on 900f #490
596 A135a 10r on 900f #494
597 A136 10r on 900f #498
598 A137 10r on 900f #502
599 A138 10r on 900f #507
600 A139 10r on 900f #511
601 A140 10r on 900f #515
602 A141 10r on 900f #519
603 A142 10r on 900f #523
604 A150 10r on 900f #576
605 A134a 12r on 850f #489
606 A135a 12r on 850f #493
607 A136 12r on 850f #497
608 A137 12r on 850f #501
609 A138 12r on 850f #506
610 A139 12r on 850f #510
611 A140 12r on 850f #514

612 A141 12r on 850f #518
613 A150 12r on 850f #575
614 A151 12r on 850f #581
615 A153 12r on 850f #586

Size and location of surcharge varies.

Yemen (PDR) Nos. 441, 443, 447, and Yemen Nos. 577-578, 583 Surcharged Type a or

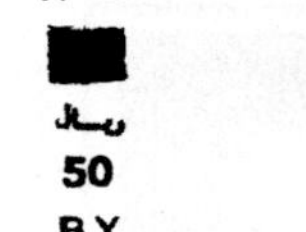


c

**1993** ***Perfs., Etc. as Before***

616 A139(a) 50r on 500f #447
617 A151(a) 50r on 225f #577
618 A151(c) 50r on 225f #577
*a.* Pair, #617-618
619 A151(a) 100r on 300f #578
620 A153(a) 100r on 300f #583
621 A139(a) 200r on 5f #441
*a.* 3-Line surcharge
621B A139(a) 200r on 20f #443

Size and location of surcharge varies.

Yemen Republic Nos. 532, 538, 573-574, 579, & 584 Surcharged

a

**1993, Sept. 1** ***Perfs., Etc. as Before***

622 A144(a) 50r on 150f #532
623 A145(a) 50r on 150f #538
624 A150(a) 50r on 375f #574
625 A151(a) 50r on 375f #579
626 A153(a) 50r on 375f #584
627 A150(a) 100r on 300f #573

Size and location of surcharge varies.
No. 623 exists with a surcharge similar to surcharge "c."

Yemen People's Democratic Republic Nos. 75, 84B, 204, 208, 216, 232, 235, 244, 267, 335-336, 347, 425, 436-437, 439 & Types Surcharged Type a and:

b

**1993, Sept. 1** ***Perfs., Etc. as Before***

628 A25(a) 8r on 100f #84B
629 A63(a) 8r on 110f #204
630 A64(a) 8r on 110f #208
631 A66(a) 8r on 110f #216
632 A72(a) 8r on 110f #232
633 A74(a) 8r on 110r #235
634 A76(a) 8r on 110r #244
635 A86(a) 8r on 110f #267
636 A105(a) 100r on 2d #347
637 A137(a) 100r on 300f #439
638 A24(a) 200r on 5f #75
639 (b) 200r on 15f
640 A105(b) 200r on 15f #335
641 (b) 200r on 20f
642 A105(b) 200r on 20f #336
643 A131(a) 200r on 20f #425 135.00 —
644 A134(a) 200r on 75f #436
645 A135(a) 200r on 250f #437

Size and location of surcharge varies.
No. 582 exists with a 50r type "b" surcharge.

No. 636 exists with a surcharge similar to surcharge "c."
Nos. 639, 641 without surcharge have not been listed in the Scott Catalogue.

Yemen Unity, 4th Anniv. — A155

Various views of govt. building, San'a.

**1994, Sept. 27** **Litho.** ***Perf. 13½x14***

646 A155 3r multicolored
647 A155 5r multicolored
648 A155 8r multicolored
649 A155 20r multicolored

**Souvenir Sheet**

650 A155 20r multi, diff.

1994 World Cup Soccer Championships, US — A156

2r, Player in yellow shirt dribbling ball, vert. 6r, Player in striped shirt dribbling, vert. 10r, Goal keeper. No. 654, Heading ball, vert.
No. 655, Tackling.

**1994, Oct. 1** ***Perf. 14x13½, 13½x14***

651 A156 2r multicolored
652 A156 6r multicolored
653 A156 10r multicolored
654 A156 12r multicolored

**Souvenir Sheet**

655 A156 12r multicolored

World Day of Environmental Protection A157

FAO, 50th Anniv. A158

***Perf. 14x13½, 13½x14***

**1995, Oct. 15** **Litho.**

656 A157 15r Arabian leopard
657 A157 20r Caracal lynx
658 A157 30r Guinea fowl, horiz.

**Souvenir Sheet**

659 A157 50r Partridge, horiz.

**1995, Oct. 16** ***Perf. 14x13½***

Emblem, field, hand holding: 10r, Plant. 25r, Seed. 30r, Fish. 50r, Grain.

660 A158 10r violet & multi
661 A158 25r claret & multi
662 A158 30r light blue & multi

**Souvenir Sheet**

663 A158 50r dark blue & multi

A159

A160

UN, 50th anniv.: Various views of Aden Dam.

**1995, Oct. 24** ***Perf. 14x13½, 13½x14***

664 A159 10r multi
665 A159 20r multi
666 A159 25r multi, horiz.

**Souvenir Sheet**

667 A159 50r multi, horiz.

***Perf. 14x13½, 13½x14***

**1995, Nov. 29**

Naseem Hamed Kashmem, world boxing champion: 10r, With champion belts. 20r, Up close. 25r, Boxing opponent, horiz. 30r, Holding up arm as winner, trainer.
50r, Boxing opponent, diff., horiz.

668 A160 10r multicolored
669 A160 20r multicolored
670 A160 25r multicolored
671 A160 30r multicolored

**Souvenir Sheet**

672 A160 50r multicolored

Souvenir Sheet

CHINA '96, 9th Asian Intl. Philatelic Exhibition — A161

Illustration reduced.

**1996, May 18** **Litho.** ***Perf. 11½***

673 A161 80r Shanghai

1996 Summer Olympic Games, Atlanta — A162

**1996, July 19** ***Perf. 14x13½, 13½x14***

674 A162 20r Wrestling, vert.
675 A162 50r High jump
676 A162 60r Running, vert.
677 A162 70r Gymnastics, vert.
678 A162 100r Judo, vert.

**Souvenir Sheet**

679 A162 150r Javelin, vert.

Landmarks A163

10r, 70r, 250r, Popular Heritage Museum, Seiyoan. 15r, 40r, 60r, 500r, Rock Palace, Wadi Dhahr, vert. 20r, 100r, 200r, Old Sana'a City. 30r, 50r, 150r, 300r, Al-Mohdhar Minaret, Tarim, vert.

***Perf. 13½x14, 14x13½***

**1996, Sept. 26** **Litho.**

680 A163 10r org yel & multi
681 A163 15r grn yel & multi
682 A163 20r lt blue & multi
683 A163 30r blue & multi
684 A163 40r salmon & multi
685 A163 50r green & multi
686 A163 60r lilac & multi
687 A163 70r violet & multi
688 A163 100r yellow & multi
689 A163 150r orange & multi
690 A163 200r rose & multi
691 A163 250r gray & multi
692 A163 300r red & multi
693 A163 500r yellow & multi

Birds — A164

Designs: 20r, Tyto alba. 50r, Alectoris philbyi. 60r, Gypaetus barbatus. 70r, Alectoris melanocephala. 100r, Chlamydotis undulata.
150r, Ixobrychus minutus, vert.

**1996, Oct. 14** **Litho.** ***Perf. 13½x14***

694 A164 20r multicolored
695 A164 50r multicolored
696 A164 60r multicolored
697 A164 70r multicolored
698 A164 100r multicolored

**Souvenir Sheet**

***Perf. 14x13½***

699 A164 150r multicolored

Rare Plants in Yemen — A165

Designs: 20r, Parodia masii. 50r, Notocatus cristata. 60r, Adenium obesum socotranum. 70r, Dracaena cinnabari. 100r, Mammillaria erythrosperma.
150r, Parodia maasii, diff.

**1996, Nov. 30** ***Perf. 13½x14***

700 A165 20r multicolored
701 A165 50r multicolored
702 A165 60r multicolored
703 A165 70r multicolored
704 A165 100r multicolored

**Souvenir Sheet**

705 A165 150r multicolored

A166

A167

Fish: 20r, Heniochus acuminatus. 50r, 150r, Cheilinus undulatus. 60r, Zebrasoma xanthurum. 70r, Pomacanthus imperator. 100r, Pomacanthus vanthometopon.

**1996, Nov. 30**

706 A166 20r multicolored
707 A166 50r multicolored
708 A166 60r multicolored
709 A166 70r multicolored
710 A166 100r multicolored

**Souvenir Sheet**

711 A166 150r multicolored

**1996, Dec. 11** ***Perf. 14x13½***

UNICEF, 50th Anniv.: 20r, Children with books. 50r, Girls clapping hands. 60r, Mother, child. 70r, Mother, three children.
150r, Child making jewelry, horiz.

712 A167 20r multicolored
713 A167 50r multicolored
714 A167 60r multicolored
715 A167 70r multicolored

**Souvenir Sheet**

***Perf. 13½x14***

716 A167 150r multicolored

1998 World Cup Soccer Championships, France — A168

Various soccer plays.

**1998, June 10 Litho. *Perf. 13x13½***

**717** A168 10r multicolored
**718** A168 15r multicolored
**719** A168 35r multicolored
**720** A168 65r multicolored
**721** A168 75r multicolored
*a.* Souvenir sheet, #717-721

Birds A169

Designs: 10r, Ardeotis arabs. 15r, Neophron percnopterus. 35r, Coracias abyssinicus. 65r, Cinnyricinclus leucogaster. 75r, Melierax metabates.

**1998, Sept. 26 Litho. *Perf. 13***

**722-726** A169 Set of 5 4.25 4.25
*726a* Sheet of 5, #722-726 4.25 4.25

Universal Declaration of Human Rights, 50th Anniv. A170

15r, Hands in air. 35r, Hands clasped in handshake. 100r, Hands reaching out.

**1998, Oct. 12**

**727-729** A170 Set of 3 3.25 3.25
*729a* Sheet of 3, #727-729 3.25 3.25

First General Conference of Yemeni Immigrants (in 1999) A171

Emblem &: 60r, Dhows. 90r, Fort, camel.

**2000, May 16 Litho. *Perf. 14½x14***

**730-731** A171 Set of 2 2.00 2.00
*731a* Souvenir sheet, #730-731 2.00 2.00

Tenth National Day — A172

Background colors: 30r, Light green. 50r, Rose lilac. 70r, Light blue. 150r, Orange.

**2000, May 22 *Perf. 14x14½***

**732-734** A172 Set of 3 1.60 1.60

**Souvenir Sheet**

**735** A172 150r multi 1.60 1.60

Plants of Socotra — A173

Designs: 30r, Euphorbia abdalkuri. 70r, Dendrosicyos socotranus. 80r, Caralluma socotrana. 120r, Dracaena cinnabari.

300r, Exacum affine.

**2000, July 15**

**736-739** A173 Set of 4 4.00 4.00

**Souvenir Sheet**

**740** A173 300r multi 4.00 4.00

2000 Summer Olympics, Sydney — A174

Designs: 50r, Judo. 70r, Runner. 80r, Hurdler. 100r, Shooting.

300r, Tennis.

**2000, Sept. 15**

**741-744** A174 Set of 4 4.00 4.00

**Souvenir Sheet**

**745** A174 300r multi 4.00 4.00

Antiquities — A175

Designs: 30r, Stone idols, 3000 B.C. 70r, Statue of Ma'adi Karib, 800 B.C. 100r, Horned griffin, Royal Palace of Shabwa, 300. 120r, Statue of King of Awsan Yasduq Eil, 100 B.C.

320r, Stele with bull's head, 100 B.C., horiz.

**2002, June 15 Litho. *Perf. 13x12¾***

**746-749** A175 Set of 4 4.25 4.25

**Souvenir Sheet**

***Imperf***

**750** A175 320r multi 4.25 4.25

No. 750 contains one 41x26mm stamp.

2002 World Cup Soccer Championships, Japan and Korea — A176

Soccer players with background colors of: 30r, Bister, vert. 70r, Green. 100r, Blue, vert. 120r, Red brown, vert.

No. 755: a, Player's foot and ball. b, World Cup trophy.

**2002, May 31 *Perf. 13x12¾, 12¾x13***

**751-754** A176 Set of 4 4.25 4.25

**Souvenir Sheet**

***Perf.***

**755** A176 160r Sheet of 2, #a-b 4.25 4.25

No. 755 contains two 28mm diameter stamps.

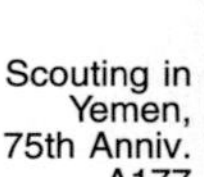

Scouting in Yemen, 75th Anniv. A177

Designs: 30r, Scout escorting man across street. 60r, Scout digging. 70r, Scouts in rowboat.

160r, Scout saluting, vert.

**2002, Apr. 30 *Perf. 12¾x13***

**756-758** A177 Set of 3 2.10 2.10

**Souvenir Sheet**

***Perf. 13x13¼***

**759** A177 160r multi 2.10 2.10

No. 759 contains one 16x26mm stamp.

Palestinian Intifada — A178

Designs: 30r, Frightened child. 60r, Bleeding child.

90r, Dome of the Rock, horiz.

**2002, Apr. 27 *Perf. 13x12¾***

**760-761** A178 Set of 2 1.25 1.25

***Imperf***

**Size: 111x78mm**

**762** A178 90r multi 1.25 1.25

Poets — A179

Revolution, 40th Anniv. — A180

Designs: Nos. 763, 30r, 765, 60r, 767a, 70r, Hussain Al-Muhdhar (1931-2000). Nos. 764, 30r, 766, 60r, 767b, 70r, Abdullah Al-Baradony (1929-99).

**2002, June 30 Litho. *Perf. 13x12¾***

**763-766** A179 Set of 4 2.25 2.25

**Souvenir Sheet**

***Perf. 13x13¼***

**767** A179 70r Sheet of 2, #a-b 1.75 1.75

No. 767 contains two 16x28mm stamps.

**2002, Sept. 26 *Perf. 13x12¾***

Background colors: 30r, Dull green. 60r, Rose.

90r, Lilac.

**768-769** A180 Set of 2 1.10 1.10

***Imperf***

**Size: 110x76mm**

**770** A180 90r multi 1.10 1.10

World Under-17 Soccer Championships, Finland — A181

Various soccer players with background color of: 30r, Red violet. 50r, Golden brown. 70r, Blue. 100r, Green.

250r, Soccer team and stadium

**2003, Aug. 13 Litho. *Perf. 12¾x13***

**771-774** A181 Set of 4 3.00 3.00

***Imperf***

**Size: 109x74mm**

**775** A181 250r multi 3.00 3.00

Antiquities — A182

Various sculptures with background colors of: 20r, Pale yellow. 40r, Lilac. 50r, Light green. 150r, Pink.

260r, Black, horiz.

**2003, Sept. 26 *Perf. 13x12¾***

**776-779** A182 Set of 4 3.00 3.00

**Souvenir Sheet**

***Perf. 12¾x13***

**780** A182 260r multi 3.00 3.00

Traditional Women's Clothing — A183

Various women with panel colors of: 30r, Purple. 60r, Yellow green. 70r, Dark green. 100r, Red violet. 150r, Brown.

410r, Purple background, horiz.

**2003, Oct. 14 *Perf. 13x12¾***

**781-785** A183 Set of 5 4.75 4.75

**Souvenir Sheet**

***Perf. 12¾x13***

**786** A183 410r multi 4.75 4.75

Children's Art — A184

Designs: 20r, Girl with flower on globe, vert. 30r, Dove over buildings, vert. 40r, Dove holding swing, vert. 50r, Children in field. 60r, Animals in field. 70r, Street and park.

**2003, Oct. 15 *Perf. 13x12¾, 12¾x13***

**787-792** A184 Set of 6 3.00 3.00

Sana'a, 2004 Arabic Cultural Capital — A185

Various buildings with frame colors of: 30r, White. 50r, Purple. 70r, Black. 100r, Dark brown. 150r Red brown.

400r, Buildings, horiz.

**2003, Nov. 30 *Perf. 13x12¾***

**793-797** A185 Set of 5 4.50 4.50

**Souvenir Sheet**

***Perf. 12¾x13***

**798** A185 400r multi 4.50 4.50

FIFA (Fédération Internationale de Football Association), Cent. — A186

**2004, May 21 Litho. *Perf. 13x12¾***
**799** A186 100r multi 1.10 1.10

Dated 2005. Stamps did not appear in marketplace until 2005.

2004 Summer Olympics, Athens — A187

Designs: 70r, Running. 80r, Shooting. 100r, Swimming.
250r, Equestrian.

**2004, Aug. 13**
**800-802** A187 Set of 3 2.75 2.75

**Souvenir Sheet**

**803** A187 250r multi 2.75 2.75

Dated 2005. Stamps did not appear in marketplace until 2005.

Telecommunications and Technology — A188

Designs: 60r, Computer chips, "@" symbol, keyboard. 70r, Computer and stylized people, vert. 100r, Yemen Mobile emblem, vert.
400r, Like 70r, vert.

***Perf. 12¾x13, 13x12¾***

**2004, Sept. 26**
**804-806** A188 Set of 3 2.50 2.50

**Souvenir Sheet**

**807** A188 400r multi 4.50 4.50

Dated 2005. Stamps did not appear in marketplace until 2005.

Spiders A189

No. 808: a, Tidarren argo. b, Scelidomachus socotranus. c, Habrocestum albopunctatum. d, Rafalus insignipalpis. e, Latrodectus hystrix. f, Atrophothele socotrana.
300r, Like No. 808b.

**2004, Oct. 14 *Perf. 12¾x13***
**808** Horiz. strip of 6 3.25 3.25
***a.-f.*** A189 50r Any single .50 .50

**Souvenir Sheet**

**809** A189 300r multi 3.25 3.25

Dated 2005. Stamps did not appear in marketplace until 2005.

Traditional Men's Clothing — A190

Men wearing various outfits with background colors of: 50r, Light yellow. 60r, Green. 70r, Pink. 100r, Blue.
360r, Orange brown.

**2004, Oct. 30 *Perf. 13x12¾***
**810-813** A190 Set of 4 3.25 3.25

**Souvenir Sheet**

**814** A190 360r multi 4.00 4.00

Dated 2005. Stamps did not appear in marketplace until 2005.

Handicrafts A191

No. 815: a, Knife maker holding hammer. b, Textile worker piecing fabric. c, Jeweler. d, Weaver at loom.
3004, Like No. 815a.

**2004, Nov. 30**
**815** Horiz. strip of 4 3.25 3.25
***a.-d.*** A191 70r multi .80 .80

**Souvenir Sheet**

**816** A191 300r multi 3.25 3.25

Dated 2005. Stamps did not appear in marketplace until 2005.

15th National Day — A192

Emblem and: 30r, Industrial plant. 60r, Dam and reservoir. 70r, Man holding flag.
90r, Buildings.

**2005, May 22**
**817-819** A192 Set of 3 1.75 1.75

**Souvenir Sheet**

**820** A192 90r multi 1.00 1.00

United Nations, 60th Anniv. — A193

Symbols of eight goals for a better Yemen: No. 821, 40r, Pregnant woman and doctor. No. 822, 40r, Woman, infant and doctor. No. 823, 40r, Woman reading book. No. 824, 40r, Mosquito, AIDS ribbon, medicine and bottle. No. 825, Man depositing trash in can, tree, smiling sun. 80r, Goats, hat seller and child. 100r, Woman, man and balance. 120r, Handshake.
130r, UN anniversary emblem.

**2005, Oct. 24 Litho. *Perf. 13x12¾***
**821-828** A193 Set of 8 5.50 5.50

**Size: 111x83mm**
***Imperf***

**829** A193 130r multi 1.50 1.50

No. 829 contains one perforated label lacking a denomination.

## AIR POST STAMPS

**Catalogue values for unused stamps in this section are for Never Hinged items.**

Plane over San'a AP1

**1947 Unwmk. Engr. *Perf. 12½***
**C1** AP1 10b bright blue 6.00 2.00
**C2** AP1 20b olive green 10.00 2.50

**Views Type of Regular Issue**

6b, 8b, View of San'a. 10b, Mocha coffee branch. 12b, Palace of the Rock, Wadi Dhahr. 16b, Palace, Ta'iz. 20b, 1i, Parade Ground, San'a.

**1951 Wmk. 277 Photo. *Perf. 14***
**C3** A14 6b blue 1.40 .50
**C4** A14 8b dark brown 1.75 .60
**C5** A14 10b dark green 2.25 1.40
**C6** A13 12b dark blue 2.50 .80
**C7** A14 16b lilac rose 3.00 .80
**C8** A13 20b orange brown 3.75 1.25
**C9** A13 1i dark red 10.00 3.00
*Nos. C3-C9 (7)* 24.65 8.35

Nos. C3 and C4 were used provisionally in 1957 for registry and foreign ordinary mail.

**Type of Regular Issue**

Designs: 12b, Palace of the Rock, Wadi Dhahr. 20b, Walls of Ibb.

**Engraved and Photogravure**

**1952 Unwmk. *Perf. 14½***
**C10** A15 12b grnsh blk, bl & brn 10.00 10.00
**C11** A15 20b indigo, bl & brn 10.00 10.00

**Flag-and-View Type**

**1952**
**C12** A16 1i dk brn, car & brt ultra 18.00 18.00

Palace in Foreground

**1952**
**C13** A16 30b yel grn, car & gray 11.00 11.00

Leaning Minaret, Mosque of Ta'iz — AP6

**1954 Photo. *Perf. 14***
**C14** AP6 10b scarlet 3.25 .90
**C15** AP6 12b dull blue 4.00 1.25
**C16** AP6 20b olive bister 6.50 2.00
*Nos. C14-C16 (3)* 13.75 4.15

Accession of King Ahmed I, 5th anniv.

**Type of Regular Issue**

**1959 Wmk. 318 *Perf. 13x13½***
**C17** A21 6b orange & blk 1.00 .70
**C18** A21 10b red & blk 1.60 1.25
**C19** A21 16b brt violet & red 2.50 2.00
*Nos. C17-C19 (3)* 5.10 3.95

**Antiquities of Marib Type**

Designs: 6b, Columns, Temple of the Moon God. 16b, Control tower and spillway of 2,700-year-old dam of Marib.

***Perf. 11½***

**1961, Oct. 14 Unwmk. Photo.**
**C20** A27 6b lt bl grn & blk 1.00 .20
**C21** A27 16b lt blue & blk 2.75 1.50

For overprints see Nos. C24, C25.

**Buildings Type**

6b, Bab al-Yemen, main gate of San'a, horiz. 16b, Palace of the Rock (Dar al-Hajar).

**1961, Nov. 15**
**C22** A28 6b blk, lt bl & grn .55 .20
**C23** A28 16b blk, rose & grn 1.40 .60

For overprints see Nos. C24A, C25A.

Nos. C20-C23 Ovptd. Like Nos. 144-158 in Dark Red or Black

***Perf. 11½***

**1963, Jan. 1 Photo. Unwmk.**
**C24** A27 (a) 6b No. C20 .70 .70
**C24A** A28 (b) 6b No. C22 .85 .85
**C25** A27 (a) 16b No. C21 1.75 1.75
**C25A** A28 (a) 16b No. C23 (B) 2.75 2.75

**Proclamation of the Republic Type**

**1963, Mar. 15 *Perf. 11x11½, 11½x11***
**C26** A34 8b Bayonette, torch 1.50 1.50
**C27** A34 10b Jet, torch, tank 2.00 2.00
**C28** A34 16b Flag, chain, torch 2.75 2.75

Nos. C27-C28 horiz.

Nos. 25-29 Ovptd. in Black

**Wmk. 258**

**1963, Sept. 1 Litho. *Perf. 12½***
**C29** A5 6b slate blue & ultra 1.50 1.50
**C29A** A5 10b fawn & ultra 1.90 1.90
**C29B** A5 14b olive & ultra 2.25 2.25
**C29C** A5 20b yel grn & ultra 3.00 3.00
**C29D** A5 1i claret & ultra 6.50 6.50
*Nos. C29-C29D (5)* 15.15 15.15

Astronauts. Set of five airmail, ¼, ⅓, ½, 4, 20b. Airmail imperf. souvenir sheet, 20b. Dec. 5. Nos. 63C01-63C06. Value, set $11, souvenir $9.

**1964**

Astronauts issue of 1963 overprinted in black or red brown "John F. Kennedy / 1917 / 1963" in English or Arabic. Set of five airmail. May 5. Nos. 64C01-64C05.

**San'a Intl. Airport Type**

***Perf. 11½x11***

**1964, Oct. 1 Photo. Unwmk.**
**C30** A40 6b Sun, buildings, aircraft .70 .70

See note after No. 203.

**APU 10th Anniv. Type**

**1964, Oct. 15 *Perf. 13½***
**C31** A41 6b blue grn & blk 1.00 .80

An imperf. souvenir sheet of one exists containing No. C31. Value $3.

**Deir Yassin Massacre Type**

**1965, Apr. 30 *Perf. 11x11½***
**C32** A44 6b ver & brt org 1.00

**Library Type**

**1965, July 7 *Perf. 11½x11***
**C33** A46 6b sepia, red & int blue .85 .55

An imperf. souvenir sheet of one exists containing No. C33. Value $2.50.

**1966**

Butterflies. Set of four airmail, 6, 8, 10, 16b. May 5. Nos. 66C01-66C04.

Lenin's Birth Centenary AP7

**1970, Aug. 15 Litho. *Perf. 12x12½***

**C34** AP7 6b Public speech 1.40 1.10
**C35** AP7 16b Meeting with Arab delegates 3.00 1.90

8th Anniv. of the Revolution — AP8

**1971, Jan. 24 *Perf. 13***

**C36** AP8 5b Country estate .75
**C37** AP8 7b Workers 1.10
**C38** AP8 16b Handshake, flag, flowers, open book 1.50
*Nos. C36-C38 (3)* 3.35

A souv. sheet of 1 exists containing No. C38. Value $5.

### Revolution Type

**1972, Nov. 25 Photo. *Perf. 13***

**C40** A80 21b lilac, blk & multi 5.00 3.50

### Al-Aqsa Mosque Type

**1973, Jan. 1 Photo. *Perf. 13½***

**C41** A82 24b lt bl, blk & multi 2.00 1.40
*a.* Min. sheet of 1, imperf.

### UNICEF Type

**1973, Jan. 15 Photo. *Perf. 13***

**C42** A83 18b lt bl, blk & multi 1.75 1.50
*a.* Min. sheet of 1, imperf. 3.25 2.50

For surcharge see No. C46.

11th Anniv. of Revolution AP10

**1973, Sept. 26 Photo. *Perf. 14***

**C43** AP10 7b Bank .50 .35
**C44** AP10 10b Cement factory .65 .55
**C45** AP10 18b Hospital 1.50 1.10
*Nos. C43-C45 (3)* 2.65 2.00

For surcharges see Nos. C47-C48.

### Nos. C42, C43, C45 Surcharged in Black with New Value and Bars

**1975, Nov. 15**

**C46** A83 75f on 18b lt bl, blk & multi 2.50 2.50
**C46A** A80 75f on 21b #C40 (R) — —
**C47** AP10 90f on 7b multi 5.50 2.75
**C48** AP10 120f on 18b multi 4.25 4.25
*a.* Overprinted in red

### Argentina 1978 World Cup Type

World cup emblem and various soccer players.

**1980, Mar. 30 Photo. *Perf. 14***

**C49** A99 60f gold & multi .80 .60
**C50** A99 75f gold & multi 1.00 .70
**C51** A99 80f gold & multi 1.25 .90
**C52** A99 100f gold & multi 1.50 1.00
*Nos. C49-C52 (4)* 4.55 3.20

Two 225f souvenir sheets exist.

### IYC Type

**1980, Apr. 1 *Perf. 13½***

**C53** A100 80f Girl, bird 3.00 1.25
**C54** A100 100f Boy, butterfly, flower 3.00 1.25
**C55** A100 150f Boy, butterfly, flower, diff. 4.50 1.75
*Nos. C53-C55 (3)* 10.50 4.25

Two 200f souvenir sheets exist.

### Scouting Type of 1980

**1980, May 1 Photo. *Perf. 13½x14***

**C56** A101 60f Bicycling 2.00 .80
**C57** A101 75f Fencing 2.40 1.10
**C58** A101 120f Butterfly catching 3.75 1.50
*Nos. C56-C58 (3)* 8.15 3.40

Two 300f souvenir sheets exist.

### Argentina 1978 Winners' Type

World cup emblem and various soccer players.

**1980, June 1 Photo. *Perf. 14***

**C59** A102 60f gold & multi 1.00 .50
**C60** A102 75f gold & multi 1.40 .65
**C61** A102 80f gold & multi 1.50 .75
**C62** A102 100f gold & multi 1.60 1.10
*Nos. C59-C62 (4)* 5.50 3.00

Two 225f souvenir sheets exist.

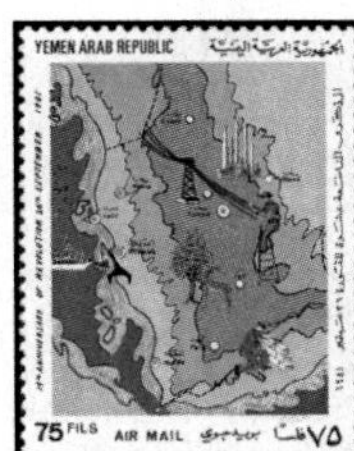


19th Anniv. of Sept. 26th Revolution (1981) — AP11

**1982, Jan. 25 Litho. *Perf. 14***

**C63** AP11 75f Map .45 .25
**C64** AP11 125f Map in sunset .70 .40
**C65** AP11 325f Dove in natl. colors 2.00 1.25
*a.* Souvenir sheet of 1 5.00 5.00
**C66** AP11 400f Jets 2.25 1.40
*Nos. C63-C66 (4)* 5.40 3.30

Al-Hasan Ibn Al-Hamadani, Writer — AP12

**1982, Feb. 1**

**C67** AP12 125f green & multi 1.25 .60
**C68** AP12 325f blue & multi 2.75 1.40

### Souvenir Sheet

**C69** AP12 375f multi 3.50 3.50

No. C69 contains one stamp (36x46mm).
For surcharge see No. C138.

World Food Day — AP13

Designs: No. C76a, Eggplants. No. C76b, Tomatoes. No. C76c, Beets, peas. No. C76d, Cauliflower, carrots. No. C77a, Dove. No. C77b, Water birds. No. C77c, Fish. No. C77d, Geese.

**1982, Mar. 1 Litho. *Perf. 14***

**C70** AP13 25f Rabbits .50
**C71** AP13 50f Rooster, Hens 1.00
**C72** AP13 60f Turkeys 1.25
**C73** AP13 75f Sheep 1.50
**C74** AP13 100f Cattle 2.00
**C75** AP13 125f Deer 2.50
*Nos. C70-C75 (6)* 8.75

### Souvenir Sheets

**C76** Sheet of 4 2.00
*a.-d.* AP13 100f, any single .50
**C77** Sheet of 4 2.50
*a.-d.* AP13 125f, any single .60

For surcharges see Nos. C139, C144.

1980 Summer Olympics, Moscow AP14

**1982, Apr. 1**

**C78** AP14 25f Gymnastics
**C79** AP14 50f Pole vault
**C80** AP14 60f Javelin
**C81** AP14 75f Running
**C82** AP14 100f Basketball
**C83** AP14 125f Soccer

Two souvenir sheets of 4 exist: 100f, picturing boxing, wrestling, canoeing, swimming, and 125f, picturing weight lifting, discus, long jump, fencing.
For surcharges see Nos. C140, C145.

Aviation — AP15

Various space and aircraft.

**1982, May 21**

**C86** AP15 25f multi
**C87** AP15 50f multi
**C88** AP15 60f multi
**C89** AP15 75f multi
**C90** AP15 100f multi
**C91** AP15 125f multi

Two souvenir sheets of 4 exist, 100f and 125f, picturing various aircraft and satellites.
For surcharges see Nos. C141, C146.

Intl. Year of the Disabled — AP16

Designs: Nos. C94-C99, Diff. flowers.
No. C100a, Emblem, natl. flag. b, Emblem on globe. c, Natl. colors, UN emblems. d, Disabled man, gifts, nurse.
No. C101a, Flags, globe and nurse. b, UN emblems, natl. flag. c, Emblem, disabled man. d, UN emblem, nurse.

**1982, June 1**

**C94** AP16 25f multi
**C95** AP16 50f multi
**C96** AP16 60f multi
**C97** AP16 75f multi
**C98** AP16 100f multi
**C99** AP16 125f multi

### Souvenir Sheets

**C100** Sheet of 4
*a.-d.* AP16 100f, any single
**C101** Sheet of 4
*a.-d.* AP16 125f, any single

For surcharge see No. C147.

Telecommunications Progress — AP17

Designs: 25f, FNRR communication center. 50f, Dish receivers, satellite, globe. 60f, Broadcast towers, dish receivers. 75f, Receivers, birds over plain. 100f, Receivers, satellite, telegraph key. No. C107, Receivers, passenger jet, Earth.
No. C108a, Receivers, Earth. b, Earth, television, flag and camera. c, Computer. d, Skyscraper, Earth, telephone.
No. C109a, Receivers, satellite, ship. b, Communication center, bolts of energy, receivers. c, Receivers, jet, ship, train, car, carriage. d, Radar.

**1982, July 1 Litho. *Perf. 14***

**C102** AP17 25f multi
**C103** AP17 50f multi
**C104** AP17 60f multi
**C105** AP17 75f multi
**C106** AP17 100f multi
**C107** AP17 125f multi

### Souvenir Sheets

**C108** Sheet of 4
*a.-d.* AP17 100f any single
**C109** Sheet of 4
*a.-d.* AP17 100f any single

For surcharges see Nos. C142, C148.

TB Bacillus Centenary — AP18

**1982 Litho. *Perf. 14***

**C110** AP18 25f multi
**C111** AP18 50f multi
**C112** AP18 60f multi
**C113** AP18 75f multi
**C114** AP18 100f multi
**C115** AP18 125f multi

### Souvenir Sheets

**C116** Sheet of 4, Fruit
*a.* AP18 100f, any single
**C117** Sheet of 4, Flowers
*a.* AP18 125f, any single

For surcharges see Nos. C143, C149.

1982 World Cup Soccer Championships, Spain — AP19

Various soccer plays.

**1982, Sept. 1 *Perf. 14***

**C118** AP19 25f multi
**C119** AP19 50f multi
**C120** AP19 60f multi
**C121** AP19 75f multi
**C122** AP19 100f multi
**C123** AP19 125f multi

Palestinian Children's Day — AP20

**1982, Oct. 20**

| | | |
|---|---|---|
| C126 | AP20 | 75f Boy |
| C127 | AP20 | 125f Girl |
| C128 | AP20 | 325f Boy and girl |
| a. | | Souvenir sheet of 1 |

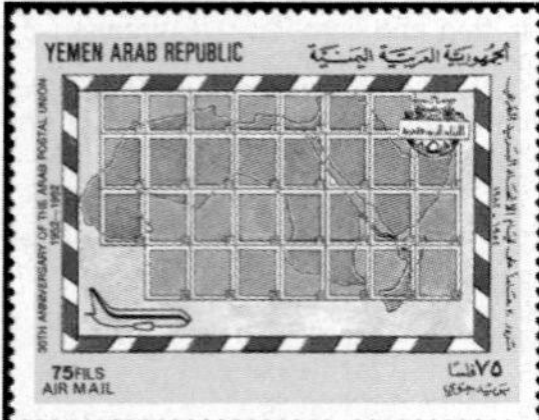

Arab Postal Union, 30th Anniv. — AP21

**1982, Dec. 1**

| | | |
|---|---|---|
| C129 | AP21 | 75f yellow & multi |
| C130 | AP21 | 125f green & multi |
| C131 | AP21 | 325f magenta & multi |
| a. | | Souvenir sheet of 1 |

1984 Summer Olympics, Los Angeles — AP22

**1984, Nov. 15**

| | | |
|---|---|---|
| C132 | AP22 | 20f Wrestling |
| C133 | AP22 | 30f Boxing |
| C134 | AP22 | 40f Running |
| C135 | AP22 | 60f Hurdling |
| C136 | AP22 | 150f Pole vault |
| C137 | AP22 | 325f Javelin throw |

Two souvenir sheets of four 75f stamps exist picturing water sports, gymnastics, weightlifting, shot put and discus throwing.

No. C67 Surcharged

Nos. 459, 461, 463, 466, 474, 483, 486, 522, C73, C75, C81, C83, C89, C91, C97, C105, C107, C113 & C115 Surcharged with New Value and "AIR MAIL"

**1993, Jan. 1** ***Perfs, etc. as Before***

| | | |
|---|---|---|
| C138 | AP12 | 3r on 125f #C67 |
| C139 | AP13 | 3r on 125f #C75 |
| C140 | AP14 | 3r on 125f #C83 |
| C141 | AP15 | 3r on 125f #C91 |
| C142 | AP17 | 3r on 125f #C107 |
| C143 | AP18 | 3r on 125f #C115 |
| C144 | AP13 | 5r on 75f #C73 |
| C145 | AP14 | 5r on 75f #C81 |
| C146 | AP15 | 5r on 75f #C89 |
| C147 | AP16 | 5r on 75f #C97 |
| C148 | AP17 | 5r on 75f #C105 |
| C149 | AP18 | 5r on 75f #C113 |
| C150 | A126 | 8r on 425f #459 |
| C151 | A127 | 8r on 425f #461 |
| C152 | A128 | 8r on 425f #463 |
| C153 | A129 | 8r on 425f #466 |
| C154 | A130 | 8r on 425f #474 |
| C155 | A132 | 8r on 425f #483 |
| C156 | A133 | 8r on 425f #486 |
| C157 | A142 | 12r on 850f #522 |

Size and location of surcharge varies.

## POSTAGE DUE STAMPS

D1

**1942 Litho. Wmk. 258** ***Perf. 12½***

| | | | | |
|---|---|---|---|---|
| J1 | D1 | 1b org & yel grn | .20 | .20 |
| J2 | D1 | 2b org & yel grn | .25 | .25 |
| J3 | D1 | 4b org & yel grn | .45 | .45 |
| J4 | D1 | 6b org & brt ultra | .55 | .55 |
| J5 | D1 | 8b org & brt ultra | .80 | .80 |
| J6 | D1 | 10b org & brt ultra | 1.00 | 1.00 |
| J7 | D1 | 12b org & brt ultra | 1.50 | 1.50 |
| J8 | D1 | 20b org & brt ultra | 3.00 | 3.00 |
| | | *Nos. J1-J8 (8)* | 7.75 | 7.75 |

Yemen had no postage due system. Nos. J1-J8 were used for regular postage.

See Nos. 66-67 for surcharges.

# YEMEN, PEOPLE'S DEMOCRATIC REPUBLIC OF

ˈpē-pəls ri-ˈpə-blik of ˈye-mən

LOCATION — Southern Arabia
GOVT. — Republic
AREA — 111,074 sq. mi.
POP. — 2,030,000 (est. 1981)
CAPITAL — Aden

The People's Republic of Southern Yemen was proclaimed Nov. 30, 1967, when the Federation of South Arabia achieved independence. It consisted of the former British colony of Aden and the protectorates. The name was changed to People's Democratic Republic of Yemen on Nov. 30, 1970. See South Arabia.

The Yemen Arab Republic and the People's Republic of Yemen planned a 30-month unification process scheduled for completion by November 1992. While government ministries merged, both currencies remained valid. A civil war in 1994 delayed the merger.

1,000 Fils = 1 Dinar

**Catalogue values for all unused stamps in this country are for Never Hinged items.**

### People's Republic of Southern Yemen

South Arabia Nos. 3-16 Overprinted in Red or Blue

جمهورية اليمن الجنوبية
الشعبية

Nos. 1-10

PEOPLE'S REPUBLIC
OF SOUTHERN YEMEN

جمهورية اليمن الجنوبية الشعبية

PEOPLE'S REPUBLIC
OF SOUTHERN YEMEN
Nos. 11-14

***Perf. 14½x14***

**1968, Apr. 1 Photo. Unwmk.**

| | | | | |
|---|---|---|---|---|
| 1 | A1 | 5f blue | .20 | .20 |
| 2 | A1 | 10f lt vio bl | .20 | .20 |
| 3 | A1 | 15f bl grn | .20 | .20 |
| 4 | A1 | 20f green | .20 | .20 |
| 5 | A1 | 25f org brn (B) | .20 | .20 |
| 6 | A1 | 30f lemon | .20 | .20 |
| 7 | A1 | 35f red brn (B) | .25 | .20 |
| 8 | A1 | 50f rose red (B) | .35 | .25 |
| 9 | A1 | 65f lt yel grn | .45 | .30 |
| 10 | A1 | 75f rose car (B) | .60 | .40 |
| 11 | A2 | 100f multi (B) | .90 | .50 |
| 12 | A2 | 250f multi | 1.75 | 1.00 |
| 13 | A2 | 500f multi (B) | 3.25 | 2.00 |
| 14 | A2 | 1d vio & multi | 8.25 | 5.00 |
| | | *Nos. 1-14 (14)* | 17.00 | 10.85 |

Globe and Flag A1

Designs: 15f, Revolutionist with broken chain and flames, vert. 50f, Aden Harbor. 100f, Cotton picking.

**1968, May 25 Litho.** ***Perf. 13x12½***

| | | | | |
|---|---|---|---|---|
| 15 | A1 | 10f multi | .20 | .20 |
| 16 | A1 | 15f multi | .20 | .20 |
| 17 | A1 | 50f multi | .30 | .30 |
| 18 | A1 | 100f multi | .65 | .65 |
| | | *Nos. 15-19 (5)* | 1.65 | 1.65 |

Independence Day, Nov. 30, 1967.

Girl Scouts at Campfire A2

Designs: 25f, Three Girl Scouts, vert. 50f, Three Girl Scout leaders.

***Perf. 13½***

**1968, Sept. 21 Litho. Unwmk.**

| | | | | |
|---|---|---|---|---|
| 19 | A2 | 10f ultra & sepia | .30 | .30 |
| 20 | A2 | 25f org brn & Prus bl | .40 | .40 |
| 21 | A2 | 50f yel, bl & brn | .80 | .80 |
| | | *Nos. 19-21 (3)* | 1.50 | 1.50 |

Girl Scout movement in Southern Yemen, established 1966 (in Aden).

Revolutionary — A3

"Freedom-Socialism-Unity" A4

King of Ausan, Alabaster Statue A5

Design: 30f, Radfan Mountains where first revolutionary fell.

**1968, Oct. 14 Unwmk.** ***Perf. 13***

| | | | | |
|---|---|---|---|---|
| 22 | A3 | 20f brn & lt bl | .25 | .25 |
| 23 | A3 | 30f grn & brn | .35 | .35 |
| 24 | A4 | 100f ver & yel | .90 | .90 |
| | | *Nos. 22-24 (3)* | 1.50 | 1.50 |

Revolution Day (revolution of Oct. 14, 1963).

**1968, Dec. 28 Litho.** ***Perf. 13***

Antiquities of Southern Yemen: 35f, African-type sculpture of a man. 50f, Winged bull, Assyrian-type bas-relief, horiz. 65f, Bull's head (Moon God), alabaster plaque, 230 B.C., horiz.

| | | | | |
|---|---|---|---|---|
| 25 | A5 | 5f olive & bister | .20 | .20 |
| 26 | A5 | 35f maroon & lt bl | .30 | .30 |
| 27 | A5 | 50f bister & blue | .65 | .65 |
| 28 | A5 | 65f lt grnsh bl & lilac | .85 | .85 |
| | | *Nos. 25-28 (4)* | 2.00 | 2.00 |

A6

A7

Martyr Monument, Steamer Point, Aden.

**1969, Feb. 11 Litho.** ***Perf. 13***

| | | | | |
|---|---|---|---|---|
| 29 | A6 | 15f yellow & multi | .20 | .20 |
| 30 | A6 | 35f emerald & multi | .20 | .20 |
| 31 | A6 | 100f orange & multi | .60 | .60 |
| | | *Nos. 29-31 (3)* | 1.00 | 1.00 |

Issued for Martyr Day.

**1969, June 1 Litho.** ***Perf. 13***

Albert Thomas Monument, Geneva, and ILO emblem.

| | | | | |
|---|---|---|---|---|
| 32 | A7 | 10f brt grn, blk & lt brn | .25 | .25 |
| 33 | A7 | 35f car rose, blk & lt brn | .75 | .75 |

50th anniv. of the ILO, and to honor founder Albert Thomas.

Classroom — A8

**1969, Sept. 8 Litho.** ***Perf. 13***

| | | | | |
|---|---|---|---|---|
| 34 | A8 | 35f orange & multi | .40 | .40 |
| 35 | A8 | 100f yellow & multi | 1.10 | 1.10 |

International Literacy Day, Sept. 8.

Mahatma Gandhi — A9

**1969, Sept. 27 Litho.** ***Perf. 13***

| | | | | |
|---|---|---|---|---|
| 36 | A9 | 35f lt ultra & vio brn | 1.10 | .40 |

Mohandas K. Gandhi (1869-1948), leader in India's fight for independence.

Family A10

**1969, Oct. 1**

| | | | | |
|---|---|---|---|---|
| 37 | A10 | 25f lt grn & multi | .50 | .40 |
| 38 | A10 | 75f car rose & multi | 1.00 | .60 |

Issued for Family Day.

UN Headquarters, NYC — A11

**1969, Oct. 24** ***Perf. 13***

| | | | | |
|---|---|---|---|---|
| **39** | A11 | 20f rose red & multi | .40 | .20 |
| **40** | A11 | 65f emer & multi | .85 | .40 |

Issued for United Nations Day.

Map and Flag of Southern Yemen — A12

40f, 50f, Tractors, flag (agricultural progress).

**1969, Nov. 30** **Litho.** **Unwmk.**

**Size: 41x24½mm**

| | | | | |
|---|---|---|---|---|
| **41** | A12 | 15f multi | .20 | .20 |
| **42** | A12 | 35f multi | .40 | .20 |

**Size: 37x37mm**

| | | | | |
|---|---|---|---|---|
| **43** | A12 | 40f blue & multi | .45 | .25 |
| **44** | A12 | 50f brown & multi | .70 | .35 |
| | | *Nos. 41-44 (4)* | 1.75 | 1.00 |

Second anniversary of independence.

Map of Arab League Countries, Flag and Emblem — A13

**1970, Mar. 22** **Unwmk.** ***Perf. 13***

| | | | | |
|---|---|---|---|---|
| **45** | A13 | 35f lt bl & multi | .75 | .25 |

25th anniversary of the Arab League.

Lenin — A14 Fighter — A15

**1970, Apr. 22** **Litho.** ***Perf. 13***

| | | | | |
|---|---|---|---|---|
| **46** | A14 | 75f multi | 1.25 | .50 |

Lenin (1870-1924), Russian communist leader.

**1970, May 15**

Designs: 35f, Underground soldier and plane destroyed on ground. 50f, Fighting people hailing Arab liberation flag, horiz.

| | | | | |
|---|---|---|---|---|
| **47** | A15 | 15f grn, red & blk | .20 | .20 |
| **48** | A15 | 35f grn, bl, red & blk | .40 | .35 |
| **49** | A15 | 50f grn, blk & red | .55 | .45 |
| | | *Nos. 47-49 (3)* | 1.15 | 1.00 |

Issued for Palestine Day.

UPU Headquarters, Bern — A16

**1970, May 22** **Litho.** ***Perf. 13***

| | | | | |
|---|---|---|---|---|
| **50** | A16 | 15f org & brt grn | .40 | .20 |
| **51** | A16 | 65f yel & car rose | .85 | .40 |

New UPU Headquarters in Bern.

Yemeni Costume — A17

Regional Costumes: 15f, 20f, Women's costumes. 50f, Three men of Aden.

**1970, July 2** **Litho.** ***Perf. 13***

| | | | | |
|---|---|---|---|---|
| **52** | A17 | 10f yel & multi | .25 | .20 |
| **53** | A17 | 15f lt lil & multi | .25 | .20 |
| **54** | A17 | 20f lt bl & multi | .40 | .20 |
| **55** | A17 | 50f multi | .85 | .30 |
| | | *Nos. 52-55 (4)* | 1.75 | .90 |

Camel and Calf — A18

Designs: 25f, Goats. 35f, Arabian oryx. 65f, Socotra dwarf cows.

**1970, Aug. 31** **Litho.** ***Perf. 13***

| | | | | |
|---|---|---|---|---|
| **56** | A18 | 15f dk brn & multi | .25 | .20 |
| **57** | A18 | 25f car rose & multi | .45 | .30 |
| **58** | A18 | 35f ultra & multi | .90 | .60 |
| **59** | A18 | 65f brt grn & multi | 1.40 | .90 |
| | | *Nos. 56-59 (4)* | 3.00 | 2.00 |

A19

35f, Natl. Front Organization Headquarters. 50f, Farm worker, 1970, battle scene, 1963.

**1970, Oct. 14** **Litho.** ***Perf. 13***

**Size: 41½x29½mm**

| | | | | |
|---|---|---|---|---|
| **60** | A19 | 25f multi | .35 | .20 |

**Size: 56½x27mm**

| | | | | |
|---|---|---|---|---|
| **61** | A19 | 35f multi | .45 | .30 |

**Size: 41x24½mm**

| | | | | |
|---|---|---|---|---|
| **62** | A19 | 50f multi | .70 | .40 |
| | | *Nos. 60-62 (3)* | 1.50 | .90 |

7th anniversary of Oct. 14 Revolution.

UN Headquarters, Emblem — A20

**1970, Oct. 24** **Litho.** ***Perf. 13***

| | | | | |
|---|---|---|---|---|
| **63** | A20 | 10f org & bl | .40 | .20 |
| **64** | A20 | 65f brt pink & bl | .85 | .45 |

25th anniversary of the United Nations.

## People's Democratic Republic of Yemen

Temples at Philae — A21

**1971, Feb. 1** **Litho.** ***Perf. 13½x13***

| | | | | |
|---|---|---|---|---|
| **65** | A21 | 5f violet & multi | .20 | .20 |
| **66** | A21 | 35f blue & multi | .40 | .25 |
| **67** | A21 | 65f green & multi | .95 | .55 |
| | | *Nos. 65-67 (3)* | 1.55 | 1.00 |

UNESCO campaign to save the monuments in Nubia.

Scales, Book and Sword A22

**1971, Mar. 1** ***Perf. 13x12½***

| | | | | |
|---|---|---|---|---|
| **68** | A22 | 10f brt pink & multi | .20 | .20 |
| **69** | A22 | 15f brt grn & multi | .20 | .20 |
| **70** | A22 | 35f lt ultra & multi | .30 | .30 |
| **71** | A22 | 50f rose & multi | .40 | .40 |
| | | *Nos. 68-71 (4)* | 1.10 | 1.10 |

First Constitution, 1971.

Men of 3 Races, Human Rights Emblem A23

**1971, Mar. 21**

| | | | | |
|---|---|---|---|---|
| **72** | A23 | 20f lt bl & multi | .20 | .20 |
| **73** | A23 | 35f grn & multi | .40 | .40 |
| **74** | A23 | 75f lt vio & multi | .65 | .65 |
| | | *Nos. 72-74 (3)* | 1.25 | 1.25 |

Intl. year against racial discrimination.

Map and Flag — A24

"Brothers' Blood" Tree, Socotra Island — A25

**1971-77** **Litho.** ***Perf. 13½***

| | | | | |
|---|---|---|---|---|
| **75** | A24 | 5f yel & multi | .20 | .20 |
| **76** | A24 | 10f grn & multi | .20 | .20 |
| **77** | A24 | 15f yel & multi | .20 | .20 |
| **78** | A24 | 20f org & multi | .20 | .20 |
| **79** | A24 | 25f bl & multi | .20 | .20 |
| **80** | A24 | 35f red org & multi | .25 | .20 |
| **81** | A24 | 40f vio & multi | .35 | .20 |
| **82** | A24 | 50f yel grn & multi | .50 | .30 |
| **82A** | A24 | 60f red & multi | 1.00 | .40 |
| **83** | A24 | 65f pale vio & multi | .65 | .45 |
| **84** | A24 | 80f org brn & multi | .75 | .55 |
| **84A** | A24 | 90f ol & multi | 1.00 | .50 |

***Perf. 13***

| | | | | |
|---|---|---|---|---|
| **84B** | A25 | 110f brn & multi | 1.50 | .65 |
| **85** | A25 | 125f ultra & multi | 1.25 | 1.10 |
| **86** | A25 | 250f org & multi | 2.25 | 1.40 |
| **87** | A25 | 500f multi | 4.50 | 2.75 |
| **88** | A25 | 1d grn & multi | 10.00 | 6.00 |
| | | *Nos. 75-88 (17)* | 25.00 | 15.50 |

Issued: #82A, 84A-84B, 10/17/77; others, 4/1/71.

See Nos. 332-333. For surcharges see Yemen Nos. 628, 638.

Machine Gun and Map A26 Arms with Wrench and Cogwheel A27

Designs: 45f, Woman fighter and flame, horiz. 50f, Fighter, factories and rainbow.

**1971, June 9** **Litho.** ***Perf. 12½x13***

| | | | | |
|---|---|---|---|---|
| **89** | A26 | 15f multi | .20 | .20 |
| **90** | A26 | 45f green & multi | .50 | .30 |
| **91** | A26 | 50f multi | .80 | .50 |
| | | *Nos. 89-91 (3)* | 1.50 | 1.00 |

Armed revolution in the Arabian Gulf.

**1971, June 22**

25f, Torch, factories, symbols. 65f, Windmill.

| | | | | |
|---|---|---|---|---|
| **92** | A27 | 15f blue & multi | *.25* | *.25* |
| **93** | A27 | 25f multi | *.75* | *.55* |
| **94** | A27 | 65f multi | *1.25* | *.75* |
| | | *Nos. 92-94 (3)* | *2.25* | *1.55* |

2nd anniversary of the revolution of June 22, 1969 (Corrective Move).

A 20f picturing a fighter holding rifle and flag, with flag colors transposed, was withdrawn on day of issue.

Revolutionary Emblem — A28

40f, Map of southern Arabia & flag of republic.

**1971, Sept. 26**

| | | | | |
|---|---|---|---|---|
| **95** | A28 | 10f yellow & multi | .20 | .20 |
| **96** | A28 | 40f lt grn & multi | .60 | .40 |

9th anniv. of the revolution of Sept. 26.

Gamal Abdel Nasser — A29

UNICEF Emblem, Children of the World — A30

**1971, Sept. 28** **Litho.** ***Perf. 12½x13***

| | | | | |
|---|---|---|---|---|
| **97** | A29 | 65f multi | .80 | .50 |

1st anniv. of the death of Gamal Abdel Nasser (1918-1970), President of Egypt.

**1971, Dec. 11** ***Perf. 13x13½***

| | | | | |
|---|---|---|---|---|
| **98** | A30 | 15f org, car & blk | .20 | .20 |
| **99** | A30 | 40f lt ultra, car & blk | .30 | .25 |
| **100** | A30 | 50f yel grn, car & blk | .50 | .40 |
| | | *Nos. 98-100 (3)* | 1.00 | .85 |

25th anniv. of UNICEF.

Pigeons A31

Birds: 40f, Partridge. 65f, Partridge and guinea fowl. 100f, European kite.

**1971, Dec. 22** ***Perf. 13½x13***

| | | | | |
|---|---|---|---|---|
| **101** | A31 | 5f bl, blk & car | .25 | .20 |
| **102** | A31 | 40f salmon & multi | .90 | .50 |
| **103** | A31 | 65f brt grn, blk & car | 2.10 | .75 |
| **104** | A31 | 100f yel, blk & car | 3.50 | 1.50 |
| | | *Nos. 101-104 (4)* | 6.75 | 2.95 |

Dhow under Construction A32

Design: 80f, Dhow under sail, vert.

**1972, Feb. 15** ***Perf. 13½x13, 13x13½***

| | | | | |
|---|---|---|---|---|
| **105** | A32 | 25f bl, brn & yel | .40 | .25 |
| **106** | A32 | 80f lt bl & multi | 1.25 | .90 |

Band — A33

Designs: 25f, 40f, 80f, Various folk dances.

**1972, Apr. 8** **Litho.** ***Perf. 13***

| | | | | |
|---|---|---|---|---|
| **107** | A33 | 10f lt grn & multi | .20 | .20 |
| **108** | A33 | 25f org & multi | .30 | .25 |
| **109** | A33 | 40f red & multi | .60 | .35 |
| **110** | A33 | 80f blue & multi | 1.10 | .75 |
| | | *Nos. 107-110 (4)* | 2.20 | 1.55 |

Palestinian Fighter and Barbed Wire — A34

**1972, May 15**

| | | | | |
|---|---|---|---|---|
| **111** | A34 | 5f emerald & multi | .25 | .20 |
| **112** | A34 | 20f blue & multi | .50 | .30 |
| **113** | A34 | 65f org ver & multi | 1.25 | .75 |
| | | *Nos. 111-113 (3)* | 2.00 | 1.25 |

Struggle for Palestine liberation.

Policemen on Parade A35

Design: 80f, Militia women on parade.

**1972, June 20** **Litho.** ***Perf. 13½***

| | | | | |
|---|---|---|---|---|
| **114** | A35 | 25f lt bl & multi | .30 | .20 |
| **115** | A35 | 80f bl grn & multi | 1.25 | .75 |
| *a.* | | Souv. sheet of 2, #114-115 | 4.25 | 4.25 |

Police Day. No. 115a sold for 150f.

Start of Bicycle Race A36

15f Parade of young women. 40f, Yemeni Guides & Scouts on parade. 80f, Acrobats, vert.

**1972, July 20** **Litho.** ***Perf. 13½***

| | | | | |
|---|---|---|---|---|
| **116** | A36 | 10f lt bl & multi | .25 | .20 |
| **117** | A36 | 15f multi | .25 | .20 |
| **118** | A36 | 40f buff & multi | .50 | .35 |
| **119** | A36 | 80f lt ultra & multi | 1.25 | .50 |
| | | *Nos. 116-119 (4)* | 2.25 | 1.25 |

Turtle A37

**1972, Sept. 2** **Litho.** ***Perf. 13***

| | | | | |
|---|---|---|---|---|
| **120** | A37 | 15f Shown | .45 | .20 |
| **121** | A37 | 40f Sailfish | .60 | .35 |
| **122** | A37 | 65f Kingfish | .75 | .45 |
| **123** | A37 | 125f Spiny lobster | 1.50 | .80 |
| | | *Nos. 120-123 (4)* | 3.30 | 1.80 |

Book Year Emblem A38

**1972, Sept. 9**

| | | | | |
|---|---|---|---|---|
| **124** | A38 | 40f red, ultra & yel | .55 | .35 |
| **125** | A38 | 65f org, ultra & yel | .85 | .60 |

International Book Year 1972.

Farm Couple and Fields A39

**1972, Nov. 23** **Litho.** ***Perf. 13***

| | | | | |
|---|---|---|---|---|
| **126** | A39 | 10f orange & multi | .20 | .20 |
| **127** | A39 | 25f rose lilac & multi | .45 | .30 |
| **128** | A39 | 40f red & multi | .75 | .50 |
| | | *Nos. 126-128 (3)* | 1.40 | 1.00 |

Lands Day, publicizing land reforms.

Militia — A40

20f, Soldier guarding village. 65f, Industrial, agricultural and educational progress, vert.

**1972, Dec. 2** **Litho.** ***Perf. 13***

| | | | | |
|---|---|---|---|---|
| **129** | A40 | 5f multi | .20 | .20 |
| **130** | A40 | 20f multi | .20 | .20 |
| **131** | A40 | 65f multi | .45 | .45 |
| *a.* | | Souv. sheet of 3, #129-131, imperf. | 1.75 | 1.75 |
| | | *Nos. 129-131 (3)* | .85 | .85 |

5th anniversary of independence.

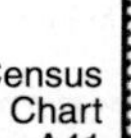

Census Chart A41

**1973, Apr. 3** **Litho.** ***Perf. 12½x13½***

| | | | | |
|---|---|---|---|---|
| **132** | A41 | 25f org, emer & ol | .20 | .20 |
| **133** | A41 | 40f rose, bl & vio | .35 | .35 |

Population census 1973.

WHO Emblem and "25" — A42

**1973, Apr. 7** ***Perf. 14x12½, 12½x14***

| | | | | |
|---|---|---|---|---|
| **134** | A42 | 5f "25" and WHO emblem, vert | .20 | .20 |
| **135** | A42 | 20f Shown | .20 | .20 |
| **136** | A42 | 125f "25" and WHO emblem | .60 | .60 |
| | | *Nos. 134-136 (3)* | 1.00 | 1.00 |

25th anniv. of the WHO.

Elephant Bay A43

Tourist Publicity: 20f, Taweels Tanks Reservoir, vert. 25f, Shibam Town. 100f, Al-Mohdar Mosque, Tarim.

**1973, June 9** **Litho.** ***Perf. 13***

| | | | | |
|---|---|---|---|---|
| **137** | A43 | 20f multi | .20 | .20 |
| **138** | A43 | 25f multi | .20 | .20 |
| **139** | A43 | 40f multi | .30 | .30 |
| **140** | A43 | 100f multi | .55 | .55 |
| | | *Nos. 137-140 (4)* | 1.25 | 1.25 |

Office Buildings and Slum, Aden — A44

Design: 80f, Intersection, Aden, vert.

**1973, Aug. 4** **Litho.** ***Perf. 13***

| | | | | |
|---|---|---|---|---|
| **141** | A44 | 20f multi | .20 | .20 |
| **142** | A44 | 80f multi | .50 | .50 |

Nationalization of buildings.

Army Unit A45

People's Army: 20f, Four marching soldiers. 40f, Sailors on parade. 80f, Tanks.

**1973, Sept. 1**

| | | | | |
|---|---|---|---|---|
| **143** | A45 | 10f multi | .20 | .20 |
| **144** | A45 | 20f multi | .20 | .20 |
| **145** | A45 | 40f multi | .30 | .30 |
| **146** | A45 | 80f multi | .50 | .50 |
| | | *Nos. 143-146 (4)* | 1.20 | 1.20 |

FAO Emblem, Loading Food A46

Design: 80f, Workers and grain sacks.

**1973, Dec. 19** **Litho.** ***Perf. 13***

| | | | | |
|---|---|---|---|---|
| **147** | A46 | 20f blue & multi | .20 | .20 |
| **148** | A46 | 80f blue & multi | .50 | .50 |

World Food Program, 10th anniversary.

Letter and UPU Emblem A47

UPU Emblem and Yemeni Flag — A48

Map of Yemen, UPU Emblem — A49

UPU cent.: 20f, "100" formed by people, and UPU emblem.

**1974, Oct. 9** **Litho.** ***Perf. 12½x13½***

| | | | | |
|---|---|---|---|---|
| **149** | A47 | 5f multi | .20 | .20 |
| **150** | A47 | 20f multi | .20 | .20 |
| **151** | A48 | 40f multi | .35 | .35 |
| **152** | A49 | 125f multi | .60 | .60 |
| | | *Nos. 149-152 (4)* | 1.35 | 1.35 |

Irrigation System — A50

Progress in Agriculture: 20f, Bulldozer pushing soil. 100f, Tractors plowing field.

**1974** **Litho.** ***Perf. 13***

| | | | | |
|---|---|---|---|---|
| **153** | A50 | 10f multi | .20 | .20 |
| **154** | A50 | 20f multi | .20 | .20 |
| **155** | A50 | 100f multi | .50 | .50 |
| | | *Nos. 153-155 (3)* | .90 | .90 |

Lathe Operator — A51

Industrial progress: 40f, Printers. 80f, Women textile workers, horiz.

**1975, May 1** **Litho.** ***Perf. 13***

| | | | | |
|---|---|---|---|---|
| **156** | A51 | 10f multi | .20 | .20 |
| **157** | A51 | 40f multi | .30 | .30 |
| **158** | A51 | 80f multi | .50 | .50 |
| | | *Nos. 156-158 (3)* | 1.00 | 1.00 |

Yemeni Woman — A52

Designs: Various women's costumes.

**1975, Nov. 15 Litho. *Perf. 11½x12***

| | | | | |
|---|---|---|---|---|
| **159** | A52 | 5f blk & ocher | .20 | .20 |
| **160** | A52 | 10f blk & vio | .20 | .20 |
| **161** | A52 | 15f blk & olive | .20 | .20 |
| **162** | A52 | 25f blk & rose lil | .25 | .25 |
| **163** | A52 | 40f blk & Prus bl | .40 | .40 |
| **164** | A52 | 50f blk & org brn | .60 | .60 |
| | | *Nos. 159-164 (6)* | 1.85 | 1.85 |

Women Factory Workers, IWY Emblem A53

**1975, Dec. 30 Litho. *Perf. 12x11½***

| | | | | |
|---|---|---|---|---|
| **165** | A53 | 40f blk & salmon | .25 | .25 |
| **166** | A53 | 50f blk & yel grn | .40 | .40 |

International Women's Year 1975.

Soccer Player and Field — A54

Designs: Different scenes from soccer.

**1976, Apr. 1 Litho. *Perf. 11½x12***

| | | | | |
|---|---|---|---|---|
| **167** | A54 | 5f lt bl & brn | .20 | .20 |
| **168** | A54 | 40f yel & green | .30 | .30 |
| **169** | A54 | 80f salmon & vio | .50 | .50 |
| | | *Nos. 167-169 (3)* | 1.00 | 1.00 |

Rocket Take-off from Moon — A55

15f, Alexander Satalov. 40f, Lunokhod on moon, horiz. 65f, Valentina Tereshkova, rocket.

***Perf. 11½x12, 12x11½***

**1976, Apr. 17 Litho.**

| | | | | |
|---|---|---|---|---|
| **170** | A55 | 10f multi | .20 | .20 |
| **171** | A55 | 15f multi | .20 | .20 |
| **172** | A55 | 40f multi | .40 | .40 |
| **173** | A55 | 65f multi | .55 | .55 |
| | | *Nos. 170-173 (4)* | 1.35 | 1.35 |

Soviet cosmonauts and space program.

Traffic Policemen A56

**1977, Apr. 16 Litho. *Perf. 14***

| | | | | |
|---|---|---|---|---|
| **174** | A56 | 25f red & blk | .30 | .30 |
| **175** | A56 | 60f yel & blk | .60 | .60 |
| **176** | A56 | 75f grn & blk | .75 | .75 |
| **177** | A56 | 110f dp bl & blk | 1.00 | 1.00 |
| | | *Nos. 174-177 (4)* | 2.65 | 2.65 |

Traffic change to right side of road.

APU Emblem — A57

**1977, Apr. 12 Litho. *Perf. 13½***

| | | | | |
|---|---|---|---|---|
| **178** | A57 | 20f lt bl & multi | .20 | .20 |
| **179** | A57 | 60f gray & multi | .40 | .40 |
| **180** | A57 | 70f lt grn & multi | .50 | .50 |
| **181** | A57 | 90f bl grn & multi | .55 | .55 |
| | | *Nos. 178-181 (4)* | 1.65 | 1.65 |

Arab Postal Union, 25th anniversary.

Congress Decree and Red Star A58

Designs: 25f, Pres. Salim Rubi'a Ali, Council members Ali Nasser Muhamed and Abdul Farta Ismail. 65f, Women's militia on parade. 95f, Aerial view of textile mill.

**1977, May Photo. *Perf. 13***

| | | | | |
|---|---|---|---|---|
| **182** | A58 | 25f grn, gold & dk brn | .20 | .20 |
| **183** | A58 | 35f red, gold & lt bl | .25 | .25 |
| **184** | A58 | 65f bl, gold & lil | .40 | .40 |
| **185** | A58 | 95f org, gold & grn | .45 | .45 |
| | | *Nos. 182-185 (4)* | 1.30 | 1.30 |

Unification Congress, 1st anniversary.

Afrivoluta Pringlei A59

Shells: 60f, Festilyria duponti, vert. 110f, Conus splendidulus. 180f, Cypraea 4broderipii.

**1977, July 16 Litho. *Perf. 13½***

| | | | | |
|---|---|---|---|---|
| **186** | A59 | 60f multi | .40 | .30 |
| **187** | A59 | 90f multi | .60 | .30 |
| **188** | A59 | 110f multi | 1.00 | .60 |
| **189** | A59 | 180f multi | 1.40 | 1.00 |
| | | *Nos. 186-189 (4)* | 3.40 | 2.20 |

Emblem and Flag — A60

Designs: 20f, Man with broken chain. 90f, Pipeline, agriculture and industry. 110f, Flag, symbolic tree and hands holding tools.

**1977, Nov. 30 Litho. *Perf. 13½***

| | | | | |
|---|---|---|---|---|
| **190** | A60 | 5f blk & multi | .20 | .20 |
| **191** | A60 | 20f blk & multi | .20 | .20 |
| **192** | A60 | 90f blk & multi | .30 | .20 |
| **193** | A60 | 110f blk & multi | .50 | .25 |
| | | *Nos. 190-193 (4)* | 1.20 | .85 |

10th anniversary of independence.

Dome of the Rock A61

**1978, May 15 *Perf. 12***

| | | | | |
|---|---|---|---|---|
| **194** | A61 | 5f multi | *.65* | *.35* |

Palestinian fighters & families. See #264A.

Congress Emblem and "CUBA" — A62

Designs: 60f, Congress emblem. 90f, Festival emblem as flower. 110f, Festival emblem, dove, young man and woman.

**1978, June 22 Litho. *Perf. 14***

| | | | | |
|---|---|---|---|---|
| **195** | A62 | 5f multi | .20 | .20 |
| **196** | A62 | 60f multi | .55 | .35 |
| **197** | A62 | 90f multi | .70 | .40 |
| **198** | A62 | 110f multi | .90 | .60 |
| | | *Nos. 195-198 (4)* | 2.35 | 1.55 |

11th World Youth Festival, Havana.

Silver Ornaments — A63

Designs: Various silver ornaments.

**1978, July 22 Litho. *Perf. 13½***

| | | | | |
|---|---|---|---|---|
| **199** | A63 | 10f blk & multi | .20 | .20 |
| **200** | A63 | 15f blk & multi | .20 | .20 |
| **201** | A63 | 20f blk & multi | .20 | .20 |
| **202** | A63 | 60f blk & multi | .20 | .20 |
| **203** | A63 | 90f blk & multi | .40 | .25 |
| **204** | A63 | 110f blk & multi | .50 | .30 |
| | | *Nos. 199-204 (6)* | 1.70 | 1.35 |

For surcharge see Yemen No. 629.

Yemeni Musical Instruments — A64

**1978, Aug. 26 *Perf. 14***

| | | | | |
|---|---|---|---|---|
| **205** | A64 | 35f Almarfaai | .20 | .20 |
| **206** | A64 | 60f Almizmar | .25 | .20 |
| **207** | A64 | 90f Alqnboos | .30 | .20 |
| **208** | A64 | 110f Simsimiya | .50 | .30 |
| | | *Nos. 205-208 (4)* | 1.25 | .90 |

For surcharge see Yemen No. 630.

"V" for Vanguard A65

Man with Palm, Factories — A66

**1978, Oct. 11 Litho. *Perf. 14***

| | | | | |
|---|---|---|---|---|
| **209** | A65 | 5f multi | .20 | .20 |
| **210** | A65 | 20f multi | .20 | .20 |
| **211** | A65 | 60f multi | .25 | .20 |
| **212** | A65 | 180f multi | .50 | .30 |
| | | *Nos. 209-212 (4)* | 1.15 | .90 |

1st Conf. of Vanguard Party, Oct. 11-13.

**1978, Oct. 14**

Designs: 10f, Palm branches, broken chains, horiz. 60f, Candle and "15." 110f, Woman and man with rifle, "15."

| | | | | |
|---|---|---|---|---|
| **213** | A66 | 10f multi | .20 | .20 |
| **214** | A66 | 35f multi | .20 | .20 |
| **215** | A66 | 60f multi | .40 | .20 |
| **216** | A66 | 110f multi | .70 | .40 |
| | | *Nos. 213-216 (4)* | 1.50 | 1.00 |

15th Revolution Day.

For surcharge see Yemen No. 631.

Child, Map of Arabia and IYC Emblem — A67

**1979, Mar. 20 Litho. *Perf. 13½***

| | | | | |
|---|---|---|---|---|
| **217** | A67 | 15f multi | .20 | .20 |
| **218** | A67 | 20f multi | .20 | .20 |
| **219** | A67 | 60f multi | .25 | .20 |
| **220** | A67 | 90f multi | .35 | .20 |
| | | *Nos. 217-220 (4)* | 1.00 | .80 |

International Year of the Child.

Sickle, Star, Tractor, Wheat and Dove — A68

Designs: 35f, Pylon, star, compass, wheat and hammer. 60f, Students, worker and clock. 90f, Woman with raised arms, doves and star.

**1979, June 22 Litho. *Perf. 14***

| | | | | |
|---|---|---|---|---|
| **221** | A68 | 20f multi | .20 | .20 |
| **222** | A68 | 35f multi | .20 | .20 |
| **223** | A68 | 60f multi | .25 | .20 |
| **224** | A68 | 90f multi | .35 | .20 |
| | | *Nos. 221-224 (4)* | 1.00 | .80 |

Corrective Move, 10th anniversary.

Yemen #52, Hill A69

Hill and: 110f, Yemen #56. 250f, Aden #12.

**1979, Aug. 27 Litho. *Perf. 14***

| | | | | |
|---|---|---|---|---|
| **225** | A69 | 90f multi | .30 | .20 |
| **226** | A69 | 110f multi | .40 | .25 |

**Souvenir Sheet**

| | | | | |
|---|---|---|---|---|
| **227** | A69 | 250f multi | 1.00 | 1.00 |

Sir Rowland Hill (1795-1879), originator of penny postage.

Book, World Map, Arab Achievements — A70

**1979, Sept. 26 Litho. *Perf. 14***

**228** A70 60f multi .25 .20

Party Emblem — A71

Cassia Adenesis — A72

**1979, Oct. 13 *Perf. 14½x14***

**229** A71 60f multi .25 .20

Yemeni Socialist Party, 1st anniversary.

**1979, Nov. 30 Litho. *Perf. 13½***

Flowers: 90f, Nerium oleander. 110f, Calligonum comosum. 180f, Adenium obesium.

| | | | | |
|---|---|---|---|---|
| **230** | A72 | 20f multi | .20 | .20 |
| **231** | A72 | 90f multi | .65 | .35 |
| **232** | A72 | 110f multi | 1.00 | .50 |
| **233** | A72 | 180f multi | 1.25 | .65 |
| | | *Nos. 230-233 (4)* | 3.10 | 1.70 |

For surcharge see Yemen No. 632.

First Anniv. of Iranian Revolution — A73

**1980, Feb. 12 Litho. *Perf. 13½***

**234** A73 60f multi .25 .25

Dido A74

**1980, Mar. 5 Litho. *Perf. 13½***

| | | | | |
|---|---|---|---|---|
| **235** | A74 | 110f shown | .65 | .30 |
| **236** | A74 | 180f Anglia | .90 | .40 |
| **237** | A74 | 250f India | 1.25 | .50 |
| | | *Nos. 235-237 (3)* | 2.80 | 1.20 |

For surcharge see Yemen No. 633.

Basket Maker, London 1980 Emblem — A75

**1980, May 6 Litho. *Perf. 14***

| | | | | |
|---|---|---|---|---|
| **238** | A75 | 60f shown | .20 | .20 |
| **239** | A75 | 90f Hubble bubble pipe maker | .30 | .20 |
| **240** | A75 | 110f Weaver | .40 | .25 |
| **241** | A75 | 250f Potter | .90 | .50 |
| | | *Nos. 238-241 (4)* | 1.80 | 1.15 |

London 1980 Intl. Stamp Exhib., May 6-14.

Hemprich's Skink — A76

**1980, May 8 Litho. *Perf. 14***

| | | | | |
|---|---|---|---|---|
| **242** | A76 | 20f shown | .20 | .20 |
| **243** | A76 | 35f Mole viper | .30 | .20 |
| **244** | A76 | 110f Carter's day gecko | .75 | .30 |
| **245** | A76 | 180f Cobra | 1.25 | .60 |
| | | *Nos. 242-245 (4)* | 2.50 | 1.30 |

For surcharge see Yemen No. 634.

Misha and Olympic Emblem — A77

Farmers Armed — A78

**1980, July 19 Litho. *Perf. 12½x12***

**246** A77 110f multi .50 .30

For overprint see No. 287.

**1980, Oct. 17 *Perf. 13½***

| | | | | |
|---|---|---|---|---|
| **247** | A78 | 50f Armed farmers working, horiz. | .30 | .20 |
| **248** | A78 | 90f shown | .45 | .30 |
| **249** | A78 | 110f Sickle (wheat) and fist | .60 | .40 |
| | | *Nos. 247-249 (3)* | 1.35 | .90 |

10th anniversary of farmers' uprising.

110th Birth Anniversary of Lenin — A79

**1980, Nov. 7 Litho. *Perf. 12***

**250** A79 35f multi .20 .20

Douglas DC-3 — A80

**1981, Mar. 11 Litho. *Perf. 13½***

| | | | | |
|---|---|---|---|---|
| **251** | A80 | 60f shown | .20 | .20 |
| **252** | A80 | 90f Boeing 707 | .40 | .20 |
| **253** | A80 | 250f DHC Dash 7 | 1.00 | .50 |
| | | *Nos. 251-253 (3)* | 1.60 | .90 |

Democratic Yemen Airlines, 10th anniv.

Ras Boradli Earth Satellite Station A82

**1981, June 22 Litho. *Perf. 12***

**257** A82 60f multi .40 .30

Conocarpus Lancifolius — A83

Supreme People's Council, 10th Anniv. — A84

**1981, Aug. 1 Litho. *Perf. 12***

| | | | | |
|---|---|---|---|---|
| **258** | A83 | 90f shown | .30 | .20 |
| **259** | A83 | 180f Ficus vasta | .70 | .40 |
| **260** | A83 | 250f Maerua crassifolia | 1.00 | .65 |
| | | *Nos. 258-260 (3)* | 2.00 | 1.25 |

**1981, Aug. 18 Litho. *Perf. 15x14½***

**261** A84 180f multi .65 .40

Desert Fox — A85

**1981, Sept. 26 Litho. *Perf. 14½***

| | | | | |
|---|---|---|---|---|
| **262** | A85 | 50f shown | .30 | .20 |
| **263** | A85 | 90f South Arabian leopard | .60 | .30 |
| **264** | A85 | 250f Ibex | 1.40 | .75 |
| | | *Nos. 262-264 (3)* | 2.30 | 1.25 |

No. 194 Redrawn

**1981, Oct. 15 Litho. *Perf. 12***

**Size: 25x27mm**

**264A** A61 5f multi .20 .20

Denomination in upper right.

Tephrosia Apollinea — A86

**1981, Nov. 30 Litho. *Perf. 13½***

| | | | | |
|---|---|---|---|---|
| **265** | A86 | 50f shown | .20 | .20 |
| **266** | A86 | 90f Citrullus colocynthis | .30 | .20 |
| **267** | A86 | 110f Aloe sqarrosa | .40 | .20 |
| **268** | A86 | 250f Lawsonia inermis | 1.00 | .60 |
| | | *Nos. 265-268 (4)* | 1.90 | 1.20 |

For surcharge see Yemen No. 635.

Intl. Year of the Disabled A87

**1981, Dec. 12 Litho. *Perf. 14½***

| | | | | |
|---|---|---|---|---|
| **269** | A87 | 50f multi | .20 | .20 |
| **270** | A87 | 100f multi | .40 | .20 |
| **271** | A87 | 150f multi | .60 | .40 |
| | | *Nos. 269-271 (3)* | 1.20 | .80 |

TB Bacillus Centenary — A88

**1982, Mar. 24 Litho. *Perf. 14½***

**272** A88 50f multi .30 .20

30th Anniv. of Arab Postal Union A89

**1982, Apr. 12 Litho. *Perf. 14***

**273** A89 100f multi .50 .30

1982 World Cup A90

Designs: Various soccer players.

**1982, June 13 Litho. *Perf. 14***

| | | | | |
|---|---|---|---|---|
| **274** | A90 | 50f multi | .25 | .20 |
| **275** | A90 | 100f multi | .50 | .30 |
| **276** | A90 | 150f multi | .70 | .45 |
| **277** | A90 | 200f multi | 1.00 | .60 |
| *a.* | | Souv. sheet of 4, #274-277 | 2.50 | 1.50 |
| | | *Nos. 274-277 (4)* | 2.45 | 1.55 |

For overprints see Nos. 281-284.

60th Anniv. of USSR A93

**1982, Dec. 22 Litho. *Perf. 12½x12***

**280** A93 50f Flags, arms .50 .35

Nos. 274-277, 277a Ovptd. with Emblem and "WORLD CUP / WINNERS / 1982 / 1st ITALY / 2nd W-GERMANY / 3rd POLAND / 4th FRANCE" in Blue

**1982, Dec. 30 Litho. *Perf. 14***

| | | | | |
|---|---|---|---|---|
| **281** | A90 | 50f multi | .20 | .20 |
| **282** | A90 | 100f multi | .40 | .40 |
| **283** | A90 | 150f multi | .60 | .60 |
| **284** | A90 | 200f multi | .70 | .70 |
| *a.* | | Souvenir sheet of 4, #281-284 | 2.00 | 2.00 |
| | | *Nos. 281-284 (4)* | 1.90 | 1.90 |

Palestinian Solidarity A94

**1983, Apr. 10 *Perf. 13½x14½***

| | | | | |
|---|---|---|---|---|
| **285** | A94 | 50f Yasser Arafat | .20 | .20 |
| **286** | A94 | 100f Arafat, Dome of the Rock | .40 | .40 |
| *a.* | | Souvenir sheet of 1, imperf. | .50 | .50 |

No. 246 Ovptd. with TEMBAL '83 Emblem in Yellow

**1983, May 21 *Perf. 12½x12***

**287** A77 110f multi .40 .40

World Communications Year — A95

Designs: 50f, Correspondent, postrider, ship. 100f, Postman, coach, telegraph. No. 290, Telephones, bus. 200f, Telecommunications. No. 292, Montage.

**1983, June 10** *Perf. 13x13½*
**288** A95 50f blk & brt bl .20 .20
**289** A95 100f multi .40 .40
**290** A95 150f multi .60 .60
**291** A95 200f multi .70 .70
*Nos. 288-291 (4)* 1.90 1.90

### Souvenir Sheet

**292** A95 150f multi 1.50 1.50

Pablo Picasso (1881-1973), Painter — A96

Paintings: No. 293, The Poor Family, 1903. No. 294, Woman with Crow. No. 295a, The Gourmet. No. 295b, Woman with Child on Beach. No. 295c, Sitting Beggar. No. 296, The Solar Family, horiz.

**1983, July 25** *Perf. 14*
**293** A96 50f multi .20 .20
**294** A96 100f multi .40 .40

### Souvenir Sheets

**295** Sheet of 3 3.50 3.50
*a.* A96 50f multi .50 .50
*b.* A96 100f multi 1.25 1.25
*c.* A96 150f multi 1.75 1.75
**296** A96 150f multi 8.00 8.00

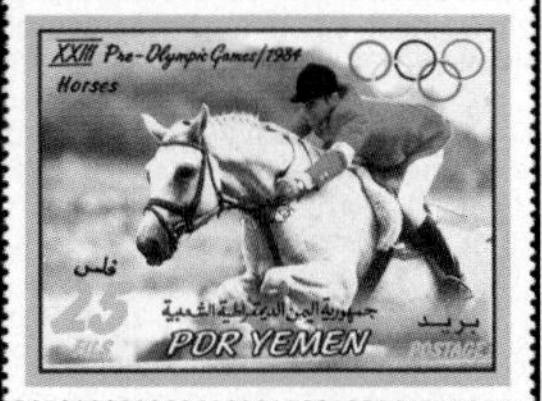

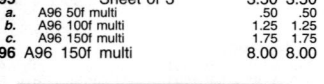

23rd Pre-Olympics Games, 1984 — A97

**1983, July 30**
**297** A97 25f Show jumping .20 .20
**298** A97 50f Show jumping, diff. .20 .20
**299** A97 100f Three-day event .40 .40
*Nos. 297-299 (3)* .80 .80

### Souvenir Sheets

**300** Sheet of 4 5.00 5.00
*a.* A97 20f Bay, vert. 1.00 1.00
*b.* A97 40f Gray, vert. 1.00 1.00
*c.* A97 60f Bay, diff., vert. 1.25 1.25
*d.* A97 80f Arabian 1.75 1.75
**301** A97 200f Show jumping, diff., vert. 6.75 6.75

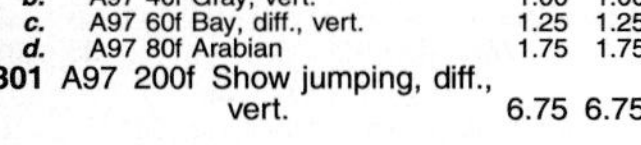

Locomotives — A98

**1983, Aug. 24** *Perf. 14½x15*
**302** A98 25f P8 steam engine, 1905 .20 .20
**303** A98 50f 880 steam, 1915 .20 .20
**304** A98 100f GT 2-4-4, 1923 .40 .40
*Nos. 302-304 (3)* .80 .80

### Souvenir Sheets

**305** Sheet of 3 9.00 9.00
*a.* A98 40f D51 steam, 1936 2.25 2.25
*b.* A98 60f 45 Series, 1937 2.25 2.25
*c.* A98 100f PT 47, 1948 4.50 4.50
**306** A98 200f P36, 1950 9.00 9.00

Natl. Revolution, 20th Anniv. A100

**1983, Oct. 15** **Litho.** *Perf. 13½x13*
**312** A100 50f shown .20 .20
**313** A100 100f Flag, freedom fighter .40 .40

1st Manned Flight, Bicent. — A101

Balloons: 100f, La Montgolfiere prototype. No. 316a, Lunardi's. No. 316b, Charles and Robert's. No. 316c, Wiseman's. No. 316d, Blanchard and Jeffries's. 200f, Five-balloon craft.

**1983, Oct. 25** *Perf. 14*
**314** A101 50f shown .20 .20
**315** A101 100f multi .40 .40

### Souvenir Sheets

**316** Sheet of 4 6.75 6.75
*a.* A101 20f multi 1.50 1.50
*b.* A101 40f multi 1.50 1.50
*c.* A101 60f multi 1.50 1.50
*d.* A101 80f multi 2.25 2.25
**317** A101 200f multi 8.00 8.00

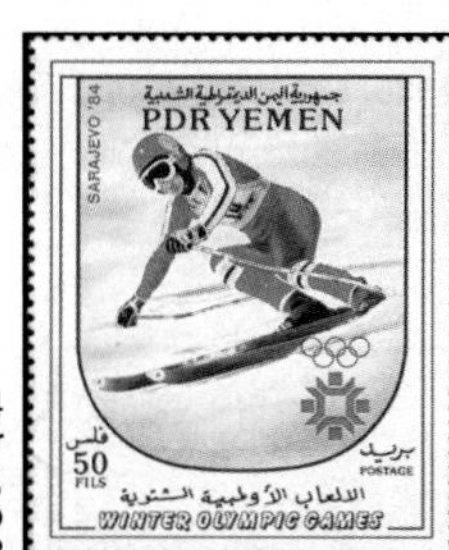

1984 Winter Olympics, Sarajevo A102

**1983, Dec. 28** **Litho.** *Perf. 14*
**318** A102 50f Men's downhill skiing .20 .20
**319** A102 100f Two-man bobsled .40 .40

### Souvenir Sheets

**320** Sheet of 2 6.50 6.50
*a.* A102 40f Ski jumping 3.25 3.25
*b.* A102 60f Figure skating 3.25 3.25
**321** A102 200f Ice hockey 6.50 6.50

1984 Summer Olympics, Los Angeles — A103

**1984, Jan. 24**
**322** A103 25f Fencing .20 .20
**323** A103 50f Fencing, diff. .20 .20
**324** A103 100f Fencing, diff. .40 .40
*Nos. 322-324 (3)* .80 .80

### Souvenir Sheets

**325** Sheet of 4 5.00 5.00
*a.* A103 20f Gymnastics 1.25 1.25
*b.* A103 40f Water polo 1.25 1.25
*c.* A103 60f Wrestling 1.25 1.25
*d.* A103 80f Show jumping 1.25 1.25
**326** A103 200f Show jumping, diff. 5.00 5.00

Nos. 83 and 84B Surcharged with Black Squares

**1984, May 26** **Litho.** *Perf. 13½, 13*
**332** A24 50f on 65f multi
**333** A25 100f on 110f multi

Fish — A105

**1984, Nov. 25** **Litho.** *Perf. 11½*
**334** A105 10f Abalistes stellaris .20 .20
**335** A105 15f Caranx speciocus .20 .20
**336** A105 20f Pomadasys maculatus .20 .20
**337** A105 25f Chaetodon fasciatus .20 .20
**338** A105 35f Pomacanthus imperator .20 .20
**339** A105 50f Rastrelliger kanagurta .20 .20
**340** A105 100f Euthynnus affinis .40 .40
**341** A105 150f Heniochus acuminatus .60 .60
**342** A105 200f Pomacanthus maculosus .80 .80
**343** A105 250f Pterois russellii 1.00 1.00
**344** A105 400f Argyrops spinifer 1.60 1.60
**345** A105 500f Dasyatis uarnak 2.00 2.00
**346** A105 1d Epinephalus chlorostigma 3.75 3.75
**347** A105 2d Drepane longimana 8.00 8.00
*Nos. 334-347 (14)* 19.35 19.35

For surcharges see Yemen Nos. 636, 640, 642.

Natl. Literacy Campaign A106

**1985, Feb. 27** *Perf. 12*
**350** A106 50f Girls writing .20 .20
**351** A106 100f Hand, fountain pen, vert. .40 .40

Victory Parade, Red Square, Moscow, 1945 — A107

12th World Youth and Students Festival — A108

**1985, May 9** *Perf. 12x12½*
**352** A107 100f multi .40 .40

Defeat of Nazi Germany, end of World War II, 40th anniv.

**1985, Aug. 3** *Perf. 12*
**353** A108 50f Emblem .20 .20
**354** A108 100f Hand holding emblem .40 .40

UNESCO World Heritage Campaign — A109

Natl. Socialist Party, 3rd Gen. Cong. — A110

**1985, Aug. 29**
**355** A109 50f Shibam city .20 .20
**356** A109 50f Close-up of buildings .20 .20
**357** A109 100f Windows .40 .40
**358** A109 100f Door .40 .40
*Nos. 355-358 (4)* 1.20 1.20

Nos. 355-357 horiz.

**1985, Oct. 10**
**359** A110 25f Energy .20 .20
**360** A110 50f Industry .20 .20
**361** A110 100f Agriculture .40 .40
*Nos. 359-361 (3)* .80 .80

UN Child Survival Campaign — A111

World Food Day — A112

**1985, Nov. 28**
**362** A111 50f Mother feeding child .20 .20
**363** A111 50f Holding child .20 .20
**364** A111 100f Feeding child, diff. .40 .40
**365** A111 100f Breastfeeding .40 .40
*Nos. 362-365 (4)* 1.20 1.20

**1986, Jan. 30**
**366** A112 20f Almihdar Mosque, Aden .20 .20
**367** A112 180f Palm trees 1.00 1.00

UN Food and Agriculture Org., 40th anniv.

Lenin, Red Square, Moscow A113

**1986, Feb. 25** *Perf. 12x12½*

**368** A113 75f multi .45 .45
**369** A113 250f multi 1.50 1.50

27th Soviet Communist Party Cong., Moscow.

Costumes Worn at the 1984 Brides Dance Festival — A114

Designs: No. 370, Bride wearing red and green costume, face markings. No. 371, Violet costume. No. 372, Veiled bride. No. 373, Unveiled bride. No. 374, Groom holding dagger. No. 375, Groom holding rifle.

**1986, Feb. 27**

**370** A114 50f multi .30 .30
**371** A114 50f multi .30 .30
**372** A114 50f multi .30 .30
**373** A114 100f multi .60 .60
**374** A114 100f multi .60 .60
**375** A114 100f multi .60 .60
*Nos. 370-375 (6)* 2.70 2.70

Revolution Martyrs A115

**1986, Oct. 15** **Litho.** *Perf. 12*

**376** A115 75f Abdul Fattah Ismail .45 .45
**377** A115 75f Ali Shayaa Hadi .45 .45
**378** A115 75f Saleh Musleh Kasim .45 .45
**379** A115 75f Ali Ahmed N. Antar .45 .45
*Nos. 376-379 (4)* 1.80 1.80

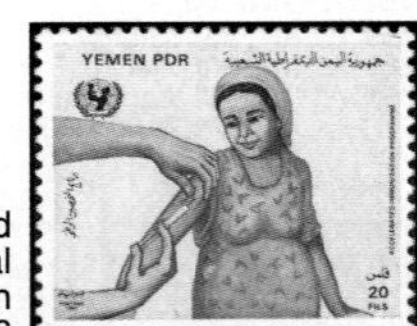


UN Child Survival Campaign A116

Infant Immunization Program.

**1987, Apr. 7** **Litho.** *Perf. 12*

**380** A116 20f Immunizing pregnant woman .20 .20
**381** A116 75f Immunizing infant .45 .45
**382** A116 140f Oral immunization .85 .85
**383** A116 150f Infant, girl, pregnant woman .90 .90
*Nos. 380-383 (4)* 2.40 2.40

1st Socialist Party General Conference — A117

**1987, July 30** **Litho.** *Perf. 12*

**384** A117 75fr multi .45 .45
**385** A117 150fr multi .90 .90

October Revolution, Russia, 70th Anniv. — A118

Monuments, Ancient City of Shabwa — A119

**1987, Nov. 7** **Litho.** *Perf. 12½x12*

**386** A118 250f multi 1.50 1.50

**1987, Nov. 18** *Perf. 12*

**387** A119 25f Royal palace and court .20 .20
**388** A119 75f Palace, diff. .45 .45
**389** A119 140f Winged lion bas-relief on stone capital .85 .85
**390** A119 150f The Moon, legend on bronze tablet .90 .90
*Nos. 387-390 (4)* 2.40 2.40

Nos. 387-388 horiz.

Natl. Independence, 20th Anniv. — A120

Designs: 5f, Students walking to school. 75f, Family, apartments. 140f, Workers, oil derrick, thermal plant. 150f, Workers, soldier, Workers' Party headquarters.

**1987, Nov. 29** *Perf. 12x12½*

**391** A120 25f multi .20 .20
**392** A120 75f multi .45 .45
**393** A120 140f multi .85 .85
**394** A120 150f multi .90 .90
*Nos. 391-394 (4)* 2.40 2.40

September 26th Revolution, 25th Anniv. A121

**1988, Feb. 27** **Litho.** *Perf. 13*

**395** A121 75f Revolution monument, San'a .45 .45

WHO, 40th Anniv. A122

**1988, Apr. 7** **Litho.** *Perf. 12*

**396** A122 40f Sanitary public water supply, vert. .25 .25
**397** A122 75f No smoking .45 .45
**398** A122 140f Child immunization .85 .85
**399** A122 250f Health care for all by the year 2000 1.55 1.55
*Nos. 396-399 (4)* 3.10 3.10

1988 Summer Olympics, Seoul A125

**1988, Sept. 17** **Litho.** *Perf. 12x12½*

**406** A125 40f Weight lifting .25 .25
**407** A125 75f Running .45 .45
**408** A125 140f Boxing .85 .85
**409** A125 150f Soccer .90 .90
*Nos. 406-409 (4)* 2.45 2.45

1st Freedom Fighter Killed at the Liberation Front, Radfan Mountains A126

*Perf. 12½x12, 12x12½*

**1988, Oct. 12** **Litho.**

**410** A126 25f Freedom fighters, flag, vert. .20 .20
**411** A126 75f shown .45 .45
**412** A126 300f Anniv. emblem, vert. 1.90 1.90
*Nos. 410-412 (3)* 2.55 2.55

October 14th Revolution, 25th anniv.

Indigenous Birds A127

**1988, Nov. 5** *Perf. 12x12½, 12½x12*

**413** A127 40f Treron waalia .25 .25
**414** A127 50f Coracias caudatus lorti, vert. .30 .30
**415** A127 75f Upupa epops, vert. .45 .45
**416** A127 250f Chlamydotis undulata macqueenii 1.55 1.55
*Nos. 413-416 (4)* 2.55 2.55

Handicrafts — A128

Designs: 25f, Incense brazier. 75f, Cage-shaped dress form. 150f, Shell and wicker lidded basket. 250f, Wicker basket.

**1988, Nov. 29** **Litho.** *Perf. 12½x12*

**417** A128 25f multi .20 .20
**418** A128 75f multi .45 .45
**419** A128 150f multi .90 .90
**420** A128 250f multi 1.55 1.55
*Nos. 417-420 (4)* 3.10 3.10

Aden Harbor and Yemen Port Authority, Cent. A129

**1988, Dec. 5** *Perf. 12x12½*

**421** A129 75f Old harbor facility .65 .65
**422** A129 300f New facility 2.75 2.75

Preservation of San'a City, a Site on the UNESCO World Heritage List — A130

**1988, Dec. 15** *Perf. 12x12½, 12½x12*

**423** A130 75f shown .45 .45
**424** A130 250f City view, diff., vert. 1.55 1.55

World Wildlife Fund — A131

**1989, May 18** **Litho.** *Perf. 12½x12*

**425** A131 20f Sand cat 1.00 .50
**426** A131 25f Cat's head 1.00 .50
**427** A131 50f Fennec fox 2.75 .60
**428** A131 75f Fox's head 3.75 1.00
*Nos. 425-428 (4)* 8.50 2.60

For surcharge see Yemen No. 643.

Military Forces — A132

Abdul Fattah Ismail — A133

Developments of the corrective movement.

**1989, Aug. 15** *Perf. 12x12½*

**429** A132 25f shown .20 .20
**430** A132 35f Industry .25 .25
**431** A132 40f Agriculture .25 .25
*Nos. 429-431 (3)* .70 .70

June 22 Corrective Movement, 20th anniv.

**1989, Aug. 28**

**432** A133 75f multi .45 .45
**433** A133 150f multi .90 .90

50th Birthday of Abdul Fattah Ismail, 1st secretary-general of the natl. Socialist Party.

Ali Anter Yemeni Pioneer Organization, 15th Anniv. — A134

*Perf. 12x12½, 12½x12*

**1989, Sept. 29** **Litho.**

**434** A134 10f Drawing by Abeer Anwer .20 .20
**435** A134 25f Girl in pioneer uniform .20 .20
**436** A134 75f Parade, Aden .45 .45
*Nos. 434-436 (3)* .85 .85

Nos. 434-435 vert.
For surcharge see Yemen No. 644.

Nehru and the Taj Mahal — A135

**1989, Nov. 14 Photo. *Perf. 14***

| | | | | |
|---|---|---|---|---|
| **437** | A135 | 250f blk & golden brn | 1.50 | 1.50 |

Jawaharlal Nehru, 1st prime minister of independent India.

For surcharge see Yemen No. 645.

Seventy-Day Siege of San'a, 1967-68 — A136

Coffee Plant — A137

**1989, Oct. 25 Litho. *Perf. 12x12½***

| | | | | |
|---|---|---|---|---|
| **438** | A136 | 150f multicolored | .90 | .90 |

**1989, Dec. 20**

| | | | | |
|---|---|---|---|---|
| **439** | A137 | 300f multicolored | 1.75 | 1.75 |

For surcharge see Yemen No. 637.

Seera Rock, Aden, and the Arc de Triomphe, Paris A138

**1989, Dec. 29 Litho. *Perf. 12½x12***

| | | | | |
|---|---|---|---|---|
| **440** | A138 | 250f multicolored | 1.50 | 1.50 |

French Revolution, bicent.

World Cup Soccer Championships, Italy — A139

Character trademark, soccer plays and flags of participants: 5f, US, Belgium, 1930. 10f, Switzerland, Holland, 1934. 20f, Italy, France, 1938. 35f, Sweden, Spain, 1950. 50f, Federal Republic of Germany, Austria, 1954. Brazil, England, 1958. 500f, Russia, Uruguay, 1962. No. 448, Soccer game.

**1990, Apr. 30 Litho. *Perf. 12½x12***

| | | | | |
|---|---|---|---|---|
| **441** | A139 | 5f multicolored | .20 | .20 |
| **442** | A139 | 10f multicolored | .20 | .20 |
| **443** | A139 | 20f multicolored | .20 | .20 |
| **444** | A139 | 35f multicolored | .25 | .25 |
| **445** | A139 | 50f multicolored | .30 | .30 |
| **446** | A139 | 60f multicolored | .35 | .35 |
| **447** | A139 | 500f multicolored | 3.00 | 3.00 |
| | | *Nos. 441-447 (7)* | 4.50 | 4.50 |

**Souvenir Sheet**

| | | | | |
|---|---|---|---|---|
| **448** | A139 | 340f multicolored | 2.00 | 2.00 |

For surcharges see Yemen Nos. 616, 621-621B.

# YUGOSLAVIA

,yü-gō-'slä-vē-ə

LOCATION — Southern Europe, bordering on the Adriatic Sea
GOVT. — Republic
AREA — 39,500 sq. mi. (est)
POP. — 11,206,847 (1999 est.)
CAPITAL — Belgrade

On December 1, 1918, Bosnia and Herzegovina, Croatia, Dalmatia, Montenegro, Serbia and Slovenia united to form a kingdom which was later called Yugoslavia. A republic was proclaimed November 29, 1945. Other listings may be found under all.

100 Heller = 1 Krone (Bosnia & Herzegovina)
100 Filler = 1 Krone (Croatia-Slavonia)
100 Paras = 1 Dinar (General Issues)

**Catalogue values for unused stamps in this country are for Never Hinged items, beginning with Scott 410 in the regular postage section, Scott C50 in the airpost section, Scott F1 in the registered letter section, Scott J67 in the postage due section, Scott RA1 in the postal tax section, and Scott RAJ1 in the postal tax due section.**

Counterfeits exist of most of the 1918-19 overprints for Bosnia and Herzegovina, Croatia-Slavonia and Slovenia.

## BOSNIA AND HERZEGOVINA

Stamps of Bosnia and Herzegovina, 1910, Overprinted or Surcharged in Black or Red

a

b

c

**1918 Unwmk. *Perf. 12½***

| | | | | |
|---|---|---|---|---|
| **1L1** | A4(a) | 3h olive green | .40 | .70 |
| **1L2** | A4(b) | 5h dk grn (R) | .20 | .20 |
| **1L3** | A4(a) | 10h carmine | .20 | .20 |
| **1L4** | A4(a) | 20h dk brn (R) | .20 | .20 |
| **1L5** | A4(a) | 25h deep blue (R) | .20 | .20 |
| **1L6** | A4(b) | 30h green | .20 | .20 |
| **1L7** | A4(b) | 40h orange | .20 | .20 |
| **1L8** | A4(b) | 45h brown red | .20 | .20 |
| **1L9** | A4(b) | 50h dull violet | .20 | .20 |
| **1L10** | A4(a) | 60h on 50h dl vio | .20 | .20 |
| **1L11** | A4(b) | 80h on 6h org brown | .20 | .30 |
| **1L12** | A4(a) | 90h on 35h myr green | .20 | .20 |
| **1L13** | A5(c) | 2k gray green | .20 | .35 |
| **1L14** | A4(b) | 3k on 3h ol grn | .80 | 1.25 |
| **1L15** | A5(c) | 4k on 1k mar | 1.40 | 1.90 |
| **1L16** | A4(b) | 10k on 2h vio | 2.25 | 2.50 |
| | | *Nos. 1L1-1L16 (16)* | 7.25 | 9.00 |

Inverted and double overprints and assorted varieties exist on the stamps for Bosnia and Herzegovina.

Bosnian Girl — A1

**1918 Typo. *Perf. 11½***

| | | | | |
|---|---|---|---|---|
| **1L17** | A1 | 2h ultramarine | .20 | .20 |
| **1L18** | A1 | 6h violet | .55 | 1.90 |
| **1L19** | A1 | 10h rose | .20 | .20 |
| **1L20** | A1 | 20h green | .20 | .20 |
| | | *Nos. 1L17-1L20 (4)* | 1.15 | 2.50 |

Imperforate stamps of this type (A1) are newspaper stamps of Bosnia.

See Nos. 1L21-1L22, 1L43-1L45.

Bosnia and Herzegovina Nos. P1-P2 (Nos. 1L17-1L18, Imperf.) Surcharged

**1918 *Imperf.***

| | | | | |
|---|---|---|---|---|
| **1L21** | A1 | 3h on 2h ultra | .20 | .20 |
| *a.* | | Double surcharge | 14.00 | |
| **1L22** | A1 | 5h on 6h violet | .20 | .20 |
| *a.* | | Double surcharge | 14.00 | |

Stamps of Bosnia and Herzegovina, 1906-17, Overprinted or Surcharged in Black or Red:

d

e

f


**1919 *Perf. 12½***

| | | | | |
|---|---|---|---|---|
| **1L25** | A23(d) | 3h claret | .20 | .50 |
| **1L26** | A23(e) | 5h green | .20 | .20 |
| **1L27** | A23(e) | 10h on 6h dark gray | .20 | .20 |
| **1L28** | A24(d) | 20h on 35h myr green | .20 | .20 |
| **1L29** | A23(e) | 25h ultra | .20 | .20 |
| **1L30** | A23(d) | 30h orange red | .45 | .90 |
| **1L31** | A24(d) | 45h olive brn | .35 | .45 |
| **1L32** | A27(d) | 45h on 80h org brown | .20 | .20 |
| *a.* | | Perf. 11½ | 3.25 | 4.00 |
| **1L33** | A24(e) | 50h slate blue | 20.00 | 24.00 |
| **1L34** | A24(e) | 50h on 72h dk blue (R) | .20 | .20 |
| **1L35** | A24(d) | 60h brown violet | .20 | .20 |
| **1L36** | A27(e) | 80h orange brown | .20 | .25 |
| *a.* | | Perf. 11½ | 24.00 | 30.00 |
| **1L37** | A27(d) | 90h dark violet | .20 | .20 |
| *a.* | | Perf. 11½ | 2.25 | 2.75 |
| **1L38** | A5(f) | 2k gray green | .20 | .25 |
| *a.* | | Imperf. | 27.50 | |
| *b.* | | Perf. 9½ | 4.50 | 5.00 |
| **1L39** | A26(d) | 3k car, *green* | .80 | .90 |
| **1L40** | A28(e) | 4k car, *green* | 1.75 | 2.50 |
| **1L41** | A26(d) | 5k dk vio, *gray* | 1.75 | 2.75 |
| **1L42** | A28(e) | 10k dk vio, *gray* | 2.00 | 2.75 |
| | | *Nos. 1L25-1L42 (18)* | 29.30 | 36.85 |

Nos. 1L32, 1L36, 1L37, 1L40 and 1L42 have no bars in the overprint.

Nos. 1L25 to 1L42 exist with inverted overprint or surcharge.

Bosnia and Herzegovina Nos. P2-P4 (Nos. 1L18-1L20, Imperf.) Surcharged

**1920 *Imperf.***

| | | | | |
|---|---|---|---|---|
| **1L43** | A1 | 2h on 6h violet | 50.00 | 70.00 |
| **1L44** | A1 | 2h on 10h rose | 20.00 | 40.00 |
| **1L45** | A1 | 2h on 20h green | 1.10 | 2.75 |
| | | *Nos. 1L43-1L45 (3)* | 71.10 | 112.75 |

## SEMI-POSTAL STAMPS ISSUES FOR BOSNIA AND HERZEGOVINA

Leading Blind Soldier — SP1

Wounded Soldier — SP2

Semi-Postal Stamps of Bosnia and Herzegovina, 1918 Overprinted

**1918 Unwmk. *Perf. 12½, 13***

| | | | | |
|---|---|---|---|---|
| **1LB1** | SP1 | 10h greenish bl | .65 | 1.00 |
| *a.* | | Overprinted as No. 1LB2 | 27.50 | 37.50 |
| **1LB2** | SP2 | 15h red brown | 1.75 | 1.75 |
| *a.* | | Overprinted as No. 1LB1 | 27.50 | 37.50 |

**Bosnian Semi-Postal Stamps of 1916 Overprinted like No. 1LB2**

| | | | | |
|---|---|---|---|---|
| **1LB3** | SP1 | 5h green | 125.00 | 140.00 |
| *a.* | | Overprinted as No. 1LB1 | 240.00 | 300.00 |
| **1LB4** | SP2 | 10h magenta | 75.00 | 95.00 |
| | | *Nos. 1LB1-1LB4 (4)* | 202.40 | 237.75 |

Inverted and double overprints exist on Nos. 1LB1-1LB4.

Mail Wagon SP3

Bridge at Mostar SP4

Scene near Sarajevo — SP5

Regular Issue of Bosnia, 1906 Surcharged in Black

**1919**

| | | | | |
|---|---|---|---|---|
| **1LB5** | SP3 | 10h + 10h on 40h org red | 1.75 | 1.90 |
| **1LB6** | SP4 | 20h + 10h on 20h dk brown | .60 | .60 |
| **1LB7** | SP5 | 45h + 15h on 1k mar | 2.50 | 2.75 |
| | | *Nos. 1LB5-1LB7 (3)* | 4.85 | 5.25 |

Nos. 1LB5-1LB7 exist with surcharge inverted. Value each $7.50.

### SPECIAL DELIVERY STAMPS ISSUES FOR BOSNIA AND HERZEGOVINA

Lightning
SD1 SD2

Bosnian Special Delivery Stamps Overprinted in Black

**1918 Unwmk. *Perf. 12½, 13***

| | | | |
|---|---|---|---|
| **1LE1** | SD1 2h vermilion | 4.75 | 5.00 |
| *a.* | Inverted overprint | 32.50 | |
| *b.* | Overprinted as No. 1LE2 | 30.00 | 35.00 |
| **1LE2** | SD2 5h deep green | 1.40 | 1.50 |
| *a.* | Inverted overprint | 18.00 | |
| *b.* | Overprinted as No. 1LE1 | 30.00 | 35.00 |

### POSTAGE DUE STAMPS ISSUES FOR BOSNIA AND HERZEGOVINA

Postage Due Stamps of Bosnia and Herzegovina, 1916, Overprinted in Black or Red:

a b

**1918 Unwmk. *Perf. 12½, 13***

| | | | | |
|---|---|---|---|---|
| **1LJ1** | D2 (a) | 2h red | .20 | .20 |
| **1LJ2** | D2 (b) | 4h red | .25 | .65 |
| **1LJ3** | D2 (a) | 5h red | .20 | .20 |
| **1LJ4** | D2 (b) | 6h red | .30 | .40 |
| **1LJ5** | D2 (a) | 10h red | .20 | .20 |
| **1LJ6** | D2 (b) | 15h red | 4.00 | 4.75 |
| **1LJ7** | D2 (a) | 20h red | .20 | .20 |
| **1LJ8** | D2 (b) | 25h red | .25 | .70 |
| **1LJ9** | D2 (a) | 30h red | .25 | .70 |
| **1LJ10** | D2 (b) | 40h red | .20 | .20 |
| **1LJ11** | D2 (a) | 50h red | .50 | .80 |

c d

| | | | | |
|---|---|---|---|---|
| **1LJ12** | D2 (c) | 1k dark blue (R) | .25 | .25 |
| **1LJ13** | D2 (d) | 3k dark blue (R) | .25 | .20 |
| | | *Nos. 1LJ1-1LJ13 (13)* | 7.00 | 9.45 |

Nos. 1LJ1-1LJ13 exist with overprint double or inverted. Value $3 to $7.

Nos. 1LJ1-1LJ11 exist with type "b" overprint instead of type "a," and vice versa. Value, each $10.

Stamps of Bosnia and Herzegovina, 1900-04, Surcharged

e f

**1919**

| | | | | |
|---|---|---|---|---|
| **1LJ14** | A2 (e) | 2h on 35h blue | .25 | 1.10 |
| **1LJ15** | A2 (e) | 5h on 45h grnsh bl | .40 | .85 |
| **1LJ16** | A2 (f) | 10h on 10 red | .20 | .20 |
| **1LJ17** | A2 (e) | 15h on 40h org | .20 | .80 |
| **1LJ18** | A2 (f) | 20h on 5h green | .20 | .20 |
| **1LJ19** | A2 (e) | 25h on 20h pink | .20 | .50 |
| **1LJ20** | A2 (f) | 30h on 30h bis brn | .20 | .45 |
| **1LJ21** | A2 (e) | 1k on 50h red lil | .20 | .20 |
| **1LJ22** | A2 (e) | 3k on 25h blue | .20 | .30 |

Postage Due Stamps of Bosnia and Herzegovina, 1904 Surcharged:

g h

| | | | | |
|---|---|---|---|---|
| **1LJ23** | D1 (g) | 40h on 6h blk, red & yel | .20 | .20 |
| **1LJ24** | D1 (h) | 50h on 8h blk, red & yel | .20 | .20 |
| **1LJ25** | D1 (h) | 200h blk, red & grn | 2.50 | 2.50 |
| **1LJ26** | D1 (h) | 4k on 7h blk, red & yel | .20 | .30 |
| | | *Nos. 1LJ14-1LJ26 (13)* | 5.15 | 7.80 |

Nos. 1LJ14-1LJ26 exist with overprint double or inverted. Value, $3 to $6.

### CROATIA-SLAVONIA

Stamps of Hungary Overprinted in Blue

A1

**1918 Wmk. 137 *Perf. 15***

**On Stamps of 1913**

| | | | |
|---|---|---|---|
| **2L1** | A1 6f olive green | 1.10 | 2.00 |
| **2L2** | A1 50f lake, *blue* | .85 | 1.75 |

A2 A3

**On Stamps of 1916**

| | | | |
|---|---|---|---|
| **2L3** | A2 10f violet | 20.00 | 27.50 |
| **2L4** | A3 15f red | 20.00 | 27.50 |

A4

**On Hungary Nos. 106-107**
**White Numerals**

| | | | |
|---|---|---|---|
| **2L4A** | A4 10f rose | 240.00 | 300.00 |
| **2L5** | A4 15f violet | 22.50 | 27.50 |
| *a.* | Inverted overprint | *125.00* | |

**On Stamps of 1916-18**
**Colored Numerals**

| | | | | |
|---|---|---|---|---|
| **2L6** | A4 | 2f brown orange | .20 | .20 |
| **2L7** | A4 | 3f red lilac | .20 | .20 |
| **2L8** | A4 | 5f green | .20 | .20 |
| **2L9** | A4 | 6f greenish blue | .20 | .25 |
| **2L10** | A4 | 10f rose red | 1.60 | 2.75 |
| **2L11** | A4 | 15f violet | .20 | .20 |
| **2L12** | A4 | 20f gray brown | .20 | .30 |
| **2L13** | A4 | 25f dull blue | .20 | .20 |
| **2L14** | A4 | 35f brown | .20 | .20 |
| **2L15** | A4 | 40f olive green | .20 | .45 |

The overprints and surcharges for Croatia-Slavonia exist inverted, double, double inverted, in wrong colors, on wrong stamps, on back, in pairs with one lacking overprint, etc.

A5

A6

| | | | | |
|---|---|---|---|---|
| **2L16** | A5 | 50f red vio & lilac | .20 | .20 |
| **2L17** | A5 | 75f brt bl & pale bl | .20 | .25 |
| **2L18** | A5 | 80f grn & pale grn | .20 | .20 |
| **2L19** | A6 | 1k red brown & cl | .20 | .20 |
| **2L20** | A6 | 2k olive brn & bis | .20 | .20 |
| **2L21** | A6 | 3k dark vio & ind | .40 | 1.00 |
| **2L22** | A6 | 5k dk brn & lt brn | 2.00 | 4.00 |
| **2L23** | A6 | 10k vio brn & vio | 7.50 | 14.00 |

Stamps of Hungary Overprinted in Blue, Black or Red

A7 A8

| | | | | |
|---|---|---|---|---|
| **2L24** | A7 | 10f scarlet (Bl) | .20 | .20 |
| **2L25** | A7 | 20f dark brown (Bk) | .20 | .20 |
| **2L26** | A7 | 25f deep blue (R) | .80 | 2.50 |
| **2L27** | A8 | 40f olive green (Bl) | .20 | .20 |
| | | *Nos. 2L6-2L27 (22)* | 15.70 | 28.10 |

Many other stamps of the 1913-18 issues of Hungary, the Semi-Postal Stamps of 1915-16 and Postage Due Stamps were surreptitiously overprinted but were never sold through the post office.

Freedom of Croatia-Slavonia
A9

**1918 Unwmk. Litho. *Perf. 11½***

| | | | | |
|---|---|---|---|---|
| **2L28** | A9 | 10f rose | 1.00 | 1.00 |
| **2L29** | A9 | 20f violet | 1.25 | 1.25 |
| **2L30** | A9 | 25f blue | 2.50 | 2.50 |
| **2L31** | A9 | 45f greenish blk | 24.00 | 24.00 |
| | | *Nos. 2L28-2L31 (4)* | 28.75 | 28.75 |

Independence of Croatia, Slavonia and Dalmatia.

#2L28-2L31 exist imperforate, but were not officially issued in this condition.

Excellent counterfeits of #2L28-2L31 exist.

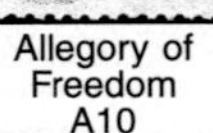

Allegory of Freedom
A10

Youth with Standard
A11

Falcon, Symbol of Liberty — A12

**1919 *Perf. 11½***

| | | | | |
|---|---|---|---|---|
| **2L32** | A10 | 2f brn orange | .20 | .20 |
| **2L33** | A10 | 3f violet | .20 | .20 |
| **2L34** | A10 | 5f green | .20 | .20 |
| **2L35** | A11 | 10f red | .20 | .20 |
| **2L36** | A11 | 20f black brown | .20 | .20 |
| **2L37** | A11 | 25f deep blue | .20 | .20 |
| **2L38** | A11 | 45f dark ol grn | .20 | .20 |
| **2L39** | A12 | 1k carmine rose | .20 | .20 |
| **2L40** | A12 | 3k dark violet | .35 | .35 |
| **2L41** | A12 | 5k deep brown | .85 | .70 |
| | | *Nos. 2L32-2L41 (10)* | 2.80 | 2.65 |

***Perf. 12½***

| | | | | |
|---|---|---|---|---|
| *2L32a* | A10 | 2f | 1.25 | 1.25 |
| *2L33a* | A10 | 3f | 1.25 | 1.25 |
| *2L34a* | A10 | 5f | 40.00 | 52.50 |
| *2L35a* | A11 | 10f | .35 | .35 |
| *2L36a* | A11 | 20f | .30 | .25 |
| | | *Nos. 2L32a-2L36a (5)* | 43.15 | 55.60 |

#2L32-2L41 exist imperf. Value, set $25.

### SEMI-POSTAL STAMPS ISSUES FOR CROATIA-SLAVONIA

SP1 SP2

SP3

**1918 Wmk. 137 *Perf. 15***

| | | | |
|---|---|---|---|
| **2LB1** | SP1 10f + 2f rose red | .30 | *2.75* |
| **2LB2** | SP2 15f + 2f dull violet | .20 | *.40* |
| **2LB3** | SP3 40f + 2f brn carmine | .20 | *.85* |
| | *Nos. 2LB1-2LB3 (3)* | .70 | *4.00* |

### SPECIAL DELIVERY STAMP ISSUE FOR CROATIA-SLAVONIA

SD1

Hungary No. E1 Overprinted in Black

**1918 Wmk. 137 *Perf. 15***

| | | | |
|---|---|---|---|
| **2LE1** | SD1 2f gray green & red | .20 | .20 |

### POSTAGE DUE STAMPS ISSUES FOR CROATIA-SLAVONIA

D1

Postage Due Stamps of Hungary Overprinted in Blue

**1918 Wmk. Crown (136) *Perf. 15***

| | | | |
|---|---|---|---|
| **2LJ1** | D1 50f green & blk | 175.00 | 175.00 |

**Wmk. Double Cross (137)**

| | | | |
|---|---|---|---|
| **2LJ2** | D1 1f green & red | 6.25 | 6.25 |
| *a.* | Inverted overprint | 22.50 | 22.50 |
| **2LJ3** | D1 2f green & red | .75 | .75 |
| **2LJ4** | D1 10f green & red | .55 | .55 |
| **2LJ5** | D1 12f green & red | 25.00 | 25.00 |
| **2LJ6** | D1 15f green & red | .45 | .45 |
| **2LJ7** | D1 20f green & red | .45 | .45 |
| **2LJ8** | D1 30f green & red | 1.10 | 1.10 |
| **2LJ9** | D1 50f green & blk | 7.75 | 7.75 |
| | *Nos. 2LJ2-2LJ9 (8)* | 42.30 | 42.30 |

### NEWSPAPER STAMPS ISSUES FOR CROATIA-SLAVONIA

N1 N2

Hungary No. P8 Overprinted in Black

**1918 Wmk. 137 *Imperf.***

| | | | |
|---|---|---|---|
| **2LP1** | N1 (2f) orange | .20 | .30 |

**1919 Litho. Unwmk.**

| | | | |
|---|---|---|---|
| **2LP2** | N2 2f yellow | .20 | .50 |

## SLOVENIA

Chain Breaker
A1 A2

3, 5, 10, 15f: Chain on right wrist is short, extending only about half way to the frame.
10f: Numerals are 8½mm high.
20, 25, 30, 40f: Distant mountains show faintly between legs of male figure.
40f: Numerals 7mm high. The upright strokes of the "4" extend to the same height; the "0" is 3mm wide.

**1919 Unwmk. *Perf. 11½***
**Lithographed at Ljubljana**
**Fine Impression**

| | | | | |
|---|---|---|---|---|
| **3L1** | A1 | 3f violet | .20 | .20 |
| **3L2** | A1 | 5f green | .20 | .20 |
| **3L3** | A1 | 10f carmine rose | .20 | .20 |
| **3L4** | A1 | 15f blue | .20 | .20 |
| **3L5** | A2 | 20f brown | .20 | .20 |
| **3L6** | A2 | 25f blue | .20 | .20 |
| **3L7** | A2 | 30f lilac rose | .20 | .20 |
| **3L8** | A2 | 40f bister | .20 | .20 |
| | | *Nos. 3L1-3L8 (8)* | 1.60 | 1.60 |

Various stamps of this series exist imperforate and part perforate. Many shades exist.
See Nos. 3L9-3L17, 3L24-3L28. For surcharges see Nos. 3LJ15-3LJ32.

Allegories of Freedom
A3 A4

King Peter I — A5

3, 5, 15f: The chain on the right wrist touches the bottom tablet.
10f: Numerals are 7½mm high.
15f: Curled end of loin cloth appears above letter "H" in the bottom tablet.
20, 25, 30, 40f: The outlines of the mountains have been redrawn and they are more distinct than on the lithographed stamps.
40f: Numerals 8mm high. The left slanting stroke of the "4" extends much higher than the main vertical stroke. The "0" is 2½mm wide and encloses a much narrower space than on the lithographed stamp.

**1919-20 *Perf. 11½***
**Typographed at Ljubljana and Vienna**
**Coarse Impression**

| | | | | |
|---|---|---|---|---|
| **3L9** | A1 | 3f violet | .20 | .20 |
| **3L10** | A1 | 5f green | .20 | .20 |
| **3L11** | A1 | 10f red | .20 | .20 |
| **3L12** | A1 | 15f blue | .20 | .20 |
| **3L13** | A2 | 20f brown | .20 | .20 |
| **3L14** | A2 | 25f blue | .20 | .20 |
| **3L15** | A2 | 30f carmine rose | .20 | .20 |
| **3L16** | A2 | 30f dp red | 2.75 | .90 |
| **3L17** | A2 | 40f orange | .25 | .20 |
| **3L18** | A3 | 50f green | .30 | .20 |
| *a.* | | 50f dark green | .30 | .20 |
| *b.* | | 50f olive green | 3.50 | 1.10 |
| **3L19** | A3 | 60f dark blue | .50 | .20 |
| *a.* | | 60f violet blue | .85 | .20 |
| **3L20** | A4 | 1k vermilion | .30 | .20 |
| *a.* | | 1k red orange | .45 | .20 |
| **3L21** | A4 | 2k blue | .30 | .20 |
| *a.* | | 2k dull ultramarine | .90 | .20 |
| **3L22** | A5 | 5k brown lake | .45 | .20 |
| *a.* | | 5k lake | 12.00 | 1.60 |
| *b.* | | 5k dull red | .60 | .20 |
| **3L23** | A5 | 10k deep ultra | 2.75 | .90 |
| | | *Nos. 3L9-3L23 (15)* | 9.00 | 4.40 |

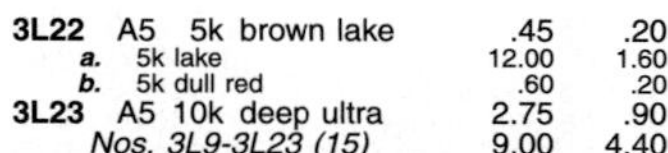

Nos. 3L9-3L23 exist imperf. Value, set $90.
Many of the series exist part perforate.
Many shades exist of lower values.
See Nos. 3L29-3L32, 3L40-3L41.

***Serrate Roulette 13½***

| | | | | |
|---|---|---|---|---|
| **3L24** | A1 | 5f light grn | .20 | .20 |
| **3L25** | A1 | 10f carmine | .20 | .20 |
| **3L26** | A1 | 15f slate blue | .20 | .20 |
| **3L27** | A2 | 20f dark brown | .30 | .20 |
| *a.* | | Serrate x straight roul. | .55 | .20 |
| **3L28** | A2 | 30f car rose | .20 | .20 |
| *a.* | | Serrate x straight roul. | .60 | .20 |
| **3L29** | A3 | 50f green | .30 | .20 |
| **3L30** | A3 | 60f dark blue | .45 | .20 |
| *a.* | | 60f violet blue | 2.25 | 1.10 |
| **3L31** | A4 | 1k vermilion | .65 | .20 |
| *a.* | | 1k rose red | .60 | .20 |
| **3L32** | A4 | 2k blue | 13.00 | 1.50 |
| | | *Nos. 3L24-3L32 (9)* | 15.50 | 3.10 |

**Roulette x Perf. 11½**

| | | | | |
|---|---|---|---|---|
| *3L24a* | A1 | 5f | 125.00 | 140.00 |
| *3L25a* | A1 | 10f | 45.00 | 47.50 |
| *3L26a* | A1 | 15f | 140.00 | 150.00 |
| *3L28b* | A2 | 30f | 45.00 | 47.50 |
| *3L29a* | A3 | 50f | 5.25 | 4.00 |
| *3L30b* | A3 | 60f | 45.00 | 47.50 |
| *3L31b* | A4 | 1k | 45.00 | 47.50 |

Thick Wove Paper

**1920 Litho. *Perf. 11½***

| | | | | |
|---|---|---|---|---|
| **3L40** | A5 | 15k gray green | 4.00 | 5.25 |
| **3L41** | A5 | 20k dull violet | 1.00 | 2.00 |

On Nos. 3L40-3L41 the horizontal lines have been removed from the value tablets. They are printed over a background of pale brown wavy lines.

Chain Breaker
A7

Freedom
A8

King Peter I — A9

Dinar Values:
Type I — Size: 21x30½mm.
Type II — Size: 22x32½mm.

Thin to Thick Wove Paper

**1920 *Serrate Roulette 13½***

| | | | | |
|---|---|---|---|---|
| **3L42** | A7 | 5p olive green | .20 | .20 |
| **3L43** | A7 | 10p green | .20 | .20 |
| **3L44** | A7 | 15p brown | .20 | .20 |
| **3L45** | A7 | 20p carmine | .75 | 1.00 |
| **3L46** | A7 | 25p chocolate | .30 | .30 |
| **3L47** | A8 | 40p dark violet | .20 | .20 |
| **3L48** | A8 | 45p yellow | .20 | .20 |
| **3L49** | A8 | 50p dark blue | .20 | .20 |
| **3L50** | A8 | 60p red brown | .20 | .20 |
| **3L51** | A9 | 1d dark brown (I) | .20 | .20 |

***Perf. 11½***

| | | | | |
|---|---|---|---|---|
| **3L52** | A9 | 2d gray vio (II) | .20 | .20 |
| **3L53** | A9 | 4d grnsh black (I) | .30 | .30 |
| **3L54** | A9 | 6d olive brn (II) | .20 | .25 |
| **3L55** | A9 | 10d brown red (II) | .30 | .35 |
| | | *Nos. 3L42-3L55 (14)* | 3.65 | 4.00 |

The 2d and 6d have a background of pale red wavy lines, the 10d of gray lines.
Counterfeits exist of No. 3L45.

## POSTAGE DUE STAMPS ISSUES FOR SLOVENIA

D1

**1919 Litho. Unwmk. *Perf. 11½***
**Ljubljana Print**
**Numerals 9½mm high**

| | | | | |
|---|---|---|---|---|
| **3LJ1** | D1 | 5f carmine | .20 | .20 |
| **3LJ2** | D1 | 10f carmine | .20 | .20 |
| **3LJ3** | D1 | 20f carmine | .20 | .20 |
| **3LJ4** | D1 | 50f carmine | .20 | .20 |

Nos. 3LJ1-3LJ4 were also printed in scarlet and dark red.

**Numerals 8mm high**

| | | | | |
|---|---|---|---|---|
| **3LJ5** | D1 | 1k dark blue | .45 | .30 |
| **3LJ6** | D1 | 5k dark blue | .65 | .50 |
| **3LJ7** | D1 | 10k dark blue | .90 | .75 |
| | | *Nos. 3LJ1-3LJ7 (7)* | 2.80 | 2.35 |

**1920**
**Vienna Print**
**Numerals 11 to 12 mm high**

| | | | | |
|---|---|---|---|---|
| **3LJ8** | D1 | 5f red | .20 | .20 |
| **3LJ9** | D1 | 10f red | .20 | .20 |
| **3LJ10** | D1 | 20f red | .20 | .20 |
| **3LJ11** | D1 | 50f red | 1.25 | .85 |

**Numerals 7mm high**

| | | | | |
|---|---|---|---|---|
| **3LJ12** | D1 | 1k Prussian blue | 1.10 | .70 |
| *a.* | | 1k dark blue | 5.00 | 4.50 |
| **3LJ13** | D1 | 5k Prussian blue | 1.60 | 1.25 |
| *a.* | | 5k dark blue | 8.00 | 6.75 |
| **3LJ14** | D1 | 10k Prussian blue | 3.75 | 3.25 |
| *a.* | | 10k dark blue | 14.00 | 15.00 |
| | | *Nos. 3LJ8-3LJ14 (7)* | 8.30 | 6.65 |

Nos. 3LJ8-3LJ14 exist imperf. Value, set $40.

No. 3L4 Surcharged in Red

**1920 *Perf. 11½***
**On Litho. Stamps**

| | | | | |
|---|---|---|---|---|
| **3LJ15** | A1 | 5p on 15f blue | .20 | .20 |
| **3LJ16** | A1 | 10p on 15f blue | .60 | .60 |
| **3LJ17** | A1 | 20p on 15f blue | .20 | .20 |
| **3LJ18** | A1 | 50p on 15f blue | .20 | .20 |
| | | *Nos. 3LJ15-3LJ18 (4)* | 1.20 | 1.20 |

Nos. 3L7, 3L12, 3L26, 3L28, 3L28a Surcharged in Dark Blue

| | | | | |
|---|---|---|---|---|
| **3LJ19** | A2 | 1d on 30f lil rose | .20 | .20 |
| **3LJ20** | A2 | 3d on 30f lil rose | .20 | .20 |
| **3LJ21** | A2 | 8d on 30f lil rose | 1.10 | .60 |
| | | *Nos. 3LJ19-3LJ21 (3)* | 1.50 | 1.00 |

**On Typographed Stamps**
***Perf. 11½***

| | | | | |
|---|---|---|---|---|
| **3LJ22** | A1 | 5p on 15f pale bl | 12.00 | 2.50 |
| **3LJ23** | A1 | 10p on 15f pale bl | 27.50 | 22.50 |
| **3LJ24** | A1 | 20p on 15f pale bl | 11.00 | 4.00 |
| **3LJ25** | A1 | 50p on 15f pale bl | 6.00 | 7.00 |
| | | *Nos. 3LJ22-3LJ25 (4)* | 56.50 | 36.00 |

***Serrate Roulette 13½***

| | | | | |
|---|---|---|---|---|
| **3LJ26** | A1 | 5p on 15f slate bl | 2.75 | .50 |
| **3LJ27** | A1 | 10p on 15f slate bl | 8.50 | 3.25 |
| **3LJ28** | A1 | 20p on 15f slate bl | 2.75 | .50 |
| **3LJ29** | A1 | 50p on 15f slate bl | 2.75 | .50 |
| **3LJ30** | A2 | 1d on 30f dp rose | 2.75 | .65 |
| *a.* | | Serrate x straight roulette | 7.00 | 4.50 |
| **3LJ31** | A2 | 3d on 30f dp rose | 5.75 | 1.75 |
| *a.* | | Serrate x straight roulette | 8.00 | 5.50 |
| **3LJ32** | A2 | 8d on 30f dp rose | 95.00 | 6.50 |
| *a.* | | Serrate x straight roulette | 90.00 | 7.50 |
| | | *Nos. 3LJ26-3LJ32 (7)* | 120.25 | 13.65 |

The para surcharges were printed in sheets of 100, ten horizontal rows of ten. There were: 5p three rows, 10p one row, 20p three rows, 50p three rows. The dinar surcharges were in a setting of 50, arranged in vertical rows of five. There were: 1d five rows, 3d three rows, 8d two rows.

## NEWSPAPER STAMPS ISSUES FOR SLOVENIA

Eros — N1

2 4 6 10

**1919 Unwmk. Litho. *Imperf.***
**Ljubljana Print**

| | | | | |
|---|---|---|---|---|
| **3LP1** | N1 | 2f gray | .20 | .20 |
| **3LP2** | N1 | 4f gray | .20 | .20 |
| **3LP3** | N1 | 6f gray | 3.25 | 4.00 |
| **3LP4** | N1 | 10f gray | .20 | .20 |
| **3LP5** | N1 | 30f gray | .20 | .20 |
| | | *Nos. 3LP1-3LP5 (5)* | 4.05 | 4.80 |

See Nos. 3LP6-3LP13. For surcharges see Nos. 3LP14-3LP23, 4LB1-4LB5.

2 4 6 10

**1920**
**Vienna Print**

| | | | | |
|---|---|---|---|---|
| **3LP6** | N1 | 2f gray | .20 | .20 |
| **3LP7** | N1 | 4f gray | 6.50 | 10.00 |
| **3LP8** | N1 | 6f gray | 1.75 | 2.75 |
| **3LP9** | N1 | 10f gray | 14.00 | 21.00 |
| **3LP10** | N1 | 2f blue | .20 | .30 |
| **3LP11** | N1 | 4f blue | .20 | .20 |
| **3LP12** | N1 | 6f blue | 90.00 | 110.00 |
| **3LP13** | N1 | 10f blue | .20 | .20 |
| | | *Nos. 3LP6-3LP13 (8)* | 113.05 | 144.65 |

Nos. 3LP1, 3LP10 Surcharged:

a

b

**On Ljubljana Print**

| | | | | | |
|---|---|---|---|---|---|
| **3LP14** | N1 | (a) | 2p on 2f gray | .25 | .40 |
| **3LP15** | N1 | (a) | 4p on 2f gray | .25 | .40 |
| **3LP16** | N1 | (a) | 6p on 2f gray | .40 | .65 |
| **3LP17** | N1 | (b) | 10p on 2f gray | .65 | .80 |
| **3LP18** | N1 | (b) | 30p on 2f gray | .65 | .85 |

**On Vienna Print**

| | | | | | |
|---|---|---|---|---|---|
| **3LP19** | N1 | (a) | 2p on 2f blue | .20 | .20 |
| **3LP20** | N1 | (a) | 4p on 2f blue | .20 | .20 |
| **3LP21** | N1 | (a) | 6p on 2f blue | .20 | .20 |
| **3LP22** | N1 | (b) | 10p on 2f blue | .20 | .20 |
| **3LP23** | N1 | (b) | 30p on 2f blue | .20 | .25 |
| | | | *Nos. 3LP14-3LP23 (10)* | 3.20 | 4.15 |

The five surcharges were arranged in a setting of 100, in horizontal rows of ten. There were: 2p three rows, 4p three rows, 6p two rows, 10p one row and 30p one row. The sheets were perforated 11½ horizontally between the groups of the different values.

## SEMI-POSTAL STAMPS ISSUE FOR CARINTHIA PLEBISCITE

SP1

Nos. 3LP2, 3LP1 Surcharged With Various Designs in Dark Red

**1920**

| | | | | |
|---|---|---|---|---|
| **4LB1** | SP1 | 5p on 4f gray | .20 | .20 |
| **4LB2** | SP1 | 15p on 4f gray | .20 | .20 |
| **4LB3** | SP1 | 25p on 4f gray | .20 | .20 |
| **4LB4** | SP1 | 45p on 2f gray | .20 | .20 |
| **4LB5** | SP1 | 50p on 2f gray | .20 | .20 |
| **4LB6** | SP1 | 2d on 2f gray | 1.25 | 1.60 |
| | | *Nos. 4LB1-4LB6 (6)* | 2.25 | 2.60 |

Nos. 4LB1 to 4LB6 have a different surcharge on each stamp but each includes the letters "K.G.C.A." which signify Carinthian Governmental Commission, Zone A.

Sold at three times face value for the benefit of the Plebiscite Propaganda Fund.

## GENERAL ISSUES

### For Use throughout the Kingdom

King Alexander — A1

King Peter I — A2

**Unwmk.**

**1921, Jan. 16 Engr. *Perf. 12***

| | | | | |
|---|---|---|---|---|
| **1** | A1 | 2p olive brown | .20 | .20 |
| **2** | A1 | 5p deep green | .20 | .20 |
| **3** | A1 | 10p carmine | .20 | .20 |
| **4** | A1 | 15p violet | .20 | .20 |
| **5** | A1 | 20p black | .20 | .20 |
| **6** | A1 | 25p dark blue | .20 | .20 |
| **7** | A1 | 50p olive green | .20 | .20 |
| **8** | A1 | 60p vermilion | .20 | .20 |
| **9** | A1 | 75p purple | .20 | .20 |
| **10** | A2 | 1d orange | .20 | .20 |
| **11** | A2 | 2d olive bister | .25 | .20 |
| **12** | A2 | 4d dark green | .40 | .20 |
| **13** | A2 | 5d carmine rose | 2.00 | .20 |
| **14** | A2 | 10d red brown | 4.00 | .55 |
| | | *Nos. 1-14 (14)* | 8.65 | 3.15 |

Exist imperf. Value, set $22.50.

For surcharge see No. 27.

Nos. B1-B3 Surcharged in Black, Brown, Green or Blue:

a

b

**1922-24**

| | | | | |
|---|---|---|---|---|
| **15** | SP1(a) | 1d on 10p | .20 | .20 |
| **16** | SP2(b) | 1d on 15p ('24) | .20 | .20 |
| **17** | SP3(a) | 1d on 25p (Br) | .20 | .20 |
| **18** | SP2(b) | 3d on 15p (G) | .80 | .20 |
| *a.* | | Blue surcharge | 1.90 | .20 |
| **19** | SP2(b) | 8d on 15p (G) | 1.40 | .20 |
| *a.* | | Double surcharge | 32.50 | 30.00 |
| *b.* | | 9d on 15p (error) | 100.00 | |
| **20** | SP2(b) | 20d on 15p | 6.50 | 1.00 |
| **21** | SP2(b) | 30d on 15p (Bl) | 13.50 | 2.50 |
| | | *Nos. 15-21 (7)* | 22.80 | 4.50 |

A3

**1923, Jan. 23 Engr.**

| | | | | |
|---|---|---|---|---|
| **22** | A3 | 1d red brown | .65 | .20 |
| **23** | A3 | 5d carmine | 3.25 | .20 |
| **24** | A3 | 8d violet | 6.25 | .25 |
| **25** | A3 | 20d green | 16.00 | .75 |
| **26** | A3 | 30d red orange | 42.50 | 2.00 |
| | | *Nos. 22-26 (5)* | 68.65 | 3.40 |

For surcharge see No. 28.

Nos. 8 and 24 Surcharged in Black or Blue

**1924, Feb. 18**

| | | | | |
|---|---|---|---|---|
| **27** | A1 | 20p on 60p ver | .25 | .20 |
| **28** | A3 | 5d on 8d violet (Bl) | 4.75 | .60 |

The color of the surcharge on No. 28 varies, including blue, blue black, greenish black and black.

A4

A5

**1924, July 1 *Perf. 14***

| | | | | |
|---|---|---|---|---|
| **29** | A4 | 20p black | .90 | .20 |
| **30** | A4 | 50p dark brown | .90 | .20 |
| **31** | A4 | 1d carmine | .35 | .20 |
| **32** | A4 | 2d myrtle green | .75 | .20 |
| **33** | A4 | 3d ultramarine | .60 | .20 |
| **34** | A4 | 5d orange brown | 2.50 | .20 |
| **35** | A5 | 10d dark violet | 8.50 | .20 |
| **36** | A5 | 15d olive green | 5.00 | .20 |
| **37** | A5 | 20d vermilion | 4.50 | .20 |
| **38** | A5 | 30d dark green | 4.50 | 1.10 |
| | | *Nos. 29-38 (10)* | 28.50 | 2.90 |

No. 33 Surcharged

**1925, June 5**

| | | | | |
|---|---|---|---|---|
| **39** | A4 | 25p on 3d ultramarine | .20 | .20 |
| **40** | A4 | 50p on 3d ultramarine | .20 | .20 |

King Alexander

A6 A7

**1926-27 Typo. *Perf. 13***

| | | | | |
|---|---|---|---|---|
| **41** | A6 | 25p deep green | .20 | .20 |
| **42** | A6 | 50p olive brown | .20 | .20 |
| **43** | A6 | 1d scarlet | .30 | .20 |
| **44** | A6 | 2d slate black | .30 | .20 |
| **45** | A6 | 3d slate blue | .40 | .20 |
| **46** | A6 | 4d red orange | 2.00 | .20 |
| **47** | A6 | 5d violet | 1.50 | .20 |
| **48** | A6 | 8d black brown | 3.75 | .20 |
| **49** | A6 | 10d olive brown | 3.50 | .20 |
| **50** | A6 | 15d brown ('27) | 6.75 | .20 |
| **51** | A6 | 20d dark vio ('27) | 8.25 | .20 |
| **52** | A6 | 30d orange ('27) | 25.00 | .45 |
| | | *Nos. 41-52 (12)* | 52.15 | 2.65 |

For overprints and surcharges see Nos. 53-62, 87-101, B5-B16.

Semi-Postal Stamps of 1926 Overprinted over the Red Surcharge

**1928, July**

| | | | | |
|---|---|---|---|---|
| **53** | A6 | 1d scarlet | 1.25 | .20 |
| *a.* | | Surcharge "0.50" inverted | | |
| **54** | A6 | 2d black | 4.00 | .20 |
| **55** | A6 | 3d deep blue | 3.00 | .35 |
| **56** | A6 | 4d red orange | 9.25 | .40 |
| **57** | A6 | 5d bright vio | 3.00 | .20 |
| **58** | A6 | 8d black brown | 4.50 | .65 |
| **59** | A6 | 10d olive brown | 6.00 | .20 |
| **60** | A6 | 15d brown | 35.00 | 2.00 |
| **61** | A6 | 20d violet | 18.00 | 2.00 |
| **62** | A6 | 30d orange | 40.00 | 4.00 |
| | | *Nos. 53-62 (10)* | 124.00 | 10.20 |

With Imprint at Foot

**1931-34 *Perf. 12½***

| | | | | |
|---|---|---|---|---|
| **63** | A7 | 25p black | .70 | .20 |
| **64** | A7 | 50p green | .60 | .20 |
| **65** | A7 | 75p slate green | .20 | .20 |
| **66** | A7 | 1d red | .65 | .20 |
| **67** | A7 | 1.50d pink | .30 | .20 |
| **68** | A7 | 1.75d dp rose ('34) | .55 | .35 |
| **69** | A7 | 3d slate blue | 3.50 | .20 |
| **70** | A7 | 3.50d ultra ('34) | 1.10 | .25 |
| **71** | A7 | 4d deep orange | 2.00 | .20 |
| **72** | A7 | 5d purple | 2.00 | .20 |
| **73** | A7 | 10d dark olive | 5.50 | .20 |
| **74** | A7 | 15d deep brown | 5.50 | .20 |
| **75** | A7 | 20d dark violet | 9.25 | .20 |
| **76** | A7 | 30d rose | 6.00 | .45 |
| | | *Nos. 63-76 (14)* | 37.85 | 3.25 |

Type of 1931 Issue Without Imprint at Foot

**1932-33**

| | | | | |
|---|---|---|---|---|
| **77** | A7 | 25p black | .20 | .20 |
| **78** | A7 | 50p green | .30 | .20 |
| **79** | A7 | 1d red | .65 | .20 |
| **80** | A7 | 3d slate bl ('33) | 1.60 | .20 |
| **81** | A7 | 4d deep org ('33) | 3.50 | .20 |
| **82** | A7 | 5d purple ('33) | 5.25 | .20 |
| **83** | A7 | 10d dk olive ('33) | 17.00 | .20 |
| **84** | A7 | 15d deep brn ('33) | 21.00 | .20 |
| **85** | A7 | 20d dark vio ('33) | 32.50 | .20 |
| **86** | A7 | 30d rose ('33) | 37.50 | .35 |
| | | *Nos. 77-86 (10)* | 119.50 | 2.15 |

See Nos. 102-115.

**ЈУГОСЛАВИЈА**

Nos. 41 to 52 Overprinted

**JUGOSLAVIJA**

**1933, Sept. 5 *Perf. 13***

| | | | | |
|---|---|---|---|---|
| **87** | A6 | 25p deep green | .20 | .20 |
| **88** | A6 | 50p olive brown | .20 | .20 |
| **89** | A6 | 1d scarlet | .40 | .20 |
| **90** | A6 | 2d slate black | 1.75 | .70 |
| **91** | A6 | 3d slate blue | 1.60 | .20 |
| **92** | A6 | 4d red orange | 1.10 | .20 |
| **93** | A6 | 5d violet | 1.60 | .20 |
| **94** | A6 | 8d black brown | 4.75 | 1.00 |
| **95** | A6 | 10d olive brown | 6.75 | .20 |
| **96** | A6 | 15d brown | 8.25 | 1.75 |
| **97** | A6 | 20d dark violet | 15.00 | .50 |
| **98** | A6 | 30d orange | 13.00 | .65 |
| | | *Nos. 87-98 (12)* | 54.60 | 6.00 |

Semi-Postal Stamps of 1926 Overprinted like Nos. 87 to 98 and Four Bars over the Red Surcharge of 1926

**1933, Sept. 5**

| | | | | |
|---|---|---|---|---|
| **99** | A6 | 25p green | .50 | .20 |
| **100** | A6 | 50p olive brown | .60 | .20 |
| **101** | A6 | 1d scarlet | 1.25 | .40 |
| | | *Nos. 99-101 (3)* | 2.35 | .80 |

Nos. 99-101 exist with double impression of bars. Value, each $5.50 unused, $4.50 used.

### King Alexander Memorial Issue

Type of 1931-34 Issues Borders in Black

**1934, Oct. 17**

| | | | | |
|---|---|---|---|---|
| **102** | A7 | 25p black | .20 | .20 |
| **103** | A7 | 50p green | .20 | .20 |
| **104** | A7 | 75p slate green | .20 | .20 |
| **105** | A7 | 1d red | .20 | .20 |
| **106** | A7 | 1.50d pink | .20 | .20 |
| **107** | A7 | 1.75d deep rose | .20 | .20 |
| **108** | A7 | 3d slate blue | .20 | .20 |
| **109** | A7 | 3.50d ultramarine | .25 | .20 |
| **110** | A7 | 4d deep orange | .40 | .20 |
| **111** | A7 | 5d purple | .45 | .20 |
| **112** | A7 | 10d dark olive | 1.90 | .20 |
| **113** | A7 | 15d deep brown | 3.25 | .20 |
| **114** | A7 | 20d dark violet | 5.00 | .20 |
| **115** | A7 | 30d rose | 3.25 | .20 |
| | | *Nos. 102-115 (14)* | 15.90 | 2.80 |

Cyrillic Characters

Latin and Cyrillic inscriptions are transposed within some sets. In some sets some stamps are inscribed in Latin, others in Cyrillic. This will be mentioned only if it is necessary to identify otherwise identical stamps.

King Peter II — A10

**1935-36 *Perf. 13x12½***

| | | | | |
|---|---|---|---|---|
| **116** | A10 | 25p brown black | .20 | .20 |
| **117** | A10 | 50p yel orange | .20 | .20 |
| **118** | A10 | 75p turq green | .20 | .20 |
| **119** | A10 | 1d brown red | .20 | .20 |
| **120** | A10 | 1.50d scarlet | .20 | .20 |
| **121** | A10 | 1.75d cerise | .20 | .20 |
| **122** | A10 | 2d magenta ('36) | .20 | .20 |
| **123** | A10 | 3d brn orange | .20 | .20 |
| **124** | A10 | 3.50d ultramarine | .20 | .20 |
| **125** | A10 | 4d yellow grn | .75 | .20 |
| **126** | A10 | 4d slate blue ('36) | .20 | .20 |
| **127** | A10 | 10d bright vio | .35 | .20 |
| **128** | A10 | 15d brown | .60 | .20 |
| **129** | A10 | 20d bright blue | 2.25 | .20 |
| **130** | A10 | 30d rose pink | 1.50 | .20 |
| | | *Nos. 116-130 (15)* | 7.45 | 3.00 |

For overprints see Nos. N12, 14, N29.

King Alexander — A11

Nikola Tesla — A12

**1935, Oct. 9 *Perf. 12½x11½, 11½***

| | | | | |
|---|---|---|---|---|
| **131** | A11 | 75p turq green | .20 | .20 |
| **132** | A11 | 1.50d scarlet | .20 | .20 |
| **133** | A11 | 1.75d dark brown | .70 | 1.00 |
| **134** | A11 | 3.50d ultramarine | .70 | 1.00 |
| **135** | A11 | 7.50d rose carmine | .70 | 1.00 |
| | | *Nos. 131-135 (5)* | 2.50 | 3.40 |

Death of King Alexander, 1st anniv.

**1936, May 28 Litho. *Perf. 12½x11½***

| | | | | |
|---|---|---|---|---|
| **136** | A12 | 75p yel grn & dk brn | .20 | .20 |
| **137** | A12 | 1.75d dull blue & indigo | .25 | .20 |

80th birthday of Nikola Tesla (1856-1943), electrical inventor.

Memorial Church, Oplenac — A13

Coats of Arms of Yugoslavia, Greece, Romania and Turkey — A14

**1937, July 1**

| | | | | |
|---|---|---|---|---|
| **138** | A13 | 3d Prussian grn | .60 | .20 |
| *a.* | | Perf. 12½ | 7.25 | 5.00 |
| **139** | A13 | 4d dark blue | .60 | .20 |

"Little Entente," 16th anniversary.

***Perf. 11, 11½, 12½***

**1937, Oct. 29 Photo.**

| | | | | |
|---|---|---|---|---|
| **140** | A14 | 3d peacock grn | .35 | .20 |
| **141** | A14 | 4d ultramarine | .45 | .30 |

Balkan Entente.

King Peter II — A16

**1939-40 Typo. *Perf. 12½***

| | | | | |
|---|---|---|---|---|
| **142** | A16 | 25p black ('40) | .20 | .20 |
| **143** | A16 | 50p orange ('40) | .20 | .20 |
| **144** | A16 | 1d yellow grn | .20 | .20 |
| **145** | A16 | 1.50d red | .20 | .20 |
| **146** | A16 | 2d dp mag ('40) | .20 | .20 |
| **147** | A16 | 3d dull red brn | .20 | .20 |
| **148** | A16 | 4d ultra | .20 | .20 |
| **148A** | A16 | 5d dk blue ('40) | .20 | .20 |
| **148B** | A16 | 5.50d dk vio brn ('40) | .20 | .20 |

| | | | | |
|---|---|---|---|---|
| **149** | A16 | 6d slate blue | .40 | .20 |
| **150** | A16 | 8d sepia | .40 | .20 |
| **151** | A16 | 12d bright vio | .70 | .20 |
| **152** | A16 | 16d dull violet | 1.00 | .20 |
| **153** | A16 | 20d blue ('40) | 1.00 | .20 |
| **154** | A16 | 30d brt pink ('40) | 2.25 | .30 |
| | | *Nos. 142-154 (15)* | 7.55 | 3.10 |

For overprints and surcharges see Nos. N1-N11, N13, N15-N28, N30-N35, Croatia 1-25.

Arms of Yugoslavia, Greece, Romania and Turkey
A17 A18

**1940, June 1**

| | | | | |
|---|---|---|---|---|
| **155** | A17 | 3d ultramarine | .65 | .35 |
| **156** | A18 | 3d ultramarine | .65 | .35 |
| *a.* | | Pair, #155-156 | 2.50 | 2.50 |
| **157** | A17 | 4d dark blue | .65 | .35 |
| **158** | A18 | 4d dark blue | .65 | .35 |
| *a.* | | Pair, #157-158 | 2.50 | 2.50 |
| | | *Nos. 155-158 (4)* | 2.60 | 1.40 |

Balkan Entente.

Bridge at Obod A19

**1940, Sept. 29** **Litho.**

| | | | | |
|---|---|---|---|---|
| **159** | A19 | 5.50d slate grn & dull grn | 1.50 | 1.75 |

Zagreb Phil. Exhib.; 500th anniv. of Johann Gutenberg's invention of printing. The first press in the Yugoslav area was located at Obod in 1493.

### Issues for Federal Republic

Types of Serbia, 1942-43, Surcharged in Green or Vermilion

**1944, Dec.** **Unwmk.** ***Perf. 11½***
**Overprinted with Pale Green Network**

| | | | | |
|---|---|---|---|---|
| **159A** | OS4 | 5d (3d + 2d) rose pink | .20 | .25 |
| **159B** | OS4 | 10d (7d + 3d) dk sl grn (V) | .20 | .25 |

Similar Surcharge on Serbia Nos. 2N37-2N39

**1945, Jan. 24** **Without Network**

| | | | | |
|---|---|---|---|---|
| **159C** | OS4 | 5d (3d + 2d) rose pink | .20 | .25 |
| **159D** | OS4 | 10d (7d + 3d) dk sl grn (V) | .20 | .25 |
| **159E** | OS4 | 25d (4d + 21d) ultra (Bk) | .20 | .25 |
| | | *Nos. 159C-159E (3)* | .60 | .75 |

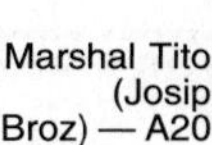

Marshal Tito (Josip Broz) — A20

Prohor Pcinski Monastery — A21

**1945** **Photo.** ***Perf. 12½***

| | | | | |
|---|---|---|---|---|
| **160** | A20 | 25p bright bl grn | .25 | .20 |
| **161** | A20 | 50p deep green | .25 | .20 |
| **162** | A20 | 1d crimson rose | 2.50 | .20 |
| **163** | A20 | 2d dark car rose | .25 | .20 |
| **164** | A20 | 4d deep blue | .50 | .20 |
| **165** | A20 | 5d deep green | .20 | .40 |
| **166** | A20 | 6d dark purple | .40 | .20 |
| **167** | A20 | 9d orange brown | .80 | .20 |
| **168** | A20 | 10d deep rose | .20 | .40 |
| **169** | A20 | 20d orange | 4.00 | 1.50 |
| **170** | A20 | 25d dark purple | .20 | .20 |
| **171** | A20 | 30d deep blue | .20 | .70 |
| | | *Nos. 160-171 (12)* | 9.75 | 4.60 |

**1945, Aug. 2** **Typo.** ***Perf. 11½***

| | | | | |
|---|---|---|---|---|
| **172** | A21 | 2d red | .60 | .20 |

Formation of the Popular Antifascist Chamber of Deputies of Macedonia, Aug. 2, 1944.

Partisans
A22 A23

Marshal Tito — A24

City of Jajce — A25

Partisan Girl and Flag — A26

**1945, Oct. 10** **Litho.** ***Perf. 12½***

| | | | | |
|---|---|---|---|---|
| **173** | A22 | 50p olive gray | .20 | .20 |
| **174** | A22 | 1d blue green | .20 | .20 |
| **175** | A23 | 1.50d orange brown | .20 | .20 |
| **176** | A24 | 2d scarlet | .20 | .20 |
| **177** | A25 | 3d red brown | .65 | .20 |
| **178** | A24 | 4d dark blue | .20 | .20 |
| **179** | A25 | 5d dark yel grn | .65 | .20 |
| **180** | A26 | 6d black | .25 | .20 |
| **181** | A26 | 9d deep plum | .25 | .20 |
| **182** | A23 | 12d ultramarine | .40 | .20 |
| **183** | A22 | 16d blue | .40 | .20 |
| **184** | A23 | 20d orange ver | 1.00 | .20 |
| | | *Nos. 173-184 (12)* | 4.60 | 2.40 |

See Nos. 211-214. For surcharges and overprints see Nos. 202-203, 273-292, 286-289, Istria 42, 44, 46, 48, 50, Trieste 5-14.

"Labor" and "Agriculture"
A27 A28

**1945, Nov. 29** **Photo.** ***Perf. 12***

| | | | | |
|---|---|---|---|---|
| **185** | A27 | 2d brn carmine | 3.00 | 3.00 |
| **186** | A28 | 2d brn carmine | 3.00 | 3.00 |
| **187** | A27 | 4d deep blue | 3.00 | 3.00 |
| **188** | A28 | 4d deep blue | 3.00 | 3.00 |
| **189** | A27 | 6d dk slate grn | 3.00 | 3.00 |
| **190** | A28 | 6d dk slate grn | 3.00 | 3.00 |
| **191** | A27 | 9d red orange | 3.00 | 3.00 |
| **192** | A28 | 9d red orange | 3.00 | 3.00 |
| **193** | A27 | 16d bright ultra | 3.00 | 3.00 |
| **194** | A28 | 16d bright ultra | 3.00 | 3.00 |
| **195** | A27 | 20d dark brown | 3.00 | 3.00 |
| *a.* | | Souv. sheet of 2, #191, 195, perf. 11½ | 8.00 | 8.00 |
| **196** | A28 | 20d dark brown | 3.00 | 3.00 |
| *a.* | | Souv. sheet of 2, #192, 196, perf. 11½ | 8.00 | 8.00 |
| | | *Nos. 185-196 (12)* | 36.00 | 36.00 |
| | | Se-tenant pairs, #185-196 (6) | 60.00 | 60.00 |

Constitution for the Democratic Federation of Yugoslavia, Nov. 29, 1945.

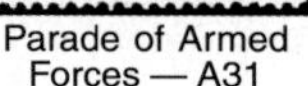

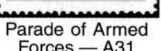

Parade of Armed Forces — A31

Svetozar Markovic — A32

**1946, May 9** **Unwmk.** ***Perf. 12½***

| | | | | |
|---|---|---|---|---|
| **199** | A31 | 1.50d org yel & red | .30 | .20 |
| **200** | A31 | 2.50d cerise & red | .45 | .25 |
| **201** | A31 | 5d blue & red | 1.25 | .90 |
| | | *Nos. 199-201 (3)* | 2.00 | 1.35 |

Victory over fascism, 1st anniv.

Type of 1945 Surcharged with New Values in Black

**1946, Apr. 1**

| | | | | |
|---|---|---|---|---|
| **202** | A26 | 2.50d on 6d bright red | .90 | .20 |
| **203** | A26 | 8d on 9d orange | .95 | .20 |

**1946, Sept. 22**

| | | | | |
|---|---|---|---|---|
| **204** | A32 | 1.50d blue green | .75 | .35 |
| **205** | A32 | 2.50d dp red lilac | .85 | .50 |

Markovic, Serbian socialist, birth cent.

People's Theater, Sofia A33

Sigismund Monument, Warsaw — A35

Designs: 1d, Prague. 2½d, Victory Monument, Belgrade. 5d, Spassky Tower, Kremlin.

**1946, Dec. 8** **Litho.** ***Perf. 11½***

| | | | | |
|---|---|---|---|---|
| **206** | A33 | ½d dk brn & yel brn | .20 | .20 |
| **207** | A33 | 1d grnsh blk & emer | .20 | .20 |
| **208** | A35 | 1½d dk car rose & rose | .20 | .20 |
| **209** | A35 | 2½d hn brn & brn org | .20 | .20 |
| **210** | A35 | 5d dark bl & blue | .30 | .20 |
| | | *Nos. 206-210 (5)* | 1.10 | 1.00 |

Pan-Slavic Congress, Belgrade, Dec. 1946.

Types of 1945

**1947, Jan. 15** **Litho.** ***Perf. 12½***

| | | | | |
|---|---|---|---|---|
| **211** | A26 | 2.50d red orange | .35 | .20 |
| **212** | A25 | 3d dull red | .35 | .20 |
| **213** | A25 | 5d dark blue | 1.10 | .20 |
| **214** | A26 | 8d orange | .90 | .20 |
| | | *Nos. 211-214 (4)* | 2.70 | .80 |

Gorski Vijenac — A38

Peter P. Nyegosh — A39

**1947, June 8** **Typo.**

| | | | | |
|---|---|---|---|---|
| **215** | A38 | 1.50d Prus grn & blk | .20 | .20 |
| **216** | A39 | 2.50d ol bis & dk car | .25 | .20 |
| **217** | A38 | 5d blue & black | .25 | .20 |
| | | *Nos. 215-217 (3)* | .70 | .60 |

Centenary of the Montenegrin national epic "Gorski Vijenac" (Wreath of Mountains) by Nyegosh.

Girls' Physical Training Classes — A40

Girl Runner — A41

Physical Culture Parade A42

**1947, June 15** **Litho.** ***Perf. 11***

| | | | | |
|---|---|---|---|---|
| **218** | A40 | 1.50d brown | .20 | .20 |
| **219** | A41 | 2.50d red | .25 | .25 |
| **220** | A42 | 4d violet blue | .40 | .35 |
| | | *Nos. 218-220 (3)* | .85 | .80 |

Natl. sports meet, Belgrade, 6/15-22/47.

Map and Star — A43

**1947, Sept. 16** **Typo.**

| | | | | |
|---|---|---|---|---|
| **231** | A43 | 2.50d dp car & dark bl | .20 | .20 |
| **232** | A43 | 5d org brn & dk grn | .20 | .20 |

Annexation of Julian Province.

Music and One-string Gusle A44

Vuk Karadzic — A45

**1947, Sept. 27** ***Perf. 11½x12, 12½***

| | | | | |
|---|---|---|---|---|
| **233** | A44 | 1.50d green | .25 | .25 |
| **234** | A45 | 2.50d orange red | .25 | .25 |
| **235** | A44 | 5d violet blue | .25 | .25 |
| | | *Nos. 233-235 (3)* | .75 | .75 |

Centenary of Serbian literature.

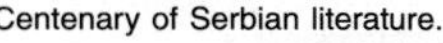

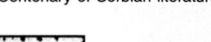

Symbols of Industry and Agriculture, Map and Flag — A46

Danube River Scene — A47

**1948, Apr. 8 Litho. *Perf. 12½***

**236** A46 1.50d grn, bl & salmon .20 .20
**237** A46 2.50d red brn, bl & salmon .20 .20
**238** A46 5d dk bl, bl & salmon .20 .20
*Nos. 236-238 (3)* .60 .60

International Fair, Zagreb, May 8-17.

**1948, July 30 Unwmk.**

**239** A47 2d green 2.25 2.25
**240** A47 3d carmine 2.25 2.25
**241** A47 5d blue 2.25 2.25
**242** A47 10d brown orange 2.25 2.25
*Nos. 239-242 (4)* 9.00 9.00

Danube Conference, Belgrade.

Marchers with Party Flag — A48

Laurent Kosir — A49

**1948, July 21 *Perf. 11½, 12½***

**243** A48 2d dark green .20 .20
**244** A48 3d dark red .25 .20
**245** A48 10d dark blue vio .35 .20
*Nos. 243-245 (3)* .80 .60

5th Congress of the Communist Party in Yugoslavia, July 21, 1948.

**1948, Aug. 21 *Perf. 12½***

**246** A49 3d claret .20 .20
**247** A49 5d blue .20 .20
**248** A49 10d red orange .20 .20
**249** A49 12d dull green .20 .20
*Nos. 246-249 (4)* .80 .80

80th death anniv. of Laurent Kosir, recognized by Yugoslavia as inventor of the postage stamp.

Arms of Bosnia and Herzegovina A50

Arms of Yugoslavia A51

**1948, Nov. 29 *Perf. 12½, 12x11½***
**Arms of Yugoslav Peoples Republics**

**250** A50 3d green .30 .30
**251** A50 3d rose lil (Macedonia) .30 .30
**252** A50 3d gray bl (Serbia) .30 .30
**253** A50 3d gray (Montenegro) .30 .30
**254** A50 3d rose (Croatia) .30 .30
**255** A50 3d orange (Slovenia) .30 .30
**256** A51 10d deep carmine 1.40 1.40
*Nos. 250-256 (7)* 3.20 3.20

The Cyrillic and Latin inscriptions are transposed on Nos. 252, 253 and 255.

Franc Presern — A52

**1949, Feb. 8 Photo. *Perf. 11½***

**257** A52 3d dark blue .30 .20
**258** A52 5d brown orange .30 .20
**259** A52 10d olive black .30 .20
*Nos. 257-259 (3)* .90 .60

Death cent. of Franc Presern, poet.

Ski Jump, Planica — A53

Ski Jumper — A54

***Perf. 12½x11½***
**1949, Mar. 20 Litho.**

**260** A53 10d magenta .75 .55
**261** A54 12d slate gray .75 .55

Intl. Ski Championships, Planica, Mar. 13-20.

Soldiers — A55

Farmers — A56

Arms and Flags of Macedonia and Yugoslavia — A57

**1949, Aug. 2 *Perf. 12½***

**262** A55 3d carmine rose .20 .20
**263** A56 5d dull blue .20 .20
**264** A57 12d red brown 2.00 2.75
*Nos. 262-264 (3)* 2.40 3.15

Liberation of Macedonia, 5th anniv.
It is reported that No. 264 was not sold to the public at post offices.
For overprints see Nos. C30-C32.

Postal Communications A58

UPU, 75th anniversary: 5d, Plane, locomotive and stagecoach, horiz.

**1949, Sept. 8 Unwmk.**

**265** A58 3d red 1.10 1.10
**266** A58 5d blue .25 .25
**267** A58 12d brown .25 .25
*Nos. 265-267 (3)* 1.60 1.60

For overprints see Trieste Nos. 15-16.

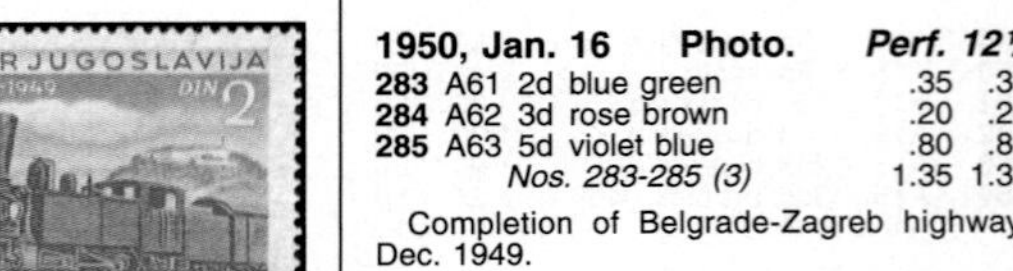
Locomotives A60

**1949, Dec. 15 Photo.**

**269** A60 2d Early steam .85 .20
**270** A60 3d Modern steam .90 .20
**271** A60 5d Diesel 2.50 .25
**272** A60 10d Electric 8.75 5.50
*Nos. 269-272 (4)* 13.00 6.15

Centenary of Yugoslav railroads.
For overprints see Trieste Nos. 17-20.

Official Stamps Nos. O7 and O8 Surcharged:

**1949 Typo.**

**272A** O1 3d on 8d chocolate .20 .20
**272B** O1 3d on 12d violet .20 .20

Stamps of 1945 and 1947 Overprinted or Surcharged in Black:

a b c d

**1949 Litho.**

**273** A22 (a) 50p olive gray .20 .20
**274** A22 (a) 1d blue green .20 .20
**275** A24 (b) 2d scarlet .20 .20
**276** A26 (c) 3d on 8d orange .20 .20
**277** A25 (d) 3d dull red .20 .20
**278** A25 (d) 5d dark blue .20 .20
**279** A23 (a) 10d on 20d org ver .25 .20
**280** A23 (a) 12d ultramarine .35 .20
**281** A22 (a) 16d blue .60 .20
**282** A23 (a) 20d orange ver .45 .20
*Nos. 273-282 (10)* 2.85 2.00

On No. 279 the surcharge includes a rule below "JUGOSLAVIJA" and "D 10" with two bars over "20D."
See Nos. 286-289.

Surveying for Highway A61

Bridge, Map and Automobile A62

Highway Completion Symbolized A63

**1950, Jan. 16 Photo. *Perf. 12½***

**283** A61 2d blue green .35 .35
**284** A62 3d rose brown .20 .20
**285** A63 5d violet blue .80 .80
*Nos. 283-285 (3)* 1.35 1.35

Completion of Belgrade-Zagreb highway, Dec. 1949.

Types of 1945 Overprinted in Black

**1950 Unwmk. *Perf. 12½***

**286** A22 (a) 1d brownish org .20 .20
**287** A24 (b) 2d blue green .20 .20
**288** A25 (d) 3d rose pink .20 .20
**289** A25 (d) 5d blue .25 .20
*Nos. 286-289 (4)* .85 .80

Marshal Tito — A64

Child Eating — A65

**1950, Apr. 30 Engr.**

**290** A64 3d red .70 .30
**291** A64 5d dull blue .70 .30
**292** A64 10d brown 4.50 3.25
**293** A64 12d olive black 1.25 .70
*Nos. 290-293 (4)* 7.15 4.55

Labor Day, May 1.

**1950, June 1 Photo.**

**294** A65 3d brown red .25 .20

Issued to publicize Children's Day, June 1.

Boy and Model Plane — A66

Map and Chess Symbols — A67

Designs: 3d, Glider aloft. 5d, Parachutists. 10d, Aviatrix. 20d, Glider on field.

**1950, July 2 Engr.**

**295** A66 2d dark green .65 .30
**296** A66 3d brown red .65 .30
**297** A66 5d violet .65 .30
**298** A66 10d chocolate .65 .30
**299** A66 20d ultramarine 5.50 4.00
*Nos. 295-299 (5)* 8.10 5.20

Third Aviation Meet, July 2-11.

**1950, Aug. 20 Photo. *Perf. 11½***

3d, Rook and ribbon. 5d, Globe and chess board. 10d, Allegory of international chess. 20d, View of Dubrovnik, knight and ribbon.

**300** A67 2d red brn & rose brown .45 .35
**301** A67 3d blk brn, gray brn & dl yellow .45 .35
**302** A67 5d dk grn, bl & buff .75 .45
**303** A67 10d cl, bl & org yel 1.10 .60
**304** A67 20d dk bl, bl & org yellow 7.75 5.00
*Nos. 300-304 (5)* 10.50 6.75

Intl. Chess Matches, Dubrovnik, Aug. 1950.

Electrification A68

Coal and Logs for Export A69

Designs: 50p, Metallurgy. 2d, Agriculture, 3d, Construction. 5d, Fishing. 7d, Mining. 10d, Fruitgrowing. 12d, Lumbering. 16d, Gathering sunflowers. 20d, Livestock raising. 30d, Book manufacture. 50d, Loading ship.

**1950-51 Unwmk. Engr. *Perf. 12½***

| | | | | |
|---|---|---|---|---|
| **305** | A68 | 50p dk brn ('51) | .20 | .20 |
| **306** | A68 | 1d blue green | .20 | .20 |
| **307** | A68 | 2d orange | .20 | .20 |
| **308** | A68 | 3d rose red | .20 | .20 |
| **309** | A68 | 5d ultramarine | .30 | .20 |
| **310** | A68 | 7d gray | .30 | .20 |
| **311** | A68 | 10d chocolate | .50 | .20 |
| **312** | A68 | 12d vio brn ('51) | 1.25 | .20 |
| **313** | A68 | 16d vio bl ('51) | 1.75 | .30 |
| **314** | A68 | 20d ol grn ('51) | 1.75 | .25 |
| **314A** | A68 | 30d red brn ('51) | 3.50 | 1.00 |
| **315** | A68 | 50d violet ('51) | 21.00 | 12.00 |
| | | *Nos. 305-315 (12)* | 31.15 | 15.15 |

See Nos. 343-354, 378-384A. For overprints see Trieste Nos. 68-75, 90-92.

**1950, Sept. 23 Photo.**

**316** A69 3d red brown .30 .20

Zagreb International Fair, 1950.

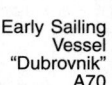

Early Sailing Vessel "Dubrovnik" A70

Partisans with Flag — A71

Designs: 3d, Partisans in boat. 5d, Loading freighter. 10d, Transatlantic ship "Zagreb." 12d, Sailboats. 20d, Naval gun and ship.

**1950, Nov. 29**

| | | | | |
|---|---|---|---|---|
| **317** | A70 | 2d brown violet | .20 | .20 |
| **318** | A70 | 3d orange brown | .20 | .20 |
| **319** | A70 | 5d dull green | .20 | .20 |
| **320** | A70 | 10d chalky blue | .30 | .20 |
| **321** | A70 | 12d dark blue | .70 | .30 |
| **322** | A70 | 20d red brown | 2.00 | 1.10 |
| | | *Nos. 317-322 (6)* | 3.60 | 2.20 |

Yugoslav navy.

**1951, Mar. 27 Engr.**

**323** A71 3d red & red brn 2.75 1.50

Yugoslavia's resistance to Nazi Germany, 10th anniv.

Stane Rozman A72

5d, Post-boy during Slovene insurrection.

**1951, Apr. 27 Photo.**

| | | | | |
|---|---|---|---|---|
| **324** | A72 | 3d brown red | .35 | .25 |
| **325** | A72 | 5d dark blue | .60 | .40 |

Slovene insurrection, 10th anniv.

Children Painting A73

**1951, June 3**

**326** A73 3d red .60 .20

Issued to publicize Children's Day, June 3.

Zika Jovanovich — A74

Serbian Revolutionists A75

**1951, July 7**

| | | | | |
|---|---|---|---|---|
| **327** | A74 | 3d brown red | .45 | .25 |
| **328** | A75 | 5d deep blue | .70 | .40 |

Serbian insurrection, 10th anniv.

Sava Kovacevich A76

Kovacevich Leading Revolutionists A77

**1951, July 13**

| | | | | |
|---|---|---|---|---|
| **329** | A76 | 3d rose pink | .70 | .25 |
| **330** | A77 | 5d light blue | 1.00 | .40 |

Montenegrin insurrection, 10th anniv.

Monument to Marko Oreskovich A78

**1951, July 27**

| | | | | |
|---|---|---|---|---|
| **331** | A78 | 3d shown | .45 | .25 |
| **332** | A78 | 5d Monument to wounded | .70 | .40 |

Croatian insurrection, 10th anniv.

Sium Bolaj — A79

Revolutionists A80

**1951, July 27**

| | | | | |
|---|---|---|---|---|
| **333** | A79 | 3d rose brown | .35 | .20 |
| **334** | A80 | 5d blue | .75 | .40 |

Revolution in Bosnia and Herzegovina, 10th anniv.

Primoz Trubar — A81

National Handicrafts — A82

12d, Marko Marulic. 20d, Tsar Stefan Duschan.

**1951, Sept. 9 Engr.**

| | | | | |
|---|---|---|---|---|
| **335** | A81 | 10d slate gray | .40 | .25 |
| **336** | A81 | 12d brown orange | .40 | .25 |
| **337** | A81 | 20d violet | 2.50 | 2.00 |
| | | *Nos. 335-337 (3)* | 3.30 | 2.50 |

Yugoslav cultural anniversaries. For overprints see Trieste Nos. 40-41.

**1951, Sept. 15 Litho. *Perf. 11½***

**338** A82 3d multicolored 1.75 .45

Zagreb International Fair, 1951.

Mirce Acev — A83

Monument at Skopje A84

**1951, Oct. 11**

| | | | | |
|---|---|---|---|---|
| **339** | A83 | 3d deep plum | .55 | .30 |
| **340** | A84 | 5d indigo | 1.10 | .65 |

Macedonian insurrection, 10th anniv.

Soldier and Emblem — A85

Peter P. Nyegosh — A86

**1951, Dec. 22 Photo. *Perf. 12½***

**341** A85 15d deep carmine .45 .20

Army Day. See No. C54.

**1951, Nov. 29 Engr.**

**342** A86 15d deep claret 2.00 .55

Death centenary of Nyegosh. See note after No. 217.

Types of 1950-51

**1951-52 Engr.**

Designs: 15d, Gathering sunflowers. 25d, Agriculture. 35d, Construction. 75d, Lumbering. 100d, Metallurgy.

| | | | | |
|---|---|---|---|---|
| **343** | A68 | 1d gray ('52) | .20 | .20 |
| **344** | A68 | 2d rose car ('52) | .25 | .20 |
| **345** | A68 | 5d orange ('52) | 1.25 | .20 |
| **346** | A68 | 10d emerald ('52) | 4.75 | .20 |
| **347** | A68 | 15d rose car ('52) | 10.50 | 1.50 |
| **348** | A68 | 20d purple | 2.25 | .20 |
| **349** | A68 | 25d yel brn ('52) | 7.00 | .20 |
| **350** | A68 | 30d blue | 1.25 | .20 |
| **351** | A68 | 35d red brn ('52) | 1.60 | .20 |
| **352** | A68 | 50d greenish bl | 1.25 | .20 |
| **353** | A68 | 75d purple ('52) | 1.90 | .20 |
| **354** | A68 | 100d sepia ('52) | 3.00 | .25 |
| | | *Nos. 343-354 (12)* | 35.20 | 3.75 |

No. 349 exists with and without printer's inscriptions at bottom, with stamps differing slightly.

Marshal Tito

A87 A88

**1952, May 25 Photo. *Perf. 11½***

| | | | | |
|---|---|---|---|---|
| **355** | A87 | 15d shown | .50 | .45 |
| **356** | A88 | 28d shown | 1.10 | .90 |
| **357** | A87 | 50d Tito facing left | 8.50 | 7.75 |
| | | *Nos. 355-357 (3)* | 10.10 | 9.10 |

60th birthday of Marshal Tito

Child with Ball — A89

**1952, June 1 Litho. *Perf. 12½***

**358** A89 15d bright rose 3.50 1.00

Issued to publicize Children's Day, June 1. For overprint see Trieste No. 60.

Girl Gymnast — A90

Split, Dalmatia — A91

**1952, July 10** *Perf. 12½*

**359** A90 5d shown .50 .35
**360** A90 10d Runner .50 .35
**361** A90 15d Swimmer .50 .35
**362** A90 28d Boxer .50 .35
**363** A90 50d Basketball 4.00 2.00
**364** A90 100d Soccer 8.50 6.25
*Nos. 359-364 (6)* 14.50 9.65

15th Olympic Games, Helsinki, 1952.
Nos. 359-364 exist imperf. Value $250.
For overprints see Trieste Nos. 51-56.

**1952, Sept. 10** **Litho.**

**365** A91 15d shown 1.10 1.10
**366** A91 28d Naval scene 1.75 1.75
**367** A91 50d St. Stefan 6.75 6.75
*Nos. 365-367 (3)* 9.60 9.60

Yugoslav navy, 10th anniv.
For overprints see Trieste Nos. 57-59.

Belgrade, 16th Century A92

**1952, Sept. 14** **Engr.** *Perf. 11½*

**368** A92 15d violet brn 6.00 5.00

1st Yugoslav Phil. Exhib., Sept. 14-20. Sold only at the exhibition.

Marching Workers and Congress Flag — A93

**1952, Nov. 2** *Perf. 11½*

**369** A93 15d red brown 1.25 1.10
**370** A93 15d dark vio blue 1.25 1.10
**371** A93 15d dark brown 1.25 1.10
**372** A93 15d blue green 1.25 1.10
*Nos. 369-372 (4)* 5.00 4.40

6th Yugoslav Communist Party Congress, Zagreb.
For overprints see Trieste Nos. 61-64.

Nikola Tesla — A94

Woman Pouring Water — A95

**1953, Jan. 7** **Unwmk.**

**373** A94 15d brown carmine .65 .20
**374** A94 30d chalky blue 2.00 .35

Death of Nikola Tesla, 10th anniv.
For overprints see Trieste Nos. 66-67.

**1953, Mar. 24** **Litho.** *Perf. 11½*

Designs: 30d, Hands holding two birds. 50d, Woman holding Urn.

**375** A95 15d dk olive green .90 .30
**376** A95 30d chalky blue .90 .30
**377** A95 50d henna brown 6.00 1.60
*Nos. 375-377 (3)* 7.80 2.20

Issued to honor the United Nations.
See Nos. RA19 and RAJ16. For overprints see Trieste Nos. 76-78.

Types of 1950-52

**1953-55** **Litho.** *Perf. 12½*

8d, Mining. 17d, Livestock raising.

**378** A68 1d dull gray .70 .20
**379** A68 2d carmine 2.50 .20
**380** A68 5d orange 3.50 .20
**381** A68 8d blue 2.50 .20
**382** A68 10d yellow green 5.50 .20
**383** A68 12d lt vio brown 25.00 .20
**384** A68 15d rose red 11.00 .20
**384A** A68 17d vio brn ('55) 2.00 .20
*Nos. 378-384A (8)* 52.70 1.60

For overprints see Trieste Nos. 68-75, 90-92.

Automobile Climbing Mt. Lovcen — A96

30d, Motorcycle & auto at Opatija. 50d, Racers leaving Belgrade. 70d, Auto near Mt. Triglav.

**1953, May 10** **Photo.** *Perf. 12½*

**385** A96 15d sal & dp plum .20 .20
**386** A96 30d bl & dark blue .30 .20
**387** A96 50d ocher & choc .45 .20
**388** A96 70d lt bl grn & ol grn 1.90 .40
*Nos. 385-388 (4)* 2.85 1.00

Intl. Automobile & Motorcycle Races, 1953.

President Tito — A97

Star and Flag-encircled Globe — A98

**1953, June 28** **Engr.** **Unwmk.**

**389** A97 50d deep purple 4.25 1.25

Marshal Tito's election to the presidency, Jan. 14, 1953.
For overprint see Trieste No. 83.

**1953, July 25** **Engr.; Star Typo.**

**390** A98 15d gray & green 2.50 2.00

38th Esperanto Cong., Zagreb, 7/25-8/1.
For overprint see Trieste No. 84.

Macedonian Revolutionary A99

Nicolas Karev A100

**1953, Aug. 2** **Litho.**

**391** A99 15d dark red brown .85 .65
**392** A100 30d dull green 3.00 1.75

Macedonian Insurection of 1903, 50th anniv.

Family — A101

Branko Radicevic — A102

**1953, Sept. 6** **Photo.**

**393** A101 15d deep green 10.00 2.50

Liberation of Istria and the Slovene coast, 10th anniv.
For overprint see Trieste No. 85.

**1953, Oct. 1** **Engr.**

**394** A102 15d lilac 4.25 1.50

10th death anniv. of Branko Radicevic, poet.
For overprint see Trieste No. 86.

View of Jajce — A103

Designs: 30d, First meeting place. 50d, Marshal Tito addressing Assembly.

**1953, Nov. 29** *Perf. 12½x12*

**395** A103 15d dark green 1.40 .70
**396** A103 30d rose car 1.90 1.10
**397** A103 50d dark brown 7.75 7.00
*Nos. 395-397 (3)* 11.05 8.80

2nd Assembly of the Natl. Republic of Yugoslavia, 10th anniv.
For overprints see Trieste Nos. 87-89.

Wildlife A104

Lammergeier A105

**1954, June 30** **Photo.** *Perf. 11½*

**398** A104 2d Ground squirrel .25 .20
**399** A104 5d Lynx .25 .20
**400** A104 10d Red deer .25 .20
**401** A104 15d Brown bear .35 .20
**402** A104 17d Chamois .35 .20
**403** A104 25d White pelican .60 .40
**404** A105 30d shown .60 .40
**405** A105 35d Black beetle .60 .40
**406** A105 50d Bush cricket 5.00 3.25
**407** A105 65d Adriatic lizard 10.00 5.00
**408** A105 70d Salamander 9.00 5.00
**409** A105 100d Trout 15.00 15.00
*Nos. 398-409 (12)* 42.25 30.45

See Nos. 497-505. For overprints see Trieste Nos. 93-104.

**Catalogue values for unused stamps in this section, from this point to the end of the section, are for Never Hinged items.**

Ljubljana, 17th Century A106

**1954, July 29** **Engr.**

**410** A106 15d multicolored 11.00 10.50

2nd Yugoslav Phil. Exhib., July 29-Aug. 8. Sold for 50d, which included admission to the exhibition.

Revolutionary Flag — A107

**Engr. & Typo.**

**1954, Oct. 3** *Perf. 12½*

**411** A107 15d shown 1.60 .45
**412** A107 30d Cannon 2.25 .80
**413** A107 50d Revolutionary seal 5.00 1.10
**414** A107 70d Karageorge 32.50 15.00
*Nos. 411-414 (4)* 41.35 17.35

1st Serbian insurrection, 150th anniv.
For overprints see Trieste Nos. 105-108.

Vatroslav Lisinski — A108

30d, Andrea Kacic-Miosic. 50d, Jure Vega. 70d, Jovan Jovanovic-Zmaj. 100d, Philip Visnic.

**1954, Dec. 25** **Engr.**

**415** A108 15d dark green 2.75 1.00
**416** A108 30d chocolate 2.75 1.60
**417** A108 50d dp claret 3.75 3.00
**418** A108 70d indigo 7.50 7.00
**419** A108 100d purple 19.00 19.00
*Nos. 415-419 (5)* 35.75 31.60

Scene from "Robinja" — A109

"A Midsummer Night's Dream" A110

**1955** **Photo.** *Perf. 12x11½, 12½*
**Glazed Paper**

**420** A109 15d brown lake 1.00 .55
**421** A110 30d dark blue 3.50 1.60

Festival at Dubrovnik.

Dragon Emblem of Ljubljana — A111

**1955 Engr. *Perf. 12½***

| | | | | |
|---|---|---|---|---|
| **422** | A111 | 15d dk grn & brn | 3.00 | .95 |

1st Intl. Exhib. of Graphic Arts, Ljubljana, July 3-Sept. 3.

Symbol of Sign Language — A112

Hops — A113

**1955, Aug. 23**

| | | | | |
|---|---|---|---|---|
| **423** | A112 | 15d rose lake | 1.75 | .45 |

2nd World Congress of Deaf Mutes, Zagreb, Aug. 23-27.

**1955, Sept. 24 Photo. *Perf. 11½***

Medicinal Plants.

| | | | | |
|---|---|---|---|---|
| **424** | A113 | 5d shown | .20 | .20 |
| **425** | A113 | 10d Tobacco | .20 | .20 |
| **426** | A113 | 15d Poppy | .20 | .20 |
| **427** | A113 | 17d Linden | .20 | .20 |
| **428** | A113 | 25d Chamomile | .20 | .20 |
| **429** | A113 | 30d Salvia | .40 | .20 |
| **430** | A113 | 50d Dog rose | 5.25 | 1.50 |
| **431** | A113 | 70d Gentian | 6.50 | 1.90 |
| **432** | A113 | 100d Adonis | 12.00 | 2.50 |
| | | *Nos. 424-432 (9)* | 25.15 | 7.10 |

"Peace" Statue, New York — A114

Woman and Dove — A115

**1955, Oct. 24 Litho. *Perf. 12½***

| | | | | |
|---|---|---|---|---|
| **433** | A114 | 30d lt bl & blk | 1.75 | 1.10 |

United Nations, 10th anniversary.

**1955, Nov. 29 Engr.**

| | | | | |
|---|---|---|---|---|
| **434** | A115 | 15d dull violet | .65 | .20 |

10th anniv. of the "New Yugoslavia."

St. Donat, Zadar — A116

Cornice, Cathedral at Sibenik A117

Yugoslav Art: 10d, Relief of a King, Split. 15d, Griffin, Studenica Monastery. 20d, Figures, Trogir Cathedral. 25d, Fresco, Sopocani Monastery. 30d, Tombstone, Radimlje. 40d, Ciborium, Kotor Cathedral. 50d, St. Martin from Tryptich, Dubrovnik. 70d, Figure, Belec Church. 100d, Rihard Jakopic, self-portrait. 200d, "Peace" Statue, New York.

**1956, Mar. 24 Photo. *Perf. 11½***

| | | | | |
|---|---|---|---|---|
| **435** | A116 | 5d blue vio | .25 | .20 |
| **436** | A116 | 10d slate grn | .25 | .20 |
| **437** | A116 | 15d olive brn | .25 | .20 |
| **438** | A116 | 20d brown car | .25 | .20 |
| **439** | A116 | 25d black brn | .25 | .20 |
| **440** | A116 | 30d dp claret | .25 | .20 |
| **441** | A117 | 35d olive grn | .60 | .20 |
| **442** | A117 | 40d red brown | 1.00 | .30 |
| **443** | A116 | 50d olive brn | 1.50 | .40 |
| **444** | A116 | 70d dk green | 5.50 | 4.00 |
| **445** | A116 | 100d dark pur | 19.00 | 12.00 |
| **446** | A116 | 200d deep blue | 45.00 | 19.00 |
| | | *Nos. 435-446 (12)* | 74.10 | 37.10 |

13th Century Tower, Zagreb A118

**1956, Apr. 20 Engr. *Perf. 11½***
**Chalky Paper**

| | | | | |
|---|---|---|---|---|
| **447** | A118 | 15d vio brn, bis brn & gray | .40 | .20 |
| *a.* | | Miniature sheet of 4 | 4.50 | 1.60 |

3rd Yugoslavia Phil. Exhib. (JUFIZ III), Zagreb, May 20-27. No. 447a was sold at the exhibition, tipped into a folder, for 75 dinars. See No. C56.

Induction Motor — A119

***Perf. 11½x12½***

**1956, July 10 Photo.**

| | | | | |
|---|---|---|---|---|
| **448** | A119 | 10d shown | .25 | .20 |
| **449** | A119 | 15d Transformer | .30 | .20 |
| **450** | A119 | 30d Electronic controls | .55 | .25 |
| **451** | A119 | 50d Nikola Tesla | 1.90 | 1.00 |
| | | *Nos. 448-451 (4)* | 3.00 | 1.65 |

Birth cent. of Nikola Tesla, inventor.

Sea Horse — A120

Paper Nautilus A121

Designs: 20d, European rock lobster. 25d, "Sea Prince." 30d, Sea perch. 35d, Red mullet. 50d, Scorpion fish. 70d, Wrasse. 100d, Dory.

**1956, Sept. 10 *Perf. 11½***
**Granite Paper**
**Animals in Natural Colors**

| | | | | |
|---|---|---|---|---|
| **452** | A120 | 10d bright grn | .20 | .20 |
| **453** | A121 | 15d ultra & blk | .20 | .20 |
| **454** | A121 | 20d deep blue | .20 | .20 |
| **455** | A121 | 25d violet blue | .30 | .20 |
| **456** | A121 | 30d brt grnsh bl | .35 | .20 |
| **457** | A121 | 35d dk bl green | .70 | .20 |
| **458** | A121 | 50d indigo | 2.75 | .80 |
| **459** | A121 | 70d slate grn | 4.50 | 1.40 |
| **460** | A121 | 100d dark blue | 12.00 | 4.00 |
| | | *Nos. 452-460 (9)* | 21.20 | 7.40 |

Runner A122

Centaury — A123

Designs: 15d, Paddling kayak. 20d, Skiing. 30d, Swimming. 35d, Soccer. 50d, Water polo. 70d, Table tennis. 100d, Sharpshooting.

**1956, Oct. 24 Litho. *Perf. 12½***
**Design and Inscription in Bister**

| | | | | |
|---|---|---|---|---|
| **461** | A122 | 10d dk carmine | .20 | .20 |
| **462** | A122 | 15d dark blue | .20 | .20 |
| **463** | A122 | 20d ultramarine | .20 | .20 |
| **464** | A122 | 30d olive grn | .20 | .20 |
| **465** | A122 | 35d dark brown | .25 | .20 |
| **466** | A122 | 50d green | .65 | .20 |
| **467** | A122 | 70d brn violet | 2.00 | 1.10 |
| **468** | A122 | 100d dark red | 4.75 | 2.25 |
| | | *Nos. 461-468 (8)* | 8.45 | 4.55 |

16th Olympic Games, Melbourne, 11/22-12/8.

**1957, May 25 Photo. *Perf. 11½***

Medicinal Plants: 15d, Belladonna. 20d, Autumn crocus. 25d, Marsh mallow. 30d, Valerian. 35d, Woolly Foxglove. 50d, Aspidium. 70d, Green Winged Orchid. 100d, Pyrethrum.

**Granite Paper**
**Flowers in Natural Colors**

| | | | | |
|---|---|---|---|---|
| **469** | A123 | 10d dk bl & grn | .20 | .20 |
| **470** | A123 | 15d violet | .20 | .20 |
| **471** | A123 | 20d lt ol grn & brn | .20 | .20 |
| **472** | A123 | 25d dp cl & dk bl | .30 | .20 |
| **473** | A123 | 30d lil rose & claret | .55 | .20 |
| **474** | A123 | 35d dk gray & dl pur | .90 | .20 |
| **475** | A123 | 50d dp grn & choc | 1.50 | .45 |
| **476** | A123 | 70d pale brn & grn | 2.75 | 1.00 |
| **477** | A123 | 100d gray & brown | 8.50 | 1.90 |
| | | *Nos. 469-477 (9)* | 15.10 | 4.55 |

See #538-546, 597-605, 689-694, 772-777.

Hand Holding Factory A124

**1957, June 25 Engr. *Perf. 12½***

| | | | | |
|---|---|---|---|---|
| **478** | A124 | 15d dark car rose | .35 | .20 |
| **479** | A124 | 30d violet blue | 1.40 | .35 |

Congress of Workers' Councils, Belgrade, June 25.

2nd Gymnastic Meet, Zagreb, July 10-14 — A125

Various gymnastic positions.

**1957, July 1 Photo.**

| | | | | |
|---|---|---|---|---|
| **480** | A125 | 10d ol grn & blk | .20 | .20 |
| **481** | A125 | 15d brn red & blk | .20 | .20 |
| **482** | A125 | 30d Prus bl & blk | .50 | .20 |
| **483** | A125 | 50d brn & black | 2.25 | 1.25 |
| | | *Nos. 480-483 (4)* | 3.15 | 1.85 |

Montenegro A126

Natl. Costumes: 15d, Macedonia. 30d, Croatia. 50d, Serbia. 70d, Bosnia and Herzegovina. 100d, Slovenia. 50d, 70d, 100d vert.

**1957, Sept. 24 Typo. *Perf. 12½***
**Background in Bister Brown**

| | | | | |
|---|---|---|---|---|
| **484** | A126 | 10d dk brn, ultra & red | .20 | .20 |
| **485** | A126 | 15d dk brn, blk & red | .20 | .20 |
| **486** | A126 | 30d dk brn, grn & red | .20 | .20 |
| **487** | A126 | 50d dk brn & green | .50 | .20 |
| **488** | A126 | 70d dk brn & black | .65 | .40 |
| **489** | A126 | 100d dk brn, grn & red | 3.25 | 1.90 |
| | | *Nos. 484-489 (6)* | 5.00 | 3.10 |

Revolutionists A127

Simon Gregorcic — A128

**Lithographed and Engraved**
**1957, Nov. 7 *Perf. 11½x12½***

| | | | | |
|---|---|---|---|---|
| **490** | A127 | 15d ocher & red | .55 | .40 |

Russian Revolution, 40th anniv.

**1957, Dec. 3 Engr. *Perf. 12½***

Famous Yugoslavs: 30d, Anton Linhart, dramatist and historian. 50d, Oton Kucera, physicist. 70d, Stevan Mokranjac, composer. 100d, Jovan Sterija Popovic, writer

| | | | | |
|---|---|---|---|---|
| **491** | A128 | 15d sepia | .45 | .20 |
| **492** | A128 | 30d indigo | .60 | .20 |
| **493** | A128 | 50d reddish brn | 1.25 | .20 |
| **494** | A128 | 70d dl violet | 9.00 | 2.50 |
| **495** | A128 | 100d olive grn | 15.00 | 13.00 |
| | | *Nos. 491-495 (5)* | 26.30 | 16.10 |

"Young Man on Fire" — A129

Stylized Bird — A130

**1958, Apr. 22** **Photo.**
**496** A129 15d deep plum .35 .20

Union of Yugoslav Communists, 7th congress, Ljubljana, Apr. 22.

Types of 1954

Game birds.

**1958, May 25** ***Perf. 11½***
**Granite Paper**
**Birds in Natural Colors**

**497** A104 10d Mallard .20 .20
**498** A104 15d Capercaillie .20 .20
**499** A104 20d Ring-necked pheasant .20 .20
**500** A105 25d Coot .20 .20
**501** A104 30d Water rail .30 .20
**502** A105 35d Great bustard .50 .20
**503** A105 50d Rock partridge 2.00 .70
**504** A104 70d Woodcock 3.50 1.75
**505** A105 100d Eurasian crane 7.50 4.00
*Nos. 497-505 (9)* 14.60 7.65

**1958, June 14** **Engr.** ***Perf. 12½***
**506** A130 15d bluish black .50 .25

Opening of Postal Museum, Belgrade.

Flag and Laurel A131

**1958, July 1** **Unwmk.**
**507** A131 15d brn carmine .40 .20

15th anniv. of victory over Germans at Sutjeska, Bosnia.

Onufrio Well, Dubrovnik A132

**1958, Aug. 10** **Litho.** ***Perf. 12½***
**508** A132 15d black & brn .55 .30

Marin Drzic, dramatist, 450th birth anniv.

Sisak Steel Works — A133

Titograd Hotel and Open-Air Theater — A134

Industrial Progress Designs: 2d, Crude oil production. 5d, Shipbuilding. 10d, Sisak steel works. 15d, Jablanica hydroelectric works. 17d, Lumber industry. 25d, Overpass, Zagreb-Ljubljana highway. 30d, Litostroy turbine factory. 35d, Lukavac coke plant. 50d, Bridge at Skopje. 70d, Railroad station, Sarajevo. 100d, Triple bridge, Ljubljana. 200d, Mestrovic station, Zagreb. 500d, Parliament, Belgrade.

**1958** **Typo.** ***Perf. 12½ Horiz.***
**509** A133 10d green 7.75 3.50
**510** A133 15d orange ver 7.75 3.50

**Engr.** ***Perf. 12½***
**511** A133 2d olive .20 .20
**512** A133 5d brown red .20 .20
**513** A133 10d green .20 .20
**514** A133 15d orange ver .20 .20
**515** A133 17d deep claret .20 .20
**516** A133 25d slate .20 .20
**517** A133 30d blue black .20 .20
**518** A133 35d rose red .20 .20
**519** A134 40d car rose .25 .20
**520** A134 50d bright bl .30 .20
**521** A134 70d orange ver .45 .20
**522** A134 100d green 2.25 .20
**523** A134 200d red brown 2.00 .20
**524** A134 500d intense bl 3.75 .30
*Nos. 511-524 (14)* 10.60 2.90

Nos. 509-510 are coil stamps.
See #555-562, 627-645, 786-789, 830-840.

Ocean Exploration A135

**1958, Oct. 24** **Unwmk.**
**525** A135 15d brown violet .50 .25

Intl. Geophysical Year, 1957-58. See #C58.

White and Black Hands Holding Scales A136

**1958, Dec. 10** ***Perf. 12½***
**526** A136 30d steel blue .55 .30

Universal Declaration of Human Rights, 10th anniv.

Dubrovnik A137

Red Flags — A138

Tourist attractions: #528, Bled. #529, Postojna grotto. #530, Ohrid. #531, Opatija. #532, Plitvice National Park. #533, Split. #534, Sveti Stefan. #535, Exhibition Hall, Belgrade.

**1959, Feb. 16** **Litho.** ***Perf. 12½***
**527** A137 10d crim rose & cit .20 .20
**528** A137 10d lt grn & lt vio bl .20 .20
**529** A137 15d grnsh bl & pur .20 .20
**530** A137 15d grn & bright bl .20 .20
**531** A137 20d lt grn & grnsh bl .20 .20
**532** A137 20d ol bis & brt grn .20 .20
**533** A137 30d yel org & purple .70 .20
**534** A137 30d lt vio bl & gray ol .70 .20
**535** A137 70d gray & grnsh bl 2.25 1.10
*Nos. 527-535 (9)* 4.85 2.70

Nos. 527, 530, 532 and 534 are inscribed in Cyrillic characters. See #650-658, 695-700.

**1959, Apr. 20** **Unwmk.** ***Perf. 12½***
**536** A138 20d multicolored .25 .20

Yugoslav Communist Party, 40th anniv.

Dubrovnik, 15th Century A139

**1959, May 24** **Engr.** ***Perf. 11½***
**537** A139 20d yel grn, dk grn & bl .85 .75

4th Yugoslavia Phil. Exhib. (JUFIZ IV), Dubrovnik.

Type of 1957

Medicinal Plants: 10d, Lavender. 15d, Black Alder. 20d, Scopolia. 25d, Monkshood. 30d, Bilberry. 35d, Juniper. 50d, Primrose. 70d, Pomegranate. 100d, Jimson weed.

**1959, May 25** **Photo.**
**Granite Paper**
**Flowers in Natural Colors**

**538** A123 10d lt bl & dk blue .20 .20
**539** A123 15d brt yel & car .20 .20
**540** A123 20d dk ol bis & mar .20 .20
**541** A123 25d ap grn & dk pur .20 .20
**542** A123 30d pink & dk bl .20 .20
**543** A123 35d bis brn & vio bl .40 .20
**544** A123 50d brn & green .95 .25
**545** A123 70d yel & ocher 1.25 .45
**546** A123 100d lt brn & brn 2.50 1.10
*Nos. 538-546 (9)* 6.10 3.00

Tug of War — A140

Sports: 15d, High jump and runners. 20d, Ring and parallel bar exercises. 35d, Women gymnasts. 40d, Sailors doing gymnastics. 55d, Field ball and basketball. 80d, Swimming. 100d, Festival emblem, vert.

**1959, June 26** **Litho.** ***Perf. 12½***
**547** A140 10d dk sl grn & ocher .20 .20
**548** A140 15d vio bl & sepia .20 .20
**549** A140 20d ol bis & dl lil .20 .20
**550** A140 35d deep cl & gray .20 .20
**551** A140 40d violet & gray .20 .20
**552** A140 55d sl grn & ol bis .20 .20
**553** A140 80d indigo & olive .75 .35
**554** A140 100d pur & bister 1.75 1.00
*Nos. 547-554 (8)* 3.70 2.55

Physical Culture Festival.

Types of 1958; Designs as before

Designs: 8d, Lumber industry. 15d, Overpass, Zagreb-Ljubljana highway. 20d, Jablanica hydroelectric works. 40d, Titograd Hotel. 55d, Bridge at Skopje. 80d, Railroad Station, Sarajevo.

**1959** **Typo.** ***Perf. 12½ Horizontally***
**555** A133 15d green 2.50 1.10
**556** A133 20d orange ver 3.00 1.10

**Engr.** ***Perf. 12½***
**557** A133 8d deep claret .25 .20
**558** A133 15d green .35 .20
**559** A133 20d orange ver .60 .20
**560** A134 40d bright blue 1.40 .20
**561** A134 55d carmine rose 2.25 .20
**562** A134 80d orange ver 3.75 .20
*Nos. 557-562 (6)* 8.60 1.20

Nos. 555-556 are coil stamps.

Athletics — A142

Hedgehog A143

Lenin, 90th Birth Anniv. — A144

Atomic Accelerator A145

Serbian National Theater, Novi Sad — A146

Fair Emblem — A141

**1959, Sept. 5** **Litho.** **Unwmk.**
**563** A141 20d lt vio bl & blk .55 .20

50th International Fair at Zagreb.

**1960, Apr. 25** ***Perf. 12½***
**564** A142 15d shown .20 .20
**565** A142 20d Swimming .20 .20
**566** A142 30d Skiing .20 .20
**567** A142 35d Wrestling .20 .20
**568** A142 40d Bicycling .20 .20
**569** A142 55d Yachting .25 .20
**570** A142 80d Horseback riding .55 .35
**571** A142 100d Fencing .70 .45
*Nos. 564-571 (8)* 2.50 2.00

17th Olympic Games.

**1960, May 25** **Photo.** ***Perf. 12x11½***
**Animals in Natural Colors**

**572** A143 15d shown .20 .20
**573** A143 20d Red squirrel .20 .20
**574** A143 25d Pine marten .20 .20
**575** A143 30d Hare .20 .20
**576** A143 35d Red fox .20 .20
**577** A143 40d Badger .20 .20
**578** A143 55d Wolf .40 .25
**579** A143 80d Roe deer .65 .35
**580** A143 100d Wild boar 1.40 1.00
*Nos. 572-580 (9)* 3.65 2.80

See Nos. 663-671.

**1960, June 22** **Engr.** ***Perf. 12½***
**581** A144 20d dk grn & slate grn .20 .20

**1960, Aug. 23** **Unwmk.**
**582** A145 15d shown .20 .20
**583** A145 20d Generator .20 .20
**584** A145 40d Nuclear reactor .30 .20
*Nos. 582-584 (3)* .70 .60

Nuclear energy exposition, Belgrade.

Ivan Cankar, Writer — A147

Designs: 20d, Woman from Croatian play. 40d, Edward Rusijan and early plane. 55d, Symbolic hand holding fruit. 80d, Atom and UN emblem.

**1960, Oct. 24** ***Perf. 12½***

**585** A146 15d gray black .20 .20
**586** A146 20d brown .20 .20
**587** A146 40d dark gray blue .20 .20
**588** A146 55d dull claret .20 .20
**589** A146 80d dark green .30 .20
*Nos. 585-589 (5)* 1.10 1.00

Serbian Natl. Theater, Novi Sad, cent. (#585); Croatian Natl. Theater, Zagreb, cent. (#586); 1st flight in Yugoslavia, 50th anniv. (#587); 15th anniv. of the Yugoslav Republic (#588); UN, 15th anniv. (#589).

**1960, Dec. 24** **Engr.** ***Perf. 12½***

Famous Yugoslavs: 20d, Silvije Strahimir Kranjcevic, poet. 40d, Paja Jovanovic, painter. 55d, Dura Jaksic, writer and painter. 80d, Mihajlo Pupin, electro-technician. 100d, Rudjer Boscovich, mathematician.

**590** A147 15d dark green .20 .20
**591** A147 20d henna brown .20 .20
**592** A147 40d olive bister .20 .20
**593** A147 55d magenta .20 .20
**594** A147 80d dark blue .30 .20
**595** A147 100d Prussian bl .60 .30
*Nos. 590-595 (6)* 1.70 1.30

International Atomic Energy Commission Emblem A148

Victims' Monument, Kragujevac A149

**Engr. & Litho.**

**1961, May 15** ***Perf. 12½***

**596** A148 25d multicolored .25 .20

Intl. Nuclear Electronic Conf., Belgrade.

Flower Type of 1957

Medicinal plants: 10d, Yellow foxglove. 15d, Marjoram. 20d, Hyssop. 25d, Scarlet haw. 40d, Rose mallow. 50d, Soapwort. 60d, Clary. 80d, Blackthorn. 100d, Marigold.

**1961, May 25** **Photo.** ***Perf. 11½***

**Granite Paper**

**Flowers in Natural Colors**

**597** A123 10d lt bl & grnsh bl .20 .20
**598** A123 15d gray & chnt .20 .20
**599** A123 20d buff & green .20 .20
**600** A123 25d lt vio & vio .20 .20
**601** A123 40d lt ultra & ultra .35 .20
**602** A123 50d lt bl & blue .35 .25
**603** A123 60d beige & dk car rose .50 .25
**604** A123 80d lt grn & green .60 .40
**605** A123 100d redsh brn & choc 1.75 .95
*Nos. 597-605 (9)* 4.35 2.85

**1961, July 3** ***Perf. 12x12½***

Monuments: 15d, Stevan Filipovic, Valjevo. 20d, Relief from Insurrection, Bozansko Grahovo. 60d, Victory, Nova Gradiska. 100d, Marshal Tito, Titovo Uzice.

**Granite Paper**

**Gold Frames and Inscriptions**

**606** A149 15d crimson & brn .20 .20
**607** A149 20d brn & ol bis .20 .20
**608** A149 25d bl grn & gray olive .20 .20
**609** A149 60d violet .25 .20
**610** A149 100d indigo & black .55 .40
*Nos. 606-610 (5)* 1.40 1.20

**Souvenir Sheet**

***Imperf***

**611** A149 500d indigo & black 60.00 60.00

Natl. Insurrection, 20th anniv.

Men of Five Races A150

National Assembly Building, Belgrade — A151

**1961, Sept. 1** **Litho.** ***Perf. 11½***

**613** A150 25d brown .20 .20

**Engr.**

**614** A151 50d blue green .20 .20
*Nos. 613-614,C59-C60 (4)* 3.80 2.65

**Miniature Sheet**

***Imperf***

**615** A150 1000d claret 12.00 12.00

Conference of Non-aligned Nations, Belgrade, Sept. 1961.

St. Clement, 14th Century Wood Sculpture — A152

**1961, Sept. 10** **Engr.** ***Perf. 12½***

**616** A152 25d sepia & olive .25 .20

12th Intl. Congress for Byzantine Studies.

Serbian Women A153

Regional Costumes: 25d, Montenegro. 30d, Bosnia and Herzegovina. 50d, Macedonia. 65d, Croatia. 100d, Slovenia.

**1961, Nov. 28** **Litho.**

**617** A153 15d beige, brn & red .20 .20
**618** A153 25d beige, red brn & black .20 .20
**619** A153 30d beige, brn & dk red .20 .20
**620** A153 50d multicolored .20 .20
**621** A153 65d brn, red & yel .30 .20
**622** A153 100d multicolored .90 .25
*Nos. 617-622 (6)* 2.00 1.25

Luka Vukalovic — A154

Hands with Flower and Rifle — A155

**1961, Dec. 15** **Engr.**

**623** A154 25d slate blue .20 .20

Centenary of Herzegovina insurrection.

**1961, Dec. 22**

**624** A155 25d red & vio blue .20 .20

20th anniversary of Yugoslav army.

Miladinov Brothers A156

**1961, Dec. 25** **Litho.**

**625** A156 25d buff & claret .20 .20

Centenary of Macedonian folksong "Koder;" Dimitri and Konstantin Miladinov, brothers who collected and published folksongs. Monument is at Struga.

Types of 1958; Designs as Before

Designs: 5d, Shipbuilding. 8d, Lumber industry. 10d, Sisak steel works. 15d, Overpass. 20d, Jablanica hydroelectric works. 25d, Cable factory, Svetozarevo. 30d, Litostroy turbine factory. 40d, Lukavac coke plant. 50d, Zenica steel works. 65d, Sevojno copper works. 100d, Crude oil production. 150d, Titograd hotel. 200d, Bridge, Skoplje. 300d, Railroad station, Sarajevo. 500d, Triple bridge, Ljubljana. 1000d, Mestrovic station, Zagreb. 2000d, Parliament, Belgrade.

**1961-62** **Typo.** ***Perf. 12½ Horiz.***

**627** A133 10d dark red brn 4.00 .55
**628** A133 15d emerald 7.00 .30

**Engr.** ***Perf. 12½***

**629** A133 5d dull orange .20 .20
**630** A133 8d gray .20 .20
**631** A133 10d dk red brn .20 .20
**632** A133 15d emerald .20 .20
**633** A133 20d violet blue .20 .20
**634** A133 25d vermilion .20 .20
**635** A133 30d red brown .20 .20
**636** A133 40d dp cl ('62) .20 .20
**637** A133 50d gray blue .25 .20
**638** A133 65d green .20 .20
**639** A133 100d yel olive 1.75 .20
**640** A134 150d carmine ('62) .40 .20
**641** A134 200d slate grn ('62) .40 .20
**642** A134 300d olive ('62) .90 .20
**643** A134 500d dull violet .90 .20
**644** A134 1000d bister brn 2.00 .20
**645** A134 2000d claret 4.50 .30
*Nos. 629-645 (17)* 12.90 3.50

Nos. 627-628 are coil stamps. For surcharges see Nos. 786, 789.

Joy of Motherhood by Frano Krsinic — A158

Isis of Kalabsha — A157

Design: 50d, Ramses II, Abu Simbel.

**1962, Apr. 7** **Engr.** ***Perf. 12½***

**646** A157 25d grnsh blk, *cream* .20 .20
**647** A157 50d brown, *buff* .35 .20

15th anniv. (in 1961) of UNESCO.

**1962, Apr. 7**

**648** A158 50d black, *cream* .30 .20

15th anniv. (in 1961) of UNICEF.

Anopheles Mosquito — A159

**1962, Apr. 7** **Unwmk.**

**649** A159 50d black, *gray* .30 .20

WHO drive to eradicate malaria.

Scenic Type of 1959

Tourist attractions: #650, Portoroz. #651, Jajce. #652, Zadar. #653, Popova Sapka. #654, Hvar. #655, Bay of Kotor. #656, Danube, Iron Gate. #657, Rab. #658, Zagreb.

**1962, Apr. 24** **Litho.**

**650** A137 15d ol & chlky bl .20 .20
**651** A137 15d blue grn & bis .20 .20
**652** A137 25d blue & red brn .20 .20
**653** A137 25d dk bl & pale bl .20 .20
**654** A137 30d blue & brn org .20 .20
**655** A137 30d gray & chlky bl .20 .20
**656** A137 50d ol & grnsh bl .45 .20
**657** A137 50d blue & olive .45 .20
**658** A137 100d dk grn & gray bl 2.00 .40
*Nos. 650-658 (9)* 4.10 2.00

#651, 653, 655-656 are inscribed in Cyrillic.

Marshal Tito, by Augustincic A160

Pole Vault — A161

Design: 50d, 200d, Sideview of bust by Antun Augustincic.

**1962, May 25** **Engr.** ***Perf. 12½***

**659** A160 25d dark green .20 .20
**660** A160 50d dark brown .20 .20
**661** A160 100d dark blue .45 .30
**662** A160 200d greenish blk 1.75 .90
*a.* Souv. sheet of 4, #659-662, imperf. 12.00 12.00
*Nos. 659-662 (4)* 2.60

70th birthday of Pres. Tito (Josip Broz).

Animal Type of 1960

Designs: 15d, Crested newt. 20d, Fire salamander. 25d, Yellow-bellied toad. 30d, Pond frog. 50d, Pond turtle. 65d, Lizard. 100d, Emerald lizard. 150d, Leopard snake. 200d, European viper (adder).

**1962, June 8** **Photo.** ***Perf. 12x11½***

**Animals in Natural Colors**

**663** A143 15d green .20 .20
**664** A143 20d purple .20 .20
**665** A143 25d chocolate .20 .20
**666** A143 30d violet blue .20 .20
**667** A143 50d dark red .20 .20
**668** A143 65d bright grn .20 .20
**669** A143 100d black .35 .30
**670** A143 150d brown .95 .95
**671** A143 200d car rose 2.25 1.25
*Nos. 663-671 (9)* 4.75 3.70

**1962, July 10 Litho. *Perf. 12½***

Sports: 25d, Woman discus thrower, horiz. 30d, Long distance runners. 50d, Javelin thrower, horiz. 65d, Shot put. 100d, Women runners, horiz. 150d, Hop, step and jump. 200d, High jump, horiz.

**Athletes in Black**

| No. | Type | Description | Unused | Used |
|---|---|---|---|---|
| **672** | A161 | 15d blue | .20 | .20 |
| **673** | A161 | 25d magenta | .20 | .20 |
| **674** | A161 | 30d emerald | .20 | .20 |
| **675** | A161 | 50d red | .20 | .20 |
| **676** | A161 | 65d vio blue | .20 | .20 |
| **677** | A161 | 100d green | .40 | .20 |
| **678** | A161 | 150d orange | .45 | .30 |
| **679** | A161 | 200d orange brn | .95 | .60 |
| | | *Nos. 672-679 (8)* | 2.80 | 2.10 |

7th European Athletic Championships, Belgrade, Sept. 12-16. See No. C61.

Child at Play — A162

**Litho. & Engr.**

**1962, Oct. 1 *Perf. 12½***

| No. | Type | Description | Unused | Used |
|---|---|---|---|---|
| **680** | A162 | 25d red & black | .30 | .20 |

Issued for Children's Week.

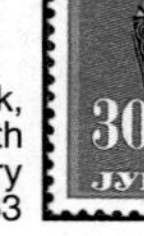

Gold Mask, Trebeniste, 5th Century B.C. — A163

Bathing the Infant Christ, Fresco, Decani Monastery — A164

Yugoslav Art Treasures: 25d, Horseman and bird, bronze vase (5th cent. B.C.). 50d, God Kairos, marble relief. 65d, "The Pigeons of Nerezi," fresco (12th cent.). 150d, Archangel Gabriel, icon (14th cent.).

**1962, Nov. 28 Photo.**

| No. | Type | Description | Unused | Used |
|---|---|---|---|---|
| **681** | A163 | 25d Prus bl, blk & gold | .20 | .20 |
| **682** | A163 | 30d gold, saph & blk | .20 | .20 |
| **683** | A164 | 50d dk grn, brn & gold | .20 | .20 |
| **684** | A164 | 65d multicolored | .35 | .20 |
| **685** | A164 | 100d multicolored | .45 | .60 |
| **686** | A163 | 150d multicolored | 1.90 | 1.10 |
| | | *Nos. 681-686 (6)* | 3.30 | 2.50 |

Parched Earth and Wheat — A165

Dr. Andrija Mohorovicic and UN Emblem — A166

**1963, Mar. 21 Engr. *Perf. 12½***

| No. | Type | Description | Unused | Used |
|---|---|---|---|---|
| **687** | A165 | 50d dark brn, *tan* | .25 | .20 |

FAO "Freedom from Hunger" campaign.

**1963, Mar. 23 Unwmk.**

| No. | Type | Description | Unused | Used |
|---|---|---|---|---|
| **688** | A166 | 50d dk blue, *gray* | .25 | .20 |

UN 3rd World Meteorological Day, Mar. 23. Dr. Mohorovicic (1857-1936) was director of the Zagreb meteorological observatory.

Flower Type of 1957

Medicinal Plants: 15d, Lily of the valley. 25d, Iris. 30d, Bistort. 50d, Henbane. 65d, St. John's wort. 100d, Caraway.

**1963, May 25 Photo. *Perf. 11½***

**Granite Paper**

**Flowers in Natural Colors**

| No. | Type | Description | Unused | Used |
|---|---|---|---|---|
| **689** | A123 | 15d gray grn & grn | .20 | .20 |
| **690** | A123 | 25d lt bl, ultra & pur | .20 | .20 |
| **691** | A123 | 30d gray & black | .20 | .20 |
| **692** | A123 | 50d redsh brn & red brn | .20 | .20 |
| **693** | A123 | 65d pale brn & brn | .30 | .20 |
| **694** | A123 | 100d slate & blk | .90 | .35 |
| | | *Nos. 689-694 (6)* | 2.00 | 1.35 |

Scenic Type of 1959

Tourist attractions: 15d, Pula. 25d, Vrnjacka Banja. 30d, Crikvenica. 50d, Korcula. 65d, Durmitor mountain. 100d, Ljubljana.

**1963, June 6 Litho. *Perf. 12½***

| No. | Type | Description | Unused | Used |
|---|---|---|---|---|
| **695** | A137 | 15d multicolored | .20 | .20 |
| **696** | A137 | 25d multicolored | .20 | .20 |
| **697** | A137 | 30d multicolored | .20 | .20 |
| **698** | A137 | 50d multicolored | .20 | .20 |
| **699** | A137 | 65d multicolored | .20 | .20 |
| **700** | A137 | 100d multicolored | .85 | .25 |
| | | *Nos. 695-700 (6)* | 1.85 | 1.25 |

Partisans on the March, by Djordje Andrejevic-Kun — A167

Sutjeska (Gorge) — A168

Design: No. 702A, As 15d, but inscribed "Vis 1944-1964." 50d, Partisans in battle.

**Engr. & Litho.; Litho. (No. 702)**

**1963-64 *Perf. 12½, 11½***

| No. | Type | Description | Unused | Used |
|---|---|---|---|---|
| **701** | A167 | 15d gray & dk sl grn | .20 | .20 |
| **702** | A168 | 25d dark slate grn | .20 | .20 |
| **702A** | A167 | 25d gray & dark car rose | .20 | .20 |
| **703** | A167 | 50d tan & purple | .20 | .20 |
| | | *Nos. 701-703 (4)* | .80 | .80 |

20th anniv. of the Partisan Battle of Sutjeska (Nos. 701, 702-703); 20th anniv. of the arrival of the Yugoslav General Staff on the island of Vis (No. 702A).

Issued: #702A, 7/27/64; others, 7/3/63.

Gymnast on Vaulting Horse — A169

Mother, by Ivan Mestrovic A170

**1963, July 6 Litho. *Perf. 12½***

| No. | Type | Description | Unused | Used |
|---|---|---|---|---|
| **704** | A169 | 25d shown | .20 | .20 |
| **705** | A169 | 50d Parallel bars | .20 | .20 |
| **706** | A169 | 100d Rings | .35 | .35 |
| | | *Nos. 704-706 (3)* | .75 | .75 |

5th Gymnastics Europa Prize.

**1963, Sept. 28 Engr.**

Sculptures by Mestrovic (1883-1962): 50d, "Reminiscences" (woman). 65d, Head of Kraljevic Marko. 100d, Indian on Horseback.

| No. | Type | Description | Unused | Used |
|---|---|---|---|---|
| **707** | A170 | 25d brown, *buff* | .20 | .20 |
| **708** | A170 | 50d sl green, *grnsh* | .20 | .20 |
| **709** | A170 | 65d grnsh blk, *grysh* | .70 | .30 |
| **710** | A170 | 100d black, *grayish* | 1.00 | .60 |
| | | *Nos. 707-710 (4)* | 2.10 | 1.30 |

Children with Toys — A171

**1963, Oct. 5 Litho.**

| No. | Type | Description | Unused | Used |
|---|---|---|---|---|
| **711** | A171 | 25d multicolored | .35 | .20 |

Issued for Children's Week.

Soldier with Gun and Flag — A172

**Litho. & Engr.**

**1963, Oct. 20 *Perf. 12½***

| No. | Type | Description | Unused | Used |
|---|---|---|---|---|
| **712** | A172 | 25d ver, tan & gold | .20 | .20 |

Yugoslavian Democratic Federation, 20th anniv.

Relief from Tombstone, Herzegovina A173

Dositej Obradovic A174

Art through the centuries: 30d, Horseback trio, Split Cathedral. 50d, King & queen on horseback, Beram Church, Istria. 65d, Archangel Michael, Dominican monastery, Dubrovnik. 100d, Man pouring water, fountain, Ljubljana. 150d, Archbishop Eufrasie, mosaic, Porec Basilica, Istria.

**1963, Nov. 29 Photo.**

| No. | Type | Description | Unused | Used |
|---|---|---|---|---|
| **713** | A173 | 25d multi | .20 | .20 |
| **714** | A173 | 30d multi, horiz. | .20 | .20 |
| **715** | A173 | 50d multi, horiz. | .20 | .20 |
| **716** | A173 | 65d multi | .20 | .20 |
| **717** | A173 | 100d multi | .25 | .20 |
| **718** | A173 | 150d multi | .95 | .60 |
| | | *Nos. 713-718 (6)* | 2.00 | 1.60 |

Issued for the Day of the Republic.

**1963, Dec. 10 Engr.**

Famous Yugoslavians: 30d, Vuk Stefanovic Karadzic, reformer of Serbian language. 50d, Franc Miklosic, Slovenian philologist. 65d, Ljudevit Gaj, reformer of Croatian language. 100d, Peter Petrovich Nyegosh, Montenegrin prince, bishop and poet.

**Variously Toned Paper**

| No. | Type | Description | Unused | Used |
|---|---|---|---|---|
| **719** | A174 | 25d black | .20 | .20 |
| **720** | A174 | 30d black | .20 | .20 |
| **721** | A174 | 50d black | .20 | .20 |
| **722** | A174 | 65d black | .40 | .20 |
| **723** | A174 | 100d black | .65 | .50 |
| | | *Nos. 719-723 (5)* | 1.65 | 1.30 |

Vanessa Io — A175

Fireman Rescuing Child — A176

Butterflies & Moths: 30d, Vanessa antiopa. 40d, Daphnis nerii. 50d, Parnassius apollo. 150d, Saturnia pyri. 200d, Papilio machaon.

**1964, May 25 Photo. *Perf. 12½***

| No. | Type | Description | Unused | Used |
|---|---|---|---|---|
| **724** | A175 | 25d multicolored | .20 | .20 |
| **725** | A175 | 30d multicolored | .20 | .20 |
| **726** | A175 | 40d multicolored | .20 | .20 |
| **727** | A175 | 50d multicolored | .20 | .20 |
| **728** | A175 | 150d multicolored | .40 | .30 |
| **729** | A175 | 200d multicolored | .65 | .40 |
| | | *Nos. 724-729 (6)* | 1.85 | 1.50 |

**1964, June 14 Litho.**

| No. | Type | Description | Unused | Used |
|---|---|---|---|---|
| **730** | A176 | 25d red & black | .25 | .20 |

Centenary of voluntary firemen.

Runner A177

**1964, July 1 Unwmk. *Perf. 12½***

| No. | Type | Description | Unused | Used |
|---|---|---|---|---|
| **731** | A177 | 25d shown | .20 | .20 |
| **732** | A177 | 30d Boxing | .20 | .20 |
| **733** | A177 | 40d Rowing | .20 | .20 |
| **734** | A177 | 50d Basketball | .20 | .20 |
| **735** | A177 | 150d Soccer | .35 | .20 |
| **736** | A177 | 200d Water polo | .60 | .35 |
| | | *Nos. 731-736 (6)* | 1.75 | 1.35 |

18th Olympic Games, Tokyo, Oct. 10-25.

UN Flag over Scaffolding A178

25d, Upheaval of the earth & scaffolding.

**1964, July 26 Engr.**

| No. | Type | Description | Unused | Used |
|---|---|---|---|---|
| **737** | A178 | 25d red brown | .20 | .20 |
| **738** | A178 | 50d blue | .20 | .20 |

Earthquake at Skopje; 1st anniv.

Serbian Women — A179

Friedrich Engels — A180

Regional Costumes: 30d, Slovenia. 40d, Bosnia and Herzegovina. 50d, Croatia. 150d, Macedonia. 200d, Montenegro.

**1964, Aug. 5** **Litho.**

**Costumes Multicolored**

| | | | | |
|---|---|---|---|---|
| **740** | A179 | 25d violet & brn | .20 | .20 |
| **741** | A179 | 30d slate & green | .20 | .20 |
| **742** | A179 | 40d redsh brn & blk | .20 | .20 |
| **743** | A179 | 50d blue & black | .20 | .20 |
| **744** | A179 | 150d dl grn & sepia | .40 | .20 |
| **745** | A179 | 200d tan, red & brn | .50 | .45 |
| | | *Nos. 740-745 (6)* | 1.70 | 1.45 |

**Litho. & Engr.**

**1964, Sept. 27** ***Perf. 11½***

| | | | | |
|---|---|---|---|---|
| **746** | A180 | 25d shown | .20 | .20 |
| **747** | A180 | 50d Karl Marx | .20 | .20 |

1st Socialist Intl., London, Sept. 28, 1864.

Children at Play — A181

**1964, Oct. 4** **Litho.** ***Perf. 12½***

| | | | | |
|---|---|---|---|---|
| **748** | A181 | 25d ver, pink & gray grn | .35 | .20 |

Issued for Children's Week.

The Victor by Ivan Mestrovic — A182

**1964, Oct. 20** **Engr.** ***Perf. 11½***

| | | | | |
|---|---|---|---|---|
| **749** | A182 | 25d gold & blk, *pnksh* | .20 | .20 |

Liberation of Belgrade, 20th anniv.

Initial from Evangel of Hilandar — A183

Hand, "Liberty and Equality" — A184

Art through the centuries: 30d, Initial from Evangel of Miroslav (musician). 40d, Detail from Cetigne octavo, 1494 (saint with scroll). 50d, Miniature from Evangel of Trogir, 13th cent. (female saint). 150d, Miniature from Hrovoe Missal, 15th cent. (knight on horseback). 200d, Miniature from 14th cent. manuscript (symbolic fight), horiz.

***Perf. 11½x12, 12x11½***

**1964, Nov. 29** **Photo.** **Unwmk.**

| | | | | |
|---|---|---|---|---|
| **750** | A183 | 25d multicolored | .20 | .20 |
| **751** | A183 | 30d multicolored | .20 | .20 |
| **752** | A183 | 40d multicolored | .20 | .20 |
| **753** | A183 | 50d multicolored | .20 | .20 |
| **754** | A183 | 150d multicolored | .35 | .20 |
| **755** | A183 | 200d multicolored | .70 | .40 |
| | | *Nos. 750-755 (6)* | 1.85 | 1.40 |

Issued for Day of the Republic.

**1964, Dec. 7** ***Perf. 12***

50d, Dove over factory, "Peace and Socialism." 100d, Smokestacks, "Building Socialism."

| | | | | |
|---|---|---|---|---|
| **756** | A184 | 25d multicolored | .20 | .20 |
| **757** | A184 | 50d multicolored | .20 | .20 |
| **758** | A184 | 100d multicolored | .40 | .25 |
| | | *Nos. 756-758 (3)* | .80 | .65 |

Yugoslav Communist League, 8th congress.

Table Tennis Player — A185

Titograd — A186

**1965, Apr. 15** **Litho.** ***Perf. 12½***

| | | | | |
|---|---|---|---|---|
| **759** | A185 | 50d shown | .20 | .20 |
| **760** | A185 | 150d Player at left | .40 | .25 |

28th Table Tennis Championships, Ljubljana, Apr. 15-25.

**1965, May 8** **Engr.**

| | | | | |
|---|---|---|---|---|
| **761** | A186 | 25d shown | .20 | .20 |
| **762** | A186 | 30d Skopje | .20 | .20 |
| **763** | A186 | 40d Sarajevo | .20 | .20 |
| **764** | A186 | 50d Ljubljana | .20 | .20 |
| **765** | A186 | 150d Zagreb | .30 | .20 |
| **766** | A186 | 200d Belgrade | .65 | .40 |
| | | *Nos. 761-766 (6)* | 1.75 | 1.40 |

Liberation of Yugoslavia from the Nazis, 20th anniv.

Young Pioneer — A187

ITU Emblem and Television Tower — A188

**1965, May 10** **Litho. & Engr.**

| | | | | |
|---|---|---|---|---|
| **767** | A187 | 25d blk & tan, *buff* | .20 | .20 |

Young Pioneer Games "20 Years of Freedom."

**1965, May 17** **Engr.**

| | | | | |
|---|---|---|---|---|
| **768** | A188 | 50d dark blue | .20 | .20 |

ITU, centenary.

Iron Gate, Danube — A189

Arms of Yugoslavia and Romania and Djerdap Dam — A190

50d, Iron Gate hydroelectric plant and dam.

**1965, May 20** **Litho.** ***Perf. 12½x12***

| | | | | |
|---|---|---|---|---|
| **769** | A189 | 25d (30b) lt bl & grn | .20 | .20 |
| **770** | A189 | 50d (55b) lt bl & dk red | .25 | .20 |

**Miniature Sheet**

***Perf. 13½x13***

| | | | | |
|---|---|---|---|---|
| **771** | A190 | Sheet of 4 | 2.50 | 2.50 |
| *a.* | | 100d multicolored | .35 | .35 |
| *b.* | | 150d multicolored | .70 | .70 |

Nos. 769-771 were issued simultaneously by Yugoslavia and Romania to commemorate the start of the construction of the Iron Gate hydroelectric plant. Nos. 769-770 were valid for postage in both countries.

No. 771 contains one each of Nos. 771a, 771b and Romania Nos. 1747a and 1747b. Only Nos. 771a and 771b were valid in Yugoslavia. Sold for 500d.

See Romania Nos. 1745-1747.

Flower Type of 1957

Medicinal Plants: 25d, Milfoil. 30d, Rosemary. 40d, Inula. 50d, Belladonna. 150d, Mint. 200d, Foxglove.

**1965, May 25** **Photo.** ***Perf. 11½***

**Granite Paper**

**Flowers in Natural Colors**

| | | | | |
|---|---|---|---|---|
| **772** | A123 | 25d deep carmine | .20 | .20 |
| **773** | A123 | 30d olive bister | .20 | .20 |
| **774** | A123 | 40d red brown | .20 | .20 |
| **775** | A123 | 50d dark blue | .20 | .20 |
| **776** | A123 | 150d violet blue | .35 | .20 |
| **777** | A123 | 200d purple | .85 | .60 |
| | | *Nos. 772-777 (6)* | 2.00 | 1.60 |

Intl. Cooperation Year Emblem A191

**1965, June 26** **Litho.** ***Perf. 12½***

| | | | | |
|---|---|---|---|---|
| **778** | A191 | 50d dk bl & dull bl | .20 | .20 |

Sibenik — A192

Cat — A193

**1965, July 6** **Unwmk.** ***Perf. 12½***

| | | | | |
|---|---|---|---|---|
| **779** | A192 | 25d Rogaska Slatina | .20 | .20 |
| **780** | A192 | 30d shown | .20 | .20 |
| **781** | A192 | 40d Prespa Lake | .20 | .20 |
| **782** | A192 | 50d Prizren | .20 | .20 |
| **783** | A192 | 150d Scutari | .30 | .20 |
| **784** | A192 | 200d Sarajevo | .60 | .55 |
| | | *Nos. 779-784 (6)* | 1.70 | 1.55 |

**1965, Oct. 3** **Litho.** ***Perf. 12½***

| | | | | |
|---|---|---|---|---|
| **785** | A193 | 30d maroon & brt yel | .45 | .20 |

Issued for Children's Week.

Nos. 630 and 634 Surcharged in Maroon and Type of 1958

Designs: 20d, Jablanica hydroelectric works. 30d, Litostroy turbine factory.

**1965** **Engr.** ***Perf. 12½***

| | | | | |
|---|---|---|---|---|
| **786** | A133 | 5d on 8d gray | .60 | .20 |
| **787** | A133 | 20d emerald | .50 | .20 |
| **788** | A133 | 30d red orange | .80 | .20 |
| **789** | A133 | 50d on 25d vermilion | .60 | .20 |
| | | *Nos. 786-789 (4)* | 2.50 | .80 |

Branislav Nusic — A194

Marshal Tito — A195

Famous Yugoslavs: 50d, Antun Gustav Matos, poet. 60d, Ivan Mazuranic, writer. 85d, Fran Levstik, writer. 200d, Josif Pancic, physician and botanist. 500d, Dimitrije Tucovic, political writer.

**1965, Nov. 28** **Engr.**

**Variously Toned Paper**

| | | | | |
|---|---|---|---|---|
| **790** | A194 | 30d dull red | .20 | .20 |
| **791** | A194 | 50d indigo | .20 | .20 |
| **792** | A194 | 60d brown | .20 | .20 |
| **793** | A194 | 85d dark blue | .20 | .20 |
| **794** | A194 | 200d dk olive grn | .20 | .20 |
| **795** | A194 | 500d deep claret | .60 | .45 |
| | | *Nos. 790-795 (6)* | 1.60 | 1.45 |

**1966, Feb. 4** **Litho.** ***Perf. 12½***

| | | | | |
|---|---|---|---|---|
| **796** | A195 | 20p bluish grn | .40 | .20 |
| **797** | A195 | 30p rose pink | .55 | .20 |

Rowing A196

30p, Long jump. 50p, Ice hockey. 3d, Hockey sticks, puck. 5d, Oars, scull.

**1966, Mar. 1** **Engr.**

| | | | | |
|---|---|---|---|---|
| **798** | A196 | 30p dk car rose | .20 | .20 |
| **799** | A196 | 50p dk purple | .20 | .20 |
| **800** | A196 | 1d gray green | .20 | .20 |
| **801** | A196 | 3d dk red brn | .35 | .20 |
| **802** | A196 | 5d dark blue | .65 | .50 |
| | | *Nos. 798-802 (5)* | 1.60 | 1.30 |

25th Balkan Games; World ice hockey championship; 2nd rowing championships.

"T" from 15th Century Psalter — A197

Radio Amateurs' Emblem — A198

Art through the Centuries (Initials from Medieval Manuscripts): 50p, Cyrillic "V," Divosh Evangel, 14th cent. 60p, "R," Gregorius I, Libri moralium, 12th cent. 85p, Cyrillic "P," Miroslav Evangel, 12th cent. 2d, Cyrillic "B," Radomir Evangel, 13th cent. 5d, "F," Passional, 11th cent.

**1966, Apr. 25 Photo. *Perf. 12***

**803** A197 30p multicolored .20 .20
**804** A197 50p multicolored .20 .20
**805** A197 60p multicolored .20 .20
**806** A197 85p multicolored .20 .20
**807** A197 2d multicolored .30 .20
**808** A197 5d multicolored .65 .60
*Nos. 803-808 (6)* 1.75 1.60

**1966, May 23 Engr. *Perf. 12½x12***

**809** A198 85p dark blue .20 .20

Union of Yugoslav Radio Amateurs, 20th anniv.; Intl. Congress of Radio Amateurs, Opatija, 5/23-28.

Stag Beetle — A199

Serbia No. 2, 1866 — A200

Beetles: 50p, Floral beetle. 60p, Oil beetle. 85p, Ladybird. 2d, Rosalia alpina. 5d, Aquatic beetle.

**1966, May 25 Photo. *Perf. 12x12½***

**810** A199 30p gray, blk & bis .20 .20
**811** A199 50p gray, emer & blk .20 .20
**812** A199 60p bluish blk, sl grn & gray .20 .20
**813** A199 85p dl org, dp org & black .20 .20
**814** A199 2d gray, ultra & blk .25 .20
**815** A199 5d tan, brn & blk .40 .40
*Nos. 810-815 (6)* 1.45 1.40

**Litho. & Engr.**

**1966, June 25 *Perf. 12½***

**816** A200 30p shown .20 .20
**817** A200 50p No. 3 .20 .20
**818** A200 60p No. 4 .20 .20
**819** A200 85p No. 5 .20 .20
**820** A200 2d No. 6 .45 .35
*Nos. 816-820 (5)* 1.25 1.15

**Souvenir Sheet**

***Imperf***

**821** A200 10d No. 1 2.00 2.00

Serbia's first postage stamps, cent.

Leather Shield with Farmer, Soldier and Woman — A201

Bishop Strossmayer and Franjo Racki — A202

**1966, July 2 *Perf. 12½***

**822** A201 20p pale grn, gold & red brown .20 .20
**823** A201 30p buff, gold & dp mag .20 .20
**824** A201 85p lt gray, gold & Prus bl .20 .20
**825** A201 2d lt bl, gold & vio .25 .25
*Nos. 822-825 (4)* .85 .85

25th anniversary of National Revolution.

**1966, July 15**

**826** A202 30p dl ol, blk & buff .20 .20

Centenary of Academy of Arts and Sciences, founded by Bishop Josip Juraj Strossmayer with Racki as first president.

Mostar Bridge, Neretva River — A203

**1966, Sept. 24 Engr. *Perf. 12½***

**827** A203 30p rose claret 1.75 .25

400th anniversary of Mostar Bridge.

Medieval View of Sibenik A204

**1966, Sept. 24**

**828** A204 30p deep plum .25 .20

900th anniversary of Sibenik.

Girl A205

Shipbuilding A206

**1966, Oct. 2 Litho.**

**829** A205 30p ultra, org, red & blk .70 .20

Issued for Children's Week.

**1966 Engr. *Perf. 12½***

Designs: 10p, Sisak steel works. 15p, Overpass. 20p, Jablonica hydroelectric works. 30p, Litostroy turbine factory. 40p, Lukavac coke factory. 50p, Zenica steel works. 60p, Cable factory, Svetozarevo. 65p, Sevojno copper works. 85p, Lumber industry. 1d, Crude oil production.

**830** A206 5p dull orange .20 .20
**831** A206 10p brown .20 .20
**832** A206 15p vio blue .20 .20
**833** A206 20p emerald .30 .20
**834** A206 30p vermilion 1.10 .20
**835** A206 40p dp claret .20 .20
**836** A206 50p gray blue .25 .20
**837** A206 60p red brown .25 .20
**838** A206 65p green .35 .20
**839** A206 85p dl purple .55 .20
**840** A206 1d yel olive .80 .20
*Nos. 830-840 (11)* 4.40 2.20

Issued: 5, 15p, 6/10; 10, 40, 50p, 6/8; 20, 30p, 4/28; 60, 65, 85p, 5/12; 1d, 6/18.
For surcharge see No. 1322.

UNESCO Emblem — A207

Santa Claus — A208

**1966, Nov. 4 Litho.**

**841** A207 85p violet blue .20 .20

20th anniversary of UNESCO.

**1966, Nov. 25 Litho. *Perf. 12½***

Designs: 15p, Stylized winter landscape. 30p, Stylized Christmas tree.

**842** A208 15p org & dk bl .20 .20
**843** A208 20p org & purple .20 .20
**844** A208 30p org & sl grn .20 .20

**1966, Dec. 23 Photo. *Perf. 12½***

**845** A208 15p gold & dk bl .30 .20
**846** A208 20p gold & red .30 .20
**847** A208 30p gold & green .30 .20
*Nos. 842-847 (6)* 1.50 1.20

Nos. 842-847 issued for New Year, 1967.

Wolf's Head Coin of Durad I, 1373 — A209

Medieval Coins: 50p, ½d of King Stefan, c. 1461 (arms of Bosnia). 60d, Dinar of Serbia (portrait of Durad Brankovic). 85p, Dinar of Ljubljana, c. 1250 (heraldic eagle). 2d, Dinar of Split, c. 1403-1413 (shield with arms of Duke Hrvoje Vukcic). 5d, Dinar of Emperor Stefan Dusan, c. 1346-1355 (Emperor on horseback).

**1966, Nov. 28 Photo.**

**Coins in Silver, Gray and Black**

**848** A209 30p ver & blk .20 .20
**849** A209 50p ultra & blk .20 .20
**850** A209 60p magenta & blk .20 .20
**851** A209 85p violet & blk .20 .20
**852** A209 2d dk ol bis & blk .20 .20
**853** A209 5d brt grn & blk .55 .35
*Nos. 848-853 (6)* 1.55 1.35

Medicinal Plants — A210

Marshal Tito — A211

**1967, May 25 Photo. *Perf. 11½***

**Granite Paper**

**854** A210 30p Arnica .20 .20
**855** A210 50p Flax .20 .20
**856** A210 85p Oleander .20 .20
**857** A210 1.20d Gentian .20 .20
**858** A210 3d Laurel .20 .20
**859** A210 5d African rue .50 .30
*Nos. 854-859 (6)* 1.50 1.30

Youth Day, May 25.

**1967, May 25 Engr. *Perf. 12½***

**Size: 20x27½mm**

**860** A211 5p orange .20 .20
**861** A211 10p dk red brown .20 .20
**862** A211 15p dk vio blue .20 .20
**863** A211 20p green .20 .20
**864** A211 30p vermilion .20 .20
**865** A211 40p black .20 .20
**866** A211 50p Prussian grn .20 .20
**867** A211 60p lilac .20 .20
**868** A211 85p deep blue .20 .20
**869** A211 1d plum .20 .20
*Nos. 860-869 (10)* 2.00 2.00

75th birthday of Pres. Tito. Sheets of 15.
Nos. 860-869 were reissued in 1967 with slight differences including thinner paper and slightly darker shades.
See #924-939. For surcharge see #1414.

Coil Stamps

**1968-69 Photo. *Perf. 12½ Horiz.***

**869A** A211 20p green .30 .20
**869B** A211 30p vermilion .40 .20
**869C** A211 50p vermilion ('69) .30 .20
*Nos. 869A-869C (3)* 1.00 .60

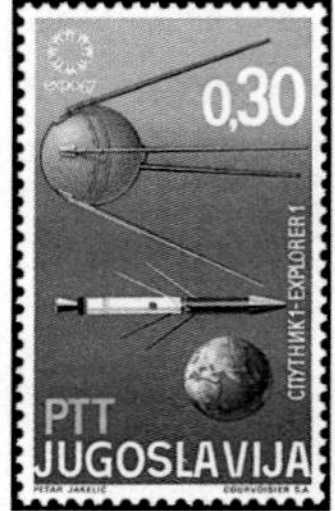

EXPO Emblem, Sputnik 1 and Explorer 1 — A212

ITY Emblem, St. Tripun's Church, Kotor — A213

Spacecraft: 50p, Tiros, Telstar and Molniya. 85p, Luna 9 and lunar satellite. 1.20d, Mariner 4, and Venus 3. 3d, Vostok, Gemini and Agena Rocket. 5d, Astronaut walking in space.

**1967, June 26 Photo. *Perf. 11½***

**870** A212 30p ultra & multi .20 .20
**871** A212 50p yel & multi .20 .20
**872** A212 85p slate & multi .20 .20
**873** A212 1.20d multicolored .20 .20
**874** A212 3d vio & multi .20 .20
**875** A212 5d blue & multi .35 .35
*Nos. 870-875 (6)* 1.35 1.35

EXPO '67, Montreal, Apr. 28-Oct. 27; 18th Congress of the Intl. Astronautical Federation, Belgrade.

**1967, July 17 Engr.**

Designs (ITY Emblem and): 50p, Municipal Building, Maribor. 85p, Cathedral, Trogir. 1.20d, Fortress gate, Nis. 3d, Drina Bridge, Visegrad. 5d, Daut-pasha's Bath, Skopje.

**876** A213 30p slate bl & lt ol .20 .20
**877** A213 50p brn & dl vio .20 .20
**878** A213 85p dk bl & dp claret .20 .20
**879** A213 1.20d dp claret & brn .20 .20
**880** A213 3d brn & slate grn .35 .20
**881** A213 5d slate grn & brn .50 .45
*Nos. 876-881 (6)* 1.65 1.45

Issued for International Tourist Year, 1967.

Partridge — A214

**1967, Sept. 22 Photo. *Perf. 14***

**882** A214 30p shown .20 .20
**883** A214 50p Pike .20 .20
**884** A214 1.20d Red deer .20 .20
**885** A214 5d Peregrine falcon .75 .70
*Nos. 882-885 (4)* 1.35 1.30

Intl. Fishing and Hunting Exposition and Fair, Novi Sad.

Congress Emblem with Sputnik 1 A215

**Litho. & Engr.**

**1967, Sept. 25 *Perf. 12½***

**886** A215 85p dk bl, lt bl & gold .20 .20

18th Congress of the Intl. Astronautical Federation, Belgrade, Sept. 25-30.

Old Theater and Castle, Ljubljana — A216

Child's Drawing: Winter Scene — A217

**1967, Sept. 29 Engr. *Perf. 12½***

**887** A216 30p sepia & dk grn .20 .20

Centenary of Slovene National Theater.

**1967, Oct. 2 Litho.**

**888** A217 30p multicolored .50 .20

International Children's Week, Oct. 2-8.

Lenin by Mestrovic A218

4-Leaf Clover A219

**1967, Nov. 7 Engr. *Perf. 12½***

**889** A218 30p dark purple .20 .20
**890** A218 85p olive gray .25 .20

**Souvenir Sheet**

***Imperf***

**891** A218 10d magenta 3.75 3.00

Russian October Revolution, 50th anniv.

**1967, Nov. 15 Photo. *Perf. 14***

30p, Chimney sweep. 50p, Horseshoe & flower.

**Dated "1968"**

**892** A219 20p shown .20 .20
**893** A219 30p Chimney sweep .20 .20
**894** A219 50p Horseshoe, flower .20 .20
*Nos. 892-894 (3)* .60 .60

New Year 1968. See Nos. 957-959.

The Young Sultana, by Vlaho Bucovac — A220

Paintings: 85p, The Watchtower, by Dura Jaksic. 2d, Visit to the Family, by Josip Petkovsek. 3d, The Cock Fight, by Paja Jovanovic. 5d, "Spring" (woman and children), by Ivana Kobilca.

***Perf. 11½x12, 12x11½***

**1967, Nov. 28 Engr. & Litho.**

**895** A220 85p multi, vert. .20 .20
**896** A220 1d multi .20 .20
**897** A220 2d multi .30 .25
**898** A220 3d multi .40 .40
**899** A220 5d multi, vert. .75 .70
*Nos. 895-899 (5)* 1.85 1.75

Issued for the Day of the Republic, Nov. 29. See Nos. 942-946, 995-1000.

Ski Jump — A221

Annunciation A222

Sport: 1d, Figure skating pair. 2d, Downhill skiing. 5d, Ice hockey.

**1968, Feb. 5 Engr. *Perf. 12½***

**900** A221 50p dk bl & dk pur .20 .20
**901** A221 1d brn & sl green .20 .20
**902** A221 2d sl grn & lake .20 .25
**903** A221 5d sl grn & dk bl .70 .35
*Nos. 900-903 (4)* 1.30 1.00

10th Winter Olympic Games, Grenoble, France, Feb. 6-18.

**1968, Apr. 20 Photo. *Perf. 13½***

Medieval Icons: 50p, Madonna, St. George's Church, Prizren. 1.50d, St. Sava and St. Simeon. 2d, Christ's descent into hell, Ohrid. 3d, Crucifixion, St. Clement's Church, Ohrid. 5d, Madonna, Church of Our Lady of the Bell Tower, Split.

**906** A222 50p gold & multi .20 .20
**907** A222 1d gold & multi .20 .20
**908** A222 1.50d gold & multi .20 .20
**909** A222 2d gold & multi .35 .25
**910** A222 3d gold & multi .50 .40
**911** A222 5d gold & multi 1.10 1.00
*Nos. 906-911 (6)* 2.55 2.25

European Bullfinch — A223

800-meter Race for Women — A224

Finches: 1d, Goldfinch. 1.50d, Chaffinch. 2d, European greenfinch. 3d, Red crossbill. 5d, Hawfinch.

**1968, May 25 Photo. *Perf. 11½***

**Birds in Natural Colors**

**912** A223 50p bister .20 .20
**913** A223 1d rose lake .20 .20
**914** A223 1.50d gray blue .20 .20
**915** A223 2d deep orange .25 .20
**916** A223 3d olive green .45 .20
**917** A223 5d pale violet .70 .45
*Nos. 912-917 (6)* 2.00 1.45

Issued for Youth Day.

**Litho. & Engr.**

**1968, June 28 *Perf. 12½***

1d, Basketball. 1.50d, Gymnast on vaulting horse. 2d, Rowing. 3d, Water polo. 5d, Wrestling.

**918** A224 50p dk brn & dk red brown .20 .20
**919** A224 1d Prus bl & blk .20 .20
**920** A224 1.50d slate & dk brn .20 .20
**921** A224 2d bis & sl grn .20 .20
**922** A224 3d blk brn & ind .25 .20
**923** A224 5d dk grn & vio blk .50 .45
*Nos. 918-923 (6)* 1.55 1.45

19th Olympic Games, Mexico City, 10/12-27.

Tito Type of 1967

**1968-72 Engr. *Perf. 12½***

**Size: 20x27½mm**

**924** A211 20p dark blue .20 .20
**925** A211 25p lake .20 .20
**926** A211 30p green .20 .20
**927** A211 50p vermilion .20 .20
**928** A211 70p black .30 .20
**929** A211 75p slate grn .40 .20
**930** A211 80p olive .40 .20
**930A** A211 80p red org ('72) .35 .20
**931** A211 90p olive .30 .20
**932** A211 1.20d dark blue .50 .20
**932A** A211 1.20d sl grn ('72) .40 .20
**933** A211 1.25d deep blue .45 .20
**934** A211 1.50d slate grn .40 .20

**Size: 20x30½mm**

**935** A211 2d sepia .60 .20
**936** A211 2.50d Prussian grn 1.60 .20
**937** A211 5d deep plum 1.40 .20
**938** A211 10d violet blk 3.00 .35
**939** A211 20d bluish black 4.25 .45
*Nos. 924-939 (18)* 15.15 4.00

The shading of the background of Nos. 924-939 has been changed from the 1967 issue to intensify the contrast around the portrait.

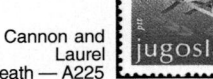

Cannon and Laurel Wreath — A225

Mother Nursing Twins, Fresco by Jan of Kastav — A226

**1968, Aug. 2 Photo. *Perf. 12½***

**940** A225 50p org brn & gold .20 .20

65th anniversary of the Ilinden uprising.

**1968, Sept. 9 Litho.**

**941** A226 50p black & multi .20 .20

Annexation of Istria and the Slovene Coast to Yugoslavia, 25th anniv.

Painting Type of 1967

Paintings: 1d, Lake Klansko, by Marko Pernhart. 1.50d, Bavarian Landscape, by Milan Popovic. 2d, Porta Terraferma, Zadar, by Ferdo Quiquerez. 3d, Mt. Triglav seen from Bohinj, by Anton Karinger. 5d, Studenica Monastery, by Djordje Krstic.

**Engr. & Litho.**

**1968, Oct. 3 *Perf. 14x13½***

**942** A220 1d gold & multi .20 .20
**943** A220 1.50d gold & multi .20 .20
**944** A220 2d gold & multi .20 .20
**945** A220 3d gold & multi .30 .20
**946** A220 5d gold & multi .80 .70
*Nos. 942-946 (5)* 1.70 1.50

Aleksa Santic (1868-1924), Poet — A227

"Going for a Walk" — A228

**1968, Oct. 5 Engr. *Perf. 12½***

**947** A227 50p dark blue .20 .20

**1968, Oct. 6 Litho.**

**948** A228 50p multicolored .20 .20

Issued for Children's Week.

Karl Marx (1818-1883), by N. Mitric — A229

Old Theater and Belgrade Castle — A230

**1968, Oct. 11 Engr.**

**949** A229 50d dk car rose .20 .20

**1968, Nov. 22 Engr. *Perf. 12½***

**950** A230 50p ol brn & sl grn .20 .20

Serbian National Theater, Belgrade, cent.

Hasan Brkic — A231

The Family, by J. Soldatovic A232

Portraits: 75p, Ivan Milutinovic. 1.25d, Rade Koncar. 2d, Kuzman Josifovski. 2.50d, Tone Tomsic. 5d, Mosa Pijade.

**1968, Nov. 28 Engr. *Perf. 12½***

**951** A231 50p violet black .20 .20
**952** A231 75p black .20 .20
**953** A231 1.25d red brown .25 .20
*a.* Souv. sheet, 2 ea #951-953 12.50 12.50
**954** A231 2d bluish black .30 .20
**955** A231 2.50d slate green .50 .25
**956** A231 5d claret 1.10 .75
*a.* Souv. sheet, 2 ea #954-956 12.50 12.50
*Nos. 951-956 (6)* 2.55 1.80

2nd Assembly of the National Republic of Yugoslavia, 25th anniv.

Type of New Year's Issue, 1967

**1968, Nov. 25 Photo. *Perf. 14***

**Dated "1969"**

**957** A219 20p Four-leaf clover .20 .20
**958** A219 30p Chimney sweep .20 .20
**959** A219 50p Horseshoe, flower .20 .20
*Nos. 957-959 (3)* .60 .60

Issued for New Year 1969.

**1968, Dec. 10 Engr. *Perf. 12½***

**960** A232 1.25d dark blue .25 .20

International Human Rights Year.

ILO Emblem — A233

Dove, Hammer and Sickle Emblem — A234

**Litho. & Engr.**

**1969, Jan. 27 *Perf. 12½***

**961** A233 1.25d red & black .25 .20

ILO, 50th anniv.

**Engr. & Photo.**

**1969, Mar. 11 *Perf. 12½***

75p, Graffiti "TITO" & 5-pointed star. 1.25d, 5-pointed crystal. 10d, Marshal Tito in 1943.

**962** A234 50p black & red .20 .20
**963** A234 75p ol bis & blk .20 .20
**964** A234 1.25d red & black .25 .20
*Nos. 962-964 (3)* .65 .60

**Souvenir Sheet**

**964A** Sheet of 9 5.50 5.50
*b.* A234 10d brown, engr. 3.00 3.00

Communist Federation of Yugoslavia, 50th anniv.; 9th party congress.
#964A contains 4 #962, 2 each #963-964, 964b.

St. Nikita, from Manasija Monastery A235

Frescoes from Monasteries: 75p, Apostles, Zakopani. 1.25d, Crucifixion, Studenica. 2d, Wedding at Cana, Kalenic. 3d, Angel at the Grave, Milseva. 5d, Pietá, Nerezi.

**1969, Apr. 7 Photo. *Perf. 13½***

| | | | | | |
|---|---|---|---|---|---|
| **965** | A235 | 50p | gold & multi | .20 | .20 |
| **966** | A235 | 75p | gold & multi | .20 | .20 |
| **967** | A235 | 1.25d | gold & multi | .20 | .20 |
| **968** | A235 | 2d | gold & multi | .20 | .20 |
| **969** | A235 | 3d | gold & multi | .45 | .45 |
| **970** | A235 | 5d | gold & multi | 1.25 | .90 |
| | | | *Nos. 965-970 (6)* | 2.50 | 2.15 |

Roman Memorial and View of Ptuj A236

**1969, Apr. 23 Engr. *Perf. 11½***

| | | | | | |
|---|---|---|---|---|---|
| **971** | A236 | 50p | violet brown | .20 | .20 |

1900th anniv. of Ptuj, the Roman Petovio. Issued in sheets of 9 (3x3).

Vasil Glavinov — A237

Thin-leafed Peony — A238

**1969, May 8 *Perf. 12x12½***

| | | | | | |
|---|---|---|---|---|---|
| **972** | A237 | 50p | ocher & rose lilac | .20 | .20 |

Vasil Glavinov, Macedonian socialist, birth cent.. Issued in sheets of 9 (3x3).

**1969, May 25 Photo. *Perf. 11½***

Medicinal Plants: 75p, Coltsfoot. 1.25d, Primrose. 2d, Hellebore. 2.50d, Violets. 5d, Anemones.

**Flowers in Natural Colors**

| | | | | | |
|---|---|---|---|---|---|
| **973** | A238 | 50p | yellow brn | .20 | .20 |
| **974** | A238 | 75p | dull purple | .20 | .20 |
| **975** | A238 | 1.25d | blue | .20 | .20 |
| **976** | A238 | 2d | brown | .20 | .20 |
| **977** | A238 | 2.50d | plum | .25 | .20 |
| **978** | A238 | 5d | green | .80 | .60 |
| | | | *Nos. 973-978 (6)* | 1.85 | 1.60 |

See Nos. 1056-1061, 1140-1145.

Eber, by Vasa Ivankovic — A239

Paintings of Sailing Ships: 1.25d, Tare, by Franasovic. 1.50d, Brig Sela, by Vasa Ivankovic. 2.50d, Dubrovnik galleon, 16th century. 3.25d, Madre Mimbelli, by Antoine Roux. 5d, The Virgin Saving Seamen from Disaster, 16th century ikon.

**1969, July 10 Photo. *Perf. 11½***

| | | | | | |
|---|---|---|---|---|---|
| **979** | A239 | 50p | gold & multi | .20 | .20 |
| **980** | A239 | 1.25d | gold & multi | .20 | .20 |
| **981** | A239 | 1.50d | gold & multi | .20 | .20 |
| **982** | A239 | 2.50d | gold & multi | .35 | .25 |
| **983** | A239 | 3.25d | gold & multi | .65 | .45 |
| **984** | A239 | 5d | gold & multi | 1.40 | 1.00 |
| | | | *Nos. 979-984 (6)* | 3.00 | 2.30 |

Dubrovnik Summer Festival, 20th anniv.

11th World Games for the Deaf, Belgrade, Aug. 9-16 — A240

**1969, Aug. 9 Engr. *Perf. 12½***

| | | | | | |
|---|---|---|---|---|---|
| **985** | A240 | 1.25d | dp claret & dl vio | .40 | .20 |

Lipice Horse A241

Horses: 75p, Bosnian mountain horse. 3.25d, Ljutomer trotter. 5d, Half-breed.

**1969, Sept. 26 Photo. *Perf. 11½***

| | | | | | |
|---|---|---|---|---|---|
| **986** | A241 | 75p | multicolored | .20 | .20 |
| **987** | A241 | 1.25d | olive & multi | .20 | .20 |
| **988** | A241 | 3.25d | brn & multi | .25 | .20 |
| **989** | A241 | 5d | multicolored | .60 | .60 |
| | | | *Nos. 986-989 (4)* | 1.25 | 1.20 |

Zagreb Veterinary College, 50th anniv.

Children and Birds, by Tanja Vucanik, 13 years A242

**1969, Oct. 5 Litho. *Perf. 12½***

| | | | | | |
|---|---|---|---|---|---|
| **990** | A242 | 50p | org, blk & gray | .20 | .20 |

Issued for Children's Week.

Arms of Belgrade — A243

Josip Smodlaka A244

Arms: #992, Skopje (bridge & mountain). #993, Titograd (bridge & fortifications).

**1969 Litho. *Perf. 12½***

| | | | | | |
|---|---|---|---|---|---|
| **991** | A243 | 50p | gold & multi | .20 | .20 |
| **992** | A243 | 50p | gold & multi | .20 | .20 |
| **993** | A243 | 50p | gold & multi | .20 | .20 |
| | | | *Nos. 991-993 (3)* | .60 | .60 |

Liberation of capitals of the Federated Republics, 25th anniv. See Nos. 1017-1020.

**1969, Nov. 9 Engr.**

| | | | | | |
|---|---|---|---|---|---|
| **994** | A244 | 50p | dark blue | .20 | .20 |

Smodlaka (1869-1956), leader in Yugoslavia's fight for independence.

Painting Type of 1967

Paintings of Nudes: 50p, The Little Gypsy with the Rose, by Nikola Martinoski. 1.25d, Girl on a Red Chair, by Sava Sumanovic. 1.50d, Woman Combing her Hair, by Marin Tartaglia. 2.50d, Olympia, by Miroslav Kraljevic. 3.25d, The Bather, by Jovan Bijelic. 5d, Woman on a Couch, by Matej Sternen.

**Photo. & Engr.**

**1969, Nov. 29 *Perf. 13½***

| | | | | | |
|---|---|---|---|---|---|
| **995** | A220 | 50p | multi, vert. | .20 | .20 |
| **996** | A220 | 1.25d | multi, vert. | .35 | .20 |
| **997** | A220 | 1.50d | multi, vert. | .45 | .20 |
| **998** | A220 | 2.50d | multi | .55 | .50 |
| **999** | A220 | 3.25d | multi, vert. | 1.10 | .90 |
| **1000** | A220 | 5d | multi | 2.00 | 2.00 |
| | | | *Nos. 995-1000 (6)* | 4.65 | 4.00 |

University of Ljubljana, 50th Anniv. A245

**1969, Dec. 9 Engr. *Perf. 11½***

| | | | | | |
|---|---|---|---|---|---|
| **1001** | A245 | 50p | slate grn | .20 | .20 |

Seal of Zagreb University A246

Jovan Cvijic, Geographer A247

**Photo. & Engr.**

**1969, Dec. 17 *Perf. 12½***

| | | | | | |
|---|---|---|---|---|---|
| **1002** | A246 | 50p | gold, bl & brn | .20 | .20 |

University of Zagreb, 300th anniv.

Common Design Types pictured following the introduction.

**Europa Issue, 1969**

Common Design Type

**1969, Dec. 20 Photo. *Perf. 11½***

| | | | | | |
|---|---|---|---|---|---|
| **1003** | CD12 | 1.25d | grnsh gray, buff & brn | 2.00 | 2.00 |
| **1004** | CD12 | 3.25d | rose lil, gray & dk bl | 6.75 | 6.75 |

Yugoslavia's admission to CEPT.

**1970, Feb. 16 Engr. *Perf. 12½***

Famous Yugoslavs: 1.25d, Dr. Andrija Stampar, hygienist. 1.50d, Joakim Krcovski, author. 2.50d, Marko Miljanov, Montenegrin patriot-hero. 3.25d, Vaca Pelagic, socialist. 5d, Oton Zupancic, Slovenian poet.

| | | | | | |
|---|---|---|---|---|---|
| **1005** | A247 | 50p | reddish brn | .20 | .20 |
| **1006** | A247 | 1.25d | brnsh black | .20 | .20 |
| **1007** | A247 | 1.50d | lilac | .20 | .20 |
| **1008** | A247 | 2.50d | slate grn | .25 | .20 |
| **1009** | A247 | 3.25d | reddish brn | .25 | .20 |
| **1010** | A247 | 5d | blue vio | .50 | .40 |
| | | | *Nos. 1005-1010 (6)* | 1.60 | 1.40 |

Punishment of Dirce, Pulj — A248

Mosaics from the 1st-4th Centuries: 1.25d, Cerberus, Bitola, horiz. 1.50d, Angel of the Annunciation, Porec. 2.50d, Hunters, Gamzigard. 3.25d, Bull and cherry tree, horiz. 5d, Virgin and Child enthroned, Porec.

**1970, Mar. 16 Photo. *Perf. 13½***

| | | | | | |
|---|---|---|---|---|---|
| **1011** | A248 | 50p | gold & multi | .20 | .20 |
| **1012** | A248 | 1.25d | gold & multi | .20 | .20 |
| **1013** | A248 | 1.50d | gold & multi | .20 | .20 |
| **1014** | A248 | 2.50d | gold & multi | .30 | .25 |
| **1015** | A248 | 3.25d | gold & multi | .55 | .35 |
| **1016** | A248 | 5d | gold & multi | 1.00 | 1.00 |
| | | | *Nos. 1011-1016 (6)* | 2.45 | 2.20 |

Arms Type of 1969

#1017, Sarajevo (arcade). #1018, Zagreb (castle). #1019, Ljubljana (dragon and tower). #1020a, Yugoslavia (embossed coat of arms.)

**1970 Litho. *Perf. 12½***

| | | | | | |
|---|---|---|---|---|---|
| **1017** | A243 | 50p | gold & multi | .20 | .20 |
| **1018** | A243 | 50p | gold & multi | .20 | .20 |
| **1019** | A243 | 50p | gold & multi | .20 | .20 |
| | | | *Nos. 1017-1019 (3)* | .60 | .60 |

**Souvenir Sheet**

| | | | | | |
|---|---|---|---|---|---|
| **1020** | | | Sheet of 7 | 4.25 | 4.25 |
| *a.* | A243 | 12d | gold & black | 2.00 | 2.00 |

Liberation of Yugoslavia, 25th anniv. No. 1020 contains Nos. 991-993, 1017-1019, 1020a + 2 labels.

Issued: #1017, Apr. 6; #1018, May 8; #1019, May 9; #1020, May 15.

Lenin (1870-1924), by S. Stojanovic A249

Basketball A250

Design: 1.25d, Lenin sculpture facing left.

**1970, Apr. 22 Engr.**

| | | | | | |
|---|---|---|---|---|---|
| **1021** | A249 | 50p | rose lilac | .20 | .20 |
| **1022** | A249 | 1.25d | blue gray | .20 | .20 |

**1970, Apr. 25**

| | | | | | |
|---|---|---|---|---|---|
| **1023** | A250 | 1.25d | plum | .25 | .20 |

6th World Basketball Championships, Ljubljana, May 10-23.

**Europa Issue, 1970**

Common Design Type

**1970, May 4 Photo. *Perf. 11½***

**Size: 32½x23mm**

| | | | | | |
|---|---|---|---|---|---|
| **1024** | CD13 | 1.25d | lt bl, dk bl & lt grnsh bl | .20 | .20 |
| **1025** | CD13 | 3.25d | rose lil, plum & gray | .55 | .55 |

Istrian Shorthaired Hound A251

Yugoslav Breeds of Dogs: 1.25d, Yugoslav tricolor hound. 1.50d, Istrian hard-haired hound. 2.50d, Balkan hound. 3.25d, Dalmatian. 5d, Shara mountain dog.

**1970, May 25 Photo. *Perf. 11½***

**Granite Paper**

| | | | | | |
|---|---|---|---|---|---|
| **1026** | A251 | 50p | tan & multi | .20 | .20 |
| **1027** | A251 | 1.25d | olive & multi | .20 | .20 |
| **1028** | A251 | 1.50d | violet & multi | .20 | .20 |
| **1029** | A251 | 2.50d | slate & multi | .25 | .20 |
| **1030** | A251 | 3.25d | multi | .45 | .20 |
| **1031** | A251 | 5d | multi | .70 | .60 |
| | | | *Nos. 1026-1031 (6)* | 2.00 | 1.60 |

Telegraph Circuit — A252

Stylized Gymnast — A254

Bird — A253

**1970, June 20 Litho. *Perf. 12½***

| | | | | |
|---|---|---|---|---|
| **1032** | A252 | 50p henna brn, gold & blk | .20 | .20 |

Telegraph service in Montenegro, cent.

**1970, Oct. 5**

| | | | | |
|---|---|---|---|---|
| **1033** | A253 | 50p multicolored | .20 | .20 |

Issued for Children's Week, Oct. 5-11.

**1970, Oct. 22 Engr.**

| | | | | |
|---|---|---|---|---|
| **1034** | A254 | 1.25d car & slate | .20 | .20 |

17th World Gymnastics Championships, Ljubljana, Oct. 22-27.

UN Emblem and Hand Holding Dove, by Makoto A255

**Litho. & Engr.**

**1970, Oct. 24 *Perf. 11½***

| | | | | |
|---|---|---|---|---|
| **1035** | A255 | 1.25d dk brn, blk & gold | .25 | .20 |

25th anniversary of the United Nations.

Ascension, by Teodor D. Kracum A256

Baroque Paintings: 75p, Abraham's Sacrifice, by Federiko Benkovic. 1.25d, Holy Family, by Francisek Jelovsek. 2.50d, Jacob's Ladder, by Hristofor Zefarovic. 3.25d, Baptism of Christ, by unknown Serbian painter. 5.75d, The Coronation of Mary, by Tripo Kokolja.

**Engr. & Photo.**

**1970, Nov. 28 *Perf. 13½x14***

| | | | | | |
|---|---|---|---|---|---|
| **1036** | A256 | 50p | gold & multi | .20 | .20 |
| **1037** | A256 | 75p | gold & multi | .20 | .20 |
| **1038** | A256 | 1.25d | gold & multi | .20 | .20 |
| **1039** | A256 | 2.50d | gold & multi | .20 | .20 |
| **1040** | A256 | 3.25d | gold & multi | .45 | .20 |
| **1041** | A256 | 5.75d | gold & multi | .75 | .70 |
| | *Nos. 1036-1041 (6)* | | | 2.00 | 1.70 |

Alpine Rhododendron — A257

European Nature Protection Year emblem and: 3.25d, Bearded vulture.

**1970, Dec. 14 Photo. *Perf. 11½***

| | | | | |
|---|---|---|---|---|
| **1042** | A257 | 1.25d multi | 2.25 | 2.25 |
| **1043** | A257 | 3.25d multi | 7.25 | 6.25 |

Sheets of 9.

Frano Supilo — A258

British, French, Canadian, Italian Satellites A259

**Litho. & Engr.**

**1971, Jan. 25 *Perf. 12½***

| | | | | |
|---|---|---|---|---|
| **1044** | A258 | 50p black & buff | .20 | .20 |

Supilo (1870-1917), Croat leader for independence from Austria-Hungary. Sheets of 9.

**1971, Feb. 8 Photo. *Perf. 13½***

75p, Satellite. 1.25d, Automated moon exploration. 2.50d, Various spacecraft. 3.25d, 1st experimental space station. 5.75d, Astronauts on moon.

| | | | | | |
|---|---|---|---|---|---|
| **1045** | A259 | 50p | multi | .20 | .20 |
| **1046** | A259 | 75p | multi | .20 | .20 |
| **1047** | A259 | 1.25d | multi | .30 | .20 |
| **1048** | A259 | 2.50d | multi, horiz. | .70 | .45 |
| **1049** | A259 | 3.25d | multi, horiz. | .95 | .85 |
| **1050** | A259 | 5.75d | multi, horiz. | 2.25 | 2.00 |
| | *Nos. 1045-1050 (6)* | | | 4.60 | 3.90 |

"Space in the service of science." Sheets of 9.

Proclamation of the Commune, Town Hall, Paris — A260

**Litho. & Engr.**

**1971, Mar. 18 *Perf. 11½***

| | | | | |
|---|---|---|---|---|
| **1051** | A260 | 1.25d bis brn & gray brn | .20 | .20 |

Centenary of the Paris Commune.

**Europa Issue, 1971**

Common Design Type

**1971, May 4 Photo. *Perf. 11½***

**Size: 33x23mm**

| | | | | |
|---|---|---|---|---|
| **1052** | CD14 | 1.50d Prus bl, pale grn & dk bl | .20 | .20 |
| **1053** | CD14 | 4d mag, pink & dk mag | .50 | .50 |

Circles — A261

Prince Lazar, Fresco, Lazarica Church — A262

**1971, May 5 *Perf. 13½***

| | | | | | |
|---|---|---|---|---|---|
| **1054** | A261 | 50p | shown | .40 | .20 |
| **1055** | A261 | 1.25d | 20 circles | 1.10 | .60 |

2nd Congress of Managers of Autonomous States.

Flower Type of 1969

Medicinal Plants: 50p, Common mallow. 1.50d, Common buckthorn. 2d, Water lily. 2.50d, Poppy. 4d, Wild chicory. 6d, Physalis.

**1971, May 25 Photo. *Perf. 11½***

**Flowers in Natural Colors**

| | | | | | |
|---|---|---|---|---|---|
| **1056** | A238 | 50p | lt ultra | .20 | .20 |
| **1057** | A238 | 1.50d | olive bis | .20 | .20 |
| **1058** | A238 | 2d | dull blue | .20 | .20 |
| **1059** | A238 | 2.50d | dark car | .30 | .20 |
| **1060** | A238 | 4d | dp bister | .40 | .25 |
| **1061** | A238 | 6d | org brown | .70 | .60 |
| | *Nos. 1056-1061 (6)* | | | 2.00 | 1.65 |

**1971, June 28 Photo. *Perf. 13½***

| | | | | |
|---|---|---|---|---|
| **1062** | A262 | 50p gray & multi | .20 | .20 |

600th anniversary of founding of Krusevac by Prince Lazar Hrebeljanovic (1329-1389).

View of Krk — A263

Views: 5p, Krusevac. 10p, Castle & church, Gradacac. 20p, Church & bridge, Bohinj. 35p, Shore & mountains, Omis. 40p, Peje. 50p, Memorial column, Krusevac. 60p, Logar Valley. 75p, Bridge & church, Bohinj. 80p, Church, Piran. 1d, Street, Bitolj. 1.20d, Minaret, Pocitelj. 1.25d, 1.50d, Gate tower, Hercegnovi. 2d, Cathedral & City Hall Square, Novi Sad. 2.50d, Crna River.

**1971-73 Engr. *Perf. 13***

| | | | | | |
|---|---|---|---|---|---|
| **1063** | A263 | 5p | orange ('73) | .20 | .20 |
| **1064** | A263 | 10p | brown ('72) | .20 | .20 |
| **1065** | A263 | 20p | vio blk ('73) | .20 | .20 |
| **1066** | A263 | 30p | ol gray ('72) | .20 | .20 |
| *a.* | | 30p | green | .85 | .20 |
| **1067** | A263 | 35p | brn car ('73) | .20 | .20 |
| **1068** | A263 | 40p | black ('72) | .20 | .20 |
| **1069** | A263 | 50p | vermilion | 1.25 | .20 |
| **1070** | A263 | 50p | green ('72) | .20 | .20 |
| **1071** | A263 | 60p | purple ('72) | .20 | .20 |
| **1072** | A263 | 75p | slate green | .20 | .20 |
| **1073** | A263 | 80p | rose red ('72) | 1.25 | .20 |
| **1073A** | A263 | 1d | violet brn | 1.25 | .45 |
| **1073B** | A263 | 1.20d | sl grn ('72) | 1.60 | .20 |
| **1073C** | A263 | 1.25d | deep blue | .90 | .20 |
| **1073D** | A263 | 1.50d | bluish blk ('73) | .25 | .20 |
| **1073E** | A263 | 2d | blue ('72) | .85 | .20 |
| **1073F** | A263 | 2.50d | dl pur ('73) | .85 | .20 |
| | *Nos. 1063-1073F (17)* | | | 10.00 | 3.65 |

Issued with and without fluorescent bars.

See type A323. See Nos. 1482-1486, 1599-1600, 1602-1603, 1717. For surcharges see Nos. 1413, 1711-1712, 1765-1766, 1769.

Emperor Constantine, 4th Century — A264

UNICEF Emblem, Children in Balloon — A265

**Tourist Issue**

Antique Bronzes excavated in Yugoslavia: 1.50d, Boy with fish. 2d, Hercules, replica after Lysippus. 2.50d, Satyr. 4d, Head of Aphrodite. 6d, Citizen of Emona, 1st century tomb.

**1971, Sept. 20 Photo. *Perf. 13½***

| | | | | | |
|---|---|---|---|---|---|
| **1074** | A264 | 50p | rose & multi | .20 | .20 |
| **1075** | A264 | 1.50d | multicolored | .20 | .20 |
| **1076** | A264 | 2d | multicolored | .20 | .20 |
| **1077** | A264 | 2.50d | lem & multi | .25 | .20 |
| **1078** | A264 | 4d | ocher & multi | .40 | .25 |
| **1079** | A264 | 6d | multicolored | .75 | .60 |
| | *Nos. 1074-1079 (6)* | | | 2.00 | 1.65 |

Sheets of 9.

**1971, Oct. 4 Litho. *Perf. 13x13½***

| | | | | |
|---|---|---|---|---|
| **1080** | A265 | 50p multicolored | .25 | .20 |

Children's Week, Oct. 3-10.

Woman in Serbian Costume, by Katarina Ivanovic A266

Portraits, 19th Century: 1.50d, The Merchant Ivanisevic, by Anastasije Bocaric. 2d, Ana Kresic, by Vjekoslav Karas. 2.50d, Pavle Jagodic, by Konstantin Danil. 4r, Luiza Pesjakova, by Mihael Stroj. 6d, Old Man and view of Ljubljana, by Matevz Langus.

**Engraved and Photogravure**

**1971, Nov. 29 *Perf. 13½x14***

| | | | | | |
|---|---|---|---|---|---|
| **1081** | A266 | 50p | gold & multi | .20 | .20 |
| **1082** | A266 | 1.50d | gold & multi | .20 | .20 |
| **1083** | A266 | 2d | gold & multi | .20 | .20 |
| **1084** | A266 | 2.50d | gold & multi | .25 | .20 |
| **1085** | A266 | 4d | gold & multi | .40 | .30 |
| **1086** | A266 | 6d | gold & multi | .90 | .80 |
| | *Nos. 1081-1086 (6)* | | | 2.15 | 1.90 |

See Nos. 1120-1125.

Letter with Postal Code, Map of Yugoslavia — A267

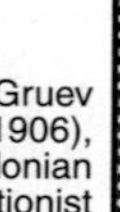

Damjan Gruev (1871-1906), Macedonian Revolutionist A268

**1971, Dec. 15 Photo. *Perf. 13½x14***

**1087** A267 50p ultra & multi .20 .20

Introduction of postal code system.

**1971, Dec. 22 Engr. *Perf. 12½***

**1088** A268 50p dark blue .20 .20

11th Winter Olympic Games, Sapporo, Japan, Feb. 3-13 A269

**Engr. & Typo.**

**1972, Feb. 3 *Perf. 11½***

**1089** A269 1.25d Speed skating .80 .50
**1090** A269 6d Slalom 3.25 2.10

Sheets of 9.

First Page of Statute of Dubrovnik A270

**Lithographed and Engraved**

**1972, Mar. 15 *Perf. 13½***

**1091** A270 1.25d gold & multi .25 .20

700th anniversary of the Statute of Dubrovnik, a legal code given by Prince Marko Justiniani.

Ski Jump Track, Planica — A271

Water Polo and Olympic Rings — A272

**1972, Mar. 21 *Perf. 11½***

**1092** A271 1.25d blk, lt bl & grn .25 .20

World Ski Jump Championships, Planica, Mar. 22-26.

**1972, Apr. 17 Litho. *Perf. 12½x12***

**1093** A272 50p shown .20 .20
**1094** A272 1.25d Basketball .20 .20
**1095** A272 2.50d Butterfly stroke .20 .20
**1096** A272 3.25d Boxing .30 .20
**1097** A272 5d Running .50 .25
**1098** A272 6.50d Yachting 1.00 .65
*Nos. 1093-1098 (6)* 2.40 1.70

20th Olympic Games, Munich, Aug. 26-Sept. 10. Sheets of 9.

**Europa Issue 1972**

Common Design Type

**1972, May 4 Photo. *Perf. 11½***

**1100** CD15 1.50d bl, grn & yel .60 .60
**1101** CD15 5d brt rose, mag & org .90 .80

Wall Creeper — A275

Marshal Tito, by Bozidar Jakac — A276

Birds: 1.25d, Little bustard. 2.50d, Red-billed chough. 3.25d, Spoonbill. 5d, Eagle owl. 6.50d, Rock ptarmigan.

**1972, May 8**

**Birds in Natural Colors**

**1102** A275 50p gray violet .20 .20
**1103** A275 1.25d ocher .20 .20
**1104** A275 2.50d gray olive .20 .20
**1105** A275 3.25d light plum .35 .20
**1106** A275 5d red brown .60 .30
**1107** A275 6.50d violet 1.25 .80
*Nos. 1102-1107 (6)* 2.80 1.90

Nature protection.

**1972, May 25 Litho. *Perf. 12½***

**1108** A276 50p cream & dk brn .20 .20
**1109** A276 1.25d gray & indigo .50 .25

**Souvenir Sheet**

***Imperf***

**1110** A276 10d gray & blk brn 2.75 2.75

80th birthday of Pres. Tito. Sheets of 9. No. 1110 printed in blocks of 4.

First Locomotive Built in Serbia, 1882 — A277

5d, Modern Yugoslavian electric locomotive.

**1972, June 12 Photo. *Perf. 11½***

**1111** A277 1.50d multicolored .20 .20
**1112** A277 5d multicolored .70 .25

Intl. Railroad Union, 50th anniv.

Glider A278

**1972, July 8 Photo. *Perf. 12½***

**1113** A278 2d bl gray, gold & blk .20 .20

13th World Gliding Championships, Vrsac Airport, July 9-23. Sheets of 9.

Pawn on Chessboard — A279

6d, Chessboard, emblems of King and Queen.

**1972, Sept. 18 *Perf. 11½***

**1114** A279 1.50d multi .20 .20
**1115** A279 6d multi .80 .70

20th Men's and 5th Women's Chess Olympiad, Skopje, Sept.-Oct. Sheets of 9.

Boy on Rocking Horse — A280

Goce Delchev — A281

**1972, Oct. 2 Litho. *Perf. 12½***

**1116** A280 80p org & multi .20 .20

Children's Week, Oct. 2-8.

**1972, Oct. 16 *Perf. 13***

**1117** A281 80p yel grn & blk .20 .20

Delchev (1872-1903), Macedonian freedom fighter.

Grga Martic, by Ivan Mestrovic A282

**1972, Nov. 3 *Perf. 12½***

**1118** A282 80p red, yel grn & blk .20 .20

Brother Grga Martic (1822-1905), Franciscan administrator, educator and poet.

Serbian National Library, Belgrade A283

**1972, Nov. 25 Engr. *Perf. 11½x12***

**1119** A283 50p chocolate .20 .20

140th anniversary of the Serbian National Library and opening of new building.

Painting Type of 1971

Still-Life Paintings: 50p, by Milos Tenkovic, horiz. 1.25d, by Jozef Pekovsek. 2.50d, by Katarina Jovanovic, horiz. 3.25d, by Konstantin Danil, horiz. 5d, by Nikola Masic. 6.50d, by Celestin Medovic, horiz.

***Perf. 14x13½, 13½x14***

**1972, Nov. 28 Engr. & Photo.**

**1120** A266 50p gold & multi .20 .20
**1121** A266 1.25d gold & multi .20 .20
**1122** A266 2.50d gold & multi .20 .20
**1123** A266 3.25d gold & multi .30 .20
**1124** A266 5d gold & multi .40 .30
**1125** A266 6.50d gold & multi .70 .50
*Nos. 1120-1125 (6)* 2.00 1.60

Battle of Stubica, by Krsto Hegedusic — A284

6d, Battle of Krsko, by Gojmir Anton Kos.

**1973, Jan. 29 Photo. *Perf. 11½***

**1126** A284 2d gold & multi .30 .20
**1127** A284 6d gold & multi 1.25 .70

Croatian-Slovenian Rebellion, 400th anniv. (2d); Beginning of the peasant rebellions in Slovenia, 500th anniv. (6d). Sheets of 9.

Radoje Domanovic (1873-1908), Serbian Writer — A285

**1973, Feb. 3 Litho. *Perf. 12½***

**1128** A285 80p tan & brn .40 .20

Sheets of 9.

Skofja Loka A286

**1973, Feb. 15 *Perf. 11½***

**1129** A286 80p brown & buff .30 .20

Millennium of the founding of Skofja Loka. Sheets of 9.

Novi Sad, by Peter Demetrovic — A287

Old Engravings: 1.25d, Zagreb, by Josef Szeman. 2.50d, Kotor, by Pierre Mortier. 3.25d, Belgrade, by Mancini. 5d, Split, by Louis-Francois Cassas. 6.50d, Kranj, by Mathaus Merian.

**Engraved and Photogravure**

**1973, Mar. 15 *Perf. 13½***

**1130** A287 50p gold, buff & blk .20 .20
**1131** A287 1.25d gold, gray & black .20 .20
**1132** A287 2.50d gold & blk .20 .20
**1133** A287 3.25d gold & blk .20 .20
**1134** A287 5d gold, buff & blk .35 .30
**1135** A287 6.50d gold & blk .50 .45
*Nos. 1130-1135 (6)* 1.65 1.55

Championship Poster A288

**1973, Apr. 5 Litho. *Perf. 13½x13***

**1136** A288 2d multicolored .35 .20

32nd Intl. Table Tennis Championships, Sarajevo, Apr. 5-15. Sheets of 9.

**Europa Issue, 1973**

Common Design Type

**1973, Apr. 30 Photo. *Perf. 11½***

**Size: 32½x23mm**

**1138** CD16 2d dk bl, lil & lt grn .35 .30
**1139** CD16 5.50d pur, cit & sal pink 1.40 1.25

Sheets of 9.

Flower Type of 1969

Medicinal Plants: 80p, Birthwort. 2d, Globe thistles. 3d, Olive branch. 4d, Corydalis. 5d, Mistletoe. 6d, Comfrey.

**1973, May 25 Photo. *Perf. 11½***
**Flowers in Natural Colors**

**1140** A238 80p orange & grn .20 .20
**1141** A238 2d dl bl & blue .20 .20
**1142** A238 3d olive & blk .25 .20
**1143** A238 4d yel grn & grn .40 .25
**1144** A238 5d org & sepia .60 .40
**1145** A238 6d lilac & grn 1.10 .75
*Nos. 1140-1145 (6)* 2.75 2.00

Anton Jansa (1734-1773), Teacher, Apiculturist and Bee — A291

**1973, Aug. 25 Engr. *Perf. 12½***
**1147** A291 80p black .20 .20

Sheets of 9.

Championship Badge A292

**1973, Sept. 1 Litho. *Perf. 13½x13***
**1148** A292 2d multicolored .30 .20

World water sport championships (swimming, water polo, water jumps, figure swimming), Belgrade, Sept. 1-9. Sheets of 9.

"Greeting the Sun," by Ivan Vucovic A293

Post Horn — A294

**1973, Oct. 1 *Perf. 12½***
**1149** A293 80p multicolored .35 .20

Children's Week, Oct. 1-7. Sheets of 9.

Coil Stamps

**1973-77 Photo. *Perf. 14½x14***
**1150** A294 30p brown .20 .20
**1151** A294 50p gray blue .20 .20
**1152** A294 80p rose red ('74) .20 .20
**1153** A294 1d yel grn ('77) .20 .20
**1154** A294 1.20d pink ('74) .30 .20
**1155** A294 1.50d rose ('77) .20 .20
*Nos. 1150-1155 (6)* 1.30 1.20

Juraj Dalmatinac, Sculptor, Architect, 500th Anniv. of Death — A295

**1973, Oct. 8 Litho. *Perf. 12½***
**1158** A295 80p grnsh gray & ol blk .20 .20

Sheets of 9.

Nadezda Petrovic (1873-1915), Self-Portrait — A296

**Lithographed and Engraved**
**1973, Oct. 12 *Perf. 11½***
**1159** A296 2d gold & multi .30 .20

Sheets of 9.

Interior, by Marko Celebonovic — A297

Paintings of Interiors by Yugoslav artists: 2d, St. Duja, by Emanuel Vidovic. 3d, Room with Slovak Woman, by Marino Tartaglia. 4d, Painter with Easel, by Miljenko Stancic. 5d, Studio, by Milan Konjovic. 6d, Tavern in Stara Loka, by France Slana.

**1973, Oct. 20 Photo. *Perf. 13½***
**1160** A297 80p gold & multi .20 .20
**1161** A297 2d gold & multi .20 .20
**1162** A297 3d gold & multi .20 .20
**1163** A297 4d gold & multi .20 .20
**1164** A297 5d gold & multi .35 .25
**1165** A297 6d gold & multi .45 .40
*Nos. 1160-1165 (6)* 1.60 1.45

Sheets of 9.

Dragojlo Dudic — A298

**Lithographed and Engraved**
**1973, Nov. 29 *Perf. 12½***
**Gray and Indigo**

**1166** A298 80p shown .20 .20
**1167** A298 80p Strahil Pindzur .20 .20
**1168** A298 80p Boris Kidric .20 .20
**1169** A298 80p Radoje Dakic .20 .20

**Gray and Plum**

**1170** A298 2d Josip Mazar-Sosa .25 .25
**1171** A298 2d Zarko Zrenjanin .25 .25
**1172** A298 2d Emin Duraku .25 .25
**1173** A298 2d Ivan-Lola Ribar .25 .25
*a.* Sheet of 8, #1166-1173 1.50 1.50

Republic Day, Nov. 29, honoring national heroes who perished during WWII.

Memorial, by O. Boljka, Ljubljana A299

Winged Globe, by D. Dzamonja, at Podgaric A300

Sculptures: 4.50d, Tower by D. Dzamonja, at Kozara. 5d, Memorial, by B. Grabulovski, at Belcista. 10d, Abstract, by M. Zivkovic, at Sutjeska. 50d, Stone "V," by Zivkovic, at Kragujevac.

**1974 Engr. *Perf. 12½***
**1174** A299 3d slate grn 1.10 .20
**1175** A299 4.50d brn lake 1.75 .20
**1176** A299 5d dark vio 1.75 .20
*b.* Perf. 13½ 5.00 .20
**1177** A300 10d slate grn 2.10 .35
**1178** A300 20d dull pur 2.50 .45
**1179** A300 50d indigo 5.50 1.40
*Nos. 1174-1179 (6)* 14.70 2.80

**1978-82 Litho.**
*1176a* A299 5d 1.90 .20
*1177a* A300 10d ('81) 1.90 .45
*1178a* A300 20d ('81) 2.75 .45
*1179a* A300 50d ('82) 3.00 .75
*Nos. 1176a-1179a (4)* 9.55 1.85

Metric Measure A301

**1974, Jan. 10 Litho. *Perf. 13***
**1180** A301 80p plum & multi .20 .20

Centenary of introduction of metric system.

European Ice Skating Championships, Jan. 29-Feb. 2, Zagreb — A302

**1974, Jan. 29**
**1181** A302 2d multicolored .65 .25

Diligence, 1874 A303

**Litho. & Engr.**
**1974, Feb. 25 *Perf. 11½***
**1182** A303 80p shown .20 .20
**1183** A303 2d New UPU headquarters .20 .20
**1184** A303 8d Jet plane .75 .50
*Nos. 1182-1184 (3)* 1.15 .90

Centenary of the Universal Postal Union.

Montenegro No. 1 — A304

**Litho. & Engr.**
**1974, Mar. 11 *Perf. 13***
**1185** A304 80p shown .20 .20
**1186** A304 6d Montenegro No. 7 .40 .20

Centenary of first Montenegrin postage stamps.

Marshal Tito — A305

Lenin, by Nandor Glid — A306

**1974 Litho. *Perf. 13***
**1193** A305 50p green .20 .20
*a.* Perf. 13x12½
**1196** A305 80p vermilion .20 .20
**1198** A305 1.20d slate green .25 .20
**1201** A305 2d gray blue .25 .20
*a.* Perf. 13x12½ .50
*Nos. 1193-1201 (4)* .90 .80

Issued with and without fluorescence.

For surcharge see No. 1415.

**1974, Apr. 20 Litho. *Perf. 13***
**1204** A306 2d blk & silver .25 .20

50th death anniv. of Lenin.

Lepenski Vir Statue, c. 4950 B.C. — A307

Europa: 6d, Widow & Child, by Ivan Mestrovic.

**1974, Apr. 29 Photo. *Perf. 11½***
**1205** A307 2d multicolored .40 .40
**1206** A307 6d multicolored 1.60 1.60

Great Tit — A308

Congress Poster — A309

**1974, May 25 Photo. *Perf. 11½***
**1207** A308 80p shown .20 .20
**1208** A308 2d Rose .55 .20
**1209** A308 6d Cabbage butterfly 1.40 1.10
*Nos. 1207-1209 (3)* 2.15 1.50

Youth Day. Issued in sheets of 9.

**1974, May 27 Litho. *Perf. 11½***
**1210** A309 80p gold & multi .20 .20
**1211** A309 2d silver & multi .20 .20
**1212** A309 6d ocher & multi .40 .40
*Nos. 1210-1212 (3)* .80 .80

10th Congress of Yugoslav League of Communists, Belgrade, May 27-30.

Radar Ground Station, Ivanjica — A311

Games Emblem and Soccer Cup — A312

**1974, June 7 Engr. *Perf. 13***

| | | | | |
|---|---|---|---|---|
| 1214 | A311 | 80p shown | .20 | .20 |
| 1215 | A311 | 6d Intelsat IV | 1.10 | .50 |

Opening of first satellite ground station in Yugoslavia at Ivanjica. Sheets of 9.

**1974, June 13 Litho. *Perf. 13***

| | | | | |
|---|---|---|---|---|
| 1216 | A312 | 4.50d vio bl & multi | 1.25 | .90 |

World Cup Soccer Championship, Munich, June 13-July 7. Sheets of 9.

Klek Mountain, Edelweiss, Mountaineers' Emblem — A313

**1974, June 15**

| | | | | |
|---|---|---|---|---|
| 1217 | A313 | 2d grn & multi | .20 | .20 |

Mountaineering in Yugoslavia, cent. Sheets of 9.

Children's Dance, by Jano Knjazovic — A314

Paintings: 2d, "Crucified Rooster," by Ivan Generalic, vert. 5d, Laundresses, by Ivan Lackovic, vert. 8d, Dance, by Janko Brasic.

**1974, Sept. 9 Photo. *Perf. 11½***

| | | | | |
|---|---|---|---|---|
| 1218 | A314 | 80p multi | .20 | .20 |
| 1219 | A314 | 2d multi | .20 | .20 |
| 1220 | A314 | 5d multi | .60 | .45 |
| 1221 | A314 | 8d multi | 1.90 | .75 |
| | | *Nos. 1218-1221 (4)* | 2.90 | 1.60 |

Yugoslav primitive art.

Cock and Flower, by Kaca Milinojsin A315

Designs (Children's Paintings): 3.20d, Girl and Boy, by Ewa Medrzecka, vert. 5d, Cat and Kitten, by Jelena Anastasijevic.

**1974, Oct. 7 Litho. *Perf. 13***

| | | | | |
|---|---|---|---|---|
| 1222 | A315 | 1.20d multi | .20 | .20 |
| 1223 | A315 | 3.20d multi | .20 | .20 |
| 1224 | A315 | 5d multi | .70 | .20 |
| | | *Nos. 1222-1224 (3)* | 1.10 | .60 |

Children's Week, Oct. 1-7, and Joy of Europe meeting in Belgrade. Sheets of 9.

Library and Primoz Trubar Statue A316

**1974, Oct. 21 Engr. *Perf. 13***

| | | | | |
|---|---|---|---|---|
| 1225 | A316 | 1.20d black | .20 | .20 |

Natl. University Library, Ljubljana, 200th anniv.

White Peonies, by Petar Dobrovic A317

Paintings of Flowers by Yugoslav artists: 2d, Carnations, by Vilko Gecan. 3d, Flowers, still-life, by Milan Konjovic. 4d, White Vase, by Sava Sumanovic. 5d, Larkspur, by Stane Kregar. 8d, Roses, by Petar Lubarda.

**1974, Nov. 28 Photo. *Perf. 11½***

| | | | | |
|---|---|---|---|---|
| 1226 | A317 | 80p gold & multi | .20 | .20 |
| 1227 | A317 | 2d gold & multi | .20 | .20 |
| 1228 | A317 | 3d gold & multi | .20 | .20 |
| 1229 | A317 | 4d gold & multi | .30 | .20 |
| 1230 | A317 | 5d gold & multi | .45 | .20 |
| 1231 | A317 | 8d gold & multi | .85 | .35 |
| | | *Nos. 1226-1231 (6)* | 2.20 | 1.35 |

Sheets of 9.

Title Page and View of Belgrade A318

**1975, Jan. 8 Litho. *Perf. 13***

| | | | | |
|---|---|---|---|---|
| 1232 | A318 | 1.20d citron | .20 | .20 |
| *a.* | | Perf. 12½ | | |

Sesquicentennial of the first publication of Matica Srpska, literary journal.

Map of Europe and Dove — A319

Svetozar Markovic, by Stevan Bodnarov A321

Gold-plated Bronze Earring A320

**1975, Jan. 30 *Perf. 12x11½***

| | | | | |
|---|---|---|---|---|
| 1233 | A319 | 3.20d bl & multi | .55 | .25 |
| 1234 | A319 | 8d multi | 1.75 | .90 |

Interparliamentary Union for European Cooperation and Security, 2nd Conference, Belgrade, Jan. 31-Feb. 6.

**1975, Feb. 25 Photo. *Perf. 14x13***

Antique jewelry in Yugoslav museums: 2.10d, Silver bracelet, 18th cent. 3.20d, Silver gilt belt buckle, 18th cent. 5d, Silver ring with Nike cameo, 14th cent. 6d, Silver necklace, 17th cent. 8d, Bronze gilt bracelet, 14th cent.

| | | | | |
|---|---|---|---|---|
| 1235 | A320 | 1.20d multi | .20 | .20 |
| 1236 | A320 | 2.10d multi | .20 | .20 |
| 1237 | A320 | 3.20d multi | .20 | .20 |
| 1238 | A320 | 5d multi | .35 | .25 |
| 1239 | A320 | 6d multi | .65 | .40 |
| 1240 | A320 | 8d multi | .80 | .75 |
| | | *Nos. 1235-1240 (6)* | 2.40 | 2.00 |

**1975, Feb. 26 Engr. *Perf. 13***

| | | | | |
|---|---|---|---|---|
| 1241 | A321 | 1.20d blue blk | .20 | .20 |

Markovic (1846-1875), writer and poet.

Fettered Woman, by Frano Krsinic A322

Street, Ohrid — A323

**1975, Mar. 8 Photo. *Perf. 14½x14***

| | | | | |
|---|---|---|---|---|
| 1242 | A322 | 3.20d gold & sepia | .30 | .20 |

International Women's Year.

**1975-77 Litho. *Perf. 13***

Views: 25p, Budva. 75p, City Hall, Rijeka (Fiume). Nos. 1245, 1246, Street, Ohrid. 1.50d, Church, Bihac. 2.10d, Street and fountain, Hvar. 3.20d, Skofja Loka. 3.40d, Main Square, Vranje. 4.90d, Mosque, Perast.

**No Inscription at Bottom**

| | | | | |
|---|---|---|---|---|
| 1243 | A323 | 25p carmine ('76) | .20 | .20 |
| 1244 | A323 | 75p purple ('76) | .20 | .20 |
| 1245 | A323 | 1d dull purple | .25 | .20 |
| 1246 | A323 | 1d dl grn ('76) | .20 | .20 |
| *a.* | | Perf. 13x12½ | .20 | |
| 1247 | A323 | 1.50d rose red ('76) | .30 | .20 |
| *a.* | | Perf. 13x12½ | 10.00 | |
| 1248 | A323 | 2.10d gray green | .50 | .20 |
| 1249 | A323 | 3.20d dull blue | .70 | .20 |
| 1250 | A323 | 3.40d gray grn ('77) | .30 | .20 |
| *a.* | | Perf. 13x12½ | 1.00 | |
| 1251 | A323 | 4.90d dl bl ('76) | .55 | .20 |
| | | *Nos. 1243-1251 (9)* | 3.20 | 1.80 |

See Nos. 1487-1491, 1598, 1601, 1603A, 1713, 1718-1719. For surcharges see Nos. 1382-1383, 1481, 1502, 1545, 1550, 1594-1597A, 1764, 1767-1768, 1770-1771, 1964, 1973.

**Europa Issue 1975**

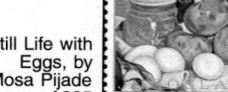

Still Life with Eggs, by Mosa Pijade A325

Painting: 8d, Three Graces, by Ivan Radovic.

**1975, Apr. 28**

| | | | | |
|---|---|---|---|---|
| 1252 | A325 | 3.20d gold & multi | .20 | .20 |
| 1253 | A325 | 8d gold & multi | .60 | .60 |

Srem Front Fighters' Monument, by Dusan Dzamonja A326

**1975, May 9 Litho. *Perf. 13½***

| | | | | |
|---|---|---|---|---|
| 1254 | A326 | 3.20d red & multi | .30 | .20 |

Victory over Fascism in WWII; liberation of Yugoslavia, 30th anniv.

Garland Flower — A327

Kayak — A328

**1975, May 24 Photo. *Perf. 14x14½***

| | | | | |
|---|---|---|---|---|
| 1255 | A327 | 1.20d shown | .20 | .20 |
| 1256 | A327 | 2.10d Garden balsam | .20 | .20 |
| 1257 | A327 | 3.20d Rose mallow | .20 | .20 |
| 1258 | A327 | 5d Geranium | .40 | .25 |
| 1259 | A327 | 6d Crocus | .55 | .30 |
| 1260 | A327 | 8d Oleander | .85 | .60 |
| | | *Nos. 1255-1260 (6)* | 2.40 | 1.75 |

Youth Day.

**1975, June 20 Litho. *Perf. 13½***

| | | | | |
|---|---|---|---|---|
| 1261 | A328 | 3.20d grnsh bl & multi | .25 | .20 |

9th World Championship of Wild Water Racing, Radika River, June 24-25, and 14th World Championship of Canoe-Slalom, Treska River, June 28-29.

Ambush, Herzegovinian Insurgents, by Ferdo Quiquerez — A329

**1975, July 9 Photo. *Perf. 13½x14½***

| | | | | |
|---|---|---|---|---|
| 1262 | A329 | 1.20d gold & multi | .20 | .20 |

Bosnian & Herzegovinian Uprising, cent.

Stjepan Mitrov Ljubisa (1824-1878) A330

Yugoslav writers: 2.10d, Ivan Prijatelj (1875-1937). 3.20d, Jakov Ignjatovic (1824-1889). 5d, Dragojla Jarnevic (1824-1889). 6d, Svetozar Corovic (1875-1919). 8d, Ivana Brlic-Mazuranic (1874-1938).

**1975, Sept. 16 Litho. *Perf. 13***

| | | | | |
|---|---|---|---|---|
| 1263 | A330 | 1.20d brick red & blk | .20 | .20 |
| 1264 | A330 | 2.10d dl grn & blk | .20 | .20 |
| 1265 | A330 | 3.20d ol bis & blk | .20 | .20 |
| 1266 | A330 | 5d brn org & blk | .35 | .20 |
| 1267 | A330 | 6d yel grn & blk | .40 | .20 |
| 1268 | A330 | 8d Prus bl & blk | .50 | .30 |
| | | *Nos. 1263-1268 (6)* | 1.85 | 1.30 |

"Joy of Europe" Children's Meeting, Oct. 2-7, Belgrade A331

Children's drawings.

**1975, Oct. 1 Litho. *Perf. 13½***

| | | | | |
|---|---|---|---|---|
| 1269 | A331 | 3.20d Young Lion | .35 | .20 |
| 1270 | A331 | 6d Baby Carriage | 1.60 | .65 |

Peace Dove A332

**1975, Oct. 10**
**1271** A332 3.20d multi .20 .20
**1272** A332 8d multi .75 .45

European Security and Cooperation Conference, Helsinki, July 30-Aug. 1.

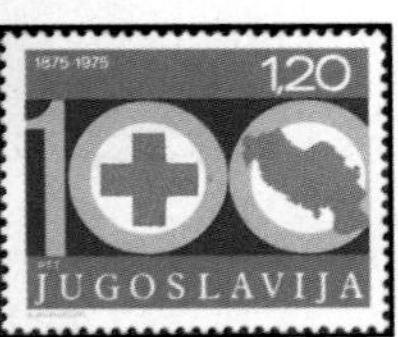

Red Cross, "100", Map of Yugoslavia A333

8d, Red Cross, people seeking help.

**1975, Nov. 1 Litho. *Perf. 13½x13***
**1273** A333 1.20d red & multi .20 .20
**1274** A333 8d red & multi .45 .30

Centenary of Red Cross in Yugoslavia.

Soup Kitchen, by Dorde Andrejevic-Kun A334

Social paintings by 20th century Yugoslav artists: 2.10d, People at the Door, by Vinko Grdan. 3.20d, Drunks in Coach, by Marijan Detoni, horiz. 5d, Workers' Lunch, by Tone Kralj, horiz. 6d, Water Wheel, by Lazar Licenoski. 8d, The Hanging, by Krsto Hegedusic.

***Perf. 14½x13½, 13½x14½***
**1975, Nov. 28 Photo.**
**1275** A334 1.20d gold & multi .20 .20
**1276** A334 2.10d gold & multi .20 .20
**1277** A334 3.20d gold & multi .20 .20
**1278** A334 5d gold & multi .20 .20
**1279** A334 6d gold & multi .30 .25
**1280** A334 8d gold & multi .55 .55
*Nos. 1275-1280 (6)* 1.65 1.60

Sheets of 9.

Diocletian's Palace, 304 A.D. — A335

3.20d, House of Ohrid, 19th cent., vert. 8d, Gracanica Monastery, Kosovo, 1321.

**1975, Dec. 10 Engr. *Perf. 13½***
**1281** A335 1.20d dark brown .20 .20
**1282** A335 3.20d bluish black .30 .20
**1283** A335 8d dk vio brown .80 .35
*Nos. 1281-1283 (3)* 1.30 .75

European Architectural Heritage Year 1975. Sheets of 9.

12th Winter Olympic Games, Feb. 4-15, Innsbruck, Austria A336

**1976, Feb. 4 Engr. *Perf. 13½***
**1284** A336 3.20d Ski jump .20 .20
**1285** A336 8d Pair figure skating .70 .40

Red Flag — A337

**1976, Feb. 14 Litho.**
**1286** A337 1.20d red & multi .20 .20

"Red Flag" workers demonstration, Kragujevac, Feb. 15, 1876.

Svetozar Miletic (1826-1901), Lawyer, Founder of United Serbian Youth — A338

**1976, Feb. 23 *Perf. 13½x13***
**1287** A338 1.20d grnsh gray & dl grn .20 .20

Borislav "Bora" Stankovic, (1876-1927), Writer A339

**1976, Mar. 31 Litho. *Perf. 13½x13***
**1288** A339 1.20d lem, ol & mar .20 .20

Sheets of 9.

### Europa Issue 1976

King Matthias, by Jakob Pogorelec, 1931 — A340

**1976, Apr. 26 Photo. *Perf. 11½***
**1289** A340 3.20d shown .20 .20
**1290** A340 8d Bowl, 14th cent .30 .30

Ivan Cankar (1876-1918), Slovenian Writer A341

**1976, May 8 Litho. *Perf. 13½x13***
**1291** A341 1.20d orange & plum .20 .20

Train on Viaduct in Bosnia A342

Design: 8d, Train on viaduct in Montenegro.

**1976, May 15 Engr. *Perf. 13½***
**1292** A342 3.20d deep magenta .20 .20
**1293** A342 8d deep blue .55 .25

Inauguration of the Belgrade-Bar railroad.

Hawker Dragonfly A343

Fresh-water Fauna: 2.10d, Winkle. 3.20d, Rudd. 5d, Green frog. 6d, Ferruginous duck. 8d, Muskrat.

**1976, May 25 Litho.**
**1294** A343 1.20d yel & multi .20 .20
**1295** A343 2.10d bl & multi .20 .20
**1296** A343 3.20d vio & multi .20 .20
**1297** A343 5d multicolored .40 .30
**1298** A343 6d multicolored .45 .40
**1299** A343 8d multicolored .75 .50
*Nos. 1294-1299 (6)* 2.20 1.80

Youth Day.

Vladimir Nazor, Croatian Writer, Birth Cent. — A344

**1976, May 29 *Perf. 13***
**1300** A344 1.20d pale lil & dl bl .20 .20

Battle of Vucji Dol, 1876 A345

**1976, June 16 Litho. *Perf. 13***
**1301** A345 1.20d gold, brn & buff .20 .20

Liberation of Montenegro from Turkey, cent.

Serbian Pitcher A346

Water Pitchers: 2.10d, Slovenia. 3.20d, Bosnia-Herzegovina. 5d, Vojvodina 6d, Macedonia. 8d, Kosovo.

**1976, June 22 Photo. *Perf. 14x13***
**1302** A346 1.20d dk car & multi .20 .20
**1303** A346 2.10d olive & multi .20 .20
**1304** A346 3.20d red & multi .20 .20
**1305** A346 5d brown & multi .30 .20
**1306** A346 6d dk grn & multi .40 .30
**1307** A346 8d dk bl & multi .85 .35
*Nos. 1302-1307 (6)* 2.15 1.45

Tesla Monument, Belgrade, and Niagara Falls — A347

**1976, July 10 Engr. *Perf. 13***
**1308** A347 5d slate grn & indigo .50 .20

Nikola Tesla (1856-1943), electrical engineer and inventor. Sheets of 9.

21st Olympic Games, July 17-Aug. 1, Montreal, Canada, A348

**1976, July 17**
**1309** A348 1.20d Long jump .20 .20
**1310** A348 3.20d Team handball .20 .20
**1311** A348 5d Target shooting .25 .20
**1312** A348 8d Single scull rowing .45 .25
*Nos. 1309-1312 (4)* 1.10 .85

Sheets of 9.

World Map and Peace Dove A349

**1976, Aug. 16 Litho. *Perf. 13***
**1313** A349 4.90d multi .30 .20

5th Summit Conference of Non-Aligned Countries, Colombo, Sri Lanka, Aug. 9-19. Sheets of 9.

Children's Train — A350

Children's drawings: 4.90d, Navy Day (submarine).

**1976, Oct. 2 Litho. *Perf. 13***
**1314** A350 4.90d multi .35 .20
**1315** A350 8d multi .90 .35

"Joy of Europe" Children's Meeting, Belgrade, Oct. 2-7.

Herzegovinian Fugitives, by Uros Predic — A351

Historical paintings by 19th-20th century Yugoslav painters: 1.20d, Battle of the Montenegrins, by Djura Jaksic, vert. 2.10d, Nikola S. Zrinjski at Siget, by Oton Ivekovic, vert. 5d, Uprising at Razlovci, by Borko Lazeski. 6d, Enthroning of Slovenian Duke at Gospovetsko Field, by Anton Gojmir Kos. 8d, Break-through at Solun Front, by Veljko Stanojevic.

***Perf. 13½x12½, 12½x13½***
**1976, Nov. 29 Photo.**
**1316** A351 1.20d gold & multi .20 .20
**1317** A351 2.10d gold & multi .20 .20
**1318** A351 3.20d gold & multi .20 .20
**1319** A351 5d gold & multi .25 .25
**1320** A351 6d gold & multi .45 .35
**1321** A351 8d gold & multi .55 .50
*Nos. 1316-1321 (6)* 1.85 1.70

Sheets of 9.

No. 839 Surcharged with New Value and 3 Bars in Rose

**1976, Dec. 8 Engr. *Perf. 12½***
**1322** A206 1d on 85p dl pur .20 .20

Mateja Nenadovic A352

Rajko Zinzifov — A353

**1977, Feb. 4 Photo. *Perf. 13½x14***
**1323** A352 4.90d multicolored .30 .20

Prota Mateja Nenadovic (1777-1854), Serbian Duke, archbishop and writer.

**1977, Feb. 10 Litho. *Perf. 13x13½***
**1324** A353 1.50d brn & sepia .20 .20

Rajko Zinzifov (1839-1877), writer.

Phlox — A354

Alojz Kraigher — A356

Croatian Music Institute, Zagreb, 150th Anniv. A355

Flowers: 3.40d, Lily. 4.90d, Bleeding heart. 6d, Zinnia. 8d, Spreading marigold. 10d, Horseshoe geranium.

**1977, Mar. 8 *Perf. 13½x13***
**1325** A354 1.50d multi .20 .20
**1326** A354 3.40d multi .25 .20
**1327** A354 4.90d multi .30 .20
**1328** A354 6d multi .35 .20
**1329** A354 8d multi .55 .20
**1330** A354 10d multi .90 .55
*Nos. 1325-1330 (6)* 2.55 1.55

**1977, Apr. 4 Engr. *Perf. 13***
**1331** A355 4.90d bl & sepia .30 .20

**1977, Apr. 11 Litho. *Perf. 13½***
**1332** A356 1.50d lemon & brn .20 .20

Kraigher (1877-1959), Slovenian writer.

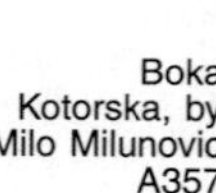

Boka Kotorska, by Milo Milunovic A357

10d, Zagorje in November, by Ljubo Babie.

**1977, May 4 Photo. *Perf. 11½***
**1333** A357 4.90d gold & multi .20 .20
**1334** A357 10d gold & multi .55 .55

Europa. Issued in sheets of 9.

Marshal Tito, by Omer Mujadzic A358

Mountain Range and Gentian — A359

**1977, May 25 *Perf. 11½x12***
**1335** A358 1.50d gold & multi .20 .20
**1336** A358 4.90d gold & multi .30 .25
**1337** A358 8d gold & multi .60 .40
*Nos. 1335-1337 (3)* 1.10 .85

85th birthday of Pres. Tito. Sheets of 9.

**1977, June 6 Litho. *Perf. 13x13½***

Design: 10d, Plitvice Lakes Falls, trees, robin and environmental protection emblem.

**1338** A359 4.90d multicolored .30 .20
**1339** A359 10d multicolored .70 .50

World Environment Day.

Petar Kocic (1877-1916), Writer A360

**1977, June 15 *Perf. 13½***
**1340** A360 1.50d pale grn & brn .20 .20

Map of Europe and Peace Dove A361

**1977, June 15 Litho. *Perf. 13½***
**1341** A361 4.90d multi .90 .90
**1342** A361 10d multi 3.75 3.75

Security and Cooperation Conference, Belgrade, June 15.

Child on Float — A362

Children's drawings: 10d, Fruit picking.

**1977, Oct. 3 Litho. *Perf. 13½***
**1343** A362 4.90d multi .35 .20
**1344** A362 10d multi .90 .40

"Joy of Europe" Children's Meeting.

Sava Congress Center, Belgrade A363

**1977, Oct. 4 Litho. *Perf. 13½***
**1345** A363 4.90d bl & multi .55 .40
**1346** A363 10d car & multi 4.00 3.00

European Security and Cooperation Conference, Belgrade.

Exhibition Emblem — A364

**1977, Oct. 20 Litho. *Perf. 13½***
**1347** A364 4.90d gold & multi .30 .20

Balkanfila 1977, 6th Intl. Phil. Exhib. of Balkan Countries, Belgrade, Oct. 24-30.

Double Flute and Shepherd A365

Landscape and Musician: 3.40d, 4.90d, 6d, Various string instruments. 8d, Bagpipes. 10d, Panpipes.

**1977, Oct. 25 Engr. *Perf. 13½***
**1348** A365 1.50d och & red brn .20 .20
**1349** A365 3.40d green & brn .20 .20
**1350** A365 4.90d dk brn & yel .25 .20
**1351** A365 6d bl & red brn .40 .20
**1352** A365 8d brick red & sep .60 .20
**1353** A365 10d sl grn & bis .90 .25
*Nos. 1348-1353 (6)* 2.55 1.25

Musical instruments from Belgrade Ethnographical Museum.

Ivan Vavpotic, Self-portrait A366

Self-portraits of Yugoslav artists: 3.40d, Mihailo Vukotic. 4.90d, Kosta Hakman. 6d, Miroslav Kraljevic. 8d, Nikola Martinovski. 10d, Milena Pavlovic-Barili.

***Perf. 13½x12½***
**1977, Nov. 26 Photo.**
**1354** A366 1.50d gold & multi .20 .20
**1355** A366 3.40d gold & multi .20 .20
**1356** A366 4.90d gold & multi .20 .20
**1357** A366 6d gold & multi .30 .20
**1358** A366 8d gold & multi .45 .20
**1359** A366 10d gold & multi .65 .65
*Nos. 1354-1359 (6)* 2.00 1.65

Festival of Testaccio, by Klovic — A367

Julija Klovic, by El Greco — A368

**1978, Jan. 14 Photo. *Perf. 13½***
**1360** A367 4.90d multicolored .20 .20
**1361** A368 10d multicolored .35 .30

Julija Klovic (1498-1578), Croat miniaturist.

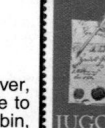

Stampless Cover, Banaviste to Kubin, 1869 — A369

Designs: 3.40d, Mailbox. 4.90d, Ericsson telephone, 1900. 10d, Morse telegraph, 1844.

**1978, Jan. 28 *Perf. 13x14***
**1362** A369 1.50d multicolored .20 .20
**1363** A369 3.40d multicolored .20 .20
**1364** A369 4.90d multicolored .25 .20
**1365** A369 10d multicolored .50 .40
*Nos. 1362-1365 (4)* 1.15 1.00

Post Office Museum, Belgrade.

Battle of Pirot A370

**1978, Feb. 20 Litho. *Perf. 13½***
**1366** A370 1.50d gold, blk & sl grn .20 .20

Centenary of Serbo-Turkish War.

Airplanes A371

**1978, Apr. 24 Litho. *Perf. 13½***
**1367** A371 1.50d S-49A, 1949 .20 .20
**1368** A371 3.40d Galeb, 1961 .25 .20
**1369** A371 4.90d Utva-75, 1976 .35 .20
**1370** A371 10d Orao, 1974 .95 .40
*Nos. 1367-1370 (4)* 1.75 1.00

Aeronautical Day.

### Europa Issue

View of Golubac A372

**1978, May 3 Photo. *Perf. 11½***
**1371** A372 4.90d shown .20 .20
**1372** A372 10d St. Naum Monastery, Ohrid .80 .80

Boxing Glove A373

Honeybee A374

**1978, May 5 Litho. *Perf. 13½***
**1373** A373 4.90d multicolored .35 .20

Amateur Boxing Championships.

**1978, May 25 Photo. *Perf. 11½***

Bees of Yugoslavia: 3.40d, Halictus scabiosae. 4.90d, Blue carpenter bee. 10d, Large earth bumblebee.

**1374** A374 1.50d multi .20 .20
**1375** A374 3.40d multi .25 .20
**1376** A374 4.90d multi .40 .25
**1377** A374 10d multi .95 .70
*Nos. 1374-1377 (4)* 1.80 1.35

Filip Filipovic (1878-1938), Radovan Radovic (1878-1906), Revolutionaries — A375

**1978, June 19 Litho. *Perf. 13½***
**1378** A375 1.50d dk pur & dl ol .20 .20

Marshal Tito — A376

Congress Emblem — A377

**1978, June 20**
**1379** A376 2d red & multi .20 .20
**1380** A377 4.90d red & multi .45 .20

**Souvenir Sheet**
***Imperf***

**1381** A376 15d red & multi 3.75 2.60

11th Congress of Yugoslav League of Communists, Belgrade, June 20-23.

Nos. 1246, 1248 Surcharged with New Value and Two Bars in Brown

**1978 Litho. *Perf. 13***
**1382** A323 2d on 1d .25 .20
**1383** A323 3.40d on 2.10d .25 .20

Issue dates: #1382, July 17; #1383, Aug. 1.

Conference Emblem over Belgrade — A378

Championship Emblem — A379

**1978, July 25 Photo. *Perf. 13½***
**1384** A378 4.90d bl & lt blue .20 .20

Conference of Foreign Ministers of Nonaligned Countries, Belgrade, July 25-29.

**1978, Aug. 10 Litho. *Perf. 13½x13***
**1385** A379 4.90d multicolored .30 .20

14th Kayak and Canoe Still Water Championships, Lake Sava, Aug. 10-14.

Mt. Triglav, North Rock — A380

Black Lake, Mt. Durmitor A381

**1978, Aug. 26 Photo. *Perf. 14***
**1386** A380 2d multicolored .20 .20

Bicentenary of first ascent of Mt. Triglav by Slovenian climbers.

**1978, Sept. 20**
**1387** A381 4.90d shown .25 .20
**1388** A381 10d Tara River .55 .30

Protection of the environment.

Night Sky A382

**1978, Sept. 30 Litho. *Perf. 13x12½***
**1389** A382 4.90d bl blk, blk & gold .20 .20

29th Congress of International Astronautical Federation, Dubrovnik, Oct. 1-8.

People in Forest A383

Children's drawings: 10d, Family around pond.

**1978, Oct. 2 *Perf. 13½x13***
**1390** A383 4.90d multi .35 .20
**1391** A383 10d multi .80 .45

"Joy of Europe" Children's Meeting.

Seal on Insurrection Declaration A384

**1978, Oct. 5 *Perf. 13½***
**1392** A384 2d gold, brn & blk .20 .20

Centenary of Kresna uprising.

Teachers' Training Institute, Sombor, Bicent. A385

**1978, Oct. 16**
**1393** A385 2d multicolored .20 .20

Croatian Red Cross, Cent. A386

**1978, Oct. 21**
**1394** A386 2d lt bl, blk & red .20 .20

Metallic Sculpture XXII, by Dusan Dzamonja A387

Modern Sculptures: 3.40d, Circulation in Space I, by Vojin Bakic, vert. 4.90d, Tectonic Octopode, by Olga Jevric, vert. 10d, Tree of Life, by Drago Trsar.

***Perf. 13½x13, 13x13½***

**1978, Nov. 4 Litho.**
**1395** A387 2d multicolored .20 .20
**1396** A387 3.40d multicolored .20 .20
**1397** A387 4.90d multicolored .25 .20
**1398** A387 10d multicolored .65 .40
*Nos. 1395-1398 (4)* 1.30 1.00

Crossing of Neretva Pass, by Ismet Mujezinovic A388

**1978, Nov. 10 Litho. *Perf. 13***
**1399** A388 2d multicolored .20 .20

35th anniversary of Battle of Neretva.

Workers Leaving Factory, by Marijan Detoni — A389

Larch Cone — A390

Engravings: 3.40d, Workers, by Maksim Sedej. 4.90d, Lumberjacks, by Daniel Ozmo. 6d, Meal Break, by Pivo Karamatijevic. 10d, Hanged Man and Raped Woman, by Djordje Andrejevic Kun.

**1978, Nov. 28 Photo. *Perf. 14x13½***
**1400** A389 2d gold, blk & buff .20 .20
**1401** A389 3.40d gold & black .20 .20
**1402** A389 4.90d gold, yel & blk .30 .20
**1403** A389 6d gold, buff & blk .40 .25
**1404** A389 10d gold, cr & blk .70 .50
*Nos. 1400-1404 (5)* 1.80 1.35

Republic day.

**1978, Dec. 11 Photo. *Perf. 13x12½***
**1405** A390 1.50d shown .20 .20
**1406** A390 1.50d Red squirrel .20 .20
**1407** A390 2d Sycamore leaves .25 .20
**1408** A390 2d Red deer .25 .20
*a.* Bklt. pane of 8 1.25
**1409** A390 3.40d Alder leaves .35 .20
**1410** A390 3.40d Partridge .35 .20
**1411** A390 4.90d Oak leaves .45 .20
**1412** A390 4.90d Grouse .45 .20
*a.* Bklt. pane of 8 3.25
*Nos. 1405-1412 (8)* 2.50 1.60

New Year 1979. Nos. 1405-1412 printed se-tenant in sheets of 25.

No. 1408a contains 4 each of Nos. 1407-1408; No. 1412a 2 each of Nos. 1409-1412, with background colors changed.

Nos. 1064, 868, 1198 Surcharged with New Value and Bars

**1978 Engr.; Litho. *Perf. 12½, 13½***
**1413** A263 35p on 10p brown .20 .20
**1414** A211 60p on 85p dp bl .20 .20
**1415** A305 80p on 1.20d sl grn .20 .20
*Nos. 1413-1415 (3)* .60 .60

First Masthead of Politika A391

**1979, Jan. 25 Litho. *Perf. 13½***
**1416** A391 2d gold & black .20 .20

Politika daily newspaper, 75th anniv.

Red Flags and Emblem A392

Child and IYC Emblem A393

**1979, Feb. 15**
**1417** A392 2d red & gold .20 .20

11th Meeting of Self-managers, Kragujevac, Feb. 15-16.

**1979, Mar. 1 Photo. *Perf. 11½x12***
**1418** A393 4.90d gold vio & bl .45 .30

International Year of the Child.

Sabre, Mace, Koran Pouch A394

Old Weapons: 3.40d, Pistol and ramrod, Montenegro. 4.90d, Short carbine and powder horn, Slovenia and Croatia. 10d, Oriental rifle and cartridge pouch.

**1979, Mar. 26 Photo. *Perf. 14***
**1419** A394 2d multicolored .20 .20
**1420** A394 3.40d multicolored .20 .20
**1421** A394 4.90d multicolored .20 .20
**1422** A394 10d multicolored .40 .40
*Nos. 1419-1422 (4)* 1.00 1.00

5-Pointed Star, Hammer and Sickle — A395

**1979, Apr. 20 Photo. *Perf. 13½***
**1423** A395 2d multicolored .20 .20
**1424** A395 4.90d multicolored .35 .20

Communist and Communist Youth Leagues, 60th anniversary.

Cyril and Methodius University and Emblem A396

**1979, Apr. 24 Litho.**
**1425** A396 2d multicolored .20 .20

Sts. Cyril and Methodius University, Skopje, 30th anniv.

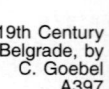

19th Century Belgrade, by C. Goebel A397

Europa: 10d, Postilion and Ljubljana, 17th century, by Jan van der Heyden.

**1979, Apr. 30 Photo. *Perf. 11½***
**1426** A397 4.90d multicolored .20 .20
**1427** A397 10d multicolored .55 .55

Blue Sow Thistles A398

Milutin Milankovic, by Paja Jovanovic A399

Flowers: 3.40d, Anemones. 4.90d, Astragalus. 10d, Alpine trifolium.

**1979, May 25 Photo. *Perf. 13½***
**1428** A398 2d multicolored .20 .20
**1429** A398 3.40d multicolored .20 .20
**1430** A398 4.90d multicolored .30 .20
**1431** A398 10d multicolored .65 .30
*Nos. 1428-1431 (4)* 1.35 .90

**1979, May 28**
**1432** A399 4.90d multi .35 .20

Milutin Milankovic (1879-1958), scientist.

Kosta Abrasevic (1879-1898), Poet — A400

**1979, May 29 Litho. *Perf. 13½x13***
**1433** A400 2d org, blk & gray .20 .20

Eight-Oared Shell A401

**1979, Aug. 28 Litho. *Perf. 13***
**1434** A401 4.90d multicolored .40 .25

9th World Rowing Championship, Lake Bled.

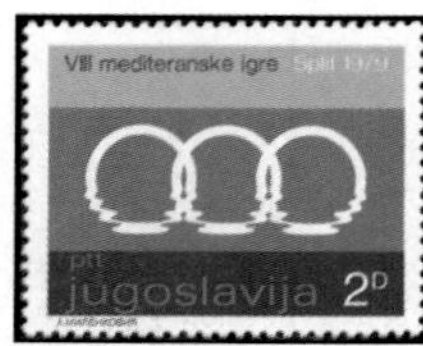


8th Mediterranean Games, Sept. 15-29, Split — A402

**1979, Sept. 10**
**1435** A402 2d Games Emblem .20 .20
**1436** A402 4.90d Mascot .30 .20
**1437** A402 10d Map, Flags .60 .30
*Nos. 1435-1437 (3)* 1.10 .70

Seal, 15th Century A403

**1979, Sept. 14 *Perf. 12½***
**1438** A403 2d multicolored .20 .20

Zagreb Postal Service, 450th anniversary.

Lake Palic — A404

Environment Protection: 10d, Lakefront, Prokletije Mountains.

**1979, Sept. 20 Photo. *Perf. 14x13½***
**1439** A404 4.90d multicolored .35 .20
**1440** A404 10d multicolored .65 .40

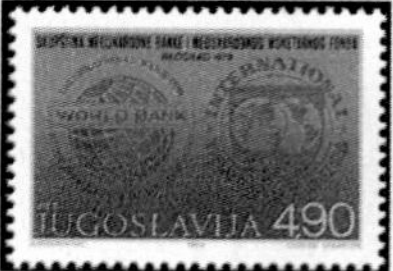


Bank and Fund Emblems A405

**Engr. & Photo.**
**1979, Oct. 1 *Perf. 13½***
**1441** A405 4.90d multicolored .40 .20
**1442** A405 10d multicolored .80 .40

Meeting of the World Bank and International Monetary Fund, Belgrade, Oct. 2-5.

"Joy of Europe" A406

Children's drawings.

**1979, Oct. 2 Litho.**
**1443** A406 4.90d shown .40 .20
**1444** A406 10d Child in yard .85 .45

Mihailo Pupin (1854-1935), Physicist, Inventor — A407

**1979, Oct. 9 *Perf. 13x13½***
**1445** A407 4.90d multicolored .40 .20

Marko Cepenkov A408

Radovan Portal, Trogir Cathedral A410

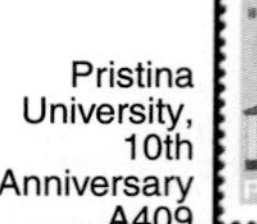

Pristina University, 10th Anniversary A409

**1979, Nov. 15 Litho. *Perf. 13½***
**1446** A408 2d multicolored .20 .20

Cepenkov (1829-1920), Macedonian folklorist.

**1979, Nov. 17**
**1447** A409 2d multicolored .20 .20

**1979, Nov. 28 Photo.**

Romanesque Sculptures: 3.40d, Choir stall, Cathedral of Split. 4.90d, Triforium, Church of the Resurrection, Decani. 6d, Buvina Portal, Cathedral of Split. 10d, Western portal, Church of Our Lady, Studenica.

**1448** A410 2d multi .20 .20
**1449** A410 3.40d multi .25 .20
**1450** A410 4.90d multi .30 .20
**1451** A410 6d multi .35 .20
**1452** A410 10d multi .70 .30
*Nos. 1448-1452 (5)* 1.80 1.10

Sarajevo University, 30th Anniversary A411

**1979, Dec. 1 Litho.**
**1453** A411 2d multicolored .20 .20

Duro Dakovic and Nikola Hecimovic, Communist Revolutionaries, 50th Death Annivs. — A412

**1979, Dec. 10**
**1454** A412 2d multicolored .20 .20

Sidewheeler Deligrad, 1862-1914 — A413

**1979, Dec. 14**
**1455** A413 4.90d shown .85 .85
**1456** A413 10d Sidewheeler Serbia, 1917-72 1.90 1.90

Danube Conference.

Milton Manaki and Camera A414

Edward Kardelj, by Zdenko Kalin — A415

**1980, Jan. 21 Litho. *Perf. 13½***
**1457** A414 2d deep bister & plum .20 .20

Manaki (1880-1964), photographer and documentary film maker.

**1980, Jan. 26**
**1458** A415 2d multicolored .20 .20

Kardelj (1910-1979), labor movement leader.

No. 1458 Overprinted in Red

**1980, Jan. 26**
**1459** A415 2d multicolored .25 .20

Ploce renamed Kardeljevo.

13th Winter Olympic Games, Feb. 12-24, Lake Placid, NY — A416

**1980, Feb. 13**
**1460** A416 4.90d Speed skating .35 .25
**1461** A416 10d Cross-country skiing .90 .50

University of Belgrade, 75th Anniversary A417

**1980, Feb. 27**
**1462** A417 2d multicolored .20 .20

22nd Summer Olympic Games, July 19-Aug. 3, Moscow A418

**1980, Apr. 21**
**1463** A418 2d Fencing .20 .20
**1464** A418 3.40d Bicycling .25 .25
**1465** A418 4.90d Field hockey .35 .35
**1466** A418 10d Archery .75 .75
*Nos. 1463-1466 (4)* 1.55 1.55

Marshal Tito, by Antun Augustincic A419

Europa: 13d, Tito, by Djordje Prudnikov.

**1980, Apr. 28 Photo. *Perf. 11½***
**Granite Paper**
**1467** A419 4.90d multi .25 .25
**1468** A419 13d multi 1.75 1.75

Marshal Tito, by Bozidar Jakac — A420

**1980, May 4 Litho. *Perf. 13½***
**1469** A420 2.50d purplish blk .20 .20
*a.* Perf. 10½ .40 .35
**1470** A420 4.90d gray black *3.00 3.00*

Marshal Tito (1892-1980) memorial. Issued in sheets of 8 plus label.

Sava Kovacevic (1905-1943), Revolutionary — A421

**1980, May 11 Litho. *Perf. 13½***
**1471** A421 2.50d multicolored .20 .20

Wood Baton and Letter A422

**1980, May 14**
**1472** A422 2d multicolored .20 .20

1st Tito Youth Relay Race, 35th anniv.

Flying Gunard — A423

Emperor Trajan Decius Coin, 3rd Cent. — A424

**1980, May 24 Photo. *Perf. 12***
**1473** A423 2d shown .20 .20
**1474** A423 3.40d Loggerhead turtle .40 .20
**1475** A423 4.90d Sea swallow .35 .25
**1476** A423 10d Dolphin .65 .50
*Nos. 1473-1476 (4)* 1.60 1.15

**1980, June 10**

3rd Century Roman Coins (Illyrian Emperors): 3.40d, Aurelianus. 4.90d, Probus. 10d, Diocletianus.

**1477** A424 2d multicolored .20 .20
**1478** A424 3.40d multicolored .25 .20
**1479** A424 4.90d multicolored .30 .20
**1480** A424 10d multicolored .60 .40
*Nos. 1477-1480 (4)* 1.35 1.00

No. 1247 Surcharged with New Value and Bars

**1980, June 17 Litho. *Perf. 13½***
**1481** A323 2.50d on 1.50d .20 .20

Types of 1971-77

Views: 5p, Krusevac. 10p, Gradacac. 20p, Church and bridge, Bohinj. 30p, Krk. 35p, Omis. 40p, Pec. 60p, Logar Valley. 2.50d, Kragujevac. 3.50d, Vrsac. 5.60d, Travnik. 8d, Dubrovnik.

***Perf. 13½, 13¼x12½ (#1487), 13¼ (#1486A)***

**1980-81**
**1482** A263 5p deep orange .20 .20
**1483** A263 10p brown .25 .20
**1483A** A263 20p purple ('78) .20 .20
**1484** A263 30p olive gray .20 .20
**1485** A263 35p brown red .20 .20
**1486** A263 40p gray .20 .20
**1486A** A263 60p purple .20 .20
**1487** A323 2.50d rose red .20 .20
**1488** A323 2.50d bl gray ('81) .20 .20
**1489** A323 3.50d red org ('81) .30 .20
**1490** A323 5.60d gray grn ('81) .40 .20
**1491** A323 8d gray ('81) .50 .20
*Nos. 1482-1491 (12)* 3.05 2.40

No. 1483A has all three numerals in denomination the same size. On No. 1065 "20" is taller than first "0."

***Perf. 13¼x12½***

*1482a* A263 5p
*1483b* A263 10p
*1483Ac* A263 20p
*1484a* A263 30p
*1485a* A263 35p
*1486b* A263 40p
*1486Ac* A263 60p
*1487a* A323 2.50d
*1488a* A323 2.50d
*1489a* A323 3.50d
*1490a* A323 5.60d
*1491a* A323 8d

400th Anniversary of Lipica Stud Farm — A425

**1980, June 25**
**1493** A425 2.50d black .25 .20

A426

A427

**1980, June 27 *Perf. 13½***
**1494** A426 2.50d magenta & red .25 .20

Tito, Basic Law of Self-management, 30th anniv.

**1980, June 28 *Perf. 13***
**1495** A427 2.50d light green .25 .20

University of Novi Sad, 20th anniv.

Mljet National Park — A428

Minerals — A429

**1980, Sept. 5 Photo. *Perf. 14***
**1496** A428 4.90d shown .25 .20
**1497** A428 13d Galicica Natl. Park .65 .40

European Nature Protection Year.

**1980, Sept. 10 Litho. *Perf. 13½***
**1498** A429 2.50d Pyrrhotine .20 .20
**1499** A429 3.40d Dolomite .20 .20
**1500** A429 4.90d Sphalerite .30 .20
**1501** A429 13d Wulfenite .65 .40
*Nos. 1498-1501 (4)* 1.35 1.00

No. 1244 Surcharged with New Value and Bars

**1980, Oct. 15 Litho. *Perf. 13***
**1502** A323 5d on 75p purple .35 .20

View of Kotor, UNESCO Emblem A430

**1980, Sept. 23 *Perf. 13½***
**1503** A430 4.90d multicolored .30 .20

21st UNESCO General Conf., Belgrade,

Children in Garden A431

Joy of Europe Children's Festival: 13d, 3 faces.

**1980, Oct. 2 *Perf. 13½x13***
**1504** A431 4.90d multi .35 .25
**1505** A431 13d multi .90 .50

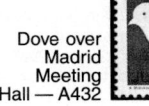

Dove over Madrid Meeting Hall — A432

**Lithographed and Engraved**
**1980, Nov. 11 *Perf. 13½***
**1506** A432 4.90d dk grn & bl grn .30 .25
**1507** A432 13d dk brn & yel brown 1.25 .75

European Security Conference, Madrid.

Federal Flag of Yugoslavia A433

Republic Day: Socialist Republic flags. Nos. 1508-1515 se-tenant. No. 1511 has Latin letters.

**1980, Nov. 28 Litho. *Perf. 12½***

**1508** A433 2.50d Bosnia & Herzegovina .20 .20
**1509** A433 2.50d Croatia .20 .20
**1510** A433 2.50d shown .20 .20
**1511** A433 2.50d Yugoslavia .20 .20
**1512** A433 2.50d Macedonia .20 .20
**1513** A433 2.50d Montenegro .20 .20
**1514** A433 2.50d Serbia .20 .20
**1515** A433 2.50d Slovenia .20 .20
*Nos. 1508-1515 (8)* 1.60 1.60

Woman with Straw Hat — A434

Paintings: 3.40d, Atelier No. 1, by Gabriel Stupica. 4.90d, To the Glory of the Sutjeska Fighters, by Ismet Mujezinovic. 8d, Serenity, by Marino Tartaglia. 13d, Complaint, by Milos Vuskovic.

**1980, Dec. 16 *Perf. 13½***
**1516** A434 2.50d multi .20 .20
**1517** A434 3.40d multi .20 .20
**1518** A434 4.90d multi .25 .20
**1519** A434 8d multi, vert. .35 .30
**1520** A434 13d multi, vert. .60 .45
*Nos. 1516-1520 (5)* 1.60 1.35

Ivan Ribar (1881-1968), Politician — A435

**1981, Jan. 21 Litho. *Perf. 13½***
**1521** A435 2.50d rose red & blk .20 .20

Cementusa Hand Bomb A436

Partisan Weapons: 5.60d, Rifle. 8d, 52-mm Cannon. 13d, Man-powered tank.

**1981, Feb. 16**
**1522** A436 3.50d brick red & blk .20 .20
**1523** A436 5.60d grn & blk .25 .20
**1524** A436 8d bis brn & blk .35 .20
**1525** A436 13d rose vio & blk .55 .30
*Nos. 1522-1525 (4)* 1.35 .90

Monastery of the Virgin, Eleousa, 900th Anniversary A437

**1981, Mar. 3**
**1526** A437 3.50d multicolored .20 .20

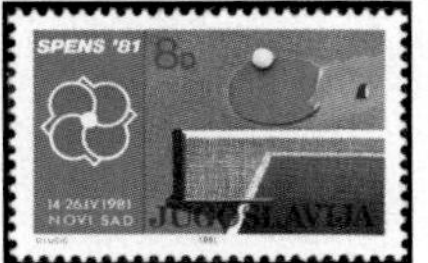

36th World Table Tennis Championship, Novi Sad, Apr. 14-26 — A438

**1981, Apr. 14 Litho. *Perf. 13½***
**1527** A438 8d multicolored .40 .25

### Europa Issue

Wedding in Herzegovina, by Nikola Arsenovic A439

Paintings by Nikola Arsenovic (1823-85): 13d, Witnesses at a Wedding.

**1981, May 5 Photo. *Perf. 12***
**Granite Paper**

**1528** A439 8d multicolored .25 .20
**1529** A439 13d multicolored .50 .35

Dimitrije Tucovic and Slavija Square, Belgrade A440

**1981, May 13 Litho. *Perf. 13½***

**1530** A440 3.50d bl vio & red .20 .20

Tucovic (1881-1914), Socialist leader.

Marshal Tito, by Milivoje Unkovic — A441

**1981, May 25 Photo. *Perf. 11½x12***
**Granite Paper**

**1531** A441 3.50d gold & dk brn *.75 .75*

Marshal Tito's 89th birth anniversary.

Sunflower A442

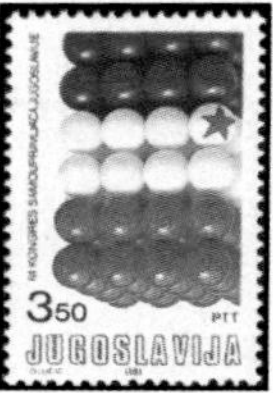

3rd Autonomous Enterprises Cong. A443

**1981, May 28 Photo. *Perf. 11½***
**Granite Paper**

**1532** A442 3.05d shown .20 .20
**1533** A442 5.60d Hops .20 .20
**1534** A442 8d Corn .30 .25
**1535** A442 13d Wheat .55 .35
*Nos. 1532-1535 (4)* 1.25 1.00

**1981, June 16 Litho. *Perf. 13½***

**1536** A443 3.50d multicolored .20 .20

Djordje Petrov (1864-1921), Macedonian Revolutionary A444

**1981, June 22**

**1537** A444 3.50d bister & black .20 .20

National Insurrection, 40th Anniv. A445

**1981, July 4 *Perf. 12½***

**1538** A445 3.50d red org & tan .20 .20
**1539** A445 8d red org & tan .35 .20

**Souvenir Sheet**
***Imperf***

**1540** A445 30d Lenin monument 1.50 1.25

800th Anniv. of Varazdin A446

**1981, Aug. 20 Litho. *Perf. 13½***

**1541** A446 3.50d multicolored .20 .20

Parliament Building, Belgrade — A447

**1981, Sept. 1**

**1542** A447 8d red & blue .35 .30

Belgrade Conference of Non-Aligned Countries, 20th anniv.

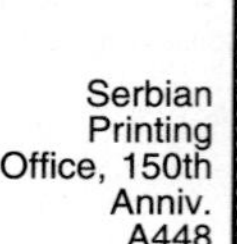

Serbian Printing Office, 150th Anniv. A448

**1981, Sept. 15**

**1543** A448 3.50d pale rose & dk bl .20 .20

Fran Levstik (1831-1887), Writer A449

**1981, Sept. 28 *Perf. 12x11½***

**1544** A449 3.50d dl red & gray .20 .20

No. 1251 Surcharged with New Value and Bars

**1981, Oct. *Perf. 13***

**1545** A323 5d on 4.90d dl bl .35 .20
*a.* Perf. 13x12½ .75

Joy of Europe Children's Festival A450

**1981, Oct. 2**

**1546** A450 8d Barnyard .30 .30
**1547** A450 13d Skiers .60 .40

125th Anniv. of European Danube Commission — A451

**1981, Oct. 28 Litho. *Perf. 13½***

**1548** A451 8d Tugboat Karlovac .30 .30
**1549** A451 13d Train hauling boat, Sip Canal .60 .40

No. 1250a Surcharged with New Value and Bars

**1981, Oct. 9 Litho. *Perf. 13x12½***

**1550** A323 3.50d on 3.40d gray grn .40 .20
*a.* on #1250

Savings Bank of Yugoslavia, 60th Anniv. — A452

Intl. Inventions Conference — A453

**1981, Oct. 31 *Perf. 11½x12***

**1551** A452 3.50d multicolored .20 .20

**1981, Nov. 4 *Perf. 13½***

**1552** A453 8d red & gold .30 .30

Nature Protection — A454

**1981, Nov. 14**

**1553** A454 8d Plant, Ruguvo Ravine .35 .35
**1554** A454 13d Lynx, Prokletjie Mountains .50 .50

August Senoa (1838-1881), Writer — A455

**1981, Dec. 12 *Perf. 11½x12***

**1555** A455 3.50d dl gray vio & gldn brn .20 .20

Still Life with a Fish, by Jovan Bijelic (1886-1964) — A456

Paintings of Animals: 5.60d, Raven, by Milo Milunovic (1897-1967). 8d, Bird on Blue Background, by Marko Celebonovic (b. 1902). 10d, Horses, by Peter Lubarda (1907-1974). 13d, Sheep, by Nikola Masic (1852-1902).

**1981, Dec. 29 Photo. *Perf. 13½***

**1556** A456 3.50d multi .20 .20
**1557** A456 5.60d multi .20 .20
**1558** A456 8d multi .25 .25
**1559** A456 10d multi .35 .35
**1560** A456 13d multi .45 .45
*Nos. 1556-1560 (5)* 1.45 1.45

40th Anniv. of Foca Regulations A457

**1982, Jan 14 Litho. *Perf. 13½***

**1561** A457 3.50d Mosa Pijade .20 .20

60th Anniv. of Communist Newspaper Borba A458

**1982, Feb. 19 Litho.**

**1562** A458 3.50d red & blk .20 .20

500th Anniv. of City of Cetinje — A459

**1982, Mar. 10**

**1563** A459 3.50d dull red brn .20 .20

Capt. Ivo Visin (1806-1868), Boka Kotorska's Map — A460

**1982, May 5 Photo. *Perf. 11½***

**1564** A460 8d shown .25 .25
**1565** A460 15d Ship Splendido .40 .40

Europa, 1st Yugoslavian circumnavigation, 1852-1859.

Male House Sparrow A461

**1982, May 24 Litho. *Perf. 13½***

**1566** A461 3.50d shown .20 .20
**1567** A461 5.60d Female house sparrow .25 .25
**1568** A461 8d Male field sparrow .40 .40
**1569** A461 15d Female field sparrow .70 .70
*Nos. 1566-1569 (4)* 1.55 1.55

See Nos. 1687-1690.

90th Birth Anniv. of Marshal Tito — A462

**1982, May 25 Photo. *Perf. 11½x12***
**Granite Paper**

**1570** A462 3.50d multicolored .20 .20

1982 World Cup — A463

Designs: Soccer ball in various positions.

**1982, June 12** *Perf. 11½*

**Granite Paper**

**1571** Sheet of 4 1.25 1.25
*a.* A463 3.50d multicolored .20 .20
*b.* A463 5.60d multicolored .20 .20
*c.* A463 8d multicolored .30 .30
*d.* A463 15d multicolored .55 .55

12th Congress of Yugoslavian Communists' League, Belgrade, June 26-29 A464

**1982 June 26** **Litho.** *Perf. 13½*

**1572** A464 3.50d orange & red .20 .20
**1573** A464 8d gray & red .25 .25

**Souvenir Sheet**

*Perf. 12½*

**1574** Sheet of 2 1.25 1.25
*a.* A464 10d like 3.50d .40 .40
*b.* A464 20d like 8d .80 .80

Dura Jaksic (1832-1878), Writer, Painter A465

**1982, July 27** **Litho.** *Perf. 14*

**1575** A465 3.50d Self-portrait .20 .20

1982 World Championships Held in Yugoslavia — A466

**1982, July 30** *Perf. 13½*

**1576** A466 8d Gymnastics .25 .25
**1577** A466 8d Kayak .25 .25
**1578** A466 8d Weightlifting .25 .25
*Nos. 1576-1578 (3)* .75 .75

Ivan Zajc (1832-1914), Composer and Conductor A467

**1982, Aug. 3**

**1579** A467 4d brown .20 .20

Breguet XIX and Potez XXV A468

**1982, Sept. 1** **Litho.** *Perf. 13½*

**1580** A468 4d shown .20 .20
**1581** A468 6.10d Super Galeb G-4 .20 .20
**1582** A468 8.80d Armed boat .35 .35
**1583** A468 15d Rocket gun boat .50 .50
*Nos. 1580-1583 (4)* 1.25 1.25

40th anniv. of Air Force/Anti-aircraft Defense and Navy.

Spruce Branch, Tara Natl. Park A469

**1982, Sept. 3**

**1584** A469 8.80d shown .35 .35
**1585** A469 15d Mediterranean monk seal, Kornati .55 .55

14th Joy of Europe Children's Festival — A470

**1982, Oct. 2**

**1586** A470 8.80d Traffic .30 .30
**1587** A470 15d In the Bath .45 .45

Small Onofrio's Fountain, 15th Cent. A471

**1982, Oct. 23**

**1588** A471 8.80d multi .25 .25

16th Universal Federation of Travel Agents' Assoc. Cong., Dubrovnik, Oct. 24-30.

600th Anniv. of Hercegnovi A472

**1982, Oct. 28**

**1589** A472 4d multicolored .20 .20

14th Winter Olympic Games, Sarajevo, Feb. 8-19, 1984 — A473

**1982, Nov. 20** *Perf. 12½*

**1590** A473 4d Bridge, Miljacka River .20 .20
**1591** A473 6.10d Minaret, Mosque .20 .20
**1592** A473 8.80d Evangelical Church .30 .30
**1593** A473 15d Street .45 .45
*Nos. 1590-1593 (4)* 1.15 1.15

Nos. 1488a and 1489a Surcharged In Red, Blue, Black or Red Violet with Two Bars or Shield

**1982-83** **Litho.** *Perf. 13x12½*

**1594** A323 30p on 2.50d (R) .20 .20
**1595** A323 50p on 2.50d (Bl) .20 .20
**1596** A323 60p on 2.50d ('83) .20 .20
**1597** A323 1d on 3.50d .20 .20
**1597A** A323 2d on 2.50d (RV) .20 .20
*Nos. 1594-1597A (5)* 1.00 1.00

*Perf. 13*

*1594a* A323 30p on #1488
*1595a* A323 50p on #1488
*1596a* A323 60p on #1488
*1597b* A323 1d on #1489

Types of 1971-77

Designs: 3d, Skofja Loka. 4d, Pocitelj. 5d, Osijek. 6.10d, like 2.10d. 8.80d, Hercegnovi. 10d, Sarajevo. 16.50d, Ohrid.

**1982-83** **Litho.** *Perf. 13x12½*

**1598** A323 3d gray bl .20 .20
**1599** A263 4d red org .20 .20
**1600** A263 5d grnsh bl ('83) .20 .20
**1601** A323 6.10d olive grn .30 .20
**1602** A263 8.80d gray .50 .20

*Perf. 13½*

**1603** A263 10d red lil ('83) .50 .20
**1603A** A323 16.50d dl bl ('83) .80 .25
*Nos. 1598-1603A (7)* 2.70 1.45

Type styles of Nos. 1600, 1603-1603A differ somewhat from illustrations.

*Perf. 13*

*1598a* A323 3d
*1599a* A323 4d
*1600a* A323 5d
*1601a* A323 6.10d
*1602a* A323 8.80d
*1603b* A323 10d
*1603c* A323 16.50d

40th Anniv. of Anti-Fascist Council A474

**1982, Nov. 26** *Perf. 13½*

**1604** A474 4d Bihac, 1942 .20 .20

The Manuscript, by Janez Bernik (b. 1933) — A475

4d, Prophet on Golden Background, by Joze Ciuha (b. 1924). 6.10d, Journey to the West, by Andrej Jemec (b. 1934). 8.80d, Black Comb with Red Band, by Riko Debenjak (b. 1908). 15d, The Vitrine, by Adriana Maraz (b. 1931).

**1982, Nov. 27**

**1605** A475 4d multi, vert. .20 .20
**1606** A475 6.10d multi, vert. .20 .20
**1607** A475 8.80d multi, vert. .25 .20
**1608** A475 10d multi .25 .20
**1609** A475 15d multi .40 .30
*Nos. 1605-1609 (5)* 1.30 1.10

Uros Predic (1857-1953), Painter — A476

Union of Pioneers, 40th Anniv. — A477

**1982, Dec. 7**

**1610** A476 4d multicolored .20 .20

**1982, Dec. 27** *Perf. 12*

**1611** A477 4d multicolored .20 .20

Articles from Museum of Applied Art, Belgrade A478

Designs: 4d, Lead pitcher, Gnjilane, 16th cent. 6.10d, Silver-plated jug, Macedonia, 18th cent. 8.80d, Goblet, 16th cent., Dalmatia. 15d, Mortar, 15th cent., Kotor.

**1983, Feb. 19**

**1612** A478 4d multicolored .20 .20
**1613** A478 6.10d multicolored .20 .20
**1614** A478 8.80d multicolored .20 .20
**1615** A478 15d multicolored .40 .30
*Nos. 1612-1615 (4)* 1.00 .90

Mount Jalovec — A479

Serbian Telephone Service Centenary — A480

**1983, Feb. 26**

**1616** A479 4d blue & lt bl .20 .20

Slovenian Mountaineering Soc., 90th anniv.

**1983, Mar. 15**

**1617** A480 3d Ericsson phone .20 .20

25th Anniv. of Intl. Org. for Maritime Navigation (OMI) — A481

**1983, Mar. 17** *Perf. 13½x14*

**1618** A481 8.80d multi .30 .30

Edible Mushrooms A482

**1983, Mar. 21** *Perf. 14*

**1619** A482 4d Agaricus campestris .20 .20
**1620** A482 6.10d Morchella vulgaris .20 .20
**1621** A482 8.80d Boletus edulis .25 .25
**1622** A482 15d Cantharellus cibarius .35 .35
*Nos. 1619-1622 (4)* 1.00 1.00

Rijeka Railway, 110th Anniv. — A483

Boro and Ramiz Monument, Landovica A484

**1983, Apr. 5**

**1623** A483 4d Steam engine series 401 .20 .20
**1624** A483 23.70d on 8.80d Thyristor locomotive 442 .35 .35

No. 1624 not issued without surcharge.

**1983, Apr. 10**

**1625** A484 4d multi .20 .20

Boro Vukmirovic and Ramiz Sadiku, revolutionary martyrs, 40th death anniv.

Ivo Andric (1892-1975), Poet, 1961 Nobel Prize Winner A485

**1983, May 5** **Photo.** ***Perf. 11½***

**Granite Paper**

**1626** A485 8.80d Medal, Travnik Chronicle text .20 .20
**1627** A485 20d Portrait, Bridge, Drina River .40 .35

Europa.

50th Intl. Agricultural Fair, Novi Sad — A486

**1983, May 13** **Litho.** ***Perf. 14***

**1628** A486 4d Combine harvester .20 .20

40th Anniv. of Battle of Sutjeska A487

**1983, May 14** ***Perf. 12½***

**1629** A487 3d Assault, by Pivo Karamatijevic .20 .20

A488

A489

**1983, May 25** ***Perf. 13½***

**1630** A488 4d Tito, Parliament .20 .20
*a.* Perf. 12½

30th anniv. of election of Pres. Tito.

**1983, May 27**

**1631** A489 4d First mail and passenger car .20 .20
**1632** A489 16.50d Mountain road, Kotor .40 .20

80th anniv. of automobile service in Montenegro.

A490

A491

**1983, June 5** ***Perf. 14***

**1633** A490 23.70d multi .60 .30

UN Conference on Trade and Development, 6th session, Belgrade, June 6-30.

**1983, June 7** ***Perf. 12½***

**1634** A491 4d Engraving by Valvasor .20 .20

Town of Pazin millenium.

Triumphal Arch, Titograd A492

**1983, June 9** ***Perf. 12½***

**1635** A492 100d Memorial to S. Filipovic, Valjevo, vert. 2.25 1.10
*a.* Perf. 13x13½
**1636** A492 200d shown 4.50 2.25
*a.* Perf. 13½x13

Skopje Earthquake, 20th Anniv. — A493

**1983, July 26** **Litho.** ***Perf. 12½***

**1637** A493 23.70d deep magenta .55 .25
*a.* Perf. 13½

For surcharge, see No. 1715.

Sculpture by Ivan Mestrovic A494

Joy of Europe A496

European Nature Protection — A495

**1983, Aug. 15**

**1638** A494 6d multicolored .20 .20

**1983, Sept. 10** **Litho.** ***Perf. 13***

16.50d, Gentian, Kopaonik National Park. 23.70d, Chamois, Perucica Gorge.

**1639** A495 16.50d multi .30 .20
**1640** A495 23.70d multi .55 .25

See Nos. 1685-1686.

**1983, Oct. 3** **Litho.** ***Perf. 13½***

Children's Paintings: 16.50d, Bride and Bridegroom by Verna Paunkonik. 23.70d, Andres and his Mother by Marta Lopez-Ibor.

**1641** A496 16.50d multi .35 .20
**1642** A496 23.70d multi .45 .25

A497

A498

**1983, Oct. 17** **Litho.** ***Perf. 12½***

**1643** A497 5d multicolored .20 .20

Kragujevac High School sesquicentenary.

**1983, Oct. 17** **Litho.** ***Perf. 13½***

**1644** A498 5d multicolored .20 .20

Timok Uprising centenary.

14th Winter Olympic Games, Sarajevo, Feb. 8-19, 1984 A499

**1983, Nov. 25** **Engr.** ***Perf. 13½***

**1645** A499 4d Ski jump .20 .20
**1646** A499 4d Slalom .20 .20
**1647** A499 16.50d Bobsledding .40 .20
**1648** A499 16.50d Downhill skiing .40 .20
**1649** A499 23.70d Speed skating .60 .30
**1650** A499 23.70d Hockey .60 .30
*Nos. 1645-1650 (6)* 2.40 1.40

**Souvenir Sheet**

***Imperf***

**1651** A499 50d Emblem 1.40 .60

Jovan Jovanovic Zmaj (1833-1904), Poet, Neven Masthead A500

**1983, Nov. 24** **Litho.** ***Perf. 12½***

**1652** A500 5d multicolored .20 .20

Peasant Wedding, by Pieter Brueghel A501

Paintings: No. 1654, Susanna with the Old Men, by the 'Master of the Prodigal Son.' No. 1655, Allegory of Wisdom and Strength, by Paolo Veronese (1528-1588). No. 1656, Virgin Mary from Salamanca, by Robert Campin (1375-1444). No. 1657, St. Ann with Madonna and Jesus, by Albrecht Dürer (1471-1528).

**1983, Nov. 26** ***Perf. 14***

**1653** A501 4d multi .20 .20
**1654** A501 16.50d multi .40 .20
**1655** A501 16.50d multi .40 .20
**1656** A501 23.70d multi .50 .25
**1657** A501 23.70d multi .50 .25
*Nos. 1653-1657 (5)* 2.00 1.10

View of Jajce — A502

Koco Racin (1908-1943), Writer — A504

World Communications Year — A503

**1983, Nov. 28** ***Perf. 13x12½***

**1658** A502 5d multicolored .20 .20

**Souvenir Sheet**

***Imperf***

**1659** A502 30d Tito 1.25 .60

40th anniv. of Second Session of the Antifascist Council of the Natl. Liberation of Yugoslavia, Jajce, Nov. 29-30.

**1983, Dec. 10** ***Perf. 13½***

**1660** A503 23.70d multi .50 .25

**1983, Dec. 22**

**1661** A504 5d multicolored .20 .20

Politika Front Page, Oct. 28, 1944 — A505

**1984, Jan. 25** **Litho.** ***Perf. 12½***

**1662** A505 5d red & black .20 .20

80th anniv. of Politika newspaper and 40th anniv. in Yugoslavia.

Veljko Petrovic (1884-1967), Poet — A506

**1984, Feb. 4** **Litho.** ***Perf. 13½***

**1663** A506 5d multicolored .20 .20

1984 Winter Olympics A507

**1984, Feb. 8**

**1664** A507 4d Biathlon .20 .20
**1665** A507 4d Giant slalom .20 .20
**1666** A507 5d Bobsledding .20 .20
**1667** A507 5d Slalom .20 .20
**1668** A507 16.50d Speed skating .40 .20
**1669** A507 16.50d Hockey .40 .20
**1670** A507 23.70d Ski jumping .60 .30
**1671** A507 23.70d Downhill skiing .60 .30
*Nos. 1664-1671 (8)* 2.80 1.80

**Souvenir Sheets**

***Imperf***

**1672** A507 50d Flame, rings 1.40 .70
**1673** A507 100d Flame, map 2.75 1.40

Natl. Heroines A508

Designs: a, Marija Bursac (1902-43). b, Jelena Cetkovic (1916-43). c, Nada Dimic (1923-42). d, Elpida Karamandi (1920-42). e, Toncka Cec Olga (1896-1943). f, Spasenija Babovic Cana (1907-77). g, Jovanka Radivojevic Kica (1922-43). h, Sonja Marinkovic (1916-41).

**1984, Mar. 8** **Litho.** ***Perf. 14***

**1674** Sheet of 8 + label 1.00 .75
*a.-h.* A508 5d any single .20 .20

Slovenia Monetary Institute, 40th Anniv. A509

**1984, Mar. 12** ***Perf. 12½***

**1675** A509 5d Bond, note .20 .20

Railroad Service in Serbia (Belgrade-Nis) Centenary — A510

**1984, Apr. 9** *Perf. 13*

**1676** A510 5d Train, Central Belgrade Station .20 .20

Jure Franko, Giant Slalom Silver Medalist, 1984 — A511

**1984, Apr. 28**

**1677** A511 23.70d multi .60 .35

Yugoslavia's first Winter Olympic medalist.

Europa (1959-84) A512

**1984, Apr. 30** *Perf. 13½*

**1678** A512 23.70d multi .30 .25
**1679** A512 50d multi .80 .50

1984 Summer Olympics, Los Angeles A513

**1984, May 14**

**1680** A513 5d Basketball .20 .20
**1681** A513 16.50d Diving .35 .20
**1682** A513 23.70d Equestrian .45 .20
**1683** A513 50d Running 1.10 .50
*Nos. 1680-1683 (4)* 2.10 1.10

Marshal Tito — A514

**1984, May 25** *Perf. 13*

**1684** A514 5d brown red .20 .20

Nature Type of 1983

Designs: 26d, Centaurea gloriosa (flower), Biokovo Mountain Park. 40d, Anophthalmus (insect), Pekel Cave, Savinja Valley.

**1984, June 11 Litho.** *Perf. 13½*

**1685** A495 26d multicolored .30 .20
**1686** A495 40d multicolored .50 .20

Bird Type of 1982

**1984, June 28**

**1687** A461 4d Great black-backed gull .20 .20
**1688** A461 5d Black-headed gull .20 .20
**1689** A461 16.50d Herring gull .25 .20
**1690** A461 40d Common tern .35 .20
*Nos. 1687-1690 (4)* 1.00 .80

19th Cent. Cradles A515

**1984, Sept. 1 Litho.** *Perf. 12½*

**1691** A515 4d Bosnia & Herzegovina .20 .20
**1692** A515 5d Montenegro .20 .20
**1693** A515 26d Macedonia .25 .20
**1694** A515 40d Serbia .35 .20
*Nos. 1691-1694 (4)* 1.00 .80

Olive Tree, Mirovica A516

**1984, Sept. 1**

**1695** A516 5d multi .20 .20

Joy of Europe — A517

Map, Concentric Waves — A519

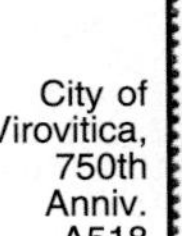
City of Virovitica, 750th Anniv. A518

Children's Drawings.

**1984, Oct. 2 Litho.** *Perf. 14*

**1696** A517 26d Traditional costumes .30 .20
**1697** A517 40d Girl with doll carriage .50 .20

**1984, Oct. 4** *Perf. 13½*

**1698** A518 5d Engraving, 17th cent. .20 .20

**1984, Oct. 10**

**1699** A519 6d Prus bl & brt grn .20 .20

Radio and telegraph service in Montenegro, 80th anniv.

Veterans Conference A520

**1984, Oct. 18**

**1700** A520 26d multicolored .30 .20
**1701** A520 40d multicolored .50 .20

Conf. of Veterans on Security, Disarmament & Cooperation in Europe, Belgrade, 10/18-20.

Liberation of Belgrade, 40th Anniv. — A521

Miloje Milojevic (1884-1946), Composer A522

**1984, Oct. 20**

**1702** A521 6d "40," arms .20 .20

**1984, Oct. 27**

**1703** A522 6d Portrait, score .20 .20

Medals Events, 1984 Summer Olympics A522a

Designs: a, Wrestling. b, Running. c, Field hockey. d, Shot put. e, Soccer. f, Basketball. g, Netball. h, Rowing.

**1984, Nov. 14 Litho.** *Perf. 13½*

**1704** Sheet of 8 2.75 2.50
*a.-h.* A522a 26d any single .30 .25

The Tahitians, by Gauguin — A523

Paintings by Foreign Artists in Yugoslav Museums: 6d, Portrait of Madame Tatichek, by Ferdinand Waldmuller (1793-1865). No. 1706, The Bathers, by Renoir (1841-1919). No. 1707, At the Window, by Henri Matisse (1869-1954). 40d, Ballerinas, by Edgar Degas (1834-1917).

*Perf. 13½x14, 14x13½*

**1984, Nov. 15**

**1705** A523 6d multi, vert. .20 .20
**1706** A523 26d multi, vert. .35 .30
**1707** A523 26d multi, vert. .35 .20
**1708** A523 38d multi .50 .30
**1709** A523 40d multi .60 .30
*Nos. 1705-1709 (5)* 2.00 1.30

Nova Macedonia Newspaper, 40th Anniv. A523a

**1984, Nov. 29** *Perf. 13½*

**1710** A523a 6d 1st & recent editions .20 .20

Nos. 1602, 1599 and 1637 Surcharged with Three Bars in Red Brown or Black, Types of 1975 and

Exhibition Center, Zagreb A524

Bird, Jet, Landscape A525

Designs: 6d, Kikinda. 26d, Korcula. 38d, Maribor. 70d, Trumpeter monument, riverside buildings in Zagreb. 1000d, bird, tail of jet on airfield.

*Perf. 13½x12½, 13 (#1713, 1717), 12½ (#1715)*

**1984-86 Litho.**

**1711** A263 2d on 8.80d .20 .20
*a.* on #1602a
**1712** A263 6d on 4d (RBr) .20 .20
*a.* on #1599a
**1713** A323 6d lt red brn .20 .20
*a.* Perf. 13x12½
**1715** A493 20d on 23.70d .20 .20
**1717** A263 26d dp ultra .25 .20
*a.* Perf. 13x12½
**1718** A323 38d dp lil rose .30 .20
*a.* Perf. 13
**1719** A323 70d brt ultra ('85) .30 .25
*b.* Perf. 13

*Perf. 14*

**1719A** A524 100d brt org yel & vio .50 .30

*Perf. 12½*

**1720** A525 500d redsh brn & multi ('85) 2.50 1.75
**1721** A525 1000d org brn & multi ('85) 5.00 3.50
*a.* Perf. 13½
*Nos. 1711-1721 (10)* 9.65 7.00

Type styles for Nos. 1717-1718 differ somewhat from illustration.

For surcharge, see No. 1973.

Museum Exhibits - Fossils A526

**1985, Feb. 4 Litho.** *Perf. 12½*

**1722** A526 5d Aturia aturi .20 .20
**1723** A526 6d Pachyophis woodwardi .20 .20
**1724** A526 33d Chaetodon hoeferi .20 .20
**1725** A526 60d Homo sapiens neanderthalensis .40 .20
*Nos. 1722-1725 (4)* 1.00 .80

40th Anniv., Monument Protection A527

**1985, Feb. 20 Litho.** *Perf. 12½*

**1726** A527 6d Hopovo church .20 .20

Ski Jumping at Planica, 50th Anniv. A528

European Nature Conservation A529

**1985, Mar. 15 Litho.** *Perf. 13½*

**1727** A528 6d Three herons in flight .20 .20

**1985, Mar. 30** *Perf. 14*

**1728** A529 42d Pandion haliaetus .35 .20
**1729** A529 60d Upupa epops .50 .20

Audubon birth bicentenary, European Information Center for Nature Protection.

A530

A531

Fresco of St. Methodius, St. Naum Monastery, Ohrid.

**1985, Apr. 6 Litho. *Perf. 11½x12***
**1730** A530 10d multicolored .20 .20

St. Methodius (d. 885), archbishop of Pannonia and Moravia.

**1985, Apr. 16 Litho. *Perf. 12½***
**1731** A531 6d Clasped hands .20 .20

Osimo Agreements, 10th anniv. Yugoslavia-Italy political and economic cooperation.

Josip Slavenski (1896-1955), Composer A532

Europa: 60d, Portrait, block flute, darabukka. 80d, Balkanophonia score, signature.

**1985, Apr. 29 *Perf. 14***
**1732** A532 60d multi .70 .70
**1733** A532 80d multi .70 .70

Joachim Vujic, by Dimitrije Avramovic (1815-1855) A533

**1985, May 8 *Perf. 12x11½***
**1734** A533 10d multi .20 .20

Joachim Vujic Theater, Kragujevac, 150th anniv.

Liberation from German Occupation Forces, 40th Anniv. — A534

**1985, May 9 *Perf. 13½***
**1735** A534 10d shown .20 .20
**1736** A534 10d Order of Natl. Liberation .20 .20

Franjo Kluz (1912-1944), Rudi Cajavec (1911-1942), Breguet-19 Fighter — A535

**1985, May 21 *Perf. 13x12½***
**1737** A535 10d multi .20 .20

Air Force Day.

Pres. Tito (1892-1980) A536

Cres-Losinj Municipal Tourism Bureau, Cent. — A537

**1985, May 25 *Perf. 13½***
**1738** A536 10d Portrait .20 .20

**1985, June 12**
**1739** A537 10d Map, town arms, villa .20 .20

UN 40th Anniv. — A538

Rowing — A539

**1985, June 26 Litho. *Perf. 12½***
**1740** A538 70d Emblem, rainbow .55 .25

**1985, June 29 Litho. *Perf. 13½***
**1741** A539 70d multicolored .55 .25

**Souvenir Sheet**

**1742** A539 100d Course map, arms .75 .35

Intl. European-Danube Rowing Regatta, 30th anniv.

Nautical Tourism — A540

**1985, July 1 Litho.**
**1743** A540 8d Sailboat .20 .20
**1744** A540 10d Windsurfing .20 .20
**1745** A540 50d Sailboat, diff. .35 .20
**1746** A540 70d Sailboat, diff. .45 .25
*Nos. 1743-1746 (4)* 1.20 .85



F1B Class Motorized Model Plane A541

**1985, Aug. 10 Litho. *Perf. 12½x13***
**1747** A541 70d multicolored .45 .35

Free Flight World Championships, Livno, Aug. 12-18.

Algae — A542

**1985, Sept. 20 *Perf. 14***
**1748** A542 8d Corallina officinalis .20 .20
**1749** A542 10d Desmarestia viridis .20 .20
**1750** A542 50d Fucus vesiculosus .30 .20
**1751** A542 70d Padina pavonia .40 .30
*Nos. 1748-1751 (4)* 1.10 .90

Intl. Federation of Stomatologists, 73rd Congress, Belgrade, Sept. 21-28 — A543

**1985, Sept. 21 *Perf. 12x11½***
**1752** A543 70d multicolored .45 .30

Children's Drawings A544

Designs: 50d, Children in a Horse-drawn Cart, by Branka Lukic, age 14, Yugoslavia. 70d, Children in Field, by Suzanne Straathof, age 9, Netherlands.

**1985, Oct. 2 *Perf. 14***
**1753** A544 50d multicolored .30 .20
**1754** A544 70d multicolored .40 .30

Croatian Natl. Theater, Zagreb, 125th Anniv. A545

**1985, Nov. 23 *Perf. 12½***
**1755** A545 10d Facade detail .20 .20

Miladin Popovic A546

Natl. Coat of Arms A547

**1985, Nov. 26 *Perf. 11½x12***
**1756** A546 10d Portrait .20 .20

Popovic (1910-1945), revolutionary.

**1985, Nov. 28 *Perf. 13½***
**1757** A547 10d multicolored .20 .20

**Souvenir Sheet**

***Imperf***

**1758** A547 100d multicolored .65 .45

Socialist Federal Republic of Yugoslavia, 40th anniv. No. 1758 contains one stamp 18x27mm.

Royal Procession, by Iromie Wijewardena, Sri Lanka — A548

Paintings from the Art Gallery of Non-aligned Countries, Titograd: 10d, Return from Hunting, by Mama Cangare, Mali. No. 1761, Drum of Coca, by Agnes Ovando Sanz De Franck, Bolivia. No. 1762, The Cock, by Mariano Rodriguez, Cuba. 70d, Three Women, by Quamrul Hassan, Bangladesh.

**1985, Dec. 2 *Perf. 14***
**1759** A548 8d multicolored .20 .20
**1760** A548 10d multicolored .20 .20
**1761** A548 50d multicolored .30 .20
**1762** A548 50d multicolored .30 .20
**1763** A548 70d multicolored .40 .30
*Nos. 1759-1763 (5)* 1.40 1.10

Nos. 1243, 1482, 1485a, 1490, 1491, 1713a, 1717a, 1603A and 1718 Surcharged in Light Red Brown, Brown or Dark Brown

**1985-86 Litho. *Perf. 13½, 13½x12½***
**1764** A323 1d on 25p (B) .20 .20
**1765** A263 2d on 5p (DB) .20 .20
*a.* on #1482a
**1766** A263 3d on 35p (DB) .20 .20
*a.* on #1485a
**1767** A323 4d on 5.60d (B) .20 .20
*b.* on #1490
**1767A** A323 5d on 8d (B) .20 .20
*c.* on #1491a
**1768** A323 8d on 6d .20 .20
*a.* on #1713
**1769** A263 20d on 26d .20 .20
*a.* on #1717
**1770** A323 50d on 16.50d (B) .40 .30
*a.* on #1603c
**1771** A323 70d on 38d .55 .40
*Nos. 1764-1771 (9)* 2.35 2.10

Issued: #1767A, 3/17/86; others, 12/85.

Natl. Automobile Assoc., 40th Anniv. A549

**1986, Feb. 25 *Perf. 12½***
**1772** A549 10d Car .20 .20
**1773** A549 70d Helicopter .40 .30

Tara River, Montenegro A550

**1986, Mar. 3 *Perf. 14***
**1774** A550 100d Canyon .55 .40
**1775** A550 150d Bridge .95 .60

European nature protection. Sheets of 9.

Studenica Monastery, 800th Anniv. — A551

**1986, Mar. 15 *Perf. 13½***
**1776** A551 10d Chapel of Our Lady .20 .20

A552

Various soccer plays.

**1986, Apr. 5 Litho. *Perf. 14***

**1777** A552 70d multi .35 .25
**1778** A552 150d multi .75 .55

1986 World Cup Soccer Championships, Mexico.

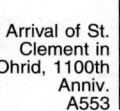

Arrival of St. Clement in Ohrid, 1100th Anniv. A553

**1986, Apr. 12 *Perf. 12½***

**1779** A553 10d Township model .20 .20

**Europa Issue**

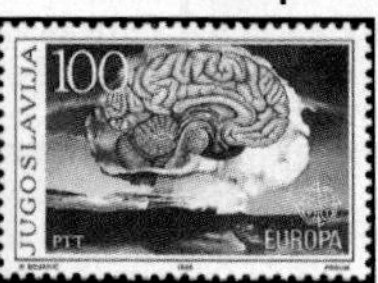


Brain, Mushroom Cloud — A554

**1986, Apr. 28 *Perf. 14***

**1780** A554 100d shown .50 .35
**1781** A554 200d Injured deer .90 .70

European Men's Senior Judo Championships, Belgrade, May 8-11 — A555

**1986, May 7 *Perf. 12½***

**1782** A555 70d multi .35 .25

Natl. Costumes A556

Yachts, Moscenika Draga Bay A557

a, Slovenia. b, Vojvodina. c, Croatia. d, Macedonia. e, Serbia. f, Montenegro. g, Kosovo. h, Bosnia & Herzegovina.

**1986, May 22 Litho. *Perf. 12x13***

**Booklet Stamps**

**1783** Bklt. pane of 8 2.25
***a.-h.*** A556 50d any single .25 .20

**1986, May 23 *Perf. 14***

**1784** A557 50d multi .25 .20
**1785** A557 80d multi, diff. .40 .20

**Souvenir Sheet**

***Imperf***

**1786** A557 100d multi .55 .50

European Sailing Championships, Croatia, May 29-June 7, Flying Dutchman Class. No. 1786 contains one stamp 22x28mm.

Marshal Tito — A557a

**1986, May 24 *Perf. 13x12½***

**1787** A557a 10d multicolored .20 .20

Moths and Butterflies A558

**1986, May 26 *Perf. 14***

**1788** A558 10d Eudia pavonia .20 .20
**1789** A558 20d Inachis io .20 .20
**1790** A558 50d Parnassius apollo .20 .20
**1791** A558 100d Apatura iris .50 .20
*Nos. 1788-1791 (4)* 1.10 .80

Ancient Manuscripts A558a

Designs: 10d, Evangelical, 18th cent. 20d, Leontijevo Evangelical, 16th cent. 50d, Astrological, Mesopotamia, 15th cent. 100d, Hebrew Haggadah, Spain, 14th cent.

**1986, June 12 Litho. *Perf. 14***

**1792** A558a 10d multicolored .20 .20
**1793** A558a 20d multicolored .20 .20
**1794** A558a 50d multicolored .30 .20
**1795** A558a 100d multicolored .60 .30
*Nos. 1792-1795 (4)* 1.30 .90

A559

A560

Designs: 20d, Postman on motorcycle. 30d, Postman, resident. 40d, Forklift, mail pallets. 50d, Mail train. 60d, Man posting letters in mailbox. 93d, Open envelope and greetings telegram form. 100d, Postman, mail van. No. 1803, Computer operator facing right. No. 1804, 140d, Computer operator facing left. 120d, Woman sending love letter. 200d, Freighter in high seas. 500d, Postal employee sorting mail. 1000d, Woman at telephone station. 2000d, Aircraft, hemispheres on world map. 30d, 60d, 93d, 106d, 120d, 140d, 500d, 1000d vert.

***Perf. 13½, 12½x13½ (20d, 40d, 50d), 14 (100d)***

**1986-88 Litho.**

**1796** A559 20d brt pink .20 .20
*a.* Perf. 13
**1797** A559 30d lt brn vio .20 .20
*a.* Perf. 13x12½
**1798** A559 40d brt red .25 .20
*a.* Perf. 13
**1799** A559 50d violet .30 .20
*a.* Perf. 13
**1800** A559 60d lt sage grn .25 .20
**1801** A559 93d ultra .25 .20
**1802** A559 100d dl magenta .65 .30
**1803** A559 106d rose red .30 .20
**1804** A559 106d brn org .20 .20
**1805** A559 120d dull blue grn .20 .20
**1806** A559 140d dull rose .20 .20
**1807** A559 200d greenish bl 1.25 .60
*a.* Perf. 12½
*b.* Perf. 12½x13½
**1808** A559 500d deep blue & beige .75 .35
**1809** A559 500d chalky blue & yel .60 .25
**1810** A559 1000d vio & blue grn 1.10 .60
*b.* Perf. 12½
**1810A** A560 2000d brt blue, red & brt vio 2.25 1.10
*Nos. 1796-1810A (16)* 8.95 5.20

Size of No. 1802: 19½x18mm.

Issued: 20d, 3/17; 50d, 200d, 6/4; 40d, 7/17; 100d, 6/12; 30d, 7/26; 60d, 6/5/87; #1803, 12/10/87; 93d, 12/16/87; #1804, 1/22/88; #1808, 4/29/88; 1000d, 7/21/88; 20d, 140d, 2000d, #1809, 9/5/88.

See Nos. 1935-1945, 2004-2007, 2013-2015, 2021. For surcharges see Nos. 1877, 1912-1913, 1947-1948, 1972, 1974-1975, 2017, 2019, 2048-2051, 2053.

13th Communist Federations Congress (SKJ) A561

**1986, June 25 *Perf. 12½***

**1811** A561 10d shown .20 .20
**1812** A561 20d Star .20 .20

**Souvenir Sheet**

***Imperf***

**1813** A561 100d Tito .50 .25

Trubar, Abecedarian Manuscript Title Page A562

**1986, June 28 Litho. *Perf. 12½x13***

**1814** A562 20d multi .20 .20

Primoz Trubar (1508-1568), Slovenian philologist and religious reformer.

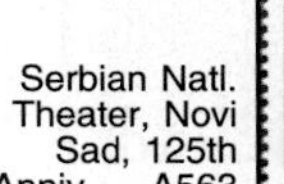

Serbian Natl. Theater, Novi Sad, 125th Anniv. — A563

**1986, July 28 *Perf. 14***

**1815** A563 40d Thalia .20 .20

Rugovo Dance, Kosovo Province — A564

1987 Universiade Games, Zagreb, July 8-19 — A565

**1986, Sept. 10**

**1816** A564 40d multi .20 .20

**1986, Sept. 22 *Perf. 13½***

**1817** A565 30d Volleyball .20 .20
**1818** A565 40d Canoeing .20 .20
**1819** A565 100d Gymnastics .45 .20
**1820** A565 150d Fencing .65 .30
*Nos. 1817-1820 (4)* 1.50 .90

18th Joy of Europe Youth Conference A566

Children's drawings: 100d, Dove, by Tanja Faletic, 14. 150d, Buildings, by Johanna Kraus, 12, DDR.

**1986, Oct. 2 *Perf. 14***

**1821** A566 100d multicolored .45 .20
**1822** A566 150d multicolored .70 .30

Rotary Switching Apparatus, Village of Bled — A567

**1986, Oct. 4 *Perf. 13½***

**1823** A567 40d multicolored .20 .20

Telephone exchanges connected with automatic switching equipment, 50th anniv.

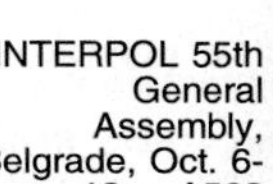

INTERPOL 55th General Assembly, Belgrade, Oct. 6-13 — A568

Intl. Brigades, 50th Anniv. — A569

**1986, Oct. 6 *Perf. 14***

**1824** A568 150d multicolored .65 .30

**1986, Oct. 21 *Perf. 13½***

**1825** A569 40d multicolored .20 .20

Intl. Peace Year — A570

**1986, Nov. 20**

**1826** A570 150d multicolored .65 .30

Serbian Academy of the Arts and Sciences, Cent. A571

**1986, Nov. 1 Photo. *Perf. 13½***

**1827** A571 40d multicolored .20 .20

Paintings by Foreign Artists in the Museum of Contemporary Art, Skopje — A572

No. 1828, Still Life, by Frantisek Muzika, Czechoslovakia. #1829, Disturance, by Rafael Canogar, England. #1830, Iol, by Victor Vasarely, France. #1831, Portrait, by Bernard Buffet, France. #1832, Woman's Head, by Pablo Picasso, Spain.

**1986, Dec. 10 Litho. *Perf. 14***

**1828** A572 30d multi .20 .20
**1829** A572 40d multi .20 .20
**1830** A572 100d multi, vert. .55 .25
**1831** A572 100d multi, vert. .55 .25
**1832** A572 150d multi, vert. .75 .40
*Nos. 1828-1832 (5)* 2.25 1.30

Wildlife Conservation A573

30d, Lutra lutra. 40d, Ovis musimon. 100d, Cervus elaphus. 150d, Ursus arctos.

**1987, Jan. 22 Litho. *Perf. 13½x14***

**1833** Strip of 4 + label 1.10 .65
*a.* A573 30d multi .20 .20
*b.* A573 40d multi .20 .20
*c.* A573 100d multi .30 .20
*d.* A573 150d multi .50 .30

Label pictures nature reserve.

Rudjer Boscovich (1711-1787), Scientist, and Solar Eclipse over Brera Observatory, Italy — A574

**1987, Feb. 13 *Perf. 14***

**1834** A574 150d multicolored .65 .30

European Nature Protection — A575

1987 World Alpine Skiing Championships, Crans Montana — A576

**1987, Mar. 9**

**1835** A575 150d shown .60 .30
**1836** A575 400d Triglav glacial lake 1.40 .75

**1987, Mar. 20 Litho. *Perf. 14***

**1837** A576 200d multicolored .75 .40

No. 1837 printed in sheets of 8 plus center label.

Natl. Civil Aviation, 60th Anniv. A577

**1987, Mar. 20 *Perf. 14***

**1838** A577 150d POTEZ-29 .60 .30
**1839** A577 400d DC-10 1.60 .80

Each printed in sheets of 8 plus center label.

Kole Nedelkovski (1912-1941), Poet, Revolutionary A578

**1987, Apr. 2 *Perf. 13½***

**1840** A578 40d multicolored .20 .20

Liberation of Montenegro from Turkey, 125th Anniv. A579

**1987, Apr. 16 *Perf. 13½***

**1841** A579 40d Battle flags, folk guitar .20 .20

Slovenian Communist Party, Cebine, 50th Anniv. — A580

**1987, Apr. 18 *Perf. 14***

**1842** A580 40d multicolored .20 .20

**Europa Issue**

Tito Bridge, Krk — A581

**1987, Apr. 30 Litho. *Perf. 14***

**1843** A581 200d shown .70 .45
**1844** A581 400d Bridges over canal 1.00 .75

Fruit Trees — A582

Tito, 1930, by Mosa Pijade — A583

**1987, May 15 Litho. *Perf. 14***

**1845** A582 60d Almond .20 .20
**1846** A582 150d Pear .30 .20
**1847** A582 200d Apple .50 .25
**1848** A582 400d Plum 1.00 .50
*Nos. 1845-1848 (4)* 2.00 1.15

**1987, May 25**

**1849** A583 60d multi .20 .20

50th anniv. of Tito's assumption of Yugoslavian communist party leadership.

Vuk Stefanovik Karadzic (1787-1864), Linguist and Historian — A584

60d, Bust by Petar Ubavkic, his Trsic residence & Vienna. 200d, Portrait by Uros Knezevic, & alphabet from Karadzic's Serbian Dictionary, 1818.

**1987, June 10**

**1850** A584 60d multi .20 .20
**1851** A584 200d multi .50 .25

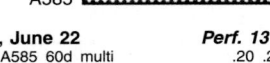

Zrenjanin Postal Service, 250th Anniv. A585

**1987, June 22 *Perf. 13½***

**1852** A585 60d multi .20 .20

UNIVERSIADE '87, Zagreb, July 8-19 — A586

**1987, July 8 Litho. *Perf. 13½***

**1853** A586 60d Hurdling .20 .20
**1854** A586 150d Basketball .30 .20
**1855** A586 200d Balance beam .40 .25
**1856** A586 400d Swimming .90 .45
*Nos. 1853-1856 (4)* 1.80 1.10

Each printed in sheets of eight plus label.

Fire Fighting A587

Monument, Anindol Park, Samobor — A588

**1987, July 20 *Perf. 14***

**1857** A587 60d Canadair CL-215 spraying forest .20 .20
**1858** A587 200d Fire boat .45 .25

Each printed in sheets of eight plus label.

**1987, Aug. 1 *Perf. 13½***

**1859** A588 60d multi .20 .20

Communist Party of Croatia, 50th anniv.

Sabac High School, 150th Anniv. A589

**1987, Sept. 10 Litho. *Perf. 13½***

**1860** A589 80d multi .20 .20

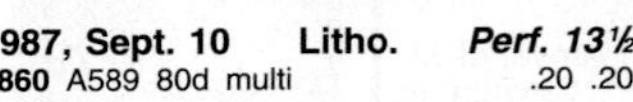

Exhibition Emblem, Balkan Peninsula, Flowers A590

Clock Tower, Petrovaradin Fortress and Novi Sad — A591

**1987, Sept. 19 *Perf. 14***

**1861** A590 250d multi .50 .25

**Souvenir Sheet**

***Imperf***

**1862** A591 400d multi .90 .80

BALKANFILA XI, Novi Sad, Sept. 19-26.

19th Joy of Europe Conference A592

Bridges A593

Children's drawings: 250d, Girls in forest, by Bedic Aranka, Juguoslavia. 400d, Scarecrow, by Schaffer Ingeborg, Austria.

**1987, Oct. 2 Litho. *Perf. 14***

**1863** A592 250d multi .65 .30
**1864** A592 400d multi 1.00 .50

Printed in sheets of nine.

**1987, Oct. 15**

**1865** A593 80d Arslanagica, Trebinje, 16th cent. .20 .20
**1866** A593 250d Terzija, Djakovica, 15th cent. .70 .35

Ship, Dunav-Tisa Channel A594

**1987, Oct. 20** ***Perf. 13½***

**1867** A594 80d multi .20 .20

City of Titov Vrbas, 600th anniv.

Astronomical and Meteorological Observatory, Belgrade, Cent. — A595

**1987, Nov. 21** ***Perf. 14***

**1868** A595 80d multi .20 .20

St. Luke the Evangelist, by Raphael A596

Paintings by foreign artists in national museums: 200d, Infanta Maria Theresa, by Velazquez. 250d, Nicholas Rubens, Painter's Son, by Rubens. 400d, Louis Laure Sennegon, Painter's Niece, by Jean-Baptiste-Camille Corot (1796-1875).

**1987, Nov. 28**

**1869** A596 80d shown .20 .20
**1870** A596 200d multi .45 .25
**1871** A596 250d multi .55 .35
**1872** A596 400d multi .90 .55
*Nos. 1869-1872 (4)* 2.10 1.35

Traditional Competitions A597

80d, Bull fighting. 200d, Ljubicevo Horse Games. 250d, Moresca game. 400d, Sinj iron ring.

**1987, Dec. 10**

**1873** A597 80d multi .20 .20
**1874** A597 200d multi .40 .20
**1875** A597 250d multi .55 .25
**1876** A597 400d multi .85 .45
*Nos. 1873-1876 (4)* 2.00 1.10

No. 1800 Surcharged

**1987, Sept. 22** ***Perf. 13½***

**1877** A559 80d on 60d sg grn .20 .20

Vinodol Codex, City of Vinodolski, Coat of Arms — A598

**1988, Jan. 6** **Litho.** ***Perf. 14***

**1878** A598 100d multi .25 .20

Vinodol Codex, 700th anniv.

Intl. Women's Golden Fox Skiing Championships, 25th Anniv. — A599

**1988, Jan. 30**

**1879** A599 350d Slalom, emblem, Mirobor City .85 .40

Printed in sheets of eight plus center label.

World Wildlife Fund — A600

Brown bears (Ursus arctos).

**1988, Feb. 1**

**1880** A600 70d Cub 1.75 1.00
**1881** A600 80d Cubs 1.75 1.00
**1882** A600 200d Adult, head 2.00 1.25
**1883** A600 350d Adult 4.25 1.50
*Nos. 1880-1883 (4)* 9.75 4.75

1988 Winter Olympics, Calgary — A601

**1988, Feb. 13** ***Perf. 14x13½***

**1884** A601 350d Slalom .85 .40
**1885** A601 1200d Ice hockey 3.00 1.50

Each printed in sheets of 8 plus center label.

Souvenir Sheet

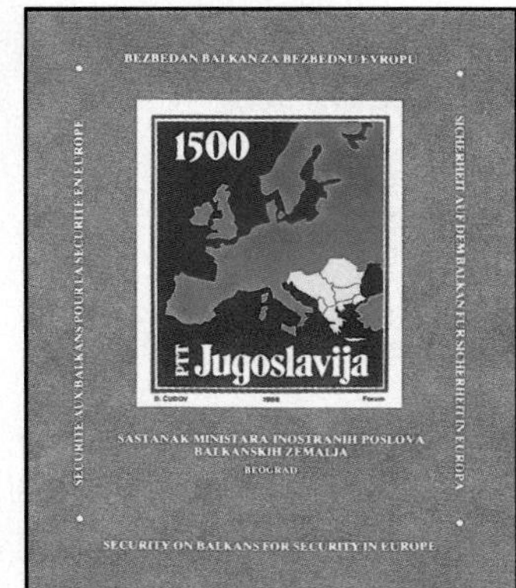


Map of Europe Highlighting Balkan Nations — A602

**1988, Feb. 24** **Litho.** ***Imperf.***

**1886** A602 1500d multi 3.00 3.00

Congress of Foreign Affairs Ministers from the Balkan Countries, Belgrade, Feb. 24-26.

1988 Summer Olympics, Seoul — A603

South Korean Landscape — A604

**1988, Mar. 21** ***Perf. 14x13½***

**1887** A603 106d Basketball .20 .20
**1888** A603 450d High jump .90 .45
**1889** A603 500d Pommel horse 1.00 .50
**1890** A603 1200d Boxing 2.40 1.25
*Nos. 1887-1890 (4)* 4.50 2.40

**Souvenir Sheet**

***Imperf***

**1891** A604 1500d multi 2.75 2.75

Nos. 1887-1890 printed in sheets of 8 plus center label.

**Europa Issue**

Telecommunications — A605

**1988, Apr. 30** **Litho.** ***Perf. 13½x14***

**1892** A605 450d shown .45 .30
**1893** A605 1200d Transportation 1.25 .80

Sea Shells — A606

**1988, May 14**

**1894** A606 106d Gibbula magus .20 .20
**1895** A606 550d Pecten jacobaeus .75 .35
**1896** A606 600d Tonna galea .80 .40
**1897** A606 1000d Argonauta argo 1.25 .65
*Nos. 1894-1897 (4)* 3.00 1.60

Trial of Tito and Five Comrades, 60th Anniv. — A607

**1988, May 25**

**1898** A607 106d black & brn .20 .20

Palace of Princess Ljubica of Serbia, 1st University Building A608

**1988, June 14** **Litho.** ***Perf. 13½***

**1899** A608 106d multi .20 .20

Belgrade University, 150th anniv.

Flowers — A609

Esperanto, Cent. — A610

**1988, July 2** ***Perf. 14***

**1900** A609 600d Phelypaea boissieri .60 .30
**1901** A609 1000d Campanula formanekiana 1.00 .50

Council of Europe.

**1988, July 14** ***Perf. 13½***

**1902** A610 600d dull vio & ol grn .60 .30

Printed in sheets of 8 plus center label.

Cargo Ships — A611

Map of the Danube Basin — A612

**1988, Aug. 18** **Litho.** ***Perf. 14***

**1903** A611 1000d multi .80 .40

**Souvenir Sheet**

***Imperf***

**1904** A612 2000d multi 1.50 1.50

Danube Conference, 40th anniv.

13th European Junior Basketball Championships, Aug. 21-28 — A613

**1988, Aug. 20** ***Perf. 14***

**1905** A613 600d multi .50 .25

1st Horse Race in Belgrade, 125th Anniv. — A614

**1988, Aug. 27**

**1906** A614 140d Thoroughbred racing .20 .20
**1907** A614 600d Steeplechase .40 .20
**1908** A614 1000d Harness racing .70 .35
*Nos. 1906-1908 (3)* 1.30 .75

Museum of Bosnia and Herzegovina, Sarajevo, Cent. A615

**1988, Sept. 10** ***Perf. 13½***

**1909** A615 140d Museum, Bosnian bellflower .20 .20

Anti-Cancer and AIDS Campaigns A616

**1988, Sept. 24** ***Perf. 14***

**1910** A616 140d Arm, lobster claw .20 .20
**1911** A616 1000d Blood, scream .80 .40

Nos. 1801 and 1804 Surcharged

**1988, July Litho.** ***Perf. 13½***

**1912** A559 120d on 93d ultra .20 .20
**1913** A559 140d on 106d brn org .20 .20

Joy of Europe Youth Conference A617

Portraits of girls by: 1000d, P. Ranosovic. 1100d, Renoir.

**1988, Oct. 1 Litho.** ***Perf. 14***

**1914** A617 1000d multi .80 .40
**1915** A617 1100d multi .85 .45

See Nos. 1987-1988.

Slovenski Academy, 50th Anniv. — A618

**1988, Oct. 13 Litho.** ***Perf. 14***

**1916** A618 200d multi .20 .20

Museum Exhibits and Places of Origin A618a

200d, Wood bassinet, traditional wedding (Galicka). #1918, Embroidery, man and woman wearing folk costumes of Vojvodina. #1919, Scimitar, flintlock, man & woman wearing folk costumes of Kotor (Bokelji). 1100d, Masks (Kurenti).

**1988, Oct. 18**

**1917** A618a 200d multi, vert. .20 .20
**1918** A618a 1000d shown .65 .35
**1919** A618a 1000d multi, vert. .65 .35
**1920** A618a 1100d multi .75 .40
*Nos. 1917-1920 (4)* 2.25 1.30

Woman with Lyre, 4th Cent. B.C. — A618b

Grecian terra cotta figurines: #1922, Eros & Psyche, 2nd cent. BC. #1923, Seated woman, 3rd cent. BC. 1100d, Woman by Stele, 3rd cent. BC.

**1988, Oct. 28**

**1921** A618b 200d multi .20 .20
**1922** A618b 1000d multi .45 .20
**1923** A618b 1000d multi .45 .20
**1924** A618b 1100d multi .50 .25
*Nos. 1921-1924 (4)* 1.60 .85

Peter II (1813-1851), Prince Bishop and Poet — A618c

Portraits and: 200d, Cetinje Monastery and frontispiece of his principal work. 1000d, Njegos Mausoleum.

**1988, Nov. 1**

**1925** A618c 200d multi .20 .20
**1926** A618c 1000d multi .80 .40

Postal Service Types of 1986 and

Telephone Receiver and Telephone Card — A619

Bird, Posthorn, Simulated Stamp — A620

Propeller Plane, Two Arrows and Map — A621

Designs: 170d, 300d, Flower, envelope, mailbox and simulated stamp. 220d, PTT emblem on simulated stamp, mail coach. 800d, Postman on motorcycle. No. 1941, Postman, resident. No. 1942, Mail train. No. 1943, Envelopes, satellite dish. No. 1944, Earth, telecommunications satellite. 100,000d, Bird, open envelope, flower. 170d, 220d, 300d, 2000d, 5000d, No. 1941 vert.

**1988-89 Litho.** ***Perf. 13¼***

**1935** A559 170d dl grn .20 .20
**1936** A559 220d brn org .20 .20
**1937** A559 300d ver .20 .20
**1938** A559 800d brt ultra .20 .20
**1939** A619 2000d multi .20 .20
**1940** A620 5000d dk red & ultra 1.00 .50
**1941** A559 10,000d org & brt lil .35 .20
**1942** A559 20,000d lt ol grn & lt red brn .35 .35

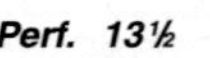

***Perf. 13½***

**1943** A560 10,000d multi 2.00 1.40
**1944** A560 20,000d multi 1.50 1.00
**1944A** A621 50,000d org & dl bl 1.60 .75
**1945** A560 100,000d org & dl grn 1.60 1.00
*Nos. 1935-1945 (12)* 9.40 6.20

***Perf. 12½***

*1937a* A559 300d .20 .20
*1938a* A559 800d .20 .20
*1939a* A619 2000d .20 .20
*1940a* A620 5000d 1.00 .50
*1941a* A559 10,000d
*Nos. 1937a-1941a (4)* 1.60 1.10

Issued: 1988 - 170d, 11/17; 220d, 12/6; 1989 — 300d, 5/11; 800d, 2000d, 7/20; 5000d, 1/20; #1941, 11/28; #1942, 12/8; #1943, 3/20; #1944, 7/19; 50,000d, 11/8; 100,000d, 12/4.

See Nos. 2008-2009, 2017, 2052. For surcharges see Nos. 1972, 1974, 2048.

Yugoslavia, 70th Anniv. — A622

**1988, Dec. 1 Litho.** ***Perf. 14***

**1946** A622 200d Krsmanovic Hall, Belgrade .20 .20

Nos. 1805-1806 Surcharged

**1988 Litho.** ***Perf. 13½***

**1947** A559 170d on 120d .20 .20
**1948** A559 220d on 140d .20 .20

Issued: #1947, Dec. 21; #1948, Dec. 15.

Miniature Sheet

Victory of Yugoslavian Athletes at the 1988 Summer Olympics, Seoul — A623

Medals and events: a, Women's air pistol. b, Team handball. c, Table tennis. d, Wrestling. e, Double sculls. f, Basketball. g, Water polo. h, Boxing.

**1988, Dec. 31 Litho.** ***Perf. 14***

**1949** Sheet of 8 + label 1.75 1.40
***a.-h.*** A623 500d any single .20 .20

Ivan Gundulic (1589-1638), Poet — A624

**1989, Jan. 7** ***Perf. 13½***

**1950** A624 220d multi .20 .20

World Wildlife Fund — A625

Ducks.

**1989, Feb. 23 Litho.** ***Perf. 14***

**1951** Strip of 4 + label 14.00 8.00
***a.*** A625 300d Anas platyrhynchos 1.25 .50
***b.*** A625 2100d Anas crecca 3.50 1.75
***c.*** A625 2200d Anas acuta 3.50 1.75
***d.*** A625 2200d Anas clypeata 3.50 1.75

Printed in sheets of 20+5 labels. Label pictures WWF emblem.

Publication of The Glory of the Duchy of Kranjska, by Johann Valvasor (1641-1693), 300th Anniv. A626

**1989, Mar. 10** ***Perf. 13½***

**1952** A626 300d Portrait .20 .20

Flowering Plants — A627

**1989, Mar. 20** ***Perf. 14***

**1953** A627 300d Bulbocodium vernum .20 .20
**1954** A627 2100d Nymphaea alba .95 .45
**1955** A627 2200d Fritillaria degeniana, vert. 1.00 .50
**1956** A627 3000d Orchis simia, vert. 1.40 .70
*Nos. 1953-1956 (4)* 3.55 1.85

6th World Air-Gun Championships, Sarajevo, Apr. 27-30 — A628

**1989, Apr. 26**

**1957** A628 3000d multi 1.50 .75

Europa 1989 — A629

**1989, Apr. 29**

**1958** A629 3000d shown .75 .60
**1959** A629 6000d Marbles 1.75 1.25

15th European Trophy for Natl. Athletic Club Champions, Belgrade, June 3-4 — A630

**1989, June 1 Litho.** ***Perf. 13½***

**1960** A630 4000d Pole vault .50 .25

Printed in sheets of 8+label picturing flags of participating nations.

Yugoslavia Motorcycle Grand Prix, Rijeka, June 9-11 — A631

Various race scenes.

**1989, June 9** ***Perf. 14***

**1961** A631 500d multi .20 .20
**1962** A631 4000d multi .60 .30

**Souvenir Sheet**

***Perf. 14x13½***

**1963** A631 6000d multi .90 .45

No. 1963 contains one 54x35 stamp.

No. 1246 Surcharged

**1989, Apr. 6 Litho. *Perf. 13***

**1964** A323 100d on 1d dull grn .20 .20
***a.*** Perf. 13x12½ .70

Tito — A632

**1989, May 25 *Perf. 13½x14***

**1965** A632 300d multi .20 .20

Early Adriatic Ships A633

a, Ancient Greek galley. b, Roman galley. c, Crusade galleon, 13th cent. d, Nava of Dubrovnik, 16th cent. e, French ship, 17th cent. f, Vessels, 18th cent. 3000d, View of Dubrovnik seaport, called Ragusa in Italian, from a 17th cent. engraving.

**1989, June 10 *Perf. 13½***

**1966** Block of 6 .90 .45
***a.-f.*** A633 1000d any single .20 .20

**Souvenir Sheet**

**1967** A633 3000d multi .45 .20

No. 1967 contains one 75x32mm stamp. Nos. 1966-1967 printed se-tenant and sold folded in booklet cover.

26th European Basketball Championships — A634

Map of Europe, basketball and flags of: No. 1968, France, Yugoslavia, Greece, Bulgaria. No. 1969, Netherlands, Italy, Russia, Spain.

**1989, June 20 Litho. *Perf. 13½x14***

**1968** A634 2000d multi .25 .20
**1969** A634 2000d multi .25 .20

Nos. 1968-1969 exist with setenant label.

Defeat of the Serbians at the Battle of Kosovo, 1389 — A635

**1989, June 28**

**1970** A635 500d multi .20 .20

Danilovgrad Library, Cent. A636

**1989, July 15 Litho. *Perf. 13½***

**1971** A636 500d multi .20 .20

Nos. 1797, 1719, 1935, 1936 Surcharged

**1989**

**1972** A559 400d on 30d lt brn vio .20 .20
**1973** A323 700d on 70d brt ultra .20 .20
**1974** A559 700d on 170d dull green .20 .20
**1975** A559 700d on 220d brn org .20 .20
*Nos. 1972-1975 (4)* .80 .80

Issued: #1975, 7/19; #1974, 8/10; #1972, 8/23; #1973, 12/13.

Kulin Ban Charter, 800th Anniv. A638

**1989, Aug. 29 Litho. *Perf. 14***

**1976** A638 500d multi .20 .20

World Rowing Championships A639

**1989, Sept. 2 *Perf. 13½***

**1977** A639 10,000d multi .75 .35

Interparliamentary Union, Cent. — A640

Architecture: No. 1978, Parliament, London (emblem at R). No. 1979, Notre Dame Cathedral (emblem at L).

**1989, Sept. 4 *Perf. 13½x14***

**1978** A640 10,000d multi .65 .30
**1979** A640 10,000d multi .65 .30

A641

View of Belgrade and Maps BEOGRAD '89 — A642

Architecture & antiquities of exhibition host cities: #1980, Belgrade '61, Cairo '64. #1981, Lusaka '70, Algiers '73. #1982, Colombo '76, Havana '79. #1983, New Delhi '83, Harare '76.

**1989, Sept. 4**

**1980** A641 10,000d multi .65 .30
**1981** A641 10,000d multi .65 .30
**1982** A641 10,000d multi .65 .30
**1983** A641 10,000d multi .65 .30
*Nos. 1980-1983 (4)* 2.60 1.20

**Souvenir Sheet**

***Perf. 14***

**1984** A642 20,000d multi 1.50 1.50

European Nature Protection A643

8000d, Paeonia officinalis, Brezovica-Jazinac Lake. 10,000d, Paeonia corallina, Mirusa Canyon.

**1989, Sept. 11 *Perf. 14***

**1985** A643 8000d multi .45 .20
**1986** A643 10,000d multi .55 .25

Joy of Europe Type of 1988

Portraits of children: No. 1987, Child with Lamb, by Jovan Popovic. No. 1988, Girl Feeding Dog, by Albert Cuyp (1620-1691).

**1989, Oct. 2 Litho. *Perf. 14***

**1987** A617 10,000d multi .60 .30
**1988** A617 10,000d multi .60 .30

Karpos Uprising, 300th Anniv. — A644

**1989, Oct. 20 Litho. *Perf. 13½***

**1989** A644 1200d ver & dark brn .20 .20

No. 1833c, Cancellation, Quill Pen, Wax Seals and Seal Device on Parchment A645

**1989, Oct. 31 *Perf. 14***

**1990** A645 1200d multicolored .20 .20

Stamp Day.

Museum Exhibits A646

**1989, Nov. 2**

**1991** A646 1200d Pack-saddle maker .20 .20
**1992** A646 14,000d Cooper .60 .30
**1993** A646 15,000d Winegrower .65 .35
**1994** A646 30,000d Weaver 1.40 .70
*Nos. 1991-1994 (4)* 2.85 1.55

Religious Paintings — A647

2100d, Apostle Matthew, vert. 21,000d, St. Barbara, vert. 30,000d, The Fourth Day of Creation. 50,000d, The Fifth Day of Creation.

**1989, Nov. 28 Litho. *Perf. 14***

**1997** A647 2100d multicolored .20 .20
**1998** A647 21,000d multicolored .65 .30
**1999** A647 30,000d multicolored .90 .45
**2000** A647 50,000d multicolored 1.50 .75
*Nos. 1997-2000 (4)* 3.25 1.70

A648

League of Communists 14th Congress — A649

**1990, Jan. 20 Litho. *Perf. 13½x14***

**2001** A648 10,000d Star .20 .20
**2002** A648 50,000d Computer .75 .35

**Souvenir Sheet**

***Imperf***

**2003** A649 100,000d Star, diff. 1.50 1.50

Postal Service Types of 1986-88

10p, Man posting letters in mailbox. 20p, Postal employee sorting mail. 30p, Postman, resident. 40p, Woman at telephone station. 1d, Mail train. 2d, Ship & envelope. 3d, Flower, mailbox, envelope & simulated stamp. 5d, Airplane, letters, map of Europe. 10d, Bird, open envelope, flower. 20d, Woman at telephone station.

Designs for other values as before.

10p, 20p, 30p, 40p, 3d, 5d vert.

**1990 *Perf. 12½***

**2004** A559 10p br yel grn & vio .20 .20
**2005** A559 20p red vio & org .20 .20
**2006** A559 30p org & yel grn .20 .20
**2007** A559 40p blue grn & red vio .20 .20
**2008** A620 50p pur & blue grn .20 .20

**2009** A619 60p red org & brt vio .20 .20
**2013** A559 1d rose lil & greenish bl .20 .20
**2014** A559 2d red lil & blue .25 .20
**2015** A559 3d org & dl blue .50 .25
**2017** A619 5d ultra & grnsh blue .75 .35
**2019** A559 10d red org & vio bl 1.75 1.25
*Nos. 2004-2019 (11)* 4.65 3.45

Issued: 10p, 20p, 2/9; 30p, 40p, 1/24; 50p, 1/29; 60p, 2/6; 2d, 2/14; 3d, 2/22; 5d, 1/31; 1d, 5/24; 10d, 6/12.

For surcharges see Nos. 2049-2053, 2168//2174.

**1990-92** ***Perf. 13¼***

*2004a* A559 10p br yel grn & vio .20 .20
*2005a* A559 20p red vio & org .20 .20
*2006a* A559 30p org & yel grn .20 .20
*2007a* A559 40p blue grn & red vio .20 .20
*2008a* A620 50p pur & blue grn .20 .20
*2009a* A619 60p red org & brt vio .20 .20
*2013a* A559 1d rose lil & greenish bl 1.60 1.25
*2014a* A559 2d red lil & blue .35 .30
*2015a* A559 3d org & dl blue> 2.00 1.75
*2017a* A619 5d ultra & grnsh blue 1.00 .85
*2019a* A559 10d red org & vio bl 4.50 4.50
**2021** A559 20d car rose & org .30 .20
*Nos. 2004a-2021 (12)* 10.95 10.05

Issued: 30p, 40p, 1/24; 50p, 1/29; 5d, 1/31; 60p, 2/6; 10p, 20p, 2/9; 2d, 2/14; 3d, 2/22; 10d, 6/12; 1d, 7/2; 20d, 1/27/92.

For surcharges see Nos. 2049a-2053a, 2170//2176.

Anti-smoking Campaign A650

**1990, Jan. 31** **Litho.** ***Perf. 13½x13***

**2034** A650 10d gry & yel brn 1.75 .85

Protected Fish — A651

**1990, Feb. 15** ***Perf. 13½***

**2035** Strip of 4 + label 5.25 2.75
***a.*** A651 1d *Esox lucius* .20 .20
***b.*** A651 5d *Silurus glanis* .85 .40
***c.*** A651 10d *Lota lota* 1.60 .80
***d.*** A651 15d *Perca fluviatilis* 2.50 1.25

Zabljak Fortress, Illuminated Manuscript, Coat of Arms — A652

**1990, Mar. 9** ***Perf. 14x13½***

**2036** A652 50p multicolored .20 .20

Enthronement of Djuradj Crnojevic, 500th anniv.

ITU, 125th Anniv. A653

**1990, Mar. 23**

**2037** A653 6.50d Telegrapher, computer 1.10 .55

1990 World Cup Soccer Championships, Italy — A654

**1990, Apr. 16**

**2038** A654 6.50d shown 1.10 .55
**2039** A654 10d multi, diff. 1.60 .80

Europa 1990 — A655

Post offices: 6.50d, PTT Central, Skopje. 10d, Telecommunications Central, Belgrade.

**1990, Apr. 23** ***Perf. 13½x14***

**2040** A655 6.50d multicolored 1.25 .55
**2041** A655 10d multicolored 2.00 .80

A656

A657

**1990, Apr. 30** **Litho.** ***Perf. 13½***

**2042** A656 6.50d multicolored 1.25 .60

Labor Day, cent.

No. 2043 exists with setenant label.

**1990, May 5** ***Perf. 14x13½***

Eurovision Song Contest: 10d, Conductor, musical score.

**2043** A657 6.50d multicolored 1.25 .60
**2044** A657 10d multicolored 1.75 .90

Tennis — A658

**1990, May 15** **Litho.** ***Perf. 14***

**2045** A658 6.50d multicolored 1.25 .60
**2046** A658 10d multicolored 1.90 .95

Tito — A659

**1990, May 25** ***Perf. 13½x14***

**2047** A659 50p multicolored .20 .20

Nos. 1938, 2004-2009a Surcharged

No. 2048

No. 2049

**1990-91** **Litho.** ***Perf. 12½***

**2048** A559 50p on 800d (#1938a) .20 .20
***a.*** Perf 13¼ (#1938) .20 .20
**2049** A559 50p on 20p (#2005) .20 .20
***a.*** Perf 13¼ (#2005a) ('91) 2.75 2.75
**2050** A559 1d on 30p (#2006) .20 .20
***a.*** Perf 13¼ (#2006a) 3.25 3.25
**2051** A559 2d on 40p (#2007), I .90 .90
***a.*** Type II, perf. 13¼ (#2007a) 1.25 .90
***b.*** Type I, perf. 13¼ (#2007a) 2.00 2.00
**2052** A619 5d on 60p (#2009) .40 .20
***a.*** Perf 13¼ (#2009a) 2.75 1.75
**2053** A559 10d on 10p (#2004) .40 .20
***a.*** Perf 13¼ (#2004a) 1.00 .45
*Nos. 2048-2053 (6)* 2.30 1.90

Type II surcharge has 3 instead of 2 bars obliterating old value, new denomination is at bottom of stamp.

Issued: #2048, 2048a, 5/24; #2050, 8/7; #2049, 2049a, 9/18; #2051-2051b, 10/2; #2050a, 1/4/91; #2053, 2053a, 12/12/91; #2052, 2052a, 12/17/91.

Public Postal Service in Serbia, 150th Anniv. A660

**1990, May 25**

**2056** A660 50p multicolored .20 .20

Pigeons A661

**1990, June 8** ***Perf. 13½***

**2057** A661 50p multicolored .20 .20
**2058** A661 5d multicolored .80 .40
**2059** A661 6.50d multi, vert. 1.10 .55
**2060** A661 10d multi, vert. 1.60 .75
*Nos. 2057-2060 (4)* 3.70 1.90

Mercury Mine at Idrija, 500th Anniv. — A662

Designs: 6.50d, Miners at work, ca. 1490.

**1990, June 22** ***Perf. 13½x14***

**2061** A662 50p multicolored .20 .20
**2062** A662 6.50d multicolored 1.10 .55

Newspaper "Vjesnik," 50th Anniv. — A663

**1990, June 23** ***Perf. 13½***

**2063** A663 60p multicolored .20 .20

Serbian Migration, 300th Anniv. — A664

**1990, Sept. 20** ***Perf. 14***

**2064** A664 1d shown .20 .20
**2065** A664 6.50d Caravan 1.25 .60

European Track & Field Championships, Split — A665

**1990, Aug. 27** ***Perf. 13½***

**2067** A665 1d Start of race .20 .20
**2068** A665 6.50d Runners' feet 1.10 .55

### Souvenir Sheet

**2069** A665 10d Runners 1.75 .90

No. 2069 contains one 54x35mm stamp. A 50p exists but no information on its postal category is available.

Joy of Europe A666

Paintings: 6.50d, Children by I. Kobilca. 10d, William III of Orange as a Child by A. Hanneman, vert.

**1990, Oct. 2** **Litho.** ***Perf. 14***

**2070** A666 6.50d multicolored 1.00 .50
**2071** A666 10d multicolored 1.75 .80

### Souvenir Sheets

29th Chess Olympics, Novi Sad — A667

**1990, Oct. 2** ***Perf. 11½***

### Granite Paper

**2072** Sheet of 4 4.50 4.50
***a.*** A667 1d shown .20 .20
***b.*** A667 5d Rook, bishop, knight 1.00 1.00
***c.*** A667 6.50d King, bishop, knght, pawn 1.25 1.25
***d.*** A667 10d Chess pieces 2.00 2.00

### *Imperf*

**2073** Sheet of 4 4.50 4.50
***a.*** A667 1d like No. 2072a .20 .20
***b.*** A667 5d like No. 2072b 1.00 1.00
***c.*** A667 6.50d like No. 2072c 1.25 1.25
***d.*** A667 10d like No. 2072d 2.00 2.00

No. 2073 has blue margin inscriptions. Emblems on Nos. 2072a-2072d are in silver, those on Nos. 2073a-2073d are in gold.

Stamp Day A668

**1990, Oct. 2** ***Perf. 14***

**2074** A668 2d multicolored .40 .20

150th anniv. of the Penny Black.

Environmental Protection A669

**1990, Nov. 16 Litho. *Perf. 14***

**2075** A669 6.50d Vransko Lake 1.25 1.25
**2076** A669 10d Gyps fulvus 1.75 1.75

Frescoes — A670

Designs: 2d, King Milutin, Monastery of Our Lady, Ljeviska. 5d, Saint Sava, Mileseva Monastery. 6.50d, Saint Elias, Moraca Monastery. 10d, Jesus Christ, Sopocani Monastery.

**1990, Nov. 28**

**2077** A670 2d multicolored .35 .35
**2078** A670 5d multicolored .80 .80
**2079** A670 6.50d multicolored 1.10 1.10
**2080** A670 10d multicolored 1.75 1.75
*Nos. 2077-2080 (4)* 4.00 4.00

Dr. Bozo Milanovic (1890-1980), Religious and Political Leader A671

**1990, Dec. 20 Litho. *Perf. 13½***

**2081** A671 2d multicolored .35 .35

Religious Carvings A672

Designs: 2d, Christ in the temple. 5d, Nativity scene. 6.50d, Flight from Egypt, horiz. 10d, Entry into Jerusalem, horiz.

**1990, Dec. 24 *Perf. 13½x14, 14x13½***

**2082** A672 2d gld, brn, & blk .35 .35
**2083** A672 5d gld, brn, & blk .90 .90
**2084** A672 6.50d gld, brn, & blk 1.10 1.10
**2085** A672 10d gld, brn, & blk 1.90 1.90
*Nos. 2082-2085 (4)* 4.25 4.25

Protected Birds — A673

Flora — A674

**1991, Jan. 31 Litho. *Perf. 14x13½***

**2086** Strip of 4 + label 4.50 4.50
*a.* A673 2d Vanellus vanellus .35 .35
*b.* A673 5d Lanius senator .95 .95
*c.* A673 6.50d Grus grus 1.25 1.25
*d.* A673 10d Mergus merganser 1.90 1.90

**1991, Feb. 20**

**2087** A674 2d Crocus kosaninii .30 .30
**2088** A674 6d Crocus scardicus .90 .90
**2089** A674 7.50d Crocus rujanesis 1.10 1.10
**2090** A674 15d Crocus adamii 2.40 2.40
*Nos. 2087-2090 (4)* 4.70 4.70

Bishop Josip J. Strossmayer (1815-1905), Founder of Academy of Arts and Sciences A675

**1991, Mar. 4 Litho. *Perf. 13½x14***

**2091** A675 2d multicolored .30 .30

Academy of Arts and Sciences, 125th Anniv.

Wolfgang Amadeus Mozart, Composer A676

**1991, Mar. 20 *Perf. 14***

**2092** A676 7.50d multicolored 1.00 1.00

Otto Lilienthal's First Glider Flight, Cent. — A677

Designs: 7.50d, Edvard Rusjan (1886-1911), pilot, aircraft designer. 15d, Otto Lilienthal (1848-1896), aviation pioneer.

**1991, Apr. 1**

**2093** A677 7.50d multicolored .90 .90
**2094** A677 15d multicolored 1.90 1.90

Printed in sheets of 8 plus label.

Lhotse I, Himalayas, South Face First Climbed by Tomo Cesen, 1990 — A678

**1991, Apr. 24 *Perf. 14x13½***

**2095** A678 7.50d multicolored .75 .75

Europa A679

Designs: 7.50d, Telecommunications satellite. 15d, Satellite, antenna, telephone.

**1991, May 6 *Perf. 14***

**2096** A679 7.50d multicolored 1.00 .60
**2097** A679 15d multicolored 2.00 1.25

Franciscan Monastery, Trsat, 700th Anniv. — A680

**1991, May 10 Litho. *Perf. 13½x14***

**2098** A680 3.50d multicolored .40 .40

Governments of Danube River Region Conf., Belgrade — A681

15d, Danube River shipping. 20d, Course of Danube, landmarks, regional animals.

**1991, May 15 *Perf. 13½***

**2099** A681 7.50d multicolored .65 .65
**2100** A681 15d multicolored 1.10 1.10

**Souvenir Sheet**

**2101** A681 20d multicolored 1.75 1.75

No. 2101 contains one 55x35mm stamp.

Opening of Karavanke Tunnel — A682

Designs: 4.50d, Passage Over Karavanke by J. Valvasor, 17th century. 11d, Entrance to new Karavanke Tunnel.

**1991, June 1 *Perf. 14x13½***

**2102** A682 4.50d multicolored .35 .35
**2103** A682 11d multicolored .90 .90

Basketball, Cent. — A683

**1991, June 15 *Perf. 13½x14***

**2104** A683 11d shown .95 .95
**2105** A683 15d Nets, "100" 1.25 1.25

Yugoslavian Insurrection, 50th Anniv. — A684

Tin Ujevic (1891-1955), Writer — A685

Designs: 4.50d, Partisan Memorial Medal, 1941. 11d, Medal for Courage.

**1991, July 4 Litho. *Perf. 14***

**2106** A684 4.50d multicolored .35 .35
**2107** A684 11d multicolored .90 .90

Yugoslav Natl. Army, 50th Anniv.

**1991, July 5 *Perf. 13½***

**2108** A685 4.50d multicolored .40 .40

Jacobus Gallus (1550-1591), Composer A686

**1991, July 18**

**2109** A686 11d multicolored .80 .80

Lighthouses of Adriatic and Danube — A687

Designs: a, Savudrija, 1818. b, Sveti Ivan na pucini, 1853. c, Porer, 1833. d, Stoncica, 1865. e, Olipa, c. 1842. f, Glavat, 1884. g, Veli rat, 1849. h, Vir, 1881. i, Tajerske sestrice, 1876. j, Razanj, 1875. k, Derdap-Danube. l, Tamis-Danube.

**1991, July 25 Litho. *Perf. 13½***

**2110** A687 10d Bklt. pane of 12, #a.-l. 10.50 10.50

Sremski Karlovci High School, Bicent. — A688

**1991, Sept. 12 Litho. *Perf. 14***

**2111** A688 4.50d multicolored .40 .40

European Nature Protection A689

**1991, Sept. 24 *Perf. 13½x14***

**2112** A689 11d Palingenia longicauda .95 .95
**2113** A689 15d Phalacrocorax pygmaeus 1.25 1.25

A690

A691

**1991, Sept. 28 *Perf. 14***

**2114** A690 4.50d multicolored .40 .40

Town of Subotica, 600th anniv.

**1991, Oct. 2**

Paintings: 15d, Little Dubravka, by Jovan Bijelic (1886-1964). 30d, Little Girl with a Cat by Mary Cassatt (1845-1926).

**2115** A691 15d multicolored 1.10 1.10
**2116** A691 30d multicolored 2.25 2.25

Joy of Europe.

33rd Intl. Apicultural Congress, APIMONDIA '91 — A692

**1991, Sept. 28 Litho.** ***Perf. 13½x14***
**2117** A692 11d multicolored .75 .75

Stamp Day, Monument to Prince Michael Obrenovich, Serbia #1 — A693

**1991, Oct. 31** ***Perf. 14***
**2118** A693 4.50d multicolored .40 .40

First Serbia Postage Stamps, 125th Anniv.

Museum Exhibits A694

Flags and medals: 20d, Vucjido battle flag, medal for courage. 30d, Grahovac battle flag and medal. 40d, Montenegrin state flag, medal for bravery. 50d, Montenegrin court flag, medal of Petrovich Nyegosh Dynasty.

**1991, Nov. 28** ***Perf. 13½x14***
**2119** A694 20d multicolored .65 .65
**2120** A694 30d multicolored 1.00 1.00
**2121** A694 40d multicolored 1.40 1.40
**2122** A694 50d multicolored 1.75 1.75
*Nos. 2119-2122 (4)* 4.80 4.80

Illustrations from Ancient Manuscripts A695

Designs: 20d, Angel carrying Sun around Earth, 17th cent. 30d, Celnica Gospel, menology for April, 14th cent. 40d, Angel from the Annunciation, 13th cent. 50d, Mary Magdalene, 12th cent.

**1991, Dec. 12**
**2123** A695 20d multicolored .65 .65
**2124** A695 30d multicolored 1.00 1.00
**2125** A695 40d multicolored 1.40 1.40
**2126** A695 50d multicolored 1.75 1.75
*Nos. 2123-2126 (4)* 4.80 4.80

Gotse Deltchev (1872-1903), Macedonian Revolutionary A696

**1992, Jan. 29 Litho.** ***Perf. 13½***
**2127** A696 5d multicolored .20 .20

Red Star, European and World Soccer Champions A697

**1992, Jan. 29 Litho.** ***Perf. 14x13½***
**2128** A697 17d multicolored .25 .20

A698

A699

**1992, Feb. 8** ***Perf. 14x13½***
**2129** A698 80d Ski jumping 1.10 .55
**2130** A698 100d Freestyle skiing 1.40 .70

1992 Winter Olympics, Albertville.

**1992, Mar. 10 Litho.** ***Perf. 14***

Protected Animals: a, 50d, Lepus europaeus. b, 60d, Pteromys volans. c, 80d, Dryomys nitedula. d, 100d, Cricetus cricetus.

**2131** A699 Strip of 4, #a.-d. + label 3.75 1.90

Madonna and Child, 14th century, Pec — A700

**1992, Mar. 14** ***Perf. 13½x14***
**2132** A700 80d multicolored 1.00 .50

Promotion of Breastfeeding.

Ski Association of Montenegro — A701

**1992, Mar. 25** ***Perf. 14x13½***
**2133** A701 8d multicolored .20 .20

Skiing in Montenegro, cent.

1860 Fountain, Belgrade — A702

A702a

A702b

A702c

A702d

A702e

A702f

A702g

A702h

A702i

A702j

5d, Griffins, 14th cent. #2136, #2139, Fisherman Fountain, Belgrade. #2138, like #2137. 300d, Kalemegdan Fountain, Belgrade. 500d, Fountain, Sremski Karlovci. #2142, Symbols of Miroslav-Evangelium, 12th cent. 3000d, Fountain, Studenica. 5000d, Fountain, Oplenzu. 10,000d, 500,000d, Health spa, Vrnjacka Banja. 50,000d, Envelopes over map of Europe. #2147, Airplane. #2148, Health spa, Bukovacka Banja.

**1992-93 Litho.** ***Perf. 13½***
**2135** A702a 5d brn & olive .30 .20
**2136** A702 50d dk bl & lt bl .30 .25
**2137** A702 50d violet .20 .20
**2138** A702 100d lil rose & pink .20 .20
**2139** A702 100d dk grn & lt grn .20 .20
**2140** A702b 300d brn & red brn .25 .20
**2141** A702c 500d dk ol & pale org .25 .20
**2142** A702d (A) red, 18x22mm .50 .25
***a.*** Perf. 12½ .90 .90
**2143** A702e 3000d red brn .25 .20
***a.*** Perf. 12½ 2.00 2.00
**2144** A702f 5000d vio & yel brn .25 .20
**2145** A702g 10,000d vio bl & grn bl .25 .20
**2146** A702h 50,000d gray & gray bl .30 .20
**2147** A702i 100,000d red & bl .50 .25
***a.*** Perf. 12½ .50 .50
**2148** A702j 100,000d brn red & brn .30 .20
**2149** A702g 500,000d bl & vio .50 .25
*Nos. 2135-2149 (15)* 4.55 3.20

Issued: #2137, 4/1/92; #2139, 5/6/92; 5d, 11/24/92; #2136, 12/15/92; #2138, 12/22/92; 300d, 12/3/92; 500d, 1/14/93; #2142, 4/5/93; #2142a, 1993; #2143, 4/23/93; 5000d, 3/18/93; 10,000d, 11/9/93; 50,000d, 6/10/93; 100,000d, 6/28/93; 100,000d, 12/6/93; 500,000d, 8/10/93.

No. 2142 was valued at 3000d on day of issue.

See No. 2386. For surcharges see Nos. 2220A-2220I, 2253-2254.

This is an expanding set. Numbers may change.

Sinking of the Titanic, 80th Anniv. — A703

**1992, Apr. 14** ***Perf. 14***
**2152** A703 150d multicolored 1.25 .80

Expo '92, Seville A704

**1992, Apr. 20**
**2153** A704 150d multicolored 1.25 .80

Discovery of America, 500th Anniv. — A705

**1992, May 5 Litho.** ***Perf. 13½x14***
**2154** A705 300d Columbus, ship 2.00 1.25
**2155** A705 500d Columbus' fleet 3.25 2.10

**Souvenir Sheet**

***Perf. 14x13½***

**2156** A705 1200d Ships in port 7.50 7.50

Europa. No. 2156 contains one 54x34mm stamp.

1992 Summer Olympics, Barcelona — A706

**1992, May 20** ***Perf. 14x13½***
**2157** A706 500d Pistol shooting 1.40 .70
**2158** A706 500d Water polo 1.40 .70
**2159** A706 500d Tennis 1.40 .70
**2160** A706 500d Handball 1.40 .70
*Nos. 2157-2160 (4)* 5.60 2.80

European Soccer Championships — A707

Various soccer plays.

**1992, June 1** ***Perf. 13½***
**2161** A707 1000d shown 2.25 1.10
**2162** A707 1000d multicolored 2.25 1.10

Domestic Cats — A708

Designs: No. 2163, Red Persian. No. 2164, White Persian. No. 2165, Yellow tabby. No. 2166, British blue short-hair.

**1992, June 25 Litho.** ***Perf. 13½x14***
**Background Color**
**Cyrillic Letters**

**2163** A708 1000d blue 1.25 .80
**2164** A708 1000d purple 1.25 .80

**Latin Letters**

**2165** A708 1000d dark purple 1.25 .80
**2166** A708 1000d brown 1.25 .80
*Nos. 2163-2166 (4)* 5.00 3.20

Steam Locomotives A709

Designs: a, JDZ 162. b, JDZ 151. c, JDZ 73. d, JDZ 83. e, JDZ 16. f, Prince Nicholas' coach.

**1992, July 3 Litho.** ***Perf. 14***

**2167** A709 1000d Booklet pane of 6, #a.-f. 12.00 10.00

Nos. 2005-2006, 2007a, 2008, 2013a, 2014a, 2015a, 2017a Surcharged

**1992** ***Perfs., Etc. as Before***

**2168** A559 2d on 30p #2006 .20 .20
**2169** A559 5d on 20p #2005 .20 .20
**2170** A559 5d on 40p #2007a .20 .20
**2171** A620 10d on 50p #2008 .20 .20
**2172** A621 10d on 5d #2017a .20 .20
**2173** A559 20d on 1d #2013a .40 .25
**2174** A621 20d on 5d like #2017,yel, bl & grn bl .40 .25
**2175** A559 50d on 2d #2014a 1.00 .70
**2176** A559 100d on 3d #2015a 2.10 1.40
*Nos. 2168-2176 (9)* 4.90 3.60

Issued: #2168, 2170, 10/26; #2169, 9/12; #2171, 9/17; #2172, 10/29; #2173, 2175-2176, 8/6; #2174, 11/9.

World Chess Champions A710

**1992, Sept. 14 Litho.** ***Perf. 14***

**2177** A710 500d Bobby Fischer 1.90 1.25
**2178** A710 500d Boris Spassky 1.90 1.25

Telephone Service in Vojvodina, Cent. A711

1892 Telephone, buildings of Novi Sad, Subotica and Zrenjanin.

**1992, Oct. 1**

**2179** A711 10d multicolored 1.00 .70

Stamp Day A712

Design: Montenegro #7, musician.

**1992, Oct. 2**

**2180** A712 50d multicolored 1.50 1.00

European Art — A713

Protection of Nature — A714

Europa: No. 2181, Ballet Dancer, by Edgar Degas (1834-1917). No. 2182, Painting of young man, by V. Knezevic.

**1992, Oct. 2**

**2181** A713 500d multicolored 1.90 1.25
**2182** A713 500d multicolored 1.90 1.25

**1992, Nov. 14** ***Perf. 13½***

**2183** A714 500d Tetrao urogallus 3.25 2.00
**2184** A714 500d Pelecanus onocrotalus 3.25 2.00

Serbian Writers Assoc., Cent. — A715

**1992, Nov. 20** ***Perf. 14***

**2185** A715 100d multicolored 1.00 .70

Traditional Architecture — A716

Designs: No. 2186, Ancient hut, Zlatibor region. No. 2187, Round house, Morava region. No. 2188, House, on stone cliff, Metohija region. No. 2189, Large estate house, Vojvodina region.

**1992, Dec. 12**

**2186** A716 500d multicolored 1.10 .75
**2187** A716 500d multicolored 1.10 .75
**2188** A716 500d multicolored 1.10 .75
**2189** A716 500d multicolored 1.10 .75
*Nos. 2186-2189 (4)* 4.40 3.00

Icons, Mosaics — A717

#2190, St. Petka, St. Petka Church, Belgrade. #2191, St. Vasilije-Ostronoski, St. Vasilije-Ostronoski Church, Montenegro. #2192, Mosaic of Simeon Nemanja with model of Blessed Virgin Church, Studenica. #2193, Mosaic of St. Lazar with model of Ravanica Monastery.

**1992, Dec. 15**

**2190** A717 500d multi 1.40 1.00
**2191** A717 500d multi 1.40 1.00
**2192** A717 500d multi, vert. 1.40 1.00
**2193** A717 500d multi, vert. 1.40 1.00
*Nos. 2190-2193 (4)* 5.60 4.00

Aviation in Yugoslavia, 80th Anniv. — A718

**1992, Dec. 24**

**2194** A718 500d Bleriot XI 1.25 .80

Diocletian's Reformation of the Roman Empire, 1700th Anniv. — A719

Design: Detail of Roman fresco.

**1993, Jan. 28 Litho.** ***Perf. 13½***

**2195** A719 1500d multicolored 1.25 .80

State Museum, Cetinje, Cent. — A720

**1993, Feb. 12** ***Perf. 14***

**2196** A720 2500d multicolored 1.25 .80

Marine Life — A721

Designs: a, Acipenser sturio. b, Scorpaena scrofa. c, Xiphias gladius. d, Tursiops truncatus.

**1993, Mar. 20** ***Perf. 13½***

**2197** A721 10,000d Strip of 4, #a.-d. + label 4.75 4.00

Serbian Money — A722

#2198, Ancient document, 10 para coins. #2199, 5 dinar banknotes, 5 dinar coins.

**1993, Mar. 30**

**2198** A722 10,000d multicolored 1.75 1.10
**2199** A722 10,000d multicolored 1.75 1.10

Restablishment of Serbian monetary system, 125th anniv. (No. 2198). Restoring dinars as Serbian currency, 120th anniv. (No. 2199).

Famous People A723

Designs: No. 2200, Milos Crnjanski (1893-1977), writer, journalist. No. 2201, Nicola Tesla (1856-1943), physicist. No. 2202, Mihailo Petrovic (1868-1943), mathematician. No. 2203, Aleksa Santic (1868-1924), poet.

**1993, Apr. 1**

**2200** A723 40,000d multicolored 1.40 1.00
**2201** A723 40,000d multicolored 1.40 1.00
**2202** A723 40,000d multicolored 1.40 1.00
**2203** A723 40,000d multicolored 1.40 1.00
*Nos. 2200-2203 (4)* 5.60 4.00

Joy of Europe — A724

Contemporary Art — A725

Children's paintings: No. 2204, Girl holding flowers, children, dove, by M. Markovski. No. 2205, Angels, birds, by J. Rugovac.

**1993, Apr. 5**

**2204** A724 50,000d multicolored 1.75 1.10
**2205** A724 50,000d multicolored 1.75 1.10

**1993, May 5**

Europa: No. 2206, Nude with a Mirror, by M. Milunovic. No. 2207, Composition, by M.P. Barili.

**2206** A725 95,000d multicolored 2.25 2.00
**2207** A725 95,000d multicolored 2.25 2.00

A726

A727

A728

A729

A730

Ancient Fortresses: No. 2208, Sutorina, Montenegro. No. 2209, Kalemegdan, Belgrade. No. 2210, Medun, Montenegro. No. 2211, Petrovaradin, near Novi Sad. No. 2212, Bar, Montenegro. No. 2213, Golubac.

**1993, July 9**

**Booklet Stamps**

**2208** A726 900,000d multicolored 1.25 .80
**2209** A727 900,000d multicolored 1.25 .80
**2210** A728 900,000d multicolored 1.25 .80
**2211** A729 900,000d multicolored 1.25 .80
**2212** A730 900,000d multicolored 1.25 .80
**2213** A730 900,000d multicolored 1.25 .80
*a.* Booklet pane, #2208-2213 7.50
Complete booklet, #2213a 7.50

Flowers A731

Colors of various flowers in vases: No. 2214, Yellow, white. No. 2215, Orange, red. No. 2216, Purple, pink, white. No. 2217, Mixed.

**1993, July 10** ***Perf. 14***

**2214** A731 1,000,000d multi 1.25 .80
**2215** A731 1,000,000d multi 1.25 .80
**2216** A731 1,000,000d multi 1.25 .80
**2217** A731 1,000,000d multi 1.25 .80
*Nos. 2214-2217 (4)* 5.00 3.20

Electrification of Serbia, Cent. A732

**1993, July 28** ***Perf. 13½***

**2218** A732 2,500,000d multi 1.00 .70

Protection of Nature A733

Designs: No. 2219, Garrulus glandarius. No. 2220, Oriolus oriolus.

**1993, Sept. 30**

**2219** A733 300,000,000d multi 3.00 2.00
**2220** A733 300,000,000d multi 3.00 2.00

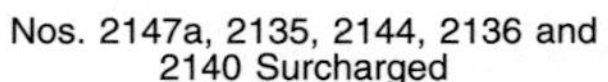
Nos. 2147a, 2135, 2144, 2136 and 2140 Surcharged

No. 2143 Surcharged

**1993** ***Perfs., Etc. as Before***

**2220A** A702i 10d on 100,000d .20 .20
**2220C** A702a 50d on 5d .20 .20
**2220D** A702f 100d on 5000d .20 .20
**2220E** A702 500d on 50d .20 .20
**2220F** A702e 1000d on 3000d .20 .20
**2220H** A702b 10,000d on 300d .60 .40
**2220I** A702a 50,000d on 5d 3.00 2.00
*Nos. 2220A-2220I (7)* 4.60 3.40

Issued: 50,000d, 11/9/93; others, 10/18/93.
Size and location of surcharge varies.

A734

Cooperation on the Danube River — A735

Designs: No. 2221, Ships on river. No. 2222, Ship going down river. 20,000d, Map showing location of Danube River.
Illustration reduced (A735).

**1993, Oct. 20** ***Perf. 14***

**2221** A734 15,000d multicolored 1.40 1.00
**2222** A734 15,000d multicolored 1.40 1.00

**Souvenir Sheet**

**2223** A735 20,000d multicolored 2.50 1.75

Post Office in Jagodina, 150th Anniv. A736

**1993, Oct. 30** ***Perf. 13½***

**2224** A736 12,000d multicolored 1.50 1.00
Stamp Day.

Joy of Europe — A737

Icons in Monasteries A738

Paintings: No. 2225, Boy with Cat, by Sava Sumanovic (1896-1942). No. 2226, Circus Rider, by Georges Rouault (1871-1958).

**1993, Nov. 26**

**2225** A737 2,000,000d multi 1.75 1.10
**2226** A737 2,000,000d multi 1.75 1.10

**1993, Dec. 15**

Designs: No. 2227, The Annunciation, Mileseva. No. 2228, Nativity, Studenica. No. 2229, Madonna and Child, Bogorodica Ljeviska. No. 2230, Flight into Egypt, Oplenac.

**2227** A738 400,000,000d multi .95 .60
**2228** A738 400,000,000d multi .95 .60
**2229** A738 400,000,000d multi .95 .60
**2230** A738 400,000,000d multi .95 .60
*Nos. 2227-2230 (4)* 3.80 2.40

Traditional Houses — A739

Publication of Oktoechos, 500th Anniv. — A740

#2231, A-frame huts, Savardak, horiz. #2232, Watchtower. #2233, Stone house on edge of river. #2234, Crmnicka house, Bar, horiz.

**1993, Dec. 31**

**2231** A739 50d multicolored .95 .60
**2232** A739 50d multicolored .95 .60
**2233** A739 50d multicolored .95 .60
**2234** A739 50d multicolored .95 .60
*Nos. 2231-2234 (4)* 3.80 2.40

**1994, Jan. 17** **Litho.** ***Perf. 13½***

**2235** A740 1000d Text .90 .60
**2236** A740 1000d Liturgists .90 .60

Raptors A741

Designs: a, Neophron percnopterus. b, Falco cherrug. c, Buteo rufinus. d, Falco naumanni.

**1994, Feb. 7**

**2237** A741 80p Strip of 4, #a.-d. + label 7.50 7.50

Intl. Mimosa Festival, Herceg-Novi A742

**1994, Feb. 28**

**2238** A742 80p multicolored 1.50 1.00

Natl. Museum, Belgrade, 150th Anniv. A743

Design: No. 2240, National Theater, Belgrade, 125th anniv., portrait of Prince Milos Obrenovic.

**1994, Mar. 19**

**2239** A743 80p multicolored 1.40 1.00
**2240** A743 80p multicolored 1.40 1.00

1994 Winter Olympics, Lillehammer — A744

a, Speed skater. b. Olympic rings, flame. c, Skier.

**1994, Apr. 11**

**2241** A744 60p Strip of 3, #a.-c. 3.75 3.75

Europa A745

Map of flight route and: 60p, Kodron C61, automobile. 1.80d, Kodron C61 in air over Belgrade.

**1994, May 5**

**2242** A745 60p multicolored 1.75 1.10
**2243** A745 1.80d multicolored 2.75 1.60

First night flight Paris-Belgrade-Bucharest-Istanbul, piloted by Louis Guidon, 1923.

Burning of Relics of Holy Sava, 400th Anniv. A746

**1994, May 10** ***Perf. 14***

**2244** A746 60p multicolored 1.75 1.10

1994 World Cup Soccer Championships, U.S. — A747

60p, Three players with arms raised in victory. 1d, Three players down on ground.

**1994, June 10** ***Perf. 13½***

**2245** A747 60p multicolored 1.40 1.00
**2246** A747 1d multicolored 2.40 1.60

A748

A749

**1994, July 8**

**2247** A748 60p Basset hound 1.10 .75
**2248** A748 60p Maltese 1.10 .75
**2249** A748 60p Welsh terrier 1.10 .75
**2250** A748 1d Husky 1.90 1.25
*Nos. 2247-2250 (4)* 5.20 3.50

**1994, July 20**

**2251** A749 60p multicolored 1.50 1.00

Assembly of Eastern Orthodox Christian nations.

Protecting the Ecology of Montenegro A750

**1994, July 28**

**2252** A750 50p Tcherna Gora Park 1.75 1.10

Nos. 2148, 2145 Surcharged

**1994, July 15** ***Perf. 13½***

**2253** A702j 10p on 100,000d .25 .20
**2254** A702g 50p on 10,000d 1.25 .80

A751

A752

Monasteries: 1p, Moraca, 13th cent. 5p, Gracanica, 14th cent. 10p, Ostrog. No. 2258-2259, Lazarica, 14th cent. 50p, Studenica, 12th cent. 1d, Sopocani, 13th cent.

**1994** **Litho.** ***Perf. 13½***

**2255** A751 1p bister & purple .20 .20
**2256** A751 5p yel brn & blue .20 .20
**2257** A751 10p magenta & slate .20 .20
**2258** A751 20p lil rose & pale vio .40 .25
**2259** A751 20p pale car & gray .40 .25
**2260** A751 50p deep pur & mag 1.00 .70
**2261** A751 1d blue & org brown 2.10 1.40
*Nos. 2255-2261 (7)* 4.50 3.20

UNESCO (#2260-2261).

Issued: 1p, 5p, #2258, 1d, 8/15; #2259, 9/10; 10p, 50p, 11/10.

Nos. 2262-2271 are unassigned.

For surcharge, see Serbia No. 195.

**1994, Sept. 10**

**2272** A752 50p multicolored 1.25 .80

St. Arsenius Seminary, Sremski Karlovci, bicent.

Protection of Nature A753

Designs: 1d, Fishing pier, Reka Bojana. 1.50d, Lake, Belgrade.

**1994, Sept. 20**

**2273** A753 1d multicolored 2.25 1.50
**2274** A753 1.50d multicolored 3.50 2.10

Painting by U. Knezevic — A754

Sailing Ships in Bottles — A755

**1994, Oct. 5** ***Perf. 14***

**2275** A754 1d multicolored 2.00 1.40

Joy of Europe.

**1994, Oct. 27** ***Perf. 13½***

a, Revenge, 1585. b, Grand yacht, 1678. c, Santa Maria, 15th cent. d, Nava, 15th cent. e, Mayflower, 1615. f, Carrack, 14th cent.

**2276** A755 50p Bklt. pane of 6, #a.-f. 6.00 5.50
Complete booklet, #2276 6.00

Stamp Day — A756

Drawings on Gravestones A757

**1994, Oct. 31**

**2277** A756 50p multicolored 2.00 1.40

**1994, Nov. 25**

#2278, Man holding umbrella, purse. #2279, 2 men. #2280, Cemetery, stone with man on horse, inscriptions. #2281, Fence, 2 gravestones, cross, man.

**2278** A757 50p multicolored 1.10 .75
**2279** A757 50p multicolored 1.10 .75
**2280** A757 50p multicolored 1.10 .75
**2281** A757 50p multicolored 1.10 .75
*Nos. 2278-2281 (4)* 4.40 3.00

Religious Art — A758

#2282, The Annunciation, by D. Bacevic. #2283, Adoration of the Magi, by N. Neskovic. #2284, Madonna and Child, by T.N. Cesljar. #2285, St. John Baptizing Christ, by T. Kracun.

**1994, Dec. 15**

**2282** A758 60p multicolored 1.25 .80
**2283** A758 60p multicolored 1.25 .80
**2284** A758 60p multicolored 1.25 .80
**2285** A758 60p multicolored 1.25 .80
*Nos. 2282-2285 (4)* 5.00 3.20

Natl. Symbols A759

**1995, Jan. 26** **Litho.** ***Perf. 13½***

**2286** A759 1d Flag 1.50 1.00
**2287** A759 1d Arms 1.50 1.00

Sheets of 8

World Chess Champions A760

#2288: a, Wilhelm Steinitz (1836-1900), Austria. b, Silhouettes of chessman. c, Emmanuel Lasker (1868-1941), Germany. d, Knight. e, Chessman, row of pawns at top. f, José Raúl Capablanca (1888-1942), Cuba. g, Chessman, rook at left. h, Alexander Alekhine (1892-1946), Russia.

#2289: a, Max Euwe, Netherlands. b, Board, pawn in center. c, Mikhail M. Botvinik, Soviet Union. d, Board, queen in middle. e, Board, bishop, knight. f, Vassili Smyslov, Soviet Union. g, Silhouette of knight, rook queen, chessboard. h, Mikhail N. Tal, Soviet Union.

**1995**

**2288** A760 60p #a.-h. + label 6.25 6.00
**2289** A760 60p #a.-h. + label 6.25 6.00

Issued: No. 2288, 2/28; No. 2289, 9/1.

Red Star Army Sport Club, 50th Anniv. A761

**1995, Mar. 4**

**2290** A761 60p bl, red & bister 1.75 1.10

Protection of Nature A762

a, Salamandra salamandra. b, Triturus alpestris. c, Rana graeca. d, Pelobates syriacus balcanicus.

**1995, Mar. 23**

**2291** A762 60p Strip of 4, #a.-d. + label 6.75 6.00

A763

A764

**1995, Apr. 20**

**2292** A763 60p multicolored 1.75 1.10

Radnicki Soccer Club, Belgrade, 75th anniv.

**1995, May 6**

Europa: 60p, Eagle, mountains. 1.90d, Girl on tricycle, elderly man, woman on park bench, horiz.

**2293** A764 60p multicolored 1.60 1.10
**2294** A764 1.90d multicolored 2.40 1.60

A765

A766

**1995, May 9**

**2295** A765 60p multicolored 1.50 1.00

End of World War II, 50th anniv.

**1995, May 28**

**2296** A766 60p multicolored 1.75 1.10

Opening of Vukov-Denkmal Subway Station, Belgrade.

Draba Bertiscea A767

a, shown. b, Plants, diff. c, Flowers, mountain. d, Plants on rock, stems at right.

**1995, June 12**

**2297** A767 60p Strip of 4, #a.-d. + label 4.50 4.00

European Nature Protection A768

Designs: 60p, Eremophila alpestris balcanica. 1.90d, Rhinolophus blasii.

**1995, July 10**

**2298** A768 60p multicolored 1.10 .65
**2299** A768 1.90d multicolored 3.50 2.10

Slovakian Folk Festival, by Zuzka Medvedova (1897-1985), Painter — A769

**1995, Aug. 3**

**2300** A769 60p multicolored 1.50 1.00

Volleyball, Cent. — A770

Church of St. Luke, Kotor, 800th Anniv. — A771

**1995, Sept. 10**

**2301** A770 90d multicolored 1.50 1.00

**1995, Sept. 20**

**2302** A771 80p multicolored 1.50 1.00

Motion Pictures, Cent. A772

Designs: 1.10d, Newsreel showing coronation of King Peter II. 2.20d, Auguste and Louis Jean Lumière, film projector.

**1995, Oct. 3**

**2303** A772 1.10d dk brn, lt red brn 1.25 .80
**2304** A772 2.20d dk brn, lt red brn 2.25 1.50

Army Sports Club "Partisan," 50th Anniv. — A773

**1995, Oct. 4**

**2305** A773 80p multi + label 1.50 1.00

UN, 50th Anniv. — A774

Stamp Day — A775

**1995, Oct. 24**

**2306** A774 1.10d multicolored 1.50 1.00

**1995, Oct. 31**

**2307** A775 1.10d multicolored 1.50 1.00

Joy of Europe — A776

Paintings: 1.10d, Young boy by Milos Tenkovic. 2.20d, Young girl by Pierre Bonnard.

**1995, Nov. 26**

**2308** A776 1.10d multicolored 1.25 .80
**2309** A776 2.20d multicolored 2.25 1.50

Children's Day.

Souvenir Sheet

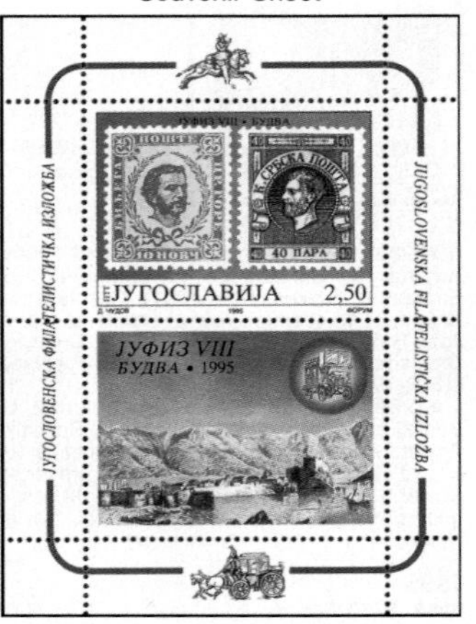

JUFIZ VIII, Natl. Philatelic Exhibition, Budva — A777

Design: Montenegro #37, Serbia #6.

**1995, Dec. 13** ***Perf. 14***

**2310** A777 2.50d Sheet of 1 + label 1.50 1.00

Christmas A778

Contemporary religious paintings: No. 2311, Flight into Egypt, by Z. Halupova. No. 2312, Nativity, by D. Milojevic, vert. No. 2313, Outdoor Christmas scene, by M. Rasic, vert. No. 2314, Indoor traditional Christmas scene, by J. Brasic.

**1995, Dec. 26** ***Perf. 13½***

**2311** A778 1.10d multicolored .60 .40
**2312** A778 1.10d multicolored .60 .40
**2313** A778 2.20d multicolored 1.10 .75
**2314** A778 2.20d multicolored 1.10 .75
*Nos. 2311-2314 (4)* 3.40 2.30

Airplanes A779

**1995, Dec. 26**

**2315** A779 1.10d Saric No. 1 .60 .40
**2316** A779 1.10d Douglas DC-3 .60 .40
**2317** A779 2.20d Fizir FN 1.10 .75
**2318** A779 2.20d Caravelle 1.10 .75
*Nos. 2315-2318 (4)* 3.40 2.30

Battle of Mojkovac, 80th Anniv. — A780

Design: Montenegrins on mountain.

**1996, Jan. 6**

**2319** A780 1.10d multicolored .45 .30

Birth of Sava Sumanovic, Cent. A781

Design: 1927 Painting, "Drink Boat."

**1996, Jan. 22**

**2320** A781 1.10d multicolored .45 .30

A782

A783

Insects: a, Pyrgomorphela serbica. b, Calosoma sycopanta. c, Formica rufa. d, Ascalaphus macaronius.

**1996, Feb. 15**

**2321** A782 2.20d Strip of 4, #a.-d. + label 2.75 2.50

Protection of nature.

**1996, Feb. 29** **Litho.** ***Perf. 12½***

Churches.

**2322** A783 5d Ljeviska 1.60 .95
**2323** A783 10d Zica 3.25 2.00
**2324** A783 20d Decani 6.50 4.00
*Nos. 2322-2324 (3)* 11.35 6.95

Chess Champions — A784

Designs: a, Tigran Petrosian, Soviet Union. b, Chess pieces, sundial, chess board. c, Boris Spassky, Soviet Union. d, Chess pieces, board, clock showing two time zones. e, Garry Kasparov, Soviet Union. f, Chess pieces, hand holding hour glass. g, Bobby Fischer, US. h, Chess pieces, six clocks. i, Anatoly Karpov, Soviet Union.

**1996, Mar. 15** **Litho.** ***Perf. 13½***

**2325** A784 1.50d Sheet of 9, #a.-i. 6.25 6.00

Olympic Games, Cent. A786

1.50d, Discus throwers. 2.50d, Runners.

***Perf. 13½x13¼***

**1996, Mar. 30** **Litho.**

**2326** A786 1.50d multi .55 .45
**2327** A786 2.50d multi 1.00 1.00

1996 Summer Olympics, Atlanta — A787

**1996, Apr. 12**

**2328** A787 1.50d shown 1.00 .75
**2329** A787 1.50d Basketball 1.00 .75
**2330** A787 1.50d Handball 1.00 .75
**2331** A787 1.50d Volleyball 1.00 .75
**2332** A787 1.50d Shooting 1.00 .75
**2333** A787 1.50d Water polo 1.00 .75
*Nos. 2328-2333 (6)* 6.00 4.50

1996 Summer Olympic Games, Atlanta — A787a

**1996, Apr. 12** **Litho.** ***Perf. 13***

**2334** A787 5d Sheet of 1 + label 2.00 1.50

Stamp Day — A788

**1996, Apr. 30** **Litho.** ***Perf. 13½***

**2335** A788 1.50d Railway mail car .65 .50

Famous Women Writers — A789

Europa: 2.50d, Isidora Sekulic (1877-1958). 5d, Desanka Maksimovic (1898-1993).

**1996, May 7** **Litho.** ***Perf. 13½***

**2336** A789 2.50d multicolored 1.10 .65
**2337** A789 5d multicolored 2.40 1.60

Serbian Red Cross, 120th Anniv. A790

**1996, May 8**

**2338** A790 1.50d Dr. Vladan Djordjevic .75 .60

Architectural Education in Yugoslavia, 150th Anniv. — A791

**1996, June 1 Litho. *Perf. 13½***

**2339** A791 1.50d multicolored .65 .50

Birds A792

**1996, June 28**

**2340** A792 2.50d Platalea leucorodia .85 .65

**2341** A792 5d Plegadis falcinellus 1.75 1.25

Prince Peter I Petrovic at Battle of Martinici, 1796 — A793

Design: 2.50d, Prince's Guard at Battle of Kruse (1796), by Valerio, vert.

**1996, July 22**

**2342** A793 1.50d multicolored .65 .50

**2343** A793 2.50d multicolored 1.00 .75

Horse Racing, Ljubicevo A794

**1996, Sept. 2 Litho. *Perf. 13½***

**2344** A794 1.50d shown .70 .55

**2345** A794 2.50d 3 horses racing 1.25 1.00

Fauna A795

Designs: a, 1.50d, Probosciger aterrimus. b, 2.50d, Goura scheepmakeri. c, 1.50d, Equus burchelli. d, 2.50d, Panthera tigris.

**1996, Sept. 25**

**2346** A795 Strip of 4, #a.-d. + label 3.75 3.50

Belgrade Zoo, 60th anniv.

Children's Day — A796

**1996, Oct. 2**

**2347** A796 1.50d multicolored .70 .55

**2348** A796 2.50d Bird 1.25 1.00

Medalists, 1996 Summer Olympic Games A797

Designs: No. 2349, Shooting, bronze. No. 2350, Shooting, gold. No. 2351, Volleyball, bronze. No. 2352, Basketball, silver.

**1996, Oct. 31 Litho. *Perf. 13½***

**2349** A797 2.50d multicolored .60 .50

**2350** A797 2.50d multicolored .60 .50

**2351** A797 2.50d multicolored .60 .50

**2352** A797 2.50d multicolored .60 .50

*Nos. 2349-2352 (4)* 2.40 2.00

Savings Accounts, 75th Anniv. — A798

**1996, Oct. 31 Litho. *Perf. 13½***

**2353** A798 1.50d multicolored .65 .55

Soccer in Yugoslavia, Cent. — A799

Archaeological Finds — A800

**1996, Nov. 8 Litho. *Perf. 13½***

**2354** A799 1.50d multicolored .60 .50

**1996, Nov. 25**

Sculptures: No. 2355, God of Autumn. No. 2356, Mother with child. No. 2357, Head of woman. No. 2358, Redheaded goddess.

**2355** A800 1.50d multicolored .60 .50

**2356** A800 1.50d multicolored .60 .50

**2357** A800 2.50d multicolored 1.00 .75

**2358** A800 2.50d multicolored 1.00 .75

*Nos. 2355-2358 (4)* 3.20 2.50

A801

A802

Christmas (Paintings): No. 2359, Annunciation. No. 2360, Mother of God with Christ. No. 2361, Birth of Christ. No. 2362, Palm Sunday.

**1996, Dec. 10**

**2359** A801 1.50d multicolored .60 .50

**2360** A801 1.50d multicolored .60 .50

**2361** A801 2.50d multicolored 1.00 .75

**2362** A801 2.50d multicolored 1.00 .75

*Nos. 2359-2362 (4)* 3.20 2.50

**1997, Jan. 24 Litho. *Perf. 13½***

**2363** A802 1.50d multicolored .35 .25

Radomir Putnik Voivode, 150th birth anniv.

25th Intl. Film Festival, Belgrade A803

**1997, Jan. 31**

**2364** A803 1.50d multicolored .35 .25

Protected Birds — A804

Designs: No. 2365, Dendrocopos major. No. 2366, Nucifraga caryocatactes. No. 2367, Parus cristatus. No. 2368, Erithacus rubecula.

**1997, Feb. 21**

**2365** A804 1.50d multicolored .35 .25

**2366** A804 2.50d multicolored .55 .40

**2367** A804 1.50d multicolored .35 .25

**2368** A804 2.50d multicolored .55 .40

*a.* Strip of 4, #2365-2368 + label 1.90 1.75

A805

A806

**1997, Mar. 17 Litho. *Perf. 13***

**2369** A805 1.50d multicolored .50 .40

St. Achilleus Church, 700th Anniv.

**1997, Apr. 3 *Perf. 13½***

Design: Prince Peter I Petrovic (1747-1830), Bishop of Montenegro.

**2370** A806 1.50d multicolored .50 .40

A807

A808

**1997, Apr. 19**

**2371** A807 2.50d multicolored .85 .70

10th Belgrade Marathon.

**1997, Apr. 22 Litho. *Perf. 13½***

**2372** A808 2.50d multicolored .90 .75

Serbian Medical Assoc., 125th anniv.

Air Mail Being Loaded at Night A809

**1997, May 3**

**2373** A809 2.50d multicolored .90 .75

Stamp Day.

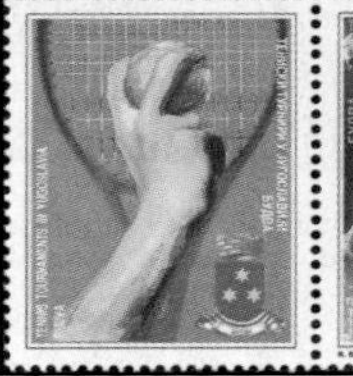

Tennis Tournaments in Yugoslavia — A810

Stylized designs: No. 2374, Player, large racket overhead, Budva. No. 2375, Player with ball flying from racket, Belgrade. No. 2376, Player with racket out in front, Novi Sad.

**1997, May 8**

**2374** A810 2.50d multi + label .90 .75

**2375** A810 2.50d multi + label .90 .75

**2376** A810 2.50d multi + label .90 .75

*Nos. 2374-2376 (3)* 2.70 2.25

Stories and Legends A811

Europa: 2.50d, Shackled Bach Chelik surrounded by creatures. 6d, Bach Chelik in chains, prince fighting with him, princess, castle.

**1997, May 30 *Perf. 11½***

**2377** A811 2.50d multicolored .90 .75

**2378** A811 6d multicolored 2.10 1.60

Each issued in sheets of 8 + label.

Nature Protection A812

**1997, June 5**

**2379** A812 2.50d Cerambyx cerdo .90 .75

**2380** A812 6d Quercus robur 2.10 1.60

Stanislav Binicki (1872-1947)
A813

Printing of Gorski Vijenac, 150th Anniv. — A814

**1997, June 7** *Perf. 13½*

**2381** A813 2.50d multicolored .90 .75

**1997, June 7**

**2382** A814 2.50d multicolored .90 .75

Flowers — A815

Designs: a, 1.50d, Pelargonium grandiflorum. b, 2.50d, Saintpaulia ionantha. c, 1.50d, Hydrangea macrophylla. d, 2.50d, Oncidium varicosum.

**1997, Sept. 10 Litho.** *Perf. 13*

**2383** A815 Strip of 4, #a.-d. + label 2.75 2.50

Souvenir Sheet

JUFIZ IX, 9th Natl. Philatelic Exhibition — A816

Design: Sculpture, by Dragomir Arambasic, in front of art gallery. Illustration reduced.

**1997, Sept. 10** *Perf. 14*

**2384** A816 5d multicolored 1.75 1.40

A817

A818

**1997, Sept. 24** *Perf. 13½x14*

**2385** A817 2.50d multicolored .85 .70

Serbian Chemical Society, cent.

Type of 1993

**1997, Oct. 2** *Perf. 14*

**Size: 18x18mm**

**2386** A702d (A) like #2142 .20 .20

Exists dated "1999."

**1997, Oct. 2**

Joy of Europe children's art works: 2.50d, 5d, Busts of people formed from collage of various food products.

**2387** A818 2.50d multicolored .85 .70
**2388** A818 5d multicolored 1.75 1.40

"May Assembly in Sremski Karlivoci," by Pavle Simic — A819

**1997, Oct. 10 Litho.** *Perf. 14*

**2389** A819 2.50d multicolored .95 .75

Matica Srpska Gallery, 150th anniv.

A820

A821

Museum exhibits: No. 2390, Two-headed statuette. No. 2391, Parade helmet. No. 2392, Terra cotta statuette. No. 2393, Virgin icon.

**1997, Nov. 12**

**2390** A820 1.50d multicolored .50 .40
**2391** A820 1.50d multicolored .50 .40
**2392** A820 2.50d multicolored .85 .65
**2393** A820 2.50d multicolored .85 .65
*Nos. 2390-2393 (4)* 2.70 2.10

**1997, Dec. 2** *Perf. 11½*

Icons (Chelandari Serbian Monastery, Mount Athos): No. 2394, Christ. No. 2395, Madonna and Child, 12th cent. No. 2396, Madonna and Child, 13th cent. No. 2397, 3-handed Madonna.

**Granite Paper**

**2394** A821 1.50d multicolored .50 .40
**2395** A821 1.50d multicolored .50 .40
**2396** A821 2.50d multicolored .85 .65
**2397** A821 2.50d multicolored .85 .65
*Nos. 2394-2397 (4)* 2.70 2.10

A822

A823

**1998, Jan. 20 Litho.** *Perf. 13½*

**2398** A822 1.50d Savina .55 .45
**2399** A822 2.50d Donji Brceli .95 .75

Monasteries of Montenegro.

**1998, Feb. 6** *Perf. 14*

**2400** A823 2.50d Figure skater .95 .75
**2401** A823 6d Skier 2.25 1.75

1998 Winter Olympic Games, Nagano.

Horses
A824

Designs: a, 1.50d, Two running. b, 2.50d, Arabian up close. c, 1.50d, Thoroughbred. d, 2.50d, Thoroughbred running on race track.

**1998, Feb. 26 Litho.** *Perf. 12x11½*

**2402** A824 Strip of 4, #a.-d. + label 3.00 2.50

Intl. Women's Day
A825

**1998, Mar. 7** *Perf. 13½*

**2403** A825 2.50d multicolored .95 .75

Yugoslav Airlines Assoc., 50th Anniv.
A826

**1998, Apr. 24**

**2404** A826 2.50d multicolored .95 .75

Europa — A827

Paintings: 6d, "Dressing the Bride," by Paja Jovanovic (1859-1957). 9d, "Bishop's Congratulations," by Pero Pocek (1878-1963).

**1998, May 4 Litho.** *Perf. 12*

**Granite Paper**

**2405** A827 6d multicolored 1.10 .90
**2406** A827 9d on 2.50d, multi 1.75 1.40

No. 2406 was not issued without the silver surcharge.

1998 World Cup Soccer Championships, France — A828

**1998, May 15 Litho.** *Perf. 13½*

**2407** A828 6d shown 1.25 1.25
**2408** A828 9d Soccer players, diff. 1.75 1.75

Souvenir Sheet

Danube Commission, 50th Anniv. — A829

Illustration reduced.

**1998, May 19** *Perf. 14*

**2409** A829 9d multicolored 1.75 1.75

Nature Protection
A830

Designs: 6d, Heracium blecicii. 9d, Mola mola, vert.

**1998, June 17 Litho.** *Perf. 13¾*

**2410** A830 6d multi — —
**2411** A830 9d multi — —

Each stamp was printed in sheets of 8 + label.

Famous People of Serbia — A831

a, Djura Jaksic (1832-78), poet, painter. b, Nadezda Petrovic (1873-1915), painter. c, Radoje Domanovic (1873-1908), writer. d, Vasilije Mokranjac (1923-1984), composer. e, Streten Stojanovic (1898-1960), sculptor. f, Milan Konjovic (1898-1993), painter. g, Desanka Maksimovic (1898-1993), poet. h, Ivan Tabakovic (1898-1977), painter.

**1998, June 30 Litho.** *Perf. 12*

**Granite Paper**

**Sheet of 8**

**2412** A831 1.50d #a.-h. + label 2.25 2.25

Souvenir Sheet

Yugoslavia, Winner of World Basketball Championships — A832

**1998, Aug. 21** *Perf. 13½*
**2413** A832 10d multicolored 2.00 2.00

Protected Animals — A833

a, 2d, Martes martes. b, 2d, Anthropoides virgo. c, 5d, Lynx lynx. d, 5d, Loxia curvirostra.

**1998, Sept. 2**
**2414** A833 Strip of 4, #a.-d. + label 2.75 2.75

Breaking of the Thessaloniki Front, 80th Anniv. A834

Designs: No. 2415, 5d, Soldiers and cannons. No. 2416, 5d, Soldiers with machine guns, binoculars.

**1998, Sept. 15** **Engr.** *Perf. 13½*
**2415-2416** A834 Set of 2 2.00 2.00

Stamp Day — A835

**1998, Sept. 28**
**2417** A835 6d Prussian blue 1.25 1.25

Serbian Philatelic Society, 50th anniv.

Joy of Europe Children's Drawings A836

Designs: 6d, Fish. 9d, Fish, diff.

**1998, Oct. 2** **Litho.** *Perf. 13¾*
**2418-2419** A836 Set of 2 3.25 3.25

Development of the Railway — A837

Trains: a, 1847. b, 1900. c, 1920. d, 1930. e, Diesel locomotive. f, 1990.

**1998, Nov. 3** **Litho.** *Perf. 13½*
**2420** A837 2.50d Booklet pane of 6, #a.-f. 3.00 3.00
Complete booklet, #2420 3.25

Paintings of Sailing Ships, Maritime Museum, Kotor A838

#2421, Veracruz, 1873. #2422, Pierino, 1883. #2423, Draghetto, 1865. #2424, Group of ships.

**1998, Nov. 11** *Perf. 12*
**Granite Paper**
**2421** A838 2d multicolored .40 .30
**2422** A838 2d multicolored .40 .30
**2423** A838 5d multicolored 1.00 .80
**2424** A838 5d multicolored 1.00 .80
*Nos. 2421-2424 (4)* 2.80 2.20

Chelandari Monastery, 800th Anniv. — A839

Views of monastery: No. 2425, Looking from center of complex, two trees. No. 2426, Group of taller buildings. No. 2427, Aerial view. No. 2428, Looking across group of buildings, crosses on turrets.

**1998, Dec. 9** *Perf. 14*
**2425** A839 2d multicolored .40 .30
**2426** A839 2d multicolored .40 .30
**2427** A839 5d multicolored 1.00 .80
**2428** A839 5d multicolored 1.00 .80
*Nos. 2425-2428 (4)* 2.80 2.20

Third Meeting of Southeast European Postal Ministers A840

**1998, Dec. 17** **Litho.** *Perf. 14*
**2429** A840 5d multicolored 1.00 .80

Souvenir Sheet

Yugoslavia, Silver Medalists at 1998 World Volleyball Championships — A841

Illustration reduced.

**1998, Dec. 19** *Perf. 13½*
**2430** A841 10d multicolored 2.00 1.60

Post and Telecommunications Museum, Belgrade, 75th Anniv. — A842

#2431, Postrider. #No. 2432, Antique telegraph equipment, museum building.

**1998, Dec. 21** **Engr.**
**2431** A842 5d olive brown & slate 1.00 .80
**2432** A842 5d red & brown 1.00 .80

Serbian Monasteries A843

**1999, Jan. 14** **Litho.** *Perf. 13¾*
**2433** A843 2d Visoki Decani .40 .30
**2434** A843 5d Grachanica 1.00 .80

Farm Animals A844

Designs: a, 2d, Pigs. b, 6d, Goat. c, 2d, Oxen. d, 6d, Long-horn sheep.

**1999, Feb. 5** **Litho.** *Perf. 13½*
**2435** A844 Strip of 4, #a.-d. + label 3.25 3.00

A845

A846

**1999, Feb. 24** **Litho.** *Perf. 13¼*
**2436** A845 6d Scouting 1.10 .90

**1999, Mar.**
**2437** A846 6d brown & buff 1.10 .90

Yugoslav Bar Association, 70th anniv.

Target
A847 A848

**1999** *Perf. 12¼x12½*
**2438** A847 (A) black .40 .30
**2439** A848 (A) black & red .40 .30

Nos. 2438-2439 sold for 2.04d when issued.

World Table Tennis Championships, Belgrade — A849

**1999, Apr.** *Perf. 13¼*
**Player colors**
**2440** A849 6d blue & red 1.10 .90
**2441** A849 6d green & red 1.10 .90

A850

A851

Europa, National Parks and Reserves: 6d, Falcon, trees, mountains, Kopaonik Natl. Park. 15d, Flowers, mountains, Lovcen Natl. Park.

**1999, May 5** **Photo.** *Perf. 11¾*
**Granite Paper**
**2442** A850 6d multicolored 3.00 2.00
**2443** A850 15d multicolored 5.00 3.50

Each printed in shhets of 8 + 1 central label.

**1999, May** *Perf. 11¾x12*

Nature protection.

**2444** A851 6d Shovel, spider web 1.10 .90
**2445** A851 15d Thumb squeezing earth 2.75 2.00

Mushrooms A852

Designs: a, Amanita virosa. b, Amanita pantherina. c, Hypholoma fasciculare. d, Ramaria pallida.

**1999, June 18 Litho. *Perf. 11¾x12***
**Granite Paper**

**2446** A852 6d Strip of 4, #a.-d., + central label 5.00 4.50

Central labels differ on sheet.

Famous Montenegrins — A853

Designs: a, Stjepan Mitrov Ljubisa (1824-78). b, Marko Milanov (1833-1901). c, Pero Pocek (1878-1963). d, Risto Stijovic (1894-1974). e, Milo Milunovic (1897-1967). f, Petar Lubarda (1907-74). g, Vuko Radovic (1911-96). h, Mihailo Lalic (1914-92).

**1999, June 30 *Perf. 13¼***

**2447** A853 2d Sheet of 8, #a.-h., + central label 2.75 2.50

UPU, 125th Anniv. A854

**1999, Sept. 15 *Perf. 13¼***

| | | | | |
|---|---|---|---|---|
| **2448** | A854 | 6d shown | 1.00 | .80 |
| **2449** | A854 | 12d Envelopes circling globe | 2.00 | 1.60 |

Joy of Europe Children's Drawings A855

**1999, Oct. 1 *Perf. 13¾***

| | | | | |
|---|---|---|---|---|
| **2450** | A855 | 6d Lion | 1.10 | .90 |
| **2451** | A855 | 15d Family, vert. | 2.75 | 2.00 |

Frédéric Chopin (1810-49), Composer A856

**1999, Oct. 15 *Perf. 13¼***

**2452** A856 10d multi 1.75 1.40

No. 2438, Mastheads of "Filatelista" A857

**1999, Oct. 18**

**2453** A857 10d multi 1.75 1.40

Stamp Day.

A858

Bridges Destroyed by NATO Air Strikes A859

Bridges: #2454, Varadinski. #2455, Ostruznica. #2456, Murino. #2457, Grdelica. #2458, Bistrica. #2459, Zezeljev.

**1999, Oct. 29 *Perf. 13¾***

| | | | | |
|---|---|---|---|---|
| **2454** | A858 | 2d shown | .30 | .25 |
| **2455** | A859 | 2d shown | .30 | .25 |
| **2456** | A859 | 2d multi | .30 | .25 |
| **2457** | A859 | 6d multi | 1.00 | .75 |
| **2458** | A859 | 6d multi | 1.00 | .75 |
| **2459** | A859 | 6d multi | 1.00 | .75 |
| | | *Nos. 2454-2459 (6)* | 3.90 | 3.00 |

Millennium A860

a, 6d, Roman altars, statue of Jupiter. b, 6d, Sculpture of Emperor Trajan and army leaders, mosaic, lamp, lead mirror. c, 6d, Mosaic of Dionysius, arch. d, 6d, Hagia Sophia, mosaic of Madonna and Child, Emperor Constantine. e, 6d, Large cross, candle, fibula, pot. f, 6d, Church, boats, manuscript. g, 15d, Nativity and crucifixion of Christ, boats, farmers.

**1999, Nov. 19**

**2460** A860 Booklet pane of 7, #a.-g., + 2 labels 9.00 8.00
Complete booklet, #2460 9.00

Size of #2460g: 105x55mm.

A861

Bomb Damage A862

#2461, Bolnice. #2462, Telecommunications complex. #2463, Refinery. #2464, Bolnice, diff. #2465, Telecommunications complex, diff. #2466, Television complex.

**1999, Nov. 27 Litho. *Perf. 13¾***

| | | | | |
|---|---|---|---|---|
| **2461** | A861 | 2d shown | .30 | .25 |
| **2462** | A862 | 2d shown | .30 | .25 |
| **2463** | A862 | 2d multi | .30 | .25 |
| **2464** | A862 | 6d multi | 1.00 | .75 |
| **2465** | A862 | 6d multi | 1.00 | .75 |
| **2466** | A862 | 6d multi | 1.00 | .75 |
| | | *Nos. 2461-2466 (6)* | 3.90 | 3.00 |

A863

Frescoes of Poganovo Monastery, 500th Anniv. — A864

Design A863 has Latin letters, A864 has Cyrillic letters.

**1999, Dec. 23**

| | | | | |
|---|---|---|---|---|
| **2467** | A863 | 6d shown | 1.00 | .75 |
| **2468** | A864 | 6d shown | 1.00 | .75 |
| **2469** | A863 | 6d Fresco, diff. | 1.00 | .75 |
| **2470** | A864 | 6d Fresco, diff. | 1.00 | .75 |
| | | *Nos. 2467-2470 (4)* | 4.00 | 3.00 |

A865

Gold Prospectors in Pec River — A866

Design A865 has Latin letters, A866 has Cyrillic letters.

**1999, Dec. 30**

| | | | | |
|---|---|---|---|---|
| **2471** | A865 | 6d shown | 1.00 | .75 |
| **2472** | A866 | 6d shown | 1.00 | .75 |
| **2473** | A865 | 6d Prospectors, diff. | 1.00 | .75 |
| **2474** | A866 | 6d Prospectors, diff. | 1.00 | .75 |
| | | *Nos. 2471-2474 (4)* | 4.00 | 3.00 |

Krusedol Monastery A867

**2000, Jan. 13 *Perf. 13¼***

| | | | | |
|---|---|---|---|---|
| **2475** | A867 | 10d shown | 1.75 | 1.40 |
| **2476** | A867 | 10d Rakovac Monastery | 1.75 | 1.40 |

Yugoslavian Archives, 50th Anniv. A868

**2000, Jan. 21**

**2477** A868 10d multi 15.00 15.00

Butterflies — A869

No. 2478: a, Nymphalis antiopa. b, Parnalius polyxena. c, Limenitis populi. d, Melanargia galathea.

**2000, Feb. 25 Litho. *Perf. 13¾***

**2478** Horiz. strip of 4 + central label 8.50 8.50
***a.-d.*** A869 10d Any single 2.00 2.00

Worldwide Fund for Nature A870

Perdix perdix: a, Pair in snow. b, Pair facing right. c, Bird on nest. d, Pair, one facing left.

**2000, Mar. 14 Litho. *Perf. 12x11¾***

**2479** A870 10d Strip of 4, #a.-d., + central label 8.00 8.00

Damage from NATO Airstrikes A871

Various destroyed buildings. Colors: 10d, Blue. 20d, Brown.

**2000, Mar. 24 Engr. *Perf. 13¼***

**2480-2481** A871 Set of 2 4.00 3.00

Souvenir Sheet

JUFIZ X Philatelic Exhibition, Belgrade — A872

Illustration reduced.

**2000, May 2 Litho.**

**2482** A872 15d multi 40.00 40.00

Nature Protection A873

Designs: No. 2483, 30d, Feeding chicks by hand. No. 2484, 30d, Map of Europe in tree's leaves, vert.

***Perf. 12x11¾, 11¾x12***

**2000, May 4 Litho.**

**2483-2484** A873 Set of 2 9.00 7.50

Europa — A874

"2000" and: No. 2485, 30d, Astronaut on moon. No. 2486, 30d, Star and mountains.

**2000, May 9** ***Perf. 11¾x12***
**2485-2486** A874 Set of 2 9.00 7.50

European Soccer Championships A875

Inscriptions in: No. 2487, 30d, Cyrillic letters. No. 2488, 30d, Latin letters.

**2000, May 20 Litho.** ***Perf. 13¾***
**2487-2488** A875 Set of 2 9.00 7.50

Postal Services in Serbia, 160th Anniv. — A876

**2000, June 7 Litho.** ***Perf. 13¾***
**2489** A876 10d multi 1.60 1.25

2000 Summer Olympics, Sydney — A877

Map of Australia and: 6d, Kangaroo. 12d, Emu. 24d, Koala and soccer ball. 30d, Parrot.

**2000, June 28**
**2490-2493** A877 Set of 4 12.00 9.00

Stamp Day — A878

**2000, Sept. 26** ***Perf. 13¼***
**2494** A878 10d multi 1.60 1.25

"Joy of Europe" A879

Children's art: 30d, Cows. 40d, Cranes, vert.

**2000, Oct. 2**
**2495-2496** A879 Set of 2 12.00 9.00

World Teachers' Day — A880

**2000, Oct. 5**
**2497** A880 10d multi 1.60 1.25

13th Apiarists Congress A881

**2000, Oct. 6**
**2498** A881 10d multi 1.60 1.25

Medals Won at 2000 Summer Olympics A882

Designs: No. 2499, 20d, Water polo (bronze). No. 2500, 20d, Shooting (silver). 30d, Volleyball, vert.

**2000, Oct. 23** ***Perf. 13¾***
**2499-2500** A882 Set of 2 6.75 5.00

**Souvenir Sheet**

**2501** A882 30d multi 10.00 10.00

No. 2501 contains one 35x46mm stamp.

Millennium A883

No. 2502: a, Ships. b, Papermaking. c, Galileo and telescopes. d, Steam locomotive and steamship. e, Nikola Tesla, invention of the telephone. f, Astronaut, outer space settlement. g, Ships, airplanes, balloons, horses.

**2000, Nov. 2 Litho.** ***Perf. 13¾***

| | | | |
|---|---|---|---|
| **2502** | Booklet pane of 7 + 2 labels | 3.50 | — |
| *a.-f.* | A883 12d Any single | .35 | .35 |
| *g.* | A883 40d multi | 1.25 | 1.25 |
| | Booklet, #2502 | 3.50 | |

Size of No. 2502g: 105x55mm.

Nativity Fresco, Pec — A884

**2000, Nov. 7 Litho.** ***Perf. 13¾***
**2503** A884 A multi .60 .30

No. 2503 sold for 3.56d on day of issue.

Serb Clothing From the 1900s — A885

Designs: 6d, Vest, Jagodina. 12d, Dresses, Metochija. 24d, Blouse, Pec. 30d, Vest, Kupres.

**2000, Dec. 7**
**2504-2507** A885 Set of 4 12.00 9.00

Montenegrin Religious Art — A886

Designs: 6d, Madonna and Child, 1573-74. 12d, Nativity, 1666-67. 24d, St. Luke, 1672-73. 30d, Madonna and Child, 1642.

**2000, Dec. 19**
**2508-2511** A886 Set of 4 12.00 9.00

A887

A887a

**2000, Dec. 29 Litho.** ***Perf. 13¾***
**2512** A887 6d multi 1.00 .75
**2513** A887a 12d multi 2.10 1.10

Resumption of Yugoslavia's membership in Organization for Security and Cooperation in Europe (#2512), and United Nations (#2513).

Vatoped Monastery, Mount Athos, Greece A888

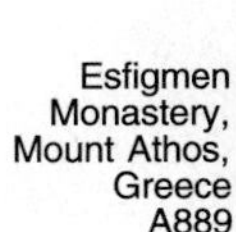
Esfigmen Monastery, Mount Athos, Greece A889

**2001, Jan. 26 Litho.** ***Perf. 13¼***
**2514** A888 10d multi .30 .30
**2515** A889 27d multi .85 .85

Matica Srpska, 175th Anniv. — A890

**2001, Feb. 16** ***Perf. 13¾***
**2516** A890 15d multi .45 .45

Animals — A891

No. 2517: a, Felis leo. b, Ursus maritimus. c, Macaca fuscata. d, Spheniscus humboldti.

**2001, Feb. 23**

| | | | |
|---|---|---|---|
| **2517** | Horiz. strip of 4 + central label | 2.25 | 2.25 |
| *a.* | A891 6d multi | .20 | .20 |
| *b.* | A891 12d multi | .35 | .35 |
| *c.* | A891 24d multi | .75 | .75 |
| *d.* | A891 30d multi | .95 | .95 |

Women's World Chess Champions — A892

No. 2518: a, Vera Menchik (1927-44). b, Lyudmila Rudenko (1950-53). c, Yelisavyeta Bykova (1953-56, 1958-62). d, Olga Rubtsova (1956-58). e, Nona Gaprindashvili (1962-78). f, Maia Chiburdanidze (1978-91). g, Zsuzsa Polgar (1996-99). h, Xie Jun (1991-96, 1999-2000).

**2001, Mar. 8** ***Perf. 13¼***
**2518** A892 10d Sheet of 8, #a-h, + label 2.50 2.50

Famous Men — A893

Designs: 50d, Stevan Mokranjac (1856-1914), composer. 100d, Nikola Tesla (1856-1943), inventor.

**2001, Mar. 19** ***Perf. 13¾***
**2519-2520** A893 Set of 2 4.75 4.75

Flowers A894

No. 2521: a, Hibiscus syriacus. b, Nerium oleander. c, Lapageria rosea. d, Sorbus aucuparia.

**2001, Apr. 13** ***Perf. 12x11¾***

| | | | |
|---|---|---|---|
| **2521** | Horiz. strip of 4 + central label | 2.25 | 2.25 |
| *a.* | A894 6d multi | .20 | .20 |
| *b.* | A894 12d multi | .40 | .40 |
| *c.* | A894 24d multi | .75 | .75 |
| *d.* | A894 30d multi | .90 | .90 |

Europa — A895

Designs: 30d, Vratna River. 45d, Jerme Canyon.

**2001, May 4** ***Perf. 11¾x12***
**2522-2523** A895 Set of 2 2.25 2.25

Serbian Mountaineering Association, Cent. — A896

**2001, June 8** ***Perf. 13¼***

**2524** A896 15d multi .45 .45

Nature Protection A897

Designs: 30d, Bird on branch, Lake Ludasko. 45d, Stork flying above Begej River.

**2001, June 22** ***Perf. 12x11¾***

**2525-2526** A897 Set of 2 2.25 2.25

14th Cent. Book Illumination A898

**2001, July 2** ***Perf. 13¼***

**2527** A898 E multi .85 .85

Sold for 28.70d on day of issue.

Souvenir Sheet

Yugoslavian Victory in European Water Polo Championships — A899

**2001, July 5** ***Perf. 13¾***

**2528** A899 30d multi .85 .85

Souvenir Sheet

Serbiafila XII Stamp Exhibition — A900

**2001, Sept. 8**

**2529** A900 30d multi .90 .90

Solar Energy — A901

**2001, Sept. 19** ***Perf. 13¼***

**2530** A901 15d multi .45 .45

Danube Commission A902

Designs: 30d, Ships, hands raising bridge. 45d, Ship, hand, clock.

**2001, Sept. 20** ***Perf. 13¾***

**2531-2532** A902 Set of 2 2.25 2.25

Joy of Europe — A903

Paintings: 30d, Child, by Marko Chelebonovic. 45d, Girl Under a Fruit Tree, by Beta Vukanovic.

**2001, Oct. 2** ***Perf. 13¼***

**2533-2534** A903 Set of 2 2.25 2.25

Yugoslavian Victories in European Sports Championships A904

Designs: No. 2535, 30d, Men's basketball. No. 2536, 30d, Men's volleyball.

**2001, Oct. 1**

**2535-2536** A904 Set of 2 1.90 1.90

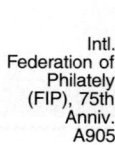

Intl. Federation of Philately (FIP), 75th Anniv. A905

**2001, Oct. 24**

**2537** A905 15d multi .45 .45

Stamp Day.

Minerals A906

**2001, Nov. 2** ***Perf. 13¾***

**2538** Horiz. strip of 4 + central label 2.25 2.25

- ***a.*** A906 7d Antimonite .20 .20
- ***b.*** A906 14d Calcite .40 .40
- ***c.*** A906 26.20d Quartz .80 .80
- ***d.*** A906 28.70d Calcite and galenite .85 .85

Pljevlja Gymnasium, Cent. — A907

**2001, Nov. 18** ***Perf. 13¼***

**2539** A907 15d multi .45 .45

Public Telephone Booths in Serbia, Cent. — A908

**2001, Nov. 20**

**2540** A908 15d multi .45 .45

Christmas A910

Paintings of the Birth of Jesus Christ: 7d, 14d, 26.20d, 28.70d.

**2001, Dec. 1** ***Perf. 13¾***

**2541-2544** A910 Set of 4 2.25 2.25

Junior World Ice Hockey Championships, Belgrade — A911

**2002, Jan. 5** ***Perf. 13¼***

**2545** A911 14d multi .45 .45

2002 Winter Olympics, Salt Lake City — A912

Designs: 28.70d, Skier. 50d, Four-man bobsled, vert.

**2002, Jan. 25** ***Perf. 13¼***

**2546-2547** A912 Set of 2 2.40 2.40

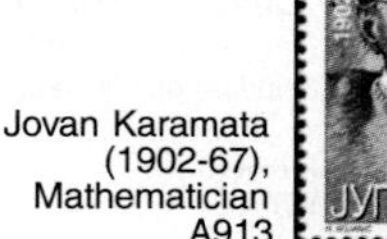

Jovan Karamata (1902-67), Mathematician A913

**2002, Feb. 1**

**2548** A913 14d multi .45 .45

Birds — A914

No. 2549: a, Saxicola torquata. b, Saxicola rubetra. c, Parus caeruleus. d, Turdus philomelos.

**2002, Feb. 22**

**2549** Horiz. strip of 4 + central label 2.25 2.25

- ***a.*** A914 7d multi .20 .20
- ***b.*** A914 14d multi .40 .40
- ***c.*** A914 26.20d multi .80 .80
- ***d.*** A914 28.70d multi .85 .85

Easter — A915

Designs: 7d, Crucifixion, fresco from Studenica Monastery, 1208. 14d, King Milutin's Veil, 1300. 26.20d, Christ's Descent to Hell, silverwork, 1540. 28.70d, Easter egg, Pec Patriarchy, 1980.

**2002, Mar. 7** ***Perf. 13¾***

**2550-2553** A915 Set of 4 2.25 2.25

Bunjevac Women's Clothing — A916

Woman with: 7d, White blouse. 28.70d, Kerchief.

**2002, Mar. 29** ***Perf. 13¼***

**2554-2555** A916 Set of 2 1.00 1.00

Zarko Tomic-Sremac (b. 1900), World War II Hero — A917

**2002, Apr. 15**

**2556** A917 14d multi .45 .45

Danube Fish — A918

No. 2557: a, Rutilus rutilus. b, Acipenser ruthenus. c, Huso huso. d, Stizostedion lucioperca.

**2002, Apr. 25** **Litho.** ***Perf. 13¼***

**2557** Horiz. strip of 4 + central label 2.25 2.25

- ***a.*** A918 7d multi .20 .20
- ***b.*** A918 14d multi .40 .40
- ***c.*** A918 26.20d multi .80 .80
- ***d.*** A918 28.70d multi .85 .85

Europa
A919

Designs: 28.70d, Trapeze artists. 50d, Tiger trainer.

| **2002, May 3** | | *Perf. 13¾* |
|---|---|---|
| **2558-2559** A919 | Set of 2 | 2.40 2.40 |

**Europa Type of 2002**
Souvenir Sheet

Design: 45d, Trained horse act.

| **2002, May 3** | **Litho.** | *Perf. 13¾* |
|---|---|---|
| **2560** A919 45d multi | | 1.40 1.40 |

No. 2560 contains one 46x35mm stamp.

Civil Aviation in Yugoslavia, 75th Anniv. A920

Designs: 7d, Potez-29. 28.70d, Boeing 737-300.

***Perf. 13¼ Syncopated***

| **2002, June 17** | | **Litho.** |
|---|---|---|
| **2561-2562** A920 | Set of 2 | 1.25 1.25 |

**Types of 1993 and 2001**

**2002, July 25 Litho. *Perf. 12½***
**Size: 19x21mm (#2563)**

| | |
|---|---|
| **2563** A702d A blue | .25 .25 |

***Perf. 13¼***
**"E" in Green**

| | |
|---|---|
| **2564** A898 E multi | 1.00 1.00 |

Nos. 2563-2564 were intended for use in Montenegro and were sold there for 13c and 52c in euro currency respectively. The stamps were valid for use in the Serbian section of Yugoslavia.

European Nature Protection A921

Designs: 28.70d, Tara National Park. 50d, Golija Nature Park.

***Perf. 13¼ Syncopated***

| **2002, June 28** | | **Litho.** |
|---|---|---|
| **2565-2566** A921 | Set of 2 | 2.60 2.60 |

Mills — A922

Designs: 7d, Windmill, Melenci. 28.70d, Water mill, Lyuberada.

| **2002, Sept. 14** | | |
|---|---|---|
| **2567-2568** A922 | Set of 2 | 1.25 1.25 |

Liberation of Niskic, 125th Anniv. — A923

| **2002, Sept. 18** | *Perf. 13¾* |
|---|---|
| **2569** A923 14d multi | .45 .45 |

Souvenir Sheet

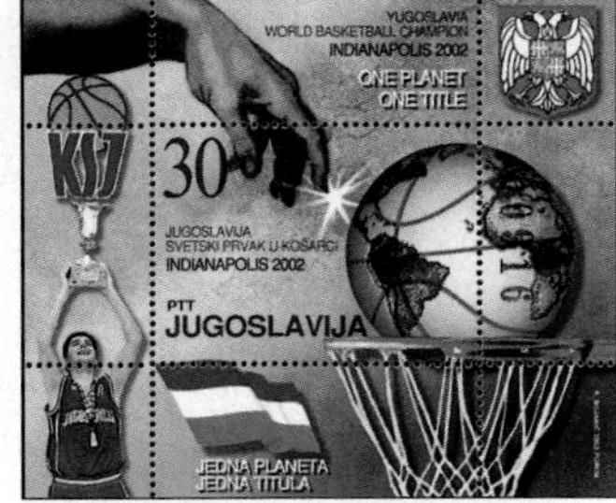

Victory in 2002 World Basketball Championships — A924

| **2002, Sept. 20** | |
|---|---|
| **2570** A924 30d multi | 1.00 1.00 |

Souvenir Sheet

JUFIZ XI Philatelic Exhibition — A925

| **2002, Sept. 23** | |
|---|---|
| **2571** A925 30d multi | 1.00 1.00 |

Joy of Europe — A926

Children's art: 28.70d, Boat. 50d, Bird.

| **2002, Oct. 2** | | |
|---|---|---|
| **2572-2573** A926 | Set of 2 | 2.60 2.60 |

Moraca Monastery, 750th Anniv. — A927

| **2002, Oct. 10** | |
|---|---|
| **2574** A927 16d multi | .55 .55 |

**Types of Nos. 2255 and 2256 Surcharged in Black or Violet**

| **2002** | | | *Perfs, etc., as Before* |
|---|---|---|---|
| **2575** A751 | 50p on 5p #2256 multi | | .20 .20 |
| **2576** A702g | 10d on 10,000d #2145 | | .35 .35 |
| **2577** A751 | 12d on 1p #2255 multi (V) | | .40 .40 |
| | *Nos. 2575-2577 (3)* | | .95 .95 |

Issued: No. 2575, 10/17; No. 2576, 11/28; No. 2577, 12/19.

For stamp like No. 2577, but with black surcharge, see Serbia and Montenegro No. 260.

Intl. Federation of Stamp Dealers Associations, 50th Anniv. — A928

| **2002, Oct. 24** | **Litho.** | *Perf. 13¾* |
|---|---|---|
| **2578** A928 16d multi | | .55 .55 |

Serbian Folk Costumes — A929

Paintings of costumes by Olga Benson in Ethnographic Institute of Serbian Academy of Sciences and Arts: a, Man, Kusadak. b, Woman with red headdress, Belgrade. c, Man, Novo Selo. d, Woman in profile, Belgrade.

| **2002, Nov. 8** | *Perf. 13¾* |
|---|---|
| **2579** Horiz. strip of 4, + central label | 3.25 3.25 |
| *a.* A929 16d multi | .55 .55 |
| *b.* A929 24d multi | .80 .80 |
| *c.* A929 26.20d multi | .90 .90 |
| *d.* A929 28.70d multi | .95 .95 |

Christmas A930

Religious art: 12d, Nativity, Stavronikita Monastery, Mount Athos, Greece, 1546. 16d, Nativity, Chilandari Monastery, Mount Athos, Greece, c. 1618. 26.20d, Nativity, Tretyakov Gallery, Moscow, 15th cent. 28.70d, Adoration of the Magi, by Sandro Botticelli.

| **2002, Dec. 2** | | |
|---|---|---|
| **2580-2583** A930 | Set of 4 | 2.75 2.75 |

Abandoned Dogs — A931

Various dogs.

| **2003, Jan. 31** | *Perf. 13¾* |
|---|---|
| **2584** Horiz. strip of 4, + central label | 3.25 3.25 |
| *a.* A931 16d multi | .55 .55 |
| *b.* A931 24d multi | .80 .80 |
| *c.* A931 26.20d multi | .90 .90 |
| *d.* A931 28.70d multi | .95 .95 |

Yugoslavia became Serbia & Montenegro on Feb. 4, 2003. See Serbia & Montenegro for subsequent issues.

## SEMI-POSTAL STAMPS

Giving Succor to Wounded SP1

Wounded Soldier SP2

Symbolical of National Unity — SP3

**Unwmk.**

| **1921, Jan. 30** | **Engr.** | *Perf. 12* |
|---|---|---|
| **B1** SP1 10p carmine | | .20 .20 |
| **B2** SP2 15p violet brown | | .20 .20 |
| **B3** SP3 25p light blue | | .20 .20 |
| *Nos. B1-B3 (3)* | | .60 .60 |

Nos. B1-B3 were sold at double face value, the excess being for the benefit of invalid soldiers.

For surcharges see Nos. 15-21.

This overprint was applied to 500,000 copies of No. B1 in 1923 and they were given to the Society for Wounded Invalids (Uprava Ratnih Invalida) which sold them for 2d apiece. These overprinted stamps had no franking power, but some were used through ignorance.

Regular Issue of 1926-27 Surcharged in Dark Red

| **1926, Nov. 1** | | *Perf. 13* |
|---|---|---|
| **B5** A6 25p + 25p green | | .20 .20 |
| **B6** A6 50p + 50p olive brn | | .20 .20 |
| **B7** A6 1d + 50p scarlet | | .20 .20 |
| **B8** A6 2d + 50p black | | .60 .20 |
| **B9** A6 3d + 50p slate blue | | .50 .20 |
| **B10** A6 4d + 50p red org | | 1.40 .20 |
| **B11** A6 5d + 50p brt vio | | .75 .20 |
| **B12** A6 8d + 50p black brn | | 1.90 .60 |
| **B13** A6 10d + 1d olive brn | | 1.75 .60 |
| **B14** A6 15d + 1d brown | | 5.00 1.00 |
| **B15** A6 20d + 1d dark vio | | 4.50 .75 |
| **B16** A6 30d + 1d orange | | 15.00 1.90 |
| *a.* Double surcharge | | |
| *Nos. B5-B16 (12)* | | 32.00 6.25 |

The surtax on these stamps was intended for a fund for relief of sufferers from floods.

For overprints see Nos. 99-101.

Cathedral at Duvno SP4

King Tomislav SP6

Kings Tomislav and Alexander SP5

***Perf. 12½, 11½x12***

**1929, Nov. 1** **Typo.**

| | | | | |
|---|---|---|---|---|
| **B17** | SP4 | 50p (+ 50p) olive green | .20 | .20 |
| **B18** | SP5 | 1d (+ 50p) red | .20 | .20 |
| **B19** | SP6 | 3d (+ 1d) blue | 1.25 | 1.10 |
| | | *Nos. B17-B19 (3)* | 1.65 | 1.50 |

Millenary of the Croatian kingdom. The surtax was used to create a War Memorial Cemetery in France and to erect a monument to Serbian soldiers who died there.

View of Dobropolje SP7

War Memorial — SP8

View of Kajmaktchalan SP9

**1931, Apr. 1** ***Perf. 12½, 11½***

| | | | | |
|---|---|---|---|---|
| **B20** | SP7 | 50p + 50p blue grn | .20 | .20 |
| **B21** | SP8 | 1d + 1d scarlet | .20 | .20 |
| **B22** | SP9 | 3d + 3d deep blue | .20 | .20 |
| | | *Nos. B20-B22 (3)* | .60 | .60 |

The surtax was added to a fund for a War Memorial to Serbian soldiers who died in France during World War I.

SP10

SP12

SP11

Black Overprint

**1931, Nov. 1** ***Perf. 12½, 11½x12***

| | | | | |
|---|---|---|---|---|
| **B23** | SP10 | 50p (+ 50p) olive grn | .20 | *.20* |
| **B24** | SP11 | 1d (+ 50p) red | .20 | *.20* |
| **B25** | SP12 | 3d (+ 1d) blue | .20 | *.20* |
| | | *Nos. B23-B25 (3)* | .60 | *.60* |

Surtax for War Memorial fund.

Rower on Danube at Smederevo SP13

Bled Lake SP14

Danube near Belgrade SP15

View of Split Harbor SP16

Zagreb Cathedral — SP17

Prince Peter — SP18

**1932, Sept. 2** **Litho.** ***Perf. 11½***

| | | | | |
|---|---|---|---|---|
| **B26** | SP13 | 75p + 50p dl grn & lt blue | .40 | 1.00 |
| **B27** | SP14 | 1d + ½d scar & lt blue | .40 | 1.10 |
| **B28** | SP15 | 1½d + ½d rose & green | .40 | 1.10 |
| **B29** | SP16 | 3d + 1d bl & lt bl | .80 | 2.00 |
| **B30** | SP17 | 4d + 1d red org & lt blue | 4.00 | 10.00 |
| **B31** | SP18 | 5d + 1d dl vio & lilac | 4.00 | 8.50 |
| | | *Nos. B26-B31 (6)* | 10.00 | 23.70 |

European Rowing Championship Races, Belgrade.

King Alexander SP19

Prince Peter SP20

**1933, May 25** **Typo.** ***Perf. 12½***

| | | | | |
|---|---|---|---|---|
| **B32** | SP19 | 50p + 25p black | 3.50 | 5.25 |
| **B33** | SP19 | 75p + 25p yel grn | 3.50 | 5.25 |
| **B34** | SP19 | 1.50d + 50p rose | 3.50 | 5.25 |
| **B35** | SP19 | 3d + 1d bl vio | 3.50 | 5.25 |
| **B36** | SP19 | 4p + 1d dk grn | 3.50 | 5.25 |
| **B37** | SP19 | 5d + 1d orange | 3.50 | 5.25 |
| | | *Nos. B32-B37 (6)* | 21.00 | 31.50 |

11th Intl. Congress of P.E.N. (Poets, Editors and Novelists) Clubs, Dubrovnik, May 25-27.

The labels at the foot of the stamps are printed in either Cyrillic or Latin letters and each bears the amount of a premium for the benefit of the local P.E.N. Club at Dubrovnik.

**1933, June 28**

| | | | | |
|---|---|---|---|---|
| **B38** | SP20 | 75p + 25p slate grn | .20 | .25 |
| **B39** | SP20 | 1½d + ½d deep red | .20 | .25 |

60th anniv. meeting of the National Sokols (Sports Associations) at Ljubljana, July 1.

Eagle Soaring over City SP22

Athlete and Eagle SP23

**1934, June 1** ***Perf. 12½***

| | | | | |
|---|---|---|---|---|
| **B40** | SP22 | 75p + 25p green | 1.75 | 1.10 |
| **B41** | SP22 | 1.50d + 50p car | 3.50 | 1.60 |
| **B42** | SP22 | 1.75d + 25p brown | 5.50 | 2.25 |
| | | *Nos. B40-B42 (3)* | 10.75 | 4.95 |

20th anniversary of Sokols of Sarajevo.

**1934, June 1**

| | | | | |
|---|---|---|---|---|
| **B43** | SP23 | 75p + 25p Prus grn | 1.60 | .90 |
| **B44** | SP23 | 1.50d + 50p car | 3.50 | 1.75 |
| **B45** | SP23 | 1.75d + 25p choc | 5.50 | 2.50 |
| | | *Nos. B43-B45 (3)* | 10.60 | 5.15 |

60th anniversary of Sokols of Zagreb.

Mother and Children SP24 SP25

***Perf. 12½x11½***

**1935, Dec. 25** **Photo.**

| | | | | |
|---|---|---|---|---|
| **B46** | SP24 | 1.50d + 1d dk brn & brown | .70 | .55 |
| *a.* | | Perf. 11½ | 11.50 | 11.50 |
| **B47** | SP25 | 3.50d + 1.50d bright ultra & bl | 1.25 | 1.00 |

The surtax was for "Winter Help."

Queen Mother Marie SP26

Prince Regent Paul SP27

**1936, May 3** **Litho.**

| | | | | |
|---|---|---|---|---|
| **B48** | SP26 | 75p + 25p grnsh bl | .40 | .40 |
| **B49** | SP26 | 1.50d + 50p rose pink | .45 | .45 |
| **B50** | SP26 | 1.75d + 75p brown | .65 | .65 |
| **B51** | SP26 | 3.50d + 1d brt bl | .50 | .50 |
| | | *Nos. B48-B51 (4)* | 2.00 | 2.00 |

**1936, Sept. 20** **Typo.**

| | | | | |
|---|---|---|---|---|
| **B52** | SP27 | 75p + 50p turq grn & red | .20 | *4.50* |
| **B53** | SP27 | 1.50d + 50p cer & red | .20 | *3.00* |

Surtax for the Red Cross.

Princes Tomislav and Andrej SP28 SP29

***Perf. 11½x12½, 12½x11½***

**1937, May 1**

| | | | | |
|---|---|---|---|---|
| **B54** | SP28 | 25p + 25p red brn | .20 | .25 |
| **B55** | SP28 | 75p + 75p emerald | .20 | .30 |
| **B56** | SP29 | 1.50d + 1d org red | .25 | .35 |
| **B57** | SP29 | 2d + 1d magenta | .25 | .35 |
| | | *Nos. B54-B57 (4)* | .90 | 1.25 |

Souvenir Sheet

National Costumes — SP30

**1937, Sept. 12** ***Perf. 14***

| | | | | |
|---|---|---|---|---|
| **B57A** | SP30 | Sheet of 4 | 1.75 | 2.75 |
| *b.* | | 1d blue green | .25 | .35 |
| *c.* | | 1.50d bright violet | .25 | .35 |
| *d.* | | 2d rose red | .25 | .35 |
| *e.* | | 4d dark blue | .25 | .35 |

1st Yugoslavian Phil. Exhib., Belgrade. Sold only at the exhibition post office at 15d each.

SP31

SP32

***Perf. 11½x12½, 12½x11½***

**1938, May 1** **Photo.**

| | | | | |
|---|---|---|---|---|
| **B58** | SP31 | 50p + 50p dark brn | .25 | .30 |
| **B59** | SP32 | 1d + 1d dk green | .30 | .35 |
| **B60** | SP31 | 1.50d + 1.50d scar | .35 | .40 |
| **B61** | SP32 | 2d + 2d magenta | .40 | .45 |
| | | *Nos. B58-B61 (4)* | 1.30 | 1.50 |

Surtax for the benefit of Child Welfare.

For overprints see Nos. B75-B78.

Bridge and Anti-aircraft Lights — SP33

**1938, May 28** ***Perf. 11½x12½***

| | | | | |
|---|---|---|---|---|
| **B62** | SP33 | 1d + 50p dk grn | .20 | .25 |
| **B63** | SP33 | 1.50d + 1d scarlet | .35 | .40 |
| *a.* | | Perf. 11½ | 17.50 | 17.50 |
| **B64** | SP33 | 2d + 1d rose vio | .45 | .50 |
| *a.* | | Perf. 11½ | 16.00 | 16.00 |
| **B65** | SP33 | 3d + 1.50d dp bl | .50 | .60 |
| | | *Nos. B62-B65 (4)* | 1.50 | 1.75 |

Intl. Aeronautical Exhib., Belgrade.

Cliff at Demir-Kapiya — SP34

Modern Hospital SP35

Runner Carrying Torch — SP36

Alexander I — SP37

***Perf. 11½x12½, 12½x11½***

**1938, Aug. 1**

**B66** SP34 1d + 1d slate grn & dp grn .45 .55
**B67** SP35 1.50d + 1.50d scar .60 .75
**B68** SP36 2d + 2d claret & dp rose .75 .85
**B69** SP37 3d + 3d dp bl .75 .85
*Nos. B66-B69 (4)* 2.55 3.00

The surtax was to raise funds to build a hospital for railway employees.

Runner SP38

Shot-Putter SP41

Hurdlers SP39

Pole Vaulter SP40

**1938, Sept. 11**

**B70** SP38 50p + 50p org brn .70 .70
**B71** SP39 1d + 1d sl grn & dp grn .90 .90
**B72** SP40 1.50d + 1.50d rose & dk mag .90 .90
**B73** SP41 2d + 2d dk blue 1.40 1.40
*Nos. B70-B73 (4)* 3.90 3.90

Ninth Balkan Games.

Stamps of 1938 Overprinted in Black

a

b

**1938, Oct. 1**

**B75** SP31(a) 50p + 50p dk brn .35 .35
**B76** SP32(b) 1d + 1d dk grn .35 .35
**B77** SP31(a) 1.50d + 1.50d scar .35 .35
**B78** SP32(b) 2d + 2d mag .50 .50
*Nos. B75-B78 (4)* 1.55 1.55

Surtax for the benefit of Child Welfare.

Postriders SP43

1d+1d, Rural mail delivery. 1.50d+1.50d, Mail train. 2d+2d, Mail bus. 4d+4d, Mail plane.

**1939, Mar. 15 Photo. *Perf. 11½***

**B79** SP43 50p + 50p buff, bis & brown .40 .50
**B80** SP43 1d + 1d sl grn & dp green .55 .75
**B81** SP43 1.50d + 1.50d red, cop red & brn car .60 .90
**B82** SP43 2d + 2d dp plum & rose lilac .70 1.25
**B83** SP43 4d + 4d ind & sl bl 1.25 1.60
*Nos. B79-B83 (5)* 3.50 5.00

Centenary of the present postal system in Yugoslavia. The surtax was used for the Railway Benevolent Association.

The Cyrillic and Latin inscriptions are transposed on Nos. B82 and B83.

Child Eating SP48

Children at Seashore — SP49

Children in Crib — SP51

Boy Planing Board SP50

**1939, May 1 *Perf. 12½***

**B84** SP48 1d + 1d blk & dp bl green 1.25 1.40
**B85** SP49 1.50d + 1.50d org brn & sal .55 1.25
*a.* Perf. 11½ 40.00 22.50
**B86** SP50 2d + 2d mar & vio rose 1.10 1.40
**B87** SP51 4d + 4d ind & royal blue 1.40 1.90
*Nos. B84-B87 (4)* 4.30 5.95

The surtax was for the benefit of Child Welfare.

Czar Lazar of Serbia — SP52

Milosh Obilich — SP53

**1939, June 28 *Perf. 11½***

**B88** SP52 1d + 1d sl grn & bl grn .55 .70
**B89** SP53 1.50d + 1.50d mar & brt car .55 .70

Battle of Kosovo, 550th anniversary.

Training Ship "Jadran" SP54

Designs: 1d+50p, Steamship "King Alexander." 1.50d+1d, Freighter "Triglan." 2d+1.50d, Cruiser "Dubrovnik."

**1939, Sept. 6 Engr.**

**B90** SP54 50p + 50p brn org .60 .70
**B91** SP54 1d + 50p dull grn .80 .95
**B92** SP54 1.50d + 1d dp rose .70 .80
**B93** SP54 2d + 1.50d dark bl .80 1.10
*Nos. B90-B93 (4)* 2.90 3.55

Yugoslav Navy and Merchant Marine. The surtax aided a Marine Museum.

Motorcycle and Sidecar — SP58

Motorcycle SP60

Racing Car SP59

Racing Car SP61

**1939, Sept. 3 Photo.**

**B94** SP58 50p + 50p multi .55 .60
**B95** SP59 1d + 1d multi .60 .70
**B96** SP60 1.50d + 1.50d multi .70 .85
**B97** SP61 2d + 2d multi 1.25 1.50
*Nos. B94-B97 (4)* 3.10 3.65

Automobile and Motorcycle Races, Belgrade. The surtax was for the Race Organization and the State Treasury.

Unknown Soldier Memorial SP62

**1939, Oct. 9 *Perf. 12½***

**B98** SP62 1d + 50p sl grn & green .60 .85
**B99** SP62 1.50d + 1d red & rose red .70 .90
**B100** SP62 2d + 1.50d dp cl & vio rose .85 1.00
**B101** SP62 3d + 2d dp bl & bl .85 1.00
*Nos. B98-B101 (4)* 3.00 3.75

Assassination of King Alexander, 5th anniv. The surtax was used to aid World War I invalids.

Postman Delivering Mail — SP64

Postman Emptying Mail Box — SP65

Parcel Post Delivery Wagon SP66

Parcel Post SP67

Repairing Telephone Wires — SP68

**1940, Jan. 1**

**B102** SP64 50p + 50p brn & deep org .50 .55
**B103** SP65 1d + 1d sl grn & blue grn .55 .70
**B104** SP66 1.50d + 1.50d red brn & scar .70 .85
**B105** SP67 2d + 2d dl vio & red lilac .85 1.40
**B106** SP68 4d + 4d sl bl & bl 1.40 1.75
*Nos. B102-B106 (5)* 4.00 5.25

The surtax was used for the employees of the Postal System in Belgrade.

Croats' Arrival at Adriatic in 640 SP69

King Tomislav — SP70

Death of Matija Gubec — SP71

Anton and Stjepan Radic SP72

Map of Yugoslavia SP73

**1940, Mar. 1 Typo. *Perf. 11½***

**B107** SP69 50p + 50p brn org .25 .30
**B108** SP70 1d + 1d green .25 .30
**B109** SP71 1.50d + 1.50d brt red .30 .30
**B110** SP72 2d + 2d dk cerise .35 .45
**B111** SP73 4d + 2d dark blue .40 .50
*Nos. B107-B111 (5)* 1.55 1.85

The surtax was used for the benefit of postal employees in Zagreb.

Children Playing in Snow SP74

Children at Seashore — SP75

**1940, May 1 Photo. *Perf. 11½, 12½***

**B112** SP74 50p + 50p brn org & org yellow .25 .30
**B113** SP75 1d + 1d sl grn & dk green .30 .40
**B114** SP74 1.50d + 1.50d brn red & scarlet .25 .30
**B115** SP75 2d + 2d mar & vio rose .35 .45
*Nos. B112-B115 (4)* 1.15 1.45

The surtax was for Child Welfare.

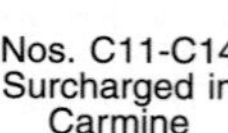

Nos. C11-C14 Surcharged in Carmine

***Perf. 11½x12½, 12½x11½***

**1940, Dec. 23**

**B116** AP6 50p + 50p on 5d .30 .30
**B117** AP7 1d + 1d on 10d .30 .30
**B118** AP8 1.50d + 1.50d on 20d .35 .45
**B119** AP9 2d + 2d on 30d .35 .45
*Nos. B116-B119 (4)* 1.30 1.50

The surtax was used to fight tuberculosis. For surcharges see Nos. NB1-NB4.

St. Peter's Cemetery, Ljubljana — SP76

Croatian, Serbian and Slovenian SP77

Chapel at Kajmaktchalan SP78

Memorial at Brezje SP79

**1941, Jan. 1 *Perf. 12½***

**B120** SP76 50p + 50p gray grn & yel green .30 .35
**B121** SP77 1d + 1d brn car & dl rose .30 .35
**B122** SP78 1.50d + 1.50d myr grn & bl green .30 .45
**B123** SP79 2d + 2d gray bl & pale lilac .40 .55
*Nos. B120-B123 (4)* 1.30 1.70

Surtax for the Ljubljana War Veterans Assoc.

Kamenita Gate, Zagreb — SP80

13th Century Cathedral, Zagreb — SP81

**1941, Mar. 16 Engr. *Perf. 11½***

**B124** SP80 1.50d + 1.50d choc .40 .80
**B125** SP81 4d + 3d blue blk .40 .80

2nd Philatelic Exhibition of Croatia, at Zagreb, Mar. 16-27.

Nos. B124-B125 exist perf. 9½ on right side. Value, each $25.

**1941, Apr.**

**B126** SP80 1.50d + 1.50d bl black 8.50 9.50
**B127** SP81 4d + 3d choc 8.50 9.50

Regional philatelic exhibition at Slavonski Brod. Nos. B126-B127 with gold overprint, "Nezavisna Drzava Hrvatska," are Croatia Nos. B1-B2.

Nos. B126-B127 exist perf. 9½ on right side. Value, each $55 unused, $70 used.

**Issues for Federal Republic**

Carrying Wounded Soldier — SP82

Child — SP83

**1945, Sept. 15 Typo. *Perf. 11½***

**B131** SP82 1d + 4d deep ultra .70 .70
**B132** SP83 2d + 6d scarlet .70 .70

The surtax was for the Red Cross.

Russia, Yugoslavia Flags SP84

**1945, Oct. 20 Photo. Unwmk.**

**B133** SP84 2d + 5d multi .80 .80

Liberation of Belgrade, 1st anniv.

Communications Symbols — SP85

**1946, May 10 *Perf. 12½***

**B134** SP85 1.50d + 1d emer 2.75 2.50
**B135** SP85 2.50d + 1.50d car rose 2.75 2.50
**B136** SP85 5d + 2d gray bl 2.75 2.50
**B137** SP85 8d + 3.50d dl brn 2.75 2.50
*Nos. B134-B137 (4)* 11.00 10.00

1st PTT Congress since liberation, May 10.

Flag and Young Laborers SP86

Handstand on Horizontal Bar SP87

**1946, Aug. 1 Litho.**

**Flag in Red or Carmine and Deep or Dark Blue**

**B138** SP86 50p + 50p brn & buff 2.25 1.40
**B139** SP86 1.50d + 1d dk grn & lt green 2.25 1.40
**B140** SP86 2.50d + 2d rose vio & rose lilac 2.25 1.40
**B141** SP86 5d + 3d gray bl & blue 2.25 1.40
*Nos. B138-B141 (4)* 9.00 5.60

The surtax aided railroad reconstruction carried out by Yugoslav youths.

**1947, Sept. 5 *Perf. 11½***

**B142** SP87 1.50d + 50p dark grn .20 .20
**B143** SP87 2.50d + 50p carmine .20 .20
**B144** SP87 4d + 50p brt blue .20 .20
*Nos. B142-B144 (3)* .60 .60

1947 Balkan Games, Sept. 5-7, Ljubljana.

Young Railway Laborers SP88

**1947, Sept. 25 Typo. *Perf. 11½x12***

**B145** SP88 1d + 50p orange .20 .20
**B146** SP88 1.50d + 1d yel green .20 .20
**B147** SP88 2.50d + 1.50d car lake .20 .20
**B148** SP88 5d + 2d deep blue .20 .20
*Nos. B145-B148 (4)* .80 .80

The surtax was for youth brigades employed in the construction of the Samac-Sarajevo railway.

Symbolizing Protection of "B.C.G." Vaccine SP89

Dying Serpent SP91

"Illness" and "Recovery" SP90

**1948, Apr. 1 Litho. *Perf. 12½***

**B149** SP89 1.50d + 1d sl blk & red .20 .20
**B150** SP90 2.50d + 2d grnsh gray, ol blk & red .20 .20
**B151** SP91 5d + 3d dk bl & car .20 .20
*Nos. B149-B151 (3)* .60 .60

Fight against tuberculosis. The surtax was for the Yugoslav Red Cross.

Juro Danicic SP92

Shot Put — SP93

Portraits: 2.50d+1d, Franjo Racki. 4d+2d, Josip J. Strossmayer.

**1948, July 28 *Perf. 11***

**B152** SP92 1.50d + 50p blk green .25 .20
**B153** SP92 2.50d + 1d dark red .25 .20
**B154** SP92 4d + 2d dark blue .25 .20
*Nos. B152-B154 (3)* .75 .60

Yugoslav Academy of Arts and Sciences, Zagreb, 80th anniv. The surtax was for the Academy.

**1948, Sept. 10 *Perf. 12½***

**B155** SP93 2d + 1d shown .25 .35
**B156** SP93 3d + 1d Hurdles .25 .35
**B157** SP93 5d + 2d Pole vault .25 .35
*Nos. B155-B157 (3)* .75 1.05

Balkan and Central Europe Games, 1948. On sale 4 days.

---

## AIR POST STAMPS

Dubrovnik AP1

Lake Bled AP2

Falls of Jaice — AP3

Church at Oplenac — AP4

Bridge at Mostar — AP5

*Perf. 12½*

**1934, June 15 Typo. Unwmk.**

**C1** AP1 50p violet brown .20 .20
**C2** AP2 1d green .20 .20
**C3** AP3 2d rose red .45 .20
**C4** AP4 3d ultramarine .50 .25
**C5** AP5 10d vermilion 1.50 1.40
*Nos. C1-C5 (5)* 2.85 2.25

**King Alexander Memorial Issue**

**1935, Jan. 1**

**Border in Black**

**C6** AP4 3d ultramarine 1.50 1.25

St. Naum Convent — AP6

Sarajevo AP8

Port of Rab — AP7

Ljubljana AP9

*Perf. 12½, 11½x12½, 12½x11½*

**1937, Sept. 12 Photo.**

**C7** AP6 50p brown .20 .20
**C8** AP7 1d yellow grn .20 .20
**C9** AP8 2d blue gray .20 .20
**C10** AP9 2.50d rose red .20 .20
**C11** AP6 5d brn violet .20 .20
**C12** AP7 10d brown lake .20 .20
**C13** AP8 20d dark green .35 .35
**C14** AP9 30d ultramarine .70 .70
*Nos. C7-C14 (8)* 2.25 2.25

For surcharges see Nos. B116-B119, NB1-NB4, NC1-NC8.

Cathedral of Zagreb AP10

Bridge at Belgrade AP11

**1940, Aug. 15 Litho.** ***Perf. 12½***

**C15** AP10 40d Prus grn & pale green .95 1.40
**C16** AP11 50d slate bl & gray bl 1.10 1.40

For overprints see Nos. NC9-NC10.

**Issues for Federal Republic**

Plane over Terrace of Kalimegdan, Belgrade AP12

Plane over Dubrovnik AP13

**1947, Apr. 21 Typo.** ***Perf. 11½***

**Cyrillic Inscription at Top**

**C17** AP12 50p ol gray & brn vio .20 .20
**C18** AP13 1d mag & ol gray .20 .20
**C19** AP12 2d blue & black .20 .20
**C20** AP13 5d green & gray .30 .20
**C21** AP12 10d olive bis & choc .35 .20
**C22** AP13 20d ultra & olive .75 .35

**Roman Inscription at Top**

**C23** AP12 50p ol gray & brn vio .20 .20
**C24** AP13 1d mag & ol gray .20 .20
**C25** AP12 2d blue & black .20 .20
**C26** AP13 5d green & gray .30 .20
**C27** AP12 10d olive bis & choc .35 .20
**C28** AP13 20d ultra & olive .75 .35
*Nos. C17-C28 (12)* 4.00 2.70

Sheets of each denomination contain alternately stamps with Cyrillic or Roman inscription at top. Value, 6 se-tenant pairs, $35.

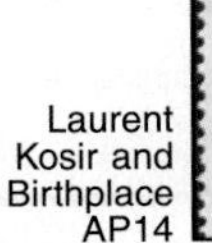

Laurent Kosir and Birthplace AP14

**1948, Aug. 27 Engr.**

**C29** AP14 15d red violet 1.00 .80

Kosir, recognized by Yugoslavia as inventor of the postage stamp, 80th death anniv. Issued in sheets of 25 stamps and 25 labels.

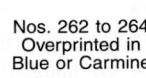

Nos. 262 to 264 Overprinted in Blue or Carmine

**1949, Aug. 25 Unwmk.** ***Perf. 12½***

**C30** A55 3d carmine rose 1.10 2.50
**C31** A56 5d dull blue (C) 1.10 2.50
**C32** A57 12d red brown 1.10 2.50
*Nos. C30-C32 (3)* 3.30 7.50

Liberation of Macedonia, 5th anniv.
It is reported that No. C32 was not sold to the public at the post office.

Souvenir Sheet

Electric Train AP15

*Perf. 11½x12½*

**1949, Dec. 15 Photo.**

**C33** AP15 10d lilac rose 35.00 19.00
*a.* Imperf. 35.00 19.00

Centenary of Yugoslav railroads.
For overprint see Trieste No. C17.

Iron Gate, Derdap AP16

Belgrade AP17

Designs: 2d, Cascades, Plitvice. 3d, Carolina. 6d, Roman bridge, Mostar. 10d, Ohrid. 20d, Gulf of Kotor. 30d, Dubrovnik. 50d, Bled.

*Perf. 12½*

**1951, June 16 Unwmk. Engr.**

**C34** AP16 1d deep org .20 .20
**C35** AP16 2d dk green .20 .20
**C36** AP16 3d dark red .20 .20
**C37** AP16 6d ultra 3.00 3.50
**C38** AP16 10d dark brn .25 .20
**C39** AP16 20d grnsh blk .30 .20
**C40** AP16 30d dp claret .50 .20
**C41** AP16 50d dk purple .90 .20
**C42** AP17 100d dk gray bl 16.00 2.50
*Nos. C34-C42 (9)* 21.55 7.40

**Souvenir Sheet**

***Imperf***

**C43** AP17 100d red brn 65.00 65.00

See Nos. C50-C53. For overprints see Nos. C44, C49, Trieste C22-C32.

Roman Bridge Type of 1951 Overprinted "ZEFIZ 1951" in Carmine

**1951, June 16** ***Perf. 12½***

**C44** AP16 6d dark green .80 .70

Nos. C43-C44 were issued for Zagreb Philatelic Exhibition, June 16-26.

View on Mt. Kapaonik AP18

Plane and Parachutists AP19

*Perf. 12½*

**1951, July Unwmk. Photo.**

**C45** AP18 3d shown .90 .65
**C46** AP18 5d Mt. Triglav .90 .65
**C47** AP18 20d Mt. Kalnik 32.50 27.50
*Nos. C45-C47 (3)* 34.30 28.80

Intl. Union of Mountaineers, 12th Assembly, Bled, July 13-18.

**1951, Aug. 16 Engr.**

**C48** AP19 6d carmine 2.25 1.10

Type of 1951 Overprinted in Carmine

**C49** AP16 50d blue 32.50 25.00

First World Parachute Championship, Bled, Aug. 16-20.

**Catalogue values for unused stamps in this section, from this point to the end of the section, are for Never Hinged items.**

Types of 1951

Designs: 5d, Cascades, Plitvice. 100d, Carniola. 200d, Roman bridge, Mostar.

**1951-52**

**C50** AP16 5d yel brn ('52) .20 .20
**C51** AP16 100d green .65 .20
**C52** AP16 200d deep car ('52) 1.00 .30
**C53** AP17 500d blue vio ('52) 2.25 .65
*Nos. C50-C53 (4)* 4.10 1.35

Marshal Tito, Tank, Factory and Planes AP20

**1951, Dec. 22 Unwmk.**

**C54** AP20 150d deep blue 5.25 3.50

Army Day, Dec. 22; 10th anniv. of the formation of the 1st military unit of "New" Yugoslavia.

Star and Flag-encircled Globe — AP21

**1953, July 30 Engr.**

**C55** AP21 300d bl & grn 160.00 160.00

38th Esperanto Congress, Zagreb, 7/25-8/1.
For overprint see Trieste No. C21.

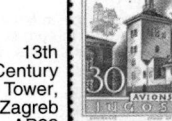

13th Century Tower, Zagreb AP22

**1956, May 20** ***Perf. 11½***

**Chalky Paper**

**C56** AP22 30d gray, vio bl & org red 1.60 .90

Yugoslav Intl. Phil. Exhib., JUFIZ III, Zagreb, May 20-27.

Workers and Cogwheel — AP23

Moon and Earth with Satellites — AP24

**1956, June 15** **Photo.**
**Glossy Paper**

| | | | | |
|---|---|---|---|---|
| **C57** | AP23 | 30d car rose & blk | 1.60 | 1.60 |

10th anniversary of technical education.

**1958, Oct. 24** **Engr.** ***Perf. 12½***

| | | | | |
|---|---|---|---|---|
| **C58** | AP24 | 300d dark blue | 4.75 | 2.00 |

Intl. Geophysical Year, 1957-58.

Types of Regular Issue, 1961
**1961, Sept. 1** ***Perf. 11½***

| | | | | |
|---|---|---|---|---|
| **C59** | A150 | 250d dark purple | .90 | .50 |
| **C60** | A151 | 500d violet blue | 2.50 | 1.75 |

Type of Athletic Regular Issue, 1962
Souvenir Sheet

Design: Army Stadium, Belgrade.

**1962, Sept. 12** **Litho.** ***Imperf.***

| | | | | |
|---|---|---|---|---|
| **C61** | A161 | 600d vio & blk | 3.25 | 2.50 |

7th European Athletic Championships, Belgrade, Sept. 12-16.

## REGISTERED LETTER STAMP

**Catalogue values for unused stamps in this section are for Never Hinged items.**

RL1

**1993, June 28** **Litho.** ***Perf. 12½***

| | | | | |
|---|---|---|---|---|
| **F1** | RL1 | (R) ultra | .50 | |

No. F1 was valued at 11,000d on day of issue.
For surcharge, see Serbia No. 194.

**Type of 1993**
**2002, July 25** **Litho.** ***Perf. 12½***

| | | | | |
|---|---|---|---|---|
| **F2** | RL1 | R red | .75 | .75 |

No. F2 was intended for use in Montenegro and was sold there for 39c in euro currency. The stamp was valid for use in the Serbian section of Yugoslavia.

## POSTAGE DUE STAMPS

King Alexander — D1

**1921** **Typo.** **Unwmk.** ***Perf. 11½***
**Red or Black Surcharge**

| | | | | |
|---|---|---|---|---|
| **J1** | D1 | 10p on 5p green (R) | .20 | .20 |
| **J2** | D1 | 30p on 5p green (Bk) | .20 | .20 |

D2

D3

**1921-22** **Typo.** ***Perf. 11½, Rough***

| | | | | |
|---|---|---|---|---|
| **J3** | D2 | 10p rose | .20 | .20 |
| **J4** | D2 | 30p yellow green | .20 | .20 |
| **J5** | D2 | 50p violet | .30 | .20 |
| **J6** | D2 | 1d brown | .35 | .20 |
| **J7** | D2 | 2d blue | .35 | .20 |
| **J8** | D3 | 5d orange | 7.50 | .40 |
| **J9** | D3 | 10d violet brown | 9.25 | .45 |
| *a.* | | Cliche of 10p in sheet of 10d | 75.00 | 100.00 |
| **J10** | D3 | 25d pink | 30.00 | 2.00 |
| **J11** | D3 | 50d green | 27.50 | 1.60 |
| | | *Nos. J3-J11 (9)* | 75.65 | 5.45 |

**1924** ***Perf. 9, 10½, 11½, Clean-cut***

| | | | | |
|---|---|---|---|---|
| **J12** | D3 | 10p rose red | .20 | .20 |
| **J13** | D3 | 30p yellow green | .45 | .35 |
| **J14** | D3 | 50p violet | .20 | .20 |
| **J15** | D3 | 1d brown | .35 | .20 |
| **J16** | D3 | 2d deep blue | .55 | .20 |
| **J17** | D3 | 5d orange | 9.25 | .20 |
| **J18** | D3 | 10d violet brown | 21.00 | .20 |
| **J19** | D3 | 25d pink | 42.50 | 1.00 |
| **J20** | D3 | 50d green | 57.50 | .85 |
| | | *Nos. J12-J20 (9)* | 132.00 | 3.40 |

Nos. J19-J20 do not exist perf 9. Nos. J18-J20 do not exist perf 11½.

Nos. J19-J20 Surcharged

**1928**

| | | | | |
|---|---|---|---|---|
| **J21** | D3 | 10d on 25d pink | 3.25 | .25 |
| **J22** | D3 | 10d on 50d green | 3.25 | .25 |
| *a.* | | Inverted surcharge | 30.00 | 18.00 |

A second type of "1" in surcharge has flag projecting horizontally. Value, each $15 unused, $3 used.

Coat of Arms — D4

Numeral of Value — D5

**1931** **Typo.** ***Perf. 12½***
**With Imprint at Foot**

| | | | | |
|---|---|---|---|---|
| **J23** | D4 | 50p violet | 1.10 | .20 |
| **J24** | D4 | 1d deep magenta | 2.00 | .20 |
| **J25** | D4 | 2d deep blue | 5.00 | .20 |
| **J26** | D4 | 5d orange | 2.00 | .20 |
| **J27** | D4 | 10d chocolate | 6.75 | .70 |
| | | *Nos. J23-J27 (5)* | 16.85 | 1.50 |

For overprints see Nos. NJ1-NJ13, Croatia 26-29, J1-J5.

**1932**
**Without Imprint at Foot**

| | | | | |
|---|---|---|---|---|
| **J28** | D4 | 50p violet | .20 | .20 |
| **J29** | D4 | 1d deep magenta | .20 | .20 |
| **J30** | D4 | 2d deep blue | .20 | .20 |
| **J31** | D4 | 5d orange | .20 | .20 |
| **J32** | D4 | 10d chocolate | .20 | .20 |
| | | *Nos. J28-J32 (5)* | 1.00 | 1.00 |

**1933** ***Perf. 9, 10½, 11½***
**Overprint in Green, Blue or Maroon**

| | | | | |
|---|---|---|---|---|
| **J33** | D5 | 50p vio (G) | .20 | .20 |
| **J34** | D5 | 1d brown (Bl) | .20 | .20 |
| *a.* | | Perf. 10½ | 3.25 | .85 |
| **J35** | D5 | 2d blue (M) | .35 | .20 |
| *a.* | | Perf. 10½ | 1.60 | .50 |
| **J36** | D5 | 5d orange (Bl) | 1.25 | .20 |
| **J37** | D5 | 10d violet brn (Bl) | 6.00 | 1.00 |
| | | *Nos. J33-J37 (5)* | 8.00 | 1.80 |

**Issues for Federal Republic**

Redrawn Type OD5, German Occupation of Serbia, Overprinted in Black

**1945** **Unwmk.** ***Perf. 12½***

| | | | | |
|---|---|---|---|---|
| **J37A** | OD5 | 10d red | .35 | .35 |
| **J37B** | OD5 | 20d ultramarine | .35 | .35 |

In the redrawn design the eagle is replaced by a colorless tablet.

Coat of Arms — D6

Torches and Star — D7

**1945** **Litho.** ***Perf. 12½***
**Numerals in Black**

| | | | | |
|---|---|---|---|---|
| **J38** | D6 | 2d brown violet | .20 | .25 |
| **J39** | D6 | 3d violet | .20 | .25 |
| **J40** | D6 | 5d green | .20 | .25 |
| **J41** | D6 | 7d orange brown | .20 | .25 |
| **J42** | D6 | 10d rose lilac | .20 | .25 |
| **J43** | D6 | 20d blue | .20 | .25 |
| **J44** | D6 | 30d light bl grn | .20 | .35 |
| **J45** | D6 | 40d rose red | .20 | .35 |

**Numerals in Color of Stamp**

| | | | | |
|---|---|---|---|---|
| **J46** | D6 | 1d blue green | .20 | .20 |
| **J47** | D6 | 1.50d blue | .20 | .20 |
| **J48** | D6 | 2d vermilion | .20 | .20 |
| **J49** | D6 | 3d violet brown | .20 | .20 |
| **J50** | D6 | 4d rose violet | .20 | .20 |
| | | *Nos. J38-J50 (13)* | 2.60 | 3.20 |

For overprints see Nos. J64-J66.

**1946-47** **Typo.** **Unwmk.**

| | | | | |
|---|---|---|---|---|
| **J51** | D7 | 50p dp orange ('47) | .20 | .20 |
| **J52** | D7 | 1d orange | .20 | .20 |
| **J53** | D7 | 2d dark blue | .20 | .20 |
| **J54** | D7 | 3d yellow green | .20 | .20 |
| **J55** | D7 | 5d bright purple | .20 | .20 |
| **J56** | D7 | 7d crimson | .25 | .20 |
| **J57** | D7 | 10d brt pink ('47) | .50 | .20 |
| **J58** | D7 | 20d rose lake ('47) | .65 | .20 |
| | | *Nos. J51-J58 (8)* | 2.40 | 1.60 |

See Nos. J67-J79. For overprints see Trieste Nos. J1-J5, J11-J18.

Nos. J47, J49 and J50 Overprinted in Black

**1950** **Litho.**

| | | | | |
|---|---|---|---|---|
| **J64** | D6 | 1.50d blue | .20 | .20 |
| **J65** | D6 | 3d violet brown | .20 | .20 |
| **J66** | D6 | 4d rose violet | .20 | .20 |
| | | *Nos. J64-J66 (3)* | .60 | .60 |

**Catalogue values for unused stamps in this section, from this point to the end of the section, are for Never Hinged items.**

Type of 1946-47
**1951-52** **Typo.** ***Perf. 12½***

| | | | | |
|---|---|---|---|---|
| **J67** | D7 | 1d brown ('52) | .20 | .20 |
| **J68** | D7 | 2d emerald | .20 | .20 |
| **J69** | D7 | 5d blue | .35 | .20 |
| **J70** | D7 | 10d scarlet | 1.75 | .20 |
| **J71** | D7 | 20d purple | 1.75 | .20 |
| **J72** | D7 | 30d org yel ('52) | 3.00 | .20 |
| **J73** | D7 | 50d ultramarine | 6.50 | .25 |
| **J74** | D7 | 100d dp plum ('52) | 6.75 | .45 |
| | | *Nos. J67-J74 (8)* | 20.50 | 1.90 |

For overprints see Istria Nos. J20-J24, Trieste J11-J18.

**1962** **Litho.** ***Perf. 12½***

| | | | | |
|---|---|---|---|---|
| **J75** | D7 | 10d red orange | 2.50 | .20 |
| **J76** | D7 | 20d purple | 2.50 | .20 |
| **J77** | D7 | 30d orange | 3.75 | .20 |
| **J78** | D7 | 50d ultramarine | 9.50 | .50 |
| **J79** | D7 | 100d rose lake | 7.75 | .70 |
| | | *Nos. J75-J79 (5)* | 26.00 | 1.80 |

## OFFICIAL STAMPS

**Issues for Federal Republic**

Arms of the Federated People's Republic — O1

***Perf. 12½***
**1946, Nov. 1** **Unwmk.** **Typo.**

| | | | | |
|---|---|---|---|---|
| **O1** | O1 | 50p orange | .20 | .20 |
| **O2** | O1 | 1d blue green | .20 | .20 |
| **O3** | O1 | 1.50d olive green | .20 | .20 |
| **O4** | O1 | 2.50d red | .20 | .20 |
| **O5** | O1 | 4d yellow brown | .35 | .20 |
| **O6** | O1 | 5d deep blue | .45 | .20 |
| **O7** | O1 | 8d chocolate | .80 | .20 |
| **O8** | O1 | 12d violet | .95 | .25 |
| | | *Nos. O1-O8 (8)* | 3.35 | 1.65 |

For surcharges see Nos. 272A-272B, Istria 43, 45, 47, 49, 51.

## POSTAL TAX STAMPS

**Catalogue values for unused stamps in this section are for Never Hinged items.**

The tax was for the Red Cross or The Olympic Fund unless otherwise noted.

Red Cross Emblem PT1

Dr. Vladen Djordjevic PT2

**Unwmk.**
**1933, Sept. 17** **Litho.** ***Perf. 13***

| | | | | |
|---|---|---|---|---|
| **RA1** | PT1 | 50p dark blue & red | .30 | .20 |

Obligatory on inland letters during Red Cross Week, Sept. 17-23.
See No. RAJ1.

**1936, Sept. 20** **Typo.** ***Perf. 12***

| | | | | |
|---|---|---|---|---|
| **RA2** | PT2 | 50p brn blk & red | .35 | .20 |

Obligatory on inland letters during Red Cross Week, Sept. 20-26.

Aiding the Wounded PT3

**1938, Sept. 18** **Litho.** ***Perf. 12½***

| | | | | |
|---|---|---|---|---|
| **RA3** | PT3 | 50p dk bl, red, yel & grn | .35 | .20 |

**1940, Sept. 15** **Redrawn**

| | | | | |
|---|---|---|---|---|
| **RA4** | PT3 | 50p slate blue & red | 1.10 | .20 |

The inscription at the upper right of this stamp and the numerals of value are in smaller characters.
Obligatory on all letters during the second week of September.

### Issues for Federal Republic

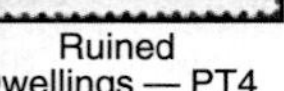
Ruined Dwellings — PT4

Red Cross Nurse — PT5

**1947, Jan. 1** **Litho.** ***Perf. 12½***
**RA5** PT4 50p brn & scarlet .20 .20

See No. RAJ2. For overprints see Trieste Nos. RA1, RAJ1.

**1948, Oct. 1**
**RA6** PT5 50p dk vio bl & red .20 .20

See No. RAJ3.

Nurse and Child — PT6

Nurse Holding Book — PT7

**1949, Nov. 5**
**RA7** PT6 50p red & brown .20 .20

See No. RAJ4. For overprints see Trieste Nos. RA2, RAJ2.

**1950, Oct. 1**
**RA8** PT7 50p dark green & red .20 .20

Obligatory Oct. 1-8, 1950.
See No. RAJ6.

Hands Raising Red Cross Flag — PT8

Nurse — PT9

**1951, Oct. 7**
**RA9** PT8 50p vio bl & red .20 .20

Obligatory Oct. 7-14.
For overprints see Trieste Nos. RA3, RAJ3.

**1952, Oct. 5** **Photo.** ***Perf. 12½***
**RA10** PT9 50p gray & carmine .20 .20

For overprint see Trieste No. RA4.

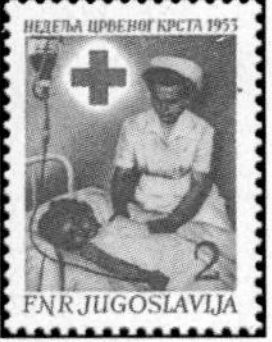
Child Receiving Blood Transfusion PT10

Youths Carrying Flags PT11

**1953, Oct. 25** **Litho.**
**RA11** PT10 2d red vio & red .20 .20

See No. RAJ8. For overprints see Trieste Nos. RA5, RAJ5.

**1954, Nov. 1**
**RA12** PT11 2d gray grn & red .20 .20

See Nos. RAJ9.

Infant — PT11a

**1954, Oct. 4**
**RA12A** PT11a 2d brn & salmon .60 1.25

The tax was for Children's Week.

Girl PT12

Nurse Opening Window PT13

**1955, Oct. 2** **Unwmk.** ***Perf. 12½***
**RA13** PT12 2d dull red .20 .20

The tax was for child welfare.
See No. RAJ10.

**1955, Oct. 31**
**RA14** PT13 2d vio blk & red .20 .20

See No. RAJ11.

Ruins in the Snow — PT14

Children and Goose — PT15

**1956, May 6** ***Perf. 12½***
**RA15** PT14 2d sepia & red .20 .20

See No. RAJ12.

**1956, Sept. 30**
**RA16** PT15 2d gray green .20 .20

The tax was for child welfare.
See No. RAJ13.

Plane over Temporary Shelter — PT16

**1957, May 5** **Litho.**
**RA17** PT16 2d lt bl, blk & car .20 .20

See No. RAJ14.

Girl and Boy Pioneers PT17

**1957, Sept. 30** **Unwmk.** ***Perf. 12½***
**RA18** PT17 2d rose & gray .20 .20

Children's Week. Obligatory Oct. 2-6.
See No. RAJ15.

Redrawn Type of Regular Issue, 1953

**1958, May 4** ***Perf. 12½x12***
**RA19** A95 2d multicolored .20 .20

On No. RA19 the UN emblem has been left out, Cyrillic inscriptions at left added, country name in Latin letters.

Playing Children — PT18

Helping Hand and Family — PT19

**1958, Oct. 5** **Litho.** ***Perf. 12½***
**RA20** PT18 2d brt yel & black .20 .20

Children's Week, Oct. 5-11.

**1959, May 3**
**RA21** PT19 2d blue vio & red .20 .20

Red Cross centenary. Obligatory May 3-9.
See No. RAJ18.

Blackboard, Flower and Fish — PT20

"Reconstruction" PT21

**1959, Oct. 5** **Unwmk.**
**RA22** PT20 2d ocher & Prus grn .20 .20

Children's Week. Obligatory on domestic mail, Oct. 5-11.
See No. RAJ19.

**1960, May 8** ***Perf. 12½***
**RA23** PT21 2d slate & red .20 .20

Obligatory May 8-14. See No. RAJ20.

Girl and Toys — PT22

Blood Donor Symbolism PT23

**1960, Oct. 2** **Litho.** ***Perf. 12½***
**RA24** PT22 2d red .20 .20

Issued for Children's Week. Obligatory on domestic mail Oct. 2-8.

See No. RAJ21.

**1961, May 7**
**RA25** PT23 2d multicolored .20 .20

Obligatory May 7-13. Exists imperf. Value $12.50.
See No. RAJ22.

Bird Holding Flower PT24

**1961, Oct. 1**
**RA26** PT24 2d orange & violet .20 .20

Children's Week. Obligatory on domestic mail, Oct. 1-7.
See No. RAJ23.

Bandages and Symbols of Home, Industry, Weather, Transportation, Fire and Flood — PT25

**1962, Apr. 30** ***Perf. 12½***
**RA27** PT25 5d red brn, gray & red .20 .20

Obligatory on domestic mail May 6-12.
See No. RAJ24.

Centenary Emblem — PT26

Parachute Drop of Supplies, Yugoslav Flag — PT27

**1963, May 5** **Unwmk.** ***Perf. 12½***
**RA28** PT26 5d dl yel, red & gray .20 .20

Intl. Red Cross, centenary. Obligatory on all domestic mail during Red Cross Week, May 5-11.
See No. RAJ25.

**1964, Apr. 27** **Litho.**
**RA29** PT27 5d blue, rose & dk bl .20 .20

Obligatory on domestic mail, May 3-9.

Children in Circle — PT28

**1965, May 2** **Litho.** ***Perf. 12½***
**RA30** PT28 5d tan & red .20 .20

Obligatory on domestic mail, May 2-8.

Arrows
PT29

**1966, Apr. 28 Litho. *Perf. 12½***
**RA31** PT29 5p gray & multi .20 .20

Obligatory on domestic mail, May 1-7.

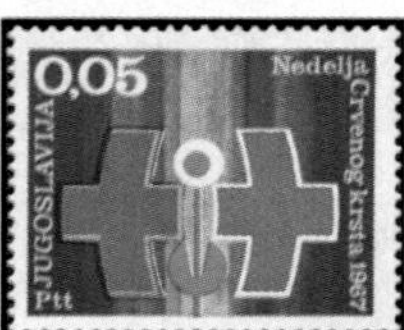


Crosses and Flower
PT30

**1967, Apr. 28 Litho. *Perf. 12½***
**RA32** PT30 5p vio, red & yel grn .20 .20

Honeycomb and Red Cross — PT31

Aztec Calendar Stone and Olympic Rings — PT32

**1968, Apr. 30 Litho. *Perf. 12***
**RA33** PT31 5p multicolored .20 .20

Obligatory on all domestic mail May 5-11.

**1968, Oct. 12 *Perf. 12½***
**RA34** PT32 10p black & multi .20 .20

Red Cross, Hands and Globe — PT33

Globe, Olympic Torch and Rings — PT34

**1969, May 18 Litho. *Perf. 12***
**RA35** PT33 20p red org, dl red & blk .20 .20

**1969, Nov. 24 Litho. *Perf. 11***
**RA36** PT34 10p gold & multi .20 .20

Yugoslav Olympic Committee, 50th anniv.

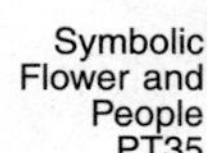

Symbolic Flower and People
PT35

**1970, Apr. 27 Litho. *Perf. 13***
**RA37** PT35 20p vio bl, org & red .20 .20

Olympic Flag — PT36

Red Cross Encircling Globe
PT37

Olympic Rings and Disk — PT38

**1970, June 10 Litho. *Perf. 13x13½***
**RA38** PT36 10p multicolored .20 .20

**1971, Apr. 26 Litho. *Perf. 12½***
**RA39** PT37 20p blue, yel & red .20 .20

**1971, June 15 Litho. *Perf. 12½***
**RA40** PT38 10p blue & black .20 .20

Red Cross and Hemispheres
PT39

**1972, Apr. 27 *Perf. 13½x13***
**RA41** PT39 20p red & multi .20 .20

Olympic Rings, TV Tower, Munich and Sapporo Emblems — PT40

**1972, May *Perf. 13x13½***
**RA42** PT40 10p ultra & multi .20 .20

Red Cross, Crescent and Lion Emblems — PT41

Globe and Olympic Rings — PT42

**1973, Apr. 24 Litho. *Perf. 13x13½***
**RA43** PT41 20p blue & multi .20 .20

**1973, June 1 Litho. *Perf. 13x13½***
**RA44** PT42 10p multicolored .20 .20

Drop of Blood, Red Cross Emblems
PT43

**1974, Apr. 25 Litho. *Perf. 13***
**RA45** PT43 20p red & multi .20 .20

Olympic Rings
PT44

**1974, June 1 Litho. *Perf. 13***
**RA46** PT44 10p blue & multi .20 .20

Red Cross, Hands
PT45

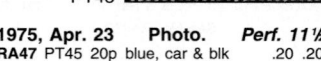

**1975, Apr. 23 Photo. *Perf. 11½***
**RA47** PT45 20p blue, car & blk .20 .20

Olympic Rings — PT46

**1975, June 2 Litho. *Perf. 13½***
**RA48** PT46 10p multicolored .20 .20

Ruin and Clock — PT47

**1975, July 26 Litho. *Perf. 13x13½***
**RA49** PT47 30p blk & dk bl .20 .20

Solidarity Week, July 26-Aug. 1. See Nos. RA61-RA62.

Red Crescent, Red Cross, Red Lion — PT48

**1976, May 8 Photo. *Perf. 12½x13***
**RA50** PT48 20p multicolored .85 .50

1984 Olympics
PT49

**1976, July 26 Litho. *Perf. 13½***
**RA51** PT49 10p intense blue .30 .20

Fight Tuberculosis, Red Cross — PT50

**1977, Sept. 14 Photo.**
**RA52** PT50 50p multicolored 5.25 5.25
**RA53** PT50 1d multicolored .80 .80

1984 Olympics
PT51

**1977, Dec. 17 *Perf. 13½x13***
**RA54** PT51 10p multicolored .22 .20

Postal Tax Stamps for use in a particular republic or republics fall beyond the scope of this catalogue and are not listed. These stamps, issued since 1977, were not intended for nationwide use. Some of these issues have designs which are similar to stamps used nationwide, most notably those using variations of the Ruin and Clock (PT47) design. Most others show the Red Cross or the Tuberculosis Cross.

Red Crescent, Red Cross, Red Lion — PT52

**1978, May 7 Litho. *Perf. 13½***
**RA55** PT52 20p on 1d bl & red .70 .35
**RA56** PT52 1d blue & red .30 .20

1984 Olympics
PT53

**1978, Sept.**
**RA57** PT53 30p multicolored .30 .25

8th Mediterranean Games, Split, Sept. 15-29 — PT54

**1979, Mar. 1 Photo. *Perf. 13½x13***
**RA58** PT54 1d violet .25 .25
**RA59** PT54 1d greenish blue .25 .25

Red Cross Week PT55

**1979, May 6** ***Perf. 13½***
**RA60** PT55 1d multicolored .25 .25

Ruin and Clock Type of 1975 Inscribed "1.-7.VI"

**1979, June 1**
**RA61** PT47 30p blk & intense bl .30 .20
Solidarity Week.

Ruin and Clock Type of 1975 Inscribed "1.-7.VI"

**1980, June 1 Litho.** ***Perf. 13x13½***
**RA62** PT47 1d black & blue .25 .25
Solidarity Week, June 1-7.

Olympic Week — PT57

**1979, Oct. 15 Photo.** ***Perf. 14***
**RA63** PT57 30p blue & red .25 .25

Sculpture, Red Cross — PT58

Olympic Week — PT59

**1980, May 4 Litho.** ***Perf. 13½***
**RA64** PT58 1d multicolored .30 .30

**1980, Oct. 20** ***Perf. 14***
**RA65** PT59 50p multicolored .25 .25

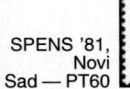

SPENS '81, Novi Sad — PT60

**1980, Dec. 20** ***Perf. 13½***
**RA66** PT60 1d multicolored .20 .20

Red Cross — PT61

Fight Tuberculosis, Red Cross — PT62

**1981, May 4** **Photo.**
**RA67** PT61 1d multicolored .20 .20

**1981, Sept. 14**
**RA68** PT62 1d multicolored .20 .20

Handshake PT63

Robert Koch PT64

Fight Tuberculosis, Red Cross — PT65

**1982, May Litho.** ***Perf. 13***
**RA69** PT63 1d black & red .20 .20

**1983, Sept. 18 Litho.** ***Perf. 13***
**RA70** PT64 1d multicolored .20 .20
For surcharge see No. RA76.

**1983, Sept. 14 Litho.** ***Perf. 13½***
**RA71** PT65 1d bluish grn, blk & red .20 .20
**RA72** PT65 2d bluish grn, blk & red .20 .20

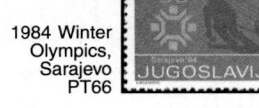

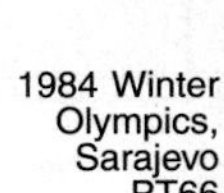
1984 Winter Olympics, Sarajevo PT66

**1983, Oct. 20 Litho.** ***Perf. 12½***
**RA73** PT66 2d greenish blue .20 .20

PLANICA 50 — PT67

**1985, Apr. 1 Photo.** ***Perf. 14***
**RA74** PT67 2d brt ultra & blue .20 .20

Ruin, Clock and Red Cross — PT68

**1987, June 1 Litho.** ***Perf. 10***
**RA75** PT68 30d multicolored .20 .20
Solidarity Week, June 1-7.

No. RA70 Surcharged in Silver

**1988, Sept. 14 Litho.** ***Perf. 13***
**RA76** PT64 12d on 1d multi .20 .20

Intl. Red Cross, 125th Anniv. — PT69

**1989, May 8 Litho.** ***Perf. 12x11***
**Without Gum**
**RA77** PT69 20d bl, sil & red .20 .20
**RA78** PT69 80d bl, sil & red .20 .20
**RA79** PT69 150d bl, sil & red .20 .20
**RA80** PT69 160d bl, sil & red .20 .20
*Nos. RA77-RA80 (4)* .80 .80

Souvenir folders with perf. or imperf. miniature sheets of 4 sold for 3200d.

Ruin, Clock and Red Cross — PT70

Building, Clock and Red Cross — PT71

**1989, June 1** ***Perf. 10***
**Without Gum**
**RA81** PT70 250d red & silver .20 .20
***Roulette 10***
**RA82** PT71 400d brt bl gray & red .20 .20

Souvenir folders with perf. or imperf. miniature sheets containing one 45x65mm stamp like RA81 sold for 3200d.

Fight TB, Red Cross — PT72

Red Cross — PT73

**1989, Sept. 14** ***Rough Perf. 10½***
**Without Gum**
**RA83** PT72 20d black & red .20 .20
**RA84** PT72 200d black & red .20 .20
**RA85** PT72 250d black & red .20 .20
**RA86** PT72 400d black & red .20 .20
**RA87** PT72 650d black & red .20 .20
*Nos. RA83-RA87 (5)* 1.00 1.00

**1990, May 8** ***Perf. 13½***
**Without Gum**
**RA88** PT73 10p green & red .20 .20
**RA89** PT73 20p green & red .20 .20
**RA90** PT73 30p green & red .20 .20
*Nos. RA88-RA90 (3)* .60 .60

Flowers — PT74

Macedonian Red Cross, 45th Anniv. — PT75

**1990, May 8** ***Perf. 10***
**Without Gum**
**RA91** PT74 20p shown .20 .20
**RA92** PT74 20p multi, diff. .20 .20
**RA93** PT75 20p multicolored .20 .20
*a.* Block of 3 + label, #RA91-RA93 .45 .45

Souvenir folders with perf. or imperf. miniature sheets of 3 + label sold for 4d.

PT76

PT77

**1990, Sept. 14 Litho.** ***Perf. 10***
**Without Gum**
**RA94** PT76 20p blue, org & red .20 .20
**RA95** PT76 25p blue, yel & red .20 .20
**RA96** PT76 50p blue, yel & red .35 .20
*Nos. RA94-RA96 (3)* .75 .60
Fight tuberculosis, Red Cross.

**1991, Sept. 14 Litho.** ***Perf. 12½***
**Without Gum**
**RA97** PT77 1.20d dk bl, yel & red .70 .35
**RA98** PT77 2.50d multicolored
Required on mail 9/14-21/91.

PT78

PT79

**1994, May 8 Litho.** ***Perf. 13½***
**RA99** PT78 10p multicolored
No. RA99 was required on mail 5/8-15/94.

**1994, Sept. 14 Litho.** ***Perf. 13x13½***
**RA100** PT79 10p multicolored
No. RA100 was required on mail 9/14-21/94.

PT80

PT81

**1995, May 8 Litho. *Perf. 13½x13***
**RA101** PT80 10p multicolored

No. RA101 was required on mail 5/8-15/95.

**1995, Sept. 9 Litho. *Perf. 13½x13***
**RA102** PT81 10p Wilhelm Röntgen

Fight Tuberculosis. No. RA102 was required on mail 9/9-14/95.

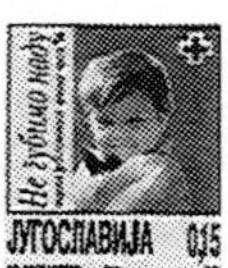

PT82

PT83

**1996, May 8 Litho. *Perf. 12x12½***
**RA103** PT82 15p multicolored

No. RA103 was required on mail 5/8-15/96.

**1996, Sept. Litho. *Perf. 12x12½***
**RA104** PT83 20p multicolored

PT84

**1997, May 8 Litho. *Perf. 13***
**RA105** PT84 20p multicolored

No. RA105 was required on mail 5/8-15/97.

Milutin Rankovic (1880-1967), Artist — PT85

**1997, Sept. 14 Litho. *Perf. 14***
**RA106** PT85 20p multicolored

Fight Tuberculosis. No. RA106 was required on mail 9/14-21/97.

PT86

**1998, May 8 Litho. *Perf. 13¾***
**RA107** PT86 20p multicolored

No. RA107 was required on mail 5/8-15/98.

Red Cross — PT87

**1999, May 8 Litho. *Perf. 13¾***
**RA108** PT87 1d multi

No. RA108 was required on mail 5/8-5/15/99.

Red Cross — PT88

**1999, Sept. 14**
**RA109** PT88 1d multi

No. RA109 was required on mail 9/14-9/21/99.

## POSTAL TAX DUE STAMPS

**Catalogue values for unused stamps in this section are for Never Hinged items.**

The tax of Nos. RAJ1-RAJ9, RAJ11-RAJ12, RAJ14 and RAJ18 was for the Red Cross.

Inscribed "PORTO."

Type of Postal Tax Stamp, 1933

**1933 Unwmk. Litho. *Perf. 13***
**RAJ1** PT1 50p dull grn & red .80 .20

Type of Postal Tax Stamp, 1947

**1947 *Perf. 12½***
**RAJ2** PT4 50p blue grn & scar .75 .20

For surcharge see Trieste No. RAJ1.

Type of Postal Tax Stamp, 1948

**1948**
**RAJ3** PT5 50p dark grn & red .75 .20

Type of Postal Tax Stamp, 1949

**1949**
**RAJ4** PT6 50p red & violet 1.10 .20

For overprint see Trieste No. RAJ2.

Cross and Map of Yugoslavia PTD2

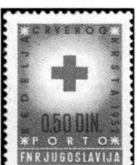

Red Cross PTD3

**1950 Unwmk. *Perf. 12½***
**RAJ5** PTD2 50p red brown & red .40 .20

Type of Postal Tax Stamp, 1951

**1951**
**RAJ6** PT8 50p emerald & red .50 .20

For overprint see Trieste No. RAJ3.

**1952 Unwmk. Photo. *Perf. 12½***
**RAJ7** PTD3 50p gray & car .60 .20

For overprint see Trieste No. RAJ4.

Types of Postal Tax Stamps, 1953-57

**1953-57 Litho.**
**RAJ8** PT10 2d yel brown & red .80 .20
**RAJ9** PT11 2d lilac & red ('54) .80 .20
**RAJ10** PT12 2d yel grn ('55) .70 .20
**RAJ11** PT13 2d dk vio brn & red ('55) .90 .20
**RAJ12** PT14 2d blue grn & red ('56) .35 .20
**RAJ13** PT15 2d violet brn ('56) .70 .20
**RAJ14** PT16 2d gray, blk & car ('57) .65 .20
**RAJ15** PT17 2d lt bl, bis & grn ('57) .50 .20
*Nos. RAJ8-RAJ15 (8)* 5.40 1.60

For overprints see Trieste Nos. RAJ5-RAJ5.

Redrawn Type of Regular Issue, 1953

**1958 *Perf. 12½x12***
**RAJ16** A95 2d multicolored .35 .20

Child With Toy — PTD4

**1958 Litho. *Perf. 12½***
**RAJ17** PTD4 2d lt ultra & blk .30 .20

Issued for Children's Week, Oct. 5-11.

Type of Postal Tax Stamp, 1959

**1959**
**RAJ18** PT19 2d yel org & red .30 .20

Type of Postal Tax Stamp, 1959

Design: Tree, cock and wheat.

**1959**
**RAJ19** PT20 2d ocher & mar .40 .20

Type of Postal Tax Stamp, 1960

**1960**
**RAJ20** PT21 2d vio brn & red .50 .20

Type of Postal Tax Stamp, 1960

Design: Boy, tools and ball.

**1960**
**RAJ21** PT22 2d Prussian blue .45 .20

Type of Postal Tax Stamp, 1961

**1961, May 7**
**RAJ22** PT23 2d multicolored .55 .20

Type of Postal Tax Stamp, 1961

**1961, Oct. 1**
**RAJ23** PT24 2d apple grn & brn .30 .20

Type of Postal Tax Stamp, 1962

**1962, Apr. 30**
**RAJ24** PT25 5d brn red, bl & red .25 .20

Type of Postal Tax Stamp, 1963

**1963, May 5**
**RAJ25** PT26 5d red org, red & gray .30 .20

## OFFICES ABROAD

King Peter II — A1

**1943 Unwmk. Typo. *Perf. 12½***
**1K1** A1 2d dark blue .20 *4.00*
**1K2** A1 3d slate .20 *4.00*
**1K3** A1 5d carmine .20 *4.00*
**1K4** A1 10d black .20 *4.00*
*Nos. 1K1-1K4 (4)* .80 *16.00*

For surcharges see Nos. 1KB1-1KB4.

V. Vodnik — A2

Peter Nyegosh — A3

3d, Ljudovit Gaj. 4d, Vuk Stefanovic Karadzic. 5d, Bishop Joseph Strossmayer. 10d, Karageorge.

**1943, Dec. 1 Engr. *Perf. 12½x13***
**1K5** A2 1d red org & black .30 *8.25*
**1K6** A3 2d yel green & blk .35 *8.50*
**1K7** A2 3d dp ultra & blk .35 *8.75*
**1K8** A3 4d dk pur & brn blk .40 *9.25*
**1K9** A2 5d brn vio & brn blk .40 *9.75*
**1K10** A3 10d brn & brown blk .45 *10.00*
*Nos. 1K5-1K10 (6)* 2.25 *54.50*

**Souvenir Sheet**
***Perf. 13½***
**Center in Black**

**1K11** Sheet of 6, #1K5-1K10 6.75

25th anniv. of the Union of Liberated Yugoslavia. Valid on ships of the Yugoslav Navy and Mercantile Marine.

Nos. 1K5-1K10 overprinted diagonally "1945" in London were not issued. In 1950, they were sold by the Yugoslav Government without postal validity. Later they appeared with the additional overprint of the outline of a plane at upper left in carmine or black.

## OFFICES ABROAD SEMI-POSTAL STAMPS

Nos. 1K1-1K4 Surcharged in Orange or Black

**1943 Unwmk. *Perf. 12½***
**1KB1** A1 2d + 12.50d dk bl .65 *8.25*
**1KB2** A1 3d + 12.50d slate .65 *8.25*
**1KB3** A1 5d + 12.50d car (Bk) .65 *8.25*
**1KB4** A1 10d + 12.50d black .65 *8.25*
*Nos. 1KB1-1KB4 (4)* 2.60 *33.00*

The surtax was for the Red Cross.

# LJUBLJANA

## (Lubiana, Laibach)

### Italian Occupation

Under Italian occupation in 1941, the western half of Slovenia was known as the Province of Ljubljana (Lubiana to the Italians, Laibach to the Germans) and a quisling administration was set up under the profascist General Rupnik.

100 Centesimi = 1 Lira

Yugoslavia Nos. 127, 128, 142-154 Overprinted in Black

**1941 Unwmk. *Perf. 12½, 13x12½***
**N1** A16 25p black .75 1.00
**N2** A16 50p orange .75 1.00
**N3** A16 1d yellow grn .75 1.00
**N4** A16 1.50d red .75 1.00
**N5** A16 2d dp magenta .75 1.00
**N6** A16 3d dl red brn .75 1.00
**N7** A16 4d ultra .75 1.00
**N8** A16 5d dark blue .75 1.00
**N9** A16 5.50d dk vio brn .75 1.00
**N10** A16 6d slate blue 1.00 1.50
**N11** A16 8d sepia 1.00 1.50
**N12** A10 10d bright vio 1.00 1.50
**N13** A16 12d brt violet 2.00 2.50
**N14** A10 15d brown 110.00 140.00
**N15** A16 16d dl violet 2.00 2.50
**N16** A16 20d blue 5.00 6.50
**N17** A16 30d brt pink 20.00 27.50
*Nos. N1-N17 (17)* 148.75 192.50

Yugoslavia Nos. 127, 142-154 Overprinted in Black

**N18** A16 25p black .60 .50
**N19** A16 50p orange .60 .50
**N20** A16 1d yellow grn .60 .50
**N21** A16 1.50d red .60 .50
**N22** A16 2d dp magenta .60 .50
**N23** A16 3d dl red brn .60 .50
**N24** A16 4d ultra .60 .50
**N25** A16 5d dark blue .60 .50
**N26** A16 5.50d dk vio brn .60 .50
**N27** A16 6d slate blue .60 .50
**N28** A16 8d sepia .60 .50
**N29** A10 10d brt violet 1.25 1.00

N30 A16 12d bright vio .60 .50
N31 A16 16d dl violet 1.25 1.00
N32 A16 20d blue 5.00 4.50
N33 A16 30d brt pink 35.00 32.50

Yugoslavia Nos. 145, 148 Surcharged in Black

N34 A16 50p on 1.50d red .50 .60
N35 A16 1d on 4d ultra .50 .60
*Nos. N18-N35 (18)* 50.70 46.20

**German Occupation**

Stamps of Italy, 1929-42, Overprinted or Surcharged in Blue, Carmine, Black or Green

a

b

c

| 1944 | Wmk. 140 | | *Perf. 14* | |
|---|---|---|---|---|
| N36 | A90(a) | 5c ol brown | .20 | *1.25* |
| N37 | A92(b) | 10c dark brn | .20 | *1.25* |
| N38 | A93(a) | 15c sl grn (C) | .20 | *1.25* |
| N39 | A91(b) | 20c rose red | .20 | *1.25* |
| N40 | A94(a) | 25c dp grn (C) | .20 | *1.25* |
| N41 | A95(b) | 30c ol brown | .20 | *1.25* |
| N42 | A93(a) | 35c dp bl (C) | .20 | *1.25* |
| N43 | A95(b) | 50c purple (C) | .20 | *2.00* |
| N44 | A94(a) | 75c rose red | .20 | *2.75* |
| N45 | A91(b) | 1 l deep vio | .20 | *2.75* |
| N46 | A94(a) | 1.25 l dp bl (C) | .20 | *1.60* |
| N47 | A92(b) | 1.75 l red org | .85 | *8.50* |
| N48 | A93(a) | 2 l car lake | .20 | *2.00* |
| N49 | A90(c) | 2.55 l on 5c ol brn (Bk) | .50 | *4.00* |
| N50 | A94(a) | 5 l on 25c dp grn | .40 | *4.00* |
| N51 | A93(b) | 10 l purple | 2.75 | *16.00* |
| N52 | A91(a) | 20 l on 20c rose red (G) | 2.75 | *16.00* |
| N53 | A93(b) | 25 l on 2 l car lake (G) | 2.75 | *27.50* |
| N54 | A92(a) | 50 l on 1.75 l red org (C) | 6.50 | *50.00* |
| | | *Nos. N36-N54 (19)* | 18.90 | *145.85* |

Krizna Jama — A1

Cerknica Lake — A2

Designs: 20c, Railroad Bridge, Borovnica. 25c, Landscape near Ljubljana. 50c, Church, Ribnica. 75c, View, Ljubljana. 1 l, Old Castle, Ljubljana. 1.25 l, Kocevje (Gottschee). 1.50 l, Borovnica Falls. 2 l, Castle, Konstanjevnica. 2.50 l, Castle, Turjak. 3 l, Castle, Zuzemperk. 5 l, View of Krk. 10 l, View of Otolac. 20 l, Farm, Carniola. 30 l, Castle and church, Tabor.

***Perf. 10½x11½, 11½x10½***

| 1945 | Photo. | | Unwmk. | |
|---|---|---|---|---|
| N55 | A1 | 5c black | .25 | *.75* |
| N56 | A2 | 10c red orange | .25 | *.75* |
| N57 | A2 | 20c brn carmine | .25 | *.75* |
| N58 | A2 | 25c dk sl green | .25 | *.75* |
| N59 | A1 | 50c deep violet | .25 | *.75* |
| N60 | A2 | 75c vermilion | .25 | *.75* |
| N61 | A2 | 1 l dark ol grn | .25 | *.75* |
| N62 | A1 | 1.25 l dark blue | .25 | *.75* |
| N63 | A1 | 1.50 l olive black | .25 | *.75* |
| N64 | A2 | 2 l ultramarine | .40 | *1.10* |
| N65 | A2 | 2.50 l brown | .40 | *1.10* |
| N66 | A1 | 3 l brt red vio | .75 | *2.25* |
| N67 | A2 | 5 l dk red brn | .75 | *2.25* |
| N68 | A2 | 10 l slate green | 1.50 | *5.25* |
| N69 | A2 | 20 l sapphire | 6.00 | *20.00* |
| N70 | A1 | 30 l rose pink | 40.00 | *150.00* |
| | | *Nos. N55-N70 (16)* | 52.05 | *188.70* |

## SEMI-POSTAL STAMPS

**Italian Occupation**

Yugoslavia Nos. B116-B119 with Additional Overprint in Black

***Perf. 11½x12½, 12½x11½***

| 1941 | | | Unwmk. | |
|---|---|---|---|---|
| NB1 | AP6 | 50p + 50p on 5d | 7.50 | 9.75 |
| NB2 | AP7 | 1d + 1d on 10d | 7.50 | 9.75 |
| NB3 | AP8 | 1.50d + 1.50d on 20d | 7.50 | 9.75 |
| NB4 | AP9 | 2d + 2d on 30d | 7.50 | 9.75 |
| | | *Nos. NB1-NB4 (4)* | 30.00 | 39.00 |

**German Occupation**

Italy Nos. E14 and E15 Surcharged in Red:

| 1944 | | | Wmk. 140 | |
|---|---|---|---|---|
| NB5 | SD4 | 1.25 l + 50 l green | 12.50 | *125.00* |
| NB6 | SD4 | 2.50 l + 50 l dp org | 12.50 | *125.00* |

The surtax aided the Red Cross.

Same, Surcharged in Blue or Green:

| | | | | |
|---|---|---|---|---|
| NB7 | SD4 | 1.25 l + 50 l grn (B) | 12.50 | *125.00* |
| NB8 | SD4 | 2.50 l + 50 l dp org | 12.50 | *125.00* |
| | | *Nos. NB5-NB8 (4)* | 50.00 | *500.00* |

The surtax aided the Homeless Relief Fund. The German and Slovenian inscriptions in the surcharges are transposed on Nos. NB6 and NB8.

Italy Nos. C12-C14, C16-C18 Surcharged "DEN WAISEN," "SIROTAM," Heraldic Eagle and Surtax in Blue or Red

| 1944 | | | Wmk. 140 | |
|---|---|---|---|---|
| NB9 | AP4 | 25c + 10 l dk grn | 6.00 | *40.00* |
| NB10 | AP3 | 50c + 10 l ol brn | 6.00 | *40.00* |
| NB11 | AP5 | 75c + 20 l org brn | 6.00 | *40.00* |
| NB12 | AP5 | 1 l + 20 l purple | 6.00 | *40.00* |
| NB13 | AP6 | 2 l + 20 l dp bl (R) | 6.00 | *40.00* |
| NB14 | AP3 | 5 l + 20 l dk grn | 6.00 | *40.00* |
| | | *Nos. NB9-NB14 (6)* | 36.00 | *240.00* |

The surcharge aided orphans.

Same, Surcharged "WINTERHILFE," "ZIMSKA POMOC," Heraldic Eagle and Surtax in Blue or Red

| | | | | |
|---|---|---|---|---|
| NB15 | AP4 | 25c + 10 l dk grn | 6.00 | *40.00* |
| NB16 | AP3 | 50c + 10 l ol brn | 6.00 | *40.00* |
| NB17 | AP5 | 75c + 20 l org brn | 6.00 | *40.00* |
| NB18 | AP5 | 1 l + 20 l purple | 6.00 | *40.00* |
| NB19 | AP6 | 2 l + 20 l dp bl (R) | 6.00 | *40.00* |
| NB20 | AP3 | 5 l + 20 l dk grn | 6.00 | *40.00* |
| | | *Nos. NB15-NB20 (6)* | 36.00 | *240.00* |

The surcharge was for winter relief.

## AIR POST STAMPS

**Italian Occupation**

Yugoslavia Nos. C7-C16 Ovptd. like Nos. NB1-NB4

***Perf. 12½, 12½x11½, 11½x12½***

| 1941 | | | Unwmk. | |
|---|---|---|---|---|
| NC1 | AP6 | 50p brown | .40 | .85 |
| NC2 | AP7 | 1d yel grn | .40 | .85 |
| NC3 | AP8 | 2d bl gray | .55 | 1.10 |
| NC4 | AP9 | 2.50d rose red | .55 | 1.10 |
| NC5 | AP6 | 5d brn vio | 1.00 | 1.75 |
| NC6 | AP7 | 10d brn lake | 1.00 | 1.75 |
| NC7 | AP8 | 20d dark grn | 8.25 | 10.00 |
| NC8 | AP9 | 30d ultra | 37.50 | 22.50 |
| NC9 | AP10 | 40d Prus grn & pale grn | 110.00 | 70.00 |
| NC10 | AP11 | 50d sl bl & gray bl | 75.00 | 45.00 |
| *a.* | | Inverted overprint | 200.00 | |
| | | *Nos. NC1-NC10 (10)* | 234.65 | 154.90 |

**German Occupation**

Italy Nos. C12-C14, C16-C19 Overprinted Types "a" and "b" in Carmine, Green or Blue

| 1944 | Wmk. 140 | | *Perf. 14* | |
|---|---|---|---|---|
| NC11 | AP4(a) | 25c dk grn (C) | 1.10 | *6.25* |
| NC12 | AP3(b) | 50c ol brn (C) | 4.25 | *30.00* |
| NC13 | AP5(a) | 75c org brn (G) | 1.25 | *8.75* |
| NC14 | AP5(b) | 1 l pur (C) | 5.25 | *24.00* |
| NC15 | AP6(a) | 2 l dp bl (Bl) | 3.00 | *20.00* |
| NC16 | AP3(b) | 5 l dk grn (C) | 3.00 | *24.00* |
| NC17 | AP3(a) | 10 l dp car (G) | 2.25 | *32.50* |
| | | *Nos. NC11-NC17 (7)* | 20.10 | *145.50* |

## AIR POST SPECIAL DELIVERY STAMP

**German Occupation**

Italy #CE3 Ovptd. Type "b" in Blue

| 1944 | Wmk. 140 | | *Perf. 14* | |
|---|---|---|---|---|
| NCE1 | APSD2 | 2 l gray blk | 3.75 | *15.00* |

## SPECIAL DELIVERY STAMP

**German Occupation**

Italy #E14 Ovptd. Type "b" in Green

| 1944 | Wmk. 140 | | *Perf. 14* | |
|---|---|---|---|---|
| NE1 | SD4 | 1.25 l green | 1.00 | *5.00* |

## POSTAGE DUE STAMPS

**Italian Occupation**

Yugoslavia Nos. J28-J32 Overprinted in Black Like Nos. N1-N17

| 1941 | Unwmk. | | *Perf. 12½* | |
|---|---|---|---|---|
| NJ1 | D4 | 50p violet | .40 | .65 |
| NJ2 | D4 | 1d rose | .40 | .65 |
| NJ3 | D4 | 2d deep blue | .40 | .65 |
| NJ4 | D4 | 5d orange | 4.50 | 5.50 |
| NJ5 | D4 | 10d chocolate | 4.50 | 5.50 |
| | | *Nos. NJ1-NJ5 (5)* | 10.20 | 12.95 |

Same Overprinted in Black

| | | | | |
|---|---|---|---|---|
| NJ6 | D4 | 50p violet | .20 | .25 |
| NJ7 | D4 | 1d rose | .20 | .25 |
| NJ8 | D4 | 2d deep blue | .40 | .75 |
| NJ9 | D4 | 5d orange | 22.50 | 30.00 |
| NJ10 | D4 | 10d chocolate | 8.00 | 10.00 |
| | | *Nos. NJ6-NJ10 (5)* | 31.30 | 41.25 |

Same Overprinted in Black

R. Commissariato Civile Territori Sloveni occupati LUBIANA

| | | | | |
|---|---|---|---|---|
| NJ11 | D4 | 50p violet | .25 | .50 |
| NJ12 | D4 | 1d rose | .50 | .70 |
| NJ13 | D4 | 2d deep blue | 9.25 | 11.50 |
| | | *Nos. NJ11-NJ13 (3)* | 10.00 | 12.70 |

**German Occupation**

Postage Due Stamps of Italy, 1934, Overprinted or Surcharged in Various Colors

d

e

f

g

| 1944 | Wmk. 140 | | *Perf. 14* | |
|---|---|---|---|---|
| NJ14 | D6(d) | 5c brown (Br) | 1.25 | *13.00* |
| NJ15 | D6(e) | 10c blue (Bl) | 1.25 | *13.00* |
| NJ16 | D6(d) | 20c rose red (R) | .20 | *.55* |
| NJ17 | D6(e) | 25c green (G) | .20 | *.55* |
| NJ18 | D6(f) | 30c on 50c vio (Bk) | .20 | *.55* |
| NJ19 | D6(g) | 40c on 5c brn (Bl) | .20 | *.55* |
| NJ20 | D6(d) | 50c violet (V) | .20 | *.55* |
| NJ21 | D7(e) | 1 l red orange (R) | 1.25 | *6.50* |
| NJ22 | D7(d) | 2 l green (Bl) | 1.25 | *6.50* |
| | | *Nos. NJ14-NJ22 (9)* | 6.00 | *41.75* |

Fiume-Kupa Zone
Italian Occupation

Four issues of 1941-42 consist of overprints on Yugoslav stamps of 1939-41: (a.) 14 stamps overprinted "ZONA OCCUPATO FIUMANO KUPA" and "ZOFK ZOFK ZOFK." (b.) 3 stamps overprinted as illustrated. (c.) 1 stamp surcharged "MEMENTO AVDERE SEMPER." "L1," etc. (d.) 3 stamps overprinted in arch: "Pro Maternite e Infanzia."

# ISSUES FOR ISTRIA AND THE SLOVENE COAST (ZONE B)

Grapes — A1

Olive Branch — A2

Sailboat, Pola — A3

Designs: 50c, Donkey. Nos. 25-26, Ruined home. 2 l, Duino Castle. 5 l, Birthplace of Vladimir Gortan. 10 l, Plowing. Nos. 33-34, Tuna. 30 l, Viaduct at Solkan, Soca River.

***Perf. 11½, 12, 10½x11½***

**1945-46** **Photo.**

| No. | Type | Description | Unused | Used |
|---|---|---|---|---|
| **23** | A1 | 25c dark green | .85 | 1.00 |
| **24** | A1 | 50c red brown | .20 | .20 |
| **25** | A1 | 1 l green | .20 | .20 |
| **26** | A1 | 1 l red | .20 | .20 |
| **27** | A2 | 1.50 l olive brown | .20 | .20 |
| **28** | A2 | 2 l dk Prus grn | .20 | .20 |
| **29** | A3 | 4 l red | .20 | .20 |
| **30** | A3 | 4 l bright blue | .30 | .40 |
| **31** | A3 | 5 l gray black | .20 | .20 |
| **32** | A3 | 10 l brown | .20 | .20 |
| **33** | A3 | 20 l blue | 1.60 | .85 |
| **34** | A3 | 20 l dark violet | 4.50 | 4.00 |
| **35** | A3 | 30 l magenta | 1.25 | .60 |
| | | *Nos. 23-35 (13)* | 10.10 | 8.45 |

The first (Ljubljana) printing is perf. 10½x11½ and consists of Nos. 23-24, 26-28, 30-32, 34-35. The second (Zagreb) printing is perf. 12 and consists of Nos. 23-25, 27-29, 31-33, 35. The third (Belgrade) printing is perf. 11½ and consists of Nos. 25, 28, 40-41.

See Nos. 40-41. For surcharges see Nos. 36-37, J1-J19.

Nos. 33 and 35 Surcharged with New Values and Bars in Black

**1946** **Unwmk.** ***Perf. 11½***

| No. | Type | Description | Unused | Used |
|---|---|---|---|---|
| **36** | A3 | 1 l on 20 l blue | .70 | .35 |
| **37** | A3 | 2 l on 30 l magenta | .65 | .35 |

Types of 1945

Design: 3 l, Duino Castle

**1946, Nov. 30**

| No. | Type | Description | Unused | Used |
|---|---|---|---|---|
| **40** | A2 | 3 l crimson | .20 | .20 |
| **41** | A3 | 6 l ultra | .20 | .20 |

Types of Yugoslavia and of Official Stamps of 1946 Surcharged in Black

On A26

On O1

**1947** **Unwmk.** ***Perf. 12½***

| No. | Type | Description | Unused | Used |
|---|---|---|---|---|
| **42** | A26 | 1 l on 9d lilac rose | .20 | .20 |
| **43** | O1 | 1.50 l on 50p blue | .20 | .20 |
| **44** | A26 | 2 l on 9d lilac rose | .20 | .20 |
| **45** | O1 | 3 l on 50p blue | .20 | .20 |
| **46** | A26 | 5 l on 9d lilac rose | .20 | .20 |
| **47** | O1 | 6 l on 50p blue | .20 | .20 |
| **48** | A26 | 10 l on 9d lilac rose | .20 | .20 |
| **49** | O1 | 15 l on 50p blue | .20 | .20 |
| **50** | A26 | 35 l on 9d lilac rose | .20 | .20 |
| **51** | O1 | 50 l on 50p blue | .20 | .20 |
| | | *Nos. 42-51 (10)* | 2.00 | 2.00 |

## POSTAGE DUE STAMPS

Nos. 23, 24 34 and 35 Surcharged in Black

**1945** **Unwmk.** ***Perf. 10½x11½***

| No. | Type | Description | Unused | Used |
|---|---|---|---|---|
| **J1** | A3 | 50c on 20 l dk vio | .50 | 1.25 |
| **J2** | A1 | 1 l on 25c dk grn | 2.75 | 3.50 |
| **J3** | A3 | 2 l on 30 l magenta | .40 | 1.00 |
| **J4** | A1 | 4 l on 50c red brn | .30 | .20 |
| **J5** | A1 | 8 l on 50c red brn | .25 | .20 |
| **J6** | A1 | 10 l on 50c red brn | 3.00 | 1.60 |
| **J7** | A1 | 20 l on 50c red brn | 3.00 | 1.60 |
| | | *Nos. J1-J7 (7)* | 10.20 | 9.35 |

Nos. 25 and 35 Surcharged in Black

**1945** ***Perf. 12***

| No. | Type | Description | Unused | Used |
|---|---|---|---|---|
| **J8** | A1 | 1 l on 1 l green | .20 | .20 |
| **J9** | A1 | 2 l on 1 l green | .20 | .20 |
| **J10** | A1 | 4 l on 1 l green | .25 | .20 |
| **J11** | A3 | 10 l on 30 l magenta | .55 | .40 |
| **J12** | A3 | 20 l on 30 l magenta | 3.00 | 1.50 |
| **J13** | A3 | 30 l on 30 l magenta | 3.00 | 1.50 |
| | | *Nos. J8-J13 (6)* | 7.20 | 4.00 |

The surcharges are arranged to fit the designs of the stamps.

No. 23 Surcharged in Black

**1946**

| No. | Type | Description | Unused | Used |
|---|---|---|---|---|
| **J14** | A1 | 1 l on 25c dark green | .60 | .70 |
| **J15** | A1 | 2 l on 25c dark green | .85 | 1.00 |
| **J16** | A1 | 4 l on 25c dark green | 1.00 | 1.10 |

No. 33 Surcharged in Black

| No. | Type | Description | Unused | Used |
|---|---|---|---|---|
| **J17** | A3 | 10 l on 20 l blue | 3.00 | .50 |
| **J18** | A3 | 20 l on 20 l blue | 5.50 | 4.00 |
| **J19** | A3 | 30 l on 20 l blue | 6.75 | 5.00 |
| | | *Nos. J14-J19 (6)* | 17.70 | 12.30 |

Type of Yugoslavia Postage Due Stamps, 1946, Surcharged in Black

**1947**

| No. | Type | Description | Unused | Used |
|---|---|---|---|---|
| **J20** | D7 | 1 l on 1d brt blue grn | .20 | .20 |
| **J21** | D7 | 2 l on 1d brt blue grn | .20 | .20 |
| **J22** | D7 | 6 l on 1d brt blue grn | .20 | .20 |
| **J23** | D7 | 10 l on 1d brt blue grn | .20 | .20 |
| **J24** | D7 | 30 l on 1d brt blue grn | .30 | .40 |
| | | *Nos. J20-J24 (5)* | 1.10 | 1.20 |

TRIESTE, ZONE A

See listing under Italy, Vol. 3.

# TRIESTE

A free territory (1947-1954) on the Adriatic Sea between Italy and Yugoslavia. In 1954 the territory was divided, Italy acquiring the northern section and seaport, Yugoslavia the southern section (Zone B).

**Catalogue values for all unused stamps in this country are for Never Hinged items.**

## ZONE B

**Issued by the Yugoslav Military Government**

100 Centesimi = 1 Lira

100 Paras = 1 Dinar (1949)

See Istria and the Slovene Coast (Zone B) for preceding issues of 1945-47.

Stylized Gymnast and Arms of Trieste — A1

**1948** **Unwmk.** **Litho.** ***Perf. 10½x11***

**Inscriptions in:**

| No. | Type | Description | Unused | Used |
|---|---|---|---|---|
| **1** | A1 | 100 l Italian | 2.50 | 1.75 |
| **2** | A1 | 100 l Croatian | 2.50 | 1.75 |
| **3** | A1 | 100 l Slovene | 2.50 | 1.75 |
| *a.* | | Strip of 3, #1-3 | 12.50 | 17.50 |
| | | *Nos. 1-3 (3)* | 7.50 | 5.25 |

May Day.

Clasped Hands, Hammer and Sickle — A2

**1949** **Photo.** ***Perf. 11½x12½***

| No. | Type | Description | Unused | Used |
|---|---|---|---|---|
| **4** | A2 | 10 l grnsh blk & ol grn | .50 | .40 |

Labor Day, May 1, 1949.

"V.U.J.A. S.T.T." are the initials of "Vojna Uprava Jugoslovenske Armije, Slobodna Teritorija Trsta" (Military Administration Yugoslav Army, Free Territory of Trieste).

Stamps of Yugoslavia, 1945-47 Overprinted in Carmine or Ultramarine

**1949, Aug. 15** ***Perf. 12½***

| No. | Type | Description | Unused | Used |
|---|---|---|---|---|
| **5** | A22 | 50p ol gray | .25 | .25 |
| **6** | A22 | 1d bl grn | .25 | .25 |
| **7** | A24 | 2d scar (U) | .25 | .25 |
| **8** | A25 | 3d dl red (U) | .25 | .25 |
| **9** | A24 | 4d dk bl | .50 | .35 |
| **10** | A25 | 5d dk bl | .50 | .35 |
| **11** | A26 | 9d rose vio (U) | 1.25 | .75 |
| **12** | A23 | 12d ultra | 3.00 | 2.00 |
| **13** | A22 | 16d blue | 3.75 | 2.50 |
| **14** | A23 | 20d org ver (U) | 5.00 | 3.00 |
| | | *Nos. 5-14 (10)* | 15.00 | 9.95 |

The letters of the overprint are set closer and in one line on Nos. 7 and 9.

Yugoslavia Nos. 266 and 267 Overprinted in Carmine

Burelage in Color of Stamp

**1949**

| No. | Type | Description | Unused | Used |
|---|---|---|---|---|
| **15** | A58 | 5d blue | 7.50 | *6.50* |
| **16** | A58 | 12d brown | 7.50 | *6.50* |

75th anniv. of the UPU.

Yugoslavia, Nos. 269 to 272, Overprinted in Carmine

**1950**

| No. | Type | Description | Unused | Used |
|---|---|---|---|---|
| **17** | A60 | 2d bl grn | 1.00 | .60 |
| **18** | A60 | 3d car rose | 1.25 | .75 |
| **19** | A60 | 5d blue | 1.75 | 1.00 |
| **20** | A60 | 10d dp org | 4.75 | 3.25 |
| | | *Nos. 17-20 (4)* | 8.75 | 5.60 |

Workers Carrying Tools and Flag — A3

Peasant on Ass — A4

**1950, May 1** **Photo.**

| No. | Type | Description | Unused | Used |
|---|---|---|---|---|
| **21** | A3 | 3d violet | .50 | .40 |
| **22** | A3 | 10d carmine | .75 | .50 |

Labor Day, May 1, 1950.

**1950** **Unwmk.** ***Perf. 12½***

Designs: 1d, Cockerel. 2d, Goose. 3d, Bees and honeycomb. 5d, Oxen. 10d, Turkey. 15d, Goats. 20d, Silkworms.

| No. | Type | Description | Unused | Used |
|---|---|---|---|---|
| **23** | A4 | 50p dk gray | .20 | .20 |
| **24** | A4 | 1d brn car | .20 | .20 |
| **25** | A4 | 2d dp bl | .20 | .20 |
| **26** | A4 | 3d org brn | .30 | .20 |
| **27** | A4 | 5d aqua | 1.00 | .20 |
| **28** | A4 | 10d brown | 1.40 | .20 |
| **29** | A4 | 15d violet | 6.75 | 4.00 |
| **30** | A4 | 20d dk grn | 2.50 | 1.50 |
| | | *Nos. 23-30 (8)* | 12.55 | 6.70 |

**1951**

| No. | Type | Description | Unused | Used |
|---|---|---|---|---|
| **31** | A4 | 1d orange brown | .35 | .20 |
| **32** | A4 | 3d rose brown | .50 | .20 |

Worker A5

**1951, May 1**

| No. | Type | Description | Unused | Used |
|---|---|---|---|---|
| **33** | A5 | 3d dark red | .55 | .40 |
| **34** | A5 | 10d brown olive | .95 | .60 |

Labor Day.

Pietro Paolo Vergerio — A7

Bicycle Race — A8

**1951, Oct. 21** **Litho.**

| No. | Type | Description | Unused | Used |
|---|---|---|---|---|
| **37** | A7 | 5d blue | .65 | .50 |
| **38** | A7 | 10d claret | .65 | .50 |
| **39** | A7 | 20d sepia | .65 | .50 |
| | | *Nos. 37-39 (3)* | 1.95 | 1.50 |

Types of Yugoslavia, 1951, Overprinted "STT VUJA"

**1951, Nov.**

| No. | Type | Description | Unused | Used |
|---|---|---|---|---|
| **40** | A81 | 10d brn org (V) | .90 | .60 |
| **41** | A81 | 12d grnsh blk (C) | .90 | .60 |

**1952** **Photo.**

| No. | Type | Description | Unused | Used |
|---|---|---|---|---|
| **42** | A8 | 5d shown | .20 | .20 |
| **43** | A8 | 10d Soccer | .20 | .20 |
| **44** | A8 | 15d Rowing | .20 | .20 |
| **45** | A8 | 28d Sailing | .70 | .50 |
| **46** | A8 | 50d Volleyball | 1.50 | .85 |
| **47** | A8 | 100d Diving | 4.00 | 2.50 |
| | | *Nos. 42-47 (6)* | 6.80 | 4.45 |

Marshal Tito
A9 A10

**1952, May 25** *Perf. 11½*
**48** A9 15d dk brn 1.75 1.00
**49** A10 28d red brn 2.25 2.00
**50** A9 50d dk gray grn 2.75 2.00
*Nos. 48-50 (3)* 6.75 5.00

60th birthday of Marshal Tito.

### Types of Yugoslavia 1952 Overprinted in Carmine "STT VUJNA"

**1952, July 26** *Perf. 12½*
**51** A90 5d dk brn & sal, *cr* .65 .40
**52** A90 10d dk grn & grn .65 .40
**53** A90 15d dk brn & bl, *lil* .65 .40
**54** A90 28d dk brn & buff, *cr* 1.50 1.00
**55** A90 50d dk brn & buff, *yel* 6.00 4.00
**56** A90 100d ind & lil, *pink* 13.50 10.00
*Nos. 51-56 (6)* 22.95 16.20

15th Olympic Games, Helsinki, 1952. Nos. 52, 54, 56 inscribed in Cyrillic characters.
The added "N" in "VUJNA" stands for "Narodna" (Peoples'). See note after No. 4.
Nos. 51-56 exist imperf. Value of set, $375.

### Yugoslavia Nos. 365 to 367 Overprinted in Carmine "STT VUJNA"

**1952, Sept. 13**
**57** A91 15d deep claret .55 .55
**58** A91 28d dark brown .75 .75
**59** A91 50d gray 3.00 3.00
*Nos. 57-59 (3)* 4.30 4.30

Formation of the Yugoslav navy, 10th anniv.

### Yugoslavia No. 358 Overprinted "STT VUJA" in Blue

**1952, June 22**
**60** A89 15d bright rose .90 .95

Children's Week.

### Yugoslavia Nos. 369-372 Overprinted "VUJNA STT" in Blue or Carmine

**1952, Nov. 4**
**61** A93 15d red brn (Bl) .50 .75
**62** A93 15d dk vio bl .50 .75
**63** A93 15d dk brn .50 .75
**64** A93 15d bl grn .50 .75
*Nos. 61-64 (4)* 2.00 3.00

Issued to publicize the 6th Yugoslavia Communist Party Congress, Zagreb, 1952.

Anchovies and Starfish — A11

**1952 Unwmk. Photo.** *Perf. 11x11½*
**65** A11 15d red brown 1.25 1.60
*a.* Souvenir sheet, imperf. 8.75 15.00

Capodistria Phil. Exhib., Nov. 29-Dec. 7.
No. 65a contains a 50d dark blue green stamp. Sold for 85d.

### Stamps or Types of Yugoslavia Overprinted "STT VUJNA" in Various Colors

**1953, Feb. 3** *Perf. 12½*
**66** A94 15d brn carmine (Bl) .30 .40
**67** A94 30d chalky blue (R) .85 .55

10th anniv. of the death of Nikola Tesla.

**1953**
**68** A68 1d gray 2.25 2.50
**69** A68 2d car (V) .45 .50
**70** A68 3d rose red (R) .45 .50
**71** A68 5d orange .45 .50
**72** A68 10d emerald (G) .45 .50
**73** A68 15d rose red (V) .90 1.10
**74** A68 30d blue (Bl) 1.90 2.00
**75** A68 50d grnsh bl (Bl) 3.50 4.00
*Nos. 68-75 (8)* 10.35 11.60

Nos. 69, 71 and 73 are lithographed.
See Nos. 90-92.

**1953, Apr. 21** *Perf. 11½*
**76** A95 15d dk ol grn (O) .35 .40
**77** A95 30d chalky blue (O) .35 .40
**78** A95 50d henna brown 1.10 1.10
*Nos. 76-78 (3)* 1.80 1.90

Issued in honor of the United Nations.

Automobile Climbing Mt. Lovcen — A12

Various automobiles and motorcycles.

**1953, June 2** *Perf. 12½*
**79** A12 15d ocher & choc .35 .20
**80** A12 30d lt bl grn & ol grn .35 .40
**81** A12 50d salmon & dp plum .35 .40
**82** A12 70d bl & dk bl .70 .75
*Nos. 79-82 (4)* 1.75 1.75

Intl. Automobile and Motorcycle Races, 1953.

### Stamps or Types of Yugoslavia Overprinted "STT VUJNA" in Various Colors

**1953, July 8** **Engr.**
**83** A97 50d grnsh gray (C) 1.90 1.50

Tito's election to the presidency, 1/14/53.

**1953, July 31**
**84** A98 15d gray & grn (C) 2.00 1.90

38th Esperanto Cong., Zagreb, July 25-Aug. 1, 1953. See No. C21.

**1953, Sept. 5**
**85** A101 15d blue (C) 3.25 2.25

Liberation of Istria & the Slovene coast, 10th anniv.

**1953, Oct. 3**
**86** A102 15d gray 1.40 1.50

Cent. of the death of Branko Radicevic, poet.

**1953, Nov. 29** *Perf. 12½x12*
**87** A103 15d gray vio (V) .45 .40
**88** A103 30d claret (Br) .65 .55
**89** A103 50d dl bl grn (Dk Bl) 1.00 .95
*Nos. 87-89 (3)* 2.10 1.90

10th anniv. of the 1st republican legislative assembly of Yugoslavia.

**1954, Mar. 5** *Perf. 12½*
**90** A68 5d org (V) .50 .40
**91** A68 10d yel grn (C) .35 .30
**92** A68 15d rose red (G) .50 .40
*Nos. 90-92 (3)* 1.35 1.10

### Overprinted in Carmine

**1954 Photo.** *Perf. 11½*
**93** A104 2d red brn, sl & cr .20 .25
**94** A104 5d gray & dk yel brn .20 .25
**95** A104 10d ol grn & dk org brn .20 .25
**96** A104 15d dp bl grn & dk org brn .20 .25
**97** A104 17d gray brn, dk brn & cr .20 .25
**98** A104 25d bis, gray bl & org yel .20 .25
**99** A105 30d lil & dk brn .20 .25
**100** A105 35d rose vio & bl blk .30 .50
**101** A105 50d yel grn & vio brn .45 .75
**102** A105 65d org brn & gray blk 2.25 3.50
**103** A105 70d bl & org brn 4.50 7.50
**104** A105 100d brt bl & blk brn 15.00 25.00
*Nos. 93-104 (12)* 23.90 39.00

### Overprinted in Various Colors

**1954, Oct. 8** *Perf. 12½*
**105** A107 15d mar, red, ocher & dk bl (Bk) .35 .35
**106** A107 30d dk bl, grn, sal buff & choc (G) .35 .35
**107** A107 50d brn, bis & red (G) .55 .55
**108** A107 70d dk grn, gray grn & choc (R) 1.40 1.25
*Nos. 105-108 (4)* 2.65 2.50

150th anniv. of the 1st Serbian insurrection.

## AIR POST STAMPS

AP1

***Perf. 12½x11½***
**1948, Oct. 17 Photo. Unwmk.**
**C1** AP1 25 l gray .75 .75
**C2** AP1 50 l orange .75 .75

Economic Exhib. at Capodistria, Oct. 17-24.

Fishermen — AP2

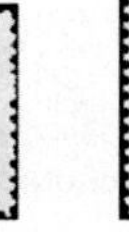


Farmer and Pack Mule — AP3

Mew over Chimneys AP4

**1949, June 1** *Perf. 11½*
**C3** AP2 1 l grnsh bl .20 .20
**C4** AP3 2 l red brn .20 .20
**C5** AP2 5 l blue .20 .20
**C6** AP3 10 l purple 1.25 .85
**C7** AP2 25 l brown 1.60 .90
**C8** AP3 50 l ol grn 1.60 .90
**C9** AP4 100 l dk vio brn 2.25 1.50
*Nos. C3-C9 (7)* 7.30 4.75

Italian inscriptions on Nos. C5 and C6, Croatian on No. C7, Slavonic on No. C8.
Nos. C3-C4 exist imperf. Value, each $135.

### Nos. C3-C9 Surcharged "DIN," or New Value and "DIN" in Various Colors

**1949, Nov. 5**
**C10** AP2 1d on 1 l (Bk) .20 .20
**C11** AP3 2d on 2 l (Br) .20 .20
**C12** AP2 5d on 5 l (Bl) .20 .20
**C13** AP3 10d on 10 l (V) .45 .40
**C14** AP2 15d on 25 l (Br) 4.75 4.50
**C15** AP3 20d on 50 l (Gr) 1.60 1.50
**C16** AP4 30d on 100 l (Bk) 1.60 1.50
*Nos. C10-C16 (7)* 9.00 8.50

On Nos. C14 and C15 the original value is obliterated by a framed block, on No. C16 by four parallel lines.

### Yugoslavia No. C33 Overprinted in Carmine and Lilac Rose Network

C17ovpt

### Souvenir Sheet

**1950** *Perf. 11½x12½*
**C17** AP15 10d lilac rose 50.00 57.50
*a.* Imperf. 50.00 57.50

Main Square, Capodístria — AP5

Lighthouse, Pirano — AP6

Design: 25d, Hotel, Portorose.

**1952 Unwmk. Photo.** *Perf. 12½*
**C18** AP5 5d brown 7.50 7.00
**C19** AP6 15d brt bl 4.75 5.50
**C20** AP5 25d green 4.75 5.50
*Nos. C18-C20 (3)* 17.00 18.00

75th anniv. (in 1949) of the UPU.

### Type of Yugoslavia, 1953 Overprinted "STT VUJNA" in Carmine

**1953, July 31**
**C21** AP21 300d vio & grn 190.00 160.00

38th Esperanto Cong., Zagreb, 7/25-8/1.
Sheets of 12 (12,000 stamps) and sheets of 8 (3,000 stamps in light violet and green).
A private red overprint was applied marginally to 250 sheets of 8: "Esperantski Kongres — 38 — a Universala Kongreso de Esperanto — Congresso del Esperanto."

### Air Post Stamps of Yugoslavia in New Colors Overprinted "STT VUJNA" in Various Colors

**1954** **Engr.**
**C22** AP16 1d dp pur gray .20 .20
**C23** AP16 2d brt grn (G) .20 .20
**C24** AP16 3d red brn (Br) .20 .20
**C25** AP16 5d chocolate .20 .20
**C26** AP16 10d bl grn .20 .20
**C27** AP16 20d brn (Br) .25 .40
**C28** AP16 30d blue .25 .40
**C29** AP16 50d olive blk .40 .55
**C30** AP16 100d scar (R) 1.10 1.50
**C31** AP16 200d dk bl vio (Bl) 2.75 3.75

***Perf. 11x11½***
**C32** AP17 500d orange (Br) 8.50 12.00
*Nos. C22-C32 (11)* 14.25 19.60

## POSTAGE DUE STAMPS

### Yugoslavia Nos. J51 to J55 Overprinted "S T T VUJA" in Two Lines in Ultramarine or Carmine

**1949 Unwmk.** *Perf. 12½*
**J1** D7 50p dp org .55 .55
**J2** D7 1d orange .55 .55
**J3** D7 2d dk bl (C) .55 .55
**J4** D7 3d yel grn (C) .55 .55
**J5** D7 5d brt pur (C) 1.10 1.10
*Nos. J1-J5 (5)* 3.30 3.30

Croakers D1

Anchovies D2

**1950** **Photo.**
**J6** D1 50p brn org .20 .20
**J7** D1 1d dp ol grn .90 .95
**J8** D2 2d dk grnsh bl .90 .95
**J9** D2 3d dk vio bl .90 .95
**J10** D2 5d plum 4.50 4.25
*Nos. J6-J10 (5)* 7.40 7.30

### Yugoslavia Nos. J67-J74 Overprinted "STT VUJNA" in Blue or Carmine

**1952**
**J11** D7 1d brown (Bl) .20 .20
**J12** D7 2d emerald .20 .20
**J13** D7 5d blue .20 .20
**J14** D7 10d scar (Bl) .20 .20
**J15** D7 20d purple .20 .20
**J16** D7 30d org yel (Bl) .20 .20

**J17** D7 50d ultra .20 .20
**J18** D7 100d dp plum (Bl) 3.00 4.50
*Nos. J11-J18 (8)* 4.40 5.90

## POSTAL TAX STAMPS

Yugoslavia No. RA5 Surcharged in Blue

**1948 Unwmk. *Perf. 12½***
**RA1** PT4 2 l on 50p brn & scar 6.50 *10.00*

Obligatory on all mail from May 22-30.

Yugoslavia No. RA7 Overprinted "VUJA STT" in Black

**1950, July 3**
**RA2** PT6 50p red & brn .35 .40

Yugoslavia No. RA9 Overprinted "STT VUJA" in Black

**1951**
**RA3** PT8 50p vio bl & red 6.50 *10.00*

Yugoslavia No. RA10 Overprinted "STT VUJNA" in Carmine

**1952**
**RA4** PT9 50p gray & carmine .20 .20

Type of Yugoslavia, 1953, Overprinted "STT VUJNA" in Blue

**1953**
**RA5** PT10 2d org brn & red .20 .30

The tax of Nos. RA1-RA5 was for the Red Cross.

## POSTAL TAX DUE STAMPS

Yugoslavia No. RAJ2 Surcharged Like No. RA1 in Scarlet

**1948 Unwmk. *Perf. 12½***
**RAJ1** PT4 2 l on 50p bl grn & scar 100.00 140.00

Yugoslavia No. RAJ4 Overprinted "VUJA STT" in Black

**1950, July 3**
**RAJ2** PT6 50p red & vio .85 1.25

Yugoslavia No. RAJ6 Overprinted "STT VUJA" in Black

**1951**
**RAJ3** PT8 50p emer & red 85.00 110.00

Yugoslavia No. RAJ7 Overprinted "STT VUJNA" in Carmine

**1952**
**RAJ4** PTD3 50p gray & car .50 .60

Type of Yugoslavia, 1953, Overprinted "STT VUJNA" in Blue

**1953**
**RAJ5** PT10 2d lilac rose & red .50 .60

# ZAIRE

zä-'ir

## (Congo Democratic Republic)

LOCATION — Central Africa
GOVT. — Republic
AREA — 905,365 sq. mi.
POP. — 50,481,305 (1999 est.)
CAPITAL — Kinshasa

Congo Democratic Republic changed its name to Republic of the Zaire in November 1971. Issues before that date are listed in Vol. 2 under Congo Democratic Republic.

100 Sengi = 1 Li-Kuta
100 Ma-Kuta = 1 Zaire
100 Centimes = 1 Franc (July 1998)

**Catalogue values for all unused stamps in this country are for Never Hinged items.**

UNICEF Emblem, Child Care — A143

UNICEF Emblem and: 14k, Map of Africa showing Zaire. 17k, Boy in African village.

***Perf. 14x13½***

**1971, Dec. 18 Unwmk.**
**750** A143 4k gold & multi .40 .20
**751** A143 14k lt bl, gold, red & grn 1.10 .65
**752** A143 17k gold & multi 1.50 .60
*Nos. 750-752 (3)* 3.00 1.45

25th anniv. of UNICEF. For surcharge see No. 1327.

Pres. Mobutu, MPR Emblem A144

**1972 Photo. *Perf. 11½***
**753** A144 4k multi 3.25 2.50
**754** A144 14k multi 3.25 2.50
**755** A144 22k multi 3.25 2.50
*Nos. 753-755 (3)* 9.75 7.50

5th anniv. of the People's Revolutionary Movement (MPR). For surcharge see #1308.

Zaire Arms — A145

Pres. Joseph D. Mobutu — A146

**1972 Litho. *Perf. 14***
**756** A145 10s red org & blk .20 .20
**757** A145 40s brt bl & multi .20 .20
**758** A145 50s citron & multi .20 .20

***Perf. 13***
**759** A146 1k sky bl & multi .20 .20
**760** A146 2k org & multi .20 .20
**761** A146 3k multi .20 .20
**762** A146 4k emer & multi .20 .20
**763** A146 5k multi .20 .20
**764** A146 6k multi .20 .20
**765** A146 8k cit & multi .45 .20
**766** A146 9k multi .55 .20
**767** A146 10k lt lil & multi .55 .20
**768** A146 14k multi .70 .35
**769** A146 17k multi .80 .45
**770** A146 20k yel & multi 1.00 .50
**771** A146 50k multi 2.40 1.00
**772** A146 100k fawn & multi 4.00 2.25
*Nos. 756-772 (17)* 12.25 6.95

For surcharges and overprints see Nos. 860, 1328, O1-O11.

Same, Denominations in Zaires

**1973, Feb. 21**
**773** A146 0.01z sky bl & multi .20 .20
**774** A146 0.02z org & multi .20 .20
**775** A146 0.03z multi .20 .20
**776** A146 0.04z multi .20 .20
**777** A146 0.10z multi .25 .20
**778** A146 0.14z multi .35 .30
*Nos. 773-778 (6)* 1.40 1.30

Inga Dam A147

**1973, Jan. 25 Litho. *Perf. 13½***
**790** A147 0.04z multi .25 .25
**791** A147 0.14z pink & multi .35 .30
**792** A147 0.18z yel & multi .60 .50
*Nos. 790-792 (3)* 1.20 1.05

Completion of first section of Inga Dam Nov. 24, 1972.

World Map A148

**1973, June 23 Photo. *Perf. 12½x12***
**793** A148 0.04z lil & multi .20 .20
**794** A148 0.07z multi .30 .20
**795** A148 0.18z multi .75 .35
*Nos. 793-795 (3)* 1.25 .75

3rd Intl. Fair at Kinshasa, June 23-July 8.
The dark brown ink of the inscription was applied by a thermographic process and varnished, producing a shiny, raised effect.

Hand and INTERPOL Emblem — A149

**1973, Sept. 28 Litho. *Perf. 12½***
**796** A149 0.06z multi .40 .20
**797** A149 0.14z multi .85 .40

50th anniversary of International Criminal Police Organization.

Leopard with Soccer Ball on Globe A150

**1974, July 17 Photo. *Perf. 11½x12***
**798** A150 1k multi .20 .20
**799** A150 2k multi .25 .20
**800** A150 3k multi .75 .35
**801** A150 4k multi .85 .45
**802** A150 5k multi 1.00 .55
**803** A150 14k multi 2.75 1.10
*a.* Souvenir sheet, 1 #803 29.00 —
*Nos. 798-803 (6)* 5.80 2.85

World Cup Soccer Championship, Munich, June 13-July 7.

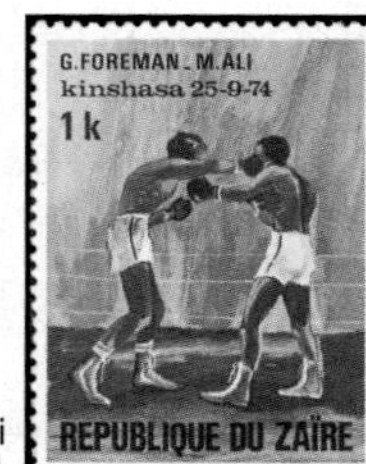

Foreman-Ali Fight — A151

**1974, Nov. 9 Litho. *Perf. 12x12½***
**804** A151 1k multi .20 .20
**805** A151 4k multi .20 .20
**806** A151 6k multi .30 .25
**807** A151 14k multi .60 .45
**808** A151 20k multi .90 .85
*Nos. 804-808 (5)* 2.20 1.95

World Heavyweight Boxing Championship match between George Foreman and Muhammad Ali, Kinshasa, Oct. 30 (postponed from Sept. 25).

Same, Type of 1974, Denominations in Zaires and Inscribed in Various Colors

**1975, Aug. Litho. *Perf. 12x12½***
**809** A151 0.01z multi (R) .20 .20
**810** A151 0.04z multi (Br) .20 .20
**811** A151 0.06z multi (Bk) .25 .25
**812** A151 0.14z multi (G) .55 .45
**813** A151 0.20z multi (Bk) .90 .85
*Nos. 809-813 (5)* 2.10 1.95

Judge, Lawyers, IWY Emblem A152

**1975, Dec. Photo. *Perf. 11½***
**814** A152 1k dull blk & multi .25 .20
**815** A152 2k dp rose & multi .25 .20
**816** A152 4k dull grn & multi .75 .35
**817** A152 14k violet & multi 1.50 .60
*Nos. 814-817 (4)* 2.75 1.35

International Women's Year 1975.

Waterfall — A153

Okapis A154

**1975 Photo. *Perf. 11½***
**818** A153 1k multicolored .20 .20
**819** A153 2k lt blue & multi .30 .20
**820** A153 3k multicolored .45 .25
**821** A153 4k salmon & multi 1.00 .55
**822** A153 5k green & multi 1.00 .55
*Nos. 818-822 (5)* 2.95 1.75

12th General Assembly of the Intl. Union for Nature Preservation (U.I.C.N.), Kinshasa, Sept. 1975.

**1975**
**823** A154 1k blue & multi .35 .20
**824** A154 2k yellow grn & multi .45 .20
**825** A154 3k brown red & multi 1.00 .20
**826** A154 4k green & multi 1.60 .35
**827** A154 5k yellow & multi 2.25 .45
*Nos. 823-827 (5)* 5.65 1.40

Virunga National Park, 50th anniversary.

Siderma Maluku Industry A155

Designs: 1k, Sozacom apartment building, vert. 3k, Matadi flour mill, vert. 4k, Women parachutists. 8k, Pres. Mobutu visiting Chairman Mao, vert. 10k, Soldiers working along the Salongo. 14k, Pres. Mobutu addressing UN Gen. Assembly, Oct. 1974. 15k, Celebrating crowd.

**1975**

| | | | | |
|---|---|---|---|---|
| **828** | A155 | 1k ocher & multi | .30 | .20 |
| **829** | A155 | 2k yel grn & multi | .30 | .20 |
| **830** | A155 | 3k multi | .60 | .20 |
| **831** | A155 | 4k multi | .85 | .20 |
| **832** | A155 | 8k dk brn & multi | 1.25 | .30 |
| **833** | A155 | 10k sep & multi | 1.90 | .40 |
| **834** | A155 | 14k bl & multi | 3.75 | .60 |
| **835** | A155 | 15k org & multi | 5.25 | .85 |
| | | *Nos. 828-835 (8)* | 14.20 | 2.95 |

10th anniversary of new government.

Tshokwe Mask — A156

Map of Zaire, UPU Emblem — A157

Designs: 2k, 4k, Seated woman, Pende. 7k, like 5k. 10k, 14k, Antelope mask, Suku. 15k, 18k, Kneeling woman, Kongo. 20k, 25k, Kuba mask.

**1977, Jan. 8 Photo. *Perf. 11½***

| | | | | |
|---|---|---|---|---|
| **836** | A156 | 2k multi | .20 | .20 |
| **837** | A156 | 4k multi | .20 | .20 |
| **838** | A156 | 5k gray & multi | .20 | .20 |
| **839** | A156 | 7k multi | .20 | .20 |
| **840** | A156 | 10k multi | .25 | .20 |
| **841** | A156 | 14k multi | .35 | .20 |
| **842** | A156 | 15k multi | .40 | .20 |
| **843** | A156 | 18k multi | .50 | .25 |
| **844** | A156 | 20k multi | 1.00 | .35 |
| **845** | A156 | 25k vio & multi | 1.10 | .45 |
| | | *Nos. 836-845 (10)* | 4.40 | 2.45 |

Wood carving and masks of Zaire.

**1977, Apr. Litho. *Perf. 13½***

| | | | | |
|---|---|---|---|---|
| **846** | A157 | 1k org & multi | .25 | .20 |
| **847** | A157 | 4k dk bl & multi | .75 | .20 |
| **848** | A157 | 7k ol grn & multi | 1.10 | .25 |
| **849** | A157 | 50k brn & multi | 5.25 | 3.25 |
| | | *Nos. 846-849 (4)* | 7.35 | 3.90 |

Cent. of UPU (in 1974).

Congo Stamps of 1968-1971 Surcharged with New Value, Bars and "REPUBLIQUE DU ZAIRE"

**1977**

| | | | | |
|---|---|---|---|---|
| **850** | A126 | 1k on 10s (#642) | .70 | .70 |
| **851** | A122 | 2k on 9.6k (#618) | .70 | .70 |
| **852** | A140 | 10k on 10s (#735) | .85 | .70 |
| **853** | A134 | 25k on 10s (#703) | 2.25 | 1.60 |
| **854** | A127 | 40k on 9.6k (#652) | 3.75 | 2.40 |
| **855** | A135 | 48k on 10s (#713) | 5.00 | 3.00 |
| | | *Nos. 850-855 (6)* | 13.25 | 9.10 |

Congo Nos. 644, 643, 635, 746 Surcharged with New Value, Bars and "REPUBLIQUE DU ZAIRE" in Black or Carmine, Zaire No. 757 Surcharged

**1977**

| | | | | |
|---|---|---|---|---|
| **856** | A126 | 5k on 30s | .70 | .70 |
| **857** | A126 | 10k on 15s (C) | .70 | .70 |
| **858** | A124 | 20k on 9.60k | 1.75 | .70 |
| **859** | A141 | 30k on 12k | 3.25 | 1.25 |
| **860** | A145 | 100k on 40s (C) | 9.50 | 5.25 |
| | | *Nos. 856-860 (5)* | 15.90 | 8.60 |
| | | *Nos. 850-860 (11)* | 29.15 | 17.70 |

Souvenir Sheet

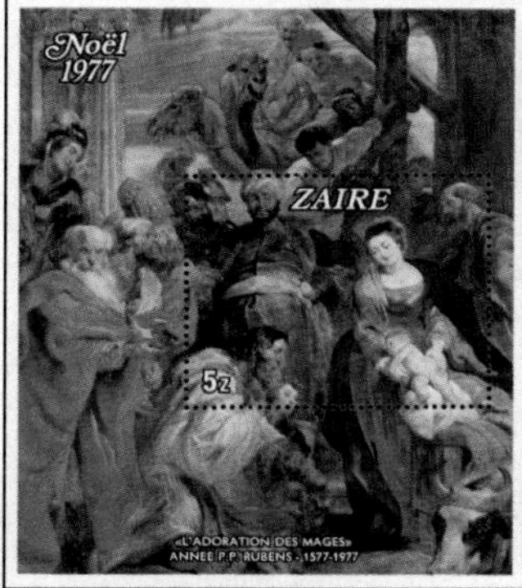

Adoration of the Kings, by Rubens — A158

**1977, Dec. 19 Photo. *Perf. 13½***

| | | | | |
|---|---|---|---|---|
| **861** | A158 | 5z multi | 100.00 | 92.50 |

Christmas 1977.

Pantodon Buchholzi A159

Soccer Game, Argentina-France A160

Fish: 70s, Aphyosemion striatum. 55, Ctenopoma fasciolatum. 8k, Malapterurus electricus. 10k, Hemichromis bimaculatus. 30k, Marcusenius isidori. 40k, Synodontis nigriventris. 48k, Julidochromis ornatus. 100k, Nothobranchius brieni. 250k, Micralestes interruptus.

**1978, Jan. 23 Litho. *Perf. 14***

| | | | | |
|---|---|---|---|---|
| **862** | A159 | 30s multi | .20 | .20 |
| **863** | A159 | 70s multi | .20 | .20 |
| **864** | A159 | 5k multi | .20 | .20 |
| **865** | A159 | 8k multi | .30 | .20 |
| **866** | A159 | 10k multi | .35 | .20 |
| **867** | A159 | 30k multi | .85 | .50 |
| **868** | A159 | 40k multi | 1.10 | .60 |
| **869** | A159 | 48k multi | 1.25 | .85 |
| **870** | A159 | 100k multi | 4.00 | 1.60 |
| | | *Nos. 862-870 (9)* | 8.45 | 4.55 |

**Souvenir Sheet**

***Perf. 13½***

| | | | | |
|---|---|---|---|---|
| **871** | A159 | 250k multi | 10.00 | 10.00 |

No. 871 contains one 46x35mm stamp. For surcharges see Nos. 1294, 1311.

**1978, Aug. 7 Litho. *Perf. 12½***

Various Soccer Games and Jules Rimet Cup: 3k, Austria-Brazil. 7k, Scotland-Iran. 9k, Netherlands-Peru. 10k, Hungary-Italy. 20k, Fed. Rep. of Germany-Mexico. 50k, Tunisia-Poland. 100k, Spain-Sweden. 500k, Rimet Cup, Games' emblem and cartoon of soccer player, horiz.

| | | | | |
|---|---|---|---|---|
| **872** | A160 | 1k multi | .20 | .20 |
| **873** | A160 | 3k multi | .20 | .20 |
| **874** | A160 | 7k multi | .20 | .20 |
| **875** | A160 | 9k multi | .20 | .20 |
| **876** | A160 | 10k multi | .20 | .20 |
| **877** | A160 | 20k multi | .30 | .20 |
| **878** | A160 | 50k multi | .85 | .50 |
| **879** | A160 | 100k multi | 1.65 | 1.00 |
| | | *Nos. 872-879 (8)* | 3.80 | 2.70 |

**Souvenir Sheets**

| | | | | |
|---|---|---|---|---|
| **880** | A160 | 500k blue & multi | 17.50 | 17.50 |
| **881** | A160 | 500k red & multi | 17.50 | 17.50 |

11th World Cup Soccer Championship, Argentina, June 1-25. Nos. 880-881 contain one stamp each (47x36mm). Stamp of No. 880 has blue frameline. Stamp of No. 881 has red frame line.

For surcharge see No. 1259.

Mama Mobutu — A161

Pres. Joseph D. Mobutu — A162

**1978, Oct. 23 Photo. *Perf. 12***

| | | | | |
|---|---|---|---|---|
| **882** | A161 | 8k multi | .20 | .20 |

Mama Mobutu (1941-77), wife of Pres. Mobutu.

**Frame Color**

**1978 Photo. *Perf. 12***

**Granite Paper**

| | | | | |
|---|---|---|---|---|
| **883** | A162 | 2k blue | .20 | .20 |
| **884** | A162 | 5k bister | .20 | .20 |
| **885** | A162 | 6k Prussian blue | .20 | .20 |
| **886** | A162 | 8k red brown | .20 | .20 |
| **887** | A162 | 10k emerald | .20 | .20 |
| **888** | A162 | 25k red | .20 | .20 |
| **889** | A162 | 48k purple | .50 | .30 |
| **890** | A162 | 1z green | .95 | .70 |
| | | *Nos. 883-890 (8)* | 2.65 | 2.20 |

See Nos. 1053, 1055-1056. For surcharges see Nos. 1313, 1333-1336.

Souvenir Sheet

Elizabeth II in Westminster Abbey — A163

**1978, Dec. 11 Photo. *Perf. 13½***

| | | | | |
|---|---|---|---|---|
| **891** | A163 | 5z multi | 10.50 | 10.50 |

Coronation of Queen Elizabeth II, 25th anniv.

Souvenir Sheet

Albrecht Dürer, Self-portrait — A164

**1978, Dec. 18 *Perf. 13***

| | | | | |
|---|---|---|---|---|
| **892** | A164 | 5z multi | 10.50 | 10.50 |

Albrecht Dürer (1471-1528), German painter and engraver.

Leonardo da Vinci and his Drawings — A165

History of Aviation: 70s, Planes of Wright Brothers, 1905, and Santos Dumont, 1906. 1k, Bleriot XI, 1909, and Farman F-60, 1909. 5k, Junkers G-38, 1929, and Spirit of St. Louis, 1927. 8k, Sikorsky S-42B, 1934 and Macchi-Castoldi MC-72, 1934. 10k, Boeing 707, 1960, and Fokker F-VII, 1935. 50k, Apollo XI, 1969, and Concorde, 1976. 75k, Helicopter and Douglas DC-10, 1971. 5z, Giffard's balloon, 1852, and Hindenburg LZ 129, 1936.

**1978, Dec. 28 Litho. *Perf. 13***

| | | | | |
|---|---|---|---|---|
| **893** | A165 | 30s multi | .20 | .20 |
| **894** | A165 | 70s multi | .20 | .20 |
| **895** | A165 | 1k multi | .20 | .20 |
| **896** | A165 | 5k multi | .25 | .20 |
| **897** | A165 | 8k multi | .25 | .20 |
| **898** | A165 | 10k multi | .55 | .20 |
| **899** | A165 | 50k multi | 2.40 | 1.00 |
| **900** | A165 | 75k multi | 3.25 | 1.25 |
| | | *Nos. 893-900 (8)* | 7.30 | 3.45 |

**Souvenir Sheet**

***Perf. 11½***

| | | | | |
|---|---|---|---|---|
| **901** | A165 | 5z multi | 12.00 | 12.00 |

For overprint and surcharges see Nos. 993, 1173-1181, 1291, 1295.

Pres. Mobutu, Map of Zaire, N'tombe Dancer — A166

Pres. Mobutu & Map: 3k, Bird. 4k, Elephant. 10k, Diamond and cotton boll. 14k, Hand holding torch. 17k, Leopard's head and Victoria Regia lily. 25k, Finzia waterfall. 50k, Wagenia fishermen.

**1979, Feb. Litho. *Perf. 14x13½***

| | | | | |
|---|---|---|---|---|
| **902** | A166 | 1k multicolored | .20 | .20 |
| **903** | A166 | 3k multicolored | .20 | .20 |
| **904** | A166 | 4k multicolored | .20 | .20 |
| **905** | A166 | 10k multicolored | .20 | .20 |
| *a.* | | Souvenir sheet of 4, #902-905 | *10.00* | — |
| **906** | A166 | 14k multicolored | .20 | .20 |
| **907** | A166 | 17k multicolored | .30 | .20 |
| **908** | A166 | 25k multicolored | .45 | .30 |
| **909** | A166 | 50k multicolored | .90 | .65 |
| *a.* | | Souvenir sheet of 4, #906-909 | *10.00* | — |
| | | *Nos. 902-909 (8)* | 2.65 | 2.15 |

Zaire (Congo) River expedition.

Phylloporus Ampliporus A167

Mushrooms: 5k, Engleromyces goetzei. 8k, Scutellinia virungae. 10k, Pycnoporus sanguineus. 30k, Cantharellus miniatescens. 40k, Lactarius phlebonemus. 48k, Phallus indusiatus. 100k, Ramaria moelleriana.

**1979, Mar. Photo. *Perf. 13½x13***

**910** A167 30s multicolored .25 .20
**911** A167 5k multicolored .30 .25
**912** A167 8k multicolored .45 .30
**913** A167 10k multicolored .60 .40
**914** A167 30k multicolored 1.25 .90
**915** A167 40k multicolored 1.50 1.00
**916** A167 48k multicolored 3.00 1.40
**917** A167 100k multicolored 4.25 2.50
*Nos. 910-917 (8)* 11.60 6.95

For surcharges see Nos. 1296, 1298, 1312, 1361-1362, 1365-1366, 1368-1369, 1372, 1375.

Souvenir Sheets

Pope John XXIII (1881-1963) A168

Popes: No. 919, Paul VI (1897-1978). No. 920, John Paul I (1912-78).

**1979, June 25 Litho. *Perf. 11½***

**918** A168 250k multi 3.50 3.50
**919** A168 250k multi 3.50 3.50
**920** A168 250k multi 3.50 3.50
*Nos. 918-920 (3)* 10.50 10.50

Boy Beating Drum — A169

IYC Emblem on Map of Zaire and: 10k, 20k, Girl, diff. 50k, Boy. 100k, Boys. 300k, Mother and child. 10z, Mother and children, horiz.

**1979, July 23 Litho. *Perf. 12½***

**921** A169 5k multi .20 .20
**922** A169 10k multi .20 .20
**923** A169 20k multi .25 .20
**924** A169 50k multi .60 .35
**925** A169 100k multi 1.25 .70
**926** A169 300k multi 3.50 1.65
*Nos. 921-926 (6)* 6.00 3.30

**Souvenir Sheet**

**927** A169 10z multi 12.00 9.25

International Year of the Child.
For surcharges see Nos. 997, 999, 1299, 1306.

Globe and Drummer A170

**1979, July 23**

**928** A170 1k multi .20 .20
**929** A170 9k multi .20 .20
**930** A170 90k multi .60 .40
**931** A170 100k multi .65 .45
*Nos. 928-931 (4)* 1.65 1.25

**Souvenir Sheet**

**932** A170 500k multi 4.75 2.75

6th International Fair, Kinshasa. No. 932 contains one 52x31mm stamp.
For overprint & surcharge see #996, 1320.

Globe and School Desk — A171

**1979, Dec. 24 Litho. *Perf. 13***

**933** A171 10k multi .25 .20

Intl. Bureau of Education, Geneva, 50th anniv.

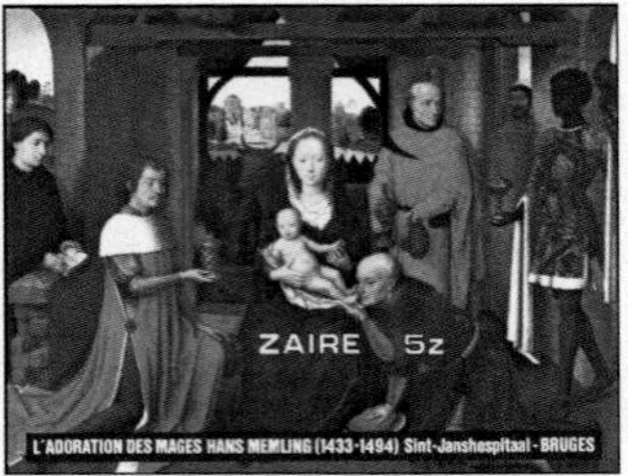


Adoration of the Kings, by Memling — A172

**1979, Dec. 24 *Imperf.***

**934** A172 5z multi 5.00 2.50

Christmas 1979.

"Puffing Billy," 1814, Gt. Britain A173

**1980, Jan. 14 Litho. *Perf. 13½x13***

**935** A173 50s shown .20 .20
**936** A173 1.50k Buddicom No. 33, 1843, France .20 .20
**937** A173 5k "Elephant," 1835, Belgium .20 .20
**938** A173 8k No. 601, 1906, Zaire .20 .20
**939** A173 50k "Slieve Gullion 440," Ireland .50 .20
**940** A173 75k "Black Elephant," Germany .75 .50
**941** A173 2z Type 1-15, Zaire 1.50 1.25
**942** A173 5z "Golden State," US 4.00 4.00
*Nos. 935-942 (8)* 7.55 6.75

**Souvenir Sheet**

**943** A173 10z Type E.D.75, Zaire 11.00 11.00

For overprints and surcharges see Nos. 991-992, 994, 1325.

Hill, Belgian Congo No. 257 A174

**1980, Jan. 28 *Perf. 13½x14***

**944** A174 2k No. 5 .20 .20
**945** A174 4k No. 13 .20 .20
**946** A174 10k No. 24 .20 .20
**947** A174 20k No. 38 .20 .20
**948** A174 40k No. 111 .35 .20
**949** A174 150k No. B29 1.00 .70
**950** A174 200k No. 198 1.25 .85
**951** A174 250k shown 1.60 1.00
*Nos. 944-951 (8)* 5.00 3.55

**Souvenir Sheet**

**952** A174 10z No. 198 8.50 8.50

Sir Rowland Hill (1795-1879), originator of penny postage.
For overprint and surcharge see Nos. 998, 1329.

Albert Einstein (1879-1955), Theoretical Physicist A175

**1980, Feb. 18 *Perf. 13***

**953** A175 40s multi .20 .20
**954** A175 2k multi .20 .20
**955** A175 4k multi .20 .20
**956** A175 15k multi .20 .20
**957** A175 50k multi .40 .25
**958** A175 300k multi 1.50 .75
*Nos. 953-958 (6)* 2.70 1.80

**Souvenir Sheet**

**959** A175 5z multi, diff. 4.50 2.50

For surcharges see Nos. 1285, 1290, 1304.

Salvation Army Brass Players — A176

50s, Booth Memorial Hospital, NYC. 4.50k, Commissioner George Railton sailing for US mission. 10k, Mobile dispensary, Masina. 20k, Gen. Evangeline Booth, officer holding infant, vert. 75k, Outdoor well-baby clinic. 1.50z, Disaster relief. 2z, Parade, vert. 10z, Gen. & Mrs. Arnold Brown.

**1980, Mar. 3 *Perf. 11***

**960** A176 50s multi .20 .20
**961** A176 4.50k multi .20 .20
**962** A176 10k multi .20 .20
**963** A176 20k multi .20 .20
**964** A176 40k multi .35 .20
**965** A176 75k multi .55 .25
**966** A176 1.50z multi 1.10 .55
**967** A176 2z multi 1.60 .80
*Nos. 960-967 (8)* 4.40 2.60

**Souvenir Sheet**

**968** A176 10z multi 7.50 5.00

Salvation Army cent. in US. No. 968 contains one 53x38mm stamp and 2 labels.

Souvenir Sheets

Pope John Paul II — A177

**1980, May 2 Litho. *Perf. 11½***

**969** A177 10z multi 14.00 14.00

Visit of Pope John Paul II to Zaire, May.

Baia Castle, by Antonio Pitloo — A178

**1980, May 5**

**970** A178 10z multi 5.50 5.50

20th International Philatelic Exhibition, Europa '80, Naples, Apr. 26-May 4.

A179

***Perf. 12½x13, 13x12½***
**1980, May 24 Litho.**

**971** A179 50k Woman, line-drawing .25 .20
**972** A179 100k Plutiarch .50 .40
**973** A179 500k Kneeling man, sculpture, vert. 2.50 1.75
*a.* Souvenir sheet of 3 3.50 2.50
*Nos. 971-973 (3)* 3.25 2.35

Rotary Intl., 75th anniv. No. 973a contains 3 stamps similar to Nos. 971-973, size: 55x35, 35x55mm. Exists imperf.
For surcharge see No. 1313.

Tropical Fish — A180

**1980, Oct. 20 Litho. *Perf. 14x13½***

**974** A180 1k *Chaetodon collaris* .20 .20
**975** A180 5k *Zebrasoma veliferum* .20 .20
**976** A180 10k *Euxiphipops xanthometapon* .20 .20
**977** A180 20k *Pomacanthus annularis* .20 .20
**978** A180 50k *Centropyge oriculus* .45 .40

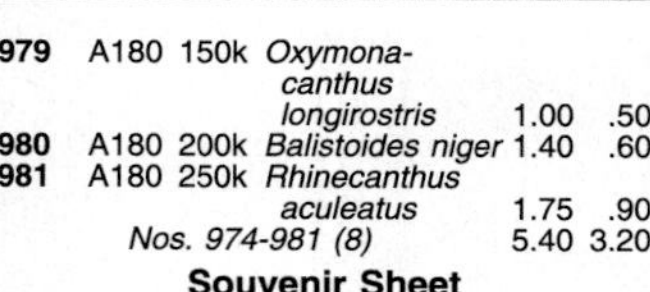

979 A180 150k *Oxymonacanthus longirostris* 1.00 .50
980 A180 200k *Balistoides niger* 1.40 .60
981 A180 250k *Rhinecanthus aculeatus* 1.75 .90
*Nos. 974-981 (8)* 5.40 3.20

**Souvenir Sheet**

981A A180 5z *Baliste ondule* 4.50 4.50

For surcharge see No. 1307.

Exhibition Emblem, Congo #365 — A181

**1980, Dec. 6 Litho. *Perf. 13***

982 Block of 4 2.00 1.60
*a.* A181 1z, UR shown .45 .35
*b.* A181 1z, UL Belgium #511 .45 .35
*c.* A181 1z, UR like #982b .45 .35
*d.* A181 1z, UL like #982a .45 .35
983 Block of 4 4.00 2.50
*a.* A181 2z, UR Congo #432 .95 .60
*b.* A181 2z, UL Belguim # B835 .95 .60
*c.* A181 2z, UR like #983b .95 .60
*d.* A181 2z, UL like #983a .95 .60
984 Block of 4 5.75 4.00
*a.* A181 3z, UR Zaire #755 1.40 .90
*b.* A181 3z, UL Belgium # B878 1.40 .90
*c.* A181 3z, UR like #984b 1.40 .90
*d.* A181 3z, UL like #984a 1.40 .90
985 Block of 4 8.00 5.00
*a.* A181 4z, UR Congo #572 1.75 1.10
*b.* A181 4z, UL Belgium # B996 1.75 1.10
*c.* A181 4z, UR like #985b 1.75 1.10
*d.* A181 4z, UL like #985a 1.75 1.10
*Nos. 982-985 (4)* 19.75 13.10

PHIBELZA, Belgium-Zaire Phil. Exhib. #982-985 can be collected as strips of 4. For surcharge see No. 1342.

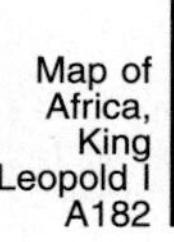

Map of Africa, King Leopold I — A182

Belgian independence sesquicentennial: 75k, Stanley expedition, Leopold II. 100k, Colonial troops, Albert I. 270k, 145k, protected animals, Leopold III. Visit of King Baudouin and Queen Fabiola.

**1980, Dec. 13 Photo. *Perf. 14***

986 A182 10k multi .25 .20
987 A182 75k multi .90 .40
988 A182 100k multi 1.40 .55
989 A182 145k multi 2.00 .70
990 A182 270k multi 3.50 1.25
*Nos. 986-990 (5)* 8.05 3.10

For surcharges see Nos. 1326, 1331, 1345, 1357, 1408-1412, 1426.

Nos. 935, 936, 898, 939, 900, 931, 925, 951, Overprinted in Red, Silver or Black: 20e Anniversaire-Independence / 1960-1980

**1980, Dec. 13 Litho.**

991 A173 50s multi .20 .20
992 A173 1.50k multi .20 .20
993 A165 10k multi .20 .20
994 A173 50k multi .55 .20
995 A165 75k multi .70 .20
996 A170 100k multi (S) 1.00 .65
997 A169 1z on 5z on 100k multi (B) 1.25 .65
998 A174 250k multi 2.50 1.40
999 A169 5z on 100k multi (B) 5.00 2.75
*Nos. 991-999 (9)* 11.60 6.45

20th anniversary of independence. For surcharges see Nos. 1300, 1316.

Nativity A183

**1980, Dec. 24 *Perf. 13***

1000 A183 10k Shepherds and angels .25 .20
1001 A183 75k Flight into Egypt .75 .40
1002 A183 80k Three kings .75 .40
1003 A183 145k shown 1.40 .60
*Nos. 1000-1003 (4)* 3.15 1.60

**Souvenir Sheet**

1004 A183 10z Church, nativity 5.50 5.50

Christmas 1980. No. 1004 contains one 49x33mm stamp. Exists imperf. For surcharges see Nos. 1301, 1317-1318.

Postal Clerk Sorting Mail, by Norman Rockwell A184

Designs: Saturday Evening Post covers by Norman Rockwell.

**1981, Apr. 27 Litho. *Perf. 14***

1005 A184 10k multi .20 .20
1006 A184 20k multi .20 .20
1007 A184 50k multi .30 .20
1008 A184 80k multi .50 .30
1009 A184 100k multi .55 .35
1010 A184 125k multi .65 .40
1011 A184 175k multi .95 .55
1012 A184 200k multi 1.10 .60
*Nos. 1005-1012 (8)* 4.45 2.80

For surcharges see Nos. 1262, 1265, 1269, 1275, 1281, 1354.

First Anniv. of Visit of Pope John Paul II A185

Scenes of Pope's visit. 50k, 500k, vert.

**1981, May 2 *Perf. 13***

1013 A185 5k multi .20 .20
1014 A185 10k multi .20 .20
1015 A185 50k multi .30 .25
1016 A185 100k multi .75 .45
1017 A185 500k multi 4.25 2.25
1018 A185 800k multi 6.00 3.75
*Nos. 1013-1018 (6)* 11.70 7.10

For surcharges see #1190-1194, 1292, 1302, 1343.

Soccer Players — A186

Designs: Soccer scenes.

**1981, July 6 Litho. *Perf. 12½***

1019 A186 2k multi .20 .20
1020 A186 10k multi .20 .20
1021 A186 25k multi .20 .20
1022 A186 90k multi .45 .25
1023 A186 2z multi .90 .60
1024 A186 3z multi 1.40 .90
1025 A186 6z multi 2.50 1.60
1026 A186 8z multi 4.00 3.00
*Nos. 1019-1026 (8)* 9.85 6.95

**Souvenir Sheet**

1027 Sheet of 2 4.75 4.75
*a.* A186 5z like #1019 2.25 2.25
*b.* A186 5z like #1025 2.25 2.25

ESPANA '82 World Cup Soccer Championship. For surcharges see Nos. 1287, 1303, 1309, 1321.

Intl. Year of the Disabled — A187

**1981, Nov. 2 Litho. *Perf. 14x14½***

1028 A187 2k Archer .20 .20
1029 A187 5k Ear, sound waves .20 .20
1030 A187 10k Amputee .20 .20
1031 A187 18k Cane braille, sunglasses .20 .20
1032 A187 50k Boy with leg braces .20 .20
1033 A187 150k Sign language .40 .25
1034 A187 500k Hands 1.10 .95
1035 A187 800k Dove 2.00 1.75
*Nos. 1028-1035 (8)* 4.50 3.95

For surcharges see Nos. 1288, 1293, 1305, 1314.

**Souvenir Sheet**

Birth Sesqui. of Heinrich von Stephan, UPU Founder — A188

**Photogravure and Engraved**

**1981, Dec. 21 *Perf. 11½x12***

1036 A188 15z purple 5.75 5.75

Christmas 1981 — A189

**1981, Dec. 21 Litho. *Perf. 14***

Designs: 25k, 1z, 1.50z, 3z, 5z, Various children. 10z, Holy Family, horiz.

1037 A189 25k multi .20 .20
1038 A189 1z multi .45 .20
1039 A189 1.50z multi .55 .25
1040 A189 3z multi 1.10 .55
1041 A189 5z multi 1.90 1.00
*Nos. 1037-1041 (5)* 4.20 2.20

**Souvenir Sheet**

1042 A189 10z multi 4.25 4.25

13th World Telecommunications Day (1981) — A190

Designs: Symbols of communications and health care delivery.

**1982, Feb. 8 Litho. *Perf. 13***

1043 A190 1k multi .20 .20
1044 A190 25k multi .20 .20
1045 A190 90k multi .25 .20
1046 A190 1z multi .25 .20
1047 A190 1.70z multi .50 .40
1048 A190 3z multi .95 .70
1049 A190 4.50z multi 1.40 .95
1050 A190 5z multi 1.60 1.10
*Nos. 1043-1050 (8)* 5.35 3.95

For surcharges see Nos. 1270, 1282.

Pres. Mobutu Type of 1978
**Frame Color**

**1982 Photo. *Perf. 12***
**Granite Paper**

1053 A162 50k purple .20 .20
1055 A162 2z bister .35 .20
1056 A162 5z Prussian blue 1.90 1.10
*Nos. 1053-1056 (3)* 2.45 1.50

20th Anniv. of African Postal Union (1981) — A191

**1982, Mar. 8 Litho. *Perf. 13***

1057 A191 1z yel grn & gold .35 .20

For surcharges see Nos. 1348, 1352.

1982 World Cup A192

Designs: Flags and players of finalists.

**1982**

1058 A192 2k multi .20 .20
1059 A192 8k multi .20 .20
1060 A192 25k multi .20 .20
1061 A192 50k multi .20 .20
1062 A192 90k multi .30 .25
1063 A192 1z multi .45 .30
1064 A192 1.45z multi .55 .45
1065 A192 1.70z multi .75 .55
1066 A192 3z multi 1.00 .90
1067 A192 3.50z multi 1.40 1.10
1068 A192 5z multi 2.25 1.60
1069 A192 6z multi 2.50 1.90
*Nos. 1058-1069 (12)* 10.00 7.85

**Souvenir Sheet**

1070 A192 10z multi 5.75 5.75

Issued: #1058-1069, July 6; #1070, Sept. 21.
For surcharges see #1289, 1315, 1322, 1344, 1435 and footnote after #1336.

9th Conference of Heads of State of Africa and France, Kinshasa, Oct. — A193

**1982, Oct. 8 Litho. *Perf. 13***

1071 A193 75k multi .20 .20
1072 A193 90k multi .20 .20
1073 A193 1z multi .20 .20
1074 A193 1.50z multi .20 .20
1075 A193 3z multi .50 .40
1076 A193 5z multi .75 .60
1077 A193 8z multi 1.25 1.00
*Nos. 1071-1077 (7)* 3.30 2.80

For surcharges see Nos. 1268, 1271, 1280, 1283, 1347, 1351.

Animals from Virunga Natl. Park — A194

**1982, Nov. 5**

**1078** A194 1z Lions .25 .20
**1079** A194 1.70z Buffalo .90 .60
**1080** A194 3.50z Elephants 2.10 1.40
**1081** A194 6.50z Antelope 3.50 2.25
**1082** A194 8z Hippopotamus 5.00 3.25
**1083** A194 10z Monkeys 5.75 3.75
**1084** A194 10z Leopard 5.75 3.75
*a.* Pair, #1083-1084 + label 12.00 12.00
*Nos. 1078-1084 (7)* 23.25 15.20

#1084a has continuous design.
For surcharge see No. 1430.

Scouting Year — A195

**1982, Nov. 29 Photo. *Perf. 11½***
**Granite Paper**

**1085** A195 90k Camp .30 .25
**1086** A195 1.70z Campfire .75 .55
**1087** A195 3z Scout 1.25 .90
**1088** A195 5z First aid 2.75 1.60
**1089** A195 8z Flag signals 5.00 3.00
*Nos. 1085-1089 (5)* 10.05 6.30

**Souvenir Sheet**

**1090** A195 10z Baden-Powell 8.50 8.50

For surcharges see Nos. 1207-1214.

Local Birds — A196

**1982, Dec. 6 Litho. *Perf. 13***

**1091** A196 25k Quelea quelea .20 .20
**1092** A196 50k Ceyx picta .20 .20
**1093** A196 90k Tauraco persa .50 .20
**1094** A196 1.50z Charadrius tricollaris .55 .35
**1095** A196 1.70z Cursorius temminckii .60 .35
**1096** A196 2z Campethera bennettii .80 .50
**1097** A196 3z Podiceps ruficollis 1.10 .65
**1098** A196 3.50z Kaupifalco monogrammicus 1.25 .70
**1099** A196 5z Limnocorax flavirostris 1.90 1.00
**1100** A196 8z White-headed vulture 3.00 1.75
*Nos. 1091-1100 (10)* 10.10 5.90

All except 3.50z, 8z horiz.
For surcharges see Nos. 1263, 1266, 1272, 1276, 1278, 1284, 1425, 1432, 1438, 1440.

Souvenir Sheet

Christmas — A197

**1982, Dec. 20 Photo. *Perf. 13½***

**1101** A197 15z Adoration of the Magi, by van der Goes 5.75 5.75

Quartz A198

**1983, Feb. 13 Photo. *Perf. 11½***
**Granite Paper**

**1102** A198 2k Malachite, vert. .20 .20
**1103** A198 45k shown .25 .20
**1104** A198 75k Gold .45 .20
**1105** A198 1z Uraninite .70 .20
**1106** A198 1.50z Bournonite, vert. 1.00 .55
**1107** A198 3z Cassiterite 2.00 1.00
**1108** A198 6z Dioptase, vert. 4.00 2.00
**1109** A198 8z Cuprite, vert. 5.00 2.75
*Nos. 1102-1109 (8)* 13.60 7.10

**Souvenir Sheet**

**1110** A198 10z Diamonds 7.50 7.50

For surcharges see Nos. 1324, 1330, 1332, 1346.

TB Bacillus Centenary — A199

**1983, Feb. 21 Litho. *Perf. 13***

**1111** A199 80k multi .25 .20
**1112** A199 1.20z multi .40 .20
**1113** A199 3.60z multi 1.25 .60
**1114** A199 9.60z multi 3.50 1.75
*Nos. 1111-1114 (4)* 5.40 2.75

For surcharges see Nos. 1319, 1356, 1358, 1360, 1433, 1436, 1441.

Kinshasa Monuments — A200

**1983, Apr. 25**

**1115** A200 50k Zaire Diplomat, vert. .20 .20
**1116** A200 1z Echo of Zaire .20 .20
**1117** A200 1.50z Messengers, vert. .30 .20
**1118** A200 3z Shield of Revolution, vert. .60 .30
**1119** A200 5z Weeping Woman .95 .50
**1120** A200 10z Militant, vert. 2.10 .95
*Nos. 1115-1120 (6)* 4.35 2.35

For surcharges see Nos. 1267, 1279, 1349-1350.

ITU Plenipotentiaries Conference, Nairobi, Sept. 1982 — A201

Various satellites, dish antennae and maps.

**1983, June 13 Litho. *Perf. 13***

**1121** A201 2k multi .20 .20
**1122** A201 4k multi .20 .20
**1123** A201 25k multi .20 .20
**1124** A201 1.20z multi .40 .20
**1125** A201 2.05z multi .65 .35
**1126** A201 3.60z multi 1.25 .60
**1127** A201 6z multi 2.00 1.00
**1128** A201 8z multi 2.50 1.40
*Nos. 1121-1128 (8)* 7.40 4.15

For surcharges see Nos. 1260-1261, 1264, 1273-1274, 1277, 1355, 1359, 1429, 1434, 1437, 1439, 1442.

Christmas 1983 — A202

Raphael Paintings; No. 1129: a, Virgin and Child. b, Holy Family. c, Esterhazy Madonna. d, Sistine Madonna. No. 1130: a, La Belle Jardiniere. b, Virgin of Alba. c, Holy Family, diff. d, Virgin and Child, diff.

**1983, Dec. 26 Photo. *Perf. 13½x13***

**1129** Sheet of 4 3.50 3.50
*a.-d.* A202 10z, any single .85 .85
**1130** Sheet of 4 5.25 5.25
*a.-d.* A202 15z, any single 1.25 1.25

Garamba Park — A203

**1984, Apr. 2 Litho. *Perf. 13***

**1131** A203 10k Darby's Eland .20 .20
**1132** A203 15k Eagles .20 .20
**1133** A203 3z Servals .20 .20
**1134** A203 10z White rhinoceros 1.25 1.25
**1135** A203 15z Lions 1.75 1.75
**1136** A203 37.50z Warthogs 4.25 4.25
**1137** A203 40z Koris bustards 4.75 4.75
**1138** A203 40z Crowned cranes 4.75 4.75
*a.* Pair, #1137-1138 + label 9.50 9.50
*Nos. 1131-1138 (8)* 17.35 17.35

Nos. 1137-1138 are narrower, 49x34mm, with continuous design.
For surcharge see No. 1428.

World Communications Year — A204

Designs: 10k, Computer operator, Congo River ferry. 15k, Communications satellite. 8.50z, Engineer, Congo River Bridge. 10z, Satellite, ground receiving station. 15z, TV camerawoman filming crowed crane. 37.50z, Satellite, dish antennas. 80z, Switchboard operator, bus.

**1984, May 14 Litho. *Perf. 13x12½***

**1139** A204 10k multi .20 .20
**1140** A204 15k multi .20 .20
**1141** A204 8.50z multi .65 .65
**1142** A204 10z multi .70 .70
**1143** A204 15z multi 1.10 1.10
**1144** A204 37.50z multi 2.75 2.75
**1145** A204 80z multi 5.75 5.75
*Nos. 1139-1145 (7)* 11.35 11.35

Hypericum Revolutum A205

Local flowers: 15k, Borreria dibrachiata. 3z, Disa erubescens. 8.50z, Scaevola plumieri. 10z, Clerodendron thompsonii. 15z, Thumbergia erecta. 37.50z, Impatiens niamniamensis. 100z, Canarina eminii.

**1984, May 28 Photo. *Perf. 14x13½***

**1146** A205 10k multi .20 .20
**1147** A205 15k multi .20 .20
**1148** A205 3z multi .20 .20
**1149** A205 8.50z multi .80 .80
**1150** A205 10z multi .90 .90
**1151** A205 15z multi 1.25 1.25
**1152** A205 37.50z multi 3.25 3.25
**1153** A205 100z multi 9.00 9.00
*Nos. 1146-1153 (8)* 15.80 15.80

1984 Summer Olympics A206

Manned Flight Bicent. — A207

**1984, June 5 Litho. *Perf. 13***

**1154** A206 2z Basketball .20 .20
**1155** A206 3z Equestrian .25 .25
**1156** A206 10z Running .75 .75
**1157** A206 15z Long jump 1.10 1.10
**1158** A206 20z Soccer 1.75 1.75
*Nos. 1154-1158 (5)* 4.05 4.05

**Souvenir Sheet**
***Perf. 11½***

**1159** A206 50z Kayak 4.25 4.25

No. 1159 contains one 31x49mm stamp.
For surcharge see No. 1427.

**1984, June 28 Litho. *Perf. 14***

10k, Montgolfiere, 1783. 15k, Charles & Robert, 1783. 3z, Gustave, 1783. 5z, Santos-Dumont III, 1899. 10z, Stratospheric balloon, 1934. 15z, Zeppelin LZ-129, 1936. 37.50z, Double Eagle II, 1978. 80z, Hot air balloons.

**1160** A207 10k multi .20 .20
**1161** A207 15k multi .20 .20
**1162** A207 3z multi .20 .20
**1163** A207 5z multi .40 .40
**1164** A207 10z multi .75 .75
**1165** A207 15z multi 1.10 1.10
**1166** A207 37.50z multi 2.75 2.75
**1167** A207 80z multi 6.00 6.00
*Nos. 1160-1167 (8)* 11.60 11.60

For surcharges see Nos. 1413-1420.

Okapi — A208

**1984, Oct. 15 Litho. *Perf. 13***

**1168** A208 2z Grazing 1.00 .50
**1169** A208 3z Resting 1.50 .50
**1170** A208 8z Mother and young 2.50 1.75
**1171** A208 10z In water 4.00 3.25
*Nos. 1168-1171 (4)* 9.00 6.00

**Souvenir Sheet**

***Perf. 11½***

**1172** A208 50z like 10z 5.00 5.00

World Wildlife Fund. No. 1172 contains one 36x51mm stamp, margin continues the design of the 10z without emblem.

Nos. 893, 896, 894-895, 898, 897, 900, 899 Ovptd. with Black Bar, Silver Emblem and Surcharged on Stamp and Margin: 60e ANNIVERSAIRE/1re LIASON AERIENNE/BRUXELLES-KINSHASAL/PAR EDMOND THIEFFRY in 3 or 5 Lines

**1985, Feb. 19 *Perf. 13, 11½***

**1173** A165 2.50z on 30s multi .20 .20
**1174** A165 5z on 5k multi .40 .40
**1175** A165 6z on 70s multi .40 .40
**1176** A165 7.50z on 1k multi .60 .60
**1177** A165 8.50z on 10k multi .60 .60
**1178** A165 10z on 8k multi .75 .75
**1179** A165 12.50z on 75k multi .95 .95
**1180** A165 30z on 50k multi 2.25 2.25
*Nos. 1173-1180 (8)* 6.15 6.15

**Souvenir Sheet**

**1181** A165 50z on 5z multi 50.00 50.00

OLYMPHILEX '85, Lausanne — A209

**1985, Apr. 19 *Perf. 13***

**1182** A209 1z Swimming .20 .20
**1183** A209 2z Soccer, vert. .20 .20
**1184** A209 3z Boxing .20 .20
**1185** A209 4z Basketball, vert. .25 .25
**1186** A209 5z Equestrian .40 .40
**1187** A209 10z Volleyball, vert. .75 .75
**1188** A209 15z Running 1.25 1.25
**1189** A209 30z Cycling, vert. 2.50 2.50
*Nos. 1182-1189 (8)* 5.75 5.75

Nos. 1013-1018, 969 Ovptd. and Surcharged with 1 or 2 Gold Bars and "AOUT 1985" in Gold or Black

**1985, Aug. 15 *Perf. 13, 11½***

**1190** A185 2z on 5k .25 .25
**1191** A185 3z on 10k .30 .30
**1192** A185 5z on 50k .45 .45
**1192A** A185 10z on 100k 1.00 1.00
**1192B** A185 15z on 500k 1.40 1.40
**1193** A185 40z on 800k 4.25 4.25
*Nos. 1190-1193 (6)* 7.65 7.65

**Souvenir Sheet**

**1194** A177 50z on 10z (B) 9.00 9.00

Second visit of Pope John Paul II.

Audubon Birth Bicent. — A210

Illustrations of North American bird species by John Audubon.

**1985, Oct. 1 *Perf. 13***

**1195** A210 5z Great egret .60 .40
**1196** A210 10z Yellow-beaked duck 1.25 .75
**1197** A210 15z Small heron 2.00 1.25
**1198** A210 25z White-fronted duck 3.50 2.25
*Nos. 1195-1198 (4)* 7.35 4.65

For surcharges see Nos. 1421-1424.

Natl. Independence, 25th Anniv. — A211

**1985, Oct. 23 Photo. *Perf. 12***

**Granite Paper**

**1200** A211 5z multi .25 .25
**1201** A211 10z multi .45 .45
**1202** A211 15z multi .70 .70
**1203** A211 20z multi 1.10 1.10
*Nos. 1200-1203 (4)* 2.50 2.50

**Souvenir Sheet**

***Perf. 11½***

**1204** A211 50z multi 2.25 2.25

UN, 40th Anniv. A212

**1985, Nov. 26**

**1205** A212 10z Flags, vert. .50 .50
**1206** A212 50z Emblem, UN building 2.50 2.50

Nos. 1087-1088, 1085-1086, 1089-1090 Surcharged

**1985, Dec. 2 *Perf. 11½***

**Granite Paper**

**1207** A195 3z on 3z multi .40 .40
**1208** A195 5z on 5z multi .55 .55
**1209** A195 7z on 90k multi .70 .70
**1210** A195 10z on 90k multi 1.00 1.00
**1211** A195 15z on 1.70z multi 1.60 1.60
**1212** A195 20z on 8z multi 2.25 2.25
**1213** A195 50z on 90k multi 5.75 5.75
*Nos. 1207-1213 (7)* 12.25 12.25

**Souvenir Sheet**

**1214** A195 50z on 10z multi 9.00 9.00

Intl. Youth Year.

Souvenir Sheet

Virgin and Child, by Titian — A213

**Photogravure and Engraved**

**1985, Dec. 23 *Perf. 13½***

**1215** A213 100z brown 5.25 5.25

Christmas 1985.

Natl. Transit Authority, 50th Anniv. — A214

**1985, Dec. 31 *Perf. 13***

**1216** A214 7z Kokolo mail ship .25 .25
**1217** A214 10z Steam locomotive .40 .40
**1218** A214 15z Luebo ferry .60 .60
**1219** A214 50z Stanley locomotive 2.00 2.00
*Nos. 1216-1219 (4)* 3.25 3.25

Postage Stamp, Cent. A215

Stamps on stamps: 7z, Belgian Congo No. 30. 15z, Belgian Congo No. B28. 20z, Belgian Congo No. 226. 25z, Zaire No. 1059. 40z, Zaire No. 1152. 50z, Zaire No. 883 and Belgium No. 1094.

**1986, Feb. 23 *Perf. 13***

**1220** A215 7z multi .50 .50
**1221** A215 15z multi 1.00 1.00
**1222** A215 20z multi 1.40 1.40
**1223** A215 25z multi 1.60 1.60
**1224** A215 40z multi 2.75 2.75
*Nos. 1220-1224 (5)* 7.25 7.25

**Souvenir Sheet**

***Perf. 11½***

**1225** A215 50z multi 2.50 2.50

No. 1225 contains one 50x35mm stamp.

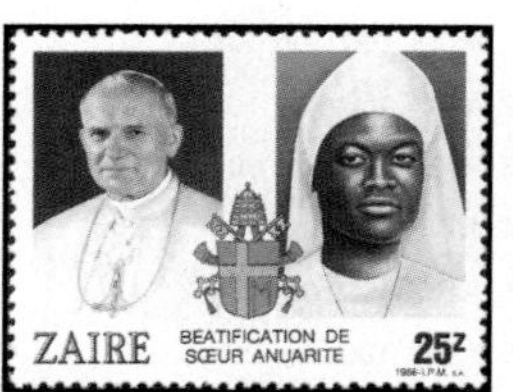


Beatification of Sister Anuarite Nengapeta, Aug. 15, 1985 — A216

**1986, Feb. 21 Litho. *Perf. 13***

**1226** A216 10z Pope John Paul II .60 .45
**1227** A216 15z Sr. Anuarite .85 .60
**1228** A216 25z Both portraits 1.25 1.00
*Nos. 1226-1228 (3)* 2.70 2.05

**Souvenir Sheet**

***Imperf***

**1229** A216 100z Both portraits, triangular 4.00 4.00

Nos. 1226-1227 vert. No. 1229 contains one quadrilateral stamp, size: 30x36x60mm.

For surcharges see Nos. 1370-1371, 1373, 1376-1377.

Congo Stamp Cent. — A217

**1986, Feb. 22 Litho. *Perf. 13***

**1230** A217 25z Belgian Congo No. 3 1.00 1.00

Imperfs exist. Value $5.

See Belgium No. 1236.

Indigenous Reptiles A218

**1987, Feb. 11 Litho. *Perf. 13***

**1231** A218 2z Dasypeltis scaber .20 .20
**1232** A218 5z Agama agama .20 .20
**1233** A218 10z Python regius .30 .30
**1234** A218 15z Chamaeleo dilepis .60 .60
**1235** A218 25z Dendroaspis jamesoni .85 .85
**1236** A218 50z Naja nigricolis 1.60 1.60
*Nos. 1231-1236 (6)* 3.75 3.75

Christmas 1987 — A219

Paintings (details) by Fra Angelico: 50z, Virgin and Child, center panel of the Triptych of Cortona, 1435. 100z, The Nativity. 120z, Virgin and Child with Angels and Four Saints, Fiesole Retable. 180z, Virgin and Child with Six Saints, Annalena Retable.

**1987, Dec. 24 Litho. *Perf. 13***

**1237** A219 50z multi .75 .75
**1238** A219 100z multi 1.50 1.50
**1239** A219 120z multi 1.90 1.90
**1240** A219 180z multi 2.80 2.80
*Nos. 1237-1240 (4)* 6.95 6.95

French Revolution, Bicent. — A220

Designs: 50z, Declaration of the Rights of Man and Citizen. 100z, Abstract art. 120z, Globe showing Africa, South America.

**1989 Litho. *Perf. 13½x14½***

1241 A220 40z multicolored .45 .45
1242 A220 50z multicolored .55 .55
1243 A220 100z multicolored 1.10 1.10
1244 A220 120z multicolored 1.40 1.40
*Nos. 1241-1244 (4)* 3.50 3.50

REGIDESCO, 50th Anniv. — A221

**1989**

1245 A221 40z Administration bldg. .40 .40
1246 A221 50z Modern factory .50 .50
1247 A221 75z Water works .75 .75
1248 A221 120z Woman drawing water 1.25 1.25
*Nos. 1245-1248 (4)* 2.90 2.90

Fight Against AIDS — A222

Designs: 40z, Bowman firing arrow through SIDA. 80z, "SIDA" on Leopard. 150z, World map with AIDS symbols.

**1989**

1249 A222 30z multicolored .90 .90
1250 A222 40z multicolored 1.25 1.25
1251 A222 80z multicolored 2.50 2.50
*Nos. 1249-1251 (3)* 4.65 4.65

**Souvenir Sheet**

***Perf. 14***

1252 A222 150z multicolored 4.50 4.50

Tourist Attractions — A223

**1990 Litho. *Perf. 13½x14½***

1253 A223 40z Waterfalls of Venus .55 .55
1254 A223 60z Rural village .85 .85
1255 A223 100z Kivu Lake 1.40 1.40
1256 A223 120z Niyara Gongo Volcano 1.75 1.75
*Nos. 1253-1256 (4)* 4.55 4.55

**Souvenir Sheet**

***Perf. 14½***

1257 A223 300z Kisantu Botanical Gardens, vert. 4.25 4.25

Souvenir Sheet

Christmas — A224

Illustration reduced.

**1990 Litho. *Perf. 14***

1258 A224 500z multicolored 3.50 3.50

Various 1971-1983 Stamps Surcharged in Gold

**1990 *Perfs., Etc. as Before***

1259 A160 20z on 20k #877 .40 .40
1260 A201 40z on 2k #1121 .40 .40
1261 A201 40z on 4k #1122 .40 .40
1262 A184 40z on 10k #1005 .40 .40
1263 A196 40z on 25k #1091 .40 .40
1264 A201 40z on 25k #1123 .40 .40
1265 A184 40z on 50k #1007 .40 .40
1266 A196 40z on 50k #1092 .40 .40
1267 A200 40z on 50k #1115 .40 .40
1268 A193 40z on 75k #1071 .40 .40
1269 A184 40z on 80k #1008 .40 .40
1270 A190 40z on 90k #1045 .40 .40
1271 A193 40z on 90k #1072 .40 .40
1272 A196 40z on 90k #1093 .40 .40
1273 A201 80z on 2k #1121 1.00 1.00
1274 A201 80z on 4k #1122 1.00 1.00
1275 A184 80z on 10k #1005 1.00 1.00
1276 A196 80z on 25k #1091 1.00 1.00
1277 A201 80z on 25k #1123 1.00 1.00
1278 A196 80z on 50k #1092 1.00 1.00
1279 A200 80z on 50k #1115 1.00 1.00
1280 A193 80z on 75k #1071 1.00 1.00
1281 A184 80z on 80k #1008 1.00 1.00
1282 A190 80z on 90k #1045 1.00 1.00
1283 A193 80z on 90k #1072 1.00 1.00
1284 A196 80z on 90k #1093 1.00 1.00
1285 A175 100z on 40s #953 1.40 1.40
1287 A186 100z on 2k #1019 1.40 1.40
1288 A187 100z on 2k #1028 1.40 1.40
1289 A192 100z on 2k #1058 1.40 1.40
1290 A175 100z on 4k #955 1.40 1.40
1291 A165 100z on 5k #896 1.40 1.40
1292 A185 100z on 5k #1013 1.40 1.40
1293 A187 100z on 5k #1029 1.40 1.40
1294 A159 100z on 8k #865 1.40 1.40
1295 A165 100z on 8k #897 1.40 1.40
1296 A167 100z on 8k #912 1.40 1.40
1298 A167 100z on 10k #913 1.40 1.40
1299 A169 100z on 10k #922 1.40 1.40
1300 A165 100z on 10k #993 1.40 1.40
1301 A183 100z on 10k #1000 1.40 1.40
1302 A185 100z on 10k #1014 1.40 1.40
1303 A186 100z on 10k #1020 1.40 1.40
1304 A175 100z on 15k #956 1.40 1.40
1305 A187 100z on 18k #1031 1.40 1.40
1306 A169 100z on 20k #923 1.40 1.40
1307 A180 100z on 20k #977 1.40 1.40
1308 A144 100z on 22k #755 1.40 1.40
1309 A186 100z on 25k #1021 1.40 1.40
1311 A159 100z on 48k #869 1.40 1.40
1312 A167 100z on 48k #916 1.40 1.40
1313 A179 100z on 50k #971 1.40 1.40
1314 A187 100z on 50k #1032 1.40 1.40
1315 A192 100z on 50k #1061 1.40 1.40
1316 A165 100z on 75k #995 1.40 1.40
1317 A183 100z on 75k #1001 1.40 1.40
1318 A183 100z on 80k #1002 1.40 1.40
1319 A199 100z on 80k #1111 1.40 1.40
1320 A170 100z on 90k #930 1.40 1.40
1321 A186 100z on 90k #1022 1.40 1.40
1322 A192 100z on 90k #1062 1.40 1.40
1324 A198 300z on 2k #1102 4.25 4.25
1325 A173 300z on 8k #938 4.25 4.25
1326 A182 300z on 10k #986 4.25 4.25
1327 A143 300z on 14k #751 4.25 4.25
1328 A146 300z on 17k #769 4.25 4.25
1329 A174 300z on 20k #947 4.25 4.25
1330 A198 300z on 45k #1103 4.25 4.25
1331 A182 300z on 75k #987 4.25 4.25
1332 A198 300z on 75k #1104 4.25 4.25
1333 A162 500z on 8k #886 7.50 7.50
1334 A162 500z on 10k #887 7.50 7.50
1335 A162 500z on 25k #888 7.50 7.50
1336 A162 500z on 48k #889 7.50 7.50
*Nos. 1259-1336 (74)* 134.85 134.85

Size and location of surcharge varies. Some surcharges show "z" before numeral.

100z on #1060 was surcharged in error.

Numbers have been reserved for additional values in this set.

Various 1980-1983 Stamps Surcharged

**1991 *Perfs., Etc., as Before***

1342 A181 1000z on 1z #982a-982d 1.40 1.40
1343 A185 1000z on 100k #1016 .35 .35
1344 A192 1000z on 1z #1063 .35 .35
1345 A182 2000z on 100k #988 .70 .70
1346 A198 2000z on 1z #1105 .70 .70
1347 A193 2500z on 1z #1073 1.00 1.00
1348 A191 3000z on 1z #1057 1.40 1.40
1349 A200 4000z on 1z #1116 2.00 2.00
1350 A200 5000z on 1z #1116 2.90 2.90
1351 A193 10,000z on 1z #1073 3.75 3.75
1352 A191 15,000z on 1z #1057 5.75 5.75
*Nos. 1342-1352 (11)* 20.30 20.30

Size and location of surcharge varies.

The editors have received from a collector mint stamps bearing the surcharges shown below. There is conflicting data as to the validity of these surcharges, and anyone with information on them is asked to contact the new issues editor.

12 - 6 - 92
6e ANNIVERSAIRE DE
OFFICE NATIONAL
DU TOUR.SME
1.000 000 Z

12 - 3 - 92
INAUGURATION
STATION POMPAGE
600.000 Z.

Du 8 au 15 - 6 - 92
2e Conférence Addis - Abeba
Virus VIH 1 - et VIH 2
EN AFRIQUE
**10.000.000 Z**

5.000.000 Z

**Conference Nationale Souveraine**
**3 mars - 4 decembre 1991 - 1992**

Nos. 989, 1010, 1112, 1124 Surcharged

**1992, Aug. 18 *Perfs., Etc. as Before***

1354 A184 50th z on 125k #1010 .30 .30
1355 A201 100th z on 1.20z #1124 .40 .40
1356 A199 150th z on 1.20z #1112 .70 .70
1357 A182 200th z on 145k #989 1.00 1.00
1358 A199 250th z on 1.20z #1112 1.25 1.25
1359 A201 300th z on 1.20z #1124 1.50 1.50
1360 A199 500th z on 1.20z #1112 2.50 2.50
*Nos. 1354-1360 (7)* 7.65 7.65

Size and location of surcharge varies. Numbers have been reserved for additional values in this set.

#1361-1366

#1368-1374

**1993, Oct. 29 Photo. *Perf. 13½x13***

1361 A167 500th z on 30s #910 .55 .55
1362 A167 500th z on 5k #911 .55 .55
1365 A167 750th z on 8k #912 .80 .80
1366 A167 750th z on 10k #913 .80 .80
1368 A167 1 mil z on 30k #914 1.10 1.10
1369 A167 1 mil z on 40k #915 1.10 1.10
1370 A167 5 mil z on 48k #916 5.25 5.25
1371 A167 10 mil z on 100k #917 10.50 10.50
*Nos. 1361-1371 (8)* 20.65 20.65

Nos. 1226-1229 Surcharged in Black or Red (#1374)

**1993, Oct. 29 Litho. *Perf. 13***

**1373** A216 3 mil z on 10z #1226 2.75 2.75
**1374** A216 3 mil z on 10z #1226
**1375** A216 5 mil z on 15z #1227 4.50 4.50
**1376** A216 10 mil z on 25z #1228 8.75 8.75

**Souvenir Sheet**

**1377** A216 10 mil z on 100z #1229 8.50 8.50

Size and location of surcharge varies.

Natl. Game Parks, 50th Anniv. A225

**1993 Litho. *Perf. 13***

**1403** A225 30k Cape eland .25 .25
**1404** A225 50k Elephants .25 .25
**1405** A225 1.50z Giant eland .70 .70
**1406** A225 3.50z White rhinoceros 1.75 1.75
**1407** A225 5z Bongo 2.40 2.40
*Nos. 1403-1407 (5)* 5.35 5.35

For surcharge see No. 1431.

Nos. 986-900 Surcharged

**1994, Apr. 23 Photo. *Perf. 14***

**1408** A182 30k on 10k .45 .45
**1409** A182 50k on 75k .90 .90
**1410** A182 1.50z on 100k 2.25 2.25
**1411** A182 3.50z on 145k 4.50 4.50
**1412** A182 5z on 270k 7.25 7.25
*Nos. 1408-1412 (5)* 15.35 15.35

Nos. 1160-1167 Surcharged

**1994, Apr. 23 Litho. *Perf. 14***

**1413** A207 30k on 10k .40 .40
**1414** A207 50k on 15k .55 .55
**1415** A207 1.50z on 3z 1.60 1.60
**1416** A207 2.50z on 5z 2.50 2.50
**1417** A207 3.50z on 10z 3.75 3.75
**1418** A207 5z on 15z 5.25 5.25
**1419** A207 7.50z on 37.50z 8.50 8.50
**1420** A207 10z on 80z 10.50 10.50
*Nos. 1413-1420 (8)* 33.05 33.05

Nos. 1195-1198 Surcharged

**1994, Apr. 23 Litho. *Perf. 13***

**1421** A210 50k on 5z 1.00 1.00
**1422** A210 1.50z on 10z 2.75 2.75
**1423** A210 3.50z on 15z 5.25 5.25
**1424** A210 5z on 25z 10.50 10.50
*Nos. 1421-1424 (4)* 19.50 19.50

Nos. 990, 1079, 1094, 1097, 1113, 1125-1126, 1133, 1155, & 1404 Surcharged in Gold

**1994, Aug. 31 *Perfs., Etc. as Before***

**1425** A196 20z on 3z #1097 .20 .20
**1426** A182 40z on 270k #990 .25 .25
**1427** A203 50z on 3z #1133 .40 .40
**1428** A206 75z on 3z #1155 .40 .40
**1429** A201 100z on 2.05z #1125 .55 .55
**1430** A194 150z on 1.70z #1079 .90 .90
**1431** A225 200z on 50k #1404 1.00 1.00
**1432** A196 250z on 1.50z #1094 1.25 1.25
**1433** A199 300z on 3.60z #1113 1.40 1.40
**1434** A201 500z on 3.60z #1126 2.25 2.25
*Nos. 1425-1434 (10)* 8.60 8.60

Size and location of surcharge varies.

Nos. 1067, 1094, 1113, 1125-1126 Surcharged in Gold

100NZ

1000 NZ

**1996 *Perfs., Etc. as Before***

**1435** A192 100z on 3.50z #1067 .25 .25
**1436** A199 500z on 3.60z #1113 .25 .25
**1437** A201 1000z on 2.05z #1125 .25 .25
**1438** A196 2500z on 1.50z #1094 .90 .90
**1439** A201 5000z on 3.60z #1126 1.60 1.60
**1440** A196 6000z on 1.50z #1094 2.10 2.10
**1441** A199 15,000z on 3.60z #1113 5.00 5.00
**1442** A201 25,000z on 3.60z #1126 8.50 8.50
*Nos. 1435-1442 (8)* 18.85 18.85

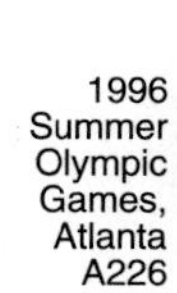

1996 Summer Olympic Games, Atlanta A226

**1996, July 29 Litho. *Perf. 11½***

**1444** A226 1000z Equestrian .20 .20
**1445** A226 12,500z Boxing .80 .80
**1446** A226 25,000z Table tennis 2.00 2.00
**1447** A226 35,000z Basketball, vert. 2.75 2.75
**1448** A226 50,000z Tennis 3.25 3.25
*Nos. 1444-1448 (5)* 9.00 9.00

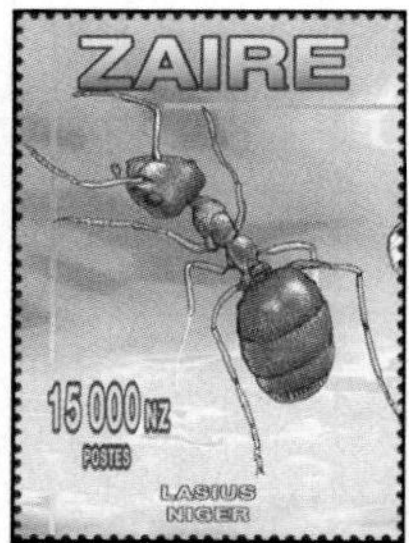


Insects & Spiders A227

No. 1449: a, Lasius niger. b, Calopterygides. c, Peucetia. d, Sphecides.

**1996 Litho. *Perf. 13½***

**1449** A227 15,000z Sheet of 4, #a.-d. 9.00 9.00

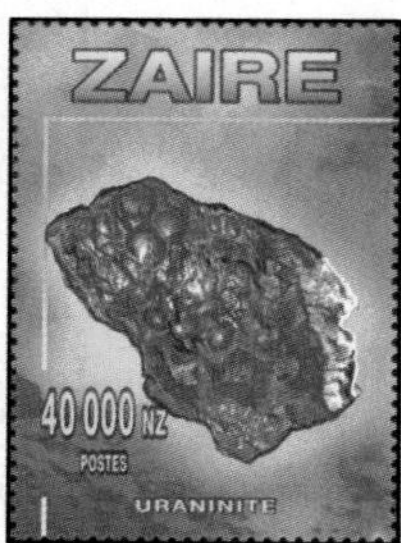


Minerals A228

No. 1450: a, Uraninite. b, Malachite. c, Ruby. d, Diamond.

No. 1452, Uranotile, cuprosklodowskite, horiz.

**1996**

**1450** A228 40,000z Sheet of 4, #a.-d. 25.00 25.00

**Souvenir Sheet**

**1452** A228 105,000z multi 11.00 11.00

A number has been reserved for an additional sheet with this set.

Raptors A229

No. 1453: a, Congo eagle. b, Crowned eagle. c, Melierax metabates. d, Urotriorchis macrourus.

**1996**

**1453** A229 50,000z Sheet of 4, #a.-d. 23.00 23.00

Butterflies A230

No. 1454: a, Cymothoe sangaris. b, Colotis zoe. c, Physcaeneura leda. d, Charaxes candiope.

**1996**

**Sheet of 4**

**1454** A230 70,000z #a.-d. 27.50 27.50

The validity of Nos. 1455-1481 and other stamps from the same time period has been questioned. The editors are attempting to find out more about these stamps.

1998 World Cup Soccer Championships, France — A231

Numbers on players: No. 1455, #12. No. 1456, none. No. 1457, #7. No. 1458, #3.

No. 1459: a, British player. b, Brazilian player.

No. 1460: a-d, Like #1455-1458, but with part of World Cup Trophy behind each player.

**1996**

**1455-1458** A231 35,000z Set of 4 9.00 9.00

**Souvenir Sheets**

**1459** A231 10,500z Sheet of 2, #a.-b. 1.25 1.25
**1460** A231 35,000z Sheet of 4, #a.-d. 9.00 9.00

No. 1459 contains 2 42x39mm stamps.

See Nos. 1467-1476.

World Wildlife Fund — A231a

No. 1466 — Pan paniscus: a, With young. b, Two in trees. c, Holding vines. d, Head.

**1997**

**1466** A231a 20,000z Block of 4, #a.-d. 5.50 5.50

1998 World Cup Soccer Championships Type of 1996

African soccer players: No. 1467, 20,000z, Soccer ball at his right. No. 1468, 20,000z, Ball at head. No. 1469, 20,000z, Yellow uniform. No. 1470, 20,000z, Ball on knee.

German soccer players, soccer ball on stamp at: No. 1471, 50,000z, UR. No. 1472, 50,000z, LL. No. 1473, 50,000z, LR. No. 1474, 50,000z, UL.

Nos. 1475a-1475d, 1476a-1476d are like Nos. 1467-1474 but with part of World Cup Trophy behind each player.

**1996 Litho. *Perf. 13½***

**1467-1470** A231 Set of 4 5.00 5.00
**1471-1474** A231 Set of 4 12.25 12.25

**Souvenir Sheets**

**1475** A231 20,000z Sheet of 4, #a.-d. 5.00 5.00
**1476** A231 50,000z Sheet of 4, #a.-d. 12.25 12.25

Boy Scouts and Lions Intl. Clubs A232

No. 1477 — Diceros bicornis: a, Walking forward. b, Walking left, left leg up. c, Facing left. d, Holding head up.

No. 1478 — Panthera leo: a, Cubs. b, Adult male. c, Adult male facing forward, mouth open. d, Adult female on fallen tree.

No. 1479 — Loxodonta africana: a, Walking right, trunk in air. b, Reaching up to tree limb with trunk. c, Walking right, trunk down. d, Mother with calf.

105,000z, Hippopotamus amphibus.

**1997 Litho. *Perf. 13x13½***

**1477** A232 40,000z Sheet of 4, #a.-d. 9.50 9.50
**1478** A232 50,000z Sheet of 4, #a.-d. 11.75 11.75
**1479** A232 70,000z Sheet of 4, #a.-d. 19.00 19.00

**Souvenir Sheet**

**1480** A232 105,000z multi 6.25 6.25

Boy Scouts (#1477, 1479-1480). Lions Intl. Clubs (#1478).

Jacqueline Kennedy Onassis (1929-94) A233

Various portraits.

**1997** **Litho.** ***Perf. 13½***

**1481** A233 15,000z Sheet of 9, #a.-i. 11.00 11.00

No. 1481 also exists imperf.

---

Stamps from this country are now being released under the previous name, "Republique Democratique du Congo," or Congo Democratic Republic, despite the resumption of civil war. We will continue to list these stamps under the country's name of Zaire until the situation is resolved.

---

Diana, Princess of Wales (1961-97) — A234 Mother Teresa (1910-97) — A235

No. 1482: a, Wearing tiara. b, In white jacket. c, In white hat. d, In polka dotted dress. e, Scarf around neck. f, Low cut evening dress.

No. 1483: a, Wearing tiara. b, Hand under chin. c, Leaning chin on both hands. d, One-shoulder-covered outfit.

No. 1484: a, Red & black dress. b, White jacket, pearls. c, Profile view. d, Wearing tiara.

No. 1485, 400,000z, In black evening dress. No. 1486, 400,000z, Holding flowers.

**1998, Aug. 6** **Litho.** ***Perf. 14***

**1482** A234 50,000z Sheet of 6, #a.-f. 9.50 5.50
**1483** A234 100,000z Sheet of 4, #a.-d. 12.50 7.50
**1484** A234 125,000z Sheet of 4, #a.-d. 17.00 10.50

**Souvenir Sheets**

**1485-1486** A234 Set of 2 35.00 17.50

**1998, Aug. 6**

**1487** A235 50,000z shown 1.50 1.00

**Souvenir Sheet**

**1488** A235 325,000z Portrait, diff. 7.50 5.00

No. 1487 was issued in sheets of 6.

100 Centimes = 1 Franc (1998)

Native Dwelling — A236

Arms — A237

Inauguration of Pres. Laurent Kabila — A238

Designs: 1.25fr, Troops and civilians in Kinshasa. 3fr, Flag, crowd, Pres. Kabila breaking chain with sword, horiz.

2.50fr, Gun, arrow, handshake, tractor. 3.50fr, Pres. Kabila.

**1999, May 12** **Litho.** ***Perf. 14***

**1489** A236 25c multi .25 .25
**1490** A237 50c multi .55 .55
**1491** A238 75c multi .80 .80
**1492** A238 1.25fr multi 1.40 1.40
**1493** A238 3fr multi 3.25 3.25
*Nos. 1489-1493 (5)* 6.25 6.25

**Souvenir Sheets**

**1494** A238 2.50fr multi 2.60 2.60
**1495** A238 3.50fr multi 3.75 3.75

Conquest of Kinshasa by troops of Laurent Kabila, 2nd anniv.

Chinese Zodiac Animals — A239

No. 1496: a, Rat. b, Ox. c, Tiger. d, Rabbit. e, Dragon. f, Snake. g, Horse. h, Ram. i, Monkey. j, Cock. k, Dog. l, Boar.

**1999, Aug. 20** ***Perf. 13¼x13½***

**1496** A239 78c Sheet of 12, #a-l 20.00 20.00

A240

A241

A242

A243

Outlaws of the Marsh — A244

No. 1497 — Sheet with text starting with "The historical novel. . .": a, 1.45fr, Men fighting. b, 1.50fr, Man uprooting tree. c, 1.60fr, Man with sword in snowstorm. d, 1.70fr, Man with sword, other men at bridge. e, 1.80fr, Three men at table.

No. 1498 — Sheet with text starting with "The main theme. . .": a, 1.45fr, Men and baskets. b, 1.50fr, Man threatening another man with sword. c, 1.60fr, Man attacking tiger. d, 1.70fr, People watching men in martial arts battle. e, 1.80fr, Battling horsemen.

No. 1499 - Sheet with text starting with "The common people. . .": a, 1.45fr, Men fighting in boat. b, 1.50fr, Man with sword fighting man with hatchets. c, 1.60fr, Men near fortified wall. d, 1.70fr, Men fighting on cobblestone street. e, 1.80fr, Archer on horseback at doorway.

No. 1500 — Sheet with text starting with "Today, it is thought. . .": a, 1.45fr, Man seated and other man standing near table. b, 1.50fr, Man setting fire to building. c, 1.60fr, Man in room. d, 1.70fr, Man lifting another man in a battle. e, 1.80fr, Man holding torn scroll.

**1999, Aug. 20** ***Perf. 13¼***

**Sheets of 5, #a-e**

**1497-1500** A240 Set of 4 42.50 42.50

**Souvenir Sheets**

***Perf. 13¼x13½***

**1501** A241 10fr multi 12.50 12.50
**1502** A242 10fr multi 12.50 12.50
**1503** A243 10fr multi 12.50 12.50
**1504** A244 10fr multi 12.50 12.50

A245

A246

African Flora and Fauna — A247

Designs: 1fr, Telophorus quadricolor. 1.50fr, Panthera pardus. No. 1507, 2fr, Colotis protomedia. No. 1508, 2fr, Kobus vardoni. No. 1509, 3fr, Canarina abyssinica. No. 1510, 3fr, Smutsia temminckii.

7.80fr, Lion.

No. 1512: a, Okapi. b, Bird, rainbow, waterfalls. c, Giraffe, rainbow, waterfalls. d, Giraffe, waterfall mist. e, Mandrill. f, Chimpanzee. g, Leopard. h, Butterflies. i, Hippopotamus. j, Bird in water. k, Flowers. l, Antelope.

No. 1513: a, Sun. b, Pieris citrina. c, Merops apiaster. d, Lanius collurio. e, Ploceus cucullatus. f, Charaxes pelias. g, Charaxes eupale. h, Giraffa camelopardalis. i, Galago moholi. j, Strelitzia reginae. k, Gazella thomsoni. l, Upupa epops.

No. 1514, 10fr, Taurotragus oryx. No. 1515, 10fr, Hippopotamus amphibus.

No. 1516, 10fr, Warthog.

***Perf. 14, 14¼x14¾ (#1511), 14¼x14 (#1516)***

**2000, Feb. 28**

**1505-1510** A245 Set of 6 8.50 8.50
**1511** A246 7.80fr multi 5.00 5.00
**1512** A247 1fr Sheet of 12, #a-l 8.50 8.50
**1513** A245 1.50fr Sheet of 12, #a-l 15.00 15.00

**Souvenir Sheets**

**1514-1515** A245 Set of 2 14.00 14.00
**1516** A247 10fr multi 7.00 7.00

No. 1516 contains one 42x57mm.

Wild Felines and Canines — A248

No. 1517, 1.50fr: a, Felis bengalensis. b, Felis aurata. c, Felis caracal. d, Felis conoclor. e, Felis nigripes. f, Panthera leo. g, Neofelis nebulosa. h, Felis wiedii. i, Acinonyx jubatus. j, Felis pardina. k, Felis yagouaroundi. l, Felis serval.

No. 1518, 2fr: a, Canis mesomelas. b, Otocyon megalotis. c, Speothos venaticus. d, Canis latrans. e, Cuon alpinus. f, Fennecus zerda. g, Urocyon cinereoargenteus. h, Canis lupus. i, Vulpes macrotis. j, Chrysocyon brachyurus. k, Nyctereutes procyonoides. l, Vulpes vulpes.

No. 1519, 10fr, Panthera pardus. No. 1520, 10fr, Alopex lagopus.

**2000, Feb. 28** ***Perf. 14***

**Sheets of 12, #a-l**

**1517-1518** A248 Set of 2 27.50 27.50

**Souvenir Sheets**

**1519-1520** A248 Set of 2 11.50 11.50

Millennium A249

**2000, June 10**

**1521** Horiz. strip of 3 16.00 16.00
*a.* A249 4.50fr multi 2.25 2.25
*b.* A249 9fr multi 4.50 4.50
*c.* A249 15fr multi 8.00 8.00

Printed in sheets containing two strips.

A250

A251

Birds
A252

Designs: No. 1522, 3fr, Alopochen aegyptiacus. No. 1523, 3fr, Ardeola ibis. No. 1524, 4.50fr, Oena capensis. No. 1525, 4.50fr, Lybius torquatus. No. 1526, 9fr, Falco tinnunculus. No. 1527, 9fr, Corythaelo cristata.

No. 1528, 4.50fr, Psephotus chrysopterygius chrysopterygius. 8fr, Amazona aestiva. No. 1530, 8.50fr, Are nobilis cumanensis. No. 1531, 9fr, Agapornis roseicollis.

No. 1532, 8.50fr, Lophornis ornata. No. 1533, 9fr, Polytrus guauvunibi.

No. 1534, 9fr: a, Euplectes orix. b, Euplectes ardens. c, Oriolus auratus. d, Plocens cucullatus. e, Amandava subflava. f, Nectarina senegalensis.

No. 1535, 9fr: a, Haleyon malimbicus. b, Tachymarptis melba. c, Haliaeetus vocifer. d, Ardea purpurea. e, Balaeniceps rex. f, Balearica regulorum.

No. 1536: a, Ertoxeres aquila. b, Aglaiolepus kinde. c, Archilochus calobris. d, Trochlus polytaus. e, Chaliostigna herrani. f, Ensifera. g, Chrysolampus mosquitus. h, Phorethornus syrmatophorus. i, Calypre hetervare.

No. 1537, 5fr: a, Eos squamata squamata. b, Aratinga guarouba. c, Aratinga aurea. d, Psuedeos fuscata. e, Agapornis fischeri. f, Aratinga nana nana. g, Aratinga mitrata. h, Trichoglossus haematodus rubitorquis. i, Cacatua galerita galerita.

No. 1538, 5fr: a, Ara macao. b, Neophema elegans. c, Loriculus vernalis. d, Aratinga solstitialis. e, Pionites melancephala. f, Bolborhynchus lineola. g, Ara severa. h, Psephotus chrysopterygius dissimilis. i, Ara militaris.

No. 1539, 15fr, Actophilornis africanus, horiz. No. 1540, 20fr, Ceryle rudis, horiz.

No. 1541, 15fr, Opopsitta diophthalma. No. 1542, 15fr, Ara ararrauna, horiz.

No. 1543, 15fr, Coeligena torgoata. No. 1544, 20fr, Campylopterus hemileicurus.

**2000, Aug. 16** — ***Perf. 14***

| | | | |
|---|---|---|---|
| **1522-1527** A250 | Set of 6 | *15.00* | *15.00* |
| **1528-1531** A251 | Set of 4 | *13.50* | *13.50* |
| **1532-1533** A252 | Set of 2 | *7.75* | *7.75* |

**Sheets of 6, #a-f**

| | | | |
|---|---|---|---|
| **1534-1535** A250 | Set of 2 | *47.50* | *47.50* |
| **1536** A252 4.50fr | Sheet of 9, #a-i | *18.00* | *18.00* |

**Sheets of 9, #a-i**

| | | | |
|---|---|---|---|
| **1537-1538** A251 | Set of 2 | *40.00* | *40.00* |

**Souvenir Sheets**

| | | | |
|---|---|---|---|
| **1539-1540** A250 | Set of 2 | *16.00* | *16.00* |
| **1541-1542** A251 | Set of 2 | *13.50* | *13.50* |
| **1543-1544** A252 | Set of 2 | *16.00* | *16.00* |

Surcharges on Unissued Stamps
A253

Designs: 10fr on 70,000z, Colotis zoe. 15fr on 25,000z, Bulbophyllum falcatum. 25fr on 20,000z, Scutellosaurus. 35fr on 15,000z, Sphecides. 45fr on 100,000z, Diamond. 50fr on 35,000z, Termitomyces aurantiacus. 70fr on 50,000z, Melierax metabates. 100fr on 40,000z, Malachite. 150fr on 25,000z, Panda.

**2000** — **Litho.** — ***Perf. 13¼***

| | | | |
|---|---|---|---|
| **1545** A253 | 10fr on 70,000z multi | — | — |
| **1546** A253 | 15fr on 25,000z multi | — | — |
| **1547** A253 | 25fr on 20,000z multi | — | — |
| **1548** A253 | 35fr on 15,000z multi | — | — |
| **1549** A253 | 45fr on 100,000z multi | — | — |
| **1550** A253 | 50fr on 35,000z multi | — | — |
| **1551** A253 | 70fr on 50,000z multi | — | — |
| **1552** A253 | 100fr on 40,000z multi | — | — |
| **1553** A253 | 150fr on 25,000z multi | — | — |

Location of surcharges varies. All surcharged stamps have white margins.

A254

Trains — A255

Designs: 1fr, Missouri-Kansas-Texas Line locomotive. 2fr, Spremberg steam locomotive. No. 1556, 3fr, King Class, Great Western Railway. No. 1557, 3fr, Crocodile locomotive. 5fr, Inner-city trains, Great Britain. 6fr, Big Boy, Union Pacific.

No. 1560, 4.50fr: a, Class SU, 2-6-2, Russia. b, Prussian locomotive. c, Zimbabwe locomotive. d, Hunslet 2-8-2, Peru. e, London, Midland & Scottish Railway locomotive. f, London Northeastern Railway locomotive.

No. 1561, 8fr: a, Denver & Rio Grande Western Railroad locomotive. b, Mikado 2-8-2, Louisville & Nashville. c, Mogul, Rio Grande. d, New York Central Railway locomotive. e, Sumpter Valley Railway steam locomotive. f, Three-truck Shay No. 7.

No. 1562, 9.50fr: a, Compagnie du Nord locomotive, France. b, Union Pacific locomotive. c, Great Northern Railway locomotive. d, Liverpool & Manchester Railway locomotive. e, Patentee 2-2-2, London & Birmingham. f, Puffing Billy.

No. 1563, 10fr: a, Chicago, Rock Island & Pacific Railway locomotive. b, Powhattan Arrow, Norfolk & Western. c, Class S-1, New York Central Hudson River Railway. d, Reading Railroad locomotive. e, Great Bear, Great Western Railway. f, Bi-polar, Chicago, Milwaukee, St. Paul & Pacific Railway.

No. 1564, 5fr: a, Beyer-Garratt 50 4-8-2+2-8-4 locomotive. b, Locomotive Express 4-6-2. c, 780CV electric locomotive. d, Electric locomotive on curve. e, Class 2-10-0 Locomotive 56001. f, Electric locomotive on straight track. g, Class 2-8-4 Locomotive 284. h, Class G 6/6 electric locomotive.

No. 1565, 8.50fr: a, Class B-B electric locomotive AE4/4. b, Class EX, Paris-Lyon-Mediterranean. c, Big Boy. d, Tourist car. e, Class 4-8-4 GS-4. f, Class 46 electric locomotive. g, Class-4-6-0 County. h, Class DA Diesel-electric locomotive.

No. 1566, 15fr, New York Central & Hudson River Railway locomotive. No. 1567, 20fr, Mohawk & Hudson Railroad locomotive. No. 1568, 20fr, Broadway Limited, Pennsylvania Railroad. No. 1569, 20fr, Trans-Europe Express.

No. 1570, 20fr, Deltic electric locomotive, Great Britain. No. 1571, 20fr, Diesel-electric locomotive, Canada Pacific.

**2001, Jan. 15** — **Litho.** — ***Perf. 14***

| | | | |
|---|---|---|---|
| **1554-1559** A254 | Set of 6 | 7.50 | 7.50 |

**Sheets of 6, #a-f**

| | | | |
|---|---|---|---|
| **1560-1563** A254 | Set of 4 | 45.00 | 45.00 |

**Sheets of 8, #a-h**

| | | | |
|---|---|---|---|
| **1564-1565** A255 | Set of 2 | 30.00 | 30.00 |

**Souvenir Sheets**

| | | | |
|---|---|---|---|
| **1566-1569** A254 | Set of 4 | 17.00 | 17.00 |
| **1570-1571** A255 | Set of 2 | 10.00 | 10.00 |

Ships
A256

Designs: 2.50fr, Clipper. 5fr, Arab bum. 20fr, Flemish galley. 21.70fr, Trabaccolo, vert. 30fr, Dutch galliot. 45.80fr, Japanese coaster.

No. 1578, 10fr: a, Trireme. b, Roman caudicaria. c, 13th cent. warship. d, Byzantine galley. e, Lateneer. f, 14th century cog. g, Arab dhow. h, Hanseatic cog. i, Portuguese galley.

No. 1579, 10fr: a, Egyptian sailing ship. b, Egyptian rowing craft. c, Egyptian seagoing ship. d, Greek galley. e, Etruscan merchantman f, Etruscan fishing skiff. g, Greek merchantman. h, Minoan passenger ship. i, Roman harbor boat.

No. 1580, 10fr: a, Flemish galleon. b, English galleon. c, Carrack. d, Chinese war galley. e, Venetian galley. f, Polacre. g, Hemmena. h, Venetian bragozzo. i, Schooner.

No. 1581, 25fr, Viking drakkar. No. 1582, 25fr, Portuguese caravel, vert. No. 1583, 25fr, HMS Endeavour, vert.

**2001, June 22** — ***Perf. 14***

| | | | |
|---|---|---|---|
| **1572-1577** A256 | Set of 6 | 14.00 | 14.00 |

**Sheets of 9, #a-i**

| | | | |
|---|---|---|---|
| **1578-1580** A256 | Set of 3 | 30.00 | 30.00 |

**Souvenir Sheets**

***Perf. 13¾***

| | | | |
|---|---|---|---|
| **1581-1583** A256 | Set of 3 | 16.00 | 16.00 |

No. 1581 contains one 50x38mm stamp; Nos. 1582-1583 each contain one 38x50mm stamp.

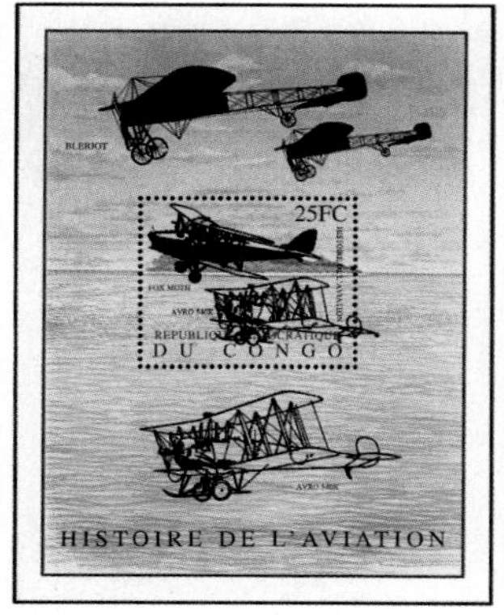

History of Aviation — A257

No. 1584: a, Montgolfier balloon (36x61mm). b, Boxkite and Tiger Moth airplanes (36x61mm). c, Gladiator. d, Eurofighter. e, Mosquito. f, Chipmunk.

No. 1585: a, Blackburn and Spartan Arrow airplanes (36x61mm). b, Tiger Moth. c, Lightning. d, Vulcan B2. e, Tornado.

No. 1586, 25fr, Fox Moth and Avro 540K airplanes. No. 1587, 25fr, Avro 504K and Fox Moth airplanes.

**2001, June 22** — ***Perf. 14¼***

| | | | |
|---|---|---|---|
| **1584** A257 10fr | Sheet of 6, #a-f | 7.00 | 7.00 |
| **1585** A257 10fr | Sheet of 6, #1584a, 1585a-1585e | 7.00 | 7.00 |

**Souvenir Sheets**

***Perf. 14¼x14½***

| | | | |
|---|---|---|---|
| **1586-1587** A257 | Set of 2 | 11.00 | 11.00 |

First Zeppelin Flight, Cent. — A258

No. 1588: a, LZ-6. b, LZ-7. c, US Navy airship Akron. c, Lindstrand HS-110 Pittsburgh Tribune-Review airship.

No. 1589, 100fr, LZ-130 Graf Zeppelin II. No. 1590, 100fr, LZ-1.

**2001, June 22** — ***Perf. 14***

| | | | |
|---|---|---|---|
| **1588** A258 60fr | Sheet of 4, #a-d | 18.00 | 18.00 |

**Souvenir Sheets**

| | | | |
|---|---|---|---|
| **1589-1590** A258 | Set of 2 | 15.00 | 15.00 |

Butterflies — A259

Designs: 5fr, Striped policeman. 21.70fr, Brown-veined white. 45fr, Common dotted border. 45.80fr, Cabbage. 50fr, African migrant. 51.80fr, Mocker swallowtail.

No. 1597, 6fr, horiz.: a, Common grass blue. b, Golden tiger. c, Palla. d, Blue diadem. e, African giant swallowtail. f, African leaf. g, Gold-banded forester. h, Small harvester.

No. 1598, 6fr, horiz.: a, Guinea fowl. b, Forest queen. c, Sweet potato acraea. d, Wanderer. e, Evening brown. f, African ringlet. g, Plain tiger. h, Monarch.

No. 1599, 8fr, horiz.: a, Broad-bordered grass yellow. b, Crimson tip. c, Orange-banded protea. d, Azure hairstreak. e, Marshall's false monarch. f, Blue swallowtail. g, Figtree blue. h, Grass jewel.

No. 1600, 25fr, Long-tailed blue, horiz. No. 1601, 25fr, Chief, horiz. No. 1602, 25fr, Large spotted acraea, horiz.

**2001, June 22**

| | | | |
|---|---|---|---|
| **1591-1596** A259 | Set of 6 | 16.00 | 16.00 |

**Sheets of 8, #a-h**

| | | | |
|---|---|---|---|
| **1597-1599** A259 | Set of 3 | 37.50 | 37.50 |

**Souvenir Sheets**

| | | | |
|---|---|---|---|
| **1600-1602** A259 | Set of 3 | 16.00 | 16.00 |

Flowers and Insects — A260

Designs; 20fr, Aconite, Brazilian frog-hopper. 21.70fr, Larkspur, Mexican cicada. 25fr, Blue orchid, dragonfly. 45.80fr, Spotted blossom orchid, buck moth.

No. 1607, 10fr, horiz.: a, Rein orchids, tiger moth. b, Ivy, Siamese wasp. c, Pink lady's slipper, goat weed emperor. d, Gletscherpetersbart, velvet ant. e, Licorice, viceroy butterfly. f, Grass pink, aphid. g, Ranunculus, spider wasp. h, Clamshell orchid, tropical bee. i, Bog orchids, mayfly.

No. 1608, 10fr, horiz.: a, Common lantana, red-spotted purple butterfly. b, Deep purple lilac, zebra swallowtail. c, Mt. Fujiyama, ruddy copper butterfly. d, Pinafore pink, red admiral butterfly. e, Argemone mexicana, purple hairstreak butterfly. f, Soapwort, sulphur butterfly. g, Lungwort, Buckeye butterfly. h, Wild thyme, pipevine swallowtail. i, Loeselia mexicana, banded purple butterfly.

No. 1609, 10fr, horiz.: a, Cymbidium Stanley Fouraker Highlander, scarlet tiger moth. b, Cymbidium Sparkle "Ruby Lips," Sumatran carpenter bee. c, Dendrobium Sussex, ant lion. d, Cymbidium Vieux Rose Loch Lomond, nachahmend butterfly. e, Cymbidium, cicada-killer wasp. f, Dendrobium Mousmee, spechosoma wasp. g, Arachnis flos-aeris, green lacewing. h, Paphiopedilum, seven-spot ladybug. i, Eulophia quartiniana, damselfly.

No. 1610, 25fr, Jolly Jocker pansy, monarch butterfly, horiz. No. 1611, 25fr, Pink peony, wasp (inscribed erroneously like No. 1610), horiz. No. 1612, 25fr, Plumbago capensis, honey bee, horiz.

**2001, June 22** — ***Perf. 14***

| | | | |
|---|---|---|---|
| **1603-1606** A260 | Set of 4 | 11.50 | 11.50 |

**Sheets of 9, #a-i**

***Perf. 14¼x14½***

| | | | |
|---|---|---|---|
| **1607-1609** A260 | Set of 3 | 30.00 | 30.00 |

**Souvenir Sheets**

| | | | |
|---|---|---|---|
| **1610-1612** A260 | Set of 3 | 16.00 | 16.00 |

Nos. 1607-1609 each contain nine 37x30mm stamps; Nos. 1610-1612 each contain one 50x37mm stamp.

Tintin in Africa — A261

Designs: 190fr, Tintin with hand above eyes. 461fr, Tintin in car with dog and native.

**2001, Dec. 31 Photo. *Perf. 11½***

**1613** A261 190fr multi 1.75 1.75

**Souvenir Sheet**

**1614** A261 461fr multi 5.00 5.00

No. 1614 contains one 48x38mm stamp.
Imperfs exist. Value: 1613, $15; 1614, $30.
See Belgium Nos. 1875-1876.

Native Handicrafts A262

Designs: 10fr, Tabwa buffalo mask. 50fr, Kongo bedpost. 60fr, Loi drum. 150fr, Kuba royal statue, vert. 200fr, Tshokwe mask, vert. 300fr, Luba mask, vert.

**2002, Mar. 7 Litho. *Perf. 11½***

**1615-1620** A262 Set of 6 9.00 9.00

Lions A263

Designs: 50fr, Lioness and cub. 75fr, Lion and dead animal. 150fr, Lioness and cubs at water's edge. 250fr, Lion and lioness. 300fr, Lion leaping in water.

**2002, Mar. 7 Litho. *Perf. 11½***

**1621-1625** A263 Set of 5 9.00 9.00

Minerals A265

Designs: 190fr, Beryl, vert. 340fr, Willemite mimetite. 410fr, Quartz chlorite. 445fr, Allophane copper. 455fr, Rhodochrosite, vert. 480fr, Zircon.

***Perf. 11½x11¼***

**2002, Aug. 30 Litho.**

| | | | | |
|---|---|---|---|---|
| **1631** | A265 | 190fr multi | 1.50 | 1.50 |
| **1632** | A265 | 340fr multi | 2.75 | 2.75 |
| **1633** | A265 | 410fr multi | 3.25 | 3.25 |
| **1634** | A265 | 445fr multi | 3.50 | 3.50 |
| **1635** | A265 | 455fr multi | 3.50 | 3.50 |
| **1636** | A265 | 480fr multi | 3.75 | 3.75 |

An additional stamp was issued in the set. The editors would like to examine it.

## OFFICIAL STAMPS

Nos. 756-772 Overprinted

**1975 Litho. *Perf. 14***

| | | | | |
|---|---|---|---|---|
| **O1** | A145 | 10s red org & blk | .20 | .20 |
| **O2** | A145 | 40s multi | .20 | .20 |
| **O3** | A145 | 50s multi | .20 | .20 |

***Perf. 13***

| | | | | |
|---|---|---|---|---|
| **O4** | A146 | 1k multi | .20 | .20 |
| **O5** | A146 | 2k multi | .20 | .20 |
| **O6** | A146 | 3k multi | .20 | .20 |
| **O7** | A146 | 4k multi | .30 | .20 |
| **O8** | A146 | 5k multi | .30 | .20 |
| **O9** | A146 | 6k multi | .45 | .20 |
| **O10** | A146 | 8k multi | .60 | .20 |
| **O11** | A146 | 9k multi | .60 | .25 |
| **O12** | A146 | 10k multi | .70 | .25 |
| **O13** | A146 | 14k multi | 1.00 | .40 |
| **O14** | A146 | 17k multi | 1.10 | .45 |
| **O15** | A146 | 20k multi | 1.10 | .45 |
| **O16** | A146 | 50k multi | 3.00 | 1.40 |
| **O17** | A146 | 100k multi | 10.00 | 3.50 |
| | | *Nos. O1-O17 (17)* | 20.35 | 8.70 |

"SP" are the initials of "Service Public."

# ZAMBEZIA

zam-'bē-zē-ə

LOCATION — A former district of the Mozambique Province in Portuguese East Africa

GOVT. — Part of the Portuguese East Africa Colony

The districts of Quelimane and Tete were created from Zambezia. Eventually stamps of Mozambique came into use. See Quelimane and Tete.

1000 Reis = 1 Milreis

King Carlos
A1 A2

***Perf. 11½, 12½, 13½***

**1894 Typo. Unwmk.**

**1** A1 5r yellow .25 .25
**2** A1 10r red violet .75 .45
**3** A1 15r chocolate 1.00 .65
*a.* Perf. 12½ 27.50 19.00
**4** A1 20r lavender 1.00 .65
**5** A1 25r blue green 2.00 1.25
*a.* Perf. 11½
**6** A1 50r lt blue 2.00 1.25
**7** A1 75r carmine 4.50 3.25
*a.* Perf. 11½ 50.00 35.00
**8** A1 80r yellow grn 5.00 2.50
**9** A1 100r brown, *buff* 4.00 1.75
**10** A1 150r car, *rose* 7.00 3.00
**11** A1 200r dk blue, *bl* 8.00 3.00
*a.* Perf. 11½ 200.00 150.00
*b.* Perf. 13½ 32.50 24.00
**12** A1 300r dk bl, *salmon* 10.00 4.50
*a.* Perf. 11½ 25.00 20.00
*Nos. 1-12 (12)* 45.50 22.50

For surcharges and overprints see Nos. 36-47, 73-74, 77-81, 84-88.

**1898-1903** ***Perf. 11½***

**Name and Value in Black or Red (500r)**

**13** A2 2½r gray .45 .45
**14** A2 5r orange .45 .45
**15** A2 10r lt green .75 .50
**16** A2 15r brown 1.25 1.00
**17** A2 15r gray grn ('03) 1.60 1.40
**18** A2 20r gray violet 1.25 1.00
**19** A2 25r sea green 1.25 1.00
**20** A2 25r carmine ('03) 1.00 .85
**21** A2 50r blue 1.25 1.10
**22** A2 50r brown ('03) 2.75 2.25
**23** A2 65r dull bl ('03) 8.00 5.50
**24** A2 75r rose 10.00 5.25
**25** A2 75r lilac ('03) 3.25 2.75
**26** A2 80r violet 5.00 3.00
**27** A2 100r dk bl, *bl* 2.00 2.00
**28** A2 115r org brn, *pink* ('03) 10.00 7.25
**29** A2 130r brn, *straw* ('03) 10.00 7.25
**30** A2 150r brn, *buff* 6.00 3.50
**31** A2 200r red vio, *pnksh* 6.00 3.50
**32** A2 300r dk bl, *rose* 8.00 3.50
**33** A2 400r dull bl, *straw* ('03) 10.00 8.50
**34** A2 500r blk, *bl* ('01) 12.00 6.75
**35** A2 700r vio, *yelsh* ('01) 15.00 8.75
*Nos. 13-35 (23)* 117.25 77.50

For surcharges and overprints see Nos. 49-68, 72, 82-83, 93-107.

Stamps of 1894 Surcharged

**1902** ***Perf. 11½, 12½***

**36** A1 65r on 10r red vio 9.00 7.00
**37** A1 65r on 15r choc 9.00 7.00
**38** A1 65r on 20r lav 9.00 7.00
**39** A1 65r on 300r bl, *sal* 9.00 7.00
**40** A1 115r on 5r yel 9.00 7.00
**41** A1 115r on 25r bl grn 9.00 7.00
**42** A1 115r on 80r yel grn 9.00 7.00
**43** A1 130r on 75r car 7.00 7.00
**44** A1 130r on 150r car, *rose* 5.25 5.25
**45** A1 400r on 50r lt bl 2.00 3.25
**46** A1 400r on 100r brn, *buff* 2.00 3.50
**47** A1 400r on 200r bl, *bl* 2.00 3.50

**Same Surcharge on No. P1**

**48** N1 130r on 2½r brn 9.00 7.00
*Nos. 36-48 (13)* 90.25 78.50

Stamps of 1898 Overprinted

**1902** ***Perf. 11½***

**49** A2 15r brown 2.00 1.40
**50** A2 25r sea green 2.00 1.40
**51** A2 50r blue 2.00 1.40
**52** A2 75r rose 6.00 3.75
*Nos. 49-52 (4)* 12.00 7.95

No. 23 Surcharged in Black

**1905**

**53** A2 50r on 65r dull blue 5.75 4.00

Stamps of 1898-1903 Overprinted in Carmine or Green

**1911**

**54** A2 2½r gray .35 .20
**55** A2 5r orange .35 .20
**56** A2 10r light green .40 .25
*a.* Inverted overprint 15.00 12.50
**57** A2 15r gray green .40 .25
**58** A2 20r gray violet .50 .30
**59** A2 25r carmine (G) 1.50 .50
**60** A2 50r brown .40 .35
**61** A2 75r lilac 1.25 .90
**62** A2 100r dk bl, *bl* 1.25 .90
**63** A2 115r org brn, *pink* 1.25 .90
**64** A2 130r brown, *straw* 1.25 .90
**65** A2 200r red vio, *pnksh* 1.25 .90
**66** A2 400r dull bl, *straw* 2.10 1.10
**67** A2 500r blk & red, *bl* 2.10 1.10
**68** A2 700r violet, *yelsh* 2.25 1.50
*Nos. 54-68 (15)* 16.60 *10.25*

Stamps of 1902-05 Overprinted in Carmine or Green

**1914**

**Without Gum**

**72** A2 50r on 65r dl bl *1,200. 800.00*
**73** A1 115r on 5r yellow 1.25 1.50
**74** A1 115r on 25r bl grn 1.25 1.50
**75** A1 115r on 80r yel grn 1.25 1.50
**76** N1 130r on 2½r brn (G) 1.25 1.50
*a.* Carmine overprint 22.50 22.50
**77** A1 130r on 75r car 1.75 1.50
*a.* Perf. 12½ 5.50 7.00
**78** A1 130r on 150r car, *rose* 1.75 1.50
**79** A1 400r on 50r lt bl 2.50 3.00
*a.* Perf. 12½ 11.00 11.00
**80** A1 400r on 100r brn, *buff* 2.50 2.50
**81** A1 400r on 200r bl, *bl* 2.50 2.50

**On Nos. 51-52**

**82** A2 50r blue 1.50 1.50
**83** A2 75r rose 1.50 1.50
*Nos. 73-83 (11)* 19.00 20.00

Preceding Issues Overprinted in Carmine

**1915**

**On Provisional Issue of 1902**

**84** A1 115r on 5r yellow .85 .45
**85** A1 115r on 25r bl grn .85 .45
**86** A1 115r on 80r lt grn .85 .45
**87** A1 130r on 75r carmine .85 .45
*a.* Perf. 12½ 4.50 2.25
**88** A1 130r on 150r car, *rose* .85 .45
**92** N1 130r on 2½r (down) .85 .45

**On Nos. 51, 53**

**93** A2 50r blue .85 .50
*a.* "Republica" inverted 15.00 15.00
**94** A2 50r on 65r dull bl 3.50 *4.50*
*Nos. 84-94 (8)* 9.45 *7.70*

Stamps of 1898-1903 Overprinted Locally in Carmine

**1917**

**Without Gum**

**95** A2 2½r gray 1.50 *3.00*
**96** A2 5r orange 7.00 6.50
**97** A2 10r light green 7.00 6.00
**98** A2 15r gray green 6.50 6.50
**99** A2 20r gray violet 7.25 6.50
**100** A2 25r sea green 13.50 15.00
**101** A2 100r blue, *blue* 4.00 2.75
**102** A2 115r org brn, *pink* 4.00 2.75
**103** A2 130r brown, *straw* 4.00 2.75
**104** A2 200r red vio, *pnksh* 4.00 2.75
**105** A2 400r dull bl, *straw* 4.50 3.50
**106** A2 500r blk & red, *bl* 5.50 3.75
**107** A2 700r vio, *yelsh* 9.00 5.25
*Nos. 95-107 (13)* 77.75 67.00

## NEWSPAPER STAMP

N1

**1894 Unwmk. Typo.** ***Perf. 12½***

**P1** N1 2½r brown .60 .35

For overprints and surcharges see Nos. 76, 92.

# ZAMBIA

'zam-bē-ə

LOCATION — Southern Africa
GOVT. — Republic
AREA — 290,586 sq. mi.
POP. — 9,663,535 (1999 est.)
CAPITAL — Lusaka

The former British protectorate of Northern Rhodesia became an independent republic Oct. 24, 1964, taking the name Zambia. See Northern Rhodesia; see Rhodesia and Nyasaland.

12 Pence = 1 Shilling
20 Shillings = 1 Pound
100 Ngwee = 1 Kwacha (1968)

**Catalogue values for all unused stamps in this country are for Never Hinged items.**

Pres. Kenneth D. Kaunda, Victoria Falls — A1

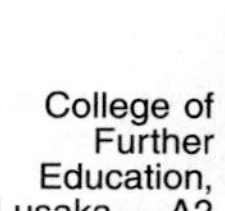

College of Further Education, Lusaka — A2

***Perf. 14½x14, 14x14½***

**1964, Oct. 24 Photo. Unwmk.**

**1** A1 3p shown .20 .20
**2** A2 6p shown .30 .20
**3** A1 1sh3p Barotse dancer .40 .30
*Nos. 1-3 (3)* .90 .70

Zambia's independence, Oct. 24, 1964.

Farmer and Silo
A3

X-Ray Technician
A4

Designs: 2p, Chinyau dancer. 3p, Woman picking cotton. 4p, Angoni bull. 6p, Communications by drum and teletype. 9p, Redwood blossoms and factory. 1sh, Night fishing on Lake Tanganyika. 1sh3p, Woman tobacco worker. 2sh, Tonga basket maker and child. 2sh6p, Elephants in Luangwa Valley Game Reserve. 5sh, Child and school. 10sh, Copper mining. £1, Makishi dancer.

**1964, Oct. 24 Photo.** ***Perf. 14½***

**Size: 23x19mm, 19x23mm**

**4** A3 ½p emerald, blk & red .20 .25
**5** A4 1p ultra, blk & brn .20 .20
**6** A4 2p orange, brn & red .20 .20
**7** A3 3p red & black .20 .20
**8** A3 4p orange & black .20 .20

***Perf. 13½x14½, 14½x13½***

**Size: 32x23mm, 23x32mm**

**9** A3 6p Prus grn, brn & org .20 .20
**10** A3 9p ultra, brn & dk car rose .20 .20
**11** A3 1sh blue, bis & blk .20 .20
**12** A4 1sh3p dk bl, ver, blk & yel .25 .20
**13** A4 2sh org, blk, brn & ultra .30 .20
**14** A3 2sh6p org yel & blk .75 .40
**15** A3 5sh emerald, blk & yel 1.10 .55
**16** A3 10sh orange & blk 4.00 4.00
**17** A4 £1 red, blk, brn & yel 2.50 4.00
*Nos. 4-17 (14)* 10.50 11.00

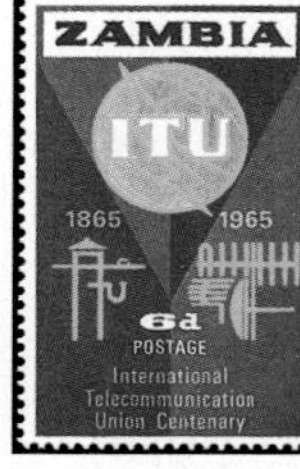


ITU Emblem, Old and New Communication Equipment — A5

**1965, July 26 Photo.** ***Perf. 14***

**18** A5 6p brt lilac & gold .20 .20
**19** A5 2sh6p gray & gold .80 1.00

Cent. of the ITU.

ICY Emblem
A6

**1965, July 26** ***Perf. 14***

**20** A6 3p grnsh blue & gold .20 .20
**21** A6 1sh3p ultra & gold .50 .40

International Cooperation Year, 1965.

Pres. Kaunda and State House, Lusaka — A7

Clematopsis — A8

Designs: 6p, Fireworks over Independence Stadium. 2sh6p, Tithonia diversifolia.

***Perf. 13½x14½***

**1965, Oct. 18** **Unwmk.**

| | | | | |
|---|---|---|---|---|
| **22** | A7 | 3p multicolored | .20 | .20 |
| **23** | A7 | 6p ind, yel & brt pink | .20 | .20 |
| | | ***Perf. 14*** | | |
| **24** | A8 | 1sh3p pink, yel & brn | .20 | .20 |
| **25** | A8 | 2sh6p brt grn, dp org & brn | .40 | .40 |
| | | *Nos. 22-25 (4)* | 1.00 | 1.00 |

1st anniv. of independence, Oct. 24.

Inauguration of WHO Headquarters, Geneva — A9

**1966, May 18** ***Perf. 14***

| | | | | |
|---|---|---|---|---|
| **26** | A9 | 3p rose brn, brt bl & gold | .20 | .20 |
| **27** | A9 | 1sh3p vio bl, brt bl & gold | .60 | .50 |

University of Zambia — A10

**1966, July 12** **Photo.** ***Perf. 14***

| | | | | |
|---|---|---|---|---|
| **28** | A10 | 3p brt green & gold | .20 | .20 |
| **29** | A10 | 1sh3p brt purple & gold | .25 | .20 |

University of Zambia opening, Mar. 17.

National Assembly Building — A11

**1967, May 2** **Unwmk.** ***Perf. 14***

| | | | | |
|---|---|---|---|---|
| **30** | A11 | 3p slate & bronze | .20 | .20 |
| **31** | A11 | 6p yellow grn & bronze | .20 | .20 |

Completion of National Assembly Building.

Lusaka Airport — A12

**1967, Oct. 2** **Photo.** ***Perf. 13½x14½***

| | | | | |
|---|---|---|---|---|
| **32** | A12 | 6p vio blue & bronze | .20 | .20 |
| **33** | A12 | 2sh6p brown & bronze | .70 | .70 |

Opening of Lusaka International Airport.

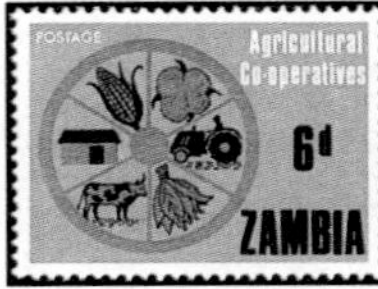


Symbols of Agriculture A13

Radio, Telephone and Television — A14

Designs: 4p, Emblem of Zambia Youth Service. 1sh, Map showing locations of Zambia coalfields. 1sh6p, Map showing Zambia-Tanzania Road.

***Perf. 14½x13½, 13½x14½***

**1967, Oct. 23**

| | | | | |
|---|---|---|---|---|
| **34** | A14 | 4p gray, red & gold | .20 | .20 |
| **35** | A13 | 6p lt vio bl, gold & blk | .20 | .20 |
| **36** | A14 | 9p dull blue, sil & blk | .25 | .25 |
| **37** | A14 | 1sh gold, red, blk & vio bl | .50 | .20 |
| **38** | A13 | 1sh6p bl grn, ultra, gold & blk | .75 | 1.00 |
| | | *Nos. 34-38 (5)* | 1.90 | 1.85 |

Issued to publicize National Development.

Lusaka Cathedral — A15

Baobab Tree — A16

Designs: 3n, Zambia Airways plane. 5n, National Museum, Livingstone. 8n, Vimbuza dancer. 10n, Woman tobacco picker. 15n, Nudaurelia zambesina butterfly. 20n, Crowned cranes. 25n, Angoni warrior. 50n, Chokwe dancer. 1k, Railroad bridge, Kafue River. 2k, Eland.

***Perf. 13½x14½, 14½x13½***

**1968, Jan. 16** **Photo.**

**Size: 26x22mm, 22x26mm**

| | | | | |
|---|---|---|---|---|
| **39** | A15 | 1n bronze & multi | .20 | .20 |
| *a.* | | Booklet pane of 6 | .20 | |
| *b.* | | Booklet pane of 4 | .20 | |
| **40** | A16 | 2n bronze & multi | .20 | .20 |
| **41** | A15 | 3n bronze & multi | .20 | .20 |
| *a.* | | Booklet pane of 6 | .60 | |
| *b.* | | Booklet pane of 4 | .40 | |
| **42** | A16 | 5n sepia & bronze | .20 | .20 |
| **43** | A16 | 8n bronze & multi | .20 | .20 |
| **44** | A16 | 10n bronze & multi | .25 | .20 |
| | | **Size: 32x26mm, 26x32mm** | | |
| **45** | A15 | 15n bronze & multi | 3.00 | .20 |
| **46** | A16 | 20n bronze & multi | 5.00 | .20 |
| **47** | A16 | 25n bronze & multi | .55 | .20 |
| **48** | A16 | 50n bronze, org & blk | .50 | .25 |
| **49** | A15 | 1k dk blue & brnz | 5.00 | .30 |
| **50** | A15 | 2k copper & blk | 3.50 | *1.25* |
| | | *Nos. 39-50 (12)* | 18.80 | *3.60* |

Used values of Nos. 48-50 are for canceled-to-order stamps. Postally used copies sell for more.

Map of Zambia, Arrow Pointing to Ndola — A17

***Perf. 14½x14***

**1968, June 29** **Photo.** **Unwmk.**

| | | | | |
|---|---|---|---|---|
| **51** | A17 | 15n brt green & gold | .25 | .25 |

Zambia Trade Fair at Ndola.

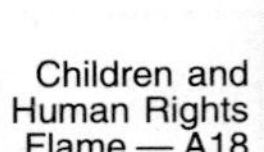


Children and Human Rights Flame — A18

WHO Emblem A19

Children A20

**Photogravure; Gold Impressed**

**1968, Oct. 23** ***Perf. 14½x14***

| | | | | |
|---|---|---|---|---|
| **52** | A18 | 3n ultra, dk bl & gold | .20 | .20 |
| **53** | A19 | 10n brt violet & gold | .20 | .20 |
| **54** | A20 | 25n brt blue, blk & gold | .50 | .50 |
| | | *Nos. 52-54 (3)* | .90 | .90 |

Intl. Human Rights Year; 20th anniv. of WHO; 21st anniv. of UNICEF (25n).

Copper Miner — A21

Map of Africa with Zambia — A22

Design: 25n, Worker poling furnace, horiz.

***Perf. 14½x13½***

**1969, June 18** **Photo.**

| | | | | |
|---|---|---|---|---|
| **55** | A21 | 3n dp violet & copper | .25 | .20 |
| **56** | A21 | 25n yellow, blk & copper | 1.25 | 1.00 |

50th anniv. of the ILO.

***Perf. 13½x14, 14x13½***

**1969, Oct. 23** **Photo.**

10n, Waterbucks, Kafue National Park, horiz. 15n, Golden perch, Kasaba Bay, horiz. 25n, Carmine bee-eater, Luangwa Valley.

| | | | | |
|---|---|---|---|---|
| **57** | A22 | 5n ultra, yel & copper | .20 | .20 |
| **58** | A22 | 10n copper & multi | .25 | .20 |
| **59** | A22 | 15n copper & multi | .50 | .30 |
| **60** | A22 | 25n copper & multi | 1.25 | 1.00 |
| | | *Nos. 57-60 (4)* | 2.20 | 1.70 |

International Year of African Tourism.

Nimbus III Weather Satellite — A23

**1970, Mar. 23** **Litho.** ***Perf. 13x11***

| | | | | |
|---|---|---|---|---|
| **61** | A23 | 15n multicolored | .30 | .50 |

Issued for World Meteorological Day.

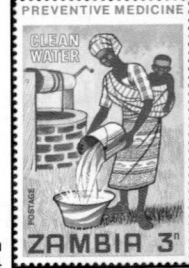

"Clean Water" — A24

Designs: 15n, "Nutrition" (infant on scale). 25n, Children's immunization and Edward Jenner, M.D.

**1970, July 4** **Litho.** ***Perf. 13x12½***

| | | | | |
|---|---|---|---|---|
| **62** | A24 | 3n multicolored | .20 | .20 |
| **63** | A24 | 15n multicolored | .50 | .50 |
| **64** | A24 | 25n multicolored | .85 | .85 |
| | | *Nos. 62-64 (3)* | 1.55 | 1.55 |

Issued to publicize preventive medicine and the "Under Five" children's clinics.

Mural by Gabriel Ellison A25

**1970, Sept. 8** **Litho.** ***Perf. 14x14½***

| | | | | |
|---|---|---|---|---|
| **65** | A25 | 15n multicolored | .35 | .35 |

Opening of the Conf. of Non-Aligned Nations in Mulungushi Hall (decorated with murals by Mrs. Ellison) in Zambia.

Ceremonial Axe — A26

Traditional Crafts: 5n, Clay pipe bowl with antelope head. 15n, Makishi mask, vert. 25n, The Kuomboka Ceremony (dancers and ceremonial boat).

**1970, Nov. 30** **Litho.** ***Perf. 14x14½***

**Size: 34x25mm**

| | | | | |
|---|---|---|---|---|
| **66** | A26 | 3n dp lil rose & multi | .20 | .20 |
| **67** | A26 | 5n dp org, blk & sepia | .20 | .20 |
| | | ***Perf. 13x13½*** | | |
| | | **Size: 30x45½mm** | | |
| **68** | A26 | 15n dp lil rose & multi | .45 | .45 |
| | | ***Perf. 12½*** | | |
| | | **Size: 71½x23½mm** | | |
| **69** | A26 | 25n violet, blue & multi | .75 | .75 |
| *a.* | | Souvenir sheet of 4, #66-69 | 10.00 | 10.00 |
| | | *Nos. 66-69 (4)* | 1.60 | 1.60 |

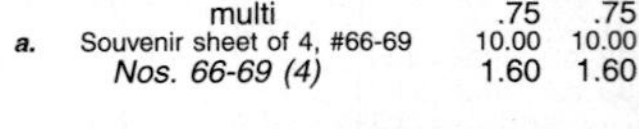

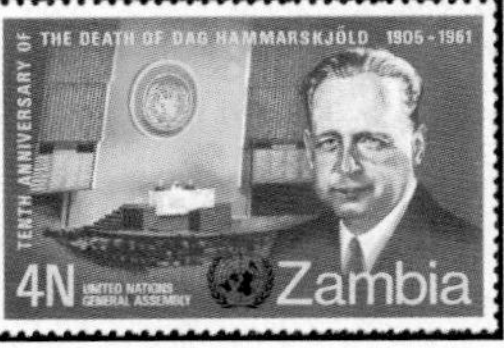


Dag Hammarskjold and UN General Assembly — A27

Hammarskjold and: 10n, Downed plane. 15n, Dove with olive branch. 25n, Plaque and flowers.

**1971, Sept. 18** ***Perf. 13½***

| | | | | |
|---|---|---|---|---|
| **70** | A27 | 4n brown & multi | .20 | .20 |
| **71** | A27 | 10n yellow grn & multi | .20 | .20 |
| **72** | A27 | 15n blue & multi | .30 | .30 |
| **73** | A27 | 25n plum & multi | .45 | .45 |
| | | *Nos. 70-73 (4)* | 1.15 | 1.15 |

10th anniv. of the death of Dag Hammarskjold, (1905-61) Secretary-General of the UN, near Ndola, Zambia.

Red-Breasted Bream — A28

**1971, Dec. 10**

| | | | | |
|---|---|---|---|---|
| **74** | A28 | 4n shown | .20 | .20 |
| **75** | A28 | 10n Green-headed bream | .60 | .50 |
| **76** | A28 | 15n Tiger fish | 1.50 | .75 |
| | | *Nos. 74-76 (3)* | 2.30 | 1.45 |

Christmas.

Cheetah — A29

Soil Conservation A30

**1972, Mar. 15** *Perf. 13½x14*

| | | | | |
|---|---|---|---|---|
| **77** | A29 | 4n shown | .30 | .20 |
| **78** | A29 | 10n Lechue | .70 | .55 |
| | | ***Perf. 14x13½*** | | |
| **79** | A30 | 15n Cape porcupine | 1.10 | .85 |
| **80** | A30 | 25n Elephant | 2.75 | 1.40 |
| | | *Nos. 77-80 (4)* | 4.85 | 3.00 |

Conservation Year.

**1972, June 30 Litho.** *Perf. 14x13½*

**Size: 18½x45mm**

| | | | | |
|---|---|---|---|---|
| **81** | A30 | 4n shown | .25 | .25 |
| **82** | A30 | 10n Forest conservation | .75 | .75 |
| | | ***Perf. 13½x14*** | | |
| **83** | A29 | 15n Water conservation (river view) | 1.10 | 1.10 |
| **84** | A29 | 25n Woman in corn field | 1.90 | 1.90 |
| | | *Nos. 81-84 (4)* | 4.00 | 4.00 |

**Souvenir Sheet**

| | | | |
|---|---|---|---|
| **85** | Sheet of 4 | 10.00 | *12.50* |
| *a.* | A30 10n Giraffe and zebra | 1.40 | |
| *b.* | A30 10n Rhinoceros | 1.40 | |
| *c.* | A30 10n Hippopotamus and deer | 1.40 | |
| *d.* | A30 10n Lion | 1.40 | |

Conservation Year. Stamp size: 27x50mm.

**1972, Sept. 22** *Perf. 13½x14*

Designs: All horizontal.

**Size: 48x35mm**

| | | | | |
|---|---|---|---|---|
| **86** | A30 | 4n Zambian flowers | .90 | .50 |
| **87** | A30 | 10n Citrus swallowtails and roses | 1.60 | 1.40 |
| **88** | A30 | 15n Bee | 3.00 | 2.00 |
| **89** | A30 | 25n Locusts in corn field | 4.50 | 3.00 |
| | | *Nos. 86-89 (4)* | 10.00 | 6.90 |

Conservation Year.

Mary and Joseph Going to Bethlehem — A31

**1972, Dec. 1 Litho.** *Perf. 14*

| | | | | |
|---|---|---|---|---|
| **90** | A31 | 4n shown | .20 | .20 |
| **91** | A31 | 9n Holy Family | .25 | .25 |
| **92** | A31 | 15n Adoration of the shepherds | .40 | .40 |
| **93** | A31 | 25n Kings following the star | .75 | .75 |
| | | *Nos. 90-93 (4)* | 1.60 | 1.60 |

Christmas.

Broken Hill Man A32

Designs: 4n, Oudenodon and rubidgea (artist's conception; vert.). 10n, Zambiasaurus. 15n, Skull of Luangwa Drysdalli. 25n, Glossoptoris (seed).

***Perf. 14x13½, 14***

**1973, Feb. 1** **Litho.**

**Size: 29x45mm**

| | | | | |
|---|---|---|---|---|
| **94** | A32 | 4n org ver & multi | .65 | .30 |
| | | **Size: 37½x21mm** | | |
| **95** | A32 | 9n org ver & multi | 1.00 | .65 |
| **96** | A32 | 10n apple grn & multi | 1.10 | .85 |
| **97** | A32 | 15n lilac & multi | 1.50 | 1.10 |
| **98** | A32 | 25n orange brn & multi | 2.75 | 2.75 |
| | | *Nos. 94-98 (5)* | 7.00 | 5.65 |

Fossils from Luangwa area (except 9n), over 200 million years old.

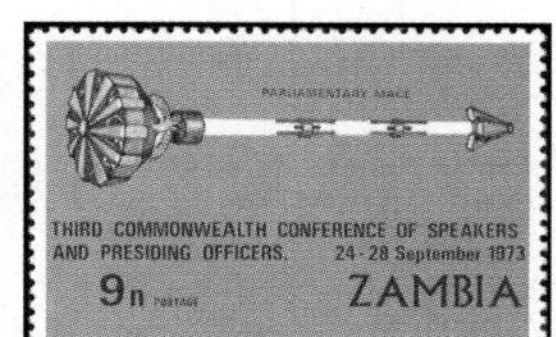

Meeting of Stanley and Livingstone at Ujiji — A33

4n, Livingstone, the missionary. 9n, Livingstone at Victoria Falls. 10n, Livingstone stopping slave traders. 15n, Livingstone, the physician. 25n, Portrait & tree in Chitumbu, marking burial place of heart.

**1973, May 1** *Perf. 13x13½*

| | | | | |
|---|---|---|---|---|
| **99** | A33 | 3n multicolored | .20 | .20 |
| **100** | A33 | 4n multicolored | .30 | .30 |
| **101** | A33 | 9n multicolored | .60 | .60 |
| **102** | A33 | 10n multicolored | .75 | .75 |
| **103** | A33 | 15n multicolored | 1.10 | 1.10 |
| **104** | A33 | 25n multicolored | 1.75 | 1.75 |
| | | *Nos. 99-104 (6)* | 4.70 | 4.70 |

Dr. David Livingstone (1813-73), medical missionary and explorer.

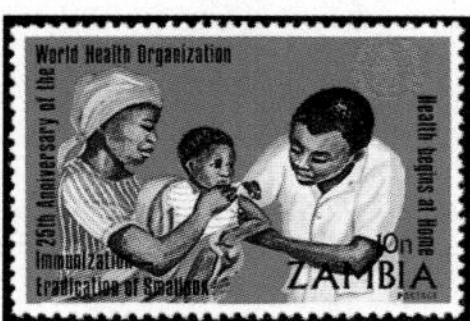

Parliamentary Mace — A34

**1973, Sept. 24 Litho.** *Perf. 13½x14*

| | | | | |
|---|---|---|---|---|
| **105** | A34 | 9n tan & multi | .70 | .70 |
| **106** | A34 | 15n gray & multi | 1.40 | 1.40 |
| **107** | A34 | 25n brt green & multi | 1.90 | 1.90 |
| | | *Nos. 105-107 (3)* | 4.00 | 4.00 |

Third Commonwealth Conference of Speakers and Presiding Officers, Lusaka.

Vaccination — A35

WHO Emblem and: 4n, Mother washing infant, vert. 9n, Nurse weighing infant, vert. 15n, Child eating cereal and fruit.

**1973, Oct. 16 Litho.** *Perf. 14*

| | | | | |
|---|---|---|---|---|
| **108** | A35 | 4n blue & multi | *60.00* | *25.00* |
| **109** | A35 | 9n orange & multi | .30 | .30 |
| **110** | A35 | 10n brt grn & multi | .40 | .40 |
| **111** | A35 | 15n violet & multi | .50 | .50 |
| | | *Nos. 108-111 (4)* | *61.20* | *26.20* |

WHO, 25th anniv.

A36

A37

Birth of the Second Republic: 4n, UNIP flag. 9n, United National Independence Party Headquarters, Lusaka. 10n, Army band. 15n, Women dancing and singing. 25n, President's parliamentary chair.

**1973, Dec. 13 Litho.** *Perf. 14x13½*

| | | | | |
|---|---|---|---|---|
| **112** | A36 | 4n multicolored | *17.50* | *7.50* |
| **113** | A36 | 9n multicolored | .25 | .25 |
| **114** | A36 | 10n multicolored | .30 | .30 |
| **115** | A36 | 15n multicolored | .45 | .45 |
| **116** | A37 | 25n multicolored | .75 | .75 |
| | | *Nos. 112-116 (5)* | *19.25* | *9.25* |

Pres. Kaunda and his Home During Struggle for Independence — A38

4n, Pres. Kaunda at Mulungushi. 15n, Pres. Kaunda holding torch of freedom.

**1974, Apr. 28 Litho.** *Perf. 14½x14*

| | | | | |
|---|---|---|---|---|
| **117** | A38 | 4n multi, vert. | .70 | .70 |
| **118** | A38 | 9n multi | .90 | .90 |
| **119** | A38 | 15n multi | 1.40 | 1.40 |
| | | *Nos. 117-119 (3)* | 3.00 | 3.00 |

50th birthday of Pres. Kenneth Kaunda.

Nakambla Sugar Estate — A39

Designs: 4n, Local market. 9n, Kapiri glass factory. 10n, Kafue hydroelectric plant. 15n, Kafue Bridge. 25n, Conference of Non-aligned Nations, Lusaka, 1970.

**1974, Oct. 24 Litho.** *Perf. 13½x14*

| | | | | |
|---|---|---|---|---|
| **120** | A39 | 3n multicolored | .20 | .20 |
| **121** | A39 | 4n multicolored | .20 | .20 |
| **122** | A39 | 9n multicolored | .40 | .40 |
| **123** | A39 | 10n multicolored | .50 | .50 |
| **124** | A39 | 15n multicolored | .70 | .70 |
| **125** | A39 | 25n multicolored | 1.10 | 1.10 |
| | | *Nos. 120-125 (6)* | 3.10 | 3.10 |

**Souvenir Sheet**

| | | | |
|---|---|---|---|
| **126** | Sheet of 4 | 8.00 | *10.00* |
| *a.* | A39 15n Academic education | 1.50 | |
| *b.* | A39 15n Teacher Training College | 1.50 | |
| *c.* | A39 15n Technical education | 1.50 | |
| *d.* | A39 15n University of Zambia | 1.50 | |

10th anniversary of indepencence.

Mobile Post Office — A40

UPU Emblem and: 9n, Rural mail service by Zambia Airways. 10n, Modern Post Office, Chipata. 15n, Ndola Postal Training Center.

**1974, Nov. 15**

| | | | | |
|---|---|---|---|---|
| **127** | A40 | 4n multicolored | .20 | .20 |
| **128** | A40 | 9n multicolored | .25 | .20 |
| **129** | A40 | 10n multicolored | .30 | .20 |
| **130** | A40 | 15n multicolored | .45 | .30 |
| | | *Nos. 127-130 (4)* | 1.20 | .90 |

Centenary of Universal Postal Union.

Radar by Day A41

**1974, Dec. 16**

| | | | | |
|---|---|---|---|---|
| **131** | A41 | 4n shown | .25 | .20 |
| **132** | A41 | 9n Radar by night | .50 | .40 |
| **133** | A41 | 15n Radar at dawn | 1.00 | .70 |
| **134** | A41 | 25n Radar station | 1.75 | 1.25 |
| | | *Nos. 131-134 (4)* | 3.50 | 2.55 |

Inauguration of Mwembeshi Earth Station, Oct. 21, 1974.

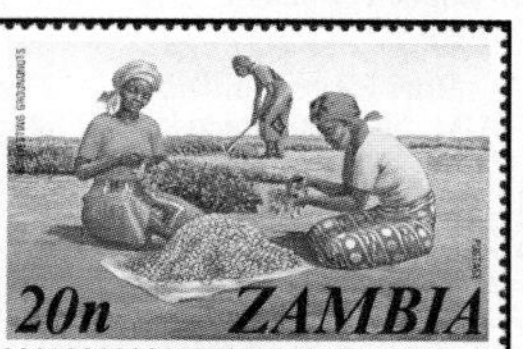

Rhinoceros and Calf — A42


Peanut Harvest — A43

**1975, Jan. 3 Litho.** *Perf. 13½x14*

| | | | | |
|---|---|---|---|---|
| **135** | A42 | 1n shown | .50 | .50 |
| **136** | A42 | 2n Guinea fowl | .50 | .50 |
| **137** | A42 | 3n Zambian dancers | .20 | .35 |
| **138** | A42 | 4n Fish eagle | .90 | .20 |
| **139** | A42 | 5n Bridge, Victoria Falls | .90 | .90 |
| **140** | A42 | 8n Sitatunga | .90 | .80 |
| **141** | A42 | 9n Elephant, Kasaba Bay Resort | 1.10 | .75 |
| **142** | A42 | 10n Giant pangolin | .20 | .20 |
| | | ***Perf. 13*** | | |
| **143** | A43 | 15n Zambezi River source, Monument | .30 | .20 |
| **144** | A43 | 20n shown | .90 | 1.25 |
| **145** | A43 | 25n Tobacco field | 1.40 | .55 |
| **146** | A43 | 50n Flying doctor service | 3.50 | 2.50 |
| **147** | A43 | 1k Lady Ross's touraco | 5.00 | 2.00 |
| **148** | A43 | 2k Village scene | 3.50 | 5.00 |
| | | *Nos. 135-148 (14)* | 19.80 | 15.70 |

For surcharges see #188-191, 319.

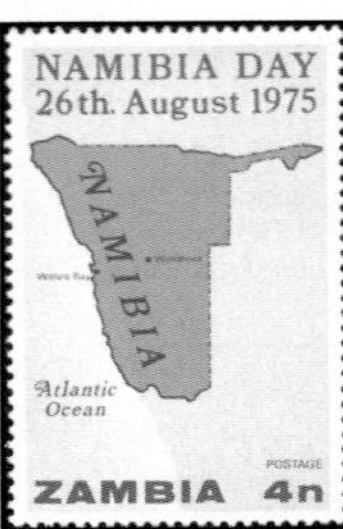


Map of Namibia (South-West Africa) — A44

**1975, Aug. 26 Litho.** ***Perf. 14x13½***

**149** A44 4n green & dk green .20 .20
**150** A44 9n dk blue & gray bl .25 .25
**151** A44 15n yellow & orange .35 .40
**152** A44 25n orange & dp orange .45 .70
*Nos. 149-152 (4)* 1.25 1.55

Namibia Day.

Sprinkler Irrigation — A45

Designs: 9n, Sprinkler irrigation over rows of vegetables. 15n, Furrow irrigation.

**1975, Dec. 16 Litho.** ***Perf. 13***

**153** A45 4n multicolored .20 .20
**154** A45 9p multicolored .50 .50
**155** A45 15n multicolored .80 .80
*Nos. 153-155 (3)* 1.50 1.50

Intl. Commission on Irrigation and Drainage, 25th anniv.

Julbernardia Paniculata — A46

Trees of Zambia: 4n, Sycamore fig. 9n, Baikiaea plurijuga. 10n, Colophospermum. 15n, Uapaca kirkiana. 25n, Pterocarpus angolensis.

**1976, Mar. 22 Litho.** ***Perf. 13***

**156** A46 3n multicolored .25 .25
**157** A46 4n multicolored .25 .25
**158** A46 9n multicolored .40 .40
**159** A46 10n multicolored .40 .40
**160** A46 15n multicolored .65 .65
**161** A46 25n multicolored .80 .80
*Nos. 156-161 (6)* 2.75 2.75

World Forestry Day, Mar. 21.

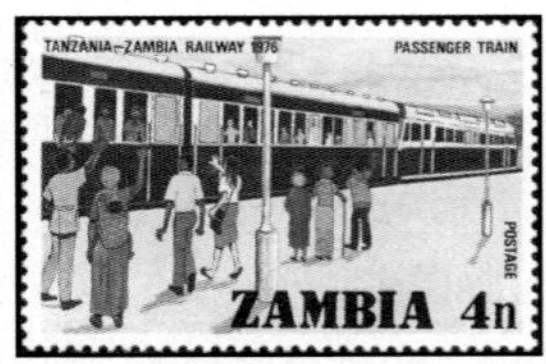


TAZARA Passenger Train — A47

9n, Train carrying copper. 10n, Clearing the bush. #164, Train carrying heavy machinery. #166b, Track laying. 20n, Reinforcing railroad track. #165, Train carrying various goods. #166d, Completed tracks.

**1976, Dec. 10 Litho.** ***Perf. 13***

**162** A47 4n multicolored .20 .20
**163** A47 9n multicolored .50 .50
**164** A47 15n multicolored .85 .85
**165** A47 25n multicolored 1.40 1.40
*Nos. 162-165 (4)* 2.95 2.95

**Souvenir Sheet**

***Perf. 13½x14***

**166** Sheet of 4 4.00 4.00
*a.* A47 10n multicolored .40 .30
*b.* A47 15n multicolored .60 .45
*c.* A47 20n multicolored .70 .50
*d.* A47 25n multicolored 1.00 .65

Completion of Tanzania-Zambia Railroad.

Kayowe Dance — A48

**1977, Jan. 18 Litho.** ***Perf. 13½x14***

**167** A48 4n shown .20 .20
**168** A48 9n Lilombola dance .25 .20
**169** A48 15n Initiation ceremony .45 .40
**170** A48 25n Munkhwele dance .75 .50
*Nos. 167-170 (4)* 1.65 1.30

2nd World Black and African Festival, Lagos, Nigeria, Jan. 15-Feb. 12.

Grimwood's Longclaw — A49

Birds of Zambia: 9n, Shelley's sunbird. 10n, Black-cheeked lovebird. 15n, Locust finch. 20n, White-chested tinkerbird. 25n, Chaplin's barbet.

**1977, July 1 Litho.** ***Perf. 14½***

**171** A49 4n multicolored .35 .20
**172** A49 9n multicolored .60 .45
**173** A49 10n multicolored .70 .45
**174** A49 15n multicolored .95 1.40
**175** A49 20n multicolored 1.50 1.50
**176** A49 25n multicolored 1.90 2.00
*Nos. 171-176 (6)* 6.00 6.00

Children Playing with Blocks A50

Designs: 9n, Women of various races dancing in circle. 15n, Black and white girls with young bird.

**1977, Oct. 20 Litho.** ***Perf. 14x14½***

**177** A50 4n multicolored .20 .20
**178** A50 9n multicolored .20 .20
**179** A50 15n multicolored .35 .35
*Nos. 177-179 (3)* .75 .75

Combat racism and racial discrimination.

"Glory to God in the Highest" A51

Christmas: 9n, Nativity. 10n, Three Kings and camel. 15n, Presentation at the Temple.

**1977, Dec. 20 Litho.** ***Perf. 14***

**180** A51 4n multicolored .20 .20
**181** A51 9n multicolored .20 .20
**182** A51 10n multicolored .20 .20
**183** A51 15n multicolored .30 .30
*Nos. 180-183 (4)* .90 .90

Elephant and Road Check A52

Designs: 18n, Waterbuck and Kafue River boat patrol. 28n, Warthog and helicopter surveillance of National Parks. 32n, Cheetah and armed wildlife guards in Parks and Game Management Areas.

**1978, Aug. 1 Litho.** ***Perf. 14x14½***

**184** A52 8n multicolored .25 .25
**185** A52 18n multicolored .50 .50
**186** A52 28n multicolored .85 .85
**187** A52 32n multicolored .90 .90
*Nos. 184-187 (4)* 2.50 2.50

Anti-poaching Campaign of Zambia Wildlife Conservation Society, Aug. 1978.

Nos. 141, 137, 145 and 143 Surcharged with New Value and 2 Bars

**1979, Mar. 15** ***Perf. 13½x14, 13***

**188** A42 8n on 9n multi .60 .20
**189** A42 10n on 3n multi .20 .20
**190** A43 18n on 25n multi .20 .20
**191** A43 28n on 15n multi .20 .20
*Nos. 188-191 (4)* 1.20 .80

Kayowe Dance A53

Designs: 32n, Kutambala dance. 42n, Chitwansombo drummers. 58n, Lilombola dance.

**1979, Aug. 1**

**192** A53 18n multicolored .35 .35
**193** A53 32n multicolored .50 .50
**194** A53 42n multicolored .50 .50
**195** A53 58n multicolored .65 .65
*Nos. 192-195 (4)* 2.00 2.00

Commonwealth Summit Conf., Lusaka, Aug. 1-9.

"Why the Zebra is Hornless" — A54

Children's Stories: 18n, Kalulu and the Tug of War. 42n, How the Tortoise got his Shell. 58n, Kalulu and the Lion.

**1979, Sept. 21 Litho.** ***Perf. 14***

**196** A54 18n multicolored .30 .20
**197** A54 32n multicolored .45 *.55*
**198** A54 42n multicolored .55 *.75*
**199** A54 58n multicolored .70 *1.00*
*a.* Souvenir sheet of 4, #196-199 3.00 3.00
*Nos. 196-199 (4)* 2.00 2.50

International Year of the Child.

Girls of Different Races Holding Emblem A55

Anti-Apartheid Year (1978): 32n, Boys and toy car. 42n, Infants and butterfly. 58n, Children and microscope.

**1979, Nov. 16 Litho.** ***Perf. 14½x15***

**200** A55 18n multicolored .25 .25
**201** A55 32n multicolored .45 .45
**202** A55 42n multicolored .65 .65
**203** A55 58n multicolored .90 .90
*Nos. 200-203 (4)* 2.25 2.25

Hill, Zambia No. 13 A56

Hill and: 32n, Mailman & bicycle. 42n, No. Rhodesia #75. 58n, Mailman & oxcart.

**1979, Dec. 20 Litho.** ***Perf. 14½***

**204** A56 18n multicolored .40 .25
**205** A56 32n multicolored .50 .50
**206** A56 42n multicolored .50 .65
**207** A56 58n multicolored .60 1.10
*a.* Souvenir sheet of 4, #204-207 3.00 3.50
*Nos. 204-207 (4)* 2.00 2.50

Sir Rowland Hill (1795-1879), originator of penny postage.

Nos. 204-207a Overprinted "LONDON 1980"

**1980, Mar 6 Litho.** ***Perf. 15***

**208** A56 18n multicolored .30 .40
**209** A56 32n multicolored .40 .55
**210** A56 42n multicolored .50 .70
**211** A56 58n multicolored .80 .85
*a.* Souvenir sheet of 4 3.00 3.50
*Nos. 208-211 (4)* 2.00 2.50

London 80 Intl. Stamp Exhib., May 6-14.

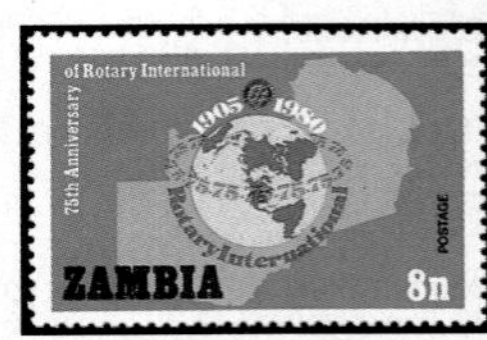


Anniverary Emblem on Map of Zambia — A57

**1980, June 18 Litho.** ***Perf. 14***

**212** A57 8n multicolored .20 .20
**213** A57 32n multicolored .60 .60
**214** A57 42n multicolored .75 .75
**215** A57 58n multicolored .95 .95
*a.* Souvenir sheet of 4, #212-215 2.75 2.75
*Nos. 212-215 (4)* 2.50 2.50

Rotary International, 75th anniversary.

Running A58

**1980, July 19 Litho.** ***Perf. 13***

**216** A58 18n shown .35 .35
**217** A58 32n Boxing .60 .60
**218** A58 42n Soccer .70 .70
**219** A58 58n Swimming 1.10 1.10
*a.* Souvenir sheet of 4, #216-219 3.00 3.00
*Nos. 216-219 (4)* 2.75 2.75

22nd Summer Olympic Games, Moscow, July 19-Aug. 3.

Zaddach's Forester — A59

**1980, Sept. 22**

**220** A59 18n shown .35 .20
**221** A59 32n Northern highflier .55 .45
**222** A59 42n Zambezi skipper .85 .95
**223** A59 58n Modest blue 1.25 1.90
*a.* Souvenir sheet of 4, #220-223 5.00 5.00
*Nos. 220-223 (4)* 3.00 3.50

Coat of Arms — A60

A61

**1980, Sept. 27 Litho. *Perf. 14½***

**224** A60 18n multicolored .30 .25
**225** A60 32n multicolored .50 .55
**226** A60 42n multicolored .60 .70
**227** A60 58n multicolored .85 1.25
*Nos. 224-227 (4)* 2.25 2.75

26th Commonwealth Parliamentary Association Conference, Lusaka.

**1980, Oct. Litho. *Perf. 14***

Nativity and St. Francis of Assisi (stained glass window), Ndola Church.

**228** A61 8n multicolored .20 .20
**229** A61 28n multicolored .50 .70
**230** A61 32n multicolored .50 .70
**231** A61 42n multicolored .80 .90
*Nos. 228-231 (4)* 2.00 2.50

Christmas and 50th anniv. of Catholic Church in Copperbelt (central Zambia).

Trichilia Emetica Seed Pods, Musikili A62

Designs: Seed Pods.

**1981, Mar. 21 Litho. *Perf. 14***

**232** A62 8n shown .20 .20
**233** A62 18n Afzelia quanzensis, Mupapa .40 .40
**234** A62 28n Erythrina abyssinica, Mulunguti .45 .65
**235** A62 32n Combretum collinum, Mulama .45 1.00
*Nos. 232-235 (4)* 1.50 2.25

World Forestry Day.

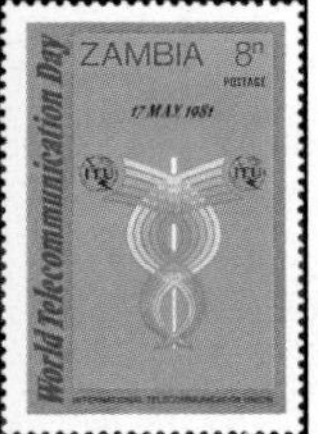
ITU Emblem — A63

Mask Maker — A64

Designs: 18n, 32n, WHO emblem.

**1981, May 15 Litho. *Perf. 14½***

**236** A63 8n multicolored .50 .50
**237** A63 18n multicolored .65 .65
**238** A63 28n multicolored .75 .75
**239** A63 32n multicolored .85 .85
*Nos. 236-239 (4)* 2.75 2.75

13th World Telecommunications Day (8n, 28n).

**1981-83**

**240** A64 1n shown .20 .20
**241** A64 2n Blacksmiths .20 .20
**242** A64 5n Potter .20 .20
**243** A64 8n Straw basket fishing .20 .20
**244** A64 10n Roof thatching .20 .20
**244A** A64 12n Picking mushrooms ('83) 3.25 2.50
**245** A64 18n Millet grinding .40 .20
**246** A64 28n Royal Barge paddler .60 .20
**247** A64 30n Makishi tightrope dancer .60 .20
**248** A64 35n Tonga-ila granary, house .65 .20
**249** A64 42n Cattle herding .65 1.10

***Perf. 14***

**Size: 37x25mm**

**250** A64 50n Traditional healer .65 .20
**251** A64 75n Carrying water jugs ('83) .65 .80
**252** A64 1k Grinding corn ('83) .65 .80
**253** A64 2k Woman smoking pipe .65 .80
*Nos. 240-253 (15)* 9.75 8.00

For surcharges see Nos. 358, 372, 499-506, 596.

Kankobele — A65

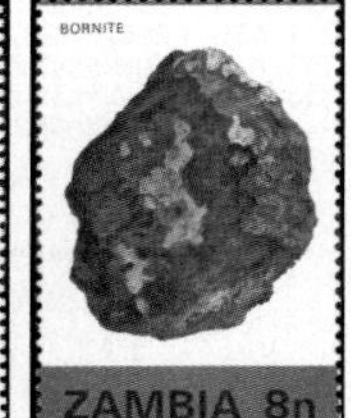
Banded Ironstone — A66

Designs: Traditional musical instruments.

**1981, Sept. 30 Litho. *Perf. 14½***

**254** A65 8n shown .55 .20
**255** A65 18n Inshingili .65 .55
**256** A65 28n Ilimba .90 1.25
**257** A65 32n Bango .90 1.50
*Nos. 254-257 (4)* 3.00 3.50

**1982, Jan. 5 Litho. *Perf. 14***

**258** A66 8n shown 1.00 .20
**259** A66 18n Cobaltocalcite 2.25 .80
**260** A66 28n Amazonite 2.75 2.25
**261** A66 32n Tourmaline 3.00 2.75
**262** A66 42n Uranium ore 3.50 4.00
*Nos. 258-262 (5)* 12.50 10.00

**1982, July 1 Litho. *Perf. 14***

**263** A66 8n Bornite 1.00 .25
**264** A66 18n Chalcopyrite 2.50 1.25
**265** A66 28n Malachite 3.25 3.50
**266** A66 32n Azurite 3.25 3.50
**267** A66 42n Vanadinite 3.75 4.00
*Nos. 263-267 (5)* 13.75 12.50

Scouting Year A67

**1982, Mar. 30 Litho. *Perf. 14***

**268** A67 8n Scouts, flag .35 .35
**269** A67 18n Baden-Powell .70 .70
**270** A67 28n Horned buffalo, patrol pennat .70 .70
**271** A67 1k Eagle, conservation badge 2.25 2.25
*a.* Souvenir sheet of 4, #268-271 4.75 5.50
*Nos. 268-271 (4)* 4.00 4.00

Drilling Rig, 1926 A68

Steam locomotives.

**1983, Jan. 26 *Perf. 14x14½***

**272** A68 8n shown .50 .25
**273** A68 18n Class B6, 1910 .75 .75
**274** A68 28n Borsig engine, 1925 1.25 2.00
**275** A68 32n 7th class, 1900 1.50 2.25
*Nos. 272-275 (4)* 4.00 5.25

Commonwealth Day — A68a

**1983, Mar. 10 Litho. *Perf. 14***

**276** A68a 12n Cotton picking .20 .20
**277** A68a 18n Miners .30 .20
**278** A68a 28n Ritual pot, dancers .25 .35
**279** A68a 1k Victoria Falls, purple-crested lorie 3.00 4.00
*Nos. 276-279 (4)* 3.75 4.75

Local Flowers — A69

**1983, May 26 Litho. *Perf. 14***

**280** A69 12n Eulophia cucullata .20 .20
**281** A69 28n Kigelia africana .50 .50
**282** A69 35n Protea gaguedi .60 .60
**283** A69 50n Leonotis nepotifolia 1.25 3.25
*a.* Souvenir sheet of 4, #280-283, perf. 12x12½ 2.50 3.75
*Nos. 280-283 (4)* 2.55 4.55

Thornicroft's Giraffes — A70

**1983, July 21 Litho. *Perf. 14***

**284** A70 12n shown .75 .75
**285** A70 28n Cookson's wildebeest 1.00 1.00
**286** A70 35n Black lechwe 1.25 1.25
**287** A70 1k Yellow-backed duiker 2.50 2.50
*Nos. 284-287 (4)* 5.50 5.50

Tiger Fish A71

**1983, Sept. 29 Litho. *Perf. 14***

**288** A71 12n shown .45 .20
**289** A71 28n Silver Barbel .75 .50
**290** A71 35n Spotted Squeaker .85 1.40
**291** A71 38n Red Breasted Bream .95 1.40
*Nos. 288-291 (4)* 3.00 3.50

For surcharge see No. 597.

Christmas — A72

**1983, Dec. 12 Litho. *Perf. 14x14½***

**292** A72 12n Annunciation .20 .20
**293** A72 28n Shepherds .35 .30
**294** A72 35n Three Kings .45 .75
**295** A72 38n Flight into Egypt .50 1.00
*Nos. 292-295 (4)* 1.50 2.25

40th Anniv. of Intl. Civil Aviation Org. — A73

**1984, Jan. 26 Litho. *Perf. 14***

**296** A73 12n Boeing 737, 1983 .20 .20
**297** A73 28n Beaver, 1954 .35 .35
**298** A73 35n Short Solent Flying Boat, 1948 .45 .45
**299** A73 1k DH-66, 1931 1.25 1.25
*Nos. 296-299 (4)* 2.25 2.25

60th Birthday of Pres. Kaunda A74

***Perf. 14½x14, 14x14½***

**1984, Apr. 28 Litho.**

**300** A74 12n Receiving greetings .40 .40
**301** A74 28n Swearing in, 1983, vert. .60 .60
**302** A74 60n Planting cherry tree 1.10 1.10
**303** A74 1k Opening Natl. Assembly, vert. 1.40 1.40
*Nos. 300-303 (4)* 3.50 3.50

1984 Summer Olympics — A75

**1984, July 18 Litho. *Perf. 14***

**304** A75 12n Soccer .20 .20
**305** A75 28n Running .45 .45
**306** A75 35n Hurdles .55 .55
**307** A75 50n Boxing .80 .80
*Nos. 304-307 (4)* 2.00 2.00

Reptiles A76

**1984, Sept. 5 Litho. *Perf. 14***

**308** A76 12n Gabon viper .30 .30
**309** A76 28n Chameleon .65 .65
**310** A76 35n Nile crocodile .80 .80
**311** A76 1k Blue-headed agama 1.75 1.75
*a.* Souvenir sheet of 4, #308-311 4.00 4.00
*Nos. 308-311 (4)* 3.50 3.50

20th Anniv. of Independence — A77

**1984, Oct. 22 Litho. *Perf. 14***

**312** A77 12n Pres. Kaunda, Mulungushi Rock .25 .25
**313** A77 28n Freedom Statue .40 .40
**314** A77 1k Produce 1.25 1.25
*Nos. 312-314 (3)* 1.90 1.90

Local Mushrooms A78

**1984, Dec. 12 Litho. *Perf. 14x14½***
**315** A78 12n Amanita flammeola 1.25 1.25
**316** A78 28n Amanita zambiana 1.50 1.50
**317** A78 32n Termitomyces letestui 2.25 2.25
**318** A78 75n Cantharellus miniatescens 3.75 3.75
*Nos. 315-318 (4)* 8.75 8.75

For surcharge see No. 600.

No. 146 Surcharged with New Value and Two Bars

**1985, Mar. 5 Litho. *Perf. 13½***
**319** A43 5k on 50n multi 2.25 2.75

Primates A79

**1985, Apr. 25 Litho. *Perf. 14***
**320** A79 12n Chacma baboon .70 .70
**321** A79 20n Moloney's monkey .90 .90
**322** A79 45n Blue monkey 1.90 1.90
**323** A79 1k Vervet monkey 3.00 3.00
*Nos. 320-323 (4)* 6.50 6.50

For surcharge see No. 604.

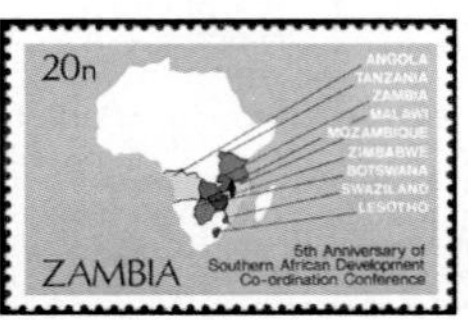

SADCC, 5th Anniv. A80

**1985, July 9 Litho. *Perf. 14***
**324** A80 20n Map .75 .75
**325** A80 45n Mining 1.90 1.90
**326** A80 1k Mulungushi Hall 2.10 2.10
*Nos. 324-326 (3)* 4.75 4.75

Southern African Development Coordination Conference.
For surcharge see No. 605.

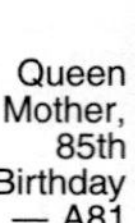

Queen Mother, 85th Birthday — A81

25n, Portrait in blue, age 80. 45n, Queen Consort at Clarence House, 1963. 55n, With Elizabeth II and Princess Margaret. 5k, With royal family, christening of Prince Henry, 1984.

**1985, Aug. 2**
**327** A81 25n multi, vert. .20 .20
**328** A81 45n multi, vert. .20 .20
**329** A81 55n multi .20 .20
**330** A81 5k multi 1.40 1.40
*Nos. 327-330 (4)* 2.00 2.00

For surcharges see Nos. 401, 406, 410, 414, 595, 606, 611.

National Anniversaries — A81a

#330A, Pres. Kenneth Kaunda, Mulungushi Rock. #330B, Kaunda, agricultural products. #330C, Freedom statue, flags.

***Die Cut Perf. 10***

**1985, Oct. 23 Embossed**
**330A-330C** A81a 5k gold *4.50 8.50*

United National Independence Party, 26th anniv. (No. 330A); Independence, 20th anniv. (Nos. 330B-330C).

Postal and Telecommunications Corp., 10th Anniv. — A82

**1985, Dec. 12 *Perf. 13½x13***
**331** A82 20n Lusaka P.O., 1958 .60 .60
**332** A82 45n Livingstone P.O., 1950 .90 .90
**333** A82 55n Kalomo P.O., 1902 1.00 1.00
**334** A82 5k Transcontinental Telegraph, 1900 3.25 3.25
*Nos. 331-334 (4)* 5.75 5.75

For surcharges see Nos. 590-593.

UN, 40th Anniv. — A83

**1985, Dec. 19 *Perf. 14***
**335** A83 20n Boy in cornfield .40 .40
**336** A83 45n Emblem .70 .70
**337** A83 1k Pres. Kaunda, 1970 1.25 1.25
**338** A83 2k Charter signing, 1945 1.90 1.90
*Nos. 335-338 (4)* 4.25 4.25

For surcharges see #594, 607.

Beetles A84

**1986, Mar. 20**
**339** A84 35n Mylabris tricolor .20 .20
**340** A84 1k Phasgonocnema melanianthe .30 .30
**341** A84 1.70k Amaurodes passerinii .50 .50
**342** A84 5k Ranzania petersiana 1.50 1.50
*Nos. 339-342 (4)* 2.50 2.50

For surcharges see #609, 612.

Common Design Types pictured following the introduction.

**Queen Elizabeth II 60th Birthday**
Common Design Type

Designs: 35n, At the Flower Ball, Savoy Hotel, London, 1951. 1.25k, With Prince Andrew at Lusaka Airport, Commonwealth Conf., 1979. 1.70k, With Dr. Kaunda observing natl. anthem. 1.95k, Wearing Queen Mary tiara, state visit to Luxembourg, 1976. 5k, Visiting Crown Agents' offices, 1983.

**1986, Apr. 21 Wmk. 384 *Perf. 14***
**343** CD337 35n scar, blk & sil .25 .25
**344** CD337 1.25k ultra & multi .35 .35
**345** CD337 1.70k grn, blk & sil .40 .40
**346** CD337 1.95k vio & multi .40 .40
**347** CD337 5k rose vio & multi .60 .60
*Nos. 343-347 (5)* 2.00 2.00

For surcharges see Nos. 402, 405, 407, 411, 415.

**Royal Wedding Issue, 1986**
Common Design Type

Designs: 1.70k, Sarah Ferguson kissing Prince Andrew. 5k, Andrew in informal dress.

**1986, July 23 Litho. *Perf. 14***
**348** CD338 1.70k multicolored .35 .35
**349** CD338 5k multicolored .90 .90

1986 World Cup Soccer Championships, Mexico — A85

Various soccer plays.

**1986, June 27 Litho. *Perf. 14½***
**350** A85 35n multicolored .75 .75
**351** A85 1.25k multicolored 2.00 2.00
**352** A85 1.70k multicolored 2.25 2.25
**353** A85 5k multicolored 3.50 3.50
*Nos. 350-353 (4)* 8.50 8.50

For surcharges see Nos. 403, 408, 412, 416.

Halley's Comet A86

Designs: 1.25k, Edmond Halley (1656-1742), by Henry Pegram. 1.70k, Giotto space probe approaching comet. 2k, Youth, astronomer. 5k, Halley's map of the southern constellations.

**1986, July 4**
**354** A86 1.25k multicolored .90 .90
**355** A86 1.70k multicolored 1.10 1.10
**356** A86 2k multicolored 1.50 1.50
**357** A86 5k multicolored 3.25 3.25
*Nos. 354-357 (4)* 6.75 6.75

For surcharges see Nos. 404, 409, 413, 417.

#244A Surchd. in Light Red Brown

**1986, July Litho. *Perf. 14½***
**358** A64 20n on 12n multi *4.00* .35

Christmas A87

Children's drawings.

**1986, Dec. 15 Litho. *Perf. 14***
**359** A87 35n Nativity .35 .35
**360** A87 1.25k Magi 1.25 1.25
**361** A87 1.60k Nativity 1.40 1.40
**362** A87 5k Angel, house, tree 3.00 3.00
*Nos. 359-362 (4)* 6.00 6.00

For surcharges see #602, 608.

Tazara Railroad, 10th Anniv. A88

Locomotive traveling various railway lines.

**1986, Dec. 22**
**363** A88 35n Overpass, Kasama .30 .30
**364** A88 1.25k Tunnel 21 vicinity .45 .45
**365** A88 1.70k Tunnels 6-7 .50 .50
**366** A88 5k Mpika Station grade separation 1.00 1.00
*Nos. 363-366 (4)* 2.25 2.25

University of Zambia A89

Designs: 35n, Pres. Kaunda shaking council member's hand. 1.25k, University crest, vert. 1.60k, University statue. 5k, Kaunda laying university building cornerstone, vert.

**1987, Jan. 27 Litho. *Perf. 14***
**367** A89 35n multicolored .35 .35
**368** A89 1.25k multicolored .75 .75
**369** A89 1.60k multicolored .90 .90
**370** A89 5k multicolored 3.00 3.00
*Nos. 367-370 (4)* 5.00 5.00

No. 137 Surcharged in Blue

**1987 *Perf. 14½***
**372** A64 25n on 8n multi .55 .40

Municipal Arms — A90

Birds — A91

**1987, Mar. 26 *Perf. 14***
**373** A90 35n Kitwe .20 .20
**374** A90 1.25k Ndola .25 .25
**375** A90 1.70k Lusaka .30 .30
**376** A90 20k Livingstone 3.00 3.00
*Nos. 373-376 (4)* 3.75 3.75

For surcharge see No. 603.

**1987-88 *Perf. 11x13***
**Size: 20x25½mm**
**377** A91 25n Long-toed fluff tail 2.00 2.00
**378** A91 30n Miombo pied barbet .20 .20
**379** A91 35n Black-and-rufous swallow 2.00 2.00

**Size: 25x38½mm**
***Perf. 14***
**380** A91 50n Slaty egret .20 .20
**381** A91 1k Bradfield's hornbill 2.00 2.00
**382** A91 1.25k Margaret's batis 2.00 2.00
**383** A91 1.60k Red-and-blue sunbird 2.00 2.00
**384** A91 1.70k Boehm's bee-eater 2.25 2.25
**385** A91 1.95k Gorgeous bush shrike 2.25 2.25
**386** A91 2k Shoebill .30 .30
**387** A91 5k Taita falcon 2.75 2.75

**Surcharged**

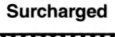

**Size: 20x25½mm**
***Perf. 11x13***
**388** A91 20n on 1n Yellow swamp warbler .25 .25
**389** A91 75n on 2n Olive-flanked robin .25 .25
**390** A91 1.65k on 30n #378 .25 .25

**Size: 25x38½mm**
***Perf. 14***
**391** A91 10k on 50n #380 .90 .90
**392** A91 20k on 2k #386 1.40 1.40
*Nos. 377-392 (16)* 21.00 21.00

Issued: #377, 379, 381-385, 387, 9/14/87; #391-392, 3/10/88; others 10/8/87.
Nos. 388-389 not issued without overprint.
See Nos. 433-435, 527-547. For surcharges see Nos. 490, 492-498.

Look-out Tree, Livingstone — A92

**1987, June 30** ***Perf. 14***

**393** A92 35n shown .30 .30
**394** A92 1.25k Rafting, Zambezi River .35 .35
**395** A92 1.70k Walking safari, Luangwa Valley 1.60 1.60
**396** A92 10k White pelicans 6.00 6.00
*Nos. 393-396 (4)* 8.25 8.25

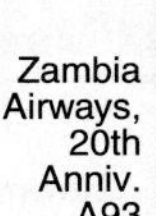

Zambia Airways, 20th Anniv. A93

**1987, Sept. 21**

**397** A93 35n De Havilland Beaver .60 .60
**398** A93 1.70k DC-10 1.40 1.40
**399** A93 5k DC-3 3.50 3.50
**400** A93 10k Boeing 707 5.50 5.50
*Nos. 397-400 (4)* 11.00 11.00

Issues of 1985-86 Surcharged in Gold or Black

**1987, Sept. 14** ***Perfs. as Before***

**401** A81 3k on 25n #327 (G) .90 .90
**402** CD337 3k on 35n #343 .70 .70
**403** A85 3k on 35n #350 .90 .90
**404** A86 3k on 1.25k #354 (G) 1.60 1.60
**405** CD337 4k on 1.25k #344 .85 .85
**406** A81 6k on 45n #328 1.60 1.60
**407** CD337 6k on 1.70k #345 1.25 1.25
**408** A85 6k on 1.25k #351 1.60 1.60
**409** A86 6k on 1.70k #355 (G) 2.50 2.50
**410** A81 10k on 55n #329 (G) 2.25 2.25
**411** CD337 10k on 1.95k #346 2.10 2.10
**412** A85 10k on 1.70k #352 2.25 2.25
**413** A86 10k on 2k #356 (G) 4.25 4.25
**414** A81 20k on 5k #330 (G) 4.50 4.50
**415** CD337 20k on 5k #347 4.50 4.50
**416** A85 20k on 5k #353 4.50 4.50
**417** A86 20k on 5k #357 (G) 7.75 7.75
*Nos. 401-417 (17)* 44.00 44.00

World Food Day — A94

Cattle.

**1987, Oct. 1** ***Perf. 14½x15***

**418** A94 35n Friesian-Holstein .20 .20
**419** A94 1.25k Simmental .40 .40
**420** A94 1.70k Sussex .40 .40
**421** A94 20k Brahma 2.00 2.00
*Nos. 418-421 (4)* 3.00 3.00

Traditional Heritage — A95

Zambian people.

**1987, Oct. 20** ***Perf. 13x12½***

**422** A95 35n Mpoloto Ne Mikobango .25 .25
**423** A95 1.25k Zintaka .40 .40
**424** A95 1.70k Mufuluhi .60 .60
**425** A95 10k Ntebwe 1.75 1.75
**426** A95 20k Kubangwa Aa Mbulunga 3.00 3.00
*Nos. 422-426 (5)* 6.00 6.00

World Wildlife Fund — A96

Wild Cats — A97

**1987, Dec. 21** **Litho.** ***Perf. 14***

**427** A96 50n Black lechwe drinking water *1.00 1.00*
**428** A96 2k Adults and young, horiz. *2.25 2.25*
**429** A96 2.50k Running, horiz. *2.25 2.25*
**430** A96 10k Male, diff. *5.50 5.50*
*Nos. 427-430 (4) 11.00 11.00*

**Souvenir Sheets**

**431** A97 20k Cheetah *7.50 7.50*
**432** A97 20k Caracal *7.50 7.50*

Bird Type of 1987

**1987** **Litho.** ***Perf. 11x13***

**433** A91 5n Black-tailed cisticola .20 .20
**434** A91 10n White-winged starling .20 .20
**435** A91 40n Wattled crane .20 .20
*Nos. 433-435 (3) .60 .60*

For surcharge see No. 491.

Intl. Fund for Agricultural Development (IFAD), 10th Anniv. — A98

**1988, Apr. 2** ***Perf. 14***

**436** A98 50n Cassava crop .20 .20
**437** A98 2.50k Net fishing .65 .65
**438** A98 2.85k Cattle breeding .75 .75
**439** A98 10k Coffee picking 2.50 2.50
*Nos. 436-439 (4)* 4.10 4.10

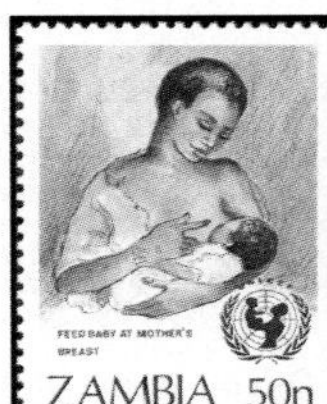


A99

A100

**1988, Sept. 12** **Litho.** ***Perf. 12½***

**440** A99 50n Breast-feeding .20 .20
**441** A99 2k Growth monitoring .55 .55
**442** A99 2.85k Immunization .75 .75
**443** A99 10k Oral rehydration 2.50 2.50
*Nos. 440-443 (4)* 4.00 4.00

UN child survival campaign.

**1988, Oct. 10** **Litho.** ***Perf. 12½x13***

**444** A100 50n Asbestos cement .20 .20
**445** A100 2.35k Textiles .60 .60
**446** A100 2.50k Tea .70 .70
**447** A100 10k Poultry 2.50 2.50
*Nos. 444-447 (4)* 4.00 4.00

Preferential Trade Area Fair.

Intl. Red Cross and Red Crescent Organizations, 125th Annivs. — A101

**1988, Oct. 20** ***Perf. 14***

**448** A101 50n Famine relief .20 .20
**449** A101 2.50k Giving first aid .60 .60
**450** A101 2.85k Teaching first aid .70 .70
**451** A101 10k Jean-Henri Dunant 2.60 2.60
*Nos. 448-451 (4)* 4.10 4.10

Endangered Species — A102

**1988, Dec. 5** **Litho.** ***Perf. 14***

**452** A102 50n Aardvark .25 .20
**453** A102 2k Pangolin .60 .50
**454** A102 2.85k Wild dog .75 .75
**455** A102 20k Black rhinoceros 7.00 7.00
*Nos. 452-455 (4)* 8.60 8.45

1988 Summer Olympics, Seoul A103

**1988, Dec. 30** **Litho.** ***Perf. 14***

**456** A103 50n Boxing .20 .20
**457** A103 2k Running .50 .50
**458** A103 2.50k Hurdling .65 .65
**459** A103 20k Soccer 5.25 5.25
*Nos. 456-459 (4)* 6.60 6.60

**Souvenir Sheets**

**460** A103 30k Tennis 6.50 6.50
**461** A103 30k Martial arts 6.50 6.50

Frogs and Toads A104

**1989, Jan. 25** **Litho.** ***Perf. 12½***

**462** A104 50n Red toad .20 .20
**463** A104 2.50k Puddle frog .50 .50
**464** A104 2.85k Marbled reed frog .60 .60
**465** A104 10k Young reed frogs 2.00 2.00
*Nos. 462-465 (4)* 3.30 3.30

Bats A105

**1989, Mar. 22** **Litho.** ***Perf. 12½x13***

**466** A105 50n Common slit-faced .20 .20
**467** A105 2.50k Little free-tailed .50 .50
**468** A105 2.85k Hildebrandt's horseshoe .60 .60
**469** A105 10k Peters' epauletted fruit 2.00 2.00
*Nos. 466-469 (4)* 3.30 3.30

A106

A107

**1989, May 2** **Litho.** ***Perf. 12½***

**470** A106 50n Map of Zambia .75 .20
**471** A106 6.85k Peace dove 3.00 3.00
**472** A106 7.85k Papal arms 3.50 3.50
**473** A106 10k Victoria Falls 5.00 5.00
*Nos. 470-473 (4)* 12.25 11.70

State visit of Pope John Paul II, May 2-4.
For surcharges see #614, 616.

**1989, July 26** **Litho.** ***Perf. 14½x15***

Edible wild fruits.

**474** A107 50n Parinari curatellifolia .20 .20
**475** A107 6.50k Uapaca kirkiana 1.40 1.75
**476** A107 6.85k Ficus capensis 1.40 1.75
**477** A107 10k Borassus aethiopum 2.50 3.00
*Nos. 474-477 (4)* 5.50 6.70

For surcharges see #613, 615.

Grasshoppers — A108

**1989, Nov. 8** **Litho.** ***Perf. 14x13½***

**478** A108 70n Phamphagid .20 .20
**479** A108 10.40k Pyrgomorphid 1.60 1.75
**480** A108 12.50k Brown katydid 2.00 2.25
**481** A108 15k Bush locust 2.50 3.25
*Nos. 478-481 (4)* 6.30 7.45

No. 480 misspelled "Catydid."

Christmas — A109

Flowers.

**1989, Dec. 6** **Litho.** ***Perf. 14½***

**482** A109 70n Fireball .20 .20
**483** A109 10.40k Flame lily 1.10 1.25
**484** A109 12.50k Foxglove lily 1.60 1.75
**485** A109 20k Vlei lily 2.60 3.25
*Nos. 482-485 (4)* 5.50 6.45

Stamp World London '90 A110

Designs: 1.20k, Lusaka Main P.O., van, mailman, bicycle. 19.50k, Zambia #220. 20.50k, Rhodesia and Nyasaland #164A, No. Rhodesia #1. 50k, Great Britain #1, Maltese Cross cancel in red.

**Unwmk.**

**1990, May 2 Litho. *Perf. 14***

**486** A110 1.20k multicolored .20 .20
**487** A110 19.50k multicolored 3.00 3.00
**488** A110 20.50k multicolored 3.00 3.00
**489** A110 50k multicolored 6.00 7.00
*Nos. 486-489 (4)* 12.20 13.20

Nos. 379, 381-387, 433 Surcharged

**1989, July 1 *Perf. 11x13***

**490** A91 70n on 35n #379 1.00 .20
**491** A91 3k on 5n #433 1.25 .40

**Size: 25x38½mm**

***Perf. 14***

**492** A91 8k on 1.25k #382 1.50 1.00
**493** A91 9.90k on 1.70k #384 1.75 1.75
**494** A91 10.40k on 1.60k #383 1.75 1.75
**495** A91 12.50k on 1k #381 2.00 2.00
**496** A91 15k on 1.95k #385 2.00 2.00
**497** A91 20k on 2k #386 3.00 3.00
**498** A91 20.35k on 5k #387 3.00 3.00
*Nos. 490-498 (9)* 17.25 15.10

Nos. 242, 244-245, 247-248 251, 253 Surcharged in Black, Orange Brown, Red Brown, or Violet

a

b

c

**1989 *Perf. 14½***

**Size: 22x26mm**

**499** A64(a) 1.20k on 35n #248 (OB) .25 .25
**500** A64(b) 3.75k on 5n #242 .40 .40
**501** A64(b) 8.11k on 10n #244 1.00 1.00
**502** A64(b) 9k on 30n #247 1.00 1.00

**Size: 37x25mm**

***Perf. 14***

**503** A64(b) 10k on 75n #251 1.00 1.00
**504** A64(c) 18.50k on 2k #253 2.00 2.00

**Size: 22x26mm**

***Perf. 14½***

**505** A64(a) 19.50k on 12n #244A (RB) 4.00 4.00
**506** A64(a) 20.50k on 18n #245 (V) 2.00 1.75
*Nos. 499-506 (8)* 11.65 11.40

Issued: #500-504, 7/1; others, 11/1.

World Cup Soccer Championships, Italy — A111

Soccer players in various positions.

**1990, July 7 Litho. *Perf. 14***

**507** A111 1.20k multicolored .20 .20
**508** A111 18.50k multicolored 2.25 2.50
**509** A111 19.50k multicolored 2.25 2.50
**510** A111 20.50k multicolored 2.25 2.50
*Nos. 507-510 (4)* 6.95 7.70

**Souvenir Sheet**

**510A** A111 50k multicolored 9.00 10.00

Southern African Development Co-ordination Conf. (SADCC), 10th Anniv. — A112

Map of SADCC members and: 1.20k, Truck. 19.50k, Telecommunications. 20.50k, Regional cooperation. 50k, Coal transport by cable car.

**1990, July 23 *Perf. 12½***

**511** A112 1.20k multicolored .30 .20
**512** A112 19.50k multicolored 2.25 2.25
**513** A112 20.50k multicolored 2.25 2.25
**514** A112 50k multicolored 7.50 7.50
*Nos. 511-514 (4)* 12.30 12.20

Independence, 26th Anniv. — A113

**1990, Oct. 23 Litho. *Perf. 14***

**515** A113 1.20k Agriculture .20 .20
**516** A113 19.50k Shoe factory 1.25 1.25
**517** A113 20.50k Satellite communications 1.40 1.40
**518** A113 50k Mother and child statue 3.00 3.00
*Nos. 515-518 (4)* 5.85 5.85

Small Carnivores — A114

**1990, Nov. 12**

**519** A114 1.20k Genet .20 .20
**520** A114 18.50k Civet 2.75 2.75
**521** A114 19.50k Serval 3.00 3.00
**522** A114 20.50k African wild cat 3.25 3.25
*Nos. 519-522 (4)* 9.20 9.20

Intl. Literacy Year — A115

Soy Beans — A116

Children's stories.

**1991, Jan. 11 Litho. *Perf. 14***

**523** A115 1.20k Bird and the Snake .20 .20
**524** A115 18.50k Hare and the Leopard 2.00 2.00
**525** A115 19.50k Mouse and Lion 2.75 2.75
**526** A115 20.50k Hare and the Hippo 3.00 3.00
*Nos. 523-526 (4)* 7.95 7.95

Bird Type of 1987

**1990-91 Litho. *Perf. 11x13***

**527** A91 10n Livingstone's fly-catcher .80 .45
**528** A91 15n Bar-winged weaver .80 .45
**529** A91 30n Purple-throated cuckoo shrike 1.25 .45
**530** A91 50n Red-billed helmet shrike 1.25 .50
**531** A91 50n like #527 1.25 .60
**532** A91 1k like #528 1.50 .20
**533** A91 1.20k Western bronze-naped pigeon 1.50 .20
**534** A91 2k like #529 1.50 .65
**535** A91 3k like #530 1.50 .65
**536** A91 5k like #533 1.75 .65

**Size: 25x38½mm**

***Perf. 14***

**537** A91 15k Corn crake 1.25 .60
**538** A91 20k Dickinson's grey kestrel 2.50 1.75
**539** A91 20.50k like #538 1.25 .85
**540** A91 50k Denham's bustard 2.00 2.00
*Nos. 527-540 (14)* 20.10 10.00

Issued: #533, 1k, 2k, 3k, 5k, 20k, 5/7/91; others, 10/30.

**1991, June 28 Litho. *Perf. 13½***

**548** A116 1k Woman cooking .20 .20
**549** A116 2k Soy bean seed .20 .20
**550** A116 5k Woman feeding child .25 .20
**551** A116 20k Malnourished, healthy children 1.50 1.50
**552** A116 50k Pres. Kaunda, child 3.00 3.00
*Nos. 548-552 (5)* 5.15 5.10

United Church of Zambia / Rotary Foundation Project.

St. Ignatius of Loyola (1491-1556), Founder of Jesuit Order — A117

1k, Chilubula Church near Kasama. 2k, Chikuni Church near Monze. 20k, Bishop Joseph Du Pont.

**1991, July 18 Litho. *Perf. 13½***

**553** A117 1k multicolored .20 .20
**554** A117 2k multicolored .20 .20
**555** A117 20k multicolored 2.50 2.50
**556** A117 50k shown 4.50 4.50
*Nos. 553-556 (4)* 7.40 7.40

Flowering Trees A118

**1991, Nov. 29 Litho. *Perf. 13½***

**557** A118 1k Baobab .20 .20
**558** A118 2k Dichrostachys cinerea .35 .20
**559** A118 10k Sterospermum kunthianum 2.00 1.50
**560** A118 30k Azanza garckeana 3.75 3.75
*Nos. 557-560 (4)* 6.30 5.65

**Queen Elizabeth II's Accession to the Throne, 40th Anniv.**

Common Design Type

***Perf. 14x13½***

**1992, Feb. 2 Litho. Wmk. 373**

**561** CD349 4k multicolored .20 .20
**562** CD349 32k multicolored 1.25 1.25
**563** CD349 35k multicolored 1.40 1.40
**564** CD349 38k multicolored 1.50 1.50
**565** CD349 50k multicolored 2.00 2.00
*Nos. 561-565 (5)* 6.35 6.35

For surcharges see Nos. 690-692.

Orchids — A119

Masks — A120

***Perf. 13x13½***

**1992, Feb. 28 Unwmk.**

**566** A119 1k Disa hamatopetala .55 .20
**567** A119 2k Eulophia paivaeana .55 .20
**568** A119 5k Eulophia quartiniana .90 .45
**569** A119 20k Aerangis verdickii 4.00 4.00
*Nos. 566-569 (4)* 6.00 4.85

**1992, Mar. 10**

**570** A120 1k Kasinja .20 .20
**571** A120 2k Chizaluke .20 .20
**572** A120 10k Mwanapweu .90 .75
**573** A120 30k Maliya 2.50 3.00
*Nos. 570-573 (4)* 3.80 4.15

Antelopes A121

**1992, Sept. 14 Litho. *Perf. 14***

**574** A121 4k Bushbuck .20 .20
**575** A121 40k Eland .85 .55
**576** A121 45k Roan antelope .85 .55
**577** A121 100k Sable antelope 1.75 2.50
*Nos. 574-577 (4)* 3.65 3.80

Airmail Services, 75th Anniv. A122

**1992, Nov. 24 Litho. *Perf. 14***

**578** A122 4k DH66 Hercules .40 .30
**579** A122 40k VC10 2.25 .90
**580** A122 45k C Class flying boat 2.25 .90
**581** A122 100k DC10 4.00 5.00
*Nos. 578-581 (4)* 8.90 7.10

1992 Summer Olympics, Barcelona — A123

**1992, Dec. 28**

**582** A123 10k 400-meter hurdles .20 .20
**583** A123 40k Boxing .70 .45
**584** A123 80k Judo 1.40 1.40
**585** A123 100k Cycling 3.50 3.50
*Nos. 582-585 (4)* 5.80 5.55

Christmas — A124

**1992, Dec. 23 Litho. *Perf. 14***

| | | | | | |
|---|---|---|---|---|---|
| **586** | A124 | 10k | Wise men | .20 | .20 |
| **587** | A124 | 80k | Nativity scene | 1.75 | 1.75 |
| **588** | A124 | 90k | Angels singing | 2.00 | 2.00 |
| **589** | A124 | 100k | Angel, shepherds | 2.00 | 2.00 |
| *a.* | | | Souvenir sheet of 4, #586-589 | 8.50 | 8.50 |
| | | | *Nos. 586-589 (4)* | 5.95 | 5.95 |

For surcharges see Nos. 658-659.

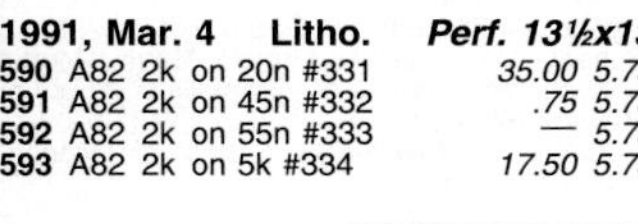

Nos. 331-334 Surcharged

**1991, Mar. 4 Litho. *Perf. 13½x13***

| | | | | | |
|---|---|---|---|---|---|
| **590** | A82 | 2k on 20n #331 | *35.00* | *5.75* |
| **591** | A82 | 2k on 45n #332 | *.75* | *5.75* |
| **592** | A82 | 2k on 55n #333 | — | *5.75* |
| **593** | A82 | 2k on 5k #334 | *17.50* | *5.75* |

Stamps of 1981-89 Surcharged in Black or Gold

***Perfs. as Before***

**1991, July 5 Litho.**

| | | | | |
|---|---|---|---|---|
| **594** | A83 | 2k on 20n #335 | *10.00* | *6.00* |
| **595** | A81 | 2k on 25n #327 (G) | *10.00* | *6.00* |
| **596** | A64 | 2k on 28n #246 | | — |
| **597** | A71 | 2k on 28n #289 | | — |
| **600** | A78 | 2k on 32n #317 | *30.00* | *8.00* |
| **601** | CD337 | 2k on 35n #343 | — | *20.00* |
| **602** | A87 | 2k on 35n #359 | *75.00* | *6.00* |
| **603** | A90 | 2k on 35n #373 | *45.00* | *6.00* |
| **604** | A79 | 2k on 45n #322 | *45.00* | *6.00* |
| **605** | A80 | 2k on 45n #325 | *60.00* | *6.00* |
| **606** | A81 | 2k on 45n #328 | *90.00* | *6.00* |
| **607** | A83 | 2k on 45n #336 | *47.50* | *6.00* |
| **608** | A87 | 2k on 1.60k #361 | *80.00* | *6.00* |
| **609** | A84 | 2k on 1.70k #341 | *47.50* | *6.00* |
| **611** | A81 | 2k on 5k #330 | *17.50* | *6.00* |
| **612** | A84 | 2k on 5k #342 | *17.50* | *6.00* |
| **613** | A107 | 2k on 6.50k #475 | *47.50* | *6.00* |
| **614** | A106 | 2k on 6.85k #471 | *62.50* | *6.00* |
| **615** | A107 | 2k on 6.85k #476 | *17.50* | *6.00* |
| **616** | A106 | 2k on 7.85k #472 | *90.00* | *6.00* |

Numbers have been reserved for additional surcharges in this set.

Waterfalls A125

**1993, Sept. 30 Litho. *Perf. 13½***

| | | | | | |
|---|---|---|---|---|---|
| **617** | A125 | 50k | Nkundalila | .20 | .20 |
| **618** | A125 | 200k | Chishimba | 1.00 | 1.00 |
| **619** | A125 | 250k | Chipoma | 1.25 | 1.25 |
| **620** | A125 | 300k | Lumangwe | 1.75 | 1.75 |
| | | | *Nos. 617-620 (4)* | 4.20 | 4.20 |

Healthy Hearts — A126

**1993, Oct. 20 Litho. *Perf. 14½***

| | | | | | |
|---|---|---|---|---|---|
| **621** | A126 | O | Runner | .75 | .75 |
| **622** | A126 | P | Heart | .75 | .75 |

No. 621 sold for 50k and No. 622 sold for 80k on date of issue.

Sunbirds A127

Designs: 20k, Bronze. 50k, Violet-backed. No. 625, Marico. No. 626, Eastern double-collared. 100k, Scarlet-chested. 150k, Bannerman's blue-headed. 200k, Oustalet's. 250k, Red and blue. 300k, Olive. 350k, Green-headed. 400k, Scarlet tufted malachite. 500k, Yellow-bellied. 800k, Copper. 1000k, Orange-tufted. 1500k, Black. 2000k, Green-throated.

**1993, May 30 Litho. *Perf. 13***

| | | | | | |
|---|---|---|---|---|---|
| **623** | A127 | 20k | multicolored | .20 | .20 |
| **624** | A127 | 50k | multicolored | .20 | .20 |
| **625** | A127 | O | multicolored | .20 | .20 |
| **626** | A127 | P | multicolored | .30 | .30 |
| **627** | A127 | 100k | multicolored | .35 | .35 |
| **628** | A127 | 150k | multicolored | .55 | .55 |
| **629** | A127 | 200k | multicolored | .65 | .65 |
| **630** | A127 | 250k | multicolored | .80 | .80 |
| **631** | A127 | 300k | multicolored | 1.00 | 1.00 |
| **632** | A127 | 350k | multicolored | 1.25 | 1.25 |
| **633** | A127 | 400k | multicolored | 1.40 | 1.40 |
| **634** | A127 | 500k | multicolored | 1.60 | 1.60 |
| **635** | A127 | 800k | multicolored | 2.75 | 2.75 |
| **636** | A127 | 1000k | multicolored | 3.50 | 3.50 |
| **637** | A127 | 1500k | multicolored | 5.25 | 5.25 |
| **638** | A127 | 2000k | multicolored | 7.00 | 7.00 |
| | | | *Nos. 623-638 (16)* | 27.00 | 27.00 |

Nos. 625 sold for 50k and 626 sold for 80k on date of issue.

For surcharge, see No. 997.

Snakes — A128

**1994, Sept. 28 Litho. *Perf. 14***

| | | | | | |
|---|---|---|---|---|---|
| **639** | A128 | 50k | Tiger snake | .20 | .20 |
| **640** | A128 | 200k | Egyptian cobra | .60 | .60 |
| **641** | A128 | 300k | African python | .90 | .90 |
| **642** | A128 | 500k | Green mamba | 1.50 | 1.50 |
| | | | *Nos. 639-642 (4)* | 3.20 | 3.20 |

For surcharge, see No. 996.

ILO, 75th Anniv. A129

**1995, Apr. 3 Litho. *Perf. 14***

| | | | | | |
|---|---|---|---|---|---|
| **643** | A129 | 100k | Road rehabilitation | .30 | .30 |
| **644** | A129 | 450k | Block making | 1.40 | 1.40 |

For surcharge see No. 781A.

Christmas Angels — A130

**1995, Aug. 29 *Perf. 14½x14***

| | | | | | |
|---|---|---|---|---|---|
| **645** | A130 | 100k | shown | .30 | .30 |
| **646** | A130 | 300k | With animals | .90 | .90 |
| **647** | A130 | 450k | Blowing horn, birds | 1.40 | 1.40 |
| **648** | A130 | 500k | Playing drum | 1.50 | 1.50 |
| | | | *Nos. 645-648 (4)* | 4.10 | 4.10 |

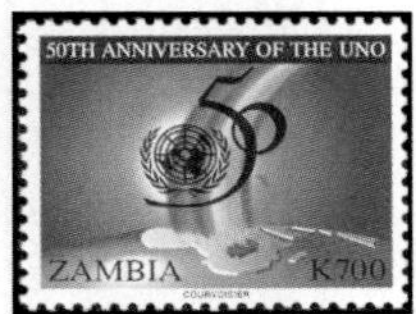

UN, 50th Anniv. A131

**1995, Dec. 30 Litho. *Perf. 11½***

**Granite Paper**

| | | | | | |
|---|---|---|---|---|---|
| **649** | A131 | 700k | multicolored | 1.50 | 1.50 |

Natl. Monuments A132

Designs: 100k, David Livingstone. 300k, Mbereshi Mission. 450k, Von Lettow-Vorbeck. 500k, Niamkolo Church.

**1996, Feb. 21 Litho. *Perf. 14***

| | | | | | |
|---|---|---|---|---|---|
| **650** | A132 | 100k | multicolored | .30 | .20 |
| **651** | A132 | 300k | multicolored | 1.00 | 1.00 |
| **652** | A132 | 450k | multicolored | 1.25 | 1.25 |
| **653** | A132 | 500k | multicolored | 1.50 | 1.50 |
| | | | *Nos. 650-653 (4)* | 4.05 | 3.95 |

World Wildlife Fund A133

Designs: 200k, Saddle-billed stork. 300k, Black-cheeked lovebird. 500k, Two black-cheeked lovebirds. 900k, Saddle-billed stork with young.

**1996, Nov. 27 Litho. *Perf. 14x14½***

| | | | | | |
|---|---|---|---|---|---|
| **654** | A133 | 200k | multicolored | .75 | .75 |
| **655** | A133 | 300k | multicolored | 1.00 | 1.00 |
| **656** | A133 | 500k | multicolored | 1.50 | 1.50 |
| **657** | A133 | 900k | multicolored | 2.50 | 2.50 |
| | | | *Nos. 654-657 (4)* | 5.75 | 5.75 |

Nos. 587-588 Surcharged

**1996 Litho. *Perf. 14***

| | | | | | |
|---|---|---|---|---|---|
| **658** | A124 | (0) | on 90k #588 | .85 | .85 |
| **659** | A124 | 900k | on 80k #587 | 1.50 | 1.50 |

No. 658 was valued at 500k on day of issue. Size and location of surcharge varies.

New Year 1997 (Year of the Ox) — A134

Disney characters posing for portrait in Chinese scene, vert.: #660: a, Clarabelle seated. b, Holding scroll. c, Playing musical instrument. d, On bicycle. e, Minnie, Mickey, Clarabelle. f, Holding mirror.

No. 661: a, 250k, Faces of Minnie, Mickey, Clarabelle Cow. b, 400k, Clarabelle seated. c, 500k, Clarabelle standing. d, 600k, Mickey, Clarabelle, Minnie dressed in Chinese outfits. e, 750k, Minnie, Clarabelle, Mickey dancing. f, 1000k, Clarabelle with parasol.

**1997, Jan. 28 Litho. *Perf. 14x13½***

| | | | | | |
|---|---|---|---|---|---|
| **660** | A134 | 500k | Sheet of 6, #a.-f. | 5.00 | 5.00 |
| **661** | A134 | | Sheet of 6, #a.-f. | 6.00 | 6.00 |

No. 660 contains six 35x61mm stamps.

Endangered Species — A135

Species of the world, each 500k: No. 662: a, Spider monkey. b, Manatee. c, Jaguar. d, Puerto Rican parrot. d, Green sea turtle. e, Harpy eagle.

Species of Africa, each 1000k: No. 663a, Black rhinoceros. b, Leopard. c, Champanzee. d, Zebra (Grants). e, Mountain gorilla. f, African elephant.

Each, 3000k: No. 664, Lion (African). No. 665, Margay cat.

**1997, Feb. 12 *Perf. 14***

| | | | | |
|---|---|---|---|---|
| **662** | A135 | Sheet of 6, #a.-f. | 5.00 | 5.00 |
| **663** | A135 | Sheet of 6, #a.-f. | 10.00 | 10.00 |

**Souvenir Sheets**

| | | | | |
|---|---|---|---|---|
| **664-665** | A135 | Set of 2 | 10.00 | 10.00 |

Deng Xiaoping (1904-97) — A136

Various portraits of Deng Xiaoping and: 800k, Flags, map of Hong Kong. 1000k, Flag, Hong Kong harbor. 2000k, Hong Kong at night, countdown clock. 2500k, World map with China highlighted.

**1997, May 26 Litho. *Perf. 14***

| | | | | | |
|---|---|---|---|---|---|
| **666** | A136 | 800k | multicolored | 1.40 | 1.40 |
| **667** | A136 | 1000k | multicolored | 1.75 | 1.75 |

**Souvenir Sheets**

| | | | | | |
|---|---|---|---|---|---|
| **668** | A136 | 2000k | multicolored | 3.25 | 3.25 |
| **669** | A136 | 2500k | multicolored | 4.25 | 4.25 |

Nos. 666-667 were issued in sheets of 3 each. No. 669 contains one 72x47mm stamp.

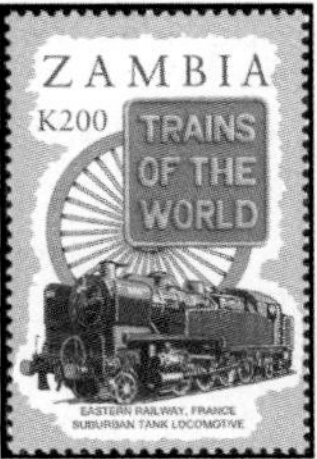

Trains — A137

A138

Locomotives: 200k, Suburban tank, Eastern Railway, France. 300k, Streamlined express, Belgian Natl. Railways. 500k, "Mountain" type express, Union Pacific Railraod. 900k, 2-8-2 "Mikado," Kenya & Uganda Railway. 1000k, 4-6-0 "Royal Scot," LM & S Railway. 1500k, 4-6-0 "Lord Nelson" type, Southern Railway.

No. 676, each 500k: a, Express, German State Railways. b, Express, "Duke of Abercorn," NCC (LMSR), Ireland. c, Heavy freight tank, Netherlands Railways. d, Express, Austrian Federal Railways. e, "Governor" class, Gold Coast Railways. f, 4-8-4 Express, Canadian Natl. Railways.

Each 3000k: No. 677, Diesel-electric passenger, Royal Siamese State Railways. No. 678, "Pacific" type, South African Railways.

**1997, June 2**

**670-675** A137 Set of 6 7.25 7.25
**676** A137 Sheet of 6, #a.-f. 5.00 5.00

**Souvenir Sheets**

**677-678** A137 Set of 2 10.00 10.00

**1997, Aug. 8 Litho. *Perf. 14***

Butterflies and Moths: 300k, No. 683a, Gaudy commodore. 500k, No. 683b, African moon moth. 700k, No. 683c, Emperor moth. No. 682, 900k, Emperor swallowtail.

**679-682** A138 Set of 4 4.00 4.00
**683** A138 900k Sheet of 4, #a.-c., #682 6.00 6.00

Queen Elizabeth II and Prince Philip, 50th Wedding Anniv. A139

No. 684, each 500k: a, Queen Elizabeth II. b, Royal arms. c, Queen wearing crown, Prince in uniform. d, Queen, Prince riding in open carriage. e, Buckingham Palace. f, Prince waving.

3200k, Queen, Prince waving from balcony.

**1997, Aug. 26 Litho. *Perf. 14***

**684** A139 Sheet of 6, #a.-f. 4.50 4.50

**Souvenir Sheet**

**685** A139 3200k multicolored 5.00 5.00

Paul P. Harris (1868-1947), Founder of Rotary, Intl. — A140

1000k, First Rotarians, Silvester Schiele, Harris, Hiram Shorey, Gus Loehr, portrait of Harris.

3200k, Zambian interactors with retirees.

**1997, Aug. 27**

**686** A140 1000k multicolored 1.50 1.50

**Souvenir Sheet**

**687** A140 3200k multicolored 5.00 5.00

Heinrich von Stephan (1831-97), Founder of UPU A141

Each 1000k, Portrait of Von Stephan and: #688a, World Postal Congress, Berne, 1874. #688b, UPU emblem. #688c, Savannah, paddle steamer, 1819.

3200k, Von Stephan, Prussian postilion, 1715.

**1997, Aug. 28**

**688** A141 Sheet of 3, #a.-c. 4.50 4.50

**Souvenir Sheet**

**689** A141 3200k multicolored 5.00 5.00

Nos. 562-564 Surcharged

**1997, Sept. 19 Litho. *Perf. 14x13½***

**690** CD349 500k on 35k .75 .75
**691** CD349 (0) on 32k .90 .90
**692** CD349 900k on 38k 1.25 1.25
*Nos. 690-692 (3)* 2.90 2.90

No. 691 was valued at 600k on day of issue.

Owls — A142

300k, #697b, Verreaux's eagle owl. 500k, #697c, Pel's fishing owl. 700k, #697a, Barn owl. #696, Spotted eagle owl.

**1997, Dec. 18 Litho. *Perf. 14***

**693** A142 300k multicolored .50 .50
**694** A142 500k multicolored .85 .85
**695** A142 700k multicolored 1.25 1.25
**696** A142 900k multicolored 1.50 1.50
*Nos. 693-696 (4)* 4.10 4.10

**Sheet of 4**

**697** A142 900k #a.-c., #696 6.00 6.00

Christmas A143

Entire paintings or details, sculpture: No. 698, 50k, Winged Victory of Samothrace. No. 699, 50k, Ognissanti Madonna, by Giotto. No. 700, 100k, Angel, by Antonio Pollaiuolo. No. 701, 100k, Angel of the Annunciation, by Jacopo da Pontormo. No. 702, 500k, No. 703. 1000k, The Virgin and Child Enthroned Among Angels and Saints, by Benozzo Gozzoli.

Each 3200k: No. 704, All of the Rebel Angels, detail, by Rubens. No. 705, The Resurrection of the Dead, by Joseph Christian.

**1997, Dec. 18 Litho. *Perf. 14***

**698-703** A143 Set of 6 2.75 2.75

**Souvenir Sheets**

**704-705** A143 Set of 2 10.00 10.00

No. 704 incorrectly inscribed "The Virgin and Child Enthroned Among Angels and Saints, by Bonozzo Gozzoli."

Diana, Princess of Wales (1961-97) — A144

Various portraits with color of sheet margin: No. 706, Pale green. No. 707, Pale yellow.

Each 2500k: No. 708, Touching hand of blind man (in sheet margin). No. 709, With Barbara Bush (in sheet margin).

**1997**

**706** A144 500k Sheet of 6, #a.-f. 4.50 4.50
**707** A144 700k Sheet of 6, #a.-f. 6.50 6.50

**Souvenir Sheets**

**708-709** A144 Set of 2 8.00 8.00

PAPU (Pan African Postal Union), 18th Anniv. A145

Designs: 500k, Kobus leche kafuensis. (O), Dove carrying letter over map. 900k, Emblem of dove carrying letter.

**1998 *Perf. 14½***

**710** A145 500k multicolored .75 .75
**711** A145 (O) multicolored .95 .95
**712** A145 900k multicolored 1.25 1.25
*Nos. 710-712 (3)* 2.95 2.95

No. 711 was valued at 600k on day of issue.

Mahatma Gandhi (1869-1948) — A146

Portraits of Gandhi: 250k, As law student in London, 1888. 500k, With Nehru, 1946. No. 715, (O), In front of Red Fort, New Dehli. 900k, At prayer.

2000k, Gandhi at 2nd Round Table Conference, London, 1931.

**1998, Jan. 30 Litho. *Perf. 13½***

**713-716** A146 Set of 4 3.25 3.25

**Souvenir Sheet**

**717** A146 2000k multicolored 3.00 3.00

No. 715 was valued at 600k on day of issue. Nos. 713, 715-717 are vert.

Flowers — A147

Designs: No. 718, Lantana camara. No. 719, Clusia rosea. No. 720, Nymphaea hybrids. No. 721, Portulaca grandiflora.

No. 722: a, Hibiscus rosa-sinensis. b, Plumeria. c, Erythrina variegata. d, Bauhinia blakeana. e, Carissa grandiflora. f, Cordia sebestena. g, Couroupita guianensis. h, Eustoma grandiflorum. i, Passiflora.

3200k, Strelitzia reginae, horiz.

**1998, Feb. 27 Litho. *Perf. 14***

**718-721** A147 500k Set of 4 3.25 3.25
**722** A147 500k Sheet of 9, #a.-i. 7.50 7.50

**Souvenir Sheet**

**723** A147 3200k multicolored 5.25 5.25

New Year 1998 (Year of the Tiger) A148

Chinese symbols and stylized tigers, each 700k: No. 724: a, Looking right. b, Looking left. c, Facing forward, denomination UL. d, Facing forward, denomination UR.

1500k, Tiger, symbols on both sides.

**1998 Litho. *Perf. 14***

**724** A148 Sheet of 4, #a.-d. 4.00 4.00

**Souenir Sheet**

**725** A148 1500k multicolored 2.10 2.10

Sites of India A149

Designs: a, Taj Mahal, Agra. b, Gateway to India, Calcutta. c, Great Imambara Mosque, Lucknow.

**1998**

**726** A149 900k Sheet of 3, #a.-c. 3.75 3.75

Art of India A150

No. 727, each 700k: a, Ragmala, School of Mewar, 17th cent. b, Babar Nama, Mogul School, 16th cent. c, Hamza Nama, Mogul School, 16th cent. d, Meghamallar, School of Mewar, 16th cent.

2500k, Hindola Raga, School of Deccan, 17th-18th cent.

**1998**

**727** A150 Sheet of 4, #a.-d. 4.00 4.00

**Souvenir Sheet**

**728** A150 2500k multicolored 3.50 3.50

1998 World Cup Soccer Championships, France — A151

No. 729, each 450k: a, Albert, Belgium. b, Bebeto, Brazil. c, Beckenbauer, W. Germany. d, Littbarski, W. Germany. e, Juninho, Brazil. f, Lineker, England. g, Lato, Poland. h, McCoist, Scotland.

No. 730, each 500k: a, Maier, W. Germany, 1974. b, Bellini, Brazil, 1958. c, Kempes, Argentina, 1978. d, Nazassi, Uruguay, 1930. e, Pele, Brazil, 1970. f, Beckenbauer, W. Germany, 1974. g, Combi, Italy, 1934. h, Zoff, Italy, 1982.

No. 731, each 500k: a, Keane, Rep. of Ireland. b, Seaman, England. c, Like #729b. d, Futre, Portugal. e, Ravanelli, Italy. f, Weah, Liberia. g, Bergkamp, Holland. h, Raducioiu, Romania.

Each 3200k: No. 732, Juninho, Brazil. No. 733, Romario, Brazil, horiz. No. 734, McCoist, Scotland, horiz.

**1998, Apr. 17 *Perf. 13½x14, 14x13½***

**Sheets of 8, #a-h, + Label**

**729** A151 multi 5.25 5.25
**730-731** A151 Set of 2 11.50 11.50

**Souvenir Sheets**

**732-734** A151 Set of 3 13.50 13.50

Parrots — A152

No. 735, each 500k: a, Rainbow lorikeet. b, Budgerigar, blossom-headed parakeet. c, Blue-yellow macaw. d, Blue-crowned parrot. e, Golden conure. f, Sulphur-crested cockatoo.

No. 736, each 1000k: a, Ara ararauna. b, Ara chloropterd. c, Pale-headed rosellas. d, Northern rosella. e, Gang-gang cockatoo. f, Palm cockatoo.
Each 3200k: No. 737, Mulda parakeet. No. 738, Major Mitchell cockatoo, horiz.

**1998, June 1 Litho. *Perf. 14***
**735** A152 Sheet of 6, #a.-f. 4.25 4.25
**736** A152 Sheet of 6, #a.-f. 8.50 8.50

**Souvenir Shets**
**737-738** A152 Set of 2 9.50 9.50

Mushrooms — A153

No. 739, 250k, Red-tufted wood tricholoma. No. 740, 250k, Chlorophyllum molybdites. No. 741, 450k, Stuntz's psilocybe. No. 742, 450k, Lepista sordida. No. 743, 500k, Lepiota. No. 744, 500k, Rosy gomphidius. No. 745, 900k, Cantharellus cybrina. No. 746, 900k, Olive-capped boletus. No. 747, 1000k, Showy volvaria. No. 748, 1000k, Sooty brown waxy cap.
No. 749, each 900k: a, Leller's boletus. b, Short-stemmed russula. c, Anise-scented clitocybe. d, Dung roundhead. e, Oak-loving collybia. f, Wine-red stropharia.
No. 750, each 900k: a, Flat-topped mushroom. b, Alice Eastwood's boletus. c, Pitted milky cap. d, Short-stemmed slippery jask. e, Rose-red russula. f, Zeller's tricholoma.
Each 3200k: No. 751, Honey mushroom. No. 752, Velvet-stemmed flammulina.

**1998, July 1**
**739-748** A153 Set of 10 8.00 8.00

**Sheets of 6**
**749-750** A153 Set of 2 15.50 15.50

**Souvenir Sheets**
**751-752** A153 Set of 2 9.00 9.00
Nos. 749-752 are continuous designs.

Traditional Stories — A154

No. 755, each 2000k: a, like #753. b, like #754.

**1998, Dec. 2 Litho. *Perf. 14***
**753** A154 300k Luchela nganga .45 .45
**754** A154 500k Kasuli .70 .70

**Souvenir Sheet**
**755** A154 Sheet of 2, #a.-b. 4.25 4.25
Christmas.

Orchids A155

Designs, vert: No. 756, 100k, Paphiopedilum callosum. No. 757, 100k, Phaius tankervilleae. No. 758, 500k, Paphiopedilum fairrieanum. No. 759, 500k, Barkeria lindleyana. No. 760, 1000k, Laelia flava. No. 761, 1000k, Masdervallia unifloria, masdervallia angulifera.
No. 762, each 900k: a, Acacallis cyanea. b, Miltoniopsis phalaenopsis. c, Dendrobium bellatulum. d, Polystachya campyloglossa. e, Pleione bulbocodioides. f, Rhynchostylis gigantea. g, Cattleya lawrenceana. h, Sopbrolaelia. i, Laelia tenebrosa.
No. 763, each 900k: a, Acacallis cyanea, diff. b, Epidendrum gastropodium. c, Laelia rubescens. d, Paphiopedilum dayanum. e, Laelia lobata. f, Dendrobium crepidatum. g, Cattleya nobilior. h, Dendrobium johnsoniae. i, Trichopilia fragrans.
Each 4000k: No. 764, Cattleya maxima, vert. No. 765, Cattleya violacea.

**1998, Dec. 23**
**756-761** A155 Set of 6 3.50 3.50

**Sheets of 9**
**762-763** A155 Set of 2 17.50 17.50

**Souvenir Sheets**
**764-765** A155 Set of 2 9.00 9.00

Classic Cars A156

Designs: 300k, Ferrari Daytona 365 GTB/4. 500k, Austin Healey Sprite. 900k, Gordon Keeble. 1000k, Alvis TD.
No. 770: a, Mercedes-Benz 300Sl. b, Chevrolet Corvair. c, AC Cobra 427. d, Aston Martin DB5. e, BMW 2002 Turbo. f, Cadillac Eldorado Brougham.
No. 771: a, Mercedes-Benz 280SE 3.5. b, Aston Martin DB2. c, Volkswagen Beetle. d, Lancia Aurelia B20 GT. e, Lamborghini 350 GT. f, Cisitalia 202 Coupe.
No. 771G: h, 1995 Ferrari 750 Pinnafarina. i, 1997 Federarri 312T2/77. j, 1983 Ferrari 208 Turbo. k, 1962 Ferrari Dino 268 SP. l, 1994 Ferrari F355 Berlinetta. m, Ferrari 250 GTE Coupe 2+2 California.
Each 4000k: No. 772, Citroen Light 15. No. 773, Austin Healey MKII 3000.

**1998, Dec. 23**
**766-769** A156 Set of 4 3.00 3.00

**Sheets of 6, #a-f**
**770-771G** A156 900k Set of 3 17.50 17.50

**Souvenir Sheets**
**772-773** A156 Set of 2 9.00 9.00

New Year 1999 (Year of the Rabbit) A157

Various rabbits, denomination at — #774 (each 700k): a, LL. b, LR. c, LL (scratching). d, LR (nose near ground).
2000k, Rabbit, vert.

**1999, Jan. 4**
**774** A157 Sheet of 4, #a.-d. 3.00 3.00

**Souvenir Sheet**
**775** A157 2000k multicolored 2.25 2.25

Trains A158

Locomotives: No. 776, (0), U20C Diesel electric, 1967. No. 777, 800k, 7th Class No. 70, 1900. No. 778, 800k, 15A Class Beyer-Garrat No. 401, 1950. No. 779, 900k, HP diesel electric, 1966. No. 780, 900k, 20th Class No. 708, 1954.
4000k, 7th Class No. 955, 1892.

**1999, Feb. 1 Litho. *Perf. 14½***
**776-780** A158 Set of 5 4.50 4.50

**Souvenir Sheet**
**781** A158 4000k multicolored 4.50 4.50
No. 776 was valued at 600k on day of issue.

No. 643 Surcharged

**Methods and Perfs as Before**

**1999, June 1**
**781A** A129 500k on 100k multi

Queen Mother (b. 1900) — A159

No. 782: a, With Princess Elizabeth, 1936. b, Lady of the Garter. c, With Prince Andrew, 1960. d, At Ascot.
5000k, Wedding photograph, 1923.

**1999, Sept. 1 *Perf. 14***
**782** A159 2000k Sheet of 4, #a.-d., + label 6.75 6.75

**Souvenir Sheet**
***Perf. 13¾***
**783** A159 5000k multicolored 4.25 4.25
No. 783 contains one 38x51mm stamp.

Dinosaurs A160

Designs: 50k, Dimetrodon. 100k, Deinonychus. 500k, Protoceratops. 900k, Heterodontosaurus. 1000k, Oviraptor. 1800k, Psittacosaurus.
No. 790, each 900k: a, Stegosaurus. b, Triceratops. c, Brontosaurus. d, Gallimimus. e, Saurolophus. f, Lambeosaurus. g, Centrosaurus. h, Edmontonia. i, Parasaurolophus.
No. 791, each 900k: a, Ceratosaurus. b, Daspletosaurus. c, Baryonyx. d, Ornitholestes. e, Troodon. f, Coelophysis. g, Tyrannosaurus. h, Allosaurus. i, Compsognathus.
Each 4000k: No. 792, Saltasaurus, vert. No. 793, Stygimoloch, vert.

**1999, Sept. 27 Litho. *Perf. 14***
**784-789** A160 Set of 6 3.75 3.75

**Sheets of 9**
**790-791** A160 Set of 2 13.50 13.50

**Souvenir Sheets**
**792-793** A160 Set of 2 7.00 7.00

Johann Wolfgang von Goethe (1749-1832), German Poet — A161

No. 794, each 2000k: a, A drinking party in Amerbach's cellar. b, Goethe and Friedrich von Schiller. c, Faust falls in love with Margaret.
5000k, Angel.

**1999, Oct. 4 Litho. *Perf. 14***
**794** A161 Sheet of 3, #a.-c. 4.25 4.25

**Souvenir Sheet**
**795** A161 5000k org brn & brn 3.75 3.75

A162

A163

Cats: 50k, White Devon Rex. 100k, Red Persian. 500k, Chartreux. 900k, Brown tabby Maine Coon.
No. 800, each 1000k, horiz.: a, Tortie point Himalayan. b, Blue mackerel tabby Scottish Fold. c, Chocolate lynx point Balinese. d, Havana Brown. e, Seal point Ragdoll. f, Silver shaded Persian.
No. 801, each 1000k, horiz.: a, Red spotted tabby Exotic Shorthair. b, Blue tortie smoke Persian. c, Brown classic tabby longhaired Scottish Fold. d, Spotted tabby American Bobtail. e, Silver spotted tabby Ocicat. f, Blue British Shorthair.
Each 4000k: No. 802, Silver tabby longhair Persian, horiz. No. 803, Tabby point Siamese.

**1999, Oct. 18**
**796-799** A162 Set of 4 1.10 1.10

**Sheets of 6, #a.-f.**
**800-801** A162 Set of 2 8.50 8.50

**Souvenir Sheets**
**802-803** A162 Set of 2 6.00 6.00

**1999, Oct. 18**

Dogs: 100k, Welsh corgi. 500k, Shetland sheepdog. 900k, Italian greyhound. 1000k, Tibetan spaniel.
No. 808, each 1000k, horiz.: a, Dalmatian. b, Shetland sheepdogs. c, Bearded collie. d, Eskimo. e, Basenji. f, Saluki.
No. 809, each 1000k, horiz.: a, Norwegian elkhound. b, Flat-coated retriever. c, St. Bernard. d, Basset hound, Pembroke Welsh corgi. e, Pembroke Welsh corgi, Pointer. f, Petit Basset Griffon Vendeen.
Each 4000k: No. 810, Whippet. No. 811, Rottweiler.

**804-807** A163 Set of 4 1.75 1.75

**Sheets of 6, #a.-f.**
**808-809** A163 Set of 2 8.50 8.50

**Souvenir Sheets**
**810-811** A163 Set of 2 6.00 6.00

11th Intl. Conference on AIDS in Africa, Lusaka — A164

Designs: 500k, Emblem, waterfalls. 900k, Emblem, close-up view of waterfalls.

**1999, Oct. 20**
**812-813** A164 Set of 2 1.00 1.00


Paintings by Zhang Daqian (1899-1983) A165

No. 814, each 500k: a, Water Lily in the Rain. b, Chinghai Tribal Girl and a Black Hound. c, Taking a Nap. d, Monkey and Old Tree. e, Bird and Tree of Chin-Chang Mountain. f, Watching Waterfalls. g, On the Way to

Switzerland and Austria. h, A Boat Brings the Wine. i, Brown Landscape. j, Nice Autumn.
No. 815: a, 1000k, White Water Lily, horiz. b, 2000k, Cloudy Waterfalls and Summer Mountain, horiz.

**1999, Oct. 21** *Perf. 13*

**814** A165 Sheet of 10, #a.-j. 3.75 3.75
**815** A165 Sheet of 2, #a.-b. 2.10 2.10

China 1999 World Philatelic Exhibition, 22nd UPU Congress, Beijing. #815 contains two 52x39mm stamps.

A166

Flora & Fauna A167

Designs: 50k, Leatherback turtle. 100k, American kestrel. No. 818, 500k, Great blue heron. 900k, Mesene phareus. 1000k, Laelio-cattleya. 1800k, Papilio cresphontes.
Each 500k: No. 822, Cairn's birdwing. No. 823, Pintail. No. 824, Rose. No. 825, Gray tree frog.
No. 826, each 700k: a, White-tailed tropicbird. b, Sooty tern. c, Laughing gull. d, Black skimmer. e, Brown pelican. f, Bottle-nosed dolphin. g, Common dolphin. h, Man in sailboat. i, Blue tang. j, Southern stingray. k, Hammerhead shark. l, Mako shark.
No. 827, each 700k: a, Heliconia. b, Purple-throated Carib. c, St. Vincent parrot. d, Bananaquit. e, prepona meander. f, Unidentified butterfly. g, Hawksbill turtle. h, Black-necked stilt. i, Banded butterflyfish. j, Porkfish. k, Seahorse. l, Chain moray eel.
No. 828: a, Baltimore oriole. b, Chipmunk. c, Blue jay. d, Monarch butterfly. e, Gray heron. f, Mallard. g, Canadian otter. h, American lotus. i, Fowler's toad. j, Bluegill sunfish. k, Rainbow trout. l, Terrapin.
Each 4000k: No. 829, Amazona guildingii. No. 830, Bottle-nosed dolphin, diff. No. 831, Fuchsia. No. 832, Red-banded pereute.

**1999, Oct. 27**

**816-821** A166 Set of 6 3.25 3.25
**822-825** A167 Set of 4 1.40 1.40

**Sheets of 12, #a.-l.**

**826-827** A166 Set of 2 12.00 12.00
**828** A167 700k multi 6.00 6.00

**Souvenir Sheets**

**829-830** A166 Set of 2 6.00 6.00
**831-832** A167 Set of 2 6.00 6.00

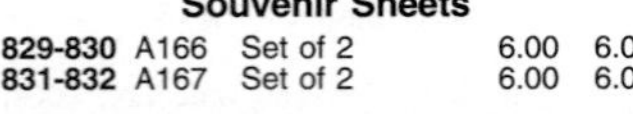

IBRA '99 — A168

Trains: 1000k, Crampton. 3200k, Post standard 2-8-4 tank locomotive.
Illustration reduced.

**1999** *Perf. 14x14¾*

**833-834** A168 Set of 2 3.00 3.00

**Souvenir Sheets**

PhilexFrance '99 — A169

Each 5000k: #835, Paris-Orleans Railway 4-4-0. #836, paris, Lyon & Mediterranean Railway 2-4-2.

**1999** *Perf. 14¼*

**835-836** A169 Set of 2 7.50 7.50

Wedding of Prince Edward and Sophie Rhys-Jones A170

No. 837: a, 500k, Sophie. b, 900k, Couple. c, 100k, Edward.
3000k, Couple kissing.

**1999** *Perf. 14*

**837** A170 Sheet of 3, #a.-c. 1.75 1.75

**Souvenir Sheet**

**838** A170 3000k multi 2.10 2.10

Birds — A171

Designs: 50k, Blacksmith plover. 100k, Sacred ibis. 200k, Purple gallinule. 250k, Purple heron. 300k, Glossy ibis. 400k, Marabou stork. 450k, African spoonbill. 500k, African finfoot. O, No. 847, Knot-billed duck. 600k, Darter. 700k, African skimmer. 800k, Spur-winged goose. 900k, Hammerkop. 1000k, White pelican. 1500k, Black-winged stilt. 2000k, Black-crowned night heron.

**1999, Dec. 20 Litho.** *Perf. 14½x15*

**839-854** A171 Set of 16 7.00 7.00

No. 847 sold for 500k on day of issue.
Design size of No. 847 is 30½mm wide. See Nos. 927-930.

Flowers A172

Various flowers making up a photomosaic of Princess Diana, each 1000k.

**1999, Dec. 31** *Perf. 13¾*

**855** A172 Sheet of 8, #a.-h. 6.25 6.25

Millennium A173

Highlights of 1950-2000: a, Venice Biennale shows Jackson Pollock and Abstract Expressionism. b, James Watson and Francis Crick piece together the structure of DNA. c, Edmund Hillary reaches the summit of Mount Everest. d, Jonas Salk's polio vaccine. e, Ghana achieves independence. f, Yuri Gagarin becomes 1st man in space. g, Rachel Carson and the beginning of the environmental movement. h, Indira Gandhi becomes Prime Minister of India. i, 1st successful heart transplant. j, Apollo 11 lands on moon. k, Microprocessor developed. l, Richard Nixon visits People's Republic of China. m, Qin Shi Huang Mausoleum discovered. n, Stephen Hawking proposes new ideas about the universe and black holes. o, Margaret Thatcher elected 1st female Prime Minister of Great Britain. p, Mikhail Gorbachev becomes leader of Soviet Union. q, Fall of the Berlin Wall. r, Nelson Mandela elected Pres. of South Africa.

**2000, Feb. 7** *Perf. 12¾x12½*

**856** A173 500k Sheet of 18, #a.-r., + label 6.25 6.25

Butterflies A174

400k, Papilio antimachus. 450k, Amauris niavius. 500k, Charaxes smaragdalis. 800k, Charaxes zelica. 900k, Cymothoe confusa. 1000k, #862, Labobunea ansorgei.
No. 863, each 1000k: a, Palla ussheri. b, Euphaedra aureola. c, Graphium cyrnus nuscyrus. d, Salamis cacta. e, Salamis parhassus. f, Charaxes pelias.
No. 864, each 1000k: a, Large Spotted Acraea. b, Palla (orange wings). c, Palla (blue wings). d, Gold-banded Forester (white wings). e, Figtree blue. f, Gold-banded Forester (pink wings).
No. 865, each 1500k: a, Colotis ione. b, Charaxes acraeoides. c, Euphaedra edwardsi. d, Colotis phisadia. e, Charaxes lydiae. f, Euphaedra eupaulus.
No. 866, each 1500k: a, Papilio zalmoxis. b, Amauris niavius. c, Salamis cytora. d, Salamis temora. e, Charaxes eupale. f, Cymothoe hypatha.
Each 5000k: No. 867, Euphaedra ceres. No. 868, Cymothoe fumana. No. 869, Euphaedra spatiosa. No. 870, Euryphene gambiae.

**2000, Feb. 8** *Perf. 14*

**857-862** A174 Set of 6 2.75 2.75

**Sheets of 6, #a.-f.**

**863-864** A174 Set of 2 8.50 8.50
**865-866** A174 Set of 2 12.50 12.50

**Souvenir Sheets**

**867-870** A174 Set of 4 14.00 14.00

No. 650 Surcharged

**Method and Perf. as Before**

**2000, Apr. 11**

**870A** A132 700k on 100k multi

Orchids — A175

Illustration reduced.
No. 871, each 1500k: a, Paphiopedilum sioux. b, Phalaenopsis amabilis hybrid. c, Thelymitza ixioides. d, Phalaenopsis schilleriana.
No. 872, each 1500k: a, Miltoniopsis pansy orchid. b, Paphiopedilum venustum. c, Odontoglossum grande. d, Vanda sanderiana alba. e, Phalaenopsis violacea. f, Pleione alishan.
No. 873, each 1500k: a, Cyrtorchis arcuata. b, Cymbioiella rhodochila. c, Unidentified orchid. d, Eulophia quartiana. e, Augraecum montanum. f, Polystacha vulcanica.
No. 874, , each 1500k, vert.: a, Catasetum splendens. b, Miltonia spectabilis. c, Stenia pallida. d, Cozacias spatulata. e, Eriopsis sceptzum. f, Paphinia cristata.
Each 6000k: No. 875, Cattleya hybrid. No. 876, Brachycorythis kalbreyeri.

**2000, May 16 Litho.** *Perf. 14*

**871** A175 Sheet of 4, #a.-d. 4.00 4.00

**Sheets of 6, #a.-f.**

**872-874** A175 Set of 3 18.00 18.00

**Souvenir Sheets**

**875-876** A175 Set of 2 8.00 8.00

The Stamp Show 2000, London.

Popes — A176

No. 877: a, Liberius, 352-66. b, Linus, 67-76. c, Lucius I, 253-54. d, Marcellinus, 296-304. e, Mark, 336. f, Pius I, 140-155.
No. 878: a, Simplicius, 468-83. b, Siricius, 384-99. c, Stephen I, 254-57. d, Urban I, 222-30. e, Zephyrinus, 199-217. f, Zosimus, 417-18.
No. 879, Silverius, 536-37. No. 880, Vigilius, 537-55.
Illustration reduced.

**2000, July 7 Litho.** *Perf. 13¾*

**Sheets of 6, #a-f**

**877-878** A176 1500k Set of 2 11.00 11.00

**Souvenir Sheets**

**879-880** A176 5000k Set of 2 6.00 6.00

Birds — A177

400k, Great Indian hornbill. 500k, Cockatiel. 600k, Amazonian umbrellabird. 1000k, Unidentified bird. 2000k, Rainbow lorikeet.

No. 886: a, Green aracari. b, Eclectus parrot. c, Crimson topaz. d, King bird of paradise. e, keel-billed toucan. f, Australian king parrot. g, Sailboat. h, Hyacinth macaw.

No. 887: a, Resplendent quetzal. b, Carmine bee-eater. c, Wattled false sunbird. d, Palm trees. e, Sulphur-crested cockatoo. f, Great blue turaco. g, Crimson rosella. h, Malabar pied hornbill.

No. 888: a, Yellow-crowned amazon. b, Green turaco. c, Butterfly and palm trees. d, Plate-billed mountain toucan. e, Scarlet macaw. f, Blue and yellow macaw. g, Guianan cock of the rock. h, Palm cockatoo.

No. 889, Red-crested pochard. No. 890, Toco toucan, horiz. No. 891, Blue and yellow macaw, horiz.

**2000, Sept. 8** *Perf. 14*

**881-885** A177 Set of 5 2.75 2.75

**Sheets of 8, #a-h**

**886-888** A177 1500k Set of 3 21.00 21.00

**Souvenir Sheets**

**889-891** A177 5000k Set of 3 9.00 9.00

Birds — A178

Designs: 700k, Red-backed shrike. 800k, Golden pipet. No. 894, 1200k, Orange-breasted sunbird. No. 895, 1400k, Eurasian goldfinch. 1500k, Red-crested turaco. 3000k, Carmine bee-eater.

No. 898, 1000k: a, Gouldian finch. b, Parrot finch. c, Purple grenadier. d, Red bishop. e, Red-crested cardinal. f, Spectacled monarch. g, Crimson chat. h, Necklaced laughing thrush. i, Chestnut-backed jewel babbler.

No. 899, 1200k: a, Lovely cotinga. b, Andean cock-of-the-rock. c, Orange-bellied leafbird. d, Pin-tailed manakin. e, Pin-tailed broadbill. f, Rufous motmot. g, American goldfinch. h, Double-barred finch. i, Golden-breasted starling.

No. 900, 1400k: a, Campo oriole. b, Hooded warbler. c, Purple honeycreeper. d, Blue-faced honeyeater. e, Scarlet tanager. f, Green-headed tanager. g, Blue-breasted fairy wren. h, Banded pitta. i, Wire-tailed manakin.

No. 901, 5000k, Pin-tailed sandgrouse. No. 902, 5000k, Black bustard.

**2000, Sept. 8** **Litho.** *Perf. 14*

**892-897** A178 Set of 6 4.75 4.75

**Sheets of 9, #a-i**

**898-900** A178 Set of 3 18.00 18.00

**Souvenir Sheets**

**901-902** A178 Set of 2 5.75 5.75

African Creation Legends A179

Designs: Nos, 903, 906a, 600k, Creation in Clay. Nos. 904, 906b, 1000k, The Chameleon and the Lizard. Nos. 905, 906c, 1400k, Why the Stones Do Not Die.

*Perf. 14¼x14½*

**2000, Nov. 10** **Litho.**

**903-905** A179 Set of 3 1.40 1.40

**With Brown Frame**

**906** A179 Horiz. strip of 3, #a-c 1.40 1.40

**Souvenir Sheet**

**No Frame Around Stamp**

**907** A179 3500k The Rooster in the Sky 1.60 1.60

No. 906 issued in sheets of 9 stamps.

Common Market for Eastern and Southern Africa A180

Designs: 600k, Map of member nations. 700k, Truck crossing border. 1000k, Exchange of money and sale of goods at border.

**2000**

**908-910** A180 Set of 3 1.10 1.10

Nos. 713-714 Surcharged

**2000** **Method and Perf. as Before**

**911** A146 1200k on 250k multi

**912** A146 1500k on 500k multi

UN High Commissioner for Refugees, 50th Anniv. — A181

Designs: 700k, Children receiving food. 1500k, Woman carrying child.

*Perf. 13¾x14¼*

**2001, Mar. 13** **Litho.**

**915-916** A181 Set of 2 1.40 1.40

A182

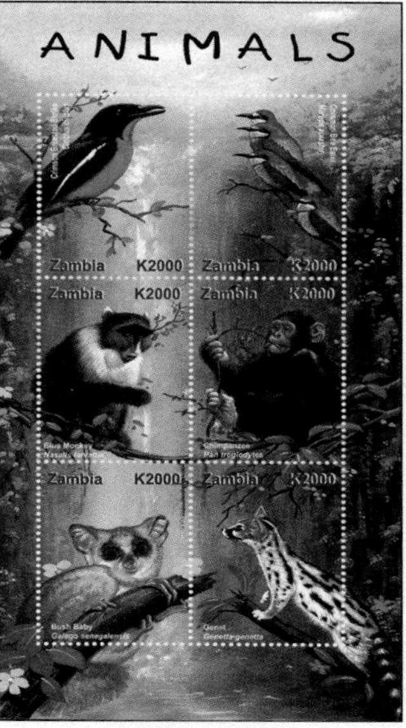

Animals — A183

Designs: 500k, African buffalo. 1000k, Cheetah, vert. No. 919, 2000k, Female elephant. 3200k, Ruffed lemur, vert.

No. 921, 2000k: a, Crimson-breasted shrike. b, Common bee-eater. c, Blue monkey. d, Chimpanzee. e, Bush baby. f, Genet.

No. 922, 2000k, horiz.: a, Defassa waterbuck. b, Crowned crane. c, Red hartebeest. d, Pygmy hippopotamus. e, White rhinoceros. f, Giant forest hog.

No. 923, 2000k, horiz.: a, Cheetah. b, Three adult, one young impala. c, Four adult impalas. d, Warthog. e, Two lions. f, Four lions.

No. 924, 6000k, Bull elephant. No. 925, 6000k, Black rhinoceros. No. 926, 6000k, Zebras, vert.

*Perf. 13¼x13½, 13½x13¼*

**2001, Mar. 30**

**917-920** A182 Set of 4 4.00 4.00

**Sheets of 6, #a-f**

**921-923** A183 Set of 3 22.50 22.50

**Souvenir Sheets**

**924-926** A182 Set of 3 11.00 11.00

**Bird Type of 1999**

Designs: No. 927, O, Knob-billed duck. No. 928, A, Blacksmith plover. No. 929, B, Sacred ibis. No. 930, C, Purple gallinule.

*Perf. 14½x14¾*

**2001, Mar. 19** **Litho.**

**927-930** A171 Set of 4 3.00 3.00

Nos. 927-930 each sold for 700k, 1200k, 1400k, and 1500k respectively on day of issue. No. 927 is dated "2000" and has a design width of 31½mm. No. 847 has no date and has a design width of 30½mm.

Total Solar Eclipse, June 21 — A184

Eclipse and: 1000k, Woman. 1500k, Bird. 1700k, Lizard. 1800k, Elephant and man. 2200k, Man.

**2001, June 1** **Litho.** *Perf. 13¾*

**931-935** A184 Set of 5 4.50 4.50

Phila Nippon '01, Japan — A185

Designs: No. 936, 500k, Senya Nakamura as Toknatsu, by Kiyomasu Torii I. No. 937, 500k, Kantaro Sanjo II and Monosuke Ichikawa I, by Okumura Masanobu, 1720. No. 938, 1000k, Kantaro Sanjo and Monosuke Ichikawa, by Masanobu, c. 1730. No. 939, 1000k, Standing Figure of a Woman, by Kiyomasu Torii I. 1500k, Ono no Komachi, by Masanobu. 1800k, Dog Bringing a Love Letter, by Shigenaga.

No. 942, 3200k: a, Matsue Nakamura as a Cat Woman, by Shunsho. b, Kantaro Sanjo With Branch of Bamboo, by Kiyomasu Torii I. c, Kinsaku Yamashika I as Peddler, by Kiyomasu Torii I. d, Portrait of an Actor, by Shunsho.

No. 943, 3200k: a, Kumetaro Nakamura I, by Shunsho. b, Actor in Female Role, by Kiyomasu Torii I. c, Kikunojo Segawa Leaning on Sugoroku Board, by Kiyomasu Torii I. d, Gennosuke Ichikawa as a Wakashu, by Kiyomasu Torii I.

No. 944, 6000k, Akashi of the Tamaya, by Ryukoku Hishikawa. No. 945, 6000k, Events of Year in the Floating World, by Moroshige, horiz.

**2001, July 4** *Perf. 14*

**936-941** A185 Set of 6 3.50 3.50

**Sheets of 4, #a-d**

**942-943** A185 Set of 2 14.00 14.00

**Souvenir Sheets**

**944-945** A185 Set of 2 6.50 6.50

SOS Children's Village A186

**2001, July 30**

**946** A186 2500k multi 1.40 1.40

Royal Navy Submarines, Cent. — A187

No. 947, horiz.: a, HMS Tabard. b, HMS Opossum. c, HMS Unicorn. d, HMS Churchill. e, HMS Victorious. f, HMS Triumph.

6000k, Lieutenant Commander Malcolm David Wanklyn.

**2001, July 30**

**947** A187 2000k Sheet of 6, #a-f 6.75 6.75

**Souvenir Sheet**

**948** A187 6000k multi 3.50 3.50

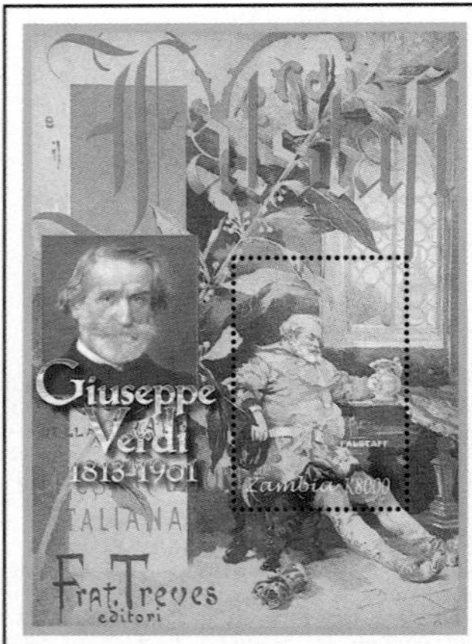


Giuseppe Verdi (1813-1901), Opera Composer — A188

No. 949 — Actors in Falstaff : a, Benjamin Luxon (without hat). b, Luxon (with hat). c, Paul Plishka. d, Anne Collin.
8000k, Falstaff.

**2001, July 30**
**949** A188 4000k Sheet of 4, #a-d 9.00 9.00

**Souvenir Sheet**

**950** A188 8000k multi 4.50 4.50

Monet Paintings — A189

No. 951, horiz.: a, The Promenade at Argenteuil. b, View of the Argenteuil Plain from the Sannois Hills. c, The Seine at Argenteuil. d, The Basin at Argenteuil.
6000k, Rouen Cathedral Portal, Overcast Weather.

**2001, July 30** ***Perf. 13¾***
**951** A189 1500k Sheet of 4, #a-d 3.50 3.50

**Souvenir Sheet**

**952** A189 6000k multi 3.50 3.50

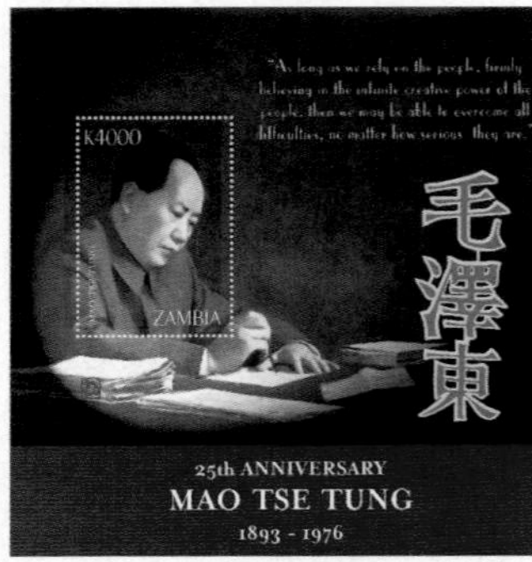


Mao Zedong (1893-1976) — A190

No. 953 — Mao in: a, 1918. b, 1945. c, 1937.
4000k, Portrait.

**2001, July 30**
**953** A190 3200k Sheet of 3, #a-c 5.50 5.50

**Souvenir Sheet**

**954** A190 4000k multi 2.25 2.25

Queen Victoria (1819-1901) — A191

No. 955: a, As child. b, Wearing black dress. c, With child. d, With Prince Albert. e, Wearing crown and red sash. f, Wearing red dress.
7000k, Portrait.

**2001, July 30** ***Perf. 14***
**955** A191 2000k Sheet of 6, #a-f 6.75 6.75

**Souvenir Sheet**

**956** A191 7000k multi 4.00 4.00

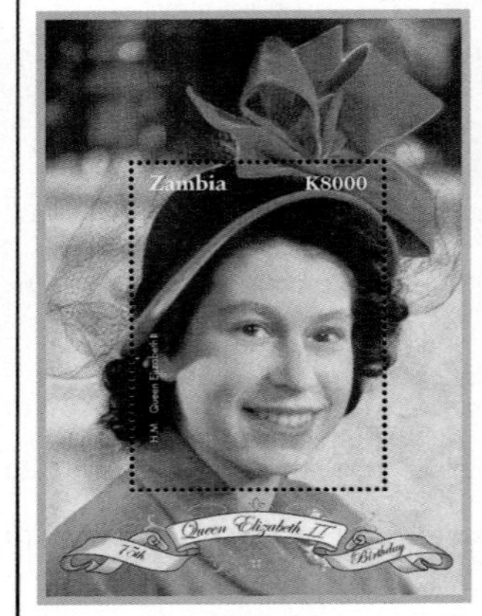


Queen Elizabeth II, 75th Birthday — A192

No. 957: a, As infant. b, As child. c, As child, in garden. d, Wearing hat.
8000k, Wearing green and black hat.

**2001, July 30**
**957** A192 4000k Sheet of 4, #a-d 9.00 9.00

**Souvenir Sheet**

**958** A192 8000k multi 4.50 4.50

No. 957 contains four 28x42mm stamps.

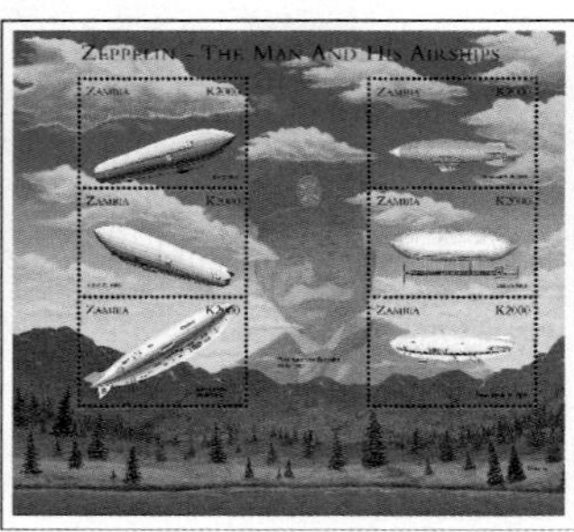


First Zeppelin Flight, Cent. — A193

No. 959: a, LZ-1. b, Parseval PL25. c, LZ-3. d, Baldwin. e, LZ-129. f, Norge Nobile N1.
No. 960, 700k, Graf Zeppelin, vert.

**2001, July 30**
**959** A193 2000k Sheet of 6, #a-f 6.75 6.75

**Souvenir Sheet**

**960** A173 700k multi .40 .40

No. 960 contains one 38x51mm stamp.

Pres. F. J. T. Chiluba — A194

Chiluba: 1000k, Recieving Master's degree. 1500k, Signing forms. 1700k, With arm raised, horiz.
6000k, Receiving Master's degree, diff.

**2001** **Litho.** ***Perf. 14***
**961-963** A194 Set of 3 2.25 2.25

**Souvenir Sheet**

**964** A194 6000k multi 3.00 3.00

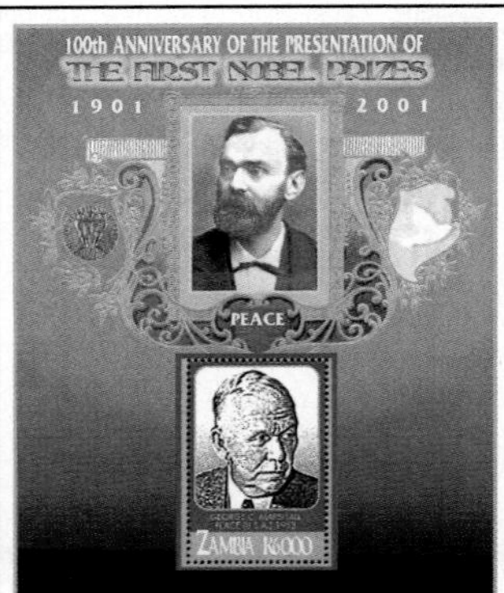


Nobel Prizes, Cent. (in 2001) — A195

No. 965, 2000k — Peace laureates: a, Norman E. Borlaug, 1970. b, Lester B. Pearson, 1957. c, Intl. Red Cross, 1944. d, Anwar Sadat, 1978. e, Georges Pire, 1958. f, Linus Pauling, 1962.
No. 966, 2000k — Literature laureates: a, Isaac Bashevis Singer, 1978. b, Gao Xingjian, 2000. c, Claude Simon, 1985. d, Naguib Mahfouz, 1988. e, Camilo Jose Cela, 1989. f, Czeslaw Milosz, 1980.
No. 967, 2000k — Literature laureates: a, Seamus Heaney, 1995. b, Toni Morrison, 1993. c, Günter Grass, 1999. d, Wislawa Szymborska, 1996. e, Dario Fo, 1997. f, José Saramago, 1998.
No. 968, 6000k, George C. Marshall, Peace, 1953. No. 969, 6000k, Gerard Debreu, Economics, 1983. No. 970, 6000k, Robert W. Fogel, Economics, 1993.

**2002, Feb. 11** **Litho.** ***Perf. 14***

**Sheets of 6, #a-f**

**965-967** A195 Set of 3 16.00 16.00

**Souvenir Sheets**

**968-970** A195 Set of 3 8.25 8.25

Souvenir Sheet

New Year 2002 (Year of the Horse) — A196

**2002, Feb. 18** ***Perf. 13¼***
**971** A196 5000k multi 2.40 2.40

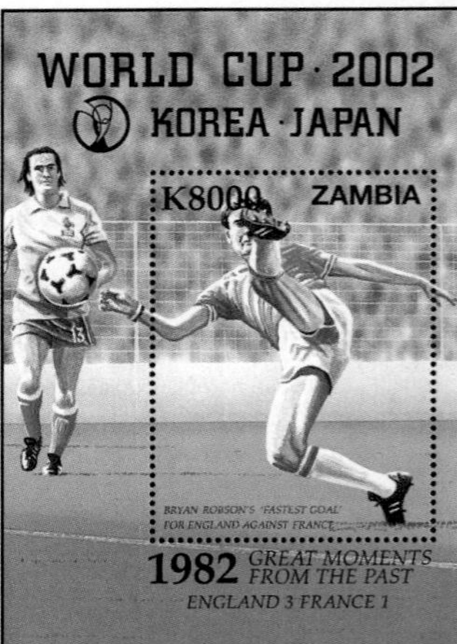


2002 World Cup Soccer Championships, Japan and Korea — A197

No. 972, 2000k: a, Poster from 1954 World Cup, Switzerland. b, Stanly Matthews and English flag. c, Scottish player and flag. d, Belgian player and flag. e, Player and Daejon World Cup Stadium, Korea, horiz.
No. 973, 2000k: a, Ferenc Puskas and Hungarian flag. b, Poster from 1962 World Cup, Chile. c, Spanish player and flag. d, English player and flag. e, Player and Jeonju World Cup Stadium, Korea, horiz.
No. 974, 8000k, Bryan Robson's goal against France, 1982. No. 975, 8000k, Salenko's fifth goal against Cameroon, 1994, horiz.

**2002, Feb. 26** ***Perf. 14***

**Sheets of 5, #a-e**

**972-973** A197 Set of 2 8.75 8.75

**Souvenir Sheets**

**974-975** A197 Set of 2 7.00 7.00

Size of Nos. 972a-972d, 973a-973d: 28x42mm.

United We Stand — A198

**2002, Feb.** ***Perf. 13½x13¼***
**976** A198 3200k multi 1.40 1.40

Issued in sheets of 4.

Reign of Queen Elizabeth, 50th Anniv. — A199

No. 977: a, Wearing blue and white hat. b, Without hat. c, Wearing scarf. d, Wearing tiara.
7500k, With Prince Philip.

**2002, July 15 Litho. *Perf. 14¼***
**977** A199 3200k Sheet of 4, #a-d 5.75 5.75

**Souvenir Sheet**

**978** A199 7500k multi 3.50 3.50

2002 Winter Olympics, Salt Lake City A200

Designs: 1000k, Ice hockey. 3200k, Cross-country skiing.

**2002, July 30 *Perf. 13¼x13¾***
**979-980** A200 Set of 2 1.90 1.90

20th World Scout Jamboree, Thailand — A201

No. 981, horiz.: a, Troop hiking. b, Knot tying. c, Archery. d, Fire making.
8000k, Camping.

**2002, July 30 *Perf. 14***
**981** A201 3200k Sheet of 4, #a-d 5.75 5.75

**Souvenir Sheet**

**982** A201 8000k multi 3.50 3.50

Intl. Year of Mountains — A202

No. 983: a, Mt. Whitney, US. b, Mt. Aconcagua, Argentina and Chile. c, Mt. Mönch, Switzerland. d, Mt. Ararat, Turkey.
9000k, Mt. Everest, Nepal and China.

**2002, July 30**
**983** A202 1500k Sheet of 4, #a-d 2.75 2.75

**Souvenir Sheet**

**984** A202 9000k multi 4.00 4.00

Birds — A203

Designs: 700k, Bee-eater. 1200k, Blue-cheeked bee-eater. 1400k, Boehn's bee-eater. 1500k, Little bee-eater.

**2002, Aug. 12**
**985-988** A203 Set of 4 2.10 2.10

Flowers, Butterflies and Mushrooms — A204

No. 989, 2500k — Flowers: a, Camel's foot. b, Christmas bells. c, Impala lily. d, Everlasting. e, Anomatheca grandiflora. f, Soldier lily.
No. 990, 2500k — Butterflies: a, False monarch. b, Golden piper. c, Blue pansy. d, Christmas tree acraea. e, Grass yellow. f, Gold-spotted sylph.
No. 991, 2500k — Mushrooms: a, Copper trumpet. b, King bolete. c, Death cap. d, Fly agaric. e, Chanterelle. f, Deadly fiber cap.
No. 992, 8000k, Arum lily. No. 993, 8000k, African monarch butterfly. No. 994, 8000k, Stump brittle-head mushrooms.

**2002, Sept. 9 Litho.**

**Sheets of 6, #a-f**

**989-991** A204 Set of 3 20.00 20.00

**Souvenir Sheets**

**992-994** A204 Set of 3 11.00 11.00

Nos. 624, 629, 645 Surcharged

**Methods & Perfs as Before**

**2002, July 1**
**996** A128 250k on 50k #639 — —
**997** A128 300k on 50k #624 — —
**998** A130 1000k on 100k #645 — —

Numbers have been reserved for three additional surcharges. The editors would like to examine any examples.

Coronation of Queen Elizabeth II, 50th Anniv. — A205

No. 999: a, Wearing crown and pearl necklace. b, Wearing tiara and jeweled necklace. c, Wearing pink and black hat.
10,000k, Wearing flowered dress and hat.

**2003, May 19 Litho. *Perf. 14***
**999** A205 5000k Sheet of 3, #a-c 6.25 6.25

**Souvenir Sheet**

**1000** A205 10,000k multi 4.25 4.25

Prince William, 21st Birthday — A206

No. 1001: a, Wearing bow tie. b, Wearing blue shirt and tie. c, Wearing yellow and black sports shirt.
10,000k, Wearing sweater.

**2003, May 19**
**1001** A206 5000k Sheet of 3, #a-c 6.25 6.25

**Souvenir Sheet**

**1002** A206 10,000k multi 4.25 4.25

Nos. 654-657 Surcharged

Nos. 639-642 Surcharged

Nos. 617-620 Surcharged

Nos. 650-653 Surcharged

Nos. 710-712 Surcharged

**Methods & Perfs. as Before**

**2003, June 26**

| No. | Type | Surcharge | Unused | Used |
|---|---|---|---|---|
| **1003** | A133 | 1000k on 200k #654 | 22.50 | 22.50 |
| **1004** | A133 | 1000k on 300k #655 | 22.50 | 22.50 |
| **1005** | A133 | 1000k on 500k #656 | 22.50 | 22.50 |
| **1006** | A133 | 1000k on 900k #657 | 22.50 | 22.50 |
| **1007** | A128 | 1700k on 50k #639 | .70 | .70 |
| **1008** | A128 | 1700k on 200k #640 | .70 | .70 |
| **1009** | A128 | 1700k on 300k #641 | .70 | .70 |
| **1010** | A128 | 1700k on 500k #642 | .70 | .70 |
| **1011** | A125 | 1800k on 50k #617 | .75 | .75 |
| **1012** | A125 | 1800k on 200k #618 | .75 | .75 |
| **1013** | A125 | 1800k on 250k #619 | .75 | .75 |
| **1014** | A125 | 1800k on 300k #620 | .75 | .75 |
| **1015** | A132 | 2200k on 100k #650 | .90 | .90 |
| **1016** | A132 | 2200k on 300k #651 | .90 | .90 |
| **1017** | A132 | 2200k on 450k #652 | .90 | .90 |
| **1018** | A132 | 2200k on 500k #653 | .90 | .90 |
| **1019** | A145 | 2500k on 500k #710 | 1.00 | 1.00 |
| **1020** | A145 | 2500k on (O) #711 | 1.00 | 1.00 |
| **1021** | A145 | 2500k on 900k #712 | 1.00 | 1.00 |
| | | *Nos. 1003-1021 (19)* | 102.40 | 102.40 |

Location of surcharges vary on Nos. 1019-1021.

Miniature Sheet

New Year 2003 (Year of the Ram) — A207

No. 1022 — Background colors: a, Green. b, Blue violet. c, Maroon. d, Purple.

**2003, July 30 Litho. *Perf. 13¼***
**1022** A207 3200k Sheet of 4, #a-d 5.50 5.50

Intl. Year of Fresh Water — A208

No. 1023: a, Cabora Bassa Dam. b, Lake Kariba. c, Mana Pools National Park.
10,000k, Victoria Falls.

**2003, July 30 *Perf. 13½x13¼***
**1023** A208 5000k Sheet of 3, #a-c 6.50 6.50

**Souvenir Sheet**

**1024** A208 10,000k multi 4.25 4.25

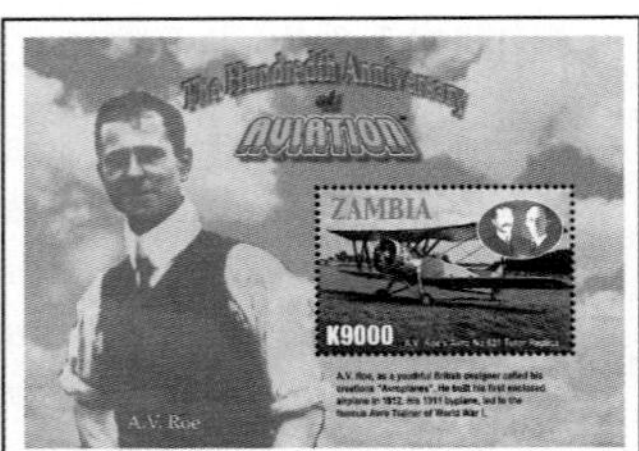


Powered Flight, Cent. — A209

No. 1025: a, Avro 547A. b, Avro 504O with floats. c, Avro 584 Avrocet. d, Avro 504M.
10,000k, Avro 621 Tutor Replica.

**2003, July 30** ***Perf. 14***

**1025** A209 4000k Sheet of 4, #a-d 6.75 6.75

**Souvenir Sheet**

**1026** A209 9000k multi 4.00 4.00

**Bird Type of 2002**

Designs: 1000k, White-fronted bee-eaters. 1200k, Little bee-eaters. 1500k, Blue-cheeked bee-eater. 1800k, Boehn's bee-eater.

**2003, Dec. 26** ***Perf. 13¼***

**Size: 25x20mm**

**1027-1030** A203 Set of 4 2.50 2.50

Rotary International in Zambia, 50th Anniv. — A210

Design: 1000k, Rotary emblem and hands.

**2003, Nov. 21** **Litho.** ***Perf. 13***

**1031** A210 1000k multi — —

**Rotary Type of 2003**

Design: 1200k, Rotary emblem.

**2003, Nov. 21** **Litho.** ***Perf. 13***

**1032** A210 1200k multi — —

Miniature Sheet

Birds — A211

No. 1033: a, 500k, African fish eagles, national bird of Zimbabwe. b, 750k, Cattle egrets, national bird of Botswana. c, 1000k, African fish eagles, national bird of Zambia. d, 1100k, Peregrine falcons, national bird of Angola. e, 1500k, Bar-tailed trogons. f, 1700k, African fish eagles, national bird of Namibia. g, 1800k, Purple-crested louries, national bird of Swaziland. h, 2200k, Blue cranes, national bird of South Africa.

**2004, Oct. 11** **Litho.** ***Perf. 14***

**1033** A211 Sheet of 8, #a-h 4.50 4.50

See Angola No. , Botswana Nos. 792-793, Malawi No. , Namibia No. 1052, South Africa No. 1342, Swaziland Nos. 727-735, and Zimbabwe No. 975.

Mammals A213

Designs: No. 1039, 2250k, Acionyx jubatus. No. 1040, 2250k, Phacochoerus aethiopicus. No. 1041, 2250k, Giraffa camelopardalis. 2700k, Syncerus caffer.

No. 1043, vert.: a, Panthera pardus. b, Pan troglodytes. c, Lycaon pictus. d, Equus burchelli.
10,000k, Diceros bicornis, vert.

**2005, June 27** **Litho.** ***Perf. 14***

**1039-1042** A213 Set of 4 4.25 4.25

**1043** A213 3300k Sheet of 4, #a-d 5.75 5.75

**Souvenir Sheet**

**1044** A213 10,000k multi 4.50 4.50

Insects — A214

Designs: 1500k, Fornasinius russus. No. 1046, 2250k, Goliathus giganteus. No. 1047, 2250k, Macrorhina. 2700k, Chelorrhina polyphemus.
No. 1048: a, Sternotomis virescens. b, Cicindela regalis. c, Goliathus meleagris. d, Mecosasms explanta.
10,000k, Meloid.

**2005, June 27**

**1045-1048** A214 Set of 4 3.75 3.75

**1049** A214 3300k Sheet of 4, #a-d 5.75 5.75

**Souvenir Sheet**

**1050** A214 10,000k multi 4.50 4.50

Butterflies — A215

Designs: No. 1051, 2250k, Ropalo ceres. No. 1052, 2250k, Morpho portis nymphalidae. No. 1053, 2250k, Phyllocnistis citrella. 2700k, H. misippus.
No. 1055: a, Colotis evippe. b, Papilio lormieri. c, Papilio dardanus. d, Papilio zalmoxis.
10,000k, Epiphora albida druce.

**2005, June 27**

**1051-1054** A215 Set of 4 4.25 4.25

**1055** A215 3300k Sheet of 4, #a-d 5.75 5.75

**Souvenir Sheet**

**1056** A215 10,000k multi 4.50 4.50

Orchids — A216

Designs: No. 1057, 1500k, Disa draconis. No. 1058, 1500k, Disa uniflora. No. 1059, 1500k, Disa uniflora orange. 2700k, Phalaenopsis penetrate.
No. 1061: a, Ansellia africana (yellow flower). b, Ansellia africana (spotted flower). c, Cattleya lueddemanniana. d, Laelia tenebrosa.
10,000k, Cymbidium.

**2005, June 27**

**1057-1060** A216 Set of 4 3.25 3.25

**1061** A216 3300k Sheet of 4, #a-d 5.75 5.75

**Souvenir Sheet**

**1062** A216 10,000k multi 4.50 4.50

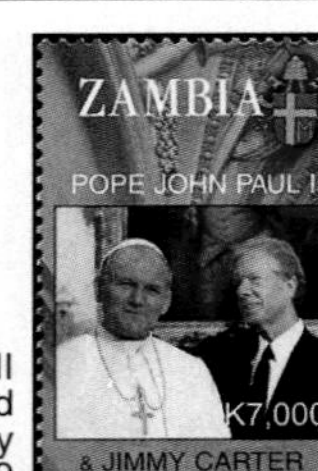
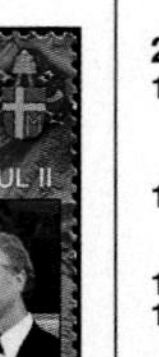


Pope John Paul II (1920-2005) and Pres. Jimmy Carter — A219

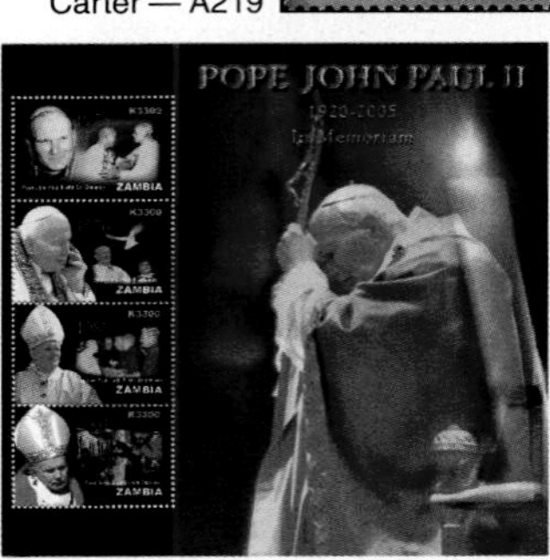


Pope John Paul II — A220

No. 1070: a, With Sri Chinmoy. b, With boy and dove. c, With Schneider brothers. d, Visiting Ukraine.

**2005, Aug. 22** **Litho.** ***Perf. 12¾***

**1069** A219 7000k multi 3.00 3.00

**1070** A220 3300k Sheet of 4, #a-d 5.75 5.75

No. 1069 was printed in sheets of 4.

A221

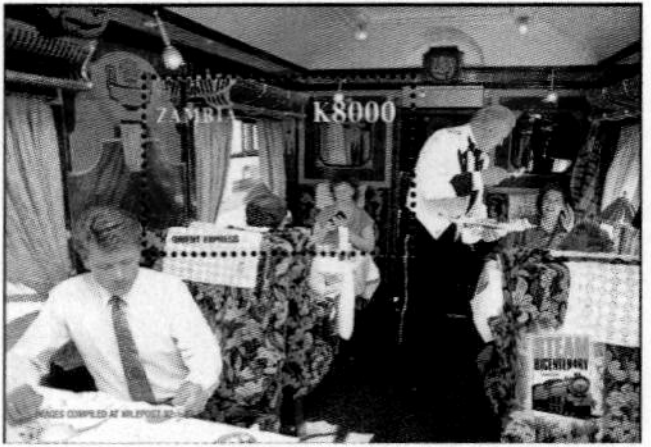


Railroads, 200th Anniv. — A222

No. 1071: a, Chinese Class KF 4-8-4. b, Indian Class WP 4-6-2. c, Irish 800 Class 4-6-0. d, French 241A Class 4-8-2.
No. 1072, 1700k: a, British Rail Class 4MT 2-6-4T. b, South African Railways Class 12A. c, Cuban sugar plantation locomotive. d, LNER A4 Pacific facing right. e, LNER A4 Pacific facing left. f, GWR City of Truro 4-4-0. g, British Rail HST Intercity 125. h, Eurostar. i, LNER A3 Flying Scotsman.
No. 1073, 1700k: a, Southern Railway King Arthur Class 4-6-0. b, Berkshire at Kaiiman's Bridge. c, Indian Railways WT Class 2-84 Suburban Tank steam locomotive. d, Ladders on shelf of railway car being built. e, Worker on knees inside railway car. f, Yellow staircase next to railway car. g, Workers looking at undercarriage of raised railway car. h, Railway car between blue machinery. i, Model of steam locomotive.
No. 1074, 1700k: a, Great Western Hall Class 4-6-0. b, Argentinian 15B Class 4-8-0. c, Mallet Meter Gauge steam locomotive. d, Worker cutting track. e, Worker and pulley. f, Workers in cherrypicker. g, Workers on tracks and in cherrypickers. h, Workers pouring cement. i, Track workers.
No. 1075, Finnish Class HV2 4-6-0.
No. 1076, 8000k, Orient Express. No. 1077, 8000k, Edinburgh to London train. No. 1078, 800k, Bernina Express.

**2005, Aug. 22**

**1071** A221 4200k Sheet of 4, #a-d 7.50 7.50

**Sheets of 9, #a-i**

**1072-1074** A222 Set of 3 20.00 20.00

**Souvenir Sheets**

**1075** A221 8000k multi 3.50 3.50

**1076-1078** A222 Set of 3 10.50 10.50

David Livingstone at Victoria Falls, 150th Anniv. A223

Designs: 1500k, Livingstone, Victoria Falls. 2700k, Statue of Livingstone, railroad bridge.

**2006, Jan. 20** **Litho.** ***Perf. 13x13¼***

**1079-1080** A223 Set of 2 2.60 2.60

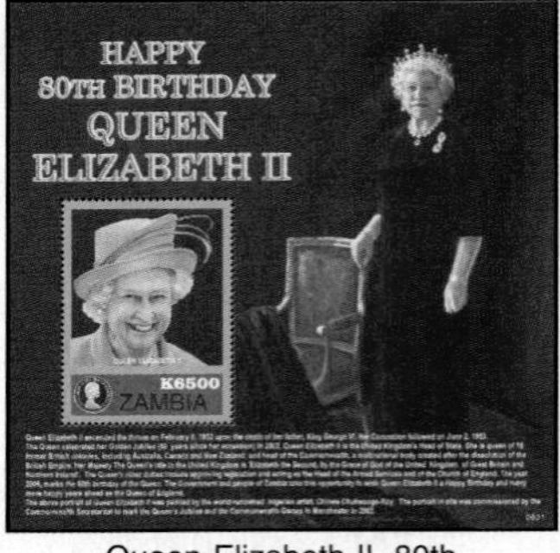


Queen Elizabeth II, 80th Birthday — A225

No. 1085 — Queen: a, Wearing crown. b, Wearing necklace. c, Wearing necklace and jacket. d, With Princess Anne.
6500k, Wearing green hat.

**2006, Aug. 8** **Litho.** ***Perf. 13¼***

**1085** A225 3200k Sheet of 4, #a-d 6.50 6.50

**Souvenir Sheet**

**1086** A225 6500k multi 3.25 3.25

Scouting, Cent. (in 2007) — A226

No. 1087, vert. — Scouting emblem, doves, Lord Robert Baden-Powell and background colors of: a, Pink and lilac. b, Yellow and orange. c, Blue and light blue. d, Light green and green.
6500k, Purple and red.

**2006, Aug. 8**

**1087** A226 3200k Sheet of 4, #a-d 6.50 6.50

**Souvenir Sheet**

**1088** A226 6500k multi 3.25 3.25

## POSTAGE DUE STAMPS

Type of Northern Rhodesia

***Perf. 12½***

**1964, Oct. 24** **Litho.** **Unwmk.**

| | | | | |
|---|---|---|---|---|
| **J1** | D1 | 1p orange | .20 | .20 |
| **J2** | D1 | 2p dark blue | .20 | .20 |
| **J3** | D1 | 3p rose claret | .25 | .25 |
| **J4** | D1 | 4p violet blue | .35 | .35 |
| **J5** | D1 | 6p purple | .50 | .50 |
| **J6** | D1 | 1sh emerald | 1.50 | 1.50 |
| | | *Nos. J1-J6 (6)* | 3.00 | 3.00 |

# ZANZIBAR

'zan-zə-ˌbär

LOCATION — Group of islands about twenty miles off the coast of Tanganyika in East Africa
GOVT. — Republic
AREA — 1,044 sq. mi. (approx.)
POP. — 354,360 (est. 1967)
CAPITAL — Zanzibar

Before 1895, unoverprinted stamps of India were used in Zanzibar.

Zanzibar was a British protectorate until Dec. 10, 1963, when it became independent. After a revolt in January, 1964, a republic was established. Zanzibar joined Tanganyika Apr. 26, 1964, to form the United Republic of Tanganyika and Zanzibar (later renamed Tanzania). See Tanzania.

12 Pies = 1 Anna
16 Annas = 1 Rupee
100 Cents = 1 Rupee (1908)
100 Cents = 1 Shilling (1935)

**Catalogue values for unused stamps in this country are for Never Hinged items, beginning with Scott 201 in the regular postage section and Scott J18 in the postage due section.**

### Watermarks

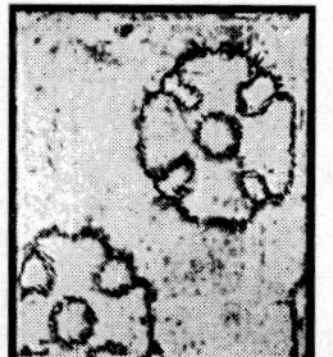

Wmk. 47 — Multiple Rosette

Wmk. 71 — Rosette

Stamps of British India Overprinted

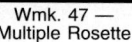

On Stamps of 1882-95

**1895 Wmk. Star (39) *Perf. 14***

**Blue Overprint**

| | | | | |
|---|---|---|---|---|
| **1** | A17 | ½a green | *15,000.* | *4,500.* |
| **2** | A19 | 1a violet brown | 2,600. | 575. |
| *a.* | | "Zanzidar" | | *17,500.* |

**1895-96**

**Black Overprint**

| | | | | |
|---|---|---|---|---|
| **3** | A17 | ½a green | 4.75 | 4.00 |
| *a.* | | "Zanzidar" | 1,350. | 725.00 |
| *b.* | | "Zanibar" | 1,350. | *1,800.* |
| *c.* | | "Zapzibar" | | |
| **4** | A19 | 1a violet brn | 4.50 | 4.00 |
| *a.* | | "Zanzidar" | — | *3,250.* |
| *b.* | | "Zanibar" | 1,750. | 2,000. |
| **5** | A20 | 1a6p bister brn | 5.25 | 3.75 |
| *a.* | | "Zanzidar" | 3,750. | 1,100. |
| *b.* | | "Zanizbar" | 1,750. | |
| *c.* | | "Zanibar" | 1,600. | 1,750. |
| *d.* | | "Zapzibar" | | |
| **6** | A21 | 2a ultra | 5.50 | 5.25 |
| *a.* | | "Zanzidar" | 4,250. | 2,100. |
| *b.* | | "Zanibar" | 4,250. | 2,100. |
| *c.* | | "Zapzibar" | | |
| *d.* | | Double overprint | 280.00 | |
| **7** | A28 | 2a6p green | 8.50 | 5.50 |
| *a.* | | "Zanzidar" | 3,750. | 1,800. |
| *b.* | | "Zanibar" | 700.00 | *1,250.* |
| *c.* | | "Zapzibar" | | |
| *d.* | | "Zanzipar" | 1,250. | |
| **8** | A22 | 3a orange | 12.50 | 11.00 |
| *a.* | | "Zanzidar" | 850.00 | *1,600.* |
| *b.* | | "Zanizbar" | 4,000. | *4,500.* |
| **9** | A23 | 4a olive grn | 12.50 | 15.00 |
| *a.* | | "Zanzidar" | 7,000. | 4,250. |
| **10** | A25 | 8a red vio | 18.00 | 24.00 |
| *a.* | | "Zanzidar" | 7,000. | 7,000. |
| **11** | A26 | 12a vio, *red* | 18.00 | 11.50 |
| *a.* | | "Zanzidar" | 6,250. | 4,250. |
| **12** | A27 | 1r gray | 85.00 | 80.00 |
| *a.* | | "Zanzidar" | 6,250. | 4,750. |
| **13** | A29 | 1r car rose & grn | 18.00 | *27.50* |
| *a.* | | Vertical overprint | 475.00 | |
| **14** | A30 | 2r brn & rose | 62.50 | *90.00* |
| *a.* | | "Zanziba" | 8,500. | 4,750. |
| *b.* | | Inverted "r" | 4,250. | 4,250. |
| *c.* | | Pair, one without overprint | | |
| **15** | A30 | 3r grn & brn | 55.00 | *67.50* |
| *a.* | | "Zanziba" | 8,500. | |
| *b.* | | Inverted "r" | 4,250. | 4,500. |
| **16** | A30 | 5r vio & blue | 62.50 | *85.00* |
| *a.* | | "Zanziba" | 8,500. | |
| *b.* | | Inverted "r" | 3,750. | *4,500.* |
| *c.* | | Dbl. ovpt., one invtd. | 950.00 | |

On Stamp of 1873-76

**Wmk. Elephant's Head (38)**

| | | | | |
|---|---|---|---|---|
| **17** | A14 | 6a bister | 21.00 | 12.50 |
| *a.* | | "Zanzidar" | 7,000. | 4,000. |
| *b.* | | "Zanzibarr" | *4,250.* | *4,000.* |
| *c.* | | "Zanibar" | 725.00 | *1,400.* |
| *d.* | | "Zapzibar" | | |
| *e.* | | Double overprint | 160.00 | |
| | | *Nos. 3-17 (15)* | 393.50 | 446.50 |

Nos. 4-6 Surcharged:

a

b

c

d

e

2½

f

**1896 Wmk. Star (39)**

**Black Surcharge**

| | | | | |
|---|---|---|---|---|
| **18** | (a) | 2½a on 1a | *175.00* | *110.00* |
| **19** | (b) | 2½a on 1a | *450.00* | *350.00* |
| **20** | (c) | 2½a on 1a | *180.00* | *125.00* |

**Red Surcharge**

| | | | | |
|---|---|---|---|---|
| **21** | (a) | 2½a on 1a | *260.00* | *675.00* |
| **22** | (b) | 2½a on 1a | *500.00* | *1,000.* |
| **23** | (c) | 2½a on 1a | *275.00* | *675.00* |
| **24** | (a) | 2½a on 1a6p | *60.00* | *50.00* |
| *a.* | | "Zanzidar" | *1,600.* | *1,400.* |
| *b.* | | "Zanizbar" | *4,250.* | *2,250.* |
| **24C** | (b) | 2½a on 1a6p | *210.00* | *500.00* |
| **25** | (c) | 2½a on 1a6p | *130.00* | *275.00* |
| **26** | (d) | 2½a on 1a6p | *150.00* | *125.00* |
| **27** | (e) | 2½a on 1a6p | *425.00* | *400.00* |
| **27A** | (f) | 2½a on 1a6p | *13,500.* | *9,000.* |
| **28** | (a) | 2½a on 2a | *110.00* | *275.00* |
| **28A** | (b) | 2½a on 2a | *225.00* | *525.00* |
| **29** | (c) | 2½a on 2a | *125.00* | *350.00* |
| **30** | (d) | 2½a on 2a | *65.00* | *35.00* |
| **31** | (e) | 2½a on 2a | *200.00* | *125.00* |
| **31A** | (f) | 2½a on 2a | *5,000.* | *2,250.* |

Certain type varieties are found in the word "Zanzibar" on Nos. 1 to 31A viz: Inverted "q" for "b," broken "p" for "n," "i" without dot, small second "z" and tall second "z." These varieties are found on all values from ½a to 1r inclusive and the tall "z" is also found on the 2r, 3r and 5r.

Stamps of British East Africa, 1896, Overprinted in Black or Red

**1896 Wmk. Crown and C A (2)**

| | | | | |
|---|---|---|---|---|
| **32** | A8 | ½a yellow grn | 35.00 | 20.00 |
| **33** | A8 | 1a carmine | 30.00 | 18.00 |
| **34** | A8 | 2½a dk blue (R) | 85.00 | 50.00 |
| **35** | A8 | 4½a orange | 50.00 | 57.50 |
| **36** | A8 | 5a dark ocher | 57.50 | 37.50 |
| **37** | A8 | 7½a lilac | 42.50 | 57.50 |
| | | *Nos. 32-37 (6)* | 300.00 | 240.50 |

A2

Sultan Seyyid Hamed-bin-Thwain
A3

**1896, Sept. 20 Engr. Wmk. 71**

| | | | | |
|---|---|---|---|---|
| **38** | A2 | ½a yel grn & red | 4.50 | 2.00 |
| **39** | A2 | 1a indigo & red | 3.00 | 1.75 |
| **40** | A2 | 2a red brn & red | 3.25 | .85 |
| **41** | A2 | 2½a ultra & red | 12.50 | 1.60 |
| **42** | A2 | 3a slate & red | 10.50 | 5.75 |
| **43** | A2 | 4a dk green & red | 7.25 | 3.00 |
| **44** | A2 | 4½a orange & red | 5.25 | 5.50 |
| **45** | A2 | 5a bister & red | 5.00 | 2.75 |
| *a.* | | Half used as 2½a on cover | | *3,750.* |
| **46** | A2 | 7½a lilac & red | 4.00 | 3.00 |
| **47** | A2 | 8a ol gray & red | 11.00 | 8.00 |
| **48** | A3 | 1r ultra & red | 15.00 | 11.00 |
| **49** | A3 | 2r green & red | 26.00 | 11.00 |
| **50** | A3 | 3r violet & red | 26.00 | 11.00 |
| **51** | A3 | 4r lake & red | 21.00 | 18.00 |
| **52** | A3 | 5r blk brn & red | 27.50 | 18.00 |
| | | *Nos. 38-52 (15)* | 181.75 | 103.20 |

No. 43 Surcharged in Red

**1897**

| | | | | |
|---|---|---|---|---|
| **53** | A2 (a) | 2½a on 4a | 67.50 | *45.00* |
| **54** | A2 (b) | 2½a on 4a | 225.00 | *200.00* |
| **55** | A2 (c) | 2½a on 4a | 85.00 | *57.50* |
| | | *Nos. 53-55 (3)* | 377.50 | *302.50* |

**1898 Engr. Wmk. 47**

| | | | | |
|---|---|---|---|---|
| **56** | A2 | ½a yel grn & red | 1.75 | .40 |
| **57** | A2 | 1a indigo & red | 2.50 | .60 |
| **58** | A2 | 2a red brn & red | 4.50 | 2.00 |
| **58A** | A2 | 2½a ultra & red | 3.25 | .35 |
| **59** | A2 | 3a slate & red | 6.25 | .65 |
| **60** | A2 | 4a dk grn & red | 3.75 | 1.10 |
| **60A** | A2 | 4½a orange & red | 8.00 | 1.25 |
| **61** | A2 | 5a bister & red | 16.00 | 2.00 |
| **61A** | A2 | 7½a lilac & red | 9.50 | 3.00 |
| **61B** | A2 | 8a ol gray & red | 13.50 | 2.50 |
| | | *Nos. 56-61B (10)* | 69.00 | 13.85 |

Sultan Seyyid Hamoud-bin-Mahommed-bin-Said
A4 A5

**1899-1901**

| | | | | |
|---|---|---|---|---|
| **62** | A4 | ½a yel grn & red | 2.25 | .65 |
| **63** | A4 | 1a indigo & red | 5.00 | .25 |
| **64** | A4 | 1a car & red ('01) | 2.25 | .25 |
| **65** | A4 | 2a red brn & red | 2.50 | .55 |
| **66** | A4 | 2½a ultra & red | 2.50 | .65 |
| **67** | A4 | 3a slate & red | 3.25 | 2.50 |
| **68** | A4 | 4a dk green & red | 3.75 | 1.60 |
| **69** | A4 | 4½a orange & red | 14.00 | 4.00 |
| **70** | A4 | 4½a ind & red ('01) | 16.00 | 13.50 |
| **71** | A4 | 5a bister & red | 3.50 | 1.40 |
| **72** | A4 | 7½a lilac & red | 3.75 | *4.25* |
| **73** | A4 | 8a ol gray & red | 3.75 | *5.00* |

**Wmk. 71**

| | | | | |
|---|---|---|---|---|
| **74** | A5 | 1r ultra & red | 21.00 | 17.50 |
| **75** | A5 | 2r green & red | 21.00 | 21.00 |
| **76** | A5 | 3r violet & red | 35.00 | *40.00* |
| **77** | A5 | 4r lilac rose & red | 55.00 | *62.50* |
| **78** | A5 | 5r gray brown & red | 62.50 | *75.00* |
| | | *Nos. 62-78 (17)* | 257.00 | *250.60* |

For surcharges see Nos. 94-98.

Monogram of Sultan Ali bin Hamoud
A6 A7

**1904, June 8 Typo. Wmk. 47**

| | | | | |
|---|---|---|---|---|
| **79** | A6 | ½a emerald | 1.75 | 1.00 |
| **80** | A6 | 1a rose red | 1.75 | .20 |
| **81** | A6 | 2a bister brown | 2.00 | .50 |
| **82** | A6 | 2½a ultra | 3.00 | .40 |
| **83** | A6 | 3a gray | 3.00 | 2.50 |
| **84** | A6 | 4a blue green | 2.75 | 1.75 |
| **85** | A6 | 4½a black | 3.75 | 2.75 |
| **86** | A6 | 5a ocher | 4.25 | 1.40 |
| **87** | A6 | 7½a violet | 5.25 | *8.00* |
| **88** | A6 | 8a olive green | 4.75 | 3.00 |
| **89** | A7 | 1r ultra & red | 24.00 | 14.00 |
| **90** | A7 | 2r green & red | 27.00 | *42.50* |
| **91** | A7 | 3r violet & red | 50.00 | *85.00* |
| **92** | A7 | 4r magenta & red | 55.00 | *100.00* |
| **93** | A7 | 5r olive & red | 55.00 | *110.00* |
| | | *Nos. 79-93 (15)* | 243.25 | *373.00* |

Nos. 69-70, 72-73 Surcharged in Black or Lake:

g

h

i

**1904**

| | | | | |
|---|---|---|---|---|
| **94** | A4 (g) | 1a on 4½a | 4.75 | *5.25* |
| **95** | A4 (g) | 1a on 4½a (L) | 5.25 | *21.00* |
| **96** | A4 (h) | 2a on 4a (L) | 16.00 | *21.00* |
| **97** | A4 (i) | 2½a on 7½a | 15.00 | *22.50* |
| *a.* | | "Hlaf" | 12,500. | |
| **98** | A4 (i) | 2½a on 8a | 19.00 | *35.00* |
| *a.* | | "Hlaf" | 11,500. | *9,000.* |
| | | *Nos. 94-98 (5)* | 60.00 | *104.75* |

Sultan Ali bin Hamoud
A8 A9

A10

Palace of the Sultan — A11

**1908-09 Engr. Wmk. 47**

| | | | | |
|---|---|---|---|---|
| **99** | A8 | 1c gray ('09) | 2.50 | .35 |
| **100** | A8 | 3c yellow grn | 6.75 | .20 |
| **101** | A8 | 6c carmine | 10.50 | .20 |
| **102** | A8 | 10c org brn ('09) | 2.75 | 2.25 |
| **103** | A8 | 12c violet | 16.00 | 3.50 |
| **104** | A9 | 15c ultra | 14.00 | .45 |
| **105** | A9 | 25c brown | 4.25 | 1.10 |
| **106** | A9 | 50c dp green | 6.75 | 4.75 |
| **107** | A9 | 75c slate ('09) | 11.50 | *14.00* |
| **108** | A10 | 1r yellow green | 27.50 | 14.00 |
| **109** | A10 | 2r violet | 21.00 | 16.00 |
| **110** | A10 | 3r yellow brown | 27.50 | *52.50* |
| **111** | A10 | 4r red | 50.00 | *85.00* |
| **112** | A10 | 5r blue | 45.00 | *62.50* |
| **113** | A11 | 10r brn & dk grn | 160.00 | *280.00* |
| **114** | A11 | 20r yel grn & blk | 350.00 | *500.00* |
| **115** | A11 | 30r dk brn & blk | 375.00 | *675.00* |
| **116** | A11 | 40r org brn & blk | 525.00 | |
| **117** | A11 | 50r lilac & blk | 450.00 | |
| **118** | A11 | 100r blue & blk | 750.00 | |
| **119** | A11 | 200r black & brn | 1,150. | |
| | | *Nos. 99-112 (14)* | 246.00 | *256.80* |

It is probable that Nos. 118 and 119 were used only for fiscal purposes.

Sultan Khalifa bin Harub — A12

Dhow — A13

Dhow — A14

**1913** **Perf. 14**
120 A12 1c gray .45 .20
121 A12 3c yellow grn .55 .20
122 A12 6c carmine 1.75 .20
123 A12 10c brown 1.25 2.10
124 A12 12c violet 1.10 .20
125 A12 15c ultra 1.40 .35
126 A12 25c black brn 1.10 1.10
127 A12 50c dk green 2.25 4.50
128 A12 75c dk gray 2.25 3.00
129 A13 1r yellow grn 8.00 10.00
130 A13 2r dk violet 12.50 27.50
131 A13 3r orange 15.00 45.00
132 A13 4r red 30.00 72.50
133 A13 5r blue 40.00 40.00
134 A14 10r brown & grn 125.00 210.00
135 A14 20r yel grn & blk 175.00 400.00
136 A14 30r dk brn & blk 190.00 475.00
137 A14 40r orange & blk 400.00 675.00
138 A14 50r dull vio & blk 375.00 675.00
139 A14 100r blue & blk 450.00
140 A14 200r black & brn 725.00
*Nos. 120-134 (15)* 242.60 416.85

**1914-22** **Wmk. 3**
141 A12 1c gray .90 .30
142 A12 3c yellow grn 1.40 .20
143 A12 6c carmine .95 .20
144 A12 8c vio, *yel* ('22) .85 4.00
145 A12 10c dk grn, *yel* ('22) .85 .40
146 A12 15c ultra 1.25 5.75
148 A12 50c dark green 5.00 4.75
149 A12 75c deep gray 3.50 26.00
150 A13 1r yellow grn 4.50 4.00
151 A13 2r dark violet 5.75 9.00
152 A13 3r brown org 18.00 37.50
153 A13 4r red 18.00 95.00
154 A13 5r blue 18.00 72.50
155 A14 10r brown & grn 125.00 450.00
*Nos. 141-155 (14)* 203.95 709.60

**1921-29** **Wmk. 4**
156 A12 1c gray .20 8.00
157 A12 3c yellow grn .55 3.75
158 A12 3c orange ('22) .35 .20
159 A12 4c green ('22) .55 .55
160 A12 6c carmine .35 .55
161 A12 6c vio, *bl* ('22) .45 .20
162 A12 10c lt brown .80 9.50
163 A12 12c violet .50 .35
164 A12 12c carmine ('22) .50 .50
165 A12 15c ultra .70 9.50
166 A12 20c dk blue ('22) 1.10 .40
167 A12 25c black brn .85 11.50
168 A12 50c blue green 1.40 4.25
169 A12 75c dark gray 2.75 57.50
170 A13 1r yellow grn 4.75 4.00
171 A13 2r dk violet 3.75 9.50
172 A13 3r ocher 4.75 8.50
173 A13 4r red 14.00 40.00
174 A13 5r blue 22.50 72.50
175 A14 10r brown & grn 110.00 275.00
176 A14 20r green & blk 225.00 450.00
177 A14 30r dk brn & blk ('29) 210.00 575.00
*Nos. 156-175 (20)* 170.80 516.25

Sultan Khalifa bin Harub ("CENTS" with Serifs) — A15

**1926-27**
184 A15 1c brown .65 .20
185 A15 3c yellow org .20 .20
186 A15 4c deep green .25 .35
187 A15 6c dark violet .35 .20
188 A15 8c slate 1.10 5.00
189 A15 10c olive green 1.10 .45
190 A15 12c deep red 1.60 .20
191 A15 20c ultra .60 .35
192 A15 25c violet, *yel* 4.75 2.75
193 A15 50c claret 2.00 .40
194 A15 75c olive brown 28.00 25.00
*Nos. 184-194 (11)* 40.60 35.10

**Catalogue values for unused stamps in this section, from this point to the end of the section, are for Never Hinged items.**

"CENTS" without Serifs — A16

Dhow — A17

Dhow — A18

**1936** **Perf. 14**
201 A16 5c deep green .20 .20
202 A16 10c black .20 .20
203 A16 15c carmine .30 .20
204 A16 20c brown org .20 .20
205 A16 25c violet, *yel* .20 .20
206 A16 30c ultra .25 .20
207 A16 40c black brown .25 .20
208 A16 50c claret .40 .20
209 A17 1sh yellow grn .65 .20
210 A17 2sh dark violet 1.25 2.00
211 A17 5sh red 17.50 6.75
212 A17 7.50sh blue 28.50 28.00
213 A18 10sh brn & grn 32.50 25.00
*Nos. 201-213 (13)* 82.40 63.55

For overprints see Nos. 222-223.

A19

A20

**1936, Dec. 9**
214 A19 10c olive grn & blk 3.00 .30
215 A19 20c red violet & blk 5.00 1.10
216 A19 30c deep ultra & blk 13.00 .75
217 A19 50c red orange & blk 13.50 4.50
*Nos. 214-217 (4)* 34.50 6.65

Reign of Sultan Khalifa bin Harub, 25th anniv.

**Perf. 14**
**1944, Nov. 20** **Engr.** **Wmk. 4**

Dhow & Map Showing Zanzibar & Muscat.

218 A20 10c violet blue .85 2.75
219 A20 20c brown orange .90 3.50
220 A20 50c Prus green .90 .35
221 A20 1sh dull purple .90 .75
*Nos. 218-221 (4)* 3.55 7.35

200th anniv. of the Al Busaid Dynasty.

Nos. 202 and 206 Overprinted in Red

**1946, Nov. 11**
222 A16 10c black .20 .20
223 A16 30c ultra .30 .30

Victory of the Allied Nations in WW II.

Common Design Types pictured following the introduction.

### Silver Wedding Issue
Common Design Types

**1949, Jan. 10** **Photo.** ***Perf. 14x14½***
224 CD304 20c orange .60 .60

**Engraved; Name Typographed**
***Perf. 11½x11***
225 CD305 10sh light brown 21.00 30.00

### UPU Issue
Common Design Types
**Engr.; Name Typo. on 30c, 50c**
***Perf. 13½, 11x11½***

**1949, Oct. 10** **Wmk. 4**
226 CD306 20c red orange .35 2.50
227 CD307 30c indigo 2.00 1.00
228 CD308 50c red lilac 1.25 2.00
229 CD309 1sh blue green 1.25 3.50
*Nos. 226-229 (4)* 4.85 9.00

Sultan Khalifa bin Harub — A21

Seyyid Khalifa Schools A22

***Perf. 12x12½, 13x12½***
**1952, Aug. 26** **Engr.**
230 A21 5c black .20 .20
231 A21 10c red orange .20 .20
232 A21 15c green .75 2.25
233 A21 20c carmine .55 .20
234 A21 25c plum 1.10 .20
235 A21 30c blue green 1.10 .20
236 A21 35c ultra .70 3.50
237 A21 40c chocolate .70 1.25
238 A21 50c purple 2.50 .20
239 A22 1sh choc & bl grn .65 .20
240 A22 2sh claret & ultra 2.50 2.75
241 A22 5sh carmine & blk 2.50 4.00
242 A22 7.50sh emer & gray 22.50 24.00
243 A22 10sh gray blk & rose red 12.00 13.00
*Nos. 230-243 (14)* 47.95 52.15

Sultan Khalifa bin Harub — A23

**1954, Aug. 26** ***Perf. 12½x12***
244 A23 15c green .20 .20
245 A23 20c scarlet .20 .20
246 A23 30c ultra .20 .20
247 A23 50c purple .30 .30
248 A23 1.25sh brown orange .75 .75
*Nos. 244-248 (5)* 1.65 1.65

The frames differ on Nos. 245 and 247. Sultan Khalifa bin Harub, 75th birth anniv.

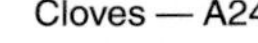
Cloves — A24

Sultan's Barge — A26

Dhows A25

Malindi Minaret Mosque — A27

Kibweni Palace — A28

Sultan Khalifa bin Harub and: 25c, 35c, and 50c Map showing location of Zanzibar. 1sh, 2sh, Dimbani Mosque.

***Perf. 11½ (A24), 11x11½ (A25), 14x13½ (A26), 13½x14 (A27), 13x13½ (A28)***

**1957, Aug. 26** **Engr.** **Wmk. 314**
249 A24 5c dull grn & org .20 .20
250 A24 10c rose car & brt grn .20 .20
251 A25 15c dk brn & grn .20 2.50
252 A26 20c ultra .20 .20
253 A26 25c blk & brn org .20 1.00
254 A25 30c int blk & rose car .20 1.00
255 A26 35c brt grn & ind .20 .20
256 A27 40c int blk & redsh brn .20 .20
257 A26 50c dull grn & bl .30 .30
258 A27 1sh int blk & brt car .30 .30
259 A25 1.25sh rose car & dk grn 4.00 .45
260 A27 2sh dull grn & org 4.00 2.50
261 A28 5sh ultra 5.75 2.25
262 A28 7.50sh green 9.00 4.50
263 A28 10sh rose carmine 10.00 7.00
*Nos. 249-263 (15)* 34.95 22.80

Sultan Seyyid Abdulla bin Khalifa — A29

Designs as before with portrait of Sultan Seyyid Abdulla bin Khalifa.

***Perf. 11½ (A29), 11x11½ (A25), 14x13½ (A26), 13½x14 (A27)***

**1961, Oct. 17** **Engr.** **Wmk. 314**
264 A29 5c dull grn & org .20 .20
265 A29 10c rose car & brt grn .20 .20
266 A25 15c dk brn & grn .80 2.75
267 A26 20c ultra .35 .35
268 A26 25c blk & brn org .65 .55
269 A25 30c int blk & rose car 3.25 1.00
270 A26 35c brt grn & indigo 2.75 3.50
271 A27 40c int blk & redsh brn .35 .20
272 A26 50c dull grn & bl 1.25 .20
273 A27 1sh int blk & brt car .45 1.10
274 A25 1.25sh rose car & dk grn 2.75 3.75
275 A27 2sh dull grn & org .65 3.75

***Perf. 13x13½***
276 A28 5sh ultra 3.50 8.00
277 A28 7.50sh green 3.75 17.50
278 A28 10sh rose carmine 3.75 6.00
279 A28 20sh dk brown 19.00 30.00
*Nos. 264-279 (16)* 43.65 79.05

For overprints see Nos. 285-300.

### Freedom from Hunger Issue
Common Design Type with Portrait of Sultan Seyyid Abdulla bin Khalifa

**1963, June 4** **Photo.** ***Perf. 14x14½***
280 CD314 1.30sh sepia 1.40 .80

### Independent State

Sultan Seyyid Jamshid bin Abdulla and Zanzibar Clove — A30

Designs: 50c, "To Prosperity," arch and sun. 1.30sh, "Religious Tolerance," composite view of churches and mosques, horiz. 2.50sh, "Towards the Light," Mangapwani Cave.

*Perf. 12½*

**1963, Dec. 10 Photo. Unwmk.**

| | | | | |
|---|---|---|---|---|
| **281** | A30 | 30c multicolored | .20 | .20 |
| **282** | A30 | 50c multicolored | .30 | .30 |
| **283** | A30 | 1.30sh multicolored | .40 | *2.00* |
| **284** | A30 | 2.50sh multicolored | .50 | *2.00* |
| | | *Nos. 281-284 (4)* | 1.40 | *4.50* |

Zanzibar's independence, Dec. 10, 1963.
For overprints see Nos. 301-304.

### Republic

Nos. 264-279 Overprinted

**1964, Feb. 28 As Before**

| | | | | |
|---|---|---|---|---|
| **285** | A29 | 5c dull grn & org | .20 | .20 |
| **286** | A29 | 10c rose car & brt grn | .20 | .20 |
| **287** | A25 | 15c dk brn & grn | .20 | .20 |
| **288** | A26 | 20c ultra | .20 | .20 |
| **289** | A26 | 25c blk & brn org | .20 | .20 |
| **290** | A25 | 30c int blk & rose car | .20 | .20 |
| **291** | A26 | 35c brt grn & ind | .20 | .20 |
| **292** | A27 | 40c int blk & redsh brn | .20 | .20 |
| **293** | A26 | 50c dull grn & blue | .20 | .20 |
| **294** | A27 | 1sh int blk & brt car | .20 | .20 |
| **295** | A25 | 1.25sh rose car & dk grn | 1.60 | .20 |
| **296** | A27 | 2sh dull grn & org | .55 | .35 |
| **297** | A28 | 5sh ultra | .75 | .50 |
| **298** | A28 | 7.50sh green | 2.25 | 1.90 |
| **299** | A28 | 10sh rose carmine | 2.25 | 1.90 |
| **300** | A28 | 20sh dark brown | 3.50 | *6.00* |
| | | *Nos. 285-300 (16)* | 12.90 | *12.85* |

The overprint was applied in England. It is in 2 lines on 40c and 1sh to 20sh. "Jamhuri" means "republic."

### Overprint Handstamped

| | | | | |
|---|---|---|---|---|
| *285a* | A29 | 5c | .25 | .25 |
| *286a* | A29 | 10c | .25 | .25 |
| *287a* | A25 | 15c | .25 | .25 |
| *288a* | A26 | 20c | .25 | .25 |
| *289a* | A26 | 25c | .25 | .25 |
| *290a* | A25 | 30c | .25 | .25 |
| *291a* | A26 | 35c | .25 | .25 |
| *292a* | A27 | 40c | .25 | .25 |
| *293a* | A26 | 50c | .25 | .25 |
| *294a* | A27 | 1sh | .25 | .25 |
| *295a* | A25 | 1.25sh | .30 | .30 |
| *296a* | A27 | 2sh | 1.50 | 1.50 |
| *297a* | A28 | 5sh | 3.50 | 3.50 |
| *298a* | A28 | 7.50sh | 6.00 | 6.00 |
| *299a* | A28 | 10sh | 6.50 | 6.50 |
| *300a* | A28 | 20sh | 8.00 | 8.00 |
| | | *Nos. 285a-300a (16)* | 28.30 | 28.30 |

This overprint was applied locally. It has one line of serifed letters. These are found diagonal, vertical, horizontal, double and inverted. See Nos. 301a-304b. Other stamps with this overprint, including postage dues, were unofficial.

Nos. 281-284 Overprinted

**1964, Feb. 28 As Before**

| | | | | |
|---|---|---|---|---|
| **301** | A30 | 30c multi | .20 | .20 |
| **302** | A30 | 50c multi | .30 | .30 |
| **303** | A30 | 1.30sh multi | .45 | .45 |
| **304** | A30 | 2.50sh multi | .75 | .75 |
| *a.* | | Green omitted | 60.00 | |
| | | *Nos. 301-304 (4)* | 1.70 | 1.70 |

One-line overprint on 1.30sh.

### Overprint Handstamped

| | | | | |
|---|---|---|---|---|
| *301a* | A30 | 30c | .20 | .20 |
| *302a* | A30 | 50c | .30 | .30 |
| *303a* | A30 | 1.30sh | .45 | .45 |
| *304b* | A30 | 2.50sh | .75 | .75 |
| | | *Nos. 301a-304b (4)* | 1.70 | 1.70 |

See note after No. 300a.

Moorish Arch, Ax, Sword and Spear — A31

Designs: 10c, 20c, Arch and arrow piercing chain. 25c, 40c, Man with rifle. 30c, 50c, Man breaking chain. 1sh, Man, flag and sun. 1.30sh, Hands breaking chain and cloves, horiz. 2sh, Hands waving flag, horiz. 5sh, Map of Zanzibar and Pemba and flag, horiz. 10sh, Flag and map of Zanzibar and Pemba. 20sh, Flag of Zanzibar, horiz

*Perf. 13x13½, 13½x13*

**1964, June 21 Litho. Unwmk.**

| | | | | |
|---|---|---|---|---|
| **305** | A31 | 5c multicolored | .20 | .20 |
| **306** | A31 | 10c multicolored | .20 | .20 |
| **307** | A31 | 15c multicolored | .20 | .20 |
| **308** | A31 | 20c multicolored | .20 | .20 |
| **309** | A31 | 25c multicolored | .20 | .20 |
| **310** | A31 | 30c multicolored | .20 | .20 |
| **311** | A31 | 40c multicolored | .20 | .20 |
| **312** | A31 | 50c multicolored | .20 | .20 |
| **313** | A31 | 1sh multicolored | .25 | .25 |
| **314** | A31 | 1.30sh multicolored | .30 | .30 |
| **315** | A31 | 2sh multicolored | .50 | .50 |
| **316** | A31 | 5sh multicolored | 1.10 | *2.00* |
| **317** | A31 | 10sh multicolored | 2.00 | *3.50* |
| **318** | A31 | 20sh multicolored | 4.25 | *17.50* |
| | | *Nos. 305-318 (14)* | 10.00 | 25.65 |

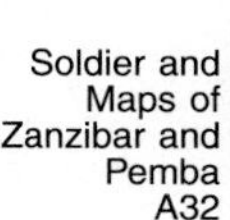

Soldier and Maps of Zanzibar and Pemba A32

Reconstruction A33

*Perf. 13½x13, 13x13½*

**1965, Jan. 12 Unwmk.**

| | | | | |
|---|---|---|---|---|
| **319** | A32 | 20c green & yel grn | .20 | .20 |
| **320** | A33 | 30c dk brn & ocher | .20 | .20 |
| **321** | A32 | 1.30sh vio blue & blue | .20 | .20 |
| **322** | A33 | 2.50sh purple & rose | .40 | .40 |
| | | *Nos. 319-322 (4)* | 1.00 | 1.00 |

First anniversary of the revolution.

### Zanzibar and Tanzania

Rice Planting A34

Design: 30c, 1.30sh, Hands holding rice.

*Perf. 13x12½*

**1965, Oct. 17 Litho. Unwmk.**

| | | | | |
|---|---|---|---|---|
| **323** | A34 | 20c blue & blk brn | .20 | *1.00* |
| **324** | A34 | 30c brt pink & blk brn | .20 | *1.00* |
| **325** | A34 | 1.30sh org & blk brn | .30 | *2.25* |
| **326** | A34 | 2.50sh emer & blk brn | .35 | *4.00* |
| | | *Nos. 323-326 (4)* | 1.05 | *8.25* |

Issued to publicize agricultural development.

Symbols of Trade, Agriculture, Industry and Education A35

Pres. Abeid Amani Karume and Vice-Pres. Abdulla Kassim Hanga A36

Designs: 50c, 2.50sh, Soldier and sunburst.

**1966, Jan. 12 Litho.** *Perf. 12½x13*

| | | | | |
|---|---|---|---|---|
| **327** | A35 | 20c ultra, red & gray | .20 | .20 |
| **328** | A35 | 50c black & yel | .20 | .20 |
| **329** | A35 | 1.30sh multicolored | .20 | .35 |
| **330** | A35 | 2.50sh black & org | .40 | *.60* |
| | | *Nos. 327-330 (4)* | 1.00 | *1.35* |

2nd anniv. of the revolution of Jan. 12, 1964.

**1966, Apr. 26 Photo.** *Perf. 13½x13*

Design: 50c, 1.30sh, Flag, laurel and hands holding Flame of the Union (inscribed: Jamhuri Tanzania Zanzibar).

| | | | | |
|---|---|---|---|---|
| **331** | A36 | 30c multicolored | .20 | .20 |
| **332** | A36 | 50c multicolored | .20 | .20 |
| **333** | A36 | 1.30sh multicolored | .30 | .30 |
| **334** | A36 | 2.50sh multicolored | .55 | 1.00 |
| | | *Nos. 331-334 (4)* | 1.25 | 1.70 |

Union of Tanganyika and Zanzibar, 2nd anniv.

Logging A37

10c, 1sh, Clove trees & man. 15c, 40c, Cabinetmaker. 20c, 5sh, Lumumba College & book. 25c, 1.30sh, Farmer & tractor. 30c, 2sh, Volunteer farm workers. 50c, 10sh, Street scene, vert.

*Perf. 13x12½, 12½x13*

**1966, June 5 Litho.**

| | | | | |
|---|---|---|---|---|
| **335** | A37 | 5c lemon & vio brn | .20 | .20 |
| **336** | A37 | 10c brt grn & vio brn | .20 | *.75* |
| **337** | A37 | 15c vio brn & bl | .20 | *.75* |
| **338** | A37 | 20c vio bl & org | .20 | .20 |
| **339** | A37 | 25c vio brn & yel | .20 | .20 |
| **340** | A37 | 30c vio brn & dl yel | .80 | .20 |
| **341** | A37 | 40c vio brn & rose | .90 | .20 |
| **342** | A37 | 50c green & yel | .90 | .20 |
| **343** | A37 | 1sh ultra & vio brn | .90 | .25 |
| **344** | A37 | 1.30sh lt bl grn & vio brn | .90 | *2.50* |
| **345** | A37 | 2sh brt grn & vio brn | .90 | .45 |
| **346** | A37 | 5sh ver & gray | 1.40 | *5.00* |
| **347** | A37 | 10sh red brn & yel | 2.50 | *17.50* |
| **348** | A37 | 20sh brt pink & vio brn | 5.00 | *30.00* |
| | | *Nos. 335-348 (14)* | 15.20 | *58.40* |

Symbols of Education — A38

**1966, Sept. 25** *Perf. 13½x13*

| | | | | |
|---|---|---|---|---|
| **349** | A38 | 50c blue, blk & org | .20 | *1.00* |
| **350** | A38 | 1.30sh blue, blk & yel grn | .25 | *1.75* |
| **351** | A38 | 2.50sh blue, blk & pink | .50 | *4.00* |
| | | *Nos. 349-351 (3)* | .95 | *6.75* |

Introduction of free education.

People and Flag A39

Design: 50c, 1.30sh, Vice-President Abdulla Kassim Hanga, flag and crowd, vert.

*Perf. 14x14½, 14½x14*

**1967, Feb. 5 Litho. Unwmk.**

| | | | | |
|---|---|---|---|---|
| **352** | A39 | 30c multicolored | .20 | *.50* |
| **353** | A39 | 50c multicolored | .20 | *.50* |
| **354** | A39 | 1.30sh multicolored | .20 | *.75* |
| **355** | A39 | 2.50sh multicolored | .25 | *2.00* |
| | | *Nos. 352-355 (4)* | .85 | *3.75* |

10th anniversary of Afro-Shirazi Party.

Volunteer Workers A40

*Perf. 12½x12*

**1967, Aug. 20 Photo. Unwmk.**

| | | | | |
|---|---|---|---|---|
| **356** | A40 | 1.30sh multicolored | .30 | *2.50* |
| **357** | A40 | 2.50sh multicolored | .55 | *6.50* |

Volunteer (Young) Workers Brigade.

All Zanzibar stamps were withdrawn July 1, 1968, and replaced with current Kenya, Uganda and Tanzania stamps.

---

### POSTAGE DUE STAMPS

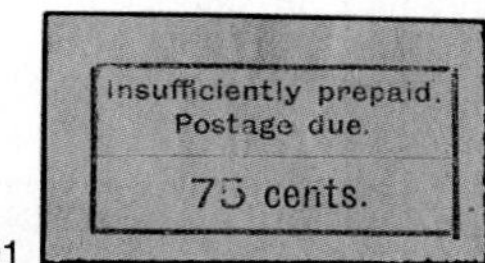

D1

*Roulletted 10*

**1931 Typeset Unwmk.**

**Thin Paper**

**Without Gum**

| | | | | |
|---|---|---|---|---|
| **J1** | D1 | 1c blk, *orange* | 12.50 | *100.00* |
| **J2** | D1 | 2c blk, *orange* | 5.50 | *60.00* |
| **J3** | D1 | 3c blk, *orange* | 5.75 | *47.50* |
| **J3A** | D1 | 6c blk, *orange* | | *8,000.* |
| **J4** | D1 | 9c blk, *orange* | 3.25 | *25.00* |
| **J4A** | D1 | 12c blk, *orange* | *10,000.* | *9,500.* |
| **J4B** | D1 | 12c blk, *green* | *1,600.* | *675.00* |
| **J5** | D1 | 15c blk, *orange* | 3.25 | *27.50* |
| **J6** | D1 | 18c blk, *orange* | 20.00 | *75.00* |
| *a.* | | 18c black, *salmon* | 5.00 | *45.00* |
| **J7** | D1 | 20c blk, *orange* | 4.50 | *65.00* |
| **J8** | D1 | 21c blk, *orange* | 4.00 | *37.50* |
| **J8A** | D1 | 25c blk, *orange* | *11,500.* | *11,500.* |
| **J8B** | D1 | 25c blk, *magenta* | *3,250.* | 1,500. |

**J9** D1 31c blk, *orange* 11.00 *85.00*
**J10** D1 50c blk, *orange* 24.00 *160.00*
**J11** D1 75c blk, *orange* 72.50 *375.00*

The variety "cent.s" occurs once on each sheet of Nos. J3 to J11 inclusive.

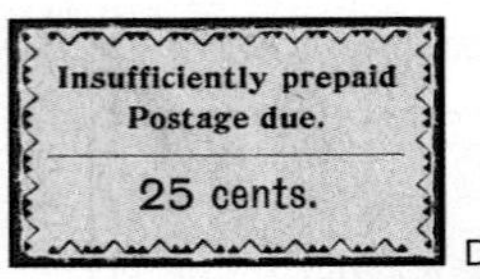

D2

D3

**1931-33** ***Rouletted 5***

**Thick Paper**

**J12** D2 2c blk, *salmon* 17.50 *32.50*
**J13** D2 3c blk, *rose* 3.50 *52.50*
**J14** D2 6c blk, *yellow* 3.50 *37.50*
**J15** D2 12c blk, *blue* 4.50 *30.00*
**J16** D2 25c blk, *pink* 11.00 *85.00*
**J17** D2 25c blk, *dull violet* 16.00 *57.50*
*Nos. J12-J17 (6)* 56.00 *295.00*

**Catalogue values for unused stamps in this section, from this point to the end of the section, are for Never Hinged items.**

**1936 Typo. Wmk. 4** ***Perf. 14***

**J18** D3 5c violet 4.75 *9.50*
**J19** D3 10c carmine 4.00 *3.25*
**J20** D3 20c green 2.50 *4.75*
**J21** D3 30c brown 9.50 *21.00*
**J22** D3 40c ultra 9.50 *27.50*
**J23** D3 1sh gray 9.50 *32.50*
*Nos. J18-J23 (6)* 39.75 *98.50*

Chalky paper was introduced in 1956 for the 5c, 30c, 40c, 1sh, and in 1962 for the 10c, 20c. Value for set of 6, unused $3.25, used $110.

See note after No. 300a.

## ZIMBABWE

zim-'bä-bwē

LOCATION — Southeastern Africa, bordered by Zambia, Mozambique, South Africa, and Botswana
GOVT. — Republic
AREA — 150,872 sq. mi.
POP. — 11,163,160 (1999 est.)
CAPITAL — Harare

Formerly Rhodesia, the Republic of Zimbabwe was established April 18, 1980.

100 Cents = 1 Dollar

**Catalogue values for all unused stamps in this country are for Never Hinged items.**

Morganite
A69

Black Rhinoceros
A70

Odzani Falls — A71

***Perf. 14½, 14½x14 (A70)***

**1980** **Litho.**

**414** A69 1c shown .20 .30
**415** A69 3c Amethyst .35 .30
**416** A69 4c Garnet .35 .20
**417** A69 5c Citrine .35 .20
**418** A69 7c Blue topaz .35 .20
**419** A70 9c shown .20 .20
**420** A70 11c Lion .20 .20
**421** A70 13c Warthog .20 .20
**422** A70 15c Giraffe .20 .20
**423** A70 17c Zebra .20 .20
**424** A71 21c shown .20 .20
**425** A71 25c Goba Falls .30 .30
**426** A71 30c Inyangombe Falls .35 .50
**426A** A71 40c Bundi Falls 7.00 4.75
**427** A71 $1 Bridal Veil Falls .50 2.00
**428** A71 $2 Victoria Falls .85 3.75
*Nos. 414-428 (16)* 11.80 13.70

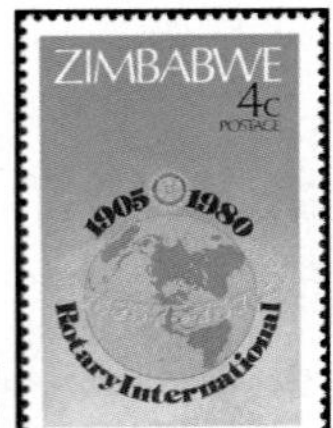

Rotary International, 75th Anniversary — A72

**1980, June 18** ***Perf. 14½***

**429** A72 4c multicolored .20 .20
**430** A72 13c multicolored .20 .30
**431** A72 21c multicolored .25 .50
**432** A72 25c multicolored .35 .75
*a.* Souvenir sheet of 4, #429-432 1.40 1.40
*Nos. 429-432 (4)* 1.00 1.75

Olympic Rings A73

**1980, July 19**

**433** A73 17c multicolored .30 .35

22nd Summer Olympic Games, Moscow, July 19-Aug. 3.

Gatooma Post Office, 1912 A74

Post Offices: 7c, Salisbury, 1912. 9c, Umtali, 1901. 17c, Bulawayo, 1895.

**1980** **Litho.** ***Perf. 14½***

**434** A74 5c multicolored .20 .20
**435** A74 7c multicolored .20 .20
**436** A74 9c multicolored .20 .20
**437** A74 17c multicolored .25 .25
*a.* Souvenir sheet of 4, #434-437 1.00 1.25
*Nos. 434-437 (4)* .85 .85

Post Office Savings Bank, 75th anniv.

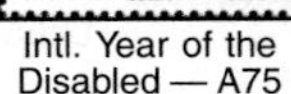

Intl. Year of the Disabled — A75

Natl. Tree Day — A76

Designs: Various disabilities. Nos. 438-441 form a continuous design.

**1981, Sept. 23** **Litho.** ***Perf. 14½***

**438** A75 5c multicolored .20 .20
**439** A75 7c multicolored .20 .20
**440** A75 11c multicolored .20 .20
**441** A75 17c multicolored .25 .25
*Nos. 438-441 (4)* .85 .85

**1981, Dec. 4**

**442** A76 5c Msasa .20 .20
**443** A76 7c Mopane .20 .20
**444** A76 21c Flat-crowned acacia .70 .70
**445** A76 30c Pod mahogany .90 .90
*Nos. 442-445 (4)* 2.00 2.00

Rock Paintings A77

Designs: 9c, Khoisan figures, Gwamgwadza Cave. 11c, Kudus, human figures, Epworth Mission. 17c, Diana's Vow, Rusape. 21c, Giraffes, Gwamgwadza Cave. 25c, Warthog, Mucheka Cave. 30c, Hunters, Shinzwini Shelter.

**1982, Mar. 17** **Litho.** ***Perf. 14½***

**446** A77 9c multicolored .75 .75
**447** A77 11c multicolored .90 .90
**448** A77 17c multicolored 1.25 1.25
**449** A77 21c multicolored 1.75 1.75
**450** A77 25c multicolored 1.75 1.75
**451** A77 30c multicolored 2.75 2.75
*Nos. 446-451 (6)* 9.15 9.15

Scouting Year — A78

**1982, July 21**

**452** A78 9c Emblem .35 .35
**453** A78 11c Campfire .40 .40
**454** A78 21c Map reading .75 .75
**455** A78 30c Baden Powell 1.00 1.00
*Nos. 452-455 (4)* 2.50 2.50

TB Bacillus Centenary A79

**1982, Nov. 17** ***Perf. 14½***

**456** A79 11c Koch 1.00 1.25
**457** A79 30c Scientist examining slide 2.00 2.25

Commonwealth Day — A80

Sculptures: 9c, Wing Woman, by Henry Mudzengerere, vert. 11c, Telling Secrets, by Joseph Ndandarika. 30c, Hornbill Man, by John Takawira. $1, The Chief, by Nicholas Mukomberanwa, vert.

**1983, Mar. 14** ***Perf. 14½***

**458** A80 9c multicolored .20 .20
**459** A80 11c multicolored .20 .20
**460** A80 30c multicolored .30 .35
**461** A80 $1 multicolored .80 1.50
*Nos. 458-461 (4)* 1.50 2.25

World Plowing Contest, May — A81

No. 463, mechanized plowing.

**1983, May 13** **Litho.** ***Perf. 14½***

**462** A81 Pair .70 .70
*a.-b.* 21c, any single .35 .35
**463** A81 Pair .90 .90
*a.-b.* 30c, any single .45 .45

World Communications Year — A82

Means of communication and transportation. Nos. 464-467 vert.

**1983, Oct. 12** **Litho.** ***Perf. 14½***

**464** A82 9c Mailman .20 .20
**465** A82 11c Signaling airplane .30 .30
**466** A82 15c Telephone operators .45 .45
**467** A82 17c Reading newspapers .60 .60
**468** A82 21c Truck on highway .70 .70
**469** A82 30c Train 1.00 1.00
*Nos. 464-469 (6)* 3.25 3.25

Zimbabwe Intl. Trade Fair, Bulawayo, May 5-13 — A83

**1984, Apr. 11** **Litho.** ***Perf. 14½***

**470** A83 9c shown .20 .20
**471** A83 11c Globe .20 .20
**472** A83 30c Emblem .50 .50
*Nos. 470-472 (3)* .90 .90

1984 Summer Olympics A84

Children's Drawings.

**1984, July 18** **Litho.** ***Perf. 14½***

**473** A84 11c Bicycling .30 .20
**474** A84 21c Swimming .65 .65
**475** A84 30c Running 1.00 1.00
**476** A84 40c Hurdles 1.40 2.25
*Nos. 473-476 (4)* 3.35 4.10

Heroes' Day A85

**1984, Aug. 8** **Litho.** ***Perf. 14½***

**477** A85 9c Heroes .20 .20
**478** A85 11c Monument, vert. .25 .25
**479** A85 17c Statue, vert. .45 .45
**480** A85 30c Bas-relief .75 .75
*Nos. 477-480 (4)* 1.65 1.65

Fish Eagle — A86

**1984, Oct. 10** **Litho.** ***Perf. 14½***

**481** A86 9c shown .75 .75
**482** A86 11c Long crested eagle .80 .80
**483** A86 13c Bateleur .90 .90
**484** A86 17c Black eagle 1.25 1.25

**485** A86 21c Martial eagle 1.50 1.50
**486** A86 30c African hawk eagle 2.10 2.10
*Nos. 481-486 (6)* 7.30 7.30

Superheat Engine No. 86, Mashonaland Railways, 1918 — A87

Steam locomotives: 11c, Engine No. 190, North British Locomotive Co., 1926. 17c, Engine No. 424, Beyer Peacock & Co., 1950. 30c, Engine No. 726, Beyer Peacock & Co., 1957.

**1985, May 15** **Litho.**

**487** A87 9c multicolored 1.00 1.00
**488** A87 11c multicolored 1.40 1.40
**489** A87 17c multicolored 2.10 2.10
**490** A87 30c multicolored 3.75 3.75
*Nos. 487-490 (4)* 8.25 8.25

INTELSAT V A88

57c, Mazowe Earth Satellite Station.

***Perf. 14½x14, 14½***

**1985, July 8** **Litho.**

**491** A88 26c multicolored 2.10 2.40

**Size: 62x23mm**

**492** A88 57c multicolored 4.25 4.75

Zimbabwe Bird and Tobacco — A89

Agriculture and industry.

***Perf. 14¾x14½***

**1985, Aug. 21** **Litho.**

**493** A89 1c shown .20 .20
*a.* Perf 14¼x13¾ — —
**494** A89 3c Corn .20 .20
**495** A89 4c Cotton .20 .20
*a.* Perf 14¼x13¾ — —
**496** A89 5c Tea .40 .20
**497** A89 10c Cattle .40 .20
*a.* Perf 14¼x13¾ — —
**498** A89 11c Birchenough Bridge 1.00 .20
**499** A89 12c Stamp mill 1.60 .20
**500** A89 13c Gold production 3.00 .20
**501** A89 15c Coal mining 2.25 .20
*a.* Perf 14¼x13¾ — —
**502** A89 17c Amethyst mining 3.00 .40
**503** A89 18c Electric train 3.00 .40
**504** A89 20c Kariba Dam 2.00 .20
*a.* Perf 14¼x13¾ — —
**505** A89 23c Elephants 3.25 .40
**506** A89 25c Zambezi River sunset .80 .40
**507** A89 26c Baobab tree .80 .25
**508** A89 30c Great Zimbabwe ruins 1.00 .40
**509** A89 35c Folk dancing .80 .40
**510** A89 45c Crushing corn 1.00 .55
**511** A89 57c Wood carving 1.00 .90
**512** A89 $1 Mbira drum 1.60 1.10
**513** A89 $2 Mule-drawn scotch cart 2.75 3.75
**514** A89 $5 Natl. coat of arms 5.00 6.50
*Nos. 493-514 (22)* 35.25 17.45

Natl. Archives, 50th Anniv. A90

Designs: 12c, Gatsi Rusere (c. 1589-1623), ruler of Mashonaland and Zambezi area; mutapa, 17th cent. 18c, Lobengula, ruler of Ndebele State (1870-94), sketch by E. A. Maund, 1889; 1888 Moffat Treaty and elephant seal. 26c, Archives exhibition hall. 35c, Archives building.

**1985, Sept. 18** ***Perf. 14½***

**515** A90 12c multicolored .20 .20
**516** A90 18c multicolored .30 .30
**517** A90 26c multicolored .45 .45
**518** A90 35c multicolored .65 .65
*Nos. 515-518 (4)* 1.60 1.60

UN Decade for Women A91

**1985, Nov. 13**

**519** A91 10c Computer operator .70 .70
**520** A91 17c Nurse, child 1.00 1.00
**521** A91 26c Engineer 1.75 1.75
*Nos. 519-521 (3)* 3.45 3.45

Harare Conference Center — A92

**1986, Jan. 29** **Litho.** ***Perf. 14½***

**523** A92 26c Facade .90 .90
**524** A92 35c Interior 1.60 1.60

Southern African Development Coordination Conference — A93

**1986, Apr. 1** ***Perf. 14½***

**525** A93 12c Grain elevators .50 .50
**526** A93 18c Rhinoceros 2.75 2.75
**527** A93 26c Map, jet 2.75 2.75
**528** A93 35c Map, flags 3.00 3.00
*Nos. 525-528 (4)* 9.00 9.00

Moths — A94

**1986, June 18** **Litho.** ***Perf. 14½x14***

**529** A94 12c Jackson's emperor 1.60 1.60
**530** A94 18c Oleander hawk 2.10 2.10
**531** A94 26c Zaddach's emperor 2.75 2.75
**532** A94 35c Southern marbled emperor 3.25 3.25
*Nos. 529-532 (4)* 9.70 9.70

8th Non-aligned Summit Conference A95

**1986, Aug. 28** **Litho.** ***Perf. 14½x14***

**533** A95 26c Victoria Falls 3.00 3.00

**Size: 66x26mm**

***Perf. 14½***

**534** A95 $1 Great Zimbabwe Enclosure 6.75 6.75

Motoring Cent. A96

**1986, Oct. 8** ***Perf. 14½***

**535** A96 10c Sopwith, 1921 .75 .75
**536** A96 12c Gladiator, 1902 .75 .75
**537** A96 17c Douglas, 1920 1.10 1.10
**538** A96 26c Ford Model-A, 1930 1.75 1.75
**539** A96 35c Schacht, 1909 2.25 2.25
**540** A96 40c Benz Velocipede, 1886 2.25 2.25
*Nos. 535-540 (6)* 8.85 8.85

A97

A98

UN Child Survival Campaign: a, Growth monitoring. b, Breast-feeding. c, Oral rehydration. d, Immunization.

**1987, Feb. 11** **Litho.** ***Perf. 14x14½***

**541** Block of 4 9.00 9.00
*a.-d.* A97 12c any single 2.00 2.00

**1987, Apr. 15** ***Perf. 14½***

Indigenous owls.

**542** A98 12c Barred 2.50 2.50
**543** A98 18c Pearl-spotted 3.25 3.25
**544** A98 26c White-faced 3.75 3.75
**545** A98 35c Scops 5.75 5.75
*Nos. 542-545 (4)* 15.25 15.25

Natl. Girl Guides Movement, 75th Anniv. — A99

**1987, June 24**

**546** A99 15c Commitment .75 .75
**547** A99 23c Adventure .95 .95
**548** A99 35c Service 1.10 1.10
**549** A99 $1 Intl. friendship 2.50 2.50
*Nos. 546-549 (4)* 5.30 5.30

Duikers and Population Maps — A100

**1987, Oct. 7** ***Perf. 14½x14***

**550** A100 15c Common gray 1.00 1.00
**551** A100 23c Zebra 1.10 1.10
**552** A100 25c Yellow-backed 1.10 1.10
**553** A100 30c Blue 1.40 1.40
**554** A100 35c Jentink's 1.40 1.40
**555** A100 38c Red 1.40 1.40
*Nos. 550-555 (6)* 7.40 7.40

Insects A101

**1988, Jan. 12** **Litho.** ***Perf. 14½***

**556** A101 15c Praying mantis 1.00 .20
**557** A101 23c Scarab beetle 1.10 .40
**558** A101 35c Short-horned grasshopper 1.60 1.25
**559** A101 45c Giant shield bug 1.90 *3.25*
*Nos. 556-559 (4)* 5.60 5.10

Natl. Gallery of Art, 30th Anniv. — A102

Aloes and Succulents A103

Sculpture and paintings: 15c, Cockerel, by Arthur Azevedo. 23c, Changeling, by Bernard Matemera. 30c, Spirit Python, by Henry Munyaradzi. 35c, Spirit Bird Carrying People, by Thomas Mukarobgwa, horiz. 38c, The Song of the Shepherd Boy, by George Nene, horiz. 45c, War Victim, by Joseph Muzondo, horiz.

***Perf. 14x14½, 14½x14***

**1988, Apr. 14** **Litho.**

**560** A102 15c multicolored .30 .30
**561** A102 23c multicolored .45 .45
**562** A102 30c multicolored .60 .60
**563** A102 35c multicolored .80 .80
**564** A102 38c multicolored .80 .80
**565** A102 45c multicolored .95 .95
*Nos. 560-565 (6)* 3.90 3.90

**1988, July 14** ***Perf. 14½***

**566** A103 15c Aloe cameronii bondana .35 .35
**567** A103 23c Orbeopsis caudata .70 .70
**568** A103 25c Euphorbia wildii .70 .70
**569** A103 30c Euphorbia fortissima .75 .75
**570** A103 35c Aloe aculeata .75 .75
**571** A103 38c Huernia zebrina .95 .95
*Nos. 566-571 (6)* 4.20 4.20

A104

**1988, Oct. 6** **Litho.** ***Perf. 14½x14***

**572** A104 15c White-faced duck .90 .20
**573** A104 23c Pygmy goose 1.00 .35
**574** A104 30c Hottentot teal 1.10 1.10
**575** A104 35c Knob-billed duck 1.25 1.25
**576** A104 38c White-backed duck 1.40 1.40
**577** A104 45c Maccoa 1.90 *2.50*
*Nos. 572-577 (6)* 7.55 6.80

Geckos A105

**1989, Jan. 10** **Litho.** ***Perf. 14½***

**578** A105 15c O'Shaughnessy's banded 1.10 1.10
**579** A105 23c Tiger rock 1.25 1.25
**580** A105 35c Tasman's 2.10 2.10
**581** A105 45c Bibron's 2.25 2.25
*Nos. 578-581 (4)* 6.70 6.70

Wildflowers
A106

**1989, Apr. 12 Litho. *Perf. 14½***

**582** A106 15c Spotted-leaved arum-lily .55 .55
**583** A106 23c Grassland vlei-lily .70 .70
**584** A106 30c Manica protea .70 .70
**585** A106 35c Flame lily .80 .80
**586** A106 38c Poppy hibiscus .90 .90
**587** A106 45c Blue sesbania 1.00 1.00
*Nos. 582-587 (6)* 4.65 4.65

Fish
A107

**1989, July 12 Litho. *Perf. 14½***

**588** A107 15c Red-breasted bream .90 .20
**589** A107 23c Chessa 1.10 .20
**590** A107 30c Eastern bottle-nose 1.25 1.00
**591** A107 35c Vundu 1.25 1.00
**592** A107 38c Largemouth black bass 1.50 1.50
**593** A107 45c Tiger fish 2.00 *2.40*
*Nos. 588-593 (6)* 8.00 6.30

See Nos. 696-701.

Endangered Species
A108

**1989 Litho. *Perf. 14½x14***

**594** A108 15c Black rhinoceros 1.75 1.75
**595** A108 23c Cheetah 2.00 2.00
**596** A108 30c Wild dog 2.25 2.25
**597** A108 35c Pangolin 2.25 2.25
**598** A108 38c Brown hyena 2.40 2.40
**599** A108 45c Roan antelope 2.50 2.50
*Nos. 594-599 (6)* 13.15 13.15

Achievements, 1980-1990
A109

**1990, Apr. 17 Litho. *Perf. 14½x14***

**600** A109 15c Unity accord .55 .20
**601** A109 23c Conference center .65 .20
**602** A109 30c Education .70 .70
**603** A109 35c Satellite dish .85 .85
**604** A109 38c Sports stadium .85 .85
**605** A109 45c Agriculture 1.40 *2.25*
*Nos. 600-605 (6)* 5.00 5.05

City of Harare, Cent.
A110

**1990, July 11 Litho. *Perf. 14½***

**606** A110 15c Runhare house, 1986 .55 .55
**607** A110 23c Market hall, 1894 .80 .80
**608** A110 30c Charter house, 1959 .85 .85
**609** A110 35c Supreme Court, 1927 .95 .95
**610** A110 38c Standard Chartered Bank, 1911 .95 .95
**611** A110 45c Town house, 1933 1.25 1.25
*Nos. 606-611 (6)* 5.35 5.35

36th Commonwealth Parliamentary Conf. — A111

**1990, Sept. 17**

**612** A111 35c Speaker's mace .60 .60
**613** A111 $1 Speaker's chair 2.10 2.10

Animals — A112

Hand Crafts — A113

Transportation — A114

***Perf. 14, 14¾x14½ (#615, 617, 619), 14½x14 (#620-625), 14¼ (#626)***

**1990, Jan. 2 Litho.**

**614** A112 1c Tiger fish .20 .20
*a.* Perf 14¾x14½ — —
**615** A112 2c Helmeted guineafowl .50 .50
**616** A112 3c Scrub hare .20 .20
*a.* Perf 14¾x14½ — —
**617** A112 4c Pangolin .20 .20
*a.* Perf 14¾x14½ — —
**618** A112 5c Greater kudu .45 .45
**619** A112 9c Black rhinoceros 1.25 1.25
*a.* Perf 14 — —
**620** A113 15c Head rest .20 .20
**621** A113 20c Hand axe .20 .20
**622** A113 23c Gourd, water pot .20 .20
**623** A113 25c Snuff box .20 .20
**624** A113 26c Winnowing basket .35 .35
**625** A113 30c Grinding stone .35 .35
**626** A114 33c Riding bicycles .80 .80
**627** A114 35c Buses 1.25 1.25
**628** A114 38c Train 1.25 1.25
**629** A114 45c Motorcycle, trailer 1.25 1.25
**630** A114 $1 Jet 2.10 2.10
**631** A114 $2 Tractor-trailer truck 2.10 2.10
*Nos. 614-631 (18)* 13.05 13.05

Animals
A115

A116

**1991, Jan. 15 Litho. *Perf. 14½x14***

**632** A115 15c Small-spotted genet 1.25 1.25
**633** A115 23c Red squirrel 1.40 1.40
**634** A115 35c Night ape 1.90 1.90
**635** A115 45c Bat-eared fox 2.75 2.75
*Nos. 632-635 (4)* 7.30 7.30

**1991, Apr. 16 Litho. *Perf. 14½***

Traditional musical instruments.

**636** A116 15c Hosho .70 .20
**637** A116 23c Mbira .75 .20
**638** A116 30c Ngororombe .85 .85
**639** A116 35c Chipendani 1.10 1.10
**640** A116 38c Marimba 1.10 1.10
**641** A116 45c Ngoma 1.25 *1.75*
*Nos. 636-641 (6)* 5.75 5.20

Wild Fruits — A117

A118

**1991, July 17 Litho. *Perf. 14x14½***

**642** A117 20c Snot-apple .70 .70
**643** A117 39c Marula .80 .80
**644** A117 51c Mobola plum .90 .90
**645** A117 60c Water berry 1.00 1.00
**646** A117 65c Northern dwaba berry 1.10 1.10
**647** A117 77c Mahobohobo 1.25 1.25
*Nos. 642-647 (6)* 5.75 5.75

See Nos. 870-875.

**1991, Oct. 16 Litho. *Perf. 14½***

**648** A118 20c Bridal Veil Falls .85 .85
**649** A118 39c Conference Emblem .85 .85
**650** A118 51c Chinhoyi Caves 1.10 1.10
**651** A118 60c Kariba Dam Wall 1.25 1.25
**652** A118 65c Victoria Falls 1.40 1.40
**653** A118 77c Balancing Rocks 1.40 1.40
*Nos. 648-653 (6)* 6.85 6.85

Commonwealth Heads of Government meeting, Harare.

Wild Cats
A119

**1992, Jan. 8 Litho. *Perf. 14½***

**654** A119 20c Lion .90 .20
**655** A119 39c Leopard 1.40 .65
**656** A119 60c Cheetah 2.10 2.10
**657** A119 77c Serval 3.00 2.75
*Nos. 654-657 (4)* 7.40 5.70

Mushrooms
A120

Birds — A121

Designs: 20c, Amanita zambiana. 39c, Boletus edulis. 51c, Termitomyces. 60c, Cantharellus densifolius. 65c, Cantharellus longisporus. 77c, Cantharellus cibarius.

**1992, Apr. 8 Litho. *Perf. 14x14½***

**658** A120 20c multicolored 1.00 1.00
**659** A120 39c multicolored 1.25 1.25
**660** A120 51c multicolored 1.40 1.40
**661** A120 60c multicolored 1.50 1.50
**662** A120 65c multicolored 1.75 1.75
**663** A120 77c multicolored 2.25 2.25
*Nos. 658-663 (6)* 9.15 9.15

**1992, July 17 Litho. *Perf. 14½***

**664** A121 25c Blackeyed bulbul .75 .75
**665** A121 59c Fiscal shrike 1.00 1.00
**666** A121 77c Forktailed drongo 1.10 1.10
**667** A121 90c Cardinal woodpecker 1.25 1.25
**668** A121 98c Yellowbilled hornbill 1.25 1.25
**669** A121 $1.16 Crested francolin 1.40 1.40
*Nos. 664-669 (6)* 6.75 6.75

Butterflies
A122

**1992, Oct. 15 Litho. *Perf. 14½x14***

**670** A122 25c Foxy charaxes 1.10 1.10
**671** A122 59c Orange & lemon 2.10 2.10
**672** A122 77c Emperor swallowtail 2.50 2.50
**673** A122 90c Blue pansy 3.00 3.00
**674** A122 98c African monarch 3.25 3.25
**675** A122 $1.16 Gaudy commodore 3.50 3.50
*Nos. 670-675 (6)* 15.45 15.45

Minerals
A123

Owls — A124

**1993, Jan. 12 Litho. *Perf. 14½x14***

**676** A123 25c Autunite 1.60 1.60
**677** A123 59c Chromite 2.40 2.40
**678** A123 77c Azurite 2.75 2.75
**679** A123 90c Coal 3.25 3.25

**680** A123 98c Gold 3.50 3.50
**681** A123 $1.16 Emerald 4.50 4.50
*Nos. 676-681 (6)* 18.00 18.00

**1993, Apr. 6 Litho. *Perf. 14½***

**682** A124 25c Wood owl 1.75 1.75
**683** A124 59c Pels fishing owl 2.25 2.25
**684** A124 90c Spotted eagle owl 3.25 3.25
**685** A124 $1.16 Giant eagle owl 4.25 4.25
*Nos. 682-685 (4)* 11.50 11.50

Household Pottery A125

Orchids — A126

**1993, July 13 Litho. *Perf. 14½x14***

**686** A125 25c Hadyana .65 .65
**687** A125 59c Chirongo .80 .80
**688** A125 77c Mbiya .95 .95
**689** A125 90c Pfuko 1.10 1.10
**690** A125 98c Tsaya 1.25 1.25
**691** A125 $1.16 Gate 1.50 1.50
*Nos. 686-691 (6)* 6.25 6.25

**1993, Oct. 12 Litho. *Perf. 14½***

**692** A126 35c Polystachya dendrobiflora .90 .90
**693** A126 $1 Diaphananthe subsimplex 1.75 1.75
**694** A126 $1.50 Ansellia gigantea 2.75 2.75
**695** A126 $1.95 Vanilla polyepis 3.50 3.50
*Nos. 692-695 (4)* 8.90 8.90

Fish Type of 1989

**1994, Jan. 20 Litho. *Perf. 14½***

**696** A107 35c Hunyani salmon .35 .35
**697** A107 $1 Barbel .75 .75
**698** A107 $1.30 Rainbow trout .90 .90
**699** A107 $1.50 Mottled eel 1.10 1.10
**700** A107 $1.65 Mirror carp 1.25 1.25
**701** A107 $1.95 Robustus bream 1.40 1.40
*Nos. 696-701 (6)* 5.75 5.75

City of Bulawayo, Cent. A127

**1994, Apr. 5 Litho. *Perf. 14½***

**702** A127 35c City Hall .50 .50
**703** A127 80c Cresta Churchill Hotel .50 .50
**704** A127 $1.15 High Court .80 .80
**705** A127 $1.75 Douslin House 1.00 1.00
**706** A127 $1.95 Goldfields Building 1.25 1.25
**707** A127 $2.30 Parkade Centre 1.40 1.40
*Nos. 702-707 (6)* 5.45 5.45

Export Flowers — A128

Christmas — A129

**1994, July 12 Litho. *Perf. 14½***

**708** A128 35c Strelitzia .65 .65
**709** A128 80c Protea .65 .65
**710** A128 $1.15 Phlox 1.00 1.00
**711** A128 $1.75 Chrysanthemum 1.50 1.50
**712** A128 $1.95 Lilium 1.60 1.60
**713** A128 $2.30 Rose 1.90 1.90
*Nos. 708-713 (6)* 7.30 7.30

**1994, Oct. 11 Litho. *Perf. 14½***

Designs: 35c, Archangel Gabriel, Virgin Mary. 80c, Mary, Joseph on way to Bethlehem. $1.15, Nativity scene. $1.75, Angel pointing way to shepherds. $1.95, Magi following star. $2.30, Madonna and child.

**714** A129 35c multicolored .60 .60
**715** A129 80c multicolored .60 .60
**716** A129 $1.15 multicolored .90 .90
**717** A129 $1.75 multicolored 1.10 1.10
**718** A129 $1.95 multicolored 1.50 1.50
**719** A129 $2.30 multicolored 1.60 1.60
*Nos. 714-719 (6)* 6.30 6.30

A130

**1995-96 Litho. *Perf. 14***

**720** A130 1c Corn .25 .25
**721** A130 2c Sugar cane .25 .25
**722** A130 3c Sunflowers .25 .25
**723** A130 4c Sorghum .25 .25
**724** A130 5c Mine workers .25 .25
**725** A130 10c Underground mining .25 .25
**726** A130 20c Coal mining .25 .25
**727** A130 30c Chrome smelting .25 .25
**728** A130 40c Opencast mining .25 .25
**728A** A130 45c Underground drilling .25 .25
**729** A130 50c Gold smelting .25 .25
**730** A130 70c Boggie Clock Tower .25 .25
**731** A130 80c Masvingo Watchtower .25 .25
**732** A130 $1 Hanging tree .30 .30
**733** A130 $2 Cecil House .60 .60
**734** A130 $5 The Toposcope 1.50 1.50
**735** A130 $10 Paper House 3.00 3.00
*Nos. 720-735 (17)* 8.65 8.65

Issued: 45c, 6/3/96; others, 1/17/95.

Insects A131

**1995, Apr. 4 Litho. *Perf. 14½***

**736** A131 35c Spider-hunting wasp .80 .80
**737** A131 $1.15 Emperor dragonfly 1.25 1.25
**738** A131 $1.75 Foxy charaxes 1.60 1.60
**739** A131 $2.30 Antlion 2.25 2.25
*Nos. 736-739 (4)* 5.90 5.90

6th All Africa Games, Harare — A132

**1995, July 11 Litho. *Perf. 14x14½***

**740** A132 35c Soccer .50 .50
**741** A132 80c Track .50 .50
**742** A132 $1.15 Boxing .75 .75
**743** A132 $1.75 Swimming 1.00 1.00
**744** A132 $1.95 Field hockey 1.10 1.10
**745** A132 $2.30 Volleyball 1.40 1.40
*Nos. 740-745 (6)* 5.25 5.25

UN, 50th Anniv. — A133

**1995, Oct. 17 Litho. *Perf. 14½***

**746** A133 35c Health .35 .35
**747** A133 $1.15 Environment .55 .55
**748** A133 $1.75 Food distribution .75 .75
**749** A133 $2.30 Education 1.00 1.00
*Nos. 746-749 (4)* 2.65 2.65

Flowering Trees — A134

**1996, Jan. 24 Litho. *Perf. 14½***

**750** A134 45c Fernandoa .30 .30
**751** A134 $1 Round leaf mukwa .30 .30
**752** A134 $1.50 Luckybean tree .50 .50
**753** A134 $2.20 Winter cassia .75 .75
**754** A134 $2.50 Sausage tree .90 .90
**755** A134 $3 Sweet thorn 1.10 1.10
*Nos. 750-755 (6)* 3.85 3.85

Dams of Zimbabwe A135

**1996, Apr. 9 Litho. *Perf. 14½***

**756** A135 45c Mazvikadei .30 .30
**757** A135 $1.50 Mutirikwi .50 .50
**758** A135 $2.20 Ncema .75 .75
**759** A135 $3 Odzani 1.00 1.00
*Nos. 756-759 (4)* 2.55 2.55

Scenic Views A136

Designs: 45c, Matusadonha Natl. Park. $1.50, Juliasdale Rocky Outcrops. $2.20, Honde Valley. $3, Finger Rocks, Morgenster Mission.

**1996, July 18 Litho. *Perf. 14½***

**760** A136 45c multicolored .45 .45
**761** A136 $1.50 multicolored .65 .65
**762** A136 $2.20 multicolored 1.00 1.00
**763** A136 $3 multicolored 1.40 1.40
*Nos. 760-763 (4)* 3.50 3.50

Wood Carvings A137

**1996, Oct. 15 Litho. *Perf. 14½***

**764** A137 45c Frog .30 .30
**765** A137 $1.50 Tortoise .45 .45
**766** A137 $1.70 Kudu .55 .55
**767** A137 $2.20 Chimpanzee .70 .70
**768** A137 $2.50 Porcupine .80 .80
**769** A137 $3 Rhinoceros .95 .95
*Nos. 764-769 (6)* 3.75 3.75

Cattle A138

**1997, Jan. 7 Litho. *Perf. 14½***

**770** A138 45c Mashona cow .40 .40
**771** A138 $1.50 Tuli cow .60 .60
**772** A138 $2.20 Nkoni bull .80 .80
**773** A138 $3 Brahman bull 1.10 1.10
*Nos. 770-773 (4)* 2.90 2.90

Convention on Intl. Trade in Endangered Species of Flora and Fauna (CITES) — A139

**1997, Apr. 15 Litho. *Perf. 14½***

**774** A139 45c Cycad .35 .35
**775** A139 $1.50 Peregrine falcon .45 .45
**776** A139 $1.70 Pangolin .55 .55
**777** A139 $2.20 Black rhinoceros .75 .75
**778** A139 $2.50 Elephant .85 .85
**779** A139 $3 Python 1.00 1.00
*Nos. 774-779 (6)* 3.95 3.95

Aspects of Rural Life A140

**1997, July 22 Litho. *Perf. 14½***

**780** A140 65c Carving .20 .20
**781** A140 $1 Winnowing .20 .20
**782** A140 $2.40 Dancing .40 .40
**783** A140 $2.50 Plowing .45 .45
**784** A140 $3.10 Stamping .55 .55
**785** A140 $4.20 Fetching water .75 .75
*Nos. 780-785 (6)* 2.55 2.55

Zimbabwe Railway, Cent. A141

**1997, Oct. 28 Litho. *Perf. 14½***

**786** A141 65c Passenger coach .35 .35
**787** A141 $1 12th Class, No. 257 .35 .35
**788** A141 $2.40 16A Class, No. 605 .60 .60
**789** A141 $2.50 El 1, No. 4107 .60 .60
**790** A141 $3.10 Jack Tar .80 .80
**791** A141 $4.20 DE 2, No. 1211 1.00 1.00
*Nos. 786-791 (6)* 3.70 3.70

Wildlife A142

**1998, Jan. 20 Litho. *Perf. 14½***

**792** A142 65c Aardwolf .40 .40
**793** A142 $2.40 Large gray mongoose .50 .50
**794** A142 $3.10 Clawless otter .70 .70
**795** A142 $4.20 Antbear (Aardvark) .85 .85
*Nos. 792-795 (4)* 2.45 2.45

Apiculture A143

Designs: $1.20, Honeybee on flower. $4.10, Queen, worker, drone. $4.70, Queen, retinue. $5.60, Rural beekeeper. $7.40, Commercial beekeepers. $9.90, Products of the hive.

**1998, Apr. 14 Litho. *Perf. 14***

**796** A143 $1.20 multicolored .25 .25
**797** A143 $4.10 multicolored .65 .65
**798** A143 $4.70 multicolored .75 .75
**799** A143 $5.60 multicolored .90 .90
**800** A143 $7.40 multicolored 1.10 1.10
**801** A143 $9.90 multicolored 1.50 1.50
*Nos. 796-801 (6)* 5.15 5.15

Fossils A144

**1998, July 21 Litho. *Perf. 14½***

**802** A144 $1.20 Fossil fish .80 .30
**803** A144 $5.60 Allosaurus footprints 1.10 .85
**804** A144 $7.40 Massospondylus 1.25 1.10
**805** A144 $9.90 Fossil wood 1.60 1.60
*Nos. 802-805 (4)* 4.75 3.85

Birds — A145

Designs: $1.20, Yellow-bellied sunbird. $4.10, Lesser blue-eared starling. $4.70, Greyhooded kingfisher. $5.60, Mombo gray tit. $7.40, Chirinda apalis. $9.90, Swynnerton's robin.

**1998, Oct. 20 Litho. *Perf. 14***

**806** A145 $1.20 multicolored .40 .40
**807** A145 $4.10 multicolored .50 .50
**808** A145 $4.70 multicolored .60 .60
**809** A145 $5.60 multicolored .75 .75
**810** A145 $7.40 multicolored .85 .85
**811** A145 $9.90 multicolored 1.10 1.10
*Nos. 806-811 (6)* 4.20 4.20

UPU, 125th Anniv. — A146

$1.20, Counter services at Post Office and Philatelic Bureau. $5.60, Postman delivering mail on bicycle. $7.40, 19th cent. runner, EMS, PTC delivery today. $9.90, Harare Central Sorting Office.

**1999, Jan. 19 Litho. *Perf. 14***

**812** A146 $1.20 multicolored .45 .45
**813** A146 $5.60 multicolored .60 .60
**814** A146 $7.40 multicolored .80 .80
**815** A146 $9.90 multicolored 1.00 1.00
*Nos. 812-815 (4)* 2.85 2.85

A147

A148

Wild cats of Zimbabwe.

**1999, Mar. 16 Litho. *Perf. 14***

**816** A147 $1.20 Serval .45 .45
**817** A147 $5.60 Cheetah .70 .70
**818** A147 $7.40 Caracal .95 .95
**819** A147 $9.90 Leopard 1.25 1.25
*Nos. 816-819 (4)* 3.35 3.35

**1999, June 8 Litho. *Perf. 14¼***

Owls.

**820** A148 $1.20 Cape eagle owl .50 .50
**821** A148 $5.60 Grass owl .75 .75
**822** A148 $7.40 Barn owl 1.00 1.00
**823** A148 $9.90 Marsh owl 1.25 1.25
*Nos. 820-823 (4)* 3.50 3.50

Tourist Activities A149

**1999, Aug. 10 Litho. *Perf. 14¼x14***

**824** A149 $2 Canoeing .30 .30
**825** A149 $6.70 Rock climbing .55 .55
**826** A149 $7.70 Microlighting .60 .60
**827** A149 $9.10 White water rafting .75 .75
**828** A149 $12 Scenic view 1.00 1.00
**829** A149 $16 Viewing game 1.40 1.40
*Nos. 824-829 (6)* 4.60 4.60

A150

A151

Christmas: $2, Christmas time - Family time. $6.70, Christmas tree in Africa. $7.70, Joy to you this Christmas. $9.10, Christmas time - Flame lily time. $12, Glory to God & Peace on Earth. $16, The House of Christmas.

**1999, Oct. 12 Litho. *Perf. 14x14¼***

**830** A150 $2 multi .30 .30
**831** A150 $6.70 multi .55 .55
**832** A150 $7.70 multi .60 .40
**833** A150 $9.10 multi .80 .80
**834** A150 $12 multi 1.00 1.00
**835** A150 $16 multi 1.40 1.40
*Nos. 830-835 (6)* 4.65 4.45

**2000, Jan. 25 Litho. *Perf. 14¾***

Designs: 1c, Nyala. 10c, Construction. 30c, Timber. 50c, Tobacco auction floors. 70c, Harare Central Sorting Office. 80c, New international airport, Harare. $1, Westgate Shopping Complex. $2, Nile crocodile. $3, Pungwe water project. $4, Zebra. $5, Mining. $7, National University of Science and Technology. $10, Ostrich. $15, Cape parrot. $20, Leather products. $30, Lilac-breasted roller. $50, Victoria Falls. $100, Tokwe Mukorsi Dam.

**836** A151 1c multi .20 .20
**837** A151 10c multi .20 .20
**838** A151 30c multi .20 .20
**839** A151 50c multi .20 .20
**840** A151 70c multi .20 .20
**841** A151 80c multi .20 .20
**842** A151 $1 multi .20 .20
**843** A151 $2 multi .20 .20
**844** A151 $3 multi .20 .20
**845** A151 $4 multi .20 .20
**846** A151 $5 multi .25 .25
**847** A151 $7 multi .35 .35
**848** A151 $10 multi .60 .60
**849** A151 $15 multi .90 .90
**850** A151 $20 multi 1.10 1.10
**851** A151 $30 multi 1.75 1.75
**852** A151 $50 multi 2.75 2.75
**853** A151 $100 multi 5.75 5.75
*Nos. 836-853 (18)* 15.45 15.45

Sports — A152

**2000, Apr. 25 Litho. *Perf. 14***

**854** A152 $2 Basketball .35 .35
**855** A152 $6.70 Lawn tennis .60 .60
**856** A152 $7.70 Netball .80 .80
**857** A152 $9.10 Weight lifting .85 .85
**858** A152 $12 Taekwondo 1.10 1.10
**859** A152 $16 Diving 1.60 1.60
*Nos. 854-859 (6)* 5.30 5.30

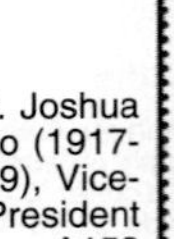

Dr. Joshua Nkomo (1917-99), Vice-President A153

Designs: $2, $12, Wearing suit. $9.10, $16, Wearing headdress.

**2000, June 27 Litho. *Perf. 14x14¼***
**Background Color**

**860** A153 $2 blue .50 .50
**861** A153 $9.10 green 1.25 1.25
**862** A153 $12 red 1.60 1.60
**863** A153 $16 orange 2.10 2.10
*Nos. 860-863 (4)* 5.45 5.45

Organizations Combatting Disease A154

Designs: $2, Ministry of Health. $6.70, Rehabilitation and Prevention of Tuberculosis (RAPT). $7.70, New Start centers. $9.10, Riders for Health. $12, Natl. Aids Coordination Program (NACP). $16, Rotary Intl.

**2000, July 18 Litho. *Perf. 14¼x14***

**864** A154 $2 multi .45 .45
**865** A154 $6.70 multi .75 .75
**866** A154 $7.70 multi .90 .90
**867** A154 $9.10 multi 1.10 1.10
**868** A154 $12 multi 1.40 1.40
**869** A154 $16 multi 1.90 1.90
*Nos. 864-869 (6)* 6.50 6.50

**Wild Fruits Type of 1991**

$2, Masawu. $6.70, Spiny monkey orange. $7.70, Bird plum. $9.10, Shakama plum. $12, Wild medlar. $16, Wild custard apple.

**2000, Oct. 24 Litho. *Perf. 14x14½***

**870-875** A117 Set of 6 4.00 4.00

Aviation A155

Designs: $8, Boeing 737-200. $12, BAe Hawk MK 60. $14, Hawker Hunter FGA-9. $16, Cessna/Reims F-337. $21, Aerospatiale Alouette III helicopter. $28, Boeing 767-200ER.

**2001, Jan. 31 Litho. *Perf. 14¼***

**876-881** A155 Set of 6 5.75 5.75

Total Solar Eclipse, June 21, 2001 — A156

Designs: $8, Solar prominences. $21, Eclipse path over Africa. $28, Eclipse phases (62x24mm).

***Perf. 14¼x14, 14½ ($28)***

**2001, Apr. 24 Litho.**

**882-884** A156 Set of 3 3.50 3.50

Folklore — A157

Designs: $8, The Hare Who Rode Horseback. $12, The Hippo Who Lost His Hair. $13, The Lion Who Was Saved by a Mouse. $16, The Bush Fowl Who Wakes the Sun. $21, The Chameleon Who Came Too Late. $28, The Tortoise Who Collected Wisdom.

**2001, July 24 Litho. *Perf. 14x14¼***

**885-890** A157 Set of 6 5.50 5.50
*a.* Souvenir sheet, #885-890 5.50 5.50

Heroes' Acre — A158

Designs: $8, Main entrance gate. $16, Statue of the Unknown Soldier. $21, General view. $28, Aerial view.

**2001, Aug. 7 Litho. *Perf. 14¼x14***

**891-894** A158 Set of 4 2.60 2.60

Year of Dialogue Among Civilizations A159

Winning stamp design entry in: $8, National competition (Three Faces, by Nation Mandla Mguni). $21, International competition.

**2001, Oct. 16 Litho. *Perf. 14¼***

**895-896** A159 Set of 2 2.40 2.40

Butterflies A160

Designs: $12, Large blue charaxes. $20, Painted lady. $25, Yellow pansy. $30, Gold-banded forester. $35, Sapphire. $45, Clear-spotted acrea.

**2001, Dec. 6 Litho. *Perf. 14¼x14***

**897-902** A160 Set of 6 10.50 10.50
*902a* Souvenir sheet, #897-902 10.50 10.50

Craftsmanship A161

Designs: $12, Knitting and crocheting. $20, Art and design. $25, Basket making. $30, Pottery. $35, Wood carving. $45, Sculpture.

**2002, Jan. 22**

**903-908** A161 Set of 6 11.00 11.00

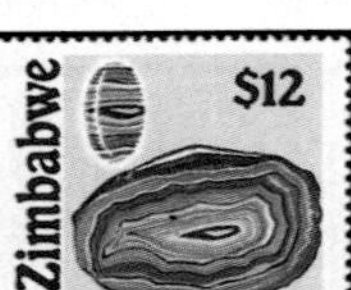

Gemstones A162

Designs: $12, Agate. $25, Aquamarine. $35, Diamond. $45, Emerald.

**2002, Apr. 23 Litho. *Perf. 14¼x14***

**909-912** A162 Set of 4 7.25 7.25

Childline
A163

Children's art: $12, Children embracing. $25, Girl on phone. $35, Teddy bear. $45, Arm with phone receiver.

**2002, June 4** **Litho.** ***Perf. 14¼x14***

| | | | |
|---|---|---|---|
| **913-916** A163 | Set of 4 | 7.25 | 7.25 |

First Lady Sally Mugabe (1931-92) — A164

Various portraits: $20, $50, $70, $90.

**2002, Aug. 6** ***Perf. 14x14¼***

| | | | |
|---|---|---|---|
| **917-920** A164 | Set of 4 | 13.50 | 13.50 |

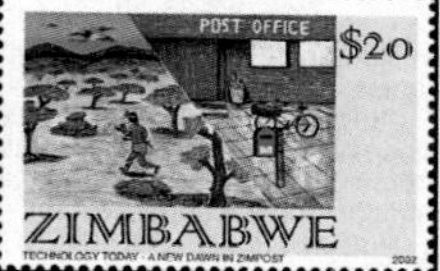


Children's Stamp Design Contest Winners A165

Designs: $20, Mail runner and bicycle at post office, by Agreement Ngwenya. $70, Mail runner and airplane, by Kudzai Chikomo.

**2002, Oct. 8** **Litho.** ***Perf. 14¼***

| | | | |
|---|---|---|---|
| **921-922** A165 | Set of 2 | 3.25 | 3.25 |

Wild Flowers A166

Designs: $20, Dissotis princeps. $35, Leonotis nepetifolia. $40, Hibiscus vitifolius. $50, Boophane disticha. $70, Pycnostachys urticifolia. $90, Gloriosa superba.

**2002, Oct. 22** ***Perf. 14¼x14***

| | | | |
|---|---|---|---|
| **923-928** A166 | Set of 6 | 16.00 | 16.00 |
| *928a* | Souvenir sheet, #923-928 | 17.00 | 17.00 |

History Society of Zimbabwe, 50th Anniv. — A167

Map of Zimbabwe and: $30, Society emblem. $80, Hourglass, books, diploma. $110, People listening to speaker. $140, Old building.

**2003, Jan. 28** **Litho.** ***Perf. 14x14¼***

| | | | |
|---|---|---|---|
| **929-932** A167 | Set of 4 | .90 | .90 |

Harare Intl. Festival of the Arts — A168

Designs: $30, Festival emblem. $80, Emblem and flower. $110, Eye and flowers. $140, Emblem and flowers.

**2003, Apr. 22** **Litho.** ***Perf. 14x14¼***

| | | | |
|---|---|---|---|
| **933-936** A168 | Set of 4 | .90 | .90 |

### Type of 2000

Designs: ($100), Bateleur eagle. $500, Goliath heron. $1000, White rhinoceros. $5000, Cheetah.

**2003, June 24** **Litho.** ***Perf. 14¾***

| | | | |
|---|---|---|---|
| **937** A151 ($100) multi | | .25 | .25 |
| **938** A151 $500 multi | | 1.25 | 1.25 |
| **939** A151 $1000 multi | | 2.50 | 2.50 |
| **940** A151 $5000 multi | | 12.50 | 12.50 |
| *Nos. 937-940 (4)* | | 16.50 | 16.50 |

Spiders A169

Designs: $150, Baboon spider. $200, Rain spider. $600, Black widow spider. $900, Wolf spider. $1250, Violin spider. $1600, Wall spider.

**2003, July 30** ***Perf. 14¼***

| | | | |
|---|---|---|---|
| **941-946** A169 | Set of 6 | 11.50 | 11.50 |
| *946a* | Souvenir sheet, #941-946 | 11.50 | 11.50 |

Women Empowerment A170

Woman in cap and gown with: $300, Globe, hoe and briefcase. $2100, Traditional woman.

**2003, Oct. 14** **Litho.** ***Perf. 14¼***

| | | | |
|---|---|---|---|
| **947-948** A170 | Set of 2 | 6.00 | 6.00 |

Endangered Medicinal Herbs — A171

Designs: $200, Wild verbena. $500, Pimpernel. $1000, African arrowroot. $3000, Bird pepper. $4200, Wild garlic. $5400, Cleome.

**2003, Oct. 28** ***Perf. 14x14¼***

| | | | |
|---|---|---|---|
| **949-954** A171 | Set of 6 | 22.50 | 22.50 |
| ***a.*** | Miniature sheet, #949-954 | 22.50 | 22.50 |

Environmental Awareness A172

Designs: $500, Environment Africa. $3000, Sondela. $4200, Water Africa. $5400, Tree Africa.

**2004, Feb. 17** **Litho.** ***Perf. 14x14¼***

| | | | |
|---|---|---|---|
| **955-958** A172 | Set of 4 | *10.00* | *10.00* |

Medals — A173

Designs: $1500, Zimbabwe Independence Medal. $9000, Bronze Cross of Zimbabwe. $13,000, Silver Cross of Zimbabwe. $16,500, Gold Cross of Zimbabwe.

**2004, Apr. 6** **Litho.** ***Perf. 14¼***

| | | | |
|---|---|---|---|
| **959-962** A173 | Set of 4 | *18.00* | *18.00* |

Aloes — A174

Designs: $1500, Aloe ballii. $3,000, Aloe rhodesiana. $9000, Aloe greatheadii. $10,000, Aloe ortholopha. $13,000, Aloe inyangensis. $16,500, Aloe arborescens.

**2004, July 20** **Litho.** ***Perf. 14x14¼***

| | | | |
|---|---|---|---|
| **963-968** A174 | Set of 6 | *20.00* | *20.00* |
| *968a* | Miniature sheet, #963-968 | *20.00* | *20.00* |

Co-Vice President Simon Vengai Muzenda (1922-2003) A175

Background colors: $2300, Red. $12,000, Yellow. $17,000, Green. $22,000, Gray.

**2004, Sept. 20** **Litho.** ***Perf. 14x14¼***

| | | | |
|---|---|---|---|
| **969-972** A175 | Set of 4 | *20.00* | *20.00* |

Conservation A176

Winning art in conservation stamp design contest: $4600, Butterfly, by Kingston Chigidhani. $33,500, Hands and wildlife, by Kudzai Chikomo.

**2004, Oct. 26** **Litho.** ***Perf. 14¼x14***

| | | | |
|---|---|---|---|
| **973-974** A176 | Set of 2 | *14.00* | *14.00* |

### Miniature Sheet

Birds — A177

No. 975: a, $500, African fish eagles, national bird of Zambia. b, $1000, Purple-crested louries, national bird of Swaziland. c, $2300, African fish eagles, national bird of Zimbabwe. d, $3000, Blue cranes, national bird of South Africa. e, $5000, Cattle egrets, national bird of Botswana. f, $9000, Peregrine falcons, national bird of Angola. g, $12,000, Bar-tailed trogons. h, $17,000, African fish eagles, national bird of Namibia.

**2004, Oct. 11** **Litho.** ***Perf. 14***

| | | | |
|---|---|---|---|
| **975** A177 | Sheet of 8, #a-h | *18.50* | *18.50* |

See Angola No. , Botswana Nos. 792-793, Malawi No. , Namibia No. 1052, South Africa No. 1342, Swaziland Nos. 727-735, and Zambia No. 1033.

Birds — A178

Designs: $500, Black-collared barbet. $5000, Gray-headed bush shrike. Z, Red-headed weaver. $10,000, Golden-breasted bunting. $20,000, Cut-throat finch. A, Cabanis's bunting. E, Miombo double-collared sunbird. R, Crested barbet. $50,000, Heuglin's robin. $100,000, Giant kingfisher.

**2005, Feb. 8** **Litho.** ***Perf. 14¾x14½***

| | | | |
|---|---|---|---|
| **976** A178 | $500 multi | *.20* | *.20* |
| **977** A178 | $5000 multi | *1.75* | *1.75* |
| **978** A178 | Z multi | *2.25* | *2.25* |
| **979** A178 | $10,000 multi | *3.50* | *3.50* |
| **980** A178 | $20,000 multi | *6.75* | *6.75* |
| **981** A178 | A multi | *10.00* | *10.00* |
| **982** A178 | E multi | *13.00* | *13.00* |
| **983** A178 | R multi | *16.50* | *16.50* |
| **984** A178 | $50,000 multi | *16.50* | *16.50* |
| **985** A178 | $100,000 multi | *32.50* | *32.50* |
| *Nos. 976-985 (10)* | | *102.95* | *102.95* |

On day of issue No. 978 sold for $6900, No. 981 sold for $30,000, No. 982 sold for $40,000, and No. 983 sold for $50,000.

Clouds A179

Designs: $6900, Cirrus. $13,800, Nimbostratus. $30,000, Altocumulus. $40,000, Cumulonimbus.

**2005, Apr. 26** ***Perf. 14¼***

| | | | |
|---|---|---|---|
| **986-989** A179 | Set of 4 | *30.00* | *30.00* |

Snakes A180

Designs: $6900, Banded Egyptian cobra. $13,800, Puff adder. $20,000, Boomslang. $25,000, Mozambique spitting cobra. $30,000, Gaboon viper. $40,000, Black mamba.

**2005, July 12** **Litho.** ***Perf. 14¼x14***

| | | | |
|---|---|---|---|
| **990-995** A180 | Set of 6 | *16.00* | *16.00* |
| *995a* | Miniature sheet, #990-995 | *16.00* | *16.00* |

Governmental Officials — A181

Designs: $6900, Josiah Tongogara (1940-79), Chief of Defense. $13,800, Herbert Chitepo (1923-75), Director of Public Prosecutions. $30,000, Bernard Chidzero (1927-2002), Minister of Economic Planning. $50,000, Moven Mahachi (1948-2001), Minister of various departments.

**2005, Aug. 4** **Litho.** ***Perf. 14x14¼***

| | | | |
|---|---|---|---|
| **996-999** A181 | Set of 4 | *12.00* | *12.00* |

UNESCO World Heritage Sites
A182

Designs: Z, Soapstone Zimbabwe bird, Great Zimbabwe National Park. $15,500, Wall, Khami Ruins. $52,000, Elephant, Mana Pools National Park. $62,000, Victoria Falls.

**2005, Oct. 6 Litho. *Perf. 14¼***

| | | | | |
|---|---|---|---|---|
| **1000-1003** | A182 | Set of 4 | *11.00* | *11.00* |

No. 1000 sold for $10,250 on day of issue.

World AIDS Day — A183

Designs: $18,000, Cooking pot, field tender, care for the ill. $80,000, Children teaching AIDS prevention.

**2005, Dec. 1 Litho. *Perf. 14¼x14***

| | | | | |
|---|---|---|---|---|
| **1004-1005** | A183 | Set of 2 | 2.60 | 2.60 |

Food — A184

Designs: $25,000, Mushrooms. $35,000, Rapoko, corn and sorghum. $50,000, Pumpkin, watermelon, spiny cucumber. $150,000, Wild fruits. $250,000, Herbs. $300,000, Sweet potato, cassava, peanuts.

**2006, Jan. 17 Litho. *Perf. 14x14¼***

| | | | | |
|---|---|---|---|---|
| **1006-1011** | A184 | Set of 6 | 16.50 | 16.50 |
| *1011a* | | Miniature sheet, #1006-1011 | 16.50 | 16.50 |

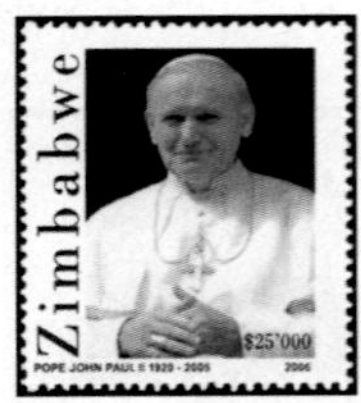


Pope John Paul II (1920-2005)
A185

Pope: $25,000, Wearing crucifix. $250,000, Holding crucifix.

**2006, Feb. 9**

| | | | | |
|---|---|---|---|---|
| **1012-1013** | A185 | Set of 2 | 5.50 | 5.50 |
| *1013a* | | Souvenir sheet, #1012-1013 | 5.50 | 5.50 |

Water Conservation
A186

Designs: $30,000, Faucet and pail. $225,000, Flood irrigation system. $375,000, Lions at waterhole. $450,000, Kariba Dam.

**2006, Apr. 25 Litho. *Perf. 14x14¼***

| | | | | |
|---|---|---|---|---|
| **1014-1017** | A186 | Set of 4 | *21.50* | *21.50* |

National Heroes — A187

Flag and: $60,000, Leopold T. Takawira (1916-70), first vice-president of Zimbabwe African National Union. $350,000, Simon C. Mazorodze (1933-81), health minister. $500,000, Herbert M. Ushewokunze (1933-95), government minister. $650,000, Tichafa S. Parirenyatwa (1927-62), deputy president of Zimbabwe African People's Union.

**2006, July 25 Litho. *Perf. 14x14¼***

| | | | | |
|---|---|---|---|---|
| **1018-1021** | A187 | Set of 4 | *31.00* | *31.00* |

Huts — A188

Designs: $100, One hut. $800, Three huts.

**2006, Oct. 24 Litho. *Perf. 14¼x14***

| | | | | |
|---|---|---|---|---|
| **1022-1023** | A188 | Set of 2 | 7.25 | 7.25 |

Bridges
A189

Designs: Z, Mpudzi River Bridge. $450, Victoria Falls Bridge. $600, Limpopo River Bridge. $750, Otto Beit Bridge. $800, Kariba Barrage Bridge. $1000, Birchenough Bridge.

**2006, Oct. 24**

| | | | | |
|---|---|---|---|---|
| **1024-1029** | A189 | Set of 6 | 30.00 | 30.00 |

No. 1024 sold for $100 on day of issue.

Trees — A190

Designs: $150, Ziziphuus mauritania. $600, Schlerochra birrea. $750, Jatropha carcus. $1000, Uaparca kirkiana.

**2006, Dec. 1 Litho. *Perf. 14x14¼***

| | | | | |
|---|---|---|---|---|
| **1030-1033** | A190 | Set of 4 | 20.00 | 20.00 |

## POSTAGE DUE STAMPS

D1

D2

**1981 Litho. *Perf. 14½***

| | | | | |
|---|---|---|---|---|
| **J20** | D1 | 1c emerald | .40 | 1.10 |
| **J21** | D1 | 2c ultramarine | .40 | 1.10 |
| **J22** | D1 | 5c lilac | .50 | 1.40 |
| **J23** | D1 | 6c yellow | .65 | 2.00 |
| **J24** | D1 | 10c red | 1.40 | 4.25 |
| | | *Nos. J20-J24 (5)* | 3.35 | 9.85 |

For surcharge see No. J30.

**1985, Aug. 21 Litho. *Perf. 14½***

| | | | | |
|---|---|---|---|---|
| **J25** | D2 | 1c pale orange | .40 | .75 |
| **J26** | D2 | 2c lilac rose | .40 | .75 |
| **J27** | D2 | 6c light green | .40 | .75 |
| **J28** | D2 | 10c tan | .40 | .75 |
| **J29** | D2 | 13c bright blue | .40 | .75 |
| | | *Nos. J25-J29 (5)* | 2.00 | 3.75 |

No. J24 Surcharged

**1990, Jan. 2 Litho. *Perf. 14½***

| | | | | |
|---|---|---|---|---|
| **J30** | D1 | 25c on 10c #J24 | *10.00* | *10.00* |

D3

D4

**1995, Jan. 17 Litho. *Perf. 14½***

| | | | | |
|---|---|---|---|---|
| **J31** | D3 | 1c yellow | .25 | .25 |
| **J32** | D3 | 2c yellow orange | .25 | .25 |
| **J33** | D3 | 5c rose lilac | .25 | .25 |
| **J34** | D3 | 10c pale blue | .25 | .25 |
| **J35** | D3 | 25c violet | .25 | .25 |
| **J36** | D3 | 40c green | .25 | .25 |
| **J37** | D3 | 60c orange | .25 | .25 |
| **J38** | D3 | $1 brown | .40 | .40 |
| | | *Nos. J31-J38 (8)* | 2.15 | 2.15 |

**2000, Jan. 25 Litho. *Perf. 14½***

Bird sculpture.

| | | | | |
|---|---|---|---|---|
| **J39** | D4 | 1c blk, lt grn & grn | .20 | .20 |
| **J40** | D4 | 10c blk, lt blue & blue | .20 | .20 |
| **J41** | D4 | 50c blk, lt brn & brn | .20 | .20 |
| **J42** | D4 | $1 blk, pink & red | .20 | .20 |
| **J43** | D4 | $2 blk, lt yel & yel | .20 | .20 |
| **J44** | D4 | $5 blk, lil & red vio | .25 | .25 |
| **J45** | D4 | $10 blk, lt ver & ver | .55 | .55 |
| | | *Nos. J39-J45 (7)* | 1.80 | 1.80 |

## ZULULAND

ˈzü-ˌlü-ˌland

LOCATION — Northeastern part of Natal, South Africa
GOVT. — British Colony, 1887-1897
AREA — 10,427 sq. mi.
POP. — 230,000 (estimated 1900)
CAPITAL — Eshowe

12 Pence = 1 Shilling
20 Shillings = 1 Pound

Stamps of Great Britain Overprinted

**1888-93 Wmk. 30 *Perf. 14***

| | | | | |
|---|---|---|---|---|
| **1** | A54 | ½p vermilion | 4.25 | 3.00 |
| **2** | A40 | 1p violet | 29.00 | 4.50 |
| **3** | A56 | 2p green & red | 17.50 | 32.50 |
| **4** | A57 | 2½p vio, *bl* ('91) | 27.50 | 22.50 |
| **5** | A58 | 3p violet, *yel* | 29.00 | 25.00 |
| **6** | A59 | 4p green & brn | 50.00 | 65.00 |
| **7** | A61 | 5p lil & bl ('93) | 100.00 | 150.00 |
| **8** | A62 | 6p vio, *rose* | 15.00 | 20.00 |
| **9** | A63 | 9p blue & lil ('92) | 100.00 | 100.00 |
| **10** | A65 | 1sh green ('92) | 125.00 | 150.00 |
| | | **Wmk. 31** | | |
| **11** | A51 | 5sh rose ('92) | 600.00 | *700.00* |
| | | *Nos. 1-10 (10)* | 497.25 | 572.50 |

Natal No. 66 Overprinted

**1888-94 Wmk. 2**

| | | | | |
|---|---|---|---|---|
| **12** | A14 | ½p green, no period | 26.00 | *45.00* |
| *a.* | | Period after "Zululand" | 62.50 | *85.00* |
| *b.* | | As "a," double overprint | 3,000. | 1,750. |
| *c.* | | As "a," invtd. overprint | 1,400. | |
| *d.* | | As "a," pair, one without ovpt. | *8,500.* | |
| *e.* | | As No. 12, double overprint | 1,600. | *1,750.* |

**Natal No. 71 Ovptd. Like Nos. 1-11**

| | | | | |
|---|---|---|---|---|
| **13** | A11 | 6p violet ('94) | 62.50 | 62.50 |

A1

A2

**1891**

| | | | | |
|---|---|---|---|---|
| **14** | A1 | 1p lilac | 3.50 | 3.50 |

By proclamation of the Governor of Zululand, dated June 27th, 1891, No. 14 was declared to be a postage stamp.

**1894-96 Typo.**

| | | | | |
|---|---|---|---|---|
| **15** | A2 | ½p lilac & grn | 3.75 | 5.00 |
| **16** | A2 | 1p lilac & rose | 5.75 | 2.25 |
| **17** | A2 | 2½p lilac & blue | 16.00 | 9.75 |
| **18** | A2 | 3p lilac & brn | 9.25 | 4.00 |
| **19** | A2 | 6p lilac & blk | 22.50 | 22.50 |
| **20** | A2 | 1sh green | 45.00 | 45.00 |
| **21** | A2 | 2sh6p grn & blk ('96) | 85.00 | *97.50* |
| **22** | A2 | 4sh grn & car rose | 125.00 | *175.00* |
| **23** | A2 | £1 violet, *red* | 550.00 | 625.00 |
| **24** | A2 | £5 vio & blk, *red* | 5,250. | *1,750.* |
| | | *Nos. 15-23 (9)* | 862.25 | 986.00 |

Numerals of #19-24 are in color on plain tablet.

**Purple or violet cancellations are not necessarily revenue cancels.** 14 of the 17 post offices and agencies used violet as well as black postal cancellations.

Zululand was annexed to Natal in Dec. 1897 and separate stamps were discontinued June 30, 1898.

# Vol. 6 Number Additions, Deletions & Changes

| Number in 2007 Catalogue | Number in 2008 Catalogue |
|---|---|
| **Spain** | |
| new | 2810a |
| new | 2811a |
| new | 2847a |
| new | 2848a |
| new | 2884a |
| new | 2885a |
| **Tanzania** | |
| 1441 | 1440e |
| **Togo** | |
| C394a | deleted |
| **Turkey in Asia** | |
| 36 | deleted |
| 36a | 36 |
| **Vatican City** | |
| new | 267a |

# Illustrated Identifier

This section pictures stamps or parts of stamp designs that will help identify postage stamps that do not have English words on them.

Many of the symbols that identify stamps of countries are shown here as well as typical examples of their stamps.

See the Index and Identifier on the previous pages for stamps with inscriptions such as "sen," "posta," "Baja Porto," "Helvetia," "K.S.A.", etc.

*Linn's Stamp Identifier* is now available. The 144 pages include more 2,000 inscriptions and over 500 large stamp illustrations. Available from Linn's Stamp News, P.O. Box 29, Sidney, OH 45365-0029.

## 1. HEADS, PICTURES AND NUMERALS

### GREAT BRITAIN

Great Britain stamps never show the country name, but, except for postage dues, show a picture of the reigning monarch.

Victoria

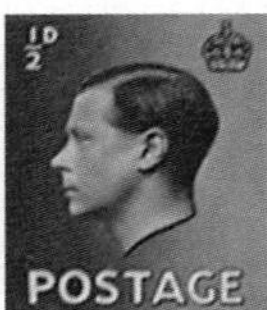

Edward VII George V Edward VIII

George VI

Elizabeth II

Some George VI and Elizabeth II stamps are surcharged in annas, new paisa or rupees. These are listed under Oman.

Silhouette (sometimes facing right, generally at the top of stamp)

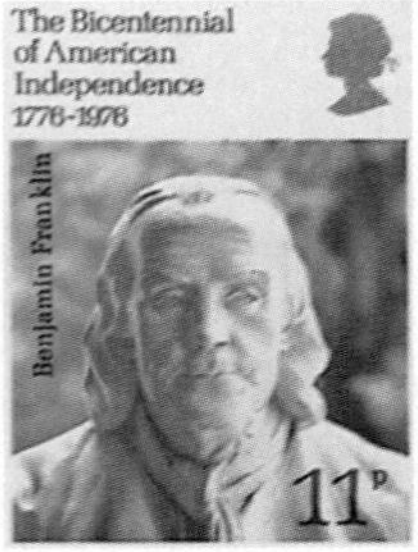

The silhouette indicates this is a British stamp. It is not a U.S. stamp.

### VICTORIA

Queen Victoria

### INDIA

Other stamps of India show this portrait of Queen Victoria and the words "Service" and "Annas."

### AUSTRIA

### YUGOSLAVIA

(Also BOSNIA & HERZEGOVINA if imperf.)

### BOSNIA & HERZEGOVINA

Denominations also appear in top corners instead of bottom corners.

### HUNGARY

Another stamp has posthorn facing left

### BRAZIL

### AUSTRALIA

Kangaroo and Emu

### GERMANY

### Mecklenburg-Vorpommern

## SWITZERLAND

## PALAU

# 2. ORIENTAL INSCRIPTIONS

## CHINA

Any stamp with this one character is from China (Imperial, Republic or People's Republic).
This character appears in a four-character overprint on stamps of Manchukuo. These stamps are local provisionals, which are unlisted. Other overprinted Manchukuo stamps show this character, but have more than four characters in the overprints. These are listed in People's Republic of China.

Some Chinese stamps show the Sun.

Most stamps of Republic of China show this series of characters.

Stamps with the China character and this character are from People's Republic of China. 人

Calligraphic form of People's Republic of China

| (一) | (二) | (三) | (四) | (五) | (六) |
|---|---|---|---|---|---|
| 1 | 2 | 3 | 4 | 5 | 6 |
| (七) | (八) | (九) | (十) | (一十) | (二十) |
| 7 | 8 | 9 | 10 | 11 | 12 |

### Chinese stamps without China character

## REPUBLIC OF CHINA

## PEOPLE'S REPUBLIC OF CHINA

Mao Tse-tung

## MANCHUKUO

Temple

Emperor Pu-Yi

The first 3 characters are common to many Manchukuo stamps.

The last 3 characters are common to other Manchukuo stamps.

Orchid Crest

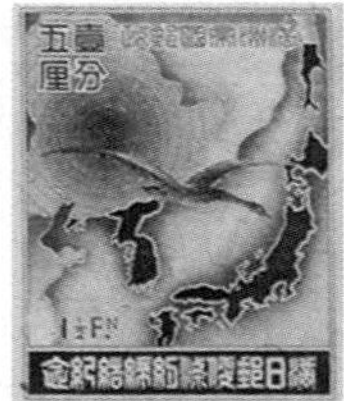
Manchukuo stamp without these elements

## JAPAN

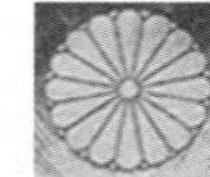
Chrysanthemum Crest

Country Name

Japanese stamps without these elements

The number of characters in the center and the design of dragons on the sides will vary.

## RYUKYU ISLANDS

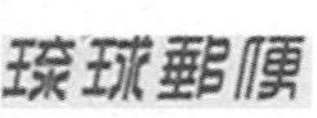
Country Name

## PHILIPPINES (Japanese Occupation)

Country Name

## NORTH BORNEO (Japanese Occupation)

Indicates Japanese Occupation

Country Name

## MALAYA (Japanese Occupation)

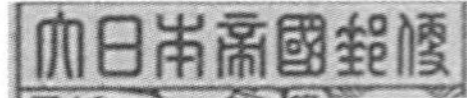
Indicates Japanese Occupation

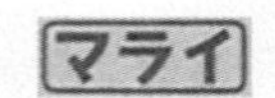
Country Name

## BURMA

## Union of Myanmar

ပြည်ထောင်စုမြန်မာနိုင်ငံတော်

Union of Myanmar

## (Japanese Occupation)

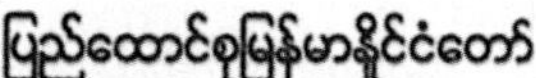

Indicates Japanese Occupation

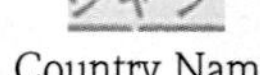
Country Name

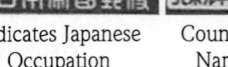

Other Burma Japanese Occupation stamps without these elements

Burmese Script

## KOREA

These two characters, in any order, are common to stamps from the Republic of Korea (South Korea) or of the People's Democratic Republic of Korea (North Korea).

This series of four characters can be found on the stamps of both Koreas. Most stamps of the Democratic People's Republic of Korea (North Korea) have just this inscription.

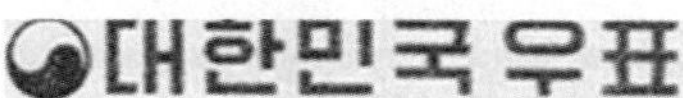


Indicates Republic of Korea (South Korea)

South Korean postage stamps issed after 1952 do not show currency expressed in Latin letters. Stamps wiith "HW," "HWAN," "WON," "WN," "W" or "W" with two lines through it, if not illustrated in listings of stamps before this date, are revenues. North Korean postage stamps do not have currency expressed in Latin letters.

Yin Yang appears on some stamps.

## THAILAND

Country Name

King Chulalongkorn

King Prajadhipok and Chao P'ya Chakri

## 3. CENTRAL AND EASTERN ASIAN INSCRIPTIONS

### INDIA - FEUDATORY STATES

**Alwar**

**Bhor**

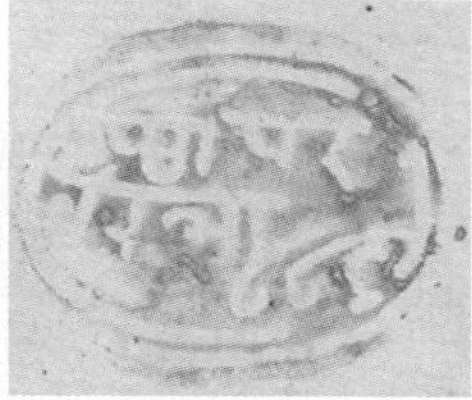

**Bundi**

Similar stamps come with different designs in corners and differently drawn daggers (at center of circle).

**Dhar**

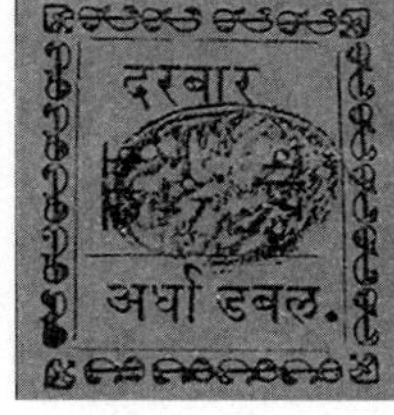


**Faridkot**

**Hyderabad**

Similar stamps exist with straight line frame around stamp, and also with different central design which is inscribed "Postage" or "Post & Receipt."

**Indore**

**Jhalawar**

A similar stamp has the central figure in an oval.

### Nandgaon

### Nowanuggur

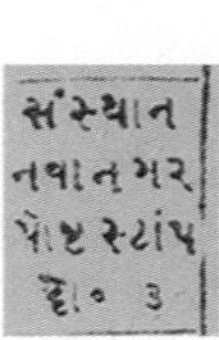

### Poonch

Similar stamps exist in various sizes

### Rajpeepla

### Soruth

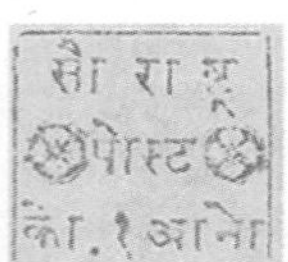

### BANGLADESH

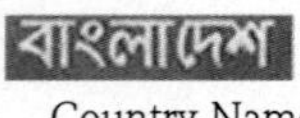


Country Name

### NEPAL

Similar stamps are smaller, have squares in upper corners and have five or nine characters in central bottom panel.

### TANNU TUVA

### ISRAEL

### GEORGIA

This inscription is found on other pictorial stamps.

Country Name

### ARMENIA

The four characters are found somewhere on pictorial stamps. On some stamps only the middle two are found.

## 4. AFRICAN INSCRIPTIONS

### ETHIOPIA

## 5. ARABIC INSCRIPTIONS

١ ٢ ٣ ٤ ٥
1 2 3 4 5

٦ ٧ ٨ ٩ ٠
6 7 8 9 0

## AFGHANISTAN

Many early Afghanistan stamps show Tiger's head, many of these have ornaments protruding from outer ring, others show inscriptions in black.

Arabic Script

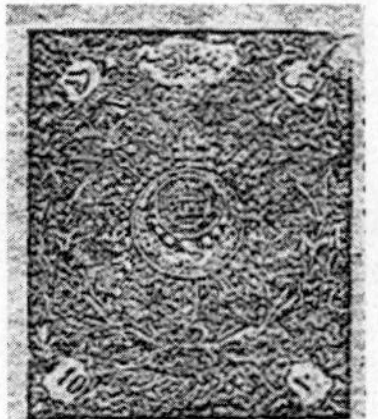

Mosque Gate & Crossed Cannons
The four characters are found somewhere on pictorial stamps. On some stamps only the middle two are found.

## BAHRAIN

## EGYPT

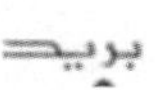

Postage

## INDIA - FEUDATORY STATES

### Jammu & Kashmir

Text and thickness of ovals vary. Some stamps have flower devices in corners.

### India-Hyderabad

## IRAN

Country Name

Royal Crown

Lion with Sword

Symbol

## IRAQ

## JORDAN

## LEBANON

Similar types have denominations at top and slightly different design.

## LIBYA

Country Name in various styles

Other Libya stamps show Eagle and Shield (head facing either direction) or Red, White and Black Shield (with or without eagle in center).

Without Country Name

## SAUDI ARABIA

Tughra (Central design)

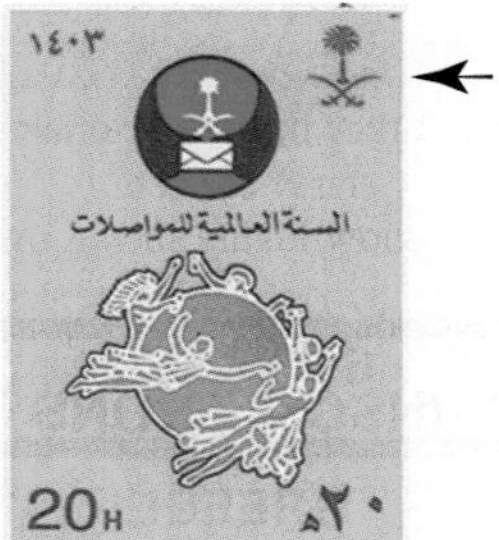

Palm Tree and Swords

## SYRIA

## THRACE

## YEMEN

## PAKISTAN

## PAKISTAN - BAHAWALPUR

Country Name in top panel, star and crescent

## TURKEY

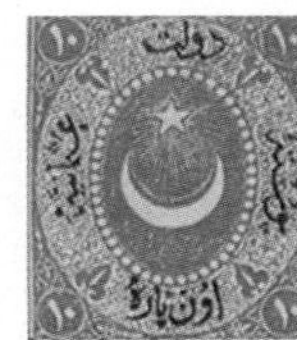

Star & Crescent is a device found on many Turkish stamps, but is also found on stamps from other Arabic areas (see Pakistan-Bahawalpur)

Tughra (similar tughras can be found on stamps of Turkey in Asia, Afghanistan and Saudi Arabia)

Mohammed V

Mustafa Kemal

Plane, Star and Crescent

## TURKEY IN ASIA

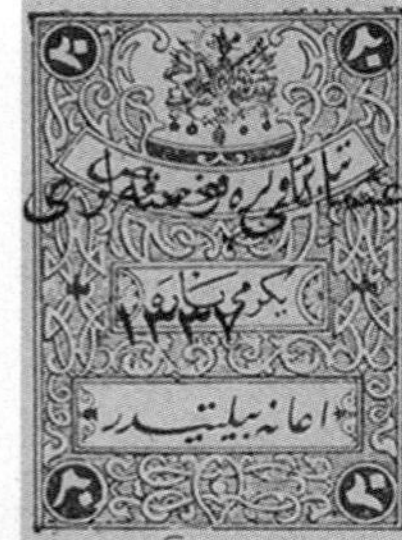

Other Turkey in Asia pictorials show star & crescent.
Other stamps show tughra shown under Turkey.

## 6. GREEK INSCRIPTIONS

### GREECE

Country Name in various styles
(Some Crete stamps overprinted with the Greece country name are listed in Crete.)

Lepta

Drachma Drachmas

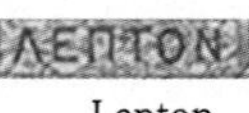

Lepton

Abbreviated Country Name ΕΛΛ.

Other forms of Country Name

No country name

### CRETE

Country Name

These words are on other stamps

Grosion

Crete stamps with a surcharge that have the year "1922" are listed under Greece.

**EPIRUS** **IONIAN IS.**

Country Name

## 7. CYRILLIC INSCRIPTIONS

### RUSSIA

Postage Stamp

Imperial Eagle

Postage in various styles

Abbreviation for Kopeck

Abbreviation for Ruble

Russian

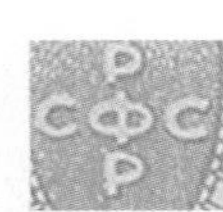

Abbreviation for Russian Soviet Federated Socialist Republic

RSFSR stamps were overprinted (see below)

Abbreviation for Union of Soviet Socialist Republics

This item is footnoted in Latvia

### RUSSIA - Army of the North

"OKCA"

### RUSSIA - Wenden

### RUSSIAN OFFICES IN THE TURKISH EMPIRE

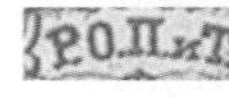

These letters appear on other stamps of the Russian offices.

The unoverprinted version of this stamp and a similar stamp were overprinted by various countries (see below).

### ARMENIA

### BELARUS

### FAR EASTERN REPUBLIC

Country Name

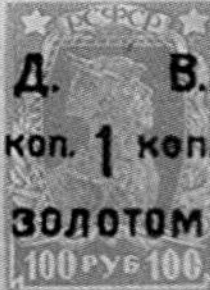

## SOUTH RUSSIA

Country Name

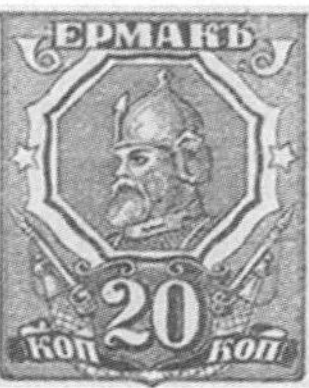

## FINLAND

Circles and Dots on stamps similar to Imperial Russia issues

## BATUM

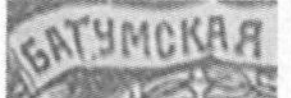

Forms of Country Name

## TRANSCAUCASIAN FEDERATED REPUBLICS

Abbreviation for Country Name

## KAZAKHSTAN

ҚАЗАҚСТАН

Country Name

## KYRGYZSTAN

КЫРГЫЗСТАН

Country Name

## ROMANIA

## TADJIKISTAN

Country Name & Abbreviation

## UKRAINE

Україні

Country Name in various forms

The trident appears on many stamps, usually as an overprint.

Abbreviation for Ukrainian Soviet Socialist Republic

## WESTERN UKRAINE

Abbreviation for Country Name

## AZERBAIJAN

Country Name

Abbreviation for Azerbaijan Soviet Socialist Republic

## MONTENEGRO

ЦРНА ГОРА

Country Name in various forms

Abbreviation for country name

No country name (A similar Montenegro stamp without country name has same vignette.)

## SERBIA

СРПСКА СРБИЈА

Country Name in various forms

Abbreviation for country name

No country name

## SERBIA & MONTENEGRO

## YUGOSLAVIA

ЈУГОСЛАВИЈА

Showing country name

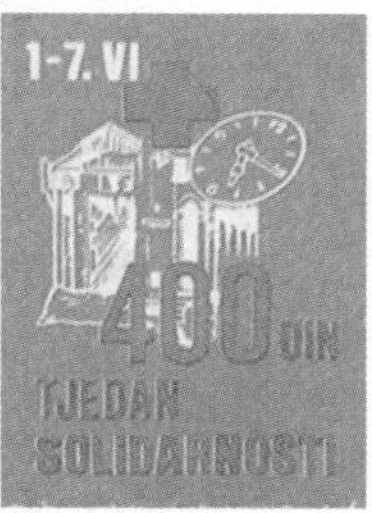


No Country Name

## MACEDONIA

МАКЕДОНИЈА

МАКЕДОНИЈА

Country Name

МАКЕДОНСКИ

Different form of Country Name

## BOSNIA & HERZEGOVINA (Serb Administration)

РЕПУБЛИКА СРПСКА

Country Name

РЕПУБЛИКЕ СРПСКЕ

Different form of Country Name

No Country Name

## BULGARIA

Country Name Postage

Stotinka

Stotinki (plural) Abbreviation for Stotinki

Country Name in various forms and styles

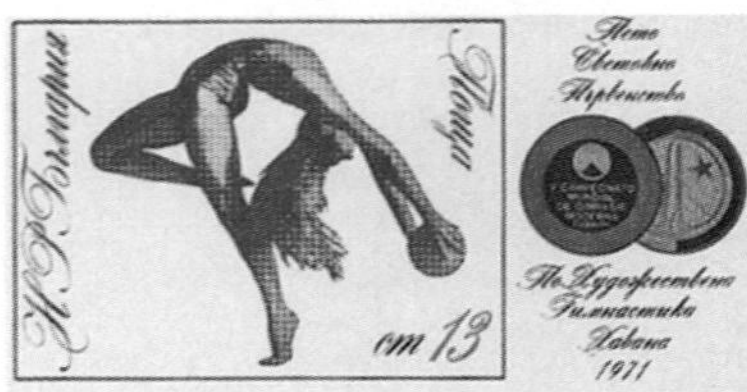

No country name

Abbreviation for Lev, leva

## MONGOLIA

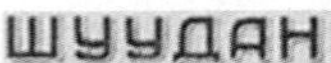

Country name in one word Tugrik in Cyrillic

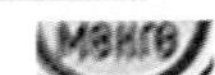
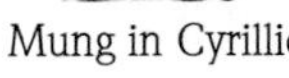

Country name in two words Mung in Cyrillic

Mung in Mongolian

Tugrik in Mongolian

Arms

No Country Name

# INDEX AND IDENTIFIER

**All page numbers shown are those in this Volume 6.**

Postage stamps that do not have English words on them are shown in the Identifier which begins on page 1164.

**D** 

**E.A.F. overprinted on stamps of Great Britain** 

**15 August 1947 (Pakistan #23)** 

# Pronunciation Symbols

ə .... banana, collide, abut

ˈə, ˌə .... humdrum, abut

ə .... immediately preceding \l\, \n\, \m\, \ŋ\, as in battle, mitten, eaten, and sometimes open \ˈō-p$^{ə}$m\, lock and key \-$^{ə}$ŋ-\; immediately following \l\, \m\, \r\, as often in French table, prisme, titre

ər .... further, merger, bird

ˈər-, ˈə-r .... as in two different pronunciations of hurry \ˈhər-ē, ˈhə-rē\

a .... mat, map, mad, gag, snap, patch

ā .... day, fade, date, aorta, drape, cape

ä .... bother, cot, and, with most American speakers, father, cart

ȧ .... father as pronounced by speakers who do not rhyme it with *bother*; French patte

aů .... now, loud, out

b .... baby, rib

ch .... chin, nature \ˈnā-chər\

d .... did, adder

e .... bet, bed, peck

ˈē, ˌē .... beat, nosebleed, evenly, easy

ē .... easy, mealy

f .... fifty, cuff

g .... go, big, gift

h .... hat, ahead

hw .... whale as pronounced by those who do not have the same pronunciation for both *whale* and *wail*

i .... tip, banish, active

ī .... site, side, buy, tripe

j .... job, gem, edge, join, judge

k .... kin, cook, ache

k̲ .... German ich, Buch; one pronunciation of loch

l .... lily, pool

m .... murmur, dim, nymph

n .... no, own

$^{n}$ .... indicates that a preceding vowel or diphthong is pronounced with the nasal passages open, as in French *un bon vin blanc* \œ$^{n}$ -bō$^{n}$ -va$^{n}$ -blä$^{n}$\

ŋ .... sing \ˈsiŋ\, singer \ˈsiŋ-ər\, finger \ˈfiŋ-gər\, ink \ˈiŋk \

ō .... bone, know, beau

ȯ .... saw, all, gnaw, caught

œ .... French boeuf, German Hölle

œ̄ .... French feu, German Höhle

ȯi .... coin, destroy

p .... pepper, lip

r .... red, car, rarity

s .... source, less

sh .... as in shy, mission, machine, special (actually, this is a single sound, not two); with a hyphen between, two sounds as in *grasshopper* \ˈgras-ˌhä-pər\

t .... tie, attack, late, later, latter

th .... as in thin, ether (actually, this is a single sound, not two); with a hyphen between, two sounds as in *knighthood* \ˈnīt-ˌhůd\

t̲h̲ .... then, either, this (actually, this is a single sound, not two)

ü .... rule, youth, union \ˈyün-yən\, few \ˈfyü\

ů .... pull, wood, book, curable \ˈkyůr-ə-bəl\, fury \ˈfyůr-ē\

ᵫ .... German füllen, hübsch

ᵫ̄ .... French rue, German fühlen

v .... vivid, give

w .... we, away

y .... yard, young, cue \ˈkyü\, mute \ˈmyüt\, union \ˈyün-yən\

$^{y}$ .... indicates that during the articulation of the sound represented by the preceding character the front of the tongue has substantially the position it has for the articulation of the first sound of *yard*, as in French *digne* \dēn$^{y}$\

z .... zone, raise

zh .... as in vision, azure \ˈa-zhər\ (actually, this is a single sound, not two); with a hyphen between, two sounds as in *hogshead* \ˈhȯgz-ˌhed, ˈhägz-\

\ .... slant line used in pairs to mark the beginning and end of a transcription: \ˈpen\

ˈ .... mark preceding a syllable with primary (strongest) stress: \ˈpen-mən-ˌship\

ˌ .... mark preceding a syllable with secondary (medium) stress: \ˈpen-mən-ˌship\

\- .... mark of syllable division

( ) .... indicate that what is symbolized between is present in some utterances but not in others: *factory* \ˈfak-t(ə-)rē\

÷ .... indicates that many regard as unacceptable the pronunciation variant immediately following: *cupola* \ˈkyü-pə-lə, ÷-ˌlō\

# INDEX TO ADVERTISERS 2008 VOLUME 6

# 2008 VOLUME 6 DEALER DIRECTORY YELLOW PAGE LISTINGS

**This section of your Scott Catalogue contains advertisements to help you conveniently find what you need, when you need it...!**

## Accessories

**BROOKLYN GALLERY COIN & STAMP, INC.**
8725 4th Ave.
Brooklyn, NY 11209
PH: 718-745-5701
FAX: 718-745-2775
info@brooklyngallery.com
www.brooklyngallery.com

## Appraisals

**COLONIAL STAMP COMPANY**
5757 Wilshire Blvd. PH #8
Los Angeles, CA 90036
PH: 323-933-9435
FAX: 323-939-9930
Toll Free in North America
PH: 877-272-6693
FAX: 877-272-6694
info@colonialstampcompany.com
www.colonialstampcompany.com

## Approvals-Personalized WW & US

**THE KEEPING ROOM**
PO Box 257
Trumbull, CT 06611
PH: 203-372-8436

## Asia

**MICHAEL ROGERS, INC.**
Mailing Address:
336 Grove Ave.
Suite B
Winter Park, FL 32789-3602
Walk-in Address:
Ranch Mall
325 S. Orlando Ave.
Suite 14
Winter Park, FL 32789-3608
PH: 407-644-2290
PH: 800-843-3751
FAX: 407-645-4434
Stamps@michaelrogersinc.com
www.michaelrogersinc.com

## Auctions

**COLONIAL STAMP COMPANY**
5757 Wilshire Blvd. PH #8
Los Angeles, CA 90036
PH: 323-933-9435
FAX: 323-939-9930
Toll Free in North America
PH: 877-272-6693
FAX: 877-272-6694
info@colonialstampcompany.com
www.colonialstampcompany.com

**DANIEL F. KELLEHER CO., INC.**
20 Walnut St.
Suite 213
Wellesley, MA 02481
PH: 781-235-0990
FAX: 781-235-0945

## Auctions

**JACQUES C. SCHIFF, JR., INC.**
195 Main St.
Ridgefield Park, NJ 07660
PH: 201-641-5566
PH from NYC: 212-662-2777
FAX: 201-641-5705

**R. MARESCH & SON LTD.**
5th Floor - 6075 Yonge St.
Toronto, ON M2M 3W2
CANADA
PH: 416-363-7777
FAX: 416-363-6511
www.maresch.com

**THE STAMP CENTER DUTCH COUNTRY AUCTIONS**
4115 Concord Pike
Wilmington, DE 19803
PH: 302-478-8740
FAX: 302-478-8779
auctions@thestampcenter.com
www.thestampcenter.com

## Auctions - Public

**ALAN BLAIR STAMPS/ AUCTIONS**
5405 Lakeside Ave.
Suite 1
Richmond, VA 23228
PH/FAX: 800-689-5602
alanblair@prodigy.net

## British Commonwealth

**ARON R. HALBERSTAM PHILATELISTS, LTD.**
PO Box 150168
Van Brunt Station
Brooklyn, NY 11215-0168
PH: 718-788-3978
FAX: 718-965-3099
arh@arhstamps.com
www.arhstamps.com

**METROPOLITAN STAMP CO., INC.**
PO Box 657
Park Ridge, IL 60068-0657
PH: 815-439-0142
FAX: 815-439-0143
metrostamp@aol.com
www.metropolitanstamps.com

**WWW.WORLDSTAMPS.COM**
242 West Saddle River Road
Suite C
Upper Saddle River, NJ 07458
PH: 201-236-8122
FAX: 201-236-8133
by mail:
Frank Geiger Philatelists
info@WorldStamps.com
www.WorldStamps.com

## Central America

**GUY SHAW**
PO Box 27138
San Diego, CA 92198
PH/FAX: 858-485-8269
guyshaw@guyshaw.com
www.guyshaw.com

## Auctions

# Schiff Auctions

**Buyers, Auctioneers & Appraisers of U.S. & Worldwide Stamps & Covers**

We have been catering to the individual buyer and seller since 1947. Let us put our **60 years** of experience to work for you when selling your stamps, covers or your collection. Whether you prefer consigning to public auction or selling outright, call us first. Describe your material before sending. Please include your address and telephone numbers.

| CATALOG SUBSCRIPTIONS | N. AMERICA | OVERSEAS |
|---|---|---|
| 1 Year Catalogs & Prices Realized | $10.00 | $18.00 |
| 1 Year Catalog Only | $7.50 | $15.00 |
| 1 Catalog with Prices Realized | $1.50 | $2.50 |
| 1 Catalog Only | $1.00 | $1.50 |

Send a self-addressed, stamped envelope for our complimentary brochure "How to auction your stamps and covers".

**JACQUES C. SCHIFF, JR., INC.**

195 Main St., Ridgefield Park, NJ 07660 USA
Telephone 201-641-5566 from NYC 212-662-2777
FAX 201-641-5705
**OFFICIAL AUCTIONEERS:**
AMERIPEX 1986.
WORLD STAMP EXPO 1989.
WORLD COLUMBIAN STAMP EXPO 1992.
AMERICAN PHILATELIC SOCIETY 2000-2003

NATIONAL STAMP DEALERS ASSN. NSDA · APS · ASDA Qualified Auctioneer

## British Commonwealth

# *The British Empire 1840-1936*

**Aden to Zululand Mint & Used**
**Most complete stock in North America**

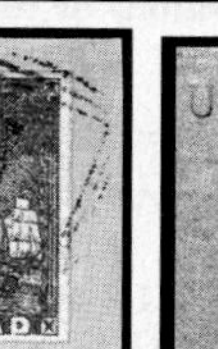

For over 30 years we have helped our customers build some of the worlds finest known collections. Our expert ***Want Lists Services*** can do the same for you. With over 40 volumes filled with singles, sets and rare stamps, I am sure we have what you need. We welcome your Want Lists in Scott or Gibbons numbers. Monthly payment plans available for larger purchases.

**Put our expertise to work for you today!**
**You'll be glad you did!!**

*Colonial Stamp Company*
5757 Wilshire Blvd., Penthouse 8
Los Angeles, CA 90036 USA
Tel: +1 (323) 933-9435 Fax: +1 (323) 939-9930
**Toll Free in North America**
**Tel: 1 (877) 272-6693 Fax: 1 (877) 272-6694**
E-Mail: *info@colonialstampcompany.com*
URL: *www.colonialstampcompany.com*

**British Empire Public Auctions Subscription: $35**

CCNY, IFSDA, INTERNATIONAL SOCIETY OF APPRAISERS

## China

**MICHAEL ROGERS, INC.**
Mailing Address:
336 Grove Ave.
Suite B
Winter Park, FL 32789-3602
Walk-in Address:
Ranch Mall
325 S. Orlando Ave.
Suite 14
Winter Park, FL 32789-3608
PH: 407-644-2290
PH: 800-843-3751
FAX: 407-645-4434
Stamps@michaelrogersinc.com
www.michaelrogersinc.com

## Cuba

**R.D.C. STAMPS**
R. del Campo
Store Address:
3131 Coral Way
Miami, FL 33145
Mailing Address:
10535 SW 96thTerrace
Miami, FL 33176
PH: 305-815-0577
PH: 305-567-3131
FAX: 305-567-1416
rdcstamps@aol.com

## Ducks

**MICHAEL JAFFE**
PO Box 61484
Vancouver, WA 98666
PH: 360-695-6161
PH: 800-782-6770
FAX: 360-695-1616
mjaffe@brookmanstamps.com
www.brookmanstamps.com

## Europe

**WWW.WORLDSTAMPS.COM**
242 West Saddle River Road
Suite C
Upper Saddle River, NJ 07458
PH: 201-236-8122
FAX: 201-236-8133
by mail:
Frank Geiger Philatelists
info@WorldStamps.com
www.WorldStamps.com

## Europe-Western

**CURTIS GIDDING STAMP STORE**
2003 Sunview Dr.
Suite 101
Champaign, IL 61821
PH: 217-359-4017
curtstamp@aol.com
www.curtisgiddingstampstore.com

## German Colonies

**COLONIAL STAMP COMPANY**
View our on-line price list
at our website!
5757 Wilshire Blvd. PH #8
Los Angeles, CA 90036
PH: 323-933-9435
FAX: 323-939-9930
Toll Free in North America
PH: 877-272-6693
FAX: 877-272-6694
info@colonialstampcompany.com
www.colonialstampcompany.com

## Germany

**HENRY GITNER PHILATELISTS, INC.**
PO Box 3077-S
Middletown, NY 10940
PH: 845-343-5151
PH: 800-947-8267
FAX: 845-343-0068
hgitner@hgitner.com
www.hgitner.com

## Insurance

**COLLECTIBLES INSURANCE AGENCY**
11350 McCormick Rd.
Suite 700
Hunt Valley, MD 21031
PH: 888-837-9537
PH: 410-876-8833
FAX: 410-876-9233
info@insurecollectibles.com
www.collectinsure.com

## Japan

**MICHAEL ROGERS, INC.**
Mailing Address:
336 Grove Ave.
Suite B
Winter Park, FL 32789-3602
Walk-in Address:
Ranch Mall
325 S. Orlando Ave.
Suite 14
Winter Park, FL 32789-3608
PH: 407-644-2290
PH: 800-843-3751
FAX: 407-645-4434
Stamps@michaelrogersinc.com
www.michaelrogersinc.com

## Korea

**MICHAEL ROGERS, INC.**
Mailing Address:
336 Grove Ave.
Suite B
Winter Park, FL 32789-3602
Walk-in Address:
Ranch Mall
325 S. Orlando Ave.
Suite 14
Winter Park, FL 32789-3608
PH: 407-644-2290
PH: 800-843-3751
FAX: 407-645-4434
Stamps@michaelrogersinc.com
www.michaelrogersinc.com

## Latin America

**GUY SHAW**
PO Box 27138
San Diego, CA 92198
PH/FAX: 858-485-8269
guyshaw@guyshaw.com
www.guyshaw.com

## Manchukuo

**MICHAEL ROGERS, INC.**
Mailing Address:
336 Grove Ave.
Suite B
Winter Park, FL 32789-3602
Walk-in Address:
Ranch Mall
325 S. Orlando Ave.
Suite 14
Winter Park, FL 32789-3608
PH: 407-644-2290
PH: 800-843-3751
FAX: 407-645-4434
Stamps@michaelrogersinc.com
www.michaelrogersinc.com

## Mexico

**AMEEN STAMPS**
8831 Long Point Road
Suite 204
Houston, TX 77055
PH: 713-468-0644
FAX: 713-468-2420
rameen03@sbcglobal.net

## New Issues

**DAVIDSON'S STAMP SERVICE**
PO Box 36355
Indianapolis, IN 46236-0355
PH: 317-826-2620
davidson@in.net
www.newstampissues.com

## New Issues - Retail

**BOMBAY PHILATELIC INC.**
PO Box 480009
Delray Beach, FL 33448
PH: 561-499-7990
FAX: 561-499-7553
sales@bombaystamps.com
www.bombaystamps.com

## British Commonwealth



## Insurance

## Publications-Collector

**THE AMERICAN PHILATELIST**
Dept. TZ
100 Match Factory Pl
Bellefonte, PA 16823-1367
PH: 814-933-3803
FAX: 814-933-6128
apsinfo@stamps.org
www.stamps.org

## South Africa

**ARON R. HALBERSTAM PHILATELISTS, LTD.**
PO Box 150168
Van Brunt Station
Brooklyn, NY 11215-0168
PH: 718-788-3978
FAX: 718-965-3099
arh@arhstamps.com
www.arhstamps.com

## South America

**GUY SHAW**
PO Box 27138
San Diego, CA 92198
PH/FAX: 858-485-8269
guyshaw@guyshaw.com
www.guyshaw.com

**WWW.WORLDSTAMPS.COM**
242 West Saddle River Road
Suite C
Upper Saddle River, NJ 07458
PH: 201-236-8122
FAX: 201-236-8133
by mail:
Frank Geiger Philatelists
info@WorldStamps.com
www.WorldStamps.com

## Sri Lanka

**COLONIAL STAMP COMPANY**
5757 Wilshire Blvd. PH #8
Los Angeles, CA 90036
PH: 323-933-9435
FAX: 323-939-9930
Toll Free in North America
PH: 877-272-6693
FAX: 877-272-6694
info@colonialstampcompany.com
www.colonialstampcompany.com

## STAMP STORES

### Arizona

**B.J.'S STAMPS**
Barbara J. Johnson
6342 W. Bell Road
Glendale, AZ 85308
PH: 623-878-2080
FAX: 623-412-3456
info@bjstamps.com
www.bjstamps.com

### California

**BROSIUS STAMP, COIN & SUPPLIES**
2105 Main St.
Santa Monica, CA 90405
PH: 310-396-7480
FAX: 310-396-7455

**COLONIAL STAMP CO./ BRITISH EMPIRE SPECIALIST**
5757 Wilshire Blvd. PH #8
(by appt.)
Los Angeles, CA 90036
PH: 323-933-9435
FAX: 323-939-9930
Toll Free in North America
PH: 877-272-6693
FAX: 877-272-6694
info@colonialstampcompany.com
www.colonialstampcompany.com

**FISCHER-WOLK PHILATELICS**
22762 Aspan St
Suite 211
Lake Forest, CA 92630
PH: 949-837-2932
fischerwolk@earthlink.net

**NATICK STAMPS & HOBBIES**
405 S. Myrtle Ave.
Monrovia, CA 91016
PH: 626-305-7333
natickco@earthlink.net

### Colorado

**ACKLEY'S ROCKS & STAMPS**
3230 N. Stone Ave.
Colorado Springs, CO 80907
PH: 719-633-1153
ackl9@aol.com

**SHOWCASE STAMPS**
3865 Wadsworth
Wheat Ridge, CO 80033
PH: 303-425-9252
kbeiner@colbi.net
www.showcasestamps.com

### Connecticut

**SILVER CITY COIN & STAMP**
41 Colony Street
Meriden, CT 06451
PH: 203-235-7634
FAX: 203-237-4915

### Florida

**R.D.C. STAMPS**
R. del Campo
Store Address:
3131 Coral Way
Miami, FL 33145
Mailing Address:
10535 SW 96thTerrace
Miami, FL 33176
PH: 305-815-0577
PH: 305-567-3131
FAX: 305-567-1416
rdcstamps@aol.com

**WINTER PARK STAMP SHOP**
Ranch Mall (17-92)
325 S. Orlando Ave.
Suite 14
Winter Park, FL 32789-3608
PH: 407-628-1120
PH: 800-845-1819
FAX: 407-628-0091
stamps@winterparkstampshop.com
www.winterparkstampshop.com

### Georgia

**STAMPS UNLIMITED OF GEORGIA, INC.**
100 Peachtree St.
Suite 1460
Atlanta, GA 30303
PH: 404-688-9161

### Illinois

**DR. ROBERT FRIEDMAN & SONS**
2029 W. 75th St.
Woodridge, IL 60517
PH: 800-588-8100
FAX: 630-985-1588
drbobstamps@yahoo.com
www.drbobfriedmanstamps.com

### Indiana

**KNIGHT STAMP & COIN CO.**
237 Main St.
Hobart, IN 46342
PH: 219-942-4341
PH: 800-634-2646
knight@knightcoin.com
www.knightcoin.com

### Massachusetts

**KAPPY'S COINS & STAMPS**
534 Washington St.
Norwood, MA 02062
PH: 781-762-5552
FAX: 781-762-3292
kappyscoins@aol.com

### Maryland

**BULLDOG STAMP COMPANY**
4641 Montgomery Ave.
Bethesda, MD 20814
PH: 301-654-1138

### New Jersey

**BERGEN STAMPS & COLLECTIBLES**
717 American Legion Dr.
Teaneck, NJ 07666
PH: 201-836-8987

**RON RITZER STAMPS INC.**
Millburn Mall
2933 Vauxhall Rd.
Vauxhall, NJ 07088
PH: 908-687-0007
FAX: 908-687-0795
rritzer@comcast.net
www.ritzerstamps.com

**TRENTON STAMP & COIN CO.**
Thomas DeLuca
Store: Forest Glen Plaza
1804 Route 33
Hamilton Square, NJ 08690
Mail: PO Box 8574
Trenton, NJ 08650
PH: 800-446-8664
PH: 609-584-8100
FAX: 609-587-8664
TOMD4TSC@aol.com

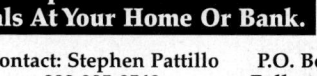

## New Issues

## Stamp Shows

## STAMP STORES

### New York

**CHAMPION STAMP CO., INC.**
432 W. 54th St.
New York, NY 10019
PH: 212-489-8130
FAX: 212-581-8130
championstamp@aol.com
www.championstamp.com

### Ohio

**HILLTOP STAMP SERVICE**
Richard A. Peterson
PO Box 626
Wooster, OH 44691
PH: 330-262-8907
PH: 330-262-5378
hilltop@bright.net

**THE LINK STAMP CO.**
3461 E. Livingston Ave.
Columbus, OH 43227
PH/FAX: 614-237-4125
PH/FAX: 800-546-5726

### Tennessee

**HERRON HILL, INC.**
5007 Black Road
Suite 140
Memphis, TN 38117
PH: 901-683-9644

### Virginia

**KENNEDY'S STAMPS & COINS, INC.**
7059 Brookfield Plaza
Springfield, VA 22150
PH: 703-569-7300
FAX: 703-569-7644
j.w.kennedy@verizon.net

**LATHEROW & CO., INC.**
5054 Lee Hwy.
Arlington, VA 22207
PH: 703-538-2727
PH: 800-647-4624
FAX: 703-538-5210

### Straits Settlements

**COLONIAL STAMP COMPANY**
5757 Wilshire Blvd. PH #8
Los Angeles, CA 90036
PH: 323-933-9435
FAX: 323-939-9930
Toll Free in North America
PH: 877-272-6693
FAX: 877-272-6694
info@colonialstampcompany.com
www.colonialstampcompany.com

### Sweden

**CURTIS GIDDING STAMP STORE**
2003 Sunview Dr.
Suite 101
Champaign, IL 61821
PH: 217-359-4017
curtstamp@aol.com
www.curtisgiddingstampstore.com

### Togo

**COLONIAL STAMP COMPANY**
5757 Wilshire Blvd. PH #8
Los Angeles, CA 90036
PH: 323-933-9435
FAX: 323-939-9930
Toll Free in North America
PH: 877-272-6693
FAX: 877-272-6694
info@colonialstampcompany.com
www.colonialstampcompany.com

### Tonga

**COLONIAL STAMP COMPANY**
5757 Wilshire Blvd. PH #8
Los Angeles, CA 90036
PH: 323-933-9435
FAX: 323-939-9930
Toll Free in North America
PH: 877-272-6693
FAX: 877-272-6694
info@colonialstampcompany.com
www.colonialstampcompany.com

### Topicals

**E. JOSEPH MCCONNELL**
PO Box 683
Monroe, NY 10949
PH: 845-496-5916
FAX: 845-782-0347
ejstamps@gmail.com
www.EJMcConnell.com

**HENRY GITNER PHILATELISTS, INC.**
PO Box 3077-S
Middletown, NY 10940
PH: 845-343-5151
PH: 800-947-8267
FAX: 845-343-0068
hgitner@hgitner.com
www.hgitner.com

### Topicals-Columbus

**MR. COLUMBUS**
PO Box 1492
Fennville, MI 49408
PH: 269-543-4755
columbus@accn.org

### Transvaal

**COLONIAL STAMP COMPANY**
5757 Wilshire Blvd. PH #8
Los Angeles, CA 90036
PH: 323-933-9435
FAX: 323-939-9930
Toll Free in North America
PH: 877-272-6693
FAX: 877-272-6694
info@colonialstampcompany.com
www.colonialstampcompany.com

### Uganda

**COLONIAL STAMP COMPANY**
5757 Wilshire Blvd. PH #8
Los Angeles, CA 90036
PH: 323-933-9435
FAX: 323-939-9930
Toll Free in North America
PH: 877-272-6693
FAX: 877-272-6694
info@colonialstampcompany.com
www.colonialstampcompany.com

### Ukraine

**MR. VAL ZABIJAKA**
PO Box 3711
Silver Spring, MD 20918
PH/FAX: 301-593-5316
vtz@comcast.net

### United States

**BROOKMAN STAMP CO.**
PO Box 90
Vancouver, WA 98666
PH: 360-695-1391
PH: 800-545-4871
FAX: 360-695-1616
larry@brookmanstamps.com
www.brookmanstamps.com

### U.S.-Collections Wanted

**DR. ROBERT FRIEDMAN & SONS**
2029 W. 75th St.
Woodridge, IL 60517
PH: 800-588-8100
FAX: 630-985-1588
drbobstamps@yahoo.com
www.drbobfriedmanstamps.com

### Want Lists

**BROOKMAN INTERNATIONAL**
PO Box 450
Vancouver, WA 98666
PH: 360-695-1391
PH: 800-545-4871
FAX: 360-695-1616
larry@brookmanstamps.com
www.brookmanstamps.com

**CHARLES P. SCHWARTZ**
PO Box 165
Mora, MN 55051
PH: 320-679-4705
charlesp@ecenet.com

### Want Lists-British Empire 1840-1935 German Cols./Offices

**COLONIAL STAMP COMPANY**
5757 Wilshire Blvd. PH #8
Los Angeles, CA 90036
PH: 323-933-9435
FAX: 323-939-9930
Toll Free in North America
PH: 877-272-6693
FAX: 877-272-6694
info@colonialstampcompany.com
www.colonialstampcompany.com

### Wanted-U.S. Collections

**THE STAMP CENTER DUTCH COUNTRY AUCTIONS**
4115 Concord Pike
Wilmington, DE 19803
PH: 302-478-8740
FAX: 302-478-8779
auctions@thestampcenter.com
www.thestampcenter.com

### Wanted-Worldwide Collections

**DR. ROBERT FRIEDMAN & SONS**
2029 W. 75th St.
Woodridge, IL 60517
PH: 800-588-8100
FAX: 630-985-1588
drbobstamps@yahoo.com
www.drbobfriedmanstamps.com

**THE STAMP CENTER DUTCH COUNTRY AUCTIONS**
4115 Concord Pike
Wilmington, DE 19803
PH: 302-478-8740
FAX: 302-478-8779
auctions@thestampcenter.com
www.thestampcenter.com

### Wholesale FDC's

**HENRY GITNER PHILATELISTS, INC.**
PO Box 3077-S
Middletown, NY 10940
PH: 845-343-5151
PH: 800-947-8267
FAX: 845-343-0068
hgitner@hgitner.com
www.hgitner.com

### Worldwide Stamps

**METROPOLITAN STAMP CO., INC.**
PO Box 657
Park Ridge, IL 60068-0657
PH: 815-439-0142
FAX: 815-439-0143
metrostamp@aol.com
www.metropolitanstamps.com

### Worldwide-Year Sets

**WWW.WORLDSTAMPS.COM**
242 West Saddle River Road
Suite C
Upper Saddle River, NJ 07458
PH: 201-236-8122
FAX: 201-236-8133
by mail:
Frank Geiger Philatelists
info@WorldStamps.com
www.WorldStamps.com

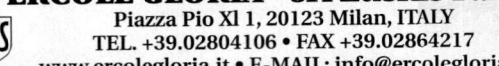

### Worldwide